Who Was Who in America

Biographical Titles Currently Published by Marquis Who's Who

Who's Who in America
Who's Who in America derivatives:
  Geographic/Professional Index
  Supplement to Who's Who in America
  Who's Who in America Classroom Project Book
Who Was Who in America
  Historical Volume (1607-1896)
  Volume I (1897-1942)
  Volume II (1943-1950)
  Volume III (1951-1960)
  Volume IV (1961-1968)
  Volume V (1969-1973)
  Volume VI (1974-1976)
  Volume VII (1977-1981)
  Volume VIII (1982-1985)
  Volume IX (1985-1989)
  Index Volume (1607-1989)
Who's Who in the World
Who's Who in the East
Who's Who in the Midwest
Who's Who in the South and Southwest
Who's Who in the West
Who's Who in American Law
Who's Who of American Women
Who's Who of Emerging Leaders in America
Who's Who in Entertainment
Who's Who in Finance and Industry
Index to Who's Who Books
Directory of Medical Specialists
Supplement to Directory of Medical Specialists

Who Was Who in America ®
with World Notables

Volume IX
1985-1989

MARQUIS **Who'sWho**

Macmillan Directory Division
3002 Glenview Road
Wilmette, Illinois 60091 U.S.A.

James J. Pfister—President
Paul E. Rose—Executive Vice President
Timothy J. Sullivan—Vice President, Finance
A. Robert Weicherding—Vice President, Publisher
Sandra S. Barnes—Group Vice President, Product Management
John L. Daniels—Product Manager

Library of Congress Catalog Card Number 43–3789
International Standard Book Number 0–8379–0217–7
Product Code Number 030491

Distributed in Asia by
United Publishers Services Ltd.
Kenkyu-Sha Bldg.
9, Kanda Surugadai 2-Chome
Chiyoda-ku, Tokyo, Japan

Manufactured in the United States of America

Table of Contents

Preface

The publication of Volume IX of *Who Was Who in America* is an important step forward in the growth of a series of biographical reference books that seek to reflect both American history and the genealogical heritages of this country. The sketches are of deceased biographees in *Who's Who in America* as well as our regional and topical library.

The *Was* books (to use the shortened form by which they are better known) display the distinctive characteristics that have made *Who's Who in America* both an internationally respected reference work, and a household word in the country of its origin. Sketches not only were prepared by information supplied by the biographees themselves, but were approved and frequently revised by the subjects before being printed in a Marquis publication. As a result, many sketches contain personal data unavailable elsewhere. The preface to the first volume of *Who's Who in America* selected this fact as one of the volume's outstanding characteristics, and stated: "The book is autobiographical, the data having been obtained from first hands." Similarly, *Who Was Who in America* is largely autobiographical. Although condensed to the concise style that Marquis Who's Who has made famous, the sketches contain essential facts. Inclusion of date of death and place of interment completes the sketches.

In continuing improvements introduced in previous volumes of *Who Was Who in America*, this volume includes sketches of some Marquis biographees known to be 95 years of age or older. Lacking current information regarding these individuals, we make such inclusions in the hope that our apologies will be accepted should errors occur. Sketches of recently deceased world notables also are included, particularly of those international figures whose careers had a direct bearing on the course of recent American history.

The result is far more than a biographical directory of some 117,000 deceased American notables within the covers of nine volumes. *Who Was Who in America* contains a vital portion of American history from the early days of the colonies to mid-1989. It is the autobiography of America.

Table of Abbreviations

The following abbreviations and symbols are frequently used in this book

*Following a sketch indicates that the published biography could not be verified

† Non-current sketches of *Who Was Who in America* biographees who were born 95 or more years ago (see Preface for explanation).

AA, A.A. Associate in Arts, Associate of Arts
AAAL American Academy of Arts and Letters
AAAS American Association for the Advancement of Science
AAHPER Alliance for Health, Physical Education and Recreation
AAU Amateur Athletic Union
AAUP American Association of University Professors
AAUW American Association of University Women
AB, A.B. Arts, Bachelor of
AB Alberta
ABA American Bar Association
ABC American Broadcasting Company
AC Air Corps
acad. academy, academic
acct. accountant
acctg. accounting
ACDA Arms Control and Disarmament Agency
ACLU American Civil Liberties Union
ACP American College of Physicians
ACS American College of Surgeons
ADA American Dental Association
a.d.c. aide-de-camp
adj. adjunct, adjutant
adj. gen. adjutant general
adm. admiral
adminstr. administrator
adminstrn. administration
adminstrv. administrative
ADP Automatic Data Processing
adv. advocate, advisory
advt. advertising
AE, A.E. Agricultural Engineer
A.E. and P. Ambassador Extraordinary and Plenipotentiary
AEC Atomic Energy Commission
aero. aeronautical, aeronautic
aerodyn. aerodynamic
AFB Air Force Base
AFL-CIO American Federation of Labor and Congress of Industrial Organizations
AFTRA American Federation of TV and Radio Artists
AFSCME American Federation of State, County and Municipal Employees
agr. agriculture
agrl. agricultural
agt. agent
AGVA American Guild of Variety Artists
agy. agency
A&I Agricultural and Industrial
AIA American Institute of Architects
AIAA American Institute of Aeronautics and Astronautics
AICPA American Institute of Certified Public Accountants
AID Agency for International Development

AIDS Acquired Immune Deficiency Syndrome
AIEE American Institute of Electrical Engineers
AIM American Institute of Management
AIME American Institute of Mining, Metallurgy, and Petroleum Engineers
AK Alaska
AL Alabama
ALA American Library Association
Ala. Alabama
alt. alternate
Alta. Alberta
A&M Agricultural and Mechanical
AM, A.M. Arts, Master of
Am. American, America
AMA American Medical Association
amb. ambassador
A.M.E. African Methodist Episcopal
Amtrak National Railroad Passenger Corporation
AMVETS American Veterans of World War II, Korea, Vietnam
anat. anatomical
ann. annual
ANTA American National Theatre and Academy
anthrop. anthropological
AP Associated Press
APO Army Post Office
apptd. appointed
Apr. April
apt. apartment
AR Arkansas
ARC American Red Cross
archeol. archeological
archtl. architectural
Ariz. Arizona
Ark. Arkansas
ArtsD, ArtsD. Arts, Doctor of
arty. artillery
AS American Samoa
AS Associate in Science
AS Associate of Applied Science
ASCAP American Society of Composers, Authors and Publishers
ASCE American Society of Civil Engineers
ASHRAE American Society of Heating, Refrigeration, and Air Conditioning Engineers
ASME American Society of Mechanical Engineers
ASPCA American Society for the Prevention of Cruelty to Animals
assn. association
assoc. associate
asst. assistant
ASTM American Society for Testing and Materials
astron. astronomical
astrophys. astrophysical
ATSC Air Technical Service Command
AT&T American Telephone & Telegraph Company
atty. attorney
Aug. August
AUS Army of the United States

aux. auxiliary
Ave. Avenue
AVMA American Veterinary Medical Association
AZ Arizona

B. Bachelor
b. born
BA, B.A. Bachelor of Arts
BAgr, B.Agr. Bachelor of Agriculture
Balt. Baltimore
Bapt. Baptist
BArch, B.Arch. Bachelor of Architecture
BAS, B.A.S. Bachelor of Agricultural Science
BBA, B.B.A. Bachelor of Business Administration
BBC British Broadcasting Corporation
BC, B.C. British Columbia
BCE, B.C.E. Bachelor of Civil Engineering
BChir, B.Chir. Bachelor of Surgery
BCL, B.C.L. Bachelor of Civil Law
BCS, B.C.S. Bachelor of Commercial Science
BD, B.D. Bachelor of Divinity
bd. board
BE, B.E. Bachelor of Education
BEE, B.E.E. Bachelor of Electrical Engineering
BFA, B.F.A. Bachelor of Fine Arts
bibl. biblical
bibliog. bibliographical
biog. biographical
biol. biological
BJ, B.J. Bachelor of Journalism
Bklyn. Brooklyn
BL, B.L. Bachelor of Letters
bldg. building
BLS, B.L.S. Bachelor of Library Science
Blvd. Boulevard
BMW Bavarian Motor Works (Bayerische Motoren Werke)
bn. batallion
B.& O.R.R. Baltimore & Ohio Railroad
bot. botanical
BPE, B.P.E. Bachelor of Physical Education
BPhil, B.Phil. Bachelor of Philosophy
br. branch
BRE, B.R.E. Bachelor of Religious Education
brig. gen. brigadier general
Brit. British, Brittanica
Bros. Brothers
BS, B.S. Bachelor of Science
BSA, B.S.A. Bachelor of Agricultural Science
BSBA Bachelor of Science in Business Administration
BSChemE Bachelor of Science in Chemical Engineering
BSD, B.S.D. Bachelor of Didactic Science
BST, B.S.T. Bachelor of Sacred Theology
BTh, B.Th. Bachelor of Theology
bull. bulletin
bur. bureau
bus. business
B.W.I. British West Indies

CA California
CAA Civil Aeronautics Administration
CAB Civil Aeronautics Board
CAD-CAM Computer Aided Design-
  Computer Aided Model
Calif. California
C.Am. Central America
Can. Canada, Canadian
CAP Civil Air Patrol
capt. captain
CARE Cooperative American Relief
  Everywhere
Cath. Catholic
cav. cavalry
CBC Canadian Broadcasting Company
CBI China, Burma, India Theatre of
  Operations
CBS Columbia Broadcasting Company
CCC Commodity Credit Corporation
CCNY City College of New York
CCU Cardiac Care Unit
CD Civil Defense
CE, C.E. Corps of Engineers, Civil
  Engineer
cen. central
CENTO Central Treaty Organization
CERN European Organization of Nuclear
  Research
cert. certificate, certification, certified
CETA Comprehensive Employment
  Training Act
CFL Canadian Football League
ch. church
ChD, Ch.D. Doctor of Chemistry
chem. chemical
ChemE, Chem.E. Chemical Engineer
Chgo. Chicago
chirurg. chirurgical
chmn. chairman
chpt. chapter
CIA Central Intelligence Agency
Cin. Cincinnati
cir. circuit
Cleve. Cleveland
climatol. climatological
clin. clinical
clk. clerk
C.L.U. Chartered Life Underwriter
CM, C.M. Master in Surgery
CM Northern Mariana Islands
C.&N.W.Ry. Chicago & North Western
  Railway
CO Colorado
Co. Company
COF Catholic Order of Foresters
C. of C. Chamber of Commerce
col. colonel
coll. college
Colo. Colorado
com. committee
comd. commanded
comdg. commanding
comdr. commander
comdt. commandant
commd. commissioned
comml. commercial
commn. commission
commr. commissioner

compt. comptroller
condr. conductor
Conf. Conference
Congl. Congregational, Congressional
Conglist. Congregationalist
Conn. Connecticut
cons. consultant, consulting
consol. consolidated
constl. constitutional
constn. constitution
constrn. construction
contbd. contributed
contbg. contributing
contbn. contribution
contbr. contributor
contr. controller
Conv. Convention
coop. cooperative
coord. coordinator
CORDS Civil Operations and
  Revolutionary Development Support
CORE Congress of Racial Equality
corp. corporation, corporate
corr. correspondent, corresponding,
  correspondence
C.&O.Ry. Chesapeake & Ohio Railway
coun. council
C.P.A. Certified Public Accountant
C.P.C.U. Chartered Property and Casualty
  Underwriter
CPH, C.P.H. Certificate of Public Health
cpl. corporal
C.P.R. Cardio-Pulmonary Resuscitation
C.P.Ry. Canadian Pacific Railway
CRT Cathode Ray Terminal
C.S. Christian Science
CSB, C.S.B. Bachelor of Christian Science
C.S.C. Civil Service Commission
CT Connecticut
ct. court
ctr. center
CWS Chemical Warfare Service
C.Z. Canal Zone

D. Doctor
d. daughter
DAgr, D.Agr. Doctor of Agriculture
DAR Daughters of the American Revolution
dau. daughter
DAV Disabled American Veterans
DC, D.C. District of Columbia
DCL, D.C.L. Doctor of Civil Law
DCS, D.C.S. Doctor of Commercial Science
DD, D.D. Doctor of Divinity
DDS, D.D.S. Doctor of Dental Surgery
DE Delaware
Dec. December
dec. deceased
def. defense
Del. Delaware
del. delegate, delegation
Dem. Democrat, Democratic
DEng, D.Eng. Doctor of Engineering
denom. denomination, denominational
dep. deputy
dept. department
dermatol. dermatological

desc. descendant
devel. development, developmental
DFA, D.F.A. Doctor of Fine Arts
D.F.C. Distinguished Flying Cross
DHL, D.H.L. Doctor of Hebrew Literature
dir. director
dist. district
distbg. distributing
distbn. distribution
distbr. distributor
disting. distinguished
div. division, divinity, divorce
DLitt, D.Litt. Doctor of Literature
DMD, D.M.D. Doctor of Medical Dentistry
DMS, D.M.S. Doctor of Medical Science
DO, D.O. Doctor of Osteopathy
DPH, D.P.H. Diploma in Public Health
DPhil, D.Phil. Doctor of Philosophy
D.R. Daughters of the Revolution
Dr. Drive, Doctor
DRE, D.R.E. Doctor of Religious Education
DrPH, Dr.P.H. Doctor of Public Health,
  Doctor of Public Hygiene
D.S.C. Distinguished Service Cross
DSc, D.Sc. Doctor of Science
D.S.M. Distinguished Service Medal
DST, D.S.T. Doctor of Sacred Theology
DTM, D.T.M. Doctor of Tropical Medicine
DVM, D.V.M. Doctor of Veterinary
  Medicine
DVS, D.V.S. Doctor of Veterinary Surgery

E, E. East
ea. eastern
E. and P. Extraordinary and
  Plenipotentiary
Eccles. Ecclesiastical
ecol. ecological
econ. economical
ECOSOC Economic and Social Council (of
  the UN)
ED, E.D. Doctor of Engineering
ed. educated
EdB, Ed.B. Bachelor of Education
EdD, Ed.D. Doctor of Education
edit. edition
EdM, Ed.M. Master of Education
edn. education
ednl. educational
EDP Electronic Data Processing
EdS, Ed.S. Specialist in Education
EE, E.E. Electrical Engineer
E.E. and M.P. Envoy Extraordinary and
  Minister Plenipotentiary
EEC European Economic Community
EEG Electroencephalogram
EEO Equal Employment Opportunity
EEOC Equal Employment Opportunity
  Commission
E.Ger. German Democratic Republic
EKG Electrocardiogram
elec. electrical
electrochem. electrochemical
electrophys. electrophysical
elem. elementary
EM, E.M. Engineer of Mines
ency. encyclopedia

Eng. England
engr. engineer
engring. engineering
entomol. entomological
environ. environmental
EPA Environmental Protection Agency
epidemiol. epidemiological
Episc. Episcopalian
ERA Equal Rights Amendment
ERDA Energy Research and Development
  Administration
ESEA Elementary and Secondary Education
  Act
ESL English as Second Language
ESPN Entertainment and Sports
  Programming Network
ESSA Environmental Science Services
  Administration
ethnol. ethnological
ETO European Theatre of Operations
Evang. Evangelical
exam. examination, examining
Exch. Exchange
exec. executive
exhbn. exhibition
expdn. expedition
expn. exposition
expt. experiment
exptl. experimental
Expwy. Expressway

F.A. Field Artillery
FAA Federal Aviation Administration
FAO Food and Agriculture Organization
  (of the UN)
FBI Federal Bureau of Investigation
FCA Farm Credit Administration
FCC Federal Communications Commission
FCDA Federal Civil Defense
  Administration
FDA Food and Drug Administration
FDIA Federal Deposit Insurance
  Administration
FDIC Federal Deposit Insurance
  Corporation
FE, F.E. Forest Engineer
FEA Federal Energy Administration
Feb. February
fed. federal
fedn. federation
FERC Federal Energy Regulatory
  Commission
fgn. foreign
FHA Federal Housing Administration
fin. financial, finance
FL Florida
Fl. Floor
Fla. Florida
FMC Federal Maritime Commission
FOA Foreign Operations Administration
found. foundation
FPC Federal Power Commission
FPO Fleet Post Office
frat. fraternity
FRS Federal Reserve System
Frwy. Freeway

FSA Federal Security Agency
Ft. Fort
FTC Federal Trade Commission

G-1 (or other number) Division of General
  Staff
GA, Ga. Georgia
GAO General Accounting Office
gastroent. gastroenterological
GATT General Agreement of Tariff and
  Trades
GE General Electric Company
gen. general
geneal. genealogical
geod. geodetic
geog. geographic, geographical
geol. geological
geophys. geophysical
gerontol. gerontological
G.H.Q. General Headquarters
GM General Motors Corporation
GMAC General Motors Acceptance
  Corporation
G.N.Ry. Great Northern Railway
gov. governor
govt. government
govtl. governmental
GPO Government Printing Office
grad. graduate, graduated
GSA General Services Administration
Gt. Great
GTE General Telephone and Electric
  Company
GU Guam
gynecol. gynecological

HBO Home Box Office
hdqrs. headquarters
HEW Department of Health, Education and
  Welfare
HHD, H.H.D. Doctor of Humanities
HHFA Housing and Home Finance Agency
HHS Department of Health and Human
  Services
HI Hawaii
hist. historical, historic
HM, H.M. Master of Humanics
HMO Health Maintenance Organization
homeo. homeopathic
hon. honorary, honorable
Ho. of Dels. House of Delegates
Ho. of Reps. House of Representatives
hort. horticultural
hosp. hospital
HUD Department of Housing and Urban
  Development
Hwy. Highway
hydrog. hydrographic

IA Iowa
IAEA International Atomic Energy Agency
IBM International Business Machines
  Corporation
IBRD International Bank for Reconstruction
  and Development

ICA International Cooperation
  Administration
ICC Interstate Commerce Commission
ICU Intensive Care Unit
ID Idaho
IEEE Institute of Electrical and Electronics
  Engineers
IFC International Finance Corporation
IGY International Geophysical Year
IL Illinois
Ill. Illinois
illus. illustrated
ILO International Labor Organization
IMF International Monetary Fund
IN Indiana
Inc. Incorporated
Ind. Indiana
ind. independent
Indpls. Indianapolis
indsl. industrial
inf. infantry
info. information
ins. insurance
insp. inspector
insp. gen. inspector general
inst. institute
instl. institutional
instn. institution
instr. instructor
instrn. instruction
internat. international
intro. introduction
IRE Institute of Radio Engineers
IRS Internal Revenue Service
ITT International Telephone & Telegraph
  Corporation

JAG Judge Advocate General
JAGC Judge Advocate General Corps
Jan. January
Jaycees Junior Chamber of Commerce
JB, J.B. Jurum Baccalaureus
JCB, J.C.B. Juris Canoni Baccalaureus
JCD, J.C.D. Juris Canonici Doctor, Juris
  Civilis Doctor
JCL, J.C.L. Juris Canonici Licentiatus
JD, J.D. Juris Doctor
jg. junior grade
jour. journal
jr. junior
JSD, J.S.D. Juris Scientiae Doctor
JUD, J.U.D. Juris Utriusque Doctor
Jud. judicial

Kans. Kansas
K.C. Knights of Columbus
K.P. Knights of Pythias
KS Kansas
K.T. Knight Templar
KY, Ky. Kentucky

LA, La. Louisiana
L.A. Los Angeles
lab. laboratory
lang. language
laryngol. laryngological
LB Labrador

LDS Church Church of Jesus Christ of Latter Day Saints
lectr. lecturer
legis. legislation, legislative
LHD, L.H.D. Doctor of Humane Letters
L.I. Long Island
libr. librarian, library
lic. licensed, license
L.I.R.R. Long Island Railroad
lit. literature
LittB, Litt.B. Bachelor of Letters
LittD, Litt.D. Doctor of Letters
LLB, LL.B. Bachelor of Laws
LLD, L.L.D. Doctor of Laws
LLM, L.L.M. Master of Laws
Ln. Lane
L.&N.R.R. Louisville & Nashville Railroad
LPGA Ladies Professional Golf Association
LS, L.S. Library Science (in degree)
lt. lieutenant
Ltd. Limited
Luth. Lutheran
LWV League of Women Voters

M. Master
m. married
MA, M.A. Master of Arts
MA Massachusetts
MADD Mothers Against Drunk Driving
mag. magazine
MAgr, M.Agr. Master of Agriculture
maj. major
Man. Manitoba
Mar. March
MArch, M.Arch. Master in Architecture
Mass. Massachusetts
math. mathematics, mathematical
MATS Military Air Transport Service
MB, M.B. Bachelor of Medicine
MB Manitoba
MBA, M.B.A. Master of Business Administration
MBS Mutual Broadcasting System
M.C. Medical Corps
MCE, M.C.E. Master of Civil Engineering
mcht. merchant
mcpl. municipal
MCS, M.C.S. Master of Commercial Science
MD, M.D. Doctor of Medicine
MD, Md. Maryland
MDiv Master of Divinity
MDip, M.Dip. Master in Diplomacy
mdse. merchandise
MDV, M.D.V. Doctor of Veterinary Medicine
ME, M.E. Mechanical Engineer
ME Maine
M.E.Ch. Methodist Episcopal Church
mech. mechanical
MEd., M.Ed. Master of Education
med. medical
MEE, M.E.E. Master of Electrical Engineering
mem. member
meml. memorial
merc. mercantile

met. metropolitan
metall. metallurgical
MetE, Met.E. Metallurgical Engineer
meteorol. meteorological
Meth. Methodist
Mex. Mexico
MF, M.F. Master of Forestry
MFA, M.F.A. Master of Fine Arts
mfg. manufacturing
mfr. manufacturer
mgmt. management
mgr. manager
MHA, M.H.A. Master of Hospital Administration
M.I. Military Intelligence
MI Michigan
Mich. Michigan
micros. microscopic, microscopical
mid. middle
mil. military
Milw. Milwaukee
Min. Minister
mineral. mineralogical
Minn. Minnesota
MIS Management Information Systems
Miss. Mississippi
MIT Massachusetts Institute of Technology
mktg. marketing
ML, M.L. Master of Laws
MLA Modern Language Association
M.L.D. Magister Legnum Diplomatic
MLitt, M.Litt. Master of Literature
MLS, M.L.S. Master of Library Science
MME, M.M.E. Master of Mechanical Engineering
MN Minnesota
mng. managing
MO, Mo. Missouri
moblzn. mobilization
Mont. Montana
MP Northern Mariana Islands
M.P. Member of Parliament
MPA Master of Public Administration
MPE, M.P.E. Master of Physical Education
MPH, M.P.H. Master of Public Health
MPhil, M.Phil. Master of Philosophy
MPL, M.P.L. Master of Patent Law
Mpls. Minneapolis
MRE, M.R.E. Master of Religious Education
MS, M.S. Master of Science
MS, Ms. Mississippi
MSc, M.Sc. Master of Science
MSChemE Master of Science in Chemical Engineering
MSF, M.S.F. Master of Science of Forestry
MST, M.S.T. Master of Sacred Theology
MSW, M.S.W. Master of Social Work
MT Montana
Mt. Mount
MTO Mediterranean Theatre of Operation
MTV Music Television
mus. museum, musical
MusB, Mus.B. Bachelor of Music
MusD, Mus.D. Doctor of Music
MusM, Mus.M. Master of Music
mut. mutual
mycol. mycological

N. North
NAACP National Association for the Advancement of Colored People
NACA National Advisory Committee for Aeronautics
NAD National Academy of Design
NAE National Academy of Engineering
NAFE National Association of Female Executives
N.Am. North America
NAM National Association of Manufacturers
NAPA National Association of Performing Artists
NARAS National Academy of Recording Arts and Sciences
NAREB National Association of Real Estate Boards
NARS National Archives and Record Service
NAS National Academy of Sciences
NASA National Aeronautics and Space Administration
nat. national
NATAS National Academy of Television Arts and Sciences
NATO North Atlantic Treaty Organization
NATOUSA North African Theatre of Operations
nav. navigation
NB, N.B. New Brunswick
NBA National Basketball Association
NBC National Broadcasting Company
NC, N.C. North Carolina
NCAA National College Athletic Association
NCCJ National Conference of Christians and Jews
ND, N.D. North Dakota
NDEA National Defense Education Act
NE Nebraska
NE, N.E. Northeast
NEA National Education Association
Nebr. Nebraska
NEH National Endowment for Humanities
neurol. neurological
Nev. Nevada
NF Newfoundland
NFL National Football League
Nfld. Newfoundland
NG National Guard
NH, N.H. New Hampshire
NHL National Hockey League
NIH National Institutes of Health
NIMH National Institute of Mental Health
NJ, N.J. New Jersey
NLRB National Labor Relations Board
NM New Mexico
N.Mex. New Mexico
No. Northern
NOAA National Oceanographic and Atmospheric Administration
NORAD North America Air Defense
Nov. November
NOW National Organization for Women

N.P.Ry. Northern Pacific Railway
nr. near
NRA National Rifle Association
NRC National Research Council
NS, N.S. Nova Scotia
NSC National Security Council
NSF National Science Foundation
NSW New South Wales
N.T. New Testament
NT Northwest Territories
numis. numismatic
NV Nevada
NW, N.W. Northwest
N.W.T. Northwest Territories
NY, N.Y. New York
N.Y.C. New York City
NYU New York University
N.Z. New Zealand

OAS Organization of American States
ob-gyn obstetrics-gynecology
obs. observatory
obstet. obstetrical
Oct. October
OD, O.D. Doctor of Optometry
OECD Organization of European
  Cooperation and Development
OEEC Organization of European
  Economic Cooperation
OEO Office of Economic Opportunity
ofcl. official
OH Ohio
OK Oklahoma
Okla. Oklahoma
ON Ontario
Ont. Ontario
oper. operating
ophthal. ophthalmological
ops. operations
OR Oregon
orch. orchestra
Oreg. Oregon
orgn. organization
ornithol. ornithological
OSHA Occupational Safety and Health
  Administration
OSRD Office of Scientific Research and
  Development
OSS Office of Strategic Services
osteo. osteopathic
otol. otological
otolaryn. otolaryngological

PA, Pa. Pennsylvania
P.A. Professional Association
paleontol. paleontological
path. pathological
PBS Public Broadcasting System
P.C. Professional Corporation
PE Prince Edward Island
P.E.I. Prince Edward Island
PEN Poets, Playwrights, Editors, Essayists
  and Novelists (international association)
penol. penological
P.E.O. women's organization (full name not
  disclosed)
pers. personnel

pfc. private first class
PGA Professional Golfers' Association of
  America
PHA Public Housing Administration
pharm. pharmaceutical
PharmD, Pharm.D. Doctor of Pharmacy
PharmM, Pharm.M. Master of Pharmacy
PhB, Ph.B. Bachelor of Philosophy
PhD, Ph.D. Doctor of Philosophy
PhDChemE Doctor of Science in Chemical
  Engineering
PhM, Ph.M. Master of Philosophy
Phila. Philadelphia
philharm. philharmonic
philol. philological
philos. philosophical
photog. photographic
phys. physical
physiol. physiological
Pitts. Pittsburgh
Pk. Park
Pkwy. Parkway
Pl. Place
Pla. Plaza
P.&L.E.R.R. Pittsburgh & Lake Erie
  Railroad
P.O. Post Office
PO Box Post Office Box
polit. political
poly. polytechnic, polytechnical
PQ Province of Quebec
PR, P.R. Puerto Rico
prep. preparatory
pres. president
Presbyn. Presbyterian
presdl. presidential
prin. principal
proc. proceedings
prod. produced
prodn. production
prof. professor
profl. professional
prog. progressive
propr. proprietor
pros. atty. prosecuting attorney
pro tem pro tempore
PSRO Professional Services Review
  Organization
psychiat. psychiatric
psychol. psychological
PTA Parent-Teachers Association
ptnr. partner
PTO Pacific Theatre of Operations, Parent
  Teacher Organization
pub. publisher, publishing, published
pub. public
publ. publication
pvt. private

quar. quarterly
qm. quartermaster
Q.M.C. Quartermaster Corps
Que. Quebec

radiol. radiological
RAF Royal Air Force
RCA Radio Corporation of America

RCAF Royal Canadian Air Force
RD Rural Delivery
Rd. Road
R&D Research & Development
REA Rural Electrification Administration
rec. recording
ref. reformed
regt. regiment
regtl. regimental
rehab. rehabilitation
rels. relations
Rep. Republican
rep. representative
Res. Reserve
ret. retired
Rev. Reverend
rev. review, revised
RFC Reconstruction Finance Corporation
RFD Rural Free Delivery
rhinol. rhinological
RI, R.I. Rhode Island
RISD Rhode Island School of Design
Rm. Room
RN, R.N. Registered Nurse
roentgenol. roentgenological
ROTC Reserve Officers Training Corps
RR Rural Route
R.R. Railroad
rsch. research
Rte. Route
Ry. Railway

S. South
s. son
SAC Strategic Air Command
SAG Screen Actors Guild
SALT Strategic Arms Limitation Talks
S.Am. South America
san. sanitary
SAR Sons of the American Revolution
Sask. Saskatchewan
savs. savings
SB, S.B. Bachelor of Science
SBA Small Business Administration
SC, S.C. South Carolina
SCAP Supreme Command Allies Pacific
ScB, Sc.B. Bachelor of Science
SCD, S.C.D. Doctor of Commercial Science
ScD, Sc.D. Doctor of Science
sch. school
sci. science, scientific
SCLC Southern Christian Leadership
  Conference
SCV Sons of Confederate Veterans
SD, S.D. South Dakota
SE, S.E. Southeast
SEATO Southeast Asia Treaty Organization
SEC Securities and Exchange Commission
sec. secretary
sect. section
seismol. seismological
sem. seminary
Sept. September
s.g. senior grade
sgt. sergeant
SHAEF Supreme Headquarters Allied
  Expeditionary Forces

SHAPE Supreme Headquarters Allied
  Powers in Europe
S.I. Staten Island
S.J. Society of Jesus (Jesuit)
SJD Scientiae Juridicae Doctor
SK Saskatchewan
SM, S.M. Master of Science
So. Southern
soc. society
sociol. sociological
S.P. Co. Southern Pacific Company
spl. special
splty. specialty
Sq. Square
S.R. Sons of the Revolution
sr. senior
SS Steamship
SSS Selective Service System
St. Saint, Street
sta. station
stats. statistics
statis. statistical
STB, S.T.B. Bachelor of Sacred Theology
stblzn. stabilization
STD, S.T.D. Doctor of Sacred Theology
Ste. Suite
subs. subsidiary
SUNY State University of New York
supr. supervisor
supt. superintendent
surg. surgical
svc. service
SW, S.W. Southwest

TAPPI Technical Association of the Pulp
  and Paper Industry
Tb. Tuberculosis
tchr. teacher
tech. technical, technology
technol. technological
Tel. & Tel. Telephone & Telegraph
temp. temporary
Tenn. Tennessee
Ter. Territory
Terr. Terrace
Tex. Texas
ThD, Th.D. Doctor of Theology
theol. theological
ThM, Th.M. Master of Theology
TN Tennessee
tng. training
topog. topographical
trans. transaction, transferred
transl. translation, translated
transp. transportation
treas. treasurer
TT Trust Territory
TV television
TVA Tennessee Valley Authority
TWA Trans World Airlines
twp. township
TX Texas
typog. typographical

U. University
UAW United Auto Workers

UCLA University of California at Los
  Angeles
UDC United Daughters of the Confederacy
U.K. United Kingdom
UN United Nations
UNESCO United Nations Educational,
  Scientific and Cultural Organization
UNICEF United Nations International
  Children's Emergency Fund
univ. university
UNRRA United Nations Relief and
  Rehabilitation Administration
UPI United Press International
U.P.R.R. United Pacific Railroad
urol. urological
U.S. United States
U.S.A. United States of America
USAAF United States Army Air Force
USAF United States Air Force
USAFR United States Air Force Reserve
USAR United States Army Reserve
USCG United States Coast Guard
USCGR United States Coast Guard Reserve
USES United States Employment Service
USIA United States Information Agency
USMC United States Marine Corps
USMCR United States Marine Corps
  Reserve
USN United States Navy
USNG United States National Guard
USNR United States Naval Reserve
USO United Service Organizations
USPHS United States Public Health Service
USS United States Ship
USSR Union of the Soviet Socialist
  Republics
USTA United States Tennis Association
USV United States Volunteers
UT Utah

VA Veterans' Administration
VA, Va. Virginia
vet. veteran, veterinary
VFW Veterans of Foreign Wars
VI, V.I. Virgin Islands
vice pres. vice president
vis. visiting
VISTA Volunteers in Service to America
VITA Volunteers in Technical Service
vocat. vocational
vol. volunteer, volume
v.p. vice president
vs. versus
VT, Vt. Vermont

W, W. West
WA Washington (state)
WAC Women's Army Corps
Wash. Washington (state)
WAVES Women's Reserve, US Naval
  Reserve
WCTU Women's Christian Temperance
  Union
we. western
W. Ger. Germany, Federal Republic of
WHO World Health Organization

WI Wisconsin
W.I. West Indies
Wis. Wisconsin
WSB Wage Stabilization Board
WV West Virginia
W.Va. West Virginia
WY Wyoming
Wyo. Wyoming

YK Yukon Territory
YMCA Young Men's Christian Association
YMHA Young Men's Hebrew Association
YM & YWHA Young Men's and Young
  Women's Hebrew Association
yr. year
YT, Y.T. Yukon Territory
YWCA Young Women's Christian
  Association

zool. zoological

Alphabetical Practices

Names are arranged alphabetically according to the surnames, and under identical surnames according to the first given name. If both surname and first given name are identical, names are arranged alphabetically according to the second given name. Where full names are identical, they are arranged in order of age—with the elder listed first.

Surnames beginning with De, Des, Du, however capitalized or spaced, are recorded with the prefix preceding the surname and arranged alphabetically under the letter D.

Surnames beginning with Mac and Mc are arranged alphabetically under M.

Surnames beginning with Saint or St. appear after names that begin Sains, and are arranged according to the second part of the name, e.g. St. Clair before Saint Dennis.

Surnames beginning with Van, Von or von are arranged alphabetically under letter V.

Compound hyphenated surnames are arranged according to the first member of the compound. Compound unhyphenated surnames are treated as hyphenated names.

Parentheses used in connection with a name indicate which part of the full name is usually deleted in common usage. Hence Abbott, W(illiam) Lewis indicates that the usual form of the given name is W. Lewis. In such a case, the parentheses are ignored in alphabetizing. However, if the name is recorded Abbott, (William) Lewis, signifying that the entire name William is not commonly used, the alphabetizing would be arranged as though the name were Abbott, Lewis.

Who Was Who in America

AACH, HERBERT, painter; b. Cologne, Germany, Mar. 24, 1923; came to U.S., 1938, naturalized, 1942; s. Leo and Frieda (Schloss) A.; m. Doris Schein, Jan. 23, 1929; children: Christopher Jeffry, John Dennis. Student, Cologne Acad. Art, 1936-37, Pratt Inst., 1940-41, Stanford U., 1942-43, Escuela de Pintura Y Escultura, Mexico, 1948-50, Bklyn. Mus. Art Sch., 1946-48, 50-51. Tech. dir. Sargent Art Material Co., Inc., Hazleton, Pa., 1954-64; tchr. Bklyn. Mus. Art Sch., 1947-48, 50-51, Kingsbridge Community Ctr., 1951-53, Hazleton Art League, 1954-64, Queens Coll., 1965-85, Scarsdale (N.Y.) Studio, 1965-85, Pratt Inst., 1965-85; chmn. dept. art Queens Coll., 1976-85; pres. Artists Tech. Research Inst., 1976-85; lectr. Mem. standing com. artists materials U.S. Govt., 1962, then mem. standard practices com. Exhibited one-man shows including Creative Gallery, 1952, 53, 54, Stroudsburg Gallery, 1957, Art Direction Gallery, 1958, Evergart Mus., 1959, Albert Landry Gallery, 1961, Pa. State U., 1962, Jacques Seligmann Gallery, 1964, 66, Hazelton Art League, 1964, Fischbach Gallery, 1966, Howard Wise Gallery, 1967, Martha Jackson Gallery, 1974, Albright Knox Mus., Buffalo, 1975, Aaron Berman Gallery, N.Y.C., 1977, Allentown Art Mus., 1978, Oberlichtsaal, Van de Welde Bldg., Weimar, German Democratic Republic, 1980, Qeens Coll., N.Y.C., 1986, Ingber Gallery, N.Y.C., 1988, numerous others; group shows include Whitney Mus., 1952, 56, Bklyn. Mus., 1956, 57, AAAL, N.Y.C., 1957, Everhart Mus., Scranton, Pa., 1958, Jacques Seligmann Gallery, N.Y.C., 1965, 69, Portland Mus. Art, Washington, 1970, Paula Cooper Gallery, N.Y.C., 1974, Bronx Mus., N.Y., 1977, Mint Mus., Charlotte, N.C., 1987, others; represented in permanent collections Met. Mus. Art, N.Y.C., Albright Knox Mus., Buffalo, Birla Acad. Art and Culture, Calcutta, India, Boston Mus., William Penn Meml. Mus., Harrisburg, Pa., Grey Gallery NYU, Corcoran Gallery Art, Washington, Harold Hart Collection, also numerous pub. and pvt. collecions; contbr. articles to profl. jours.; contbg. editor: Color Engring., 1962-85, Arts mag., 1966-85. With AUS, World War II. Recipient 1st prize Creative Gallery, 1951, Hazelton Art League Annual, 1956, 63, Roberson Meml. Ctr. Annual, 1959, numerous others. Mem. Artists Workshop Club, Intersoc. Color Council, Coll. Art Assn., Nat. Art Edn. Assn., Ea. Art Edn. Assn., Inst. Study of Art in Edn., U.S., N.Y. cacti and succulent socs., Color Forum (founding). Home: New York N.Y. Died Oct. 13, 1985; cremated.

AAGRE, CURT, merchandise broker; b. Grimstad, Norway, Oct. 11, 1909; (parents Am. citizens); s. George and Tecla (Nilsen) A.; m. Helen Winter, Oct. 19, 1946; children—Kim O'Connor, Dee Zeitounian. Student, Columbia U., N.Y.C., 1927-28, NYU, N.Y.C., 1929-30; Grad., Pace Inst., N.Y.C., 1933; postgrad., Harvard U., 1948. Various positions to asst. div. sales mgr. Corn Products Refining Co. (now C.P.C. Internat.), N.Y.C., 1926-40; fgn. rep. Corn Products Refining Co. (now C.P.C. Internat.), Mexico, 1947-48, Europe, 1949-52; asst. sales mgr. Hubinger Co., N.Y.C., 1953-59; sales mgr. Connell Rice & Sugar Co., Westfield, N.J., 1960-63; sales mgr. nat. accounts Olavarria & Co., N.Y.C., 1963; asst. v.p. Lamborn & Co. Inc., N.Y.C., 1964-69, v.p., mgr. diversification program, from 1969; activated Curt Aagre Co., Westfield, N.J., pres.; mgr. Sweetener div. All Star Dairy Assn. Trustee, Westfield Adult Sch. Served from pvt. to acting col. AUS, 1941-46. Decorated D.S.M., Bronze Star; Philippine Govt. decorations; Grand Marshall Westfield, N.J. Meml. Day Parade, 1984, 86. Mem. Harvard Alumni Assn., Am. Inst. Mgmt., Nat. Confectioners Salesman Assn., N.Y. Sugar Club, N.Y. Preservers Assn., Sales Exec. Club, Candy Execs., VFW, Am. Legion, Nat. Sugar Brokers Assn. Presbyterian. Club: Harvard Bus. Sch. Lodge: Rotary (Westfield). Died Jan. 6, 1987; buried Fairview Cemetery, Westfield, N.J.

AAMODT, OLAF SVERRE, agronomist; b. St. Paul, Aug. 9, 1892; s. August and Julia (Hagen) A.; m. Monica Evelyn Jones, Oct. 27, 1923; children: Phyllis Monica, Joan Gura. BS, U. Minn., 1917, MS, PhD, 1927. Student asst. Coll. Agr. U. Minn., 1912; sci. asst. cereal div. U.S. Dept. Agr., St. Paul, 1917; plant pathologist U.S. Dept. Agr., 1920-28; prof. genetics and plant breeding U. Alta., Edmonton, Can., 1928-35, head dept. field crops, 1930-35; prof. agronomy and chmn. dept. U. Wis., 1935-39; head div. forage crops and diseases U.S. Dept. Agr., Washington, 1939-52, plant sci. specialist Agrl. Rsch. Svc., 1952-55; cons. ICA, 1955-56, chief party U. Ky. Coll. Contract-ICA, 1957-60; cons. agrl. prodn. and edn., from 1961; exploratory investigations agr. problems, Alaska, 1946; made survey agrl. rsch. in Western Europe, Brit. Isles and Scandynavian countries, agrl. economy Uruguay for Internat. Bank and UN, 1950, agrl. survey Mediterranean area for FAO and Orgn. European Econ. Cooperation, 1951-52, tech. cooperation and agrl. survey Middle and Far East countries for Fgn. Ops. Adminstrn., 1953-54. With U.S. Army, 1917-20. Contbr. sci. articles. Fellow AAAS, Am. Soc. Agronomy (pres. 1948); mem. Genetic Soc. Am., Am. Naturalists, Acacia, Alpha Zeta, Sigma Xi, Gamma Alpha, Gamma Sigma Delta. Home: Hyattsville Md. †

AARON, CHARLES, lawyer; b. N.Y.C., Dec. 28, 1890; s. Abraham S. and Fannie (Charness) A.; m. Geraldine S. Weisfeldt, Feb. 2, 1964. JD, John Marshall Law Sch., 1911. Bar: Ill. 1912. Pvt. practice Chgo., from 1912; sr. ptnr. Aaron, Aaron, Schimberg & Hess and predecessors, Chgo., 1922-77, of counsel, 1977-86; bd. dirs. Mangood Corp., Beatty Machine and Mfg. Co., Erman Corp., Inc., also other corps. Bd. dirs., past pres. USO, Chgo. Jewish Fedn. Chgo. (Julius Rosenwald Gold Medal award), Nat. Jewish Welfare Bd., Jewish Community Ctrs. of Chgo.; founder, life mem. bd. dirs. Lincoln Park Zool. Soc.; former dir., mem. exec. com. Chgo. chpt. ARC: mem. citizens bd. U. Chgo., past mem. vis. com. Law Sch. Fellow Brandeis U.; recipient Distinguished Alumnus award John Marshall Law School. Fellow Chgo. Bar Found.; mem. ABA, Ill. Bar Assn. (sr. councillor), Chgo. Bar Assn. (bd. mgrs. 1927-29), Assn. of Bar of City of N.Y., Northwestern U. Assocs., Commercial, Mid-Day, Standard, Tavern, Lake Shore Country, Northmoor Country. Home: Chicago Ill. Died Sept. 25, 1986; interred Rosehill Mausoleum, Chgo.

ABBETT, ROBERT WILLIAM, consulting engineer; b. Jamesport, Mo., Dec. 23, 1902; s. Phillip Allen and Virginia Abbett; m. Ruth Virginia Bloomer, Oct. 1953; 1 son, Robert William. B.S., U. Mo., Rolla, 1927; C.E., U. Mo., 1933; M.S., Yale, 1932; ScD (hon.), Gettysburg Coll., 1953. Surveyor, designer, engr. constrn. rys., mcpl. projects, bridges, bldgs. for various pvt. and govt. agys., 1923-29; instr. dept. civil engring Yale, 1929-33; assoc. prof. civil engring. Union Coll., Schenectady, N.Y., 1933-39; assoc. Parsons, Klapp, Brinckerhoff & Douglas, also Waddell & Hardesty (cons. engrs.), N.Y.C., 1938-40; asst. prof. civil engring. Columbia U., 1940-41; founding ptnr. Tippets Abbett McCarthy Stratton (engrs. and architects), N.Y.C., from 1945; cons. engr. U.S. and fgn. rys., hwys., bridges, port devel., harbor works, mineral devel. projects. Author: Engineering Contracts and Specifications; editor in chief: American Civil Engineering Practice; contbr. articles to profl. mags. Served to comdr. C.E., USNR, 1941-45. Mem. ASCE, Am. Cons. Engrs. Council, Yale Club, Univ. Club, Anglers Club, Sigma Xi. Home: New York N.Y. Deceased.

ABBOTT, CHARLES CORTEZ, university dean; b. Lawrence, Kans., Oct. 30, 1906; s. Wilbur Cortez and Margaret Ellen (Smith) A.; m. Louise Slocum, 1934; children: Margaret Ellen, Louise Austin, Charles C., William S., Preston H. AB, Harvard U., 1928, AM, 1930, PhD, 1933. Instr. econs. Harvard U., Cambridge, Mass., 1931-37, asst. prof. bus. econ. Grad. Sch. Bus. Adminstrn., 1937-40, assoc. prof., 1940-46, prof., 1946-54; dean Darden Grad Sch. Bus. Adminstrn., U. Va., Charlottesville, 1954-72; with War Shipping Adminstrn., 1942-43; bd. dirs. Chesapeake Corp. of Va. Author: The New York Bond Market, 1920-30, 1937, Financing Business During the Transition, 1946, Management of the Federal Debt, 1946; editor: Basic Financial Research: Needs and Prospects, 1966; contbr. articles to profl. jours. Trustee Conn. chpt. Nature Conservancy. Mem. Phi Beta Kappa. Clubs: Harvard (N.Y.C.); Union (Boston). Home: Pomfret Center Conn. Died May 8, 1986.

ABBOTT, CHESTER G., banker; b. Lynn, Mass., June 1, 1890; s. Lewis H. A.; m. Olive Barnes, Oct. 16, 1915; children: Nancy B. Abbott Thompson, Mary L. Abbott Samp. AB, Bowdoin Coll., 1913; LLD, U. Maine. Salesman Henley-Kimball Co., Portland, Maine, 1914-16, state mgr., 1916-25, v.p., gen. mgr., 1924-29; gen. sales mgr. Hudson Motor Car Co., Detroit, 1929-31, asst. gen. mgr., 1931-34, dir., 1929-35; pres. Transport Co., 1935-42; v.p. 1st Portland Nat. Bank, 1942-49, pres. from 1950, chmn. exec. com., also bd. dirs.; bd. dirs. Haverford Bros. Co., Oxford Paper Co., Maine Bonding and Casualty Co., Portland Stove Foundry. Pres. bd. overseers Bowdoin Coll.; pres. Portland Community Chest. Mem. Am. Bankers Assn. (exec. com. nat. bank div.), Maine Bankers Assn. (pres.), C. of C. (pres.). Home: Falmouth Maine. †

ABBOTT, LAWRENCE, author, economist; b. Cornwall, N.Y., July 9, 1902; s. Ernest Hamlin and May Louise (Kleberg) A.; m. Ann Sands Tatham, Oct. 22, 1932; children: Vaighan, Sarah Tatham, Pauline Sands (Mrs. Kenneth E. McMurtry);m. Marie Bohrn Lamnert, Dec. 9, 1966. AB in Music cum laude, Harvard U., 1924; AM, Columbia U., 1945, PhD, 1951. Advt. writer, publicity writer and mgr. country inn 1924-33; mem. writing staff program dept. NBC, 1934-42; mem. faculty Hotchkiss Sch., 1943-47; instr. econs. Columbia U., N.Y.C., 1947-51; assoc. prof. econs. Mt. Holyoke Coll., South Hadley, Mass., 1951-53; assoc. prof. econs. Union Coll., 1953-56, prof., 1956-68, prof. emeritus, 1968-85, chmn. dept. econs., 1962-66; Fulbright lectr. Pierce Coll., Athens, Greece, 1966-67. Contbr. monthly music rev. column Rolls and Discs, 1925-28; contbg. editor Time mag., 1942-43; author: (books) Student's Workbooks and Teacher's Guide, 1936-41, Approach to Music, 1940, Listener's Book on Harmony, 1941, Quality and Competition, 1955, Economics and the Modern World, 1960, rev. edit., 1967, World Federalism: What? Why? How?, 1975, rev. edit., 1982; (song) The Ghost of John McCrae, 1928. Mem. Am. Econ. Assn., AAUP, Royal Econ. Soc., World Federalists Assn. (chmn, publs. com. Edn. Fund 1973-85, bd. dirs. 1975-85, exec. com. 1979-85, sec. 1982, editor jour. 1981-85, del. Tokyo Congress 1980, Netherlands Congress 1983), Century Club. Home: Coventry Conn. Died Dec. 8, 1985.

ABBOTT, TALBERT WARD, educator; b. Otwell, Ind., Aug. 21, 1892; s. McCrillis and Emma (Haupt) A.; m. Hazel Ervin, Dec. 20, 1930; children, Ellen, Frank. AB, U. Ind., 1918; AM, Harvard U., 1922; PhD, U. Ill., 1928. Rural instr. pub. schs. of Ind., 1912-18; asst. in chemistry Harvard U., 1921-22; prof. chemistry So. Ill. U., Carbondale, from 1928, dir. extension, 1938-45, dir. placements, 1944-45, dean Coll. Liberal Arts and Scis., from 1945, acting dean academic affairs, 1960-61. Author: (with others) Experimental General Chemistry, 1940, rev. ed., 1949. Cpl. Signal Corps, AEF, 1918-19. Mem. AAAU, Am. Chem. Soc., Ill. Edn. Assn. (2d v.p. of so. div.), Masons, Jackson County Country Club (Carbondale), Sigma Xi, Phi Kappa Phi, Phi Lambda Upsilon, Alpha Chi Sigma, Gamma Alpha. Republican. Presbyterian. Home: Carbondale Ill. †

ABEL, CHARLES, author, editor, publisher; b. London, Eng., Oct. 12, 1891; s. Juan Carlos and Anna Augusta Eliza (Griepenkerl) A.; m. Florence E. Lunte, Oct. 4, 1929 (dec.). Student pub. schs. and, DeWitt Clinton High Sch., N.Y.C. Pres. Charles Abel Inc.; editor, pub. The Profl. Photographer, from 1914, The Comml. Photographer, 1925-50, various other photog. periodicals; sec. O-M-I Internat. Photog. Assn., 1927-32; exec. mgr. Photographers Assn. Am., 1933-49; officer numerous other state and local photog. orgns., 1925-33. Author, co-author or compiler more than 30 books, latest being: Photography: Careers and Opportunities for You, 1960; numerous booklets and articles on photog. subjects; owner large collections photog. lit. Dir. Nat. Code Authority for Portrait and Comml. Photog. Industry; life trustee Winona Sch. Photography, Winona Lake, Ind.; mem. adv. com. Rochester (N.Y.) Inst. Tech. Maj. U.S. Army, 1917-19; recommd. lt. col. A.G. Res. 1919-29; apptd. col. Staff Gov. La., 1950. Decorated D.S.M., 1945; recipient hon. degree M. Photography, Photographers Assn. Am., 1939, Nat. Award placque, 1959. Fellow Royal Photog. Soc. Gt. Brit.; mem. Photog. Soc. Am. (assoc.), Profl. Photog. Am. (hon., life), Profl. Photog. Soc. Ohio (hon., life), Conn. Profl. Photog. Assn., (hon., life), Ky. Photog. Assn. (hon, life), S.E. Mass. Photog. Guild (hon, life), Cleve. So. Profl. Photographers (hon., life), Ohio Profl. Photographers Assn., Cleve. Athletic Club, Shrine Luncheon Club (pres. 1945), City Club, Masons (32 deg.), Shriner. Home: Cleveland Ohio. †

ABEL, I(ORWITH) W(ILBUR), labor union official; b. Magnolia, Ohio, Aug. 11, 1908; s. John Franklin and Mary Ann (Jones) A.; m. Bernice N. Joseph, June 27, 1930; children: Karen, Linda. Grad., Canton (Ohio) Actual Bus. Coll. With Am. Sheet & Tin Plate Co. (now subsidiary, U.S. Steel Corp.), Canton, 1925-33; staff United Steelworkers Am., 1937-87; sec.-treas. nat. orgn., 1953-65, pres. nat. orgn., 1965-77; v.p. AFL-CIO, after 1965. Mem. War Manpower Commn., War Labor Bd., World War II. Democrat. Lutheran. Home: Pittsburgh Pa. Died Aug. 10, 1987.

ABEL, WALTER, actor; b. St. Paul, June 6, 1898; s. Richard Michael and Christine (Becker) A.; m. Marietta Bitner, Sept. 24, 1926; children: Jonathan , Michael. Student, Am. Acad. Dramatic Arts, N.Y.C., 1916-18, U. Wis., 1923. Debut in N.Y.C. in Forbidden, 1919, has since appeared in numerous plays including Back to Methuselah, 1919, S.S. Glencairn, 1924, Mourning Becomes Electra, 1931, When Ladies Meet, 1932, Merrily We Roll Along, 1934, The Wingless Victory, 1938, The Pleasure of His Company, 1957, Saturday, Sunday, Monday, 1974, Trelawny of the Wells, 1976; toured in In Praise of Love, summer 1975; first film appearance The Three Musketers, 1934, has since appeared in 80 films including Arise My Love, 1942, Hold Back the Dawn, 1943, Fury, 1943, Mr. Skeffington, 1944, Skylark, 1944, 13 Rue Madleine, 1944, The Fabulous Joe, 1944, Kiss and Tell, 1945, Man Without a Country, 1973; star film We Have Come of Age; numerous radio and TV appearances, including The American Woman: Portraits in Courage, 1976. Mem. Nat. Council Sr. Citizens, Screen Actors Guild (council 1937-47), Actors Equity (dir. 1932-34, 58-67), ANTA (pres. 1966-67, v.p. 1969-87), Dutch Treat, Players. Home: Ivoryton Conn. Died Mar. 26, 1987.

ABELES, CHARLES TAUSSIG, railroad attorney; b. St. Louis, July 22, 1891; s. J. David and Emily (Taussig) A.; m. Sally Pope Taylor, May 8, 1926; children: Charles Calvert, Sally Taylor. AB, Harvard U., 1913, LLB, 1916. Bar: Mo. 1916. With Boyle & Priest, St. Louis, 1916-17; atty. S.A.L. Ry., Norfolk, Va., 1919-26, solicitor, 1926-34, asst. gen. solicitor, 1934-38, gen. atty., 1938-43, sr. gen. atty., 1943; gen. solicitor S.A.L. Ry. Co. and its subs., from 1956. Pres. Norfolk Forum, 1946-50, Norfolk Servicemen's Club; chmn. Norfolk Commn. on Higher Edn.; bd. dirs. Mus. Arts and Scis., DePaul Hosp., Norfolk and Community Concerts Assn., Richmond Red Cross; trustee Hermitage Found., Norfolk. Mem. ABA, Va. Bar Assn., Mo. Bar Assn., Assn. ICC Practitioners, Newcomen Soc., Virginia Club (Norfolk), Princess Anne Country Club, Commonwealth Club, Yacht Club (Norfolk), Country Club (Norfolk), Harvard Club (N.Y.C.).,. Home: Richmond Va. †

ABELSON, HAROLD HERBERT, educator; b. N.Y.C., Sept. 25, 1904; s. Max and Jennie (Bernstein) A.; m. Lucie Bernard, Aug. 24, 1926; children: Jane Frances Abelson Wildhorn, Robert Bernard. Student, Townsend Harris Hall, 1917-20; B.E., CCNY, 1924; A.M., Columbia U., 1925, Ph.D., 1927. Tutor dept. edn. CCNY, 1924-28, instr., 1928-35, asst. prof., 1935-42, assoc. prof., 1942-48, prof., 1948-66, dir. ednl. clinic, 1941-52, dean Sch. Edn., 1952-66; acting dean tchr. edn. CUNY, 1966-67, prof. div. tchr. edn., 1967-74, prof., dean emeritus, 1974-89; dir. ednl. clinic CCNY, 1941-52; sr. research assoc. Human Interaction Research Inst., Los Angeles, 1974-89; prof. U. Colo., summer 1938, Cornell U., summer 1949-50, Hunter Coll., summer 1952-58; vis. lectr. New Sch. Social Research, 1948-60, Lehman Coll., 1967-74; expert cons. adj. gen. office War Dept., summer 1944; pres. Interstate Tchr. Edn. Conf., 1962; chmn. adv. bd. Emeritus Coll., Santa Monica Coll., 1974-76. Author: Art of Educational Research; co-author: Putting Knowledge to Use; contbr. articles to profl. jours. Recipient Townsend Harris medal City Coll. Alumni Assn., 1962. Fellow Am. Psychol. Assn., AAAS; mem. Am. Edn. Research Assn., Western Psychol. Assn., City Coll. Alumni Assn., Columbia Grad. Sch. Alumni Assn., Phi Beta Kappa, Kappa Delta Pi. Home: Santa Monica Calif. Died Feb. 6, 1989.

ABERASTAIN, JOSE MANUEL, ballet master; b. San Luis, Argentina, May 14, 1938; came to U.S., 1970; s. Ladislao and Margarita Maria (Quiroga) A. Student, U. Buenos Aires, Teatro Colon. Mem. faculty Washington Sch. Ballet, 1970-72, Pa. Ballet Sch., 1972-74, Va. Intermont Coll., 1974-76; asst. prof. ballet Dallas Ballet Acad., So. Methodist U., from 1981; guest tchr., master classes U.S. and abroad; choreographer, 1971. Dancer, Teatro Colon ballet co., 1959-62, Nat. Ballet Cuba, 1962-64, Classical Ballet Mex., 1964-66, Chilean Nat. Ballet, 1966-68, Stuttgart (W. Ger.) Ballet, 1968-70, ballet master, Ohio Ballet, 1976-81; prin. works include Divergence, performed by Washington Ballet and, Bristol Concert Ballet, Children's Games, Bristol Concert Ballet. Deceased.

ABERNETHY, JOHN LEO, chemistry educator; b. San Jose, Calif., Mar. 6, 1915; s. Elmer Robert and Margaret May (Scott) A. B.A., UCLA, 1936; M.S., Northwestern U., 1938, Ph.D., 1940. Instr. U.Tex., 1940-42, asst. prof., 1942-44, assoc. prof., 1944-45; fellow Northwestern U., Evanston, Ill., 1946; mem. faculty Washington and Lee U., 1948-49, Calif. State U., 1947-59; research assoc. UCLA, 1959-69; prof. chemistry Calif. State Poly. U., Pomona, 1969—. Author: Principles of Organic Chemistry, 1949. Mem. editorial bd. Jour. Chem. Edn., 1956—. Contbr. articles to chem. jours. Adv., Intervarsity Christian Fellowship, 1956-59. Fulbright fellow San Marcos U., Lima, Peru, 1962-63. Mem. Am. Chem. Soc., Am. Sci. Affiliation, Calif. Assn. Chemistry Tchrs. (editor proc. 1966—) Sigma Xi (local pres.), Alpha Chi Sigma, Phi Lambda Upsilon. †

ABRONS, LOUIS W(ILLIAM), business executive; b. Russia, June 16, 1887; came to U.S., 1894; naturalized, 1898; s. Simon and Kate A.; m. Anne Schroeder, Aug. 4, 1911 (dec.); children: Herbert, Rita Abrons Aranow, Alan, Richard; m. 2d, Marguerite S. Baer, May 23, 1958. BSCE, U. Mich., 1908. Govt. engr. The Philippines, 1908-10; asst. to pres. Rutland (Vt.) Mfg. Co., 1911-14; treas. Harby Abrons & Melius Builders, 1917-28; pres. Gen. Realty & Utilities Corp., 1929-40; bd. dirs. Beaunit Mills, Inc., Cen. Nat. Corp., Barbizon-Pla. Hotel., Sterling Stores, Inc., 1st Westchester Nat. Bank. Trustee New Rochelle Hosp. Mem. Univ. Mich. Club, Quaker Ridge Golf Club. Home: New Rochelle N.Y. †

ACCURSO, ANTHONY SALVATORE, artist. s. Carl Joseph and Mary Civita (Iannella) A. Student, Bklyn. Mus. Art Sch., 1950-52, Sch. Art and Design, N.Y.C., 1954-57, Pratt Inst., 1961-69, Sch. Visual Arts, N.Y.C., 1977. Exhibited group show, Bronx Mus. Arts in Cooperation with Met. Mus. Art, N.Y.C., 1972, Notre Dame U. Law Sch., 1973, Harbor Gallery, L.I., N.Y., 1975, Syracuse U., 1976, Huntsville Mus. Art, Ala., 1976, Galerie Mouffe, Paris, 1978, Galerie Vallombreuse, Biarritz, France, 1977, John Jay Coll. Criminal Justice, 1987; illustrator: Sci. Digest mag., N.Y.C., 1960-67; illustrator-corr., trial-courtroom-news media artist: ABC-TV World News Tonight, Washington, N.Y.C., Chgo. and Atlanta, 1969-87, WABC-TV Eyewitness News, N.Y.C., 1969-87, Nightline ABC-TV News, N.Y.C., 1980, Cable News Network, N.Y. bur., 1980, MacNeil-Lehrer Report, PBS-TV, 1979, RAI Italian TV, 1985, Newsday, N.Y.C., 1986; illustrator: Newsweek mag., 1974-87; TV program ABC-TV series Close up, 1980; artist-actor: TV series All My Children, 1979, 81, 85, One Life to Live, 1985; illustrator: book Man's Contact with UFO's, 1974; motion picture Mysteries From Beyond Earth, 1975. Recipient Gold medal Accademia Italia delle Arti del Lavoro, Parma, Italy, 1980, Recommendation Knights of Malta, 1985. Home: Brooklyn N.Y. Died Oct. 23, 1987.

ACHILLES, THEODORE CARTER, international organization official; b. Rochester, N.Y., Dec. 29, 1905; s. Henry Lawrence and Gertrude (Strong) A.; A.B., Stanford U., 1925; postgrad. Yale U., 1926-28; m. Marian Field, June 4, 1933; children—Marian Achilles O'Brien, Theodore Carter, Daphne, Stephen. Newspaper work in Calif. and Japan, 1928-31; vice-consul, Havana, 1932, Rome, 1933; assigned to Dept. State, 1935; sec. Am. embassy, London, 1939; chargé d'affaires ad interim near govts. Poland, Belgium, Netherlands and Norway, 1940; assigned Dept. State, Washington, 1941, asst. chief. div. Brit. Commonwealth Affairs, 1944, chief, 1944; 1st sec. Am. embassy, London, 1945, Brussels, 1946; dir. Western European Affairs, Dept. State, 1947; U.S. vice dep. NATO, London, 1950-52; minister, Paris, 1952-60; ambassador to Peru, 1956-60; counselor Dept. State, Washington, 1960, spl. asst. to sec. of state, dir. Ops. Center, 1961-62; cons. NASA, 1963-68; vice chmn. Atlantic Council U.S., from 1962; vice-chmn. Internat. Mgmt. and Devel. Inst., from 1965; gov. Atlantic Inst., Paris, 1969-73; mem. U.S. del. ILO Conf., 1941, UN Conf. on Food and Agr., 1943, UN Conf. on Internat. Orgn., San Francisco, 1945, Council Fgn. Ministers, London, 1945, first session UN Assembly, London, 1946, 2d session, N.Y., 1947; Paris Conf., 1946, North Atlantic Pact Negotiations, 1948-49, NATO, 1950-52, 60, CENTO, SEATO and Colombo Plan Confs., 1960. Mem. Beta Theta Pi. Clubs: Metropolitan, Chevy Chase, Alibi (Washington); Yale, Brook (N.Y.C.). Co-editor Atlantic Community Quar., 1963-75. Home: Washington D.C. Died Apr. 8, 1986; interred columbarium of St. Johns Church Lafayete Iguere, Washington.

ADAMS, CARROLL P(ARKER), organization executive; b. Plymouth, Mich., Jan. 18, 1892; s. Frank B. and Mary S. (Bryant) A.; m. Hazel Gould, Oct. 1917 (div. 1933); 1 dau., Barbara Nancy Adams Jones; m. 2d, Olive Smith Bigelow, July 1, 1934 (dec. 1942); m. 3d, Franc Stannard Prine, Oct. 23, 1942. Student, U. Mich., 1911-13. Sales exec. Detroit Steel Products Co., 1916-28; exec. sec. U. Mich. Alumni Club, Detroit, 1928-33; mem. staff domestic rels. div. Wayne County Cir. Ct., Ind., 1933-41; mem. staff indsl. dept. Detroit Bd. Commerce, 1941-42; office mgr. Strong, Carlisle & Hammond Co., 1942-44; internat. exec. sec. Soc. Preservation and Encouragement Barbershop Quartet Singing Am., Inc. 1944-53, emeritus from 1953; exec. sec. Bennington County Indsl. Corp., 1953-59, Vt. Rep. State Com., from 1959. Mem. Assn. Male Choruses Am. (v.p. 1944-48), Midwest Conf. Male Choruses (bd. govs., pres.), Mich. Male Choruses Assn. (sec.-treas. 1927-51), SAR, Soc. Preservation and Encouragement Barber Shop Quartet Singing Am. (nat. v.p. 1940-41, nat. pres. 1941-42, nat. sec. 1942-44), Orpheus Club, Lost Lake Woods Club, Adcraft Club, Economic Club, Bohemians Club, Toastmasters Club, Masons, Rotary, Pi Upsilon Rho. Congregationalist. Home: Montpelier Vt. †

ADAMS, EARL CLINTON, lawyer; b. San Jose, Calif., May 12, 1892; s. John F. and Alice (Sinclair) A.; m. Ilse Downey, Oct. 14, 1922; children: Nancy Adams Holliday, Robert Pierce. AB, Stanford U., 1916, JD, 1920; postgrad., Harvard U., 1916-17. Bar: Calif. 1920. Practiced in L.A., from 1924; sr. ptnr. Adams, Duque & Hazeltine, from 1946; asst. commr. corps. State of Calif., 1923-26; bd. dirs. L.A. Steel Casing Co., L.A. By-Products Co. Mem. exec. com. L.A. chpt. Nat. Found. 2d lt. F.A., U.S. Army, World War I. Mem. ABA, Calif. Bar Assn., L.A. Bar Assn., Stock Exchange Club, Calif. Club, L.A. Club, Phi Delta Phi, Delta Tau Delta. Home: San Marino Calif. Deceased.

ADAMS, ELEANOR N., college president; b. Lebanon, Ohio; d. John Mortimer and Eleanor (Maxwell) Adams, m. Randolph Matthews, 1929. BA, U. Cin., 1902, MA, 1904; rsch. student, Oxford U., Eng., 1904, 07, 10; PhD, Yale U., 1914. Tchr. pvt. schs., Cin., util 1911; instr. English U. Cin., 1911-12; prof. English Oxford (Ohio) Coll. for Women, 1915-18, pres., 1918-28. Author: Old English Scholarship in England, 1917; editor: The Old Flatboatmen's Trail (by Sarah Sullivan), 1935. Mem. League of Am. Pen Women, MLA Am., Am. Acad. Polit. Sci., Kappa Alpha Theta. Home: Cincinnati Ohio †

ADAMS, FREDERICK JAY, oil executive; b. Salem, Tex., July 26, 1892; s. George and Orinda (Scott) A; m. Lena Brown, Oct. 11, 1920; 1 dau., Jackie Adams Manning. Student, Beaumont Bus. Coll., 1909, Harvard U., 1951. Joined Gulf Oil Corp., Gulf Refining Co., Beaumont, Tex., 1910; asst. to v.p. in charge ops. Ft. Worth dist. Gulf Oil Corp., Gulf Refining Co., 1918-24, gen. agt. in charge ops., 1924-50, v.p. in charge Ft. Worth div., 1950-54; ret., independent oil operator Ft. Worth, Tex., 1954; bd. dirs. Southwest Expn. and Fat Stock Show; trustee Mary Couts Burnett Trust; mem. expansion program com., Tex. Christian U. 2d lt., U.S.A., 1917-18. Mem. Tex. Mid-Continent Oil and Gas Assn. (bd. dirs.), Am. Petroleum Inst., Am. Inst. Mining and Metall. Engrs., Masons, Ft. Worth Club (bd. govs.). Home: Fort Worth Tex. †

ADAMS, GEORGE PLIMPTON, professor of philosophy; b. Northboro, Mass., Oct. 7, 1882; s. Edwin Augustus and Caroline Amelia (Plimpton) A.; m. Mary Knowles Woodle, June 30, 1908: children: George Plimpton, Cornelia Sheldon, John Edwin. Student, Lewis Inst., Chgo., 1897-1900; AB, Harvard U., 1903, AM, 1906, PhD, 1911; LLD, U. Calif., 1954. Instr. biology Lewis Inst., Chgo., 1903-05, 1906-08; instr. philosophy U. Calif., 1908-09, asst. prof., 1909-12, assoc. prof., 1912-18, prof., 1918-32, Mills prof. mental and moral philosophy, 1932-54, prof. emeritus, chmn. of dept. of philosophy, 1933-35, dean Coll. Letters and Sci., from 1943; Messenger lectr. Cornell U., 1939; Woodbridge lectr. and vis. prof. philosophy Columbia U., 1946. Author: Idealism and the Modern Age, 1918, Man and Metaphysics, 1948; edited U. Calif. publs. in philos., 17 vols., 1923-40. Mem. Am. Philos. Assn., Phi Beta Kappa. Home: Berkeley Calif. †

ADAMS, J(AMES) DONALD, editor, writer; b. N.Y.C., Sept. 24, 1891; s. James and Mary Louise (Barron) A.; m. Elvine Georgievna Simeon, Dec. 1921 (div.); 1 child, Mary Louise Adams Orth-Pallavicini; m. Jacqueline Winston Holt, June, 1953. AB cum laude, Harvard U., 1913. Mem. U.S. Geol. Survey, Mt. Ranier, Wash., summer 1913; tchr. English U. Wash., 1913-14; reporter New Bedford (Mass.) Evening Standard, 1915, Seattle Post Intelligencer, 1916-17; reporter Providence Jour., 1916-17, asst. Sunday editor, 1919; reporter, then editorial writer N.Y. Sun and Herald, 1920-24; asst. editor N.Y. Times Book Rev., 1924-25, editor, 1925-43, contbg. editor, condr. Page Two, weekly columnist "Speaking of Books", from 1943; editorial adviser E.P. Dutton & Co., 1945-46. Author: The Shape of Books to Come, 1944, Literary Frontiers, 1951, Copey of Harvard: A Biography of Charles Townsend Copeland, 1960, The Magic and Mystery of Words, 1963; editor: The Treasure Chest: An Anthologhy of Contemplative Prose, 1945, The New Treasure Chest, 1953, Triumph Over Odds: An Anthology of Man's Unconquerable Spirit, 1957 (Christopher award 1958). Chancellor Am. Acad. Poets. With U.S. Army, 1917-19. Mem. PEN (del. Edinburgh Congress, 1934, Buenos Aires, 1936), Poetry Soc. Am. (pres. 1945-46), Pilgrims Soc., Authors Guild Authors' League Am., Soc. Silurians, Explorers Club, Century Club, Harvard Club, Dutch Treat Club. †

ADAMS, JAMES FAIRCHILD, business executive; b. N.Y.C., Nov. 9, 1892; s. William Crittenden and Grace Fairchild (James) A.; m. Katharine Place, Nov. 9, 1916; children: Grace Joy (Mrs. Joe Jones), Catherine Curtis (Mrs. C. Paul Mailloux), Jean Place (Mrs. John Ballard Blake), James Crittenden. BS, Princeton U., 1915; LLD, Union Coll., 1959. Apprentice Aluminum Co. Am., New Kensington, Pa., 1915-17; rsch. engr. Manning Abrasive Co. (name now Norton Co.), Troy, N.Y., 1919-22; gen. mgr. John A. Manning Paper Co., Inc. (name now Manning), 1922-38, bd. dirs., 1923-69, v.p., gen. mgr., 1930-38, pres., gen. mgr., 1938-58, chmn. bd., 1958-69; pres. Internat. Purchasing Co., Boston, 1943-63, v.p., 1963-69; bd. dirs. Eberhard Faber, Inc. Pres. bd. trustees Albany (N.Y.) Med. Coll., 1953-64, v.p., 1964-67; trustee Dudley Obs., Albany, Vassar Coll., Poughkeepsie, N.Y., 1939-47; gov. Union U., 1939-49, 53-64. 1st lt. C.W.S., U.S. Army, 1917-18. Mem. Newcomen Soc. Eng. (Am. br.), Am. Legion, Schuyler Meadows Club, Century Assn. †

ADAMS, JOHN CRANFORD, college president; b. Boston, Oct. 11, 1903; s. John Davis and Mary (Cranford) A.; m. Alice deBois Murray, July 2, 1929; children: Charles Murray, Joan deBois. AB, Cornell U., 1926, PhD, 1935; student, King's Coll., Cambridge, Eng., 1926-28; LLD, NYU, 1958. Instr. English

Syracuse U., 1928-29; instr. English Cornell U., 1930-37, asst. prof., 1937-43, assoc. prof., 1943-44; pres. Hofstra Coll., since July 1944; sec.-treas. Assn. Colls. and Univs. of State N.Y., 1947-50, pres., 1950-52; mem. State Exam. Bd. State Edn. Dept. N.Y., 1945-52; commr. Instns. Higher Edn., Middle States Assn., 1956-86; mem. adv. bd. U.S. Mcht. Marine Acad., Kings Point, N.Y.; trustee Met. Ednl. TV Assn., 1954-86; mem. Commn. on Non-Tax Supported Colls. and Univs. of State N.Y., 1957-86. Author: The Globe Playhouse, 1942. Built 1/12 scale model of Globe Playhouse now on exhibit at Shakespeare Library. Contbr. to lit. jours. Bd. dirs. Nassau County ARC; mem. joint com. ednl. television Am. Council on Edn., Ednl. TV programs Inst.; chmn. TV com. Am. Council on Edn., 1953-57, 2d vice chmn. council, 1957-58. Sr. research fellow Folger Shakespeare Library, Washington, 1937-38. Mem. Modern Language Assn. (trustee 1955-86), Nat. Multiple Sclerosis Soc. (bd. trustees Nassau Co. chpt.), Malone Soc. (Eng.), Andiron (hon. assoc.), Grolier, University, Cherry Valley, Garden City Golf, Hempstead Golf, Phi Beta Kappa, Phi Kappa Phi, Chi Phi. Republican. Unitarian. Home: Garden City N.Y. Died Nov. 24, 1986.

ADAMS, JOHN QUINCY, insurance company executive; b. Dover, Mass., Dec. 24, 1922; s. Arthur and Margery (Lee) A.; m. Nancy Motley, Feb. 1, 1947; children: Nancy Barton, John Quincy, Margery Lee, Benjamin Crowninshield. Student, St. Paul's Sch., 1941; A.B., Harvard U., 1945. With John Hancock Mut. Ins. Co., 1947-87, 2d v.p., 1961-65, v.p., 1965-68, sr. v.p., 1968-87; dir., chmn. John Hancock Venture Capital Mgmt., Inc.; dir. Zurn Industries, John Hancock Growth Fund, John Hancock Advisers, Inc., John Hancock U.S. Govt. Securities Fund, John Hancock Investors, John Hancock Income Securities, Mass. Bus Devel. Corp., Independence Investment Assocs., Tucker Anthony Holding Corp.; trustee John Hancock Tax-Exempt Trust, Provident Instn. for Savs., Real Estate Investment Trust, John Hancock Cash Mgmt. Trust. Mem. com. on univ. resources Harvard; bd. dirs. New Eng. Historic Seaport; mem. corp. Mus. of Sci.; bd. overseers Boston Symphony Orch. Home: Dover Mass. Died July 20, 1987; buried Highland Cemetery, Dover, Mass.

ADAMS, LOUISE HARDING, publisher; b. Gallipolis, Ohio, Oct. 29, 1902; d. Arthur Robert and Marilla Jeanette (Vincent) Harding; m. Ivan Rupert Adams, July 3, 1929 (dec. 1956); children—Kathryn Adams Kirn, Joanne (dec. 1952). B.A., B.S., Ohio State U., 1925. Acct. A.R. Harding Pub. Co., Columbus, Ohio, 1925-30; bus. and circulation mgr. A.R. Harding Pub. Co., 1930-82, pub., from 1983. Chmn. tour com. YWCA, Columbus, 1961-73, bd. dirs., 1960-64; trustee Broad St. Presbyterian Ch., Columbus, 1973-76; pres. Columbus City Panhellenic Assn., 1928; bd. dirs. River Ridge Riding Club, Columbus, 1960-66. Mem. Altrusa (bd. dirs. 1970-71). Presbyterian. Home: Columbus Ohio. Died Sept. 26, 1986, buried Jamestown, Ohio.

ADAMS, PARK, III (PEPPER ADAMS), musician; b. Highland Park, Mich., Oct. 8, 1930; s. Park II and Cleo (Coyle) A.; m. Claudette Nadra, Feb. 14, 1976; 1 stepson, Dylan Foster Hill. Student, Wayne State U., 1948-50. pres. Excerent Music (music pubs.). Profl. baritone saxophonist/clarinetist, 1944-86, appearances with, Stan Kenton, Thelonious Monk, Benny Goodman, Dizzy Gillespie, others; co-leader, Quintet with Donald Byrd, 1958-62, rec. artist for, Blue Note, Spotlight, ENJA Muse, Uptown records, with Thad Jones-Mel Lewis Orch., 1966-77, albums include, Encounter!, Ephemera, 1973, Reflectory, 1978, Urban Dreams, 1981, Live at Fat Tuesdays, 1984. Served with AUS, 1951-53, Korea. Recipient New Star award Down Beat mag., 1957; Talent Deserving of Wider Recognition award Down Beat mag., 1967; All-Star's All-Star award Playboy mag., 1975; winner Down Beat Reader's Poll, 1982, 86, winner Down Beat Critic's Poll, annually, 1979-86; Grammy nominee for best jazz soloist, 1979-81, 84. Mem. Nat. Acad. Rec. Arts and Scis. (gov. 1978-84), ASCAP. Home: Brooklyn N.Y. Died Sept. 10, 1986.

ADAMS, SHERMAN, former governor of New Hampshire; b. East Dover, Vt., Jan. 8, 1899; s. Clyde H. and Winnie Marion (Sherman) A.; m. Rachel Leona White, July 28, 1923 (dec. 1979); children—Marion Adams Freese, Jean Adams Hallager, Sarah, Samuel. A.B., Dartmouth Coll., 1920, A.M., 1940; LL.D., U. N.H., 1950; D.C.L., New Eng. Coll., 1951; LL.D., Coll., St. Lawrence U., 1954, Center Coll., Ky., 1955, U. Maine, Middlebury Coll., 1957. Treas. Black River Lumber Co. Vt., 1921-22; mgr., timberland and lumber operations The Parker-Young Co., Lincoln, N.H., 1928-45; former dir. Pemigewasset R.R., Concord; pres. Loon Mountain Recreation Corp., 1966-79, chmn. bd., 1980-86; mem. N.H. Ho. of Reps., 1941-44, chmn. com. on labor, 1941-42, speaker of house, 1943-44; mem. 79th Congress, 1945-47, 2d N.H. Dist.; gov. N.H., 1949-53; asst. to Pres. U.S., 1953-58; Chmn. Conf. N.E. Govs., 1951-52. Author: First Hand Report, 1961; also articles in Life; other mags.; Lectr. Pres. White Mountain Center for Music and Arts; chmn. Mt. Washington Commn., 1971-86; Dir. (life) Northeastern Lumber Mfrs. Assn. Del. Rep. Nat. Conv., 1944, 52, Eisenhower floor leader 1952 conv. Served with USMCR, 1918. Recipient N.H. Outstanding Citizen of Year award Boy Scouts Am. Mem. (sr.) Soc. Am. Foresters, S.A.R. (N.H. soc.), Sigma Alpha Epsilon. Republican. Club: Mason (33rd deg.). Home: Lincoln N.H. Died Oct. 27, 1986; buried Riverside Cemetery, Lincoln.

ADAMS, WILLIAM W., clergyman, educator; b. Chelsea, Ala., Sept. 16, 1892; s. William Ferguson and Nancy Rebecca (Martin) A.; children: William Walter, Bert Newton. AB, Howard Coll., Birmingham, Ala., 1919; ThM, So. Bapt. Theol. Sem., Louisville, 1922, ThD, 1925; DD (hon.), William Jewell Coll., 1946. Student pastorates various chs. 1915-25; prof. N.T. interpretation and Greek exegesis Eastern Bapt. Theol. Sem., Phila., 1925-46; pres., prof. N.T interpretation Cen. Bapt. Theol. Sem., Kansas City, Kans., 1946-54; James Buchanan Harrison prof. N.T. interpretation So. Bapt. Theol. Sem., from 1954. Author scripture expn. for The Bapt. Leader, 1938-41; assoc. editor The Christian Rev., 1932-36; contbr. articles to religious pubs. Mem. No. Bapt. Ednl. Assn. (pres. 1945-46), Masons. Home: Louisville Ky. †

ADDABBO, JOSEPH PATRICK, congressman; b. Queens County, N.Y., Mar. 17, 1925; s. Dominick and Anna (Polizzo) A.; m. Grace Salamone, June 12, 1949; children: Dominic, Dina, Joseph. Student, Coll. City of N.Y., 1942-44; LLB, St. John's Law Sch., 1946. Bar: N.Y. 1947. Pvt. practice Ozone Pk., N.Y., 1948-86; mem. 87th Congress 5th Dist., N.Y.; mem. 88th, 97th Congresses 7th Dist., N.Y.; mem. 98th Congress 6th Dist., N.Y. Mem. bldg. com. Ozone Pk. Jewish Ctr.; regional chmn. Bishop's Diocesan Drive for High Sch. and Old Age Home; past pres. Ferrini Welfare League of Cath. Charities. Mem. Ozone Park Men's Assn. (past pres.), Queen's County Bar Assn., Kiwanis. Democrat. Home: Ozone Park N.Y. Died Apr. 1986.

ADDAMS, CHARLES SAMUEL, cartoonist; b. Westfield, N.J., Jan. 7, 1912; s. Charles Huey and Grace M. (Spear) A.; m. Barbara Day, May 29, 1943 (div. Oct. 1951); m. Barbara Barb, Dec. 1, 1954 (div. 1956); m. Marilyn Matthews, May 31, 1980. Student, Colgate U., 1929-30, U. Pa., 1930-31, Grand Central Sch. Art, N.Y.C., 1931-32; D.F.A. (hon.), U. Pa., 1980. Exhibited in, Fogg Art Mus., R.I., Sch. Design, Mus. City N.Y., 1956, Pa. U. Mus., 1957, Met. Mus. Art, war exhbn., print exhbn.; cartoons appear in New Yorker, 1935-88; TV show The Addams Family based on original cartoon characters; drawings in biennial New Yorker Album and The New Yorker War Album, 1942, Mus. Modern Art, N.Y.C.; author: Drawn & Quartered, 1942, Addams and Evil, 1947, Monster Rally, 1950, Home Bodies, 1954, Nightcrawlers, 1957, Dear Dead Days, 1959, Black Maria, 1960, The Groaning Board, 1964, The Charles Addams Mother Goose, 1967, My Crowd, 1970, Monster Rally, 1975, Favorite Haunts, 1976, Creature Comforts, 1981. Served with AUS, 1943-46. Recipient Humor award Yale Record, 1954, spl. award Mystery Writers Am., 1961. Clubs: Coffee House, Vintage Car Club of Am, Armor and Arms, Century Assn. Died Sept. 29, 1988.

ADELMANN, HOWARD BERNHARDT, educator; b. Buffalo, May 8, 1898; s. Charles Michael and Louise Henrietta (Kohler) A.; m. Dorothy May Schullian, July 6, 1978. A.B., Cornell U., 1920, A.M., 1922, Ph.D., 1924; student, U. Freiburg, Germany, 1927; Sc.D. honoris causa, Ohio State U., 1962; M.D. honoris causa, U. Bologna, Italy, 1972. Asst. histology and embryology Cornell U., 1919-21, instr., 1921-25, asst. prof., 1925-37, prof., 1937-88, chmn. dept. zoology, 1944-59, faculty rep. bd. trustees, 1947-51. Author: The Embryological Treatises of Hieronymus Fabricius (Crofts prize Cornell U. Press 1942), Marcello Malpighi and the Evolution of Embryology, 5 vols, (Pfizer award History of Science Soc. 1966); editor: The Correspondence of Marcello Malpighi, 5 vols, 1975; Asso. editor: Jour. Morphology, 1948-51; Contbr. sci. papers to profl. jours. NRC fellow biol. sci., 1927-28; Recipient Galileo Galilei prize U. Pisa, Italy, 1972; decorated Order Star Italian Solidarity Italy, 1962; hon. citizenship Crevalcore, Italy, 1977. Fellow Institut Internat. d'Embryologie (Amsterdam); mem. Am. Assn. Anatomists, Am. Soc. Zoologists, Hist. Sci. Soc., Am. Assn. History Medicine (William H. Welch medal 1967), Internat. Acad. History Medicine, Phi Beta Kappa, Sigma Xi, Phi Kappa Phi. Republican. Lutheran. Home: Ithaca N.Y. Died July 25, 1988.

ADKERSON, J(OSEPH) CARSON, mining engineer; b. Lynchburg, Va., Feb. 10, 1892; s. Alonza Thomas and Lizzie Lillian (Carson) A.; m. Anne Winfield Clower, Mar. 11, 1961. Registered profl. mining engr., Va., D.C. Asst. engr. Piedmont-Manganese Corp., Lynchburg, 1912-13, Oxford Mining & Manganese Corp., 1913-14; engr., mgr. Powells Fort Manganese Mines, Woodstock, Va., 1915-19; v.p., engr., mgr. Hy-Grade Manganese Co., Woodstock, 1919-36; v.p., engr. Hy-Grade Manganese Prodn. & Sales Corp., Woodstock, 1929-32, Nat. Metals Corp., Damascus, Va., 1940-42; pres. Raw Materials Nat. Council, 1936-68; cons. engr. Cuban Am. Manganese Corp., N.Y.C., 1940-45; chmn. Joint Conf. of Unfair Russian Competition, 1930-33; investigator, researcher manganese, tungsten, other strategic materials. Mem. session Woodstock Presby. Ch., 1978-80. Recipient Outstanding Citizen award Woodstock C. of C., 1979. Mem. Am. Manganese Producers Assn. (pres. 1927-62), Masons, Shriners, Rotary. Home: Woodstock Va. Died Mar. 15, 1985; buried Massanutten Cemetery, Woodstock.

ADLER, DAVID, physicist; b. Bronx, N.Y., Apr. 13, 1935; s. Saul and Betty (Kopelman) A.; m. Alice Joan Salzman, June 8, 1958; children: Kyle, Andrew, Carrie. B.S., Rensselaer Poly. Inst., 1956; A.M. (Leeds and Northrup fellow), Harvard U., 1958, Ph.D. (NSF Coop. Grad. fellow), 1964. Research assoc. U.K. Atomic Energy Research Establishment, Harwell, Eng., 1964-65; research assoc. MIT, 1965-67, asst. prof. elec. engring., 1967-69, assoc. prof., 1969-75, prof., 1975-87; lectr. Franco-Russian Summer Sch., Montpellier, France, 1971, Queen's U., 1974, Latin Am. Summer Sch., Venezuela, 1976, U. Campinas, Brazil, 1976, McMaster U., 1977, U. N.C., 1979, NATO, 1979, Kyoto (Japan) Summer Inst., 1980, U. Montreal, 1981, Caracas, Venezuela, 1982, U.N.C.C., 1983, Nile Winter Coll., Khartoum, Sudan, 1985; lectr. Beijing Inst. Aeros. and Astronautics, China, 1983, hon. adviser, 1984-87; chmn. Solar Photovoltaic Panel, Solar Energy Workshop, 1975; mem. com. basic research NRC, 1973-76; mem. organizing com. Internat. Symposium on Electronic Properties of Oxides, 1974, 6th Joint U.S.-USSR Symposium on Theory of Condensed Matter, 1976; co-chmn. 8th Internat. Conf. on Amorphous and Liquid Semiconductors, 1978; chmn. 1st Workshop on Threshold Switching, 1980; mem. external rev. com. NSF-MRL program Purdue U., 1978-81; chmn. various confs. Soc. Photo-Optical Instrumentation Engrs., 1983, 86. Author: Amorphous Semiconductors, 1971, Tokei Rikigaku oyobi Netsu Rikigaku, 1983, Ryoshi Butsurigaku, 1983; editor: Sci. and Tech. in Non-Crystalline Semicondrs., 1982; Physical Properties of Amorphous Materials, 1985, Physics of Disordered Systems, 1985, Tetrahedrally Bonded Amorphous Semiconductors, 1985; editorial bd. Jour. Nonmetals, 1971-76, Semicondrs. and Insulators, 1976-87, Jour. Applied Physics, 1979-82, Applied Physics Letters, 1979-82; regional editor: Jour. Non-Crystalline Solids, 1981-87; assoc. editor: Materials Research Bull., 1983-87. Treas. Community Nursery Sch., Lexington, Mass., 1971-73, Maria Hastings PTA, Lexington, 1974-75. Recipient McKinney prize Rensselaer Poly. Inst., 1954, Gold medal Soc. Actuaries, 1955. Fellow Am. Phys. Soc. (exec. com. div. solid state physics, chmn. program com. conf. 1984); mem. IEEE (sr.), Materials Research Soc. (co-chmn. symposia 1985, 86), Am. Assn. Physics Tchrs., Am. Vacuum Soc. (sr.). Home: Lexington Mass. Died Mar. 31, 1987.

ADLER, FRANCIS HEED, retired medical educator; b. Phila., Feb. 4, 1895; s. Lewis H. and Emma Augusta (Heed) A.; m. Emily Anne MacDonald, July 7, 1970; children by previous marriage: Jeanne Adler Morris, Lynn. A.B., U. Pa., 1916, M.S., 1918, M.D., 1919. Diplomate: Am. Bd. Ophthalmology (sec.-treas. 1965-81, chmn. 1955). Intern Hosp. U. Pa., 1919-21; mem. faculty U. Pa. Med. Sch., 1921-77, prof. ophthalmology, 1937-60, emeritus, from 1960. Author: Physiology of the Eye, 1950, Text Book of Ophthalmology, 1941; cons. editor: Jour. Ophthalmology, 1960-65. Served with U.S. Army, World War I. Recipient Lucian Howe medal U. Buffalo, 1960, Proctor medal Assn. Research Ophthalmology, 1967. Mem. Am. Opthal. Soc. (chmn. 1962, Howe medal 1951), AMA (medal ophthalmology 1959, editor-in-chief), Archives Ophthalmology (1950-60), Am. Acad. Ophthalmology and Otolaryngology (pres. 1969). Clubs: Union League (Phila.), Cricket (Phila.). Home: Philadelphia Pa. Died Aug. 14, 1987; cremated.

ADLER, KURT HERBERT, conductor; b. Vienna, Austria, Apr. 2, 1905; came to U.S., 1938, naturalized, 1941; s. Ernst and Ida (Bauer) A.; m. Diantha Warfel, July 7, 1940 (div. Dec. 1963); children: Kristin Diantha, Ronald Huntington; m. Nancy Miller, Aug. 23, 1965. Student, Vienna State Acad. Music, 1922-26, U. Vienna, 1923-27; Mus.D. (hon.), Coll. of Pacific, 1956, U. San Francisco, 1976. Coach, accompanist, chorus dir., instr., condr. Max Reinhardt's theatres, Vienna, 1925-28, various opera houses, Germany and Italy, 1928-34; condr. Volksoper, Vienna, 1934-36, Vienna Concert Orch., 1934-36; asst. condr. to A. Toscanini Salzburg Festival, 1936; instr. Salzburg Mozarteum, 1936-37; condr. opera and radio Czechoslovakia, 1936-38; condr. Chgo. Opera Co., 1938-43, Grant Park Concerts, Chgo., 1941-42; guest condr. Ill. Symphony Orch., 1942; with San Francisco Opera Co., 1943-81, asst. to gen. dir., 1952, artistic dir., 1953-56, gen. dir., 1956-81; condr. ann. Midsummer Music Festival San Francisco Opera and Symphony, 1944-81; with New Opera Co., N.Y.C., 1945; lectr., guest condr. symphony orch. U. Calif., Berkeley, 1949-50; artistic advisor San Francisco Conservatory Music, 1949-52; condr. youth concerts San Francisco Symphony, 1949-52; guest condr. Standard Hour Symphony Broadcasts, NBC, Pacific Music Camp, 1952-61, Hollywood Bowl, 1954-56; supr. Merola Opera Program, San Francisco, 1957-88; guest condr. San Carlo Opera, Naples, 1958; founder artistic supr. Western Opera Theater, 1967-88, Spring Opera Theater of San Francisco, 1961-88, Brown Bag Opera, 1974-88, Music Ctr. Opera Assn., Los Angeles, 1969; mem. profl. com. Central Opera Service; bd, dirs. Nat. Opera Inst.;

v.p. bd. dirs. Opera Am.; mem. opera sect. adv. panel Nat. Endowment for Arts. Decorated Star of Solidarity (Italy), 1957; Officer's Cross (Germany), 1959; cavaliere Italian Republic, 1965; Great Medal of Honor (Austria), 1961; comdr.'s cross Order Merit (Fed. Republic Germany), 1969; 1st Am. recipient Bolshoi Theatre medal (USSR), 1972; recipient St. Francis of Assis award City of San Francisco, 1973, Highest honor citation U. Calif. at Berkeley, 1976, hon. title of prof. Fed. Govt. Austria, 1976. Home: Ross Calif. Died Feb. 9, 1988.

ADLER, SELIG, history educator; b. Balt., Jan. 22, 1909; s. Joseph G. and Della (Rubenstein) A.; m. Janet M. Sukernek, Aug. 26, 1936; children: Ellen Adler Krantz, Joseph G. BA, U. Buffalo, 1931; MA, U. Ill., 1932, PhD, 1934. Tchr. high schs. Buffalo, 1934-47; lectr. history SUNY-Buffalo (formerly U. Buffalo), 1941-84, prof. history, 1952-84, Samuel P. Capen prof. Am. History, 1959-75, Disting. Service prof., 1975-80, Disting. prof. emeritus, 1980-84; vis. prof. Cornell U., summer 1951, spring 1959, U. Rochester, 1952-53; historian, archivist Jewish Fedn. Greater Buffalo, 1980-84. Author: The Isolationist Impulse, 1957, (with T.E. Connolly) From Ararat to Suburbia, 1960, The Uncertain Giant, 1921-41, 1965; also profl. articles; contbg. editor: Judaism, 1956-84. Mem. N.Y. State Kosher Law Adv. Bd., 1952-79. Mem. Am. Jewish Hist. Soc. (hon. life mem. exec. council), Phi Beta Kappa. Home: Buffalo N.Y. Died Nov. 8, 1984; buried Elmlawn Cemetery, Buffalo.

ADLUM, MERLE DANIEL, union official; b. Friday Harbor, Wash., Feb. 21, 1919; s. Jack Daniel and Anna Ruth (Barene) A.; m. Virginia L. Schultz, Mar. 8, 1940 (div. Oct. 1986); children: Virginia (Mrs. Clifford Houser), Joan (Mrs. James Chandler), Judy (Mrs. Del Blanks), Merle Daniel (dec.), Jacquelyn Stropple, John E. (dec.), Cynthia A. Larsen; m. Miriam Del Duca Lippincott, Oct. 9, 1986. Grad. high sch. Ofcl. Masters, Mates and Pilots Union, 1954-65; ofcl. Inland Boatmen's Union of the Pacific, Seattle, 1954-79; pres. Inland Boatmen's Union of the Pacific, 1967-79; v.p. Seafarers Internat. Union N. Am., 1969-79; trustee Puget Sound Maritime Trades Dept., 1961-86, v.p., 1976-78, pres., 1978-86; pres. North by Northwest Adventureres, Inc., Seattle, 1969-72, Northwest Marine Tng. Program; mem. Port Seattle Commn., 1963-83, pres., 1967, 71, 75, 80; mem. Wash. Canal Commn., 1965-86; now chmn.; mem. Mayor's Maritime Adv. Com., 1956-86, chmn., 1970-86; mem. statewide task force Alternatives for Washington; sec. Seattle King County Econ. Devel. Adv. Com., 1972-80; now chmn.; chmn. Econ. Devel. Adv. Com., Marine Firemen Protection Working Com.; bd. dirs. Econ. Devel. Dist. Central Puget Sound, Econ. Devel. Council, Evergreen Safety Council, ARC, Council for Washington's Future, Downtown Coordinating Com., Washington State Trade Fair, Seattle Opportunities Industrialization Council. Trustee Nat. Multiple Sclerosis Soc., 1967-86; trustee Coast Guard Mus. N.W. Served with U.S. Navy, 1937-39. Named Maritime Man of Year Puget Sound Maritime Press Assn., 1972; recipient Outstanding Citizen award Muny League, 1967. Mem. Wash. Pub. Ports Assn., Pacific Coast Assn. Port Authorities (dir. 1964-83), Northwest Waterways Assn., Seattle C. of C. (trustee 1971-86, mem. exec. com.), Navy League, Japan Am. Soc., World Affairs Council, Puget Sound Maritime Hist. Soc. Clubs: Propeller Club, China Club. Home: Seattle Wash. Died Oct. 10, 1986; buried Forest Lawn Cemetery, Seattle.

ADRIANI, JOHN, physician, emeritus educator; b. Bridgeport, Conn., Dec. 2, 1907; s. Nicola and Lucia (Caseria) A.; m. Eleanor Anderson, Dec. 1936 (div. Feb. 1947); 1 child, John Nicholas; m. Irene Miller, Sept. 7, 1953. A.B., Columbia U., 1930, M.D., 1934. Diplomate Am. Bd. Anesthesiology, (dir. 1960-72, chmn. exams. com. 1963-88, pres. 1967-68). Intern surgery French Hosp., N.Y.C., 1934-36; resident anesthesiology Bellevue Hosp., N.Y.C., 1936-37; fellow N.Y.U., 1937-39, instr. anesthesiology dept. surgery, 1939-41; asst., then asso. clin. prof. surgery La. State U. Sch. Medicine, 1941-54, clin. prof. surgery and pharmacology, 1954; asst. prof., later asso. prof. anesthesiology Loyola Sch. Dentistry, New Orleans, 1945-56; prof. gen. anesthesiology Loyola Sch. Dentistry, 1956-71; prof. surgery Tulane U., 1947-75, emeritus, 1975-88; prof. anesthesiology La. State Med. Center, 1975-88; dir. dept. anesthesiology Charity Hosp., 1941-75, emeritus dir., 1975—; dir. dept. inhalation therapy, 1941-69, dir. blood plasma bank, 1944-70, asst. dir., 1960-64; clin. prof. oral surgery Sch. Dentistry, La. State U., 1971-88; assoc. dir. Charity Hosp., 1966-76, center chmn. regional med. program, 1967-70; cons. anesthesiologist Flint-Goodridge, VA, USPHS, Ochsner Found. hosps., Hotel Dieu, New Orleans; cons. anesthesiology, pharmacology and medico-legal problems La. Health and Human Resources Adminstrn., 1975-82; cons. to Touro Infirmary, New Orleans; mem. adv. com. div. investigational drugs FDA, 1963-65, 72-88, chmn. adv. com. on anesthetic and respiratory drugs, 1968-70, mem. adv. panel topical analgesics over-the-counter drugs, 1972-78, mem. adv. panel oral cavity preparations, 1974-80, cons. consumer protection div., 1980-88; cons. FTC; mem. founders group expansion program Holy Cross Coll., 1963; mem. revision com., chmn. com. on anesthesia, subcom. on scope U.S. Pharmacopoeia, 1960-70; mem. U.S. Pharmacopeal Conv., 1970-88, Nat. Formulary Admissions Com., 1970-88. Author: Pharmacology of Anesthetic Drugs, rev. edit, 1970, Chemistry of Anesthesia, 1946, Techniques and Procedures of Anesthesia, 3d edit., 1964, Nerve Blocks, 1954, Selection of Anesthesia, 1955, General Anesthesiology For Students and Practitioners of Dentistry, 1958, The Recovery Room, 1958, Chemistry and Physics of Anesthesia, 1962, Appraisal-Current Concepts Anesthesiology (Mosby), Vol. 1, 1961, Vol. 2, 1964, Vol. 3, 1966, Vol. 4, 1969, Revision of Labat's Region Anesthesia, 1967, edit. 4, 1985, also numerous scientific and med. papers.; Editor: American Lecture Series in Anesthesiology; cons. editor: The Resident G. P. Survey Anesthesiology; editor: Anesthesiology, 1958-67; cons. editor: Dorland's Illustrated Med. Dictionary, 1969-88, Internat. Corr. Soc. Anesthesiology. Bd. dirs. Cancer Soc., New Orleans; mem. Met. Action Com. of New Orleans, Public Affairs Research Council, Bur. of Govtl. Research of La., Italian-Am. Culture Center, Piazza Italiana, New Orleans.; trustee, mem. acad. bd. St. George's U. Med. Ctr., Granada, W.I.; life v.p. Civil Service League La. Named hon. col. staff Gov. La., 1965; hon. dep. atty. gen. State of La., 1980; hon. dep. Sheriff La Fourche Parish, 1980; recipient Disting. Service award Am. Soc. Anesthesiologists, 1949, Disting. Service award Internat. Anesthesiology Research Soc., 1957; Guedel medal for anesthesiology, 1959; Gold medal Assn. Alumni Coll. Physicians and Surgeons, Columbia, 1967; silver medal for achievements in medicine Columbia U. Sch. Medicine; Ralph M. Waters award internat. achievements in anesthesiology, 1968; decorated knight comdr. Order of Merit, Italy, 1969; named Nat. Italian Am. of Year, 1969; recipient Hon. Alumnus award Tulane Sch. Medicine, 12, Cert. of Honor Library of Congress, 1973; Monte M. Lemann award Civil Service League La., 1975; named hon. senator La. Legislature, 1975, hon. atty. gen. State of La., 1980; recipient William McQuiston award Ill. Soc. Anesthesiology, 1982, NYU Med. Coll. Alumni award, 1982; Disting. Service award So. Med. Assn., 1986. Fellow Am. Soc. Clin. Pharm. and Chemotherapy, Am. Soc. Clin. Pharmacology and Therapeutics, Am. Coll. Anesthesiologists (gov. 1944-50, 56-60); mem. Am. Heart Assn., Assn. Colonic Surgeons, AAAS, Soc. Exptl. Biology and Medicine, So. Soc. Clinical Research, Internat. Anesthesia Research Soc., NRC, Columbia U. Alumni Assn., Am. Hosp. Assn., Assn. Univ. Anesthesiologists (pres. 1955), Assn. Univ. Anesthesiology Departmental Chmn., AMA (mem. council on drugs 1964-72, vice chmn. 1967, chmn. 1967-71), 50 Yr. Club AMA, La. Med. Soc. (50 yr. pin and cert.), Internat. Soc. Comprehensive Medicine, Am. Soc. Anesthesiologists, La. Soc. Anesthesiologists (pres. 1950), New Orleans Soc. Anesthesiology (hon. mem. 1982), So. Soc. Anesthesiologists (pres. 1952-53, cert. of recognition 1975), Acad. Anesthesiology (pres. 1985-86, exec. com., citation of merit 1982), Cuban Soc. Anesthesiologists (hon.), Venezuelan Soc. Anesthesiologists (hon.), So. Med. Assn., Southeastern Surg. Congress, Am. Soc. Regional Anesthesia (hon.), History of Anesthesiology Soc. (hon.), Am. Soc. Regional Anesthesia (Gaston Labat award 1980), History of Medicine Club, Am. Coll. Angiology, Am. Surg. Assn., Mexican Soc. Anesthesiology (hon. pres. 1954), La. Thoracic Soc., Yucatan Soc. Anesthesiology (hon. pres. 1966), Philippines Acad. Anesthesiology, Alton Ochsner Med. Found. Soc. (advisor), John Jay Assocs. Columbia Coll., Samuel Bard Assocs. of Columbia U. Coll. Physicians and Surgeons, Civil Service League La. (dir.), Assn. Wild-life and Fisheries of La., Sigma Xi, Alpha Omega Alpha. Clubs: Thoracophilis Horse Shoe, Century (Phys. and Surg.), Columbia U. Alumni New Orleans; 1834, Emeritus (Tulane U.). Home: New Orleans La. Died June 14, 1988.

ADRIAN OF CAMBRIDGE, BARON, educational administrator, university chancellor; b. London, Nov. 30, 1889; s. Alfred Douglas and Flora Lavinia (Barton) A.; m. Hester Agnes Pinsent, June 15, 1923 (dec. 1966); 3 children. Ed., Westminister Sch., Trinity Coll.; MA, MD, Cambridge U.; hon. degrees various univs. Lectr. in physiology Cambridge U., 1920-29, prof., 1937-51, master Trinity Coll., 1951-65, chancellor, from 1967; chancellor U. Leicester, 1957-70; pres. Royal Soc. Medicine, 1960-62. Author: The Basis of Sensation, 1928, The Mechanism of Nervous Action, 1932. Capt. M.C., Royal Army, 1916-19. Decorated Order of Merit, Chevalier Legion of Honour (France); recipient Nobel prize for physiology and medicine, 1932. Fellow Royal Soc. (Foulerton rsch. prof. 1929, fgn. sec. 1946, pres. 1950-55), Academia del Lincei; mem. Am. Physiol. Soc., Nat. Acad. Medicine (Argentina), Acad. Nacional de Medicine (Mex.), NAS (fgn. assoc.), Am. Acad. Arts and Scis., Royal Acad. Medicine (Belgium), Royal Acad. Sci. (Amsterdam), Royal Flemish Acad. Sci., Acad. Sci. (corr.), Acad. Medicine (fgn. assoc.), Kungl. Vetenshaps Soc., Am. Philos. Soc. Home: Cambridge England †

AGAR, FREDERICK ALFRED BAILEY, clergyman; b. Ponders End, County Middlesex, Eng., Nov. 30, 1871; came to U.S., 1889; s. Frederick A. and Sophia (Dennis) A.; m. Harriett Louise Caldwell, Dec. 20, 1893 (dec.). Student, Louisville Theol. Sem. (did not grad. because called to Africa in emergency); D.D., Franklin Coll., 1921. Ordained to ministry Bapt. Ch., 1893. Med. missionary Congo Free State, 1893-94; pastor Wheatland, Calif., 1895-97, Ellensburg, Wash., 1897-99, Bellingham, Wash., 1900-03; supt. missions Mont., 1904-08, Wash. and Idaho, 1908-12; co-pastor 1st Ch., Portland, ORe., 1912-13; efficiency and methods sec. Northern Bapt. Conv., 1913-1938; cons. to local Protestant churches. Author: Church Finance, 1915, Dead or Alive, 1916, Help Those Women, 1917, Personality and Possessions, 1917, Democracy and the Church, 1918, Church Officers, 1918, The Stewardship of Life, 1919, Modern Money Methods, 1920, Manual of Church Methods, 1921, The Deacon at Work, 1922, The COmpetent Church, 1924, The Local Church, 1926, Enlisting Laymen, 1927, Church Profit Making, 1928; co-author: Workers Together, 1931, The Minister and His Opportunity, 1932, Church Women at Work, 1937; also 40 tech, pamphlets on ch. methods. Republican. Home: New York N.Y. Died Dec. 19, 1969; inurned Lone Fir Masonic Cemetery, Portland, Oreg.

AGARWAL, PAUL DHARAM, electrical engineer, manufacturing company executive; b. Ambala, India, Jan. 21, 1924; came to U.S., 1947, naturalized, 1959; s. Dina Nath and Sherbati Honi A.; m. Mary M. Glenn, Dec. 22, 1951 (div. 1974); children—Rani Lisa, Karen Lee, Paul Douglas, Deborah Anne; m. Mary Underdown, Feb. 15, 1987. B.S.E.E. with honors, Benares Hindu U., 1944, M.E., 1944; M.S.E.E., Ill. Inst. Tech., 1949; Ph.D., Bklyn. Poly. Inst., 1958. Asst. prof. elec. engring. Bklyn. Poly. Inst., 1951-57; prof. elec. engring. U. Mass., 1957-61; head electric power and propulsion Gen. Motors Defense Labs., Santa Barbara, Calif., 1961-66; head elec. engring. Gen. Motors Defense Labs., 1967-84; head electromech. systems dept. Gen. Motors Research Labs., Warren, Mich., 1984-85; exec. engr., head electromech. systems Gen. Motors Advanced Engring. Staff, 1985—; cons. to Gen. Electric Co., 1954-61; mem. adv. coms. NSF and Dept. Commerce, 1958-67. Contbr. papers to profl. publs. and confs. Mem. vis. com. U. Tex.-Austin, chmn. edn. and research subcom., 1985—. Recipient prize paper awards Am. Inst. Elec. Engrs., 1960, 62; NSF grantee, 1960. Fellow IEEE (vice chmn. ednl. activities bd. 1975-77, chmn. induction motor com. 1976); mem. Soc. Automotive Engrs. (exec. com. passenger car activity 1970), Sigma Xi (award 1960, various paper awards). Clubs: Cranbrook, Tennis. Home: Troy Mich. Deceased.

AGLE, CHARLES KLEMM, architect, city planner; b. Bloomington, Ill., Oct. 19, 1906; s. Charles F. and Clara (Klemm) A.; divorced; children: Charles H., Kenneth C., Alan P.; m. Jo Ann Sayers, June 22, 1968. Grad., Choate Sch., 1923-25; A.B., Princeton U., 1929; M.F.A., Princeton, 1931; student, Am. Sch., Fontainebleau, France, 1931. Asso. Henry Wright, Sr. (city planner), N.Y.C., 1931-34; dir. planning Fed. Pub. Housing Authority, 1934-43, Harrison, Ballard & Allen, N.Y.C., 1946-52; propr. own firm in city planning and architecture Princeton, N.J., 1953-87; mem. faculty community planning U. Pa., 1953-54; Princeton Grad. Sch., 1956-66. Editor, contbr.: Rehousing Urban America, 1934, An Approach to Urban Planning, 1953; Author: Zoning, 1965, Community Appearance, 1969, Planned Residential Neighborhoods, 1970, The Energy Crisis and Community Planning, 1974. Served with USNR, 1943-46. Recipient, 1968; Design award U.S. Dept. Housing and Urban Devel. Fellow AIA; mem. Am. Inst. Certified Planners, Am. Planning Assn., Regional Plan Assn. N.Y., Lambda Alpha. Home: Princeton N.J. Died Dec. 2, 1987.

AGNEW, JOHN CURRY, oil company executive; b. Phila., Dec. 14, 1892; s. Samuel and Sarah (McClenahan) A.; m. Pearl Van Stone, June 14, 1919; children: John Curry, Jane Agnew McDonald. Student, Alexander Hamilton Inst. With U.S. Shipping Bd., Emergency Fleet Corp., 1917-19; auditor, dept. mgr. Sun Oil Co., Phila., 1920-47, asst. sec. and treas., 1947-49, sec., treas., bd. dirs., from 1949. Bd. dirs. Phila. United Fund, Phila. Community Chest, Phila. chpt. Boy Scouts Am., Phila. Jr. Achievement; trustee Wood Sch., Langhorne, Pa.; hon. mem. Vet. Guard Pa. N.G. Mem. Phila. C. of C. (bd. dirs.), Friends of Franklin. Republican. Presbyterian. Home: Bryn Mawr Pa. †

AGOPOFF, AGOP MINASS, sculptor; b. Sliven, Bulgaria, May 15, 1905; came to U.S., 1929; s. Minass Agop and Anna-Efrate Caplanian (Avakian) A. Student, Columbia U., 1930, Nat. Acad. Design, 1931-33. Fellow Hudson Valley Art Assn., Allied Artists of Am., Acad. Artists Assn., Am. Artists Profl. League, Nat. Sculpture Soc.; mem. Nat. Acad. Design. Home: Denville N.J. Died 1983.

AGUS, JACOB BERNARD, rabbi, Jewish philosophy educator; b. Swislocz, Poland, Nov. 8, 1911; came to U.S., 1927, naturalized, 1929; s. Judah Leib and Bela (Bereznitsky) Agushewitz; m. Miriam Shore, June 16, 1940; children—Zalman, Edna (Mrs. Lawrence Povich), Robert, Deborah (Mrs. Robert Kleinman). A.B., Yeshiva U., 1933; A.M., Harvard U., 1938, Ph.D., 1939; D.D. (hon.), Balt. Hebrew Coll., D.H.L. (hon.), 1983. Ordained rabbi 1935; rabbi Temple Ashkenaz, Cambridge, Mass., 1935-39, Agudas Achim North Shore, Chgo., 1939-41; Beth Abraham United, Dayton, Ohio, 1942-50, Beth El Congregation, Balt., from 1950; adj. prof. religion, history of Jewish thought Temple U., 1968-71; prof. Rabbinic Judaism reconstructionist Rabbinical Coll., 1969-71; vis. prof. modern Jewish philosophy Dropsie U., from 1971; Bd. dirs. Balt. br.

NCCJ, Balt. br.; Am. Jewish Com., Balt. Asso. Jewish Charities and Welfare Fund; bd. regents Morgan State U., from 1976. Author: Modern Philosophies of Judaism, 1940, Guideposts in Modern Judaism, 1954, Banner of Jerusalem, 1946, The Evolution of Jewish Thought, 1959, The Meaning of Jewish History, 2 vols, 1963, The Vision and the Way, 1966, Dialogue and Tradition, 1971, Jewish Identity in an Age of Ideologies, 1978, The Jewish Quest, 1983; Mem. bd. editors Judaism quarterly, from 1950; cons. editor for: works on Judaism, Jewish history Ency. Britannica, 1957-68. Fellow Jewish Acad., Acad. Jewish Thought; mem. Rabbinical Assembly Am., United Synagogues Am., Acad. Jewish Theol. Sem. Club: B'nai B'rith (nat. urban commn.). Home: Baltimore Md. Died Sept. 26, 1986; buried Beth El Meml. Park, Balt.

AHERN, JAMES FRANCIS, insurance crime prevention institute administrator; b. New Haven, Jan. 24, 1932; s. James Patrick and Mary (Walsh) A.; m. Janet Margaret Wyatt, Feb. 14, 1952; children: Susan Eileen, Mary Elizabeth, Sheila W., Sandra S.; m. Jennifer Ahern, 1979. Student, St. Thomas Sem., 1949-50, Gonzaga U., 1950-52; A.A., U. New Haven, 1962, B.B.A., 1964. Patrolman New haven Police Dept., 1954-62; sgt. New Haven Police Dept., 1962-67, lt., 1967-68, chief of police, 1968-71; dir. Ins. Crime Prevention Inst., Westport, Conn., 1971-86; law enforement cons. Dept. Justice; mem. Pres.'s Commn. Campus Unrest, 1970. Author: Police in Trouble: Our Frightening Crisis in Law Enforcement, 1972. Mem. Democratic Nat. Policy Council, 1971-72; mem. security adv. com. Dem. Nat. Com., 1972; mem. adv. commn. spl. com. youth edn. for citizenship ABA, 1972-73; bd. dirs. Inst. Effective Criminal Justice, Lower East Side Action Project, N.Y.C. Mem. Am. Soc. Assn. Execs. Roman Catholic. Home: Wilton Conn. Died Feb. 28, 1986, buried Hillside Cemetery, Wilton.

AHERN, THOMAS EDWARD, JR., lawyer; b. Cambridge, Mass., Jan. 11, 1920; s. Thomas Edward and Nora (McLean) A.; m. Virginia Holmes Hinch, Feb. 2, 1946; children—Sharon Ann, Mary Helen, Joan Nora, Thomas Edward III. A.B. cum laude, Harvard U., 1941, LL.B., 1944. Bar: N.Mex. 1945. Mem. firm Wilson & Ahern, Albuquerque, 1947-54; mem. firm Wilson, Ahern & Montgomery, Albuquerque, 1954-70, Ahern, Montgomery & Albert, Albuquerque, 1970-72, Ahern & Montgomery, Albuquerque, 1972-86; chmn. Legal Aid to Indigents Com., 1966-67; mem. N.Mex. Bd. Bar Commrs., 1969-76; adj. prof. law U. N.Mex., 1973-74, also vis. lectr.; vis. prof. law, dean. admissions Nat. U. Sch. Laws, San Diego, 1980-86. Editor Albuquerque Bar Jour., 1960-62. Mem. N.Mex. Arts and Crafts Bd., 1966-69; chmn. Fine Arts Adv. Bd., 1974-86; div. capt. Community Fund; vice-chmn. Met. Boundaries Commn., 1967-78; chmn. ethics and grievance com. State of N.Mex., 1971-72, chmn. new admissions com., 1974-75, chmn. auditing com., 1974-75; mem. N.Mex. Jud. Council, 1969-73, chmn., 1971-73. Mem. N.Mex. State Bar Assn. (pres. 1972-73), ABA (standing com. on profl. discipline 1973-74, com. on membership 1974-76), Albuquerque Bar Assn. (pres. 1964-65, dir. 1962-64). Club: Country (Albuquerque). Lodge: Elks. Home: Albuquerque N.Mex. Died Oct. 16, 1986; cremated.

AHERNE, BRIAN, actor; b. Kings Norton, Worcestershire, Eng.; s. William deLacy and Louise (Thomas) A.; M. Eleanor de Liagre. Student, Malvern Coll., U. London, Eng. Appeared on English stage, in Brit. films, 1924-86; appeared on N.Y. stage in The Barretts of Wimpole Street, Lucrece, Romeo and Juliet, St. Joan, Othello, The French Touch, Escapade, The Constant Wife, Quadrille, My Fair Lady, Dear Liar; starred in motion pictures in What Every Woman Knows, I Live My Life, The Constant Nymph, Beloved Enemy, The Great Garrick, Merrily We Life, Juarez, Captain Furry, My Son, My Son, The Lady in Question, Hired Wife, The Man Who Lost Himself, Skylark, Smilin' Through, My Sister Eileen, A Night to Remember, What A Woman, Smart Woman, The Swan, Titanic, The Best of Everyhing, Susan Slade. Home: Boca Grande Fla. Died Feb. 10, 1986.

AHLSTROM, SYDNEY ECKMAN, educator; b. Cokato, Minn., Dec. 16, 1919; s. Joseph T. and Selma (Eckman) A.; m. Nancy Ethel Alexander, Aug. 8, 1953; children: Joseph Alexander, Promise Ann, Constance Burton, Sydney Eckman. MA, U. Minn., 1946; PhD, Harvard U., 1952; DHL honoris causa, Upsala Coll., 1975; DLitt, Susquehanna U., 1976. Tutor history Harvard U., 1948-51, instr., 1952-54; mem. faculty Yale U., 1954-84, prof. Am. history and modern history, 1964-84; chmn. Am. Studies Program, 1967-71, 73; mem. faculty Salzburg Seminar Am. Studies, 1949-52; vis. prof. Princeton, spring 1962; trustee Gustavus Adolphus Coll., 1962-71. Author: (with G.H. Williams, editor) The Harvard Divinity School, 1954, (with J.W. Smith, editor) The Shaping of American Religion, 1961, The American Protestant Encounter with World Religions, 1962, (with G.L. Hunt, editor) Calvinism and the Political Order, 1965, Theology in America, 1967; A Religious History of the American People, 1972 (Nat. Book award); also articles. Capt. Transp. Corps, AUS, 1942-46. Mem. Am. Hist. Assn., Am. Soc. Ch. History, Am. Studies Assn., Am. Acad. Arts and Scis., Mass. Hist. Soc. (corr.). Lutheran. Home: New Haven Conn. Died July 3, 1984.

AIKEN, (JOHN) NEWTON, newspaperman; b. Cleveland, Tenn., Feb. 21, 1892; s. Samuel James and Carrie (Webb) A.; m. Margaret Louise Wirth, Aug. 21, 1917. AB, Duke U., 1912. Reporter Richmond (Va.) Times-Dispatch, 1912-13; dep. clk. U.S. Dist. Ct., Chattanooga, Tenn., 1913-16; reporter Norfolk (Va.) Ledger-Dispatch, 1919-23; editorial writer Norfolk-Virginian Pilot, 1923-29; mem. Washington staff Balt. Sun, 1929-31, editorial writer, 1931-34, corr., London, Eng., 1934-36, editorial writer, 1936-43; editor Balt. Evening Sun, from 1943. Contbr. articles on pub. affairs to nat. publs. With Troop B, Tenn. N.G., 1916-17, 6 mos. Mex. border; lieut., later capt., 306th ammunition train 81st div., U.S. Army, 1917-19; with AEF 10 mos. Mem. Kappa Sigma. Democrat. Presbyterian. Home: Baltimore Md. †

AKERS, SUSAN GREY, librarian; b. Richmond, Ky., Apr. 3, 1889; d. James Tazewell and Clara Elizabeth (Harris) A. AB, U. Ky., 1909; cert., Library Sch., U. Wis., 1913; PhD, U. Chgo., 1932. Tchr. grade and high schs. 1909-11; with pub. library br. Louisville, 1911-12; librarian Dept. Hygiene, Wellesley Coll., 1913-20; cataloger U. N.D. Library, 1920-22; instr., asst. prof. library sci. U. Wis., 1922-28; also field visitor Wis. Free Library Commn.; assoc. prof. library sci. U. N.C., 1931-32, acting dir., prof., 1932-35, dir., prof., 1935-41, dean, prof. Sch. Library Sci., 1942-54, prof., dean emeritus, from 1954; vis. lectr. library sci. U. Tehran, Iran, 1954-55; part-time summer instr. several univs.; cons. Civil Info. and Edn. Sect. U.S. Army, Tokyo, 1950-51; mem. U.S. State Dept. Internat. Edn. Exchange Program. Author: Simple Library Cataloging, 1927, 6th edit., 1977, Spanish transl., 1962. Mem. ALA (Mann citation 1956), N.C. Library Assn. Home: Chapel Hill N.C.

ALAJALOV, CONSTANTIN, artist; b. Rostov on the Don, Russia, Nov. 18, 1900; came to U.S., 1923, naturalized, 1928; s. Ivan and Izabella (Avramov) A. Student, Gymnasium, Rostov, 1912-17, U. of Petrograd, 1917. teacher, lectr. Archipenko's L'Ecole d'Art, Phoenix Art Inst., etc. 1st participation in exhbn., 1916; drafted by Soviet Govt. as artist to paint murals, portraits, posters, 1920, sent to Persia, 1921, left Russia for Constantinople, 1921; painted murals in U.S., 1923; with The New Yorker, since 1926, worked on Vanity Fair, Vogue, Town and Country, Fortune, Life, and others, covers, Saturday Evening Post, 1945; painted murals for S.S. America, also, Sherry-Netherland Hotel; one-man shows, Hollywood, 1936, N.Y.C., 1942, Dallas, 1951, Art Mus., Wichita, Kan., 1972, N.Y.C., 1985, Boston U. Library, 1987; paintings represented in Dallas Art Mus., Bklyn. Mus., Mus. Modern Art, Phila. Mus. of Fine Arts, Mus. of City of N.Y., Library of Congress, Boston U., and others; painter: numerous portraits including Countess E. Bismark, Duke and Duchess of Windsor, John Sherman Cooper, Mrs. Angier Biddle Duke, others, 1964; Alajalov collection established Syracuse U., 1964, The Constantin Alajalov Manuscript Collection established at, The Archives of Am. Art, Smithsonian Instn., 1980, Boston U., 1981. illustrated: books George Gershwin Song Book, 1932, Our Hearts Were Young and Gay, by Cornelia Otis Skinner, 1942, Cinderella, by Alice Duer Miller, 1943, Conversation Pieces, A Collection of Alajalov's Paintings and Drawings, text by Janet Flanner, 1942. Died Oct. 24, 1987.

ALBEE, GRACE ARNOLD, artist; b. Scituate, R.I., July 28, 1890; m. Percy F. Albee, May 10, 1913 (dec. 1959); children: Edward F. II, John F., Nathaniel E., William C., Percy F. Jr. Painter and engraver; represented in Bklyn. Mus. (Purchase award 1947), R.I. Sch. Design, Library of Congress, Met. Mus. N.Y.C., Carnegie Inst. Mus., Pitts., Okla. A&M Coll., Stillwater, Nat. Mus. Art, Stockholm, Cleve. Mus. Art, Kansas City Mus. John Herron Art Mus., N.Y, Boston Pub. Library, Newark Pub. Library, Phila. Mus., Melrose (Mass.) Library, Pa. State Library, Harrisburg, Nat. Gallery Art, Washington, Bethlehem Library, Peacham (Vt.) Library, Lynchburg (Va.) Art Club, collection of King Victor Emmanuel of Italy (1940), Cayuga Mus. History and Art, Auburn, N.Y., Albany (N.Y.) Print Club (Bowen Purchase award 1967), Norton Mus., West Palm Beach, Fla., Portland (Maine) Mus. Art, Nat. Bezalel Mus., Jerusalem, Culver Mil. Acad., Notre Dame U., various pvt. collections; one-woman show wood engravings Bklyn. Mus., 1976; reproductions in numerous publs. Nat. Academician, 1946; recipient numerous awards including Eugenia F. Atwood Purchase prize Phila. Print Club, 1949, prize Hunterdon County Art Ctr., 1959, Trenton Mus. Purchase prize, R.I. Sch. Design Alumni Assn. prize, 1965, Best of Yr. award drawing Non-Profl. Inst. Pa., 1965, numerous others. Fellow Am. Artists Profl. League (chmn. jury selection and awards, 1968, prizes 1965, Gold medal for wood engraving 1961, first prize in graphics 1974); mem. NAD (chmn. graphic art membership com. from 1953, mem. jury 1974, print prize 1959, prizes 1959, 62, Samuel Finley Breeze Meml. award 1962, 72), Conn. Acad., Providence Water Color Club (life, Oake-on-the-Hill prize 1964), Albany Print Club(Bowen purchase award 1967, Purchase award 1976), Providence Art Club (medal and citation contbn. visual arts, paiting and wood engraving 1965), Boston Printmakers, Acad. Artists Assn. (Helen Gould Kennedy award 1968), Met. Mus. N.Y. (life). Home: East Providence R.I. Deceased.

ALBJERG, VICTOR L., educator, historian; b. Fergus Falls, Minn., Jan. 24, 1892; s. Niels M. and Karen (Johansen) A.; m. Marguerite Hall, Aug. 13, 1927; 1 child, Patricia Parks (Mrs. Loren Graham). Student, Hamline U., 1914-17; AB, U. Minn., 1918; AM, U. Wis., 1924, PhD, 1926; LLD (hon.), St. Norbert Coll., 1967. Supt. city schs. Gary, S.D., 1920-22; asst. prof. Purdue U., 1926-29, assoc. prof., 1929-37, prof., 1937-62, prof. emeritus; vis. prof. George Peabody Tchrs. Coll., summers 1929, 30, 31, St. Norbert Coll., 1963-66. Author: (with C.R. Fish) Foundations of American Neutrality; (with Marguerite Albjerg) From Sedan to Stresa, 1951; Richard Owen, 1945, Europe Since 1914, 1951, Winston Churchill, Herald of Victory, 1971; contbr. articles to profl. jours. With USN, World War I. Hay-Whitney fellow. Mem. Am., Ind. hist. assns., Torch Club, Parlor Club, Reamer Club, Phi Beta Kappa, Phi Delta Kappa, Sigma Beta Kappa, Alpha Phi Omega. Home: West Lafayette Ind. †

ALBRECHT, ARTHUR EMIL, educator; b. N.Y.C., Aug. 19, 1894; s. Marx and Louise (Krogman) A.; m. Laura C. Hayden, June 18, 1921; children: June Louise Albrecht Atwood, Helen Gwendolyn Albrecht Morgenreth. BA, Coll. City N.Y., 1916; MA, George Washington U., 1917; PhD, Columbia U., 1923. Expert spl. agt. U.S. Dept. Labor, 1916-19; instr. dept. econs. Coll. City N.Y., 1919-23, successively instr., asst. prof., assoc. prof., 1931-44, prof. dept. econs. and bus. adminstrn., 1945-64; chmn. bus. adminstrn. Baruch Sch. Bus. and Pub. Adminstrn., 1940-64; dir. N.Y. office State Dept. Agr., 1923-31; Fulbright prof. Turku Finland, spring 1958. Contbr. articles nat. mags. Trustee Rockdale Inst., N.Y.C. Mem. Am. Assn. U. Profs., Am. Marketing Assn., Beta Gamma Sigma. Home: Bronxville N.Y. Died May 12, 1986.

ALBRIGHT, ARTHUR S(TANLEY), utilities executive; b. Columbus, Ohio, June 13, 1889; s. James G. and Helen (Twiss) A.; m. Dorothea Becker, Sept.15, 1916; 1 child, Joyce Albright Greig. MEE, Ohio State U., 1912. Elec. engr. statis. and meter depts. Detroit Edison Co., 1912-18, successively supt. meters, acting chief rsch., controller, treas., v.p., then exec. v.p., 1953, ret., 1954. Past pres. Better Bus. Bur., Detroit; trustee Better Bus. Bur. Rsch. Found.; active Ga. Heart Assn., Thomas County chpt. ARC; mem. bd. appeals City-County Zoning Commn. Recipient D.S.M. 425th Inf. Mich. N.G. Fellow IEEE; mem. Fin. Execs. Inst., Engring. Soc. Detroit, SAR, Newcomen Soc. N.Am., Detroit Athletic Club, Glen Arven Country Club (Ga.), Rotary, Phi Gamma Delta, Eta Kappa Nu, Tau Beta Pi. Republican. Congregationalist. Home: Thomasville Ga. †

ALBRIGHT, HORACE MADDEN, conservationist, consultant; b. Bishop, Calif., Jan. 6, 1890; s. George L. and Mary (Marden) A.; m. Grace Marian Noble, Dec. 23, 1915; children: Robert (dec.), Marian Albright Schenck. BL, U. Calif., 1912, LLD (hon.), 1951; LLB, Georgetown U., 1914; LLD (hon.), U. Mont., 1956, U. N.Mex., 1962. Bar: D.C. 1914, Calif. 1914. Asst. in econs. U. Calif., 1912-13; mem. staff of sec. Interior Dept., Washington, 1913-16, asst. atty. assigned to nat. park affairs, 1915-17; asst. dir. Nat. Park Service, Washington, 1917-19, acting dir., 1917-18, asst. dir. field and supt. Yellowstone Nat. Park, 1919-29, dir. of the service and mem. Nat. Capitol Park and Planning Commn., 1929-33; v.p., gen. mgr. U.S. Potash Co., 1933-46, pres., gen. mgr., dir., 1946-56, ret.; mem. Nat. Parks Adv. Council, from 1958; mem. adv. council Nat. Outdoor Recreation Resources Rev. Com., 1959-62; bd. dirs. N.Am. Phillips Co., Phillips Trust, 1953-61, Arnold Bakers, 1956-61. Author: (with F.J. Taylor) Oh Ranger; also numerous articles on conservation, nat. parks. Bd. dirs. Grand Teton Lodge Co.; trustee Colonial Williamsburg Found., 1934-58, Jackson Hole Preserve, Inc., Mills Coll., 1939-42, 51-59; mem. Palisades Interstate Park Com., N.Y. and N.J., 1945-61, Council Save-the-Redwoods League, natural resources com. Hoover Commn. to Organize Exec. Br. of Govt., 1948-49. Decorated Order of the Northern Star (Sweden), 1926; named Alumnus of Yr. U. Calif. Alumni Assn., 1952; recipient Conservation award Interior Dept., 1952, Frances K. Hutchinson medal Garden Club Am., 1959, Theodore Roosevelt Disting. Service medal, 1959, Neasham medal for historic preservation Calif. Hist. Soc., 1976; Berkeley fellow, 1968. Mem. Nat. Audubon Soc. (Audubon medal 1969), Am. Forestry Assn. (Disting. Service award 1962), Theodore Roosevelt Assn. (trustee, hon. v.p.), Nature Conservancy, Nat. Trust Hist. Preservation, Am. Scenic and Hist. Preservation Soc. (hon. pres., trustee, Pugsley Gold medal 1933), Nat. Parks Assn., Wilderness Soc., Desert Protective Council, Resources for Future (dir., chmn. 1952-61), Am. Plan and Civic Assn. (pres. 1936-46), Death Valley 49ers (hon. dir.), Pacific Tropical Bot. Garden (pres. 1964-71, trustee), Am. Pioneer Trails Assn. (v.p.), Cosmos Club (Washington) (award 1974), Sierra Club (San Francisco), Boone and Crockett Club, Explorers Club, Century Club, Camfire Club of Am. (hon., N.Y.C., Gold medal 1962), UCLA Faculty Ctr. Club, Masons, Phi Delta Phi, Beta Gamma Sigma. Deceased.

ALBRITTON, ERRETT C(YRIL), medical research administrator; b. Mayfield, Ky., Dec. 14, 1890; s. Samuel Pope and Azalea Ruth (JOnes) A.; m. Rietta

Glassell Garland, Dec. 20, 1919; children: Rogers Garland, Heloise Ruth. AB, U. Mo., 1916; MD, Johns Hopkins U., 1921. Instr. anatomy Tulane U. Med. Sch., 1917-18; intern Henry Ford Hosp., Detroit, 1921-22; assoc. in physiology U. Buffalo Med. Sch., 1924-26; prof. physiology, pharmacology and biochemistry (auspices Rockefeller Found.) Govt. Med. Sch., Bangkok, 1926-32; tchr. statis methods to med. students 1926-56; prof., exec. officer dept. physiology George Washington U. Sch. Medicine, 1932-51, Fry prof. physiology, 1951-56; asst. sci. dir. div. rsch. grants NIH, 1956-58, project rev. officer, 1958-60, chief rsch. accomplishments, 1960-67; lectr. in biostats. Walter Reed Army Inst. Rsch., 1956; exec. sec. com. Hanbook Biol. Data, NRC, 1949-54. Author: Experiment Design and Judgement of Evidence, 1948, Physiological Techniques, 1946; editor: Standard Values in Blood, 1952, Standard Values in Nutrition and Metabolism, 1954. Active govt. reform Montgomery County, Md. NRC fellow, 1922-24. Fellow AAAS; mem. Acad. Medicine (sec. 1936-60), Am. Physiol. Soc., Biometric Soc., Phi Beta Kappa, Sigma Xi, Theta Kappa Psi. Home: Chevy Chase Md. †

ALCORN, PAUL, librarian; b. Minden, Nebr., July 27, 1892; s. William A. and Isabelle (Showwalter) A.; m. Helen Sprecher, Dec. 24, 1918; children: Barbara, Paul. AB, U. Nebr., 1933; diploma, U. Wis. Libr. Sch., 1934. Pub. Daily Reporter, Lincoln, Nebr., 1922-29; bookstore propr. Lincoln, 1929-34; dir. of librs. U. Conn., Storrs, from 1934. Author: Specimens of Printing Type of John Baskerville, 1939. Mem. Conn. Libr. Assn. (pres. 1939), Conn. Acad. Arts and Scis., Conn. Hist. Soc., Columbiad Club of Conn., Phi Beta Kappa. Democrat. Congregationalist. Home: Mansfield Center Conn. †

ALCOTT, JOHN, cinematographer. Films include A Clockwork Orange, Barry Lyndon (Acad. award 1975), March or Die, Who Is Killing the Great Chefs of Europe?, Terror Train, Ft. Apache the Bronx, 2001: A Space Odyssey, Vice Squad, Triumph of a Man Called Horse, Under Fire, The Shining, Greystoke the Legend of Tarzan. Died July 28, 1986.

ALDERMAN, LOUIS CLEVELAND, JR., college president; b. Douglas, Ga., Aug. 12, 1924; s. Louis Cleveland and Minnis Amelia (Wooten) A.; m. Anne Augusta Whipple, Dec. 31, 1952; children: Amelia Anne, Louis Cleveland III, Fielding Dillard, Jonathan Augustus. A.A., South Ga. Coll., 1942; A.B., Emory U., 1946; M.S., U. Ga., 1949; postgrad., Columbia U., summers 1951-54; Ed.D. (Ford Found. fellow), Auburn U., 1959; postgrad. Pres.'s Inst., Harvard U., 1965; postgrad. TransAtlantic Inst., Oxford U., 1982-84. USPHS grad. research asst. U. Ga., 1948-49; instr. biology Rome Center, 1949-50; dir., asst. prof. biology Savannah Center, 1950-51, Rome Center, 1951-56, Columbus Center, 1956-59; dir. Henderson Coll., U. Ky., 1959-64; pres. Middle Ga. Coll., Cochran from 1964; Trustee Middle Ga. Coll. Found., pres., 1982—; mem. adv. council Univ. System of Ga., from 1964; bd. dirs. Bleckley County Hosp. Authority, 1969-79, Cochran Community House, 1964-79; trustee Ga. Rotary Student Fund, 1975-78, 81-84, 85-87; chmn. Cochran-Bleckley Bicentennial Com.; pres. Bleckley-Cochran Bicentennial Celebration, Inc.; chmn. 8th dist. Ga. State C. of C. Travel Council; dist. chmn. Rotary Found.; lt. col., aide-de-camp Gov.'s Staff State of Ga. Author: Focus on Change, 1964, Fifty Years as Middle Georgia College, 1967, Education in the American Colonies, 1971, History of Old Richland Church, 1972, Signers of the Declaration of Independence, 1974, The Sureties for Magna Charta, 1980; Contbr. articles to profl. jours. Served to sgt. U.S. Army, 1942-46, PTO. Recipient Good Citizenship award Civitan Club, 1955, Club Service award Rotary Internat., 1968-69, Outstanding Rotarian award, 1976; Paul Harris fellow Rotary Club, Will Watt fellow. Mem. Am. Assn. Jr. and Community Coll. Pres.'s Acad., Assn. Higher Edn., Ga. Hist. Soc., Nat. Hist. Soc., Ga. Geneal. Soc., SAR, Order Ky. Cols., NEA, Ga. Assn. Colls. (bd. dirs., v.p. 1981-82, pres. 1982-83), Ga. Assn. Educators, Ga. Assn. Jr. Colls. (exec. com. 1967-70, pres. 1968-69), Pulaski Hist. Commn. (v.p., bd. dirs. 1976-87), Ga. Heart Assn. (12th dist. chmn. and cabinet mem. 1976-81), Cochran-Bleckley C. of C. (1st v.p., dir., v.p.), SAR (Kendall award 1980), Nat. Soc. SAR (trustee 1984-85, nat. chmn. Douglas G. High Sch. hist. oration contest 1985-87), Ga. Soc. SAR (bd. mgrs. 1979-82, v.p. 1981-82, pres. 1983-84), Middle Ga. Chpt. SAR (organizing pres. 1979-80, pres. 1980-83, bd. dirs. 1985-87), Magna Charta Barons (regent Ga. div. from 1986), Descs. Order Knights of Garter, Descs. of Founders of Hartford, Order Founders and Patriots Am., Soc. Friends St. George's Chapel, Order of Washington, Plantagenet Soc., Order of Crown, Ams. of Royal Descent, Ancient and Honorable Arty. Co. of Mass., Hospitaller Order, Knights St. John of Jerusalem (sec. central and Gulf states priory 1985-86), Phi Delta Kappa, Phi Theta Kappa, Gamma Beta Phi, Sigma Nu, Phi Beta Lambda, others. Democrat. Baptist (deacon, chmn. bd. deacons 1982-83). Clubs: Rotary (v.p. Cochran 1966-67, pres. 1967-68, gov. dist. 692 1976-77; trustee Ga. student program 1984-87), Uchee Trail Country. Died Dec. 13, 1987, buried Cedar Hill Cemetery, Cochran, Ga.

ALDRICH, HENRY RAY, geologist; b. Boston, June 8, 1891; s. Arthur Wilbur and Abbie Clarinda (Perkins) A.; m. Louise Clement, June 11, 1918; children: Richard Wayland, Robert Clement. BS in Mining Engring., MIT, 1914; MS in Econ. Geology, U. Minn., 1917; PhD, U. Wis., 1931; DSc (hon.), Tufts U., 1955. Instr. in mining and metallurgy Northwestern U., 1914-16; asst. geologist Wis. Geol. Survey, summer 1916, geologist, 1917; asst. U. Minn., 1916-17; statistician non-ferrous metals War Industries Bd., 1917-19; instr. ore dressing MIT, 1920; geologist Wis. Geol. Survey, 1919-34, chief of field parties, 1919-25, asst. state geologist, 1925-34; asst. sec., editor in chief Geol. Soc. Am., 1934-40, sec., councilor, editor in chief from 1941. Author of numerous bulletins and sci. papers; co-inventor (with William O. Hotchkiss, John P. Foerst and Noel H. Stearn) of Hotchkiss Super Dip. 1st lt. (unattached), U.S. Army, 1918-19; assigned to War Industries Bd. Mem. Geochem. Soc., Am. Inst. Mining and Metall. Engrs., Mineralogical Soc. Am., Geol. Soc. Am., Am. Assn. Petroleum Geologists, AAAS (v.p., chmn. sect E. 1948), Soc. Econ. Geologists (mem. exec. com. 1944), Am. Geog. Soc., Am. Geophys. Union, Mens Faculty Club (Columbia), Cosmos Club, Sigma Xi, Gamma Alpha. Home: Leonia N.J. †

ALDRICH, MALCOLM PRATT, foundation executive; b. Fall River, Mass., Oct. 1, 1900; s. Stanley A. and Jane S. (Pratt) A.; m. Ella F. Buffington, June 20, 1925; children: Joan Aldrich Knowlton, Shirley Aldrich Daiger, Malcolm. BMC, Durfee Sch., Fall River, 1918; AB, Yale U., 1922. Began in finance and philanthropy with Edward S. Harkness; hon. chmn. Commonwealth Fund., N.Y.C.; hon. mem. bd. trustees Am. Museum, Met. Museum Art. Spl. asst. to asst. sec. of Navy for Air, USN, 1942-45; disch. rank capt. Mem. Maidstone, Links, Century Assn., Links Golf. Republican. Home: East Hampton N.Y. Died July 31, 1986; buried Cedar Lawn Cemetary, East Hampton, N.Y.

ALDRICH, NELSON WILMARTH, architect; b. N.Y.C., Apr. 6, 1911; s. William Truman and Dorothea (Davenport) A.; m. Eleanor Tweed (div.); 1 child, Nelson Wilmarth; m. Frances Turner, Nov. 9, 1940; children—Frances D. Maher, Abigail Cheever, Rosalie C. West. A.B., Harvard, 1934, M.Arch., 1938; L.H.D. (hon.), Tufts U., 1956; LL.D., Emerson Coll., 1962. Designer Harrison & Abramoviz, 1939-40; project planner U.S. Housing Authority, 1940-42; partner Campbell, Aldrich & Nulty, Boston, 1947-74; pres. Aldrich, Pounder & Assos., Inc., Boston, 1974-86; cons. architect Dartmouth, Bradford Jr. Coll., Phillips Exeter Acad.; assoc. architect Boton City Hall; architect, developer Portsmouth (N.H.) Urban Renewal Project.; Co-founder, chmn. Boston Arts Festival, 1952-64; dir. Boston Archtl. Center, 1968-72; chmn. Boston Art Commn., 1955-75; mem. Planning Bd. Town of Marblehead, Mass., 1979-85; pres. Inst. Contemporary Art, 1947-60, trustee, 1960-64; mem. archtl. design adv. com. Boston Redevel. Authority, Boston, 1959-68. Mem. Mass. Bd. Regional Community Colls., 1961-72; trustee Boston Mus. of Fine Arts, 1954-86, Radcliffe Coll., 1957-71, vice chmn., 1961-66; v.p. Met. Boston Arts Center, 1958-60, pres., 1960-63; bd. dirs. New Eng. Hist. Seaport, 1977-85. Served as lt. comdr. USNR, 1942-46; charge combat aircraft service units, Pacific. Fellow AIA, Am. Acad. Arts and Scis.; mem. Boston Soc. Architects, Mass. Assn. Architects (dir. 1950-58), Harvard Alumni Assn. (dir. 1962-65). Club: Tavern (Boston). Home: Marblehead Mass. Died Sept. 16, 1986; buried Swan Point Cemetery, Providence, R.I.

ALDRICH, RICHARD STODDARD, producer; b. Boston, Aug. 17, 1902; s. Edward Irving and Mary Pickering (Joy) A.; m. Helen Beals, Nov. 5, 1927 (div. 1936); children: Richard Stoddard, David Beals; m. Gertrude Lawrence, July 4, 1940 (dec. Sept. 1952); m. Elizabeth Boyd, June 18, 1955; children: Susan, Mary Joy. AB cum laude, Harvard Coll., 1925. Dep. dir. U.S. Econ. Mission, Madrid, Spain, 1955-56, dir., 1956-62; minister econ. affairs Am. Embassy, Madrid, 1957-62; dir. U.S. Agy. Internat. Devel., Morocco, 1962-65. Gen. mgr. Richard Boleslavsky and his Am. Lab. Theatre, 1926; co-presented plays: La Gringa, 1928, Twelfth Night, 1929, Art and Mrs. Bottle, 1930, Lean Harvest, 1931, The Lady with a Lamp, 1931, Springtime for Harry, 1932, Three Cornered Moon, 1933, By Your Leave, 1934, Pure in Heart, 1934, Petticoat Fever, 1935, Fresh Fields, Aged 26, 1936, Tide Rising, 1937, Be So Kindly, 1937, Lorelei, 1938, The Importance of Being Earnest, 1939, My Dear Children, 1939, Margin for Error, 1939, Cue for Passion, 1940, Plan M, 1942; produced Pygmalion (mng. dir. Theatre Inc.), 1945, Playboy of the Western World, 1946, It Takes Two, 1947, Macbeth, 1948, Goodbye My Fancy, 1948-50, Caesar and Cleopatra, 1949-50, The Devil's Disciple, 1950, The Guardsman, 1950-51, The Moon is Blue, 1951-53, The Love of Four Colonels, 1953, A Girl Can Tell, 1953, Sailor's Delight, 1954-55; presented Tallulah Bankhead in Dear Charles, 1954-55; brought Old Vic Theatre from London, 1946, Habimah Players from Tel Aviv, The Dublin Gate Theatre from Ireland, 1948; operated 3 summer theatres: Cape Playhouse, Dennis, Mass., Falmouth Playhouse, Coonamessett, Mass., Cape Cod Music Circus, Hyannis, Mass.; operator Nat. Theatre, Washington 1952-72;dir. A Doll's House, Central City (Colo.) Festivals, 1937, Ruy Blas, 1938; author: Gertrude Lawrence as Mrs. 'A', 1955; (motion picture)

Star, 1968. Bd. dirs. Nat. Theatre and Acad., City Center Music and Drama Inc. Decorated Grand Cross Isabella the Catholic (Spain). Mem. Soc. Colonial Wars, Soc. Mayflower Descendants, SAR. Clubs: Union, Harvard, Players, Coffe House, Badminton, Dutch Treat (N.Y.C.); Buck's (London); Metropolitan, Army and Navy (Washington); The Travellers (Paris); Farmington Country (Charlottesville, Va.). Home: Dennis Mass. Died Mar. 31, 1986.

ALEXANDER, CHARLES P(AUL), professor of entomology; b. Gloversville, N.Y., Sept. 25, 1889; s. Emil and Janet (Parker) A.; m. Mabel M. Miller, Nov. 10, 1917. BS, Cornell U., 1913, PhD, 1918; DSc, U. Mass., 1959. Asst. in entomology Cornell U., 1911-13, instr., 1915-17; curator entomology collection U. Kans., 1917-19, Ill. State Natural History Survey Collections, Urbana, 1919-22; asst. prof. entomology U. Mass., 1922-30, prof., from 1930, head dept. entomology and zoology, 1938-48, 52-58, acting dean sch. of sci., 1945-46, dean, 1946-52. Author: The Craneflies of New York, part 1, 1919, part 2, 1920, Cranflies of the Baltic Amber, 1931; author of Part I Craneflies in Diptera of Patagonia and South Chile, 1929; contbr. to entomol. jours. in U.S. and fgn. countries. Decorated Order Bernardo O'Higgins (Chile). Fellow Entomol. Soc. Am. (pres. 1942-43), Entomol. socs. London, France; mem. Am. Entomol. Soc. (corr. mem.), Sigma Xi, Phi Kappa Phi, Alpha Gamma Rho, Gamma Alpha. Republican. Methodist. Home: Amherst Mass. †

ALEXANDER, HARRY LOUIS, physician; b. N.Y.C., Feb. 16, 1887; s. Henry and Minnie A.; m. Laura Stryker, Apr. 17, 1917 (div.); children: Lewis McElwain, Beverly Gertrude; m. Janet Holmes, Dec. 23, 1929; children: Janet Marjorie, Andrew Holmes. AB, Williams Coll., 1910, DSc (hon., 1956; MD, Columbia U., 1914. House officer Presbyn. Hosp., N.Y.C., 1914-16; asst. resident physician Peter Bent Brigham Hosp., Boston, 1916-17; instr. medicine Cornell U., 1919-24; assoc. prof. medicine Washington U., St. Louis, 1924-36, assoc. prof. clin. medicine, 1936-41, prof. clin. medicine, 1941-52, prof. emeritus, 1952; assoc. physician Barnes Hosp., St. Louis from 1924; asst. vis. physician Bellevue Hosp., N.Y.C., 1919-24; cen. com. cons. VA, 1950-54; mem. adv. com. Nat. Inst. Allergy and Infectious Diseases, NIH, 1957-61; chmn. Mayor's Adv. Com. on Health and Hosps. Author: Bronchial Asthma, 1928, Synopsis of Allergy, 1941, 2d edit., 1946; Reactions with Drug Therapy, 1955, also chpts. on allergy systems of medicine; editor Jour. of Allergy, 1929-50; co-editor: Immunological Diseases, 1965; contbr. articles to profl. jours. Capt. M.C. U.S. Army, 1917-18; maj. med. service Am. Expeditionary Force, 1918-19. Decorated Officer d'academie; recipient Alumni Faculty award Washington U., 1964; Harry L. Alexander ann. vis. professorship established in his name, 1964. Fellow ACP, Internat. Congress Allergology (hon.), Am. Acad. Allergy (hon.); mem. Am. Assn. Physicians, AMA, Soc. Exptl. Biology amd Medicine, Am. Soc. Clin. Investigation, Soc. Study Asthma and Allied Conditions (pres. 1934), Harvey Soc., Soc. Française d'allergie (hon.), Soc. Argentina para el estudio de la Alergia (hon.). Home: Saint Louis Mo. †

ALEXANDER, HERBERT M., publisher; b. N.Y.C., Sept. 1, 1910; s. Max and Therese (Rothschild) A.; m. Greta Maren Hinterauer, May 8, 1942; 1 child, Thomas P. BA, NYU, 1931. Publishers' traveler 1932-34; social worker City of N.Y., 1935-36; editor N.Y. Graphic Soc., 1936-39; copy chief Norman Warren & Co., 1939-42; assoc. editor Pocket Books, Inc., 1947, editor-in-chief, from 1948, v.p., after 1953, pub., dir., until 1974; exec. v.p. Washington Sq. Press, from 1959; pres. Trident Press, from 1963; v.p., dir. Simon & Schuster, from 1966; free-lance editor various cos. including Playboy Press, William Morrow & Co., from 1974. Author translations, articles and short stories. 2d lt. USAAF, 1942-46. Mem. Player's Club, Phi Beta Kappa, Pi Lambda Phi. Home: New York N.Y. Died Nov. 23, 1988.

ALEXANDER, PARK JACOBUS, lawyer; b. Bridgeport, Ohio, Apr. 12, 1879; s. William and Sarah Jane (Park) A. AB, Washington and Jefferson Coll., 1900, AM, 1904; LLD, LLB, Harvard U., 1903. Bar: Pa. 1904. Pvt. practice Pitts., from 1904; counsel Fidelity Trust Co., Pitts. Trustee, pres. emeritus bd. trustees Washington and Jefferson Coll.; trustee Presbyn. Hosp., Pitts. Lt. coast arty., later instr. in arty. fire, U.S. Army, AEF, World War I. Mem. Am., Pa., and Allegheny County bar assns., Masons, University Club, Duquesne Club, Pittsburgh Athletic Club, Oakmont Country Club, Beta Theta Pi. Republican. Presbyterian. Home: Pittsburgh Pa. †

ALEXANDER, WILLIS WALTER, trust company executive; b. Trenton, Mo., Jan. 2, 1919; s. Willis W. and Ethel Claire (Newmeyer) A.; m. Doris Vosburg, June 20, 1942 (div. May 1975); children: Eric Willis, Barbara Louise Alexander, Patricia Ann Alexander; m. Sandra Skidmore, Oct. 1975; children: Margaret Claire, Mary Katherine. B.A., U. Mo., 1940; M.B.A., U. Pa., 1941. Asst. sec. to exec. v.p. Trenton Trust Co., 1947-60, pres., 1960-74, chmn. bd., from 1974; pres. state bank div. Am. Bankers Assn., Washington, 1966-67; v.p. Am. Bankers Assn., 1967-68, pres., 1968-69, exec. v.p., 1969-85; co-pub. Trenton Republican Times, from

1963; exec. v.p. Internat. Monetary Conf., 1971-85. Served to lt. comdr. USNR, 1941-47. Mem. Mo. Bankers Assn. (pres. 1959-60). Died Oct. 27, 1985; buried Trenton, Mo.

ALEXION, JOHN COULON, former university dean, educator, corporate director, consultant; b. N.Y.C., Jan. 2, 1916; s. Alexander John and Madeleine C. (Coulon) A.; m. Grace E. Bunn, Oct. 15, 1938; 1 dau., Karen Alexion Scheidt. Student, Poly. Inst. N.Y., 1937-41; B.Sc. in Mgmt., NYU, 1945, M.B.A., 1945, Ph.D., 1964. Vice pres. corporate devel. Liggett Drug Co., Stamford, Conn., 1956-59; pres. Gens, Jarboe, Inc., N.Y.C., 1959-61; v.p. adminstrn. Va. Metal Products, Inc., Orange, 1961-63; chmn. dept. fin. and law Adelphi U., Garden City, N.Y., 1963-66; v.p. bus. and career-oriented programs, dean Coll. Bus. Adminstrn. St. John's U., Jamaica, N.Y., 1966-85, v.p., spl. asst. to pres. for bus. and career oriented programs, 1985-86; cons. Irvin Industries, Inc., N.Y.C., 1964-82, dir., 1964-80; chmn. bd. State-Wide Ins. Co., Great Neck, N.Y., 1966-86; dir. spl. projects Va. Metal Industries, Inc., Orange, 1983-86; pres. Alexion & Assocs., mgmt. cons., Glen Oaks, N.Y., 1973-86; cons. Mobil Oil Corp., N.Y.C., 1972-83. Pres. Am. Hellenic Inst., Washington, 1982. Served to capt. Supply Corps USNR, 1949-76; to rear adm. N.Y. Naval Militia, 1981-86. Decorated Navy Commendation medal; decorated Joint Service Commendation medal, medal for Disting. Civilian Service Dept. Army, 1982, Pres.'s medal St. John's U., 1977, Legion of Merit award, 1985, Outstanding Adminstrv. Achievement award St. John's U., 1985. Mem. ASME (sr.), Soc. Am. Mil. Engrs., Naval Res. Assn. (chpt. v.p. adminstrn. 1981-86), Naval Order U.S., Mil. Order World Wars, Vets. 7th Regt. (life), Beta Gamma Sigma. Republican. Home: Glen Oaks N.Y. Died Sept. 6, 1986.

ALEXOPOULOS, CONSTANTINE JOHN, mycologist, educator; b. Chgo., Mar. 17, 1907; s. John Constantine and Chrysoula (Panagopoulou) A.; m. Juliet Catherine Dowdy, Aug. 26, 1939. BS in Agr. with honors, U. Ill., 1927, MS in Horticulture, 1928, PhD in Botany, 1932. Instr. botany U. Ill., 1934-35; instr. Kent State U., 1935-36, asst prof., 1936-40, assoc. prof., 1940-43; plant pathologist Institut N. Canellopoulos, Piraeus, Greece, 1938-39; staff RFC Rubber Devel. Program, Amazon Valley, Brazil, 1943-44; officer agrl rehab., dep. dir. div. agr. and fisheries UNRAA Mission to Greece, 1944-47; assoc. prof. botany Mich. State U., 1947-52, prof., 1952-56; prof., head dept. botany U. Iowa, 1956-62; prof. botany U. Tex., Austin, 1962-77, prof. emeritus, 1977-86, acting chmn. dept. botany, 1965; Fulbright sr. rsch. scholar U. Athens, Greece, 1954-55; 4th Bessey lectr. Iowa State U., 1972; mem. NSF Systematic Biology Panel, 1962-65; trustee Am. Type Culture Collection, 1965-71. Author: Introductory Mycology, 1952, 2d edit., 1962 (trans. 6 fgn. langs.), 3d edit. (with C.R. Mims), 1979, (with H. C. Bold) Algae and Fungi, 1967, (with W. D. Gray) The Biology of the Myxomycetes, 1968, (with G. W. Martin) The Myxomycetes, 1969, (with Bold and T. Delevoryas) Morphology of Plants and Fungi, 1980, (with G.W. Martin and M.L. Farr) The Genera of the Myxomycetes, 1983; mem. editorial bd. Brittonia, 1963-66, Llyodia, 1963-71; contbr. McGraw Hill Ency. Sci. and Tech., Ency. Biol. Scis., Ency. Biochemistry, Ency. Brit., also articles to profl. jours. Mem. Bot. Soc. Am. (pres. 1963, cert. merit 1967), Iowa Acad. sci. (chmn. botany 1960), Internat. Mycol. Assn. (pres. 1971-77, hon. pres. 1983), Mycol. Soc. Am. (pres. 1959, 19th ann. lectr. 1968, Disting. Mycologists award 1981, W.H. Weston award for teaching excellence in Mycology 1983). Am. Acad. Arts and Scis., Acad. Athens (corr. mem.), Brit. Mycol. Soc. (hon. mem. 1983), Ohio Acad. Sci. (v.p. 1943), Indian Mycol. Soc., Mycol. Soc. Japan, Mich. Acad. Sci. Arts and Letters (chmn. botany 1954), Torrey Bot. Club, Sigma Xi, Alpha Zeta. Greek Orthodox. Home: Austin Tex. Died May 15, 1986; interred Capitol Meml. Park.

ALFORD, NEWELL GILDER, mining engineer, consultant; b. Phila., Dec. 11, 1887; s. Reuben Gilder and Mary Ellen (DuBree) A.; m. Caroline Farren Atkinson, June 27, 1912; children: Newell Gilder, Frances Lydia. AB, Swarthmore Coll., 1909; BS and ME, U. Pitts. With engrng. corps U.S. Coal & Coke Co., Gary, W.Va., summers, 1907-08; with Ill. Steel Co., Joliet, 1909; with St. Bernard Mining Co., Earlington, Ky., 1910-20, mine supt. and asst. chief engr., 1913-19, chief engr., asst. to pres., 1920; owner firm cons. mining engrs. from 1920; individual cons. practice, coal property appraisal, devel., ops. in N.Am.; gen. mgr., treas., bd. dirs. Clover Splint Coal Co., 1923-44; trustee Pitts. Terminal Coal Corp., 1939-40. Author numerous pamphlets, brochures, etc., on mining and econs. Mem. AIME (bd. dirs. 1949-51, chmn. coal div. 1942, 1st chmn. coal div. com. on coal mining engrng. scholarships 1937-41), Coal Mining Inst. Am. (pres. 1940), Am. Mining Congress (chmn. com. mining depreciation study), Am. Standards Assn. (chmn. mining standards bd.), Ill. Mining Inst., Engrs. Soc. Western Pa., Minig Soc. N.S., Mine Rescue Vets., W.Va. Mining Inst., Ky. Hist. Soc., Soc. War of 1812, University Club, Duquesne Club, Book and Key Club (Swarthmore), Soc. Friends, Delta Upsilon. Home: Pittsburgh Pa. †

ALIOTO, ROBERT FRANKLYN, school system administrator; b. San Francisco, Nov. 22, 1933; s. Michael P. and Evelyn (Blohm) A.; m. Dominica Ann Deuel, June 28, 1980; children: Deborah Ann, Robert Franklyn, David R., Diane A. AA, Hartnell Coll., 1953; BE, San Jose State Coll., 1958, MA, 1961; EdD, Harvard, 1968. Tchr. elem. and jr. high schs. Greenfield, Calif., 1956-60; prin. Carneros Elem. Sch., Napa, Calif., 1960-62; supt. Shurtleff Elementary Sch. Dist., Napa, 1962-65; adminstrv. asst. Ctr. for Rsch. and Devel. on Ednl. Differences, Harvard U., 1965-66; dir. Inst. Tng. Selected Tchrs. Liaison Role, 1966-67; supt. schs. Pearl River (N.Y.) Sch. Dist., 1966-71, Yonkers (N.Y.) City Sch. Dist., 1971-75, San Francisco Unified Sch. Dist., from 1975. Author: (with J.A. Jungherr) Operational PPBS for Education, 1971. Deceased.

ALLAN, THOMAS A., lawyer; b. Ont., Can., 1884. LLB, Golden Gate Coll. Law, 1909. Bar: Calif. 1909. Ptnr. Allan, Miller, Groezinger, Keesling & Martin, San Francisco. Mem. ABA, State Bar Calif., Bar Assn. San Francisco. Home: San Francisco Calif. †

ALLEE, JOHN GAGE, English educator; b. Helena, Mont., Feb. 28, 1918; s. John and Pearla (Townshend) A.; m. Harriet Dow, Apr. 17, 1943 (dec. 1983); children: John Gage, Stephen Dole; m. Frances Colby, Aug. 25, 1985. B.A., George Washington U., 1939, M.A., 1940; Ph.D., Johns Hopkins U., 1955. Jr. instr. Johns Hopkins U., Balt., 1945-49; asst. prof. English George Washington U., Washington, 1949-56, assoc. prof., 1956-62, prof., 1962-85; prof. emeritus George Washington U., 1986-87, asst. dean div. univ. students, 1953-58, assoc. dean univ. students, 1958-62, dean univ. students, 1962-79; lectr. Fgn. Service Inst., Smithsonian Instn., 1975-76; lectr. Scandinavian countries including Iceland and Greenland, 1980, 84, 85. Served with U.S. Army, 1941-45. Fulbright grantee Iceland, 1961, 69-70. Mem. Soc. Advancement Scandinavian Study, Mediaeval Acad. Am., Linguistic Soc. Am., Icelandic Archaeol. Soc., Am. Name Soc., New Chaucer Soc., Tudor and Stuart Club, Phi Beta Kappa. Home: Albany N.Y. Died Jan. 1, 1987; cremated.

ALLEGRO, JOHN MARCO, author, scholar; b. London, Feb. 17, 1923; s. John Marco and Mable Jessie (Perry) A.; B.A. with honors, Manchester U., 1951, M.A. in Oriental Studies (David Bles Hebrew prize 1950), 1953; m. Joan Ruby Lawrence, June 17, 1948; children—Judith Anne, John Mark. Lectr., Oriental and O.T. studies U. Manchester, 1954-70; 1st Brit. rep. Internat. Dead Sea Scrolls editing team, 1953-88; adv. Jordanian Govt. on Dead Sea Scrolls, 1961-88; trustee, adv., hon. sec. Dead Sea Scrolls Fund, 1962-70; author: Dead Sea Scrolls, 1956, rev. edit. 1964; People of the Dead Sea Scrolls, 1958; Treasure of the Copper Scroll, 1960; Search in the Desert, 1964; The Shapira Affair, 1965; Discoveries in the Judean Desert, vol. V, 1968; The Sacred Mushroom and The Cross, 1970; The End of a Road, 1970; The Chosen People, 1971; Lost Gods, 1977; Dead Sea Scrolls and the Christian Myth, 1979; All Manner of Men, 1982; Physician, Heal Thyself, 1985. Served with Brit. Navy, 1941-46. Recipient Leverhulme Research award, 1958. Life mem. Soc. O.T. Study; mem. Explorers Club. Home: Cheshire, England. Died Feb. 17, 1988; cremated.

ALLEN, AUSTIN FLETCHER, insurance company executive; b. Bunkie, La., Feb. 22, 1892; s. William T. and Isadora (Sims) A.; m. Sadie Stephens, June 16, 1915; children: Ruth Isadora, Sarah Elizabeth. Student pub. schs., Tex. Clk. Roberts & Corley, Beaumont, Tex., 1910-11, Trezevant & Cochran, Dallas, 1912-13; asst. sec., asst. treas., later sec., v.p. and sales mgr., exec. v.p., pres. and gen. mgr. Tex. Employers Ins. Assn., Dallas, 1914-38, pres. and dir., 1938-56, chmn. bd., from 1956; pres., dir. Employers Casualty Co., Dallas, 1938-56, chmn. bd., from 1956; pres., dir. Employers Nat. Ins. Co., 1957-56, chmn. bd., from 1956; chmn. bd. Employers Nat. Life Ins. Co., from 1961; bd. dirs. Republic Nat. Bank. Mem. Dallas Country Club, City Club, Masons, Rotary. Congregationalist. Home: Dallas Tex. †

ALLEN, BEN (WILLIAM BENJAMIN), lawyer, business executive; b. Elizabethton, Tenn., Oct. 29, 1891; s. William Robert and Sarah Margaret (Smith) A.; m. Corinne Crawford Renfro, June 27, 1928; children: Robert Renfro, Elizabeth. LLB, Cumberland U., 1921. Bar: Tenn. 1921. Pvt. practice Elizabethton, Tenn., 1921-26; mem. firm Allen & Allen, , dist. atty. gen., State of Tenn., judge, 1st judicial cir., State of, Tenn., v.p., dir. N.Am. Rayon Corp., 1946-57; pvt. practice Elizabethton, Tenn., from 1957; chmn. bd. Carter County Meml. Hosp., from 1957. Pres. Sequoyah Coun., Boy Scouts Am., 1941-42; mem. nat. Protestant lay com. on scouting. Mem. ABA, Am. Legion, Masons, Rotary, Metropolitan Club (Washington). Republican. Baptist. †

ALLEN, BYRON GILCHRIST, assistant secretary of agriculture; b. Lauren, Iowa, Sept. 13, 1901; s. Joseph Holmes and Grace (Gilchrist) A.; m. Elsa Ellanora Erickson, Dec. 18, 1928; children: Virginia Allen Flemming, Joseph (dec.), Eric. G. BS, Iowa State Coll., 1924. Farmer in state S.D., 1924-26; farm owner, mgr. Detroit Lakes, Minn., since 1940; supt. Iowa Div. Old Age Assistance, 1934-39; Minn. commr. agr. until 1961; asst. to U.S. sec. of agr. Washington, 1961-88; mem. Iowa Ho. of Reps. from Pocahontas Co., 1927-32; sec. State Senate Iowa, 1933-34; sec. to Senator Smith W. Brookhart of Iowa 1932; Dem. candidate for Congress, Iowa, 1940; nominee for gov., Minn., Dem.-Farmer-Labor Party, 1944; dem. nat. committeeman, Minn., 1948-55; nominee for Minn. State Senate, 1946, 50; del. Dem. Nat. Convs., 1944, 52, chmn. Minn. Delegation, 1944; head Agrl. Speakers Bur. Dem. Nat. Com., 1940; trustee Minn. Found. for Polit. Edn. Editor, pub. Pocahontas Democrat, 1926-31; contbr. social sci., farm coop. polit. sci. publs. Mem. Mason Lodge, Phi Delta Theta, Delta Sigma Rho. Home: Detroit Lakes Minn. Died June 10, 1988.

ALLEN, FRED HAROLD, JR., physician, educator; b. Holyoke, Mass., Feb. 23, 1912; s. Fred Harold and Harriet (Ives) A.; m. Frances Williams Brown, July 16, 1938; children: Philip Brown, Mark Harold, Barbara Allen Sandersen, Dwight Bickford (dec.). A.B., Amherst Coll., 1934, D.Sc. (hon.), 1984; M.D., Harvard U., 1938. Intern Children's Hosp., Boston, 1938-42; practice pediatrics Holyoke, Mass., 1946-47; asso. dir. Blood Grouping Lab. Boston, 1947-63; sr. investigator N.Y. Blood Center, 1963-86, sr. investigator emeritus, 1986; clin. asso. prof. pediatrics Cornell U. Med. Coll., 1963-86. Author: (with L. K. Diamond) Erythroblastosis Fetalis, 1958; also articles.; Chief editor for N. and S. Am.: Vox Sanguinis, 1963-76; Assoc. editor: Transfusion. Served to maj., M.C. AUS, 1942-46. Recipient Karl Landsteiner Meml. award Am. Assn. Blood Banks, 1963; Joseph P. Kennedy Internat. award research mental retardation, 1966; Philip Levine award Am. Soc. Clin. Pathology, 1976; Buffalo award State U. N.Y. at Buffalo, 1976; Schweitzer Research award Greater N.Y. Acad. Prosthodontics, 1978. Home: Groton Mass. Died, Mar. 12, 1987; buried Westford, Mass.

ALLEN, HAROLD BYRON, English language educator; b. Grand Rapids, Mich., Oct. 6, 1902; s. Arthur Kingsbury and Edith (Welch) A.; m. Elizabeth Mitchell, June 19, 1934; children: Marjorie Lyle (Mrs. Alexander G. Russell), Susan Kingsbury (Mrs. David Stevenson). B.A., Kalamazoo Coll., 1924; M.A., U. Mich., 1928, Ph.D., 1941. From asst. prof. to prof. rhetoric, also asst. to pres. Shurtleff Coll., Alton, Ill., 1925-34; asst. editor Early Modern English Dictionary, 1934-39, Middle English Dictionary, 1939-40; asst. prof. English San Diego State Coll., 1940-43; mem. faculty U. Minn., 1944—, prof. English, 1958-68, prof. English and linguistics, 1968-71, prof. emeritus, 1971—, lectr. in linguistics, 1976-77, 86; vis. summer prof. Mills Coll., 1943, U. So. Calif., 1961, U. Victoria, Can., 1973, 74, 75, Moorhead State U., 1976, Chadron State Coll., 1978; Fulbright lectr. U. Cairo, Egypt, 1954-55; Smith-Mundt vis. prof. linguistics UAR Ministry of Edn., Cairo, 1958-59; Fulbright-Hayes lectr. Kossuth Lajos U., Debrecen, Hungary, 1972; dir., editor Linguistic Atlas of Upper Midwest, 1947—; linguistic cons. Economy Co., 1967-83, 87—, Ency. of the States, 1980; adv. bd. Doubleday dictionaries, 1975—; mem. nat. adv. council Teaching English as Fgn. Lang., 1962-65, 69-77, chmn., 1974-77; English lang. cons. U. Tehran, Iran, 1971, 73; chmn. lang. arts adv. com. Minn. Bd. Edn., 1962-67; chmn. English lang. adv. panel USIA, 1986—. Author: An Introduction to English Sound Structure, 1960, TENES-A Survey of the Teaching of English to Non-English Speakers in the U.S, 1966, Linguistic Atlas of the Upper Midwest, Vol. 1, 1973, Vol. 2, 1975, Vol. 3, 1976, Pathways to English, 1984; also articles.; Editor, compiler in field. Recipient Disting. Alumnus award Kalamazoo Coll., 1980; Am. Council Learned Soc. fellow, summers, 1938-40; fellow Fund Advancement Edn., 1951-52. Mem. ACLU, AAUP, Nat. Council Tchrs. English (pres. 1961, dir. commn. English lang. 1964-68, chmn. Conf. Coll. Composition and Communication 1952, Distinguished service award 1969, David Russell award for research 1973), Tchrs. English to Speakers of Other Langs. (pres. 1966-67, Distinguished service citation 1970), Linguistic Soc. Am., Am. Dialect Soc. (mem. exec. council 1963-68, pres. 1971, 72, disting. scholar award 1986), Am. Name Soc. (bd. mgrs. 1961-63), Canadian Linguistic Assn., Internat. Assn. U. Profs. English, Speech Communication Assn., Minn. Group Linguistics (chmn. 1948, 64-67, 74), Phi Delta Kappa, Phi Kappa Phi, Pi Kappa Delta, Sigma Tau Delta, Theta Alpha Phi. Died July 27, 1988.

ALLEN, RAYMOND BERNARD, educator, physician, former government official; b. Cathay, N.D., Aug. 7, 1902; s. Anthony J. and Ellen (Faulkner) A.; m. Dorothy Sheard, Aug. 29, 1931 (div. Dec. 1963); children: Charles Anthony, Raymond Bernard, Willard Sheard (dec.) Blanche E. (dec.), Dorothy, Barbara Jean; m. Emmy Portman Stone, Aug. 13, 1968. BS, U. Minn., 1924, MA, 1925, MB, MD, 1928, PhD, 1934; LLD, Tulane U., 1946, U. Ill., 1946, Lake Forest Coll., 1946, U. Hawaii, 1948, Boston U., 1948, Gonzaga U., 1949, U. So. Calif., 1951; DSc., Whitman Coll., 1947. Fellow Mayo Found., 1930-33; gen. med. practice Minot, N.D., 1928-30; assoc. dean in charge grad. studies Coll. Physicians and Surgeons, Columbia U., 1934-36; assoc. dir. N.Y. Post-Grad. Med. Sch. and Hosp., Columbia U., 1933-36; dean Wayne U. Coll. Medicine, 1936-39; exec. dean medicine, dentistry and pharmacy Chgo. Colls. U. Ill., 1939-46; dean Coll. of Medicine, 1943-46; pres. U. Wash., Seattle, 1946-52; dir. Psychol. Strategy Bd., 1952; chancellor UCLA, 1952-59;

dir. U.S. Operations Missions to Indonesia, 1959-61; chief office research coordination Pan Am. Health Orgn., Washington, 1962-66, chief office of health and population dynamics, 1966-67, cons. health, edn., population dynamics, 1967-86; cons. Project to Strengthen Health Profl. Schs. of Bangladesh, Asia Found., 1972-86; clin. prof. community medicine and internat. health Georgetown U. Coll. Medicine, 1967-70, lectr., 1970-86; cons. health, edn., population dynamics AID, State Dept., 1969-86; dir. med. services Office Sec. of Defense, 1949 (on leave from U. of Wash.), dir. Salary Stblzn. Bd., 1951; nat. cons. U.S. Air Force; bd. dirs. Transp. Assn. Am., Freedoms Found., Los Angeles World Affairs Council, pres. 2d World Conf. Med. Edn., 1959; chmn. bd. trustees Ednl. Testing Service, 1951; trustee Carnegie Found. for Advancement Teaching, 1948-59, Am. Com. on United Europe; mem. Com. (Eberstadt) on Nat. Security Orgn. (Hoover Commn. 1948-49); cons. emeritus Nat. War Coll. Contbr. articles on profl. and mgmt. activity. Fellow A.C.P. (emeritus); mem. Cosmos Club, Sigma Xi, Alpha Omega Alpha, Phi Delta Kappa, Phi Beta Kappa (hon.). Republican. Home: Flint Hill Va. Died Mar. 15, 1986.

ALLEN, ROBERT DAY, educator, biologist; b. Providence, Aug. 28, 1927; s. Richard Day and Mary (Cottrell) A.; m. Margaret Dampman, Dec. 23, 1950 (div. 1970); children: Elizabeth, Wayne; m. Nina Strömgren, Sept. 12, 1971; 1 dau. Barbara. AB, Brown U., 1949; PhD, U. Pa., 1953. Asst. instr. zoology U. Pa., 1950-51; instr. zoology U. Mich., 1954-56; asst. prof., then assoc. prof. biology Princeton U., 1956-66; prof. biology dept. SUNY, Albany, 1966-74, chmn., 1966-72; prof., chmn. dept. biol. scis. Dartmouth Coll., 1975-78, Ira Allen Eastman prof. biology, 1978-86; cons. industry, 1963-86l lectr. Eng., Japan, Mexico, USSR, Poland, East and West Germany, France, Sweden, Denmark; vis. prof. Osaka (Japan) U., Japan Soc. for Promotion of Sci., 1974. Editor: Primitive Motile Systems in Cell Biology, 1964, Cell Motility, 1980-86; assoc. editor: Jour. Mechanochem. and Cell Motility, 1971-75; editor: Microscopica Acta, 1977-86; contbr. articles to U.S. and fgn. jours. Trustee Marine Biol. Lab., Woods Hole, Mass., 1966-74. Guggenheim fellow, 1961, 66; recipient Golden Eagle award for non-theatre motion picture Mitosis Coun. Internat. Non-Theatrical Events, 1965; USPHS predoctoral fellow U. Pa., 1951-53; USPHS postdoctoral fellow, Sweden and Italy, 1953-54. Fellow AAAS (coun. 1976-79, com. on fellows 1977-86, nominating com. 1978), Royal Micros. Soc.; mem. Soc. Gen. Physiologists (treas. 1963-65, pres. 1973-74), Am. Soc. for Cell Biology (coun. 1973-74), Biophys. Soc. Home: Hanover N.H. Died Mar. 23, 1986.

ALLEN, ROGER, architect; b. Grand Rapids, Mich., June 23, 1892; s. Frank Payne and Mary Francis (O'Connor) A.; m. Margaret Katherine Sullivan, Nov. 24, 1923; children: Mary Margaret (Mrs. Robert Peckham), Bridget Irene (Mrs. Irving G. Hunsberger). Student pub. schs., Grand Rapids; LLD, Cen. Mich. Coll., 1956; DSc (hon.), Ferris Inst., 1957. Pvt. practice Grand Rapids, from 1921. Works include Cen. Mich. Coll., Ferris Inst., Big Rapids, Mich., Mulick Park Elem. Sch., Hall Elem. Sch., Grand Rapids Pub. Mus., St. Thomas the Apostle Cath. Ch., Grace Episcopal Ch., Holland, Mich., Mt. Pleasant (Mich.) State Home and Tng. Sch.; columnist Fired at Random, Grand Rapids Press, from 1940; contbr. articles to profl. jours. Lt. USN, 1918-21. Fellow AIA; mem. Mich. Soc. Architects (pres. 1948-49, gold medal 1954), Mich. Engring Soc., Archtl. League N.Y., Torch Club, Peninsular Club. Episcopalian. Home: Grand Rapids Mich. †

ALLEN, WILLIAM M., airplane manufacturing company executive, lawyer; b. Lolo, Mont., Sept. 1, 1900; s. Charles and Gertrude M. (Hughes) A.; m. Dorothy Dixon, Apr. 15, 1927 (dec. Nov. 1943); children: Nancy Dudley, Dorothy Dixon; m. Mary Ellen Agen, Dec. 28, 1948. AB, Mont. State U., 1922, LLD, 1954; LLB, Harvard U., 1925; LLD, Seattle U., 1957. Bar: Wash. 1926. Pvt. practice Seattle, 1926-45; assoc. Donworth, Todd and Higgins, Seattle, 1925-30; ptnr. Holman, Sprague and Allen, Seattle, 1930-45; pres. The Boeing Co., Seattle, 1945-70; chmn. bd. The Boing Co., Seattle, 1970-72; chmn. emeritus The Boeing Co., Seattle, 1972-85, hon. chmn., 1977-85. Mem. ABA, Wash. State Bar Assn., Seattle Bar Assn., Seattle Golf, Rainier, University, Sigma Chi. Home: Seattle Wash. Died Oct. 29, 1985; buried Missoula, Mont.

ALLISON, EVERETT E., insurance company executive; b. Hall, Ind., June 21, 1891; s. James Simpson and Sarah (Armstrong) A.; m. Helen Kathryn Sharpe, Jan. 22, 1918. Ed. pub. and bus. schs. Mem. Allison, Steinhart & Zook, Inc., Indpls., from 1919; bd. dirs. Grain Dealers Mut. Ins. Co., from 1947, chmn. bd., from 1962. Mem. Ind. State Office Bldg. Commn.; trustee Franklin (Ind.) Coll. Lt. U.S. Army, World War I. Mem. Indpls. Bd. Trade, Nat. Assn. Feed Dealers, Rotary. Baptist (deacon, trustee). Home: Zionsville Ind. †

ALLISON, STANLEY FREDERICK, corporate consultant; b. Mpls., Apr. 5, 1917; s. Carl J. and Amelia (Marohn) A.; m. Elizabeth H. Spielman, May 15, 1942; children: Richard B., David R., Thomas R. BBA, U. Minn., 1939. With Ohio Boxboard Co., 1945-58, v.p., 1953-58; v.p. Packaging Corp. Am., Evanston, Ill., 1958-63; sr. v.p. Packaging Corp. Am., Evanston, 1963-66, dir., 1965-85, pres., chief exec. officer, 1966-74, chmn. bd., 1974-77; sr. v.p. Tenneco Inc., 1966-74, exec. v.p., 1974-82; dir. Tenn. River Pulp & Paper Co., 1969-74, chmn. bd., 1970-74; trustee Paperboard Packaging Council, 1969-72, Inst. Paper Chemistry, 1974-77. With USNR, 1942-45. Mem. Fiber Box Assn. (bd. dirs. 1958-68, pres. 1966), Am. Paper Inst. (bd. dirs. 1967-74), Fourdrinier Kraft Bd. Inst. (chmn. bd. 1971-72), Rice U. Shepherd Soc. (governing council), Mid-Am., Lyford Cay, Houston Club. Home: Houston Tex. Died May 17, 1985.

ALLOTT, GORDON LLEWELLYN, senator, lawyer; b. Pueblo, Colo., Jan. 2, 1907; s. Leonard John and Bertha Louise (Reese) A.; m. Welda O. Hall, May 15, 1934; children: Roger Hall, Gordon Llewellyn Jr. BA, U. Colo., 1927, LLB, 1929; LLD (hon.), Colo. Coll., 1963, Colo. State U., 1968; Dr Eng (hon.), Colo. Sch. Mines, 1967. Bar: Colo. 1929. Pvt. practice Lamar, Colo.; county atty. Lamar, 1934, 41-46, city atty., 1937-41; dist. atty. 1946-49, lt. gov. of Colo., 1950-54, U.S. senator from Colo., 1955-73; U.S. senator from Colo. mem. appropriations and interior coms., 1955-72; atty., dir. First Fed. Savs. & Loan Assn. Lamar, 1934-89; local counsel specializing in irrigation, trial and probate law Amity Mut. Irrigation Co., Brown Lumber Co., Kan.-Colo. Utilities, Inc., C.H. Habern, Inc., State Bank of Wiley (Colo.), Town of Wiley and various ins. cos.; mem. Colo. Bd. Bar Examiners. Vice chmn. Am. del. Inter-Parliamentary Union; U.S. rep. 17th Assembly UN; Am. del. Inst. d'Etudes Politiques, Vaduz, Lichtenstein; mem. Nat. Monuments Commn.; nat. chmn. Young Rep. Nat. Fedn., 1941-46 Maj. USAAF, PTO, World War II. Mem. ABA, Colo. Bar Assn. Southeastern Colo. Bar Assn. (pres. 1940-42), Am. Legion, VFW, Airplane Owners and Pilots Assn., Mason, Rotary, Phi Gamma Delta, Delta Sigma Pi. Episcopalian. Home: Lamar Colo. Died Jan. 17, 1989.

ALLRED, ORAN H(ENDERSON), government official, lawyer; b. Childress, Tex., Dec. 2, 1892; s. Renne and Mary (Henson) A.; m. Katherine Miller, June 3, 1922; children: John C., Katherine (Mrs. Joseph R. Harris). Bar: Tex. 1920. Practice Breckenridge, 1920-25; atty. Stephens County, Tex., 1925-29; pvt. practice Ft. Worth, 1929-34; regional adminstr. SEC, Ft. Worth, from 1935. Sgt. inf. U.S. Army, A.E.F., 1917-19. Mem. Ft. Worth Bar Assn., State Bar Assn. Tex. Home: Fort Worth Tex. †

ALLRICH, ROBERT WILLIAM, advertising agency executive; b. Chgo., July 13, 1924; s. Robert Dobson and Irma (Grauer) A.; m. Mary Lynn Seder, Aug. 7, 1948; children: Martha Allrich Fuller, Stephen, Nancy, Margaret. Student, Yale U., 1943; BA cum laude, Brown U., 1948. Free-lance illustrator 1948-51; research dir. McFarland-Aveyard & Co., Chgo., 1951-56; account supr. Maxon Inc., Chgo. and Detroit, 1959-64; pres. Earle Ludgin & Co., Chgo., 1964-70; v.p. mktg., dir. Clinton E. Frank, Inc., Chgo., 1970-72; pres. Hurvis, Binzer & Churchill, Inc., Chgo., 1972-86, chmn. bd., chief exec. officer, 1976-86. Contbr. to advt. jours. With USMCR, 1943-46. Recipient award Artists Guild Chgo., 1949. Mem. Chgo. Advt. Club (chmn. mktg. workshop 1964), Alpha Delta Phi. Democrat. Home: Northbrook Ill. Died Mar. 20, 1986.

ALLTOP, JAMES HOWARD, insurance company executive; b. cb. Glenville, W.Va., Nov. 28, 1905; s. Evan and Ida and (Miller) A.; m. Lillian O'Bannon, June 11, 1930 (dec. July 7, 1978); children—James H., William O'Bannon; m. Helen Gragg Perlin, Dec. 1, 1979. A.B., Ind. U., 1929. With Eli Lilly Co., 1929-31, Am. United Life Ins. Co., Indpls., 1931-86; personnel dir. Am. United Life Ins. Co., 1932-52, sec., 1952-61, sr. v.p., dir., 1961-86; lectr. Butler U., 1936-52. Gen. chmn. Community Chest, Indpls., 1953-54. Mem. Ind. U. Alumni Assn. (past pres.), Beta Theta Pi. Home: Indianapolis Ind. Died Oct. 25, 1986.

ALMIRALL, LLOYD VINCENT, lawyer; b. Bklyn., Nov. 9, 1907; s. Juan A. and Emma (Kuntz) A.; m. Catherine Lewerth, Sept. 17, 1937; children—Danne, Jan (Mrs. Robert Grigas), Paul L., Irene (Mrs. Wayne Hobin). A.B., Hamilton Coll., Clinton, N.Y., 1929; LL.B., Harvard, 1932. Bar: N.Y. bar 1932. Since practiced in N.Y.C.; partner firm Breed, Abbott & Morgan, 1946-76, ret. Trustee Lenox Sch., N.Y.C., 1946-59, pres., 1951-56; trustee Harvey Sch., Katonah; N.Y., 1948-76, Hamilton Coll., 1958-64. Mem. Mr. Haight Jr.'s Litchfield County Hounds (M.F.H.), Chi Psi. Clubs: Players (N.Y.C.), Harvard (N.Y.C.). Home: Ridgefield Conn. Died May 4, 1987; buried The Green-Wood Cemetery, Bklyn.

ALMOND, JAMES LINDSAY, JR., judge; b. Charlottesville, Va., June 15, 1898; s. James Lindsay and Eddie Nicholas (Burgess) A.; m. Josephine Katherine Minter, Aug. 15, 1925. LLB, U. Va., 1923; LLD, Coll. William and Mary, 1959, Roanoke Coll., 1982, Christopher Newport Coll., 1982. Bar: Va. 1921. Pvt. practice Roanoke, 1923-32; prin. Zoar High Sch., Roanoke, 1921-22; asst. pros. atty. Roanoke, 1930-33, Judge Hustings Ct., Roanoke, 1933-45; mem. 79th Congress, 2d session; elected 80th Congress; mem. post office and civil svc. com., atty. gen. Va. Roanoke, 1948-57; gov. State of Va., 1958-62; interim judge U.S. Ct. Customs and Patent Appeals, Washington, 1962-63, assoc. judge, 1963-73, sr. judge, 1973-82; sr. judge U.S. Ct. Appeals for Fed. Cir., Washington, 1982-86. Served with U.S. Army, World War I. Recipient DAR medal of honor Nat. Soc. DAR, 1983. Mem. ABA (hon.), Va. Bar Assn., Richmond Bar Assn., United Comml. Travelers, Raven Soc., Masons (32 degree), Shriners, Delta Theta Phi, Alpha Kappa Psi, Omicron Delta Kappa. Democrat. Lutheran (tchr. men's Bible class). Home: Richmond Va. Died April 14, 1986; buried Evergreen Cemetery, Roanoke, Va.

ALSTON, PHILIP HENRY, JR., ambassador, lawyer; b. Atlanta, Apr. 19, 1911; s. Philip Henry and May (Lewis) A.; m. Elkin Goddard, June 27, 1939; children: Elkin Goddard (Mrs. James E. Cushman), John Goddard. A.B., U. Ga., 1932; LL.B., Emory U., 1934; student, Harvard Law Sch., 1935. Bar: Ga. 1934. Then practiced in Atlanta; with firm Alston & Bird; ambassador to Australia, Nauru, 1977-81; Past mem. Atlanta advisory bd. Citizens and So. Nat. Bank; former dir. Triton Inc., Ansell Inc. Former trustee Charles Loridans Found., Vasser Woolley Found.; past bd. regents Univ. System Ga. Served to lt. USNR, World War II. Mem. U. Ga. Alumni Soc. (pres. 1963-64), Sigma Alpha Epsilon. Episcopalian (past sr. warden). Home: Sea Island Ga. Died Mar. 2, 1988.

ALTFILLISCH, CHARLES, architect; b. Bellevue, Iowa, Mar. 27, 1892; m. Leila Marsh, 1921; 1 child, Mrs. Philip W. Tone. Student, U. Iowa, 1910-14, Carnegie Tech., 1926; LLD, Luther Coll. Registered architect, Iowa, Minn., Wash.; lic. engr. With Hanson & Altfillisch, 1921-31; pvt. practice Decorah, Iowa, 1931-61; then sr. mem. firm Altfillisch, Olson, Gray & Thompson, architects and engrs., Decorah. Prin. works include the girls' dormitory Luther Coll., Decorah, 1946, boys dormitory, 1955, Crippled Children's Hosp., U. Iowa, 1950, Hancock County Hosp., girls' dormitory and press box State U. Iowa. Mem. Decorah Planning Commn., pres., from 1952; mem. Iowa Bldg. Code Commn. Decorated St. Olaf Medal (Norway). Fellow AIA (pres. Iowa chpt. 1936, chmn. fin. com. 1955); mem. Decorah C. of C. (pres. 1927), Am. Legion, Elks, Oncota Golf and Country Club (past pres.). Home: Decorah Iowa. †

ALTHAUS, JOHN CARL, credit bureau executive; b. Columbus, Ohio, Mar. 21, 1892; s. John C. and Barbara A. (Heinlein) A.; m. Caroline M. Meyer, Oct. 1, 1913; children: J. William, Robert K., Elizabeth B., Donald C., Carolyn V., Patricia A. With The Credit Bureau, Inc., Washington, from 1935, gen. mgr., sec. treas. Mem. Northeastern Credit Burs. Inc. (past pres.), Assn. Credit Burs. Am. Inc. (dir., pres. 1964-65), Kiwanis. Home: Silver Spring Md. †

ALTUS, WILLIAM DAVID, psychologist; b. Burlington, Kans., May 28, 1908; s. Samuel Abraham and Cora Jane (Burch) A.; m. Mary Agnes Atkinson, Dec. 14, 1929 (div. 1948); m. Grace Merriman Thompson, Dec. 24, 1951; children: Martha, Elizabeth, Deborah. A.B., B.S., Kans. State Tchrs. Coll., 1930, M.S., 1932; Ph.D., N.Y. U., 1941. Instr. Santa Barbara Coll., 1941-44; asst. prof. U. Calif. at Santa Barbara, 1944-47, asso. prof., 1947-54, prof., 1954-75, prof. emeritus, from 1975; chmn. dept. psychology, 1950-55, faculty research lectr., from 1961. Contbr. over 60 articles to profl. jours. Served from 2d lt. to capt. AUS, 1942-46. Fellow Am. Psychol. Assn., AAAS; mem. Sierra Club. Clubs: Univ. Calif. Faculty, Channel City. Died Sept. 12, 1985; buried Santa Barbara Cemetery.

ALVAREZ, LUIS W., physicist; b. San Francisco, June 13, 1911; s. Walter C. and Harriet S. (Smyth) A.; m. Geraldine Smithwick, 1936; children: Walter, Jean; m. Janet L. Landis, 1958; children: Donald and Helen. B.S., U. Chgo., 1932, M.S., 1934, Ph.D., 1936, Sc.D., 1967; Sc.D., Carnegie-Mellon U., 1968, Kenyon Coll., 1969, Notre Dame U., 1976, Ain Shams U., Cairo, 1979, Pa. Coll. Optometry, 1982. Research asso., instr., asst. prof., asso. prof. U. Calif., 1936-45, prof. physics, 1945-78, prof. emeritus, 1978-88; asso. dir. Lawrence Radiation Lab., 1954-59, 75-78; radar research and devel. Mass. Inst. Tech., 1940-43, Los Alamos, 1944-45. Recipient Collier Trophy, 1946; Medal for Merit, 1948; John Scott medal, 1953; Einstein medal, 1961; Nat. Medal of Sci., 1964; Michelson award, 1965; Nobel prize in physics, 1968; Wright prize, 1981; Rockwell medal, 1986; Enrico Fermi award U.S. Energy Dept., 1987; named Calif. Scientist of Year, 1960; named to Nat. Inventors Hall of Fame, 1978. Fellow Am. Phys. Soc. (pres. 1969); mem. Nat. Acad. Scis., Nat. Acad. Engring., Am. Philos. Soc., Am. Acad. Arts and Scis., Phi Beta Kappa, Sigma Xi; asso. mem. Institut D'Egypte. Home: Berkeley Calif. Died Aug. 31, 1988.

AMAYA, MARIO ANTHONY, art administrator, editor, writer; b. N.Y.C., Oct. 6, 1933; s. Mario A. and Maria Sophia (Garofalo) A. B.A. in Art and English Lit, Bklyn. Coll.; postgrad., London (Eng.) U. Editor, author, art critic, exhbn. organizer 1956-69; art adviser, founding asso. editor Royal Opera House mag., 1962-68; founding editor Art and Artists Mag., London, 1965-68; chief curator Art Gallery of Toronto, Ont., Can., 1969-72; dir. N.Y. Cultural Center, Farleigh Dickinson U.,

1972-76, adj. prof., 1972-76; Am. editor Connoisseur mag., 1976-79; dir. Chrysler Mus., Norfolk, Va., 1976-79; pres. Fine Arts Collection Services, Inc., art cons., 1979; head of devel. NAD, 1980-86; vis. prof. SUNY-Buffalo, 1971-72; lectr. abroad USIS. Organizer opening exhbn., Inst. Contemporary Arts, London, 1968; guest dir., Queens Mus., Flushing Meadow, 1976; organizer exhbns.: The Obsessive Image, London, 1968, Sacred and Profane in Symbolist Art, Toronto, 1969, (with Pierre Rosenberg) French 17th and 18th Century Master Drawings, Toronto, 1973, Blacks: USA: Now, 1973, Women Choose Women, 1973, (with Robert Isaacson) Bouguereau, 1975, Man Ray, N.Y.C., London, Rome, 1974-75, Art Deco, Can., 1974; Author: Pop as Art, 1965, Art Nouveau, 1966, Tiffany Glass, 1967; numerous exhbn. catalogues; Am. editor: Connoisseur, 1977-79; contbg. editor: Archtl. Digest, 1977-82; Am. editor, mktg. dir. Studio Internat., 1982-85; contbr. articles to profl. jours. Home: London England. Died June 29, 1986.

AMES, JOHN DAWES, banker; b. May 7, 1904; s. K.L. and A.S. A.; m. Charlotte Schoonmaker, Nov. 9, 1928; children: John D., William S., Knowlton; m. Constance Hasler, Oct. 1, 1949. Grad., Princeton, 1928. Pres. Chgo. Jour. Commerce, 1929-50; exec. dir. Midwest div. Dow Jones & Co., Inc.; pubs. Wall Street Jour., 1951-87; partner Bacon, Whipple & Co. Served as lt. col. AUS, World War II. Decorated Bronze Star. Episcopalian. Home: Lake Forest Ill. Died Apr. 27, 1987.

AMES, ROBERT BARBOUR, machinery manufacturing executive; b. Dover-Foxcroft, Maine, July 7, 1924; s. John Everett and Bertha Janet (Barbour) A.; m. Veda Harriet Morin, Aug. 28, 1946; children: Robert J., Anne E., Mary E., Jahn E., Jane V., Roberta K. Successively mktg. mgr., mgr. engring., mgr. mfg., gen. mgr., v.p. Gen. Electric Co., Phila., 1950-72; successively v.p. and gen. mgr., staff v.p., regional v.p. Allis Chalmers Corp., N.Y.C., 1972—; dir. Foodsales Inc. Mem. bd. visitors Berry Coll.; devel. council U. Maine. With AUS, 1944-46. Mem. IEEE, Sigma Xi. Republican. Roman Catholic. Home: Summit N.J. Deceased.

AMES, VAN METER, educator; b. De Soto, Iowa, July 9, 1898; s. Edward Scribner and Mabel (Van Meter) A.; m. Betty Breneman, June 12, 1930; children: Sanford Scribner, Christine (Mrs. Judson E. Cornish), Damaris. Ph.B., U. Chgo., 1919, Ph.D., 1924. Mem. faculty U. Cin., Cin., 1925-85, head dept. philosophy, 1959-85, Obed J. Wilson prof. ethics, 1960-66, Obed J. Wilson prof. ethics emeritus, 1966-85, fellow grad. sch., 1957-85; vis. prof. Cornell U., summer 1931, U. Tex., 1934-35, U. Hawaii, 1947-48, Faculté des Lettres U. Aix-Marseille, France, spring 1949, Columbia, summer 1957; mem. 2d East-West Philosophers Conf., U. Hawaii, summer 1959. Author: Aesthetics of the Novel, 1928, Introduction to Beauty, 1931; (poetry) Out of Iowa, 1936; Proust and Santayana, 1937, Andre Gide, 1947, (with Betty B. Ames) Japan and Zen, 1961, Zen and American Thought, 1962; editor: (with Betty B. Ames) Beyond Theology: The Autobiography of Edward Scribner Ames, 1959, The Prayers and Meditations of E.S. Ames, 1970. Rockefeller grantee, France, 1948; Fulbright research prof. philosophy Komazawa U., Tokyo, 1958-59; Humanist fellow, 1976. Mem. Am. Philos. Assn. (pres. western div. 1959-60), Am. Soc. Aesthetics (pres. 1961-62), Am. Humanist Assn. Home: Cincinnati Ohio. Died Nov. 5, 1985.

AMIOKA, SHIRO, educator; b. Honolulu, Oct. 26, 1922; s. Tsurumatsu and Reye (Yoshimura) A.; m. Toshiko Watanabe, July 25, 1956. EdB, U. Hawaii, 1949, EdM, 1952; PhD, U. Ill., 1959; postgrad., U. Minn., 1951-52; 5, U. Tokyo, Japan, 1962-63, 69-70; PhD, Ashiya U., Japan, 1978. Instr. edn. U. Ill., Urbana, 1954-55, 58-59; instr. edn. U. Hawaii, Honolulu, 1955-57, asst. prof., 1957-63, assoc. prof., 1963-66, prof., from 1966, chmn. dept. ednl. founds., from 1981, asst. dean summer session, 1960-65, assoc. dean summer session, 1965-71; chancellor community colls., 1975-77, supt. edn. Hawaii State Dept. Edn., Honolulu, 1971-74. With AUS, 1943-47. Mem. Philosophy of Edn. Soc., John Dewey Soc., Hawaiian Acad. Sci., AAUP, Assn. for Asian Studies, History Edn. Soc., Soc. Profs. Edn., Nat. Soc. for Study Edn., John Dewey Soc. of Japan, Phi Kappa Phi, Phi Delta Kappa, Kappa Delta Pi. Home: Honolulu Hawaii. Deceased.

AMIS, EDWARD STEPHEN, chemistry educator; b. Himyar, Ky., Nov. 9, 1905; s. Jack and Artie (Southard) A.; m. Annie Velma Birdwhistle, Sept. 2, 1934; children: Edward Stephen, Velma Dianne. B.S., U. Ky., 1930, M.S., 1933; Ph.D., Columbia U., 1939. Mem. faculty La. State U., 1939-45, asso. prof., 1943-45; staff Carbide & Carbon Chems. Corp., Oak Ridge, 1945-47; prof. chemistry U. Ark., Fayetteville, from 1947; Mem. bd. alumni Union Coll., Barbourville, Ky., from 1979. Author: Kinetics of Chemical Change in Solution, 1949, A Book of Verse and Prose, 1965, Solvent Effects on Reaction Rates and Mechanisms, 1966, Russian edit., 1968, (with James F. Hinton) Solvent Effects on Chemical Phenomena, 1973, Saga of Racehorse and Other Items, 1969, A Novice in Europe and Other Writings, 1971, Beautiful But Dangerous and Other Poetry, 1977; numerous articles. Recipient Distinguished Research award U. Ark., 1967. Fellow N.Y. Acad. Scis.; mem. Am. Chem. Soc. (So. Chemist award 1959, S.W. award 1960, Tour Speaker plaque 1975), Am. Inst. Chemists (La., Ark., Miss. sect. honor scroll 1975), Ark. Acad. Scis., Sigma Xi, Alpha Chi Sigma, Pi Mu Epsilon, Phi Lambda Upsilon, Sigma Pi Sigma. Deceased.

AMMIDON, HOYT, banker; b. Balt., June 30, 1909; s. Daniel Clark and Estelle H. (Hoyt) A.; m. Elizabeth MacI. K. Callaway, May 19, 1933; children: Hoyt, Lee. Student, Loomis Sch., Windsor, Conn., 1923-25, 1926-28, Le Rosey Sch., Rolle, Switzerland, 1925-26; B.A., Yale U., 1932; LL.D., Hofstra U., 1968. With Central Hanover Bank (now Mfrs. Hanover Trust Co.), 1932-88, asst. sec., 1937-43, v.p., 1950-52, trustee, 1957; chief exec. officer Vincent Astor, 1952-58; pres. U.S. Trust Co., N.Y.C., 1958-62, chmn., 1962-74; chmn. bd. U.S. Internat. Adv. Co., 1966-74; dir., exec. com., chmn. audit com. Perkin-Elmer Corp., 1967-79; dir. Alliance: Balanced Shares, Divident Shares, Insured Calif. Tax.-Ex. Shelter Inc., Tax-Free Shares, Inc.,Alliance Bond Fund, Mortgage Securities Income Fund and Tax-Free Income Fund, Tax-Free, Pacific Gen. Devel. Co.; former chmn. bd. WestAm. Properties, S.A.; mem. N.Y. Banking Bd., 1963-67; commr. Port N.Y. Authority, 1969-72, vice chmn., 1970-72, chmn. operations com., 1970-72. Hon. chmn., founding mem. Am. Friends Can. Com., Inc.; mem. nat. businessmen's com. A Better Chance, 1969-73; Mem. devel. bd. Yale U.; mem. adv. bd. YMCA, Huntington Twp., N.Y.; former bd. dirs. Meml. Hosp.; mem. com. N.Y. Clearing House Assn.; bd. dirs. emeritus Lincoln Center Performing Arts; bd. dirs. Fed. Hall Meml. Assocs., N.Y.C., 1959-74, N.Y.C. Nat. Shrines Assocs., 1969-74, N.Y. div. Am. Cancer Soc., 1969-73; bd. govs. Hundred Year Assn. of N.Y., 1963-71; trustee, pres. emeritus bd. Loomis Sch.; trustee emeritus Cooper Union Advancement Sci. and Art; trustee, founding mem. Bus. Com. for the Arts, Inc.; life fellow Met. Mus. Art; fellow Pierpont Morgan Library, 1962-74; pres. bd. dirs. adv. council Am. Ditchley Found.; adv. com. Marine Hist. Assn.; mem. council Fedn. Protestant Welfare Agys., Inc.; bd. govs. N.Y. Coll. Osteo. Medicine. Served as lt. USCGR, 1942-45. Decorated grand ofcl. Order Crown of Italy; Fundacion Internacional Eloy Alfaro Panama; officer Am. Soc. Most Venerable Order of Hosp. of St. John of Jerusalem; hon. comdr. Order Brit. Empire; recipient Medal of Merit St. Nicholas Soc. City N.Y., 1969; Gold medal St. Paul's Cathedral, London; Distinguished Service award Loomis-Chaffee Sch. Mem. Soc. Colonial Wars, Soc. Mayflower Descs., Am. Inst. Banking (adv. council N.Y. chpt. 1959-74), Grad. Club Assn. New Haven, Assn. Internat. Anciens Roseens, Pilgrims, U.S. Srs. Golf Assn. (former dir.), Chi Psi. Clubs: Economic (N.Y.C.); Cove Neck Tennis Courts, Cruising of America, Elihu (Yale) (grad. pres. 1958-60), River, Links, Piping Rock, St. Nicholas Hockey, Mory's Assn; Royal and Ancient Golf of St. Andrews (Scotland). Home: Glen Head N.Y. Died Mar. 13, 1988.

AMOS, JOHN ELLIS, lawyer; b. Charleston, W.Va., July 16, 1905; s. John Ellison and Louise Hampton (Delaney) A.; m. Edith Johnston, Oct. 5, 1935; children: John Delaney, Mary Johnston Amos. Student, Augusta Mil. Acad.; LL.B., W.Va. U., 1929. Bar: W.Va. 1929. Practiced in Charleston.; Dir. Vulcan Materials Co., Birmingham, Ala.; Mem. W.Va. Ho. Dels. from Kanawha County, 1935-47, speaker, 1943-45, 47; mem. W.Va., Senate, 1947-56; Mem. Dem. Nat. Com. from W.Va., 1959-68; Pres. W.Va. Bd. Regents, 1969, sec., 1970. Mem. Am. Trucking Assn. (pres. 1965, chmn. bd. 1966, v.p. at large). Home: Charleston W.Va. Died May 8, 1986.

ANDERSEN, MARTIN, publisher; b. Greenwood, Miss., Jan. 12, 1898; s. Martin and Amelia (Katra) A.; m. Jane Bludworth, 1928 (div. Dec. 1949); children: Marcia, Doris; m. Gracia Warlow Barr, July 1950. Pres. Sentinel Star Co.; founder, pres. Good Fellows Inc. Democrat. Episcopalian. Home: Orlando Fla. Died May 5, 1986.

ANDERSON, CHARLES ARNER, physician; b. Cortland, Ohio, June 13, 1907; s. James Cossatt and Halle Lenore (Clark) A.; m. Mary Pond Hughes, July 9, 1949; children: Charles Arner, David James, Grayson Carroll, Warren Rice. Student, Miami U., 1927, cleve. Coll., 1928, Ohio Wesleyan, 1929-31; M.B., Ch.B., U. Edinburgh, 1937, L.R.C.P., 1938, D.N.B., 1939. Postgrad. tng. urology Genesse Hosp., U. Rochester, St. Francis Hosp., Peoria, Watts Hosp., U. N.C., 1937-42; assoc. urology St. Louis U., 1946-47; pvt. practice urology Warren, Ohio, 1947-85; chief urology svc. St. Joseph Riverside Hosp., Warren, Ohio, 1948-62, assoc. staff, 1962-85, staff urologist, 1964-85, chief urol. svc., 1973-76; pres., treas. Warndeer Land Co. Inc., 1962-76, Denusurg. Corp., 1967-85. Pres. Patriotic Edn. Inc., 1968-68, chmn., 1970-85; mem. Ohio Republican Cent. Com. Capt. M.C. AUS, 1942-46; chief urol. and surg. svc. 29th Evac. Hosp. Recipient Minute Man award Nat. Soc. S.A.R.; named Ky. col., Miss. col. Mem. Am. Urol. Assn., Trumbull County Hist. Soc. (v.p. 1964-68, pres. 1969-78), AMA, Ohio, Trumbull County med. socs., Am. Soc. Clin. Hypnosis, SAR (nat. pres. 1962-63), Order Ky. Cols., Order Miss. Cols., Symposiarchs (nat. pres. 1968-69), Masons, Shriners (Jester), Buckeye Club, Trumbull Country Club, Kappa Sigma (dist. grand master 1964-67, 73-85, nat. alumni commr. 1967-70). Home: Warren Ohio. Died 1985.

ANDERSON, CHARLES BURROUGHS, bookseller; b. Washington, Iowa, Mar. 4, 1905; s. Marion T. and Lucy (Burroughs) A.; m. Herta Lindke, Sept. 16, 1938 (div.); m. Frances L. Wallace, May 28, 1946. PhB, U. Chgo., 1926; MA, Columbia U., 1929; student, U. Paris, France, 1931; diplomiert, U. Berlin, Germany, 1932. Faculty Edgewood Sch., 1926-28; instr. English Columbia U., 1929-31; faculty Horace Mann Sch., 1934-45; supr. Coll. Entrance Exam. Bd., 1933-39; chmn. bd. Anderson's Book Shop, Inc., Larchmont, N.Y., from 1946; lectr. Grad. Inst. Book Pub. NYU, 1959-62. Author: Guide to Good Pronunciation; co-translator: World History of Dance (Sachs), 1938; editor: Bookselling in America and the World; editor-in-chief ABA Publs., 1972-75; contbr. articles to profl. publs. Bd. dirs. Am. Booksellers Assn., 1954-62, 64-74, pres. 1958-60, chmn. bd. dirs., 1960-62; bd. judges Carey-Thomas Book award, 1958; bd. dirs. Library Club Am., 1959; steering com. Nat. Library Week, 1958-61; bd. dirs. Nat. Com. for Florence Agreement, 1960-68; Am. del. Internat. Community Booksellers, Wiesbaden, Germany, 1962; rep. R.R. Bowker Co. to Internat. Book Fair, Frankfurt, 1965-70. Mem. English Grad. Union (Columbia), Lions (pres. 1951), Columbia University, Princeton (N.Y.C.), Larchmont Shore, Halifax (Daytona Beach, Fla.) clubs, Alpha Delta Phi. Home: Ormond Beach Fla. Died Jan. 20, 1985.

ANDERSON, CORTLAND EDWIN, JR., educational administrator; b. Laurelton, N.Y., Oct. 10, 1935; s. Cortland Edwin and Helen (O'Krinsky) A.; m. Fidella Purdin, Feb. 2, 1958; children: Laura, Sharon, Mary. AB in English, Fla. So. Coll., Lakeland, 1958. Editor, v.p. Suffolk (N.Y.) Sun, 1966-69; asst. v.p. public relations N.Y. Telephone Co., 1970-76; exec. v.p. Corp. for Public Broadcasting, Washington, 1977-79; v.p. Washington Post Co., 1979-81; dir. E.W. Scripps Sch. Journalism Ohio U., Athens, 1981-85; cons. Time Inc., Internat. Assn. Bus. Communicators; mem. editorial adv. bd. Sci. 83 Mag., adv. bd. Children's Express, N.Y.C. Mem. energy com. Atlantic Council; mem. adv. bd. Third Sector Project, Washington. Episcopalian. Home: Athens Ohio. Died Dec. 25, 1985, buried Clarks Chapel Cemetery, Athens.

ANDERSON, EDWIN JOHN, professional football executive; b. Rockford, Ill., Aug. 3, 1902; s. John A. and Emma (Wallin) A.; m. Isabelle B. Bort, Mar. 31, 1928; children: Suzanne Jane Anderson Stenglein (dec.), Marynell Anderson Williams. AB, Beloit Coll., 1927. Advt. mgr. ABC Washing Machine Co., Peoria, Ill., 1927; with Goebel Brewing Co., Detroit, 1938-87; pres. Goebel Brewing Co. of Calif., Oakland, 1941-58; bd. dirs., mem. adv. bd. Kemper Co.; pres., gen. mgr. Detroit Lions Football Co., 1949-62, exec. v.p., 1962-73, sr. v.p., 1973-87. Former mem. bd. dirs. Detroit Community Found., United Found., Detroit Bd. Commerce, Met. Bldg. Com. Detroit; past pres. Children's Hosp. of Mich., Birmingham Community House. Mem. Detroit Athletic, Bloomfield Hills Country, Detroit Club, Seven Lakes Country, Racquet. Episcopalian. Home: Bloomfield Hills Mich. Died Feb. 2, 1987; buried ChristChurch Cranbrook, Bloomfield Hills.

ANDERSON, ERNEST GUSTAVE, educator; b. Concord, Nebr., Mar. 3, 1891; s. Andrew G. and Ellen (Rosenberg) A.; m. Florence Larson, May 4, 1941; 1 child, Jean Elizabeth. BSc, U. Nebr., 1915; PhD, Cornell U., 1920. Research assoc. Carnegie Instn., Washington, 1920-22; instr. biology CCNY, 1922-23; NRC fellow U. Mich., 1923-26, asst. prof. botany, 1926-27, Lloyd fellow in sci., 1927-28; assoc. prof. genetics Calif. Inst. Tech., 1928-46, prof., 1946-61, then emeritus; vis. prof. U. Ill., 1961-62, U. Mo., Columbia, from 1962; assoc. prof. U. Minn., 1936-37. Mem. AAAS, Am. Soc. Naturalists, Am. Genetics Assn., Am. Soc. Agronomy, Genetics Soc. Am., Bot. Soc. Am. Home: Columbia Mo. †

ANDERSON, FLORENCE, foundation consultant; b. Bklyn., Oct. 29, 1910; d. Charles Albert and Florence (Gould) A. AB, Mt. Holyoke Coll., 1931, LHD (hon.), 1972; spl. student, NYU, New Sch. Social Research; LLD (hon.), Western Coll. for Women, 1967. With Carnegie Corp., N.Y.C., 1934-85, adminstrv. asst., 1939-47, asst. sec., 1947-51, assoc. sec., 1951-54, sec., 1954-75, cons., 1975-85. Sec. Carnegie Found. for Advancement of Teaching, 1955-74; trustee Virginia Gildersleeve Internat. Fund for Univ. Women. Capt. USMCR, 1943-45. Mem. Cosmopolitan Club (N.Y.C.), Mt. Holyoke Club (N.Y.C.), Washington Club (Conn.). Home: New York N.Y. Died Dec. 16, 1985.

ANDERSON, HAROLD H., publisher; b. Princeton, Ill., June 26, 1901; s. A. Clarence and Hilda (Linder) A.; m. Virginia Copeland, Feb. 20, 1926 (dec. Mar. 1988); 1 child, Carolyn. BS, Northwestern U., 1924. Sales mgr. Assoc. Editors Inc., Chgo., 1924-25; ptnr. Pubs. Syndicate, Chgo., 1925-62; pres., exec. editor Pubs. Newspaper Syndicate, 1963-67; chmn. Pubs.-Hall Syndicate, 1967-68; co-founder Am. Inst. Pub. Opinion, 1935. Trustee Northwestern U., Northwestern Meml. Hosp.; bd. dirs. Wesley Hosp. Harold and Virginia Anderson Hall named in his honor Northwestern U. Mem. University Club, Chicago Club, Glen View Golf Club,

Indian Hill Club, Country Club of Fla., Phi Gamma Delta. Home: Wilmette Ill. Died Jan. 24, 1988.

ANDERSON, HERBERT L., physicist; b. N.Y.C., May 24, 1914; s. Joseph and Sima (Goldberg) A.; m. Mary Elizabeth Kearns, June 16, 1978; children by previous marriage—Faith, Clifton, Kelley, Dana. A.B., Columbia U., 1935, B.S.E.E., 1936, Ph.D. in Physics, 1940; Sc.D. (hon.), Allegheny Coll., 1976. From asst. prof. to assoc. prof. physics U. Chgo., 1946-47, 47-50, dir. Enrico Fermi Inst., 1958-62, prof. physics, 1950-77, Disting. Service prof. physics, 1977-82, Disting. service prof. physics emeritus, 1982-88; sr. fellow Los Alamos Nat. Lab., 1978-85, staff mem., 1985-88; sr. fellow Eleanor Roosevelt Inst., 1985-88. Recipient Fermi award U.S. Dept. Energy, 1983; Guggenheim fellow, 1955, Fulbright fellow, 1956-57. Fellow Am. Acad. Arts and Sci.; mem. Nat. Acad. Scis. Home: Los Alamos N.Mex. Died July 16, 1988.

ANDERSON, HERBERT WALFRED, business executive; b. Everett, Mass., Dec. 13, 1892; s. O. Alfred and Elena (Wade) A.; m. Helen Barrett Gehris, July 17, 1940; 1 child, Peter Barrett; m. 2d, Alice Newman Ingersoll, Jan. 20, 1940. Indsl. engr. United Shoe Machinery Corp., Boston, 1916-20; ptnr. K.W. Freund and Assoc., Bklyn., 1920-23; pres., gen. mgr. Fidelity Machine Co., Phila., 1923-47, Haskell-Dawes Machine Co., Phila., 1947-63; mem. N.E. adv. bd. Provident Tradesmens Bank and Trust Co., Phila., from 1964. Copntbr. articles to profl. periodicals. Former trustee N.E. Boys Club, Frankford Hosp. Assn. Served with U.S. Army, 1 yr. Received Service award U.S. Dept. Treasury, 1943; awarded Army-Navy E five times during WWII. Mem. N.E. Phila. C. of C. (chmn. bd. 1950-52), MIT of Phila. Club (pres. 1945, 46), Huntingdon Valley Country, Frankford Exchange clubs. Episcopalian. Home: Prospectville Pa. †

ANDERSON, J. JOSEPH, banker; b. Cortland, N.Y., Apr. 12, 1938; s. Edward J. and Agnes E. A.; m. May B. Marovich; children: Daniel F., George P., Mark E. B.B.A., U. Notre Dame, 1960; M.B.A., U. Chgo., 1968. Bar: C.P.A., Ill. Gen. acct. UARCO Bus. Forms, Inc., 1960-63; with Continental Ill. Nat. Bank and Trust Co., from 1963, 2d v.p., 1968, operating rep. methods research, 1969, v.p., 1970; auditor Continental Bank and parent co., 1972, v.p., 1974, sr. v.p., 1975, head multinat. banking services, 1976, head controller's and systems, 1980, controller, 1980, exec. v.p., from 1981; past mem. faculty Loyola U., Chgo.; mem. acctg. adv. bd. U. Ill.-Chgo. Bd. dirs. A.R.C., Cath. Charities Chgo.; bd. advisers Dartmouth Inst., Dartmouth Coll.; bd. dirs. Ill. Benedictine Coll; trustee Morehouse Coll., Atlanta. Served with U.S. Army, 1961-62. Mem. Ill. Soc. C.P.A.s. Clubs: Bankers, Economic. Home: Chicago Ill. Deceased.

ANDERSON, JESSE THOMAS, superintendent of education; b. Timmonsville, S.C., Oct. 26, 1892; s. Ervin and Frances Letitia (Thomas) A.; m. Hazel Prickett, Jan. 19, 1921; children: Mary Louise (Mrs. Earle Rice), Frances Letitia (Mrs. Frank Fulton), Hazel-Ann. AB, Furman U., 1914, LLD, 1951; MA, U. S.C., 1942; grad. work, Peabody Coll., U. Chgo. Prin. sch. at Elm, 1914-16; supt. schs. of Olanta, 1916-17, Blacksburg, 1917-18; supt. of edn. Florence County, 1929-46, state supt. of edn., after 1946; sec. and exec. officer State Bd. Edn., after 1946; former bd. trustees U. S.C., The Citadel, Winthrop Coll., S.C. Sch. for the Deaf and Blind. Served as pvt., later 2d lt., U.S. Army, WWI. Mem. NEA, Am. Assn. Sch. Adminstrs., Nat. Council of Chief Sch. Officers, Am. Legion (past post comdr.), 40 and 8, S.C. Edn. Assn. (past pres.), County Supts. Assn. of S.C. (past pres.), Bapt. Assn. Florence (past moderator), Phi Beta Kappa, Delta Sigma Phi. Baptist. Lodge: Masons. Club: Lions. Home: Columbia S.C. †

ANDERSON, JOHN, gas transmission company executive. Pres., chief exec. officer, dir. Westcoast Transmission Co. Ltd., Vancouver, B.C., Can.; chmn. Pacific No. Gas Ltd., Vancouver, B.C., Can., Westcoast Petroleum Ltd. Died Aug. 13, 1987.

ANDERSON, JOSEPH JAMES, state librarian; b. Dubuque, Iowa, June 28, 1932; s. George James and Agnes Irene (Melroy) A. B.A., St. Mary's U., San Antonio, 1953. Library asst. Bolt Hall Sch. of Law Library U. Calif., Berkeley, 1960-61; tech. librarian Lockheed Missiles & Space Co., Van Nuys, Calif., 1961-64; mgr. tech. processing Ampex Corp., Redwood City, Calif., 1964-67; dir. reference services Nev. State Library, Carson City, 1967-70; state librarian Nev. State Library, 1970-86; chmn. western states adv. council edn., 1974-76; state coordinator Nev. State Hist. Records Adv. Bd., 1977-86; mem. Western State Com. on Higher Edn., 1970-77. Lt. comdr. USNR, 1954-66. Mem. ALA, Mountain Plains Library Assn. (pres. 1980), Spl. Libraries Assn., Nev. Library Assn., Calif. Library Assn., Western Council State Libraries (past pres., treas. 1978-86). Republican. Roman Catholic. Home: Carson City Nev. Died June 23, 1986.

ANDERSON, KENNETH EUGENE, education educator; b. Mpls., Mar. 2, 1910; s. Peter Wilhelm and Alma Annette (Ekstrum) A.; m. Dorothy Woodruff Smith, Aug. 1, 1934; children: Peter Alden, Philip Norman. BS, U. Minn., 1932, MA, 1934, PhD, 1949. Tchr., adminstr. pub. schs., Minn., 1934-44; instr. U. Minn. High Sch., 1944-46, dir., 1946-47; prin. Campus High Sch., Iowa State Tchr.'s Coll., 1947-48; asst. prof. edn. U. Kans., Lawrence, 1948-50, assoc. prof. edn., dir. bur. edn. research service, 1950-52, prof edn., 1952-85, dean sch. edn., 1952-69; exec. dir. Kans. Master Planning Commn. on Post High Sch. Edn., 1970-73. Author: Anderson-Fisk Chemistry Test, 1966, (with Collister, Ladd) The Educational Achievement of Indian Children, 1953, (with others) The Indian Child Goes to School, 1957, (with H.A. Smith) Topics in Statistics for Students of Education, 1959; exec. editor: Bull. Edn. and Kans. Studies in Edn., 1953-68; contbr articles to profl. jours. Recipient Outstanding Achievement award U. Minn., 1965, Master Tchr. award Kans. State Tchr.'s Coll., Emporia, 1971; Fulbright-Hays scholar, Colombia, summer 1974. Fellow AAAS (v.p. sect. Q 1961-62); mem. NAt. Assn. Research Sci. Teaching (pres. 1954-55), North Cen. Assn. Colls. and Secondary Schs. (dir., exec. com. 1961-65), Nat. Soc. Study Edn., Am. Statis. Assn., Am. Ednl. reserach Assn. (pres. 1959), Fulbright Alumni Assn., Sigma Xi. Home: Lawrence Kans. Died Oct. 15, 1985; buried Pioneer Cemetery, Lawrence, Kans.

ANDERSON, PAUL F., bishop; b. Boston, Apr. 20, 1917; s. Philip Leo and Mary Elizabeth (Doyle) A. B.A., St. John's Sem., Brighton, Mass., 1943. Ordained priest Roman Cath. Ch., 1943; pastor Sioux Falls (S.D.) Cath. Diocese, 1946-68; coadjutor bishop of Duluth, 1968-69; bishop 1969-82; aux. bishop of Sioux Falls, S.D., 1982-87. Home: Sioux Falls S.D. Died Jan. 4, 1987.

ANDERSON, ROBERT BERNARD, chemical engineering educator; b. Moline, Ill., Aug. 31, 1915; s. Gustav Adel and Hilda (Benson) A.; m. Jane Elizabeth Udden, July 3, 1942; children: Robert Udden, Susan Jane. A.B., Augustana Coll., 1938; M.S., State U. Iowa, 1940, Ph.D., 1942. Grad. asst., instr. chemistry dept. State U. Iowa, 1938-42; NDRC project dept. chem. engring. Johns Hopkins, 1942-44; phys. chemist U.S. Bur. Mines, Pitts., 1944-64; Petroleum Research Fund fellow 1965; prof. chem. engring. McMaster U., Hamilton, Ont., Can., 1965-81; prof. emeritus McMaster U., 1981-87; Spinks lectr. U. Sask., 1982; Mem. NRC grants awards com., 1967-70; mem. adv. bd. Petroleum Research Fund, 1958-61; co-chmn. 9th Internat. Congress Catalysis, Calgary, Alta., 1988; plenary speaker Bahia Catalysis Symposium, Salvador, Brazil, 1986. Author: (with others) The Fischer-Tropsch and Related Syntheses, 1951, the Fischer-Tropsch Synthesis, 1984; editor: (with others) Experimental Methods in Catalytic Research, vol. I, 1968, vol. II, vol. III, 1976; contbr. to Emmett's Catalysis, vol. IV, 1956; editorial bd. Jour. Catalysis, 1960-87; contbr. numerous articles to jours. Recipient Pitts. award, 1960, Outstanding Alumni award Augustana Coll., 1961, Distinguished Service award U.S. Dept. Interior, 1966, Catalysis award Pitts. Catalysis Soc., 1983. Fellow Chem. Inst. Can. (chmn. div. catalysis 1971, Catalysis award 1979, honored by Anderson Fischer-Tropsch Symposium 1984), Royal Soc. Can.; mem. Am. Chem. Soc. (Ipatieff prize 1953, chmn. Pitts. sect. 1959), Catalysis Soc. Home: Ancaster, Ont. Canada. Died Oct. 24, 1987, buried Whitechapel Meml., Hamilton, Ont., Can.

ANDERSON, ROBERT CLETUS, educator, consultant; b. Birmingham, Ala., July 18, 1921; s. Allie Cletus and Dana (Hilliard) A.; m. Evalee R. Pilgrim, 1977; children by previous marriage: Margaret Campbell, William Robert. B.S., Auburn U., 1942; M.A., U. N.C., 1947; Ph.D., N.Y. U., 1950. Research asst. Inst. Research in Social Sci., U. N.C., 1946-47; asst. to dean Sch. Edn., N.Y. U., 1948-50; dean Grad. Sch., Memphis State U., 1950-53; exec. assoc. So. Regional Edn. Bd., 1953-55, assoc. dir., 1955-57, dir., 1957-61; exec. v.p. Auburn U., 1961-65; v.p. research U. Ga., Athens, 1965-84; prof. sociology U. Ga., 1965-87, Univ. prof., 1984-87, spl. asst. to pres., 1984-86; pres. U. Ga. Research Found., 1978-84; prof. emeritus, v.p. research emeritus 1987; dir. So. Regional Project on Ednl. TV, So. Regional Edn. Bd., 1952, So. Regional Conf. on Edn. Beyond the High Sch., 1957; mem. Surgeon Gen.'s cons. group on Med. Edn., 1958-59, W.K. Kellogg Found. Ednl. Adv. Com., 1960-64, Joint Council on Ednl. Telecommunications, 1961-70, v.p., 1965-67; mem. council for research policy and adminstrn. Nat. Assn. State Univs. and Land-Grant Colls., 1965-87, chmn., 1965-67; mem. exec. com. Nat. Conf. Advancement Research, 1981-85; mem. Nat. Council Univ. Research Administrs., 1965-87, mem. exec. com., 1982-85, editor newsletter, 1985; dir. Nat. Conf. Future Univ. Research, 1984-85, prof., 1984-87; mem. Nat. Inst. Higher Edn., 1986-87. Mem. editorial bd. Soc. Research Adminstrs., 1981-84. Served from 2d lt. to capt. AUS, 1942-46, ETO. Decorated Purple Heart. Fellow Nat. Acad. Univ. Research Adminstrn (charter, pres. 1985-86); mem. AAAS, N.Y. Acad. Scis., Am. Council on Edn. (council on fed. relations 1963-67), Am. Assn. Higher Edn., Phi Kappa Phi, Alpha Tau Omega, Alpha Kappa Delta, Kappa Delta Pi, Omicron Delta Kappa, Phi Delta Kappa, Phi Eta Sigma, Pi Gamma Mu. Home: Athens Ga. Died Aug. 28, 1987.

ANDERSON, STEWART WISE, foreign service office; b. Chgo., June 10, 1912; S. Emil Bernard and Harriett (Going) A.; m. Marguerite Giraud, June 21, 1940; children: Stewart Going, Susan, Marilyn. Grad., Harvard Sch. for Boys, Chgo., 1930; AB, Dartmouth Coll., 1934; certificat, Ecole Superieure de Commerce, Neuchatel, Switzerland, 1935; AM, Fletcher Sch. Law and Diplomacy, Medford, Mass., 1938. Jr. auditor Arthur Young & Co., N.Y.C., 1935-36; traveling auditor Am. Radiator & Standard Sanitary Corp., N.Y.C., 1936-37; fgn. svc. officer Dept. State, from 1940; vice consul Dept. State, Toronto, Can., 1940; assigned Fgn. Svc. sch., Washington, 1941; 3d sec., vice consul Fgn. Svc. sch., Montevideo, 1941-47; 3d sec., vice consul Fgn. Svc. sch., Rio de Janeiro, 1947, 2d sec., vice consul, 1947-49, 2d sec., consul, 1949-50; 2d sec., consul Fgn. Svc. sch., Bogatá, Colombia, 1950-52; mem. staff regional office Inst. Internat. Edn., Denver, 1952-53; 2d sec., consul Inst. Internat. Edn., Manila, P.I., 1953-56, 1st sec., consul, from 1956. Ensign USNR, 1938-40. Mem. Fgn. Svc. Assn., Kenwood Golf and Country Club. Home: Chevy Chase Md. †

ANDERSON, WALLACE LUDWIG, language educator; b. Hartford, Conn., Sept. 9, 1917; s. Ludwig and Greta (Askerbloom) A.; m. Mary Elizabeth Belden, Mar. 10, 1943; children: Hale, Whit. BA, Trinity Coll., Conn., 1939, MA, 1945; PhD, U. Chgo., 1948. Tchr. pub. schs. Conn., 1939-42; asst. prof. English U. No. Iowa, Cedar Falls, 1948-54, assoc. prof., 1954-58, prof., 1958-72, asst. dean instrn., 1959-63, assoc. dean instrn., 1963-65, dean undergrad. studies, 1965-72; prof. English Bridgewater (Mass.) State Coll., 1972-82, prof. emeritus, from 1983, acad. dean, 1972-78, v.p. acad. affairs, 1978-83. Author: (with N.C. Stageberg) Poetry as Experience, 1952, Introductory Readings on Language, 1962, Edwin Arlington Robinson: A Critical Introduction, 1967; contbr. articles to profl. jours. Mem. intercultural edn. com. Edn. and World Affairs. With USAAF, 1942-45. Fulbright award The Netherlands, 1957-58; Guggenheim fellow, 1967-68. Mem. MLA. Home: Bridgewater Mass. Deceased.

ANDERSON, WILLIAM ERNEST, lawyer; b. Chgo., July 31, 1895; s. Andrew and Mary (Lofqvist) A.; m. Marjorie Allen, June 18, 1927; children: Laurel Joyce, Lois Winifred; m. Beatriz Hernandez del Valle. LL.B., Webster Coll., 1920; LL.M., Loyola U., Chgo., 1926. Bar: Ill. 1920. Since practiced in Chgo.; specializing in patents, unfair competition, trade-marks and copyrights; counsel to firm Fitch, Even, Tabin & Flannery (and predecessor firm), Chgo., 1931-86; U.S. claims commr. for, Morocco, Algeria, Tunisia, 1943-45. Author: Spanish Adjectives and Adverbs, 1941. Served to lt. col. AUS, 1942-46. Mem. Inter-Am., Am., Ill., Chgo. bar assns., Am., Chgo. patent law assns. Club: Union League (Chicago). Home: River Forest Ill. Died Nov. 18, 1986.

ANDERSON, WILLIAM OTIS, banker; b. Columbus, Ohio, Mar. 3, 1918; s. William Orville and Florence Bryson (Berger) A.; m. Clara L. Heil, May 16, 1947; children: Susan Lynn, William David. BSc, Ohio State U., 1939, MBA, 1941, PhD, 1950. With BancOhio Nat. Bank., Columbus, 1939-88, sr. v.p., 1967-88, sec. bd. dirs., 1968-88, bd. dirs, 1976-88; lectr. banking Ohio State U., Columbus, 1950-59. Bd. dirs. Franklin County chpt. ARC, 1965-76. Franklin County Soc. for Crippled Children, 1968-77, Columbus Symphony Orch., 1974, Citizens Research Inc., 1972, Childrens Hosp., 1974; trustee Episcopal Diocese So. Ohio, 1979; mem. Trinity episcopal Ch., Columbus (jr. and sr. warden). With USAAF, 1942-46. Recipient Disting. Service award Coll. Adminstrv. Sci., Ohio State U., 1970. Mem. Am. Bankers Assn. (econ. adv. com. 1978), Newcomen Soc., Am. Econs. Assn., Mason, Shriner, Ohio State U. Pres.'s Club, Ohio State U. Pacesetters Club, Lambskin, Phi Eta Sigma, Beta Gamma Sigma. Home: Worthington Ohio. Died Jan. 10, 1988; buried Jersey Cemetery.

ANDES, JOHN WILBUR, medical association executive; b. Knoxville, Tenn., July 18, 1928; s. John Wilbur and Irene (Garrett) A.; m. Patricia Jane Guy, Nov. 20, 1954; children: Alan Patrick, Jane Alison. A.B., Princeton U., 1948. Claims mgr. Blue Cross-Blue Shield of Fla., Jacksonville, 1948-50, 52-57, profl. relations dir., 1955-57; asst. exec. sec. Am. Soc. Anesthesiologists, Park Ridge, Ill., 1957-58, exec. sec., from 1958. Served with U.S. Navy, 1950-52. Mem. Am. Assn. Med. Soc. Execs., Profl. Conv. Mgmt. Assn., Park Ridge C. of C., Am. Soc. Assn. Execs., Chgo. Soc. Assn. Execs. Club: Princeton (Chgo.). Died Nov. 11, 1987; buried Ridgewood Cemetery, Des Plaines, Ill.

ANDREWES, CHRISTOPHER HOWARD, pathologist; b. London, June 7, 1896; s. Frederick William and Phyllis Mary (Hamer) A.; m. Kathleen Helen Lamb, Mar. 26, 1927; children: John Frederick, Michael Robert, David Anthony. M.B., B.S., U. London, 1921, M.D., 1923; LL.D., Aberdeen U., 1963. House physician, clin. asst. St. Bartholomews Hosp., London, 1921-23, 25-26; asst. resident physician Rockefeller Hosp., N.Y.C., 1923-25; mem. sci. staff Nat. Inst. for Med. Rsch., London, 1927-61, dep. dir., 1952-61. Author: Viruses of Vertebrates, 1964, The Common Cold, 1965; over 200 articles on influenza and common cold viruses. With Royal Naval Vol. Res., 1918-19. Created knight bachelor, 1961; recipient Bisset-Hawkins medal Royal Coll. Physicians, Steward prize Brit. Med. Assn., 1952; William Julius Mickle fellow U. London,

1931. Fellow Royal Soc., Royal Entomol. Soc.; mem. NAS (fgn. assoc.), Am. Philos. Soc. (fgn.), Soc. for Gen. Microbiology (hon., U.K.), Soc. Pathology. Home: Salisbury England. Died Dec. 31, 1988.

ANDREWS, ALBERT H., JR., physician; b. Chgo., June 20, 1907; s. Albert H. and Hattie (Frazey) A.; m. Jane Olson, June 25, 1938. BS, Northwestern U., 1929, MS in Physiology, 1932, MD, 1933. Diplomate Am. Bd. Otolaryngology. Intern St. Luke's Hosp., Chgo., 1932-33; practice medicine specializing in bronchoesophagology and laryngeal surger; clin. asst. Northwestern U., Chgo., 1933-38, research asst., 1933-40; mem. faculty Coll. Medicine, U. Ill., Chgo., 1939-86, clin. assoc. prof. bronchoesophagology, 1955-63, clin. prof., 1963-65, prof., 1965-86, head dept. otolaryngology, 1967-75; mem. staff Presbyn.-St. Lukes Hosp., Childrens Meml. Hosp., VA West Side Hosp., Skokie Valley Community Hosp.; cons. Edgewater Hosp., Englewood Hosp., St. Francis Hosp., DuPage County Tb Case and Treatment Bd. Lt. comdr. M.C., USNR, 1942-45, ETO. Fellow AMA, Am. Coll. Chest Physicians (treas., past pres. Ill.), Inst. of Medicine of Chgo.; mem. Chgo. Med. Soc., Ill. Med. Soc., Am. Acad. Opthalmology and Otolaryngology, Am. Laryngological, Rhinological and Otological Soc., Am. Broncho-esophagological Assn., Am. Laryngological Assn., Am. Council Otolaryngology, Collegium Medicorum Theatri, Internat. Broncho-esophagological Soc., Pan.-Am. Assn. Oto-Rhino-Laryngology and Bronchoesophagology, Chgo. Laryngological and Otological Soc. (pres. 1962-63), AAAS, Am. Registry Inhalation Therapists Inc. (pres. bd. trustees 1960-71), Am. Assn. Inhalation Therapy (mem. bd. med. advisors 1954-66), Kansas City Soc. Opthalmology and Otolaryngology (hon.), Am. Med. Writers Assn., Union League. Home: Chicago Ill. Died Sept. 26, 1986.

ANDREWS, ELMORE LYNNWOOD, lawyer; b. Mpls., Nov. 19, 1892; s. Frederick Grove and Jennie (Kelly) A.; m. Florence C. Stafford, Sept. 14, 1920 (dec. 1942); children: Stafford E., David L.; m. Ruth S. Moak, Apr. 23, 1945. Student, U. Mich., 1912-13; LLB, U. Va., 1916. Bar: Va. 1916, Ohio 1916. Mem. Thompson, Hine & Flory, from 1916, ptnr., from 1926, sr. ptnr., from 1960; bd. dirs. Medusa Portland Cement Co., Osborn Mfg. Co., Land Title Guarantee & Trust Co., Curtis Noll Corp., Motch & Merryweather Machinery Co., Am. Vitrified Products Co., Cleve. Punch & Shear Works Co., Clauss Cutlery Co., Parsons & Co., Inc. Past pres., trustee Citizens League Cleve.; mem. vis. com. Western Res. U. Law Sch. With U.S. Army, 1917-19. Mem. ABA, Ohio, Cleve. bar assns., Raven Soc., Order of Coif, Union Club, Nisi Prius Club, Country Club (Pepper Pike, Ohio), Hunting Valley Gun Club. Home: Shaker Heights Ohio. †

ANDREWS, FLETCHER REED, educational administrator, lawyer; b. N.Y.C., Jan. 22, 1894; s. Addison Fletcher and Ella (Reed) A.; m. Marguerite Jeavons, Aug. 8, 1917; children: Jeanne (Mrs. Jacob. B. Perkins), Fletcher Reed, Jr. AB, Dartmouth Coll., 1916; LLB, Case Western Reserve U., 1925; JSD, Yale U., 1941. Bar: Ohio 1925. With advt. dept. Crowell Pub. Co., 1916-17; asst. to gen. mgr. J.H.R. Products Co., Willoughby, Ohio, 1919-22; assoc. Copeland and Quintrell, Cleve., 1925-27; prof. law Case Western Reserve U., Cleve., 1927-64, dean, 1948-58; impartial chmn. Thompson Products Inc. Pension Bd., 1952-58; referee Probate Ct., 1961-74; adv. spl. com. bar exam Supreme Ct., Ohio; Ohio annotator REstatement of Conflict of Laws. Assoc. editor: Throckmorton's Ohio General Code, 1929; editor: Baldwins Ohio Law Rev., 1931; also several chpts. in Ohio Annotations to the Restatement of Conflict of Laws, 1935-38; contbr. articles to law jours. V.p. Cleve. Community Fund, Council World Affairs, 1st Unitarian Ch., 1955-58; pres. League Ohio Law Schs., 1949; mem. Dartmouth Coll. Alumni Council , 1935-41; gen. chmn. Cleve. Community Fund, 1941-42; mem. exec. com. Legal Aid Soc. Cleve., 1935-40, treas. 1963-65; trustee Cleve. Bar Found., Univ. Sch., Cleve., Bennett Jr. Coll., Millbrook, N.Y.; fiscal trustee Dorcas Soc., 1955-72. With U.S. Army, 1917-19; lt. col. JAGC, U.S. Army 1942-45. Decorated medal of Honor (France), Legion of Merit; recipient Disting. Service award Cleve. Community Fund, 1943, Alumni award Dartmouth Coll., 1957; Sterling fellow Yale U., 1941. Mem. ABA, Cleve. Bar Assn. (pres. 1960-61, chmn. uniform comml. code com.), Ohio Bar Assn. (mem. com. on banking and comml law), Cuyahoga County Bar Assn., Am. Arbitration Assn. (mem. arbitration law com. 1955-58), Am. Law Inst. (mem. council 1947-52), Union Club, Cleve. Country Club, Order of Coif, Alpha Delta Phi, Phi Delta Phi. Republican. Home: Cleveland Ohio. Died Aug. 30, 1982; buried Knollwood Mausoleum, Mayfield Heights, Ohio.

ANDREWS, FONNIE JACKSON, drug manufacturer; b. Chatham County, N.C., 1892; s. Franklin and Augusta (Norwood) A.; m. Phyllis Mitchell, Mar. 1, 1930; 1 dau., Heather Margaret. AB, Franklin and Marshll Coll., 1923, LHD (hon.), 1952. With Emerson Drug Co., Balt., from 1919; Canadian mgr. Emerson Drug Co., 1919-51, pres., dir., from 1951; chmn., dir. Bromo-Seltzer Ltd., Toronto, Can., Alkalithia Co., Balt.; dir. Md. Glass Corp., Balt., N.C. Pharm. Rsch. Found. Mem. U.S. C. of C., Nat. Assn. Mfrs., Kappa Psi. Presbyterian. Home: Baltimore Md. †

ANDREWS, GEORGE CLINTON, dermatologist; b. Tarrytown, N.Y., Nov. 26, 1891; s. George Clinton and Julia (Biers) A.; m. Emmie Donner, May1, 1925; children: George, Peter, Richard; m. Pauline Peterka, June 18, 1940; children: Pauline, Barbara. AB, Cornell U., 1912; MD, Columbia U., 1918. Intern Presbyn. Hosp., N.Y.C., 1919-20; resident Presbyn. Hosp. and Sloane Maternity Hosp., 1920-21; pvt. practice N.Y.C., from 1921; mem. staff Presbyn. Hosp., Roosevelt Hosp.; cons. dermatologist Columbia Presbyn. Med. Ctr., 1950-60; clin. prof. dermatology Columbia Coll. Physicians and Surgeons, 1950-60. Author: Disease of the Skin, 5th edit., 1962, Spanish transl., 1960. Bd. dirs. ann. appeal Salvation Army, N.Y.C., 1955-65. With U.S. Army, World War I. Mem. Am. Dermatol. Assn. (pres. 1961), Am. Acad. Dermatology (bd..dirs. 1959-62), N.Y. Acad. Medicine (life), N.Y. Acad. Sic., N.Y. Hist. Soc. (life), Am. Legion; hon., corr. mem. dermatol. socs. in Britain, Australia, Mex., Cuba, Venezuela, Argentina, Brazil, Germany, France, Swededn, Denmark, India, Poland, Iran. Home: New York N.Y. also: Lake Placid N.Y. †

ANDREWS, J. FLOYD, airline executive; b. 1919; married. Student, Wichita U., Friends U. Co-founder Pacific S.W. Airlines, 1949, pres., chief exec. officer, bd. dirs., from 1962, ret.; bd. dirs. San Diego Gas & Electric Co., Bank of La Jolla, So. Calif. First Nat. Bank. With USAAF, 1944-48. Home: San Diego Calif. Died Jan. 24, 1989.

ANDREWS, WAYNE, author, art history educator, photographer; b. Kenilworth, Ill., Sept. 5, 1913; s. Emory Cobb and Helen (Armstrong) A.; m. Elizabeth A. Hodges, June 12, 1948; 1 dau., Elizabeth Waties. Grad., Lawrenceville Sch., 1932; A.B., Harvard U., 1936; Ph.D., Columbia U., 1956. Curator manuscripts N.-Y. Hist. Soc., 1948-56; editor Charles Scribner's Sons, 1956-63; Archives of Am. Art prof. Wayne State U., 1964-84; Phi Beta Kappa vis. lectr., 1975-76. Author: The Vanderbilt Legend, 1941, Battle for Chicago, 1946, Architecture, Ambition and Americans, 1955, rev. edit., 1978, Architecture in America, 1960, rev. edit., 1977, Germaine: A Portrait of Madame de Staël, 1963, Architecture in Michigan, 1967, rev. edit., 1982, Architecture in Chicago and Mid-America, 1968, Architecture in New York, 1969, Siegfried's Curse: The German Journey from Nietzsche to Hesse, 1972, Architecture in New England, 1973, American Gothic, 1975, Pride of the South-A Social History of Southern Architecture, 1979, Voltaire, 1981; pseudonym Montagu O'Reilly: Who Has Been Tampering With These Pianos?, 1948 English edit., 1988; editor: Concise Dictionary of American History, 1962, Best Short Stories of Edith Wharton, 1958. Co-trustee Joseph and Robert Cornell Meml. Found., 1982. Mem. Société Chateaubriand (Paris). Club: Cliff Dwellers. Home: Chicago Ill. Died Aug. 17, 1987; buried Ch. of the Holy Cross, Stateburg, S.C.

ANDUZE-FARIS, GUSTAVE, shipowner; b. Toulouse, France, Dec. 23, 1892; s. Henri and Marguerite (Astrie-Rolland) Anduze-F.; m. Arlette Grosos, July 24, 1923. Student, Ecole Polytechnique. Dir. Marine Marchande et des Transports Maritimes a Alger, 1943-44, sec.-gen., 1944-48; pres. Compagnie des Messageries Maritimes, 1948-61; chmn. bd. Compagnie Generale Transatlantique (French Line). Served with French Navy. Decorated Comdr. Legion of Honor, Comdr. Mérite Maritime, Comdr. Mérite Touristique, Comdr. Order l'Economie Nationale, Croix de Guerre, 1914-18, Croix des Services militaire voluntaires, Medal of Freedom (U.S. and U.K). Mem. Comité Central des Armateurs France (v.p.), Sté Centrale de Sauvetage des Naufragés (v.p.), L'Académie de Marine (pres. 1956-57, sec.), L'Institut de Commerce Nationale (pres.). Home: Paris France. †

ANGEL, J(OHN) LAWRENCE, physical anthropologist; b. London, Mar. 21, 1915; s. John and Elizabeth Day (Seymour) A.; m. Margaret Seymour Richardson, July 1, 1937; children—Elizabeth Richardson Angel Cohen, Stephen Bearne, Jonathan Seymour. A.B. magna cum laude, Harvard U., 1936, Ph.D., 1942. Instr. anthropology U. Calif.-Berkeley, 1941-42; asst. prof. U. Minn., Mpls., 1942-43; mem. faculty Thomas Jefferson Med. Coll., Phila., 1942-62, prof. anatomy and phys. anthropology, 1962; curator phys. anthropology Smithsonian Instn., Washington, 1962-86; cons. surg. anatomy U.S. Naval Hosp., Phila., 1953-62; prof. phys. anthropology George Washington U., Washington, 1965-86; vis. prof. Johns Hopkins U. Sch. Pub. Health, Balt., 1966-86; pres. Am. Bd. Forensic Anthropology, 1980-85; cons. forensic anthropology FBI, U.S. Army, U.S. Air Force, U.S. Navy, Police Dept. Washington, 1962-86. Author: Troy, the Human Remains, 1951; The People of Lerna, 1971. Contbr. articles to profl. jours. Recipient Pomerance medal Archaeol. Inst. Am., 1983; Guggenheim fellow, 1949, 65; grantee Am. Philos. Soc., 1954, 57, 65, NIH, 1953, 64. Fellow Am. Athrop. Assn., AAAS; mem. Am. Assn. Phys. Anthropologists (sec., v.p.), Assn. Anatomists, Soc. Human Genetics, Archeol. Inst. Am., Am. Acad. Forensic Scis. phys. anthropology sect. award 1983. Democrat. Unitarian. Clubs: Harvard, Cosmos. Avocations: photography, church choir, walking. Home: Washington, DC. Died Nov. 3, 1986. Home: Washington D.C.

ANGELL, JAMES WATERHOUSE, economist; b. Chgo., May 20, 1898; s. James Rowland and Marion Isabel (Watrous) A.; m. Jane Norton Grew, Oct. 19, 1923 (dec.); children: James Grew, Edward Dexter (dec.). AB, Harvard U., 1918, AM, 1921, PhD, 1924. Asst. in econs. U. Chgo., 1919-20; instr. in econs. Harvard U., Cambridge, Mass., 1921-24; lectr. in econs. Columbia U., N.Y.C., 1924-26, assoc. prof., 1926-31, prof., 1931-66, prof. emeritus, 1966-86; vis. prof. New Sch. Social Research, 1966-67; with Office Civilian requirements, WPB and predecessor units, 1941-43; with Fgn. Econ. Adminstrn., 1943-45, asst. adminstr., 1945; U.S. rep. with rank of minister Allied Commn. on REparations, Germany, 1945-46; dir. United Funds-Can. Internat., 1961-70; vice chmn. Anthracite Coal Industry Commn., Pa., 1937-38; tech adv. U.S. del. to UN Monetary-Fin. Conf., 1944; U.S. del. Paris Conf. on Reparations, 1945; cons. NAt Security REsources Bd., 1948-50, UN, 1951. Author: The Theory of International Prices, 1926, The Recovery of Germany, 1929, 32, Der Wiederaufbau Deutschlands, 1930, Financial Foreign Policy of the U.S., 1933, The Behavior of Money, 1936, Investment and Business Cycles, 1941; (with others) Measures for International Economic Stability, 1951; contbr. articles to profl. jours. Fellow Am. Acad. Arts and Scis.; mem. Am. Econ. Assn. (v.p. 1940), Royal Econ. Soc. (Eng.), Acad. Polit. Sci., Council Fgn. Relations, Century Assn., Phi Beta Kappa. Home: West Chop Mass. Died Mar. 29, 1986.

ANGELL, PHILIP HAROLD, lawyer; b. Newark Valley, N.Y., Mar. 21, 1896; s. Charles Everett and Adelaide C. (Turner) A.; m. Ethel F. Chappelka, Sept. 14, 1921; children: Dorothy F., Philip Harold. BA, U. Calif., 1919; LLB, HArvard U., 1921. Bar: Calif. 1922. Ptnr. Athearn, Chandler, Hoffman & Angell, San Francisco, 1922-50; sr. ptnr. Angell, Holmes & Lea and predecessor firm, San Francisco, 1950-77, of counsel, 1977-85; bd. dirs. Fidelity Savs. & Loan Assn., Fidelity Fin. Corp., Ancora-Verde Corp.; pres., bd. dirs. Tracy Drilling Corp.; sec. Fastener Supply Co.; mem. Calif. Bd. Bar Examiners, 1942-45, chmn. 1944-45. Mem. Berkeley (Calif.) Bd. Edn., 1935; chmn. adv. panel Calif. Youth Correction Authority, 1941-42; mem. personnel bd., Berkeley, 1937-59, chmn. 1937-58; former vice chmn. nat. loyalty bd., 12th regional office, CSC. Mem. ABA, State Bar Calif. (bd. govs. 1939-42, pres. 1941-42), San Francisco Bar Assn., Am. Judicature Soc., Nat. Legal Aid Assn., Calif. Alumni Assn., Harvard Law Sch. Assn., Harvard Club, Olympic Club, Lawyers Club, Lambda Chi. Home: Berkeley Calif. Died Jan. 8, 1985.

ANGULO, CHARLES, lawyer; b. Havana, Cuba, Nov. 4, 1890. Student, Georgetown Prep. Sch., Washington; AB, Georgetown U., 1911; LLB, Columbia U., 1914. Bar: N.Y. 1914. Pvt. practice N.Y.C., from 1914; mem. firm Angulo, Cooney, Marsh & Ouchterloney, N.Y.C., from 1914. Mem. Assn. Bar City N.Y., N.Y. County Lawyers Assn., Am., N.Y. bar assns. Home: New York N.Y. †

ANOFF, ISADOR SAMUEL, corporation executive; b. Cin., 1892. Pres. Albert Pick Co., Chgo., 1932-58; exec. v.p. Equipment Mfg. Co., Chgo.,; v.p. Franklin Products Corp., Chgo. Chmn. exec. com. Food Svc. Equipment Industry; mem. indsl. adv. com., Nat. Sanitation Found.; v.p. and trustee Bellefaire (Cleve.); exec. v.p. Off-the-Street Club, Chgo.; past pres., dir. Jewish Children's Bur., Chgo., past pres., dir. Chgo. Conv. Bur. Mem. Standard Club. Home: Chicago Ill. †

ANTHONY, GRAHAM HUDSON, manufacturer; b. Shelby, N.C., Apr. 2, 1892; s. John Alston and Ollie (Gardner) A.; m. Elizabeth Johnson, Apr. 27, 1916 (dec. 1953); 1 child, James I.; m. 2d, Mrs. Mary Alice Kaiser, Dec. 20, 1954. Engaged as factory clk. Mason Machine Works, Taunton, Mass., 1914-15; supt. Gilbert Clock Co., Winsted, Conn., 1915-17; sec. and factory mgr. Allen Mfg. Co., 1918-28; assoc. with Veeder-Root Inc., Hartford, Conn., 1928-64, v.p., dir., 1928-32, pres., 1932-44, chmn. bd., 1944-54, chmn. exec. com., 1954-56; pres. Colt's Co., 1944-49, chmn. bd., 1949-54, chmn. exec. com., 1954-56; chmn. bd. Holo-Krome Screw Corp., 1950-61; hon. dir. Hartford Nat. Bank & Trust Co., Hartford Electric Light Co.; former mem. adv. bd. Chem. Bank N.Y. Trust Dirs. Pres. Jr. Achievement, Hartford, 1960-62; trustee Hartford YMCA; also life trustee Kingswood Sch., West Hartford. Mem. ASME, Newcomen Soc. of England, St. Andrews Soc. N.Y., Sigma Nu, Phi Kappa Phi, Masons, Hartford Gold, 20th Century, Hartford Gun, Metropolitan, Economic of N.Y. clubs. Home: Hartford Conn. †

ARAMANY, MOHAMED ABDELAL, prosthodontist, educator; b. Cairo, Mar. 24, 1935; m. Janet Jacqueline Young, July 31, 1964; children: Jacqueline, Elizabeth, Andrew, Richard. P.N.S., Cairo U., 1954, D.D.S., 1958; M.S., U. Pitts., 1963, D.M.D., 1973. Am. Bd. Prosthodontics cert. N.E. Regional Dental Bd., lic. dentist, Pa. Intern Univ. Hosp., Cairo, 1958-59, instr. Sch. Dentistry, 1959-60, asst. prof. Sch. Dentistry, 1964-68; resident in prosthodontics U. Pitts. Sch. Dental Medicine and Hosps., 1961-63, teaching fellow, 1961-63, asst. prof., 1968-71, assoc. prof., 1971-75, prof., 1975-85;

resident in maxillofacial prosthetics Tex. U. Dental Br., M.D. Anderson Hosp. and Tumor Inst., Houston, 1969-70; dir. Regional Ctr. for Maxillofacial Rehab., Eye and Ear Hosp., Pitts., 1973-85; dir. dept. maxillofacial prosthodontics VA Hosp., Pitts., Mercy Hosp., Pitts. Fellow Internat. Coll. Dentists; mem. Am. Cleft Palate Assn., Internat. Assn. Dental Research, Am. Prosthodontic Soc., ADA, Pa. Dental Assn., Odontol. soc. Western Pa., Am. acad. Maxillofacial Prosthetics, Internat. Assn. for Study of Dento Facial Abnormalities, Am. Coll. Prosthodontics, Am. Assn. Dental Schs. Home: Pittsburgh Pa. Died Nov. 12, 1985.

ARAND, LOUIS A., educator; b. Pitts., Nov. 3, 1892; s. Jacob J. and Josephine M. (Arand) A. AB, AM, STB, St. Mary's Sem., U. Balt., 1912-17; STL, Cath. U. Am., 1919; postgrad., Paris, 1919-20; STD, Angelico U., Rome, 1921. Prof. philosophy St. Mary's U., 1921-24; prof. dogmatic theology Sulpician Sem., Washington, 1924-39, prof. sacramental theology, 1926-39; pres. Div. Coll. Cath. U., from 1932, prof. dogmatic theology, from 1936, trustee. Author: (with Father Tangueroy) Doctrine and Devotion, 1933; editor: The Spiritual Life, 1932, St. Augustine: Faith, Hope and Charity, 1947. Republican. †

ARANOW, HENRY, JR., medical educator; b. N.Y.C., May 5, 1913; s. Harry and Dora (Bittman) A.; m. Doris Elaine Jones, Apr. 26, 1941; children: Peter Jones, Philip Thompson, Michael Henry, Robert Bittman. Grad., Horace Mann Sch. Boys, 1930; AB magma cum laude, Harvard U., 1934; MD, Columbia U., 1938, DMS, 1944. Intern Presbyn. Hosp., N.Y.C., 1938-40; Harlow Brooks fellow N.Y. Acad. Medicine, Johns Hopkins Hosp., Balt., 1941-42; resident Presbyn. Hosp., N.Y.C., 1942-44, mem. staff, adminstrn., from 1944, acting dir. med. svc., 1970-71, 75-76, attending physician, from 1969; mem. faculty Columbia Coll. Physicians and Surgeons, N.Y.C., assoc. prof. clin. medicine, 1960-67, prof., from 1967, Samuel W. Lambert prof. medicine, 1976-78, Lambert prof. emeritus, from 1978, acting chmn. dept. medicine, 1970-71, 75-76; sr. adj. assoc. Inst. Soc. Ethics and Life Scis., from 1981; dir., mem. exec. com., hon. counselor Group Health, Inc.; trustee Mary Imogene Bassett Hosp., Cooperstown, N.Y., from 1977, chmn. bd. trustees, pres., from 1982; bd. visitors Helen Hayes Rehab. and Rsch. Hosp., N.Y., from 1978. Assoc. editor: Man and Medicine; mem. editorial bd. The Pharos, from 1979; contbr. articles to profl. jours. Benjamin Franklin fellow Royal Soc. Arts, London, Eng., 1970. Mem. Am. Thyroid Assn., Endocrine Soc., N.Y. Acad. Medicine, Harvey Soc., Century Assn., Phi Beta Kappa, Alpha Omega Alpha. Home: Hastings-on-Hudson N.Y. Deceased.

ARANYOS, ALEXANDER SANDOR, international operations executive; b. Zilina, Czechoslovakia; s. Ludwig and Ethel (Wilhelm) A.; m. Gertrude Reisman, Aug. 22, 1937; children: Alexander Paul, Vivian Jane. Degree Comml. Engring. cum laude, Grad. Sch. Commerce U. Prague, 1931. Adminstrv. asst. to pres. and export mgr. Coburg Mining & Foundry Co., Bratislava, Czechoslovakia, 1940-41; mgr. import div. Gen. Motors Distbrs., Republic of Panama, 1940-41; mgr. Latin Am. div. Van Raalte Co., N.Y.C., 1941-53; with Fruehauf Corp., Detroit, 1953-87; v.p. internat. ops. Fruehauf Corp., 1956-87, dir., 1973-87; pres., dir. Fruehauf Internat. Ltd., 1957, chmn., dir., 1976-82, hon. chmn., 1982-87; mem. adminstrv. council Viaturas PNV-Freuhauf S.A., Sao Paulo, Brazil; assoc. dir. Fruehauf Trailers (Australasia) Pty. Ltd.; bd. dirs. Fruehauf Finance Corp. (Pty.) Ltd., Melbourne, Australia, Fruehauf France, S.A., RIS-ORANGIS, France, Fruehauf de Mexico, S.A., Coacalco, Nippon Fruehauf Co., Ltd., Tokyo, Henred-Fruehauf Trailers (Pty.) Ltd., Johannesburg, S. Africa, Fruehauf S.A., Madrid, Spain. Mem. regional export expansion council U.S. Dept. Commerce, 1970-73. Decorated French Legion of Honor. Mem. Research Inst. Am., AIM, Detroit Bd. Commerce, Internat. Execs. Assn. N.Y., World Trade Club Detroit, Am. Australian Assn. N.Y., C. of C. U.S. (internat. com.). Clubs: Rotary (N.Y.C.), Rockefeller Center Luncheon (N.Y.C.). Home: Sands Point N.Y. Died Dec. 11, 1987; buried Nassau Knolls, Port Washington, N.Y.

ARBUCKLE, ERNEST COMINGS, banker, educator; b. Lee, N.H., Sept. 5, 1912; s. Frank Albert and Ernestine C. (Weeden) A.; m. Katherine Norris Hall, Dec. 10, 1942; children: Ernest C., Joan. Katherine, Susan. AB, Stanford U., 1933, MBA, 1936; Dr. h.c., U. Centroamericana, 1970; LLD, Golden Gate U., 1973. Personnel specialist Standard Oil of Calif., 1937-41, orgn. analyst, 1945-46; dir. procurement, asst. to pres. Golden State Co. Ltd., 1946-50; exec. v.p. Pacific Coast div. W.R. Grace & Co., 1950-58; dean Grad Sch. Bus., Stanford U., 1958-68, dean emeritus, 1968-86; Bd. dirs. Stanford Research Inst., 1966-86, chmn. 1966-70; chmn. bd. dirs. Wells Fargo Bank, San Francisco, 1968-77, dir. emeritus, 1977-86; chmn. bd. dirs. Saga Corp., Menlo Park, Calif., chmn. exec. com., 1982; bd. dirs. Owens-Ill. Inc., Hewlett -Packard Co., Utah Internat. Inc., A. Johnson & Co. Inc.; mem. adv. com. Export-Import Bank U.S., 1972-75; mem. commn. on White House Fellows, 1964-68; mem. Adv. Com. on Pvt. Enterprise in Fgn. Aid, 1964-65, Pres.'s Commn. on Internat. Trade and Investment Policy, 1970-71; mem. industry adv. council Dept. Def., 1969-72; mem. Trilateral Commn., 1973-77. Bd. dirs. Bay Area Council Inc., chmn., 1976-77; chmn. Community Found. Santa Clara County, 1982-86; trustee Stanford U., 1968-76, Packard Found., 1970-86, Calif. Acad. Scis., 1979-86. Lt. comdr. USNR, 1941-45. Decorated Silver Star; recipient Freedom Found award, 1950, Adminstrv. Excellence award Stanford Bus. Sch. Assn., 1968, Bus. Leadership award U. Mich. Grad. Sch. Bus. Adminstrn., 1969, Disting. Achievement medal Stanford Athletic Bd., 1971, Bus. Statesman award Harvard Bus. Sch. Alumni Assn., 1975. Mem. Pacific Union Club, Bohemian Club. Republican. Home: Menlo Park Calif. Died Jan. 17, 1986.

ARCHER, JOHN DALE, physician, medical editor; b. Brady, Tex., Mar. 10, 1923; s. John Andrew and Mattie Rae (Willis) A.; m. Dora Alice Bullard, June 10, 1952; children: Linda Dale, Diana Lee. B.A., U. Tex., 1950, M.D., 1952, postgrad. Sch. Law, 1954-57. Intern Brackenridge Hosp., Austin, Tex., 1952-53; research asso. dept. pharmacology and toxicology U. Tex. Med. Br., Galveston, 1951-52; instr. U. Tex. Med. Br., 1952-53, asst. prof., 1953-55; team physician dept. intercollegiate athletics U. Tex., Austin, 1955-57; staff physician Student Health Center, 1955-57; asst. med. dir. State Dept. Pub. Welfare, Austin, 1957-58; med. officer div. new drugs FDA, HEW, Washington, 1958-61; dep. dir. FDA, HEW, 1961-62, acting dir., 1962; staff physician med. service VA Center, Temple, Tex., 1962-64; asst. dir. dept. of drugs, div. of science activities AMA, Chgo., 1964-67; dir. drug evaluation sect. AMA, 1967-72, asst. dir. dept. of drugs, 1972; sr. editor Jour. of AMA, Chgo., 1972-86; contbg. editor Jour of AMA, 1986-87. Author: The Archer Method of Winning at 21, 1973, also other trade books; Contbr. articles to med. jours. Served with USMC, 1941-45. Mem. Drug Info. Assn. (pres. 1972-73), Am. Med. Writers Assn., Research Soc. Am., Am. Acad. Clin. Toxicology, Am. Soc. for Clin. Pharmacology and Therapeutics, Phi Beta Kappa, Phi Eta Sigma. Club: Elks. Home: Park Forest Ill. Died Aug. 5, 1988.

ARCHER, LAIRD, foundation administrator; b. Argonia, Kans., 1892; s. John James and Ida (Miller) A.; m. Mary E. Balderston, 1919 (div. 1946); m. 2d, Evangeline Pratt Waterman, Oct. 10, 1947; children (adopted): Boris, Julian. Editorial staff Henry J. Allen Publs., Kansas, 1910-17; regional bus. officer War Work Council, France, 1917-19; dep. sr. officer, same, Greece, 1919-20; editor, sec. Gov. Henry J Allen, Kans., 1920-22; survey rehab. Assyrians for League of Nations, Persia, refugee problems, Russia, Turkey, Iraq, Syria, for Near East Found., Athens, Greece, 1930-53, ret., 1953; gen. chmn. Am. Repatriation Com., Greece, 1941; chmn. coordination com. Am. agys. for reconstrn. planning Greek govt., N.Y.C., 1942-43; lectr. on rehab., Columbia U., Cornell U., Antioch Coll., 1942-43; chief U.S. Office Fgn. Relief and Rehab. Ops., Cairo, Egypt, 1943-44; chief of Greece Mission, UNRRA, 1944-45. Panel participant Tulane U. So. Assembly, 1957, 58, 59; opened new Cordell Hull lectr. series Memphis State U., 1957; lectr. fgn. affairs Stephens Coll., 1959, 60, U. Ark. Coll. Edn., 1961-62, Chgo. Greek Heritage Found. annual symposium, Athens, 1964, to civic clubs, Oklahoma City, Dallas, Little Rock, others. Author: Balkan Journal. Mem. Nat. resolutions com. ARC, 1959, disaster service chmn., Washington County chpt. Decorated Grand Comdr. Order Phoenix, Order of Redeemer (Greece), Comdr. Order of Scanderberg (Albania). Mem. World Neighbors Inc. Home: Fayetteville Ark. †

ARENTS, CHESTER ABBO, engineer, educator; b. Leonardville, Kans., Apr. 19, 1910; s. Abbo Edward and Hazel Amanda (Johnson) A.; m. Edna Louisa Van Vleet, Feb. 18, 1935. B.S., Oreg. State U., 1932, M.S., 1946; M.E., 953; D.Sc., Marshall U., 1968. Registered profl. engr., Oreg., W.Va. Test engr. (automotive) City of Portland, Oreg., 1936-41; asso. elec. engr. Bonneville Power Adm., 1941-43; asst. prof. mech. engring. Oreg. State Coll., 1943-46; asso. prof. mech. engring. in charge machine design and heat power engring. Mont. State Coll., 1946-47; asso. prof. mech. engring. and asst. dept. dir. Ill. Inst. Tech., Chgo., 1947-49; asst. dean engring. Ill. Inst. Tech., 1949-51, coordinator research and prof. mech. engring. in charge sponsored research program, 1951-55; dean Coll. Engring. W.Va. U., 1955-75, dean emeritus, 1975-86, tech. cons., engring. analyst, 1975-86; dir. of engring. Expt. Sta. Cons. div. air pollution NIH; past sec. Nat. Conf. Indsl. Hydraulics; mem. Bldg. Research Adv. Bd.; mem. bd. rev. Marine Engring. Lab., U.S. Navy; mem. Pub. Land Corp. W.Va.; past pres. W.Va. Registration Bd. Profl. Engrs.; Past dir. N.E. zone Nat. Council State Bd. Engring. Examiners; pres. Nat. Council Engring. Examiners, 1970-71. Author manuals on insulation. Mem. W.Va. Soc. Profl. Engrs., ASME, Am. Soc. Engring. Edn., Nat. (dir.), W.Va. socs. profl. engrs.), Morgantown C. of C. (pres. 1962), Morgantown Community Assn. (trustee), Sigma Xi, Pi Tau Sigma, Tau Beta Pi, Eta Kappa Nu, Alpha Pi Mu. Mem. Pentecostal Ch. Home: Morgantown W.V. Died Oct. 24, 1986; buried Lenardville, Kans.

AREY, LESLIE BRAINERD, anatomist, educator; b. Camden, Maine, Feb. 15, 1891; s. Arthur Brainerd and Mary Josephine (Page) A.; m. Mary E. Holt, 1926. A.B., Colby Coll., Waterville, Maine, 1912, D.Sc., 1937; Ph.D., Harvard, 1915; LL.D., Chgo. Med. Sch., 1934; L.H.D., Ill. Coll. Podiatric Medicine, 1983. Asst. in zoology Harvard, 1912-13, teaching fellow, 1913; asst. in zoology Radcliffe, 1913-14, instr. anatomy, 1915-17, assoc. prof., 1917-19, prof. microscopic anatomy, 1919-24; Robert L. Rea prof. anatomy, chmn. dept. anatomy Northwestern U. Med. Sch., 1924-56, emeritus prof. anatomy, 1956-88; mem. staff Wesley Meml. Hosp., Passavant Hosp., Children's Meml. Hosp; spl. cons. NIH.; sometime investigator U.S. Bureau Fisheries; sometime chmn. Com. Basic Scis., White House Conf. on Child Health and Protection; sometime guest lectr. Chgo. Jr. Colls; vis. prof. U. P.R., 1963, 64; chmn. Internat. Com. on Embryological Terminology, 1962-88; pres. Internat. Anatomical Nomenclature Com., 1975-80; sec.-treas. Interfraternity Confs., 1938-42, pres., 1944-47; mem. exec. com. Profl. Interfraternity Conference, 1942-44. Author: Tratado de Endocrinologia Clinica, 1951, Word Book Encyclopedia, 1949, Morris Human Anatomy, 1966, Developmental Anatomy, 1974, Human Histology, 1974, Medical Dictionary, 1974, Anatomia Desarrollo, 1958, Histologia Humana, 1958, Centennial History of Northwestern University Medical School, 1959, Northwestern University Medical School, 1979, Histologia Humana, 1976. Assoc. editor: Excerpta Medica. Editor: Northwestern U. Med. Sch. Mag, 1963-74. Writer papers and monographs on anatomy and physiology. Contbr. to 13 books and 6 encys. Recipient Alumni medal Northwestern U., 1959, Service award, 1973, Hamilton Interstate Teaching award, 1973; Coll. award Am. Coll. Obstetrics and Gynecology, 1975; William H. Byford Northwestern award, 1980; Disting. Alumnus award Colby Coll., 1980; named to City of Chgo. Hall of Fame, 1967. Fellow Chgo. Acad. Sci. (pres. 1956-73, pres. emeritus 1973-88, trustee 1973-88); mem. Am. Soc. Zoologists (sec. 1928, treas. 1925-30), Am. Assn. Anatomists (exec. com. 1930-34, v.p. 1942-46, pres. 1952-54, Henry Gray award 1974), Phi Beta Kappa, Sigma Xi, Delta Upsilon, Phi Beta Pi (praetor 1932-34, 40-47, supreme archon 1934-41, trustee and supreme councillor 1934-73, supreme editor 1942, moderator 1951-88), Alpha Omega Alpha (hon.), Pi Kappa Epsilon, Pi Delta. Republican. Clubs: Mason (K.T., 32 deg.), Shriner, University, Chaos. Home: Chicago Ill. Died Mar. 23, 1988; buried Meml. Pk. Mausoleum, Skokie, Ill.

ARIETI, SILVANO, psychiatrist; b. Pisa, Italy, June 28, 1914; came to U.S., 1939, naturalized, 1942; s. Elio and Ines (Bemporad) A.; m. Marianne Thompson, Oct. 24, 1965; children by previous marriage: David, James. BA, Lyceé Galileo, Pisa, 1932; MD, Med. Sch. Pisa, 1938; diploma in psychoanalysis, William Alanson White Inst., 1952. Intern St. Chiara Hosp., Pisa, 1938-39; resident Pilgrim State Hosp., West Brentwood, N.Y., 1941-44; practice medicine specializing in psychiatry, psychoanalysi; fellow neuropathology N.Y. State Psychiat. Inst., N.Y.C., 1939-41, Yale U., New Haven, CT, 1940; clin. assoc. prof. psychiatry SUNY, 1954-61; clin. prof. N.Y. Med. Coll., 1961-81. Author: Interpretation of Schizophrenia, 1955, rev. edit., 1974 (Nat. Book award 1975), The Intrapsychic Self, 1967, The Will To Be Human, 1972, Creativity: The Magic Synthesis, 1976, Sever and Mild Depression, 1978, The Parnas, 1979, Understanding and Helping the Schizophrenic, 1979; editor: The American Handbook of Psychiatry, 1959, 2d edit., 1974. Recipient Gold Medal award Milan (Italy) Group for Advancement of Psychotherapy, 1964, Frieda Fromm-Reichmann award for contbn. to knowledge of schizophrenia Am. Acad. Psychoanalysis, 1968, Sigmund Freud award Am. Assn Psychoanalytic Physicians, 1978. Mem. William Alanson White Psychoanalytic Soc. (pres. 1964), Soc. Med. Psychoanalysts (pres. 1970), Am. Acad Psychoanalysis (editor jour. 1973-81, pres. 1978), Am Psychiat. Assn., Am. Assn. Neuropathologists, Am Psychopathol. Assn., Assn. Advancement Psychotherapy, (Emil A. Gutheil meml. award 1978), AMA. Home: New York N.Y. Died Aug. 7, 1981.

ARLEN, HAROLD, composer; b. Buffalo, Feb. 15, 1905; s. Samuel and Celia (Orlin) Arluck; m. Anya Taranda, 1937. Student pub. schs., Buffalo. Profl. pianist at age 15 Buffalo; arranger, pianist, singer Arnold Johnson, band leader, N.Y.C., 1927. First composition (with Ted Koehler) Get Happy, 1930, and since wrote songs for Cotton Club revues, etc.; collaborated with various lyricists including E.Y. Harburg, Johnny Mercer, Ira Gershwin; composer numerous songs including Over The Rainbow (Acad. award 1939), It's Only a Paper Moon, Let's Fall in Love (complete score for motion picture), I Love A Parade, I've Got the World on a String, Stormy Weather, Last Night When We Were Young, Wizard of Oz complete score for motion picture, A Day at the Circus (motion picture), Let's Take the Long Way Home (for Bing Crosby), So Long Big Time (for Tony Bennett), The Silent Spring (for Lena Horne); Acad. award nominee for Blues in the Night, 1941, That Old Black Magic, 1942, My Shining Hour, 1943, Ac-cen-tchu-ate the Positive, 1944, The Man that Got Away, 1954; broadway shows including Americana, Hooray for What, St. Louis Woman Saratoga, Free and Easy (a blue opera), also several editions Earl Carroll's Vanities; motion pictures include Star Spangled Rhythm, Love Affair, The Sky's the Limit, A Star is Born, The Country Girl, Gay Purr-ee contbr. article to book on George Gershwin. Home New York N.Y. Died Apr. 23, 1986.

ARMBRUSTER, CHRISTIAN HERMAN, lawyer; b. Yonkers, N.Y., Mar. 14, 1921; s. Christian and Helen (Sergel) A. B.A., Columbia U., 1942, LL.B., 1947. Bar: N.Y. 1948. Assoc. Spence, Hotchkiss, Parker & Duryea, N.Y.C., 1947-48; pvt. practice Bronxville, N.Y., 1948-86. Supr., Westchester County, N.Y., 1949-59; mem. N.Y. State Assembly, 1959-66, N.Y. State Senate, 1967-68; trustee Yonkers Gen. Hosp.; adv. com. Pace Coll., Westchester. Served to maj. USAAF, 1943-46. Mem. Am. Legion. Mem. Reformed Ch. Lodge: Masons. Home: Bronxville N.Y. Died Feb. 24, 1986.

ARMENTANO, ANTHONY JOHN, state supreme court justice; b. Hartford, Conn., June 12, 1916; s. Joseph and Rosina (DiDonato) A.; m. Mary Fraticelli, Feb. 6, 1943; children: Frank J., James A. B.S., Boston U., 1938, J.D., 1941. Bar: Conn. bar 1941. Mem. Conn. Senate, 1957-63, pres. pro tempore, 1959-61; lt. gov. State of Conn., 1961-63; judge of Ct.of Common Pleas, 1963-65; judge Superior Ct., 1965-81; asso. justice Conn. Supreme Ct., Hartford, from 1981. Served to capt. U.S. Army, 1942-46. Mem. Am. Bar Assn., Conn. Bar Assn., Hartford County Bar Assn. Democrat. Roman Catholic. Home: Hartford Conn. Deceased.

ARMISTEAD, GEORGE H(ARRISON), JR., lawyer; b. Franklin, Tenn., 1891; s. George Harrison and Jessie (Parkes) A.; m. Jane Eve Buckner, Apr. 30, 1919; 1 child, Wilson Buckner. AB, Vanderbilt U., 1914, LLB, 1916. Pvt. practice Nashville; v.p. Nashville & Decatur R.R. Lt. U.S. Army, World War I. Mem. AMA, Tenn. Bar Assn. (past pres.), Nashville Bar Assn. (past pres.), Belle Meade Country Club, Cumberland Club (Nashville), Phi Delta Phi, Sigma Chi. Home: Nashville Tenn. †

ARMOUR, NORMAN, ambassador; b. Brighton, Eng., Oct. 14, 1887; s. George Allison and Harriette (Foote) A.; m. Princess Myra Koudacheff, Feb. 2, 1919; 1 son, Norman. Prep. edn., St. Paul's Sch., Concord, N.H.; AB, Princeton U., 1909, AM, 1915, LLD (hon.), 1947; LLB, Harvard U., 1913. Attaché U.S. Embassy, Paris, 1915; 3d sec. U.S. Embassy, Petrograd, Russia, 1916, 2d sec., 1917-18; 2d sec. U.S. Embassy, Brussels, Belgium, 1919-20; lst sec. of legation The Hague, Netherlands, 1920-21, Montevideo, Uruguay, 1921-22; asst. to under sec. state Washington, 1922-24; 1st sec. U.S. Embassy, Rome, 1924-25; counselor of embassy Tokyo, Japan, 1925-28, Paris, 1928-32; U.S. minister Canada, June 1935; ambassador Chile, 1938, Argetina, 1939, Spain, 1944-45; asst. sec. of state Washington, 1947-48; ambassador Venezuela, 1950-51, Guatemala, 1954-55. Mem. Princeton Club, Brook Club, Century Club (N.Y.C); Metropolitan Club, Alibi Club, Chevy Chase Club (Washington). Episcopalian. Home: New York N.Y. †

ARMSTRONG, CLYDE WILSON, lawyer; b. New Kensington, Pa., Apr. 22, 1926; s. Clyde Allman and Ethlyn Wilson (Logan) A.; m. Jean Marvin Forncrook, June 12, 1948; children: Cathy Mitchell, Melissa Anne, Christopher Lee. AB, Princeton U., 1948; LLB, U. Pa., 1951. Bar: Pa. 1951, U.S. Dist. Ct. 1951. Assoc. Thorp, Reed & Armstrong, Pitts., 1951-57, ptnr., 1957-85; dir. Shannopin Mining Co., Delray Connecting R.R. Co., Mitchell Plastics, Michael D. Baker C. V.p. Community Chest of Allegheny County, 1971-73, United Way of Allegheny County, 1974-75; bd. dirs. Community Services of Pa., 1973-79, v.p. 1977-78; deacon, trustee Shadyside Presbyn. Ch.; trustee Shadyside Acad., Winchester-Thurston Sch. Served with USNR, 1944-46. Mem. ABA, Am. Law inst., Am. Coll. Trial Lawyers, Pa. Bar Assn., Allegheny County Bar Assn., Am. Bar Found., Duquesne Club, Longue Vue County Club. Home: Pittsburgh Pa. Died Apr. 15, 1985; cremated.

ARMSTRONG, HARRY LACEY, academic administrator; b. Logan, Ohio, July 19, 1888; m. Mildred Tomlinson, Sept. 3, 1914 (dec. May 1959). BS, Ohio Wesleyan U., 1909; AM, Cumberland U., 1925, LLD, 1959; grad., Peabody Coll. Tchrs., 1925. Instr. math. Castle Heights Mil. Acad., Lebanon, Tenn., 1909-14, headmaster, 1914-19, supt., 1919-21, pres., from 1929; prin. high sch., Lebanon, 1923-24; prof. math., dean Cumberland U., 1925-29. Mem. Assn. Mil. Colls. and Schs. U.S. (pres. 1942), Mid-South Assn. Pvt. Schs. (pres. 1943), Masons, Rotary (dist. gov. 1953-54), Sigma Alpha Epsilon. Democrat. Methodist. Home: Lebanon Tenn. †

ARMSTRONG, HERBERT W., evangelist; b. Des Moines, July 31, 1892; married; children: Richard David (dec.), Garner Ted, Beverly Gott, Dorothy Mattson. Ordained to ministry, 1931. Founder Worldwide Ch. of God, 1933, Ambassador Found.; broadcaster Radio Ch. of God (now World Tomorrow), 1934-86. Author: The Autobiography of Herbert W. Armstrong, 1967, The United States and British Commonwealth in Prophecy, 1967, Incredible Human Potential, 1978, The Missing Dimension in Sex, 1964, 71, 81, The Wonderful World Tomorrow, 1979; editor: The Plain Truth, 1934-86, The Good News, Youth, 83. Chmn. bd. Ambassador Coll. Home: Pasadena Calif. Died Jan. 16, 1986.

ARMSTRONG, ROBERT PLANT, editor, educator; b. Wheeling, W.Va., May 19, 1919; s. Clarence Warren and Dorothy Johanna (Green) A. B.A., U. Ariz., 1944; M.A., U. Iowa, 1946; Ph.D., Northwestern U., 1957. Traveler Houghton Mifflin & Co., 1945-46; instr. English Mont. State U., Missoula, 1946-50; field editor Harper and Bros., 1956-58; editor Alfred A. Knopf, N.Y.C., 1958-59; dir. publs. U. Ariz. Press, 1959-60; dir. Northwestern U. Press, 1960-73, prof. Coll. Arts and Scis., 1967-73; prof. anthropology U. Tex. at Dallas, 1974-84; vis. prof. art history State U. N.Y., Buffalo, summer 1970; vis. curator African art Buffalo Mus. Sci., summer 1970; vis. prof. U. Ibadan, Nigeria, 1972-73; also vis. dir. Univ. Press. Columnist: Book Forum, 1975-84; author: The Affecting Presence: An Essay in Humanistic Anthropology, 1971, Forms and Processes in Africa, 1970, Wellspring: On the Myth and the Source of Culture, 1975, The Powers of Presence: Myth, Consciousness, and Affecting Presence, 1981; chmn. editorial bd.: Book Forum; mem. editorial bd.: Arts Inquiry; cons. editor: Studies in Visual Communications; contbr. numerous articles to profl. jours. Served with USNR, 1940-43. Fellow African Studies Assn., Am. Anthrop. Assn. Home: Richardson Tex. Died Aug. 9, 1984.

ARMSTRONG, R(OBERT) WRIGHT, railway executive; b. Brownwood, Tex., Dec. 18, 1892; s. Walter David and Mary Elizabeth (Wright) A.; m. Nannie Pauline Lusher, Apr. 23, 1918; children: Mary Elizabeth, Robert Wright, Pauline. Student, Kemper Mil. Sch., Boonville, Mo., 1904-05, Mo. Mil. Acad., Mexico, 1906-08. Gen. agt. Trinity & Brazos Valley Ry., Ft. Worth, 1924-28, Burlington-Rock Island R.R., Houston, 1928-34, C.B.&Q R.R., New Orleans, 1934-36; gen. freight agt. C.B.&Q R.R., Denver, 1936-38, St. Louis, 1938-43; exec. asst. Ft. Worth & Denver Ry. Co., Houston, 1945-47; v.p. Ft. Worth & Denver Ry. Co., Ft. Worth, from 1948; pres. Union Terminal Co., Dallas, from 1953. Bd. dirs. Tex. Tech. Coll., Lubbock; trustee Tex. A&M Rsch. Found. Mem. West Tex. C. of C. (pres. 1952-53), 36th Div. Assn. Club. Home: Fort Worth Tex. †

ARMSTRONG, ROY FRASER, administrative consultant; b. St. Andrews, N.B., Can.; s. Robert E. and Margaret (Paterson) A.; m. Muriel S. Smith, Sept. 5, 1923; children: Donald Fraser, Helen Margaret Armstrong Baker. BS, U. N.B., 1910; spl. study, McGill U., 1913; hon. degree, Queen's U., 1957. Engaged in constrn. and design 1910-17; town mgr. Woodstock, N.B., 1919-23; mcpl., hosp. and indsl. surveys, 1923-25; gen. supt. Kingston Gen. Hosp., 1925-58; counsellor in adminstrv. and planning svcs., from 1958. Pres. Can. Hosp. Coun., Kingston Community Chest; bd. dirs. Ont. Hosp. Assn., Ont. Plan for Hosp. Care; mem. cen. fin. com. Kingston Dist. for 9 War Loans. With Can. Expeditionary Forces, 1917-18. Decorated Mil. Cross; recipient George Findlay Stephens award Can. Hosp. Assn., 1957. Fellow Am. Coll. Hosp. Adminstrs. (regent 1947, 49, 56, 57). Home: Kingston, Ont. Canada. †

ARNASON, HJORVARDUR HARVARD, art historian; b. Winnipeg, Man., Can., Apr. 24, 1909; came to U.S., 1927, naturalized, 1940; s. Sveinbjorn and Maria (Bjarnadottir) A.; m. Elizabeth Hickcox Yard, July 25, 1936; children: Eleanor Atwood, Jon Yard. Student, U. Man., 1925-27; B.S., Northwestern U., 1931, A.M., 1937; M.F.A., Princeton U., 1939. Instr. Northwestern U., 1936-38; research asst. and lectr. Frick Collection, N.Y.C., 1938-42; lectr. Hunter Coll, 1939-42; field rep. OWI, Iceland, 1942-44; asst. dep. dir. for Europe OWI, hdqrs. Washington, 1944-45; chief program planning and evaluation unit Office of Internat. Info. and Cultural Affairs, Dept. State, Washington, 1945-46; vis. asso. prof. art U. Chgo., 1947; prof., chmn. dept. art U. Minn., 1947-61; dir. Walker Art Center, Mpls., 1951-61; v.p. for art adminstrn. Solomon R. Guggenheim Found., N.Y.C., 1961-69; former cons. Guggenheim Mus.; Fulbright fellow, France, 1955-56; Carnegie vis. prof. U. Hawaii, 1959; sr. research fellow NEH, 1971-72; U.S. rep. Prep. Commn. on UNESCO, London and Paris, 1946. Author: Modern Sculpture, 1962, Conrad Marca-Relli, 1962, Sculpture by Houdon, 1964, Alexander Calder, 1966, History of Modern Art, 1968, 2d, 1977, Jacques Lipchitz: Fifty Years of Sketches in Bronze, 1969, (with Ugo Mulas) Alexander Calder, 1969, (with Jacques Lipchitz) Jacques Lipchitz: My Life in Sculpture, 1972, The Sculptures of Houdon, 1975, Jean-Antoine Houdon, French edit., 1976, (with Barbaralla Diamonstein) Robert Motherwell: New & Revised, 1982, Robert Motherwell, 1977; also monographs, catalogues, articles on medieval, 18th century and modern art. Trustee Adolph Gottlieb Found.; mem. exec. bd., chmn. adv. com. Internat. Found. for Art Research. Decorated chevalier de l'Ordre des Arts et des Lettres (France); knight Order St. Olav (Norway), Order of Falcon (Iceland). Mem. Coll. Art Assn., Am. Assn. Mus., AAUP, Am. Soc. 18th Century Studies, Société Française d'Étude du 18ème Siècle. Clubs: Century (N.Y.C.), Princeton (N.Y.C.). Home: New York N.Y. Died May 28, 1986.

ARNAZ, DESI, actor, producer; b. Santiago, Cuba, Mar. 2, 1917; s. Desidero Alberto Arnaz y de Acha and Delores A.; m. Lucille Ball, Nov. 30, 1940 (div. May 1960); children: Lucie, Desi, Jr.; m. Edith Mack Hirsch. Student pub. schs., Miami, Fla. Appeared Roney Plaza Hotel, Miami, 1936; introduced La Conga dance to U.S. Miami, 1938; starred La Conga Club N.Y.C., 1938; with R.K.O. Hollywood, Calif., 1940; MGM Studios, 1942; music dir. Bob Hope Radio Show, 1946; under contract to Columbia Records 1953; star (with Lucille Ball) TV show I Love Lucy, CBS-TV, 1950-57; star (with Lucille Ball) Long, Long, Trailer, 1953, Forever Darling, 1955; former co-star Lucille Ball-Desi Arnaz Show (for Westinghouse); host Westinghouse Desilu Playhouse; pres. Desilu Productions until 1962; independent producer; pres. Desi Arnaz Prodns., Inc; guest appearances TV, 1962-86. With AUS, 1944-46. Home: Culver City Calif. Died Dec. 2, 1986.

ARNEST, BERNARD PATRICK, artist; b. Denver, Feb. 19, 1917; s. Bernard Patrick and Marie Josephine (Kaelin) A.; m. Barbara Irene Maurin, June 5, 1948; children: Paul, Lisa, Mark. Student, Colorado Springs Fine Arts Center, 1936-39. Instr. Mpls. Sch. Art, 1947-49; asst. prof., assoc. prof. art U. Minn., Mpls., 1949-57; prof. art Colo. Coll., Colorado Springs, 1957-82, chmn. dept., 1957-71, 79-82; initiator advanced placement in art Coll. Entrance Exam Bd., 1966-72, co-chmn. examining com., 1966-72; cons. Coll. Art Programs, Ford Found., 1965. One-man shows, San Francisco Mus. Art, Mpls. Inst. Art, Walker Art Center, U. Minn. Galleries, Denver Art Mus., Colorado Springs Fine Arts Center, Kraushaar Galleries, N.Y.C., group shows, Whitney Annual, Pitts. Internat., Corcoran Biennial, Am. Acad., Mpls. Art Inst., Walker Art Center, Denver Art Mus., Colorado Springs Fine Arts Center. Served to 1st lt. U.S. Army, 1941-45, ETO. Guggenheim fellow, 1940; U.S. State Dept. grantee, 1960. Mem. Coll. Art Assn., AAUP, Artists Equity (head Mpls. chpt. 1948-50). Died June 5, 1987.

ARNOLD, ELTING, lawyer; b. Staatsburg, N.Y., Aug. 1, 1912; s. Harry and Adelaide (Elting) A.; m. Hannah Burr Polk, Aug. 24, 1936; children: Sarah Burr, Patricia. AB, Williams Coll., 1934; LLB, Columbia U., 1937. Bar: N.Y. 1938, D.C. 1949. Assoc. Root, Clark, Buckner and Ballantine, N.Y.C., 1937-39; atty. U.S. Treasury Dept., Washington, 1939-47, chief counsel Fgn. Funds Control, 1947, asst. to asst. gen. counsel, 1947-48, asst. gen. counsel in charge internat. fin. and monetary matters, 1948-60, acting. dir. Fgn. Assets Control, 1950-60; gen. counsel Inter-Am. Devel. Bank, 1960-71; spl. asst. to gen. counsel U.S. Treas. Dept., 1971-73, sr. counselor to gen. counsel, 1973-75; counselor Inter-Am. Devel. Bank, 1975-77; ptnr. Wolf, Arnold & Cardoso, Washington, 1978-88. Mem. Am. Soc. Internat. Law, D.C. Bar Assn., Am. Ornithologists Union, Defenders of Wildlife (treas.), Phi Beta Kappa. Home: Chevy Chase Md. Died Dec. 28, 1988.

ARNOLD, GAYLE WILLIAM, railroad official; b. Owen County, Ky., July 12, 1889; s. Jasper Oliver and Mary Ellen (True) A.; m. Lutie Pearl Gardner, Oct. 6, 1909; 1 son, Gayle G. Student, secondary and high schs., Ky. With transp. and sales depts. Procter & Gamble Co., 9 yrs.; with transp. svc. Southern Ry., Chesapeake & Ohio R.R., 5 yrs.; with Baltimore & Ohio, Alton and Baltimore & Ohio Chgo. Terminal R.Rs., from 1919; cons. to Chief of Ordnance, U.S. Army, 1940-44; dir. indsl. svcs. Nat. Security Rsch. Bd., 1948. Author articles in various tech. jours.; lectr. on indsl. location, indsl. and govtl. dispersion, plant location and related subjects. Mem. Am. Ry. Devel. Assn. (past pres.), Indsl. Corp. Balt. (v.p.), Am. Indsl. Devel. Counc. (past pres.), Urban Land Inst. (trustee, mem. exec. group indsl. coun.), Am. Ordnance Assn., Soc. Am. Mil. Engrs., Md. Hist. Soc., Md. Acad. Sci., Am. Soc. Traffic and Transp. (founder mem.), Balt. Assn. Commerce, C. of C. U.S., Soc. Indsl. Realtors, Masons (33 degree A.A.S.R., K.T. (past comdr.), F.&A.M. (past master), Nat. Sojourner, Shriners, Royal Order of Scotland), Merchants Club (Balt.); Wall St. Club (N.Y.C.); Midday Club (Phila.). Home: Baltimore Md. †

ARNOLD, H. PARK, lumber and manufacturing executive; b. Lebo, Coffee County, Kans., May 25, 1892; s. John Thomas and Belle (Parke) A.; m. Mayme Frances Swan, Aug. 5, 1912; children: Richard Keith, Betty Sanders. Grad. high sch. Pres. Precision Processing Co. Dep. procurement officer Civil Def., State of Calif.; pres. bd. edn. Glendale Unified Sch. Dist.; trustee, vice chmn. exec. com. U. Redlands; signing founder Glendale Community Found.; pres. Glendale YMCA; mem. adv. bd. Glendale and State of Calif. Salvation Army. Mem. Kiwanis (internat. pres., trustee, bd. dirs., pres. Glendale chpt.). Home: Glendale Calif. †

ARNOLD, ROBERT OLIVER, textile manufacturer; b. Hampton, Ga., Oct. 24, 1888; s. Robert Johnson and Nellie (Curry) A.; m. Florence Turner, Mar. 20, 1930. BS, U. Ga., 1908; LLD (hon.), Mercer U., 1961. With Arnold Grocery Co., Athens, Ga., 1908-14, Athens Mattress & Spring Bed Co., 1908-17; sec. Hampton (Ga.) Cotton Mills, 1919, pres., 1920-24; v.p., gen. mgr. Mallison Braided Cord Co., Athens, 1924-32; treas., gen. mgr. Covington (Ga.) Mills, 1932-45, pres., from 1945, also bd. dirs.; dir. Ga. Railroad & Banking Co., 1935-83, Cotton-Textile Inst., N.Y.C., 1944-47, Mobile (Ala.) Gas Service Corp., 1945-83, chmn. bd. 1970-83; dir. Atlanta Gas-Light Co., 1948-83, Henry Grady Hotel Corp., Phoenix Ins. Corp., Phoenix Investment Co., Atlanta; former trustee First Atlantic Realty Rund. Mayor, Athens, 1916-17; trustee Ga.

Baptist Children's Home; chmn. bd. regents U. Ga., 1949-63. Capt. U.S. Army, 1917-19. Mem. Cotton Mfrs. Assn. Ga. (pres. 1939-40), Am. Legion (past commdr.), Newcomen Soc. Eng. Baptist. Home: Covington Ga. Died Jan. 25, 1983; buried Covington, Ga.

ARONSON, DAVID, rabbi; b. Vitebsk, Russia, Aug. 1, 1894; came to U.S., 1906, naturalized, 1918; s. Jekuthiel Zalman and Yetta (Kudritzin) A.; m. Bertha Friedman, May 1, 1927; children—Raphael, Hillel. A.B., N.Y. U., 1916; A.M., Columbia, 1917; Rabbi, Jewish Theol. Sem. of Am., 1919, D.H.L. (honoris causa), 1946; D.D., U. Judaism, 1969. Served with Jewish Welfare Bd.; camp rabbi Camp Upton, L.I., 1917-19; rabbi Salt Lake City, 1920-22, Duluth, Minn., 1922-24; rabbi Beth El Synagogue, Mpls., 1924-59; since emeritus; prof. rabbinics grad. sch. U. Judaism, Los Angeles, 1959-88; vis. lectr. Jewish Theol. Sem.; Mem. Gov.'s Human Relations Commn., 1943-59, Mayor's Council on Human Relations, Citizen's Charter Commn.; rep. Am. Jewish Conf., 1943; pres. Rabbinical Assembly, 1948-50; bd. dirs., bd. overseers Jewish Theol. Sem. and others. Author: The Jewish Way of Life; Asso. editor of the: Am. Jewish World, 1930-59; Contbr. articles relating to Jewish affairs to profl. jours. Recipient Outstanding Service award Mpls. Jewish Fedn., 1959, Distinguished Service award City of Mpls., 1959; Prime Minister's award State of Israel, 1976; Mordecai M. Kaplan medal of honor U. Judaism, 1981. Home: L.A. Calif. Died Oct. 20, 1988; buried Beth El Meml. Pk., New Hope, Minn.

ARONSON, J(OHN) HUGO, former governor; b. Gallstad, Sweden, Sept. 1, 1891; came to U.S., 1911; s. Aron Johannson and Fredericka (Ryding) A.; m. Matilda Langagne, June 3, 1919 (dec. Mar. 1, 1936); m. 2d Rose Myrtle McClure, Sept. 25, 1944; 1 dau., Rika. Student, pub. schs., Sweden. Dir. Toole County Bank, Shelby, Mont., from 1927, pres., from 1940; mem. Ho. of Reps. Mont. State Legislature, 1939-45, mem. Senate, 1945-53; gov. Mont., from 1953. With C.E., U.S. Army, 1917-19, overseas France. Mem. Am. Legion, VFW, Mont. Bankers Assn., Elks, Moose, Masons (Shriner), Lions Club. Home: Helena Mont. †

ARPS, LESLIE HANSEN, lawyer; b. Leipzig, Germany, July 14, 1907; s. George F. and Alice (Black) A.; m. Ruth Collicott, Oct. 26, 1959. A.B., Stanford, 1928; LL.B., Harvard, 1931. Bar: N.Y. bar 1932. Asso. Root, Clark, Buckner & Ballantine, N.Y.C., 1931-42, 46-48; mem. firm Skadden, Arps, Slate, Meagher & Flom, N.Y.C., 1948-87; spl. asst. atty. gen. State of N.Y.; asst. chief counsel N.Y. State Crime Commn., 1951-52; asso. gen. counsel to N.Y. State Moreland Commn. to Investigate State Agys. in relation to Pari-Mutuel Harness Racing, 1953-54; cons. N.Y. State Moreland Commn. on Alcoholic Beverage Control law, 1963-64. Chmn. bd. trustees Gateway Sch. N.Y., 1965-67; trustee The Gunnery, Inc., 1978-84; bd. visitors Stanford U. Law Sch., Fordham U. Sch. Law. Served to lt. col. USAAF, 1942-45. Mem. ABA, N.Y. State Bar Assn. (chmn. bicentennial film com. 1986-87), N.Y.C. Bar Assn. (chmn. exec. com. 1973-74, v.p. 1974-75), N.Y. County Lawyers Assn., Am. Bar Found., Am. Judicature Soc., Fed. Bar Council, Merc. Library Assn. (dir.), Am. Arbitration Assn. (dir.), Phi Beta Kappa. Clubs: Union League (N.Y.C.), Sky (N.Y.C.), Harvard (N.Y.C.). Home: New York N.Y. Died July 15, 1987.

ARTZ, FREDERICK BINKERD, historian; b. Dayton, Ohio, Oct. 19, 1894; s. J. Elam and May (Binkerd) Artz. AB summa cum laude, Oberlin Coll., 1916, DLitt, 1966; student, U. Toulouse, 1919, U. Paris, 1922-23; PhD, Harvard U., 1924; DLitt, Carthage Coll., 1970. Instr. history Antioch Coll., 1916-17, Harvard U., 1923-24; prof. history Oberlin Coll., from 1924; vis. prof. Harvard U., 1930-31; lectr. Havard U. summer sch., 1931, 34. Author: France Under the Bourbon Restoration, 1931, Reaction and Revolution, 1814-32, W.L. Langer series of Rise of Modern Europe The Intellectual History of Europe from St. Augustine to Marx-a Guide, 1951, The Mind of the Middle Ages, 200-1500 A.D., an Historical Survey, 1954, 3d rev. edit., 1980, From the Renaissance to Romanticism A.D. 1300-1830, 1962; also Japanese transl. Memoirs, 1964, The Enlightenment in France, 1968; contbr. to: Ency. of Soc. Scis.; mem. bd. editors: Jour. Modern History, 1932-35. With Am. Expeditionary Force, 1917-19, France. Mem. Am. Hist. Assn., AAUP, Royal Hist. Soc., Sociëtē d'Histoire Moderne, Phi Beta Kappa. Home: Oberlin Ohio. Deceased.

ASCH, MOSES, record company executive. Owner, founder, head Folkways Records, N.Y.C., 1948-86. Home: New York N.Y. Died Oct. 19., 1986.

ASHBY, MABEL KATHLEEN, writer; b. Tysoe, Warwickshire, Eng., May 16, 1892; d. Joseph and Hannah Ashby. BA, U. Birmingham, 1914; MEd, U. Manchester, 1930. Engaged in rural edn. Eng., 1915-19, tchr. tng. colls., 1925-28; prin. Hillcroft Coll., Surbiton, Eng., 1933-46; Pres. Womens Inst., Bledington, Oxford, Eng., from 1960. Author: The Country School, 1929, Joseph Ashby of Tysoe, 1961 (James Tait Black prize for biography 1962, Leverhulme rsch. award 1962). Chmn. coun. Bledington Parish, 1958-61. Home: Oxford England. †

ASHE, DAVID I(RVING), lawyer; b. Bklyn., Nov. 13, 1910; s. Morris and Bessie (Newman) A.; m. 1934 (div. 1959); children: Judith Ashe Handelman, Deborah Lucy Ashe Warheit; m. Amelia H. Wexler, Dec. 26, 1962 (dec. 1985); stepchildren: Richard Wexler, Susan Wexler Lahn. B.S.S. magna cum laude, CCNY, 1929; J.D., Columbia U., 1932. Bar: N.Y. 1933. Practiced in N.Y.C; specializing in law of labor relations and representing internat. and local labor unions; mem. firm Ashe & Rifkin, 1940-86; instr. labor law and labor problems Trade Union Inst. of Rand Sch. Social Sci., 1936-45, dir., 1940-44; mem. bd. dirs. New Leader (pub.), 1944-50; labor law cons. ACLU. Author: Yellow Dog Contracts, Legal and Social Aspects, 1931, The Taft-Hartley Law: How It Affects Unions and Workers, 1947, The Labor-Management Reporting and Disclosure Act of 1959, An Analysis, 1959; adv. editor: Parents mag., 1948-50; contbr. to labor ednl. publs. Mem. state adv. com. for study of vocat. edn. in N.Y. City Schs., 1949-52, mem. com. (N.Y. City Bd. Edn.) to study impact of increased birth rate on N.Y. City Schs., 1948-49; mem. N.Y. Gov.'s Task Force Aid to Edn., 1974-75; adv. bd. Center Advanced Study in Edn., 1975-81; mem. adv. bd. Nat. Center for Study of Collective Bargaining in Higher Edn., 1972-80; mem. adminstrv., nat. exec. coms. Jewish Labor Com., 1965-86, chmn. N.Y. div., 1966-86; mem. exec. com. Nat. Jewish Community Relations Adv. Council, 1965-86; mem. exec. com. Jewish Community Relations Council of N.Y., 1977-86, v.p., 1980-86; mem. adv. com. Robert F. Wagner Labor Archives; mem. edn. com. United Negro Coll. Fund, 1960-62; mem. com. on legis. Citizens Union, N.Y.C., 1960-64; pres. Musicians Service Corp.; mem. Bd. Higher Edn. N.Y.C., 1966-73; bd. dirs. Research Found. CUNY, v.p., 1975-77, pres., 1977-81; bd. dirs. Italian-Am. Inst. to Promote Higher Edn., 1977-80; bd. dirs., chmn. nat. com. Fund for Open Society, 1977-86; exec. com. City U. Faculty Welfare Trustees, 1967-86. Mem. Am. Arbitration Assn. (nat. panel arbitrators), Workers Def. League (nat. com. 1956-58), Nat. Planning Assn. (nat. council), Workmen's Circle (gen. counsel), Alumni Assn. Columbia Sch. Law, Bar Assn. N.Y.C. (labor and social security legis. com. 1951-54, 67-70, com. on post admission legal edn. 1971-74), Alumni Assn. City Coll., United Parents Assns. N.Y.C. (counsel, past pres., chmn. exec. council and legis. com. and v.p.), Pub. Edn. Assn. (legis. and sch. adminstrn. com. 1950-62), N.Y. County Lawyers Assn. (com. labor relations 1976-82), Phi Beta Kappa. Home: White Plains N.Y. Died Oct. 25, 1986; buried New Montefiore Cemetery, Pinelawn (Babylon) N.Y.

ASHTON, FREDERICK (WILLIAM MALLANDAINE), choreographer; b. Guayaquil, Ecuador, Sept. 17, 1904; s. George and Georgiana (Fulcher) A. Ed. The Dominican Fathers, Lima, Peru, Dover Coll.; studied dance with Léonide Massine, Marie Rambert; DLitt (hon.), U. Durham, 1972, U. East Anglia, 1967; DMus (hon.), U. London, 1970, U. Hull, 1971, Oxford U., 1976. Choreographer, dancer Ballet Rambert, 1926-33; with Ida Rubinstein Co., Paris, 1929-30; founder, choreographer Royal Ballet, London, 1933-70, prin. choreographer, 1933-70, dir., 1963-70. Ballets choreographed include: Les Patineurs, Apparitions, Horoscope, Symphonic Variations, Facade, Wedding Bouquet, Scenes de Ballet, Cinderelle, Illuminations, Sylvia, Romeo and Juliet, Ondine, La Fille Mal Gardee, Les Deux Pigeons, Marguerite and Armand, The Dream, Sinfonietta, Jazz Calendar, Enigma Variations, Walk to the Paradise Garden, Birthday Offering, A Month in the Country, Rhapsody; choreographer, appeared as Mrs. Tiggywinkle in film: The Tales of Beatrix Potter, 1971. Served as flight lt. RAF. Decorated Order Brit. Empire, Legion of Honor (France), Order of Dannebrog (Denmark); recipient Queen Elizabeth II Coronation award Royal Acad. Dancing, 1959, Freedom of City of London, 1981. Subject of publs.: Frederick Ashton: a Choreographer and His Ballets, by Z. Dominic and J.S. Gilbert, 1971, Frederick Ashton and His Ballets, by D. Vaughan, 1977. Home: Suffolk, Eng. Died Aug. 18, 1988.

ASHTON, SAMUEL COLLIER, research institute executive; b. Hohenwald, Tenn., Sept. 26, 1922; s. Arch Will and Lulu Earle (Collier) A.; m. Rita Jane Anderson, Oct. 18, 1947; 1 son, Craig Collier. B.S.E.E., U.S. Naval Acad., 1945. Head cryogenic lab. The Tex. Co., Long Beach, Calif., 1947-48; asst. dir. phys. sic. div. Stanford Research Inst., Menlo Park, Calif., 1948-59; corp. v.p. Research Triangle Inst., Research Triangle Park, N.C., 1959—. Co-patentee continuous ion exchange sugar beet refining. Served to engisn USN, 1945-47, PTO. Mem. Am. Def. Preparedness Assn. (chmn. Carolinas chpt. 1965). Republican. Episcopalian. Club: Hope Valley Country (Durham, N.C.). Died Aug. 2, 1987; buried St. Stephen's Episcopal Ch., Durham, N.C.

ASPLUNDH, LESTER, tree care company executive; b. Bryn Athyn, Pa., 1901. Grad., Swarthmore Coll., 1923. Chmn. bd. Asplundh Tree Expert Co., Inc., Willow Grove, Pa., also dir.; chmn. Utilities Line Constrn. Co. Home: Willow Grove Pa. Died May 3, 1984.

ASTAIRE, FRED, actor, dancer, songwriter; b. Omaha, May 10, 1899; s. Frederic and Ann (Geilus) Austerlitz; m. Phyllis Baker, July 12, 1933 (dec. 1954); children: Fred, Ava, Peter Potter (step-son); m. Robyn Smith, June 22, 1980. Ed. pub. schs. Co-starred with sister as team of Fred and Adele (Mrs. Kingman Douglass) Astaire, 1916-32; appeared in Funny Face, Over the Top, Passing Show of 1918, Apple Blossoms, Lady Be Good, The Bandwagon; following sister's marriage to Lord Charles Cavendish starred alone in musical comedies on stage and screen; films include: Gay Divorcee, Roberta, Follow the Fleet, Swingtime, Top Hat, Shall We Dance?, Damsel in Distress, Carefree, The Story of Vernon and Irene Castle, Broadway Melody of 1940, Second Chorus, You'll Never Get Rich, Holiday Inn, You Were Never Lovelier, The Sky's the Limit, The Ziegfield Follies, Yolanda and the Thief, Blue Skies, Easter Parade, Barkleys of Broadway, Three Little Words, Let's Dance, Royal Wedding, The Belle of New York, The Bandwagon, Daddy Longlegs, Silk Stockings, Funny Face, On the Beach, The Pleasure of His Company, Notorious Lady, Finnian's Rainbow, 1967, Midas Run, 1968, That's Entertainment, 1974, The Towering Inferno, 1974 (Acad. award nominee), That's Entertainment, Part Two, 1976, Ghost Story, 1981; TV show Fred Astaire Show, 1968; appeared on TV in It Takes A Thief; starred in TV spls.; host, occasional star: Alcoa Premier; appeared in TV in Santa Claus Is Coming to Town, 1970, The Easter Bunny Is Coming to Town, 1977, A Family Upside Down, 1978 (Emmy award); author: Steps In Time, 1959; composer (songs) Life is Beautiful, You Worry Me, City of the Angels, Closing Theme for Carson Show. Recipient 9 Emmy awards; Acad. award for raising standards all musicals, 1949; Lifetime Achievement award Am. Film Inst., 1981; Kennedy Center Honor, 1978. Episcopalian. Clubs: Racquet and Tennis, Lambs, The Brook (N.Y.C.). Home: Los Angeles Calif. Died June 22, 1987.

ASTMAN, JOSEPH GUSTAV, educator; b. Willimantic, Conn., Nov. 1, 1916; s. Joseph and Helen (Mueller) A.; m. Dorothy Rennie, Dec. 31, 1941; children: Joseph Gustav, William Rennie, Dorothe Rennie, Selda. BA, Trinity Coll., Hartford, Conn., 1938; MA, Yale U., 1942, PhD, 1948. Tchr. German Trinity Coll., 1941-42, 46-48; tchr. English and German Avon (Conn.) Old Farms Sch., 1942-43; tchr. German St. Joseph Coll., West Hartford, Conn., 1947-48; mem. faculty Hofstra U., Hempstead, N.Y., 1948-85; prof. German, chmn. dept. fgn. langs. and lit. Hofstra U., 1954-66, dean Coll. Liberal Arts and Scis., 1966-72; on leave 1972-73; prof. comparative lit. and langs. Hofstra U., 1973-85, dir. univ. ctr. for cultural and intercultural study, 1975-85, dir. Cultural Ctr., 1982-85; dir. NDEA Summer Lang. Inst., 1960-63; assoc. Yale U. Library, 1955-85; dir. testing MLA, N.Y.C., 1964-65; mem. Woodrow Wilson fellowship selection com., 1966-70, Middle-States Evaluation Teams. Contbr. articles to profl. publs. Bd. dirs. Friends Nassau County Mus., former treas.; bd. fellows Trinity Coll., Hartford, 1964-71. With AUS, 1944-46; ETO. Recipient Dean's award for excellence Hofstra U., 1977, Alumni medal Trinity Coll., 1983; Am. Council Learned Socs. grantee U. Mich., summer 1956, NEH grantee U. Calif.-Berkeley, summer 1981, 1983; named Hon. Alumnus Hofstra U., 1983. Mem. AAUP (pres. Hofstra chpt. 1951-52), MLA, Assn. Tchrs. Slavic E. European Langs. (v.p. N.Y. State 1951-55), Nat. Assn. Standard Med. Vocabulary, Am. Legion (past post vice comdr.), Early Trades and Crafts Soc., Maynard Hill Hist. Soc. (charter), Am. Soc. 18th Century Studies, Sigma Kappa Alpha, Sigma Delta Pi. Home: Levittown N.Y. Died Sept. 2, 1985; buried Pine Lawn L.I. Nat. Cemetery.

ASTOR, MARY LUCILLE LANGHANKE, actress; b. Quincy, Ill., May 3, 1906; d. Otto and Helen (Vasconcellos) Langhanke; m. Kenneth Hawks, Feb. 28, 1928 (dec. 1930); m. Franklyn Thrope, June 29, 1931 (div. 1935); 1 dau., Marylyn Hauoli; m. Manuel del Campo, Feb. 18, 1937 (div. 1942); 1 son, Anthony Paul; m. Thomas G. Wheelock, Dec. 24, 1945. Student pub. schs. and pvt. tutors. Appeared in numerous motion pictures since 1920 including Beau Brummel, Ladies Love Brutes, Lost Squadron, Red Dust, World Changes, Page Miss Glory, Dodsworth, The Prisonr of Zenda, The Hurricane, 1937, Listen Darling, Midnight, 1938, Brigham Young Frontiersman, 1940, The Great Lie (Acad. award best supporting role) 1941, Maltese Falcon, Across the Pacific, 1942, Fiesta, Claudia and David, Meet Me in St. Louis, Desert Fury, The Rich Full Life, Act of Violence, Little Women, Return to Peyton Place, Hush, Hush, Sweet Charlotte; actress appearing various roles in stage plays; Among the Married, Tonight at Eight Thirty, The Male Animal, Time of the Cuckoo, Don Juan in Hell (on the road), Starcross Story (on Broadway); dramatic roles TV shows, 1953-87; author: Mary Astor, My Story; The Incredible Charlie Carewe, The Image of Kate; The O'Conners; Goodbye Darling-Be Happy; Place Called Saturday, 1968; A Life on Film, 1971. Home: Malibu Calif. Died Sept. 25, 1987.

ATHERTON, JAMES PEYTON, JR., tenor; b. Montgomery, Ala., Apr. 27, 1943; s. James Peyton and Anna Avery (Thomas) A. B.Music, Peabody Conservatory Music, Balt., 1965, M.Music, 1966. Debuts include Met. Opera, N.Y.C., 1977, Gyndebourne Festival, 1979, Holland Festival, 1976, mem., Santa Fe Opera, 1973-78, Met. Opera, from 1977, appeared also with San Francisco Opera, Houston Grand Opera, Miami Opera, Dallas Opera, Canadian Opera.

Recipient Nat. Opera Inst. award, 1972. Home: New York N.Y. Died 1987.

ATKINSON, CARROLL HOLLOWAY, education educator; b. Fairbury, Nebr., Oct. 24, 1896; s. Charles Raymond and Florence (Bennie) A.; m. Ruby Baker, Aug. 23, 1921 (dec. 1925); children—Yvonne Dorothy, Carroll Holloway; m. Mary Hansen, 1926 (dec. 1941); m. Carol Mary Gonzales, 1959; children—Ardith Anne, Alicia Arthurita, Arthur Amigo. A.B., Lawrence Coll., 1920; student, U. Grenoble, France, 1919, Pacific U., 1922, U. Oreg., 1922, U. Wash., 1923, U. Calif. Los Angeles, 1926, U. So. Calif.; M.A., U. Tex., 1937, George Peabody Coll. for Tchrs.; Ph.D., 1937-38. Jr. clerk Met. Life Ins. Co., 1915-16; steno. Sheridan (Wyo.) Iron Works, 1917-18; statistician Kimberly-Clark Paper Co., Wis., 1920-21; athletic coach Lawrence Coll., 1915-17, 9-21; prof. and athletic coach Coll. of Idaho, 1921-22; rin. and coach Forest Grove, Oreg., 1922-23, Thorp, Wash., 1923-24, North Bend, Oreg., 1924-25; salesman Acme Fast Freight Service, 1925-26; tchr. Pasadena ob. Schs., 1926-30; prin. and coach San Luis Obispo, Calif., 1930-35; ednl. adviser Civilian Conservation Corps, 1935-36; asso. prof. North Tex. State Tchrs. Coll., 1936-37, Edinboro (Pa.) State Tchrs. Coll., 1938-9; asso. prof. and dir. radio Jersey City and Newark N.J.) State Tchrs. colls., 1939-41; dir. Nelson and McLucas Meml. Libraries, Detroit, 1941-45; pub. relations dept. Key System., Oakland, Calif., 1945-46; columnist Honolulu Star-Bull. (and radio producer), 946-47, Santa Fe New Mexican, 1951-52; dean of men outhwestern U., 1947-49; dir. tchr. tng. Dakota Wesleyan U., 1949-51; lectr. St. Michaels Coll., Santa Fe, 951-54, also summer; supervising prin. pub. schools Cojoaque, N.Mex., 1951-54; tchr. (summers) U. Wash., 940, U. Wyo., No. Mont. Coll. and Eastern Mont. tate Normal Sch., 1941, U. Utah, 1943, N.Mex. Highands U., 1949; supervising prin. Belen (N.Mex.) pub. chs., 1954-57; tchr. pub. schs. Grants, N.Mex., 1957-0; prof. edn., psychology Tex. Luth. Coll., Sequin, ex., 1960-61; instr. history Fla. Meml. Coll., 1964-66; asso. rof. edn. Bethune-Cookman Coll., 1966-72; Extension taff faculty N.Mex. Western Coll., 1954-57; radio roducer, 1931-88; with Wally Gluck Enterprises. Author 20 books, 1938-88, including, Intellectual ramp, 1955, Story of Education, 1962, 65, The Show Must Go On—Even For Children, 1977. Mem. exec. om. Boy Scouts Am. Served with A.E.F., World War I. Life mem. NEA; mem. AAAS, Tex. Acad. Sci., Texas sychol. Assn., Am. Assn. Sch. Adminstrs., Soc. Advancement Learning, Am. Legion, Acad. Polit. Sci., Jnited Comml. Travelers, Portland Psychol. Assn., Am. ssn. of Croix de Guerre, VFW, AAUP, Daytona each Psychol. Assn., Internat. Platform Assn., Vets. us. Men's Club. Methodist. Home: Daytona Beach la. Died Aug. 1, 1988; buried Ormond Meml. Cemetery.

ATKINSON, HUGH CRAIG, university library administrator; b. Chgo., Nov. 27, 1933; s. Craig and Margaret (Ritchey) A.; m. Mary Nugent, Jan. 12, 1957; children—George, Mary Susan, Ann. Student, St. Benedict's Coll., 1951-53, U. Chgo., 1953-57; M.A., Grad. Library Sch., 1959. Certificate in archival administrn. U.S. Nat. Archives, 1958. Asst. in rare books J. Chgo. Library, 1957-58; reader's service librarian Pa. Mil. Coll. Library, 1958-61; with State U. N.Y. at Buffalo, 1961-67, asst. dir., 1964-67; with Ohio State Univs. ibraries, 1967-76, prof. and dir., 1971-76; prof. and niv. librarian U. Ill., Urbana, 1976-86; Mem. adv. com. or research in info. scis. Ohio Project for Research in nfo. Sci., 1972-73; chmn. com. direct borrowing Ohio Coll. Library Center, 1973-76, trustee, 1978-86, chmn. udit com., 1978-79, nominating com., 1985-86. Author IEW report: Optimum Speed of Library Access as Related to Optimum Size Library Collections, 1970; ontbg. author: Advances in Librarianship, 1974; ditor: (with Joseph Katz, Richard A. Ploch) Twenty-ne Letters from Hart Crane to George Bryan, 1968, with William White gen. editor) Theodore Dreiser: a hecklist, 1971; Compiler: (with William White gen. ditor) The Merrill Checklist of Theodore Dreiser, 1969; ontbg. compiler; (with William White gen. ditor) The Bowker Annual of Library and Book Trade nformation, 16th-23d edits, 1971-78; Contbr. (with Villiam White gen. editor) articles to profl. jours. rustee Interuniv. Communications Council, 1976-79. Iem. ALA, Ill. Library Assn., Assn. Research Libraries od. dirs. 1982-86, task force sch. com. 1982-86, govt. elations com. 1986), Center Research Libraries, U. hgo. Grad. Library Sch. Alumni Assn. (pres. 1974-75), AAUP. Home: Urbana Ill. Died Oct. 24, 1986.

ATKYNS, (WILLIE) LEE, (JR.), artist, museum rector; b. Washington, Sept. 13, 1913; s. Willie Lee nd Marion Amelia (Van Horn) A. Retouch artist, egative cutter Bur. Engraving & Printing, Washington, 936-42; map maker, retouch artist Army Map Service, alcavilia, Md., 1942-45; tchr. Lee Atkyns Art Sch., Vashington, 1945-47, Lee Atkyns Studio, Puzzletown, a., 1946-50, Lee Atkyns Art Mart, Johnstown, Pa., 948-50, Lee Atkyns Little Bohemia, Indiana, Pa., 1947-, Lee Atkyns Art Sch., Altoona, Pa., 1948-50, Lee tkyns Art Studio, Washington, 1950-75; dir. Lee tkyns Studio Gallery (Puzzletown) Duncansville, Pa., om 1975. Exhibited group shows, Corcoran Art Galry, Smithsonian Inst., Catholic U. Am., American U.,

George Washington U., exhibited, Balt. Mus., Nat. Acad. Design, Carnegie Inst. Art, Butler Art Inst., Phillips Meml. Gallery, Md. U., Wilson Tchrs. Coll., LDM Sweat Meml. Mus., Hagerstown Mus., Hirshon Galleries; one-man exhbns. include So. Alleghenies Mus., Loretto and Hollidaysburg, Pa., 1987-88. Recipient numerous awards profl. assns. Mem. Artists Equity, Internat. Platform Assn., Soc. Washington Artists, Landscape Club, Arts Club, Water Color Club (past pres.), Puzzletown Artists Guild, Art for the Home Group. Republican. Deceased.

ATTERBERG, KURT MAGNUS, composer, conductor, critic, violoncellist; b. Göteborg, Sweden, Dec. 12, 1887; s. Anders Johan and Elvira (Uddman) A.; m. Margareta Dalsjo, 1925. Studies with Anders Hallén, 1910-11; diploma in elec. engring., Royal Tech. High Sch., Stockholm, 1911. Condr. Dramatic Theatre, Stockholm, 1915-21; music critic Stockholm-Tidningen, 1919-57; sec. Royal Swedish Acad. Music, 1940-53; condr. orchs. in Sweden, Berlin, Hamburg, heidelberg, Helsingfors, Vienna, Wiesbaden, Paris, Warsaw, Bremen, Braunschweig, Dresden, Oslo, Bergen, Brussels, Ostende, Vicy; composer 9 symphonies (Symphony No. 6 received Schubert Centenary Meml. Contest award); (operas) Herwarth the Harper, 1919, Bäckahästen, 1925, Fanal, 1934, Aladdin, 1941, The Tempest, 1948; (pantomime ballets) The Wise and the Foolish Virgins, 1920, Peter the Swineherd, 1921; incidental music to Shakespeare's Tempest; (cantatas) Requiem, Jarnbaraland and Songen; 8 suties for orch.; 5 concertos for solo instruments with orch.; various chamber music and chorus works. Recipient decorations govts. of Sweden, Denmark, Finland, Austria, France, Germany, Norway. Mem. Soc. Swedish Composers (a founder, hon. pres. 1947), Fedn. Confédération Internat. des Sociétés d'Auteurs et Compositeurs (hon. pres.). Home: Stockholm Sweden. †

ATWOOD, FREDERICK H., lawyer, business executive; b. Allegheny, Pa., July 19, 1891; s. Moses and Jane Wilson (Baird) A.; m. Alice Thompson, Dec. 1, 1919; children: Eleanor Atwood Clowney, John Baird. Student, Allegheny Prep. Sch., 1897-1909; AB, Princeton U., 1913; LLB, U. Pitts., 1916. Bar: Pa. 1916. Pvt. practice Pitts., 1916-18, 19-27; with Harbison Walker Refractories Co., Pitts., 1927-56, dir., gen. counsel, from 1956. Pres. borough coun., Sewickley, Pa. With U.S. Army, 1918-19. Mem. Allegheny County Club, Edgeworth Club, Phi Beta Kappa. Home: Sewickley Pa. †

AUGELLI, ANTHONY THOMAS, automotive company executive, chief federal judge; b. Orsara, Italy, Mar. 27, 1902; brought to U.S., 1904, naturalized, 1910; s. Lorenzo and Lucia (Aquilino) A.; m. Mary Carroll, Oct. 28, 1936; children: Kathleen, Robert, Marie, Patircia. LLB, N.J. Law Sch., 1929; LLM, Mercer Beasley Sch. Law, Newark, 1934; LLD, Seton Hall U., 1971. Bar: N.J. 1930, U.S. Supreme Ct. 1939, other fed. and state cts. Assoc. Milton, Augelli & Keane and predecessors, Jersey City, 1930-61, ptnr., 1935-61; U.S. dist. judge for N.J. 1961-73, chief judge, 1968-72, sr. judge, 1972-74; umpire, dealer relations plan Gen. Motors Corp., Newark, 1974-85; mem. Jud. Conf. Com. on Adminstrn. Probation System, 1969-71; dir. Hudson County Nat. Bank, Jersey City, 1943-61; park commnr. Hudson County, 1955-61. Mem. ABA, N.J. Bar Assn., Hudson County Bar Assn., Dante Alighieri Soc., Elks. Home: Newark N.J. Died Oct. 24, 1985.

AULT, WARREN ORTMAN, historian; b. Lenexa, Kans., Jan. 8, 1887; s. Addison and Mary Aleja (McElwain) A.; m. Myrtle Lavina Wilcock, June 12, 1931; children: Addison, Mary Myrtle. AB, Baker U., 1907, LLD (hon.), 1937; BA, Oxford U., Eng., 1910, MA, 1917; PhD, Yale U., 1919; LittD (hon.), Boston U., 1960. Instr. history Boston U., 1913-19, asst. prof., 1919-24, William Edwards Huntington prof. history, chmn. dept., 1924-57, emeritus from 1957, Bacon lectr. 1933, Univ. lectr., 1951-52; vis. prof. Kansas City Regional Council Higher Edn. Author: Private Jurisdiction in England, 1923, Court Rolls of the Abbey of Ramsey and the Honor Clare, 1927, Europe in the Middle Ages, 1932, Europe in Modern Times, 1947, Open-Field Husbandry and the Village Community, 1965, Open-Field Farming in Medieval England, 1972, Boston University College of Liberal Arts, 1873-1973, 1973; contbr. to profl. jours. With M.C., then 2d lt. F.A., U.S. Army, 1919. Rhodes scholar, Oxford U., 1907-10; Univ. fellow in history Yale U., 1911-13, Guggenheim fellow, 1926-27; Disting. scholar-in-residence Baker U., 1968-69; hon. fellow Jesus Coll., Oxford U., 1971; recipient spl. award Gen. Alumni Assn. Boston U., 1973. Fellow Am. Acad. Arts and Scis., Royal Hist. Soc.; mem. Am. Hist. Assn., N.E. History Tchrs. Assn. (pres. 1934-36), University Club, Appalachian Mountain Club (Boston), Phi Beta Kappa, Zeta Chi. Home: Waban Mass. Deceased.

AURIN, FRITZ LOVE, consulting geologist; b. Prescott, Ark., Dec. 18, 1891; s. Frederick Karl and Theresa Emma (Abbott) A.; m. Clara Bawden, Dec. 14, 1917; children: Fred Bawden, Joan. Geologist Empire Gas & Fuel Co. and geol. chemist Okla. Geol. Survey, 1914-16; field geologist 1916-17, asst. dir., 1918; resident geologist Empire Oil Co., 1918-19; asst. chief geologist Marland Oil Co., 1919-25, chief geologist, 1925-28; chief

geologist Southland Royalty Co., Ft. Worth, Tex., 1928-33, v.p., 1933-38, pres., 1938-55, exec. v.p., 1955-58, consulting geologist, after 1958. Mem. AAAS, Tex. Acad. Sci., Ft. Worth, Tulsa, Kans. geol. socs., Geol. Soc. Am., Am. Assn. Petroleum Geologists, Lambda Chi Alpha, Phi Beta Kappa, Masons, Rivercrest Country, Ft. Worth clubs. Home: Fort Worth Tex. †

AUSTAD, MARK EVANS, diplomat, broadcast executive; b. Ogden, Utah, Apr. 1, 1917; s. Jacob and Signe (Anderson) A.; m. Lola Brown, Aug. 20, 1941; children: Nancy Austad Roth, Penny Austad Davis, Wendy Austad Durfee. Student, Weber State Coll., HHD (hon.), 1973. With Sta. KSL, Salt Lake City; commentator CBS, Sta. WTOP, Washington, 1950-60; founding trust mem. Metromedia, Inc., Washington and N.Y.C., v.p., 1961-81; U.S. rep. Gen. Assembly UN, N.Y.C., 1973; ambassador to Finland Helsinki, 1974-77; ambassador to Norway Oslo, 1980-84; lectr. Nat. Geog. Soc., Washington, from 1960. Producer full length travel films: Visit with Albert Schweitzer, The Soviet Union, Machu Pichu to Sao Paulo, U.S. Nat. Parks, others. Chmn. Washington Cherry Blossom Festival, 1964-65, presdsl. inaugural balls, 1968-72; vice chmn. inauguration com., 1972. Decorated Order of White Rose, Finland; named Outstanding Citizen State of Wash. Mem. Burning Tree Club; Paradise Valley Club; Bald Peak Club; Broadcast Pioneers Club, Rotary. Died Oct. 20, 1988.

AUSTIN, JOHN PAUL, beverage company executive; b. La Grange, Ga., Feb. 14, 1915; s. Samuel Yates and Maude (Jernigan) A.; m. Jeane Weed, July 12, 1950; children: John Paul, Samuel Weed. AB, Harvard U., 1937, LLB, 1940. Bar: N.Y. 1940. Practiced in N.Y.C. 1940-41, 45-49; mem. legal dept. Coca-Cola Co., 1949-50, exec. v.p., 1961-62, pres., dir., 1962-83, chief exec. officer, 1966-81, chmn. bd., 1970-81; exec. v.p. Coca-Cola Export Corp., 1958-59, pres., dir., from 1959. Lt. comdr. USNR, 1942-45. Mem. Racquet and Tennis (N.Y.C.), Blind Brook Golf (Purchase, N.Y.), Capital City, Peachtree Golf, Links clubs. Home: Atlanta Ga. Died Dec. 27, 1985.

AUSTIN, KENNETH RALPH, insurance executive; b. Keosauqua, Iowa, Mar. 15, 1920; s. James Clayton and Nancy M. (Landreth) A.; m. LaVerne Eleanor Turin, May 9, 1942; children: Marilyn Ruth, Alan Karl. B.C.S., Drake U. 1941; M.S., U. Iowa, 1942. With Equitable Life Ins. Co. Iowa, Des Moines, 1947-85; asst. sec. Equitable Life Ins. Co. Iowa, 1953-59, supt. policy issue, 1959-60, agy. v.p., 1960-64, v.p., controller, 1964-66, exec. v.p., 1966-69, pres., 1969-81, chief exec. officer, 1970-83, chmn., 1981-85. Bd. dirs. Drake U.; past bd. dirs. Simpson Coll., Marycrest Coll., South Iowa Methodist Homes, Am. Assn. Homes for Aging; bd. govs. Iowa Coll. Found. Served to comdr. USNR, 1942-45. Fellow Life Mgmt. Inst.; mem. Life Office Mgmt. Assn. (past dir.), Am. Council Life Ins. (past dir.). Home: Des Moines Iowa. Died June 26, 1987; buried Glendale Cemetary, Des Moines.

AVERILL, LAWRENCE AUGUSTUS, professor of psychology; b. Alna, Maine, May 1, 1891; s. Augustus B. and Etta M. (West) A.; m. Esther M. Cunningham, Dec. 25, 1915 (dec.); m. 2d, Marion P. Haggett, 1950. AB, Clark Coll., 1913; AM, Clark U., 1914, PhD, 1915. Diplomate Am. Bd. Examiners Profl. Psychology. Instr. modern langs. Clark Coll., 1912-14; prof. psychology and head dept. Worcester State Tchrs. Coll., Worcester, Mass., 1915-50; instr. U. Maine, extension div. Author: introductory Psychology, 1945, Psychology of the Elementary School Child, 1948, Psychology Applied to Nursing, 5th edit., 1956, (with Marion P. Averill) Pie for Breakfast, 1953; assoc. editor: the Ensign; contbr. articles, revs. to ednl. and psychol. mags., jours. Pastor Sheepscot Community Parish. Fellow Am. Psychol. Assn.; mem. AAUP, Eastern, N.E., Maine psychol. assns.; Nat. Soc. Coll. Tchrs. Edn., Boston Authors Club, Wiscasset Yacht Club (commodore), Pi Gamma Mu, Kappa Delta Pi. Republican. Methodist. Home: Wiscasset Maine. †

AXMAN, LAURENCE HENRY, lawyer; b. Kansas City, Mo., July 30, 1890; s. Charles David and Sophia (Cahn) A. AB, Columbia U., 1911, LLB, 1913. Bar: N.Y. 1913, U.S. Supreme Ct. 1923, D.C. 1958. Pvt. practice N.Y.C., 1913-17, 1919-42; asst. U.S. atty So. Dist. N.Y., 1917-19; spl. asst. to U.S. atty. gen. in charge trial sect. 1948-52; trial atty. civil div. Dept. Justice, Washington, 1952-61, employment policy officer, 1957-61; pvt. practice Washington, from 1962; tech. cons. White Conf. on Children and YOuth, 1960; mem. adv. com. hearing examiners Civil Service Commn. Mem. Fed. Bar Assn. (pres. 1957-58, mem. nat. council, vice chmn. com. ct. claims, vice chmn. com. juvenile and youth problems, chmn. 50th Anniversary Commn. 1970, chmn. constrn. and bylaws com., mem. jud. selections, ethics coms.), Internat. Bar Assn. (v.p. 1958), D.C. Bar Assn., Assn. Bar of City of N.Y., Nat. Lawyers Club. Home: Washington D.C. Deceased.

AYALA Y AYALA, RAFAEL, bishop; b. Coatepec de Harinas, Mex., Oct. 25, 1913. Ordained priest Roman Cath. Ch., 1942. Elevated to bishop 1962, named bishop of Tehuacán, 1962. Home: Tehuacán Mexico. Deceased.

AYERS, LORENZ KNEEDLER, manufacturing executive; b. Easton, Pa., Apr. 15, 1891; s. Charles Pearson and Emma C. (Williams) A.; m. Anna M. Spackman, Sept. 27, 1919; children: Helen Spackman, Barbara. Chemist, later departmental supr. severl prodn. units C.K. Williams & Co., Easton, Pa., 1913-17; v.p. George S. Mepham Corp., East St. Louis, Ill., 1919-31, pres., 1931-48; pres. Point Milling & Mfg. Co., 1945-48, firms consol. to form C.K. Williams & Co., East St. Louis, Ill., from 1948; pres. Midwest Mining Co., Acme Barite Co., Victorville Lime Rock Co; area dir. Am. Mutual Liability Ins. Co.; bd. dirs. St. Louis Capital, Inc. 1st lt., A.S., U.S. Army, 1917-19. Mem. Ill. Mfrs. Assn. (pres. 1952), Am. Chem. Soc., Racquet Club, Mo. Athletic Club, Bellerive Country Club, Noonday Club, Northampton Country Club, Chemists Club, University Club (St. Louis); Union League Club (Chgo.). Republican. Presbyterian. Home: Saint Louis Mo. †

BAAR, EMIL N., lawyer; b. Vienna, Austria, Sept. 9, 1891; came to U.S., 1893; s. Jacob and Fannie (Sonnenschein) B.; m. Amelia A. Wasch, June 19, 1919 (dec. 1966); m. Grace Arenson, 1974 (dec. 1984). AB, Columbia U., 1913, JD, 1915; DHL (hon.), Hebrew Union Coll., 1965. Bar: N.Y. 1915. Mem. firm Baar, Bennett & Fullen, N.Y.C., 1926-74, Palmer, Series & Baar, N.Y.C., 1974-78; counsel Baar, Bennett & Metz, N.Y.C., 1978-81, Keenan, Powers & Andrews, N.Y.C., 1981-85; justice N.Y. State Supreme Ct., 1951; spl. asst. State Atty. Gen., 1955; v.p., dir. JHMCB Nursing Home Co Inc; hon. trustee Met. Savs. Bank, Bklyn. Hon. life chmn. bd. Interfaith Med. Ctr.; hon. life trustee Bklyn. Inst. Arts and Scis.; trustee United Hosp. Fund N.Y., Jewish Braille Inst. Am., hon. pres., Fedn. Jewish Philanthropies; governing com. Bklyn. Mus.; hon. life pres. Union Temple; hon. gov. Hebrew Union Coll., Jewish Inst. Religion; hon. life v.p., gov. World Union for Progressive Judaism Ltd. Served with 49th Inf. AUS, World War I. Adopted as hon. chief Algonquin Tribe of Am. Indians of Bklyn., 1951. Mem. Union Am. Hebrew Congregations (hon. life chmn. bd.), Am., N.Y. State, Bklyn. bar assns., Assn. Bar City N.Y., Am. Legion (county comdr. 1925), Masons (32 deg.), Elks, Sojourners Club, Unity Club (Bklyn.) (dir.), Fresh Meadow Country Club (pres., chmn. bd. 1936-46). Home: New York N.Y. Died Nov. 11, 1985.

BABBITT, DEAN, corporation executive; b. Cin., July 10, 1888; s. Dean Richmond and Adelaide Marcella (Karrmann) B.; m. Georgia Harmon Warren, Oct. 18, 1911; m. 2d, Estelle A. Van Son, Feb. 20, 1940; children: Dean, Ann Richmond. Student, Holbrook Mil. Acad., Peekskill Mil. Acad. Book agt., clk., jewelry salesman, furniture salesman 1904-07; mgr. mail order sales Shaw-Walker Co., Muskegon, Mich., 1907-08; asst. advt. mgr. The Gobe-Wernicke Co., Cin., 1909; mgr. office furniture dept. Gibson and Perin Co., Cin., 1910-11; with Safe-Cabinet Co., Marietta, Ohio, 1911-25, serving as br. mgr., Dallas, dist. mgr. State of Tex., gen. sales and advt. mgr., dir. sales and advt., sec. co., bd. dirs.; gen. sales mgr. Safe Cabinet div. Remington-Rand, Inc., Buffalo, 1925-28, also mem. gen. sales adv. gabinet; v.p., treas. Jackson-Babbitt, Inc., comml. rsch. engrs., N.Y.C., 1929-1931; v.p., exec. sales mgr., L.C. Smith and Corona Typewriters, Inc., 1931-1933; v.p., gen. sales mgr. Sonotone Corp., N.Y.C., 1933-36, pres., 1936-47; pres., ea. distbr., bd. dirs. Carry-Cab, Corp., from 1947; chmn. bd., pres., dirs. sales Belmar Electric Corp.; bd. dirs. Stereo Pictures Corp., Norcor Mfg. Co. Mem. indsl. adv. com. State N.H. Mem. N.Y. Sales Mgrs. Club, Bankers Am. Club, Mktg. Execs. Soc., Sales Execs. of N.Y. Club, Costograph Corp. Execs. Club (pres.), Masons. Home: Ashland N.H. †

BABCOCK, CHARLES DWIGHT, JR., aeronautical engineer; b. Indpls., June 17, 1934; s. Charles Dwight and Helen (Flanagan) B.; m. Janet Elaine York, June 14, 1958; children: Cynthia Lynne, Linda Christine. BS in Aeros., Purdue U., 1957; MS, Calif. Inst. Tech., 1958, PhD, 1962. Research fellow Calif. Inst. Tech., Pasadena, 1962-63, asst. prof. aeros., 1963-68, assoc. prof., 1968-74, prof., 1974-87. Contbr. tech. articles to profl. jours. Mem. ASME, Am. Inst. Aeros. and Astronautics., Soc. for Exptl. Stress Analysis, Sigma Xi. Home: Altadena Calif. Died July 1, 1987.

BABCOCK, PERVIN LATHROP, banker; b. Syracuse, N.Y., Aug. 8, 1892; s. Howard Noyes and Caroline Comstock (Lathrop) B.; m. Eleanor R. Severance, Jan. 27, 1940; children: Susan, Peter Lewis, Severance. Pub. acct., Syracuse, 1919-38; with Onondaga County Savs. Bank, from 1938, pres., 1943-59, chmn. bd., from 1959. Home: Cazenovia N.Y. †

BABCOCK, ROBERT SHILLINGFORD, educator; b. Chgo., July 22, 1915; s. Oliver M. and Martha (Shillingford) B.; m. Alice-Anne Hanchett, Aug. 20, 1940; children: Robert Shillingford, Ann, Julie, Peter Trowbridge, Martha Rena. AB, U. Rochester, 1937; BA, Oxford U., Eng., 1939; MA, Oxford U., 1943; PHD, Northwestern U., 1949; LLD, Marlboro Coll., 1957. Instr. Black Mountain Coll., N.C., 1940-42; econ. analyst Treasury Dept., Washington, 1942; mem. Bd. Econ. Warfare, Washington, 1942-43; asst. prof. polit. sci. U. Vt., Burlington, 1946-54, assoc. prof., 1954-59, prof. polit. sci., 1961-85; provost, pres. Vt. State Colls., 1965-85; mem. Vt. Sen. 1951, 53, 57, pres. pro tem. 1957-59; sec. to gov. Vt., 1955; lt. gov. Vt. 1959-61. Author: State and Local Governmnet and Politics, 1957, rev. edit., 1962. Lt. (j.g.) USNR, 1943-46. Rhodes scholar, 1937. Mem. Am. Polit. Sci. Assn., Phi Beta Kappa. Home: South Burlington Vt. Died Sept. 1, 1985.

BACKMAN, GUSTAVE POLLARD, association executive; b. Salt Lake City, Nov. 11, 1891; s. Gustave Hilmer and Grace Baily (Pollard) B.; m. Annie Irene Davis, June 12, 1912; children: Gustave Leroy, Pollard Davis, William Davis. Ed. pub. schs.; LLD (hon.), U. Utah, 1958. Assoc. G.H. Backman & Sons (abstractors and attys.), 1910-21, mgr., 1923-24; collection mgr. Zion's Coop. Merc. Inst., Salt Lake City, 1921-23, asst. sec., 1925, sales mgr., 1926-27, asst. gen. mgr., 1928-29, sec., mgr., 1929-30; exec. sec. Salt Lake City C. of C., 1930-64; pres. Utah Hotel Co., Bonneville Speedway Assn., Jordan Fur & Reclamation Co.; chmn. exec. com. Zions Savs. & Loan Assn.; bd. dirs. Newspaper Agy. Corp., Zions 1st Nat. Bank, Denver & Rio Grande R.R., Wasatch Lawn Cemetery Assn., Pro-Utah, Inc. Mem. Alta Winter Sports Assn. (sec.-treas.), University Club, Ambassador Club, Alta Club, Country Club, New State Gun Club, Elks, Rotary. Home: Salt Lake City Utah. †

BACON, JOHN BAPTISTE FORD, chemist; b. Jacksonville, Fla., Aug. 24, 1891; s. Mark Reeves and Mary (Ford) B.; m. Helois Lysle, Oct. 24, 1925; children: Heloise L. Bacon Power, John Baptiste Ford, Mark A. Student, Phillips Exeter Acad.; PhB, Yale U., 1915. With Ford Bldg. Co., Detroit, from 1937, v.p., from 1948, also bd. dirs.; with Wyandotte (Mich.) Chemicals Corp., from 1951, then bd. dirs. Author: Elements of Aviation Engines, 1918. Treas., bd. dirs. Pasadena YMCA, from 1935. Mem. Annandale Golf Club, Calif. Club (L.A.), Detroit Athletic Club, Yale Club (N.Y.C.). Home: Pasadena Calif. †

BACON, PEGGY, artist, writer; b. Ridgefield, Conn., May 2, 1895; d. Charles Roswell and Elizabeth (Chase) B.; m. Alexander Brook, May 4, 1920 (div.); children: Belinda, Alexander Bacon. Diploma, Kent Place Sch., 1913; student Art Students League, Sch. Fine and Applied Arts, N.Y.C. Artist 1920-87; tchr. art Fieldston Sch., N.Y.C., 1933-39; former tchr. life drawing, painting and composition Art Students League; tchr. drawing Hunter Coll., Stella Elkins Tlyer Coll. Fine Arts, Phila., Corcoran Art Sch., Washington; past tchr. New Sch. Social Research, New Art Ctr., Kennebunk, Maine, summers; tchr. Summer Sch. Music and Art, Stowe, Vt. Work represented in permanent collection Met. and other museums, retrospective exhbn. Smithsonian Inst., 1975-76; author and illustrator: The True Philosopher, 1919, Funeralities, 1925, Lion-hearted Kitten, 1927, Mercy and the Mouse, 1928, Ballad of Tangle Street, 1929, The Terrible Nuisance, 1931, Animosities, 1931, Mischief in Mayfield, 1933, Off with Their Heads, 1934, The True Philosopher, 1919, Catcalls, 1935, The Mystery of East Hatchett or Eric the Pink Viking, 1939, Starting from Scratch, 1945, The Good American Witch, 1957, The Magic Touch, 1968; author: (novel) The Inward Eye, 1952, The Oddity, 1962, The Ghost of Opalina, 1967; illustrator more than 60 books; contbr. verse, drawings and stories to leading mags. Guggenheim fellow, 1934; grantee Nat. Acad. Arts and Letters, 1942; recipient Gold medal for graphic art Am. Acad. and Inst. of Arts and Letters, 1980. Mem. Nat. Inst. Arts and Letters. Died Jan. 4, 1987.

BADDELEY, HERMIONE, actress; b. Broseley, Shropshire, Eng., Nov. 13, 1908; d. W.H. Clinton and Louise (Bourdin) B.; m. J.H. Willis. Stage appearances included La Boite a Joujoux, Court Theatre, London, 1918, 1919-23, Makebelieve, Lyric, Hammersmith, 1920, West End parts, Florrie Small in The Likes of Her, St. Martin's, 1923, Punchbowl revue, Palace, 1924; joined the Co-Optimists, London Pavilion, 1925; continuous appearances in West End theatres in varied plays including The Greeks Had a Word for It, Nine Sharp, Rise About It, Sky High, Brighton Rock; entertained the troops A La Carte, Grand National Night, Fallen Angels, Far East and Middle East tour in Cabaret, 1955-56, A Taste of Honey, U.S. tour, 1961-62, The Milk Train Doesn't Stop Here Any More, N.Y.C., 1963, The Kinning of Sister George, St. Martin's, 1966, The Threepenny Opera, Prince of Wales, 1972; debut in comml. TV, 1956, appeared in films and TV, 1957-61, U.S. TV Julia (Golden Globe award 1976), Mrs. Naugutuck in Maude (Emmy nomination 1976); films include Caste, Kipps, It Always Rains on Sunday, Brighton Rock, No Room at the Inn, Quartet, Passport to Pimlico, Scrooge, The Belles of St. Trinians, Midnight Lace, Room at the Top (Oscar nomination), Mary Poppins, The Unsinkable Molly Brown, Marriage on the Rocks, Harlow, Do Not Disturb, The Black Windmill; author: autobiography The Unsinkable Hermione Baddeley. Died Aug. 19, 1986.

BADGER, WALTER IRVING, JR., lawyer; b. Cambridge, Mass., Sept. 16, 1891; s. Walter Irving and Elizabeth Hand (Wilcox) B.; m. Jane Whitman Bullard, June 2, 1917 (dec. June 1956); children: Walter Irving III (dec.), Jane Hallett Badger Newell; m. 2d, Olive Folsom Langsdale, Apr. 5, 1957. Student, Browne & Nichols Sch., Cambridge, 1900-05, St. Paul's Sch., Concord, N.H., 1905-08; BA, Yale U., 1913, MA, 1913; LLB, Harvard U., 1916. Bar: Mass. 1916. Pvt. practice Boston, from 1916; mem. firm Badger, Parrish, Sulliva[n] & Frederick and predecessor firms, Boston, from 1922 sr. ptnr., from 1942; 1st v.p. Nat. Braille Press, Boston 1944-45, pres. from 1956. 1st lt. M.I. Div., Gen. Staff U.S. Army, 1918-19; capt. and adj. 1st Moto[r] Squadron, Mass. State Guards (1st Corps Cadets), 1940-46. Mem. ABA, Mass. Bar Assn., Am. Rowing Assn (steward), Bostonian Soc., Mil. Order of World Wars Soc. Colonial Wars, Union Boat Club, The Countr[y] Club (Brookline) Harvard Club, Down-Town Clu[b] (pres. from 1956) (Boston); Yale Club (N.Y.C.) Longwood Cricket Club (Chestnut Hill), Phi Bet[a] Kappa, Delta Kappa Epsilon. Home: Boston Mass. †

BADSKEY, LORIN JUSTIN, farm machinery an[d] marine company executive; b. Ind., Sept. 23, 1914; s Fred John and Mary (Badger) B.; m. Ruby Mari Lepley, May 2, 1937; children: Jerry L., Jane L. Owner Badskey's Standard Service, Nort[h] Manchester, Ind., 1935-47; pres., dir. LML Corp Columbia City, Ind., 1947-71; chmn., bd. dirs. LM[L] Corp., Columbia City, Ind., 1971-80; ptnr. Badskey Schubert-Reiff Realty, Columbia City, 1953-80, Bad skey-Badskey Realty, North Webster, Ind., 1968-80; v.p Carefree Travel Inc., Chgo., 1973-80; bd. dirs. Countin[g] House Bank, North Webster and Warsaw, Ind., 1972-80. Author: (under pseudonym Justin Lee) unaccus tomed as i am, 1974. Mem. Riley Meml. Hosp. Assn Indpls., 1957-80; treas., mem. exec. com. local counc[il] Boy Scouts Am., Marion, Ind., 1948-57; bd. dirs Kiwanis Ind. Found., Shelbyville, 1957-62, pres., 1962-71, North Manchester Community Found., Futur[e] Farmers of Am. Found., Indpls., Kiwanis Interna[t.] Found., Chgo., 1970-73, Internat. Palace of Spor[ts] Found., North Webster. Mem. Internat. Farm Equip ment Mfrs. Assn. (dir. St. Louis 1952-54, internat. pre[s.] 1954-55), Boating Industry Assn., Chgo., Nort[h] Manchester C. of C. (pres. 1944), Mason (32 deg Shriner), Kiwanis (internat. trustee 1966-74, internat pres. 1972-73). Republican. Mem. Brethren Ch. Home: North Webster Ind. Died Dec. 13, 1980; interre[d] Fairview Cemetery.

BAILEY, CLEVELAND MONROE, congressman; b St. Mary's, W.Va., July 15, 1886; s. Albert and Mar[y] Jane (Stead) B.; m. Maud Agatha Rigby, Dec. 25, 1908 children: Joslyn Rigby, Wanda Fern, Agatha Baile[y] Massie, Audrey Lee Bailey Zakaski, Jared Blackwel[l] Donald C. Student, West Liberty State Coll., Genev[a] Coll., Beaver Comml. Coll. Clk. Jones-Laughlin Ste[el] Co., Pitts., 1908-10; high sch. prin., dist. supt. sch[s.] 1910-18; editor daily newspaper, Clarksburg (W.Va Pub. Co., 1918-33; asst. state auditor, 1933-41; state di[r.] budget, 1941-44; mem. 79th Congress from 3d W.Va dist., 1945-47, 81st-87th Congresses from 3d W.Va dist.; state tax statistician, 1947-48. Dist. clk. draft bd 1917-18. Mem. Coun. State Gkovts., Nat. Assn. Sta[te] Auditors, NEA, Nat. Assn. Sch. Fin. Officers, Kiwanis Elks, Knights of Pythias. Democrat. Home: Clark sburg W.Va. †

BAILEY, EDD HAMILTON, railroad official; b Elmo, Mo., Sept. 13, 1904; s. Larkin A. and Iol[a] (Hamilton) B.; m. Mabel Lavinia Parker, May 24, 1926 children: Hugh Parker, Laura May Bailey Richard son. Grad. high sch. With Union Pacific R.R., fro[m] 1922, succesively car checker mech. dept., transp. dep[t.] brakeman. trainmaster, asst. supt., supt., gen supt., ge[n.] mgr. Northwestern dist., 1922-53, gen. mgr. Easter[n] dist., 1954-57, v.p. ops., 1957-64, pres., 1965-71, chi[ef] exec. officer, 1965-70, also bd. dirs. Mem. Omaha C. o[f] C., Masons, Shriners. Republican. Methodist. Hm[e:] Omaha Nebr. Died Sept. 11, 1988.

BAIN, READ, professor of sociology; b. Woods, Oreg Oct. 20, 1892; s. Alexander Thomas and Fanny Ma (Fletcher) B.; m. Florence Virginia Davis, July 14, 192[5] 1 dau., Sheila. AB, Willamette U., 1916, LLD, 194[1] AM, U. Oreg., 1921; PhD, U. Mich., 1926; student, U Chgo., 1922. Tchr. Oreg. high schs., 1916-20; asst. pro[f.] sociology U. Oreg., 1921-23; fellow U. Mich., 1923-24 asst. prof. U. Wash., 1924-27; assoc. prof. of sociolog[y] Miami U., Oxford, Ohio, 1927-29, prof. of sociology from 1929; tchr. U. So. Calif., summer 1927, U. Tex summer 1929, Brigham Young U., summer 1933, U Minn., summer 1934; vis. prof. Harvard U., 1937-39, U Idaho, 1938, U. Wash., 1946, Reed Coll., 1947-4[8] Humboldt State Coll., 1953. Author: A Socialize[d] State, 1921; editor and contbr.: Trends in America[n] Sociology, 1929; contbr.: Social Progress and Soci[al] Process, 1933, Fields and Methods of Sociology, 193[4] Marriage and the Family, 1942, Marriage, Family an[d] Parenthood, 1948, Mensch Geschlecht, Gesellschaf[t] 1954, Einmal Eins de Glücklichen Lebens, 1955; edito[r] Critiqes of Research in Social Science, 3 vols., 1939-4[?] editor in chief: Am. Sociol. Rev., 1938-42; poetry edito[r] The Humanist, 1953-57, contbg. editor, from 1957. 2[d] lt., flying instr., U.S. Army, 1918-19; mem. Office[rs] Res., 1919-34. Mem. AAAS, AAUP, Am. Sociol. So[c.] (1st v.p. 1944), Sociol. Rsch. Assn. (exec. com., pre[s.] 1945), Ohio Valley Sociol. Soc. (pres. 1934), Alph[a] Kappa Delta (nat. pres. 1930-34). Home: Oxford Ohio.

BAIONE, LUKE A., banker; b. N.Y.C., Aug. 23, 192[?] s. Dominick and Mary (Marotta) B.; m. Juliet F. Bu lard, Aug. 26, 1944; children: Mary, Dominick. B.B.A CCNY, 1942. With Crossland Savs. FSB (former revoort Savs. Bank and Met. Savs. Bank), Bklyn., from 946; pres. Crossland Savs. FSB (formerly Brevoort avs. Bank and Met. Savs. Bank), 1969-71, chmn. bd., om 1971, dir., from 1967; dir. Savs. Banks Trust Co.; em. Bklyn. adv. bd. Mfrs. Hanover Trust Co. bd. rs. St. Francis Coll., Bklyn. Bur. Community Services; em. bishop's lay com. Diocese of Bklyn. Served with SAAF, 1942-46. Decorated Bronze Star. Mem. Nat. ouncil Savs. Instns., Savs. Banks Assn. (dir.). Clubs: ichmond County Country, Brooklyn, Metropolitan. ome: Staten Island N.Y. Died Jan. 6, 1989, buried oravian Cemetery, S.I., N.Y.

AIRD, FREDERICK H., railroad executive; b. Buflo, Aug. 14, 1892; s. Fred Holmes and Blanche laxwell) B.; m. Ruth Llewellyn, Apr. 9, 1921; chilen: Richard Llewellyn, Beverly Maxwell. Student ib. schs., Buffalo. Operating dept. Lake Shore & ich. So. Ry., Buffalo, 1909-13, passenger traffic dept., 913-16, city passenger agt., 1916-20; with N.Y.C. R.R., nce 1920; with N.Y.C. R.R., Cleve., 1920-29, div. assenger agt., 1929-30, asst. gen. agt., 1930-32; asst. n. agt. N.Y.C. R.R., Cin., 1932-34, gen. passenger t., 1934-37, asst. passenger traffic mgr., 1937, pasnger traffic mgr., 1937-40; gen. passenger traffic mgr. .Y.C. R.R., N.Y.C., 1940-51, asst. v.p. passenger affic, N.Y., 1951-56, asst. v.p. passenger sales and rvice, N.Y., from 1956. Served as 2d lt., 307th achine Gun Bn., 78th div. A.E.F., WWI. Mem. Am. assengers Traffic Officers (pres. 1955), Union League, iverside Yacht clubs. Home: Riverside Conn. †

AIRD, HENRY WELLES, III, pediatric neurologist; Fort Leavenworth, Kans., Oct. 10, 1922; s. Henry elles and Elizabeth (Tower) B.; m. Eleanora C. ordon, Apr. 21, 1950; children: Henry Welles IV, ouglas G., Bruce C., Matthew C. BS, Yale U., 1945, D, 1949. Fellow, resident neurology and pediatrics emple U. Sch. Medicine, Phila., 1950-53; faculty pedirics Temple U. Sch. Medicine, 1953-87, assoc. prof., 963-68, prof. pediatrics, 1968-84; practice medicine ecializing in pediatric neurology Phila., 1953-87; atnding pediatrician St. Christopher's Hosp. for Chilen, Phila., 1966-84. Author: The Child with Convulons, 1972, Neurologic Evaluation of Infants and Chilen, 1983; Mem. editorial bd.: Devel. Medicine and ild Neurology, 1971-87, editor, 1977-87; contbr. arles to profl. jours. Served to capt. M.C. AUS, 1950- . Mem. Soc. Pediatric Research, Am. Acad. Pediacs, Am. Acad. Cerebral Palsy. Home: Wynnewood . Died Apr. 7, 1987; buried Rosehill Cemetery, olumbia, Tenn.

AIRD, JULIAN BRADEN, banker; b. St. Paul, Nov. , 1892; s. John and Etta (Redington) B.; m. Helen all, Nov. 29, 1916; children: Duncan H., John B., Jane iird Evans. PhB, Yale U., 1915. With Nat. City ank of N.Y., 1915-17, Nat. City Co., St. Paul Office, 919-20; with First Nat. Bank of St. Paul and affiliated s., 1920-57, v.p., 1936, pres., 1945-54, chmn. bd., 954-57, from 1961; under sec. for monetary affairs easury Dept., 1957-61; bd. dirs. Discount Corp. of Y., 1st Bank Stock Corp., First Trust Co. (St. Paul). es. Amherst H. Wilder Found., St. Paul. With U.S. rmy, 1918-19. Mem. Reserve City Bankers Assn., innesota Club (St. Pul), Century Assn. (N.Y.C.). ome: Saint Paul Minn. †

AIRD, WILLIAM BRITTON (BIL BAIRD), pupteer; b. Grand Island, Nebr., Aug. 15, 1904; s. Wilm Hull and Louise (Hetzel) B.; m. Evelyn Schwartz, 32 (div. 1934); m. Cora Burlar, Jan. 13, 1937 (dec. ec. 1967); children: Peter Britton, Laura Jenne Baird; Patricia Courtleigh, June 1969 (div. 1972); m. sanna Lloyd, Dec. 1974 (div. 1984); 1 dau., adeleine. AB, U. Iowa, 1926. toured, India, Nepal, ghanistan for; State Dept., 1962, Russia, 1963; toured, dia and Turkey for; U.S. AID, 1970. Began with, ny Sarg Marionettes, 1928-33; started: Bil Baird's arionettes at, Chgo. World's Fair, 1934; appeared in: udeville, nightclubs, 4 Broadway shows including egfeld Follies, 1943-44, Flahooley, 1951; produced: udeville, nightclubs, 4 Broadway shows including Ali ba and the Forty Thieves, 1956; Davy Jones' Locker, 59, Man in the Moon, 1963, Chrysler Show Go ound, N.Y. World's Fair, 1964-65; Puppet sequence, ker Street, 1965, govt. films, World War II; films rty Lines, 1946, Telezonia AT&T, 1949, Strange Case osmic Rays, 1953; starred in: films H.B.O. Spl. Puppet evue, 1979; produced: TV series for CBS Snarky rker, 1950-51; Whistling Wizard, 1951-52, Bil Baird ow, 1953; appeared on: Morning Show, 1954; apared in: Peter and the Wolf, 1958, 59-60, Sorcerer's pprentice, 1959, Winnie the Pooh, 1960, O'Halloran's ck, 1961; film The Sound of Music, 1965; opened: ith Cora Baird) Bil Baird Theater, N.Y.C., 1967; esented: People Is, 1967, Winnie the Pooh, 1967-68, izard of Oz, 1968-69, Sultan of Tuffet, 1969-70, Ali ba, 1970-71, Peter and the Wolf, 1971-72, Davy nes' Locker-Band Wagon revue, 1972-73; produced: nocchio, 1973-74, Alice in Wonderland, 1975, Winnie Pooh, 1975-76, Once Upon A Dragon at Busch rdens, 1977-78, Histoire du Soldat, films for, Social curity Adminstrn., 1973, over 400 commls.; Author: e Art of the Puppet, 1966, Puppets and Population, 69. Del. Planned Parenthood Fedn., London, 1972; dirs. World Edn., Presidium Unima. Lt. O.R.C., 26. Recipient Jennie Heiden award for excellence in profl. children's theater Am. Theater Assn., 1974. Mem. Internat. Puppet Fedn. (dir.), Nat. Acad. TV Arts and Scis. (gov. 1957-61), Sigma Chi, Omicron Delta Kappa. Clubs: Lotos, Salmagundi. Home: New York N.Y. Died Mar. 18, 1987; cremated.

BAIRD, WILLIAM CAMERON, foundry executive; b. Buffalo, Apr. 20, 1907; s. Frank B. and Flora (Cameron) B.; m. Marjorie B. Mitchell, July 19, 1930 (div. 1945); 1 child, Barbara (Mrs. Joseph Jay Palladino). Grad., Phillips Exeter Acad., 1925; BA, Williams Coll., 1929; LHD, D'Youville Coll., 1979, SUNY-Buffalo, 1984. Treas. Buffalo Pipe & Foundry Corp., 1930-49, pres., 1949-67, chmn. bd., 1967-72; chmn. bd. Gruber Supply Corp., 1973-85; pres., chief exec. officer Central Foundry Co., 1966-67; dir. Mfrs. & Traders Trust Co., 1937-77, Cathedral Sq., Inc. Chmn. Peace Bridge Authority, 1939-60; Pres. Brent Manor, Inc., 1967-70, Niagara Frontier Housing Devel. Corp., 1968-70, Boys' Clubs of Niagara Frontier, 1956-58; bd. dirs. Boys' Clubs of Buffalo, 1933-83, pres., 1962-63; chmn. council State U. Buffalo, 1970-77; Trustee Community Chest; bd. dirs. Forest Lawn Cemetery, Millard Fillmore Hosp., 1937-83. Served to lt. comdr. USNR. Recipient Bishop's Cross Diocese Western N.Y., 1963; Canisius Coll. Disting. award, 1969; Red Jacket award Buffalo Hist. Soc., 1975; Chancellor's Medal State U. Buffalo, 1978; Disting. Citizen award SUNY; named Man of Year Buffalo Evening News, 1969; named Man of Year Buffalo C. of C., 1977. Mem. Soc. Alumni Williams Coll. (pres. 1955-56), C. of C. (past pres.), Delta Upsilon. Episcopalian (dep. gen. conv. 1937, 40, 49, 52, 61, 67, 69, 70, ch. warden). Clubs: Buffalo, Buffalo Yacht, Buffalo Canoe, Buffalo; Williams (N.Y.C.). Home: Williamsville N.Y. Died Jan. 31, 1987; buried Forest Lawn Cemetery.

BAKER, A. B., neurologist; b. Mpls., Mar. 27, 1908; s. Solomon and Molly (Greenspan) B.; m. Rose Witzman, Aug. 6, 1933; children: Lowell Howard, Elaine Frances, Eleanor Jean, Judith Ann. BA, U. Minn., 1928, BS, 1929, MB, 1930, MD, 1931, MS, 1932, PhD, 1934. Diplomate Am. Bd. Psychiatry and Neurology. Intern Robert Packer Hosp., Sayre, Pa., 1930-31; clin. asst. in neuropsychiatry U. Minn., 1934-36, instr. in neuropsychiatry, 1936-37, asst. prof., 1937-40, assoc. prof., 1940-47, prof. neurology, 1947-88, Regents' prof. neurology, 1973-76, prof. emeritus, 1976-88; dir. dept. neurology, 1946, head dept., 1968-76; spl. cons. USPHS Neurol Inst.; council Nat. Inst. Neurol Diseases and Blindness. Editor: Clinical Neurology, 4 vols., 1962, 3d edit., 3 vols., 1971. Felow Am. Acad. Neurology (past pres.); mem. AMA, Am. Neurol Assn. (past pres.), Epilepsy Found. Am. (past chmn. bd.), Am. Assn. Neuropathologists, Am. Assn. Expt. Pathology, Minn. Soc. Neurology and Psychiatry, Minn. Pathol. Assn., Phi Beta Kappa, Sigma Xi, Alpha Omega Alpha. Home: Minneapolis Minn. Died Jan. 18, 1988.

BAKER, CARLOS HEARD, educator, author; b. Biddeford, Maine, May 5, 1909; s. Arthur Erwin and Edna May (Heard) B.; m. Dorothy Thomasson Scott, Aug. 22, 1932; children: Diane, Elizabeth, Brian. AB, Dartmouth Coll., 1932, LittD, 1957; AM, Harvard U., 1933; PhD, Princeton U., 1940; HHD, U. Maine, 1974; LHD, Monmouth Coll., 1977. Tchr. English Thornton Acad., Saco, Maine, 1933-34, Nichols Sch., Buffalo, 1934-36; mem. faculty Princeton U., 1937-87, prof. English, 1951-77, emeritus, 1977-87, dept. chmn., 1952-58, 74-75; Fulbright lectr. Oxford U., 1957-58; Guggenheim fellow, 1965-66. Author: Shelley's Major Poetry, 1948, Hemingway: The Writer as Artist, 1952, TheEchoing Green: Essays by Carlos Baker, 1984; (novels) A Friend in Power, 1958, The Land of Rumbelow, 1963, The Gay Head Conspiracy, 1973; (poems) A Year and a Day, 1963; (biography) Ernest Hemingway: A Life Story, 1969; (short stories) The Talismans and Other Stories, 1976; editor: Wordsworth's Prelude, etc., 1948, Shelley's Poetry and Prose, 1950, Fielding's Joseph Andrews, 1960, Hemingway and His Critics, 1961, Keats's Poetry and Letters, 1962, Hudson's Green Mansions, 1963, Coleridge's Poetry and Prose, 1965, Ernest Hemingway Selected LEtters 1917-61, 1981; (with others) American Issues, 1941, Major English Romantic Poets, 1957, Modern American Usage, 1966; contbr. Dictionary American Biography, Literary History of U.S., various periodicals, newspapers. Mem. AAUP, MLA, Century Assn., Phi Beta Kappa, Theta Delta Chi. Home: Princeton N.J. Died Apr. 18, 1987; buried Princeton, N.J.

BAKER, CHET, trumpeter, singer; b. Yale, Okla., Dec. 23, 1929. Student, El Camino Coll., 1948-50. Jazz trumpeter, singer 1952-88. Trupmteter with marching and dance bands before 1948; played at Bop City, San Francisco, 1950-52; musician with Charlie Parker, 1952, Gerry Mulligan Quartet, Lee Konitz, Art Pepper, coleader band with Russ Freeman; rec. artist: (with Charlie Parker) Bird on the Coast, (with Art Pepper) Playboys, (with Paul Bley) Diane, (solo albums) Chet Baker in Paris, Peace, The Touch of Your Lips, Daybreak, This is Always. With U.S. Army, 1946-48, 50-52; mem. 298th Army Band, Berlin, Federal Republic of German, also Presidio Army Band, San Francisco. Recipient Down Beat Critics poll, 1953, 54, Met. poll, 1954-55, Melody Maker poll, 1955, German Jazz Echo poll, 1956, 58, Playboy poll, 1958. Died May 13, 1988.

BAKER, EVERETT G., railroad official; b. Poole, Ky., Dec. 19, 1891; s. Nelson Grant and Martha Anna (Allen) B.; m. Gertrude May Marks, Dec. 23, 1914; children: Dorothy Louise Baker Walker, Virginia Mary Baker Figgemeier, Betty Ann Baker Kirkpatrick. With St.L.-S.F. R.R., from 1914, beginning as sta. passenger agt. and ticket clk., St. Louis, becoming passenger traffic mgr., 1944, gen. passenger traffic mgr., 1947-50, gen. traffic mgr., 1950-54; v.p. fiscal St.L.-S.F. R.R., N.Y.C., 1954-57; v.p. hdqrs. St.L.-S.F. R.R., Birmingham, Ala., from 1957. Bd. dirs. St. Louis Youth Activities Coun., 1948-49. Mem. Nat. Freight Traffic Assn., Fedn. for Ry. Progress, Am. Assn. Passenger Rate Men, Nat. Def. Transp. Assn., Am. Assn. R.R. Ticket Agts. (hon.), Am. Soc. Traffic and Transp. Inc., Am. Assn. Passenger Traffic Officers (pres. 1951-52), Ala. R.R. Assn., Fla. R.R. Assn., Ala. C. of C., Birmingham C. of C., Westborough Countrdy Club (pres. 1949), Sertoma Civic Club (pres. St. Louis 1938-39), Passenger Traffic Club (St. Louis), Traffic Club (Kansas City, Mo.), Passenger Traffic Club (New Orleans), The Club, Downtown Vestavia Club, Masons, Kiwanis, Delta Nu Alpha. Baptist. Home: Birmingham Ala. †

BAKER, JAMES ADDISON, JR., lawyer, banker; b. Houston, Nov. 3, 1892; s. James Addison and Alice (Graham) B.; m. Ethel Bonner Means, Aug. 4, 1917; children: James Addison III, Bonner Means Moffitt. AB, Princeton U., 1915; LLB, U. Tex., 1917. Bar: Tex. 1919. Pvt. practice Houston, from 1919; sr. ptnr. Baker, Botts, Shepherd & Coates, Houston; pres., dir. Graham Realty Co., Houston; adv. dir., chmn. exec. com. Tex. Nat. Bank Commerce, Houston; pres., dir. Trinity Petroleum Trust. Trustee Norman Meldrum Children's Libr. Fund, McManis Mission Tust. Served from 2d lt. to capt. 359th Inf., 90th Div., U.S. Army, 1917-19. Decorated comdr. Brit. Empire (hon.). Mem. English-Speaking Union (dir.), C. of C. (past dir., treas.), Am., Houston bar assns., Ex-Student's Assn. U. Tex., Eagle Lake Rod and Gun Club, River Oaks Country Club, Houston Country Club, Houston Club (Houston), Phi Delta Theta. Home: Houston Tex. Deceased.

BAKER, REX GAVIN, lawyer; b. Big Valley, Tex., Aug. 29, 1891; s. John Berrien and Octavia (Weaver) B.; m. Edna Estelle Heflin, Aug. 16, 1917; children: Robert H., Rex Gavin, John H., Elizabeth Ann. AB, U. Tex., 1917, LLB, 1917. Bar: Tex. 1916. Practiced in Beaumont, Tex., 1919-20; mem. law dept. Humble Oil & Refining Co., Houston, 1920-56, gen. counsel, 1943-56, v.p., 1951-56, also bd. dirs.; bd. dirs. Humble Pipe Line Co. Mem. Tex. Commn. on Higher Edn.; chmn. Com. 75 U. Tex.; trustee Houston Bapt. Coll. Mem. Am. Petroleum Inst., Tex. Bar Assn., Houston Bar Assn., Houston Club, River Oaks Country Club, Friar Soc., Phi Beta Kappa. Democrat. Baptist. Home: Houston Tex. †

BAKER, WAKEFIELD, business executive; b. San Francisco, Dec. 22, 1892; s. Wakefield and Coralie (Thomas) B.; m. Margaret Madison, Sept. 7, 1921; children: Wakefield, Joan (Mrs. Robert B. Linscott), Cynthia (Mrs. Robert B. Linscott). Grad., Phiilips Exeter Acad.; student, Harvard, 1915. Pres., dir. Baker & Hamilton, from 1935, Payne's Bolt Works, from 1949, 91 Land Co., from 1933, Bollibokka Land Co.; dir., mem. exec. com. Pacific Cement & Aggregates, Fiberboard Paper Products Corp.; bd. dirs. Baker Estates Co., W.P. R.R. Co., Wells Fargo Bank-Am. Trust Co. Mem. San Francisco Distbrs. Assn. (dir.), Pacific Union Club, Bohemian Club (San Francisco), Burlingame (Calif.) Country Club. Home: San Rafael Calif. †

BAKER, WARREN LOWE, engineer, government official; b. Washington, May 9, 1892; s. Charles Ayres and Emma Brooks (Knapp) B.; m. Myrtle Richards, June 15, 1911; 1 son, Charles Ayres. BA M.E., Cornell U., 1911. Pres. Baker-Hopkins Co., Balt., 1911-13; engr. Vacuum Oil Co. (later Socony Vacuum Oil Co. Inc.), Phila., 1919-20; gen. sales and advt. mgr. Glenn L. Martin Co., Balt., 1929-33; engr. Socony-Vacuum Oil Co. Inc., 1933-43; gen. mgr. aviation dept. Socony-Vacuum Oil Co. Inc., N.Y.C., from 1943; formerly fuel specialist on aviation Dept. of Def.; dep. dir. Office Tech. Svcs., Air Rsch. and Devel. Command, Dept. of Def. from 1956. Exec. com., v.p. and bd. dirs., chmn. fuels and lubricants com. (aviation sect.), dir. aviation sect. N.Y. Bd. of Trade Inc. Served with French Fgn. Legion and Lafayette Escadrille, 1915-16; capt. USAAF. 1917-19. Decorated Croix de Guerre with 2 palms, DFC, Order of Leopold of Belgium; del. to 4th, 5th and 6th Pan. Am. Union Confs., Washington, 1929, 30, 31. Mem. SAR, Wings Club, Air Power League, Whitehall Club (N.Y.C.), Westchester Country Club (Larchmont); Bonnie Briar Country Club (Westchester), Colony Club (Bronxville), Delta Kappa Epsilon. Republican. Home: Baltimore Md. †

BAKER, WILLIAM C., railway executive; b. Balt., Feb. 18, 1891; s. Henry and Josephine (Haffer) B.; m. Elizabeth Gauche, May 11, 1935; children: W. Stuart, L. Doris, J. Elbert, Jeanne Ann. Student, pub. schs., Balt., Balt. Bus. Coll. Mem. clerical staff Baltimore & Ohio R.R., Balt., 1906-17, asst. train master, 1917-24, train master, 1924-26, asst. supt., 1926-29, supt., 1929-42, gen. supt. transp., 1942-46, gen. mgr., 1946-48, asst. v.p. ops. and maintenance, 1948-49, v.p. ops. and maintenance, from 1949. Mem. Masons, Baltimore Country Club. Democrat. Episcopalian. Home: Baltimore Md. †

BAKER, WOOLFORD BALES, biology educator; b. Las Vegas, N.Mex., Dec. 30, 1892; s. Carey Lavega and Susan Adeline (Coulter) B.; m. Bernice Hall, Dec. 21, 1916; children: Frances Adeline Baker Gladden, Woolford Bakes Jr. (dec.), Betty Lou Baker Prior. AB, Henderson-Brown Coll., 1913; AM, Emory U., 1920. Prof. sci. in acad. Henderson-Brown Coll., Arkadelphia, Ark., 1913-14, headmaster acad., 1914-15, prof. sci. in coll., 1915-19; instr. biology Emory U., 1919-22, asst. prof., 1922-24, assoc. prof., 1924-26, prof., from 1926, prof. biology, dir. Emory Mus., from 1955; acting prof. biology, head dept. Agnes Scott Coll., 1922-24; asst. biol. Columbia U., 1924-25, Inst. Woods Hole, summer 1926; on staff U. Va., summers 1952, 55; dir. Sci. Curriculum Conf. Ga., 1957, 58. Author: (with Lucien Harris Jr. and Wallace Rogers) Southern Nature Stories, Books I, II and III, 1938, 39, 40; contbr. sci. articles. Mem. com. tchr. certification Ga. Dept. Edn., Ga. Edn. Coun., So. States Ednl. Work Conf., 1959, steering com., 1959-60; vice chmn. Druid Hills Sch. Dist., 1937-46, chmn., 1946-47. With Students Tng. Corps, Ft. Sheridan, Ill., 1918. Recipient Meritorious Teaching award Southwestern Biologists, 1955; Rosenwald travelling fellow Kaiser Wilhelm Inst., Berlin, 1931-32. Fellow AAAS, Ga. Acad. Sci. (pres. 1944-42); mem. Am. Bot. Soc., AAUP, Torrey Bot. Club, Men's Garden Club, Ga. Naturalists Club, Emory Faculty Club, Phi Sigma, Kappa Phi Kappa, Sigma Xi, Phi Beta Kappa, Sigma Chi, Omicron Delta Kappa. Democrat. Methodist. Home: Atlanta Ga. †

BAKWIN, RUTH MORRIS, pediatrician; b. Chgo., June 3, 1898; d. Edward Morris and Helen (Swift) Nelson; m. Harry Bakwin, Feb. 2, 1925; children: Edward Morris, Patricia Anne Bakwin Selch, Barbara Swift Bakwin Rosenthal, Michael. BA, Wellesley Coll., 1919; MD, Cornell U., 1923; MA, Columbia U., 1929; postgrad., grad. schs., Vienna and Berlin, 1924-25. Diplomate Am. Bd. Pediatrics. Intern Fifth Ave. Hosp., 1923-24; instr. pediatrics Columbia U., 1927-30; instr. pediatrics NYU, 1930-40, asst. prof. clin. pediatrics, 1940-49, assoc. prof. clin. pediatrics, 1949-60, prof. clin. pediatrics, from 1961; asst. pediatrician Bellevue Hosp., 1927-43, asst. vis. physician, 1943-48, assoc. vis. physician children's medical svc., 1948-55, vis. physician, from 1955, dir. child guidance clinic, pediatric dept., 1931-65; asst. pediatrician Fifth Ave. Hosp., 1925-35; assoc. pediatrician N.Y. Infirmary, 1954, dir. emeritus, from 1955, trustee, from 1962, co-dir. dept. pediatrics, 1966-67; courtesy staff pediatrics Univ. Hosp. Author: Psychologic Care During Infancy and Childhood, 1942, Clinical Management of Behavior Disorders in Children, 1953, 60, 66, 72, Behavior Disorders in Children; also numerous papers. Mem. com. on child health White House Conf., 1960; mem. Nat. Com. Children and Youth, 1964-67; vol. pediatrician Care-Medico, Honduras, Indonesia. Recipient N.Y. Infirmary award of merit, 1960, Med. Woman of Yr. award N.Y. State Med. Soc., 1971. Mem. AAAS, Pan Am. Med. Women's Alliance, World Med. Assn., Am. Acad. Pediatrics (state chmn. 1965-67), Med. Women's Internat. Assn., AMA, N.Y. Acad. Medicine, Child Study Assn. Am., Soc. Rsch. Child Devel., Am. Med. Women's Assn. (Elizabeth Blackwell award 1950), Women's Med. Soc. N.Y. State, Women's Med. Soc. N.Y.C., Nat. Assn. for Mental Health, Inc. (adv. coun. on childhood mental illnesses, from 1962, dir. 1962-66), Cornell Women's Club of N.Y., Cosmopolitan Club, Wellesley Club, Alpha Phi (award 1952). Died July 31, 1985.

BALAGOT, REUBEN CASTILLO, anesthesiologist; b. Manila, July 28, 1920; came to U.S., 1949, naturalized, 1955; s. Pedro G. and Ambrosia (Castillo) B.; m. Lourdes Ramirez, July 10, 1946; children: Joseph, Edgar, Victoria Balagot Hermann, Ophelia Balagot Julien. B.S., U. Philippines, 1941, M.D., 1944. Diplomate: Am. Bd. Anesthesiology. Intern Philippines Gen. Hosp., Manila, 1943-44; resident U. Ill., Chgo., 1949-50; research fellow U. Ill., 1951, clin. instr., 1952-54, asst. prof., 1954-56, asso. prof., 1956-60, prof., from 1960, chmn. dept., 1974; chmn. dept. anesthesiology Chgo. Med. Sch., Downey, Ill., from 1975; head div. anesthesiology Grant Hosp., 1956-66, Ill. Masonic Hosp., 1966-67; pres. St. Luke's Hosp., Chgo., 1967-71, Hines (Ill.) VA Hosp, 1971-75; chmn. dept. anesthesiology Cook County Hosp., Chgo., from 1981. Contbr. articles to profl. jours. Served with AUS, 1944-46. Named distinguished physician of yr. Philippine Med. Assn., 1968; Outstanding Filipino Overseas in Med. Research award, 1977. Fellow Am. Fedn. Clin. Research; mem. AMA, A.C.S., AAUP, AAAS, N.Y. Acad. Sci., Ill., Chgo. med. socs., Am. Soc. Anesthesiologists, Ill. Soc. for Med. Research, Am. Writers Research, Am. Assn. Med. Instrumentation, Sigma Xi. Home: Chicago Ill. Died Apr. 16, 1986.

BALDRIDGE, C(YRUS) LE ROY, artist, author; b. Alton, N.Y., May 27, 1889; s. William and Charity (Burghdorf) B.; m. Caroline Singer, 1921. PhB, U. Chgo., 1911; studied art with Frank Holme, Chgo. Newspaper corr. German occupation of Belgium, 1914. Represented in permanent collections West African drawings, Samuel Insull Collection, Fisk U., Nashville; various paintings, exhbns. in Art Mus., N.Mex., 1956; artist Stars and Strips; illustrator spl. edits.; designer, typographer, art instr.; author: Code of Ethics for Graphic Arts Industry of the U.S. for the NRA, 1932, (autobiography) Time and Chance. With French Army, 1917, Am. Expeditionary Forces, 1918-19. Recipient Soc. Etchers publ. prize, 1938, Prairie Print Makers publ. prize, 1944, U. Chgo. Alumni citation for pub. svc., 1944, Recognition award China Relief Legion, 1944. Home: Santa Fe N.Mex. †

BALDRIGE, MALCOLM, former U.S. secretary of commerce; b. Omaha, Oct. 4, 1922; s. Howard Malcolm and Regina (Connell) B.; m. Margaret Trowbridge Murray, Mar. 31, 1951; children: Megan Brewster, Mary Trowbridge. BA, Yale U., 1944. With Eastern Co. (formerly Eastern Malleable Iron Co.), 1947-62; mng. dir. Eastern Co. (Frazer & Jones div.), 1951-57, v.p. co., 1957-60, pres., 1960-62; now dir.; exec. v.p. Scovill Mfg. Co., 1962-63, pres., chief exec. officer, 1963-69, chmn. bd., 1969-81; sec. commerce Washington, 1981-87; Co-chmn. Yale Nat. Bus. Gifts Com.; mem. Conn. Republican Fin. Com. Mem. Woodbury Rep. Town Com.; bd. dirs., past chmn. Waterbury ARC; trustee U.S. council Internat. C. of C. Served to capt., F.A. AUS, 1943-46. Mem. Bus. Council, Council for Fgn. Relations, Rodeo Cowboys Assn. Deceased.

BALDWIN, JAMES, writer; b. N.Y.C., Aug. 2, 1924; s. David and Berdis Emma (Jones) B. Ed. high sch. Author: Go Tell It on the Mountain, 1953; essays Notes of a Native Son, 1955; Giovanni's Room, 1958, Nobody Knows My Name, 1960, Another Country, 1962, The Fire Next Time, 1963, Blues for Mr. Charlie; play The Amen Corner, 1955, 1964, Going to Meet the Man, 1966, Tell Me How Long the Train's Been Gone, 1968, (with Margaret Mead) A Rap on Race, 1971, No Name In the Street, 1972, One Day When I Was Lost, 1973, If Beale Street Could Talk, 1974; Little Man, Little Man, 1975; essays The Devil Finds Work, 1976, Just Above My Head, 1979, The Evidence of Things Not Seen, 1985, Price of the Ticket, 1985; Jimmy's Blues: Selected Poems, 1986; contbr. numerous articles to nat. mags. Mem. nat. adv. bd. Congress Racial Equality, Nat. Com. for Sane Nuclear Policy, lectr. civil rights. Saxton fellow, 1945; Rosenwald fellow, 1948; Guggenheim fellow, 1954; Partisan Rev. fellow, 1956; recipient Nat. Inst. Arts and Letters award, 1956; Ford Found. grant-in-aid, 1959; recipient George K. Polk award, 1963. Mem. Actors Studio, Nat. Inst. Arts and Letters. Home: Saint Paul de Vence France. Died Nov. 30, 1987.

BALDWIN, RAYMOND EARL, senator, governor, judge; b. Rye, N.Y., Aug. 31, 1893; s. Lucian Earl and Sarah Emily (Tyler) B.; m. Edith Lindholm, June 29, 1922; children: Lucian Earl II, Raymond Earl, Tyler. AB, Wesleyan U., 1916, LLD, 1939; LLB, Yale U., 1921; LLD, Trinity Coll., 1940, Bloomfield Coll. and Sem., N.J., 1953, Fairfield U., 1953, U. Hartford, 1957; HHD, Lincoln Meml. U. Bar: Conn. 1921. Assoc. Philip Pond, lawyer, New Haven, 1922-24; assoc. Pullman & Comley, New Haven, 1924-28, mem. firm, 1928-39, 1941-43, 1947-49; pros. atty., judge Town Court of Stratford, 1927-33; mem. Ho. of Reps. Conn. Gen. Assembly, 1931, 1933; gov. of Conn. 1939-41, 43-46, mem. U.S. Senate, 1946-49; judge Supreme Ct. of Errors, Conn., 1949-59; chief justice 1959-1963; bd. dirs. Middlesex Mut. Assurance Co. Author: Let's Go Into Politics. Chancellor P.E. Ch., Diocese of Com., lay del. to Pan-Anglican Congress, 1954; trustee Wesleyan U., Conn. Coll. for Women, 1960-86. Served to lt. (j.g.) USN, 1917-18. Mem. University Club (Bridgeport); Hartford Club; Cupheag (Stratford); Masons, Delta Tau Delta, Phi Delta Phi. Republican. Home: Middletown Conn. Died Oct. 4, 1986; buried Indian Hill Cemetery, Middletown, Conn.

BALDWIN, ROBERT CHESTER, philosophy educator; b. Seymour, Conn., June 21, 1905; s. Herbert York and Ida Mae (Fisher) B.; m. Catherine A. Roche, June 23, 1932; children: Mary Baldwin Spector, James York, Robert Chester. AB, Wesleyan U., Middletown, Conn., 1929, MA, 1930; PhD, Yale U., 1932. Faculty U. Conn., Storrs, 1932-61, prof. philosophy, 1950-61, chmn. dept., 1932-61; prof. philosophy, chmn. dept. Am. Internat. Coll., Springfield, Mass., 1961-73, prof. emeritus, from 1973; vis. prof. Wesleyan U., 1946-47, Conn. Coll. Women, 1947, Springfield Coll., 1964-65. Editor: (with James A.S. McPeek) An Introduction to Philosophy Through Literature, 1950. Mem. Am. Philos. Assn., Metaphys. Soc. Am., Internat. Platform Assn., Conn. Acad. Arts and Scis., Realistic Philosophy Soc., Delta Sigma Rho, Phi Kappa Phi. Home: Storrs Conn. Died Nov. 11, 1988.

BALL, DUARD DANIEL, army officer; b. McAlester, Okla., Oct. 11, 1930; s. Lemuel Franklin and Bertha (Shepherd) B.; m. Marion Dods, May 4, 1957; children: Lisa E., Julia L., Daniel R. BS, Okla. A&M Coll., 1953; MBA, Babson Inst., Wellesley, Mass., 1962. Commd. 2d lt. U.S. Army, 1953, advanced through grades to maj. gen., 1979; service in Korea, Taiwan, Vietnam and Europe; comdg. gen., comdt. U.S. Army Ordnance and Chem. Center and Sch., Aberdeen (Md.) Proving Ground, 1977-79; comdg. gen. White Sands Missile Range, 1979-80; program mgr. XM-1 Tank System, Warren, Mich., 1980-83; comdg. gen. U.S. Army Tank Automotive Command, Warren, Mich., 1983-84; def. program cons. 1984-86. Decorated Legio of Merit, Soldier's medal, Bronze Star, Meritorious Se vice medal with 3 oak leaf clusters, Joint Service Com mendation medal, Army Commendation medal with oak leaf clusters. Mem. Assn. U.S. Army, Soc. Missil and Space Pioneers, Am. Def. Preparedness Assn., Soc Automotive Engrs. Home: Tucson Ariz. Died Apr. 1986; buried Arlington Nat. Cemetery, Arlington, Va

BALL, JOHN DUDLEY, JR., writer; b. Schenectady N.Y., July 8, 1911; s. John Dudley and Alena (Wiles B.; m. Patricia Hamilton, Aug. 22, 1942; 1 son, Joh David. B.A., Carroll Coll., Waukesha, Wis., 193 L.H.D., 1978. Mem. editorial staff Fortune mag., 1937 40; asst. curator Hayden Planetarium, N.Y.C., 1940-4 with Columbia Rec. Corp., 1945-47; music editor Bklyn Eagle, 1946-51; columnist N.Y. World Telegram, 195 52; dir. pub. relations Inst. Aero. Scis., 1958-61; edito in-chief DMS, Inc., 1961-62; author 1963-88. Autho Records for Pleasure, 1947, Operation Springboard 1958, Spacemaster I, 1960, Edwards: USAF Flight Te Center, 1962, Judo Boy, 1964 (Jr. Lit. Guild selection In the Heat of the Night, 1965 (Edgar award, Critic award, London, Acad. award Best Picture of Yr. 1968 Arctic Showdown, 1966, Rescue Mission, 1966, Th Cool Cottontail, 1966 (Mystery Guild selection Dragon Hotel, 1968, Miss 1000 Spring Blossoms, 196 (Readers Digest Condensed Book Club selection Johnny Get Your Gun, 1969, Last Plane Out, 1969, Th First Team, 1971, Five Pieces of Jade, 1972 (Detectiv Book Club selection), The Fourteenth Point, 1973, Mar One-The Dummy, 1974 (Detective Book Club selection The Winds of Mitamura, 1975, The Eyes of Buddha 1976, Phase Three Alert, 1977 (Mil. Book Club selec tion), Police Chief, 1977 (Detective Book Club selec tion), The Killing in the Market, 1978, The Murde Children, 1979, Then Came Violence, 1980, Trouble fo Tallon, 1981, Ananda, 1982, Chief Tallon and th S.O.R., 1984, Singapore, 1986, The Kiwi Target, 198 The Van, 1989; editor: Cop Cade, 1978, The Myster Story, 1976. Served with Air Transport Comman 1942-45. Mem. Mystery Writers Am., PEN, Baker S Irregulars, All Am. Karate Fedn., Japanese-Am. C tizens League, Calif. Aikido Assn. (black belt), Ox- Club, Mensa, Civil Air Patrol (lt. col.). Lutheran. Home: Encino Calif. Died Oct. 15, 1988.

BALL, MUNGER T(HOMAS), transportation execu tive; b. Elm Creek, Nebr., Jan. 14, 1886; s. Thomas and Eva Augusta (Munger) B.; m. Kate Harper, Jan. 1 1912; children: Leslie Munger, Ralph Harper, Doroth Belle. Student bus. adminstrn., Southwestern La. Inst 1901-02. Marine engr. Sabine, Tex., 1908; pres., ge mgr. Sabine Towing Co. Inc., Port Arthur, Tex., fro 1908, Sabine Transp. Co. Inc., Port Arthur, Tex., fro 1925; vice chmn. bd. dirs. First Nat. Bank; dir. Radi Sta. KPAC, Port Arthur; mem. U.S. delegation 19 Internat. Aviation Congress, Brussels, 1935; U.S. de Conf. Sci. Rsch. Conservation and Utilizatio Resources, Lake Success, N.Y., 1949. Contbr. articl to profl. publs. Mem. adv. com. Nat. Petroleum Coun Office Def. Transp., Naval Rsch. Adv. Coun., Weste Rivers panel USCG; dir. Lower Neches Valle Authority; v.p. Intracoastal canal Assn. La. and Tex chmn. bd., dir. Tex. Soc. Crippled Childen Inc.; vi chmn. Jefferson County chpt. Nat. Found. Infanti Paralysis; mem. bd. dirs. Port Arthur Salvation Arm mem. exec. com. United Fund, Port Arthur. Mem. Tex.,. Port Arthur (dir.) C.s of C., Tex: Water Ccon servation Assn. (dir.), Soc. Naval Architects, Nat. A Soc., Am. Assn. Port Authorities, Am. Assn. Sma Bus., Am. Waterways Operators, Am. Mcht. Marin Inst., Am. Petroleum Inst., Mason (33 degre K.C.C.H., K.T., past comdr., Shriner; past potentat Intendant gen. Red Cross Constantine; Jester, Grott Cabiri), Port Arthur Club, Shriners, Rotary (past pres. Propeller (past pres. Port of Sabine, past nat. v.p. Country Club, Hunting Club, Propeller (Port Arthur Town Club (Beaumont, Tex.), Austin Club (Tex. Whitehall Club (N.Y.C.), Athletic Club (Galveston Petroleum Club, Cork Club (Houston). Home: Po Arthur Tex. †

BALL, ROBERT HAMILTON, English educato theatre historian, author; b. N.Y.C., May 21, 1902; George Martin and Flora Cristene (Hill) B.; m. Esthe Marshall Smith, June 26, 1928; 1 child, Marcia M. Ba Weatherstone. AB, Princeton U., 1923, AM, 192 PhD, 1928. Instr. English and dramatic art Princeto (N.J.) U., 1927-31, asst. prof., 1931-39, curator Willia Seymour Theatre Collection, 1936-39; asst. prof. Englis Queen's Coll., Flushing, N.Y., 1939-43, assoc., prof 1944-51, prof., 1951-71, emeritus, from 1971, chm dept., 1941-47, 60-64, chmn. arts div., 1949-55; esta lished chair, 1st prof. of Am. Lit., U. Ankara, Turke 1955-56; vis. prof. U. Colo., NYU, UCLA. Author: Th Amazing Career of Sir Giles Overreach, 1939, (wit T.M. Parrott) A Short View of Elizabethan Drama, re edit., 1960, (with W.P. Bowman) Theatre Languag 1961, Shakespeare on Silent Film, 1968; editor: Th Plays of Henry C. DeMille, 1941; adv. bd. editor America's Lost Plays, 20 vols., 1939-42; contbr. to Co lier's Ency., Ency. Americana, also jours.; cons. theat terms Random House Dictionary of English Language Mem. arts adv. council Port Washington (N.Y.) Pu Library; adv. council Folger Shakespeare Library; pa dir. pub. relations Port Washington Civil Def.; pa mem. exec. bd. Port Washington br. ARC. Charlot

Elizabeth Proctor fellow Princeton U., 1926-27, Guggenheim fellow, 1946-47; Rockefeller Found. grantee, 1955-56. Mem. MLA, Shakespeare Assn. Am., Modern Humanities Rsch. Assn., Theatre Library Assn. (former chmn. theatre documents bd., former exec. bd.), AAUP (past chpt. pres.), Am. Soc. Theatre Rsch. (exec. com.), Internat. Fedn. Theatre Rsch. Home: Port Washington N.Y. Died Nov. 10, 1988.

BALL, VAUGHN CHARLES, educator, lawyer; b. St. Louis, Jan. 3, 1915; s. Charles Joseph and Bird (Vaughn) B.; m. Mary Ellen Miller, Aug. 31, 1940. JD, Washington U., St. Louis, 1937, AB, 1947. Bar: Mo. 1937, Ohio 1954. Pvt. practice St. Louis, 1937-42; atty. office of solicitor U.S. Dept. Labor, 1942-46; asst. prof. Washington U., St. Louis, 1946; asst. prof. Ohio State U., Columbus, 1948, assoc. prof., 1949-51, 53, prof., 1954-65; dep. div. counsel Office Price Stblzn., 1951; asst. gen. counsel Office Def. Moblzn., 1951-52, dep. gen. counsel, 1952; Legion Lex prof. U. So. Calif., Los Angeles, 1965-74; Thomas Reade Rootes Cobb prof. law U. Ga., Athens, 1974-85; mem. faculty Nat. Jud. Coll., 1966-75, Am. Acad. Jud. Edn., 1974-78. Author: Materials on Trial Practice, 1957, Materials on Selected Evidence Problems, 1966, rev. edit. (with Gilmore), 1973; author: (with others) McCormick, Hornbook on Evidence, rev. edit., 1972, supplement, 1978. With USAAF, 1943-46. Mem. Order of Coif. Home: Athens Ga. Died Dec. 2, 1985.

BALLANTINE, GEORGE W., banker; b. Denver, Aug. 17, 1892; s. George W. and Ida (Winne) B.; m. Marie Wilson, Mar. 14, 1917; 1 dau., Jane Ballentine McCotter. BCE, U. Mich., 1914. Bond salesman Internat. Trust Co., Denver, 1915-16, various positions, 1920-34, v.p., 1934-51, exec. v.p., dir., 1951-58; dir., sr. v.p. First Nat. Bank, Denver, from 1958; ptnr. Bosworth Chanute & Co., 1916-20. Home: Denver Colo. †

BALLER, WARREN ROBERT, educational psychologist; b. Trenton, Nebr., June 19, 1900; s. Albert Ernest and Mary Louise (Taylor) B.; m. Dorothy Gwendolyn Jensen, Mar. 15, 1941; children: William Warren, John Timothy, Elizabeth Claire. AB, York Coll., 1923; MA, U. Nebr., 1927, PhD, 1935; student, Columbia U., 1930, U. Minn., 1932; LLD, George Williams Coll., 1961. Prin. Callaway (Nebr.) High Sch., 1923-24; supt. schs. Cheney, Nebr., 1925-28; tchr. York Coll., 1928-34, dean, 1933-34; asst. prof. ednl. psychology U. Nebr., 1936-38, assoc. prof., 1938-43, prof., 1943-67, chmn., 1961-67, dir. jr. div., 1948-50; vis. prof. edn. U. Calif. at Los Angeles, 1955-57, prof. ednl. psychology Calif. Western U., 1967-68, U.S. Internat. U., San Diego, 1968-88; fellow gen. edn. bd. U. Chgo., 1940-41; vis. prof. George Peabody Coll., summer 1941, Northwestern U., summer 1941, U. Fla., summer, 1950, U. Calif., summer, 1951, U. Tex. spring, 1949; cons. child behavior and devel., Lincoln, 1938-88. Author: Psychology of Human Growth and Development, 1961, 2d edit., 1968, Readings in the Psychology of Human Growth and Development, 1962, 2d edit., 1969, Nocturnal Enuresis (Bedwetting)) Origins and Treatment, 1975. Mem. Am. Psychol. Assn., Soc. Profs. of Edn. (past pres.), Midwestern Psychol. Assn., Western Psychol. Assn., Sigma Xi. Democrat. Presbyterian. Home: Spring Valley Calif. Died Jan. 25, 1988; interred Blair, Nebr.

BALLS, ARNOLD KENT, biochemist; b. Toronto, Apr. 2, 1891; s. Alfred Z. and Amelia C. (Arnold) B.; m. Elizabeth Charlotte Franke, Apr. 2, 1922; 1 child, Kent F. BS, U. Pa., 1912; PhD, Columbia U., 1917; postgrad., Univs. Munich, Graz, Prague, 1928-30. Instr. bacteriology acting in charge dept. Columbia U., 1917; assoc. in chemistry U. Pa., 1922-27; Privatdocent fur Biochemie deut. tech. Hochschule, Prague, 1930-31; adj. prof. enzymology George Washington U., 1935-51; indsl. biochemist 1919-21; sr. chemist U.S. Dept. Agr., 1931-37, prin. chemist, 1937-40, head chemist, enzyme research lab., 1940-51; prof. biochemistry Purdue U., Lafayette, Ind., 1951-62, prof. emeritus, from 1962. Author numerous papers on sci. subjects and patents on microbiology, metabolism, enzyme action. Entire lab. cited for superior service by sec. of agr., 1949, 52. Del. of U.S. to fgn. sci. congresses, Rome, 1932, Paris, Madrid, 1993; spl. investigator for U.S. Dept. Agr., Hawaii, 1937, Germany and Switzerland, 1938, Puerto Rico, 1940-41, occupied territories in Europe, 1945. Recipient McCollum award, 1959; Nicholas Appert award, 1962; Charles F. Spencer award, 1962. Mem. Am. Soc. Biol. Chemists (sec. 1941-46, councillor-at-large 1946-49), Inst. of Food Technologists (councillor-at-large 1949-51), Soc. Exptl. Biology and Medicine (chmn. Washington sect. 1941), Washington Acad. Medicine, Nat. Acad. Sci., Sigma Xi, Cosmos Club. †

BALTZLY, ALEXANDER, history educator; b. Fond du Lac, Wis., Jan. 10, 1892; s. John and Mary W. (Baugher) B.; m. Josephine Tucker, Aug. 11, 1923; 1 child, Deborah. AB, Harvard U., 1912, AM, 1913; LHD (hon.), Pace Coll., N.Y.C., 1966. Assoc. editor Am. Lawe Tennis Assn., 1912-13; English and history instr. MIT, 1919-22; mem. faculty NYU, 1922-57, prof. emeritus, from 1957; adj. prof. Pace Coll., from 1959; vis. prof. Lehigh U., 1958, Gettysburg Coll., 1958-59; asst. dean Washington Sq. Coll., 1928-51. Author: (with F.A. Woods) Is War Diminishing?, 1915, (with J.F. Scott) Readings in European History since 1814, 1930, (with A.W. Salomone) Readings in Twentieth Century History, 1950. Home: New York N.Y. †

BAMBERGER, FRITZ, college administrator; b. Frankfurt-am-Main, Germany, Jan. 7, 1902; came to U.S., 1939; naturalized, 1944; s. Max and Amalie (Wolf) B.; m. Kate Schwabe, Mar. 21, 1933 (dec.); children: Michael Albert, Gay; m. Maria E. Nussbaum, Sept. 29, 1963. PhD, U. Berlin, 1923; DHL (hon.), Hebrew Union Coll., 1982. Research prof. Acad. for Jewish Research, Berlin, Germany, 1926-33; prof. philosophy Coll. Jewish Studies, Berlin, 1933-34; mem. Bd. Edn. for Jews, Berlin, 1934-38; pres. Jewish Tchrs. Coll. of Prussia; mem. Bd. Jewish Edn., Chgo.; mem. faculty Coll. Jewish Studies, 1939-44; dir. research Coronet and Esquire mags., 1942-48; editorial dir. Coronet mag., 1948-52, editor, 1952-56; exec. dir. Esquire and Coronet mags., 1956-61; cons. Esquire mag., 1962-71; prof. intellectual history, asst. to pres. Hebrew Union Coll., N.Y.C., 1962-79, emeritus prof., 1979-84; mem. exec. com. scholars. Inst. Advanced Studies in Religion and Humanities; v.p. Leo Baeck Inst. Author: Entstehung des Wertproblems, 1924, Moses Mendelssohn, 1929, Das System des Maimonides, 1935, Das neunte Schuljahr, 1937, Zunz's Conception of History, 1941, Leo Baeck: The Man and the Idea, 1958, The Philosophy of Julius Guttmann, 1960, Hebrew edit., 1976, Books are the Best Things, 1962; editor or compiler: Lehren des Judentums, 1928-30, Moses Mendelssohn's Gesammelte Schriften, 1929-32, rev. edit., 1971-81, Denkmal der Freundschaft, 1929, Das Buch Zunz, 1932, Herder's Blaetter der Vorzeith, 1936; contbr. articles to various publs. Mem. governing body World Union for Progressive Judaism; bd. dirs. Selfhelp Community Services, United Help. Home: New York N.Y. Died Sept. 22, 1984; buried N.Y.C.

BANCROFT, THEODORE ALFONSO, statistics educator; b. Columbus, Miss., Jan. 2, 1907; s. Frank Hammond and Laura Louise (Cox) B.; m. Lenore Springer, Dec. 1, 1933; children: Alice Muriel, Lenore Louise. B.A., U. Fla., 1927; M.A., U. Mich., 1934; Ph.D., Iowa State U., 1943. Teaching asst. math. Vanderbilt U., 1937-38; head math. dept. Mercer U., 1938-41; assoc. prof. math. U. Ga., 1946-47; dir. statis. lab. Auburn U., 1947-49; assoc. prof. Iowa State U., Ames, 1949; prof. Iowa State U., 1950-77, prof. emeritus, 1977-86, dir., head statis. lab., dept. stats., 1950-72; UN assignment, Middle East, India, 1954, Mexico, 1955, Univ. tng. command, Italy, 1945, Japan Soc. Promotion Sci. vis. prof., 1973; vis. prof. U. Philippines, 1973, Cath. U., Chile, 1975; Disting. vis. prof. San Diego State U., 1980. Author: (with R.L. Anderson) Statistical Theory in Research, 1952, Topics in Intermediate Statistical Methods, vol. 1, 1968; Editor: (with Kempthorne, Gowen, Lush) Statistics and Mathematics in Biology, 1954, 64; statistical papers in Honor of George W. Snedecor, 1971, (with C.P. Han) Statistical Theory and Inference in Research, 1981; contbr. articles to profl. jours., article to Ency. Americana. Recipient Wilton Park award Iowa State U., 1976. Fellow Am. Statis. Assn. (pres. 1970), Inst. Math. Statistics, AAAS; mem. Internat. Statis. Inst., Biometric Soc. (mem. council, past pres.), NRC, Sigma Xi, Phi Kappa Phi, Mu Sigma Rho (nat. dir.). Home: Ames Iowa. Died July 26, 1986.

BANEN, DAVID MERTON, physician; b. Kiev, Russia, June 1, 1904; came to U.S., 1906, naturalized, 1935; s. Harry and Lena (Hecht) B.; m. Ruth N. Schwartz, May 7, 1939; 1 dau., Elsa Harriet (Mrs. Revan A.F. Tranter). BS, U. Ill., 1926, MD, 1930. Diplomate: Am. Bd. Psychiatry and Neurology. Intern Cook County Hosp., Chgo., 1930-32; served as col., M.C. U.S. Army, 1935-38, 41-47, USPHS, 1938-41; chief of staff VA, Brockton, Mass., 1947-66; supt. Cushing Hosp., Mass. Dept. Mental Health, Framingham, 1966-75; asst. clin. prof. psychiatry Tufts U., 1953; del. White House Conf. on Aging, 1961, 71; mem. Calif. Gov.'s Council on Aging, 1976. Contbr. articles to profl. jours. Cons. Jewish Vocat. Service.; Mem. Mass. Commn. on Aging, 1968. Decorated Purple Heart, Bronze Star. Fellow Am. Geriatric Soc., N.E. Soc. Gerontologic Psychiatry, Am. Psychiat. Assn. (life); mem. AMA (life), No. Calif. Psychiat. Soc. Jewish (pres., chmn. bd. temple). Home: Walnut Creek Calif. Died Jan. 13, 1987; cremated.

BANK, ARNOLD, graphic artist, educator; b. N.Y.C., Mar. 31, 1908; s. Wolf and Rose (Springer) B.; m. Rose Sokolow, Oct. 18, 1931; 1 child, Stephen. Student, Art Students League, N.Y.C., N.Y. State U., 1935-38. Freelance designer, letterer 1935-86; art dir. promotion dept. Time Inc., 1941-47; tchr. art colls., N.Y. and Oreg., 1944-60; sr. Fulbright fellow Royal Coll. Art, London, 1954-57; prof. graphic arts Carnegie-Mellon U., Pitts., 1960-85. Author: Lettering Portfolio, 1951. Contbr. articles to profl. jours. Participant numerous exhbns. in graphic arts. Art commns. include Life Mag., Rockefeller Ctr. Credo (inscription), N.Y.C., P. Morgan Library, N.Y.C., others. Recipient spl. medal Type Directors Club, N.Y.C., 1979. Died Feb. 1986.

BANK, THEODORE PAUL, JR., anthropologist; b. Patterson, La., Aug. 31, 1923; s. Theodore Paul and Madlyn (Huber) B.; m. Janet Fowler, Sept. 1948 (div. Oct. 1953); 1 son, Theodore Paul; m. Shirley Waterman, May 1954 (div. Oct. 1962); m. Trina Paula Lindenstein, Apr. 20, 1963; 1 dau., Kristin Kara. Student (Harvard Club scholar), Harvard U., 1941-43; BS in Forestry, U. Mich., 1947, MS in Ethnobotany, 1950, postgrad. in anthropology, 1947-53. Field dir. Aleutian-Bering Sea Expdns. U. Mich., 1948-55, U.S. Office Naval Research, 1948-49; research assoc. Mus. Anthropology U. Mich., Ann Arbor, 1956-57; exec. dir. Am. Inst. Exploration Inc., Kalamazoo, The Dalles, Oreg., Dutch Harbor, Alaska, from 1954; asst. prof. anthropology Chgo. Tchrs. Coll. North, 1961-63; social research analyst Agnews State Hosp., San Jose, Calif., 1964-65; vis. lectr. anthropology Coll. San Mateo (Calif.), 1965-66; asst. prof. anthropology Seven Seas Div. Chapman Coll., 1967; asst. prof. social sci. Western Mich. U., Kalamazoo, 1967-73, assoc. prof. social sci., from 1973, chmn. world explorations program, from 1973; U.S. del., convenor symposium on ethnobotany SE Asia, 9th Pacific Sci. Congress, Bangkok, 1957; exec. producer ednl. TV series on non-Western World, 1968-69; conducted anthrop. expdns. to SE Asia, 1957, Argentina and W. Africa, 1967; expdns. to Aleutian Islands, 1948-54, from 1969; dir. Aleutian Bering Sea Insts. Program, from 1969; leader Joint Japanese-Am. expdns. to Aleutian Islands, from 1975; mem. sci. adv. bd. Am. Heritage Research, Calif., from 1974; hon. adviser Our World-Underwater, Chgo., from 1974; mem. adv. bd. Expdn. Tng. Inst., Boston, from 1976; leader Joint Brit.-Am. Expdn. to Bering Sea, 1977-78; lectr. various univs. U.S. and abroad. Author: Birthplace of the Winds, 1956, Student Manual for Cultural Anthropology, 1966, People of the Bering Sea, 1971, Ethnobotany as an Adjunct to Archaeology, 1977; (script and narration) Canoeing into the Past, 1979; contbg. editor Explorers Jour., from 1959, mem. editorial bd. from 1974; editorial adv. bd. Mariah mag., from 1976; assoc. editor Current Field Reports (Anthropology), from 1968; contbr. articles on Alaska, Aleutian Islands, Japan and others to various publs. Chmn. U.S. Com. for Clark Meml. Student Ctr., Hokkaido U., 1958-60. With USNR, 1945-46. Fulbright research scholar, vis. lectr. anthropology Hokkaido (Japan) U., 1955-56. Fellow AAAS, Am. Anthrop. Assn.; mem. Am. Inst. for Exploration Inc. (trustee), Pacific Sci. Assn. (chmn. sub-com. ethnobotany 1954-57), Soc. Am. Archaeology, Current Anthropology (assoc.), Am. Ecol. Soc., Polar Soc., Oceanic Soc., Japan Soc., Japan-Am. Soc. Sapporo, Internat. Platform Assn., Explorers Club (N.Y.C.), Harvard Club (Mich.), Sigma Xi, Phi Sigma. Home: Kalamazoo Mich. Deceased.

BANKS, EDWIN MELVIN, biological sciences educator; b. Chgo., Mar. 21, 1926; s. David Louis and Eleanor (Johnson) B.; m. Hilda Markoff, June 20, 1950; children: Daniel, Ronald, Ellen. PhB, U. Chgo., 1948, BS, 1949, MS, 1950; PhD, U. Fla., 1955. Asst. prof. biology U. Ill., 1955-60, assoc. prof., 1960-63, prof. ethology, head dept., from 1965; assoc. prof. zoology U. Toronto, 1963-65. Author: Vertebrate Social Organization, 1977, Animal Behavior, 1977; contbr. articles in field. With USNR, 1943-46. Guggenheim Found. grantee, 1977-78. Fellow AAAS, Animal Behavior Soc. (pres. 1972); mem. Am. Soc. Zoologists, Am. Soc. Mammalogists, Ecol. Soc. Am., Internat. Ethological Soc., Soc. Study of Aggression, Rotary, Sigma Xi. Jewish. Home: Champaign Ill. Died Mar. 24, 1985, buried Mt. Hope Cemetery, Champaign.

BANKS, VIRGINIA, artist; b. Norwood, Mass., Jan. 12, 1920; d. Henry Lewis and Ottilie (Rietzel) B. AB, Smith Coll., 1941; MA, State U. Iowa, 1944. Instr. art State U. Iowa, 1942-47, Albright Art Sch., 1947-48, U. Buffalo, 1947-48, N.Y. State Tchrs. Coll., 1947-48, U. Wash., 1949, Cornish Art Sch., Seattle, 1951-52; area chmn. capital campaign Smith Coll., 1968-70. One-woman shows include Grand Central Moderns, N.Y.C., 1950, 52, 56, 59, 65, Dusanne Gallery, Seattle, 1952, 58, Collectors Gallery, Bellevue, Wash., 1965, Foster-White Gallery, Seattle, 1977, 80; exhibited nat. and internat. shows 1946-85; represented in permanent collections, U. Ill., Seattle Art Mus., IBM Coll., U. Oreg., San Francisco Mus. Art, Springfield (Mo.) Art Mus., Davenport (Iowa) Mcpl. Art Gallery, Plattsburg (N.Y.) State Tchrs. Coll., State U. Iowa, U. Notre Dame, Cornell U., Rainier Nat. Bank, Peoples Nat. Bank, Seattle, Pacific NW Bell collection, Seattle, U. Wash. Med. Sch., Seattle, Duxbury (Mass.) Art Complex, Mass. Sheldon Meml. Art Gallery, U. Nebr., Lincoln, Ency. Brit. Collection Contemporary Am. Painting, Safeco Ins. Hdqrs., Seattle. Recipient award Pepsi-Cola Competition, 1948, Hallmark Internat. Art award, 1949. Mem. Smith Coll. Club (Seattle) (pres. 1960-61, hon. bd. mem. 1967-68), Alpha Phi Kappa Psi, Pi Lambda Theta. Home: Seattle Wash. Died Feb. 7, 1985; cremated Seattle, Wash.

BANKS, WILLIAM VENOID, lawyer, radio and TV executive; b. Geneva, Ky., May 6, 1903; s. Richard Dennis and Clara Ann (Barnett) B.; m. Rose Glassman, 1932; m. Ivy Burt, 1963; children: Tenicia Ann, Harumi, Alterio Alhanen. BA, Detroit Coll. Law, 1929; DD, Detroit Bapt. Coll., 1956; LLD, Detroit Coll. Law, 1968. Bar: Mich. 1930. Pvt. practice Detroit, 1929-50; supreme grand master Internat. Masons, 1950-85; pres. WGPR Radio, Detroit, 1964-85; pres., gen. mgr. TV 62, Detroit, 1975-85. Pres. 1st Rep. Dist., Detroit, 1974-77; del. Rep. Nat. Conv., 1972, 76. Recipient awards Ho. of Reps., 1973, U.S. Senate, 1974, Booker T. Washington Businssman's award, 1974, Trailblazer award

Assn. Bus. Sci. Engring. Professions, 1974, award Common Council of Detroit, 1975, others. Mem. Wolverine Bar Assn., Nat. Assn. Black Broadcasters (dir.), NAACP, Masons. Baptist. Home: Detroit Mich. Died Aug. 24, 1985.

BANNARD, WILLIAM NEWELL, III, investment banker; b. Hazelton, Pa., June 12, 1918; s. William Newell Jr. and Emily (Markle) B.; m. Marion H. Sutphen, Oct. 22, 1942; children: Marie S. (Mrs. Charles Lockwood), David N., Barbara M. (Mrs Christopher Haller). Grad., Hill Sch., 1937; BA, Yale U., 1941. With Graham, Parsons & Co., N.Y.C., 1946-50; v.p., chmn. exec. com. Am. Securities Corp., 1950-87, pres., dir. With USNR, 1942-46. Decorated Silver Star. Mem. Nat. Assn. Dealers (vice chmn. dist. bd.), N.Y. Soc. Security Analysts, Huntinton Country Club (dir.), Bond Club (gov.) (N.Y.C.), Mid-Ocean Club, Piping Rock Club, Kappa Beta Phi (mem. council), Chi Psi. Home: Cold Spring Harbor N.Y. Died Nov. 11, 1987.

BANNERMAN, ROBIN MOWAT, physician, educator; b. Alton, Eng., Feb. 2, 1928; came to U.S., 1963; s. Robert George and Charlotte (Mowatt) B.; m. Franca Angela Eleonora Vescia, Oct. 31, 1953; children: Catherine Eleanora, Francesca Mowat, Isabella Bianca. B.A., Christ Ch. Coll., Oxford U., Eng., 1949; B.M., B.Ch., Christ Ch. Coll., Oxford U., 1952, M.A., D.M., 1960; postgrad., St. Thomas' Hosp. Med. Sch., London, 1949-52. House officer St. Thomas' Hosp., London, 1952-54, med. registrar, 1955-57; fellow in medicine Washington U., St. Louis, 1957-58, Johns Hopkins U. Hosp., Balt., 1958-59; lectr. medicine, med. tutor Radcliffe Infirmary, Oxford U., Eng., 1960-63; assoc. prof. medicine SUNY, Buffalo, 1963-70, prof. medicine, 1970-85, prof. pediatrics, 1976-85; vis. prof. hematology St. Thomas' Hosp., 1971. Author: Thalassemia, A Survey, 1961. Mem. nat. med. adv. bd. Cooley's Anemia Found., 1964-85, March of Dimes, Western N.Y., 1966-85, others. Radcliffe traveling fellow, 1957-58; recipient Mod. Med. Monographs prize, 1961. Fellow ACP, Royal Coll. Physicians (London); mem. Brit., Am., Internat. socs. hematology, Cen. Soc. Clin. Research, Am. Soc. Human Genetics, Soc. Exptl. Biology and Medicine, Am. Fedn. Clin. Research, Brit. Med. Assn., AAAS. Home: Buffalo N.Y. Died Mar. 8, 1985, cremated.

BANNON, JOHN FRANCIS, clergyman, educator; b. St. Joseph, Mo., Apr. 28, 1905; s. William Joseph and Clara (Shortle) B. AB, St. Louis U., 1928, AM, 1929, STL, 1936; PhD, U. Calif., 1939; DHL, Rockhurst Coll., Kansas City, Mo., 1973. Ordained priest, Roman Catholic Ch., 1935. Entered SJ 1922; instr. history St. Louis U., 1939-41, asst. prof., 1941-44, assoc. prof., 1944-49, prof. history, 1949-73, prof. emeritus, 1973-86, chmn. dept. history, 1943-71; vis. lectr. in history Marquette U., summers 1936, 74, U. San Francisco, summers 1939, 47, Mount Saint Mary's Coll., Calif., summer 1964, U. Colo., Boulder, summer 1965, 74, U. Calif. at Santa Barbara, 1967-68, U. N.Mex., 1971-72, Utah State U., 1972, Marquette U., 1974, U. Colo., 1974; pres. Jesuit Hist. Conf., 1947-48; chmn. conf. on Latin Am. History, 1955; dir. Inst. on Fgn. Trade of Export Mgrs. Club of St. Louis. Author: Epitome of Western Civilization, 1942, Colonial North America, 1946, (with P.M. Dunne) Latin America: An Historical Survey, 1947, rev. edits. 1958, 63, 4th edit. (with R.R. Miller) 1977, History of the Americas, 2 vols., 1952, rev. edit. 1963, The Mission Frontier in Sonora, 1955, Nat. ETV series: The U.S.A., 1955, The Spanish Conquistadors, Men or Devils?, 1960, Bolton and the Spanish Borderlands, 1964, Indian Labor in the Spanish Indies, 1966, The Spanish Borderlands Frontier, 1970, The Missouri Province Society of Jesus: A Mini-History, 1976, Herbert Eugene Bolton: The Historian and the Man, 1978; editor The Hist. Bull., 1943-50; The American West series and reprint series, 1962-86; editorial bd. Hispanic Am. Hist. Rev., 1954-60; Manuscripta, 1957-86, Arizona and the West, 1959-73, St. Louis Archdiocesan Bicentennial Series, 1964-65, Red River Valley Hist. Rev., 1974-86, Am. Indian Quar., 1974-86, Western Hist. Quar., 1976-86. Mem. Am. Hist. Assn., Am. Cath. Hist. Assn. (v.p. 1972-73), Orgn. Am. Historians, Cath. Commn. Intellectual and Cultural Affairs, Acad. Am. Franciscan History (corr. mem.), St. Louis Council World Affairs (chmn. Inter-Am. div. 1949-62), Western History Assn. (exec. council 1962-69, pres. 1965-66), Alpha Sigma Nu, Phi Alpha Theta, Gamma Theta Upsilon, Phi Kappa Theta. Home: Saint Louis Mo. Died June 5, 1986; buried Calvary Cemetery, St. Louis.

BANTHIN, JOHN FREDERICK, mechanical engineer; b. N.Y.C., Oct. 19, 1897; s. John Frederick and Anna Marie (Geibner) B.; m. Clare P. Reuther, Nov. 8, 1923; children: John Frederick, Clifford Richard, Mary Ann Banthin Wood. BS in Mech. Engring., Pa. State U., 1921. Mech. engr. Gen. Electric Co., 1921-24; plant layout and prodn. engr. Gen. Motors Corp., 1924-27; with Ford, Bacon & Davis, cons. and mgmt. engrs., 1927-30; pres. Banthin Engring. Co., Bridgeport, Conn., 1930-78. Patentee high speed printing machinery. With A.C., U.S. Army, 1918-19. Fellow ASME (chpt. pres. 1946-47); mem. Am. Soc. Mil. Engrs., Am. Ordnance Assn., Nat. Aero. Assn., Conn. Bus. and Industry Assn., NAM, Bridgeport Mfrs. Assn., Aircraft Owners and Pilots Assn., Lions, Jesters, Shriners, Brooklawn Country Club, University Club. Home: West Redding Conn. Died Feb. 9, 1988; interred Mt. Grove Cemetery, Fairfield, Conn.

BARBEAU, ANDRE, physician, educator; b. Montreal, Que., Can., May 27, 1931; s. Antonio and Rachel (Jodoin) B.; m. Lise Trudeau, June 16, 1956; children: Claire, Claude, Michel, Dany. BA, U. Paris, 1948; MD, U. Montreal, 1956. Intern Hotel Dieu Hosp., Montreal, 1955-56, resident, 1956-57; resident U. Chgo.-Billings Hosp., 1957-59, Montreal Neurol. Inst., 1959-60; with dept. histology U. Montreal, 1960-61, dir. lab. neurology, 1961-67, prof. neurology, from 1970, chmn. dept. neurology, from 1976; dir. dept. neurobiology Clin. Rsch. Inst. Montreal, from 1967; prof. exptl. medicine McGill U., Montreal, from 1970. Editor 28 books; contbr. articles to profl. jours. Decorated officer Order of Can.; recipient Can. Mental Health Assn. award, 1965, United Parkinson Found. award of merit, 1965, Gold medal Can. Parkinson Found., 1965, Rsch. prize Assn. des Medecins de Langue Francaise du Canada, 1974, M. Piché prize, 1979, Pariseau prize French Can. Assn. Advancement Scis., 1980. Fellow Royal Coll. Physicians, Royal Soc. Can.; mem. Am. Acad. Neurology, Am. Neurol. Assn. Roman Catholic. Home: Montreal Can. ied Mar. 9, 1986; buried Côte des Neiges Cemetery, Montreal, Can.

BARBER, AZRO LUCIEN, lawyer; b. Syracuse, N.Y., May 5, 1885; s. Vincent A. and Rose (Fisher) B.; m. Laura Harton, Mar. 7, 1917; children: Rebecca Barber Sadler, Martha, Vincent Harton. AB, Syracuse U., 1907; LLB, George Washington U., 1912. Bar: Ark. 1914. Prin. Minetto (N.Y.) High Sch., 1907-09; clk. U.S. Civil Svc. Commn., Washington, 1909-14; ptnr. Barber, Henry & Thurman, Little Rock, Ark., from 1914. Del. Rep. Nat. Conv., 1940, 44, 48, 52; chmn. Ark. Rep. Com., 1953-54. Mem. ABA, Am. Coll. Trial Lawyers, Ark. Bar Assn. Home: Little Rock Ark. †

BARCLAY, ROBERT HAMILTON, consulting engineer; b. St. Louis, Aug. 10, 1887; s. Robert and Minnie Genie (Hamilton) B.; m. Bobbey Elizabeth Timberlake, Apr. 19, 1937. Student elec. engring., Washington U., St. Louis, 1906-08, 1911-12. Cert. Nat. Bur. Engring. Registration; lic. profl. engr., N.Y., Fla., Maine, Mich., Mo. Tex. Chief draftsman and supt. power plants and bldgs. Southwestern Bell telephone Co., St. Louis and kansas City Mo., 1908-11; asst. elec. engr. Kansas City Terminal Ry. Co., 1912-15, Bklyn. Rapid Transit Co., 1915-17; chief elec. engr. The Foundation Co., N.Y.C., 1917-22, Starrett & Van Vleck, architects, N.Y.C., 1922-24; elec. engr. Stone & Webster Engring. Corp., Boston, 1924-31; pres. McClelland Barclay Art Products Inc., Boston, 1931-34; regional dir. Fed. Power Commn., 1934-41; chief exec. officer in charge N.Y. Regional Office, chief elec. engr. The J.G. White Engring. Corp., N.Y.C., 1941-50, engring. mgr., 1950-53, v.p., dir., 1953-57; pvt. practice cons. engr. N.Y.C., from 1957. Fellow AIEE (life mem., mem. marine com., 1917-19, bd. of examiners from 1942, chmn. 1946-48), Radio Club Am., Inst. Elec. Engrs Gt. Britain (hon. sec. in U.S. from 1953), Engrs. Joint Coun. (vice chmn. com. on practice engring. 1957; mem. planning com. from 1958), Nat. Soc. Profl. Engrs., Engring. Socs. Libr. Bd., 1942-48 (chmn. 1946-48); mem. Soc. Am. Mil. Engrs., S.R., Soc. Colonial Wars, Com. on Profl. Recognition, Engrs. Coun. for Profl. Devel. from 1946 (chmn. 1949-53), Newcomen Soc., Washington Univ. Club (pres. 1934-35), Engineers Club, Midday Club, City Club (N.Y.C.), Masons, Theta Xi. Episcopalian. Home: New York N.Y. †

BARCLAY, THOMAS SWAIN, political scientist; b. St. Louis, Jan. 26, 1892; s. George Reppert and Lillie (Swain) B. AB, U. Mo., 1915, AM, 1916, LLD (hon.), 1962; PhD, Columbia U., 1924. Fellow U. Chgo., 1916-17; scholar in pub. law Columbia U., 1920-21; instr. polit. sci. U. Mo., 1920, asst. prof., 1922-26, assoc. prof., 1926-27; assoc. prof. Stanford U., 1928-37, prof., 1937-57; vis. prof. U. N.C., summer 1921, U. Mo., 1930, Syracuse U., 1931, U. Wash., 1935, 40, 57, Cornell U., 1936, 41, U. Minn., spring 1936, u. Idaho, summer 1946; cons. fellow Brookings Instn., 1931-33; acting prof. U. Mich., 1949-50, U. Ill., 1947-48; leader Des Moines Pub. Forums, 1936; mem. Alien Enemy Hearing Bd., Calif., 1942-45, Nat. Alien Enemy Hearing Bd., 1943-45; acting prof. Columbia U., 1950, mem. com. on award Bancroft Prizes, 1955-56; with internat. law div. Am. Commn. to Negotiate Peace, sec. to Henry White, Paris, 1919; mem. coun. Calif. Congl. Recognition Plan, 1958-70. Author: Liberal Republican Movement in Missouri, 1926, The Movement for Municipal Home Rule, 1943, A Home Rule Charter of 1876, 1962; mem. bd. editors Am. Polit. Sci. Rev., 1941-44, 47-50, Nat. Mcpl. Rev. Calif. Law Rev., Mo. Hist. Rev., Dictionary Am. Biography, Dictionary Am. History, Western Polit. Quar.; contbr. to Ency. Brittania, mags. Bd. dirs. George D. Hart Found. Del. Dem. Nat. Conv., 1936, 44, 48; presdl. elector for Calif., 1944; mem. Dem. county and state coms., 1932-50. Mem. Am. Polit. Sci. Assn. (exec. coun. 1932-35, v.p. 1939-40), Am. Acad. Polit. Sci., Nat. Mcpl. League, AAUP, State Hist. Soc. Mo., Am. Hist. Assn., Soc. Calif. Pioneers, Bohemian Club, Commonwealth Club, Cosmos Club, Phi Beta Kappa (senator 1949-51, vis. scholar 1958-59), Beta Theta Pi. Democrat. Episcopalian. Home: Stanford Calif. †

BARDES, PAUL METZNER, insurance company executive; b. Wilkinsburg, Pa., July 21, 1929; s. Paul Metzner and Lillian (Schreiber) B.; m. Evelyn Kay Record, Nov. 1, 1976. Student, U. Pitts., 1947-48; BBA, Tulane U., 1957, JD, 1959. Bar: La. 1959; CLU, CPCU. Chpt. counselor Sigma Pi, Elizabeth, N.J., 1948-51, 53; dist. claims mgr. Allstate Ins. Co., Northbrook, Ill., 1959-67; atty. Erie Ins. Exchange, Erie, Pa., 1967-72; v.p., gen. counsel, sec. Am. States Ins. Cos., Indpls., from 1972; underwriter Am. States Lloyds Ins. Cos., Dallas, from 1972; sec.-treas. Ind. Ins. Guaranty Assn.; dir. City Ins. Agy., Inc. Bd. dirs. Young Reps., Allegheny County, Pa., 1950-51. With USMC, 1951-53. Mem. Rotary, Sigma Pi. Home: West Plainfield Ind.

BARGER, HERMAN H., foreign service officer, international organization executive; b. Springfield, Mass., Nov. 28, 1915; s. Paul and Rose (Barger) B.; m. Dolly King, May 3, 1943; children: Lesli Kristine, Brian King. BA cum laude, Harvard U., 1937; JD, George Washington U., 1955. Bar: D.C. 1955. Fgn. corr. newspapers and news agys., Japan, China, Argentina, 1937-42; various fgn. service positions U.S. Dept. State, Buenos Aires, LaPaz, Bolivia, 1942-58; with Naval War Coll., Newport, R.I., 1957; counselor of embassy econ. affairs Am. Embassy, Djarkata, Indonesia, 1958-60; dep. spl. asst. to undersec. of state for econ. affairs U.S. Dept. State, Washington, 1960-61, dep. dir. office Internat. Trade and Fin., 1961-63; counselor of embassy for econ. affairs Am. embassy, Mexico City, 1963-66; coordinator AID, 1964-66; alternat dir. Asian Devel. Bank, Manila, 1966-68; minister, counsel econ. affairs Tokyo, 1968-70; dep. asst. sec. state for East Asian and Pacific affairs 1970-73; rep. Inter-Am. Devel. Bank, Asuncion, Paraguay, 1974-75, Santiago, Chile, 1975-77; sr. policy officer Washington, 1977-80; ptnr. Buddie Products Co. Greenfield, Mass., 1947-48. With USNR, 1944-46, ETO, PTO; lt. (j.g.) USNR ret. Recipient commendable service award U.S. Dept. State, 1950. Mem. Fgn. Service Assn., Am. C. of C. of Japan (hon.). Home: Bethesda Md. Died June 15, 1987; interred Rock Creek Cemetery, Washington, D.C.

BARGER, THOMAS CHARLES, petroleum company executive; b. Mpls., Aug. 30, 1909; s. Michael Thomas and Mary (Donohue) B.; m. Kathleen Elizabeth Ray, Nov. 18, 1937 (dec. Dec. 1971); children: Ann, Michael, Timothy, Mary, Norah, Teresa; m. Kathleen Vachreau Loeb, Aug. 14, 1972. Student, St. Mary's Coll., 1926-28, D Bus. and Commerce (hon.), 1974; BS, U. N.D., 1931, LLD, 1966. Engr. Lake Shore Mines Ltd., Kirkland Lake, Ont., Can., 1931-34, Bear Exploration & Radium, Contact Lake, N.W.T., 1934-35; assoc. prof. mining U. N.D., 1935-37; with Arabian Am. Oil Co., N.Y.C., 1937-69, geologist, govt. relations mgr., 1954-69, chief exec. officer, 1961-69; v.p., dir. Aramco, 1958-69, pres., 1959-68, chmn., 1968-69; cons. to pvt. corps.; bd. dirs. Calif. First Bank, Kratos Corp., Northrop, Offshore Tech. Corp., W-D 40 Corp. Author: Energy Policies of the Arab States of the Persian Gulf, 1975. Trustee U. San Diego; bd. overseers U. Calif., San Diego. Decorated knight comdr. Order St. Gregory the Great, knight Grand Cross Order Holy Sepulchre. Mem. Am. Inst. M.E., Council Fgn. Relations, Alumni Assn. U. N.D. (trustee), Explorers Club (N.Y.C.), University Club (San Diego), Sigma Xi, Sigma Tau, Kappa Sigma. Roman Catholic. Home: La Jolla Calif. Died June 30, 1986.

BARKER, CARL, corporate executive; b. Selma, Ala., May 18, 1891; s. William and Alice (Schermerhorn) R.; m. Della Batson, Sept. 10, 1910; children: Alice Batson, Mary Edna, Carl. Grad., Dallas Acad. and Ala. Poly. Inst. Asst. county engr. Jefferson County, Ala., 1908-10; asst. city engr., Birmingham, Ala., 1910; asst. engr. T.C.I. & R.R. Co., Birmingham, 1911, U.S. War Dept., 1914; co. engr., Ala., 1915; various positions with Shell Oil Co., from 1917, apptd. asst. to pres., 1948, retired by co., 1953; v.p., chmn. investment com. Associated Fund Inc., St. Louis, from 1953; pres. Shell Aviation Corp., from 1931, Interstate Petroleum Communications Inc., from 1937. Former pres. Tax Inst. Inc., Princeton, N.J.; mem. St. Louis Security Analysts Assn., Am. Soc. Mil. Engrs., 25 Yr. of Petroleum Industry, Rotary, Missouri Athletic clubs. Home: Kirkwood Mo. †

BARKER, CREIGHTON, physician; b. New Milford, Conn., Jan. 15, 1892; s. James C. and Adelaide (DeWitt) B.; m. Juliette B. Beach, Nov. 17, 1917; children: Merritt B., Stanton DeWitt. MD, Dartmouth Coll., 1913; student, U. Edinburgh. Diplomate Am. Bd. Otolaryngology; mem. exec. com. Nat. Bd. Med. Examiners. Pvt. practice specializing in otolaryngology New Haven, from 1921; bd. dirs. C.M. Beach co., Conn. Med. Svc., U.S. adv. com. Am. Specialties; mem. Gov.'s Commn. on Med. Edn.; chmn. Gov.'s Commn. Treatment Chronically Sick, 1939-40; sec. Med. Exam. Bd. 1st lt. M.C., AEF; maj. M.C., Conn. Nat. Guard. Mem. Conn. Med. Soc. (exec. sec.), AMA (mem. adv. bd. med. specialists), Graduate Club, Lawn Club, New Haven Club, Hartford Club, Sigma Xi. Home: New Haven Conn. †

BARKER, ROBERT WHITNEY, lawyer, business executive, church official; b. Ogden, Utah, July 9, 1919; s. George Simon, Jr. and Florence Emily (Dee) B.; m. Amy Vera Thomas, June 30, 1942; children: Amy Ann Barker Wilson, Robert Whitney, Paul Thomas, Philip

Dee, Jeffrey Cutler, Brian Thomas. BS with honors, U. Utah, 1941; JD, Georgetown U., 1947, postgrad. Georgetown Law Ctr., 1949-50. Bar: Utah 1948, D.C. 1949, U.S. Supreme Ct 1951. Partner firm Barker & Barker, Ogden, Utah, 1948; assoc. Ernest L. Wilkinson, Washington, 1948-50; adminstrv. asst. to U.S. Senator Wallace F. Bennett, 1951-53; ptnr. firm Wilkinson, Cragun & Barker, Washington, 1953-82, Wilkinson, Barker, Knauer & Quinn, Washington, 1982-87; dir., sec. Barlow Corp., 1969-87; sr. v.p., sec., gen. counsel, dir. Bonneville Internat. Corp., 1964-85; v.p. Bonneville Holding Co.; v.p., sec., gen. counsel Radio N.Y. Worldwide, Inc., 1964-85, Radio Skokie Valley, Inc., 1970-76, Bay Area Broadcasting Co., 1976-85; dir. WCLR Bldg. Corp., Bonneville Satellite Corp., 1979-85; Mem. nat. adv. council U. Utah; bd. visitors Brigham Young U. Law Sch., 1971-78; gen. counsel Presdl. Inaugural Com., 1969, 73, dep. gen. counsel, chmn. law commn., 1985; dir. Honor Am. Day, Am. Hist. and Cultural Soc., 1970-87; mem. continuing legal edn. adv. bd. Georgetown U. Law Ctr., 1979. Editorial bd.: Georgetown Law Jour, 1947-48. Pres. Weber County (Utah) Young Republican Club, 1948; mem. exec. bd. Nat. Capitol Area Council Boy Scouts Am., 1966-79. Served to maj., F.A. AUS, 1941-46, MTO, ETO. Decorated Bronze Star with two oak leaf clusters. Fellow Am. Bar Found., Am. Coll. Trial Lawyers; mem. ABA (chmn. Indian matters, chmn. adminstrv. law sect. 1957-59), Fed. Bar Assn. (dep. chmn. Indian law com. 1966-72), D.C. Bar Assn. (chmn. legis. com. 1963-65, chmn. U.S. Ct. of Claims com. 1965-67), Utah Bar Assn., Fed. Communications Bar Assn. Mem. Ch. of Jesus Christ of Latter-day Saints (bishop 1953-57, 2d counselor Washington Stake presidency 1957-59, first counselor Washington stake presidency 1959-67, regional rep. Council of Twelve 1967-75, 77-79, pres. Washington Temple 1986-87). Home: Kensington Md. Died Dec. 31, 1987.

BARKEY, PATRICK TERRENCE, librarian, consultant; b. Flint, Mich., Feb. 11, 1922; s. James Daniel and Damie Ann (Terwilliger) B.; m. Mary Ann Schutte, Nov. 18, 1960; children: Susan, Brian, Leslie, Daniel. BA, Pomona Coll., 1948; MLS, U. Mich., 1949. Audio-visual librarian Flint Pub. Library, 1949-57; head circulation dept. U. Notre Dame Library, 1957-60, Eastern Ill. U. Library, 1960-64; head librarian Tex. A. and I. U., Kingsville, 1964-67; dir. libraries U. Toledo, 1967-74, Claremont (Calif.) Coll., 1974-88; pres. Claremont Library Cons., Inc., 1983-88; dir. OCLC Western Service Center, 1975-82, OCLC Pacific Network, 1982-86, OCLC Exec. Office Assocs., 1986-88. Contbr. articles to profl. jours. Served with USNR, 1942-44. Mem. ALA, Calif. Library Assn. Roman Catholic. Club: Zamorano. Home: Claremont Calif. Died May 17, 1988, buried Oak Park Cemetery, Claremont.

BARKLEY, FREDERICK R., writer, business executive; b. Watertown, N.Y., May 18, 1892; s. Reuben E. and Josephine (Workman) B.; m. Claire Coyle, Nov. 22, 1916; m. Lillian M. Simpson, Sept. 8, 1959. Grad. high sch., Watertown, 1913. Reporter Watertown Standard, 1913-14; asst. sports editor Springfield Republican, 1914-15; telegraph editor Geneva (N.Y.) Times, 1915, Providence Jour. and Evening Bull., 1916-17, Detroit Free Press, 1917-18, Detroit News, 1918-21; editor Detroit Forum, 1919-20; exec. sec. Washington City Club, 1921-23; Washington corr. Balt. Evening Sun, 1923-38, N.Y. Times, 1938-46; editor-analyst Bur. Prisons, Dept. Justice, 1946-48; bus., real estate and constrn. editor St. Petersburg (Fla.) Times, 1949; sales and promotion mgr. Fla. Modern Crete, Inc., 1949-50, also bd. dirs., sec. - treas., from 1952; ptnr. Alexander Assocs., advt. agy., 1950; sec.-treas. Cast-Crete Corp. Fla., St. Petersburg, Tampa and Winter Garden, from 1955. Reporter exclusive exposé in newspapers and mags. articles on the nature of the Palmer "red raids" in Detroit, 1920, also first exposés of power, aluminum monopolies to appear in quality mags., 1930-31; author: (with Ray Tucker) Sons of the Wild Jackass, 1932. Mem. Nat. Press Club, Penquin Club (sec.-treas. 1924-25, pres. 1925-26). Republican. Home: South Gulfport Fla. †

BARNES, DONALD GROVE, history educator; b. Albion, Nebr., May 21, 1892; s. Cass Grove and Isabella (Smith) B.; m. Margaret MacGregor, June 15, 1925 (dec. July 1940). AB, U. Nebr., 1915; postgrad., U. Pa., 1917-18; AM, Harvard U., 1917; postgrad., London Sch. Econs., 1920-21, King's Coll., Cambridge U., 1922; PhD, Harvard U., 1924. Instr. in history Milton (Mass.) Acad., 1918-20; asst. prof. history U. Oreg., 1922-26, prof., 1926-30; prof. history U. Wash., 1930-34; prof. history Western Res. U., 1934-60, Haydh prof. history, from 1960; vis. prof. summers U. Minn., 1923, 26, Western Res. U., 1931, 32, UCLA, 1939, 47, U. Mich., 1945. Author: A History of English Corn Lawa, 1660-1846, 1930, George III and William Pitt, 1783-1806, 1939; bd. editors Pacific Hist. Rev., 1932-34, Jour. Modern History, 1938-41. Thayer fellow Harvard U., 1916-17, Bayard Cutting traveling fellowship, 1920-21, Parker traveling fellow, 1921-22, Harrison fellow U. Pa., 1917-18, Guggenheim fellow 1928-29. Mem. Am. Hist. Assn., Royal Hist. Soc., AAUP, Phi Beta Kappa. Home: Cleveland Heights Ohio. †

BARNES, DORIS MARIAN (MRS. FRANK SCOTT BARNES), Republican national committeewoman; b. Portland, Oreg., Aug. 27, 1891; d. Oakes M. and Jessie B. (Kribs) Plummer; m. Frank Scott Barnes, Mar. 20, 1912 (dec. Oct. 11, 1940); children: Frank P., Marian E. (Mrs. Clarence E. Henning), Dorianne (Mrs. Arthur C. Salonek). Student, U. Oreg., 1910-12. Ins. agt. Wrangell, Alaska, from 1940. Chmn. Wrangell Charter Commn., 1960; mem. city council Wrangell, 1944-46, mayor, 1946-48, and from 1960; mem. Alaska Ho. Reps., 1949-53, mem. Senate, 1953-57; mem. 1st Alaska Interim Legislative Council; Republican nat. committeewoman for Alaska, 1955-57, and from 1964; mem. Rep. State Com., S.E. Dist., 1959-62, vice chmn., 1960-64; vice moderator Presbyn. Ch., Synod of Wash., 1958-59; mem. adv. com. Sheldon Jackson Jr. Coll. Recipient Jessen's Weekly award for Outstanding Alaskan, 1948. Mem. Arctic Inst. N.A. (charter assoc.), Alaska Ins. Agts. Assn. (exec. bd. 1955), Wrangell C. of C. (past pres.), Alaska Fedn. Women's Clubs (past pres.), Alaska Fedn. Bus. and Profl. Women's Clubs (pres. 1955-57), Beta Sigma Phi (hon.). Presbyterian. Home: Wrangell Alaska. †

BARNES, IRSTON ROBERTS, educator, economist; b. New Haven, Feb. 14, 1904; s. Niar and Mabel Jane (Roberts) B.; m. Lidorra Holt Putney, June 30, 1936 (dec. Mar. 1983); 1 son, Chaplin Bradford. Ph.B., Yale, 1926, Ph.D. in Econs, 1928. Faculty Yale, 1928-41, asst. prof. polit. economy, 1932-41; fellow Pierson Coll., 1935-41; cons. economist antitrust div. Dept. Justice, 1941-44; dir. econ. bur. CAB, 1944-45, econ. adviser to bd., 1945-48; economist FTC, 1948-52, 54-60, chief div. econ. evidence, 1952-54; professorial lectr. George Washington U., 1954-55; vis. lectr. Columbia Grad. Sch. Bus., 1949-50, prof. polit. economy, 1960-63; econ. cons. antitrust and govt. regulation 1960-81. Author: Public Utility Control in Massachusetts, 1930, Cases on Public Utility Regulation, 1938, The Economics of Public Utility Regulation, 1942; Contbr. articles to profl. jours.; weekly column The Naturalist in Washington Post, 1951-76. Mem. Am. Econ. Assn., Am. Ornithologists Union, Audubon Soc. Central Atlantic States (pres. 1946-61, chmn. bd. 1961-68), Phi Beta Kappa. Clubs: Graduates (New Haven); Cosmos (Washington); Yale (N.Y.C.). Home: Westerly R.I. Died Jan. 19, 1988; buried Grove St. Cemetery, New Haven, Conn.

BARNES, WILLIAM ALEXANDER, organ architect, business executive; b. Chgo., Nov. 10, 1892; s.Charles Osborne and Nettie Ann (Shedd) B.; m. Edith McMillan Robinson, Oct. 22, 1927. AB, Harvard U., 1914; MusD (hon.), Park Coll., 1931, Baylor U., 1945; student piano, 1902; studied organ with, Wallace Goodrich, Clarence Dickinson. V.p., treas. A.R. Barnes & Co. (printers), from 1916; bd. dirs. First Nat. Bank & Trust Co., Evanston, chmn. exec. com., from 1948. Builder ch. size organ at age 15; organist Ch. of the Ascension, Chgo., 1909,Epworth M.E. Ch., Chgo., 12 yrs., Wilmette (Ill.) Bapt. Ch., 4 yrs., 1st Bapt. Ch., Evanston, Ill., 1928-52; as organ architect, planned and supervised constrn. organs for 200 chs. and colls. throughout U.S; organ recitalist; author: The Contemporary American Organ, 1930, The Odyssey of an Organ Enthusiast and His Wife, 1932. Pres. Northwestern U. Settlement Assn., 1928-36; trustee Evanston Hosp. Assn., from 1933, George Williams Coll., 1944-58; dir. YMCA Hotel, 1928-54, chmn. bd., from 1951; chmn. Chgo. Sch. Printing, 1935-45; with Com. on Classification of Personnel of the Army, Office Adj. Gen., Washington, World War I. Mem. Ill. chpt. Am. Guild Organists (ex-dean), Chgo. Artists Assn. (former pres.), Cliff Dwellers Club (Chgo.), University Club (Evanston), Westmoreland Country Club (Wilmette), Bohemian Club (San Francisco), Masons, Phi Mu Alpha. Home: Evanston Ill. †

BARNES, WILLIAM P., investor, lawyer; b. Marlin, Tex., May 31, 1920; s. William P. and Katharine E. (Horne) B.; m. Sally Temple, Oct. 20, 1950; children: William P., Joseph L., James H., Thomas L. B.A., So. Meth. U., 1947, LL.B., 1949. Bar: Tex. 1949. Practiced law Dallas, 1949-53; atty. Gen. Am. Oil Co. Tex., 1953-54, v.p., 1955-60, exec. v.p., gen. counsel, 1960-66, dir., 1960-83, pres., 1966-83, chmn. bd., 1978-83, chmn. exec. com., 1978-83; chmn. bd. Meadows Bldg. Corp., 1966-83; dir. Republic Bank Corp., Stockton, Whatley, Davin & Co., 1964-83. Editor in chief: Southwestern Law Jour., 1948. Trustee So. Meth. U., 1976-84, Southwestern Med. Found., from 1977; v.p., bd. dirs. The Meadows Found., 1966-83. Served to maj. AUS, 1942-46. Mem. Tex. Bar Assn., Kappa Sigma, Phi Alpha Delta, Blue Key. Clubs: Petroleum (Dallas), City (Dallas). Died Aug. 22, 1986; buried Restland Cemetery, Dallas.

BARNETT, BERNARD HARRY, lawyer; b. Helena, Ark., July 13, 1916; s. Harry and Rebecca (Grossman) B.; BA U. Mich., 1934-36; JD, Vanderbilt U., 1940; m. Marian Spiesberger, Apr. 9, 1949; 1 son, Charles Dawson. Bar: Ky. 1940, D.C. Practiced in Louisville, 1940-42; assoc. firm Woodward, Dawson, Hobson & Fulton, 1946-48; partner firm Bulitt, Dawson & Tarrant, 1948-52, firm Greenbaum, Barnett, Wood & Doll, 1952-70, firm Barnett & McConnell, 1972, firm Barnett, Greenebaum, Martin & McConnell, 1972-74, firm Barnett, Alagia, Greenebaum, Miller & Senn, 1974-75; sr. ptnr. Barnett & Alagia, 1975-87; bd. dirs. Fuqua Industries, Inc., Hasbro, Inc., Advanced World Techs. Inc., U.S. Container Corp.; mem. adv. group Joint Com. on Internal Revenue Taxation, U.S. Congress, 1953-55, Com. on Ways and Means, U.S. Ho. of Reps., 1956-58. Chmn., Louisville Fund, 1952-53; mem. Louisville and Jefferson County Republican Exec. Com., 1954-60; chmn. Ky. Rep. Fin. Com., 1955-60; nat. exec. com., nat. campaign cabinet United Jewish Appeal, 1959-71, nat. chmn., 1967-71, campaign chmn., Louisville, 1968-69; trustee Spalding Coll., Louisville, 1975-82, Benjamin N. Cardozo Sch. Law, 1979-84, Ford's Theatre, 1981-87; bd. dirs. Norton Gallery and Sch. Art, 1980-87. Served as lt. USNR, 1942-45. Mem. ABA, D.C. Bar, Louisville Bar Assn., Ky. Bar Assn., Fellows of Am. Bar Found. Died Dec. 10, 1987. Home: Palm Beach, Fla.

BARNETT, DAVID, pianist, composer; b. N.Y.C., Dec. 1, 1907; s. Samuel and Bertha (Margolis) B.; m. Josephine Wolff, Dec. 31, 1929; 1 son, Jonathan. Diploma, Juilliard Sch. Music, 1925, Ecole Normale de Musique, 1928; B.A., Columbia U., 1927; Mus.D., Elon Coll., 1953. Mem. faculty Wellesley Coll., 1935-65, Harvard U., 1955-59, New Eng. Conservatory Music, 1946-65, Columbia U., summers 1946-62; prof. music U. Bridgeport, Conn., from 1967; vis. lectr. Assn. Am. Colls.; lectr. WGBH, Boston; Bd. dirs. Boston Old South Meeting House. Pianist on concert tours in the, east and mid-west, also Gt. Britain; recitalist, Carnegie Hall, Town Hall, Jordan Hall, Gardner Mus., Salle Pleyel, soloist with, Boston, St. Louis, Cin., Bridgeport symphony orchs., Orchestre Symphonique de Paris, dir., Wellesley Concert Series, Westport Friends of Music.; Composer: song Rhapsody and Scherzo for Violin and Piano; recorded: (with Josephine Barnett, narrator.) song Three Cycles of Robert Schumann, Complete Etudes and Preludes of Chopin; author: song The Performance of Music; contbr. articles profl. jours. and mags. Mem. Am. Music Centre, Conn. State Music Tchrs. Assn. (pres.), Coll. Music Soc., Am. British socs. aesthetics, Pi Kappa Lambda, Kappa Gamma Psi, Tau Zeta Epsilon. Home: Weston Conn. Deceased.

BARNETT, HAROLD JOSEPH, economist, educator; b. Paterson, N.J., May 10, 1917; s. Abraham and Lena (Schiff) B.; m. Mildred Denn, Aug. 4, 1940; children: Peter, Alexander, Katherine. BS, U. Ark., 1939; MS, U. Calif. - Berkeley, 1940; MA (Social Sci. Research Council fellow), Harvard U., 1948, PhD, 1952. Teaching asst. U. Calif., Berkeley, 1939-40; economist Treasury Dept., 1941-42, Dept. State, also Dept. Interior, 1946-52, Rand Corp., Washington, 1952-55; economist, dir. econ. growth studies Resources For Future, Washington, 1955-59; cons. Resources For Future, 1959-87; prof. econs., chmn. dept. Wayne State U., 1959-63; prof. econs. Washington U., St. Louis, 1963-87; chmn. dept. Washington U., 1963-66; cons. White House Task Force on Communication Policy, NSF, U.S. Office Edn., Com. for Econ. Devel., Nat Acad. Scis.-NRC. Author: Energy Uses and Supplies, 1950, Malthusianism and Conservation, 1959, (with C. Morse) Scarcity and Growth, 1963, Wired City monographs, 1968-73, Population Problems—Myths and Realities, 1971, Energy, Resources, and Growth, 1974, Atomic Energy in U.S. Economy, 1979, also monographs.; Contbr. articles to profl. jours. Served to maj. U.S. Army, 1943-46. Mem. Am. Econ. Assn., Assn. Environ. and Resource Economists, AAUP. Home: Clayton Mo. Died Feb. 11, 1987; buried Jefferson Barracks Nat. Cemetery, Mo.

BARNETT, ROSS R., governor; b. Carthage, Miss., 1898. BA, Miss. Coll.; LLB, Vanderbilt U.; LLD, U. Miss. Bar: Miss. 1926. Mem. Barnett, Montgomery, McClintock & Cunningham; gov. State of Miss., 1959-64; pvt. practice Jackson, Miss., 1964-87. Mem. Am. (law reform com., legal and lawyer reference com., agrl. com.), Jackson and Hinds County (pres. 1940-43, 47-49), bar assns., Miss. State Bar (pres. 1943-44). Died Nov. 6, 1987.

BARNETT, SOLOMON MEYER, retail executive; b. Evansville, Ind., Mar. 28, 1896; s. Samuel and Teresia (Meyer) B.; m. Jeannette Hofheimer, Oct. 18, 1908 (dec. 1983); children: Jane Abraham, Richard Meyer. With Reliable Stores Corp., Balt., 1916-58; pres. Columbia, Md., 1958-80; chmn. Reliable Stores Corp., Columbia, Md., 1980-85; now hon. chmn. RelStores, Inc. (formerly Reliable Stores Corp.). Pres. Aaron Straus and Lillie Straus Found. Inc. Served as ensign USN, 1917-21. Republican. Jewish. Club: Woodmont Country (Washington) (bd. dirs. 1958-60). Home: Washington D.C. Died Dec. 2, 1986.

BARNHART, HUGH ARTHUR, telephone company executive, newspaper publisher; b. Rochester, Ind., July 14, 1892; s. Henry A. and Louretta (Leffel) B.; m. Martha Anspaugh, June 25, 1928. Student, U. Notre Dame, 1911; AB, Ind. U., 1915. Pres. Rochester Sentinel Corp., 1919-68, chmn. bd., 1968-76; pres. Rochester Telephone Co., 1932-67, chmn. bd., 1967-76. Dir. Ind. Excise Dept., 1937-41, Ind. Dept. Conservation, 1941-45, Ind. Hwy Dept., 1932-33; dir. Bus. and Def. U.S. Services Adminstrn., Dept. Communications, Dept. Commerce, 1955; Dem. nominee 2d Congl. Dist. Ind., 1936; mem. adv. bd. Ind. U., 1950-53. 1st lt. F.A., U.S. Army, 1917-19. Recipient Disting. Alumni Service award Ind. U., 1971; named Sagamore of the Wabash, 1959. Mem. U.S. Ind. Telephone Assn. (pres. 1959, dir. Service award 1971), Ind. C. of C. (bd. dirs.), Rochester

C. of C. (pres. 1942-44), Ind. Soc. Chgo. (v.p. 1970-86), Am. Legion (post comdr.), Fulton County Hist. Soc. (pres. 1967-69), Masons, Elks, Moose, Odd Fellows, Kiwanis (pres. Rochester chpt. 1929), Delta Tau Delta, Indpls. Athletic Club. Baptist. Home: Rochester Ind. Died Feb. 16, 1986.

BARNSLEY, ALAN GABRIEL See **FIELDING, GABRIEL**

BARONE, PAUL LOUIS, retired hospital administrator, physician; b. Paterson, N.J., Oct. 11, 1902; s. Joseph and Jennie (Iozia) B.; m. Martha Watkins, Jan. 20, 1940; children: Joe A., Jean Ann. B.S., Alfred U., 1926; M.D., Royal U., Naples, Italy, 1936. Intern St. Joseph (Mo.) Hosp., 1937, resident, 1938-39; practice medicine, specializing in psychiatry Nevada, Mo., from 1939; staff physician Mo. State Hosp., from 1939, asst. supt., 1943-48, supt., 1948-70, 72-83; clin. dir. Nevada State Hosp, Mo., 1970-83; supt. Nevada State Hosp, 1972-83, clin. dir., 1975-83. Fellow Am. Geriatric Soc., Am. Psychiat. Assn. (life mem., certified mental hosp. adminstr.); mem. AMA, West Central Mo. Counties Med. Assn., Am. Assn. Psychiat. Adminstrs., Am. Assn. Grads. Italian Med. Schs., Mo. Med. Assn., Mid Continent Psychiat. Assn. (life), Western Mo. Psychiat. Assn. (counselor, past pres.). Lodges: Elks, Rotary. Deceased.

BARONI, MONSIGNOR GENO C., government official; b. Acosta, Pa., Oct. 24, 1930; s. Guido and Josephine (Tranquillini) B. BA, Mt. St. Mary Coll., 1952; postgrad., Mt. St. Mary Sem., 1952-56; 5 hon. doctoral degrees. Ordained priest Roman Cath. Ch., 1956. Asst. pastor, high sch. tchr. Johnstown and Altoona, Pa., 1956-60; asst. pastor Sts. Paul and Augustine Ch., Washington, 1960-65; exec. dir. office urban affairs Archdiocese of Washington, 1965-67; dir. urban poverty task force U.S. Cath. Conf., 1967-70; pres. Nat. Ctr. for Urban Ethnic Affairs, 1971-77; asst. sec. for neighborhood, voluntary assns. and consumer protection HUD, Washington, 1977-81. Author numerous articles on neighborhoods, cities and ethnicity. Mem. Italian-Am. Found., Cath. Com. Urban Ministry, Robert F. Kennedy Meml. Found., Miners Legal Def. Fund. Democrat. Roman Catholic. Home: Washington D.C. Died Aug. 27, 1984.

BARR, J. MCFERRAN, banker; b. Louisville, Oct. 17, 1892; s. John W. Jr. and Margaret (McFerran) B.; m. Anita Lawton Carrington, Aug. 31, 1918; children: Anita Barr Watkins, John Watson III, Margaret Barr Matton. AB, Princeton U., 1916. With Ky. Wagon Mfg. Co., 1916-21; v.p. E.D. Morton Co., Louisville, 1921-26, Ky. Title Co., 1927-36; v.p., also bd. dirs. First Nat. Bank, 1928, Ky. Trust Co., from 1928; pres. First Nat. Bank, 1944-57; pres. Cave Hill Investment Co.; bd. dirs. Louisville Gas & Electric Co., Louisville Cement Co., First Nat. Lincoln Bank of Louisville, The Mengel Co., Commonwealth Life Ins. Co.; v.p., bd. dirs. Price Chem. Co.; bd. dirs., mem. exec. com. The Pullman Co. Trustee The Hill Sch., 1943-54, Louisville Presby. Theol. Sem., Centre Coll., Princeton U., 1936-40; mem. exec. com., trustee Am. Printing House for Blind; bd. dirs., chmn. fin. com. Community Chest Louisville and Jefferson County. Mem. Ivy Club (Princeton, N.J.), Princeton Club (N.Y.), Louisville Country Club, Pendennis Club (Louisville). Home: Louisville Ky. †

BARR, RICHARD DAVID, theater producer; b. Washington, Sept. 6, 1917; s. David Alphonse and Ruth Nanette (Israel) Baer. AB, Princeton U., 1938. Formed prodn. co. Theatre 1960 (became Theatre of the Absurd), 1962; pres. League N.Y. Theatres, from 1967. Appeared with Orson Welles' Mercury Theatre War of the Worlds Program; exec. asst. to Orson Welles on prodn. Citizen Kane, 1938-41; dir. Volpone, City Center, N.Y.C., 1948, Richard III, Booth Theatre, N.Y.C., 1949; Arena Theatre prodns. Arms and the Man, 1950-52; producer Broadway plays Hotel Paradiso, Fallen Angels, All In One, 27 Wagons Full of Cotton, 1950's, nat. cos. Auntie Mame, 1952-59, off-Broadway shows including Dutchman, Boys in the Band, 1968, Zoo Story, Krapp's Last Tape, others, 1959-64; producer on Broadway plays Who's Afraid of Virginia Woolf, 1962-63, Tiny Alice, 1964, Malcolm, 1966, A Delicate Balance (Pulitzer prize), 1966-67, Johnny No-Trump, Everything in the Garden, 1968, All Over, 1971, The Grass Harp, 1972, The Last of Mrs. Lincoln, 1972, Noel Coward in Two Keys, 1973, Seascape, 1974, P.S. Your Cat is Dead, 1975, Sweeney Todd (Tony award best musical), 1979, The Lady from Dubuque, 1980, Home Front, 1985; established Playwrights Unit workshop for young Am. playwrights presenting Up to Thursday by Sam Shepard, Home Free! by Lanford Wilson, others; also presented Am. premiers of works by Samuel Beckett and Eugene Ionesco. Served to capt. USAAF, 1941-46. Home: New York N.Y. Died Jan. 9, 1989.

BARRAGÁN, LUIS, architect; b. Guadalajara, Jalisco, Mex., 1902. Hon. doctorate, Autonomous U. Guadalajara, 1984. Practice architecture Mexico City, 1936-88; ptnr. Luis Barragán and Raöl Ferrera Arquitectos, S.C., Mexico City, 1979-83, aesthetic counselor, 1983-88; owner real estate properties Avenida San Jerónimo, Mexico City, Pedregal de San Angel; developer Jardines del Pedregal de San Angel S.A. Prin. works include apt. bldgs., Cuauhtémoc, Mexico City, gardens and ornamental work Jardines del Pedregral de San Angel S.A., Mexico City, convent and chapel, Tlalpan, urban devels., Manzanillo zone, Mex., gardens and ornamental works Jardines del Bosque, Guadalajara, gardens Pierre Marquez Hotel, Acapulco, Mex., symbol for Satellite City, Mexico, ornamental works and landscape architecture Las Arboledas S.A., State of Mexico, residential zone Lomas Verdes, State of Mexico, residences and horse stables Los Clubes, Gilardi's House, Mexico City, Gárate's House, (with Raöl Ferrera) projects for Menil Found., U.S.A., Calvin Klein, monument for C. of C. in cen. plaza, Monterrey, Nuevo León, 1984, Valdáz House, 1985; exhbns. include (slide exhibit) Mus. Modern Art, N.Y.C., 1976, (full exhibit works) Museo Rufino Tamayo, Mex., 1985, various others; subject of numerous articles and books. Recipient Art Nat. prize Mex., Pres. Luis Echeverría Alvarez, 1976, Pritzker prize, 1980, Jalisco Architecture award State of Jalisco Coll. Architects, 1985, Jalisco Prize for Plastic Arts, 1985. Fellow AIA (hon.); mem. Mex. Acad. Architects, N.Y. Acad. Arts and Lit., World Acad. Architecture. Home: Mexico City Mex. Died Nov. 22, 1988.

BARRETT, HARRY OKE, retired university administrator; b. Brantford, Ont., Can., Aug. 26, 1908; s. Charles and Elizabeth (Cook) B.; m. Isabel Alford Weddell, Aug. 10, 1946; children—Charles Alexander, Judith Isabel (Mrs. William John McCreery), John William. B.A., U. Toronto, Ont., 1931, B.Paed., 1938, D.Paed., 1948. Asst. prin. St. Paul's Sch. for Boys, Toronto, Ont., 1935-39; head of guidance Eastern High Sch. Commerce, Toronto, 1939-58, North Toronto Collegiate Inst., 1958-62; prof. ednl. psychology U. Toronto, 1962-66, asst. dean. Faculty Edn.,, 1966-73, acting dean, 1973-74, dean, 1974, exec. asst., 1974-76, prof. emeritus, from 1976; Bd. dirs. Harshman Found. Author: A Job For You, 1960, Status of the Secondary School Teacher in Ontario, 1963, Here and There in Teacher Education, 1974; Editor: book series Student, Subject and Careers, 1972—; author: series book English, 1972, History, 1980; Contbr. numerous articles to profl. jours., popular mags. Served to maj. Can. Army, 1940-46. Fellow Ont. Tchrs. Fedn. (pres. 1959-60); mem. Ont. Secondary Sch. Tchrs. Fedn. (pres. from 1959, life), Ont. Ednl. Research Council (pres. from 1961, sec. from 1962), Can. Psychol. Assn. (life), Faculty Club of U. Toronto. Progressive Conservative. Clubs: Masons, Knight Hospitaller, mem. Order of St. John of Jerusalem. Deceased.

BARRETT, WILLIAM EDMUND, author; b. N.Y.C., Nov. 16, 1900; s. John Joseph and Eleanor Margaret (Flannery) B.; m. Christine Rollman, Feb. 15, 1925; children: Marjorie Christine, William Edmund. Student, Manhattan Coll.; LittD (hon.), Creighton U., 1961. Cons. in aerospace Denver Pub. Library, 1941-86; civilian lectr. for Army Air Forces, 1942. Author: Woman on Horseback, 1938, Flight from Youth, 1939, Son-of-a-Gun Stew, 1945, Denver Murders, 1946, The Last Man, 1946, The Evil Heart, 1946, The Number of My Days, 1946, Man From Rome, 1949, The Left Hand of God, 1951, Shadows of the Images, 1953, Sudden Strangers, 1956, The Empty Shrine, 1958 (5 Acad. awards for motion picture), The Edge of Things, 1960, The First War Planes, 1960, Lilies of the Field, 1962 (Acad. award for motion picture), The Fools of Time, 1963, Shepherd of Mankind, 1964, The Red Lacquered Gate, 1967, The Glory Tent, 1967, The Wine and the Music, 1968, A Woman in the House, 1971, The Shape of Illusion, 1972, Lady of the Lotus, 1975; contbr. serials to Red Book, Cosmopolitan, others. Recipient citation Regis Coll., 1956, Accomplishment in Communication of Arts award Manhattan Coll., 1972. Fellow Internat. Inst. Arts and Letters; mem. P.E.W., Authors League Am., The Players Club, Nat. Press Club, Denver Press Club, Denver Athletic Club, Colo. Authors League (pres. 1943-44). Roman Catholic. Home: Denver Colo. Died Sept. 14, 1986; buried Mt. Olivet Cemetery, Denver.

BARRON, ALEX E., investment trust executive; b. Paris, Ont., Can., Aug. 4, 1918; s. Frederick and Ethel (Rutherford) B.; m. Nina Marion Burrows, June 1, 1946 (dec. July 1976); children—Paul, James; m. Beverley Mollett, May 5, 1978. In investment bus. from 1935; with Fry & Co. Ltd., 1938-59, pres., 1955-59; officer Can. Gen. Investments Ltd., Toronto, Ont., 1959-87, now vice chmn., dir.; bd. dirs. Can. Reassurance Co., Can. Reins. Co., Stelco Inc., Halliburton Co., Dallas, Overseas Venture Capital Ltd., Dome Mines Ltd., Can. Trust Co., Can. Trustco Mortgage Co.; vice-chmn., dir. Can. Gen. Investments Ltd., Third Can. Gen. Investment Trust Ltd., Toronto. Clubs: Toronto, Rosedale, Granite of Toronto. Died Sept. 18, 1987.

BARRON, DEAN JAMES, lawyer, retired government official; b. Peoria, Ill., Dec. 21, 1919; s. James and Alberta (Sprague) B.; m. Anna Belle Bristol, July 27, 1940; children: Deanna A., Stephanie G. Student, Bradley U.; J.D., Am. U., 1959. Bar: Va. 1960, Pa. Supreme Ct. 1969, U.S. Supreme Ct 1970, D.C. 1972; C.P.A., Ill. Assoc. internal service Treasury Dept, 1942-74, dir. internat. ops., 1959-60; dir. audit div. Treasury Dept, Washington, 1960-62; regional commr. Treasury Dept, Phila., 1962-70; asst. commr. data processing Treasury Dept, Washington, 1970-71, asst. commr. accounts, collection and taxpayer service, 1971-73; asst. commr. planning and research Treasury Dept, 1973-74; ret. 1974; sole practice law Fairfax, Va., from 1975, State College, Pa. Author article. Chmn. Phila. Fed. Exec. Bd., 1964. Mem. Am., Fed., Pa., Phila., Fairfax, D.C. bar assns., Va. State Bar, Ill. Soc. C.P.A.s. Died Sept. 2, 1986.

BARROWS, C(HARLES) STORRS, architect; b. Springfield, Mass., Jan. 10, 1889; s. Charles Storrs and Evelyn (Snow) B.; m. Valerie Emerson, May 8, 1918 (dec. Jan. 1927); children: Valerie Barrows Clithero, Charles Storrs, Dorothy Barrows Pallesen; m. Winifred Smith, Nov. 12, 1928. Student, De Veaux Sch., 1903-08, U. Rochester, 1909-10. Pvt. practice architecture Rochester, 1912-17, 1919-42; chief engr. Arcadia Trailer Corp., Newark, N.Y., 1917; ptnr. Carpenter & Barrows, 1945-52; prin. C. Storr Barrows & Assocs., 1952-57, Barrows, Parks, Morin, Hall & Brennan, 1958-66. 2d lt. inf. U.S. Army, 1918-19, ETO; lt. col. USAAF, 1942-45. Decorated Bronze Star, Croix de Guerre with star (France). Fellow AIA; mem. Fla. Assn. Architects, Res. Officers Assn., Air Force Assn., Soc. First Div., Sarasota (Fla.) Shrine Lunch Club, Forest Lakes Country Club, Masons, Shriners, Psi Upsilon, Theta Nu Epsilon. Home: Sarasota Fla. †

BARRY, ROBERT RAYMOND, business executive, former congressman; b. Omaha, May 15, 1915; s. Ralph and Ethel (Thomas) B.; m. Anne Rogers Benjamin, July 19, 1945; children: Cynthia Herndon Bidwell, Henry Huttleston Rogers. Student, Hamilton Coll., 1933-36, Dartmouth Coll., 1936-37, Sch. Finance, NYU, 1938, Law Sch., 1946-47. Investment banker Kidder Peabody & Co., 1937-38; with Mfrs. Trust Co., 1938-40; mgr. exec. Bendix Aviation Corp., 1940-44; asst. to pres. Yale & Towne Mfg. Co., 1945-50; pres. Calicopia Corp., from 1965; engaged in ranching and land devel. Coachella Valley, Calif.; also in mining Quincy, Calif.; mem. 86th-88th Congresses from 27th Dist. N.Y.; mem. coms. govt. operations 88th Congress from 25th Dist. N.Y., 1959-61, post office and civil service, 1959-65, fgn. affairs, 1961-65. Former mem. nat. council Boy Scouts Am.; active campaign Dewey for dist. atty., 1937, Willkie presdl. campaign; mem. N.Y. Republican County Com., 1945; del. coordinator, statistician for Dewey, Rep. Nat. Conv.; mem. Rep. Nat. Campaign Com., Washington, 1948; personal staff Eisenhower campaign tour, Denver, Chgo., 1952; chmn. finance com. N.Y. State Congl. Campaign Com., Citizens for Eisenhower, 1954; chmn. Yonkers Citizens Eisenhower Com., 1956; U.S. del. NATO Parliamentarian Conf., 1959, 60, UNESCO Conf., 1963; Rep. nominee for congress 38th Calif. Dist.; mem. Nixon-Agnew Nat. Staff, 1968; dir. Calif. Rep. Central Com., 1966-68; Former mem. bd. dirs. Greater N.Y. YMCA; appointee Pres. Reagan's Peace Corps Adv. Council, active community, civic affairs; chmn. adv. council Humane Soc. of the Desert. Mem. Alpha Delta Phi Internat. (pres.). Presbyterian. Clubs: Eldorado Country (Indian Wells, Calif.), St. Andrews Golf (Hastings, N.Y.), Economic of N.Y. (N.Y.C.), Metropolitan (N.Y.C.), Metropolitan (Washington), Capitol Hill (Washington). Home: Woodside Calif. Died June 14, 1988; buried Redwood City, Calif.

BARTHOLOMEW, HARLAND, city planner; b. Stoneham, Mass., Sept. 14, 1889; s. Aden Luther and Harriet Mary (Lewin) B.; m. Lillian R. Barton, Dec. 1911 (dec. Aug. 1954): 1 child, Herbert Melvin;m. Frances Ball, Nov. 21, 1955 (dec. Jan. 1963; m. Gladys B. funsten, May 15, 1968 (dec. May 1971). C.E. course, Rutgers Coll., 1921, DSc, 1952; LLB, Carthage Coll., 1978. Formerly cons. engr. City Plan Commn., St. Louis; formerly cons. Mo. State Planning Bd.; prof. civic design U. Ill.; former chmn. Nat. Capital Planning Commn., Washington; cons. Harland Bartholomew & Assocs. (civil engrs., city planners and landscape architects), St. Louis; adviser preparation city plans and zoning ordinances numerous Am. and Can. cities, including St. Louis, Washington, Williamsburg, Va., Pitts., Louisville, Memphis, New Orleans, Omaha, Mpls., Dallas, Los Angeles, Portland, Vancouver, B.C. Author: Urban Land Uses, 1932, Land Uses in American Cities, 1955. Former pres. Am. Inst. Planning, Nat. Conf. on City Planning, Am. Planning and Civil Assn. Urban Am. Mem. ASCE (hon.), Am. Inst. Cons. Engrs., Am. Soc. Landscape Architects (hon.), Am. Soc. Planning Ofcls., Bellerive Country Club, University Club (St. Louis), Cosmos Club (Washington), Zeta Psi, Tau Beta Pi. Republican. Congregationalist. Home: Saint Louis Mo. Deceased.

BARTLEY, S. HOWARD, psychobiologist, educator; b. Pitts., June 19, 1901; s. Edward G. and Mary Agnes (Byers) B.; m. Velma Himebaugh, Aug. 19, 1924; children: Samuel Howard, Katherine Joyce, Jeanne Antoinette; m. Leola Sarah Bevis, June 25, 1938. BS, Greenville Coll., 1923; MA, U. Kans., 1928, PhD, 1931. Tchr. Miltonvale Wesleyan Coll., Kans., 1924-25; asst. instr. U. Kans., Lawrence, 1926-31; fellow, research assoc. Washington U., St. Louis, 1931-42; prof., dir. research Dartmouth Eye Inst., Hanover, N.H., 1942-47, Mich. State U., E. Lansing, 1947-71; disting. research prof. Memphis State U., 1972-88. Author: Vision: A Study of Its Basis, 1941, Fatigue and Impairment in Man, 1947, Principles of Perception, 1958, Beginning Experimental Psychology, 1960, The Human Organism as a Person, 1967, Perception in Everyday Life, 1972. NRC fellow, 1931-33; recipient Apollo award Am. Optometric Assn., 1970, Prentice medal Am. Acad. Optometry, 1972. Mem. Am. Acad. Optometry, Am. Psychol. Assn., Optical Soc. Am., Am. Physiol. Soc., Sigma Xi, Beta Sigma Kappa. Christian Ch. Home: Memphis Tenn. Died June 1, 1988; buried Meml. Park, Memphis.

BARTON, HELEN, university professor; b. Balt., Aug. 9, 1891; d. James Sheridan and Mary Irene (Eichelberger) Barton. AB, Goucher Coll., Balt., 1913; AM, Johns Hopkins U., 1922, PhD, 1926. Asst. in physics Goucher Coll., 1913-14; head dept. physics and chemistry Salem Coll., 1915-19; instr. math. Wellesley Coll., 1919-21; assoc. prof. math., dean of women Albion (Mich.) Coll., 1921-25; prof. and head dept. math. Ala. Coll., 1926-27; assoc. prof. math. Woman's Coll., Univ. N.C., 1927, prof. and head dept., from 1928. Contbr. articles to profl. mags. Recipient Western High Sch. Alumnae scholarship, 1909-11, Goucher Coll. fellowship, 1914-15, Johns Hopkins U. scholarship, 1925-26. Mem. Am. Math. Soc., Math. Assn. Am., N.C. Edn. Assn., N.C. Acad. Sci., AAUW, Phi Beta Kappa, Sigma Xi. Methodist. Home: Greensboro N.C. †

BARTON, JACKSON MOUNCE, petroleum company executive; b. Shawnee, Okla., Jan. 12, 1917; s. Jesse Downy and Elizabeth (Mounce) B.; m. Dorothy King Benedict, May 9, 1942; children: Jackson M., Charles D., Elizabeth B. Student, Phillips U., 1934-36; B.S., U. Okla., 1938; postgrad., Yale U., 1939-41. Geologist Magnolia Petroleum Co., 1938-47; div. geologist Coop. Refinery Assn., Kansas City, Mo., 1947-49; chief geologist Coop. Refinery Assn., 1949-50, exploration mgr., 1950; mgr. geol. dept. Deep Rock Oil Corp., Tulsa, 1950-53; exploration mgr. to v.p., gen. mgr., dir. No. Natural Gas Producing Co., 1953-65; gen. mgr. Glover Hefner Kennedy Oil Co., Oklahoma City, 1965-68; exec. v.p., dir. Royal Resources Corp.; also exec. v.p. Royal Resources Exploration, Inc., 1968-70; exec. v.p., dir. Champlin Petroleum Co., Ft. Worth, 1970-71; cons. geologist 1971-72; pres., dir. Home-Stake Prodn. Co., Tulsa, 1972-73; v.p. Terra Resources, Inc., 1973-77; asst. to pres. Warrior Drilling & Engring. Co., Inc., 1977-78, v.p. adminstrn., sec. and treas., 1978-80; pres., dir. Carless Resources, Inc., 1980-85, Murray Hill Oil & Gas Co. of U.S.A., from 1986; dir. Union Pacific Resources Corp., 1970-71, Carless, Capel & Leonard, London, 1984, New Ct. Natural Resources of London, from 1986. Contbr. articles to profl. jours. Bd. dirs. Omaha Planned Parenthood, 1963-65; Mem. Westside Community Schs. Bd. Edn., 1955-65, pres., 1962-65; Mem. alumni adv. council Sch. Geology of U. Okla., from 1968. Fellow Geol. Soc. Am., AAAS; mem. Am. Assn. Petroleum Geologists, Am. Inst. Mining and Metall. Engrs., Soc. Exploration Geophysicists, Am. Geol. Inst., Am. Geophys. Union, Am. Inst. Profl. Geologists, Rocky Mountain Oil and Gas Assn. (past pres. Nebr. sect.), Ind. Petroleum Assn. Am., Am. Petroleum Inst., Am. Gas Assn., Ind. Natural Gas Assn., Mid-Continent Oil and Gas Assn., Omaha C. of C. Unitarian (pres. bd. trustees). Home: Tuscaloosa Ala. Died June 29, 1986; cremated.

BARTON, THOMAS FRANK, SR., geographer, educator, writer; b. Cornell, Ill., Dec. 3, 1905; s. Frank Douglas and Martha (Gamlin) B.; m. Erselia M.A. Monticello, Sept. 26, 1931; 1 son, Thomas Frank Monticello. Diploma, Ill. State U., 1929, BEd, 1930, LLD (hon.), 1977; PhM, U. Wis., 1931; PhD, U. Nebr., 1935. Rural sch. tchr. 1925-27; grad. teaching asst., dept. geography U. Wis., 1930-32, U. Nebr., 1932-34; asst. prof. geography Memphis State Coll., summers 1933, 34; assoc. prof. social studies Nebr. State Tchrs. Coll., 1934-35; prof. geography, head geography-geology dept., So. Ill. U., 1935-48; vis. prof. geography U. Nebr., summer 1947; assoc. prof. Ind. U., 1947-51, prof. geography, from 1951, on leave, 1955-57; vis. prof. geography and social studies Sri Nakharinwirot U., Bangkok, Thailand, 1955-57; supr. U.S. Airway Weather Sta., So. Ill. U., 1941-47. Author: Living in Illinois, 1941, Patrick Henry: Boy Spokesman, 1960, John Smith: Jamestown Boy, 1966, Lyndon Baines Johnson: Texas Boy, 1973, (with others) Southeast Asia in Maps, 1970, (with Sedman P. Poole and Clara Belle Baker) Through The Day, 1947, From Season to Season, 1947, In Country and City, 1947, (with Sedman P. Poole and Irving Robert Melbo) The World About Us, 1948; co-author: Geography of the North American Midwest, 1955, Curriculum Guide for Geographic Education, 1963, Methods of Geographic Instructions, 1968, An Overall Economic Development Study of Southeastern Indiana, 1970, World Geography, 1972, Southeast Asia: Realm of Contrasts, 1974; senior author: An Economic Geography of Thailand, 1958; assoc. editor Jour. Geography, 1940-45, asst. editor, 1948-50, editor, 1950-65, land surface wall map series, 1952, including world, U.S., Europe, S.Am., Africa, Eurasia, N.Am.; editor: series maps and globes Pictorial Relief with Emerging Color; contbr. chpts. tech. publs., articles profl. jours. One of 4 dels. representing U.S. at 6 week UNESCO seminar McDonald Coll., St. Anne de Bellevue, Que., Can., July-Aug. 1950; sec. Internat. Geog. Union Commn. on Teaching Geography in Schs., 1952-55; ednl. motion picture collaborator and adviser. Mem. Ill. Reserve Militia; ground instr. meterology Civilian Pilot Tng. Program; geography instr. Army A.C. Tng. Program, all 1942-43. Recipient Disting. Alumni award Alumni Assn. Ill. State U., 1976, Rocking Chair award Sigma Delta Chi of Ind. U., 1976, Disting. Svc. award Geog. Soc. Chgo., 1978. Fellow AAAS, Nat. Coun. Geog. Edn. (disting. svc. award 1965), Nat. Coun. Geography Tchrs. (pres. 1948); mem. Am. Geog. Soc., AAUP, Assn. Am. Geographers, Royal Geog. Soc., Nebr. Coun. Geography Tchrs. (pres. 1935), Ill. Coun. Geography Tchrs. (pres. 1939-40), Ind. Coun. Geography Tchrs. (pres. 1961-63), Ill. Acad. Social Sci., Ind. Acad. Social Sci. (pres. 1972-73), Ill. Edn. Assn., Ind. State Tchrs. Assn., Sigma Xi, Phi Delta Kappa, Kappa Phi Kappa, Pi Kappa Delta, Kappa Delta Pi, Phi Gamma Mu, Gamma Theta Upsilon. Home: Bloomington Ind. Died Aug. 26, 1985, buried Valhalla Meml. Garden.

BASEHART, RICHARD, actor; b. Zanesville, Ohio; s. Harry T. and Mae (Wetherald) B.; m. Stephanie Klein, Jan. 14, 1940 (dec.); m. Diana Lotery; children: Jenna, Gayla. Appeared Hedgerow Theatre, Moylan, Pa., 1938-42, on Broadway in Counterattack, 1943, Othello, 1944, Take It as It Comes, 1944, The Hasty Heart, 1945 (N.Y. Drama Critics award), The Survivors, 1948, The Day the Money Stopped; motion pictures: He Walked by Night, The House on Telegraph Hill, Decision Before Dawn, Fixed Bayonets, Portrait in Black, 1960, The Good Die Young, Il Dibone, The Brothers Karamozov, Moby Dick, Time Limit, LaStrada, The Island of Dr. Moreau, Being There, 1979; TV shows: Voyage to the Bottom of the Sea, 1964-68, W.E.B., 1978; TV films: Andersonville Trial, The Satan Bug, Four Days in November: The Trial of Lt. William Calley, Flood, 21 Hours at Munich, Eric Hoffer—The Crowded Life, Marilyn—The Untold Story, The Ten Thousand Day War. Named Best Actor Nat. Bd. Rev., 1951. Died Sept. 17, 1984.

BASSETT, BEN, journalist; b. Topeka, Oct. 30, 1909; s. William T. and Sophia (Hoffman) B.; m. Eileen Ewing; children: Elizabeth E., Jonathan, W. Brian. Reporter Topeka State Jour., 1925-27; copy editor New Bedford (Mass.) Standard-Times, 1928-30; wire editor AP, Kansas City, Mo., 1930-35; news editor New Bedford Standard-Times, 1935-36; successively assigned AP, Cleve., Washington and N.Y.C., 1936-48; fgn. news editor AP, N.Y.C., 1948-73, cons., 1973-74. Club: Nat. Press (Washington). Home: Larchmont N.Y. Died Oct. 14, 1987.

BASTEDO, FRANK LINDSAY, lieutenant governor; b. Bracebridge, Ont., Can., Sept. 10, 1886; s. David Edgar and Elizabeth Ann (Oaten) B.; m. Alma Anderson, July 12, 1911 (dec. May 1935); children: Dorothy Bastedo Cavers, Edgar F., Jean Anne, Donald L.; m. 2d, Lillian Michaelis, Sept. 10, 1938. LLB, U. Toronto. Bar: Ont. 1909, Saskatchewan, 1911, King's Counsel, 1927. Pvt. practice, counsel numerous ct. cases Cts. of Saskatchewan, Supreme Ct. of Can., jud. com. Privy Coun.; lt. gov. Saskatchewan, Can., from 1958. Contbr. articles to legal jours. Named Knight of Grace and Justice of Order of St. John. mem. Law Soc. Saskatchewan (past pres.), Can. Bar Assn. (v.p. for Saskatchewan 1949-50), Regina Fed. Conservative Assn. (pres. 1921-24), Regina Orchestral Soc. (past pres.), Masons, Canadian Club (past pres.), Assiniboia Club (Regina), Delta Chi. Mem. United Ch. of Can. Home: Regina, Sask. Canada. †

BASTEDO, PHILIP, lawyer; b. N.Y.C., Dec. 13, 1908; s. Walter A. and Helen Russell Kip (Priest) B.; m. Helen C. Wilmerding, Feb. 4, 1937; children: Philip R., W. Bayard, Cecily, Christopher K. AB, Princeton U., 1929; JD, Harvard U., 1932. Bar: N.Y. 1933. Since practiced in N.Y.C.; mem. Wickes, Riddell, Bloomer, Jacobi & McGuire, 1941-70, of counsel, 1970-78; dep. dir. Office Civilian Def., Washington, 1942-43. Trustee Hosp. Spl. Surgery, pres., 1958-72; trustee United Hosp. Fund, chmn., 1978-84; treas., trustee Am. Acad. Rome, 1977-87; trustee MacDowell Colony. Served with USNR, OSS, 1943-45. Mem. Council Fgn. Relations, Pilgrims, Bar Assn. City N.Y. Episcopalian. Clubs: River, Century. Home: New York N.Y. Died Feb. 19, 1987.

BATES, CLAUDE ELLSWORTH, territory commander Salvation Army; b. Woodward Hill, Pa., Apr. 5, 1892; s. Christian Melancthon and Mary Elizabeth (Kisner) B; m. Edith Marie Holz, Oct. 13, 1915; children: Louise Marie Bates Seiler, Edward Christian, John Joseph. Student, Baptist State Bd. Religious Edn., Wilkes Barre, 1907-08, Wilkes Barre Coll. of Bus., 1908-09, Salvation Army Officers Tng. Coll., N.Y., 1912. Chief acct. Morris & Co., Wilkes Barre, 1910-12; sec. religious work Salvation Army, Phila., 1912-14; comdg. officer Salvation Army, West Chester, Pa., 1914-16; sec. for naval and mil. ops. Salvation Army, Phila., 1916; sec. in territorial fin. dept. Salvation Army, N.Y.C., 1917, pvt. sec. to terr. comdr., 1918-n22; sec. for youth work Salvation Army, Buffalo, 1922-25; divisional comdr. Salvation Army, Cin., 1925-35; territorial sec. for youth work Salvation Army, N.Y.C., 1935-40; prin. Officers Tng. Coll. Salvation Army, 1940-42, field sec. for all personnel, 1942-47; chief sec. for the West Salvation Army, San Francisco, 1947; comdr. of Salvation Army work in 11 Western states, including alaska, Hawaii and the P.I. Salvation Army, 1948-53, cen. territorial comdr., 1953-62. Recipient Long Svc. medal The Salvation Army, 1937, silver star to badge, 1947. Mem. USO, Nat. Coun. Rotary. Home: Oak Park Ill. †

BATES, G(EORGE) WALLACE, organization executive, lawyer; b. Battle Lake, Minn., May 17, 1908; s. George Wilson and Anna (Burke) B.; m. Frances E. Trump, June 25, 1932 (dec. 1978); children: Elizabeth B. (Mrs. Robert Zenowich), Anne W. AB, U. Minn., 1928, LLB, 1930; LLM, Columbia U., 1931. Bar: Minn. 1930, N.Y. 1936, Mo. 1950. With firm Root, Clark, Buckner & Ballantine, N.Y.C., 1931-43; atty. Am. Tel. & Tel. Co., N.Y.C., 1943-50; gen. atty. Am. Tel. & Tel. Co., 1953-57; gen. counsel Southwestern Bell Telephone Co., St. Louis, 1950-53; v.p., gen. counsel, dir. N.Y. Telephone Co. and Empire City Subway Co., Ltd., 1958-73; pres. Bus. Roundtable, N.Y.C., 1973-83. Bd. dirs. Police Athletic League, Center for Public Resources, Inc. Mem. N.Y. C. of C. (exec. com. 1968-70, pres. 1970-71), Am. Law Inst., ABA (ho. of dels. 1973-75), N.Y. State Bar Assn. (v.p. 1974-75, exec. com. 1969-72, ho. of dels. 1972-75), Assn. Bar City N.Y. Clubs: Indian Harbor Yacht (Greenwich); University (N.Y.C.). Home: Greenwich Conn. Oct. 11, 1987.

BATES, HENRY GEORGE, clergyman; b. Snodland, Eng., Nov. 17, 1919; came to U.S., 1929, naturalized, 1947; s. Henry Philippe and Annie (Parker) B.; m. Ruby Maxine Younce, Jan. 27, 1945; children—Maxine Bates Craver, Nancy Bates McGraw, Lillian Bates Mellott, Mary Ellen Bates Dulaney. Student, Temple U., 1940-41, Park Coll., 1942-43; A.B., Ashland (Ohio) Coll., 1944; B.D., Ashland Theol. Sem., 1946; S.T.M., Gettysburg Luth. Sem., 1948. Ordained to ministry Brethren Ch., 1946; pastor St. James (Md.) Brethren Ch., 1946-48; prof. O.T. and Hebrew Ashland Theol. Sem., 1948-55; pastor North Manchester (Ind.) Brethren Ch., 1955-59, Vinco (Pa.) Brethren Ch., 1959-71, Wayne Heights Brethren Ch., Waynesboro, Pa., 1971-88; part-time prof. O.T. and Christian edn. Broadfording Christian Coll., Hagerstown, Md., 1976-81; past mem. Pa. Dist. Bd. Evangelists; moderator Pa. Dist. of Brethren Ch., 1961, 69, Gen. Conf., 1973, mem. rules and orgn. com. Gen. Conf.; bd. dirs. Camp Peniel, Brethren Care Retirement Village, Riverside Christian Tng. Sch., 1961-69. Writer: Sunday Sch. Quar, 1952-75; Author: Old Testament Hebrew for Beginning Students, 1951, The Old Testament in Perspective, 1953. Home: Waynesboro Pa. Died June 4, 1988.

BATES, J. W., SR., oil company executive; b. 1889; married. Grad., Dartmouth Coll., 1910. With Reading & Bates Co., from 1937; vice chmn. bd. Reading & Bates Offshore Drilling Co., Tulsa. With USAAF, World War II. †

BATOR, PAUL MICHAEL, lawyer, educator; b. Budapest, Hungary, July 2, 1929; came to U.S., 1939; naturalized, 1945; s. Victor and Franciska Elisabeth (Sichermann) B.; m. Alice Garrett Hoag, June 2, 1956; children—Thomas Ewing, Michael G., Julia F. Grad., Groton Sch., 1947; AB, Princeton U., 1951; MA in History, Harvard U., 1953, LLB, 1956. Bar: N.Y. bar 1958. Law clk. to Supreme Ct. Justice Harlan, 1956-57; assoc. firm Debevoise, Plimpton & McLean, N.Y.C., 1957-59; asst. prof. law Harvard Law Sch., 1959-62, prof., 1962-85, assoc. dean, 1971-75, Bromley prof., 1981-85; dep. solicitor gen., counselor Solicitor Gen. of U.S., 1983-84; John P. Wilson prof. of law U. Chgo., 1985-89; of counsel Mayer, Brown & Platt, Chgo., 1985-89; vis. prof. law U. Calif., Berkeley, 1966, Stanford U., 1971-72, U. Chgo., 1978-79. Co-author: Hart and Wechsler's Federal Courts and the Federal System, 3d edit, 1988; author: The International Trade in Art, 1983. Fellow Am. Acad. Arts and Sci.; mem. Am. Law Inst. Home: Chicago Ill. Died Feb. 24, 1989.

BATOR, PETER ANTHONY, lawyer; b. Budapest, Hungary, July 2, 1929; s. Victor and Franciska (Sichermann) B.; m. Mary C. Bigelow, May 19, 1951 (div. 1967); children: Francesca Bradley Bator Johnson, Anthony Bigelow (dec.); m. Joanna C. Sturges, Sept. 12, 1969; children: Alexa S., Timothy C. A.B. magna cum laude, Harvard U., 1951, LL.B. magna cum laude, 1954, Sheldon fellow, 1954-55. Bar: N.Y. 1955. Assoc. Davis Polk & Wardwell, N.Y.C., 1955-61; ptnr. Davis Polk & Wardwell, 1961-84; dir. ICI Americas Inc. (and predecessors), N.Y.C., 1969-84, Kreutoll Realization Corp., N.Y.C., 1969-78. Editor: Harvard Law Rev. V.p., trustee N.Y. Infirmary-Beekman Downtown Hosp., N.Y.C., 1972-84; mem. alumni standing com. Groton (Mass.) Sch., 1975-77. Mem. Harvard Law Sch. Assn. N.Y.C. (trustee 1974-76), Am., N.Y. State bar assns., Bar Assn. City N.Y., Am. Law Inst., Am. Inst. Internat. Law, Internat. Law Soc., Council Fgn. Relations, Incorporated Proprietors of Nauquitt, Inc. (pres. 1980-82), Phi Beta Kappa. Clubs: Knickerbocker (N.Y.C.), River (N.Y.C.), Downtown Assn. (N.Y.C.), Wall St. (N.Y.C.), Meadow Brook (N.Y.C.). Home: New York N.Y. Died Jan. 13, 1984; buried South Dartmouth, Mass.

BATT, GEORGE KENNETH, industrialist; b. New Albany, Ind., 1894; s. George and Nettie (Markland) B.; m. Margaret Robinson Dugan, Oct. 11, 1921; children—Peggy (Mrs. Solon Palmer Jr.), Mary (Mrs. Arnett B. Taylor). Student, Purdue U., 1913-15; LL.D., Bloomfield Coll. and Sem. Exec. staff R.H. Macy Co., N.Y.C., 1919-25; 1st asst. controller to v.p. and treas.

Dugan Bros., 1925-62; Past dir. N.J. Bell Telephone Co.; past exec. com. Montclair Nat. Bank & Trust Co.; indsl. mem. NWLB, Washington, 1943-44; now mem. QED, LaJolla, Calif. Mem. Pres.'s Cost of Living Commn., 1943-44; vice chmn. Gov. War Transp. Commn., Gov. Human Resources Commn.; chmn. Ann. Rutger Bus. Forum, 1950; chmn. citizens council N.J. Jet Port Assn., 1960-61; mayor City of Montclair, N.J., 1944-48; chmn. N.J. Republican Fin. Commn., 1945-48; dir. Morristown Meml. Hosp., Bloomfield Coll; trustee Vineland Tng. Sch. Served to 1st lt. U.S. Army, 1917-19. Recipient Man of the Yr. award Notre Dame Alumni Assn., 1946; named Man of the Yr. in N.J. Agr. and Industry, 1962. Mem. N.J. C. of C. (pres. 1941-43), Beta Gamma Sigma, Theta Xi. Presbyterian. Clubs: QED, LaJolla Country. Deceased.

BATTEN, JOHN HENRY, III, manufacturing executive; b. Chgo., Jan. 16, 1912; s. Percy Haight and Lisa (Stockton) B.; m. Katherine Vernet Smith, June 30, 1938; children: Edmund Peter Smith, Michael Ellsworth, Linda Vernet. Grad., Phillips (Andover) Acad., 1931; A.B., Yale U., 1935; Cert. M.E., U. Wis. Extension, 1949. With Twin Disc, Inc., Racine, Wis., 1935-89; dir. Twin Disc, Inc., 1937-89, asst. treas., 1942-43, v.p., asst. gen. mgr., 1943-45, exec. v.p., 1945-48, pres., chief exec. officer, 1948-76, chmn., chief exec. officer, 1976-83, chmn. bd., 1983-89; chmn. dir. Twin Disc Pacific, Albury, Australia, Twin Disc, S.Africa, Twin Disc (Far East) Ltd., Singapore; dir., former chmn. Twin Disc Internat. S.A., Nivelles, Belgium; dir. emeritus Walker Forge, Racine, Wausau Ins. Cos., M&I Am. Bank & Trust Co., Racine, Giddings & Lewis, Fond du Lac; former dir. Bell & Gossett Corp., Northbrook, Ill., Gorton Machine Co., Racine, Niigata Converter Co., Tokyo, Nordberg Mfg. Co., Milw. Author: Skyline Pursuits, The Formidable Game, The Forest and the Plain; editor: The Best of Sheep Hunting, The Best of Tiger Hunting. Mem. Bd. Edn., 1936-46. Mem. N.A.M. (former Midwest v.p., dir.), Wis. Mfrs. Assn. (past dir.), Soc. Automotive Engrs., Chief Execs. Forum, SAR, Phi Beta Kappa. Episcopalian. Died Feb. 14, 1989. †

BATTEY, PAUL LEON, consulting engineer; b. Marion, Kans., Mar. 11, 1876; s. Alvan D. and Rubie C. (Griswold) B.; m. Anna L. Trent, Sept. 4, 1912; 1 dau., Rubie Eleanor. Student engring. dept., U. Kans., 1898-99. With Edison Electric Illuminating Co., Topeka, 1893-1900, asst. supt., 1900; power switchboard designer Western Electric Co., Chgo., 1900-1901; draftsman, later chief engr., v.p. Arnold Electric Power Station Co., The Arnold Co., Chgo., 1901-1919; cons. engr. Willys Overland Co. and subs., Chgo., 1919-21; pvt. practice Chgo., 1921-22, organizer, 1922; pres., treas., cons. Battey & Kipp Inc., from 1922. Trustee Village of Glencoe, Ill., 1916-19; pres. Park Bd., 1920-34. Mem. AIEE, ASME, Am. Concrete Inst., Am. Soc. Agrl. Engrs., Western Soc. Engrs., Masons (32 degree, Shriner), Union League Club. Mem. Glencoe Union Ch. Home: Mundelein Ill. †

BATTSON, LEIGH MCMASTER, petroleum executive; b. Springfield, Mo., June 25, 1891; s. Jesse J. and Vernie (McMaster) B.; married; 1 dau., Alice Mullally; m. 2d, Lucy Smith Doheny, Feb. 18, 1932. Student, pub. schs., Springfield, Mo. With investment securities bus., 1913-38; ind. operator oil bus., from 1938; pres. Los Nietos Co. until 1949; bd. dirs. Union Oil Co. of Calif., MCA Inc. Mem. Eldorado Country Club (Palm Desert), California Club, Los Angeles Country Club, Bel Air Country Club (Los Angeles); Pacific Union Club (San Francisco); Metropolitan Club (Washington); The Links Club (N.Y.C.). Home: Beverly Hills Calif. †

BAUDOUX, MONSIGNOR MAURICE, archbishop; b. La Louvière, Belgium, July 10, 1902; arrived in Can., 1911; s. Norbert and Marie (Moreau) B. Student, Coll. de St.-Boniface, Can., 1919-23, St. Joseph's Sem., Edmonton, Can., 1923-27; STD, Grand Seminaire et U. Laval, Can., 1929, D. es L. (hon.), 1952; PhD (hon.), U. Montreal, 1957; DD (hon.), United Coll., Winnipeg, Can., 1967; LLD (hon.), U. Man., Can., 1967; DCL (hon.), St. John's Coll., Winnipeg, 1972. Ordained priest Roman Cath. Ch., 1929. Asst. Prud'homme, Sask., Can., 1929-31, pastor, 1931-48; domestic prelate Sask., Can., 1944; bishop of St.-Paul Alta., Can., 1948-52; archbishop coadjuctor St.-Boniface, 1952-55, archbishop, 1955-74. Died July 1, 1988; entombed in the St. Boniface Cathedral, St. Boniface, Man., Canada.

BAUERS, ELOI, lawyer, association executive; b. Osseo, Minn., Aug. 5, 1890; s. Casper and Anna Frances (Jacomet) B.; m. Mary F. O'Malley, July 27, 1911 (dec. May 31, 1966; children: Catherine A. Kimball, Helen M. Mahoney, Mary J. Boulav. LLB, U. Minn., 1913. Bar: Minn. 1913. Pvt. practice Mpls., from 1913; mem. firm Bauers & Kelly, Mpls., 1959-74; of counsel Mahoney, Dougherty and Mahoney, Mpls., from 1974; exec. v.p. Am. Coll. Allergists, 1953-76; field v.p. sales Americana Hotels, 1960-72; gen. counsel Profl. Conv. Mgmt. Assn., from 1975; spl. counsel. conv. cons. USA, Air France, 1972-75, Hyatt Corp., from 1972; mem. adv. bd. Paris Conv. Ctr., 1972-74; bd. dirs. Gen. Securities, Inc., Mpls. 2d lt., field arty., U.S. Army, World War I. Decorated knight comdr. with shell Equestrian Order Holy Sepulchre, Jerusalem, Knight Grand Holy Sepulchre; recipient Bronze medal Le bureau du Conseil de Paris, 1975; first recipient Profl. Conv. Mgmt. Assn.; Disting. Svc. award, 1978. Disting. fellow Am. Coll. Allergists (pub. emeritus Annals of Allery, 1976); mem. Am., Minn., Hennepin County bar assns., Am. Legion, Mpls. Club, Athletic Club, Phi Delta Phi, Delta Sigma Rho. Roman Catholic. Home: Minneapolis Minn. Deceased.

BAUGHMAN, HARRY FRIDLEY, clergyman, academic administrator; b. Everett, Pa., Jan. 23, 1892; s. George W. and Elizabeth (Schafhirt) B.; m. Jo Liller, Oct. 17, 1916; 1 child, Peter Fridley. AB, Gettysburg Coll., 1910, DD (hon.), 1931, LLD (hon.), 1960; student, Luth. Theol. Sem., Gettysburg, Pa., 1910-13; LHD (hon.), Muhlenberg Coll., 1953. Ordained to ministry Luth. Ch., 1913. Pastor Trinity Luth. Ch., Keyser, W.Va., 1913-18, St. Stephen Luth. Ch., Pitts., 1918-25, Trinity Luth. Ch., Germantown, Pa., 1925-41; prof. art of preaching Luth. Theol. Sem., Gettysburg, from 1941, pres., from 1951; mem. bd. publs. United Luth. Ch., 1934-40; mem. bd. Deaconess Work, 1944; pres. bd. mgmt. Balt. Deaconess House, from 1950; mem. exec. bd. United Luth Ch. Author: Jeremiah For Today, 1947, Preaching From the Prophets, 1949, Commentaries on Jonah and Epsitle to Philippians; contbr. articles to religious publs. Mem. Phi Beta Kappa. Home: Gettysburg Pa. †

BAUMAN, HELEN WOOD, educator, editor; b. St. Joseph, Mo., Nov. 17, 1891; d. Horace W. and Mary (Vance) Wood; m. Oscar George Bauman, Jan. 1, 1922. Musical edn. with, Arthur Foote, Boston; student, Tobias Mattay Sch., London, 1928; master classes, Thomas Whitney Surette Sch., Concord, Mass., 1927. C.S. practitioner C.S. Ch., Boston, from 1932, c.S. tchr., 1946-65. Assoc. editor publs. C.S. Pub. Soc., 1948-59, editor-in-chief, 1958-70; tchr. normal class Mother Ch., 1958, pres., from 1963; editor C.S. Jour., 1959-70, C.S. Sentinel, 1959-70, C.S. Herald (in 12 langs. in Braille), 1959-70. Mem. DAR. Home: Boston Mass. Deceased.

BAUMANN, FRIEDA, internist, educator; b. Scranton, Pa., Apr. 28, 1887; d. Anthony and Ida Elizabeth (Hooker) Baumann. Grad., Mansfield State Tchrs. Coll., 1906; MD, Women's Med. Coll. Pa., 1917. Diplomate Am. Bd. Internal Medicine. Student's physician Women's Med. Coll. Pa., 1920-22, asst. prof. medicine, assoc. prof. applied therapeutics, 1937-83, prof. applied therapeutics and clin. medicine, 1938-42, prof. therapeutics, 1942, prof. medicine in charge nutrition and metabolism, 1947-51, Hannah E. Longshore prof. medicine, 1951-59, prof. emeritus; pvt. practice Phila., from 1928; vis. physician Hosp. of Women's Med. Coll. Pa., from 1931; vis. physician Phila. Gen. Hosp., from 1922, cons. med. service, from 1933; examining physician AT&T Co., Phila., 1922-29. Contbr. articles to profl. jours. Fellow ACP, Phila. Coll. Physicians; mem. Am. Med. Women's Assn. (editor jour. 1957), Alumnae Assn. Women's Med. Coll. Pa. (pres. 1930-32), Zeta Phi (nat. pres. 1937). Home: West Chester Pa. †

BAUR, JOHN IRELAND HOWE, art consultant, former museum director; b. Woodbridge, Conn., Aug. 9, 1909; s. Paul V.C. and Susan (Whiting) B.; m. Louise W. Chase, Jan. 8, 1938; children: Susan, Arthur M., Jean E. BA, Yale U., 1932, MA, 1934. Supr. edn. Bklyn. Mus., 1934-36, curator paintings and sculpture, 1936-52; curator Whitney Mus. Am. Art, N.Y.C., 1952-58, assoc. dir., 1958-66, dir., 1966-74, ret., 1974; cons. Terra Mus. Am. Art, Evanston, Ill., 1979-87. Author: 18 books including Revolution and Tradition in Modern American Art, 1951, American Painting in the 19th Century, 1953, Philip Evergood, 1960, Joseph Stella, 1971, The Inlander: Life and Work of Charles Burchfield, 1982; editor: Am. Art Jour. Books, 1980-87. Served with U.S. Army, 1944-45. Home: Katonah N.Y. Died May 15, 1987; cremated.

BAXTER, ANNE, actress; b. Michigan City, Ind., May 7, 1923; d. Kenneth Stuart and Catherine (Wright) B.; m. John Hodiak, July 7, 1946; 1 child, Katrina; m. Randolph Galt, Feb. 18, 1960; children: Melissa, Maginel; m. David Klee, Jan. 30, 1977. Ed. pub. schs.; student, Theodora's Irvine's Sch. of the Theater, White Plains, Chappaqua and Bronxville (N.Y.), 1934-36, The Lenox Sch., 1937, The Brearley Sch., 1938-39, Studio Sch. 20th Century Fox, 1940; studied with Ouspenskaya. - Author: Intermission, 1976; appeared in Seen But Not Heard, 1936, There's Always A Breeze, 1937, Madame Capet, 1937, Susan and God, Summer Playhouse, Dennis, Mass., 1938, Spring Meeting Cape Playhouse, 1939; Broadway play The Joshua Tree, London; motion pictures: The Razor's Edge, 1946 (Acad. award for best supporting actress), All About Eve, 1951 (Acad. award nominee), The Ten Commandments, Cimarron, 1960, Walk on the Wild Side, 1961, Mix Me a Person, 1962, The Tall Women, 1980, The Busy Body, 1980, Jane Austen in Manhattan, 1980; 5 months tour John Brown's Body, 1955-56; Noel Coward in Two Keys, 1975; appeared in Cause Celebre, 1979-80; TV series Hotel, 1983. Recipient Fgn. Press award, 1947. Presbyterian. Home: Easton Conn. Died Dec. 12, 1985.

BAY, HOWARD, stage and film designer; b. Centralia, Wash., May 3, 1912; s. William D. and Bertha A. (Jenkins) B.; m. Ruth Jonas, Nov. 23, 1932; children: Ellen, Timothy. Student, U. Wash., 1928, U. Colo., 1929, Marshall Coll., 1929-30, Carnegie Inst. Tech., 1930-31, Westminster Coll., 1931-32, Chappell Sch. of Art, Denver, 1928-29; study in, Europe, 1939. Vis. instr. Purdue U., 1962; instr. Circle-in-the-Square Theatre Sch., 1962-63, CCNY, 1979; guest designer, dir., instr. Ohio U., 1964; lectr. Cooper-Hewitt Mus., 1976; Andrew W. Mellon guest dir. Carnegie-Mellon U., 1963; dir. theatre, prof. theatre arts Brandeis U., 1965-86; also Alan King prof., chmn. theatre arts dept.; vis. prof. Yale, 1966-67; instr. Banff Ctr. of the Arts, 1980; mem. adv. bd. Internat. Theatre Inst. Designed: Food Pavillion, St. Louis Mid-Am. Jubilee, 1956; designer settings for 170 Broadway stage shows; also designer for TV shows; staged and designed: As the Girls Go, 1948; puppets and settings for Pete Roleum film, 1939; resident designer settings for Bucks County Playhouse, 1941, designer-dir., Universal-Internat. Pictures, 1946-48; designer: settings for My Mother, My Father and Me, 1963; opera Natalia Petrovna, 1964, Man of La Mancha, Odyssey for Broadway, Poor Murderer, Utter Glory of Morrissey Hall, Oedipus Rex, Volpone, Fanny, London prodn. of Little Foxes, 1983; art dir.: film Balanchine's Midsummer Night's Dream; ballet; television series Mr. Broadway, 1964, Pueblo Incident, 1973; Pal Joey, 1977; Author: U.S. Navy Handbook, Navy on Stage, 1944, Staging and Stage Design sect. Ency. Brit, 1973, Stage Design, 1973, Broadway sect. Contemporary Stage Design U.S.A, 1974. Guggenheim fellow, 1940-41; cited for year's best setting by Donaldson Awards for best designs for musicals, N.Y. stage, 1943-44, 44-45 seasons; Antoinete Perry award for best setting, 1960, 66; Maharam award for best settings, 1966. Mem. United Scenic Artists Am. (pres.), Nat. Soc. Interior Designers (nat. bd.). Club: Players. Home: New York N.Y. Died Nov. 21, 1986.

BAYARD, ALEXIS IRÉNÉE DUPONT, lawyer; b. Wilmington, Del., Feb. 11, 1918; s. Thomas F. and Elizabeth (duPont) B.; m. Jane Brady Hildreth, Apr. 24, 1944 (dec. July 10, 1960); children: Alexis Irenee duPont, Eugene H., Richard H., Jane Bayard Curley, John F., William B. B.A., Princeton U., 1940; LL.B., U. Va., 1947. Bar: Del. bar 1948. Since practiced in Wilmington; sr. partner firm Bayard, Brill & Handelman, from 1965; dir. Girard Bank Del.; mem. Nat. Commn. on Uniform Laws, 1962-71. Chmn. Delaware River and Bay Authority, 1967-69; bd. dirs. Del. Project Hope, from 1962, Blood Bank of Del., 1955-70, Del. region NCCJ, from 1964; bd. overseers Del. Law Sch.; trustee Widener Univ.; state chmn. Nat. Found. March of Dimes, from 1966; lt. gov. State of Del., 1949-53; campaign chmn. Del. Democratic Com., 1954, chmn., 1967-69; chmn. Del. Citizens for Kennedy and Johnson, 1960, Del. Citizens for Johnson-Humphrey, 1964; mem. fin. com. Nat. Dem. Com., from 1970. Served from pvt. to 1st lt. USMCR, 1942-45. Decorated Purple Heart. Mem. Am., Del. bar assns., Am. Judicature Soc., Soc. Mayflower Descs., SAR, Del. Swedish Colonial Soc., Hist. Soc. Del., Marine Res. Officers Assn., Mil. Order World Wars, Am. Road Bldg. Assn., Am. Acad. Polit. and Social Sci. Episcopalian. Clubs: Wilmington, Wilmington Country, Greenville, Univ. Home: Wilmington Del. Deceased.

BAYER, HERBERT, painter, designer, architect; b. Haag, Austria, Apr. 5, 1900; came to U.S., 1938, naturalized, 1943; s. Maximilian and Rosa (Simmer) B.; m. Joella Bayer, 1944; 3 stepsons. Studied design with architects Schmidthammer, Emmanuel Margold, Darmstadt, Fed. Republic Germany, 1920; studies with Kandinsky, 1921; student, Bauhaus, Weimar, 1921-23, U. Graz, Austria, 1978, Phila. Coll. Art, Art Ctr. Coll. Design, 1979. Tchr. graphic design and typography Bauhaus, Dessau, 1925-28; dir. advt., typography, painting, photography, exhbn. planning Dorland Studio, Berlin, 1928-38; art dir. Gt. Ideas of Western Man; cons. Aspen Inst. Humanistic Studies, 1949-66; chmn. dept. design Container Corp. Am., 1956-65; cons. on architecture, art and design Atlantic Richfield Co., 1965-85. As painter represented in museums throughout U.S., Europe; one-man exhbns. in N.Y.C., Berlin, Paris, London, San Francisco and other major cities; retrospective exhibit 33 Years of Herbert Bayer's Work in Nûrnberg, Munich, Zûrich, Amsterdam, Brussels, Berlin; designed: Earth Sculpture, Marble Garden, 1955, Anderson Park, Aspen, Colo., 1973, Double Ascension; fountain sculpture, Los Angeles, 1972, tile mural and park, Phila. Coll. Art, 1976, articulated wall hwy. constrn. for 1968 Olympics, Mexico City; archtl. works include bldgs. of Aspen Inst. for Humanistic Studies, indsl. bldgs. for Container Corp. Am.; interiors for Atlantic Richfield Co. in N.Y.C., Los Angeles, Chgo., Denver, Dallas, Newtown Square, Pa.; designed many posters, exhbn. installations including, Bauhaus Exhbn., 1938, Mus. Modern Art Airways to Peace, 1943, traveling shows for coordinator Inter-Am. Affairs, 1942, traveling exhbn., 50 yrs. Bauhaus Exhbn., Stuttgart, London, Amsterdam, Paris, Chgo., Toronto, Pasadena, Tokyo, 1968-71. Editor, designer: World Geo-Graphic Atlas, 1953, Herbert Bayer Book of Drawings, 1961; portfolio Bayer, 1965; suite of lithographs, 8 monochromes, 1965, portfolio of 6 silk screens, 1968; pub. portfolios: 10 fotomontages, 10 fotoplastiken, 1936; books of his work The Way Beyond Art, The Work of Herbert Bayer, 1947, Herbert Bayer-Visual Concepto Total, 1975, Herbert Bayer: The Complete Work, 1984. Decorated Austrian Honor Cross; recipient awards including Ambassador's award for excellence, London, 1968; Kulturpreis, Cologne, Fed. Republic Germany, 1969; Gold medal for excellence Am. Inst. Graphic Arts, 1970; Adalbert Stifter Preis, Austria, 1971; President's Fellow award R.I. Sch. Design, 1984. Hon. fellow Royal Acad. Fine Arts (Netherlands); mem. Art Dirs. Club (Hall of Fame). Home: Montecito Calif. Died Sept. 29, 1985, cremated, buried Aspen, Colo.

BAYLEY, FRANK SAWYER, lawyer; b. Seattle, June 7, 1910; s. Frank S. and Mary (Bass) B.; m. Frances A. Stimson, June 24, 1938 (div. 1958); children: Frank Sawyer, Thomas S., Douglas C.; m. Margaret M. Hayes, Nov. 28, 1958; children: Margaret A., Colby J. BA, Harvard U., 1932; JD, U. Wash., 1936. Bar: Wash. 1936. Practiced in Seattle 1936-82; ptnr. Jones, Grey & Bayley, 1966-82; cons. ECA, 1948; regional counsel NPA, 1951. Bd. dirs. Ryther Child Ctr., 1947-76, pres., 1952-54; bd. dirs. Child Welfare League Am., 1954-57, v.p., 1957. Capt. USNR, 1941-45. Decorated Navy Cross. Mem. ABA, Wash. Bar Assn., Seattle Golf Club, Orcas Island Yacht Club, Harbor Club, University Club. Home: Seattle Wash. Died 1982.

BEACH, FRANK AMBROSE, psychobiologist, emeritus educator; b. Emporia, Kans., Apr. 13, 1911; s. Frank Ambrose and Bertha (Robinson) B.; m. Anna Beth Odenweller, Mar. 1935 (dec. June 1971); children: Frank Ambrose, Susan Elizabeth; m. Noel Ann Gaustad, Apr. 1972. BS, Kans. State Tchrs. Coll., 1933, MS, 1934; PhD, U. Chgo., 1940; ScD, McGill U., 1966, Williams Coll., 1968; LHD (hon.), Emporia State U., 1988. Research asst. to Dr. K.S. Lashley dept. psychology Harvard U., 1935-36; asst. curator dept. exptl. biology Am. Mus. Natural History, 1936-41, asst. curator in charge, 1941-42, assoc. curator in charge dept. animal behavior, 1942, chmn. and curator dept. animal behavior, 1942-46; prof. psychology Yale U., 1946-58, Sterling prof., 1952-58; prof. psychology U. Calif.-Berkeley, 1958-78, prof. emeritus, 1978-88; research assoc. Am. Mus. Natural History. Fellow N.Y. Zool. Soc., Am. Psychol. Assn.; mem. Am. Soc. Naturalists, Nat. Acad. Sci., Soc. Exptl. Psychologists, Am. Philos. Soc., Western Psychol. Assn., Phi Beta Kappa (hon.), Sigma Xi. Home: El Cerrito Calif. Died June 15, 1988.

BEACHAM, WOODARD DAVIS, physician, medical historian; b. McComb, Miss., Apr. 10, 1911; s. Woodard D. and Ida (Felder) B. B.A., U. Miss., 1932, B.S., 1933; M.D., Tulane U., 1935. Diplomate: Am. Bd. Obstetrics and Gynecology. Intern Charity Hosp. of La., New Orleans, resident in ob-gyn, sr. resident in urology, 1939-40, later sr. vis. surgeon; past pres. surg. staff Charity Hosp., New Orleans, then cons.; prof. clin. gynecology and obstetrics Tulane U. Sch. Medicine, New Orleans, 1949-81, emeritus prof. ob-gyn, from 1981; assoc. staff Tulane Med. Center Hosp., from 1976; obstetrician and gynecologist So. Bapt. Hosp., pres. staff, 1961, chmn. condolence com., 1976; practice medicine specializing in obstetrics and gynecology from 1940; cons. Beacham Meml. Hosp., Magnolia, Miss., Meth. Hosp., Hotel Dieu Sisters Hosp., New Orleans; chmn. internat. relations com. 10th World Congress of Ob-Gyn, 1982; pres. Beacham Corp.; Surgeon USPHS, 1943-48. Author: (with Robert J. Crossen and Dan. W. Beacham) Synopsis of Gynecology, (5th edit.), (with Dan. W. Beacham) 6-10th edits.) Synopsis of Gynecology,, 1963, 67, 72, 77, 82; Editor for gynecology and obstetrics: Stedman's Med. Dictionary, 23d edit, 1976; Contbr. articles to tech. jours. Chmn. bd. trustees Carrollton United Meth. Ch., 1980, chmn. pastor-parish relations com., 1980, chmn. adminstrv. bd., 1981; mem. planning com. Internat. House, 1983; mem. New Orleans Tourist and Conv. Commn., New Orleans Mus. of Art, Internat. Trade Mart. Recipient John Herr Musser award Tulane U. Sch. Medicine, 1933; Distinguished Service award So. Med. Assn., 1974; Distinguished Alumnus award U. Miss. Alumni Hall of Fame, 1976; Plaque of appreciation So. Bapt. Hosp. Dept. Ob-Gyn, 1979; Outstanding Alumnus Cert. of Appreciation, Tulane U. Med. Ctr., 1986. Fellow ACS (gov. 1955-63, adv. council 1963-67, chmn. 1967, 2d. v.p. 1972-73, Med. Records prize 1943, pres. La. chpt., mem. com. on med. devices, presiding officer symposium 1983), Am. Gynecol. Soc. (mem. council 1959-60), Am. Assn. Obstetricians and Gynecologists (v.p. 1970-71, mem. Found.), Am. Coll. Obstetricians and Gynecologists (1st pres. 1951-52, com. on liaison with Internat. Fedn. Gynaecology and Obstetrics from 1973, del. VIIIth World Congress Obstetrics and Gynaecology 1976, Distinguished Service award 1976, Award of Excellence 1986, chmn. Library for History of Obstetrics and Gynecology, mem. task force on geriatric gynecology, com. on devel.), Silver Badge Club; mem. Am. Gynec-Ob Soc., So. Gynec-Ob Soc. (pres. 1967), AMA (chmn. sect. obstetrics and gynecology 1957-58), So. Med. Assn. (chmn. sect. on obstetrics 1949, mem. council 1961-63, 2d v.p. 1972, 1st v.p. 1973), Fifty Year Club of Am. Medicine, La. C. of C., Orleans Parish med. socs., New Orleans Grad. Med. Assembly (past pres., adv. council from 1965, chmn. long range planning com. 1976-77), New Orleans Gynecol. and Obstet. Soc. (past pres.), Am. Cancer Soc., Royal Soc. Medicine, Ole Miss. Loyalty Found., Conrad G. Collins Obstetric and Gynecologic Soc. Tulane U. (1st pres.), Central Assn. Obstetricians and Gynecologists (asst. sec. 1950-52), Am. Assn. Med. Colls. (emeritus), Am. Fertility Soc. (charter asso. mem.), Tulane Med. Alumni Assn. (dir. 1970-71, sec. 1971-73, 2d v.p. 1973-74, 1st v.p. 1974-75, pres. 1976-77), Sociedad Peruana De Obstetricia y Gynecologia (corr. fgn. mem.), Sociedad Paraquaya De Ginecologia y Obstetricia (hon.), U. Miss. Alumni Assn. (dir. 1962-65, past pres. New Orleans chpt.), Philippine Obstet. and Gynecol. Soc. (hon.), AAAS, U. Miss. Guardian Soc., Doctors Club Internat., Assn. Profs. Gynecology and Obstetrics, Emeritus Club of Tulane U., Sigma Xi, Alpha Omega Alpha, Phi Chi (grand presiding sr., nat. pres. 1969-73, exec. trustee from 1973), Beta Theta Pi. Clubs: Plimsoll, New Orleans Country, Circumnavigators, Tulane Green Wave, Internat. House (founding mem., exec. dir. from 1977), World Trade of New Orleans (founder). Died May 2, 1987.

BEACHER, LAWRENCE LESTER, optometrist, homeopathic physician, research scientist, author and lecturer; b. Cherne, Czechoslovakia, Aug. 18, 1905; came to U.S., 1921, naturalized, 1921; s. Frank A. and Jenny (Berger) B.; m. Sylvia Budoff, Jan. 12, 1930 (dec.); 1 child, Melvin M.; m. Eugenie Cruz, Dec. 18, 1967; 1 dau., Lillian Gonzalez. OD, Pa. Coll. Optometry, 1927; D Ocular Sci. (hon.), Ill. Coll. Optometry, 1937; PhD, Phila. Coll. and Infirmary Osteopathy, 1945; LittD, Sem. St. Francis of Assisi, 1947; MD, McCormick Med. Coll., 1948; MA, Philathea Coll., London, Ont., Can., 1959, LHD, 1961, PhD, 1962; ScD, Dearborn Coll. Physicians and Surgeons, 1946, Studiorum Colegium Academicum, 1967, Cambridge (Eng.) Coll. Applied Sci., 1968, Ind. No. U., 1972; LLD, Nat. Police Acad., 1970, London Coll. Applied Sci., 1970; EdD, Ohio Coll. Podiatric Medicine, 1968; MD (hon.), Homeopathic Med. Coll., S.Africa, 1975. Diplomate: Am. Bd. Examiners in Psychotherapy. Instr. geometrical optics Pa. State Coll. Optometry, 1927-29, asst. prof., 1929-31; chief staff, head ednl. div. Bronx County Optometrical Clin. Service, 1929-31; lectr. contact lens impression methods Optometric Found., 1944-50; prof. psychology Philathea Coll., 1957-72, chancellor, 1967-72, emeritus, 1972-87; vis. lectr. Pa. State Coll. Optometry, 1962-71, emeritus, 1971-87; also mem. vis. clin. staff; prof. ophthalmology and contact lens therapy McCormick Med. Coll., 1946-52; vis. lectr. Ill. Coll. Optometry, 1944-68, So. Coll. Optometry, 1962-64; vis. prof. Ind. No. U., 1972-73. Author: Ocular Refraction and Diagnosis, 1931, 2d edit., 1980, Practical Optometry, 1934, Contact Lens Technique, 1941, 5th edit., 1974, Your Precious Eyesight, 1952, Corneal Contact Lenses, 1956, A Study of Practical Psychology, How Can I Improve Myself, 1962, Psychological Manifestations in Ocular Science, 1968, Happiness and Success in Marriage, 1979, (autobiography) The Rise of an Immigrant to National Fame, 1985; also over 100 articles. Served with USAF-CAP, 1945-62; maj. Res. ret. Decorated grand cross Eloy Alfano Internat. Found. Panama; Maltese Cross Order St. John Jerusalem; recipient Martin Buber award Midway Counseling Ctr.; Nathan W. Collier award Fla. Meml. Coll., 1965; award Mass. Gov.'s Council, 1971; Wisdom Hall of Fame award Wisdom Soc., 1971; Good Citizenship medal Nat. Soc. SAR, 1971; Archbishop Benjamin C. Eckardt award, 1971; Humanitarian award J.F. Kennedy Library for Minorities, 1978; named to Hall of Fame Nat. Police Acad., Venice, Fla. Fellow Am. Psychotherapy Assn. (pres. 1971-72), Am. Assn. Clin. Physicians and Surgeons, Assn. Social Psychology, Disting. Service Found. Optometry, Am. Acad. Optometry (diplomate contact lens bd.), AAAS, Philos. Soc. Eng., Am. Coll. Clinic Adminstrs., Internat. Soc. Psychologists (Eng.), Internat. Coll. Ocular Sci. (dir. edn.), Am. Coll. Homeopathic Physicians (diplomate, life, hon. mem.), Am. Acad. Med. Adminstrs., N.J. Acad. Sci.; mem. N.Y. Acad. Scis., Essex County Optometric Soc., Am. Optometric Assn., N.Y. State Optometric Assn., N.Y. County Optometric Assn. (hon. life mem.), N.J. Optometric Assn. (past chmn. contact lens sect., sci. achievement award with honor 1975), Hahnemann Med. Soc., Western Homeopathic Med. Soc. Ariz. (hon. life mem.), Fla. Soc. Homeopathic Physicians, Assn. Mil. Surgeons of U.S., La. Psychol. Assn. (life), Circolo Italiano U. Conn. and U. South Fla., Beta Sigma Kappa (chmn., ret. bd. regents sci. sect., gold medal 1976), Phi Delta Alpha. Jewish. Lodges: Masons; Order of Foresters. Home: West Orange N.J. Died Jan. 7, 1987; buried Hackensack, N.J.

BEAGLE, CHARLES WELLINGTON, civil engineer; b. Media, Pa., Oct. 25, 1910; s. John Andrew and Ella Mae (Hartman) B.; m. Alice Rosa Rigg, July 6, 1946; children: Joann Beagle Bricks, Rosana Beagle McGill, Charles Andrew, Ruth Ella Beagle Jerome. BS, Pa. State U., 1933, CE, 1939. Jr. civil engr. U.S. Forest Svc., Pa., 1933-39; chief constrn. engr. Bendix Aviation Corp., Teterboro, N.J., 1940-44; project engr. George M. Brewster, Inc., Bogota, N.J., 1945-49; pres. R.& B. Constrn. Co., South Plainfield, N.J., 1950-55; mcpl. engr. City of South Plainfield, N.J., 1955-60, City of New Providence, N.J., 1960-62; mcpl. engr., dir. pub. works City of Woodbridge, N.J., 1962-76. Vice chmn. South Plainfield Redevel. Agy., 1967-70. With U.S. Army, 1939-40, USNR, 1944-45. Recipient Industry Recognition award Nat. Asphalt Pavement Assn., 1965, Asphalt Leadership award Poly. Inst. Bklyn., 1972, Pioneer award N.J. Asphalt Pavement Assn., 1974, Outstanding Contbn. award Rutgers U. Asphalt Paving Conf., 1976; charter mem. elected to Hot Mix Asphalt Hall of Fame, Nat. Asphalt Pavement Assn. Mem. Transp. Rsch. Bd., Am. Rd. Builders Assn., Assn. Asphalt Paving Technologists (dir., pres. 1974), Am. Pub. Works Assn. (Pub. Works Man of Yr. 1966), NSPE, N.J. Soc. Profl. Engrs. (Engr. of Yr. 1971, Govt. Profl. Devel. award 1974), N.J. Soc. Mcpl. Engrs. (Merit award 1961), Internat. Inst. Community Svc. (honor roll 1976), Asphalt Inst. Internat. Platform Assn., Water Pollution Control Fedn., Am. Arbitration Assn., Am. Legion, VFW, Elks, Alpha Sigma Phi. Home: South Plainfield N.J. Died Jan. 8, 1984; buried Hillside Cemetery, Scotch Plains, N.J.

BEAHAN, JOHN M., bishop; b. Ottawa, Ont., Can., Feb. 14, 1922. Ordained priest Roman Catholic Ch., 1946. Auxiliary bishop of Ottawa, 1977-88. Died Mar. 14, 1988; buried Notre Dame Cemetery, Ottawa.

BEAL, RICHARD SMITH, government official, political scientist, educator; b. Washington, Nov. 27, 1945; s. George Max and Virginia (Smith) B.; m. Ruth Sorensen, Jan. 31, 1969; children: Emily Longstroth, Jason Richard, Trevor Max, Melinda Ruth, Quincy Frodesen. BA, Brigham Young U., 1970, MA (fellow), 1970; PhD (Herman fellow), U. So. Calif., Los Angeles, 1977. Translator and cons. devel. lang. materials Lang. Tng. Ctr., Brigham Young U., Provo, Utah, 1968-69; grad. teaching asst. dept. polit. sci. Brigham Young U., Provo, Utah, 1969-70, adminstrv. asst. internal relations program, 1969-70, rsch. assoc., 1971-72, instr. dept. polit. sci., 1970-72, asst. prof. polit. sci., 1975-78, coordinator internat. relations program, 1975-78, 79-80, assoc. prof. internat. relations and polit. sci., 1978-82; spl. asst. to pres. for nat. security affairs, sr. dir. for crisis mgmt. systems and planning NSC, Washington, 1983-84; polit. analyst and cons. Decision/Making/Info., Santa Ana, Calif., 1973; rsch. assoc. Sch. Internat. Relations, U. So. Calif., 1973; project study dir., 1973-75; vis. prof. internat. relations, summer, 1977; vis. scholar dept. systems sci. City U. London, 1978; vis. fgn. fellow Indian Inst. Advanced Studies, summer 1979; vis. Fulbright-Hays scholar Jawaharial Nehru U. Sch. Internat. Studies, New Delhi, 1979; dir. Polit. Info. System, Reagan-Bush Com., Arlington, Va., 1980; asst. dep. dir. planning and evaluation Office of Pres.-elect, Washington, 1980-81; spl. asst. to Pres. U.S. and dir. Office of Planning and Evaluation, White House, 1981-83; cons. compensatory edn. participation project Decima Inc., U.S. Office Edn., 1977-79; cons. lang. indicators project Lang. Rsch. Ctr. and Eyring Rsch. Inst., 1977—; spl. cons. computing U.S. Senate select Com. on Intelligence, 1978-79. Author: (with K.P. Misra) international Relations Theory, 1978, Systems Analysis of International Crises, 1979; contbr. numerous articles on internat. relations to profl. jours. Mem. Am. Polit. Sci. Assn., Internat. Polit. Sci. Assn., Internat. Studies Assn., Phi Kappa Phi, Pi Sigma Alpha. Mem. Ch. Jesus Christ of Latter-day Saints. Home: Herndon Va. Died Nov. 2, 1984.

BEALL, PAUL RENSSELAER, educator, communications consultant, editor; b. Des Moines, Aug. 28, 1909; s. Ollie Monroe and Helen May (Paul) B.; m. Helen Minerva Wadsworth, Sept. 18, 1937; children: Helen Wadsworth Beall Gerken, Sarah Evarts Beall Garcia y Vaz, Christopher Wadsworth Paul, Nancy Patch Beall Hendren. AB, Grinnell Coll., 1932; student law, Harvard U., 1935-36; AM, U. Mich., 1940; PhD, Pa. State U., 1948, spl. courses indsl. engring., 1948-50. Eastern states sales mgr. Morrison-Shults Mfg. Co. (leather products), 1932-39; teaching fellow speech U. Mich., 1939-41; from instr. to assoc. prof. speech and rhetoric Pa. State U., 1941-50, lectr. indsl. engring. extension, 1941-50, summer sch. lectr. in communications problems in mgmt., 1951-57; dir. info., research and devel. bd. Dept. Def., 1950-51; sci. adviser to comdg. gen. Air Research and Devel. Command, 1952, to comdg. gen. for operations USAF, 1953, to comdg. gen. USAF-Far East, 1955, 57, to comdr.-in-chief U.S. Strike Command, 1969; lectr. Joint U.S.-NATO commands, in Europe, intermittently 1955-58; cons. to founding faculty USAF Acad.; communications cons. in indsl. and mil. mgmt. (aerospace projects), 1953-87; pres. Oglethorpe U., Atlanta, 1964-67; vis. prof. Rollins Coll., 1977-79; cons. to under sec. Dept. Energy, 1979. Contbr. articles to tech. mags. Trustee Aerospace Edn. Found.; cons. Community Welfare Dr., Greater Balt., 1955-57; mem. bd. Annapolis Roads (Md.) Property Owners Assn., 1958, 62; mem. visitors adv. council Grinnell Coll., 1962-67; mem. pres.'s council Rollins Coll., 1968-72; mem. tech. adv. com. Atlanta-Fulton County Econ. Opportunity Authority, 1965-68; bd. dirs. Atlanta chpt. UN Assn. U.S., 1964-67. Mem. Nat. Conf. Adminstrn. Research (pres. 1961), U.S. Air Force Assn., Nat. Space Inst. (charter, life). Episcopalian. Clubs: Country (Orlando, Fla.); Cosmos (Washington); Explorers (N.Y.C.); Racquet (Winter Park, Fla.). Lodges: Masons, Rotary. Home: Winter Park Fla. Died Sept. 26, 1987, buried Des Moines.

BEAMAN, BERRY NELSON, tool manufacturing executive; b. Jackson, Mich., Aug. 15, 1890; s. Fred J. and Grace A. (Berry) B.; m. Lucretia C. Comstock, Aug. 24, 1915; children: Nelson, James. Student, George Washington U., 1910-12; D Bus. Adminstrn. Chmn. bd. Universal Vise & Tool Co., Parma, Mich., from 1942. Mem. Mich. State Corrections Commn., 1942-45, Fed. Prison Industries Bd., from 1953, Mich. Racing Commn., 1963-66.; del. Mich. Constl. Conv., 1961-62l fin. chmn. Mich. of Rep. Nat. Com., 1948-54. Mem. Jackson Country Club, Jackson Town Club, Burr Oak Golf Club, Elks, Sigma Chi. Home: Jackson Mich. Deceased.

BEAN, STEPHEN SIBLEY, government official; b. Woburn, Mass., June 17, 1892; s. George F. and Maria (Blodgett) B.; m. Frieda M. MacQuarrie, Feb. 25, 1939. AB, Brown U., 1914. Bar: Mass. 1919. Pvt. practice Boston, 1924-49; trial examiner NLRB, Washington, 1950-54, mem., from 1955; judge Mil. Govt. Ct., Berlin, 1945-46. Mayor Woburn, Mass., 1923-25. Sgt. Inf. AEF, World War I; lt. col. 3d Army, AUS, World War II. Mem. Delta Upsilon. Republican. Congregationalist. Home: Silver Spring Md. †

BEAN, WILLIAM BENNETT, physician; b. Manila, Philippines, Nov. 8, 1909; s. Robert Bennett and Adelaide Leiper (Martin) B.; m. Abigail Shepard, June 17, 1939; children: Robert Bennett, Margaret Bean Bayog, John Perrin. B.A., U. Va., 1932, M.D., 1935; L.H.D. (hon.), Thomas Jefferson U., 1985. Diplomate: Am. Bd. Internal Medicine, Am. Bd. Nutrition. Intern Johns Hopkins Hosp., 1935-36; asst. resident physician Boston City Hosp., 1936-37; sr. med. resident Cin. Gen. Hosp., 1937-38, asst. attending physician, 1941-46, clinician out-patient dept., 1946-48, attending physician, 1946-48; asst. prof. medicine U. Cin. Med. Coll., 1940-47, asso. prof., 1947-48; prof. medicine, head dept. internal medicine U. Iowa Coll. Medicine, 1948-70; physician-in-chief Univ. Hosps., 1948-70, Sir. William Osler prof. medicine, 1970—, prof. emeritus, 1980-89; Kempner prof., dir. Inst. for Med. Humanities U. Tex., Galveston, 1974-80, acting head dept. dermatology, 1977-78; vis. prof. medicine and history of medicine U. Va., 1968-72; Frank and Tommye Rose vis. prof. medicine U. Ala., 1976; sr. med. cons. VA, from 1947. Author: Sir William Osler: From His Bedside Teachings and Writings, 3d edit, 1968, Vascular Spiders and Related Lesions of the Skin, 1958, Aphorisms from Latham, 1962, Rare Diseases and Lesions: Their Contribution to Clinical Medicine, 1967, Walter Reed: A Biography, 1982; contbr. 300 articles to profl. jours.; author 500 book revs.; editor: Monographs in Medicine, 1951-52; book review editor of Archives of Internal Medicine, 1955-62; editor in chief, 1962-67; editorial cons. Modern Medicine, 1964-67, Stedman's Med. Dictionary, Familiar Medical Quotations; editor: Current Med. Dialog, 1967-75; editor-in-chief: Tex. Reports Biology and Medicine, 1976-80. Bd. regents Nat. Library Medicine, 1957-61, 1965-69, chmn., 1960-61. Served from capt. to lt. col. M.C. AUS, 1942-46. Recipient John Horsley Meml. prize U. Va., 1944; Groedel medal, 1961; Gold-Headed Cane, 1964; McCollum award, 1974; Disting. Head of Medicine award, 1982; named Ky. col.; hon. adm. Tex. Navy. Fellow Am. Coll. Chest Physicians (past gov. Iowa), Am. Med. Writers Assn., AAAS, ACP (past gov. Iowa, master 1971); mem. Am. Coll. Cardiology (past gov. Iowa), Nat. Assn. Standard Med. Vocabulary (dir.), Nockian Soc., AMA, Soc. Exptl. Biology and Medicine, Soc. Med. Cons. to Armed Forces, Am. Coll. Sports Medicine (charter), N.Y. Acad. Scis., Am. Acad. Polit. and Social Sci., Archeology Inst. Am. (pres. Iowa chpt. 1955-57), Am. Clin. and Climatol. Assn. (pres. 1967-68), Am. Assn. Study Liver Diseases (charter), Am. Assn. Med. History, Am. Soc. Tropical Medicine, Am. Heart Assn. (exec. com., sci. council), Iowa Heart Assn. (pres. 1950), Iowa Med. Soc., Assn. Mil. Surgeons, Med. and Jockey Soc. Interior Valley N.Am., Tb and Health Assn., Central Interurban Clin. Club (pres. 1959-61), Am. Soc. Clin. Nutrition (pres. 1962-63), John Fulton Soc. (charter mem.), Iowa Clin. Soc., World Med. Assn., Am. Osler Soc. (charter, 1st pres. 1970), Assn. Am. Physicians, Central Soc. Clin. Research (councilor 1946-49, pres. 1951), Sociedad Mexicana Historia y Filosofia de Medicina, Phi Beta Kappa, Sigma Xi, Alpha Omega Alpha. Episcopalian. Clubs: Cosmos (Washington); Stuart and Tudor (Johns Hopkins); Artillery (Galveston). Home: Iowa City Iowa. Died Mar. 1, 1989.

BEAR, STANLEY HERMAN, physician, air force officer; b. Newville, Pa., June 6, 1921; s. Samuel Herman and Elsie Claire (Ginter) B.; m. Jacqueline Jarman Silver, Nov. 17, 1951; children: Susan Jarman, Vicki Lee, Nancy Claire, Stanley David. BS in Biology, Bucknell U., 1943; MD, Temple U., 1946. Diplomate Am. Bd. Otolaryngology. Intern Temple U. Hosp., Phila., 1946-47; resident in otolaryngology Ill. Eye and Ear Infirmary, Chgo., 1952-54, chief resident, 1953-54; advanced through grades to brig. gen. USAF, 1972; mem. Air Rescue Svc. staff Westover AFB, Mass., 1948-49; with Flight Surgeon Sch., Randolph AFB, Tex., 1949; chief aviation medicine Westover AFB, Mass., 1949-50; flight surgeon 20th Fighter Bomber Group, Eng. and Shaw AFB, S.C., 1950-51; chief otolaryngology and aviation medicine Maxwell AFB, Ala., 1954-59; chief otolaryngology Weisbaden, Federal Republic of Germany, 1959-61; hosp comdr., dir. bioastronautics Edwards AFB, Calif., 1961-66; vice-comdr. Sch. Aerospace Medicine Brooks AFB, Tex., 1966-67; surgeon 7th Air Force, Vietnam, 1967-68; dep. surgeon Pacific Air Forces, Hawaii, 1968-69; asst. physician Pres. U.S., Washington, 1969-71; chief med. inspn. Hdqrs. Norton AFB, Calif., 1971-72; surgeon Mil. Airlift Command Scott AFB, Ill., 1972-73; ret. USAF, 1973; clin. instr. head and neck surgery UCLA, 1974; dir. otolaryngology San Bernardino County Med. Ctr., 1975-85; teaching asst. in otolaryngology U. Ill., Chgo., 1952-53, instr., 1953-54; cons. in otolaryngology Surgeon USAF Europe, 1959-61. Chm. Community Fund Drive, Edwards, Calif., 1963. Decorated D.S.M., Legion of Merit, D.F.C., Air Medals; recipient Disting. Alumni award Bucknell U., 1976. Fellow Aerospace Med. Assn. (exec. 1965), ACS, Internat. Coll. Surgeons, Coll. Preventive Medicine, Am. Acad. Otolaryngology and Ophthalmology; mem. AMA, Am. Coun. Otolaryngology, Soc. USAF Flight Surgeons (pres. 1965), USAF Clin. Surgeons (treas. 1965), Soc. Mil. Otolaryngolist (pres. 1957), Air Force Assn., Bucknell U., Temple U., Alumni assns., Otolaryngol. Alumni Assn. U. Ill. (pres. 1965, 73P, Muroc Lake Golf Club (pres. bd. govs. 1964), Delta Upsilon, Phi Chi. Home: Redlands Calif. Died July 3, 1985; buried Riverside Nat. Cemetery.

BEARDEN, JOYCE ALVIN, educator; b. Greenville, S.C., Oct. 19, 1903; s. Joseph Sylvester and Annie (Haley) B.; m. Lillian S. Singleton, June 6, 1923; 1 child, Alan Joyce. AB, Furman U., 1923, DSc, 1951; PhD, U. Chgo., 1926. Fellow U. Chgo., 1925, asst., 1926, instr. physics, 1926-29; assoc. Johns Hopkins U., 1929-32, assoc. prof., 1932-39, prof., 1939-86, dir. Radiation Lab., 1943-55, chmn. dept., 1947; physicist Carnegie Instn., Washington, 1941-42, Applied Physics Lab., Washington, 1942-46; cons. Nat. Def. Research Com., 1940-42. Col. U.S. Army, 1944-45, ETO. Fellow Am. Physics Soc., AAAS; mem. Am. Phys. Soc. (council 1946-50), Phi Beta Kappa, Sigma Xi. Home: Baltimore Md. Died July 28, 1986; buried Lorraine Park Cemetery.

BEARDEN, ROMARE HOWARD, artist; b. Charlotte, N.C., Sept. 2, 1914; s. Howard R. and Bessye (Johnson) B.; m. Nanette Rohan, Sept. 4, 1954. BS, NYU, 1935; postgrad., Art Students League, 1937; D of Arts (hon.), Pratt Inst., Bklyn., 1973, Carnegie-Mellon U., Pitts., 1975. art dir. Harlem Cultural Council.; vis. lectr. African and Afro-Am. art and culture Williams Coll., 1969. Exhibited in one-man shows at Kootz Gallery, N.Y.C., 1945-47, Niveau Gallery, N.Y.C., 1949, Barone Gallery, N.Y.C., 1955, Michel Warren Gallery, N.Y.C., 1960, Cordier-Ekstrom, N.Y.C., 1961, 64, 67, 69, 73, 75, 77, Corcoran Gallery, Washington, 1965, Carnegie Inst. Tech., 1966, Bundy Mus., Vt., 1966, Mus. Modern Art, 1971, Albert Loeb Gallery, Paris, 1975, Birmingham Mus. Art, McIntosh Gallery, Atlanta, Contemporary Arts Ctr., New Orleans, Mass. Coll. Art, Boston, Seventeen Wendell St., Cambridge, Malcolm Brown Gallery, Shaker Heights, Ohio, 1982, U. Mass., Amherst, Concept Art Gallery, Pitts., 1984, U. No. Iowa, London Arts, Detroit, Cordier and Ekstrom, N.Y.C., others; exhibited in Mint. Mus. Art, Charlotte, N.C., 1981, Balt. Mus., 1981, Mus. State Va., 1981, Bklyn. Mus., 1981; two-man show, Phila. Art Alliance, 1971; exhibited numerous group shows in Europe, S.Am.; author: (with Carl Holty) The Painter's Mind, 1969, (with Harry Henderson) 6 Black Masters of American Art. Served with AUS, 1942-45. Recipient award Nat. Inst. Arts. and Letters, 1966, purchase award Am. Acad. Arts and Letters, 1970, Gov.'s medal State of N.C., 1976, Nat. Arts Medal, 1987; Guggenheim fellow, 1970-71. Mem. Nat. Inst. Arts and Letters. Home: New York N.Y. Died Mar. 11, 1988.

BEASLEY, THEODORE PRENTIS, insurance executive; b. Mt. Ayr, Iowa, June 29, 1900; s. Clarence H. and Ada (Prentis) B.; m. Beulah F. Porter, June 21 1921 (dec. Dec. 1969); children: Ronald Rex, Betty Jean; m. Mary Evans Carsey, Sept. 9, 1972. Student pub. schs., Iowa, Kans.; LLD, Tex. Christian U., 1968; LHD (hon.), George Williams Coll., 1984. Founder Joplin (Mo.) Life Ins. Co., 1928; sec., gen. mgr. Pub. Nat. Life Ins. Co., Little Rock, 1935-37; pres. Republic Nat. Life Ins. Co., Dallas, 1937-61, chmn. bd., 1961-84; bd. dirs. Merc. Nat. Bank Dallas. Trustee Tex. Christian U.; bd. dirs. Nat. City Christian Ch. Corp., Washington, Dallas Community Chest, Dallas met. bd. YMCA; v.p. Greater Dallas Council Chs.; U.S. mem. World's Council, mem. nat. com., U.S. and Can.; chmn. adv. bd. Salvation Army, Dallas Citizens Council, Greater Dallas Planning Council; mem. Greater Dallas Community of Chs.; hon. trustee, vice chmn. George Williams Coll. Sgt. U.S. Army, 1918-20. Recipient Lay Churchman of Yr. award, 1952, Nat. Brotherhood citation NCCJ, 1965. Mem. Oak Cliff C. of C. (pres.), Dallas C. of C. (bd. dirs.), Am. Life Ins. Assn., Tex. Life Ins. Assn., Ins. Econ. Soc. Am. (v.p.), Health Ins. Assn. Am., Life Insurers Conf., Masons (32 deg., 33 deg.), Shriners, Kiwanis, Dallas Country Club, Lancers, Dallas Club, Brook Hollow Golf Club, Austin Club. Home: Dallas Tex. Died July 23, 1984; buried Sparkman-Hillcrest Park, Dallas.

BEATY, ROBERT COLDER, university dean; b. Ripley, Miss., Apr. 23, 1890; s. John Sadler and Martha Lou (Hodges) B.; m. Marjorie Junia Vories, Aug. 30, 1924; children: Marjorie Roberta, Robert Colder. BS, Miss. Coll., 1917; AM, Vanderbilt U., 1920, YMCA Grad. Sch., 1921; postgrad., Columbia U., 1927, U. N.C., summers 1934, 35, 37. Pub. sch. tchr. 1912-14; sec. Ga. Sch. Tech., 1921-24; with U. Fla., Gainesville, from 1925, prof. sociology, asst. dean students, 1928-37, dean students, 1939-40, dean of men, 1949-56, dean of student personnel, 1956-60, dir. Alumni Assn. Loyalty Fund, 1960-65, cons. Univ. Found., from 1965. Bd. dirs. Rodeheaver Ranch for Boys, U. Fla. Found.; state dir. Nat. Youth Adminstrn. of Fla., 1935-36, chmn. So. Regional Coll. Work Council of Nat. Youth Adminstrn., 1941-43, chmn. Nat. Work Council, 1941-43; v.p. Fla. State Housing and Scholarship Found. Sgt. U.S. Army, World War I. Mem. So. Sociol. Soc., Nat. Assn. Student Personnel Adminstrs (v.p. 1950-51), So. Assn. Deans of Men (chmn. steering com. 1951-52), Fla. Blue Key Club, Rotary, Phi Eta Sigma, Alpha Phi Omega, Phi Kappa Tau. Democrat. Baptist. Home: Gainesville Fla. †

BEAU, LUCAS V., military officer; b. N.Y., Aug. 3, 1895; m. Dulcie Steinhardt. Grad., A.C. Tactical Sch., 1934. With N.Y.N.G., 1916; pvt. aviation sect. Signal Corps, 1917; commd. 2d lt. 1918, advanced through grades to maj. gen., 1943; flight instr. World War I France; comdr. San Bernardino Air Depot, Calif.; comdg. gen. Mediterranean Air Transport Service, Naples, Italy, 1945, European Air Transport Command, Wiesbaden, Germany; nat. comdr. CAP, USAF, Washington, 1947-56; v.p. in charge fgn. ops. Consol. Diesel Electric Corp., Stamford, Conn., 1956-86. Decorated Bronze Star, Legion of Merit; Order of Nicken Ifilkyar (Tunisia); St. Maurice Lazarus, grand officer Order of Crown, knight comdr., grand officer Order of St. Hubert (Italy); comdr. Brit. Empire (Gt. Britain); Legion of Honor de Chevalier (France); War Cross (Czechoslovakia); Grand Cross of Aero. Merit (Spain). Mem. Air Force Assn., Nat. Aerospace Assn., Fedn. Aeronautique Internats., Nat. Press Club, Wings Club, Quiet Birdmen, Columbia Country Club, Washington Aviation Club. Died Oct. 22, 1986.

BEAUMONT, WORTHAM CONKLING, advertising executive; b. Mayfield, Ky., Sept. 24, 1892; s. Edgar Samuel and May Viola (Wortham) B.; m. Helen Rountree, July 4, 1915; children: Campbell A., Jeanne Beaumont Featherstone, Judith Beaumont Pine; m. Elphye Maye Hayes, Nov. 18, 1942; children: Richard H., Henry Wortham. Student, West Ky. Coll., 190608, U. Ky., 1909, 1913, Acad. Fine Arts, Chgo., 1914. With Armour & Co., 1914-18; founder Advt. Art Studio, Calif., 1918; founder, later chmn. Beaumont & Hohman. Inc., advt. agy., Fresno, Calif., 1920. Mem. Am. Jersey Cattle Club, Bel-Air Country Club (Beverly Hills, Calif.), Jonathan Club (L.A.), Olympic Club, Lakeside Country Club, San Francisco Comml. Club, Sigma Alpha Epsilon. Home: Healdsburg Calif. †

BEAVER, CLOYD SYLVESTER, business executive; b. McClure, Pa., Sept. 28, 1891; s. Joseph A. and Susana M. (Peters) B.; m. Grace Morrisey, Feb. 20, 1920; children: William M., Thomas J. Student, Susquehana U., 1908-09, Rutgers U., 1923-25, Fawcett Sch. Indsl. Arts, 1923. Sch. tchr. 1909-10, telegraph operator, 1910-23; with indsl. arts dept. Plainfield (N.J.) Bd. Edn., 1923-29; with Am. Marietta Co., from 1929, plant mgr., 1929-35, div. gen. mgr., 1935-42, v.p., from 1942, also bd. dirs. With Signal Corps, U.S. Army, 1917-19. Mem. Masons. Presbyterian. Home: High Point N.C. †

BEAVER, ROBERT PIERCE, clergyman, educator; b. Hamilton, Ohio, May 26, 1906; s. Joseph Earl and Caroline (Neusch) B.; m. Wilma Manessier, Aug. 22, 1927; children: Ellen (dec.), David Pierce, Stephen Robert. AB, AM, Oberlin Coll., 1928; PhD, Cornell U., 1933; postgrad., U. Munich, Yale U. Div. Sch., Coll. Chinese Studies at Peking, Union Theol. Sem., Columbia U.; DD (hon.), Concordia Sem., 1972. Ordained to ministry Evang. and Ref. Ch. (now United Ch. of Christ), 1932. Pastor Evang. Ref. Ch. of Oakley, Cin., 1932-36, Huber Meml. Ch., Balt., 1936-38; mem. China Mission Evang. and Ref. Ch., 1938-47; prof. Cen. China United Theol. Sem., 1940-42; prof. missions and ecumenics Theol. Sem. of Evang. and Ref. Ch., Lancaster, Pa., 1944-48; dir. Missionary Research Library, N.Y.C.; research sec. div. fgn. missions Nat. Council Chs., 1948-55; lectr. Union Theol. Sem., 1949-55; prof. missions Bibl. Sem., N.Y.C., 1950-55; prof. missions Div. Sch., U. Chgo., 1955-71, prof. emeritus, 1971-87; dir. Overseas Ministries Study Ctr., Ventnor, N.J., 1973-76; adj. prof. Fuller Theol. Sem. Pasadena, Calif., 1974-87; vis. lectr. Princeton Theol. Sem., 1974-76; vis. prof. Christian Theol. Sem., Indpls., 1981. Author: American Protestant Women in World Mission, 1980, Mission Today and Tomorrow, Introduction to Native American Church History, 1983; mem. editorial bd. Jour. Ch. and State; editor: World Christian Mission Books; contbr. articles to profl. publs. Trustee Found. for Theol. Edn. in S.E. Asia, Cook Christian Tng. Sch. Mem. Am. Soc. Ch. History, S.E. Asia Soc. Ch. History and Ecumenics (hon. pres. 1968-87), Am. Soc. Missiology (exec. com. 1972-76, chmn. bd. publs. 1979-87), Assn. Profs. Missions (pres. 1956-58), Deutsche Gesellschaft für Missionswissenschaft, Phi Beta Kappa, Phi Kappa Phi. Home: Green Valley Ariz. Died Nov. 20, 1987; buried Green Valley (Ariz.) Cemetery.

BECHER, JOHN C., actor; b. Milw.; s. John and Katherine (Schmidt) B.; m. Margaret Becher, Aug. 7, 1945. B.S., Milw. State Tchrs. Coll., 1938; B.F.A., Goodman Sch. Theatre, Chgo., 1941. Appeared in numerous Broadway plays including Mame, 1966-69, Gypsy, 1974; appeared in numerous films including Up the Sandbox, 1972, Deathwish, 1974, Next Stop Greenwich Village, 1975, Below the Belt, 1980, Honky Tonk Freeway, 1981, Gremlins, 1984, Mass Appeal, 1984,

Murphy's Romance, 1985; TV series Remington Steele, Different Strokes, Murder She Wrote, Benson, Newhart, others. Served to capt. AUS, 1941-46. Mem. Actors Equity, Screen Actors Guild, AFTRA, Motion Picture Acad. Arts and Scis., Pacific Pioneer Broadcasters. Home: Los Angeles Calif. Died Sept. 23, 1986; buried Forest Lawn Cemetery, Glendale, Calif.

BECK, CLIFFORD KEITH, physicist; b. nr. Salisbury, N.C., Apr. 12, 1913; s. Arthur Bradley and Zelma Pauline (Weant) B.; m. Mary Elizabeth Lassetter, May 28, 1943; children: Mary, Clifford K., Barbara, Jon. AB cum laude, Catawba Coll., 1933, DSc (hon.), 1951; MS, Vanderbilt U., 1940; PhD, U. N.C., 1943. Research scientist Manhattan project Columbia, 1943-45; tech. aide to mgr. of Gaseous Diffusion Project Oak Ridge, Tenn., 1945-46, dir. research, 1946-49; head physics dept. N.C. State Coll., Raleigh, 1949-56; on leave to AEC 1957-58; sci. adviser to dir. Div. Civilian Applications; chief reactor safety evaluation, coordinator for safety research AEC, 1957-60, asst. dir. Div. Licensing and Regulation, 1960-61, dep. dir. regulation, 1961-72, dir. office govt. liaison and regulation U.S., 1972-74, spl. asst. to dir. regulation, 1974-86; bd. dirs., v.p. Oak Ridge Inst. Nuclear Studies; mem. nuclear standards bd. Am. Nuclear Standards Inst., 1966-72; U.S. mem. Reactor Safety Tech., European Nuclear Energy Assn., 1966-86; mem. standards com. USA Standards Inst., 1960-66; mem. U.S. del. World Conf. on Peaceful Uses Atomic Energy, Geneva, 1956, 58, 64, 71. Trustee Montgomery Jr. Coll., 1960-69, pres., 1966-68; mem., pres. bd. edn. Montgomery County, Md., 1960-69; pres. Md. Bd. for Community Colls., 1969-86; bd. mgrs. Ministers and Missionaries Retirement Fund, Am. Bapt. Conv., 1970-86. Fellow Am. Phys. Soc.; mem. Am. Nuclear Soc. (bd. dirs. 1955-56). Home: Boyds Md. Died Apr. 17, 1986.

BECK, GEORGE FREDERICK, geologist; b. Alvord, Iowa, Dec. 26, 1892; s. Lawrence Casper and Mary (Moeller) B.; m. Sue B. Slusser, May 8, 1917; children: Katherine Beck Havnaer, Virginia Beck Michel, Shirley Ann Beck Poage. Student, U. Wash., 1914-16, 34-35, M.S., 1947; BS, Wash. State Coll., 1931; MS, U. Calif., 1940. High sch. tchr. Moses Lake, Wash., 1916-17, Warden, Wash., 1917-19, Ephrata, Wash., 1919-20, Hartline, Wash., 1920-22, Yakima, Wash., 1922-25; assoc. prof., prof. geology Cen. Wash. Coll. Edn., from 1925. Student and author concerning tertiary fossil woods of Western Am.; discoverer, founder Ginkgo Petrified Forest of Cen. Wash.; authority on identification of Western Am. fossils. Mem. AAAS, Northwest Sci. Assn., Paleontol. Soc., Soc. of Vertebrate Paleontolog6, Kiwanis, Phi Kappa Sigma. †

BECK, JULIAN, director, writer, scenic designer, actor, producer; b. N.Y.C., Mar. 31, 1925; s. Irving and Mabel (Blum) B.; m. Judith Malina, Oct. 30, 1948; 2 children. Student, Yale U., 1942-43, CCNY, 1946-49. Cofounder: (with Judith Malina) The Living Theatre; designer: The Thirteenth God, 1951; producer, designer: Doctor Faustus Lights the Lights, 1951, Ladies Voices, 1951, He Who Says Yes and He Who Says No, 1951, Childish Jokes, 1951, Dialogue of the Manikin and the Young Man, 1951; producer, designer, dir.: Beyond the Mountains, 1951, An Evening of Bohemian Theatre, 1952, Faustina, 1952, The Heroes (also acted in) and Ubi Roi, 1952, Desire Trapped by The Tail, Ladies Voices, Sweeny Agonistes, 1952, Ticklish Acrobat, 1954; producer, designer, actor: The Age of Anxiety, 1954, The Spook Sonata, 1954, Orpheus', 1954, The Idiot King, 1954, Tonight We Improvise, 1955, Phedre, 1955; dir.: The Young Disciple, 1955; designer: operas Voices for a Mirror and the Curious Fern, 1957, Dances Before a Wall, 1958; designer, producer, dir.: Many Loves, 1959, The Cave at Machpelah, 1959, The Connection, 1959, Tonight We Improvise; also acted in, 1959, The Marrying Maiden and The Women of Trachis, 1960, The Election, 1960, In The Jungle of the Cities, 1960, The Mountain Giants, 1961, The Apple, 1961, Man is Man, 1962, The Brig, 1963, Mysteries and Smaller Pieces, 1964, The Maids, 1965, Frankenstein, 1965, Antigone, 1967, Paradise Now, 1968, The Legacy of Cain, 1970, 71, 73, 74, 75, Seven Meditations on Political Sadomasochism, 1973, Six Public Acts, 1975, European tour of some prodns., 1961, 62, 64-70, 75-80, The Money Tower, 1975, Prometheus, 1978, Antigone, 1979, Masse Mensch, 1980; film performances The Brig (Venice documentary prize 1964), Narcissus, 1957, Living and Glorious, 1965, Amore, Amore, 1966, Agonia, 1967, EdipoRe, 1967 (Living Theatre received Lola D'Annunzio award 1959) Cotton Club, 1984, Poltergeist II, 1985; author: (poetry) Songs of the Revolution 1-35, 1963, 36-89, 1974, Paradise Now, 1971, The Life of The Theatre, 1972, Seven Meditations on Political Sadomasochism, 1977, others. Mem. N.Y. Com. for Gen. Strike for Peace, 1961-63; vice chmn. U.S. com. for Justice to Latin Am. Polit. Prisoners, 1973-74; sponsor Am. Friends of Brazil. Recipient Page One award Newspaper Guild N.Y., 1960, Obie award, 1960, 64, 69, 75, Brandeis U. Creative Arts award, 1961, Grand Prix de Theatre de Nations, 1961, medallion Paris Theatre Critics Circle, 1961, Prix de l'Universite, 1961, New Eng. Theatre Conf. award, 1962, Olympio award (Italy), 1967, Maharam award (stage design), 1969. Mem. Actors Equity Assn. Home: New York N.Y. Died Sept. 14, 1985; buried Cedar Park Cemetery, Emerson, N.J.

BECKER, ERNEST LOVELL, physician, educator; b. Cin., Jan. 13, 1923; s. Ernest Louis and Sarah (Lovell) B.; m. Margaret Webb Thompson, Oct. 22, 1949 (div. 1970); children: James T., Margaret W., Frank L.; m. Eleanor Holden, July 14, 1972. AB, Washntgon and Lee U., 1944; MD, U. Cin., 1948. Diplomate: Am. Bd. Internal Medicine. Asst. pharmacology U. Cin. Coll. Medicine, 1946-47; intern Christ Hosp., Cin., 1948-49; jr. asst. resident Med. Coll. Va. Hosp., Richmond, 1949-50, sr. asst. resident, 1950-51, asst. medicine, 1950-51; instr. physiology NYU Coll. Medicine, 1951-53; investigator Mt. Desert Island Biol. Lab., Salisbury Cove, Maine, summers 1951-52, 55; asst. prof. medicine Med. Coll. Va., 1955-57; asst. prof. medicine Cornell U. Med. Coll., 1957-62, assoc. prof., 1962-69, prof., 1969-78, adj. prof., 1978-86; dir. dept. grad. med. evaluation AMA, 1978-86; dir. Eugene F. DuBois Pavilion, N.Y. Hosp.-Cornell Med. Ctr., 1960-73, chief nephrology and hypertension service, dept. medicine, 1967-73; asst. attending physician 2d Cornell med. div. Bellevue Hosp., 1957-68; clin. asst. medicine Meml. Hosp., 1964-81; dir. medicine Beth Israel Med. Ctr., N.Y.C., 1981-84; cons. U.S. Naval Hosp., St. Albans, N.Y., 1960-73; asst. attending physician N.Y. Hosp., 1957-65, assoc. attending physician, 1965-69, attending physician, 1969-78; asst. vis. physician James Ewing Hosp.; sec.-gen. Internat. Co. Nomenclature and Nosology Renal Disease; mem. rsch. adv. com. Health Rsch. Coun., N.Y.C., also mem. metabolic study sect., 1965-78; chmn. ad hoc com. establishing criteria chronic renal disease ctrs. Regional Med. Programs, 1972; sci. adv. com. artificial kidney-chronic uremia program Nat. Inst. Arthritis and Metabolic Diseases, 1971-78; mem. steering com. listing program specialized clin. svcs., chmn. kidney rsch. com. Joint Commn. Accreditation Hosps., 1972-73; chmn. adv. com. renal provisions HR-1, Social Security Adminstrn., 1972-73. Editorial cons: Am. Jour. Medicine, 1971-86, Clin. Nephrology, 1971; editorial adv. bd.: Current Contents, 1972-86; contbr. articles to profl. jours. Pres. Nat. Kidney Found., 1970-73. Capt. USAF, 1953-55. Recipient Lederle Med. Faculty award, 1960-63; Markle scholar med. scis., 1955-60; WHO fellow, 1974, 78. Fellow AAAS, Royal Soc. Medicine, N.Y. Acad. Scis., Royal Soc. Tropical Medicine and Hygiene, ACP; mem. Am. Soc. Nephrology (fin. chmn.), Am. Heart Assn. (exec. com. renal sect. coun. circulation 1965-67), N.Y. Heart Assn. (bd. dirs. 1965-70), AMA, Soc. Exptl. Biology and Medicine, N.Y. County Med. Soc., N.Y. Med. and Surg. Soc., Chgo. Med. Soc., Am. Physiol. Soc., Harvey Soc., Am. Clin. and Climatol. Assn., Chgo. Soc. Internal Medicine, So. Soc. Clin. Rsch., Explorers Club N.Y., Century Assn., Union Club, Cosmos Club (Washington), Sigma Xi. Home: New York N.Y. Died Feb. 1986.

BECKER, R(AYMOND) B(ROWN), university professor; b. Clermont, Iowa, Dec. 13, 1892; s. August George and Emma Lorette (Brown) B.; m. Harriet J. Horn, July 1926 (dec. Nov. 1947); children: Elizabeth Becker Mitchell, George F., Ann M. Becker Herrick. BS, Iowa State Coll., 1916, MS, 1920; PhD, U. Minn., 1925; student of dairy cattle breeds in Brit. Isles and Europe, 1938. Instr. Kans. State Coll., 1920-23, U. Minn., 1924-25; assoc. prof. dairy husbandry Okla. A&M Coll., 1925-28; assoc. dairy husbandman U. Fla. Agrl. Expt. Sta., 1929-34, prof. dairy husbandry and animal nutrition, from 1935. Author: Dairy Cattle Breeds: Origin and Development. Mem. subcom. on dairy cattle nutrition NRC. Sgt. Inf. 91st Div., AEF, 1917-18. Recipient Borden award in dairy prodn., 1953. Mem. Am. Dairy Sci. Assn. (v.p. 1950, pres. 1951, exec. bd. 1952, sec. So. sect. 1929, 41, vice chmn. 1930, 42, chmn. 1931, 1943-46, award of honor 1962), Am. Soc. Animal Sci., Fla. Acad. Sci, Rotary, Eckles Club, Sigma Xi, Phi Kappa Phi, Alpha Zeta Gamma, Sigma Delta, Phi Sigma. Presbyterian. Home: Gainesville Fla. †

BECKERMAN, BERNARD, English literature educator; b. N.Y.C., Sept. 24, 1921; s. Morris and Elizabeth (Scheftel) B.; m. Gloria Brim, Aug. 21, 1940; children: Jonathan, Michael. BSS, CCNY, 1942; MFA, Yale U., 1943; PhD, Columbia U., 1956. Mem. faculty Hofstra Coll., 1947-65; organizer, dir. Ann. Hofstra Shakespeare Festival, 1950-64, chmn. dept. drama and speech, 1957-65; mem. faculty Columbia U., 1957-60, 65-85, prof., chmn. dept. theatre arts, 1965-81, Brander Matthews prof. dramatic lit., from 1976, chmn. dept. English and comparative lit., 1983-85, dean, 1972-76; Fulbright lectr. U. Tel-Aviv, 1960-61; Andrew Mellon prof. Tulane U., spring 1983; disting. lectr. Kyoto Am. Studies Seminar, summer 1983. Author: Shakespeare at the Globe, 1599-1609, 1962, Dynamics of Drama, 1970; also articles, revs. Bd. dirs. L.I. Arts Ctr., 1963-64. With inf. AUS, 1943-45, ETO. Decorated Bronze Star; recipient 7th Ann. award Am. Shakespeare Festival Theatre and Acad., 1962. Fellow Am. Theatre Assn.; mem. L.I. Speech Assn. (v.p. 1953-54), N.Y. Dist. Theatre Conf. (pres. 1961-62), ANTA (dir. 1963-68), Am. Soc. Theatre Rsch. (dir., chmn. 1973-79), Nat. Theatre Conf. (trustee), Shakespeare Assn. Am. (trustee, pres. 1981-82). Home: Sag Harbor N.Y. Died Oct. 7, 1985.

BECKETT, GARNER ARTHUR, cement corporation executive; b. San Francisco, Oct. 13, 1891; s. Frederick Arthur and Frances Mason (Bowen) B.; m. Lillian Hazlewood Chichester, Oct. 11, 1917; children: Patricia Ann, Jean Alice, Garner Arthur. BS in Civil Engring., U. Pa.; PhD (hon.), Claremont Men's Coll., 1958. Various positions Riverside Cement Co. div. Am. Cement Corp., 1921-36, pres., 1936-57; hon. chmn. bd. dirs. Am. Cement Corp.; bd. dirs. Union Bank, Warner Resort Co., Cyprus Mines Corp. Trustee Southwest Mus., Resthaven Psychiat. Hosp.; dir. Welfare Fedn., Los Angeles Area, from 1945, pres. 1954-57, campaign chmn., 1952-53; mem. bd. fellows Claremont U. Coll.; chmn. bd. and founding trustee Claremont Men's Coll.; trustee Barlow Found., Southwest Mus., Hoover Instn. War, Revolution and Peace, City of Hope; founding trustee Harvey Mudd Coll.; dir. So. Calif. and Ariz. Tng. within Industry, War Man Power Commn.; mem. Portland Cement adv. com. WPB, and cement industry adv. com. OPA, World War II. With U.S. Army, 1917-19, AEF. Recipient hon. citation NCCJ, 1957. Mem. California Club, Zamroano Club, Sunset Club, Los Angeles Country Club, Bel-Air Bay Club. Home: Beverly Hills Calif. †

BECKLEY, THOMAS MALLOY, railroad executive, lawyer; b. Mpls., Mar. 2, 1922; s. Miles and Rosemary (Malloy) B.; m. Nancy M. Arntsen, 1950; children: Rosemary Beckley Everson, Margaret Beckley Herrmann, Nancy, Kathryn. B.S., Yale U., 1942; LL.B., Harvard U., 1948. Bar: Minn. 1948, Mich. 1955. Practiced law Mpls., 1948-60; assoc. firm Stinchfield, Mackall, Crounse & Moore, 1948-52; gen. counsel, sec. Duluth, South Shore & Atlantic R.R., Mpls., 1953-60; asst. to pres., sec. Soo Line R.R., Mpls., 1961-68; v.p., sec. Soo Line R.R., 1968-78, pres., dir., 1978-83, chmn., chief exec. officer, dir., 1983-85, cons., dir., from 1985. Bd. dirs. Minn. Citizens Council Crime and Justice; trustee Dunwoody Indsl. Inst. Served to 1st lt. Adj. Gen. Dept., AUS, 1943-46. Mem. Assn. Am. R.R.s (dir.), Western R.R. Assn. (dir.). Clubs: Mpls. (Mpls.), Minikahda (Mpls.). Home: Minneapolis Minn. Died Jan. 31, 1987.

BECKMAN, BEN, interior designer; b. N.Y.C., Nov. 7, 1927; s. Max and Bessie (Buchman) B.; m. Amoree Cynthia Garden, May 17, 1953; children: Joel Seth, Karen Eeta, Eric Blair. BBA, Coll. City N.Y., 1949; certificate, N.Y. Sch. Interior Design, 1955. Prin. Ben Beckman, F.A.S.I.D., N.Y.C., from 1955; asst. prof. interior design dept. Fashion Inst. Tech., SUNY, N.Y.C., from 1975, also mem. adv. council. Designer furniture, carpets, men's accessories. Chmn. South Bronx Prospect Ave. Rehab. Coop. With U.S. Army, 1945-46. Recipient Presdl. citation NAt. Soc. Interior Designers, 1969, Gold medal, 1970. Fellow Am. Soc. Interior Designers (nat. chmn. bd. 1971, past pres. met. chpt. N.Y., nat. dir.). Home: Riverdale N.Y. Deceased.

BECKMAN, HARRY, physician, educator; b. Louisville, Aug. 14, 1892; s. Julius Victor and Florence (Stuber) B.; m. Jane Smith, Mar. 6, 1943; children: Thomas Howell, John Ross. Student, U. Ky., 1911-12; M.D., U. Louisville, 1921; grad. study, U. Vienna, 1930-31. Intern N.Y. Skin and Cancer Hosp., N.Y.C., 1921-23; instr. physiology and pharmacology, Sch. Medicine Marquette U., 1923, asst. prof., 1923-25, assoc. prof., acting dir. dept. pharmacology, 1925-26, chmn., 1926-61, emeritus, from 1961; investigator malariology, NIH, 1937-62; cons. physician Milw. County. and Columbia hosps., Milw.; hon. physician St. Mary's Hosp., Milw.. Author: Treatment in General Practice, 1930, Pharmacology in Clinical Practice, 1952, Drugs: Their Nature, Action and Use, 1958, Pharmacology: The Nature, action and Use of Drugs, Dilemmas in Drug Therapy, 1967; contbrs article to med. jours; editor: Year Book of Drug Therapy, 1949-69; contbg. editor Wis. Med. Jour., 1936-69; mem. editorial adv. bd. The New Physician of Student AMA. Houghton fellow clin. rsch. Columbia Hosp., Milw.; recipient State Med. Soc. Wis. Coun. award, 1959, Marquette U. teaching excellence award, 1960. Fellow AAAS, AMA; mem. Internat. Pharmacopoeia of WHO (expert adv. panel), N.Y. Acad. Scis., Milw. Acad. Med. (pres. 1949), Wis., N.H. (hon.), Milw. County mned. socs., Soc. Exptl. Biology and Medicine, Am. Soc. Pharmacology and Exptl. Therapeutics (pres. 1956-57), Fedn. Am. Socs. Exptl. Biology, Cen. Soc. Clin. Rsch., Am. and Wis. heart assns, Milw. Soc. Internal Medicine, Am., Royal socs. tropical medicine and hygiene, University Club (Milw.), Sigma Xi, Alpha Omega alpha, Phi Chi, Alpha Tau Omega. Home: Center Sandwich N.H. Died Sept. 16, 1981, buried Rural Cemetery, Center Sandwich.

BEEBE, ALEXANDER MITCHELL, utilities executive; b. Rochester, N.Y., Oct. 17, 1892; s. James Hoyt and Henrietta Rebecca (Mitchell) B.; m. Ethel Benton, June 29, 1918; 1 child, Alexander MacWhorter. MEE, Cornell U., 1915. With GE Corp., Rochester, from 1916, gen. supt. gas div., 1927-43, also bd. dirs., v.p., 1945-47, pres., 1947-56, chmn. bd., chief exec. officer, 1956-57, chmn. exec. com., 1957-65, chmn. exec. and fin. com., from 1965; past pres. Caneasea Power Corp.; bd. dirs. Lincoln Rochester Trust Co., Graflex, Inc., Assn. Edison Illuminating Cos.; exec. dir. Empire State Utilities Power Resources Assocs., 1960-66; bd. dirs. Inst. Gas Tech., Assn. Industries N.Y. State. Mem. nat. adv. com. Office Price Adminstrn. and Solid Fuels for War, 1943-45; pres., bd. dirs. Rochester Conv. and Publicity Bur., 1962; bd. dirs. Indsl. Mgmt. Council, Community Chest Rochester, Rochester YWCA, Rochester Civic Music Assn., Rochester Mus. Arts and Scis., Founders Com. of Rochesterians, George Eastman

Trustees, Rochester Inst. Tech; mem. Cornell U. Council and univ. Council Engring. Colls. Recipient Fuertes Meml. prize Cornall U., 1915, Rochester Rotary award, 1961. Mem. Am. Gas Assn. (Beale medal 1938, past mem. adv. council), Rochester Engring. Soc. (pres. 1945), Rochester C. of C. (pres. 1954), Am. Chem. Soc., Newcomen Soc., Cornell Club, Genesee Valley Country Club, University Club, Automobile Club Rochester (pres. 1966-67), Sigma Nu, Tau Beta Pi. Home: Rochester N.Y. †

BEELER, JOHN WATSON, physician, educator; b. Indpls., July 2, 1921; s. Raymond Cole and Myra (Watson) B.; m. Marcella Thorson, Jan. 13, 1951; children: John Cole, Richard Thorson, Thomas Watson. Student, Wesleyan U., Middletown, Conn., 1939-41; B.S., Ind. U., 1942, M.D., 1944; M.S. in Radiology, U. Minn., 1950. Diplomate Am. Bd. Radiology. Intern Phila. Gen. Hosp., 1945; fellow radiology Mayo Found., 1947-50; pvt. practice radiology Indpls., 1950-64, 66-87; chmn. dept. radiology Methodist Hosp., Indpls., 1963-66, dir. dept., 1964-66; asst. prof. radiology Ind. U. Sch. Medicine, 1960-81, assoc. prof., 1981-87; mem. courtesy staff Community Hosp., Indpls., 1956-87; radiologist Hancock Meml. Hosp., Greenfield, Ind., 1954-87; sec. exec. staff Marion County Gen. Hosp., Indpls., 1956-58; dir. dept. radiology Winona Meml. Hosp., 1970-81. Bd. dirs. Nat. Bd. Med. Examiners, 1977-81. Served with M.C., USAAF, 1945-47; with med. dept. AUS, 1953-54. Fellow Am. Coll. Radiology (councilor for Ind. 1961-66, speaker of council 1967-69, mem. bd. chancellors 1969-75, v.p. 1976-77); mem. AMA (interspecialty adv. bd. 1976-80, alt. del. 1978-86, del. 1986-87, exec. com. 1980-87, exec. com. Forum Med. Affairs 1981-87), Ind. Med. Assn. (mem. ho. dels. 1958-66, 68-75, speaker 1974-75, pres. 1976-77, exec. com. 1975-79, chmn. 1978), Radiol. Soc. N.Am. (counselor for Ind. 1961-66, 1st v.p. 1969-70, dir. 1970-75, chmn. bd. dirs. 1972-87, pres. 1975, councilor to Am. Coll. Radiology 1978-1980), Ind. Roentgen Soc. (chmn. exec. council 1958, pres. 1961), Marion County Med. Soc. (dir. 1956-58, 68-81, chmn. 1969-70), Am. Roentgen Ray Soc., Council Med. Splty. Socs., Eastern, Rocky Mountain radiol. socs., Orgn. State Med. Assn. Pres. (pres. 1977). Clubs: Rotary, Indianapolis Athletic. Home: Indianapolis Ind. Died Jan. 15, 1987; buried Indianapolis.

BEELER, RAYMOND COLE, radiologist; b. Charlestown, Ind., Jan. 20, 1888; s. George Theodore and Eva (Cole) B.; m. Myra Watson, Oct. 16, 1915 (dec. 1947); 1 child, John Watson. AB, Ind. U., 1910, MD, 1912. Intern Indpls. City Hosp., 1912-13; pvt. practice Indpls., from 1913; attending staff Long Hosp., Univ. Hosp.; radiologist Meth. Hosp., 1919-25; emeritus prof. radiology, chmn. sect. Ind. U. Med. Sch., from 1956. Beeler lectureship in radiology Ind. U. Fellow Am. Coll. Radiology (bd. chancellors); mem. AMA (chmn. sect radiology 1941), Am. Roentgen Ray Soc. (pres. 1946-47), Radiol. N.Am., Ind. Med. Soc., Indpls. Med. Soc., Ind. Roentgen Soc. (1st pres.), Columbia Club, Athenaeum Club, Rotary. Republican. Home: Indianapolis Ind. †

BEEMAN, WILLIAM WALDRON, physicist, emeritus educator; b. Detroit, Oct. 21, 1911; s. Joseph John and Mary E. (Waldron) B.; m. Eleanor Mildred Coswell, June 22, 1940; children: Ann Margaret, Richard William, John Michael and David Kevin (twins). Student, Wayne U., 1929-35; BS in Math, U. Mich., 1937; PhD in Physics, Johns Hopkins U., 1940. Research physicist Gen. Motors Research Labs., Detroit, 1940-41; instr. physics U. Wis., Madison, 1941-44, asst. prof., 1944-47, asso. prof., 1947-52, prof., 1952-82, prof. emeritus, 1982-87, chmn. dept., 1951-52, chmn. grad. com. biophysics, 1956-75, dir. biophysics lab., 1963-70; Sci. adviser to gov. Wis., 1963-64; adv. com. Wis. Dept. Resource Devel., 1963-64; cons. Argonne Nat. Lab., Lemont, Ill., Los Alamos Nat. Lab., 1947-52. Editorial bd.: Rev. Sci. Instruments, 1958-61; Contbr. numerous research articles to profl. publs. Citizen mem. Madison Plan Com., 1957-63; Alderman, Madison, 1955-57; Trustee Madison Gen. Hosp., 1955-57. Fellow Am. Phys. Soc.; mem. Am. Crystallographic Assn., Biophys. Soc., Phi Beta Kappa, Sigma Xi. Died Feb. 7, 1987; buried Amherstburg, Ont., Can.

BEERS, DAVID MONROE, railroad executive; b. Pelham, N.Y., July 12, 1934; s. Ernest Monroe and Jean (Thoman) B.; m. Jean Marie Tubbs, Dec. 28, 1965; children: Terri, Mia. B.A., Wesleyan U., 1955; M.P.A., Syracuse U., 1956, postgrad., 1962-63; postgrad., Yale Div. Sch., 1959-61. Exec. dir. University Hill Corp., Syracuse, 1963-67; dir. Joint Legis. Com. Housing and Urban Devel., N.Y. Legislature, 1968-69; pres. Crouse-Irving Meml. Hosp., Syracuse, 1969-80; cons., acting chief exec. officer Cortland Meml. Hosp., from 1985; chmn. Ont. Midland R.R., Ont. Eastern R.R., Ont. Central R.R., Rail Mgmt. Services, Inc., from 1979; former chmn. bd. Va. & Md. R.R., Md. & Del. R.R.; former chmn. bd. Health Mgmt. Services Corp. of Central N.Y.; dir. Norstar Bank Upstate N.Y.-Central Region; cons. Peace Corps, 1961. Served with AUS, 1957. Methodist. Home: Syracuse N.Y. Deceased.

BEGG, JOHN MURRAY, real estate investment executive; b. San Jose, Costa Rica, Jan. 5, 1903; s. John William and Blanche Eugenie (Bowns) B.; m. Jeanne Frederique van den Bosch, June 27, 1940. Student, Clifton (Eng.) Coll., 1916-19; AB, Harvard, 1924; B.A., Magdalen Coll., Oxford, Eng., 1925; MA, Oxford (Eng.) U., 1965. Pub. relations writer Internat. Tel. & Tel. Co., 1926-27; producer ednl. films Calif., 1927-28; asst. editor and Far Eastern dir. Fox Movietone News, 1928-30; editor Newsreel Theatres, Radio News and Newsreels, Pathe, 1930-36; v.p. Motion Picture Merchandising Corp., 1936-40; asst. to pres. Phillips Lord, Inc. (radio program producers), 1940-41; with Dept. State, 1941-53, asst. chief cultural relations, 1941, acting chief motion picture and radio div., 1944, chief internat. information div., 1944-46, chief internat. motion pictures div., 1946; alternate U.S. rep. subcom. on edn. Com. for Strengthening Democratic Processes, Far Eastern Commn., 1946; cons. U.S. Delegation, London Preparatory Commn. UNESCO, 1946; asst. dir. (media) Office Internat. Info. and Cultural Affairs, 1947, dir. pvt. enterprise coop. staff internat. inform. adminstrn., 1948-53; vice chmn. U.S. Delegation to Internat. High Frequency Broadcasting Conf., Atlantic City, N.J., 1947; spl. asst. to U.S. ambassador to The Netherlands, 1949; dep. examiner Bd. Examiners for Fgn. Service, 1952-53; dep. dir. Office Pvt. Coop. USIA, 1953-60; pres. Islands Investment Corp. (Realtors), Washington, 1960-76, Begg Disher Assos. Inc., Washington, 1966-71; v.p. Begg Internat. Inc. (Realtors), 1973-85. Recipient Merit citation Nat. Civil Service League, 1956; Superior Service award USIA, 1956; Wisdom award of honor Wisdom Soc. Mem. U.S. Fgn. Service Assn., Washington, V.I., Nat., Internat. real estate bds., Nat. Steeplechase and Hunt Assn. (sr.). Episcopalian. Clubs: Harvard (N.Y.C.); Metropolitan (Washington); Costa Smeralda Yacht (Sardinia, Italy); Gibson Island (Md.); Marlborough Hunt (Upper Marlboro, Md.); Sprat Bay (V.I.). Home: Davidsonville Md. Died Oct. 5, 1985; buried Rock Creek Cemetery, Washington, D.C.

BEHRE, CHARLES HENRY, JR., geologist, educator; b. Atlanta, Mar. 16, 1896; s. Charles H. and Emilie (Schumann) B.; m. H. Jeanette Allen, June 25, 1921 (dec. June 1979). Student, U. Wis., 1914-16; BS, U. Chgo., 1918, PhD, 1925; DSc (hon.), Franklin and Marshall Coll., 1949. Geologist, tchr. 1915; field geologist Wis. Geol. Survey, 1916-17; part-time asst., assoc., sr. geologist U.S. Geol. Survey, 1921-45; asst. zoology and geology U. Chgo., 1917, 19-20; instr. geology Lehigh U., Bethlehem, Pa., 1921-23; co-operating geologist Pa. Geol. Survey, 1922-46; asst. prof. U. Cin., 1924-30; assoc. prof. Northwestern U., 1930-35, prof., 1935-41, chmn. dept. geology and geography, 1933-37; prof. Columbia U., 1941-64, prof. emeritus, 1964-86, exec. officer geology dept., 1956-59; cons. Behre Dolbear & Co., 1946-86, pres., 1961-68, v.p., sr. geologist, 1968-71, sr. cons., 1971-86; Disting. lectr. Assn. Petroleum Geologists, 1950, Am. Geol. Inst., 1962; John A. Bownocker lectr. Ohio State U., 1962; gen. cons., tech. adviser metal Govt. Union Burma, 1949, Govt. of Haiti, 1951, Govt. of Algeria, 1968; chmn. com. geog. exploration Joint Research and Devel. Bd., 1946-47; mem. U.S. Nat. Com. on Geology, 1968-69. With M.C., U.S. Army, World War I. Recipient Posepny medal Cxechoslovak Acad. Scis., 1968; Guggenheim fellow, 1937-38. Fellow AAAS, Mineral. Soc. Am., Geol. Soc. Am. (council 1940-42); mem. Am. Inst. Mining and Metall. Engrs. (sr., chmn. divs. indsl. minerals and mineral econs.), Am. Assn. Geographers, Chgo. Acad. Sci., Ill. Acad. Sci. (v.p. 1933, pres. 1934), Ohio Acad. Sci. (v.p.), Assn. Petroleum Geologists, Nat. Assn. Geology Tchrs. (Miner citation 1958), Soc. Econ. Geologists (councillor 1936-39, sec. 1942-46, chmn. com. on research, v.p. 1963, pres. 1967-68), Am. Geog. Soc. (hon.), Assn. des Ingenieurs Sortis de Liège (hon.), Soc. Géologique de Belgique (corr.), Deutsch and Ak Leopoldina (Halle), Sigma Xi (pres. Columbia U. chpt. 1960-61). Home: Leonia N.J. Died Feb. 18, 1986.

BEHRENS, ROLAND CONRAD, banker; b. St. Louis, June 29, 1898; s. Charles Henry and Emma (Windhorst) B.; m. Ruth Gertrude Barrett, Aug. 7, 1928; 1 dau., Jeanne Elizabeth Behrens Lewi. Ed., St. Louis U. Sch. Law, 1927, extension div. Washington U. With St. Louis Union Trust Co., 1917-24, asst. sec., 1924-30, v.p., 1930-56, sr. v.p., 1956-65; now asso. dir.; dir. Pilot Knob Ore Co., St. Louis. Mem. Mo. Bar Assn., Newcomen Soc. N.Am. Clubs: Media (St. Louis), Univ. (St. Louis). Home: Saint Louis Mo. Died Feb. 11, 1988; interred Valhalla Mausoleum.

BEHRENS, WILLIAM WOHLSEN, JR., oceanographer, engineer, research company executive, educator, naval officer; b. Newport, R.I., Sept. 14, 1922; s. William Wohlsen and Nell (Vasey) B.; m. Betty Ann Taylor, June 22, 1946; children: Elizabeth Behrens Garland, William Wohlsen III, Charles Conrad, Susan Raker. BS, U.S. Naval Acad., 1943; postgrad., U.S. Submarine Sch., 1943, U.S. Naval Nuclear Power Sch., 1955-56, Nat. War Coll., 1963; MA, George Washington U., 1964; ScD, Gettysburg Coll., 1974. Commd. ensign USN, 1943, advanced through grades to vice adm., 1972, ret., 1974; combat duty 6 submarine patrols Pacific, World War II; comdr. 4 submarines 1953-63, founding dir. Navy's Nuclear Power Sch., 1955, AEC qualified nuclear chief reactor operator, 1956; spl. asst. AEC, 1956-57; dir. NATO nuclear planning strategic plans Office Chief Naval Ops., 1964-66, dir. politico-mil. policy, 1969-70; dep. asst. sec. state, mem. policy planning council 1966-67; comdr. Amphibious Force, Vietnam, 1967-69; oceanographer of Navy 1970-72, U.S. del. on Law of Sea, 1970-74; assoc. adminstr. and naval dep. NOAA, 1972-74; founder, dir. Fla. State Inst. Oceanography, 1977-86; sr. v.p. J. Watson Noah Inc., Arlington, Va.; pres. Earth Resources Applications Inst., Inc., Washington; sci. adviser Wheeler Industries, Inc., Washington. V.p. Am. Oceanic Orgn., 1976; trustee SEA Edn. Assn., Boston, 1974-78; bd. dirs. Fla. Inst. for Oceanography; mem. Com. of 100, Pinellas County, Fla.; bd. govs. Sci. Ctr., Inc., Pinellas County, 1975-81; mem. Port Commn., St. Petersburg, Fla.; mem. exec. bd. St. Petersburg Progress, Inc. Decorated D.S.M., Silver Star, Legion of Merit with 4 gold stars and combat V, Navy Bronze Star with combat V, Army Bronze Star with combat V, other U.S. and fgn. decorations. Mem. AAAS, IEEE, N.Y. Acad. Scis., U.S. Naval Inst. (life), U.S. Naval Acad. Alumni Assn. (life), U.S. Naval Acad. Found., Navy-Marine Corps-Coast Guard Residence Found., Naval Acad. Athletic Assn., Explorers Club, U.S. Navy League, Soc. Am. Mil. Engrs., Inst. Navigation, Marine Tech. Soc., Am. Geophys. Union, Internat. Oceanographic Found., Internat. Game Fish Assn., Arctic Inst., Am. Soc. Naval Engrs., Smithsonian Instn. Nat. Assocs., Ret. Officers Assn. (life), N.Y. Yacht Club, U.S. Naval Sailing Assn. (commodore 1975), Nat. Propeller Club, Army Navy Club. Home: Saint Petersburg Fla. Died Jan. 21, 1986; buried Arlington Nat. Cemetery, Washington.

BEIGHTLER, ROBERT SPRAGUE, state agency administrator, army officer; b. Marysville, Ohio, Mar. 21, 1892; s. William Peter and Joana (Sprague) B.;m. Claire Springer; children: Marjorie Anne Beightler Taylor, Robert Sprague. Student, Ohio State U., 1909-12; grad., Command and Gen. Staff Coll., 1926, Army War Coll., 1930; HHD (hon.), U. Ryukyus. Registered profl. engr. Civil engr. 1912; dep. county engr. Union County, Ohio; also asst. city engr. Marysville, Ohio, 1912-16; div. engr. Ohio Hwy. Dept., 1920-24, chief engr. bur. constrn., 1924-27, chief engr., 1928-30; ptnr. Stellhorn & Beightler, contracting engr., Columbus, Ohio, 1930-46; dir. Ohio Hwy. Dept., 1939-40; exec. dir. Ohio Turnpike Com., 1953-55, sec. treas., from 1955; enlisted Ohio inf. N.G. U.S. Army, 1911, commd. 2d lt., 1914, advanced through grades to maj. gen., 1944, served on Mexican border, 1916-17, with 166th inf., 42d Div., World War I, with army of occupation, Europe, 1918-19, served with 37th Div., World War II, commd. maj. gen. USNG, 1940, comdg. gen. Luzon Area Command, 1945, mem. staff War Dept., Washington, 1932-36, comd. 5th Service Command, 1946-47, pres. Army Personnel Bd., 1947-48, comdg. gen. Camp Chaffee, Ark., also 5th Armored Div., 1948-49, comdg. gen. Marianas Bonins Command, 1949, comdg. gen. and gov., Rycom, Okinawa, 1950-53, ret. Decorated D.S.C., D.S.M. with oak leaf cluster, Legion of Merit with oak leaf cluster, Silver Star, Bronze Star with oak leaf cluster, Purple Heart, Phillipine Legion of Honor, others. Mem. Masons, Eagles (hon. life), Sigma Alpha Epsilon. Home: Worthington Ohio. †

BEILFUSS, BRUCE FREDERICH, state chief justice; b. Withee, Wis., Jan. 8, 1915; s. Walter W. and Elsie (Dodte) B.; m. Helen B. Hendrickson, May 29, 1941 (dec. May 1, 1960); 1 son—Mark; m. 2d, DeEtte H. Knowlton, Oct. 17, 1961. B.A., U. Wis.-Madison, 1936, J.D., 1938. Bar: Wis. 1938, U.S. Dist. Ct. (we. dist.) Wis. 1938. Supr. county bd., Clark County, Wis., 1940; dist. atty. Clark County, Wis., 1940-48; judge U.S. Ct. Appeals (17th cir.), 1948-64; justice Wis. Supreme Ct., 1964-83, chief justice, 1976-83. With USN, 1943-46. Mem. Wis. State Bar Assn., Dane County Bar Assn., ABA., Inst. for Jud. Adminstrn., Am. Law Inst., Am. Judicature Soc., Conf. Chief Justices, Am. Legion, VFW, Madison Club. Home: Middleton, Wis. Died Aug. 18, 1986.

BELCHER, BENJAMIN MOORE, paint manufacturing company executive; b. Montclair, N.J., June 30, 1912; s. Ward C. and Ella (Moore) B.; m. Nancy Knapp, May 19, 1934; 3 sons, 2 daus. Student, U. Va. With Benjamin Moore & Co., 1934-88, pres., 1952-70, chmn. bd., chief exec. officer, 1955-84, chmn. exec. com.; staff Chem. Bur., WPB, 1942-45, chief paint sect., 1942-45; cons. NPA. Mem. Nat. Paint and Coatings Assn. (chmn. 1958, 65, dir., mem. exec. com. 1958, 65, 69-71). Home: Lakeville Conn. Died Oct. 23, 1988.

BELCHER, FRANK BAKER, lawyer; b. Carrolton, Mo., Oct. 6, 1891; s. George L. and William A. (Beazley) B.; m. Ruth B. Reynolds, May 29, 1917; children: Dorothy J. (Mrs. J. Addison Sawyer), Frank Baker II, Nancy B. (Mrs. Philip Watson). AB, Stanford U., 1913; postgrad., U. So. Calif. Law Sch., 1913-14. Bar: Calif. 1914. Mem. Jennings & Belcher, L.A., 1914-48, Belcher, Kearney & Fargo, 1948-57, Belcher, Henzie & Fargo, 1957-63, Belcher, Henzie & Bregenzahn, L.A., from 1963; v.p. Bank L.A.; bd. dirs. Bell Petroleum Co.; mem. Calif. Bd. Bar Examiners, 1943-48. Exec. officer Sheriff's Aero Squadron, L.A. County. Maj. inf. U.S. Amry, 1917-19. Fellow Am. Coll. Trial Lawyers; mem. Am. (ho. of dels. 1941-43), Calif. (pres. 1943), L.A. County (pres. 1938) bar assns., Am. Bar Found., Res. Officers Assn. (pres. L.A. chpt. 1928). Home: L.A. Calif. †

BELDEN, CLARK, business association executive, writer, educator; b. Canaan, Conn., Apr. 4, 1896; s. John H. and Frances M. (Clark) B.; m. Alice Bradford

Chapman, Aug. 1, 1931; 1 child, Constance Chapman (dec.). Student, Brown U., 1914-15, 16-17, Cornell U., summer 1914, Northwestern U., summers 1926, 27. Reporter Hartford (Conn.) Courant, 1915-16; spl. reporter Providence Jour., 1916-17; with advt. and publicity dept. Travelers Ins. Co., 1919-23, Aetna Life Ins. Co., 1923-24, Hartford Fire Ins. Co., 1924; mgr. legis. bur. Conn. C. of C., 1924-25, asst. sec., 1925-26, acting sec., later sec., 1926-27, exec. v.p., sec., bd. dirs., 1927-29; dir. pub. relations and employee edn. Nat. Electric Power Co., N.Y.C., 1929-32; exec. sec., later mng. dir. New Eng. Gas Assn., 1932-65; Faculty for trade assn. insts. Northwestern U., 1944, 46, Yale U., 1949, 55; lectr. pub. relations MIT, Boston U. Sch. Pub. Relations and Communications, Harvard Bus. Sch., Harvard Sch. Edn.; lectr. Mass Dept. Edn., Boston; mem. bd. mgrs. Northeastern Inst., Yale U., 1951-54. Author several books, 1935-49; contbr. mags. and profl. jours. Corp. mem. New Eng. Bapt. Hosp., Boston, 1955-62; mem. numerous advt. and pub. relations groups for pvt. and govtl. purposes, N.E. and nat. areas; donor with wife Constance Chapman Belden Meml. Fund and lectureship for research on systemic lupus erythematosus Mayo Found.; benefactor student scholarships, Mayo Clinic, Yale U., Harvard U.; donor specialized equipment, exhibits, funds Georgetown U., N.E. Bapt. Hosp., Boston, Rochester Meth. Hosp. Recipient Spl. Recognition award Georgetown U./Am. Security Council Edn. Found/Pentagon Edn. Ctr.; Named (with wife) maj. benefactor Mayo Clinic, 1970-80. Mem. Pub. Relations Soc. Am. (bd. dirs. 1950-52, 54-57, exec. com. 1952, ea. v.p. 1954, pres. N.E. chpt. 1953), Am. Security Council (nat. adv. bd.), Am. Soc. Assn. Execs. (bd. dirs. 1939-42, pres. Boston Chpt. 1940-41), Masons. Home: Washington D.C. Died Apr. 20, 1984; buried Salisbury (Conn.) Cemetery.

BELFORD, LEE ARCHER, clergyman, educator; b. Savannah, Ga., Oct. 14, 1913; s. William Thomas and Minnie (Archer) B.; m. Cora Louise McGee, Apr. 12, 1939; children: Fontaine Maury, Mildred Humphreys Okino. BA, U. of the South, 1935, MDiv, 1938, DD, 1978; STM, Union Theol. Sem., N.Y.C., 1947; PhD, Columbia U., 1953. Ordained to ministry Episcopal Ch., 1938. Vicar Douglas and Fitzgerald, Ga., 1938-41; rector Brunswick, Ga., 1941-43; assoc. Ch. of Epiphany, N.Y.C., 1948-80; lectr.-prof. Sch. Edn. NYU, 1949-79, chmn. dept. religious edn., 1954-74, chaplain, 1974-79. Author: The Christian and His Jewish Neighbor, 1959, Introduction to Judaism, 1961; editor: The Church in Georgia, 1949-53; trustee, assoc. editor The Churchman, 1958-88. Served as chaplain USNR. 1943-46. Mem. Religious Edn. Assn., Nat. Council Chs., Am. Acad. Religion, Soc. Sci. Study Religion, Delta Tau Delta, Sigma Upsilon. Home: Leland Miss. Died June 12, 1988, buried Greenville, Miss.

BELL, DANIEL W., commercial banker; b. Kinderhook, Ill., July 23, 1891; s. Daniel Morgan and Otis (Hardy) B.; m. Sarah Agnes Killeen, June 22, 1921; 1 child, Mary Kathleen. LLB, Nat. U. Law, Washington, 1924; BCS, Southeastern U., 1927, LLD, 1957; MA (hon.), Princeton U., 1940. Began as stenographer and bookkeeper Treasury Dept., 1911, acct. in charge fgn. loans, 1919-20, exec. asst. to assist. sec. Treasury, 1920-24, asst. commr. accounts and deposits, 1924-31, asst. to sec. of treasury on financial and accounting matters, 1935-40, acting dir. of budget, 1934-39, undersec., 1940-45; pres. Am. Security and Trust Co., 1946-59, chmn., from 1954; mem. Price Decontrol Bd., 1946-47; spl. amb. to Philippines, 1950; acting chmn. pub. adv. bd. Mut. Security Adminstrn., 1952-53; bd. dirs. Nat. Press Bldg. Corp., People's Drug Stores, Peoples Life Ins. Co., B. F. Saul Co., Security Storage Co., Washington Gas Light Co. Mem. bus. adv. bd. Am. U. Sch. Bus. Adminstrn.; active Boy Scouts Am., ARC; bd. dirs. Columbia Hosp. Women, Madeira Sch.; trustee Brookings Instn. Pvt. U.S. Army, 1918-19. Decorated Legion of Honor (France). Mem. Am. Automobile Assn. (treas.), Am. Bankers Assn., Chevy Chase Club, Sulgrave Club, Alfalfa Club, Met. Club, Nat. Press Club, Ponte Verde (Fla.) Club, Farmington Country Club (Va.). Home: Washington D.C. †

BELL, DOROTHY MAY, junior college president; b. Elyria, Ohio, May 29, 1903; d. William Frederick and Lois Elizabeth (Dickinson) B. AB, Oberlin Coll., 1925, LLD, 1957; AM, Smith Coll., 1929; student, Am. Sch. Classical Studies, Athens, Greece, summer 1932; also studied, Columbia U. Tchr. Latin Amherst (Ohio) High Sch., 1925-28; critic tchr. in Latin Oberlin (Ohio) High Sch., 1929-32, 33-34; asst. in exptl. work in Latin Tchrs. Coll., Columbia U., N.Y.C., 1932-33; head Latin dept. The Berkeley Inst., Bklyn., 1934-38; instr. in classics Oberlin Coll., 1938-40; pres. Bradford (Mass.) Jr. Coll., 1940-67. Mem. Mass. Bd. of Collegiate Authority (4 4-yr. terms). Awarded Trustee fellowship Smith Coll., 1928, Aeolian fellowship Oberlin Coll., 1932, 40. Mem. Am. Assn. Jr. Colls. (past pres.), New Engl. Assn. of Colls. and Secondary Schs. (exec. com.), Phi Beta Kappa. Congregationalist. Home: Elyria Ohio. Died Apr. 8, 1988.

BELL, HOWARD WILLIAM, petroleum company executive; b. Hays, Kans., July 8, 1918; s. Myron Judson and Alice (Chambers) B.; m. Dorothy Leslie Goodrick Crosno, July 3, 1976; children: Brenda Bell Jenner, Sherron Bell Mullin. Student, U. So. Calif., 1937-41. With Standard Oil Co., Calif., 1936-83; asst. treas. Standard Oil Co., San Francisco, 1961-67, v.p. fin., 1968-83, bd. dirs., 1971-83; officer Iranian Oil Consortium, Teheran, 1954-61; v.p., sec. Chevron Oil Europe, N.Y.C., 1967-68. Bd. regents St. Mary's Coll., Moraga, Calif., from 1978. Mem. Fin. Officers No. Calif., Nat. Planning Assn., Am. Petroleum Inst., Bankers Club, Pacific Union Club, San Francisco Golf Club, Stock Exchange of San Francisco. Republican. Deceased.

BELL, JOSEPH RAYMOND, lawyer, government official; b. New Orleans, Jan. 7, 1908; s. Harry and Anna B.; m. Jeanne Viner, Dec. 15, 1974; children: Carol Johnston, Bonnie Sauve, Joseph Raymond, Melodie Macklin. Grad., NYU, 1928; LLB, Atlanta Law Sch., 1930. Bar: N.Y., D.C., Ga. Reporter Georgian-Am., 1928-30, Detroit Times, 1930-33; dir. publicity and advt. Loew's Washington Theatres, 1933-42; ea. publicity mgr. Metro-Goldwyn-Mayer, N.Y.C., 1942-44; dir. pub. relations Capital Airlines, Washington, 1944-47; v.p. Columbia Pictures Industries Inc., 1949-72; mem. firm Wyman, Bautzer, Rothman & Kuchel, 1973; chmn. Fgn Claims Settlement Commn. U.S., Washington, 1973-77, 81-83; bd. dirs. MacMillen Ring Free Oil Co., WHDH Corp., Miami Hotel Corp., Palm Beach. Bd. dirs. Palm Beach Symphony; dir. polit. communications Reagan-Bush Com., 1980; chmn., dir. Heart Fund, D.C. Cancer Drive. Recipient Exceptional Service award USAF, Patriotic Service award U.S. Army, Good Guy award Am. Legion. Mem. Pub. Relations Soc. Am. (dir., pres. N.Y. chpt., D.C. chpt., nat. v.p., presdl. citation), Air Force Assn. (pres. chpt., Man of Yr.), Advt. Club Washington (v.p.), Assn. of Bar of City of N.Y., Bar Assn. D.C., Ga. Bar Assn., Fed. Bar Assn., ABA, Metropolitan Club, Cosmos Club, Overseas Press Club, Nat. Press Club, Army and Navy Club, Congl. Country Club, Pisces Club, Nat. Lawyers Club. Republican. Methodist. Home: Washington D.C. Died Sept. 6, 1983.

BELL, TYREE LEWIS, JR., contracting company executive; b. Horse Cave, Ky., Mar. 26, 1891; s. Tyree Lewis and Martha (Hardy) B.; m. Alta Harrison, Jan. 18, 1921; 1 dau., Patricia (Mrs. John T. Miller). BSCE, Tex. A&M Coll., 1913; student, U. Glasgow (Scotland), 1919. Registered profl. engr., Tex. With Vicksburg (Miss.) dist. U.S. Corps. Engrs., 1913-17; Southwestern mgr. Lakewood Engring Co., Cleve., 1919-22; gen. supt. F. P. McElwrath Constrn. Co., Corsicana, Tex., 1922-33; pres. Austin Road Co., Dallas, then cons. dir.; pres., dir. Austin Paving Co., Dallas, from 1950, Austin-Worth Constrn. Co., Dallas, from 1947; v.p., trustee Worth Constrn. Co., Dallas, from 1952; dir. Lone Star Steel Co., Tex. Power & Light Co., Austin Bridge Co., Austin Bldg. Co., Servis Equipment Co., Lakewood State Bank, Superior Ins. Co. Chmn. street and hwy. com. Greater Dallas Planning Coun., from 1950; adv. com. Tex. Transp. Inst., from 1960; pres. Cotton Bowl Athletic Assn., 1948-49; mem. Dallas Citizens Coun.; v.p., dir. Tex. A&M Coll. System, 1947-52, councilor Rsch. Found., from 1950; bd. dirs. State Fair Tex., from 1948. Maj. C.E., U.S. Army, 1917-19, AEF in France and Eng. Mem. ASCE (life), Soc. Am. Mil. Engrs., Nat. Soc. Profl. Engrs., Assoc. Gen. Contractors (past pres. Tex.), Dallas Salesmanship Club, Assn. Former Students Tex. A&M Coll. (pres. 1942), Dallas Club, Dallas Athletic Club, City Club, Chaparral Club, Koon Kreek Club (Athens, Tex.), Fin & Feather Club (Hutchins, Tex.), Pi Beta Tau. Home: Dallas Tex. †

BELL, WILLIAM RAYMOND, trade association executive; b. Concord, N.C., Sept. 10, 1892; s. William L. and Maggie J. (Leslie) B.; m. Beatrice M. Cast, Sept. 7, 1921; children: Jean Bell Andrews, Sallie Bell Potter, Leslie Cast (dec.). AB summa cum laude, Trinity Coll. (now Duke U.), 1911. Mgr. export dept., various other positions Cannon Mills, Inc., 1911-17, mgr. sheets and pillowcase dept., 1922-29; exec. v.p. Cotton Textile Inst., N.Y., 1929-32; sec. Assn. Cotton Textile Mchts., N.Y., 1932-34, pres., from 1934; mem. Cotton Textile Industry Code Authority, 1934-35; mem. Gen. Arbitration Council Textile Industry, from 1936, chmn., from 1949; chief textile div. Nat. Def. Adv. Commn., 1940, textile div. Office Procurement Mgmt., 1941. Author: Ten Years of Cotton Textiles, 1932, ann. edits., from 1933, Worth Street Rules, 1936, rev. edit., 1941; contbr. articles to Jour. Commerce, Daily News Record, textile pubs. With N.Y. N.G., 1916, capt. inf., U.S. Army, 1917-18. Mem. Am. Trade Assn. Execs., Trade Assn. Execs. of N.Y. (v.p. 1948), Mchts. Club, Town of Scarsdale Club, Scarsdale Golf Club, N.Y. So. Soc. (exec. com. 1947-48), N.C. Soc. (N.Y.). Home: Hartsdale N.Y. †

BELLAMY, ALBERT WILLIAM, university professor and dean; b. Yukon, Okla., June 30, 1892; s. Charles W. and Etta J. (Martindale) B.; m. Anna L. Gish., June 19, 1913; children: Anna Louise Bellamy Henry, Dorothy Marie Bellamy Wright, Evelyn Grace Bellamy Robbins. BS, Kans. State Coll., 1914; fellow, U. Chgo., 1916-90, PhD summa cum laude, 1919. Asst. Kans. State Coll., Manhattan, 1914-16; instr. U. Chgo., 1919-23, asst. prof., 1923-24; asst. prof. UCLA, 1924-27, assoc. prof., 1927-37, prof., from 1937, dean Div. Life Scis., 1946-49, prof. of biophysics, 1948-59, emeritus, acting dept. chmn. Med. Sch., from 1959; staff mem. Radiation Lab., MIT (radar rsch.), 1943-44; radiolog. safety sect.; Operation Crossroad, 1946; chief of sect. Atomic energy project U. Cal., from 1947; chief Radiol. Safety Svc. State Office Civil Def., 1951-55; lectr. on mil. and peacetime implications of nuclear energy, population densities in relation to natural resources. Dir. Los Angeles County br. Am. Cancer Soc. Mem. AAAS, Am. Soc. Zoology, Sigma Xi, Gamma Alpha. Home: North Hollywood Calif. †

BELLINGER, BURDETTE W., business executive; b. Battle Creek, Mich., Sept. 28, 1892; s. Arthur Frederick and Lena Belle (Willison) B.; m. Vera Eddins, Apr. 20, 1929; children: Dan Eddins, Barbara Bellinger Platt. BS, Mich. State Coll., 1920. Engr. Colombia, S.Am., 1920-23; gen. mgr. mining co. Mex., 1925-31; various positions Tampa (Fla.) div. Tenn. Corp., 1931-51, v.p., dir., 1951-56, exec. v.p., from 1955; bd. dirs. Tenn. Copper Co., New Haven Copper Co., Capitol Fertilzer Co., U.S. Phosphoric Products Corp., Tenn. Trading Co. 1st lt. F.A. U.S. Army, 1917-19. Mem. Am. Chem. Soc., Greenwich (Conn.) Country Club, Indian Harbor Yacht Club (Greenwich), Atlanta Club, Athletic Club, Tampa Yacht and Country Club, Palma Ceia Golf Club (Tampa), Masons, Tau Beta Pi, Psi Upsilon. Republican. Episcopalian. Home: Greenwich Conn. †

BELLOT, HUGH HALE, history educator; b. Addlestone, Surrey, Eng., Jan. 26, 1890; s. Hugh Hale Leigh and Beatrice Violette (Clarke) B. BA, Oxford U., 1913; LLD (hon.), U. London, 1957. Temp. master Battersea Poly. Secondary Sch., Bedales Sch., 1915-17; asst. dept. history Univ. Coll., U. London, 1921-26; sr. lectr. Univ. Coll., London, 1926; reader modern history U. Manchester, 1927-30; Commonwealth Fund prof. Am. history U. London, 1939-55, mem. senate, 1938-56, mem. ct., 1948-53, vice chancellor univ., 1951-53; Sir George Watson lectr., Birmingham, Eng., 1938; acting prin. Bd. Trade, 1940-44, mem. council U. Coll., Ibadan, Nigeria, 1948-57. Author: The Study of American History, 1932, American History and American Historians, 1952, Woodrow Wilson, 1955. Fellow Royal Hist. Soc. (hon. sec. 1934-52, pres. 1952-56). Home: London Eng. †

BELTZ, LEROY DUANE, university dean; b. Pierce, Nebr., Apr. 25, 1924; s. Adolph and Caroline (Rohde) B.; m. Glenda Marie Reese, Jan. 21, 1944; children—Judith Ann, Glen Duane, David Scott, Keith Stuart. B.Sc. in Pharmacy with distinction, U. Nebr., 1951; Ph.D. in Pharm. Chemistry, U. Conn., 1956. Instr. pharmacy U. Conn., 1952-56; asst. prof. pharmacy U. Fla., 1956-58; asso. prof., then prof. Ferris State Coll., 1958-66; prof. pharmacy, dean Coll. Pharmacy, Ohio No. U., Ada, from 1966. Served with USN, 1941-47. Mem. Am., Ohio pharm. assns., Am. Inst. History of Pharmacy, Sigma Xi, Rho Chi, Phi Lambda Upsilon, Beta Beta Beta, Phi Eta Sigma, Phi Kappa Phi, Kappa Psi, Omicron Delta Kappa, Alpha Zeta Omega, Gamma Sigma Epsilon, Phi Delta Chi, Kappa Epsilon. Republican. Mem. Christian Ch. Deceased.

BENADE, ARTHUR HENRY, physicist, educator; b. Chgo., Jan. 2, 1925; s. James Martin and Miriam (McGaw) B.; m. Virginia Lee Wassall, June 9, 1948; children: Judith Anne, Martin Daniel. AB, Washington U., 1948, PhD, 1952. Design engr. McDonnell Aircraft, St. Louis, 1952; instr. physics Case Western Res. U., Cleve., 1952-54, asst. prof., 1954-60, assoc. prof., 1960-69, prof. physics, 1969-87; vis. prof. Indian Inst. Tech., Kanpur, 1964-65, U. Mich., 1974; cons. instrumentation, musical and archtl. acoustics. Author: Horns, Strings and Harmony, 1960, Fundamentals of Musical Acoustics, 1976. Pres. Cleve. Chamber Music Soc., 1980-81. Served with USAAF, 1943-46. Fellow Acoustical Soc. Am. (v.p. 1974-75, Gold medal 1988), AAAS; mem. Am. Phys. Soc., Galpin Soc., Catgut Acoustical Soc. (pres. 1969-72), Am. Assn. Physics Tchrs. Home: Shaker Heights Ohio. Died Aug. 4, 1987; cremated.

BENDER, LAURETTA, child psychologist; b. Butte, Mont., Aug. 9, 1897; d. John Oscar and Katherine Parr (Irvine) B.; m. Paul Ferdinand Schilder, 1936 (dec. Dec. 1940); children: Michael, Peter, Jane; m. Henry B. Parkes, 1967 (dec. Jan. 1972). BS, U. Chgo., 1922, MA in Pathology, 1923; MD, State U. Iowa, 1926. Diplomate Am. Bd. Psychiatry and Neurology. Intern, resident in neurology Billings Hosp., U. Chgo., 1927-28; psychiat. resident Boston Psychopathic Hosp., 1928-29; research assoc. Phipps Clinic, Johns Hopkins Hosp., Balt., 1929-30; sr. psychiatrist Bellevue Hosp., N.Y.C., 1930-56, charge children's service, 1934-56; with NYU, 1930-58, prof. clin. psychiatry, 1951-58, sr. cons. VA tng. program, 1940-58; psychiat. cons. children N.J. State Neuropsychiat. Inst., 1954, attending psychiatrist, 1969-73; cons. child psychiatry N.Y. State Dept. Mental Hygiene, 1956-67; dir. research child psychiatry Creedmor State Hosp., 1959-67; attending psychiatrist N.Y. State Psychiat. Inst., 1969-74; clin. prof. psychiatry Columbia Coll. Physicians and Surgeons, 1959-62, U. Md. Sch. Medicine, 1975-87; cons. Childrens Guild Inc. Author, editor Bellevue Studies in Child Psychiatry. Served on various civic orgn. coms. for child welfare. Recipient Adolph Meyer award, 1953, Med. Woman of Yr. award for N.Y., 1958, Alumni Profl. Achievement award U. Chgo., 1972. Mem. Am. Psychiat. Assn. (Agnes Purcell McGavin award 1969), Am. Neurol. Assn., Am. Orthopsychiat. Assn., Am. Psychopath.

Assn., Acad. Child Psychiatry, Am. Assn. for Mental Deficiency. Home: Annapolis Md. Died Jan. 4, 1987.

BENDER, MYRON LEE, chemist, educator; b. St. Louis, May 20, 1924; s. Averam Burton and Fannie (Leventhal) B.; m. Muriel Blossom Schulman, June 8, 1952; children: Alec Robert, Bruce Michael, Steven Pat. BS with highest distinction, Purdue U., 1944, PhD, 1948, DSc honoris causae, 1969; postdoctoral student, Harvard, 1948-49; AEC fellow, U. Chgo., 1949-50. Chemist Eastman Kodak Co., 1944-45; instr. U. Conn., 1950-51; from instr. to assoc. prof. Ill. Inst. Tech., 1951-60; mem. faculty Northwestern U., 1960-88, prof. chemistry, 1962-85, prof. biochemistry, 1975-85, prof. emeritus, 1985-88; cons. to govt. and industry, 1959-88; vis. fellow Merton Coll., Oxford U., 1968; J.S.P.S. vis. lectr., Japan, 1974; vis. prof. U. Queensland, Australia, 1979, Nankai U., China, 1982, univs. Tokyo and Kyoto, Japan, 1982. Recipient Midwest award Am. Chem. Soc., 1972; Sloan fellow, 1959-65; Fulbright Hays disting. prof. Zagreb, Yugoslavia, 1977. Fellow Am. Inst. Chemists; mem. Am. Chem. Soc., AAUP, Chem. Soc. (London), Am. Soc. Biol. Chemists, Assn. Harvard Chemists, AAAS (councilor chemistry sect.), Nat. Acad. Scis., Phi Beta Kappa, Sigma Xi, Phi Lambda Upsilon. Home: Evanston Ill. Died July 29, 1988.

BENEDICT, MURRAY REED, economist; b. Neillsville, Wis., Jan. 23, 1892; s. Julius Sidney and Celia Ruth (Reed) B., m. Elizabeth Tucker, 1916 (dec. 1930); children: Bruce Tucker, Elizabeth Jean; m. 2d Martha Scott Epps, June 21, 1933; 1 dau., Barbara Lee. BS, U. Wis., 1916; PhD (Social Sci. Rsch. fellow), Harvard U., 1928, PhD (Ricardo prize fellowship), 1929; Rockefeller Found. grantee, Europe, 1939; LLD (hon.), U. Calif., 1961. Instr. in agr. Boscobel, Wis., 1913-14, Aurora, Minn., 1916-17; farm advisor Blue Earth Co., Mankato, Minn., 1918-19; sec. S.D. Farm Bur. Fedn., 1921; sec.-treas. Coop. Wool Growers of S.D., 1921-28; asst. commr. agr. S.D. Dept. Agr., half-time 1921-25; prof. agrl. economics, head of dept. S.D. State Coll., 1921-28; lectr. on economics Harvard U., 1930-31; prof. agrl. economics, agrl. economist Gianni Found. and agrl. economist exptl. sta., U. Calif., Berkeley, 1931-61, emeritus, from 1961; mem. resident staff Com. on Govt. Statistics and Info. Svcs., Washington, 1933-34; mem. com. 1934-37; vis. prof. U. Ariz., 1965; chmn. faculty Salzburg Seminar in Am. Studies, Salzburg, Austria, 1966. Author: Farm Policies of the United States, 1790-1950, 1953, Can We Solve the Farm Problem, 1955, (with O.C. Stine) The Agricultural Commodity Programs: Two Decades of Experience, 1956, (with E.K.Bauer) Farm surpluses: U.S. Burden or World Asset, 1960; author bulls., pamphlets; contbr. articles to profl. jours. Econ. advisor Calif. Farm Debt Adjustment Commn., 1935-39; dir. San Francisco Bay and Richmond-Vallejo Def. Rental Areas, 1942; spl. staff cons. on foods, Lendlease Adminstrn., 1943; cons. on foods, Fgn. Econ. Adminstrn., 1944; chmn. spl. com. of consultants to recommend plans for reorgn. FCA, 1944, to recommend plans for fed. forest credit program, 1945; cons. WSB, Washington, 1951; rsch. dir. farm policy study Twentieth Century Fund, 1951-56. Fellow Am. Statis. Assn. (mem. adv. com. to dir. census 1937-54, pres. San Francisco chpt. 1937), AAAS, Am. Farm Econ. Assn. (exec. com. 1942-44, v.p. 1928, pres. 1941, chmn. joint com. on agr. census with Social Sci. Rsch. Coun., 1935); mem. Social Sci. Rsch. Conf. of Pacific Coast (sec. 1940), Western Farm Econ. Assn. (pres. 1040), Nat. Planning Assn. (mem. agrl. com. from 1943), Am. Econ. Assn., Cosmus Club (Washington). Home: Berkeley Calif. Deceased.

BENETAR, DAVID L., lawyer; b. N.Y.C., Nov. 19, 1906; s. Morris and Estella B.; m. Beatrice Dalsimer, June 26, 1934; children: Carol Ann, Richard D. Student, NYU, 1923-25, postgrad. lawa, 1928-29; LLB, Bklyn. Law Sch., 1928. Bar: N.Y. 1929. Pvt. practice N.Y.C., 1929-86; mem. firm Nordlinger, Riegelman, Benetar & Charney, N.Y.C., 1933-70; prin. mediation officer, dir. disputes div. 22d region, mem. pub. panel U.S. War Labor Bd., Washington and N.YC., 1942-45; mem. firm Aranow, Brodsky, Bohlinger, Benetar & Einhorn, N.Y.C., 1971-78, Benetar Isaacs Bernstein & Schair, 1979-86. Mem. Gov.'s Labor-Mgmt. Adv. Panel Mediation Bd., N.Y., 1969-79; bd. dirs. Econ. Devel. Coun., N.Y.C. Inc., 1968-79; chmn. bd. edn. Mt. Pleasant Dist. Schs., Hawthorne, N.Y., 1950-56; pres. Jewish Bd. Guardians, 1956-60, chmn. exec. com., 1960-78, hon. pres., 1980-86; trustee Fedn. Jewish Philanthropies, N.Y., 1956-86. Mem. ABA (mem. labor law sect. 1965-86), Fed. Bar Assn. (chmn. labor com. Empire State chpt. 1971-77, chpt. pres. 1977-79), Assn. Bar City N.Y. (mem. exec. com. 1957-60), N.Y. Chamber Commerce and Industry (mem. exec. com. 1958-74, dir. 1974-79) U.S. C. of C. (mem. labor relations com. 1965-69), Edward Corsi Labor-Mgmt. Relations Ins. Pace Univ. (chmn. exec. com. 1969-86), Cornell Club. Home: New York N.Y. Died 1986.

BENEVENTANO, THOMAS CARMINE, radiologist, educator; b. Maspeth, N.Y., Mar. 20, 1932; s. Joseph Anthony and Mildred Carmela (Citera) B.; m. Marilyn Louise Rarrick, June 15, 1957; 1 son, Thomas Martin. A.B., N.Y. U., 1953; M.D., SUNY, 1957. Diplomate: Am. Bd. Radiology. Intern Kings County Hosp., Bklyn., 1957-58; resident in radiology Kings County Hosp., 1960-63; radiologist Montefiore Hosp. and Med. Center, Bronx, N.Y., 1963—; prof. radiology Albert Einstein Coll. Medicine, 1978-88, acting chmn. dept. radiology, 1986-88. Co-author: Radiologic Examination of the Orohypopharynx and Esophagus, 1977. Served to capt. M.C., U.S. Army, 1958-60. Fellow Am. Coll. Radiology, N.Y. Acad. Gastroenterology, N.Y. Acad. Medicine; mem. Radiol. Soc. N.Am., Am. Roentgen Ray Soc. (chmn. exec. council 1984-85, 2d v.p. 1985-86), N.Y. Roentgen Soc. (pres. 1980-81), AMA, N.Y. Med. Soc., Bronx County Med. Soc., Soc. Gastrointestinal Radiologists (sec./treas. 1986-87, pres.-elect 1987—), Assn. Univ Radiologists, Am. Bd. Radiology (trustee). Died Apr. 28, 1988.

BENFIELD, WILLIAM AVERY, JR., clergyman; b. Greenville, W.Va., July 5, 1915; s. William Avery and Mamie Etta (Bonds) B.; m. Eunice Byrnside, Aug. 31, 1938; children: William Avery III, Robert Byrnside, John Milne. AB, Davidson Coll., 1936, DD, 1949; BD, Louisville Presbyn. Theol. Sem., 1939, ThM, 1940; ThD, So. Bapt. Sem., 1943; DD, Morris Harvey Coll., 1970; LHD, Davis and Elkins Coll., 1979. Ordained to ministry Presbyn. Ch., 1939; pastor Beechmont Presbyn. Ch., Louisville, 1940; prof. Hebrew and old testament Louisville Presbyn. Theol. Sem., 1940-44, v.p., 1945-49; sr. minister Highland Presbyn. Ch., Louisville, 1949-58; sr. minister First Presbyn. Ch., Shreveport, La., 1958-63, Charleston, W.Va., 1963-80; adj. prof. theology U. Charleston, 1980; Moderator Gen. Assembly Presbyn. Ch. U.S., 1970-71; chmn. gen. council, chmn. bd. annuities and relief; mem. exec. com. Consultation on Ch. Union. Co-author: Understanding the Books of the Old Testament, 1944, The Church Faces the Isms, 1958. Trustee Davis and Elkins Coll., Centre Coll., Southwestern at Memphis, Austin Presbyn. Theol. Sem., Louisville Presbyn. Theol. Sem., Union Theol. Sem., Richmond, Va. Recipient Disting. Alumnus award Louisville Presbyn. Theol. Sem., 1986, Citizen of Yr. award WV Chpt.of Nat. Assn. of Social Workers, 1988; William A. Benfield Jr. Professorship in Evangelism and Global Mission, Louisville Presbyn. Theol. Sem.,1988. Mem. Beta Theta Phi. Democrat. Presbyn. Club: Juniper Hunting and Fishing (Astor, Fla.); Southern Cross Fishing (Little Cayman, B.W.I.). Lodge: Rotary. Home: Charleston W.Va. Died Dec. 9, 1987; buried Boone Meml. Park, Madison, W.Va.

BENJAMIN, BURTON RICHARD, producer, writer; b. Cleve., Oct. 9, 1917; s. Sam and Ruth (Bernstein) B.; m. Aline L. Wolff, Apr. 5, 1942; children: Ann Norma, Jane Ruth. BA, U. Mich., 1939. Newspaperman U.P. and NEA Service, Cleve. and N.Y.C., 1939-42, NEA Service, N.Y.C., 1945-46; writer, producer documentary films RKO-Pathe, N.Y.C., 1946-55; exec. producer World War I CBS News, 1965; sr. exec. producer CBS News, N.Y.C., 1968-75; exec. producer Evening News CBS News, 1975-78; v.p. and dir. news CBS, 1978-81, sr. exec. producer, 1981-85; writer documentary and dramatic scripts for TV from 1955; Lectr. polit. sci. Manhattanville Coll., Purchase, N.Y.; Howard R. Marsh vis. prof. journalism U. Mich., 1976, 87. Author: Fair Play, 1988; producer TV series Twentieth Century, CBS News, 1957; exec. producer TV series The 21st Century, CBS News, 1957 (Emmy award, Lasker award 1968-69), CBS news spls. Justice Black and the Bill of Rights Aftermath, Martin Luther King Assassination, 1968 (ABA award, Emmy award), Justice in Am., 1972 (Emmy award), CBS Reports spls. The Rockefellers (Emmy award), Solzhenitsyn, 1974 (Emmy award). Trustee Scarborough Sch. Served to lt. USCGR, 1942-45. Recipient Peabody award Overseas Press Club; Gannet Ctr. Media Studies sr. fellow Columbia U., 1986-87. Mem. Writers Guild Am., Authors Guild. Club: Century Assn. Died Sept. 18, 1988.

BENNETT, WILLARD HARRISON, physicist, emeritus educator; b. Findlay, Ohio, June 13, 1903; s. Harry and Elsie Mae (Ward) B.; m. Mona D. Sheets, Sept. 8, 1928; children: Willard Harrison, Barbara, Bruce, Steven; m. Helen Mae Sawyer, Oct. 24, 1948; children: Charles, Ward, Rebecca. Student, Carnegie Inst. Tech., 1921-22; AB, Ohio State U., 1924; MS, U. Wis., 1926; PhD, U. Mich., 1928. NRC fellow Calif. Inst. Tech., 1928-30; faculty Ohio State U., 1930-38; dir. research Electronics Research Corp., 1938-41; dir. applied research Inst. Textile Tech., 1945; physicist, sect. chief Nat. Bur. Standards, 1945-50; prof. physics U. Ark., 1950-51; br. head, div. cons. U.S. Naval Research Lab., 1951-61; Burlington prof. physics N.C. State U., 1961-76, prof. emeritus, 1976-87; cons. Los Alamos Sci. Lab., 1953-87. Contbr. articles to profl. jours.; co-author textbook. Served to lt. col. AUS, 1941-45. Fellow Am. Phys. Soc., Washington Acad. Sci. Presbyterian (ruling elder). Home: Raleigh N.C. Died Dec. 28, 1987; buried Arlington Nat. Cemetery.

BENSON, OSCAR ALGOT, church executive; b. Derry, Pa., Apr. 7, 1891; s. Andrew B. and Albertina (Johnson) B.; m. Elfie Hanson, July 29, 1920; children: Hilvie Elizabeth, Philip Andrew. AB, Upsala Coll., East Orange, N.J., 1912; AM, Augustana Coll., Rock Island, Ill., 1914; BD, Augustana Sem., 1915; student, Columbia U., 1921-25; PhD, U. Pitts., 1933; DD, Upsala Coll., 1943, Bethany Coll., 1956. Ordained to ministry Luth. Ch., 1915. Pastor successively Luth. Ch., Albert City, Iowa, Montclair, N.J. and Ridgeway, Pa., 1915-31, Salem Ch., Chgo., 1931-42; pres. Ill. Conf. of Augustana Luth. Chs., 1940-49; pastor Trinity Ch., Worcester, Mass., 1949-51; v.p. Augustana Luth. Ch. 1941-51; v.p. Augustana Luth.Ch., 1941-51, pres., 1951-59; pastor Salem Ch, Omaha, 1961, Emanuel ch., Mt. Vernon, N.Y., 1962, Christ Ch., Mt. Vernon, from 1963; pres. Nat. Luth. Coun., 1953-56. Mem. AAAS. Home: Mount Vernon N.Y. †

BENSON, ROBERT DALE, management consultant; b. Little River, Kans., June 4, 1912; s. Leslie Robert and Vernena (Sherer) B.; m. Nelle Malick Payne, Dec. 23, 1933 (dec.); children: Robert Payne (dec.), Robin Sherwood; m. Gertrude Marie Trudeau, June 21, 1975. Grad., Hutchinson (Kans.) Jr. Coll., 1932; student, Northwestern U., 1939-40; grad., Army Indsl. Coll., 1944. Chief acct. Associated Dairies, Wichita, Kans., 1933-34; chief acct., comptroller Steffen Ice and Ice Cream Corp., Wichita, 1936; with Spurrier & Wood (CPAs), Wichita, 1935; partner Spurrier, Wood & Benson (accts. and auditors), Hutchinson, 1941-43; with firm P.H. Willems (accts. and auditors), McPherson, Kans., 1937; partner Willems & Benson (accts. and auditors), McPherson, 1937-43; chief fixed price audits, chief spl. audits, chief termination audits brs. Hdqrs. USAAF, 1943-47; chief spl. audits br., asst. chief indsl. audits div. Hdqrs. Army Audit Agy., 1947-48; dep. auditor gen. USAF, 1948-53; dep. for acctg. and fin. mgmt. to asst. sec. Air Force, 1953-58, dep. asst. sec., 1958-69, prin. dep. asst. sec., 1969-71; chmn. bd. dirs. Internat. Finance & Mgmt. Corp., Washington, 1971-72; pres. Robert D. Benson & Assos. (mgmt. cons.), Washington, 1972-86; guest lectr. George Washington U., 1953-56. Asso. editor: Future mag, Chgo., 1944. Pres. Kans. Jr. C. of C., 1942-43; bd. dirs. Kans. C. of C., 1942-43; v.p. U.S. Jr. C. of C., 1943-44, treas., 1944-45; mem. Bd. U.S. Civil Service Examiners, 1955-71. Named Outstanding Young Man Kans., 1942; recipient Exceptional Civilian Service decoration Dept. Air Force, 1953, 55, 69, 71. Mem. Am. Acctg. Assn., Air Force Assn., Assn. Govt. Accts., Kans. Soc. Lic. Mcpl. Public Accts., Ordre Des Compagnons Du Bontemps-Medoc et Graves (Bordeaux, France; hon. comdr.), Internat. Wine and Food Soc., Les Amis du Vin, Kans. State Soc., Washington Met. Golf Assn. (pres. 1984). Clubs: Kenwood Country (Bethesda, Md.); Nat. Aviation (Washington). Died Aug. 23, 1986; buried Parklawn Meml. Pk., Rockville, Md.

BENSTEAD, HORACE MELVILLE, printing company executive; b. Arlington, N.J., Mar. 13, 1891; s. Charles Robert and Henrietta (Butcher) B.; m. Jessie I. Jordan, June 30, 1926; children: Horace M., Dorothy J. Student, NYU. Asst. treas. Thomas A. Edison Industries, West Orange, N.J., 1910-17; asst. to pres. Franklin Automobile Co., Syracuse, N.Y., 1919-23; ptnr. E. Naumburg & Co., N.Y.C., 1923-32; bd. dirs. Western Publ. Co., Racine, Wis., from 1933, mem. exec. com., from 1952, chmn., 1952-67; chmn. bd. Horlicks Corp., Racine; bd. dirs. 1st Wis. Bankshares Corp., 1st Nat. Bank & Trust Co., Racine. Trustee Cove Schs., Racine; pres. St. Lukes Hosp., Racine, Kemper Hall, Kenosha, Wis., Athens (Greece) Coll., Ripon Coll.; hon. trustee Anatolla (Greece) Coll. 1st lt. Signal Corps, AUS, 1917-19. Recipient Founders award Ripon Coll., 1967. Mem. Am. Legion, Wis. Hist. Soc. (curator), Milw. Country Club, Milwaukee Club, Racine Country Club, Somerset Club, Bucks Club, American Club, Racquet and Tennis Club. Episcopalian. Home: Racine Wis. †

BENTON, JOHN FREDERIC, history educator; b. Phila., July 15, 1931; s. Frederic Elmon and Anna Josephine (Moffett) B.; m. Elspeth Baillie Hughes, Dec. 31, 1953; children: Helen Benton Metzler, Josephine Benton Soliz, Anna G. Benton Williams, Laura E. AB, Haverford Coll., 1953; MA, Princeton U., 1955, PhD, 1959. Fulbright fellow U. Dijon, 1956-57; Instr. Reed Coll., 1957-59; Instr. U. Pa., 1959-60, asst. prof., 1960-65; asst. prof. Calif. Inst. Tech., Pasadena, 1965-66; assoc. prof. Calif. Inst. Tech., 1966-70, prof. history, 1970-87, Doris and Henry Dreyfuss prof., 1987-88, exec. officer for humanities, 1981-83; Fulbright prof. U. Reims (France), 1972; research assoc. Medieval and Renaissance Center, UCLA, 1977-88; prof. history grad. dept. U. So. Calif., Los Angeles, 1973-74. Author: Town Origins, 1968, Self and Society in Medieval France, 1970; contbr. articles to profl. jours. Pres. Westside Community Council, Phila., 1960-61; mem. Pasadena Commn. on Human Need and Opportunity, 1969-70; bd. dirs. Pasadena Minority History Found., 1986-88. Guggenheim fellow, 1963-64; MacArthur prize fellow, 1985-88. Fellow Medieval Acad. Am. (councillor 1969-72), Am. Hist. Assn. (councillor 1986-88), Medieval Assn. of Pacific (v.p. 1980-82, pres. 1982-84), Internat. Courtly Lit. Soc. (hon. pres.). Home: Pasadena Calif. Died Feb. 25, 1988; buried Mt. View Cemetery, Pasadena.

BEN-ZION, artist; b. Stary Constantin, Ukraine, Russia, July 8, 1897; came to U.S., 1920, naturalized, 1936; m. Lillian Dubin, 1949. Ed., Art Acad., Vienna, Austria. Prepared for rabbinical career until 1917, engaged in Hebrew letters, 1917-31, painter, 1931-87; art instr. Cooper Union, 1946-53. Exhibited in one-man shows at, Balt. Mus., Portland (Oreg.) Mus., Taft Mus., Cin., San Francisco Mus., Iowa U., St. Louis Mus., Smithsonian Inst.; exhibited, Am. Artists Gallery, 1936, East River Gallery, 1937, exhibitor at, Bonestell Gallery, spring 1939, Jewish Mus. N.Y., 1948, 52, 59, Brandeis U., 1969, Nat. Maritime Mus. Haifa, 1975, Haifa Mus., 1978; represented in traveling exhbn. circulated by Am. Fedn. Art, 1953-54, permanent collections, Mus. Modern Art, N.Y.C., Whitney Mus., N.Y.C., Dept. State Art Abroad, Art Inst. Chgo., Duncan Phillips Gallery, Washington, Met. Mus. Art, N.Y.C., Newark Mus., St. Louis Mus., Tel Aviv Mus., Bezalel Mus., Jerusalem, New Art Circle, J.B. Neumann and Goodyear collections, Marian Willard Gallery, Bertha Schaefer and Buchholz galleries, exhbns., Duveen-Graham Gallery, 1955-56; author of: poetry, drama and fairy tales in Hebrew Portfolio of Biblical Etchings, 1950; author of: poetry, drama and fairy tales in Hebrew Portfolio of Prophets, 1953, Portfolio of Ruth, Job, Song of Songs, 1954; drawings: The Wisdom of the Fathers, 1960, Judges and Kings; portfolio of etchings, 1964, The Life of A Prophet, 1965, The Epic of Gilgamesh and Enkidu, 1967, In Search of Oneself, 1968, The Thirty-Six; portfolio of 36 etchings, 1972, numerous others; author: (poetry) Hebrew Songs of Ben-Zion, vols. I-V, The Thirty-Six Unknown (Hebrew and English); (plays in Hebrew) King Solomon, The Street, Advertisement; (epics in Hebrew) Gilgamesh & Enkidu, In Those Days, Adam Alone, In the Beginning; (essays in English) Reflections on Symbolism, The Abstract, On the Inner Life; biographies (Hebrew) In Those Days, In the Primeval Forest; essasys on art: An Artist's View of a Jewish Museum, 1963, Reflections on Symbolism and the Abstract, 1982, On the Inner Life, 1983. Recipient art award Congress for Jewish Culture. Mem. United Am. Artists, Artists Congress. Home: New York N.Y. Died Jan. 23, 1987; buried Haifa, Israel.

BERENSEN, BERTRAM MELVIN, university dean; b. Santa Ana, Calif., Dec. 13, 1928; s. Milo Loren and Sadie (Singer) B.; children: Katharine Sarah, Robert Lawrence. BA in Architecture, U. Calif., Berkeley, 1953, MA, 1954. Dir. div. architecture Hampton (Va.) Inst., 1965-70; dir. Sch. Environ. Devel. U. Nebr., Lincoln, 1970-72; dean Coll. Architecture and Art U. Ill., Chgo., 1972-74; prof., dean Coll. Design, Architecture and Art U. Cin., 1975-85; cons. in field. Prin. works include Cerebral Palsy Ctr., Baton Rouge, 1965, Geriatric Ctr. Med. Bldg., San Diego, 1964-67, Betts residence, Chgo., 1975, Caruso residence, Baton Rouge, 1963, Claire residence, Baton Rouge, 1969; author: The Planned Environment: An Educational Tool, 1968; also articles, chpts. in books. With USN, 1954-56. Recipient AIA award, 1962, 63. Mem. Assn. Collegiate Schs. Architecture (pres. 1975-76), Cliff Dwellers Club, Arts Club. Home: Cincinnati Ohio. Died Dec. 28, 1985.

BERESFORD, JOHN PERCIVAL, advertising executive; b. Short Hills, N.J., July 22, 1917; s. Percival and Ethel (Addenbrooke) B.; m. Solita Arbib, Apr. 5, 1965; children: Sheila, Bridget, Stephen, Charles. Grad., Lawrenceville Sch., 1935; student, Yale U., 1936. V.p. Cecil & Desbrey Inc., N.Y.C., 1950-54; exec. v.p., dir. McCann-Erickson Inc., N.Y.C., 1954-65; exec. v.p. Advt. Measurements Inc., N.Y.C., 1965-67; pres. Data Base Corp., N.Y.C., 1967-69; chmn. exec. com., dir. Norman, Craig & Kummel Inc., N.Y.C., 1969-80; dir. NCK Orgn. Ltd., 1980-86. Capt. AUS, 1944-47, ETO. Home: Coral Gables Fla. Died Sept. 17, 1986.

BERGEN, JULIUS, foundation executive; b. Chgo., Nov. 7, 1896; s. Sophus Theodor and Marie (Tecklenburg) Bergenholz; m. Mary Elizabeth Wood, Feb. 14, 1927; children: Barbara Marie, Ann. Student, Ill. Bus. Coll., also extension courses; D.Bus. Adminstrn. (hon.), U. Nev., 1956. With Fleischmann Co., Chgo., 1912-21, sec. mfg. dept., 1920-21; with Fleischmann Co. and Standard Brands Inc., N.Y.C., 1921-41, asst. to chmn. bd., 1925-41; bus. mgr., agt. Max C. Fleischmann enterprises, 1941-51; agt. for estate, also chmn., trustee Max C. Fleischmann Found., Reno, 1951-80; bd. dirs. Security Nat. Bank, Reno, Haida Corp., J.V. Oil Corp. Mem. Reno chpt. NCCJ; bd. dirs. Council Founds., Inc.; adv. investment com. U. Nev.; trustee Santa Barbara Mus. Natural History, Western Speleological Inst.; hon. mem. Nev. State Mus. Served with USCGR, World War II. Mem. Reno C. of C., Reno Execs. Club, Rotary, Elks, Channel City Club, Hidden Valley Country Club. Republican. Episcopalian (vestry). Home: Reno Nev. Died Jan. 19, 1987; encrypted Santa Barbara, Calif.

BERGEN, WILLIAM BENJAMIN, aerospace engineer; b. Floral Park, N.Y., Mar. 29, 1915; s. Oldfield and Hazel (Zernico) B.; m. Eleanor M. Bergen, Dec. 14, 1968; children by previous marriage: William Benjamin, Lynn Louise. BS, MIT, 1937; D.Engring., Drexel Inst. Tech., 1963. With The Martin Co. (aerospace div. Martin Marietta Corp.), Balt., 1937-68, successively vibrations engr., chief flight test engr., chief pilotless aircraft sect., dir. spl. weapons dept., chief engr., v.p., v.p. ops., 1937-55, exec. v.p., 1955-59, pres., 1959-67; group v.p. space and propulsion N.Am. Aviation (now Rockwell Internat.), 1967, pres. space div., 1967-70, corp. v.p., group v.p. aerospace, 1970-71, group pres. aerospace div., 1971-78. Contr. tech. articles. Alumni term mem. exec. com. MIT; trustee St. Paul's Sch., Brooklandville, Md. Served as 1st lt. U.S. CAC Res., 1937-38; cadet Md. N.G., 1938-40. Recipient Sperry award Inst. Aerospace Scis., 1944, 2 Pub. Service awards NASA, 1969. Fellow Am. Inst. Aeros. and Astronautics; mem. Am. Astronautical Soc. (dir.), Air Force Assn., Aerospace Industries Assn. (hon. chmn. internat. commn.), Nat. Space Club, Soc. Automotive Engrs., Armed Forces Communication Assn., Holland Soc. N.Y., Conquistadores del Cielo. Home: Saint Michaels Md. Died Oct. 9, 1987.

BERGMAN, EDWIN ALFRED, aluminum company executive, civic leader; b. Chgo., July 18, 1917; s. Sigmund and Eda (Eisenstadt) B.; m. Betty Jane Lindenberger, July 10, 1940; children: Carol Ann Bergman Cohen, Robert Henry, Betty Lynn. BA in Bus. Adminstrn., U. Chgo., 1939. V.p. S.A. Bergman Inc., Chgo., 1939-86; pres. U.S. Reduction Co., East Chicago, Ind., 1940-81; bd. dirs. Am. Can Co., Pittway Corp. Pres. Young Men's Jewish Council, Chgo., 1950, Mus. Contemporary Art, Chgo., 1974-86, also founder, vice chmn.; mem. vis. com. humanities U. Chgo., 1955-86, chmn., 1977, univ. trustee, 1975-86, chmn. bd. trustees, 1981-86; pres. Soc. Contemporary Art, 1967-86; trustee Michael Reese Hosp., Chgo., 1952-86, St. Catherine's Hosp., East Chicago, 1965-86, Chgo. Hort. Soc., 1970-86, Whitney Mus., 1977-86; trustee, chmn. print and drawing com. Art Inst. Chgo., 1977-86. Mem. Aluminum Assn. (pres. from 1960), Standard Club (dir. 1960-86), Ravisloe Country Club. Home: Chicago Ill. Died Feb. 17, 1986.

BERGMAN, ELMER OTTO, civil and mechanical engineer; b. Kimball, Nebr., Jan. 21, 1892; s. Andrew and Hannah (Sjoblom) B.; m. Helen Frances Webber, Feb. 11, 1922; children: Charles Andrew, Patricia Jean (Mrs. H.J. Conacher), Margaret Ann (Mrs. W.J. Ansell). AB, Creighton U., 1920; BS, U. Colo., 1925, MS, 1926, CE, 1932; PhD, Stanford U., 1938. Instr. U. Colo., 1924-26, asst. prof., 1926-32, assoc. prof., 1932-37; stress analyst C.F. Braun & Co., Alhambra, Calif., 1938-40, chief research, 1940-44, staff cons., 1944-58; sr. staff Nat. Engring. Sci. Co., Pasadena, Calif., from 1959; consulting engr. from 1958. Author: (with H.J. Gilkey) Materials Testing, 1941. Fellow ASME (mem. boiler code com. 1949-64, dir. codes and standards 1954-62, pres. 1964-65), ASCE; mem. Am. Welding Soc., Am. Soc. Metals, Am. Soc. Testing Materials, Inst. Mech. Engrs., Sigma Chi, Tau Beta Pi, Chi Epsilon, Engineers Club N.Y.C. Home: San Marino Calif. †

BERGMAN, JULES, broadcast journalist; b. N.Y.C., Mar. 21, 1929; s. Irving and Ruth B.; m. Joanne Bergman, Jan. 11, 1953; children: David, Beth, Karen. Student, CCNY, 1946, Ind. U., 1947, Columbia U., 1948-50; postgrad. (Sloan-Rockefeller Advanced Sci. Writing fellow), Sch. Journalism, 1960-61. News desk asst. CBS News, N.Y.C., 1947-48; writer trainee Time mag., N.Y.C., 1948-50; asst. news dir. Sta.-WFDR, N.Y.C., 1950-51; jr. writer ABC News, N.Y.C., 1953; sr. writer, reporter ABC News, 1955-59, sci. editor, 1961-87; tech. adv. Inst. Sports Medicine and Athletic Trauma, Lenox Hill Hosp. Author: 90 Seconds to Space, 1962, Anyone Can Fly, 1965, rev. edit., 1978; writer, narrator: documentary Fire, 1974 (Emmy award 1975), Weekend Athletes, 1975, Danger in Sports, 1975, Dupont, 1982, Crashes, Illusions of Safety, 1975, Asbestos: The Way to Dusty Death, 1978. Mem. Nat. Assn. Sci. Writers., Aviation Writers Assn. Club: Wings (v.p. 1976). Home: New York N.Y. Died 1987.

BERGREN, GUSTAV WALTER, engineering educator; b. S.I., N.Y., Sept. 10, 1917; s. Axel L. and Gudrun (Strom) B.; m. Virginia Wilkinson Trice, Sept. 15, 1942; children: Walter W., Paul L. BS in Mech. Engring., Colo. State U., 1940; MS, Purdue U., 1948. Registered profl. engr., Ind. Grad. asst. Purdue U., 1940-41, mem. faculty, 1945-81, prof. mech. engring., adminstrv. dean for regional campuses, 1966-81. Served with USNR, 1941-45. Decorated Letter of Commendation. Mem. Am. Soc. Engring. Edn., ASME, Rotary. Home: Lafayette Ind. Died June 29, 1981; buried Tippecanoe Memory Gardens, West Lafayette, Ind.

BERKINSHAW, RICHARD COULTON, business executive; b. Toronto, Ont., Can., Sept. 2, 1891; s. Robert James and Emma (Coulton) B.; m. Marjorie Brown (dec.); 1 child, William Robert; m. Ora Kitchen, June 11, 1925. BA, Trinity Coll., Toronto, 1913; LLD, Osgoode Hall Law Sch., 1916; LLD (hon.), U. Toronto, 1952. Bar: Ont. 1916. Barrister, solicitor Tilley, Johnston, Thomson & Parmenter, Toronto, 1919-20; with legal dept. Goodyear Tire & Rubber Co. of Can., Ltd., Toronto, 1920, asst. sec., 1921, sec., gen. counsel, 1926, asst. to pres., 1931, treas., 1932, gen. mgr., treas., 1933, dir., v.p., gen. mgr., 1945-52, pres., gen. mgr., 1952-59, chmn. bd., 1959-61, bd. dirs., from 1961; v.p., bd. dirs. Crown Trust Co., Mut. Life Assurance Co. Can.; bd. dirs. Maple Leaf Mills Ltd., Gen. Steelwares Ltd., Triarch Corp., Stein Roe and Farnham Internat. Fund, Inc., Bank Montreal Can., dep. chmn. Econ. Investment Trust Ltd.; chmn. bd. Toromont Indsl. Holdings Ltd.; past pres. Toronto Bd. Trade. Mem., past pres. Nat. Council Boy Scouts Can.; past pres., dir. Queen Elizabeth Hosp., Toronto; hon. pres. Met. Toronto Indsl. Commn.; chmn. bd. Toronto Mendelsohn Choir; bd. govs., past pres. Can. council Internat. C. of C.; past pres., mem. nat. exec. council Can. Mfrs. Assn.; past pres., mem. exec. com. Citizen's Rsch. Inst. Can.; life dir., past pres. Can. Nat. Exhbn.; mem. exec. com. Corp. of Trinity U., chancellor of U. Trinity Coll. Maj. Can. Engrs., World War I. Created Comdr. Order of the Brit. Empire, 1946. Mem. Royal Order Scotland, Toronto Art Gallery, Rideau Club (Ottawa, Can.), Natrional Club, York Club, Toronto Club, Totonto Hunt Club, Mt. Royal Club (Montreal, Can.), Granite Club, Wedgewood Hunting and Fishing Club, Can. Progress Club (past pres.), Empire and Can. Club, Masons, Shriners, KT. Home: Toronto, Ont. Canada. †

BERKMAN, IRVING JAY, steel company executive, lawyer; b. Chgo., Feb. 8, 1915; s. Louis and Jessie (Bell) B.; m. Jeanette Fisher, Aug. 11, 1935 (dec.); m. Elaine P. Friedlander, Aug. 17, 1985. LLB, Ill. Inst. Tech., 1937. Bar: Ill., 1938. Pvt. practice Chgo., 1938-42; exec. v.p. Follansbee Steel Corp. (W.Va.), 1954-87; exec. v.p. Ampco-Pitts Corp., Pitts., 1961-87, also bd. dirs, pres. Wyckoff Steel div. Mem. Ill. Bar Assn., Steubenville Country Club, Covenant Club, Standard Club, Franklin Hills Country Club, Westmoreland Country Club, Concordia Club, Masons, Shriners. Home: Pittsburgh Pa. Died Apr. 27, 1987; buried Steubenville, Ohio.

BERLIN, ELLIN, author; b. Roslyn, N.Y., Mar. 22, 1903; d. Clarence Hungerford and Katherine (Duer) Mackay; m. Irving Berlin, Jan. 4, 1926; children: Mary Ellin Berlin Barrett, Linda Louise Berlin Emmet, Elizabeth Irving Berlin Peters. Student, Sch. of Holy Child, Suffern, N.Y., 1915-18; grad., St. Timothy's Sch., Catonsville, Md., 1921; LittD (hon.), U. Nev., 1959. Author: (novels) Land I Have Chosen, 1944, Lace Curtain, 1948, Silver Platter, 1957, The Best of Families, 1970, also articles for the New Yorker, short stories for Saturday Evening Post, Ladies' Home Jour., other popular mags. Roman Catholic. Home: New York N.Y. Died July 29, 1988.

BERLIN, RICHARD E., publisher; b. Omaha; s. Richard and Sarah (Noonan) B.; m. Muriel (Honey) Johnson, Dec. 21, 1938; children: Brigid, Ritchie, Christina, Richard E. Jr. Grad. high sch., Omaha. With Hearst Corp., 1919-73, pres. mag. div., 1934-41, head mgmt. team, 1941-43, corp. pres., 1943-73, chief exec. officer, 1951-73. Bd. dirs. Boys Clubs Am.; trustee Roosevelt Hosp., N.Y.C., Am. Heritage Found., Freedoms Found., Valley Forge; commr. Saratoga Springs commn. With U.S. Navy, World War I. Recipient Henry Johnson award, 1966. Mem. Knights of Malta, Book Club, Apawamis Club, Deepdale Golf Club. Home: Rye N.Y. Died Jan. 28, 1986.

BERMAN, EDGAR FRANK, surgeon, writer; b. Balt., Aug. 6, 1915; s. Isaas Isaac and Sarah (Katz) B.; m. Phoebe Rhea, Nov. 22, 1952. MD, U. Md., 1939. Diplomate Am. Bd. Surgery. Intern Sinai Hosp., Balt., 1939-40; resident in surgery Lutheran Hosp., Johns Hopkins Hosp., Balt.; cons. surgeon Albert Schweitzer Hosp., Lambarene, Gabon, 1960, Med. Aspects of Community Devel., Colombia, 1961; chief cons. State Dept. AID on Latin Am. Health, 1962-67; coordinator rural health projects AID, Cen. Am., 1962-65; dir. Haiti Med. Pilot Project, 1960-61; cons. to White House Task Force, Medicare, 1962-63; dir. med. survey southeast Asia, 1960-61; advisor to V.P. of U.S., 1965-69. Author: Teilhardian Philosophy, 1966, The Unchanging Woman, 1967, Population and Foreign Policy, 1965, Population and Politics, 1969, The Politician Primeval, 1974, The Solid Gold Stethescope, 1976, Hubert - The Triumph and Tragedy of the Humphrey I Knew, 1979, The Compleat Chauvinist: A Guide for the Bedeviled Male, 1982; editor: The Carroll County Times, 1964-70; columnist: N.Am. Newspaper Alliance, 1970-71, USA Today. Bd. dirs. Pub. Welfare Found., Washington, 1960, Care/Medico, N.Y.C., pres., 1959-65; bd. dirs. Balt. County Gen. Hosp., 1965, Balt. Symphony Orch. Assn., 1960-65, Balt. Opera Soc., 1962-67, May Inst. of Autistic Children, Chatham, Mass., 1964, Latin Am. Commn., State of Md., 1967, Sino-Am. Ctr. Internat. Studies, 1982; trustee Md. State Coll. and Univs., 1970-87; coordinator Nat. Physicians Com. for Johnson and Humphrey, 1964. Lt. USN, 1943-46. Recipient Moscow Internat. Fellowship, 1957, fellowships from various German univs., 1952-55, U. Basel, Switzerland, 1957, U. Paris, 1957. Fellow ACS; mem. AMA, Nat. Pub. Health Assn., Internat. Coll. Surgeons (regent 1957-62), N.Y. Acad. Scis. Democrat. Jewish. Home: Lutherville Md. Died Nov. 25, 1987.

BERMAN, EMILE ZOLA, lawyer; b. N.Y.C., Nov. 3, 1902; s. Eli and Elizabeth Berman; m. Alice R. Gaines, Oct. 20, 1944 (dec.); children: Eliza, Eli; m. Virginia Anne Berman. BS, NYU, 1923, LLB, 1924. Bar: N.Y. 1925. Practice law N.Y.C., 1926-81; mem. firm Emile Z. Berman & A. Harold Frost, N.Y.C., 1956-81; lectr. trial tactics Practicing Law Inst., 1935-41, 46-81; lectr. law grad. div. NYU, 1950-55, Columbia U. Law Sch., 1950-51, 55, Law Sci. Inst., U. Tex., 1954-55. Author: Foundations for Evidence (Trial Practice Series), 1956; contbr. articles to profl. jours. Mem. nat. adv. council Law-Medicine Research Inst., Boston U. Fellow Am. Coll. Trial Lawyers; mem. Assn. of Bar of City of N.Y., ABA, N.Y. Bar Assn. (past exec. com.), Met. Trial Lawyers Assn. (past pres., dir.), Internat. Acad. Trial Lawyers (past pres., trustee), Bklyn.-Manhattan Trial Counsel Assn. (past pres.), Fedn. Ins. Counsel (past gov.), Internat. Assn. Ins. Counsel. Home: New York N.Y. Died July 3, 1981.

BERMAN, LOUIS KEVA, mechanical engineer; b. N.Y.C., Dec. 25, 1885; s. Jacob and Anna (Kaeplus) B.; m. Marie Kellner, June 6, 1923; children: James K.,

Virginia Berman Slaughter, Richard L. BS, CCNY, 1903. Registered profl. engr., N.Y., N.J. With Raisler Corp. and predecessor, N.Y.C., from 1905, pres., 1930-47, chmn. bd., from 1957. Mem. Am. Soc. Heating and Ventilating Engrs.(life), NSPE, N.Y. Soc. Profl.Engrd. †

BERMAN, MORTON MAYER, rabbi; b. Balt., Aug. 23, 1899; s. Morris and Rose (Frommer) B.; m. Grayce Sunchine Hofheimer, Oct. 21, 1925 (dec. 1949); 1 son, John Simon; m. Elaine Ruth Siegel Levy, June 27, 1950; children: Susanna, Stephen, David. BA, Yale U., 1921; MHL, Jewish Inst. Religion, 1926, DD, 1946; postgrad., Columbia U., 1922-30, U. Grenoble, France, 1926, Hebrew U., Palestine, 1926-27, Hochschule für die Wissenschaft des Judentums, Berlin, 1927. Ordained rabbi, 1926. Student rabbi Danbury, Conn., 1923-26; rabbi Temple Emanuel, Davenport, Iowa, 1927-29; assoc. rabbi, dir. edn. Free Synagogue, N.Y.C., 1929-37; dir. field activities Jewish Inst. Religion, 1929-37; rabbi Temple Isaiah Israel, Chgo., 1937-57, rabbi emeritus; hon. dir. dept. English speaking countries Keren Hayesod United Jewish Appeal, Jeruslaem, Israel. Author: A Jew's View of the Crucifixion, 1929, Index to Mielziner's Introduction to the Talmud, 3d. edit., 1925, Role of the Rabbi, 1941, Our First Century, 1952, The Bridge to Life, 1971, Zionist Reminiscences, 1976; editor: Negro Community to the West, 1940; editor Am. Jewish Congress Bull., 1933-34; past editor Opinion; contbr. articles to Jewish Forum, Unity, and Congress Weekly; mem. editorial adv. bd. P.F. Collier & Sons; asst. editor Ency. Judaica. Past nat. v.p., former chmn. adminstrv. com., past pres. Chgo. div. Am. Jewish Congress; former chmn. Zionist Council Chgo.; hon. pres. Chgo. council Jewish Nat. Fund; past mem. exec. com. World Jewish Congress; past pres. Chgo. Rabbinical Assn.; mem. Central Conf. Am. Rabbis; trustee AMLI Central Music Library, Israel, Zionist Gen. Council. Chaplain USNR, 1943-46, Okinawa. Decorated Bronze Star; Guggenheim fellow. Mem. Masons (32 deg.), B'nai B'rith, Phi Beta Kappa, Phi Alpha. Home: Jerusalem Israel. Died Jan. 23, 1986.

BERNARDI, HERSCHEL, actor; b. N.Y.C., Oct. 30, 1923. Actor appearing in films including Green Fields, 1937, Crime, Inc., 1945, Miss Susie Slagle's, 1946, Stake Out on Dope Street, 1958, The Savage Eye, 1960, A Cold Wind in August, 1961, Irma La Douce, 1963, Love With the Proper Stranger, 1964, The Honey Pot, 1967, No Deposit No Return, 1976, The Front, 1976; TV credits include Peter Gunn series, 1958-61, Arnie, 1970-72, But I Don't Want to Get Married, 1971, No Place to Run, 1972, Hail to the Chief, 1984, Indestuctible Man, 1984, Going Home, 1986, Murder She Wrote, 1985; Broadway appearances include Bajour, 1968, The Goodbye People, 1979, Fiddler on the Roof, as Tevye, Zorba the Greek, as Zorba. Home: Los Angeles Calif. Died May 10, 1986; buried Mt. Sinai at Forest Lawn.

BERNHARD, ARNOLD, investment adviser, publisher; b. N.Y.C., Dec. 2, 1901; s. Bernhard and Regina (Steigelfest) B.; m. Janet Marie Kinghorn, Dec. 21, 1929; children: Jean Haxton (Mrs. Edgar M. Buttner), Arnold Van Hoven. BA, Williams Coll., 1925; LLD; LHD, Skidmore Coll., U. Bridgeport., Colby Coll. Newspaper reporter 1926-28, securities analyst, 1928-31, investment counsel, 1931-87; founder, chief exec. officer, chmn. Arnold Bernhard & Co., Inc., 1935-87; chief exec. officer, chmn. The Value Line, Inc., N.Y.C., 1983-87. Mem. Metropolitan Club N.Y.C., Phi Beta Kappa, Delta Sigma Rho, Delta Upsilon. Died Dec. 22, 1987.

BERNHEIM, EMILE, retail business executive; b. Mulhouse, France, Oct. 18, 1886; s. Julien and Marie (Meyer) B.; m. Suzanne Yvonne Chabot, Oct. 17, 1923. With Les Grands Magasins A l'Innovation, Brussels, from 1901, comml. dir., early 1900's, mng. dir., 1923, later, pres., also bd. dirs.; pres. Priba chain stores, Brussels, 1953; pres. Le Manteau. Mem. spl. mission to study comml. edn. in U.S., 1927; bd. dirs. Brussels U. Ctr. for Bus. Adminstrn.; gen. dir. Belgian Ministry of Food Supplies, 1919-20, leader Belgian del. Rye Conf., 1944; v.p. Hopital Francais Reine Elizabeth; hon. v.p. Les Enfants de la Patrie; bd. dirs. Belgian Industry Univs. Found. Bus. Adminstrn. With Belgian Army. 1914-18. Decorated Comdr. de l'ordre de Leopold, Officier de la Legion d'Honneur, Grand Officier de l'Ordre Couronne, Commandeur de l'Ordre du Merite Commercial (France), Comdr. de l'Ordre de la Rose Blanche (Finland), Comdr. de l'Ordre du Merite italien; named to Hall of Fame in Distbn. Boston Conf. on Distbn. Mem. Internat. C. of C. (bd. dirs., mem. Belgian nat. com.), Internat. Distbn. Commn. (hon. chmn.), Internat. Assn. Dept. Stores (pres.), Assn. des Grandes Enterprises de Distbn. de Belgique (past pres.), Nat. Belge de l'Orgn. Sci. (v.p.), Caisse de Compensation pour Allocations Familiales des Grands Magasins de Belgique (pres.), Caisse Nat. Belge Magasins de Belge d'Assurance (bd. dirs.), Internat. Fedn. Distbrs. (pres.), Internat. Acad. Mgmt., Nat. Retail Mchts. Assn. (bd. dirs.). Home: Brussels Belgium. †

BERNSTEIN, HAROLD JOSEPH, research chemist; b. Toronto, Ont., Can., Aug. 26, 1914; s. Benjamin and Molly (Cohn) B.; m. Dorothy Snipper, Nov. 11, 1948; children: Lee, Mark, Susan. BA, U. Toronto, 1935, MA, 1936, PhD, 1938. With NRC Can., Ottawa, 1947-78, prin. research officer, 1957-78. Co-editor Jour. Raman Spectroscopy, 1973-78; mem. editorial adv. bd. Jour Molecular Structure, 1971-84; contbr. articles to profl. jours. Recipient medal Chem. Inst. Can., 1974, Queens Jubilee medal, 1977, Herzberg award Can. Spectroscopy Soc., 1978, award Pitts. Spectroscopy Soc., 1980. Fellow Royal Soc. Can., Chem. Inst. Can., Rideau View Golf and Country Club. Jewish. Home: Ottawa, Ont. Canada. Died Dec. 14, 1984; buried Ottawa.

BERRY, EDWIN CARLOS (BILL), association executive, civic leader, business executive; b. Oberlin, Ohio, Nov. 11, 1910; s. John A. and Kitty Berry; student Oberlin Coll.; BA in Edn., Duquesne U.; postgrad. U. Pitts., Western Res. U.; LL.D., Western Mich. U., 1973; L.H.D., Chgo. State U., 1973; LL.D., Northwestern U., 1975; m. Betsy Gordon Bell; children—Joseph, Melanie Fraser; foster children—Myron Wahls, Charles Carter, Westina Mathews. With Nat. Urban League, Pitts., 1937-45, Portland, Oreg., 1945-56, Chgo., 1956-69; spl. asst. to pres., urban affairs officer, corp. cons. Johnson Products Co., Chgo., 1970-87; treas., adminstrv. officer George E. Johnson Found., George E. Johnson Ednl. Fund. Moderator People to People program WGN-TV, Chgo. Mem. fund raising com. Chgo. Urban League, Chgo. Community Fund, Leadership Council for Met. Open Communities, Woodlawn Devel. Corp., Chgo. United, Chgo. Alliance Businessmen, Nat. Com. Against Discrimination in Housing; chmn. Harold Washington for Mayor campaign; chmn. Mayor Washington's Transition Team, Chgo. Recipient John F. Kennedy award Cath. Interracial Council; Citation of Honor Stateway Mother's Soc.; Citation for outstanding service and leadership in black community The Woodlawn Orgn.; Golden Oil Can award Chgo. Econ. Devel. Corp.; named Chicagoan of the Year Chgo. Jr. Assn. Commerce and Industry; Man of Yr. Ada S. McKinley House; Laureate Lincoln Acad. Mem. UN Assn. of U.S.A. (chmn. Ralph Bunche awards panel). Mem. editorial bd. The Chicago Reporter. Home: Chicago Ill. Died May 13, 1987.

BERRY, GEORGE PACKER, physician, educator; b. Troy, N.Y., Dec. 29, 1898; s. George Titus and Carrie Electa (Packer) B.; m. Elizabeth L'Estrange Duncan, July 10, 1923 (dec. Mar. 1926); children: Caroline Elizabeth (Mrs. Cloyd Laporte), Mary. AB with highest honors, Princeton U., 1921; MD, Johns Hopkins U., 1925; AM (hon.), Harvard U., 1949; ScD (hon.), Union Coll., 1950, Princeton U., 1951, Harvard U., 1954, NYU, 1955, U. Rochester, 1955, Boston U., 1963, U. Pa., 1965, Dartmouth, 1965; Litt.D. (hon.), Tufts U., 1952; LHD (hon.), Jefferson Med. Coll., 1955, Brandeis U., 1964; LLD, Hobart and William Smith Coll., 1949, U. Calif., 1966, Loyola U., 1966; MSD, Brown U., 1969. Diplomate Am. Bd. Internal Medicine. Resident house officer Johns Hopkins Hosp., Balt., 1925-27; asst. resident physician in medicine Johns Hopkins U., Balt., 1927-28, instr. in medicine, 1928-29; asst. Rockefeller Inst. Med. Research, 1929-31, assoc., 1931-32; prof. bacteriology, head of dept., assoc. prof medicine U. Rochester Sch. Medicine and Dentistry, 1932-49, asst. dean, 1941-47, assoc. dean, 1947-49; dean of faculty and dean Harvard Med. Sch., 1949-65, prof. bacteriology, 1949-65, prof. emeritus bacteriology, 1965-86; pres. Harvard Med. Ctr., 1956-65; spl. cons. to pres. Princeton, 1966-86; cons. med. research and edn. HEW, 1957-68; mem. adv. com. Mass. Dept. Pub. Health, 1957-68; cons. medicine Peter Bent Brigham Hosp., Boston, 1963. Mem. editorial bd. Jour. Bacteriology; assoc. editor Jour. Immunol. and Bact. Revs.; contbr. numerous papers to med. and ednl. jours. Chmn. adv. council dept. biol., mem. grad. council Princeton, 1941-56; ednl. cons. Council Rochester Regional Hosps., 1946-49; bd. dirs. Josiah Macy Found., 1943-65, Nat. Health Council, 1956-57; trustee Am. U. Beirut, 1952-86; charter trustee Princeton, 1956-86; mem. med. sch. grants adv. com. Ford Found., 1956-57; v.p. Sex Information and Edn. Council of U.S., 1964-86; trustee Worcester Found. Exptl. Biology, 1965-68; mem. adv. com. edn. VA, 1952-86; mem. med. adv. com. Boston Mus. Sci., 1952-86; mem. sci. adv. com. Howard Hughes Med. Inst., 1956-68; mem. adv. med. bd. Am. Hosp. Paris, 1961-68. With USNR, 1941-53. Fellow AAAS, Am. Pub. Health Assn., Rochester Mus. Arts and Scis.; mem. Johns Hopkins Med. Assn., Am. Soc. Clin. Investigation, Assn. Am. Med. Colls. (chmn. com. research and edn. 1947-61, mem. exec. council 1947-52, pres 1951-52), Harvey Soc. N.Y., Soc. Exptl. Biology and Medicine, Soc. Am. Bacteriologists (chmn. Cen. N.Y. br. 1934-35, mem. council 1935-40), Boylston Med. Soc. (trustee 1961-62), Am. Assn. Immunologists (council 1938-45, pres. 1939-40), Am. Assn. Pathologists and Bacteriologists, Am. Assn. History Medicine, SAR, Century Assn. of N.Y., Princeton Club (N.Y.), Newcomen Soc., Fortnightly Club, Genesee Valley Club, Harvard Club of Boston, Martha's Vineyard Club, New York Club, Aesculapian, Roxbury Clin. Record, St. Botolph, Cosmos Club, Phi Beta Kappa, Omicron Kappa Upsilon, Alpha Omega Alpha, Sigma Xi, Kappa Pi Eta. Republican. Presbyterian. Home: Princeton N.J. Died Oct. 5, 1986.

BERRY, J(AMES) RAYMOND, lawyer; b. Newark, Aug. 30, 1901; James Aloysius and Frances Irene (Heery) B.; m. Adelaide Cecilia Poulson, Oct. 3, 1928; children: James Raymond, Adelaide P. Berry Tietje, Joseph Michael. AB, Princeton U., 1922; LLB, Columbia U., 1925. Bar: N.J. 1926, U.S. Supreme Ct. 1936, N.Y. 1943. Pvt. gen. practice Newark, 1926-42; gen. counsel Nat. Bd. Fire Underwriters, 1943-63, Am. Ins. Assn., 1964-67, N.J. Ins. Underwriting Assn., N.J. Med. Malpractice Reins. Assn.; of counsel Lum Biunno & Tompkins, Newark, 1968-75; ptnr. Francis & Berry, 1977-82. Treas., counsel Twenty Two Found., Princeton; candidate N.J. State Senate, 1941. Recipient Gold medal Gen. Ins. Brokers Assn., 1960. Mem. Dial Lodge, Nassau Club (Princeton), Iota Nu Sigma, Psi Upsilon. Home: Summit N.J. Died Feb. 24, 1982.

BERRY, LEVETTE JOE, microbiologist; b. Birmingham, Ala., June 17, 1910; s. Levette J. and Elizabeth (Fitzgerald) B.; m. Virginia Lee Goolsby, May 28, 1934; 1 son, James Goolsby. BS, S.W. Tex. State Coll., 1930; PhD, U. Tex., 1939. Instr. U. Tex., 1939-40; faculty Bryn Mawr Coll., 1940-70, asso. prof., 1946-52, prof., 1952-70, chmn. dept. biology, 1965-70, sec. faculty, 1964-69, acting provost, 1969-70; prof. U. Tex., Austin, 1970-87; chmn. dept. microbiology U. Tex., 1970-75; research assoc. nutrition clinic Hillman Hosp., Birmingham, 1943-45; cons. infectious diseases com. VA, 1960-71, chmn., 1968-71; cons. bacteriology and mycology study sect. NIH, 1963-87, chmn., 1966-67, cons. internat. fellowship rev. com., 1970-73, chmn., 1971-73; cons. bacteriology and mycology Lunar Receiving Lab., NASA Space Center, Houston, 1969-71, chmn., 1971-87; adv. com. Army Chem. Corps, 1960-63; cons. life scis. research evaluation com. Office Naval Research, 1970-73; chmn. sci. adv. com. Alfred I. DuPont Inst., 1977-84; Found. for Microbiology lectr., 1976-77; chmn. life scis. panel associateship program NRC, mem. rev. bd. and adv. com., 1982-87. Editorial bd. Infection and Immunity, 1970-87, editor Jour. Bacteriology, 1964-68. Named disting. alumnus Southwest Tex. State U., 1983. Fellow Am. Acad. Microbiology (bd. govs. 1969-75, 86-89, chmn. 1970-71), AAAS; mem. Am. Soc. Microbiology (hon. mem.; councilor-at-large, council policy com., chmn. bd. edn. and tng. 1971-81, chmn. bacterial infections and pathogenesis div. 1976-77; pres. Tex. br. 1984-85), Am. Physiol. Soc., Reticuloendothelial Soc. (hon. life; chmn. internat. com.; pres. 1966-68, adv. editorial bd. 1973), Soc. Exptl. Biology and Medicine, Royal Acad. of London (assoc.), Sigma Xi. Home: Austin Tex. Died Feb. 26, 1987.

BERRY, RAYMOND H., lawyer; b. Pennsboro, W.Va., June 28, 1891; s. Charles Albert and Martha Florence (Ward) B.; m. Eska Ethelyn Eckels, Sept. 5, 1916; 1 child, Martha Jane Berry Silliere. LLB, Nat. U., Washington, 1914. Bar: D.C. 1915, Mich. 1924. Pvt. practice 1928-32; ptnr. Berry and Moorman; bd. dirs. Buell Die and Machine Co., C.P.A. Co., Metal Mouldings Corp., Detroit, Ferry-Morse Seed Co., Detroit and San Francisco, Leonard Refineries, Inc., Alma, Mich., Standard Products Co., Cleve., Vernors Ginger Ale, Inc., Detroit, French Mortgage & Bond Co., Detroit; asst. in orgn., then asst. cashier Dupont NAt. Bank, Washington, 1916; head tax dept. Detroit Trust Co., 1920; sec. spl. commn. of inquiry taxation State of Mich., 1929. Co-author Mich. state sales tax law, 1933. Mem. ABA, Mich. Bar Assn., Detroit Bar Assn., Fed. Bar Assn., Detroit Bd. Commerce, U.S. C. of C., Nat. Tax Assn., Econ. Club Detroit, Detroit Athletic Club, Country Club, Question Club Detroit, Masons, Sigma Nu Phi. Home: Grosse Point Mich. †

BERTOLETTE, NORMAN B(OONE), public utilites executive; b. Norristown, Pa., Jan. 28, 1891; s. Daniel A. and Alice J. (Dutlinger) B.; m. Katherine Marie Schweyer, Sept. 6, 1916; children: Robert (dec.), Reed. ME, Drexel Inst. Tech., 1911. Engr., div. mgr. Phila. Suburban Gas & Electric Co., 1912-28; div. mgr. Phila. Electric Co., 1928-30; pres. Harrisburg (Pa.) Gas Co., 1930-36; pres. Hartford (Conn.) Gas Co., 1936-57, chmn. bd., 1957-60, cons., dir., from 1960; pres., dir. Jefferson St. Med. Bldg., from 1960; hon. dir. Conn. Bank & Trust Co; hon. trustee Soc. Savs. Bd. dirs. Hartford Hosp. Recipient Alumni citation Drexel Inst. Tech., 1951. Mem. Conn. Electric and Gas Assn. (past pres.), Am. Gas Assn., N.E. Gas Assn. (past pres.), Mfrs. Assn. Hartford County, Hartford C. of C. (past pres.), Soc. Gas Engrs. N.Y. (past pres.), Newcomen Soc., Twentieth Century Club, Hartford Club (past pres.), Hartford Golf Club, Masons. Congregationalist. Home: Hartford Conn. †

BERTRAM, JOHN ELWOOD, computer company executive; b. Bedford, Pa., May 3, 1927; s. John Franklin and Mildred Rachel (King) B.; m. Lucy Virginia Keen, June 22, 1952; 1 son, John David. B.S.E.E., Washington U., St. Louis, 1952; M.S., Columbia U., 1955, Ph.D., 1958. Staff engr. Research div. IBM, Yorktown Heights, N.Y., 1958-65, dir. computer sci., 1965-67; assoc. dir. advanced computer systems System Devel. div. IBM, Menlo Park, Calif., 1967-68, asst. gen. mgr. Advanced Systems Devel. div., 1968; acting lab. mgr. Systems Lab IBM, Mohansic, N.J., 1968; gen. mgr. Advanced Systems Devel. div. IBM, San Jose, 1968-70; dir. engring. programming IBM, White Plains, N.Y., 1970-73, v.p., pres. Advanced Systems div., 1973-75, v.p., pres. Systems Product div., 1975-78, v.p., pres. Data Systems div., 1978-83; v.p., pres. Gen. Products div. IBM, San Jose, Calif., 1983-86. Home: San Jose Calif. Died Apr. 12, 1986.

BETHKE, ROBERT HARDER, investment banker; b. Chgo., Mar. 12, 1916; s. William and Florence (Gaumnitz) B.; m. Patricia Davis, Dec. 16, 1939; children: Robert Davis, William Milford. BS, U. Chgo., 1937. With J.P. Morgan & Co., N.Y.C., 1937-39; with Discount Corp. of N.Y., 1939-87, pres., 1974-87, chmn. exec. com., dir., 1967-87, chmn. bd., 1978-81; ind. counsellor U.S. Steel and Carnegie Pension Fund, N.Y.C., 1976-86; dir. Chem. Fund, Inc., Internat. Investors Inc., World Trends Fund, Discount Corps. N.Y. and D.C., Union Cash Mgmt. Fund, Inc., N.Y.C.; speaker in field treasury financing and money markets; mem. financial adv. com. U.S. Postal Service, 1973-77. Mem. planning bd. North Castle, N.Y., 1953-63; Pres., trustee North Castle Free Library, Armonk, N.Y., 1955-60; vice chmn., Greenburgh (N.Y.) Bd. Edn., 1950-52; mem. finance com. N.Y.C. Mission Soc., 1961-78; mem. fin. com. Nat. Council Chs., N.Y.C. Served to lt. col. AUS, 1942-46. Decorated Legion of Merit; recipient Alumni Citation U. Chgo., 1960. Mem. Am. Finance Assn., Am. Econ. Assn., Pub. Fin. Assn., Securities Industry Assn. (past chmn. and mem. U.S. Treasury and fed. agy. com. 1966-80), Assn. Primary Dealers in U.S. Govt. Securities (dir. 1977-80), Pilgrims of Am., Alpha Delta Phi. Clubs: Whippoorwill Country (Armonk); Economic (N.Y.C.). Home: Armonk N.Y. Deceased.

BETTENBENDER, JOHN I., theater educator; b. Chgo., Apr. 18, 1921. PhD, Loyola U., Chgo., 1943; MFA, Cath. U. Am., 1948. Asst. prof. speech and drama, chmn. dept. speech and drama Loyola U., 1948-55; asst. prof. Jersey State Coll., 1959-64; assoc. prof., chmn. dept. speech and theater St. Joseph's Coll.; prof., chmn. dept. theater Oberlin (Ohio) Coll., 1969-70; prof., chmn. dept. theater arts Rutgers U., New Brunswick, N.J., 1970-88, dean Mason Gross Sch. Arts, 1976-88. Contbr. articles to profl. jours. Mem. Am. Theatre Assn., AAUP. Home: New Brunswick N.J. Died June 24, 1988.

BETTS, EMMETT ALBERT, psychologist, author; b. Elkhart, Iowa, 1903; s. Albert Henry and Grace L. (Greenwood) B.; m. Katherine P. Betts. B.S., Des Moines U., 1925; M.S., U. Iowa, 1928, Ph.D., 1931; LL.D., Sioux Falls (S.D.) Coll., 1972. Vocat. dir. indsl. arts and agr. Orient, Iowa, 1922-24; staff physics dept. Des Moines U., 1924-25; supt. schs. Northboro, Iowa, 1925-29; research asst. U. Iowa, 1929-31; sch. psychologist, elementary prin. Shaker Heights, Ohio, 1931-34; dir. tchr. edn., dir. summer sessions State Tchrs. Coll., Oswego, N.Y., 1934-37; research prof., dir. reading clinic sch. edn. Pa. State U., 1937-45; prof. psychology, dir. reading clinic, dept. psychology Temple U., 1945-54; dir. Betts Reading Clinic, Haverford, Pa., 1954-61; research prof. dept. psychology (Sch. Edn.), Miami U., Coral Gables, Fla., 1961; vis. prof. numerous colls. and univs. U.S., 1930-87. Editor,contbr.: My Weekly Reader, 1938-69; editor in chief Education, 1957-69; assoc. editor: Jour. Ednl. Research; adv. editor: Highlights for Children; contbg. editor: Jour. Exptl. Edn.; reading editor Education, 1948-69, mem. editorial bd., 1948-57, 69-87; contbg. editor: Reading Tchr. jour, Internat. Reading Assn., 1971-87; author vision tests; author: Foundation of Reading Instruction, rev. edit, 1957, Betts Basic Readers, 1970, others; contbr. articles to profl. jours. V.p., bd. dirs. Nat. Aerospace Edn. Council, 1956-87; Chmn. adv. bd. Winter Haven Lion's Research Found., Inc., 1963-87; bd. dirs., chmn. state orgn. com. Internat. Council for Improvement of Reading Instruction; trustee Lake Placid (N.Y.) Edn. Found., 1968-87. Recipient Apollo award, 1962; Founders award Internat. Reading Assn., 1971; citation of merit, 1971; Gold medal Phonemic Spelling Council; Crown Circle award Nat. Congress Aerospace Edn.-FAA-NASA-USAF-CAP, 1979; 1977; others. Fellow Am. Psychol. Assn. (diplomate sch. psychology, mem. com. sch. psychol. services for exceptional children), Distinguished Service Found. Optometry, Grad. Soc. Optometry; mem. Soc. Advancement Edn., Nat. Council Research in English (chmn. editorial com.), Nat. Conf. Research Elementary Sch. English (co-founder 1932), Nat. Soc. Study of Edn., Internat. Reading Assn. (life), Nat. Council Tchrs. English, Eastern Psychol. Assn., Internat. Council Exceptional Children (adv. com.), NEA, AAUP, Am. Assn. Sch. Adminstrs. (life), Am. Assn. Applied Psychology, Am. Edn. Research Assn., Nat. Aeronautics Assn., Aircraft Owners and Pilots Assn., AAUS, Silver Wings (hon. life), Assn. Childhood Edn., Fla. Psychol. Assn., Dade County Psychol. Assn., Pa. Psychol. Assn., Internat. Council Exceptional Children, Linguistic Soc. Am., N.Y. Acad. Sci., Pa. Acad. Sci., Pa. Edn. Research Assn., Greater Miami Aviation Assn., LuLu Flying Squadron, Nat. Pilots Assn., Lafayette Escadrille, Delaware Valley Reading Assn. (hon. life mem.), Nat. Aerospace Edn. Assn. (hon. dir. 1972-87), Simpler Spelling Assn. (dir. 1966, pres. 1967-71), Phonemic Spelling Council (pres. 1970-87), Phi Delta Kappa, Phi Theta Pi Beta, Sigma Kappa, Psi Chi. Clubs: Masons, Shriners; Jockey (Miami); Lake Region Yacht and Country. Home: Winter Haven Fla. Died Mar. 10, 1987; cremated.

BEUKEMA, JOHN CHARLES, business association executive; b. Muskegon, Mich., Aug. 11, 1888; s. Charles John and Wyke (Banninga) B.; m. Jantina Klomp, July 20, 1910; children: Charles Robert, John Lewis (dec. 1944). Ed., Calvin Coll., Grand Rapids, Mich.; LLD (hon.), Cen. Ind. Coll., 1959. Newspaper reporter, edito, bus. mgr. Muskegon News, 1906-17; sec. Manistee (Mich.) Bd. of Commerce, 1917-22; sec., mgr. Muskegon C. of C., 1922-53; bd. dirs. Naph-Sol Refining Co.; chmn. Muskegon Fed. Savs. & Loan Assn. Author: (under name John Charles Beechame) The Argus Pheasant, 1916, The Yellow Spider, 1917; contbr. articles to bus. jours. Sec. Muskegon Progress and Devel. Fund; mem. Mich. Tax Study Commn, 1938, Mich. Commn. on Reorgn. Govt., 1938, Mich. Civil Service Commn., 1940-52, Muskegon Harbor Commn., Muskegon Parks and Recreation Commn.; chmn. exec. council St. Lawrence Nat. Seaway Council; adv. bd. St. Lawrence Seaway Devel. Corp., 1953-61; trustee, dir. Muskegon YMCA. Decorated Knight of Orange-Nassau (Netherlands); recipient Mich. Frontiersman award, 1959; named Mich. Indsl. Ambassador. Mem. Elks, Rotary. Republican. Congregationalist. Home: Muskegon Mich. †

BEVERIDGE, GEORGE DAVID, JR., bank communications executive; b. Washington, Jan. 5, 1922; s. George David and Lillian Agnes (Little) B.; m. Betty Jean Derwent, June 6, 1944; children: Barbara J., Deborah A., David C. Student, George Washington U., 1939. Copy boy Washington Star, 1940, news reporter, 1942-63, editorial writer, 1963-74, asst. mng. editor, 1974-75, ombudsman, 1976-81, assoc. editor, 1980-81; asst. to chmn. Allbritton Communications Co., Washington, 1981-84; sr. v.p. communications Riggs Nat. Bank, Washington, 1984-87. Served to lt. AUS, 1942-46. Recipient Pulitzer prize for reporting in local news category, 1958. Democrat. Presbyterian. Home: Bethesda Md. Died Feb. 14, 1987; buried Arlington Nat. Cemetery.

BEYCHOK, SHERMAN, biochemist, educator; b. N.Y.C., Sept. 10, 1931; s. Abe and Miriam (Schiffman) B.; m. Martha Marcus, Mar. 25, 1950; 1 dau., Cori Bess. BS, CCNY, 1951; PhD, NYU, 1957. Guest chemistry MIT, 1956-60; research assoc. Children's Cancer Research Found. and Harvard Med. Sch., 1960-61; mem. faculty Columbia U., N.Y.C., 1962-85, Alan H. Kempner prof. biol. scis., 1975-85, chmn. dept. biol. scis., 1968-79; vis. prof. faculty medicine U. Paris; mem. panel on molecular biology NSF, 1979-82, adv. com. on physiology, 1982-85; cons. NIH; trustee Cold Spring Harbor Lab., 1968-79; mem. Louisa Gross Horwitz Prize Com., 1980-85; cons. in field. Mem. editorial adv. bd. Internat. Jours., The Netherlands; contbr. articles to profl. jours. Mem. Am. Soc. Biol. Chemists, Harvey Soc., Am. Chem. Soc. Home: New York N.Y. Died Oct. 2, 1985.

BEYER, CLARA MORTENSON, government official; b. Middletown, Calif., Apr. 13, 1892; d. Morten and Mary (Frederickson) Mortenson; m. Otto S. Beyer, July 30, 1920 (dec.); children: Morten, Donald, Richard. BA, U. Calif., 1915, MS, 1916. Instr. U. Calif., 1915-17, Bryn Mawr Coll., 1917-18; exec. asst. War Labor Policies Bd., 1918-19; exec. sec. D.C. Minimum Wage Bd., 1919-21; economist Children's Bur. Dept. Labor, 1928-31, dir. indsl. div., 1931-34; assoc. dir. Bur. Labor Standards, 1943-57, acting dir., 1957-58; tech. assistance program adviser ICA, from 1959; advisor in labor law adminstrn. AID, from 1961; chmn. Fed. Com. on Apprentice Tng., 1934-44; U.S. govt. adviser ILO Ann. confs., 1938-53; U.S. govt. del. Inter-Am. Conf. Social Security, Buenos Aires, 1951; sec.-tres. Internat. Assn. Govtl. Labor Ofcls., 1946-58. Bd. dirs. Overseas Edn. Found., McLean Civic Assn. Mem. Nat. Consumers League, Nat. Child Labor Com., LWV, Am. Mgmt. Assn., McLean Civic League. Home: McLean Va. †

BIBLE, ALAN, United States senator; b. Lovelock, Nebr., Nov. 20, 1909; s. H.H. and Isabel (Welsh) B.; m. Loucile Jacks, Nov. 17, 1939; children: Debra Watkins, Paul Alfred, William Alan, David Milton. AB, U. Nev., 1930; LLB, Georgetown Law Sch., 1934, LLD; LLD, Rider Coll., U. Nev., 1970. Bar: Nev. 1935. Dist. atty Storey County, Nev., 1935-38, dep. atty. gen., 1938-43; atty. gen. Nev., 1943-51, U.S. senator, 1954-74. Mem. Masons, Eagles. Democrat. Methodist. Home: Zephyr Cove Nev. Deceased.

BICKHAM, THOMAS MARION, JR., city official; b. Blanchard, La., Sept. 21, 1915; s. Thomas Marion and Mary Emma (Flowers) B.; m. Mildred Freeman, Mar. 22, 1941; 1 dau., Nancy Elizabeth. Grad., La. State U., 1938; postgrad., Centenary Law Sch., 1948-50. Mem. trust dept. 1st Nat. Bank of Shreveport, La., 1938-41; mgmt. analyst VA, Shreveport, 1946-51; asst. dir. VA Hosp., 1955-69; mayoral exec. officer City of Shreveport, from 1971. Col. U.S. Army, 1941-46, 51-54. Decorated Legion of Merit, others. Mem. Nat. League Cities, U.S. Conf. Mayors, La. Municipal Assn., Lions. Methodist. Home: Shreveport La. Deceased.

BICKLE, JOHN MARCHER, sales executive; b. Racine, Wis., Feb. 21, 1892; s. John F. and Cora B. (Marcher) B.; m. Mary Dupuy, June 23, 1917; children: Barbara M. Bickle Nolan, Jane M. Bickle Morris. BA, U. Wis., 1916. Asst. sales mgr. Curtiss Aeroplane & Motor Corp., 1919-21; advt. rep. Curtis Pub. Co., 1921-27; sales mgr. Holmes Refrigerator Co., 1928-29; with Carrier Corp., Syracuse, N.Y., from 1929, sales mgr. Carrier-Lyle Corp. div., 1929, merchanising mgr. Carrier Corp., dir. post-war planning, eastern regional mgr., 1929-52; v.p., gen. sales mgr. unitary equipment div. Carrier Corp., from 1952. Sgt. U.S. Army, 1917-18. Mem. Extrapolators (founder, moderator), N.Y. Sales Mgrs. Club. Home: Skaneateles N.Y. †

BICKMORE, LEE SMITH, food products executive; b. Paradise, Utah, June 5, 1908; s. Danford M. and Sarah Jane (Smith) B.; m. Ellen McMinn, June 30, 1939; children: Beverlee, Elizabeth Kay (Mrs. William Blake Sonne). BS, Utah State U., 1931; cert. in advanced mgmt. program, Harvard Bus. Sch., 1949; hon. degrees, Brigham Young U., St. Joseph's U., Utah State U., St. John Fisher U., Colgate Coll., Pace U. With J.C. Penney Co., 1927-32; office, warehouse staff Nat. Biscuit Co. (now Nabisco), 1933-35, salesman, 1935-40; spl. salesman Nat. Biscuit Co. (now Nabisco), Salt Lake City, 1940-43; br. mgr., Pocatello, Idaho Nat. Biscuit Co. (now Nabisco), 1943-45; asst. mdse. mgr. Nat. Biscuit Co. (now Nabisco), N.Y.C., 1946-47; dist. sales mgr. N.J. Nat. Biscuit Co. (now Nabisco), 1947-49, adminstrv. asst. to v.p., 1949-50, v.p. sales, advt., 1950, sr. v.p., 1957-59, exec. v.p., mem. exec. com., 1959-60, pres., 1960-61, chief exec. officer, 1961-73, chmn. bd., 1969-73, chmn. exec. com., 1973-86, also bd. dirs; officer and/or dir. Nabisco subs.; bd. dirs. Bankers Trust Co., Western Electric Co. Carrier Corp., Mut. N.Y., Hart Schaffner & Marx, Chgo., Radio Sta. WRFM. Contbr. articles to various publs. Hon. trustee Pace Coll.; fellow Brandeis U. Decorated chevalier Legion of Honor (France), Merit of Honor (Italy); recipient Brotherhood award NCCJ. Mem. Conf. Bd., Am. Mgmt. Assn. (chmn. exec. com., bd. dirs.), Grocery Mfrs. Am. (past chmn., bd. dirs.), Def. Supply Assn., Biscuit and Crackers Mfrs. Assn., UN Assn. of U.S.A. (past bd. dirs.), University Club, Links Club, Balustrol Golf Club, Pauma Valley Country Club, Alpha Kappa PSi. Died June 7, 1986; buried Paradise Cemetery, Paradise, Utah.

BIDDLE, THEODORE WILLIAM, educator; b. Donora, Pa., Mar. 2, 1906; s. Rev. Richard Long and Mary Jane (Pitcock) B.; m. Ruby Anne Meyer, July 7, 1934; children: Susanna, Theodore Long. BS, U. Pitts., 1929, EdM, 1936; EdD, Waynesburg Coll., 1952. Asst. dean men U. Pitts., 1929-41, acting dean men, 1941-42, dean men, 1942-58; pres. U. Pitts. at Johnstown, 1958-71, pres. emeritus, prof.-at-large, 1971-86; Trustee Johnstown Savs. Bank.; Mem. Greater Johnstown Com. Contbr. articles to ednl. jours. Bd. dirs. Johnstown United Community Chest, Met. YMCA, Pitts. Mem. Greater Johnstown C. of C. (dir.), Am. Arbitration Assn., Nat., Eastern assns. (deans and advisers of men), Pitts. Personnel Assn., Nat. Assn. Student Personnel Adminstrs., NEA, Pa. Soc., Assn. Higher Edn., Eastern Assn. Coll. Deans (pres. 1950-52), Alpha Phi Omega, Pi Kappa Alpha, Omicron Delta Kappa, Phi Eta Sigma, Scabbard and Blade, Druids. Presbyterian. Clubs: University (Pitts.), Faculty (Pitts.), Bachelor's (Johnstown), Sunnehanna Country (pres. 1978), Club (Johnstown). Home: Johnstown Pa. Died Aug. 2, 1986.

BIGGAR, EDWARD SAMUEL, lawyer; b. Kansas City, Mo., Nov. 19, 1917; s. Frank Wilson and Katharine (Rea) B.; m. Susan Bagby, July 9, 1955; children: John, Julie, Nancy, William, Martha Susan. AB, U. Mich., 1938, JD with distinction, 1940. Bar: Mo. 1940. Assoc. firm Stinson, Mag & Fizzell, Kansas City, 1948-50; ptnr. Stinson, Mag & Fizzell, 1950-83, of counsel, 1983-87; dir. Western Chem. Co., Cereal Food Processors, Inc., Lumber Products Sales Co., Mission Hills Bank, N.A. Trustee Sunset Hill Sch., Kansas City, 1970-76; mem. com. of visitors U. Mich. Law Sch., 1977-81. Editor: Mich. Law Rev, 1939-40. Pres. Met. Kansas City YMCA, 1979-81; pres. Kansas City (Mo.) unit Am. Cancer Soc., 1968-69, Kansas City (Mo.) Bd. Police Commrs., 1981-85; mem. Kansas City (Mo.) Met. Planning Commn., 1974-75; chmn. Citizens Assn. Kansas City (Mo.), 1960-61. Served to 1st lt. AC U.S. Army, 1942-45, New Guinea, Philippines. Named Man of Yr. Phi Delta Theta Alumni Assn., Kansas City, 1968; recipient Disting. Service award YMCA, 1985. Mem. ABA, Mo. Bar, Lawyers Assn. Kansas City (pres. 1966-67), Kansas City Bar Assn., Order of Coif, Phi Beta Kappa, Phi Delta Theta, Phi Delta Phi. Republican. Presbyterian. Clubs: Kansas City Country, Mission Hills Country, Univ. of Kansas City, Mercury of Kansas City. Home: Kansas City Mo. Died Jan. 5, 1987.

BILBY, RALPH WILLARD, lawyer; b. Concho, Ariz., Sept. 15, 1891; s. John and Ann Wallrade (Whipple) B.; m. Marguerite Mansfield, May 16, 1914 (dec. Feb. 1956); children: Ralph M. (dec.), Kenneth W., Margaret Ann (Mrs. William A. Drake), Richard M.; m. Ethel Parker McChesney, June 10, 1957. LLB, U. Ariz., 1920. Bar: Ariz. 1917. Since practiced in Tucson; mem. firm Bilby, Shoenhair Warnock & Dolph, profl. corp., 1946-87; asst. U.S. atty. for Ariz. 1922-23; chmn. Ariz. Oil and Gas Conservation Commn. Del. Republican Nat. Conv., 1928, 48. Recipient U. Ariz. Distinguished Citizen award. Fellow Am. Coll. Trial Lawyers; mem. ABA, Pima County Bar Assn., State Bar Ariz. (pres. 1948-49), Alumni Assn. U. Ariz. (past pres.), Order of Coif, Phi Kappa Phi. Clubs: El Rio Golf and Country (Tucson) (past pres.), Old Pueblo (Tucson) (past pres.), Tucson Country (Tucson) (past pres.), Sunshine Climate (Tucson) (past pres.). Home: Tucson Ariz. Died Aug. 28, 1987.

BILLINGS, DOROTHY BAKER, interior designer; b. Columbia, S.C., 1918; d. James Alpheus and Ethel Vivian (Ogg) Baker; m. Robinson Billings, June 11, 1943. AB, Queens Coll., Charlotte, N.C., 1939; postgrad., N.Y. Sch. Interior Design, 1946. Cryptographer Air Transp. Command., Gt. Falls, Mont., 1942-43; with Irene's Interiors, Charlotte, 1947-48; propr. Dorothy Baker Billings, Inc. (interiors), Charlotte, 1948—; liaison between designers and mgrs., ednl. and pub. relations promotor Am. Inst. Interiors Designers (now Am. Soc. Interior Designers), 1959-73; pres. Carolinas chpt., 1964, 70, nat. bd. govs., 1963-66, chmn. coms., 1959-77, nat. chmn. hist. preservation, 1977-87; dir. Hadley Peoples Mfg. Co., 1958-87; tchr. interior design Queens Coll., 1967; cons. Hezekia Alexander Restoration, 1967-87, Latta Place, Inc., 1975-87. Designer: Jefferson Standard Broadcasting Co. rooms, Charlotte, 1960-62; 18th century period room, Mint Mus. Art, Charlotte, 1967, room for, Nat. Home Fashion League, So. Furniture Market Center, High Point, Celanese House, N.Y.C., 1970; Celanese House/South, Charlotte, 1977, N.C., 1969; design work appears in major feature mags. Fellow Am. Soc. Interior Designers; mem. Hist. N.C. Preservation Soc., Mus. Early Decorative Arts, Nat. Trust. Presbyterian. Clubs: Charlotte Country; Linville Country, Grandfather Golf and Country (Linville, N.C.). Home: Linville N.C. Died Nov. 1987.

BILLS, BENJAMIN FRANKLIN, business consultant, lawyer, realtor, author; b. Genesco, Ill., June 10, 1889; s. Clarence M. and Alice M. (Wagner) B.; m. Beryl Gilbert, 1916 (dec. 1923); children: Betty Alice, Gilbert Clarence (dec. 1942); m. Marguerite Hanford, Aug. 15, 1925. PhB, U. Chgo., 1911, JD, 1913. Bar: Ill. 1914. Pvt. practice Chgo., until 1919; mem. faculty Williams Coll., Williamstown, Mass., 1918-19; mem. law faculty U. Chgo., 1919-20; trust officer Continental & Comml. Trust & Savs. Bank, Chgo., 1920-22; pres. The Bills Realty, Inc., 1925-28, chmn. bd., from 1928; chmn. bd. Bills Securities Corp., Bills Bros., Inc.; head B. Franklin Bills and Assocs.; sales and exec. cons.; profl. lectr. Sch. Commerce, Northwestern U. Author: Principles of Persuasion, 1935, Persuasion in Business, 1937, Selling Sense, 1939, Action, How to Get It, 1949, Business Conference Leadership, 1952, Ways to Successful Business and Professional Persuasion, 1959, Salesman to Salesman, 1962, Bank Paper Problems-Solutions, 1963, Recordings on More Effective Personal Persuasiveness, 1964, Guidelines to Successful Persuasion. Recipient citation U. Chgo. Alumni Assn. Mem. Chgo. Real Estate Bd., Nat. Assn. Real Estate Bds., John Howard Assn. (pres.), Land Developers Assn. (pres.), University Club Evanston (Ill.), Union League Club (Chgo.), Westmoreland Country Club, (Ill.), Sigma Alpha Epsilon, Phi Alpha Delta, Delta Sigma Rho, Phi Beta Kappa. Home: Glenview Ill. †

BINFORD, THOMAS PETER, publishing company executive; b. Portland, Oreg., Oct. 28, 1914; s. Peter Alvin and Sylvia Jane (Munkers) B.; m. Janet Elizabeth Walker, May 7, 1941; 1 son, David Peter. BS, U. Oreg., 1937. Gen. mgr. Met. Press, Portland, Oreg., 1938-39; gen. mgr. Binford & Mort, Pubs., Portland, 1946-59, pres., from 1947; pres., chmn. bd. dirs. Met. Printing Co., Portland, 1959-74, Peter Binford Found. With U.S. Army, 1940-46. Decorated Purple Heart; recipient Rounce and Coffin award for best books produced graphically, 1976. Mem. Oreg. Hist. Soc., Oreg. Archeol. Soc., Portland Art Mus., Hudson's Bay Record Soc., Printing Industries of Pacific, Freinds of Library U. Oreg., U.S. Power Squadron, Portland Yacht Club, Multnomah Athletic Club, Sigma Delta Chi. Home: Portland Oreg. Deceased.

BING, R. H., educator, mathematician; b. Oakwood, Tex., Oct. 20, 1914; s. Rupert Henry and Lula May (Thompson) B.; m. Mary Blanche Hobbs, Aug. 26, 1938; children: Robert H., Susan Elizabeth, Virginia Gay, Mary Patricia. BS, S.W. Tex. State Tchrs. Coll., 1935; MEd, U. Tex., 1938, PhD, 1945. Tchr. high sch. Tex., 1935-42; instr., then asst. prof. math. U. Tex., 1942-47, vis. prof., 1971-72, prof., 1973-86, chmn. dept., 1975-77, Ashbel Smith prof., 1979-86; mem. faculty U. Wis., Madison, 1947-73, prof., 1952-64, rsch. prof., 1964-68, Rudolph E. Langer prof., 1968-73, chmn. dept., 1958-60; acting prof. U. Va., 1949-50; dir. Summer Inst. on Set Theoretic topology, Madison, 1955; mem. Inst. Advanced Study, Princeton, 1957-58, 62-63, 67. Mem. AAAS (v.p., chmn. sect. A 1959), Nat. Sci. Bd. (chmn. div. math. 1968-74), NAS (chmn. math. sect. 1970-73, councilor 1977-80), Math. Assn. Am. (pres. 1963-64, vis. lectr. 1954-55, 61-62, chmn. Wis. sect. 1952), Am. Math. Soc. (councilor 1952-54, 58-60, v.p. 1967-68, pres. 1977-78), NRC, Conf. Bd. Math. Sci. (chmn. 1965-66), Pi Mu Epsilon (vice dir. gen. 1960-63). Presbyterian. Died Apr. 28, 1986; buried Capitol Meml. Park Cemetery, Austin, Tex.

BINGHAM, BARRY, editor; b. Louisville, Feb. 10, 1906; s. Robert Worth and Eleanor (Miller) B.; m. Mary Clifford Caperton, June 9, 1931; children: Worth (dec.), Barry Jr., Sallie, Jonathan (dec.), Eleanor (Mrs. Rowland Miller). Student, Middlesex Sch., Concord, Mass., 1921-23; AB magna cum laude, Harvard U., 1928; LLD, U. Ky.; LLD (hon.), Kenyon Coll., Bellarmine Coll., Ind. U., Spalding Coll., Edgecliff Coll.; LittD (hon.), U. Louisville, U. Cin., Centre Coll., Alfred U., Berea Coll. With Courier-Jour. & Louisville Times Co., 1930-86, editor, pub., 1945-71, chmn. bd., 1971-86, ret., 1986. Trustee Berea Coll., 1938-76; trustee Nat. Portrait Gallery; bd. overseers Harvard U.; dir. Asia Found.; chmn. Internat. Press Inst., 1964-66; hon. life mem. Chief of mission to France, ECA, 1949-50; Nat. chmn. Vols. for Stevenson-Kefauver, 1956. Served to comdr. USNR, 1941-45. Decorated comdr. Order Brit. Empire; comdr. Legion of Honor; recipient Sullivan award U. Ky.; William Allen White Journalism award U. Kans.; Roger W. Straus award NCCJ. Mem. English-Speaking Union U.S. (chmn. bd. trustees 1974-77). Democrat. Episcopalian. Clubs: River Valley, Wynn-Stay, Jefferson (Louisville); Century (N.Y.C.). Home: Glenview Ky. Died Aug. 15, 1988.

BINGHAM, JONATHAN BREWSTER, former congressman, lawyer; b. New Haven, Apr. 24, 1914; s. Hiram and Alfreda (Mitchell) B.; m. June Rossbach, Sept. 20, 1939; children: Sherrell Bingham Downes, June Mitchell Bingham Esselstyn, Timothy Woodbridge, Claudia Rossbach (now Gurunam Bhajan Kaur Khalsa). B.A., Yale U., 1936, J.D., 1939. Bar: N.Y. 1940. Practiced in N.Y.C. 1939-41, 46-51, 53-54, 59-61, 83—; with O.P.A., 1941-42; chief Alien Enemy Control Sect., Dept. State, 1945-46, asst. dir. Office Internat. Security Affairs, 1951; dep. adminstr. Tech. Coop. (Point Four), 1951-53; mem. firm Goldwater & Flynn, 1959-61; sec. to gov. N.Y. State, 1955-58; U.S. rep. in UN Trusteeship Council, 1961-62, pres., 1962; prin. adviser to U.S. ambassador to UN on colonial and trusteeship questions, 1961-62; U.S. rep. with rank ambassador UNECOSOC, 1962-63; also alt. rep. 15th-18th Gen. Assemblies; mem. U.S. mission UN, 1961-64, 89th-92d congresses from 23d Dist. N.Y., 93d-97th congresses from 22d Dist. N.Y.; mem. fgn. affairs and interior and insular affairs com., chmn. subcom. on internat. econ. policy and trad; spl. counsel Pryor, Cashman, Sherman & Flynn N.Y.C., from 1983; lectr. Columbia U. Sch. Law. Author: Shirt Sleeve Diplomacy-Point 4 in Action, 1954, (with Alfred M. Bingham) Violence and Democracy, 1970; also articles. Bd. dirs. People for Am. Way, UN Devel. Corp., Inst. Internat. Edn.; bd. dirs. U.S. Com. UNICEF, Population Crisis Com.; cochmn. FDR Four Freedoms Found.; pres. Bronx County Soc. Mental Health, 1960-62; mem., past pres. Bronx Boys' Club; trustee emeritus 20th Century Fund. Served to capt. AUS, 1943-45. Yale Corp. fellow, 1949-51; recipient Staff citation War Dept., 1945. Mem. Assn. Bar City N.Y., Council Fgn. Relations N.Y.C. Club: Century Assn. (N.Y.C.). Home: Bronx N.Y. Died July 3, 1986; buried Salem, Conn.

BINGHAM, WOODBRIDGE, history educator; b. Cambridge, Mass., Nov. 24, 1901; died May 2, 1986; s. Hiram and Alfreda (Mitchell) B.; m. Ursula W. Griswold, June 28, 1928; children: Anne Bingham Wright, Clarissa Bingham Junge, Evelyn Bingham Goodman, Marian Bingham Hubbell. A.B., Yale U., 1924; A.M., Harvard U., 1929; Ph.D., U. Calif., 1934. Instr., Yale-in-China, Chang-sha, China, 1924-25; instr. Far Eastern history U. Calif., 1937-40, asst. prof., 1940-46, assoc. prof., 1946-52, prof., 1952-69, prof. emeritus, 1969-86, dir. Inst. East Asiatic Studies, 1949-57; vis. prof. Centre of Asian studies, U. Hong Kong, 1970-71. Author: The Founding of the T'ang Dynasty: The Fall of Sui and Rise of T'ang, 1941, (with Hilary Conroy, Frank W. Iklé) History of Asia, vol. I: Formation of Civilizations from Antiquity to 1600, 1964, rev. edit., 1974, vol. II, Old Empires, Western Penetration and the Rise of New Nations, since 1600, 1965, rev. edit., 1974. Served as lt. USNR, 1943-45. Mem. Nat. Com. U.S.-China Relations., Assn. Asian Studies, Am. Hist. Assn., Am. Oriental Soc., Psi Upsilon. Club: University (San Francisco). Deceased.

BINKLEY, JAMES SAMUEL, surgeon, oncologist, radiologist; b. Guymon, Okla., July 31, 1908; s. James Garfield and Nellie Irene (Keller) B.; m. Kathrine Bretch, Mar. 8, 1941; children: Donald James, Keith Bretch. BS, U. Okla., 1929, AB, 1930; MD, Harvard U., 1932. Chief resident surgeon, Rockefeller Clinic fellow Meml. Hosp., N.Y.C., 1939, research fellow, 1936-40; med. dir. Am. Soc. for Control Cancer Inc., Am. Cancer Soc., 1940-46; mem. surg. staff chest dept. Meml. Cancer Ctr.; pvt. practice N.Y.C., 1940-42; organizer Cancer Ctr., Bethesda Naval Hosp. and Long Beach Naval Hosp., 1942-46; sr. surgeon Los Angeles Tumor Inst., 1946-50; assoc. prof. surgery U. Okla. Med. Sch., Oklahoma City, 1950-80; mem. staff Bapt. Meml., Mercy, Presbyn. and Univ. hosps.; med. dir. Standard Life & Accident Ins. Co.; cons. to ins. industry. Contbr. articles to med. jours. Lt. Comdr. M.C., USNR, 1942-46. Mem. ACS, AMA, Okla. Med. Soc., Calif. Med. Soc., N.Y. Med. Soc., Los Angeles Med. Soc., N.Y.C. Med. Soc., Oklahoma City Med. Soc., County Med. Soc., Oklahoma City Surg. Soc., Soc. Head and Neck Surgeons, Am. Radium Soc., James Ewing Soc., Kiwanis, Lake Aluma Club, Phi Beta Kappa, Phi Beta Phi. Phi Delta Theta. Home: Oklahoma City Okla. Died Mar. 14, 1980; buried Meml. Park, Oklahoma City.

BINNS, JAMES HAZLETT, industrial executive; b. Salida, Colo., Dec. 23, 1912; s. Hazlett C. and May (Lacey) B.; m. Ruamie Hill, Dec. 29, 1936; 1 son, James Hazlett Jr. AB, U. Denver, 1934. Dir. placement and field work U. Denver, 1934-35; with Armstrong Cork Co. (name changed to Armstrong World Industries, Inc.), Lancaster, Pa., from 1935, successively sales trainee floor div., salesman floor div., Atlanta, acting dist. mgr., dist. mgr., asst. sales mgr., Lancaster. Pa., asst. gen. mgr. munitions div., asst. gen. sales mgr. floor div., gen. sales mgr., 1935-60, v.p., gen. mgr. floor and indsl. ops., 1961-62, sr. v.p., 1962-68, pres., 1968-78, chmn., 1978-82, also dir.; dir. Campbell Soup Co., Woodstream Corp., Lititz, Pa. Mem. NAM (dir., chmn. fin. com.), Newcomen Soc. N.Am., Lancaster Country, Hamilton, Skytop, Goodyear Golf and Country (Ariz.) clubs, Omicron Delta Kappa, Kappa Sigma. Home: Lancaster Pa. Died Apr. 30, 1985; cremated.

BIRD, WILLIAM C., consumer products company executive; b. Rockland, Maine, July 1, 1888; s. Hanson and Jennie (Willey) B.; m. Julia Coleman, Mar. 16, 1933. Student, Phillips Exeter Acad., 1908; BS, MIT, 1912. Asst. chief engr. Tex., Okla. and Easter R.R., 1913-16; gen. mgr. Knox Co., electric co., 1916-20; gen. supt., v.p. Rockland & Rocport Lime Co., 1920-28; indsl. engr. Bond & Goodwin, N.Y.C., 1928-30; pres. Pro-phy-lac-tic Brush Co.; bd. dirs. Warner-Lambert Pharm. Co. Home: Longmeadow Mass. †

BIRKHAHN, N. STEVEN, public relations executive. BA in Fin., Am. U. Ptnr., dir. investment community liaison activities The Fin. Relations Bd., N.Y.C. Deceased.

BIRKHAUG, KONRAD ELIAS, bacteriologist; b. Bergen, Norway, Oct. 12, 1892; came to U.S., 1911; naturalized, 1917; s. Karl Anderssen and Elise Marie (Olsen) B.; m. Marie Mustad Berner, Mar. 8, 1938 (div. 1944). Student, Jamestown (N.D.) Coll. Acad., 1912-14; AB, Jamestown Coll., 1917; MD, Johns Hopkins U., 1924; MS, Rochester U., 1927; postgrad., U. Berlin, U. Hamburg, Germany, summers 1922, 24, 32. Diplomate Am. Bd. Preventive Medicine and Pub. Health. Hosp. sec. Internat. YMCA, Russia, 1917-18; prisoner of war relief Internat. YMCA, Verdun, France, 1919-20; interne Sydenham Hosp., Balt., 1923-24; asst. medicine and Charlton fellow in med. rsch. Johns Hopkins Hosp., Balt., 1924-25; assoc. in bacteriology U. Rochester, 1925-26, asst. prof., 1925-28, assoc. prof., 1928-34; resident bacteriologist Strong Meml. Hosp., Rochester, 1925-32; sous-chef Institut Pasteur Lab Tb, Paris, 1932-35; mem. Christian Michelsen Inst., Bergen, 1935-45; dir. Norwegian Nat. Tb Vaccine (BCG) Lab., Bergen, 1937-45; bacteriol. adviser Sahlgrenska Hosp., Gothenburg, Sweden, 1945-46; assoc. med. bacteriologist dir. Tb Vaccine (BCG) Lab. N.Y. State Dept. Health, Albany, 1946-50, prin. med. bacteriologist, 1950-53; assoc. prof. pathology and bacteriology Albany Med. Coll., 1954; cons. USPHS; v.p. 1st Internat. BCG Congress, Paris, 1948. Exhibitor sculptures, aquarelles; author books including: Telavaag, 1946, It Happened in Norway, 1967, Physician at the End of the Road, 1968; also articles relating to field; sculptor, water-colourist. Active ARC, Norway, World War II. Recipient awards Tb, Red Cross Work, Diploma of Honor, Am. Acad. Tb Physicians, 1949. Fellow AAAS, ACP, AMA; mem. N.Y. State Pub. Health Assn., N.Y. State Assn. Pub. Health Labs., N.Y. State Med. Soc., Med. Soc. City Albany, Am. Trudeau Soc., Am. Assn. Immunologists, Internat. Leprosy Assn., Am. Assn. Pathologists and Bacteriologists, Am. Soc. Bacteriology, Soc. Exptl. Biology and Medicine, Sigma Xi; also fgn. socs. Home: Bergen Norway. Deceased.

BIRREN, FABER (GREGOR LANG), color consultant, author; b. Chgo., Sept. 21, 1900; s. Joseph Pierre and Crescentia (Lang) B.; m. Wanda Martin, Apr. 25, 1934; children: Zoe Kirby, Fay Koedel. Student, Chgo. Art Inst., 1914-18, U. Chgo., 1919-20; MS (hon.), Arnold Coll., 1941. In devel. spl. color code for industry 1942-43; pres. Am. Color Trends, rsch. orgn., N.Y.C., 1942-88; rsch. psychol. and visual aspects of color. Author: Color in Modern Packaging, 1935, Wonderful Wonders of Red-Yellow-Blue, 1937, Story of Color, 1941, Selling with Color, 1945, American Colorist, 1948, Your Color and Your Self, 1952, New Horizons in Color, 1955, Selling Color to People, 1956; fiction written under pseudonym: Terra, An Allegory, 1953, The Unconsidered, 1955, Make Mine Love, 1958. U.S. rep. World Conf. on Prevention Indsl. Accidents, Rome, 1955; researcher on functional uses of color in submarine, surface vessels OSRD, World War II. Mem. Optical Soc. Am., Chgo. Art Inst. Alumni Assn. Home: Stamford Conn. Died Dec. 30, 1988.

BISHOP, ISABEL (MRS. HAROLD G. WOLFF), artist; b. Cin., Mar. 3, 1902; d. John Remsen and Anna Bartram (Newbold) B.; m. Harold George Wolff, Aug. 9, 1934; 1 son, Remsen. Ed., Wicker Art Sch., Detroit, 1917-18, N.Y. Sch. Applied Design for Women, 1918-20, Art Students League N.Y., 1920-22, 1927-30; AFD (hon.), Moore Inst., Phila.; DFA (hon.), Bates Coll., 1979, Mt. Holyoke Coll., 1982. Instr. life painting and composition Art Students League, N.Y.C., 1936-37; instr. Snowhegan Sch. Painting and Sculpture, 1957, lectr., 1957, 60, 62, 64, 66. Represented in, Mus. Bibliothèque Nationale, Paris, Victoria and Albert Mus., London, Brit. Mus., London, Des Moines Art Center, also art galleries, collections, Paul Sachs, Johnson Collection, others; exhibited at expns., 10 one-man shows in, N.Y.C., also at, Berkshire Mus., Pittsfield, Mass., 1957, retrospective exhbns., Whitney Mus. Art, 1975, U.

Ariz., 1974, Wichita (Kans.) State U., 1974, group shows, Bklyn. Mus., 1977, Hayward Gallery, 1977, N.Y. U., 1977, Am. embassy, London, 1977, Wichita State U., 1979. Recipient awards including; W.A. Clark prize; Bronze medal Corcoran Gallery, Washington, 1945; Mrs. H. S. Noyes and Am. Artists Group prizes, 1947; Forsythia award Bklyn. Bot. Garden, 1979; Benjamin Franklin fellow Royal Soc. Art, 1965; first Altman prize N.A.D., 1967; asso. mem. N.A.D., 1940; elected Nat. Academician, 1941. Fellow Royal Soc. Arts London; mem. Nat. Inst. Arts and Letters, Am. Acad. Arts and Letters, Am. Soc. Painters, Sculptors and Gravers, Soc. Am. Etchers, Nat. Arts Club, Phila. Water Color Club, Am. Group Cosmopolitan Club. Home: Bronx N.Y. Died Feb. 19, 1988.

BISHOP, JIM, author; b. Jersey City, Nov. 21, 1907; s. John Michael and Jenny Josephine (Tier) B.; m. Elinor Margaret Dunning, June 14, 1930 (dec. Oct. 1957); children: Virginia Lee, Gayle Peggy; m. Elizabeth Kelly Stone, May, 1961; children: Karen, Kathleen. Student, Drakes Secretarial Coll., 1923; LittD, St. Bonaventure U., 1958, Belmont Abbey Coll., 1968, St. Peter's Coll., 1978, St. Thomas of Villanova U., 1984; LHD (hon.). Copy boy N.Y. News, 1929-30; reporter N.Y. Daily Mirror, 1930-32; asst. to Mark Hellinger, columnist, 1932-34; rewriteman, feature writer Daily Mirror, 1934-43; asso. editor Colliers mag., 1943-44, war editor, 1944-45; exec. editor Liberty mag., 1945-47; dir. lit. dept. Music Corp. Am., 1947-49; founding editor Gold Medal Books, 1949-51; exec. editor Catholic Digest; founding editor Catholic Digest Book Club, 1954-55. Author: The Glass Crutch, 1945, The Mark Hellinger Story, 1952, Parish Priest, 1953, The Girl in Poison Cottage, 1953, The Making of a Priest, 1954, The Day Lincoln Was Shot, 1955, The Golden Ham, 1956, The Day Christ Died, 1957, Go With God, 1958, Some of My Very Best, 1960, The Day Christ Was Born, 1960, The Murder Trial of Judge Peal, 1962, Honeymoon Diary, 1963, A Day in the Life of President Kennedy, 1964, Jim Bishop; Reporter, 1965, A Day in the Life of President Johnson, 1967, The Day Kennedy was Shot, 1968, The Days of Martin Luther King, Jr, 1971, F.D.R.'s Last Year, 1974, the Birth of the United States, 1976, A Bishop's Confession, 1980; Columnist, King Features Syndicate.; Contbr. nat. mags. Recipient Journalism in Life award Ency. Brit., 1979. Home: Delray Beach Fla. Died July 26, 1987; buried Palm Beach Meml. Park, Lantana, Fla.

BISHOP, WILLIAM WARNER, JR., legal educator; b. Princeton, N.J., June 10, 1906; s. William Warner and Finie Murfree (Burton) B.; m. Mary Fairfax Shreve, July 19, 1947; 1 dau., Elizabeth Shreve. AB, U. Mich., 1928, JD, 1931; postgrad., Harvard U., 1928-29, Columbia U., 1938-39. Bar: Mich. 1931, U.S. Supreme Ct 1941. Asst. reporter Harvard Research Internat. Law, 1932-35, mem. exec. com., 1949-87; asso. Root, Clark, Buckner & Ballantine, N.Y.C., 1935-36; lectr. politics Princeton U., 1936-38; asst. legal adv. Dept. State, 1939-47; vis. prof. internat. law Law Sch., U. Pa., 1947-48, Columbia U., 1948; research, teaching asst. Law Sch., U. Mich., 1931-35, prof. law, 1948-76, prof. emeritus, 1977-87; Legal adviser to U.S. delegation Council Fgn. Ministers and Paris Peace Conf., 1946; lectr. Hague Acad. Internat. Law, 1961, 65; mem. Permanent Ct. of Arbitration, 1975-81. Author: International Law Cases and Materials, 1951, 1962, 71; Contbr. articles to legal jours.; Bd. editors: Am. Jour. Internat. Law, 1947-87; editor-in-chief, 1953-55, 62-70; contbg. editor: Ann. Digest of Pub. Internat. Law Cases, 1931-40. Mem. Mich. State Bar, Am. Soc. Internat. Law (v.p. 1960-61, 65-66, hon. v.p. 1969-82, 84-87, hon. pres. 1982-84), Internat. Law Assn. Home: Ann Arbor Mich. Died Dec. 29, 1987; buried Forrest Hill Cemetery, Ann Arbor, Mich.

BISSELL, BETTY CHAPMAN, public utility holding company executive; b. Pelzer, S.C., Mar. 23, 1932; d. Harold T. and Beulah (Hunt) Chapman; m. George Humphrey Bissell, Dec. 27, 1952; 1 child, George Anthony. BA in Bus. Adminstrn., Furman U., 1954. Asst. sec. SCE&G Co., Columbia, S.C., 1982-83, corp. sec., 1983-87; corp. sec. SCANA & Cos., Columbia, S.C., 1984-87. Pres. Am. Lung Assn. S.C., Columbia, 1984-87. Recipient Tribute to Women in Industry award YWCA, Columbia, 1985. Mem. Am. Soc. Corporate Secs. Episcopalian. Home: Columbia S.C. Deceased.

BISSELL, CUSHMAN BREWER, lawyer; b. St. Marys, Ohio, July 20, 1900; s. John Winthrop and Rowena (Brewer) B.; m. Marion Bremner, July 3, 1928; children: Denorah, Cushman B. AB, U. Ill., 1923; LLB, Harvard U., 1926; JD, John Marshall Law Sch., 1927; LLD (hon.), Loyola U., Chgo., 1965. Bar: Ill. 1926. Assoc. Lord, Wire & Cobb, 1926-28; pvt. practice 1928-31; ptnr. Lord, Lloyd & Bissell, 1931-38, Lord, Bissell & Brook, Chgo., from 1938; pres. NW Nat. Bank Chgo., 1943, chmn. bd. dirs., 1944-63, bd. dirs., from 1963; gen. counsel, dir. Gen. Outdoor Advt. Co., from 1942; bd. dirs. Nova Chrome Inc., Waylite Co. Mem. exec. com. Nat. Cath. Community Service from 1950, Ill. Assn. for Crippled from 1946, U.S.O., 1951-54, United Def. Fund Inc., 1951-57; mem. Chgo. Crime Commn., from 1944, dir. 1946-64; pres. Cath. Charities Chgo., 1949-53, bd. dirs., mem. exec. com. from 1953; pres., bd. dirs. Chgo. Charitable Found. from 1949; v.p. Chgo. Community Fund, 1949-54; trustee U. Ill., 1952-59, U. Retirement System of Ill., 1953-59, Art. Inst., Chgo. from 1952, Loyola U. from 1960; organizer, dir. Citizens Greater Chgo. Inc.; mem. U. Ill. Found. from 1970; bd. dirs. Joyce Found. from 1974; mem. council Harvard Law Sch., 1956-60. Decorated knight Order St. Gregory by Pope Pious XII. Mem. Nat. Conf. Realtors and Lawyers, ABA, (chmn. law list com. 1942-45), Ill. Bar Assn., Chgo. Bar Assn. (pres. 1951-52), Harvard Law Sch. Assn. (council), Chgo. Club, Attic Comml. Club, Law Club, Lincoln Inn, Pi Kappa Alpha, Phi Alpha Delta, Alpha Alpha Alpha. Home: Chicago Ill. Deceased.

BISSELL, PATRICK, ballet dancer; b. 1958. Attended, Nat. Acad. Dance, Champaign, Ill., N.C. Sch. Arts, Sch. Am. Ballet. Dancer with Boston Ballet; corps mem. Am. Ballet Theatre, N.Y.C., 1977-78, soloist, 1978-79, prin., 1979-81, 82-87; guest dancer Stars of World Ballet, 1979, Nat. Ballet of Can., 1980, Edinburgh Festival, 1980, others. Died Dec. 29, 1987.

BISSON, WHEELOCK ALEXANDER, physician; b. Key West, Fla., 1898; s. George Henry and Sarah Jane (Kemp) B.; m. Maude Lee Voorhies, June 2, 1930. BS, Fla. A&M U., 1922; MD, Meharry Med. Coll., 1929. Intern Royal Circle Hosp., Memphis, 1931-33; pvt. practice Memphis, 1931-85; clinician Memphis and Shelby County Health Dept., 1932-85. Mem. Cynthia Milk Fund Com., Memphis; active YMCA, Boy Scouts Am. Named Tenn. Dr. of Yr. by Vol. State Med. Assn., 1962, 63; recipient Meritorious Achievement award Fla. A&M U., 1964, citation and Key to City, plaque Memphis and Shelby County Health Dept., 1965, Practitioner of Yr. award Nat. Med. Assn., 1967. Fellow Intercontinental Biog. Assn.; mem. AAAS, Am. Thoracic Soc., Nat. Pub. Health Assn., Nat. Rehab. Assn., NAACP (life), Internat. Platform Assn., Tenn. Acad. Sci., Am. Acad. Pediatrics, Tenn. Acad. Pediatrics, AMA, Tenn. Med. Assn., Nat. Med. Assn. (2d v.p. 1966-85, mem. nat. sickle cell anemia com. pediatric sect.), Vol. State Med. Assn. (past pres., chmn. bd. trustees, treas., chmn. Tb com., chmn. legislative com.), Bluff City Med. Soc. (sec.), Memphis Med. Soc., Shelby County Med. Soc., Masons (33 deg.), Elks (past state pres.), Omega Psi Phi. Episcopalian. Home: Memphis Tenn. Died Oct. 23, 1985.

BITNER, LYNN NEVIN, newspaperman; b. Lancaster, Pa., Jan. 31, 1904; s. Henry Franklin and Cora Catherine (Murray) B.; m. Beatrice K. Stohrer, Feb. 25, 1932; children: Laurence M., Carol C. (Mrs. David W. Loysen), Susan F. Student, Bucknell U., 1920-22. Newspaperman various ind. papers and Hearst papers, 1925-28; with Gannett newspapers, 1928-66; advt. mgr. Gannett newspapers, Ogdensburg, N.Y.; nat. advt. mgr. then advt. mgr. Gannett newspapers, Rochester, N.Y., 1933-41; gen. mgr. Elmira (N.Y.) Star Gazette Gannett newspapers, 1941-52; bus. mgr. Gannett newspapers, Rochester, 1952-55, gen. mgr., dir., 1955-61, v.p., 1961-66. Trustee Frank E. Gannett Newspaper Found. Inc., Rochester Inst. Tech. Mem. Am. Newspaper Pubs. Assn. (dir. bur. advt. 1949-55), N.Y. State Publishers Assn. (exec. com.), Rochester Club, Oak Hill Country Club, Binghamton Club. Home: Hilton Head Island S.C. Died Apr. 23, 1986.

BITTLEMAN, ARNOLD, artist, educator; b. N.Y.C., July 4, 1933; s. Max and Jean (Rosenblatt) B.; m. Dolores Dembus, June 8, 1958; children: Davis, Sarah. B.F.A., Yale U., 1956, M.F.A., 1958. Mem. faculty Yale U., 1958-63, Parsons Sch. Design, N.Y.C., 1958-60, Skidmore Coll., 1964-66; prof. art Union Coll., Schenectady, 1966-85. One man shows include: Kanegis Gallery, Boston, 1958, 61, 65, Schenectady Mus., 1971, 75, 76, Webb & Parsons, Bedford, N.Y., 1974; exhibited in group shows at Genesis Gallery, N.Y.C., 1980, Borgenicht Gallery, N.Y.C., 1959-60, Milliken Gallery, N.Y.C., 1981, Mus. Modern Art, N.Y.C., 1978, Whitney Mus. Am. Art, N.Y.C., 1971, Naples (Fla.) Art Gallery, 1979-80, Am. Embassy. Moscow; represented in permanent collections Mus. Modern Art, N.Y.C., Whitney Mus. Am. Art, Bklyn. Mus., Boston Mus., Fogg Mus., Cambridge, Brandeis U., Waltham, Mass., Addison Gallery Am. Art, Andover, Mass., Munson-Williams-Proctor Inst., Utica, N.Y., Schenectady Mus. Alice Kimball English traveling fellow, 1956-57. Died Apr. 6, 1985; buried N.Y.C.

BITZER, CHARLES W., banker; b. Bridgeport, Conn., 1892. Sec., asst. treas, dir. Bridgeport Storage Warehouse Co., Conn.; bd. dirs. Bridgeport Gas Co. Home: Bridgeport Conn. †

BJORNSON, VAL (KRISTJAN VALDIMAR), state treasurer; b. Minneota, Minn., Aug. 29, 1906; s. Gunnar B. and Ingibjorg Augustine (Hurdal) B.; m. Gudrun Jonsdottir, Feb. 20, 1946; children: Helga, Kristin, Jon, Valdimar, Maria. BA summa cum laude, U. Minn., 1930. With Minneota Mascot, 1918, editor, 1925-27, 31-35; radio commentator Sta. KSTP, St. Paul-Mpls., 1935-42; editorial writer Mpls. Jour., 1935-36, Mpls. Tribune, 1937-41; assoc. editor St. Paul Pioneer Press and Dispatch, 1947-50, 55-56; treas. State of Minn., 1951-55, 57-75. Mem. nat. bd., former pres., then treas. Minn. chpt. Am.-Scandinavian Found.; hon. consul for Iceland, Minn., 1942, 47-50; Rep. nominee for U.S. senator, 1954. Lt. comdr. USN, 1942-46, ETO. Decorated comdr. Order of Falcon (Iceland), 1946; knight 1st class Order St. Olav, 1949. Mem. Phi Beta Kappa, Delta Sigma Rho, Sigma Delta Chi, Masons. Lutheran. Home: Minneapolis Minn. Died Mar. 10, 1987.

BLACK, EDWIN FAHEY, international business consultant; b. New Orleans, Aug. 17, 1915; s. Edwin Gregory and Lillian (Fahey) B.; m. Margaret Cobey, Nov. 26, 1945; children: Star, Christopher, Noel, Nicholas, Brian, Bruce. BSCE, U.S. Mil. Acad., 1940; MA in Internat. Relations, George Washington U., 1962; grad., Nat. War Coll., 1962. Commd. 2d lt. U.S. Army, 1940, advanced through grades to brig. gen., 1965; with OSS, Europe, World War II; comdg. officer 2d bn. 505th Airborne Inf. 82d Airborne Div., Ft. Bragg, N.C., 1950-51; comdg. officer 2d battle group 19 Ind., 25th Div., Schofield Barracks, Honolulu, 1957-58; mil asst. to dep. sec. Dept. Def., Washington, 1959-61; comdg. gen. U.S. Army Support Command, Thailand, 1967-69; asst. div. comdr. 25th Inf. Div., Vietnam, 1969; asst. chief of staff U.S. Army Pacific, Honolulu, 1970; ret. U.S. Army, 1970; exec. v.p. Freedoms Found., Valley Forge, Pa., 1970-71; dir. bus. plans S.E. Asia LTV Aerospace Corp., Bangkok, 1971-74; mng. dir. KRA Canal Survey Office, Bangkok, 1972-76; dir. internat. bus. devel. LTV Corp., 1974-75; dir. indsl. devel. Govt. of Am. Samoa; cons. on econ. devel. Trust Ters. of Pacific Islands, 1976-77; v.p. internat. bus. devel. I.R.A.S. Devel. Corp., White Plains, N.Y., 1980-85; spl. asst. to pres. Radiation Tech., Inc., Rockaway, N.J., 1983-85. Contbr. articles on polit.-mil. affaris to mags. and profl. jours. Decorated Legion of Merit with 2 oak leaf clusters, Bronze Star; Order Crown (Thailand); Cross of Gallantry with palm and star (Republic of South Vietnam). Mem. Council Fgn. Relations, Outrigger Canoe Club, Waialae Country Club, Royal Bangkok Sports Club, Army-Navy Country Club, Army-Navy Club (Washington). Home: Honolulu Hawaii. Died Apr. 15, 1985.

BLACK, JAMES HAY, chemical engineering educator; b. Pitts., Aug. 14, 1921; s. Alexander and Ruth (Hay) B.; m. Mary Lucretia Garland, Feb. 4, 1950; children: Ruth Hay Black McKinzey, Alexander Chisholm, Patricia Anne. AB in Chemistry, Cornell U., 1943; B.S., U. Pitts., 1948, MS, 1949, PhD, 1954; PhD hon. alumnus, Carnegie Mellon U., 1954. Registerd profl. engr., Pa. Rsch. chemist Koppers Co. Inc., Pitts., 1943; instr. U. Pitts., 1950-52; fellow Mellon Inst. Indsl. Rsch., Pitts., 1952-54; asst. project engr. Standard Oil Co., Ind., 1954-55; sr. technologist, supervising technologist U.S. Steel Corp., Monroeville, Pa., 1955-62; prof., head chem. engring. U. Ala., 1962-85; exec. sec. Am. Assn. Cost Engrs., 1964-71, dir., 1972-74, v.p., 1974, pres. 1975; cons. in field. Co-author: Cost and Optimization Engineering, 1983, Cost Engineering Planning Techniques for Management, 1984; univ. contbg. author: Environmental Engineer's Handbook, 1973; contbr. articles to prof. jours. Mem. Nat. air Pollution Techniques Adv. Com., HEW, Washington, 1969; cons. Tuscaloosa (Ala.) Envir. Quality Control Com., 1969-85; mem. Tuscaloosa Environ. Health Adv. Com.; mem. tech. panel U.S. Office Coal Rsch., Washington. 1st lt. AUS, 1943-46. Fellow Am. Inst. Chem. Engrs., Am. Assn. Cost Engrs., Am. Inst. Chemists; mem. Am. Chem. Soc., Soc. History Tech., Universtiy Club, Sigma Xi, Tau Beta Pi, Sigma Tau, Phi Lambda Upsilon, Omega Chi Epsilon. Episcopalian. Home: Tuscaloosa Ala. Died Dec. 17, 1985; buried Pitts.

BLACK, JOHN WILSON, speech educator; b. Veedersburg, Ind., Feb. 9, 1906; s. George Keys and Hattie Lee (Wilson) B.; m. Helen Harrington, Aug. 21, 1936; children: Caroline (Mrs. Philip Utley), Richard Willis, Constance (Mrs. Dennis Nagle), Charlotte. A.B., Wabash Coll., 1927, D.H.L. (hon.), 1977; M.A., U. Iowa, 1930, Ph.D., 1935; D.Sc. (hon.), Bowling Green State U., 1977; D.H.L. (hon.), Ohio State U., 1982. Prof. speech and rhetoric Adrian (Mich.) Coll., 1927-35; instr. English Kenyon Coll., Gambier, Ohio, 1935-36; prof. speech 1936-49, Ohio State U., Columbus, 1949-66; regents prof. speech Ohio State U., 1966-76, emeritus, 1976-87; vis. prof. U. Minn., summer 1946, Mich. State U., 1977, Tex. So. U., 1978-79, U. Tex. Health Sci. Center, Houston, 1980; Emons prof. Ball State U., 1976; project dir. voice communication lab. Nat. Def. Research Council, Waco, Tex., 1943-45; exec. sec. Ohio Coll. Assn., 1946-53; cons. Vocat. Rehab. Adminstrn., 1962-66. Author: (with Wilbur C. Moore) Speech: Code, Meaning, and Communication, 1955, American Speech for Foreign Students, 1963, 2d edit., 1983, Multiple-Choice Intelligibility Tests, 1963, 2d edit., entitled Word Discrimination, 1985; (with Ruth B. Irwin) Voice and Diction, 1969, (with Cleavonne S. Stratton, Alan C. Nochols, Marian A. Chavez) Use of Words in Context: The Vocabulary of College Students, 1985; (with others) Language and Hearing Journal Titles, 1954-78, 1979; Editor: Speech Monographs, 1959; mem. editorial bd.: Jour. Speech, 1948-53, Jour. Communication Disorders, 1967-87, Folia Phoniatrica, 1970-87, Jour. Psycholinguistic Research, 1971-87. Recipient Presdl. certificate of merit, 1949; Fulbright scholar, 1954-55; NSF postdoctoral fellow, 1961; Japanese Soc. for Promotion Sci. fellow Chiba U., 1976. Fellow AAAS, Acoustical Soc. Am., Am. Speech and Hearing Assn. (v.p. 1964, certificate of merit 1968); mem. Speech Communication Assn. (pres. 1966), Am. Psychol. Assn., Linguistic Soc.

Am., AAUP, Internat. Coll. Exptl. Phonology (pres. 1971), Internat. Soc. Phonetic Scis. (hon. v.p. 1983-87), Aerospace Med. Assn., Phi Beta Kappa. (hon.). Home: Columbus Ohio. Died Dec. 5, 1987, buried Osborn Prairie Cemetery, Veedersburg, Ind.

BLACK, MAX, philosophy educator; b. Baku, Russia, Feb. 24, 1909; came to U.S., 1940, naturalized, 1948; s. Lionel and Sophia (Divinska) B.; m. Michal Landsberg, Aug. 21, 1933; children: Susan Naomi, Jonathan. B.A., Queens Coll., U. Cambridge, 1930; student, U. Göttingen, 1930-31; Ph.D., U. London, 1939, D.Lit., 1955. Lectr., tutor U. London Inst. Edn., 1936-40; prof. philosophy U. Ill., 1940-46; prof. philosophy Cornell U., 1946, Susan Linn Sage prof. philosophy and humane letters, 1954-77; prof. emeritus Cornell, 1977-88; chmn. program for Andrew D. White profs.-at-large, 1965-78; dir. Soc. for Humanities, 1965-70; sr. mem. program Sci. Tech. and Soc., 1971—; vis. prof. U. Washington, 1951-52; vis. mem. Princeton Inst. Advanced Study, 1970-71; vis. fellow St. John's Coll., Oxford and Clare Hall, Cambridge, 1978; Tarner lectr. Trinity Coll., Cambridge, Eng., 1978. Author: (with others) Philosophical Studies, 1948, Science and Civilization, 1949, Language and Philosophy, 1949, The Nature of Mathematics, 1950, Critical Thinking, rev. edit., 1952, Translations from the Philosophical Writings of Gottlob Frege, (with P. T. Geach), 1952, Problems of Analysis, 1954, Models and Metaphors, 1962, A Companion to Wittgenstein's Tractatus, 1964, The Labyrinth of Language, 1968, Margins of Precision, 1970, Caveats and Critiques, 1975, The Prevalence of Humbug and Other Essays, 1983; Editor: Philos. Rev, 1946—, Philosophical Analysis, 1950, The Social Theories of Talcott Parsons, 1961, The Importance of Language, 1962, Philosophy in America, 1965, The Morality of Scholarship, 1967, Problems of Choice and Decision, 1975. Guggenheim fellow, 1950-51. Fellow Am. Acad. Arts and Scis.; mem. Am. Philos. Assn. (pres. 1958), Aristotelian Soc., Internat. Inst. Philosophy (v.p. 1970, pres. 1981-84). Died Aug. 27, 1988.

BLACK, RALPH, performing arts executive; b. Knoxville, Tenn., July 11, 1919; s. Ernest Watson and Margaret Marie (Caston) B.; m. Eva Landsberger, Aug. 1, 1950; children—Johana, Eric, Ralph II, Dean. Student, Houghton Coll., 1937-41. Gen. mgr. Chattanooga Symphony, 1950-51, Buffalo Philharmonic, 1951-55, Nat. Symphony, Washington, 1955-60, Balt. Symphony, 1960-63, Nat. Ballet, Washington, 1963-73; v.p. Am. Symphony Orch. League, Vienna, Va., 1955-59; exec. dir. Am. Symphony Orch. League, 1973-81; gen. dir. Shenandoah Valley Music Festival, Woodstock, Va., 1974-78. Author: The Best of Black Notes, 1983, More Black Notes, 1986. Recipient Louis Sudler disting. svc. award, 1982; Fulbright scholar, 1986. Mem. Assn. Am. Dance Cos. (founding chmn.), Am. Arts Alliance (dir. Washington), Nat. Music Coun. (dir. N.Y.C.), Congl. Country Club. Home: Bethesda Md. Died Feb. 13, 1989.

BLACK, ROBERT FOSTER, geology educator; b. Dayton, Ohio, Feb. 1, 1918; s. Stanley C. and Margaret (Martin) B.; m. Hernelda R. Lone, Feb. 12, 1944; children: John R., Dean S. BA, Coll. Wooster, 1940; MA, Syracuse U., 1942; postgrad., Calif. Inst. Tech., 1942-43; PhD, Johns Hopkins U., 1953. Geologist Roosevelt Wildlife Conservation Dept., N.Y., 1941-42, U.S. Geol. Survey, 1943-59; assoc. prof. geology U. Wis., 1956-59, prof., 1959-70; prof. U. Conn., Storrs, 1970-83; cons. in field, 1942-83. Contbr. papers in field. Recipient Alexander Winchell Disting. Alumni award Syracuse U. Fellow Geol. Soc. Am., Arctic Inst. N. Am.; mem. AAAS, Soc. Econ. Geologists, Am. Geophys. Union, Am. Soc. Photogrammetry, Assn. Engring. Geologists, Assn. Profl. Geol. Scientists, Soc. Econ. Paleontologists and Mineralogists, Internat. Glaciol Soc., Am. Quaternary Assn. Home: Willimantic Conn. Died Oct. 25, 1983.

BLACK, THOMPSON, JR., educator; b. Barwick-upon-Tweek, Eng., Sept. 20, 1909; came to U.S., 1913, naturalized, 1919; s. Thompson and Agnes (Percy) B.; m. Katherine Anntoinette Becker, June 16, 1935; children: Robert Thompson, Virginia, Ruth Ann, Bruce Richard. BS, U.S. Naval Acad., 1933; MA, UCLA, 1949, PhD, 1954. Commd. ensign USN, 1933, advanced through grades to comdr., 1944; asst. prof. naval sci. U. Notre Dame, 1941-43; injured during Anzio campaign 1944; assoc. prof. naval sci. UCLA, 1944-45; exec. officer Naval ROTC, 1945-46; ret. 1947; teaching fellow UCLA, 1948-49; faculty Calif. State Coll. at Los Angeles, 1949-86, prof. polit. sci., 1959-67, prof. govt., 1967-74, emeritus, 1974-86, chmn. dept. govt., 1955-61, chmn. div. social scis., 1961-64, acting dean letters and sci., 1964, coordinator social scis., 1965-73, dir. coll. found., 1951-66; chmn. Joint Coll. Fed. Service Council, 1959-60. Decorated Purple Heart. Mem. Assn. Calif. State Coll. Profs. (sec. 1958-61), Am. Soc. Legal History (chmn. Pacific Coast br. 1960), So. Calif. Polit. Sci. Assn. (chmn. 1959), Los Angeles World Affairs Council, Calif. Employees Assn., U.S. Naval Inst., Blue Key, Pi Sigma Alpha, Phi Delta Kappa. Home: Westlake Village Calif. Died Apr. 25, 1986.

BLACK, WILLIAM MCNAUGHTON, manufacturing executive; b. Pender, Nebr., Mar. 25, 1892; s. Thomas P. and Luella M. (McNaughton) B.; m. Margaret Marian Fox, Aug. 25, 1917. Student, U. Chgo., 1910. With Am. Brake Shoe Co., from 1912, v.p., 1942-61, in charge sales relations all divs., 1952-61, ret.; pres. Am. Manganese Steel div., 1940-52, Electro-Alloys div., Elyria, Ohio, 1951-52; bd. dirs. Plunkett Chem. Co., Chgo. Bd. dirs. 6901 Oglesby Ave. Apt. Bldg. Corp., Chgo. Mem. Mfrs. Assn. Chgo. Heights, Olympia Fields (Ill.) Country Club, Chgo. Club., Chgo. Athletic Assn. (pres.), South Shore country Club (Chgo.). Home: Chicago Ill. †

BLACKWELL, LLOYD PHALTI, forester, employment consultant; b. Lynchburg, Va., Nov. 4, 1910; s. Allen Owen and Mary Elizabeth (Martin) B.; m. Eva Ray Mackey, June 30, 1938; 1 dau., Mary Ellen. B.A., Lynchburg Coll., 1931, Va. collegiate teaching certificate, 1932; M.F., Yale U., 1937. Field and staff asst. U.S. Forest Service, Lynchburg, Va., Elkins, W. Va., Charleston, S.C., Columbia, S.C., 1931-35; forester and woodlands mgr. The Urania Lumber Co. Ltd., La., 1937-46; prof., dir. Sch. Forestry, Coll. Life Scis., La. Tech. U., 1946-76, prof., dir. emeritus, 1976-87; chmn. bd. Driggers & Blackwell Personnel, Inc., 1976-87, Driggers & Blackwell Enterprises, Inc., 1985-87; nat. landowner assistance advisor to pres. La. Pacific Corp., 1981-87. Author: Selective Land Utilization in the Piedmont Region of South Carolina, 1936, Puerto Rico and Its Forests, 1937; co-author: Effects of Thinning on Yield of Loblolly Pine in Central Louisiana, 1972; editor: Handbook of Trees, Shrubs and Vines along Caroline Dorman Nature Trail, 1978; Compiler, pub.: Louisiana Forest Laws; Contbr. to trade jours, on forestry and related subjects. Permanent sec. Yale Forestry Class, 1937; Pres. Presbyn. Young Peoples Conf. for State of Va., 1928; Chmn. La. Tree Farms System, 1950-55; U.S. del. internat. meeting Soc. of Foresters, Helsinki, 1974. Served with USNR, 1942-45; transport duty Pacific and Atlantic; personnel duty Dunkeswell, Eng. Recipient ann. award Forest Farmers Assn. Forestry and Conservation, 1986. Fellow Soc. Am. Foresters (mem. nat. com. of income taxation 1949, chmn. La. chpt. Gulf States sect. 1961-62, Outstanding La. Forester Gulf States sect., 1963, John Beale Outstanding Service award 1986); mem. La. Forestry Assn. (bd. dirs., exec. com. 1947-87, chmn. N. La. group foresters 1941-76), Assn. State Coll. and Univ. Forest Research Orgn. (nat. exec. com., So. regional chmn. 1968-76), Am. Legion (dir. 1947, vice comdr. 1948), Phi Kappa Phi, Tau Kappa Alpha, Alpha Psi Omega. Presbyn. Clubs: Mason, Masquers of Hollywood (hon. mem. 1942-43), Kiwanis (past pres.). Home: Ruston La. Died July 9, 1987; buried Forest Lawn Cemetery, Ruston.

BLADEN, RONALD, sculptor; b. Vancouver, B.C., Can., July 13, 1918; s. Kenneth Wells and Muriel Beatrice (Tylcott) B. Ed., Vancouver Sch. Art, Calif. Sch. Fine Arts, San Francisco. instr./lectr. Yale U., Columbia U., Parsons Sch. Design. Exhibited sculpture shows at Guggenheim Mus., Whitney Mus., Corcoran Gallery, Walker Art Ctr., Vancouver Art Gallery, Mus. Modern Art, N.Y.C., San Francisco Mus. Art, Jewish Mus. N.Y., Washburn Gallery, N.Y.C., also in The Hague, Netherlands and Kassel, Fed. Republic Germany; commns. included Mus. Modern Art, Patrick Lanin Found., Fla., Marine Midland Bank, Buffalo, Fed. Res. Bank, Boston, King Saud U., Riyadh, Saudi Arabia, State Office Bldg., Albany, N.Y. NEH grantee, 1964; fellow Guggenheim Found., 1968, Mark Rothko Found., 1975. Home: New York N.Y. Died Feb. 3, 1988.

BLADY, JOHN VALENTINE, surgeon, educator; b. Milw., Dec. 16, 1905; s. Valentine and Kathryn (Grolewski) B.; m. Mary Esther Fisher, Aug. 9, 1939 (dec. 1962) children: John Fisher, Kathryn Diane Blady McNeill; 1 stepchild, Mary Frances Dina Pomerantz; m. Rose Dina Cadman, Oct. 20, 1962. BS, U. Wis., 1929; MD, Duke U., 1932. Surg. intern Duke Med. Sch., 1932-33; resident radiology Temple U. Hosp., 1933-35; surg. resident, postgrad. cancer surgery Rockefeller fellow Meml. Hosp., N.Y.C., 1936-39; pvt. practice Phila., 1939-85; dir. tumor clinic Temple U. Med. Ctr., 1940-70; clin. prof. surgery Temple U. Health Scis. Ctr., 1950-76, prof. emeritus, 1976-85; attending surgeon Paoli (Pa.) Meml. Hosp., 1976-85; mem. grant rev. com. United Fund of Phila. Bd. dirs. Phila. div. Am. Cancer Soc., 1945-71, pres., 1959-60, hon. life mem., 1971-85. Recipient award Am. Cancer Soc., 1950. Mem. AMA, ACS, Phila. County Med. Soc. (bd. dirs. 1956-68, pres. 1967), Soc. Surg. Oncology (pres. 1947-48), Wainwright Tumor Clinic Assn. (pres. 1957-58), Am. Radium Soc. (sec. 1968, pres. 1971-72), Soc. Head and Neck Surgeons, Pa. Med. Soc. (pres. 1977-78), Phila. Coll. Physicians (council 1972-75), Phila. Acad. Surgery, Med. Club Phila., Am. Soc. for Contemporary Medicine, Def. Orientation Conf. Assn., Drs. Golf Assn. Phila. (pres. 1968). Clubs: Phila. Country, Union League (Phila.); Atlantic City Country. Home: Villanova Pa. Died Nov. 24, 1985.

BLAIR, WILLIAM FRANKLIN, zoologist; b. Dayton, Tex., June 25, 1912; s. Percy Franklin and Mona (Patrick) B.; m. Fern Antell, Oct. 25, 1933. BS, U. Tulsa, 1934; MS, U. Fla., 1935; PhD, U. Mich., 1938. Research assoc. Lab. Vertebrate Biology, U. Mich., 1937-46; prof. zoology U. Tex., 1946-85; mem. adv. panel environ. biology NSF, 1958-62, mem. adv. com. div. biology and medicine, 1967-69; chmn. U.S. na com. Internat. Biol. Program, 1968-72, mem. spl. i ternat. com., 1968-74, v.p., 1969-74, mem. internat. e viron. programs Com. NAS/NRC, 1970-76, mem. exe com., 1971-76; mem. monitoring commn. spl. com. c problems of the environment Internat. Council Sc Unions, 1970-72; chmn. adv. panel U.S. Bur. Reclama tion, 1971-85. Author: The Rusty Lizard, 1960; s author: Vertebrates of the United States, 1957, rev. edit 1968, Big Biology: The US/IBP, 1977; editor: Vertebra Speciation, 1961, Evolution in the Genus Bufo, 1972 Fellow AAAS; mem. Am. Soc. Ichthyologists ar Herpetologists (bd. govs. 1951-55, 56-61, 62-63, v. 1955), Am. Soc. Mammalogists, Am. Soc. Naturalis (editorial bd. 1957-58), Am. Inst. Biol. Scis. (panel i ternat. law and global environment 1969—), Ecol. So Am. (editorial bd. 1960-62, pres. 1963, chmn. pub. a fairs com. 1967-68), Am. Soc. Zoologists (chmn. ecolog sect. 1965), Genetics Soc. Am., Soc. Study Evolutic (council 1959-61, pres. 1962, assoc. editor 1961-62), So Systematic Zoology (council 1968-71). Home: Austi Tex. Died Feb. 9, 1985.

BLAISDELL, THOMAS CHARLES, JR., economis educator; b. Pitts., Dec. 2, 1895; s. Thomas Charles an Kate (Christy) B.; m. Catharine L. Maltby, Dec. 2 1921; 1 son, Thomas Maltby. Student, Alma (Mich Coll., 1912-13, 1914-15, Köigstädtische Oberealschul Berlin, 1913-14; BA, Pa. State Coll., 1916; grad., N.Y Sch. Social Work, 1922; MA, Columbia U., 1922, PhD 1932. History tchr. Ewing Christian Coll., Allahaba U., U.P., India, 1916-19; traveling sec. Student Vo Movement, 1919-20; industrial social workerand tch sociology and econs. Internat. Com., YMCA an Yenching U., Peking, 1922-25; tchr. econs. Columb U., 1925-33; asst. dir. Consumers Coun. Agrl. Adjus ment Adminstrn., 1933-34; exec. dir. Consumers Ad Bd. NRA, 1934-35; econ. advisor to adminstr. Rese tlement Adminstrn., 1935-36; asst. dir. Bur. Rsch. an Stats. Social Security Bd., 1936-38; dir. monopoly stud SEC, 1938-39; asst. dir. Nat. Resources Planning Bd 1939-43, chmn. Indsl. Com., 1942-43; mem. plannin com. War Prodn. Bd., 1942-43; dir. Orders and Regula tions Bur., 1943-44; dir. Bur. of Program and Stat Office of War Mobilization and Reconversion, 194 chief, with rank of minister Mission for Econ. Affair London, 1945-46; dir. Office of Internat. Trade Dept. c Commerce, 1947-49; asst. sec. of commerce 1949-51 prof. poli. sci., dir. Bur. of Internat. Relations U. c Calif., 1951-63, emeritus, 1963-88; dir. Internat. Con on Agrl. and Coop. Credit, Berkeley, Calif., 1953; con to chmn. Tech. Assistance Bd., UN, 1952, Ford Found 1962; mem. Am. adv. bd. Ditchely Found. Autho (with C.C. Chu) Peking Rugs and Peking Boys, 1924 Federal Trade Commission and Experiment in Contr of Business, 1932; contbr. to govt. bulls., coll. textbook govt. reports, etc. Bd. dirs. Harry S. Truman Libr. Ins Recipient Exceptional Svc. award Dept. Commerc 1951. Mem. Am. Polit. Sci. Assn., Am. Assn. for Asia Studies, No. Calif. World Affairs Coun. (trustee Round Hill Country Club (Alamo, Calif.), Phi Delt Theta, Phi Kappa Phi. Home: Berkeley Calif. Died De 27, 1988.

BLAKE, ALFRED GREENE, mining company exec tive; b. Pitts., June 22, 1902; s. William F. and Blanch (Johnson) B.; m. Mildred I. Cordeaux, July 27, 192 children: Johnson C., Phyllis I. C.E., Lehigh U., 192 D. Engring. (hon.), 1980; postgrad., U. Pa., 1933-34. Spl. rep. Standard San. Mfg. Co., Pitts., 1925-32; mg dealer div. Phila. Gas Works Co.,, 1932-37; mgr. E ops. Ruud Mfg. Co., Pitts., 1937-45; ptnr. Rogers & Slade, N.Y.C., 1945-50; v.p. Edgar Bros. Co., Metuche N.J., 1950-54, exec. v.p., mem. exec. com., bd. dirs 1954-60; exec. v.p., bd. dirs., mem. exec. com. minera and chems. div. Philipp Corp., 1960-64; pres., chief exe officer div. Engelhard Minerals & Chems. Corp. (merge Philipp Corp. and Englehard Industries 1967), 1964-6 exec. v.p., 1967-71, chmn. bd., 1971-75, ret. chmn. bd 1975-85, bd. dirs., mem. exec. com., 1967-76, dir. emer itus, 1976-85, pres. minerals and chems. div., 1967-6 chmn. div., 1969-71; v.p., bd. dirs. Porocel Corp., 1954 67, pres., bd. dirs., 1967-70, chmn. bd., 1970-75, re chmn. bd., 1975-85; v.p., bd. dirs. Chemstone Corp 1955-67, pres., bd. dirs., 1967-70, chmn. bd., 1970-7 ret. chmn. bd., 1975-85; v.p., bd. dirs. Cuyahoga Lim Co., 1955-67, pres., bd. dirs., 1967-70, chmn. bd., 197 75, ret. chmn. bd., 1975-85; pres., bd. dirs. Ea. Magnesi Talc Co., 1967-70, chmn. bd., 1970-75, ret. chmn. bd 1975-85; bd. dirs. Commonwealth Bank Metuchen, N.J mem. adv. bd. 1st Nat. Bank N.J. Bd. dirs. emerit Syracuse U. Pulp and Paper Found., pres., 1970-7 mem. exec. com.; dir. ops. tng. within industry div. U.S War Manpower Commn., 1942-45; former truste Lehigh U., Ind. Coll. Fund N.J. Mem. TAPPI, Lehig U. Alumni Assn. (bd. dirs., mem. exec. com., pres 1969-70). Home: Plainfield N.J. Died Aug. 1985.

BLAKE, EUGENE CARSON, church official; b. St Louis, Nov. 7, 1906; s. Orville P. and Lulu (Carson) B m. Jean Ware Hoyt, June 14, 1974. AB, Princeton U. 1928, DD (hon.), 1952; postgrad., New Coll Edinburgh, Scotland, 1929-30; ThB, Princeton Theo Sem., 1932; DD, Occidental Coll., 1941, Lake Fore Coll., 1954, Lafayette Coll., 1959, U. Pitts., 1961 Grinnell Coll., 1962, Yale U., 1962, Morgan State U 1962, Dickinson Coll., 1974, Coll. of Wooster, 1979 HHD, Coll. Idaho, 1951, Ohio Wesleyan U., 196

LD, Mo. Valley Coll., 1951, Macalester Coll., 1961, lma Coll., 1962, Fordham U., 1966, LaSalle Coll. nila., 1969; LittD, Beaver Coll., 1952; DCL, Bloom-eld Coll. and Sem., 1952; LHD, Parsons Coll., 1955; TD, Maryville Coll., 1958. Tchr. Forman Christian oll., Lahore, India, 1928-29; asst. pastor Collegiate Ch. . Nicholas, N.Y.C., 1932-35; pastor 1st Presbyn. Ch. lbany, 1935-40, Pasadena Presbyn. Ch., 1940-51; ated clk. Gen. Assembly, Presbyn. Ch. U.S.A., 1951-3, Gen. Assembly, United Presbyn. Ch. in U.S.A., 958-66; gen. sec. World Council Chs., Geneva, 1966-2; pres. Bread for the World, 1974-78; vis. lectr. religion Williams Coll., 1938-40; pres. Nat. Council Chs. hrist U.S.A., 1954-57. Author: He is Lord of All, hallenge to the Church, The Church in the Next De-de, 1966. Former trustee Princeton Sem., Occidental oll., San Francisco Theol. Sem., Princeton U. ecipient Woodrow Wilson award Princeton U., 1967; amed Clergyman of yr. Religious Heritage Am., 1967. ome: Stamford Conn. Died July 31, 1985.

LAKE, NELSON MOREHOUSE, historian; b. nr. ewoka, Indian Ter., May 21, 1901; s. William Packer nd Loula (Gangwer) B. AB, George Washington U., 926; AM, Duke U., 1929, PhD, 1932. Sec. Washington MCA, 1926-28; with manuscript div. Duke U., 1932-4; tchr. Durham (N.C.) High Sch., 1934-35; dept. examiner Nat. Archives, Washington, 1935-38, chief div. avy Dept. archives, 1938-42, with hist. project, 1946-, asst. chief war records br., 1947-54, chief Navy sect., 950-55; ind. hist. research 1955-58; asst. prof. history nd polit. sci. U. Balt., 1958-71; with Office Naval ecords and Library, 1942-46. Author: William lahone of Virginia, Soldier and Political Insurgent, 935; complier, editor (with Richard Spencer Palmer): he Vaughn Bible Class: A Fifty-Year History, 1940. es. Soc. Sponsors, Washington, 1952-53, Washington ound Table, 1949-50. Lt. comdr. USNR, 1942-46. lem. Am. Hist. Soc., So. Hist. Soc., Okla. Hist. Soc., .C. Library Assn., Soc. Am. Archivists, Naval Hist. ound., Am. Legion (1st past comdr. 1948-49, chaplain .C. dept. 1954-55), Civil War Round Table, The incoln Group, Round Table Club (internat. pres. 1952-3), Odd Fellows, Tau Kappa Alpha. Baptist. Home: akoma Park Md. Died Aug. 27, 1986; buried Fort incoln Cemetery, Brentwood, Md.

LAKEY, RICHARD WATSON, lawyer; b. Rock ounty, Wis., Oct. 17, 1911; s. Richard Watson and an (White) B.; m. Dorothy Jean Jones, May 17, 1941; ildren: Jean Clare, Richard Watson. BA, Beloit Coll., 933; LLB, U. Wis., 1936. Bar: Wis. 1936, Nev. 1945. vt. practice Beloit, Wis., 1936-42, Reno, 1946-47, 51—; igation atty. OPA, Nev., 1944-45; dep. city atty. City Reno, 1947-51; mem. McCarran, Rice, Wedge & lakey, 1951-55, Woodburn, Wedge, Blakey & Jeppson, 955-85; Mem. adv. com. rules of civil procedure ipreme Ct. Nev., 1951-85; mem. Reno CSC, 1963-76. rustee Nev. Children's Found., 1947-73, 75-85. Mem. BA, Washoe County Bar Assn. (pres. 1954-55), State ar Nev. (chmn. bd. bar examiners 1955-63, bd. govs. 962-72, pres. 1971-72), Am. Judicature Soc., Nat. ssn. R.R. Trial Counsel, Am. Law Inst., Am. Coll. rial Lawyers, Am. Bd. Trial Advs., Hidden Valley ountry Club, Prospectors Club. Home: Reno Nev. ied Mar. 7, 1985; cremated.

LAKNEY, GEORGE PETTIT, banker; b. Milw., Dec. 1892; s. John S. and Daisy Jane (Pettit) B.; m. Janet ierce, Oct. 22, 1921; 1 child, Barbara Blakney rumder. BS, U. Wis., 1915. Supt. Northwestern Malable Iron Co., 1919-26; co-mgr. Merrill Lynch, Pierce, enner & Smith, 1927-43; v.p. Marine Nat. Exchange ank, Milw., 1943-57, ret. Pres. Milw. Art Ctr., 1956-9; treas., bd. dirs. Milw. Community Chest; bd. dirs. lilw. Blood Ctr., Lakeside Children's Ctr., corp. mem. lilw. Children's Hosp., Columbia Hosp., Curative orshop. Capt. U.S. Army, World War I. Mem. niversity Club Milw. (past pres.). Home: Wickenburg riz. †

LANK, SHELDON HAAS, educator; b. Mt. Carmel, ., Sept. 17, 1896; s. Solomon Henry and Byrde (Haas) ; m. Amy Kirchberger, July 21, 1926; children: liriam, Elizabeth. AB, U. Cin., 1918, AM, 1920; PhD, . Jena, Germany, 1925. Ordained rabbi, 1923. Mem. culty Hebrew Union Coll., Cin., 1926-89, prof. Bible, om 1936, later Nelson Glueck prof. Bible emeritus, imn. faculty, 1947-55. Author: Prophetic Faith in aiah, 1958, Jeremiah: Man and Prophet, 1961, Understanding the Prophets, 1969, Prophetic Thought: Essays nd Addresses, 1977; sci. articles on Hebrew Scriptures; litor Hebrew Union Coll. Ann., from 1973. Mem. m. Oriental Soc. (pres. Middle West br. 1937-38), Soc. bl. Lit. and Exegesis (pres. Midwest sect. 1947, nat. es. 1952). Home: Cincinnati Ohio. Died Feb. 14, 989.

LANSHARD, BRAND, philosopher, educator; b. redericksburg, Ohio, Aug. 27, 1892; s. Francis G. and mily (Coulter) B.; m. Frances Bradshaw, Nov. 3, 1918 lec. 1966); m. Roberta Yerkes, June 6, 1969. AB, U. lich., 1914; AM, Columbia U., 1918; BS, Oxford ng.) U., 1920; PhD, Harvard U., 1921; LittD, warthmore Coll., 1947, Concord Coll., 1962, Albion oll., 1966; LHD, Bucknell U., 1954, Colby Coll., 1956, rinity Coll., 1957, Roosevelt U., 1959, Simpson Coll., 961, Kenyon Coll., 1961, U. N.Mex., 1968; LLD, Oberlin Coll., 1956, U. St. Andrew's, Scotland, 1959. Asst. prof. philosophy U. Mich., 1921-25; assoc. prof. Swarthmore Coll., 1925-28, prof., 1928-45; prof. Yale U., 1945-61, chmn. dept. philosophy, 1945-50, 59-61; Dudleian lectr. Harvard U., 1945, Noble lectr., 1948, Whitehead lectr., 1961; Gifford lectr. St. Andrews U., 1952-53; Hertz lectr. Brit. Acad., 1952; Adamson lectr. U. Manchester, Eng., 1953; Howison lectr. U. Calif., Berkeley, 1954; Matchette lectr. Wesleyan U., Middletown, Conn., 1957, Bklyn. Coll., 1962; Carus lectr. Am. Philos. Assn., 1959; vis. prof. U. Minn., 1962. Author: The Nature of Thought, 2 vols., 1939, On Philosophical Style, 1954, Reason and Goodness, 1961, Reason and Analysis, 1962, The Uses of a Liberal Education, 1973, Reason and Belief, 1974, The Philosophy of Brand Blanshard, 1980, Four Reasonable Men: Aurelius, Mill, Renan, Sidgwick, 1984; (with others) Philosophy in American Education, 1945, Preface to Philosophy, 1946; editor: Education in the Age of Science, 1959. Sec. Brit. YMCA, Mesopotamia and India, 1915-17. With U.S. Army, 1918-19; AEF in France. Recipient Humanist Pioneer award, 1979; Rhodes scholar, 1913-15, 1919-20; Guggenheim fellow, 1929-30; fellow Ctr. Advanced Studies, Wesleyan U., 1961-62; recipient Sr. award Am. Council Learned Socs., 1959; Medal of Honor Rice U., 1962; hon. fellow Merton Coll., Oxford U. Corr. fellow Brit. Acad.; mem. Am. Theol. Soc. (pres. 1955-56), Am. Philos. Assn. (pres. Ea. div. 1942-44), Am. Philos. Soc., Am. Acad. Arts and Scis., Aristotelian Soc. (London, hon.), Phi Beta Kappa. Mem. Soc. Friends. Home: New Haven Conn. Died Nov. 8, 1987.

BLASIER, ROBERT DALTON, business executive; b. Jesup, Iowa, Jan. 3, 1911; s. William W. and Ula E. (Dalton) B.; m. Helen J. Talbott, Aug. 20, 1935; children: Susan Elizabeth (Mrs. John Butler), Diane Talbott (Mrs. Stanton F. Grushkin), Marcia Jean (Mrs. Dirk Schindel), Robert Dalton, William Eugene. AB, Grinell Coll., 1932; JD cum laude, Harvard, 1935. Bar: N.Y. 1937. With Cravath, Swaine & Moore (formerly Cravath, de Gersdoeff, Swaine & Wood), 1935-42; sr. atty. law dept. Westinghouse Electric Corp., 1942-48, asst. to v.p. law dept., 1948-52, v.p. indsl. rels., ret., 1973. Mem. ABA, Harvard Law Sch. Assn., Am. Acad. Polit. Sci., Masons (Shriner), Duquesne Club (Pitts.), Lakeciew Ciountry Club (Morgantown, W.Va.), Palmetto Pine Country Club (Cape Coral, Fla.), Indian Lake (Pa.) Golf Club, Phi Beta Kappa. Home: Fort Myers Beach Fla. also: Central City Pa. Died Oct. 31, 1982; buried Jefferson Meml. Pk., Pleasant Hills, Pa.

BLATT, SOLOMON, state legislator; b. Blackville, S.C., Feb. 27, 1895; s. Nathan and Mollie Blatt; m. Ethel Green, Mar. 18, 1920. LLB, U. S.C., 1917. Mem. Blatt & Fales, Barnwell, S.C.; mem. S.C. Ho. of Reps., Columbia, 1933-86, speaker pro tem, 1935-37, speaker of house, 1937-47, 51-86; speaker emeritus S.C. Ho. of Reps., 1973-86. Trustee Barnwell Sch., U. S.C., 1936-48. With U.S. Army, World War I. Home: Barnwell S.C. Died May 14, 1986; buried Barnwell, S.C.

BLEITZ, DONALD LOUIS, engineer, author, ornithologist, naturalist; b. Los Angeles, Oct. 1, 1915; s. Louis Rollin and Violet Mae (Trout) B. Owner, operator photog. mfg. firms, pharm. mfg. plant, various tech. labs. and optical mfg. concerns; founder, pres. Bleitz Wildlife Found., from 1952; Mem. faculty tng. program Vet. Medicine Comml., Pet, and Wild Birds.; mem. adv. bd. Reys Bird Obs., San Francisco Bay Bird Obs. Author: 22 folio vols. in compilation Birds of the Americas; Contbr.: feature articles (in color) Ariz. Hwys, Readers Digest, Saturday Evening Post; also various sci. jours., news media periodicals.; color photographs, descriptive manuscripts over 3500 species birds of Americas, 1940—; produces and shows slides; lectures sci. ornithol. groups; exhibited traveling show of plates from Birds of Am., at various museums including, San Diego Mus. Natural History, Pacific Grove and Santa Cruz Mus. Natural History, 1973. Mem. Los Angeles County Mus.; pres. San Pedro Heart Found.; bd. dirs. Hollywood Chorale, Hollywood Heritage. Recipient award Am. Acad. Achievement, 1964, award of honor Calif. Conservation Council. Fellow Explorers Club, Cleve. Zool. Soc.; mem. Nat. Audubon Soc. (life), Cooper Ornithol. Soc. (life), Wilson Ornithol. Club (life), Am. Ornithologists Union (elective life mem.), Calif., So. Calif. acads. sci., Internat. Soc. Bird Protection, Western Bird Banding Assn. (life), Eastern Bird Banding Assn., Inland Bird Banding Assn., League of Ams. (bd. dirs., pres.), Hancock Park Art Council, AAAS, Los Angeles Heart Inst., Lepidopterists Soc., Am. Soc. Mammologists, Phila. Zool. Soc. (hon. life), Bromeliad Soc., San Diego Zool. Soc., Am. Orchid Soc., Malibu Orchid Soc., Windsor Sq.-Hancock Park Hist. Soc. (trustee, founding mem.), N.Y. Acad. Scis., Am. Soc. Naturalists, Avicultural Soc., Pacific Hort. Soc. Clubs: Thunderbird Country, Los Angeles (founder, pres., dir.), Los Angeles Men's Garden (elective life mem., founder, pres., dir.). Deceased.

BLESH, RUDI (RUDOLPH PICKETT), author, artist; b. Guthrie, Okla., Jan. 21, 1899; s. Abraham Lincoln and Theodora Bell (Pickett) B.; m. Editha Tuttle, Feb. 22, 1925; 1 child, Editha Hilary; m. Barbara Lamont, July 1939. Student, Dartmouth Coll, 1917-20; BS with honors, U. Calif., 1924. Prof. emeritus music Queens Coll.; prof. emeritus Am. arts NYU; furniture, archtl., indsl. designer 1924-43; jazz critic N.Y. Herald Tribune; founder, v.p. Circle Sound Inc., N.Y.C.; creator phonograph documentation of Afro-Am. music. Author: This is Jazz, 1943, Shining Trumpets: A History of Jazz, 1946; (with Harriet Janis) They All Played Ragtime, 1950, Modern Art USA, 1956, De Kooning, 1960, Stuart Davis, 1960, Collage, 1962, Keaton, 1966, Combo USA, 1971; editor (with Harriet Janis) O Susanna, 1960; writer, narrator (radio programs) Dimensions of Jazz, This is Jazz, Our Singing Land; one-man show included Art of This Century, N.Y.C., 1946. Mem. Phi Gamma Delta, Pi Delta Epsilon. Home: New York NY Died Aug. 25, 1985.

BLETTNER, EDWARD FREDERICK, banker; b. Chgo., Dec. 9, 1907; s. Edward Frederick and Mary (Klaner) B.; m. Margaret Maw, Mar. 19, 1943 (dec. July 1982); children: Margaret Jean Blettner Angell, Elizabeth Mary; m. Beverly Dowls, Dec. 30, 1983. AB, Harvard U., 1928, MBA, 1930; JD, John Marshall Law Sch., 1935. Various positions First Nat. Bank of Chgo., 1930-62, exec. v.p., 1962-67, pres., 1968-69, vice chmn. bd., 1969-73, hon. dir., 1973-78; Bd. dirs. Internat. Minerals and Chems. Corp., Zenith Radio Corp., Pabst Brewing Co., Ecodyne Corp., Genesco Inc. Bd. dirs. Lyric Opera of Chgo.; trustee Newberry Library, Chgo.; trustee Rush-Presbyn. St. Luke's Med. Ctr., Chgo.; governing mem. Art Inst. of Chgo. Served to lt. col. AUS, 1942-45. Congregationalist. Clubs: Chgo., Comml. (Chgo.), Old Elm (Lake Forest, Ill.). Home: Chicago Ill. Died Oct. 23, 1987.

BLINKEN, MAURICE HENRY, investment company executive; b. Kiev, Ukraine, Apr. 26, 1900; (father Am. citizen); s. Mayer and Anna (Turefskoy) B.; m. Ethel Horowitz, Oct. 9, 1924; children: Donald M., Robert J., Alan J. BCS, NYU, 1921, LLB, 1924, LLM, 1925. Bar: N.Y., 1925, U.S. Supreme Ct.; CPA, N.Y. Ptnr. Blinken, Eisner & Philip, N.Y.C., 1921-25; pvt. practice law 1925-45; co-founder Mite Corp., New Haven, 1954-62, treas., 1962-85; U.S. rep. Marks & Spencer, 1939-51. Mem. Yonkers (N.Y.) Bd. Edn., 1934-35, pres., 1935; trustee Horace Mann Sch. Boys, N.Y.C., 1936-52, Yonkers Pub. Library, 1936; pres., bd. dirs. Am. Palestine Inst., 1940-52. With U.S. Army, 1918. Mem. Assn. of Bar of City of N.Y., Delta Mu Delta (past pres.), Tau Delta Phi (past pres.), Masons, B'nai B'rith. Home: Palm Beach Fla. Died July 13, 1986.

BLISS, DOROTHY ELIZABETH, zoologist; b. Cranston, R.I., Feb. 13, 1916; d. Orville Thayer and Sophia Topham (Farnell) B. A.B., Brown U., 1937, Sc.M., 1942, Sc.D. (hon.), 1972; Ph.D., Radcliffe Coll., 1952. Sci. tchr. Milton (Mass.) Acad., 1942-49; teaching fellow biology Harvard, 1947-51, research fellow, 1952-55; asst. curator Am. Mus. Natural History, N.Y.C., 1956-62; asso. curator Am. Mus. Natural History, 1962-67, curator, 1967-80, curator emerita, 1980-87, chmn., curator dept. fossil and living invertebrates, 1974-77; research asst. prof. anatomy Albert Einstein Coll. Medicine, 1956-64, vis. research asso. prof., 1964-66; adj. prof. biology City U. N.Y., 1971-80; adj. prof. zoology U. R.I., 1980-87; mem. adv. com. respiration and circulation, biol. handbooks Fedn. Am. Socs. Exptl. Biology, 1968-71; Mem. corp. Bermuda Biol. Sta. for Research, Inc. Author: Shrimps, Lobsters and Crabs; Editor-in-chief: The Biology of Crustacea; Mem. editorial bds.: Natural History Press, 1966-70, Am. Zoologist, 1967-72, Curator, 1968-79, Jour. Exptl. Zoology, 1970-73, Natural History Mag, 1970-79, Gen. and Comparative Endocrinology, 1974-78; Contbr. articles sci. jours. NSF grantee, 1957-78. Fellow AAAS (chmn. sect. biol. scis. 1973, mem. council 1973, mem. com. council affairs 1973-75, chmn. nominating com. 1973-74); Mem. Am. Soc. Zoologists (pres. 1978, chmn. div. invertebrate zoology 1970), Am. Inst. Biol. Scis. (chmn. com. biosci. 1974-75), Assn. for Women in Sci., Crustacean Soc., Phi Beta Kappa., Sigma Xi. Home: Wakefield R.I. Died Dec. 26, 1987.

BLOCH, HENRY SIMON, economist; b. County Kehl, Baden, Germany, Apr. 6, 1915; came to U.S., 1937, naturalized, 1943; s. Edward and Claire (Bloch) B.; 1 dau., Miriam Bloch Feuerstein. Dr. Laws (Econs.), U. Nancy, 1937; Dr.h.c. in Econs., Polit. Social Scis, Free U. of Brussels, 1969; fellow, Acad. Internat. Law, The Hague, summer 1937. Research asst. U. Chgo., 1938; lectr. Inst. for Mil. Studies, 1941-42, instr. econs., 1943; research supr. Civil Affairs Tng. Sch. for Army and Navy Officers, 1943-45; cons. Fgn. Econ. Adminstrn., 1945; economist Treasury Dept., 1945-46; mem. Treasury del. for tax treaty negotiations Treasury Dept., France, U.K., Benelux, 1946; sect. chief UN, 1947-49, dir. fiscal and financial br., 1955-62; acting dir. Bur. Econ. Affairs, 1958-59; dir. Bur. Tech. Assistance, 1959-62, dep. commr. for tech. assistance, 1961-62; pres. Zinder Internat. Ltd., 1962-66; v.p., dir. E.M. Warburg & Co., Inc., 1967-70; sr. v.p. E.M. Warburg, Pincus & Co., Inc., 1970-75, exec. v.p., 1976-81, mng. dir., 1982-88; vis. prof. econs. Yale U., 1955; lectr. Columbia U., 1955-63, adj. prof. law and internat. relations, 1963-85, prof. emeritus, 1985-88, mem. internat. adv. bd. Schcool Internat. and Pub. Affairs, 1986-88. Author: The Challenge of the World Trade Conference, 1965, Financial Strategy for Developing Nations, 1969, Export Financing Emerging as a Major Policy Problem, 1976, Foreign Risk Judgement for Commercial Banks, 1977, Society and Business after the

Great Reschedulings: A Futuristic Essay, 1984; co-author: Yale Law Journal Symposium on World Organization, 1946, Legal-Economic Problems of International Trade, 1961, The Global Partnership, 1968, Financial Integration in Western Europe, 1969; contbg. author: Multinational Banking: Theory and Regulation, 1978; contbr. to econ., legal jours. Mem. bd. applies econs. inst. U. Brussels, 1980-88; bd. govs. Tel-Aviv U., 1984-88. Decorated comdr. Order of Leopold II (Belgium); hon. assoc. fellow Berkeley Coll., Yale U., 1977-88. Mem. Am. Econ. Assn., Council Fgn. Relations, Soc. Royale d'Economie Politique de Belgique (hon.). Club: Faculty (Columbia). Home: New York N.Y. Died Feb. 28, 1988.

BLOCK, IRVING ALEXANDER, artist, art educator; b. N.Y.C.; s. Abraham and Frieda (Weinberg) B.; m. Gilda Klein, Mar. 10, 1960; children: Gregory, Francesca. BS magna cum laude, NYU, 1933; student, NAD, 1935, Grande Chaumiere, Paris, 1947. Artist, writer major motion picture studios Hollywood, Calif., 1945-60; prof. art Calif. State U., Northridge, 1962-80, prof. emeritus, 1980-86, mem. adj. faculty, 1980-85; vis. prof. various univs. in Calif.; illustrator works by Dickens, Updike, Francesca Block, Santa Susana Press, others, 1980-86. Exhibited works in numerous one-man shows, including Ankrum Gallery, L.A., 1962-81, Calif. State U., Northridge, 1980; richly represented (paintings and drawings) in collections of Hirshhorn Mus., Washington, Wichita Art Mus., San Diego Mus. of Art, Harvard U., NYU, Victoria and Albert Mus., London, Oakland Mus., Calif.; producer: documentary films Goya, World of Rubens. Recipient Disting. Prof. award Calif. State U., 1967, Outstanding Prof. award Calif. State Univ. System, 1980, Gold medal Academia Italia delle Arti e Del Lavoro, Ranger Fund Purchase award Nat. Acad. Design, 1986; Hirshhorn Found. grantee, 1970. Mem. Academia Internazionale Tommaso Campanella, Phi Kappa Phi. Home: Studio City Calif. Died Mar. 3, 1986; cremated.

BLOCK, LEIGH B(LOOM), steel company executive; b. Chgo., Apr. 7, 1905; s. Leopold E. and Cora (Bloom) B.; m. Margaret Byfield, Apr. 30, 1927; children: Mary Lee, James A.; m. Mary Lasker, Oct. 1942. Student, Cascadilla Sch., 1921-23, U. Chgo., 1923-24. Assoc. Inland Steel Co., Indiana Harbor, Ind., 1924, with purchasing dept., 1927, agt. works purchasing, 1928-32, with sales flat rolled steel div., 1932-34, asst. v.p., asst. mgr. sales, 1934-39, v.p.-in-charge purchases, 1939-87, also bd. dirs., 1948-87. Dir. Med. Research Inst., Michael Reese Hosp.; trustee Northwestern U., Chgo. Symphony Orch.; v.p., trustee Art Inst. Chgo.; v.p., chmn. fin. com. Orchestral Assn. Mem. Newcomen Soc. N.Am., Lake Shore Country Club, Midday Club, Tavern Club, Comml. Club. Died Dec. 9, 1987.

BLOCK, PAUL, JR., newspaper publisher, chemist; b. N.Y.C., May 11, 1911; s. Paul and Dina (Wallach) B.; m. Eleana Barnes Conley, 1940 (div. 1947); 1 son, Cyrus P.; m. Marjorie McNab Main, May 26, 1948 (dec. Sept. 1960); children—Allan James, John Robinson; m. Mary Gall Petok, 1965; 3 children by previous marriage. Grad., Hotchkiss Sch., Lakeville, Conn., 1929; A.B., Yale, 1933; postgrad., Columbia, 1933-34, Ph.D., 1943; postgrad., Harvard, 1934-35. Reporter Toledo Blade, 1935, became polit. writer, 1938, asst. editor, 1941, co-pub., 1942; co-pub. Pitts. Post Gazette, 1944-87; fellow Mellon Inst. Indsl. Research, Pitts., 1943-44; hon. fellow dept. pharmacology Yale U., 1948-49. Chmn. Toledo Devel. Com., 1975-79; chmn. bd. trustees Med. Coll. Ohio at Toledo, 1964-70; mem. U.S. Metric Bd., 1978-80. Mem. Am. Chem. Soc., Am. Soc. Newspaper Editors, Internat. Press Inst. (chmn. Am. com. 1958-61), Sigma Xi. Home: Toledo Ohio. Died Mar. 15, 1987; buried Valhalla, N.Y.

BLOCKER, TRUMAN GRAVES, JR., surgeon; b. Westpoint, Miss., 1909. MD, U. Tex., 1933. Diplomate Am. Bd. Plastic Surgery, Am. Bd. Surgery. Intern Pa. Gen. Hosp., 1933-35; resident in surgery, then attending surgery and plastic surgery John Sealy Hosp., Galveston, Tex., 1935-36; med. adminstr., then dean clin. faculty Univ. Br. Hosps., 1950-55; instr. Columbia Coll. Physicians and Surg., 1936-37; faculty U. Tex. Med. Sch., 1937-84, prof. surgery, 1946-84, chmn. dept., 1960-64, exec. dir., dean, 1964-67, pres., 1967-74, pres. emeritus, 1974-84; pres. U. Tex. Health Sci. Ctr. at Houston, 1977-79. Col. M.C., U.S. Army, 1942-46; brig. gen. Res. Fellow ACS (v.p.), Am. Assn. Plastic Surgery; mem. AMA, Am. Surg. Assn. (v.p.), So. Surg. Assn., Am. Assn. Plastic and Reconstructive Surgery. Home: Galveston Tex. Died May 17, 1984.

BLOIS, MARSDEN SCOTT, physician, educator; b. San Antonio, Jan. 5, 1919; s. Marsden Scott and Miriam (Eckart) B.; m. Jean McCanna, Dec. 24, 1941; children: Marsden, Byron, Stephen, Philip, Miriam. BS, U.S. Naval Acad., 1941; MS, Stanford U., 1950, PhD, 1952, MD, 1959. Ensign USN, 1941-53, advanced through grades to commdr., 1953; research assoc. Stanford (Calif.) U., 1953-61, assoc. prof., 1961-69; prof. U. Calif., San Francisco, 1969-88. Author: Information and Medicine, 1984; editor Free Radicals in Biological Systems, 1959; contbr. articles to sci. jours. Recipient Gold, Silver, Bronze awards for research Am. Acad. Dermatology. Fellow Am. Coll. Med. Informatics (pres. 1984-86), N.Y. Acad. Scis., AAAS; mem. Am. Assn. Med. Systems and Infosystems, Am. Phys. Soc. Roman Catholic. Home: San Francisco Calif.

BLOOMFIELD, MORTON WILFRED, educator; b. Montreal, Que., Can., May 19, 1913; came to U.S., 1936, naturalized, 1943; s. Samuel and Hanna Mai (Brown) B.; m. Caroline Lichtenberg, Mar. 16, 1952; children: Micah Warren, Hanna Ellen Bloomfield Rubins, Samuel John. B.A., McGill U., 1934, M.A., 1935; grad. study, U. London, 1935-36; Ph.D., U. Wis., 1938; A.M., Harvard U., 1961; H. Litt. D., U. Western Mich., 1982; Litt. D., SUNY, Binghampton, 1986; PhD (hon.), Bar Ilan U., Ramat Gan, Israel, 1986. Faculty McGill U., 1934-35, U. Wis., 1936-39, U. Akron, 1939-46; asst. prof. English Ohio State U., 1946-51, assoc. prof., 1951-54, prof. English, 1954-61; prof. English, Harvard U., 1961-83, chmn. dept. English, 1968-72, Arthur Kingsley Porter prof. English, 1972-83, Arthur Kingsley Porter prof. emeritus, 1983-87; Henry W. and Albert A. Berg prof. English and Am. lit. Washington Sq. Coll., NYU, 1955-56; Fannie Hurst vis. prof. lit. Washington U., St. Louis, 1977, Brandeis U., 1978; Disting. vis. prof. humanities Stanford U., 1981, 83, 84, 85, 86; Spl. civilian cons. Sec. War, 1945-46; mem. exec. com., trustee Nat. Humanities Center, 1973; chmn. bd. trustees, 1973-76; trustee Center for Applied Linguistics, 1966-68; supervising com. The English Inst., 1975-78. Author: The Seven Deadly Sins, An Introduction to the History of a Religious Concept, 1952, Piers Plowman as a Fourteenth-Century Apocalypse, 1962, (with Leonard Newmark) A Linguistic Introduction to the History of English, 1963, Essays and Explorations, Studies in Language and Literature, 1970; also articles; editor: (with R.C. Elliott) Ten Plays, 1951; rev. as Great Plays: Sophocles to Brecht, 1965, Great Plays: Sophocles to Albee, 1975; (with E. Robbins) Form and Idea, 1953, rev. edit., 1961, The Interpretation of Narrative, 1970, In Search of Literary Theory, 1972; (with E. Haugen) Language as a Human Problem, 1974, Incipits to Latin Works on the Virtues and Vice, 1979, The Interpretation of Narrative: Theory and Practice of Allegory, Myth and Symbol, 1981; editorial adv. bd., contbr.: Am. Heritage Dictionary; editorial bd.: Jour. History Ideas, 1976-79; editorial adv. bd.: Viator. Served with AUS, 1942-45. Decorated Bronze Star; Moyse fellow, 1935-36; Guggenheim fellow, 1949-50, 64-65; Elizabeth Clay Howald fellow, 1953-54; hon. research assoc. U. Coll., U. London, 1953-54; Am. Council Learned Socs. grantee, 1958-59, 76; fellow Center for Advanced Study in Behavorial Scis., Stanford U., 1967-68; fellow Princeton Inst., 1972; Am. Philos. Soc. grantee, 1973; research fellow Australian Nat. U. Humanities Center, 1978. Fellow Mediaeval Acad. Am. (Haskins medal 1964, v.p. 1975-76, pres. 1976-77), Am. Acad. Arts and Scis. (councillor 1969-72, v.p. 1972-76), Am. Philos. Soc., Brit. Acad. (corr.), Medieval Soc. South Africa (corr.); mem. MLA (exec. com. 1966-69), Renaissance Soc. Am., Am. Dialect Soc., Can. Linguistic Assn., Dante Soc. Am. (mem. council 1971-74, 79-82), Internat. Assn. Univ. Profs. English (cons. com. 1962-87), Modern Humanities Research Assn. (mem. Am. com. 1976-83), Soc. Internationale pour l'étude de la Philosophie Medievale, Linguistic Soc. Am., Phi Beta Kappa (hon.). Home: Cambridge Mass. Died Apr. 14, 1987; buried West Roxbury, Mass.

BLOUGH, ROGER M., lawyer, steel company executive; b. Riverside, Pa., Jan. 19, 1904; s. Christian E. and Viola (Hoffman) B.; m. Helen Martha Decker, June 13, 1928; children: Jane Blough French, Judith Ann Wentz. AB, Susquehanna U., 1925, LLD, 1953; JD, Yale U., 1931; LLD (hon.), Baylor U., 1955, Washington and Jefferson Coll., 1956, Rollins Coll., 1958, Trinity Coll., 1958, Syracuse U., 1959, Roanoke Coll., Gettysburg Coll., Allegheny Coll., 1960, Wartburg Coll., 1963, Washington U., 1966, Dickinson Sch. Law, 1967, Akron U., 1970; DCS, U. Pitts., 1957; DCL, U. of the South, 1958, Bucknell U., 1961; HHD, Pace Coll., 1964, Wagner Coll., 1965. Bar: N.Y., Pa., U.S. Supreme Ct. Assoc. White & Case, N.Y.C., 1931-42, ptnr., 1969-75; gen. solicitor U.S. Steel Corp. Del., 1942-51; exec. v.p. law, sec. U.S. Steel Corp., 1951, vice chmn., 1952-55, dir., mem. fin. com., 1952-76, gen. counsel, 1953-55, chmn. bd., chief exec. officer, 1955-69, mem. exec. com., 1956-76; chmn. bd. 1st State Bank, Hawley, Pa. Fellow Pierpont Morgan Library; assoc. fellow Timothy Dwight Coll., Yale U.; trustee U.S. Steel Found., 1955-76, Grand Cen. Art Galleries, Presbyn. Hosp., N.Y.C.; trustee, chmn. fin. com. Hawley Library Assn.; bd. dirs. comml. Union; trustee, exec. com. Internat. C. of C.; chmn., councilor Conf. Bd.; chmn. bd. Council for fin. Aid to Edn.; bd. dirs., founding mem. Bus. Com. for Arts; chmn. emeritus nat. adv. bd. Nat. Football Found. and Hall of Fame. Fellow Inst. Jud. Adminstrn. (pres.), Am. Bar Found; mem. Met. Mus. Art, Pa. Soc. (pres., council), Bus. Council (chmn.), Am., N.Y. State, Allegheny, Pike, Wayne County bar assns., Am. Iron and Steel Inst. (hon. v.p.), Yale Law Sch. Assn. (hon. mem. exec. com.), Acad. Polit. Sci., Assn. of Bar of City of N.Y., N.Y. County Lawyers Assn., Am. Forestry Assn., Legal Aid Soc., Constrn. User Anti-Inflation Roundtable (chmn.), Bus. Roundtable (co-chmn.), Com. for Econ. Devel. (hon. trustee), Japan Iron and Steel Fedn. (hon.), Pine Valley Golf Club, Links, The Board Room, Recess Club, Cotton Bay Club, Lords Valley Country, Blooming Grove Hunting and Fishing Club, Skytop Club. Home: Hawley Pa. Died Oct. 8, 1985, buried Hawley, Pa.

BLUMENFELD, M. JOSEPH, judge; b. South S Paul, Minn., Mar. 23, 1904; s. David and Lena (Lase B.; m. Rebecca Meyers, July 29, 1929. B.A., U. Minn 1925; LL.B., Harvard U., 1928; LL.D. (hon.), U Hartford, 1985, U. Hartford, 1985. Bar: Conn. 1928 Practiced in Hartford, 1928-61; spl. asst. to U.S. atty 1942-45; U.S. dist. judge for Conn. Hartford, 1961-8 chief judge 1971-74. Mem. Am., Conn., Hartfo County bar assns., Am. Judicature Soc. Home: Bloom field Conn. Died Nov. 5, 1988.

BOAL, ARTHUR MCCLURE, lawyer; b. Cherry Tre Pa., Feb. 14, 1889; s. William McClure and Hanna Waller (Camp) B.; m. Sara Elizabeth Metzner, Apr. 1921; children: Elizabeth (Mrs. William R. Hogan Arthur. AB, Harvard U., 1914, LLB, 1916. Bar: Mas 1917, N.Y. 1930. Assoc. William J.E. Sander, Bosto 1917, Whipple, Sears & Ogden, 1917-19; admiralty att U.S. Shipping Bd., Washington, 1919-23, asst. admiral counsel, 1923-25, admiralty counsel, 1925-29; mer Chapman, Snider, Duke & Boal, 1930-32; ptnr. Boa McQuade & Fitzpatrick (and predecessor firms), 193 72, Boal, Doti & Larsen, 1972-84. Contbr. article Encyclopaedia Britannica, 14th edit. Mayor Village Pelham, N.Y., 1949-53; chmn. adjudication, arbitratio internat. cts. Southwestern Legal Found.; dir. Pelha Community Chest, campaign mgr., 1940-41, pres., 194 43; chmn. Pelham Red Cross War Fund campaig 1945-46; vice chmn. Westchester County chpt. AR 1946-49; mem. Pelham Bd. Edn., 1960-67, pres., 196 67; mem. Coast Arty. Sch., 1918. Mem. Maritime La Assn. U.S. (pres. 1958-60, chmn. com. on Comité Mar time Internat., 1960—, v.p. Comité 1969—), N.Y. Ba Assn., Internat. Law Assn., Assn. of Bar of City of N.Y (com. on judiciary 1962-64), Royal Soc. Arts and Sc (London), Downtown Assn., Harvard Club, Author Club, Men's Club (pres. local chpt. 1943-44), Pelha Country Club. Home: Pelham N.Y. Died July 7, 198 buried Pelham, N.Y.

BOARDMAN, EUGENE POWERS, educator; b Aurora, Ill., Oct. 5, 1910; s. Charles Watkins and Irm gard (Heth) B.; m. Elizabeth Reynolds Jelinek, June 2 1940 (div. June 1969); children—Susan, Sarah, Chri topher, Erika, Andrew, Benjamin. B.A., Beloit (Wis Coll., 1932; M.A., U. Wis., 1937, Harvard U., 193 Ph.D., Harvard U., 1947. Tchr. English prep. dep Am. U., Beirut, Lebanon, 1932-35; tchr. social studie French Delavan (Wis.) High Sch., 1935-36; prof. charg courses, grad. work East Asian history U. Wis Madison, 1946-81; Lobbyist with U.S. Congress for New China Policy under auspices Friends Com. Na Legislation, 1965-66. Author: Madison, 1952. Serve as maj. USMCR, 1941-46. Decorated Legion of Merit Mem. Assn. for Asian Studies (past program chmn. Phi Beta Kappa, Sigma Pi, Delta Sigma Rho. Mem Soc. of Friends. Deceased.

BOATWRIGHT, JAMES, III, language professiona educator, editor; b. Augusta, Ga., Sept. 28, 1933; James and Dorothy (Lee) B. B.A. in Journalism, U Ga., 1954, M.A. in English, 1956. Instr. Washington & Lee U., Lexington, Va., 1960-64, asst. prof., 1964-6 assoc. prof., 1968-73, prof., 1973-88. Editor She nandoah, Lexington, 1962-88; contbr. articles to prof jours. Recipient Editors' award Coordinating Counc of Literary Mags., 1980. Democrat. Home: Lexingto Va. Died Sept. 18, 1988.

BOBER, HARRY, humanities-history of art educato b. N.Y.C., Sept. 2, 1915; s. Hyman and Fann (Newman) B.; m. Phyllis Barbara Pray, Aug. 11, 194 (div. 1973); children: Jonathan P., David H. B.A CCNY, 1955; cert., Institut d'Art et d'Archeologie-U Paris, 1938, Free U., Brussels, 1939; M.A., Inst. Fin Arts-NYU, 1940, Ph.D., 1949; H.H.D. hon, Oaklan U., Rochester, Mich., 1979. Reader, tutor CCNY 1935-42; instr. Queens Coll., 1947-49; asst. prof. Smit Coll., Northampton, Mass., 1949-50; lectr. Inst. Fin Art-NYU, N.Y.C., 1950-51, assoc. prof., 1954-61, prof 1961-65, Avalon Found. prof. humanities, 1965—; ass prof. Washington Sq. Coll., 1950-51, Harvard U Cambridge, Mass., 1951-54; Disting. vis. prof. humani ties Johns Hopkins U., Balt., 1964-65; Disting. pro CCNY, 1970-71; Messinger lectr. Cornell U., Ithaca N.Y., 1973-74; mem. vis. coms. medieval dept. an Photog. Library Met. Mus. Art, N.Y.C., 1969— founder Internat. Found. Art Research, 1968—. Author: The St. Blasien Psalter, 1963, Medieval Art i the Guennol Collection, 1975, Jan Van Vliet's Book o Crafts and Trades, 1981; editor: Astrological an Mythological Illuminated Manuscripts of the Lati Middle Ages in the English Libraries, 2 vols., 195 Religious Art in France (Emile Mâle), English edit., vols., 1978-83. Served to lt. USN, 1942-45, Caribbean Guggenheim fellow, 1947; fellow Bollingen Found 1953-58, Am. Council Learned Socs., 1960; researc fellow Warburg Inst., U. London, 1949-62. Fello Warburg. Inst. (hon. life); mem. Internat. Ctr. Medieva Art (founding, dir.), Medieval Acad. Am. (counc 1959), Assn. Belgian Am. Found. Fellows (founde pres. 1963-72), Coll. Art Assn. Am. (dir. 1966-73), So N. Am. Goldsmiths (hon.). Home: New York N.Y Died June 17, 1988; interred Wellwood Cemetery, L.I N.Y.

BOBER, MANDELL MORTON, educator; b. Russi Nov. 15, 1891; s. Leo Myer and Anna (Gevierts) B.; m lga Enoch, Apr. 15, 1922. BS, U. Mont., 1917; udent, U. Lyons, France, 1919; PhD, U. Lyons, 1925; LD, Grinnell Coll., 1956. Asst. in econs. Harvard U., 920-24, instr. and tutor, 1924-27, vis. instr., 1927-32; ctr. in econs. Northeastern U., Providence, 1921-24; str. in econs. Radcliffe Coll., 1924-25; lectr. in econs. oston U., 1925-27; assoc. prof. Lawrence Coll., 1927-), prof., 1929—; vis. prof. of econs. U. Buffalo (on ave), 2d semester, 1938-39, 1950-51, U. Ill. summer ssion, 1951; on leave of absence to act as prin. onomist Office Price Adminstrn., Washington, 1942-; vis. prof. summer session U. Wis., 1947, Harvard U., 959. Author: Karl Marx's Interpretation of History, 927 (rev. 2d edit. 1948), Intermediate Price and Income heory, 1955; contbr. to profl. jours. Served in Intelgence Corps, AUS, AEF. World War I. Fellow Royal con. soc.; mem. Am. Econ. Assn., Econometric Soc., AUP (mem. coun. 1942-44), Mid-West Econ. Assn. ast v.p., pres. 1949-50), Phi Beta Kappa, Phi Kappa au. Home: Appleton Wis. †

OBRINSKOY, GEORGE VLADIMIR, educator; b. ula, Russia, Jan. 23, 1901; came to U.S., 1923, aturalized, 1942; s. Vladimir Alexeivitch and Maria likonowa) B.; m. Theodora Platt, Sept. 2, 1931; chilen: Helen (dec.), George Vladimir Jr., Theodora obrinskoy Shepherd. Cert. graduation, Mt. Airy Luth. m., Phila., 1923-26; grad., U. Pa., 1926, Yale U., 1928. nstr., teaching fellow Yale U., 1927-28; mem. faculty . Chgo., 1928-85, prof. Sanskrit, 1959-67, dean udents div. humanities, 1954-67, chmn. com. South sian studies, 1959-67, chmn. dept. linguistics, 1951-66, of. emeritus, 1967-85. Author: Graded Russian eaders, 1961; also numerous articles. With Denikin's hite Army, Russian Civil War. Mem. Am. Oriental oc., Linguistic Soc. Home: Greenfield Mass. Died ov. 17, 1985, buried Chgo.

ODE, HENDRIK WADE, research engineer, edutor; b. Madison, Wis., Dec. 24, 1905; s. Boyd Henry d Bernice (Ballard) B.; m. Barbara Poore, Nov. 18, 933; children: Katharine Anne, Beatrice Anne athaway. BA, Ohio State U., 1924, MA, 1926, DSc on.), 1970; PhD, Columbia U., 1935; DSc (hon.), U. ., 1977. With Bell Telephone Labs., 1926-67; beginng with research elec. network theory and application long distance communications facilities, successively evel. electronic fire control devices, in charge math. search group, dir. math. research, 1944-55, dir. search phys. scis., 1955-58, v.p. mil. devel. and sysms engring., 1958-67; Gordon McKay prof. systems gring., Harvard U., 1967-74, prof. emeritus, from 974; trustee Research Analysis Corp. Author: etwork Theory and Feedback Amplifier Design, nergy: Technical Integration and Technological Inovation in the Bell System; also tech. papers; holder atents in fields electric cir. theory, mil. devices. Mem. rious govt. mil. adv. groups. Recipient Presdl. cert. of erit, 1948; Oldenburger medal ASME, 1975. Fellow EE (Edison medal 1969), Am. Acad. Arts and Scis., m. Phys. Soc.; mem. Nat. Acad. Engring., Nat. Acad. i., Am. Math. Soc., Phi Beta Kappa. Home: Washgton D.C. Deceased.

ODEMER, CHARLES WILLIAM, scientific hisrian; b. Denison, Iowa, Jan. 4, 1927; s. Herman and anche Orpha (Nicola) B.; m. Sheila Campbell Hedley, ne 22, 1948; children: Karen Hedley, Eric Charles, ett William; m. Susanne Maria Lilja, July 14, 977. AA, San Francisco City Coll., 1949; BA magma m laude, Pomona Coll., 1951; MA, Claremont Grad. h., 1952; PhD, Cornell U., 1956. Teaching fellow artmouth Coll., Hanover, N.H., 1952-53; mem. faculty . Wash., Seattle, 1956-85, prof. biomed. history, 1967-, dir. research tng. program, 1960-65, assoc. dean, 963-67, chmn. dept. biomed. history, 1964-85. Author: odern Embryology, 1968; contbr. articles to profl. urs. With USMC, 1944-47. Decorated Purple Heart. em. Academie Internationale d'Histoire de la edecine, Am. Assn. History Medicine (sec., treas. 964-71), History Sci. Soc., Am. Assn. Anatomists, ociété Internationale d'Histoire de la Medecine, Sigma i. Home: North Bend Wash. Died Feb. 3, 1985; uried Seattle.

ODEN, ROBERT FRANCIS, lawyer, educator; b. ilw., June 4, 1928; s. Francis X. and Edith A. (Ebert) ; m. Patricia M. Gill, July 10, 1954 (dec. Nov. 979). PhB, Marquette U., 1950, JD, 1952; LLD, arthage Coll., 1975. Bar: Wis. 1952. Assoc. Quarles, ence & Quarles, Milw., 1952-56; gen. practice Milw., 956-63; lectr. U. Marquette Law Sch., 1959-63, asst. of., 1963-65, assoc. prof., 1965-71, prof., 1971-84, acng dean, 1965-66, dean, from 1966; chmn. adminstrn. justice com. State Bar Wis., 1970-75, rsch. reporter editor-debtor law revision project, 1971-75; pres. Law rojects, Inc., 1970-76; mem. Gov.'s Spl. Com. on Jud. rgn., from 1971; mem. Wis. Jud. Coun., 1961-71, mn., 1963-65; mem. Milw. Police Edn. Study Com., 967-69; chmn. Wis. Garnishment Law Revision Com. 968-69, Wis. Supreme Ct. Chief Judge Study Com., 974-75, Gov.'s Jud. Appointment Adv. Commn., 1978-). Author: Bankruptcy Practice in Wisconsin, 1966, isconsin Creditor-Debtor Law, 1971, Basic Banuptcy Law, 1973; editor Wis. Continuing Legal Edn. ur., 1964-70; contbr. articles to profl. jours. Bd. dirs. ilw. Legal Aid Soc., 1969-74. Fellow Am. Bar Found. oun. on legal edn. and bar admission 1970-76, spl. com. on legal assts. 1974-76); mem. Am. Law Inst., Am. Judicature Soc., Wis. Bar Assn., Milw. Bar Assn., Delta Theta Phi, Alpha Sigma Nu. Home: Waukesha Wis. Died Feb. 3, 1984.

BODENSIECK, JULIUS H(ENRY), clergyman; b. Hameln, Germany, June 19, 1894; came to U.S., 1910, naturalized, 1926; s. Ernst August and Minna (Niemack) B.; m. Elma Sommer, June 19, 1918 (dec. Nov. 1936); children: Mathilde Bodensieck Fritschel, Justus; m. Justine Henkelmann, May 7, 1938. Grad., Wartburg Theol. Sem., Dubuque, Iowa, 1917; ThD, U. Muenster, 1951; LLD (hon.), Wartburg Coll., 1965. Ordained Lutheran (Iowa Synod) minister, 1917. Pastor St. Paul, to 1918; prof. Latin and Greek Wartburg Coll., Waverly, Iowa, 1918-21; prof. New Testament theology Wartburg Theol. Sem., Dubuque, Iowa, 1921-30; pres. Wartburg Theol. Sem., Dubuque, 1940-48, prof. Bible, 1954-64; assoc. pastor St. Matthew Luth Ch., Aurora, 1965-86; mem. cent. com. faith and order World Council Chs., 1952-62; Luth. World Fedn. theol. commr. in Europe, 1949-53; apptd. by Fed. Council Chs. Christ, U.S. Protestant Liason Rep. with Office of Mil. Govt. for Germany, 1946-48. Editor: Lutheran Herald, 1926-30, Kirchenblatt, 1931-40; editor-in-chief Luth. World Ency., 1954-65; contbr. theol. articles to various publs. Republican. Home: Aurora Colo. Died Apr. 28, 1986; buried Fairmount Cemetery, Denver.

BODLEY, RONALD VICTOR COURTENAY, author; b. Paris, Mar. 3, 1892; S. J. E. C. and Evelyn (Bell) B.; m. Harriet Moseley, Nov. 1949. Student, Eton Coll., Windsor, Eng., Royal Mil. Coll., Sandhurst, Eng. War corr. London Sphere, 1932-34; mil. attaché Brit. embassy, Paris, taking part in in Peace Conf., 1919; while there became friend of Lawrence of Arabia and as a result left army and went to live among nomad Arabs in desert, remaining 7 years; then set out on long series of voyages to Dutch Indies, China, Japan, Manchuria, Korea, Mongolia and South Sea Islands; came to U.S. and wrote screen plays for several years for Metro-Goldwyn-Mayer, Charlie Chaplin; returned to Europe in 1939 and remained until German invasion; escaped to Spain, then Portugal, eventually reaching U.S. Author: The Messenger, 1946, The Quest, 1947, The Warrior Saint, 1953, In Search of Serenity, 1955, The Soundless Sahara, 1968; contbr. numerous articles on travels to Am. and Brit. newspapers. Col. King's Royal Rifle Corps, Brit. Army. Decorated Mil. Cross, Legion of Honor, Crown of Rumania, Mons Star, and others. Mem. Garrick Club, Marylebone Cricket Club, Naval and Mil. Club. Mem. Ch. of England. Home: Newburyport Mass. †

BODMAM, HENRY TAYLOR, banker; b. Detroit, Jan. 26, 1906; s. Henry Edward and Florence (Taylor) B.; m. Marie-Louise McMillan, May 8, 1930; children: Henry E. II (dec.), Thayer B. Cluett, Richard S. Student, Detroit U. Sch., Hotchkiss Sch., Lakeville, Conn., 1922-24; BS cum laude, Princeton U., 1928. With Guardian Detroit Bank and affiliated instns., 1928-33; asst. cashier Nat. Bank of Detroit, asst. v.p., asst. trust officer, v.p., 1945-46, v.p., asst. to pres., 1949, gen. v.p., 1950-58, pres., 1958-64, chmn., 1964-70, dir., 1953-70; dir. Nat. Steel Corp. Contbr. articles on econ. subjects. Bd. dirs., hon. trustee Henry Ford Hosp.; trustee Citizens Research Council Mich.; bd. overseers Hoover Instn., Stanford; chmn. bd. trustees Earhart Found.; bd. dirs. RFC Washington, 1946-48. Served from maj. to col., ordnance, AUS, 1942-46. With OPM Washington, 1941-42. Decorated Legion of Merit. Mem. Assn. Res. City Bankers (hon. pres.), Bloomfield Hills Country, Grosse Pointe, Detroit, Country, Yondotega, Chevy Chase clubs. Republican. Episcopalian. Home: Grosse Pointe Mich. Died June 16, 1987.

BOE, ARCHIE R., retail and insurance company executive; b. Estherville, Iowa, Feb. 27, 1921; s. Berge B. and Regina B. (Nelson) B.; m. Elaine B. Jansson, May 11, 1973; 1 child, Michael; stepchildren: Constance Day, Randee Gregos. BCS, Drake U., 1941, LLB (hon.), 1976; MBA, U. Chgo., 1950. With Allstate Ins. Co., 1941-84, v.p., sec., 1960-66, pres., 1966-68, vice chmn., 1968-72; v.p., sec. Allstate Enterprises, Inc., 1960-66, pres., 1966-68, vice chmn., 1968-72; chmn., chief exec. officer Allstate Ins. and Allstate Enterprises, 1972-84; pres. Sears, Roebuck & Co., 1982-84, also bd. dirs.; bd. dirs. NICOR Inc., No. Ill. Gas Co., U.S. Gypsum Co., William Wrigley Jr. Co., Alberto-Culver Co., Continental Ill. Corp., Continental Ill. Nat. Bank and Trust Co. of Chgo., Delta Air Lines, Inc., Stewart-Warner Corp. Bd. dirs. Library Council of Northwestern U., Lyric Opera Co. Chgo., Protestant Found. Chgo., Found. for Teaching Econs., Am. Trauma Soc. Served with USNR, 1942-45. Mem. Newcomen Soc. N.Am. Clubs: Chicago (Chgo.), Commercial (Chgo.), Executives (Chgo.), Economic (Chgo.), Mid-America (Chgo.); Tavern, Glen View Country. Home: Chicago Ill. Died Jan. 2, 1989.

BOECKEL, RICHARD MARTIN, editor; b. Phila., Oct. 17, 1892; s. Richard Martin and Lennie (Ford) B.; m. Florence Murheid Brewer, Jan. 10, 1916; children: Richard Martin, John Hart. Ed., N.E. Manual Tng. Sch., Phila. Reporter Albany (N.Y.) Knickerbocker Press, 1908-09, Newburgh (N.Y.) News, 1909-10, Kingston (N.Y.) Leader, 1910-11, Poughkeepsie (N.Y.) News-Press, 1911-13; mgr. Pitts. bur. Internat. News Service, 1914-16, corr. Washington bur., 1916-18; publicity dir. Indsl. Bd., U.S. Dept. Commerce, 1919; corr. Washington bur. N.Y. Tribune, 1920-21; Washington corr. The Independent, 1922-23; co-founder, ptnr., editorial dir. Editorial Research Reports (daily and weekly newspaper service), Washington, from 1923; dir. emeritus; Paul Block Found. lectr., Yale U., 1938. Author: Labor's Money, 1923, Presidential Politics, 1928. Council mem. Nat. Civil Service Reform League. Mem. Nat. Press Club (Washington), Manor Club (Norbeck, Md.). Home: Washington D.C. †

BOGLE, HENRY CHARLES, lawyer; b. Ann Arbor, Mich., 1892; s. Thomas A. and Alice (Burgard) B.; m. Mathilde Masson, Oct. 15, 1927; children: Suzanne, David, Peter. LLB, U. Mich., 1915. Bar: Mich. 1915. Pvt. practice Detroit, from 1915; mem. firm Bodman, Longley, Bogle, Armstrong & Dahling, Detroit, from 1933. Author: Who Murdered Aikenhead?, 1973. Lt. U.S. Army, 1917-19. Mem. Am., Detroit bar assns., State Bar Mich., founders soc. Detroit Inst. Arts., Detroit Zool. Soc., Detroit Club, Country Club of Detroit, Phi Delta Phi, Psi Upsilon. Home: Grosse Pointe Mich. Deceased.

BOIES, LAWRENCE RANDALL, otolaryngologist, educator; b. Renville, Minn., Nov. 7, 1898; s. Walter Randall and Gertrude (Olufsen) B.; m. Louise Marty, Sept. 11, 1928; children: Lawrence Randall, David Blandford, William (dec.). AB, U. Wis., 1922, AM, 1923; MD, Columbia U., 1926; postgrad., Harvard U., 1929. Resident physician in otolaryngology Mass. Eye and Ear Infirmary, 1929-31; practice medicine specializing in otolaryngology Mpls., from 1931; instr. otolaryngology U. Minn. Med. Sch., 1931-36, clin. asst. prof., 1933-39, clin. assoc. prof., 1939-41, dir. div. otolaryngology, 1941-67, clin. prof., 1942-55, prof., head dept., 1955-67, emeritus, from 1967; dir. med. affairs Deafness Rsch. Found., 1967-70. Author: sect. diseases the ear in Specialties in Medical Practice, 1943, Fundamentals of Otolaryngology, 1949; contbr. numerous articles to profl. jours. Dir., Am. Bd. Otolaryngology, pres., 1963-68. With U.S. Army, 1917-18. Mem. Am. Acad. Ophthalmology and Otolaryngology (bd. secs. 1947-56, pres. 1962), Minn., Mpls. acads. medicine, Minn. Acad. Ophthalmology and Otolaryngology, AMA (chmn. sect. laryngology, otology, rhinology 1961), Am. Laringol., Rhinol. and Otol. Soc. (pres. 1957-58), Am. Otol. Soc. (pres. 1962), Am. Laryngol. Assn. (pres. 1967), Am. Broncho-Esophological Soc., Hennepin County Med. Soc. (pres. 1946-47), Alpha Kappa Lambda, Alpha Kappa Kappa. Home: Hopkins Minn. Died July 5, 1986.

BOIVIN, BERNARD, botanist; b. Montreal, Que., Can., May 7, 1916; s. Alexis and Marie L. (Tremblay) B.; m. Cosette Marcoux, Dec. 26, 1946; children: Lilian, Helene, Jacques. BA, U. Montreal, 1937, LSc, 1941; PhD, Harvard U., 1943. Botanist Nat. Mus., Ottawa, Ont., Can., 1946-47; research assoc. Harvard U., 1947-48; research scientist Can. Agr., Ottawa, 1948-65, 67-81; vis. prof. Laval U., 1965-66, lectr., 1981-85; vis. prof. U. Toronto, 1969-70. Author: American Thalictra, 1944, Enumeration des Plantes du Canada, 1967, Flora of the Prairie Provinces, 5 vols., 1967-81, Survey of Canadian Herbaria, 1980. With Can. Army, 1943-46. Guggenheim fellow, 1947-48. Fellow Royal Soc. Can.; mem. New Eng. Bot. Club, Ottawa Field Naturalists Club. Roman Catholic. Home: Quebec Canada. Died May 9, 1985; buried Quebec, Canada.

BOLAND, EDWARD R.A., librarian; b. San Francisco, Jan. 10, 1892; s. Richard Joseph and Julia (Brosnahan) B. MA, Gonzaga U., 1918; postgrad., St. Louis U., 1921-25. Ordained priest Roman Cath. Ch. Head history dept. U. Santa Clara (Calif.), 1926-40, librarian, from 1940. Home: Santa Clara Calif. †

BOLD, HAROLD C., botany educator; b. June 16, 1909. B.A., Columbia U., 1929; M.S., U. Vt., 1931; Ph.D., Columbia U., 1933. Instr. botany U. Vermont, 1929-31; instr. biology Vanderbilt U., 1932-39; vis. lectr., asst. prof. botany Barnard Coll., Columbia U., 1940-42; assoc. prof. Vanderbilt U., 1946-49, prof. biology, 1949-57; prof. botany U. Tex., 1957-75, chmn. dept., 1962-68, chmn. biol. scis., 1969-71, sec. gen. faculty, 1972-74, C.L. Lundell prof. systematic botany, 1975-78, C.L. Lundell prof. emeritus, 1978—; instr. in charge phycology course Chesapeake Biol. Lab., 1934-37; instr. marine botany course Marine Biol. Lab., Woods Hole, Mass., 1930, 48, instr. in charge, 1954-58. Author: Morphology of Plants, 1957, 2d edit., 1967, 3d edit., 1973, The Plant Kingdom, 1961, 2d edit., 1964, 3d edit., 1970, 4th edit., 1977, 5th edit., 1987, Algae and Fungi, 1967, Morphology of Plants and Fungi, 4th edit., 1980 co-author (with Whaley, Breland, Heimsch, Phelps, Schrank and Wyss): Principles of Biology, 1964, (with M.J. Wynne): Introduction to the Algae, 1978, 2d edit., 1985. Fellow AAAS; mem. Nat. Acad. Scis., Am. Acad Arts and Scis., Bot. Soc. Am. (sec. 1955-58, editor in chief Am. Jo. of Botany, 1958-65, pres. 1966), Phycol. Soc. Am. (past pres.), Torrey Bot. Club (corresponding sec. 1940-41), Internat. Phycol. Soc., Brit. Phycol. Soc., Assn. Southeastern Biologist, Southwestern Assn. Naturalist, Tex. Acad. Sci. Home: Austin Tex. Died Dec. 17, 1987; interred Cedar Hill Cemetary, Abilene.

BOLES, RUSSELL SAGE, physician; b. Phila., Sept. 27, 1889; s. George H. and Rhoda (Borden) B.; m. Mary McNeely, Nov. 29, 1916; children: Mary Laird McIlvain, Russell Sage. MD, U. Penna., 1912; post-grad., U. Halle, Germany, Berlin, Vienna, Austria, Hungary, 1914. Diplomate in Gastroenterology, Am. Bd. Internal Medicine. Intern Phila. Gen. Hosp., 1912-13, chmn. med. div., 1940-43, pres. med. bd., 1943-47, vis. physician, 1929-55, sr. med. chief, Dept. Medicine, 1952-55, hon. cons. Dept. Medicine, 1955; assoc. prof. medicine Grad. Sch. U. Pa., 1947-52, prof. clin. medicine, 1952-55, emeritus prof. clin. medicine, from 1955; chief gastroenterology Bryn Mawr (Pa.) Hosp., 1937-41; spl. cons. Nat. Cancer Inst. USPHS; mem. sci. com. Rsch. Coun. on Problems of Alcohol, adv. com. Nat. Com. for Edn. on Alcoholism; del. 1st Internat. Congress Gastroenterology, Brussels, 1935. Author articles in sci. books, jours., lay mags.; mem. gen. com. revision U.S. Pharmacopoeia, 1950-60; book rev. editor Gastroenterology. Mem. adv. bd. Woods Sch., Langhorne, Pa.; mem. bd. dirs. Phila. Civic Opera Co. Lt. M.C., USN, World War I; cons. Pa. Adv. Bd. I, World War II. Recipient Julius Friedenwald medal Am. Gastroent. Assn., 1959; Russell S. Boles Med. Rsch. Fund established U. Pa., 1959. Fellow ACP (life), Phila. Coll. Physicians; mem. Am. Gastroent. Assn. (sec. 1933-39), v.p. 1940-41, pres. 1942), World (founder mem. U.S. com.), Pan-Am. (pres. sect. gastroenterolgy 1953, Am. (chmn. sect. gastroenterology and proctology 1950), Pa., Montgomery County, Phila. County med. assns, AAAS, Musical Fund Soc. (mem. bd.), Rittenhouse Club, Phila. Country Club, The Orpheus Club, Univ. Pa. Faculty Club. Republican. Episcopalian (vestryman). Home: Narbeth Pa. Deceased.

BOLGER, RAY, actor; b. Boston, Jan. 10, 1904; s. James Edward and Anne (Wallace) B.; m. Gwendolyn Rickard, July 9, 1929. Ed. pub. schs., Boston; DFA (hon.), U. Conn., 1986. sr. cons. U. Conn. Center for Instructional Media and Tech., 1977; lectr., throughout U.S. Began acting career with Bob Ott Repertory Co., 1923-25, with Ralph Sanford as A Pair of Nifties, vaudeville; with Gus Edwards in vaudeville Ritz Carlton Nights, 1926-28; appeared on Broadway in Shubert revue The Merry Whirl, 1925; revues Heads Up, 1929, George White's Scandals of 1931, (with Bert Lahr) Life Begins at 8:40, 1934; starred in On Your Toes, 1936; under MGM picture contract made Rosalie, Sweethearts, Wizard of Oz, 1938-40; starred on Broadway in: Keep Off the Grass, 1940, By Jupiter, 1942; with MGM, 1941-42, 45-87; appeared in: The Harvey Girls, 1945; starred in: Three to Make Ready, 1946, and in, Warner Bros.; film Silver Lining; starred on Broadway in: (produced by wife, Gwen Rickard) Where's Charley?, 1948-51, filmed film, 1951; co-starred in: film April in Paris, 1952; star: motion picture Babes in Toyland, 1961, NBC, That's Dancing, MGM 60th anniversary film, 1984; TV debut Comedy Hour, 1952; filmed weekly: Ray Bolger Show, ABC-TV, 1953-55, Washington Square, NBC-TV series, 1956; appeared in: TV series The Partridge Family; starred in: Broadway mus. All American, 1962, Come Summer, 1968-69; summer theatres The Happy Time, 1969; appeared in: one-man show a Musical Comical Concert; various concert halls and nightclubs; appeared: TV programs The Entertainer, 1975, Captains and Kings, 1976, Boston Pops Concert, 1976; appeared in concert with, Sarasota Symphony Orch., Kansas City Philharmonic Orch., Amarillo Symphony Orch., 1977; film The Runner Stumbles, 1979; instr. media and tech. film A Time for Living (prize winner Internat. Film Festival N.Y., 1975). Recipient Silver medal for Treasury activities during World War II; Antoinette Perry award, 1948-49; 2 Donaldson award for best performances; drama critics poll best musical comedy performance, 1946; N.Y. Newspapers Guild Page One award, 1943, 50; Decency in Entertainment award Notre Dame Club, Chgo., 1967; Medallion of Valor State of Israel, 1970; named to Theatrical Hall of Fame, 1980. Clubs: Players; Bel-Air Country (Calif.); Valley (Montecito); Bohemian (San Francisco); Burlingame Country (Calif.); Swallows (Pebble Beach, Calif.). Home: Beverly Hills Calif. Died Jan. 15, 1987; interred Holy Cross Mausoleum.

BOLTON, WILLIAM E(RNEST), railroad executive; b. Toronto, Oct. 7, 1891; came to U.S., 1917, naturalized, 1924; s. William J. and Janet (Plaxton) B.; m. Mary Lee Johnson, Apr. 24, 1935; children: William Johnson, George Anthony. Student pub. schs., Wells Coll., Toronto. With Canadian No. Ry., Toronto, 1909-16, S.A.L. Ry., Norfolk, Va., 1916-17; sec. to v.p. C.R.I.& P. Ry., 1919-25, asst. to v.p. charge ops., 1925-38, indsl. commr., 1938-46, asst. to pres., 1946-51, v.p., 1952-54, ret. Served with USN, 1917-19. Mem. Culver Fathers Assn. (former v.p.), Ill., Chgo. C.'s of C., Soc. Four Arts, Palm Beach Artists League, Am. Legion, Skokie Country, Union League, Chicago Curling clubs. Republican. Episcopalian. Home: Orangeville Pa. †

BOMZER, HERBERT WALLACE, computer and information science educator; b. N.Y.C., Sept. 23, 1925; s. David and Bertha (Brettschneider) B.; m. Estie Ann Lipman, Nov. 21, 1951; children: Charles Alan, Sue Merle, David Jay. BA in Math., Bklyn. Coll., 1948; MA in Stats., U. Del., 1950; PhD in Bus., U. Ill., 1974. Statistician, Aberdeen Proving Ground (Md.), 1948-50; project mgr. Ford Instrument Co., Queens, N.Y., 1950-57; dir. ops., asst. v.p. Autometric Corp., N.Y.C., 1957-63; head dept. Gen. Precision, Little Falls, N.Y., 1963-68; dir. systems Magnavox, Urbana, Ill., 1968-69; asst. dir. data processing U. Ill., Champaign, 1970-77; assoc. prof. bus. adminstrn. Ill. State U., Normal, 1974-77; prof., chmn. dept. info. and systems analysis Central Mich. U., Mt. Pleasant, 1977-84; prof., chmn. dept. computer and info. sci. Fordham U., Bronx, N.Y., 1984-86; dir. Data Basic, Inc., Mt. Pleasant; cons. in field. Author: Managing the Data Processing Center, 1980; contbr. articles to profl. jours.; patentee in field. Vice pres. Shelter Rock Community Ctr., N.Y., 1952-54; advisor to bd. Herricks Sch. Dist., 1953-57; bd. dirs. Eagle Rock council Boy Scouts Am., N.Y.C., 1959-62, Community Chest, Champaign, Ill., 1974-77; pres. Hillel Found. U. Ill., Champaign, 1975-77; chmn. computer adv. com. Mt. Pleasant High Sch., from 1980; chmn. Mt. Pleasant Computer Literacy Com., 1983-84. Served with U.S. Army, 1943-46. Mem. IEEE, Data Processing Mgmt. Assn., Am. Statis. Assn., Assn. Computing Machinery. Jewish. Lodge: B'nai B'rith (v.p. 1978-79). Home: Bayside, N.Y. Died: May 1986.

BOND, DONALD FREDERIC, educator; b. Franfort, Ind., Nov. 27, 1898; s. Jesse Fred and Almeda (Norris) B.; m. Judith Strohm, Sept. 1, 1927; children: James, Deborah Bond Falk. PhB, U. Chgo., 1922, AM, 1923, fellow, 1929, PhD, 1934. Instr. English Washington U., St. Louis, 1923, asst. prof., 1924-28; mem. faculty U. Chgo., 1930-67, asst. prof., 1940-47, assoc. prof., 1947-52, William H. Colvin research prof., 1961-62, prof. emeritus, 1963-87; vis. prof. No. Ill. U., 1969-71. Author: A Reference Guide to English Studies, 1962, 2d edit., 1971, The Spectator, a critical edit., 5 vols., 1965, The Age of Dryden, 1970, Critical Essays from the Spectator, 1970; editor: A Critical Bibliography of French Literature (Vol. 4, with G.R. Havens), 1951; editorial bd. Modern Philology, 1952-59, editor, 1959-67; contbr. articles and revs., profl. jours. Mem. Palos Park (Ill.) Library Bd., 1943-58; chmn. com. on curriculum Citizens Com. Edn., 1949; mem. bd. edn. Cook County High Sch. Dist. 230, 1948-58. Guggenheim fellow, 1958-59, 66-67. Mem. Modern Humanities Research Assn., Bibliog. Soc., Internat. Assn. U. Profs. English, Modern Lang. Assn., Phi Beta Kappa, Lambda Chi Alpha. Republican. Episcopalian. Home: El Cerrito Calif. Deceased.

BOND, GEORGE WILLIAM, educator; b. Summers, Ark., Apr. 6, 1891; s. William Elijah and Martha Irene (Simpson) B.; m. Mary Elizabeth Bost, Sept. 29, 1923. Licentiate of Instruction, U. of Ark., 1916, BS, 1920; AM, U. Chgo., 1928; EdD, Columbia U., 1938. Supt. schs. Cane Hill, Ark., 1917-18, Bauxite, Ark., 1920-22; prin. Sr. High Sch., Texarkana, Ark., 1923-24; prof. rural edn. La. Poly. Inst., Ruston, 1924-26, dean Coll. of Edn., 1926-28, pres., 1928-36; dean Southeastern La. Coll., Hammond, 1938-44, acting pres., 1944-45, 1944-45; dean Sch. of Edn. La. Poly. Inst., 1945-56; prof. edn. Harding Coll., Searcy, Ark., from 1956. Author: Eight Years of Progress, 1936, A Program for Control of Teacher Certification in Louisiana, 1938, George and Mary Ann Simpson: Their Family, 1958. With U.S. Army, World War I; disch. with rank of sergt.; commd. maj., La. State Guard, 1943. Mem. NEA, Am. Assoc. Sch. Adminstrs., Nat. Soc. Study Edn., Masons (Order Eastern Star), Rotary, Phi Delta Kappa, Kappa Delta Pi. Home: Searcy Ark. †

BOND, HIRAM E., petroleum company executive; b. 1924; married. With Atlantic Richfield Co., Los Angeles, from 1948, tech. trainee, then product foreman, dist. foreman, 1948-57, engr., then region product supt., then adminstrv. asst. to mgr. fgn. exploration, then adminstrv. asst. to v.p. & prodn. mgr., then dist. mgr. Mid Continent & Rocky Mountain dists. & mgr. synthetic crude & mineral ops., 1957-72, v.p. synthetic crude & mineral div., 1972-78, corp. sr. v.p., 1978-79, sr. v.p. & pres. ARCO Coal Co. (subs.), 1979-81, sr. v.p. & pres. ARCO Transp. Co., 1981-87. Served with USNR, 1943-46. Deceased.

BOND, RICHARD GUY, civil engineer, educator; b. Beecher Falls, Vt., Dec. 9, 1916; s. Richard Henry and Annie (Bassett) B.; m. Betty Telford Wells, Sept. 29, 1953. BS in Civil Engring., U. N.H., 1938; MS in San. Engring., U. Iowa, 1940; MPH, U. Minn., 1948. Registered profl. engr., Minn., Iowa; Diplomate Am. Acad. Environ. Engrs. Pub. health engr. Iowa Dept. Health, 1940-47; vis. lectr. U. Minn. Sch. Pub. Health, 1943-45, 47-48; asst. prof. civil engring. Cornell U., 1947-49; faculty U. Minn., Mpls., 1949-79, prof., 1958-79, prof. emeritus, 1980-85, dir. environ. health and safety, 1949-62, dir. environ. health div., 1962-73; cons. in field, from 1958, Office Surgeon Gen. Army, 1962-74, U.S. Bur. Prisons, from 1976; chmn. planetary quarantine adv. com. Am. Inst. Biol. Scis., 1966-75; lectr. seminar community health workers from overseas Cen. Coun. Health Edn., Britain, 1964; mem. 3d Nat. Conf. Pub. Health Tng., 1967, health planning adv. coun. Minn. Planning Agy., 1967-72, campus safety assn. Nat. Safety Coun., 1955-62, coun. pub. health cons. Nat. Sanitation Found., 1970-78; mem. life scis. com. NASA, 1971-74. Co-editor: Environmental Health and Safety in Health Care Facilities, 1973. Mem. U.S. Nat. Com. on Vital Health Statistics, 1972-74; mem. health care adv. com. Minn. Dept. Corrections, 1974-79. Recipient Outstanding Achievement award U. N.H. Coll. Tech., 1973; WHO travel fellow, S.E., Asia, 1960. Fellow Am. P Health Assn. (gov. coun. 1962-65, 69-74, chmn. h facilities com. 1955-65), ASCE, Royal Soc. He Britain (hon.); mem. AAAS, Pub. Health Insps. A Britain (hon.), Am. Coll. Health Assn. (gov. coun., e bd. 1958-64, Ruth E. Boynton award 1968, Hitchc award 1977), Health Physics Soc., Nat. Soc. P Engrs., Minn. Soc. Profl. Engrs., Campus Club Minn.), Sigma Xi, Alpha Tau Omega. Episcopali Home: Minneapolis Minn. Died Oct. 25, 1985.

BOND, ROBERT MCGEHEE, air force officer; Trenton, Tenn., Dec. 16, 1929; s. Robert U. Dorothy (McGehee) B.; m. Betty Renick, Aug. 14, 1 children: Susan Hurry, Michael, Pamela Lun Stephen. Student, Marion (Ala.) Mil. Inst., U. M Air Command and Staff Coll., 1966. Enlisted in US 1951; commd., advanced through grades to lt. gen.; comdr. 23 Tactical Fighter Wing, 1972-73; dep. Gen. Purpose Forces Directorate, Office of Dept. C of Staff Research and Devel., Hdqrs. USAF, 1973 comdr. Armament Devel. and Test Ctr., Eglin A Fla., 1978-81; vice comdr. Air Force Systems C mand, Andrews AFB, 1981-84. Decorated Meritori Service medal, Silver Star, Air medal with 13 oak clusters. Home: Andrews Md. Died May 2, 1984.

BONDURANT, HERBERT W(ILLIAM), business ecutive; b. Union City, Tenn., Aug. 19, 1892; s. Lo Walter and Melinda (Beaird) B.; m. Maude Biss Campbell, Sept. 12, 1947; 1 child by previous marri Herbert William II. Ed. pub. schs., Tenn. Chief c service traffic dept. So. Ry. System, Nashville, Te 1912, chief clerk, Dallas, 1916, traveling freight ag Little Rock, July 1916, freight traffic rep., Nashv 1920, comml. agt., Nashville, 1922, dist. freight a Memphis, 1925, dist. freight agt., Phila., 1928, freight agt., Charlotte, N.C., 1931, asst. freight tra mgr., Atlanta, 1935, freight traffic mgr., Cin., 1938, a v.p., Washington, 1940, v.p., resident exec., Atla from 1945; pres. Atlanta Terminal Co., Columbia (S Union Station Co., Meridian (Mis..) Terminal North Charleston (S.C.) Terminal Co., Tallulah F Ry. Co., Cornelia, Ga.; v.p. Chattanooga Sta. Co. Atlanta chpt. ARC. Mem. Newcomen Soc. of Engla Huguenot Soc. pf Founders of Mahakin in Colony Va. (Va. br.), Capital City Club, Piedmont Driv Club. Democrat. Episcopalian. Home: Atlanta Ga.

BONGIOVANNI, ALFRED MARIUS, physic educator; b. Phila., Sept. 22, 1921; s. Joseph Natha and Elisa (DiSilvestro) B. B.S., Villanova U., 1 M.D., U. Pa., 1943. Diplomate Am. Bd. Pediatri Investigator Marine Lab., Woods Hole, Mass., 1939 instr. pharmacology Phila. Coll. Pharmacy and 1947-49; asst. physician Rockefeller Inst., 1949-51; a prof. Johns Hopkins Sch. Medicine, Balt., 1950 faculty U. Pa. Sch. Medicine, Phila., 1952-86; p pediatrics, chmn. dept. U. Pa. Sch. Medicine, 1963 prof. pediatrics, dir. pediatric endocrine div., 1973 prof. pediatrics and ob-gyn, 1980-86; physician-in-c Children's Hosp., Phila., 1963-72; prof., chmn. d pediatrics Sch. Health Sci., U. Ife, Nigeria, 1974 dean Sch. Medicine, Cath. U. P.R., Ponce, 1977 prof. pediatrics U. P.R., San Juan, 1978-80, Pa. Ho Phila., 1980-86; adj. prof. pediatrics Thomas Jeffer Med. Sch., 1980-86; mem. staff Hosp. U. Pa., Pa. Ho Children's Seashore House, Atlantic City; pediatric Elwyn Inst.; mem. sci. adv. bd. St. Jude's Ho Memphis; mem. com. research Am. Cancer Soc.; c HEW. Editorial staff: Jour. Steroid Biochemis contbr. articles to profl. jours. Chmn. child devel. mental retardation tng. rev. com. NIH; sci. adv. Child Devel. Group Miss.; trustee South Jersey M Research Found. Recipient award League of Childr Hosp., Phila., 1962, Shaffrey medal St. Joseph's C Phila., 1965, Mendel medal Villanova U., 1968. Fel N.Y. Acad. Scis., ACP; mem. Endocrine Soc. (C award 1956), Endocrine Soc. P.R., Am. Soc. Clin. vestigation, Am. Pediatric Soc., Am. Acad. Pediat (Mead Johnson award 1957, drug dosage com.), Pe tric Research Soc., Endocrine Soc. Peru, Pediatric Guatemala, Assn. Am. Physicians, Royal Soc. Medi (affiliate), Wilkins Pediatric Endocrine Soc. (pres. 1 86), U.S. Pharmacopoeia, Alpha Omega Alpha (hon Roman Catholic. Club: Union League (Phila.). Ho Philadelphia Penn. Died Aug. 10, 1986; buried H Cross Cemetery, Phila.

BONILLA, CHARLES FRANCIS, chemical nuclear engineer, educator; b. Albany, N.Y., July 1909; s. Rodrigo and Lucy E. (Smith) B.; m. Sig Isabel Johnson, Oct. 28, 1938 (dec. May 26, 19 children: Laurence Huguet, Elisabeth Blair. Cuenca Inst., Spain, 1925, Columbia U., 1928; BS Elec. Engring., Columbia U., 1929, PhD, 1933. Re tered profl. engr., N.Y., Md. Tutor chem. engr CCNY, 1932-37; from asst. prof. to prof. chem. engr Johns Hopkins, Balt., 1937-49, chmn. dept. chem. er ing., 1943-49; prof. chem. engring. Columbia N.Y.C., 1948-78, chmn. dept., 1974-77, prof. nuc engring., 1950-78, emeritus prof. chem. and nuclear gring., 1978-87, dir. nuclear engring. program, 1950 TRIGA reactor program, 1960-87; founder, dir. Liq Metals Research Lab., 1948-87, sr. cons., 1978-87; founder Nuclear Heat Transfer Research Facility, 1 dir., 1960-78; cons. Bd. Econs. Warfare, Fgn. Ec Adminstrn., Washington, 1942-46; mem. US. In ission to Brazil, 1942, U.S. Tech. Mission to Cuba, 43, Atoms for Peace Missions to South Am., 1956; clear exchange specialist to Spain, 1956, Nat. Acad. i. mission to Chile, 1960; cons. Phillips Petroleum Co., artlesville, Okla., 1942-46, U.S. Naval Engring. Expt. a., 1946-51, Brookhaven Nat. Lab., 1948-56, Knolls tomic Power Lab., Schenectady, 1952-55, E.I. du Pont e Nemours & Co. (Engring. Research Lab.), 1955-62, ettis Atomic Power Lab., 1956-62, Atomic Power evel. Assn., 1960-68, Gen. Electric Co., 1960-75, 78, at. Lead Co., 1961-69, Argonne Nat. Lab., 1956-59, -87, Kaiser Engrs. 1977-78; v.p. research Chlormetals, c., 1964-67; dir. Belfort Instrument Co., Balt., 1956- , chmn. bd., 1962-72; dir. P.R. Nuclear Ctr., AEC, 57-59; mem. ASME coms. K-13, K-7, 1956-87, chmn. -7,1968-71; co-chmn. Nat. Heat Transfer Conf. (Am. st. Chem. Engr. and ASME), 1983; OAS lectr. U. ex., 1972; invited speaker on sodium research tech. ternat. Assn. for Hydraulics Research, 1983; dir. search projects Rubber Res., Air Force, NASA, AEC, llison div. Gen. Motors, others; hon. mem. AEC of ru, 1956-87; invited speaker on sodium research tech. ternat. Assn. Hydraulics Research, 1983. Editor, co- thor: Nuclear Engineering, 1957; editor: Nuclear En- ing. and Design Jour., 1966-87; contbr. articles on dsl. chemistry, chem. and nuclear engring., heat ansfer, liquid metals; patentee in field. Home: Tenafly .J. Died Oct. 31, 1987.

OOKHOLT, WILLIAM JOHN, lawyer, accountant; Paterson, N.J., Aug. 30, 1916; s. James and Bella an Haste) B.; m. Marian E. Bell, June 30, 1943; chil- en: Robert G., Barbara G. Diploma acctg. and bus. ministrn., Pace Coll., 1939; student, Rutgers U., 1938- , Newark U., 1945; J.D., Woodrow Wilson Coll. Law, tlanta, 1950; postgrad., U. Ga., 1951-52. Bar. Ga. bar 50; C.P.A., Ga. Field auditor Equitable Life As- rance Soc N.Y., 1935-41; with IRS, 1946-72; dist. dir. RS, Atlanta, 1958-59, regional commr., 1959-72; pvt. actice, Atlanta, 1972-88. Served to capt. AUS, 1941- . Mem. Ga. Soc. C.P.A.s (Key award 1951, Out- anding Pub. Service award 1956, 72), Ga. Bar Assn. ome: Decatur Ga. Died Oct. 19, 1986, Decatur.

OONE, WILLIAM COOKE, clergyman; b. Bowling reen, Ky., Feb. 8, 1892; s. Arthur Upshaw and Eddie elle (Cooke) B.; m. Ruth Harvey Trotter, Sept. 1, 1915; ildren: Ruth Trotter (Mrs. Warner E. Fusselle), artha Maria (Mrs. Jack S. Foust), Arthur Upshaw, an Eager (Mrs. Chas. B. Arendall Jr.), William ooke. AB, William Jewell Coll., 1912, AM, 1913; udent, So. Bapt. Theol. Sem., 1912-14, Columbia U, mmer 1923; DD, Georgetown (Ky.) Coll., 1928. astor Bapt. Ch., Hernando, Miss., 1914-16; prin. high h., Hernando, 1914-16; pastor Bapt. Ch., Marianna, rk., 1916-18, Owensboro, Ky., 1918-27, Roanoke, Va., 27-30; pres. Okla. Bapt. U., 1930-32; pastor First apt.Ch., Jackson, Tenn., 1932-40, Crescent Hill Bapt. h., Louisville, 1940-45. Author: What God Hath ined Together, What We Believe. V.p. So. Bapts. onv., 1931; chmn. exec. bd. Gen. Assn. of Bapts. in y., 1941-44, gen. sec., treas., exec. bd. 1946—. Mem. asons, K.T., Kiwanis, Sigma Nu. Home: Anchorage y. †

OOTH, WARREN S., newspaper publisher; b. De- oit, Apr. 18, 1894; s. George Gough and Ellen Warren cripps) B.; m. Alice Sedgwick Newcomb, May 14, 21; children: Barbara Booth Craig, Marjorie Booth och (dec.), Sally Booth Fitzgerald, Dorothy Booth scher, Peter. Clk. advt. dept. Detroit News, 1916-17, st. bus. mgr., 1919-25; dir. Evening News Assn. (pub. etroit News, owners, licenses Sta. WWJ-AM-FM-TV), 25-70, treas., 1927-52, pres., pub., 1952-63, chmn., 63-70, counselor to bd. dirs., 1970-87; dir. Booth ewspapers, Inc., 1932-69, v.p 1935-46, pres., 1946-52. ommd. 1st lt. F.A., 329th F.A., 85th Div. Camp uster, Mich., Aug. 15, 1917; capt., battalion adj., Mar. , 1918; saw action Meuse-Argonne, Metz, World War Mem. Detroit, Bloomfield Hills Country, Grosse ointe, Orchard Lake Country, Old, Bayview Yacht, cean, Key Largo Anglers, Ocean Reef and Crown olony Clubs. Republican. Episcopalian. Home: earborn Mich. Died Jan. 4, 1987.

OOTH, WILLIAM WALLACE, lawyer; b. Al- gheny, Pa., Nov. 2, 1896; s. Harry J. and Ella oungson) B.; m. Adelaide Skelton Lanz, June 27, 25; children: William Wallace, James Youngson, ynthia S. Booth Jennings. BS in Econs., U. Pitts., 20, LLB, 1922. Bar: Pa. 1922. Practiced in Pitts., om 1922; mem. Reed, Smith, Shaw & McClay, from 35. Chmn. alumni com. on trustees elections U. tts., 1940, mem. alumni counc., 1941-47, trustee, then neritus from 1969, mem. exec. com., 1955-68; trustee esbyn. U. Hosp., 1955-70, emeritus, from 1970; under Bellefield Ednl. Trust, 1952. 2d lt. A.C., U.S. rmy, 1917-19. Mem. ABA, Pa. Bar Assn., Allegheny ounty Bar Assn., Am. Judicare Soc., Scottish-Am. oc., University Club (pres. 1957-58), Duquesne Club itts.), Rolling Rock Club (ligonier, Pa.), Ox 5 Club l., Masons (Jester), Omicron Delta Kappa, Sigma pha Epsilon, Beta Gamma Sigma, Phi Delta Phi, der of Daedalians. Presbyterian. Home: Pittsburgh . Died Oct. 21, 1986, buried Homewood Cemetery, tts.

BORCHERS, ROBERT HARLEY, meat packing ex- ecutive; b. Bigelow, Mo., Feb. 8, 1906; s. Henry A. and Maude (McKee) B.; m. Josephine Reece, May 29, 1931; children: Robert Reece, Judith Lee, Amy Catherine; m. Mary B. Brown, May 7, 1983. Student, Mo. U., 1925. With Armour & Co., 1926-71; successively clk., foreman, salesman, head provision dept., plant mgr. Armour & Co., Indpls.; mgr. Armour & Co., Oklahoma City; asst. to v.p. Armour & Co., Chgo., v.p. in charge pork operations, 1926-55, group v.p. food operations, 1956-57, exec. v.p., 1957-71, dir., 1959-71; bd. dirs. Am. Meat Inst., Found. for Am. Agr. Mem. Chgo. Athletic Assn., Rolling Green Country Club, Elks. Home: Laguna Hills Calif. Died Nov. 30, 1987, buried All Saints Cemetery, Chgo.

BORGES, JORGO LUIS, author, educator; b. Aug. 24, 1899. Ed. in Switzerland, also Cambridge (Eng.) and Buenos Aires (Argentina) univs. Prof. English and North Am. lit. Buenos Aires U.; early opponent of Argentine politician Juan Peron, was removed from his post as a Buenos Aires mcpl. librarian in 1946; dir. Nat. Library Buenos Aires, resigned after Peron returned to power in 1973. Author: Luna de Enfrente, Cuaderno San Maritn, Historia de la Eternidad, Antologia Clasica de la Literatura Argentina, (with Margarita Guerrere) El Marin Fierro, La Poesia Gauchesca, El Aleph, El Jardin de Desiderios que se bifurcan, Inquisiciones, Otras Inqu- siciones, Historia de la Eternidad, Historia Universal de la Infamia, Fervor de Buenos Aires, Ficciones, Labyrinthe, Libro de Cielo y del Infierno (poems), 1960, El Hacedor, 1960, Antologia personal, 1961. Recipient Premio de Honor, 1961, Fondo de les Artes, 1963; co- recipient Prix Formentor, 1961; named hon. knight Brit. Empire. Mem. Acad. Argentina de Letras. Home: Buenos Aires Argentina. Died June 14, 1986.

BORGLUM, JAMES LINCOLN DE LA MOTHE, sculptor, photographer; b. Stamford, Conn., Apr. 9, 1912; s. John Gutzon and Mary (Montgomery) B.; m. Louella Jones, Dec. 16, 1937 (dec. Nov. 1963); children: Anna Mary April, James Gutzon; m. Mrs. Richard Ells- worth, Apr. 9, 1964; children: Richard, Paul, Robert Ellsworth. Student, Lukin Mil. Acad., San Antonio, Tex., 1925-27, Valley (Wyo.) Ranch Sch. 1928-30; studied sculpture under father for, 1929, 31. Apprentice West Tex. Pub. Utilities Co., Abilene, 1931; with Mt. Rushmore Nat. Meml., Black Hills, S.D. 1929-41, charge measurements and enlarging models, 1934-38; apptd. supt. Meml. by Mt. Rushmore Meml. Commn., 1938, apptd. sculptor to complete Meml. following his father's death, 1940, mem. commn., 1960-86; apptd. supt. by Nat. Park Service U.S. Dept. Interior, 1942; tech. advisor in carving worlds largest known sapphires in likeness: Washington, Jefferson, Eisenhower; designed carving for world's largest known ruby; executed statue: Our Lady of Loreto, La Bahia Mission, Goliad, Tex.; bust Pres. Johnson, near Keystone, S.D.; bronze Statue of founder, Gladys Porter Zoo, Brownsville, Tex.; has exhibited color photography work in salons at Milw., Rochester, N.Y., N.Y.C.; colored photographs used for covers of This Week and Sat. Eve. Post; author: My Father's Mountain, 1965; co-author: Borglum's Unfin- ished Dream, Mt. Rushmore, 1976, Mount Rushmore, The Story Behind the Scenery, 1977. Hon. mem. Lincoln Sesquicentennial Commn., S.D. Bicentennial Commn.; trustee Mt. Rushmore Nat. Meml. Soc. Black Hills, Rapid City, S.D.; pres. Whopping Crane council Girl Scouts U.S.; mem. Beeville City Council, 1955-61. Mem. So. Tex. Hereford Assn., Rotary. Home: La Feria Tex. Died Jan. 27, 1986.

BORGMANN, DMITRI ALFRED, research company and loan brokerage firm executive, investment firm company executive, church official; b. Berlin, Germany, Oct. 22, 1927; s. Hans and Lisa (Kalnitzkaya) B.; brought to U.S., 1936, naturalized, 1943; Ph.B., U. Chgo., 1946; D.D. Universal Life Ch., 1976; Ph.D., Sussex Coll. Tech. (Eng.) 1979; m. Iris Sandra Sterling, Oct. 27, 1962; 1 son, Keith Alan. Policy change supr. Central Standard Life Ins. Co., Chgo., 1946-61; ac- tuarial asst. Harry S. Tressel & Assos., Chgo., 1961-65; ind. writer, columnist, researcher, Chgo., 1965-71; owner RC Research Co., also Jackpot Jubilee, Chgo., 1970-72, Dayton, Wash., 1972-75, Research Unltd., Dayton, 1975-85, Intellex, Dayton, 1976-85, Service Unltd., Dayton, 1976-85; corporate identity cons., 1967-85; co- owner Crossword Cash, 1970-85; ordained minister Universal Life Ch., Modesto, Calif., 1976; founder, pres. Divine Immortality Ch., Dayton, 1978-85; loan broker 1980-85; pres. Myriagon, Inc., 1983-85. Mem. Life Of- fice Mgmt. Assn. Inst., Word Guild, Mensa, Nat. Puz- zlers League. Author: Language on Vacation, 1965; Beyond Language, 1967; Curious Crosswords, 1970. Founding editor, contbr. Word Ways, 1968-85; columnist Books, 1966, Puzzle Lovers Newspaper, 1968- 71, Chgo. Tribune Mag., 1973-74, Games Mag., 1979- 80. Home: Dayton, Wash. Died Dec. 7, 1985.

BORKLAND, ERNEST WALDERMAR, JR., investment banker; b. Hartford, Conn., June 20, 1905; s. Ernest W. and Alma W. (Ericson) B.; m. Caroline Whidbee Powell, Aug. 22, 1937; 1 dau., Barbara Legh Borkland Uzielli. BS, U. Pa., 1929; grad. Wharton Sch. Fin. and Commerce, 1929. With Dillon Read & Co., N.Y.C., 1929-31, J&W Seligman & Co., 1931-37; with Tucker, Anthony and R.L. Day, N.Y.C., from 1937,

ptnr., from 1949. Mem. University, Recess clubs. Home: New York N.Y. Died Apr. 9, 1986.

BORNE, MORTIMER, artist; b. Rypin, Poland, Dec. 31, 1902; came to U.S., 1916, naturalized, 1921; s. Harry and Lena (Warshaw) B.; m. Rachel Zipes, Feb. 28, 1929. Student schs. U.S. and abroad. lectr. Sweet Briar Coll., 1945; lectr. art New Sch. Social Research, N.Y.C., 1945-67. Exhibited major graphic exhbns., 1926-87, in- cluding, Brit. Mus., London, 1980; one-man shows, New Gallery, Jerusalem, 1935, Internat. Coll., Springfield, Mass., 1940, Cedar Rapids (Iowa) Art Assn., 1940, Corcoran Gallery of Art, Washington, 1941, Mus. Fine Arts, Montreal, Can., 1942, Grand Central Art Gal- leries, N.Y.C., 1943, Smithsonian Instn., Washington, 1944, Currier Gallery, Manchester, 1945, Connoisseur Gallery, N.Y.C., 1959, Tel-Aviv, 1965, Tappan Zee Art Center, Nyack, N.Y., 1962, 69, Shulamit Gallery, Tel Aviv, 1980, N.Y. Hist. Soc. Mus., 1980; Author: The Visual Bible: Ninety-two Drawings, 1976, Meet Moses: 54 Drawings, 1978, Drypoints, Etchings, Color Dry- points, 88 Reproductions, 1980; also articles on art; works reproduced various mags., newspapers; represented in permanent collections, Mus. Modern Art, Library of Congress, Nat. Mus., Smithsonian Inst., N.Y. Public Library, Rosenwald Collection, (100 etchings and drypoints) Met. Mus. Art, N.Y.C., U. Judaism, Los Angeles, Brit. Mus., Israel Mus., Jerusalem, Tel Aviv Mus., Boston Public Library, Bklyn. Mus., Phila. Mus. Art, Nat. Gallery Art, Washington, Mus. Fine Arts, Houston, Victoria and Albert Mus., London, Boymans Mus., Rotterdam, Wadsworth Atheneum, N.Y. Hist. Soc., Detroit Inst. Art, San Francisco Mus., Boston Mus. Fine Arts, Fogg Art Mus., Fort Lauderdale Mus., N.Y. Pub. Library, Herbert F. Johnson Mus., Ithaca, N.Y., Family of Peoples (chromatic wood sculpture), Mcpl. Mus., Ramat-gan, Israel, Birmingham Mus. Art, High Mus. Art, Milw. Art Mus., Portland Art Mus., Dallas Mus. Fine Arts, St. Louis Art Mus., Ga. Mus. Art, Santa Barbara Mus. Art, New Britain Mus. Am. Art, Minn. Mus., Nat. Mus. History and Tech., Everson Mus. Art, Jewish Mus. Recipient J. Frederick Talcott prize Soc. Am. Etchers 1939, Noyes prize for best print Soc. Am. Etchers 28th Ann. Exhbn., 1943. Home: Nyack N.Y. Died Oct. 17, 1987.

BORWELL, ROBERT CRANE, insurance executive; b. Oak Park, Ill., May 4, 1902; s. Francis J.C. and Elizabeth Mary (Carne) B.; m. Mary Emma Vette, June 24, 1931; children: Robert Carne, Elsie V. Borwell Revenaugh; m. Naomi Borwell. BS, Dartmouth U., 1925. With Marsh & McLennan, Inc., Chgo., 1927-67, v.p., 1941-59, sr. v.p., 1959-67, also bd. dirs.; dir. chmn. exec. com. First United Fin. Services (5 bank holding co.), from 1967; bd. dirs. Stanray Corp. Trustee, exec. com. Presbyn.-St. Luke's Hosp., donor to hosp. Robert C. Borwell Chair for Multiple Sclerosis Rsch.; trustee Union League Found. Boys Clubs; donor rsch. bldg. Dartmouth Med. Sch. Mem. Execs. Club (bd. dirs.), Chgo. Club., Chgo. Yacht Club, Union League Club, Univ. Club (Chgo.), Economic Club (Chgo.), Univ. Club (Milw.), Oak Park Country Club, Crown Colony Club (Bahamas), Crystal Downs Country Club, Crystal Lake Yacht Club (Frankfort, Mich.). Episcopalian. Home: Oak Park Ill. and: Frankfort Mich. Died Feb. 25, 1989.

BOSS, EDWIN AUGUST, hotel executive; b. Bismark, Mo., Mar. 21, 1891; s. August Daniel and Sophia (Seitz) B.; m. Ethel Hartman, June 5, 1919; children: Donald A., Betty Louise, Reilly John. Ed. pub. schs. Pres. Boss Hotels. Sgt. U.S. Army, World War I. Mem. Am. Hotel Assn., Iowa Hotel Assn., Rotary. Home: Des Moines Iowa. †

BOSTON, ORLAN WILLIAM, educator, consultant; b. Nashville, Mich., July 16, 1891; s. William and Adaline (Vinkle) B.; m. Stella R. Roth, Aug. 27, 1916; 1 son, Filbert Roth. BSME, U. Mich., 1914, MSE, 1917. Registered mech. engr. Instr. in engring. U. Mich., 1914-17; indsl. engr. Cleve. Tractor Co., 1919-21; asst. prof. engring. shop U. Mich. 1921-23, assoc. prof. and acting dir., 1923-25, prof. and chmn. dept. metal processing, 1926-51, prof. mech. engring. and prodn. engring., chmn. dept. prodn. engring., 1951-56; cus- todian of Detroit Ordnance Gage Lab., U. Mich., 1936- 56; prof. emeritus mech. and prodn. engring. Detroit Ordnance Gage Lab., from 1956; ednl. supervision ordnance inspection, aircraft inspection, and ordnance inspection, aircraft inspection, and ordnance engring. aides courses, 1941-44. Adviser to Nat. Acad. Scis., Materials Adv. Bd., on development mfg. processes for aircraft materials. Author 7 books before 1950; Metal Processing, 1951; editor and prin. author ASME manual on Cutting of Metals, 1953; author over 300 sci. papers. Served as lt. (j.g.) Ordnance Dept., USN, 1917-19 (designed submarine mines). Recipient Worcester Reed Warner gold medal ASME, 1950, Blackall award, 1956; gold medal Am. Soc. Tool Engrs., 1955. Mich. fellow ASME (chmn. research com. on metal processing 1952); mem. Am. Soc. Metals, Am. Soc. Engring. Edn., Am. Soc. Tool Engrs., Am. Ordnance Assn. (life), Engring. Soc. Detroit, Sigma Xi, Sigma Rho Tau, Phi Kappa Phi, Pi Tau Sigma (hon.), Vulcans (hon.), Alumni, Union, Research clubs. Home: Ann Arbor Mich. †

BOSWELL, ELMER E., hotel executive; b. Canton, Ill., Feb. 2, 1891; s. Charles and Cora Alice (MacElwee) B.; m. Juanita L. Querry, Mar. 2, 1916; children:

Barbara Boswell Lynch, Frances Boswell Willcox. Bell boy, advancing through various positions Sheraton Corp. Am.., Boston, to 1943, v.p. in charge all hotel ops., gen. mgr., from 1943; exec. v.p., gen. mgr. Sheraton Hotels Ltd., Montreal, Can., from 1952; v.p. or v.p. and dir. 14 subs. Sheraton Hotels Corp. Mem. Am. Hotel Assn., Masons (Shriner). Home: Weston Mass. †

BOSWELL, GUY THOMAS, psychology educator; b. Lincoln, Nebr., Jan. 21, 1891; s. William Mann and Malissa Mary (Harritt) B.; m. Eva May Stuckey, 1917; children: Margaret Mary, John Thomas. AB, York Coll., 1913, LLD, 1946; AM, U. Chgo., 1916, PhD, 1926; LLD, U. Nebr., 1948. Instr. edn. York Coll., 1916-18; asst. prof. ednl. psychology Hamline U., St. Paul, 1919-20; asst. prof. ednl. psychology U. Chgo., 1920-23, assoc. prof., 1924-26, prof., 1927-49; prof. ednl. psychology U. Calif., Berkeley, 1949-58, then prof. emeritus; spl. asst. to dean Sch. Edn., U. Calif., 1963-64; vis. prof. Johns Hopkins U., 1958; exec. sec. Am. Ednl. Research Assn., 1960-62. Recipient citation for research on reading Internat. Reading Assn., 1963. Author several monographs including: Non-Oral Reading, 1945; Patterns of Thinking in Solving Problems, 1956. Mem. Am. Psychol. Assn. (pres. div. ednl. psychology 1954), Ednl. Research Assn. (pres. 1953), Soc. Coll. Tchrs. Edn., Phi Beta Kappa, Phi Delta Kappa. Congregationalist. Home: Berkeley Calif. †

BOUDLEAUX, BRYANT, songwriter; b. Shellman, Ga., Feb. 13, 1920; m. Felice Scaduto; children: Del, Dane. Musician with Atlanta Philharm., various jazz group, songwriter, 1949-87. Songs written include: (with Felice Bryant) Country Boy, Hey Joe, I've Been Thinking, The Richest Man, Bye Bye Love, Wake Up Litte Susie, Problems, Bird Dog, All I Have to Do is Dream, Poor Jenny, Take a Message to Mary, Let's Think About Living, Mexico, Baltimore, Come Live With Me, Rocky Top (named official Tenn. state song in 1981). Home: Nashville Tenn. Died June 25, 1987.

BOUDREAU, JAMES CLAYTON, artist; b. Framingham, Mass., Dec. 25, 1891; s. Louis Calbert and Ada Augusta (Houghton) B.; m. Helen Lucille Cronenwett, Apr. 11, 1922; 1 child, Rene Leon; m. Margaret Bennett Stephenson, Dec. 12, 1956. Grad., Mass. Normal Art Sch., Boston, 1913; BS, Mass. Sch. Art, 1945; DFA, Pratt Inst., 1956; student, Columbia U., U. Pitts, Alfred U. Lic. comml. pilot. Art tchr. Pitts Acad., 1913-16, U. Pitts., 1916-17, Schenley High Sch., Pitts., 1919-20, Carnegie Inst. Tech., Pitts., summers 1925, 26, Extension div. Pa. State Coll., 1925-28; dir. art Pitts. Pub. Schs., 1920-28; dean Art Sch. Pratt Inst., Bklyn., 1928-56; lectr. on fine and applied arts; painter, lithographer; lectr. Gulf Coast Art Ctr., Belleair, Fla. Author: (brochure) (with Harriet Cantrall) Art in Daily Activities, 1929, (with Florence Fitch and Elmer Stephan) Inspirational Art (series 8 elem. art textbooks), 1932, History of Base No. 17, Coastal Air Patrol, 1943. Lt. USAAF, 1918-19; maj. Coastal Air Patrol, 1941-46, pilot active duty, 1942-43. Benjamin Franklin fellow Royal Soc. Arts, 1960. Mem. NEA, Eastern Art Assn., Western Art Assn., Am. Fedn. Art, Art Dirs. Club, Soc. Illustrators, Am. Legion, Royal Soc. Arts London, Coop. Club (life), Aero Club (Pitts.), Q-B's (N.Y.), Phi Delta Kappa. Home: Belleair Fla. †

BOUGHTON, WALTER LEROY, theater educator; b. Toledo, Dec. 27, 1918; s. Solon James and Theodora Ferguson (Prince) B.; m. Georgia Dagmar Aune, June 9, 1950; 3 sons. A.B., Brown U., 1941, M.A., 1949, M.F.A., 1951. Instr. speech and drama English dept. Brown U., Providence, R.I., 1947-49; Fulbright scholar Shakespeare Inst., Straford, Eng., 1951-52; chmn. drama dept. Ripon Coll., Wis., 1953-56; vis. dir. theater U. Calif-Berkeley, 1956-57; dir. Kirby Meml. Theater Amherst Coll., Mass., 1957-88; chmn. dept. dramatic arts Amherst Coll., 1957-58; dir. Keuka Coll. Summer Theater, 1950-53, Casino Theater, Holyoke, Mass., summer 1960; producer, dir. Weston Playhouse, Vt., from 1972; actor summer stock, from 1950; actor in film supporting role Universal Studios, 1969. Served to capt. USAAF, 1941-46. Mem. Amherst Edn. Assn.; chmn. summer theater project (1959-61); mem. Am. Theater Assn., Am. Nat. Theater Assn. Home: Amherst Mass. Died Jan. 13, 1988; buried Amherst, Mass.

BOURNE, GEOFFREY HOWARD, anatomist, primatologist, medical school administrator; b. Perth, Western Australia, Nov. 17, 1909; came to U.S., 1957, naturalized, 1962; s. Walter Howard and Ann (Mellon) B.; m. Maria Nelly Golarz, Oct. 31, 1964; children by previous marriage: Peter, Merfyn. B.Sc., U. Western Australia, 1930, B.Sc. with honors, 1931, M.Sc., 1932, D.Sc., 1935; D.Phil., U. Oxford, Eng., 1943. Biologist Australian Inst. Anatomy, Canberra, 1934-35; biochemist Australian Advisory Council on Nutrition, 1936-37; demonstrator in physiology U. Oxford, 1941-47; reader in histology U. London, 1947-57; chmn. anatomy Emory U., 1957-62; dir. Yerkes Regional Primate Research Center, 1962-78; vice chancellor St. Georges U. Sch. Medicine, Grenada, W.I., 1978-88; cons. Sch. Aerospace Medicine, 1964-88. Author: books, including Starvation in Europe, 1943, Biochemistry and Physiology of Bone, 1956, Structure and Function of Muscle, 1962, Division of Labour in Cells, 1962, Structure and Function of Nervous Tissue, 1969, Ape People, 1970, Primate Odyssey, 1974, The Gentle Giants: The Gorilla Story, 1975; contbr. numerous articles to profl. publs.; editor: Cytology and Cell Physiology, 1941; founder, editor-in-chief Internat. Rev. Cytology, 1952—, World Review of Nutrition and Dietetics, 1962—. Beit Meml. Research fellow, 1939-41; Mackenzie Mackinnon Research fellow, 1941-43. Fellow Royal Soc. Medicine, Gerontology Soc., Zool. Soc. London, Inst. Biology; mem. nat. socs. U.S., U. K., gerontol. socs. U.S., U.K., Am. Rocket Soc., Aerospace Med. Assn., Internat. Primatology Soc., Internat. Soc. Cell Biology. Home: Atlanta Ga. Died July 19, 1988.

BOUTELL, CLARENCE BURLEY (CLIP), editor, columnist; b. Washington, Feb. 8, 1908; s. Roger Sherman Gates and Avis (Burley) B.; m. Helen Paulsen, May 25, 1935; children: Patricia Carley (Mrs. S. W. G. Denlinger), William Burley, Christine Blodgett (Mrs. Ed R. Raynor III). Student, Stanford U., 1926-27. Advt. mgr. Alfred A. Knopf, 1930-32; promtion mgr. Saturday Rev. Lit., 1933-37; advt. and publicity mgr. G.P. Putnam Sons, Coward-McCann and John Day, 1937-43; author syndicated lit. column Authors Are Like People N.Y. Post, other newspapers, 1943-47; editor Fiction Book Club, 1947-48; copy chief Denhard & Stewart, 1953-55, Christian Herald, 1955-65, Famous Writers Sch., Westport, Conn., 1965-67. Author: The Fat Baron, 1946; co-editor: Speak of the Devil, 1945; contbr. articles to mags. Original organizer, 1st chmn. Coun. on Books in Wartime. Home: Georgetown Conn. Died July 29, 1981.

BOW, KATHY O'CONNOR, public relations consultant; b. Dayton, Ohio, Oct. 2, 1948; d. Grover William and Laura Louise (Storm) O'C.; m. Stephen T. Bow, July 2, 1982; children: Jarod William, Jonathan Stephen. Student, Miami U. Newscaster Sta. WING-Radio, Dayton, 1970-76, Sta. WDTN-TV, Dayton, 1976-79; owner, v.p., dir. Kathy O's, Kettering, Ohio, 1978-80; pub. relations rep. Am. Income Life, Waco, Tex., 1980-82; pvt. practice cons. San Francisco, from 1983; mgr. staff Reagan-Bush 84, San Francisco. Contbr. med. related articles to Kettering Mag., 1981. Campaign or pub. relations mgr. 16 polit. campaigns, Dayton, 1970-83; chmn. Citizens for Am., San Francisco, 1986. Home: San Rafael Calif. Deceased.

BOWDEN, BURNHAM, business executive; b. Melrose, Mass., Sept. 22, 1900; s. Frederick Prescott and Mary Eunice Lord (Burnham) B.; m. Margaret Loughridge Cornelison, July 24, 1929; children: Mary Alice Bowden Lyman, Elizabeth Forsyth Bowden Freimer, Burnham, Margaret Loughridge Bowden Murray. AB, Harvard U., 1922, MBA, 1923. with Lord & Burnham Co., 1923-85, v.p., 1927-85, Burnham Boiler Corp., 1932, pres., 1933-85, Burnham Corp. (consolidation Lord & Burnham Co., Burnham Boiler Corp.), 1933-69, 72, chmn. bd., 1969-85; treas. J.C. Turner Lumber Co. (now Turner Corp.), 1933-65, v.p., 1933-69, dir., 1921-81, chmn. bd., 1970-81; mem. Mid-Atlantic adv. bd. Arkwright-Boston Mut. Ins. Co., 1961-76; dir. Felters Co. Mem. N.Y. Florists, Harvard Bus. Sch., Appalachian Mountain Club, Corinthians, Huguenot Yacht Club. Republican. Unitarian. Home: Irvington N.Y. Died May 24, 1985; buried Sleepy Hollow Cemetery, Tarrytown, N.Y.

BOWDERN, THOMAS STEPHEN, education educator; b. St. Louis, Nov. 3, 1892; s. Thomas Stephen and Ellen (Hardy) B. AB, St. Louis U., 1915, AM, 1917, PhD, 1936. Joined Soc. Jesus, 1910, ordained priest Roman Cath. Ch., 1924. Tchr. classics, librarian St. Ignatius High Sch., Chgo., 1917-21; instr. history Loyola U., Chgo., 1921-22; instr. edn. St. Louis U., 1923-24, asst. prof., acting dir. dept. edn., 1927-28, acting dean Sch. Edn., 1927-28, regent Jr. Corp. Colls. of univ., 1927-28, asst. supr. student tchrs. and grad. students, 1928-31, prof. edn., 1955-57; dean Grad. Sch., Univ. Coll. and summer session Creighton U., 1931-43, prof. edn., 1931-43, 1951-55, pres., 1943-46; assoc. dir. Inst. Social Order, 1946-47; dir. dept. social edn. and summer sch., also assoc. editor The Queen's Work and Action Now Cath. Action of Sodality of Our Lady, 1947-51; prof. edn. Rockhurst Coll., Kansa City, Mo., from 1957. Contbr. articles to profl. and religious publs. Mem. commn. on religious orgns., NCCJ, from 1951; chmn. editorial com. Nebr. High Sch. Improvement Com.; mem. High Sch. Work Council of Nebr., Nat. Youth Authority, 1940-41, mem. Coll. Work Council, 1941-43; ednl. adviser Omaha Deanery, Nat. Council Cath. Women. Mem. Kansas City Soc. Theol. Studies (v.p. 1963-64), Philosophy of Edn. Soc., History Edn. Soc., Jesuit Edn. Assn., Nat. Cath. Edn. Assn., Nebr. State Tchrs. Assn., Nebr. Assn. Ch. Colls. (past v.p.), Nat. Conf. Church-related Colls. (past chmn. West Cen. area), Omaha Adult Edn. Council (past pres.), Nebr. Council Adult Edn. (commr.). Home: Kansas City Mo. †

BOWEN, CHARLES CORBIN, management consultant, accountant; b. Monson, Calif., May 20, 1897; s. William Lee and Serepta Jane (Wicker) B.; m. Mildred Virginia Moore, Feb. 5, 1928; 1 dau., Jane. BS, U. Calif., 1921; MBA, Harvard U., 1923. econ. statistician USDA, spl. assignments Europe and Asia, 1923-24; expert mgr. Sun Maid Raisin Growers, Fresno, Calif., 1924-25; head research dept. Tucker, Hunter, Dulin & Co., Los Angeles, 1926-28; chief Calif. Bur. Commerce, Sacramento, 1929-30; v.p., dir. Am. Trust Co., affiliates, San Francisco, 1931-33; exec. v.p. Bishop Trust Co Honolulu, 1935-37; asst. to dir. RFC, Washingto 1934; C.P.A., mgmt. cons. Charles C. Bowen & Co., Sa Francisco, 1938-87; exec. v.p., dir. Empire Factors, Sa Francisco; pres., dir. Pacific Assocs., Inc., Sa Francisco, Portland Transit Co.; pres., treas., d Landport Co., Inc., Portland, Oreg.; pres., treas., d Rose City Transit Co., Portland, 1956-87; civilian e pert, cons. U.S. Army Engrs. and Q.M. Corps, 1942-4 mem. U.S. Senatorial Adv. Bd., 1980-87. Contbr. a ticles to profl. jours. Ordnance officer AEF, U.S. Arm 1918-19. Mem. Am. Pub. Transit Assn. (dir., pa pres.), SAR, Am. Inst. C.P.A.'s, Calif. Soc. C.P.A. Olympic Club, Merchants Exchange Club, Californ Club, Arlington Club, Multnomah, Harvard Clu Capitol Hill Club, Mason, Phi Sigma Kappa, Be Alpha Psi, Alpha Kappa Psi. Republican. Home: Sa Francisco Calif. Died Oct. 23, 1987; buried Golden Ga National Cemetery, San Bruno, Calif.

BOWLES, CHESTER, government official; Springfield, Mass., Apr. 5, 1901; s. Charles Allen ar Nellie (Harris) B.; m. Dorothy Stebbins, Feb. 22, 193 children: Barbara, Chester Jr., Cynthia, Sal Samuel. Student, Choate Sch., 1919; BS, Yale U., 192 LLD, 1968; LLD, Howard U., 1955, Oberlin Co 1957, R.I. U., 1958, U. Mich., 1961, Bard Coll., 19 Davidson Coll., 1972. with Springfield Rep., 1924-2 George Batten Co., 1925-29; established Benton Bowles, Inc., N.Y.C., 1929, chmn. bd., 1936-41; tioning adminstr. State of Conn., 1942; Conn. dir. OP 1942-43, gen. mgr., Washington, 1943; price adminst 1943-46; chmn., dir. Econ. Stblzn. Bd., 1946; me WPB and Petroleum Council for War, 1943-46; spl. as to sec. gen. UN, 1947-48; gov. Conn., 1949-51; amba sador to India and Nepal, 1951-53; Shaw lectr. Br Mawr Coll., 1953-54; Berkeley lectr. U. Calif., 19 Godkin lectr. Harvard, 1956; Chubb lectr. Yale, 195 mem. 88th U.S. Congress from 2d Dist. of Conn.; fg policy adv. to Pres. Kennedy, 1959-60; under sec. state, 1961; Pre.'s spl. rep. for Asian, African and Lat Am. affairs, 1961; ambassador to India, 1963-69 Author: Tomorrow Without Fear, 1946, Ambassado Report, 1954, The New Dimensions of Peace, 19 American Politics in a Revolutionary World, 19 Africa's Challenge to America, 1956, Ideas, People, a Peace, 1958, The Coming Political Breakthrough, 19 The Conscience of a Liberal, 1962, The Makings of Just Society, 1963, A View from New Delhi, 19 Promises to Keep--My Years in Public Life, 1971, M sion To India, 1974. Am. del. UNESCO Conf., Par 1946; mem. nat. commn. for UNESCO, 1946-47; Co del. Democratic Nat. Conv., 1940, 48, 56; Conn. elec for Franklin D. Roosevelt, 1940; platform chmn. De Nat. Conv., 1960; bd. dirs. Franklin D. Roosev Found., Eleanor Roosevelt Meml. Found., Woodr Wilson Found.; chmn. adv. com. Yale Center For Ec Growth, Rockefeller Found. Mem. Asia Soc., Co Grange, Essex Yacht Club, Cruising Club of Am Home: Essex Conn. Died May 25, 1986.

BOWLES, LUANNA JANE, educator; b. Nor Branch, Kans., Sept. 18, 1892; d. Levi and Hann Elizabeth (Mendenhall) Bowles. AB, Penn Coll., O kaloosa, Iowa, 1923; AM, Peabody Coll. Tchrs., 193 grad. student, Am. U., also Columbia; LHD (hon William Penn Coll., 1964. Tchr. history Westtown Sc Pa., 1923-27; tchr. English, Friends Girls Sch., Tok 1927-28; exec. sec. to pres., dir. publicity Fisk U., 19 41; assoc. editor-writer U.S. Office Edn., Washingto 1942-46; advisor sec. edn. Ministry Edn., Tokyo, 194 50; advisor tchr. edn. and fundamental edn. Ministry Edn. in Iran, U.S. Ops. Mission, Tehran, 1952-59; a visor Ministry Edn., U.S. Agy. for Internat. Deve Nepal, 1959-64; consultant ednl. materials AID, Was ington, from 1964. Author: The Story of Music at Fi University, 1938; Off to Japan—Lessons for Interme ates, 1950; also articles on edn. Trustee S.E. Settleme House, Washington, 1944-45. Disting. Pub. Servi award AID, 1963. Home: Washington D.C. †

BOYCE, CARROLL WILSON, editor, transportati consultant; b. Montclair, N.J., Dec. 20, 1923; Benjamin Knowlton and Gladys (Wilson) B.; m. Je Corrin Compton, June 15, 1946; children: Dav Compton, Barbara Ann (dec. 1953), Linda Corri Wilson Keith. B.S. in Bus. and Engring. Adminstr MIT, 1946. Editorial asst. to mng. editor Factory ma 1946-58; editor-in-chief Fleet Owner mag., McGra Hill, Inc., N.Y.C., 1959-69, 73-77; emeritus Fleet Own mag., McGraw-Hill, Inc., 1977-87; dir. truck div. Mot Vehicle Mfrs. Assn., Washington, 1969-73; editor-i chief Trucks 26-Plus mag., McGraw-Hill, Inc., N.Y. 1977-79; pres. Transp. Forecasts & Planning, Inc., 197 82, Abney Graphics, Inc., North Ft. Myers, Fla., 19 asso. pub. Milner Assos., North Ft. Myers, 1981; co to adminstr. Def. Prodn. Adminstrn., Washington, 19 vis. lectr. MIT, 1950-51; chmn. motor transp. conf. N Safety Council, 1969-70, chmn. pub. info. conf., 1973-7 bd. dirs., 1963-79, hon. life mem., 1979-87. Autho How to Plan Pensions, 1950, Materials Handli Casebook, 1951; contbr. numerous articles to perio cals. Recipient Pub. Service to Safety award Nat. Safe Council, 1963, 64, 65; Jesse H. Neal award for ou standing bus. journalism, 1957, 65, 67; Golden Knig award Internat. Assn. State and Provincial Safe Coordinators, 1965; Uniroyal Hwy. Safety Journalis award, 1975. Mem. Am. Bus. Press (chmn. editor

/. 1967-68), Soc. Automotive Engrs., ASME, Regular ommon Carrier Conf. (maintenance com. 1975-79), stern Bus Maintenance Men's Conf., Philatelic und., Royal, Am., Gt. Britain philatelic socs., Soc. ilatelic Americans, Brit. Philatelic Fedn., Nat. Press ub, Met. Ft. Myers C. of C. (com. on area devel. 80-82). Presbyterian. Club: Collectors (N.Y.C.). me: North Fort Myers Fla. Died Dec. 10, 1987.

)YCE, EARNEST, civil and sanitary engineer; b. interset, Iowa, July 11, 1892; s. Marcus James and race (Smith) B.; m. Elsie Jane Green, Sept. 21, 1919; 1 n, James Earnest. B.S., Iowa State Coll., 1917, C.E., 30; M.S.E., Harvard U., 1932. Diplomate Am. Acad. n. Engrs. Mem. staff sch. engring. U. Kans., 1920-41; . div. sanitation, chief engr. Kans. State Bd. Health, 24-41; chief sanitation facilities sect., san. engring. div. SPHS, Washington, 1941-44; prof. municipal and san. gring., coll. engring., prof. pub. health engring., sch. b. health U. Mich., 1944-61, chmn. dept. civil engr- ., 1947-61; cons. san. and pub. health engr. from 61; Mem. Pub. Health Planning Team, Germany, y-Aug. 1951; mem. WHO vis. team, Indonesia, Apr.- ay 1953; san. engring. cons. WHO, Western Pacific gion, from 1958, ICA, India and Pakistan, 1960; cons. Pan Am. Health Orgn. in Latin Am., and WHO, neva, 1962-67. Contbr. to tech. jours. Served to ot. U.S. Army, World War I, AEF. Recipient Charles vin Emerson medal Water Pollution Control Fedn., 57; Marston gold medal Iowa State U. Coll. Engring., 77. Fellow ASCE (hon. mem.); mem. Water Pollution ntrol Fedn. (Gordon M. Fair award 1976, hon., past s.), Am. Pub. Health Assn. (v.p. 1961-62), Am. ater Works Assn. (life), Am. Soc. Engring. Edn. (life), gring. Soc. Detroit (pres. 1956), Am. Pub. Works sn., Mich. Engring. Soc. (hon.), Sigma Xi, Phi Kappa i, Delta Omega, Tau Beta Pi, Chi Epsilon. esbyterian. Club: Rotary (Paul Harris fellow). Home: n Arbor Mich. Deceased.

)YCE, FRANK GORDON, educator; b. Binghamton, Y., Apr. 8, 1917; s. Clarence and Ethel (Wilcox) B.; Joan A. Sweet, Sept. 5, 1941; children: Frank ordon, Jonathan (dec.), Johanna. A.B., Colgate U., 39, A.M., 1948; LL.D. (hon.), Middlebury Coll., 52, Cornell Coll., Mt. Vernon, Iowa, 1966; L.H.D. n.), Elmira Coll., 1962; LL.D. (hon.), Colgate U., 36. Reporter, feature writer Binghamton Sun, 1939- asst. to pres. Colgate U., 1946-50; pres. (Expt. in ernat. Living), Brattleboro, Vt., 1950-74; pres. emer- s (Expt. in Internat. Living), 1974-87; sec. gen. (In- nat. Expt.), 1956-72; exec. dir. Vt. Fedn. Ind. Colls., 76-83; dir. internat. programs Nathaniel Hawthorne ll., 1976-79; internat. counselor Nasson Coll., ingvale, Maine., Green Mountain Coll., 1983-87; first div. pvt. and internat. orgns. Peace Corps, 1961; m. ad hoc com. to advise gov. and legislature on el. Coll. V.I., 1961; pres. (Council Student Travel), 51-55; mem. U.S. commn. for UNESCO, 1965-70. ustee Colgate U., 1963-69, Coll. V.I., 1962-74; bd. s. Colgate U. Alumni Corp., 1957-62, pres., 1969-71, mem., 1973-87. Served to lt. USNR, 1941-45. corated officer's cross Order Merit (Fed. Republic rmany); Legion de O'Higgins award Chile, 1968; ipient The Experiment citation, 1970; Order of the red Treasure Japan, 1972. Mem. Delta Phi Alpha, pha Tau Omega. Congregationalist. Home: West attleboro Vt. Died Dec. 9, 1987; buried Meeting use Hill Cemetery, Brattleboro, Vt.

YD, ALAN WILSON, lawyer; b. Indpls., Mar. 11, 97; s. John Anderson and Mabel (Conduitt) B.; m. rothy Lee, Oct. 24, 1923; children: Alan C., Thomas AB, U. Mich., 1918, JD, 1921. Bar: Ind. 1921, U.S. preme Ct. 1934. Practiced in Indpls. 1921—; mem. n Noel, Hickam & Boyd, 1923-26, Noel, Hickam, yd & Armstrong, 1926-40, Barnes, Hickam, Pantzer Boyd, 1940—; mem. Indpls. Bd. Sch. Commrs., 1935- pres., 1937; mem. Ind. Bd. Bar Examiners, 1937-42. th USMC, 1918-19. Mem. ABA, Ind. Bar Assn., pls. Bar Assn. (pres. 1948), Am. Judicare Soc., Am. w Inst., Bar Assn. 7th Fed. Cir., Ind. Soc. Chgo., der of Coif, Woodstock, Indpls. Athletic Club, Con- porary Club, Lawyers Club, University Club, son, Delta Upsilon, Phi Delta Phi. Home: Indi- polis Ind. Deceased.

YD, CHESTER EUGENE, retail company execu- ; b. Gaylord, Kans., Dec. 4, 1924; s. Roy and Ella tilda (Mattson) B.; m. Betty Jayne Berg, June 10, 0; children: Linda, Gary, Ronald, James, thy. BS, U. Nebr., 1949. With S.S. Kresge Co. (K rt Corp.), 1949-87, v.p. auto div., 1968-72, gen. v.p. rnat. hdqrs., 1972-78; chmn. bd., chief exec. officer Mart Enterprises Inc., Troy, Mich., 1978-87. With S, 1943-46. Mem. Am. Legion, Elks. Republican. me: Troy Mich. Died Dec. 1987.

YD, DREXELL ALLEN, dentist, educator; b. rshfield, Mo., Apr. 1, 1910; s. John Barnes and ble (Allen) B.; m. Jean Boesinger, July 24, 9. Student, DePauw U., 1928-29; D.D.S., Ind. U., 4; postgrad. tng., Forsyth Infirmary, Boston, 1935, Iowa Hosp., 1936. Faculty Ind. U., Indpls., 1937-87; oc. prof. pedodontics, dir. dept. Ind. U., 1937-48, f. operative dentistry, 1948-87; in dentistry practice pls., 1940-48; Vis. prof. dentistry U. Rio de Janeiro, 1. Fellow Am. Coll. Dentistry; mem. Internat. Assn. Dental Research, Beta Theta Pi, Delta Sigma Delta. Democrat. Club: Mason. Home: Indianapolis Ind. Died Nov. 15, 1987.

BOYD, JAMES, consulting geologist; b. Kanowna, West Australia, Dec. 20, 1904; s. Julian and Mary (Innes) Cane B.; m. Ruth Ragland Brown, Aug. 17, 1932 (dec. 1979); children: James Brown, Harry Bruce, Douglas Cane, Hudson; m. Clemence De Graw Jandray, 1980. B.S., Calif. Inst. Tech., 1927; M.Sc., Colo. Sch. Mines, 1932, D.Sc., 1934. Instr. geology Colo. Sch. Mines, Golden, 1929-34; asst. prof. mineralogy Colo. Sch. Mines, 1934-37, assoc. prof. econ. geology, 1938-41, dean faculty, 1946-47; asst. to sec. interior chmn. interdeptl. com. (Resources for Marshall Plan), 1947; dir. Bur. Mines, 1947-51, Def. Minerals Adminstrn., 1950-51; exploration mgr. Kennecott Copper Corp., 1951-55, v.p. exploration, 1955-60; pres. Copper Range Co., 1960-70, chmn. bd. dirs., 1970-71; exec. dir. Nat. Commn. on Materials Policy, Washington, 1971-73; pres. Materials Assos., 1974-78; geologist U.S. Geol. Survey, 1933-34; cons. geology, mining and geophysics, 1935-40; pres., gen. mgr. Goldcrest Mining Co., 1939-40; dir. engrs. Joint Council and United Engring.; Trustees, 1969-71; chmn. com. on mineral research NSF, 1952-57; vice chmn. Engrs. Commn. on Air Resources, 1970-71; chmn. sec. interior's adv. com. on non-coal mine safety, 1971-74; chmn. materials com. Office Tech. Assessment, 1974-79; mem. nat. materials adv. bd. NRC, 1975-77, mem. mineral and energy resources bd., 1977-80, mem. mineral resources bd., 1973-75, chmn. com. on surface mining and reclamation, 1978-79; mem. tech. adv. com. Office of Nuclear Waste Isolation, 1979-82, engring. rev. group, 1983-87 Bd. dirs. Watergate S. Corp., 1972-79, pres., 1976-77. First reader Carmel Christian Sci. Ch., 1983-85. Served from capt. to col. AUS, 1941-46. Decorated Legion of Merit with oak leaf cluster; recipient Distinquished Service medal Colo. Sch. Mines, 1949; Distinguished Alumni award Calif. Inst. Tech., 1967; Hoover medal, 1975. Mem. Mining and Metall. Soc. Am. (pres. 1960-63), Am. Inst. Mining Engrs. (Rand gold medal 1963, pres. 1969), Nat. Acad. Engring., Am. Soc. Econ. Geologists, Geol. Soc. Am., Am. Inst. Profl. Geologists (Parker Meml. medal 1973, v.p. 1965-66), Australasia Inst. Mining and Metallurgy (hon.), Acad. Polit. Sci. Clubs: Cosmos (Washington). Died Nov. 24, 1987, buried Estes Park, Colo.

BOYD, MARK FREDERICK, malariologist; b. St. Paul, Minn., May 21, 1889; s. William Samuel and Maria (Moench) B.; m. Bertha Beard, Jan. 8, 1913 (dec. Sept. 1963); children: Jean Beard (Mrs. George Winchester), Mary Elizabeth (Mrs. Edgar Krause), Ruth Dorothea (Mrs. John A. Henderson); m. 2d, Nancy Ruth Harris, Apr. 24, 1965. MD, State U. Iowa, 1911, MS, 1913, cert. of accomplishment, 1947; Cert. of Pub. Health, Harvard U. and MIT, 1914; MPH, Harvard U., 1947; ScD (hon.), Fla. State U., 1950. Instr. in pathology and bacteriology State U. Iowa, 1911-12; health officer Oskaloosa, Iowa, 1912-13; C. F. Folsom teaching fellow Harvard U., 1913-14; assoc. prof. bacteriology and hygiene U. Nev., 1914-15; assoc. prof. preventive medicine State U. Iowa, 1915-17; epidemiologist Iowa State Bd. Health, 1915-17; prof. bacteriology and preventive medicine U. Tex., 1917-21; mem. staff Internat. Health div. Rockefeller Found., 1921-46; dir. field studies malaria Internat. Health div. Rockefeller Found., Brazil, 1922-25, Leesburg, Ga. and Edenton, N.C., 1925-28, Cen. Bd. of Health, Jamaica, B.W.I., 1928-29, Miss. State Bd. Health, 1929-31; dir. Sta. Malaria Rsch. Internat. Health div. Rockefeller Found., 1931-46; mem. Fla. Bd. Health, 1947-52; mem. expert adv. malaria panel WHO; mem. adv. sci. bd. Gorgas Meml. Inst.; del. several internat. confs. Author: Preventive Medicine, 7th edit., 1945; (with others) Malariology, 1949; (with H. G. Smith and J. W. Griffin) Here They Once Stood, 1951. Recipient Prix de Brumpt, U. Paris Faculty of Medicine, 1953. Fellow Iowa (emeritus), Fla. acads. sci., Am. Acad. Tropical Medicine (pres. 1945); emeritus mem. Am. Pub. Health Assn., Am. Soc. Tropical Medicine (pres. 1938), Nat. Malaria Soc. (sec.-treas. 1930-45, pres. 1946), Fla. Pub. Health Assn. (ex-pres.); hon. mem. several Am., fgn. socs. Home: Tallahassee Fla. †

BOYD, THOMAS MUNFORD, lawyer, educator; b. Roanoke, Va., Sept. 25, 1899; s. James and Emma (Munford) B.; m. Dorothy Pilkington, Sept. 10, 1929; 1 son, Thomas Munford. BS, U. Va., 1920, LLB, 1923. Bar: Va. 1923. Pvt. practice Charlottesville, Va., 1923-40; judge Juvenile and Domestic Relations Ct. of Charlottesville and Albemarle County, 1925-30; legal staff Nat. Def. Adv. Commn., Office Prodn. Mgmt., War Prodn. Bd., Washington, 1940-43; ptnr. Christian, Barton, Parker & Boyd, Richmond, 1943-48, counsel, 1948-70; counsel Paxson, Marshall & Smith, Charlottesville, 1970-73; ptnr. Paxson, Smith, Boyd, Gilliam and Gouldman (P.C.), Charlottesville, 1973-81, Paxson, Smith, Boyd & Gilliam (P.C.), Charlottesville, 1982-84; counsel Wood, Wood & Wood, Charlottesville, 1984-85, Pippin & Pippin, Norton, Va., 1979-85; lectr. law U. Va., 1946-47, prof. law, 1947-65, Doherty prof. law, 1965-70, prof. emeritus, 1970-85; (on leave) chmn. appeals bd. Nat. Prodn. Authority, Washington, 1951-52; adv. counsel Va. Code Commn., 1953-58, cons., 1972-77; pres. Stetinius Fund. Inc., 1947-66; dir., gen. counsel Am. and Fgn. Enterprises, Inc., N.Y.C., 1947-85; vis. prof. Washington and Lee U., 1961-62. Author: Burk's Pleading and Practice, 4th edit., 1952, Cases on Virginia Procedure, 1958, rev. edit., 1969, (with others) Virginia Civil Procedure, 1982. bd. dirs. Va. Soc. for Prevention Blindness, 1968-73; mem. Am. Council of the Blind. Recipient Thomas Jefferson award U. Va., 1957, Raven award, 1961; T. Munford Boyd chair established U. Va. Law Sch., 1977; Disting. Service award Va. Trial Lawyers Assn., 1978. Fellow Am. Bar Found.; mem. ABA (Jour. adv. com. 1962), Va. Bar Assn., Va. State Bar, Am. Judicature Soc., Am. Blind Lawyers Assn., Order of Coif, Commonwealth Club, Redland Club, Phi Beta Kappa, Phi Kappa Psi, Phi Delta Phi. Episcopalian. Home: Charlottesville Va. Died Sept. 2, 1985.

BOYLAN, J. RICHARD, banker; b. New Rochelle, N.Y., June 25, 1928; s. James Owen and Ethel (King) B.; m. Hildegarde W. Scheffler, Apr.14, 1956; children: Cynthia Ann, James Richard. B.A., Johns Hopkins U., 1950; exchange student, U. Oslo, Norway, 1947; postgrad., Stonier Sch. Banking, 1961. With Provident Nat. Bank, Phila., from 1954, now vice chmn.; chmn. bd., dir. Provident Instl. Mgmt. Corp.; pres., dir. Provident Nat. Investment Corp.; exec. v.p. Independence Sq. Income Securities, Inc.; mng. dir. Shearson Internat. Dollar Res. Fund; vice chmn., dir. PNC Fin. Corp., Colonial Penn Group, Inc.; S. Chester Tube Co., Tatnall Corp.; mem. investment policy com. Gen. Accident Fire & Life Assurance Corp., Ltd. Bd. mgrs. Friends Hosp.; trustee Johns Hopkins U., Widener U. Mem. Am. Bankers Assn. (chmn. trust div. 1984-85). Club: Phila. Union League (Phila.). Home: Devon Pa. Died Mar. 30, 1986; buried Lansdowne, Pa.

BOYLE, ROBERT WILLIAM, physician; b. St. Paul, Feb. 11, 1908; s. William Henry and Gertrude May (Ritsch) B.; m. Daphne Jennette Connell, Nov. 26, 1931; children—William Charles, Jeanne Marguerite Boyle Hanks and Georgianna Phyllis Boyle Gunaji (twins). Student, Hamline U., 1924-26; B.P.E., YMCA Coll., Chgo., 1929, M.P.E., 1937; Ph.B., U. Chgo., 1930; M.A., Coll. City Detroit, 1933; Ph.D., U. Minn., 1936; M.D., U. Ark., 1940; Baruch fellow, Mayo Clinic, 1946-47. Diplomate Am. Bd. Phys. Medicine and Rehab. Phys. dir. Eau Claire (Wis.) YMCA, 1930-31; instr. physiology, coach freshman football Coll. City Detroit, 1931-32; teaching fellow physiology U. Minn. Sch. Medicine, 1933-36; asst. prof., later prof., head dept. physiology and pharmacology U. Ark. Sch. Medicine, 1936-44; chief phys. medicine and rehab., later chief profl. services VA Hosp., Ft. Thomas, Ky., 1947-54; prof. phys. medicine and rehab. Med. Coll. Wis., Milw., 1954-78; prof. emeritus Med. Coll. Wis., 1978-87, chmn. dept. phys. medicine and rehab., 1965-73; dir. dept. phys. medicine and rehab. Milw. County Hosp., 1954-78; chmn. rehab. div. Commn. State Dept. (Wis. Med. Soc.), 1956-59; exec. com. health services (United Community Service), Milw., 1958-60, 62-69; dept. Christian social action Episcopal Diocese Milw., 1960-74; cons. VA Center, Wood, Wis., 1954-78; staff physician Cardiopulmonary Rehab. Center, 1978-84; participant Internat. Congress Phys. Medicine and Rehab., Washington, 1960, Paris, 1964, Montreal, Que., Can., 1968, Barcelona, Spain, 1972, Rio de Janeiro, Brazil, 1976, Stockholm, 1980. Contbr. articles to profl. jours., chpt. in book. Served as capt., M.C. AUS, 1944-46. Fellow ACP, Am. Coll. Chest Physicians; mem. Am. Acad. Phys. Medicine and Rehab. (bd. govs. pres. 1961-62, sec. 1967-82), Am. Congress Rehab. Medicine, Assn. Acad. Physiatrists, AAUP, AAAS, AMA (sect. council phys. medicine and rehab. 1976-78, alt. mem. intersplty. adv. bd. 1968-76, 77-80), Pan Am. Med. Assn., Internat. Soc. Rehab. Disabled, Nat. Rehab. Assn., Am. Heart Assn., Am. Rheumatism Assn., Am. Geriatrics Soc., Royal Soc. Health, Wis. Soc. Phys. Medicine and Rehab. (Disting. Clinician award 1984), Sigma Xi, Phi Beta Pi, Alpha Omicron Alpha. Episcopalian. Home: Wauwatosa Wis. Died Apr. 21, 1987; buried Germantown, Wis.

BRACE, CLAYTON H., broadcasting company executive; b. Topeka, Aug. 8, 1923; s. Clayton Henry and Gladys (Hawley) B.; B.; student U. Denver, 1940-41, U. Colo., 1941; m. Jeanne Haney, Sept. 10, 1947 children—Kimball William, Dianne, Lynne, Kerry. With KLZ Radio, Denver, 1941-50, prodn. mgr., 1950-53; dir. TV research, program dir. KLZ-TV, 1953-57; asst. to pres. Time-Life Broadcast, Inc., Denver, 1957-61, v.p., gen. mgr. KOGO-TV-AM-FM, San Diego, 1963-72; ops. mgr. Compagnie Lebanaise de TV, Beirut, 1961-63; v.p. McGraw-Hill Broadcasting Co., Inc., KGTV 10, San Diego, 1972-86 . Bd. dirs. Donald N. Sharp Meml. Community Hosp., World Affairs Council; mem. nat. adv. com. Mexican-Am. Edn., 1967-69; chmn. adv. com. San Diego State U.; chmn. San Diego United Way Campaign, 1978; mem. San Diego Crime Commn., 1980. Served with Signal Corps, AUS, 1943-45. Recipient Try San Diego First award 1964. Mem. Nat. Assn. Broadcasters Code Authority, chmn. TV Code 1981-83), Calif. Broadcasters Assn. (chmn. bd. 1969-70), Broadcast Edn. Assn. (adv. bd. leadership devel. program), ABC-TV Affiliates Assn. (chmn. bd. govs. 1984-85), U. Calif.-San Diego Chancellor's Assocs. (chmn. 1982-83), San Diego C. of C. (pres. 1969-70), Sigma Delta Chi. Clubs: Rotary (pres. San Diego 1970-71). Home: San Diego, CA. Died June 20, 1986; buried El Camino Meml. Park. Home: San Diego Calif.

BRACE, LLOYD D., banker; b. Lincoln, Nebr., Feb. 26, 1903; s. DeWitt B. and Elizabeth (Wing) B.; m. Helen Rhodes, Oct. 6, 1928; children: Robert D., Lloyd DeWitt, Richard G., Ann Barnes. BS, Dartmouth Coll., 1925; LLD (hon.), Northeastern U., Bowdoin Coll. With First Nat. Bank of Boston, 1925-86; bd. dirs. A.T.&T., Gen. Motors, John Hancock Mutual Life Ins. Co., Stone & Webster Inc., other major corps. Fellow Am. Acad. Arts. and Scis. ; mem. Corp. of MIT, Mass. Soc. Prevention of Cruelty to Animals (investment adv. com.), Coordinating Com. (Boston). Home: Needham Mass. Died Apr. 20, 1986; buried Dover, Mass.

BRACELAND, FRANCIS JAMES, psychiatrist; b. Phila., July 22, 1900; s. John J. and Margaret (L'Estrange) B; m. Hope Van Gelder Jenkins, June 1, 1938; children: John Michael, Mary Faith Kerrigan. AB, LaSalle Coll., Phila., 1926; ScD, LaSalle Coll., 1941; LHD, Canisius Coll., 1956; ScD, Coll. of Holy Cross, 1956; LittD, 1965, Cath. U. Am., 1957, Northwestern U., 1957, Trinity Coll., Hartford, Conn., 1958, Fairfield U., 1961, U. Hartford, 1964; ScD, Georgetown U. Sch. Medicine, 1977. Diplomate Am. Bd. Psychiatry and Neurology (sec.-treas. 1945-52, pres. 1952). Resident physician Jefferson Med. Hosp., Phila., 1930-32; clin. dir., asst. physician Pa. Hosp. for Mental Disease, Phila., 1932-35, clin. dir., 1937-38; asst. physician Burgholzi Hosp., Zurich, Switzerland, 1935-36, Nat. Hosp., Queen Sq, London, 1936; psychiatrist Inst. of Pa. Hosp., Phila., 1937-41, Phila. Gen. Hosp., 1940-41; instr. psychiatry U. Pa. Med. Sch., 1936-38; asst. prof. psychiatry, Grad. Sch. Medcine U. Pa., 1938-41; dean Sch. Medicine U. Chgo., 1941-46; prof. psychiatry, Grad Sch. U. Minn., 1946-51; head sect. psychiatry Mayo Clinic, Rochester, Minn., 1946-51; psychiatrist-in-chief Inst. of Living, Hartford, Conn., 1951-65, sr. cons., 1965-84, ret., 1984; clin. prof. psychiatry Yale U., 1951-68; lectr. psychiatry Harvard U., 1960-66; vis. prof. dept. psychiatry U. Conn. Health Ctr., 1974-84; cons. Hartford Hosp., St. Francis Hosp., 1952-84, v.p. World Psychiat. Assn., 1961-66. Editor: Am. Jour. Psychiatry, 1965-78, editor emeritus, 1978-84; sr. editor Year Book of Psychiatry and Applied Mental Health, 1968-76; mem. internat. editorial bd. World Biennial Book of Psychiatry and Psychotherapy, 1966-84; editorial dir. Med. Insight, 1970-74, Psychiat. Annals, 1971-84; mem. sci. adv. bd. MD Mag. 1956-84, contbg. editor, 1979-84. Chmn. Nat. Health Forum, 1957. Capt. M.C. USNR, 1942-46; rear adm. Res. ret.; chief neuropsychiat. div. Bur. Medicine and Surgery, Navy Dept., 1944-46; cons. psychiatrist to Surgeon Gen., U.S. Navy; cons. Spl. Med. Adv. Bd, VA; appointed Armed Forces Med. Adv. Com., 1949. Recipient Disting. Pub. Service award State Bar Conn., 1961, Stritch medal Loyola U., 1965, Laetare medal Notre Dame U., 1962, E.B. Bowis award Am. Coll. Psychiatrists, 1971, Edward B. Allen gold medal Am. Geriatrics Soc., 1972, William C. Porter award Assn. Mil. Surgeons, 1974, Gold medal Mount Airy Found., 1976, Nolan D.C. Lewis award Carrier Found., 1978; named comdr. Knights of St. Gregory; decorated Legion of Merit. Fellow ACP, Coll. Physicians Phila., Am. Psychiat. Assn. (pres.1957, Disting. Service award 1976); mem. World Psychiat. Assn. (v.p. 61-66, Disting. Service award 1971, AMA, Assn. for Research in Nervous and Mental Disease (pres. 1957, chmn. bd.trustees 1969-70, Disting. Service award 1970), N.Y. Acad. Scis., N.Y. Acad. Medicine (hon. mem., chmn. Salmon com. on psychiatry and mental hygiene 1959-76, Salmon medal for disting. service to psychiatry 1972); hon. mem. Royal Coll. Psychiatrists, Spanish, German, Peruvian psychiat. assns. Home: Hartford Conn. Died Feb. 27, 1985; buried Arlington Nat. Cemetery, Va.

BRACKEN, JOHN ROBERT, educator, landscape architect; b. Duquesne, Pa., Aug. 25, 1891; s. Edward Speare and Margaret Jane (Caughey) B.; m. Margaret Waldie Baird, July 25, 1917. BS, Pa. State U., 1914; BLD, U. Mich., 1933, PhD, 1945. Designer, field supr. Paul & Ford, Landscape Architects, Phila., 1916-20; landscape architect, city planner Thomas W. Sears, 1920-24; asst. prof. landscape architecture Pa. State U., 1924-26, prof. landscape architecture, head dept., 1926-57, prof. emeritus, from 1957; vis. prof. U. Wis., 1957-62; con. in field; landscape cons. govt., state, pvt. projects. Author: Principles of Landscape Planting Design, 3d edit., 1957. Mem. State Coll. (Pa.) Shade Commn., 1927-29. With U.S. Army, 1918. Fellow Am. Soc. Landscape Architects; mem. AAUP, Masons, Alpha Zeta, Phi Epsilon Phi, Pi Alpha Xi, Pi Gamma Alpha. Republican. Methodist. Home: State College Pa. Deceased.

BRADEN, CHARLES SAMUEL, clergyman, educator, author; b. Chanute, Kans., Sept. 19, 1887; s. George Washington and Flora Jane (Birt) B.; m. Grace Eleanor McMurray, Oct. 24, 1911 (dec. May 1951); children: George William (dec.), Grace E., Charles McM.; m.. 2d, La Venia Craddock Ulmer, June 16, 1956. AB, Baker U., 1909, DD, 1943; student, Columbia U., 1911-12; BD, Union Theol. Sem., 1912; PhD, U. Chgo., 1926. Ordained ministry M.E. Ch., 1914. Missionary M.E. Ch., Bolivia, S.Am., 1912-15, Chile, S.Am., 1916-22; editor El Heraldo Cristiano; prof. and pres., mgr. Union Book Store Union Theol. Sem., Santiago, Chile, 1923-25; asst. sec. Meth. Bd. Fgn. Missions, 1923-25; sec. Meth. Life Svc. Commn., Chgo., 1923-25; asst. prof. history and lit. of religions Northwestern U., 1926-36, assoc. prof., 1936-43, prof., 1943-54, prof. emeritus, from 1954; John C. Schaffer lectr., 1955; vis. prof. Perkins Sch. Theology, Dallas, summer 1954, 59, Iliff Sch. Theology, Denver, summer 1954; vis. prof. Scripps Coll., 1954-56, Facultad Evangelica de Teologia, Buenos Aires, 1957; Fondren lectr., Scarritt Coll. for Christian Workers, 1954. Author books including: The Scriptures of Mankind, 1952, War, Communism and World Religion, 1953, Jesus Compared, 1956, Christian Science Today, 1958, Spirits in Rebellion, The Rise and Development of the New Thought Movement, 1963; founder and editor of World Christianity--A Digest, 1937-39; contributing editor Protestant Digest, 1939-42, Guide to Historical Literature, 1960; contributor to thesymposium Protestantism, 1944, Annals of Am. Acad. Polit. and Social Sci., symposium Organized Religion in America; contributing editor Ency. of Religion, 1945; editorial bd. Jour. Bible and Religion, 1943-49; contbr. to Ency. Bit., Grolier's Ency., others. Mem. Am. Theol. Soc. (pres. 1940-41), Am. Oriental Soc. (pres. Midwest Br. 1933), Chgo. Soc. Bibl. Rsch. (pres. 1936-37), AAUP, Nat. Assn. Bibl. Instr. (pres. 1952). Home: Dallas Tex. †

BRADFORD, RALPH, business organization consultant, lecturer, writer; b. Kirby, Pa., 1892; s. John M. and Ida (Miller) B.; m. Hazel Munger, June 16, 1925; 1 son, Ralph Gordon. Ed., high sch. and Bay View (Tex.) Coll.; LLD (hon.), Elon Coll., 1950. Lectr. for Agrl. Svc. Internat. Harvester Co., 1913-14; tchr. of history Bay View Coll., 1915-16; with U.S. Army, 1918-19; with sales dept. Lehigh Portland Cement Co., 1919; circulation mgr. and spl. writer Sheridan (Wyo.) Post, 1919-20; salesman Am. Cement Plaster Co., 1921-23; mgr. C. of C., Corpus Christi, Tex., 1924-29; asst. dept. mgr., later dept. mgr. C. of C. of U.S.A., 1929-38, sec., 1938-42, gen. mgr. and sec., 1942-47, exec. v.p., 1947-50, internat. v.p., 1950-57; lectr. on adminstrn. of bus. orgns. Western Inst. at Stanford U., 1933-38, Nat. Inst. of Northwestern U., 1931-42 (mem. bd. mgrs. Nat. Inst., 1936-50); lectr. Stanford, 1956, U. N.C., 1956, and others; mem. bd. dirs. Washington Loan & Trust Co., 1944-56, Internat. Bank, Washington, 1956-60; adv. dir. Riggs Nat. Bank, from 1954. Author: The Purple Robe, 1929, The White Way, 1931, In the Image of Man, 1932, Brief Interludes, 1934, After the Passage of Winter, 193, Three Men of Persia, 1935, Legend of the River People, 1937, Reprieve, 1940, A Bit of Christmas, 1941, Along the Way, 1949, One There Was in Palestine, 1949, Heritage, 1950, Bright Star, 1953, Prologue for Tomorrow, 1956. Del. to Inter-American Coun. of Commerce and Industry, Montevideo, 1947, Plenary, Chgo., 1948, Congress Internat. Chamber, Lisbon, 1951, Vienna, 1953, first Postwar Plenary of Internat. Chamber, Switzerland, 1947, Lima (Peru) Plenary, Inter-American Coun., 1952, and Mexico City, 1954; adviser to Coun., Internat. Chamber, Paris, 1948, mem. Coun., 1952-55; del. to biennial congress, Tokyo, 1955, dir. U.S. Coun., 1952-55; trustee U.S. Inter-American Coun. of Commerce and Prodn., 1952-57; spl. rep. U.S. Chamber, to the Hemispheric Ins. Conf., Mexico, 1948. Awarded Medal of Honor, Am. C. of C. in France, 1954. Hon. life mem. Am. C. of C. Execs. Assn., Am. Soc. of Assn. Execs., Nat. Assn. Execs. Club (hon. mem.). Home: McLean Va. †

BRADFORD, WILLIAM PARKINSON, investment banker; b. Oakland, Calif., Aug. 8, 1920; s. William Martin and Minnie (Gray) B.; m. Mariana Welch, Nov. 22, 1946; children: Mariana Bradford Longstreth, Suzanne Bradford Smith, William Parkinson, Pamela Bradford Andrews. BBA, U. Calif., Berkeley, 1942. Salesman Dean Witter & Co. Inc., San Francisco, 1946-58, ptnr., br. mgr., 1958-68, 1st v.p., asst. div. mgr., 1968-70, sr. v.p., dir., 1970-72, sor. v.p. fin., 1972-73, exec. v.p., treas., 1973-85; dir. Dean Witter Orgn. Inc. and assoc. affiliates, Surety Life Ins. Co., San Francisco. Lt. comdr. USNR, 1942-46. Mem. Mchts. Exchange, Pacific-Union (San Francisco), Burlingame Country Club. Home: San Francisco Calif. Died Dec. 2, 1985; buried Oakland Mountain View Cemetery, Oakland, Calif.

BRADLEY, VAN ALLEN, rare book and autograph dealer, journalist; b. Albertville, Ala., Aug. 24, 1913; s. Van A. and Lula (Montgomery) B.; m. Patricia Elaine Thompson, Nov. 5, 1939 (div.); children: Van Allen III, Pamela Star, Susan; m. Sharon Lee Luedke, Dec. 3, 1966 (div.); 1 child, Gremlyn Angelica. Student, Harding Coll., 1930-32; BJ, U. Mo., 1933. Reporter Nashville Tennessean, 1934-35; reporter, columnist, chief copy desk Omaha Bee-News, 1935-37; copy editor Chgo. Herald Examiner, 1937-38; copy editor, asst. picture editor Chgo. Tribune, 1938-42; copy editor, book columnist, chief copy desk Chgo. Sun (now Sun-Times), 1942-48; lit. editor Chgo. Daily News, 1948-71, editorial writer, 1953-60, ret., 1971; pres. Heritage Book Shop Inc., Chgo., 1964-72; pres. Van Allen Bradley Inc., Lake Zurich, Ill., 1972-78, Scottsdale, Ariz., 1978-84; author syndicated rare book column Gold in Your Attic, 1957-71; lectr., tchr. Northwestern U. Medill Sch. Journalism, 1942-54; platform lectr. books, current lit. Author: Music for the Millions, 1957, Gold in Your Attic, 1958, More Gold in Your Attic, 1961, The New Gold in Your Attic, 1968, The Book Collector's Handbook of Values, 1972, 4th edit., 1982; editor: How To Predict What People Will Buy, 1957,. Founder mem. Lincolnwood (Ill.) Little Theatre Inc., pres. 1957-58; mem. Lincolnwood Bd. Edn., 1950-60, pres., 1953-60; mer Citizens Com. for Chgo. Pub. Libr.; mem. poetry ar lit. adv. coms. Ill. Arts Coun.; bd. dirs. Friends Chg Pub. Libr.; pres. Friends Barrington (Ill.) Pub. Lib 1975-77. Recipient award for meritorious service letters Chgo. Found. for Lit., 1956. Mem. Soc. Midlar Authors (dir., pres. 1955-57), Friends Lit. (adv. coun Chgo. Press Vets. Assn., Tavern Club. Home: Scot sdale Ariz. Died Dec. 25, 1984.

BRADSHAW, THORNTON FREDERICK, busine consultant; b. Washington, Aug. 4, 1917; s. Frederi and Julia V. (See) B.; m. Sally Davis, 1940 (div. 197 children: Nancy M. (Mrs. Thomas Poor), Priscilla (Mrs. Richard Page, Jr.), Jonathan G.; m. Patricia Salt West, May 11, 1974; children: Jeffrey D. West, Nichol S. West, Andrew P. West, Eric R. West. AB, Harva U., 1940, MBA, 1942; DCS, Harvard, 1950; LL (hon.), Pepperdine U., 1974, Southampton Coll., 198 DSocial Sci. (hon.), Villanova U., 1975; LLD (hon Dickinson Coll., 1986. Assoc. prof. Grad. Sch. Bu Adminstrn., Harvard U., Cambridge, Mass., 1942- ptnr. Cresap, McCormick & Paget, N.Y.C., 1952- v.p., dir. Atlantic Richfield Co. (formerly Atlan Refining Co.), Los Angeles, 1956-62, exec. v.p., 1962-6 pres., 1964-80, mem. exec. com., 1966-81; chmn. b RCA Corp., N.Y.C., 1981-86; bd. dirs. NBC, Fi Boston, Inc., Brooks Fashion Stores, Inc., Gen. Elect Co.; overseer Harvard Coll., 1978-84. Trustee Co servation Found.; trustee Rockefeller Bros. Fund, In Internat. Edn., Inst. Advanced Study; chmn. bd. Asp Inst. Humanistic Studies Aspen Inst.; chmn. Ctr. f Communication, The Lauder Inst. of Mgmt. and ternat. Studies; chmn. vis. com. The Loeb Drama C Harvard U.; chmn. bd. dirs. John D. and Catherine MacArthur Found. Served to lt. (j.g.) USNR, 1943-4 Mem. Am. Petroleum Inst. Died Dec. 6, 1988.

BRADY, BERNARD VINCENT, lawyer; b. Wi neconne, Wis., Feb. 24, 1891; s. Owen W. and Ma (Roddy) B.; m. Amybelle Halbert, July 2 1922. Student, Marquette U. Law Sch., 1910-13. B Wis. 1913. Sr. ptnr. Brady, Tyrrell, Cotter & Cutl from 1957; bd. dirs. Briggs & Stratton Corp., Lad Co., Ladish Malting Co., Milw. Devel. Group, Inc. lt. Ordnance Corps, U.S. Army, 1917-19. Mem. AB Wis., Milw. bar assns. Home: Milwaukee Wis. †

BRAINERD, JOHN G., electrical engineer, educat b. Phila., Aug. 7, 1904; s. John Austin and Mat (Grist) B; m. Carol Paxson, Sept. 6, 1930. BS, U. P 1925, ScD, 1934; cert., MIT, 1941, 54. Reporter T N.Am., Phila., 1922-25; faculty Moore Sch. Elec. Eng ing., U. Pa., Phila., 1925-88, prof., 1954-88, Univ. pro 1979-88, dir., 1954-70; chmn. div. phys. scis. U. Grad. Sch., Phila., 1942-48; engr. acting state dir. PW 1935-37; cons. engr. govt. agencies; project su ENIAC Project (large-scale digital gen. purpose el tronic computer, completed) , 1946; mem. sci. adv. co Nat. Bur. Standards, 1959-65, U.S. nat. com. Expe Internat. Electrotech. Commn.; chmn. sci. and arts co Franklin Inst., 1979-88; mem. engring. coll. accredi tion com., regional chmn. ECPD; public speaker energy and world food supply, 1974-88. Co-auth Ultra High Frequency Techniques, 1942; book review Tech. and Culture, 1969-88; contbr. articles to pro Jours. Recipient numerous profl. awards. Fell AAAS, IEEE (chmn. nat. com. for elect. engring. film chmn. awards com., dir. Founders Gold medal), Ro Soc. Arts, Fellows in Am. Studies; mem. Soc. for H tory Tech. (pres. 1974-76, treas. 1976-88), Engrs. Jo Council, AAUP, Jovians (pres.), Am. Standards As (standards council 1949-5), Faculty Club (Phila.), Sig Xi, Tau Beta Pi. Home: Kennett Square Pa. Died F 1, 1988.

BRAMELD, THEODORE, educator; b. Neillsvi Wis., Jan. 20, 1904; s. Theodore and Minnie (Dange B.; children: Katherine Alice Greene, Kristin Elizab Melton, Patricia Gene; m. Midori Matsuyama. B Ripon Coll., 1926; Ph.D. (fellow), U. Chgo., 1931; Ed (hon.), R.I. Coll., 1959; LittD (hon.), U. Vt., 197 Field sec. Ripon Coll., Ripon, Wis., 1926-28; ins philosophy L.I. U., N.Y., 1931-35; asst. prof. Adel U., Garden City, N.Y., 1935-38, assoc. prof., 1938- assoc. prof. ednl. philosophy U. Minn., Mpls., 1939- prof., 1945-47; prof. ednl. philosophy NYU, 1947- prof. ednl. philosophy Boston U., 1958-69, prof. em itus, 1969-87; vis. assoc. prof. edn. Columbia U., su mers 1939, 45; vis. lectr. Sch. for Workers, U. Haw 1970-72; lectr. New Sch. for Social Research, Willi Alson White Inst. Psychiatry; vis. lectr. Dartmou Coll., 1953-54; vis. prof. U. P.R., 1955-58; vis. special Dept. State, Japan, Korea, 1962-63; Fulbright resea scholar, Japan, 1964-65; sr. fellow East-West Ctr., 19 72; vis. prof. CUNY, 1973-74; World Campus Aflo 1975, U. Vt., 1974-75. v.p. Am. Edn. Fellowship, 19 53; sec. treas. Philosophy of Edn. Soc., 1941-47, pr 1947-48; Am. del. Internat. Conf. New Edn. Fellowsh Australia, 1946; mem. exec. bd. Council for Stu Mankind, 1969-87; Boston U. lectr., 1969. Author Philosophic Approach to Communism, 1933, Minor Problems in the Public Schools, 1945, Design America, 1945, Ends and Means in Education - Midcentury Appraisal, 1950, Patterns of Educatio Philosophy, 1950, rev. 1971, Philosophies of Educati in Cultural Perspective, 1955, Toward a Reconstruc Philosophy of Education, 1956, Cultural Foundations

ucation - An Interdisciplinary Eploration, 1957, The
:making of a Culture - Life and Education in Puerto
co, 1959, Education for the Emerging Age, 1965,
lucation as Power, 1965, The Use of Explosive Idea in
lucation - Culture, Class and Evolution, 1965, Japan:
ılture, Education and Change in Two Communities,
68, The Climactic Decades: Mandate to Education,
70, The Teacher as World Citizen, 1974. Editor, co-
thor: Workers' Education in the U.S., 1941, Values in
nerican Education, 1964. Co-author: Tourism as
ıltural Learning, 1977. Mem. Philosophy of Edn.
c., Am. Philos. Assn., Soc. for Ednl. Reconstruction,
n. Ednl. Studies Assn., Internat. Ctr. for Integrative
ln. (internat. council), Planetary Citizens (adv. bd.),
ppa Delta Pi (Laureate chpt.). Home: Lyme Center
H. Died Oct. 18, 1987.

RAMSTEDT, WILLIAM FREDERICK, foundation
ecutive; b. Manila, P.I., Aug. 21, 1905; s. William and
rah (McBride) B.; m. Margaret Martin (dec.); chil-
en: Eric, Sally; m. 2d, Margaret Weaver, May 27,
50. BS, U. Calif., 1926. Engr. Standard Oil Co.,
lif., 1927-28; various positions Richmond refinery,
28-40; v.p., dir. Standard Oil Co., B.C., Vancouver,
40-43, Standard oil Co. of Alaska, 1943-45; supt.
andard Oil Refinery, El Segundo, Calif., 1945; in
arge crude oil sales Arabian Am. Oil Co., 1945-47;
. Calif.-Tex. Oil Corp., 1947-49, exec. v.p., 1949,
es., 1949-57, chmn. bd. dirs., 1957-63; v.p. Standard
Co. of Calif., 1963-70; vice chmn. nat. devel. Asia
und., San Francisco, from 1970. Mem. Rockefeller
ncheon Club (N.Y.C.); Silverado Country Club
apa, Calif.). Home: San Francisco Calif. Died Sept.
1988.

AND, DONALD DILWORTH, educator; b.
clayo, Peru, Mar. 6, 1905; s. Willis C. and Martha
an (Dilworth) B.; m. Joy Morenci Erickson, Sept. 16,
32; children: Donald Dilworth, Joy Beverly (Mrs.
lliam J. Doughty). AB, U. Calif., 1929; traveling
ow, 1930-31; PhD, U. Calif., 1933. Teaching fellow
Calif., 1931-33, instr., 1934, lectr. geography, 1934;
. prof. U. N.Mex., 1934-35, assoc. prof., 1935-39,
f. anthrop. geography, 1939-47, head dept. anthro-
ogy, 1935-43, 46-47; cultural geographer Smithsonian
t. Mexico, 1944-46; prof. geography U. Mich., 1947-
U. Tex., Austin, 1949-75; emeritus U. Tex., 1975-84;
anized dept. geography, 1949, chmn. dept. ge-
aphy, 1949-60. Author: Quiroga, A Mexican
nicipio, 1951, Coastal Study of Southwest Mexico, 2
s, 1957, 58, Coalcoman and Motines del Oro-An Ex-
rito of Michoacán Mexico, 1960, Mexico, Land of
shine and Shadow, 1966; monographs; contbr. chpts.
books, tech. articles to profl. jours. and encys.
low AAAS, Am. Anthrop. Assn., Explorers Club;
n. Assn. Am. Geographers, Soc. History Discoveries,
in-Am. Studies Assn., Soc. for Am. Archeology, Soc.
xicana de Antropologia, Current Anthropology (as-
, Phi Beta Kappa, Sigma Xi, Phi Kappa Phi. Home:
stin Tex. Died July 21, 1984.

ANDEL, PAUL WILLIAM, lawyer, business ex-
:ive; b. Chgo., Oct. 7, 1911; s. Carl P. and Christine
nnson) B.; grad. North Park Acad., Chgo., 1928;
l. North Park Coll. 1930, LL.D., 1972; J.D., Chgo.
nt Coll. Law, 1933; LL.D., Trinity Coll., 1968, Ill.
edictine Coll., 1973; m. Bernice Peterson Stege, Jan.
1976; 1 dau., Carola Ruth (Mrs. Loren Anderson).
nitted to Ill. bar, 1933, since practiced in Chgo.;
r. firm Brandel & Johnson; dir. Barrington State
k, Countryside Bank; pres. Paul W. Brandel Enter-
es, Inc. Chmn. bd. Stone-Brandel Center; bd. dirs.
erlocken Music Acad., Religious Heritage Am.; life
stee Ill. Inst. Tech.; adv. bd. Salvation Army,
odwill Industries. Decorated commdr. Kungl.
rdstjärneorden (Sweden). Mem. Am., Ill., Chgo. bar
ns., Gideons. Mem. Evangelical Covenant Ch.
erica Clubs: Union League, Mich. Shores, Svithoid,
rdic Law, Chgo. Athletic Assn., Swedish (Chgo.);
derdale Yacht; Everglades (Palm Beach, Fla.);
vanis. Home: Northbrook, Ill. Died June 30, 1986;
ed Ridgewood Cemetery, Des Plaines, Ill.

ANDENBURG, DAVID JOHN, educator; b.
.C., June 7, 1920; s. Joseph Franklin and Josephine
e (Baker); m. Millicent Louise Harcourt, June 24,
4; children: John Gifford, Guy Franklin, Ann
emary. BS, Bowdoin Coll., 1943; MA, Columbia
1947, PhD, 1954. Tchr. Riverdale Country Sch.,
.C., 1944-46; lectr. history Columbia U., N.Y.C.,
7-48; mem. faculty Am. U., Washington, 1948-87,
. history, 1957-87, chmn. dept., 1967-77; vis. prof.
sh. State U., summer 1970. Author: Early Modern
es, 3d edit., 1975; (with M. H. Brandenburg) The
de la Rochefoucauld-Liancourt's Visit to the
eral City in 1797: A New Translation, 1976; also
cles. Fulbright research grantee, France, 1959;
shington Eve. Star faculty grantee, 1959. Mem. Am.
. Assn., Columbia Hist. Soc., Soc. French Hist.
dies, Agrl. History Soc., Société d'histoire moderne.
ne: Washington D.C. Died Oct. 24, 1987.

ANDT, MARY RICHARDS, physician, medical
sultant and writer; b. Chgo., Sept. 26, 1921; d. Rus-
Dean and Anna Elizabeth (Isham) Robinson; m.
ph Samuel Richards, Dec. 18. 1943 (div. 1968);
dren—Anne Leslie, Kathleen Elizabeth; m. Melville
en Brandt, Dec. 27, 1982. B.S., Purdue U., 1944;
M.D., U. Ill., Chgo., 1947. Diplomate Am. Bd. Pediatrics. Intern Cook County Hosp., Chgo., 1947-48; resident Mcpl. Contagious Hosp., La Rabida, Children's Meml. Hosp., Chgo., 1948-50; pvt. practice pediatrics Glenview, Ill., 1950-52, Tenafly, N.J., 1957-64; clin. fellow Babies Hosp., N.Y.C., 1952-54; sr. v.p., group med. dir. Sudler & Hennessey Inc., N.Y.C., 1964-69, 1971-85; assoc. med. dir. Syntex Labs., Palo Alto, Calif., 1969-71; free lance med. cons., writer, 1985-88. Contbr. articles to profl. jours. Fellow Am. Acad. Pediatrics; mem. Am. Med. Writers Assn., Pharm. Advt. Council, Babies Hosp. Alumni Assn., Alpha Omega Alpha, Kappa Kappa Gamma. Episcopalian. Clubs: Englewood Field, Knickerbocker Country. Home: Tenafly N.J. Deceased.

BRANNEN, BARRY, lawyer; b. Tucson, Feb. 14, 1902; s. Phillip Cornelius and Elizabeth (Barry) B. AB, U. Calif.-Berkeley, 1922; LLB, Harvard, 1925. Bar: Calif. 1925. Practiced in Los Angeles, 1930-55, Beverly Hills, 1955-75, Santa Monica, 1975-87. Author articles. Served with USNR, 1942-46. Decorated Legion of Merit, Purple Heart; Sovereign Order White Eagle Yugoslavia; medal of merit V.F.W.; recipient Meritorious Pub. Service citation U.S. Navy (2). Mem. Navy League U.S. (v.p. 1956, dir. 1955, adv. council 1956-87). Home: Santa Monica Calif. Died Mar. 24, 1987; interred Mausoleum of Calvary Cemetery, Los Angeles County.

BRANOM, FREDERICK KENNETH, geography educator, author; b. Waverly, Ill., July 27, 1891; s. John Douglas and Ella Mae (Canatsey) B.; m. Laurana Edgerton, Aug. 2, 1922; children: Elsi Arline, Berton Edgerton (dec.), Curtis Douglas, Shirley Ann. BE, Ill. State Normal U., 1915; MS, U. Chgo., 1916; PhD, Clark U., 1923. Tchr. then. prin. and supt. various pub. schs. Ill., 1908-16; instr. Tuley High Sch., Chgo., 1917-19; prof., chmn. dept. geography and social scis. Chgo. Tchrs. Coll., 1919-56; vis. prof. De Kalb State Tchrs. Coll., Miami U., Hyannis State Normal Sch., U. Pa., St. Xavier Coll., summers 1919, 21, 22, 23, 45. Author: (with M. Branom) Teaching of Geography, 1921, Pupil's Workbook on the Geography of Ill., 1922, Use of Maps and Use of Globes, 1925, (with H. Ganey) Social Geography Series, 1928-48, (with Ganey) Study Lesson Books, 1932-38, (with Ganey) Our Earth and Our Needs, 1938, The Teaching of the Social Studies in a Changing World, 1955, (with J.L. Shea, Mary Lambert) Christian Living in Our Economic World, 1944, (with Ganey, Juliana Bedier, O. McVey) The Catholic Geography Series, from 1948; editor: New Pictorial Atlas of the World, 1941, New Internat. Census Atlas of the World, 1948; contbg. editor Comml. and Library Atlas of the World, 1955; contbr. to mags. With U.S. Army, World War I. Fellow AAAS; mem. Nat. Coun. Geography Tchrs., Nat. Coun. for Social Studies, Nat. Soc. Study of Edn., NEA, Ill. State Tchrs. Assn., Geog. Soc. Chgo., Ill. State Acad. Sci., Sigma Xi. Home: Chicago Ill. †

BRANTON, WILEY AUSTIN, lawyer; b. Pine Bluff, Ark., Dec. 13, 1923; s. Leo Andrew and Pauline (Wiley) B.; m. Lucille McKee, Feb. 1, 1948; children: Richard, Toni Cheryl (dec.), Wylene Branton Wood, Wiley Austin, Beverly Lucille, Debra Branton Levy. BS, U. Ark.-Pine Bluff, 1950; JD, U. Ark., 1953. Bar: Ark. 1952, U.S. Supreme Ct 1956, Ga. 1962, D.C. 1967, other fed. cts. Practiced in Pine Bluff, 1952-62; dir. voter edn. project So. Regional Council, 1962-65; spl. asst. to atty. gen. of U.S. 1965-67; exec. dir. United Planning Orgn., 1967-69, Council United Civil Rights Leadership, 1963-65; dir. community and social action Alliance for Labor Action, 1969-71; ptnr. Dolphin, Branton, Stafford & Webber, Attys., Washington, 1971-77; of counsel Walker, Kaplan & Mays, Little Rock, 1971-78; dean Sch. Law, Howard U., Washington, 1978-83; counsel Sidley & Austin, Washington, 1983-84, ptnr., 1985-88; bd. dirs. Columbia First Fed. Savs. and Loan Assn., Consol. Ry. Corp.; chmn. D.C. Jud. Nomination Commn. Bd. dirs. Africare, Lawyers Com. for Civil Rights Under Law, NAACP Legal Def. and Edn. Fund. Served with AUS, 1943-46. Named one of 100 most important young men or women in U.S. Life mag., 1962; one of America's 100 most influential Negroes Ebony mag., 1963; recipient numerous awards for participation civil rights litigation including: Henry W. Edgerton award ACLU, 1977, Whitney North Seymour award Lawyers Com. for Civil Rights Under Law, 1987, 1st Martin Luther King Jr. Leadership award Washington Pub. Library, 1988. Fellow Am. Bar Found.; mem. ABA (council of sect. on legal edn. and admissions to bar), Nat. Bar Assn. (C. Francis Stratford award 1958), D.C. Bar Assn. (unified), Bar Assn. of D.C. (Lawyer of Yr. 1986), Washington Bar Assn. (Charles Hamilton Houston medallion 1978), NAACP, Nat. Urban League, Omega Psi Phi, Sigma Pi Phi, Phi Alpha Delta. Club: Mason. Home: Washington D.C. Died Dec. 15, 1988; buried Pine Bluff, Ark.

BRANTON, WILLIAM COLEMAN, lawyer; b. Greenville, Miss., June 30, 1914; s. William Coleman and Marybelle (Crittenden) B.; m. Mary Shaw, Apr. 12, 1947; children: Leslie, Page. BS cum laude, Davidson Coll., 1936; JD, U. Miss., 1939. Bar: Miss. 1939, Mo. 1946. Practiced in Greenville, Miss., 1939-40, Kansas City, Mo., 1946-65; sr. v.p. City Nat. Bank & Trust Co., Kansas City, 1965-70; chmn. bd. Plaza Bank & Trust Co., Plaza Bancshares, Inc., Kansas City, 1970-79; of counsel Slagle & Bernard, Kansas City, from 1979; vice chmn. Traders Bank of Kansas City, 1980-82; civilian aide Sec. of Army, 1979-81; bd. dirs., mem. exec. com. Mo-Ark. Flood Control Assn. Mem. Civic Coun. Kansas City; bd. govs. Nelson Mus. Art; founding trustee Mo. Repertory Theater, Inc., pres., 1978-81; trustee Parker B. Francis Found., Kansas City Mus. Sci. and Industry, Midwest Rsch. Inst., U. Kansas City, P.B. Francis III Found., Kansas City Assn. Trusts and Founds., 1978-81; founding trustee Greater Kansas City Community Found.; founding trustee Clearinghouse for Midcontinent Founds., pres., 1976-79; hon. trustee, pres. Barstow Sch., Kansas City; bd. dirs. Starlight Theatre Assn., Kansas City, Liberty Meml. Assn., St. Luke's Hosp.; chmn. U. Kansas City, 1976-78; bd. visitors Davidson Coll., from 1980. Served to col. AUS, 1936-66; PTO. Decorated Legion of Merit, Bronze Star with cluster and combat V, Air medal. Mem. ABA, Mo. Bar Assn., Kansas City Bar Assn., Lawyers Assn. Kansas City, Kansas City C. of C. (dir.), Assn. U.S. Army (pres. Leavenworth chpt. 1973), N.G. Assn. Mo. (pres. 1954), Mil. Order World Wars (comdr. 1964), Kansas City Country Club, University Club, Mercury Club, Blue Key, Phi Beta Kappa, Phi Gamma Delta, Phi Delta Phi, Omicron Delta Kappa. Episcopalian. Home: Kansas City Mo. Died Sept. 11, 1985; buried Mt. Washington Cemetery, Kansas City, Mo.

BRASHARES, CHARLES WESLEY, bishop; b. Williamsport, Ohio, Mar. 31, 1891; s. Isaiah Mark and Clara Emma (McBroom) B.; m. Julia E. Merrill, Dec. 20, 1916; children: Charles Merrill, Wesley Emerson, Robert Mark. AB, Ohio Wesleyan U., 1914, DD, 1927; STB, Boston U. Sch. Theology, 1917; student, Harvard U. and Boston U., 1917-18; LLD, Cornell Coll., 1945, Boston U., 1948; LHD, Simpson Coll., 1949, Ill. Wesleyan U., 1954; DLitt, Iowa Wesleyan Coll., 1951. Ordained ministry M.E. Ch., 1917. Successively pastor Orient Heights (E. Boston), Gorham, Maine, and Newton, Mass. M.E. Chs., 1917-22; pastor Grace Ch., Dayton, Ohio, 1922-34; pastor and dir. Wesley Found. First Ch., Ann Arbor, Mich., 1934-44; bishop M.E. Ch., Des Moines area, 1944-52, Chgo. area, 1952-58, from 1960, Ill. area, 1956-60; del. Gen. Conf. Meth. Ch., 1928, 32, 40, 44; last fraternal del. of M.E. Ch. to Gen. Coun. of United Ch. of Can., 1938; del. World Coun. Chs. 2d Assembly, Evanston; mem. Bd. Edn., chmn. Coordinating Coun., 1952-60; mem. Bd. Missions, Nat. Coun. Chs., Ecumenical Meth. Coun.; past pres. Coun. of Bishops (all of Meth. Ch.); v.p. Ch. Fedn. Greater Chgo., 1962-64; mem. Mayor's All-Chgo. Citizens. Com., Chgo. Fedn. Settlements and Neighborhood Ctrs., U. Ill. Citizens Com.; trustee Wesley Meml. Hosp., Chgo., Lake Bluff Children's Home, Ill. Wesleyan U., Northwstern U.; dir. Kendall Coll.; mem. bd. Trustees McKendree Coll., Lebanon, Ill.; trustee Wesley Found., U. Ill. Contbr. to mags. Mem. Ill. Coun. of Chs. (pres.), Union League Club (Chgo.), Kiwanis, Phi Beta Kappa, Delta Sigma Rho. Home: Chicago Ill. †

BRASTED, ROBERT CROCKER, chemistry educator; b. Lisbon, N.D., Aug. 26, 1915; s. Alva Jennings and Ada (Crocker) B.; m. Corinne Beaudry Mense, Oct. 17, 1942; children: Mary Frances, Barclay Mense, Donald More, Robert Crocker. BS, George Washington U., 1938, MA, 1939; PhD, U. Ill., 1942. Asst. in instrn. George Washington U., 1935-39, U. Ill., 1939-42; phys. research chemist Celanese Corp., Cumberland, Md., 1942-43; asst. prof. U. Hawaii, 1943-47; prof. chemistry, dir. gen. chemistry program U. Minn., Mpls., 1947-86; operations research chemist Johns Hopkins, 1949; guest prof. Poona U., India, U. Heidelberg, 1961, U. Costa Rica, 1961, Jadavpur U., India, 1964; guest prof., lectr. Taiwan Nat. U., 1970; guest prof., Fulbright lectr. Stuttgart U., 1971; guest prof. Calif. State Coll., Bakersfield, 1972, U. Tokyo, 1977, U. Natal, South Africa; Disting. vis. prof. U.S. Mil. Acad., 1986-87. Author: (with Sneed and Maynard) General College Chemistry, 1955, (with others) The Chemistry of Coordination Compounds, 1958, Comprehensive Inorganic Chemistry, 8 vols, 1953-62, (with Conroy and Tobias) Laboratory Operations, 3d edit., 1977, (with E. Fluck) Allgemeine und Anorganische Chemie, 1973, rev., 1984; co-author: A Guide to Chemical Education in the U.S. for Foreign Students, 1981; contbr. articles to profl. jours. Sanders fellow, 1939; Fulbright fellow, 1961, 71; NSF fellow, 1961; recipient Distinguished Tchr. award Inst. Tech., U. Minn., 1969, Morse award Council on Liberal Edn. of U. Minn., 1970, medal for teaching excellence, Catalyst award Mfg. Chemists Assn., 1971, Distinguished Alumni award George Washington U., 1975, George Taylor award in Edn. U. Minn., 1975, 79; vis. scholar award Japan Soc. Promotion of Sci., 1977. Fellow AAAS (del.); mem. Am. Chem. Soc. (chmn. Minn. sect. 1962, chmn. div. chem. edn. 1965, com. on edn. 1968-86, com. on nominations and elections 1971-86, council policy com. 1981, chmn. gen. chemistry exams. com. 1973-86, award in chem. edn. 1973, internat. activities com. 1975, bd. council com. on publs. 1979-86, bd. dirs. region 1986-88, Coll. Tchr. award Minn. sect. 1979, mem. com. edn., 1986, com. profl. tng. 1986, com. grants and awards, 1986; Minn. award 1980, James Flack Norris Northeastern sect. award 1980, Carol and Harry Mosher award Santa Clara Valley sect. 1981), Minn. Acad. Sci., Sigma Xi, Omicron Delta Kappa, Phi Lambda Upsilon, Alpha Chi Sigma. Home: Saint Paul Minn. Died Oct. 18, 1986.

BRATT, FLOYD CLARENCE, physician; b. Clarence Center, N.Y., Nov. 19, 1903; s. Clarence Almon and Agnes Ruth (Eshelman) B.; m. Arline Swift Downey, Oct. 12, 1929 (dec. Aug. 1969); 1 dau., Marilyn (Mrs. R. Bruce Kirkwood). BS, Denison U., 1924; MD, U. Buffalo, 1928. Intern Buffalo City Hosp., 1928-29; family practice of medicine Hamburg, N.Y., 1929-31, Rochester, N.Y., 1931-81; med. staff Highland Hosp., Park Ave. Hosp., Rochester, mem. Pres. Eisenhower's People-to-People Com. on Health Professions which sponsored Project HOPE; rep. meeting of World Med. Assn., Copenhagen, 1958; cons. mem. orgn. com. Internat. Conf. on Gen. Practice, Montreal, Que., Can., 1964. Contbr. articles to profl. jours. Bd. dirs. Am. Acad. Family Physicians Found., Nat. Health Council, 1961-64. Recipient citation for outstanding achievements and services Denison U., 1962. Mem. Am. Acad. Family Physicians (pres. 1961, v.p., chmn. bd. 1959, mem. congress of dels., past dir. , past mem. exec. com., chmn. com. on internat. affairs 1962-63, rep. to planning conf. gen. practice orgns. 1964), N.Y.Sate (pres. 1952), Rochester acads. family physicians, A.M.A., World, Pan. Am. med. assns., Med. Soc. State N.Y. (chmn. subcom. gen practice of council com. on pub. health and edn 1950-59, past sec., chmn. gen. practice sect.; mem. council com. on legislation., Presdl. citation for outstanding community service 1963), Monroe County Med. Soc., Rochester Acad. Medicine, Am. Geriatrics Assn., Rochester Path. Soc., Am. Med. Soc. of Vienna (life), Brit. Coll. Gen. Practice (corr. assoc.), Mason (Shriner), Kiwanis (past lt. gov. N.Y. dist., past pres. Rochester club), Century (Rochester), Nu Sigma Nu. Methodist (trustee emeritus local ch.; trustee Genesee conf.). Home: Clarence Center N.Y. Died Nov. 16, 1983; buried Evergreen Lawn Cemetery, Akron, N.Y.

BRATTAIN, WALTER HOUSER, physics educator; b. Amoy, China (parents Am. citizens), Feb. 10, 1902; s. Ross R. and Ottilie (Houser) B.; m. Keren Gilmore, July 5, 1935 (dec. Apr. 1957); 1 child, William G.; m. Emma Jane Miller, May 10, 1958. BS, Whitman Coll., 1924, DSc (hon.), 1955; MA, U. Oreg., 1926; PhD, U. Minn., 1929; DSc (hon.), U. Portland, 1952, Union Coll., 1955, U. Minn., 1957, Gustavus Adolphus Coll., 1963; LHD (hon.), Hartwick Coll., 1964. With radio sect. Bur. Standards, 1928-29; research physicist Bell Telephone Labs., Murray Hill, N.J., 1929-67; with div. war research Columbia U., N.Y.C., 1942-43; vis. lectr. Harvard U., 1952-53; vis. prof. Whitman Coll., Walla Walla, Wash., 1962-72; overseer emeritus Whitman Coll., 1972-87. Recipient Stuart Ballantine medal Franklin Inst., 1952; John Scott award City of Phila., 1955; (with William Shockley and John Bardeen) Nobel prize in Physics, 1956; named to Nat. Inventors Hall of Fame, 1974, Disting. Alumnus, U. Oreg., 1976. Fellow Am. Phys. Soc., AAAS, Am. Acad. Arts and Scis., Explorers Club; mem. Swedish Royal Acad., IEEE (hon.), Franklin Inst., Nat. Acad. Scis., Phi Beta Kappa, Sigma Xi. Club: Walla Walla Country. Home: Walla Walla Wash. Died Oct. 13, 1987; inurned; Pomeroy, Wash.

BRAUDE, ABRAHAM ISAAC, physician, educator; b. Chgo., June 15, 1917; s. Benjamin and Lillian (Schiff) B.; m. Gita Siegel, Jan. 5, 1942; children: Claire, Kathryn. BS, U. Chgo., 1937; MD, Rush Med. Coll., 1940; PhD, U. Minn., 1950. Diplomate Am. Bd. Internal Medicine. Intern Michael Reese Hosp., Chgo., 1940-41; resident in internal medicine U. Minn., 1945-48, instr. internal medicine, 1948-50; hosp. bacteriologist Univ. Hosp. (U. Mich.), 1950-53; assoc. prof., then prof. medicine, also dir. microbiology Southwesten Med. Sch., U. Tex., Dallas, 1953-57; prof. medicine and pathology, chief div. infectious diseases, dir. microbiology U. Calif. Med. Sch., San Diego, 1969-84; chmn. bacteriology mycology study sect. NIH, 1969-71; mem. Anglo-Am. Amoeba Commn. to India, 1982; mem. exam. com. on microbiology Nat. Bd. Med. Examiners, 1974-78; vis. scientist London Sch. Hygiene and Tropical Medicine, 1981-82. Author: Antimicrobial Drug Therapy, 1976; editor: International Textbook of Medicine, 1981, Microbiology and Infectious Diseases, vol. II, 1981. Recipient Kaiser Teaching award, 1973, Maxwell Finland award, 1981; grantee NIH, 1951-84; Macy Faculty scholar, 1981-82. Mem. Am. Soc. Clin. Investigation, Am. Assn. Physicians, Am. Assn. Immunologists, Infectious Disease Soc. Am. (pres.), ACP, Am. Soc. Microbiology. Home: La Jolla Calif. Died Dec. 5, 1984; buried San Diego, Calif.

BRAUER, ALFRED T(HEODOR), mathematician; b. Berlin, Federal Republic of Germany, Apr. 8, 1894; came to U.S., 1939; naturalized, 1944; s. Max and Caroline Lilly (Jacob) B.; m. Hildegard Franziska Wolf, Sept. 4, 1934; children: Ellen Evelyn Brauer Kaplan, Carolyn Toni Brauer Hudson. Student, U. Heidelberg (Germany), 1913, U. Berlin, 1913-14, 19, 25; PhD, U. Berlin, 1928; LLD (hon.), U. N.C., 1972. Asst. U. Berlin, Germany, 1926-35, privadocent, 1932-35; asst. Inst. Advanced Study Princeton U., N.J., 1939-42; lectr. NYU, 1940-42; instr. U. N.C., Chapel Hill, 1942, asst. prof., 1942-43, assoc. prof., 1943-47, prof., 1947-59, Kenan prof., 1959-66, prof. emeritus, 1966-85; vis. prof. U. Colo., summer 1963, 67, Wake Forest U., 1965-75. With German Army, 1914-19. Recipient Sci. Research award Oak Ridge Inst. Nuclear Studies, 1948, Tanner award U. N.C., 1963, Hegel medal Humboldt U., Berlin, 1971; Alfred T. Brauer Library at U. N.C. named in his honor., 1976. Mem. Am. Math. Soc., Math. Assn. Am., N.C. Acad. Sci., Elisha Mitchell Sci. Soc., Deutsche Math. Verein, Sigma Xi. Home: Chapel Hill N.C. Died Dec. 24, 1985.

BRAUN, ARMIN CHARLES JOHN, educator; b. Milw., Sept. 5, 1911; s. Adolph and Ella (Schreiber) B. BS, U. Wis., 1934; predoctoral study, European sci. labs., 1936-37; PhD, U. Wis., 1938. With Rockefeller U., N.Y.C., 1938-86, successively fellow, asst., assoc., assoc. mem., assoc. prof., 1938-59, mem. and prof., 1959-86, head dept. plant biology, 1955-86; mem. sci. panel biology and medicine NSF, 1958-61; mem. sci. adv. bd. Inst. Cancer Research Phila., 1959-65; sci. adv. panel Brookhaven Nat. Lab., 1960-64; mem. adv. com. Aspen Biol Inst., 1965-68. Author numerous sci. papers, books. Capt. AUS, 1943-46. Recipient Newcomb Cleveland award AAAS, 1949, Charles Leopold Mayer prize French Acad. Scis., 1982; Jenkinson Meml. lectr. Oxford U., 1978. Fellow Am. Bot. Soc. (hon.), Am. Phytopath. Soc. (hon.); mem. Am. Acad. Arts and Scis., Nat. Acad. Scis., Harvey Soc. (hon.), Internat. Soc. Developmental Biologists, AAAS, Soc. Developmental Biology, Sigma Xi, Phi Sigma, Alpha Zeta, Delta Theta Sigma. Home: Princeton N.J. Died Sept. 2, 1986; buried Forest Home Cemetery, Milwaukee, Wis.

BRAWLEY, PAUL HOLM, editor; b. Granite City, Ill., Sept. 27, 1942; s. Paul Virgil and Lucille Melba (Holm) B. B.A. in English, So. Ill. U., 1965; M.S. in L.S, Simmons Coll., Boston, 1968. Recs. librarian Boston Pub. Library, 1965-66, audio-visual librarian, 1966-68; nonprint revs. editor Booklist (A.L.A.), Chgo., 1969-73; editor-in-chief, art dir. Booklist (A.L.A.), 1973-88; Guest lectr. library sci. Kent State U., L.I. U., Dalhousie U., Halifax, N.S., Syracuse U., U. Wash., Seattle. Active Hunger Project. Mem. ALA, Sigma Pi. Home: Chgo. Ill. Died Oct. 2, 1988.

BRAYMAN, HAROLD, public relations consultant; b. Middleburgh, N.Y., Mar. 10, 1900; s. Channing and Minnie C. (Feeck) B.; m. Martha Witherspoon Wood, Jan. 25, 1930; children: Harold Halliday, Walter Witherspoon. AB, Cornell U., 1920; LLD (hon.), Gettysburg Coll., 1965. Tchr. English and history Ft. Lee (N.J.) High Sch., 1920-22; reporter Albany (N.Y.) Evening Jour., 1922-24; asst. legislative corr. N.Y. Evening Post, 1924-26, corr., 1926-1928, Washington corr., 1928-33; Washington corr. Phila. Evening Ledger; writer syndicated column Daily Mirror of Washington, 1934-40; Washington corr. Houston Chronicle and other newspapers, 1940-42; spl. corr. in, London, 1925, covered all nat. convs. and nat. polit. campaigns, 1928-40; asst. dir., public relations dept. E.I. du Pont de Nemours & Co., 1942-44, dir., 1944-65; corporate exec. in residence Am. U., 1968; bd. visitors Sch. Pub. Relations and Communications, Boston U., chmn., 1961-71. Editor: Pub. Relations Jour, 1956; author: Corporate Management in a World of Politics, 1967, Developing a Philosophy for Business Action, 1969, (with A.O.H. Grier) A History of the Lincoln Club of Delaware, 1970, The President Speaks Off-the-Record, 1976. Mem. Cornell U. Council, chmn., 1961-63; mem. Cornell Centennial planning com., also chmn. adv. council grad. sch. bus. and pub. adminstrn., 1960-65; trustee emeritus Gettysburg Coll.; trustee Found. for Pub. Relations Research and Edn., 1956-62, Wilmington Med. Center.; mem. sponsoring com. Pub. Relations Seminar, 1952-61. Recipient citation Pub. Relations Soc. Am., 1963; Golden Plate award Am. Acad. Achievement, 1965. Mem. U.S. C. of C. (com. on taxation 1954-60, com. on govt. ops. and expenditures 1964-66), Am. Acad. Achievement (v.p. 1966-74), Mfg. Chemists Assn. (pub. relations adv. com. 1951-56, chmn. 1951-53), Mencken Soc. of Del. (pres. 1980-81), Ams. for the Competitive Enterprise System (life bd. dirs.). Clubs: University (N.Y.C.), Gridiron (pres. 1941), Nat. Press (pres. 1938), Overseas Writers (Washington), Wilmington, Wilmington Country (dir. 1952-64), Greenville Country (Wilmington, Del.). Lodge: Rotary. Home: Wilmington Del. Died Jan. 3, 1988.

BREATHED, JOHN WILLIAM, food products executive; b. Chgo., May 25, 1891; s. Edward McGill and Nettie (Little) B.; m. Rachel Woods, Dec. 8, 1920; 1 son, John W. BS, U. Chgo., 1915. With Borden Milk Co., N.Y.C., 1919-20; with Cudahy Packing Co., Chgo., from 1920, v.p. and dir., from 1944; pres. Am. Salt Corp., from 1943; bd. dirs. Am. Salt Corp., Western Engraving & Embossing Co. 1st lt., Inf., AEF, U.S. Army, 1917-19. Mem. Delta Kappa Epsilon. Home: Omaha Nebr. †

BRECHER, GERHARD ADOLF, physician, educator; b. Goldap, Germany, June 14, 1909; came to U.S., 1948, naturalized, 1955; s. Otto Ernst and Hedwig (Wulst), B.; m. Eleanor Baker, Apr. 23, 1941; children: Armin G., M. Herbert, Elisabeth E. Student, U. Hamburg, 1928-28, PhD, 1932; MA, Duke U., 1930; postgrad., U. Prague, 1932-34, U. Berlin, 1934-35; MD, U. Kiel, 1937. Instr. physiology U. Kiel, 1937-38; intern U. Calif. Hosp., San Francisco, 1938-41; asst. resident Orange Meml. Hosp., Orlando, Fla., 1939-40; resident Brewster Hosp., Jacksonville, Fla., 1940-41; sr. instr. physiology U. Prague, 1941-45; asst. prof. Western Res. U., Cleve., 1948-54, assoc. prof., 1954-55; prof., dir. Inst. Research in Vision Ohio State U., Columbus, 1955-57; prof. physiology Emory U., Atlanta, 1957-66, chmn. dept., 1957-66, chief clin. physiology, dept. internal medicir 1966; med. cons. Gen. Electric Co., Clevel, 1954-8 Tuskegee Inst. Sch. Vet Medicine, 1963-67; disting. pr U. Okla. Med. Ctr., Oklahoma City, 1967-88. Auth Venous Return, 1956, (with P.M. Galletti) Heart Lu Bypass, 1962; contbr. numerous articles to sci. publs Fellow Am. Coll. Cardiology; mem. Am. Physiol. So Assn. for Research in Ophthalmology, Am. Hea Assn., Am. Soc. Physiology (disting. mem. circulati group), Am. Illuminating Soc. Home: Atlanta Ga. Di Feb. 25, 1988; buried Atlanta.

BREDELL, HAROLD HOLMES, lawyer; b. Indpl June 18, 1907; s. Jesse Bailey and Flora E. (Glasscoc B.; m. Victoria Schreiber, Apr. 20, 1939 (dec. D 1975); children: Harold H., Philip K. AB, Butler U 1929; LLB, Harvard U., 1932. Bar: Ind. 1932. Lec Ind. Law Sch., 1938-40; mem. Bredell, Mart McTurnan & Meyer, 1947-80; chmn. Vernon Fire Casualty Ins. Co., Vernon Gen. Ins. Co.; pres., bd. di Vernon Fin. Corp., Ins. Investment Corp. Contbr. legal jours. Bd. dirs. Festival Music Soc., 1978-82. USNR, 1944-46. Mem. ABA (treas., bd. govs. 1949-5 bd. dirs. endowment 1959-75, treas. 1959-65, v.p. 19 71, pres. endowment 1971-73), Ind. Bar Assn., Indp Bar Assn., C. of C., Ind. Soc. Chgo., Ind. Harvard L Assn., Lawyers Club, Harvard Club, Columbia Cl (Indpls.), Highland Country Club, Traders Point Hu Club. Republican. Episcopalian. Home: Indianapo Ind. Died Feb. 23, 1982.

BREED, FRANCES, association executive; b. N.Y. Feb. 21; d. Henry Eltinge and Ethel (Burns) B.; 1 da Ann. Artist's diploma, Juilliard Sch. Music, 1936; A cum laude, Barnard Coll., 1940; postgrad., Berksh Music Ctr., 1940, Ind. U. Grad. Sch. Bus. Adminstr 1965, New Sch. Social Research, 1966, Brookings Ins 1968, Columbia U. Grad. Sch. Bus., 1969. Dir. a minstrn. Planned Parenthood-World Populati N.Y.C., 1960-66; assoc. dir. community services S Info. and Edn. Council U.S., N.Y.C., 1966-69; ex Harold L. Oram, Inc., N.Y.C., 1969-70; dir. devel. a pub. relations Nat. Audubon Soc., N.Y.C., 1971- v.p., from 1977; mgr. population program from 19 rep. UN Conf. on Human Environment, Stockhol 1972, Nat. Council Philanthropy, 1974-75, Intern Conf. Family Planning, Indonesia, 1981, UN Exp Working Group, Geneva, 1983. Mem. Nat. Inst. Soc Scis., Nat. Soc. Fund Raising Execs. (dir. N.Y.C. chp Conf. UN Reps. of UN Assn. U.S. (exec. com. 198 Council Non-Govt. Orgns. Deceased.

BREEN, JOSEPH SYLVESTER, university de clergyman; b. Phila., Mar. 29, 1918; s. Joseph Mich and Anna Mary (Phelan) B. Student, St. Joseph's Co Princeton, N.J., St. Vincent's Sem., Phila., Mary I maculate Sem., Northampton, Pa.; MA in Ma Columbia U., 1948; MA in Philosophy, Cath. U. A 1950, PhD, 1952. Joined Soc. of Vincentians, 19 ordained priest Roman Cath. Ch., 1944. Instr. ma Niagara (N.Y.) U., 1944-45, instr. math. a philosophy, 1952-57, exec. sec. nat. alumni assn., 19 58, asst. to pres. univ., 1958-60, dir. recruitment, 19 60; tchr. math. St. John's U. Prep. Sch., Bklyn., spri 1945-46; instr. math. St. John's U., 1946-49, philosop 1960-61, dean Colls. Liberal Arts and Scis., from 19 also trustee. Author: Civilization and God, 1950, R gion and Secularism in the Light of Thomis Philosophy, 1952, Hello, Brother, 1955; editor: Cent nial (1956-1956) History of Niagara University, 19 Formula for Progress, 1957; mem. editorial bd. Niag U. Eagle, 1958-60. Mem. nat. adv. bd. Nat. Fedn. Ca Colls. Mem. Am. Assn. Coll. Deans, Scabbard a Blade, Alpha Phi Omega. Home: Jamaica N.Y. D Feb. 6, 1989.

BREESKIN, ADELYN DOHME, senior curato adviser, former art museum director, art adviser; Balt., July 19, 1896; d. Alfred R.L. and Emmie (Blu mer) Dohme; m. Elias Breeskin, Apr. 12, 1920; child Jean (Mrs. Clayton Timbrell), Dorothy (Mrs. Doro B. Brown), Gloria (Mrs. Cornelius Peck). Grad., R cliffe Coll., 1918, Sch. Fine Arts, Crafts and Decora Design, Boston, 1918; LD, Goucher Coll., Balt., 19 DFA, Washington Coll., 1961, Wheaton Coll., 19 Hood Coll., 1966, Morgan State Coll., 1966. As print dept. Met. Mus. Art, N.Y.C., 1918-20; with B Mus. Art, 1930-62, acting dir., 1942-47, dir., 1947 dir. Washington Gallery Modern Art, 1962-64; cura graphic art, lectr. U.S.A. and abroad; curator 20th C tury painting and sculpture Nat. Collection of F Arts, Smithsonian Instn., Washington, 1968-74, curatorial advisor, 1981-86. Author: Catalo Raisonne, Graphic Works of Mary Cassatt, 2d ec 1979, Catalogue Raisonne of Paintings, Past Watercolors and Drawings by Mary Cassatt, 197 Decorated Star of Solidarity by Italian Govt., 19 recipient Disting. Service award U. Md., 1962, U commr. Am. Pavilion, Venice Exhbn., 1960. M Assn. Art Mus. Dirs. (sec.-treas. 1953-56, pres 19 57), Internat. Graphic Arts Soc. (mem. Am. jury selection, 1955-65), Print Council Am. (sec. 1956 Home: Washington D.C. Died July 24, 1986.

BREITENSTEIN, JEAN SALA, judge; b. Keok Iowa, July 18, 1900; s. George J. and Ida M. (Sala) m. Helen Collamore Thomas, July 8, 1925; c dren—Eleanore Thomas (Mrs. George M. Wilfl

:er Frederick. A.B., U. Colo., 1922, LL.B., 1924, ..D., 1965; LL.D., U. Denver, 1960. Bar: Colo. 1924. st. atty. gen. Colo., 1925-29, asst. U.S. dist atty., 30-33; practice law Denver, 1933-54; atty. State Colo. interstate water matters 1940-54; U.S. dist. judge lo., 1954-57; U.S. circuit judge 10th Circuit, Denver, 57-70; sr. circuit judge 10th Circuit, 1970-86. Mem. 3A, Colo. Bar Assn., Denver Bar Assn., Order of if, Phi Beta Kappa. Republican. Episcopalian. ıbs: Mason (33 deg.), Law, Denver Country, Denver; iversity. Home: Denver Colo. Died Jan. 30, 1986.

:EMNER, JOHN BURTON, journalist; b. Brisbane, stralia, Dec. 28, 1920; came to U.S., 1950, natural- d, 1960; s. Norman Frederick and Pauline Marcia ıcas) B.; m. Mary Ann McCue, Dec. 23, 1968. STB, opaganda Fide U., Rome, 1941; MS, Columbia U., 52; PhD, U. Iowa, 1965. Ordained priest Roman tholic Ch., 1943-68; nat. sec. Pontifical Mission Aid :s., Australia, 1945-48; editor Cath. Missions, Holy ild, Apostolatus, Australia, 1945-48; insp. schs. sbane (Australia) Archdiocese, 1948-49; assoc. editor . Cath., 1953-54; polit. columnist Los Angeles Tid- s, 1954-56; assoc. prof. English, asst. to pres. U. San go, 1957-61; asst. prof. journalism U. Iowa, 1965-68; oc. prof. U. Kans., Lawrence, 1969-72; prof. U. ns., 1972-85, Oscar S. Stauffer prof. journalism, 1976- journalism prof. emeritus, 1986-87; newspaper cons., '3-87. Author: HTK - A Study in News Headlines, '5, Words on Words - A Dictionary for Writers and ıers Who Care About Words, 1980. Pulitzer veling fellow, 1952-53; recipient Amoco Disting. ıching award, HOPE award U. Kans., 1971; Gannett ınd. grantee for nat. editing seminars, 1980-81, 83-84; ster tchr. William Allen White Found. award U. ns., 1985. Mem. Sigma Delta Chi (Disting. Teaching ournalism award 1985), Phi Beta Kappa, Kappa Tau oha. Republican. Home: Ponce Inlet Fla. Died July 1987; buried Lawrence, Kans.

ENNAN, JOSEPH CANTWELL, banker; b. slyn, N.Y., Sept. 26, 1910; s. Joseph P. and Evange- (Walsh) B.; m. Anne C. Patterson, Sept. 7, 1935; 1 d, Constance C. Student, LaSalle Mil. Acad., 1929; B., Georgetown U., 1933. With Mfrs. Trust Co., 3-45, asst. sec., 1940-45; asst. treas. Bankers Trust , 1946-49, asst. v.p., 1949-51, v.p., 1951-52; v.p., . to pres. Emigrant Savs. Bank, N.Y.C., 1953-56; :. Emigrant Savs. Bank, 1957-67, chmn. bd., 1967-78, ın. exec. com., 1979-83, also trustee; dir. St. Joseph's on, S.I., Patterson Fuel Oil Co., Floral Park, N.Y.; cons. Vatican State, Rome, from 1982. Mem. dinals Com. of the Laity; dir. Cath. Youth Orgn., '.C.; bd. dirs. United Hosp. Fund N.Y.; trustee Coll. Mt. St. Vincent, Riverdale, N.Y. Served as lt. comdr. NR, 1942-46. Decorated Bronze Star medal; pient Nat. Brotherhood award NCCJ, 1969; Gold lal Cath. Youth Orgn., 1974; Good Scout award Boy uts Am., 1975; Knight of Malta. Mem. Friendly s of St. Patrick (treas.). Club: Seaview Country. ne: New York N.Y. Died Nov. 12, 1987.

ENNER, ROBERT, government official, safety ex- ; b. Atlantic City, May 20, 1922; s. Samuel and ıie (Erien) B.; m. Esther Fairmont, Dec. 18, 1955; dren: Richard Aaron, Ruth Andrea, Sharon n. BS in Mech. Engring., U. Pa., 1943; MS in En- g., U. Calif. at Los Angeles, 1949, PhD, 1962. Re- ered profl. engr., Calif. Designer Lockheed Aircraft , 1943-44; plant engr. Am. Can. Co., 1946048; mem. lty U. Calif. at Los Angeles, 1949-66; cons. Dept. ımerce, Washington, 1966, dep. dir. Nat. Hwy. ty Bur., 1966-86, acting dir. Nat. Hwy. Safety Bur.,)-70, chief scientist Nat. Hwy. Safety Bur., 1971-86; :. in field. Author articles in field. Mem. exec. com. ional Plan Assn. S. Calif., 1965-66; mem. accident vention panel NIH, 1962-64; sec. hwy. safety com. /. Research Bd., 1960-65; mem. com. traffic safety W, 1967; U.S. del. to CCMS NATO Rd. Safety Pilot ly, 1969-86. With AUS, 1944-46; USA, 1950-53. ıed Calif. Hwy. Safety Man of Yr., 1967. Mem. Automotive Engrs. (tech. bd. 1970-73), Am. Pub. th Assn., Sigma Xi, Tau Beta Pi. Home: Rockville Died Oct. 25, 1986.

:W, JOHN OTIS, archeologist, educator; b. den, Mass., Mar. 28, 1906; s. Michael Parker and ı (Fryer) B.; m. Evelyn Ruth Nimmo, June 11,); children: Alan Parker, Lindsay Edward. BFA, tmouth Coll., 1928; student, Harvard Grad Sch. , and Scis., 1928-31; PhD, Harvard U., 1941; LLD ıternat. Relations, U. Liberia, 1970. Fellow arche- y U. Chgo. Expdn., 1930; mem. staff Harvard U. ody Mus., 1930-88, asst. to dir., 1930-47, asst. tor, 1941-45, curator, 1945-48, dir., 1948-67, tor, 1945-48, Peabody Prof. Am. Archeol. and ıol., 1949-72, prof. emeritus, 1972-88, asst. to dir., , dir. field seasons, 1935-39, mem. staff, 1937-88, curator, 1941-45, curator, 1945-48, dir., 1948-67, ged in archeol. reconnaissance for mus. in N.Mex. Ariz., 1946-47, Peabody prof. Am. archeology and ology, 1949-72, prof. emeritus, 1972-88; mem. bd. ics Harvard U. Press; vis. prof.So. Meth. U., 1972- 'is. lectr. U. Calgary, Alta., Can., fall 1977; archeol. . TVA; chmn. UNESCO comm. for Monuments stic and historic sites and archeol excavations); . adv. bd. Nat. Park Service, 1952-58, Nat. Park ce Adv. Council, 1968-88; bd. dirs. Human Relations Area Files, chmn. bd., 1954-57; chmn. U.S. Nat. Com. for Preservation of Monuments of Nubia; mem. internat ctr. com. Adv. council Historic Preservation, 1966-88; field work: sci. dir. Claflin-Emerson Expdn., 1931; dir. Southeastern Utah Expdn., 1931-33; asst. to dir. Harvard Irish Expdn., 1934; dir. Awatovi Expdn., 1935-39; reconnaissance in N.Mex. and Ariz., 1946-47; co-dir. Upper Gila Expdn., 1948-53,. Contbr. articles to jours. and to papers of Peabody Mus. Trustee Fruitlands and the Wayside Museums. Donations for Edn. in Liberia, 1958-88; trustee Plymouth Plantation Inc. Recipient Viking fund medal for anthropology, 1947, Conservation Service award Dept. Interior; decorated grand comdr. Star of Africa. Fellow Am. Acad. Arts and Scis.; mem. Soc. Am. Archeology (council 1944-46, pres. 1949-50), Internat. Inst. for Conservation Mus. Objects, Internat. African Inst. (exec. council), Mass. Archaeol. Soc. (exec. council 1941-44, trustee 1949-52, Tree Ring Soc., Soc. Applied Archaeology, Am. Assn. Museums (council 1956-60), Colonial Soc. Mass., Acad. Am. Francisco Hist. (corr. mem.), S.W. Mus. (hon.), Los Angeles, No. Ariz. Soc. Hist. Sci. and Art., Am. Antiquarian Soc., Mass Hist. Soc., German Archeol. Inst., Soc. Antiquaries, London, Prehistoric Soc. (U.K.), Am. Anthrop. Assn. (pres. 1951), Harvard Faculty Club (pres. 1951-55), Odd Volumes (pres. 1964-69), Cosmos Club (Washington). Home: Cambridge Mass. Died Mar. 19, 1988.

BREWER, JOHN WITHROW, political science educator; b. Boston, Mar. 26, 1904; s. Daniel Chauncey and Genevieve (Withrow) B.; m. Thelma Lillian Martin, Aug. 22, 1943. A.B. maxima cum laude, Princeton U., 1926, M.A., 1930, Ph.D., 1932; student, Harvard Law Sch., 1926-28. Instr. polit. sci. George Washington U., Washington, 1933-34, assoc. prof. internat. law, 1939-46, prof., 1946-73, prof. emeritus internat. law and polit. sci., from 1973, head dept. polit. sci., 1946-63; prof. dept. history Harvard U., Cambridge, Mass.; instr. Dartmouth Coll., 1934-35; asst. prof. polit. sci. Conn. State Coll., 1935-38, assoc. prof., 1938-39; vis. prof. U. So. Calif., from 1950. Served with U.S. Army, 1942-46. Decorated Legion of Merit. Mem. Phi Beta Kappa. Deceased.

BREWER, WILMA DENELL, educator; b. Riley, Kans., Oct. 18, 1915; d. Benjamin Clarence and Rosetta (James) B. BS, Kans. State U., 1935; MS, Wash. State U., 1939; PhD, Mich. State U., 1950. Instr. Simpson Coll., Indianola, Iowa, 1939-40; from instr. to asst. prof. U. N.H., Durham, 1940-43; mem. faculty Mich. State U., E. Lansing, 1943-57, prof., 1954-57; prof. nutrition Iowa State U., Ames, 1957-81, prof. emeritus, 1981-85, dept. head, 1961-77. Mem. Am. Inst. Nutrition, Am. Dietetic Assn., Am. Home Econs. Assn., Am. Chem. Soc., AAAS. Methodist. Home: Berkeley Calif. Died Aug. 9, 1985.

BREWSTER, ELLIS WETHRELL, manufacturing executive; b. Plymouth, Mass., July 13, 1892; s. William W. and Annie L. (Barnes) B.; m. Ellen Hatch, Apr. 11, 1916; children: William S., Lois, Spencer H., Lydia, Benjamin B. BS, MIT, 1913. With Bemis Br. Bag Co., St. Louis and Seattle, 1913-14; asst. MIT, 1914-15; with Plymouth Cordage Co., 1915-61, treas., 1938, pres., 1942, also bd. dirs., chmn. bd., 1951-61; bd. dirs. Plymouth Cordage Industries, Plymouth Nat. Bank, N.Eng. Tel. & Tel. Co., State St. Bank and Trust Co., Plymouth Cordage Co. of Can. Ltd. Mem. Pilgrim Soc. (pres.), Old Colony Club, Union Club, Algonquin Club. Unitarian. Home: Plymouth Mass. †

BREWSTER, KINGMAN, lawyer; b. Longmeadow, Mass., June 17, 1919; s. Kingman and Florence (Besse) B.; m. Mary Louise Phillips, Nov. 30, 1942; children: Constance, Kingman III, Deborah, Alden, Riley. A.B., Yale U., 1941; LL.B., Harvard U., 1948; numerous hon. degrees. Chmn., Yale Daily News, 1940-41; spl. asst. to coordinator Inter-Am. affairs, 1941; research asso. dept. econs. MIT, 1949-50; asst. prof. law Harvard U., 1950-53, prof. law, 1953-60; prof., provost Yale U., 1961-63, pres., 1963-77; ambassador to U.K. 1977-81; counsel Winthrop, Stimson, Putnam & Roberts, N.Y.C., 1981-83, resident ptnr. in charge London office, 1984-86; counsel Winthrop, Stimson, Putnam & Roberts, 1986—; chmn. English-Speaking Union of U.S., 1981-84; master Univ. Coll. Oxford U., Eng., 1986—; chmn. internat. bd. United World Coll., 1986—; asst. gen. counsel Office U.S. Spl. Rep. in Europe, 1948-49; cons. Pres.'s Materials Policy Commn., 1951, Mut. Security Agy., 1952; mem. Pres.'s Commn. on Law Enforcement and Adminstrn. Justice, 1965-67, Pres.'s Commn. on Selective Service, 1966-67; chmn. Nat. Policy Panel UN, 1968. Author: Anti-trust and American Business Abroad, 1959, rev. edit. (with Atwood), 1981, (with M. Katz) Law of International Transactions and Relations, 1960. Former mem. corp. Belmont Hill Sch.; former pres. bd. dirs. Buckingham Soc.; past bd. dirs. Ednl. TV and Radio Ctr.; adv. com. on higher edn. HEW; bd. dirs. Salzburg Seminar in Am. Studies; former mem. bd. dirs. Common Cause; cons. NEH; mem. policy rev. bd. Pub. Agenda Found.; former mem. corp., trustee Carnegie Endowment Internat. Peace; mem. internat. adv. council Population Inst. Served as lt., aviator USNR, 1942-46. Hon. bencher Middle Temple; hon. fellow Clare Coll., Cambridge. Fellow Am. Bar Found.; mem. Mass. Bar, N.Y. Bar, Am. Philos. Soc., Am. Council Learned Socs. (past dir.), Am. Council Edn., Am. Acad. Arts and Scis., Council Fgn. Relations. Clubs: Metropolitan (Washington); Athanaeum, Buck's (London); Tavern (Boston); Yale, Century Assn. (N.Y.C.). Died Nov. 8, 1988.

BREWSTER, RAY QUINCY, educator; b. nr. Guthrie, Okla., Nov. 27, 1892; s. Nathan Augusts and Agnes Adaline (Jones) B.; m. Ida Fay Stewart, Jan. 29, 1919; children: Charles Stewart (dec.), Doris Jean (Mrs. Paul Swift), Nita Agnes (Mrs. Paul Griers), Ina May (Mrs. Donald Fakhoury). AB, Ottawa U., 1914, DSc (hon.), 1959; AM, U. Kans., 1915; PhD, U. Chgo., 1919. Asst. prof. U. Kans., 1919-21, assoc. prof., 1921-27, prof., from 1927, chmn. dept. chemistry, 1940-56; Fulbright lectr. chemistry U. Alexandria, Arab Republic of Egypt, 1952. Author: A Brief Course in Organic Chemistry, 1959; (with W. E. McEwen) Organic Chemistry, 1961; (with C. A. Vanderwefr, W. E. McEwen) Unitized Experiments in Organic Chemistry, 1959. Recipient Midwest medal, 1957. Fellow Am. Inst. Chemists; mem. AAAS, Am. Chem. Soc., Kiwanis, Sigma Xi, Gamma Alpha. Republican. Baptist. Address: Lawrence Kans. †

BREYER, FRANK GOTTLOB, chemical and metallurgical engineer; b. Balt., Dec. 21, 1886; s. Gottlob and Sophia Regina (Smith) B.; m. Marjorie Baker, Dec. 27, 1910; children: Marjorie Love (Mrs. J.A. Singmaster Jr.), Elizabeth Jane (Mrs. W.A. patterson Jr.), Ann Maxwell (Mrs. Ian Ritson). AB, Johns Hopkins U., 1908, MA, 1910; hon. degree, Clarkson Coll. Registered profl. engr., N.Y., Conn. Rsch. worker, then chief chemist N.J. Zinc Co., 1910-17, chief R&D, 1971-27; ptnr. Singmaster & Breyer, N.Y.C., 1927; sr. ptnr., chmn. adv. com. Singmaster & Breyer, Inc.; chmn. bd. Chem. Enterprises, Inc.; bd. dirs. Fluor Corp., Ltd. Patentee in field. Decorated Order of Falcon (Iceland); recipient Modern Pioneer award NAM, 1940. Mem. AIME, ASTM, Am. Inst. Chemists (hon.), Am. Inst. Chem. Engrs., Am. Chem. Soc., Electro-chem. Soc., Assn. Cons. Chemists and Chem. Engrs., Dirs. Indsl. Rsch., U.S. Naval Inst., U.S. Naval Acad. Assn. (hon.), Am. Ordnance Assn., Mining Club, Cheists Club, Pinnacle Club, Clayton Yacht Club. Home: Wilton Conn. †

BRICKER, JOHN WILLIAM, lawyer, former governor; b. Madison County, Ohio, Sept. 6, 1893; s. Lemuel Spencer and Laura (King) B.; m. Harriet Day, Sept. 4, 1920 (dec. June 1, 1985); 1 son, John Day. AB, Ohio State U., 1916, LLB, 1920, LLD, 1939. Solicitor Grandview Heights, Ohio, 1920-28; asst. atty. gen. Ohio, 1923-27; mem. Pub. Utilities Commn., 1929-32; atty. gen. Ohio, 1933-37; mem. firm Bricker & Eckler, Ohio, 1939-45; dir. Buckeye Fed. Savs. & Loan Assn. Ohio, 1939-45; gov. Columbus, Ohio, 1939-45; Republican candidate for vice pres. U.S. 1944; mem. from Ohio U.S. Senate, Washington, 1946-58; Past trustee Ohio State U., Dennison U., Defiance Coll. 1st. lt. U.S. Army, World War I. Mem. ABA, Ohio Bar Assn., Columbus Bar Assn., Am. Legion, Masons (33 degree Supreme Council), Shriners, Rotary, Faculty (Ohio State U.), Torch Club, Athletic Club, Kit-Kat Club, University Club, Order of Coif, Delta Chi, Delta Sigma Rho. Republican. Mem. Community Ch. Home: Columbus Ohio. Died Mar. 22, 1986.

BRICKMAN, WILLIAM WOLFGANG, teacher educator; b. N.Y.C., June 30, 1913; s. David Shalom and Chaya Sarah (Shaber) B.; m. Sylvia Schnitzer, Feb. 26, 1958; children: Joy (Mrs. Gary Poupko), Chaim M., Sara V. (Mrs. Shlomo Sudry). BA, CUNY, 1934, MS in Edn, 1935; PhD, NYU, 1938; MA (hon.), U. Pa., 1972. Instr. edn. NYU, 1940-42, 46-48, lectr. in edn., 1948-50, asst. prof., 1950-51, asso. prof., 1951-57, prof., 1957-62; prof. ednl. history and comparative edn. U. Pa., Phila., 1962-81; prof. emeritus U. Pa., 1981-86; dean Touro Coll., N.Y.C., 1977-79; vis. prof. univs. in, U.S., South Africa, Germany, and Israel.; Pres.'s research fellow in history Brown U., 1950-51. Author: Two Millenia of International Relations in Higher Education, 1975, Educational Histiography: Tradition, Theory and Technique, 1983, Educational Roots and Routes in Western Europe, 1985; co-author: The Changing Soviet School, 1960, Conflict and Change on Campus, 1970, A Bibliography of American Educational History, 1975, others; Editor: Intellect (formerly School and Society), 1953-76, Western European Education, 1979-86; contbr. articles to encys., yearbooks, jours. Mem. Comparative and Internat. Edn. Soc. (pres.). Home: Cherry Hill N.J. Died June 22, 1986; buried Jerusalem, Israel.

BRIGGS, LEON EUGENE, automotive executive; b. Syracuse, N.Y., Jan. 31, 1892; s. Samuel and Ida (Chase) B.; m. Noreene Crane, Aug. 28, 1945; children: Patricia Ann, Lenore Ida. Student, Northwestern U. Sch. Commerce, 1917-20. With Ford Motor Co., from 1914, stenograph, Chgo. br., 1914-16, asst. comptroller, 1918-20; travelling auditor Detroit, 1920-24; comptroller, Des Moines, 1924-25; travelling auditor assigned to Europe, 1925-29; successively asst. gen. auditor and gen. auditor Ford Motor Co., Dearborn, Mich., 1946-57; ret. trustee Detroit Inst. Cancer Research; trustee Mich. Cancer Found. Served wtih USN, WWI. Mem. Detroit Bd. Commerce, Nat. Assn. Accts., Newcomen Soc. Republican. Mason. Clubs: Detroit, Economic, Oakland Hills Country. Home: Birmingham Mich. †

BRIGGS, MARVIN JAMES, farm association executive; b. Macy, Ind., June 2, 1892; s. Albert M. and Ida (Lovett) B.; m. Sylvia True Lowry, Nov. 22, 1924. Student, Rochester (Ind.) Normal, 1908, Ind. U., 1908-10; spl. student, Purdue U. Tchr. Rochester (Ind.) Schs., 1911-14; mem. staff extension dept., agrl. coll. Purdue U., 1913-18; treas., asst. gen. mgr. Ind. Farm Bur. Coop. Assn. Inc., 1927-46, gen. mgr., 1946-57, cons., 1957-59; past sec. Ind. Grain Coop. Inc.; pres., dir. Cockshutt Farm Equipment Inc.; bd. dirs. FCA, Louisville, 1936-53; mem. Fed. Farm Credit Bd., chmn. from 1956. Recipient citation DePauw U., 1952, Purdue Agrl. Alumni Assn. award, 1955, Disting. Svc. to Agr. award Mo. Farmers Assn., 1960. Mem. Nat. Coun. Farmer Coops. (exec. com., chmn. farm credit com., pres. 1955-56), Am. Farm Rsch. Assn. (dir.), Masons, Columbia Club (Indpls.), Highland Golf and Country Club. Mem. Christian Ch. Home: Indianapolis Ind. †

BRIGGS, MITCHELL PIRIE, educator; b. Le Mars, Iowa, Feb. 23, 1892; s. William Henry and Elizabeth (Goldie) B.; m. Mary Elizabeth Bradford, July 31, 1920. AB, Morningside Coll., 1914; MA, U. Wis., 1917; PhD, Stanford U., 1930; LLD, Golden Gate Coll., 1965. Tchr. Pierre (Iowa) High Sch., 1912-13; prin. Lake Preston (S.D.) High Sch., 1914-15; tchr. Sheldon (Iowa) High Sch., 1915-16, Fresno High Sch., Jr. Coll., 1917-28; instr. history Stanford, 1929-30; instr. Fresno State Coll., 1928-29, prof. history, 1930-54, dean of men, dean summer sessions, 1930-48, dean instrn., 1948-54; exec. sec.-treas. Western Coll. Assn., 1954-65. Author: George D. Herron and the European Settlement, 1932; (with Betty Allen) Behave Yourself, 1938; If You Please, 1942, Mind Your Manners, 1956; Central Eastern Europe (with Joseph S. Roucek et al), 1946. Mem. Am. Hist. Assn. Republican. Congregationalist. Home: Fresno Calif. †

BRIGGS, ROGER THOMAS, holding corporation executive; b. Greenwich, Conn., Mar. 6, 1929; s. Alfred Charles and Therese (Golden) B.; m. Elizabeth Dickson, Oct. 28, 1950; children: Teresa Bridgman, Roger Jr., Patricia. BBA, U. Miami, Fla., 1952. CPA, N.Y., Ill. Mgr. Price Waterhouse & Co., N.Y.C., 1952-64; contr. Sterling Drug Co., N.Y.C., 1964-68; v.p. Hartwell Mgmt. Corp., N.Y.C., 1968-70; vice chmn. Esmark, Inc., Chgo., 1970-84; ptnr. Kelly Briggs & Assocs., Chgo., 1984-86; exec. v.p., chief fin. officer, dir. Beatrice Cos., Inc., Chgo., 1986-87; exec. v.p., chief fin. officer E-II Holdings, Inc., Chgo., 1987-88, also bd. dirs.; bd. dirs. Instl. Liquid Assets, Inc., Chgo., Playtex Co., Stamford, Conn. Trustee Glenwood (Ill.) Sch. for Boys; bd. dirs. Evanston (Ill.) Hosp. Mem. Am. Inst. CPA's, Fin. Execs. Inst. Roman Catholic. Clubs: Econ., Tavern, Univ. (Chgo.); North Shore Country (Glenview, Ill.); Bob O'Link Golf (Highland Pk., Ill.); Sky (N.Y.C.). Home: Wilmette Ill. Died Feb. 11, 1989.

BRIGHTMAN, HAROLD WARREN, department store president; b. Fall River, Mass., Nov. 5, 1889; s. Charles and Abbie J. (Albert) B.; m. Florence Pennington, Jan. 28, 1914; children: Emerson Eliot, Robert Lloyd. AB, Harvard U., 1911. Stockboy Wm. Filenes Sons Co., Boston, 1911-12, various positions merchandising div., 1912-18, asst. to gen. mdse. mgr., 1918-21, div. mdse. mgr., 1921-24; div. mdse. mgr. Abraham F. Strauss, Bklyn., 1924-27, Gimbel Bros., N.Y.C., 1927-30; dir. mdse. mgr. L. Bamberger & Co., Newark, 1930-35, v.p. and gen. mdse. mgr., 1935-44; exec. mdse. dir. Meir & Frank, Portland, Oreg., 1944-45; sr. v.p. Lit Bros., Phila., 1945-47, pres., 1947-54; chmn. bd. Swern & Co., Trenton, N.J., 1947-54; v.p., dir., mem. exec. com. City Stores Co., N.Y.C.; mem. adv. com. Tradesmen's Land Title Bank & Trust Co., Phila.; dir. Bonwit Teller (Phila.), Bankers Securities Corp., Phila. Transp. Co. Contbr. articles in field. Hon. chmn. bd. Nat. Consumer-Retailer Coun., N.Y.C.; v.p., dir. Phila. Better Bus. Bur.; mem. retail adv. bd. Drexel Heritage Found., N.Y.C.; mem. adv. bd., Phila. Coun. Chs.; mem. fin. adv. com. Phila. YWCA; chmn. Phila. div. Nat. Conf. Christians and Jews. Recipient civilian cert. of award for disting. pub. svc. to USN from sec. of navy. Mem. C. of C. (past chmn., dir., mem. exec. com.), Harvard Club (N.Y.C.); Union League Club (Phila.); Smoke Rise Club (Butler, N.J.). Home: Butler N.J. †

BRINCKERHOFF, CHARLES M., mining company executive; b. Mpls., Mar. 15, 1901; s. William H. and MaryBelle (Sharp) B.; m. Florence M. Andreen, Oct. 11, 1926; 1 child, Carol B. Brinckerhoff Kietzman. B.A., Columbia U., 1922, Metall. Engr., 1925; Sc.D. (hon.), U. Ariz., 1967. With Phelps-Dodge Corp., Inspiration Consol. Copper Co. and Andes Copper Mining Co., 1925-48; gen. mgr. Chile Exploration Co., 1948-56; v.p. Andes Copper Mining Co., Chile Exploration Co., 1956-57, exec. v.p., 1957-58; pres., dir. Anaconda Co., 1958, vice chmn. bd., chief exec. officer, 1964-65, chmn. bd., chief exec. officer, 1965-69, chmn. exec. com., cons., from 1969, dir., chmn. bd., pres. subs. and affiliated cos.; dir. Nat. Mines Service Co., Pitts.; mining advisor Govt. of Iran, others. Contbr. articles to profl. jours. Served with U.S. Army, World War I. Decorated Bernardo O'Higgins Order of Merit (Chile); recipient George Vincent Wendell medal Columbia U., also Egleston medal; Gold medal Chilean Mining Soc.; Hoover medal, 1974. Mem. Mining and Metall. Soc. Am., AIME (hon.; Saunders medal), Holland Soc. of N.Y. (trustee from 1967, Gold medal), Nat. Acad. Engring., Sigma Xi. Presbyterian. Clubs: University, Mining (N.Y.C.). Died Apr. 22, 1987.

BRINK, ROYAL ALEXANDER, educator; b. Woodstock, Ont., Can., Sept. 16, 1897; came to U.S., 1920, naturalized, 1933; s. Royal Wilson and Elizabeth Ann (Cuthbert) B.; m. Edith Margaret Whitelaw, Dec. 27, 1922 (dec. May, 1962); children: Andrew Whitelaw, Margaret Alexandra; m. Joyce Hickling, Oct. 19, 1963. BSA, Ont. Agrl. Coll., 1919; MS, U. Ill., 1921; DSc, Harvard U., 1923; postgrad. (NRC fellow), Institut für Vererbungsforschung, Berlin and Birmingham U., U.K., 1925-26, Calif. Inst. Tech., 1938-39. Chemist Western Can. Flour Mills, Winnipeg, Man., Can., 1919-20; Emerson fellow in biology Harvard U., Boston, 1921-22; asst. prof. genetics U. Wis., Madison, 1922-27, assoc. prof., 1929-31, prof., 1931-68, emeritus prof. genetics, 1969-84, chmn. dept., 1939-51. Editor: Heritage from Mendel, 1967; mng. editor: Genetics, 1952-56; contbr. numerous researh papers to biol. jours. Haight Traveling fellow U. Wis., 1960-61; NSF Sr. Postdoctorate fellow, 1966-67. Fellow AAAS: mem. Am. Genetics Assn., Genetics Soc. Am. (pres. 1957), Bot. Soc. Am., Am. Acad. Arts and Scis., Am. Soc. Naturalists (pres. 1963), Nat. Acad. Scis., Wis. Acad. of Scis., Arts and Letters, Univesity Club, Sigma Xi (pres. Wis. chpt. 1940-41), Phi Sigma, Phi Eta. Home: Madison Wis. Died Oct. 3, 1984; buried Woodstock, Ont., Can.

BRISCOE, WILLIAM ALEXANDER, physician, physiology educator; b. London, May 26, 1918; s. Henry Vincent and Rebecca Kirkwood (Stevenson) B.; m. Anne Briscoe, Aug. 20, 1955. B.A., Oxford U., 1939, M.A., 1940, B.M., B.Ch., 1942, D.M., 1950. Intern, resident, chief resident Royal Postgrad. Med. Sch., London, 1947-51; fellow chest service Columbia U. Div., Bellevue Hosp., N.Y.C., 1951; fellow dept. physiology U. Pa., Phila., 1952; mem. pneumoconiosis research unit Cardiff, Wales, 1953-55; asst. prof. physiology U. Pa., 1955-56; asst. prof. medicine Columbia U., N.Y.C., 1956-61; assoc. prof. Columbia U., 1961-68; prof. medicine Cornell U. Med. Coll., N.Y.C., from 1971; clin. prof. physiology Cornell U. Med. Coll., from 1975; cons. in pulmonary medicine Burke Rehab. Ctr.; mem. med. adv. bd. Will Rogers Inst. Author: (with others) The Lung: Clinical Physiology, 1955, 3d edit., 1985. Trustee Stony Wold-Herbert Fund. Served to capt. M.C. Brit. Army, 1943-46. Fellow Royal Coll. Physicians, Am. Coll. Chest Physicians, A.C.P.; mem. Am. Physiol. Soc., Am. Thoracic Soc., Am. Soc. Clin. Investigation, Assn. Am. Physicians, Undersea Med. Soc., N.Y. Lung Club (pres. 1971—). Home: New York N.Y. Deceased.

BRISTOL, BENJAMIN HIEL, banker; b. Naugatuck, Conn., June 19, 1896; s. Edgar H. and May C.(Rexford) B.; m. Lida C. Brannon, June 24, 1933; children: Edgar H., Eleanor C., William L. BS, MIT, 1918. With Foxboro Co., Foxboro, Mass., 1919-87, pres., dir., 1944-62, chmn. bd., 1962-67; with Foxboro Nat. Bank, Foxboro, 1938-87, v.p., 1942-63, pres., 1963-67, chmn. bd., dir., 1967-87; dir. Sentry Co.; trustee Worcester Acad., Mass. Meml. Hosp.; trustee, former pres. bd. trustees Norwood Hosp. With USN, 1918-19. Mem. Sci. Apparatus Makers Am., Instrument Soc. Am. (hon.). Home: Foxboro Mass. Died Jan. 18,1987; buried Rockhill Cemetery, Foxboro, Mass.

BRISTOL, REXFORD ALLYN, automation company executive, banker; b. Naugatuck, Conn., June 25, 1903; s. Bennet B. and Gertrude (Rexford) B.; m. Margaret E. Chickering, Sept. 15, 1926; children: Betsy B., Margaret A. and Barbara A. (twins). B.A., Amherst Coll., 1924; S.B., Mass. Inst. Tech., 1926; D.C.S., Suffolk U., 1951; LL.D., Curry Coll., 1976. Engaged in mfg. 1926-30, engring., 1930-40, engring. and sales, 1940—; with Foxboro Co., Mass., from 1926; treas. Foxboro Co., 1943-57, exec. v.p., 1958-62, pres., 1962—, chmn. bd., 1968-71, chmn. exec. com., from 1971; pres. Foxboro Nat. Bank, 1945-63, v.p., from 1963; also dir.; dir. emeritus Arkwright Boston Ins. Co., New Eng. Mchts. Bank, Robertson Factories, Inc., Taunton, Mass.; dir. Sentry Co., Foxboro.; Mem. Mass. Adv. Council on Vocat. and Tech. Edn. Trustee emeritus Suffolk U.; trustee Stadium Realty Trust, Shaeffer Stadium, Foxboro, 1971-82; chmn. bd. Mass. Taxpayers Found., 1966-69; past pres., trustee Retina Found., Dean Jr. Coll.; mem. corp. Northeastern U., Mus. Sci. Wentworth Inst., Boston. Recipient Silver Beaver award Boy Scouts Am., award Sci. Apparatus Mfrs. Assn., 1977. Mem. Elec. Mfrs. Club, Instrument Soc. Am. (hon.), Mass. Taxpayers Fedn. (past chmn.), Norfolk Trout Club (pres. 1978-80), Chi Psi. Clubs: Algonquin (Boston), University (Boston). Home: Foxboro Mass. Died Sept. 13, 1988.

BRITTON, WILLIAM EVERETT, law educator; b. Bible Grove, Ill., Mar. 23, 1887; s. Joseph Walter and Lucretia Ada (Morgan) B.; m. Sarah Myrtle Castile, July 28, 1916; children: Kent Gunnell, John Mansfield; m. Helen G. Ross, July 30, 1949 (dec. 1957). AB, McKendree Coll., 1909, LLD (hon.), 1955; AM, U. Ill., 1910, JD, 1914. Bar: Ill. 1914. Pvt. practice Chgo., 1914-1916; instr. in law U. Ill., 1916-19, asst. prof. law, 1919-21, prof., 1924-54, prof. emeritus, from 1954, legal counsel, 1945-50; prof. law Ind. U., 1921-24, Hastings Coll. Law, U. Calif., San Francisco, from 1954; vis. prof. summer sessions various univs.; mem. Nat. Co Commrs. on Uniform State Laws, 1922-25. Auth Hornbook on the Law of Bills and Notes, 1943; cont articles to profl. jours. and revs. Mem. ABA, Ill. B Assn., Am. Law Inst., Am. Judicare Soc., AAUP (n pres. 1954-60), Law Club, University Club, Co monwealth Club of Calif., Pi Kappa Alpha, Phi Alp Delta, Phi Beta Kappa, Beta Gamma Sigma, De Sigma Rho, Order of Coif. Republican. Presbyterian.

BROADLEY, SIR HERBERT, United Nations offici b. Louth, Lincolnshire, Eng., Nov. 23, 1892; Stephenson S. and Clara Hollingsworth (Furnish) B.; Kathleen May Moore, Apr. 30, 1927. Ed., King E ward VI Grammar Sch., Louth, Birbeck Coll., London. Entered U.K. Civil Service, 1912; in mil. de India Office, 1912-20; sec. Imperial Customs Con 1921, German Repatriation Act Com., 1921, Imper Econ. Com., 1925-26; with W. S. Crawford Ltd., ad agy., London, 1927, mng. dir. Berlin br., 1927-32, charge distbn. and rsch. dept., 1932-39; joined U. Ministry of Food, 1939, apptd. asst. sec., 1939, pr asst. sec., 1940, dep. sec., 1941, 2d sec., 1945; lea U.K. del. Internat. Wheat Conf., 1947, 48; dep. dir.-g FAO of the UN, 1948-58, acting dir.-gen., 1956; rep. U.K. UNICEF, from 1958. Author: (with Sir Willi Crawford) The People's Food, 1938. Mem. U.K. n com. Freedom from Hunger Campaign, 1961; h fellow Birkbeck Coll., U. London, gov., from 196 Decorated knight comdr. Order Brit. Empire; com Order Crown Belgium; made Freeman, Borough Lou Lincolnshire, by Borough Coun., 1961. Hor Farnham, Surrey England. †

BROCE, THOMAS EDWARD, foundation and ec cational consultant; b. Fort Meade, Md., Oct. 27, 19 s. Thomas Louis and Arlene Derma (Seifert) B.; Barbara Lynn Barnes, Nov. 25, 1960; children: Ash Beth, Thomas Allan, David Edward. BA, Baylor 1957; MA, U. N.C., Chapel Hill, 1965; PhD, U. Ok 1970. Reporter Waco Tribune-Herald, Tex., 1953- dir. pub. relations and devel. Little Rock U., 1959- dir. devel. Duke U., Durham, N.C., 1961-67; v.p. Meth. U., 1967-69; exec. asst. to pres. U. Ok Norman, 1969-73; pres. chmn. bd. Phillips U., En Okla., 1973-78; pres. The Kerr Found., Oklahoma Ci 1979-83; dir. Am. Exchange Bank, Norman; cons. W ford Coll., Spartanburg, S.C., 1972-75, Rice U., 1974, South Fla., 1976-78, Westmont Coll., 1977-81, A Coll., 1978-80, Coker Coll., 1978-80, Okla. M Research Found., 1978-80, Central Meth. Coll., 19 86, Ursuline Acad., 1980-87, Southwestern Coll., 19 84, Wesley Theol. Sem., 1981-88, Milw. Sch. Engrir 1981-88, Austin Coll., 1982-88, Frank Lloyd Wri Found., 1984-88, U. Tex. Health Sci. Ctr., Houst 1986-88, St. Edward's U., 1987-88, Iliff Sch. of T ology, 1987-88. Author: Fund Raising: The Guide Raising Money from Private Sources, 1986, Directory Oklahoma Foundations, 1981; contbg. auth Handbook Higher Education Adminstration, 1970. dirs. Inst. Resource Devel., 1972-88; bd. visitors Ba U.; bd. advisors Regis. Coll.; trustee Fellowship Christian Athletes, Okla. Med. Research Found., Cr Acad., Rocky Mountain Heart Research Inst. Ser with USAF, 1957-59. Mem. Nat. Soc. Fund Rais Execs. (dir.), Sigma Delta Chi, Phi Delta Kappa. Clu Rotarian, Men's Dinner, Petroleum (Oklahoma Ci Died Apr. 4, 1988; buried The Mountains, Evergr Colo.

BROCK, VENTRESS NOLAN, college administra b. Rochester, Tex., Aug. 12, 1924; s. Robert Lawre and Lamiza Pearl (Brown) B.; m. Mary June Po June 22, 1952; children: Roderick Mark, Lisa Jun ne. BA magna cum laude, Hardin-Simmons U., 19 MEd, U. Tex., 1957; EdD, Tex. Tech U., 1970. T Sweetwater (Tex.) High Sch., 1949-64, dir. publs., 19 64, vice prin., 1954-64; prin. Snyder (Tex.) High S 1964-69; dean, exec. v.p. Western Tex. Coll., Sny 1970-85; Guest lectr. Columbia U., N.Y.C., 1964; gu expert-lectr. U. Mo., 1957; lectr. U. Tex., 1961. Con articles to profl. jours. Vice pres. United Way, Sny 1963-64; pres., trustee Scurry County div. Am. H Assn., 1981-86; chmn. Snyder Bicentennial, 1975; dirs. Scurry County Mus., 1986. Served with Sig Corps AUS, 1943-46. Decorated Bronze Star me recipient Gold Key award Columbia U., 1963; na Outstanding Young Man in Sweetwater, 1956, O standing Journalism Tchr. in Tex., 1964. Mem. T Assn. Jr. Coll. Instructional Adminstrs. (sec.-tr 1980-81, pres. 1983-84), Tex. Jr. Coll. Tchrs. Assn., Delta Kappa. Democrat. Baptist (deacon-trust Clubs: Gold Coats (pres. 1984), Rotary (pres. 1963- dir. 1963-65). Home: Snyder Tex. Died May 2, 19 buried Hillside Meml. Gardens, Snyder.

BROCKMAN, EARL HUGO, agriculture coopera executive; b. Rushville, Nebr., Oct. 22, 1892; s. Aug and Florence (King) B.; m. Pearl O. Cook, Apr. 1925; 1 child, Earl Francis. Student, U. Ca Berkeley, 1914-15, U. Idaho, 1915-16. Clk. hardw store Weiser, Idaho, 1912-14; farmer 1920-22; br. m Idaho Egg Producers, Pocatello and Twin Falls, 19 29; gen. mgr. Idaho Egg Producers, Caldwell, f 1930; bd. dirs. Nat. Coun. Farmer Coops., Washingt Bd. dirs. Fed. Farm Credit Bd., from 1953; pres. cc Boy Scouts Am., 1940-42; sec. fin. com. Idaho R Cen. Com., 1942-52. Capt. U.S. Army, 1916-1 corated Croix du Guerre (France). Mem. Norbest rkey Growers Assn. (bd. dirs. 1930-39, pres. 1934-, Idaho Coop. Coun. (pres. 1931), Pacific Dairy and ultry Assn. (v.p. 1950), Masons, Elks, Kiwanis (pres. al chpt. 1942), Phi Delta Theta. †

ODE, ROBERT B., physicist; b. Walla Walla, sh., June 12, 1900; s. Howard Stidham and Martha therine (Bigham) B.; m. Bernice Hedley Bidwell, Sept. 1926; children: William (dec.), John Howard. BS, itman Coll., 1921, DSc, 1954; PhD, Calif. Inst. ch., 1924; postgrad. (Rhodes scholar), Oxford U., g., 1924-25; Internat. Edn. Bd. fellow, Göttingen U., rmany, 1925-26; NRC fellow, Princeton U., 1926-27; D, U. Calif., Berkeley, 1970. Assoc. physicist U.S. r. Standards, 1924; asst. prof. physics U. Calif., keley, 1927-30, assoc. prof., 1930-32, prof., 1932-67, f. emeritus, 1967-1986; vis. prof. MIT, 1932; Gugheim fellow London and Cambridge, 1934-35; ysicist dept. terrestrial magnetism Carnegie Inst., 1; sect. T., applied physics lab. OSRD, Johns pkins, U., 1942-43, supervising research and devel. proximity fuse and fire control equipment; group der Los Alamos Atomic Bomb Lab., 1943-46, rvard, summer 1948; mem. physics div. NRC, 1951- v.p. Internat. Union Pure and Applied Physics, 4-60, U.S. del. Internat. Council Sci. Unions, rway, 1955, Washington, 1958; assoc. dir. NSF, 8-59; mem. bd. fgn. scholarships Dept. State, 1963- Contbr. articles to profl. publs. Recipient Fulbright ard, Manchester, 1951-52. Fellow Am. Phys. Soc., AS (v.p. 1949, pres Pacific div. 1956); mem. Am. n. Physics Teachers, Am. Assn. U. Profs. (2d v.p. 0-61), Am. Assn. Rhodes Scholars, Am. Acad. Arts Scis., Nat. Acad. Scis., Phi Beta Kappa, Sigma Xi. me: Berkeley Calif. Died Feb. 19, 1986;.

ODIE, BERNARD BERYL, pharmacologist, edur; b. Liverpool, Eng., Aug. 7, 1907; s. Samuel and her (Ginsburg) B.; m. Anne Lois Smith, Aug. 30, 0. B.S., McGill U., 1931; Ph.D., N.Y.U., 1935; c. (hon.), U. Paris, France, 1963, Phila. Coll. rmacy and Sci., 1965, U. Barcelona, 1967, N.Y. d. Coll., 1970, U. Louvain, Belgium, 1971, U. Ariz., 5; M.D. (hon.), Karolinska Inst., 1968, U. Cagliari, y, 1973. Asst. prof. pharmacology N.Y.U. Med. ., 1943-47, asso. prof. biochemistry, 1947-50; chief chem. pharmacology Nat. Heart Inst., 1950-70, ret., 0; sr. cons. Hoffmann-LaRoche Inc., 1971-89; vis. f. pharmacology Pa. State U. Coll. Medicine, 1975- Vis. prof. George Washington U. Med. Sch., 1950- prof. pharmacology U. Ariz. Med. Center, Tucson, 2-75, 82-89; cons. Nat. Heart and Lung Inst., NIH, hesda, Md., 1971-89; Carl Wilhelm Scheele lectr. al Pharm. Inst., Stockholm, 1967; Paul Lamson r. Vanderbilt U., 1971; Rosemary Cass Meml. lectr. Dundee, Scotland, 1971. Author: Metabolic Factors trolling Duration of Drug Action, 1963, Drug Ene Interactions, 1964, Concepts in Biochemical rmacology, vols. I and II, 1972, Bioavialability of gs, 1973; Founder, chmn. editorial bd.: Life nces, Internat. Jour. Neuropharmacology; editor, coder: Pharmacology; Contbr. numerous articles to l. jours. Served with Canadian Army, 1926-28. ipient Disting. Svc. award HEW, 1958; Shionogi nmemoration lectr. Japan, 1962; Karl Beyer award, 2; Julius Sturmer Meml. lectr., 1962; Torald mann award Am. Pharmacology Soc., 1963; Disting. ievement award Modern Medicine med. jour., 1964; ert Lasker award for basic med. research, 1967; Nat. dal of Sci., 1968; Claude Bernard prof. U. Montreal, 9; Schmiede-Plakette German Pharmacol. Soc., 1969; ar B. Hunter Meml. award Am. Pharm. Soc., 1970; earch Achievement award for stimulation research d. Pharm. Scis., 1972; Intrascis. medalist, 1972; al for research U. Turku, Finland. Mem. Nat. d. Scis., Inst. Medicine, Internat. Pharm. Soc., Am. Neuropsychopharmacology (pres. 1965), Am. Soc. Chemists, Am. Soc. Pharmacology and Exptl. rapeutics, Harvey Soc., N.Y., Washington acads. , Royal Soc. Medicine. Died Feb. 27, 1989.

DDSHAUG, MELVIN, communication consultant; Davenport, N.D., May 22, 1900; s. Ole and Kaja king) B.; m. Alpha Madeline Boe, Dec. 27, 1927; dren: Joan Barbara, Karin Sandra. BS, N.D. State 1932, LittD, 1958; MA, U. Chgo., 1927; PhD, mbia U., 1931. Prin. Arnegard (N.D.) Consol. , 1923-25, supt. schs., 1925-28; research assoc. ERPI ure Consultants, N.Y.C., 1930-37; dir. research I Classroom Films, N.Y.C., 1937-45; v.p. charge rch Ency. Britannica Films, Wilmette, Ill., 1945-48, charge prodn. devel., 1948-53; dean Sch. Pub. Rens and Communications Boston U., 1954-62; dir. on U. Film Library, 1962-65; prof., cons. Norfolk State Coll. 1965-88; producer of ednl. motion picseries; communication counsel; motion picture .; market research analyst. Mem. bd. dirs. Teaching s Custodians Inc.; trustee Village of Wilmette, -54. Mem. NEA (dept. audio-visual instrn.), Ro- (Boston), Phi Kappa Phi, Phi Delta Kappa, Kappa a Pi. Mem. Old South Ch. Home: Harwich Port s. Died May 18, 1988.

DERSMA, SYBRAND, physics educator; b. ingen, Netherlands, Sept. 20, 1919; came to U.S., , naturalized, 1957; s. Jacob and Johanna nenburg) B. Candidaats in Physics, Leiden U., 1939, Doctoraal, 1941; D.Sc. cum laude in Physics, Delft Inst. Tech., 1947. Research asso. Columbia, 1947; instr. U. Toronto, 1948; prof. physics U. Indonesia, Bandung, 1949-51; asst. prof. physics Northwestern U., 1952-58; prof. physics U. Okla., from 1959; adj. prof. materials research U. Tex. at Dallas, 1967-70. Author: Magnetic Measurements on Organic Compounds, 1947, Elementary Physics Laboratory Manual, 1963; collector of native arts. Internat. exchange fellow Northwestern U., 1947; NSF grantee, 1956-68. Mem. Am., Netherlands, European phys. socs., AAUP, Sigma Xi. Died Dec. 1987.

BROOKMAN, HERMAN, architect; b. N.Y.C., July 2, 1891; s. Joseph and Dorothy (Israelson) B.; m. Sophie Elson, Dec. 7, 1911; children: Bernard, Emanuel, Dorothy Rose. Student, Art Student's League, N.Y.C., 1912-13, Beaux Arts, 1913-14. Registered architect, N.Y., Oreg. Draftsman Harry T. Lindberg, N.Y.C., 1909-18, designer, 1918-23; pvt. practice architecture Portland, Oreg., from 1924. Fellow AIA (pres. Oreg. chpt.); mem. Oreg. Hist. Soc., Portland Art Mus., Portland C. of C., Civic Club. Jewish. Home: Portland Oreg. †

BROOKS, ERNEST, JR., foundation executive; b. N.Y.C., Dec. 5, 1907; s. Ernest and Jeanne L. (Marion) B.; m. Mary Caroline Schoyer, June 23, 1934; children: Joan (Mrs. John R. McLane III), Peter Preston, Howard Turner, Ernest III. BA, Yale U., 1930; LLB, Harvard U., 1933. Bar: N.Y. 1934. Assoc. Breed, Abbott & Morgan, N.Y.C., 1933-48; Officer Old Dominion Found., N.Y.C., 1948-69, trustee, 1948-69, pres., 1956-69; cons. Andrew W. Mellon Found., 1969-71; trustee Anne S. Richardson Fund, Nat. Humanities Faculty, 1969-76; bd. dirs. Nat. Audubon Soc., 1957-63, sec., 1959-60, v.p., 1969-80; trustee Conservation Found., 1956-84, chmn., 1972-84; trustee New Canaan (Conn.) Country Sch., 1955-64, Putney Sch., 1965-71, Stamford Mus. and Nature Ctr., 1971-73; Assn. for Protection Adironacks, 1978-84; bd. govs. Nature Conservancy, 1954-61, 69-73. With OSS, 1943-46. Fellow Berkeley Coll., Yale U.; mem. Country Club (New Canaan), Century Assn. (N.Y.C.), Phi Beta Kappa. Home: New Canaan Conn. Died Dec. 7, 1984; buried Starksboro, Vt.

BROOKS, JOHN WOOD, chemical manufacturer; b. N.Y.C., Oct. 9, 1917; s. Arthur and Mary TenEyck (Oakley) B.; m. Margaret O. Magoun, July 19, 1958; children: Sylvia B., John W., Laurence O., Anne Strong, Mary Strong, Selina Strong. Grad., Groton Sch., 1935; AB, Harvard U., 1939. Various sales, sales exec. positions fiber industry, 1939-53; v.p., gen. sales mgr. Spring Mills Inc., 1953-54; gen. mdse. mgr., fibers div. Celanese Corp., N.Y.C., 1955, dir. mktg. fibers div., 1955-56, v.p., gen. mgr. fibers div., 1956-59, exec. v.p. domestic ops., 1960-61, exec. v.p. ops., 1961-65, pres., 1965, chief exec. officer, 1968-77, chmn., 1971-80, chmn. exec. com., dir., 1980-89; bd. dirs. ACF Industries Inc., Bankers Trust Corp., Dun & Bradstreet Cos. Inc. Co-chmn. bd. trustees Presbyn. Hosp. at Columbia-Presbyn. Med. Ctr., N.Y.C. Mem. Bedford Golf and Tennis Club (N.Y.), University Club, Links Club, Economists Club, Union Club. Home: Bedford Hills N.Y. Died Jan. 4, 1989.

BROOKS, LAWRENCE GRAHAM, judge, church official; b. Roxbury, Mass., Feb. 21, 1881; s. John Graham and Helen Lawrence (Appleton) B.; m. Susan Morris Hallowell, Oct. 12, 1912; children: John Graham, Helen Lawrence (dec.), Ann, Charlotte Hallowell, Catherine Lawrence. AB, Harvard, 1902, AM, 1903, LLB, 1905; LHD (hon.), Tufts U., 1966. Bar: Mass. 1905. Practice Boston; counsel U.S. R.R. Labor Bd., Chgo., 1920-21; city solicitor Medford, Mass., 1923-27; sr. spl. justice 1st Dist. Ct. of East Middlesex, 1928-48, presiding justice, from 1948; presiding justice appellate div. Mass. Dist. Cts., from 1958; pres. Prentiss, Brooks & Co., 1927-42; dir. Middlesex County Nat. Bank, Montan Pole Co. V.p. Medford Community Chest and Coun.; vice moderator Unitarian Universalist Assn. Mem. Am. (exec. sec. war service com. Washington 1918-19), Mass., Boston (mem. council) bar assns., Cosmos Club (Washington), Union Club (Boston). Republican. Home: West Medford Mass. †

BROOKS, LEE M(ARSHALL), sociologist; b. Norwood, Mass., May 31, 1891; s. Marshall Ezra and Isabel (Ross) B.; m. Evelyn M. Cheney, Feb. 16, 1916; 1 son, Robert Lee. AB, Boston U., 1925; MA, U. N.C., 1926, PhD, 1929. Clk. Atkinson, Haserick & Co., textile machinery, Boston, 1906-12; salesman Atkinson, Haserick & Co., textile machinery, Boston and New Bedford, 1914-17; dir. young men's work Eliot Congl. Ch., Boston, 1918-22; instr. U. N.C., 1926-30, asst. prof., 1930-35, assoc. prof., 1936-46, prof., 1946-55, prof. emeritus, from 1955, chmn. dept. sociology, 1950-54; vis. prof. Ala. Coll., 1935-36, La. State U., 1940-41, U. Wash., spring 1945, U. Hawaii, 1947-48, 1955, Whittier Coll., Calif., from 1955; summer study tours, U.S., 1930, British Isles, 1934, Nova Scotia, 1938, Army YMCA, sec. Camp Devens, 1918. Author: (with G.W. Blackwell and S.H. Hobbs) Church and Community in the South, 1949, (with A.L. Bertrand) History of the Southern Sociological Society, 1962; contbr. chpt. in North Carolina Chain Gang, 1927, Aspects of Democracy, 1941, Successful Marriage, 1947; contbr. articles and book revs. to sociol., ednl. and religious jours.; assoc. editor: Social Forces, 1946-55. Dir. Western Carolina TV Literacy Program. Mem. Am. Sociol. Soc., So. Sociol. Soc. (pres. 1949-50), So. Regional Coun., Phi Beta Kappa. Home: Webster N.C. †

BROPHY, JAMES EDWARD, association executive; b. St. Louis, Feb. 9, 1921; s. James L. and Emma (Rathmann) B.; m. Delphine E. Wolfe, Oct. 11, 1947. BA, Washington U., St. Louis, 1946. Exec. sec. Greater St. Louis Dental Soc., 1948-61; exec. dir. Am. Assn. Orthodontists, St. Louis, from 1961, dir. communications, from 1968, editor newsletter, from 1964; cons. to ADA and other health orgns., 1962—; producer dental edn. series Sta. KETC-TV, St. Louis, 1952-55; mem. bd. control Am. Assn. Orthodontists Found., from 1968; bd. dirs. Mo. Dental Service Corp., 1959-61; trustee Am. Fund for Dental Health, from 1979. Contbr. articles to dental assn. and bus. jours. Recipient Disting. Service scroll Am. Assn. Orthodontists, 1971. Hon. fellow Am. Coll. Dentists; mem. ADA (hon.), Am. Soc. Assn. Execs., Am. Assn. Dental Editors, Profl. Conv. Mgmt. Assn., Assn. of Dental Exec. Secs. (pres. 1958-59), Southwestern Soc. Orthodontists (hon. mem.), St. Louis Soc. Assn. Execs. (pres. 1968-69, chmn. various coms.), Rotary, K.C., Media. Home: Webster Groves Mo. Died Dec. 5, 1985; buried St. Louis.

BROTEMARKLE, ROBERT ARCHIBALD, professor of psychology; b. Lonaconing, Md., Nov. 12, 1892; s. Clinton and Laura Jane (Somerville) B.; m. Bernice W. Rorer, Sept. 28, 1918; children: Richard Gordon, Alene Frances Brotemarkle Snedaker. Student, Mercersburg Acad., 1910-12; AB, Princeton U., 1916, AM, 1918; PhD., U. Pa., 1923. Diplomate Clin. Psychology, Am. Bd. Examiners in Profl. Psychology, Feb. 1948. Asst. instr. in psychology U. Pa., 1919-20, instr., 1920-26, asst. prof., 1926-35, assoc. prof., 1935-40, prof., from 1940; coll. personnel officer, 1926-43, chmn. dept. of psychology, 1943-57; dir. psychol. lab. and clinic, 1943-57, clin. psychologist since 1920. Served as mem. emergency com. in psychology Nat. Rsch. Coun., 1940-44; expert cons. to Sec. of War, 1941-45. Editor: Clinical Psychology. Studies in Honor of Lightner Witmer, 1931; contbr. numerous articles on psychology, personality, coll. personnel problems to profl. jours. Fellow Am. Psychol. Assn., AAAS; mem. Am. Assn. for Applied Psychology (v.P. 1938), Assn. Consultin Psychologists (pres. 1938), Am. Coll. Personnel Assn., Ea. Psychol. Assn., Ea. Assn. of Coll. Deans and Advisors, Pa. Assn. Psychologists, Sigma Xi. Republican. Presbyterian. Home: Merion Station Pa. †

BROUGH, KENNETH JAMES, educator, librarian; b. Scotch Grove, Iowa, Aug. 22, 1906; s. R.A. and Sarah (Metcalf) B.; m. Ruth Bloomer, May 22, 1933. AB, Grinnell Coll., 1927; AM, U. Colo., 1931; BLS, Columbia U., 1942; PhD, Stanford U., 1949. Tchr. Portales (N.Mex.) High Sch., 1927-34; librarian, dir. instrn. Eastern N.Mex. U., 1934-43; asst. reference librarian Stanford U., 1946-49; prof. bibliography, librarian San Francisco State Coll., 1949-72, ret.; mem. N.Mex. Library Planning Com., 1940-42, N.Mex. Library Commn., 1946. Author: Scholar's Workshop, 1953; contbr. articles to profl. jours. With U.S. Army, 1943-46. Mem. ALA, NEA, N.Mex. Library Assn. (pres. 1935-36), Calif. Library Assn., Masons, Phi Beta Kappa, Phi Delta Kappa. Presbyterian. Home: Palo Alto Calif. Died May 3, 1984.

BROWER, HORACE W., life insurance executive; b. Kansas City, Mo., Aug. 10, 1900; s. William N. and Elsie Ann (Chambers) B.; m. Margurette Hamell, Jan. 20, 1923. Engaged as bookkeeper Continental Bank, Los Angeles, 1920-22; successively gen. bookkeeper, note teller, asst. sec., asst. cashier and asst. v.p. Bank of Italy (later Bank of Am. Nat. Trust & Savs. Assn.), 1922-33; mgr. mortgage loan dept. Occidental Life Ins. Co. of Calif., 1933-35, asst. sec., 1935-43, v.p., 1943-46, exec. v.p., 1946-51, pres., 1951-64, chmn., chief exec. officer, from 1964, chmn. of exec. com., from 1965; former chmn. Transamerica Corp.; former chmn. exec. com. Transamerica Financial Corp. Former mem. exec. com. Am. Life Conv.; trustee Nat. Found.; dir., mem. Better Bus. Bur. Los Angeles Ltd.; dir. Calif. Traffic Safety Found., Los Angeles chpt. Nat. Safety Council, Jr. Achievement; nat. council USO Club. All-Year of So. Calif. Home: Los Angeles Calif. †

BROWN, CECIL, television and radio news commentator, educator, lecturer; b. New Brighton, Pa., Sept. 14, 1907; m. Martha Brown, July 20, 1938. Student, Western Res. U., 1925-27; BS, Ohio State U., 1929; LittD (hon.), Union Coll. Sailed as seaman to S. Am., Russia, West Africa; wrote stories of experience, pub. in Youngstown (Ohio) Vindicator, 1928-29; reporter for United Press, Los Angeles, 1931-32; editor Prescott (Ariz.) Jour.-Miner, 1933; staff Pitts. Press, 1934-36, Newark Ledger, 1936-37; freelance writer Europe, North Africa, 1937-38; with Internat. News Service, 1938-39; news broadcast for CBS, Rome, 1940-41, Yugoslavia, Cairo, Singapore, 1941-42, Australia, N.Y.C., from 1943; news commentator over MBS, 1944-57; news commentator ABC, 1957-58; Far East bur. chief NBC, Tokyo, 1958-62; TV-radio news commentator NBC, Los Angeles, 1962-64; dir. news and pub. affairs, commentator Community TV of So. Calif., KCET-28, Los

Angeles, 1964-67; TV cons. Ency. Brit., 1967-68; prof. communications and internat. affairs Calif. State Poly. U., Pomona, 1968-80. Author: Suez to Singapore, 1942; Introduction to ltd. edits., Club edit. Carlyle's The French Revolution, 1956; chpt. on Japan in Memo to J.F.K; Contbr. to mags. Recipient awards for distinguished radio news reporting from abroad during 1941 from Sigma Delta Chi, Overseas Press Club, Nat. Council for Edn. by Radio, Nat. Headliners Club, The George Foster Peabody Award, Motion Picture Daily's award, winner World-Telegram poll for outstanding single broadcast of 1942, Alfred I. Dupont award for best TV news commentary, 1965; awards for commentary A.P., 1965, 66; named Distinguished Tchr. Calif. State Poly. U., Pomona, 1973-74, Outstanding Prof., 1979-80. Mem. Overseas Press Club (past pres.), Soc. Profl. Journalists. Home: Los Angeles Calif. Died Oct. 25, 1987, cremated.

BROWN, DANIEL L(UCIUS), lawyer, banker; b. Norwich, Conn., June 23, 1891; s. Lucius and Hannah (Larrabee) B.; m. Bettina T. Savage, Apr. 24, 1926; children: Lucia, Deborah, Betsy T., Eric. AB, Brown U., 1912, LLD (hon.), 1962; LLB, Harvard, 1919. Bar: Mass. 1919. Practice Boston; ptnr. Hale & Dorr, from 1924; v.p., trustee Boston 5 Cent Savs. Bank; dir. Fidelity Fund, S.A.L. R.R. Trustee Brown U. Home: Milton Mass. †

BROWN, DONALD ERWIN, banker; b. Anderson, S.C., Oct. 28, 1891; s. Elijah William and Lena Moss (Salley) B.; m. Eleanor Alberta Brock, Apr. 26, 1917; children: Eleanor Brown Sewell, Caroline Brown Bumbarger. Student, Davidson (N.C.) Coll., 1909-12. Bookkeeper, then asst. cashier Peoples Bank of Anderson, S.C., 1912-17; asst. cashier to pres. Carolina Nat. Bank, Anderson, 1922-55; chmn. bd. First Nat. Bank S.C., Columbia, 1955-62; hon. chmn. bd., dir. First Nat. Bank S.C., from 1962. Mem. U.S. Army adv. com., Anderson County, from 1955; chmn. U.S. Savs. Bd., Anderson County, from 1949; chmn. Anderson County chpt. ARC, 1935-41. 2d lt. U.S. Army, 1917-19. Mem. Am. (v.p. S.C. 1948-49), S.C. (pres. 1946-47) bankers assns., Anderson C. of C. Presbyerian (life elder). Home: Anderson S.C. †

BROWN, DOUGLASS VINCENT, educator; b. Wilkes-Barre, Pa., May 16, 1904; s. George Henry and Frederica (Beinert) B.; m. Mary A. Nuss, Dec 2, 1933 (dec. 1984); children: Deborah, Constance. AB, Harvard U., 1925, AM, 1926, PhD, 1932. Instr., tutor econ. Harvard U., 1927-33; asst. prof. med. econ. Harvard Med. Sch., 1933-38; asst. prof., assoc. prof. and prof. indsl. rels. MIT, Cambridge, 1938-46, Alfred P. Sloan prof. indsl. mgmt., 1946-69, prof. emeritus, 1969-86; various positions with adv. commn. to Council of Nat. Def. and OPM, 1940-41; staff mem. Harriman-Beaverbrook Mission to Russia, 1941; cons. to War Dept., 1942-43; pub. mem. Nat. War Labor Bd., Region I, 1943-45. Author: (with others) Economics of the Recovery Program, 1934, Industrial Wage Rates, Labor Costs and Price Policies, Temporary National Economic Committee, Monograph 5, 1940. Fellow Am. Acad. Arts and Sci.; mem. Indsl. Relations Research Assn., Nat. Acad. Arbitrators. Home: Brookline Mass. Died Mar. 21, 1986; buried Walnut Hills Cemetery, Brookline, Mass.

BROWN, EDGAR ALLAN, lawyer, political leader; b. nr. Aiken, S.C., July 11, 1888; s. Augustus Abraham and Elizabeth (Howard) B.; m. Annie Love Sitgreaves, Dec. 30, 1913; 1 dau., Emily McBurney (Mrs. Richard M. Jefferies Jr.). Student, Graniteville Acad., 1902-06; LLB (hon.), Clemson Coll., 1955. Bar: S.C. 1910. Ct. reporter 2d S.C. Cir., 1908-18; sr. mem. Brown, Jefferies & Mazursky, Barnwell, S.C.; v.p. The Bank of Barnwell; dir. North Augusta Banking Co., State Bank & Trust Co., Cooper Motor Lines. Life trustee Clemson Coll., S.C.; mem., past chmn. bd. mgrs. Coun. of State Govts.; chmn., gen. counsel Clark's Hill Authority of S.C.; mem. State Budget and Control Bd.; del.-at-large Nat. Dem. Conv., N.Y.C., 1924, Phila., 1948, Chgo., 1952; candidate for U.S. Senate, 1926, 38; mem. nat. exec. com. Dem. Party of S.C., 1953; chmn. county Dem. exec. com., mem. state Dem. exec. com., from 1914; mem. S.C. Ho. of Reps., 1921-26, speaker, 1925-26; mem. S.C. State Senate, from 1929, pres. pro tempore, also chmn. senate fin. com., from 1942. Mem. Am., S.C. (former pres.) bar assns., Carolina Motor Club (former chmn. bd.), Masons, Shriners. Methodist (trustee). Home: Barnwell S.C. †

BROWN, EDITH PETRIE, physician; b. Conneaut Lake, Pa., June 7, 1900; d. William and Hattie Elnina (Shontz) Petrie; m. William H. Brown, Sept 13, 1928; children: Margaret Elizabeth (Mrs. John Fleming), William Stanley. BS with honors, Westminster Coll., New Wilmington, Pa., 1923; DH, Westminster Coll., 1963; MD with distinction, George Washington U., 1927. Intern Grace Hosp., Detroit, 1927-28; pediatric resident Children's Hosp., Washington, 1929; asst. physician Rochester (Minn.) State Hosp., 1929; resident physician Sunny Acres Tb Sanatorium, Warrensville, Ohio, 1929-31; pvt. practice Bedford, Ohio, 1937-63; sec. staff Bedford Mcpl. Hosp. 1945-51, chief staff, 1954-60; vice chief staff Woman's Hosp., Cleve., 1947-48, 55-56; exec. com. Bedford Community Hosp. Corp., 1957-63; physician, field rep. Joint Commn. on Accreditation Hosps., 1964-68; staff mem. Sage Meml. Hosp., Ganado, Ariz., 1968-69, Pima County Hosp., So. Ariz. Mental Health Ctr., 1969-70, Carl Hayden Community Hosp., 1970; organizer, adminstr. measles immunization program in Kenya, 1971; staff Christian Meml. Hosp., Sialkot, Pakistan, 1971-85, Tumu Tumu Hosp., Kenya, 1972; med. group mission Chr. Med. Soc. to Liberia, 1974; contract physician Newton County Med. Ctr., Jasper, Ark., 1874-85. Contbr. articles to med. jours. Mem. Corp. Cleve. Ctr. on Alcoholism; hon. mem. governing bd. Woman's Hosp., Cleve. Recipient Alumni Achievement award Westminster Coll. Alumni Assn., 1973. Fellow Acad. Psychosomatic Medicine, Am. Acad. Family Practice; mem. Assn. Am. Physicians and Surgeons, Am. Physicians Art Assn., AMA, Am. Med. Women's Assn. (br. pres. 1943-44; nat. pres. 1962, founder, pres. Tucson br. 1970), Ariz. Acad. Gen. Practice, George Washington U. Med. Soc., Am. Heart Assn., Cleve. Acad. Medicine, Ohio Med. Assn., Christian Med. Soc., Med. Women's Internat. Assn., Internat. Platform Assn., World Med. Assn., Bedford Hist. Soc. (charter mem.), Nat. Council on Alcoholism, United World Federalists, Internat. Soc. Christian Endeavor, Nat. Resuscitation Soc., Cleve. Mus. Art, Cleve. Health Mus. (life mem.), Zonta Internat. Home: Russellville Ark. Died June 14, 1985.

BROWN, EDWARD MCLAIN, JR., lawyer; b. Balt., Apr. 26, 1929; s. Edward McLain and Rita Virginia (House) B.; m. Patsy Sue Millikan, Jan. 28, 1956; children: Carol Lorraine, Ruth Virginia, David William. Student, U. Pa., 1946-47; B.B.A., U. Tex., 1958, LL.B., 1960. Bar: Tex. 1960, U.S. Supreme Ct. 1965. Assoc. firms Karl Cayton, Lamesa, Tex., 1960-62, Lyne, Blanchette, Smith & Shelton, Dallas, 1962-65; partner firms Brown, Elliott & Brown, Dallas, 1965-70, Brown & Moore, Dallas, 1970-75, Brown, Moore & Lee, Dallas, 1975-79, Brown & Walker, Dallas, 1980-81; sole practice Dallas, 1981-85; sec., dir. Fas-Pak Inc., Pat Jetton Inc., Ranchmen's Mfg. Co., Inc.; pres. dir. Courtland Devel. Co., Inc.; sec., dir. Woodcraft Constrn. Co. Inc., Phalanx Corp. Mem. charter com. Farmers Br., Dallas, 1967-70, chmn., 1969-70, mem. library bd., 1964-68, chmn. library bd., 1967-68, mem. indsl. devel. com., 1971. Served with USAF, 1950-56. Mem. Dallas Bar Assn., State Bar Tex., Tex. Trial Lawyers Assn., Farmers Br.-Carrollton Lawyers Assn. (pres. 1973). Republican. Episcopalian (sr. warden 1967). Clubs: Rotary, Lions. Home: Dallas Tex. Died Aug. 31, 1985; buried Carrollton, Tex.

BROWN, FRANK EDWARD, archeologist; b. La Grange, Ill., May 24, 1908; s. Philip Sidney and Rose Louise (Swain) B.; m. Jaquelin Goddard, July 21, 1935. AB, Carleton Coll., 1929; postgrad. (fellow), Am. Acad., Rome, 1931-33; PhD, Yale U., 1938; LittD, Carleton Coll., 1968. Asst. dir. Yale Excavations, Dura-Europos, 1932-35, dir., 1935-37; research asst., asst. prof. Yale U., 1938-42, prof. classics, 1952-63; master Jonathan Edwards Coll., 1953-56; gen. rep. O.W.I., Syria, Lebanon, 1942-45; Mellon prof. in charge, dir. excavations Am. Acad. Rome, 1947-52, 63-76, dir. acad., 1963-69, 73. Editor and contbr.: Excavations at Dura-Europos (vols. 6-9), 1936-52, Fasti Archeologici (vols. 1-5), 1946-52, Pubs. of Am. Acad. in Rome, 1951-60, Roman Architecture, 1962, Cosa, The Making of A Roman Town, 1979. Mem. Internat. Fedn. Socs. Classical Studies (past v.p.), Internat. Assn. Classical Archaeology (past v.p.), Archeol. Inst. Am. (exec. com.), Am. Schs. Oriental Research (past sec.), Am. Philol. Assn., Am. Oriental Soc., Instituto de Studi Etruschi ed Italici, German Archaeol. Inst., Pontif. Acad. Archaeology, Am. Acad. Arts and Scis., Century Assn. Club. Home: Rome Italy. Died Feb. 28, 1988.

BROWN, GEORGE HAROLD, radio engineer; b. North Milwaukee, Wis., Oct. 14, 1908; s. James Clifford and Ida Louise (Siegert) B.; m. Julia Elizabeth Ward, Dec. 26, 1932; children: James Ward and George H. (twins). B.S., U. Wis., 1930, M.S., 1931, Ph.D., 1933, E.E., 1942; Dr.Eng. (hon.), U. R.I., 1968. With RCA, 1933-37, 38-73; successively rsch. engr. RCA, Camden, Princeton, N.J.; dir. Systems Rsch. Lab. RCA; chief engr. Comml. Electronic Products div. RCA, Camden; chief engr. indsl. electronic products RCA, 1933-59, v.p. engring., 1959-61, v.p. research and engring., 1961-65, exec. v.p. research and engring., 1965-68, exec. v.p. patents and licensing, 1968-72; dir. Trane Co., 1967-79, cons. engr., 1937-87; dir. RCA Global Communications, 1962-71, RCA, 1965-72, RCA Internat., Ltd., 1968-72; Shoenberg Meml. lectr. Royal Instn., 1972; Marconi Centenary lectr. AAAS, 1974. Author: (with R.A. Bierwirth and C.N. Hoyler) Radio Frequency Heating, 1947, And Part of Which I Was, 1982; contbr. articles to sci. jours. Exec. bd. George Washington council Boy Scouts Am.; bd. govs. Hamilton Hosp. Recipient Silver Beaver and Silver Antelope awards Boy Scouts Am.; citation Internat. TV Symposium, Montreux, Switzerland, 1965; DeForest Audion award, 1968; David Sarnoff award for outstanding achievements in radio and TV U. Ariz., 1980; Engring. Achievement award Nat. Assn. Broadcasters, 1986. Fellow IEEE (Edison medal 1967, Centennial medal 1984), AAAS, Royal TV Soc., Radio Club Am. (Armstrong medal 1986); mem. Nat. Acad. Engring., Am. Mgmt. Assn., Nassau, Springdale clubs, Sigma Xi, Tau Beta Pi, Eta Kappa Nu (eminent mem.). Home: Princeton N.J. Died Dec. 11, 1987.

BROWN, HARRISON SCOTT, chemist, educator;
Sheridan, Wyo., Sept. 26, 1917; s. Harrison H. a
Agatha (Scott) B.; m. Adele Scringer, 1938; 1 son, E
Scott; m. Theresa Tellez, 1975. BS, U. Calif., 19
LLD, 1970; PhD, Johns Hopkins U., 1941; LLD,
Alta., 1961; ScD, Rutgers U., 1964, Amherst Co
1966, Cambridge U., 1969. Instr. chemistry Joh
Hopkins U., 1941-42; asst. dir. chemistry Clinton Lab
Oak Ridge, 1943-46; research assoc. plutonium proj
U. Chgo., 1942-43; asst. prof. Inst. Nuclear Studi
1946-48, assoc. prof., 1948-51; prof. geochemistry Ca
Inst. Tech., 1951-77, prof. sci. and govt., 1967-77; d
Resource Systems Inst., East-West Center, Honolu
1977-83. Author: Must Destruction Be Our Destin
1946, The Challenge of Man's Future, 1954, The N
Hundred Years, 1957, The Cassiopeia Affair, 1968, T
Human Future Revisited, 1978, Learning How To L
in a Technological Society (Ishizaka lectures, Japa
1979; editor-in-chief Bull. Atomic Scientists, 1985-8
Recipient Lasker Found. award, 1958, N.Y. Acad. Sc
award, 1978. Mem. Nat. Acad. Scis. (fgn. sec. 1962-
chmn. world food and nutrition study 1975-77),
ternat. Council Sci. Unions (pres. 1974-76), Am. Che
Soc. (award in pure chemistry 1952), Geol. Soc. Ar
AAAS (ann. award 1947), Am. Geophys. Union,
Beta Kappa, Sigma Xi. Home: Albuquerque N.M
Died Dec. 8, 1986, buried Albuqueque.

BROWN, HARRY PETER MCNAB, JR., author;
Portland, Maine, Apr. 30, 1917; s. Harry McNab a
Beth Maude (Hiles) B.; m. 3d, June Jollie, Dec.
1959; one son, Jared Jollie Clark Brown. Stude
Harvard U., 1940. With Time mag., 1939, New York
mag., 1939-40; attached to Yank Army newspap
N.Y.C., 1942. Author: The End of a Decade, 1941; T
Poem of Bunker Hill, 1941; The Violent, 1943; A W
in the Sun, 1944; Poems, 1941-44 (Eng.) 1945; Ar
Greengroin, 1945; A Sound of Hunting, 1946; The Be
in His Hunger, 1948; The Stars in their Courses, 19
A Quiet Place to Work, 1968; The Wild Hunt, 19
The Gathering, 1977; also numerous film scripts
cluding Arch of Triumph, 1947; Sands of Iwo Jin
1949; The Sniper, 1952; Between Heaven and Hell, 19
Ocean's 11. With AUS, 1941-45. Recipient You
Poets' prize, 1935, Lloyd McKim Garrison awa
Harvard U., 1937, Shelley award, 1939, award Co
monwealth Club, Calif., 1949, Acad. award for b
screenplay A Place in the Sun, 1952. Mem. Acad. M
tion Picture Arts and Scis., Nat. Rifle Assn., Writ
Guild Am. Home: Beverly Hills Calif. Died Nov.
1986.

BROWN, HENRY SEABURY, industrial physici
and surgeon; b. Providence, Sept. 12, 1891; s. Arn
Cleveland and Gretchen Margaret (Leonhardt) B.;
Dorothy Adams Trites, Dec. 7, 1921; children: Nar
Seabury (Mrs. Frederick W. Sanders), Barbara Arn
(Mrs. Russell V. Allman). Grad., Classical High Sc
Providence, 1909; student, Brown U., 1913; MD, Tu
Med. Coll., 1917. Intern Robert B. Brigham Ho
Boston, Mass., 1917-18, R.I. Hosp., Providence, 19
gen. practice medicine and surgery Detroit, from 19
indsl. physician and surgeon Gen. Accident Ins. C
1921-24; indsl. physician and surgeon Mich. Bell
Co., from 1924, med. dir., from 1930; staff surg
Harper and Florence Crittendon Hosps.; instr. in
medicine Wayne U., from 1928. Lt. M.C., U.S. Na
1918-19; lt. comdr. USNR, 1919-39. Fellow Am. P
Health Assn., Am. Assn. Indsl. Physicians and Surge
(dir. 1943-45, 2d v.p., 1945, v.p., 1946, pres. 1947),
ternat. Coll. Surgeons; mem. AMA, Am. Assn.
Surgeons, Soc. Mayflower DEscendants, SAR, Detr
Golf Club. Home: Detroit Mich. †

BROWN, IRVING JOSEPH, labor union official;
N.Y.C., Nov. 20, 1911; s. Ralph and Fannie (Singer)
m. Lillie Smith, Mar. 13, 1934; 1 son, Rob
Manuel. AB, NYU, 1932. Internat. rep. UAW, A
Fedn. of Labor, 1937-40, mem. exec. bd., 1939-40, r
Am. Fedn. of Labor, 1940-42; dep. vice chmn. la
War Prodn. Bd., 1942-45; dir. labor and manpower d
enemy br., Fgn. Econ. Adminstrn., Apr.-Sept. 19
European rep. Am. Fedn. of Labor, 1945-55, AFL-C
from 1955; sr. adviser to Lane Kirkland, pres. A
CIO, 1986-89. Home: Paris France Died Feb. 10, 19

BROWN, J(AMES) DOUGLAS, economist;
Somerville, N.J., Aug. 11, 1898; s. James and Ella
(Lane) B.; m. Dorothy Andrews, June 18, 1923; c
dren: Martha Jane, Dorothy Andrews, James Doug
Elizabeth Andrews (dec.). AB, Princeton U., 19
AM, 1921, PhD, 1928; LittD, Rutgers U., 1947; LH
Kenyon Coll., 1954; LLD, Union Coll., 1955; Pe
(hon.), Franklin and Marshall Coll., 1966. In
Princeton U., 1921-23, N.Y.U., 1923-25; dir. indsl. r
tions sect. Princeton U., 1926-55, asst. prof. eco
1927-34, prof. econs., 1934-66, dean faculty, 1946-
provost, 1966-86; vis. asst. prof. U. Pa., 1932-33; ser
on many N.J. and Fed. commns. and adv. coms.
cluding development and revisions of fed. social secu
program, N.J. unemployment ins. law and formulat
of nat. manpower policies, 1930-86; cons. NSRB, 19
53; mem. sci. adv. bd. Chief of Staff USAF, 1950-
mem. com. specialized personnel ODM, 1951; cons.
sec. of labor, 1954-55; mem. mobilization program a
com. for Office of Def. Mobilization, 1955-58; m
Fed. Adv. Council on Social Security Financing, 19
59, Fed. Adv. Council on Social Security, 1963-64; m

adv. com. to sec. of HEW on revision Nat. Def. Edn. Act., 1960-61; mem. adv. com. on Social Security Adminstrn., 1961; mem. commn. on acad. affairs Am. Council Edn., 1962-66, adv. com. Inst. Coll. and Univ. Adminstrs., 1966-68; cons. to Office of Spl. Internat. Programs Nat. Sci. Found., 1960-64; dir. McGraw-Hill Pub. Co. Author: (with Eleanor Davis) The Labor Banking Movement in U.S., 1929; also articles on indsl. relations, social ins. and higher edn.; joint author, editor of reports on indsl. relations, pub. by indsl. relations sect., Princeton, 1926-55. Former trustee U. Rochester (N.Y.). With 167th Inf., 42d Div., A.E.F., U.S. Army, World War I. Fellow Am. Acad. Arts and Scis.; mem. Assn. Am. Colls. (chmn. commn. on faculty and staff benefits 1960-63), Indsl. Relations Research Assn. (pres. 1952), Am. Econ. Assn., Am. Mgmt. Assn., N.J. Assn. Coll. and Univs. (pres. 1952-53), Phi Beta Kappa. Presbyterian. Home: Hightstown N.J. Died Jan. 19, 1986.

BROWN, JAMES WILSON, educator; b. Hanford, Wash., Sept. 18, 1913; s. Harrison and Sophia Estelle (Tuttle) B.; m. Winifred Louise Weersing, Dec. 31, 1940 (dec. Mar. 1977); children: Martha Lee, Pamela Jean, Gregory James; m. Shirley Marie Stromme Norman, Nov. 5, 1977. Student, U. Wash., 1931-32; BA, Central Wash. Coll., 1935; MA, U. Chgo., PhD, 1947. Marine radio operator 1930-31; Gen. Edn. Bd. fellow motion picture project Am. Council Edn., 1940; state supr. teaching materials Va. Dept. Edn., Richmond, 1941-42, 1945-46; asst. prof. edn. Syracuse U., 1947-48; supr. Univ. Film Center, U. Wash, 1948-53; info. specialist U.S. Dept. State OSR, Paris, 1951-52; prof. edn., dean grad. studies and research San Jose State U., 1953-78, prof. instnl. tech., 1972-78; former mem. adv. panels Far West Regional Lab. for Research and Devel., also Stanford U. Center for Research and Devel. in Teaching; asso. dir. ERIC Clearinghouse on Info. Resources, Stanford, 1974-76. Author: Virginia Plan for Audio-Visual Education, 1947, New Media in Public Libraries, 1976; co-author: AV Instruction, Technology, Media and Methods, 1959, 64, 69, 73, 77, 83, New Media in Higher Education, 1963, Going to College in California, 1965, New Media and College Teaching, 1968, Administering Educational Media, 1972, College Teaching: A Systematic Approach, 1971; editor: Educational Media Yearbook, 1973-83, Before You Go to Great Britain: A Resource Directory and Planning Guide, 1986. Served to lt. comdr. USNR, 1942-45, ETO. Mem. NEA (v.p. 1950-51, pres. dept. audio-visual instrn. 1952-53), Western Assn. Grad. Schs. (chmn. 1963-64), Phi Delta Kappa, Phi Kappa Phi. Home: San Jose Calif. Died Apr. 2, 1987; buried Oak Hill Cemetery, San Jose.

BROWN, JOSIAH, physician, educator; b. Centerfield, Utah, Dec. 19, 1923; s. Nathan and Sophie (Lederman) B.; m. Pearl Holen, Oct. 21, 1944; children: Jeffrey Josiah, Celia Lynn, Todd Evan. AB, UCLA, 1944, MD, 1947. Intern San Francisco City and County Hosp., 1947-48; jr. resident Mallory Inst. Pathology, Boston City Hosp., 1948-49; resident medicine Cin. Gen. Hosp., 1949-51; mem. faculty U. Calif. Sch. Medicine, Los Angeles, 1956-85, prof., chief div. endocrinology, 1966-85, chmn. ednl. policy and curriculum com., 1968-70. Author: (with C.M. Pearson) Clinical Uses of Adrenal Steroids, 1962. With USPHS, 1951-53. Hon. fellow Courtauld Inst. Biochemistry, Middlesex Hosp. Med. Sch., 1964-65. Mem. Am. Soc. Clin. Investigation, AAAS, Endocrine Soc., Diabetes Assn. So. Calif. Home: Los Angeles Calif. Died Aug. 30, 1985.

BROWN, MARGARET CHRISTINA, educator; b. St. Lambert, P.Q., Can., Sept. 1, 1891; d. James Gentles and Sarah (Gibson) Brown. Grad., St. Lambert Acad., Can., 1908; student, Sch. for Teachers, Macdonald Coll., Can., 1908-09, Sch. of Phys. Edn., Chautauqua, N.Y., 1912, McGill U., Montreal, 1920-21; BS in edn., Rutgers U., 1930, EdM, 1936; EdD, NYU, 1944. Tchr. elem. grades Montreal Pub. Schs., 1909-12, tchr. phys. edn., 1912-21; asst. dir. and registrar Newark Normal Sch. of Phys. Edn. and Hygiene, 1921-26; tchr. phys. edn. State Summer Normal Sch., Rutgers U., 1926-32; dean and supr. student teaching Panzer Coll. Phys. Edn. and Hygiene, East Orange, N.J., 1926-32, pres., 1932-58; Del. Internat. Fedn. of Gymnastics, Berlin, 1936, Prague, 1938, Helsinki, 1952. Author articles in profl. jours. Recipient Anderson Merit award Am. Assn. Health, Phys. Edn. and Recreation, 1953; named Woman of Yr., Essex County Women's Svc. Clubs, 1953, Honor Award Fellow, 1956; recipient awards Girl Scouts of the Oranges, N.J. Phys. Edn. Assn., 1958. Mem. NEA, Am. Assn. for Health and Physical Recreation (chmn. com. profl. ethics, ea. dist.), Suprs. of Student Teaching, N.J. Assn. Health and Phys. Edn., Bus. and Profl. Women of the Oranges (dir.), Altrusa of Essex County (dir.). Home: East Orange N.J. †

BROWN, MILTON FLEMING, banker; b. Ennis, Tex., 1892. Pres., then dir. Mercantile Nat. Bank, Dallas; chmn., then dir. First Fed. Savs. & Loan Assn.; dir. Southwestern Pub. Service Co. Mem. Masons, Shriners. Home: Dallas Tex. †

BROWN, RALPH MANNING, JR., insurance company executive; b. Elizabeth, N.J., July 1, 1915; s. Ralph Manning and Anna Alethea (Rankin) B.; m. Margrette Burnham, Oct. 6, 1950; children: Anne Alethea Brown Durney, Ralph Manning. Grad., Gilman Sch., 1932; AB, Princeton U., 1936. With Gen. Motors Acceptance Corp., 1936-51; asst. v.p. N.Y. Life Ins. Co., N.Y.C., 1951-53, v.p., 1953-55, v.p. in charge real estate and mortgage loan dept., 1955-62, exec. v.p., 1962-69, pres., chief adminstrv. officer, 1969-72, chmn. bd., chief exec. officer, 1972-81, dir., 1981-85; bd. dirs. La. Land & Exploration Co., Assoc. Dry Goods Corp., Avon Products Inc., J.P. Morgan & Co Inc., Union Camp Corp., Union Carbide Corp.; trustee Princeton U. Bd. dirs. Union Theol. Sem.; trustee Princeton U., 1963-85, chmn. bd. trustees, 1970-85; trustee Met. Mus. Art, Alfred P. Sloan Found., Lincoln Ctr. Fund, John Simon Guggenheim Meml. Fund. Maj. inf. U.S. Army, World War II. Mem. Univ. Links Club (N.Y.C.); Pretty Brook Tennis Club (Princeton), Bay Head yacht Club, Manasquan River Golf Club, Springdale Golf Club, Nassau Club. Home: Princeton N.J. Died Oct. 19, 1985; buried All Sts. Cemetery, Princeton, N.J.

BROWN, REX IVAN, power and light company official; b. Lowell, Mich., Aug. 22, 1889; s. Edwin Henry and Nettie (Myers) B.; m. Blanceh Dinges, Dec. 25, 1911 (dec. Jan. 1959); 1 child, Charles Edwin. Ed. pub. schs. of Ark.; LLD, Millsaps Coll., Jackson, Miss. With Ark. Power & Light Co. and predecessor cos., 1908-32; v.p., gen. mgr., dir. Miss. Power & Light Co., 1932-36, pres., dir., 1936-54, chmn., 1954-59, chmn. emeritus, 1959-64. Chmn. City Planning Bd.; trustee Belhaven Coll. (chmn. bd. 1959), Am. Humanics Found., Miss. Fedn. Med. Research and Devel. (treas.); dir. Goodwill Industries Missl; mem. nat. exec. bd. Boy Scouts Am.; mem. adv. bd. Jackson Meml. Hosp.; state chmn. War Fin. Com., U.S. Treasury, WWII, chmn. state adv. com. def. bonds div.; chmn. Jackson army adv. com. Mem. N.Am. br. Newcomen Soc. Eng. (state chmn.), Omicron Delta Kappa, Delta Sigma, Beta Sigma Gamma, Rotary, Capital City, Petroleum clubs. Home: Jackson Miss. †

BROWN, ROBERT COLEMAN, lawyer, educator; b. Nichols, N.Y., Sept. 14, 1892; s. Charles W.M. and Adele (Sydney) B.; m. Iva George Rigsby, Sept. 16, 1922. AB, Wesleyan U., Middletown, Conn., 1914; LLB, Harvard U., 1917, SJD (hon.), 1930. Bar: Hawaii 1917. Assoc. Frear, Prosser, Anderson & Marx, Honolulu, 1917-18, McAdoo, Cotton & Franklin, N.Y.C., 1919-26; asst. prof. law Ind. U., 1926-27, assoc. prof., 1927-30, prof., 1930-43; assoc. Wright, Gordon, Zachry, Parlin & Cahill, N.Y.C., 1943-46; prof. law U. Fla., 1946-47; prof. law U. Pitts., 1947-58, emeritus, from 1958; advisor Pa. Joint Govt. Commn., 1948-54. Author: Cases and Materials on the Law of Taxation, 1938, supplement, 1949; contbr. articles to profl. jours. With U.S. Army, 1918-19. Mem. ABA (coun. sect. taxation 1941-45), Nat. Tax. Assn., Order of Coif, Delta Upsilon, Phi Beta Kappa, Phi Beta Kappa Assocs., Delta Sigma Rho, Phi Delta Phi. Home: Chevy Chase Md. †

BROWN, STERLING WADE, clergyman, educator; b. Cookville, Tex., Dec. 28, 1907; s. Charles A. and Pludie (Bready) B.; m. Mary Jeanne Murray, Sept. 8, 1938; children: Charlene Ann, Vicki Sue. AB, Tex. Christian U., 1930, BD, 1932; PhD, U. Chgo., 1936; LLD, Eureka Coll., 1965, Tex. Christian U., 1966. Ordained to ministry Disciples of Christ Ch., 1928. Prof. religion U. Okla., 1936-40; chmn. dept. religion Drake U., 1940-43; dir. Vassar Intergroup Workshop, Poughkeepsie, N.Y., 1945-46; field supr. Nat. Conf. Christians and Jews, St. Louis, Chgo., 1943-45; asst. to pres. Nat. Conf. Christians and Jews, N.Y.C., 1945-47; gen. dir. Nat. Conf. Christians and Jews, 1949-53, exec. v.p., 1953-65, pres., 1965-73, pres. emeritus, spl. cons. to pres., 1973-84; adj. prof. human relations U. Okla., 1973-84. Author: Changing Functions of Disciple Colleges, 1936, Developing Christian Personality, 1944, Primer on Intergroup Relations, 1946. Mem. staff Mil. Govt., 1947-49, Germany. Mem. Alpha Tau Omega. Democrat. Home: Norman Okla. Died Dec. 17, 1984; buried Oklahoma City.

BROWN, T. DAWSON, banker; b. Providence, 1891. Former pres. Indsl. Nat. Bank, Providence, exec. v.p., bd. dirs.; 1st v.p., bd. dirs. Indsl. Trust Co.; bd. dirs. Providence Gas Co., Nicholson File Co., Am. Bleached Goods Co., Inc., Ponemah Mills, Sayles Finishing Plants, Inc., Sayles Biltmore Bleacheries, Inc. Home: East Providence R.I. †

BROWN, TRAVIS WALTER, oil field drilling equipment company executive; b. Oklahoma city, June 18, 1934; s. H. Travis and Irene (Robison) B.; m. Marilynn Davis, June 1, 1957; children: Deborah Sue, Travis Carson, Thomas Walter, Darla Lynn. B.B.A., Okla. U., 1956; J.D., Oklahoma city U., 1962. Bar: Okla. 1956. Pres. Geolograph Co. and related cos., Oklahoma City, 1948-79; ptnr. Robinwood Farms, Oklahoma City, 1968; pres. Geolograph-Pioneer div. Geosource, Inc., Oklahoma City, 1979-84, XIT Oil Tool Co., from 1984, Robinwood Auction Co., from 1984; chmn. bd. Robinwood's Poor Boy Feed co., Edmond, Okla., from 1980; pres., chmn. bd. Geolograph Pioneer Inc., Oklahoma City, from 1984, Geolograph (U K) Ltd., from 1984, Geolograph Service Ltd., from 1984; owner S.W. Am. Pub. Co., from 1982; pres. XIT Robinwood Pub. Co., pubs. Horse Digest, Leesburg, Va., 1982-87; cons. Jr. Achievement, from 1983. Author: Sub Surface Geology, 1976, Freeze Branding of Cattle, Horses and Mules, 1982; contbr. articles to profl. jours. Bd. dirs. Am. Cattle Breeders Hall of Fame, 1985—Served to lt. (j.g.) USN, 1956-57. Recipient Wall St. Jour. award, 1956; recipient Disting. Service award Cosmopolitan Internat. Civic Club, 1964, 67; inducted into Am. Cattle Breeders Hall of Fame, 1979. Mem. Internat. Grapho analysis Soc., Internat. Assn. Oilwell Drilling Contractors (surface equipment co-chmn.), Am. Soc. Petroleum Engrs., Can. Inst. Mining and Metallurgy, Am. Mining Congress, Can. Diamond Drilling Assn., Ind. Petroleum Assn, Nomads (pres. 1984-85), Palomino Horse Breeders Am. (nat. pres. 1981-82, Hall of Fame), Internat. Brangus Breeders (co-chmn. promotion com. 1984-86), Am. Quarter Horse Assn., Am. Horse Shows Assn. (Palomino com.), Indian Nations Brangus Breeders Assn., ABA, Golden Saddlebred Assn., Okla. Bar Assn. (Disting. Service award 1964), Okla. Petroleum Assn., Okla. Palomino Horse Breeders Assn. (pres. 1979-80), Okla. Brangus Breeders Assn. (pres. 1982-83), Okla. Horse Council (pres. 1983-86), Western Okla. Brangus Breeders (sec.-treas. 1982-84), Okla. Beef Inc. (dir.), Okla. County Cattleman's Assn. (pres. 1974-75), Okla. Quarter Horse Assn., Okla. County Beef Com., Okla. Poultry Fedn., Oklahoma County Bar Assn., Antique Aircraft Assn., N.W. Okla. Brangus Breeders Assn., Midcontinent Oil and Gas Assn., Ind. Petroleum Producers Assn. Republican. Methodist. Clubs: Petroleum (Oklahoma City); Serlion. Died June 26, 1987; buried Meml. Pk. Cemetery., Oklahoma City.

BROWN, WALTER HAROLD, JR., lawyer; b. Johnson City, Tenn., May 20, 1910; s. Walter H. and Constance (Malone) B.; m. Phyllis Elizabeth Barnard, June 6, 1935; children: Walter Barnard, Phyllis Deborah (Mrs. George J. Pillorgé). B.A., Birmingham-So. Coll., 1931; LL.B., Columbia U., 1934. Bar: N.Y. 1935, U.S. Supreme Ct. Assoc. firm Willkie, Farr & Gallagher (and predecessors), 1934-43, ptnr., 1943-80, counsel, 1980-85, retired sr. ptnr., from 1985; gen. counsel Seaboard Coast Line R.R. Co., 1965-70; spl. counsel to maj. life ins. cos. in pvt. placement investments; co-counsel Penn Central Trustees, 1978; reorgn. mgr. Mo. Pacific R.R. Co., 1956, Instl. Investors Penn Central Group, 1970-78, Erie Group, 1973-80. Trustee Finch Jr. Coll., 1943-53. Fellow Am. Bar Found. (life); mem. ABA, N.Y. State Bar Assn., Sigma Alpha Epsilon, Omicron Delta Kappa. Clubs: University (N.Y.C.); Port Washington (N.Y.) Yacht. Home: Port Washington N.Y. Deceased.

BROWN, WINTHROP GILMAN, government official; b. Seal Harbor, Maine, July 12, 1907; s. William Adams and Helen Gilman (Noyes) B.; m. Peggy Ann Bell, Dec. 28, 1946; children: Winthrop, Julia, Anne. BA, Yale U., 1929, LLB, 1932. Mem. firm Bleakley, Platt & Walker, N.Y.C., 1938-41; in office of gen counsel Lend Lease Adminstrn., Washington, 1941; exec. officer Harriman Mission U.S. embassy, London, 1941-43, U.S. Lend Lease Mission to India, 1943; exec. officer Harriman Mission Mission for Econ. Affairs, U.S. embassy, London, 1943-45, acting chief, 1945; chief Div. Comml. Policy Dept. State, Washington, 1945-48, acting dir. Office Internat. Trade Policy, 1947-48, dir., 1948-50, dir. Office Internat. Materials Policy, 1950-52; dep. to minister for econ. affairs U.S. embassy, London, 1952-55; minister econ. affairs, dir. U.S. operations mission 1955-57; minister-counsellor, dep. chief mission Am. embassy New Delhi, 1957-60; U.S. ambassador to Laos 1962-64; dep. comdt. for fgn. affairs Nat. War Coll., Washington, 1962-64; U.S. ambassador to Korea 1964-67, spl. asst. to Sec. State for liaison with state govs., 1967-68; dep. asst. sec. for East Asian and Pacific Affairs State Dept., 1968-72; ret. 1972. Recipient Superior Service award Dept. State, 1952, Meritorious Service award, 1956, Pres.'s medal for Disting. Fed. Civilian Service, 1963, Disting. Service award, 1972. Mem. Sco. Scroll and Key, Zeta Psi, Met. Club, Chevy Chase Club, Yeamans Hall. Home: Washington D.C. Died May 5, 1987.

BROWNE, DUDLEY, corporate executive; b. Washington, July 10, 1891; s. Francis Littleton and Lena Delano (Johnson) B.; m. Eva O. Clore, Oct. 29, 1925. Student, Georgetown U. V.p. Am. Home Products Corp., also bd. dirs. With U.S. Army, World War I, AEF. Mem. Am. Patent Law Assn., Chartered Inst. Patent Agts. (London), N.Y. Acad. Scis., U.S. Trademark Assn. (pres., dir.), Engrs. Club (Montreal, Que., Can.). Home: New York N.Y. †

BROWNE, FRANCIS CEDRIC, judge; b. Cleve., Jan. 22, 1915; s. William Henry and Anna Loretta (Ginley) B.; m. Elizabeth Ann Cullen, July 3, 1937; children: Richard C., James F., Barbara Ann Browne Elliott, Martha Louise Browne Schwartz, David F. Student, Ohio State U., 1935; AB, U. Akron, 1936; JD, Cleve. State U., 1942; postgrad., George Washington U., 1942, 50. Bar: D.C., Md. Patent lawyer Washington, 1945-75; ptnr. Browne, Beveridge, DeGrandi & Kline and predecessors; patent solicitor Indsl. Rayon Corp., Cleve., 1938-41; trial judge U.S. Ct. Claims, 1975-80, sr. trial judge, 1981-82, sr. judge, from 1982. Patent atty. USAF, 1945; col. Judge Adv. Gen. Dept., USAF res. ret. Mem. ABA, Fed. Bar Assn., D.C. Bar Assn., Am. Patent Law Assn., Thomas More Soc. (treas. 1961-72), Delta Theta Phi, Phi Delta Theta (pres. Washington alumni 1962-63), Omicron Delta Kappa, Pi Kappa Delta, KC (4th deg.), Nat. Lawyers Club (gov. 1959-80, sec. 1959-75), Kenwood Golf and Country Club, Cosmos CLub. Home: Chevy Chase Md. Deceased.

BROWNE, HARRY L., lawyer; b. South Bend, Ind., July 27, 1911; s. Alex and Lena (Godfried) B.; m. Helen Liberman, Apr. 16, 1942; 1 child, Douglas F. BS, Ind. U., 1934, JD, 1936; postgrad., Columbus U., 1939. Bar: Ind. 1936, Mo. 1948, U.S. Supreme Ct. 1948. Pvt. practice South Bend, 1936-38; atty. NLRB, 1938-49, regional atty. 6th region, 1948-49; mem. Spencer, Fane, Britt & Browne, 1951-85; past chmn. Kansas City Personnel Appeal Bd. Contbr. articles to profl. jours. Bd. dirs. Starlight Theatre Assn., Kansas City, Mo., Menorah Hosp., Kansas City, Planned Parenthood, Greater Kansas City Sports Commn., Heart of Am. United Way Campaign, Kansas City Amateur sprots Hall of Champions; bd. govs., trustee Kansas City Philharm. Assn.; hon. trustee Rockhurst Coll., Kansas City U., Truman Med. Ctr., Kansas City Conservatory; hon. fellow Truman Library Inst. Lt. USNR, 1942-45, PTO. Mem. ABA (co-chmn. com. on relations between lawyers and agys. and depts. in field labor law 1965-72, com. on practice and procedure under Nat. labor Relations Act), Kansas City Bar Assn. (chmn. labor com. 1960-63), Mo. Bar (chmn. labor com. 1957-61), Am. Judicature Soc., Lawyers Assn. Kansas City (bd. dirs.), Kansas City C. of C., Nat. Retail Mchts. Assn., Am. Retail Fedn., Indsl. Relations Rsch. Assn., Downtown, Inc., Rotary (past dir., sec.-treas., pres. Kansas City chpt. 1970-71). Home: Kansas City Mo. Died June 8, 1985.

BROWNE, SECOR DELAHAY, industrial engineer, educator, consultant; b. Chgo., July 22, 1916; s. Aldis Jerome and Elizabeth (Cunningham) B.; m. Mary Denise Giles, Aug. 23, 1945; children: Patrick R., Giles C.; m. Constance Ely Haden, Sept. 6, 1970; stepchildren: Dana M., Sabra I., Russell L., C. Keller, Chesley E., Kinard E. AB, Harvard U., 1938. Engr. draftsman Kroeschell Engring. Co., Chgo., 1938-42; engr. salesman Barber-Colman Co., Rockford, Ill., 1939-42, mgr. aircraft prodn., 1946-51; with Clifford Mfg. Co., Waltham, Mass., 1951-55; pres., chmn. bd. Browne & Shaw Co., 1955-69, Browne & Shaw Rsch. Corp., 1963-68; assoc. prof. MIT, 1958-69, prof., 1973-75; v.p. Bolt, Beranek and Newman, Inc., Cambridge, Mass., 1968-69; asst. sec. for rsch. and tech. Dept. Transp., 1969; chmn. CAB, 1971-73; cons. Secor D. Browne Assocs. Inc., from 1973. Contbr. articles. Mem. Lincoln (Mass.) Rep. Town Com., 1962-68; chmn. Flight Safety Found. Served to maj. USAAF, 1942-46. Decorated Bronze Star. Fellow Royal Aero. Soc., Royal Soc. Arts, AIAA (assoc.); mem. Soc. Automotive Engrs., Royal Commonwealth Soc., Harvard (N.Y.C.), Wings (N.Y.C.), Metropolitan, Nat. Aviation, Atheneum, American (London) clubs. Home: Washington D.C. Died Mar. 23, 1986.

BROWNLEE, OSWALD HARVEY, economist, educator; b. Moccasin, Mont., Apr. 14, 1917; s. William and Sarah (Fyffe) B.; m. Lela McDonald, June 11, 1939; children—Barbara, Richard. B.S., Mont. State Coll., 1938; M.A., U. Wis., 1939; Ph.D., Iowa State U., 1945. Prof. econs. Iowa State Coll., 1943-47, Carnegie Inst. Tech., 1947-48, U. Chgo., 1948-50; prof. econs. faculty U. Minn., 1950—; dep. asst. sec. Treasury, 1973-74; economist ICA mission to Chile, 1956-57; vis. prof. econs. Cath. U. Chile, 1967-69; vis. scholar Office Comptroller of Currency, 1965; cons. in field, from 1947. Author: (with J.A. Buttrick) Consumer and Social Choice, 1968, (with Robert I. Chien) Issues in Pharmaceutical Economics, 1979, Taxing the Income from U.S. Corporation Investment Abroad, 1980; also articles. Farm Found. fellow, 1941-42; Ford faculty fellow, 1958. Mem. Am. Econ. Assn., Econometric Soc., Phi Kappa Phi. Died Aug. 6, 1985.

BROWNSON, CHARLES BRUCE, editor, publisher, government relations executive; b. Jackson, Mich., Feb. 5, 1914; s. Charles Matthew and Helen Gray (Oxby) B.; m. Anna Louise Harshman, Nov. 23, 1966; Children: Dwight C., Bruce B., Guy David, Catharine Andrea Lunsford, Scott Malcolm. AB, U. Mich., 1935; LLB, Butler U., 1955; grad., Nat. War Coll. Pres. Cen. Wallpaper & Print Corp., Indpls., 1936-59; mem. 82d, 85th Congresses from 11th dist. Ind. 1951-59; asst. commr. public affairs, congl. liaison Housing and Home Fin. Agy., Washington, 1959-60; prin. Charles Brownson Assocs., 1960-80; gen. ptnr. Brownson Properties (Va.), 1980-88; founder, pub. Congl. Staff Directory, Ltd., Washington, 1959-88; profl. assoc. East-West Ctr. Editor, pub. Congressional Staff Directory, 1959-88; advance locator Capitol Hill, 1964—, Fed. Staff Directory, 1980—, Judicial Staff Directory, 1986—; lectr. seminars on such topics as: Pacific Prospects in Gobal prespective, 1978, Energy Interdependence and Growth Problems, 1978, Comparative Studies of U.S. Congress and Japanese Diet, 1981; also participated in Johnson Found. Seminars U.S. and UN., Racine, Wis., 1977; hist. papers in Bentley Library, Ann Arbor, Mich. Official observer Zimbabwe-Rhodesian elections, 1979. Served to lt. col. AUS, 1941-45, ETO, World War II; col. Res. ret., 1974. Decorated 5 battle stars, Legion of Merit, Medaille de Reconnaissance (France); named one of Outstanding Young Men Am. Indpls. Jaycees, 1947; recipient Disting. Alumnus award Delta Sigma Rho, Tau Kappa Alpha, 1982, tribute publ. in Congl. Record by Sen. Strom Thurmond, 1988. Mem. Former Mems. Congress (charter, pres. 1978-79), Pub. Relations Soc. Am., Ind. Soc. Washington, Fla. State Soc. Washington, Am. Acad. Polit. and Soc. Sci., Sigma Nu, Fusaliers (pres. 1972-77, treas. 1977-88), Internat. Oceanographic Found., Fairchild Tropical Gardens Assn., Nat. Trust Hist. Preservation, Washington Direct Mktg. Assn., (bd. dirs. 1973-75), Smithsonian Assn., Assocs. Corcoran. Republican. Presbyterian. Clubs: Athletic (Indpls.); Higgins Lake Property Owners Assn.; Lodges: Masons, Mystic Tie. Home: Mount Vernon Va. Died Aug. 1988, buried Arlington Nat. Cemetery, Va.

BROYHILL, JAMES EDGAR, furniture manufacturing executive, member Republican National Committee; b. Wilkes County, N.C., May 5, 1892; s. Isaac and Margaret (Parsons) B.; m. Satie L. Hunt, June 21, 1921; children: Allene Stevens, Paul, James T., Bettie Gortner. Student, Appalacian Tng. Sch., Boone, N.C., 1913-17. With Lenoir Furniture Corp., 1919; organized Lenoir Chair Co., 1926; exec. head Broyhill Furniture Factories, Lenoir Furniture Corp., Lenoir Veneer Co., Nat. Veneer Co., Harper Furniture Co., Lenoir Furniture Forwarding Co., Lenoir, Whitmel, N.C., Lenoir Chair Co. 5, Taylorsville, N.C., Conover Furniture Co., Conover, N.C., Otis L. Broyhill Furniture Co., Marion, N.C.; bd. dirs. Lenoir Chair Co., Arcadia, La., Wachovia Bank & Trust Co., Charlotte, N.C., C.&N.W. Ry.; mem. adv. bd. Am. Mut. Liability Ins. Co., Charlotte. Bd. govs. Am. Furniture Mart, Chgo.; mem. Rep. Nat. Com., from 1948; del. Rep. Nat. Conv. 8 times; trustee Wake Forest Coll., Southeastern Bapt. Theol. Sem.; bd. dirs. Caldwell Meml. Hosp., Lenoir. With U.S. Army, World War I. Recipient Man of Yr. plaque by bd. govs. Am. Furniture Mart, 1946, Free Enterprise award, 1961, James T. Ryan award So. Furniture Mfrs. Assn., 1967. Mem. So. Furniture Mfrs. Assn. (pres. 1943-46), Masons, Shriners, K.P. (past chancellor), Charlotte Country Club, Charlotte City Club, Sedgefield (N.C.) Country Club, Boone (N.C.) Golf Club, Biltmore (N.C.) Club, Forest Country Club, Mimosa Golf Club (Morganton, N.C.), Blowing Rock (N.C.) Golf Club, Lenoir (N.C.,) Golf Club, Lenoir Country Club. Home: Lenoir N.C. Deceased.

BROZ, JOSSIP See TITO, MARSHALL

BRUCE, HAROLD ROZELLE, political science educator; b. Clinton, Wis., Oct. 13, 1890; s. Walter Louis and Sarah Adrina (Mayberry) B.; m. Katherine Alfreda Cook, Dec. 26, 1918; 1 child, Donald Walter (dec. 1944). AB, Beloit (Wis.) Coll., 1912; AM, U. Wis., 1919, PhD, 1920; MA (hon.), Dartmouth Coll., 1923. Instr. in pub. speaking Pomona Coll., Claremont, Calif., 1912-14, John Hay Whitney vis. prof. govt., 1958-59, vis. prof. govt., 1959-61; traveling rep. MacMillan Pub. Co., 1914-18; asst. in polit. sci. U. Wis., 1919-20; asst. prof. polit. sci. Dartmouth Coll., 1920-23, prof., 1923-44, prof. govt., 1944-58, emeritus, from 1958; prof. polit. sci. N.Y. State Coll. for Tchrs, Albany, summers 1938-42; mem. N.H. State Liquor Survey Commn., 1936-37, N.H. Constl. Conv., 1948; moderator Precinct of Hanover, 1957-58; corp. mem. Dartmouth Savs. Bank. Author: American Parties and Politics, 3d edit., 1936, American National Government, 1952, rev. edit., 1957; co-author: The American Political Scene, 1938, Our Living Government, 1960. State chmn. N.H. Am. United for World Orgn., 1944; trustee N.H. Congl. Conf., 1931-37, Thetford (N.Y.) Acad.; moderator Grafton-Orange Assn. Congl. Chs., 1923-58; interoim minister 1st Presbyn. Ch., Barre, Vt., 1944-47, Congl. Ch., 1953, N. Congl. Ch., St. Johnsbury, Vt., 1954. Lt. F.A., U.S. Army, 1918. Mem. Phi Beta Kappa, Delta Upsilon, Delta Sigma Rho. Home: Hanover N.H. †

BRUCE, HARRY WILLIAM, JR., dentist, dental association executive; b. Nashville, July 19, 1920; s. Harry W. and Ethel (Scruggs) B.; m. Grace Brooks, June 12, 1944; children: Harry William III, Neal Irvin. BS, Carson Newman Coll., 1943; DDS, U. Tenn., 1946; MPH, U. Mich., 1950; LHD (hon.), Loyola U., Chgo., 1970, Des Moines Coll. Osteopathic Medicine and Surgery, 1971, Med. U. of S.C., 1977; LLD, Creighton U., 1981; ScD, Georgetown U., 1981. Pvt. practice 1946-84; dental officer Chattanooga-Hamilton County Health Dept., Tenn., 1947-48; dental trainee Pub. Health Service, Atlanta, 1954-56; regional pub. health cons. Charlottesville, Va., 1956-61; dental officer USPHS, 1961, asst. surgeon gen., 1971-84; assoc. dir. ops. Bur. of Health Manpower, Health Resources Adminstrn., Bethesda, Md., 1973-75; exec. dir. Am. Assn. Dental Schs., Washington, 1975-84; Lister Hill lectr. U. Ala., 1980; mem. adv. com. dental radiology Nat. Ctr. for Health Care Tech., 1980-81; mem. nat. adv. com. hosp. dental program Robert Wood Johnson Found., 1979-82. Contbr. articles to profl. jours. With U.S. Army, 1942-44. Recipient Disting. Service award USPHS, 1975, Award of Merit Georgetown U. Sch. Dentistry, 1971, Fairleigh Dickinson U., 1971; named Outstanding Alumnus U. Tenn., 1981. Fellow Am. Pub. Health Assn., Am. Coll. Dentists; mem. ADA (cons. 1975-84), Am. Assn. Dental Schs., Am. Assn. Pub. Health Dentists. Democrat. Baptist. Home: Bethesda Md. Died Jan. 7, 1984; buried Parklawn Meml. Park, Rockville, Md.

BRUCE, IMON ELBA, college president; b. Blevins, Ark., Dec. 9, 1910; s. Jewell Joseph and Ada Lee (Wortham) B.; m. Catherine Coles, Dec. 24, 1938; children—Catherine Jane, Carolyn Louise, Elizabeth Ann. B.A., Henderson State Coll., 1932; M.S., La. State U., 1937; D.Ed., Ind. U., 1952. Tchr. math. and sci. Hope (Ark.) High Sch., 1932-33; tchr. math and sci. Fordyce (Ark.) High Sch., 1933-36; supt. schs. Fordyce, 1937-49; teaching fellow math. La. State U., 1936-37; dir. student teaching Ark. State Tchrs. Coll., Conway, 1949-53; supt. schs., Hot Springs, Ark., 1953-59; pres. So. Ark. U., Magnolia, 1959-76, pres. emeritus, 1976-88; summer vis. lectr. Ind. U., 1955, U. Ark., 1956, 57, U. N.Mex., 1958. Mem. NEA, Ark. Edn. Assn., Am., Ark. (past pres.) assns. sch. adminstrs., Magnolia C. of C. (past pres.), Phi Delta Kappa. Methodist. Club: Rotarian (past pres.). Home: Magnolia Ariz. Died Jan. 5, 1988, buried Meml. Park Cemetery, Magnolia, Ariz.

BRUCE, WILLIAM HENRY, JR., consulting engineer; b. Bradford, England, June 3, 1908; s. William Henry and Isabella (Lowe) B.; m. Ruth Hope Short, July 27, 1940; children: William Henry, Ruth Marina, Richard David. BCE, Northeastern U., 1930. Constrn. engr. various cos., 1930-39; constrn. engr., chief field engr. Parsons, Brinckerhoff, Hall & MacDonald, 1939-54; from ptnr. to sr. v.p., then pres. Parsons, Brinckerhoff, Quade & Douglas, Inc., N.Y.C., 1954-73, dir., also cons., from 1973. Treas., trustee N.J. Citizens Hwy. Com.; bd. dirs. Nat. Council Northeastern U.; mem. corp. Northeastern U. With USNR, 1944-46; PTO. Recipient Disting. Attainment citation Northeastern U., 1973. Fellow Am. Cons. Engrs. Council (past nat. del.); mem. ASCE, Nat. Soc. Profl. Engrs., Soc. Am. Mil. Engrs., Cons. Engrs Council N.J. (past pres.), Hopewell Country Club, Bedens Brook Club, Seaview County Club, Honeywell Twp. Lions (past sec., past pres.), Masons, Shriners. Home: Pennington N.J. Died Dec. 28, 1985; buried Pennington.

BRUGLER, FRANK RUSSELL, comptroller; b. Columbia, N.J., Oct. 19, 1892; s. Frank and Laura (Uhler) B.; m. Miriam E. Walters, 1915; 1 child, Marguerite (Mrs. James A. Worrell). Student, Pace Inst. Accounting, N.Y.C., 1915. With Alpha Portland Cement Co., Easton, Pa., 1913-18; with Bethlehem (Pa.) Steel Co., from 1918, successively in comptroller's dept., asst. to comptroller, asst. comptroller, 1918-55, comptroller, dir., from 1955; mem. various coms. War Prodn. Bd., Washington, World War II. Mem. Am. Iron and Steel Inst., Comptroller's Inst. Am., Saucon Valley Country Club, Bethlehem Club. Lutheran. Home: Bethlehem Pa. †

BRUHN, ERIK BELTON EVERS, dancer; b. Copenhagen, Oct. 3, 1928; s. Ernst Emil and Ellen (Evers) B.; student Royal Danish Ballet Royal Theater, Copenhagen. Made debut with Danish Ballet, 1946, premiere danseur, 1949, 58-61; guest artist Met. Ballet, London, 1947-49; dancer Am. Ballet Theatre, 1949-58, N.Y.C. Ballet, 1959; guest Bolshoi Ballet, Moscow, 1961, Danish Ballet, 1961, Royal Ballet, London, 1962; dir. Royal Swedish Ballet, Stockholm, 1967-71; resident producer Nat. Ballet Can., Toronto, Ont., 1973-76, artistic dir., 1983-86; ptnr. with Jeanmaire in movie Hans Christian Andersen, 1952; appeared as ptnr. with Alicia Markova, Alicia Alonso, Nora Kayo, Mary Ellen Moylan, Mia Slavenska, Rosella Hightower; tours with Ballet Theatre Europe, North Africa; author: Bournonville and Ballet Technic. Named Ridder of Danebrog by King Denmark, 1963; recipient Narslav Nifinsky prize Paris, 1963, Damcemagazine award, 1968, Diplôme d'honneur (Can.), 1974, Litteris et Artibus medal King Carl Gustaf of Sweden, 1980. Mem. Royal Danish Ballet Union, Equity (London), Am. Guild Mus. Artists, Screen Actors Guild. Choreographer: Concertette (Morton Gould), 1953. Died Apr. 1, 1986.

BRUNET, MEADE, manufacturing company executive; b. Petersburg, Va., June 21, 1894; s. Robert Edward and Sally (Minson) B.; m. Edythe Redman, Oct. 2, 1925; children: Sally (Mrs. K.H. Beyan), Stuart. B.E., Union Coll., 1916, LLD, 1966. Prodn. clk. GE, Schenectady, N.Y., 1915-16, Sperry Gyroscope Co., 1916-17; comml. engr. pub. utility dept. GE, 1919-22; with RCA, 1922-66; dist. mgr. RCA, Chgo., 1923-25, asst. sales mgr. in charge merchandising, 1925-28; v.p. Radio Victor, 1928-29; sales mgr. radiotron div. RCA, 1929-32, v.p. mfg., Washington rep., 1939-45; mgr. engring. products dept. Victor div. RCA, 1945-46; v.p. RCA, 1946-66; mng. dir. RCA Internat. Div., 1946-57. Author: History of the 56th Engineers in First World War. Dir. Nat. Fgn. Trade Coun., 1946-67, PAn. Am. soc.; chmn. Bus. Coun. Internat. Understanding, 1957-60; mem. adv. bd. Internat. and comparative Law Ctr.; chmn. bd. trustees Union Coll., Schenectady, 1963-69, acting pres., 1966; past trustee U.S. Inter Am. coun., Far East Coun.; adviser internat. bus. program Rutgers Grad. Sch. Bus. Adminstrn.; gov. Union U., Albany, 1956-69; mem. adv. bd. Internat. Assn. Students in Econs. and Industry; former mem. bus. and industry adv. com. OECD; past mem. N.J. Rep. Fin. Com.; trustee Speedwell Village, Morristown, N.J. 1st lt. 56th Engrs., World War I; mil. combat service with French VIII Army and 1st Am. Army AEF. Decorated officer Cruzeiro do Sul (Brazil); Order El Merito (Chile). Fellow Radio Club Am.; mem. Internat. C. of C. (exec. com., trustee U.S. coun.), Arbitration Assn., NAM (chmn. internat. econs. affairs com. 1962-63, dir.), IEEE (life), Acad. Polit. Sci. (life), Conf. Nat. Orgns. (hon.), Univ. Club (N.Y.C.), Army and Navy Club (Washington), Somerset Hills (Bernardsville, N.J.), Farmington Country Club (Charlottesville, Va.), Radio Pioneers Club (life), Sigma Phi, Sigma Xi, Tau Beta Pi. Home: Mendham N.J. Deceased.

BRUNET, MICHEL, historian, educator, consultant; b. Montreal, Que., Can., Aug. 24, 1917; s. Leo and Rose (De Guise) B.; m. Berthe Boyer, May 17, 1945 (dec. 1974); m. Leone Dussault, Dec. 5, 1975. BA, U. Montreal, 1939, B Pedagogie, 1941, MA, 1947; PhD, Clark U., 1949. Tchr. Commn. des Ecoles Catholique de Montreal, 1941-49; asst. prof. dept. history U. Montreal, 1949-50, assoc. prof., 1950-59, prof., 1959-83, chmn. dept. history, 1959-67, prof. emeritus, 1983-85; vis. prof. Sorbonne, 1972, U. Poitiers, 1976; sec. Faculty of Letters, U. Montreal, 1961-66, vice-dean, 1966-67; pres. Inst. History of French Am., 1970-72. Author: Histoire du Canada, 1963, Les Canadiens après la Conquete 1759-1775, 1969 (Gov. Gen. Lit. prize 1969, France-Que. prize 1970); of hist. essays. Sec. gen. Soc. St. John the Baptist, Montreal, 1957-61, v.p. 1961-63. Recipient Duvernay prize, Montreal, 1969. Mem. Hist. Soc. Can., Hist. Soc. Montreal (recipient medal 1978). Roman Catholic. Home: Laval P.Q., Canada. Died Apr. 4, 1985.

BRUNINGS, KARL JOHN, chemist, research executive, government official, educator; b. Balt., Dec. 4, 1913; s. Johann Karl and Eleanor Marie (Meyrahl) B.; m. Helen Medcalf; children: Frieda (Mrs. Geoffrey Gardner), Laura (Mrs. Edwin C. Hoffman, Jr.). Student, U. Heidelberg, Germany, 1935-36; PhD, Johns Hopkins U., 1939; grad., Harvard Bus. Sch. Advanced Mgmt. Program, 1960. Chemist Eastman Kodak Co., 1939-41; research fellow, instr. Johns Hopkins, 1941-44; assoc. prof. Johns Hopkins U., Balt., 1946-48; asst. prof. NYU, N.Y.C., 1944-46; dir. chem. research and devel. Chas. Pfizer & Co., Inc., 1948-61, adminstrv. dir. research, 1961-62; pres. Geigy Research div. Geigy Chem. Corp., 1962-68; sr. v.p., dir. medicinal research Geigy Pharms. div. Geigy Chem. Corp., 1968-71; sr. v.p. pharm. research CIBA-Geigy Corp., Ardsley, N.Y., 1971-77; program dir. and cons. Office Tech. Assessment, U.S. Congress, 1977-78; prof. U. Rochester Med. Sch., part time 1979-80, cons. chem. and sci. policy, 1980-87; Rennebohm lectr. U. Wis., 1965; chmn. 1st Internat. Pharmacology Meeting, Stockholm, Sweden, 1961; participant seminar series NRC-Dept. Commerce, 1976; I.R.I. advisor Dept. Commerce, 1983-87. Contbr. articles to profl. jours. Bd. dirs. Westchester div. Am. Cancer Soc.; adv. council Westchester (N.Y.) Office Aging, 1978-80. Mem. Pharm. Mfrs. Assn. (chmn. subcom. 1965-67), AAAS (chmn. medicinal chem. sect.), Am. Chem. Soc. (corp. assoc., dir. N.Y. sect.; mem. subcom. sci. exhibits centennial 1976, chmn. pharm. task force on health, congl. sci. counselor 1981), Indsl. Research Inst. (chmn. tellers com., bd. editors; chmn. bd. editors, adv. editorial bd., chmn. emeriti com. Research Mgmt. 1972-87, dir. 1975-78, bd. rep. mid-mgmt. groups com. 1975-76, edn. com. 1976), Soc. Chem. Industry (hon. sec. 1959, exec. com. 1960-63), Assn. Research Dirs., Am. Inst. Chemists (honor scroll award), Chamber Music Assn. N.Y. Club: Chemists (N.Y.C.). Home: Scarsdale N.Y. Died Jan. 29, 1987; buried Balt.

BRUNSDALE, C(LARENCE) NORMAN, former governor, farmer; b. Sherbrooke, N.D., July 9, 1891; s. Knute H. and Margaret (Nordgaard) B.; m. Carrie Lajord, Aug. 30, 1924; children: Margaret Marie (Mrs. Edson G. Larson), Helen Lucille (Mrs. P. D. Williams). AB, Luther Coll., Decorah, Iowa, 1913. Mem. N.D. State Senate, 1927-34, 41-51, pres. pro tem, 1943, majority floor leader, 1945, 47; gov. State of N.D., 1951-56; U.S. senator from N.D. 1959-60. Mem. N.D. Rep. organizing com. from 1946, chmn., 1946; N.D. nat. Rep. committeeman, 1948-52. Mem. Am. Farm Bur. Lutheran. Home: Mayville N.D. †

BRUSKI, GEORGE, retail executive; b. Paris, 1888. Ed., John Marshall Law Sch., 1914. Treas. Goldblatt Bros., Inc. Home: Chgo. Ill. †

BRUTON, PAUL WESLEY, law educator; b. Woodland, Calif., Aug. 1, 1903; s. Philip and Nancy (Gilstrap) B.; m. Margaret Perry, Sept. 2, 1931; children—Margaret Jane (Mrs. Duane R. Batista), David, Laura (Mrs. L. Wallace Clausen). AB, U. Calif., 1929, LLB, 1929; JSD, Yale U., 1930; MA (hon.), U. Pa., 1971. Bar: Calif. bar 1930, Pa. bar 1943, Supreme Ct. U.S 1935. Sterling fellow law Yale U., New Haven, Conn., 1929-30, instr. law, 1930-32; assoc. prof. law Duke U., 1932-35; atty., office chief counsel Bur. Internal Revenue, Washington, 1935-37; vis. assoc. prof. law U. Pa., Phila., 1937-38, assoc. prof., 1938-39, prof., 1939-88, acting dean, 1951-52, Ferdinand Wakeman Hubbell prof. law, 1964-69, Algernon Sidney Biddle prof. law, 1969-74, emeritus, 1974-88; assoc. firm Ballard, Spahr, Andrews & Ingersoll, Phila., 1943-44; tax cons. law firm MacCoy, Evans & Lewis, Phila., 1953-62; Vis. prof. Stanford, 1941, 52, U. Tex., 1947, McGill U., 1961; spl. asst., gen. counsel A.A.A., 1934; chief price atty. Phila. region OPA, 1942-43; Chmn. Phila. Tax Rev. Bd., 1953-59; mem. Task Force on Revision Pa. Tax Law. Editor: Cases on Taxation, 1941, 2d edit., 1949, Cases on Federal Taxation, 1950, (with R.J. Bradley, 1953, 55), (with Edward L. Barrett and John Honrold) Cases and Materials on Constitutional Law, 1959, 4th edit., 1973. Mem. Juristic Soc. Phila., Phi Beta Kappa, Pi Sigma Alpha, Delta Sigma Rho, Order of Coif. Democrat. Mem. Soc. of Friends. Clubs: Franklin Inn, Penn Faculty. Home: Philadelphia Pa. Died July 16, 1988.

BRYAN, ALBERT VICKERS, judge; b. Alexandria, Va., July 23, 1899; s. Albert and Marion (Beach) B.; m. Marie Gasson, Dec. 1, 1923; children—Albert Vickers, Henry Gasson. LLB, U. Va., 1921. Bar: Va. 1920. Sole practice Alexandria, Va., 1921-47; judge U.S. Dist. Ct. (ea. dist.) Va., 1947-61, from 1961, U.S. Ct. Appeals (4th cir.), 1961-72; mem. Va. Bd. Corrections, 1943-45, Va. Bd. Law Examiners, 1944-47. Bd. visitors U. Va., 1956-64, rector, 1960-64. Mem. ABA, Va. Bar Assn., Am. Law Inst., Raven Soc., Phi Beta Kappa, Phi Kappa Sigma, Phi Delta Phi, Omicron Delta Kappa. Died Mar. 13, 1984.

BRYAN, ARTHUR EVAN, business executive; b. Barrie, Ont., Can., Mar. 11, 1892; s. J. Ingram and Emma (Arnold) B.; m. Evelyn May Boag, May 4, 1916; children: Harold, Elizabeth, Margaret. Student, Ridley Coll., St. Catherine, Ont., 1903-10, U. Toronto (Ont.), 1910-14; BA, McMaster U., 1915. With fgn. trade service Can. Dept. Trade and Commerce, from 1916, trade commr., Yokahama, Japan, 1917-23, trade commr., Kobe, Japan, 1923-25, trade commr., Liverpool, Eng., 1939-46, inspector trade commn. offices abroad, 1925-29, 35-39; comml. counsellor for Can. London, 1946-50; dep. consul gen. (comml.), N.Y.C. and Detroit 1950-54, ret.; bd. dirs. Poritts and Spencer, Ltd., Can. Mem. Consitutional Club, Palatine Club, Lyceum Club, Royal Golf Club (Liverpool), Royal Automobile Club, Woodcote Golf Club (London), The Hamilton Club, Hamilton Golf and Country Club, Psi Upsilon. Episcopalian. Home: Grimsby, Ont. Canada. †

BRYAN, JACK YEAMAN, former diplomat, author, photographer; b. Peoria, Ill., Sept. 24, 1907; s. James Yeaman and Regina (Gibson) B.; m. Margaret Gardner, June 21, 1934; children: Joel Yeaman, Guy Kelsey, Donna Gardner, Kirsten Stuart (Mrs. Winkle-Bryan). Student, U. Chgo., 1925-27; B.A. with high distinction, U. Ariz., 1932, M.A., 1933; postgrad. (fellow philosophy), Duke U., 1933-35; Ph.D., U. Iowa, 1939. Research analyst Fed. Emergency Relief Adminstrn., Washington, 1935-36; from instr. English to prof., head dept. journalism U. Md., 1936-48; pub. relations adviser OCD, 1942-43; dir. pub. relations Welfare Fedn. Cleve., 1943-45; pub. info. officer UNRRA, 1945-46; cultural attaché Am. Embassy, Manila, 1948-51; chief program planning Internat. Exchange Service, State Dept., 1951-53; pub. affairs officer USIS, Bombay, India, 1953-54, Bangalore, India., 1954-55; cultural affairs officer embassy Cairo, Egypt, 1956, Tehran, Iran, 1956-58; cultural attaché, chief cultural affairs officer embassy Karachi, Pakistan, 1958-63; personnel officer for Africa USIA, 1964-65; officer in charge Project AIM, U.S. Dept. State, Washington, 1965; officer-in-charge spl. recruitment program Bur. Edn. and Cultural Affairs, 1965-67; chief cultural affairs adviser USIA, 1968; ret. 1968; lectr. creative photography U. Calif. at Riverside, 1968-80. Author: novel Come to the Bower, 1963, 1986, Cameras in the Quest for Meaning, 1986; contbr. short stories, articles, photographs to numerous mags.; Photog. exhibits one man shows, Pakistan, 1961-62, U.S., 1964, 66, Perspectives Eastward on tour U.S., 1968-71. Chmn. publs. bd. U. Md., 1946-48; chmn. bd. dirs. U.S. Ednl. Founds, Philippines, 1949-51, Pakistan, 1958-63; exec. dir. Iran Am. Soc. in Tehran, 1956-58; founder, exec. dir. Pakistan-Am. Cultural Center, 1959-60, 62-63. Recipient ann. prize for best novel Tex. Inst. Letters, 1964, Summerfield Roberts award, 1964, award for best short story, 1974. Mem. Am. Soc. Mag. Photographers, Friends of Ctr. for Tex. Studies, Tex. Inst. Letters, Tex. Hist. Assn., Am. Mus. Natural History, Am. Fgn. Service Assn., Wilderness Soc., Nature Conservancy, Audubon Soc., Sierra Club, Phi Delta Theta, Delta Sigma Rho, Phi Gamma Mu. Home: Riverside Calif. Died May 22, 1988.

BRYNGELSON, BRYNO, speech pathologist; b. Otisco, Minn., Apr. 22, 1892; s. August and Ida Sofia (Nelson) B.; m. Arminda Mowre, Sept. 13, 1922; 1 child, William Mowre. BA, Carleton Coll., 1916; student grad. sch. divinity, Yale U., 1920-21; MA, U. Iowa, 1926, PhD, 1931. With speech staff U. Iowa, 1921-22, 24-26; prof. speech Hanover Coll., 1922-24; staff mem. U. Wis., 1925-26; dir. speech and hearing clinic U. Minn., 1927-51, clin. prof. pediatrics, from 1931, prof. speech, from 1943, dir. speech pathology, from 1951; prof. U. Colo. summers, 1938-42, Northwestern U., summer 1946, U. Fla., 1950; cons. VA Aphasia Clinic, Ft. Snelling Hosp., Mpls.; cons. personnel office speech pathology, World War II. Author: Speech in the Classroom, 1941, (with others) Know Yourself, 1944, (with Mikalson) Speech Correction Through Listening, 1959; contbr. articles to profl. jours. With inf., U.S. Army, 1917-18. Mem. Am. Med. Writers Assn., Am. Speech and Hearing Disorder Assn. (treas. 1932-40, pres. 1943-44), Midwest Speech Assn. (bd. assoc. editors), N.W. Pediatric Soc. (hon.), Minn. Assn. Speech Clinicians, Sigma Xi, Psi Chi. Home: Minneapolis Minn. †

BRYNNER, YUL, actor; b. Sakhalin (Island), Japan, July 11, 1920; came to U.S., 1940; m. Virginia Gilmore, Sept. 6, 1944; 1 son, Rock; m. Doris Kleiner (div.); m. Jacqueline de Croisset (div.); m. Kathy Lee, 1983. Ed. chiefly in France including the Sorbonne. Connected with entertainment field since 12 yrs. old; made debut in circus and on legitimate stage in Paris; first appeared on U.S. Stage, 1941; in Shakespearean role with Michael Chekhov company; debut on Broadway stage in Lute Song, 1946; later on tour throughout U.S. in same prodn.; appeared abroad in Dark Eyes, 1947-48; also as entertainer in Paris night clubs; actor, producer, dir. 1st TV talk show for NBC, 1948; became TV dir. CBS programs; on legitimate stage in The King and I, 1951-54; star of play, 1952-54; also on tour in film prodns. as Ramses in the Ten Commandments, 1955; as the king in The King and I, 1956; co-star with Ingrid Bergman in Anastasia, 1956; other films Brothers Karamazov, 1958, Journey, Sound and the Fury, 1959, Solomon and Sheba, 1959, Once More With Feeling, Magnificent Seven, 1960, Cast a Giant Shadow, 1966, Triple Cross, 1967, The Long Duel, 1967, The Double Man, 1968, The Madwoman of Chaillot, 1969, Flight of the Golden Goose, 1969, The Battle of Neretva, 1971, The Light at the Edge of the World, 1971, Fuzz, 1972, Westworld, 1973, Futureworld, 1976; TV series Anna and the King, 1972; toured with prodn. of the King and I, through 1984; author: Bring Forth the Children, 1960; served as radio announcer and commentator (in French) OWI, 1942-46. Active anti-smoking campaigner. Recipient Donalson award for best actor 1951, Nat. Bd. Rev. Motion Pictures award for best performance in The King and I, 1956, Acad. award, 1957, Tony award, 1952, Critics Circle award. Home: New York N.Y. Died Oct. 10, 1985.

BUCHANAN, JESSE EVERETT, civil engineer; b. nr. Algona, Iowa, Apr. 22, 1904; s. Sophus and Jessie Ann (Samuelson) B.; m. Leah Rachel Tuttle, June 10, 1929; children: Nancy Tuttle, John Austin. BS, U. Idaho, 1927, MS, 1929, C.E., 1936, LHD, 1951, ScD, 1953. Instr. civil engring., testing engr. U. Idaho, Idaho Bur. Hwys., Moscow, 1927-29; asst. prof., testing engr. U. Idaho, Moscow, 1929-36, dean Coll. Engring., dir. engring. expt. Sta., prof. civil engring., 1938-42, pres., 1946-54; research engr. Asphalt Inst., College Park, Md., 1936-38, pres., 1954-69, cons., 1969-86. Mem. Idaho Bd. Engring. Examiners, 1939-48; sec. Automotive Safety Found., Washington, 1956-69; sec., treas. Road Information Program Inc., 1970-86. Lt. col. C.E. AUS, 1942-46, CBI. Decorated Legion of Merit. Mem. Nat., Idaho, Md. socs. profl. engrs., ASCE, Am. Rd. and Transp. Builders Assn., Washington Soc. Engrs. (hon.), Phi Beta Kappa, Sigma Xi, Tau Beta Pi, Sigma Tau. Home: Coeur d'Alene Idaho. Died Feb. 2, 1986; buried Arlington Nat. Cemetery.

BUCHANAN, WILEY THOMAS, JR., ambassador, corporation executive; b. Myrtle Hill, Tex., Jan. 4, 1914; s. Wiley T. and Lilla A. (Youngblood) B.; m. Ruth Elizabeth Hale, Apr. 12, 1940; children: Bonnie Ruth (Mrs. C.T. Matheson), Diane Dow, Wiley Thomas III. Student, So. Meth. U., George Washington U.; LLD, Alma Coll.; HHD, Dickinson Coll., Wiley Coll. Sec.-treas. Nat. Agrol. Co., 1942-50; v.p. Berks Parachute Co., Reading, Pa., 1943-46; dir. metal cutting tool dept. NPA 1950-52, minister to Luxembourg, 1953-55, ambassador, 1955-57, chief protocol U.S. with rank of ambassador, 1957-61, ambassador to Austria, Vienna, 1975-86; bd. dirs. Nat. Savs. & Trust Bank, Washington, Mut. Broadcasting Corp., L'Enfant Plaza Corp. Author: Red Carpet at the White House, 1964. Bd. dirs. Fed. City Council; trustee George Washington U., Landon Sch. for Boys, Bethesda, Md. Exec. sec. machine tool br. intelligence investigating com. Joint Chiefs of Staff, World War II. Decorated by govts. of Belgium, Luxembourg, Denmark, P.I., Thailand; comdr. Legion of Honor (France), knight comdr. Order of Merit (Germany). Mem. Everglades Club, Met. Club, 1925 F Street Club, Chevy Chase Club, Dallas Country Club, Brook Hollow Country Club, Travelers Club, Reading Room, Spouting Rock Beach CLub, Clambake Club. Methodist. Home: Washington D.C. Died Feb. 16, 1986.

BUCHER, CHARLES AUGUSTUS, physical education educator; b. Conesus, N.Y., Oct. 2, 1912; s. Grover C. and Elizabeth (Barr) B.; m. Jacqueline N. Dubois, Aug. 24, 1941; children: Diana Bucher Grantz, Richard, Nancy Bucher MacCarrick, Gerald. B.A., Ohio Wesleyan U., 1937; M.A., Columbia, 1941; Ed.D., N.Y. U., 1948; post-grad., Yale, 1948-49. Tchr. pub. schs. N.Y., 1937-41; asso. prof. New Haven State Coll., 1946-50; prof. edn. N.Y. U., 1950-79, dir. Sch. Health, Phys. Edn., Recreation and Dance, 1981-86; prof. U. Nev., Las Vegas, 1980-88; editor Appleton-Century-Crofts, N.Y.C.; Am. specialist U.S. State Dept., 1962; del. Pres. Eisenhower's White House Conf. on Youth Fitness, 1956; cons. Pres.'s Council on Phys. Fitness and Sports, 1972-88, Nat. Fitness Found.; chmn. nat. adv. bd. Am. Fitness Club; pres. Nat. Fitness Leaders Assn. Author: Methods and Materials in Physical Education and Recreation, 1954, Foundations of Physical Education, rev. edit, 1983, Recreation for Today's Society, 1984, Methods and Materials Secondary School Physical Education, rev. edit, 1983, Physical Education in Modern Elementary School, rev, 1971, College Ahead, rev. edit, 1961, Athletics in Schools and Colleges, 1965, Guiding Your Child toward College, 1967, Physical Education for Life, 1969, Dimensions of Physical Education, 2d edit, 1974, Administration of Health and Physical Education Programs, 1983, Administrative Dimensions of Health and Physical Education Programs, 1971, The Foundations of Health, 1976, Physical Education for Children: Movement Foundations and Experiences, 1979, Physical Education: Change and Challenge, 1981, Health, 1981, Fitness for College and Life, 1985, Foundations of Physical Education and Sport, 1987, Management of Physical Education and Athletic Programs, 1987; columnist and contbr. articles to profl. jours.; columnist Los Angeles Times Syndicate. Trustee, chmn. scholarship com. Coll. Scholarship Plan, Inc., 1959-88. Served to capt. USAAF, 1941-46. Recipient Sch. Bell award, 1960; named One of 10 Ams. who have contributed most to nation's health and fitness Jaycees, 1982. Fellow A.A.H.P.E.R., Am. Coll. Sports Medicine, Am. Sch. Health Assn.; mem. N.E.A. Home: Las Vegas Nev. Died July 14, 1988.

BUCHHEISTER, CARL WILLIAM, conservationist; b. Balt., Jan. 20, 1901; s. George Albrecht and Mary Hermine (Koch) B.; m. Harriet Nettleton Gillilan, Dec. 26, 1924; children: Harriet Ann (Mrs. Louis C. Reggio), Mary Carol, (Mrs. Robert L. Massonneau), Elizabeth Clare (Mrs. Thomas C. Shortell). BA, Johns Hopkins U., 1923, postgrad. Latin and Greek, 1923-25; LLD, Pace Coll.; HHD, Bowdoin Coll. Tchr. Lation, Park Sch., Balt., 1925-26, Lawrence Sch., Hewlitt, L.I., N.Y., 1927-36; founder, dir. Camp Mocassin, pvt. boys' camp, Lochmere, N.H., 1926-34; dir. Audubon Camp of Maine for tchrs., adult leaders, Medomak, 1936-57; exec. dir. Mass. Audubon Soc., 1936-39; asst. dir. Nat. Audubon Soc., 1940-44, sr. v.p., 1944-59, pres., 1959-67, pres. emeritus, 1967-86. Pres. Edward Ball Wildlife Found., Nat. Audubon So., Greenwich, Conn., Alice Rich Northrop Assn., 1950-60, past hon. pres.; bd. dirs. Chewonki Found., Inc., Can. Audubon Soc., 1960-67. Mem. Nat. Parks Assn. (past dir.), Am. Forestry Assn. (hon. v.p. 1963), Am. Ornithologists' Union, Wilson Ornithol. CLub, N.Y. Zool. Soc., Linnaean Soc. N.Y., Johns-Hopkins Alumni Assn. (pres. N.Y., N.J., Conn. 1958-60), Omicron Delta Kappa, Century Assn. Club, Johns Hopkins Club of N.Y.C. Home: Chapel Hill N.C. Died July 25, 1986.

BUCK, CLIFFORD HOWARD, olympic official, sports administrator; b. Rushville, Ill., Apr. 22, 1901; s. Nathaniel C. and Blanche (Pollock) B.; m. Isabel McFerran, Dec. 1923 (div. 1947); children: John N., Nancy Jean Buck Brown. BA, Iowa Wesleyan Coll., 1923; postgrad., U. Iowa, 1925, U. Mich., 1926. Dir. athletics, phys. edn., head coach football, basketball Salida (Colo.) High Sch., 1925-27; with Wilson Sporting Goods Co., 1927-63, mgr. Rocky Mountain sales div., 1930-40, 46-62, Tex. sales div., 1940-46; with AAU, Denver, 1946-67, nat. basketball tournament com., 1946-67, nat. exec. com., 1957-67, fgn. rels. com., 1956-67, pres., 1964-66. V.p. Internat. Amateur Basketball Fedn., from 1962, AAU, from 1962, mem. Cen. Bur., from 1962; bd. dirs. U.S. Olympic Com., pres., 1969-73. Mem. Mt. Vernon Country Club (Golden, Colo.), Boulder Country Club, Lakewood Country Club. Methodist. Home: Denver Colo. Died Feb. 7, 1989.

BUCKLEY, JOHN BEECHER, lawyer, chemical pharmaceutical manufacturing executive; b. N.Y.C., Aug. 31, 1923; s. John B. and Emily (Enstrom) B.; m. Ruth N. Eck, Aug. 23, 1947; children—John B., Beverly P. Buckley Toth, Alison M. Buckley Bruland, Denis E. B.A., Rutgers U., 1950, LL.B. cum laude, 1950; LL.M., N.Y. U., 1951. Bar: N.Y. 1953, Ind. 1959. Instr. law N.Y. U., 1951-53; trial atty. and spl. assignments as spl. asst. to Atty. Gen. U.S. Dept. Justice, 1953-57; with Miles Labs., Inc., Elkhart, Ind., 1957-83; v.p., gen. counsel Bayer USA Inc., Pitts., 1983-87; pvt. practice Elkhart, 1988. Contbr. to law reviews and jours. Served to capt. AC AUS, 1943-46. Mem. ABA, Elkhart City Bar Assn. Home: Elkhart Ind. Died Feb. 19, 1988; buried Rice Cemetery, Elkhart, Ind.

BUCKLEY, JOHN RAYMOND, government official; b. Washington, Iowa, July 21, 1891; s. John D. and Mary Jane (Cross) B.; m. Dorothy Davenport, Sept. 15, 1926. Student, U. Chgo. Asst. to pres. charge sales and advt. Beaver Board Cos., 1920-25; advt. mgr., pub. Cosmopolitan mag., 1926-41; pub. Good Housekeeping mag., 1941-54; gen. mgr. mag. div. Hearst Corp., 1954-56; nat. dir. U.S. Savs. Bonds div. U.S. Treasury, 1955-58; chmn. Econ. Stablzn. Com. (civil def.), V.I., from 1961. Mem. Nat. Better Bus. Bur. (past dir.), Mag. Advt. Bur. (past dir.), Assn. Better Bus. Burs. (past chmn.), Periodical Pub. Assn. (past dir.); hon. mem. Rotary Club St. Thomas. Home: Saint Thomas V.I. †

BUCKLEY, WARREN BOWMAN, lawyer; b. Chgo., Aug. 21, 1891; s. Walter B. and Catherine (Baumann) B.; m. Clara Wright Jackson, June 16, 1934; children: Irving G. Jackson, Robert W. Jackson, Mary Elizabeth Jackson. Student, U. Ill., 1909-11, Northwestern U. Law Sch., 1913. Bar: Ill. 1913. Pvt. practice Chgo., from 1913. Mem. 1st ROTC, Ft. Sheridan, Ill.; lt. 333d F.A., 86th Div. in U.S. and A.E.F., World War I. Mem. ABA, Ill. State Bar Assn. (pres. 1943), Chgo. Bar Assn., University Club, Exmoor Country Club, Law Legal Club (ex-pres.), Phi Gamma Delta, Phi Delta Phi. Home: Chicago Ill. †

BUEDING, ERNEST, educator, biochemist, pharmacologist; b. Frankfust am Main, Germany, Aug. 19, 1910; came to U.S., 1939, naturalized, 1944; s. Frederick and Katia (Margoulieff) B.; m. Raya Palzeff, Apr. 3, 1940; 1 son, Robert. BA, Goethe Coll., Frankfurt, 1928; MD, U. Paris, France, 1936. Fellow Pasteur Inst., Paris, 1933-35; asst. biochemistry U. Istanbul, Turkey, 1936-38; rsch. fellow Coll. Medicine, NYU, 1939-44; asst. prof. pharmacology, then assoc. prof. Western Res. U. Med. Sch., 1944-54; prof. pharmacology, chmn. dept. Sch. Medicine, La. State U., 1954-60; prof. pathobiology Sch. Hygiene and Pub. Health, Johns Hopkins, from 1960, dir., from 1969, prof. pharmacology and exptl. therapeutics, from 1966; vis. Fulbright prof. U. Oxford, Eng., 1959; Guggenheim fellow Oxford, summer 1963; investigator OSRD, 1941-45; mem. bd. Nat. Vitamin Found., 1949-52; mem. commn. parasitology Armed Forces Epidemiol. Bd., 1953-72; cons. to Surgeon Gen. Dept. Army. from 1973; mem. study sect. tropical medicine and parasitology NIH, 1956-60; mem. panel metabolic biology NSF, 1962-65; cons. WHO, 1961, 63, mem. expert com. schistosomiasis, 1959, 62, expert adv. panel parasitic diseases (Bilharziasis), 1963-75; mem. parasitic diseases panel U.S.-Japan Coop. Med. Sci. Program, 1965-71; chmn. U.S. Schistosomiasis del. to Peoples Republic of China, Apr. 1975. Contbr. articles to profl. jours., revs., also chpts. in bokks; mem. editorial bd.; Exptl. Parasitology, 1952-63, Biochem. Pharmacology, 1958-68, Molecular Pharmacol., 1969-86, The Johns Hopkins Mag., 1971-73. Founder Cleve. Chamber Music Soc., 1949, pres. 1953-54; founder New Orleans Friends Music, 1955, counselor, 1955-60; pres. Shriver Hall Concert Series, Johns Hopkins, 1965-78. Recipient Nat. Svc. award Chamber Music Am., N.Y.C., 1984, Paul Ehrlich award, Frankfurt am Main Gold medal, 1985. Fellow AAAS; mem. Am. Acad. Arts and Scis., Am. Soc. Biol. Chemists, Am. Soc. Pharmacology and Exptl. Therapeutics (recipient 1st Theodor Weicker Meml. award 1978), Am. Chem. Soc., Brit. Biochem. Soc., Brit. Pharmacol. Soc. (assoc.), Brazilian Soc. Tropical Medicine (hon.), Phi Beta Kappa. Home: Baltimore Md. Died Apr. 18, 1986.

BUEHL, LOUIS HARRY, III, career military; b. Pitts., Sept. 18, 1932; s. Louis Harry and Marcella Marie (McGraw) B.; m. Georgia M. Warwick, June 7, 1954; children: Marcella Marie, Heidi Susan, Megan Elesbeth, Jennifer Liane. BS, Miami U., Oxford, Ohio, 1954; MS, U. Mich., 1968; student, Brown U., 1968; student J.F. Kennedy Sch. Govt., Harvard U., 1986; student, Command and Staff Sch., 1967-68, Air War Coll, 1975-76. Commd. 2d lt. USMC, 1954, advanced through grades to lt. gen., 1987; dep. chief. of staff, sec. joint staff U.S. Forces Hdqrs., Japan, 1976-79; chief of staff Fleet Marine Force Pacific USMC, Hawaii, 1979-80; CO 3d Marine Regiment, 1st Marine Brigade USMC, Kaneohe Bay, Hawaii, 1980-82; comdg. gen. USMC, Camp LeJeune, N.C., 1984-85; dir. facilities, services div. I&L USMC Hdqrs., Washington, 1982-84, dep. chief of staff res. affairs, 1985-86; sr. mil. asst. to dep. sec. def. Office Sec. Def., Washington, 1986-87; chief of staff USMC, Washington, 1987-88. Decorated D.S.M., Def. Superior Service medal, Bronze Star with Combat V, Legion of Merit; recipient Vietnam Service award, Republic of Vietnam Meritorious Unit Citations, Republic of Vietnam Campaign, Vietnam Armed Forces Honor, Vienamese Cross of Gallantry (Republic of Vietnam). Mem. Marine Corps Assn., 3d Marine Div. Assn., Res. Officers Assn., Nat. Def. Transportation Assn., Retired Officers Assn., Navy Mutual Aid Assn., Phi Delta Theta, Army-Navy Club. Died Oct. 5, 1988; buried Arlington (Va.) Nat. Cemetery.

BUEHRIG, EDWARD HENRY, political science educator; b. Minier, Ill., Oct. 4, 1910; s. Edward S. and Emma (Kuhfuss) B.; m. Margaret E. Masters, June 18, 1935; children: Edward M., Robert M. PhB, U. Chgo., 1932, MA, 1934, PhD, 1942. Instr. polit. sci. U. Ind., Bloomington, 1934-42, asst. prof., 1942-46, assoc. prof., 1946-53, prof., 1953-63, Univ. prof., 1963-86, acting chmn. dept., 1966-67; officer Dept. State, 1944-46; faculty Nat. War Coll., 1951; with Brookings Instn., 1952; vis. prof. Am. U., Beirut, 1957-58; vis. mem. Inst. for Advanced Study, Princeton, N.J., 1948. Author: Woodrow Wilson and the Balance of Power, 1955, The UN and the Palestinian Refugees, 1971, The Perversity of Politics, 1986; editor: Wilson's Foreign Policy in Perspective, 1957, Essays in Political Science, 1966; contbr. articles to profl. jours. Recipient Smith-Mundt award, 1957-58; grantee Social Sci. Research Council, 1965-66. Mem. Am. Polit. Sci. Assn., Am. Soc. Internat. Law. Home: Bloomington Ind. Died Aug. 31, 1986; buried Valhalla Cemetery, Bloomington, Ind.

BUEK, CHARLES WELLES, banker; b. Glenbrook, Conn., Oct. 27, 1911; s. Thomas C. and Katharine Taintor (Welles) B.; m. Marjorie Ann Pinckney, Apr. 19, 1941; children: Ann P. Buek Beggs, Thomas Welles. Grad., Phillips Acad., Andover, Mass.; AB, Yale U., 1933. With U.S. Trust. Co. of N.Y., 1933-76, successively analyst, asst. sec., asst. v.p., 1933-51, v.p., 1953-58, exec. v.p., 1958-59, 1st v.p., 1959-62, pres., 1962-74, chief exec. officer, 1971-76, chmn. bd., pres., 1974-76, trustee (hon.), 1959-77; dir. Gen. Reins. Corp., Equitable Assurance Soc. of U.S., Continental Oil Co; past pres. bd. trustees, nat. bd. YMCA, N.Y.C.; bd. dirs. corp. of Presbyn. Hosp., Royal Globe Ins. Cos. N.Y. investment com.; bd. trustees NYU; past pres. N.Y. State Bank Fiduciary Fund; adj. faculty Stonier Grad. Sch. of Banking. Mem. Am. Bankers Assn. (pres. trust div. 1968-69, chmn. com. trust investments), Assn. of Res. City Bankers, N.Y. State Bankers Assn. (trust div. exec. com.). Home: Darien Conn. Died July 18, 1988; buried Spring Grove Cemetery, Darien.

BUELL, EUGENE F(RANKLIN), lawyer; b. Elrama, Pa., Dec. 3, 1916; s. Frank Currey and Altina (Ecklund) B.; m. Elizabeth Ellen Foster, Dec. 28, 1940; children: Ellen E. (dec.), Erik Foster. B.S., St. Vincent's Coll., 1938; grad., Carnegie Inst. Tech., 1938-40, U. Pitts., 1941, Johns Hopkins U., 1942; J.D., Duquesne U., 1944. Bar: D.C. 1949, Canadian Patent Office 1949, U.S. Supreme Ct. 1952. Chemist U.S. Steel Corp., 1938-42; chief chemist Homestead works, 1942-45; with Stebbins, Blenko & Webb, 1945-48; partner firm Blenko, Hoopes, Leonard & Glenn, 1949-52; Blenko, Hoopes, Leonard & Buell Pitts., 1953-66; Blenko, Leonard & Buell 1966-72; partner firm Blenko, Buell, Ziesenheim & Beck (P.C.), 1973-79; pres., chmn. Buell, Blenko, Ziesenheim & Beck, P.C., 1979-84, Tartan Industries Inc.; chmn., pres. Buell, Ziesenheim, Beck & Alstadt, P.C., 1984-88; treas. Pitts. Performance Products, Inc.; instr. Law Sch. U., Pitts., 1954-59, adj. prof. law, 1959-88. Past pres. Richland Com. for Better Govt., Babcock Sch. Dist. Dirs.; chmn. Richland Sch. Authority; mem. Sch. Bd. Richland Twp. Mem. Am. Bar Assn., Am. Patent Law Assn., Engrs. Soc. Western Pa., Pa. Soc., Assn. Bar City N.Y., Licensing Exec. Soc., Am. Arbitration Assn., Am. Soc. Metals, Interam. Bar Assn., Am. Judicature Soc., Pa. Bar Assn., Allegheny County Bar Assn., U.S. Trademark Assn., Chartered Inst. Patent Agts., Asia-Pacific Lawyers Assn., Assn. Internationale pour la Protection de la Propriete Industrielle, Order of Coif. Clubs: Duquesne, Elks, Masons, Press, Allegheny, Rivers, Amen Corner. Home: Gibsonia Pa. Died Jan. 4, 1988.

BUERKI, ROBIN CARL, medical administrator, hospital consultant; b. Black Earth, Wis., July 25, 1892; s. Otto C. and Katherine Ann (Kuntz) B.; m. Louise Matthews, Oct. 6, 1918; 1 son, Robin Carl. BS, U. Wis., 1915; MD, U. Pa., 1917, DSc (hon.), 1951. Chief resident physician Univ. Hosp., U. Pa., 1917-18; pvt. practice Boise, Idaho, Burn, Oreg., 1920-23; prof. hosp. adminstrn. U. Wis., 1923-41; supt. State of Wis. Gen. Hosp., U. Wis., 1923-41, Wis. Orthopedic Hosp. for Children, 1931-41; chmn., exec. sec. Med. Sch., 1935-41, dir. study of commn. on grad. med. edn., 1938-40; dean, dir. hosps. Grad. Sch. Medicine, U. Pa., 1941-48; v.p. charge med. affairs Grad. Sch. Medicine, 1948-51; exec. dir. Henry Ford Hosp., Detroit, 1951-64, cons., emeritus trustee, from 1965; spl. lectr. Columbia U. Sch. Pub. Health, 1946-49. Mem. Adv. Bd. Med. Spltys., from 1934, pres., 1947-50; mem. Fed. Hosp. Coun., 1946-50; mem. numerous adv. coms. to govl. agys., asssns., hosps.; mem. Albert and Mary Lasker Found. com. on Awards of Nat. Com. for Mental Health Inc., 1948; chmn. com. on edn. and publ. Nat. Found. for Infantile Paralysis, 1948-58; trustee, mem. exec. com. Mich. Hosp. Svc., v.p., 1954-61; bd. dirs., mem. adv. com. task force on comprehensive health care Nat. Commn. on Community Health Svcs., 1963-66; mem. hosp. constrn. adv. coun. VA, 1963-68; chmn. Conf. on Group Practice, 1967. 1st lt. M.C. U.S. Army, 1918-19; spl. cons. surgeon gen. U.S.. Army, from 1953.,. Recipient Wis. Hosp. Assn. Award of Merit, 1942, Am. Hosp. Assn. Award of Merit, 1947, Tri-State Hosp. Assn. Award of Merit, 1948, Silver award, City of France Chevaliers du Tastevin, Chateau du Clos de Vougeot en Bourgogne, 1st Gold Medal award Am. Coll. Hosp. Adminstrs, 1964. Mem. Founders Group Am. Bd. Preventive Medicine and Pub. Health; founding fellow Am. Coll. Hosp. Adminstrs. (pres. 1938-39, bd. regents 1953-59); mem. AMA, state and local med. assns., Am. Hosp. Assn. (pres. 1935, chmn. coun. govt. relations 1957-59, 60-61), Internat. Hosp. Fedn. (bd. mgmt.), Inter-Am. Hosp. Assn. (chmn. 1955-60), U. Mich. Program in Hosp. Asminstrn. Alumni Assn. (hon.), state and local hosp. assns., various spl. med. groups, Detroit Club, Grosse Point Club (Mich.). Home: Grosse Pointe Farms Mich. Deceased.

BULEY, HILTON CLIFFORD, college president; b. Waverly, N.Y., Dec. 25, 1903; s. Joseph Myron and Nora Belle (McCutcheon) B.; m. Arline Besse, Aug. 30, 1930; children: Hilton M., David R. BS, Hobart Coll., 1927; postgrad., Cortland State Tchrs. Coll., 1928; MA, Cornell U., 1934; postgrad., Syracuse U., 1939-40; EdD, Columbia U., 1947; LHD, Hobart Coll., 1963. Tchr. sci., athletic coach Brewster, N.Y., 1927-30, Milw. Country Day Sch., 1930-34; supervising prin. Spencer Central Sch., 1934-38, Vestal Central Sch., N.Y., 1938-42; supt. schs. Gloversville, N.Y. and Bound Brook, N.J., 1942-48; commr. edn. State of N.H., 1948-54; pres. So. Conn. State Coll., 1954-71; lectr.; cons. Commn. Tchr. Edn. and Profl. Standards, 1950, N.H. Bd. Nursing Edn.; dir. N.H. Council Tchr. Edn. Author profl. publs., articles profl. jours. Past pres. Community Chest; mem. dist. council Boy Scouts Am.; dir. N.H. League Arts and Crafts; cons. N.H. Jackson Meml. Found. for Cancer Research; state coordinator edn. N.H. Civil Def.; trustee Community Libraries; hon. mem. bd. dirs. New Haven Opera Soc.; mem. Conn. Com. on Edn. of Gifted, Conn. Accreditation Council. Recipient State citation for outstanding service to citizenship edn. VFW, State citation for exceptional service to pub. edn., N.H. Wisdom award of honor Wisdom Soc., 1969, first medal of excellence Hobart Coll. Alumni Assn., 1970. Mem. NEA, Am. Assn. Sch. Adminstrs., N.H. State Tchrs. Assn., N.E. Supts. Assn., Am. Assn. State Colls. and Univs. (dir., treas., pres. 1971), Nat. Chief State Sch. Officers U.S., Nat. Soc. for Study Edn., Conn. Edn. Assn., Am. Assn. Coll. for Tchr. Edn. (chmn. com. on TV and tchr. edn.; citation exceptional service and studies in new media of instrn.), Greater New Haven C. of C. (past dir.), Phi Delta Kappa, Phi Phi Delta, Chimera, Kappa Delta Phi, Rotarian (dist. gov. 1972-73, Paul Harris fellow 1977). Congregationalist. Home: Gilford N.H. Died Jan. 17, 1987.

BULKLEY, WILLIAM FRANCIS, archdeacon; b. Tashua, Conn., Apr. 21, 1881; s. William Howard and Annie F. (Pemberton) B.; m. Fanny Douglas Lees, Feb. 14, 1914; 1 child, William Lees. Student, Detroit Ch. Acad., 1899-1901; BA, Trinity Coll., Hartford, Conn., 1905; BD, Berkeley Div. Sch., Middletown, Conn., 1908; DD, Ch. Div. Sch. of Pacific, 1943. Ordained to ministry Protestant Episcopal Ch. as deacon, 1908, as priest 1909. City missionary Salt Lake City, 1908-14; chaplain St. Mark's Hosp., 1908-14; priest-in-charge St. Mary's Ch., Provo, 1914-29; gen. missionary Utah, 1917-24, archdeacon, 1924-49; ret. 1949; del. many ch. confs., synods. Author: St. Mark's Cathedral, a Spiritual Force, 1947, The Episcopal Church in Utah, 1949. Active many local and national civic activities; sec. Interdenom. Intermountain Area Conf., 1937-49; mem. Utah Commn. Physically Handicapped, from 1952; mem. exec. com. Salt Lake Safety Coun. Mem. Utah Soc. UN (dir.), Utah Social Hygiene Assn. (dir.), SAR (Minute Man award 1958), Soc. Mayflower Descs., Masons, K.T., Shriners, Provo Rotary Club, Phi Gamma Delta. Home: Salt Lake City Utah. †

BULL, WILLIAM LYLE, shipping company executive; b. Bklyn., Oct. 25, 1892; s. Frank A. and Florence Mary (Greene) B.; m. Jessie Marguerite Douglass, Sept. 8, 1919; children: William Lyle II, Patricia Beverly (Mrs. Theodore G. Bergmann). Engaged in shipping industry from 1909; v.p., gen. mgr., dir. Mallory Transp. Lines, also sec. C. D. Mallory & Co., 1919-24; gen. mgr. Richmond-N.Y.C. Steamship Co., 1924-26; asst. 1st v.p. Eastern Steamship Lines, 1926-41; head dept. ship mgmt. U.S. Mcht. Marine Acad., 1943-50; comml. shipping adviser to comdr. Mil. Sea Transp. Services, Dept. Navy, 1950-59; exec. v.p., dir. Am. Export Esbrandtsen Lines Inc., from 1959; spl. mission to Egypt for U.S. Shipping Bd., 1921-22; cond. ship mgmt. course Sch. Fgn. Service, Georgetown U., 1920-21, 53-59, mem. sch. adv. coun., from 1962. Capt. U.S. Army, 1917-19, AEF in France. Recipient Disting. Civilian Service medal Navy Dept., 1958. Mem. AAUP, Soc. Naval Architects and Marine Engrs., Marine Hist. Assn. Home: Washington D.C. †

BULLITT, DOROTHY STIMSON, broadcasting executive; b. Seattle, Feb. 5, 1892; d. Charles Douglas and Harriet Mary (Overton) Stimson; m. Alexander Scott Bullitt, May 16, 1918 (dec.); children: Stimson, Dorothy Priscilla (Mrs. Josiah Collins), Harriet Overton (Mrs. William R. Brewster Jr.). Student, pub. and pvt. schs., Seattle, Mrs. Dow's Sch., Briarcliff Manor, N.Y.; LHD, Pacific U., 1960. Pres. Bullitt Co. (formerly Stimson Realty Co.), Seattle, 1929-55; pres. King Broadcasting Co., Seattle, 1947-65, chmn. bd., from 1965; v.p. Krem Broadcasting Co., Spokane, 1958-59, pres., 1960-65, chmn. bd., from 1965; dir. Gen. Am. Corp., mem. exec. com. from 1936; dir. Pacific Nat. Bank, Seattle, mem. trust, investment and discount coms., from 1943. Mem. gov.'s emergency relief adminstrn., Seattle, 1932-34; state chmn. Nat. Women's Com. Moblzn. for Human Needs, 1933; mem. mayor's civic unity com., 1944-46; pres. Bullitt Found.; mem. Seattle Pub. Libr. Bd., from 1956, Fgn. Policy Assn., 1957-58; trustee Children's Orthopedic Hosp., 1921-56, Seattle Art Mus., from 1938; assoc. coun. Mills Coll., 1939-40; regent U. Wash., from 1958; mem. exec. com. War Commn. State of Wash.; chmn. bd. Service Women's Club, World War II. Recipient community service awards B'nai B'rith Women, 1954, Seattle Bus. and Profl. Women's Club, 1945, disting. citizen award Seattle Real Estate Bd., 1959. Mem. Am. Women in Radio and TV, Am. Rocket Soc., Seattle Jr. League, Washington Athletic Club, Tennis Club, Golf Club, Seattle Yacht Club, Sunset Club, Cosmopolitan Club (N.Y.C.), Radio and TV Execs. Soc. (N.Y.C.), Town Club (Portland, Oreg.). Home: Seattle Wash. †

BULLITT, JOHN C., lawyer; b. Phila., June 6, 1925; s. Orville H. and Susan B. (Ingersoll) B.; m. Lelia M. Wardwell, Nov. 20, 1954 (div.); children: Thomas W., Clarissa W.; m. Judith Ogden Cabot, May 15, 1976; stepchildren: Elizabeth, Edward, Timothy. B.A., Harvard, 1950; LL.B., U. Pa., 1953. Bar: N.Y. 1956. Assoc. Shearman & Sterling, N.Y.C., 1953-60, ptnr., then sr. ptnr., 1969-88, ptnr. in charge Hong Kong Office, 1978-81; dep. asst. sec. internat. affairs U.S. Treasury, Washington, 1961-62; asst. sec. internat. affairs U.S. Treasury, 1962-64; U.S. exec. dir. Internat. Bank Reconstrn. and Devel., 1962-65; dir. N.J. Office Econ. Opportunity, 1964-67; asst. adminstr. for East Asia AID, Dept. State, 1967-69. Served with inf. AUS, World War II. Mem. Council Fgn. Relations. Clubs: N.Y. Yacht, Century Assn. (N.Y.C.); Fed. City (Washington); Philadelphia; Royal Hong Kong Yacht, Shanghai Frat. Assn. (Hong Kong). Home: Princeton N.J. Died May 14, 1988.

BULLITT, JOHN MARSHALL, educator; b. Seattle, July 9, 1921; s. Keith Logan and Dorothy (Terry) B.; m. Sarah Cowles, Aug. 11, 1948 (div.); children: Elizabeth, Margaret, Sarah, John; m. Sandra Merrihue, June 27, 1969; 1 son, David, 1 stepson, Jeffrey Merrihue; m. Brianna Punton. AB, Harvard, 1943, PhD, 1950. Mem. faculty English dept. Harvard U., 1946-85, assoc. porf., 1956-62, prof., 1962-85; master Quincy House, 1957-66; assoc. dir. Peace Corps, Bolivia, 1966-68; pres. Elmasar Inc., 1977-85. Author: Jonathan Swift and the Anatomy of Satire, 1953; editor: Pamela-Shamela, 1980; co-editor: Samuel Johnson, The Idler and the Adventurer, 1963, 18th Century Poetry and Prose, 1973. Served to capt. inf. AUS, 1943-46. Mem. MLA, U.S. Power Squadron (chief chart instr. Pequosette div. 1977-80), Manchester Yacht Club, Cambridge Tennis Club, Phi Beta Kappa. Home: Marblehead Mass. Died Aug. 9, 1985.

BULLOCK, MARIE LEONTINE (MARIE LEONTINE GRAVES), civic leader; b. Paris, France, June 30, 1911; d. William Leon and Florence Christmas (Eno) Graves; m. Hugh Bullock, Apr. 5, 1933; children—Florence Eno (Fleur) Bullock Weymouth, Fair Alice Seymour (Mrs. Peter H. McCormick). Grad. student, Sorbonne, Paris and Columbia U., 1933-37, Julliard Sch. Music, 1937; mem., Tchrs. Astronomy Course, Hayden Planetarium, 1952-53; L.H.D., Williams Coll., 1975. Founder of Acad. Am. Poets, 1934, pres., 1939-86; bd. dirs. Edward MacDowell Assn., 1945-79; ex-officio mem. pres. adv. com. on arts John F. Kennedy Center Performing Arts, 1960; hon. trustee Theodore Roosevelt Assn.; hon. fellow Pierpont Morgan Library. Chmn. belles lettres com. Office Cultural Affairs, City of N.Y., 1964; mem. Citizens Advisory Commn., 1963; Mem. vis. com. dept. astronomy Harvard Coll., 1968-74, 75-81, 82-86. Council fellows Pierpont Morgan Library, 1969-73; recipient King's medal for service in cause of freedom; Distinguished Service award National Inst. Arts and Letters, 1963; Gold medal Nat. Inst. Social Scis., 1961; Mayor's award of honor for arts and culture, 1982; decorated dame Order St. John of Jerusalem. Mem. Nat. Soc. Colonial Dames, Poetry Soc. Am. (exec. bd. 1938-39), Nat. Inst. Social Sci. (gold medal 1961), Hroswitha Club, Philharm. Symphony Soc, English Speaking Union. Episcopalian. Clubs: Colony (N.Y.C.) (bd. govs. 1968-76, mem. com. lit. and art 1966, chmn. library com. 1973, chmn. sub-com. for hon. visitors 1976-86), River (N.Y.C.); Sulgrave (Washington). Home: New York N.Y. Died Dec. 25, 1986, buried Royalston, Mass.

BUMGARDNER, ALBERT ORIN, architect; b. Springfield, Ill., Jan. 3, 1923; s. Alfred Orin and Florence (Lonas) B. Student, Ill. State U., 1941-43, City Coll. N.Y., 1943-44; B.Arch. summa cum laude, U. Ill., 1949. Pvt. practice architecture Seattle, 1953-61; partner firm A. O. Bumgardner & Partners, Seattle, 1961-70; prin. The Bumgardner Partnership, Seattle, 1970-87; cons. editor Architecture*West, 1957-71; vis. lectr. U. Wash., 1961, 67, Mont. State U., 1967; Mem Municipal Art Commn. Seattle, 1965-69; chmn. Design Commn. Seattle, 1969-71; mem. exec. bd. Commn. 2000, Seattle, 1972-87. Served with USAAF, 1943-46. Recipient Sunset mag. Design awards, 1965, 69; Seattle chpt. AIA Honor awards for Excellence of Design, 1954, 56, 58, 60, 63, 65, 67, 69, 70, 73, 75, 83. Fellow AIA (pres. Seattle 1962-63); mem. Alpha Rho Chi. Home: Seattle Wash. Died July 10, 1987.

BUMP, BOARDMAN, investment manager; b. Pittsfield, Mass., Dec. 8, 1908; s. Charles Henry and Esther Elizabeth (Boardman) B; m. Eleanor Myrick, June 28, 1933; children: Carolyn Bump Marsh, Daniel Boardman, Susan Bump Vancura, Jonathan. AB magna cum laude, Amherst Coll., 1930; MBA, Harvard U., 1932. Asst. purchasing agent Mt. Holyoke Coll., 1932-34, comptroller, 1934-51, asst. treas., 1939-42, treas., 1942-73, v.p., 1951-54, trustee, 1955-65, 66-76; ptnr. Morrison & Bump, 1955, Morrison, Bump & Morse, 1956-63, Bump, Morse & Marsh, Boston, from 1963; mng. gen. ptnr. Vance, Sanders Exchange Fund, from 1976; hon. dir. Liberty Mut. Ins. Co. Recipient Disting. Service medal Bd. Trustees Mt. Holyoke Coll., 1976. Mem. Phi Beta Kappa, Harvard Club of Boston. Home: Putney Vt. Deceased.

BUMPUS, HERMON CAREY, JR., urologist; b. Dorchester, Mass., Aug. 9, 1888; s. Hermon Carey and Lucy Ella (Nightengale) B.; m. Helen McBurnie, Dec. 29, 1915; children: Nancy Bumpus Urquhart, William, Frank. Student, U. Chgo., 1911, U. Wis., 1911-12; PhB, Brown U., 1912; MD, Harvard U., 1915; MS in Urology, U. Minn., 1920. Mem. staff Mayo Clinic, Rochester, Minn., 1915-33; assoc. prof. urology Mayo Found., U. Minn., 1925-33; prof. urology Coll. Med. Evangelists, 1933-45; pvt. practice Pasadena, Calif., 1934-45; chief urol. service L.A. County Gen. Hosp., 1934-45; chief of staff St. Luke's Hosp., Pasadena, 1939-45. Contbr. articles to profl. jours. Treas., dir. Laird Norton County, Winona, Minn., 1943; pres. Historic Winslow House Assn., Marshfield, 1952-58; trustee Brown U., 1950-56. With U.S. Army, World War I, lt. comdr. M.C. USNR, 1945-46. Fellow ACS; mem. AMA (chmn. urology sect. 1930), ho. dels. 1931-33), Am. Assn. Genito-Urinary Surgeons, L.S. Acad. Medicine, Internat. Urol. Soc., Pan-Am. Med. Soc., L.A. Surg. Soc., Am. Geog. Soc., Minn. Hist. Soc., Duxbury Rural and Hist. Soc., Harvard Travelers Club, Sigma Xi, Delta Phi. Home: Duxbury Mass. †

BUNGER, WILLIAM BOONE, chemistry educator; b. Alta Vista, Kans., Feb. 14, 1917; s. Harry T. and Lila (Beagel) B.; m. Ida Margaret Chitwood, May 29, 1941; 1 dau., Jane Margaret Bunger Winn. BS, Washburn Coll., 1940; MS, Kans. State U., 1941, PhD, 1949. Chemist Hill Packing Co., Topeka, 1939, Hercules Powder Co., Topeka, 1941-45; instr. chemistry Kans. State U., 1947-49; asst. prof. then assoc. prof. Auburn U., 1949-65; prof. chemistry, chmn. dept. Ind. State U., Terre Haute, 1965-82, prof. and chmn. emeritus, 1982-84; vis. prof. Oak Ridge Nat. Lab., 1951, 53, Ala. State Chem. Lab., 1955, Humble Oil and Refining Co., 1957. Author: (with others) Organic Solvents, 3d edit., 1971, (with others) Organic Solvents, 4th edit., 1986 (completed by Dr. Theodore K. Sakano, Rose Hulman Inst. of Tech.). Mem. AAAS, Am. Chem. Soc. (chmn. Auburn sect. 1953-54), Ind. Acad. Sci., Sigma Xi, Phi Lambda Upsilon. Home: Terre Haute Ind. Died Nov. 5, 1984; buried Moss Springs Cemetery, Alta Vista, Kans.

BUNKER, GEORGE M, manufacturing company executive; b. Chgo., 1908; married. BS, MIT, 1937. V.p. mfg. Kroger Co., 1942-49; pres. Trailmobile Inc., 1949-52; chmn. Martin Marietta Corp., 1952-77; chmn. bd. Bunker Ramo Corp., 1975-85. Home: Washington D.C. Died Nov. 5, 1985.

BUONO, VICTOR CHARLES, actor, author; b. San Diego, Feb. 3, 1938; s. Victor Francis and Myrtle Bell (Keller) B. Student, Villanova U., 1956-57. Appeared in 5 seasons of Shakespeare, 5 seasons of contemporary plays, San Diego Jr. Theatre and Old Globe Theatre, Stratford-on-Avon, Eng., 1956-78; numerous stage, motion picture and TV appearances including: movies Whatever Happened to Baby Jane?, 1962, Hush, Hush, Sweet Charlotte, 1965, The Greatest Story Ever Told, The Evil, 1978, The Man with Bogart's Face, 1980; TV Sunset Strip; Author: book It Could Be Verse; performer, author poems, also recs. book; lectr., performer, condr. workshops at colls., univs., 1960-82 (Recipient Atlas award for acting Old Globe Theatre 1956, 57, 60, Los Angeles Critics Circle award 1975, Entertainer of Yr. award San Diego Press Club 1978). Mem. Screen Actors Guild, Actors Equity Assn., AFTRA, Acad. Motion Picture Arts and Scis. Roman Catholic. Home: Apple Valley Calif. Died Jan. 1, 1982.

BURCH, FRANCIS BOUCHER, lawyer; b. Balt., Nov. 26, 1918; s. Louis Claude and Constance (Boucher) B.; m. Mary Patricia Howe, Apr. 12, 1947; children: Francis Boucher, Catherine Howe Jenkins, Richard Claude, Constance B. McGrain, Edwin Howe, Robert Stuart, Mary Patricia Burch Farrell. PhB summa cum laude, Loyola Coll., Balt., 1941; LLB, Yale U., 1943; LLD, U. Balt., 1976. Bar: Md. 1943, U.S. Supreme Ct 1943. Pres. Balt. CSC, 1960-61; mem. Balt. Bd. Estimates, 1961-63, Gov.'s Crime Commn., 1970-78; city solicitor Balt., 1961-63; ins. commr. Md., 1965-66, atty gen., 1966-78; mem. firm Siskind, Burch, Grady & Rosen; instr. bus. law Loyola Coll. Evening Sch., 1945-57; ptnr. Sheraton Fontainebleau Hotel, Ocean City, Md., 1972-85, Family Entertainment Ctrs., Fla., 1981-87, Cove Road Joint Venture, Stuart, Fla. Author: On Calling of a Constitutional Convention, 1950. Chmn. bd. Lauderdale '70, Inc., Ft. Lauderdale, Fla., 1964-68; mem. bd. Balt. Credit Union, 1961-63; mem. Pension Study Com. Balt., 1962; chmn. Mayor Balt. Com. Scholarship Program, 1961, Mayor Balt. Com. Mass. Transit, 1961; mem. Standard Salary Bd. Md., 196O-61, Mayor Balt. Com. Conflict of Interest, 1960; chmn. Md. Cancer Crusade, 1967-68, Constl. Prayer Found., 1963-66; pres. Balt. Safety Council, 1963-65, chmn. exec. com., 1965-67, v.p., 1958-62; lay chmn. Papal Volunteers Com. Latin Am., Archdiocese Balt., 1962-65; vice chmn. Alumni div. Loyola Coll. Devel. Program, 1957, chmn. spl. gifts div., 1971; chmn. Md. Cath. Lawyers Retreat, 1957-59; pres. Reciprocity Club Balt., 1956-57, bd. dirs., 1954-59; bd. dirs. Legal Aid Bur. Balt., 1954, Goodwill Industries Balt., 1959-65; trustee Loyola Coll., Balt., 1974-75, Camp Fire Girls Balt., 1960-65; chmn. maj. gifts div. Loyola and Notre Dame Coll. (Balt.) Library Devel. Dr., 1972; vice chmn. devel. drive Loyola Coll., 1981. Served with USCGR, 1944-45. Recipient Pope John XXIII medal, 1965, Spiritum award Cardinal Gibbons High Sch., Balt., 1966; Man of Year award Hibernian Soc. Md., 1967; Pub. Servant award Md. Cath. War Vets., 1967; Humanitarian award Nu Beta Epsilon, 1967; Nat. Jewish Hosp. award, 1969; Alumnus of Year award Loyola Coll., 1970; Andrew White medal for distinguished citizenship Loyola Coll., 1973. Mem. ABA, Md. Bar Assn., Balt. Bar Assn., Am. Arbitration Assn. (panel 1954-87), Nat. Assn. Attys. Gen. (pres. 1970-71, exec. com. 1969-78, Wyman award 1975), Council State Govts. (exec. com. 1971-78), So. Md. Soc., Hibernian Soc. Md., St. Thomas More Soc. (pres. Md. 1962-63), St. Georges Soc. Md., Friendly Sons of St. Patrick. Clubs: Paint and Powder (bd. govs. 1957-63), Baltimore Country (Balt.); Tri-State

Anglers (Md.-Del.-Va.); Sawgrass, TPC (Ponte Vedro, Fla.). Home: Baltimore Md. Died June 1, 1987.

BURCH, GEORGE E., cardiologist, scientist, clinician, educator, author; b. Edgard, La., 1910; s. George Edward and Lottie Edith (Monroe) B.; m. Vivian Ann Gerard, Sept. 16, 1932; children: Vivian Anna, Janet Vivian, George Edward III, Bryan George. MD, Tulane U., 1933, BS, 1935. Diplomate Am. Bd. Internal Medicine. Intern Charity Hosp., New Orleans, 1933-34; asst. dept. medicine Tulane U., New Orleans, 1934-35, instr., 1935-42, asst. prof., 1942-43, assoc. prof., 1943-47, prof., chmn. dept., 1947-75, prof. emeritus, 1975-86; asst. Rockefeller Inst. Hosp., 1939-41; asst. vis. physician Charity Hosp., 1934-36, vis. physician, 1936-44, sr. vis. physician, 1944-47, cons. in medicine Tulane unit, 1975-86; mem. exptl. adv. com. cardiovascular diseases WHO, 1960-86. Editor Am. Heart Jour., 1959-86. Capt. La. N.G., 1936-40; capt. Med. Res. Corp., U.S. Army, Tulane Unit Base Hosp. No. 23, 1940-42. Commonwealth Fund fellow, 1939-41. Master ACP, Am. Coll. Clin. Pharmacology and Chemotherapy, Am. Coll. Cardiology (pres. 1968); mem. AMA, Assn. U. Cardiologists (founder), Assn. Am. Physicians, Am. Heart Assn., Am. Soc. for Clin. Investigation, AAAS, Harvey Soc., Am. Fedn. Clin. Research, Central, So. Socs. for Clin. Research, N.Y. Acad. Medicine, So. Med. Assn., Soc. for Exptl. Biology and Medicine, Am. Therapeutic Soc., Royal Soc. Medicine. Home: Metairie La. Died Apr. 16, 1986; cremated.

BURCHAM, LESTER ARTHUR, retail merchandising executive; b. Lancaster, Ohio, Apr. 26, 1913; s. Arthur L. and Estella (Grannan) B.; m. Zora M. Gray, Apr. 20, 1935; 1 son, James Edward. Student pub. schs. Dist. mgr. F.W. Woolworth Co., 1931-58, v.p., 1958-62, exec. v.p., 1962-64, pres., 1965-69, chmn. bd., 1970-77, chief exec. officer, 1970-77, former dir.; past dir. Kinney Shoe Corp., F.W. Woolworth Co. Ltd. (Eng.), Woolworth Espanola, S.A. (Spain), Richman Bros. Co., Charter N.Y. Corp., Western Electric Co. Mem. Pres.'s Adv. Council on Minority Bus. Enterprise; mem. nat. corps. com. United Negro Coll. Fund; chmn. retail merchandising industry U.S. Indsl. Payroll Savs. Com., 1973; past dir. Econ. Devel. Council N.Y.C.; bd. dirs. Nat. Multiple Sclerosis Soc., Greater N.Y. Fund. Mem. Nat. Retail Merchants Assn. (past dir.), Newcomen Soc. N.Am., Economic Club, Scarsdale Golf Club, Indian Harbor Yacht Club, Presidents Club. Home: New York N.Y. Died Jan. 24, 1987.

BURCHARD, WALDO WADSWORTH, sociologist, educator; b. Satanta, Kans., Nov. 28, 1916; s. Charles and Jennie Grace (Swink) B.; m. Rachael Caroline Ballenger, May 24, 1945; children: Gina Michel, Petrea Celeste, Stuart Gregory, Margot Theresa. AB, U. Calif., Berkeley, 1949, MA, 1951, PhD, 1953. Instr. sociology U. Denver, 1952-53, U. Kans., 1953-55; asst. prof. sociology Hollins Coll., 1955-58; assoc. prof. No. Ill. U., 1958-61, prof., from 1961, head dept. social scis., 1959-61, head dept. sociology and anthropology, 1961-68. Contbr. articles to profl. jours. With USMC, 1942-46. Mem. Am. Sociol. Assn., Midwest Sociol. Soc. (chmn. publs. com., exofficio dir.), So. Sociol. Soc., North Cen. Sociol. Soc. (exec. com.), Soc. Sci. Study Religion, Ill. Sociol. Assn. (hon. pres.), Religious Rsch. Assn., Assn. Sociology Religion. Home: DeKalb Ill. Died Dec. 3, 1985; buried Afton Cemetery, De Kalb, Ill.

BURD, HENRY ALFRED, business consultant; b. Armstrong, Ill., July 12, 1889; s. William Frazee and Mary Elizabeth (Bass.) B.; m. Jennie E. Heckerson, Dec. 25, 1912; children: Jacqueline Burd Reid, Miriam Burd Donaldson, Sherman Kay. BS, Ill. Weslyan U., 1910, LLD (hon.), 1957; MA, U. Ill., 1911, PhD, 1915. Instr. English U. Wis., 1915-17; exec. sec. Wis. State Council Def., 1917-19; sec.-treas. Ellwood Tractor Co., 1919-23, Rosen Heating Co., 1923-24; assoc. prof. bus. adminstrn. U. Wash, Seattle, 1924-27, prof. mktg., head dept mktg., transp. and fgn. trade, 1927-54, emeritus prof., from 1954, acting dean grad. sch., 1955-59, dir. summer quarter, 1927-45, acting dean coll. bus. adminstrn., 1948-49; faculty Banff Sch. Advanced Mgmt., from 1954; mem. staff Wash. State Internat. Mktg. Conf., 1954-56. Author: Joseph Ritson, 1961, (with R.S. Butler) Commercial Correspondence, 1920, (with C. J. Miller) Business Letters, 1930; contbr. to Marketing in the West, 1946; author articles and revs. Bd. dirs. Wesley Found., 1927-31; edn. dir. Seattle Stock Exchange Inst., 1929-30; bd. dirs. Inst. Retailing, 1929-31, Inst. Distbn., 1940, Seattle Traffic and Safety Coun., 1936-43; regional cons. Office Civilian Requirements, War Prodn. Bd., 1942-45; trustee U. Wash. YMCA, 1931-39, chmn. bd., 1936-39; trustee, chmn. bd. U. Wash. Bookstore, 1940-54. Mem. Am. Mktg. Assn., AAUP, Am. Arbitration Assn., N.W. Univ. Bus. Schs. Assn. (bd. dirs., pres. 1949-50), Seattle Advt. and Sales Club, Univ. Comml. Club (Seattle), Lions, Masons, Phi Beta Kappa, Phi Kappa Phi, Phi Eta, Phi Kappa Delta, Alpha Delta Sigma, Beta Gamma Sigma, Tau Kappa Epsilon. Home: Edmonds Wash. †

BURGER, OTHMAR JOSEPH, university dean; b. Jasper, Ind., May 23, 1921; s. August and Katherine (Lechner) B.; m. Elizabeth Ann Evans, Aug. 21, 1943; children: Thomas Glen, Robert Howard, David William. B.S., Purdue U., 1943, M.S., 1947, Ph.D., 1950. Prof. agronomy W.Va. U., 1950-57, asst. dean agr., 1959-68, asst. to provost for instrn., 1968-69; prof. agronomy Iowa State U., 1957-59; dean Sch. Agr. and Home Econs., Calif. State U., Fresno, 1969-88; prof. agronomy. Sch. Agr. and Home Econs., Calif. State U. Cubmaster local council Boy Scouts Am., 1956-58; Bd. dirs. United Fund, Morgantown, W.Va., 1953-55. Served with USMCR, World War II, PTO. Decorated Bronze Star, Purple Heart. Fellow Am. Soc. Agronomy, Crop Sci. Soc. Am.; mem. Nat. Assn. Colls. and Tchrs. of Agr. (pres. 1978-79, Disting. Educator award 1982), Gamma Sigma Delta, Phi Lambda Upsilon, Alpha Zeta. Lodge: Kiwanis. Home: Fresno Calif. Died Mar. 18, 1988.

BURGOON, NORMAN AARON, JR., surety bond and insurance company executive; b. Balt., Oct. 27, 1916; s. Norman Aaron and Nellie (Ricker) B.; m. Doris Hunter, June 30, 1939; children: Norman Richard, Harvey Ronald, Alan Charles, Michele Doris. Student, Balt. City Coll., 1931-34; JD, U. Balt., 1939. Bar: Md. 1940. With Fidelity & Deposit Co., Balt., 1935-79, exec. v.p., 1966-79, also bd. dirs., mem. exec. com.; atty., gen. counsel Nat. Assn. Surety Bond Producers, 1979-84; past v.p., bd. dirs. Bur. Contract Info. Inc.; mem. exec. com., bd. dirs., past pres. Commerce and Industry Combined Health Appeal, Balt., 1967-80; mem. fin. com. Presbyn. Hosp., Balt., 1955-84. Bd. dirs. Greater Balt. Med. Ctr., 1966-84, United Fund, 1974-80; trustee U. Balt., 1971-74. Served with AUS, World War II. Mem. Am. Ins. Assn., Am. Mgmt. Assn., Surety Assn. Am. (chmn. exec. com.), Md. Hist. Soc. Presbyn. (ruling elder). Club: Md. (Balt.). Home: Baltimore Md. Died Dec. 17, 1984.

BURK, DEAN, biochemist; b. Oakland, Calif., Mar. 21, 1904; s. Frederic and Caroline (Frear) B.; m. Mildred Chaundy; children: Diana Burk Barker, Wendy Burk Maiorana, Frederic Chaundy. BS, U. Calif., 1923, PhD, 1927. Fellow NRC and Internat. Edn. Bd. U. London (Univ. Coll.), 1927-29, Kaiser Wilhelm Inst. for Biology, 1927-29, NRC and Internat. Edn. Bd., Harvard U., 1927-29; assoc. phys. chemist Fixed Nitrogen Rsch. Lab. Dept. Agr., Washington, 1929, chemist, 1937-39; sr. chemist Nat. Cancer Inst., NIH, Bethesda, Md., 1939-48, prin. chemist, 1948-51, head chemist, 1951-58, chief chemist, 1958-74; assoc. prof. biochemistry Cornell U. Med. Coll., 1939-41; rsch. master grad. faculty George Washington U., 1947-88; guest rsch. worker USSR Acad. Scis. (Biochem. Inst.), Moscow, 1935. Author, editor: Cancer, 1945, Approaches to Tumor Chemotherapy, 1947, Cell Chemistry, 1953; assoc. editor: Record Chem. Progress, 1943-88, Proc. Soc. Exptl. Biology and Medicine, 1948-53, Enzymologia, 1937-88; contbr. to sci. jours. Pres. Dean Burk Found. Inc. Recipient Domagk prize for cancer rsch., 1965, Nat. Health Fedn. Humanitarian award, 1971, Wisdom award Honor, 1973, Humanitarian award Cancer Control Soc., 1973; decorated knight comdr. Med. Order Bethlemen; knight Mark Twain. Fellow AAAS (organizer, chmn. rsch. confs. on cancer 1942-45); mem. Am. Chem. Soc. (Hillebrand award 1952), Am. Soc. Biol. Chemists, Am. Assn. Cancer Rsch., Am. Soc. Plant Physiologist, Soc. Exptl. Biology and Medicine (chmn. 1949-50, sec.-treas. 1948-49), N.Y., Washington acads. sci., Soc. Gen. Physiology, L.I. Biol. Assn., Harvey Soc., Chem. Soc. Washington, Max Planck Assn. Munich, Inst. for Cell Physiology Berlin, Royal Soc. Medicine London, Nat. Trust Gt. Britain, Dolmetsch Found. Haslemere (fgn.), Max Planck Inst. Biochemistry Munich, Soc. Calif. Pioneers, Cosmos Club (Washington), commonwealth Club (Calif.), Sigma Xi, Gamma Alpha. Died Oct. 6, 1988.

BURKARD, RALPH FREDERICK, chain store executive; b. Boston, Dec. 5, 1892; s. Anthony John and Mary Ann (Frehauf) B.; m. Etta O. Houg, Nov. 24, 1920; children: Ursula Burkard Keleher, Elise Burkard O'Brien. Student, Pub. Schs. Boston. Chief acct. F.L. Ames Estate, Boston, 1918; treas., dir. John T. Connor Co., Boston, 1918-25; asst. treas., dir. 1st Nat. Stores Ind., Boston, 1925-35, mem. exec. com., 1935-43, dir., mem. exec. com., from 1943; dir., mem. exec. com. State St. Trust Co.; dir. Power Condenser and Electronics Corp., Boston Garden Corp., Boston Profl. Hockey Assn.; trustee Charleston Savs. Bank, Corporator Symmes Hosp., Arlington, Mass. Mem. Nat. Assn. Food Chains (dir., treas., mem. exec. com.), Algonquin Club (Boston); Easten Yacht Club (Marblehead, Mass.); Winchester Country Club (Mass.). Home: Arlington Mass. †

BURKE, LLOYD HUDSON, judge; b. Oakland, Calif., Apr. 1, 1916; s. James H. and Edna L. (Taylor) B.; m. Virginia Joan Kerchum, Apr. 27, 1941; children—Brian Hudson, Bruce Thomas. A.B., St. Mary's Coll. of Calif., 1937, LL.D. (hon.); LL.B., U. Calif., 1940, J.D. (hon.), 1972. Dep. dist. atty. Alameda County, Calif., 1940-53; sr. criminal trial dep. 1950-53, U.S. atty. for No. Calif., 1953-58; U.S. dist. judge No. Dist. Calif., 1958-88. Served with U.S. Army, 1942-46; capt. Res., to 1951. Mem. Phi Delta Phi. Home: Piedmont Calif. Died Mar. 15, 1988.

BURNET, FRANK MACFARLANE, immunologist; b. Traralgon, Australia, Sept. 3, 1899; s. Frank and Hadassah (Mackay) B.; ed. Geelong Coll.; MD, Melbourne U., 1922; PhD, London U., 1928; m. Edith Linda Marston Druce, July 10, 1928 (dec. 1973); children: Elizabeth Burnet Dexter, Ian, Deborah Burnet Giddy. m. 2d, Hazel Foletta Jenkin, 1976. Beit Meml. fellow Lister Inst., London, 1926-27; asst. dir. Walter and Eliza Hall Inst. Med. Research, 1928-31, 34-44, dir., also prof. exptl. medicine U. Melbourne, 1944-65, prof. emeritus 1966-85, Rowden White research fellow Sch. Microbiology, 1966-67. Chmn. Med. Research Adv. Com., Papua, New Guinea, 1962-69. Recipient Lasker Found. award, 1952; Von Behring prize Marburg U. 1952; Nobel prize in physiology and medicine (with P. Medawar), 1960; knighted, 1951; decorated Order of Merit (U.K.). Fellow Royal Soc., mem. Australian Acad. Sci. (pres. 1965-69), Australian Med. Assn., Pathol. Soc. U.K. Author: Virus as Organism, 1945; (with F.J. Fenner) The Production of Antibodies, 1949; Viruses and Man, 1955; The Clonal Selection Theory of Acquired Immunity, 1959; Principles of Animal Virology, 1960; (with D. O. White) Natural History of Infectious Diseases, 4th edit., 1972; Integrity of the Body, 1962; (with I.R. Mackay) Autoimmune Diseases, 1963; (autobiography) Changing Patterns, 1968; Cellular Immunology, 1969; Immunological Surveillance, 1970; Dominant Mammal, 1971; Auto-immunity, 1972; Intrinsic Mutagenesis, 1974; Immunology, 1976; Immunity, Aging & Cancer, 1976; Endurance of Life, 1978. Research, publs. on cultivation of viruses in chick embryo; genetics of influenza virus; clin. studies on autoimmune diseases. Home: Melbourne, Australia. Died Aug. 31, 1985.

BURNHAM, JAMES, author, philosopher, educator; b. Chgo., Nov. 22, 1905; s. Claude George and Mary May (Gillis) B.; m. Marcia Lightner, Mar. 31, 1934; children: Marcia, James Bernard, John Lightner. BA, Princeton U., 1927, Oxford U., Eng., 1929; MA, Oxford U., Eng., 1932. Prof. philosophy Washington Sq. Coll., NYU, N.Y.C., 1929-53. Author: (with Philip E. Wainwright) Introduction to Philosophical Analysis, 1931, The Managerial Revolution, 1941, The Machiavellians, 1943, The Struggle for the World, 1947, (with Andre Malraux) The Case for De Gaulle, 1948, The Coming Defeat of Communism, 1950, Containment or Liberation?, 1953, The Web of Subversion, 1954, Congress and the American Tradition, 1959, Suicide of the West, 1964, The War We Are In, 1967; editor: (with Philip Wainwright) The Symposium, 1930-33, What Europe Thinks of America, 1953; mem. editorial bd. Nat. Rev., 1955-87. Home: Kent Conn. Died July 28, 1987.

BURNS, ARTHUR EDWARD, economist; b. Oakland, Calif., Sept. 3, 1908; s. William Thomas and Anne (Bruns) B.; m. Marcella Eugenie Wyss, Oct. 30, 1933; 1 son, Robert Lee. A.B., U. Calif., 1931, M.A., 1934; Ph.D., George Washington U., 1935. Instr. George Washington U., 1934-35, asst. prof., 1935-37, assoc. prof., 1937-40, adj. prof., 1940-45, prof. econs., 1945-74, prof. emeritus, 1974-86; acting dean Sch. Govt., 1946-49, dean, 1949-57, dean, chmn. grad. council, 1957-67; dean Grad. Sch. Arts and Scis., 1967-74; dir. acad. planning Consortium of Univs., Washington, 1974-75; econ. cons. on profit renegotiation 1972-86; Vis. prof. econs. U. Calif., summer 1949, Getulio Vargus Found.; nat. faculty econ. scis. U. Brazil, Rio de Janeiro, 1952; Economist Fed. Emergency Relief Adminstrn., 1934-35; economist, asst. dir. research WPA, 1935-40, adviser, 1941-42; spl. cons. OPA, 1942-43; dep. dir. Office of Materials and Facilities, War Food Adminstrn., 1943-45; cons. White House Office, 1957-60, Renegotiation Bd., 1961-72, U.S.-P.R. Status Commn., 1965-66; vis. lectr. Indsl. Coll. Armed Forces, 1950-86; pub. mem. Fgn. Service Selection Bd., Dept. State, 1951; cons. Fgn. Operations Adminstrn., ICA, 1953-57, Operations Research Office, 1951-60, Italian Govt., Rome, 1955. Author: (with Neal and Watson) Modern Economics, 1948, rev. edit. 1953, Arabic edit., 1960, (with D.S. Watson) Government Spending and Economic Expansion, 1940, (with E.A. Williams) Federal Work, Security, and Relief Programs, 1941; Contbr. articles and revs. to profl. jours., govt. publs. Mem. Am. Econ. Assn., Artus, Delta Phi Epsilon (nat. pres. 1948-50). Club: Cosmos. Home: Washington D.C. Died Dec. 15, 1986; interred Mt. View Mausoleum, Oakland, Calif.

BURNS, ARTHUR F., ambassador, economist; b. Stanislau, Austria, Apr. 27, 1904; m. Helen Bernstein, Jan. 25, 1930; children: David S., Joseph M. A.B., Columbia U., 1925, A.M., 1925, Ph.D., 1934; LL.D., Lehigh U., 1952; L.H.D., Rutgers U., 1955; LL.D., Brown U., 1956, Dartmouth Coll., 1956, Oberlin Coll., 1956, Wesleyan U., 1958, Swarthmore Coll., 1958, L.I.U., 1960, U. Chgo., 1960, Rikkyo U., Tokyo, 1965, Fordham U., 1969, Columbia U., 1970, NYU, 1970, U. Calif., 1970, The Cath. U., 1973, George Washington U., 1973, Ill. Coll., 1974, Yeshiva U., 1974, U. Akron, 1975, Washington U., 1976, S.C. U., 1977, Carnegie Mellon U., 1977, Notre Dame U., 1977, Gonzaga U., 1977, Ripon Coll., 1978, U. Vt., 1979, Chapman Coll., 1979, Fairleigh Dickinson U., 1979, U. So. Calif., 1979, Hofstra U., 1980, Allegheny Coll., 1980, Xavier U., 1981; Sc.D., U. Pa., 1958, U. Rochester, 1963, Fla. Inst. Tech., 1976, Lake Forest Coll., 1978; other hon. degrees. Asst. stats. Columbia U., 1926, Gilder fellow, 1926-27; instr. econs. Rutgers U., 1927-30, asst. prof., 1930-33, assoc. prof., 1933-43, prof., 1943-44; research assoc. Nat. Bur. Econ. Research, 1930-31, mem. research staff, 1933-69, dir. research staff, 1945-53, chmn., 1967-68; chief statistician Ry. Emergency Bd., 1941; chief statistician Columbia U., 1941-42, vis. prof. econs., 1942-44, prof., 1944-58; chmn. Pres. Adv. Bd. on Econ. Growth and Stability, 1953-56, Pres. Council Econ. Advisers, 1953-56, Cabinet Com. Small Bus., 1956; mem.. Adv. Council on Social Security Financing, 1957-58; John Bates Clark prof. econs. Columbia U., 1959-69, prof. emeritus, 1969-87; mem. Temporary State Commn. on Econ. Expansion, N.Y., 1959-60, Pres. Adv. Com. on Labor-Mgmt. Policy, 1961-66; chmn. Nat. Bur. Econ. Research, 1967-68; mem. Gov.'s Com. on Minimum Wage, N.Y., 1964; vis. prof. econs. Stanford U., 1968; counsellor to Pres. U.S. 1969-70; chmn. bd. govs. Fed. Res. System, 1970-78; alt. gov. IMF, 1973-78; disting. scholar in residence Am. Enterprise Inst., 1978-81, 85-87; disting. professorial lectr. Georgetown U., Washington, 1978-81; ambassador to Fed. Republic of Germany 1981-85; bd. dirs. Nat. Bur. Econ. Research, 1945-87, hon. chmn., 1969-87; Anheuser-Busch disting. guest lectr. St. Louis U., 1980; Kathleen Price Bryan lectr. U. N.C., 1981; Founders' Day lectr. Xavier U., Cin., 1981. Recipient Jefferson award Am. Inst. Pub. Service, 1976; recipient Alexander Hamilton award U.S. Treasury Dept., 1976, Am. Democratic Legacy award Anti-Defamation League, B'nai B'rith, 1978, award Fed. City Club, Washington, 1978, award Econ. Club, N.Y.C., 1978, Grand Cross of Order of Merit W.Ger., 1978, Am. Eagle award Invest-in-Am. Nat. Council, 1978, McMahon Meml. award Fordham U. Club Washington, 1978, award Citizens Budget Commn., N.Y.C., 1978, Frank E. Seidman Disting. award, 1978, George Washington award Am. Hungarian Found., 1978, Gold Medal award Inst. Social Scis., 1978, Francis Boyer award Am. Enterprise Inst. Pub. Policy Research, 1978, medal for disting. achievement Am. Soc. French Legion of Honor, 1978; Per Jacobsson Lectr. Belgrade, Yugoslavia, 1979. Fellow Am. Econ. Assn. (pres. 1959), Am. Statis. Assn., Econometric Soc., Am. Acad. Arts and Scis., Acad. Polit. Sci. (pres. 1962-68); mem. (bd. dirs. 1957-87), Am. Philos. Soc., Council Fgn. Relations, Pilgrims Soc., Institut de Sci. Economique Appliquee (corr.), Phi Beta Kappa. Clubs: Cosmos, City Tavern (Washington); Century Assn. (N.Y.C.). Home: New York N.Y. Died June 26, 1987.

BURNS, EVELINE M(ABEL), economist; b. London, Mar. 16, 1900; came to U.S., 1926; d. Frederick Haig and Eveline Maud (Falkner) Richardson; m. Arthur Robert Burns, Apr. 8, 1922. BS in Econs., U. London, 1920, PhD, 1926; DHL (hon.), Western Coll., 1962; LLD (hon.), Western Reserve U., 1963; LHD (hon.), Adelphi U., 1968, Columbia U., 1969; postgrad., N.Y. Sch. Social Work, Columbia U., 1946-67. Adminstrv. asst. Ministry Labour, London, 1917-21; asst. lectr. London Sch. Econs., 1921-26; asst. editor Economica, London, 1923-26; Laura Spelman Rockefeller fellow traveling in the U.S. 1926-28; lectr. grad. dept. econs. Columbia U., N.Y.C., 1928-42; sr. staff mem. com. on social security Social Sci. Research Council, 1937-39; chief econ. security and health section Nat. Resources Planning Bd., 1939-43; cons. on social security Nat. Planning Assn., 1943-45; prof. social work emeritus 1967-85; prof. social work Grad. Sch. Social Work NYU, N.Y.C., from 1968; cons. N.Y. State Dept. Labor, U.S. Treasury Dept., Com. on Econ. Security, Fed. Reserve Bd., Social Security Bd. Author: Wages and the State, 1926, (with Arthur Robert Burns) The Economic World, 1927, Toward Social Security, 1936, British Unemployment Programs 1920-38, 1941, The American Social Security System, 1949, Social Security and Public Policy, 1956; contbr. to encys. U.S. Ambassador to Jordon, from 1966. Recipient Adam Smith medal for outstanding econ. research, 1926, Florina Lasker award, 1960, Blanche Ittelson award, 1968; Guggenheim fellow, 1954-55, hon. fellow London Sch. Econs., 1964-85. Episcopalian. Home: New York N.Y. Died Sept. 2, 1985.

BURNS, LAWRENCE, lawyer; b. Corning, Ohio, May 3, 1910; s. Lawrence and Anna (Amberge) B.; m. Elinor Bresnahan, Oct. 8, 1935; children: Lawrence (dec.), David William. Student, Aquinas Coll., Columbus, Ohio, 1928; J.D., Ohio State U., 1933. Bar: Ohio 1933. Practice of law Coshocton, from 1933; atty. Bank-One, Coshocton, Ohio, Conrail, Ohio Power Co.; dir. Bank-One of Dover, Ohio, Novelty Advt. Co., Buckeye Fabric Finishing Co., Auto Supply Co., Muskingum Valley Lumber Co., Coshocton. City solicitor, Coshocton, 1942-44; chmn. Republican County Exec. Com., 1943-62. Trustee Coshocton Found., Ohio Legal Center, Columbus. Served to lt. (s.g.) USNR, 1942-46. Mem. ABA, Ohio Bar Assn. (pres.), Coshocton County Bar Assn., Am. Judicature Soc., Ohio State U. Alumni Assn., C. of C., Internat. Assn. Ins. Counsels, Am. Coll. Probate Counsel. Rotarian. Home: Coshocton Ohio Deceased.

BURNS, VINCENT LEO, church rector; b. Catasauqua, Pa., May 11, 1891; s. William John and Hannah Cecelia (McGee) B. AB, St. Charles Sem., Phila., 1917; J.C.B., Cath. U., Washington, 1927, AM, 1928; DSc, La Salle Coll., Phila., 1935; PhD, U. Pa., 1936. Ordained priest Roman Cath. Ch., 1917. Lic. radio sta. operator. Curate Holy Cross Ch., Phila., 1917-20; dean St. Charles Sem., Phila., 1920-26, Mission House Cath. U., Phila., 1926-28, grad. dept. St. Charles Sem., Phila., 1928-31; rector Our Lady of Mercy Ch., Phila., 1931-32; prof. biology and moral theology St. Charles Sem., Phila., 1932-35; pres. Immaculata (Pa.) Coll., 1935-36, St. Charles Sem., Overbrook, Phila., 1935-46, Immaculata (Pa.) Coll., 1946-55; rector St. Joan of Arc Ch., Phila., from 1955. Apptd. Domestic Prelate by Pope Pius XI, June 22, 1936. Home: Philadelphia Pa. †

BURNS, W(ILLIAM) HAYDON, public official, businessman; b. Chgo., Mar. 17, 1912; s. Harry Haydon and Ethel Emma (Burnett) B.; m. Mildred Carlyon, 1934; children: Eleanor Burns Watkins, William Haydon Burns Jr. Student, Babson Coll. Mayor City of Jacksonville, Fla., 1949-65; gov. State of Fla., 1965-67; pres. Haydon Burns & Assocs., Jacksonville, 1967-79; pres. U.S. Conf. Mayors, 1959. Lt. (j.g.) USN, 1941-46. Mem. Masons, Shriners, Royal Order of Jesters. Democrat. Methodist. Home: Jacksonville Fla. Died Nov. 22, 1987; buried Oaklawn Cemetery, Jacksonville.

BURR, DAVID ANTHONY, university official; b. Columbus, Kans., Apr. 19, 1925; s. Hugh Henry and Grace Elizabeth (Mitchell) B.; m. Carol Jean Robinson, Nov. 18, 1962; children: Michael James, Kathleen Elizabeth, Thaddeus Mitchell. A.A., Northeastern Agrl. and Mech. Coll., 1948; B.A., U. Okla., 1952; LL.D. (hon.), Pepperdine U., 1981. Editor Sooner Mag. U. Okla., Norman, 1950-57, asst. to pres., 1957-59, asst. to pres., dir. univ. relations and devel., 1959-68, v.p., dir. univ. community, 1968-71, v.p. devel., 1971-77, v.p. univ. relations and devel., 1977-79, v.p. univ. affairs, 1979-87; coordinator, dir. U. Okla. leadership program, 1961; dir. Editorial Projects Edn., Inc. Dir. Okla. Gov.'s Opportunity Program, 1964; mem. Civic Improvement Council, Norman, 1965; deacon 1st Presbyn. Ch., Norman, 1968-69, elder. Served to lt. U.S. Army, 1944-46. Recipient Sibley award, 1956; named Outstanding Alumnus Northeastern A&M U., 1971, Disting. Service citation U. Okla., 1983. Mem. Council Advancement and Support of Edn., Okla. Higher Edn. Alumni Council, U. Okla. Assn., Norman C. of C. (dir. 1968-70, 81-84), Lambda Chi Alpha. Democrat. Home: Norman Okla. Died Aug. 6, 1987.

BURR, SAMUEL ENGLE, JR., retired educator; b. Bordentown, N.J., Dec. 6, 1897; s. Samuel Engle and Elizabeth (Thompson) B.; m. Ella Mount, Oct. 11, 1980; children: Evelyn Anne, Samuel Engle. LittB, Rutgers U., 1919; MA, U. Wis.-Madison, 1928; MA, Columbia U., 1932; EdD, U. Cin., 1936. Supt. schs. Glendale Pub. Schs., Ohio, 1930-35, New Castle Pub. Schs., Del., 1935-40, Rye Neck Pub. Schs., Mamaroneck, N.Y., 1940-42; prof. edn. Am. U., Washington, 1947-69; vis. prof. history Weatherford Coll., Tex., 1969-72. Author: China: A.P.O., 1982, The Aaron Burr Lectures, 1983; 37 Years of ABA, Vol. I, 1983, Vol. II, 1983. Bd. dirs. Inst. World Affairs, Washington, 1948-69, Inst. Problems in Edn., 1955-60. Served to lt. col. U.S. Army, 1942-47. Decorated Bronze Star, Purple Heart, Medale de la France Libre. Mem. Aaron Burr Assn. (founder), Mil. Order of Purple Heart, Order St. John Jerusalem, Phi Kappa Phi. Club: Country of Fairfield. Lodges: Rotary, K.P. Avocations: horseback riding, canoeing. Home: Hightstown, N.J. Died Nov. 16, 1987.

BURROWS, CHARLES ROBERT, former U.S. ambassador; b. Detroit, Feb. 25, 1910; s. John Robert and Martha (Schultz) B.; m. Lucy Mullin, June 12, 1940; children: James Christian, Joan Davidson. AB, Otterbein Coll., 1931; MS, NYU, 1932; postgrad. law sch., George Washington U., 1934-35; postgrad., Nat. War Coll., 1952-53; PhD, Otterbein Coll., 1964. Adminstrv. asst. U.S. Dept. Agr., Washington, 1936-39; appointed fgn. service officer U.S. State Dept., Washington, 1939; vice counsul Havana 1939, 3d sec., vice counsul La Paz, 1940-43, 2d sec. Buenos Aires, 1943-47, 1st sec., counsul, charge d'affaires Cuidad Trujillo, 1947-49, 1st sec., polit. counselor Mexico City, 1949-51; dir. Middle Am. affairs U.S. State Dept., 1953-54; counselor, dep. chief mission Am. Embassy, Manila, 1954, minister-counselor, 1955; minister-counselor Am. Embassy, Caracas, Venezuela, 1956-60; ambassador to Honduras 1960-65; dir. Cen. Am. affairs U.S. State Dept., 1965-69; pvt. cons. Latin Am. relations Standard Fruit & S.S. Co.; Washington rep. Castle & Cooke. Bd. dirs. Found. Coop. Housing, Washington, Washington Inst. Fgn. Affairs. Clubs: Internat. Washington, Cosmos, DACOR. Home: Washington D.C. Died Sept. 6, 1986; buried Rock Creek Cemetery, Washington.

BURT, ARTHUR HARTWELL, paint manufacturing executive; b. Cleve., Aug. 6, 1892; s. Arthur Edwin and Sarah (Jones) B.; m. Gladys Hopkins Tilden, June 22, 1918 (dec. Mar. 1940); children: Mary B. Coppedge, Sarah B. Moore, Nancy Louise; m. 2d, Dorothy Whitelaw, June 14, 1941. Student, Pub. Schs., Cleve. With advt. dept. The Sherwin-Williams Co., Cleve., 1912-14, salesman, 1915-16, archtl. rep., 1916, mgr. archtl. sales, 1918-24, Cleve. div. sales mgr., 1924-30, nat. dealers sales mgr., 1930-42, gen. mgr. trade sales, 1942-46, regional dir. North Central, 1946-52, gen. sales mgr., 1952-53, v.p. mktg. and dir., from 1953; bd. dirs. Ozark Mining & Smelting Co., The Lowe Bros. Co., John Lucas & Co., Martin-Senour Co. Capt. U.S. Army, 1917-18. Mem. Cleve. Sr. Coun. Citizen's League, Am. Soc. Sales Execs., Nat. Paint, Varnish and Lacquer Assn., Cleve. Advt. Club, Pilgrims of U.S., Pepper Pike Club, Canterbury Golf Club, Midday Club, Rotary (Cleve.). Home: Shaker Heights Ohio. †

BURTON, JOSEPH ASHBY, chemist; b. Onley, Va., Aug. 22, 1914; s. Vernon Swanger and Loleta (Boggs) B.; m. Denison Laws, Aug. 29, 1936; children: Delano (Mrs. Leroy M. May), W. Butler, John D. BS, Washington and Lee U., 1934; PhD in Chemistry, Johns Hopkins U., 1938. Mem. tech. staff Bell Telephone Labs., Murray Hill, N.J., 1938-76, head semicondr. physics research dept., 1954-58, dir. chem. physics research, 1958-71, dir. phys. research, 1971-76. Mem. Am. Phys. Soc. (treas., exec. com. 1969-86). Home: Chatham N.J. Died Aug. 31, 1986; buried St. George's Cemetery, Pungoteague, Va.

BURTON, MALCOLM KING, clergyman, author; b. Mpls., Mar. 28, 1905; s. Charles Emerson and Cora (King) B.; m. Carol Berkemeier, Feb. 24, 1930. BA, Carleton Coll., 1927; postgrad., Chgo. Theol. Sem., 1927-29. Ordained to ministry Congl. Ch., 1928. Pastor Massena, N.Y., 1929-33, Pelham, N.Y., 1933-38, New London, Conn., 1938-52, Pontiac, Mich., 1952-71; assoc. pastor Springfield, Mass., from 1973; exec. vice chmn., dir. com. on continuation Congl. Christian Chs. in U.S., from 1954; chaplin Police Protective Assn., Massena, 1930-33; moderator Nat. Assn. Congl. Chs., 1968-69, historian, 1973-77. Author: Destiny for Congregationalism, 1953, Constitution for Congregationalism?, 1954, How Church Union Came, 1966, Sermons on Special Days of the Church Year-Vol. I, 1977, Vol. II, 1980, (with A.H. Abbott) Early Merger Pamphlets, 1978, Disorders in the Kingdom, 1978, 2d edit., 1981, Sermons on the Mysteries of Life and Death, 1980, Sermons on Controversial Subjects, 1981, Bible Sermons on God, 1981, Bible Sermons with Unique Insights, 1981; also numerous pamphlets and articles. Served as chaplin AUS, 1945. Mem. Delta Sigma Rho. Club: Conn. Valley Congl. (pres. 1977-79). Home: Agawam Mass. Deceased.

BURTT, EDWIN ARTHUR, author, university professor; b. Groton, Mass., Oct. 11, 1892; s. Edwin Palmer and Harriet Louis (Jerome) B.; m. Mildred Caroline Camp, Sept. 25, 1916 (div.); children: Edith Jerome, Dorothy Newell, Harriet Virginia, Winifred Jane Burtt Brinster.; m. 2d. Marjorie Frances Murray, June 16, 1951. AB, Yale U., 1915; BD, Union Theol. Sem., N.Y.C., 1920; S.T.M., Union Theol. Sem., 1922; PhD, Columbia U., 1925; LHD (hon.), U. Chgo., 1951. Instr. philosophy Columbia U., N.Y.C., 1921-23; instr. philosophy U. Chgo., 1923-24, asst. prof., 1924-27, prof., 1928-31; prof. philosophy Cornell U., 1932-41, Susan Linn Sage prof. of philosophy, from 1941; vis. lectr. in philosophy, Harvard U., 1927-28, Stanford U., 1931-32. Author: Metaphysial Foundations of Modern Physical Science, 1925, Types of Religious Philosophy, 1939, Man Seeks the Divine, 1957, others; co-author: Essays in Honor of John Dewey, 1929, others; editor: The English Philosophers from Bacon to Mill, 1939. Recipient Nicholas Murray Butler medal in silver Columbia U., 1958. Mem. Am. Philos. Assn., Am. Theol. Assn., Phi Beta Kappa, Delta Sigma Rho, Beta Theta Pi. Home: Ithaca N.Y. †

BURYAN, EDMUND FREDERICK, manufacturing company executive; b. N.Y.C., Aug. 24, 1913; s. William and Mary (Berndt) B.; m. Elizabeth Taylor, Aug. 23, 1941 (dec. 1975); children: Elizabeth, Richard T.; m. Naomi Kissling; children: Richard B. Esser, Carolyn Wilson. BA, Columbia U., 1936, postgrad. Grad. Sch. Bus., 1937. Gen. mgr. Revlon Internat. Corp., N.Y.C., 1949-56; mktg. cons. Booz, Allen & Hamilton, N.Y.C., 1956-57; v.p. mktg. W. A. Sheaffer Pen Co., Ft. Madison, Iowa, 1957-60; pres., chief exec. officer, bd. dirs. Mpls.-Moline Co. and Motec Industries Inc., 1960-62; spl. cons. to adminstrn. NASA, Washington, from 1962, mem. inventions and contbns. bd., from 1963. Mem. Am. Ordnance Assn., Def. Orientation Conf. Assn. Presbyn. Clubs: Am. (London), Univ., Columbia Varsity (N.Y.C.), Union League (Chgo.), Mpls. Lodges: Masons, Shriners. Home: Scarsdale N.Y. Died May 12, 1986.

BUSA, PETER, artist; b. Pitts., June 23, 1914; s. Salvatore and Ernestine (Chrispo) B.; m. Jeanne Juhl, June 26, 1943; children: Christopher, Stephen, Paul, Marianne, Nicholas. Student, Carnegie Inst. Tech., 1929-30, Art Students League, N.Y.C., 1934-37; studied with Raymond Simboli, Sam Rosenberg, Harry Sternberg, Thomas Benton, Hans Hofmann. With WPA Art Project, N.Y.C., 1935-40; mem. faculty dept. art U. Minn., Mpls., 1961-63, prof., 1963-81, prof. emeritus, 1981; tchr. Cooper Union, 1945-53, La. State U., 1958-59, SUNY, Buffalo, 1954-57; vis. artist U. Mich., 1960, Kans. State U., 1972. One-man exhbns. include Bertha Schaefer Gallery, Parrish Mus., 1972, Walker Art Ctr., 1962-67, U. Minn. Gallery, 1966, Tweed Gallery; represented in permanent collections: Peggy Guggenheim, Walker Art Ctr., Whitney Mus. Am. Art, Met. Mus., Smithsonian Instn., others. Recipient Ford Found. Purchase award, 1962, Disting. Tchr. award Coll. Liberal Art U. Minn., 1975, Guggenheim award, 1976-77. Mem. Coll. Art Assn., Artist Equity Assn. (past pres.), Art Students League N.Y. (life). Home: Easthampton N.Y. Died 1981.

BUSCH, NOEL, author, editor; b. N.Y.C., Dec. 27, 1906; s. Briton Niven and Christine (Fairchild) B.; m. Mary Smart, June 5, 1950 (dec. 1981); children: Mary Fairchild, Beatrix Akiko. Student, Princeton U., 1925-

27. Assoc. editor Time mag., 1927-38; sportswriter N.Y. Daily News, 1928-31; sr. editor Life mag., 1938-42, war corr., 1942-45, sr. writer, 1945-52; rep. The Asia Found., Tokyo, 1952-54; rep. The Asia Found., Bangkok, 1954-58, spl. asst. to the pres., 1958-59; staff writer Reader's Digest, 1959-76. Author: My Unconsidered Judgement, 1944, What Manner of Man (a biography of Franklin Delano Roosevelt), 1944, Lost Continent, 1945, Fallen Sun: A Report on Japan, 1948, Briton Hadden: a biography of the co-founder of Time, 1949, Thailand: An Introduction to Modern Siam, 1958, Two Minutes to Noon: the Story of the Great Tokyo Earthquake, 1962, T.R.: The Story of Theodore Roosevelt, 1963, The Emperor's Sword, 1969, A Concise History of Japan, 1972, Winter Quarters: George Washington at Valley Forge, 1974; contbr. articles to periodicals. Mem. Am. Hist. Soc. Clubs: PEN, Princeton, Century Assn., Racquet and Tennis (N.Y.C.), Millbrook Golf and Tennis. Home: Millbrook N.Y. Died Sept. 7, 1985.

BUSH, IAN ELCOCK, research scientist; b. Bristol, Eng., May 25, 1928; came to U.S., 1964; s. Gilbert B. and Jean (Elcock) B.; m. Alison Pickard, Aug. 26, 1951 (div. 1966); children: Charles Fabian, Philippa, Caroline; m. Joan Morthland, Sept. 16, 1967 (div. 1972); children: Andrew, Georgia; m. Mary Johnson, Feb. 15, 1982. BA, U. Cambridge, Eng., 1949, PhD., 1952, M.B., B.Chir., 1957. Med. rsch. coun. scholar Cambridge Nat. Inst. Med. Rsch., London, 1949-52; Commonwealth fellow U. Utah Mass. Gen. Hosp., Boston, 1952-53; rsch. assoc. St. Mary's Hosp., Boston, 1952-53, St. Mary's Hosp. Med. Sch., London, 1953-56; grad. asst. U. Oxford, Eng., 1956-60; prof., chmn. dept. physiology U. Birmingham, Eng., 1960-64; sr. scientist Worcester Found. Exptl. Biology, 1964-67; prof., chmn. dept. physiology Med. Coll. Va., 1967-70; v.p. rsch. and devel. Cybertek Inc., 1970-71, pres., chief exec. officer, 1971-72; sr. rsch. assoc. dept. medicine Dartmouth Med. Sch., 1974-77, prof. psychiatry and physiology, 1977-86; assoc. chief staff rsch. VA Hosp., 1977-88; cons. in field, 1949-88; past mem. panels NSF, Am. Cancer Soc., Med. Rsch. Coun. Eng. Author: Chromatography of Steroids, 1961, The Siberian Reservoir, 1983; also papers. Fellow Am. Acad. Arts and Scis.; mem. Am. Eng. physiol. socs., Am. Eng. endocrine socs., AAAS, The Players. Home: Woodstock Vt. Died Nov. 1, 1986; buried S. Woodstock, Vt.

BUSTAMANTE Y RIVERO, JOSE LUIS, judge; b. Arequipa, Peru, Jan. 15, 1894; s. Manuel Bustamente y Barreda and Vitoria Rivero de Bustamente; m. Maria Jesös Rivera de Bustamente, Dec. 16, 1923; children: Beatriz (Mrs. St. Ricardo Bouroncle), Jose Luis. D.Law, U. San Agustin, Arequipa, 1918, D.Polit. Scis., 1929; D.Philosophy and Letters, U. San Antonio Abad, Cuzco, 1918. Practice law Arequipa, 1918-34, Lima, Peru; substitute judge, substitute atty. Ct. Arequipa, 1925-33; prof. Faculty Letters U. Arequipa, 1921, prof. civil law, 1930-34; spl. envoy and M.P. to Bolivia, 1934-38, to Uruguay, 1939-42; spl. ambassador to Bolivia, 1942-45, to Paraguay, 1939; minister justice and instrn. 1930-31; pres. Peruvian del. to Congreso de Jurisconsultos, Montevideo, 1939-40; constl. pres. Peru, 1945-48; dean Coll. Lawyers of Lima, 1960; judge Internat. Ct. of Justice, The Hague, Netherlands, 1960-70, pres., 1967-70, ret.; del. Colegio de Abogados de Lima to V and XI confs. Inter-americanas de Abogados, Rio de Janeiro and Miami, Fla., 1943, 59; mem. Peru, 1960. Author: La ONU en el Palacio de Chaillot, 1952, Panamericanismo e Ibero-americanismo, 1953, La subestimación del Deracho en el mundo moderno, 1954, Las clases sociales en el Peru, 1959. Mem. Interam. Bar Assn. (hon.), Sociedad Peruana de Derecho Internat., Instituto Hispano-Luso-Americano de Derecho Internat. (Founder), Asociación Francisco de Vitoria de Derecho Internacional de Madrid, Academia Peruana de la Lengua. Home: Lima Peru. Died Jan 11, 1989.

BUTCHER, FANNY (MRS. RICHARD DRUMMOND BOKUM), literary critic; b. Fredonia, Kans., Feb. 13, 1888; d. L. Oliver and Hattie May (Young) Butcher; m. Richard Drummond Bokum, Feb. 13, 1935. Prep. edn., Lewis Inst., Chgo,; AB, U. Chgo., 1910. Soc. editor, asst. woman's editor, spl. corr., lit. editor, writer Lit. Spotlight. Chgo. Tribune, 1913-63; Past sec. to first little theatre movement in Am.; former owner Fanny Butcher-Books (bookshop). Author: (autobiography) Many Lives--One Love, 1972. Recipient Friends of Lit. Non-Fiction award, 1972, Constance Lindsay Skinner award, 1955, Communicator of Yr. award U. Chgo., 1964, citation Alliance of Bus. and Profl. Women, 1964, Merit award The Cliff Dwellers, 1976. Mem. Soc. Midland Authors (Patron Saint award 1973), Adult Edn. Coun. (dir.), Modern Poetry Assn. (hon. dir.), Internat. PEN Club (past pres. Chgo. chpt.), Friends of Am. Writers (hon.), Officer d'Academie de France, Friends of Chgo. Pub. Library (hon. chmn. bd.), Friday Club, Fortnightly Club, Press Club, Kappa Phi Delta. Home: Chicago Ill. Deceased.

BUTCHER, RAYMOND M., architectural engineering company executive; b. 1924; married. BSME, U. Mo., 1948. With Babcock & Wilcox Co.; then with Black & Veatch, Kansas City, Mo., from 1949; then exec. ptnr. Black & Veatch, Kansas City, also bd. dirs. Served with U.S. Army, 1944-46. Deceased.

BUTLER, ALLAN MACY, physician; b. Yonkers, N.Y., Apr. 3, 1894; s. George P. and Ellen (Mudge) B.; m. Mabel H. Churchill, June 1921 (dec. 1981); children: Margaret B., Allan C., Beverly A. LittB, Princeton U., 1916; MD, Harvard U., 1926. With Cunard S.S. Co., N.Y.C., 1919-21; research asst. Rockefeller Inst., 1926-28; tutor prof. pediatrics, biochem. scis. Harvard U., Cambridge, Mass., 1928-30, staff mem. dept. pediatrics, 1930-42, prof. pediatrics, 1942-60, prof. emeritus, 1960-86; chief children's med. service Mass. Gen. Hosp., Boston, 1942-60; dir. med. clinics, chief pediatric service Met. Hosp. Clinics, Detroit, 1960-62; spl. cons. Calif. Dept. Pub. Health, 1962-63; lectr. Stanford U. Med. Sch., 1963-66; cons. AID, 1964-65; med. cons. Head Start, Office Econ. Opportunity, 1965-69, Chgo. Bd. Edn., 1969-71; dir. med. edn. St. Lukes Hosp., San Francisco, 1965-66; fellow Ctr. for Study Dem. Instns., Santa Barbara, Calif., 1966-67. Assoc. editor New Eng. Jour Medicine, 1936-38, Jour. Clin. Investigation, 1940-46; contbr. articles to profl. jours. Mem. Soc. for Pediatric Research, Am. Soc. Clin. Investigation, Am. Acad. Arts and Scis., Assn. Am. Physicians, Am. Pediatrics Soc. (pres. 1955, Howland award1969), Am. Acad. Pediatrics, Com. Physicians for Improvement Med. Care (sec., treas.), Physicians Forum (chmn. 1960), Nat. Council Infant and Child Care (pres. 1958). Home: Tisbury Mass. Died Oct. 7, 1986.

BUTTERFIELD, CHARLES WILLIAM (BILLY), composer, musician; b. Middletown, Ohio, 1916; m. Dotty Smith; children: Debby, Judy (twins). Student, Transylvania U., Lexington, Ky. With Bob Crosby Orch., 1937, later with Artie Shaw; with Benny Goodman, 1940-41; recordings with Gramercy Five; organized Billy Butterfield and His Orch., toured U.S.; recordings: RCA-Victor, Capitol, Decca, Essex, Westminster. Served with U.S. Army. Died Mar. 18, 1988.

BUTTERWECK, JOSEPH SEIBERT, educator; b. Allentown, Pa., Oct. 9, 1891; s. Wesley and Alice Jane (Seiber) B.; m. Reba Godfrey, Nov. 7, 1917; children: Marjorie Mary Burns, Janet Schwab Blatt; m. 2d, Grace Otto Thomas, Jan. 22, 1937; 1 child, Joseph Sebring. BS, U. Pa., 1922, MA, 1924; PhD, Tchrs. Coll., Columbia U., 1926. Tchr. of sci. Moorestown (N.J.) High Sch., 1910-14; real estate bus. Camsden and Moorestown, 1914-18; tchr. of sci. Media (Pa.) High Sch., 1918-20, prin., 1920-22; prin. Haddon Heights (N.J.) High Sch., 1922-24; asst. in rsch. Lincoln Sch., Columbia, 1925-26; asst. prof. edn. Temple U., Phila., 1926-30, prof. edn., dir. dept. secondary edn., 1930-53, acting dean tchrs. coll., 1953-54, dir. exptl. program in tchr. edn., 1954-59, emeritus prof. edn. and ednl. cons., from 1961; dir. East Pa. Ednl. Fedn., 1959-61; supr. grad. tchr. edn. State Dept. Pub. Instrn., Harrisburg, Pa., 1961-67; ednl. cons. Lehigh U., from 1967; cons. Akila Hebrew Acad., Phila. Music Acad. Author books including: General Education for Teachers, 1959, Preparing Teachers for Secondary Schools, 1960; contbr. articles to mags. Mem. NEA, Pa. State Edn. Assn., Schoolmen's Club of Pa. (sec. 1942-62). Democrat. Baptist. Home: Lederack Pa. †

BUTWELL, RICHARD LEE, university president; b. Portland, Maine, Apr. 19, 1929; s. Walter and Jenny (Petersen) B.; m. Charlene B., Dec. 18, 1965; children: Michael, Scot, John, Ann. BA, Tufts U., 1951; MA, Ind. U., 1952; PhD, Oxford U., 1954. Reporter Gannett Newspapers, Portland, Maine, summers 1944-51; from asst. to prof. polit. sci. U. Ill., Urbana, 1958-65; prof. polit. sci., dir. W.A. Patterson Sch. Diplomacy and Internat. Commerce U. Ky., Lexington, 1965-68; prof. S.E. Asian politics Am. U., Washington, 1968-71, dir. Bus. Council for Internat. Understanding Program, Sch. Internat. Service, 1968-71; prof., chmn. dept. polit. sci. SUNY-Brockport, 1971-74; dean arts and scis., prof. polit. sci. SUNY, Fredonia, 1974-78; v.p. acad. programs, prof. polit. sci. Murray State U., Ky., 1978-82; v.p. acad. affairs, prof. polit. sci. U. S.D., Vermillion, 1982-84; pres. univ., prof. polit. sci. Calif. State U., Dominguez Hills, from 1984; dir. Asian studies program Nat. Def. Coll., Washington, 1970-71; social scis. field rep. Rockefeller Found., Philippines, 1964-65; vis. lectr. Nat. Def. Coll., 1969, 70, 72-77; lectr. Indsl. Coll. Armed Forces, Air U., Naval War Coll., Army War Coll., Fgn. Service Inst. (Dept. State); reviewer grant proposals Fulbright Found., others; chmn. Calif. State U. Pacific Rim Commn., from 1985. Author: (with Amry Vandenbosch) Southeast Asia Among the World Powers, 1958, (with Amry Vandenbosch) The Changing Face of Southeast Asia, 1966, U Nu of Burma, 1969, Southeast Asia Today and Tomorrow, 1969, Southeast Asia, a Political Introduction, 1975; editor: Foreign Policy and the Developing State, 1969; (monograph) Southeast Asia, a Survey, 1968; contbr. numerous chpts. to books, articles to scholarly jours.; mem. editorial bd. Asian Survey, Current History. Served to lt. (j.g.) USN, 1955-58. Fulbright scholar, 1952-54; Fulbright prof. U. Rangoon, Burma, 1959-60; SEATO research fellow, Bangkok, Thailand, 1962; Am. U. travel grantee, 1970; Am. Enterprise Inst.-Hoover Instn. grantee, 1972; State Dept. travel grantee, 1969, 71, 73, 74. Mem. Asia Soc. (Philippine and Burma councils), Phi Beta Kappa, Pi Sigma Alpha, Phi Delta Kappa. Deceased.

BYE, RAYMOND TAYLOR, economist; b. Phila., Jan. 30, 1892; s. Andrew Moore and Alva May (Tayor) B.; m. Jane W. Twining, Oct. 22, 1917 (dec. Aug. 1918); m. 2d, Virginia Lippincott Higgins, Sept. 7, 1922; children: Doris (Mrs. John C. Ferm), Elinor (Mrs. David W. Harry), Florence (Mrs. Ronald H. Brown). Student, George Sch., Pa., 1904-10; AB, Swarthmore Coll., 1914; AM, Harvard U., 1915; PhD, U. Pa., 1918. Instr. econs. U. Pa., 1916-20, asst. prof., 1920-26, prof. econs., 1926—; chmn. grad. econs. group, 1956-59. Author several books including: Principles of Economics, 1924 (fifth edit., 1956), Social Economy and the Price System, 1950, (with W.W. Hewett) The Economic Process, 1952; contbr. to jours. Sec., dir. Lake Paupac Corp., 1949-57; former mem. Phila. Interracial Commn. Mem. Am. Econ. Assn., Am. Civil Liberties Union, Esperanto Assn. of N. Am. (v.p. 1926-27), Soc. of Friends (chmn. Young Friends Movement of Phila. 1919-20, chmn. com. on interests of the colored race of Phila. yearly meeting of Friends, 1921-24, chmn. Race Relations sect., Am. Friends Svc. Com. 1925-29), Phi Beta Kappa, Delta Sigma Rho, Pi Gamma Mu. Home: Moylan Pa. †

BYRNE, BRENDAN, public affairs consultant; b. N.Y.C., Dec. 28, 1908; s. Thomas J. and Clara (Janson) B.; m. Rena H. Faecher, July 1, 1937; children: Mary P., Michael K., Judith A. A.B. magna cum laude, Fordham U., 1930, M.A., 1936. Chmn. social studies dept. John Adams High Sch., N.Y.C., 1931-42; editor Facts mag., Read mag., New Books Digest, 1946; research dir., copywriter Grady Advt. Agy., 1947; dir. programs Am. Heritage Found., 1947-50, assoc. dir., 1956, exec. dir., 1956, 1957-65; public affairs cons. ITT Fed. Electric Corp., from 1965; pres. Richmond Hill Devel Corp., from 1982; trustee Richmond Hill Savs. Bank, from 1969; Pub. relations dir. Nat. Citizens Commn. for Better Schs., 1950; v.p. Valley Forge Found., 1951-52; exec. v.p. Goldby & Byrne. Inc. (philanthropic cons.), N.Y.C., 1954-55; pub. affairs cons. Author: Guide to the Study of History, 1936, American Heritage Manual, 1950, Alert America Public Relations Guide, 1951, Three Weeks to a Better Memory, 1951, Let's Modernize Our Horse-and-Buggy Election Laws, 1961, How to Help or Hurt Your Country, 1963; Contbr. articles to profl. jours. Mem. Pres.'s Commn. on Registration and Voter Participation, 1962-65; vice chmn. N.Y. Commn. on Hist. Observances, 1960-63; dir. Nat. Conf. on Citizenship, 1962—; dir. nationwide campaign Contribute to Your Polit. Party, 1958-65, nonpartisan program to modernize archaic election laws, 1957-65, Register, Inform Yourself and Vote Program, 1957-65; mem. N.Y.C. Bd. Edn., 1961-64, N.Y.C. Nat. Shrines Com., 1969—. Served from lt. (j.g.) to lt. comdr. USNR, 1942-45, ETO. Decorated Sec. of Navy Letter of Commendation; recipient Freedoms Found. George Washington honor medal for pub. speaking, 1963; S.A.R. Gold Good Citizenship medal, 1948. Mem. Pub. Relations Soc. Am., N.Y. Hist. Soc., Am. Polit. Sci. Assn., Authors League Am., Authors Guild, Am. Mgmt. Assn., Am. Acad. Polit. Scis., Nat. Municipal League, Adult Edn. Assn., Advt. Club N.Y.C., Fordham U. Alumni Assn. (bd. dirs.), Am. Polit. Sci. Assn. Club: Naval Reserve Officers (N.Y.C.). Home: Richmond Hill N.Y. Deceased.

BYRNS, RICHARD HOWARD, English educator, author, counselor; b. Willits, Calif., Aug. 11, 1915; s. Walter Herbert and Dorothy (Meier) B.; m. Theo Ella Thompson, Aug. 26, 1939; children: Richard Howard, Theo Anne. BA, U. No. Colo.; MA, U. Calif.-Berkeley; Ph.D., U. Edinburgh, Scotland, 1955. Cert. marriage and family counselor, Nev. Asst. prof. English U. Alaska, 1947-49, assoc. prof., 1949-51, dir. mil. brs., 1950-51; research student U. Edinburgh, 1951-52; prof. English U. Alaska, 1953-57; editorial cons. Geophys. Inst., 1953-57; assoc. prof. So. Oreg. Coll., 1957-59, prof. English, 1959-66, head dept. English, 1965-66; prof. English, chmn. dept. U. Nev., 1966-67, prof. English, 1971-86, dean Coll. Humanities, 1967-71; pres. Richard H. Byrns MFC, Ltd., 1982-87. Author: Current Research in Alaska, 1954; also short stories.; contbr. articles scholastic jours. Mem. MLA, Philol. Assn. Pacific Coast, Am. Comparative Lit. Assn., Rocky Mountain Modern Lang. Assn., Am. Assn. Marriage and Family Therapy (clin.), Alpha Psi Omega, Pi Kappa Delta, Phi Lambda Alpha, Phi Kappa Phi. Home: Las Vegas Nev. Died July 1, 1986.

CABANA, GEORGES, archbishop; b. Granby, Can., Oct. 23, 1894; s. Joseph and Marie V. (Desgrés) C. Student, St. Charles Coll., Sherbrooke, 1908-10, St. Hyacinthe Sem., 1910-14; BA, Laval U., 1914; B Canon Law, Sem. Theology, Montreal, 1917; DCL, Bishop's U.; LLD, Bishop's U., Lennoxville, Sherbrooke U. Ordained as priest Roman Cath. Ch., 1918. Prof. St. Hyacinthe Sem., 1918-21, St. Augustine's Sem., Toronto, 1921-31; prof., asst. St. Hyacinthe and Sorel, 1931-34; chaplain St. Charles Hosp., 1935; spiritual dir. St. Hyacinthe Sem. of Man., Can., 1941-52; archbishop of Sherbrooke, Que., 1952-68; titular See, from 1968; chancellor Sherbrooke U., 1954-68. Home: Sherbrooke Que. Died Feb. 6, 1986.

CADY, ERNEST ALBERT, newspaper editor; b. Newark, Ohio, Oct. 25, 1899; s. Charles Adelbert and Bird Lenore (Bollwine) C.; m. Frances D. Fairchild, June 11, 1923; children: Charles Sherman, Jocelyn Sue Cady Ritter, Judith Ann Cady Wiggins, Jerilou. Grad., Ohio State U., 1920-22. Mem. staff Columbus (Ohio) Dispatch, 1922-77, editorial writer, asst. editor editorial page, 1936-65, lit. editor, columnist, 1948-77, book reviewer; mem. book awards com. Ohioana Library Assn., 1950-85, chmn. 1965, 67, 69, 71, 73. Author: We Adopted Three, 1952, (with Frances Cady) How to Adopt a Child, 1956; also articles. Co-incorporator, trustee Ohio Children's Soc., pvt. adoption agy., 1953-85. Recipient Nat. Freedoms Found. award editorial writing, 1971, Ohioana library citation for service to Ohio journalism, 1974. Mem. Nat. Book Critics Circle (charter), Ohio Press Club, Gridiron, Columbus Dispatch Country Club, Sigma Delta Chi (organizing pres. Cen. Ohio profl. chpt. 1950, Disting. Service award 1980). Republican. Methodist. Home: Columbus Ohio. Died July 30, 1985; cremated.

CAGLE, FREDRIC WILLIAM, JR., chemistry educator; b. Metropolis, Ill., Dec. 17, 1924; s. Fredric William and Hattimay (Stalcup) C. B.S., U. Ill., 1944, M.S., 1945, Ph.D., 1946. Mem. Sch. Math. Inst. for Advanced Study, Princeton, N.J., 1947-48; fellow in chemistry U. Utah, 1948-49, research asst. prof., 1949-53, asst. prof., 1953-54, asso. prof., 1954-60, prof., 1960-88; cons. Pacific Northwest Pipeline Corp., 1958-61, Dow Chem. Co., 1963-67. Mem. Am. Chem. Soc., Am. Crystallographic Assn., Sigma Xi, Phi Kappa Phi, Sigma Pi Sigma. Home: Salt Lake City Utah. Died May 1, 1988; interred Masonic Cemetery, Metropolis, Ill.

CAGNEY, JAMES, actor; b. N.Y.C., July 17, 1899; m. Frances Vernon, 1922; children: James Jr., Cathleen. Ed. grammar sch. Began in vaudeville 1924, worked in motion pictures, 1931-61; pres. Cagney-Montgomery Prodns., L.A.; v.p. Cagney Prodns., 1942. Has appeared in: many pictures among which were Sinner's Holiday, 1930, Doorway to Hell, 1930, The Millionaire, 1931, Other Men's Women, 1931, The Public Enemy, 1931, Smart Money, 1931, Blonde Crazy, 1931, Taxi, 1932, The Crowd Roars, 1932, Winner Take All, 1932, Hard to Handle, 1933, Picture Snatcher, 1933, The Mayor of Hell, 1933, Footlight Parade, 1933, Lady Killer, 1934, Jimmy the Gent, 1934, He Was Her Man, 1934, Here Comes the Navy, 1934, The St. Louis Kid, 1934, Devil Dogs of the Air, 1935, G Men, 1935, The Irish in Us, 1935, A Midsummer Night's Dream, 1935, Frisco Kid, 1935, Ceiling Zero, 1936, Great Guy, 1937, Something to Sing About, 1937, Boy Meets Girl, 1938, Angels with Dirty Faces, 1938, The Oklahoma Kid, 1939, Each Dawn I Die, 1939, The Roaring Twenties, 1939, The Fighting 69th, 1940, Torrid Zone, 1940, City for Conquest, 1940, Strawberry Blonde, 1941, The Bride Came C.O.D., 1941, Captains of the Clouds, 1942, Yankee Doodle Dandy (best actor award Critics' Circle 1942), Johnny Come Lately, 1943, Blood on the Sun, 1945, 13 Rue Madeleine, Point Story, 1950, Come Fill the Cup, 1951, Starlift, 1951, What Price Glory, 1952, A Lion Is in the Streets, 1953, Run for Cover, 1955, Love Me or Leave Me, 1955, The Seven Little Foys, 1955, Mister Roberts, 1955, Tribute to a Bad Man, 1956, These Wilder Years, 1956, Man of a Thousand Faces, 1957, Never Steal Anything Small, 1959, Shake Hands with the Devil, 1959, The Gallant Hours, 1960, One, Two, Three, 1961, Ragtime, 1981; TV appearances include Terrible Joe Moran, 1984. Recipient Academy award as best actor, 1942, Life Achievement award Am. Film Inst., 1974, Medal of Freedom award, 1984, Kennedy Ctr. honor award, 1984. Mem. Screen Actor's Guild (pres. 1942-43). Home: Millbrook N.Y. Died Mar. 30, 1986.

CAHNERS, NORMAN LEE, publisher; b. Bangor, Maine, June 5, 1914; s. James A. and Katherine L. (Epstein) C.; m. Helene Rabb, May 15, 1941; children: Robert M., Andrew P. (dec.), Nancy L. Grad., Harvard Coll., 1936; MA (hon.), Colby Coll., 1969; LLD (hon.), Franklin Pierce Coll., 1969; DHL (hon.), Suffolk U., 1970; DBA (hon.), Husson Coll., 1972; LHD (hon.), Northeastern U., 1983. Founder, chmn. Cahners Pub. Co., Boston, 1946-86; bd. dirs. John Hancock Mut. Life Ins. Co., Boston, Stop & Shop Cos. Inc., Boston, SYR Corp., Santa Barbara, Calif.; vice chmn. Reed Holdings Inc., N.Y.C. Chmn. Mus. Sci., Boston; vice chmn. Northeastern U.; mem. overseers com. on univ. resources Harvard U.; mem. overseers vis. com. Harvard and Radcliffe Colls., 1968-74, Dept. Athletics, 1974-80, Grad. sch. Bus. Adminstrn., 1974-80; trustee Colby Coll., 1969-75; bd. overseers Children's Hosp. Med. Ctr.; trustee New Eng. Med. Ctr., USS Constitution Mus.; life trustee Beth Israel Hosp., Boston, Combined Jewish Philanthropies Greater Boston Inc.; mem. corp., mem. medicine vis. com. Mass. Gen. Hosp.; mem. Corp. Affiliated Hosps. Ctr. Inc.; bd. dirs. U.S. Coast Guard Acad. Found., Boys and Girls Clubs Boston, Boston-Fenway Program Inc.; mem. exec. bd. Mass. Bay Federated Couns. Inc., Boy Scouts Am. Recipient Bus. Statesman awardHarvard Bus. Sch. Assn., 1977, Theodore Storer Meml. award Boy Scouts Am., 1978, Ralph Lowell Disting. Citizen award Boy Scouts Am., 1981, Honor Scroll, Am. Bus. Press, 1984, Disting. Citizen award NCCJ, 1986 (posthumously), Reed Apple award Material Handling Edn. Found. Inc. 1986 (posthumously);, named to Harvard Varsity Club Hall of Fame, 1986 (posthumously); fellow Am. Acad. Arts and Scis., Brandeis U. Mem. Greater Boston C. of C. (v.p. 1973-76), Comml. Club, Algonquin Club, St.Botolph Club, Harvard U. Club, University Club (Boston), Harvard Varsity Club, N.Y. Yacht Club, Camden Yacht Club, Boca Rio Club (Boca Raton, Fla.), Belmont Country Club. Home: Boca Raton Fla. Died Mar. 14, 1986.

CAINE, LYNN, author, lecturer; b. N.Y.C.; d. Saul and Sally (Bialkin) Shapiro; children: Jonathan, Elizabeth. Student pub. schs., N.Y.C. Publicity dir. Farrar, Straus & Giroux, N.Y.C., 1955-64; publicity mgr. N.Y.C. office Little, Brown & Co., 1967-76; free lance author, lectr. N.Y.C., 1976—; mem. faculty Human Relations Center, New Sch. Social Research. Author: Widow, 1974, Lifelines: Living Alone Without Being Lonely, 1978, What Did I Do Wrong: Mothers, Children and Guilt, 1985. Mem. adv. bd. Women's Center, YWCA, N.Y.C. Recipient Christopher award, 1974. Mem. Womens' Media Group, Friends of Scarlett O'Hara, Authors Guild, PEN, Pub.'s Publicity Assn. (co-founder). Jewish. Home: New York N.Y. Died Dec. 19, 1987.

CAIRNS, HUNTINGTON, lawyer, author; b. Balt., Sept. 1, 1904; s. James Duncanson and Helen Huntington (Heath) C.; m. Florence F. Butler, May 29, 1929. Grad., Balt. City Coll., 1922; LL.B., U. Md., 1925; LL.D., N.Y. U., St. Andrews U., Johns Hopkins, U. Md.; L.H.D., Tulane U., Kenyon Coll. Bar: Md. 1926, D.C. 1943. Assoc. Piper, Carey & Hall, 1926-37, ptnr., 1933-37; spl. legal adviser U.S. Treasury Dept., 1934-37, 43-65; Lectr. taxation U. Md. Law Sch., 1935-37; chmn. radio program Invitation to Learning, 1940-41; asst. gen. counsel U.S. Treasury, 1937-43; mem. com. on practice Treasury Dept., 1944-52; Sec., mem. Am. Commn. for Protection and Salvage of Artistic and Historic Monuments, War Areas, 1943-46; sec., treas., gen. counsel Nat. Gallery Art, 1943-65; James Schouler lectr. polit. sci. Johns Hopkins, 1947, lectr. criticism, 1949-59; mem. Md. Tax Revision Commn., 1938-41. Author: Law and the Social Sciences, 1935, The Theory of Legal Science, 1941, Invitation to Learning, (with Allen Tate and Mark Van Doren), 1941, (with John Walker) Masterpieces of Painting from the National Gallery of Art, 1944, The Limits of Art, 1948, Legal Philosophy from Plato to Hegel, 1949, Law and its Premises, 1962, This Other Eden, 1973; Editor: (with John Walker) Tax Laws of Maryland, 1937, Malinowski, A Scientific Theory of Culture, 1944, Saintsbury, French Literature and Its Masters, 1945, Lectures in Criticism, 1949, Great Paintings from the National Gallery of Art, 1952, (with Edith Hamilton) The Collected Dialogues of Plato, 1961, (with John Walker) Treasures from the National Gallery of Art, 1962, H.L. Mencken; The American Scene, A Reader, 1965, What Is Law?, 1970, On Mencken, 1980, Shakespeare's Herbs, 1982; translator: (Plato) Minos, 1970; contbr. to various mags., symposia, Dictionary Am. Biography. Trustee Bollingen Found., Textile Mus.; mem. Dumbarton Oaks adminstrv. com. Harvard; bd. dirs. Jr. History of Ideas; mem.-at-large Am. Council Learned Socs. Benjamin N. Cardozo lectr., 1962; John Randolph Tucker lectr., 1970; Recipient Civic medallion for most significant contbn. to progress of Balt. in field professions and sci., 1935, Rockefeller Pub. Service award. Mem. ABA, D.C. Bar Assn., Md. Bar Assn. (hon. life mem.), Am. Law Inst., Am. Philos. Assn., Am. Acad. Arts and Scis., Phi Beta Kappa. Clubs: Hamilton Street, Maryland, Cosmos, Wranglers. Died Jan. 19, 1985.

CALDERONE, FRANK ANTHONY, physician; b. N.Y.C., 1901; s. Salvatore and Rosaria C.; m. Mary Steichen, Nov. 1941; children: Francesca Calderone-Steichen, Maria S. MD, NYU, 1924; MPH, Johns Hopkins U., 1937. Diplomate Am. Bd. Preventive Medicine. Med. dir. health svc. UN, 1951-54; pres. Occupational Health Inst., N.Y.C., 1955-57; exec. dir. U.S. Cancer Com., 1949; dir. hdqrs. office WHO, 1946-49; dep. commr. health N.Y.C., 1944-46, sec. dept. health, 1942-44, dist. health officer, 1938-42; then cons. pub. and indsl. health; trustee L.I. chpt. Medic Alert. Donated Adelphi Calderone Theatre to Adelphi U., 1978. Fellow Am. Pub. Health Assn.; mem. Alpha Omega Alpha. Home: Old Brookville N.Y. Died Feb. 10, 1987; buried Greenfield Cemetery, Hempstead, N.Y.

CALDWELL, ERSKINE, author; b. Moreland, Ga., Dec. 17, 1903; s. Ira Sylvester and Caroline Preston (Bell) C.; m. Helen Lannigan, Mar. 3, 1925; children—Erskine Preston, Dabney Withers, Janet; m. Margaret Bourke-White, Feb. 27, 1939; m. June Johnson, Dec. 21, 1942; 1 child, Jay Erskine; m. Virginia Moffett Fletcher, Jan. 1, 1957. Student, Erskine Coll., S.C., 1920, 21, U. Va., 1922, 25, 26, U. Pa., 1924. Newspaper writer 1925; cotton picker, stage hand, profl. football player, book reviewer, lectr., editor; motion picture screen writer Hollywood, Calif., 1933-34, 42-43; corr. Mexico, Spain, Czechoslovakia, 1938-39, China, Mongolia, Turkestan, 1940; editor Am. Folkways, 1940-55; war corr. Life mag., PM, CBS, Russia, 1941. Author: The Bastard, 1929, Poor Fool, 1930, American Earth, 1931, Tobacco Road, 1932, God's Little Acre, 1933, We Are The Living, 1933, Journeyman, 1935, Kneel to the Rising Sun, 1935, Some American People, 1935, (with Margaret Bourke-White) You Have Seen Their Faces, 1937, Southways, 1938, (with Margaret Bourke- White) North of the Danube, 1939, Trouble in July, 1940, Jackpot, 1940, (with Margaret Bourke-White) Say, Is This the U.S.A.?, 1941, All-Out on the Road to Smolensk, 1942, Moscow Under Fire, 1942, All Night Long, 1942, Georgia Boy, 1943, Stories, 1944, Tragic Ground, 1944, A House in the Uplands, 1946, The Sure Hand of God, 1947, This Very Earth, 1948, Place Called Estherville, 1949, Episode in Palmetto, 1950, Call It Experience, 1951, The Courting of Susie Brown, 1952, A Lamp for Nightfall, 1952, The Complete Stories of Erskine Caldwell, 1953, Love and Money, 1954, Gretta, 1955, Erskine Caldwell's Gulf Coast Stories, 1956, Certain Women, 1957, Molly Cottontail, 1958, Claudelle Inglish, 1959, When You Think of Me, 1959, Jenny by Nature, 1961, Close to Home, 1962, The Last Night of Summer, 1963, (with Virginia M. Caldwell) Around About America, 1964, In Search of Bisco, 1965, The Deer at Our House, 1966, In The Shadow of The Steeple, 1966, Writing in America, 1966, Miss Mamma Aimee, 1967, Deep South, 1968, Summertime Island, 1968, The Weather Shelter, 1969, The Earnshaw Neighborhood, 1971, Annette, 1973, (with Alexander Calder) The Sacrilege of Alan Kent, 1976, (with Virginia M. Caldwell) Afternoons in Mid-America, 1976, Stories of Life North and South, 1983, With All My Might: An Autobiography, 1987; Contbr. to mags. Decorated L'Ordre du Merite Culturel (Poland); comdr. L'Ordre des Arts et des Lettres (France); recipient Yale Rev. $1,000 award for fiction, 1933. Mem. Authors League Am., Am. Acad. and Inst. Arts and Letters, Internat. P.E.N., Euphemian Lit. Soc., Raven Soc. Clubs: Phoenix Press, San Francisco Press. Home: Scottsdale Ariz. Died Apr. 11, 1987; buried Scenic Hills Meml. Park, Ashland, Oreg.

CALDWELL, GUY A., orthopedic surgeon; b. Alcorn County, Miss., Jan. 24, 1891; s. Rufus Lusk and Frances (Hill) C.; m. Lettie Mae Wheat, Oct. 26, 1934; children: Marie Muriel (Mrs. Lem Wootten), Mignon (Mrs. Charles W. Morse Jr.), Marjorie Cade (Mrs. Thomas R. Howell), Marc. BS, U. Miss., 1911; MD, Columbia U., 1914. Diplomate Am. Bd. Surgery (past pres.). Instr. fractures Emory U., 1919-22; asst. surgeon Scottish Rite Hosp., Atlanta, Ga., 1919-22; chief surgeon Shriners' Hosp. for Crippled Children, Shreveport, La., 1922-23; vis. orthopedic surgeon Shreveport Charity Hosp., 1923-38; prof. orthopedics Tulane U., 1939-50, prof. emeritus, from 1957, chmn. orthopedic div., 1950-54; sr. vis. orthopedic surgeon Charity Hosp. and Touro Infirmary, New Orleans, 1939-44; head dept. orthopedics Ochsner Clinic, from 1942, Found. Hosp., from 1944. Chmn. emeritus surg. adv. bd. Shriners Hosps. for Crippled Children; trustee Alton Ochsner Med. Found. Fellow ACS; mem. AMA (mem. coun. on med. edn. and hosps.), Am. Acad. Orthopedic Surgeons (past pres.), Am. Orthopedic Assn., Am. Surg. Soc., So. Surg. Assn., Internat. Soc. Orthopedic Surgeons, Internat. Soc. Surgery, Mexican Soc. Orthopedic Surgeons (hon.), Boston Club. Democrat. Presbyterian. Home: New Orleans La. †

CALDWELL, (JANET MIRIAM) TAYLOR, author; b. Manchester, Eng., Sept. 7, 1900; came to U.S., 1906; d. Arthur F. and Anna (Marks) Caldwell; m. William Fairfax Combs, May 27, 1919 (div. 1931); 1 child, Mary Margaret Combs Fried; m. Marcus Reback, May 12, 1931 (dec. Aug. 1970O; 1 child, Judith Ann Reback Goodman; m. William E. Stancell, June 1972 (div. 1973); m. William Robert Prestie, July 1978. AB, U. Buffalo, 1931; LittD, D'Youville Coll., 1964; LHD, Niagara U., 1971. Ct. reporter Workmen's Compensation div. N.Y. Dept. Labor, Buffalo, 1923-24; sec. Spl. Bd. Inquiry, U.S. Immigration and Naturalization Service, Dept. Justice, Buffalo, 1924-31. Author: Dynasty of Death, 1938, Melissa, 1948, Let Love Come Last, 1949, The Balance Wheel, 1951, The Devil's Advocate, 1952, Never Victorious, Never Defeated (Grand Prix, Prix Chatrain, Paris), 1956, Tender Victory, 1956, The Sound of Thunder, 1957, Dear and Glorious Physician, 1959, The Listener, 1960, A Prologue to Love, 1961, Grandmother and the Priests, 1963, A Pillar of Iron, 1965, No One Hears But Him, 1966, Dialogues with the Devil, 1967, Testimony of Two Men, 1968, Great Lion of God, 1970, Captains and Kings, 1972, Glory and the Lightning, 1974, Ceremony of the Innocent, 1976, Bright Flows the River, 1978, Answer as a Man, 1981. Yeomanette USNR, 1918-19. Fellow Internat. Inst. Arts and Letters; mem. Am. Legion, St. Francis Guild, Nazareth Guild, Legion of Mary. Republican. Roman Catholic. Home: Greenwich Conn. Died Aug. 30, 1985.

CALDWELL, WILLIAM ANTHONY, editor; b. Butler, Pa., Dec. 5, 1906; s. William Arthur and Johanna Marie (DeLeuw) C.; m. Dorothy C. Alexander, Oct. 22, 1938; children: Toni (Mrs. Daniel Cohen), Alix (Mrs. Thomas McArdle), William Alexander. LittD, Rutgers U., 1967, Fairleigh Dickinson U., 1973; LHD, William Paterson Coll., 1972. Reporter, editor The Record (formerly Bergen Evening Record), Hackensack, N.J., 1926-72; editorial page columnist Vineyard Gazette, Edgartown, Mass., 1972-86. Author: In the Record, 1971; editor: How to Save Urban America, 1972. Mem. lay judicial com. Bergen County Med. Soc., 1962-72; pres. Bergen County unit Am. Cancer Soc., 1950-64, pres. N.J. div., 1962-64; chmn. bd. trustees William Paterson Coll. of N.J., 1967-70. Recipient Bronze medal Am. Cancer Soc., 1961, medal for editorial writing Soc. Silurians, 1964, Pulitzer prize for commentary, 1971. Republican. Presbyterian. Home: Martha's Vineyard MAss. Died Apr. 11, 1986; buried Edgartown Cemetery, Edgartown, Mass.

CALIGUIRI, RICHARD S., mayor; b. Pitts., Oct. 20, 1931; m. Jeanne Conte; children—Greg, David. Grad.,

Pitts. Tech. Inst. Mem. City Council, Pitts., 1970-77; mayor City of Pitts., 1977-88. Served with USAF, 1950-54. Home: Pittsburgh Pa. Died May 7, 1988.

CALKINS, FRANCIS JOSEPH, business administration educator; b. Chgo., Oct. 15, 1910; s. Frank M. and Anna (Masilko) C.; m. Rose Marie Schreiber, June 24, 1944; children: Edward J., Richard F., Anne R., Timothy J. A.B., Loyola U., Chgo., 1932, A.M., 1933; Ph.D., Northwestern U., 1947. Statistician, asst. supr. WPA, Chgo., 1933-38; analyst Standard & Poor's Corp., N.Y.C., 1938-39; asst. prof. econs., finance U. Notre Dame, 1939-45; prof. finance Marquette U., 1945-65, chmn., 1949-61; prof., chmn. banking, finance Western Res. U., 1965-67; prof. banking, finance Case Western Res. U., Cleve., 1967-69; prof. finance Cleve. State U., 1969-76, prof. emeritus, from 1976; Hightower prof. bus. adminstrn. Emory U., Atlanta, from 1976; vis. prof. banking and fin. U. Nebr., Omaha, 1978-79, Wichita U., 1979-82. Author: Case and Problems in Investments, 1955, (with Dowrie and Fuller) Investments, 1961. Trustee Cons. Credit Counseling Service Greater Cleve., 1969-76. Mem. Am. Finance Assn., Am. Econ. Assn., Atlanta Soc. Fin. Analysts, Chartered Financial Analysts, Blue Key, Alpha Kappa Psi, Pi Gamma Mu, Beta Gamma Sigma. Deceased.

CALKINS, JOHN UBERTO, JR., lawyer; b. San Francisco, Apr. 26, 1889; s. John Uberto and Harriet Louise (Bates) C.; m. Deborah Dyer (Dec. 21, 1916; children: Deborah Hathaway, John Uberto III; m. 2d, Lucile Dougherty, Feb. 25, 1933; l dau. Sally Jane. BL, U. Calif., 1911, JD, 1913. Bar: Calif. 1913, U.S. Supreme Ct. 1935. Asst. city atty. Oakland, Calif., 1916-17; asst. dist. atty. Alameda County, Calif., 1919-22; atty. for regents U. Calif., 1923-55; lectr. U. Calif. Sch. Jurisprudence, 1914-40; law prof. Hastings Coll. Law, U. Calif., 1956-59. Assoc. editor: Calif. Law Rev., 1914-40 (co-founder, 1st student editor-in-chief); 1st chmn. editorial com. Calif. State Bar Jour. Mem. Calif. Crime Commn., 1924-25, Crime Problem Adv. Com. Calif., 1931-32; trustee Calif. Coll. Arts and Crafts, 1947-57, mem. adv. bd. from 1957. 1st lt. US. Army, 1917-1919; AEF in France, 1918-19; maj. gen. AUS, 1941-46; participated in campaigns Bismarck Archipelago, New Britain, New Guinea, Leyte, Luzon; with Army of Occupation, Japan; brig. gen. asst. div. comdr. 52d Div., N.G., 1946-48; maj. gen. comdg. 49th Div., 1948-49. Decorated D.S.M., Legion of Merit, Bronze Star with cluster, Combat Inf. badge, Medal of Merit with cluster (Calif.). Mem. Am., Calif. bar assns., Ry. and Locomotive Hist. Soc., Am. Judicature Soc., Am. Legion (charter), Am. Arbitration Assn. (arbitrator), Order of Coif, Marine Meml. Club (San Francisco, Faculty Club (U. Calif.), Rotary, Elks, Phi Delta Phi, Phi Kappa Sigma. Home: Saint Helena Calif. Deceased.

CALLAHAN, GEORGE HAROLD, insurance company executive, lawyer; b. Glen Ridge, N.J., July 13, 1920; s. George Leo and Katherine (Higgins) C.; m. Regina Heslin, Feb. 17, 1943; children: Kevin, Jeanne, Jill, Barbara, John. BS, Seton Hall Coll., 1942; LLB, Harvard U., 1948. Bar: N.J. 1948. Pvt. practice Newark, 1948-60; asst. gen. counsel Colonial Life Ins. Co. Am., East Orange, N.J., 1960-62, gen. counsel, 1962-83, sr. v.p., 1970-80, vice chmn., gen. counsel, sec., 1979-83, bd. dirs., 1970-83; vice chmn., gen. counsel, sec., bd. dirs. Chubb Life Ins. Co. Am., Parsippany, N.J., 1981-84, United Life and Accident Ins. Cos., Concord, N.H., 1981-84. Mcpl. atty. Glen Ridge, 1958-84; asst. counsel Essex County, N.J., 1958-60. Lt. USNR, 1942-45, PTO. Decorated Silver Star medal with bar. Mem. ABA, N.J. State Bar Assn., Essex County Bar Assn., Harvard U. Law Sch. Assn. N.J. (pres. 1963). Democrat. Roman Catholic. Club: Glen Ridge Country. Home: Glen Ridge N.J. Died Dec. 3, 1984.

CALLAHAN, KENNETH, artist; b. Spokane, Wash., Oct. 30, 1906; s. John Lafayette and Martha Anna (Cross) C.; m. Margaret Macauley Bundy, Oct. 11, 1930 (dec. 1961); 1 son, Brian Tobey; m. Beth Inge Gotfredsen, 1964. Student, U. Wash., 1922-25; spl. study in, Mexico, 1931, Paris, London and Florence, Italy, 1936. Asst. dir. Seattle Art Mus., 1931-35, curator, 1935-53; Guggenheim fellow creative painting 1954-55; art writer Seattle Times, 1932-53; free lance writer art mags. from 1932. One-man show Am.-Brit. Art Ctr., N.Y.C., 1946; exhibited Whitney Mus. Contemporary Am. Painting, Carnegie Inst. Painting in U.S., 1946; exhibited France, England, Germany, Italy, Denmark, Formosa, Japan, Australia, New Zealand, Philippines, 1957; work in permanent collections Met. Mus. Art, Mus. Modern Art, Bklyn., Phila. and Springfield art museums, Whitney Mus. Art, Pa. Acad. Art, others. Home: Seattle Wash Died May 1, 1986.

CALLAN, WILLIAM WOODY, motor carrier executive; b. Valley Mills, Tex., 1905; ed. Baylor U. Chmn., Central Freight Lines, Inc., Waco, Tex.; chmn. Am. Bank, Waco, Curry Motor Freight Inc., Express Inc., KWTZ, Waco, Western Nat. Bank, Bryan, Tex., Matthews, Callan & Texhoma Broadcasting Co., Waco, Victoria Broadcasting Co. (Tex.); dir. KBTX, Bryan. Home: Waco TX. Died Mar. 1987.

CALLEN, IRWIN R., physician; b. Chgo., May 3, 1919; s. Harry and Esther (Levey) C.; student U. Chgo., 1936-39; B.S., U. Ill., 1941, M.D., 1943; M.S., 1949; m. Rose P. Cohen, Aug. 10, 1941; children—Jeffrey P., James Jay. Intern, Ill. Research and Ednl. Hosps., U. Ill., 1943, fellow dept. internal medicine, 1946-47, electrocardiographer, assoc. attending physician, 1948-51; resident dept. internal medicine, McCloskey Gen. Hosp., Temple, Tex. 1944; dept. of internal medicine and cardiology regional hosp., Camp Maxey, Tex., 1944-45; practice medicine specializing in internal medicine and cardiology, Chgo., 1947-72, North Miami Beach, Fla., from 1973;instr. medicine U. Health Scis., Chgo., 1951-56, assoc. dept. internal medicine, 1956-66, assoc. prof. medicine, 1966-72, prof. clin. medicine, 1972-77; prof. medicine, cardiology Cook County (Ill.) Hosp. Grad. Sch., from 1958; mem. staff and bd. of dirs. Miami Heart Inst., Miami Beach, Fla., from 1976, also hon. attending physician in cardiology; mem. staff Edgewater hosp., Chgo., from 1947, pres., 1967-69, bd. dirs., 1969-73, dir. cardiology, 1965-73; mem. staff, v.p. Weiss Meml. Hosp., Chgo., 1955-71; cons. in cardiology Forkosh Meml. Hosp., Chgo., from 1950. Served as capt. M.C., AUS, 1944-45. Diplomate Am. Bd. Internal Medicine, also Sub-Bd. Cardiology. Fellow Am. Coll. Cardiology (sec. Chgo. roundtable 1963), ACP, Am. Coll. Chest Physicians, Am. Assn. Bioanalysts; mem. Ill. Soc. Med. Research, Am. Heart Assn. (fellow Council Clin. Cardiology), Ill. Heart Assn., Chgo. Heart Assn., Am. Heart Assn. of Greater Miami (bd. dirs. from 1975), Chgo. Diabetes Assn., Am., Ill., Chgo., Dade County (Fla.) med. assns., N.Y. Acad. Scis., Fla. Soc. Internal Medicine, AAAS, Brain Research Found. Guest editor symposia Med. Clinics of N.Am., Jan. and Mar. issues, 1980; contbr. numerous articles to med. jours. Died Apr., 1986, buried Chgo.

CALLIS, HAROLD BAKER, hotel executive; b. Indpls., Nov. 14, 1892; s. Theodore O. and Genevieve (Baker) C.; m. Blanche Cole, May 17,1919 (dec.); children: Edward Cole, Harold Baker, Robert Henry; m. 2d, Doris C. Huseman, June 4, 1956. Student, Ohio Wesleyan U., 1911-12. With Hotel Statler, Detroit, 1915-17, mem. exec. office staff, 1919—; asst. sec. Hotels Statler Co. Inc., 1923-37, in chg. purchases, 1933, v.p. in charge maintenance, 1937, v.p., sec., dir., 1945-54, sr. v.p., 1951-54; organized Statler Studios Inc., 1939; in charge plans and constrn. Hotel Statler, Washington, 1943, Los Angeles, 1952, Hartford, Conn., 1954; in charge plans and constrn. Conrad Hilton opening, Dallas, 1955; mng. dir. Statler Found., N.Y.C.; hotel cons.; made study of tourism and hotels in Israel for Govt. Israel; cons. hotel properties, Copenhagen, London, Rome, Athens. Trustee, mayor Munsey Park, 1933-35. 1st lt. U.S. Army, World War I. Mem. Am. Legion, Cornell Soc. Hotelmen, Ye Hosts Hotel Frat., Engineers Club (trustee N.Y.C.); The Family Club (San Francisco): Ye Hosts Square Club, North Hempstead Country Club, Phi Gamma Delta. Mem. Christ Ch. Home: New York N.Y. †

CALLMANN, RUDOLF, lawyer; b. Cologne, Germany, Sept. 29, 1892; came to U.S., 1936; naturalized, 1943; s. Max and Claire (Meyer) C.; m. Marie Hess, Apr. 19, 1919 ; 1 dau., Ellen. LL.D., U. Frieburg, Germany, 1920; LL.B., Harvard U. (rsch. fellowship), 1939. Pvt. practice Cologne, Germany, 1926-36; pvt. practice specializing in law unfair competition, trade marks, copyrights and anti-trust N.Y.C., 1943—; hon. prof. law U. Cologne, 1959. Author: The Law of Unfair Competition and Trade Marks, 5 vols., 1945, 2d edit., 1950. Mem. Am., N.Y. State and N.Y.C. bar assns., Am. Assn. Internat. Law, N.Y. Patent Law Assn., U.S. Trade Mark Assn. Home: Kew Gardens N.Y. †

CALMER, NED, author, journalist; b. Chgo., July 16, 1907; s. Henry Edgar and May (Regan) C.; m. Priscilla A. Hatch, Mar., 1929; 1 dau., Alden; m. Carol Church, Aug. 1957, 1 son, Regan; m. Gloria F. Hercik, Oct. 1974. Student, U. Va., 1930. Reporter, fgn. corr. Paris edits. Chgo. Tribune and N.Y. Herald-Tribune, 1927-34; fgn. news editor in N.Y. for Agence Havas, France, 1934-40; news editor, broadcaster CBS, 1940-67; war corr. with U.S. armed forces Eng., France, Belgium, Germany, Holland, Italy, 1944-45; Mediterrenean corr. 1951-53; reporter, corr. You Are There, 1955; broadcaster CBS Views the Press; anchor CBS World News Roundup. Author: Beyond the Street, 1934, When Night Descends, 1936, The Strange Land, 1950, All the Summer Days, 1961, The Anchorman, 1970, The Avima Affair, 1973, Late Show, 1974, Madam Ambassador, 1975, The Peking Dimension, 1976, Bay of Lions, The Winds of Montauk, 1980; creator documentaries (TV show) See It Now. Club: Players. Home: Lawrence N.Y. Died Mar. 9, 1986; buried Trinity-St. Johns Churchyard, Hewlett, N.Y.

CALVERT, ROBERT S., state official; b. Tex., Apr. 27, 1892; s. Cleon H. and Sallie (Neff) C.; m. Josie Moody, Mar. 24, 1920; 1 child, Josephine (Mrs. Leonard Baker). Student, Howard Payne Coll., 1909. Asst. cashier 1st Nat. Bank Sweetwater, Tex., 1917-30; statistician for state compt. State of Tex., Austin, 1930-44, chief clk., 1944-49, state compt., from 1949; bd. dirs. Fedn. Tax Adminstrs. With U.S. Army, World War I. Named Man of Yr. Howard Payne Coll., 1957. Mem. VFW, SAR, Am. Legion, Son. Confederacy, Nat. Assn. State Auditors, Compts. and Treas., Nat. Tax Assn., Austin C. of C., Masons, Lions. Mem. Christian Ch. Home: Austin Tex. †

CAMACHO FLORES, FELIXBERTO, bishop; b. Agana, Guam, Jan. 13, 1921. Ordained priest Roman Catholic Ch., 1949; apptd. apostolic adminstr. Diocese of Agana, Guam, 1969; apptd. titular bishop of Stonj 1970, consecrated bishop of Agana, 1970, apptd. 1st archbishop, 1984. Deceased.

CAMERON, CHARLES FRANKLIN, electrical engineer; b. Enid, Okla., Jan. 22, 1898; s. William J. and Carrie (Nelson) C.; m. Helen Fash, June 28, 1920 (dec. 1950); children: Jean Cameron Levy, Joanna Cameron Pipkin; m. Eleanor Drummond Hanna, 1951 (dec. 1969); m. Mildred Faye Nelson, Oct. 11, 1975. Diploma, Northwestern state Coll., Okla., 1919; student, U. Okla., 1920-21; BS, Okla. A&M Coll., 1923, BEE, 1936; MSE, Purdue U., 1939; postgrad., Iowa State Coll., summers 1927, 29, 30, Colo. Agrl. Coll., 1928. Instr. electronics high sch., Rock Springs, Wyo., 1923-28, dir. insdl. edn., 1928-41; dir. war tng. trade sch., 1941; asst. prof. elec. engring. Okla. State U., Stillwater, 1941-44, assoc. prof., 1944-47, prof. elec. engring. specializing in power machinery, 1947-51, Rsch. prof. elec. engring., 1951-63, prof. emeritus, from 1963, acting head Sch. Elec. Engring., 1959-61; cons. engr.; cons. electric projects; researcher electromagnetic relays; v.p. Internat. Conf. Electromagnetic Relays, 1963, chmn. com., 1965; vis. prof.elec. engring. Assiut U., Egypt. Author engring. dept. sta. bulls., sci. articles. Mem. IEEE, Am. Soc. Engring. Edn., NSPE, Okla. Soc. Profl. Engrs., Acacia, Sigma Xi, Eta Kappa Nu, Sigma Tau. Republican. Home: Stillwater Okla. Died July 23, 1988, buried Capron, Okla.

CAMERON, RICHARD RAY, psychiatrist; b. Wheeling, W.Va., Sept. 17, 1910; s, Albert Ernest and Zoe Shockley (Barker) C.; m. Ellen Irene Jones, Mar. 2, 1935; children: Richard Douglas, Bonnie Jean, Bruce Robin, Heather Anne, Scott Kenneth. BA, W.Va. U., 1932; MD, Jefferson Med. Coll., 1936. Diplomate Am. Bd. Psychiatry and Neurology. Rotating intern George F. Geisinger Meml. Hosp., Danville, Pa., 1936-37; instr. pathology U. Ark. Sch. Medicine, 1937-38; commd. lt., M.C. U.S. Army, 1938, advanced through grades to col., 1954; assigned Philippines, 1945-46; resident in psychiatry Fitzsimons Army Hosp., 1948-51, chief dept. psychiatry, 1951-52; asst. chief psychiat. cons. div. Office Surgeon Gen., U.S. Army, 1952-53; sr. resident neurology Walter Reed Army Hosp., 1953-54; chief psychiatry and neurology service Ft. Dix, N.J., 1954-55; chief psychiat. service Brooke Army Hosp., Ft. Sam Houston, Tex., 1955-56, chief dept. neuropsychiatry, 1956-58; ret. U.S. Army, 1958; clin. dir. Mental Health Inst., Independence, Iowa, 1958-59; pvt. practice Cedar Rapids, Iowa, 1959-60; dir. psychiat. services for correctional and juvenile instns. Iowa Dept. Mental Health, 1960-61; profl. lectr. George Washington Sch. Medicine, 1952-53, 53-54; assoc. clin. prof. psychiatry U. Tex. Med. Sch. San Antonio, from 1970. Contbr. articles to profl. jours. Fellow Am. Psychiat. Assn. (life); mem. Phi Beta Kappa, Delta Phi Alpha, Alpha Kappa Kappa, Kappa Beta Phi. Home: San Antonio Tex. Died Nov. 27, 1985; buried Ft. Sam Houston Nat. Cemetery.

CAMP, WOFFORD BENJAMIN, farmer; b. Gaffney, S.C., Mar. 14, 1894; s. John Clayton and Mary Jane (Atkins) C.; m. Georgia Anna App, December, 14, 1921 (dec.); children: Wofford Benjamin, Donald Max; m. Louise Phifer Wise, Jan. 18, 1956; children: Addie Louise Segars, George W. Wise, Sarah Cory. B.S., Clemson Agrl. Coll., 1916; Dr. Agrl. Industries (hon.), 1951; postgrad., U. Calif.; LL.D., Limestone Coll., 1955, Whittier Coll., 1958; H.H.D., Gardner-Webb Coll., 1974. Head coop. testing field crops U.S. Dept. Agr., S.C., 1916-17; founder cotton San Joaquin Valley, Calif., 1917; agronomist charge cotton breeding and growing expts. San Joaquin Valley, others, 1917-28; established, charge U.S. Expt. Sta., Shafter, Calif., 1922-28; head agr. appraiser Bank of Am. Nat. Trust & Savs. Assn., 1929; mgr. Calif. Lands, Inc., Bank Am. subsidiary, 1929-33; head agrl. economist, asst. dir. cotton div. and So. region A.A.A., Washington, 1933-36; pres., owner Georgianna Farms, Inc., 1937-45; pres. W.B. Camp & Sons, Inc., from 1946; co-owner Calolina Farms and; Calolina Cotton Ginning Co.; founder Calif. Cotton Planting Seed Distbrs.; co-founder Calif. Cotton Coop. Assn.; Mem. com. on conservation and devel. soil and water resources U.S. Dept. Agr.; bd. dirs. Nat. Indsl. Conf. Bd. Author: Calif. One-variety Cotton law; Author several agrl. bulls.; Contbr. articles to mags., newspapers. Founder W.B. Camp Found. (scholarship); bd. dirs. Nat. Rivers and Harbors Congress, co-chmn. com. conversions and uses saline water; trustee Bur. Water Resources, S.C. Conservation Dists. Found., Whittier Coll., Freedom's Found., Valley Forge; exec. com. Religious Heritage Am.; bd. govs. Agrl. Hall of Fame and Nat. Center, also chmn. nat. devel. com.; mem. pres.'s bd. Pepperdine Coll.; mem. adv. bd. Sch. Bus., Am. U.; hon. life dir. Clemson U. Found. Recipient George Washington medal Freedoms Found. at Valley Forge, 1965; Calif. chpt. award Am. Soc. Agronomy, 1974; Agr. award Religious Heritage Am., 1975; Horatio Alger award, 1978; inducted into Order of Knights Hospitallers of St. John Knights of Malta, 1979; Right to Work Com. named its new bldg. in his and his wife's honor, 1980. Mem. Kern County Potato

Seed Assn. (founder, pres.), Nat. Potato Council (co-founder, v.p.), Asso. Farmers Calif. (past pres.), Kern County Mus. Assn., Am. Cancer Soc. (Kern County dir.), Crippled Children Soc. Calif., Farm Bur. U.S. C. of C. (v.p., treas., dir., chmn. agrl. com., chmn. vol. unionism com.), Farm Labor Research Com. (chmn.), Right to Work Com. (dir.), Blue Key, Phi Kappa Phi. Baptist. Clubs: Mason (San Francisco), Rotarian. (San Francisco), Commonwealth (San Francisco); California (Los Angeles); Capitol Hill (Washington). Died Aug. 1, 1986.

CAMPBELL, ALBERT ANGUS, social psychologist; b. Leiters, Ind., Aug. 10, 1910; s. Albert Alexis and Orpha (Brumbaugh) C.; m. Jean Winter, June 29, 1940; children: Bruce, Joan, Carol. BA, U. Oreg., 1931, MA, 1932; PhD, Stanford U., 1936. Instr. dept. psychology Northwestern U., Evanston, Ill., 1936-39; research fellow Social Sci. Research Council, 1939-40, asst. prof. psychology, 1940-42; asst. head div. program surveys U.S. Dept. Agr., 1942-46; assoc. prof. psychology and sociology U. Mich., Ann Arbor, 1946-49, prof., from 1949. Fellow Am. Acad. Arts and Scis.; mem. Am. Psychol. Assn., Am. Sociol. Assn., Am. Assn. Pub. Opinion Research, Soc. Psychol. Study Social Issues. Nat. Acad. Scis. Home: Ann Arbor Mich. Died Dec. 15, 1980.

CAMPBELL, ARCHIE JAMES, comedian, recording artist; b. Bulls Gap, Tenn., Nov. 7, 1914; m. Mary Lee Lewis; children: Stephen Archie, Phillip Edward Lee. Student, Mars Hill (N.C.) Coll. Appeared on Barn Dance and Mid-Day Merry-Go-Round, Knoxville, Tenn., 1936-37, Sta. WDOD, Chattanooga, 1937-41, Sta. WNOX, Knoxville, 1949, Sta. WATE-TV, Knoxville, 1952-58, Sta. WSM Grand Ole Opry, Nashville, from 1958; writer, performer TV Series Hee Haw, from 1969. Albums include: Bedtime Stories for Adults, Joker is Wild. Served with USN. Named Comedian of the Yr., Country Music Assn., 1969. Home: Bulls Gap Tenn. Died Aug. 29, 1987, buried Powell, Tenn.

CAMPBELL, C. WILLIAM, lawyer; b. Plumer, Pa., Nov. 3, 1891; s. George M. and Ella (Emery) C.; m. Edith Scharpf, June 20, 1918; 1 child, Virginia. AB, Grove City Coll., 1911, LLD, 1955; postgrad., U. Philippines, 1912-13; LLB, U. Pitts., 1916. Bar: Pa. 1916. Ptnr. Campbell, Thomas & Burke (name now Tucker, Burke, Campbell & Arensberg), from 1924; bd. dirs. emeritus N.Am. Rockwell Corp.; with mgmt. com. Coraopolis office Union Nat. Bank Pitts. Home: Pitts. Pa. †

CAMPBELL, GRETNA, painter; b. N.Y.C., Mar. 23, 1922; d. John and Gretna (Koppe) Campbell); m. Louis Finkelstein, Feb. 3, 1945; children—Martha, Henry. Student, Cooper-Union, 1939-43, Art Students League, 1943-45. One-woman shows, Pyramid Gallery, N.Y.C., 1947, 49, Artists' Gallery, N.Y.C., 1950, 52, 54, Zabriskie Gallery, N.Y.C., 1956-57, Green Mountain Gallery, 1970, 73, 75, Ingber Gallery, N.Y., 1976, 77, 78, 79, 80, 81, 85-86, N.Y. Studio Sch., 1977, 79, Wright State Mus., Dayton, Ohio, 1980, Rutgers U., 1985, Coll. William & Mary, 1987, numerous others, group shows include, Chgo. Art Inst., 1944, Mus. Modern Art, N.Y.C., 1945, Riverside Mus., N.Y.C., 1949, 52, Whitney Mus., 1949, 52, 54, Phila. Mus. Art, 1958, 62, 65, Bklyn. Mus., 1956, Pa. Acad., Phila., 1967, N.Y. Cultural Center, 1973, Fordham U., 1973, Ciba-Geigy Collection, 1972, Weatherspoon Gallery, 1974, Squibb Gallery, 1975, Maine State Mus., Augusta, 1976, Am. Acad. Arts and Letters, 1978, 87, Landmark Gallery, N.Y.C., 1980, 81, others; tchr., Phila. Coll. Art, 1963-71, N.Y. Studio Sch., 1971-73, 76-80, Md. Art Inst., 1972-73, Pratt Inst., 1980-81, Yale U., 1972-87, Nat. Acad., 1986, NAD, 1987; vis. artist, Ind. U., 1977, Wright State U., 1980, Jersey City Mus., 1982, NAD, 1982, Phila. Coll. Art, 1983, Nat. Inst. Arts and Letters, 1984, others. (Pearl Fund fellow 1946-49, Fulbright fellow), France, 1953-54 (Louis Comfort Tiffany Found. fellow 1952); elected assoc. Nat. Acad., 1987. Recipient Am. Acad. Arts & Letters awards, 1978, 87, NAD Altman prize, 1987, Ranger Fund purchase prize, 1987. Home: New York N.Y. Died July 14, 1987.

CAMPBELL, HARVEY J., association executive; b. Yale, Mich., Jan. 2, 1890; s. Hugh J. and Mina (Atkinson) C.; m. Mabel Emily Thosteson, June 3, 1909 (dec.); 1 dau., Ruth (Mrs. Wilfred D. Gmeiner). Hon. alumnus, U. Mich., 1949; LLD, Wayne State U., 1952; HHD, Lawrence Inst. Tech., 1953, Hillsdale Coll., 1959. With Detroit Photo-Engraving Co., 1905-15; ptnr. Apel-Campbell advt. designers, 1915-19; dir. Bd. of Commerce, 1919; with Greater Detroit Bd. Commerce, from 1922, exec. v.p., from 1940; bd. dirs. Evans Products Co., Ryerson & Haynes Inc. Treas. regional planning commn., Detroit Met. Area, 1948-49; dir. Detroit Zool. Soc., Great Lakes States Indsl Devel. Coun., Mich. Heart Assn., USO orgns. of Detroit, Boys' Club of Detroit, Detroit Symphony Soc.; trustee Detroit Civic Light Opera Assn., Mich. Colls. Found., Met. Detroit Bldg. Fund; trustee, exec. com. Nat. San. Found. Mem. Am. Speakers Bur., Am C. of C. Execs. (past dir.), St. Andrew's Soc., Automobile Old Timers, Masons, Economic Club (dir.), Detroit Athletic Club, Detroit Club, Recess Club, Adcraft Club (past pres.) The Players Club (past pres.), The Hundred Club, Orpheus Club (Detroit); Nat. Press Club (Washington). Home: Detroit Mich. †

CAMPBELL, JOSEPH, author, educator; b. N.Y.C., Mar. 26, 1904; s. Charles William and Josephine (Lynch) C.; m. Jean Erdman, May 5, 1938. Grad., Canterbury Sch., 1921; student, Dartmouth, 1921-22; A.B., Columbia, 1925, M.A., 1927; postgrad., U. Paris, 1927-28, U. Munich, 1928-29. Tchr. Canterbury Sch., 1932-33; mem. faculty dept. lit. Sarah Lawrence Coll., Bronxville, N.Y., 1934-72; lectr. Fgn. Service Inst. Dept. State, Washington, 1956-73, Columbia, 1959. Author: (with Jeff King, Maud Oakes) Where The Two Came to Their Father: A Navaho War Ceremonial, 1943, Grimm's Fairy Tales, Folkloristic Commentary, 1944, (with Henry Morton Robinson) A Skeleton Key to Finnegans Wake, 1944, The Hero with a Thousand Faces, 1949, The Masks of God, Vol. I, Primitive Mythology, 1959, Vol. II, Oriental Mythology, 1962, Vol. III, Occidental Mythology, 1964, Vol. IV, Creative Mythology, 1968, The Flight of the Wild Gander, 1969, Myths To Live By, 1972, The Mythic Image, 1974, Historical Atlas of World Mythology, Vol. I. The Way of the Animal Powers, 1983, Vol. II, The Way of the Seeded Earth, 1987, The Inner Reaches of Outer Space, 1986; Editor: The Viking Portable Arabian Nights, 1952, Papers from the Eranos Yearbooks (vols. 1 to 6), 1954, 55, 57, 60, 64, 69, Myths, Dreams and Religion, 1970, Viking Portable Jung, 1972, (with Heinrich Zimmer) Myths and Symbols in Indian Art and Civilization, 1946, The King and the Corpse, 1948, Philosophies of India, 1951, The Art of Indian Asia, 1955; Contbr. articles to profl. publs. Pres. Creative Film Found., 1954-63, Found. for Open Eye, 1973-87; trustee Bollingen Found., 1960-69. Mem. Am. Inst. Arts and Letters, Soc. for Arts, Religion and Contemporary Culture (dir.), Am. Soc. Study Religion (pres. 1972-75), Am. Acad. Arts and Letters. Home: Honolulu Hawaii. Died Oct. 30, 1987; buried Honolulu.

CAMPBELL, LESLIE HARTWELL, college president; b. Buie's Creek, N.C., Apr. 3, 1892; s. James Archibald and Cornelia (Pearson) C.; m. Viola Haire, 1914 (dec.); 1 child, Arthur Hartwell; m. 2d, Ora Green; children: Catherine McLean, Elizabeth Pearson, Ora Green, James Archibald. AB, Wake Forest Coll., 1911, AM, 1916, LLD (hon.), 1955; student summer sch., U. N.C., 1912-26, Columbia U., 1913, 24. Began as tchr. Buie's Creek Acad., 1911; dean Campbell Coll., 1926-34, pres., 1934-67, pres. emeritus, from 1967. Moderator Little River Bapt. Assn., 1937-54; v.p. Bapt. State Conv., 1940; pres. Harnett County Centennial Assn., 1955; bd. dirs. Good Hope Hosp., Erwin, N.C.; pres. Eastern N.C. Colls. Inc., from 1966. Mem. Harnett County Hist. Soc. (pres. 1956), Civic Club. Democrat. Home: Buies' Creek N.C. †

CAMPBELL, ROBERT ARGYLL, economics educator; b. Gurnee, Ill., Nov. 20, 1879; s. JAmes and Mary (Doak) C.; m. Harriet Josephine Imhoff, Feb. 7, 1912; 1 child, Jean Doak (Mrs. T. F. Schreier). AB, U. Wis., 1906. Asst. U. Wis., 1906-08, fellow, 1909-10; fellow Cornell U., 1908-09; libr. Legis. Reference Libr., Calif., 1910-11; sec. Wis. State Bd. Pub. Affairs, 1911-14; researcher Alexander Hamilton Inst., 1914-15; lectr. Cornell U., 1915-19; prof. econs. Rochester U., 1919-22; with Inst. of Econs., Washington, 1923-27; head dept. econs. Vanderbilt U., 1927-40, prof. econs., 1940-49, prof. emeritus, from 1949; vis. prof. econs. George Pepperdine Coll., 1950-59. Mem. Scorpion, Artus, Pi Delta Epsilon, Omicron Delta Kappa. Home: Los Angeles Calif. †

CAMPBELL, ROBERT ERLE, business executive; b. Storm Lake, Iowa, Mar. 13, 1888; s. John and Minna (Bentley) C.; m. Dorothy Tibbets Miller, June 27, 1912; children: Robert E., John M., Dorothy Campbell Hurtz. BS, U. Nebr., 1910. Asst. to gen. mgr. sales Nat. Electric Lamp div. GE Co., Cleve., 1910-15; sec., gen. mgr. Miller & Paine, Lincoln, Nebr., 1915-38, later chmn. bd.; chmn. bd. 1st Trust Co. (merged with Nat. Bank Commerce), Lincoln, 1956-61; bd. dirs. Omaha br. Fed. Res. Bank Kansas City, 1934-41, Security Mut. Life Ins. Co., Lincoln Devel. Co. Mem. Lincoln City Council, 1937-41; mayor of Lincoln, 1940-41; chmn. bd. commrs. Housing Authority, Lincoln, 1946-52; mem. exec. com. Nebr. Resources Found., from 1947; pres. Lincoln Community Chest, 1931, U. Nebr. Found.; trustee Cooper Found. Mem. U.S. C. of C. (bd. dirs. 1937-40), Lincoln C. of C. (pres. 1929), Nebr. Reclamation Assn., Nat. Retail Dry Goods Assn., Nat. Better Bus. Bur., U. Nebr. Alumni Assn. (pres. 1925), Country Club Lincoln, University Club, Masons, Alpha Tau Omega, Beta Gamma Sigma, Alpha Kappa Psi. Republican. Presbyterian. Home: Lincoln Nebr. Deceased.

CAMPBELL, ROLLA DACRES, lawyer; b. Huntington, W.Va., Jan. 5, 1895; s. Charles William and Jennie Elena (Ratliff) C.; m. Ruth Cammack, Jan. 1, 1918 (dec. Sept. 23, 1979); children: Rolla Dacres, William C.; m. Patience McNulty, June 8, 1980. B.A., Harvard, 1917, J.D. cum laude, 1920. Practice law 1920-87; sr. partner firm Campbell, Woods, Bagley, Emerson, McNeer and Herndon (and predecessors), 1935-87; pres., dir. Dingess-Rum Coal Co., Huntington, chmn. bd., 1985-87; pres., dir. C.W. Campbell Co.; v.p. dir. Caldwell-Campbell Co.; v.p., dir. D-R Stores, Inc.; gen. and cons. counsel Island Creek Coal Co., and affiliated cos., 1935-62; founder, pres., dir. Nat. Council Coal Lessors, Inc., Washington, 1951-71. Mem. editorial bd.: Harvard Law Rev. (vol. 33), 1919-20. Mem. ABA (past chmn. natural resources sect., past mem. ho. of dels.). Episcopalian. Clubs: D.U. (Harvard Coll.), Inst. of 1770 (Harvard Coll.), Speakers (Harvard Coll.), Varsity (Harvard Coll.); Guyan Golf and Country (Huntington), City (Huntington); Everglades (Palm Beach, Fla.), Beach (Palm Beach, Fla.), Governor's (Palm Beach, Fla.), Bath and Tennis (Palm Beach, Fla.). Home: Palm Beach Fla. Died Apr. 15, 1987, buried Huntington, W.Va.

CAMPBELL, ROY E(LLIOTT), entomologist; b. Orange, Calif., Mar. 31, 1890; s. David Frank and Julia Ferris (Shaw) C.; m. Florence Marie Gitchell, Mar. 19, 1914. BS, U. Calif., 1913, MS, 1925; student, U. Minn., 1930. Asst. in entomology U. Calif., 1914; sci. asst. Bur. Entomology and Plant Quarantine, USDA, 1914-21, assoc. entomologist, 1921-29; entomologist charge field sta. Bur. Entomology and Plant Quarantine, USDA, Alhambra, Calif., 1929-51; entomologist charge field sta. for entomology rsch. br. USDA, Whittier, Calif., from 1952. Pres. Alhambra Community Chest, 1938; dir., 1939-47. Mem. AAAS, Entomol. Soc. Am., Ecol. Soc. Am., Am. Assn. Econ. Entoniologist (pres. 1951), chmn. Pacific slope br., 1931, sec. 1924-30, 1939-50), Rotary (pres. 1933), Entomological Club of So. Calif. (pres. 1928, sec. 1940-51), Alpha Zeta, Phi Sigma, Gamma Alpha, Phi Sigma Kappa. Republican. Presbyterian. Home: Whittier Calif. †

CAMPBELL, SAMUEL JONES, printer, publisher; b. Mt. Carroll, Ill., June 18, 1892; s. Robert H. and Susan (Miles) C.; m. Ileen Bullis, Oct. 10, 1914. AB, Stanford, 1914; LLD, Lincoln Meml. U., 1939, Beloit (Wis.) Coll., 1963. Pres. First Carroll County State Bank, Mt. Carroll, 1914-29; ptnr. Blake Bros. Co., Chgo., 1929-30; treas. Kable Bros. Co., Mt. Morris, Ill., 1929-35; then chmn. Kable News Co., Mt. Morris; mem. policy holders exam. com. Northwestern Mutual Life Ins. Co., 1953-54; chmn. bd. Catalina Savs. & Loan Assn., Tucson; dir. Lumbermens Mut. Casualty Co., Am. Farmers Mutual Ins. Co., Fed. Mut. Ins. Co., Economy Fire & Casualty Co.; dir., mem. exec. com. Fidelity Life Assn.; adv. bd. Ill. Mfrs. Ins. Co. Dist. chmn. WPB, 1945-46; hon. trustee Shimer Coll.; life trustee, chmn. bd. trustees Beloit Coll.; bd. dirs. Grant Hosp., Chgo., U. Ariz. Found., So. Ariz. Heart Found., Hosp. Planning Coun. Greater Tucson Inc.; trustee Grand Central Art Galleries, N.Y.C., Amerind Found., Dragoon, Ariz.; adv. coun. Pres.'s Club, U. Ariz. Lt. comdr. USNR, 1942-45. Mem. Newcomen Soc. N.Am., Chgo. Club, Exec. Club, Tavern Club, Casino Club, Union League, Univ. Club (Chgo.), N.Y. Athletic Club, Old Pueblo Club, Tucson Country Club, Mountain Oyster Club (Tucson), Tucson Nat. Golf Club. Home: Tucson Ariz. also: Mount Carroll Ill. †

CAMPBELL, STUART BLAND, JR., lawyer; b. Wytheville, Va., July 30, 1916; s. Stuart Bland and Mary (Miles) C.; m. Janet Reed Sutherland, Aug. 14, 1953; children: Stuart Bland III, Arthur Reed, Martha Miles. AB, Presbyn. Coll., Clinton, S.C., 1937; LLB, U. Va., 1941. Bar: Va. 1940. Ptnr. Campbell & Campbell, 1941-42; sec. State Dept. Bd. Appeals on Visa Cases, 1942-44; div. dir. UNRRA Greece Mission, 1944-47; U.S. fgn. service officer 1949-53; ptnr. Campbell, Young & Crewe (and predecessors), Wytheville, Va., from 1953; mem. adv. bd., bd. dirs. Wytheville br. 1st Nat. Exchange Bank Va., 1971-87. Fellow Am. Coll. Trial Lawyers, Am. Bar Found.; mem, ABA, Am. Law Inst., Va. Bar Assn. Home: Wytheville Va. Died Sept. 3, 1987; buried Wytheville, Va.

CAMPBELL, WILLIAM J., judge; b. Chgo., Mar. 19, 1905; s. John and Christina (Larsen) C.; m. Marie Agnes Cloherty, 1937; children—Marie Agnes (Mrs. Walter J. Cummings), Karen Christina (Mrs. James T. Reid), Heather Therese (Mrs. Patrick Henry), Patti Ann (Mrs. Peter V. Fazio, Jr.), Roxane (Mrs. Wesley Sedlacek), William J., Christian Larsen, Thomas John. J.D., Loyola U., 1926, LL.M., 1928, LL.D., 1955; LL.D., Lincoln Coll., 1960; Litt.D., Duchesne Coll., 1965; J.C.D., Barat Coll., 1966. Bar: Ill. 1927. Partner Campbell and Burns, Chgo., 1927-40; Ill. adminstr. Nat. Youth Adminstrn., 1935-39; U.S. dist atty. No. Dist. Ill., 1938-40; judge U.S. Dist. Ct., 1940-88; chief judge No. Dist. Ill., 1959-70; Mem. Jud. Conf. U.S., 1958-62; chmn. Jud. Conf. Commn. Budget, 1960-70; asst. dir., chmn. seminars Fed. Jud. Center, 1971-88. Mem. nat. exec. bd. Boy Scouts Am., 1934-88, mem. regional exec. com., 1937-88; mem. exec. bd. Chgo. council, 1930-88; Trustee Barat Coll., Lake Forest, Ill.; mem. citizens bd. U. Chgo., Loyola U., Chgo.; bd. dirs. Cath. Charities Chgo. Recipient award of merit Citizens of Greater Chgo., 1966; named Chicagoan of Year, 1965; Lincoln laureate in law State of Ill., 1970; Devitt Disting. Service to Justice award, 1986. Clubs: Ill. Athletic (Chgo.), Union League (Chgo.), Standard (Chgo.), Mid-America (Chgo.); La Coquille (Palm Beach, Fla.). Home: Manalapan Fla. Died Oct. 19, 1988.

CAMPBELL, WILLIAM STUART, glass company executive; b. Chatham, Ont., Can., June 1, 1927; s. William S. and Mary (Shannon) C.; m. Della Huff, Sept. 15,

1951; 1 dau., Amy Victoria. M.T.C., U. Western Ont., 1966. With Imperial Bank of Commerce, Chatham, Ont.; div. mgr. Rockwell Internat., Chatham; v.p., gen. mgr. plastics Rockwell Internat., Toronto, Ont.; v.p., gen. mgr. metals Consumers Glass Co. Ltd., Toronto; exec. v.p. corp. mktg. and devel. Consumers Glass Co. Ltd., Etiobicoke, Ont., Can., from 1970; dir. Dennison Mfg. Ltd., 1982-83; mem. Ont. Bus. Adv. Coun. Pres. Licensing Exec. Soc., Inc., U.S.A., Can., 1982-83; mem. exec. council Toronto Bd. Trade, 1980-83, immediate past pres.; pres. Toronto Area Indsl. Devel. Bd., 1981-83; v.p. On. C. of C., 1978-81; chmn. Econ. Com. Met. Toronto, 1982-83. Recipient CanPlast Leadership award Soc. Plastics Ins., 1980. Mem. SAE, Licensing Execs. Soc. Conservative Party. Anglican. Club: Rotary (dir. 1976-77). Deceased.

CAMPION, DONALD RICHARD, editor, publisher; b. Bklyn., Aug. 29, 1921; s. Richard Michael and Josephine (Gayne) C. AB, St. Louis U., 1945, PhL, 1946, MA, 1949; STL, Woodstocxk (Md.) Coll., 1953; PhD, U. Pa., 1960. Joined Soc. of Jesus, 1939, ordained priest Roman Cath. Ch., 1952. Tchr. Xavier High Sch., N.Y.C., 1946-47; instr. LeMoyne Coll., Syracuse, N.Y., 1947-49; assoc. editor America, 1957-65, editor-in-chief, 1968-75; nat. dir. self-evaluation Soc. of Jesus, 1965-68; editor Catholic Mind, 1968-75; dir. info. Soc. of Jesus, Rome, 1976-78; sec. for info. and communications Jesuit Conf., Washington, 1978-88; lectr. Woodstock Coll., Inst. Religious and Social Studies, Union Theol. Sem., Fordham U. Contbr. to numerous books. Mem. adv. bd. Vera Found., 1962-64; trustee, sec. bd. Fordham U., 1966-78, 80-88; trustee Woodstock Coll., 1968-88, Holy Cross Coll., 1969-76, Boston Coll., 1980-88; bd. dirs. Appeal of Conscience Found., 1971-88, Inst. Religious and Social Studies, 1970-88. Mem. Am., Am. Cath. sociol. assns., Religious Edn. Assn. (bd. dirs. 1964-88), Coun. Religion and Internat. Affairs (bd. dirs. 1970-88). Home: Washington D.C. Died Dec. 11, 1988.

CANADAY, JOHN EDWIN, writer, art critic; b. Ft. Scott., Kans., Feb. 1, 1907; s. Franklin and Agnes F. (Musson) C.; m. Katherine S. Hoover, Sept. 19, 1935; children: Rudd Hoover, John Harrington. BA, U. Tex., 1929; MA, Yale U., 1933. Tchr. art history, dept. architecture U. Va., 1938-50; head sch. art Newcomb Coll. Tulane U., New Orleans, 1950-52; chief div. edn. Phila. Mus. Art, 1953-59; art critic N.Y. Times, 1959-77; vis. prof. U. Tex.-Austin, 1977. Author: (24 portfolios) The Metropolitan Seminars In Art, Mainstreams of Modern Art, 1959, Embattled Critic, 1962, Culture Gulch: Notes on Art and Its Public in the 1960's, 1969, (with Katherine H. Canaday) Keys to Art: Lives of the Painters, 4 vols., Baroque Painters, 1972, Late Gothic to Renaissance Painters, 1972, Neo-Classic to Post-Impressionist Painters, 1972, Artful Avocado, 1973, What is Art, 1981; 7 mystery novels under pseudonym Matthew Head. With USMCR, 1944-45. Home: New York N.Y. Died July 19, 1985.

CANFIELD, CASS, publishing company executive; b. N.Y.C., Apr. 26, 1897; s. August Cass and Josephine (Houghteling) C.; m. Katharine Emmet, May 24, 1922; children: Cass, Michael Temple; m. Jane White Fuller, May 27, 1938 (dec.). Student, Groton Sch., 1909-15; AB, Harvard, 1919; postgrad., Oxford U., Eng., 1919-20; LLD (hon.), Wagner Coll. With Harris Forbes & Co., 1921-22, N.Y. Evening Post, 1922-23, Fgn. Affairs, 1923-24; mgr. London office Harper & Bros., 1924-27, with N.Y.C. office, 1927-62; chmn. exec. com. and Harper editorial bd. Harper & Row, N.Y.C., 1962-67, sr. editor, from 1967; hon. chmn. Harpers Mag., Inc., 1965-75. Author: The Publishing Experience, 1969, Up and Down and Around, 1971, The Incredible Pierpont Morgan, 1974, Samuel Adams' Revolution, 1976, The Iron Will Of Jefferson Davis, 1978, Outrageous Fortunes, 1981, The Six, 1983. Chmn. exec. com. Planned Parenthood Fedn. Am.-World Population Emergency Campaign, 1962-67; chmn. governing body Internat. Planned Parenthood Fedn., 1963-69, hon. chmn., 1969-86; trustee Woodrow Wilson Fellowship Found.; mem. N.Y. State Coun. on Arts, 1960-64; mem. bd. Econ. Warfare, Washington, 1942-43; spl. adviser to Am. ambassador, London, in charge Econ. Warfare div.; dir. O.W.I., France, 1945. 2d lt. World War I. Recipient Albert Lasker award. Mem. Am. assn. UN (dir.), Nat. Assn. Book Pubs. (pres. 1932-34), Century Assn., Phi Beta Kappa (hon.). Home: Bedford Village N.Y. Died Mar. 27, 1986.

CANFIELD, FAYETTE CURTIS, drama educator; b. Bridgeport, Conn., July 29, 1903; s. Andrew A. and Elizabeth M.C.V. (O'Connor) C.; m. Katherine Fitz Randolph Newbold, May 21, 1927; 1 child, Sylvia Huntington Canfield Winn. AB, Amherst Coll., 1925; MA (hon.), Yale U., 1954; LHD (hon.), Amherst Coll., 1955; LLD (hon.), Emerson Coll., 1956. Instr. dramatics Amherst Coll., 1927, prof., 1938, Stanley King prof. dramatic arts, 1952-54, dir. Kirby Meml. Theatre, 1938-54; prof. drama, chmn. dept., dir. Univ. Theatre Yale U., New Haven, Conn., 1954-65, 1st dean drama sch., 1955-65; prof. drama U. Pitts., 1965-73. Author: The Seed and the Sowers, 1955, Plays of the Irish Renaissance 1929, Plays of Changing Ireland, 1936, The Craft of Play Directing, 1963. Trustee Am. Shakespeare Festival Theatre and Acad., 1963-86. Served as lt. comd. USNR, World War II. Home: Amherst Mass. Died June 8, 1986, buried Wildwood Cemetery, Amherst.

CANFIELD, JANE WHITE, sculptor; b. Syracuse, N.Y., Apr. 29, 1897; d. Ernest Ingersol and Katharine Curtin (Sage) White; m. Charles F. Fuller, Sept. 9, 1922; children: Jane Sage Fuller Cowles, Isabel Fuller Fox, Blair Fuller; m. Cass Canfield, May 27, 1938. Student, N.Y. Art Students League, 1918-20, Borglum Sch., 1920-22. Exhibited one-artist shows: Am.-Brit. Art Gallery, N.Y.C., 1951, County Art Gallery, Westbury, L.I., N.Y., 1960, FAR Gallery, N.Y.C., 1965; exhibited World's Fair, 1939, Archtl. League, Knoedler Gallery, Am. Acad.; executed figure for ch., Locust Valley, N.Y., figures for Miss Porter's Sch., Farmington, Conn., six figures Paul Mellon estate; author: The Frog Prince, 1970, Swan Cove, 1977. Chmn. bd. dirs. Bedford-Rippowam Sch., 1933-38; bd. dirs. ARC Arts and Skills, Washington, 1942-45, Planned Parenthood, 1945-55, Internat. Planned Parenthood, 1955-65, Margaret Sanger Bur., 1965-84, Swan Cove, 1978-84. Home: Bedford N.Y. Died May 23, 1984; buried St. Mathews Ch., Bedford, N.Y.

CANHAM, ROBERT ALLEN, association executive; b. Virden, Ill., Jan. 3, 1921; s. Howard Ambrose and Rhoda Ann (Hancline) C.; m. Margie Lu Bruton, Dec. 21, 1951 (dec. 1986); children—Patricia Canham Schuler, Robert Allen, Jane Canham Ritchie. B.S. in Civil Engring., Purdue U., 1942, M.S. (Nat. Polio Found. fellow), 1947. Registered profl. engr., Del., Ind.; diplomate Am. Acad. Environ. Engrs. Civil engr. M.W. Kellogg Co., 1942-47; san. engr. Nat. Canners assn., 1947-57; assoc. editor Water Pollution Control Fedn., Washington, 1957-64; asst. sec., editor Water Pollution Control Fedn., 1964-69, exec. dir., 1969-86; cons. 1987-88; adj. prof. san. engring. Howard U., Washington, 1967-88; cons. food canning industry, 1957-88; cons. USPHS, 1962-65; mem. adv. group U.S. Geol. Service, 1957-88, EPA, 1971-76. Editor Jour. Water Pollution Control Fedn., 1957-69; contbr. articles to profl. jours. Pres., P.T.A., 1966; treas. Fairfax County Council P.T.A.'s, 1970-88; citizen adviser Fairfax County Sch. Bd., 1968-88. Served to lt. (j.g.) USNR, 1944-46. Recipient Environ. award Assn. Met. Sewerage Agys., 1987. Fellow Instn. Pub. Health Engrs. (U.K.) (hon.), Inst. Water Pollution Control (U.K.) (hon.); mem. Water Pollution Control Fedn. (hon.), ASCE, Am. Water Works Assn. (hon.), Va. Water Pollution Control Assn., Inter-Am. Assn. San. Engrs., Am. Acad. Environ. Engrs. (Gordon M. Fair medal 1987), Internat. Assn. Water Pollution Research, New Zealand Water Supply and Disposal Assn. (life), Sigma Nu. Methodist. Clubs: Cosmos, Engrs. (Balt.). Home: Falls Church Va. Died May 1988; buried Ft. Lincoln Cemetery, Washington.

CANIFF, MILTON ARTHUR, cartoonist; b. Hillsboro, Ohio, Feb. 28, 1907; s. John William and Elizabeth (Burton) C.; m. Esther Parsons, Aug. 23, 1930. A.B., Ohio State U., 1930, L.H.D., 1974; LL.D. (hon.), Atlanta Law Sch.; A.F.D. (hon.), Rollins Coll., U. Dayton. Began as cartoonist summer 1921; successively on Dayton (Ohio) Jour.-Herald, Miami (Fla.) Daily News, Columbus (Ohio) Dispatch, A.P. Feature Service, N.Y.C., Chgo. Tribune-N.Y. News Syndicate, N.Y.C., 1934-46, King Features. Creator of Dickie Dare, Terry and the Pirates, Male Call, and Steve Canyon. Recipient Scroll of Merit Dayton Art Inst.; War Dept. citation for Male Call; Billy DeBeck Meml. award (now Reuben award), 1947; Disting. Service award Sigma Delta Chi, 1950; Freedoms Found. award, 1950; certificate of merit, 1953; Medal of Merit award Air Force Assn., 1952; Arts and Letters award, 1953; U.S. Treas. citation, 1953; Ohioana Career medal, 1954; USAF exceptional service award, 1957; Ohio gov.'s award, 1957; Silver Beaver award Boy Scouts Am., 1960; Silver Buffalo award, 1976; Silver medallion N.Y. World's Fair, 1964; Goodwill Industries award, 1965; N.Y. Philanthropic League award, 1965; Aerospace Edn. Council award, 1966; named Man of Yr. USAF Assn., 1966; YMCA Service-to-Youth award, 1966; Freedoms Found. Nat. Service medal, 1967; Freedoms Found. George Washington Honor medal, 1969; Distinguished Eagle award Boy Scouts Am., 1969; Elzie Segar Cartoon award, 1971; Second Reuben award, 1972; San Diego Inkpot award, 1974; 4th Estate award; Good Guy award Am. Legion, 1978; Spirit of Am. Enterprise award, 1981, Golden Brick award, 1981; named to Nat. Comic Strip Hall of Fame, 1981. Mem. Newspaper Features Council, Soc. Illustrators, Nat. Cartoonists Soc. (pres. 1948- 49, now hon. chmn., recipient Golden Scroll 1964), Air Force Assn., Arnold Air Soc. (hon. nat. comdr.), Exec. Order Ohio Commodores (charter), Air Force Assn. (Maxwell Kriendler Man of Yr. 1981, past pres. Iron Gate chpt.), Sigma Chi (Significant Sig 1940, Order of Constantine 1976), Sigma Delta Chi. Clubs: Players (N.Y.C.), N.Y. Press (N.Y.C.), Dutch Treat (N.Y.C.), Silurians (N.Y.C.); Nat. Press (Washington), Nat. Aviation (Washington). Home: New York N.Y. Died Apr. 3, 1988.

CANNON, ABRAM H., radiologist, educator; b. Salt Lake City, Nov. 30, 1915; s. Calude Qualye and Emily (Barnes) C.; m. Aino Sylvia Marsell, Mar. 30, 1942; children: James Qualye, Margaret Carol. BA, U. Utah, 1938; MD, Northwestern U., 1941. Assoc. radiologist Chgo. Wesley Meml. Hosp., 1949-50, chmn. dept., from 1950; mem. faculty, then assoc. prof. radiology Northwestern U. Med. Sch., from 1949. Served to maj. USAAF, 1942-46. Mem. AMA, Am. Roentgen Ray Soc., Radiol. Soc. N.Am., Am. Coll. Radiology. Home: Park Ridge Ill. Died Jan. 12, 1986.

CANNON, GEORGIUS YOUNG, architect; b. Salt Lake City, Mar. 6, 1892; s. George Quayle and Caroline (Young) C.; m. Phyllis Winder, Dec. 1, 1921 (dec. June 1953); 1 child, Dorothy Cannon Webb. Student, U. Utah, 1909-11; BArch, MIT, 1918. Mormon missionary Germany and Switzerland, 1911-14; office mgr. Wallace Neff, Pasadena, Calif., 1925-30; pvt. practice architecture Pasadena, 1935-41; with L.A. Shipyards, San Pedro, Calif., 1941-43; draughtsman 20th Century Fox Studio, Hollywood, Calif., 1943-45, MGM Studio, Hollywood, 1945-46; pvt. practice architecture Pasadena, 1946-53, Salt Lake City, 1953-75, ret., 1975. Archtl. adivser new Symphony Concert Hall and Fine Arts Ctr., Salt Lake City, 1976; mem. Salt Lake City Preservation Com.; area chmn. MIT Ednl. Council, 1955-65. 2d lt. U.S. Army, 1918. Recipient Merit Honor award U. Utah Emeritus Club. Fellow AIA (pres. Utah chpt. 1957-58, award of appreciation 1975), Utah Heritage Found. (life); mem. Am. Soc. Interior Designers, Alta Club, Alpha Tau Omega.

CANNON, PAUL ROBERTS, pathologist; b. Lexington, Ill., Aug. 25, 1892; s. William H. and Clara Belle (Roberts) C.; m. Joyce Tobin, Dec. 24, 1917; 1 child, Paul R. Student, Eureka (Ill.) Coll., 1911-13; AB, James Millikin U., 1915; PhD, U. Chgo., 1921; MD, Rush Med. Coll., 1925. Began as bacteriologist, 1915; instr. bacteriology U. Chgo., 1919-20, asst. prof. pathology, 1925-32, prof., 1932-57, chmn. dept., 1940-57; prof. pathology U. Miss., 1920-23; mem. com. on pathology, food protection com. NRC (mem. food nutrition bd. 1947-51); mem. Nat. Influenza Commn.; mem. Am. Bd. of Pathology, 1937-43. Chief editor AMA Archives of Pathology, 1954-64. Served as 1st lt. San. Corps, U.S. Army, WWI. Recipient Groedel medal Am. Coll. Cardiology, 1958. Mem. Am. Soc. Pathologists and Bacteriologists (pres. 1942-43), Assn. Immunologists (ex-pres.), Chgo. Pathol. Soc. (ex-pres.), Nat. Acad. Scis., Am. Soc. Exptl. Pathology (pres. 1946-47; Burdick award 1948), Tau Kappa Epsilon. Mem. Christian (Disciples) Ch. Home: Yorkville Ill. †

CANTEY, JAMES WILLIS, banker; b. Columbia, S.C., Mar. 3, 1917; s. J.M. and Elizabeth (Childs) C.; m. Nancy Moorer, Apr. 19, 1941; children—James Willis, Joseph Moorer, John Childs. B.A., U. S.C., 1938. With Columbia Outdoor Advt., Inc., 1945-58, pres., 1947-58, chmn. bd., from 1973; with Citizens & So. Nat. Bank S.C., Charleston, 1958-74; pres. Citizens & So. Nat. Bank S.C., 1960-71, chmn. bd., 1971-74, also dir.; dir. Liberty Life Ins. Co., Carolina Freight Carriers Corp., State-Record Newspaper, Standard Bldg. & Loan Assn., Charlotte br. Fed. Res. Bank, 1967-72. Chmn. S.C. Ports Authority, 1956-64. Served with inf. AUS, World War II. Decorated Silver Star (3), Bronze Star (4), Legion of Merit, Purple Heart; Croix de Guerre France). Mem. S.C. Bankers Assn. (pres. from 1966), Sigma Alpha Epsilon. Episcopalian. Club: Kiwanian. Home: Columbia S.C. Deceased.

CAPOTE, TRUMAN, author; b. New Orleans, Sept. 30, 1924; s. Joseph G. and Nina (Faulk) C. Author: Other Voices, Other Rooms, 1948, (short stories) Tree of the Night, 1949, Observations, 1949, Local Color, 1950, The Grass Harp, 1953, The Muses Are Heard, 1956, Breakfast at Tiffany's, 1958, Selected Writings, 1963, In Cold Blood, 1965, A Christmas Memory, 1966, (with H. Arlen) House of Flowers, 1968, Thanksgiving Visitor, 1969, Trilogy: An Experiment of Multimedia, 1971, The Dogs Bark: Private Places and Public People, 1973, Then It All Came Down: Criminal Justice Today Discussed by Police, Criminals and Correction Officers with Comments by Truman Capote, 1976, Music for Chameleons, 1980; contbr. short stories, non-fiction to nat. mags. Recipient O. Henry award for short story, 1946, 48, 51. Mem. Nat. Inst. Arts and Letters (creative writing award 1959). Home: New York N.Y. Died Aug. 25, 1984; cremated.

CARDOZO, MANOEL, historian, educator; b. Ribeiras, Pico, Azores, Dec. 24, 1911; came to U.S., 1915, naturalized, 1944; s. José Silveira and Rosalina Soares (de Sousa) C. BA, Stanford U., 1931, MA, 1934, PhD, 1939. Teaching asst. U. Calif., Berkeley, 1935-36; curator Oliveira Lima Library Cath. U. Am., Washington, from 1940, prof. history, 1954-78, head. dept., 1961-71; Smith-Mundt lectr. Portugal, 1958; lectr. in Am., Brazil, Portugal, Peru, Argentina, Azores; assoc. sec. gen. 1st Internat. Colloquium Luso-Brazilian Studies, Washington, 1950; participant Internat. Congress Hist. Socs., Moscow, 1970, San Francisco, 1975, Internat. Colloquium on 18th Century and Brazil, Brasilia, 1984; lectr. on tour of Brazil, 1981, Mus. Diplomacy, Rio de Janeiro, 1984; guest lect. Alexandre de Gusmáo Found., Brasilia, 1984. Author: The Portugese in America, 590 B.C.—1974, A Chronology and Fact Book, 1976, numerous other hist. studies; translator Brazilian poetry; contbr. articles to profl. jours., encys. Decorated Chevalier Order So. Cross, Brazil; recipient Rio Branco medal Brazilian Fgn. Office, 1945, Benemerenti medal Holy See Cath. Ch., 1974; Inst. de Alta Cultura fellow, Lisbon, Portugal, 1936-38; grantee

Social Sci. Rsch. Council, Am. Philos. Soc., OAS, Inst. de Alta Cultura, Gulbenkian Found., 1984. Mem. Am. Cath Hist. Assn. (pres. 1962) Am. Hist. Assn., Soc. de Geografia (Lisbon), Inst. Histórico (Azores), Inst. Histórico Geográfica (São Paulo and São Luis do Marahhão), Inst. do Ceará, Cath. Commn. Intellectual and Cultural Affairs, Inter-Am. Council (pres. Washington 1964-65), Soc. Peruana de Historia. Home: Washington D.C. Died Dec. 14, 1985.

CAREY, HARVEY LOCKE, lawyer; b. Parkin, Ark., Jan. 19, 1915; s. Gregory and Willie Belle)Locke) C.; m. Katie Elizabeth Drew, Oct. 15, 1933 (div.); children: Richard Drew, Thomas Drew, Gregory, Katie Lucile; m. Nellie A. Deatherage, Apr. 14, 1956 (dec. Nov. 1957). Student, U. Ark., 1932-34, La. Poly. Inst., 1934-35; JD, Tulane U., 1939; postgrad., Dartmouth Coll., 1942, Princeton U., 1943. Bar: La. 1939, U.S. Dist. Ct. La. 1940, U.S. Ct. Appeals 1940, U.S. Supreme Ct 1943. Practice in Shreveport, La., from 1940; as Harvey L. Carey, Atty., from 1950; spl. asst. atty. gen. La. 1948, U.S. dist. atty. for Western Dist. La., 1950-52; spl. counsel Caddo Levee Bd., from 1948; judge ad hoc Shreveport City Ct., from 1968. Clk. La. Ho. of Reps., 1948-50; mem. Caddo Parish Dem. Exec. Com., 1948-50; candidate for U.S. rep. from La., 1948; ind. hearing officer La. Dept. Edn., from 1978. Lt. comdr. USNR, 1943-46. Mem. ABA, La. Bar Assn., Shreveport Bar Assn., Am. Judicare Soc., Assn. ICC Practitioners, Am. Legion, VFW, DAV, Mil. Order of Purple Heart (local comdr. 1949, state comdr. 1950, 56-57, nat. vice comdr. 1962-63), Phi Delta Phi, Sigma Phi Epsilon. Methodist. Home: Jamestown La. Died Jan. 8, 1984, buried Hill Crest Meml. Cemetery, Shreveport.

CARHART, ARTHUR HAWTHORNE, author, conservationist, landscape architect; b. Mapleton, Iowa, Sept. 18, 1892; s. George William and Ella Louise (Hawthorne) C.; m. Vera Amelia VanSickle, Aug. 16, 1918 (dec. Jan. 1966). BS, Iowa State Coll., 1916. On Midland Chautauqua Circuit 1916; recreational engr. U.S. Forest Service, Denver, 1919-22; mem. firm McCrary, Culley & Carhart, land architects and city planners, 1923-31; freelance writer 1931-38; co-ordinator Fed. Aid in Wildlife Restoration, Colo., 1938-43; regional information exec. O.P.A., 1944-46; cons. Conservation Collection Denver Pub. Libr. Author: Fresh Water Fishing, Fishing is Fun, Fishing in the West, 1950, Water-or-Your-Life, 1951, Son of the Forest, 1952, The Outdoorsman's Cookbook, 1955, Timber in Your Life, 1955, The National Forests, 1959, Planning America's Wildlands, 1961; editor: Conservation Please, 1950; contbr. articles to mags. Mem. Citizens com. for the ORRC Report (L. Rockefeller commn. report, from 1963; mem. com. Am. Motors Conservation Awards Program; trustee J.N. Darling Found.; bd. dirs. Desert Protective Coun. Ednl. Found. 1st lt. San. Corps., U.S. Army, 1917-19. Recipient Founders award Izaak Walton League Am., 1956, Conservation award Outdoor Writers Am. Assn., 1958; named Conservationist of Year, Am. Forest Products Industries, 1966. Mem. Colo. Author's League (1st pres.), Outdoor Writers Am. Assn., Rocky Mountain Assn. Landscape Architects, Am. Forestry Assn. (hon. v.p. from 1963), Gamma Sigma Delta. Home: Denver Colo. †

CARLETON, JOHN WALKER, insurance company executive; b. Alameda, Calif., July 8, 1914; s. Harry M. and Beulah (Potts) C.; m. Phoebe Rawles, Oct. 21, 1939; children: Catherine Carleton Washburn, Elizabeth Carleton Smith. With Fireman's Fund Idemnity Co., 1935-39, State Compensation Ins. Fund, San Francisco, 1939-41; with Liberty Mut. Ins. Co., 1941-79, v.p., 1955-68, sr. v.p., 1968-79, ret., 1979. Served with USNR, 1944-46. Fellow Casualty Actuarial Soc. Home: Annandale Va. Died Apr. 21, 1982; buried Oakland, Calif.

CARLIN, EDWARD AUGUSTINE, educator; b. Gardiner, N.Y., Sept. 21, 1916; s. Edward A. and Mary (Mulligan) C.; m. Eleanor Helen Bigos, Feb. 20, 1943; children—Mary Ellen, Edward Augustine. B.S., NYU, 1946, M.A., 1947, Ph.D., 1950. Instr. econs. and govt. Packard Bus. Coll., 1946-47; asst. prof. Mich. State U., 1947-51, asso. prof., 1952-56, asst. dean, prof., 1956, dean Univ. Coll., 1956-78, prof. econs., 1978-82, ret., 1982; cons. to Coll. Gen. Studies, U. Nigeria, 1961, 62. Co-editor: Curriculum Building in General Education, 1960; Contbr. numerous articles to profl. jours. Served to 1st lt., inf. AUS, 1942-46. Decorated Purple Heart. Mem. Am. Econ. Assn., Assn. Gen. and Liberal Studies (pres. 1963-64), Am. Acad. Polit. and Social Sci., AAUP, Pi Gamma Mu. Died Aug. 21, 1986; buried Holy Sepulchre Cemetery, Coram, New York.

CARLIN, LEO JOSEPH, lawyer; b. Grodno, Russia, Dec. 25, 1895; came to U.S., 1901, naturalized, 1906; s. Joseph and Rachel (Carlin) C.; m. Celia Cohn, Aug. 15, 1920; children: Florence E. (Mrs. Chester M. Epstein), Jerome Edward. Ph.B., U. Chgo., 1917, J.D., 1919; LL.D., Chgo. Med. Sch., 1969. Bar: Ill. 1919. Practiced in Chgo.; with firm Sonnenschein, Carlin, Nath & Rosenthal (and predecessors), 1919-87, ptnr., 1926-87. Hon. life dir. Mt. Sinai Hosp. (pres. 1955-58); trustee Chgo. Med. Sch. (vice chmn. bd.), Francis W. Parker Sch., all Chgo., Retina Found., Boston; founding pres., life trustee Five Hosp. Homebound Elderly Program, Chgo.; mem. exec. adv. bd. St. Joseph Hosp.; mem. vis. com. Div. Sch., U. Chgo., bd. of govs.; past pres. Anshe Emet synagogue; sustaining fellow Art Inst. of Chgo. Recipient nat. award for disting. service Jewish Theol. Sem. Am.; citation for pub. service U. Chgo.; Sundial award Eye Research Inst. of Retina Found.; Dr. Sol B. Kositchek Interfaith award Lake View Council on Religious Action. Mem. Am., Ill., Chgo. bar assns., Order of Coif, Phi Beta Kappa. Jewish. Clubs: Bryn Mawr Country (pres. 1941-43), Standard (pres. Chgo. 1952-54), Metropolitan, Carlton. Home: Chicago Ill. Died Nov. 17, 1987.

CARLSON, FRANK, U.S. senator; b. near Concordia, Kans., Jan. 23, 1893; s. Charles E. and Anna (Johnson) C.; m. Alice Frederickson, Aug. 26, 1919; children: Millard E. Ross (foster son), Eunice Marie Carlson Rolfs. Student, Kans. State Coll. Farmer, stockman from 1914; mem. Kans. State Legislature, 1929-33; served 6 terms as mem. U.S. Ho. Reps., Washington; gov. Kans., 1947; U.S. senator from 1951. Served U.S. Army, World War I. Mem. Am. Legion. Republican. Baptist. Lodge: Masons. Home: Concordia Kans. Died May 30, 1987.

CARLSON, WALTER, architect; b. Wilmington, Del., June 12, 1892; s. Oscar and Caroline (Peterson) C.; m. Esther Elizabeth Olson, Oct. 20, 1915; children: Milford Walter, Marion Elizabeth. Student, Drexel Inst., Phila., 1909-10. Draftsman, student architect's office, 1910-15; mem. staff engring dept. E. I. duPont Co., Wilmington, Del., 1915-22; practicing architect Raleigh, N.C., 1922-23; designer various archtl offices, Wilmington and Phila., 1923-27; practicing architect Wilmington, Del., from 1927; mem. firm Carlson and Fagnini, Wilmington; pres. Carlson-Denn, rsch, and mfr. new bldg. materials. Projects include large residences, comml. bldgs., hosps., schs., and indsl. plants. Recipient cert. of award Nat. Coun. Archtl. Registration Bds. Fellow AIA; mem. Del. Archtl. Registration Bd., Nat. Coun. Archtl. Registration Bds. Home: Wilmington Del. †

CARLSON, WILLIAM FITTS, college president; b. Bornholm, Denmark, Nov. 22, 1892; s. Frederick and Joanna F. (Stone) C.; m. Olga E. Abramson, Aug. 30, 1915 (dec. 1965); children: Paul E., F. Roy, Edward W.; m. 2d, Helen Scott, June 9, 1966. AB, Harvard, 1915; PhD, U. Louvain, 1948. Headmaster Milton (N.H.) Acad., 1916-18; head history dept. Brookline (Mass.) High Sch., 1918-22; headmaster Woodward Sem., Quincy, Mass., 1922-28; pres. Fuller Sch., Ossining, N.Y., 1928-34, Posse Coll., Kendal Green, Mass., 1934-39; pres. Mount Ida Inc. jr. coll. for women, Newton, Mass., 1939-62, later chmn. bd.; pres. Mt. Ida Coll., Palm Beach, Fla., from 1962. Chmn. Help the Retarded, Palm Beach. Mem. ALA, Nat. Aeronautic Assn., Mass. Schoolmasters Club, Sailfish Club, Harvard Club (Palm Beach), Charles River Country Club, Moose Trail Lodge. Home: Newton Mass. also: Palm Beach Fla. †

CARMICHAEL, EMMETT BRYAN, biochemist, educator; b. Shelbyville, Mo., Sept. 4, 1895; s. George Frank and Amelia Grant (Tingle) C.; m. Lelah Marie Van Hook. Student, Central Coll., 1914-16; AB, U. Colo., 1918, MS, 1922; PhD, U. Cin., 1927; DSc (hon.), Cen. Meth. Coll., 1979, U. Ala., 1981; postgrad. summers, Northwestern U., 1935, Harvard U., 1936. Instr. organic chemistry U. Colo., 1919-24; instr. biochemistry U. Cin., 1924-26; bacteriologist William S. Merrill Co., Cin., 1926-27; asst. prof., head dept. physiol. chemistry U. Ala., 1927, assoc. prof., 1928-32, prof., 1932-45; prof. biochemistry Med. Coll. Ala., 1945-66, Sch. Dentistry, 1948-66; asst. dean Med. Coll. Ala., Sch. Dentistry, 1959-66, prof. biochemistry emeritus, asst. dean emeritus, 1966. Assembler, editor bibliographies of faculty mems. U. Ala., 1937, ann. supplements, 1935-40; mem. editorial adv. bd. Scalpel of Alpha Epsilon Delta, 1938-40; editor Phi Beta Pi Quar., 1945-49, Ala. Jour. Med. Scis., 1964-66; cons. to editorial bd., 1966-73; contbr. articles to sci. jours. Chmn. N. Cen. Ala. Regional Sci. Fair, 1954-57; trustee Wesley Found. U. Ala., 1938-58; trustee Gorgas Scholarship Found., 1947-73, chmn., 1957-73, hon. chmn., from 1973; acting sec.-mgr. So. Med. Assn., 1948. With Ordnance Dept. U.S. Army, 1918-19, 2d lt. Res., 1919-29. Recipient citations Cen. Coll., 1954, U. Ala., 1966, William Crawford Gorgas award Med. Assn. Ala., 1966; named to Ala. Acad. Honor, 1973; apptd. hon. lt. col. a.-d.-c. Ala. Militia, 1976. Fellow AAAS (chmn. acad. conf. 1933), Am. Inst. Chemists (hon., nat. councilor 1952-54, pres. Ala. 1962-73, nat. pres. 1967-69, chmn. bd. 1969-71, Gold medal 1971, dir.-at-large 1971-73), Internat. Coll. Anesthetists; mem. AMA, Am. Assn. Clin. Chemists (chmn. edn. com. 1954-58, mem. nat. exec. com. 1956-57), Am. Bd. Clin. Chemistry, Am. Chem. Soc. (So. Chemist award Memphis sect. 1965, vice chmn. Ala. sect. 1932-34, chmn. 1934-35), Am. Soc. Biol. Chem., Soc. Exptl. Biology, Med. (vice chmn. So. sect.), Am. Physiol. Soc., Ala. Acad. Sci. (pres. 1930-31, editor jour. 1942-48, trustee from 1970, hon. mem.), Am. Assn. Hist. Med., Masons (32 deg.), Shriners, Acacia Club (Order of Pythagoras 1966), Sojourners Club, Mark Twain Club, Sigma Phi Epsilon (alumni citation 1967, dist. gov. 1942-46, Order of Golden Heart 1973), Sigma Xi (1st pres. Ala. chpt. 1939-40), Alpha Chi Sigma, Alpha Epsilon Delta (disting. svc. award 1966, grand pres. 1932-38, So. councilor 1938-40, nat. councilor 1940-51), Gamma Sigma Epsilon, Phi Beta Pi (So. praetor 1934-39, mem. coun. 1943-67, Man of Yr. 1954, supreme archon 1950-52). Democrat. Methodist. Home: Birmingham Ala. Died Nov. 14, 1985; buried Elmwood Cemetery, Birmingham.

CARMICHAEL, HARRY JOHN, manufacturing company executive; b. New Haven, Sept. 29, 1891; became Canadian citizen, 1916; s. William A. and Mary Ann (Moran) C. Ed. pub. schs., New Haven. With Sargent & Co., New Haven, 1908-12; with McKinnon Industries Ltd., St. Catharines, Ont., Can., 1912-41, pres., gen. mgr., 1929-41; v.p., gen. mgr. Gen. Motors of Can. Ltd., 1936-41; v.p., dir. Conroy Mfg. Co. Ltd., St. Catharines, 1918, Toronto Dominion Bank, 1932, Hiram Walker-Gooderham & Worts Ltd., 1946; owner, operator Garden City Stable, thoroughbred racing horses, from 1943; coordinator prodn. Munitions and Supplies Office, 1941-45; pres., dir. War Supplies Ltd., 1942-45; chmn. Can. sec. Joint War Prodn. Com. Can. and U.S., 1943-45. Pres. Niagara Dist. Baseball Assn., 1914-30, St. Catharines Boy Scouts Assn., 1918-52. Bd. govs. Ridley Coll., St. Catharines. Decorated comdr. St. Michael and St. George, 1943; recipient Medal of Freedom, 1944; named Knight of Malta, 1963. Mem. Am. Soc. Automotive Engrs., St. Catharines C. of C. (former pres.), Newcomen Soc., St. Catharines, St. Catharines Golf, Niagara-on-the-Lake, Granite, Turf clubs. Home: Saint Catharines Can. †

CARMICHAEL, JOHN P., sports editor; b. Madison, Wis., June 6, 1902; s. George J. and Margaret (Mooney) C.; m. Kay Naughton, Dec. 27, 1956; children: John P., Joan Marie. Student, Campion Coll., Praire du Chien, Wis., U. Wis. Reporter Milw. Jour.; reporter, columnist Milw. Leader; sports reporter Chgo. Herald-Examiner; Barber Shop columnist, sports editor Chgo. Daily News, until 1971. Author: Biggest Days in Baseball; editor (with Marshall B. Cutler): Who's Who in the Major League, 1950. Lodge: K.C. Home: Chicago Ill. Died June 6, 1986.

CARPENTER, LEROY LEONIDAS, clergyman, editor; b. Carpenter, N.C., Nov. 29, 1891; s. Rufus Jackson and Elizabeth (Rogers) C.; m. Lucile O'Brian, Sept. 2, 1919: children: Robert O'Brian, William Levy. AB, Wake Forest (N.C.) Coll., 1913; ThM, So. Baptist Theol. Sem., Louisville, 1916; ThD, So. Baptist Theol. Sem., 1918; PhD, Yale U., 1927. Ordained to ministry Baptist Ch., 1912. Instr. in N.T. interpretation and theology So. Bapt. Theol. Sem., Louisville, 1916-18; pastor Forest Ave. Bapt. Ch., Greensboro, N.C., 1919-21; chaplain and prof. Bible U. S.C., 1921-26; assoc. prof. religious edn. Furman U., 1926-27, prof. religion, 1927-30; head of dept. religion Limestone Coll., 1930-36; assoc. prof. Bible Baylor U., 1936-42; editor Biblical Recorder, jour. Bapt. State Coll. of N.C., from 1942. Author: the Upward Look, 1936, The Quest for God through Understanding, 1937, A Program of Religious Education, 1937, A Survey of Religious Education, 1940. Mem. Com. on World Peace; chmn. Commn. on Relocation of Chaplains of So. Baptist Convention. Chaplain Fort Howard, Md., April-Dec., 1918. Fellow Nat. Coun. Religion in Higher Edn.; mem. Religious Edn. Assn., Nat. Assn. Bible Instrs., Assn. So. Bapt. Tchrs. of Bible and Religious Edn. (pres. 1932-34, 40-42), Assoc. Ch. Press. So. Bapt. Press Assn. (past pres.), Raleigh Rotary Club. Democrat. Home: Raleigh N.C.†

CARPENTER, STANLEY SHERMAN, government official; b. Boston, Feb. 27, 1917; s. Lloyd and Adeline (Sherman) C.; m. Alice Luken, June 7, 1941; children: Wendell Sherman, Terry Ann. AB, Wheaton Coll., 1940; AM, U. Ill., 1941, PhD, 1943; student, U. Mich., 1943. Fgn. service officer 1947-81; vice consul Am. consulate Kobe, Japan, 1948-49; consul, 2d sec. Am. embassy Tokyo, Japan, 1949-52; 1st sec. 1955-59; consul, 2d sec. Am. embassy London, Eng., 1953-55; assigned Nat. War Coll., 1959-60; dep. chief personnel operations Dept. State, 1960-62; dep. chief mission Am. embassy Copenhagen, Denmark, 1962-65; dir. Performance Evaluation Program, Dept. State, 1965-67; civil adminstr. Ryukyu Islands, 1967-69; exec. dir. Bur. European Affairs, Dept. State, 1969-71; dept. asst. sec. for territorial affairs Dept. Interior, 1972-74; sr. fgn. service insp. 1974-77; U.S. sr. commr. S. Pacific Commn., 1974-81. Served to 1st lt. AUS, 1943-47. Decorated Disting. Civilian Service award U.S. Army, 1969; Superior Honor award Dept. Interior, 1973; Superior Honor award Dept. State, 1977. Mem. Phi Beta Kappa, Sigma Pi Sigma. Home: Arlington Va.

CARR, ARCHIE F., biologist, educator; b. Mobile, Ala., June 16, 1909; s. Archibald Fairly and Louise Gordon (Deaderick) C.; m. Marjorie Harris, Jan. 1, 1937; children: Marjorie, Archie III, Stephen, Thomas, David. BS, U. Fla., 1932, MS, 1934, PhD, 1937. Mem. faculty, then grad. research prof. zoology U. Fla., Gainesville, from 1937; prof. biology Escuela Agricola Panamericana, Honduras, 1945-49; research assoc. Am. Mus. Nat. History, from 1951; tech. dir. Caribbean Conservation Corp., 1961, exec. v.p., tech. dir., from 1968; various expdns. to Panama, Costa Rica, Trinidad 1953; NSF expdn. Cen. Am., 1955, Brazil, French West Africa, Portugal and Azores, 1956, Union South Africa, Argentina, Chile, 1958, Africa, Madagascar, 1963, Caribbean, yearly from 1960; prin. investigator marine turtle migrations project NSF, from 1955. Author:

Handbook of Turtles, 1952, High Jungles and Low, 1952, The Windward Road, 1955, (with Coleman Goin) Amphibians and Freshwater Fishes of Florida, 1956, Guideposts of Animal Navigation, 1962, The Reptiles, 1963, Ulendo, 1964, African Wildlife, 1964, So Excellent a Fishe: A Natural History of Sea Turtles, 1967, The Everglades, 1973. Decorated Officer Order Golden Ark, The Netherlands; recipient Daniel Giraud Elliot medal Nat. Acad. Sci., O. Henry award for prize stories, 1956, Edward H. Browning award for outstanding achievement in conservation Smithsonian Instn., 1975, John Burroughs medal for exemplary nature writing, 1st ann. research award Sigma Xi, U. Fla., merit award Fla. Audubon Soc., 1961, Gold medal World Wildlife Fund N.Y. Zool. Soc., 1973, Archie F. Carr medal established in his honor Fla. State Mus., 1979, Archie F. Carr postdoctoral fellowship established in his honor U. Fla. Dept. Zoology, 1983. Fellow Linnean Soc. London; mem. Am. Soc. Ichthyologists and Herpetologistsm Am. Soc. Naturalists, Fla. Acad. Sci., Internat. Union Conservation Nature (chmn. marine tutle specialists group from 1966), Phi Beta Kappa, Sigma Xi. Home: Micanopy Fla. Died May 21, 1987; buried Evergreen Cemetery, Gainesville, Fla.

CARR, WILLIAM HENRY, naturalist; b. Astoria, L.I., N.Y., Apr. 11, 1902; s. William Henry and Elva L. (Bell) C.;. Asst. then assoc. curator pub. edn. Am. Mus. Nat. History, 1926-44; dir., builder Bear Mountain State Park Trailside Museums, Nature Trails and Zoo; park naturalist Bear Mountain State Park for Palisades Interstate Park Commn. N.Y., N.J. and N.Y. State Conservation Dept., 1926-44; dir. camp leadership courses Columbia U., N.Y.C., 1932-33; tech. editor Expt. Sta., U.S. Forest Service Tucson, 1946; founder Ariz. Sonora Desert Mus., 1952, then dir. emeritus, trustee; v.p. Charles Lathrop Pack Forestry Found., from 1960; designer, creator tunnel and watershed expns. Ariz. Sonora Desert Mus.; established Ghost Ranch Mus., Abiquiu, N.Mex., 1959. Author: Stir of Nature, 1930, African Shadows, 1932, Glimpses of Familiar Birds, 1933, Desert Parade, 1946; contbr. articles to profl. jours. Mem. nat. council Boy Scouts Am., from 1962. Recipient medal Am. Scenic and Hist. Preservation Soc., 1938, award Assn. Interpretive Naturalists. Fellow Explorers Club; mem. Ariz. Wildlife Fedn. (pres. 1947-50), Am. Nature Assn. (dir. outdoor edn. 1959), San Diego Zool. Soc., Wilderness Soc., Am. Forestry Assn. (award 1959), Am. Mus. Natural History (hon. life), Newcomen Soc. N.Am., Am. Assn. Museums, Ecol. Soc. Am. Presbyn. (elder). Home: Tucson Ariz. Died Oct. 25, 1985.

CARRADINE, JOHN RICHMOND, actor; b. N.Y.C., Feb. 5, 1906; s. William Reed and Genevieve Winifred (Richmond) C.; children: Bruce John, John Arthur, Christopher John, Keith Ian, Robert Reed. Student, Episcopal Acad., Phila., Graphic Arts Sch., Phila. Actor: (debut) St. Charles Theater, New Orleans, 1925, (films) including The Prisoner at Shark Island, 1936, Under Two Flags, 1936, Gateway, 1938, Stagecoach, 1939, The Hound of the Baskervilles, 1939, Captain Fury, 1939, The Grapes of Wrath, 1940, Western Union, 1941, The Kentuckian, 1955, Desert Sands, 1955, Court Jester, 1958, The Good Guys and the Bad Guys, 1969, Everything You Always Wanted to Know About Sex, 1972, The Shootist, 1976, The Last Tycoon, 1977, The Sentinel, 1977, Zorro, The Gay Blade, 1981, The Secret of NIMH, 1982, Satan's Mistress, 1982, The Ice Pirates, 1984, (TV movies) including The Daughter of the Mind, 1969, Crow Haven Farm, 1970, The Night Strangler, 1973, The Cat Creature, 1973, Stowaway to the Moon, 1975, Death at Love House, 1976, Captains and the Kings, 1976, Tail Gunner Joe, 1977, Christmas Miracle in Canfield, USA, 1977, The Seekers, 1979, Goliath Awaits, 1981, House of the Long Shadows, Evils of the Night, Monster in the Closet, Revenge, 1986; founder, organizer own repertory co. playing Othello, Hamlet, Shylock. Mem. AFTRA, Actors Equity Assn., Screen Actors Guild. Clubs: Players, Channel Island Yacht. Died Nov. 27, 1988.

CARRIERE, CHARLES MONTBRUN, food company executive; b. New Orleans, July 2, 1908; s. Victor Montbrun and Eveline (D'Aquin) C.; m. Mary Augusta Barnett, Jan, 13, 1934; children: Mary Evelyn Carriere Ruch, Elizabeth Rosemary Carriere Nadeau, Jean Louise, Charles Montbrun, Victor Montbrun, Janet A. Carriere Harrison, Carolyn Judith. Student, Loyola U. of South, 1929-33. CPA, La. Clk. So. Oil Co., 1925-34, then v.p., treas., gen. mgr.; prof. acctg. Loyola U. South, 1933-40; acct. So. Shell Fish Co., 1934-39, office mgr., 1934-44, asst. sec., 1939-44, v.p., bd. dirs., 1944-48, then exec v.p., treas., bd. dirs.; treas., asst. sec. Wesson Oil and Snowdrift Co. Inc., 1948-56, v.p., treas., 1956-60; v.p. Hunt Foods and Industries Inc., from 1960; v.p., treas. S. Tex. Cotton Oil Co.; v.p., gen. mgr. So. Cotton Oil Inc., 1972-81. Mem. La. Soc. CPAs, Am. Inst. Accts., C. of C., Fin. Execs. Inst. (pres. New Orleans control 1956-57), Budget Execs. Inst. (pres. New Orleans chpt. 1962-63), Holy Name Soc., Cath. Evidence Guild, Nat. Cottonseed Processors Assn. (dir., mem. old guard), Nat. Canners Assn. (old guard 1972). Lodge: K.C.

CARRINGTON, PHILIP, archbishop; b. Lichfield, Eng., July 6, 1892; s. Charles Walter and Margaret Constance (Pugh) C.; m. Gwendolen Smith, Dec. 1, 1918. Student, Christ's Coll., Christchurch, New Zealand, 1901; MA, LittD., Canterbury U. Coll., Christchurch, New Zealand, 1908-13; MA, Selwyn Coll., Cambridge, Eng., 1913-16; DCL (hon.), Bishops U., Lennoxville, 1933; STD (hon.), Seabury-Western Theol. Sem., Evanston, Ill., 1933; DD (hon.), Kings Coll., Nova Scotia, 1940, Trinity Coll., Toronto, Wycliffe Coll., Toronto, Durham U., Eng., 1958. Ordained deacon Anglican Ch., 1917, priest, 1918. Curate St. Luke's, Christchurch, 1917-21; incumbent Lincoln, New Zealand, 1921-23; warden St. Barnabas Coll., Adelaide, South Australia, 1924-27; dean of divinity Bishop's Coll., Lennoxville, Que., Can., 1927-35; bishop of Quebec 1935-44, archbishop of Quebec, from 1944. Author: The Boy Scouts Camp Book, 1918, Christian Apologetics in the Second Century, 1921, The Soldier of the Cross, 1930, The Sign of Faith, 1930, The Meaning of the Revelation, 1930, The Road to Jerusalem, 1938, The Pilgrim's Way, 1937, The Primitive Christian Catechism, 1940, A Church History for Canadians, 1947, The Primitive Christian Calendar, 1952, The Story of the Christ, 1956, The Early Christian Church, 2 vols., 1957. Home: Quebec City Canada. †

CARRIUOLO, CHRISTOPHER WILFRED, savings and loan executive; b. Brockton, Mass., Oct. 12, 1920; s. Joseph W. and Emily (Larocca) C.; m. Florence M. Picanzi, Oct. 12, 1947; children: Carol Lynne, Peter Michael. BSBA, Boston U., 1942; postgrad. Advanced Mgmt. Program, Harvard U., 1944. With House of Seagrams, N.Y.C., 1948-59, nat. sales mgr., 1959; v.p. liquor sales Heublein Inc., Hartford, Conn., 1960-64, sr. v.p. liquor mktg. div., 1964-68, gen. mgr. spirits and wine div., sr. v.p., 1968-71, group v.p., 1972-75, exec. v.p., from 1975; v.p., bd. dirs. Vinifera Devel. Corp., 1970-71; pres. Beaulieu Vineyards, San Francisco, 1970-71, Smirnoff Beverage & Import Co., from 1971, United Vintners, from 1971, Theodore Hamm Co., from 1971; chmn., chief exec. officer Hartford Fed. Savs. and Loan Assn., from 1981. Bd. dirs. Hartford Symphony Soc., Conn. Opera Assn., Hartford Stage Co., Avon Old Farms Sch., Sky Ranch for Boys; trustee Wheelock Coll., Wadsworth Atheneum; mem. adv. council Bacchus. Served with AUS, World War II, ETO. Decorated Air medal. Mem. Greater Hartford C. of C. (bd. dirs.), Am. Mktg. Assn., Sales and Mktg. Execs. Internat. (trustee Grad. Sch. Sales Mgmt. and Mktg.), Sales Execs. Club N.Y., Sales and Mktg. Club Hartford, Sales Promotion Execs. Assn. N.Y., Distilled Spirits Inst. (bd. dirs.). Club: Hartford (bd. govs.). Home: Hartford Conn. Died Mar. 31, 1986.

CARROLL, GRAYSON, physician, surgeon; b. Dallas, Feb. 10, 1895; s. Washington Irving and Lettie Catherine (Mosher) C.; m. Thelma Hayman, Nov. 20, 1924; children: Gaye Carroll Voges, Elizabeth Carroll Hensley. Student, Austin Coll., 1913-14, U. Tex., 1914-15; MD, U. Tex., Galveston, 1919. Diplomate Am. Bd. Urology. Intern Bellevue Hosp., N.Y.C., 1919-21; urologist U.S. VA Hosp., Jefferson Barracks, Mo., 1921-24; asst. urologist Baylor U. Med. Sch., Dallas, 1924-26; assoc. with Bransford Lewis St. Louis, 1926-41; asst. prof. urology St. Louis U., 1945-50, assoc. prof., 1950-58, prof., from 1958; cons. urology St. Louis City Hosp.; urologist St. John's Hosp. from 1933, assoc. chief staff from 1952, chief urol. staff from 1959; cons. urologist Jewish Hosp. Mem. AMA (chmn. sect. urology 1947), ACS, Am. Urol. Assn. (pres. 1962-63, Hugh Young award 1971), So. Med. Assn. (past chmn. urol. sect.), Soc. Genito Urinary Surgeons (v.p. 1974), Internat. Soc. Urologists, Delta Tau Delta. Presbyn. Clubs: Bellerive Country, Univ. Home: Saint Louis Mo. Died Dec. 19, 1982, buried Oak Grove Cemetery, St. Louis.

CARROLL, RICHARD C., retired educational administator; b. Burlington, Vt., Mar. 16, 1909; s. Carl H. and Lena Nina (Cushman) C.; m. Esther Helen Peck, Aug. 2, 1935; children: Richard C., Nana. AB, Yale U., 1932, MA, 1940. Asst. dean Yale U., New Haven, 1939-43, dean army students, 1943-48, assoc. dean, 1948-49, dean students, 1949-51, dean undergrad. affairs, 1957-68, assoc. sec. univ., 1969-74. Trustee Hopkins Grammar Sch., pres. bd. , 1961-72; bd. dirs. Prospect Hill Sch., 1957-59, Conn. Radio Found. Inc. Mem. Zeta Psi. Home: New Haven Conn. Died July 22, 1986.

CARSON, ROBERT GORDON, JR., university dean; b. Seneca, S.C., Mar. 29, 1918; s. Robert Gordon and Sue Ellen (Hunter) C.; m. Mary Elizabeth White, Aug. 17, 1941; children: Robert Gordon III, Mary Elizabeth, Virginia Sue. BS, Clemson U., 1939; MS, Ga. Tech. Inst., 1950; PhD, U. Mich., 1953. Registered profl. engr., N.C. Jr. engr. Callaway Mills, LaGrange, Ga., 1939-42; plant mgr. Carwood Mfg. Co., Cornelia, Ga., 1946-47; asst. prof. to assoc. prof. Sch. Textiles Clemson U., 1947-55; prof., head indsl. engring. dept. N.C. State U., 1955-57, assoc. dean engring., 1957-75. Contbr. articles to profl. jours. Served to capt. inf. AUS, 1942-46, CBI. Fellow Am. Inst. Indsl. Engrs. (regional v.p. 1964-65); mem. Nat. Acad. Arbitrators, Alpha Pi Mu (nat. pres. 1960-62). Home: Raleigh N.C. Died Aug. 9, 1987.

CARTER, LAUNOR FRANKLIN, former science administrator, consultant; b. Friday Harbor, Wash., Jan. 23, 1914; s. Alvia F. and Hazel Agnes (Shull) C.; m. Mary Ann Wickersham, Feb. 14, 1941; 1 son, James Franklin. B.S., U. Wash., 1936, M.S., 1939; Ph.D., Princeton U., 1941; cert. Exec. Tng. Program, UCLA, 1961. Chief examiner Wash. State Dept. Social Security Merit System Office, 1937-38; personnel technician Social Security Bd., Washington, 1940-41, Adj. Gen. Office, Dept. Army, 1941-42; research psychologists Aero-Med. Lab., Wright Field, Ohio, 1946; asst., then asso. prof. psychology U. Rochester, 1946-52; dir. research Human Research Unit 2, Continental Army Command, Ft. Ord, Calif., 1952-55; v.p., dir. research System Devel. Corp., Santa Monica, Calif., 1955-62; v.p., mgr. pub. systems div. System Devel. Corp., 1963-73, v.p. civil devel., 1973-81, v.p. studies and evaluation, 1975-81; chief scientist USAF, 1962-63; pvt. cons. 1981-86; Mem. USAF Sci. Adv. Bd., 1955-68; adv. com. dept. psychology Princeton, 1962-68; mem. Nat. Adv. Commn. Libraries, 1966-68; mem. sci. information council NSF, 1965-69; mem. computer sci. and engring. bd. Nat. Acad. Sci.; chmn. com. on socio-econ. research and earthquake prediction; bd. dirs., treas. Council for Applied Social Research, 1977-82. Cons. editor: Psychol. Bull, 1955-60, Jour. Abnormal and Social Psychology, 1955-68, Evaluation Quar, 1976-86; asso. editor: Sociometry, 1955-64; contbr. numerous articles to profl. jours. Served with USAAF, 1942-46. Benjamin Franklin fellow Royal Soc. Arts. Fellow AAAS; mem. Am. Psychol. Assn. (rec. sec., dir. 1955-61, 71, chmn. program com. 1953, chmn. ad hoc conv. com. 1954), Western Psychol. Assn., Soc. for Psychol. Study Social Issues, Am. Fedn. Scientists, Council Applied Social Research (treas. 1976-86). Club: Riviera Country. Home: Pacific Palisades Calif. Died Dec. 7, 1986; buried Westwood Meml. Park, West Los Angeles, Calif.

CARTER, TIM LEE, JR., former congressman, physician; b. Tompkinsville, Ky., Sept. 2, 1910; s. James Clark and Idru (Tucker) C.; m. Kathleen Bradshaw, Nov. 15, 1931. AB, Western Ky. U.; MD, U. Tenn., 1937. Pub. sch. tchr. 1927-32; intern U.S. Marine Hosp., Chgo. Maternity Ctr., 1937-39; practice medicine Tompkinsville, 1939-42, 46-65; mem. 89th-96th U.S. Congresses from 5th dist. Ky., mem. interstate and fgn. commerce com., mem. small bus. com. Washington; owner T.L. Carter Devel. Co.; chief staff Monroe County Meml. Hosp. Served to capt. M.C. AUS, 1942-46. Decorated Bronze Star; recipient Benjamin Rush award for citizenship and community service, Tom Wallace award for conservation. Mem. AMA, Ky. Med. Assn., Am. Acad. Gen. Practice, Ky. Acad. Gen. Practice, Alpha Omega Alpha. Baptist. Lodges: Masons (33 degree), Shriners. Home: Tompkinsville Ky. Died Mar. 27, 1987.

CARTER, VINCENT, lawyer; b. St. Clair, Pa., Nov. 6, 1891; s. William J. and Julia Anna (Clarke) C.; m. Helen Carlson, July 2, 1921 (dec.); 1 child, James Vincent (dec.); m. Mary Crowley, Aug. 13, 1929; children: Helen, Jerome, Roch. Ed., Cath. U., Washington, Fordham U. Bar: Wyo. 1919. Dept. atty. gen. State of Wyo., 1919-23, state auditor, state purchasing agt., 1923-29; mem. 71st to 73d Congresses, 1929-35; former pres. Golconda Oil Co. Mem. Bd. Charities and Reform, Wyo., 1923-29; Wyo. Rep. nominee for U.S. Senate, 1934. Lt. USMC, World War I, capt. Wyo. N.G. Mem. Am. Legion, Elks, Pi Gamma Mu. Home: Albuquerque N.Mex. †

CARTER, WALTER COLQUITT, lawyer; b. Atlanta, June 12, 1904; s. Walter Colquitt and Nannie Sue (Hill) C.; m. Marion Cobb Bryan, June 4, 1930; children: Florence Bryan, Nancy Hill. AB, U. Ga., 1924; LLB, Harvard U., 1927. Bar: Ga. 1927. Ptnr. Carter, Ansley, Smith & McLendon, Atlanta; Bd. dirs. DeKalb Fed. Savs. & Loan Assn. Contbr. articles to profl. jours. Mem. ABA (life ins. law com. 1941-52, legal aid com. 1941-42), Ga. Bar Assn. (v.p. 1936), Atlanta Bar Assn., Am. Law Inst., Am. Judicature Soc., Phi Beta Kappa, Phi Kappa Phi, Chi Phi (nat. v.p. 1941-42). Democrat. Episcopalian. Clubs: Lawyers (pres. 1943-44), Harvard (pres. 1945-47), Piedmont Driving (Atlanta), Capital City. Home: Atlanta Ga. Died Jan. 30, 1988; buried Crestlawn Cemetery, Atlanta.

CARTON, JOHN VICTOR, lawyer; b. Asbury Park, N.J., Feb. 7, 1900; s. James D. and Mary M. (Ludlow) C.; m. Joan E. McGregor, June 20, 1939; children: Malcolm V., Gail T., Joan E. Carton Carmody, Kerry P. Carton McGreevy, Michael R. AB, Georgetown U., 1922; LLB, Columbia U., 1925. Bar: N.J. 1926. Pvt. practice Asbury Park, 1926-35; ptnr. Durand, Ivins & Carton, Asbury Park, 1935-63, Carton, Nary, Witt & Arvanitis, Asbury Park, 1964-82; dir. counsel Keystone Savs. & Loan Assn., Asbury Park; asst. pros. atty. of the Pleas, Monmouth County, N.J., 1930-35; county pros. atty. Monmouth County, 1945-55. Fellow Am. Bar Found.; mem. N.J. Bar Assn., Am. Coll. Trial Lawyers, Deal, Golf and Country Club. Home: Neptune City N.J. Died Jan. 19, 1982; buried St. Catharines Cemetery, Spring Lake Heights, N.J.

CARVER, EUGENE PENDLETON, JR., lawyer; b. Arlington, Mass., Nov. 9, 1891; s. Eugene P. and Clare (Porter) C.; m. Dorothy Bell, Sept. 20, 1917. AB, Harvard U., 1913, LLB, 1916; postgrad., U. London, 1919. Bar: Mass. 1916. Pvt. practice Boston. Mem. bd. selectmen Town of Brookline, Mass., 1942-60. 1st lt. U.S. Army, 1917-18. Mem. VFW (past comdr.-in-chief), SAR (past nat. pres. gen.), DAV, Soc. War 1812 (past nat. pres. gen.), Mass. Soc. Mayflower Descendants, Masons, Shriners, Elks (past exalted ruler, dest. dept.). Home: Brookline Mass. †

CARVER, RAYMOND, author, poet; b. Clatskanie, Oreg., May 25, 1938; s. Clevie Raymond and Ella Beatrice (Casey) C.; m. Maryann Burk, June 7, 1957 (div. Oct. 1982); children: Christine LaRae, Vance Lindsay; m. Tess Gallagher, June 17, 1988. A.B., Humboldt State U., 1963; M.F.A., U. Iowa, 1966; LittD (hon.), U. Hartford, 1988. Lectr. creative writing U. Calif., Santa Cruz, 1971-72; vis. prof. English U. Calif., Berkeley, 1972-73; vis. lectr. Writers' Workshop, U. Iowa, 1973-74; mem. faculty writing program Goddard Coll., 1977-78; vis. disting. writer U. Tex., El Paso, 1978-79; prof. English Syracuse (N.Y.) U., 1980-83. Author: (poetry) Near Klamath, 1968, Winter Insomnia, 1970, At Night The Salmon Move, 1976, Where Water Comes Together with other Water, 1985, Ultramarine, 1986, A New Path to the Waterfall, 1989; (short stories) Put Yourself in My Shoes, 1974, Will You Please Be Quiet, Please?, 1976, Furious Seasons, 1977, What We Talk About When We Talk About Love, 1981, Cathedral, 1983, Where I'm Calling From: New and Selected Stories, 1988; (essays, poetry, short stories) Fires, 1983; (screenplay) Dostoevsky: The Screenplay, 1985; editor: The Best American Short Stories, 1986, Am. Short Story Masterpieces, 1987. Recipient Strauss Living award Am. Acad. and Inst. Arts and Letters, 1983-88, Creative Arts Award citation Brandeis U., 1988; inducted Am. Acad. and Inst. Arts and Letters, 1988; Nat. Endowment Arts fellow in poetry, 1971; fellow in fiction, 1980; Wallace Stegner fellow, 1972-73; Guggenheim fellow, 1979-80. Mem. PEN, Author's Guild. Home: Port Angeles Wash. Died Aug. 2, 1988; buried Ocean View Cemetery, Port Angeles.

CARVER, THOMAS RIPLEY, physicist, educator; b. Rochester, N.Y., Mar. 6, 1929; s. Emmett Kirkendall and Ruth (Ripley) C.; m. Eleanore Bie Benson, Feb. 5, 1951; children: Davis Benson, Alison. AB, Harvard U., 1950; PhD, U. Ill., 1954; MA, Oxford (Eng.) U., 1964. Instr. U. Ill., 1954; faculty Princeton U., 1954-81, prof. physics, 1967-81; cons. to industry, 1954-81; vis. research scientist Royal Radar Establishment, Eng., 1974-75. Sloan fellow, 1956-58, Guggenheim fellow, 1964-65. Fellow Am. Phys. Soc.; mem. Am. Assn. Physics Tchrs., N.Y. Acad. Scis. Research on dynamic nuclear polarization, gas cell atomic clocks, spin transmission resonance, magnetic resonance, optical pumping, solid state physics, low temperature phenomena. Home: Princeton N.J. Died Aug. 8, 1981.

CASE, LELAND DAVIDSON, editor; b. Wesley, Iowa, May 8, 1900; s. Herbert Llewelyn and Mary Ellen (Grannis) C.; m. Josephine Altman, July 28, 1931. city editor Lead (S.D.) Call, 1923-25; staff Paris edit. N.Y. Herald-Tribune, 1926-27; instr. Medill Sch. Journalism, Northwestern U., 1925-26, asst. prof., 1927-28; co-pub. Evening Star, Hot Springs, S.D., 1928-34; editor Rotarian mag., 1930-50, field editor, 1952-54; founder-editor Together mag., 1956-63; dir. Pacific Ctr. Western Hist. Studies, U. Pacific, 1965-67; editor Pacific Historian, 1965-68; assoc. cons. U.S. Dept. of State at UN Conf., San Francisco, 1945; adv. council to chmn. Am. Revolution Bicentennial Commn., 1972. Author: (with George C. Bastian) Editing the Day's News, 1932, (with G.C. Bastian, R.E. Wolsely) Around the Copydesk, 1933, Guidebook to the Black Hills and theBadlands, 1949; contbg. author The Black Hills, 1952; editor: (series) A World to Live In, 1942, Peace Is a Process, 1944, Peace Requires Action, 1946, (with Edith Grannis) New Hampshire to Minnesota, 1962, Reader's Choice Treasury, 1964. Co-founder Friends of Middle Border, 1939, Westerners, 1944; pres. Westerners Internat., 1969-73. Recipient Alumni merit awards Macalester Coll., 1949, Nortwestern U., 1951, Dakota Wesleyan U., 1962, St. George's award, 1963, citation Southwestern Coll., 1964; named hon. citizen of LaGrange (Ga.). Mem. Soc. Midland Authors, Western Hist. Assn. (hon. life), Bibliog. Soc. Am., Tucson Lit. Club, Masons, Rotary, Acacia Club, Sigma Tau Delta, Pi Kappa Delta, Delta Sigma Rho, Sigma Delta Chi. Republican. Methodist. Home: Tucson Ariz. Died Dec. 16, 1986; buried Tucson.

CASEY, EUGENE BERNARD, engineering company executive; b. Washington, June 13, 1904; s. Michael B. and Rose (O'Neill) C.; m. Helon Stokes, Aug. 29, 1924; children—Virginia, Nancy, Betsey, Eugene; m. Charlotte Sereikas, July 29, 1945; children—Douglas, Margaret; m. Betty Brown, Feb. 8, 1955. Student, Pa. State Coll., 1922-24, Georgetown U., 1924-26; D.Eng. (hon.), Washington Coll., Chestertown, Md., 1983. Prin. Casey Engring. Co., 1931-86; owner, operator cattle and grain farms Montgomery County, Md., Wis., Va., Minn. and S.D.; dep. gov. FCA, 1940-41; exec. asst. to Pres. Roosevelt and Truman 1941-53. trustee Patrick Henry Meml Assn.; past pres. Young Men's Democratic Club. Served with USNR, 1944-45; in battles of Philippines, Iwo Jima, Okinawa, 1st and 2d air strikes on Tokyo. Mem. ASME, Am. Soc. Heating and Ventilating Engrs., Am. Soc. Mil. Engrs., Nat. Com. for Agr. (sec.-treas.), Am. Farm Bur. (dir.), Nat. Grange, Newcomen Soc., Am. Legion, U.S. Naval Res. Officers Assn., Navy League, Delta Upsilon, Lambda Sigma. Roman Catholic. Clubs: Nat. Press; Winchester Golf and Country (Va.); Washingtonian Country. Lodge: Rotary. Home: Berryville Va. Died July 26, 1986.

CASEY, WILLIAM JOSEPH, lawyer, government official; b. Elmhurst, Queens, N.Y., Mar. 13, 1913; s. William J. and Blanche (La Vigne) C.; m. Sophia Kurz, Feb. 22, 1941; 1 child, Bernadette. B.S., Fordham U., 1934; postgrad., Cath. U. Am.; J.D., St. John's U., 1937. Chmn. bd. editors Research Inst. Am., Washington, 1938-49; with OSS, U.S. Army Intelligence, U.S. Navy, 1941-46; spl. counsel small bus. com. U.S. Senate, Washington, 1947-48; assoc. gen. counsel Marshall Plan, 1948; lectr. tax law NYU, 1948-62; lectr. Practicing Law Inst., N.Y.C., 1950-62; partner firm Hall, Casey, Dickler & Howley, N.Y.C., 1957-71; mem. Gen. Adv. Com. on Arms Control, 1970-71; chmn. SEC, Washington, 1971-73; undersec. state econ. affairs Dept. State, Washington, 1973-74; pres., chmn. Export-Import Bank U.S., 1974-75; mem. Pres. Ford's Fgn. Intelligence Adv. Bd., Washington, 1976; counsel Rogers & Wells, 1976-81; chmn. Task Force on Venture Capital, SBA, Washington, 1976-80; campaign mgr. Ronald Reagan Presdl. Campaign, 1980; dir. Cen. Intelligence, Washington, 1981-87; statutory adviser Nat. Security Council, 1981-87. Author: Lawyers Desk Book, 1965, Tax Sheltered Investments, 1952, Estate Planning Book, 1956, Forms of Business Agreements, 1966, Accounting Desk Book, 1967, Armchair Guide to American Revolution, 1976. Trustee Fordham U., 1966-71; pres. L.I. Assn., 1968-71; pres. Internat. Rescue Com., 1970-71; mem. Presdl. Task Force Internat. Devel. Mem. Am. Bar Assn., Nassau County Bar Assn., Assn. Bar City N.Y. Home: New York N.Y. Died May 6, 1987; buried Holy Rd. Cemetery, Westbury, N.Y.

CASKEY, JOHN LANGDON, archaeologist; b. Boston, Dec. 7, 1908; s. Lacey Davis and Elsie Langdon (Stern) C.; m. 2d, Miriam Ervin, 1967. BA, Yale U., 1931; PhD, U. Cin., 1939. Mem. staff excavations at Troy U. Cin., 1932-38, univ. instr. classics, 1939-42, asst. prof., 1946-48, prof. classical archaeology, 1959-79, emeritus, 1979-81, head dept. classics, 1959-72; fellow Grad. Sch., from 1961; field dir. univ. excavations in Keos, from 1960; asst. dir. Am. Sch. Classical Studies, Athens, 1948-49, dir., 1949-59, vis. prof., 1975-76, vice chmn. mng. com., 1966-75; field dir. excavations at Heraion of Argos, 1949, Lerna, 1952-58, Eutresis, 1958. Co-author, co-editor Troy, from 1950; contbr. chpts. on Early and Middle Bronze Age, Cambridge Ancient History, 3d edit., Vols. I, II, 1971, 73, also articles to profl. jours., reports in field. Lt. col. AUS, 1942-46. Decorated Legion of Merit; named comdr. Royal Order Phoenix (Greece); hon. citizen Athens (Greece). Fellow Archeol. Soc. Athens (hon.); mem. Archeol. Inst. Am. (Gold medal for disting. archeol. achievement 1980), Am. Philol. Assn., Vergilian Soc., Am. Philos. Soc., Assn. Field Archaeology, Classical Assn. Can., Soc. Promotion Hellenic Studies, German Archeol. Inst., Soc. Cycladic Studies (hon.)(Greece), Phi Beta Kappa. Home: Cincinnati Ohio. Died Dec. 4, 1981.

CASPARY, VERA, writer; b. Chgo.; d. Paul and Julia (Cohen) C.; m. Isadore Goldsmith, Oct. 5, 1949 (dec. 1964). Student, Chgo. pub. schs. Author: The White Girl, 1929, Thicker than Water, 1932, Laura, 1942, Bedelia, 1944, Stranger than Truth, 1976, The Weeping and the Laughter, 1950, Thelma, 1957, The Husband, 1957, Evvie, 1950, A Chosen Sparrow, 1964, The Man Who Loved His Wife, 1966, The Rosecrest Cell, 1967, Final Portrait, 1971, The Dreamers, 1975, Elizabeth X, 1978, (autobiography) The Secrets of Grown-ups; plays include: (with Winifred Lenihan) Blind Mice, 1930, (with George Sklar) Laura, 1946, Wedding in Paris (in London), 1954; original screen stories and adaptations: Night of June 13, 1932, Easy Living, 1936, Bedelia, 1946, Letter to Three Wives, 1949, Three Husbands, 1951, Les Girls, 1958, others. Mem. Authors Guild, Dramatists Guild, Writers Guild West. Home: New York N.Y. Died June 14, 1986; cremated.

CASSARETTO, FRANK, educator; b. Chgo., Dec. 5, 1906; s. Joseph J. and Marie (Leonard) C.; m. Agnes Louise Neary, Dec. 26, 1931; children: Mary Cassaretto Simon, Toni Ann Cassaretto Perille, Gemma Cassaretto Allen. BS, Loyola U., Chgo., 1930, PhD, 1948; MS, U. Chgo., 1939. Mem. faculty Loyola U., Chgo., 1930-42, 46-72, assoc. prof., 1946-55, prof. chemistry, 1955-72. Contbr. profl. jours. Frank P. Cassaretto medal created in his honor, Loyola U., 1972. Mem. Am. Chem. Soc. (dir., chmn. edn. dept. Chgo. sect.), Blue Key, Sigma Xi. Capt. USAAF, 1942-46. Home: Evanston Ill. Died Mar. 27, 1987.

CASSAVETES, JOHN, actor, director; b. N.Y.C., Dec. 9, 1929; m. Gena Rowlands, Mar. 19, 1958; children: Nicholas, Alexandra, Zoe. Ed., Mohawk Coll., Colgate U., N.Y. Acad. Dramatic Arts. Actor in stock co.; asst. stage mgr. Broadway play Fifth Season; TV credits include Elgin Playhouse; actor in films Night Holds Terror, 1955, Crime in the Streets, 1956, Taxi, Edge of the City, Fever Tree, The Dirty Dozen, 1965 (nominated best supporting actor Acad. Awards), Rosemary's Baby, Machine Gun, 1970, Two-Minute Warning, 1976, Brass Target, 1978, The Fury, 1978, Whose Life Is It Anyway, 1981, The Incubus, 1982, The Tempest, 1982, Love Streams, 1984, I'm Almost Not Crazy, 1984, Marvin and Tige, 1984, Mickey and Nicky, 1984; writer-dir. films Shadows, 1960, Faces, 1968 (nominated best writer original screenplay Acad. Awards), Too Late Blues, 1962, Husbands, 1970, A Woman Under the Influence, 1974 (nominated best dir. Acad. Awards), Killing of a Chinese Bookie, 1976, One Summer Night, 1979, Gloria, 1980; writer-dir.-actor Minnie & Moskowitz, 1971, Opening Night, 1977; dir. films A Child is Waiting, 1962,G 1980 (Golden Lion award Venice Film Festival), Big Trouble, 1986; appeared in TV movie Flesh and Blood, 1979; writer of plays Knives, Woman of Mystery. Died Feb. 3, 1989.

CASTELLANO, RICHARD S., actor, producer; b. Bronx, N.Y., Sept. 4, 1933; m. Margaret Tiernan, 1953; 1 child, Margaret Castellano Moller.; m. Ardell Sheridan. Student, Columbia U. Pres. own constrn. co., 1956-62; actor N.Y. Yiddish Theatre, 1963. Starred off Broadway in A View From the Bridge, 1965-66; on Broadway in The Investigation, 1966, That Summer, That Fall, 1966, Mike Downstairs, 1967, Why I Went Crazy, 1968, Sheep on the Runway and Lovers and Other Strangers (Tony award nominee); film appearances include A Fine Madness, 1966, Lovers and Other Strangers, 1970 (Oscar nominee), Night of the Juggler, 1980 The Godfather, 1972; TV shows include NYPD, Incident on a Dark Street, The Super, Honor Thy Father, Joe and Sons, Gangster Chronicles. Home: North Bergen N.J. Died Dec. 10, 1988.

CASTROVIEJO, RAMON, ophthalmologist; b. Logrono, Spain, Aug. 24, 1904; came to U.S., 1928; naturalized, 1936; s. Ramon and Maria Ana (Briones) C.; m. Cynthia Warren Smith, Jan. 30, 1946; children: Cynthia, Ramon. BA and BS, Inst. Arts and Scis. of Logrono, U. Zaragoza, Spain, 1919; MD, U. Madrid, 1927; hon. doctorate, U. San Marcos de Lima, Peru, 1940, U. Santo Domingo, 1945, U. Salamanca, Spain, 1965, U. Granada, Spain, 1966, U. Santa Maria, Brazil, 1969, U. of East, Manila, Philippines, 1972. Asst. ophthalmology Red Cross Hosp., Madrid, 1927; attending ophthalmologist Chgo. Eye, Ear, Nose and Throat Hosp., 1928-30; spl. fellow research and lab. work Mayo Clinic, 1930-31; with Columbia Presbyn. Med. Ctr., N.Y.C., 1931-52; then prof. clin. ophthalmology NYU Post Grad. Med. Sch.; chief emeritus ophthalmology St. Vincent's Hospital and Med. Ctr., N.Y.C.; clin. prof. dept. ophthalmology Mt. Sinai Med. Sch.; attending ophthalmic surgeon Mt. Sinai Hosp., N.Y.C.; hon. dir. dept. spl. corneal surgery, N.Y. Eye and Ear Infirmary; cons. ophthalmologist Lincoln Hosp., St. Clare's Hosp.; mem. adviser ophthalmology Bur. Hearings and Appeals, Social Security Adminstrn.; hon. prof. U. Santo Tomas, Manila, 1972. Author: Atlas of Keratectomy and Keratoplasty, 1966; contbr. over 250 articles Am. Jour. Ophthalmology, other med. jours. Decorated grand cross Order Isabel La Catolica, Alfonso El Sabio, Sanidad Civil, Merito Militar con Distintive Blanco (Spain); Nunez de Balboa (Panama); Sol (Peru); gold medal Soc. Journalists, Oviedo (Spain), Centro Riojano, Madrid. Mem. AMA, N.Y. County Med. Soc., N.Y. State Med. Soc., N.Y. Acad. Medicine, Am. Ophthal. Soc., N.Y. Ophthal. Soc. (pres. 1972), Am. Soc. Plastic and Reconstructive Surgery, Am. Biol. Assn., Assn. Research Ophthalmology, Assn. Advancement Med. Instrumentation, Biol. Photog. Assn., Royal Med. Soc. (Gt. Britain), Spanish-Am. Med. Assn., Sociedad Medica Hispano-Americana of U.S., Société Francaise d'Ophthalmolgie (France), Sociedad Oftalmologica Espanola (Spain), N.Y. Athletic, Sewanhaka Corinthian Yacht, Oyster Bay, Piping Rock clubs; also hon. mem. ophthalmic socs. in India, Colombia, Brazil, Argentina, Chile, Peru, Panama, Costa Rica, Mexico, Cuba, Greece, Egypt, Israel, South Africa, Australian Coll. Ophthalmologists, Oxford Ophthal. Congress (Eng.). Home: New York N.Y. Died Jan. 1, 1987.

CASWELL, HOLLIS L., academic administrator; b. Woodruff, Kan., Oct. 22, 1901; s. Hollis Leland and Lotta (Hood) C.; m. Ruth Allen, Feb. 12, 1928; children: Hollis Leland, Allen Edward. Student, Kans. State Coll., Hays, 1918-20; AB, U. Nebr., 1922, LLD (hon.), 1955; MA, Columbia U., 1927, PhD, 1929; LLD (hon.), Tufts U., 1955, Northwestern U., 1956; D of Pedagogy (hon.), Havana U., 1956. High sch. prin. Auburn, Nebr., 1922-24; supt. schs. Syracuse, Nebr., 1924-26; asst. prof. George Peabody Coll., Nashville, 1929-31, prof., 1931-37, assoc. dir. div. Surveys Field and Studies, 1929-37; prof. Tchrs. Coll. Columbia U., from 1937, dir. div. instrn., 1938-50, dir. Tchrs. Coll. Schs. and Sch. Experimentation, 1943-48, assoc. dean, 1946-49, dean, 1949-54, pres., 1954-62, pres. emeritus, from 1962, Marshall Field Jr. prof. edn., 1962-67; cons. numerous state edn. depts., mcpl. sch. systems; Burton lectr., Harvard U., 1955; Steinmetz Meml. lectr., 1952; cons. pre-induction tng. br. War Dept., 1943, acting chief program sect.; chmn. exec. com. Soc. for Curriculum Study, 1936-37; dir. United Community Def. Services, 1951, v.p. 1951-55. Author: Program-Making in Small Elementary Schools, 1930, 2 textbooks (with D.S. Campbell) Curriculum Development, 1935 and Readings in Curriculum Development, 1937, Education in the Elementary Schools, 1942, (with others) Curriculum Improvement in Public Schools, 1950; chmn. editorial adv. bd., World Book Ency., 1947-67, World Book Atlas, 1962-67, World Book Yearbook, 1962-67; contbr. articles to profl. jours. Recipient Disting. Service medal N.J. State Coll. Newark, 1961, Disting. Service medal Columbia U., 1962, John Dewey Soc. award,

1973. Mem. NEA (nat. commn. on instrn. 1961-63, pres. Dept. Supervision and Curriculum Devel. 1944-46), Am. Ednl. Rsch. Assn. (v.p. 1936-37, award 1981), Phi Delta Kappa, Kappa Delta Pi. Home: Santa Barbara Calif. Died Nov. 22, 1988.

CATHEY, CORNELIUS OLIVER, educator; b. Davidson, N.C., Apr. 15, 1908; s. Albert Marcellus and Nancy (McAuley) C.; m. Beulah M. Proctor, June 15, 1929. AB, Davidson Coll., 1928, MA, 1929; PhD, U. N.C., 1948. Tchr. Am. history in jr. colls., 1929-36; camp comdr. Civilian Conservation Corps., 1936-39; mem. faculty U. N.C., 1947-74, prof. history, 1957-74, chmn. univ. scholarship com., 1956-63, campus coordinator Peace Corps, 1968-72, dean student affairs, 1963-72; prof. history Rutherford Coll., 1929-33, Brevard Coll., 1933-36; vis. prof. Columbia U., 1950-51. Author: Agricultural Developments in North Carolina 1783-1860, 1956; also articles; editor: A Woman Rice Planter, 1961. Mem. Agrl. History Soc. (exec. com. 1962-63, chmn. book award com. 1963-64), N.C. hist. assns., U. United Meth. Ch., Chapel Hill-Carrboro C. of C. (charter mem.), Chapel Hill Rotary. Col. AUS, 1940-46. Home: Chapel Hill N.C. Died Aug. 8, 1986; buried Mimosa Cemetery, Davidson, N.C.

CATTELL, ROSCOE ARNOLD, petroleum engineer; b. New Sharon, Iowa, Jan. 6, 1892; s. Harvey George and Ardilla Jane (Arnold) C.; m. Ruth Brown, Dec. 26, 1926; children: Betty Ruth (Mrs. William H. Williams), Robert Arnold. Grad. high sch., Pasadena, Calif., 1910; BSCE, U. of Calif., 1916. With Pacific Oil Co., Sunset-Midway Oil Fields, Kern County, Calif., 1916-17; petroleum engr. U.S. Bur. Mines, Muskogee, Okla., 1917-18, S. Pearson & Son and Société des Recherches et d'Exploitation des Petroles en Algerie, Chesterfield, Eng. and St. AimÉ, Algeria, 1919-20; with U.S. Bur. Mines, from Feb. 1921, successively nat. gas. engr., asst. supt, supt. Petroleum Expt. Sta., Bartlesville, Okla., chief of helium div., 1925-33, chief petroleum & natural gas div., 1933-55, chief div. of petroleum, from 1955. Author of various Bur. of Mines publs. on petroleum, natural gas, helium and oil shale. With Transp. Corps U.S. Army, AEF, 1918-19. Recipient Gold medal Dept. Interior, 1952, merit citation Nat. Civil Svc. League, 1959. Mem. Am. Inst. Mining Metall. and Petroleum Engrs., Am. Petroleum Inst., Am. Gas Assn., Masons, Delta Sigma Phi. Republican. Presbyterian. Home: Washington D.C. †

CAUDILL, REBECCA (MRS. JAMES AYARS), writer; b. Poor Fork, Ky., Feb. 2, 1899; d. George Washington and Susan (Smith) C.; m. James Sterling Ayars, Sept. 8, 1931; children: James Sterling (dec.), Rebecca Jean. AB, Wesleyan Coll., Macon, Ga., 1920; MA, Vanderbilt U., 1922. Tchr. Collegio Bennett, Rio de Janeiro, 1922-24; Alumnae trustee Wesleyan Coll., 1949-52; trustee Pine Mountain Settlement Sch., 1967-74. Author: Barrie & Daughter, 1943, Happy Little Family, 1947, Tree of Freedom, 1949, Schoolhouse in the Woods, 1949, Up and Down the River, 1951, Saturday Cousins, 1953, House of the Fifers, 1954, Susan Cornish, 1955, Schoolroom in the Parlor, 1959, Time for Lissa, 1959, Higgins and the Great Big Scare, 1960, The Best Loved Doll, 1962, The Far-Off Land, 1964 (Friends Am. Writers juvenile award 1965), A Pocketful of Cricket, 1964, A Certain Small Shepherd, 1965 (Soc. Midland Authors juvenile award 1966), Did You Carry the Flag Today, Charley?, 1966, My Appalachia, 1966, (with James Ayars) Contrary Jenkins, 1969, Come Along, 1969, Somebody Go and Hang a Drum, 1974, Wind, Sand, and Sky, 1976. Recipient Nancy Bloch Meml. award Intercultural Library, Downtown Community Sch., N.Y.C., 1956, award for disting. service in children's reading Chgo. Children's Reading Round Table, 1969, Ill. Author of Year award Ill. Assn. Tchrs. English, 1972. Mem. Delta Kappa Gamma, Theta Sigma Phi. Mem. Soc. of Friends. Home: Urbana Ill. Died Oct. 2, 1985, buried Mt. Hope Cemetery, Urbana.

CAVANAGH, EDWARD FRANCIS, JR., corporate executive, lawyer; b. N.Y.C., Aug. 18, 1906; s. Edward Francis and Mae (Masterson) C.; m. Nancy Miller, Mar. 26, 1940; children: Edward Francis III, Nannette Christine, Roderick Anthony, Mae Angela. B.A., Georgetown U., 1929; postgrad., Harvard U., 1930-31; LL.B., St. Lawrence U., 1933. Bar: N.Y. 1933, U.S. Supreme Ct. 1938. Practice in N.Y.C., 1933-86; counsel Curtiss-Wright Corp., N.Y.C., Woodbridge, N.J., 1945-47; dep. commr. N.Y.C. Dept. Marine and Aviation, 1947-49, commr., 1950-54; dep. commr., acting commr. Dept. Hosps., 1949-50; commr. Fire Dept., 1954-62; exec. dep. mayor N.Y.C., 1962-65; v.p. Baker Industries, Inc., 1966-71, dir., 1966-79; dir. Wells Fargo Armored Transport Corp., 1966-70, Wells Fargo Armored Service Corp., Tenn., 1966-70, Wells Fargo Armored Service Corp. Miss., 1966-70, Wells Fargo Armored Service Corp. Del., 1966-70; v.p. Wells Fargo Armored Service Corp. Mass., Pacific Plant Protection, Shane & Assocs.; dir. Wells Fargo Armored Service Fla., James Cavanagh Corp., Personal Investments, N.Y.C. Mem. Gov.'s Emergency Adv. Com.; chmn. Mayor's Chaplaincy Bd., Mayor's Com. on Harlem Affairs; mem. Mayor's Task Force on Markets; chmn. Interagy. Relocation Coordinating Com.; mem. exec. com. World's Fair, 1964-65; treas. Mercy Hosp., Hempstead, N.Y., 1950-56; chmn. bd. layman's adv. com. Bellevue Hosp., N.Y.C.; mem. exec. com. Post Coll., L.I. U.; Vice pres., dir. Thannawaga Democratic Orgn., N.Y.C.; chmn. N.Y. County Dem. Com.; Bd. dirs. Neighborhood House, Glen Cove, L.I., Library Presdl. Papers; trustee L.I. U. Served to col. USAAF, 1942-45. Decorated Legion of Merit U.S.; knight grand cross Order Holy Sepulchre of Jerusalem Papal; Order St. George Greece; Order Rebuen Dario Nicaragua; cavaliere ufficiale Order of Merit Italy; chevaller Order of Crown Belgium; Ecomeinda of Order of Isabella Catolica Spain; medal of Merit Iran).; Recipient William Randolph Hearst gold medal award Downtown Lower Manhattan Assn., 1954; Cath. War Vet award; Achievement award Interfaith Movement, 1964; Anti-Defamation League award, 1965. Mem. Assn. Bar City N.Y., Nat. Fire Protection Assn., Am. Legion (comdr. Air Service Post 1952-53, Distinguished Service award N.Y. dept. 1955), Phi Delta Phi. Roman Catholic. Clubs: Racquet and Tennis, Lotos, Whitehall (N.Y.C.); Piping Rock, Beaver Dam Winter Sports (Locust Valley, N.Y.); Harvard of N.Y; Spouting Rock Beach Assn., Clambake (Newport, R.I.). Home: Boca Raton Fla. Died June 17, 1986.

CAVANAUGH, WILLIAM THOMAS, association executive; b. Newark, Apr. 24, 1921; s. Daniel John and Anna E. (McGotty) C.; m. Elizabeth Louise McCann, June 24, 1950; children: Mary Cavanaugh Bloom, Dennis, Elizabeth, William, Peter. BS, Seton Hall U., 1942; postgrad., Columbia U., 1947-50. Instr., asst. prof. Seton Hall U., 1947-50; asst. exec. dir. Engrs. Joint Council, N.Y.C., 1953-56; exec. dir., sec. Engring. Manpower Commn., N.Y.C., 1956-59; mem. Adminstrv. Mgmt. Soc., Willow Grove, Pa., 1959-66; exec. dir. Met. Package Stores Assn., N.Y.C., 1966-67; dir. field ops. Am. Soc. Testing Materials, Phila., 1967-68, dep. mng. dir., 1968-70, mng. dir., 1970-85, pres., 1980-85; mem. council, mem. exec. standards council Am. Nat. Standards Inst. Mem. Am. Soc. Assn. Execs., United Bus. Schs. Assn. (nat. hon. life), Council Engring. and Sci. Soc. Execs. (exec. com.). Lt. comdr. USNR, 1942-46, comdr. 1950-53. Home: Warrington Pa. Died Apr. 18, 1985; buried Whitemarsh Meml. Park, Ambler, Pa.

CAVERS, DAVID FARQUHAR, educator; b. Buffalo, Sept. 3, 1902; s. William Watt and Elizabeth Mitchell (Farquhar) C.; m. Lelia Yeaman, Sept. 8, 1931; 1 son, David Farquhar. BS, U. Pa., 1923; LLB, Harvard U., 1926; JSD, Suffolk U., 1957; LLD, Chuo U., Tokyo, 1964, Duke U., 1979. Bar: N.Y. 1928, Mass. 1958. With N.Y.C. law firm, 1926-29; instr. Harvard U., 1929-30; asst. prof. W.Va. U. Coll. Law, 1930-31; asst. prof. Duke U. Sch. Law, 1931-32, prof. law, 1932-45; prof. Harvard Law Sch., 1945-88, Fessenden prof. law, 1952-69, emeritus, 1969-88, assoc. dean, 1951-58; pres. Walter E. Meyer Research Inst. Law, 1958-69; pres. Council Law-Related Studies, 1969-76; vice-chmn. bd. trustees Ctr. for Law and Social Policy, 1970-77, mem., 1977-88; vis. prof. law Yale U. Sch. Law, 1936-37, U. Chgo. Law Sch., 1940-41; lectr. Hague Acad. Internat. Law, 1970; asst. gen. counsel OPA, Washington, 1943-45, assoc. gen. counsel, 1945-46; legal adviser U.S. Dept. Agr. in drafting food and drug bills, 1933-34; spl. asst. to U.S. Atty. Gen., 1938; mem. research adv. bd. Com. for Econ. Devel., 1943-51; mem. Commn. for Revision N.C. Law Estates, 1935-36; exec. com. Assn. Am. Law Schs., 1967-68; U.S. del. Hague Conf. on Pvt. Internat. Law, 1941-73. Author: (with J.R. Nelson) Electric Power Regulation in Latin America, 1959, The Choice-of-Law Process, 1965, Contemporary Conflicts Law in American Perpective, 1970; editor: Law and Contemporary Problems, 1933-45; contbr. articles to jours. Fellow Ctr. for Advanced Study in the Behavioral Scis., 1958-59. Mem. Am. Acad. Arts and Scis., Phi Beta Kappa, Delta Upsilon, Beta Gamma Sigma. Home: Cambridge Mass. Died Mar. 4, 1988; buried Mt. Auburn Cemetery, Cambridge, Mass.

CAVERT, WALTER DUDLEY, clergyman; b. Charlton, N.Y., Jan. 18, 1891; s. Walter I. and Elizabeth (Brann) C.; m. Harriet Harrer, July 17, 1916; children: Elizabeth Harrer (Mrs. Howard C. Adams), Harriet Morrison (Mrs. Clyde H. McDaniel Jr.). AB, Union Coll., Schenectady, N.Y., 1911, DD, 1931; BD, Union Theol. Sem., N.Y.C., 1915. Ordained to ministry Presbyn. Ch., 1915. Asst. pastor 1st Congl. Ch., Willimantic, Conn., 1915-16; pastor Stamford, N.Y., 1916-20, North Presbyn. Ch., Elmira, N.Y., 1921-24, Grace Presbyn. Ch., Oswego, N.Y., 1925-36, Presbyn. Ch. (union of Grace and First chs.), Oswego, 1936-39; supt. Christian edn. Synod of N.Y., 1939-57; pastor North Ch., Syracuse, 1959-66; dir. pub. rels. Charlton Sch., N.Y., 1967-71; vis. prof. Christian edn. McCormick Theol. Sem., 1957-58, St. Paul's United Theol. Coll., Kenya, 1969; moderator Synod of N.Y., 1956-57; vice moderator U.P. Gen. Assembly, 1961-62; pres. Syracuse Area Coun. Chs., 1961-62; del. Presbyn. Gen. Assembly, 1929, 35; internat. exchange preacher, Eng., summer 1934. Author: Story Sermons from Literature and Art, 1939, Remember Now, 1944, With Jesus on the Scout Trail, 1951, Ours in the Faith, 1960, Prayers for Youth, 1962, Prayers for Scouts, 1964, In the Days of Thy Youth, 1971; contbr. articles to religious mags. Bd. dirs. N.Y. State Coun. Chs. and Religious Edn., Charlton Sch., N.Y. Served as chaplain, 1st lt. AUS, 1918; chaplain. capt. ORC, resigned. Mem. Phi Beta Kappa. Republican. Home: Syracuse N.Y. †

CEHANOVSKY, GEORGE, baritone; b. Petersburg, Russia, Apr. 14, 1892; came to U.S., 1922; naturalized, 1929; s. Vincent P. and Sophie (Burago); adopted s. Vera Cehanovska; m. Elisabeth Rethberg Saettler, June 23, 1956 (dec. 1976); m. 2d Sylvia. Student, St. Petersburg Naval Acad., 1912-16; pupil of Vera Cehanovska at, St. Petersburg Conservatory, 1918-22. Mem. De Feo Opera Co., Balt., 1923-24, San Carlo Opera Co., N.Y.C., other cities, 1924-25, Met. Opera Co., 1926-86, San Francisco Opera Co., 1936-56; recording artist for RCA Victor, Columbia records. Home: Yorktown Heights N.Y. Died Mar. 25, 1986.

CENNAMO, RALPH, labor union official; b. Bridgeport, Conn., Jan. 19, 1919; m. Anna Mae, 1943; 3 children. mem. Internat. Leather Goods, Plastics and Novelty Workers Union, N.Y.C., 1937-85, dir. orgn., 1961-85, gen. sec.-treas., 1980-85; sec.-treas. local 22 Internat. Ladies's Handbag, Pocketbook and Novelty Workers Union, Bridgeport, 1937-39, bus. agt., 1939-41; organizer Pocket and Novelty Workers Union, N.Y.C., 1946-51, internat. rep., 1951-61. With U.S. Army, 1941-45. Home: New York N.Y. Died June 26, 1985.

CHABRIER, JACQUES RENE, financial consultant; b. Nancy, France, Jan. 15, 1921; came to U.S., 1946; naturalized, 1954; s. R. Charles and Simone (Huber) C.; m. Marie Anne Smith, May 27, 1948; 1 dau., Yvonne Vasquez. BA, Rennes U., 1939; BL, U. Paris, 1942; grad., Ecole des Sciences Politiques, Paris, 1942. Staff asst. S.N. Pathe Cinema, Paris, 1942-43, exec. asst. prodn., studio v.p., 1944-45, Am. rep., 1946-47; pres. Pathe Cinema Corp.,.1947-51, Paris Theatre Corp. N.Y., 1948-51; mem. staff investment dept. Hartford Nat. Bank & Trust Co., 1951, supr., 1952-55, asst. trust officer, 1956, trust officer, 1956-58, v.p., 1958-61, exec. v.p., 1961-68; pres., dir. Chappell & Co., Inc., N.Y.C., 1968-73; chmn., dir. Chappell & Co. Ltd., London, 1968-73; exec. v.p., dir. Polygram Corp., N.Y.C., 1973-74; fin. cons. N.Am. Philips Corp., N.Y.C., 1974-85, Mandes Gans Bank, N.V., Amsterdam, 1975-85, Drexel-Burnham-Lambert Group, N.Y.C., 1976-85; dir., mem. investment com. Mut. Ins. Co., Hartford, Covenant Ins. Co. Hartford, Ensign Bickford Industies, Inc., Simsbury, Drexel Burnham Lambert Realty Inc., N.Y.C.; dir. Davey-Bickford Smith & Co., Rouen, France, D.B.L. Realty Corp.; v.p., dir. Importers Motion Picture Orgn. N.Y., 1950-51; film adviser French embassy, Washington, N.Y.C., 1948-52. Trustee Harford Coll. for Women, Nat. Health and Welfare Retirement Assn., Edward W. Hazen Found.; bd. dirs. Children's Village, Dobbs Ferry, N.Y., Circle Repertory Theatre, N.Y.C. Mem. Nat. Music Publs. Assn. (dir.), ASCAP (dir. 1968-74), French C. of C. in U.S. (treas. 1949-51), Knickerbocker Club. Home: New York N.Y. Died Nov. 1985.

CHAIT, FREDERICK, lawyer, newspaper executive; b. Newark, Sept. 20, 1913; s. Boris and Clara (Wolpe) C.; m. Helen Sporn, Sept. 22, 1938. A.B., Coll. City N.Y., 1932; LL.B., Columbia, 1935, J.D., 1967. Bar: N.Y. State bar 1935, Pa. bar 1952. Atty. Social Security Bd., Washington, 1936-37; asso. firm Konta, Kirchwey and Engel, N.Y.C., 1937-42; chief counsel rationing depts. OPA, 1942-44; war legislation litigation and claims div. U.S. Dept. Justice, 1944-45; gen. counsel UNRRA, 1946-48; counsel Triangle Publs., Inc., also Phila. Inquirer, 1948-69; gen. mgr. Phila. Inquirer and Phila. Daily News, 1958-69; pres. Phila. Newspapers, Inc., 1970-75; v.p. Knight-Ridder Newspapers, Inc., 1971-80, spl. counsel, cons., 1981-88. Co-author: Monopoly vs. Competition, 1935; Legal Controls on Competitive Practices, 1936, Copyright Law, 1939. Bd. dirs., mem. planning com. Phila. Mus. Art; bd. mgrs. Pa. Hosp. Mem. Pa., N.Y.C. bar assns. Home: Philadelphia Pa. Died May 7, 1988; cremated.

CHALKLEY, GLADYS BRANEGAN (MRS. CHARLES A. CHALKLEY), home economics educator, college administrator; b. Disko, Ind., June 23, 1891; d. Robert and Sophrona (Lukens) Branegan; m. Charles A. Chalkley, Dec. 18, 1954 (dec. Nov. 1958). BS, U. Wis., 1913; MA, Columbia U., 1920, PhD, 1929; ScD, Mont. State Coll., 1957. Tchr. Niobrara (Nebr.) Grade Schs., 1909-10, Madison (Wis.) High Sch., 1913-15, Platteville (Wis.) State Normal Sch., 1915-17, State Coll. for Women, Denton, Tex., 1917-19; home mgmt. specialist Mont. Extension Svc., 1920-21; state supr. home econs., Mont., 1920-22; head home econs. dept. Mont. State Coll., 1921-31, dean, 1931-45, on leave as vis. prof. home econs. Hunter Coll., N.Y.C., 1944-45; dir. Sch. Home Econs. Ohio State U., 1945-55, then prof. emeritus; vis. prof. So. Ill. U., 1960-61; cons., lectr. home econs. Author: Home Economics Teacher Training Under the Smith Hughes Act, 1917-27, 29, (with others) Home Economics in Higher Education, California Home Economics Association Yesterday, Today and Tomorrow, 1962; contbr. to mags. Mem. AAAS, Am. Home Econ. Assn. (nat. pres. 1940-42), Nat. Coun. Family Rels. (Ohio pres.), Nat. Edn. Assn., MOnt. Edn. Assn., Am. Dietetics Assn., Child Study Assn., AAUW (pres. Mont. div. 1928-30), Nat. Coun. Women, League Women Voters, Near East Coll. Assn., Fgn. Policy Assn., DAR, Mortar Board, Omicron Nu, Phi Upsilon Omicron, Phi Kappa Phi, Alpha Gamma Delta, Delta Kappa Gamma. Republican. Methodist. Home: Riverside Calif. †

CHAMBERLAIN, HERBERT W., manufacturing executive; b. Rochester, N.Y., 1890; 2 children. Pres., chmn. exec. com. Gen. Ry. Signal Co., Rochester, N.Y. Mem. Masons. Home: Saint Petersburg Fla. †

CHAMBERLAIN, KATHERINE MCFARLANE, scientist; b. Saginaw, Mich., June 28, 1892; d. Fenton Durfee and Elizabeth (McFarlane) Chamberlain. AB, U. Mich., 1914, AM, 1919, ScD, 1924; postgrad. rsch. student, Cavendish Lab., U. of Cambridge, Eng., 1925-26. Inst. Colls. City of Detroit, 1924-25, asst. prof. math., 1925-27, assoc. prof. physics, 1927-33; assoc. prof. physics Wayne U., 1933-45, prof. physics, from 1945; lectr. on social implications of atomic energy. Author: Darkroom Handbook, 1948, An Introduction to the Science of Photography, 1951. Recipient Ellen Richards rsch. grant, 1925, Bronze medal of Disting. Svc. Found. of Optometry, 1937. Mem. Am. Assn. Physics Tchrs., Optical Soc. of Am. (vice chmn. Detroit chpt., 1949-50), Photog. Soc. of Am., United World Federalists (bd. dirs. Detroit chpt. 1947), Women's Internat. League, Intergroup Coun. for Women as Pub. Policy Makers (vice chmn. Intergroup Coun. 1947-49), Engring. Soc. of Detroit, Women's City Club (bd. dirs. 1946-49), Soroptomists, Phi Beta Kappa, Sigma Xi, Sigma Pi Sigma, Collegiate Sorosis, Delta Kappa Gamma. Episcopalian (bldg. commn.). Home: Detroit Mich. †

CHAMBERS, MERRITT MADISON, educator; b. Knox County, Ohio, Jan. 26, 1899; s. Rufus Ward and Etta Amelia (Miller) C. Student, U. Fla., Harvard U.; BA, Ohio Wesleyan U., 1922; MA, Ohio State U., 1927, PhD, 1931; LittD, Eastern Ky. U., 1969. Tchr. prin. high schs. 1922-26; with Am. Council on Edn., 1935-42, 45-51; cons. U.S. Office Edn., 1952-53; owner-operator Lafayette Farms, Mt. Vernon, Ohio, 1951-58; vis. prof. higher edn. U. Mich., 1958-63; exec. dir. Mich. Council State Coll. Pres.'s, 1961-62; prof. higher edn. Ind. U., 1963-69; prof. ednl. adminstrn., cons. on higher edn. Ill. State U., Normal, 1969-85; participant surveys of higher edn., Mass., Ill., 1949, Conn., Wis., Ia., 1950, N.Y.C., 1961, Ky., 1962, Md., 1963; cons. Com. on Govt. and Higher Edn., 1957; chmn. Long-Range Study Higher Edn., Ky., 1965-66; cons. So. Ill. U. and Mich. State Bd. Edn., 1966. Author: Youth-Serving Organizations, rev. edit., 1947, The Campus and the People, 1960, Voluntary Statewide Coordination in Public Higher Education, 1961, Chance and Choice in Higher Education, 1962, Financing Higher Education, 1963, The Colleges and the Courts Since 1950, 1964, Freedom and Repression in Higher Education, 1965, Bibliography of Higher Education, 1966, The Colleges and the Courts, 1962-66, 1967, Higher Education: Who Pays?, Who Gains?, 1968, Higher Education in the Fifty States, 1970, Above High School, 1970, The Developing Law of the Student and the College, 1972, Faculty and Staff Before the Bench, 1973, Higher Education and State Governments, 1974, Keep Higher Education Moving, 1976; editor: various works including Charters of Philanthropies, 1948, Universities of the World Outside U.S.A., 1950; contbr. articles to ednl., legal publs. Recipient awards Nat. Orgn. on Legal Problems, 1970, Nat. Colloquium on Higher Edn., 1971; presdl. citation Am. Coll. Pub. Relations Assn., 1972; medalha promundi beneficio Brazilian Acad. Humanities. Fellow AAAS; mem. Knox County Farm Bur. (pres. 1957-58), NEA (life), Delta Sigma Rho, Phi Delta Kappa, Alpha Sigma Phi. Maj. USAAF, 1942-46. Home: Normal Ill. Died Nov. 15, 1985; buried Park Hill Cemetery, Bloomington, Ill.

CHAN, SHAU WING, educator; b. Canton, China, Apr. 4, 1907; s. Chan Chi-Tong and Tsui Wan-Ying; m. Anna Mae Chan, July 27, 1935; children—Wayne Lyman, Loren Briggs. A.B., Lingnan U., China, 1927; A.M., Stanford, 1932, Ph.D., 1937. Instr. English Nat. Sun Yat-Sen U., Canton, China, 1927-30; lectr. Chinese Kwangtung Provincial Normal Sch. for Women, Canton, 1928-30; U. fellow in English Stanford, 1932-34; apptd. prof. English Nat. U. Shantung, Taingtao, China, 1937; spl. lectr. Utah State Agrl. Coll., summer 1941; vis. prof. U. Utah, summer 1944; Pomona Coll., summers 1945, 1946, 1950, 1951; instr. in Chinese lang. and lit. Stanford, 1938-39, asst. prof. Chinese and English, 1939-42, asst. prof. Chinese and humanities, 1942-45, asso. prof. Chinese and humanities, 1945-50, prof. Chinese, 1950-72, emeritus, 1972-86; acting exec. head Stanford (Dept. Asiatic and Slavic exec. head dept. Asian langs.), 1958-62; dir. human relations area files China Research Project, Stanford, 1955-56; cons. hist. research Com. for Free Asia, 1951-52; cons. Stanford Research Inst., 1951-53; established soldier-training program in Chinese Stanford, 1943, dir., 1943-45; dir. Chinese-Japanese Lang. and Area Center, 1956-86; research assoc. Hoover Instn. Lang.; cons. Internat. Secretariat, UN Conf., San Francisco. Author: Chinese Reader for Beginners, 1942, Concise English-Chinese Dictionary, 1946, Elementary Flash Cards, 1944, Elementary Chinese, 1951, 2d edit., 1961; co-author: China's Men of Letters Yesterday and Today. Chmn. bd. library trustees, City of Menlo Park. Mem. Am. Oriental Soc., Phi Delta Kappa. Conglist. Clubs: Kiwanian, Commonwealth of Calif. Home: Menlo Park Calif. Died Apr. 12, 1986.

CHANDLER, EDGAR HUGH STORER, clergyman, religious association official; b. Providence, Aug. 17, 1904; s. Henry Joseph and Christiana (Toms) C.; m. Ruth Doggett, Apr. 18, 1927; children: Hugh S., Marjorie Ann, Constance Elsie, Christopher Norris, David Luscombe. BS, Boston U., 1928, DD, 1961; postgrad., U. London, 1928-31; BD, Andover Newton Theol. Sch., 1933; postgrad., Harvard Div. Sch., 1933-35; DD, Northland Coll., 1952; LLD, Loyola U., 1965, Iowa Wesleyan Coll., 1967; laureate, Lincoln Acad., 1966. Ordained to ministry Conglist. Ch., 1927. pastor, Jamaica Plain, Boston, 1933-42; dir. Conglist. Service Com., 1946-49, Refugee Service, World Council Chs., 1949-60; exec. dir. Ch. Fedn. Greater Chgo., 1960-69; exec. dir. Worcester (Mass.) Area Council Chs., 1969-75; adviser religious affairs USIA, 1960-66; lectr. Chgo. Theol. Sem., 1962-63, Boston U. Sch. Theology, 1972; instr. philosophy N.H. Coll., 1976-88; interim preacher Exeter (N.H.) United Ch. of Christ, 1976-88; pres. Internat. Conf. Vol. Agys. Working for Refugees, 1956-60; observer del. Vatican 11, 1966; mem. bd. John XXIII Ctr. for Ecumenical Studies, 1966. Author: The High Tower of Refuge, 1960; contbr. numerous articles to religious jours. Decorated Order Brit. Empire, grand cross Order of Merit (West Germany), gold cross Royal Order King George of Greece, knight-officer Order of Orange Nassau (Netherlands); named Chicagoan of Yr. in Religion, 1964; recipient Thomas Wright award City of Chgo., 1965, medal of merit City of Chgo., 1969. Comdr. Chaplains Corps, USNR, 1942-46. Home: Raymond N.H. Died May 7, 1988.

CHANDLER, RALPH JOSEPH, shipping executive; b. nr. L.A., Feb. 25, 1891; s. Fred and Rachel (Jacques) C.; m. Lenore E. Gantt, Aug. 28, 1920; children: Ralph J., Andrew Frederick. Student pub. schs., L.A. So. Calif. distbr. ALCO trucks and cars, L.A., 1910-13; v.p., sec. Star & Crescent Boat Co., San Diego, 1914-57, San Diego Marine Constrn. Co., 1915-57; v.p., gen. mgr. Ralph J. Chandler Shipbuilding Co., Wilmington, Calif., 1916-20, L.A. S.S. Co., Wilmington, 1920-31; v.p., sec. Star & Crescent Oil Co., San Diego, 1921-55; pres. L.A. S.S. Co. (affiliated Matson Nav. Co. 1931), 1932-34; So. Calif. mgr. Matson Nav. Co., L.A., 1935-44, v.p., 1945-62, also bd. dirs.; bd. dirs. Oceanic Steamship Co.; ptnr. Star & Crescent Investment Co., San Diego, 1943-57; bd. dirs., exec. com. Citizens Nat. Trust & Savs. Bank, L.A. Mem. Pacific Coast gen. com. Am. Bur. Shipping, N.Y.C., from 1937. Mem. Mchts. and Mfrs. Assn. L.A. (bd. dirs.), Pacific-Am. Steamship Assn., L.A. Steamship Assn. (pres.), Calif. C. of C., L.A. C. of C. (bd. dirs.), Wilmington C. of C., Long Beach C. of C., San Diego C. of C., All-Year of So. Calif. Club (bd. dirs.), Propeller Club U.S., Wilshire Country Club (L.A.), Bohemian Country Club (San Francisco), Cuyamaca Club (San Diego), San Gabriel Country Club (Calif.). Home: Pasadena Calif. †

CHAPMAN, ARDENIA, college dean; b. Keytesville, Mo., Nov. 17, 1892; d. Charles Alexander and Ardenia (Elliott) C. AA, Stephens Coll., 1913; BS, U. Mo., 1918; AM, Columbia, 1923. Instr. home econs. Stephens Coll., 1914-18, Warrensburg (Mo.) State Tchr.'s Coll., summer 1918; assoc. prof. home econs. Tex. State Coll. for Women, 1919-24; asst. prof. Drexel Inst. Tech., 1924-27, assoc. prof., 1927-33, prof., 1933-45, dean Coll. Home Econs., from 1945. Contbr. articles to profl. jours. Recipient honor award Stephens Coll., Columbia, Mo., 1933, Alumnae citation, 1953. Mem. AAUW, Am., Phila. (past pres.) home econs. assns., Am. Standards Assn. (past bd. dirs.), NEA, Am., Phila. (past pres.) dietetics assns., World Affairs Coun., Phila. Art Alliance, Altrusa Club (past pres.), Drexel Women's Club (past pres.), Delta Gamma, Phi Kappa Phi, Omicron Nu. Democrat. Baptist. Home: Philadelphia Pa. †

CHAPMAN, CHARLES CULLEN, clergyman; b. Aspen, Colo., May 18, 1891; s. Luke and Jane Ann (Cullen) C. Student, Boston Coll., 1916-17; AB, Gonzaga U., Spokane, 1923, AM, 1924; PhD, Fordham U., 1934; course in econs., NYU, 1935. Joined Jesuit Order, 1918, ordained priest Roman Cath. Ch., 1928. Lectr. in ancient history Fordham U., 1929, Spring Hill Coll., 1930-31; spl. studies 1931-34; asst. prof. Am. history Loyola U. of the South, 1934-37, assoc. prof., 1937-40, prof., from 1940, head dept. history and polit. sci., from 1940; exchange prof. St. Louis U., summer 1942. Author: The Development of American Business and Banking Thought, 1936, A History of Western Civilization, 1960. Mem. Am. Hist. Assn., Am. Polit. Sci. Assn., Am. Acad. Polit. and Social Sci., Am. Jesuit Hist. Conf. (pres. 1940), Cath. Hist. Assn., Cath. Econ. Assn. Home: New Orleans La. †

CHAPMAN, LAURA BERNICE, nursing educator; b. Wayne, Nebr., Sept. 23, 1909; d. William Henry and Lorena Augusta (Curtis) C. Diploma, Grinnell (Iowa) Community Hosp., 1930; BS in Nursing Edn., U. Minn., 1935; MA, Columbia U., 1952, postgrad., 1961-63. Staff nurse Community Hosp., Grinnell, 1930-32; sci. instr. Jennie Edmunson Hosp., Council Bluffs, Iowa, 1935-38; nursing arts instr. Abbott Hosp., Mpls., 1938-42; sci. instr. Broadlawns Hosp., Des Moines, 1942-43; clin. instr. Wesley Meml. Hosp., Chgo., 1943-48, asst. dir. Sch. Nursing, 1949-51; asst. prof. Sch. Nursing U. Ill., 1952-54; dean Coll. Nursing, Brigham Young U., 1954-61; dean Coll. Nursing, Rutgers, The State U., Newark, 1964-73. Mem. Am. Nurses Assn., N.J. Nurses Assn., Tchrs. Coll. Alumni Assn., Kappa Delta Pi, Sigma Theta Tau. Home: Piscataway N.J. Died Jan. 1, 1988.

CHAPMAN, WAYNE ELLSWORTH, lawyer; b. Chgo., Aug. 30, 1932; s. John William and Eva (Reece) C.; m. Helen M. Boyes, Sept. 23, 1961; children: Steven, Karen, Paul, Emily. B.A., U. Mich., 1954; LL.B., Columbia U., 1957. Bar: N.Y. 1957. Mem. Cravath, Swaine & Moore, N.Y.C., 1957-64, ptnr., 1965-87. Mem. ABA, Assn. Bar City N.Y., N.Y. State Bar Assn. Clubs: Wall St. (N.Y.C.); Quogue Beach, Shinnecock Yacht; Quogue Field (Quogue, N.Y.). Home: New York N.Y. Died Apr. 11, 1987; cremated.

CHARLES, DANE WEST, banker; b. Greenfield, Ohio, July 29, 1930; s. Forest Ray and Mary Jane (West) C.; m. Judith Ann Warner, Nov. 18, 1959; children—Sharon, Christopher, Amy. B.S. in Bus. Adminstrn., Ohio State U., 1952, M.B.A., 1956. C.P.A., Ohio. Staff accountant to ptnr. Touche Ross & Co., Dayton, Cin. and N.Y., 1952-83; sr. v.p. Sun Banks, Inc., Orlando, Fla., 1983-85; 1st v.p. SunTrust Banks, Inc., Atlanta,, Ga.,, 1985-87. Author: Accountants SEC Practice, 1976, 78. Served to 1st lt. USAF, 1952-54. Mem. Am. Inst. C.P.A.s (mem. coms.), Ohio Soc. C.P.A.s (mem. coms.), N.Y. State Soc. C.P.A.s, Fla. Inst. C.P.A.s, Inst. Internal Auditors. Methodist. Club: Citrus (Orlando). Lodge: Mason. Home: Atlanta Ga. Died Jan. 22, 1987.

CHARLEY, MICHAEL FRANCIS, pharmaceutical manufacturer; b. La Salle, Ill., Sept. 6, 1891; s. Michael J. and Sarah Elizabeth (Tracey) C.; m. Carolyn Sommers, Dec. 7, 1912. Grad., Ill. Coll. Pharmacy, 1909. Pharm. chemist from 1909, retail druggist, 1909-12, wholesale druggist, 1912-15; with Standard LAb., 1915-27; with Standard Pharmacal Co., Chgo., from 1927, successively sec., gen. mgr., pres., from 1934. Mem. Chgo. Plan Commn., 1949. Mem. Chgo. Drug and Chem. Assn. (pres. 1942), Am. Pharm. Mfrs. Assn. (pres. 1952-54), Chgo. Athletic Assn., Evanston Golf Club. Home: Chicago Ill. †

CHASE, ANTHONY GOODWIN, lawyer; b. San Francisco, Feb. 15, 1938; s. Goodwin and Gudrun M. (Mack) C.; m. Mary Costa, Mar. 22, 1981; children by previous marriage: Betsy Marie, Whitney Marie, Goodwin Samuel, Anthony Joseph. B.A., U. Wash., 1960; J.D., Georgetown U., 1967. Bar: D.C. 1967, Wash. 1969. Nat. bank examiner U.S. Treasury Dept., 1962-65; asst. to U.S. Comptroller of Currency, 1965-67; individual practice law 1967-69; asst. to U.S. sec. of commerce, 1969-70; gen. counsel SBA, Washington, 1970-71; dep. adminstr. SBA, 1971-73; ptnr. Brownstein, Zeidman Schomer and Chase, Washington and Los Angeles, 1973-78, Tufo, Johnston, Zuccotti & Chase, Washington and N.Y.C., 1978-80, Drinker Biddle & Reath, Washington, Phila. and N.Y.C., 1980-82; mng. ptnr. Trammell, Chase, Lambert & Martindale, Washington, from 1982; adj. prof. corp. law Georgetown U.; lectr. Georgetown U. (Practising Law Inst.), from 1971; Wharton Sloan lectr. Wharton Sch. Bus., U. Pa., 1973; lectr. Sr. Bank Mgmt. Seminar, Columbia U., from 1971, N.Y. Law Jour., from 1974, Am. Law Inst., from 1980; dir. VSE Corp., Alexandria, Va., Digital Switch Corp., Dallas, 1980-81; sec. Nat. Adv. Com. on Banking Policies and Practices, 1966; mem. Adminstrv. Conf. U.S., Fed. Adv. Council Regional Econ. Devel.; adv. com. on indsl. issuers SEC, 1972-73; fed. state programs coordinator State of Wash., 1967; mem. nat. devel. com. Georgetown U., from 1970; mem. bd. control U. Wash., 1960. Author: Small Business Financing, 1983; Co-editor: Wests Fed. Practice Manual, from 1974; mem.: Georgetown Law Rev, 1964-65; Contbr. articles to profl. jours. Served as lt. USMC, 1960-62; capt. Res. Named Outstanding Young Man of Year Wash. Jr. C. of C., 1968; recipient Fed. Silver medal for meritorious service, 1970, Fed. Gold medal for disting. service, 1971; Disting. Service to Am. Bus. award Nat. Assn. Small Bus. Investment Cos., 1972; Outstanding Service to Am. Small Bus. Community award Nat. Small Bus. Assn., 1974. Mem. ABA, Fed. Bar Assn., Pa. Bar Assn., D.C. Bar Assn., Wash. Bar Assn., Am. Judicature Soc., Nat. Lawyers Club, Beta Theta Pi. Republican. Episcopalian. Clubs: Union League (N.Y.C.); Pisces (Chevy Chase, Md.); Georgetown; Mid-Ocean (Tuckerstown, Bermuda). Office: The Estate of Anthony Chase Mr Goodwin Chase 11417 Gravelly Lake Dr SW Tacoma WA 98499 Deceased.

CHASE, LUCIA, ballet dancer; b. Waterbury, Conn., 1908; d. Irving Hall and Elizabeth Hosmer (Kellogg) C.; m. Thomas Ewing Jr. (dec. 1933); children: Thomas III, Alexander Cochran. Student, St. Margaret's Sch., Waterbury, Theatre Guild Sch., N.Y.C.; LHD (hon.), U. Wis., 1969; DFA, Williams Coll., 1977, L.I. U., 1979. Ballerina Mordkin Ballet, 1937-39, Am. Ballet Theatre, N.Y.C., 1940-60; co-dir. Am. Ballet Theatre, 1945-80. Recipient Dance Mag. award, 1957, 17th ann. Capezio Dance award, 1968, Mayor's Arts and Culture award N.Y.C. Commn. Cultural Affairs, 1978, Presdl. Medal of Freedom, 1980. Home: New York N.Y. Died Jan. 9, 1986.

CHASE, SAMUEL WOOD, educator; b. Lowell, Mass., May 27, 1892; s. Francis Nelson and Emma Isabelle (Wood) C.; m. Hilda Elizabeth Roehm, June 28,

1922; children: Martha Cowles, Ruth Bradley. AB, Bowdoin Coll., 1914; AM, Harvard U., 1916, PhD, 1921. Mem. faculty Western Res. U. Sch. of Medicine and Sch. of Dentistry, Cleve., from 1920, prof. histology and embryology, from 1945. 2d lt. Air Svc., U.S. Army, 1917-19; overseas with 41st Aero Squadron, 5th Pursuit Group as pilot, 1918-19. Mem. Internat. Assn. for Dental Rsch. (pres. 1946-47), Am. Assn. Anatomists, Am. Soc. of Zoologists, Ohio Acad. Scis., Sigma Xi, Omicron Kappa Upsilon (hon.) Delta Upsilon. Home: Cleveland Heights Ohio. †

CHASE, STUART, economist, writer; b. Somersworth, N.H., Mar. 8, 1888; s. Harvey Stuart and Aaronette (Rowe) C.; m. Margaret Hatfield, July 5, 1914; children: Robert, Sonia; m. 2d, Marian Tyler, 1930. LittD (hon.), Am. U., Washington, 1950, Emerson Coll., Boston, 1970, New Haven U., 1974. Ptnr. Harvey S. Chase Co., C.P.A.'s, Boston, until 1917; investigating the meat industry and the packers, under FTC, 1917-22; with Labor Bur., Inc., 1922-39; cons. Nat. Resources Com., 1934, Resettlement Adminstrn., 1935, SEC, 1939, TVA, 1940-41, UNESCO, 1949. Author: The Tragedy of Waste, 1925, (with F.J. Schlink) Your Money's Worth, 1927, Men and Machines, 1929, Prosperity Fact or Myth, 1930, The Nemesis of American Business, 1931, (with Marian Tyler) Mexico, A Study of Two Americas, 1931, A New Deal, 1932, The Economy of Abundance, 1934, Government in Business, 1935, Rich Land, Poor Land, 1936, The Tyranny of Words, 1938, The New Western Front, 1939, Idle Money, Idle Men, 1941, A Primer of Economics, 1941, The Road We Are Traveling, 1942, Goals for America, 1942, Where's the Money Coming From?, 1943, Democracy Under Pressure, 1945, Men at Work, 1945, Tomorrows's Trade, 1945, For This We Fought, 1956, The Proper Study of Manking, 1948, rev. edit., 1963, Roads to Agreement, 1951, Power of Words, Guides to Straight Thinking, 1956, Some Things Worth Knowing, 1958, Live and Let Live, 1960, Probable World, 1968, Danger, Men Talking, 1969; contbr. to mags. and periodicals. Sec. Redding Planning Commn., 1952-69. Mem. Am. Acad. and Inst. Arts and Letters, Harvard Club, Phi Gamma Delta, Phi Beta Kappa. Home: Redding Conn. Died Nov. 16, 1985; buried Umpawaug Cemetery, Redding.

CHASINS, ABRAM, pianist, composer, author; b. N.Y.C., Aug. 17, 1903; s. Saul and Elizabeth (Hochstein) C.; m. Constance Keene, 1949. Student, Ethical Culture Sch., 1914-18, Columbia U., 1920-22. Toured Europe, Am. in recital, also orchestral-soloist, 1925-46; featured performer, recording artist, speaker nat. radio networks, Chasins Music Series, 1932-38; faculty Curtis Inst., 1926-35, Berkshire Ctr., 1939-40; dir. music N.Y. Times radio sta. WQXR, 1943-65; musician-in-residence U. So. Calif., 1972-73, artistic dir. radio sta. KUSC, 1973-77; composer over 100 pub. works performed by leading orchs., soloists; dir. Annual Music Edn. projects, judge internat. competitions; then writer, lectr. Author: Speaking of Pianists, 1947, The Van Cliburn Legend, 1959, The Appreciation of Music, 1966, Music at the Crossroads, 1972, Stoki, the Incredible Apollo (biography of Stokowski); contbr. articles Sat. Rev., N.Y. Times, McCall's, Ladies' Home Jour., Hi-Fidelity. Mem. ASCAP (mem. steering com. West Coast chpt.), Nat. Fedn. Am. Composers, Juilliard Alumni Assn. (dir.), Curtis Alumni Assn., Bohemians, Musicians, Manhattan Chess. Home: New York N.Y. Deceased.

CHATFIELD, CHARLES HUGH, aeronautical engineer; b. Waterbury, Conn., Sept. 8, 1892; s. William F. and Mary F. (Cairns) C.; m. Grace M. Scofield, Nov. 10, 1920 (dec. 1951); m. 2d, Lois M. Wells, May 8, 1954; 1 dau., Deborah Mary. BS, MIT, 1914, MS, 1915, grad. work in aero. engring., 1918. Registered profl. engr., Conn. Aeronautics engr. Wright Aeronautics Corp., Paterson, N.J., 1921-26; assoc. prof. aeronautics MIT, 1926-29; rsch. engr. United Aircraft Corp., East Hartford, Conn., 1929-41, sec., from 1941; bd. dirs. Mfrs. Aircraft Assn. Author: (with C.F. Taylor and S. Ober) The Airplane and Its Engine, 1928. Aero. engr. USNRF, 1917-21. Fellow Inst. Aero. Scis., Royal Aero. Soc. (assoc.); mem. Soc. Automotive Engrs. Home: West Hartford Conn. †

CHAUNCEY, A. WALLACE, chemical corporation executive; b. Bklyn., Apr. 6, 1891; s. George W. and Adelaide (Sheldon) C.; m. Louise G. Ruxton, June 3, 1919. Student, Bklyn. Latin Sch., Pomfret (Conn.) Sch.; PhB, Yale U.; student, Columbia Law Sch. With William A. Read & Co. (later Dillon, Read & Co.), 1915-16; ptnr. Chauncey, Hayes & Lord, investment bankers, 1919-22; sec., dir. Philip Ruxton Inc., 1922-28; mem. exec. com., dir. Internat. Printing Ink Corp., 1928-37; vice chmn. exec. com, dir. Interchem. Corp., N.Y.C., 1937-59, mem. exec. com., dir., cons., from 1959; pres., dir. Greenwood Cemetery, Bklyn.; bd. dirs. Chauncey Real Estate Corp., Millprint, Inc., Internat. Printing Ink Ltd., Ault & Wiborg Corp., Ruxton Products. Past trustee Village of East Hampton, L.I., N.Y., Pomfret Sch. Capt. F.A., A.E.F., World War I. Decorated Silver star, Conspicuous Svc. cross, State of N.Y. Hon. mem. Internat. Printing Pressmen and Assts. Union of N.Am., A.F. of L.; mem. Champlain Soc. (U. Toronto), Pilgrims of the U.S., Newcomen Soc. of Eng. in N.Am., Soc. of Colonial Wars, Sons of the Revolution State N.Y., Mil. Order Fgn. Wars. U.S., Mil. Order World Wars., Soc. Am. Wars., Elizabethan Club (Yale U.), Yale Club, Union Club, N.Y. Yacht Club (N.Y.C.); Maidstone Club (East Hampton, L.I.); National Golf Link of Am. (Southampton, L.I.); Triton Fish and Game Club, Garrison (Quebec, Can.), Masons, Delta Phi, Aurelian Honor Soc. Episcopalian (past treas. and mem. vestry, Ch. of Ascension, City of N.Y.; vestryman, St. Luke's Ch., E. Hampton, L.I.). Home: East Hampton N.Y. †

CHEATHAM, JOHN MCGEE, textile manufacturing executive; b. Easley, S.C., May 15, 1913; s. John Henry and Jayne (Jackson) C.; m. Elizabeth Mathis, June 15, 1939; children: John McGee, Elizabeth M., Harvey M., Jackson Kelley. Student, Furman U., 1930-32, Ga. Tech., 1932-33. With Dundee Mills, Griffin, Ga., 1933-83; successively clk., jr. salesman, asst. to pres., v.p. Dundee Mills, Griffin, 1941-50, pres., 1950-79, chmn., chief. exec. officer, 1979-83; chmn. Hartwell Mills, Ga.; dir. Trust Co., Ga., Bibb Co. Lt. (j.g.) USNR, 1944-46. Mem. Textile Mfrs. Inst., Inc. (pres. 1960-61), Rotary. Baptist. Home: Griffin Ga. Died May 6, 1985; buried Griffin.

CHENOWETH, J. EDGAR, congressman; b. Trinidad, Colo., Aug. 17, 1897; s. Thomas Beaseman and Esther Rebecca (Shamberger) C.; m. Ruth Ollevia Crews, Dec. 25, 1919; children: William Beaseman, Wanda Elizabeth, John Edgar, James Richard, Ruth Anne. Student, U. Colo., 1915-16. Bar: Colo. 1925. With Colo. & So. Ry. Co., 1916-17, Continental Oil Co., 1917-20, Colo. Supply Co., 1920-26; police magistrate Trinidad, 1925-27; asst. dist. atty. 3d Jud. Dist. Colo., 1929-33; county judge Las Animas Co., 1933-41; mem. 77th-80th, 82d to 88th U.S. Congress, from 3d Colo. Dist.; chmn. Rep. State Cent. Com. of Colo., 1937-40. Trustee Colo. Woman's Coll. Mem. Masons, Eagles, Elks, Trinidad Rotary. Republican. Baptist. Home: Trinidad Colo. Died Jan. 2, 1986.

CHERNISS, HAROLD F., educator; b. St. Joseph, Mo., Mar. 11, 1904; s. David B. and Theresa (Hart) C.; m. Ruth Meyer, Jan. 1, 1929. AB, U. Calif., 1925, PhD, 1929; student, U. of Göttingen, Berlin, 1927-28; LHD, U. Chgo., 1950, Johns Hopkins U., 1965, Brown U., 1976; Laurea honoris causa, U. Rome, 1978. Assoc. in Greek U. Calif., 1928-29; instr. in classics Cornell U., 1930-33; lectr. in Greek Johns Hopkins U., 1932, assoc. in Greek, 1933-36, assoc. prof., 1936-42; prof. Greek U. Calif., 1946-48; prof. Inst. for Advanced Study Princeton U., 1948-74, prof. emeritus, 1974-87; Sather Found. lectr. U. Calif., 1942; mem. mng. com. Am. Sch. Classical Studies, Athens. Author books; asst. editor Am. Jour. of Philology, 1936-40, editor, 1940-42; contbr. articles to profl. jours. Corr. fellow Brit. Acad., Royal Acad., Arts and Scis. of Gotëborg, Académie Royale Flamande des Scis., Lettres et Beaux Arts de Belgique; mem. Am. Acad. Arts and Scis., Am. Philol. Assn., Am. Philos. Soc., Classical Assn. (Great Britain). Capt. AUS, 1942-46. Home: Princeton N.J. Died June 18, 1987.

CHESTON, CHARLES STEELE, business executive; b. Phila., Jan. 3, 1892; s. Radcliffe and Eugenia (Morris) C.; m. Harriet M. Frazier, June 5, 1919; children: George Frazier, Eugenia Cheston Sullivan, Harriet Cheston Klosson, Cornelia Cheston Worsley, Charles Steele. Student, St. George's Sch., Newport, R.I., U. Pa. Ptnr. Smith, Barney & Co. (and predecessor firms), 1919-1944; bd. dirs., chmn. fin. com. Philco Corp., Monsanto Chem. Co., bd. dirs., mem. exec. com. Ins. Co. N.Am.; bd. dirs. J.P. Morgan & Co., Mead Corp., Provident Mut. Life Ins. Co., Western Saving Fund Soc., Phila. Nat. Bank, Kans., Okla. & Gulf Ry. Co., Muskogee Co; bd. dirs., mem. fin. com. Am. Airlines, Inc.; bd. dirs. Indemnity Ins. Co. of N.Am., Phila. Fire & Marine Ins. Co., Chemstrand Corp., Monsanto Can. Ltd. Mem. bus. adv. coun. Dept. Commerce, from 1947. Capt. 56th F.A., AUS, World War I.; brig. gen. Army Specialist Corps. 1942; asst. dir. OSS, 1943-45. Mem. Philadelphia Club, Links Club (N.Y.C.); Metropolitan Club (Washington). Home: Bluebell Pa. †

CHICOINE, LIONEL MASON, automotive company executive; b. Detroit, Apr. 21, 1927; s. Lionel Mason and Ann P. (Hester) C.; m. Marian Elizabeth Bennett, Feb. 10, 1951; children: Carolyn, John. A.B., U. Mich., 1950; M.S., Mass. Inst. Tech., 1967. With Ford Motor Co., 1953—, asst. gen. mgr. supply assembly div., 1974-75, dir. body and assembly purchasing, 1975-76, v.p. purchasing, 1976-79, v.p. purchasing and supply, from 1979. Bd. dirs. Jr. Achievement S.E. Mich., Nat. Jr. Achievement. Served with U.S. Army, 1945-47. Alfred P. Sloan fellow, 1966-67. Clubs: Grosse Pointe, Detroit Country, Renaissance. Home: Grosse Pointe Shores Mich. Deceased.

CHILTON, WILLIAM EDWIN, III, journalist; b. Kingston, N.Y., Nov. 26, 1921; s. William Edwin and Louise (Schoonmaker) C.; m. Elizabeth Easley Early, Apr. 5, 1952; 1 dau., Susan Carroll. B.A., Yale U., 1950; H.H.D. (hon.), W.Va. State Coll., 1966, Colby Coll., 1982. Promotion mgr. Charleston Gazette, 1952-55, asst. to pub., 1955-61, pub., 1961-87; pres. Daily Gazette Co., 1961-87; gen. mgr. Charleston Newspapers, 1962-68, chmn. bd., 1968-87, also editorial writer; Mem. W.Va. Ho. of Dels., 1952-60; 1st vis. prof. journalism W.Va. U., 1969; weekly guest commentator WCHS-TV, 1971-72, W. Va. Pub. Broadcasting Radio, 1982-87; vis. journalism prof. Fuden U., Shanghai, People's Republ China, 1984, 86. Mem. W.Va. Centennial Commn 1956-64; chmn. W.Va. Lincoln-Kennedy Mem Commn.; mem. Kanawha County Library Bd., 1957-7 Kanawha County Parks and Recreation Commn., 196 70, Citizens Adv. Commn. on W.Va. Legislature, 196 70, Worth Bingham Meml. Found.; W.Va. dir. Crusac for Freedom, 1958; mem. exec. com. Com. of 10C W.Va. del. at large Dem. Nat. Conv., 1960; mem. Den nat. platform com., 1964; Trustee Morris Harvey Col mem. adv. bd. Handgun Control Affiliation. Served wit USAAF, 1941-45, CBI. Recipient Elijah Lovejc award, 1982. Mem. Chi Phi. Episcopalian. Club Edgewood; Pink Sands (Harbour Island, Bahamas). Home: Charleston W.Va. Died Feb. 7, 1987.

CHIOU, JIUNN PERNG, mechanical engineerin educator, laboratory administrator; b. Nanking, Chin July 29, 1933; m. Rita Chiou; children—Derel Jeff. B.S. in Mech. Engring., Nat. Taiwan U., 195 M.S. in Mech. Engring., Oreg. State U., 1960; Ph.D., U Wis., 1964. Mech. engr. Keelung Harbor Bur., Taiwa 1955-58; research asst. U. Wis., Madison, 1960-62, inst mech. engring., 1963-64; engring. specialist AiResearc Mfg. Co., Los Angeles, 1964-69; prof. mech. engring. U Detroit, from 1969, dir. Heat Transfer Lab., from 1969 Editor: Military Vehicle Power Plant Cooling, 197 Solar Energy in Cold Climates, 1977, Heat Transfer an Fluid Flow in Solar Energy System, 1985, Automobi Heating and Cooling, 1986, Heat Transfer in Was Heat Recovery and Heat Rejection Systems, 1986. Named Engring. Tchr. of Yr., U. Detroit, 1983. Mem Am. Soc. Mech. Engr. (chmn. 1979-86, exec. com. sol energy div. from 1986), Soc. Automotive Engrs. (chmr climate control com., passenger car activity, from 198 Forest R. McFarland award 1987), Internat. Sol Energy Soc., Phi Tau Sigma, Sigma Xi, Tau Beta P Deceased.

CHOPE, HENRY ROY, inventor, engineer; b. Louis ville, July 19, 1921; s. Henry Roy and Ameli (Guterman) C.; m. Lois Elizabeth Sherman, June 1 1954; children: Elizabeth Ann, David Roy, Ameli Louise, Charles Sherman. BEE, Ohio State U., 194 MS, Calif. Inst. Tech., 1948; SM, Harvard U., 1950. Registered profl. engr, Ohio. Electronic scientist rock devel. USAF, 1949-50, atomic scientist, 1950-53; exe v.p., dir. AccuRay Corp., Columbus, Ohio, 1952-8 dir., 1981-85, mem. exec. com., tech. adv. com.; bd. dir AccuRay Internat., Bell P.A. Systems, Columbus, 196 79, Medicon Corp., 1978-79, Danniger Med. Tech., Inc 1983-85; mem. labor-mgmt. adv. com. AEC, 1965-7 adv. com. isotopes and radiation devel., 1966-67; mem Ohio Atomic Energy Adv. Bd., 1967-69; mem. adv com. innovation Pres.'s Office Sci. and Tech., 1964; adv com. state tech. services Ohio Bd. Regents, 1967-7 adv. com. on health care Am. people AMA, 1970-7 engring. steering com., com. for tomorrow Ohio State U Coll. Engring. Patentee nuclear energy instrumentatio process control. Contbr. tech. papers to profl. jours. Trustee Riverside Meth. Hosp., Columbus, Riversid Meth. Hosp. Med. Rsch. Found., Ohio Weslyean U. 1971-79, Columbus Mus. Art, Columbus Symphon Orch., Ctr. Sci. and Industry; commr. Franklin Count Hosp., from 1978; bd. dirs. Buckeye Boys Ranch, Grov City, Ohio, 1976-77, Ohio State U. Rsch. Found., 1969 74. Recipient Disting. Alumnus award Ohio State U. 1961, Alumni Centennial award, 1970. Fellow AAAS Instrument Soc. Am. (Albert F. Sperry award 1972 mem. IEEE (sr., Morris E. Leeds award 1967), Am Nuclear Soc. (sr.), NSPE, U.S. C. of C. (bd. dirs. 1967 72, chmn. sci. and tech. com. 1968-70), Ohio C. of C (bd. dirs.), Columbus C. of C. (bd. dirs. 1967-74 Newcomen Soc. Am., Scioto Country Club (Columbus) Harvard Club (N.Y.C., Cen. Ohio), Rotary, Tau Beta P (pres., chmn. exec. com. 1966-70), Eta Kappa Nu, Thet Tau, Pi Kappa Alpha. Home: Columbus Ohio. Die Oct. 16, 1985, buried Union Cemetery, Columbus.

CHOUINARD, JULIEN, judge Supreme Court o Canada; b. Quebec, Que., Can., Feb. 4, 1929; s. Julier and Berthe (Cloutier) C.; m. Jeannine Pettigrew, Sept. 6 1956; children—Julien, Lucie, Nicole. B.A., U. Laval Quebec, 1948, LL.L., 1951; M.A. in Law, U. Oxford Eng., 1953. Bar: Called to Que. bar 1953, create queen's counsel 1965. Ptnr. firm Prevost, Gagne, Flynn Chouinard & Jacques, Quebec city, 1953-65; dep minister of justice Province Que., Quebec, 1965-68; sec gen. of exec. council 1968-75; judge Ct. of Appeal, 1975 79, Supreme Ct. of Can., Ottawa, Ont., 1979-87; lectr. i corp. law U. Laval, 1959-66. Co-commr. Roya Commn. of Inquiry into Bilingual Air Traffic Service in, Que., 1976-79. Decorated Centennial medal, office Order Can.; recipient Vanier medal Inst. Public Ad minstrn. Can., 1972; Rhodes scholar, 1951. Home: Ot tawa, Ont. Canada. Died Feb. 6, 1987.

CHRISTENSEN, GLENN JAMES, educator; b Canton, Ohio, Dec. 15, 1907; s. James Garfield an Emma (Lynch) C.; m. Mildred Balmer, Sept. 8, 1931; son, Gregory Balmer (dec.). BA, Coll. of Wooster 1935; PhD in English, Yale U., 1939; LLD, Coll. Notr Dame of Md., 1966. Instr. English Lehigh U. Bethlehem, Pa., 1939-42, asst. prof., 1942-46, assoc prof., 1946-55, prof., assoc. dean Coll. Arts and Scis. 1955, dean, 1956-62, v.p., provost, 1962-69, Univ. Dist ing. prof., 1969-76, prof. emeritus, 1976-88; pres. Lehigh Valley Ednl. TV Corp., 1962-66, then dir; vis. Carnegi

›oc. prof. English, Columbia U., 1951-52; dir. ›search Better Schs., Inc., 1966-67; cons. Inter Am. U. R., 1969-77. Mem. Commn. on Higher Edn., 1960- ; pres. Middle States Assn., 1968-69; chmn. bd. trus-›s Northampton County Area Community Coll., 1966- . Mem. Phi Beta Kappa. Home: Bethlehem Pa. Died ›b. 27, 1988.

IRISTENSEN, PARLEY ALMA, educator; b. ›arfield, Utah, May 15, 1888; s. Mads and Hannah hristiansen) C.; m. Ruth Jones, June 2, 1915; children: ›race Jones, Margaret Christensen Sorensen, Betty ›th Christensen Parker, Harold Parley. Student, ›gham Young Coll., 1906-13; BS, Utah State Agrl. ›ll., 1914; AM, Stanford U., 1925. Prin., tchr. Box ›der County schs., North Elwood, Utah, 1911-12, ›rland, Utah, 1914-15; instr. English Box Elder High ›., Brigham City, Utah, 1915-17, Brigham Young ›ll., Logan, Utah, 1917-25; prof. English Brigham ›ung U., from 1927, head dept., 1933-59. Author: All a Teacher's Day (essays), 1948. Recipient Freedom ›und. award for article, On Liberty in Our Time: ›lton and Mill., 1952, award for outstanding ›ievement Utah Acad. Sci., Arts and Letters, 1949. ›m. Medieval Acad. Am., MLA, Coll. English Assn., ›t. Coun. English Tchrs. Home: Provo Utah. †

IRISTIANSON, EDWARD GEORGE, oil company ›cutive; b. Chgo., Aug. 4, 1916; s. Oren Alfred and ›sta (Dishmaker) C.; m. Olive Yvonne Bayne, Mar. , 1940; children: George B., Mary Karen, Charles BS in Mining Engring., U. Wis., 1937. With Shell Co., 1938-70; v.p. Shell Oil Co., Houston, 1964-67; ›c. v.p., dir. Shell Oil Co., N.Y.C., 1967-70; exec. v.p. ›nerada Hess Corp., N.Y.C., 1971-74, also dir.; dir. ›tro-Lewis Corp., Denver, up to 1986; cons. in the ›troleum industry. Mem. Mid-Continent Oil and Gas ›sn. (dir. 1966), Am. Petroleum Inst., Economic, ›iversity, Winged Foot clubs, Masons. Home: Wash-›ton D.C. Died June 28, 1986.

IRISTIE, AMOS, physician, educator; b. Eureka, ›lif., Aug. 13, 1902; s. Frederick and Edna (Davis) C.; Margaret Cunningham Clarke, July 14, 1934; 1 dau., ›nda Davis. BS, U. Wash., 1924; MD, U. Calif., 1929. Diplomate Am. Bd. Pediatrics. Rotating intern ›ameda County Hosp., 1928-29; pediatric intern Babies ›sp., Coll. Physicians and Surgeons Columbia, 1929- ; vis. pediatrician San Francisco Juvenile Ct. and In-›t Shelter, 1931-35; research assoc. Johns Hopkins U., 36-37, asst. vis. pediatrician and obstetrician, 1936-37; ›ecialist in pediatrics Children's Bur. U.S. Dept. Labor, ›ashington, 1936-37; asst. prof. pediatrics U. Calif., 37-39, lectr. pub. health, 1938-39, assoc. prof. pedia-›cs, 1939, acting head dept., 1940; asst. dir. med. and ›alth services ARC, Washington, 1942-43; prof. pedia-›cs Vanderbilt U., Nashville, 1943-70, emeritus, 1970- , Harvie Branscomb Disting. prof., 1964. Contbr. ›icles to profl. jours. Mem. Cal. State Bd. Health, 40-42. Recipient John Phillips Meml. award ACP, 58, Abraham Jaconi award AMA pediatric section, 71. Mem. Soc. Pediatric Research, Am. Acad. Pedia-›cs, Am. Pediatric Soc. (v.p. 1955), Tenn. Pediatric ›c. (pres. 1953-54), Nashville Pediatric Soc. (pres. 54), Am. Pub. Health Assn., Nashville Acad. ›edicine, Assn. Am. Physicians, So. Med. Assn. (chmn. ›diatric sect. 1954), Sigma Xi, Alpha Omega Alpha. ›ome: Nashville Tenn. Died Feb. 8, 1986.

IRISTIE, ROBERT WAYNE, business executive; b. ›arion, Ky., Aug. 3, 1929; s. Elliot and Charlotte C.; Arden Furlong, Aug. 2, 1974; children: Susan Lynn, ›avid, Robert, Elizabeth, Mark. Grad., Robert Morris ›ll., 1951. With Pitts. Nat. Bank, 1960-75, asst. ›shier, 1961-62, asst. compt., 1962-63, compt., 1963-65, ›., compt., 1965-68, sr. v.p., compt., 1968-71, sr. v.p., ›mintrv. asst. to chmn., pres., 1971-75; exec. v.p. Pitts. ›t. Corp., 1972-82; vice chmn., chief exec. officer The ›ssell Co., Pitts., 1975-76, pres., chief exec. officer, 76-78, chmn., pres., chief exec. officer, 1978-81, ›mn., chief exec. officer, from 1981, also bd. dirs.; bd. ›s. PNC Funding Corp., PINACO, Inc., Pitts. Nat. ›e Ins. Co. Mem. Am. Inst. CPA's, Pa. Inst. CPA'S, ›n. Execs. Inst., Duquesne Club, St. Clair Country ›ub, Springfield Country Club. Home: Pittsburgh Pa. ›ceased.

IRISTOPHER, JOHN BARRETT, history edu-›tor; b. Phila., Nov. 20, 1914; s. John and Gertrude ›arrett) C.; m. Marjorie Gilles, Dec. 21, 1957. A.B., ›averford Coll., 1935; A.M., Harvard U., 1936, Ph.D., '42. Instr. history Haverford Coll., 1938; teaching ›low Harvard U., 1938-41; instr. Duke U., 1941-42; ›alyst U.S. Dept. State, 1945-46; asst. prof. history U. ›chester, 1946-52, assoc. prof., 1952-65, prof., 1965- , prof. emeritus, 1980-88. Author: (with others) A ›story of Civilization, 1955, rev. edit., 1976, Modern ›vilization, 1957, rev. edit., 1973, Civilization in the ›est, 1964, rev. edit., 1981, Lebanon Yesterday and ›day, 1966, The Islamic Tradition, 1972. Served with S. Army, 1942-45. Fund for Advancement of Edn. ›low, 1955-56. Mem. Am. Hist. Assn., AAUP, Middle ›st Inst., Middle East Studies Assn., Soc. for French ›st. Studies (v.p. 1960), N.Y. State Assn. European ›storians (pres. 1957). Democrat. Died Apr. 12, 1988.

IRISTOPHERSON, PAUL, lawyer; b. Long Prairie, ›inn., Aug. 12, 1902; s. Conrad H. and Effie (Jacobsen) C.; m. Edna M. Belgum, Jan. 11, 1945; children: Paul Conrad, David Lee, John Alfred. BA, Carleton Coll., 1923; student, Oxford (Eng.) U., 1926, BCL, 1927, MA, 1953; student, U. Minn. Law Sch., 1927-28. Bar: Minn. 1928. Pvt. practice Mpls., 1928-35; ptnr. Faegre & Benson, from 1935; spl. asst. Office Surgeon Gen., War Dept., 1943-44. Trustee Carleton Coll., 1951-68. Mem. ABA, Minn. Bar Assn., Inner Temple (London), Minneapolis Club, Minneapolis Athletic Club, Minikahda, Phi Beta Kappa, Phi Delta Phi. Republican. Episcopalian. Home: Minneapolis Minn. Died Apr. 5, 1987; buried St. Mark's Cathedral, Mpls.

CHRYSLER, WALTER P., JR., art collector. m. Marguerite Sykes, Apr. 29, 1933 (div.); m. Jean Esther Outland, Jan. 13, 1945. Ed., Dartmouth Coll., 1933. Organizer York Pub. House, 1926; dir. Madison Sq. Garden Corp., 1929-55; pres., chmn. bd. Cheshire House, Inc. (Pubs.), N.Y.C., 1930; founded Airtemp div. Chrysler Corp., 1934, dir. corp., 1935-56; pres. Chrysler Bldg., N.Y.C., 1935-53; dir. Chrysler Bldg., 1932-53; pres. Chrysler Mus. Provincetown, Mass., 1958; chmn., trustee Chrysler Mus., Norfolk, Va., from 1971; chmn. emeritus, dir. Chrysler Mus., 1971-77; dir. Va. Opera Assn., from 1971; trustee Norfolk Mus. Arts and Scis., 1969-71; cons. on comml. relations Office Coordinator Inter-Am. Affairs, Washington, 1941; corp. mem. Mus. Modern Art, N.Y.C. Presented: Broadway prodn. The Strong are Lonely; Eng. prodn. The Hanging Judge; movie The Joe Louis Story; paintings and sculpture in collections, shows in, Richmond, Va. and Phila., 1941, Old Masters and Modern French Sch., Portland, Oreg., Seattle, San Francisco, Los Angeles, Mpls., St. Louis, Kansas City, Mo., Detroit, Boston, 1956-57, Flemish, Dutch and German paintings, Washington, Atlanta, Dallas, New Orleans, West Palm Beach, Chattanooga, 1957-58, Inaugural Exhbn., Provincetown, Mass., 1958, French paintings 1789-1929, Dayton, Ohio, 1960, The Controversial Century 1850-1950, Provincetown, Mass., Ottawa, Can., 1962, Italian Renaissance and Baroque paintings, Norfolk, 1967-68. Mem. SAR, SR, Beta Theta Pi. Clubs: N.Y. Athletic, N.Y. Yacht, Harbor, Norfolk Yacht and Country, Virginia, Cedar Point, Princess Anne Country. Died Sept. 17, 1988.

CHURCH, MARGUERITE STITT, congresswoman, lecturer, writer; b. N.Y.C., Sept. 13, 1892; m. Ralph E. Church, Dec. 21, 1918 (dec.); children: Ralph Edwin Jr., William Stitt, Marjory Church Barnum. AB, Wellesley Coll., 1914; AM, Columbia U., 1917; LLD (hon.), Russell Sage Coll., 1958, Lake Forest Coll., 1960, Northwestern U., 1962; DHL (hon.), Nat. Coll. Edn., Evanston, Ill., 1963. Cons. psychologist State Charities Aid Assn., N.Y.C.; instr. Wellesley Coll., 1915; lectr., writer; U.S. del. to Gen. Assembly UN, 1961; mem. planning bd. White Ho. Conf. on Aging, 1971. Del. Republican Nat. Conv., 1964. Mem. U.S. Capitol Hist. Soc. (v.p., dir.), Nat. Alumnae Assn. Wellesley Coll. (pres. 1940-42), Bus. and Profl. Womens Club, Congrl. Club (pres. 1948-50), Zonta, Women's Athletic Glenview (Ill.), Sheridan Shore Yacht Club (Chgo.), Phi Beta Kappa, Kappa Gamma, Beta Sigma Phi. Deceased.

CHUTE, (BEATRICE) JOY, author; b. Mpls., Jan. 3, 1913; d. William Young and Edith Mary (Pickburn) C. Extension student, U. Minn., 1931-33. Assoc. in English Barnard Coll., N.Y.C., 1964-66, adj. assoc. prof., 1966-77, adj. prof., 1977-87; fiction judge Nat. Book Awards, 1960, children's book judge, 1971. Author: Blocking Back, 1938, Shattuck Cadet, 1940, Camp Hero, 1942, Shift to the Right, 1944, Teen-Age Sports Parade, 1949, The Fields are White, 1950, The End of Loving, 1952, Greenwillow, 1956, The Blue Cup and Other Stories, 1957, Journey to Christmas, 1958, The Moon and the Thorn, 1961, One Touch of Nature and Other Stories, 1965, The Story of a Small Life, 1971, Katie: An Impertinent Fairy Tale, 1978, The Good Woman, 1986; also short stories and articles in mags. Vol. worker Civilian Def., Police Athletic League, N.Y.C.; dir. Books Across the Sea. Mem PEN (pres. Am. Ctr. 1959-61), Authors League, LWV. Home: New York N.Y. Died Sept. 6, 1987.

CIARDI, JOHN, poet; b. Boston, June 24, 1916; s. Carmin and Concetta (di Benedictis) C.; m. Myra Judith Hostetter, July 28, 1946; children: Myra Judith, John Lyle, Benn. Student, Bates Coll., 1934-36; AB magna cum laude, Tufts U., 1938, D.Litt., 1960; MA, U. Mich., 1939; HD, Wayne U., 1963; LLD, Ursinus Coll., 1964; LHD, Kalamazoo Coll., 1964, Bates Coll., 1970, Washington U., 1971, Ohio Wesleyan Coll., 1971; DHL, Kean U., 1975, U. Mo., Kansas City, 1983. Instr. English U. Kansas City, 1940-42, 46; instr. Harvard, 1946-48, Briggs Copeland asst. prof., 1948-53; lectr. Am. poetry Salzburg Seminar in Am. Studies, 1951; staff lectr. poetry Bread Loaf Writers Conf., 1947-73, dir., 1955-72; lectr. English Rutgers U., 1953-54, assoc. prof. English, 1954-56, prof. English, 1956-61. Poetry editor Saturday Rev., 1956-73; contbg. editor World Mag., 1972-73; author: Homeward to America, 1940, Other Skies, 1947, Live Another Day, 1949, Mid-Century American Poets; anthology, 1950, From Time to Time, 1951, As If, Poems New and Selected, 1955, I Marry You, 1958, The Reason for the Pelican, 1959, 30 Poems, 1959, How Does a Poem Mean?, 1959, Scrappy the Pup, 1960; children's poems I Met A Man, 1961, The Man Who Sang the Sillies, 1961, You Read to Me, I'll Read to You, 1962, J.J. Plenty and Fiddler Den, 1963, You Know Who, 1964, Someone Could Win a Polar Bear, 1970, Fast and Slow, 1975; poems In the Stoneworks, 1961, In Fact, 1962, Person to Person, 1964, An Alphabestiary, 1966, This Strangest Everything, 1966, Lives of X, 1971, The Little That is All, 1974; translations The Inferno of Dante, 1954, Dante's Purgatorio, 1961, Dante's Paradiso, 1970, The Divine Comedy, 1977; story for children The Wish-Tree, 1962; critical essays Dialogue with an Audience, 1963; for children The Monster Den, The King Who Saved Himself From Being Saved, 1965; occasional pieces Manner of Speaking, 1972, (with Isaac Asimov) Limericks, 1978, For Instance, 1979, A Browser's Dictionary, 1980. Served with USAAF, 1942-45. Recipient Avery Hopwood award in Poetry, 1939, Blumenthal prize Poetry mag., 1944, Eunice Tietjens award, 1945, Levinson prize, 1947, Harriet Monroe Meml. award, 1955, Prix de Rome; Am. Acad. Arts and Letters, 1956. Fellow Am. Acad. Arts and Scis., Nat. Inst. Arts and Letters; mem. Nat. Coll. English Assn. (dir. 1955-57, pres. 1958-59), N.E. Coll. English Assn. (past dir.), Phi Beta Kappa. Home: Metuchen N.J. also: Key West Fla. Died Mar. 31, 1986.

CLAAS, GERHARD, religious organization executive; b. Wetter, Germany, Aug. 31, 1928; s. Ernst and Anna (Schroeder) C.; m. Irmgard Lydia Saffran, July 29, 1954; children—Regina, Gabriele, Martin. Diploma, Bapt. Theol. Sem., Rüschlikon, Switzerland, 1951, Bapt. Theol. Sem., Hamburg, Germany, 1953; D.D., Ouachita Bapt. U., Ark., 1974, Alderson-Broaddus Coll., 1985. Ordained to ministry German Bapt. Union, 1953; pastor 1st Bapt. Ch., Duesseldorf, W. Ger., 1953-58; youth sec. German Bapt. Union, Hamburg, 1958-64; gen. sec. German Bapt. Union, 1967-76; pastor J. G. Oncken Bapt. Ch., Hamburg, 1964-67; asso. sec. for Europe, Bapt. World Alliance, 1976-80; gen. sec. Europe, Bapt. World Alliance, Washington, 1980-88; tchr. religion Jacobi Gymnasium, Dusseldorf, 1953-58; dir. Youth Leaders Sem., 1958-64; chmn. exec. bd. Bapt. Theol. Sem., Ruschlikon, 1975-80. Author: Missionary Church Work, 1960; editor: b to y: Working Material for Youth Workers, 1958-64. Mem. exec. bd. Bread for the World, 1967-76; bd. dirs. Albertinen Hosp., Hamburg, 1964-80; chmn. exec. bd. Evang. Free Ch., Social Work, Hanover, W. Ger., 1967-80. Mem. Evang. Free Ch. Pastors Assn. Home: McLean Va. Deceased.

CLAGGETT, STRABO V(IVIAN), finance company executive, consultant; b. Montevideo, Minn., May 26, 1892; s. Strabo Francis and Rose Abbie (Phoenix) C.; m. Nellie M. Charlson, June 10, 1919 (div. 1958); children: Strabo Vivian, Carolyn Rose Claggett Blakeman, Florence Julia Claggett Clodius; m. Hazel K. Beery, May 7, 1962. Student, Carleton Coll., 1910-11; AB, Stanford U., 1914; LLB, Harvard Law Sch., 1917. Salesman Hemphill, Noyes & Co., 1920-21, New Eng. mgr., 1921-23; v.p. McClelland, Claggett Co., 1923-24; pres. Strabo V. Claggett & Co., 1924-30, Charles F. Noyes & Co., 1931-32; v.p. White, Claggett & Co., 1933-36; pres. Whitney-Phoenix Co., Inc., 1936-58, Whitney-Phoenix, Can., Ltd., 1949-58. Mem. Franklin D. Roosevelt's Com., sponsoring nomination for Pres., 1932; chmn. Mass. Dem. Fin. Com., 1928, 30; Dem. nominee for state auditor Mass., 1924, 26; presdl. elector Mass. pledged to Alfred E. Smith, 1928; del.-at-large Dem. Nat. Conv., Houston, 1928; Dem. nominee for lt. gov. Mass., 1930; head membership div. Food Administrn. under Herbert Hoover. With USN, 1917-19, promoted ensign, 1918; officer in charge contract sect. Navy Dept., 1918-19. Mem. Am. C. of C., Masons, Harvard Club, Stanford clubs of N.Y., N.J., Conn., Chi Psi. Episcopalian. Home: New York N.Y. †

CLAGUE, EWAN, economist; b. Prescott, Wash., Dec. 27, 1896; s. John and Eleanor Christian (Cooper) C.; m. Dorothy Vermilya Whipple, May 29, 1923; children: Ewan (dec.), Anne Vermilya, Llewellyn Whipple, Christopher Karran. AB, U. Wash., 1917, AM, 1921; PhD, U. Wis., 1929. Instr. in econs. U. Wash., 1919-21, U. Wis., 1921-26; commr. of conciliation Bur. Labor Statistics, Dept. Labor, 1926-28; research asst. Bus. Research Bur., Met. Life Ins. Co., 1928-29, Inst. Human Relations, Yale U., 1930; dir. research and prof. social research Pa. Sch. Social Work, Phila., 1931-36; assoc. dir. Bur. Research and Statistics and Social Security Bd., 1936-37, dir., 1937-40; dir. Bur. Employment Security, Social Security Bd., 1940-46; commr. labor statistics Dept. Labor, 1946-54, 55-65, spl. asst. to sec. labor, 1954-55, cons. to sec. labor, 1966-68; sr. assoc. Leo Kramer Inc., Washington, 1968-77; lectr. in labor statistics various univs.; mem. U.S. nat. com. on UNESCO. Author: The Bureau of Labor Statistics, 1968; (with others) An All-Volunteer Army, 1970; The Older Worker and the Union, 1971; The Health-Impaired Miner Under the Black Lung Legislation, 1973. With U.S. Army, 1917-19. Named one of top ten govt. career men in fed. govt. Nat. Civil Service League, 1958. Mem. Am. Statis. Assn., Am. Econ. Assn. Home: Washington D.C. Died Apr. 12, 1987; buried Laconia, N.H.

CLANCY, MAURICE LEE, pharmaceutical company executive; b. Carter, Okla., Dec. 8, 1915; s. Byron Hall and Lilly (Finch) C.; m. DeAnn Peterson, Dec. 31, 1966; children—Maurice Lee, Brian Carl. B.A., U. Okla., 1937; Ph.D. (hon.), Colo. Christian Coll., 1973. Product mgr. Westvaco Chem. Co., 1939-44; with

Wyeth Internat. Ltd., from 1944, v.p., then exec. v.p., 1952-69; pres., chief exec. officer Wyeth Internat. Ltd., Phila., from 1969; dir. Wyeth Japan Corp., Wyeth Labs., Eng.; Bd. dirs. Pa. Mental Health Assn., 1952-53; bd. govs. Pa. Export Corps, 1954. Mem. Phila. Advt. Golf Assn. (pres. 1979-80), Phi Beta Kappa, Delta Tau Delta. Republican. Presbyterian. Clubs: Merion Cricket (Haverford, Pa.); Overbrook Golf (Bryn Mawr, Pa.). Home: Villanova Pa. Deceased.

CLAPP, ALFRED COMSTOCK, lawyer; b. N.Y.C., June 8, 1903; s. Alfred C. and Anna (Roth) C.; m. Catharine Shotwell, June 11, 1932; children—Alfred C. Jr., Edward S., John W., Roger S. PhB, U. Vt., 1923, JD, Harvard U., 1927, LLD, U. Vt., 1957. Bar: N.J. 1927, N.Y. 1931. Mem. faculty Mercer Beasley Law Sch., Newark, 1929-30; dep. surrogate, adv. master orphan's ct. Essex County, 1939-47; mem. N.J. State Senate, 1947-53; prin. draftsman rules civil procedure, cts. of N.J., 1947-48; drafted revision N.J. statutes on adminstrn. justice, 1950-53; mem. law sch. faculty, NYU, 1947-52; prof., dean Rutgers Law Sch., 1951-53, lectr., from 1971; presiding judge Appelate Div. N.J. Superior Ct., 1953-58; sr. ptnr. Clapp and Eisenberg, Newark, 1958-88; counsel to Legislature on drafting N.J. Constn., 1944; chmn. N.J. Real Property, Probate and Trust Sect., 1975; chmn. N.J. Supreme Ct. Civil Practice Com., 1947-87, Rules Com., 1959-74, Inst. Continuing Legal Edn., 1962-86; draftsman Jud. article N.J. Constn., 1947, 66. Del. Rep. Nat. Conv., 1960; state chmn. Rep. candidate for U.S. senator, 1960; state campaign mgr. Rep. candidate for gov., 1961; pres. Brookside Sch., Montclair, 1945-47; past pres. Family Welfare Soc., Montclair; regent Am. Coll. Probate Counsel from 1969. Mem. ABA, N.J. Bar Assn., Essex County Bar Assn. (past pres.), Newark Bar Assn., Am. Law Inst., Am. Judicature Soc., Inst. Practicing Lawyers N.J. (pres.), Constl. Conv. Assn. (Pres. 1959), Phi Beta Kappa (past pres. North Jersey), Sigma Nu, Phi Delta Phi. Presbyterian. (elder). Author: Will Service Manual of New Jersey, 1964, Wills and Administration-N.J. (7 vols.), 1982, Post Mortem Tax Planning, 1982; editor N.J. Law Jour., 1942-53, 1970-84. Home: Montclair, N.J. Died May 23, 1988.

CLAPP, LEALLYN BURR, chemistry educator; b. Paris, Ill., Oct. 13, 1913; s. Ivan Burr and Blanche (Tate) C.; m. Florence Cottingham, Aug. 28, 1940; children—Peter, Jean. B.Ed., E.Ill. U., 1935, Pd.D. (hon.), 1956; M.A., U. Ill. at Urbana, 1939, Ph.D., 1941; LL.D. (hon.), R.I. Coll., 1964. Tchr. math. Paris (Ill.) High Sch., 1935-38; mem. faculty Brown U., 1941-83, prof. chemistry, 1956-83, 88; lectr. chemistry, Chile, 1961, Nigeria, 1962, India, 1965, 68, 71, Uruguay, 1967, Pakistan, 1970, South Korea, 1974, Mex., 1976; disting. vis. prof. Baylor U., 1977, 84-85, 87-88, Wellesley Coll., 1985-86, Earlham Coll., 1986-87. Author: Chemistry of the Covalent Bond, 1957, Chemistry of the OH Group, 1967, Portuguese edit. 1967, Japanese 1968, French 1969; co-author: General, Organic, and Biochemistry, 1980; editor: Organic Modules, 1972-86. Recipient award Mfg. Chemists Assn., 1973; Sci. Apparatus Makers award in chem. edn., 1976; Disting. Alumnus award Eastern Ill. U., 1978. Mem. New Eng. Assn. Chemistry Tchrs. (sec. 1952-57, pres. 1961-63, John Timm award 1974), Am. Chem. Soc. (vis. scientist 1956-67, com. prof. tng. 1958-67, chmn. div. chem. edn. 1959-60, award western Conn. sect. 1969). Home: Providence R.I. Died Nov. 28, 1988; interred Providence, R.I.

CLARK, BYRON BRYANT, pharmacologist; b. Temple, Tex., Apr. 5, 1908; s. Oscar W. and Ida (Hansen) C.; m. Gladys Lawson, Jan. 26, 1931; children: Barbara Clark Riter, Jack, Kenneth. BA, Baylor U., 1930; MS, Iowa State U., 1932, PhD, 1934. Instr. physiology and pharmacology Albany Med. Coll., 1936-39, asst. prof., 1939-40, assoc. prof., 1940-47; prof. pharmacology, chmn. dept. Med. Sch. Tufts U., from 1947; dir. pharmacology and chemotherapy Mead Johnson Research Ctr., Evansville, Ind., 1957-62, v.p., 1962-68; dir. pharmacology-toxicology program Nat. Inst. Gen. Medicine Scis., NIH, Bethesda, Md., 1968-79; cons. pharmacologist N.E. Ctr. Hosp.; mem. com. on drug safety, drug research bd. Nat. Acad. Scis.-NRC. Contbr. chpts. in books, articles in profl. jours. Recipient NIH Dir.'s award, 1977, Sec. HEW cert. merit, 1979. Fellow AAAS; mem. Am. Soc. Pharmacology and Exptl. Therapeutics, Soc. Exptl. Biology and Medicine, Soc. Toxicology, N.Y. Acad. Scis. Home: Cincinnati Ohio. Died Jan. 3, 1985; buried Rest Haven Cemetery, Blue Ash, Ohio.

CLARK, CHARLES MARTIN, JR., investment banker; b. Summit, N.J., Nov. 2, 1905; s. Charles Martin and Bessie (Milligan) C.; m. Valerie Graham, Aug. 1, 1939 (dec. Apr. 1971); children: Ann Valer (Mrs. Josiah T. Austin), Cecily Martin, John Sheldon; m. Helen M. Lonergan, Aug. 3, 1972. Grad., Hotchkiss Sch., 1924; B.S., Harvard U., 1928; hon. diploma, U.S. Mcht. Marine Acad., 1945. Reporter Bradstreet Co., 1928-29; statistician Second Nat. Bank, Boston, 1930-33; pres. Martin Co. (printers), Boston, 1934-35; partner Charles Clark & Co.; mems. N.Y. Stock Exchange, 1937-47; engaged in estate mgmt. and directorship cos. 1948-61; partner Sullivan & Co.; mems. N.Y. Stock Exchange, 1962-64; ltd. partner Estabrook & Co., 1965-69; chmn. bd. Estabrook & Co., Inc., 1970-72; pres., dir. Sherwood Investors, Inc.; dir. Dun & Bradstreet, Inc., 1935-76; U.S. adviser N. Atlantic Planning Bd. Ocean Shipping, 1952. Trustee Kips Bay Boys Club, N.Y.C.; trustee, v.p. Hewitt Sch., to 1983. Served to lt. (s.g.) U.S. Maritime Service, 1942-44. Presbyn. Clubs: Down Town Assn. (N.Y.C.), Union (N.Y.C.); Piping Rock (Locust Valley, L.I.); Seawanhaka Corinthian Yacht (Oyster Bay); Jupiter Island (Hobe Sound, Fla.); Everglades (Palm Beach, Fla.); Portmarnock Golf (Dublin, Ireland). Deceased.

CLARK, GEORGE L., banker; b. 1938; married. BBA, U. Tex., 1961; MBA, Stanford U., 1963. Exec. v.p. Schneider, Bernet & Hickman, 1967-75; v.p. Merc. Nat. Bank, Dallas, 1975-76, sr. v.p., head metroplex banking, 1976-78, exec. v.p. adminstrn., 1978-79; pres. Merc. Nat. bank, Dallas, 1979-81; chmn. bd., chief exec. officer Merc. Nat. Bank, Dallas, from 1981, also bd. dirs.; v.p. Merc. Tex. Corp. Home: Dallas Tex. Died June 28, 1987; buried Sparkman-Hillcrest Cemetery, Dallas.

CLARK, SIR GEORGE NORMAN, historian; b. Halifax, Eng., Feb. 27, 1890; s. James Walker and Mary (Midgley) C.; m. Barbara Keen, 1919. MA, Balliol Coll., Oxford (Eng.) U., 1915, DLitt, 1947; LLD, Aberdeen U., 1936; LittD, U. Utrecht, 1936, U. Dublin, 1950, Durham U., 1950, Sheffield U., 1951, Columbia U., 1954, Hull U., 1955; LittD (hon.), Cambridge U., 1961. Fellow All Souls Coll., Oxford, 1912-19, 31-43, from 1961; fellow Oriel Coll., 1919-31, provost, 1947-57; prof. econ. history Oxford U., 1931-43; Regius prof. modern history, fellow Trinity Coll., Cambridge, Eng., 1943-47; mem. staff various govt. depts., 1939-45. Author: The Seventeenth Century, rev. edit., 1947, The Later Stuarts, rev. edit., 1955, Science and Social Welfare in the Age of Newton, rev. edit., 1970, History of the Royal College of Physicians, Vol. 1, 1964, Vol. 2, 1966, English History, a Survey, 1971. Fomer trustee Brit. Mus. Capt. Royal Army, 1914-19. Decorated comdr. Order Orange-Nassau, created knight, 1953; hon. fellow Balliol and Oriel colls. Oxford Trinity Coll., Cambridge, Trinity Coll., Dublin. Fellow Royal Coll. Physicians (hon.); mem. Am. Hist. Assn. (hon.), Brit. Acad. (pres. 1954-58), Royal Danish Acad. (fgn.), Netherlands Acad., Am. Acad. Arts and Scis. Home: Oxford England. †

CLARK, JOHN CLINTON, business executive; b. Binghamton, N.Y., Nov. 4, 1891; s. John P.E. and Grace Amelia (Harding) C.; m. Kathryn Moore, Feb. 14, 1927; children: John Clinton, Jean C. Clark Dellay. Student, Binghamton Cen. High Sch., 1906-10. With candy mfg. bus., Hess-Clark Co., 1910-15; pres. Ames Chem. Co., Binghamton, 1915-19, Clark Assocs., Inc., Binghamton and N.Y.C., 1919-55; owner Clinton-Williams Ltd., Sydney, Australia, and Auckland, New Zealand, 1920-55; bd. dirs. Marine Midland Trust Co. So. N.Y., Endicott Johnson Corp., Clark-Cleve., Inc., Security Mut. Life Ins. Co.; pres. Hialeah Race Course, 1940-55; trustee N.Y. Racing Assn., Inc. Del. Rep. Nat. Presdl. Conv., mem. exec. com. N.Y. State, 1936; mem. Turf Com. Am.; trustee U. Miami. Mem. Thoroughbred Racing Assn. U.S. (pres. 1942, 43), Turf and Field Club, United Hunts Club, Racquet and Tennis Club, Jockey Club, all N.Y.C., Surf Club, Bath Club, Indian Creek Club, all Miami Beach. Home: Binghamton N.Y. †

CLARK, JOHN HENRY, surgeon; b. Moab, Utah, Apr. 7, 1910; s. Robert Cecil and Alice Elberta (Gaines) C.; m. Doris Mildred Colburn, June 14, 1935; children: Cecile Clark Hulquist, John Henry II. AB, U. Utah, 1932; MD, U. Chgo., 1935. Diplomate Am. Bd. Surgery. Pvt. practice Salt Lake City; asst. surgeon Tulane U. Med. Sch., 1945-47; assoc. clin. prof. surgery, U. Utah, from 1955; bd. dirs. St. Mark's Hosp., Salt Lake City, from 1969; chmn. Utah Physicians Licensing Bd., 1968-80. Contbr. articles to profl. jours. Bd. dirs. Utah chpt. Am. Cancer Soc., 1948-52; mem. regional adv. group Intermountain Regional Med. Program, Salt Lake City, 1964-69. Lt. col. M.C. AUS, 1941-45, PTO. Decorated Legion of Merit, Purple Heart; recipient Best Vis. Physician award U. Utah, 1958-59. Fellow ACS (pres. Utah chpt. 1962-63), Southwest Surg. Congress (pres. 1968-69); mem. Fedn. State Med. Bds. (flex test com. 1968-81, bd. dirs. from 1977, pres. 1982-83), Western Surg. Assn. (sr. v.p. 1980), Utah Med. Assn. (trustee 1959-66, 76-80), Salt Lake Surg. Soc. (pres. 1960), Salt Lake County Med. Soc. (pres. 1960), Ambassador Club, Alta Club, Masons, KT, Shriners. Home: Salt Lake City Utah. Died Jan. 8, 1986.

CLARK, MARSH, journalist; b. St. Louis, Nov. 19, 1928; s. Bennett Champ and Miriam (Marsh) C.; m. Pippa F.A., Dec. 29, 1969; children: James Bennett, Mary Marsh, Elizabeth Lee, Martha Ann. AB, Washington and Lee U., 1950. Reporter St. Joseph (Mo.) News-Press, 1950-51; reporter, then polit. editor St. Louis Globe Democrat, 1953-62; with Time mag., 1962-85; bur. chief Time mag., Jerusalem, 1970-72, N.Y.C., 1972-75, Moscow, 1975-80, Johannesburg, Republic of South Africa, 1980-85. With U.S. Army, 1951-53. Mem. Sigma Chi, Sigma Delta Chi. Episcopalian. Home: Johannesburg Republic of South Africa. Died Aug. 27, 1985.

CLARK, MARTIN, music critic, journalist; b. Beaumont, Tex.; s. John Franklin and Katherine (Hooper) C.; m. Nancy Linda Grayson, Dec. 26, 1958 (div. 1970); m. Maria P. Grant. Aug. 15, 1975. BA, U Tex.; postgrad., San Francisco Conservatory Music. Mng. editor Sandy (Oreg.) Post, 1951-53; wire servic Enterprise-Courier, Oregon City, 1953-55; staff write UP Internat., Portland, Oreg., 1955-56; music edito daily columnist Oreg. Jour., Portland, 1956-82; musi critic The Oregonian (merger Oregonian and Ore Jour.), Portland, from 1982. Tenor, San Francisc Opera, 1946-48; recitalist stage and radio, 1949-51; ap peared on radio talk show Sta. KLIQ-AM-FM, Portland, 1966-70. Served with USNR, 1942-46, PTO. Home: Portland Oreg. Died Aug. 18, 1983.

CLARK, RUSSELL, business executive; b. New Orleans, 1891. Grad., Georgetown U., 1912. V.p. Merrill, Lynch, Pierce, Fenner and Smith Inc., New Orleans office. Home: New Orleans La. †

CLARK, WILBER DALE, banker; b. Fillmore, Mo Apr. 26, 1892; s. Samuel Milton and Catherine Lane (Sayres) C.; m. Ethel Johnston, Aug. 31, 1915 (dec. Jul 1955); children: Russell D., Jessie E., Walter W.; m Katherine Doorly Young, Nov. 29, 1958. Ed. high sch St. Joseph, Mo. With 1st Nat. Bank, St. Joseph, 190 asst. cashier 1st Nat. Bank, Tarkio, Mo., 1913-1 cashier Stock Yards Nat. Bank, Denver, 1915-19; v.p Omaha Nat. Bank, 1919-29, pres., 1929-49, chmn. bd 1949-62; bd. dirs. World Pub. Co., from 1960; bd. dirs Omaha br. Fed. Res. Bank, Kansas City, , Union Pacific R.R.; mem. fed. adv. coun. Fed. Res. Banks, 1941-43. Pres. Omaha Community Chest, 1935-36; bd. dirs. U.S C. of C., 1935-36; mem. bus. adv. coun. Dept. Commerce, 1938-42; pres. bd. regents Mcpl. U. Omaha 1944; chmn. Nebr. War Fin. Com., 1943-46. Mem Omaha C. of C. (pres. 1932), Masons (33 degree) Shriners, Omaha Club, Omaha Country Club. Republican. Methodist. Home: Omaha Nebr. †

CLARKE, BRUCE COOPER, army officer; b. Adams N.Y., Apr. 29, 1901; s. Matthew John and Isola Venet (Stevens) C.; m. Bessie Mitchell, June 12, 1925 (dec 1956); children: Bruce Cooper, David Arthur, Gordon Mitchell, Elisabeth Jean. BS, U.S. Mil. Acad., 192 MCE, Cornell U., 1927; LLB, LaSalle Extension U. 1936; grad., Engr. Sch., 1928, Command and Gen. Staf Sch., 1940, Armored Sch., 1949; LLD, Baylor U., 1961 D. in Internat. Law, Parsons Coll., 1963. Commd. 2 lt. U.S. Army, 1925, advanced through ranks to ger (temporary), 1958, promoted to gen., 1962; mem. Gen Staff Corps, 1942-43; combat comdr. 7th and 4th Armored Divs., 1943-45; mem. staff Hdqrs. Army Ground Forces, 1945-48; asst. comdt. Armored Sch 1948-49; comdg. gen. 2d Constabulary Brigade, 1949-51 1st Armored Div., 1951-53; comdg. gen. I and X Corps and dep. comdr. 8th Army, Korea, 1953-54; comdg gen. U.S. Army, Pacific, 1954-56, 7th U.S. Army Europe, 1956-58, U.S. Continental Army Commanc hdqrs., Ft. Monroe, Va., 1958-60; comdr. in chief U.S Army in Europe, 1960-62, ret., 1962; Gen. Dougla MacArthur prof. mil. sci. U.S. Army Engr. Sch. Mem exec. council Boy Scouts Am. Decorated D.S.C. D.S.M. with 2 oak leaf clusters and V, Air medal, Conspicuous Service Cross and medal N.Y.; Companion o Bath (Gt. Britain); comdr. Legion of Honor, Croix d Guerre with palm (France); Croix de Guerre with palm grand officer Order of the Crown (Belgium); D.S.M with 2 Silver Stars, Order Service Merit Medal, 1st Class (Korea); Meritorious medal (Columbia); Grand Cross Order Merit (Fed. Republic Germany); various other medals and citations; named hon. senator U. Heidelberg (Germany). Mem. 4th Armored Div. Assn. (past pres.) 1st Armored Div. Assn. (hon. pres.), Nat. Sojourners Scabbard and Blade, Cosmos Club, Mason (33 deg. K.T.), Tau Beta Pi, Lambda Chi Alpha. Home McLean Va. Died Mar. 17, 1988.

CLARKE, JAMES WHYTE, clergyman, lecturer; b Glasgow, Scotland, Sept. 13, 1891; s. Herbert anc Margaret (Whyte) C.; m. Maria Mason, Dec. 1, 191 (dec. 1951); children: Margaret Lennox, Blanche Reid James William (dec.), George Carson. BD, McGill U. 1922; DD, United Coll., Winnepeg, 1940. Student missionary Presbyn. Ch., Man., Can., 1910-11; ministe country ch. Presbyn. Ch., 1922-26, moderator of th Presbytery, 1924; participator in union of Methodist Conglist., and Presbyn. Chs. 1925; pastor Rosemont anc Westmount Chs., Montreal, 1927, Knox Ch., Winnepeg 1932; preacher All Can. Number of Christian Centur Pulpit, 1969; prof. homiletics Presbyn. Theol. Sem. Chgo., 1941; minister Second Presbyn. Ch., St. Louis 1944; prof. homiletics Princeton Theol. Sem.; speake Chgo. Sunday Evening Club. Pres. bd. dirs Lindenwood Female Coll., St. Charles, Mo.; mem. bd dirs. Westminster Coll., Fulton, Mo. Served in Worlc War I. overseas. Decorated Mil. Cross. Mem. Nat Christian Mission Team. Home: Princeton N.J. †

CLAUSON, ANDREW GUSTAV, JR., banker; b. Por Richmond, N.Y., July 1, 1895; s. Andrew Gustav an Marie (Olson) C.; m. Esther Larsen, Sept. 25, 1920 (dec 1981); children: Ralph Andrew, Barbara C. AAS SUNY, 1947; LLD, Upsala Coll., 1948, Wagner Coll. 1950. CPA, N.Y. Acct. Richmond Light and R.R Co., 1913-17; with Haskins & Sells CPA's, 1919-23 comptroller J.H. Schroeder Banking Corp., 1924-27 United Wallpapers Inc., 1928; founder, ptnr. Bayer & CLausen, CPA's, 1929-64, ret., 1964; pres., chmn. bd Richmond County Savs. Bank, S.I., 1964-73; trustee chmn. emeritus Richmond County Savs. Bank, 1973-83; pres. Obelisk Trading Corp. Mem. N.Y.C. Bd. Edn., 1945-61, pres. 1946-49, 51-53; chmn. emeritus bd. trustees S.I. Hosp.; trustee emeritus Wagner Coll.; pres. Wingate Meml. Found.; chmn. adv. bd. Salvation Army, S.I. With U.S. Navy, 1917-19. Decorated Legion of Honor (France); knight 1st class Royal Order N. Star (Sweden); recipient Disting. Citizenship award Wagner Coll., 1948. Mem. N.Y. State Soc. CPA's, Am. Inst. CPA's, Naval Order U.S., Am. Legion, N.Y. Acad. Pub. Edn., S.I. Inst. Arts and Scis., S.I. Hist. Soc., S.I. Tchrs. Assn. (life), Am.-Scandinavian Found., LaGuardia Meml. Found., Richmond County Jurors ASsn., John Erickson Soc., Tall Cedars of Lebanon, Lawyers Club, Richmond County Country Club, Mason, Beta Alpha Psi, Tau Phi Sigma. Home: West New Brighton N.Y. Died Aug. 17, 1983; buried Moravian Cemetery, Staten Island, N.Y.

CLAYTON, CHARLES CURTIS, journalist; b. Cambridge, Nebr., June 3, 1902; s. Curtis Stanton and Clara Clyde (Richardson) C.; m. Elizabeth Elliott, June 3, 1925; children—Carol Roma (Mrs. William G. Hill), Charles Stephen. Student, U. Nebr., 1919-22; B.J., U. Mo., 1925. Reporter St. Louis Globe Democrat, 1925-29, asst. city editor, 1929-39, lit. editor, 1937-39, city editor, 1939-40, editorial writer, 1940-54, exec. asst. to publisher, 1954-55; prof. journalism So. Ill. U., from 1956; on leave to establish Sch. Journalism and Mass Communications Center at Chinese U. of Hong Kong, 1965-66; lectr. journalism Washington U., St. Louis, 1928-29, Webster Coll., 1937-40, Lindenwood Coll., St. Charles, Mo., 1940-52, sch. journalism U. Mo., 1947-50; chmn. publ. bd. Quill, 1951-53; editor The Quill, 1956-61; vis. prof. journalism, grad. sch. journalism Nat. Chengchi U., Taipei, Formosa, 1961-62, 70-71; hon. prof. for life; dir. Yenching Inst., 1970-71; leader Seminar Chinese Studies, 1976. Author: books including Newspaper Reporting Today, 1947, Fifty Years for Freedom, 1959, Little Mack: Joseph McCullah of the St. Louis Globe-Democrat, 1969, (with others) The Asian Newspapers' Reluctant Revolution, 1971, A Twinge of Nostalgia, 1979; also mag. articles. Bd. dirs. Walter Williams Found. in Journalism, 1936-38. Recipient U. Mo. Honor Medal for distinguished service to journalism, 1952; Ministry Def. medal Republic China, 1976. Mem. U. Mo. Journalism Alumni Assn. (pres. 1936-38), State Univs. Annuitants Assn. Ill. (pres. 1977-78, dir. from 1977), Sigma Delta Chi (exec. council from 1947, chmn. 1952-53, nat. pres. 1951-52), Kappa Tau Alpha, Alpha Epsilon Rho. Clubs: Circumnavigators, Rotary. Died Apr. 29, 1988; cremated.

CLEARY, JOHN JOSEPH, journalist; b. Cleve., Mar. 7, 1905; s. John Joseph and Susan Ann (MacLain) C.; m. Mary Barden, Dec. 29, 1973. L.H.B., Cath. U. Am., 1927. Asst. fin. editor Cleve. News, 1928-36, marine editor, 1936-46, bus. editor, 1946-49, fin. editor, 1949-60, columnist, 1946-60; gen. bus. editor Cleve. Plain Dealer, 1960-72; account exec. Dix & Eaton, Inc., Cleve., 1972-76; freelance writer 1976-87. Served to 1st lt. AUS, 1942-46. Mem. Sigma Delta Chi (pres. Cleve. chpt. 1957-58). Home: Lakewood Ohio. Died Jan. 30, 1987; buried Calvary Cemetery, Cleve.

CLELAND, GEORGE L., educational administrator; b. Hoyt, Kans., Feb. 9, 1904; s. Frank Estel and Laura Elizabeth (White) C.; m. Virginia Penick, July 27, 1930; children: John David, Joseph Lee. AB, Baker U., 1926, D Pedagogy (hon.), 1959; AM, Columbia U., 1935; EdD, Kans. U., 1958. Country sch. tchr. Whiting, Kans., 1922-24; math. tchr., coach Effingham, Kans., 1926-31; dir. extracurricular activities Atchison, Kans., 1931-35; prin. Atchison Jr.-Sr. High Sch., 1935-52; dir. secondary edn. Kans. Dept. Edn., 1952-65, asst. commr. edn., 1965-71; vis. lectr. Kans. State Coll., Manhattan, summer 1948-49; mem. Nat. Com. on Secondary Edn., from 1965. Contbr. articles to profl. jours. John Hay fellow U. Oreg., 1962. Mem. Kans. State Activities Assn. (legis. council 1944-48, control bd. 1952), , Kans. Prins. Assn (pres. 1949), Nat. Assn. Secondary Sch. Prins. (exec. com. 1952-58, pres. 1956-57, field cons. 1973-80), NEA, Nat. Com. Devel. Sci. and Engrs., Council Advancement Secondary Edn., Nat. Com. Exptl. Projects Secondary Edn., Masons, Kiwanis (lt. gov. 1948), Educators Club, Phi Delta Kappa, Kappa Sigma. Republican. Methodist. Home: Topeka Kans. Died Dec. 6, 1985, buried Mt. Hope Cemetery, Topeka.

CLEMENTS, SIR JOHN, actor, producer; b. London, Apr. 25, 1910; s. Herbert William and Mary Elizabeth (Stevens) C.; m. Kay Hammond, Aug. 21, 1946 (dec. 1980). Ed., Cambridge U. Debut at Lyric Hammersmith, London, 1930; founder intimate theatre in N. London, 1935; appeared opposite wife, also produced and directed numerous plays in London, 1943-88, including Private Lives, 1944, The Kingmaker, 1946, Marriage a la Mode, 1946, The Beaux Stratagem, 1949, Man and Superman, 1951, The Happy Marriage, 1952, Pygmalion, 1953, The Little Glass Clock, 1954, The Rivals, 1956, The Way of the World, 1956, The Rape of the Belt, 1957, Gilt and Ginger Bead, 1958, Marriage Go Round, 1959; appeared with Old Vic in London as Coriolanus, 1947, Petrichio, 1947, Dunois, 1947, in N.Y.C. as Macbeth, 1962, Warwick, 1962; appeared in London in The Affair, 1961-62, The Tulip Tree, 1962-63; producer, dir., appeared in the Masters, 1963; motion pictures include Knight Without Armour, 1936, South Riding, 1927, Four Feathers, 1938, Convoy, 1940, Ships With Wings, 1941, Silent Enemy, 1959, The Mind Benders, 1962, Oh What a Lovely War, 1969, Gandhi, 1982; dir. Chichester Festival Theatre, 1966-88. Decorated comdr. Brit. Empire, 1956. Home: Brighton England. Died Apr. 6, 1988.

CLIFFORD, SISTER ADELE, biologisy educator, academic administrator; b. Chillicothe, Ohio, Aug. 29, 1906; d. Timothy and Ellen (Murphy) Clifford. AB, Coll. Mt. St. Joseph, 1933; MS, Fordham U., 1946, PhD, 1949. Elem. sch. tchr. Cleve., 1930-33; elem. sch. prin. Royal Oak, Mich., 1933-35; high sch. tchr. Cin., 1935-42; instr. biology Coll. Mt. St. Joseph, Ohio, 1942-67, prof. biology, from 1972, pres., 1967-72, pres. emeritus, from 1974; researcher Marine Biol. Lab., Woods Hole, Mass., 1946-48, summers 1961-67, 73-75. Named one of Ten Women of Achievement Cin. Bus. and Profl. Women's Club, 1973. Mem. Am. Inst. Biol. Scis., Bot. Soc. Am., Biology Tchrs. Conf. (sec. 1966-67), Am. Soc. Zoologists, AAAS, Ohio Acad. Sci., Am. Genetic Assn., Zonta (sec. Cin. club 1975-76). Home: Mount Saint Joseph Ohio. Died Jan. 28, 1989.

CLINCHY, EVERETT ROSS, clergyman, educator; b. N.Y.C., Dec. 16, 1896; s. James Hugh and Lydie (Stagg) C.; m. Winifred Marcena Mead, Sept. 21, 1918; children: Ross, Eleanor Clinchy Reinhardsen, Barbara Clinchy Sutton. Student, Wesleyan U., Middletown, Conn., 1916-18, DD (hon.), 1950; BS, Lafayette Coll., 1920, DD (hon.), 1951; postgrad., Union Theol. Sem., 1920-21, Yale U., 1922-23; MA, Columbia U., 1921; PhD in Edn., Drew U., 1934; LLD (hon.), Fla. So. Coll., 1946, Washington U., 1955; LHD (hon.), Mo. Valley Coll., 1949, Wilberforce Coll., 1958, Hartwick Coll., 1959; LittD (hon.), St. Mary's Coll., 1981. Ordained to ministry Presbyn. Ch., 1921. Minister Ch. of Christ, Wesleyan U., 1923-28; sec. Fed. Council Chs. of Christ Am., 1928-33; pres. NCCJ, 1928-58, mem. Council on World Tensions, World Brotherhood; founder Inst. Man and Sci., Rensselaerville, N.Y., 1963, pres., 1963-72, chmn. exec. com., from 1972; gen. sec. program improving understanding between Islam and West under auspices UNESCO, from 1977, v.p., from 1979; v.p., exec. dir. Roger Williams Straus Found.; mem. extension winter faculty U. Calif., Riverside, 1966-72; originator sem. confs. for study of Cath., Protestant, Jewish relations, also priest-rabbi-minister trio dialogue teams; dir. Williamstown Inst. Human Relations, summers 1935, 37, 39, 41; mem. Joint Army and Navy Com. on Welfare and Recreation, Washington. Author: All in the Name of God, 1934, The World We Want to Live In, 1942, A Handbook on Human Relations, 1949, Intergroup Relations Center, 1950; contbr. articles to religious, ednl. publs. Chmn. Harlem Sch. Arts, 1972-75. 2d lt. F.A. U.S. Army, World War I. Mem. Council on Fgn. Relations, Am. Sociol. Soc., Am. Acad. Polit. Sci., AAAS, Cosmos Club (Washington), Yale Club (N.Y.C.), Alpha Delta Phi. Home: Guilford Conn. Died Jan. 22, 1986, buried Fairmount, N.J.

CLOKE, JOHN BENJAMIN, chemistry educator; b. Hoosick, N.Y., Oct. 31, 1897; s. John and Sarah (Murphy) C.; m. Mary Elizabeth Hagan, Mar. 26, 1927; children: Elizabeth Ruth, Sandra Hale. Grad. in pharmacy, Union U., 1917; student, Rensselaer Poly. Inst., 1917-18; BS, Syracuse U., 1925; PhD, U. Chgo., 1931. Asst. in chemistry Rensselaer Poly. Inst., Troy, N.Y., 1918-19, mem. faculty, 1919-63, prof. organic chemistry, 1931-63, head dept. chemistry, 1949-63; cons. and researcher in synthetic and physico-organic chemistry. Author books on organic chemistry; contbr. articles to profl. jours. Mem. Am. Chem. Soc., AAAS, Am. Soc. Engring. Edn., English Speaking Union, Sigma Xi, Phi Lambda Upsilon. Home: Brockport N.Y. Died Dec. 9, 1985.

CLOSE, FREDERICK JACOB, aluminum manufacturing executive; b. Pitts., June 21, 1905; s. Clarence William and Lyda (Bushfield) C.; m. Lillian Roberts, Aug. 30, 1930; 1 son, Frederick Jacob III. BA, Pa. State U., 1928. With Aluminum Co. of Am., 1929-70, beginning as mem. archtl. sales dept., N.Y.C., successively staff collapsible tube, screw machine products, impact extrusions depts., Edgewater, N.J., mgr. forge shop, Cleve., industry mgr. archtl. sales, mgr. market devel., gen. mgr. sales devel. and comml. rsch., 1929-59, v.p., gen. mgr. industry sales and sales devel., 159-62, v.p. charge mktg., 1962-63, exec. v.p., 1963-66, chmn. bd., 1966-70, then bd. dirs.; bd. dirs. Alcoa Svc. Corp. Mem. gen. adv. com. Harmarville (Pa.) Rehab. Ctr. Mem. Pa. State U. Alumni Assn., Duquesne Club, University Club, Pitts. Athletic Assn., Fox Chapel Golf Club (Pitts.), Sky Club (N.Y.C.), Rolling Rock Club, Laurel Valley Golf Club, Madison (Ohio) Golf and Country Club, Blue Key, Beta Theta Pi. Home: Painesville Ohio Died Feb. 6, 1989.

COAKLEY, JOSEPH CHARLES, lawyer; b. Cleve., June 10, 1928; s. John A. and Marie (Beckman) C.; m. Patricia Hunkin, July 6, 1949; children: Patricia Coakley Oppmann, Joseph Charles, M. Sean, Lisa F. Coakley Tippit. BS, John Carroll U., 1948; LLB, Cleve. State U., 1951. Bar: Ohio 1951. Pvt. practice Cleve., from 1951; ptnr. Squire, Sanders & Dempsey, Cleve., 1971-73; chmn. bd. dirs. Union Commerce Corp., 1970-81; bd. dirs. Minster Machine Co., Marjon Co.; pres. M-F Securities Inc.; v.p. Cleve. Industries Inc.. Trustee Musical Arts Assn.; chmn. bd. trustees John Carroll U., 1975-79. Mem. Union Club, Kirtland Club, Tavern Club, Chagrin Valley Hunt Club (Cleve.); Brook Club (N.Y.C.); Rolling Rock Club (Ligonier, Pa.). Home: Gates Mills Ohio. Died Apr. 10, 1985; buried Gates Mills (Ohio) Cemetary.

COATES, ALBERT, government and law educator; b. Johnston County, N.C., Aug. 25, 1896; s. Daniel Miller and Nancy (Lassiter) C.; m. Gladys J. Hall, June 23, 1928. AB, U. N.C., 1918; LLB, Harvard U., 1923; LLD (hon.), Wake Forest Coll., 1960, Duke U., 1971, U. N.C., 1974. Teaching fellow in English U. N.C., Chapel Hill, 1919-20, asst. prof. law, 1923-25, assoc. prof., 1925-27, prof., 1927-69, emeritus, from 1969, founder, dir. Inst. of Govt., 1931-62. Author: What the University of North Carolina Means to Me, 1969, Talks to Students and Teachers, The Structure and Workings of Government in the Cities and the Counties and the State of North Carolina, 1971, Rule of Law and the Role of Government in North Carolina, 1972, Problems and Leaders in North Carolina, 1972, Bridging the Gap between Government in Books and Government in Action, 1974; editor Popular Govt. mag., 1931-62; contbr. articles to profl. jours. 2d lt. U.S. Army, 1918. Recipient Di-Phi award, 1951, Gardner award, 1952, U. N.C., Pub. Svc. award, State of N.C., 1967. Mem. N.C. Bar Assn. (Parker award 1964), Tau Kappa Alpha, Sigma Upsilon, Order of Coif, Phi Delta Phi. Democrat. Methodist. Home: Chapel Hill N.C. Died Jan. 28, 1989.

COATES, JAMES OTIS, lawyer; b. Cin., Feb. 13, 1914; s. Charles Houston and Bessie Lee (Becraft) C.; m. Shirley Jane Ripley, Sept. 4, 1937 (dec. May 1973); children: James Houston, Thomas Ripley, Virginia Lee; m. Clare M. Haller, Mar. 15, 1974. A.B., Princeton U., 1935; J.D., Harvard U., 1938; postgrad., Columbia U., 1958. Bar: Ohio 1939. Practiced in Cin.; assoc. firm Dinsmore, Shohl, Sawyer & Dinsmore, 1938-43, ptnr., 1946-61; sr. ptnr. Dinsmore, Shohl, Barrett, Coates & Deupree, 1961-67, Dinsmore, Shohl, Coates & Deupree, 1967-82, Dinsmore & Shohl, 1982-86; counsel South-Western Pub. Co., Senco Products Inc., 1975-86; former dist. atty. L. & N. R.R. Co. Dist. chmn. United Appeal, 1958-59; pres. local chpt. Am. Field Service, 1962-64; trustee Legal Aid Soc., Cin., 1970-74. Served to lt. (j.g.) USNR, 1943-46. Decorated Bronze Star. Mem. Internat., Am., Ohio, Cin. bar assns., Princeton Alumni Assn. So. Ohio, Cin. Hist. Soc., Am. Soc. Internat. Law, Harvard Law Sch. Assn., Literary, Torch, University, Cin. Country, Hyde Pk. Country clubs, Phi Beta Kappa. Presbyn. Home: Cincinnati Ohio. Died Oct. 28, 1986; buried in Cin.

COATSWORTH, ELIZABETH (MRS. HENRY BESTON), author; b. Buffalo, May 31, 1893; d. William T. and Ida (Reid) C.; m. Henry Beston, June 18, 1929; children: Margaret Coatsworth (Mrs. Dorik Mechau), Catherine Maurice (Mrs. Richard Barnes). Prep. edn., Buffalo Sem.; A.B., Vassar Coll., 1915; M.A., Columbia U., 1916; Litt.D., U. Maine, 1955; L.H.D., New Eng. Coll., 1958. (Recipient Newbery medal 1931, Golden Rose award New Eng. Poetry Club 1967, Maine Arts and Sci. award, 1st runner-up Hans Christian Anderson award 1968); Author: 7 other books of verse Mountain Bride, and; 4 other novels; 3 books essays, numerous childrens books including The Cat Who Went to Heaven; the 5 Sally books beginning with Horses, Dogs and Cats, 1957; book of collected verse, 1957; novel The White Room, 1958, The Peaceable Kingdom, The Cave, 1958, Indian Encounters, 1960, Lonely Maria, 1960, Desert Dan, 1960, The UNICEF Christmas Book, 1960, The Noble Doll, 1961, Ronnie and the Chief's Son, 1962, The Princess and the Lion, 1963, Jock's Island, 1963, Cricket and the Emperors Son, 1965, The Secret, 1965, The Hand of Apollo, 1965, The Sparrow Bush; poetry, 1966, The Fox Friend, 1966, The Place, 1966, (with Henry Beston) Chimney Farm Bedtime Stories, 1966, Maine Memories, 1968, Bess and the Sphinx, 1968, Lighthouse Island, 1968, George and Red, 1969, Indian Mound Farm, 1969, Grandmother Cat and the Hermit, 1970, Good Night, 1972, The Wanderers, 1972, Daisy, 1973, Pure Magic, 1973, All of a Sudden Susan, 1974, Marra's World, 1975, Personal Geography of Elizabeth Coatsworth, 1976, Under the Green Willow, 1984, Books pub. in, England, Germany, Norway, Sweden, other countries.; Editor: (with Henry Beston) Henry Beston's Especially Maine, 1970. Fellow Internat. Inst. Arts and Letters; mem. Phi Beta Kappa. Home: Damariscotta Maine. Died Aug. 31, 1986; buried Hall Cemetery, Nobleboro, Maine.

COCHRANE, ERIC, history educator; b. Oakland, Calif., May 13, 1928; s. Eric and Adelaide (Griffith) C.; m. Lydia Steinway, Dec. 23, 1953; children: John, Nicholas. BA, Yale U., 1949, PhD, 1954. Instr. Stanford U., 1953-54; mem. faculty U. Chgo., from 1957, prof. history, from 1966; guest lectr. U. Perugia, 1969-70; sec. Renaissance Sem. Chgo., 1961-67. Author: Tradition and Enlightenment in the Tuscan Academies, 1961, The Late Italian Renaissance, 1970, Florence in the Forgotten Centuries (1527-1800), 1973, Historians and Historiography in the Italian Renaissance, 1981; contbr. articles to profl. jours. Trustee Newberry Library, Chgo.; sec. St. Thomas Apostle Parish Council, 1979-81. Fulbright scholar for study in Italy, 1951-53; Guggenheim fellow, 1960-61, Am.

Council Learned Socs. fellow, 1965-66, 77-78. Mem. Soc. for Italian Hist. Studies, Cath. Hist. Assn. (v.p. 1973, pres. 1974), Renaissance Soc. Am., Societa Colombaria, Accademia Arte del Disegno, Deputazione Storia Patria Toscana. Home: Chicago Ill. also: Florence Italy. Died Nov.29, 1985.

COCO, JAMES, actor; b. N.Y.C., Mar. 21, 1930; s. Felice and Ida (Di Testai) C. Student, Uta Hagen Bergdorf Studios, 1960. Broadway appearances include Last of the Red Hot Lovers, 1969, The Devils, 1965, Passage to India, 1963, Man of La Mancha, 1967, Arturo Ui, 1968, Everybody Loves Opal, 1966, Little Me, 1982, Wally's Cafe, 1982, You Can't Take It With You, 1983; off-Broadway appearances; appeared in films Only When I Laugh, The Muppets Take Manhattan, 1984; TV miniseries The French Atlantic Affair, 1979; TV shows Raquel Welch Special (recipient Obie awards.), St. Elsewhere (Emmy award), Who's the Boss; author: The James Coco Diet. Home: New York N.Y. Died Feb. 25, 1987; buried St. Gertrude's Cemetery, N.J.

COE, EARL, state official; b. Mpls., Sept. 12, 1892; s. Winfield Scott and Cora (Haryell) C.; m. Birdie Miller, Nov. 20, 1912. Fruit grower and shipper Coe & Co., White Salmon, Wash., 1926-39; lumber mill opererator Nordby Lumber and Box Co., White Salmon, 1939-46; mem. Wash. Ho. of Reps., 1938-40, state senator, 1944-48; sec. State of Wash., 1948-56; dir. Dept. Conservation and Devel., from 1957. Dem. state chmn., 1946-48; State chmn. YMCA youth legislature. Mem. Freedom Found., Am. Heritage Found., Elks, Eagles, Masons (Shriner). Congregationalist. Home: Olympia Wash. †

COFER, HENRY JACKSON, JR., business executive; b. Washington, Ga., Nov. 23, 1926; s. Henry Jackson and Ruby (Ray) C.; m. Allie Padgett, Aug. 25, 1947; children: Jacqueline Carole, Rebecca Gale, Leslie Claire. Student, Clemson U., 1944-45, Draughton's Bus. Sch., Atlanta, 1947-48. Engring. asst. Dupont de Nemours Inc., Wilmington, Del., 1952-55; with SeaPak Corp, St. Simons Island, Ga., 1955-69; pres., chief exec. officer Rich-SeaPak Corp., St. Simons Island; bd. dirs. Rich Products Corp., Buffalo, Coastal Bank of Ga., Brunswick; mem. Atlantic states marine fisheries commn.; mem. nat. adv. com. oceans and atmosphere. With U.S. Merchant Marine. Mem. Brunswick-Glynn County C. of C., Nat. Frozen Food Assn. (bd. dirs.), Nat. Fisheries Inst. (pres. 1972, bd. dirs.), Nat. Shrimp Breaders and Processors Assn., Southeastern Fisheries ASsn., Jaycees (past pres.), River Club, Sea Island Beach and Golf Club. Home: Saint Simons Island Ga. Deceased.

COFFEY, JOHN JOSEPH, JR., management consultation executive; b. Chgo., June 1, 1903; s. John Joseph and Catherine (Newitt) C.; m. Ann Sweeney, 1934 (dec. 1976); children: John Joseph III, Susan Coffey Kehm, Ann C., Edward C., Patricia J.; m. vivian English Clark, Apr. 22, 1978. LLB, Loyola U., Chgo., 1928. Bar: Ill. 1930. Stenographic sec. Peabody Coal Co., Chgo., 1920-25; sec., credit mgr. Consumers Co., Chgo., 1925-31; with trust dept. Prairie State Bank, Oak Park, Ill., 1932-33; with George S. May Internat. Co., Chgo., 1933-81; div. mgr. George S. May Internat. Co., N.Y.C., 1940-43; exec. sec. George S. May Internat. Co., Park Ridge, Ill., 1944-81; editor co. publ. May Trends George S. May Internat. Co. Mem. Ill. Bar Assn., KC (past grand knight). Died Nov. 17, 1985; buried All Sts. Cemetery, Des Plaines, Ill.

COFFIN, JOSEPH JOHN, business consultant; b. Indpls., Nov. 26, 1911; s. Joseph H. and Nona V. (Albright) C.; m. Marjorie M. Holcomb, Nov. 16, 1933; children—J. Robert, Joan Louise Coffin Close, William H. Student, DePauw U., 1929-31, Butler U., 1940-41. Sales and sales dist. mgr. J.B. Simpson Inc., Chgo., 1932-36; dist. rep. Alemite Sales Co., Chgo., 1936-38; agt., agy. supr. J.R. Townsend Agy. of Equitable Life Ins. of Iowa, Indpls., 1938-45; agy. mgr. Commonwealth Life Ins. Co. of Louisville, Indpls., 1945-48; sales mgr., v.p., gen. mgr., pres. J.I. Holcomb Mfg. Co., 1948-73; v.p. public relations Top Quality Chems. Co., Indpls., 1975-84; cons. Top Quality Chems. Co., 1984—; chmn. bd. Mut. Hosp. Ins. Co., Inc. (Blue Cross of Ind.), Indpls., 1971-85; bus. cons.; dir. Assoc. Ins. Cos. Inc. Mem. adv. council Christian Theol. Sem., 1967—; bd. dirs. Suemma Coleman Home for Unwed Mothers, 1960-71, pres., 1970-71; bd. dirs. Found. for Religious Studies, 1970—. Served with USCG, 1942-45. Recipient Brotherhood citation NCCJ, 1965; honoree City of Hope, 1975. Mem. Chem. Spltys. Mfg. Assn. (bd. govs. 1962-71), Meridian Kessler Neighborhood Assn., Rotary (Indpls.) (pres. 1960-61); Rotary (dist. gov. 1973-74); Indpls. Athletic, Masons (32 degree) (Indpls.). Republican. Quaker. Home: Indianapolis Ind. Deceased.

COGGESHALL, LOWELL T., retired medical educator, investigator, administrator; b. Saratoga, Ind., May 7, 1901; s. William Evart and Flossie Ann (Warren) C.; m. Louise Holland, May 15, 1930 (dec. 1966); children: Richard Edwin, Diane, Carol; m. Rebecca Clark Dobson, Apr. 20, 1967 (dec. Nov. 1987). AB, Ind. U., 1924, AM, 1925, MD, 1928, LLD (hon.), 1948; LLD (hon.), Lake Forest U., 1961; DSc (hon.), Chgo. Med. U., 1963, Union U., 1964. Intern, asst. prof. medicine U. Chgo. Hosp., 1928-35; mem. staff for research in tropical diseases, internat. health div. Rockefeller Found., Rockefeller Inst., N.Y.C., 1935-40; prof. preventive medicine Sch. Pub. Health, U. Mich., 1940-41, chmn. dept. tropical diseases, 1942-44; sr. med. officer Pan-Am. Airways-Africa, 1941-42; chmn. dept. medicine U. Chgo., 1946-47, dean div. biol. scis., 1947-50; spl. asst. to Sec. Dept. HEW, 1956-57; mem. cons. com. to survey med. edn. and research 1957-58; v.p. U. Chgo., 1960-66, acting pres., 1965, retired as Disting. Service prof. medicine, 1966; formerly cons. to Sec. of Navy, chmn. med. cons. to Sec. of Def.; mem. adv. com. South Baldwin Hosp., chmn., 1975; bd. dirs. Field Found. III, chmn. 1961-65; bd. dirs. Gaylord and Dorothy Donnelley Found., 1980; med. cons. Chgo. Community Trust, 1965. Author: Planning for Medical Progress Through Education, 1961; contbr. numerous papers on infections, tropical diseases, med. edn. Former mem. City of Chgo. Bd. Health, mem. exec. bd. Am. Cancer Soc. (pres. 1958); former trustee Chgo. Mus. Served with M.C., USNR, 1944, later promoted capt. Recipient Jesuit Centennial citation as one of Chgo.'s 100 outstanding citizens; Gorgas medal Assn. Mil. Surgeons, 1945; John M. Russell medal Assn. Am. Med. Colls., 1967; Gold Key, U. Chgo., 1967; George Coleman medal Inst. Medicine, Chgo., 1965; Abraham Flexner award Assn. Am. Med. Colls., 1963. Fellow ACP; mem. Nat. Acad. Scis., AAAS, Am. Philos. Soc., Sigma Xi, Alpha Omega Alpha, Delta Omega. Died Nov. 1987.

COHEN, ARTHUR ALLEN, author, publisher; b. N.Y.C., June 25, 1928; s. Isidore Meyer and Bess (Junger) C.; m. Elaine Firstenberg Lustig, Oct. 14, 1956; 1 dau., Tamar Judith. B.A., U. Chgo., 1946; M.A., 1949; M.A. fellow Jewish philosophy, Jewish Theol. Sem. Am., 1951-53. Co-founder, pres. Noonday Press, N.Y.C., 1951-54; founder, pres., exec. editor Meridian Books, Inc., N.Y.C., 1954-60; (acquired by World Pub. Co., 1960); v.p. World Pub. Co., 1961; dir. religion dept. Holt, Rinehart, and Winston, Inc., 1962-64, editor-in-chief, v.p. gen. books div., 1964-68; mng. editor The Document of 20th Century Art Viking Press, 1968-75; founder, pres. Ex Libris (div, T.J. Art, Inc.), 1974-86; vis. lectr. in Religion, Brown U., 1972, in Theology, Jewish Inst. Religion, 1977; del. Tisch lectures in Judaic Theology, Brown U., 1979, lectures, coloquia or readings at Harvard Coll., Yale U., Columbia U., U. Chgo., Northwestern U., Syracuse U., numerous others; mem. Farvaltung, Yivo Inst. Jewish Research 1983-86, chmn. 1985-86. Author: (fiction) The Carpenter Years, 1967, 68, In the Days of Simon Stern, 1973, 74 (Edward Lewis Wallant award 1973), A Hero in His Time, 1976, Acts of Theft, 1980 (Quality Paperbacks Book of the Month Club), 1981, An Admirable Woman, 1983, 85 (Nat. Jewish Book award 1984, featured Alternate Book of the Month Club), 1985, Artists and Enemies (3 novellas), 1987; (non-fiction) Martin Buber, 1957, London edit., 1957, The Natural and the Supernatural Jew: An Historical and Theological Introduction, 1962, The Myth of the Judeo-Christian Tradition, 1971, A People Apart: Hasidism in America, 1971, (with Mordecai Kaplan) If Not Now, When?, 1973, Osip Emilevich Mandelstam: An Essay in Antiphon, 1974, Sonia Delaunay, 1975, The Tremendum: A Theological Interpretation of the Holocaust, 1981, Herbert Bayer: The Complete Works, 1984 (George Wittenborn Meml. award 1986); contbr. to: Am. Catholics: A Protestant-Jewish View, 1959, Christianity: Some Non-Christian Appraisals, 1964, Sacramentum Mundi, 1964; others. Editor: Anatomy of Faith, 1960, Humanistic Education and Western Civilization, 1964, Arguments and Doctrines: A Reader in Jewish Thinking, 1970, The New Art of Color: The Writings of Robert and Sonia Delaunay, The Jew: Essays from Martin Buber's Journal Der Jude, 1980, (with Paul Mendes Flohr) Contemporary Jewish Religious Thought, 1986; contbr. articles to religious publs., Harper's mag., N.Y. Times Book Review, others. Mem. PEN (bd. dirs. Am. Ctr. 1977-86). Home: New York N.Y. Died Oct. 31, 1986; buried N.Y.C.

COHEN, JEROME BERNARD, economist, educator; b. N.Y.C., Jan. 18, 1915; s. Charles Kenneth and Estelle (Bauland) C.; m. Mina Salmon, June 18, 1934; 1 dau., Carla Lee. BSS, CCNY, 1934; AM, Columbia U., 1935, PhD, 1947. Prof. econs. and finance Bernard M. Baruch Coll., CUNY, 1956-71, prof. emeritus, 1971-86, dean grad. studies, dean Sch. Bus., 1968-71, dean emeritus, 1971-86, acting pres., 1970-71; research assoc. Am. Inst. Banking, summer 1937, Brookings Instn., summer 1938; vis. prof. statistics So. Meth. U., summer 1939; vis. prof. econs. State Coll. Wash., summer 1940, U. P.R., summer 1941; economist, coordinator Inter-Am. Affairs, 1941-42; asst. regional adminstr. for ters. and possessions OPA, 1942-43; mem. Tax Mission to Japan, 1949; chief S. Asia br. Office Intelligence Research U.S. Dept. State, 1950-51; research assoc. Ctr. Internat. Studies, MIT, summer 1953. Author: Japan's Economy in War and Reconstruction, 1949, Economic Problems of Free Japan, 1952, Personal Finance: Principles and Case Problems, 6th edit., 1979, Japan's Postwar Economy, 1958, (with S.R. Robbins) The Financial Manager, 1966, (with E. Zinbarg, A. Zeikel) Investment Analysis and Portfolio Management, 3d edit., 1977, Guide to Intelligent Investing, 1977; editor: Pacific Partnership: United States-Japan Trade, 1972; contbr. articles to jours.; sr. editor Bankers Mag., 1972-86. Served as Japanese specialist with rank of lt. Intelligence Corps, USNR, 1943-46. Recipient Rockefeller Found grant for new study of Japan's economy, 1956, Social Sc Research Council grant, 1963-64, Townsend Harri medal, 1967. Mem. Fin. Mgmt. Assn., Am. Econ Assn., Met. Econ. Assn., Am. Fin. Assn., Am. Stati Assn., Council Fgn. Relations, Japan Soc., AAUP, Na Assn. Bus. Economists, N.Y. Soc. Security Analysts, Pl Beta Kappa (chpt. pres. 1970-71), Beta Gamma Sigma Home: New York N.Y. Died Nov. 29, 1986.

COHEN, SAMUEL NATHAN, diversified compan executive; b. Winnipeg, Man., Can., July 9, 1919; s Alexander and Rose (Diamond) C.; children: Charle Frank, Mark David, Sharon Edith. LLD (hon.), U Man., Winnipeg, 1979. Chmn., chief exec. officer Saa Stores Ltd.; pres. Gendis Inc.; vice chmn., bd. dirs. Me Stores Can., Ltd.; bd. dirs. Greenberg Stores Ltd., Me Stores (MTS) Ltd. Mem. adv. com. Royal Trust Corp Can.; bd. dirs. St. Boniface Gen. Hosp. Research Found Recipient Canada Medal, 1980. Mem. Glendal Country Club. Home: Winnipeg Man., Canada. Die July 28, 1988.

COHEN, SIDNEY, physician; b. N.Y.C., June 7, 191(s. Adolph and Esther (Gordon) C.; m. Illse Annalouis Franke, Feb. 27, 1934; children—Dorothy Elizabeth Richard Sidney. Ph.D., Columbia, 1930; postgrad Coll. City N.Y., 1930-32, Bonn (Germany) U., 1932-38. Diplomate: Am. Bd. Internal Medicine. Intern Jamaic (L.I.) Hosp., 1938-40; resident VA Hosp., Los Angeles 1946-49; chief research Brentwood Hosp., Los Angeles 1949-59; chief psychosomatic medicine Wadsworth VA Hosp., Los Angeles, 1959-68; chief Center Studie Narcotics and Drug Abuse NIMH, Chevy Chase, Md 1968-87; assoc. clin. prof. medicine U. Calif. at Lo Angeles, 1956-87; All Univ. lectr. U. Calif., 1965; William Harvey Taylor lectr. Am. Therapeutic Soc., 1964 cons. Suicide Prevention Center, Alcoholism Researc Clinic, Central Office Research Psychiatry, Neurolog and Psychology.; Mem. sci. adv. bd. Am. Schizophreni Found.; dir. Los Angeles Med. Research Found. Author: Chemopsychotherapy, 1963, LSD, 1964, Th Drug Dilemma, 1969, The Therapeutic Potential o Marijuana, 1976, Encyclopedia of Drug Abuse, 1985 also numerous articles.; Editor-in-chief: Mind, Psychi atry in Private Practice, 1963-64; editorial bd Psychosomatics, 1964-87; editor: Jour Psychopharmacology, 1967. Served to col. M.C. AUS 1941-46. Mem. Soc. Biol. Psychiatry, Am., Calif., Lo Angeles County med. assns., Los Angeles Soc Neurology and Psychiatry, Calif. Med. Research Assn. Home: Los Angeles Calif. Died May 8, 1987.

COHEN, WILBUR JOSEPH, former government of ficial, public affairs educator; b. Milw., June 10, 1913; s Aaron and Bessie (Rubenstein) C.; m. Eloise Bittel, Apr 8, 1938; children: Christopher, Bruce, Stuart. Ph.B., U Wis., Madison, 1934; LL.D., U. Wis., 1966; L.H.D. Adelphi Coll., 1962, Cleve. State U., 1970, Ohio Stat U., 1970; LL.D., Yeshiva U., 1967, Brandeis U., 1968 Detroit U., Kenyon Coll., 1969, Mich. State U., 1975 Central Mich. U., 1976; D.S.S., U. Louisville, 1969 D.H., Fla. State U., 1972, Roosevelt U., 1978; D.P.S. Eastern Mich. U., 1982, No. Mich. U., 1983; D.H.L. Fla. Internat. U., 1985, Rutgers U., 1986, U. Wis. Milw., 1986. With Com. Econ. Security, 1934-35; with Social Security Adminstrn., 1935-56; dir. div. research and statistics 1953-56; prof. pub. welfare adminstrn. U Mich., 1956-69, 72-80; asst. sec. HEW, 1961-65, under sec., 1965-68, sec., 1968-69; prof. edn. U. Mich., 1969-80; dean U. Mich. (Sch. Edn.), 1969-78; mem. exec. bd Inst. Social Research, 1969-76; co-chmn. Inst. Gerontology, U. Mich.-Wayne State U., 1969-76; vis. prof UCLA, 1957; lectr. Catholic U., 1961-62; Sid W Richardson prof. pub. affairs L.B.J. Sch. Public Affairs U. Tex., 1980-83, prof. pub. affairs, 1983-87; dir research Pres.'s Com. Universal Tng., 1947; chmn. com on health and pensions Wage Stablzn. Bd., 1951-52 cons. aging to U.S. Senate Com. Labor and Pub Welfare, 1956-57, 59, to UN, 1956-57; chmn. Pres.'s Task Force on Health and Social Security, 1960; mem Adv. Council Pub. Assistance, 1959, Nat. Com. Social Security, 1978-81; chmn. Nat. Com. on Unemployment Compensation, 1978-80, Pres.'s Com. on Mental Retardation, 1968, Pres.'s Com. on Population and Family Planning, 1968; del. Gen. Assembly Internat Social Security Assn., Turkey, 1961, U.S., 1964, vice chmn. council, 1964; rep. U.S. Govt. at Internat. Confs Social Security, Internat. Conf. Social Work, Internat. Labor Conf.; chmn. U.S. del. UN Conf. Ministers Responsible Social Welfare, 1968; co-chmn. Health Vols. for Carter-Mondale, 1976; advisor Study Group on Social Security. Author: Retirement Policies in Social Security, 1957, (with William Haber) Readings in Social Security, 1948, Social Security, Programs, Problems and Policies, 1960, (with Milton Friedman) Social Security: Universal or Selective'9, 1972, (with Charles F. Westoff) Demographic Dynamics in America, 1977; co-author: Income and Welfare in the United States, 1962, Toward a Social Report, 1969; editor: The New Deal: Fifty Years After, 1984, The Roosevelt New Deal, 1986, also numerous articles. Trustee J.F. Kennedy Center Performing Arts, 1968; bd. govs. Haifa U. 1971-87; co-chmn. Save Our Security, 1979-87. Recipient Distinguished Service award HEW, 1956 Arthur J. Altmeyer award, 1972, award Group Health Assn., 1956, Florina Lasker award, 1961; Blanche Ittelson award, 1962; award Nat. Assn. Mentally Retarded Children, 1965; award Assn. Phys. Medicine

65; Bronfman Pub. Health prize, 1967; Rockefeller b. Service award, 1967; award Am. Assn. Hosp. anning, 1967; Murray-Green award, 1968; Wilbur 'ard Golden Ring Council Sr. Citizens, 1968; Wis. ate U.-Stevens Point award, 1968; Forand award Nat. uncil Sr. Citizens, 1969; Jane Addams-Hull House 'ard, 1975; Merrill-Palmer award, 1975; Internat. sn. Social Security award, 1979; Burden Ctr. Aging ard, 1982. Mem. Am. Pub. Welfare Assn. (Terry eml. Merit award 1961, dir. 1962-65, pres. 1975-76), t. Conf. Social Welfare (Distinguished Service award 57, pres. 1969), Council Social Work Edn. (ho. of s. 1959-62, 74-77), Nat. Assn. Social Workers, Indsl. lations Research Assn. (exec. bd. 1969-72), Am. on. Assn., Inst. Medicine of Nat. Acad. Scis., Am. sp. Assn. (hon.), Am. Pub. Health Assn. Home: stin Tex. Died May 17, 1987.

)HN, ALVIN GILBERT, musician, jazz composer; b. Y.C., Nov. 24, 1925; s. David Emanuel and Gertrude ; m. Flora Ann Morse, Aug. 23, 1963; children: chael, Peter, Danna, Lisa, Joseph. Student, public s., N.Y.C. Saxophonist, Buddy Rich, Woody rman, Artie Shaw, arranger, orchestrator, Ray arles, Andy Williams, Tony Bennett; orchestrator: oadway shows Music! Music!; TV Anne Bancroft Spl, phisticated Ladies (3 Grammy nominations); rec. ar- Concord Records; tours included, Japan, Eng., S. n., Can., Senegal, South Africa, France, Holland, nmark, Sweden, Norway, Switzerland. Mem. Am. dn. Musicians, ASCAP. Democrat. Jewish. Home: ncord Calif. Died Feb. 15, 1988.

)HN, ROY MARCUS, lawyer; b. N.Y.C., Feb. 20, 27; s. Albert and Dora (Marcus) C. B.A., Columbia , 1946, LL.B., 1947. Bar: N.Y. 1948. With U.S. dist. y.'s office, N.Y.C., 1947-52; asst. U.S. atty. U.S. dist. y.'s office, 1948-50; confidential asst. to U.S. atty. 50-52; spl. asst. to U.S. atty. gen. McGranery, 1952; ief counsel U.S. Senate Permanent investigations sub- m., 1953-54; assoc. firm Saxe, Bacon & Bolan (and edecessor firms), N.Y.C., 1959-86; adj. prof. law N.Y. w Sch., 1957-86. Author: Mc Carthy, 1968, A Fool a Client, 1970, The Answer to Tail Gunner Joe, 77, How To Stand Up for Your Rights—and Win!, 81. Pres. Am. Jewish League Against Communism; . regents St. Francis Coll., N.Y.C.; chmn. spl. projects imane Soc.; chmn. bd. Prisoner's Art Program; dir. st Side Conservative Club, N.Y.C., Western Goal's und.; trustee Roy M. Cohn Found.; Capt. N.Y. State G. Recipient ann. award lawyers div. Fedn. Jewish ilanthropies, 1952, Americanism award Am. Legion Y. State, 1956, Patriotism award Cath. War Vets., 70, Leadership award N.Y. County Conservative rty, 1975, Achievement award Jewish Nat. Fund, 81, City of Peace award B'nai B'rith and State of ael Bonds, 1983, Young Republicans of Am. award, 85, Cath. War Vets. ann. award, 1985. Mem. Am., onx County bar assns. Home: Greenwich Conn. Died ig. 2, 1986.

)LBURN, DE FOREST SMITH, cement manufac- ring executive; b. Marinette, Wis., Apr. 4, 1890; s. ed Smith and Louis (Duket) C.; m. Josephine L. pp, Mar. 18, 1933; children: De Forest, ary. Student, Lake Forest Coll., 1912-13. Bldg. con- ctor 1914-24; svc. mgr. Marquette Cement Mfg. Co., go., 1924-33, v.p., 1933-51, exec. v.p., 1951-56, v.p., ns., from 1956; trustee The 800 Lake Shore Dr. Trust. 'rustee Lake Forst Coll. Mem. Masons (Shriner), go. Engrs. Club, Union League Club, Adventurers ub, Exmoor Golf Club, Tower Club, Lake Shore ub. Home: Chicago Ill. †

)LE, ALAN Y., lawyer; b. N.Y.C., Oct. 7, 1922; s. urry I. and Gertrude (Strauchler) C.; m. Gloria H. aston, Sept. 18, 1946; children: Charles Glaston, obert Barry. BA, Columbia U., 1942; LLB, Yale U., 49. Bar: D.C. 1949. Spl. asst. to atty. gen. Dept. stice, Washington, 1949; law sec. to Assoc. Justice obert H. Jackson U.S. Supreme Ct., Washington, 49-50; asst. gen. counsel Office Def. Mobilization, 51; pvt. practice Washington, 1952-64; founder, sr. r. Cole & Groner, Washington, 1965-84; mem. nat. nel arbitrators Am. Arbitration Assn., 1954-84; mem. l. conf. D.C. Cir., 1964, 68, 73-76; mem. adv. bd. Fed. ntracts Report, 1971-84. Co-author: Moore's Federal actice, vol. 1A, 2d edit.; editor Yale Law Jour., 1948- ; sr. contbg. editor and gen. editor Fed. Bar Jour., 57-66. Served to warrant officer AUS, 1943-46, ETO, uremberg War Trials. Fellow Am. Coll. Trial wyers, Internat. Soc. Barristers, Nat. Coll. Criminal f. Lawyers and Pub. Defenders (vice chmn. bd. gents 1976-77); mem. ABA (ho. of dels. 1974-76, mn. sect. criminal justice 1976-77), Fed. Bar Assn. imn. com. rules of civil procedure 1965-66), Nat. sn. Criminal Def. Lawyers (life) (pres. elect 1976-77), n. Soc. Writers Legal Subjects, Cosmos Club, Nat. wyers Club, Yale Club of N.Y.C. Home: Bethesda d. Died Sept. 25, 1984; buried Washington.

)LE, ALPHAEUS PHILEMON, artist; b. Jersey ty Heights, N.J., 1876; s. Timothy and Annie (Carter) ; m. Margaret Ward Wamsley, Aug. 15, 1903 (dec. 03); m. Anita Rio Higgins, Apr., 1962 (dec. 73). Ed., Italy; studied with, Benjamin Constant and in Paul Laurens, Julian Acad. and Eléve des Beaux ts, Paris. Portraitist; work in permanent collections Nat. Portrait Gallery, London, Bklyn. Mus., several univs.; author: (with Margaret Ward Cole) Timothy Cole, Wood Engraver, 1936. Recipient various awards including Archer M. Huntiongton award Hudson Valley Art Assn., 1956. Mem. Am. Water Color Club (pres. N.Y. Water Color Club prior to merger), Grand Cen. Art Gallery Assn., Allied Artists Am. (pres. 1952-53, hon., prize for oil 1972), NAD (mem. coun.), Old Lyme Art Assn., Nat. Arts Club, Salmagundi Club (prize 1943). Home: New York N.Y. Died Nov. 25, 1988.

COLE, ELBERT CHARLES, educator; b. Northampton, Mass., Apr. 2, 1891; s. George Elbert and Alice Landon (French) C.; m. Ida Nell Ainsworth, Oct. 28, 1916; children: Gerald Ainsworth, Elbert Charles, Phillis Anne (Mrs. W.A.R. Deming); m. 2d, Margaret Caldwell Grierson, July 20, 1933. AB, Middlebury Coll., 1915; AM, Trinity Coll., 1918; PhD, Harvard U., 1924. Asst. in biology Middlebury Coll., 1914-15; instr. biology Hartford (Conn.) High Sch., 1915-22, Trinity Coll., 1918-19; Austin teaching fellow Harvard U., 1922-24; asst. prof. biology Williams Coll., 1924-28, assoc. prof., 1928-32, prof., 1932-45, Samuel Fessenden Clarke prof. biology, 1945-46, emeritus, from 1956; propr. Cole Enterprises, publicity svc.; mem. corp. Marine Biol. Lab., Woods Hole; life trustee Middlebury Coll., sec. of corp., from 1959; trustee of the Porter Hosp.; dir. Berkshire Frozen Foods Lockers Inc. from 1944. Author books, articles in sci. jours. Mem. Commn. for Standardizationof Biol. Stains; bd. dirs. Williamstown Boys Club, 1930-48. With first Inf., Conn. Nat. Guard, 1915-17; with Machine Gun Co, corpl., Mex. border svc., 1916, U.S. Army, 1917. Mem. AAAS, Am. Assn. Anatomists, Am. Assn. Zoologists, AAUP, Faculty Club, Williams Club, Phi Beta Kappa, Gamma Alpha, Alpha Sigma Phi. Republican. Congregationalist. Home: Middlebury Vt. †

COLE, FRED CARRINGTON, educator, academic administrator; b. Franklin, Tex., Apr. 12, 1912; s. Robert Wiley and Elizabeth (Taylor) C.; m. Lois Ferguson, Aug. 22, 1937; children: Caroline Cole Cornwell, Fred Carrington, Robert Grey, Taylor Morris. AB, La. State U., 1934, AM, 1936, PhD, 1941; LLD (hon.), Union Coll., 1961, Washington and Lee U., 1968. Editorial assoc. Jour So. History La. State U., 1936-41, mng. editor, 1941-42, co-editor So. Biography Series, 1938-45, hist. editor La. State U. Press, 1938-42; assoc. prof. history Tulane U., 1946-47, prof., 1947-59, dean, 1947-55, acad. v.p., 1954-59; pres. Washington and Lee U., 1959-67, Council on Library Resources, Inc., Washington, 1967-78, also bd. dirs.; assoc. editor Miss. Valley Hist. Rev., 1946-53; staff assoc. edn. Ford Found., 1954-55; cons. med. rsch. and edn. HEW, 1957-58; cons. to surgeon-gen. on med. manpower, 1958-59; mem. Com. on Internat. Exchange of Persons, 1963-70. Trustee United Negro Coll. Fund, George C. Marshall Found.; bd. dirs. Ford Motor Co. Fund Scholarship Program, 1965-70; pres. Va. Found. Ind. Colls.; chmn. adv. com. div. instl. programs NSF, 1957-63; chmn. adv. council coop. rsch. Office Edn., 1965-67; chmn. hist. adv. com. Dept. Army, 1963-67. Served with USNR, 1942-46. Recipient spl. commendation surgeon gen. USN, 1945, Outstanding Service award Dept. Army, 1967, medals Internat. Council Archives, Internat. Fedn. Library Assns., 1977. Mem. ALA (hon. mem., Centennial citation 1976), Am. Hist. Assn., So. Hist. Assn., Miss. Valley Hist. Assn., Am. Polit. Assn., So. Polit. Assn., Acad. Polit. Sci., Cosmos Club (Washington), Century Club (N.Y.C.), Phi Beta Kappa Assocs. (chmn. council nominating com. 1964-67) Sigma Chi, Phi Kappa Phi, Pi Sigma Alpha, Omicron Delta Kappa. Home: Chapel Hill N.C. Died May 6, 1986.

COLE, GORDON HENRY, labor union official, editor; b. Providence, Jan. 11, 1912; s. Albert Jourdan and Margaret Cooper (Ricketts) C.; m. Malvine Gescheidt, Sept. 19. 1939; children—Stephen Adams, Jeremy David; m. Morag Douglas Macintyre, Dec. 19, 1952; children—Gordon Macintyre, Susan Douglas, Margaret Cooper. A.B., Syracuse U., 1934. Newspaper reporter 1934-37; assoc. editor Labor Relations Reporter Bur. Nat. Affairs, 1937-39; labor editor U.S. News, 1939-42, U.S. News (Washington bur., newspaper PM), 1942-43; with civilian psychol. warfare br. 12th U.S. Army Group OSS, 1943-45; commr. conciliation U.S. Dept. Labor, 1946-47; cons. Bur. Internat. Labor Affairs, 1978-80; editor The Machinist, 1947-77; pub. relations dir. Internat. Assn. Machinists, AFL-CIO, 1947-77; cons. AFL-CIO Labor Studies Center, 1977-86. Decorated Medal of Freedom, Croix de Guerre. Mem. Internat. Labor Press Assn. (pres. 1955-57), Am. Newspaper Guild (v.p. 1943-44), Washington Newspaper Guild (pres. 1942), Nat. Press Club, Sigma Delta Chi. Democrat. Presbyterian. Home: Clifton Va. Died Apr. 29, 1988; cremated.

COLE, ROBERT LEE, corporation executive; b. Rockport, Mo., May 4, 1929; s. Branchie Ray and Mary (Clevenger) C.; children: Brenda Lynn (Mrs. Hill), Bradford Lee. A.A. summa cum laude, Fullerton (Calif.) Jr. Coll., 1949; A.B. cum laude, U. Calif. at Berkeley, 1951. Registered profl. engr., Calif. Asst. to plant mgr., staff indsl. engr. Rheem Mfg. Co., Downey, Calif., 1951-55; asst. to pres., chief prodn. control Longren Aircraft Co., Torrance, Calif., 1955-58; div. mgr. Aerojet-Gen. Corp., Fullerton, 1960-62; mgr. indsl. engring. Downey, 1962-63; exec. asst. to corp. v.p., gen. mgr. Downey, El Monte, Calif., 1963-64; corp. mgr. real estate and constrn. dept. Litton Industries, Inc., Beverly Hills, Calif., 1964-67; treas. Litton Industries, Inc., 1967-69; v.p. Litton Internat., 1967-69; treas. Litton Industries Found., 1967-69; pres. Litton Power Transmission, West Hartford, Conn., 1969-86; corporate v.p. Litton Industries; pres. Rust Engring. Co., 1971; group v.p., div. pres. Wheelabrator-Frye, Inc., 1972-73; dir. operations analysis United Techs. Corp. (name formerly United Aircraft Corp.), Hartford, Conn., 1973-74; corp. v.p., pres. United Techs. Corp. (Power Systems div.), 1974-76, corp. v.p., 1974-86; sr. v.p., pres. N.Am. elevator ops. Otis Elevator Co. subs., N.Y.C., 1976-81; exec. v.p. Power Group, 1981-86; pres. Allied Info. Systems Co., Hartford, Conn.; group v.p. Allied Corp., Morristown, N.J.; pres. Hartford Grad. Ctr., 1985-86; dir. Conn. Bank & Trust Co., CBT Corp. Bd. dirs. Inst. Living, Hartford Grad. Center; trustee Wadsworth Atheneum. Mem. Hartford, Hartford Gun, University (Hartford); Avon (Conn.) Country, Duquesne (Pitts.); University (N.Y.C.) clubs. Home: West Hartford Conn. Died Oct. 14, 1986.

COLE, SANDFORD STODDARD, engineer; b. Cuba, N.Y., Nov. 24, 1900; s. John Browning and Inez (Bassett) C.; m. Frances Halderman, July 11, 1925; children—Sandford Stoddard, David Lee, Stephen Hervey. B.S., Alfred (N.Y.) U., 1923, M.S., 1933, Ceramic Engr., 1950, D.Sc. (hon.), 1981; Ph.D., Pa. State U., 1934. Registered profl. engr., N.J., Pa. Fellow Mellon Inst., 1923-32; with titanium div. Nat. Lead Co., 1934-65, asst. mgr. research, 1948-65; cons. engr. 1966-86; Trustee Alfred U., 1958-61; bd. dirs. Engring. Found. Confs., 1966-84. Editorial bd.: Indsl. Minerals and Rocks, 3d edit, 1960; author tech. papers. Recipient Alumni citation Alfred U., 1952, Recognition award, 1973. Fellow Am. Ceramic Soc., Am. Inst. Chemists; mem. Soc. Mining Engrs. (distinguished mem.; bd. dirs. 1960-66, pres. 1964-65), Am. Inst. Mining Metall. and Petroleum Engrs. (dir. 1963-66, v.p. 1965-66), Am. Chem. Soc., Nat. Inst. Ceramic Engrs., Keramos, Sigma Xi, Phi Kappa Phi. Home: Hightstown N.J. Died July 21, 1986; buried Cuba, N.Y.

COLEMAN, FRANCIS CARTER, physician, educator; b. Jackson, Miss., May 14, 1915; s. Francis Marion and Emma (Carter) C.; m. Ruth Yvonne Ellzey, Sept. 2, 1937; children: Nancy Ruth, Stephen Carter, John Timothy, Jeanne Laurie. B.A., Miss. Coll., 1935; M.D., Tulane U., 1941. Diplomate Am. Bd. Pathology (sec.-treas., 1973, pres., 1974-75, life trustee, 1976-88). Intern Touro Infirmary, New Orleans, 1941-42; resident pathology Touro Infirmary, 1942-45; individual practice medicine Des Moines, 1946-64; dir. dept. pathology Mercy Hosp., Des Moines, 1946-64; asst. clin. prof. pathology U. Nebr. Coll. Medicine, 1951-88; clin. prof. pathology U. Iowa Coll. Medicine, 1964-65; pvt. practice Tampa, Fla., 1964-88; dir. Tampa Sch. Med. Tech., 1965-77; mem. staff Tampa Gen. Hosp., Centro-Espanol Hosp., Tampa, St. Joseph's Hosp., Tampa, Univ. Community Hosp., Tampa, Carrollwood Community Hosp., Tampa, AMI Town and Country Med. Ctr., Tampa clin. prof. pathology U. South Fla., 1972-88; pres., med. dir. Patterson Coleman Labs., Tampa, 1964-77; Mem. Health Services Industry Com., Phase II, 1972-73; mem. nat. manpower adv. com. U.S. Dept. Labor, 1973-74; pres. Drug Abuse Comprehensive Coordinating Office, Tampa, 1973-74; mem. spl. com. on nation's health care needs C. of C. of U.S., 1977-79; bd. regents Uniformed Services U. of Health Scis., from 1982, vice chmn. bd. 1986-87, acting chmn., 1987-88, chmn., 1988. Bd. govs. Fla. Orch., pres., 1975-76, chmn. master bd., 1978-79, mem. Pres.' Council, 1988; life mem. Pres.'s Council, 1981 and mem. Founders Soc., 1987, U. South Fla., 1981; bd. fellows U. Tampa, 1980-88. Recipient Sci. Products award for outstanding service to pathology, 1965, Disting. Service award Am. Soc. Clin. Pathologists and Coll. Am. Pathologists, 1978; Spl. award Am. Pathology Found., 1979, recognition award Internat. Coll. Surgeons, 1985, disting. service award Fla. Soc. Pathologists, 1985. Fellow Coll. Am. Pathologists (life; pres. 1960-61, chmn. council on govt. affairs 1972-78, vice chmn. 3d party reimbursement com. 1979-81, archivist and historian 1979-88, pres.'s adv. council 1981-86, advisor to Council on Govt. and Profl. Affairs 1985-88, Frank W. Hartman Meml. award 1986), Am. Soc. Clin. Pathologists, ACP, Am. Coll. Chest Physicians; mem. AMA (chmn. council legislative activities 1963-64, chmn. polit. action com. 1965-66, chmn. subcom. certification, registration and licensure of council health manpower 1967-73, chmn. council on health manpower 1973-74, Physician's recognition award in continuing med. edn. from 1971, mem. adv. panel to spl. task force on profl. liability and ins. 1986—), Am. Assn. Blood Banks (pres. 1968-69), Soc. Nuclear Medicine, Fla. Med. Assn. (chmn. com. blood 1969-73, alt. del. to AMA 1967-85, del. 1986-87, chmn. council on legislation 1979-80, vice chmn. council 1980-83, chmn. com. on nat. legislation 1980-83, 86-87, pres. Fla. med. polit. action com. 1980-83, exec. com. of bd. govs. 1981-82, 83-86, pres.-elect 1983-84, pres. 1984-85), Hillsborough County Med. Assn. (life, ex-council 1967-70, pres. 1979-80), Fla. Assn. of Blood Banks (pres. 1970-71), Fla. Soc. Pathologists (pres. 1987-88), Fla. Soc. Pathologists (pres.-elect 1986-87), Greater Tampa C. of C. (Pres. award 1974, chmn. health care council 1969-74, gov. 1974-77), Tampa World Trade

Council (exec. com. 1978-79). Club: Rotarian. Died June 5, 1988; buried Tampa, Fla.

COLEMAN, GEORGE ANTHONY, dentist; b. Hoytville, Pa., Aug. 31, 1891; s. Patrick and Mary (O'Donnell) C.; m. Mary L. Noble, June 17, 1920; children: Martha Coleman McCall, Jeanne Coleman DeVries, Margaret Coleman Casey. Student, Lock Haven Tchrs. Coll., 1909-10, U. Pa. Sch. Dentistry, 1913; DDS, Phila. Postgrad. Sch., 1915. Pvt. practice Phila., from 1915; mem. faculty U. Pa. Postgrad. Sch., 1940-55; trustee U. Pa. Capt., Dental Corps., U.S. Army, World War I. Recipient award of merit Gen. Alumni, Dental Alumni socs., U. Pa.; named Friar of the Yr., 1958. Mem. Am., Pa. (pres. 1932, 33) dental socs., Pa. Assn. Dental Surgeons (pres. 1926), Am. Acad. Restorative Dentistry (pres.), Alumni Friars Soc. (pres.), Internat. Coll. Dentists (master), N.Y. Acad. Prosthodontics, Xi Psi Phi (nat. pres. 1936, 39), Omicron Kappa Upsilon. Home: Wynnewood Pa. †

COLEMAN, GEORGE HOPKINS, chemistry educator; b. Evansville, Wis., Oct. 5, 1891; s. John Emory and Mary Louise (Hopkins) C.; m. Leah Estelle Rose, Aug. 26, 1927; children: Robert Vincent, Joseph Emory, George Lawrence. AB, Greenville (Ill.) Coll., 1915; MS, U. Ill., 1919, PhD, 1921. Instr. in sci. A.M. Chesbrough Sem., N.Y.C., 1915-17; asst. in chemistry U. Ill., 1917-21; instr. organic chemistry U. Iowa, 1921-22, assoc., 1922-24, asst. prof., 1924-28, assoc. prof., 1929-30, prof. organic chemistry, 1930-46; dean grad. work Inst. Textile Tech., Charlottesville, Va., 1946-50; prof. chemistry Wayne State U., Detroit, 1950-61, prof. emeritus, from 1962, chmn. dept., 1952-62; dir. Friends of the Kresge-Hooker Sci. Library, Wayne State U., 1950-53. Author lab. manual in organic chemistry; editor Jour. Organic Chemistry, 1952-61, cons. editor, 1961-63, mem. bd. editors, from 1964; contbr. articles to profl. jours. Recipient cert. appreciation for work during Wrold War II, U.S. Army and USN; Giggenheim fellow study in France and Germany, 1928-29. Mem. Am. Chem. Soc., AAAS, Phi Beta Kappa, Sigma Xi, Phi Lambda Upsilon, Gamma Alpha. Home: Sarasota Fla. †

COLEMAN, SHELDON, business executive; b. Ft. Worth, Nov. 15, 1901; s. William Coffin and Fanny (Sheldon) C.; m. Georgia Cleveland, Dec. 20, 1923 (div. 1949); children: Virginia Lee, Carolyn; m. Galey Dater, May 22, 1951; 1 child, Sheldon. ME, Cornell U., 1925; hon. degree, Ottawa U. Engr. Coleman Co., Inc., Wichita, Kans., 1925-32, mgr. gen. works, 1932-40, became exec. v.p. and gen. mgr., 1940, later pres., chmn. bd.; bd. dirs. Bank IV, Wichita. Past vice chmn. bd. govs. ARC.; mem. Outdoor Recreation Policy Rev. Group; mem. President's Commn. on Outdoor Ams. Outdoors, 1985. Inducted into Sporting Goods Hall of Fame, 1981; recipient Chief Exec. Officer of Yr. bronze award Fin. World, 1985; Mountain of Jade award Outdoor Writers' Assn., 1986. Mem. Gas Appliance Mfrs. Assn. (past pres.), Inst. Appliance Mfrs. (past pres.), N.A.M. Republican. Baptist. Home: Wichita Kans. Died Sept. 21, 1988.

COLES, JOHN WILLIAM, banker; b. Olmstead, Ky., Sept. 17, 1905; s. John T. and Nell Elizabeth (Adams) C.; m. Margaret Swaney, Oct. 11, 1934; children: William S., John Read. Grad., Bowling Green Coll. Commerce, 1925, Am. Inst. Banking, 1933, Rutgers U. Grad. Sch. Banking, 1947; LLB, YMCA Law Sch., 1934. Bar: Tenn. 1934. With 1st Am. Nat. Bank, Nashville, 1926-86, v.p., trust officer, head trust dept., 1966-86. Past pres. Nashville Estate Planning Coun. Mem. Davidson County Bar Assn., Tenn. Bankers Assn. (past pres. fiduciary sect.), Masons (33 degree), Shriners, Richland Country Club. Baptist. Home: Nashville Tenn. Died Oct. 26, 1986; buried Gallatin, Tenn.

COLKET, MEREDITH BRIGHT, JR., genealogist, local historian; b. Strafford, Pa., Aug. 18, 1912; s. Meredith Bright and Alberta (Kelsy) C.; m. Julia Beatrice Pelot, June 29, 1945; children: William Currie, Meredith Bright III, John Pelot. BA cum laude, Haverford (Pa.) Coll., 1935, MA, 1940; LittD (hon.), Baldwin-Wallace Coll., 1974. Asst. in govt. Haverford (Pa.) Coll., 1936; archivist Nat. Archives, Washington, 1937-57; lectr. Am. U., Washington, 1950-59; dir., then exec. dir. Western Res. Hist. Soc., Cleve., 1957-80, emeritus, 1980-85; founder, dir. Am. Inst. Geneal. Research, 1950-59; mem. Cleveland Heights, (Ohio) Landmarks Commn., 1974-85, chmn. 1978-82; v.p. Nationalities Service Ctr., Cleve., 1974-78; lectr. in field, 1944-85. Compiler: The Marbury Ancestry, 1936, The Jenks Family of England, 1956; co-compiler: Guide to Genealogical Records in the National Archives, 1964, Founders of Early American Families, 1975; assoc. editor Am. Genealogist, 1937-50; contbr. articles to profl. jours. Fellow Soc. Am. Archivists, Soc. Genealogists (London), Am. Soc. Genealogists (hon. pres. 1969); mem. Internat. Soc. Brit. Genealogy and Family History (a founder, dir.), Columbia Hist. Soc. (hon. mem., past curator, v.p.), New Eng. Historic Geneal. Soc., Nat. Trust Historic Preservation, Nat. Geneal. Soc., Ohio Geneal. Soc., Geneal. Soc. Pa., Hist. Soc. Pa. (life), Acad. Costarricense de Ciencias Genealogicas, Costa Rica (hon.), Rowfant Club, Philosophical Club. Home: Cleveland Heights Ohio. Died May 19, 1985; buried Laurel Hill Cemetery, Phila.

COLLIER, ROBERT ARTHUR, lawyer; b. Wichita Falls, Tex., Apr. 3, 1917; s. Robert H. and Lulu (Cross) C.; m. Jeanne Claybrook, Sept. 19, 1942; children: Claybrook, Deborah Leigh. LLB, U. Tex., 1940. Bar: D.C. 1954. Practice Wichita Falls; mem. firm McDaniel & Luecke, Wichita Falls, 1940-41; ptnr. Collier, Shannon, Rill & Scott (and predecessors), Washington, 1956-84; chmn. bd. dirs. MacMillan Ring-Free Oil Co., N.Y.C., 1963-84; mem. Pres.'s Com. on Mental Retardation, 1972-75, Pres.'s Com. on Employment of Handicapped, 1975-79; mem. nat. adv. com. Jobs for Vets., 1970-84. Mem. Masons, Shriners, Burning Tree Club, Metropolitan Club. Home: Alexandria Va. Died Aug. 16, 1984.

COLLINGWOOD, CHARLES (CUMMINGS), radio, TV commentator; b. Three Rivers, Mich., June 4, 1917; s. George Harris and Jean Grinnell (Cummings) C.; A.B., Cornell U., 1939; postgrad. New Coll., Oxford, Eng., 1939-40; m. Louise Allbritton, May 13, 1946 (dec. 1979); m. Tatiana Angelini Jolin. War corr. United Press, London, 1939-41; commentator CBS, 1941-46, UN corr., 1946-48, White House corr., 1948-52, radio, TV commentator, 1952-82, chief CBS news bur., London, 1957-60, chief fgn. corr., London, 1966-75; spl. asst. to dir. Mut. Security Agy., 1951. Author: The Defector, 1970. Recipient Headliners award, 1942, 48; Peabody award for best fgn. reporting, 1943, for tour White House with Mrs. John Kennedy, 1963; Alexander Hadden medal for promoting world understanding, 1954; Better Understanding award English Speaking Union, 1957; decorated chevalier Legion of Honor (France); comdr. Order of Brit. Empire; Rhodes Scholar, 1939-40. Mem. Assn. Radio News Analysts, English Speaking Union (nat. bd. dirs., exec. com. 1976-85). Clubs: Century Assn., Nat. Press; Beefsteak, Garrick (London). Home: New York, NY. Died Oct. 3, 1985.

COLLINS, CARR P., JR., corporate executive; b. Dallas, Feb. 9, 1918; s. Carr P. and Ruth (Woodall) C.; m. Calvert Keoun, Dec. 24, 1941; children: Carr P. III, Richard Howell, Christy Calvert; m. 2d Yyronne Deakins, Jan. 1 ,1968; children: Mark Bond, Brad Bond. BS in Commerce, So. Meth. U., 1939; grad. bus. study, Harvard U., 1939-40; LLD, Howard Payne Coll., 1965. C.L.U. Pres. Investment Trust Co., 1949-85, S.W. Bank & Trust Co., 1955-56, Nat. Petro-Sonics Inc., 1968; v.p., dir. Fidelity Union Life Ins. Co., Dallas, 1949-85; v.p. Elaboradora Farmaceutica S.A., Nicaragua, 1965-70; vice consul Italy, 1962-72; mem. panel arbitrators N.Y. Stock Exchange, 1957-85; mem. U.S. Trade Mission to Pakistan, 1960. Mem. adv. bd. Italian-U.S. Ctr. Jud. Studies, 1965-85. Maj. USAAF, 1940-45, PTO. Decorated Purple Heart, Air medal; knight officer Order of Merit (Italy); recipient Freedom medal Douglas MacArthur Acad. Freedom, 1965. Fellow Am. Soc. Psychial Research; mem. Masons (32 deg.), Shriner, Idlewild Club, Petroleum Club, Brook Hollow Golf Club, Phi Delta Theta, Alpha Kappa Psi. Home: Dallas Tex. Died Aug. 13, 1985.

COLLINS, CARR PRITCHETT, insurance executive; b. Chester, Tex., May 12, 1892; s. Vincent Allen and Elizabeth (Hopkins) C.; m. Ruth Woodall, Nov. 21, 1914; children: James Mitchell, Carr Pritchett, Ruth (Mrs. Charles S. Sharp). Student, S.W. State Tchrs. Coll., 1909; LLD, Baylor U., 1952. Chmn. bd., pres. Fidelity Union Life Ins. Co., Dallas, from 1927; founder, pres. Bapt. Found. Tex., from 1931; bd. dirs. 1st Nat. Bank Dallas. Donator Carr P. Collins award Tex. Inst. Letter, 1946, Ruth Collins Hall, Baylor U., 1957, Carr P. Collins Convalescent Care Hosp., Dallas, 1967, Carr P. Collins Chapel, Bishop Coll., 1967, Carr P. Collins Chair of Fgn. Affiars, Howard Payne Coll., 1966; past trustee Baylor U., Bishop Coll., Wadley Blood Rsch. Ctr., Dallas; bd. dirs. So. Bapt. Conv.; deacon Bapt. Ch. Recipient Horatio Alger award, 1964, Douglas MacArthur Freedom medal, 1966, Disting. Alumnus award S.W. State Tchrs. Coll., 1966, Univ. medal Hardin-Simmons U., 1967, Holden Plate award Am. Acad. Achievement, 1968, Disting. Am. Citizen award Harding Coll., 1968, Am. Citizen award Harding Coll., 1968. Home: Dallas Tex. †

COLLINS, CHARLES JOSEPH, investment consultant; b. Lake City, Fla., Dec. 7, 1894; s. Thomas Currie and Sarah Frink (Spencer) C.; m. Hazel Beatrice Wharton, Dec. 25, 1919; children: Anne W. Collins Husted, Josephine S. Collins Penberthy. BA, Va. Mil. Inst., 1916. Investment analyst E.E. MacCrone & Co., Detroit, 1919-23, ptnr., 1923-63; chmn., dir. Investment Counsel, Inc., 1930-59, mem. adv. bd., from 1962; trustee Investment Co. Am., 1927-32; former bd. dirs. Am. Midland Co., Investment Rsch. Corp., Am. Industries Corp., Am. Industries Securities Co.; mem. N.Y. Stock Exchange, 1929-30. Author: Fortune's Before You, 1937, The Coming Battle for World Sovereignty, 1971; editor, pub. Investment Letters, Inc., 1934-63; contbr. articles to profl. jours. Trustee Va. Mil. Inst. Maj. U.S. Army, 1917-19. Mem. Fin. Analysts Soc. Detroit (pres. 1952, bd. dirs. 1951-53), Nat. Fedn. Fin. Analysts Socs. (bd. dirs. 1950-52), Va. Mil. Inst. Alumni Assn. (bd. dirs. 1938-64), Detroit Club, Country Club Grosse Point (Mich.), Kappa Alpha (So.). Home: Grosse Point Mich. Died Dec. 24, 1982.

COLLINS, JAMES A., JR., physician, educator; b. Hazleton, Pa., Sept. 5, 1916; s. James A. and Mary E.
(Herron) C.; B.S., Pa. State U., 1937; M.D., Thor
Jefferson U., 1941; diplomate Am. Bd. Inter
Medicine; m. Virginia Troxell, Jan. 24, 1953; 1 s
George. Rotating intern Geisinger Meml. Ho
Danville, Pa., 1941-42, resident in internal medici
1942-43, asst. to staff, 1943, asso. staff dept. inter
medicine, 1944-53, head sect. gastroenterology, 1953-
dir. dept. internal medicine, 1954-74, chmn. div. m
depts., 1974-78, dir. internal medicine reside
program, 1958-78, sr. cons. internal medicine and g
troenterology, from 1978; sr. cons. internal medicine,
v.p. research Giesinger Clinic, Geisinger Med. Cen
Danville, pres. Inst. for Med. Edn. and Research, 19
82; clin. prof. medicine Pa. State U. Coll. Medici
Hershey, from 1975; vis. fellow Mayo Clinic, 1947; m
dir. Maria Joseph Home for Aged, Danville, from 19
Vice chmn. bd. Pa. Blue Shield, from 1979, mem. co
from 1974; pres. Danville Bd. Health, 1945-
councilman Riverside Borough, from 1981. Fellow A
Phila. Coll. Physicians; mem. Pa. Med. Soc. (pres. C
tinuing Edn. Inst. 1972-75), Montour County M
Soc., AMA (intersplty. adv. bd. 1976-78), Am. S
Clin. Pharmacology and Therapeutics, Pa. Soc. Inte
Medicine (pres. 1969-70), Am. Soc. Internal Medic
(pres. 1979-80). Contbr. articles to publs.; mem. AM
Joint Rev. Com. on Ednl. Programs for Physici
Assts., 1972-78, chmn., 1975-78, mem. federated cou
internal medicine, 1978-79, 81-82, AMA reside
review com. for internal medicine, from 1983. Repu
can. Roman Catholic. Home: Riverside, Pa. Deceas

COLLINS, JAMES DANIEL, educator, philospher;
Holyoke, Mass., July 12, 1917; s. Michael Joseph a
Mary Magdalen (Rooney) C.; m. Yvonne Marie S
ford, June 6, 1945; 1 son, Michael. AB, Cath. U. A
1941, AM, 1942, PhD, 1944. Leo research fell
Harvard U., Cambridge, Mass., 1944-45; mem. facu
St. Louis U., 1945-85, prof. philosophy, 1956-85; Sua
lectr. Fordham U., 1953; Aquinas lectr. Marquette
1962; Thomas More lectr. Yale U., 1963. Author: T
Existentialists, 1952, The Mind of Kierkegaard, 1953
History of Modern European Philosophy, 1954, God
Modern Philosophy, 1959, The Lure of Wisdom, 19
Three Paths in Philosophy, 1962, The Emergence
Philosophy of Religion, 1967, Descartes' Philosophy
Nature, 1971, Interpreting Modern Philosophy, 19
Spinoza on Nature, 1984; mem. editorial bd. So. Jo
Philosophy, Am. Philos. Quar., Cross Currents,
ternat. Archives for History of Ideas, Internat. Stuc
in Philosophy, History of Philosophy Quarterly, Mod
Schoolman. Penfield fellow Cath. U. Am., 1944-
Guggenheim fellow, 1963-64; recipient Cardi
Newman medal Newman Found., 1962, Cath.
Alumni award, 1962, award for scholarship N
Council Cath. Men, 1961, 29th Ann. Christian Cult
medal U. Windsor. Mem. Am. Philos. Assn., A
Cath. Philos. Assn. (pres. 1954, Aquinas medal 196
Metaphys. Soc. Am. (pres. 1962). Home: Saint Lo
Mo. Died Feb. 19, 1985; buried St. Louis.

COLLINS, JAMES FRANCIS, military officer;
N.Y.C., Sept. 2, 1905; s. Thomas William and Ar
Cecilia (Flanagan) C.; m. Marian McLaughlin, June
1932; 1 child, Patricia M. Collins Bowman. BS, U
Mil. Acad., 1927; grad., Nat. War Coll., 1947. Comr
2d lt. U.S. Army, 1927, advanced through grades
gen., 1961, commdg. gen. I Corps Arty., 1945-
faculty mem., dir. dept. personnel Command and G
Staff Sch., 1947-50, faculty Army War Coll., 1950, ex
to asst. sec. def. for manpower and personnel, 1950-
comdg. gen. U.S. Army, Alaska, 1954, comdg. gen. 7
Div., 1954-55, 2d Inf. Div., 1956, dep. chief staff p
sonnel, 1958-60, comdr. in chief U.S. Army, Paci
1961-64, ret.; pres. ARC, Washington, 1964-70; bd. di
Am. Security & Trust Co. Decorated D.S.M. with c
leaf cluster, Legion of Merit, Bronze Star, Air meda
Mem. Army-Navy Town Club, Army-Navy Coun
Club, Chevy Chase Country Club, Metropolitan Cl
(Washington). Home: Arlington Va. Died Jan.
1989.

COLLINS, WILLIAM HOWES, marketing a
communications company executive; b. East Oran
N.J., Apr. 27, 1908; s. William French and Alice De
(Howes) C.; m. Dorothy Jane Walker, Oct. 18, 19
children: William Walker, Kent Howes, Derfla Je
Collins Patterson. BA cum laude, Williams Coll., 19
Mng. editor, asst. treas. Howed Publ. Co., N.Y.
1929-31; dir. univ. service Hapag-Lloyd (Steamsh
N.Y.C., 1932-37; asst. advt. mgr. Scott Paper C
Chester, Pa., 1927-47; dir. advt. Dravo Corp., Pit
1947-55; world-wide mktg. exec. Standard-Vacuum
Co., White Plains, N.Y., 1955-62; dir. advt. and mar
research Mobil Petroleum Co., N.Y.C., 1962-64; chn
bd., pres. Intercontinental Assocs. Inc., Essex, Con
1964-85; advisor U.S. del. 5th Internat. Conf. Pub.
fairs, Geneva, 1936; mem. U.S. Trade Devel. Mission
Brazil, 1967, Dept. Commerce Regional Export Expa
sion Council, 1966-85, U.S. Nat. Def. Exec. Res., 19
85. Contbr. articles to profl. jours. Mem. Bd. Ed
Essex, 1967-72; mem. U.S.S. Nathan Hale Com., Con
1970-85; bd. dirs. Pitts. YMCA, 1947. Served to ca
USNR, 1937-68. Mem. Pub. Relations Soc. Am. (pr
Pitts. chpt. 1953-55), Assn. Nat. Advertisers (dir. 19
58), Soc. Mayflower Descendants Pa. (dep. gov. 19
55), Eastern Indsl. Advertisers Phila. (pres. 1945-4
SAR (auditor Conn., v.p. Nathan Hale br., 1983-8
English Speaking Union, Essex Art Assn., Newcom

., Naval Res. Assn., Pa. Soc., Ret. Officers Assn., ssasoit and Essex Hist. Soc., U.S. Naval Inst., Order inders and Patriots of Am., Mason, Circumnavi- rs Club, Williams Club (N.Y.C.), Mile Creek Club, al Club (London), Phi Beta Kappa, Beta Theta Pi, ta Phi Epsilon. Home: Essex Conn. Died June 6, 5; buried Arlington Nat. Cemetery.

LNON, STUART JAMES, coal company executive; Chgo., June 20, 1903; s. John Edward and Helen emes) C.; m. Rosalie Frances McMahon, June 22, 0; 1 child, Joan Colnon Dolan. With John E. non & Co., realtors, Chgo., 1921-86, also chmn., pres. Freeman Coal Mining Corp., 1946-57; past ., dir. Bell & Zoller Coal Co.; chmn., chief exec. er Zeigler Coal & Coke Co., Des Plaines, Ill., 1958- Mem. Nat. Coal Assn. (chmn. 1966-67). Home: ay Beach Fla. Died Mar. 8, 1986.

LSKY, JACOB, physician; b. Memphis, Dec. 5, 1; s. Abraham Samuel and Jennie (Shefsky) C.; m. e Vivian Belen, July 26, 1953; children: Liane Caryl, hur Spencer, Andrew Evan. Student, Memphis e Coll., 1938-40; MD, U. Tenn., 1944. Diplomate . Bd. Internal Medicine, Am. Bd. Med. Oncology. rn Jackson Meml. Hosp., Miami, Fla., 1944-45; w, then instr. preventative medicine Johns Hopkins Med. Sch., 1947-51; acting asst. chief clin. research Nat. Cancer Inst., Balt., 1950-51, asst. chief, 1951- asst. physician outpatients Johns Hopkins Hosp., 7-52; assoc. dir. medicine Maimonides Hosp., Bklyn., 2-57; assoc. attending physician Kings County Hosp. l. Ctr., 1955-57; from instr. to assoc. prof. medicine NY Med. Sch., N.Y.C., 1952-57; pvt. practice Miami, 7-82; mem. faculty U. Miami Med. Sch., 1957-82, prof. medicine, 1973-82, prof. oncology, 1975-82; n. staff Cedars of Lebanon Hosp., Jackson Meml. p.; cons. Baptist Hosp., Mt. Sinai Hosp., VA Hosp.; med. oncology sect., dept. medicine U. Miami and kson Meml. Hosp., 1960-70; chief med. oncology . Cedars of Lebanon Hosp., 1972-82, chief medicine, 7-78; sr. investigator Eastern Coop. Oncology up, 1960-82, exec. com., 1971-73; pres. Med. ology and Chemotherapy Found., Miami, 1970-73; dirs. Papanicolaou Cancer Research Inst., 1969-82. tbr. numerous articles to profl. jours. Capt. AUS, 5-47. Fellow N.Y. Acad. Medicine, ACP; mem. . Acad. Scis., AAAS, Am. Fedn. Clin. Research, . Assn. Cancer Research, Am. Geriatrics Soc., kemia Soc. (state bd. dirs. 1970-82), Am. Cancer (county bd. dirs. 1968-71), Fla. Med. Soc., Internat. Lung Cancer (a founder), Am. Soc. Clinical ology (a founder); affiliate Royal Soc. Medicine. ne: Miami Fla. Died May 18, 1982; buried Miami,

LSTON, J. A. CAMPBELL, surgeon; b. Balt., Oct. 1886; s. Frederick Morgan and Clara (Campbell) C.; Harriet Lippincott Zell, Nov. 9, 1922; children: derick Campbell, J.A. Campbell, Anne. PhB, Yale 1907; MD, Johns Hopkins U., 1911. Pvt. practice n 1916, pvt. practice specializing in urology, from 9; asst. in urology Johns Hopkins Hosp., Balt., 1919- instr., 1923-28, assoc., 1928-34, assoc. prof., from 4. Assoc. editor Jour. of Urology, 1934-35, editor in f from 1945; contbr. articles to med. jours. Mem. dirs. Lyric Theater, Balt. Med. officer, ARC, nce, 1914-15; capt. bn. med. officer 46th field ambu- e, 7/8th bn. King's Own Scottish Borderers; 13th Royal Scots, 6th bn. Queen's Own Cameron High- ders, B.E.F., 1915-17; maj. M.C., A.E.F., 1918-19. ow AMA; mem. Clin. Soc. Genito-urinary Surgeons st pres.), Am. Urol. Assn. (pres. 1953). So. Med. n., Société Internationale d'Urologie, Balt. City Med. , Gibson Island Club, Maryland Club, Hamilton St. b, Elkridge Club, Phi Beta Kappa, Delta Psi, Alpha ega Alpha. Home: Gibson Island Md. †

LVER, ALICE ROSS (MRS. FREDERIC B. LVER), writer; b. Plainfield, N.J., Aug. 28, 1892; d. is Runyon and Sarah Greenleaf (Wyckoff) Ross; m. deric Beecher Colver, Sept. 8, 1915; children: deric Ross, Jean, John Richard. AB, Wellesley ., 1913; student, Dr. Savage's Normal Sch. Phys. . Author: Babs Series for Girls, 4 vols., 1917-20, ne Series for Girls, 4 vols., 1920-24, numerous other ks including Kingsridge, 1949, Joan Foster, Junior, 9, Joan Foster, Senior, 1950, The Parson, 1951, Joan ter in Europe, 1951, Joan Foster, Bride, 1952, The asure of the Years, 1954, There is a Season, 1957, ere Goes the Heart, 1958, Susan, Nurse's Aide, 1964, Moore, Physical Therapist, 1965, Vicky Barnes, or Hospital Volunteer, 1966, also short stories and cles. Mem. Authors' League Am., AAUW, Assn. nen for World Peace, Dramatists Guild, Pen and sh Club, Zeta Alpha. Presbyterian. Home: Tenafly †

MAY, AMOS, corporate executive; b. N.Y.C., Mar. 1915; s. Joseph and Nellie (Schorr) C.; m. Ethel nay, Dec. 31, 1935; children: Sholom David, orah Esther. Ptnr. F.&B. Woodenware Co., Pitts., 7-46; v.p. Action Industries, Pitts., 1946-50, pres., 0-68, chmn., 1968-87, chief exec. officer, 1968-82. . Nat. Found. for Jewish Culture, 1978-82; v.p. ted Jewish Fedn. Pitts., 1977-79; bd. dirs., exec. com. Jewish Joint Distbn. Com., 1977-87; bd. dirs. ncil Jewish Fedns., 1974-78; nat. exec. com. United Jewish Appeal, 1970-77. With USNR, 1945-46. Democrat. Died Nov. 12, 1987.

COMBES, W. ELMER, finance company executive, consultant; b. N.Y.C., Dec. 28, 1891; s. Clarence E. and Caroline (Walker) C.; m. Ethel R. Saill, Nov. 4, 1914; 1 dau., Ethel Ruth. Student pub. schs. Successively asst. sec., comptroller, v.p., 1st v.p., vice chmn. bd. dirs., then cons. Am. Bank Note Co. Home: Great Neck N.Y. †

COMER, DONALD, JR., textile company executive; b. Birmingham, Ala., May 18, 1913; s. Donald and Gertrude (Miller) C.; m. Isabel Anderson, Oct. 29, 1936; children: Donald III, Isabel Anderson. With Avondale Mills, Sylacauga, Ala., from 1932; exec. v.p. Avondale Mills, 1954-70, pres., chief exec. officer, treas., 1970-75, chmn. bd., 1979-84, chmn. exec. com., 1984-85, chmn. emeritus, from 1986, also dir.; with Cowikee Mills, Eufaula, Ala., from 1943, treas., pres., 1956-67, chmn. bd., 1967-75; chmn. 1st Fed. Savs. & Loan Assn., Sylacauga, Ala. Fed. Savs. & Loan Assn., Birmingham, Am. Mut. Liability Ins. Co., Wakefield, Mass., Associated Industries Ala.; dir. Am. South Bancorp.; adv. bd. Chem. Bank, N.Y.C. Past bd. dirs. Birmingham YMCA; bd. govs. Ala. Assn. Ind. Colls.; past pres. Chocolocco council Boy Scouts Am.; bd. dirs. Ala. Inst. mem. exec. com. Southeastern Region; trustee So. Research Soc., Am. Bible Soc.; dir. Ala. div. Laymen's Nat. Bible Com.; mem. adminstrv. bd. First United Meth. Ch., Sylacauga; chmn., bd. dirs. Sylacauga Recreation Dept.; bd. visitors U. Ala., mem. pres.'s council, Birmingham. Recipient Silver Beaver award, Silver Antelope award Boy Scouts Am.; Textile award N.Y. Bd. of Trade, 1974; Ala. Acad. of Honor award; Textileer award Ala. Textile Mfrs. Assn. Mem. Am. Textile Mfrs. Inst. (pres. 1973-74, 83-84), Internat. Textile Mfrs. Inst. (1st v.p.), Birmingham C. of C. (past dir.), Ala. C. of C. (pres. 1980, 81). Home: Sylacauga Ala. Deceased.

COMO, WILLIAM MICHAEL, magazine editor; b. Williamstown, Mass., Nov. 10, 1925; s. Michael and Janet (Caporale) C. Merit certificate, Am. Acad. Dramatic Arts, 1947. Sales mgr. Dance Mag., N.Y.C., 1954-60; advt. mgr. and asst. to pub. Dance Mag., 1961-69, editor in chief, 1970-89; editor in chief After Dark, the Nat. Mag. of Entertainment, N.Y.C., 1968-79; lectr. on dance. Dancer, actor, N.Y., Calif., 1948-53; editor: Raoul Gelabert's Anatomy for the Dancer, 1964. Served with AUS, 1944-46. Recipient award Dance Tchrs. Club of Boston, 1974; named Hon. Lt. Col. Aide-de-Camp Gov. of Ala., 1981; Dancing Ambassadors of Friendship, 1977; honoree Dance Masters of Am., Inc., 1979; A Celebration of Men in Dance, 1981; Dance Masters of Am. ann. award, 1986; Charlie award Nat. Assn. of Dance and Affiliated Artists, 1987. Home: New York N.Y. Office: Danad Pub Co Dance Mag 33 W 60th St New York NY 10023 Died Jan. 1, 1989; buried Williamstown, Mass.

COMPTON, FRED A(RTHUR), business executive; b. Ft. Wayne, Ind., Aug. 22, 1891; s. Andrew Jasper and Ellen (Deibel) C.; m. Virginia Lothrop Smith, June 17, 1919; children: William A., Mary Ellen Compton McLaughlin, Robert A. BS, U. Mich., 1914. Engr. Detroit Edison Co., 1914-17, 19-23, asst. purchasing agt., 1923-40, purchasing agt., 1940-46, sales mgr., 1946, v.p., 1949-56; v.p. Harlan Electric Co., 1956-59; cons. Office War Utilities, War Prodn. Bd., 1942-45; bd. dirs. Hinehman Corp., Mich. Fire & Marine Ins. Co., Essex County Light & Power Co., Ltd., Can. Bd. dirs. Detroit Bd. Commerce. Mem. ASME, Engring. Soc. Detroit, Masons, Detroit Athletic Club, Detroit Yacht Club, Detroit Club. Home: Detroit Mich. †

COMPTON, RANDOLPH PARKER, investment banker; b. Macon, Mo., Mar. 18, 1892; s. William R. and Caroline (Parker) C.; m. Dorothy Danforth, Oct. 11, 1917 (dec.); children: W. Danforth (dec.), James Randolph, Ann Randolph (Mrs. Ellis M. Stephens), John Parker (dec.). Grad., Smith Acad., St. Louis, 1911; LL.B., Princeton, 1915; postgrad., Harvard Bus. Sch., 1943. Vice pres. charge N.Y. office William R. Compton Co., 1919-29; propr. mcpl. bond firm N.Y.C., 1929-34; v.p. charge mcpl. bond dept. Lazard Freres & Co., N.Y.C., 1934-41, Union Securities Corp., N.Y.C., 1941-42; corp. relations mgr. Republic Aviation Co., Ltd., Farmingdale, L.I., N.Y., 1943-44; v.p. Kidder, Peabody & Co., Inc. (Investment bankers), N.Y.C., 1945-87. Past treas., trustee Scarsdale (N.Y.) Found.; hon. trustee, mem. bd. Meharry Medical Coll.; chmn. emeritus, trustee Fund for Peace, N.Y.C. Served as ensign USN, World War I. Republican. Congregationalist (trustee). Club: Meadow Tennis (Scarsdale, N.Y.). Home: Scarsdale N.Y. Died Sept. 15, 1987; buried Mount Auburn Cemetery, Cambridge, Mass.

COMROE, JEROME HIRAM, JR., medical educator, medical historian; b. York, Pa., Mar. 13, 1911; s. Julius Hiram and Mollie (Levy) C.; m. Jeanette Wolfson, June 30, 1936; 1 dau., Joan Von Gehr. AB, U. Pa., 1931, MD, 1934, DSc (hon.), 1978; MD (hon.), Karolinska Inst., Stockholm, 1968; DSc (hon.), U. Chgo., 1968. Intern Hosp. of U. Pa., 1934-36; instr. in pharmacology U. Pa. Med. Sch., 1936-40, assoc., 1940-42; asst. prof. 1942-46; prof. physiology and pharmacology U. Pa. Grad. Sch. Medicine, 1946-57; prof. physiology, dir. Cardiovascular Research Inst. U. Calif. Med. Ctr., San Francisco, 1957-73, Herzstein prof. biology, 1973-78; chmn. teaching inst. Assn. Am. Med. Colls., 1953, 61; chmn. Physiology Study sect., 1955-58; mem. bd. sci. counselors Nat. Heart Inst., 1957-61; mem. Nat. Adv. Mental Health Council, 1958-62, Nat. Adv. Heart Council, 1963-67, Nat. Adv. Heart & Lung Council, 1970-74, Pres.'s Panel Heart Disease, 1972; mem. adv. com. to dir. NIH, 1976-78; cons. med. research div. CWS, 1944-46. Author: Physiological Basis for O2 Therapy, 1950, Methods in Medical Research, vol. 2, 1950, The Lung: Clinical Physiology and Pulmonary Function Tests, 1955, 62, Physiology of Respiration, 1964, 74, Pulmonary and Respiratory Physiology (Dowden), 1976, Retrospectroscope—Insights to Medical Discovery, 1977, Exploring the Heart, 1983; editor: Physiology for Physicians, 1963-66, Circulation Research, 1966-70, Ann. Rev. Physiology, 1971-75; assoc. editor Am. Rev. Respiratiry Disease, 1973-79; mem. editorial bd. Proc. Nat. Acad. Scis., 1977-84. Recipient travel award Am. Physiol. Soc., 1938, Research Achievement award Am. Heart Assn., 1968, Coll. medal Am. Coll. Chest Physicians, 1970, Trudeau award, 1974, Wiggers award, 1974, Gold Heart award Am. Heart Assn., 1975, Kovalenko medal Nat. Acad. Scis., 1976, Sci. Contbns. award ACP, 1977, Daggs award Am. Physiol. Soc., 1977, medal U. Calif., San Francisco, 1978, Eugene Morelli award Accademia dei Lincei, Rome, 1979, Abraham Flexner award in med. edn. Am. Assn. Med. Colls., 1979; Commonwealth Fund fellow Nat. Inst. Med. Research, London, 1939. Fellow Am. Coll. Cardiology (hon.), Royal Coll. Physicians (London), Royal Soc. Medicine (London); mem. Assn. Am. Physicians, Am. Physiol. Soc. (pres. 1960-61), Am. Soc. for Pharmacology and Exptl. Therapeutics (Councilor 1953-56), Nat. Acad. Scis. (mem. bd. medicine 1967-70), Inst. Medicine (exec. com. 1970), Am. acad. Arts and Scis., Harvey Soc. (hon.), Am. Soc. for Clin. Investigation, Phi Beta Kappa, Sigma Xi, Alpha Omega Alpha. Died Dec. 7, 1984.

CONFER, OGDEN PALMER, feed and flour mill executive; b. Mpls., Nov. 14, 1921; s. Ogden Armour and Ruth (Palmer) C.; m. Elizabeth McElhenny, Dec. 20, 1941; children: Ogden William, Kay Confer Lamb, Richard Palmer, Carol Confer Greenwald. Student, Westminster Coll., Mo., 1939-40; B.B.A., U. Minn., 1943. Mgr. feed div., v.p. Hubbard Milling Co., Mankato, Minn., 1946-58, pres., 1958-70, chmn. bd., chief exec. officer, 1970-88. Trustee Gustavus Adolphus Coll. Mem. N.W. Feed Mfrs. Assn. (past pres.), Am. Feed Industry Assn. (dir., chmn. bd. 1970), Millers Nat. Fedn. (past dir.), Mankato C. of C. (past dir.). Presbyterian (trustee, elder). Club: Mankato Golf (past dir.). Lodges: Kiwanis; Elks. Home: Mankato Minn. Died Sept. 23, 1988; buried Glenwood Cemetery.

CONGDON, SIDNEY BISHOP, banker; b. Beaver Dam, Wis., Oct. 3, 1891; s. George Conant and Carrie (Pyle) C.; m. Marie Bunn; children: Robert Sherman, Sidney Bishop, Helen Congdon VanEpps. Sec. to compt. currency, Washington, 1914-18; nat. bank examiner, 1918-23; v.p. Bank Pitts. N.Am., 1923-31; chief examining div. Reconstrn. Fin. Corp., 1932; pres. Nat. City Bank Cleve., 1933-57, chmn., 1957-59, hon. chmn., 1959-61, hon. dir., from 1962; bd. dirs. Tremco Mfg. Co. Chmn. bd. trustees U. Circle Devel. Found., St. Lukes's Hosp. Assn.; trustee Case Inst. Tech. Mem. Res. City Bankers, Union Club, Tavern Club, Country Club, Pepper Pike Club. Republican. Episcopalian. Home: Cleveland Ohio. †

CONGDON, WRAY HOLLOWELL, language and education educator; b. Bradford, Pa., July 29, 1892; s. Lafayette and Anna (Kingsley) C.; m. Anna May Stuart, July 29, 1918 (dec. Aug. 1964); children: June Congdon Wily, Ednagene W. Congdon Herbert. AB, Syracuse U., 1914, MA, 1915; PhD, U. Mich., 1929. Instr. English Peking U., China, 1915-18; head English dept. Hui Wen Boys' Acad., Tientsin, China, 1919-21, prin., 1926-28; prin. Hui Wen Boys' Acad., Changli, China, 1923-26; asst. dir., bur. cooperation with ednl. instns., also asst. prof. ednl. adminstrn. and supervision, Sch. Edn. U. Mich., 1929-34; dir. admisssions Lehigh U., Bethlehem, Pa., 1934-38, dean undergrads., from 1938, dean students, dir. student personnel svcs., 1948-58, asst. to pres. and dean grad. sch., 1958-61, dean emeritus, from 1961, also prof. edn.; vis. specialist German univs., U.S. Dept. State, 1952-53; cons. in higher edn. Pa. Dept. Pub. Instrn.; administrv. dir. Historic Bethlehem, Inc. Author: (with Charles Le Roy Anspach) Problems in Educational Sociology, 1934. Chmn. Bethlehem chpt. ARC, Redevelop, Authority, Bethlehem Authority. Grad. fellow Sch. Edn. U. Mich., 1921-23, 28-29. Mem. Fgn. Policy Assn. (Lehigh Valley br.), Rotary (pres.), Scabbard and Blade Club, Delta Upsilon, Phi Delta Kappa, Omicron Delta Kappa, Phi Eta Sigma. Episcopalian (vestryman). Home: Bethlehem Pa. †

CONKLIN, CLARENCE ROBERT, lawyer; b. Arcadia, Kan., Aug. 18, 1899; s. Thomas C. and Elizabeth (Yoos) C.; m. Ellen Gleason Birkhoff, Aug. 20, 1932 (dec. May 1972); children: Robert D. Birkhoff (stepson), Adrienne Diane Conklin Stephens, Thomas William, Ellen Melissa Conklin Pedersen. Student, Phillips U., 1919-1921, Okla, State Coll., 1923; A.B., Drake U., 1925; J.D., U. Chgo., 1928. Bar: Ill. 1928. With Nat. Surety Corp., claims atty. 1929-1937; with Toplis &

Harding, 1937-1945; partner law firm of Heineke & Conklin, and Heineke Conklin & Schrader, 1945-67; of counsel Conklin & Adler Ltd., Chgo., from 1979; counsel various ins. underwriters. Recipient Double D award Nat. D Club of Drake U., 1986. Mem. Internat. Assn. Ins. Counsel, Am., Ill., Chgo. bar assns., Maritime Law Assn. U.S., Beta Theta Pi, Phi Alpha Delta. Clubs: Union League (Chgo.); Hinsdale (Ill.) Golf; Misquamicut (Watch Hill, R.I.); Cypress Lake Country (Ft. Myers, Fla.). Deceased.

CONKLIN, EVERETT LAWSON, environmental horticulturist; b. Farmingdale, N.Y., Jan. 11, 1908; s. George and Grace (Williams) C.; student N.Y. U.; m. Ruth Purick, June 20, 1931; children—Everett George, Patricia (Mrs. Thomas Clinton, Jr.), Betty Jane (Mrs. William Baxter III). Cert. interior horticulturist, profl. nurseryman. Oostrom & Conklin, Syosset, N.Y., 1936-38; div. mgr. Bobbink & Atkins, East Rutherford, N.J., 1938-54; div. mgr., dir. Bobbink Nurseries, Inc., East Rutherford, 79, 81, pres. Everett Conklin & Co., Inc., Montvale, N.J., 1957-82, chmn., 1982-85, Everett Conklin-West, Inc., Tustin, Calif., 1974-85, Everett Conklin Can., Ltd., Montreal, Que., 1975-85; hort. cons. Sterling Forest Gardens, Tuxedo, N.Y., 1958-69; ann. designer, stager R.H. Macy & Co. Ann. Flower Show, N.Y.C., 1975-82; designer, stager floral decorations Four Seasons Restaurant, N.Y.C., from 1959; silver medal, planter interior gardens Frick Mus., N.Y.C., 1969-77; planter interior gardens Ford Found. Bldg., N.Y.C., 1967-83, Crown Center Hotel, Kansas City, from 1973, Winter Garden Rainbow Ctr., Niagara Falls, N.Y., 1977-82; ofcl. hort. adviser Winter Olympic Games, Lake Placid, N.Y., 1980, lectr. in field. Mem. N.J. Rural Adv. Commn., 1955-60; pres. Bergen County Bd. Agr., 1957-58; chmn. floral decorations com. Pres. Nixon Inaugural Ball, 1969, 73; adv. U.S. Dept. Agr., from 1971. Bd. dirs. Internat. Flower Show, N.Y.C., 1958-73. Recipient numerous hort. awards including Nat. AAN Landscape award, 1960, 61, 68, 69, 71, 72, 73, 75, 76, 77, 78, 79, 81, Internat. Floral Achievement award, 1965, Florists' Transworld Delivery Assn. award, 1971, Florafax award, 1971, Teleflora award, 1971, 75, Golden Flower award, 1971, Asso. Landscape Contractors Am. nat. award, 1971-76, Am. Inst. Interior Designers ann. Man of Year award, 1973, Nat. Environ. Awareness award, 1976, Fla. State Landscape award; spl. award Am. Soc. Landscape Architects, 1968; Olympic Participants silver medal, 1980; named to Floricultural Hall of Fame, Washington, 1980, Nat. Foliage Hall of Fame, Disney World, 1979; citation Can. Minister of Agr., 1980. Fellow Internat. Acad. Poets; mem. N.J. Florists Assn. (pres. 1954-55, Man of Yr. award 1974), Am. Acad. Florists (trustee, awards 1967-72), N.Y. Florists Club (pres. 1958, Eminent Merit award 1966, 69), Met. Retail Florists Assn. (pres. 1966), Soc. Am. Florists (pres. 1971-73, Endowment Trustee Safegardian award 1971-74, 77, Nat. award of recognition 1968, Spl. award of recognition 1971), Am. Hort. Soc. (dir. 1977—), Soc. Archtl. Historians, Am. Forestry Assn., IPA Acad. Poets. Author: A Guide to Interior Planting, 1970; (with others) Handbook of Specialty Elements in Architecture, 1982. Died Mar. 19, 1985. Home: Rutherford N.J.

CONLEY, PHEBE BRIGGS, college trustee; b. Sacamento, Calif., Nov. 8, 1892; d. William Ellery and Grace (Rideout) Briggs; m. Carlos K. McClatchy, Jan. 18, 1918 (dec. 1933); children: James Briggs, William Ellery, Charles Kenny; m. Philip Conley, Oct. 23, 1958; 1 stepchild, Philip R. AB, Vassar Coll., 1916. Mem. bd. trustees Calif. State Colls., from 1962. Active local Community Chest, ARC, Fresno Art Assn., Guide Dogs for Blind. Recipient Carnegie Silver medal for saving 3 lives, 1913. Home: Fresno Calif. †

CONNELLY, JOHN PETER, physician, educator; b. Boston, May 12, 1926; s. Thomas J. and Bridget (Finnegan) C.; m. Martha T. Cronin, June 24, 1950; children: Maureen, Martha, Eileen, Marie, Cathleen, John, Michael. BS, Boston Coll., 1951; MD, Georgetown U., 1955. Diplomate Am. Bd. Pediatrics. Intern Royal Victoria Hosp., Montreal, Que., Can., 1955-56; jr. resident children's service Mass. Gen. Hosp., Boston, 1956-57, asst. resident, 1957-58, chief resident, 1961-62; sr. resident in pediatrics Johns Hopkins Hosp., Balt., 1957-58; practice medicine specializing in pediatrics Boston, 1958-73; asst. pediatrician children's service Mass. Gen. Hosp., 1961-64, chief children's ambulatory clinic, 1963-64, chief ambulatory div., 1964-69, pediatrician, 1967-73, med. dir. pediatric nurse practitioner program, 1964-73; exec. dir. Bunker Hill Health Ctr., 1967-73; vis. physician Lying-In div. Boston Hosp. for Women, 1961-69, cons. maternal and children health, 1968-69; teaching fellow in pediatrics Harvard U., 1957-58, 61-62, instr., 1962-64, assoc. in pediatrics, 1964-67, asst. clin. prof. pediatrics, 1967-69, assoc. prof. pediatrics, 1969-73; chief pediatrics Foster McGaw Hosp., Loyola U., Maywood, Ill., 1972-76, prof., chmn. dept. pediatrics Stritch Sch. Medicine Loyola U.; sr. lectr. Sch/ Social Adminstrn. and Policy, U. Chgo., 1979-86; chmn. dept. health service devel. Am. Acad. Pediatrics, Evanston, Ill., 1976-83; dep. asst. commr. health City of Boston, 1969-73; cons. Boston Children's Service Assn., 1966-73, Nat. Ctr. for Health Services Research and Devel. HEW, 1970-72, Office Asst. Sec. Health and Sci. Affairs, HEW, 1971-73; civilian cons. in pediatrics U.S. Naval Hosp., Chelsea, Mass.; dir. Mass. Dental Service Corp., 1971-73; mem. Mass. Gov.'s Adv. Coun., Comprehensive Planning Agy., 1971-73, Harvard Ctr. for Community Health and Med. Care, 1968-73. Author: (with L. Berlow) You're Too Sweet— A Manual for Juvenile Diabetics, 1969, (with J.D. Stoeckle and R.M. Farrisey) The Nurse Clinician, 1974; contbr. chpts. to books, articles to profl. jours. Bd. dirs. Mass. Soc. for Prevention of Cruelty to Children, 1967-73, Orphans of Italy Inc., 1962-73, Cath. Charitable Bur., Boston, 1968-70, cons., 1970-73. Served with AUS, 1944-45; served to capt. M.C. USAF, 1958-61; served to rear adm. M.C. USNR, 1961. Decorated Knight Order of Malta. Mem. Mass. Med. Soc., Chgo. Med. Soc., New Eng. Pediatric Soc., Am. Fedn. Clin. Research, Am. Acad. Pediatrics (coun. on practice, chmn. liaison com. with Am. Nurses Assn. 1970-72), Assn. for Ambulatory Pediatric Services, Logan-Brophy Soc. Oral Surgery (hon.), Am. Diabetes Assn., New Eng. Diabetes Assn., Royal Coll. Medicine (London), Irish and Am. Pediatric Soc. (sec./treas. 1968-70, exec. coun. 1970-86, pres. 1976-77), U.S. Naval Inst., Am. Legion, Alpha Omega Alpha, Union Boat Club, Appalachian Mountain Club, Harvard Club, Chgo. Athletic Club. Home: Riverside Ill. Died Apr. 8, 1986, buried Arlington Nat. Cemetery.

CONNOLLY, JOHN L(AWRENCE), mining and manufacturing executive; b. Carver County, Minn., 1892; s. John J. and Rose (Daly) C.; m. Marie D. Stevens, Sept. 30, 1924; 1 child, John S. LLB, St. Paul Coll. Law, 1919. Cons. to legal dept. Minn. Mining & Mfg. Co., from 1937. 2d lt. inf. U.S. Army, 1918. Mem. Nat. Tax Assn., U.S. C. of C., NAM, St. Paul Assn., Burning Tree Country Club (Bethesda, Md.), Minn. Club, St. Paul Athletic Club, Town and Country Club (St. Paul, Delta Theta Phi. Congregationalist. Home: Saint Paul Minn. †

CONNORS, EDWARD JOSEPH, railway official; b. Albany, N.Y., May 4, 1892; s. James J. and Anna E. (McManus) C.; m. Cornelia Krueger, Nov. 28, 1918; 1 child, Edward K. Sta. helper N.Y.C. R.R., 1907, clerical and supervisory positions, 1908-15, yardmaster, 1916-18; wage schedule expert U.S. R.R. Adminstrn., 1918-20; examiner U.S. R.R. Labor Bd., 1920-22; asst. to v.p. Union Pacific R.R., 1923-37, asst. to pres., 1937-41, v.p. in charge of ops., 1941-45, v.p., 1945-58; mem. Nat. Conf. on r.r. labor, wages, working conditions, employment, retirement and coordination; dir. transport personnel and rail ops. Office Def. Transp., 1944-45; adv. to Pres. U.S. on R.R. labor problems, Feb.-July, 1945. Mem. Omaha Club, Union League (Chgo.). Home: Whitefield N.H. also: Omaha Nebr. †

CONNORS, GERALD ANTHONY, business executive; b. Janesville, Wis., June 13, 1927; s. Anthony G. and V.E. (Cress) C.; m. Lila Elizabeth Ligocki, June 19, 1948; children: Michael, Lynn, Timothy, Kevin. B.S., Marquette U., 1951. With Emery Air Freight, 1951-72, sr. v.p., gen. mgr., 1969-72; pres., chmn. bd. Air Express Internat.-Wings & Wheels Express, Inc., Jamaica, N.Y., 1972-74; pres. Connors Enterprises, St. Germain, Wis., 1974-88. Active various civic affairs. Served with inf. AUS, 1944-47, ETO. Home: Saint Germain Wis. Died May 19, 1988.

CONOVER, FREDERIC L(EROY), chemist; b. Madison, Wis., July 28, 1892; s. Frederic King and Grace (Clark) C.; m. Alene Gray Wharton, June 25, 1938. AB, U. Wis., 1915, PhD (asst. fellow and Du-Pont fellow 1919-23), 1923; student, Cornell U., 1940. Geologist Wis. State Hwy. Commn., 1920; asst. prof. chemistry Vanderbilt U., 1923-27, assoc., 1927-44, prof. chem., from 1944; rsch. participant Oak Ridge (Tenn.) Nat. Lab. 1st lt. and capt., engrs., and maj. Chem. Warfare Svc., U.S. Army, 1917-19, with A.E.F., France, and Army of Occupation, Germany; participated in Somme, St. Mihiel and Meuse-Argonne offensives; war gas cons. and dir. Civilian Def. Schs., Tenn., 1942-45. Contbr. to sci. publs. Mem. Am. Chem. Soc., Tenn. Acad. Sci., Masons, Phi Beta Kappa, Sigma Xi, Phi Lambda Upsilon, Alpha Chi Sigma, Gamma Alpha, Scabbard and Blade. Unitarian. Home: Nashville Tenn. †

CONRATH, PHILIP ALLEN, medical illustrator, educator; b. Jefferson City, Mo., Jan. 22, 1892; s. Julius H. and Lucy (Schultz) C.; m. Mary Sanburn Russell, Aug. 3, 1920; children: Philip R., Frank J. Student, U. Mo., 1911-12, Sch. Fine Arts Washington U., 1912-15. Med. illustrator Washington U., 1920-36; med. illustrator St. Louis U. Med. Sch., 1936-49, asst. prof., 1949-52, assoc. prof., 1952-61, prof. emeritus, from 1961. Contbr. articles to profl. jours. Mem. hort. coun. Mo. Bot. Garden. With U.S. Army, 1917-19. Fellow Royal Hort. Soc.; mem. Assn. Med. Illustrators (pres. 1955-56, bd. govs. 1951-56, 59-63, chmn. bd. govs. 1952-54, editorial bd. jour.), Am. Legion, Men's Garden Clubs Am. (pres. Webster Groves 1953-55, pres. St. Louis regional coun. 1955-58, nat. dir. 1959-62, nat. pres. 1965-66, bronze medal), Phi Kappa Psi, Phi Chi. Home: Webster Groves Mo. †

CONSTANT, GEORGE ZACHARY, artist; b. Greece, Apr. 2, 1892; came to U.S., 1910, naturalized, 1936; s. Zachary and Zaphire (Argiopoulos) Constantinopoulos; m. Calliroe Lakakis, Sept. 18, 1942; 1 child, Georgette Constant Preston. Student fine arts, Washington U., St. Louis, 1912-14, Art Inst. Chgo., 1914-18. Exhibited in over 40 one-man shows, from 1927; numerous gro exhbns. including Met. Mus. Art, Chgo. Art Ins Bklyn. Mus., Va. Mus. Fine Arts, Mus. Modern A Carnegie Inst., Whitney Mus., Pa. Acad. Fine Arts, Mex., L.A., N.Y. World's Fair, 1939, San Francis Golden Gate Exhbns., 1939, U. Iowa, Stedalijk Mu Amersterdam, The Netherlands, Musee d'Art Moderr Paris, Cocoran Gallery Art, Walker Art Ctr., Library Congress, Salle Franklin, Bordeaux, France, Mus Cantini, Marseille, France, De Beyard, Breda, German Galleria Nazionale D'arte Moderna Valle Gralia, Ron Mus. Fine Arts, Santiago, Chile, Parrish Art Mu Southampton, N.Y., 1917; represented in permane collections Met. Mus. Art, Andover (Mass.) Mus. A Art, Auburn U., Brandeis U., Bklyn. Mus., Balt. Mu Am. Art, Butler Inst. Am. Art, Dayton (Ohio) A Inst., Isaac Delgado Mus. Art, Detroit Inst. A Library of Congress, Pa. Acad. Fine Arts, Phila. Mu Art, Stedljk Mus., Tel-Aviv Mus., U. Nebr., Walk Art Ctr., NYU Art Collection, Norfolk (Va.) Mus. A and Scis., Ball State U., San Francisco Mus., Smit sonian Instn., Whitney Mus. Am. Art, Guild Hall Mu Hirshhorn Mus., Griffiths Art Ctr., State Dept., Dayt Art Inst., 1919-21. Recipient Shilling purchase pri 1939, 43, 56, Frank G. Logan prize and medal Art In Chgo., 1943, Library of Congress purchase prize, 194 Audubon Artists prize, 1946, first prize Guild Ha Easthampton, N.Y., 1963, 66, first prize Parrish A Mus., Southampton, 1950, 51; Mark Rothko Four grantee, 1970; decorated Phoenix Cross of Taxiarch Greece, 1963. Mem. Fedn. Modern Painters a Sculptors (past pres.), Audubon Artists (Emily Lo award 1968, Michael M. Engel Sr. Meml. award 1973 Home: New York N.Y. Deceased.

CONTOIS, DAVID ELY, microbiology educator; Battle Creek, Mich., Jan. 18, 1928; s. Ely Joseph a Grace (Gillard) C.; m. Lois Warren Swiggett, Sept. 1952; children—Michael J., Charles D. Student, Mich., 1945-47; B.A., U. Cal. at Los Angeles, 19 M.S., U. Hawaii, 1952; Ph.D., U. Cal. at San Dieg 1957. Asst. research microbiologist Scripps Inst. Oc nography, U. Cal. at San Diego, 1953-58; asst. pr microbiology U. Hawaii, 1958-64, asso. prof., 1964- prof., 1968-88, chmn. dept., 1962-64, dir. biolo program, 1961-64, asst. dean, 1964-66, asso. dean, 19 69; dean U Hawaii Coll. Arts and Scis., 1969-88, inter provost, 1980-88; cons. microbiologist, 1958-64; chm steering com. Foundational Approaches to S Teaching, 1966-88; mem. Hawaii Curriculum Coun 1966-68; cons. on sci. adminstrn. NIH, 1984, hea scientist adminstr., 1984-85. Served with AUS, 1947- NIH grantee, 1958-60; NSF grantee, 1962-64. Me AAAS, Am. Soc. Microbiology, Soc. Gen. Micro ology, Sigma Xi, Theta Chi. Home: Honolulu Haw Died Apr. 28, 1988.

CONWAY, TIMOTHY J., food merchant; b. Clev Aug. 13, 1892; s. Daniel and Bridget (O'Malley) C.; Margaret Nelson, Feb. 20, 1911 (dec. 1948); childre Mary, Robert, John, Timothy, Richard, William, Jam Jerry, Thomas, Terry, Neil, Peggy. Student pub. sch Cleve. Bookkeeper Fisher Bros. Co., Cleve., 1917, offi mgr., 1921, sec., 1928, treas., v.p., 1931, pres., fr 1949; bd. dirs., mem. exec. com. Clevite Corp.; bd. di Society Nat. Bank. Trustee Cath. Charities, Clev Cleve. Zoo. Mem. Nat., Ohio, Cleve. C.'s of C., N Assn. Food Chains (exec. com.), Ohio Coun. Ret Mchts. (v.p., trustee), Union Club, Rotary Club, Cle Athletic Club. Home: Shaker Heights Ohio. †

CONWELL, RUSSELL HERMAN, clergyma lawyer, university president; b. Worthington, Mas Feb. 15, 1843; s. Martin and Miranda C.; m. Jane Hayden, 1865 (dec.); m. Sarah J. Sanborn, 1873. E Wilbraham Acad.; entered, Yale law dept., 1862; LL Albany Law Sch., 1865; DD and LLD, Temple Col Bar: 1865; ordained Baptist Ch., 1881. Pvt. practi Minneapolis, 1865-68; immigration agt. State of Min Germany, 1867-68; feature corr. Boston Traveler, 186 70; pvt. practice Boston, 1872-81; pastor Grace Bapt Ch., Phila., 1882-1925; founder, then pres. Temple Phila., 1884; founder Samaritan Hosp.; Lyceum a Chautauqua lectr. 1870-1925. Author 44 books. Ca Union Army, Civil War, 1862-64. Home: Philadelph Pa. Died Dec. 6, 1925; buried Founder's Gard Temple U., Phila.

COOGAN, PETER FRANCIS, lawyer; b. Watertow Wis., Dec. 3, 1904; s. William and Eleanor (McFarlan C.; m. Barbara Tracy, June 4, 1942; children: Elean Coogan Merrill, Rosalind Coogan Anderson, Pe Weston, Matthew Allen. Student, Marquette U., 192 26; LL.B., Case Western Res. U., 1939; M.A., Bost U., 1941; LL.M., Harvard U., 1942. Bar: Mass. 194 U.S. Dist. Ct. Mass. 1942, U.S. Ct. Appeals (1st ci 1942. Assoc. Ropes & Gray, Boston, 1942-50, ptn 1950-77, of counsel, 1977-85; lectr. Yale U. Law Sc Harvard U. Law Sch.; practitioner-in-residence Du U.; disting. vis. prof. U. Va., U. Ga., U. So. Calif., Houston, Vt. Law Sch.; scholar-in-residence Murph Weir & Butler, San Francisco, 1980-85; mem. permane editorial bd. Uniform Comml. Code, 1953-85; me Nat. Bankruptcy Conf., 1955-85; del. U.S. State De Conf. on Internat. Leasing, 1977; lectr. continuing le edn. program Am. Law Inst.-ABA. Prin. author: (w Hogan and Vagts) Secured Transactions Under Uniform Commercial Code, 4 vols., 1963-85; bd. ov ers (Case Western Res. U.), 1969-72. Chmn. vis. com. ase Western Res, U. Law Sch., 1965-71; bd. overseers ase Western Res. U., 1969-72. Mem. Boston Bar ssn., N.Y. Bar Assn., ABA, Am. Law Inst., ABA Soc. ellows, Fellows Mass. Bar, Soc. Benchers (Case Western Res. U.). Club: Harvard (Boston and N.Y.C.). ome: Quechee Vt. Died June 20, 1985, buried S. Strafrd, Vt.

OOK, GEORGE THOMAS, newspaper executive; b. dpls., Apr. 12, 1921; s. James Merkle and Mary Harp) C.; m. Mary Frances Berry, May 3, 1952; chilren—Frances Ellen, Christopher Alan. A.B. in urnalism, U. Ala., 1949. Reporter Birmingham (Ala.) ost-Herald, 1949-62, state editor, 1962-65, city editor, 965-66, mng. editor, 1966-80, assoc. editor, 1980-86. erved to 1st lt., inf., Military Police, Transp. Corps US, 1940-46. Methodist. Home: Birmingham Ala. ied Feb. 18, 1987; buried Elmwood Cemetery, rmingham, Ala.

OOL, RODNEY LEE, physicist, educator; b. Platte, D., Mar. 8, 1920; s. George E. and Muriel (Post) C.; . Margaret E. MacMillan, June 21, 1949; children: len, John, Mary Lee, Adrienne. B.S., U. S.D., 1942; .A., Harvard U., 1947, Ph.D., 1949. Research ysicist Brookhaven Nat. Lab., Upton, L.I., N.Y., 949-59; dep. chmn. high energy physics Brookhaven at. Lab., 1960-64, asst. dir. high energy physics, 1964-, asso. dir., 1966-70, sec. high energy adv. com., 1960-, chmn., 1967-70; prof. exptl. high energy physics ockefeller U., N.Y.C., 1970-88; Mem. policy com. anford Linear Accelerator Center, 1962-67, 76-80; em. Asso. Univs. High Energy Panel, Asso. Univs., c., 1963-70; mem. Walker panel, com. on sci. and pub. licy Nat. Acad. Sci., 1964; mem. Princeton-Pa. Acerator Sci. Com., 1966-68; mem. high energy physics v. panel AEC, 1967-70; chmn. physics adv. com. Nat. ccelerator Lab., 1967-70; mem. adv. panel for physics SF, 1970-73; sci. assoc. European Ctr. Nuclear esearch, 1973-88; trustee Univs. Research Assn., 1977-; mem. rev. com. Argonne Univs. Assn., 1978-80. Coitor: Advances in Particle Physics, vols. I and II, 68; contbr. articles to profl. jours. Served to maj., gnal Corps AUS, 1942-46. Decorated Bronze Star edal. Fellow Am. Phys. Soc. (program cons. div. parles and fields 1968-70); mem. Nat. Acad. Scis., Phi ta Kappa, Sigma Xi. Home: New York N.Y. Died or. 16, 1988; buried Marblehead, Mass.

OOLEY, GEORGE RALPH, investment banker; b. oy, N.Y., May 29, 1896; s. Wallace Willard and Ruby Vebb) C.; m. Myra Taylor, Oct.1, 1919; children: rbara Cooley Dudley, Dorothy Cooley Mulleneaux, net Cooley Sloss, Robin Cooley McAllister. Student, lgate U., 1921, LLD; DSc (hon.), U. So. Fla. lesman Dillon, Read & Co., N.Y.C., 1918-24; pres., . George R. Cooley & Co. Inc., Albany, N.Y., 1924-; research fellow Gray Herbarium Harvard U., 1954-; dir., chmn. fin. com. North Am. Cement Corp., 36-48; bd. dirs. Pioneer Fund, Inc., Pioneer II Inc. em. Nature Conservancy, v.p., bd. govs.; bd. dirs. lgate-Rochester Div. Sch., 1950-70, Pioneer Enterse Fund; trustee U. So. Fla. Found., Tampa, 1959-69. erved as 2d lt. Engrs., U.S. Army, 1918. MEm. merous sci. orgns., Fort Orange Club, University Club, gma Nu. Home: Rensselaerville N.Y. Died Sept. 27, 86.

OOLEY, ROBERT NELSON, radiologist, educator; Woodlawn, Va., Mar. 12, 1911; s. Elmer Jackson and zabeth Lee (Clark) C.; m. Eula Grace Jarnagin, July 1948; children: Helen Hope, Caroline Elizabeth, obert Nelson. M.D., U. Va., 1934. Diplomate: Am. . Radiology (trustee, pres. 1974). Intern Bellevue osp., N.Y.C., 1934-36, Mary McClelland Hosp., mbridge, N.Y., 1936; resident Johns Hopkins Hosp., lt., 1941-42, 46-48; pvt. practice, specializing in radigy Balt., 1948-53, Galveston, Tex., 1953-88; mem. ffs U. Tex. Med. Br. Hosps., Galveston; asst. prof., diology Johns Hopkins U. Sch. Medicine, Balt., 1948-; asso. prof. Johns Hopkins U. Sch. Medicine, 1950-; prof. U. Tex. Med. Br., 1953-88, chmn. dept. radiogy, 1953-76. Author: (with R.D. Sloan, M.H. hreiber) Radiology of Heart and Great Vessels, 1956, edit., 1966, 3d edit., 1979; contbr. (with R.D. Sloan, H. Schreiber) articles to profl. jours. Served from 1st to maj. M.C. AUS, 1942-46. Fellow Am. Coll. diology (Gold medal); mem. AAUP, Am. Heart sn., Am. Roentgen Ray Soc., AMA, Assn. U. Radigists (Gold medal), Galveston County Med. Soc., x. Med. Assn., Tex. Radiol. Soc. (Gold medal), diol. Soc. N.Am. Presbyn. (elder). Home: Knoxville nn. Died Jan. 27, 1988; buried Monticello Meml. rden, Charlottesville, Va.

OON, BYRON S., corporate executive; b. LeRoy, Ill., r. 2, 1903; s. James S. and Rose O. (Rike) C.; mard 1924; children: James Aubert, Audrey; m. Maurine ylor, 1931; children: Thomas Taylor, Byron gene. Grad., Northwestern U., 1925. Engaged in age and real estate bus. 1923; with Gen. Finance rp., Chgo., 1930-63, collector, 1930, pres., from 1940, nn. bd. dirs., 1948-63, hon. chmn. bd. dirs., 1963-36; pres. Gen. Fin. Loan, 1948-63. Bd. dirs. Jr. hievement, Chgo. Mem. Northwestern U. Alumni sn. (v.p.), Chgo. Athletic Assn., Execs. Club, Electric ub, Tavern Club, Tower Club, Westmoreland Country Club, Minocqua Country Club, Key Largo Anglers Club, John Evans Club (cofounder, bd. dirs.), Benchwarmers Club (cofounder), Delta Upsilon. Home: Fort Lauderdale Fla. Died July 4, 1986.

COON, LELAND A(VERY), musician, educator; b. Leonardsville, N.Y., June 30, 1892; s. Almeron Morell and Martha Estelle (Avery) C.; m. Jeanne Louise Fayard, Aug. 24, 1920. BA, Alfred U., 1914, MA, 1932; piano soloist diploma, New Eng. Conservatory of Music, 1916; pupil, DeVoto, Casadesus, Philipp, Matthay and Faughé. Asst. prof. piano Kingfisher Coll., 1916-17, U. Oreg., 1919-22, Fontainebleau and Paris, France, 1922-23; assoc. prof. music U. Wis., 1923-36, prof., 1936, chmn. Sch. Music, 1946-52; London, Eng., summer 1936. With Co. C, 7th Inf., U.S. Army, World War I. Mem. Music Tchrs. Nat. Assn. (chmn. com. on colls., univs.; exec. com., treas. 1952-59, Music Educators Nat. Conf., Am. Musicol. Soc. (dir. Midwest chpt.), Wis. Acad. Sci., Art, Lit, Phi Mu Alpha, Pi Kappa Alpha, Pi Kappa Lambda. Home: Lake Mendota Wis. †

COONEY, JOSEPH PATRICK, lawyer; b. Hartford, Conn., Aug. 30, 1906; s. Jeremiah and Margaret (Dwyer) C.; m. Mary M. Malliet, June 28, 1933 (dec. Jan 1974); children: Jane (Mrs. V.J. Dowling), Edwina (Mrs. H.T. Gillis), Margaret (Mrs. B.J. Coughlin), Anne, Joseph Patrick, Mary Alice (Mrs. Edgar A. Belden), Barbara (Mrs. Robert G. Oliver); m. Marion Cobden, May 29, 1976. LLB, Georgetown U., 1929. Mem. Conn. State Senate from 2d senatorial dist., 1931-33, 37, 41; asst. U.S. Dist. atty. 1941-43; ptnr. Cooney, Scully & Dowling, Hartford; mem. Hartford Aviation Commn., 1930-31, Hartford County Commn., 1933-39, Hartford County grievance com., 1961-65; chmn. Conn. gov.'s ad hoc com. jud. nominees, 1975-77. Trustee Catholic Family Services St. Agnes Home, St. Joseph Coll.; bd. dirs. St. Francis Hosp., Conn. Hosp. Assn., pres. 1961-62, Mt. St. Benedict. Cemetery, Conn. Inst. for Blind, Hosp. Council Greater Hartford, 1962-63; bd. incorporators Inst. Living, Mt. Sinai Hosp. Recipient John Carroll award Georgetown U., 1965. Fellow Am. Coll. Trial Lawyers; mem. Internat. Soc. Barristers, ABA (ho. dels. 1966-67), Hartford County Bar Assn. (pres. 1946-48), Knights of St. Gregory. Home: West Hartford Conn. Died Aug. 25, 1984.

COOPER, IRVING S., neurosurgeon; b. Atlantic City, July 15, 1922; s. Louis and Eleanor Lillian (Cooper) C.; m. Mary Dan Frost, Dec. 15, 1944; children: Daniel Alan, Douglas Paul, Lisa Frost; m. Sissel Holm, Jan. 31, 1970; children: David Louis, Erik Holm, Charles Spencer. BA, George Washington U., 1942, MD, 1945; MS, U. Minn., 1951, PhD, 1951; DSc (hon.), Trinity Coll., Hartford, Conn., 1974, Fordham U., 1974. Diplomate Am. Bd. Neurology and Psychiatry, Am. Bd. Neurol. Surgery. Intern U.S. Naval Hosp., St. Albans, N.Y., 1945-46; fellow neurosurgery Mayo Found., 1948-51; mem. faculty NYU Med. Sch., 1951-64, prof. clin. neurosurgery, 1954-64, research prof. neurosurgery; research prof. neuroanatomy N.Y. Med. Coll.; dir. Inst. Neurosci. St. Barnabas Hosp., N.Y.C., 1954-78; prof., dir. Ctr. for Physiol. Neurosurgery Westchester County-N.Y. Coll. Med. Ctr., Valhalla, N.Y., 1978-85; pres. Naples (Fla.) Inst. for Advanced Studies in Medicine and Humanities; spl. research devel., practice, teaching specialized brain operations for treatment Parkinsonism, related diseases, devel. cryogenic surgery; Eliza Savage vis. prof., Australia, 1962; vis. prof. Mayo Found., 1974, Nat. Hosp., U. London, Eng., 1974. Author: The Neurosurgical Alleviation of Parkinsonism, 1956, Parkinsonism: Its Medical and Surgical Therapy, 1961, Involuntary Movement Disorders, 1968, The Victim is Always the Same, 1973, The Pulvinar-LP Complex, 1973, The Cerebellum, Epilepsy and Behavior, 1973, Living with Chronic Neurological Disease, 1976, It's Hard to Leave While the Music's Playing, 1977, Cerebellar Stimulation. Lt. (j.g.) M.C., USNR, 1946-48. Recipient Lewis Harvey Taylor award Am. Therapeutic Soc., 1957, St. Barnabas Hosp. award, 1959, Modern Medicine award, 1960, award in medicine N.Y. Philanthropic League, 1960, Civic award in medicine Bronx Bd. Trade, 1961, Humanitarian award Nat. Cystic Fibrosis Found., 1962, Gold medal Worshipful Soc. Apothecaries, London, 1967, Bronze award Am. Congress Rehab. Medicine, 1967, Comenius medal U. Bratislava, Czechoslovakia, Alumni Achievement award U. Minn., 1965. Fellow A.C.S., Am. Geriatric Soc., N.Y. Acad. Medicine, N.Y. Acad. Sci.; mem. Harvey Cushing Neurosurg. Soc., AMA (Hektoen Bronze medal 1957, 58, Certificate of Merit 1961), Neurosurg. Soc. Am., Am. Acad. Neurology, Soc. Cryobiology (gov.), Soc. Cryosurgery (pres.), Am. Fedn. Clin. Research, Pan Am. Soc. U.S., Am. Congress Phys. Medicine and Rehab., Amytrophic Lateral Sclerosis Soc. Am. (trustee), Scandinavian Neurosurg. Soc., Med. Honor Soc., Czechoslovak Neurosurg. Soc., Alpha Omega Alpha; hon. mem. Neurol. and Neurosurg. Soc. Argentina, Egyptian Neurosurg. Soc., Soc. Neurology and Neurosurgery Cuba, Neurol. Soc. Czechoslovakia, Luther Rice Soc., Authors Guild, Brit. Soc. Neurol. Surg., Sigma Xi. Home: Naples Fla. Died Oct. 30, 1985.

COOPER, KENNETH EZELLE, lawyer; b. Wynne, Ark., July 7, 1892; s. Coy J. and Cora (Browne) C.; m. Grace McCleskey, Oct. 1, 1916; children: Kenneth M., Elaire Cooper Fletcher, Coy Mack, Erlin Cantey. Student, So. U., Greensboro, Ala., 1911-14; LLB, U. Ala., 1916. Bar: Ala. 1916. Practiced in Birmingham, Ala., from 1916; mem. firm Cabaniss & Johnston, from 1935. Chmn. bd. Meth. Children's Home, Selma, Ala., from 1940; bd. dirs., chmn. exec. com. Carraway Meth. Hosp., Birmingham, from 1945; organizer Meth. Home for Aging, Birmingham, 1956. Named to Meth. Hall of Fame, 1954; recipient Boss of Yr. award Legal Secs. Assn., 1963. Mem. ABA, Ala. State Bar Assn., Birmingham Bar Assn., Kiwanis (pres. Birmingham Club 1955), Omicron Delta Kappa (hon.), Kappa Alpha. Home: Birmingham Ala.

COPELAND, CLARENCE EDMUND, hospital administrator; b. Richmond, Va., June 11, 1891; s. Edward and Clara (Giessler) C.; m. Gladys Pearl Wolf, July 18, 1919; children: William Henry, Ruth Elaine (Mrs. Carr C. Krueger), Robert Wayne. Student, Watters Bus. Coll., 1908-09, Alexander Hamilton Inst., 1911-13. Sec. Bus. Svc., St. Louis, 1920-28; pres. Copeland & Hasselbring, real estate, 1928-32; exec. sec. St. Louis County Relief Com., Clayton, Mo., 1932-36; fin. sec. Mo. Bapt. Hosp., St. Louis, 1936-38, dir. pub. relations, 1938-43, adminstr., from 1943. Moderator St. Louis Bapt. Assn., 1944; pres. Mo. Bapt. Brotherhood, 1941, 42; Mo. rep. Bapt. Brotherhood of South, 1946-47. 2d lt., U.S. Army, World War I. Fellow Am. Coll. Hosp. Adminstrs; mem. Am. (ho. of dels. 1952-53), Mo. (pres. 1950-51), Am. Protestant (pres. 1954-55, treas. 1957-61), S.W. Bapt. (pres. 1951-52), Midwest (pres. 1960-61) hosp. assns., Masons. Home: Webster Groves Mo. †

CORDELL, HOWARD WILLIAM, librarian, university administrator; b. Industry, Ill., June 13, 1921; s. Collen Francis and Ara Gladys (Snowden) C.; m. Margaret Wilson, Aug. 30, 1952; children: John Laughton, Ann Snowden. BS, Western Ill. U., 1944, MS, 1949; MLS, U. Ill., 1957. Acquisitions librarian Western Ill. U., Macomb, 1951-62; instr. Sch. Library Sci., U. Ill., Urbana, 1962-63; assoc. dir. libraries Fla. Atlantic U., Boca Raton, 1963-66; reference dept. head U. Ill., Chgo., 1966-67; dir. library services Cornell Coll., Mt. Vernon, Iowa, 1967-70; founding dir. libraries and media services Fla. Internat. U., Miami, 1970-86. With USAAF, 1946-48, USAF, 1950-51. Mem. ALA, Southeastern Library Assn., Dade County Library Assn. Democrat. Episcopalian. Home: Gainesville Fla. Died Oct. 21, 1987; buried Evergreen Cemetery, Gainesville, Fla.

CORDOVA, VALDEMAR A., judge; b. Phoenix, Dec. 6, 1922; s. Louis H. and Carmen A. C.; m. Gloria Orduno, July 18, 1945; children: Kenneth, Valerie, Lexia. JD, U. Ariz., 1950. Bar: Ariz. 1950. Practiced in Phoenix, 1950-65, 67-76; ptnr. Renaud, Cook, Miller & Cordova, 1967-76; judge Superior Ct. Ariz., Phoenix, 1965-67, 76-79, U.S. Dist. Ct., Phoenix, 1979-88. Mem. Phoenix City Council, 1956-59, Phoenix Civil Service Bd., 1962-65, Phoenix Adjustment Bd., 1954-56. Served with USAAF, 1940-45. Decorated Air medal, Purple Heart. Mem. Am., Ariz., Maricopa County bar assns., Ariz. Judges Assn., Am. Legion. Democrat. Roman Catholic. Club: Vesta. Home: Phoenix Ariz. Died June 18, 1988.

COREY, MERTON LEROY, management consultant; b. York County, Nebr., Feb. 23, 1883; s. Alfred G. and Mary C (Gilmore) C.; m. Lela V. Lewis, Aug. 21, 1906; children: Gerald M. (dec.), Rogene Lois Corey Jackson, Margaret L. (dec.). LLB, U. Nebr., 1907. Bar: Nebr. 1907, U.S. Supreme Ct. 1919. Practiced in Clay Ctr., Nebr.; registrar, gen. counsel Fed. Land Bank, Omaha, 1917-23; mem. Fed. Farm Loan Bd., Washington, 1923-24; fiscal agt. various coops. including Tobacco Growers Coop. Assn., Fla. Citrus Growers Clearing Ho. Assn., Fla. United Growers Coop. N.Y.C., from 1924; coop. mktg. adviser Govt. Puerto Rico, 1931-32; v.p. Am. Gen. Agys., Inc., 1933-35; spl. counsel Nat. Assn. Food Chains, 1938-39; agrl. counsel Carl Byoir & Assocs., Inc., 1939-52; with Rogers, Slade & Hill, 1952-54, 60-61; cons. Edward Thomas Assocs., Inc., pub. relations, N.Y.C., from 1961; v.p. Am. Nat. Foods, 1954-60; dir. Nat. Farm Chemurgic Council, 1954-66, pres., 1963-66; orgn. counsel Fla. Citrus Mut., 1948; bd. dirs. Fla. Citrus Rsch. Found., from 1960. Author articles on coop. mktg., farm fin., econs. Mem. nat. speakers bur. ARC, 1943, 44. Mem. Am. Mktg. Assn., Am. Acad. Polit. and Social Sci., Nat. Republican Club (agrl. and nat. affairs com.), Scarsdale Town Club (pub. info. com.), White Plains Old Guard Club, Theta Kappa Nu, Delta Sigma Rho, Phi Delta Phi. Home: Scarsdale N.Y. †

CORNELLIER, PHILIP, clergyman and educator; b. St. Remi, Napierville County, Quebec, Can., Nov. 20, 1892; s. Louis M. and Marie (O'Gleman) C. BA, Licentiate in Philosphy, U. Ottawa, 1913, PhD, 1915; B.C.L., Gregorian U., Rome, Italy; DD, Oblates of Mary Immaculate Novitiate, Lachine, Can., 1913-14. Tchr. high sch. dept. U. Ottawa, 1919, prof. theology, 1920-28, prof. philosophy (psychology, ethics and history of philosophy), 1928-42, prof. philosopy of sci., 1932-42, registrar of the univ., 1933-39, vice rector, 1939-42, rector, 1942-46; rector St. Paul's Sem., 1946-52; vice rector U. Ottawa, 1952-55, prof. med. ethics, from 1955. Mem. Oblates of Mary Immaculate, Soc. Thomiste (Ottawa), Polish Inst. Arts and Scis. in Am.,

Académie St. Thomas d'Aquin, Am. Geog. Soc. of N.Y. Home: Ottawa Canada. †

CORNETT, OLIVE BYRAM, radio corporation executive; b. Ellisville, Ill., Dec. 20, 1891; d. Daniel Amzi and Josephine (Van Decar) Byram; m. Marshall E. Cornett, June 25, 1922 (dec. Oct. 1947). Student pub. schs., Ill., Nebr. Legal stenographer Rees, Turpin, Haff, Meservey, German & Michaels, also Harrington, Howard & Ash, Kansas City, Mo., 1910-19; office mgr. Klamath Forest Protective Assn., Klamath Falls, Oreg., 1926-45; dir. Inland Radio Inc., Baker, Oreg., from 1944, v.p., 1944-47, sec.-treas., from 1947; pvt. sec. Marshall Cornett, 1945-47. Mem. State Coun. on Aging, from 1959; chmn. com. community svcs., del. White House Conf. on Agine, 1960; mem. Rep. Nat. Com., 1948-56, exec. com., 1948-52. Recipient citation for civilian def. activities Gov. of Oreg. Mem. Am. Legion Auxiliary, Daughters of Nile, Oreg. C. of C., Soroptimists, Klamath County Bus. and Profl. Women's Club, Nile Club (pres. 1946-47) (Klamath Falls). Home: Klamath Falls Oreg. †

CORNETTE, JAMES P., English educator; b. Charleston, Miss., Nov. 17, 1908; s. Albieus Marvin and Winnie Jane (Johnston) C.; m. Mary Lawson, Feb. 26, 1930; children: Marvin Brister, James Lawson, William Richard. AB, Ky. Wesleyan Coll., 1929; AM, U. Va., 1930; PhD, George Peabody Coll. for Tchrs., Nashville, 1938. Tchr., athletic coach Clark County (Ky.) High Sch., 1928-29, Mattoon (Ky.) High Sch., 1930; assoc. prof. English Western Ky. State Coll., Bowling Green, 1930-45; dean Baylor U., Waco, Tex., 1945-48; pres. West Tex. State U., Canyon, 1948-73, chancellor, 1973-74, pres. emeritus, 1974-86; pres. Am. Assn. State Colls. and Univs., 1966-67. Author: A Biography of John Henry Clagett, 1938, A History of the Western Kentucky State Coll., 1941, (with A. L. Crabb) Modern Language Handbooks, Grades V-VIII, 1941. Mem. NEA, Masons, Rotary Club, Phi Delta Kappa, Pi Delta Kappa. Democrat. Home: Canyon Tex. Died Nov. 16, 1986; buried Dreamland Cemetery, Canyon.

COROMINAS SEGURA, RODOLFO, monetary fund executive; b. Argentina, Oct. 28, 1891. Student, Colegio Nacional Central, Buenos Aires, U. Burnos Aires Sch. Laws and Social Scis. Clk. Supreme Ct., Providence of Mendoza, 1914; sec. Cmml. Ct. of First Instance, 1917-18; counsel Anglo-Sud-Americano, Londres y Rio de la Plata banks, 1923-28, Buenos Aires & Pacific Ry. Co., 1928-32, 36-38, dep. Nat. Congress, 1932-36, 36-40; assoc. justice Fed. Ct. Dist. of Mendoza, 1929, govt. Providence of Mendoza, 1938-41; author by-laws, legal adviser Stock Exchange, Mendoza, 1942-47; pres. Transports Corp., City of Buenos Aires, 1942-43; assoc. justice Fed. Ct. Appeals, Cuyo Dist., 1943, Fed. Supreme Ct., Cuyo Dist., 1944; exec. dir. Internat. Monetary Fund, Argentina, Bolivia, Chile, Ecuador, Paraguay, Uruguay, from 1956; Argentine del. 5th conf. Inter-Am. Bar Assn. Contbr. articles to newspapers, mags. Decorated Order of Merit (Chile). Mem. Argentine Fedn. Lawyers (governing bd. 1932-38), Bar Assn. Mendoza , Bar Assn. Buenos Aires, Argentine Fedn. Bar Assns. (2d v.p. 1933-38), Argentine Inst. Legislative Studies (1st v.p. 1933-38). Home: Mendoza Argentina. †

CORRADI, PETER, construction and engineering consultant; b. Bklyn., Nov. 24, 1910; s. Manlis and Mary (Bosco) C.; m. Helena Olive Corley, Jan. 23, 1937; children—Peter R., Patricia, Carol. B.S. in Civil Engring, N.Y.U., 1936, Sc.D., 1966. Design engr. Port of N.Y. Authority, 1934-39; commd. lt. (j.g.) USN, 1940, advanced through grades to rear adm., 1961, dep. chief Bur. Yards and Docks, also dep. chief civil engr., 1958-62, chief bur., chief civil engrs., 1962-65; ret.; v.p., gen. mgr. Gibbs & Hill, Inc., cons. engrs., 1965-66, pres., chief exec. officer, 1966-69; exec. v.p., dir. Raymond Internat., Inc., N.Y.C., 1969-72; chmn. bd. Raymond Internat., Inc., Houston, 1972-76, chmn. fin. com., 1976; cons. Naples, Fla., from 1976. Decorated D.S.M., Bronze Star. Mem. Nat. Soc. Profl. Engrs., ASCE (hon.), Soc. Am. Mil. Engrs. (past pres.), Moles (past pres., mem. exec. com. award for outstanding achievement in constrn. industry 1976). Clubs: Royal Poinciana Golf, Naples Athletic; Army Navy (Arlington, Va.). Home: Naples Fla. Deceased.

CORRIGAN, JAMES JOSEPH PATRICK, lawyer; b. Cleve., July 27, 1901; s. Patrick and Norah (Walsh) C.; m. Nancy McGuinness, Feb. 26, 1948. AB, John Carroll U., 1922; JD, Georgetown U., 1925. Bar: D.C. 1925, Ohio 1926. Pvt. practice Cleve., 1926-56; judge Ct. Common Pleas, Cleve., 1957-63, Ct. Appeals, 1963-69; justice Ohio Supreme Ct., 1969-77; ptnr. Marshman, Snyder & Corrigan, Cleve., from 1978; instr. trial practice Cleve.-Marshall Law Sch., 1963-69. Trustee Notre Dame Coll., Cleve., 1964-70; bd. advisers St. John's Hosp., Cleve, from 1963. Served AUS, World War II. Decorated Bronze Star. Fellow Ohio Bar Found.; mem. ABA, Ohio Bar Assn., Cleve. Bar Assn., Cuyahoga County Bar Assn., Inst. Jud. Adminstrn., Am. Judicature Soc., Am. Legion, Delta Theta Phi. Republican. Clubs: Univ. (Cleve.), Rowfant, Columbus, Athletic, University (Columbus), Avon Oaks Country. Home: Cleveland Ohio. Died Apr. 1982; buried Lakewood Cemetery, Cleve.

CORRIN, BROWNLEE SANDS, political scientist, educator; b. Bellevue, Pa., Mar. 25, 1922; s. John Grimshaw and Alice (Turkington) C.; m. Mary Elizabeth Dyer, May 18, 1946; children: Adaline Elizabeth, Rebecca Sands, David Montgomery, John Brownlee. AB, Stanford U., 1947, MA, 1950, PhD, 1959. Teaching asst. Stanford U., 1949-52; mem. faculty Goucher Coll., Towson, Md., 1952-85, prof. polit. sci., 1965-76, prof. communication, 1976-85, chmn. dept. polit. sci., 1958-73, chmn. dept. internat. relations, 1958-69, 73-77, dir. communication program, 1976, chmn. faculty history and social scis., 1966-69; dir. Field Politics Ctr., 1954-76; elections analyst ABC, 1964-76; producer Politics of Laughter, WCTV-FM, Balt., 1976-78; issue analyst WJZ-TV, Balt., 1975-78; vis. lectr. Johns Hopkins U., 1962, U. Md., 1962-68; cons. Md. Constl. Conv. Common, 1965-67; dir. edn. WTOW-FM-AM, Balt., 1968-70; dir. BSCR&D (pub. affairs and communication); chmn. working com. New Eng. Conf. Teaching Fgn. Langs., 1966. Contbr. articles to profl. jours. Mem. Balt. County Coun. Charter Rev. Com., 1961-62; mem. Md. Legis. Com. Campaign Costs, 1964; bd. govs. WJHU-FM, Balt., 1979-85; mem. bd. Library Trustees Baltimore County, 1968-80, v.p. bd., 1973, pres., 1974-77; precinct leader, chmn. Balt. County Rep. Dist. Exec. Com., 1952-63; chmn. Md. Rep. Arts and Scis. Com., 1962; treas. for candidate to Md. Constnl. Conv., 1967; mem. Rep. Nat. Arts and Scis. Com.; cons. Rep. House Conf. Com., 1963-64; bd. dirs. UN Assn. Md., 1956-66. Served to maj. AUS, 1942-47, CBI. Mem. Am. Humor Studies Assn., Biofeedback Soc. Am., Ea. Communications Assn., Am. Polit. Sci. Assn., AFTRA, Am. Soc. Internat. Law, Am. Soc. Pub. Adminstrn., Speech Communication Assn., Internat. Communications Assn., Internat. Inst. Space Law, Internat. Studies Assn., Popular Culture Soc., Nat. Coun. Social Studies, Nat. Fedn. Local Cable Programmers, World Future Soc., Pi Sigma Alpha, Sigma Alpha Epsilon, Army and Navy Club. Episcopalian. Home: Lutherville Md. Died Jan. 5, 1985; buried Timonium, Md.

CORRINGTON, LOUIS EARLE, JR., banker; b. Chgo., Nov. 8, 1916; s. Louis Earle and Katrina (Oller) C.; m. Marjorie E. Hayn, Dec. 31, 1955; 1 dau., Margo Louise. Clerical positions various banks 1934-40; asst. cashier Am. Nat. Bank & Trust Co., Chgo., 1940-54; v.p. S.E. Nat. Bank, Chgo., 1955-56; pres. Guaranty Bank & Trust Co., Chgo., 1956-62; pres., dir. Merc. Nat. Bank of Chgo., 1962-67; pres. Coran, Inc., Chgo., 1967-87; mng. ptnr. Corrington Farms (thoroughbred horses), Midway, Ky., 1983-87. Served to capt. USAAF, 1942-46. Club: Barrington Hills Country. Home: Inverness Ill. Died Feb. 1, 1987; buried Memory Gardens Cemetery and Mausoleum, Arlington Heights, Ill.

CORRSIN, STANLEY, mechanical engineering educator, fluid dynamicist; b. Phila., Apr. 3, 1920; s. Herman and Anna (Schor) C.; m. Barbara Daggett, Sept. 25, 1945; children—Nancy Eliot, Stephen David. B.S., U. Pa., 1940; M.S., Calif. Inst. Tech., 1942, Ph.D. in Aeros., 1947; Docteur honoris causa, Universite Claude Bernard, France, 1974. Research and teaching asst. in aeros. Calif. Inst. Tech., 1940-45, instr., 1945-47; asst. prof. aeros. Johns Hopkins U., Balt., 1947-51, assoc. prof., 1951-55, prof. mech. engring., chmn. dept. mech. engring., 1955-60, prof. fluid mechanics, 1960-86. Recipient disting. alumnus citation U. Pa. Sch. Engring., 1955. Fellow Am. Phys. Soc. (chmn. div. fluid dynamics 1964, Fluid Dynamics prize 1983), Am. Acad. Arts and Scis., ASME, Nat. Acad. Engring.; mem. AIAA, AAUP (pres. Johns Hopkins chpt. 1964-65), AAAS, Phi Beta Kappa, Sigma Xi, Tau Beta Pi, Pi Tau Sigma. Home: Riderwood Md. Died June 2, 1986.

COSGROVE, WILLIAM HUGH, manufacturing executive; b. Braddock, Pa., July 30, 1892; s. Thomas and Mary (Flanagan) C.; m. Elizabeth Kuhn, Jan. 9, 1924; children: Thomas, John Casey, Mary Margaret, William Hugh, Mark. ME, Cornell U., 1915. With Am. Sheet & Tin Plate Co., 1915-19, William Swindell & Bros., 1919-30; v.p. Swindell-Dressner Corp., Pitts., 1930-47, pres., 1947-59, chmn. bd., 1959-62, cons., 1962-67; bd. dirs. Pitts. Testing Labs., Union Nat. Bank, Pitts., Pa. Mfg. Assn. Ins. Co. Mem. Pitts. Bd. Edn., 1945-56; trustee Duquesne U., Found.; pres. adv. bd., trustee Mercy Hosp., Pitts.; mem. adv. bd. St. Vincent Coll., Latrobe, Pa., Duquesne U. 1st lt. A.C., U.S. Army, 1917-19. Mem. Pa. Mfg. Assn. (bd. dirs.), Am. Iron and Steel Inst., Assn. Iron and Steel Engrs., Engrs. Soc. Western Pa., Duquesne Club, Longvue Cluib, Pitts. Field Club, University Club, Cornell Club N.Y. Republican. Roman Catholic. Home: Pittsburgh Pa. †

COSTA, JOSEPH, press photographer; b. Caltabelotta, Sicily, Italy, Jan. 3, 1904; s. Giuseppi and Francesca (Stravalli) C.; m. Marguerite Macdonell, Oct. 18, 1930 (dec.); 1 dau., Frances Joyce; m. Margaret H. King, Nov. 22, 1967. Ed. pub. schs., N.Y.C.; LL.D. (hon.), Ball State U., 1985. Staff photographer N.Y. Morning World, 1920-27, N.Y. News, 1927-46; photo supr., King Features Syndicate; chief photographer Sunday Mirror Mag., 1946-63; exec. editor Nat. Press Photographer mag., N.Y.C., 1946-67; editor emeritus Nat. Press Photographer mag., 1967-88; illustrations editor World Book Ency. Sci. Service, Inc., Houston, 1967-69; guiding faculty Famous Photographers Sch., Westport, Conr vis. prof. Sch. Journalism and Graphic Arts, E. Te State U., Commerce, 1974-75; lectr. journalism Ba State U., Muncie, Ind., 1977-85. Author weekly pho feature for newspapers, 1968-70; head, Photography f Publ., also cons.; Host: weekly TV show Photo Horizons, Dumont Network, N.Y.C., (1946-47 Author: Beginner's Guide to Color Photography, 195 editor: Complete Book of Press Photography, 1950 Recipient Merit award Press Photographers Assn. N.Y 1947; asso. Photog. Soc. Am., 1949; fellow, 1956; Fe lowship award and Sprague award Nat. Pre Photographers Assn., 1949; Robin G. Garland educat award Nat. Press Photographers Assn., 1980; citatic Kent State U., 1949; Germain G award, 1952; U. M Honor medal, 1954; spl. citation in journalism Ball Sta U., 1980; Quill and Scroll award Internat. Hon. Sc High Sch. Journalists, 1983; Photog. Adminstrs. awa for Edu. in Photography, 1983; Ind AP Broadcaste Assn. award, 1984; named to Ball State U. Journalis Hall of Fame. Mem. Press Photographers Assn. N.Y Nat. Press Photographers Assn. (founder, 1st pre chmn. bd. dirs. 1948-64), Soc. Profl. Journalists, Sign Delta Chi. Home: Carmel Calif. Died Aug. 1, 198 buried Paific Grove, Calif.

COTLOW, LEWIS NATHANIEL, explorer; b. Bklyr Feb. 5, 1898; s. Nathaniel and Lena (Greene) C.; r Charlotte Faith Messenheimer, Dec. 18, 1966. Studer George Washington U., NYU. Traveling rep. U. Shipping Bd., vis. and reporting on important harbors Far East, Near East and S. Am., 1919-21; extensi travels throughout world gathering lecture materi 1930-35; Lecturer. Author: Passport to Adventur 1942, Amazon Head-hunters, 1953, Zanzabuku, 1956, Search of the Primitive, 1966, The Twilight of the Prir itive, 1971. Served with U.S. Army, World War Served with U.S. Naval Intelligence, World War II Recipient gold medal Adventurers Club, N.Y.C., 193 Spl. Recognition award Explorers Club, 1975. Fello Royal Geog. Soc. Gt. Britain. Clubs: Ends of the Eart Explorers (gold medal 1977) (N.Y.C.), Adventure (N.Y.C.) (past pres.), Circumnavigators (N.Y.C.) (pa pres., Magellan award 1977), Dutch Treat (N.Y.C Bohemian (San Francisco); Palm Beach Round Tab (dir.); Old Port Yacht (North Palm Beach). Deceased.

COTNER, F(RANK) B(OYD), botany educator; Washingtonville, Pa., Jan. 20, 1891; s. James Dallas a Josephine (Stout) C.; m. Anita Clark, Sept. 1, 192 children: James Clark (dec.), Robert Boyd. AB, Mich., 1916, AM, 1917, PhD, 1930. Instr. biolo Bloomsburg State Normal Sch., 1911-13; grad. asst. Mich., 1916-17, 20-21, assoc. prof. botany, summ 1931; prof. botany P.R. Coll. A&M, 1919-20; asst. pr Albion (Mich.) Coll., 1921-22; asst. prof. Montana Sta Coll., Bozeman, 1922-25, assoc. prof., 1925-30, pro from 1931, dir. student health service, 1932-59, asst. dean sci. div., 1943-44, dean div. sci., 1944-57, hea dept. botany and bacteriology, 1944-57; Served bacte iol., seriological labs. U.S. Army, U.S. and Franc 1917-19; sci. officer, acting chief fundamental rsch. t Sci. and Tech. div. Supreme Command Allied Powe Tokyo, 1946-47. Contbr. articles to sci. mags. Felc AAAS; mem. Am. Mycol. Soc., Soc. Am. Bacteriol gists, Bot. Soc. Am, N.W. Assn. Secondary and High Schs. (mem. higher commn. 1952-58), Bozeman C. of (past dir.), Sigma Xi, Gamma Alpha, Phi Kappa P Phi Sigma, Elks. Home: Bozeman Mont. †

COTTON, JOHN, realtor; b. San Diego, Mar. 2 1913; s. Oscar W. and Violet (Savage) C.; m. Marga Georgia McNeil, Sept. 26, 1936; children: Lawrence M Margaret Cotton Harris, Joan Cotton Cair cross. Student, Calif. State U. at San Diego, 1931, 3 Stanford, 1931, 32, 34. Salesman O.W. Cotton Co., S Diego, 1934-46, ptnr., 1946-88; pres., chmn. bd. Cotto Ritchie Corp. (formerly Cotton Property Mgmt. C Realtors), San Diego, 1977-88; real estate broker, a praiser, counselor, property mgr. San Diego; me Pres.'s Real Estate Adv. Commn., U. Calif., 1954-5 65-72; chmn. San Diego Housing and Appeals B 1962-69, mem. 1962-88; mem. State Calif Real Esta Commn., 1967-76; lectr. in field. Recipient Bron medal City of Paris, 1975. Mem. Nat. Assn. Realtc (bd. dirs. 1955-87, exec. com. 1960-61, pres. 19 founder Legal Action Fund 1972, chmn. legal acti com. 1978, 81, counsel emeritus to com. 1984-88), Ca Assn. Realtors (bd. dirs. 1948-87, pres. 1956), S Diego Bd. Realtors (bd. dirs. 1948-87, pres. 1951), I ternat. Real Estate Fedn. (bd. dirs. Am. chpt. 1960- chmn. resoultions com. 1967-69, mem. exec. com. 19 76, chmn. fin. com. 1970-75, chmn. World Congre 1976, pres. Am. chpt. 1973, dep. world pres. 1973- chief of protocol 1981-82, Disting. Service award 19 Nat. Inst. Real Estate Mgmt. (pres. San Diego ch 1948, governing council 1948-49, regional v.p. 195 Am. Inst. Real Estate Appraisers (pres. San Diego ch 1962, governing council 1964-65, 67-68, nat. 1st v 1966, chmn. appraisal rev. com. 1967, Lifetir Membership award 1986), Am. Soc. Real Estate Cou selors (bd. govs. 1978-80), Realtors Nat. Mktg. In (governing council 1957-59), Nat. Apt. Owners As (pres. 1944-46, exec. com. 1950-52), Calif. Apt. Owne Assn. (pres. 1948-49), San Diego Apt. Owners As (pres. 1944-46), San Diego Downtown Assn. (pr 1961), Am. Arbitration Assn. (nat. panel arbitratc 1967-88), San Diego C. of C. (bd. dirs. 1970-74, v nning 1974), Lions Club. Presbyterian (elder). Died y 25, 1988.

TTON, NORRIS, U.S. senator; b. Warren, N.H., y 11, 1900; s. Henry Lang and Elizabeth (Moses) C.; Ruth Isaacs, May 11, 1927 (dec. 1978); m. Eleanor olidge Brown, 1980. Student, Phillips Exeter Acad., 6-18, Weslyan U., Middletown, Conn., 1919-21; D, George Washington U., 1927; hon. degrees, U. H., U. Vt., New Eng. Coll., Belknap Coll. Bar: N.H. 28. Ptnr. Cotton, Tesreau & Stebbins, Lebanon, H., until 1955; mem. 80th-83d U. S. Congresses from dist. N.H., 1946-54; mem. U.S. Senate, 1954-74 and weeks, 1975, mem. appropriations com., commerce n.; former pros. atty. Grafton County; justice Mcpl. Lebanon, 1939-44; former majority leader, speaker H. Ho. of Reps. Home: Lebanon N.H. Died Feb. 24, 9.

UCH, JOHN NATHANIEL, botanist; b. Prince ward County, Va., Oct. 12, 1896; s. John Henry and lie Love (Terry) C.; m. Else Dorothy Ruprecht, May 1927; children—John Philip, Sally Louise Couch oder. Student, Trinity Coll. (Duke U.), 1914-17; 3., U. N.C., 1919, A.M., 1922, Ph.D., 1924; student, Nancy (France), spring 1919, U. Wis., summer, 1923. str. botany U. N.C., 1917-18; sci. tchr. high sch. apel Hill, N.C., 1919-20, Charlotte, N.C., 1920-21; r. botany U. N.C., Chapel Hill, 1922-25; asst. prof. N.C., 1927-28, assoc. prof., 1928-32, prof., 1932-45, nan prof. botany, 1945-67, Kenan prof. botany emer-, 1967-86; NRC fellow in botany Carnegie Instn., d Spring Harbor, N.Y., 1925-26, Mo. Bot. Garden, 26-27; with Johns Hopkins Bot. Exploration, Jamaica, V.I., summer, 1926; vis. prof. Johns Hopkins, winters, 3-35, U. Va., summer, 1933; cultural exchange cialist U.S. Dept. State, India, 1961; mem. N.C. v.'s Sci. Adv. Com., 1961-64; v.p. XI Internat. Bot. ngress, Seattle, 1969; Spl. adviser to chmn. OSRD, 4. Author: (with W.C. Coker) The Gasteromycetes the Eastern United States and Canada, 1928, The nus Septobasidium, 1938; assoc. editor: Mycologia, 7-39; editor (with C.E. Bland) the Genus elomoniyces, 1985; editor Jour. Elisha Mitchell Sci. , 1946-60; Contbr. articles on bot. subjects to profl. rs. Served with U.S. Army, 1918-19. Recipient lker grand prize Boston Soc. Natural History, 1939; ritorious Tchrs. award Assn. Southeastern Biologists, 4; certificate of merit Bot. Soc. Am., 1956; first N.C. rd in sci., 1964. Fellow A.A.A.S. (v.p., chmn. any sect. 1962); mem. Nat. Acad. Sci. India (hon. mem.), Bot. Soc. Am. (chmn. Southeastern section 1), Am. Mycol. Soc. (pres. 1943), Nat. Acad. Sci. S.A.), Am. Mosquito Control Assn., N.C. Acad. Sci. es. 1946-47, Jefferson award, Poteat medal 1937), ian Phytopath. Soc., Elisha Mitchell Sci. Soc. (pres. 7-38), Sigma Xi. Democrat. Baptist. Home: Chapel N.C. Died Dec. 16, 1986; buried Chapel Hill netery.

ULETTE, HENRI ANTHONY, English educator, hor; b. Los Angeles, Nov. 11, 1927; s. Robert Roger Geneveive (O'Reilly) C.; m. Jacqueline Meredith, . 27, 1950. BA, Los Angeles State Coll., 1952; A, U. Iowa, 1954, PhD, 1959. Instr. Writers Work-p, U. Iowa, 1957-59; mem. faculty Calif. State U., Angeles, 1959-88; then prof. English Calif. State U.; try readings at univs. and museums. Author: The of the Secret Agents, 1966, The Family ldschmitt, 1971; editor: (with Philip Levine) aracter and Crisis, 1966, The Unstrung Lyre, 1971. ved with AUS, 1945-46. Decorated Order of Black se (Poland); recipient Lamont poetry award Acad. . Poets, 1965, James D. Phelan award for poetry, 6. Mem. Am. Fedn. Tchrs., PEN. Democrat. me: Pasadena Calif. Died Mar. 26, 1988.

ULTER, VICTOR ALDINE, chemist; b. Newton, ., July 15, 1892; s. John Summey and Sarah hronia (Herman) C.; m. Magaret McLean, Aug. 16, 6. BS, U. N.C., 1913, MS, 1914, PhD, 1916; post-d., Cambridge U., Eng., 1919, Columbia U., summer 7. Instr. in chemistry U. N.C., 1916-17; rsch. mist Armstrong Cork Co., Pitts., 1917; with U. ss., from 1920, asst. prof. chemistry, 1920-25, assoc. f. chemistry, 1925-26, prof. phys. chemistry, 1926-47, f. chemistry, from 1947, dean Coll. of Liberal Arts, 6-57, head dept. chemistry, 1946-47. Contbr. to sci. rs. 1st lt. to capt. U.S. Army, 1917-19; in Med. ps, Engrs. and Chem. Warfare Svc.; assigned as asst. gas officer, 39th Div., 77th Div., 4th Corps and div. officer, 90th Div.; capt. Chem. Warfare Svc., U.S. . Mem. Am. Chem. Soc., Am. Legion, Res. Officers n., NRA, Masons, Phi Beta Kappa, Sigma Xi, ha Chi Sigma. Demiocrat. Presbyterian. Home: ord Miss. †

UPER, EDGAR WILLIAMS, banker; b. Boonville, ., Feb. 14, 1899; s. Walter T. and Ruth D. (Wil-ns) C.; m. Esther H. Watrous, Sept. 24, 1921; chil-n: Richard W., Katharine Couper Watrous. AB, milton Coll., 1920, LLD, 1953; LHD, Manhattan l., 1962; LLD, Hofstra U., 1963, L.I. U., 1964, twick Coll., 1965, Columbia U., 1968; LittD, Elmira l., 1967; LLD, Colgate U., 1969. Ofcl. Couper-Ack-an-Sampson Inc. (and predecessor firm), 1920-53; ., bd. dirs. 1st Nat. Bank Binghampton (N.Y.), 4-55; pres., bd. dirs. 1st City Nat. Bank Binghampton, 1955-64, chmn. bd. dirs., 1964-70, dir. emeritus, 1970-88; dir. emeritus N.Y. State Electric and Gas Corp. Mem. bd. regents N.Y. State Ednl. Dept., 1951-68, vice chancellor, 1957-61, chancellor, 1961-68; trustee Hampton Coll., 1937-61, 68-69, trustee emeritus, 1969—. Recipient Alfred E. Smith award N.Y. State Tchrs. Assn., 1962. Home: Binghampton N.Y. Died Jan. 17, 1988.

COUPER, LOUISE PETTIGREW, librarian; b. Portland, Oreg., Aug. 17, 1892; d. Robert and Mary A. (Webster) Pettigrew; m. Samuel Couper, Aug. 26, 1919 (dec. Dec. 18, 1972); children: Robert W.S. (dec.), Jack Edward (dec.). RN, Good Samaritan Hosp. Nurses Tng. Sch., 1910; student, Columbia U., 1915-16. Insdl. nurse 1914-15; chief clk. Md. Vets. Commn., 1932-40; tchr. Colgate Sch., Balt. County, 1944-46; supr. elections for Balt. County 1946-50; librarian State of Md., 1950-68. Chairperson Balt. County dist. Am. Cance Soc., from 1948; mem. Human Relations Commn., from 1969, later commr. Served as nurse Am. Expeditionary Forces, 1918-19. Recipient citation Med. and Surg. Faculty State Md., citation for community service Md. Gov., citation Am. Cancer Soc. Mem. Navy Mothers, Daughters Am. (past pres. Balt.), Bus. and Profl. Women's Club, Alexander Hamilton Club (pres. Balt.), Dundalk Club (Md.), Consolidated Club (pres.). Home: Baltimore Md. Deceased.

COURNAND, ANDRE F., physician; b. Paris, France, Sept. 24, 1895; came to U.S., 1930, naturalized, 1941; s. Jules and Marguerite (Weber) C.; m. Sibylle Blumer (dec. 1959); children: Muriel, Marie-Eve, Marie Claire; m. Ruth Fabian, 1963 (dec. 1973); m. Beatrice Bishop Berle, 1975. BA, Sorbonne U., Paris, 1913, PCB in Sci, 1914; MD, U. Paris, 1930; honorary doctorate, U. Strasbourg, 1957, U. Lyon, 1958, U. Brussels, 1959, U. Pisa, 1960, Columbia U., 1965, U. Brazil, 1965, U. Nancy, 1969; DSc (hon.), U. Birmingham, 1961; D.Sc., Gustavus Adolphus Coll., 1963. Prof. emeritus medicine Coll. Phys. & Surg., Columbia. Served with French Army, 1915-19. Decorated Croix de Guerre (France); recipient Laureate (silver medal), faculty medicine U. Paris; Andrea Retzius silver medal Swedish Soc. Internal Medicine; Lasker award USPHS; winner (with Dr. Dickinson W. Richards and Dr. Werner Forssman) of 1956 Nobel Prize in medicine and physiology; recipient Jiminez Diaz prize, 1970. Fellow Royal Soc. Medicine; mem. Nat. Acad. Scis. U.S.A., de l'Academie Nationale de Medecine (fgn.) (France), Academie Royale de Medecine de Belgique, Am. Physiol. Soc., Assn. Am. Physicians, Brit. Cardiac Soc., Swedish Soc., Internal Medicine, Soc. Medicale Hopitaux de Paris, Academie des Sciences, Institut de France (fgn. mem.). Clubs: Century Assn, Am. Alpine. Home: New York N.Y. Died Feb. 19, 1988; buried Great Barrington Cemetery.

COURTRIGHT, HERNANDO, hotel executive; b. Coeur d'Alene, Idaho, 1904; m. 3d, Marcelle Eva Llaca Cuillery; children: Hernando Patrick, DeVigne Francois, Carina Kelley. Propr. Beverly Wilshire Hotel; then chmn. bd. Courtright Corp.; chmn. bd., chief exec. officer El Camino-Rodeo Corp.; bd. dirs. United Financial Corp. Bd. regents St. John's Hosp. Mem. Calif. Vintage Wine, So. Calif. Bordeaux Soc. (co-maitre), Beverly Hills Wine and Food Soc. (co-chmn.), Chevaliers du Tastevin Calif. (founder, grand officer), Escoffier, Chaine des Rotisseurs, L'Ordre de Grand Coteaux. Home: Beverly Hills Calif. Died Jan. 22, 1986.

COUSINS, FRANK, British government official; b. Bulwell, Eng., Sept. 8, 1904; m. Annie Elizabeth Judd, 1930. Student, King Edward Sch., Doncaster, Eng. Organizer road transp. sect. T.W.G.U., 1938, nat. officer sect., 1944, nat. sec. sect., 1948, asst. gen. sec. union, 1955; mem. gen. coun. Trades Union Congress; former mem. Parliament; mem. Privy Coun., from 1964, minister tech., 1964-66; mem. Brit. Joint Consultative Coun., 1955-63; minister labour Nat. Joint Adv. Coun., 1956-64, 66-69; mem. exec. coun. Internat. Transp. Workers Fedn., 1956-64, pres., 1958-60, 62-64; mem. Colonial Labour Adv. Com., 1957-62, London Travel Com., 1958-60, Coun. Sci. and Indsl. Research, 1960-66; mem. adv. coun. Export Guarantee Dept., 1962; mem. Nat. Econ. Devel. Coun., 1962-69. Mem. bd. govs. Nat. Inst. Econ. and Social Research. Mem. Inst. Transp., Polit. Economy Club. Home: Surrey England. Died June 12, 1986.

COUSINS, WILLIAM E., archbishop; b. Chgo., Aug. 20, 1902; s. Norman B. and Theresa (Hartery) C. Student, Quigley Prep. Sem., 1916-21; MA, St. Mary of the Lake Sem., 1927; LLD (hon.), DePaul U. Ordained priest Roman Cath. Ch., 1927. Asst. St. Bernard's parish, Chgo., 1927-32, Holy Name Cathedral, Chgo., 1932-33; superior Diocesan Mission Band, 1933-46; pastor St. Columbanis Ch., Chgo., 1946-52; consecrated aux. bishop of Chgo. 1949-52; bishop of Peoria Ill., 1952-59; archbishop of Milw. from 1959, ret.; epsic. chmn. social action dept. Nat. Cath. Welfare Conf., 1961; chmn. Nat. Office for Decent Lit.; mem. Second Vatican Council, Rome. Home: Milwaukee WI Died Sept. 14, 1988, buried St. John The Evangelist Cathedral, Milw.

COUSLEY, PAUL SPARKS, newspaper publisher; b. Alton, Ill., Feb. 2, 1908; s. Paul Bliss and Mary Esther (Sparks) C.; m. Hope Jackson, Sept. 17, 1932; 1 dau., Hope Cousley Apple. BS in Journailism, U. Ill., 1929. Reporter Alton Telegraph, 1924-28, corr., editor, 1929-35, wire editor, 1935-42, asst. gen. mgr., 1942-47, editor, 1947-60, then pub. Bd. dirs. Assn. Commerce, Alton; mem. Ill. Mississippi River Scenic Hwy. Commn. Home: Alton Ill. Died Apr. 6, 1986.

COVELL, WILLIAM EDWARD RAAB, foreign business consultant; b. Washington, Nov. 29, 1892; s. Luther and Lefa Ann (Ransom) C.; m. Vera Henshaw, July 18, 1917 (dec. Dec. 1948); 1 child, Beverly Covell Ferguson; m. 2d, Kathleen Fraley Geitner, Apr. 8, 1951 (dec. Nov. 1956); m. 3d, Elva McFarlin Van Meter, Mar. 26, 1957. BS, U.S. Mil. Acad., 1915; BSCE, MIT, 1923; student, Army Engring. Sch., 1919-20, Command and Gen. Staff Sch., 1928-30. Commd. 2d lt. U.S. Army Corps of Engrs., 1915, promoted through grades to lt. col., 1936; comdg. officer 2d Engr. Regt., 2d Div., Am. Expeditionary Force, 1918; with U.S. Engrs., 1918-40; gen. mgr. and dir. Crossett-Ark. Cos., 1940-41; recalled to active duty June 1, 1941, promoted to brig. gen., 1943; mem. Construction div. Office of Q.M. Gen., 1941-42; div. engr. Caribbean Div., 1942-43; promoted to maj. gen. 1943; dir. fuels and lubricants Office of Q.M. Gen., 1943-45; comdg. gen. Services of Supply, China-Burma-India, 1943-45; retired 1946; ptnr. Parsons, Brinckerhoff, Hall & MacDonald, N.Y.C., 1946-50, cons. ptnr., from 1950; dir. gen. Damon, Dinerman, & Cia, S.A., Buenos Aires, 1948-52. Term mem. of corp. MIT, 1937-42. Decorated D.S.M. with oak leaf cluster; Hon. Companion Most Eminent Order of Indian Empire (C.I.E.); voted hon. citizen of Johnstown, Pa., 1940. Mem. Hurlingham Club, Am. Club (Buenos Aires), Monterey Peninsula Country Club (Pebble Beach, Calif.), Masons. Home: Carmel Calif. †

COVER, JOHN HIGSON, economist, statistician; b. Johnstown, Pa., Oct. 29, 1891; s. Charles Blair and Carrie Louise (Higson) C.; m. Mary Leyman, Dec. 16, 1938; children from previous marriage: Evlyn June, John Higson. Student, Ohio State U., 1911-12; BS, Columbia U., 1915, AM, 1919, PhD, 1927. Spl. attaché Am. Embassy, Vienna, Austria, 1915-16; with U.S. Food Adminstrn., Washington, 1917-18; instr. Columbia U., N.Y.C., 1921-23; prof. Colo. Coll., 1923-24; prof., dir. Bur. Bus. and Social Rsch. U. Denver, 1924-27; prof., dir. Bur. Bus. Rsch. U. Pitts., 1927-30; prof. U. Chgo., 1928-40; on leave of absence, with Com. on Govt. Stats. and Info. Service, Washington, 1933, U.S. Dept. Commerce, 1939; cons. economist 1940-41; economist, exec. officer Lend-Lease Adminstrn., Dept. State, UNRRA, Fgn. Econ. Adminstrn., Dept. Commerce, 1942-46; dir. Bur. Bus. and Econ. Rsch., U. Md., 1946-61; UN econ. planning expert to govts. of Syria, 1962-63, Barbados, 1964-65; head bus. adminstrn. dept. Army Univ. Ctr., Biarritz, France, 1945-46; vis. lectr. U. Rotterdam, 1945; Fulbright lectr. rsch. and study of planning, India, 1952-53; dir. South Asia Project, U. Calif., 1955-56; chmn. bd. Inst. on World Orgn. Author: Business and Personal Failure and Readjustment in Chicago, 1933, Retail Price Behavior, 1935, Asia is Our Business, 1955, India in World Affairs, 1957, Business Research, 1941, Economic Planning and Policies in Syria, 1963, Economic Procedural and Policy Papers for Barbados, 1965, New Industries: Analytical Consideration, 1965, Location Factors and Criteria, 1965; co-author: Some Problems of Small Business, 1941, Regulation of Economic Activities in Foreign Countries, 1941, Economy of India, 1956, Economy of Nepal, 1956, also titles under Studies in Business and Economics, 1947-61. Fellow emeritus AAAS; mem. Am. Econ. Assn., Am. Stats. Assn., Econometric Soc., Nat. Assn. Am. Composers and Condrs. (v.p. Washington chpt. 1959-61), Nat. Parks and Conservation Assn. (sec. 1960-72, trustee from 1960), Omicron Delta Gamma, Alpha Kappa Psi, Delta Upsilon. Home: Yellow Springs Ohio. Deceased.

COVERT, FRANK MANNING, lawyer, corporate executive; b. Canning, N.S., Can., Jan. 13, 1908; s. Archibald Menzies and Minnie Alma (Clarke) C.; m. Mary Louise Covert, Aug. 25, 1934; children: Michael, Susan, Peter, Sally. BA, Dalhousie U., 1927, LLB, 1929. Bar: N.S. 1930. Practice in Halifax, N.S., Can., 1930-40, 45-87; sr. ptnr. Stewart, MacKeen & Covert, Halifax, N.S., Can., 1963-87; asst. gen. counsel Dept. Munitions and Supply, 1940-42; pres. Ben's Holdings, Ltd., 1956-87; chmn. bd. Maritime Paper Products Ltd., 1959-87; bd. dirs. Bowater Mersey Paper Co. Ltd., Eastern Tel. & Tel. Co., Minas Basin Pulp & Power Co. Ltd., Can. Keyes Fibre Co. Ltd., Nat. Sea Products Ltd. With RCAF, 1942-45. Decorated D.F.C., Order Brit. Empire, officer Order of Cordoba. Home: Halifax, N.S. Canada. Died Nov. 1, 1987; buried Hunt's Point, N.S.

COVINGTON, JAMES EDWARD, business executive; b. Reidsville, Rockingham County, N.C., Apr. 21, 1891; s. James F. and Elizabeth (Oliver) C.; m. Annie Marshall James, Sept. 22, 1928; children: Annie Wilson, Elizabeth Oliver, James Edward. Student, pub. schs. N.C. With Brit. Am. Tobacco Co., 1917-22; pres. Universal Leaf Tobacco Co. of China, Fed., Inc. 1926-40, chmn. bd., 1940-59; exec. v.p., then bd. dirs. Universal Leaf Tobacco Co.; v.p. Can. Leaf Tobacco Co., Ltd., Chatham, Ont.; bd. dirs. J.P. Taylor Col, Southwestern Tobacco Co. Bd. dirs. Far-East Am. Coun. Commerce and Industry, N.Y.C. Mem. Country

Club Va., Commonwealth Club, Rotunda Club (Richmond), Farmington Country Club (Charlottesville, Va.). Presbyterian. Home: Martinsville Va. †

COWAN, LESLIE, business executive; b. Sweetwater, Tex., Aug. 28, 1888; s. William H. and Elizabeth (Hudson) C.; m. Mary Chambers, Aug. 13, 1923; 1 child, Frances. BS, U. Mo., 1913. Registered profl. engr., Mo., Tex. Registrar U. Mo., Columbia, 1917-18, exec. sec. to pres., 1918-21, sec. univ. bd. curators, 1920-54, v.p. charge bus. ops., 1944-56, v.p. emeritus, from 1957, appraiser univ. lands, 1956-58; pvt. real estate operato; constrn. supt. Ward Investment Co., Kansas City, Mo., 1925-26. Mem. staff Council Nat. Def., Washington, 1917-18; asst. to dir. fgn. ops. ARC, Athens, Greece, 1921-22; mem. joint nat. com. bus. officers of Assn. Land-Grant Colls. and Univs., 1949-55. Decorated Cross of Chevalier of Redeemer of Greece, King of Greece, 1923. Mem. NSPE, Mo. Soc. Profl. Engrs. (pres. cen. chpt. 1959-60, dir. 1960-61), Rex. Soc. Profl. Engrs., Mo. Sch. Mines Alumni Assn., State Hist. Soc. Mo. Home: Columbia Mo. †

COWAN, ROBERT GEORGE, banker; b. Lake Linden, Mich., Feb. 25, 1905; s. William Robert and May Agnes (Harrison) C.; m. Hazel Witherall Damon, May 29, 1930. Student, Phillips Exeter Acad., MIT; BS, NYU, 1930; grad., Grad. Sch. Banking, Am. Bankers Assn., 1940; LLD, Upsala Coll., 1955. Statistician rsch. dept., bank examiner, chief analysis div. of bank exams. div. Fed. Res. Bank N.Y., 1927-38; cashier Nat. Newark & Essex Banking Co., Newark, 1938-40, pres., dir., from 1940; chmn. Nat. Newark & Essex Bank, 1962-70; former mgr. Howard Savs. Inst. Past pres. Greater Newark Devel. Coun.; past trustee Marcus L. Ward Home, Newark Mus., Victoria Found. Mem. N.J. C. of C. (past dir.), Essex Club, Somerset Hills Country Club. Home: Bernardsville N.J. Died Apr. 25, 1985.

COWGILL, CLINTON HARRIMAN, architect; b. Sterling, Kans., Sept. 6, 1899; s. Elias Branson and Rena (Harriman) C.; m. Mabel Claire Huey, Jan. 19, 1918. Student, Washburn Coll., Topeka, Kans., 1910-11; BArch, U. Ill., 1916, MArch, 1923. Instr. architecture Okla. A&M Coll., 1916-17; office mgr. Reinhart and Donovan Co., contractors, Oklahoma City, 1917-18; designer Shepard and Wiser, architects, Kansas City, Mo., 1918-19; assoc. prof. archtl. engring. Iowa State Coll., 1920-28; prof. archtl. engring. Va. Poly. Inst., from 1928, head dept., 1928-56; mem. Va. State Bd. for Exam. and Cert. Profl. Engrs., Architects and Land Surveyors, 1932-48, v.p., 1933, pres., 1934-37; pres. nat. council Nat. Archtl. Accrediting Bd., 1949-52, mem. commn. to survey archtl. edn. and registration; mem. rsch. com. Va. State Bd. Edn. Author: Architectural Practice: Building for Investment; editor AIA Handbook of Archtl. Practice, from 1956. Fellow AIA; mem. Cosmos Club, Shriners, Alpha Rho Chi, Phi Kappa Phi. Home: Washington D.C. †

COWGILL, DONALD OLEN, sociologist, educator; b. Wood River, Nebr., May 10, 1911; s. Olen and Gertrude (Quisenberry) C.; m. Mary Catherine Strain, Sept. 1, 1935; children—Martha Jane Cowgill Burns, Donald Franklin, Catha Jean Cowgill Overstreet. A.B. with high honors in spl. field, Park Coll., 1933; A.M. (Van Blarcom scholar 1934-35, U. fellow 1935-36), Washington U., 1935; Ph.D. (George Leib Harrison fellow), U. Pa., 1940; postgrad., U. Minn., summer 1941, U. Mo., 1942-43. Asst. prof. sociology Drury Coll., 1937-40, assoc. prof., head dept. sociology, 1940-42, dean men, dir. counseling, 1941-42; sr. research analyst Mo. Social Security Commn., 1942-43; research asst. to v.p. Studebaker Corp., 1943-45; prof., head dept. sociology Drake U., 1945-46, Wichita State U., 1946-67; prof. U. Mo., Columbia, 1967-81; chmn. depts. sociology and rural sociology U. Mo., 1970-72; vis. prof. U. Mo., summers 1948, 66; lectr. Mindolo Ecumenical Ctr., Kitwe, Zambia, summer 1962; Fulbright lectr. Chiengmai U., Thailand, 1964-65; resident cons. Mahidol U., Thailand, 1968-69; research cons. Wichita Community Planning Council, 1946-1967. Author: Residential Mobility of An Urban Population, 1935, Mobile Homes: A Study of Trailer Life, 1941, Methodology of Planning Census Tracts, 1949, Wichita Street Index for Census Tracts, 1951, Religious Preferences of the Families of Wichita, 1958, People of Wichita, 1960, Aging and Modernization, 1972, Aging Around the World, 1986; author articles on population, urban sociology, social gerontology. Inter-Univ. Council on Aging fellow, summer 1959; Midwest Council on Aging fellow, summer 1961. Fellow Am. Sociol. Assn., Gerontol. Soc.; mem. Population Assn. Am., Midwest Sociol. Soc. (pres. 1952-53), Midwest Council for Social Research on Aging (pres. 1962-64), Pi Kappa Delta, Alpha Kappa Delta. Home: Columbia Mo. Died Apr. 22, 1987; buried Parkville, Mo.

COWLES, DONALD HARRY, army officer; b. Westfield, Mass., Sept. 10, 1917; s. Harry Andrew and Edna (Quance) C.; m. Lois Rogers Macomber, Apr. 25, 1942; children: Donald Thurston, Constance Hollister. BS, U. Mass., 1939; MF, Yale U., 1941; grad., Army Armor Sch., 1948, Command and Gen. Staff Coll., 1952, Army War Coll., 1958. Commd. 2d lt. U.S. Army, 1942, advanced through grades to lt. gen., 1972; with 4th Armored Div., 1942-45; comdr. 81st Reconnaissance Bn. and 1st Tank Bn., 1st Armored Div., 1952-54; mem. staff Dept. Army, 1954-57, 65-66, Orgn. Joint Chiefs of Staff, 1966-67, Office Sec. of Def., 1967-68; comdr. 3d Cavalry Regt., 1961-63, 3d Armored Div., 1968-69; asst. chief staff ops. U.S. Mil. Assistance Command Vietnam, 1970-71, chief staff, 1971-72; dep. chief staff mil. ops. Dept. Army, 1972-75; with BDM Corp. (now div. Ford Motor Co.), McLean, Va., from 1975. Decorated Silver Star, Legion of Merit, Bronze Star, D.S.M. Mem. Lambda Chi Alpha. Episcopalian. Home: Alexandria Va. Died Feb. 4, 1989.

COWPERTHWAITE, LOWERY LEROY, speech educator; b. Princeton, Kans., Mar. 22, 1917; s. Lowery Isaac and Lynne Bondell (Fish) C.; m. Margaret Elizabeth Farmer, Aug. 11, 1949; children: Thomas, Joseph. BA, Ottawa (Kans.) U., 1939; MA, U. Iowa, 1946, PhD, 1950. Tchr. high schs. Kans., 1939-42; instr. speech U. Iowa, 1948-49; assoc. prof. speech Richmond Area U. Ctr., 1949-54; prof. speech, dir. sch. speech Kent (Ohio) State U., 1954-85; co-founder Va. Speech and Drama Assn., 1950, pres., 1953. Contbr. articles to profl. jours., chpts. to books. Served with USAAF, World War II. Mem. Speech Communication Assn., Assn. for Communications Adminstrn., Cen. States Speech Assn., Speech Communication Ohio, Sigma Chi, Pi Kappa Delta, Delta Sigma Rho, Tau Kappa Alpha, Alpha Psi Omega, Omicron Delta Kappa. Episcopalian. Lodge: Masons. Home: Kent Ohio. Died Oct. 19, 1985; buried Standing Rock Cemetery, Kent, Ohio.

COX, AINSLEE, conductor; b. Big Spring, Tex., June 22, 1936; s. William Arthur and Mardilla (Taylor) C. Student, Westminster Choir Coll., 1953-57; B. Mus., U. Tex., 1959, M. Music in Composition, 1960. Condr. ch. choirs, choral festivals Tex., N.J., 1950-62; prof. music S.W. Tex. State Coll., San Marcos, 1960-62; guest condr. Goldman Band, N.Y.C., 1968; asst. condr. Goldman Band, 1969, asso. condr., 1970-74, co-condr., 1975-79, music dir., 1980—; orchestral, opera condr. Spoleto Festival, 1965; asst. condr. Am. Symphony Orch., 1967-68, asso. condr., 1968-72; guest condr., rec. artist U.S., Europe, from 1970; asst. condr. N.Y. Philharm. Orch., 1973-75; music. dir., condr. Okla. Symphony Orch., Oklahoma City, 1974-78, Chamber Opera Theatre of N.Y., 1980-82; lectr. in field, also cons. Mem. adv. panel Okla. Arts and Humanities Council, 1975-78. Composer choral, organ works.; contbg. editor: Music Jour. mag., from 1963. Recipient ASCAP award for service to contemporary music, 1975, 76, 77, 78. Mem. Condrs. Guild Pi Kappa Lambda. Home: New York N.Y. Died Sept. 5, 1988; interred Myrtle Cemetery, Ennis, Tex.

COX, ALLAN V., geophysicist, educator, former university dean; b. Santa Ana, Calif., Dec. 17, 1926; s. Vernon D. and Hilda (Schultz) C. B.S., U. Calif., 1955, M.A., 1957, Ph.D., 1959. Geol. field asst. U.S. Geol. Survey, Alaska, 1950, 51,54; geophysicist U.S. Geol. Survey, Menlo Park, Calif., 1959-87; research assoc. Stanford, 1962-67, prof. geophysics, 1967-87; dean Stanford (Sch. Earth Sci.), 1979-87. Mem. Nat. Acad. Sci., Am. Acad. Arts and Scis., Geol. Soc. Am., Am. Philos. Soc., Am. Geophys. Union, Am. Assn. Petroleum Geologists, AAAS, Sigma Xi. Home: Woodside Calif. Died Jan. 27, 1987; cremated.

COX, ALLYN, mural painter; b. N.Y.C., June 5, 1896; s. Kenyon and Louise H. (King) C.; m. Ethel H. Potter, Apr. 30, 1927. Student, N.A.D., 1911-16, Art Students League N.Y., 1915-16; fellowship in painting, Am. Acad. in Rome, 1916-20. Mural painter 1921—; painter mem. N.Y.C. Art Commn., 1952-57; tchr. Art Students League, Nat. Acad. Design.; lectr. in field. Prin. works include ceilings W.A. Clark Jr. Library, Los Angeles, 1924-27; panels Law Bldg., U. Va., 1930-34; decorations Nat. City Co., N.Y., 1928, Continential Bank, 1932, Cosmopolitan Club, N.Y.C., 1940, S.S. America, 1940; fresco-frieze Rotunda Nat. Capitol, Washington, 1952, repaired and restored ceiling frescom 1959; altar pieces and other decorations for the armed forces, 1942-44; murals Guaranty Trust Co., N.Y.C., 1946; George Washington Masonic Meml., Alexandria, 1948-56; portrait Senate Reception Room, Nat. Capitol, 1958; mosaics and inlaid stone panels Am. Cemetery, Luxembourg, 1960; wall and ceiling murals east corridor House Wing, 1974; master plan for decorating remaining House corridors, 1975, decoration of central corridor, 1979; installed series of 3 mosaics for Gen. U.S. Grant Nat. Meml., N.Y.C.; represented in Nat. Collection Fine Arts, Washington. Trustee Abbey Fund; bd. dirs. Ernest Peixotto Meml. Fund. Served as 1st lt. A.R.C., Italy, 1918. Recipient Gold Medal of Honor for mural paintings Archtl. League N.Y., 1954, Triennial gold medal for achievement in the arts Gen. Grand chpt. Royal Arch Masons U.S., 1966. Fellow Am. Acad. in Rome; mem. N.A.D., Am. Artists Profl. League, Nat. Soc. Mural Painters (hon. pres.), Fine Arts Fedn. N.Y., Century Assn. Club, Cosmos Club. Home: New York N.Y. Died Sept. 26, 1982.

COX, EDWARD HILL, chemist; b. Richmond, Ind., May 3, 1892; s. Jefferson Drius and Mary Bee (Kepler) C.; m. N. Jane Boyd, June 11, 1928. BS, Earlham Coll., 1914; MS, U. Louisville, 1916; AM, Harvard U., 1920; ScD, U. Geneva, Switzerland, 1922; postdoctoral study, U. Berlin, 1923; Dr. Honoris Causa, U. Montpellier, France, 1955. Asst. U. Louisville, 1914-16, U. 1916-17; asst. prof. Oberlin Coll., 1917-19; chief chem Sharp & Dohme, 1923-26; mem. faculty Swarthm (Pa.) Coll., from 1926, Edmund Allen prof., head de chemistry, from 1949; Carl Schurz fellow, Germa 1933-34; Fulbright lectureship, France, 1952, U. C laslongkorn, Thailand, 1958; tech. cons. Air Fo London, Paris, 1944-45; cons. Bur. Ordnance, US from 1948; edn. cons. NSF, 1957-58. Contbr. artic tech. publs. Sci. attaché Am. Embassy, Paris, fr 1950. Lt., C.W.S., U.S. Army, 1917-18. Fellow N Acad. Sci.; mem. Am. Chem. Soc. (councillor 1945-5 Home: San Francisco Calif. †

COX, GARDNER, artist; b. Holyoke, Mass., Jan. 1906; s. Allen Howard and Katherine Gilbert (Abb C.; m. Phyllis Moyra Byrne, Dec. 3, 1937; childr Benjamin, Katherine Gilbert Abbot (dec.), James Byr Phyllis Byrne. Student, Art Students League, N.Y 1924, Harvard U., 1924-27, Boston Mus. Sch., 1928- MIT, 1929-31; DFA(posthumously), Tufts U., 198 head dept. painting Boston Mus. Fine Arts Sch., 19 55; artist-in-residence Am. Acad. in Rome, 1961; chr Blanche Colman Award Jury, 1961-84; exec. cc Boston Arts Festival, 1959-67; mem. Mass. Fine A Commn., 1965-88. Work exhibited, Carnegie Intern 1941, Va. Mus. Fine Arts, 1946, 1948, Art Inst. Chg 1948, 49, 51, Met. Mus. Art, 1950, U. Ill., 1950-51, In Contemporary Art, Boston, 1953, one-man sho Farnsworth Mus., Rockland, Maine, 1956, Newp (R.I.) Art Assn., 1966, Corcoran Gallery, Washingt 1975, Boston Athenaeum, 1981; represented perman collections, Boston Mus. Fine Arts, Fogg M Harvard U., Addison Gallery, Andover, Mass., W sworth Atheneum, Hartford, Conn., Yale U., Welles Coll., Wabash Coll., MIT, Mt. Holyoke Coll., Bos Athenaeum, Santa Barbara (Calif.) Art Mus., De State, Dept. Army, Dept. Def., Dept. Labor, Dept. Force, Dept. Transp., FAA, Middlebury Coll., N Gallery Washington, Nat. Portrait Gallery, Collection U.S. Supreme Ct., Brandeis U., Princeton U., U.S. Appeals, Boston, State House, Boston, permanent lections, Clark Art Inst., Williamstown, Mass., othe Trustee Am. Acad. in Rome, 1962-88, St. Gaud Meml., Cornish, N.H., 1959-88. Served with AUS, 19 45. Recipient M.V. Kohnstamm prize Am. Exh Water Colors, Art Inst. Chgo., 1949, Norman W Harris Bronze medal 60th Ann. Am. Exhibit, 195 Mem. Am. Acad. Arts and Scis., Nat. Inst. Arts Letters, NAD (academician), Phi Beta Kappa (hon Clubs: Tavern (Boston), St. Botolph (Boston); Cent (N.Y.C.). Home: Cambridge Mass. Died Jan. 14, 19 buried Mt. Auburn Cemetery, Cambridge, Mass.

COX, JAMES CHARLES, librarian; b. Chgo., July 1927; s. Ora Clay and Maude Emily (White) C.; Dorothy Jean Watters, Aug. 22, 1953. Ph.B., Loy U., Chgo., 1950, postgrad., 1952-53; M.A. in Rosary Coll., River Forest, Ill., 1956; postgrad., Chgo., 1971-72. Mem. faculty Loyola U., Chgo., 19 87; asst. librarian Loyola U. (univ. library at L Towers), 1953-55; librarian Loyola U. (Sch. Dentist 1955-56; asst. librarian univ. Loyola U. (Cud Library), 1956-58, assoc. librarian univ. libraries, 19 59, dir. libraries, 1959-71; asst. librarian Lewis Tow Library, Loyola U., Chgo., 1972-74; chief libra Loyola U. Med. Center, 1974-85, on leave, 1985-8 Contbr. articles to profl. jours. Served with USN 1945-46, 50-52. Mem. ALA, Cath. Library As (chmn. Ill. 1962-63, program chmn. 1961-63, chr cataloging and classification sect. 1965-67, mem. e bd. 1967-73, pres. 1975-77), Bibliog. Soc. Am., Bibli Soc. (London). Roman Catholic. Home: Chicago Died July 31, 1987; buried All St.'s Cemetery, Plaines, Ill.

COX, JOHN PAUL, astrophysicist, educator; b. Myers, Fla., Nov. 4, 1926; s. James B. and Bess (Tollette) C.; m. Jane B. Blizard-Cox, July 1972. Ind. U., 1949, MS, 1950, PhD, 1954. Mem. facu Cornell U., 1954-62; vis. scientist Courant Inst. M Scis., NYU, N.Y.C., 1962-63; vis. fellow Joint Inst. L Astrophysics, Boulder, Colo., 1963; assoc. prof. trophysics U. Colo., Boulder, 1963-65, prof., 1965- vis. prof. dept. math. Monash U., Melbourne, Austra 1972; cons. Smithsonian Astrophys. Obs., Cambrid Mass., 1957, 59, 60, Los Almos Sci. Lab., 1960-84; a engr. Pratt & Whitney Aircraft Corp., East Hartfo Conn., 1958. Mem. Am. Phys. Soc., Am. Astron. S N.Y. Acad. Scis., Colo.-Wyo. Acad. Scis., Internat. tron. Union, Royal Astron. Soc., Astron. Soc. Pac Sigma Xi, Phi Eta Sigma. Home: Boulder Colo. D Aug. 18, 1984; buried Boulder, Colo.

COX, WILLIAM HAROLD, judge; b. Indian Miss., June 23, 1901; s. Adam Charles and Lillie Em (Ray) C.; m. Edwina Berry, June 30, 1927; c dren—William Harold, Joanne Cox Bellenger. B LL.B., U. Miss., 1924. Bar: Miss. bar 1924. Practi in Jackson, 1924-61; U.S. dist. judge So. Dist. M 1961-88, chief judge, 1962-71, sr. judge; mem. Miss. Bar Admissions, 1932-36. Chmn. Hinds Cou Democratic Exec. Com., 1950-61, presdl. elector, 19 Home: Jackson Miss. Died Feb. 25, 1988.

CRABBÉ, PIERRE, chemist, educator; b. Bruss Dec. 29, 1928; s. Francois and Simone (Doutreligne) m. Lucie de Guchteneere, Apr. 25, 1956; child manuel, Marie-Noelle, Veronique. Tech. Chem. gr., Institut Meurice-Chimie, Brussels, 1952; Chimie, U. Paris, 1954; D.Sc., U. Strasbourg, 1967. tr. Inst. Meurice-Chimie, Brussels, 1959-60; dir. m. research Syntex S.A., Mexico City, 1964-73; prof. Iberoamericana, Mexico City, 1962-73, U. Nacional tonoma Mex., 1965-74; hon. prof. Inst. Tech. nterrey, Mex., from 1968; vis. prof. Ga. Inst. Tech., anta, 1968; prof. U. Grenoble, France, 1973-79; f., chmn. dept. chemistry U. Mo., Columbia, from '9; cons. WHO, UNESCO.; sec. gen. Internat. Orgn. Chem. Scis. in Devel., 1981-85; dir. IOCD, from 5. Author: (with G. Ourisson, O. Rodig) Tetracyclic terpenes, 1964, Optical Rotatory Dispersion and cular Dichroism, 1965, Introduction to Chiroptical thods, 1972, Prostaglandin Research, 1977; contbr. cles to profl. jours. Mem. Mexican Acad. Sci., N.Y. ad. Scis., Am. Chem. Soc., Belgian Chem. Soc., em. Soc. (London). Deceased.

ADDOCK, JOSEPH DOUGLAS, insurance comy executive; b. Lanigan, Sask., Can., June 29, 1918; ne to U.S., 1964, naturalized, 1971; s. Wilbur Lee and ry Edith (Tucker) C.; m. Helen Damiani, May 15, '1; children: David, Constance, Scott, Sta- Student, Cen. Collegiate Inst., Regina, Sask., Can., 2-36. Sr. v.p. Ins. Co. N.Am., Phila., 1945-75; nn. bd. dirs. Horace MAnn Educators Corp., ingfield, Ill., 1975-85, Educators Life Ins. Co. Am., ll-Care Inc.; vice-chmn., chief exec. officer, dir. race Mann Ins. Co., Horace Mann Life Ins. Co., ucators Mktg. Svcs. Corp., Tchrs. Ins. Co., Pub. ployees Ins. Co.; pres., dir. Insuror Mgmt. Co. rs. Ins. Underwriters; bd. dirs. Ill. Nat. Bank. Bd. s. Meml. Med. Ctr., Springfield Downtown Parking ., Springfield Cen. Area Devel. Assn., Ill. Heart n.; mem. Sangamon State U. Found. With Can. ny, 1942-45. Fellow Ins. Inst. Can.; mem. Illini untry Club, Sangamo Club, Phila. Curling Club, sons. Home: Springfield Ill. Died Sept. 2, 1985; mated.

AIG, ALBERT BURCHFIELD, oil company extive; b. Allegheny, Iowa, Oct. 1, 1891; s. George L. Henrietta (Burchfield) C.; m. Elizabeth W. Gibson, . 8, 1918; children: Henrietta Craig Frederick, Mary ig Griffiths, Albert Burchfield. AB, Princeton U., 5. Geologist Greensboro Gas Co., 1915-26; with rters Oil Co., Pitts., from 1917, geologist, gen. mgr., n v.p., 1925-44, pres., from 1944, also bd. dirs.; bd. . Nat. Union Fire Ins. Co., Nat. Union Indemnity , Natco Corp., Brownsville Water Co., Calif. Water Trustee Sewickley Valley Hosp., Staunton Farm. h USN, 1917-21. Mem. AIME, Pa. Holstein Assn. dirs.). Presbyterian. Home: Sewickley Pa. †

AIG, WALTER EARLY, U.S. district judge; b. land, Calif., May 26, 1909; s. Jubal Early and Marie aig) C.; m. Meta Elizabeth Jury, Oct. 25, 1935; chil- : William Early, Meta Lucille. A.B., Stanford U., 1, LL.B., 1934; LL.D., Ariz. State U., 1963, U. San go, 1964; S.J.D., Suffolk U., 1964. Bar: Calif. 1934, . 1936. Legal dept. regional office HOLC, 1934-36; . Fennemore, Craig, Allen & Bledsoe, Phoenix, 6-55, Fennemore, Craig, Allen & McClennen, 1955- U.S. judge Ariz. dist., from 1963, chief judge, 1972- Mem. Ariz. Code Commn., 1951-56; appeal agt. ricopa County Selective Service, 1945-64; mem. Ariz. . Council, 1950-63; spl. counsel Pres.'s Commn. on assination of Pres. Kennedy, 1963-64; chmn. Nat. f. Fed. Trial Judges, 1972-73. Bd. dirs. Sun Angel nd.; exec. com. planning county hosp., 1952-60; bd. tors Stanford U. Sch. Law, 1958-63; bd. dirs. Mar- a County Hosp. Devel. Assn., 1955-62, Am. Bar lowment; pres., 1979-81, Ariz. State U. Found., Ariz. nmunity Found.; chmn. bd. visitors Ariz. State U. . Law; trustee Forensic Scis. Found., 1972-75, Harry Truman Ednl. Found., 1975-79. Served with USN, rld War II. Decorated Order So. Cross Brazil). ow Am. Bar Found.; mem. Am. Law Inst., ABA te chmn. jr. bar conf., ho. dels. 1947—, bd. govs. 8-61, pres. 1963-64), Ariz. Bar Assn. (pres. 1951-52), ricopa County Bar Assn. (pres. 1941), Am. Judica- Soc. (dir. 1951-61), Inter-Am. Bar Assn. (council), rnat. Bar Assn. (council), Can. Bar Assn. (hon. n.), Assn. Bar of City N.Y., Am. Acad. Forensic ., Ariz. Acad., Ariz. State U. Law Soc. (pres. 1972- Ninth Circuit Dist. Judges Assn. (pres. 1973-75), El tre y Nacional Colegio de Abogados de Mexico .), Barra Mexicana (hon.), El Colegio de Abogados a Ciudad de Buenos Aires (hon.), Colegio de Abo- os del Uruguay (hon.), Western States Bar Council s. 1956-57), Am. Legion, Phi Gamma Delta, Phi ta Phi. Clubs: Arizona (Phoenix), Phoenix Country enix), Kiva (Phoenix), Stanford (Phoenix) (past .), Thunderbirds (Phoenix) (past pres.). Lodges: Elks enix); Rotary (Phoenix). Home: Phoenix Ariz. eased.

AIGIE, PETER CAMPBELL, religion educator; b. caster, Eng., Aug. 18, 1938; s. Hugh Brechnin and a Campbell (Murray) C.; m. Elizabeth Alexander, . 5, 1964; children: Cregor John, Gillian. MA with ors, U. Edinburgh, Scotland, 1965; MTh, U. rdeen, Scotland, 1968; PhD, McMaster U., 1970. . prof. dept. religion Carleton U., Ottawa, Ont., ., 1970-71, McMaster U., 1971-74; assoc. prof. dept. gious studies U. Calgary, Alta., Can., 1974-85, chmn. dept. religious studies, 1977-85. Author: Commentary on the Book of Deuteronomy, 1976; contbr. articles to profl. jours. Mem. Am. Acad. Religion, Soc. Bibl. Lit., Can. Soc. Bibl. studies (sec.-treas. 1971-72, exec. sec. 1975-78). Home: Calgary, Alta. Canada. Died Sept. 1985.

CRAIGIE, WALTER WILLIAMS, SR., investment broker-dealer; b. Richmond, Va., Nov. 7, 1904; s. Frank John and Mary Hooper (Williams) C.; m. Helen Pendleton Walker, June 19, 1926; children: Harriet Craigie Van Houten, Walter Willson, Carter W. Student pub. schs., Richmond; hon. doctorate, Randolph Macon Coll. Lic. securities dealer, Va., W.Va., N.Y., N.C., Calif. Clk. Nat. State & City Bank, Richmond, 1917-18; jr. dept. head Fed. Res. Bank, Richmond, 1918-22; gen. mgr. Richmond Car Works, 1922-27; sr. partner F. W. Craigie & Co. (Municipal bonds), Richmond, 1932-65; pres. Craigie Inc. (stocks and bonds), Richmond, 1965-72; chmn. bd. Craigie Inc. (stocks and bonds), 1972-80, chmn. exec. com., 1980-88. Former pres. Episcopal Churchmen Diocese Va.; trustee St. John's Ch. Found., Richmond; hon. alumnus Randolph-Macon Coll.; hon. trustee Va. Union U.; trustee Richmond Meml. Hosp.; mem. advisory com. YWCA, Richmond. Mem. Richmond Soc. Fin. Analysts (former pres.), Investment Bankers Assn. Am. (former v.p.), Richmond C. of C. Clubs: Deep Run Hunt (Richmond) (former pres.); Commonwealth, Downtown. Home: Richmond Va. Died Feb. 10, 1989; buried Hollywood Cemetary, Richmond.

CRAIGMYLE, RONALD M., investment banker; b. Toronto, Ont., Can., June 19, 1896; s. James M. and Jessie (Gregory) C.; m. Louise de Rochemont, Apr. 10, 1923; children: Ronald M., Mary Louise Magee, Robert de Rochemont. AB, Columbia U., 1920, BS in Bus., 1921. With Minsch, Monell & Co., 1920-24; ptnr. Burley, Peabody & Craigmyle, N.Y.C., 1924-26, Craigmyle & Co. (later Craigmyle, Pinney & Co., then Fahnestock & Co.), N.Y.C., from 1926; ret. chmn. Giant Portland & Masonry Cement Co.; v.p. Intercollegiate Flying Assn., 1919-21. Mayor Village of Matinecock, N.Y., 1954-67; trustee Columbia U., 1957-63. Mem. Psi Upsilon. Republican. Episcopalian. Clubs: Piping Rock, Met., Univ., N.Y. Stock Exchange Luncheon, Pilgrims Soc., St. Andrews Soc., Beach (Palm Beach, Fla.), Creek, Everglades, Bath and Tennis. Home: Locust Valley N.Y. Died Sept. 26, 1986; buried New Rochelle, N.Y.

CRANDON, ALBERT SEABURY, consulting civil engineer; b. Acushnet, New Bedford, Mass., Mar. 1, 1893; s. Philip Howland and Emma Frances (Winslow) C.; m. Grace Monro Scully (dec. Feb. 1956); children: Mary M. Crandon Baker, Albert Seabury; m. Margaret May Banker, Mar. 9, 1957; m. Matilda Foster Marsh, Sept. 29, 1971. BS, Worcester (Mass.) Poly. Inst., 1914. Instr. civil engring Worcester Poly. Inst., 1914-16; engr. Am. Bridge Co., 1916-17, field engr., 1919-21; field engr. Am. Window Glass Co., Pitts., 1921-37, exec. v.p., 1942-45, pres., 1945-55, chmn. bd., 1955-58; glass furnace engr. Hartford Empire Co., 1937-42; cons. to pres. ASG Industries Inc (formerly Am.-St. Gobain Corp.), from 1958. Capt. C.E., 79th Div. U.S. Army, 1917-19. Mem. Am. Ceramic Soc., Duquesne Club, Pitts. Athletic Assn., Quequechan Club (Fall River, Mass.), Acoaxet Club (Westport, Mass.), Tau Beta Pi, Sigma Xi. Home: Little Compton R.I. Deceased.

CRARY, ALBERT PADDOCK, geophysicist; b. Pierrepont, N.Y., July 25, 1911; s. Frank J. and Ella (Paddock) C.; m. Mildred Reade Rogers, Feb. 16, 1968; 1 son, Frank. BS magna cum laude, St. Lawrence U., 1931; MS, Lehigh U., 1933. Oil prospector Ind. Exploration Co., Columbia, 1938-40; in Eng., Venezuela, Bahrein Island for United Geophys. Co., 1942-46; geophysicist Cambridge Research Ctr. USAF, 1946-60; chief scientist U.S. Anarctic Research Program NSF, 1959-67, dep. dir. div. environ. scis., 1967-69, dir. div., 1969-77, chief scientist IGY Program in Anarctica, 1957-59. Contbr. articles to profl. jours. Recipient Navy Distinguished Pub. Service award, 1959, Mass. Civil Servant of Yr. award, 1959, Cullum Geog. medal Am. Geog. Soc., 1960, Disting. Service award Dept. Def., 1959, Patron medal Royal Geog. Soc., 1960, Acad. Achievements Golden Plate award, 1966, Vega medal Swedish Soc. Anthropology and Geography, 1972, medal USSR Acad. Scis., 1985. Fellow Arctic Inst. N.Am.; mem. AAAS, Internat. Glaciology Soc. (hon.), Antarctian Soc., Soc. Exploration Geophysicists, Am. Meteorol. Soc., Am. Geog. Soc., Seismol. Soc. Am., Am. Geophys. Union, Cosmos Club, Phi Beta Kappa, Sigma Xi. Home: Bethesda Md. Died Oct. 29, 1987; interred Pierrepont, N.Y.

CRAWFORD, CHERYL, theatrical producer; b. Akron, Ohio, Sept. 24, 1902; d. Robert K. and Luella Elizabeth (Parker) C. Student, Buchtel Coll.; AB cum laude, Smith Coll., 1925, LittD, 1966. Produced plays while at Smith Coll.; casting dir. Theatre Guild, N.Y.C., 1926-30; one of the founders and dirs. The Group Theatre, 1930-37; produced Awake and Sing by Clifford Odets; produced independently: (with Judith Anderson) Oh Men, Oh Women, 1954, Comes a Day, Camino Real, Shadow of a Gunman, Rivalry, Sweet Bird of Youth, Period of Adjustment, 1960, Andorra, Jennie, Brecht on Courage, 1962, Mother Courage and Her Children, 1963, Double Talk, Celebration, 1969, Colette, 1970, Yentl by Isaac Basheviz Singer. Named Women of the Yr., 1959; recipient achievement medal Brandeis U., 1964. Home: New York N.Y. Died Oct. 7, 1986.

CRAWLEY, THOMAS EDWARD, English educator; b. Prospect, Va., Mar. 7, 1920; s. Charles William and Camilla Virginia (Taylor) C.; m. William Roberta Armistead, June 3, 1952. BA, Hampden-Sydney Coll., 1941; MA, U. N.C., 1953, PhD, 1965. Mem. faculty Hampden-Sydney (Va.) Coll., 1946-84, prof. English, 1965-84, dir. music, 1946-76, dean students, 1956-64, Hurt prof. English, 1968-84. Author: The Structure of Leaves of Grass, 1970, also articles on Whitman and Poe; editor: Four Makers of the American Mind, 1976. Served to lt. USNR, 1941-46. Decorated Bronze Star; recipient Cabell Disting. Prof. award Hampden-Sydney Coll., 1968; Bicentennial research grant, 1973. Mem. Modern Lang. Assn., Briery Country Club, Commonwealth Club, Phi Beta Kappa, Omicron Delta Kappa, Kappa Alpha Order. Democrat. Presbyterian. Home: Hampden-Sydney Va. Died Apr. 11, 1984; buried Hampden-Sydney.

CREANZA, JOSEPH, language and music educator; b. N.Y.C., Mar. 1, 1905; s. Peter and Maria (Pappalardi) C.; m. LaVerne Engeson, June 12, 1943; children: Carol Marie Creanza Freeman, Kathleen Creanza Hastings, Adrienne Creanza Palmer, Philip. BS, Lewis Inst., 1932; AM, U. Chgo., 1935. Instr. French Lewis Inst., Chgo., 1932-38; prof., chmn. modern lang. dept. Central YMCA Coll., 1938-44; prof. modern langs., chmn. dept. Roosevelt U., 1944-45, dir. sch. music, 1945-70, trustee, dean Chgo. Mus. Coll., 1954-70; founder, dir. Chgo. Folk Festival, 1940-46. Contbr. articles to profl. jours. Trustee Hinsdale (Ill.) Hosp. and Sanitarium. Mem. NEA, Modern Lang. Assn., French Tchrs. Nat. Assn., Nat. Assn. Schs. Music, Music Tchrs. Nat. Assn., Music Educators Nat. Conf. Home: Sun City Ariz. Died Feb. 21, 1986; cremated.

CREIGHTON, WILLIAM FORMAN, bishop; b. Phila., July 23, 1909; s. Frank Whittington and Maud R. (Hawk) C.; m. Marie-Louise Forrest, June 2, 1934; children: William Wendel, Michael Whittington, Maxwell Forrest. BA, U. Pa., 1931; STB, Phila. Div. Sch., 1934, DD, 1957; DD, Va. Theol. Sem., 1959; LHD, Rikkyo U., Tokyo, 1964. Ordained to ministry Episcopal Ch. as deacon, as priest, 1934. Vicar St. Mark's, Oakes, N.D., 1934-37; rector St. Clement's Ch., St. Paul, 1937-43, St. Johns Ch., Bethesda, Md., 1946-59; bishop co-adjutor Diocese of Washington, 1959-62, bishop, 1962-77; bishop in residence St. John's Ch., Lafayette Sq., Washington, 1977-87. Bd. dirs. Church Pension Fund. Served as chaplain USNR, 1943-46. Home: Washington D.C. Died May 20, 1987.

CRESSEY, DONALD RAY, sociology educator; b. Fergus Falls, Minn., Apr. 27, 1919; s. Raymond Wilbert and Myrtle Athelma (Prentiss) C.; m. Elaine Smythe, Dec. 16, 1943; children: Martha J. Lind, Ann K. Colomy, Mary. B.S., Iowa State U., 1943; Ph.D., Ind. U., 1950. Sociologist Ill. State Penitentiary, Joliet, 1949, U.S. Penitentiary, Terre Haute, Ind., 1951; from lectr. to prof. sociology UCLA, 1949-59, vice chmn. dept. anthropology and sociology, 1957-58, chmn. dept., 1958-61, dean div. social sci., 1960-61; vis. prof. Trinity Coll., Cambridge U., 1961-62, U. Oslo, 1965, U. Washington, summer, 1968, U. Minn., summer 1969, Churchill Coll., Cambridge U., 1970-71, Australian Nat. U., 1973, 86, U. Minn. Law Sch., 1974; dean Coll. Letters and Sci., U. Calif.-Santa Barbara, 1962-67, prof. sociology, 1962-86, faculty research lectr., 1978-86, prof. emeritus, 1986-87; dir. research Wells and Assocs., Austin, Tex., 1984-87; pres. Inst. for Fin. Crime Prevention, Austin, 1985-87; mem. mental health tng. com. NIMH, 1963-67, chmn., 1966-67, mem. policy and planning bd., tng. and manpower resources br., 1964-67; mem. ABA Commn. on Juvenile Justice Standards, 1972-76; cons. Pres.'s Commn. on Law Enforcement and Adminstrn. Justice, 1965-66, Nat. Commn. Causes and Prevention Violence, 1968, Nat. Inst. Criminal Justice, 1969-79, Calif. Council on Criminal Justice, 1969-72, (also others). Author: Other People's Money, a Study in the Social Psychology of Embezzlement, 1953, (with Edwin H. Sutherland) Principles of Criminology, 5th edit, 1955, 10th 1978, (with Richard A. Cloward, others) Theoretical Studies in Social Organization of the Prison, 1960, Delinquency, Crime and Differential Association, 1964, Functions and Structure of Confederated Crime, 1967, Theft of the Nation, 1969, (with David A. Ward) Delinquency, Crime and Social Process, 1969, Criminal Organization: Its Elementary Forms, 1972, (with Arthur Rosett) Justice by Consent: Plea Bargains in the American Courthouse, 1976, (with James W. Coleman) Social Problems, 1980, 3d edit., 1986, (with Charles A. Moore) Corporation Codes of Ethical Conduct, 1980; editor: The Prison, Studies in Institutional Organization and Change, 1961, Crime and Criminal Justice, 1971; assoc. editor: Am. Sociol. Rev, 1953-56, Am. Jour. Sociology, 1958-61, 80-83, Transaction: Soc. Sci. and the Community, 1963-69, Harper and Row Social Problems Series, 1965-75, Social Problems, 1968-74; contbr. articles to profl. jours. Served with USAAF, 1943-45. Recipient Research prizes Ill. Acad. Criminology, 1964, Am. Soc. Criminology, 1967, 80, Sociol. Research Assn., 1972, U. Calif.-Santa Barbara, 1978, Disting. Alumnus award Ind. U., 1974, Citation of Merit Iowa State U.,

1977, others.; Russell Sage Found. research grantee, 1955-56; travel grantee Am. Council Learned Socs., 1960; research grantee Ford Found., 1960, Peat, Marwick, Mitchell Found., 1979; others. Fellow Law and Soc. Assn., Am. Sociol. Assn. (council 1961-63, vis. scientist 1963-65, chmn. criminology sect. 1966-67), AAAS; mem. Am. Soc. Criminology, Pacific Sociol. Assn. (pres. 1959-60), Sociol. Research Assn., Am. Correctional Assn., Soc. for Study Social Problems. Club: Earl of Derby (Cambridge, Eng.) (pres. 1962-63). Home: Santa Barbara Calif. Died July 21, 1987; buried Santa Barbara Cemetery.

CRÊTE, MARCEL, chief justice of Quebec; b. La-Tuque, Que., Can., May 31, 1915; s. Alphida and Jeanne (Paquin) C.; m. Berthe Godin, June 14, 1941; children—Louis, Marie, Lucile, Raymonde. LL.D., Laval U., Que., 1937. Bar: Que. Assoc. Auguste Desilet et al, Grand Mere, Que., Can., 1938-66; judge Superior Court, Trois-Riveres, Que., Can., 1966-72, Court of Appeal, Montreal, Que., Can., 1972-80; chief justice Court of Appeal, Province of Que., Montreal, Que., Can., 1980-88. Home: Grand-Mer, Que. Canada. Died Mar. 11, 1988.

CROCKETT, CAMPBELL, university dean; b. Nicholasville, Ky., Apr. 25, 1918; s. O.B. and Catherine (Campbell) C.; m. Genevieve Kuntz, Oct. 22, 1942 (div.); children: Peter Campbell, Catherine Kuntz. AB, U. Cin., 1940, AM, 1941, PhD, 1949. From instr. to prof. U. Cin., 1949-60, dean, fellow, 1959-67; dir. Inst. Rsch., Tng. Higher Edn., 1967-71, dean, 1971-76; dir. edn. Palm Beach (Fla.) Inst. Found., 1977-85; lectr. Conservatory Music, 1949-54, Art Acad. Cin., 1958-60; fellow Nat. Tng. Labs. Contbr. articles to profl. publs. Bd. dirs. Cin. Playhouse in the Park; adv. bd. Inquiry. With USAAF, 1942-46. Ford faculty fellow U. Mich. and Harvard, 1951-52; Fulbright rsch. scholar U. Oslo, 1853-54. Mem. Am. Soc. Aesthetics, Am. Philos. Assn., ACLU, AAUP, Am. Assn. Humanistic Psychology. Home: Cincinnati Ohio. Died Sept. 13, 1985.

CRONE, NEIL LOUIS, physician; b. Marshalltown, Iowa, May 10, 1903; s. Charles Francis and Agnes May (Pendleton) C.; m. Katharine Griswold, June 5, 1930; children: Katharine Standish, Anne Brewer, Peter Griswold. AB, Grinnell Coll., 1925; BA, Oxford U., Eng., 1927, MA, 1929, PhD, 1929; MD, Harvard U., 1931. Instr. biochemistry, tutor physiology Oxford U., 1927-29; chief resident phys. MAss. Gen. Hosp., 1936-37; asst. in medicine Harvard Med. Sch., 1937-40, instr. medicine, 1940-41; assoc. prof. Harvard Bus. Sch., 1946-50, prof. bus. adminstrn., 1950-85; dir. Harvard Bus. Sch. Health Service; physician, dept. hygiene, Harvard, from 1940; pvt. practice medicine, Boston, 1937-41; physician Mt. Auburn Hosp., Cambridge, Mass., from 1946; asst. in medicine Peter Bent Hosp., Boston, from 1947. Col. U.S. Army, 1941-45, ETO, PTO. Decorated Bronze Star, Army Commendation ribbon; Croix de Guerre with Palm (Belgium); Rhodes scholar, 1925-27. Fellow AMA, Am. Coll. Physicians; mem. Soc. Med. Cons. World War II, Harvard Club, Faculty Club of Harvard, St. Botolph Club, Aesculapian Club, Phi Beta Kappa, Alpha Omega Alpha. Home: Belmont Mass. Died Nov. 24, 1985; buried Belmont Cemetery, Belmont, Md.

CRONIN, JOSEPH EDWARD, baseball executive; b. San Francisco, Oct. 12, 1906; s. Jeremiah and Mary (Carolin) C.; m. Mildred June Robertson, Sept. 1934; children: Thomas, Michael, Kevin, Maureen. Grad. high sch., San Francisco. Profl. baseball player Am. League, 1928-45; mgr. Washington Senators, 1933-34; mgr. Boston Red Sox, 1935-47, gen. mgr., 1948-58; pres. Am. League Profl. Baseball Clubs, 1958-73, chmn., from 1973. Co-founder, dir. MAss. Com. Catholics, Protestants and Jews. Named to Baseball Hall of Fame, 1956. Mem. Variety Club (recipient Great Heart award for work in Jimmy Fund, Boston), Knights of Malta. Home: Osterville Mass. Died Sept. 7, 1984.

CROSBY, JAMES M., hotel company executive; b. Great Neck, N.Y., May 12, 1927; s. John F. and Emily M. Crosby. Student Franklin and Marshall Coll., 1945, Bucknell Coll., 1945-46; BA, Georgetown U., 1948; postgrad., Georgetown U. Law Sch., 1948-49. Shipping rep. Internat. Paint Co., 1949-51; rep. Smith Barney Harris Upham & Co., 1951-58; dir. acquisitions Col. Gustave Ring, Washington, 1958; pres., chief exec. officer Unexcelled Chem. Corp., 1958-67; with Resorts Internat. Inc., Miami, Fla., 1958-86, chmn. bd., chief exec. officer. Bd. govs. Atlantic City Med. Ctr. With USN, 1945-46. Recipient Brotherhood award NCCJ, 1979. Mem. Jockey Club, Surf Club, Palm Bay Club, N.Y. Athletic Club. Home: New York, N.Y. also: Atlantic City, N.J. also: Paradise Island, The Bahamas. Died Apr. 10, 1986.

CROSBY, LAURENCE ALDEN, sugar corporation executive; b. Bangor, Maine, Dec. 20, 1892; s. James and Emily (Alden) C.; m. Aileen Mary O'Hea, Sept. 5, 1923; children: James O'Hea, John O'Hea. BA, Bowdoin Coll., 1913, Oxford (Eng.) U., 1915; BCL, Oxford (Eng.) U., 1916, MA, 1919; LLB, Columbia U., 1917. Bar: N.Y. 1917. Pvt. practice N.Y.C., 1919-46; mem. Sullivan & Cromwell, 1927-46; pres. Cen. Violeta Sugar Co., 1936-58, Cuban Atlantic Sugar Co., 1937-59; vice chmn. Atlantic del. Golfo Sugar Co., from 1959; chmn. U.S. Cuban Sugar Coun., 1954-60. Author: (with Frank Aydelotte) Oxford of Today, 1922. 1st lt. U.S. Army, 1917-19. Decorated comdr. Cuban Order Carlos Manuel de Cespedes, Grand Cross Cuban Order Agrl. Ind. Merit. Mem. N.Y.C. Bar Assn., Am. C. of C. of Cuba (pres. 1949-53), Down Town Assn., havana Yacht Club, Havana Country Club. Roman Catholic. Home: Santa Fe N.Mex. †

CROSSON, JAMES D., judge; b. Newberry, S.C., Mar. 8, 1909; s. Henry H. and Sallie (Spearman) C.; m. Jane T. Garland, Dec. 31, 1948; 1 child, J. David. AA, Jewish People's Inst., Chgo., 1934; student, Lewis Inst. Tech., 1936; LLB, John Marshall Law Sch., 1940, LLM, 1947; cert. traffic, Northwestern U. Law Sch., 1956, Fordham U. Law. Sch., 1957; grad., Nat. Coll. State Trial Judges, U. Colo. Bar: Ill. 1942. Pvt. practice Chgo., 1942, 46-54; mem. firm. Gassaway, Crosson, Turner & Parsons, Chgo., 1955-59; referee Chgo. Municipal Ct., 1954-61, adminstrv. asst. to chief justice, 1961-62; judge Cir. Ct. Cook County (Ill.), Chgo., 1962-80; law mem. panel Ill. Bd. Appeals, SSS of No. Ill., 1954-80. Active NAACP; trustee John Marshall Law Sch., 1963-87, treas., 1967-87; trustee Met. YMCA, Chgo., 1969-87, 1st v.p., 1970-87. Maj. AUS, 1942-46, ETO. Recipient citation of merit John Marshall Law Sch., 1966. Mem. ABA, Fed. Bar Assn., Cook County Bar Assn. (bd. dirs.), Chgo. Bar Assn., Am. Judicature Soc., Original Forty Club, Masons, Alpha Psi. Congregationalist. Home: Chicago Ill. Died Jan. 6, 1987.

CROTHERS, BENJAMIN SHERMAN (SCATMAN), actor; b. Terre Haute, Ind., May 23, 1910; m. Helen Sullivan, 1937; 1 dau., Donna. Began career as nightclub musician; film debut in Meet Me at the Fair, 1949; other films include Hello Dolly, 1969, The Great White Hope, 1970, Lady Sings the Blues, 1972, The King of Marvin Garden, 1972, One Flew Over the Cuckoo's Nest, 1975, The Fortune, 1975, The Shootist, 1976, Silver Streak, 1977, Scavenger Hunt, 1979, Bronco Billy, 1980, The Shining, 1980, Zapped!, 1982, The Rats, 1982; appeared in TV series Chico and the Man, 1974-78, Roots, 1977; other TV appearances include Beulah, One of the Boys, 1982, Missing Children: A Mother's Story, 1982; voice on cartoon voiceovers. Home: Los Angeles Calif. Died Nov. 22, 1986; buried Forest Lawn Cemetery, Los Angeles.

CROTTY, LEO ALAN, drugstore chain executive; b. Chgo., Nov. 2, 1929; s. Michael Leo and Helen Marie (Toole) C.; m. Frances Mary Tauscheck, Sept. 1, 1956; children—Robert, Daniel, Kimberly, Lisa, Matthew. B.S., U. Ill., 1958. C.P.A., Ill. Mem. firm Arthur Young & Co. (C.P.A.'s), Chgo., 1958-63, Comml. Trades Inst., Chgo., 1964-66; with Walgreen Co., Chgo., 1966-88; controller Walgreen Co., 1971-78, v.p. adminstrn., 1978-88. Served with USAF, 1950-54. Mem. Chgo. Retail Fin. Execs. Assn. (dir. 1974-81), Ill. Soc. C.P.A.'s, Am. Inst. C.P.A.'s, Fin. Execs. Inst. (bd. dirs. 1987—). Home: Deerfield Ill. Died May 17, 1988; buried Santa Barbara, Calif.

CROW, JANE HANES, educator; b. Monroe, N.C., Oct. 16, 1916; d. Edward Wilson and Mary (Hanes) C. BS, Salem Coll., 1937; MS, U. Md., 1938; PhD, Cornell U., 1961; summer student, Colubia Tchrs. Coll., U. Va. Instr. home econs. Salem Coll., 1938-44; mem. faculty U. Md., 1944-60, assoc. prof. home econs., head dept. home and instl. mgmt., 1956-60; rsch. asst. Cornell U., 1959-60; prof. home econs., dir. Sch. Home Econs., U. Maine, 1961-65; prof. home econs., head dept. housing, mgmt. and family econs. U. N.C., Greensboro, 1965-88; spl. home demonstration agt. N.C. Coop. Extension Service, 1943; instr. U. Va., summers 1955, 56. Mem. adv. com. consumer credit counseling service Family Service-Travelers Aid Assn.; bd. dirs., mem. edn. com. N.C. Consumer Coun. Recipient citations U. Md. Home Econs. Alumnae Assn., 1957, Maine Home Econs. Assn., 1965, Md. Home Econs. Assn., 1976. Mem. Am. Home Econs. Assn., Md. Home Econs. Assn. (chmn. membership 1949-51, councilor 1952-54, pres. 1956-58), N.C. Home Econs. Assn. (chmn. family econ. com., sec. 1969), Bus. and Profl. Women's Club, N.C. Dietetic Assn. (v.p., publicity chmn. 1942, pres. 1943), AAAS, AAUW, Am. Assn. Housing Educators (pres. 1975-76), Iluminating Engring. Soc., Omincron Nu, Phi Kappa Phi, Pi Lambda Theta. Home: Mocksville N.C. Died Jan. 18, 1988; buried Mocksville.

CROWELL, ALBERT DARY, physicist, educator; b. Dover, N.H., Feb. 12, 1925; s. Milton Frederick and Esther Ann (Dary) C.; m. Janet Louise Wright, June 21, 1947; children: Judith Ann, Susan Wright, Cynthia Dary. BS in Engring. summa cum laude, Brown U., 1946, PhD in Physics, 1950; MS in Applied Physics, Harvard U., 1947. Instr., then asst. prof. Amherst Coll., 1950-55; mem. faculty U. Vt., Burlington, 1955-85, prof. physics, 1961-85, chmn. dept., 1961-75; regional counselor physics State of Vt., 1963-67; vis. prof. phys. chemistry U. Bristol, Eng., 1968; vis. prof. physics U. Southampton, Eng., 1976. Author: (with D.M. Young) Physical Adsorption of Gases, 1962. Trustee Brownell Pub. Library, Essex Junction, Vt. With USNR, 1943-46. Mem. AAAS, Am. Phys. Soc., Am. Assn. Physics Tchrs., Am. Vacuum Soc., Sigma Xi. Home: Essex Junction Vt. Died Sept. 21, 1985; buried Memory Gardens, St. James Episcopal Ch., Essex Junction, Vt.

CROWELL, LUCIUS, artist; b. Chgo., Jan. 22, 1911; Lucius Alfred and Grace (Gapen) C.; m. Priscilla An Bromley, Dec. 22, 1936; children—Brigit, Geoffr Nicholas, Christopher. Student, Williams Coll., 192 30, Pa. Acad. Fine Arts, 1930-33. Exhbns. include, A Inst. Chgo., 1931, Boston Mus. Art, 1949, Phila. M Art, Pa. Acad. Fine Arts, U. Mich., Calif. Palace Legion of Honor, 1951, Concord Mus., 1955, Worces Mus., Boston Soc. Ind. Artists, 1956, Columbus Mu Widener U.; represented in permanent collectio Boston Mus., Phila. Mus. Art, U. Pa., U. Del., Tem U., Northfield Mus., Pa. Acad. Fine Arts. Served w AUS, 1944-46. Recipient Medal of honor Conco Mus., 1954; May Audubon Post prize Pa. Acad. Fi Arts, 1983. Mem. Phila. Art Alliance, Coll. Art Ass Phila. Water Color Club, Chester County Art Ass Artists Equity. Clubs: Williams (N.Y.C.); Peale (Phila Edgemere (Dingman's Ferry, Pa.). Home: Phoenixvi Pa. Died Mar. 9, 1988.

CROWLEY, DANIEL FRANCIS, publishing compa executive; b. Yonkers, N.Y., Nov. 23, 1915; s. Corneli Daniel and Elizabeth M. (Treacy) C.; m. Margaret Murphy, June 8, 1946; children: Margaret Mary, Dan Francis. AB, Columbia U., 1936, MS, 1937. Me staff Haskings & Sells, CPAs, N.Y.C., 1937-42, 46- with McGraw-Hill Inc., 1947-80, corporate controll v.p., controller publs. div., 1963-68, sr. v.p. finance, d processing, 1968, exec. v.p. finance, 1970-80, also dirs., chmn. fin. policy com., until 1981. Mem. a com. athletics Columbia U., 1966-85; mem. joint a minstrv. bd. Columbia-Presbyn. Hosp., 1970-81; tre Columbia-Presbyn. Med. Ctr. Fund, Inc., 1971- alumni trustee Columbia U.; trustee Fin. Acctg. Foun 1976-79. Comdr. USNR, World War II. Mem. F Execs. Inst. (pres. N.Y.C. chpt. 1967-68, dir.-at-la 1977-85), Am. Inst. CPAs, Alumni Assn. Colum Grad. Sch. Bus. (past pres.), Columbia Alumni Fe (past sec.-treas.), Am. Legion, Friendly Sons St. Patri St. Andrews Golf Club, Columbia Varsity Club (p pres.), Knights of Malta. Home: Hastings-on-Huds N.Y. Died Mar. 23, 1985; buried Mt. Hope Cemete Hastings, N.Y.

CROWN, IRVING, investment company executive; Chgo., Dec. 9, 1894; s. Arie and Ida (Gordon) C.; Rose Seltzer, Jan. 10, 1928; 1 dau., Suzanne Cro Goodman. LLD, Lewis U., 1964; postgrad. (fello Brandeis U., 1973. V.p. Freeman Coal Mining Co Chgo., 1947-67, Marblehead Lime Co., Chgo., 1948- pres. Material Ser. Corp., Chgo., 1955-60, chmn., 19 87; vice-chmn. Material Service div. Gen. Dynam Corp., Chgo., 1960-67, Henry Crown & Co., Ch from 1967; bd. dirs. Lemont Shipbldg. & Repair Co Sioux City and New Orleans Barge Lines. Bd. dirs. Sinai Hosp. Med. Ctr., Chgo., Anshe Emet Synagogu Mem. Western Soc. Engrs., Soc. Mining Engrs., Exe tive Club, Standard Club, Covenant Club, Prope Club, Bryn Mawr Country Club, Navy League Cl Variety Club, Carlton Club, Shriners. Home: Chica Ill. Died Mar. 1, 1987.

CRUMPACKER, SHEPARD J., JR., judge, form congressman; b. South Bend, Ind., Feb. 13, 1917; Shepard J. and Grace (Dauchy) C.; m. Marjorie Patt Feb. 18, 1950; 1 son, Richard Owen. BS, Northwest U., 1938; JD, U. Mich., 1941. Bar: Ind. 1941. practice South Bend, 1946-50, 56-77; mem. 82d-8 Congresses from 3d Ind. dist., 1950-56; judge St. Jose County (Ind.) Superior Ct., 1977-85; city atty., So Bend, 1969-71; U.S. del. NATO Parliamentary Co Paris, 1955; mem. U.S. del. Internat. Copyright Co 1952. Chmn. bd. dirs. Michiana Coll. Commerce, 19 78; bd. dirs. Jr. Achievement South Bend, 1976-86. lt. U.S. Army, 1941-46; maj. USAF Res., ret. Mem. Force Assn. (local past comdr. No. Ind. chpt.), Iz Walton League Am. (past pres. St. Joseph Cou chpt.), Masons, Rotary (South Bend pres. 1973-74 Home: South Bend Ind. Died Oct. 14, 1986; bur South Bend.

CRUTCHFIELD, FINIS ALONZO, JR., bishop; Henrietta, Tex., Aug. 22, 1916; s. Finis Alonzo a Callie (Blair) C.; m. Benja Lee Bell, Jan. 21, 1941; 1 s Charles Newton. BA, So. Meth. U., 1937; BD, D U., MDiv.; DD, Oklahoma City U.; LittD, U. Tuls Ordained to ministry Meth. Ch. Pastor Goodw Okla., Elk City, Okla., Muskogee, Okla.; pas McFarlin Meml. United MEth. Ch., Norman, Ok Boston Ave. United Meth. Ch., Tulsa, 1960-72; bish La. area United Meth. Ch., New Orleans, 1972- bishop Tex. Conf. United Meth. Ch., Houston, 1976- pres. bd. edn. Okla. Conf. United Meth. Ch.; pres. evangelism, pres. South Cen. Jurisdictional Coun; me gen. bd. edn., mem. gen. commn. on ecumenical affa mem. World Meth. Coun.; del. Assembly on Faith a Order, World Coun. Chs., New Delhi, 1961. Form mem. Okla., Nat. coms. to employ handicapped; form mem. Pkla. Com. on Religion and Medicine; form pres. bd. trustees Oklahoma City U., Meth. Home Children, Tahlequah, Okla., Frances Willard Hor Tulsa; former mem. vis. com U. Okla. Recipient D ing. Alumnus award So. Meth. U., citation NCC Mem. Masons, K.T. Home: Houston Tex. Died M 21, 1987.

CRUZ, RAMON ERNESTO, former president Honduras; b. Oct. 18, 1903; married; 3 children. E inceton, Harvard. Pres. Honduras, 1971-72. Home: egucigalpa Honduras. Died Aug. 6, 1985.

UBER, JOHN FRANK, sociologist, educator; b. ngo., Aug. 31, 1911; s. John Charles and Lillian omacka) C.; m. Armine Gulessian, Dec. 10, 1949 iv.); 1 child, Armine Anne; m. Peggy Buckwater Harff, Dec. 15, 1964 (div.); m. Marilyn Soule, Aug. 26, 79. AB, Western Mich. Coll. Edn., 1932; PhD, U. ich., 1937. Chmn. dept. econs. and sociology Sioux alls Coll., 1935-36; asst. prof. Marietta Coll., 1936-37; st. prof. Kent State U., 1937-39, assoc. prof., 1939-41, of. sociology, 1941-44; assoc. prof. Ohio State U., olumbus, 1944-46, prof. sociology, 1946-72, emeritus, 72-88; prof. summer sessions U. Chgo.-U. Mich.-Kelgg Found., 1941-42, U. Calif., 1949; bd. dirs. Nat. oun. Family Relations, 1948-53. Author: Sociology: A nopsis of Principles, 1947, rev. edit., 1968, (with R.A. arper) Problems of American Society, 1948, rev. edits. 51, 64, Marriage Counseling Practice, 1948, (with illiam Kenkel) Social Stratification in the U.S., 1954, ith Peggy B. Harroff) Readings in Sociology: Sources d Comment, 1962, The Significant Americans: A udy of Sexual Behavior Among the Affluent, 1965. em. Am. Sociol. Soc., Ohio Valley Sociol. Soc. (sec.-eas. 1940-41), AAUP, Soc. for Study Social Problems, i Beta Kappa. Home: Mount Gilead Ohio Died Dec. , 1988.

UDDY, LUCY HON, banker; b. Waldron, Ark., Aug. 1889; d. Daniel and Maggie (Gaines) Hon; m. Warren Cuddy, Aug. 15, 1917; children: David Warren, aniel Hon. AB, U. Ark, 1911. Tchr. high schs., Ark. d Alaska, 1911-17; bd. dirs. 1st NAt. Bank, nchorage, from 1942, chmn. bd. dirs., from 1958. mn. bd. dirs. Anchorage coun. Girl Scouts U.S., 35-41; chmn. 1st drive Anchorage United Good eighbors, 1956; bd. regents U. Alaska, 1957-63. ecipient Disting. Alumna citation U. Ark., 1961. em. Cook Inlet Hist. Soc., Anchorage Women's Club on.) (chmn. art show 1952). Democrat. Home: nchorage Alaska. Died May 10, 1982, buried nchorage.

ULBERT, TAYLOR, college dean; b. Bklyn., Sept. , 1917; s. Isaac Taylor and Fannie (Blauvelt) C.; m. ne Clark, Aug. 25, 1949; children—Jane Lindsay, hn Taylor, Robert Alan. A.B., Yale, 1939; M.A., U. ch., 1947, Ph.D., 1957. Mem. faculty Ohio U., 1953- , prof. English, 1965-87; dean Ohio U. (Grad. Coll.), 65-70, v.p., dean faculties, 1969-73, exec. v.p., dean ulties, 1973-75, provost, 1975-76, Trustee prof. English, 1976-87; pres. Ohio Univ. Press, 1964-87. Served maj. AUS, 1940-46. Home: Athens Ohio. Died July 1987; cremated.

ULBERTSON, HORACE COE, insurance executive; L.A., Apr. 24, 1924; s. Henry Coe and Irene A. ood) C.; m. Janet Ann Fadley, Dec. 27, 1949; chilen: Timothy Coe, Gary Dan, William Craig. Student, So. Calif., 1948; AB, Occidental Coll., 1949. With delity and Deposit Co. Md., from 1949, exec. v.p., 66-74, pres., chief exec. officer, 1974-80, chmn., chief ec. officer, 1981-84, chmn. bd. dirs., from 1984, also em. exec. com.; bd. dirs., mem. exec. com. Union ncorp Md., 1968-74, Title Guarantee Co. Md., 1962- , pres., bd. dirs. SwissRe Holding N.Am. Inc., Y.C.; bd. dirs. Md. Nat. Corp., SwissRe Advs. Inc., vissRe Corp., SwissRe Mgmt. Co., N.Am. Reins. orp., N.Am. Reassurance Co., Gen. Surety & uarantee Co. Ltd.; instr. UCLA, 1953-54. First v.p. akefield Home Improvement Assn., 1972; mem. eater Balt. Commn., from 1974; trustee, mem. exec. m. Community Chest, Balt., 1968-73; bd. dirs. Balt. nited Appeal, 1972, Balt. Area Coun. Alcoholism, 69-78. ARC Balt., 1970-76; solicitor Balt. Symphony, 68-69; trustee St. Jospeh Hosp., from 1980. With SNR, 1943-46. Mem. Nat. Assn. Casualty and Surety ecs., Surety Assn. Am. (rep. exec. com. 1969-79), Am. . Assn. Am. (rep. exec. com. 1968), Surety Underiters Assn. So. Calif. (pres. 1964), Ins. Info. Inst. (alt. . 1970-71), Beavers Heavy Engring. Contractors sn. (dir. 1970-75), Met. Balt. C. of C. (v.p. 1972, dir.), n. Legion, Newcomen Soc., Balt. Country Club, nter Club (bd. dirs. from 1978), Maryland Club, wson Golf and Country Club, Alpha Tau Omega. ome: Baltimore Md. Died Nov. 20, 1984, buried Duey Meml. Garden, Timonium, Md.

JMBERLEGE, GEOFFREY FENWICK CELYN, publisher; b. Lindfield, Eng., Apr. 18, 1891; Henry Mordaunt and Blanche P.G. (Fenwick) C.; m. ra Gladys Gibbons, Nov. 30, 1927; children: zabeth, Geoffrey, Patrick, Francis. MA, Worcester ll., Oxford U., 1913; DCL (hon.), Durham U., 1953. th Oxford Press, 1919-56, mgr. Indian brs., Bombay, lcutta and Madras, 1919-28, mgr. and v.p., N.Y.C., 28-34, asst. pub., London, 1934-45, pub. to the U. ford, 1945-56; vice chmn. Osford U. Press, Inc., Y.C., 1945-56. Hon. fellow Worcester Coll. Mem. henaeum Club. Home: Haywords Heath England. †

JMMING, HUGH SMITH, JR., diplomat; b. chmond, Va., Mar. 10, 1900; s. Hugh Smith and Lucy (Booth) C.; m. Winifred Burney West, Sept. 21, 1935 c. Jan. 1978). Student, Va. Mil. Inst., 1917-20, U. , 1920-24. Bar: Va. Banker London, Bombay, Sinpore, Peking, 1924-27; tech. adviser Dept. State, 1928; asst. to U.S. delegation Internat. Econ. Conf., London, and 7th Pan-Am. Conf. Montevideo, 1933; exec. asst. to sec. of state 1934; detailed to U.S. consulate Geneva; in connection Italo-Ethiopian affairs 1935-36; spl. mission to Scandinavia and Netherlands, 1939; mem. exec. com. U.S. Antarctic Service 1939-41; spl. mission Greenland, 1941; mem. Econ. Warfare Mission, also U.S. del. Internat. Whaling Conf. London, 1943; spl. mission to Sweden, 1943, 45; rep. State Dept. on Anglo-Swedish-Am. Commn., and chief div. No. European Affairs 1944; polit. liaison officer U.S. delegation UN Conf. on Internat. Orgn. San Francisco, 1945; spl. mission Iceland, 1946; counselor Am. embassy Stockholm 1947-50; counselor Am. embassy with personal rank of minister Moscow, 1950-52; dep. sec. gen. for polit. affairs NATO Paris, 1952-53; ambassador to Indonesia, 1953-57; spl. asst. to sec. of state, dir. intelligence Dept. State, 1957-61, spl. asst. to sec. of state, 1961, cons., 1961-64; Chmn. John Foster Dulles oral history project Princeton. Past mem. bd. dirs. Columbia Hosp. for Women, Washington; trustee Meridian House Found., Family and Child Services Washington, Washington Inst. Fgn. Affairs, Washington Cathedral; chmn. bd., pres. Bath County Community Hosp., Hot Springs, Va.; bd. dirs. Historic Georgetown, Inc., Garth Newel Music Center Found., Hot Springs; past pres. Nat. Cathedral Assn. Served as 2d lt. U.S. Army, 1918. Recipient Raven award U. Va., 1984. Mem. U. Va. Law Sch. Assn., Mil. Order World Wars, S.A.R., Raven Soc., Diplomatic and Consular Officers Ret. (past pres.), Zeta Psi. Episcopalian. Clubs: Metropolitan (Washington) (past pres.), Cosmos (Washington), Alibi (Washington), Sulgrave (Washington); Chevy Chase (Md.); Farmington (Charlottesville, Va.); Old Capitol (Monterey, Calif.); Royal Swedish Yacht; Sallskapet (Stockholm). Home: Washington D.C. Died Nov. 24, 1986; buried St. John's Ch., Hampton, Va.

CUMMINGS, PARKE, writer; b. West Medford, Mass., Oct. 8, 1902; s. Henry Irving and DeVoo P.; m. Mary Virginia Obear, Apr. 6, 1935; children—John Obear, Patricia Ann. Grad., Mercersburg Acad.; B.S., Harvard U., 1925. Free-lance writer humor, sports articles 1925—. Author: The Whimsey Report, 1948, The Dictionary of Sports, 1949, The Dictionary of Baseball, 1950, I'm Telling You Kids for the Last Time, 1951, American Tennis, 1957, Baseball Stories, 1959, The Fly in the Martini, 1961, (with Nora Lapin) Fairfield County: An Insiders Guide, 1975; contbr. articles and verse to popular mags. Home: Westport Conn. Home: Westport Conn. Deceased.

CUMMINGS, TILDEN, banker; b. Chgo., Sept. 18, 1907; s. William Charles and Frances May (Stevens) C.; m. Hester Harton Browne, Mar. 29, 1933 (dec.); children: Hester Hollyday (Mrs. Karl Jensen), Richard, Tilden, Douglas. BS, Princeton, 1930; MBA, Harvard, 1932. With Continental Ill. Nat. Bank and Trust Co., Chgo., 1932-73, pres., 1960-73; bd. dirs. Abex Corp., Consol. Foods Corp., Canteen Corp., Chgo. Milw. Corp., C.M. St.P. & P. R.R. Life trustee Northwestern U.; bd. dirs. Mid-Am. chpt. ARC; chmn. Crusade of Mercy of Met. Chgo., 1972, pres., 1975. Named Banker of the Yr., Finance mag., 1972. Mem. Old Elm Club, Commercial Club, Economic Club, Commonwealth Club, LaSalle St. Club, Chgo. Club, Glenview Club, Augusta (Ga.) Nat. Golf Club, Princeton Club (N.Y.C.), Bohemian Club (San Francisco), Delta Kappa Epsilon. Home: Winnetka Ill. Died July 22, 1986.

CUMMINS, ALBERT SHELDON, public utilities executive; b. Chgo., Jan. 24, 1892; s. James Sheldon and Alice Charlotte (Byllesby) C.; m. Myrna Linquist, Feb. 10, 1917 (dec.); children: James Sheldon, Charlotte. Student, U. Chgo. Pres. Calif. Oreg. Power Co., merged into Pacific Power and Light Co., then vice chmn. bd. Mem. Rogue River Valley Univ. Club, Rogue Valley Golf Club, Arlington Club (Portland, Oreg.), Psi Upsilon. Home: Medford Oreg. †

CUMMINS, GEORGE MANNING, JR., physician; b. Davenport, Iowa, May 24, 1914; s. George Manning and Edna Eugenia (Eckstein) C.; m. Merlene Virginia Anderson, June 11, 1941; children—George Manning III, Gregory M., Gilbert M., Cynthia H. B.S., St. Ambrose Coll., 1935; M.D., Rush Med. Sch., 1941; M.S., Northwestern U., 1947. Diplomate Am. Bd. Internal Medicine. Practice medicine specializing in internal medicine Chgo., 1946; chief gastrointestinal sect. Chgo. Wesley Meml. Hosp.; asst. prof. medicine Northwestern U. Sch. Medicine, 1955—. Contbr. articles to profl. jours. Served with AUS, 1942-46. Fellow ACP; mem. AMA, Ill. Med. Soc., Chgo. Med. Soc., Chgo. Inst. Medicine, N.Y. Acad. Scis., Alpha Omega Alpha. Clubs: Mid-Am. (Chgo.); Kenosha Country (Wis.). Home: Kenosha Wis. Deceased.

CUPP, PAUL J., business executive; b. Johnstown, Pa., 1902; m. Louise Cupp; children: Marilyn Cupp Krumhansl, Jane Cupp Wilcox, Louann Cupp Geiger. Grad., Wharton Sch., U. Pa., 1924; LLD (hon.), Bloomfield Coll., Eastern Bapt. Coll. With Am. Stores Co., now Acme Markets Inc., 1929-74, chmn. bd., 1961-74; bd. dirs. Phila. Nat. Bank, Provident Mut. Life Ins. Co., John Wanamaker Phila, Chem. Leaman Tank Lines, Inc., Western Savs. Fund Soc. Bd. dirs. Greater Phila. Movement; trustee U. Pa. Mem. Phila C. of C., Union League Club, Phila. Home: Bryn Mawr Pa. Died Aug. 15, 1988.

CURRAN, EDWARD MATTHEW, federal judge; b. Bangor, Maine, May 10, 1903; s. Michael J. and Mary A. (Callanin) C.; m. Katherine C. Hand, June 6, 1934 (dec. Mar. 1960); children—Eileen Curran Monahan, Mary Catherine, Ann Curran Schmidtlein, Edward Michael Jr.; m. Margaret V. Carr, Dec. 30, 1963. A.B., U. Maine, Orono, 1928; LL.B., Cath. U. Am., Washington, 1927, LL.D. (hon.), 1967; LL.D. (hon.), U. Maine, Orono, 1970, Georgetown U., Washington, 1971. Bar: D.C. 1929. Assoc. Milton W. King, Washington, 1929-34; asst. corp. counsel D.C., 1934-36; judge Police Ct. D.C., 1936-40; U.S. atty. D.C., 1940-46, U.S. dist. judge, 1946; chief judge U.S. Dist. Ct. D.C., Washington, 1966-71, sr. U.S. dist. judge, 1971-88; instr. Sch. of Law, Cath. U. Am., 1930-35; prof. law Georgetown U. Sch. of Law, Washington, 1943-46, Columbia U., Washington. Mem. Met. Police Boys Club, Washington, Merrick Boys Club, Washington; mem. Adv. Bd. Cath. U. Sch. of Law, Washington; v.p., bd. dirs. Ridgely Sch. Exceptional Children, Md. Recipient "M" award Maine State Soc. of D.C.; Judiciary award Assn. Fed. Adminstrs., 1967; Disting. Service award Bar Assn. of D.C., 1971. Mem. ABA, D.C. Bar Assn., Fed. Bar Assn. (past 1st v.p.), John Carroll Soc. (Washington chpt.), Gamma Eta Gamma, Phi Kappa (pres.). Democrat. Roman Catholic. Lodges: Friendly Sons of St. Patrick (Washington pres.), K.C. Home: Washington D.C. Died Jan. 10, 1988; buried Mt. Olivet Cemetery, Washington.

CURRIE, GEORGE SELKIRK, accountant; b. Glencoe, Ont., Can., Oct. 17, 1889; s. Dugald and Eliza Cowan (Cross) C.; m. Louisa Hope Napier, Mar. 3, 1927; children: George Napier McDonald, Frances Louise, Mary Ann, Gordon Selkirk. BA, McGill U., 1911. Co-founder McDonald, Currie & Co., 1914; ptnr. internat. firm Coopers & Lybrand; pres. The Bowater Corp. N.A. Ltd.; bd. dirs. Bowater's Nfld. Pulp & Paper Mills, Ltd., Bowater Power Co., Ltd., Bowater Pulp & Paper Corp. N.A. Ltd., Bowater's Mersey Paper Co., Ltd. With Princess Patricia's Can. Light Inf., dep. asst. Q.M.C., 4th Can. Div., World War I; exec. asst. Min. Nat. Def., Can., 1940-42, dep., 1942-44. Decorated Companion Disting. Svc. Order, Mil. Cross, Companion St. Michael and St. George. Mem. Mt. Royal, University, Montreal, Canadian (N.Y.C.) clubs. Home: Westmount, Que. Canada. †

CURRY, ANDREW GIBSON, investment banker; b. Windsor, N.S., Can., Apr. 6, 1901; came to U.S., 1930, naturalized, 1949; s. Rufus and Cornelia (Faulkner) C.; m. Dorothy Dawson Page, Jan. 14, 1938; children: John Page, Cornelia (Mrs. Thomas A. Thornber). Student, Kings Coll. Sch., Windsor, N.S., St. Andrew Coll., Toronto; BA, U. Toronto, 1922. With A.E. Ames & Co., 1922-66, ptnr., 1955-65, pres., bd. dirs., 1951-65, chmn. bd. dirs., 1965-68. Mem. CAn. Soc. N.Y., Pilgrims U.S., Downtown Exec. Club, Bond Club N.Y., Can. Club, Metropolitan Club (N.Y.C.), Fox Meadow Tennis Club (Scarsdale, N.Y.), Scarsdale Golf Club, Chester Yacht Club, Phi Gamma Delta. Republican. Home: Hartsdale N.Y. also: Chester, N.S. Canada. Died Dec. 17, 1984, buried Elmsford, N.Y.

CURRY, BRYCE QUENTION, lawyer, banker; b. Hartselle, Ala., Nov. 9, 1923; s. James Gordon and Grace Flossy (Sparkman) C.; m. Carolyn Jetty Evans, Sept. 2, 1970; children: James Bryce, Evan Andrew; 1 dau. by previous marriage, Janet Susan. BA, George Washington U., 1951, JD with honors, 1955. Page Ho. of Reps., Washington, 1941-43, legis. clk. to Ho. majority whip, 1946; legis. clk. to Senator John J. Sparkman 1947-50; legis. rsch. asst. U.S. Senate, 1950-53; dir. rsch. Nat. Savs. & Loan League, 1953-56, asst. gen. counsel, 1956-59, gen. counsel, 1959-63; pres. Fed. Home Loan Bank N.Y., N.Y.C., from 1963. Mem. editorial bd. George Washington U. Law Rev. Mem. bd. regents Seton Hall U. Lt. USNR, 1943-46. Mem. D.C. Bar Assn., N.Y. County Lawyers Assn., World Trade Center Club. Democrat. Home: New York N.Y. Died July 1, 1985.

CURRY, EDWARD THOMAS, lawyer; b. Homestead, N.J., July 7, 1890; s. Thomas Edward and Annie (Ryan) C.; m. Ethel Vincent Reeve, Apr. 8, 1916; children: Ethel Emma (Mrs. James E. Sturgis), Edward Thomas. LLB, U. Pa., 1913. Bar: N.J. 1913. Assoc. Grey & Archer (name changed to Norman Grey), Camden, N.J., 1913-24; ptnr. Curry, Purnell & Greene; counsel Brown, Connery, Kulp, Wille, Purnell & Greene, Camden; spl. asst. to atty. gen. of U.S. 1950-58, hearing officer, from 1958. 2d lt. U.S. Army, 1917-19. Fellow Am. Bar Found.; mem. ABA, N.J. (pres. 1953-54, gen. coun. from 1954), Camden County (pres. 1940) bar assns., Am. Judicature Soc., Am. Legion, Masons, Tavistock Country Club (bd. dirs.), Sigma Phi Sigma. Presbyterian. Home: Haddonfield N.J. †

CURTIS, CHARLOTTE MURRAY, columnist; b. Chgo.; d. George Morris and Lucile (Atcherson) C.; m. William Hunt; 3 stepchildren. B.A. in Am. History, Vassar Coll., 1950; L.H.D., St. Michael's Coll., 1974, Bates Coll., 1977; LL.D., Denison U., 1976; Litt.D. (hon.), Union Coll., 1979. Reporter, soc. editor Columbus (Ohio) Citizen, 1950-61; reporter N.Y. Times,

1961-87, women's news editor, 1965-72, Family style editor, 1972-74, assoc. editor paper, 1974-87, editor Op-Ed page, 1974-82, columnist, 1982-87; free-lance writer, 1950-87; tchr. narrative and short story writing Columbus YWCA, 1952-54; radio commentator Sta. WMNI, Columbus, 1959-60, Sta. WQXR, N.Y.C. Author: First Lady, 1963, The Rich and Other Atrocities, 1976; contbr. to: The Soviet Union: The Fifty Years, 1967, The Mafia: U.S.A, 1972, Assignment: U.S.A, 1974. Founder, pres. Young Assocs. Columbus Symphony Orch.; chmn. edn. Columbus Jr. League, 1958-60; mem. N.Y. Jr. League, 1964-87. Recipient various awards for reporting, writing and editing N.Y. Newspaper Women's Club, various awards for reporting, writing and editing Ohio Newspaper Women's Assn., various awards for reporting, writing and editing Am. Newspaper Women's Club, also awards N.Y. and Los Angeles chpts. Women in Communications; Ohio. Gov.'s award for journalism; U. So. Calif. Newspaper Journalism award. Mem. Am. Newspaper Guild (v.p. Columbus local 13 1956-60). Clubs: National Press; Cosmopolitan (N.Y.C.). Home: New York N.Y. Died Apr. 16, 1987.

CURTIS, EDWARD PECK, corporate executive; b. Rochester, N.Y., Jan. 14, 1897; s. Guerney T. and Alice (Peck) C.; m. Agness Bartlett, Oct. 25, 1924; children: Diane (Mrs. Sherwood Francis), Ruth (Mrs. C.F. Hoffman), Edward Peck. Student, Williams Coll., 1914-16, MA (hon.), 1941; LLD (hon.), Hobart Coll., 1949, U. Rochester, 1949; DSc (hon.), Stevens Inst. Tech., 1957. Joined Eastman Kodak Co., Rochester, 1921, sales mgr. motion picture film dept., 1929, v.p. in charge motion picture film bus., supr. gen. bus. Europe, 1945-62, also bd. dirs.; chmn. exec. com. Security Trust Co., Rochester; bd. dirs. Mohawk Airlines; dir. Nat. Fgn. Trade Coun. apptd. spl. asst. to Pres. Eisenhower for aviation facilities planning, 1956. Bd. dirs. Rochester Community Chest; bd. govs. ARC; bd. visitors Air Force Acad. Served to maj. USAAF, 1916-19; maj. gen., World War II. Decorated DSC, DSM, Legion of Merit, Silver Star, Bronze Star medal; companion of Bath (Great Britain); Russian Order of St. Anne; Legion of Honor, Croix de Guerre (France); recipient Collier trophy Nat. Aero. Assn., 1958. Mem. Rochester C. of C. (trustee), Rochester Assn. of UN (dir.), Air Force Assn. (bd. dirs.), Country Club, Genesee Valley Club, University Club (N.Y.C.) Wings Club (N.Y.C.), Bucks Club (London), Travellers Club (Paris), Metropolitan Club (Washington). Home: Rochester N.Y. Died Mar. 13, 1987; buried Rochester.

CURTIS, KENT KRUEGER, science adminstrator, consultant, researcher; b. Charles City, Iowa, Jan. 24, 1927; s. James Hubert and Lydia Ethel (Krueger) C.; m. Sidnee Smith, 1956; children—Greta, Christian, Sandra; m. Herta Kley, June 7, 1971; children—Celia, Katherine. B.S. in Math., Yale U., 1948; M.A. in Physics, Dartmouth Coll., 1950; postgrad., U. Calif.-Berkeley, 1955. Head div. math. and computing Lawrence Berkeley Lab., Calif., 1955-67; head computer sci. sect. NSF, Washington, 1967-83, dir. div. computer research, 1983; cons. Livermore Nat. Lab., Los Alamos Nat. Lab., Swedish Tech. Devel. Union; lectr. U. Calif.; research scientist Courant Inst. Math. Scis., N.Y.C. Contbr. articles to profl. jours. Named Disting. lectr. Computer Soc. of IEEE. Mem. Assn. Computing Machinery, IEEE, AAAS. Home: Washington D.C. Died Dec. 17, 1987.

CURTIS, LOUIS, business executive; b. Nahant, Mass., Aug. 6, 1891; s. Louis and Fanny L. (Richardson) C.; m. Mary S. Colt, June 11, 1921. AB, Harvard U., 1914. Ptnr. Brown Brothers & Co., 1921-31, Brown Brothers Harriman & Co., 1931-62, ltd. ptnr., from 1962; trustee Provident Instn. Savs. Boston. Trustee Vincent Meml. Hosp., Wentworth Inst., Boston Legal Aid Soc. Mem. Somerest Harvard Club (Boston), Country Club, Essex Country Club (Manchester, Mass.). Home: Brookline Mass. †

CURTIS, ROGER ERNEST, transportation and tire company executive; b. Greenwood, Ark., Mar. 26, 1928; s. Ernest Marshall and Nell (Rogers) C.; m. Charlene McCoy, May 4, 1947; children: Roger E., Terry Curtis Cialone, Sally Caroline. Student pub. schs., Ft. Smith, Ark. Bookkeeper Tucker Duck & Rubber Co., Ft. Smith, 1949-54; office mgr. Ross Motor Co., Ft. Smith, 1954-56; mgr. People's Loan & Investment (Tucker Duck & Rubber Co.), 1956-59; v.p. customer service ABF Freight Systems, Inc., 1959-67; v.p., pres. ABC, ABF-Ark. Bandag ABF Systems, Inc., 1967-79, sr. v.p., pres. ABC, ABF-Treadco, 1979-87; chmn. Traffic Safety Council, Ft. Smith, 1969-71. Adv. bd. dirs. Sparks Regional Med. Ctr., Ft. Smith, 1972-74; bd. dirs. Ft. Smith Girls' Club, 1979-87; justice of peace Sebastian County Quorum Ct., Ft. Smith, 1967-76; mem. Com. of 21, United Fund of Ft. Smith, 1971-73. Mem. Ft. Smith C. of C. Methodist. Club: Hardscrabble (Ft. Smith). Home: Fort Smith Ark. Died Jan. 26, 1987.

CUSHING, HERBERT LEWIS, college president; b. Ord, Nebr., Oct. 30, 1890; s. Francis Marion and Katherine Adelaide (Bassett) C.; m. Annie Laurie Van Broekhoven, Sept. 17, 1915; children: Thomas Caleb (dec.), Mae Margatet, Herbert Louis. BA, Grand Island Coll., 1914, U. Chgo., 1922; MA, U. Nebr., 1931; EdD (hon.), Nebr. Wesleyan U., 1937. Rural sch. tchr. 1908-10; county supt. pub. instrn. Valley County, Nebr., 1914-17; sec. Nebr. Food, Drug, Dairy and Oil Commn., 1917-19; farming and live stock bus. editor Ord Jour., story writer for Ord Quiz, 1919-22; supt. schs., Ord, 1922-27; dir. cert., acting dir. adult edn., dep. state supt. pub. instrn., dir Fed. Emergency Ednl. Program for Nebr., 1927-36; pres. Nebr. State Tchrs. Coll., Kearney, from 1936. Author: Manual of Physical Education, School Officers Manual. Pres. Nebr. Soc. for Crippled Children, 1947; chmn. Nebr. Crippled Children's Com., 1935-36; chmn., state cons. Ednl. Policies Commn. Mem. NEA (com. on tax edn.), Am. Assn. Sch. Adminstrs., Nebr. State Edn. Assn., Native Sons and Daughters Nebr. (pres. 1939), Nebr. Vocational Guidance Assn. (pres. 1934), Nebr. Assn. Colls. and Univs. (pres. 1953-54), Kearney C. of C. (pres. 1944), Kearney Country Club, University Club (Lincoln), Schoolmaster Club, Elks, Phi Delta Kappa. Home: Kearney Nebr. †

CUSHMAN, MARTELLE LOREEN, education educator; b. Kalamazoo, Mar. 9, 1908; s. Clifton L. and Stella M. (Doty) C.; m. Florence S. Haas, June 20, 1933; children: Cedric A., Clifton E., Marnita L., Marlene L. AB, Western Mich. U., 1932; MA, U. Mich., 1937; PhD, Cornell U., 1943. Prin. High Sch., Ellsworth, Mich., 1928-31; coach, tchr. W.K. KEllogg Sch., Augusta, Mich., 1932-35; supt. schs. Cedarville, Mich., 1935-38, Richmond, Mich., 1938-41; prof. edn. Iowa State U., 1945-54; dean, prof. Coll. Edn., U. N.D., Grand Forks, 1954-72, dean emeritus, 1972-82; adj. prof. higher edn. So. Ill. U., Carbondale, from 1977; vis. prof. edn. U. Nebr., 1952, U. Tex., 1954, U. Ill., 1972-73, So. Ill. U., 1974; pres. Internat. High Sch. Music Camp Ltd., from 1956. Author: The Governance of Teacher Education, 1977, Pilgrims of the Fruit Belt, 1980; contbr. numerous articles to mags. Lt. col. Civil Air Patrol, N.D. Wing, dep. edn., 1958-72. Mem. NEA (pres. rural dept. 1953-54), Am. Assn. Coll. Tchr. Edn. (chmn. studies com. 1961), Nat. Assn. State Univs. and Land Grant Colls. (mem. exec. com. assn. deans edn. 1968-71), Phi Delta Kappa (pres. 1955-57). Home: Port Charlotte Fla. Died Dec. 28, 1982.

CUTLER, MAX, surgeon; b. Jitomar, Russia, May 9, 1899; came to U.S., 1907, naturalized, 1914; s. Sam and Esther (Tchudnowsky) C.; m. Bertie Burger, Apr. 12, 1946; children: Nina Maxine, Nancy Max, Helen Suzette. BS, U. Ga., 1918; MD, Johns Hopkins U., 1922; postgrad., Curie Inst., Paris, Radiumhemmet, Stockholm. Res. house surgeon Johns Hopkins Hosp., 1922-23; instr. pathology Cornell U. Med. Sch. and Meml. Hosp., N.Y.C., 1924-26; Rockefeller fellow in cancer rsch. Meml. Hosp., N.Y.C., 1926-30; dir. N.Y. C. Cancer Inst., 1930-31; founder, dir. Tumor Clinic, Michael Reese Hosp., Chgo., 1931-37; cons. in cancer, dir. cancer rsch. Edward Hines VA Hosp. and U.S. VA, 1931-46; assoc. in surgery Northwestern Med. Sch., 1935-40; vis. prof. surgery Peking (China) Union Med. Coll., 1936-37; mem. surg. staff Cedars of Lebanon Hosp., L.A., 1952-79, emeritus, 1979-84; mem. staff St. Johns Hosp., Santa Monica, Calif., 1952-68; breast cons. dept. radiology UCLA, 1976-79, Century City Hosp., Brotman Meml. Hosp., 1967-79; dir. Beverly Hills Cancer Rsch. Found., 1966-79; 1st pres. Am. Assn. Neoplastic Diseases, 1933-34; mem. Nat. Adv. Cancer Coun., 1939-42. Author: (with Sir George Lenthal Cheatle) Tumors of the Breast, 1931, Cancer, Its Diagnosis and Treatment, 1938, Tumors of the Breast: Their Pathology, Symptoms, Diagnosis and Treatment, 1961; contbr. articles to profl. jours. With U.S. Army, World War I. Mem. N.Y. Acad. Medicine, Chgo. Inst. Medicine, Am. Radium Soc., Am. Assn. Cancer Rsch., AMA, L.A. County Med. Soc., Internat. Coll. Surgeons, Soc. Surg. Oncology, Masons, Phi Epsilon Pi, Phi Delta Epsilon, Phi Beta Kappa, Alpha Omega Alpha; hon. mem. Cuban Radiol. Soc., Radiol. Soc. Chile. Jewish. Home: Camarillo Calif. Died July 6, 1984, buried Hillside Meml. Park, L.A.

CUYLER, LEWIS B(AKER), foundation executive; b. Princeton, N.J., Apr. 11, 1902; s. John P. and Juliann (Stevens) C.; m. Margery Pepperrell Merrill, July 30, 1932; children: Lewis Carter, Juliane Stevens, George Grenville, David LeRoy, Margery Stuyvesant. AB, Princeton, 1924. Tchr. South Kent (Conn.) Sch., 1925-28; joined First Nat. City Bank of N.Y. (now Citibank), 1928, asst. cashier, 1939, asst. v.p., 1945, v.p. in charge of personnel adminstrn., 1946, sr. v.p., 1958-64; pres. Assn. Aid Crippled Children (now Found. Child Devel.), 1962-67; mem. task force on personnel and civil service Hoover Commn., 1953. Alumni trustee at large Princeton U., 1949-53; trustee South Kent Sch., 1953; bd. dirs. Eden Inst. Col. USAAF, 1942-43. Decorated Legion of Merit with oak leaf cluster. Mem. Ivy Club (Princeton), Pine Valley Golf Club, Springdale Golf Club, Princeton Club (N.Y.C.). Republican. Episcopalian (vestryman). Home: Princeton N.J. Died Mar. 2, 1988; buried Trinity Ch., Princeton, N.J.

CZECH, BRUNO C., retail chain executive; b. Englewood, N.H., Dec. 19, 1934; s. Carl and Katie Czech; m. Audrey Czech, June 2, 1956; children: Bruce, Christopher. BS, Fordham U., 1956; MBA, Fairleigh Dickinson U., 1964. V.p. personnel credit card div. Am. Express, Indian Head Co., N.Y.C., Kaufmann's, Pitts.; sr. v.p. human resources Zayre Corp., Framingham, Mass.; vis. prof. Eastern Conn. State Coll.; mem. coms. EEO. With USMCR, 1956-58. Mem. U.S. C. of C Home: Weston Conn. Deceased.

DACOSTA, MORTON, director, producer, actor; Phila., Mar. 7, 1914; s. Samuel and Rose (Hulnic Tecosky. BS in Edn., Temple U., 1936, LHD (hon 1958. Broadway acting debut in: The Skin of O Teeth, 1942; dir. nat. tour Sabrina Fair, 1950's; di Broadway plays including The Gray Eyed People, 195 Plain and Fancy, 1955, No Time for Sergeants, 195 Auntie Mame, 1956, The Music Man, 1957, (libret and co-producer, Tony award for show) Saratoga, 195 The Wall, 1960, To Broadway with Love, 1964, (c author) Maggie Flynn, 1966, Show Me Where the Go Times Are, 1970, The Women, 1973, A Musical Jubile 1975, Doubles, 1986; plays at City Center, N.Y.C. i cluding She Stoops to Conquer, 1949; Captain Bras bound's Conversion, 1950, Dream Girl and the Wi Duck, 1951; dir., producer: films Auntie Mame, 195 The Music Man, 1961, Island of Love; conceived ar directed: To Broadway with Love, Tex. Pavillion, N. World's Fair, 1964, Doubles, 1985. Recipient Gold Globe award Fgn. Press Assn., 1963. Mem. Soc. Sta Dirs. and Choreographers (treas. 1971-74), Dirs. Gui Am., Dramatists Guild Am., Actors Equity Assn Democrat. Jewish. Home: West Redding Conn. Di Jan., 1989.

DAGLEY, STANLEY, biochemist, educator; b. Burto on-Trent, Eng., Apr. 1, 1916; came to U.S., 196 naturalized, 1976; s. Arthur and Agnes Susann (Walker) D.; m. Pasca Alice Stretton, June 24, 19 children—Michael, Pauline Dagley White, Jane Dagl Bellion, Helen. B.A., U. Oxford, 1937, B.Sc., 19 M.A., 1946; M.Sc., U. London, 1948, D.Sc., 1955. lectr. chemistry Sir John Cass Coll., London, 1945-4 lectr. biochemistry U. Leeds, Eng., 1947-52; reader Leeds, 1952-62, prof., 1962-66; vis. prof. U. Ill., 196 64; prof. dept. biochemistry U. Minn., St. Paul, 1966-8 Regents' prof. U. Minn., 1980-87. Author: (wi Nicholson) An Introduction to Metabolic Pathway 1970; co-editor Biochem. Edn, 1974-85; contbr. articl to profl. jours. Recipient Horace T. Morse award f outstanding contbns. to undergrad. edn. U. Minn., 196 NSF Sr. Fgn. Scientist fellow, 1963. Mem. Bioche Soc., Soc. for Gen. Microbiology, Am. Soc. Micro ology, Am. Soc. Biol. Chemists (com. on ednl. affa 1974-82), Internat. Union Biochemistry (edn. com. 197 82). Episcopalian. Home: Saint Paul Minn. Died O 31, 1987; cremated, ashes interred St. Peter's Churc Leckhampton, Gloucestershire, Eng.

DAGNESE, JOSEPH MARTOCCI, librarian; Worcester, Mass., Oct. 10, 1927; s. Gennaro Francis a Carmella Veronica (Martocci) D.; divorced; childre Joseph Michael, Paul Andrew, Edward Peter. B Boston Coll., 1949; MA, Catholic U. Am., 1951, ML 1952; postgrad., Heidelberg (Germany) U., 1954-55 Cataloger Cath. U. Am., 1955-57; librarian Nucle Metals, Inc., Concord, Mass., 1957-60; head acquisitio dept. MIT, 1960-62, sci. librarian, head circulati dept., 1962-66, asst. dir. tech. services, 1966-72; pr library scis., dir. libraries Purdue U., West Lafayet Ind., 1972-89; cons. Birla Inst. Tech., Pilani (Rajasthar India, 1966-67, Delhi U., India, 1970; bd. dirs. Cent for Research Libraries, 1981-84; v.p., pres.-ele Universal Serials and Book Exchange, 1984, pres., 198 Contbr. articles to profl. jours. Served with U.S. Arm 1952-54. Fellow Spl. Libraries Assn. (pres. Boston ch 1964-65, chpt. liaison officer 1970-72, John Cotton Da lectr. 1972, chmn. com. on positive action 1972-74, d 1974-77, pres.-elect 1978-79, pres. 1979-80, posthumo Hall of Fame award 1989); mem. Assn. Resear Libraries. Home: Lafayette Ind. Died Jan. 27, 19 buried Tippecanoe Memories Garden, Lafayette.

DAHL, THOMAS MOORE, engineering and co struction company executive; b. Mpls., Aug. 8, 1918; Walter H. and Helen (Moore) D.; m. Gail Gilje, F 20, 1943; children: Susan, Janet. V.p. United Engrs. Constructors Inc., Phila., 1958-71, pres., chief operati officer, 1971-76, chmn. bd., chief exec. officer, 1976-8 past dir. Atomic Indsl. Forum, Jackson & Morelar Internat., UE&C Internat., United Mid-East In Piccon Inc; bd. dirs. Med. Coll. Pa. Mem. Assn. Ir and Steel Engrs., IEEE, Aronimink Gold Club, Uni League, Masons. Home: Phila. Pa. Died May, 1986

DAHLBERG, EDWIN LENNART, artist; b. Belo Wis., Sept. 20, 1901; s. Edwin Tore D. and Anna Sop Eckholm; m. Gertrude Ernestine Seligman, Dec. 1927; children: Eric Charles, Karen Dahlbe VanderVen, Clare Anna Dahlberg Horner. Grad., A Inst., Chgo., 1924. Illustrator Graumen-Jennin Studio, Chgo., 1925-32; free-lance illustrator N.Y. 1932-59; painter watercolors Nyack, N.Y., 1959-85 Recipient medal of honor Knickerboker Artists, 197 Mem. Am. Watercolor Soc. (Gold medal 1972), Alli Artists Am., Nat. Acad. Design, Hudson Valley A Assn. (Gold Medal of Honor and others 1974). Hon Nyack N.Y. Died Nov. 19, 1985.

DAHLBERG, EDWIN THEODORE, clergyman; Fergus Falls, Minn., Dec. 27, 1892; s. Elof and Christi (Ring) D.; m. Emilie Louise Loeffler, Aug. 27, 19 children: Margaret Emilie, Bruce Theodore, Ke Ramel. BA, U. Minn., 1914; BD, Rochester The Sem., 1917, postgrad., 1918; DD, Keuka Coll., 19

Denison U., Kalamazoo Coll.; LLD, Franklin Coll. Ordained to ministry, Baptist Ch., 1918. Pastor First Ch., Potsdam, N.Y., 1918-21, Maple St. Ch., Buffalo, 1921-31; pastor First Bapt. Ch., St. Paul, Minn., 1931-39, Syracuse, N.Y., 1939-50; pastor Delmar Bapt. Ch., St. Louis, 1950-62, pastor emeritus, 1962-86; preacher in residence Crozer Theol. Sem., Chester, Pa., 1963-86; pres. No. Bapt. Convention, 1946-48; mem. Central Com. World Council Chs. 1948-54; pres. Nat. Council Chs. of Christ in USA, 1957-60; bd. mem. Am. Bapt. Home Mission Soc., pres. 1955-56; mem. exec. com. Bapt. World Alliance, 1947-55; trustee Colgate-Rochester Div. Sch.; dir. Ministers' Life and Casualty Union, 1937-65. Author: Youth and the Homes of Tomorrow: Which Way for a Christian?, This Is the Rim of East Asia; editor: Herald of the Gospel. Mem. Iron Wedge (U. Minn.). Home: Chester Pa. Died Sept. 6, 1986.

DAHLING, LOUIS FERDINAND, lawyer; b. Boseman, Mont., Oct. 20, 1892; s. John Hugo and Louise (Kraud) D.; m. Catherine S. Vaughn, Oct. 20, 1926; 1 child, William D. Student, Mont. Agrl. Coll. (now Mont. State Coll.), 1910-13; JD, U. Mich., 1917. Bar: Mich. 1920. Practiced in Detroit, from 1920; ptnr. Bodman, Longley, Bogle, Armstrong & Dahling (later Bodman Longely & Dahling), from 1942. Trustee James and Lynelle Holden Fund, Detroit Zool. Soc. With USN, 1917-19. Mem. ABA, Mich. Bar Assn., Detroit Bar Assn. (pres. 1956-57), Renaissance Club, Country Club of Detroit, Univ. Club of Detroit, Order of Coif. Home: Grosse Point Mich. Died Feb. 5, 1982, buried Woodlawn Cemetery, Detroit.

D'ALESANDRO, THOMAS, JR., government official, mayor; b. Balt., Aug. 1, 1903; s. Thomas and Mary Anne (Foppiano) D'A.; m. Annuciata M. Lombardi, Sept. 30, 1928; children: Thomas III, Nicholas, Franklin D. Roosevelt, Nicholas J., Hector, Joseph, Annunciata. Student, Calvert Bus. Coll., Balt. Owner, pres. D'Alesandro Jr. & Sons, Balt.; mem. Md. Ho. of Dels., 1926-33; gen. dep. collector IRS, 1933-34; mem. Balt. City Council, 1935-38; mem. 76th to 80th congresses from 3d Md. Dist, mayor Balt., 1947-59, Dem. nat. committeeman Md., 1952-56, del. nat. convs., mem. renegotiation bd., 1961-69. Mem. U.S. Conf. of Mayors (chmn. standing com. on legis.), Advt. Club Md., Md. Hist. Soc., Vincent dePaul Soc., Holy Name Soc., St. Leo's Confrat., K.C. (40), Elks, Moose, Hickory Club. Home: Baltimore Md. Died Aug. 23, 1987.

DALEY, JOSEPH T., bishop; b. Connerton, Pa., Dec. 21, 1915. Ed., Charles Borromeo Sem., Phila.; DD. Ordained priest Roman Cath. Ch., June 4, 1941. titular bishop Barca and aux. bishop, Harrisburg, 1963-67, coadjutor bishop with right of succession, 1967-71, bishop Harrisburg, Pa., from 1971. Home: Harrisburg Pa. Died Sept. 2, 1983.

DALI, SALVADOR, artist; b. Figueras nr. Barcelona, Spain, May 11, 1904; s. Salvador and Felipa (Domeneck) D.; m. Gala Dali, Sept., 1935. Student pub. and pvt. schs., Bros. of Marist Order, Figueras; student, Sch. Fine Arts, Madrid, 1921-26. Influenced by Italian Futurists, 1923-25; became a Surrealist, Paris, 1929; designed jewelry, furniture and art nouveau decorations, 1929-31; designer films of Luis Bunuel; symbolic interpretations of legend of William Tell and Millet's The Angelus, 1934; series of beach scenes at Rosas, Spain, literal pictures of his dreams, 1934-46; decorated residence of Edward James, London, 1936; designed Dali's Dream House, N.Y. World's Fair, 1939; designed ballets including Bacchanale, Met. Opera, 1939; Labyrinth book, costumes, scenery; Cafe de Chiuita, Spanish Festival, Met. Opera, 1942; one-man shows include Julien Levy Gallery, N.Y.C., 1933, Arts Club, Chgo., 1941, Dalzell Hatfield Galleries, Los Angeles, Mus. Modern Art, N.Y.C., Knoedler Gallery, N.Y.C.; exhibited in numerous group shows, Paris, London, Barcelona, N.Y.C.; retrospective exhbn., Rotterdam, 1970-71; author: (autobiography) Secret Life of Salvador Dali, 1942, Diary of a Genius, 1965, The Unspeakable Confessions of Salvador Dali, 1976. Recipient $5000 Huntington Hartford Found. award, 1957. Home: Cadaqués Spain. Died Jan. 23, 1989.

DALTON, JOHN NICHOLS, lawyer, former governor Virginia; b. Emporia, Va., July 11, 1931; s. Ted R. and Mary (Turner) D.; m. Edwina Jeanette Panzer, Feb. 18, 1956; children: Katherine Scott, Ted Ernest, John Nichols, Mary Helen. A.B., Coll. William and Mary, 1953; J.D., U. Va., 1957. Bar: Va. 1957. Ptnr. Dalton & Jebo, Radford, Va., 1957-7[illegible]; lt. gov. Va. 1974-78, gov., 1978-82; ptnr. McGuire Woods & Battle, Richmond, 1982-86. Pres. Young Republican Fedn. Va., 1960; treas. Va. Rep. Com., 1960, gen. counsel, 1961-72; mem. Va. Ho. of Dels., 1966-72, Va. Senate, 1973. Served to 1st lt. AUS, 1954-56. Mem. Am. Legion, Sigma Alpha Epsilon. Clubs: Masons (33 deg.), Shriners (past potentate). Home: Richmond Va. Died July 30, 1986.

DALY, E. A., publisher; b. Tuscaloosa, Ala., Nov. 16, 1891; s. Ralph F. and Lillie L. (Floyd) D.; m. Lillian Madora Hilton, June 3, 1919. Student, Talladega Coll., 1911-13, Morris Brown Coll., 1914-18. Lic. real estate broker. Editor, pub., owner Calif. Voice, Oakland, from 1926. Active Little League Baseball, YMCA; hon. life mem. NAACP; no. Calif. chmn. Jess Unruh for gov., also Senator Allen Cranston campaign, 1965-70. With U.S. Army, 1918-19. Mem. Masons, Shriners, KP. Mem. A.M.E. Ch. Home: Oakland Calif. †

DAMON, CATHRYN, actress; b. Seattle, Sept. 11. Broadway debut in By The Beautiful Sea, 1954, followed by The Vamp, Shinbone Alley, A Family Affair, Foxy, Flora The Red Menace, UTBU, Come Summer, Criss-Crossing, A Place for Polly, Last of the Red Hot Lovers, The Prisoner of Second Avenue, Sweet Bird of Youth, The Cherry Orchard; off-Broadway appearances include: Secret Life of Walter Mitty, Effect of Gamma Rays on Man-in-the-Moon Marigolds, Prodigal, Siamese Connections, The Boys from Syracuse; numerous other theatrical appearances; TV appearances include: The Love Boat; appeared as Mary Campbell on TV Series Soap (Emmy award 1980), 1977-81. Home: New York N.Y. Died May 4, 1987.

DAMON, TERRY ALLEN, museum director, retired naval officer; b. Washington, Dec. 8, 1930; s. Norman Clare and Madeline Bates (Hoag) D.; m. Janet T. Ryon, Apr. 12, 1980; children: Diane Clare, Denise Yvonne, Andrew Allen, Charles Ronald, Richard Teeple, David Shea. BS, U. Mich., 1953. Commd. ensign U.S. Navy, 1955, advanced through grades to comdr., 1968; asst. naval attache, attache for air Am. Embassy, Tehran, Iran, 1961-63; pilot Heavy Attack Squadron 4 Naval Air Sta., Whidbey Island, Wash., 1963-66; maitenance officer, flight instr. Attack Sqaudron 128 1968-69; weapons officer Comdr. Carrier Div. 9, 1969-71; prodn. mgmt. specialist Def. Intelligence Agy., 1971-76; asst. dir. Navy Meml. Mus., Washington, 1976-78, dir., from 1978; pres. Damon Galleries Ltd., 1974-81. Decorated 4 Air medals. Mem. Council Am. Maritime Mus., Profl. Picture Framers Assn., Alpha Tau Omega. Republican. Episcopalian. Died Oct. 25, 1984, buried Arlington (Va.) Nat. Cemetery.

DAMPIER, JOSEPH HENRY, clergyman, educator; b. Guelph, Ont., Can., Mar. 7, 1908; came to U.S., 1925, naturalized, 1940; s. Robert Alexander and Elizabeth (Hindely) D.; m. Ione Margaret Chandler, 1928 (dec. 1960); 1 dau., Phyllis (Mrs. Harry E. Fontaine); m. Mildred Feagans, 1963. AB, Cin. Bible Sem., 1931; EdM, U. Pitts., 1941; DD, Atlanta Christian Coll., 1952; LLD, Johnson Bible Coll., 1957. Pastor Christian Ch., Alfordsville, Ind. and Antioch, Ind., 1927-28, Lawrenceburg, Ind., 1929-34; pastor First Christian Ch., McKeesport, Pa., 1934-41, First Ch., Johnson City, Tenn., 1941-58; provost Milligan Coll., Tenn., 1958-65; dean Emmanuel Sch. of Religion, 1965-69; prof. Christian ministries, 1969-82; pres. North Am. Christian Conv., 1950-51; mem. Commn. of Restudy, Disciples of Christ; external lectr. Maritime Christian Coll., Charlottetown, P.E.I., Can. Author: Workbook on Christian Doctrine, 1943; mem. pub. com., Standard Pub. Co., Cin.; contbr. to religious mags. Recipient Fide et Amore award Milligan Coll., 1980. Mem. Am. Acad. Religion, Disciples of Christ Hist. Soc., Masons (32 deg.), K.T., Kiwanian (past pres.). Home: Johnson City Tenn. Died Dec. 7, 1984; buried Monte Vista Cemetery, Johnson City, Tenn.

DANA, EDWARD, railway executive; b. Bernardston, Mass., July 28, 1886; s. Edward Livingston Underwood and Lucy (Merrill) D. AB, Harvard U., 1908. With Boston Elevated Ry., from 1907, pres., gen. mgr., 1937-47; bd. dirs. Union Freight R.R.; gen. mgr. Met. Transit Authority from 1947; incorporator Suffolk Savs. Bank, Charleston Five Cents Savs. Bank; bd. dirs. Mass. Safety Coun. (pres. 1928-30, 1942), Nat. Safety Coun. (v.p. 1930-32), Transit Rsch. Corp., 1941-45, Transit Mut. Ins. Co., Mass. Hosp. Svc., 1927-47; mem. Northeastern U. Corp. Author articles relating to transp.; contbr. to indsl. publs. Dir. local transport div. Office Def. Transp., 1942-45; industry dir. Region I, War Labor B., 1943-45; bd. dirs. Am. Nat. Red Cross, chmn. fin. com., 1946-54; mem. Boston War Transp. Conservation com., Mass. and Boston com. of pub. safety, 1942-45, Indsl. Relation Coun. (exec. com.), U.S. Conciliation Svc. Labor-Mgmt. Advt. Com., 1946; bd. dirs. Community Fedn. of Boston. Mem. Am. Transit Oper. Assn. (pres. 1927-28), Am. Mgmt. Assn. (dir. 1928), Am. Transit Assn. (pres. 1935-36); chmn. labor-mgmt. com. 1947), U.S. C. of C. (labor relations com.), Soc. Colonial Wars, Soc. of the War of 1812 (pres. 1942), Mass. Soc. Mayflower Descendants (gov. 1942), SAR (pres. 1948; mem. bd. mgrs.), Mass. Soc. Founders and Patriots Am., Harvard Club, Newcomen Soc., Engineers Club (pres. 1937), New England Transit Club (pres. 1921-22), Commercial Club (pres. 1942). Home: Boston Mass. †

DANGERFIELD, GEORGE, author; b. Newbury, Berkshire, Eng., Oct. 28, 1904; came to U.S., 1930, naturalized, 1943; s. George and Ethel Margaret (Tyrer) D.; m. Helen Mary Deey Spedding, June 28, 1928; m. Mary Lou Schott, June 29, 1941; children: Mary Jo, Hilary, Anthony. Student, Forest Sch., Walthamstow, Essex, Eng., 1916-22; B.A., Hertford Coll., Oxford U., 1927; M.A., Oxford U., 1968. Asst. editor Brewer, Warren & Putnam, N.Y.C., 1930-32; lit. editor Vanity Fair mag., 1933-35; writer, lectr. 1935-86; lectr. history U. Calif. at Santa Barbara, 1968-72. Author: Bengal Mutiny, 1933, The Strange Death of Liberal England, 1935, Victoria's Heir, 1941, The Era of Good Feelings, 1952, Chancellor Robert R. Livingston of New York, 1960, The Awakening of American Nationalism, 1815-1828, 1965, Defiance to the Old World, 1970, The Damnable Question, 1976, (with Otey M. Scruggs) Henry Adams' History of the United States, 1963; contbg. author: (Allan Nevins) Times of Trial, 1958, (John A. Garraty) Quarrels That Have Shaped the Constitution, 1963, Interpreting American History, 1970. Served 102d inf. div. AUS, 1942-45. Recipient Bancroft prize in Am. history Columbia U., 1953, Pulitzer prize in Am. history, 1953; Benjamin D. Shreve fellow Princeton U., 1957-58; Guggenheim fellow, 1970. Fellow Soc. Am. Historians; mem. Common Cause, ACLU, Friends of Montecito Pub. Library, Am. Antiquarian Soc. Home: Santa Barbara Calif. Died Dec. 27, 1986.

DANIEL, PRICE, SR., justice Texas Supreme Ct., former Texas governor; b. Dayton, Tex., Oct. 10, 1910; s. Marion Price and Nannie (Partlow) D.; m. Jean Houston Baldwin, June 28, 1940; children: Price, Jean, Houston, John. AB, Baylor U., 1931, LLB, 1932, LLD, 1951. Bar: Tex. 1932. Reporter Ft. Worth Star Telegram, 1926-27, Waco (Tex.) News Tribune, 1929-31; pvt. practice Liberty, Tex., 1932-43; mem. Tex. Ho. of Reps. 1939-43, speaker of Ho., 1943, atty gen. State of Tex., 1946-53; pvt. practice Austin, Tex., 1963-70; justice Tex. Supreme Ct. 1971-88; co-pub. Liberty Vindicator and Anahuac Progress, 1939-72; former chmn. So. Govs. Conf., Interstate Oil Compact Commn.; dir. Office Emergency Planning, Presdl. asst. fed.-state relations, 1967-69; past mem. Adv. Commn. Inter-Govtl. Relations, Washington, Nat. Security Council, sr. emergency planning com. NATO; chmn. U.S. sect. U.S.-Mexico Com. on Emergency Planning for Mut. Assistance in Case of Disaster, Washington, 1967-69. Author: Texas Publication Laws, 1951, Texas Election Laws, 1952; author treaties on Tex. Ownership of Submerged Lands and Annexation Agreement between Tex. and U.S.; editor Lariat, daily newspaper, 1930-31, Round-Up, 1931-32. Mem. Tex. Dem. Exec. Com., 1939-41; trustee Baylor U., Baylor Med. Sch., Houston. With AUS, 1943-46; PTO. Mem. ABA, Am. Soc. Internat. Law, Internat. Law Assn., State Bar Tex., Liberty C. of C. (pres. 1939-41), Sigma Delta Chi, Pi Kappa Delta, Masons, Shriners, Elks, Woodmen of World, Rotary. Home: Liberty Tex. Died Aug. 25, 1988.

DANIELS, DOMINICK VINCENT, congressman; b. Jersey City, Oct. 18, 1908; s. John and Carmela (De Stefano) D.; m. Camille Curcio, Sept. 15, 1935; children: Delores D. Maragni, Barbara D. Coleman. Student, Fordham U.; LLB, Rutgers U., 1929. Bar: N.J. 1930. Magistrate Jersey City Mcpl. Ct., 1952-58; past mem. 86th-94th Congresses 14th Dist. N.J.; former city chmn. Po Valley Flood Relief Com.; vice chmn. Jersey City Civil Rights Com., 1952-55. Mem. N.J. Bar Assn., Hudson County Bar Assn., Elks, K.C. (4 deg.), Univ. Club of Hudson County. Died July 17, 1987.

DANIELS, ELMER HARLAND, sculptor, architect; b. Owosso, Mich., Oct. 23, 1905; s. H. J. and Blanche (Tuthill) D.; m. Madge Kuhn, 1933; children: Stephen, Carol, Richard, Julia. Student, Grand Rapids (Mich.) Coll., 1924-25, John Herron Art Inst., Indpls., 1925-27, Beaux Arts Inst. Design, N.Y.C., 1927-29; study in, Europe, Eng., France and Italy (sculpture), 1931; student, Columbia, summer 1930. Tchr. Art Center Sch., Indpls., 1935-38; conducted pvt. studio classes Indpls, 1938-40; organized Daniels Assos. (archtl. firm), 1943-50, Daniels and Zermack Assos., Ann Arbor, 1950-72. Indsl. designer murals, Oakland (Calif.), 1942—; designer, Domore Furniture Co.; designed bank buildings, Mich., Ohio, Ind., Ill; important works include Lincoln Meml., Lincoln City, Ind., (now owned by U.S. Dept. Interior and operated by Nat. Park Service), commd. State of Ind., 1941, Heroic Head of Lincoln in Ala. marble, State Capitol Bldg, Indpls., 1939, Three Heroic Stone Figures, St. Joseph Ch., Jasper, Ind., 1941, six stone panels for Arts Bldg., Ball State Tchrs. Coll., Muncie, Ind., 1933, Brotherhood of Maintenance of Way meml, Detroit, Bay County War Meml, Bay City, Mich., Family Group, Detroit & No. Savs. & Loan, Flint, Mich., 5 terra figures, Loma Linda Restaurant, Ann Arbor, Mich., mural in oil, Union Bank, Steubenville, Ohio, also banks and instns. in, Indpls., Monroe, Mich., Grand Rapids, Mich., Petoskey, Mich., Pasadena, Calif. and Scottsdale, Ariz.; Portraits include Paul V. McNutt; bronze Ernest Hemmingway, Albert Switzer, Albert Einstein,; Indsl. designer for, Kaiser Industries, Kaiser Aluminum, Kaiser Steel, Kaiser Community Homes, Kaiser Engrs., Standard Gysum, Heywood Wakefield Co., Plomb Tool Co., Steelcase, Inc., Stow-Davis Furniture Co., Bear Archery Co., etc., series bronze portraits of great fighting Indian chiefs of West; exhibited at, Deligny Galleries, Ft. Lauderdale, Fla., Chgo. (Recipient Harry Johnson award 1931, Ind. Artists Sculpture prize 1938, C. V. Hickox prize 1942, Grand prize Standard Oil Co. float Tournament of Roses.); Contbr.: articles on sculpture and art in gen., to Mich. Tradesman; Sculpture work; exhibited in: Sat. Eve. Post. Mem. Am. Soc. Indsl. Designers, Nat. Sculpture Soc., Archtl. League N.Y., Ind. Artists, Painters and Sculptors of N.J., Ind. Lincoln Union, Lincoln Fellowship of So. Calif. (hon. mem. 1944), Mich. Acad Sci., Arts and Letters, Pasadena, Palm Beach, Ann Arbor art assns., Washtenaw, Mich. hist. socs., Ann Arbor, Mich.,

Pompano Beach, Fla. chambers of commerce. Clubs: University of Pasadena, Pasadena Maestros; Miscowabik (Calumet, Mich.) (life); Ann Arbor (Mich.); Town, Barton Hills Country. Deceased.

DANIELS, FRANK ARTHUR, newspaper executive; b. Raleigh, N.C., June 8, 1904; s. Josephus and Addie Worth (Bagley) D.; m. Ruth Aunspaugh, Nov. 20, 1929; children: Frank Arthur Jr., Patricia Daniels Woronoff. AB, U. N.C., 1927. With mech. circulation, advt. depts. News and Observer, Raleigh, 1927-32, treas., 1932-56, gen. mgr., from 1942, pres., from 1956, pub., from 1966, chmn. bd., from 1971; mem. Raleigh bd. dirs. N.C. Nat. Bank, 1969-73; bd. dirs. AP, 1964-67, Atlantic & East Carolina Ry. Co., 1968-72. Past pres. Community Chest, Raleigh; chmn. N.C. Bd. Pub. Welfare, 1949-56; mem. N.C. Tax Study Commn., 1955-56; bd. dirs. Rsch. Triangle Inst., 1960-74; chmn. bd. trustees Rex Hosp., Raleigh, 1950-68; past trustee U. N.C., Chapel Hill. Mem. Am. Newspaper Pubs. Assn. (bd. dirs. 1956-64), So. Newspaper Pubs. Assn. (pres. 1951-52), Raleigh C. of C. (past pres.), Capital City Club, Carolina Country Club, Sphinx Club (Raleigh), Delta Kappa Epsilon. Home: Raleigh N.C. Died May 5, 1986; buried Oakwood Cemetery, Raleigh, N.C.

DANIS, PETER GODFREY, pediatrician, educator; b. Ottawa, Ont., Can., Apr. 12, 1909; s. Peter Godfrey and Helene (Burns) D.; m. Katherine Kramer, Apr. 6, 1931; children: Peter Godfrey, Richard, Joanne, Mary Katherine, James, Laura, David, Timothy and Thomas (twins), Deborah. Student, Gonzaga Coll.; BS, St. Louis U., 1929, MD, 1931, MS, 1935. Diplomate Am. Bd. Pediatrics. Intern St. Louis U. Group Hosps., 1931-32, fellow pediatrics, 1932-34; chmn. dept. pediatrics St. Louis U., 1947-57, assoc. prof. pediatrics, 1948-51, prof. clin. pediatrics, 1951-79, emeritus prof. clin. pediatrics, 1979-85, emeritus chmn. dept., 1979-85; former chief staff Cardinal Glennon Meml. Children's Hosp.; honor staff St. Mary's Hosp., 1969; former chief pediatric cons., dir. health services Spl. Edn. St. Louis County. Bd. dirs. health and hosp. div. Social Planning Council, 1946-49; exec. bd. Cath. Charities, St. Louis, also past med. dir. children's dept. Decorated Knight of Malta, Vatican; recipient Alumni Honor award St. Louis U., 1968, Staff award, 1974, Merit award St. Mary's Hosp., 1969, Health Care award Hosp. Assn. Met. St. Louis, 1974. Mem. Am. Acad. Pediatrics (state chmn. 1949-53, chmn. nat. com. hosps. and dispensaries 1950-52, gen. chmn. spring meeting 1971), St. Louis Med. Soc., St. Louis Pediatirc Soc., AMA, Am. Acad. Cerebral Palsy, Am. Acad. Neurology (assoc.). Home: Saint Louis Mo. Deceased 1985.

DANNER, MAX SMITH, retail company executive; b. North Vernon, Ind., May 16, 1925; s. Harry Cleo and Genevieve Rose (Smith) D.; m. Joan B. Yeager, June 8, 1945 (div. 1961); children: Mark, Christopher, Jay, Lynn; m. Barbara E. Davis, Sept. 5, 1975; children: Derrik, Janalee, Bryan. Student, Wabash Coll., 1943-44, Harvard U., 1945; BS, Ind. U., 1947, postgrad., 1958. Various positions with Danners, Inc., Indpls., 1940-45, 46-50, 50-62, pres., chmn., 1962-82, chmn., chief exec. officer, 1982-85; bd. dirs. Ind. Retail Council, Indpls., Blue Cross. Bd. dirs. Indpls. Indians Baseball Club, from 1962, Ind. Repertory Theatre, from 1977, 500 Festival Assocs., from 1980, Indpls. Kiwanis Found.; former bd. dirs. United Way, Better Bus. Bur., Boy Scouts Am., Indpls. Zoo, Jr. Achievement; bd. dirs., past pres. Bosy Club of Indpls.; bd. dirs., trustee YMCA. Mem. Assn. Gen. Mdse. Chains (dir. from 1963, vice chmn. 1983), Nat. Mass Retailers Inst., Ind. Pres.' Orgn., Ind. State C. of C. (dir. from 1963), Downtown Club Indpls, Kiwanis, Skyline Club Indpls., Beta Gamma Sigma. Republican. Methodist. Home: Indianapolis Ind. Died Apr. 27, 1985, buried Crown Hill Cemetery, Indpls.

DANOWSKI, THADDEUS STANLEY, physician, educator; b. Wallington, N.J., Sept. 6, 1914; s. Anton and Theresa (Kosciuh) D.; m. Phyllis Little, June 22, 1949; 1 son, Stanley T. BA, Yale U., 1936, MD magna cum laude, 1940. Diplomate Nat. Bd. Med. Examiners, Am. Bd. Internal Medicine. Intern in medicine New Haven Hosp., 1940-41; prof. medicine sch. medicine U. Pitts., 1947-87; physician in charge Renziehausen Meml. Ward and Clinic, 1948-56; sr. staff physician Presbyn. Woman's and Children's Hosps. of Pitts., 1947-87, Elizabeth Steel Magee Hosp., 1949-87. Contbr. articles to profl. jours. Mem. Med. Mission to Japan, 1950; mem. NRC panel, Com. on Growth, 1951; pres. Pa. div. Am. Cancer Soc., 1961-62. Fellow Berkeley Coll., Yale U., 1943-47; named Jr. C. of C. Med. Man of Yr., Pitts., 1948; Guggenheim fellow, 1953-54; recipient Jurzykowski award 1969. Fellow ACP, AMA, AAAS, Am. Diabetes Assn. (pres. 1965); mem. Am. Soc. Clin. Investigation, Am. Physiol. Soc., Fedn. of the Am. Investigation, Am. Physiol. Soc., Fedn. Am. Socs. for Exptl. Biology, Thyroid Assn., N.Y. Acad. Scis., Allegheny County Med. Assn., Pa. State Med. Soc., Clinic Soc. of the Pitts. Diabetes Assn. (pres. 1950-51), Polish Acad. Sci., Cracow Acad. Medicine, Polish Med. Assn., Soc. Polish Internists, Phi Beta Kappa, Sigma Xi, Alpha Omega Alpha, Interurban Clin. Club. Home: Pittsburgh Pa. Died Sept. 12, 1987.

D'ARBELOFF, DIMITRI VLADIMIR, separations technology manufacturing executive; b. Paris, Oct. 8, 1929; naturalized, 1944; s. Vladimir A. and Catherine (Tiepolt) d'A; m. Sybil Coe, Aug. 6, 1955; children: Melinda, John, Nicholas. AB, Harvard U., 1951, MBA, 1955. Rsch. asst. Harvard U. Grad. Sch. Bus. Adminstrn., 1955-57; pres. United Rsch. Inc., Cambridge, Mass., 1957-62; v.p., then exec. v.p. Millipore Corp., Bedford, Mass., 1962-71, pres., chief exec. officer, 1971-80, chmn., chief exec. officer, 1980-84, chmn., from 1984; bd. dirs. Rexnord Inc., Mass. Fin. Services, Cambridge Trust Co., Black & Decker; bd. dirs., chmn. Mass. High Tech. Coun.; vice chmn. Am. Bus. Conf.; mem. Bus.-Higher Edn. Forum. Trustee Johns Hopkins U.; bd. dirs. Mass. Gen. Hosp.; chmn. trustees com. Applied Physics Lab., John Hopkins U., Balt. Served with USNR, 1951-53. Mem. Health Industry Mfrs. Assn. (dir.), Harvard Club, Comml. Club, Cambridge Tennis Club, N.Y. Yacht Club, N.E. Harbor Fleet Club (Bar Harbor, Maine). Deceased.

DARBY, ALFRED ELLERY, retail executive; b. Providence, June 28, 1892; s. Alfred John and Elizabeth Agnes (Collins) D.; m. Irma Mae Craft, May 1, 1920; children: Thelma Elizabeth, Alfred Ellery. Student, pub. schs. and bus. sch. Profl. violinist, 1912-27; acct. Outlet Co., dept. store, Providence, 1915-17, v.p., gen. mdse. mgr., 1945-50, pres., 1950-60, then mem. exec. com., also bd. didrs.; bd. dirs. Indsl. Nat. Bank. Contbr. articles to Dry Goods Economist, Women's Wear. 1st musician, radio electrician USN, 1917-19. Mem. Nat. Retail Dry Goods Assn. (bd. dirs.), Providence C. of C. (hon. dir.), Am. Legion, Masons (32 deg.), Shriners, Rotary, Eastern Star Club. Republican. Baptist. Home: Rumford R.I. †

DARBY, HARRY, U.S. senator, manufacturing company executive; b. Kansas City, Kans., Jan. 23, 1895; s. Harry and Florence Isabelle (Smith) D.; m. Edith Marie Cubbison, Dec. 17, 1917; children: Harriet Darby Gibson, Joan Darby Edwards, Edith Marie Darby Evans, Marjorie Darby Alford. B.M.E., U. Ill., 1917, M.E., 1929; LL.D., St. Benedict's Coll., Atchison, Kans., Westminster Coll., Fulton, Mo., Kans. State U., Manhattan and Washburn U., Topeka; D.C.S., Baker U., Baldwin City, Kans. With Mo. Boiler Works Co., Kansas City, 1911-19; with Darby Corp., 1920-87; chmn. bd., owner; founder, chmn. Leavenworth Steel, Inc.; now chmn. bd., owner; founder, chmn. Darby Ry. Cars, Inc.; dir. numerous corps; U.S. senator from Kans., 1949-50. Active 4-H Club, Boy Scouts Am.; mem. Republican Nat. Com. for Kans., 1940-64; trustee various cultural instns., assns.; trustee, chmn. Eisenhower Found., Abilene, Kans.; chmn. Eisenhower Presdl. Library Commn., Abilene; chmn. emeritus Am. Royal Livestock and Horse Show; mem. exec. com. Kans. Livestock Assn., Agrl. Hall of Fame; dir., trustee Nat. Cowboy Hall of Fame. Served from 2d lt. to capt., F.A. U.S. Army, 1917-19; with AEF. Recipient numerous awards for civic activities. Fellow ASME; mem. Navy League U.S., Kansas City Crime Commn., Kans. Registration Bd. Profl. Engrs., U. Ill. Found., ASCE, Nat., Kans. soc. profl. engrs., Am. Hereford Assn., Am. Nat. Livestock Assn., Soc. Am. Mil. Engrs., Am. Soc. Agrl. Engrs., VFW, Am. Legion, 40 and 8, Mil. Order World Wars. Episcopalian. Clubs: Masons (32 deg.), Shriners, Jesters, Kansas City, Automobile of Mo., Saddle and Sirloin, Rotary, River, Terr., Man of the Month (Kansas City, Kans.); Chicago; Chevy Chase, Capitol Hill (Washington). Home: Kansas City Kans. Died Jan. 17, 1987.

DARCY, DONALD, banker; b. N.Y.C., Apr. 21, 1918; s. Michael Stephen and Marie J. (Ryan) D.; m. Geraldine K. Kindermann, Sept. 10, 1943; children: Dwight, Keith, Joan Sorgi. B.A., Fordham Coll., 1942. Exec. sec. Bronx Bd. Trade, N.Y.C., 1948-53; v.p. Bronx County Trust Co., N.Y.C., 1953-55; chmn., chief exec. officer North Side Savs. Bank, N.Y.C., from 1956; mem. Bronx adv. bd. Mfrs. Hanover Bank, N.Y.C., from 1979; trustee Savs. Banks Retirement System, from 1982. Bd. dirs. UN Devel. Corp., N.Y.C., 1982; chmn. bd. trustees Bronx Rotary Found., 1975; sr. v.p., trustee St. Barnabas Hosp., 1977; chmn. Bronx div. U.S. Savs. Bond Program, 1981. Recipient Good Scout award Greater N.Y. councils Boy Scouts Am., 1965; recipient Bronze Pelican award Greater N.Y. councils Boy Scouts Am., 1966, Human Rights Citation N.Y. State Div. Human Rights, 1970, Humanitarian award Albert Einstein Med. Coll., 1976. Club: N.Y. Athletic. Home: New York N.Y. Died Jan. 11, 1985, buried Woodlawn Cemetery, N.Y.C.

D'ARISTA, ROBERT AUGUSTUS, artist; b. N.Y.C., July 2, 1929; s. Umberto and Caroline (Maruzzella) D'A.; m. Jane Webb, Oct. 30, 1954; children: Carla, Peter, Thomas, Antonia. Student, NYU, 1948-50, Columbia U., 1950-52. Art instr. Wash. Bd. Edn., 1961; mem. teaching staff Am. U., 1961-84; vis. prof. Boston U., summer 1970, 71, spring 1973, 78, mem. teaching staff, 1984-87. Self-employed as artist, 1954-61; one-man shows, N.Y.C., 1955, 56, 59, 62, 64, 67, 68, Boston, 1971, Washington, 1957, 62, 77, 80, 81, 86, 87, group shows include, Carnegie Internats., Whitney Anns., Pa. Acad., Art Inst. Chgo., Guggenheim Mus., Ill. Biennial, Bogota Biennial, Detroit Mus., Bklyn. Mus., others; represented in permanent collections, Toledo Mus., Yale U., Hirshorn Mus., Neuberger., Nat. Collection. Fulbright scholar, Florence, 1955; recipient Richard and Hinda Rosenthal Found. award Nat. Inst. Arts and Letters, 1967. Home: Ashland Mass. Died Oct. 11, 1987; buried Wildwood Cemetery, Ashland, Mass.

DARLING, CHARLES DOUGLAS, psychiatrist; b. Walkerton, Ind., July 7, 1905; s. Charles Davis and Gertrude (Peebles) D.; m. Ruth Walton, July 11, 1938; children—Charles (dec.), Barbara. B.S. summa cum laude, Lafayette Coll., 1929; M.D., U. Pa., 1933. Intern Presbyn. Hosp., Phila., 1933-35; physician George School, 1935-37; grad. tng. Pa. Hosp., Phila., 1937-38; mem. faculty Cornell U., from 1938, prof. clin. medicine (Ithaca) and head mental hygiene div. dept. univ. health services, 1944-69, prof. psychiatry emeritus, from 1969; practice medicine specializing in psychiatry from 1969; attending physician Cornell U. and clinic, from 1940; cons. physician Tompkins County Meml. Hosp., from 1941; Mem. Med. Adv. Bd., World War II; Participated in insts. on mental and public health; lectr. Fellow Am. Psychiat. Assn. (life, chmn. com. on acad. edn. 1958-61); mem. N.Y. State Soc. Mental Health (pres.), AMA, N.Y. State Med. Soc. (life), Phi Beta Kappa. Home: Ithaca N.Y. Deceased.

DARLINGTON, CHARLES FRANCIS, JR., government official, economist; b. N.Y.C., Sept. 13, 1904; s. Charles Francis and Letitia Craig (O'Neill) D.; m. Alice Nelson Benning, Nov. 3, 1931; children: Charles Francis III, Alice Letitia, Christopher Nelson. Grad., St. Mark's Sch., Southborough, Mass., 1922; AB, Harvard U., 1926; postgrad., New Coll. Oxford (Eng.) U., 1926-27, U. Geneva, 1928-29. Mem. fin. sect. League Nations Secretariat, Geneva, 1929-31; mem. central banking dept. Bank Internat. Settlements, Basle, Switzerland, 1931-34; asst. chief trade agreements div. Dept. State Washington, 1935-39; fgn. exchanges mgr. overseas ops. Gen. Motors Corp., N.Y.C., 1940-41; sec. exec. steering, coordination and jurists coms. San Francisco Conf. on UN, 1945; with Socony Vacuum Oil Co., Inc. 1946-61; chmn. Standard Fuel Oil Co., 1949-53; dir. Iraq Petroleum Co. and assoc. cos., 1949-53; v.p., dir. Socony Vacuum Corp., 1953-58; alternat dir. Iranian Consortium, 1955-56, A.E. and E.P. to Rep. Gabon, 1961-65; personal rep. of pres. Kennedy to independence ceremonies Kingdom Burundi, 1962. Author: (with wife) African Betrayal, 1968; also articles. Bd. dirs. Boys Club, Mount Kisco, N.Y., 1942-61; trustee Bedford-Rippowam Sch., Bedford, N.Y., 1946-49. With USNR, 1943-44. Mem. St. Nicholas Soc. N.Y., Huguenot Soc. Am. (hon.), Council Fgn. Relations, Brook's Club, Cosmos Club, Leander Club. Democrat. Home: Mount Kisco N.Y. Died Apr. 11, 1986; buried Mount Kisco, N.Y.

DARRELL, ROBERT DONALDSON, writer; b. Newton, Mass., Dec. 13, 1903; s. Ernest Willis and Elizabeth (Donaldson) D.; m. Emma Cartwright Bourne, Sept. 30, 1930 (div. 1936). Student, Harvard U., 1922, New Eng. Conservatory Music, 1923-26. Staff writer, record reviewer Phonograph Monthly Rev., Boston and Cambridge, Mass., 1926-30, editor, pub., 1930-31; freelance writer 1932-34; assoc. editor, reviewer Music Lovers' Guide, N.Y.C., 1932-34; record researcher Gramophone Shop, N.Y.C., 1934-39; editor Gramophone Shop Supplement, 1937-39, Steinway Rev. Permanent Music (later syndicated Rev. Recorded Music), N.Y.C., 1939-43; sr. writer, then supervising editor instrn. book dept. Hazeltine Electronics Corp., Little Neck, N.Y., 1943-46; editor Rev. Recorded Music, 1947-50; record revs. Down Beat mag., 1952; audio columnist Saturday Rev., 1953-55; columnist High Fidelity mag., 1955-87, contbg. editor, 1956-87; contbg. editor Audiocraft mag., 1955-58; record revs. Am. Record Guide, 1986-88, Phono-Mus. Retrospects, Opus, 1987-88; discographic cons. music div. N.Y.C. Pub. Library, 1952. Author: The Highroad to Musical Enjoyment, 1943, Good Listening, 1953; compiler: Gramophone Shop Encyclopedia of Recorded Music, 1936, Schirmer's Guide to Books on Music and Musicians, 1951, Tapes in Review, 1963; contbr. articles to profl. publs. Guggenheim fellow, 1939. Fellow Radio Club Am.; mem. Audio Engring. Soc., Acoustical Soc. Am., Ulster County Hist. Soc., Assn. Recorded Sound Collections. Democrat. Home: Stone Ridge N.Y. Died May 1, 1988, cremated.

DARROW, KARL KELCHNER, physicist; b. Chgo., Nov. 26, 1891; s. Edward Everett and Helen (Kelchner) D.; m. Elizabeth Marcy, 1943. BS, U. Chgo., 1911, PhD, 1917; postgrad., U. Paris, U. Berlin; Docteur es Sciences, Universite de Lyon, 1949. Mem. tech. staff Bell Telephone Labs., 1917-56; acting prof. physics Stanford U., summer 1929, U. Chgo., summer 1931, Columbia U., 1932, William Allan Nielson prof. Smith Coll., 1941, 42. Author: Atomic Energy, 1948, Introduction to Contemporary Physics, Renaissance of Physics, others; contbr. sci. articles. Decorated Chevalier de la Legion d' Honneur. Mem. Am. Phys. Soc. (sec. from 1941), Am. Philos. Soc., Am. Acad. Arts and Scis., fgn. sci. socs., Century Assn. Club. Home: New York N.Y. †

DART, HENRY P., JR., lawyer; b. New Orleans, July 22, 1883; s. Henry P. and Mary L. (Kernan) D.; m. Suzanne Dupaquier, June 9, 1915; children: Henry P. III, Eugenie L., Suzanne Micheline Dart McCutcheon, Edward D. AB, Tulane U., 1903, LLB, 1905. Bar: La. 1905. Pvt. practice New Orleans, from 1905; sr. mem. Dart & Dart. Mem. ABA (state del. La. 1936-40), La.

ar Assn. (pres. 1949), New Orelans Bar Assn., Am. aw Inst., La. Law Inst., Am. Judicare Soc., Comml. aw League Am., New Orleans C. of C., Boston Club, ound Table of New Orleans (pres. 1942-43), Rotary, der of Coif, Sigma Alpha Epsilon. Home: New leans La. †

ART, RAYMOND ARTHUR, anatomist; b. oowong, Brisbane, Australia, Feb. 4, 1893; s. Samuel d Eliza Anne (Brimblecombe) D.; m. Marjorie ordon Frew, 1936; children: Galen, Diana Dart raham. BSc, U. Queensland, 1913, MSc, 1915; MB, dney U., 1917, MD, 1927; DSc (hon.), U. Natal, 956, Witwatersrand, 1964, LaSalle, 1968. Demonstrator anatomy, acting vice prin. St. Andrew's Coll., dney, 1917; house surgeon Royal Prince Alfred osp., Sydney, 1917-18; sr. demonstrator anatomy niv. Coll., London, 1919-20, 21-22, lectr. histology, 921-22; fellow Rockefeller Found., 1920-21; prof. natomy U. Witwatersrand, Johannesburg, Republic of outh Africa, 1923-58, dean faculty medicine, 1925-43, meritus prof., 1959-88; United Steelworkers Am. prof. nthropology Inst. Achievement Human Potential, hila., 1966-88. Author: Cultural Status of the South frican Man-Apes, 1956, The Osteodontokeratic Culre of Australopithecus prometheus, 1957; (with Dennis raig) Adventures with the Missing Link, 1959, Africa's ace in the Emergence of Civilisation, 1960; editor: frica's Place in the Human Story, 1954. Mem. Inrnat. Commn. on Fossil of Man, 1929-88. Recipient . Capt. Scott Meml. medal South African Biol. Soc., 955, Viking medal and award for phys. anthropology enner-Gren Found. N.Y., 1957, Silver medal Med. ssn. South Africa, 1972. Fellow Royal Soc. South frica (v.p.), Linnean Soc. London (fgn.); mem. South frican Assn. for Advancement Sci. (pres. 1953), South frican Archaeol. Soc. (pres. 1951), South African Mus. ssn. (pres. 1961-62), South African Soc. Physiotherapy res. 1961-67), Inst. Biology (life), other profl. assns. ome: Sandhurst Sandton Transvaal Died Nov. 22, 988.

A SILVA, HOWARD, actor; b. Cleve., May 4, 1909; Benjamin and Bertha (Sohon) Silverblatt; m. Jane aylor, 1941 (div. 1947); m. Marjorie Nelson, 1950 (div. 960); m. Nancy Nutter, June 30, 1961. Student, arnegie Inst. Tech., 1928. Formerly with Group heatre, Civic Repertory Theatre, Theatre Union roup, Mercury Theatre; plays include Master Builder, lice in Wonderland, Three Sisters, Alison's House, liom, A Doll's House, Sailors of Cattaro, Golden Boy, he Cradle Will Rock, 1776, Abe Lincoln in Illinois, klahoma!, Fiorello; films include Once in a Blue oon, 1936, Abe Lincoln in Illinois, 1940, Sea Wolf, ergeant York, Nine Lives Are Not Enough, Wild Bill ickok Rides Again, Steel against the Sky, 1941, Big hot, Omaha Trail, Tonight We Raid Calais, Keeper of e Flame, 1942, The Lost Weekend, 1945, Duffy's avern, Two Years before the Mast, 1946, The Blue ahlia, 1946, Unconquered, 1947, They Live by Night, 948, The Great Gatsby, 1949, Underworld Story, hree Husbands, 1950, Fourteen Hours, M, 1951, avid and Lisa, 1962, The Outrage, 1964, Nevada mith, 1966, 1776, 1972, dir. N.Y. prodn. Cradle Will ock, 1965, Purlie Victorious, My Sweet Charlie, The orld of Sholom Aleichem., Tevya and His Daughters, andhog, Mommie Dearest, 1981, Garbo Talks, 1984, n Actor in the Ensemble: Howard da Silva, 1985; adio) for Great Classics series, Fed. Theatre project, 936; performed in plays of Arch Oboler and Norman orwin, also radio, 1940; appeared in TV spl. The Mises of October, 1974, Stop Thief, 1976, episodes of TV ries including The Fugitive, TV movies Smile Jennie, ou're Dead, 1974, Hollywood on Trial, 1977, Verna: SO Girl, 1978 (Emmy award); author: (with Felix eon) play The Most Dangerous Man in America. ome: Ossining N.Y. Died Feb. 16, 1986.

AUGHERTY, CARROLL ROOP, economist, labor bitrator; b. Annville, Pa., Dec. 3, 1900; s. Benjamin ranklin and Della Frances (Roop) D.; m. Miriam raiglow, 1928; children: James Carroll, David Henry; . Marion Roberts, 1940; 1 dau., Frances Maon. A.B., Lebanon Valley Coll., 1921; A.M., U. Pa., 924, Ph.D., 1927. Instr. Mercersburg (Pa.) Acad., 921-23, Wharton Sch., U. Pa., 1925-28; prof. econs. U. a., 1928-31, U. Pitts., 1931-40; prof. econs., chmn. ept. Hunter Coll., 1940-46; prof. labor relations orthwestern U., 1946-68, chmn. dept., 1948-58; labor bitrator, cons.; prin. economist for labor productivity udies U.S. Bur. Labor Statistics, 1936; chief economist age and Hour div., U.S. Dept. Labor, 1938-40; mem. om. on Postwar Price Problems, Nat. Bur. Econ. esearch, 1944-46; nat. wage stblzn. dir. Nat. War abor Bd., 1942-45; lend lease dir. in New Zealand for ept. State, 1945-46; chmn. Pres.'s steel-labor factnding bd., 1949; Pres.'s R.R. labor emergency bds., 951-52; referee Nat. R.R. Adjustment Bd., 1952-75; hr. mgmt. devel. U.S. and abroad. Author: Labor roblems in American Industry, 1933, 34, 38, 41, 48, abor Under NRA, 1934; co-author: books including conomics of Iron and Steel Industry, 1937, Principles Political Economy, 1950, Labor Problems of American Society, 1952, Conflict and Cooperation, 1968. ecipient Disting. Alumnus award Lebanon Valley oll., 1965, Lifetime Achievement award Am. Arbitraon Assn., 1986. Benjamin Franklin fellow Royal Soc. r Arts; mem. Indsl. Relations Research Assn. (exec. bd. 1954-56), Nat. Acad. Arbitrators, Lincoln Acad. Ill., Alpha Sigma Phi, Delta Sigma Pi, Beta Gamma Sigma. Home: La Jolla Calif. Died May 11, 1988; buried St. James-by-the-Sea Meml. Garden, La Jolla, Calif.

DAVENPORT, LOUISE STRONG, civic leader; b. Bklyn., Sept. 25, 1885; d. Robert Grier and Harriet Lydia (Zabriskie) Strong; m. Henry J. Davenport, June 1, 1909; 1 son, John J. BA, Wells Coll., 1906. Pres. New Canaan (Conn.) Garden Club, 1914-18, Bklyn. Bot. Garden aux., 1920-26, Civitan Club Bklyn., 1933-37; chmn. Boston Symphony Orch. Com. for Bklyn., 1929-40; chmn. vols. Bklyn. chpt. ARC, 1941-47, trustee chpt., 1947-55, hon. trustee, from 1955; trustee Bklyn. Inst. Arts and Scis., from 1942; mem. aux. N.Y. Philharm. Soc. Home: New York N.Y. †

DAVID, EDWARD M., lawyer; b. Phila., Dec. 26, 1916; s. William Morris and Frances Amelia (Cutler) D.; m. Mary Elizabeth Gass, Aug. 28, 1948; children—William, Peter, Elizabeth, Nancy. A.B., Princeton U., 1938; LL.B., U. Pa., 1941. Bar: Pa. bar 1942, U.S. Supreme Ct. bar 1972. Mem. firm Saul, Ewing, Remick & Saul, Phila., from 1941; partner Saul, Ewing, Remick & Saul, from 1951. Author, editor: Course Materials on Lifetime and Testamentary Estate Planning, 4th edit, 1982; editor: The Shingle, 1961; contbr. articles to profl. jours. Bd. dirs. Woodmere Art Gallery.; Trustee, former pres. bd First Presbyn. Ch. of Germantown. Served to lt. comdr. USNR, 1941-46. Mem. Am. Bar Assn., Pa. Bar Assn. (past chmn. real property, probate and trust law sect.), Phila. Bar Assn. (past chmn. orphans ct. com.), Am. Law Inst., Am. Coll. Probate Counsel. Club: Phila. Cricket. Home: Phila. Pa. Deceased.

DAVIDSON, HERBERT MARC, publisher, editor; b. N.Y.C., Nov. 8, 1895; s. Julius and Rose (Scharles) D.; m. Liliane Refregier, June 14, 1919; 1 child, Herbert Marc. B.Lit., Columbia U., 1918; LL.D. (hon.), Bethune-Cookman Coll., 1953. Reporter Kansas City (Mo.) Star, 1917, Portland (Oreg.) Jour., 1919, Fourth Estate, 1920, Los Angeles Examiner, 1920-21, Paris bur. Internat. News Service, 1922; rewrite man editorial writer, feature editor Chgo. Daily News, 1922-28; editor Daytona Beach (Fla.) News-Jour., 1928-62; v.p. News-Jour. Corp., Daytona Beach, 1928-62; pres., editor, pub. News-Jour. Corp., 1962-85. Past bd. dirs. Daytona Beach chpt. A.R.C.; past pres. Daytona Beach Community Chest, 1953-54, Unitarian-Universalist Soc., Daytona Beach Area; trustee Bethune-Cookman Coll. Served with U.S. Army, 1918-19; Served with AEF in, France. Life fellow So. Regional Council; mem. Am. Soc. Newspaper Editors, Fla. Pubs. Assn. (past pres.), Am. Legion, Civic League Halifax Area, Sigma Delta Chi. Democrat. Club: Daytona Beach Rotary (past pres.). Home: Daytona Beach Fla. Died July 26, 1985.

DAVIDSON, IRWIN DELMORE, congressman, judge; b. N.Y.C., Jan. 3, 1906; s. Lafay and Tillie (Bechstein) D.; m. Berenice Feltenstein, June 4, 1936; children: James Sylvan, Mark Lewis; m. 2d, Marion Doniger, May 31, 1965. Bar: N.Y. 1929. Pvt. practice N.Y.C., 1929-81; of counsel N.Y. State Bill Drafting Commn., 1935-36; sec. Sen. Wagner, 1938; mem. N.Y. State Assembly, 1936-49; ranking Dem. mem. judiciary com. 1944-48, sec. legis. investigating com., 1945-46; justice Ct. Spl. Sessions, City of N.Y., 1949-55; mem. 84th Congress from 20th N.Y. Dist; judge Ct. of Gen. Sessions, N.Y. County, 1957-62; justice Supreme Ct., State of N.Y. Author: The Jury is Still Out, 1959. Past dir. Mem's League in Aid of Crippled Children; trustee Fedn. for Support Jewish Charities, United Jewish Appeal. Mem. ABA, N.Y. Bar Assn., Assn. of Bar of City of N.Y., N.Y. County Lawyers Assn. Jewish. Home: New York N.Y. Died Aug. 1, 1981.

DAVIDSON, JOHN FREDERICK, naval officer, superintendent U.S. Naval Acad.; b. Olean, N.Y., May 3, 1908; s. Perry Allen and Annie Marie (Smith) D.; m. 1 dau., Diane Raguet (Mrs. William T. Ross Jr.); stepdau., Nancy Brindupke (wife of William Sterling Cole Jr., USN); m. 2d, Ann Dorsey Rogers, May 10, 1947. BS, U.S. Naval Acad., 1929; student, Can. Nat. Def. Coll., 1950-51; LLD, Allegheny Coll., 1962. Commd. ensign USN, 1929, advanced through grades to rear adm., 1956, assigned battle ships, 1929-33, assigned submarines, 1934-36, with Bur. Personnel, Navy Dept., 1936-38, 45-47, comdg. officer submarines S-44, Mackerel, Blackfish, 1938-44, comdr. submarine div., Submarine Tender Orion, submarine squadron, 1947-50; head dept English, history, govt. U.S. Naval Acad., 1951-54, supt., 1960-62; comdr. tng. command U.S. Pacific Fleet USN, from 1962, comdg. officer USS Albany, 1954-55; dep. dir. and dir. politico-mil. policy div. Office Chief Naval Ops., 1955-57; comdr. Cruiser Div. 5, Pacific Fleet, 1957-58, chief naval group Joint U.S. Mil. Mission for Aid to Turkey, 1959-60,. Decorated Silver Star, Legion of Merit. Mem. U.S. Naval Inst. (bd. control 1951-54, v.p. 1960-89), Army and Navy Club (Washington); Army-Navy Country Club (Arlington, Va.). Episcopalian. Home: San Diego Calif. Died Jan. 21, 1981.

DAVIDSON, VANDA ARTHUR, JR., obstetrician, gynecologist; b. Dubach, La., Oct. 9, 1918; s. Vanda Arthur and Flossie (Rainwater) D.; m. Earline Givens, Sept. 12, 1945; children: Vanda Lewis, Darrell Dale, Elizabeth Dianne. BS, La. Poly. Inst., 1938; MD, Tulane U., 1942. Diplomate Am. Bd. Ob-Gyn. Intern Charity Hosp. of La., New Orleans, 1942-43; resident Tulane service Charity Hosp. La., 1946-49; pvt. practice Dallas, 1949-85; former mem. staff Baylor U. Med. Ctr., Dallas, Parkland Hosp., Presbyn. Hosp. of Dallas, Gaston Episcopal Hosp.; asst. clin. prof. U. Tex. Health Sci. Ctr., Dallas, 1951-85; mem. original bd. dirs. Ling Electric, 1955; also on bds. Ling Electronics, 1958, Ling Temco and Vaught, mem. exec. com., 1956-70, chmn. compensation com. and mem. exec. com. of bd., 1961-70; builder, chmn. bd. Med. Tower, 1962-69; founding mem., chmn. bd. Morgan Maxfield and Assocs., 1964; chmn. bd. Sta. KVIL, 1968-69; bd. govs. Tulane U. Med. Ctr., 1967-85; dir. UTL, 1971-85. Maj. U.S. Army, 1943-46. Decorated Bronze Star, Legion of Merit. Fellow ACS, Am. Coll. Ob-Gyn., Internat. Coll. Surgeons; mem. AMA, Central Assn. Ob-Gyn., Tex. Ob-Gyn. Soc., Dallas-Ft. Worth Ob-Gyn. Soc., N.Mex. Ob-Gyn. Soc. (hon.), Conrad G. Collins Ob-Gyn. Soc. (pres. 1958), Am. Fertility Soc., Explorers Club, Chaparral Club, 2001 Club, Dallas Gun Club, Hurricane Creek Country Club, Tex. Game Fishing Club, Safari Club, Game Coin Internat. Club. Republican. Home: Dallas Tex. Died Sept. 30, 1985; buried Restland Cemetery, Dallas.

DAVIES, CLARENCE EBENEZER, mechanical engineer; b. Utica, N.Y., Mar. 15, 1891; s. Caleb and Lucy (Jones) D. Student, Utica Free Acad., 1903-07; ME, Renselaer Poly. Inst., 1914; DEng, Clarkson U., 1948, Drexel U., 1950. Time and prodn. clk., tool designer, rate setter Smith Premier Works of Remington Typewriter Co., 1914-17, prodn. supr., 1919-20; with Am. Soc. Mech. Engrs., 1920-57, assoc. editor, 1920-21, asst. sec. and mng. editor, 1921-31, exec. sec., 1931-34, sec., 1934-57; exec. dir. United Engring. Ctr., N.Y.C., 1957-61; consulting engr., from 1961. Life trustee Renselaer Inst. Capt. U.S. Army, 1918, col., 1940-45. Fellow AAAS (v.p. from 1950); mem. ASME (hon.), Am. Soc. Engring. Edn., Engring. Inst. Can. (hon), Newcomen Soc. (pres. 1940), Inst. Mech. Engrs. (Eng.), Inst. Engrs. (Australia), Engineers Club, Century Assn. Univ. Glee, Army and Navy Club (Washington), Sigma Xi, Tau Beta Pi, Pi Tau Sigma, Pi Kappa Phi. Republican. Home: New York N.Y. †

DAVIES, DAVID LLOYD, lawyer; b. Falls City, Nebr., Oct. 17, 1903; s. David Morris and Alice (Griffiths) D.; m. Barbara Coit Elliott, Sept. 10,1930; children: Barbara Ann (Mrs. John H.V. Davies), David Coit. AB, Stanford U., 1925, JD, 1927. Bar: Oreg. 1927. Practiced in Portlan; assoc. Stoel, Rives, Boley, Fraser & Wyse and predecessors, 1927-86; past dir. Leupold & Stevens, Inc. Trustee emeritus Med. Research Found. of Oreg.; past pres. Portland Art Assn., Portland Community Chest; past pres. and dir. Oreg. Hist. Soc.; past. pres. and bd. dirs. Library Assn. Portland; overseer emeritus Whitman Coll.; trustee Jackson Found. Mem. ABA, Oreg. Bar Assn., Multnomah County Bar Assn., Am. Law Inst., Automobile Club of Oreg. (past dir. and treas.), Arlington Club, Univ. Club, Century Club. Republican. Presbyn. Home: Portland Oreg. Died Feb. 15, 1986; buried Walla Walla, Wash.

DAVIES, STANLEY POWELL, social worker; b. Phila., June 22, 1892; s. Abner James and Ida May (Davis) D.; m. Ramona Lenington, Dec. 22, 1917; children: Mary Frances, David Lenington. AB, Bucknell U., 1912, LHD (hon.), 1939; PhD, Columbia U., 1923. Instr. Broaddus Coll., Philippi, W.Va., 1912-13; exec. sec. State Com. Mental Hygiene, State Charities Aid Assn., 1919-23; prof. sociology Bucknell U., 1923-24; assoc. sec. State Charities Aid Assn., 1924-33; gen. dir. Charity Orgn. Soc., N.Y.C., 1933-39, Community Svc. Soc. N.Y., 1939-57; dep. dir. planning N.Y. State Dept. mental hygiene, 1964-68; past pres., chmn. rsch. com. Family Svc. Assn. Am.; past pres. N.Y. State Mental health. Author: The Mentally Retarded in Society, 1959, Toward Community Mental Health, 1960; contbr. articles to profl. jours. Capt. San. Corps, U.S. Army, 1917-19. Fellow Am. Assn. Mental Deficiency; mem. Nat. Assn. Social Workers (pres. 1932-34), Phi Beta Kappa, Delta Upsilon. Congregationalist. Home: White Plains N.Y. †

DAVIS, CURTIS WHEELER, television producer and executive; b. New Haven, June 14, 1928; s. Malcolm Waters and Harriet Ide (Eager) D.; m. Julie Patricia Karras, Feb. 14, 1958; children: James Wheeler, Melissa Nina. B.A. with spl. distinction in music, Columbia, 1949; composition studies with, Nikolai Lopatnikoff, 1943-45; Jerzy Fitelberg, 1948, 1945-46, Dante Fiorillo, 1946-47, Edgard Varese, 1948, Otto Luening, 1948-49. Prodn. mgr. W-N Recorder Corp., 1949-50; prodn. asst. and prodn. mgr. Louis de Rochemont Assos., 1953-58; prodn. mgr. Council Humanities, Boston, 1958-59; with Nat. Ednl. TV, N.Y.C., 1959-72; dir. cultural programs Nat. Ednl. TV, 1965-72; ind. producer 1972-86; exec. producer ARTS, ABC Video Enterprises, 1981-82; dir. programs Arts, Hearst/ABC, 1982-83; v.p. programs Arts & Entertainment Network, 1984-86; cons. Met. Opera, Cable Arts Found., Miss. Authority for Ednl. TV, Conn. Pub. TV, Fla. Pub. TV, TCR, Paris. Exec. producerAn American Family, NET Playhouse, NET Opera, Vibrations, USA: Arts; writer, producer TV series The Music of Man for CBC, Toronto; producer, dir., writer: TV spl. Bartok for CBC, Toronto and MTV, Budapest; author: (with Yehudi Menuhin) The Music of Man, 1979 (Book of Month selection 1980), Leopold Stokowski; composer: Three Pictures for Piano, 1949, Concerto for Orchestra, 1949-53, Quintet for Harp and Strings, 1951, String Quintet, 1955, Recollections, 1969, Four Sonnets for Soprano and Orchestra, 1974-75 (premiere Festival Miami 1985). Served with AUS, 1951-53. Recipient Emmy award, 1969, 70, 71, Peabody award, 1967, 69, Am. Film Festival award, 1966, Anik award, 1979; recipient award Am. Council Better Broadcasting, 1981; Am. Council Edn. award, 1984, 85. Mem. Broadcast Music, Nat. Assn. TV Arts and Scis. Episcopalian. Clubs: Century Assn. (N.Y.C.); American (London). Home: New York N.Y. Died May 31, 1986, buried Southold, L.I., N.Y,

DAVIS, DARREY ADKINS, lawyer; b. Lawtey, Fla., Mar. 14, 1910; s. Darrey Deoma and Ora Lee (Adkins) D.; m. Mary Sue Weakley, Nov. 23, 1940; children: John Weakley, Susan Davis Logan. LLB, U. Fla., 1934. Bar: Fla. 1934. Mem. firm Meyer, Davis & Weiss, 1934-45, Cleveland, Sibley & Davis, 1946-48, Sibley & Davis, 1948-57; county atty. Dade County, Fla., 1957-64; mem. firm Hector, Faircloth & Davis, 1964-66, Steel, Hector & Davis, Miami, Fla., 1966-86; mem. circuit ct. commn. 11th Jud. Dist Fla., 1946-50. Vice chmn. long term capital improvement com. City of Miami, 1948-50; trustee, 1st v.p. Greater Miami Coalition; trustee United Fund Dade County, Dade County Law Library; chmn. bd. trustees Miami Beach Law Library, 1947-48. Lt. USNR, 1943-45. Recipient Disting. Service award Stetson U., 1956. Fellow Am. Bar Found.; Am. Coll. Trial Lawyers; mem. Am. Judicature Soc. (dir.), Fla. C of C. (bd. dirs. 1954-55), ABA (Ho. dels. 1951-60), Fla. Bar Assn. (bd. govs., 1949-55, exec. com. 1952-53, pres. 1954-55), Dade County Bar Assn. (bd. dirs. 1942, 46-49, sec. 1946-47, pres. 1948-49), Miami Beach Bar Assn. (bd. dirs. 1946-58, v.p. 1946-47), Riviera Country Club, Miami Club, Bankers Club. Home: Coral Gables Fla. Died 1986.

DAVIS, EDDIE, jazz tenor saxophonist; b. N.Y.C., Mar. 2, 1921. Leader various jazz groups, N.Y.C., 1942-52; played with Cootie Williams, Andy Kirk, Louis Armstrong, others; with Count Basie Orch., 1952-53, 57, 66-73; co-leader groups with Zoot Sims; also played with Shirley Scott, Harry Edison, Johnny Griffin; albums include I Only Have Eyes For You, Heavy Hiller, Jaws Blues, Montreux '77, Stolen Moments, Straight Ahead, Sweet and Lovely. Home: New York N.Y. Died Nov. 3, 1986.

DAVIS, GEORGE PHILIP, lawyer; b. Waltham, Mass., Mar. 19, 1892; s. John F. and Carrie G. (Smith) D.; m. Edith F. Totten, June 12, 1917; children: Priscilla Davis Hoye, Lydia Davis Scarborough. AB, Harvard U., 1914, LLB, 1917. Bar: Mass. 1917. Assoc. Nutter. McLennon & Fish and predecessor firm, Boston, 1919-29, ptnr., from 1929; v.p. Waltham Savs. Bank, 1948-65, hon. trustee, from 1965. Author: Massachusetts Conveyancers' Handbook, 1956, 2d edit., 1966; contbr. articles to profl. jours. Pres. Leland Home, Waltham, 1934-54, chmn., from 1954; chmn. Mass. Council for Aging, 1954-60; life mem. Nat. Council on Aging, panel mem. Fed. Council on Aging, 1956, White Ho. Conf. Aging, 1961; mem. Mass. Conglist. Fund, 1952-69; pres. Sr. Living, Nat. Fedn. for Elderly; founder, trustee Hiram Francis Mills Fund, Frank Huntington Beebe Trust Assn. Mass. Homes for Aging. Lt. (j.g.) USN, 1917-19; ret. lt. comdr. USNR, 1942. Mem. ABA, Mass. Bar Assn., Boston Bar Assn., Masons, Weston Golf Club, Union Club (Boston), Phi Beta Kappa. Home: Weston Mass. Died June 2, 1983.

DAVIS, GLENN ROBERT, lawyer, former congressman; b. Vernon, Wis., Oct. 28, 1914; s. Charles W. and Jennie (Wachendorf) D.; m. Kathryn J. McFarlane, Nov. 29, 1942; children—Kathleen, Margaret, James, Janet, Elizabeth. B. Edn., U. Wis.-Platteville, 1934; J.D., U. Wis.-Madison, 1940. Bar: Wis. bar 1940. Practiced in Waukesha, 12 yrs; mem. firm Love, Davis & McGraw, 1957-64; mem. Wis. Assembly from Waukesha County, 1941-42, 80th-84th Congresses 2d Dist. Wis., 89th-93rd Congresses 9th Dist. Wis.; Pres., dir. New Berlin State Bank, 1959-65; cons. Potter Internat., Inc., Washington, 1975-83. Served with USNR, 1942-45. Named one of ten outstanding young men U.S. Jr. C. of C., 1947. Mem. Order of Coif. Clubs: Mason (Shriner), Kiwanian. Died Sept. 21, 1988, buried Praire Home Cemetery, Waukesha, Wis.

DAVIS, HALE VIRGINIUS, clergyman; b. Lamar, Mo., Apr. 3, 1892; s. Arden V. and Florence (Viola) D.; m. Berta Cordelia Hawkins, Sept. 9, 1918 (dec. June 1934); children: Berta Cordelia, Hale Virginius, Florence Mary; m. Hazel Schuyler, Jan. 27, 1935; 1 son, William Vincent. Student, Southwestern Bapt. Theol. Sem., 1920-21; AB, Okla. Bapt. U., 1925, DD, 1932; AM, Okla. U., 1926. Ordained to ministry Bapt. Ch., 1916. Pastor Exchange Ave. Ch., Oklahoma City, 1918-32; pres. Okla. Baptist U., 1932-34; pastor Downtown Bapt. Ch., Oklahoma City, 1934-38; pres. Colo. Bapt. Coll., 1952-53; with Peters, Writer & Christensen, Inc., securities; organized Perpetual Life Ins. Co., Denver, 1956; organized Radio Sta. KFXR, Oklahoma City, 1923, mgr. to 1932; managed and developed KGFG, Oklahoma City, 1934-36. Contbr. articles to Bapt.

publs. Mem. Fgn. Mission Bd., So. Bapt. Conv., 1930-32; pres. and operator Samaritan Hosp., Oklahoma City, 1928-32; dir. city mgr. movement, Oklahoma City, 1926, resulting in ten million dollar civic ctr. Chaplain 387th Inf. AUS, World War I; capt., chaplain USAR, 1923. Mem. SAR (state chaplain 1933), Am. Legion (directed Denver half million bldg. campaign 1946), Oklahoma City C. of C. (bd. dirs. 1928-32), Masons (32 deg.), Shriners, Rotary, Kiwanis (pres. 1929-32), Delta Kappa, Phi Kappa Delta. Home: Denver Colo. †

DAVIS, HAMILTON SEYMOUR, anesthesiologist, educator; b. Pitts., Oct. 28, 1920; s. Karl Eugene and Vassie Sophia (Miller) D.; m. Marjorie Jean Wright, July 5, 1946; children: Eric Templeton, Scott Harold, Kim Elizabeth, Christopher Quay. AB cum laude, Colgate U., 1942; MD, Case Western Reserve U., 1945. Diplomate Am. Bd. Anesthesiology. Intern Grassland Hosp., Valhalla, N.Y., 1945-46, resident anesthesiology, 1948-50; assoc. anesthesiologist VA Hosp.; also temporary chmn. dept. anesthesiology St. Mary's Hosp., Grand Junction, Colo., 1950-51; mem. faculty Case Western Reserve U. Sch. Medicine, 1952-66; attentind anesthesiologist Met. Gen. Hosp., 1953-66; formerly cons. Cleve. VA Hosp., Lake County Meml. Hosp; team physician Kenston Sch. Dist., 1957-66; mem. jet injection immunization programs, Cleve., 1955-66; prof. anesthesiology U. Calif. at Davis Sch. Medicine, 1966-86, chmn. dept., 1966-79, 81-83; dir. dept. anesthesia U. Calif. at Davis-Sacramento Med. Ctr., 1966-79, chief of staff, 1976-77. Editor Jour. Anesthesiology, 1965-71; contbr. numerous articles to profl. jours. Camp physician Golden Empire council Boy Scouts Am., 1967-69; pres. bd. dirs Chagrin Falls Park Community Ctr., 1960-66; v.p. Geauga County Econ. Opportunities Council, 1966; founder, bd. dirs Chagrin Falls Park Well-Baby Clinic, 1959-66. Capt. M.C AUS, 1946-48. Mem. AMA, Ohio Med. Assn., Cuyahoga County Med. Assn., Cleve. Acad. Medicine (pres. sect. anesthesiology 1957), Am. Standards Assn. (chmn. com z-79 1956-63, vice chmn. 1963-66), Am. Soc. Anesthesiologists (chmn. com. standardization and equipment 1956-63), Ohio Soc. Anesthesiologists, Cleve. Soc. Anesthesiologists (pres. 1956), Internat. Anesthesia Research Soc., Am. Coll. Anesthesiologists (past mem. bd. govs.), Assn. Univ. Anesthetists, Soc. Acad. Anesthesia (past chmn.), Royal Soc. Medicine, Calif. Med. Soc. (sec. 1967, vice chmn. 1968, chmn. 1969, anesthesiology sect.), Yolo County Sacramento Med. Socs., Calif. Soc. Anesthesiologists. Home: Davis Calif. Died Feb. 2, 1986; buried Davis, Calif.

DAVIS, HAROLD EUGENE, historian, educator; b. Girard, Ohio, Dec. 3, 1902; s. Henry E. and Katherine (Zeller) D.; m. Audrey Hennen, Aug. 31, 1929; 1 child, Barbara Lee. A.B., Hiram (Ohio) Coll., 1924; A.M., U. Chgo., 1927; Ph.D., Case-Western Res. U., 1933. Prof. history, polit. sci. Hiram Coll., 1927-47, dean adminstrn., 1944-47; dir. div. edn. and tchr. aids (Office Inter-Am. Affairs), 1943-45; instr. Latin-Am. history Am.-Army U., Biarritz, France, 1945-46; organizer (Washington Semester program with cooperating colls. and univs.), 1947; prof. history and govt., chmn. div. social studies Am. U., Washington, 1947-59; prof. Latin Am. history, govt. Am. U., 1959-63, Univ. prof. Latin Am. Studies, 1963-73, dean Coll. Arts and Scis., 1952-57; univ. prof. emeritus Am. U. (Coll. Arts and Scis.), 1973-88; lectr., cons. Washington Internat Sch., 1975-76; lectr. U. Md., 1974-76, Washington Internat. Center; cons. Cin. Council on World Affairs Faculty Enrichment Program Latin Am. with cooperating colls., 1969-71, U.S. Armed Forces Inst.; Fulbright lectr. U. Chile, 1958-59; vis. prof. U. Mexico, 1962, India Sch. Internat. Studies, New Delhi, 1965-66; lectr. Inter-Am. Def. Coll., Nat. War Coll., Army War Coll., Fgn. Service Inst., Def. Intelligence Agy.; mem. Internat. team observers Dominican Republic elections, 1962; mem. Gov.'s Commn. on History Ohio, World War II. Author: Makers of Democracy in Latin America, 1945, 68, Origins and Consequences of World War II, (with others), 1948, Latin American Leaders, 1949, 68, Social Science Trends in Latin America, 1950, The Americas in History, 1953, (with others) Contemporary Social Science, 1953, (with others) Development of Historiography, 1954, Development of Social Thought in Latin America, 1956, Government and Politics in Latin America, 1958, Material and Spiritual Factors in American History, 1958, Latin American Social Thought, 1961, 63, 66, The United States in History, 1968, (with Harold Durfee) The Study of Philosophy in the United States, 1964, Os Estados Unidos na História, 1966, Los Estados Unidos en la historia, 1967, History of Latin America, 1968, Points of Focus-Latin America, 1970, Hinsdale of Hiram, 1971, Latin American Thought—A Historical Introduction, 1972, 73, Report of Conference on Latin American Thought, 1972, Revolutionaries, Traditionalists and Dictators in Latin America, 1973, (with Larman Wilson and others) Latin American Foreign Policies, 1975, (with J. Finan and F.T. Peck) Latin American Diplomatic History, 1977, Selected Poems, 1978, 150 Years of The American Peace Society, 1978, (with others) Homenaje a Luis Alberto Sánchez, 1981, Notes for a Dictionary of Ohio Indian Place Names, 1979, Homenaje a Luis Recasens Siches, 1982; editor: Inter-American Conferences, 1826-1954 (S.G. Inman), 1965, Autobio-bibliography, 1981, History and Power, 1983, Metaphysics of History or Metahistory, 1986; contbr. to: Brit. encys. Americana, yearbooks

Biog. Dictionary Internationalists; contbr. articles t profl. jours.; cons: New Jefferson Ency.; chmn. bc editors: World Affairs. Decorated Order of Coló Dominican Republic; recipient Disting. Service awar Ohio Acad. History, 1978, Disting. Service award Inte Am. Council, 1978. Fellow Garfield Soc. Hiram; mem Instituto Indigenista Interamericano, Am. Hist. Assn Latin Am. Studies Assn., Am. Polit. Sci. Assn., In stituto de Historia del Derecho Ricardo Levene (Arger tina, corr.), Instituto Histórico y Geográ fico de Uruguay (corr.), Omicron Delta Kappa, Phi Alph Delta, Phi Kappa Phi, Phi Sigma Alpha, Phi Alph Theta. Mem. Disciples Christ Ch. Club: Cosmo (Washington). Home: Chevy Chase Md. Died Sept. 1 1988.

DAVIS, HARRY DOUGLAS, banker; b. N.Y.C., Nov 26, 1891; s. Harry M. and Lillie (Marsh) D.; m Marjorie Schoeffel, Apr. 2, 1929; children: Anne Erwi (dec.), Joan Davis Eckert. Ed. pub. schs. Wit Plainfield (N.J.) Trust State Nat. Bank, from 1909 chmn. bd., 1962-65, dir., mem. exec. com., from 1965 Mem. N.J. Banking Adv. Bd., 1950-59; chmn. Union County (N.J.) U.S. Savs. Bond Com., 1961-65; bd. govs Muhlenberg Hosp., Plainfield, from 1953. Mem. Am Bankers Assn. (exec. com. 1945-48), N.J. Bankers Assr (pres. 1940-41), N.J. Taxpayers Assn. (bd. dirs. 194C 63). Presbyterian (elder). Home: Plainfield N.J. †

DAVIS, OSCAR HIRSH, judge; b. N.Y.C., Feb. 2 1914; s. Jacob and Minnie (Robison) D. AB, Harvar U., 1934; LLB, Columbia U., 1937. Bar: N.Y. 1938. Pvt. practice N.Y.C., 1937-39; with Dept. Justice, 1939 42, 46-62, first asst. to solicitor gen., 1954-62; assoc judge U.S. Ct. Claims, 1962-82, acting chief judge, 1977 78; judge U.S. Ct. Appeals (fed. cir.), 1982-88. Serve to capt. USAAF, 1942-46. Mem. Am., Fed. bar assns Am. Law Inst., N.Y. County Lawyers Assn., N.Y. Stai Bar Assn. Home: Washington D.C. Died June 19, 1988

DAVIS, RALPH OTIS, diocese administrator, nava officer; b. Litchfield, Ill., Jan. 19, 1891; s. Edward Richard and Mary (Grubbs) D.; m. Anita Bithia Cresap Apr. 22, 1915 (dec.); children: Ralph Cresap, Fran McDowell Leavitt (dec.), m. Dorothy Benson, Oct. 9 1923; 1 son, Otis Benson. BS, U.S. Naval Acad., 1914 grad., Naval War Coll., 1942. Commd. ensign, USN 1914; advanced through grades to rear adm., 1942 served in U.S.S. New Jersey (Vera Cruz), 1914; sub marine officer, European waters, 1917-18; comd. sub marines U.S. and Asiatic waters, 1918-24; filled desk c Island Govts. in Operation, Navy Dept., 1935-38; exec officer U.S.S Indianapolis, 1938-40; chief staff U.S.! Naval Acad., 1940-42; comdg. U.S.S. Chicago (sunk in action 1943), 1942-43, U.S.S. New Orleans, 1943 comdr. Amphibious Group 13, Pacific Fleet, 1945 comdr. amphibious tng. command Pacific Fleet, 1944 45; comdr. Amphibious Group 2, Atlantic Fleet, 1946 comdr. Amphibious Force, Atlantic Fleet, 1946-48 comdt. 5th Naval Dist., 1949-52; ret. as vice adm., 1953 exec adminstr. Episcopal Diocese So. Va., 1953-56. Bd govs. U.S. Naval Inst., 1941-42; trustee Norfolk Acad Norfolk Mus. Art, Norfolk Forum. Decorated Legio of Merit (Army) with 2 gold stars from Navy; Mexica campaign (Vera Cruz) Victory with star; Am. Def. wit star; Am. Area Campaign, Asiatic-Pacific Are Campaign with star and Philippine Liberation medals Bronze medal with combat V; comdr. Order of Bri Empire. Mem. Ret. Officers Assn. (pres., bd. dirs Hampton Roads chpt.), Navy League (bd. dirs. Norfol chpt.), Princess Anne Country Club. Episcopalian (s. warden 1951-52, 62, vestryman). Home: Virginia Beach Va. †

DAVIS, THURSTON M., clergyman; b. Phila., Oct 12, 1913; s. Noble Thurston and Rose Mary (Carey D. A.B., Georgetown Coll., 1937; S.T.L., Woodstoc Coll., 1943; A.M., Harvard U., 1946, Ph.D., 1947 Litt.D., LaSalle Coll., 1959, Loyola Coll., Balt., 1964. Joined S.J., 1931; ordained priest Roman Catholic Ch 1942; tchr. Regis High Sch., N.Y.C., 1938-39; inst grad. sch. arts and scis. Fordham U., 1947-49; dea Fordham Coll., 1949-53; dir. John LaFarge Inst., 196 Courtney Murray Forum, 1967-70, 76-86; with com munications dept. U.S. Cath. Conf., N.Y.C., 1970-78. Contbg. editor America, 1953-54, assoc. editor, 1954-55 editor-in-chief, 1955-68; editor-in-chief Cath. Mind 1955-68; editor: A John LaFarge Reader, 1956, Betwee Two Cities, 1962. Club: Harvard (N.Y.C.). Home New York N.Y. Deceased.

DAWSON, CHRISTOPHER HENRY, philosophe author; b. Hay, Wales, Oct. 12, 1889; s. Henry Philip and Mary (Bevan) D.; m. Valery Mills, Aug. 9, 1916 children: Juliana, Christina Dawson Scott Philip. Student, Winchester Coll., 1903-04, Trinit Coll., Oxford, 1908-11; BA, Trinity Coll., Oxford, MA. Lectr. history culture Univ. Coll., Exeter, Eng., 1930 Forwood lectr. in philosophy religion Liverpool, Eng. 1934; Gifford lectr. Edinburgh U., Scotland, 1947-48 Stillman chair Roman Cath. studies Harvard U., 1958. Author: The Age of the Gods, 1928, Christianity an the New Age, 1931, Progress and Religion, 1931, Th Making of Europe, 1932, Enquiries into Religion an Culture, 1933, The Modern Dilemma, 1933, The Spirit the Oxford Movement, 1933, Medieval Religion, 1935 Religion and the Modern State, 1935, Beyond Politics 1939, The Judgement of the Nations, 1942, Religion an

Culture, 1948, Religion and the Rise of Western Culture, 1950, Understanding Europe, 1952, Medieval Essays, 1954, Dynamics of World History, 1957, Movement of World Revolution, 1959, The Historic Reality of Christian Culture, 1960, The Crisis of Western Education, 1961. Fellow Brit. Acad. Home: Cambridge Mass. †

DAWSON, DANA, bishop; b. Cherokee County, Iowa, Apr. 18, 1892; s. Jay F. and Nettie (Armstrong) D.; m. Grace Elizabeth Lewis, Aug. 7, 1912; children: La Verne Dawson Mason, Dana; m. 2d, Delma Millikan, Nov. 2, 1926. D.D., Morningside Coll., 1950; student, U. Chgo.; DD, Centenary Coll. of La., 1936; LLD, Kans. Wesleyan U., 1949; LittD, Southwestern Coll., Winfield, Kans., 1949; LHD, Baker U., 1955. Ordained to ministry Meth. Episcopal Ch. So., 1915. Pastor Okla. City, 1921-26, Fort Smith, Ark., 1927-34, Shreveport, La., 1934-48; exchange preacher Paris and Liverpool, 1937; elected bishop Meth. Ch., Kans., Nebr., 1948-52. Mem. Bd. of Missions and Ch. Extension, Meth. Ch. Bd. of Edn., Meth. Ch. Gen. Bd. of Lay Activities, bd. of trustees, S. Meth. U. (Dallas), Kans. Wesleyan U. (Salina), Southwestern Coll. (Winfield, Kans., Baker U. (Baldwin, Kans.), Nat. Coll. Christian Workers, Kansas City, Mo., Gen. Bd. Temperance Meth. Ch., Theta Pi. Home: Topeka Kans. †

DAWSON, JOHN PHILIP, lawyer, educator; b. Detroit, July 24, 1902; s. John Philip and Cecile (Frumveller) D.; m. Emma Van Nostrand McDonald, Aug. 20, 1927; children: John Philip, David Michael, Peter McDonald. AB, U. Mich., 1922, JD, 1924, LLD, 1968; DPhil, Oxford U., Eng., 1930; LLD, U. Edinburgh, U. Chgo., 1972, U. Frankfurt, 1977, U. Boston, 1978. Bar: Mich. 1924. Asst. prof. law U. Mich., 1927-30, assoc. prof., 1930-36, prof., 1936-57; prof. Harvard U. Law Sch., 1956-73, Boston U. Law Sch., 1973-81; vis. prof. law U. Chgo., 1955, U. Colo., 1981; Storrs lectr. Yale U. Law Sch., 1978; chief counsel rent sect. Office Pub. Affairs, 1942-43; chief Middle East div. Fgn. Econ. Adminstrn., 1943-45, spl. rep. Middle East area, 1945-46; dir. Fgn. Trade Adminstrn., Greek Govt., 1947-48; Dem. candidate for Congress, 2d Dist. Mich., 1950 52; sec.-treas. Assn. Am. Law Schs., 1947. Author: Unjust Enrichment, A Comparative Analysis, 1951, A History of Lay Judges, 1960, (with George E. Palmer) Cases on Restitution, 1958, 69 (with William B. Harvey) Cases on Contracts, 1958, 69, 77, The Oracles of the Law, 1968, Gifts and Promises, A Comparative Study, 1979; contbr. articles to law rev. Corr. fellow Brit. Acad.; mem. Am. Assn. Arts and Scis., Phi Delta Phi, Order of the Coif (pres. 1956-58). Home: Cambridge Mass. Died Oct. 19, 1985.

DAY, GEORGE H., lawyer; b. Hartford, Conn., Sept. 22, 1891; s. George H. and Katherine (Beach) D.; m. Grace Phelps Allen, Apr. 18, 1917; children: George H. (dec.), Jean Allen, Mary Phelps. BA, Yale U., 1913; LLB, Harvard U., 1916. Bar: Conn. 1916. Ptnr. Shipman & Goodwin, Hartford, 1919-66, counsel, from 1967; judge City Police Ct., Hartford, 1923-27. Mem. Conn. Bar Assn., Soc. Mayflower Descs. in Conn., Soc. Colonial Wars, Hartford Club, Twilight Club. Republican. Episcopalian. Home: Hartford Conn. †

DAY, JAMES VINCENT, government official; b. Brewer, Maine, Nov. 27, 1914; s. Thomas Patrick and Mary Ellen (Ryan) D.; m. Deima Irene McCormick, July 11, 1946; children: Teresa (Mrs. John P. Lynch), Daniel, James Vincent, Thomas, Timothy, Mary. Edn. cert., Wash. State Tchrs. Coll., 1934, U. Maine at Machias, 1971. Sales supr. H.J. Heinz Co., 1936-41; pres. Spillers, Inc., Kennebunk, Maine, 1951-55; nat. dir. pub. relations Am. Legion, 1956-61; vice chmn. Fed. Maritime Commn., Washington, 1961-80, commr., 1980-86; bd. advisers Blinded Vets Assn., 1964-86; past mem. bd. visitors Maine Maritime Acad., Castine; Maine Rep. candidate for Congress, 1956. 1st lt. AUS, World War II. Named col. mil. staff Gov. Maine, 1955; recipient Pres.'s award Am. Legion Press Assn., 1961, ann. Golden Record award best services in nat. def., 1960, Big M award State of Maine Soc., 1965. Mem. Am. Legion (nat. vice comdr. 1956-86), Maine Soc. Washington (pres. 1963), Pub. Relations Soc. Am., Kappa Delta Phi. Home: Washington D.C. Died Aug. 8, 1986.

DAY, WÖRDEN, sculptor, printmaker; b. Columbus, Ohio; d. Daniel E. and Amelia (Worden) D. M.A., NYU; student, Maurice Sterne, Vytlacil, Hoffmann, Hayter. Tchr. Va. Commonwealth U., U. Wyo., State U. Iowa, Pratt Inst., New Sch., Art Students League N.Y. Exhibited solo shows, Perls Gallery, Bertha Schaefer Gallery, Krasner Gallery, Grand Central Moderns, Smithsonian Instn., U. Minn., Cin., Norfolk and Balt. museums art, Va. Mus. Fine Arts, Phila. Art Alliance, Sculpture Center, N.Y., 1972, duo exhbn. sculpture, Montclair Art Mus., 1970; represented permanent collections, Mus. Modern Art, N.Y.C., Nat. Mus. Am. Art, Washington, Whitney Mus., Bklyn. Mus., Library of Congress, Phila. Mus. Art, Met. Mus. Art, many others. Guggenheim-Rosenwald fellow, 1951-53, 61-62. Mem. Fedn. Modern Painters and Sculptors, Sculptors Guild. Home: Montclair N.J. Deceased.

DEADERICK, FRANKLIN VON ALBADE, paper company executive; b. Knoxville, Tenn., Apr. 13, 1891; s. John Franklin and Virginia Bothwell (Hughes) D.; m. Hazel Adele Bawden, 1914; children: John B., William B. Student, U. Mo., 1913. With Bemis Bros. Bag. Co., from 1918, v.p., from 1957, also bd. dirs. Mem. Papers Shipping Sack Mfrs. Assn., Textile Bag Mfrs. Assn. Home: Saint Louis Mo. †

DEAK, NICHOLAS LOUIS, banker; b. Hateg, Hungary, Oct. 8, 1905; came to U.S., 1939, naturalized, 1943; s. Louis and Malvine (Billitz) D.; m. Liselotte Maria Potter, Dec. 21, 1939; 1 son, Robert Leslie. Grad., Acad. World Trade, Vienna, 1925; Ph.D. in Econs. and Finance, U. Neuchatel, Switzerland, 1929. With Royal Hungarian Trade Inst., 1930-35; mgr. Hungarian and Rumanian subsidiaries Brit. Overseas Bank, 1935-37; with econs. dept. League of Nations, Geneva, 1937-39; prof. econs. and internat. affairs Perkiomen Coll. Prep. Sch., Pennsburg, Pa., 1940-41; trustee Perkiomen Coll. Prep. Sch., 1969-85, chmn. bd. trustees, 1972; instr. econs. Coll. City N.Y., 1941-42; with Dept. State, 1945-46; chmn. Deak & Co., Inc., N.Y.C., 1946-80; chmn. bd. Deak & Co., Inc., 1980-85; pres. Deak Nat. Bank, Fleischmanns, N.Y., 1958-85; chmn. bd. Perera Co., Inc., 1953-85; prin. Bankhaus Deak & Co. Ltd., Vienna, 1968-85; adj. prof. internat. finance Fairleigh Dickinson U., Teaneck, N.J., 1970-72; mem. faculty Am. Bankers Assn. Sch., U. Okla., 1972-79; adj. prof. N.Y. Law Sch., 1975; Vice pres. Internat. Comml. Exchange N.Y., 1970-74; bd. mgrs. N.Y. Produce Exchange, 1974; bd. dirs. N.Y. Futures Exchange of N.Y. Stock Exchange, 1980-83; mem. N.Y. Merc. Exchange, Chgo. Internat. Monetary Market of Merc. Exchange Chgo. Bd. dirs. Am.-Hungarian Found., Portuguese Am. Soc. Served to maj. AUS, 1942-46. Mem. Am. Bankers Assn. (chmn. internat. comml. lending div. 1974-76), AAUP, N.Y. C. of C. and Industry (chmn. export finance com.), Brit.-Am. (former dir.), Danish chambers commerce, Am. Portuguese Cultural Soc., Newcomen Soc. N.Am., Econ. Research Round Table, Vets. of OSS (pres. 1974-75). Clubs: Downtown Athletic (N.Y.C.), N.Y. Athletic (N.Y.C.); Westchester Country, Touring de France (U.S. del.). Home: Scarsdale N.Y. Died Nov. 18, 1985.

DE ALVAREZ, RUSSELL RAMON, obstetrician, gynecologist, educator; b. N.Y.C.; s. John and Isidora (Torres y Sanchez) de A.; m. Betty Jane Casey, Sept. 11, 1943; children: Ann, Russell Ramon (dec.). B.S., U. Mich., 1931, M.D., 1935, M.S., 1940. Diplomate: Am. Bd. Obstetrics and Gynecology (asso. examiner). Intern U. Mich. Hosp., 1935-36, resident gynecologist, 1937-38, lectr. maternal and child health, 1939-44, attending staff, 1938-44, asst. prof. obstetrics-gynecology; assoc. attending gynecologist U. Oreg. Hosps., 1946-48; 1st prof. and chmn. dept. obstetrics and gynecology U. Wash. Med. Sch., 1948-64; prof., chmn. dept. obstetrics and gynecology Temple U.; also obstetrician, gynecologist-in-chief Temple Univ. Hosp., Phila., 1964-87; obstetrician and gynecologist in chief U. Wash. Hosps., King County Hosp., Harborview, 1948-64; cons. Phila. Gen. Hosp., VA Hosp.; cons. in obstetrics-gynecology to surgeon gen. U.S. Army, HEW; cons. toxemia task force NIH (also high blood pressure edn. research program); cons. Commn. on Profl. and Hosp. Activities; cons. on gynecology Phila. Health Dept.; Bd. dirs. Planned Parenthood Assn. of Southeastern Pa., 1976-87; bd. dirs. Family Planning Council of Southeastern Pa.; treas. Phila. div.; mem. vis. com. U. Mich. Med. Center, 1978-87. Editorial bd.: Am. Jour. Obstetrics and Gynecology; editor-in-chief: Quar. Rev. Obstetrics and Gynecology; editor: Clinical Obstetrics and Gynecology; editor-in-chief: Textbook of Gynecology, The Kidney in Pregnancy; co-editor: Textbook of Obstetric-Gynecologic Terminology; assoc. editor: Textbook of Obstetrics and Perinatology; contbr. numerous articles to med. and profl. publs. Served as lt. comdr. USNR, 1944-46. Fellow A.C.S., Am. Coll. Obstetricians and Gynecologists (asst. sec. 1958-59), Soc. Gynecologic Investigation (founder, pres. 1959); mem. AMA (cons. Current Procedural Terminology, 3d and 4th edits.), Am. Assn. Obstetricians and Gynecologists, Soc. E-P-H Gestosis (U.S. chmn.), Am. Fedn. Clin. Research, Central Assn. Obstetrics and Gynecology, Wash. Soc. Obstetrics and Gynecology (hon. mem.), Ore. Soc. Obstetrics and Gynecology, Seattle Gynecol. Soc. (hon. life, pres. 1961-62), Pan Am. Med. Assn. (U.S. v.p. for Ob-Gyn), Western Soc. Clin. Research, Obstet. Soc. Phila. (council 1968-71, 1st v.p. 1970-71, pres. 1972-73), Pacific Northwest Soc. Obstetricians and Gynecologists (pres. 1962-63, hon. life mem.), Am. Gynecol. Soc. (v.p.), Am. Coll. Obstetricians and Gynecologists (asst. sec., sponsor history of obstetrics-gynecology, mem. exec. bd., founding fellow), Nurses Assn. Am. Coll. Obstetricians and Gynecologists (exec. bd.), Research Soc. U. Wash., Norman F. Miller Gynecologic Soc. (pres. 1962-63), Pa., Phila. County med. socs., Am. Soc. Human Genetics, Soc. Obstetrics and Gynecology Can., Washington Obstet. Soc., Reno Surg. Soc., Assn. Profs. Gynecology and Obstetrics, Am. Nephrology Soc., Soc. Reprodn., AAUP, Venezuelan Obstet. and Gynecol. Soc. (hon. mem.), N.J. Obstet. and Gynecol. Soc. (hon. mem.), Pacific Coast Obstet. and Gynecol. Soc., S.W. Obstet. and Gynecol. Soc., Los Angeles Obstet. and Gynecol. Soc., Pacific Northwest Obstet. and Gynecol. Soc. (hon. life mem.), Honolulu Obstet. and Gynecol. Soc., AAAS, Hollywood (Calif.) Acad. Medicine, Pacific N.W. Obstet. and Gynecol. Assn. (pres. 1962), U. Mich. Med. Alumni Soc. (bd. govs., mem. vis. com.), Am. Legion, Sigma Xi, Alpha Omega Alpha, Nu Sigma Nu. Clubs: Doctors Golf, Wayfair (pres. 1976-78), Phila. Country. Home: Villanova Pa. Died Dec. 25, 1987; buried Calvary Cemetery, Phila.

DEAN, ARTHUR HOBSON, lawyer, government official; b. Ithaca, N.Y., Oct. 16, 1898; s. William Cameron and Maud J.J. D.; m. Mary Marden, June 25, 1932; children: Nicholas B. Marden, Patricia Campbell (Mrs. Leonidas Manolis). AB, Cornell U., 1921, JD, 1923; LLD, Hamilton Coll., Allegheny Coll., 1954, Rutgers-The State U., 1958, Wash. U., 1958, Brown U., Dartmouth U., Bowdoin Coll., 1962, C.W. Post Coll., 1963, Adelphi U., 1964, Otterbein Coll., 1964; DCL, Hofstra Coll., 1961; LHD, Wash. Coll., 1963; DLitt, Lafayette Coll., 1968. Bar: N.Y. 1923. Pvt. practice N.Y.C., 1923-87; ptnr. Sullivan & Cromwell, 1929-76, of counsel, 1976-79; past dir., mem. exec. com. Am. Bank Note. Co.; past dir. Nat. Union Electric Corp; former adv. dir. El Paso Co.; Dickinson lectr. Harvard U., 1950; rep., chmn. dels. of U.S. to UN Confs. on Law of Sea, Geneva, 1958, 60; represented U.S. And 16 other nations contbg. troops in post-armistice negotiations at Panmunjom; spl. U.S. ambassador to Korea, 1953-54; exdep. to sec. of state for polit. conf. envisaged by Korean Armistice; del. 16th, 17th Gen. Assemblys of UN; chmn. U.S. del. Conf. on Discontinuance of Nuclear Weapons Tests, Geneva, 1961-62; chmn. U.S. del. 18-Nation Disarmament COnf., Geneva, 1962; former mem. Lawyers' Com. Civil Rights under law. Writer and lectr. on fin. subjects, reorgn., internat. law, nuclear test ban and disarmament. Mem. emeritus joint adminstrv. bd. N.Y. Hosp.-Cornell Med. Ctr.; mem. coordinating bd. Sloan-Kettering div. Cornell Med. Coll.; dir. emeritus N.Y. Hosp.-Cornell Med. Ctr. Fund, Inc.; trustee emeritus, presdl. councillor Cornell U., past chmn. library assocs., hon. curator Franco-Am. Collection; former trustee Hochschild Found., Planting Fields Found. With USN, World War I. Chubb fellow Yale U., 1955; decorated officer French Legion of Honor; recipient Disting. Service medal Theodore Roosevelt Assn., 1962. Fellow Am. Coll. Trial Lawyers Assn.; mem. ABA, Acad. Polit. Sci., N.Y. State Bar Assn. (Gold medal 1962), Asia Soc., Internat. C. of C., Am. Judicature Soc., Am. Soc. Internat. Law (pres. 1961-62), Fellows ABA, Am. N.Y. Law Insts., Assn. of Bar of City of N.Y., Cornell Law Assn., Council Fgn. Relations (dir. emeritus), Japan Soc., Inc. (hon.), N.Y. County Lawyers Assn., Pilgrims U.S., France-Am. Soc., Nantucket Ornithol. Assn. (past trustee), Cornell U. Alumni Assn. N.Y.C., Century Assn., Univ. Club, Recess Club, Met. Club., Piping Rock Club, Mill Reef Club, Tower Club. Home: Oyster Bay N.Y. Died Nov. 30, 1987; buried St. John's Cemetery, Cold Spring Harbor, N.Y.

DEARDEN, JOHN FRANCIS CARDINAL, former archbishop of Detroit; b. Valley Falls, R.I., Oct. 15, 1907; s. John S. and Agnes (Gregory) D. Grad., St. Mary's Sem., Cleve., 1929, N.Am. Coll., Rome, Italy, 1934; S.T.D., Gregorian U., Rome, 1934. Ordained priest Roman Catholic Ch., 1932; rector St. Mary's Sem., Cleve., 1944-48; apptd. papal chamberlain with title very rev. monsignor 1945, consecrated coadjutor bishop Pitts., titular bishop Sarepta, 1948; bishop Pitts., 1950-58; archbishop Archdiocese Detroit, 1959-80, apostolic adminstr., 1980-81. elevated to cardinal, 1969. Mem. Nat. Conf. Cath. Bishops (pres. 1966-71). Home: Detroit Mich. Died Aug. 1, 1988.

DEATHERAGE, FRED E., biochemistry educator; b. Waverly, Ill., Dec. 30, 1913; s. Fred E. and Marian Eve (Sevier) D.; m. Nellie Lou Carothers, Jan. 3, 1942; children: Fred Sevier, Catherine Margaret, Marilyn Nan. A.B., Ill. Coll., 1935, D. Sc., 1960; A.M., U. Ill., 1936; Ph. D., U. Iowa, 1938; Ph. D. fellow, Ohio State U., 1940-42. Instr. biochemistry U. Iowa, 1938-40; chemist Kroger Food Found., Cin., 1942-46; asst. prof. Ohio State U., 1946-48, asso. prof., 1949-51, prof., 1951-81, prof. emeritus biochemistry, 1981-86, chmn. dept. agrl. biochemistry, 1951-64; asst. dept. animal sci. Ohio Agrl. Expt. Sta., 1949-51, asso., 1951-53, prof., 1953-86; food scientist, technologist AID, Brazil, 1964-68; lectr. State U. of Campinas, 1974; cons. in field. Author: Food for Life, 1975. Mem. Am. Chem. Soc., Am. Inst. Nutrition, Inst. Food Technologists; AAAS Soc. for Nutrition Edn., Am. Meat Sci. Assn. Am. Soc. Biol. Chemists, Am. Soc. Animal Sci., Phi Beta Kappa, Sigma Xi, Sigma Pi, Phi Lambda Upsilon. Home: Dublin Ohio. Died Oct. 20, 1986.

DEBERRY, ROY THOMAS, mathematics educator; b. Humboldt, Tenn., May 4, 1892; s. William Thomas and Nancy Almedia (Turner) DeB.; m. Velma Grace Hamilton, Nov. 18, 1917; children: Millard Thomas (dec.), James Turner, Frances Marion (dec.), Velma Nelle DeBerry Evans, Edith Mable DeBerry Jones, Maxine, Dorothy DeBerry Gibson. Student, Union U., 1909-10; BS, Laneview Coll., Trenton, Tenn., 1912. Prin. high sch., Gibson County, Tenn., 1911-16; instr. in math., Summerlin Inst., Bartow, Fla., 1916-17; prin. consol. sch., Grenada County, Miss., 1922; tchr. math., high sch., Grenada, 1922; proprietor and headmaster Jr. Mil. Acad., Bloomington Springs, Tenn., from 1922. Home: Bloomington Springs Tenn. †

DEBO, ANGIE, author, historian, educator; b. Beattie, Kans., Jan. 30, 1890; d. Edward Peter and Lina

Elbertha (Cooper) Debo. AB, U. Okla., 1918, PhD, 1933; AM, U. Chgo., 1924. Rural sch. tchr. nr. Marshall, Okla., 1907-10, 13-15; supt. schs. North Enid, Okla., 1918-19; tchr. history Enid High Sch., 1919-23; mem. faculty Stephen F. Austin State Tchrs. Coll., Nacogdoches, Tex., summer 1935; state supr. Fed. Writers Project, 1940-41; mem. faculty history dept. Okla. State U., Stillwater, summers 1945, 46, 1957-58, mem. library staff, 1947-55. Author: numerous books including: (with J. Fred Rippy) The Historical Background of the American Policy of Isolation, 1924; The Rise and Fall of the Choctaw Republic (John H. Dunning prize), 1934; And Still the Waters Run, 1940; The Road to Disappearance, 1941; Tulsa: From Creek Town to Oil Capital, 1943; Prairie City, 1944; Oklahoma: Foot-loose and Fancy-Free, 1949; A History of the Indians of the United States, 1970; Geronimo: The Man, His Time, His Place, 1976; also editor books. Mem. Okla. Bicentennial Commn., 1975-76; bd. dirs. ACLU Okla., 1973-76. Alfred A. Knopf History fellow, 1942; Rockefeller fellow U. Okla., 1946-47. Mem. Assn. Am. Indian Affairs (dir. 1956-66), Rebekah Lodge, Marshall Woman's Club. Democrat. Mem. United Ch. Christ (commn. higher edn. 1957-62). Home: Marshall Okla. Died Feb. 21, 1988.

DE BROGLIE, LOUISE VICTOR PIERRE RAYMOND, physicist; b. Dieppe, France, Aug. 15, 1892; s. Victor and Pauline (d'Armaille) de B. B, U. Sorbonne, Paris, 1909; license in sci., U. Paris, 1913, DSc, 1924. Lectr. faculty scis. U. Paris, 1926-28; prof. theoretical physics Henri Poincare Inst., from 1928; founder ctr. of studies in applied math., 1943; established concept of connection between particles and waves known as de Broglie wave length, 1923, established theory of photon, 1943. Author: Matter and Light, 1946, The Revolution in Physics, A Non-Mathematicla Survey of Quanta, 1953. Counselor French High Commn. Atomic Energy, 1945. With French Engring. Corps, 1913-19. Decorated Albert I Grand Prize of Monaco, 1932; Order Leopold of Belgium; recipient Nobel prize in physics, 1929, Kalinga prize, 1952, grand prize Soc. Engrs. France, 1953. Mem. Academie des Scis. (sec. from 1942, Henri Poincare medal 1929), Academic Francaise, Institut France, Royal Soc. Home: Paris France. †

DE BUTTS, JOHN DULANY, telephone company executive; b. Greensboro, N.C., Apr. 10, 1915; s. Sydnor and Mary Ellen (Cutchin) deB.; m. Gertrude Willoughby Walke, Nov. 4, 1939; children: Talbot (Mrs. Tyler Cain), Mary Linda (Mrs. R. Collins Couch). B.S. in Elec. Engring., Va. Mil. Inst., 1936; LL.D. (hon.), Knox Coll., 1966, Northwestern U., 1966, Lehigh U., 1975, Loyola U., Chgo., 1967, Hampden-Sydney Coll., 1978, Columbia U., 1978; Sc.D. (hon.), Clarkson Coll. Tech., 1973; D.C.S. (hon.), Pace Coll., 1977; Eng.D. (hon.), Lafayette Coll., 1977, Worcester Poly. Inst., 1979; L.H.D. (hon.), St. Augustine Coll., 1978. With Chesapeake & Potomac Telephone Co., 1936-49, 51-55, 59-62, v.p. ops. and engring., dir., 1959-62; with AT&T, N.Y.C., 1949-51, 55-57, 66-86; asst. v.p. govt. relations AT&T, Washington, 1957-58; exec. v.p. AT&T, N.Y.C., 1966-67; vice chmn. bd. AT&T, 1967-72, chmn. bd., chief exec. officer, 1972-79, dir., 1967-81; gen. mgr. Westchester area N.Y. Telephone Co., 1958-59; pres., dir. Ill. Bell Telephone Co., 1962-66; dir. Hosp. Corp. Am., U.S. Steel Corp. Trustee Duke Endowment, 1973-86, vice chmn., 1975-81; chmn. Va. Mil. Inst. Found., 1981-86; vice chmn. Bus. Council, 1975-76, chmn., 1976-78, mem. exec. com., 1972-86, chmn. membership com., 1979-80; bd. govs. United Way Am., 1972-79; bd. visitors Grad. Sch. Bus. Adminstrn., Duke U., 1974-81; hon. trustee Chicago Mus. Sci. and Industry; hon. life mem. bd. lay trustees Loyola U., Chgo.; trustee Tax Found., 1973-79; co-chmn. Bus. Roundtable, 1974-77, mem. exec. com., policy com., 1972-79, mem. sr. exec. council Conf. Bd., 1973-79, mem. policy com., 1974-79, vice chmn., 1974-79; mem. nat. com. Assn. Episc. Colls., 1966-79; Mem. O.R.C., 1936-39, U.S. N.G., 1939-40. Recipient Silver Beaver award Boy Scouts Am., 1964, Silver Antelope award, 1971; Silver Medal Brotherhood award NCCJ, 1966; Gold medal Brotherhood award, 1972; Charles Evans Hughes award, 1976; Washington award Engring. Socs., 1974; Ann. citation Midwest Research Inst., 1974; Gold medal USO, 1974; Founders Day award Loyola U., 1965; S. Byard Colgate award Jr. Achievement, 1970; Gold Achievement award, 1970; Highest Honor Leadership award, 1972; Corporate Man of Year award B'nai B'rith, 1973; Family of Man award Council of Chs., 1974; Distinguished Service award Va. Mil. Inst., 1975; Bus. Statesman award Harvard Bus. Sch., 1976; St. La Salla medal Manhattan Coll., 1977; medal of merit St. Nicholas Soc., 1977; Bus. Leadership award U. Mich., 1977; C. Walter Nichols award N.Y. U., 1978; Leaders in Mgmt. award Pace U., 1978; Disting. Citizens award Boy Scouts Am., 1978; Disting. Citizens award Va. C. of C., 1979; Public Service award Advt. Council, 1978; N.C. award, 1978; Fairless Meml. medal, 1979; New Market medal Va. Mil. Inst., 1984. Mem. Western Soc. Engrs. (hon.), Navy League U.S., Northwestern U. Assos., Kappa Alpha (disting. achievement award), Beta Gamma Sigma (hon.). Republican. Episcopalian. Clubs: Metropolitan (Washington); Links (N.Y.C.); Commonwealth (Richmond, Va.). Home: Upperville Va. Died Dec. 17, 1986.

DEER, ROY BURTON, clergyman; b. Harbor Beach, Mich., Dec. 16, 1891; s. John Jacob and Margaret Ann (Crecine) D.; m. Emilie Spencer, Sept. 14, 1915 (dec. 1958); children: Gordon Spencer, Margaret Emily Deer Rodgers, Donald Spencer; m. 2d, Hazel J. Jones, May 9, 1959. PhB, Denison U., 1915, DD, 1938; BD, Rochester Theol. Sem., 1919. Ordained to ministry Baptist Ch., 1919. Pastor Maple St. Ch., Buffalo, 1919-21; pastor 1st Ch., Terre Haute, Ind., 1921-29, Lansing, Mich., 1930-36; mem. bd. promotion and exec. com. Ind. Bapt. Conv., 1921-29, chmn. dept. evangelism, 1922-29; mem. com. on Conf. with Gen. Bapts., Am. Bapt. Conv., 1929-32, adminstrv. com. Coun. Missionary Cooperation, 1938-44, pres. Home Mission Agys., 1942-43, mem. post-war planning com., 1943-46, Crusade for Christ through Evangelism com., 1947-49; mem. bd. mgrs. Mich. Bapt. Conv., 1931-32, 35-36, chmn. centennial com. on evangelism, 1934-36; exec. sec. and dir. state missions and evangelism Pa. Bapt. Conv., 1936-43, missionary promotion N.J. Bapt. Conv., 1943-48; spl. rep. coun. on missionary coop. Am. Bapt. Conv., 1948-53; assoc. dir. field svc. Colgate-Rochester Div. Sch., 1953-58. Author: Evangelism for the Whole Church; contbr. articles to religious jours. Pres. Bapt. Young People's Union, Buffalo, 1920-21, Lansing Coun. Religious Edn., 1936; mem. hdqrs. com. Mich. Anti-Saloon League, 1935-36. Mem. Acad. Polit. and Social Sci. Republican. Home: Rochester N.Y. †

DEFFERRE, GASTON, mayor; b. 1910. Ed. Coll. de Nimes, Aix-en-Provence U. Practiced law Marseilles, before World War II; dir. Le Provencal, 1944; mayor Marseilles 1945, 53-86; dep. from Bouches du Rhne to Constituent Assemblies, 1945-46, Nat. Assembly, 1946-58; sec. of state Presidence du Conseil, 1946; under-sec. of state Overseas France, 1945-46; minister Mcht. Marine, 1950-51; minister Overseas France, 1956-57; senator, 1959-62; dep. Nat. Assembly, 1962-86. Socialist candidate for pres. Republic, 1964. Decorated officer Legion d'Honneur, Croix de Guerre, Rosette de la Resistance, King's medal for Courage in Cause of Freedom. Home: Marseilles France. Died May 7, 1986; buried Marseilles, France.

DE KIEWIT, CORNELIS WILLEM, university president, historian; b. Rotterdam, Holland, May 21, 1902; naturalized U.S. citizen, 1939; m. Lucas Maian Hejinian, Aug. 22, 1930; children: Marie, Christina (dec.), John. AB, U. Witwatersrand, 1923, AM, 1924; PhD, U. London, 1927; postdoctorate, U. Paris, 1927-28, U. Berlin, 1928-29; LLD, Syracuse U., 1951, N.Y.U., 1951, Hull U., McGill U., Northwestern U., 1958; LHD, Hobart and William Smith Colls., 1952, Colgate U., 1959; LittD, Rennes U., 1958, Natal U., 1960. Tchr. Afrikaans and history Southern Rhodesia, 1923-25; asst. prof. history State U. Iowa, 1929-35, assoc. prof., 1935-37, prof., 1937-41; prof. modern European history Cornell U., Ithaca, N.Y., 1941-86, dean. coll. arts and scis., 1945-48, provost, 1948-49, acting pres., 1949-51; pres. U. Rochester, N.Y., 1951-61, pres. emeritus, 1961-86; hon. trustee; chmn. com. on edn. in tropical Africa, NRC, 1960-86; mem. council on higher edn. N.Y.U. Commn. on Human Resources and Advanced Trig., 1951-54; adv. com. underdeveloped areas Mut. Security Agy., 1950-52; former mem. Ford Found. African screening com, Can.-U.S. com. Am. Council Edn. Author: British Colonial Policy and the South African Republics, 1929; The Imperial Factor in South Africa, 1937; A History of South Africa, 1941; The Anatomy of South African Misery, 1956; co-editor Dufferin-Carnarvon correspondence; also articles in profl. jours. Past mem., bd. dirs. George Eastman House, Lincoln-Rochester Trust Co.; former trustee Corning Mus. Glass. Decorated Officer Legion of Honor. Mem. Am. Hist. Assn., Am. Council Learned Socs. (chmn. bd. dirs. 1952-54), Assn. Am. Univs. (pres. 1956-58), Assn. Colls. and State N.Y. (sec.-treas. 1953), Council Fgn. Relations, Inc., Phi Beta Kappa, Century Club, Univ. Club, Country Club, Genessee Valley Club. Home: Bryans Road Md. Died Feb. 15, 1986.

DE KOONING, ELAINE, artist; b. N.Y.C., Mar. 12, 1918; d. Charles Frank and Mary Ellen (O'Brien) Fried; m. Willem de Kooning, Dec. 9, 1943. DFA (hon.), Western Coll. Women, Oxford, Ohio, 1964, Moore Coll. Art, Maryland Inst.; DHL, Adelphi U.; DFA, Md. Inst., Balt., 1986. One-woman shows include Stable Gallery, N.Y.C., 1954, 56, Tibor de Nagy Gallery, N.Y.C., 1957, Graham Gallery, N.Y.C., 1960, 61, 63, 65, 75, U. N.Mex., 1957, Mus. N.Mex., Santa Fe, 1959, Gump's, San Francisco, 1959, Washington Gallery Modern Art, presdl. portraits, 1964, Lyman Allen Mus., New London, Conn., retrospective, 1959, Montclair (N.J.) Art Mus., 1973, Benson Gallery, Bridgehampton, N.Y., 1973, Ill. Wesleyan U., Bloomington, 1975, Coll. St. Catherine, St. Paul, 1975, Tampa Bay Arts Ctr., 1975, Grimaldis Gallery, Balt., 1980, 84, 85, Gruenebaum Gallery, N.Y.C., 1982, 86, Adelphi U., N.Y., 1984, Vered Gallery, N.Y., 1984, Gallery Silvia Menzel, Berlin, 1986, Guggenheim Gallery, Miami, Fla., 1986, Wenger Gallery, Los Angeles, 1987, Fischback Gallery, N.Y.C., 1988, others; represented in permanent collections Mus. Modern Art Loeb Ctr., N.Y.C., Kennedy Library, Cambridge, Mass., Truman Library, Independence, Mo., Elmira (N.Y.) Coll., Ark. Arts Ctr., Little Rock, Jewish Community Ctr., Bayonne, N.J., Montclair (N.J.) Art Mus., Ciba-Geigy Corp., Ardsley, N.Y., Neuberger Mus., Purchase, N.Y., Albright-Knox Gallery, Buffalo, Corcoran Gallery of Art, Washington, Hirshorn Mus. Art, Washington, Washington Gallery of Modern Art, also pvt. collections; commd. portrait John F. Kennedy for Truman Library, Independence, Mo., 1962; instr., U. N.Mex., 1959, Pa. State U., 1960, Contemporary Art Assn., Houston, 1952, U. Calif. at Davis, 1963-64, Yale, 1967, Mellon chair Carnegie-Mellon U., 1969-70, U. Pa., 1970-72, Wagner Coll., 1970, U. Pa., from 1971, N.Y. Studio Sch., Paris, France, 1974, Parsons Sch. Fine Art, 1974-76, Lamar Dodd chair U. Ga., Athens, 1976-78, Mellon chair Carnegie-Mellon Inst., 1969-70, Mellon chair Cooper-Union, N.Y.C., 1976, Milton and Sally Avery chair Bard Coll., 1982. Home: East Hampton N.Y. Died Feb. 1, 1989; buried Green River Cemetery, East Hampton, N.Y.

DE LA CHAPELLE, CLARENCE EWALD, cardiologist, educator; b. N.Y.C., Dec. 6, 1897; S. Maximilien G. Hugo and Mathilde (Koenig) de la C.; m. Lillian L. Buckman, Jan. 29, 1925; children: Donald Clarence, Norman Frederic. Student, St. Johns Coll., Fordham U., 1916-18; BS, N.Y.U., 1921, MD, 1922. Diplomate Am. Bd. of Internal Medicine with subsplty in cardiovascular diseases. Instr. in pathology N.Y.U. Coll. Medicine, 1924-26, instr. in medicine, 1926-32, asst. prof., 1932-38, acting chmn. dept. medicine, 1937-38, prof. clin. medicine, 1938-48, asst. dean, 1942-45, assoc. dean, dir. postgrad. div., 1945-48; prof. medicine N.Y.U. Post Grad. Med. Sch., assoc. dean, 1948-63, cons. postgrad. med. edn., 1963-87; dir. Div. Affiliated and Regional Hosps., N.Y.U. Med. Ctr., 1950-63; assoc. vis. physician Lenox Hill Hosp., 1933-45, chief cardiac clinic, 1933-45, attending cardiologist, 1945-48, dir. medicine, 1948-60, cons. physician, 1960-87; physician Bellevue Sch. Nursing, 1925-45; cons. physician St. Luke's Hosp., Newburgh, 1935-52, Fitkin Meml. Hosp., Neptune N.J., 1945-51; cons. physician in internal medicine Vassar Bros. Hosp., Poughkeepsie, N.Y., 1948-63; cons. med. edn. Surgeon Gen. USAF, 1958-64; cons. cardiologist Community Hosp., Glen Cove, 1945-52, 58-87, New Rochelle (N.Y.) Hosp., 1950-87, Nassau Hosp., Mineola, 1950-52, North Shore Hosp, Manhasset, 1955-87; mem. adminstrs. med. adv. panel FAA, 1965-68. Author: Diseases of the Heart and Blood Vessels, 1964; contbr. profl. pubs.; editor: New York Heart Association, Origins and Development, 1915-65, 1966; mem. editorial bd. Am. Heart Jour., 1946-50, Circulation, 1950-61. Commd. lt. comdr. USNR, 1933-37; cons. in cardiology SSS, cons. and adviser to war dept. in profl. edn., 1942-44. Fellow AMA, ACP, NY Acad. Medicine (v.p. 1964-66); mem. Am. Heart Assn. (dir. 1937-48, 55-57), Interam. Soc. Cardiology (dir. 1960-68), Am. Assn. Pathologists and Bacteriologists, NY Heart Assn. (council 1928-45, bd. dirs. 1945-87, v.p. 1947-49), Internat. Acad. Pathology, Harvey Soc., NY Pathol. Soc., Sigma Xi, Alpha Omega Alpha, Univ. Club. Home: New York N.Y. Died June 13, 1987.

DELACOUR, JEAN THEODORE, naturalist; b. Paris, Sept. 26, 1890; naturalized citizen of U.S., 1946; s. Theodore and Marguerite (Rousseau) D. Ed. Jesuit Sch., Rue de Madrid, Paris; Lic.S., U. Lille, 1914. ex-dir. dept. history, sci., arts Los Angeles County; research assoc. Am. Mus. Natural History, N.Y.C., 1942-60; former collaborator Fish and Wildlife Service, Dept. Interior; past pres. Ligue Française pour la Protection des Oiseaux; past v.p. Sociētē Nationale D'Acclimatation de France, Avicultural Soc. London; past pres. Avicultural Soc. Am.; mem. com. Am. Com. for Internat. Wildlife Protection; council Zool. Soc. London (hon.), Sociētē Ornithologique et Mammalogique de France (editor 1920-40), Sociētē Zoologique de France; past v.p. Council Internat. de la Chasse, Acadēmie des Sciences, Arts et Belles-Lettres de Rouen, NY and Phila. Zool. Socs., Brit. Ornithologists Union, Ornithol. Soc. Japan. Engaged in work as naturalist since 1908-85; maintained world's largest private zoo and aviary on his estate, Chateau de Clères, Normandy, as site of gardens and buildings for living collections of rare animals and birds obtained on own expeditions and by special collectors throughout the world, 1919-39; the collections were practically destroyed with records and library during World War II, now restored; editor: L'Oiseau et la Revue Française d'Ornithologie (mag.), 1920-40; author of numerous scientific books and articles relating to ornithology and mammalogy published in learned jours. of France, Eng., U.S. and Germany. Mem. Knickerbocker Club, Century Assn., Explorers, Coffee House Club, Calif. Club. Roman Catholic. Home: Los Angeles Calif. Deceased.

DELAHANTY, DAVID, university president, educational administrator; b. N.Y.C., July 27, 1935; s. Patrick D. and Eileen (Keating) O'Connor. B.A., Catholic U., 1958; M.A., U. Detroit, 1961; M.S., Syracuse U., 1966, Ph.D., 1972. Tchr. St. Joseph High Sch., Detroit, 1958-62; tchr., prin. Christian Bros. Acad., Syracuse, N.Y., 1962-69; asst. prof. Manhattan Coll., Bronx, N.Y., 1970-75, assoc. prof., 1975-82, chmn. edn. dept., 1978-82, acting dean, 1979-80; pres. Lewis U., Romeoville, Ill., 1982-87. Author: Helping Teachers Grow, 1975; editor: Manhattan College Self-Study, 1981. Trustee LaSalle Mil. Acad., Oakdale, N.Y., Christian Bros. Coll., Memphis, Manhattan Coll., N.Y.C. Syracuse U. fellow, 1969-70. Mem. Am. Assn. Higher Edn., Assn. Cath. Colls. and Univs., Nat. Cath. Edn. Assn., Fedn. Ind. Ill. Colls. and Univs., Phi Beta Kappa, Kappa Delta Pi.

Roman Catholic. Lodge: Rotary/Joliet, Ill. Home: Romeoville Ill. Died Oct. 13, 1987.

DELANEY, JAMES J., congressman; b. N.Y.C., Mar. 19, 1901; m. Lola Mathias, 1939 (dec. 1972); 1 child, Patrick. LLB, St. John's U., 1932. Asst. dist. atty. Queen's County, N.Y., 1936-44; mem. 79th Congress from 7th dist. N.Y., 1947-49, 81st-87th Congresses from 7th dist. N.Y., 1951-65, 88th-95th Congresses from 9th dist. N.Y., 1965-79; chmn. rules com. Democrat. Died May 24, 1987.

DELANY, WALTER S(TANLEY), government official, former military officer; b. Reading, Pa., Jan. 21, 1891; s. Erwin F. and Mary E. (Dunkle) DeL.; m. Lou Sharman, Oct. 2, 1915; children: Katherin DeLany Fawkes, Walter Stanley. Grad., U.S. Naval Acad., 1912; LLD (hon.), Wagner Coll., 1952. Commd. USN, 1912, advanced through grades to vice adm., 1946, duty USS Minn. during occupation Vera Cruz, Mex., 1915, also staff regtl. comdr., Naval Occupation Force, with destroyer force, Queenstown, Ireland, 1917-18, various capacities on destroyers, battleships and fleet auxs., 1918-30, also duty chief naval ops. and U.S. Naval Acad., asst. chief staff, ops. officer staff comdr. in chief, Pacific Fleet, 1941, comdr. cruiser New Orleans, 1942, asst. chief staff, ops. staff comdr. in chief, U.S. Fleet, 1942, later asst. chief staff readiness to comdr. in chief, comdr. battleships and cruisers, Pacific Fleet, USS St. Paul, 1946, comdr. 3d naval dist., 1948-52, comdr. Eastern sea frontier, also comdr. Atlantic res. fleet, 1952, comdr. U.S. Atlantic Western sub-area under NATO, ret., 1953; dep. adminstr. Mut. Def. Assistance Control Act, 1953-61. Decorated Legion of Merit with Gold star, other U.S. medals, Order of Yun Hui (China). †

DELAPLANE, STANTON HILL, newspaper columnist; b. Chgo., Oct. 12, 1907; s. Frank Hugh and Marion (Hill) D.; m. Miriam Moore, Dec. 6, 1940 (div. 1958); children: Kristin Moore, Thomas; m. Susan Aven, Feb. 2, 1961 (div. May 1973); children: Andrea Aven, John Berry Hill; m. Laddie Marshack, Oct. 19, 1979. Student, Hyde Park, Chgo., Santa Barbara, Cal., Monterey high schs., 1922-26. Editor Aperitif Mag. (pub. by Baroness Emily Von Romberg), 1933-36; reporter San Francisco Chronicle, 1936-88, editor women's dept., 1937; now columnist; also columnist Chronicle Features, San Francisco; Organizer Calif. Young Democrats; and editor The Young Democrat, 1933-34; U.S. war corr. San Francisco Chronicle, 1944-45. Author: Pacific Pathways; Contbr. to: etc. Served to lt. comdr. USMC, Maritime Commn., 1942-44, Washington. accredited corr. U.N. Conf., 1945; Recipient Pulitzer prize for regional reporting of movement of Calif.-Oreg. border counties to secede and form the 49th state, 1941, Nat. Headlines journalism award for feature series titles, Ding Dong Daddy of the D Car Line, 1946; Nat. Headlines award, 1959; 1st Ann. Writers award for best N. Am. article on sea travel Transpacific Passenger Conf. Club: San Francisco Press (pres. 1970-71, dir). Home: San Francisco Calif. Died Apr. 18, 1988, cremated.

DELAUNAY, SONIA TERK, artist; b. Ukraine, Russia, 1885; m. Robert Delaunay, 1910 (dec.). Greatly influenced by Cubism; paintings include Prismes Electriques; also works in bookbinding, collages, fabric design and illus. poem Transsiberien; a founder First Salon des Realites Nouvelles; retrospective exhbns. in mus. of Grenoble, Bielefeld, Turin, Lyon and Paris. Home: Paris France. †

DE LIAGRE, ALFRED GUSTAV ETIENNE, JR., theatrical producer, director; b. Passaic, N.J., Oct. 6, 1904; s. Alfred and Frida (Unger) de L.; m. Mary M. Howard; children: Nicolas, Christina. AB, Yale U., 1926. In various bus., including banking, real estate, pub., aviation, writing 1926-31, asst. stage mgr. with Jane Cowl in Twelfth Night, 1930. Editor: Sportsman Pilot, 1929; co-producer, dir. (with Richard Aldrich) Three Cornered Moon, 1933, numerous others; producer, dir.: Yes, My Darling Daughter, 1937, Voice of the Turtle, 1943 (Critics Prize play), The Druid Circle, 1947, The Madwoman of Chaillot, 1948, Second Threshold, 1950, Cupid and Psyche, 1951, The Deep Blue Sea, 1952, Escapade, 1953, The Golden Apple, 1954; Producer: Janus, 1955, Nature's Way, 1957, Girls in 509, 1958, J.B., 1959, Kwamina, 1961, Photo Finish, 1963, (play) The Irregular Verb to Love, 1963. Chmn. council Sch. of the Drama, Yale U., also mem. campaign; chmn. theatre div. Salvation Army; trustee Guild Hall of East Hampton; v.p. Actors Fund Am.; bd. dirs. Nat. Repertory Theatre, Am. Shakespeare Festival Theatre and Acad., Council Living Theatre, Theatre Devel. Fund; v.p. Am. Theatre Wing; trustee French Inst./Alliance Française. Decorated chevalier French Legion of Honor; recipient Pulitzer prize for play, 1959. Mem. Am. Theatre Soc. (trustee), Nat. Book Com., France-Am. Soc., League N.Y. Theatres (gov.), Com. Theatrical Producers (bd. dirs.), Renaissance Found., ANIA (exec. producer, sec. 1977-87), Nat. Cultural Ctr., Beta Theta Pi, Maidstone Club, Pilgrims Club, Pundits Clubs, Century Assn., River Club. Home: New York N.Y. Died Mar. 5, 1987; buried Cathedral of St. John the Divine, N.Y.C.

DELONG, DWIGHT MOORE, entomology educator; b. Corning, Ohio, Apr. 6, 1892; s. George W. and Addie (Moore) DeL.; m. Fannie Merchant, Dec. 22, 1917; children: Joan Elizabeth, Eleanor Jane, George Wesley. BSc, Ohio Wesleyan U., 1914, DSc, 1941; MSc, Ohio State U., 1916, PhD, 1922. Asst. dept. zoology and entomology Ohio State U., 1914-17, instr., 1918, asst. prof. entomology, 1921-23, prof., from 1923; assoc. dir. Ohio Biol. Survey, from 1943; supr. Sherwin Williams insecticide rsch. investigation, 1934-48; supr. Pitts. coal carbonization rsch. project, 1938-39; scientific expdns. to Mex., 1939, 41, 45; responsible investigator OSRD rsch. project, 1943-45; Nat. Rsch. Acad. and Q.M.C. project, 1945-48. Contbr. numerous tech. bulls., monographs to sci. jours.; patentee insect bait trap. NIH grantee from 1948. Fellow Entonological Soc. of Am., AAAS; mem. Am. Assn. Econ. Entomologists, Ohio Acad. Sci. (pres. 1959-60), Masons, Sigma Xi, Gamma Alpha, Gamma Sigma Delta, Phi Mu Delta, Delta Theta Sigma. Home: Columbus Ohio. †

DELOR, CAMILLE JOSEPH, gastroenterologist; b. Sandusky, Ohio, Jan. 24, 1907; s. Cahrles J. and Amelia (Biron) D.; m. Eleanor B. Diltz, Sept. 2, 1932; children: Nancy DeLor Bringardner, Susan DeLor Baas. AB, U. Mich., 1928; MS, Ohio State U., 1934, MD, 1934. Intern St. Francis Hosp., Columbus, Ohio, 1934-35; resident Ohio State U. Hosp., Columbus, 1935-37; pvt. practice Columbus, 1937-82; mem. staff Ohio State U. Hosp; prof. medicine Ohio State U., 1948-76, Warner M. and Lora KAys Pomerene prof. medicine, 1976-77, prof. medicine emeritus, 1977-82. Contbr. articles to profl. jours. Fellow A.C.P.; mem. Am. Fedn. Clin. Research, Am. Gastroenterol. Assn. (sr.), Sigma Xi, Alpha Omega Alpha, Alpha Kappa Kappa. Home: Columbus Ohio. Died Nov. 9, 1982; buried Columbus, Ohio.

DELP, MAHLON HENRY, internist, educator; b. Lenora, Kans., Nov. 26, 1903; s. Henry Alexander and Alice Belle (Breeden) D.; m. Florence Elizabeth Aldrich, Nov. 15, 1924; 1 child, Virginia Elizabeth. BS, MD, U. Kans., 1934. Diplomate Am. Bd. Internal Medicine. Intern U. Kans. Med. Ctr., Kansas City, 1934-35, resident in internal medicine, 1935-38, assoc. physician, 1938-42; pvt. practice Kansas City, from 1938; asst. prof. U. Kans., Kansas City, 1942-48, assoc. prof., 1948-51, prof., 1951-60, Bohan prof. medicine, from 1960, chmn. dept. postgrad. med. edn., asst. dean, 1952-60, chmn. dept. internal medicine, 1960-69. Co-author: (textbook) Physical Diagnosis; contbr. articles to profl. jours. Col. M.C., U.S. Army, 1942-46. Fellow ACP; mem. AMA, Kansas City Acad. Medicine, Am. Clin. Climatol. Soc., Milburn Country Club, Delta Upsilon, Phi Chi, Alpha Omega Alpha. Republican. Episcopalian. Home: Merriam Kans. Died Jan. 29, 1989.

DEL REY, JUDY-LYNN, publishing executive; b. N.Y.C., Jan. 26, 1943; d. Zachary Harold and Norma Victoria (Breslau) Benjamin; m. Lester Del Ray, Mar. 21, 1971. BA, Hunter Coll., 1965. Mng. editor Galaxy mag., UPD Pub. Corp., N.Y.C., 1969-73; sr. editor Random House Inc., Ballantine Books, N.Y.C., 1973-77, v.p., from 1978; editor-in-chief Del Rey Books, 1977-82, pub., 1982-86. Editor: The Celtic Bull: Essays on James Joyce's Ulysses, 1966, (book series) Stellar Science Fiction, vols. 1-7, 1974-81, Stellar Short Novels, 1976; sci. fiction cons., contbr. World Book Ency, 1972, 77. Named to Hall of Fame Hunter Coll., 1972. Home: New York N.Y. Died Feb. 20, 1986; cremated.

DELUCA, GEORGE BENJAMIN, lawyer, banker; b. N.Y.C., Sept. 20, 1889; s. Mariano and Catherine (Bonetti) DeL.; m. Mary M. Reilly, Apr. 24, 1916; children: John J., George B., Robert W. BS, CCNY, 1909; LLB, Columbia U., 1912. Bar: N.Y. 1911. Pvt. practice N.Y.C., 1912-20; asst. dist. atty. Bronx County, N.Y., 1920-30; magistrate N.Y.C., 1930-37; assoc. justice Ct. Spl. Sessions, N.Y.C., 1937-46, chief justice, 1946-50; dist. atty. Bronx County, 1950-55; lt. gov. N.Y., 1955-58; v.p. Comml. Bank N.Am., N.Y.C., from 1959. Mem. ABA, N.Y. Bar Assn., Bronx County Bar Assn., CCNY Alumni Assn., Columbia Law Alumni Assn., Moose, Elks, Phi Beta Kappa, Alpha Delta Phi. Roman Catholic. Home: New York N.Y. †

DELUCA, MARLENE ANDEREGG, biochemist, educator; b. LaCrosse, Wis., Nov. 10, 1936; s. Ruben H. and Yerda T. (Harris) Anderegg; m. William D. McElroy, Aug. 28, 1967; 1 child, Eric Gene. BS, Hamline U., 1958; PhD, U. Minn., 1962. Postdoctoral fellow Johns Hopkins U., Balt., 1962-64, asst. prof., 1965-69; asst. prof. biochemistry Georgetown U., Washington, 1969-72; assoc. prof. U. Calif. San Diego, La Jolla, 1972-78, prof., from 1978. Editor: Methods in Enzymology, 1978, Methods in Enzymology Bioluminescence and Chemiluminescence Part B, 1986, Basic Chemical and Analytical Applications, 1981; contbr. articles to profl. jours. Recipient Career Devel. awards NIH, 1967-69, 72-73; named one of Outstanding Young Women in Am. Mem. Am. Chem. Soc., Am. Soc. Biol. Chemistry, Am. Soc. for Photobiology, Sigma Xi. Democrat. Congregationalist. Home: La Jolla Calif. Deceased.

DE LUCCA, JOHN, educator; b. Bklyn., Oct. 8, 1920; s. Carlo and Adela (Ianniello) De L.; m. Margaret Louise Williams, June 10, 1956; children—Danielle S., David J. B.B.A., CCNY, 1941; M.A., New Sch. for Social Research, 1950; postgrad., Harvard U., 1952-53; Ph.D. (Univ. fellow), Ohio State U., 1955. Lectr. philosophy Pace Coll., 1950-52; acting instr. English Ohio State U., 1955-56; instr. philosophy Wash. State U., 1956-58, asst. prof., 1958-62; asst. prof. philosophy U. Victoria, B.C., Can., 1962-64; assoc. prof. U. Victoria, 1964-68, first chmn. dept., 1963-68; prof. philosophy Queen's U., Kingston, Ont., 1968-86; prof. emeritus philosophy Queen's U., 1986; pres., gen. mgr. Johart Internat. Corp., N.Y.C., 1946-51. Editor: Reason and Experience: Dialogues in Modern Philosophy, 1973; translator, editor: René Descartes' Meditations on First Philosophy, 1974, rev. edit., 1975; contbr. articles to profl. jours., numerous book reviews. Served with AUS, 1942-45. Mem. Am. Philos. Assn. (mem. exec. com. Pacific div. 1965-67, program chmn. 1967), Can. Philos. Assn., Am. Assn. Advancement of Humanities (charter mem.), Philosophy of Sci. Assn., N.W. Conf. on Philosophy (pres. 1959-60), Humanities Assn. Can., Beta Gamma Sigma. Home: Kingston Ont., Canada Died Sept. 8, 1986.

DELUE, DONALD HARCOURT, sculptor; b. Boston, Oct. 5, 1897; s. Harry Thornton and Ida Martha (DeLue) Quigley; m. Martha Naomi Cross, Oct. 5, 1931 (dec. 1981). Student, Boston Mus. Fine Arts Sch.; D. hon., Monmouth Coll., West Long Branch, N.J. Commns. include: The Rocket Thrower, World's Fair, N.Y.C., 1964-65, Boys Scout Meml. Tribute, Washington, three Confederate Memls., Gettysburg, Pa., Fed. Court House, Phila., Fourteen Stations of Cross Loyola Jesuit Sem., Shrub Oak, N.Y., four bronze figures at Alamo, San Antonio, Edward Hull Crump Meml., Memphis, Harvey Firestone Meml., Akron, Ohio, Lions of Judah Germantown Jewish Ctr., Phila., Chemistry Bldg., U. Pa., Meml. Urn., City Hall, Stockholm, Sweden, Bronze Door, Woodmont Shrine, Phila., 10 bronze statues of George Washington (Masonic) in various cities, also medals and replicas. Recipient Citations for Hist. Work DAR, United Daus. of Confederacy; recipient J. Sanford Saltus medal, others, Guggenheim Found fellow; Nat. Inst. Arts and Letters fellow. Fellow Am. Numismatic Soc. (Sculptor of Yr. 1979), Nat. Sculpture Soc. (pres. 1945-48, hon. pres. from 1979, Gold medals 1964, 66, 74); mem. Am. Inst. Commemorative Art (hon.), Archtl. League (recipient Avery prize), Am. Artists Profl. League (dir., Gold medal), NAD (recipient Samuel B. Morse Gold medal), Allied Artists Am., Royal Soc. Arts (London), Nat. Inst. Arts and Letters. Died Aug. 26, 1988.

DEL VECCHIO, GIORGIO, philosopher, jurist, educator; b. Bologna, Italy, Aug. 26, 1878; s. Giulio and Ida (Cavalieri) Del V.; m. Tina Valabrega, Mar. 30, 1930. Student univs., Genoa, Rome, Berlin; D Jurisprudence, U. Genoa, 1900. Prof. philosophy law at univs. Ferrara, 1903, Sassari, 1906, Messina, 1909, Bologna, 1911; prof. philosophy law U. Rome, 1920-53, prof. emeritus, from 1953, rector, 1925-27, dean faculty law, 1930-38. Author: Evoluzione ed involuzione nel diritto, 1945, La Giustizia, 5th edit., 1959, Lezioni di Filosofia del diritto, 10th edit., 1958, Lo Stato, 1953, Diritto ed Economia, 2d edit., 1954, La Verità nella morale e nel diritto, 3d edit., 1954, Diritto naturale e unita europea, 1958, (in English) Justice, 1952, Philosophy of Law, 1953, General Principles of Law, 1956, others; editor Rivista internazional de Filosofia del diritto, from 1921. Mem. Institut Internationale de Philosophie du Droit (pres.), Societa Italiana de Filosofia del Diritto (pres.), Am. Acad. Arts and Scis. Home: Rome Italy. †

DEMMON, ELWOOD LEONARD, forester; b. Kendallville, Ind., Sept. 23, 1892; s. Elwood Frank and Blanche (Voorheis) D.; m. Doris May Oppermann, June 27, 1925; children: Elwood Leonard, Doralese Demmon Robinson, Carol Evelyn. AB, U. Mich., 1914, MF, 1916; ScD (hon.), N.C. State Coll., 1955. Forester, tech. advisor Goodyear Tire & Rubber Co., Sumatra, Dutch East Indies, 1916-23; spl. investigator Firestone Tire & Rubber Co., Cen. Am., 1924; silviculturist So. Forest Expt. Sta., Asheville, N.C., 1951-56; forestry cons. U.S. Internat. Coop. Adminstrn. Mut. Security Mission to China (Formosa), 1956-57, in Asheville, from 1957; cons. So. Regional Edn. Bd. Atlanta, 1958-59. Contbr. articles on rubber culture and forestry. Mem. La. Agrl. War Bd., 1942-44, Minn. Agrl. War Bd., 1944-45; mem. forest products rsch. adv. com. Mich. Coll. Mining & Tech., 1947-51; mem. Gov.'s Conservation Adv. Com., Minn., 1950-51, adv. com. N.C. State Coll. Sch. Forestry, from 1952, Forest Farmers Assn. Coop., Atlanta, forestry commn. Asheville Agrl. Devel. Coun., from 1963; pres. Asheville-Biltmore Bot. Gardens, from 1965. Recipient U. Mich. Disting. Alumni Svc. medal, 1954, U.S. Dept. Agr. Disting. Svc. award, 1956, merit citation Nat. Civil Svc. League, 1956. Fellow Soc. Am. Foresters; mem. AAAS (rep. coun. 1946-49, NRC rep. div. biology and agrl. 1951-55, pres. 1954-55), Am. Forestry Assn. (bd. dirs. 1954-55), N.C. Forestry Assn. (bd. dirs.), Forest History Soc. (bd. dirs.), N.C. Forestry Coun., U. Mich. Foresters Assn. (pres. 1948-50), U. Mich. Alumni Assn. (bd. dirs.), Rotary. Home: Asheville N.C. †

DE MOSS, RALPH DEAN, microbiologist, educator; b. Danville, Ill., Dec. 29, 1922; s. Guy and Ruby (Walker) DeM.; m. Patricia H. Day, June 2, 1946 (dec.); children: Susan L., G. Newton, Guy R., Kurt S.; m. Shirley R. Siedler, Nov. 22, 1975. Student, Clemson

Coll., 1943; AB, Ind. U., 1948, PhD, 1951; PhD, St. Louis U., 1943-44. AEC postdoctoral fellow Brookhaven Nat. Lab., 1951-52; asst. prof. McCollum-Pratt Inst., Johns Hopkins U., 1952-56; assoc. prof. microbiology U. Ill., Urbana, 1956-59, prof., 1959-85, head dept., 1971-85; mem. microbiology tng. com. NIH, 1967-69, chmn., 1969-71, mem. microbial chemistry study sect., 1976-80, chmn., 1978-80; mem. biomed. scis. panel NRC, 1976-80. Editor Jour. Bacteriology, 1965-70. With AUS, 1942-46, ETO. Mem. Am. Soc. Microbiology, Am. Acad. Microbiology, Am. Soc. Biol. Chemists, Soc. Gen. Microbiology. Died Aug. 11, 1985.

DEMPSEY, ERNEST COOK, lawyer; b. Cleve., 1890. AB, Kenyon Coll., 1911, LLD, 1945; BA, Yale U., 1912; LLB, Harvard U., 1916. Bar: Ohio 1917. Mem. Squire, Sanders & Dempsey, Cleve. †

DEMPSEY, WILLIAM JAMES, lawyer; b. Bklyn., Feb. 22, 1906; s. John Joseph and Kathryn Theresa (McCarthy) D.; m. Mildred Christine Garrett, Jan. 17, 1931 (dec.); children: William James Jr. (dec.), John Joseph II (dec.), Mary Catherine, Joanne (Mrs. William J. Walsh). BS, Georgetown U., 1927, MA, 1929, LLB, 1931. Bar: D.C. 1930, N.Y. 1932, U.S. Supreme Ct. 1935, Mass. 1966. Tchr. math and physics Georgetown Coll., Washington, 1927-29; pvt. practice law N.Y.C., 1931-32; atty. PWA, 1933-34, counsel, 1934-37; asst. gen. counsel Fed. Power Commn., 1937; special counsel FCC, 1937-38, gen. counsel, 1938-40; pvt. practice Washington, 1940-88; mem. firm Dempsey & Koplovitz; prof. fed. communications law Georgetown U., 1954-56. Mem. ABA, D.C. Bar Assn., Fed. Communications Bar Assn., Fed. Bar Assn., University Club, Columbia Country Club, Burning Tree Golf Club. Democrat. Roman Catholic. Home: Washington D.C. Died Feb 16, 1988; buried Fort Lincoln Cemetery.

DENBESTEN, LAWRENCE, surgeon; b. Corsica, S.D., Oct. 4, 1926; s. Ed and Jennie DenB.; m. Shirley Langeland, June 12, 1952; children—Pamela K., David Lawrence. B.A., Calvin Coll. and Sem., Grand Rapids, Mich., 1949, B.S., 1952, Th.M., 1952; M.D., U. Iowa, 1956. Intern Hurley Hosp., Flint, Mich., 1956-57; chief surgeon, med. dir. Takum Hosp., Nigeria, 1957-60, Mkar Hosp., Nigeria, 1964-66; prof. surgery, vice chmn. dept. U. Iowa Hosps., 1966-67; prof. surgery, chief sect. gastrointestinal surgery UCLA Hosp. and Clinics, 1977-88, vice chmn. dept., 1977-81; chief surg. services VA Center, Sepulveda, Calif., 1977-81; career investigator VA, 1972-88. Author articles, abstracts in field, chpts. in books. Served with USNR, 1944-46. Advanced clin. fellow Am. Cancer Soc., 1964. Mem. A.C.S., Am. Surg. Assn., Am. Gastroenterol. Assn., Central Surg. Assn., Pacific Coast Surg. Assn., Western Surg. Assn., Alpha Omega Alpha. Home: Santa Monica Calif. Deceased.

DENEBRINK, FRANCIS COMPTON, naval officer; b. Chgo., June 22, 1896; m. Fanny McCook, July 28, 1936; 1 child, Joyce Ann. BS, U.S. Naval Acad., 1917; grad., Naval War Coll., 1932. Enlisted U.S. Navy, 1913, advanced through grades to vice adm., 1952, sr. aide to chief naval ops., 1942; comdr. U.S.S. Brooklyn, 1942-43; chief of staff to comdr. fleet operational tng. Atlantic Fleet, 1943-44; comdr. fleet operational tng. command U.S. Pacific Fleet, 1944-45; comdr. Cruiser Div. 5 engaged in occupation No. Japan, 1945-47; comdr. naval forces Eniwetok for atomic tests Operation Sandstone, 1947-48; Navy dir., mil. council Munitions Bd., 1948; comdr. Service Force PAcific Fleet, 1949-52, Mil. Sea Transp. Service, 1953-56; ret. 1956. Decorated Navy and Marine Corps medal, 3 Legion of Merit medals, D.S.M., Commendation ribbon (U.S.); chevalier Royal Order of Cambodia (France); Special Collar Order of Tao Ping and Yun Hui medal (China). Home: San Francisco Calif. Died Apr. 8, 1987.

DENISON, ROBERT HOWLAND, paleontologist; b. Somerville, Mass., Nov. 9, 1911; s. William Kendall and Florence Letchworth (Howland) D.; m. Marion Swift, June 29, 1940 (div. 1948); children: John Howland, David Oldmixen; m. Mary S. Maynard, Aug. 3, 1965; 1 child, Robert Wells. AB, Harvard U., 1933; MA, Columbia U., 1934, PhD, 1938. Asst. curator sch. mus. Dartmouth Coll., 1937-47, instr. zoology, 1938-42, asst. prof., 1943-47; paleontologist African expdn. U. Calif., 1947-48; curator fossil fishes Field Mus. Nat. History, Chgo., 1948-70, rsch. assoc., 1971-73; assoc. Mus. Comparative Zoology, Harvard U., from 1973; lectr. evolutionary biology, U. Chgo., 1965-72; field trips in U.S., Can., Europe, Africa, from 1931. Contbr. articles to profl. jours. Guggenheim fellow, 1953-54. Fellow AAAS; m. Soc. Vertebrate Paleontology (pres. 1962-63), Paleontol. Soc., Mass. Audubon Soc. Home: Lincoln Mass. Died Sept. 7, 1985.

DENNIS, CLYDE AVERY, biology educator; b. Bloomdale, Ohio, Feb. 23, 1900; s. Charles Ellsworth and Etta Mae (Frederick) D.; m. Helen Good, Aug. 26, 1924 (dec. Oct. 1971); 1 dau., Patricia Ann (Mrs. Harry Cole); m. Mabel S. Faulds, Nov. 14, 1972. BS, Coll. Wooster, 1923; MS, Ohio State U., 1928, PhD, 1937. Instr. Bloomingdale High Sch., 1923-24; from instr. to prof. biology Tusculum Coll., Greenville, Tenn., 1924-44, chmn. dept., 1937-44, v.p., 1944-45; field rep. Curtis Pub. Co., 1945-48; prof., chmn. dept. biology Milliken U., 1948-61, dean Coll. Arts and Scis., 1961-66. Contbr. articles to scholarly jours. Mem. Rotary, Sigma Xi, Phi Kappa Phi. Republican. Presbyterian. Home: Morristown Tenn. Died June 9, 1988.

DENNY, EMERY BYRD, lawyer; b. Pilot Mountain, N.C., Nov. 23, 1892; s. Gabriel and Sarah Delphina (Stone) D.; m. Bessie Brandt Brown, Dec. 27, 1922; children: Emery Byrd, Betty Brown, Sarah Catherine Denny Williamson, Jean Stone Denny Ashley. Ed., Gilliam's Acad., U. N.C., U. N.C. Law Sch.; LLD (hon.), U. N.C. Law Sch., 1946, Wake Forest Coll., 1947. Bar: N.C. 1919. Ptnr. Denny & Gaston, 1919-21, Mangum & Denny, 1921-30; pvt. practice 1930-42; apptd. assoc. justice Supreme Ct. N.C., Feb. 1942, elected, Nov. 1942, reelected, 1950, 58, chief justice, from 1962; bd. dirs. United Spinners Corp., Lowell, N.C. Mayor Gastonia, 1929-37; chmn. State Dem. exec. com., 1940-42. With Signal Corps U.S. Army, 1917-19. Fellow Am. Bar Found.; mem. ABA, N.C. Bar Assn., Am. Judicature Soc., Executives Club, Masons, Phi Delta Phi. Baptist. Home: Raleigh N.C. †

DENSLOW, JOHN STEDMAN, osteopath; b. Hartford, Conn., Dec. 19, 1906; s. George H. and Maud (Stedman) D.; m. Mary Jane Laughlin, Aug. 22, 1934; children: Martha, George, Peter. DO, Kirksville (Mo.) Coll., 1929; DO (hon.), Chgo. Coll. Osteopathy, 1941. Asst. dir. clinic Chgo. Coll. Osteopathy, 1933-38; pvt. practice Kirksville, from 1938; prof. osteopathic technic Kirksville Coll. Osteopathy and Surgery, from 1940, chmn. dept. osteopathic technic, dir. rsch. affairs, 1938-65, v.p. coll., 1965-77, cons. to pres., from 1977; dir. Still Meml. Rsch. Trust; mem. USPHS Rev. Com. Basic and Spl. Project Grants for MD and DO Schs. Mem., chmn. Mo. Bd. Health; mem. Mo. Gov.'s Adv. Coun. for Comprehensive Health Planning; cons. USPHS Nat. Ctr. for Health Stats.; mem. governing body Area II Health Systems Agy. Mo., from 1976. Mem. Am. Physiol. Soc., Am. Assn. Colls. Osteopathic Medicine (pres. 1973-74, gov. from 1972), Am. Osteopathic Assn., Mo. Assn. Osteopathic Physicians and Surgeons, Rotary. Episcopalian. Home: Kirksville Mo. Died Dec. 19, 1982, buried Kirksville.

DENT, JOHN H(ERMAN), congressman; b. Johnetta, Pa., Mar. 19, 1908; s. Samuel and Genevieve Dent; m. Margaret R. Dent, Apr. 4, 1924; children: Patricia (Mrs. Donald Sarp), John Frederick. LHD, Alliance Coll., 1965. Mem. Pa. Ho. of Reps., 1934-36; mem. Pa. Senate, 1936-58, also floor leader; mem. 85th-95th Congresses from 21st Pa. dist., 1958-79; mem. local council United Rubber Workers, 1923-27, then pres. of local, mem. exec. council, also mem. internat. council. With Air Corps, USMC, 1924-28. Democrat. Died Apr. 9, 1988.

DENTON, EUGENE KENNETH, retail executive, cattleman; b. Williamson County, Tenn., May 27, 1888; s. William and Mary Virginia (Boyd) D.; m. MArie Helen Silcott, Feb. 11, 1914 (dec.). Student, McCreery's Sch. Merchandising, 1910. With Castner-Knott, Nashville, 1908-09, James McCreery & Co., N.Y.C., 1911-12, George W. McAlpin Co., Cin., 1912-14, Denton Co., Cin., 1914-19; owner Tailored Woman Inc., N.Y.C., 1919-67, exec. v.p., mng. dir., 1919-26, pres., 1926-67; sole owner Jonasson's Inc., Pitts. and North Hills, Pa.; owner, cattle breeder White Gates Farm, Flanders, N.J. Mem. Better Bus. Bur. N.Y., N.Y. Bd. Trade, Fifth Ave. Assn., Am. Aberdeen-Angus Breeders' Assn., Nat. Retail Dry Goods Assn., Metropolitan Club, Madison Square Garden Club, Everglades Club, Duquesne Club. Home: Boonton N.J. Died May 25, 1988.

DEPALMA, JOHN T., banker; b. N.Y.C., 1911; m. Miriam DePalma; children: Jack Jr., Sister Jude Miriam, Mary E. DePalma Burke, Miriam DePalma Heck. G-rad., Rutgers Grad. Sch. Banking, 1954. With Chase Manhattan Bank; pres., treas. Kings Lafayette Bank, Blyn.; chmn. Kings Lafayette Corp. Home: Cranford N.J. Died Mar. 19, 1988.

DERBY, ETHEL ROOSEVELT, civic worker; b. Oyster Bay, L.I., Aug. 13, 1891; d. Theodore and Edith K. (Carowe) Roosevelt; m. Richard Derby, Apr. 4, 1918; children: Richard (dec.), Edith Derby Williams, Sarah Derby Gannett, Judith Derby Ames. Chmn. Nassau County (N.Y.) chpt. ARC, 1944-45, mem. bd. from 1924, Sagamore Hillcom. Theodore Roosevelt Assn., 1954-57; charter mem. Nat. Trust Preservation Hist. Sites, from 1947; chmn. Oyster Bay Meml. Pk., 1938-57; vice chmn. Cavendish (Vt.) Hist. Soc., from 1955; mem. Oyster Bay Community Ctr.; women's com. Union Theol. Sem., 1954-55; trustee Am. Mus. Natural History, from 1952. Republican (chmn. Oyster Bay club 1936-40). Episcopalian. Home: Oyster Bay, L.I. N.Y. †

DERBY, PALMER PORTNER, electronics company executive; b. Washington, May 23, 1920; s. Claude Palmer and Hildegarde Rose (Portner) D.; m. Marnie Holmes Osborn, Dec. 29, 1941; children: Susan Palmer Derby Cox, Sally Margaret Derby Duffy. Student, Va. Poly. Inst., 1939-40, MIT, 1940-42. Registered profl. engr., Mass. With Raytheon Co., from 1942, jr. engr., Waltham, Mass., 1942, various mgmt. positions in engring., rsch., mktg., 1942-62, asst . gen. mgr. microwave and power tube div., 1962-76, v.p., asst. gen. mgr., 1967-76; v.p., dir. new bus. analysis Raytheon Co., Lexington, Mass., from 1976; pioneer in devel. magnetron tubes for microwave ovens, microwave tubes for radar, electronic countermeasures missile and communications application. Recipient Commendation medal, Raytheon Co., 1947. Mem. Assn. Home Appliance Mfrs. (assoc. exec. bd. from 1969). Died June 22, 1986.

DE ROUGEMONT, DENIS, author; b. Neuchatel, Switzerland, Sept. 8, 1906; s. Georges and Alice (Bovet) de R.; m. Anabite Repond, Feb. 2, 1952; children: Nicholas, Martine. Literary and philos. studies, Neuchatel, Vienna and Geneva, 1929. Pub. Paris, 1931-85; active in creation movement 1932-85; lectr. French lit. U. Frankfurt, Germany, 1935-36, l'Ecole libre des Hautes Etudes, N.Y.C., 1942; script writer Voice Am., 1942-43; active in creation European federalists movement 1946-50; founder Ctr. European de la Culture, Geneva, 1950, also bd. dirs.; pres. exec. com. Congres pour la Liberté de la Culture, 1951-66; pres. Assn. Européene des Festivals de Musique, 1951-85, Tables Rondes du Conseil de l'Europe, 1953, 55; prof. Inst. universitaire d'Etudes Européenes, Geneva, 1963-85. Author: Le Paysan du Danube, 1932, Politique de la Personne, 1934, Penser avec les mains, 1936, Journal d'un intellectuel en chomâge, 1937, Journal d'Allemagne, 1938, L'Amour et l'Occident, 1939 (pub. in English as Love in the Western World, 1940, Passion and Society, 1940), Nicolas de Flue, 1939, Mission ou démission de la Suisse, The Heart of Europe, 1941, La part du Diable, 1944 (pub. in English as The Devil's Share, 1945, Talk of the Devil, 1946), Les Personnes du Drame, 1946 (pub. in English as Dramatic Personages, 1964), Lettres sur la Bombe Atomique, 1946 (pub. in English as The Last Trump, 1946), Vivre en Amerique, 1947, Doctrine Fabuleuse, 1947, Suite Neuchateloise, 1948, L'Europe en Jeu, 1948, Journal des Deux Mondes, 1948, La Confédération Suisse, 1953, L'Aventure Occidentale de l'homme, 1957 (pub. in English as Man's Western Quest, 1957), Comme toi-meme, 1961 (pub. in English as Love Declared, 1963, The Myths of Love, 1964), Vingt-Huit Siecles d'Europe, 1961 (pub. in English as The Idea of Europe, 1966), Les Chances de l'Europe, 1962 (pub. in English as The Meaning of Europe, 1965), The Christian Opportunity, 1963, La Suisse on l'historie d'un peuple heureux, 1965, Journal d'un époque, 1968. Recipient prix Schiller, 1960, prix E. Delacroix, 1957, prix de Monaco, 1963, Grand prix Littéraire de Genève, 1967. Home: Fenny-Voltaire, Ain France. Died Dec. 6, 1985.

DERRICK, WILLIAM SHELDON, physician; b. Millville, Pa., Mar. 5, 1916; s. Bruce Berger and Margaret (Mosteller) D.; m. Alice Marie Cowing, May 30, 1942; children: Lynn Sheldon, Bruce William. B.A., George Washington U., 1940, M.D., 1942. Diplomate: Am. Bd. Anesthesiology. Intern Allegheny Gen. Hosp., 1942-43; fellow in surgery Cleve. Clinic Found., 1943; resident in anesthesiology Walter Reed Gen., Mt. Alto VA, Gallinger Mcpl., also George Washington U. hosps., 1945-48; assoc. anesthesiology Harvard U. Med. Sch., also head sect. anesthesiology Peter Bent Brigham Hosp., Boston, 1948-54; cons. anesthesia VA Hosp., Rutland Heights, Mass., Murphy Army Hosp., Waltham, Mass., also VA Hosp., West Roxbury, Mass., 1950-54; head dept. U. Tex. System Cancer Center, M.D. Anderson Hosp., Houston, 1954-77; cons. St. Joseph's Hosp., Houston, 1955-77; prof. anesthesiology U. Tex. Med. Sch., 1954-86; mem. staff Center Pavilion Hosp., 1967-77; vis. mem. grad. faculty Tex. A&M U., 1968-71; prof. U. Tex. Med. Sch., 1968-86. Served to maj. M.C., AUS, 1943-46. Recipient Alumni Achievement award George Washington U., 1957, scholarship MIT, 1960, award for service as trustee Am. Registry Inhalation Therapists, 1972. Mem. Am. Coll. Anesthesiologists, Tex. Gulf Coast Anesthesia Soc. (pres. 1959-60), So. Soc. Anesthesiologists (pres. 1965-66, 83-84), New Eng. Soc. Anesthesiologists (pres. 1982-83), So. Med. Assn. (chmn. sect. anesthesiology 1967), Doctors Club Houston (pres., gov. 1969), Tex. Med. Found. (charter), AAUP (pres. Houston chpt. 1980-81), Cleveland Clinic Found. Alumnus Assn. (regional v.p. 1983-86), Ambulatory Hosps. Am. (bd. dirs. 1983-86), U. Tex.-M.D. Anderson Hosp. Assocs. (chmn. 1983-84), Aesculapian (Harvard U.), Bayou Rifles, Greater Houston Gun Club, Harvard Club, Racquet, Tennis Patrons, Knife and Fork, Les Amis du Vin (pres. 1971), University, U. Tex. Faculty (Houston) (pres. 1969-71), Congl. Country, George Washington U. (Washington) clubs. Presbyterian. Home: Houston Tex. Died May 25, 1986; buried Meml. Oaks Cemetery, Houston.

DERRY, DUNCAN RAMSAY, consulting geologist; b. Croydon, Surrey, Eng., June 27, 1906; came to Can., 1927; s. Douglas Erith and Margaret (Ramsay) D.; m. E. Alice Langstaff, 1935; children—Ramsay, Douglas. B.A., Cambridge U., Eng., 1927; M.A., U. Toronto, Ont., Can., 1928; Ph.D., U. Toronto, 1931, LL.D. (hon.), 1984. Geologist Ventures Ltd., Toronto, 1935-40; chief geologist Ventures Ltd., 1945-54; v.p. exploration Rio Algom Mines, Toronto, 1954-60; ptnr. Derry, Michener, Booth & Wahl, Toronto, 1960-87. Author: World Atlas of Geology & Mineral Deposits, 1980. Served with Royal Can. Air Force, 1940-45. Named Officer of Order of Can., 1982; recipient Penrose medal (posthumously), 1987. Fellow Geol. Assn. Can. (pres. 1953-54, 71-72), Geol. Soc. Am.; mem. Soc. Econ. Geologists (pres. 1960); University Club (Toronto).

Home: Mississauga, Ont. Canada. Died Jan. 29, 1987; buried Trinity Ch., Port Credit, Ont.

DESMOND, CHARLES S., judge; b. Buffalo, Dec. 2, 1896; s. Patrick and Katherine (Jordan) D.; m. Helen Marie Ryan, June 28, 1928 (dec. 1958); children: Ryan (dec.), Sheila, Kathleen, Patricia. AB, Canisius Coll., Buffalo, 1917, AM, 1918; LLB, U. Buffalo, 1920; hon. degrees, several colls. and univs. Bar: N.Y. 1920. Assoc. then ptnr. Thomas C. Burke, Buffalo, 1920-40; judge N.Y. State Supreme Ct., 1940-41; assoc. judge N.Y. State Ct. Appeals, 1941-60, chief judge, 1960-66; mem. law faculty Cornell U., SUNY; lectr. various law schs.; chmn. N.Y. Jud. Conf., 1960-66. Author 2 law books; contbr. articles and revs. to profl. jours. Pres. Legal Aid Soc., Buffalo; mem. adv. bd. Sisters Hosp. of Buffalo; mem. N.Y. State Bd. Social Welfare, 1936-40; mem. adv. council U. Notre Dame Law Sch.; chmn. bd. trustees Canisius Coll. Mem. ABA, N.Y. State Bar Assn., Erie County Bar Assn., Am. Law Inst., K.C., Fort Orange Club, Buffalo Club, Buffalo Athletic Club, Wanakah Country Club, Century Club, Order of Coif, Phi Delta Phi. Home: Eden N.Y. Died Feb. 9, 1987.

DESMOND, JOHNNY ALFRED, singer, actor; b. Detroit, Nov. 14, 1921; s. Peter and Lillian (Brucia) De Simone; m. Ruth Keddington, Jan. 3, 1942; children: Diane, Patti. Singer with Bob Crosby Orch., 1939, Gene Krupka Orch., 1940, Glen Miller USAF Orch., 1943; numerous appearances on NBC, CBS, MBS, ABC radio stas., 1946-85; actor on TV programs Philco Playhouse, Climax, Robert Montgomery Presents, Don MacNeill Breakfast Club, Hit Parade, Music on Ice, numerous others; Broadway appearance in Say Darling, 1959; motion pictures include Desert Hill, Escape from San Quentin, Calypso Heatwave, China Doll, Caribbean Hawk; recording artist for M-G-M, Coral, Columbia, RCA. With USAAF, World War II. Home: Los Angeles Calif. Died Sept. 6, 1985.

DESMOND, ROBERT WILLIAM, journalist, educator; b. Milw., July 31, 1900; s. William John and Lillian Amy (Wilce) D.; m. Dorothy Christian, 1927 (div.); 1 son, Richard; m. Emily V. Wall, 1949; children: Christopher, Carolyn. With Milw. Jour., 1922-25, Miami (Fla.) Herald, 1925-26, N.Y. Herald (Paris edit.), 1926-27; with Christian Science Monitor, 1933-38, London, 1936; mem. faculty journalism U. Mich., 1927-28, U. Minn., 1928-32, Medill Sch. Journalism, Northwestern U., 1938-39; prof. journalism U. Calif., Berkeley, 1939-68, prof. emeritus, 1968-85, chmn. dept., 1939-54, 62-63, 67; vis. prof. Stanford U., spring 1938; acad. dir. Fgn. Assignment tour, Europe, 1952; Fulbright lectr. U. Amsterdam, 1955-56, U. Baghdad, Iraq, 1965-66, U. Tejeran, Iran, 1968-69; lectr. Internat. Ctr. Advanced Instrn. in Journalism, U. Strasbourg (France), 1956, 58, 60; on fgn. news desk N.Y. Times, summer 1941; news commentator radios sta. KFSO, San Francisco, 1941-42; on staff San Francisco examiner, 1951, Louisville Courier -Jour., summer 1955, NANA, Europe, 1956, San Francisco Chronicle, 1968, San Diego Union, 1969-74; columnist Copley News Service, 1971-74; cons. Ency. Americana, 1959-60, Internat. Press Inst., Zurich, 1960-62, Hartford (Conn.) Times, summer 1964. Author: Press and World Affairs, 1937, The Information Process, 1978, others; contbr. articles to mags. MEm. UNESCO Commn. on Tech. Needs of Mass MEdia, Paris, 1947, 49. With U.S. Army, 1918; to maj. AUS, ETO, 1943-44, OWI and UN Information Office, 1944-45. Recipient citations U. Calif., Calif. Senate, 1968. Mem. Am. assn. Schs. and Depts. Journalism (pres. 1947), Assn. Edn. Journalism, Sigma Delta Chi (Key Club). Home: La Jolla Calif. Died Dec. 21, 1985.

DE TAKATS, GEZA, surgeon; b. Budapest, Hungary, Dec. 9, 1892; came to U.S., 1923, naturalized, 1929; s. Emile de Grosz and Margaret de Takats; m. Carol Beeler, Oct. 22, 1924. MD, U. Budapest, 1915, MS, 1918. House surgeon U. Budapest, 1915, asst. in surgery, 1916-18, assoc. in surgery, 1918-21, asst. prof. surgery, 1921-23; special fellow Mayo Clinic, Rochester, Minn., 1924; pvt. practice Chgo., from 1925; assoc. surgery Northwestern Med. Sch., 1926-27, asst. prof. surgery, 1927-35; clin. prof. surgery U. Ill., 1952-61; cons. surgeon Presbyn.-St. Luke's Hosp., chmn. dept., 1950-53, attending surgeon, 1941-61; cons. vascular surgery Great Lakes Naval Hosp., Ill. Author: Local Anesthesia, 1928, Thromboembolism, 1955, Vascular Surgery, 1959; contbr. articles to med. jours. Day proclaimed in his honor Dec. 2, 1976 Mayor Richard Daley, Chgo. Fellow A.C.S.; mem. Internat. Surg. Soc., Chgo. Surg. Soc., Chgo. Heart Assn. (pres.), Soc. Vascular Surgery, Internat. Cardiovascular Soc. (N.Am. chpt.), Inst. Medicine, Cen. Soc. Clin. Rsch., Chicago Club, Literary Club, Tavern Club, Univ. Club, Pentwater Yacht Club, Sigma Xi, Phi Beta Pi; hon. mem. St. Paul, Mpls. Surg. Soc., New Orleans Surg. Soc., Lyon Surg. Soc., Internat. Soc. Anesthesia. Home: Evanston Ill. Died Oct. 3, 1985.

DETMAR, CHARLES F., JR., lawyer; b. Staten Island, N.Y., Sept. 4, 1905; s. Charles F. and Helen A. (Powers) D.; m. Rose McCormick, Nov. 23, 1940; children: Catherine, Charles III, John Thomas. AB, Columbia, 1927, LLB, 1929. Bar: N.Y. 1929. Assoc. Peaslee & Brigham, 1929-32; assoc. Wright, Gordon, Zachry, Parlin & Cahill, N.Y.C., 1932-40, mem., 1940-41; spl. asst. to under sec. and sec. Navy Dept. Navy, Washington, 1941-44; mem. firm Cahill, Gordon, Reindel & Ohl, N.Y.C. Mem. The Recess, University Club, Metropolitan Club, Sigma Alpha Epsilon. Democrat. Home: Westhampton N.Y. Died Mar. 10, 1986.

DETZER, KARL, writer; b. Fort Wayne, Ind., Sept. 4, 1891; s. August J. and Laura (Goshorn) D.; m. Clarice Nissley, Nov. 26, 1921 (dec.); children—Karl (dec.), Mary-Jane (Mrs. J.C. Moench). L.H.D. (hon.), Ind. U., 1979. Reporter, photographer Ft. Wayne newspapers 1909-16; advt. writer Chgo., 1920-23; screen play writer and tech. dir. Hollywood, 1934-36; roving editor Reader's Digest, 1939-42, 46-77; pub. Enterprise-Tribune, Leland, Mich., 1947-51. Author: books and screen plays; latest book Myself When Young, 1968; Contbr. articles to leading mags. Mem. Mich. State Corrections Council, 1948-49; chmn. Mich. Citizens Com. on Reorgn. State Govt., 1950-51, spl. adviser to Mil. Govt., Berlin, Germany, 1948. Served from pvt. to capt., inf. U.S. Army, 1916-1919; from maj. to col. Gen. Staff Corps. AUS, 1942-46. Decorated D.S.M. Mem. Authors League Am., Internat. Assn. City Mgrs., Mich. State Police (hon.), V.F.W. (hon. Floyd Gibbons Post, N.Y.C.), Deadline (N.Y.C.), Nat. Press, Overseas Press clubs. Democrat. Unitarian. Home: Leland Mich. Died Apr. 28, 1987.

DEVENDORF, GEORGE E., utilities executive; b. Eldora, Iowa, June 30, 1891; s. Luther A. and Anna J. (McCall) D.; m. Adelina Spinetti. Student, Cornell Coll., Iowa, Harvard U. Sch. Bus. Adminstrn. Fgn. br. mgr. Nat. City Bank N.Y., 1915-26; with Am. Founders Corp., 1926-35; pres. Gen. Investment Corp., 1932; chmn. Consol. Electric & Gas Co.; chmn. bd. Patchogue Electric Light Co. Home: New York N.Y. †

DE VILBISS, LYDIA ALLEN (MRS. GEORGE HENRY BRADFORD), public health educator; b. Allen County, Ind.; d. William Fletcher and Naomi (Ridenour) De Vilbiss; m. George Henry Bradford, Mar. 29, 1920. MD, Ind. U., 1907. postgrad. work NYU, U. Pa.; practiced in Ohio, 5 yrs.; dir. div. child hygiene Kans. State Bd. Health, 1915-19; organized child hygiene in R.I., Mo. and Ga.; prof. pub. health adminstrn. Woman's Med. Coll., Phila.; lectr. Sch. Social and Health Work, Phila.; dir. mothers health clinics Fla. Author various monographs on pub. health. Commd. surgeon res. USPHS, 1920. Mem. AMA, Pan-Am. Med. Assn., Am. Pub. Health Assn., AAUW, Women's City Club, Coll. Women's Club. Home: Miami Fla. †

DEVOE, JENNER HIGBEE, manufacturing executive; b. Ft. Loudon, Pa., 1891; s. John H. and Ada B. (Smith) D.; m. Elsie Lemaster, Oct. 26, 1916; 1 child, John M. Grad., Pa. State Coll., 1912. With Wagner Electric Corp., St. Louis, from 1912, v.p., 1941-50, pres., dir., from 1950; bd. dirs. Sangamo Co. Ltd., Leaside, Ont., Sangamo Electric Co., Mercantile Trust Co., St. Louis. Dir. United Fund of St. Louis. Mem. St. Louis C. of C. (dir.), NAM (regional v.p.), Mo. Athletic Club, Univ. Club, Raquet Club, Detroit Athletic Club, Detroit Club, Nat. Club (Toronto, Can.). Home: Saint Louis Mo. †

DE VRIES, HENRY PETER, lawyer; b. Willemstad, Curacao, Netherlands Antilles; came to U.S., 1925, naturalized, 1935; s. Hendrik Pieter and Emma (Riedel) de V.; m. Irene Hamar, May 23, 1943; children—Diane, Suzanne; m. 2d, Kathleen Ann Costigan, May 30, 1978. A.B., Columbia U., 1934, J.D., 1937. Bar: N.Y. 1938, U.S. Dist. Ct. (so. dist.) N.Y. 1940, U.S. Supreme Ct. 1965. Assoc., Sullivan & Cromwell, N.Y.C., 1937-42, 46-48; assoc. prof. Columbia U. Law Sch., N.Y.C., 1948-51, prof., 1952-81, prof. emeritus, 1981-86; ptnr. Hyde & de Vries, N.Y.C., 1954-59; ptnr. Baker & McKenzie, N.Y.C., 1960-86, sr. ptnr., 1980-86; asst. atty. gen. State of N.Y., 1947. Pres., Netherlands-Am. Found., 1952-55. Served to lt. col., AUS, 1942-46. Mem. ABA, Assn. of Bar of City N.Y., Internat. Bar Assn., Am. Fgn. Law Assn. (pres. 1978-81), Am. Soc. Internat. Law, Am. Arbitration Assn. (internat. arbitration com.), Council on Fgn. Relations, Phi Beta Kappa. Clubs: Columbia U. Faculty; Patterson (Fairfield, Conn.). Author: The French Legal System, 1958; The Law of the Americas, 1979; Civil Law and the Anglo-American Lawyer, 1981. Home: New York, NY. Died Sept. 23, 1986.

DEWEY, FRANCIS HENSHAW, JR., lawyer; b. Worcester, Mass., May 19, 1887; s. Francis H. and Lizzie Davis (Bliss) D.; m. Dorothy F. Bowen, Feb. 1, 1913; children: Elizabeth B., Francis H., Dorothy, Harry B. AB, Williams Coll., 1909; LLB, Harvard U., 1912. Bar: Mass. 1912. Practiced in Worcester, 1912-33; sr. ptnr. Dewey & O'Brien, from 1940; chmn. bd. Mechanics Nat. Bank, Worcester; pres. Norwich & Worcester R.R.; trustee, bd. investment Worcester Mechanics Savs. Bank; bd. dirs. Guarantee Mutual Ins. Co., Worcester St. Ry. Co. Asst. dir. War Trade Bd.; mem. exec. and fin. coms. Worcester Community Chest; v.p., bd. dirs. Home for Aged Men; trustee Meml. Hosp., Clark U., Worcester Art Mus.; bd. dirs. Mass. Soc. Prevention Cruelty to Children. Mem. Am. Hist. Soc., Am. Antiquarian Soc., Newcomen Soc., Worcester Club, Tatnuck County Club, University Club, Williams Club (N.Y.C.), Kappa Alpha. Republican. Home: Worcester Mass. †

DEWITT, JOSEPH HENRI, parole official; b. Duluth, Minn., Mar. 15, 1888; s. Henri and Bertha (Heising) DeW.; m. Magdalen A. Rosskopf, Dec. 26, 1924. BS, U. Minn., 1910. Asst. instr. U. Minn., 1911-12; dir. parole Minn. State Tng. Sch. for Boys, 1912-17; state parole officer Minn. State Bd. Parole, State Prison and State Reformatory, 1921-30; supr. Minn. State Parole and Probation Dept., 1930-43; agt. U.S. Secret Svc., St. Paul, 1944; chief Internat. Security, War Relocation Authority, Washington, 1945; chmn. U.S. Army Clemency and Parole Bd., Washington, 1946-48; mem. U.S. Bd. Parole, 1949-54; administrv. officer Fgn. Claims Settlement Commn., 1954-60; mem. D.C. Bd. Parole, from 1960. 1st lt. U.S. Army, 1918-19. Mem. Am. Prison Assn., Nat. Parole and Probation Assn., Internat. Assn. Chiefs Police, Am. Legion, Minn. State Mental Hygiene Soc., United Community Svcs. Washington, Minn. Alumni Assn., Boys' Club Met. Police, Kenwood Golf and Country Club (Bethesda, Md.), Washington Figure Skating Club, Phi Delta Chi. Home: Washington D.C. †

DEWOLF, L. HAROLD, clergyman, educator; b. Columbus, Nebr., Jan. 31, 1905; s. Lotan R. and Elsie (Cook) DeW.; m. Martha P. Monkman, Aug. 5, 1925 (dec. Feb. 1939); children: Donald J., Elaine L. (Mrs. Francis V. Lombardi); m. Madeleine E. Marsh, June 15, 1940; children: Daniel L., Edward M. Student, York Coll., 1920-22; AB, Nebr. Wesleyan U., 1924, STD, 1948; STB, Boston U., 1926, PhD, 1935; postgrad, U. Nebr., 1929-30. Ordained to ministry Meth. Ch., 1926. Pastor Nebr. Conf., 1926-31, Dracut, Mass., 1931-36; from lectr. to prof. philosophy Boston U., 1934-44, prof. systematic theology Sch. Theology, 1944-65, univ. lectr., 1960-61; dean, prof. systematic theology Wesley Theol. Sem., 1965-72, emeritus, 1972-86; researcher on ethics and criminal justice, 1972-86; vis. prof. U. So. Calif., summer 1950, Fla. So. Coll., 1975-77, disting. theologian in residence, 1977-86; spl. cons. theol. edn. Cen. and East Africa for Meth. Ch. and Internat. Missionary Council, 1955-56, for World Council of Chs., 1962-63, East and Southeast ASia for Found. for Theol. Edn. in Southeast Asia, 1967; vis. lectr. Wellesley Coll., 1957-58; mem. faculty Meth. Theol. Inst., Lincoln Coll., Oxford, Eng., 1958; Cole Lectr. Vanderbilt U., 1960; Colliver lectr. on Christian Edn., Coll. of the Pacific, 1960; Mendenhall lectr. DePauw U., 1962; spl. lectr. Facultad Evangelica de Teologia, Buenos Aires, 1963. Author: Issues Concerning Immortality in Thirty Ingersoll Lectures, 1896-35, 1935, The Religious Revolt Against Reason, 1949, A Theology of the Living Church, 1953, rev. edits. 1960, 68, Trends and Frontiers of Religious Thought, 1955, The Case for Theology in Liberal Perspective, 1959, Present Trends in Christian Thought, 1960, The Enduring Message of the Bible, 1960, Teaching Our Faith in God, 1963, A Hard Rain and a Cross, 1966, Responsible Freedom: Guidelines to Christian Action, 1971, Galatians: A Letter for Today, 1971, Crime and Justice in America: A Paradox of Conscience, 1975, What Americans Should Do About Crime, 1976; contbr. chpts. to books, articles to profl. jours. Mem. nat. bd. SANE, 1961-72; pres. bd. Offender Aid and Restoration of U.S.A., 1975-78. Mem. Am. Theol. Soc. (pres. 1961-62), Am. Soc. Christian Ethics, Am. Acad. Religion, Am. Soc. Criminology, Phi Kappa Phi, Pi Kappa Delta. Home: Lakeland Fla. Died May 24, 1986.

DEYOUNG, RUSSELL, rubber company executive; b. Rutherford, N.J., Apr. 3, 1909; s. Abram and May (Thompson) DeY.; m. Lois E. Bishop, May 1, 1937; children: Bruce Russell, Ralph Earl, Janet Lois (Mrs. James Mungo). B.S., Akron U., 1932, D.Sc., 1960; M.S., M.I.T., 1940. With Goodyear Tire & Rubber Co., Akron, Ohio, 1928-79; v.p. Goodyear Tire & Rubber Co., 1956-58, pres., 1958-64, chmn. bd., 1964-74, chief exec. officer, 1964-74, chmn. exec. and finance com., 1974-79; dir. First Fla. Banks. Life mem. MIT Corp. Mem. Portage Country (Akron), Naples (Fla.) Yacht, Royal Poinciana Golf (Naples) clubs. Home: Naples Fla. Died May 31, 1988, buried Rose Hill Burial Park, Akron, Ohio.

DIACUMAKOS, ELAINE G., cell biologist; b. Chester, Pa., Aug. 11, 1930; d. Gregoris G. and Olga (Dezes) D.; B.S. in Zoology, U. Md., College Park, 1951; M.S. in Cell Physiology and Embryology, N.Y. U., 1955, Ph.D. in Cell Physiology and Embryology, 1958; postdoctoral fellow in biochem. genetics Rockefeller U., N.Y.C., 1962-64; m. James Chimonides, Nov. 24, 1958. Research asso. N.Y. U., 1956-64, teaching asst., 1957, research asst., 1952-53; research asso. Sloan-Kettering div. Grad. Sch. Med. Scis., Cornell U., N.Y.C., 1959-63, instr., 1963-71; research assoc. Sloan-Kettering Inst. Cancer Research, 1958-60, asso., 1960-71, asso., sect. head, 1965-71; guest investigator biochem. genetics, spl. USPHS fellow, Rockefeller U., 1962-64, sr. research asso. biochem. genetics, 1971-75, sr. research assos., head Lab. of Cytobiology, 1976-84; cons. Lab. Molecular Hematology, Nat. Heart, Lung and Blood Inst., 1978-84, Lab. Cellular and Molecular Biology, Nat. Cancer Inst., 1979, Lab. Tumor Virus Genetics, 1980-84, Lab. Molecular Virology-Microbiology sect. Frederick Cancer Research Center, 1980, Standard Oil Ohio, 1982-84. Bd. dirs. Faculty and Students Club Rockefeller U., 1980-84; adv. bd. Vis. Guest Scholars Program of Fulbright-Hays Act, Met. N.Y., 1980-83; bd. dirs. Children's Sch., Rockefeller U.,

1981-84; pres. Rockefeller U. Faculty House Tenants Assn., 1982-84. Recipient Founders Day award N.Y. U., 1958, Outstanding Woman Scientist award Met. N.Y., Am. Women Inst. Scientists, 1984; spl. postdoctoral fellow USPHS, 1962-64. Mem. AAAS, Am. Genetic Soc., Am. Soc. Cell Biology, Genetics Soc. Am., Internat. Cell Cycle Soc., Harvey Soc., N.Y. Acad. Scis., Sigma Xi. Greek Orthodox. Contbr. numerous articles to profl. jours. jours.; editorial bd. Anticancer Research; Internat. Jour. Cancer Research and Treatment, 1982-84. Died June 13, 1984; buried Maple Grove, Queens, N.Y. Home: New York N.Y.

DIAMOND, HERBERT MAYNARD, economics educator; b. Dansville, N.Y., May 21, 1892; s. Frank J. and Mary (Brus) D.; m. Margaret Lake, Dec. 28, 1915; children: Maynard Lake, Jack Lake. BA, Yale, 1914, PhD, 1917. Instr. in social sci. Goucher Coll., 1917-18; chief clk., later supt. New Haven office U.S. Employment Service, U.S. Dept. Labor, 1918-19; asst. sec. and legislative rsch. worker Conn. Child Welfare Commn., 1919-20; asst. prof. econs., asst. dir. Wall St. div. NYU, 1920-25; prof. econs. and dean Sch. Bus. Adminstrn. U. Md., 1925-26; assoc. prof. NYU, 1926-27; prof. econs. Lehigh U., from 1927, head dept. econs. and sociology, 1936-58, Macfarlen prof. econs., 1956; mem. staff Pa. State Coll., summers 1929-31. Author: Religion and the Commonweal, 1928; author and editor: Credits and Collections, 1928, Introduction to Social Science, 1953; also monographs; contbr. to Dictionary of American History, various periodicals; mem. reviewing staff Quarterly Book Review. Mem. adv. rsch. com. on child welfare Pa. State Joint Govtl. Commn., 1937-38, 46; former pres. Children's Aid Soc. Northampton County, Pa.; v.p. Children's Aid Soc. Pa.; pres. Child Guidance Clinic of Lehigh Valley; mem. Gov.'s Com. on White House Conf., 1950; mem. Bethlehem Community Coun. Recipient R. R. and E. C. Hillman award, 1955. Mem. Indsl. Rels. Rsch. Assn., Am. Econs. Assn., Pi Gamma Mu, Phi Beta Kappa, Delta Sigma Pi, Omicron Delta Kappa, Beta Gamma Sigma. Episcopalian. Home: Bethlehem Pa. †

DIAMOND, ISIDORE, screenwriter; b. Ungheni, Rumania, June 27, 1920; came to U.S., 1929; s. David and Elca (Waldman) D.; m. Barbara Bentley, July 21, 1945; children—Ann Cynthia, Paul Bentley. B.A., Columbia, 1941. Screenwriter, Hollywood, Calif., 1941-88, collaborator with Billy Wilder, 1955-88 (Recipient Acad. award 1960, N.Y. Film Critics award 1960), (Writers Guild award 1957, 59, 60, Laurel award 1980); Screenwriter: Love in the Afternoon, 1957, Some Like It Hot, 1959, The Apartment, 1960, One, Two, Three, 1961, Irma La Douce, 1963, Kiss Me, Stupid, 1964, The Fortune Cookie, 1966, Cactus Flower, 1969, The Private Life of Sherlock Holmes, 1970, Avanti, 1972, The Front Page, 1974, Fedora, 1978, Buddy Buddy, 1981. Mem. ASCAP, John Jay Assos. Columbia. Home: Beverly Hills Calif. Died Apr. 21, 1988; buried at sea.

DIBBLE, JOHN REX, lawyer, educator; b. Kaysville, Utah, Mar. 28, 1911; s. Rudolph K. and Myrtle (Owen) D.; m. Elda W. Wilson, Oct. 18, 1930; children: Barbara, Toni. BS, Utah State Agrl. Coll., 1932; LLB, Stanford U., 1936. Bar: Calif. 1936. Assoc. Williamson, Hoge & Judson, Los Angeles, 1936-41; ptnr. Miller, Chevalier, Peeler & Wilson, Los Angeles, 1941-48; assoc. Hill, Farrer & Burrill, Los Angeles, 1949-54; pvt. practice Los Angeles, 1954-78; asst. counsel War Dept. Price Adjustment Bd., 1944-46; counsel Los Angeles Extension Air Force div. Armed Services Renegotiation Bd., 1951; mem. Los Angeles Regional Renegotiation Bd., 1952; intermittent prof. law Loyola U., Los Angeles, 1937-65, acting dean Law Sch., 1960-62, dean, 1962-65, prof. 1965-79; lectr. constl. law and taxation. Maj. U.S. Army, 1943-46. Mem. Am. Law Inst., Los Angeles Bar Assn., Order of Coif, Phi Delta Phi, Sigma Chi. Republican. Mormon. Home: Pasadena Calif. Died Nov. 3, 1981; buried Pasadena, Calif.

DIBBLE, LEWIS ACKER, manufacturing executive; b. New Haven, Apr. 18, 1885; s. Samuel E. and Elizabeth (Davis) D.; m. Doris Rudman, Oct. 24, 1929. Ed., Yale U., 1907. With C. Cowles & Co., New Haven, 1903, bd. dirs., from 1936; became affiliated with Oakville Co., Waterbury, Conn., 1909, with Risdon Mfg. Co., from 1913, pres., bd. dirs., 1927-61, chmn., from 1961, also chief exec. officer; bd. dirs., chmn. bd. and chief exec. officer Eastern Co.; bd. dirs. Colonial Trust Co., Naugatuck Savs. Bank, Torrington (Conn.) Co., Conn. Light & Power Co. Bd. dirs. Naugatuck Valley Indsl. Coun. Mem. NAM (v.p. N.E. coun., bd. dirs.), Conn. C. of C. (bd. dirs.), Harford Club, Waterbury Club, Waterbury Country Club, East Haddam Fish and Game Club, Metropolitan Club (N.Y.C.). Home: Naugatuck Conn. †

DICKERSON, EARL BURRUS, insurance company executive; b. Canton, Miss., June 22, 1891; s. Edward and Emma (Garrett) D.; m. Kathryn Kennedy, June 15, 1930; 1 dau., Diane. A.B., U. Ill., 1914; J.D., U. Chgo., 1920; H.H.D., Wilberforce U., 1961; LL.D., Northwestern U., 1977, U. Ill.-Chgo., 1984. Bar: Ill. 1920. Exec. v.p. Supreme Life Ins. Co. of Am., 1954-55, gen. counsel, 1921-55, gen. mgr., 1955-62, pres., also chief exec. officer, 1955-71, chmn. bd., 1971-73, hon. chmn. bd., financial cons., 1973-86; asst. corp. counsel, City of Chgo., 1923-27, asst. atty. gen., Ill., 1933-39. Mem. City Council Chgo., 1939-43; dir. emeritus Hyde Park Fed. Savs. & Loan Assn.; Bd. dirs. S.E. Chgo. Commn., 1953-86; mem. Pres.'s Com. Fair Employment Practice, 1941-43; Trustee emeritus La Rabida Jackson Park Sanitarium. Served as lt. inf. AEF, World War I. Recipient citation for pub. service Alumni Assn. U. Chgo., 1961; Legal Def. award NAACP, 1975; Olive H. Crosthwait award Chgo. Ins. Assn., 1976; Humanitarian award Abraham Lincoln Center, 1977; Humanitarian award Henry A. Booth House, affiliate Hull House Assn., 1981; Disting. Legislator award Black Ill. Legis. Lobby, 1979; award for community service Negro Joint Appeal, 1970; Black Businessman of Yr. Black Book, 1971; James H. Tilghman award Washington Park and Wabash Ave YMCAs, 1979; Illini Achievement award U. Ill., 1981; Heritage award DuSable Mus. African Am. History, 1982. Mem. Chgo. Urban League (past pres.), NAACP (dir. emeritus), ABA, Ill. Bar Assn., Cook County Bar Assn. (Presdl. award 1979, spl. honoree 25th ann. lawday 1983), Chgo. Bar Assn., Nat. Lawyers Guild (past pres.), U. Ill. Alumni Assn. (Earl B. Dickerson achievement award 1982), Northwestern U. Alumni Assn., U. Chgo. Law Sch. Assn., Am. Legion (founder), Original Forty (Man of Yr. award 1976) (Chgo.), Kappa Alpha Psi (past grand polemarch). Episcopalian. Home: Chicago Ill. Died Sept. 1, 1986; buried Burr Oak Cemetery, Chgo.

DICKERSON, NORVIN KENNEDY, contractor, investor; b. Louisville, Mar. 3, 1917; s. Norvin Kennedy and Clara (Mertinkate) D.; m. Sara McCarten Craig, June 7, 1939; children: Norvin Kennedy III, Ann Gillam. Educated pub. schs., Louisville. From gen. supt. to southeastern mgr. R.B. Tyler Co., Louisville, 1935-45; founder Dickerson Inc., Monroe, N.C., 1945, pres., 1945-58, chmn. bd. dirs., 1958-86; chmn. bd. dirs. 5 other corps.; bd. dirs. N.C. Nat. Bank, Monroe, Comml. Products Inc., Monroe; chmn. bd. dirs. Dickerson Group Inc.l ptnr. Wilson Woods Real Estate co.; owner Sally Mae Greenhouses; co-owner Ridgewood Devel. Co., Monroe, Monroe Devel. Assn. Inc. Mem. council Boy Scouts Am., past pres. Cen. N.C. council; mem. N.C. State Engring. Found.; past jr. and sr. warden St. Paul's Episcopal Ch., Monroe, sr. warden emeritus; trustee St. Mary's Coll., Raleigh, N.C. Symphony; bd. visitors Johnson C. Smith U. Mem. Assn. Gen. Contractors Am. (hon. life dir., dir. past chmn. hwy. div., past pres. Carolinas br.), N.C. Arts Assn., N.C. Soc. Engrs., Charlotte City Club, Capitol City Club, Country Club of N.C., Rolling Hills Country Club, Hounds Ears Club. Home: Monroe N.C. Died Oct. 17, 1986; buried Monroe, N.C.

DICKINSON, ALICE BRAUNLICH, mathematics educator; b. N.Y.C., Apr. 11, 1921; d. Hans and Dorothy (Harding) B.; m. David J. Dickinson, Dec. 10, 1944; children: Sara, Dan. B.A., U. Mich., 1941, Ph.D., 1952; M.A., Columbia U., 1947. Asst. project engr. Sperry Gyroscope Co., Garden City, N.Y., 1942-44; mem. staff MIT Radiation Lab., Cambridge, 1944-45; lectr. Pa. State U., 1950-56; vis. prof. U. Baroda, India, 1962, 68, 77, U. Aligarh, India, 1961-62; mem. faculty Smith Coll., 1959-87, prof., 1970-81, prof. emeritus, 1981-87, chmn. math. dept., 1970-73, dean of coll., 1973-77; cons. Hampshire Coll., 1965-68. Author: Differential Equations: A Study in Time and Motion, 1972. Recipient Hampshire Coll. Founders award, 1970. Mem. Ely Ringing Guild, N.Am. Guild Change Ringers, AAUW. Home: Ashfield Mass. Died June 25, 1987.

DICKINSON, RAYMOND L., philanthropic consultant; b. Shellsburg, Ia., Feb. 2, 1890; s. Herbert and Nellie Isabel (Sherman) D.; m. Kathleen Miller, Oct. 6, 1917; children: Richard L., Mary Louise (Mrs. Richard S. Bentley), Robert M. Student, Tilford Collegiate Acad., Iowa State Tchrs. Coll.; BSCE, Iowa State Coll., 1915; LHD, Muskingham Coll., 1953. Prin. schs. Brandon, Iowa, 1908-11; community sec. Cedar Falls, Iowa, 1915-16; instr. math. Iowa State Tchrs. Coll., Cedar Falls, 1916-17; indsl. sec., exec. sec. South Side br., exec. sec. Central br., assoc. gen. exec. YMCA, Columbus, Ohio, 1917-32; exec. sec. Community Fund, Columbus, 1932-33; exec. Ohio area Nat. Coun. YMCA's, 1934-42; exec. v.p. YMCA, N.Y.C., 1942-56, nat. treas., 1956-66; philanthropic cons. Hanover Bank, N.Y.C., 1956-59. Mem. Protestant Coun.; mem. world's com. YMCA, 1947-57, exec. com. nat. bd.; hon. life mem. Springfield Coll. Corp. Mem. Assn. Secs. YMCA, Rotary, Quill Club (N.Y.C.), Tau Beta Pi, Phi Kappa Phi, Sigma Delta Chi. Republican. Home: Rossmoor-Jamesburg N.J. †

DICKSON, HORATIO LOVAT, author; b. Lawlers, Western Australia, Jan. 30, 1902; s. Gordon Fraser and Mary Josephine (Cunningham) D.; m. Marguerite Brodie, Dec. 26, 1934; 1 child, Jonathan. M.A., U. Alta., Can., 1929; LL.D. (hon.), U. Alta., U. Western Ont., Can.; D. Litt. hon., York U., Toronto, Ont. Editor Fortnightly Rev., London, 1929-32, Rev. of Revs., London, 1931-32, Lovat Dickson's Mag., London, 1934-37; mng. dir. Lovat Dickson Ltd., Pubs., London, 1932-38; dir. Macmillan & Co., London, 1938-64. Author: (biography) H.G. Wells, Richard Hillary, Wilderness Man, Radclyffe Hall, The Museum-Makers, 1986; (autobiography) The Ante Room, The House of Words. Decorated Order of Can. Fellow Royal Soc. Can. Home: Toronto Ont., Canada. Died Jan. 2, 1987; cremated.

DICKSON, JAMES G(ERE), plant pathology educator; b. Yakima, Wash., Feb. 7, 1891; s. Nelson J. and Alethe-Rose (Conrad) D.; m. Leah Alice Dodds, June 24, 1915; children: James Gere, Alan N. (dec.), Nevelle-Leah Dickson Heckman, Charlotte-Mae Dickson Fitzgerald. BS in Botany and Chemistry, Wash. State Coll., 1915; MS, U. Wis., 1917, PhD in Botany and Organic Chemistry, 1920. Asst. soil chemist, asst. librarian Wash. State Coll., 1915-16; faculty U. Wis., 1916-17, and from 1919, prof. plant pathology, from 1926; plant pathologist field crops Dept. Agr., from 1918; charge wheat moblzn. and movement to Europe, World War I; with alcohol prodn. br. Office Sci. Rsch and Devel., 1941-44; rsch. coord. European and Asiatic Expdn., 1929-30; agrl. adviser Mexican, Cen. and S.Am expdns., 1950-59; sci. adviser rsch. Philippines and Spain, from 1959. Author: Diseases of Field Crops of Northern United States, 3d edit., 1934, Diseases of Field Crops, 2d edit., 1956, also sects. in books, articles. Recipient Cin. achievement award Malting and Brewing Industries, 1941. Fellow AAAS; mem. Am. Phytopath. Soc. (pres. 1953), Am. Inst. Biol. Scis. (gov. bd. from 1954, exec. com. from 1955, pres. 1959-60), Am. Acad. Microbiologists, Am. Bot. Soc., Micological Soc. Am., Am. Soc. Agronomy, Am. Statis. Assn., Torrey Bot. Club, Sigma Xi, Gamma Alpha, Phi Sigma. Home: Madison Wis. †

DICKSON, ROBERT CLARK, physician, educator; b. St. Marys, Ont., Can., Sept. 24, 1908; s. William M. and Mabel Earl (Clark) D.; m. Constance Fraser Grant, Sept. 16, 1939 (div. 1983); children: William Fraser, Shelagh Margaret, Jane Alice Constance. MD, U. Toronto, Ont., 1934, LLD, 1983; LLD (hon.), Dalhousie U., 1978. Jr. asst. physician dept. medicine U. Toronto, 1939-56; from assoc. prof. to prof., head dept. medicine Dalhousie U., Halifax, N.S., Can., 1956-78, prof. emeritus, from 1979. Chmn. Can. Armed Forces Med. Council, 1971-83. Lt. col. M.C., Can. Army, 1939-45, ETO, NATOUSA. Decorated comdr. Order of Can., Order of Brit. Empire. Fellow Royal Coll. Physicians and Surgeons Can. (council 1960-68, pres. 1968-70); mem. Can. Med. Assn., Med. Soc. N.S. Conservative. Mem. United Ch. Can. Home: Vancouver B.C., Canada. Deceased.

DIECKMANN, HERBERT, educator; b. Duisburg, Germany, May 22, 1906; came to U.S., 1938, naturalized, 1945; s. Gottfried and Amanda (Wehrhahn-MacDonald) D.; m. Liselotte Neisser, May 1930 (div. 1955); children: Beate, Martin; m. Jane Kennan Marsh, June 1959; children: Margaret K., Judith R. Student, U. Heidelberg, 1925-26, 27-28, U. Paris, 1926-27, U. Munich, 1928-29; PhD, U. Bonn, 1930; MA, Harvard, 1950; LittD, U. Exeter (Eng.), 1965. Notgemeinschaft Deutscher Wissenschaft fellow 1930-33, Subvention Dutch Emergency Coun. for Refugees, 1933-34; lectr. Turkish State U., Istanbul, 1934-37; asst. prof. Washington U., St. Louis, 1938-46, assoc. prof., 1946-48, prof., chmn. dept. romance langs., 1948-49; assoc. prof. French Harvard, 1950-52, prof., chmn. dept. romance langs., 1952-57, Smith prof. French and Spanish langs., 1957-65; prof. French and comparative lit. Cornell U., Ithaca, N.Y., 1966-74, Avalon Found. prof., 1967-74, prof. emeritus. Decorated Legion of Honor (France); Soc. for Humanities sr. fellow, 1969-70; Guggenheim fellow, 1948, 49, 51; Fulbright lectr., 1956-57. Mem. Am. Acad. Arts and Scis., MLA Am., Phi Beta Kappa. Home: Ithaca N.Y. Died Dec. 16, 1986.

DIEFENDORF, ADELBERT, civil engineer, educator; b. Newark, May 19, 1891; s. Adelbert and Alice (Sexton) D.; m. May V. Frame, Apr. 28, 1913; children: John Stuart, Randall Alonzo. BCE, Ohio Northern U., 1911, MCE, 1914; postgrad., Ia. State Coll., summers 1932-33, U. Ill., 1921-24; DSc (hon.), U. San Carlos, Guatemala, 1952, U. Costa Rica, 1955, U. Mex., 1956. Lic. profl. engr., N.Y., S.D., Utah. With Am. Bridge Co., Gary, Ind., 1911-14; engr. structures Guggenheim Co., N.Y., 1914-16; chief engr. Krajewski-Pesant Corp., Havana, Cuba, 1916-17; plant maintenance engr. Semet Solvay Co., Syracuse, N.Y., 1917-20; chief engr. Lackawanna Bridge Co., Buffalo, 1920-21; instr. U. Ill., 1921-24; asst. prof. civil engring. S.D. State Sch. Mines, 1924-27; prof. and head dept. civil engring. U. N.Mex., 1927-30, prof. civil engring. U. Pitts., 1930-39; prof., head dept. civil engrin. U. Utah, 1939-57; dean sch. engring. U. Pacific, from 1957; cons. engr. Dept. Communications, Pub. Works, Mexico, summer 1940; cons. engr. Republic of Cuba, Min. Pub. Works, from 1947; mem. engring. mission to Guatemala for U.S. Dept. State and govt. Guatemala, 1952, 59, Costa Rica, 1955, 59, Mexico, 1956, Nicaragua, 1959; chmn. state bd. registered profl. engrs. and land surveyors. Mem. State Bd. for Land Use, com. on transp. and econs. Hwy. Rsch. Bd., Nat. Rsch. Coun.; chmn. Utah State Bd. Registration for Profl. Engrs. and Land Surveyors, constn. com. Nat. Bd. Engr. Examiners. Mem. ASCE (pres. intermountain sect.), Am. Rd. Builders Assn. (pres. ednl. div., v.p. at large, chmn. scholarship com. Pan-Am. div.), Soc. for Promotion Engring. Edn. (chmn. constrn. edn. com.), Utah Soc. Profl. Engrs. (pres.), Masons, Scabbard and Blade, Sigma Tau, Sigma Phi Epsilon, Chi Epsilon. Episcopalian. Home: Stockton Calif. †

DIERKER, CHARLES EDWARD, lawyer; b. Oklahoma City, July 10, 1891; s. Bernard and Magdalena (Jerick) D.; m. Edna Margaret Wagner, June

28, 1922; children: Helen Frances Dierker Holstead, John Wagner, Patricia Ann Dierker Kearney. Grad., Draughons Bus. Coll., Oklahoma City. Bar: Okla. 1914. Practiced Shawnee, Okla., 1914-38; dist. atty. U.S. Dist. Ct. (we. dist.) Okla., 1938-47; spl. counsel to gov. Okla., 1955-59; asst. atty. gen. Okla., 1919. With U.S. Army, 1918-19. Mem. Am. Legion (comdr. Shawnee Post 1923), Shawnee C. of C. (bd. dirs.), Men's Dinner Club, Gibbons Dinner Club, Kiwanis (pres. 1950, lt. gov. 1952), K.C. (state dep. 1920-22), Elks (exalted ruler Shawnee lodge 1927). Democrat. Roman Catholic. Home: Oklahoma City Okla. †

DIETRICH, ETHEL BARBARA, federal official; b. Racine, Wis., Oct. 16, 1891; d. Charles Matthias and Kittie Rose (Packard) D. AB, Vassar Coll., 1913; AM, U. Wis., 1914, PhD, 1921; LHD (hon.), Mt. Holyoke Coll., 1962. Instr. history Bronell Hall, Omaha, 1914-17; instr. econs. Mt. Holyoke Coll., 1917-19, asst. prof., 1921-23, assoc. prof., 1923-30, prof. econs. and sociology, 1930-41; with various depts. U.S. Govt., from 1945, mem. del. to Paris Conf. on Reparations, 1945-46, econ. advisor Trade and Commerce br., Office Mil. Govt. for Germany, 1946-47, dep. for fgn. trade negotiations, Mil. Govt. for Germany, 1947-49, chief fgn. trade sect., Office Spl. Rep., Econ. Control Agy., 1949-52, dir. fgn. trade div. Office U.S. Rep. to NATO and other regional orgns. in Europe, Paris, 1952-61; cons. Bur. African Affairs State Dept., Washington, from 1962; U.S. del. Conf. Gen. Agreement on Tariffs and Trade, Geneva, Switzerland, 1955; spl. adviser to ambassador Rabat, Morocco, 1965-66. Author: World Trade, 1939, Far Eastern Trade of the United States, 1940; contbr. articles to bus. and profl. jours. Recipient merit citation Nat. Civil Service League, 1957, award Nat. Civil Service, 1960; Vassar Coll. fellow, U. Wis. fellow. Mem. AAUW, Phi Beta Kappa, Delta Gamma (Disting. Service award 1955). Home: Winnetka Ill. †

DIETRICH, RONALD M., lawyer; b. Hammond, Ind., Nov. 23, 1933; s. Emil and Bertha (Fritzen) D.; m. Nancy Bennett; 1 child, Inslee Austin; children from previous marriage—Thomas, Peter. B.S., Colo. U., 1955; J.D., U. Mich., 1961. Bar: D.C., Ill., Pa. Ptnr. firm McBride and Baker, Chgo., 1961-70; gen. counsel OEO, Washington, 1971, FTC, Washington, 1971-73; ptnr. Pepper, Hamilton & Scheetz, Washington, 1973-76, mng. ptnr., 1978-86, exec. ptnr., 1986-88; v.p. law Consol. Ry., Phila., 1976-78; mem. Adminstrv. Conf., Washington, 1978-82; bd. dirs. Nat. Cons. Law Ctr., Boston, 1974-76; cons. anti-trust law rev. Australian Govt., Canberra, New South Wales, 1973. Contbr. articles to profl. jours. Bd. govs. Opportunity Funding Corp., Washington, 1983. Served to lt. USNR, 1955-58. Recipient Outstanding Achievement award FTC, Washington, 1972. Mem. ABA, D.C. Bar Assn., Pa. Bar Assn. Republican. Clubs: Army-Navy Country, Georgetown, River Bend Country. Home: Great Falls Va. Died Oct. 17, 1988; buried Oak Hill Cemetary, Washington.

DIEUAIDE, FRANCIS RAYMOND, clinical medicine educator; b. N.Y.C., Oct. 22, 1892; s. Thomas Mortimer and Jane Snow (Raymond) D.; m. Ruth A. Guy, 1929. AB, CCNY, 1913; student, Columbia U., 1915-17; MD, Johns Hopkins Med. Sch., 1920; postgrad., med. schs. in Europe, 1928-29, 35. Mem. staff Johns Hopkins Med. Sch. and Hosp., 1920-24; went to Far East for China Med. Bd., becoming mem. staff Peiping Union Med. Coll., 1924, prof., head dept. medicine, also chief physician, 1926-39; prof. clin. medicine, Harvard U., also vis. physician Mass. Gen. Hosp., Boston, 1939-46; clin. prof. medicine Columbia U., 1946-58. Author: Civilian Health in Wartime, 1942; contbr. profl. articles on med., edn., and clin. medicine, especially heart disease, to sci. publs. Sci. dir. Life Ins. Med. Rsch. Fund, 1946-61; mem. joint Bd. for Coordination Malaria Studies, 1943-46. Col. M.C. AUS, 1943-46. Mem. AMA, Assn. Am. Physicians, Am. Soc. for Clin. Investigation, Am. Heart Assn., Chinese Med. Assn., Chinese Physiol. Soc., Mass. Med. Soc., Cosmos Club (Washington). Home: New York N.Y. †

DILL, DAVID BRUCE, physiologist, educator; b. Eskridge, Kans., Apr. 22, 1891; s. David White and Lydia (Dunn) D.; m. Olive Lillian Cassel, June 10, 1915; children: Elizabeth Cassel Dill Horvath, David Bruce; m. Chloris Luella Fuller Gillis, Jan. 3, 1946. BS, Occidental Coll., 1913, DSc, 1959; MA, Stanford U., 1914, PhD, 1925. Asst., assoc. chemist, Bur. Chemistry U.S. Dept. Agr., 1918-25; food rsch. fellow, Stanford U., 1923-25; Nat. Rsch. fellow Harvard U., 1925-27, asst. prof. biochemistry, 1927-36, assoc. prof. indsl. physiology, 1936-38, prof., 1938-47, dir. rsch. Fatigue Lab., 1927-47, vis. lectr., 1950-61; sci. dir. med. div. Army Chem. Ctr., Md., 1947-61, ret., 1961; rsch. scholar Ind. U., from 1961; leader physiol. exploratory expedns. to Andes, Canal Zone, Colo. Desert. Author: Life, Heat, and Altitude, 1938, (with A.V. Bock), Physiology of Muscular Exercise, 1931; editor: Adaptation to the Environment, 1960; editorial bd. Jour Sports Medicine and Fitness. Lt. col. AC U.S. Army, 1941-43; lt. col. in rsch. and devel. Q.M.C., 1943-46; col. USAAF Res., 1946-53, ret., 1953. Decorated Legion of Merit. Fellow AAAS; mem. Am. Coll. Cardiology (hon.), Armed Forces Chem. Assn., NAS-NRC (mem. exec. com. div. biology and agr. 1955-58) Am. Soc. Biol. Chemists, Fedn. Am. Socs. Exptl. Biology (chmn. bd. 1951-52), Am. Physiol. Soc. (mem. coun., treas. 1946-50, pres. 1950-51), Am. Acad. Arts and Scis., Am. Acad. Phys. Edn., Aero-Med. Assn., Am. Chem. Soc., Am. Coll. Sports Medicine (pres. 1960-61), Polish Assn. Sports Medicine (hon.), Phi Beta Kappa, Sigma Xi, Phi Delta Kappa, Phi Lambda Upsilon. Republican. Presbyterian. Home: Bloomington Ind. †

DILLER, THEODORE CRAIG, lawyer; b. Pitts., Aug. 3, 1904; s. Theodore and Rebecca (Craig) D.; m. Barbara Cox, May 16, 1936; children: Anne Cox Diller Sterling, Rebecca Crossette Diller Howe, Deborah Howard Diller Triant. PhB, Kenyon Coll., 1925; LLB, Harvard U., 1928. Bar: Pa. 1928, Ill. 1929. Practiced in Chgo., 1929-85; ptnr. Lord, Bissell & Brook, 1946-85; sec. Magnaflux Corp., 1940-59. Mem. ABA, Ill. Bar Assn., Chgo. Bar Assn., Law Club Chgo., Legal Club Chgo. Republican. Episcopalian. Clubs: University. (Chgo.), Mid-Am. (Chgo.). Home: Kenilworth Ill. Died Jan. 9, 1989, buried Rosehill Cemetery, Chgo.

DILLING, ALBERT WALLWICK, civil engineer, lawyer, consultant; b. Salt Lake City, Jan. 17, 1892; s. William Ferdinand and Kristine (Huseby) D.; m. Elizabeth Eloise Kirkpatrick, Aug. 12, 1918 (div.); children: Kirkpatrick, Elizabeth Jane; m. Charlotte Niebuhr, Oct. 1943. Student spl. course civil engring., Armour Inst. Tech., Chgo., 3 yrs.; LLB, Chgo.-Kent Coll. Law, 1917. Bar: Ill. 1917, also D.C., U.S. Supreme Ct. With engring. dept. C.,M.&St.P. Ry., 1912-17; field engr. Universal Portland Cement Co., 1917-20; engring. asst. to commr. pub. work, Chgo., 1920, also in charge for city Union Sta. devel., acting engr. bridges, 1920; chief engr. Sanitary Dist. Chgo., 1921-22; pvt. practice, from 1922; pres. Riverton Uranium Corp., Chgo and Riverton, Wyo.; supr. engr. West Chicago Pk. Commn., 1927-28; founder Activated Sludge Processes Am., trust estate, 1924; confidential assoc. Richard Fitzgerald, 1924-35; has represented many large contractors as cons. and atty. in connection with claims; has traveled abroad extensively, including visit to USSR, 1931. Asst. to pres. Rep. Citizens Fin. Com. Ill., 1947-48. Mem. ABA, ASCE, Am. Assn. Port Authorities, Western Soc. Engrs., Ill. Bar Assn., Chgo. Bar. Assn., Belgian Draft Horse Corp. Am., Holstein-Friesian Assn. Am., Order Ea. Star, Chgo. Athletic Club, Executives Club, Mason (32 deg.), K.T., Shriners, Delta Chi. Presbyterian. Home: Chicago Ill. †

DILLINGHAM, LOWELL SMITH, diversified company executive, state legislator; b. Honolulu, June 17, 1911; s. Walter Francis and Louise Olga (Gaylord) D.; m. Harriet Barbour, June 12, 1936; children—Gail Louise Dillingham Williams, Heather Barbour Dillingham Suhr. Grad., Harvard U., 1930-34. With Dillingham Corp. and subs., Honolulu, 1934-87; pres. Dillingham Corp. and subs., 1955-70, pres., chief exec. officer, 1969-70, chmn. bd., chief exec. officer, 1971-77, chmn. bd., 1977-87, vice chmn., dir. and dir. subs.; former mem. Hawaii Ho. of Reps., Honolulu; dir. Hawaiian Western Steel Ltd., Nat. Properties, Inc., Econ. Devel. Corp. Honolulu; mem. internat. adv. bd. Pan Am. World Airways, 1984-87. Trustee Punahou Sch., Hawaii, 1963-86; trustee emeritus Pacific Tropical Bot. Garden, N.Y. and Hawaii; mem. sr. adv. council Japan-Am. Soc. Honolulu, 1976-87. Recipient award for outstanding achievement in constrn. The Moles, 1969. Mem. Oahu Country, Outrigger Canoe and Pacific, Pacific Union clubs. Republican. Home: Honolulu Hawaii. Died Aug. 14, 1987; buried Oahu Cemetery, Honolulu, Hawaii.

DILLON, THOMAS CHURCH, advertising executive; b. Seattle, Mar. 27, 1915; s. Thomas J. and Clarissa (Church) D.; m. Georgiana Adams, Nov. 8, 1939 (dec. May 1964); children: Thomas Adams, Victoria Caroline, George Anthony; m. Patricia Doran, 1965. Student, Harvard U., 1933-36. With Batten, Barton, Durstine & Osborn, Inc., 1938-80; copywriter Mpls.; creative head San Francisco and Los Angeles, 1938-48; v.p. 1948-59, mgr. Los Angeles office, 1957-58, treas., 1958-62, exec. v.p., 1959-64, gen. mgr., 1962-64, pres., 1964-75, chief exec. officer, 1967-77, chmn. bd., 1975-86; pres. BBDO Internat. Inc., 1971-75, chief exec. officer, 1971-77, chmn. bd., 1975-80; pres. Mintaka, Inc., 1980-86; bd. dirs. MTC Properties, Inc., Midwest Radio-TV, Inc. Elected to Advt. Hall of Fame, 1980. Mem. Economic Club, Harvard Club (N.Y.C.). Home: New York N.Y. Died Mar. 7, 1986; buried Gate of Heaven Cemetery, Hawthorne, N.Y.

DILUZIO, NICHOLAS ROBERT, educator, physiologist; b. Hazleton, Pa., May 4, 1926; s. Nicholas and Carmela (Searfella) DiL.; m. Gertrude Alma Dezagottis, June 10, 1948; children—Nicholas Mark, Tamara Ann, Daniel Val. B.S., U. Scranton, 1950; Ph.D. (USPHS fellow), U. Tenn., 1954. Investigator Dorn Lab. for Med. Rsch., Bradford, Pa., 1954, Oak Ridge Nat. Lab., 1956, U.S. Naval Radiol. Def. Lab., 1958; mem. faculty U. Tenn. Med. Units, Memphis, 1955-68; prof. U. Tenn. Med. Units, 1962-64, chmn. physiology and biophysics dept., 1965-68; prof., chmn. dept. physiology Tulane U. Med. Sch., 1968-86. Editor: Advances in Experimental Medicine and Biology; Contbr. articles profl. jours. Mem. Tenn. Adv. Com. on Atomic Energy, 1958-68; mem. sci. adv. bd. Nat. Council on Alcoholism, 1963-68. Recipient Lederle Med. Faculty award, 1958-61. Mem. AAAS, Am. Physiol. Soc., Am. Heart Assn., Soc. for Exptl. Biology and Medicine, Reticuloendotheliel Soc. (pres. 1966-68). Home: Gretna La. Died July 2, 1986.

DIMAND, MAURICE SVEN, art museum curator; b. Austria, Aug. 2, 1892; came to U.S., 1923, naturalized, 1931; s. William and Betty (Rosengren) D.; m. Avis E. Wood, Sept. 20, 1924. PhD, U. Vienna, 1916. Rsch. asst. Inst. Fine Arts, U. Vienna, 1916-18; asst. Met. Mus. Art, N.Y.C., 1923-25, asst. curator, 1925-30, curator Near Ea. art, from 1930; lectr. mus., univs. and clubs. Author: A Handbook of Muhammadan Art, 1930, Ceramic Art of the Near East, 1931, Islamic Miniature Painting, 1933, The Ballard Collection of Oriental Rugs, 1935, Oriental Rugs and Textiles, 1935; contbr. articles to art jours. Mem. Am. Oriental Soc., Irano-Am. Soc., Am. Turkish Soc., Athenaeum, Hajji Baba Club. Home: New York N.Y. †

DIMMICK, WILLIAM ARTHUR, bishop, seminary president; b. Paducah, Ky., Oct. 7, 1919; s. James Oscar and Annis Amanda (Crouch) D. BA, Berea Coll., 1946; MDiv, Yale U., 1949; MA, George Peabody Coll., 1955; DD, Berkeley Div. Sch., 1975; DCS, Christian Bros. Coll., Memphis, 1982; D of Canon Law, Seabury-Western Theol. Sem., 1984. Ordained priest Episcopal Ch., 1955. Rector St. Philips Ch., Nashville, 1955-60; dean St. Mary's Cathedral, Memphis, 1960-73; rector Trinity Ch., Southport, Conn., 1973-75; bishop Episcopal Diocese No. Mich., Marquette, 1975-82; asst. bishop Episcopal Ch., Mpls., 1981-84; interim dean, pres. Seaburg Western Theol. Sem., Evanston, Ill., 1983-84; asst. bishop Episcopal Diocese Ala., 1984; mem. standing liturgical commn. Episcopal Ch. Assoc. Parishes. Pres. Memphis and Shelby County Health and Welfare Planning Coun., 1970-73. Home: Birmingham Ala. Died Oct. 19, 1984; buried Maplelawn Cemetery, Paducah.

DIMOCK, EDWARD JORDAN, judge; b. Elizabeth, N.J., Jan. 4, 1890; s. George Edward and Elizabeth (Jordan) D.; m. Constance Bullard, June 20, 1912; children: Constance D. (Mrs. Frank H. Ellis), Mary D. Robbins, Elizabeth D. (Mrs. William B. Ryan), Lucy D. Lieberfeld, Emily D. (Mrs. Ignatius G. Mattingly). Student, Pingry Sch., Elizabeth, N.J., 1901-06; A.B., Yale U., 1911; hon. mem, Princeton U., 1910; LL.B., Harvard U., 1914. Bar: N.Y. 1914. Mem. Hawkins, Delafield & Longfellow, N.Y.C., 1918-41; state reporter editing ofcl. law reports State N.Y., Albany, 1942-45; chmn. appeal bd. Office Contract Settlement, Washington, 1945-48; mem. appeal bd. Office Contract Settlement, 1948-51; U.S. dist. judge So. N.Y. 1951-61, sr. dist. judge, 1961—; Lectr. law municipal corps. Yale Law Sch., 1941-46; Asso. fellow Berkeley Coll., Yale. Chmn. joint com. N.Y.C. Bar Assns., 1937-39, Yale Alumni U. Fund, 1938-40; rep. U.S. Dist. Cts. 2d Circuit on Jud. Conf., 1957-59. Mem. Assn. Bar City N.Y. (exec. com. 1938-42), N.Y. State Bar Assn., Fed. Bar Assn., Sullivan County Bar Assn., ABA (ho. of dels. 1943, bd. editors Jour. 1944-68, bd. govs. 1948-51), Am. Law Inst. (past mem. council), N.Y. County Lawyers Assn., Harvard Law Sch. Assn. (past pres. N.Y.C.) Psi Upsilon. Democrat. Episcopalian. Clubs: Century (N.Y.C.); Elihu (Yale), Elizabethan (Yale). Home: Forestburgh N.Y. Deceased.

DINGEMAN, JAMES HERBERT, industrial executive, consultant; b. Detroit, July 31, 1917; s. Harry J. and Bessie (Schafer) D.; m. Ann R. McGillivray, Apr. 26, 1941; children: Patricia D. (Mrs. Thomas J. Moran), James Herbert, Peter J., Mary Ann. LL.B., U. Detroit, 1939. Bar: Mich. 1939. Practice in Detroit, 1939-43; mem. firm Dingeman & DeGalan, 1939-43; legal adviser Fed.-Mogul Corp., Detroit, 1943-46; asst. dir. indsl. relations Fed.-Mogul Corp., 1946-60, dir. orgn. planning exec. devel., 1960-68, sec., 1965-68; v.p. legal and corp. planning affairs, sec. Parke, Davis & Co., 1968-70, group v.p. legal and corp. planning affairs, sec., 1970-71, v.p. adminstrn., sec., 1971-77, dir., 1970-86; v.p. Warner-Lambert Co., 1970-77, cons., 1977-86; dir. Bank of Commerce, Mich. Consol. Gas Co., Security Bancorp, Inc., Detroit Ball Bearing Co., Bush Mfg. Co., Genova Corp., Primark Corp., Commerce Bancorp; instr. Detroit Coll. Law, 1940, Walsh Inst. Accountancy, 1945. Founder Little League Baseball, Grosse Pointe Farms, 1952, pres., 1954-55; area chmn. United Fund, 1965; Mem. Republican Fin. Com., 1950-86, councilman, Grosse Pointe Farms, 1966-86, mayor pro-tem, 1969-75, mayor, 1975-86; mem. exec. bd. Detroit Area council Boy Scouts Am.; trustee St. John Hosp., Citizens Research Council, Community Found. Southeastern Mich., Harrison Hosp. Corp., St. Clair Ambulatory Care Corp., Affiliated Health Services, Oxford Inst., Detroit Sci. Center, U. Detroit, Grosse Pointe Farms Found., St. Clair Health Services Corp.; pres. Bus./Edn. Alliance, 1975-77. Mem. Am., Mich. bar assns., Assn. Gen Counsel, Am. Soc. Corp. Secs., Nat. Health Lawyers Assn., Am. Mgmt. Assn., Greater Detroit C. of C. (dir.), Lambda Sigma (past nat. pres.), Detroit Athletic (dir.), Detroit Country, Cardinal (Detroit), Otsego Ski (Gaylord, Mich.), The Little (Gulfstream, Fla.), Delray Beach (Fla.), Port Huron (Mich.) Golf clubs, Delta Theta Phi. Home: Grosse Pointe Farms Mich. Died Sept. 18, 1986.

DINGMAN, REED OTHELBERT, surgeon, educator; b. Rockwood, Mich., Nov. 4, 1906; s. Wilbert Alva and

Gertrude (Scherer) D.; m. Thelma Agnes Muir, Nov. 24, 1932; children: David Lyons, Sue Muir, Sally Fae. AB, U. Mich., 1928, DDS, 1931, MS, 1932, MD, 1936; DSc, U. Miami, 1974. Diplomate Am. Bd. Oral Surgery, Am. Bd. Plastic Surgery. Oral and plastic surgeon Gelsinger Meml. Hosp., Danville, Pa., 1937-39; pvt. practice Washington, 1939-40; asst. prof. oral surgery U. Mich., 1940-45, assoc. prof., 1945-85, prof. surgery, head sect. plastic surgery Med. Sch., 1965-76, prof. emeritus, 1976-85, acting head sect., 1982-85; chief dept. plastic surgery St. Joseph Mercy Hosp., Ann Arbor, Mich., 1960-75. Author: (with Paul Natvig) Surgery of Facial Fractures; editor Jour. Oral Surgery, 1948-52; assoc. editor: Year Book of Plastic Surgery; contbr. articles to med., dental publs. Fellow ACS, Am. Coll. Dentists; mem. ADA, AMA, Am. Soc. Oral and Maxillofacial Surgeons, Am. Soc. Plastic and Reconstructive Surgeons (pres., dir. found., pres. 1963-64), Western surg. socs., Am. Assn. Plastic Surgeons, Am. Cleft Palate Soc., Am. Soc. Maxillo-facial Surgeons (pres. 1952), Am. Soc. Trauma, South African Soc. Plastic Surgeons (hon.), Am., Internat. socs. aesthetic plastic surgeons. Home: Ann Arbor Mich. Died Dec. 24, 1985; buried Ann Arbor.

DIRKS, JOHN EDWARD, educator; b. Iowa, July 18, 1919; s. John and Henrietta (Smit) D.; m. Annabelle B. Voigt, June 14, 1943; children: Christopher, Timothy, Nicholas, Rebecca. BA, U. Dubuque, 1940; student, McCormick Theol Sem., Chgo., 1940-42; BD, Yale U., 1943; PhD, Columbia U., 1947. Ordained to ministry United Presbyn. Ch., 1947. Mem. religious teaching staff Columbia U., 1944-49; prof. philosophy Lake Forest (Ill.) Coll., 1949-55; assoc. dir. commn. on higher edn. Nat. Council Chs., 1953-54; Stephen Merrill Clement prof. Christian methods Yale Div. Sch., 1955-67; staff spl. research project Edward W. Hazen Found., 1955-60; v.p. Danforth Found., St. Louis, 1967-73; prof., dean humanities U. Calif., Santa Cruz, 1973-81; sec. univ. tchrs. com. World Student Christian Fedn., Geneva, Switzerland, 1953-60. Author: The Critical Theology of Theodore Parker, 1947; founder, editor Christian Scholar until 1967. Trustee Am. U., Cairo, 1955-71. Mem. Soc. for Values in Higher Edn. (mem. cen., bd. dirs. 1974-81), Am. Philos. Soc., Am. Acad. Religion, AAUP. Home: Santa Cruz Calif. Died Apr. 5, 1981; buried Holland, Iowa.

DIVELY, GEORGE SAMUEL, communications and information processing equipment manufacturing company executive; b. Claysburg, Pa., Dec. 17, 1902; s. Michael A. and Martha A. (Dodson) D.; m. Harriett G. Seeds, June 30, 1933 (dec. Aug. 1968); 1 son, Michael A.; m. Juliette Gaudin, Feb. 1969. B.S. in E.E, U. Pitts., 1925, D.Sc. in Engring. (hon.), 1962; M.B.A., Harvard U., 1929; D.Eng. (hon.), Case-Western Res. U., 1961; D.Sc. (hon.), Fla. Inst. Tech., 1972. With Harris Corp., 1937-88, successively asst. to sec.-treas., asst. treas., sec.-treas., dir., v.p. and gen. mgr., 1937-47, pres., 1947-61, chief exec. officer, 1952-68, chmn. bd., 1954-72, chmn. exec. and fin. com., 1972-78, hon. chmn. bd., 1972-88. Author: The Power of Professional Management. Hon. trustee Case Western Res. U.; trustee Ednl. TV Met. Cleve.; dir. assocs. Harvard Grad. Sch. Bus. Adminstrn. Fellow Am. Mgmt. Assn. (life mem.). Clubs: Masons (Cleve.), Pepper Pike Country (Cleve.), The Country (Cleve.), Union (Cleve.), Harvard (Cleve.), Royal Palm Yacht and Country (Fla.). Home: Cleveland Ohio. Died Nov. 1, 1988.

DIX, GEORGE OSCAR, lawyer; b. Prairie Creek, Ind., May 26, 1874; s. Benajah H. and Nancy E. (Harness) D.; m. Helen G. Layman, Jan. 19, 1905. LLB, Ind. Law Sch. of Indpls., 1898; LLD, Ind. State U. Bar: Ind. 1898. Practiced in Terre Haute; mem. Dix, Dix, Patrick, Ratcliffe & Adamson; mem. Ind. Judicial Coun., 1935-37; bd. dirs. Smith-Alsop Paint & Varnish Co. Bd. dirs. Ind. State Univ. Found.; commr. Terre Haute (Ind.) Park Bd., 1917-21; mem. Bd. Edn., Terre Haute, 1912-15, Ind. Corps. Survey Commn., 1927-58;lt. col. staff Gov. of Ind., 1916-20. Mem. ABA, Ind. State Bar Assn. (pres. 1925-26), SAR (pres. Ind. Soc. 1915-16), Terre Haute C. of C., Univ. Club Terre Haute, Country Club Terre Haute, Columbia Club (Indpls.), Masons (32 deg.). Republican. Congregationalist. Home: Terre Haute Ind. †

DOBBINS, CHARLES GORDON, educator, editor; b. Greensboro, Ala., Aug. 15, 1908; s. John Gordon and Mantie Edgar (Wolf) D.; 1 child, Peter Young. A.B., Samford U., 1929; M.A., Columbia, 1931; postgrad., U. Wis., 1931-33; L.H.D., Judson Coll., 1967; Litt.D., Jamestown Coll., 1971; LL.D., Coll. St. Francis, 1973. Reporter Birmingham Age-Herald, 1929; instr. English U. Wis., 1931-34; dir. Fed. Emergency Relief Adminstrn. Transient Camp, Ft. McClellan, Ala., 1935; dist. dir. Nat. Youth Adminstrn., Gadsden, Ala., 1936; asst. prof. English, asst. to pres. Ala. Coll., 1936-39; editor, pub. Anniston (Ala.) Times, 1939-42; editor Montgomery (Ala.) Advertiser, 1946-47; editor, pub. Montgomery Examiner, 1947-55; staff asso. Am. Council on Edn., 1956-62, dir. commn. on fed. relations, 1962-63, exec. sec., 1963-73, dir. acad. adminstrn. internship program, 1967-73; cons. Acad. Edn. Devel., 1974-75, Am. Council on Edn., 1975-77, Office Sec. HEW, 1976-77. Author: American Council on Education: Leadership and Chronology, 1918-1968, 1968, American Council on Education, Programs and Services, 1958-75, 1976; Editor: Educational Record, 1968-73; The Strength to Meet our National Need, 1956, Expanding Resources for College Teaching, 1956, Higher Education and the Federal Government: Programs and Problems, 1963, The University, The City, and Urban Renewal, 1964; co-editor: Whose Goals for American Higher Education?, 1968; Contbr.: articles to Ency. Americana; others. Pres. Ala. Press Assn., 1942; v.p., exec. dir. Nat. Home Library Found., 1978-88; dir. OPS, Ala., 1951-53; mem. Nat. Planning Assn. (Com. of South), 1946-55, Ala. Bd. Edn., 1951-59; bd. visitors Eckerd Coll., 1968-72; trustee Judson Coll., 1942-58, Alderson Broaddus Coll., 1975-81. Served with USNR, 1942-46. Mem. Omicron Delta Kappa, Sigma Delta Chi, Sigma Nu. Democrat. Baptist. Club: Cosmos (Washington). Died Nov. 6, 1988.

DOBBS, S. A., railroad executive; b. Chester, Miss., July 23, 1888; m. Dimple Dobbs, Oct. 24, 1922. Student, Miss. Coll., 1905-06. With G., M. & O. R.R., from 1909; successively telegraph operator, train dispatcher, chief train dispatcher, trainmaster, gen. agt., exec. gen. agt., asst. v.p. G.M.&O. R.R., 1909-45, v.p., from 1945. Home: Chicago Ill. †

DOBSON, HERBERT GORDON, management consultant; b. Can., Dec. 19, 1900; came to U.S., 1919, naturalized, 1938; s. Joseph Bent and Minnie (Steves) D.; m. Frances Garland Roberts, June 21, 1930; children: Ann Garland, Jane Frances. Student publ. schs., N.B. Auditor Can. Nat. Rys., 1918-19; insp. Bank Am. Nat. Trust Savs. Assn., Los Angeles, 1920-43; v.p., controller Occidental Life Ins. Co., Los Angeles, 1943-62, sr. v.p., 1962-65; pres. Angeles/Cardillo Travel Agy., 1965-67, mgmt. cons., 1969-85. Pres. Episcopal Ch. Home for Children, 1965-69, 70-72; coordinator Episcopal Ch. Cathedral Project, 1970-71, Vis. Nurse Assn., 1972-85. Home: Ojai Calif. Died May 10, 1985; buried San Gabriel Cemetery, Calif.

DODD, DAVID LEFEVRE, economist, educator, investment consultant; b. Berkeley County, W.Va., Aug. 23, 1895; s. David Henry and Mary Virginia (Shaffer) D.; m. Elise Marguerite Firor, Aug. 9, 1924; 1 dau., Barbara Anderson. BS, U. Pa., 1920; MS, Columbia U., 1921, PhD, 1930. Rsch. asst. to economist Nat. Bank of Commerce, N.Y.C., 1921-22; instr. econs. Columbia U., 1922-25, instr. fin., 1925-30, asst. prof. fin., 1930-38, assoc. prof., 1938-47, prof., 1947-61, prof. fin. emeritus, from 1961, charge courses bus. and econs., 1926-45, assoc. dean Grad. Sch. Bus., 1948-52; cons. expert on valuation of securities, pvt. clients, from 1928; ltd. ptnr. Newman & Graham, 1950-58, gen. ptnr. Graham-Newman & Co., 1958-59; dir. Criterion Ins. Co., Govt. Employees Ins. Co., Govt. Employees Life Ins. Co., Govt. Employees Corp.; dir. Govt. Employees Fin. Corp., vice chmn. profit-sharing plan of all cos. listed 1960-63. Author: Stock Watering, 1960, (with Benjamin Graham, Sidney Cottle, Charles Tatham) Security Analysis, 4th rev. edit., 1962. Mem. investment com. Social Sci. Rsch. Coun., 1959-65. Served from boatswain to lt. (j.g.) USN, 1917-19. Mem. Am. Fin. Assn. (v.p. 1946-47), N.Y. Soc. Security Analysts, Beta Gamma Sigma, Phi Gamma Delta, Alpha Kappa Psi, Phi Chi Theta. Home: Portland Maine. Died Sept. 18, 1988.

DODD, EDWARD HOWARD, JR., publishing executive, author; b. N.Y.C., June 25, 1905; s. Edward Howard and Mary Elizabeth (Leggett) D.; m. Roxana Foote Scoville, Aug. 6, 1932 (div. May 1950); children: Louise Dodd Nicholson, Roxana Dodd Laughlin, Edward H. III; m. Camille O. Gilpatric, Oct. 1952 (dec. 1981). AB, Yale U., 1928. With Dodd, Mead & Co. (pubs.), N.Y.C., 1929-82, head editorial dept., from 1937, also bd. dirs., v.p., 1941, pres., 1953-57, chmn., 1966-76, chmn. editorial bd., 1976-82; with OSS, Washington, 1942-45. Author: Great Dipper to Southern Cross: The Cruise of the Schooner Chance through the South Seas, 1930, The First Hundred Years: A History of Dodd, Mead & Co, 1939, Of Nature, Time and Teale, 1960, Tales of Maui, 1964, Polynesian Art, 1967, Polynesian Seafaring, 1972, Polynesia's Sacred Isle, 1976, The Rape of Tahiti, 1983. Trustee Marlboro Sch. Music. Served with Squadron A, 101st Cav. N.Y. N.G., 3 yrs. Mem. Elihu Soc., Alpha Delta Phi. Clubs: Century (N.Y.), Yale (N.Y.). Home: Putney Vt. Died Dec. 19, 1988.

DODDS, JOHN RICHARD, publishing company executive; b. Sacramento, July 29, 1922; s. G. Fulton and Theresa (Carr) D.; m. Vivian Vance, Jan. 16, 1961 (dec. 1979). BA, U. Calif., Berkeley, 1944. Sr. editor William Morrow & Co., 1956-58; head trade div. G.P. Putnam's Sons, pubs., San Francisco, 1966-70, editor-in-chief, exec. v.p., 1972-86, dir., 1972-77; sr. editor West, Simon & Shuster, 1977-86; owner McIntosh McKee Dodds, lit. agy., N.Y.C., 1960-66; editor-in-chief Holt, Rinehart-Winston, N.Y.C., 1970-72. Nat. bd. Santa Fe Opera, 1970-86, St. Johns Coll., Annapolis and Santa Fe, 1970-72. With USNR, 1941-44. Mem. Coffee House, Doubles, Knickerbocker, Bohemian. Home: Belvedere Calif. Died Oct. 9, 1986.

DODGE, M(ARCELLUS) HARTLEY, manufacturing executive; b. 1881; s. Norman W. and Emma (Hartley) D.; m. Geraldine Rockefeller, Apr. 18, 1907; 1 son, M. Hartley. Founder Union Metallic Cartridge Co.; owner, pres. Remington Arms Co.; chmn. bd. Remington Arms Co., Inc.; then hon. chmn. Bd. dirs. Equitable Life Assurance Soc. U.S.; trustee Columbia U., from 1907, clk. bd., 1923-57; trustee Hartley Dodge Found.; trustee emeritus Hartley House. Mem. Columbia, Down Town, Racquet and Tennis, Morris County Golf, Morristown, Pilgrims, Essex Fox Hounds, University clubs. Home: Madison N.J. †

DOEBLER, ERROL W(EBER), utilities executive; b. Williamsport, Pa., Nov. 10, 1892; s. Henry A. and Alice (Weber) D.; m. Mildred Maidment, June 8, 1918 (dec.); children: Barbara, Carol Doebler Golden, Henry Maidment; m. Muriel Taft, Dec. 26, 1965. BCE, Cornell U., 1915. Engr. Hazen, Whipple & Fuller, cons. engrs., N.Y.C., 1916-22; cons. engr. Weston E. Fuller, Swarthmore, Pa., 1922-27; comml. mgr. L.I. Lighting Co and affiliates, Mineola, N.Y., 1927-37, gen. operating mgr., 1937-40, v.p., 1941-53, also bd. dirs., pres., 1953-57, chmn. bd., from 1957, chief exec. officer, 1957-60; instr., then asst. prof. engring. Swarthmore Coll., 1922-27; v.p., dir. State Bank of Sea Cliff, 1935-49, Queens Borough Gas & Electric Co., 1944-50, Nassau & Suffolk Lighting Co., 1946-50, Long Beach Gas Co., 1946-50, Utilities Mut. Ins. Co.; v.p., trustee Power Reactor Devel. Co.; mem. com. Empire State Utilities Power Resources Assn, 1959-66; mem. L.I. Bridge Study Commn.; v.p. Empire State Atomic Devel. Assn., exec. com., dir., 1955-59.,. Trustee, sec. United Fund L.I., Inc.; trustee Nat. Indsl. Conf. Bd.; trustee, chmn. L.I. Industry Fund; bd. dirs. Nassau Hosp. Assn., Mineola. Mem. ASCE, Soc. Gas Lighting, Edison Elec. Inst. (dir. 1957-61), Am. Gas Assn., Am. Standards Assn. (dir. 1958-59), Nat. Golf Links Am. Club, North Fork Country Club, Garden City Golf Club, Engrs. Club N.Y.C., Masons. Home: Southold N.Y. †

DOHERTY, ROBERT P(ACE), banker; b. Ft. Worth, Jan. 23, 1891; s. William and Catherine (Pace) D.; m. Ada Honan, Jan. 14, 1915; children: Robert P., Wilfred Lansing, Mary Patricia. Student, S. Thomas Coll., Houston, 1902-06, St. Michael's Coll., Toronto, Ont., Can., 1907-08. Asst. cashier 1st State Bank, Kingsville, Tex., 1916-21; auditor Nat. Bank Commerce, Houston, 1921-23, asst. v.p., 1923-28, v.p., 1928-34, exec. v.p., 1934-48, then chmn. bd.; v.p., bd. dirs. Gulf Bldg. Corp., Houston, from 1929; pres., bd. dirs. Main Rusk Realty Corp., from 1934. Trustee Rice Inst., Baylor Med. Found. Mem. Am. Bankers Assn., Res. City Bankers Assn., Tex. Bankers Assn., Newcomen Soc., Houston Club, River Oaks Country Club, Ramada Club, Petroleum Club, K.C. Democrat. Roman Catholic. Home: Houston Tex. †

DOISY, EDWARD ADELBERT, biochemist; b. Hume, Ill., Nov. 13, 1893; s. Edward Perez and Ada (Alley) D.; m. Alice Ackert, July 20, 1918 (dec. 1964); children—Edward Adelbert (dec.), Robert Ackert, Philip Perez, Richard Joseph (dec.); m. Margaret McCormick, Apr. 19, 1965. A.B., U. Ill., 1914, M.S., 1916; Ph.D., Harvard U., 1920; D.Sc., Washington U., 1940, Yale U., 1940, U. Chgo., 1941, Central Coll., 1942, U. Ill., 1960, Gustavus Adolphus Coll., 1963; LL.D., St. Louis U., 1955; Docteur Honoris Causa, U. Paris, 1945. Asst. in biochemistry Harvard Med. Sch., 1915-17; instr., asso. and asso. prof. biochemistry Washington U. Sch. Medicine, St. Louis, 1919-23; prof. biochemistry, dir. dept. St. Louis U. Sch. Medicine, 1923-65, Distinguished Service prof. biochemistry, emeritus, also dir. emeritus Edward A. Doisy dept. biochemistry, 1965-86; adminstrv. bd.; dir. dept. biochemistry, biochemist St. Mary's Hosp., St. Louis, 1924-86; Several named lectures at various univs. and soc. meetings.; Mem. League of Nations com. for standardization sex hormones, London, 1932, 35. Author: (with Edgar Allen and Charles H. Danforth) Sex and Internal Secretions, 1939; Contbr. articles on blood buffers, sex hormones, vitamin K, and antibiotic compounds to profl. jours. Served to 2d lt. U.S. Army, 1917-19. Recipient Gold medal St. Louis Med. Soc., 1935; Philip A. Conne medal Chemists Club N.Y., 1935; St. Louis award, 1939; Willard Gibbs medal, 1941; Am. Pharm. Mfg. Assn. award, 1942; Squibb award, 1944; Barren Found. medal, 1972. Mem. Am. Soc. Biol. Chemists (council 1926-27, 34-37, 40-45, pres. 1943-45), Am. Chem. Soc., Nat. Acad. Scis., Am. Philos. Soc., Pontifical Acad. Scis., Am. Acad. Arts and Scis., Phi Beta Kappa, Sigma Xi, Phi Kappa Phi, Alpha Omega Alpha. Home: Webster Groves Mo. Died Oct. 23, 1986, buried Oak Hill Cemetery, Webster Groves.

DOLAN, PATRICK, advertising executive; b. Eng., Aug. 14, 1911; Came to U.S., 1929, naturalized; s. Joseph Thomas and Mary Josephine (Hayes) D.; m. Britta Salen, Mar. 5, 1949; children: Patrick Sean, Christina Lisa. Student, St. Joseph's Coll., Upholland, Lancashire, Eng., 1924-29. With Chgo. Times, 1936-38, CBS, 1938-41; European v.p. Foote, Cone & Belding Inc., 1946-48; chmn. Patrick Dolan & Assocs., pub. relations, N.Y.C., London; also chmn. Dolan, Davies, Whitcombe & Stewart, advt., London, 1949-60; pres. Batten, Barton, Durstine & Osborn Internat. Inc., N.Y.C., 1960-67, Malta Free Port, 1968-87; chmn. Moray Firth Maltings Ltd., Inverness, Scotland, 1968-87; dir. Combustion Combustion Power, Inc., Palto Alto, Calif. Cons. Brit. Fishing Industry, 1955-58, Western Region Govt. Nigeria, 1958-63, Dutch Bulb Industry, 1948-60, U.K. Horserace Betty Levy Bd., 1963-67, State Dept., 1965-69, Hambro Bank, London, 1967-87. With OSS, AUS, 1941-46, ETO. Decorated Silver

Star, Legion of Merit; comdr. Order White Lion (Czechoslovakia); officier Croix de Guerre (France). Mem. President's, Boodle's, Royal Thames Yacht, Pilgrims, Special Forces Ends of Special Forces Ends of Earth, American, Sky. Democrat. Roman Catholic. Home: New York N.Y. Died Dec. 31, 1987.

DOLE, HOLLIS MATHEWS, geologist; b. Paonia, Colo., Sept. 4, 1914; s. Edwin Enyart and Mary Velma (Mathews) D.; m. Ruth Josephine Mitchell, Sept. 29, 1942; children—Michael Hollis, Stephen Eric. B.S., Oreg. State Coll., 1940, M.S., 1942; student, U. Calif., 1941, U. Utah, 1951-52; D.Engring., Mont. Tech., 1972. With U.S. Bur. Mines, 1942, U.S. Geol. Survey, 1946; staff Oreg. Dept. Geology and Mining Industry, 1946-69, successively field geologist, geologist, asst. dir., 1946-55, acting dir., 1955-56, state geologist, 1956-69; asst. sec. mineral resources Dept. Interior, Washington, 1969-73; gen. mgr. Colony devel. operation Atlantic Richfield Co., Denver, 1973-76; Washington rep. Atlantic Richfield Co., 1976-79; mineral resource cons. 1980-87; instr. geology Vanport Coll., Oreg. Extension, 1949-52; adj. prof. Portland State U., 1969-73, Oreg. State U., 1980-87; mem. Nat. Petroleum Council, 1973-79, Law of Sea Adv. Commn., U.S. State Dept., 1974, 79, Antarctic sect. Ocean Affairs Adv. Commn., 1978-80; mem. fed. energy adv. com. U.S. Dept. Energy, 1974-78; govt. rep. SEA USE Council, 1979-85; mem. adv. com. OSU Sea Grant, 1980-85; mem. bd. mineral and energy resources NRC, 1981-87; mem. commn. on paleontol. guidelines NRC-Nat. Acad. Scis., 1985-86. Councilor AGI Minority Commn., 1974-87. Lt. USN, 1942-46. Recipient Gold medal hon. award U.S. Dept. Interior, 1972; Disting. Service award Oreg. State U., 1973. Mem. Soc. Mining Engrs. of AIME, Am. Assn. Petroleum Geologists, Geol. Soc. Am., Soc. Econ. Geologists, Can. Inst. Mining, Assn. Am. State Geologists, Oreg. Acad. Sci., Sigma Xi, Sigma Gamma Epsilon, Kappa Kappa Psi, Delta Sigma Phi. Republican. Presbyterian. Home: Lake Oswego Oreg. Died July 20, 1987; buried Portland, Oreg.

DONAHO, GLYNN ROBERT, naval officer; b. George, Tex., Mar. 25, 1905; s. George Robert and Ennis Cornelius (McGill) D.; m. Louise S. Stebbings, Nov. 26, 1932. BS, U.S. Naval Acad., 1927, postgrad. applied communications, 1935-36; grad., Nat. War Coll., 1951. Commd. ensign USN, 1927, advanced through grades to vice adm., 1964; comdr. Mil. Sea Transp. Service, 1964-67, ret., 1967; pres. Oetiker, Inc., Livingston, N.J., 1968. Decorated Navy Cross with 3 oak leaf clusters, Silver Star medal with oak leaf cluster, D.S.M. Mem. Navy League, Sons Republic Tex., N.Y. Yacht, Army-Navy Country, Arlington, Army and Navy, Masons. Home: McLean Va. Died May 28, 1986.

DONAHUE, LESTER, concert pianist; b. L.A., Jan. 1, 1892; s. Charles E. and Jennie Margaret (McCarthy) D. Pvt. study with, Martin Krause, Egon Petri, Rudolph Ganz, Berlin, Germany. Protege of Polish actress Mme. Helena Modjeska, playing before Paderewski, 1907; U.S. tour with Ellen Beach Yaw, soprano, 1910-11; debut Beethoven Saal, Berlin, 1913; concerts, London, Paris, and numerous German cities, 1913-14; N.Y. debut Aeolian Hall, 1915; appearances, U.S. and abroad, 1916-48; introduced Tonal Pedal (invented by John Hays Hammond Jr.) in 10 concerts, Phila. Orchestra, conducted by Stokowski, Phila., Carnegie Hall, N.Y.C., Chgo., Pitts., Cleve., Toledo, Detroit, Washington, 1925; soloist, introducing Rachmaninoff's Second Piano Concerto to Pacific Coast audiences, conducted by Alfred Hertz, Hollywood (Calif.) Bowl, 1927; European tour with Hammond piano, Hamburg, Berlin, Leipzig, Munich, Germany, Vienna, Austria, Paris, 1928; annual concerts London, Paris, 1920-28; played Da Falla's Nights in the Gardens of Spain with Wallenstein, L.A. and Long Beach, Calif., 1947. Mem. L.A. Mcpl. Art Commn., pres. 1948-53. Home: Los Angeles Calif. †

DONALDSON, ETHELBERT TALBOT, educator; b. Bethlehem, Pa., Mar. 18, 1910; s. Francis and Anne H. (Talbot) D.; m. Christine H. Hunter, June 24, 1941 (div. 1967); 1 child, Deirdre H.; m. Jacqueline Sissa Filson, Mar. 23, 1967 (div. 1969); m. Judith H. Anderson, May 18, 1971. B.A., Harvard U., 1932; Ph.D., Yale U., 1943; Litt.D. (hon.), Lehigh U., 1980. Tchr. French, English, Latin and Greek Kent Sch., Conn., 1932-38, 39-40; faculty Yale U., 1946-67, 70-74, research instr. to assoc. prof., 1946-56, prof., 1956-66, Bodman prof. English, 1966-67, 70-74; acting master of Saybrook Coll., Yale U., 1963; prof. English Columbia U., 1967-70, Ind. U., Bloomington, 1974-76; Disting. prof. English Ind. U., 1976-80, emeritus, 1980-87; vis. prof. U. Coll., London, 1951-52, King's Coll., London, 1971-72, U. Mich., 1973-74; Mary Flexner lectr. Bryn Mawr Coll., 1981. Author: Piers Plowman: The C-Text and Its Poet, 1949, Speaking of Chaucer, 1970, The Swan at the Well, 1985; also articles in profl. jours.; editor: Chaucer's Poetry, 1958, (with George Kane) B Version of Piers Plowman, 1975. Served to capt. USAAF, 1943-46. Guggenheim fellow, 1951-52, 77-78. Fellow Mediaeval Acad. (pres. 1980-81, Haskins medal 1978), Am. Acad. Arts and Scis., Brit. Acad. (corr.); mem. MLA, Conn. Acad. Arts and Scis. (pres. 1966-67), Acad. Lit. Studies, New Chaucer Soc. (pres. 1978-79), Phi Beta Kappa. Club: Savage (London). Home: Bloomington Ind. Died Apr. 13, 1987.

DONN, WILLIAM L., research scientist, consultant; b. Bklyn., Mar. 2, 1918; s. Nathan and Tina D.; m. Renee M. Brilliant, Jan. 2, 1960; children—Matthew, Tara. B.A., Bklyn. Coll., 1939; M.A., Columbia U., 1946, Ph.D., 1951. Sr. research scientist Lamont-Doherty Obs. Columbia U., Palisades, N.Y., 1951-85; special research scientist Columbia U., Palisades, 1985-87; instr. to prof. geology Bklyn. Coll., 1946-63; prof. geology CCNY, N.Y.C., 1963-77; research cons. Woods Hole Oceanographic Instn., Mass., 1947-49; mem. faculty meteorology sect. U.S. Mcht. Marine Acad., 1942-45; aerologist Naval Air Navigation Sch., 1945; geologist N.Atlantic Dist. C.E. U.S. Army, 1941-42, del. Aqueduct Program, 1941; cons. various indsl. and legal orgns., 1951-87; White House cons. Office Sci. and Tech., Washington, 1979-81; mem. com. on long waves ASCE, commn. on microseisms Internat. Union Geodesy and Geophysics; mem. rev. com. prevention and mitigation of flood losses NRC. Author textbooks: Meteorology With Marine Applications, 1946, 4th edit., 1975; Graphic Methods in Structural Geology, 1958; The Earth, 1973. Editor: Glossary of Geology, 4th edit., 1980; International Geophysics Series, 1979-87. Contbr. research articles to profl. publs. Trustee village bd. Grand View-on-Hudson, N.Y., 1968-87, dep. mayor, 1975-87, police commr., 1968-87. Served with USCGR, 1942; served to lt. (s.g.) USNR, 1942-46. Disting. nat. lectr. Am. Assn. Petroleum Geologists, 1960, Soc. Exploration Geophysicists, 1960; NSF sr. postdoctoral fellow, 1959-60; fellow in geology, Bklyn. Coll., 1940-41; chief scientist, prin., co-prin., dir. projects and grants, 1941-87. Fellow AAAS, Geol. Soc. Am., Explorers Club; mem. Seismol. Soc. Am., Am. Geophys. Union, N.Y. Acad. Scis. (council 1950-52, chmn. sect. oceanography and meteorology 1950-52), Am. Meteorol. Soc. (profl., chmn. com. on paleoclimatology 1965), Phi Beta Kappa, Sigma Xi. Home: Grand View on Hudson N.Y. Died June 30, 1987; buried Rockland Cemetery, Sparkill, N.Y.

DONNELLAN, THOMAS A., archbishop; b. N.Y.C., Jan. 24, 1914; s. Andrew and Margaret (Egan) b. A.B., Cathedral Coll., 1933; student, St. Joseph's Sem., 1933-39; J.C.D., Catholic U. Am., 1942. Ordained priest Roman Catholic Ch., 1939; synodal judge Marriage Tribunal, 1950-58; vice chancellor Archdiocese N.Y., 1947-50, chancellor, 1958-62, vocation dir., 1957-62; rector St. Joseph's Sem., 1962-64; bishop of Ogdensburg, N.Y., 1964-68; archbishop of Atlanta, 1968-87; also chaplain del., vicar gen., mil. ordinariate for Ga., Fla., N.C., S.C., 1972-87; Treas., com. Hispanic affairs Nat. Conf. Catholic Bishops; Treas., com. capitalism and Christianity 1982-87, com. pro-life activities, mem. adminstrv. bd. U.S. Catholic Conf.; mem. exec. bd. Catholic Near East Relief., adv. bd. Fellowship Cath. Scholars Commn.; bd. govs. Cath. Ch. Extension Soc. Decorated knight comdr. Knights Holy Sepulchre. Home: Atlanta Ga. Died Oct. 15, 1987, buried Arlington Cemetery, Washington.

DONNELLEY, DIXON, government official, public affairs consultant; b. Forest Hills, N.Y., July 29, 1915; s. Patrick John and Katherine Marie (Dixon) D.; m. Lucia Tarquinio de Sousa, Mar. 27, 1943; 1 dau., Leigh Patricia. Student, Columbia U., 1934-37. Jr. reporter N.Y. Daily News, 1936-37; city editor Havana (Cuba) Post, 1937-40; asst. city editor Washington Daily News, 1941-42; news editor Office Coordinator Inter-Am. Affairs, 1942; press attache Am. embassy Mexico City, 1946-47; asst. pub. affairs officer Am. embassy Santiago, Chile, 1947-48; press attache Am. embassy Buenos Aires, Argentina, 1948-50; information officer Am. republics area State Dept., 1950; editor, pub. Vision News mag., Rio de Janeiro, Brazil, 1950-52; editorial dir. com. juvenile delinquency U.S. Senate, 1955; public relations dir. Kefauver Presdl. Campaign, 1955-56; cons. information Pres. Com. Scientists and Engrs., 1956-58; spl. asst. to under sec. state, 1958-61; spl. asst. to sec. treasury, Treasury Dept., 1961-66, 69-70; asst. sec. of state for pub. affairs, Dept. State, 1966-69; cons. Inter-Am. Bank, 1972-74, Atlantic Council, 1974-82; del. numerous nat. and internat. confs. Author: Establishing and Operating a Small Newspaper, 1946; also mag. articles. With USAAF, 1942-46. Mem. Fgn. Service Assn., Metropolitan, Nat. Press, Federal City, International, Foreign Service, Overseas Press. Home: Bethesda Md. Died Jan. 6, 1982.

DONNELLY, PERCY JOHN, agriculturist; b. Grafton, N.D., Sept. 26, 1892; s. John and Mary (Desautel) D.; m. Helen Stewart, Oct. 11, 1917; children: Mary Helen, Eugene Dublin, Martha Louise, John S., Johann. Student, N.D. Agrl. Coll., 1908-11. An organizer Grafton Prodn. Credit Assn., 1934, pres., 1939-40, dir., 1938; organizer Nodak Rural Elec. Cooperative Inc., 1937, pres. and dir., 1937-41; organizerzer Minn-Kota Power Coop., 1940, pres. and dir., 1940-46; an organizer N.D. State Rural Electrification Adminstrn. Assn., 1939, pres., 1939-42; organizer N.D. Council for Agrl. Rsch. and Edn., 1946, pres., from 1946; organizer N.D. Farm Bur., 1942, past pres., dir., 1942-48; state dir. for N.D. Nat. Rural Elec. Coop. Assn., 1942-52; dir. Northwestern Bell Tel. Co.; mem. adv. com. on field crops Am. Farm Bur. Mem. N.D. Bd. Higher Edn. Mem. Greater N.D. Assn., C. of C., Elks, Modern Woodman. Home: Grafton N.D. †

DONNER, FREDERICK G., financial executive; b. Three Oaks, Mich., Oct. 4, 1902. AB with honors, U. Mich., 1923. With General Motors Corp., 1926-27, asst. treas., 1934-37, gen. asst. treas., 1937-41, v.p., 1941-56, exec. v.p., chmn. financial policy com., 1956-58, chmn., bd., chief exec. officer, 1958-67, dir., 1942-86, mem. fin. com., 1958-86; chmn. bd. Alfred P. Sloan Found., 1968-86; dir. Communications Satellite Corp. Home: Greenwich Conn. Deceased.

DONOGHUE, JOHN DANIEL, judge; b. Springfield, Mass., May 12, 1909; s. John F. and Margaret Ellen (Curran) D.; m. Rosemary Lynch, Sept. 15, 1936 (dec. 1979); children: John W., Mary Frances (Mrs. John M. Collins), James D., Michael.; m. Faith Williams Durbrow, Apr. 12, 1982. AB, St. Michael's Coll., 1932, MA, 1961, JD (hon.), 1981. Announcer WMAS, Springfield, 1932-34; reporter, editor, critic Springfield Daily News, 1934-44; dir. pub. relations, faculty St. Michael's Coll., Winooski Park, Vt., 1947-66; acting chmn. journalism dept. St. Michael's Coll., 1974-75, adj. prof. journalism, from 1983, now emeritus prof. journalism; asst. to provost Vt. State Colls., 1966-69; editor Vt. Catholic Tribune, 1969-74; asst. judge Superior Ct., Chittenden County, 1975-83; Music critic Burlington Free Press, 1952—. Editor: Assistant Judges, handbook. Sch. dir., South Burlington, 1952-67; chmn. Task Force on Vt. Parochial Schs., 1967-68; charter mem. Vt. Ednl. TV Broadcast Council, 1968-75; Justice of Peace, South Burlington, 1968-75; Asso. trustee St. Michael's Coll. Served with AUS, 1944-46. Decorated Army Commendation medal; named Alumnus of Yr. St. Michael's Coll., 1972, presdl. citation, 1978; Layman of Yr. Vt. Edn. Assn., 1960. Mem. New Eng. Press Assn. (dir.), Am. Coll. Pub. Relations Assn. (past New Eng. dir.), Vt. Sch. Dirs. Assn. (past pres.). Roman Catholic. Club: K.C. Home: South Burlington Vt. Died July, 29, 1986, buried Merrill Cemetery, Winooski, Vt.

DONOVAN, GERALD, lawyer; b. Providence, Aug. 3, 1891; s. Joseph and Margaret Barrett (Fitzgerald) D.; m. Louise Priddie, Oct. 27, 1920; children: Richard, Geraldine (Mrs. Robert Lenehan), William, Daniel Gerald. AB, Brown U., 1912; JD, NYU, 1916. Bar: N.Y. 1916, R.I. 1917. Assoc. Nicoll, Anable, Fuller & Sullivan (name now Sullivan, Donovan, Hanrahan, McGovern & Lane), N.Y.C., 1919-24; atty. N.Y. Soc. Prevention of Cruelty to Children, from 1932. Bd. dirs., past pres. Home for Aged of New Rochelle, N.Y. Maj. F.A., USAR, World War I. Mem. Assn. of Bar of City of N.Y., NYU Law Alumni Assn. (bd. dirs., past pres.), Brown U. Club (bd. dirs.), Down Town Assn., Links, Wykagyl Country Club, Garden City Golf Club, The Dundas Club, Pt. Judith Country Club, Phi Beta Kappa. Roman Catholic. Home: New Rochelle N.Y. †

DONOVAN, JOHN CHAUNCEY, political science educator; b. N.Y.C., Feb. 9, 1920; s. Michael James and Myrtie (Tucker) D.; m. Beatrice Florence Witter, Sept. 9, 1947; children: Carey, Christine, Martha, John. AB, Bates Coll., 1942; MA, Harvard U., 1948, PhD, 1949. Teaching fellow Harvard U., 1946-49; mem. faculty Bates Coll., Lewiston, Maine, 1949-59; prof. govt., chmn. social sci. div. Bates Coll., Lewiston, 1957-59; adminstrv., asst. to U.S. Senator Muskie 1959-62, exec. asst. to sec. labor Wirtz, 1962-65; DeAlva Stanwood Alexander prof. govt. Bowdoin Coll., Brunswick, Maine, 1965-84; chmn. dept. govt. and legal studies 1967-69, 70-84. Author: The Politics of Poverty, 1967, 2d edit., 1973, 3d edit., 1980, The Policy Makers, 1970, The Cold Warriors, 1974, Democracy at the Crossroads, 1978, (with R.E. Morgan and C.). Potholm) American Politics: Directions of Change, Dynamics of Choice, 1979, The 1960's: Politics and Public Policy, 1980, (with Richard E. Morgan And Christian P. Potholm) People, Power and Politics, 1981; contbr. articles to profl. jours. Chmn. New Eng. Regional Manpower Adv. Com., 1965-69, Maine Bd. Arbitration and Conciliation, 1955-56; chmn. Maine Adv. Council on Vocational Edn., 1969-72, Maine Dem. Com., 1957-58; candidate for U.S. Congress, 2d dist. Maine, 1960; overseer Bates Coll.; trustee U. Maine. With USNR, World War II, PTO. Mem. Am. Polit. Sci. Assn., New Eng. Polit. Sci. Assn. (pres. 1983-84), Phi Beta Kappa. Home: Brunswick Maine. Died Oct. 3, 1984; cremated.

DOOLING, MAURICE T., JR., state justice; b. Hollister, Calif., Nov. 13, 1889; s. Maurice T. and Ida M. (Wagner) D.; m. Mary M. Devlin, Apr. 25, 1916; children: Marjorie Dooling Burkett, Alma Dooling Deitweiler. AB, Santa Clara U., 1909; JD, Stanford U., 1913. Bar: Calif. 1913. Pvt. practice San Francisco, from 1913; judge Calif. Superior Ct., San Benito County, 1928-45; justice Dist. Ct. Appeals, San Francisco, 1945-61; assoc. justice Supreme Ct. Calif., from 1961; pres. Conf. Calif. Judges, 1934. Mem. Stanford Law Soc. (pres. 1931-32), Santa Clara Law Soc. (pres. 1952-54), Elks, KC, Commonwealth Club (pres. 1952-54). Democrat. Roman Catholic. Home: Hollister Calif. †

DOOLITTLE, GILLUM HOTCHKISS, lawyer; b. Burton, Ohio, Aug. 14, 1883; s. James Clement and Philena (Townsley) D.; m. Marta E. Habicht, June 8, 1912; children: Marloe J. (Mrs. James Jamieson), Philene (Mrs. Carl Engel), Bruce F. Bar: Ohio 1908. Dir. law City of Akron, 1932-33; ptnr. Buckingham,

Doolittle & Burroughs, from 1934. Mem. Summit County (Ohio) Rep. Exec. Com., 1925-35, Ohio Rep. Fin. Com., 1934. Fellow Ohio Bar Assn. Found.; mem. ABA, Ohio (past mem. exec. com.), Akron (past pres.) bar assns., Am. Judicature Soc., Akron C. of C. (bd. dirs.). Home: Akron Ohio. †

DORATI, ANTAL, composer, conductor; b. Budapest, Hungary, Apr. 9, 1906; came to U.S., 1941, naturalized, 1947; s. Alexander and Margit (Kunwald) D.; m. Klara Korody, 1929 (div.); 1 dau., Antonia; m. Ilse von Alpenheim, 1971. Student composition and piano, Acad. of Music, Budapest, diploma, 1924; student, U. Vienna, Austria, 1923-25; D.Mus., Macalester Coll., 1957; hon. doctorates, George Washington U., 1975, U. Md., 1976. Condr., Budapest Royal Opera House, 1924-28, Dresden State Opera, 1928-29, Munster State Opera, 1929-32, Ballet Russe de Monte Carlo, 1933-37, mus. dir. original, Ballet Russe, 1938-40, Ballet Theatre, 1940-44, mus. dir., Dallas Symphony Orch., 1945-49, Mpls. Symphony Orch., 1949-60, chief condr., BBC Symphony Orch., London, 1962-66, Stockholm Philharmonic, 1966-74, music dir., Washington Nat. Symphony, 1969-77, sr. condr., Royal Philharmonic Orch., London, 1974-78, condr. laureate, Royal Philharmonic Orch., 1978-81, music dir., Detroit Symphony Orch., 1977-81, condr. laureate, 1981-88, condr. laureate, Stockholm Symphony, 1981-88; guest condr. all maj. orchestras, U.S., Europe, Latin Am., Australia; compositions include string quartet, quintet for oboe and strings, divertimento for small orchestra, Am. serenades for string orchestra, cello concerto The Way; cantata The Two Enchantments of Li Tai Pe; lyric scene for baritone and small orchestra Symphony; for large orch. Missa brevis; for mixed choir and percussion instruments Magdalena; ballet Madrigal Suite; chorus and orch. Chamber Music for Soprano and String Orchestra; night music for flute and small orch. Bartok Variations; piano solo The Voices; opera The Chosen; song cycle; ballet arrangements include Harvest Time; recs. for, Mercury Record Co., EMI, Philips, RCA-Victor, London-Decca, 32 Prix Des Disques. Decorated Royal Order of Vasa (Sweden); chevalier Ordre des Arts et Lettres (France); Order Arts and Letters (Austria). Mem. Royal Acad. Music London (hon.). Home: Gerzensee Switzerland. Died Nov. 13, 1988; buried Gerzensee.

DORFMAN, RALPH ISADORE, biochemist; b. Chgo., June 30, 1911; s. Aron and Anna (Schwartzman) D.; m. Adeline Smith, Sept. 5, 1933 (dec. 1964); children: Gerald Allen, Ronald Arthur; m. Margaret Cameron, Feb. 19, 1965. BS in Chemistry, U. Ill., 1932; PhD in Physiol. Chemistry, U. Chgo., 1934. Research fellow in physiol. chemistry U. Chgo., 1932-33, research asst., 1933-35; instr. pharmacology La. State U., 1935-36; instr. physiol. chemistry Yale U., New Haven, Conn., 1936-39, asst. prof., 1939-41; asst. prof. biochemistry Western Reserve U., 1941-50, assoc. prof., 1950-51; assoc. dir. labs. Worcester Found. Exptl. Biology, Shrewsbury, Mass., 1951-56, dir. lab., 1956-64; prof. chemistry Clark U., 1955-64; research prof. biochemistry Boston U., 1951-67; dir. Inst. Hormone Biology, 1964-69; sr. v.p. Syntex Research Ctr., Palo Alto, Calif., 1969-72, exec. v.p., 1972, pres., 1973-76; vis. prof. pharmacology Stanford U. Sch. Medicine, 1967-73, cons. prof., 1973-85. Fellow N.Y. Acad. Sci., AAAS, Am. Acad. Arts and Scis., Chilean Med. Assn. (hon.); mem. Am. Chem. Soc., Soc. Exptl. Biology and Medicine, Am. Assn. Cancer Research, Am. Soc. Biol. Chemists, Nat. Acad. Sci., Endocrine Soc. (council), Pan Am. Med. Assn., Danish Soc. Endocrinology, Mex. Endocrine Soc., Nat. Acad. Medicine Mex., Peruvian Endocrine Soc. (hon.), Argentinian Soc. Endocrinology and Nutrition (hon.), Statis. Soc., Royal Soc. Medicine (affiliate), Portuguses Endocrinology Soc. (hon.), Soc. Francaise Endocrinologie, Internat. Soc. for Research in Biology of Reproduction, Sigma Chi, Phi Lambda Epsilon. Home: Los Altos Hills Calif. Died Nov. 18, 1985; buried Mt. Mayriv Cemetery, Chgo.

DORN, FRANCIS EDWIN, former congressman, lawyer; b. Bklyn., Apr. 18, 1911; s. Jacob Joseph and Adelaide (Leman) D.; m. Dorothy McGann, Feb. 28, 1944; children: Thomas More, Therese Adelaide, Karen-Patricia Emily, Steven Joseph, Vincent George. AB, Fordham U., 1932, LLB, 1935; postgrad., NYU, 1936. Bar: N.Y. 1936. Pvt. practice N.Y.C., 1936-40; mem. N.Y. State Assembly, Albany, 1940-42; asst. atty. gen. N.Y. State, Albany, 1946-50; ptnr. Dorn & Smith, N.Y.C, from 1950; mem. 83d-86th U.S. Congresses, 12 congl. dist. N.Y., Washington. Lt. comdr. USNR, 1942-46. Mem. ABA, Bklyn. Bar Assn., Cath. Lawyers Guild, Disabled War Vets., Park Slope Cath. War Vets. (past. comdr.), VFW, Am. Legion, St. Vincent DePaul Soc. (pres. St. Augustine conf.), Eagles, Elks, Moose, KC. Home: Brooklyn N.Y. Died Sept. 17, 1987.

DORR, JOHN A., JR., geologist, educator; b. Grosse Pointe Park, Mich., Oct. 25, 1922; s. John A. and Velma (Read) D.; m. Ruth Muriel Pritchett, Nov. 4, 1943; children: John A. III, James, Robin. BS, U. Mich., 1947, MS, 1949, PhD, 1951. Curator vertebrate paleontology Carnegie Mus., Pitts., 1951-52; prof. U. Mich., Ann Arbor, 1952-86, chmn. geology dept., 1966-71; research assoc. Mus. Paleontology, 1952-86; dir. Geol. Expdns., 1965-78, Rocky Mountain Field Sta., 1978-86. Author: (with Donald F. Eschman) Geology of Michigan, 1970; contbr. articles to profl. jours. Fellow Geol. Soc. Am.; mem. Soc. Vertebrate Paleontology (past pres.), Paleontol. Soc. Mich., Sigma Chi, Phi Kappa Phi. Home: Ann Arbor Mich. Died Apr. 6, 1986; buried Washtenong Meml. Gardens, Ann Arbor.

DORSEY, RAY, public relations executive; b. Phila., July 29, 1913; s. Rudolph Raymond and Marjorie (Conner) D.; m. Bettie Arnette Brunn, Oct. 27, 1940; 1 son, Noel Michael. B.A., Dartmouth, 1936; M.S. in Journalism, Columbia, 1937. Gen. assignment and beat reporter Cleve. Plain Dealer, 1937-46, city hall reporter, 1946-56, polit. editor, 1956-63, asso. editor, editorial writer, 1964, chief editorial writer, editor editorial page, 1964-71; owner pub. relations bus. from 1971; Mem. 1967 Pulitzer Prize Journalism Jury. Chmn. Oceanside-Carlsbad br. Am. Cancer Soc., 1977-79. Ray Dorsey Endowed Scholarship fund established in his name Cleve. State U. Mem. Am. Soc. Newspaper Editors, Alpha Sigma Phi. Home: Oceanside Calif. Died Sept. 17, 1986; cremated.

DORSEY, THOMAS BROOKSHIER, media and communications executive; b. Keokuk, Iowa, Apr. 30, 1928; s. Frank Blinn and Johanna (Brookshier) D.; m. Helen Danner, June 30, 1951; children: Diana, Frank Blinn. Student, DePauw U., 1946-47, State U. Iowa, 1947-50. Corr., Des Moines Register, 1949-51; chief European corr. Times Pub. Co., 1954-56; nat. affairs editor Am. Weekend, Washington, 1956-57; editor, gen. mgr. N.Y. Herald Tribune News Service, 1957-59; v.p. Barnet & Reef Assos., Inc., N.Y.C., 1959-63; v.p., dir. internat. div. John Moynahan & Co., N.Y.C., 1963; dir., editor Newsday Spls. (syndicate) Newsday Inc., 1964-69; v.p., editor Chgo. Tribune-N.Y. News Syndicate, Inc., N.Y.C., 1969-74; sales mgr. Knight News Wire, 1972-74; dir., editor Los Angeles Times Syndicate, 1975-77; dir. Los Angeles Times/Washington Post News Service, 1975-77; chmn., chief exec. officer Dorsey Communications, Inc., Diana Prodns., Blinn Books, Los Angeles, 1977-88; writer Times of London Syndicate, N.Am. Syndicate, 1987—; econ. devel. and pub. affairs counsel Govt. Eastern Nigeria, Nigerian Outlook newspaper, 1959-63; assoc. producer Adlai Stevenson Reports (ABC-TV), 1962-63. Served with USAF, 1951-54. Mem. Aviation/Space Writers Assn., Newspaper Comics Council, Internat. Radio and TV Soc., Internat. Platform Assn., Am. Film Inst., Sigma Delta Chi. Clubs: Nat. Press (Washington); Deadline (exec. bd. dir.). Home: Los Angeles Calif. Died Aug. 17, 1988, cremated, buried at sea.

DORSKY, STEPHEN MICHAEL, publishing company executive; b. Bangor, Maine, Nov. 7, 1947; s. Benjamin James and Priscilla (Raynes) D. Student, Rutgers U., 1966-70. Dir. sales Viking Penguin, San Francisco and N.Y.C., 1971-79; v.p. mktg. Holt-Rinehart—CBS, N.Y.C., 1979-83; v.p., dir. mktg. Simon & Schuster, N.Y.C., 1983-85. Mem. Am. Assn. Pubs. Home: New York N.Y. Died Oct. 10, 1985.

DOTT, ROBERT HENRY, SR., geologist; b. Sioux City, Iowa, Jan. 8, 1896; s. Richard M. and Delia (Rood) D.; m. Esther Reed (dec.); children: Esther, Robert H. Jr. BS, U. Mich., 1917, AM, 1920. Geologist Empire Gas and Fuel Co., 1917-19, Standard Oil Co. N.J., 1920-22, Carter Oil Co., 1922-26, Mid-Continent Petroleum Corp., 1926-29, Sunray Oil Co., 1929-31; cons. geologist 1931-35; dir. Okla. Geol. Survey, Norman, 1935-52; exec. dir. Am. Assn. Petroleum Geologists, 1952-63, editorial cons., from 1963. Contbr. articles to profl. jours. Served USAAF, 1918. Mem. Geol. Soc. Am., Am. Assn. Petroleum Geologists (hon.), Sigma Xi. Home: Tulsa Okla. Died Feb. 2, 1988; inurned; Rose Hill Cemetery, Tulsa.

DOTTER, CHARLES THEODORE, radiologist, educator; b. Boston, June 14, 1920; s. John Maury and Rosalind (Allin) D.; m. Pamela Beattie, Sept. 30, 1944; children: Barbara Allin, Jeffrey Churchill, Jane Huntington. AB, Duke U., 1941; MD, Cornell U., 1944. Diplomate Am. Bd. Radiology. Instr. medicine Cornell U. Med. Coll., N.Y.C., 1948-52, instr. radiology, 1948-51, asst. prof. radiology, 1951-52; mem. faculty, then prof. radiology, chmn. dept. Oreg. Health Scis. U., Portland, 1952-85. Author: (with Israel Steinberg) Angiocardiography; contbr. over 300 articles to periodicals. Served lt. (j.g.) USNR, 1944-45, surgeon USMC, 1945-46, CBI. Fellow Am. Coll. Angiology, Am. Coll. Radiology; mem. Am. Heart Assn., AMA, Am. Roentgen Ray Soc., Assn. Univ. Radiologists, Czechoslovak Med. Soc. (hon.), Internat. Cardiovascular Soc., Internat. Soc. Angiology, Multnomah County Med. Soc., Oreg. Heart Assn., Oreg. Radiol. Soc., Oreg. Med. Soc., Oreg. Thoracic Soc., Pacific NW Radiol. Soc., Radiol. Soc. N.Am., Soc. Chairmen Acad. Radiology Depts., Soc. Cardiovascular Radiology, Western Angiography Soc., Am. Alpine Club, Mazmas Club. Home: Portland Oreg. Died Feb. 15, 1985; interred Portland, Oreg.

DOUDNA, QUINCY VON OGDEN, university president; b. Poynette, Wis., Jan. 16, 1907; s. Frank I. and Lenore (Emery) D.; m. Winifred Zimmerman, Mar. 22, 1930; children: Lonnie Bruce, Gary Kent. BA, Carroll Coll., 1927; MA, U. Wis., 1930, PhD, 1948; LLD (hon.), Carroll Coll., 1960, Ea. Ill. U., 1985. Sci. tchr. Antigo (Wis.) High Sch., 1927-34; supervising prin. Lone Rock (Wis.) High Sch., 1934-37; prin. Richland (Wis.) County Normal Sch., 1937-40, Door Kewanee Rural Normal Sch., Algoma, Wis., 1940-45; dir. rural edn. Wis. State Coll., Stevens Point, 1945-47, dean adminstrn., 1947-56; pres. Ea. Ill. U., Charleston, 1956-71. Contbr. articles to profl. jours. Mem. Rotary Club, Phi Delta Kappa, Kappa Delta Phi, Alpha Phi Omega, Phi Mu Alpha, Phi Theta Pi. Methodist. Home: Charleston Ill. Died Apr. 21, 1987; buried Charleston, Ill.

DOUGHERTY, DAVID MITCHELL, educator; b. Wilmington, Del., Aug. 6, 1903; s. George Myers and Jennie (Mitchell) D.; m. Edna M. Rettew, June 22, 1927 (dec. 1963); children: David M. Jr., Philip R.; m. Jean Bruere Jones, May 15, 1964. AB, U. Del., 1925; AM, Harvard U., 1927, PhD, 1932; student, U. Paris, 1923-24, 29. Tchr. Manlius (N.Y.) Sch., 1926-28; instr. French, MIT, 1929-30; instr. and tutor romance langs. Harvard U., 1929-31; asst. prof., assoc. prof., prof. romance langs. Clark U., 1931-46, chmn. dept., 1942-46; dir. A.S.T.P. unit, 1943-44, chmn. Acad. Council, 1943-45; dir. U. Del. Jr. Plan, Paris, 1939, Geneva, 1946-47; prof. romance langs. U. Oreg., 1947-72, head dept. fgn. langs., 1947-64; dir. NDEA summer inst., Tours, France, 1961-68, exec. officer modern and classical langs. div., 1964-67, head dept. romance langs., 1967-69. Author: (with R. Picard and L. Wawrzyniak) Year Abroad, 1953, (with D. Hernried) Perspectives de la Littérature Française, 1961; editor: (with E.B. Barnes) La Geste de Monglane, 1966, Le Galien de Chèltenham, 1981; contbr. articles to ednl. jours., book revs. Trustee Episcopal Diocese of Oreg., 1973-76, v.p., 1974-76. Decorated Chevalier Legion of Honor, Medal of City of Tours France. Mem. Modern Lang. Assn., Am., Medieval Acad. Am., Am. Assn. Tchrs. Spanish, Philol. Assn. Pacific Coast (pres. 1961-62), Socieété Rencesvals, Theta Chi. Episcopalian. Home: Eugene Oreg. Died Mar. 3, 1985.

DOUGHERTY, GREGG, educator; b. Steubenville, Ohio, Nov. 14, 1892; s. William A. and Sallie (Gregg) D.; m. Grace E. Bassett, Dec. 18, 1924; children: James, Robert Ely. BS, Princeton, 1917, MS, 1919, PhD, 1921. Charlotte Elizabeth Procter fellow inchemistry Princeton, 1920, mem. faculty, from 1921, prof. chemistry, from 1946; cons. various indsl. orgns. Contbr. articles on organic chemistry to profl. jours. Mem. Am. Chem. Soc., Century Assn. (N.Y.C.), Univ. Cottage Club, Pretty Brook Tennis Club, Old Lyme (Conn.) Beach Club, Old Lyme Country Club, Phi Beta Kappa, Sigma Xi. Home: Princeton N.J. †

DOUGHERTY, PHILIP HUGH, journalist, radio reporter; b. N.Y.C., Dec. 21, 1923; s. Philip Hugh and Helen Flavia (O'Callaghan) D.; m. Dorothy Patt Tuomey, Jan. 15, 1953; children—Paul John, Peter Dyer, Margaret Dru. Student, Columbia U. Sch. Gen. Studies, 1947-51. With N.Y. Times, N.Y.C., 1942—; soc. reporter N.Y. Times, 1950-63, gen. assignment reporter, 1963-66, advt. news columnist, from 1966; reporter WQXR, N.Y.C., from 1981. Served with Mil. Police U.S. Army, 1943-46. Roman Catholic. Home: Forest Hills N.Y. Died Sept. 27, 1988.

DOUGHERTY, RICHARD, journalist, author; b. Bolivar, N.Y., Aug. 7, 1921; s. John Peter and Elizabeth (Crelly) D.; m. Cynthia Abbott, Apr. 23, 1966; 1 dau. by previous marriage, Lisa. A.B., Columbia U., 1948. Reporter N.Y. Herald Tribune, 1948-51; press officer N.Y.C. Govt., 1951-56; corp. pub. relations counsel 1956-60; nat. polit. writer Washington Bur., N.Y. Herald Tribune, 1964-66; N.Y. bur. chief Los Angeles Times, 1966-72; press sec. McGovern Presdl. Campaign, 1972; v.p. pub. affairs Met. Mus. Art, 1974-84. Author: novels A Summer World, 1960, Duggan, 1962, The Commissioner, 1962, We Dance and Sing, 1971; nonfiction Goodbye, Mr. Christian: A Personal Account of McGovern's Rise and Fall, 1973; play Fair Game for Lovers, 1964. Served with USAAF, 1942-45. Democrat. Club: Century Assn. (N.Y.C.). Home: Quogue N.Y. Died Dec. 30, 1986, buried Quogue.

DOUGLAS, DONALD WILLS, JR., business executive; b. Washington, July 3, 1917; s. Donald Wills and Charlotte Marguerita (Ogg) D.; m. Molly McIntosh, May 1, 1939 (deceased); children: Victoria, Holly; m. Jean Ashton, Aug. 17, 1950 (deceased); m. Linda Alstead, Nov. 29, 1986. Student, Stanford U., 1934-38. Engr. Douglas Aircraft Co., Inc., Santa Monica, Calif., 1939-43; chief flight test group Douglas Aircraft Co., Inc., 1943-51, dir. contract adminstrn., 1948, in charge research labs. Santa Monica div., 1949, v.p. mil. sales, 1951-57, pres., 1957-67; pres. Douglas Aircraft Co. div. McDonnell Douglas Corp. (merger Douglas Aircraft Co., Inc. and McDonnell Co.), 1967-68, v.p. and sr. v.p. adminstrn. parent co., 1967-71, also mem. exec. com., 1969-71; now dir.; chmn., pres. Douglas Aircraft Co., Can., Ltd., 1968-71; pres. Douglas Devel. Co., 1972-74; chmn. Capistrano Nat. Bank, from 1975, Biphase Energy Systems, Inc. (subs. Research-Cottrell, Inc.), 1977-80, Biphase Energy Systems, Inc. (joint venture Research-Cottrell and Transam. Delaval), 1980-81; chmn., chief exec. officer Douglas-Culbert-Orange-Riverside County Partners (DCOR Partners, Inc.), 1979-80, Douglas Energy, from 1982, Douglas-Thomas Cons., from 1987; sr. cons. mktg. devel. Biphase Energy Systems subs. Transam. Delaval, Inc., 1982-86; chmn. bd. Vuebotics Corp., 1982-86; chmn. bd., dir. Aerotech

Cons., Inc., from 1982; pres. Douglas Energy Co., from 1981; bus. cons., from 1974; dir. Hilton Hotels Corp., from 1966, Partners Real Estate, Inc., from 1978. Bd. dirs. Naval Aviation Mus. Assocs., Inc.; chmn. adv. com. Gt. Western council Boy Scouts Am., from 1980; chmn. Donald Douglas Mus. and Library, from 1975; trustee Air Force Mus. Assocs. Decorated chevalier Legion of Honor France; officiale Order Merit Republic of Itlay). Asso. fellow AIAA; mem. Aerospace Industries Assn. (bd. chmn. 1964), Nat. Def. Transp. Assn. (nat. v.p. 1958-63), Air Force Assn., Assn. U.S. Army, Navy League U.S. (life), Phi Gamma Delta. Home: Pacific Palisades Calif. Deceased.

DOUGLAS, GILBERT FRANKLIN, obstetrician, gynecologist; b. Pushmatah, Ala., Jan. 13, 1888; s. George Washington and Sarah Belinda (Grace) D.; m. Mary Rachael Griffin, June 26, 1912; children: Mary Elizabeth, Gilbert Franklin, Sarah Frances, George Capers, Lillian Miriam, William Wesley. Grad., Meridian Coll.; MD, U. Ala., 1910. Diplomate Am. Bd. Obstetrics and Gynecology. Asst. physician East Miss. Insane Hosp., Meridian, 1911-16; with postgrad. tng. N.Y. Polyclin. Med. Sch. and Hosp., 1914, 17, Harvard U. Grad. Sch. Medicine, 1916, N.Y. Lying-In Hosp., 1917, U. Paris, 1919; mem. staff South Highlands Infirmary, Birmingham Bapt. Hosps., Univ. Hosp., Carraway Meth. Hosp., East End Meml. Hosp., Birmingham; assoc. prof. clin. gynecology Med. Coll. Ala. Contbr. articles to profl. jours. Served capt. M.C., U.S. Army, 1917-19. Fellow Internat. Coll. Surgeons, ACS, Southeastern Surg. Congress, Am. Soc. Study Sterility, Internat. Fertility Assn., Am. Coll. Ob-Gyn; mem. AMA, So. Med. Assn., Med. Assn. Ala., Jefferson County Med. Assn., Temple Academia, Cen. Assn. Ob-Gyn, Ala. Assn. Ob-Gyn, Birmingham Ob-Gyn Soc., Birmingham Acad. Surgeons, So. Soc. Cancer Cytology, Am. Cancer Soc., Soc. Obstetricians and Gynecologists Dominican Republic. Methodist. Home: Birmingham Ala. Died Jan. 23, 1985.

DOUGLAS, JAMES H., JR., lawyer; b. Cedar Rapids, Iowa, Mar. 11, 1899; s. James Henderson and Inez (Boynton) D.; m. Grace Farwell McGann, Nov. 26, 1927(dec. Feb. 1949); children: James Henderson III, Robert Stuart, John Bruce, David Ogden; m. Elinor Thompson Donaldson, Sept. 2, 1950. AB, Princeton U., 1920; postgrad., Cambridge U.; LLB, Harvard U., 1924; LLD, Princeton U., 1960, Grinnell Coll., Lake Forest (Ill.) Coll. Bar: Ill. 1925, D.C. 1945. Pvt. practice Chgo.; assoc. Winston, Strawn & Shaw, until 1929; with Field, Gore & Co. investment bankers, 1929-32; fiscal asst. sec. tresury 1932-33; under sec. Dept. Air Force, Washington, 1953-57, sec. of air force, 1957-59, dep. sec. def., 1959-61; ptnr., then counsul Gardner, Carton, Douglas, Chilgren & Waud, 1934-53, 61-72. Served col. USAAF. Mem. ABA, Ill. Bar Assn., Chgo. Bar Assn. Republican. Presbyn. Home: Lake Forest Ill. Died Feb. 24, 1988.

DOUGLAS, PAUL HOWARD, educator, former U.S. senator; b. Salem, Mass., Mar. 26, 1892; s. James Howard and Annie (Smith) D.; m. Dorothy S. Wolff, 1915 (dec. 1930); children: Helen Douglas Klein, John, Dorothea Douglas John, Paul; m. Emily Taft, 1931; 1 dau., Jean Douglas Bandler. AB, Bowdoin Coll., 1913; AM, Columbia U., 1915, PhD, 1921; postgrad., Harvard U., 1915-16; LLD, MacMurray Coll., Bates Coll., DePaul, St. Ambrose, Lake Forest Coll., William and Mary U., Oberlin Coll., New Sch. for Social Research, Bowdoin Coll., U. Rochester, Knox Coll., Bryant Coll., Bucknell U., Amherst; LittD, Rollins Coll.; LHD, Lincoln Coll., U. So. Ill., U. Ill. Instr. econs. U. Ill., 1916-17; instr., asst. prof. econs. Reed Coll., Portland, Oreg., 1917-18; assoc. prof. econs. U. Wash., 1919-20; asst. prof. indsl. relations U. Chgo., 1920-23, assoc. prof., 1923-25, prof., 1925-48; U.S. senator 1949-66; faculty New Sch. Social Research, N.Y.C., 1966-69; vis. prof. Amherst Coll., 1924-27; Indsl. relations work with Emergency Fleet Corp., 1918-19; acting dir. Swarthmore Unemployment Study, 1930; sec. Pa. Commn. on Unemployment, 1930; econ. adviser N.Y. Commn. on Unemployment, 1930; mem. Ill. Housing Commn. 1931-33, Consumers' Adv. Bd., NRA, 1933-35, Adv. Com. to U.S. Senate and Social Security Bd. on Fed. Social Security System, 1937; chmn. Pres.'s Commn. on Urban Problems, 1967-68. Author: American Apprenticeship and Industrial Education, 1921, (with others) Worker in Modern Economic Society, 1923, Wages and the Family, 1925, (with others) Adam Smith (1776-1926), 1928, Real Wages in the United Stats (1890-1926), 1930, Economy in the National Government, 1952, America in the Market Place, 1966, Standards of Unemployment Insurance, 1933, The Theory of Wages, 1934, Controlling Depressions, 1935, Social Security in the United States, 1936, Ethics in Government, 1952, In Our Time, 1968, In the Fullness of Time, 1972, (with others) Movement of Real Wages, (1926-28), 1930, The Problem of Unemployment, 1931; contbr. to Am. Econ. Rev., Jour. Polit. Economy, Polit. Sci. Quar., others. Del.-at-large Dem. Nat. Convs., 1948, 52, 56, 64, 68; alderman 5th ward Chgo. City Council, 1939-42; chmn. bd. trustees Freedom House, 1967-69. Lt. col. USMC, 1942-46. Decorated Bronze Star; recipient Sidney Hillman award, 1957, John F. Kennedy award Cath. Interracial Council, 1970; Guggenheim fellow, 1931. Fellow Econometric Soc., Am. Acad. Arts and Scis.; mem. Am. Econ. Assn. (pres. 1947), Am. Statis. Assn., Am. Philos. Soc., Federal City, Chgo. Literary, Phi Beta Kappa, Delta Upsilon. Unitarian, Quaker. Home: Washington D.C. Died Sept. 26, 1976.

DOUGLAS, THOMAS CLEMENT, Canadian government official; b. Falkirk, Scotland, Oct. 21, 1904; s. Thomas and Annie (Clement) D.; m. Irma M. Dempsey, Sept. 3, 1930; children: Shirley Jean Douglas Sutherland, Joan Diane Douglas Tulchinsky. BA, Brandon Coll., Manitoba, Can., 1930; MA, McMaster U., Hamilton, Ont., 1933; postgrad., U. Chgo., 1931. Ordained to ministry Baptist Ch., 1930; served in Weyburn, Sask., 1930-35. rep. Constituency of Weyburn to Parliament, 1935-44; mem. Legislative Assembly for Weyburn to 1961; premier of Sask., 1944-61, minister pub. health for Sask., 1944-49, minister coops., 1949-60; elected federal leader New Dem. Party, founding conv., Ottawa, 1961, served until 1971; rep. Nanaimo-Cowichan-The Islands to Canadian Parliament, 1971-79. Died Feb. 24, 1986.

DOUGLASS, HARL ROY, education educator, consultant; b. Richmond, Mo., June 22, 1892; s. Joseph Allen and Gorda Ann (Lester) D.; m. Zanna Mae Mitchell, Aug. 1912; children: Harl Gentry, Dorothy Ann, Zanna Marian. BS, U. Mo., 1915, AM, 1921; PhD, Stanford U., 1927; LHD, U. Maine, 1960. Tchr. math. U. Mo. High Sch., 1913; prof. secondary edn., supt. U. Oreg. High Sch., 1919-23, 24-28; supt. schs. Perry, Mo., 1914-17, Ontario, Oreg., 1917-19; acting assoc. prof. edn. Stanford U., 1923-24; profl. lectr. U. Pa., 1928-29; prof. secondary edn., U. Minn., 1929-38; Kenan prof. edn., dir. div. edn. U. N.C., 1938-40; dir. Coll. Edn. U. Colo., 1940-59. Author: many textbooks in elem. and secondary sch. math., also coll. textbooks on secondary edn.; editor The High School, 1922-28; contbg. editor Jour. Exptl. Edn.; assoc. editor Jr.-Sr. High Sch. Clearing House, Jour. Ednl. Rsch. Mem. staff Am. Youth Commn., 1936. Mem. numerous nat. ednl. orgns., Rotary, Tau Psi Epsilon, Phi Delta Kappa, Kappa Delta Pi. Home: Boulder Colo. †

DOUGLASS, PAUL F., lawyer, former university president; b. Corinth, N.Y., Nov. 7, 1904; s. Rev. George C. and Mabel (Parker) D.; AB, Wesleyan U., 1926, LLD, 1946; AM, U. Cin., 1929, PhD (Taft fellow), 1931; student U. Chgo., 1928, U. Berlin, 1931-33. Reporter Cin. Post, 1926-27, ednl. editor, 1927-28; corr. Chgo. bur. Christian Sci. Monitor, 1928-30; dir. study of cts. of ltd. jurisdiction and Cin. Municipal Ct. for Inst. of Law, Johns Hopkins, in Hamilton County, Ohio, 1930-31; ordained to ministry M.E. Ch., 1933; pastor Meth. Ch., Poultney, Vt., 1933-41; pres. Am. U., Washington, 1941-52; prof. polit. sci. Rollins Coll., also dir. Center for Practical Politics (Falk Found.), 1956-71; dir. Mgmt. Corp. of Americas; gen. counsel Nat. League Postmasters, 1971-78, also Middle Americana, Inc.; adviser to pres. of Republic of Korea and counsel to ministry of fgn. affairs, 1952-55; chmn. nat. adv. com. on recruitment, tng. and placement recreation personnel Nat. Recreation Assn., 1952-58; v.p., chmn. finance com. Am. Recreation Found., 1960-65; mem. Pa. Gov.'s Recreation Council, 1956-58; chmn. Settlement Ho. Study Com., United Community Services, Wash., 1951-53; chmn. Christian Friends of Korea; trustee Nat. Recreation and Park Assn., 1965-75; chmn. task force on leisure Nat. Council of Chs., 1965-67; mem. arbitration panel Fed. Mediation and Conciliation Service. Decorated Haakon VII Cross (Norway), 1948; Order of Ascending Star with Rosette (China), 1948; Order of Taiguk (Korea), 1950. Admitted Vt., N.Y., D.C. bars. Mem. Vt. Ho. Reps., 1937-39, 39-41, Vt. Senate, 1941-43. Mem. numerous profl. assns. and orgns., past officer several. Clubs: National Press, Cosmos (Washington). Author several books, later ones including Six Upon the World, 1954; The Group Workshop Way, 1956; Communication through Reports, 1957; Teaching for Self Education at a Life Goal, 1960; How to be an Active Citizen, 1960; The ABC of Industrial Parks, 1960; Inside Isthmus America, 1971; Black Apostle to Yankeeland, 1972; Planning the Farm Estate, 1979. Editor several books, latest, Recreation in Age of Automation, 1957. Contbr. to Ency. Americana. Home: Granville, N.Y. Died Aug. 7, 1988.

DOUGLASS, RALPH BENJAMIN, corporate executive; b. Alexander City, Ala., May 6, 1891; s. Frazier Michel and Georgia Emma (Barnes) D.; m. Renova Beard, May 20, 1912 (dec. Jan. 1951); children: Dorothy Douglass Kellam, Rebecca Douglass Mapp. Student, Massey Bus. Coll., Birmingham, Ala., 1908. V.p. Ea. Cotton Oil Co., Norfolk, 1920-27; v.p. Smith-Douglass Co., Inc., Norfolk, 1927-50, pres., 1950-57, chmn. bd. dirs., 1957-64; bd. dirs. Seaboard Citizens Nat. Bank. Co-founder Plant Food Inst. N.C. and Va., Raleigh, N.C., bd. dirs., 1938-50, pres., 1945; bd. dirs. Va. Poly. Inst. Ednl. Found., Agrl. Found. N.C. State Coll., Norfolk Found.; bd. dirs., mem. exec. com. Norfolk Gen. Hosp., Norfolk Community Fund; trustee Old Dominion Coll. Ednl. Found.; mem. Norfolk City Planning Commn.; cons. chem. div. War Prodn. Bd., War World II. Mem. Newcomen Soc. N.Am., Navy League U.S., Va. Mfrs. Assn. (div. mem. exec. com.), Princess Anne Country Club (Virginia Beach, Va.), Norfolk Yacht and Country Club, Commonwealth Club (Richmond, Va.). Home: Norfolk Va. †

DOW, ALDEN BALL, architect; b. Midland, Mich., Apr. 10, 1904; s. Herbert Henry and Grace A. (Ball) D.; m. Vada Bennett, Sept. 16, 1931; children: Michael Lloyd, Mary Lloyd, Barbara Alden. Student, U. Mich., 1923-26, DArch (hon.), 1960; BArch, Columbia U., 1931; D Fine Arts (hon.), Hillsdale Coll., 1960, Albion Coll., 1964, Mich. State U., 1966; D Hon. Humanities, Northwood Inst., 1969, Saginaw Valley State Coll., 1969. Registered architect, Ariz., Ohio, Mich, N.Y., N.C., Tex., Fla. Architect, chmn. bd. Alden B. Dow Assocs., Inc., Midland, 1933-83; mem. Mich. Cultural Commn., 1961-63, Mich. Council for Arts, 1963-65; mem. environmental arts com., 1967. Author: Reflections, 1970. Prin. works include 1st Meth. Ch., Nortwood Inst., Midland Ctr. for Arts. (all Midland), Ann Arbor (Mich.) City Hall., Inst. for Social Research and Adminstrv. Office Bldg. at U. Mich,. 1970 Facility at Kalamazoo Valley Community Coll., Phoenix Mus. Addition (Theatre), Greek Orthodox Ch., Birmingham, Mich., Corson Auditorium, Interlocken, Mich., Powers Office Bldg., Ann Arbor, Greenhill Sch., Ann Arbor, Dow Gardens Greenhouse, Midland, Traverse City (Mich.) Holiday Inn. Diplome de Grand Prix for residential architecture in U.S., Paris Internat. Expn., 1937. Fellow AIA (pres. Saginaw Valley chpt. 1948-49); mem. Nat. Council Archtl. Registration, Am. Soc. Architects, Mich. Soc. Architects (past pres., dir.), Mich. Engring. Soc., Guild for Religious Architecture, Archtl. League N.Y., Country, Saginaw, Saginaw Bay Yacht, Theta Delta Chi, Alpha Rho Chi. Home: Midland Mich. Died Aug. 20, 1983; buried Midland.

DOWD, THOMAS NATHAN, lawyer; b. Sioux City, Iowa, Mar. 29, 1917; s. Daniel Thornton and Eva (Willett) D.; m. Mary Catherine Majure, July 18, 1940; children—Margaret Majure, Catherine Eva. A.B., George Washington U., 1939, J.D. with distinction, 1942. Bar: D.C. 1942, Md. 1958. U.S. Supreme Ct.; With FBI, 1939-40; practice in Washington, 1942-86; ptnr. Pierson, Ball & Dowd and predecessor, 1945-77, counsel, 1977-86; dir. Potomac Valley Bank.; operator horse and Angus cattle farm, 1958-86. Served to maj. USMCR, 1942-46. Mem. Am., D.C., FCC bar assns., Phi Beta Kappa, Order of Coif, Phi Eta Sigma, Phi Delta Delta, Pi Kappa Alpha. Clubs: M.F.H, Potomac Hunt. Home: Dickerson Md. Died Nov. 18, 1986.

DOWELL, AUSTIN ALLYN, agricultural economics educator; b. Gaynor City, Mo., Sept. 27, 1891; s. John B. and Annette (Allyn) D.; m. Isabel Dyer, Sept. 6, 1916; children: Hannah, Margaret Dowell Gravatt, Ruth Dowell Myers, Annette. BS, Iowa State Coll., 1915; MS, U. Minn., 1925, PhD, 1932; grad. study, U. Chgo., summer 1932. Instr. animal husbandry Iowa State Coll., 1915-17; prof., chief dept. animal and dairy husbandry U. Alta., Can., 1917-22; livestock extension specialist U. Minn., 1922-27, prof., supt. N.W. Sch. Agr. and Agrl. Exptl. Sta., 1927-37, prof. agrl. econs., 1937-52, dir. resident instrn. and asst. dean Coll. Agr., Forestry and Home Econs., 1952-60, dir., asst. dean, prof. emeritus, from 1960. Author: (with Oscar B. Jesness) The American Farmer and the Export Market, 1934, (with Knute Bjorka) Livestock Marketing, 1941, also numerous expt. sta. bulls. and reports; editor The Northwest Monthly, 1927-37. Mem. Alta. Commn. to Study Livestock Mktg. in Gt. Brit., 1921; conducted spl. study livestock mktg. for Bur. Agrl. Econs. U.S. Dept. Agr., 1933-34, spl. study Europe and Asia of fgn. outlets for farm, products and land tenure problems for U. Minn., 1950; mem. North Cen. Regional livestock mktg. rsch. com., 1939-53, North Cen. Land tenure rsch. com., 1949-53. Fellow AAAS; mem. Am. Farm Econ. Assn., Am. Soc. Farm Mgrs. and Rural Appraisers, Campus Club (Mpls.), Delta Tau Delta, Alpha Zeta, Phi Kappa Phi, Gamma Sigma Delta. Home: Saint Paul Minn. †

DOWNEY, JOHN IRVING, banker; b. N.Y.C., July 8, 1876; s. John Robert and Mary Louise (Fisher) D.; m. sarah F. Read, Jan. 7, 1903 (dec.); 1 dau., Sarah Louise Downey Soutter. PhB, Yale U., 1897. Pvt. practice N.Y.C., 1897-1913; pres. John I. Downey, Inc., 1913-27; v.p., bd. dirs. Bankers Trust Co., 1927-41; v.p., bd. dirs. The Fifth Ave. Bank N.Y. (merger Bank N.Y. and Fifth Ave. Bank), ret. vice chmn., then trustee; trustee Franklin Savs. Bank, N.Y., from 1911; bd. dirs. Met. Life Ins. Co.; bd. dirs., exec. com. N.Y. Telephone Co. Chmn. bldg. trades com. Red Cross Dr., 1918; exec. sec. facilities div. War Industries Bd., 1918; trustee Provident Loan Soc. N.Y., Presbyn. Hosp.; hon. trustee United Hosp. Portchester, N.Y. Mem. N.Y.C. C. of C., Soc. Colonial Wars, SAR, St. Andrew's Soc., Pilgrims, New Eng. Soc., Downtown Assn. Club, Century Assn. Club, Union Club, University Club, Union League Club, Yale Club, Apawamis Club, Manursing Island Club. Presbyterian. Home: New York N.Y. †

DOWNEY, MORTON, company executive; b. Wallingford, Conn., Nov. 14, 1901; s. James Andrew and Elizabeth (Cox) D.; m. Peggy Schulze, Oct. 17, 1950 (dec. May 1964); children: Michael Joseph, Sean Morton, Lorelle Anne, Anthony Patrick, Kevin Peter; m. Ann Van Gerbig, Feb. 5, 1970. Performer radio shows for Coca-Cola Co. 1943-85; pres. Coca-Cola Bottling Co. New Haven Inc., 1949-85; cons. Coca-Cola Co. Composer, writer numerous popular songs including Wabash Moon, That's How I Spell Ireland; vocalist on radio for over two decades; made more than one thousand five hundred recordings from 1916.

Decorated Grand Cross of Merit of Soverign Order of Malta. Mem. Everglades, Madison Square Garden, River, Bath and Tennis. Roman Catholic. Home: Wallingford Conn. Died Oct. 25, 1985; buried Wallingford.

DOWNS, CORNELIA MITCHELL, bacteriology educator; b. Kansas City, Kans., Dec. 20, 1892; d. Henry Mitchell and Lily (Campbell) Downs. AB, U. Kans., 1915, AM, 1920, PhD, 1924; postgrad., U. Chgo., 1920-21. Mem. faculty U. Kans., from 1917, successively instr., asst. prof., assoc. prof., prof. bacteriology, from 1935; vis. investigator Rockefeller Inst., 1939-40; civilian expert bacteriology CWS, Camp Detrick, Md., 1934-45, cons., from 1945. Contbr. sci. articles to profl. jours. Rsch. grantee Office Naval Rsch., 1947-54, USPHS, 1947-51, 52-54, 59-60, Army Chem. Corps, 1949-51, NSF, 1959. Fellow N.Y. Acad. Scis.; mem. Am. Assn. Immunologists, Am. Soc. Pathology and Bacteriology, Soc. Am. Bacteriologists, AAAS, AAUP, Sigma Xi, Delta Delta Delta, Phi Sigma. Republican. Home: Lawrence Kans. †

DOYLE, JAMES EDWARD, judge; b. Oshkosh, Wis., July 6, 1915; s. James Edward and Agnes (McCarthy) C.; m. Ruth Bachhuber, Aug. 10, 1940; children: Mary Eileen, James Edward, Catherine Margaret, Anne Malloy. A.B., U. Wis., 1937, LL.D. hon., 1983; LL.B., Columbia U., 1940. Bar: Wis. 1940. Also U.S. Supreme Ct.; atty. criminal div. Dept. Justice, 1940-41; law clk. to assoc. justice James F. Byrnes, U.S. Supreme Ct., 1941-42; cons. Office War Moblzn. and Reconversion, 1945; asst. to counselor State Dept., 1945-46; asst. U.S. atty., Madison, Wis., 1946-48; ptnr. LaFollette, Sinykin & Doyle, Madison, 1948-65; U.S. judge Western Dist. Wis., 1965-80, sr. judge, 1980-87; lectr. U. Wis. Law Sch., 1951-53, 58; Mem. Jud. Conf. U.S., 1972-75. Bd. editors, Columbia Law Rev., 1938-40. Nat. co-chmn. Americans for Democratic Action, 1953-55; Chmn. Wis. Democratic Party, 1951-53; exec. dir. Nat. Stevenson for Pres. Com., 1960. Served to lt. USNR, 1942-45. Mem. Dane County Bar Assn. (pres. 1962-63). Home: Madison Wis. Died Apr. 1, 1987.

DOYLE, RICHARD EDWARD, classicist, priest, university administrator; b. Bklyn., Dec. 22, 1929; s. Walter Francis and Dorothy Helen (Brassell) D. A.B., Bellarmine Coll., 1953, Ph.L., 1954, M.A., 1955; S.T.B., Woodstock Coll., 1959, S.T.L., 1961; Ph.D., Cornell U., 1965. Joined S.J., 1947; ordained priest Roman Cath. Church, 1960; tchr. Xavier High Sch., N.Y.C., 1954-57; prof. Fordham U., N.Y.C., 1965-87; chmn. classics dept. Fordham U., 1970-77; dean Grad. Sch. Arts and Sci., 1979-85, dean faculty, 1979-85, acad. v.p., 1985-87; prof. Santa Clara U., summer 1967; exec. com. Am. Acad. in Rome, 1974-77. Author: Ate: Its Use and Meaning, 1984. Editor: Traditio; book rev. editor: Classical World; contbr. articles and revs. to publs. in field. Nat. Endowment for Humanities fellow, summer 1970; Fordham faculty fellow, 1974, 78-79. Mem. Am. Philol. Assn., Archaeol. Inst. Am. (exec. com. N.Y. Soc. 1974-79), Classical Assn. of Empire State, N.Y. Classical Club, Phi Beta Kappa, Phi Kappa Phi. Club: Cornell of N.Y. Home: Bronx N.Y. Died Mar. 21, 1987, buried Jesuit Retreat Ho. and Martyrs Shrine, Auriesille, N.Y.

DOZIER, CARROLL THOMAS, bishop; b. Richmond, Va., Aug. 18, 1911; s. Curtis M. and Rose A. (Conaty) D. AB, Holy Cross Coll., 1932, LLD (hon.), 1973; postgrad., N.Am. Coll., Gregorian U., Rome. Ordained priest Roman Cath. Ch., 1937. Curate St. Vincent's Ch., Newport News, Va., 1937-41, St. Joseph's Ch., Petersburg, Va., 1941-45; dir. Soc. Propagandization of the Faith, 1945-54; pastor Christ the King Ch., Norfolk, Va., 1954-71; first bishop of Memphis from 1970, mem. lay apostolate com., from 1972. Author pastoral letters. Named papal chamberlain, 1954, domestic prelate, 1962, proto apostolate, 1967; recipient Bill of Rights award ACLU, 1972, Cath. Human Relations award, Memphis, 1973. Home: Memphis Tenn. Died Dec. 7, 1985; buried Calvary Cemetery, Memphis.

DRAKE, GEORGE LENTON, JR., research chemist; b. Georgiana, Ala., Mar. 16, 1923; s. George Lenton and Katie Lou (Lane) D.; m. Jeanette Woodruff Pickens, Sept. 10, 1949; children: George Lenton III, Curtis Lee. BS in Chemistry, U. Ga., 1944, MS, 1949. Chemist Cities Service Refining Corp., Lake Charles, La., 1944; asst. prof. chemistry U. Ga., 1949; research leader So. Regional Research Lab. Dept. Agr., New Orleans, 1949-84. Author: Flame Resistant Cotton, 1971, Textile Flammability Handbook, 1974; also chpts. in books, articles; patentee in field. Leadership tng. chmn. New Orleans Area council Boy Scouts Am., 1972-84. With AUS, 1944-46. Decorated Bronze Star, Army Commendation medal, Combat Inf. Badge; recipient Distinguished Service award Dept. Agr., 1964, Superior Service award, 1960, 64, 68, 69, 73, Certificate of Merit, 1963, 67, Civil Servant of Year award New Orleans Fed. Bus. Assn., 1962, Silver Beaver award Boy Scouts Am., 1968, Ednl. award, 1974. Mem. Am. Assn. Textile Chemists and Colorists (Olney medal 1976), Am. Chem. Soc. (Herty medal 1969), Fiber Soc., Internat. Brotherhood Magicians, So. Am. Magicians, Zeus Carnival, Pistol, City Park Golf, Sigma Xi. Democrat. Baptist. Home: Metairie La. Died Apr. 20, 1984; buried Garden of Memories, Metairie, La.

DRAKE, JOSEPH FANNING, college president; b. Auburn, Ala., Mar. 25, 1892; s. John Henry and Narcis (Freeman) D.; m. Annie Quick, Sept. 14, 1920; children: Harold Fanning, Miriam Yvonne. AB, Talledega (Ala.) Coll., 1916; AM, Columbia U., 1926; PhD, Cornell U., 1938. Tchr. high sch. Corsicana, Tex., 1916-18; tchr. Avery Normal Inst., Charleston, S.C., 1919-20; prin. high sch. State Tchrs. Coll., Montgomery, Ala., 1920-24, dean jr. coll., 1924-27; pres. Ala. Agrl. and Mech. Coll., Normal, from 1927. Trustee, sec. Talladega Coll.; chmn. Negro div. Tenn. Valley coun. Boy Scouts Am.; pres. Conf. Pres.'s Land-Grant Colls. Cpl. Am. Expeditionary Forces, France, 1918-19. Mem. Am. Tchrs. Assn., Assn. Sch. Administrs., Masons (32 deg.), Alpha Phi Alpha. Home: Normal Ala. †

DRAKE, MAYO, library director, educator; b. Tallahassee, June 9, 1924; s. Josh Steven and Lillia (Harvey) D. B.S. in Pub. Adminstrn., Fla. State U., 1954, M.S.L.S., 1957. Asst. acquisitions librarian Fla. State U., Tallahassee, 1955-56; asst. social sci. reference librarian U. Fla., Gainesville, 1956-57; acting head-librarian J. Hillis Miller Med. Library, Gainesville, 1957-67; prof., head librarian La. State U. Med. Sch., Shreveport, from 1968; cons. in field. Author: Checklist of Periodical Titles, 1967; also articles. Served with U.S. Army, 1940-46, 50-51; PTO, Korea. Mem. Med. Library Assn., La. Library Assn., Fla. Health Sci. Assn., La. Assn. Acad. Health Sci. Library Dirs. Republican. Baptist. Lodges: Shriners, Masons (Shreveport). Home: Shreveport La. Died Dec. 21, 1986.

DRAPER, CHARLES STARK, consulting aeronautical engineer; b. Windsor, Mo., Oct. 2, 1901; s. Charles Arthur and Martha Washington (Stark) D.; m. Ivy Willard, Sept. 7, 1938; children: James, Martha , Michael, John Clayton. Student, U. Mo., 1917-19; AB, U. Stanford, 1922; BS in Elec. Chem. Engring., MIT, 1926, MS in Aero. Engring., 1928, ScD in Physics, 1938; hon. degree, Eidgenossische Technische Hochschule, Zurich, Switzerland, 1967; hon. doctorate, U. Portland, 1970. operated lab. to develop infra-red signaling devices for USN, 1927; research asst. in aero. engring. MIT, 1929-30, research assoc., 1930-35, asst. prof., 1935-38, assoc. prof., 1938-39, prof., 1939-86, head aeros. and astronautics dept., until 1966, Inst. prof., 1966, then prof. emeritus, dir. Charles Stark Draper Lab. (formerly Instrumentation Lab.), pres. lab., 1970-73; Wilbur Wright Meml. lectr. Royal Aero. Soc., May 1955, Wright Brothers lectr., 1966; mem. Sci. Adv. Bd.; cons. USN, also USAF, and comml. orgns. in field of aeros. and control; chmn. bd. govs. Mass. Sci. and Tech. Found. Contbr. articles in field of aero. instruments to tech. jours. Commnd. 2d lt. U.S. Army Air Corps, Tng. Ctr., Brooks Field, Tex., 1926, Tng. Middletown Air Depot, 1931-32, 35, Wright Field, Ohio, 1936, 1st lt. U.S. Army Air Corps Res., 1926-42. Awarded Exceptional Civilian Service award Dept. of Air Force, 1951, Navy Distinguished Pub. Service award, 1956, Airpower award of Mass. Wing. Air Force Assn., Thurlow award Inst. Nav.; Airpower trophy Air Force Assn.; Magellanic medal Am. Philos. Soc., 1959; Godfrey L. Cabot award Aero Club New Eng., 1959; William Proctor prize Sci. Research. Soc. Am., 1959; Exceptional Service award Dept. Air Force, 1960; Potts medal, 1960; Navy Distinguished Pub. Service award Dept. Navy, 1961, Golden Plate award Acad. Achievement, 1961, Mo. Honor award U. Mo., 1962, Louis W. Hill Space Transp. award, 1962, Comdrs. award Ballistic System div. USAF, 1964, Montgomery award Nat. Soc. Aerospace Profls. and Aerospace Mus., 1965, Vincent Bendix award, 1966; Guggenheim medal, 1967; Distinguished Pub. Service medal NASA, 1967, J.B. Laskowitz Gold medal N.Y. Acad. Scis., 1967; Exceptional Civilian Service award USAF, 1968, 69, Sylvanus Albert Reed award; Inst. Aero Scis. Medal for Merit; Naval Ordnance Devel. award for devel. maj. improvements in antiaircraft fire control equipment, N.E. Award for 1947 given by Engring. Socs. of N.E., NASA Pub. Service award, 1969, Apollo Achievement award, 1969, Elmer A. Sperry award, 1970; Distinguished Civilian Service medal Dept. Def., 1970, Founders medal Nat. Acad. Engring., 1970, Charles F. Kettering award PTC Research Inst. George Washington U., 1970, Lovelace award Am. Astron. Soc., 1971, John Scott award Bd. Dirs. City Trusts, City of Phila., 1971. Fellow N.Y. Acad. Scis., Am. phis. Soc., Am. Acad. Arts and Sci., ASME, (Holley medal 1957, Rufus Oldenburger medal 1971), AIAA, AAAS, Am. Astron. Soc., Nat. Acad. Engring., IEEE (Lamme medal award 1973); hon. fellow Canadian Astronautical Soc. (1962 Space Flight award 1963), Inst. Aero. Scis., Brit. Instn. Mech. Engrs., Brit. Interplanetary Soc., Royal Aero. Soc.; mem. German Soc. Guidance and Nav. (hon.), Brit. Inst. Nav. (hon.), Instrument Soc. Am. (hon.), Am. Soc. Engring. Edn., Internat. Acad. Astronautics (pres.), Mass. Soc. Profl. Engrs., Soc. Automotive Engrs., Nat. Inventors Council (chmn.), Nat. Acad. Scis., Am. Ordnance Assn. (Blandy medal 1958, Distinguished Service citation 1971), Am. Inst. Cons. Engrs. (award merit 1972), Sigma Xi, Tau Beta Pi, Sigma Alpha Epsilon. Home: Newton Mass. Died July 25, 1987.

DRAPER, FREDA, opera and concert singer; b. Kansas City, Mo.; d. Frederick and Leila (Burleigh) Faulkner; student Chgo. Mus. Coll.; studied voice Edna Forsythe, Kansas City, Mo.; operatic work Dino Bigalli, Chgo.; scholarship pupil Mary Garden; m. Vernon Gerhardt, 1947. Tour soloist Ballet Russe de Monte Carlo, Chgo. Opera Co., 1937-42; sang world premier Bride of Bagdad, winner Am. Opera Soc.'s 1st award, 1940; vocal faculty Northwestern U., 1941-44; with Chgo. Opera Co., 1937-42; appeared as soloist with leading symphony orchs. U.S., guest nat. radio programs; made seven months tour P.I. as soloist before armed forces, 1945; appeared in concert and opera on 3 continents, 1952-55; coached oratorio with Chas. Baker, N.Y.C.; light opera appearances St. Louis Municipal Opera, Hollywood Prodns., Inc. Recipient Presdl. citation, Medal of Freedom, 1947; Hon. Dau. Mark Twain award for contbn. to Am. music. Hon. mem. Women's C. of C. Kansas City, Sigma Alpha Iota, Beta Sigma Phi (internat. hon.). Home: Independence MO. Deceased.

DRAPER, WALTER ADAMS, street railway official; b. Portsmouth, Ohio, Nov. 20, 1870; s. Francis Asbury and Elizabeth Jane (Adams) D.; m. Elizabeth Denver McRea, June 16, 1897; children: Lucy (Mrs. William Maxwell Fuller), Isabelle, Edgar F. AB, Ohio Wesleyan U., 1893; LHD (hon.), U. Cin., 1956. Reporter Cin. Enquirer, 1893-1902; assoc. editor and pub. The Observer, 1900-01; sec. Cin. Zool. Co., 1902-07; sec. Cin. Traction Co., Ohio Traction Co., Cin. Car Co., 1907-13, v.p., 1913-25; pres. Cin. St. Ry. Co., 1925-48, former chmn.; bd. dirs. Ohio Nat. Life Ins. Co., United States Shoe Corp. Dir. Coun. Social Agys., 1913-14; pres., trustee Herman Schneider Found. Ohio Inst.; pres. The Alfred Bettman Found.; trustee Zool. Soc. of Cin., Christ Hosp.; trustee, pres. Thomas J. Emery Meml. Mem. Cin. C. of C. (pres. 1911-13), Am. Transit Assn. (pres. 1932-33), Literary Club (pres. 1928-29), Sons of Vets., Newcomen Soc. of Eng., Queen City Club, Optimists Club, Commercial Club, Literary Club, Commonwealth Club, Cincinnati Club, Cuvier Press Club, Delta Tau Delta. Republican. Episcopalian. Home: Cincinnati Ohio. †

DRAY, WILLIAM JOHN, religious and social services organization officer; b. London, Eng., Apr. 23, 1891; came to U.S., 1952; s. William Thomas and Elizabeth (Hillsden) D.; m. Florence Jones, July 6, 1920; children: William Herbert, Ruth, Marg (Mrs. J. Ham), Howard. Student pvt. and pub. schs. Commd. officer Salvation Army, Toronto, Ont., Can., 1910; field ops. Salvation Army, Toronto, Ont., 1910-13; mem. staff territorial hdqrs. Salvation Army, Toronto, Ont., Can., 1913, with colonization dept., 1913-40; resident sec. colonization Salvation Army, Montreal, Que., Can., 1927-40, in charge Can. war svcs., 1940-47, pub. rels. sec. to nat. campaign dir., 1945-48, chief sec. for. Can., Nfld., Bermuda, 1948-50, chief sec. for Brit. Ty., 1950-52; head internat. pub. rels. bur., dir. immigration and colonization dept., sec. parliamentary affairs Salvation Army, London, 1952; territorial comdr. So. U.S. Salvation Army, Atlanta, 1952-57; chief of staff internat. hdqrs. Salvation Army, London, from 1957; vice chmn. Salvation Army Trustee Co., London. Decorated Order Brit. Empire. Fellow Royal Empire Soc.; mem. English Speaking Union, Central Rotary Club (London). Home: Beckenham Kent, England. †

DREXLER, ARTHUR JUSTIN, museum director; b. N.Y.C., Mar. 13, 1925; s. Louis Alva and Claire (Tettelbaum) D. Student, Cooper Union Coll., 1942. Designer George Nelson Assos., N.Y.C., 1947-48; archtl. editor Interiors Mag., N.Y.C., 1948-50; curator dept. architecture and design Mus. Modern Art, N.Y.C., 1951-56; dir. Mus. Modern Art, 1956-87; architect and exhibition designer Drexler & Henshell, N.Y.C.; trustee Inst. Architecture and Urban Studies, N.Y.C., chmn. bd. trustees, 1967-74; lectr. various univs. Author: Built in the U.S.A.: Postwar Architecture, 1952, The Architecture of Japan, 1955, Introduction to 20th Century Design from the Collection of the Museum of Modern Art, 1959, Ludwig Mies van der Rohe, 1960, The Drawings of Frank Lloyd Wright, 1962, Architecture of Skidmore, Owings & Merrill 1963-73, 1974, Transformations in Modern Architecture, 1979, The Mies vander Rohe Archive of Mus. Modern Art, 4 vols., 1986; editor: Architecture of the Ecole des Beaux Arts, 1977. Served with C.E. U.S. Army, 1943-45. Recipient Medal for archtl. history Am. Inst. Architects, 1977. Fellow Soc. Arts Religion Contemporary Culture. Home: New York N.Y. Died Jan. 16, 1987, cremated.

DRINKARD, DONALD, textile and floor covering company executive; b. Trenton, Mo., Mar. 29, 1919; s. Harry and Carrie (Kirk) D.; m. Helen C. Polson, Sept. 29, 1939; children: Judith D. Pearsall, Donald Dwight. Student, Kansas City (Mo.) Jr. Coll. With Fitts Dry Goods Co., Kansas City, Mo., 1937-53; v.p., gen. mgr. Fitts Dry Goods Co., 1949-53, William R. Moore, Inc., Memphis, 1953-54; pres. William R. Moore, Inc., 1954-58, pres., chmn. bd., 1958-85; dir. Washington Industries, Inc., Nat. Commerce Bancorp., Nat. Bank Commerce, Memphis, Meth. Hosp. Gen. chmn. Fed. Express St. Jude Classic; dir., past pres. Liberty Bowl Festival; past pres. Nat. Assn. Textile and Apparel Wholesalers, Memphis Cotton Carnival Assn., Memphis Cerebral Palsy Assn.; past chmn. Memphis and Shelby County Auditorium Commn.; mem. chancellor's roundtable U. Tenn. Med. Units; pres.'s council Memphis State U., Southwestern U.; Trustee William R. Moore Sch. Tech., Memphis U. Sch. Served to 1st lt. AUS, 1943-46. Mem. Memphis C. of C. (dir.),

Memphis Country Club, Masons, Shriners. Home: Memphis Tenn. Died Aug. 16, 1986; buried Meml. Pk., Memphis.

DRISCOLL, JOHN LYNN, banker; b. Craig, Nebr., May 3, 1891; s. John and Hannah Matilda (Hill) D.; m. Rachael Louise Kellogg, Spet. 16, 1916; children: John Lynn (dec.), Harriet Lenore. BA, U. Nebr., 1914. With Overland Nat. Bank, Boise, Idaho, 1915-19; asst. to pres. Live Stock Exchange Nat. Bank Chgo. and its successor, Stock Yards Nat. Bank of Chgo., 1919-25; v.p. Boise Live Stock Loan Co. of Chgo., 1919-29, Chgo. Live Stock Loan Co., 1927-29; pres. 1st Security Bank of Boise, 1929-33; elected exec. v.p. and dir. 1st Security Bank Idaho (consolidation of 14 banks), 1933, pres. and dir. nat. assn., 1944-56, chmn. bd. dirs. nat. assn., 1956-68, chmn. exec. com., 1968-69; dir. 1st Security Corp. of Ogden, Utah; pres. Ida. State Sheep Commn., 1925-37; pres. State Predatory Animal Bd., 1928-37; mem. adv. com. Salt Lake City br. RFC, 1932-38; mem. com. Boise br. Regional Agrl. Credit Corp., 1932-38. Pres. bd. trustees Boise Ind. Sch. Dist. No. 1, 1931-38; pres. bd. dirs. Boise Jr. Coll., 1943-50; chmn. Idaho Permanent Bldg. Fund Adv. Council, 1961-64; bd.dirs., pres. Children's Home Soc. Idaho; v.p., dir. St. Luke's Hosp. and Nurses Tng. Sch. Ltd., Boise; mem. exec. coun. Am. Bankers Assn., 1944-47. Mem. Idaho Bankers Assn. (pres. 1951-52), Boise C. of C. (pres.), Arid Club, Hillcrest Country Club, Masons, Phi Kappa Psi. Republican. Home: Boise Idaho. †

DRISCOLL, JUSTIN ALBERT, bishop; b. Bernard, Iowa, Sept. 30, 1920; s. William J. and Agnes (Healey) D. BA, Loras Coll., 1942; postgrad., Cath. U. Am., 1945, PhD, 1952. Ordained priest Roman Cath. Ch., 1945. Tchr. Loras Acad., Dubuque, Iowa, 1945-48; sec. to Archbishop Rohlman, 1948-49, Archbishop Binz, 1952-53; supt. schs. Dubuque, 1953-67; chaplain St. Francis Convent Motherhouse, Dubuque, 1954-67; pres. Loras Coll., 1967-70; bishop Diocese of Fargo, N.D., from 1970; dir. Confraternity Christian Doctrine, Dubuque, 1953-67; moderator Council Women, Dubuque, 1953-67; chmn. U.S. Cath. Sch. Supts. Assn. U.S. Cath. Conf., 1966-67; mem. Iowa N.Central Sch. Com., 1957-67. Author: We Pray for Our Priests, 1965, The Pastor and the School, 1966, With Faith and Vision: Schools of the Archdiocese of Dubuque, 1936-66, 1967; contbr. articles to profl. jours.; mem. adv. bd. Cath. Sch. Jour. Mem. Cath. Bus. Edn. Assn. (bd. drs.), Alumni Assn. Theol. Coll. Cath. U. Am. (1st v.p. from 1965), Nat. Cath. Edn. Assn. (exec. bd.), KC (4th deg.). Home: Fargo N.D. Died Nov. 19, 1984.

DRISCOLL, ROBERT SWANTON, banking, investment company executive; b. N.Y.C., Jan. 12, 1912; s. Clarence Uler and Elizabeth (Pinchbeck) D.; m. Jane Word, Sept. 30, 1936; children—Robert Swanton IV, Steven Word, David Christopher. A.B. with honors, Columbia, 1933. Investment counselor 1934-40; with Research & Mgmt. Council, Inc. (subs. Lord, Abbett & Co.), 1941-47, v.p., 1942, pres., 1944; v.p. Lord, Abbett & Co., 1948, partner, 1949-64, 78-79, mng. partner, 1964-78, 79-80; v.p. Lord Abbett U.S. Govt. Securities Fund, Inc. (formerly Lord, Abbett & Co.), N.Y.C., 1949-61; exec. v.p. Lord Abbett Income Fund, Inc., 1961-64, pres., chief exec. officer, 1964-80, dir., 1949-86; pres., chief exec. officer Lord Abbett Developing Growth Fund, Inc., 1973-80, dir., 1973-87; v.p. Affiliated Fund, Inc., N.Y.C., 1948-61, exec. v.p., 1961-64, pres., chief exec. officer, 1964-77, chmn., 1977-78, chmn., chief exec. officer, 1979-80, dir., 1948-87; pres., chief exec. officer Lord, Abbett Bond-Debenture Fund, Inc., 1971-79, chmn., chief exec. officer, 1979-80; dir., 1971-87; chmn. bd., pres. Am. Utility Shares, Inc. (merged into Lord Abbett U.S. Govt. Securities Fund, Inc., 1985), 1975-78; pres., chief exec. officer Lord Abbett Cash Res. Fund, Inc., 1979-80, dir., 1979-86; bd. drs. Lord Abbott Calif. Tax-Free Income Fund, Inc., 1985-87, Lord Abbott Tax-Free Income Fund, Inc., 1984-86, Lord Abbott Value Appreciation Fund, Inc., 1983-87, Depository Trust Co., 1974-78, Whittaker, Clark & Daniels, Inc.; former mem. SEC rules com. Investment Co. Inst., also former mem. exec. com. and bd. govs. Commr. Washington Irving council Boy Scouts, 1951-61, pres., 1961-64, v.p., 1964-87; trustee Securities Industry Found. for Econ. Edn. Former mem. Nat. Assn. Securities Dealers (long range planning com., com. on consumer affairs, past chmn. arbitration com., past gov.), Securities Industry Assn. (chmn. investment cos. com. 1977-78); mem. N.Y. Soc. Security Analysts, Amateur Fencers League (treas. 1947-52). Clubs: Fencers School (N.Y.C.) (pres. 1949-58, v.p. 1958-87), Broad St. (N.Y.C.); Capitol Hill (Washington); Mount Kisco (N.Y.); Country. Home: Chappaqua N.Y. Died Jan. 13, 1987.

DRIVAS, ROBERT, actor; b. Chgo., Oct. 7; s. James and Harriet (Cunningham Wright) D. Student, U. Chgo. Theatrical appearances include Night Must Fall, 1957, Sweet Bird of Youth, 1957, Tea and Sympathy, 1957, The Lady's Not for Burning, 1957, Death of a Salesman, 1957, Thieves Carnival, 1957, A View From the Bridge, 1957, The First Born, 1958, One More River, 1960, The Wall, 1960, Different, 1961, Mrs. Dally Has a Lover, 1962, Lorenzo, 1963, The Irregular Verb to Love, 1963, Where Has Tommy Flowers Gone, 1971; numerous TV appearances; mem. Yale Repertory theatre, 1971-72. Recipient Theatre World award, 1963. Home: New York N.Y. Died June 29, 1986.

DRIVER, DONALD, author, director; b. Portland, Oreg., Oct. 21, 1922; s. Herbert Leslie and Edna Mae (Luke) D.; m. Doris Margaret Atkinson, Dec. 24, 1953; children: Shan Fleming, Dion Luke. Student, Pomona Coll., 1945-47. Actor-dancer, 1950-57; dir., 1958-88; dir. over 50 popular musicals, 1958-66, Princeton Repertory Co., 1964-65; artistic dir. Shakespeare Festival, Washington, 1963-66; Broadway dir. Marat de Sade, 1967, Mike Downstairs, 1968, Jimmy Shine, 1969, Our Town, 1970; author, dir. Your Own Thing, 1968, Status Quo Vadis, 1971; writer, dir. film The Naked Ape, 1973. Recipient Drama Critics Circle award, Vernon Rice award, Outer Circle Critics award, all for Your Own Thing, 1967-68. Home: New York N.Y. Died July 27, 1988.

DRIVER, L. ROBERT, tax and financial consultant; b. Harrisonburg, Va., Mar. 2, 1886; s. A.B. and Fannie (Curry) D.; m. Therese Johnson, Mar. 4, 1916 (dec. 1954); 1 child, L. Robert. Student, Randolph Macon Coll. Editor, publisher Central Virginian, Louisa, Va., 1912-13, Hanover Progress, Ashland, Va., 1914-16; spl. rep. of Gov. of Va. Hopewell Investigation, 1915-16; with U.S. Treasury Dept., 1916-18; tax and fin. cons. N.Y.C., 1919-33, 43-51; with gen. counsel's office U.S. Treasury Dept., 1933-34; with SEC, 1934-43; rsch. assoc. Senate Minority Policy Com., 1952; tax and fin. cons. Washington, from 1952. Contbr. numerous articles and editorials to nat. mags. and profl. jours. Mem. Acad. Polit. Sci., Nat. Press Club, Kappa Sigma. Presbyterian. Home: Washington D.C. †

DROZAK, FRANK, union executive. Student pubs. schs. Shipyard worker Mobile, Ala.; organizer Port of Mobile, Seafarers Internat. Union; port agt. for union Seafarers Internat. Union, Phila., 1964-88; rep. West Coast Seafarers Internat. Union, San Francisco, v.p., 1965-88; v.p. in charge contracts Seafarers Internat. Union, Camp Springs, Md., 1972-88; pres. maritime trades dept. AFL-CIO and Seafarers Internat. Union N.Am., 1980-88; mem. AFL-CIO Exec. Council; chmn. Gen. Pres. Offshore Com.; dir. Nat. Maritime Council; hon. chmn. Am. Trade Union Council for Histadrut; mem. labor adv. bd. Am. Income Life Ins. Co. Active United Way of Tri-State N.Y.; trustee Human Resources Devel. Inst.; nat. bd. dirs. A. Philip Randolph Inst. Died June 11, 1988.

DRY, JOHN MARION, lawyer; b. Mexico, Mo., Dec. 12, 1907; s. John Wesley and Margaret (Sappington) D.; m. Jean Arrowsmith, Sept. 6, 1935 (dec.); 1 dau., Sarah Bradford; m. Isabelle Heard Bland, Dec. 26, 1948; 1 dau., Marion Marshall. AB, U. Mo., 1929; LLB, Harvard U., 1932. Bar: Mass. 1932. Assoc. Nutter McClennen & Fish, Boston, 1932-41, ptnr., 1941-43; asst. to pres. United-Carr Inc., Boston, 1943-45, sec., 1945-70, v.p., 1946-70, dir., 1951-70; gen. counsel United-Carr Divs. TRW Inc., 1970-73; asst. sec. TRW Inc., 1971-73; dir. Cambridge Trust Co. (Mass.). Chmn. library com. Harvard Law Sch. Fund.; pres. Cambridge Council Chs.; exec. bd. Cambridge council Boy Scouts Am.; bd. dirs. Cambridge Home for Aged; pres. The Avon Home, Cambridge; trustee Cambridge Family and Children's Service; mem. corp. New Eng. Deacones Hosp., Boston, Mt. Auburn Hosp., Cambridge; chmn. Beautify Cambridge Com. Mem. CAmbridge C. of C., Rotary, Cambridge, Harvard Faculty, Beta Theta Pi. Episcopalian. Home: Cambridge Mass. Died Nov. 25, 1985, buried Mt. Auburn Cemetery, Cambridge.

DUBORD, FREDERICK HAROLD, judge; b. Waterville, Maine, Dec. 14, 1891; s. Harry M. and Mary (Poulin) D.; m. Blanche Letourneau, May 14, 1917; children: Richard Joseph, Robert Paul, Elisabeth Anne. Student, Colby Coll., 1910-12; LLB, Boston U., 1922, LLD (hon.), 1960. In clothing and shoe bus. 1913-22, practice law, 1922-55; justice Maine Superior Ct., 1955-56; assoc. justice Maine Supreme Jud. Ct., from 1956. Mem. Waterville Bd. Edn., 1917-26, city coun., 1913, mayor, 1928-33; mem. Dem. Nat. Com., 1932-48. Mem. ABA, Elks, K.C., Lambda Chi Alpha, Phi Delta Phi. Roman Catholic. Home: Waterville Maine. †

DU BOSE, CHARLES, architect; b. Savannah, Ga., Aug. 16, 1908; s. Charles S. and Augusta (Wood) DuB.; m. Ruth Bogaty, Mar. 26, 1937; 1 dau., Pamela Barry (Mrs. Brian A. McIver). B.S. in Architecture, Ga. Inst. Tech., 1929; M. Arch., U. Pa., 1930; diploma, Fontainebleau, France, Sch. Fine Arts, summers 1928, 30. Pvt. practice architecture N.Y.C., 1936-48, Hartford, Conn., from 1958; instr. archtl. design U. Pa., 1931; partner Frank Grad & Sons (architects and engrs.), Newark, 1948-56; pres. F.H. McGraw & Co. of Can., Montreal, Que., 1956-58; chmn. DuBose Assocs., Inc., Architects, Hartford, from 1980; AIA rep. on urban planning commn. Union Internationale des Architectes, del. assembly, Sofia, Bulgaria, 1972, Venice, 1975; rep. at UN.; AIA rep. Federacion Panamerica de Asociaciones de Arquitectos. Prin. works include Constitution Plaza, Hartford, Pratt and Whitney Aircraft, East Hartford, Conn., Founders Plaza, East Hartford, for, Phoenix Mut. Life Ins. Co., IBM Corp, Springfield, Mass., Hartford Nat. Bank & Trust Co, Conn. Bank & Trust Co, Travelers Ins. Co, Aetna Life & Casualty Co, U.S. Post Office, Hartford, U.S. VA, U.S. Navy, Air N.G, Monmouth Park Jockey Club, Oceanport, N.J., U.S. Air Force Bases in, France. Mem. Am. bd. trustees Ecoles d'Art Americaines, Fontainebleau, from 1947, pres., 1947-53, treas., from 1953. Winner internat. competition for design nat. capitol Ecuador, 1946; awards of Merit for design AIA and U.S. Urban Renewal Adminstrn., 1964; honor awards Conn. chpt. AIA and; n. Bldg. Congress. Fellow AIA; mem. Am. Assn. Housing and Redevel. (mem. internat. com.), Sociedad Interamericana de Planificacion, Archtl. League N.Y., NAD, Chi Phi, Tau Sigma Delta. Clubs: Hartford, Hartford Golf. Home: West Hartford Conn. Deceased.

DUDLEY, RAYMOND AUGUR, church executive; b. Guilford, Conn., Feb. 18, 1890; s. Horace Francis and Mary Eliza (Augur) D.; m. Katherine Ellen Clark, June 1, 1918; children: Winston Clark, Constance Mary (Mrs. Donald H. Rumely), Robert Augur, Richard Eldridge. AB, Yale U., 1916, BD, 1919; MA, Kennedy Sch. of Missions, 1937; LLD, Olivet (Mich.) Coll., 1954. Ordained to ministry Congl. Ch., 1919. Appt. missionary Am. Bd. Commrs. for Fgn. Missions, 1919; mem. Am. Madura Missions, South India, 1919-44; assoc. sec. Am. Bd. Commrs. for Fgn. Missions, 1944-46, sec., 1946-57; cons. on staff Inter Ch. Aid and Service to Refugees div. World Coun. Chs., Geneva, Switzerland, 1958—; del. Internat. Missionary Coun., Willingen, Germany, 1952; chmn., v.p. Fgn. Missions div. Nat. Coun. Chs. of Christ, 1952-53. Home: Geneva Switzerland. †

DUFF, FRATIS LEE, air force officer, physician; b. Randlett, Okla., July 7, 1910; s. George E. and Mae E. (McNeill) D.; m. Beryl Hilborne, Sept. 18, 1937 (dec.); children—Dennis E., Randolph L.; m. Bess Kellogg, Oct. 10, 1984. B.S. in Chemistry, U. Okla., 1933, M.D. with honors, 1939; M.P.H., Johns Hopkins, 1950, D.P.H., 1953; grad. various service schs. Diplomate: Am. Bd. Preventive Medicine. Intern Colo. Gen. Hosp., 1939-40; commd. 1st lt., M.C. USAAF, 1940; advanced through grades to brig. gen. USAF, 1963; various assignments U.S., Egypt and Japan, 1940-48; chief profl. services br. (Command Surgeon's Office FEAF), Japan, 1948-49; prof. mil. sci. and tactics Johns Hopkins, 1949-51; chief preventive medicine div. Surgeon's Gen. Office, USAF, 1951-53; comdr. (Gunter br. Sch. Aviation Medicine), 1953-59; dep. surgeon (USAF Europe), Weisbaden, Germany, 1959-62; command surgeon (Air Force Systems Command), Andrews AFB, Md., 1962-63, (Tactical Air Command), Langley AFB, Va., 1964-68; ret.; dir. planning Tex. Dept. Health, 1968-69, dep. commr. for program planning, 1969-73, dep. commr., 1973-75; dir. Tex. Dept. Health Resources, Austin, 1975-77; commr. health Tex. Dept. Health, 1977-80. Author articles. Decorated Legion of Merit with 2 oak leaf clusters; recipient certificate of achievement Surgeon Gen. USAF, 1962. Home: Austin Tex. Deceased.

DUFFIN, JOHN HENRY, electrical and chemical engineering educator; b. Easton, Pa., June 18, 1919; s. George Thomas and Agatha (Rose) D. B.Ch.E., Lehigh U., 1940; Ph.D., U. Calif.-Berkeley, 1959. Research chemist High Explosives Lab., Hercules Powder Co., Kenvil, N.J., 1940-42, Bacchus, Utah, 1942-44; shift supr., tech. adviser Tenn. Eastman Corp., Oak Ridge, 1944-46; research engr. Allied Chem. and Dye Corp., Buffalo, 1946-52; research engring. supr. Allied Chem. and Dye Corp., 1949-52; sr. research engr. Battelle Meml. Inst., Columbus, O., 1952-54; teaching asst U. Calif.-Berkeley, 1954-57, instr., 1957-59; asst. prof. chem. engring., dir. Computer Center San Jose State Coll., 1959-62; assoc. prof. chem. engring. Naval Postgrad. Sch., Monterey, Calif., 1962-66; prof. Naval Postgrad. Sch., 1966-72, prof. elec./chem. engring., 1972-88, chmn. dept. material sci. and chemistry, 1969-72; cons. Naval Air Rework Facility, San Diego, 1972-88. Contbr. articles to sci. jours. Fellow Am. Inst. Chemists; mem. Am. Inst. Chem. Engrs., N.Y. Acad. Scis., Sigma Xi. Home: Carmel Calif. Died Mar. 13, 1988.

DUFFY, EDWARD WILLIAM, manufacturing company executive; b. LaSalle, Ill., Sept. 25, 1919; s. Edward J. and Margaret (Brunick) D.; m. Rosemary G. Dee, June 28, 1941; 1 dau., Jill Anne. Grad., LaSalle-Peru Jr. Coll., 1938; student, Loyola U., Chgo.; also exec. devel. program, Cornell U. Research chemist 1941-45, engaged in sales, mdsg. and sales mgr., 1945-63; v.p. U.S. Gypsum Co., 1963-69, exec. v.p., 1969-71, pres., 1971-81, vice-chmn., 1981-83, chmn., chief exec. officer, 1983-85, dir., 1969-85; bd. dirs. W. W. Grainger Co. Home: Glenview Ill. Died Aug. 22, 1988.

DUGAN, FRANK JOSEPH, educator; b. Clinton, Mo., Sept. 26, 1911; s. Frank C. and Hannah (Cunningham) D.; m. Frances L. Neubeck, Apr. 11, 1943; children: Mary, Christopher, Paul, John. AB, Rockhurst Coll., Kansas City, Mo., 1935; LLB, Georgetown U., 1938. Bar: D.C. 1938. Law clk. Judge Jackson U.S. Ct. Customs and Patent Appeals, 1938-39; atty. Dept. Justice, 1939-43; prof. law Georgetown U., 1946-88; former dean Grad. Sch. Law. Served as capt. with judge Adv. Gen. Dept., AUS, 1943-46. Mem. ABA. Home: Silver Spring Md. Died Jan. 1, 1988.

DUGAN, RICHARD TAYLOR, telephone company executive; b. Newark, Jan. 23, 1919; s. Fred Taylor and Ethel Charity (Burroughs) D.; m. Marion Higgins, Feb. 21, 1942; children: Richard W., William B., Nancy F. AB in Sci., Montclair State Coll, 1940; postgrad., Williams Coll., 1956, Columbia U., 1961. Tchr. sci. and math. high schs., N.J., 1940-42; civil service radio engring. instr. 1942-43; with AT&T, from 1946; v.p. Cin. Bell. Inc., 1973, pres., from 1974, chmn., chief exec. officer, from 1983; bd. dirs. Multimedia Inc., Cin., The Central Bancorp, Union Central Life Ins. Co., Sencorp, West Shell Inc. Bd. dirs. Cin. Children's Hosp., Xavier U., Cin., Cin. United Appeal, Cin. Salvation Army, Nat. Council Alcoholism. With USAAF, 1943-46. Mem. Ohio C. of C. (bd. dirs.), Bankers Club, Queen City Club, Cin. Country Club, Hundred Club, Comml. Club, Recess Club. Home: Cincinnati Ohio. Deceased.

DUGGAN, ANDREW, actor; b. Franklin, Ind., Dec. 28, 1923; s. Edward Dean and Annette (Beach) D.; m. Elizabeth Logue, Sept. 20, 1953; children—Richard, Nancy, Melissa. B.A., Ind. U., 1943. Broadway appearances include Dream Girl, 1946, The Innocents, 1949, Rose Tattoo, 1952, Paint Your Wagon, 1952, Gently Does It, 1953, Anniversary Waltz, 1954, Fragile Fox, 1955, Third Best Sport, 1957; film appearances include Patterns, 1954, Decision at Sundown, 1957, The Bravados, 1958, Merrill's Marauders, 1962, Chapman Report, 1962, Seven Days in May, 1965, The Glory Guys, 1968, In Like Flint, 1969, Incredible Mr. Limpet, 1962, Secret War of Harry Frigg, 1970, Bone, 1972, It's Alive, 1974, The Bears and I, 1974, Skin Game, 1975; TV films include The Last Angry Man, 1974, Two on a Bench, 1972, The Pueblo, 1974, The Missiles of October, 1975, Tail Gunner Joe, 1978, Backstairs at the Whitehouse, 1979, Fire in the Sky, 1979, Overboard, 1979; numerous appearances on TV series, 1950-88. Served with USAAF, 1943-46. Home: Los Angeles Calif. Died May 8, 1988.

DUGGAN, JOHN MICHAEL, college president, educational association executive; b. Bridgeport, Conn., June 8, 1928; s. John Hanley and Mary (Dixon) D.; children: Michael, Christopher, Paul, Timothy, John; m. Joan Holland, 1987. A.B., Coll. of Holy Cross, 1950; M.A., Yale, 1955, Ph.D., 1957, L.H.D. (hon.), L.L.D. (hon.). Instr. Canterbury Sch., New Milford, Conn., 1950-51, U. Bridgeport, 1951-53; asst. dean of freshmen Yale U., 1953-57; dir. guidance services Coll. Entrance Exam. Bd., 1957-60, dir. program devel., 1960-63, v.p., 1963-68; v.p. student affairs prof. psychology Vassar Coll., 1968-75; pres. St. Mary's Coll., Notre Dame, Ind., 1975-85, Washburn U., Topeka, 1988. Clubs: Univ., Yale (N.Y.C.). Died Nov. 30, 1988; buried Stratford, Conn.

DUKE, CHARLES MARTIN, JR., civil engineer; b. Wellsville, N.Y., Oct. 25, 1917; s. Charles Martin and Delia Applebee (Kerr) D.; m. Saga May Immonen, May 24, 1942; 1 dau., Jenny Maria. BS, U. Calif., Berkeley, 1939, MS, 1941. Registered profl. engr., Calif. Instr. civil engring. U. Calif., Berkeley, 1939-45; structural designer Austin Co., Oakland, Calif., 1945-46; testing engr. Pacific Islands Engrs., Guam, 1946-47; mem. faculty UCLA, 1947-88, prof. engring., 1956-88, chmn. dept., 1961-67, assoc. dean Coll. Engring., 1957-67, exec. sec. U. Calif. engring. master plan study, 1964-65, acting dean, 1973-74; Fulbright research prof. Tokyo U., 1956-57; vis. prof. U. Chile, 1966-67. Contbr. articles in field; designer civil engring. works. Mem. ASCE (pres. Los Angeles 1963, Ernest E. Howard award 1973, chmn. tech. council on lifeline earthquake engring., 1974-75), Am. Soc. Engring. Edn. (chmn. Pacific S.W. sect. 1953), Earthquake Engring. Research Inst. (pres. 1970-74), Seismological Soc. Am., Soc. Exploration Geophysicists, Structural Engrs. Assn. Calif. Home: Los Angeles Calif. Died Apr. 26, 1988.

DUKE, PHILLIP R., real estate developer; b. Indpls., May 24, 1935; s. Russell C. and Dorothy E. D.; m. Marcia L. DeWitt, June 15, 1958 (div. Jan. 1980); children—Jon R., Linda E., Christine E., Nancy A.; m. Pamela S. Pearson, Jan. 14, 1984. B.S. in Bus. Adminstrn., Butler U., 1959. C.P.A., Ind. Acct. Berns Constrn Co., Indpls., 1958-61; ptnr. Bettis Woodruff & Duke's Cleaners, Indpls., 1962-66; with C. W. Jackson Cos., Indpls., 1966-72; pres., gen. mgr. C. W. Jackson Cos., until 1972; ptnr. Phillip R. Duke & Assocs., Indpls., 1972-86. Bd. dirs. Indpls. Econ. Devel., Indpls. Conv. and Visitors' Assn., Greater Indpls. Progress Com., Corp. Community Council, Indpls. Symphony Orch., Indpls. Mus. Art, Indpls. Civic Theatre, St. Vincent's Hosp. Found., United Way, Starlight Musicals, Indpls. Entrepreneurship Acad.; trustee Butler U., Indpls. Served with U.S. Army, 1953-55. Mem. Indpls. C. of C. (chmn. bd. dirs.), Ind. State C. of C. (bd. dirs.), Associated Gen. Contractors (bd. dirs.), Delta Tau Delta (pres. Butler U. chpt. 1957-58). Republican. Methodist. Home: Indianapolis Ind. Died July 22, 1986.

DULIN, EDGAR SHELTON, consultant, former manufacturing executive; b. San Diego, Nov. 4, 1892; s. Edgar G. and Jean B. (Garrettson) D.; m. Sueadele Miles, Nov. 10, 1915. Ed., U. Calif., 1912-14. Began with Blankenhorn-Hunter Co., real estate, ins. and investments, 1914, v.p., dir., 1915-19; v.p., dir. Blankenhorn-Hunter-Dulin Co., investment securities (firm name changed to Hunter, Dulin & Co., 1922), 1919-29; v.p., dir. Byron Jackson Co., mfrs. centrifugal pumps and oil well tools, L.A., pres., gen. mgr., 1929-55, chmn., 1954; pres. Byron Jackson div. Borg-Warner Corp., 1955-58, chmn., 1958-60; bus. cons. from 1960; dir. Lockheed Aircraft Corp., DiGiorgio Fruit Co., others. Pres., dir. Bonsall Heights Water Dist. Mem. Calif. Club, L.A. Country Club, Wilshire Country Club, Bohemian Club, Delta Kappa Epsilon. †

DULIN, ROBERT M(UNSON), judge; b. Garden City, Kans.; s. Frank and Fannie May (Carr) D.; m. Marjorie Ada Howe, May 28, 1913; 1 child, Marjorie E. Dulin Walsh. AB, U. Denver, 1910, student law sch., 1927-28; student, Blackstone Inst. of Law, 1927; LLD (hon.), L.A. U. Applied Edn., 1945. With Continental Trust Co., Denver, 1910-11, Interstate Trust Co., 1911-15; treas. Howe-Allen Mercantile Co., 1915-18; dir. purchases Gates Rubber Co., 1919-28; mgr. Pacific coast retail stores Fireston Tire & Rubber Co., L.A., 1929-30; asst. purchasing agt. Goodrich Rubber Co., L.A., 1930-31; treas. Pollok Schultz Boyd, 1931-32; staff atty. Salisbury & Robinson, 1932-35; ptnr. Kibby, Cooper and Dulin, 1935-37; pvt. practice Beverly Hills, Calif., 1937-43; hearing commr. Office Adminstrv. Hearings, Office Price Adminstrn., from 1943, chief hearing commr., from 1944; instr. sch. law Golden Gate Coll., 1944-45; judge Mcpl. Ct., Beverly Hills, from 1962. Author: Collection Letters, 1924, Credit Letters, 1924. Mem. Beverly Hills Bd. Edn., from 1938, sec., from 1942; mem. Calif. State Bd. Edn., 1941, pres. from 1942; Beverly Hills City Council, from 1960. 1st lt. Q.M. U.S. Army, 1916-19. Mem. Colo. Bar Assn., Calif. Bar Assn., L.A. Bar Assn., Beverly Hills Bar Assn. (gov.), Law Forum Beverly Hills (founder, pres.), Am. Legion, Men's Club Beverly Hills, Masons, KP, Gamma Eta Kappa, Phi Delta Theta, Phi Delta Phi. Democrat. Episcopalian. Home: Beverly Hills Calif. †

DULSKI, THADDEUS J., congressman; b. Buffalo, Sept. 27, 1915; married; 5 children. Student, Canisius Coll. and U. Buffalo. With Bur. Internal Revenue, Treasury Dept., 1940-47; entered pvt. practice as acct. and tax cons. 1947; spl. agt. Price Stablzn. Adminstrn., 1951-53. Mem. 86th to 94th Congresses, 37th (formerly 41st) N.Y. Dist. Councilman, Walden Dist., 2 terms; councilman-at-large Buffalo, 4 yrs. Democrat. Home: Buffalo N.Y. Died Oct. 11, 1988.

DUMAS, HAL STEPHENS, telephone company executive; b. Macon, Ga., Sept. 19, 1892; s. William Jefferson and Ida (Anderson) D.; m. Genevieve Burt, Oct. 3, 1914; children: Hal Stephens, Anderson Dumas Wallace. BS, Ala. Poly. Inst., 1911. Traffic mgr. So. Bell Tel. & Tel. Co., Atlanta, 1911-34, asst. v.p., 1934-36, gen. plant mgr., 1936-38, v.p. ops., dir., 1938-43, pres., 1943-51; exec. v.p., dir. Am. Tel. & Tel. Co., 1951-56. With U.S. Army, 1918. Mem. U.S. C. of C., Am. Legion, Capital City Club, Piedmont Driving Club (Atlanta), Peachtree Golf Club, Gulf Stream Golf Club, Sapphire Valley Club, Wildcat Cliffs Golf Club (N.C.), Tau Beta Pi. Episcopalian. Home: Delray Beach Fla. Deceased.

DUMOND, JESSE WILLIAM MONROE, physicist; b. Paris, France, July 11, 1892; (parents Am. citizens); s. Frederick Melville and Louise Adele (Kerr) DuM.; m. 2d, Louise Marie Baillet; children by previous marriage: Adele I. (Mrw. W.K.H. Panofsky), Andree Desiree. BS, Calif. Inst. Tech., 1916, PhD, 1929; MS, Union Coll., 1919. Engr. GE, 1916-18, French Thomson-Houston Co., 1919-20; asst. elec. engr. Bur. of Standards, 1920-21; teaching fellow physics Calif. Inst. Tech., 1921-29, rsch. fellow, 1929-31, rsch. assoc., 1931-38, assoc. prof., 1938-46, prof. physics, from 1946; mem. com. fundamental phys. constants and conversion factors, chmn. sub-com. atomic constants NRC, from 1946. Contbr. articles to tech. publs. With OSRD, World War II. Fellow Am. Phys. Soc.; mem. AAUP, Societe Francaise de Physique (Paris). Home: Pasadena Calif. †

DUNBAR, CARL OWEN, paleontologist; b. Hallowell, Kans., Jan. 1, 1891; s. David and Emma (Thomas) D.; m. Lora Beamer, Sept. 18, 1915; children: Carl Owen, Lora Louise. Grad., Cherokee County (Kans.) High Sch., 1909; BA, U. Kans., 1913; PhD, Yale, 1917. Instr. geology U. Minn., 1918-20; asst. prof. hist. geology Yale, 1920-27, assoc. prof., 1927-30, prof. paleontology and stratigraphy, from 1930; asst. curator invertebrate peleontology Peabody Mus. Nat. History, 1920-26, curator, from 1926, dir., 1942-59, emeritus, from 1959; vis. prof. U. Kans., 1962-63. Author: Brachiopoda of the Penna. System in Nebraska, 1932; (with John W. Skinner) Permian Fusulindae of Texas, 1937; (with L. G. Heubest) Pennsylvania Fusulipsidae of Illinois, Historical Geology, 1960; (with John Rodgers) Principles of Stratigraphy, 1955; assoc. editor Am. Jour. Sci.; contbr. sci. articles to jours. Recipient Hayden medal Phila. Acad. Scis. Mem. NAS, Am. Philos. Soc., Paleontol. Soc., Geol. Soc. Am., AAAS, Soc. Econ. Paleontologists and Mineralogists, Am. Acad. Arts and Scis., Geol. Soc. London, Geol. Soc. Mexico, Skytop Club, Dunedin country Club, Sigma Xi. Home: Dunedin Fla. †

DUNCAN, CLARENCE AVERY, JR., savings and loan association executive; b. LaGrange, Ga., Jan. 28, 1917; s. Clarence Avery and Maude (Borders) D.; m. Lucy Carolyn Watson, Nov. 14, 1981; children: John Davis, David Ray, Lea Ann, Lucy Carroll, Dempse Sneed, Melanie Ann. Student, San Angelo Jr. Col (Tex.), 1935-37, U. Tex., 1937-39. With Farm & Hom Savs. Assn., Nevada, Mo., 1945-87, v.p., 1950-56, pres dir., 1956-84, chmn. bd., 1968-86. Mem. U.S. Savs. an Loan League (pres. 1966). Episcopalian. Clu Rotarian. Home: Dallas Tex. Died Dec. 21, 198 buried Sparkman Hillcrest Cemetery, Dallas.

DUNCAN, DONALD, educator; b. Marietta, Minn Jan. 31, 1903; s. Henry and Clara (Olson) D.; m. Ma garet Aileen Eberts, Sept. 18, 1924; children—Mary J anne (Mrs. Ronald Arthur Welsh), Margaret Carolir (Mrs. Nester Paul Arceneaux), Kathleen Elizabeth (Mr William Moten Edwards). B.A., Carleton Coll Northfield, Minn., 1923; M.A., U. Minn., 1927, Ph.D 1929. Asst. prof. anatomy U. Utah, 1929-30; asst. pro anatomy U. Buffalo, 1930-32, prof., head dept., 1942-4 prof. La. State U., 1943-46; asso. prof. anatomy U. Te Med. Br., 1932-42, prof., chmn. dept., 1946-68, Ashb Smith prof. anatomy, 1968-87, asso. dean grad. studie 1952-69; vis. prof. anatomy Stanford, 1975, 76, 7 Mem. adv. com. med. student research NIH, 1961-6 anat. tng., 1960-65; chmn. expert adv. panel chiropract and naturopathy USPHS, 1968. Editor: Am. Jou Anatomy, 1960-68; Contbr. articles profl. jours. Recipient Henry Gray award for distinguished service i anatomy, 1971. Mem. Tex. Acad. Sci. (pres. 1962), Ar Assn. Anatomy (pres. 1967), Phi Beta Kappa, Sigma X Nu Sigma Nu, Alpha Omega Alpha. Episcopalian. Home: Austin Tex. Died Feb. 17, 1987; burie Litchfield, Minn.

DUNCAN, JOHN JAMES, congressman; b. Sco County, Tenn., Mar. 24, 1919; married; 4 chi dren. Asst. state atty. gen. 1947-56; dir. law Knoxvill Tenn., 1956-59; mayor 1959-64; mem. 89th to 100 Congresses, 2d Dist. Tenn., 1965-88; mem. Ways an Means com. Pres. Knoxville Profl. Baseball Club, 195 59; past pres. So. Baseball League. Served with AU 1942-45. Mem. Am., Tenn., Knoxville bar assns., Ar Legion (comdr. Tenn. 1954), VFW. Republica Presbyterian. Home: Knoxville Tenn. Died June 2 1988.

DUNCAN, ROBERT EDWARD, poet; b. Oaklan Calif., Jan. 7, 1919; s. Edward Howard and Margueri (Wesley) D. Student, U. Calif., Berkeley, 1936-38, 4 50. Editor Exptl. Rev., 1938-40, Phoenix, Berkel Miscellany, 1948-49; tchr. Black Mountain Coll., N.C 1956. Author: Selected Poems, 1959, The Opening the Field, 1960, Roots and Branches, 1964, Wine, 196 Uprising, 1965, A Book of Resemblances, Poems, 195 53, Of the War: Passages 22-27, 1966, The Years a Catches, First Poems 1939-46, 1966, Fragments of Disordered Devotion, 1966, Bending the Bow, 1967, Th Cat and the Blackbird, 1967, Epilogos, 1967, Christma Present, Christmas Presence!, 1967, Selected Poem 1940-50, 1968, My Mother Would be a Falconess, 196 Names of People, 1968, Derivations, Selected Poem 1950-56, 1968, Play Time, Pseudo Stein, 1969, Achille Song, 1969, Tribunals, Passages 31-35, 1970, Poet Disturbances, 1970, Bring It Up from the Dark, 197 In Memorian Wallace Stevens, 1972, Dante, 1974, A Ode and Arcadia, 1974, The Venice Poem, 1975, Peipir Municipality and the Diplomatic Order, 1980, Th Noise: Notes from a Rock 'n' Roll Era, 1984, Groun Work: Before the War, 1984, Faust Fontu, 1985, Ficti Certainties, 1985, Ground Work : In The Dark, 198 Only The Good Die Young, 1985. Recipient Civic an Arts Found. prize Union League, 1957; Harriet Monrc Meml. prize Poetry mag., 1961; Lovinson prize, 196 grantee Nat. Endowment Arts, 1966-67; Guggenhei fellow, 1963. Home: San Francisco Calif. Died Feb. 1988.

DUNCAN, WILFRID EBEN PINKERTON, trans engineer; b. Glasgow, Scotland, Mar. 2, 1891; Ebenezer and Isabella (Pinkerton) D.; m. Beatric Panton, July 24, 1919; children: Kenneth, Ia Malcolm. Student, Glasgow Acad.; BSc, Glasgow U 1913. Engr. constrn. dept. C.P. Ry., 1910-14; eng gen. contractor 1919-21; engr. structures Toron Transit Commn., 1921-38, gen. supt., chief engr., op mgr., 1938-52, gen. mgr., 1952-59, gen. mgr. subwa constrn., 1959-61, cons., from 1961. Maj. Royal Engrs 1915-19, Royal Can. Engrs., 1939. Mem. Am. Trans Assn. (past pres.), Can. Transit Assn. (past pres.), On Safety League (v.p.), Assn. Profl. Engrs. Ont., Engrin Inst. Can., Electric Club (past chmn.), National Club Home: Toronto Ont., Canada. †

DUNCOMBE, CHARLES GROSS, engineer, educato b. Gordonsville, Va., Mar. 14, 1889; s. George Herbe and Mertie V. (Gross) D.; m. Mary Dolores Laffert Sept. 3, 1918; children: Mary Lenore, Payette, Charl Albertus. Student, Gettysburg Coll., 1905-0 BChem.Engring., Ohio State U., 1916, MS, 1929, PhI 1931. Profl. engr., Ohio and Mich. With Firestone Ti and Rubber Co., Akron, Ohio, 1916-21; storage batte engr. Prest-O-Lite Co., Indpls., 1921-26; instr. and ass prof. chem. engring. Ohio State U., 1927-36; prof. cher engring. U. Detroit, 1936-63, chmn. dept., 1936-59, di Univ. Rsch. Coun., dir. Rsch. Inst. Sci. and Engring 1957-62; cons. chem. engr., Detroit. Mem. Am. Ins Chem. Engrs., Am. Soc. Engring. Edn., Engring. Soc. Detroit, Sigma Xi, Phi Lambda Upsilon, Phi Del

Theta. Republican. Roman Catholic. Home: Detroit Mich. †

DUNHAM, DOWS, museum curator; b. Irvington, N.Y., June 1, 1890; s. Carroll and Margaret (Dows) D.; m. Marion J. Thompson, 1930; children: Philippa (Mrs. Judson T. Shaplin), Lawrence D., Margaret B. (Mrs. Cornelius Lansing). AB cum laude, Harvard U., 1913; spl. student, Oriental Inst., U. Chgo., 1916. Field asst. Harvard U. Mus. Fine Arts Egyptian Expdn., 1914-27; with Mus. Fine Arts, Boston, from 1915, successively asst., asst. curator, curator Egyptian, curator, 1942-55, curator emeritus, from 1956. Author: Royal Cemeteries of Kush, I, II, III, IV, Second Cataract Forts, Vol. I. Fellow Soc. Antiquaries (London); mem. AIA, Am. Acad. Arts and Scis., Am. Rsch. Ctr. Egypt (treas.). Home: Cambridge Mass. †

DUNIWAY, BENJAMIN CUSHING, U.S. judge; b. Stanford, Calif., Nov. 21, 1907; s. Clyde A. and Caroline M. (Cushing) D.; m. Ruth Mason, Oct. 28, 1933; children—Anne (Mrs. Anne Barker), Carolyn (Mrs. Edward P. Hoffman), John M. B.A., Carleton Coll., 1928, LL.D., 1981; LL.B., Stanford, 1931; B.A. (Rhodes scholar), Oxford U., 1933, M.A., 1964. Bar: Calif. bar 1931. Practice in San Francisco, 1933-42, 47-59; partner firm Cushing, Cullinan, Duniway & Gorrill, 1947-59; regional atty. OPA, San Francisco, 1942-45; regional adminstr. OPA, 1945-47; asst. to adminstr. OPA, Washington, 1945; justice Dist. Ct. Appeals, 1st Appellate Dist. Calif., San Francisco, 1959-61; U.S. circuit judge 9th Circuit Ct. Appeals, 1961-76, sr. judge, from 1976; judge Temp. Emergency Ct. Appeals U.S., from 1979; mem. com. trial practice and techniques Jud. Conf. U.S., 1969-74, mem. com. jud. stats., 1970-76; dir. Schlage Lock Co., 1951-59. Author: (with C.J. Vernier) American Family Laws, Vol. II, 1932. Chmn. Gov.'s Commn. Met. Area Problems, 1958-59; pres. Community Chest San Francisco, 1956-57, Calif. Conf. Social Work, 1950, Family Service Agy. San Francisco, 1950-51, Urban League San Francisco, 1952; Trustee Carleton Coll., 1958-71, Stanford, 1962-72; trustee James D. Phelan Found., 1957-71, pres., 1969-71; trustee Rosenberg Found., 1960-75, pres., 1964, 68-70; bd. dirs. Legal Aid Soc. San Francisco, 1955-70, Family and Children's Agy. San Francisco, 1948-51; life gov. Mill Hill Sch., Eng., from 1933. Recipient Presdl. Cert. of Merit, 1947, Award of Merit Stanford U. Law Sch., 1986. Mem. Am. Bar Assn., Am. Judicature Soc., Am. Law Inst., Conf. Calif. Judges, Bar Assn. San Francisco (treas. 1958, sec. 1959), Soc. Calif. Pioneers, World Affairs Council San Francisco, Order of Coif, Phi Beta Kappa, Delta Sigma Rho. Clubs: Chit Chat (San Francisco), Commercial (San Francisco). Home: Menlo Park Calif. Deceased.

DUNKEL, WILBUR DWIGHT, educator, author; b. Elwood, Ind., Feb. 15, 1901; s. Joel Ambrose and Lulu Dell (Baker) D.; m. Georgia Osborn, Aug. 29, 1925; children—Patricia Ann, Robert Osborn. A.B., Ind. U., 1922; A.M., Harvard, 1923; Ph.D., U. Chgo., 1925. Fellow in English U. Chgo., 1923-25; mem. faculty U. Rochester, 1925-66, prof. English, 1947-66, Roswell S. Burrows prof. English, 1934-66, prof. emeritus, 1966-87, chmn. dept., 1958-60; vis. prof. English U. Hull, Eng., 1955-56. Author: The Dramatic Technique of Thomas Middleton, 1926, Sir Arthur Pinero, 1941, William Lambarde Elizabethan Jurist, 1536-1601, 1965; also newspaper column Literature and Life, 1942-45; Mem. editorial bd.: also newspaper column Theology Today; reviewer: also newspaper column U.S. Quar. Book List; Contbr. edn. and religious jours. Fellow Folger Shakespeare Library, 1960-61. Mem. Modern Lang. Assn., Council Tchrs. English, Coll. English Assn., Am. Assn. U. Profs., Soc. Theatre Research (London), Beta Theta Pi. Republican. Presbyn. Club: Mountain View Country (Greensboro, Vt.). Home: Rochester N.Y. Died June 10, 1987; buried Rochester, N.Y.

DUNKLE, WILLIAM FREDERICK, JR., clergyman; b. McAlester, Okla., May 16, 1911; s. William F. and Nell (Munn) D.; m. Olga Carolyn Watson, June 12, 1936; children: Amelia Ann Dunkle Libby, William F. III, Zillah Beth. AB, U. Fla., 1934; BD, Emory U., 1936; ThM, Union Theol. Sem., 1948; DD(hon.), Am. U., 1951; LLD (hon.), McMurray Coll., 1968. Ordained to ministry Meth. Ch., 1937. Pastor Pinecastle and Conway, Fla., 1936, Fernandina, Fla., 1936-41, Jacksonville, Fla., 1941-44; pastor Barton Heights Ch., Richmond, Va., 1944-48, Grace Meth. Ch., Wilmington, Del., 1948-66; sr. minister Wilmette (Ill.) Trinity Parish Ch., 1966-76, Greenwood (Fla.) Ch., from 1976; prof. polity, vis. lectr. Crozer Theol. Sem., Chester, Pa., 1958-59; vis. prof. liturgical theology Garrett Theol. Sem., Evanston, Ill., 1969-73; chaplain Va. Senate, 1946; exchange minister, London, 1950; rep. Am. Meth. World Meth. Conf., Oxford U., 1951, Oslo, 1961, London, 1966, Dublin, 1976; speaker Chgo. Sunday Evening Club; mem. commn. on worship Gen. Conf. Meth. Ch., 1940-46, sec., 1964-68, v.p., 1968-74; mem. bd. evangelism Fla. Conf. Meth. Ch., 1940-42, Peninsula Conf., 1950, pres. bd. Christian edn., 1960-64, trustee, 1960-66; del. Meth. Gen. Conf., 1964, Northeastern Jurisdictional Conf., 1960, 64; sec. com. Episcopacy, 1964; sec. Nat. Commn. on Worship Meth. Ch., 1964-72; mem. adv. com. Meth. Ch. sch. curriculum. Author: Church Year Values for Evangelical Churches, 1959, The Office of a Methodist Stweard, 1963; editor: Companion to the Methodist Book of Worship, 1970, Splendor of God's Glory, 1978; mem. editorial council Meth. Story; contbr. articles to religious pubs. Del. White Ho. Conf. on Children and Youth, 1950; adv. bd. Del. Youth Services Commn., Del. Commn. on Aging; mem. clergy adv. council Wesley Theol. Sem., Washington; mem.-at-large Nat. council Boy Scouts Am., 1950-60, bd. dirs. Del-Mar-Va.council, 1950-60, N.E. Ill. council, 1970-74; bd. dirs. Goodwill Industries, 1950-60; chmn. Wesley Found., U. Del., Washington Coll., 1956-60; mem. Bd. Ministerial Tng., 1967-75, Meth. Student Ctr. Northwestern U., 1967-70, Meth. Bd. Homes and Services, 1974, Bd. Edn. Ill. Meth. Conf., 1967-70; trustee Meth. Found. Ill., from 1968; Wesley Coll., Drew U., Madison, N.J., Am. U. Recipient Order of Merit Nat. council Boy Scouts Am., 1956, Silver Beaver award, 1962. Mem. Nat. Council Chs., Del. Council Chs. (pres. 1959-60), Wilmington Council Chs. (pres. 1956-58), Hymn Soc. Am., Masons (32 deg., Del. grand chaplain 1955-56), Rotary, Lincoln Club of Del., Univ. Club, Torch Club, Union League Club (Chgo.), Mich. Shores Club, Westmoreland Country Club, Univ. Club of Evanston, Phi Delta Theta. Home: Marianna Fla. Died Nov. 13, 1984.

DUNLAP, GEORGE WESLEY, electrical engineer; b. Gardnerville, Nev., Apr. 13, 1911; s. Fred Sherwin and Rhoda (Early) D.; m. Alice Catherine Lloyd, Mar. 2, 1935 (dec. Nov. 1966); children—Barbara Rae, George Wesley, John Frederick, James Lloyd; m. Maude Harnden Gray, Apr. 20, 1968; stepson, Christopher G. Gray. A.B., Stanford, 1931, E.E., 1933, Ph.D., 1936. Registered profl. engr. With Gen. Electric Co., Schenectady, 1935-76; student engr. Gen. Electric Co., 1935-36; elec. engr. high voltage and impulse sect. Gen. Engring. Lab., 1936-45; asst. div. engr. high voltage and nucleonics div. Gen. Engring. & Cons. Lab., 1945-51, div. engr., 1951-53, mgr. instrument and nuclear radiation engring. services, 1953-55, mgr. engring. physics and analysis lab., 1955-61, sr. engr., 1961-66; cons. engr. Research and Devel. Center, 1966-76; pvt. cons., 1976-86; vis. Webster prof. elec. engring. Mass. Inst. Tech., 1955-56. Contbr. tech. jours. Recipient Harris J. Ryan High Voltage Research fellowship, 1932-35; Alfred Noble prize, 1943. Fellow IEEE (life); mem. Am. Phys. Soc., Am. Nuclear Soc., N.Y. State Soc. Profl. Engrs., Sigma Xi, Tau Beta Pi. Home: Schenectady N.Y. Died Feb. 6, 1986; buried Memory's Garden, Albany, N.Y.

DUNN, DANIEL FRANCIS, state official; b. Natick, Mass., May 26, 1928; s. John M. and Mary (Murphy) D.; m. Isabel Maureen Burns, June 18, 1952; children: Maureen Dunn Harvey, Daniel Francis, Kathleen Dunn Lockhart, Patricia Elaine. AB, Harvard U., 1950; JD, Boston Coll., 1953. Bar: Mass. 1953. Spl. agt. FBI, Cleve., Atlanta, Pitts., 1956-79; commr. Pa. State Police, Harrisburg, 1979—. With CIC, AUS, 1945-48. Mem. FBI Ex-Agts., Internat. Chiefs of Police Assn., Pa. Chiefs of Police Assn. Roman Catholic. Home: Bethel Park Pa. Deceased.

DUNN, ESTHER CLOUDMAN, English educator; b. Portland, Maine, May 5, 1891; d. Charles Jr. and Grace E. (Walton) D. AB, Cornell U., 1913; PhD, U. London, 1922; LittD (hon.), Smith Coll., 1956. Instr. English Bryn Mawr Coll., 1913-17, instr. and dir. English composition, 1917-19; with Smith Coll., from 1922, asst. prof. English, until 1924, assoc. prof., 1924-26, prof., from 1927, also chmn. dept. English, Mary Augusta Jordan chair of English, from 1944. Author: Ben Jonson's Art—Elizabethan Life and Literature as Reflected Therein, 1925, The Literature of Shakespeare's England, 1936, Shakespeare in America, 1939, Pursuit of Understanding, 1945, (with M. E. Dodd) Trollope Reader, 1947; contbr. articles to mags. Mem. AAUW, MLA Am., Am. and English Shalespeare assns., Cosmopolitan Club (N.Y.C.). Home: Northampton Mass. †

DUNN, JAMES CLEMENT, U.S. career ambassador; b. Newark, Dec. 27, 1890; s. John Henry and Mary Emma (Delaney) D.; m. Mary Augusta Armour, Dec. 8, 1914; children: Marianna Armour Dunn, Cynthia Louise Dunn Estherichner. Ed. privately. Practiced as architect 1913-17; asst. naval attaché Havana, 1917-19; 3d sec. embassy Madrid, Spain, 1920-22; charge d'affaires Port au Prince, Haiti, 1922-24; 1st sec. Am. embassy, Brussels, Belgium, 1924-27; dir. ceremonies at White House, Washington, 1924-30, chief Div. of Internat. Conf. and Protocol, 1928-30, 31-35; counselor to Commn. for Study of Haiti, 1930; 1st sec. Am. embassy, London, 1930; sec. del. 4th Pan-Am. Comml. Conf., Washington, 1931; sec. gen. Am. del. 1st stage Gen. Disarmament Conf., Geneva, 1932; also asst. 1st meeting expert's prep. com. Internat. Monetary and Econ. Conf., Geneva; sec. gen. Am. del. Internat. Monetary and Econ. Conf., London, 1933; sec. gen. Am. del. 7th Internat. Conf. Am. States, Montevideo, 1933; spl. asst. to sec. of State, 1934, chief Div. Western European Affairs, 1935-37, advisor on polit. rels., 1937-44, dir. Office of European Affairs, 1944, apptd. asst. sec. of State, 1944; mem. U.S. group Dumbarton Oaks Conversations on Internat. Orgn., Washington, 1944; advisor U.S. del. UN. Conf., San Francisco, 1945; chief polit. advisor Berlin Conf., 1945; dep. to U.S. mem. meetings of Coun. of Fgn. Ministers, London, Paris, N.Y.C., 1945-46, Paris Peace Conf., 1946; ambassador to Italy, 1946-52, France, 1952-53, Spain, 1953-55, Brazil, 1955-56. With USNR, 1917-19. Decorated Victory medal, Order Leopold II (Belgium); grand cross Order of Knights of Malta; grand crosss Order Star of Italy; grand cross Order Isabell II of Spain; grand cross Order So. Cross Brazil; D.S.M., U.S. Dept. State. Mem. clubs: Metropolitan (gov.), Alibi, Chevy Chase (Washington), Knickerbocker, River, Regency, Whist (N.Y.C.). Deceased.

DUNN, JUSTIN STEPHEN, investment company executive; b. New Haven, Nov. 30, 1904; s. John E. and Elizabeth (Welch) D.; m. Ann H. Knudsen, July 22, 1942; stepchildren: Earl D., Eugene R. Knudsen. BS cum laude, Yale U., 1927. With A. Iselin & Co., Inc., 1928-37, Dominick & Dominick, 1937-41; with E.W. Axe & Co., Inc., 1941-82, sr. v.p., 1964-67, pres., 1967-73, chmn. bd., chief exec. officer, 1973-82; pres., dir. Axe-Houghton Fund B, Inc.; v.p., dir. Axe-Houghton Income Fund, Inc., Axe-Houghton Stock Fund, Inc.; bd. govs. Investment Co. Inst. Mem. Sleepy Hollow Country. Roman Catholic. Home: Briarcliff Manor N.Y. Died Mar. 4, 1987; buried Gate of Heaven, Valhalla, N.Y.

DUNPHY, JOHN ENGLEBERT, surgeon, educator; b. Northampton, Mass., Mar. 31, 1908; s. Michael M. and Katherine C. (Duggan) D.; m. Nancy Stevenson, Sept. 8, 1936; children: Sara Catherine, Elizabeth Ann, Mary Jane, John Englebert. AB, Coll. of Holy Cross, 1929, DSc (hon.), 1964; MD, Harvard U., 1933; LHD (hon.), Seton Hall U., 1964; LLD, U. Glasgow, Scotland, 1965, U. Manchester, Eng., 1973; DSc (hon.), Ohio State U., 1972, Georgetown U., 1978; MD (hon.), U. Lund, Sweden, 1976. Diplomate Am. Bd. Surgery. Surg. intern Peter Bent Brigham Hosp., Boston, 1933-34, asst. resident surgeon, 1934-35, intern pathology, 1935-36, resident surgeon, 1936-38, 39-40, assoc. surgery, 1940-42, sr. assoc. surgery, 1945-48, surgeon, 1949; fellow surgery Lahey Clinic, 1938; George Gorham Peters traveling fellow 1938; Arthur Tracy Cabot fellow surgery Lab. Surg. Research Harvard U., 1938-39; instr. surgery Harvard Med. Sch., 1937-40, assoc. surgery, 1940-47, asst. prof., 1947-50, assoc. clin. prof. surgery, 1950-53, clin. prof., 1953-55, prof., 1955-59; dir. 5th surg. service and Sears Surg. Lab. Boston City Hosp., 1959; Kenneth A.J. MacKenzie prof., chmn. dept. U. Oreg., 1959-64; prof., chmn. dept. U. Calif. Sch. Medicine, San Francisco, 1964-75, prof. emeritus, 1975-81; assoc. chief staff for edn. VA Med. Ctr., San Francisco, 1975-79. Author: Physical Examination of the Surgical Patient, 1953, Current Surgical Diagnosis and Treatment, 1973; editor: Repair and Regeneration, 1969, Surgery of the Gall Bladder and Bile Ducts, 1980; contbr. articles to profl. jours. Lt. col. M.C., U.S. Army, 1942-45. Fellow ACS (pres. 1963, chmn. bd. regents 1971-73), Am. Surg. Assn., Royal Coll. Physicians and Surgeons Can. (hon.); mem. AMA, Royal Coll. Surgeons Eng. (hon.), Internat. Surg. Group (pres. 1978), Assn. surgeons Gt. Britain and Ireland (hon.), Royal Coll. Surgeons Edinburgh (hon.), Royal Australasian Coll. Surgeons (hon.), Philippine Coll. Surgeons (hon.), Soc. for Surgery Alimentary Tract, So., Western, New Eng., Pacific Coast surg. assns., Soc. Univ. Surgeons, Royal Soc. Medicine (hon.), Internat. Fedn. Surg. Colls., Sociètè Internat. de Chirurgie, King James IV Assn. Surgeons, Assn. Am. Med. Colls., Am. Acad. Arts and Scis., Soc. U.S. Med. Cons. World War II, AAAS. Republican. Roman Catholic. Clubs: Aescupalpian, Harvard, Bohemian, St. Francis Yacht, University. Home: San Francisco Calif. Died Dec. 24, 1981.

DUNTON, A. DAVIDSON, university president; b. Montreal, Que., Can., July 4, 1912; s. Robert Andrew and Elizabeth (Davidson) D.; m. Kathleen Bingay, June 30, 1944; children: Darcy, Deborah. Student, Lower Can. Coll., 1922-26, U. Grenoble, 1928-29, McGill U., 1930-31; LLD (hon.), McGill U.; student, Cambridge U., 1931-32, U. Munich, 1932-33; DSc (hon.), Laval U.; LLD (hon.), U. Sask., Queen's U., B.C., Can., U. Toronto. With Montreal Star, 1935-37, assoc. editor, 1937-38; editor Montreal Standard, 1938; asst. gen. mgr. Wartime Info. Bd., Ottawa, Ont., Can., 1943-44, gen. mgr., 1944; chmn. Can. Broadcasting Corp., 1945-58; pres. Carleton U., Ottawa, 1958-72. Co-chmn. Royal Commn. on Billingualism and Biculturalism. Home: Ottawa Ont., Canada. Died Feb. 7, 1987.

DU PONT, PIERRE SAMUEL, III, business executive; b. Wilmington, Del., Jan. 1, 1911; s. Lammot and Natalie (Wilson) Du P.; m. Jane Holcomb, June 24, 1933; children: Pierre Samuel IV, Jane de Doliete, Michele Wainwright. With engring. dept. E.I. du Pont de Nemours & Co., Inc., 1934-39, with devel. dept., 1940-41, indsl. sales mgr. sales dept. nylon div., 1942-45, asst. dir. trade analysis div., 1945-47, dir., 1948-51, asst. dir. sales, rubber chems. div., 1951-54, sec., 1954-63, mem. fin. com., 1959-63, v.p., mem. exec. com., 1963-65; v.p., bd. dirs. Christiana Securities Co., 1952-65; bd. dirs. Wilmington Trust Co. Trustee Tower Hill Sch., 1944, pres., 1952-77, chmn., 1977-88. Mem. Am. Chem. Soc., Wilmington Club, Wilmington Country Club, N.Y. Yacht, Cruising Club of Am. Home: Rockland Del. Died Apr. 9, 1988.

DU PRÉ, JACQUELINE, violoncellist; b. 1945. Student, London Cello Sch.; studies with, William Pleeth at Guildhall Sch., Paul Tortelier, Paris,

France, Rostropovich, Moscow, USSR; LittD (hon.), U. Salford, 1978; MusD (hon.), U. London, 1979, Open U., 1979, U. Sheffield, 1980, Leeds, 1982, Durham, 1983, Oxford, 1984. Tchr. music London. Made debut at Wigmore Hall, London, 1961; soloist with prin. orchs. and condrs. in Eng., Europe, U.S. and Eastern Europe; rec. artist for Angel Records. Decorated Order of the Brit. Empire; recipient Suggia Internat. Cello award, 1956, Queen's prize, 1960; Guildhall Sch. of Music fellow, 1975, St. Hilda's Coll. hon. fellow, Oxford, 1984. Fellow Royal Coll. Music, Royal Acad. Music (hon.). Home: London England. Died Oct. 19, 1987, buried Hoop Ln. Reform Cemetery, N. London.

DUPREY, JOHN PAUL, photographer; b. Bronxville, N.Y., Aug. 8, 1927; s. Paul T. and Florence C. Duprey; m. Ruth Lois West, Aug. 14, 1948; children: Diane, James, Janet, Daniel, Dennis, Jean, Jacqueline, Jerilyn. Student pub. schs., N.Y.C. Copy boy N.Y. Daily News, 1946-51, photographer, 1951-71, chief photographer, 1971-77, photog. mgr., 1978-82; judge photog. contests; lectr. in field. With USN, 1944-46. Recipient numerous awards. Mem. Nat. Press Photographers Assn., N.Y. Photographers Assn., Photog. Adminstrs. Club. Roman Catholic. Home: Beach Lake Pa. Died July 24, 1985; buried Beach Lake Cemetery, Beach Lake, Pa.

DUPUIS, CHARLES W(ILLIAM), banker; b. Cin., June 25, 1876; s. William and Ottilie (Albrecht) D.; m. Lillie Deremo, Aug. 23, 1904; children: John D., Betsy (Mrs. E.L. Hill). Ed., Coll. of Commerce, U. Cin.; MA (hon.), U. Cin., 1922, DSC, 1956. Messenger Western Bank, Cin., 1892; cashior, v.p. 2d Nat. Bank of Cin., 1913-18; pres. Citizens NAt. Bank, 1920-27; pres. Central Trust Co., 1927-49, chmn. bd. dirs., from 1949; chmn. bd. dirs. Cin. Union Stock Yard Co.; bd, dirs. Cin. & Suburban Bell Telephone Co., Cin. Milling Machine Co., F. H. Lawson Co., Union Central Life Ins. Co., The Kroger Co., Mfrs. and Mchts. Indemnity Co. Pres., trustee Endowment Fund Assn., U. Cin.; an organizer of Am. Inst. Banking and Cin. Coll. Finance. Mem. Ohio Bankers Assn. (former pres.), Queen City Club, Bankers Club, Comml. Club, Commonwealth Club, Cin. Club, Cin. Country Club, Masons (33 deg.). Episcopalian. Home: Cincinnati Ohio. †

DUPUIS, ROBERT NEWELL, chemist, management consultant; b. Indpls., June 4, 1910; s. Arthur J. and Veronica (Cox) DuP.; m. Eleanor Thomsen, June 29, 1935; children: Robert Thomsen, Eleanor Joan. AB, U. Ill., 1931; PhD in Organic Chemistry, NYU, 1934. Research chemist Miner Labs., Chgo., 1935-45, asst. dir., 1945-47; mgr. research and devel. S.C. Johnson & Son, Inc., 1947-52; dir. research and devel. Philip Morris, Inc., Richmond, Va., 1952-55, v.p. research, 1955-60, dir., 1957-63; v.p. tech. Gen. Foods Corp., 1960-67; mgmt. cons. 1968-86. Editor: Research Management, 1967-70; contbr. to patent lit., sci. publs. Trustee Sunnyside Presbyn. Home, Harrisonburg, Va. Mem. Am. Chem. Soc., Chemists Club, Downtown Club, Phi Beta Kappa, Sigma Xi, Alpha Chi Sigma. Home: Richmond Va. Died July 8, 1986.

DUQUE, ERNEST ELOY, business executive; b. L.A., 1892. Grad., U. Calif., 1916. Pres., dir. Calif., Portland Cement Co.; bd. dirs. Citizens Nat. Bank. Home: Los Angeles Calif. †

DUQUE, JOSE LUCIANO, diplomat; b. Panama, Republic of Panama, Sept. 17, 1892; s. Jose Gabriel and Felicia (Pajaro) D.; m. Josefa Sanchiz, July 12, 1913; children: Josefina Gabriela, Tomas Alberto. Grad., Clason Point Mil. Acad., Westchester, N.Y., 1909; student, McGill U., Montreal, Can., 1909-10. Gen. supt. pub. works, specializing sanitary engring. Republic of Panama, later mem. consular service; successively consul gen. Hamburg, Germany; consul. gen. L.A.; vice dean Consular Corps, L.A. Mem. Asociacion Consular Latino-Americana of L.A. (v.p.), L.A. County Mus. (hon.). †

DURHAM, HARRY DIXON, insurance executive; b. Lamont, Iowa, Nov. 25, 1892; s. George F. and Alice (Chesley) D.; m. Neva M. Maddux, Mar. 22, 1924; 1 child, Richard H. Student, Grinell Coll., 1909-12. Examiner Ins. Dept. of Iowa, 1919-22; mgr. accounting and statis. dept. Iowa Nat. Mutual Ins. Co., Cedar Rapids, 1922-24, asst. sec., agy. supr., 1931-41, sr. v.p., 1941-52, sec., 1941-52, gen. mgr., 1951-58, pres., 1952-58, chmn. exec. com., from 1958, also bd. dirs.; auditor, examiner Miles M. Dawson & Sons, actuaries and accountants, N.Y.C., 1924; asst. treas. Lynton T. Block. & Co., St. Louis, 1925-31; v.p., dir. Premium Fin. Co.; dir. Am. Mutual Ins. Alliance. Mem. Ins. Inst. of Am. (bd. govs.), U.S. C. of C. (mem. ins. com.), C. of C. (past pres.), Nat. Assn. Automotive Mut. Ins. Cos. (past pres., dir.), Am. Legion, Masons, K.T., Shriners, Elks, Cedar Rapids Country Club, Pickwick Club. Home: Cedar Rapids Iowa. †

DURUFLE, MAURICE, organist, composer; b. 1903. Ed., Paris Conservatory. Organist St.-Etienne-du-Mont; asst. prof. Paris Conservatory, 1942-43, prof. d'harmonie, 1943-86. Composer: (organ) Scherzo, 1929, Prélude Adagio et Choral Varié sum le Veni Creator, 1931, Suite, 1934, Prelude et Fugue, 1942; (chamber music) Trio pour Flute, Alto et Piano; Quatre Motets sur des themes grégorius for choir a cappella, 1960; (orch.) Trois Danses, 1935, Andante et Scherzo, 1940, Requiem pour Soli, Choeurs, Orchestre et Orque, 1947; Messe Cum Jubilo for baritone solo, baritone choir, orch. and organ, 1967. Home: Paris France. Died June 16, 1986.

DUSTMAN, ROBERT BARCLAY, educator; b. Youngstown, Ohio, Jan. 9, 1892; s. George Simon and Christina (Barclay) D.; m. Gay Zinn, July 27, 1917; children: Robert B. Jr., Mary Jean (Mrs. Richard H. Ross). BS in Agriculture, Ohio State U., 1915; MS, U. Chgo., 1923, PhD, 1924. High sch. tchr. Shinnston, W.Va., 1915-16; extension agronomist W.Va. U., 1916-18; asst. prof. soils extension Ohio State U., 1919-22; asst., assoc. and prof. of agrl. chemistry, agrl. chemist Expt. Sta. W.Va. U., 1924-47, chmn. grad. coun., 1947-49, dean grad sch., from 1949. Mem. Am. Chem. Soc., AAAS, Am. Soc. Plant Pathologists, Sigma Xi, Phi Lambda Upsilon. Home: Morgantown W.Va. †

DUTCHER, CLINTON HARVEY, hospital administrator; b. Colorado Springs, Colo., July 27, 1909; s. Oliver Harry and Elsie (Taylor) D.; m. Elizabeth Bryant, July 28, 1931; 1 son, Clinton Harvey Jr. Ed. pub. schs. Enlisted USN, 1927, commd. warrant officer, 1942, advanced through grades to lt. comdr. Med. Service Corps., 1954, ret., 1957; bus. mgr. Cen. Fla. Tb Hosp., Orlando, 1957-60; bus. mgr. Sunland Hosp., Orlando, 1960-63, adminstr., from 1963. Decrated Purple Heart. Mem. Am. Assn. Mental Deficiency, Ret. Officers Assn., Sojourners, Heroes of 76, Legion of Honor, Navy League, Masons, Shriners, Lions. Home: Inverness Fla. Deceased.

DUVOISIN, ROGER ANTOINE, artist, illustrator; b. Geneva, Aug. 28, 1904; came to U.S., 1927, naturalized, 1938.; s. Jacques Jonas and Judith E. (Morè) D.; m. Louise Fatio, July 25, 1925; children: Roger Clair, Jacques Alfred. Student, Ecole Professionalle, Geneva, 1915-17, Ecole des Arts et Mètiers, 1917-24; LittD (hon.), Kean Coll. N.J., 1979. Mgr. decorative pottery Ferney, France, 1924-26; illustrator books, designer scenery for Geneva Opera, other prodns; textile designer Lyons and Paris, France, 1927, Mallinson Silk Co., 1927-31; mag., book illustrator, writer juvenile books 1932-80. Exhibited Am. Inst. Graphic Art in 50 Best Books of Yr., 1933, 38, 39, 45-50; ALA in 9 Best Children's Books of Yr., 1937; N.Y. Times 10 best books, 1952, 54, 55, 61, 65, 66; Am. Inst. Graphic Art exhbn. best books, 1953-54, 55-57, 58-60, 61-62, 65-66, 67-68; author numerous books including the Petunia series, Veronica series, 1960-80; The Happy Hunter, 1961, The Missing Milkman, 1966, Tulip, 1969, The Crocodile in the Tree, 1972-73, Jasmine, 1973, See What I Am, 1975 (N.Y. Acad. Sci. award), Periwinkle, 1976, Crocus, 1977, Snowy and Woody, 1978, Crocus' Problem, 1979; (with Louise Duvoisin) The Happy Lions Books, Red-Bantam, Hector Penguin, 1973, contbr. to New Yorker mag., other mags. Home: Gladstone N.J. Died June 30, 1980.

DUWEZ, POL EDGARD, materials science educator; b. Mons, Belgium, Dec. 11, 1907; s. Arthur and Jeanne (Delcourt) D.; m. Nera Faisse, Sept. 4, 1935; 1 dau., Nadine. Metall.E., Sch. Mines, Mons, 1932; D.Sc., U. Brussels, 1933; D.Sc. (research fellow), Calif. Inst. Tech., 1935. Instr., prof. Sch. Mines, Mons, 1935-40; research engr. Calif. Inst. Tech., Pasadena, 1941-45; chief materials sect. jet propulsion lab. Calif. Inst. Tech., 1945-54, assoc. prof. materials sci., 1947-52, prof., 1952-78, prof. emeritus, 1978; Campbell Meml. lectr., 1967; mem. sci. adv. bd. to chief of staff USAF, 1945-55. Contbr. articles to profl. jours. Recipient Charles B. Dudley award ASTM, 1951; Francis J. Clamer medal Franklin Inst., 1968; Gov. Cornez prize Belgium, 1973; Paul Lebeau medal French Soc. for High Temperature, 1974; Heyn medal Deutsche Gesellschaft für Metallkunde, 1981; W. Hume-Rothery award Metall. Soc. of AIME, 1981. Fellow AIME (C.H. Mathewson Gold medal 1964), Am. Soc. Metals (Albert Sauveur Achievement medal 1973); mem. Nat. Acad. Scis., Nat. Acad. Engring., Am. Ceramic Soc., Am. Acad. Arts and Scis., Am. Phys. Soc. (internat. prize for new materials 1980), AAAS, Brit. Inst. Metals, Société Francaise des Ingenieurs Civils, Sigma Xi. Home: Pasadena Calif. Died Dec. 31, 1984.

DWINELL, BRUCE, lawyer; b. Washington, Ill., Oct. 12, 1891; s. Orvis Turner and Annie (McAlilly) D.; m. Ellis Coffin, Dec. 20, 1930; children: Anne, Carolyn. Student, Bradley Poly. Inst., 1910-12; AB, Northwestern U., 1914, LLB, 1916. Bar: Ill. 1916. Practice Peoria, 1916-27; gen atty. law dept. Rock Island Lines, 1927-51, gen. solicitor, 1951-52, then v.p. exec. dept.; represented Western railroads in cases involving railraod employees, 1940-50; mem. Nat. R.R. Adjustment Bd., 1947. Lt. inf. U.S. Army 1917-19. Home: Chicago Ill. †

DYE, JOSEPH A., physiologist, educator; b. Basalt, Idaho, Mar. 8, 1892; s. Joseph Henry and Nellie Dora (Child) D.; m. Dorothy Charlotte Young, Sept. 6, 1917; children: Joseph Gordon, Howard Spencer, Harold Wesley, Dorothy Elizabeth (Mrs. James W. Spencer), Richard Wilder. Student, Ricks Acad., Rexburg, Idaho, 1910-13; AB, Brigham Young U., 1916; student, U. Chgo., summer 1916; PhD, Cornell U., 1925. With dept. physiology Cornell, asst., 1916-19, instr., 1923-26, asst. prof., 1926-41, assoc. prof., 1941-46, prof. physiology, from 1946; fellow in physiology Harvard Med. Sch., 1933; resident in research Cornell U. Med. Coll., 1941; travel and visits to European univs., 1933. Author books and chpts. on physiology; cotnbr. articles to sci. publs. Mem. Am. Physiol. SOc., Soc. Exptl. Biology and Medicine, AAUP, Sigma Xi, Phi Kappa Phi. Mem. Ch. of Jesus Christ of Latter-day Saints. Home: Ithaca N.Y. †

DYER, IRBY LLOYD, lawyer; b. Pecos, Tex., Aug. 26, 1916; s. Freeman Irby and Katie (Lloyd) D.; children—Irby III (dec.), Deborah Frances Dyer Gutting; m. Margaret Pondrom Wilson, 1979. Student, Schreiner Inst., 1934-36, U. Tex., 1936-40. Bar: Tex. 1940. Assoc. Hubbard & Kerr, Pecos, 1940-42; ptnr. Turpin, Smith, Dyer, Saxe & MacDonald, Midland, Tex., 1945-87; Gen. counsel, mem. exec. com., dir. Central Airlines Inc., Ft. Worth, 1963-68; pres. DST Exploration Corp., Midland, 1957-87, White Sands Oil & Gas Corp., Midland and Corpus Christi, 1960-72; gen. counsel, dir. PED Oil Corp., Midland, Tex., 1967-87; Adobe Oil & Gas Corp., Midland, 1976-85. Chmn. ARC, Midland County, 1948. Served with USAAF, 1942-45. Decorated Bronze Star, Air medal. Mem. ABA, Tex. Bar Assn., Midland County Bar Assn. (past pres.), Midland Jr. C. of C. (past pres.). Presbyterian. Clubs: Midland Petroleum, Midland Country. Home: Midland Tex. Died Dec. 7, 1987.

DYKE, GEORGE EDWARD, manufacturing executive; b. Chelsea, Mass., Feb. 14, 1892; s. George D. and M. Eugenie (Curtis) D.; m. Madeline Gibson, July 13, 1920; children: Emily G., George E., Gibson V. BS, Dartmouth, 1915. Advt. salesman Internat. Mag. Corp., 1915-16; pres. First Nat. Bank of Merrick (N.Y.), 1923-25; broker Russell, Miller & Carey, 1930-33, DeVoe, Dyke & Sperry, 1933-37; joined Robert Gair Co. Inc., 1939, pres., 1939-56, chmn. bd., 1941-56; vice chmn. Continental Can Co. Inc., 1956-57, dir., mem. exec. com., from 1956. Chmn. bd. govs. Nat. Coun. for Stream Improvement. Mem. Nat. Paperboard Assn. (pres. 1946-51, then dir.). Home: Stonington Conn. †

DYKES, CHARLES EDWIN, corporation executive; b. Springfield, Ohio, July 23, 1912; s. Otis Edwin and Winifred Bertha (Hodge) D.; m. Doris E. Smallridge, Aug. 20, 1938; 1 child, Susan (Mrs. David V. Black). Diploma, Tenn. Mil. Inst., 1932; BS, Cornell U., 1936, postgrad., 1936-37; postgrad., Harvard U., 1955. Acct. Gen. Electric Co., 1937-39; acct., controller Coop. G.L.F. Exchange, Inc., Ithaca, N.Y., 1939-57; v.p., controller Avon Products, Inc., N.Y.C., 1958-67; v.p. fin., then exec. v.p. U.S. Gypsum Co., Chgo., 1967-77, also bd. dirs.; bd. dirs. Clow Corp., Kewaunee Sci. Equipment Corp., Dr. Scholl Found. Campaign chmn. Community Chest, Ithaca, 1954; pres. Tompkins County Meml. Hosp.; bd. govs. Chgo. Heart Assn., 1969-72, gen. campaign chmn., 1970; bd. dirs. Ill. chpt. Arthritis Found., 1974-77; trustee Cornell U., 1968-73. Recipient Disting. Service award Ithaca Jr. C. of C., 1947, Disting. Service award N.Y. Jr. C. of C., 1947. Mem. Fin. Execs. Inst. (treas. 1965-67), Chgo. Council Fgn. Relations (bd. dirs. 1970-73), Masons, Chicago Club, Country Club N.C., Beta Theta Pi. Presbyterian. Home: Pinehurst N.C. Died May 16, 1984; buried Pinelawn Meml. Park.

DYKSTRA, FRANCIS EARL, real estate company executive; b. Pella, Iowa, Nov. 3, 1905; s. John F. and Josephine (Thomassen) D.; m. Virginia Warner, Jan. 18, 1936. BCS, Drake U., 1927. Field rep. Stern Fin. Co., Des Moines, 1927-28; br. mgr. Midwest Comml. Credit Co., Sioux City and Mason City, Iowa, 1928-29; with Interstate Fin. Corp., Dubuque, Iowa, 1929-42; br. mgr., Madison, Wis., 1931-42; custodian alien property U.S. Govt., N.Y.C., 1942-44; with Thorp Fin. Corp., Wis., 1944-54; v.p. Marathon Fin. Corp. subs., Wausau, Wis., 1948-54; pres. Rock Fin. Co., Green Bay, Wis., 1954-61; with Sunrise (Fla.) Golf Devel. Corp. (and affiliated cos.), 1961-85, pres., 1965-85; pres. Pub. Utilities Corp., 1965-69, Uniflow Gas Co., Inc., 1965-73; mem. exec. com. Plantation 1st Nat. Bank, 1973-85, bd. dirs.; bd. dirs. Landmark Bank of Sunrise, chmn. bd., 1974-77; bd. dirs., chmn. audit com. Landmark 1st Nat. Bank Ft. Lauderdale, Fla. Mem. city council Sunrise, 1961-66. Mem. Wis. Assn. Fin. Cos. (pres.), Wis. Consumer Fin. Assn. (bd. dirs.), Am. Fin. Conf., Am. Indsl. Bankers Assn., Greater Plantation C. of C. (bd. dirs.), Sunrise C. of C. (founder, chmn.), Elks, Rotary, Delta Sigma Pi, Tau Kappa Epsilon. Home: Fort Lauderdale Fla. Died May 6, 1985.

DYRNESS, ENOCK CHRISTEN, education educator; b. Chgo., Aug. 23, 1902; s. Christen T. and Hilda (Erickson) D.; m. Grace Evelyn Williams, Nov. 27, 1924; children: Virginia (dec.), Christen Theodore, William Arthur. AB, Wheaton Coll., 1923; AM, U. Chgo., 1924; LLD, Houghton Coll., 1945. Asst. prof. edn., prin. Practice Sch. Wheaton (Ill.) Coll., 1924-27, acting dean Wheaton Acad., 1927, assoc. prof., 1927-35, registrar, dir. summer sch., 1928-86, v.p. acad. adminstrn., 1934-47, prof., 1934-85. Author: Aspects of Specialized Social Agencies, 1924. Sec., bd. dirs. Evang. Alliance Mission, Wheaton. Mem. NEA, Chgo. Assn. Commerce (com. on edn.), Nat. Assn. Christian Schs. (pres.), Am. Assn. Coll. Registrars and Admissions Officers

.p. 1954-57, assoc. editor jour. 1934-44), Wheaton oll. Scholastic Honor Soc., Ill. Assn. Coll. Registrars res.), Wheaton Club, Beltionian Assn., Chi Sigma heta. Home: Walnut Creek Calif. Died Jan. 15, 1986.

ZIEWIATKOWSKI, DOMINIC DONALD, iochemist, educator; b. Chgo., Feb. 20, 1915; s. Alexder and Philomena (Zukowska) D.; m. Naomi J. oosevelt, Mar. 6, 1942; children: jane Ann, Samuel amren Jr. BA, Western State Tchrs. Coll., 1939; MS, . Mich., 1941, PhD, 1943. Instr. biochemistry anderbilt U., 1943-46; assoc. prof. Johns Hopkins U., 946-48; assoc., assoc. prof. Rockefeller U., N.Y.C., 948-67; prof. biol. chemistry and dentistry U. Mich., nn Arbor, 1967-87; dir. Dental Research Inst., 1967-2; mem. Soc. Biol. Chemists, Soc. Exptl. Biology and Iedicine, Soc. Complex Carbohydrates, AAAS, Harvey ., Internat., Am. assns. dental research, Sigma Xi. lome: Ann Arbor Mich. Died Sept. 29, 1987.

ADIE, THOMAS, telephone company executive; b. ttawa, Can., 1898. BCE, McGill U. Chmn. Trans an. Telephone System, 1952-58; dir. Bell Telephone o. Can.; dir. (hon.) Royal Trust Co. Home: Westmont ue., Canada. Deceased.

AGEN, MICHAEL JOHN, state chief justice; b. ermyn, Pa., May 9, 1907; s. Michael J. and Sarah Nallin) E.; m. Helen Fitzsimmons, June 27, 1935; children: Helen Marie (Mrs. Thomas J. Foley), Michael hn Jr., Jeremiah William, James. BA, St. Thomas oll. (now U. Scranton), Scranton, Pa., 1927; student, arvard Law Sch., 1927-28; LLD (hon.), U. Scranton, 955, Dickinson Sch. Law, 1977; DHL, St. Joseph's oll., 1978. Bar: Pa. 1931. Pvt. practice 1931-41; dist. ty. Lackawanna County, 1934-41, judge ct. common eas, 1942-59; justice Supreme Ct. Pa., 1960-77, chief istice, 1977-80. Pres. Coll. of Presdl. Electors of Pa., 940, Lackawanna United Fund, 1955-59. Decorated night Equestrian Order Holy Sepulchre; recipient olden Deeds award Exchange Club of Scranton, 1950, mericanism award B'nai B'rith, 1969, award for outanding community service Friendly Sons of St. Patrick Lackawanna, Scranton-Dunmore Community Chest ward, 1944, award ARC, 1944, Lackawanna United und award, 1958, award Am. Legion, 1959, Distuished Pa. award, 1978. Mem. ABA, Pa. Bar Assn., ackawanna County Bar Assn., Am. Law Inst. Clubs: lk (past local exalted ruler), Moose. Home: Scranton a. Died July 7, 1987.

AKIN, FRANK, educator; b. Emlenton, Pa., Dec. 24, 885; s. James Alexander and Sarah Margaret (Perry) .; m. Mabel Mechlin, June 12, 1913; children: Lloyd ussell, Paul Mechlin, Frank, Eleanor Josephine; m. lildred Olivia Moody, Mar. 28, 1931. AB magna cum ude, Grove City Coll., 1910; grad., Western Theol. em., Pitts., 1913, BD, 1915; student, U. Marburg, 914, U. Glasgow, 1914-15; PhD magna cum laude, U. hgo., 1922. Ordained to ministry Presbyn. Ch., 1913. chr. history North Washington (Pa.) Inst., 1908-09; astor Glenfield and Haysville, Pa., 1913-14; instr. N.T. reek Western Theol. Sem., 1915-23, assoc. prof. N.T. ept., 1923-25, prof. ecclesiastical history and history of octrine, 1925-27, also libr., 1919-27; lectr. in N.T. artford Theol. Sem., 1927-28; pres. Item Pub. and rinting Co., Millburn, N.J., 1932-33; prof. history ssex County Jr. Coll., Newark, N.J., 1933-35; engaged freelance literary and ednl. work from 1935. Author: ith Mildred M. Eakin) The Church-School Teacher's b, 1949, Sunday School Fights Prejudice, 1953; Bible udy for Grownups, 1956, others; contbr. to religious nd ednl. publs. Home: DeBary Fla. †

AKIN, MILDRED OLIVIA MOODY (MRS. RANK EAKIN), religious educator; b. Wilson, N.Y., lar. 28, 1890; d. Alfred James and Mary Evelyn (Pet-) Moody; m. Frank Eakin, Mar. 28, 1931. Grad., ilson Acad., 1906; AB, Syracuse U., 1910; AM, NYU, 934; postgrad., Syracuse U., U. Chgo., Drew U., NYU. chr. high sch., Wilson, 1910-16; dir. children's activies WCTU, 1916-19, assoc. nat. dir., 1919; dir. elemn. for 7 states Bd. Edn. M.E. Ch., 1919-21; supt. dept. em. edn. at cen. office Bd. Edn. M.E. Ch., Chgo., 921-32; teaching fellow religious edn. Drew U., 1932-, instr. religious edn., 1934-48, asst. prof. religious n., 1948-55, dir. demonstration sch., religious edn. ept., 1937-55. Author: (with Frank Eakin): The hurch-School Teacher's Job, 1949, Sunday School ghts Prejudice, 1953, others; contbr. articles to reious and ednl. publs. Mem. Religious Edn. Assn., hild Study Assn. Am., Alpha Chi Omega. Home: eBary Fla. †

AMES, PAUL VAN, lumberman; b. Frontenac, linn., Apr. 10, 1887; s. Harry O. and Rose (Mills) E.; Vera VanMeter Hurlbut, Sept. 10, 1908; children: uane Harry M., Virginia Ruth (Mrs. Emery M. Elngson), Peggy Lou (Mrs. Eugene J. Seiberlich). Grad., ongfellow High Sch., Morris, Minn., 1904; student, U. linn., 1904-06. Successively stenographer, pvt. sec., st. sec. and sec. Shevlin, Carpenter & Clarke Co., rs. lumber, Mpls., 1908-25, v.p., 1925-32, pres., 1932-; chmn. bd. dirs. McCloud Lumber Co. (successor elvin Carpenter & Clarke Co.), from 1952; chmn. ec. com. McCloud River Lumber Co.; pres. Monarch imber Co., Bldg. Service Inc.; bd. dirs. 1st Nat. Bank,

1st Bank Stock Corp., Lumbermen's Underwriting Alliance, Kansas City. Mem. Nat. Lumber Mfrs. Assn. (Washington) (bd. dirs.), Mpls. Club, Minikahda Club, Masons (32 deg.), Shriners. Republican. Methodist. Home: Minneapolis Minn. †

EAMES, RAY, designer; b. Sacramento; d. Alexander Kaiser and Edna Mary (Evans) Burr; m. Charles Eames, June 20, 1941; 1 dau., Lucia Eames Demetrios. MA (hon.), May F. Bennett Sch., 1960; DFA (hon.), Art Ctr. Coll. Design, 1977, U. Cin., 1978, Otis Parsons Sch. Design, 1984, Mass. Coll. Art, 1986; student of painting, with Hans Hofmann, 1933-39. Designer (with Charles Eames), 1941-78, design cons. IBM; co-founder basic design course for beginning architecture, U. Calif.-Berkeley, 1953; contbr. to books, exhbns., furniture, films. Co-recipient 1st One Man Show of Furniture Mus. Modern Art, 1946, co-recipient First Ann. Kaufmann Internat. Design Award, 1960, Emmy award, 1960, First Domus Obelisk award, 1963, Art Ctr. Coll. of Design 50th Anniversary award for Disting. Lifetime Achievement, 1980, Disting. Lifetime Achievement award Modern & Contemporary Council, Los Angeles County Mus. Art, 1982. Mem. Am. Abstract Artists (founding 1936), Alliance Graphique Internationale, Am. Council for Arts in Edn. (arts and Ams. panel 1975-88), Acad. Motion Picture Arts and Scis., AIA (hon. assoc. So. Calif. chpt.), Am. Inst. Graphic Arts. Home: Pacific Palisades Calif. Died Aug. 21, 1988.

EAMES, S. MORRIS, philosopher, educator; b. Silex, Mo., June 5, 1916; s. Jesse S. and Velma (Morris) E.; m. Elizabeth Ramsden, Aug. 21, 1952; children: Ivan Lee, Anne. AB, Culver-Stockton Coll., 1939; MA in Philosophy, U. Mo., 1941, MA in Sociology, 1952; PhD, U. Chgo., 1958; D Litt, Bethany (W.Va.) Coll., 1968. Mem. faculty Culver-Stockton Coll., 1942-44, U. Mo., 1944-50, Washington U., St. Louis, 1951-63; mem. faculty So. Ill. U., 1963-86, prof. philosophy, 1968-86; Oreon Scott lectr. Bethany (W.Va.) Coll., 1965; mem. editorial bd. Coop. Research Project for Dewey Publs., 1963-86. Author: The Philosophy of Alexander Campbell, 1966; co-author: Logical Methods, rev. edit., 1971, Pragmatic Naturalism, 1977, Poems of Love and Peace, 1984; co-author: Lectures in the Far East, 1980; co-editor, contbr. Guide to the Works of John Dewey, 1970, John Dewey: The Early Works, 1882-1898; contbr. articles, poems, revs. to profl. jours., mags. Mem. Am. Philos. Assn., Mo. Philos. Assn. (pres. 1961-62), John Dewey Soc., C.S. Peirce Soc., Metaphysical Soc. Am., Mind Assn., Disciples of Christ Hist. Soc. Home: Carbondale Ill. Died Sept. 18, 1986.

EARLE, WILLIAM ALEXANDER, II, philosopher; b. Saginaw, Mich., Feb. 18, 1919; s. James Hudson and Elsie (Goeschel) E. B.A., U. Chgo., 1941, Ph.D., 1951; Docteur de l'Universite, U. Aix-Marseilles, France, 1948. Mem. faculty Northwestern U., 1948-85, prof. philosophy, 1961-85; vis. lectr. Yale U., 1956, Harvard U., 1959. Author: Objectivity, 1956, Autobiographical Consciousness, 1972, Public Sorrows and Private Pleasures, 1976, Mystical Reason, 1981, Evanescence, 1984, Imaginary Memoirs, 1986, A Surrealism The Movies, 1987; co-author: Christianity and Existentialism, 1963. Served to 1st lt. AUS, 1941-45. Rockefeller fellow, 1947-48; Carnegie grantee, 1965-66. Mem. Am. Philos. Soc., Soc. Phenomenology and Existential Philosophy, Hegel Soc., Am. Aesthetics Soc., Am. Metaphys. Soc. Home: Chicago Ill. Died Oct. 16, 1988, body donated to Northwestern U. Med. Sch.

EARLING, ROY BROWN, mining consultant; b. Milw., May 19, 1887; s. H. B. and Edna (Brown) E.; m. Mary L. Gazzam, Sept. 2, 1919; children: Mary Lou, Nancy, Barbara. Student, Mich. Coll. Mines, 1905-08. With U.S. Smelting, Refining & Mining Co., Fairbanks, Alaska, 1925-52, v.p., gen. mgr. Alaska ops., 1933-52; mining cons. Seattle, from 1952. Mem. AIME, Rainier, Washington Athletic Club, Arctic Club (Seattle), Masons. Home: Port Blakely Wash. †

EARP, CLAUDE CALLAHAN, state government official; b. Barton County, Mo., Aug. 9, 1886; m. Ruth Phillips, Oct. 7, 1914. Ed. pub. schs., student extension courses. V.p. Southwest Mail Printing Co. pub. daily and weekly newspapers, Nevada, Mo., 1928-41; adj. gen. of Mo. 1936-37; chmn. Mo. State Hwy Commn., 1937-41; state dir. SSS, Mo., 1940-47. Dep. fund vice chmn. ARC, 1960. Col. AUS. Decorated D.S.M.; named Man of Yr. by Nevada Rotary Club, 1964. Mem. Masons, K.T. Democrat. Methodist. Home: Nevada Mo. †

EAST, JOHN PORTER, U.S. senator; b. Springfield, Ill., May 5, 1931; s. Laurence J. and Virginia (Porter) E.; B.A. in Polit. Sci., Earlham Coll., 1953; LL.B., U. Ill., 1959; M.A. in Polit. Sci., U. Fla., 1962, Ph.D., 1964; m. Priscilla Sherk, Sept. 26, 1953; children—Kathryn, Martha. Bar: Fla. 1959. Prof. polit. sci. E. Carolina U., Greenville, N.C., 1964-80; mem. U.S. Senate from N.C. 1980-86. Del. to Republican Nat. Conv., 1976, 80, nat. committeeman, 1976-86. Served to lt. USMC, 1953-55. Nat. Def. fellow 1961-64. Mem. Am. Polit. Sci. Assn., Fla. Bar Assn., So. Polit. Sci. Assn., Am. Legion, Phi Beta Kappa. Methodist. Author: Council-Manager Government: The Political Thought of Its Founder, Richard S. Childs, 1965, The American Conservative Movement; contbr. numerous articles on American

polit. thought to scholarly jours.; contbr. book revs. to lit. jours.; mem. editorial bd. Polit. Sci. Reviewer, 1970-86, Modern Age, 1975-86. Died June 29, 1986; buried Arlington Nat. Cemetery. Home: Greenville N.C.

EASTERBROOK, ERNEST FRED, army officer; b. Ft. Worden, Wash., Aug. 6, 1908; s. Edmund P. and Fannie (Luscombe) E.; m. nancy Stilwell, Sept. 9, 1938; children: John Edmund, Nancy, James S. BS, U.S. Mil. Acad., 1931. Commd. 2d lt. U.S. Army, 1931, advanced through grades to maj. gen., 1959; comdr. 475th Inf. Regt., CBI, 7th Inf. Regt., Republic of Korea, 1953; mem. staff and faculty U.S. Inf. Sch., 1946-49, Can. Army Staff Coll., 1949-51, U.S. Command and Gen. Staff Coll., 1954-55; assigned G-3 Allied Land Forces Cen. Europe, SHAPE, 1955-57; dir. army aviation ODCSOPS, Dept. Army, 1957-59; comdg. gen. U.S. Army Aviation Ctr., 1959-61, 25th Inf. Div., 1961-63; chief Joint U.S. Mil. Adv. Group, Thailand, 1963-65; dep. comdg. gen. 6th U.S. Army, 1965-67. Decorated Silver Star, Broze Star, Legion of Merit, Combat Inf. badge; Mil. Cross 1st class (Belgium). Died Feb. 19, 1989.

EASTLAND, JAMES O., lawyer, senator; b. Doddsville, Mizz., Nov. 18, 1904; s. Woods Caperton and Alma (Austin) E.; m. Elizabeth Coleman, July 6, 1932; children: Nell, Anne, Sue, Woods Eugene. Student, U. Miss., 1922-24, Vanderbilt U., 1925-26, U. Ala., 1926-27; LLD (hon.), Miss. Coll., 1971. Bar: Miss. 1927. Practiced law Forest, Miss. and Sunflower County, from 1934; mem. Miss. Ho. of Reps., 1928-32; apptd. to fill vacancy in U.S. Senate June-Sept., 1941, U.S. senator from Miss., 1943-78, senate pres. protem, 1972-78, chmn. judiciary com., 1956-78, former mem. agr. and forestry com., Dem. policy com., commn. on art and antiquities. Home: Doddsville Miss. Died Feb. 19, 1986.

EATON, GEORGE S(AMUEL), trade association executive; b. Liberty, Ind., Dec. 30, 1892; s. George Winfield Scott and Laura Matilda (Osborne) E.; m. Nathalie B. Souther, July 28, 1917 (dec. Aug. 1955); 1 child, Margaret. BS, Purdue U., 1914, CE, 1917; student evening courses, Sch. Commerce, Northwestern U., 1925-26. Instr. engring. Lawrence Coll., Appleton, Wis., 1914-16; asst. prof. civil engring. Clemson Coll., 1916-17; asst. div. engr. Universal Portland Cement Co., Chgo., 1917-19; rsch. engr. Assoc. Gen. Contractors, Chgo., 1919-20; mgr. gen. ednl. bur., asst. mgr. advt. and pub. bur. Portland Cement Assn., Chgo., 1920-28; sec.-treas. Am. Face Brick Assn., Chgo., 1928-34; exec. sec. Code Authority for Structural Clay Products Industry, Washington, 1934-35; v.p., gen. mgr. Brick & Tile Sales Corp., Pitts., 1935-38; assoc. mgr. Assoc. Industries of Cleve., 1938-42; asst. chief, later chief forging sect. aluminum and magnesium div. WPB, Washington, 1943-44; exec. sec. Nat. Tool & Die Mfrs. Assn., Cleve., 1944-57; exec. v.p. Nat. Tool & Die Mfrs. Assn., 1957-61; exec. sec. Nat. Inst. Jig and Fixture Component Mfrs., from 1961, Nat. Assn. Punch Mfrs., from 1963. Contbr. articles to trade and tech. mags. Mem. Am. Soc. Assn. Execs., Western Soc. Engrs., Tau Beta Pi. Home: Oakland Calif. †

EBBS, JOHN DALE, English language educator; b. Carbondale, Ill., Sept. 26, 1925; s. Charles and Dora (Fox) E.; m. Dorothy Ruth Churchwell, Mar. 14, 1953; children: Laura Ebbs Benjamin, Charles Curtis. AB, U. N.C.- Chapel Hill, 1948; MA, U. N.C.-Chapel Hill, 1949, PhD, 1958. Tchr. English Clinton (N.C.) High Sch., 1949-50; instr. English Tex. A&M U., 1950-54; grad. instr. English U. N.C., Chapel Hill, 1955-58; assoc. prof. English High Point (N.C.) Coll., 1958-59; asst. prof. Tex. A&M U., College Station, 1959-60; assoc. prof. East Carolina U., Greenville, N.C., 1960-63, prof. English, 1963-87, dir. 'Pockets of Excellence project, 1973-87; dep. dir. BIFAD program East Carolina U., 1982-87; supr. English for State N.C., 1966-67; vis. prof. English U. Nebr., Lincoln, 1967-68; faculty advisor Phi Eta Sigma, 1975-87. Author: The Principle of Poetic Justice Illustrated in Restoration Tragedy, 1973, Manual of Style for Research Writing, 1976, rev. edit., 1980, 3d edit., 1986; editor: Early Methodism in Greenville, North Carolina: A History of the Jarvis Memorial United Methodist Church, 1979; contbr. articles, revs. to state, nat. jours. Treas. Jarvis Meml. United Meth. Ch., 1984-87; mem. com. for Outdoor Drama at Bath (N.C.), 1975-87; mem. exec. bd., 1983-86, sec., 1983-86 Served with USAAF, 1943-45. Decorated D.F.C., Air medal with five oak leaf clusters; named Outstanding Tchr. E. Carolina U., 1978; grantee to Eng. Z Smith Reynolds Found., 1973. Mem. MLA, Mediaeval Acad., Am. Council Tchrs. English, Nat. Council Tchrs. English, NEA, N.C. Assn. Educators, Phi Delta Kappa, Phi Kappa Phi (chpt. treas. 1982-85). Democrat. Methodist. Club: Exchange (Greenville, N.C.). Home: Greenville N.C. Died May 21, 1987; buried Pineview Cemetery, Greenville.

EBERLE, ALFRED M., college dean; b. Chgo., Oct. 8, 1892; s. Theodore F. and Julia (Ditt) E.; m. Mary Dolve, Apr. 21, 1933; children: Gretchen, Julia Ann, Benjamin. BS, Mont. State Coll., 1915; student, Ia. State Coll., 1928-29; MS, U. Minn., 1939. County agrl. agt. Perkins County, S.D., 1922-25, Clark County, S.D., 1925-28; mktg. specialist 1928-33; dir. agrl. extension S.D. State Coll., 1933-40, dean of agriculture, from

1940; part time dir. Resettlement Adminstrn. and mgr. Rural Rehab. Corp., 1933-35; sec. Cooperative Wool Growers, State Coun. of Agriculture; state rep. Nat. Resources Planning Com.; mem. State Land Use Program Com.; vice chmn. Natrual Resources Commn.; state chmn. coordinating com. Mo. Basin Devel.; vice chmn. Pres.'s Adv. Com. on Weather Control. Recipient Disting. Service award Epsilon Sigma Phi. Mem. Masons, K.T., Shriners, Alpha Zeta. Methodist. Home: Brookings S.D. †

EBERLEIN, WILLIAM FREDERICK, mathematician, educator; b. Shawano, Wis., June 25, 1917; s. Michael Gustave and Lora Elizabeth (Rather) E.; m. Mary Barry, May 29, 1943 (div. Jan. 1952); children—Patrick, Kathryn, Michael, Robert; m. Patricia James, June 23, 1956 (div. Sept. 1976); children—Kristen, Sarah, Mary. A.B., Harvard U., 1938, Ph.D., 1942; M.A., U. Wis., 1939. Instr. Purdue U., 1946, U. Mich., 1946-47; mem. Inst. for Advanced Study, Princeton, N.J., 1947-48; asst. prof. U. Wis., Madison, 1948-54; asso. prof. U. Wis., 1954-55; vis. prof. Wayne U., Detroit, 1955-56; mem. Courant Inst., NYU, N.Y.C., 1956-57; prof. math. U. Rochester (N.Y.), 1957-82, prof. emeritus, from 1982. Contbr. articles to profl. jours. Mem. Democratic Com., Rochester, 1958-60. Served with USNR, 1942-46. Office Naval Research grantee, 1957-62; NSF grantee, 1962-69. Mem. Am. Math. Soc., Math. Assn. Am. Club: Harvard (Rochester). Home: Rochester N.Y. Died June 13, 1986.

EBLE, CHARLES E., utilities executive; b. N.Y.C., Nov. 23, 1900; s. Gottfried and Louise (Eble) E.; m. Roselind Canning, Feb. 12, 1922 (dec. 1973); 1 son, Charles Robert. Student, Alexander Hamilton Sch. Bus. Adminstrn., 1921-22; LLD (hon.), Union Coll., 1961. Joined Consol. Gas Co. (named changed to Consol. Edison 1936), N.Y.C., 1916, asst. controller, 1935, controller, 1946, v.p., 1953-57, pres., trustee, 1957-66, chmn. bd., chief exec. officer, 1966-67; dir. East River Savs. Bank, Empire State Atomic Devel. Assocs., Inc. Trustee Nat. Indsl. Conf. Bd., N.Y.C. Mus. Sci. and Tech., Voorhees Tech. Inst., N.Y.C. Mem. Controller's Inst., Commerce and Industry Assn. N.Y., Inc. (past dir.), N.Y. C. of C. (past v.p., dir.), Seaview Country Club, Saratoga Golf Club. Home: New York N.Y. Died July 21, 1987.

EBY, MARGARETTE FINK, university administrator, musician; b. Detroit, Feb. 8, 1931; d. Christian Gotthilf and Martha Frieda (Noack) Fink; m. Stewart Leon Eby, Aug. 25, 1950; children: Dayle Marlene, Mark Douglas, Jonathan Stewart, Margaret Lynn. Student, Wheaton Coll. (Ill.), 1947-49; B.A., Wayne State U., 1955, M.A., 1962; Ph.D., U. Mich., 1971. Prof. music U. Mich., Dearborn, 1972-77, chmn. dept. humanities, 1975-77; dean Coll. Humanities and Fine Arts U. No. Iowa, Cedar Falls, 1977-81; provost, vice chancellor U. Mich., Flint, 1981-83, spl. asst. to chancellor, from 1983; pres. Flint Community Cultural Festivals, from 1983; cons., evaluator Nort Central Assn. Colls. and Schs., Chgo., from 1982; dir. Flint Inst. Music, 1981-83, Waterloo-Cedar Falls Symphony Orch., 1979-81; artistic dir. Fair Lane Music Guild, Dearborn, 1973-77; piano and harpsichord recitalist, Mich., Wis., Iowa. Chmn. U. Mich.-Flint United Way, 1982; regent Wartburg Coll., Waverly, Iowa, 1980—. Rackham research grantee, 1968; fellow Inst. Adminstrv. Advancement, Ford Found. and Carnegie Corp., 1975. Mem. Am. Assn. Higher Edn. Home: Flint Mich. Deceased.

ECCLES, WILLARD L., banker; b. Logan, Utah, Feb. 12, 1909; s. David and Ellen (Stoddard) E.; m. Ruth Pierpont, Aug. 20, 1930; children: Barbara, Susan. Student, U.S. Agrl. Coll., Oreg. State Coll., Babson Inst. With First Security Bank of Utah (N.A.), 1932-85, sr. v.p., sec., dir.; v.p., sec., dir. First Security Corp.; v.p., dir. First Security Bank of Rock Springs, Wyo.; dir. Eccles Investment Co., Anderson Lumber Co., Pioneer Wholesale Supply Co., Western Mfg. Co., Browning Arms Co., Willard Bay Devel. Corp. Bd. dirs. Pacific Coast Banking Sch. Mem. Bank Mktg. Assn., C. of C., Alta Club, Weber Club, Ogden Golf and Country Club, Sigma Chi. Mem. Ch. Jesus Christ of Latter-day Saints. Home: Ogden Utah. Died Mar. 18, 1985.

ECHOLS, WILLIAM GRAHAM, clergyman, educator; b. Tuskegee, Ala., Nov. 11, 1892; s. John Thomas and Lillie (Ware) E.; m. Virginia Hale, May 26, 1916; children: Mary L. Echols Blackmarr, William Graham, John Hale. AB, U. Ala., 1914; student, Emory U. and Ga. Inst. Tech., 1914-15; AM, Birmingham So. Coll., 1924; DD, Athens Coll., 1934. Ordained to Meth. ministry, 1916. Pastor Brandon Ch., St. John's Ch., 67th St. Ch., Fountain Hieghts Ch., N. Highlands Ch., Mt. Vernon Ch., 1912-33; mem. faculty Athens Coll., 1918-19, Birmingham So. Coll., 1928-30; univ. minister, dir. Wesley Found., 1933-58; mem. faculty U. Ala., 1933-58; pulpit minister Broadway Temple, N.Y.C., 1925; dean S.E. Jurisdiction Meth. Student Movement; dean. dir. Ala. Meth. Students; founder, pres. Pilgrimage Assocs., Inc., ednl. travel tour co.; cruise lectr. Mediterranean and the Holy Land.; lectr. pastor's schs., leadership schs., federated and civic clubs. Mem. exec. council Boy Scouts Am., chmn. conf. commn. on vacat. guidance. Mem. Nat. Soc. Biblical Lit. and Exegesis, Nat. Soc. Biblical Instrs., Am. Schs. Oriental Rsch., Am. Oriental Soc., Middle East Inst., Am. Rsch. Ctr. Egypt, So. Council Internat. Relations, So. Soc. for Philosophy of Religion, NaT. Triennial Soc. Univ. pastors (v.p.), Pi Tau Chi (founder), Omicron Delta Kappa, Kiwanis. Home: University Ala. †

ECKERT, RUTH ELIZABETH (MRS. JOHN H. MCCOMB), educator; b. Buffalo, Apr. 2, 1905; d. Edward Lee and Elizabeth Margaret (Fix) E.; m. Eric Edwin Paulson, Apr. 2, 1941 (dec. Dec. 1962); m. John Hess McComb, Nov. 23, 1973. AB cum laude, U. Buffalo, 1930, MA, 1932; EdD, Harvard U. (Austin fellowship), 1937; LittD (hon.), Houghton Coll., 1962; HHD, Drake U., 1964. Research assoc. U. Buffalo, 1932-36; research adviser Am. Council Edn., 1937-38; assoc. prof. edn. U. Minn., 1938-45, coordinator ednl. research, 1940-50, prof. higher edn., 1945-73, Regents' prof. higher edn., 1973-87; staff mem. charge studies secondary sch. students N.Y. Regents Inquiry, 1936-38; staff mem. Joint Legis. Com. Survey N.Y.C. Pub. Colls., 1943; chmn. work com. charge studies higher ednl. needs in Minn., Minn. Commn. Higher Edn., 1945-49; former ednl. cons. to individual coll. staffs in North Central area; mem. Nat. Adv. Com. on Presbyn. Colls., 1952-56, adv. com. on research U.S. Office Edn., 1956-58; mem. com. on research Ednl. Testing Service. Author: (with T.O Marshall) When You Leave School, 1938; Outcomes of General Education, 1943; (with R.J. Keller) A University Looks at its Program, 1954; (with John E. Stecklein) Job Motivations and Satisfactions of College Teachers, 1961; (with Robert T. Alciatore) Minnesota Ph.D's Evaluate Their Training, 1968; (with howard Y. Williams) College Faculty Members View Themselves and Their Jobs, 1972; (with Marcia S. Hanson) The University of Minnesota Senate and Its Committees, 1973; also chpts. in edn. books; editor: Studies in Higher Education, 1941, 43; Higher Education in Minnesota, 1950; contbr. articles to profl. jours. Mem. NEA (ednl. policies commn. 1956-60), Am. Ednl. Research Assn., Nat. Soc. Study Edn., Nat. Soc. Profs. Edn. (exec. com. 1951-56, 63-65, pres. 1954-55), Assn. for Higher Edn. (exec. com. 1947-49, 63-66), AAUP, Phi Beta Kappa. Home: Minneapolis Minn. Died Feb. 1, 1987.

ECKMAN, JAMES RUSSELL, medical editor, technical historian; b. Sioux City, Iowa, Apr. 25, 1908; s. James Abram and Katherine Russell (Letts) E.; m. Frances Elizabeth Kadlec, June 12, 1937. BA, U. Minn., 1932; MA, Georgetown U., 1944, PhD, 1946. Asst. editor Jour.-Lancet (med. jour.), Mpls., 1934-38; mem. sect. publs. Mayo Clinic, Rochester, Minn., 1938-87; press officer Mayo Clinic, 1948-65, sr. cons. sect. publs., 1965-87; asst. prof. history medicine Mayo Found., U. Minn., 1960-73; hist. editor Printing Impressions, 1960-72; owner Doomsday Press, Rochester, 1939-87; cons. Assn. Med. Illustrators, 1965. Author: Jerome Cardan, 1946, Sterling P. Rounds and His Printers Cabinet, 1962, The Heritage of the Printer, Vol 1, 1965; also articles on hist. research tech. aspects printing methods.; Editor: (Sterling P. Rounds) Among the Craft: Notes by the Way, 1968; editor, annotator: History of Typefounding in the United States (David Bruce), 1981. Bd. dirs. Rochester (Minn.) Civic Theatre, 1967. Served to capt. AUS, 1943-45. Mem. Mediaeval Acad. Am., Am. Inst. Graphic Arts, Soc. Typographic Arts Chgo., Gutenberg Gesellschaft (Mainz, Germany), Minn. Hist. Soc. (exec. council 1973), Omlsted County Hist. Soc. (sec. 1955-65), Printing Hist. Soc. (Eng.), Sigma Xi, Sigma Delta Chi, Phi Alpha Theta, Chi Phi. Clubs: Grolier, Typophiles (N.Y.C.); Press (Mpls.); Ampersand (Mpls.-St. Paul). Home: Rochester Minn. Died Apr. 28, 1987; buried in Rochester.

EDLUND, ROSCOE CLAUDIUS, association executive, management and business consultant; b. Bklyn., July 30, 1888; s. Claudius and Emma (Anderson) E.; m. Esther Gillette Alling, May 2, 1916 (dec. Apr. 5, 1965); 1 son, Harold Alling. AB, Cornell U., 1909; postgrad., N.Y. Sch. Social Work, 1913-14. Sec. to pres. Cornell U., 1909-12, dir. publs., 1909-12; asst. to gen. dir. Russell Sage Found., 1912-14; asst. sec. Cleve Community Chest, 1914-15; mng. dir. Balt. Community Chest, 1916-19, Hampden County Improvement League, Springfield, Mass., 1920-26; mgr. Nat. Assn. Am. Soap and Glicerine Producers, 1927-48; plans bd. chmn. Fred Rudge, Inc., N.Y.C., 1948-50; prin. Roscoe C. Edlund Assocs., mgmt. cons., N.Y.C., 1950-65, Kansas City, Mo., 1965-74; assoc. Rogers, Slade & Hill, Inc., mgmt. cons., N.Y.C., 1954-65. Author: To-Day's Challenge to Trade Associations, 1938, Ratio of Members Dues to Members Sales in 243 Trade Associations, 1954. Bd. dirs., sec., v.p. Eastchester (N.Y.) Community Fund, 1952-65, sec. Balt. Fund, 1916-19; chmn. McCoy Hall Recreation Commn. for Soldiers and Sailors, Balt., 1916-19; organizer, dir., treas. Am. Fat Salvage Com., N.Y.C., 1942-48; bd. govs. Lawrence Hosp., Bronxville, N.Y., 1954-59, v.p., 1959; mem. adv. bd. Christian Crusade, Tulsa; mem. men's com. Japan Internat. Christian U. Found., from 1967; hon. bd. dirs. Rockhurst Coll., from 1979; historian Class of 1909, Cornell U. Recipient Wisdom award of honor Wisdom Soc., Hon. Alumnus award Coll. Agr. and Life Scis. Cornell U., Notable Ams. award, 1978-79; honored guest Nat. Wholesale Druggists Assn. 100th Anniv. Conv., 1977; contbd. toward videotape teaching ctr.
named Roscoe Co. Edlund Videotape Room in dep
communication arts Cornell U. Fellow Harry
Truman Library Inst. (hon.); mem. Am. (sec.-treas
v.p., pres., chmn., hon. life), N.Y. (sec.-treas., v.p., pre
chmn., hon. life), Kansas City socs. assn. execs., NA
(chmn. assn. exec. group 1936), C. of C. U.S. (mer
assns. svc. com.), Assn. Mgmt. Consultants (trust
1970-72, award of honor 1974, hon. life mem.), Brita
nica Soc., Am. Viewpoint Inc. (dir. 1945-73, sec. 195
59), Laymen's Nat. Bible Com. (adv. com. from 1945
Am. Bible Soc. (bd. mgrs., 1952-65), Kansas City I
ternat. Rels. Coun., Kansas City People-to Peop
Coun., Friends of Art Nelson Gallery, Interna
Platform Assn., UN Assn. Common Cause, Siwanc
Country Club (Bronxville, N.Y.), Tower Club, Phi Be
Kappa, Delta Sigma Rho, Alpha Chi Rho. Bapti
(Mo. area dir. world mission campaign Am. Bapt. Con
1966-67). Home: Kansas City Mo. Deceased.

EDMONDS, FRANK NORMAN, JR., astonome
educator; b. Mpls., Sept. 2, 1919; s. Frank Norman an
Irene (Radcliffe) E.; m. Joan Mary McKinney, Mar. 2
1945; children: Cynthia Ann Edmonds Torkelso
Christopher Norman. AB, Princeton, 1941; PhD, U
Chgo., 1950. Asst. prof. astronomy U. Mo.-Columbi
1950-52; mem. faculty U. Tex., Austin, 1952-86; ass
prof. astronomy U. Tex., 1958-65, prof., 1965-86; Mem
naval adv. com. astronomy NRC, 1958-61, chmn., 196
61. Served to capt. AUS, 1941-45; Served to cap
USAAF, 1945-46. Guggenheim fellow, 1962-63. Mem
Internat. Astronom. Union, Am. Astron. Soc., Sigm
Xi. Home: Austin Tex. Died Sept. 3, 1986; burie
Austin.

EDMONDSON, HUGH ALLEN, physician; b. May
ville, Ark., Jan. 3, 1906; s. James Turner and Julia An
(Phillips) E.; m. Dorothy E. Mossman, July 14, 193
children: Hugh Allen, James Paul, Marian An
Marjorie Jean. AB, U. Okla., 1926; MD, U. Chgo
1931; LLD (hon.), U. So. Calif., 1977. Instr. patholog
U. So. Calif. Med. Sch., 1938-41, asst. prof. patholog
1941-43, assoc. prof., 1943-48, prof., 1948-86, hea
dept., 1951-72; dir. labs. and pathology Los Angel
County-U. So. Calif. Med. Center, 1968-72; attendin
staff Los Angeles County Hosp., 1939-86. Contbr. a
ticles med. publs. Trustee Estelle Doheny Eye Found
1971-86, pres. bd., 1972-84; chmn. bd. Estelle Doher
Eye Hosp., 1983-86; trustee Eisenhower Med. Cente
Palm Desert, Calif., 1974-86. Recipient Prof
Achievement award U. Chgo. Alumni Assn., 1979.
Fellow ACP; mem. AMA (chmn. sect. pathology an
physiology 1963-64), Coll. Am. Pathologists, Gastroen
Assn., Cal. Med. Assn. (past chmn. sec. patholog
sect.), Am. Assn. Pathologists and Bacteriologists, An
Soc. Clin. Pathologists, Internat. Acad. Patholog
(council 1960-63), Sigma Xi, Sigma Alpha Epsilon, N
Sigma Nu. Club: Valley Hunt (Pasadena). Home: Sa
Marino Calif. Died June 12, 1986.

EDMUNDS, PALMER DANIEL, lawyer, educator;
Terre Haute, Ill., Oct. 29, 1890; s. Amos and Mary An
(Campbell) E.; m. Margaret Burton, June 29, 1932 (de
1964); m. Sarah Shepard Brown, 1970. A.B., Kno
Coll., 1912, LL.D., 1945; LL.B., Harvard U., 191
LL.D., John Marshall Law Sch., 1973, Piedmont Col
1975. Bar: Ill. 1915. Practiced in Chgo.; dir., couns
Ill. Service Recognition Bd., 1922-25; mem. firm Dod
Matheny & Edmunds, 1925-29; commr. Supreme C
Ill., 1929-32; mem. Dodd & Edmunds, Chgo., 1932-5
lectr. conflict of laws and Ill. practice John Marsha
Law Sch., Chgo., 1926-58; prof. law John Marshall La
Sch., 1958-86, lectr. fed. practice, 1938-58; dir. Lawye
Inst.; vis. prof. law Knox Coll., 1944-57; complian
commr. WPB and Civilian Prodn. Adminstrn., 1944-4
hearing commr. NPA, 1951-53. Author: (with W.
Dodd) Illinois Appellate Procedure, 1929, Edmund
Common Law Forms, 1931, Illinois Civil Practi
Forms, 1933, Edmunds Federal Rules of Civ
Procedure, 1938, Cyclopedia of Federal Procedu
Forms, 1939, Law and Civilization, 1959; co-autho
(with W. F. Dodd) Encyclopedia of Federal Procedur
2d edit, 1944, Edmunds Conflict of Laws, 1948; Edito
compiler: (with W. F. Dodd) Jones Illinois Statute
Annotated, vols. 18-22, 24. Charter mem. World Peac
Through Law Center.; Trustee John Marshall Law Sch
Past comdr. Black Hawk Post, Am. Legion, Chgo.; pas
historian Dept. of Ill. First lt. A.E.F., 1917-19; cap
O.R.C. Mem. Am. Polit. Sci. Assn., Am. Acad. Poli
and Social Sci., Fgn. Policy Assn., Am., Ill., Chgo
Internat. bar assns., India Soc. Internat. Law, Ill. His
Soc., S.A.R., Nat. Sojourners, Am. Bantam Assn
Sebright Club Am., 40 and 8, Soc. of 28th Div., Con
for Continuation Congl. Christian Chs. U.S., P
Gamma Delta, Delta Sigma Rho. Democrat. Conglis
Clubs: Mason (Chgo.), Elk. (Chgo.), Harvard (Chgo.)
Home: Gilman Ill. Died Jan. 8, 1986.

EDWARDS, BILLY MATT, health care administrato
b. Mt. Pleasant, Tex., Dec. 3, 1920; s. William Hampto
and Dovie E. (Johnson) E.; m. Martiel Evelyn Austi
Feb. 22, 1941; children: Sandra Augusta (Mrs. Parke
Council), Billie Sharon (Mrs. Robert Shettlesworth
Barry Michael. Student, Washington Sch. Art, 1945-4
diploma hosp. adminstrn., Nat. Naval Med. Ctr
Bethesda, Md., 1955; LLB, LaSalle U., 1956; JD, U
Chgo., 1967. Enlisted as seaman U.S. Navy 193
commd. ensign, 1951, advanced through grades to l
comdr., 1961, served with Marine Corps at Guada

nal, Tulagi, Okinawa, other S. Pacific areas, ret., 1962, ed. adviser to Republic China, 1960-62; pres. Edwards nterprises, Inc., Keokuk, Iowa, 1962-71; adminstr. enn. Psychiat. Hosp. and Research Inst., Memphis, 963-71; v.p. Tranquillaire Health Facilities, Inc., Iemphis, 1970-72; exec. v.p. Americare, Inc., Atlanta, 972-75; exec. dir. CONALCOL (cons. in alcohol), Iemphis, 1967-77; former dir. BEM Ednl. Enterprises; roject cons. Hosp. Affiliates Internat., Inc., Nashville, 976-78; health care specialist Mgmt. Recruiters, Iemphis, 1978-79; regional health care adminstr. State Tenn., Memphis, 1980-81; mem. Tenn. Long Term sychiat. Care Co.; Memphis dist. adviser to hosp. grs.; mem. Gov.'s Commn. Mental Retardation. uthor: Kandid Kartoon Kapers, 1965, No Tears for ommy, 1979; composer songs. Bd. dirs. Memphis-ielby County Blood Bank; vice chmn. mayor's drug uncil. Recipient citation comdr.-in-chief Republic hina Navy, 1962, commendation chief U.S. Mil. Adv. roup, Taiwan, 1962. Mem. Tenn. Hosp. Assn., Iemphis-Shelby County Hosp. Council, Coast Guard ux., Memphis Yacht Club, Shriners. Methodist. ome: Memphis Tenn. Died May 29, 1981; buried Iemphis.

DWARDS, BRYAN C., gas company execu-ve. Chmn. AMOCO Gas Co., Chgo. Home: Burr idge Ill. Died Mar. 26, 1984.

DWARDS, CARLETON BAILEY, chemical anufacturing executive; b. Hamilton, Wash., Sept. 22, 392; s. Joshua Pennington and Ella (Bailey) E.; m. live Frances Modlin, Oct. 1, 1919; children: Richard Iodlin, Lois Ann Edwards Guinnup. AB, Earlham oll., 1915, MA, 1917. Head dept. chemistry Guilford oll., 1915-18; rsch. chemist E.I. duPont de Nemours & o., 1918-21; with Republic Creosoting Co. and Reilly ar & Chem. Corp., Indpsl., from 1921, rsch. chemist, r. rsch., gen. mgr., then pres., dir., 1952-60, chmn. l., from 1960; bd. dirs. Grain Dealers Mut. Ins. Co., t Fed. Savs. & Loan Assn. Patentee in field. Pres. bd. ustees Town of Meridian Hills, Ind., 1947-53; sec. dir. arlham Found.; trustee Earlham Coll. Mem. Am. hem. Soc., Mfg. Chemists Assn. (bd. dirs.), Columbus lub (Indpls.), Meridian Hills Country Club, Rotary. Iem. Soc. of Friends. Home: Indianapolis Ind. †

DWARDS, CHARLES MUNDY, JR., management onsultant, former university dean; b. Richmond, Va., ov. 2, 1903; s. Charles Mundy and Lelia Le Moyne Gahagan) E.; m. Nancy Blow Rawls, Apr. 2, 1931 (dec. ov. 1968); children: Charles M. III, Richard Franklin; . Marie Elizabeth Flannery, Oct. 10, 1969. BS in Bus. dminstrn., U. Richmond, 1925, LLD (hon.), 1963; MS Retailing, NYU, 1930, DCS, 1936. Instr. English, ead track coach Staunton Mil. Acad., Va., 1925-29; ith mgmt. div. James McCreery & Co., N.Y.C., 1929-); merchandising and sales promotion exec. Frederick oeser & Co., Bklyn., 1930-31; with Inst. Retail Mgmt. YU, 1930-85, successively lectr., instr., asst. prof., as-c. prof., prof., 1943-63, Mchts. Council prof. retail gmt., 1964-70, dean, 1946-70, sr. dean univ., 1959-70, ean emeritus, prof. emeritus, 1970-85; cons. retailers d mfrs., 1936-85; sr. v.p. Search Assocs., Inc., ımmit, N.J.; dir. Russ Togs, Inc., Concord Fabrics, c., Old Deerfield Fabrics, Inc. Author: (with William Howard) Retail Advertising and Sales Promotion, 936, rev. edit. 1943, 3d edit (with Russell A. Brown) 959, 4th edit. (with Carl F. Lebowitz) 1981, The Retail dvertising Budget, 1950, rev. edit. 1952; editor: The etail Series, 1946-63; chmn. editorial bd.: Jour. etailing, 1946-73. 2d lt. to capt. U.S. Army Res., 924-37; organizer, dir. Army Exchange Service Sch.; TO; with assimilated rank col., 1945. Decorated evalier Ordre Du Comml., France; named One of All-me Greats in retail sales promotion, 1969; named to etail Advt. Hall of Fame, 1958, Retail Educators Hall Fame, 1981. Mem. Nat. Retail Mchts. Assn. (dir. 951-53, Gold medal 1958), Am. Mktg. Assn., Am. ollegiate Retail Assn. (founding mem., pres. 1948-49), appa Alpha, Omicron Delta Kappa, Eta Mu Pi, Alpha elta Sigma. Methodist. Home: Summit N.J. Died ct. 31, 1985; buried Fair Mt. Cemetery, Chathamm, ew Jersey.

DWARDS, EDWARD EVERETT, finance educator; Bloomfield, Ind., July 15, 1908; s. Lewis Baker and lta Ethel (Terrell) E.; m. Louise Robinson, Sept. 2, 933; children: Robert Alan, Margaret Louise. BS, U. d., 1928, MS, 1934. Methods investigator Western ectric Co., 1928-31; statistician Ind. Dept. Fin. In-ns., 1933-36; Ind. dir. Nat. Youth Adminstrn., 1935-; asst. prof. U. Ind., Bloomington, 1936-41, assoc. of., 1941-48, prof. fin., 1948-62, Fred. T. Greene prof. ., 1962-73, prof. fin. emeritus, 1973-84, assoc. dir. rad Sch. Savs. and Loan, 1946-62; v.p. Bus. and Real state Trends, Inc., 1949-84; cons. to chmn. Fed. Home oan Bank Bd., 1961-62; dir. Irwin Union Bank, olumbus, Ind., 1963-81, Gt. N.W. Fed. Savs. and Loan ssn.; vis. prof. Ariz. State U., 1968-69, 1980; adv. com. 950, 1960 Census of Housing; cons. White House, Sec. ef., Sec. Army, 1948-50, Fed. Home Loan Bank Bd., 961-63, FDIC, 1964-65, Commn. Fin. Structure and egulation, 1970-72; dir. Fed. Home Loan Bank, dpls., 1963-64. Cons. editor Mortgage Guaranty Ins. orp., 1968-76. Capt. to lt. col. fin. dept., AUS, 1942-. Mem. Am. Fin. Assn. (sec.-treas. 1947-51, pres. 952), Am. Econ. Assn., Am. Savs. and Loan Inst., Beta Gamma Sigma, Delta Sigma Pi. Democrat. Methodist. Home: Bloomington Ind. Died Dec. 8, 1984.

EDWARDS, JAMES ELLIS, publisher; b. Eagle Grove, Iowa, Dec. 3, 1892; s. John Ellis and Florence Helena (Hicks) E.; m. Esther Stebbins Baker, Nov. 28, 1919; children: Shirley, Marilyn, James, Barbara. Student, The Cedar Rapids (Iowa) Bus. Sch., 1910-11. Adv. rep. Kimball's Dairy Farmer hdqrs., Waterloo, Iowa, 1911-13; with Prairie Farmer-WLS, Chgo., from 1913; pres. Prairie Farmer Pub. Co., WLS Inc.. oper. radio sta. WLS, Chgo., from 1948; pres. Wallace Homestead Co., Des Moines, Wis. Farmer Co., from 1957. Mem. Agrl. Pubs. Assn. (pres.), Chgo. Athletic Assn., La Grange (Ill.) Country Club. Congregationalist. Home: Hinsdale Ill. †

EDWARDS, JOHN S., orchestra manager; b. St. Louis, 1912. AB, U. N.C., 1930; MA, Harvard U., 1932; D Musical Arts (hon.), Cleve. Inst. Music, 1978; LHD, DePaul U., 1979. Began as music reviewer St. Louis Globe-Democrat; staff St. Louis Symphony Orch., later mgr.; formerly bus. mgr. Los Angeles Philharm. Orch., Hollywood Bowl; asst. mgr. Pitts. Symphony Orch., 1945-48; mgr. Balt. Symphony Orch., Washington Nat. Symphony, 1948-55, Pitts. Symphony Orch., 1955-67; mgr. Chgo. Symphony Orch., 1967-84, exec. v.p., 1975; past mem. adv. com. Nat. Cultural Ctr., Washington, Commonwealth Pa. Council of Arts; bd. dirs. Am. Symphony Orch. League, Vienna, Va., past pres., chmn. bd., 1968-73; charter mem. Chgo. Council on Fine Arts, 1978-84. Recipient Gold Baton award Am. Symphony Orch. League, 1975. Home: Chicago Ill. Died Aug. 10, 1984.

EDWARDS, LENA FRANCES, gynecologist/obstetrician; b. Washington, Sept. 17, 1900; d. Thomas W. and Marie (Cookley) E.; m. L. Keith Madison, June 7, 1924 (dec. 1980); children: Marie S. (Mrs. Victor Metoyer), Edward K., Genevieve A., Thomas A., John J., Paul F. BS, Howard U., 1921, MD, 1924. Diplomate Am. Bd. Ob-Gyn. Asst. attending obstetrician Margaret Hauge Maternity Hosp., Jersey City, 1931-54, 1965-70; asst. attending gynecologist Jersey City Med. Ctr., 1949-54; asst. prof. ob-gyn. Howard U. Coll. Medicine, 1954-60; operator St. Joseph's Maternity Clinic, Hereford, Tex., 1960-65; gynecologist Jersey City Women's Job Corps of the Poverty Program; attending obstetrician, gynecologist Freedman Hosp.; ret.; vol. health screening programs; participated numerous panels on sex edn. for schs., chs.; bd. dirs. Lona Whippen Home for Unwed Mothers. Named Woman Doctor of Yr. N.J. br. Am. Med. Women's Assn., 1955; recipient Medal of Freedom, 1964. Fellow Inter. Coll. Surgeons, Am. Coll. Ob-Gyn.; mem. N.J. League of Women Voters, Nat. Fedn. Colored Women's Clubs, Delta Sigma Theta. Home: Lakewood N.J. Died Dec. 3, 1986.

EELLS, HOWARD PARMALEE, JR., business executive; b. Cleve., Aug. 25, 1892; s. Howard P. and Alice Maud (Stager) E.; m. Adele Chisholm, June 7, 1919. AB, Williams Coll., 1915; LLD (hon.), U. Nev., 1953. With Cen. Nat. Bank and Superior Savs. & Trust Co., Cleve., 1915; with acctg. dept. Dolomite Products Co., 1916; with Basic Inc. and predecessor cos., from 1919, v.p. and gen. mgr., later cons., also bd. dirs., chmn. various subs. cos. Trustee Mus. Arts Assn., Lake View Cemetery Assn., Western Res. Hist. Assn. With NG, 1916-17, Mex. Border, 2d. lt. F.A. U.S. Army, ETO, 1918-19. Home: Cleveland Ohio. †

EELLS, JOHN SHEPARD, JR., educator, author; b. San Francisco, Mar. 31, 1906; s. John Shepard and Mario (Coffin) E.; m. Juliet Guion Oakes, July 30, 1938; children: Guion Oakes, Marion Coffin. BA, Yale U., 1928; LLB, JD, Stanford U., 1931; MA, U. Calif., 1939, PhD, 1943. Bar: Calif. 1932. Assoc. Orrick, Palmer & Dahlquist, San Francisco, 1931-35; faculty mem. Thacher Sch., 1935-38, Pamona Coll., 1943-44, U. Chgo., 1944-45; prof. English Beloit Coll., 1945-55; prof. English Winthrop Coll., 1955-71, disting. prof., 1967-85, chmn. honors council, 1960-71, faculty rep. on bd. trustees, 1970, cons. to pres., 1971-73; pres. Nat. Collegiate Honors Council, 1970-71. Author: Telling Time, The Touchstones of Matthew Arnold; contbr. to: Atlantic Monthly; contbr.: works Kenyon Rev., others. Mem. MLA, State Bar Calif., Am. Soc. Psychical Research, Phi Beta Kappa, Elizabethan (Yale) Club, Rock Hill Country Club. Home: Rock Hill S.C. Died Mar. 28, 1985; cremated.

EGAN, WILLIAM JOHN, physician; b. Hurley, Wis., Oct. 30, 1892; s. Timothy Francis and Mary (Murray) E.; m. Viola Forster, Sept. 25, 1919; children: William John, James Forster, Vi (Mrs. Richard A. Candee). BS, U. Mich., 1914, MD, 1916. Diplomate Am. Bd. Internal Medicine. Intern Milw. Hosp., 1916-17; fellow Mayo Clinic; practice internal medicine from 1919; staff mem. Milw. Hosp., Columbia Hosp., Milwaukee County Hosp.; asst. prof. internal medicine Marquette U., 1919-66, assoc. prof. internal medicine emeritus, from 1966; former mem. bd. control Nat. Wholesale Druggists Assn.; chmn. Crandon Drug Co., Miami, Fla.; pres. Yahr-Lange Wholesale Drugs, Milw., La Crosse Wis., Rockford, Ill. Author med. publs. and papers on personnel mgmt. Former chmn. Milw. chpt. ARC, dir. blood bank, 1944, exec. com. from 1934; former bd. govs. Am. Nat. Red Cross, 1946; vice chmn. Milw. Safety Commn. Capt. Med. Res. Corps Red Cross, AEF, France, 1918-19. Hon. mem. faculty U. Guatemala, 1937. Mem. ACP, AMA, Am. Rheumatism Assn., Wis. (councilor), Milwaukee County med. socs., Wis. Rheumatism Assn., Milw. Acad. Medicine, Milw. Soc. Internists, Am. Legion, Mil. Order of Fgn. Wars, Mil. Order of World War Officers, Milw. Club, City Club, K.C., Phi Rho Sigma, Alpha Omega Alpha. Roman Catholic. Home: Milwaukee Wis. †

EGBERT, LESTER DARLING, insurance company executive; b. Jersey City, Mar. 4, 1892; s. James Chidester and Emma (Pennington) E.; m. Beatrice Valerie Cook, May 14, 1921 (dec. 1982); children: John Pennington, Richard Cook. Asst. dept. mgr., Fidelity & Casualty Co. N.Y., 1914-16; with, Brown, Crosby & Co., Inc., 1916-87, dir., 1924-87, sec., 1934-40, v.p., 1940-47, pres., 1947-58, chmn. bd., 1958-64. dir. E.U.C. Corp., 1927-64. Past commr. Redevel. Agy, Montclair, N.J.; past trustee Community Chest, Montclair, Leonard Wood Meml., Columbia U; bd. dirs. Matheson Found., Inc. 1st lt., 22d Area Squadron, AUS, World War I. Mem. Ins. Soc. N.Y. (past pres.), Nat. Assn. Ins. Brokers, Ins. Brokers Assn. N.Y. (past pres.), N.Y. C. of C., Acad. Polit. Sci., Alumni Fedn. Columbia U. (past pres.), Nat. Inst. Social Scis., Zeta Psi, Columbia U. Club, Downtown Assn., Univ. Club of N.Y.C., Rock Spring Country Club, Bay Head Yacht Club, Montclair Golf Club, Spring Lake Golf Club, Pilgrims Club. Episcopalian. Home: Upper Montclair N.J. Deceased 1987.

EHLERS, JOSEPH HENRY, civil engineer, lawyer; b. Hartford, Conn., Dec. 31, 1892; s. C. Julius and Caroline T. (Sauer) E.; m. Marcellite Edwards Hardy, Feb. 15, 1945 (dec. Apr. 1964). B.S., Trinity Coll., 1914; M.S. in Civil Engring, U. Calif., 1915; M.C.E., Cornell U., 1916. Registered profl. engr., D.C. Chief insp. for Modjeski & Angier, Pitts., 1919; prof. structural engring. Pei Yang U., China, 1920-24; constrn. engr. Asia Devel. Co. on diversion of Yellow River, 1923; U.S. trade commr. on earthquake reconstrn. and tech. devel. of Japan 1926-30; acting comml. attache Am. embassy Tokyo, 1929; tech. dir. Nat. Conf. on Constrn., Washington, 1931-33; asst. to dep. adminstr. Fed. Emergency Adminstrn. Pub. Works, Washington, 1933-38; chief cons. engring. div. Fed. Works Agy. (War Pub. Works Program), 1942-46; cons. engr., atty. Washington, 1946-88; exec. dir. Nat. Conf. on Pub. Works, 1955-56; san. engring. dir. USPHS Res. Corps, ret.; asst. commr. tech. services Urban Renewal Adminstrn., Washington, 1955-58; housing coordinator ICA, Yemen, 1960-61; cons. UN, 1962-63; tech. adviser Govt. of Iraq Ministry Works at Baghdad. Author: Letters of Travel, 1965, Far Horizons-The Travel Diary of An Engineer, 1966; Editor: Jour. Chinese and Am. Engrs. Assn, 1923-24; Contbr. articles to profl. mags. Mem. organizing com., del. World Engring. Congress, Tokyo, 1929; chmn. adv. com. engrs. U.S. Civil Service Commn., 1950-57; pres. Joseph H. Ehlers Found., Russellville, Ky., 1971. Decorated Order Brilliant Star (China).; Recipient medal for excellence Trinity Coll., 1974; Founder's gold medal Phi Tau Phi; Scholastic Honor Soc. China; award Washington Soc. Engrs., 1982. Fellow ASCE (Washington rep. 1949-55, sec. city planning div.); mem. D.C. Bar Assn. (com. Internat. law), D.C. Soc. Prof. Engrs. (dir.), AIA (hon.), Explorers Club, Phi Beta Kappa. Club: University (Washington). Lodge: Rotary. Home: Washington D.C. Died June 23, 1988, buried Russellville, Ky.

EHRENPREIS, IRVIN, language educator; b. N.Y.C., June 9, 1920; s. Louis and Edith (Lipman) E. m. Anne Willard Henry, Aug. 19, 1961 (dec. 1978); 1 son, David Henry; m. Mary Louise Kemp, 1983. BA, CCNY, 1938; MA, Columbia U., 1939, PhD, 1944; Docteur Honoris Causa, U. Besançon, France, 1965. With dept. English Ind. U., 1945-65, prof., 1961-65; prof. English, U. Va., from 1965, Commonwealth prof. English, 1967-75, Linden Kent prof. English, from 1975; vis. prof. Brandeis U., 1961, Harvard Summer Sch., 1962, U. Minn. Summer Sch., 1960, U. Wash. Summer Sch., 1964, U. Münster, Germany, summer 1983; Beckman prof. U. Calif. at Berkeley, spring 1978; seminar leader Folger Inst., fall 1981; vis. fellow All Souls Coll., Oxford (Eng.) U., 1981-82; vis. rsch. fellow Merton Coll., Oxford (Eng.) U., 1968. Author: The Types Approach to Literature, 1945, The Personality of Jonathan Swift, 1958, Swift, Vol. I, 1962, Vol. II, 1967, vol. III, 1983, Fielding: Tom Jones, 1964, Wallace Stevens: A Critical Anthology, 1972, Literary Meaning and Augustan Values, 1974, Acts of Implication, 1980; co-editor: J. Swift, Prose Works, VIII, 1953, XIV, 1968; contbr. N.Y. Rev. Books. Fulbright fellow Oxford (Eng.) U., 1949-50, Guggenheim fellow, 1955-56, 62-63, Am. Coun. Learned Socs. fellow, 1958-59, NEH sr. fellow, 1967-68. Fellow Am. Acad. Arts and Scis. Home: Charlottesville Va. Died July 3, 1985.

EICHHORN, GEORGE CARL, foundation executive; b. Norfolk, Va., Apr. 8, 1901; s. George Jacob and Katherine Elizabeth (Marburger) E.; m. Hermene Wharton Warlick, Aug. 2, 1926; children—Charles Richard, Mary Louise Eichhorn Simons. Student pub. schs., Greensboro, N.C. City clk., treas. City of Greensboro, 1924-37; with Richardson-Merrell Inc. (formerly Vick Chem. Co.), Wilton, Conn., 1937-66; pres. Richardson-Merrell Inc. (Vick Mfg. div.), 1951-63, corp.

v.p. for mfg., 1964-66, ret., 1966; asst. to pres. Smith Richardson Found., Inc., Greensboro, 1967-70, asst. sec.-treas., 1970-74, adminstrv. v.p., treas., 1974-81, trustee, 1974-83. Bd. dirs. United Arts Council, Greensboro, 1966-76, pres., 1968-70; bd. dirs. Greensboro Preservation Soc., 1971-78; trustee Bus. Found. N.C., Chapel Hill, 1959-71, Excellence Fund, U. N.C., Greensboro, 1966-83; bd. visitors Guilford Coll., 1968-74; sr. warden Holy Trinity Episcopal Ch., 1949-51. Clubs: Rotary (Greensboro) (pres. 1952-53), Greensboro Country (Greensboro). Home: Greensboro N.C. Died. Nov. 1, 1983; interred Holy Trinity Church, Greensboro, N.C.

EIDMAN, KRAFT WARNER, lawyer; b. Liberty Hill, Tex., Jan. 17, 1912; s. Kraft H. and Vera (Bates) E.; m. Julia Mary Bell, Aug. 31, 1940; children: Kraft Gregory, Dan Kelly, John Bates. Student, Rice U., 1929-30; A.B., U. Tex., 1935, LL.B., 1935. Bar: Tex. 1935. Practiced in Housto; sr. partner Fulbright & Jaworski (and predecessors), from 1947; lectr. law sci. insts., medico-legal insts., state bar meetings.; v.p., dir. Def. Research Inst.; mem. centennial commn. U. Tex. Editor: Ins. Counsel Jour., 1961-63; contbr. articles to legal jours. Life trustee, pres. U. Tex. Law Sch. Found.; trustee, past chmn. U. Tex. Health Sci. Center Found. at Houston; mem. exec. com., chancellor's council U. Tex.; former trustee, mem. exec. com. Inst. Rehab. and Research; bd. dirs. Tex. Med. Ctr., Houston, Houston chpt. ARC; v.p., trustee M.D. Anderson Found. Served to lt. comdr. USNR, 1942-45. Named Disting. Alumnus, U. Tex., 1978. Fellow Am. Coll. Trial Lawyers (regent 1972-76, pres. elect 1976-77, pres. 1977-78), Am., Tex. bar founds.; mem. Anglo-Am. Exchange, Am. Counsel Assn., ABA (vice chmn. trial tactics coms.), Tex. Bar Assn. (chmn. tort and compensation law), Houston Bar Assn. (pres. 1960-61), Internat. Assn. Ins. Counsel (exec. com. 1957-60, 51-66, pres. 1964-65), Houston C. of C., U. Tex. Law Sch. Alumni Assn. (pres., Disting. Alumnus 1980), T Assn., Chancellors, Friar Soc. Democrat. Roman Catholic. Clubs: KC, Kiwanis (pres. S.W. Houston 1958), Houston, Colonneh, Houston Country, Briar (pres. 1952), Chaparral (Dallas); Lakeway Country (Austin), University (Austin), Capital (Austin), Tarry House (Austin). Home: Houston Tex. Died Oct. 19, 1986.

EISELE, DONN FULTON, investment counselor, former astronaut; b. Columbus, Ohio, June 23, 1930; s. Herman E. and June (Davisson) E.; m. Susan H. Hearn, Aug. 2, 1969; children: Melinda Sue, Donn Hamilton, Jon, Kristin, Andrew. BS, U.S. Naval Acad., 1952; MS in Astronautics, USAF Inst. Tech., 1960. Commd. 2d lt. USAF, 1953; advanced through grades to col.; assigned USAF, Rapid City, S.D., 1953-55, Wheelus AFB, Libya, 1955-58; missile systems engr. Wright-Patterson AFB, Ohio, 1960-61; student test pilot Aerospace Research Pilot Sch., Edwards AFB, Calif., 1962; exptl. flight test officer Kirtland AFB, N.Mex., 1962-63; astronaut NASA Manned Spacecraft Center, Houston, 1964-70; command module pilot Apollo Seven, 11-day maiden Apollo flight NASA Manned Spacecraft Center, 1968; backup crew mem. NASA Manned Spacecraft Center (Apollo Ten); tech. cons. Langley Research Center, Hampton, Va., 1970-72; ret. USAF, 1972; dir. Peace Corps, Bangkok, Thailand, 1972-74; dir. sales Eastern U.S. Marion Power Shovel Co., 1975-79; exec. v.p. Trans Carib Air, 1979-80; v.p. investments Drexel Burnham Lambert, Lauderhill, Fla., 1980-81; v.p. instl. and pvt. accounts Oppenheimer & Co., Ft. Lauderdale, Fla., 1981-87; v.p. Prudential Bache Securities, Ft. Lauderdale, 1987. Decorated D.F.C., Legion of Merit; recipient Exceptional Service medal NASA, Diplome de Record FAI; Haley Astronautics award.; TV Emmy award. Fellow Am. Astronautical Soc., Explorers Club; mem. Soc. Exptl. Test Pilots, AFTRA, Tau Beta Pi. Home: Fort Lauderdale Fla. Died Dec. 1, 1987; cremated.

EISEMAN, FLORENCE, fashion designer, clothing manufacturer; b. Mpls., Sept. 27, 1899; m. Laurence H. Eiseman, Nov. 24, 1927 (dec. 1967); children: Laurence H., Robert D. Ed. pub. schs., Mpls. Engaged in children's clothing bus. Milw., 1945-88; v.p., pres., chmn. Florence Eiseman, Inc., Milw., 1945-88, Florence Eiseman Knits, Inc., Milw., 1960-88. Recipient Disting. Contbn. to Fashion award Neiman Marcus Co., 1955, Swiss Fabrics award, 1956. Mem. Council Fashion Designers Am., Zonta Internat. Home: Milwaukee Wis. Died Jan. 8, 1988.

EISENBERG, LEONARD STERLING, real estate executive; b. Chgo., Mar. 4, 1923; s. Louis and Anna (Feingold) E.; m. Sydelle Resnick, June 29, 1947; children: Richard Brant, Russell Scott, Lisa Jane. PhD in Econs., U. Wis., 1946. V.p. Mother Hubbards Cake Co., Chgo., 1946-57; property mgr. G.R. Bailey & Co., Real Estate, Chgo., 1957-60; property mgr. Arthur Rubloff & Co., Real Estate, Chgo., 1960-82, v.p., mgr. gen. brokerage dept., 1967-71, adminstrv. v.p., 1971-73, sr. v.p., mgr. gen. brokerage dept., 1973-76, dir. property mgmt., 1976-79, dir., exec. com., 1972-82, dir. corp. adminstrn., 1979-82; v.p., sec. Gateway Ctr. Parking, Inc., Chgo., 1964-82; lectr. real estate. Contbr. articles to profl. trade jours. Trustee, chmn. No. Suburban Mass Transit Dist.; past pres. Friends Glencoe (Ill.) Pub. Library, Glencoe Blue Ribbon Com. With OSS, AUS, 1943-45. Mem. Michigan Blvd. Assn. (pres., dir. 1965-82), Nat. Assn. Realtors (mem. editorial com. 1973-76), Glencoe Hist. Soc., Realtors Nat. Mktg. Inst. (mem. governing council 1972-74), Inst. Real Estate Mgmt., Ill. Assn. Realtors, Chgo. Real Estate Bd. (dir. 1976-82, treas. 1978-79, v.p. 1979-82), Greater N. Michigan Ave. Assn., Chgo. Assn. Commerce, W. Central Assn., Bldg. Owners Mgrs. Assn., Lambda Alpha (treas. 1979-80, sec. 1980-82, chpt. pres. 1981-82), Pi Lambda Phi, Standard Club, Execs. Club. Home: Glencoe Ill. Died Dec. 17, 1982; buried Palatine, Ill.

EITEMAN, WILFORD J., economics educator, author; b. Rock Island, Ill., Feb. 13, 1902; s. Wilford Lee and Elida (Palmer) E.; m. Sylvia F. Chmelik, June 15, 1927; children: David Kurt, Dean Spencer. MB, Chgo. Mus. Coll., 1922; AB, Ohio Wesleyan U., 1926, MA, 1928; PhD, Ohio State U., 1931. Instr. econs. Ohio Wesleyan U., 1926-28; prof. acctg. Miami-Jacobs Coll., 1928-29; asst. instr. econs. Ohio State U., 1929-31; prof. econs. Albion Coll., 1931-37; Social Sci. Research Council fellow 1932-33; asst. prof. econs. Duke U., 1937-44, assoc. prof., 1945-46; assoc. prof. fin. Sch. Bus. Adminstrn. Rutgers U., 1946-47; prof. fin. U. Mich., 1947-86; vis. prof. econs. U. Ceylon, 1954-55; economist zinc, tin, and lead div. OPA, 1942, territorial price exec., Alaska, 1942-43; instr. Army U. Ctr., Biarritz, France, 1945-46; ednl. adviser European Productive Agy., Paris, 1959-60; Carnegie vis. prof. fin. U. Hawaii, 1964; vis. prof. fin. U. Fla., 1968, Ariz. State U., 1970; staff mem. Twentieth Century Fund Inc., stock market investigation, 1933-34; chmn. econs. sect. Mich. Acad. Arts, Scis. and Letters, 1937-38; mem. State Mich. Pension Com., 1969-74. Co-author: Stock Market Control, 1934, The Security Markets, 1935; author: Corporation Finance, 1948, Price Determination, Theory and Practice, 1949, Graphic Budgets, 1949, (with Frank Smith) Investment Advice for Professional Men, 1951, (with others) Essays in Business Finance, 1951, (with C.S. Davidson) The Lease, 1951, Personal Finance and Investment, 1952, Business Forecasting, 1954, Essentials of Accounting Theory, 1961, Price Determination by Oligopolists, 1961, (with D.K. Eiteman) The Stock Market, 4th edit. 1966, World Leading Stock Exchanges, 1966, Perfect Competition vs. Competitive Activity, 1966, (with S.C. Eiteman) Nine Leading Stock Exchanges, 1968, Causes and Cures of Depression, 1970; contbr. articles to profl. jours. Mem. Am. Econ. Assn., Delta Sigma Pi, Beta Gamma Sigma, Phi Mu Alpha, Delta Sigma Pi. Home: Sarasota Fla. Died Jan. 23, 1986; buried Ann Arbor, Mich.

EKMAN, ANDERS LUNDIN, banker; b. Tampa, Fla., Nov. 14, 1919; s. P.G. and Olga C. (Lundin) E.; m. Winifred E. Parham, Oct. 6, 1951; 1 dau., Holly Ekman Holt. Student pub. schs. With Holtsinger Motor Co., 1936-64, gen. mgr., to 1964; with First Nat. Bank Fla./First Fla. Banks, Inc., Tampa, 1965-80; exec. v.p. First Fla. Banks, Inc.; former pres., vice chmn., chmn., dir. First Nat. Bank Fla.; chmn. Lee County Bank, Ft. Myers, Fla.; former dir. Nat. Bank of Collier County, Marco Island, Fla., Inter City Nat. Bank, Bradenton, Fla., First Nat. Bank, Plant City, Fla., Lakeland, Fla., First Am. Bank, Pensacola, Fla. Capt. USAAF, 1941-45. Decorated D.F.C., Bronze Star, Air medal with 3 oak leaf clusters, Naval Commendation plaque; recipient numerous citations and mgmt. awards. Mem. Fla. Assn. Registered Bank Holding Cos., Tampa Exec. Club (past pres.), Greater Tampa C. of C., Tampa Yacht and Country Club, Tower Club of Tampa. Home: Tampa Fla. Deceased.

ELDERFIELD, ROBERT COOLEY, chemistry educator; b. Niagra Falls, N.Y., May 30, 1904; s. Charles James and Nellie (Cooley) E.; m. Mary Elizabeth Betts, Aug. 7, 1930; children: Margaret Helen, Anne Elizabeth. AB, Williams Coll., 1926, DSc, 1952; PhD, M.I.T., 1930. Instr. chemistry Colby Coll., 1930; asst. Rockefeller Inst. Med. Research, 1930-32, assoc., 1932-36; asst. prof. chemistry Columbia U., 1936-37, assoc. prof., 1937-41, prof., 1941-52; prof. chemistry U. Mich., Ann Arbor, 1952-70, prof. emeritus, 1970-78; instr. chemistry U. Ill., summer 1938; sect. mem. Nat. Def. Research Com., 1941-45; exec. sec. panel on synthesis Bd. for Coordination Anti-malarial Studies, 1943-46; mem. malaria study sect., cons., Nat. Insts. of Health, USPHS, 1946-49; sci. cons. Sloan-Kettering Inst., 1952-55; chmn. panel on synthesis Cancer Chemotherapy Nat. Service Ctr., Nat. Cancer Inst., 1956-60; cons., mem. chemistry adv. com. Walter Reed Army Inst. Research, 1964-70; mem. malaria commn. Armed Forces Epidemiol. Bd., 1964-78; cons. to surgeon gen. Dept. Army, 1964-78; Am. Inst. Biol. Scis. exobiology adv. panel NASA, 1964-78; adv. bd. mil. personnel supplies Nat. Acad. Scis.-NRC, 1964-67; vis. scientist Nat. Research Council, Ottawa, Can., 1959-60; Sigma Xi Nat. Lectr., 1959. Author, editor: Treatise on Heterocyclics (9 vols.), 1950; editor Jour. Organic Chemistry. Recipient Presdl. Cert. of Merit, 1948, Disting. Faculty Achievement award U. Mich., 1969. Mem. Am. Chem. Soc. (chmn. organic chemistry div. 1952, dir. 1960-66), Am. Soc. Biol. Chemists, Nat. Malaria Soc., Nat. Acad. Sci., Sigma Xi, Phi Lambda Upsilon, Alpha Chi Sigma, Delta Kappa Epsilon. Home: Ann Arbor Mich. Died Dec. 1978; buried Laurel Hills Cemetery, Phila.

ELDRIDGE, FLORENCE (MRS. FREDERIC MARCH), actress; b. Bklyn., Sept. 5, 1901; d. James
and Clara Eugenie McKechnie; m. Frederic March, M
30, 1927; adopted children: Penelope, Anthony. E
high sch., Bklyn. Acting debut in stock play Sev
Days Love; first Broadway appearance in chorus
musical comedy Rock-a-Bye Baby, 1918; Theatre Gui
appearance in Ambush, 1921; other plays include C
and the Canary, 1922, Daisy in The Great Gatsby, 192
The Swan, 1927; toured with husband Theatre Gui
Repertory Co., 1927-28; motion picutre debut in Stud
Murder Case, other pictures include Les Miserabl
1935, Mary of Scotland, 1936, Another Part of t
Forest, Inherit the Wind; co-star with husband on sta
in The American Way, 1939, Hope for a Harvest, 194
The Skin of Our Teeth, 1942, Years Ago, 1946, Chri
topher Columbus, 1949, Now I Lay Me Down to Slee
1950, An Enemy of the People, 1950, The Autum
Garden, 1951, as Mary Tyrone in Long Day's Journ
Into Night, 1956 (Drama Critics Circle award). Di
Aug. 1, 1988.

ELDRIDGE, PAUL, author, educator; b. Phila., M
5, 1888; s. Leon and Jeanette (Lefleur) E.; m. Sylvet
De Lamar. BS, Temple U., 1909; MA, U. Pa., 191
Docteur de l'Université, Université de Paris, 1913.
Lectr. Am. Lit. Sorbonne, Paris, 1913; tchr. Roman
langs. high sch., N.Y.C., 1914-46. Author: books
verse, stories, plays and novels including My First Tw
Thousand Years, 1928, Salome, 1930, Cobwebs ar
Cosmos (verse), 1930, The Invincible Adam, 1932, O
Man Show (stories), 1933, If After Every Tempe
(novel), 1941, I Bring a Sword (verse), 1945, Men ar
Women, 1946, Two Lessons in Love, 1946, And Th
Shalt Teach Them, 1947, The Bed Remains (play), 194
The Crown of Empire (The Story of New York State
1957, Tales of the Fortunate Isles, 1959, The Secor
Life of John Stevens, 1959, Seven Against the Nig
(essays), 1960, The Tree of Ignorance (novel), 196
Maxims for a Modern Man, 1965, The Homecomir
(novel), 1966, Parables of Old Cathay (verse), 1969, T
Story-Tellers (essays), 1970, Francois Rabelais (essay
1971, The Revolt of the Ancients (stories), 1976; contb
to mags. Mem. Author's League Am., Dramatis
League. Home: New York N.Y. Deceased.

ELDRIDGE, (DAVID) ROY, trumpeter; b. Pitts., Ja
30, 1911; s. Alexander and Blanche (Oakes) E.; m. Vio
Lee Fong, Jan. 24, 1936; 1 child, Carc
Elizabeth. Student high sch., Pitts. Drumme
trumpeter; musician with numerous bands, 1928-8
band leaders including Horace Henderson's Dix
Stompers, Zach White, Speed Webb, Cecil Scott, Elm
Snowden, McKinney's Cotton Pickers, Teddy Hi
Fletcher Henderson, Gene Krupa, Artie Shaw, Benr
Goodman, Count Basie; formed own band in Chgc
1936, joined Gene Krupa's band, 1941; rec. artist wi
numerous band leaders including Dizzy Gillespie, Sta
Getz, Lester Young, Buddy Tate, Buddy Rich, Ger
Krupa, Oscar Peterson, Johnny Hodges, Art Tatum, Jc
Turner, Count Basie; rec. artist: (solo album) The Nif
Cat, also Mercury Records; with Jazz at th
Philharmonic, 1945-51, on tour of Europe, 1949-51.
Recipient Citation of Merit Muscular Dystrophy Assr
Down Beat mag. award, Westinghouse Trophy awar
others; named to Downbeat Hall of Fame, 1971.
Presbyterian. Died Feb. 26, 1989.

ELGIN, JOSEPH CLIFTON, chemical engineer, ed
cator; b. Nashville, Feb. 11, 1904; s. John C. ar
Elizabeth (Vogely) E.; m. Anne Marjorie Wilkins, Sep
18, 1929 (dec. Apr. 1959); children: Alice Elgin Bisho
Sarah Elgin Timberlake, Joseph Clifton; m. 2d, Elean
Hite Bradley, July 20, 1960; 1 stepson, William Bradle
Jr. ChemE, U. Va., ., 1924; MS, U. Va., 1926; PhI
Princeton U., 1929. Asst. prof. U. Va., 1926-27; mer
faculty Princeton U., from 1929, prof. chem. engring
1939-72, emeritus, from 1972, chmn. dept., 1936-54, a
soc. dean engring., 1951-54, dean of engring., 1954-7
emeritus, from 1972; cons. and ofcl. investigator NDR
and OSRD, 1940-44; chief polymer devel. br., Rubb
Dirs. Office, WPB, 1942-44; div. chief SAM Labs
Manhattan project, Columbia, 1944-45; dir. emerit
U.S. Rubber Reclaiming Co.; cons. AEC, 1946-5
mem. grants com. Rsch. Corp., 1952-63, then dir. eme
itus; mem. spl. commn. on synthetic rubber rsch. NS
1955; chmn. sect. indsl. and engring. chemistry XII
Internat. Congress Pure and Applied Chemistry, 1951
Contbr. articles to chem. and sci. jours. Trust
Princeton U. Press, 1952-56, Princeton Country Da
Sch., 1951-54, Procter Found., 1953-57, 62-66; trust
Assoc. Univs., Inc., 1950-62, 68-71, chmn. bd., 1957-5
dir. Textile Rsch. Inst., 1965-71. Recipient Founde
award, 1972, Warren K. Lewis award, 1975. Fello
Am. Inst. Chem. Engrs. (dir., William H. Walker awa
1958); mem. Am. Chem. Soc., Am. Soc. Engring. Ed
(exec. bd. engring. coll. adminstrv. coun., Lamme awa
1969), NRC (exec. com. div. chem. and tech. 1946-56
Raven Soc., Sigma Xi, Tau Beta Pi, Sigma Phi Epsilo
Alpha Chi Sigma. Home: Princeton N.J. Died Nov. 1
1988.

ELIADE, MIRCEA, historian, author; b. Buchares
Romania, Mar. 9, 1907; s. Gheorghe and Ion
(Stonenescu) E.; m. Georgette C. Cottescu, Jan.
1950. MA, U. Bucharest, 1928, PhD, 1932; student, U
Calcutta, 1928-31. Assoc. prof. faculty letters Buchare
U., 1933-39; cultural attache Romanian legatio
London, Eng., 1940-41; cultural conseiller Romania
legation, Lisbon, Portugal, 1941-44; vis. prof. Ecole d

Hautes Etudes, Sorbonne, Paris, 1946-48; pres. Centre Roumain de REcherches, Paris, 1950-55; Haskell lectr. U. Chgo., 1956, vis. prof. history religion, 1956-57, prof., 1958-86, Swell L. Avery disting. prof., 1963-86; lectr. univs. Rome, Lund, Marburg, Munich, Frankfurt, Strasbourg, Padua; dir. Zalmoxis Revue des études religieuses, Paris, Bucharest, 1938-42. Author: Yoga, 1936, Techniques du Yoga, 1948, Traité d'Histoire des Religions, 1949, Le Chamanisme, 1951, Images et Symboles, 1952, The Myth of the Eternal Return, 1954, Forêt Interdite, 1954, Forgerons et Alchimistes, 1956, Patterns in Comparative Religions, 1958, Birth and Rebirth, 1958, Myths, Dreams and Mysteries, 1959, Images and Symbols, 1960, The Forge and the Crucible, 1962, Myth and Reality, 1963, Shamanism, 1964, The One and the Two, 1965, From Primitives to Zen, 1967, The Quest, 1969, Zalmoxis, the Vanishing God, 1972, Australian Religions, 1973, Occultism, Witchcraft and Cultural Fashions, 1976, No Souvenirs, 1977, The Forbidden Forest, 1978, A History of Religious Ideas, vol. 1, 1979. Mem. Am. Soc. for Study Religion (pres. 1963-67), Romanian Writers Soc. (sec. 1937), Société Asiatique, Frobenius Institut. Home: Chicago Ill. Died Apr. 22, 1986.

ELIOT, MARTHA MAY, pediatrician, educator; b. Dorchester, Mass., Apr. 7, 1891; d. Christopher Rhodes and Mary Jackson (May) E. AB, Radcliffe Coll., 1913; MD, Johns Hopkins U., 1918; hon. degrees LHD, ScD, LLD. House officer Peter Bent Brigham Hosp., 1918-19; intern, then asst. resident in pediatrics St. Louis Children's Hosp., 1919-20; asst. in pediatrics Out-Patient Dept. Mass. Gen. Hosp., 1920-21; resident in pediatrics New Haven Hosp., 1921-23; instr. pediatrics Yale U., 1921-27, asst. clin. prof. pediatrics, 1927-32, assoc. clin. prof., 1932-35, lectr., 1935-38; attending pediatrician New Haven Hosp. and New Haven Dispensary, 1923-34; dir. Div. Child and Maternal Health, Children's Bur., U.S. Labor Dept., 1924-34, asst. chief Children's Bur., 1934-41, assoc. chief, 1941-49, chief, 1951-58; prof., head. dept. maternal and child health Sch. Pub. Health, Harvard U., 1957-60, prof. emeritus, from 1960; mem. U.S. del. 1st World Health Assembly, Geneva, 1948; asst. dir. gen. WHO, Geneva, 1949-51, chmn. expert com. on maternal and child health, 1949; vice chmn. U.S. del. Internat. Health Conf., 1946; chief med. cons. UN Internat. Children's Emergency Fund, 1947; U.S. rep. exec. bd. UN Children's Fund, 1952-57; chmn. Mass. Com. on Children and Youth; pres. Nat. Conf. Social Welfare, 1950. Trustee Radcliffe Coll., 1932-38. Recipient Lasker award, 1948, Sedgwick Meml. medal Am. Pub. Health Assn., 1958, Founders award Radcliffe Coll., 1965, Eleanor Roosevelt Meml. award Women's Nat. Press Club, 1966. Mem. Nat. Assn. Social Workers, Am. Acad. Pediatrics, Am. Inst. Nutrition, Am. Pediatrics Soc. (John Howland award 1967), Am. Pub. Health Assn. (pres. 1947-48), Mass. State Med. Soc., Soc. Rsch. in Child Devel., Cosmopolitan Club (N.Y.C.), Phi Beta Kappa, Alpha Omega Alpha. Home: Cambridge Mass. †

ELLENBERG, MAX, physician, medical educator; b. N.Y.C., Jan. 29, 1911; s. Philip and Sarah (Yablon) E.; m. Mary M. Lemon, Dec. 1, 1942; children: Richard Dennis, William Arthur. BS, CUNY, 1931; MD, NYU, 1935. Diplomate: Am. Bd. Internal Medicine. Intern Mt. Sinai Hosp., N.Y.C., 1931-34; resident in medicine 1935-38, research asst. in chemistry, 1940-51, chief diagnostic clinic, 1951-55, attending physician for diabetes, 1969-84; instr. medicine Columbia U. Coll. Physicians and Surgeons, 1940-52; clin. prof. medicine Mt. Sinai Med. Center, 1970-84. Editor: Diabetes Mellitus, Theory and Practice, 1970, 3d edit., 1983; contbr. numerous articles to med. jours. Served to lt. col. M.C. AUS, 1942-46. Recipient Prof. Frank Meml. award Turkish Diabetes Assn., 1978. Mem. Am. Diabetes Assn. (pres. 1974-75, dir. 1972-84, Banting medal 1975), Internat. Diabetes Fedn., ACP, Am. Soc. Internal Medicine, Am. Med. Writers Assn., Internat. Soc. Internal Medicine, AMA, N.Y. Acad. Scis. (chmn. sect. bio-medicine 1979-84), N.Y. Diabetes Assn. (pres. 1964-65, dir. 1950-84), Mt. Sinai Alumni Assn. (pres. 1962-63, Abraham Jacobi medallion 1964). Jewish. Club: Vaccabuc Country. Home: New York N.Y. Died July 1984.

ELLEY, HAROLD WALTER, research chemist; b. Madison, Nebr., May 16, 1891; s. W. C. and Emeline (Field) E.; m. Sarah Palmer Caswell, Sept. 26, 1916; children: Carolyn Elley Long, Elizabeth Elley Newton. BS, U. Nebr., 1912, AM, 1913; PhD, Cornell, 1916. Rsch. chemist E. I. duPont de Nemours & Co., 1916-29, chem. dir. organic chemicals dept., 1929-56, ret.; vice chmn. Del. State Commn. on Rsch. and Tng. in Mental Health; mem. rsch. com. Del. Mental Health Dept. Patentee in field. Mem. engring. coll. council Cornell, 1940-50; pres. Psychiat. Found., N.Y., 1948-50, Wilmington Community Concerts Assn., 1942-57; dir. Wilmington Symphony Orch., 1956-57, Welfare Coun. Del., 1960-63; bd. govs. Menninger Found., from 1957. Mem. Am. Chem. Soc., Am. Inst. Chem. Engring., Nat. Assn. Mental Health (chmn. bd. 1950-57, mem. bd. 1950-62, chmn. rsch. com. 1958-60, pres. rsch. found. 1960-62, trustee rsch. found. 1962-63), Am. Guild Organists, Nat. Health Coun., Mental Health Assn. Del. (hon. dir.), Sigma Xi, Gamma Alpha, Alpha Chi Sigma. Republican. Presbyterian. Home: Kennett Square Pa. Also: Heron Island Maine. †

ELLIN, STANLEY BERNARD, author; b. Bklyn., Oct. 6, 1916; s. Louis William and Rose (Mandel) E.; m. Jeanne Michael, Nov. 23, 1937; 1 dau., Susan Ellin Brown. BA, Bklyn. Coll., 1936. Author: novels Dreadful Summit, 1948, The Key to Nicholas Street, 1952, The Eighth Circle, 1958, The Winter After This Summer, 1960, The Panama Portrait, 1962, House of Cards, 1967, The Valentine Estate, 1968, The Bind, 1970, Mirror, Mirror on the Wall, 1972, Stronghold, 1974, The Luxembourg Run, 1977, Star Light, Star Bright, 1979, The Dark Fantastic, 1983, Very Old Money, 1985; short story collections include Mystery Stories, 1956, The Blessington Method, 1964, The Specialty of the House, 1980. Served with U.S. Army, 1945-46. Recipient Edgar Allan Poe awards, 1954, 56, 58, Grandmaster award Mystery Writers Am., 1981, Grand Prix France, 1975, Foley/Burnett award, 1960. Mem. Mystery Writers Am., Crime Writers Assn. Eng., PEN Am. Ctr., Authors League, Authors Guild. Quaker. Home: Brooklyn N.Y. Died July 31, 1986.

ELLINGTON, HAROLD S(LAIGHT), engineer; b. Chgo., Jan. 24, 1886; s. Ernest Elwell and Harriet Elizabeth (Bond) E.; m. Harriet Louise Axtell, Oct. 19, 1910; children: Townley Axtell, William Bond (dec.). BSCE, Armour Inst. Tech., 1908. Licensed profl. engr., Mich., Ohio, Pa., N.J., N.Y., Tex., R.I., Ind., Ill., Minn., Wis., Ont. Constrn. engr. Chgo., 1908-12; plant engr. Stroh Brewery Co., Detroit, 1912-16; constrn. mgr. Book Estate, 1917-18; pvt. practice architecture and engring. from 1918; mem. Giaver, Dinkelberg & Ellington, 1919-23, Weston & Ellington, 1923-33, Harley & Ellington, 1933-46; then pres. Harley, Ellington, Cowin and Stirton Inc. Designer comml., indusl., monumental bldgs., also processing plants. Chmn. planning commn. City of Grosse Pointe Park, Mich.; past commr. Detroit and Met. Area Planning Commn.; life trustee Rackham Engring. Found.; past trustee Ill. Inst. Tech. Mem. ASCE, Nat. Soc. Profl. Engrs., Mich. Engring. soc., Engring. Soc. Detroit (past pres.), Am. concrete Inst., Detroit Bd. Commerce, Detroit Athletic Club, Econ. Club, Grosse Pointe Yacht Club, Masons, Delta Tau Delta, Tau Beta Pi, Pi Delta Epsilon. Republican. Home: Grosse Pointe Park Mich. †

ELLIOTT, MARTHA VIRGINIA BEGGS, artist; b. Birmingham, Ala., Dec. 17, 1892; d. John Phiilip and Amy Cletus (Etter) Beggs; m. Jan. 19, 1913; 1 child, Jane (Mrs. Mandeville C. Smith). Student, Howard Coll., summer 1915; pupil of Wayman Adams, summers 1937-40. Portrait painter from 1930; tchr. small art group, Birmingham, 1932-33, pub. schs., Jefferson County and Birmingham, studio, N.Y.C., 1940-50. One woman exhbns. in Dallas, East Hampton, L.I., Laurence Gallery, Montgomery, Ala., Pensacola, Fla., 1940, Panama City (Fla.) City Auditorium and Gallery Art, 1973; represented in Edward Benjamin Collection, Ala. Archives and History, Fla. Ho. Reps., Wash. Wildlife Fedn.; artist Govt. War Bond poster, 1945. Recipient 1st award IBM competition, 1940, Ala. Art League, 1941, also purchase awards in local art shows. Mem. Tchrs. Coun. Jefferson County (pres.), Birmingham Tchrs. Assn. (pres.); So. States Art Assn. (bd. dirs. 1938), Panama City Art Assn. Home: Panama City Fla. †

ELLIOTT, MARTIN ANDERSON, consulting energy technologist; b. Balt., Feb. 21, 1909; s. Walter and Lillian (Kesmodel) E.; m. Mary Helen Parker, June 23, 1934; children: James Parker, Virginia Layfield; m. Shirley Multhauf Whitlock; children: Timothy Scott Whitlock, J. William Whitlock, Rebbecca Ann Whitlock. B Engring., Johns Hopkins U., 1930, PhD, 1933. Instr. dept. gas engring. Johns Hopkins U., Balt., 1933-34; asst. to supt. gas mfg. Balt. Gas & Electric Co., 1934-38; gas engr., prin. chem. engr., asst. chief explosives div. U.S. Bur. Mines, Pitts., 1938-46, asst. chief and chief synthetic liquid fuels research, 1946-52; research prof. mech. engring. Ill. Inst. Tech., Chgo., 1952-56, dir. inst. gas tech., research prof. chem. engring., 1956-61, acad. v.p., 1961-67; corp. sci. adviser Tex. Eastern Transmission Corp., Houston, 1967-74, cons. energy and fuel technologist, 1974-88. Contbr. articles to tech. jours. Trustee Chgo. Planetarium Soc., 1961-67. Recipient Disting. Service medal Dept. Interior, Bur. Mines, 1952. Fellow ASME (Percy Nicholls award fuel div. 1968), Inst. Fuel (U.K.); mem. Am. Inst. Chem. Engrs., Am. Gas Assn. (1st ann. Gas Industry Research award 1975), Soc. Automotive Engrs., Am. Soc. Engring. Edn., Nat. Acad. Engring., Sigma Xi (Disting. Faculty lectr. award 1965), Tau Beta Pi, Pi Tau Sigma, Omicron Delta Kappa, Alpha Tau Omega. Clubs: University (Chgo.), Cosmos (Washington), Houston. Home: Eugene Oreg. Died Aug. 5, 1988.

ELLIS, PERRY EDWIN, fashion designer; b. Mar. 3, 1940; s. Edwin L. and Winifred (Roundtree) E.; 1 child, Tyler Alexandra Gallagher Ellis. BS, Coll. William and Mary, 1961; M Retailing, NYU, 1963. Buyer Miller & Rhoads, Richmond, Va., 1963-67; design dir. John Meyer Co., Norwich, Conn., 1967-74; designer PortfolioCo., Vera Co., N.Y.C., 1974-79; pres., designer Perry Ellis Co., N.Y.C., 1979-86. Served with USCG, 1961-62. Recipient Nieman Marcus award, 1979, Winnie award Am. Fashion Critics, Men's Fashion award Council Fashion Designers of Am., 1983; named to Coty Hall of Fame and recipient citation, 1984; named Outstanding U.S. Designer Cutty Sark Men's Fashion Awards, 1984. Died May 30, 1986.

ELLMANN, RICHARD, English literature educator; b. Highland Park, Mich., Mar. 15, 1918; s. James Isaac and Jeanette (Barsook) E.; m. Mary Donahue, Aug. 12, 1949; children: Stephen Jonathan, Maud Esther, Lucy Elizabeth. BA, Yale U., 1939, MA, 1941, PhD, 1947; BLitt, Trinity Coll., Dublin, Ireland, 1947; MA, Oxford U., Eng., 1970; DLitt (hon.), Northwestern U., 1980, Nat. U. Ireland, 1976, Emory U., 1979, McGill U., 1986; PhD (hon.), U. Gothenburg, 1978; DHL (hon.), Boston Coll., 1979, U. Rochester, 1981. Instr. Harvard U., 1942-43, 47-48, Briggs-Copeland asst. prof. English composition, 1948-51; prof. English Northwestern U., Evanston, Ill., 1951-64, Franklin Bliss Snyder prof., 1964-68; prof. English Yale U., 1968-70; Goldsmiths'prof. English lit. Oxford U., Eng., 1970-84; Frederick Ives Carpenter vis. prof. U. Chgo., 1959, 67, 75-77; Woodruff prof. Emory U., 1982-87; mem. U.S.-U.K. Ednl. Commn., 1970-85. Author: Yeats: The Man and the Masks, 1948, The Identity of Yeats, 1954, James Joyce, 1959 (Nat. Book), Eminent Domain, 1967, Literary Biography, 1972, Ulysses on the Liffey, 1972, Golden Codgers, 1973, The Consciousness of Joyce, 1977, Four Dubliners: Wilde, Yeats, Joyce, and Beckett, 1986; editor: Selected Writings of Henri Michaux, 1951, My Brother's Keeper (Stanislaus Joyce), 1958; (with others) English Masterpieces, 1958; The Symbolist Movement in Literature (Arthur Symons), 1958; (with Ellsworth Mason) The Critical Writings of James Joyce: Edwardians and Late Victorians, 1960; (with Charles Feidelson) The Modern Tradition, 1965: Letters of James Joyce, Vols. II and III, 1966; Giacomo Joyce (James Joyce), 1968, The Artist as Critic (Oscar Wilde), 1969, Oscar Wilde (Twentieth Century Views), 1970; (with Robert O'Clair) Norton Anthology of Modern Poetry, 1973; Selected Letters of James Joyce, 1976, New Oxford Book of American Verse, 1976; (with Robert O'Clair) Modern Poems, 1976, Four Dubliners, 1986, Oscar Wilde, 1987. Served with OSS, USNR, 1943-46. Rockefeller fellow in humanities, 1946-47; Guggenheim fellow, 1950, 57, 70; Kenyon Rev. fellow in criticism, 1955, Am. Philos. Soc. grantee; NEH grantee, 1977-78; fellow Sch. Letters, Ind. U., 1956, 60, sr. fellow, 1966-72; fellow New Coll., Oxford U., 1970-84, hon. fellow, 1984-87, extraordinary fellow Wolfson Coll., 1984-87. Fellow Am. Acad. and Inst., Brit. Acad., Royal Soc. Lit.; mem. English Inst. (chmn. 1961-62), MLA (exec. council 1961-65, mem. editorial com. publs. 1968-73), Elizabethan Club, Phi Beta Kappa, Chi Delta Theta, Signet, Athenaeum. Home: Oxford England. Died May 13, 1987; buried Wolvercote Cemetery, Oxford.

ELLSWORTH, HARRIS, congressman; b. Hoquiam, Wash., Sept. 17, 1899; s. Elmer Elbridge and Eva Catherine (Forbes) E.; m. Helen Evangeline Dougherty, June 21, 1923; children: Mary Margaret, Patricia Jane. BS, U. Oreg., 1922. Advt. mgr. Eugene (Oreg.) Register, 1923-25; mgr. 4-L Lumber News, 1926-28, Oreg. State Editorial Assn., 1928; editor, mgr., part owner Roseburg (Oreg.) Daily News-Review, radio sta. KRNR; mem. 78th-84th Congresses from 4th Oreg. Dist, chmn. U.S. Civil Service Commn. 1957-86; apptd. mem. Oreg. State Senate, 1941 session. Pvt., SATC, World War I. Mem. Oreg. Ednl. Commn., U. Oreg. Alumni Assn. (past pres.), Oreg. Newspaper Pubs. Assn., Oreg. C. of C., NRC, Am. Legion, The Grange, Kappa Sigma, Sigma Delta Chi, Sigma Upsilon, Phi Mu Alpha, Elks, Eagles, Rotary, Roseburg Country Club. Home: Roseburg Oreg. Died Feb. 7, 1986.

ELONEN, ANNA SIVIA, psychologist, educator; b. Laihia, Finland, Feb. 25, 1904; came to U.S., 1910, derivative citizen; d. Herman M. and Susanna (Lyyski) Elonen. BA, Lawrence Coll., 1925; MA, U. Minn., 1927; PhD, U. Chgo., 1948. Psychologist Minn. Bd. Control, 1927-37; instr., then asst. prof. U. Chgo., 1937-50; prof. psychology U. Mich., Ann Arbor, 1950-72, prof. emeritus, 1972-82; clin. assoc. Inst. for Study Mental Retardation and Related Disabilities, 1972-75; Fulbright lectr., Finland, 1953-55; Fulbright research worker, Finland, 1958-59; program dir. Mott Found. and Lang. for Deaf Children thru Parent Edn., 1968-69; cons. in field, 1950-82. Author articles in field. Grantee Founds. Fund Research Psychiatry, 1966. Mem. Assn. Mental Deficiency, Am. Psychol. Assn., Mich. Psychol. Assn., Soc. Research Child Devel., Am. Orthopsychiat. Assn., Council Exceptional Children. Home: Green Valley Ariz. Died Aug. 9, 1982.

ELSASSER, THEODORE HERMAN, surgeon; b. Union City, N.J., Dec. 19, 1899; s. Adolph Otto and Mary (Klein) E.; m. Elise Valentine Zibetti, Mar. 17, 1924; children: Elise Theodora, Mary Ellen, Elaine Delores; m. Margaret Grogan, Apr. 1946; children: Elizabeth, Theodore. Student, NYU, 1919-20, MD, 1924, postgrad. surg. course, 1927-30. Diplomate Am. Bd. Abdominal Surgery. Intern North Hudson Hosp., Weehawken, N.J., 1924-25; instr. surgery NYU Coll. Medicine, 1928-85; assoc. surgeon Jersey City Med. Ctr., Christ Hosp., Jersey City; assoc. with prof. George B. Wallace, dept. pharmacology NYU, in cancer research, 1930-85; asst. prof. surgery Seton Hall U., Jersey City, 1959. Contbr. articles to med. jours. Exec. chmn. Hudson County unit Am. Cancer Soc.; med. del. to N.J. div. bd. trustees Am. Cancer Soc. With ROTC,

1919. Named Outstanding Citizen VFW, 1974-75, Citizen of Yr., 1975. Fellow ACS; mem. Clin. and Postgrad. Surg. Soc. NYU, AMA, Hudson City and North Hudson Physicians Soc., Sigma Xi, Phi Alpha Sigma. Home: North Bergen N.J. Died Apr. 18, 1985.

ELSON, ROBERT T., journalist; b. Cleve., June 21, 1906; s. John Truscott and Katharine (Logue) E.; m. Georgina E. MacKinnon, Dec. 28, 1928; children: John Truscott, Katharine Ellen, Elizabeth, Brigid Mary, Robert Anthony. Student, U. B.C. Reporter Vancouver (B.C.) Daily Province, 1924-28; promotion mgr. Winnipeg (Man.) Tribune, 1930-32; sports editor Vancouver Daily Province, 1932-34, news editor, 1934-39; editor, pub. Vancouver News-Herald, 1939; Washington corr. Southam Newspapers of Can., 1941-43, London Daily Mail; assoc. editor Time Mag., 1943-44; Washington chief Time, Inc., 1944-48, chief corrs., 1949-50; asst. mng. editor Life, 1950-54, dep. mng. editor, 1954-60, gen. mgr., 1957-60; London chief corr. Time, Life, Fortune, Sports Illustrated mags., 1960-87; former corp. historian. Author: 2 vols. Prelude to War, Time-Life series. Mem. Fullbright Commn. of U.K., Council Fgn. Relations, Reform Club, St. James Press Club, Nat. Press Club, Overseas Writers Club, Met. Club of Washington. Home: East Hampton N.Y. Died Mar. 11, 1987.

ELVIDGE, FORD QUINT, former governor of Guam; b. Oakland, Calif., Nov. 30, 1892; s. Fred H. and Cora A. (Quint) E.; m. Anita Emily Miller, 1918; children: Marthanna (Mrs. John Veblen), Robert, Carolyn Eaton. Studied law, Vancouver, B.C. and U. Wash. Bar: Wash. 1918. Practice Seattle, from 1919; mem. firm Elvidge, Watt, Veblen & Tewell; apprd. spl. asst. to atty. gen. State of Washington, 1949; gov. of Guam 1953-56. Active in civic work, Seattle. Lt. inf. U.S. Army, 1918-19. Mem. Seattle Bar Assn. (pres. 1941), Wash. State Bar Assn. (gov. 1943-46), ABA, English-Speaking Union (past pres.), U. Wash. Law Sch. Alumni Assn. (past pres.), Am. Legion, Rainer Club, College Club (past pres.), Masons (33 deg.), Sigma Alpha Epsilon, Phi Delta Phi. Republican. Congregationalist. Home: Seattle Wash. †

EMBREE, WILLIAM DEAN, lawyer; b. Humboldt, Kans., 1880; s. William N. and Laura (Fee) E.; m. Etta Parsons, Mar. 9, 1912; children: Catherine, William Dean. B.L., Berea (Ky.) Coll., 1899, LL.D., 1933; A.B., Yale, 1902, LLB, 1905, A.M. in Italian lang. and lit., 1910. Bar: Conn. 1905, N.Y. 1906. Asst. dist. atty. N.Y. County, 1906-17; an organizer, chief counsel Voluntary DEfenders Com. for Criminal Cts., 1917-20; then mem. firm Milbank, Tweed, Hadley & McCloy; owner, operator cattle ranch nr. Laramie, Wyo.; dir. Legal Aid Soc. of N.Y.; in charge state-wide graft investigation, 1914; conductor prosecution of criminal charges involving charity orgns. of N.Y.C., 1916; apptd. bd. mgrs. N.Y. State Reformatory for Women, 1920; apptd. spl. dep. atty. gen. to prosecute election frauds, 1922. Mem. Citizens Com. on the Cts. Inc., Commn. on Inter-group Relations, N.Y.C., bd. dirs., mem. subcom. on removal of judges; trustee Berea Coll., Yale-in-China; bd. dirs. Katy Ferguson Home for Colored Girls, Soc. for Italian Immigrants; chmn. bd. trustees Tenafly (N.J.) Free Pub. Libr., William Nelson Cromwell Found. Lt. col. remount div., O.R.C., U.S. Army. Recipient Townshend oratorical prize Yale, 1905. Mem. Am. and N.Y. State bar assns., Assn. Bar City of N.Y., N.Y. County Lawyers Assn. (pres. and dir.), Yale Law Sch. Assn. (pres.), Am. Pioneer Trails Assn. (chmn. exec. com.), Timothy Dwight Coll. Yale U. (assoc. fellow), Civil Service Reform Assn. of N.Y. (pres.), Am. Law Inst. (mem. Coun., exec. com., treas.), Century Assn., Explorers Club, Yale Club, Bankers Club, Broad St. Club, Downtown Athletic Club, Oraworth Polo Club, Knickerbocker Country Club, Graduate Club (New Haven, Conn.). Republican. Congregationalist. Home: Tenafly N.J. †

EMERSON, EARL ARTHUR, manufacturing executive; b. Cin., Aug. 19, 1887; s. Dudley and Adele (Simpson) E.; m. Mary James, 1913; children: Adele (Mrs. Jack Cotton), James Dudley (dec.); m. Liette Renson, 1950. Student, Cornell, 1910. Electrician apprentice Am. Rolling Mill Co., 1904-08, lab. chemist, electrician, 1908-09, rsch. chemist, 1909; spl. apprentice Westinghouse Electric Corp., 1910; salesman Armco, 1911, Brazilian rep., 1912-15, mgr. San Francisco office, 1915, export mgr., 1916-18, 1919-24; v.p., mng. dir. Armco Internat. Corp., 1924-31, became pres., dir., 1931, then dir.; bd. dirs. Armco Propriety Ltd., Calcutta, India; Am. rep. steel survey Brit. Dominions, WPB, 1943. With U.S. Army, 1918. Winner John Pottinger World Trade Trophy, 1952. Mem. Def. Orientation Conf. Assn. (dir.), Circumnavigators Club, Export Managers Club, Bankers Club, India House Club (N.Y.). Home: Cincinnati Ohio. †

EMERY, ALBERT WALDRON, JR., advertising executive; b. Denver, Jan. 15, 1923; s. Albert Waldron and Margaret (Grimson) E.; m. Lucille E. Eye, Oct. 22, 1948; children: Linden, Lisa, Thomas, Alan, Courtney. Student, DePauw U., 1943-44; BS, U. Va., 1948. Sales promotion asst. Westinghouse Electric Corp., 1948-50, advt. acct. rep., 1950-53; div. mgr. Gen. Products Advt., 1953-54, Indsl. Products Advt., 1954-55; account exec. Harris D. McKinney, Inc., Phila., 1955-56, v.p., account supr., 1956-59, exec. v.p., 1960-62, pres., from 1962, chmn. bd., from 1964. Srved with USNR, 1940-46. Mem. Franklin Inst., Poor Richard Club, Virginia Club, Union League Club Phila., Tucson Nat. Golf Club, Sigma Chi. Home: Tucson Ariz. Died Apr. 19, 1985.

EMILE, ANDERS, educator; b. Arendal, Norway, June 17, 1892; came to U.S., 1914, naturalized, 1918; s. Andreas Olsen and Caroline (Larsen) E.; m. Thordis J. Johnson, Oct. 13, 1923; children: Thelma Evangeline (Mrs. Samuel W. Hunter), Robert Anders. Diploma, Oslo Cons. Music., 1914; BS in Music, NYU, 1930, AM in Music, 1932; MusD (hon.), N.Y. Coll. Music, 1945. Organist, choir dir. Sunset Park Meth. Ch., Bklyn., 1914, 41; mem. faculty Hunter Coll., from 1937, prof. music., from 1950, chmn. dept., from 1962; founder, 1950, since dir. Richmond Choral Soc.; dir. music Gustavus Adolphus Ch., N.Y.C., 1941-47. Composer: (opera) King Harald (grantee George Tollefsen Fund 1947), 1949. Mem. music com. S.I. Mus.; bd. dirs. S.I. Symphony. With U.S. Army, World War I. Mem. AAUP, N.Y. Musicians, Nat. Assn. Tchrs. Singing, Nat. Assn. Am. Composers and Conductors, Am. Scandinavian Found., Phi Delta Kappa; hon. mem. Academia Nicional de Artes y Letras Havana. Methodist. Home: Staten Island N.Y. †

EMME, EARLE E(DWARD), educator; b. Kankakee, Ill., Jan. 31, 1891; s. William Henry and Ella Emeline (Hertz) E.; m. Ada Julia Morlock; children: Eugene Morlock, Lois Virginia. AB, Northwestern U., 1916; AM, Columbia (spl. diploma as supr. edn.), 1918; PhD, U. Chgo., 1932. Prof. edn. Lawrence Coll., 1920-23; supt. Meth. Bd. Edn., Wis., 1923-26, Nebr., 1926-29; prof. Nebr. Wesleyan U., 1926-29; prof. psychology, chmn. personnel, head psychology dept. Morningside Coll., 1934-43, dir. downtown div., 1943-44; dean, prof. psychology and edn., dir. personnel and summer sch. Dakota Wesleyan U., 1944-46; assoc. prof., acting chmn. psychology Bowling Green (Ohio) State U., 1946-48; prof. psychology Bradley U., Peoria, 1948-56, prof. psychology and religion, also coordinator religious affairs, from 1953, chmn. lecture art programs, 1949-53; vis. prof. psychology Fla. So. Coll., Lakeland, from 1956; dean Ch. Leaders Inst., Mitchell, S.D., Peoria Community Leadership Sch.; chmn. exec. com. Rural Life Conf. Author: (with Paul R. Stevich) Introduction to the Principles of Religious Education, 1926; The Adjustment Problems of College Freshman, 1932, College Students Examine Personality and Religion, 1953, rev., 1954; contbr. articles to profl. publs. Recipient award for rsch. on superstitions Iowa Acad. Sci., 1941. Fellow Am. Psychol. Assn.; mem. S.D. Coll. Assn. (pres., head edn. depts.), Iowa Acad. Sci. (past chmn. psychology), Midwestern, Ill. psychol. assns., AAUP, Religious Edn. Assn., Northwest Ohio Psychology Club (pres.), Phi Kappa Phi, Psi Chi (hon. mem. nat. coun.), Phi Delta Kappa, Pi Gamma Mu, Tau Kappa Alpha, Pi Kappa Delta. Home: Lakeland Fla. †

EMMONS, PETER KENNETH, clergyman; b. Monmouth Junction, N.J., May 9, 1892; s. Peter Dénise and Emma Catherine (Kennedy) E.; m. Helen Augusta West, May 19, 1915; children: Roberta West, Doris Elizabeth, Mary Alice, Helen Patricia. AB, Princeton U., 1912, DD, 1956; grad., Princeton Theol. Sem., 1915; DD, Washington & Jefferson Coll., 1937, Grove City Coll., 1937. Ordained to ministry Presbyn. Ch., 1915. Pastor Brisge St. Presbyn. Ch., Catasauqua, Pa., 1915-16; pastor First Presbyn. Ch., Stroudsburg, Pa., 1916-19, Trenton, N.J., 1919-27; pastor Westminster Presbyn. Ch., Scranton, Pa., 1927-58; pastor emeritus West Ch., Scranton. Mem. exec. com. Delaware Valley area Boy Scouts Am.; bd. dirs. Monroe County YMCA, Stroudsburg; served with YMCA, World War I; pres. bd. trustees Princeton Theol. Sem.; past mem. Commn. Ecumenical Mission and Rels. United Presbyn. Ch. U.S., mem. coun. theol. edn.; mem. Monroe County Hist. Soc. Mem. Nat. Exch. Club (hon.), Irem Temple Country Club, Rotary Internat. (former gov. 36th dist.), Masons (32 degree), Shriners. Home: Stroudsburg Pa. †

ENDERS, JOHN FRANKLIN, virologist; b. West Harford, Conn., Feb. 10, 1897; s. John Ostrom and Harriet Goulden (Whitmore) E.; A.B., Yale, 1920, Sc.D. (hon.), 1953; M.A., Harvard, 1922, Ph.D., 1930, Sc.D., Trinity, 1955, Northwestern, 1956, Western Res. U., 1958, Tufts U., 1960; LL.D., Tulane U., 1958; L.H.D., Hartford U., 1960; D.Sc., Jefferson Med. Coll., 1962, U. Pa., 1964, U. Ibadan, 1968, Oxford U., 1975, Duke U., 1976; m. Sarah Frances Bennett, Sept. 17, 1927 (dec.); children—John Ostrom II, Sarah; m. 2d, Mrs. Carolyn Keane, May 12, 1951; 1 stepson, William Edmund Keane. Asst. dept. bacteriology and immunology Harvard, 1929-30, instr., 1930-32, faculty instr., 1932-35, asst. prof., 1935-42, asso. prof., 1942-56, prof., 1956-62, Univ. prof., 1962-67, emeritus, 1967-85. Civilian cons. to sec. of war on epidemic diseases, 1942-46; mem. Commn. on Viral Infections, Armed Forces Epidemiological Bd.; sci. adv. bd. Armed Forces Inst. Pathology; chief of research div. infectious diseases. Children's Hosp., Boston, 1947-80, chief virus research unit and cons. in virology. Lt. (j.g.) Naval Res., 1917-20. Decorated comdr. Ordre Nat. de la Republic de Haute Volta; recipient Passano Found. award for culturing poliomyelitis viruses in living tissues, 1953; Lasker Award, 1954; Kimball award, 1954; Nobel Prize in Medicine and Physiology, 1954; Dyer award USPHS, Chapin medal, 1955; Bruce award ACP, 1956; Cameron prize U. Edinburgh, 1961; Howard Taylor Ricketts Meml. award U. Chgo., 1962; New Eng. Israel Freedom award, 1962; Diesel Gold medal, 1962; Robert Koch medal, 1962 (Germany); Sci. achievement award A.M.A., 1963; Presdl. Medal of Freedom, 1963. Fellow Am. Acad. Arts and Scis.; mem. Nat. Acad. Scis., Harvey Soc., Am. Philos. Soc., Soc. Gen. Microbiology (hon.), Soc. Am. Bacteriologists, Am. Assn. Immunologists (pres. 1952-53), Soc. Exptl. Biology and Medicine, Am. Pub. Health Assn., A.A.A.S., Mass. Med. Soc. (asso.), Royal Soc. (fgn.), Academie des Sciences de l'Institut de France (hon.), Sigma Xi, Alpha Omega Alpha (hon.). Clubs: Harvard, Tavern (Boston); Brookline (Mass.) Country. Author: (with Hans Zinsser and Leroy D. Fothergill) Immunity: Principles and Application in Medicine and Public Health, 1939; contbr. to Virus and Rickettsial Diseases, 1958, 64; editorial bd. Jour. of Immunology, Jour. Bacteriology, Jour. Virology, others. Home: Brookline, Mass. Died Sept. 8, 1985; buried Hartford, Conn.

ENERSEN, LAWRENCE ALBERT, architect; b. Lamberton, Minn., July 5, 1909; s. Albert Hovesoe and Ethel (Rice) E.; m. Eleanore Cullinan Vail, Nov. 23, 1939; children: David, Stephen, Philip. AB, Carleton Coll., 1931; MLA, Harvard U., 1935, 1936-37; DFA (hon.), Doane Coll., 1980. Designer, draftsman Olmsted Bros., Brookline, Mass., 1937-38; instr. U. Mich., 1939-42; asst. prof. Harvard U., 1942-43; prof. U. N.C., 1947-52; prin. firm Clark & Enersen, Lincoln, Nebr., 1946-72, treas., 1972-83; mem. Lincoln Ctr. Devel. Assn., 1960-83, Lincoln Housing Authority, 1966-68; sec. Captial Murals Commn., 1960-83; chmn. Mayor's Com. on Urban Design, 1969-83; co-chmn. C.E. Adv. Com. in Environ. Planning, 1967-83. Mem. Gov.'s Com. on Employment Handicapped, 1972-83; co-chmn. Better Lincoln Com., 1957-59; pres. Lincoln Arts Council, 1966-68; mem. exec. com. Arbor Day Found., 1971-83; adv. bd. St. Elizabeth Hosp., 1960-71. With USNR, 1943-46. Recipient Conservationist award Lower Platt S. Natural Resource Dist., 1974, Disting. Service medal Kiwanis Club, 1977, Gov.'s Art award, 1979. Fellow AIA, Am. Soc. Landscape Architects; mem. Nebr. Bd. Landscape Architects, Masons, Sertoma Club, Univ. Club, Torch Club. Home: Lincoln Nebr. Died July 9, 1983; buried Lincoln (Nebr.) Meml. Park.

ENGEL, LYLE KENYON, book producer; b. N.Y.C., May 12, 1915; s. George Shandor and Beatrice (Michaels) E.; m. Gertrude Warshaw; 1 son, George S.; m. Marjorie Helen Ray, June 14, 1975. Student, NYU, N.Y. Coll. Music. Editor, pub. Song Hits mag., 1938-49; ind. promotion cons. 1950-52; pres., exec. producer Book Creations Inc., Canaan, N.Y., 1973-83, chmn. bd., 1984-86. Originator, producer series: Nick Carter Killmaster, 1962, Richard Blade, 1968; creator: Fred Astaire Dance Book, 1961, Pearl S. Buck's Fairy Tales of the Orient, 1963, Pearl S. Buck's People of Japan, 1964, Pearl S. Buck's Oriental Cook Book, 1965, Pearl S. Buck's Story Bible, 1965, Pearl S. Buck's Book of Christmas, 1971, Kent Family Chronicles, 1973, Creole Surgeon, 1975, Windhaven, 1976, Roselynde Chronicles, 1976, Oakhurst, 1977, Eve, 1977, Inheritors of the Storm, 1977, Wagons West, 1977, The Australians, 1977, White Indian, 1978, Children of the Lion, 1979, Heiress, 1979, Royal Dynasty, 1979, Saga of the Southwest, 1979, American Patriot, 1980, The Centurions, 1980, Rakehell Dynasty, 1980, Northwest Territory, 1982, Yankee, 1982, Stagecoach, 1982, Daimyo, 1983, Worldshakers, 1983, Haakon, The Viking, 1984, Taming of the West, 1986, America 2040, 1986, The Ropedancer, 1986, Belle Marie, 1987, The Badge, 1987, Wolves of the Dawn, 1987, Torka, The First American, 1987; originator term book producer; promoted original Today Show, 1950; creator: The Song from Moulin Rouge, 1952. Recipient Best of Industry award Direct Mail Advt. Assn., 1952. Mem. ASCAP, Broadcast Music. Deceased.

ENGELBART, ROGER WILLIAM, banker; b. Ft. Dodge, Iowa, Apr. 28, 1923; s. William Eberhard and Julia Kathryn (Faulstick) E.; m. Elizabeth Emma Affleck, Sept. 20, 1947; 1 son, Roger Warren. Student, Kansas City (Mo.) Jr. Coll., 1942. Bookkeeper Woolf Bros. Clothing Store, Kansas City, 1942-43; with United Mo. Bank of Kansas City (N.A.), 1946-86, cashier, 1971-86. Mem. Friends Am. Field Service scholarships, 1970-86. With AUS, 1943-46. Mem. Greater Kansas City C. of C., Mail Users Council Greater KAnsas City, Bank Adminstrn. Inst., Am. Security Council (nat. adv. bd.). Republican. Lutheran. Home: Prairie Village Kans. Died Mar. 9, 1986; buried Forest Hill Cemetery, Kansas City.

ENGGAS, CARL E., lawyer; b. Kansas City, Mo., June 3, 1900; s. Main C. and Eva M. (Killip) E.; m. Jane M. Greene, Feb. 4, 1925; 1 dau., Marion Jane (Mrs. John H. Kreamer). A.B., U. Mich., 1923, J.D., 1925. Bar: Mo. bar 1925. Since practiced in Kansas City; asso. Ingham Hook, 1925-31, Watson, Gage, Ess, Groner & Barnett, 1931-36; mem. firm Watson, Ess, Marshall & Enggas (and predecessors), from 1936. Mem., sec. Kansas City Bd. Election Commrs., 1961-65; mem. Jackson County Charter Commn., 1957-58. Served with U.S. Army, World War I. Fellow Am. Coll. Trial Lawyers; mem. Am. Bar Assn., Mo. Bar, Lawyers Assn. Kansas City, Lawyers Club Ann Arbor (Mich.), Am.

udicature Soc., C. of C., Order of Coif, Alpha Tau Omega. Clubs: River; University (Kansas City) (past pres.). Home: Kansas City Mo. Died July 12, 1986.

ENGLEHART, O(TTO) T(HEODORE), lawyer, corporation executive; b. Brazil, Ind., Aug. 2, 1892; s. Theodore Wilhelm and Maggie (Oswalt) E.; m. Lucia E. Kerfoot, June 8, 1918; children: Otto T., Gordon Kerfoot, Lucia Knight Marsh. AB, Ind. U., 1915. Bar: Ind., U.S. Supreme Ct., U.S. Dist. Ct. Washington, other U.S. Dist. Cts. History tchr., athletic dir. Brazil (Ind.) High Sch., 1915-17; gen. practcie law Brazil, 1919-30, city atty., 1920-28; trial atty. Va., Washington, 1930-33; spl. asst. to atty. gen. Dept. Justice, 1933-45; gen. practice law Washington, from 1945; acting pres. the Beryllium Corp., 1947-52, pres., mem. bd., 1948-52; chmn. Bellanca Corp., from 1959; pres., chmn. Gen. Devel. Corp., Elkton, Md., from 1959; bd. dirs. Cuban-Am. Minerals Corp.; mem. additive alloys adv. com. U.S. Munitions Bd. 1st lt. inf., U.S. Army, A.E.F., 1917-19. Mem. Am. Legion (past comdr.), University Club, Berkshire Country Club, Wyomissing Club, Wesley Heights Club, Masons, Elks, Sigma Delta Chi, Delta Tau Delta. Democrat. Presbyterian. Home: Washington D.C. †

ENGLISH, HAROLD MEDVIN, psychiatrist, hospital administrator; b. Martinsburg, W.Va., May 20, 1923; s. Harold C. and Sara Kathryn (Bowers) E.; m. Patricia Maud Dougherty, Dec. 4, 1948; children: Eric Harold, Dorilyn, Evan Allen, Daylanne Kathryn. Student, Washington Coll., 1941-44; MD, George Washington U., 1949. Intern St. Elizabeth's Hosp., Washington, 1949-51; resident in psychiatry U.S. Naval Hosp., Bethesda, Md., 1952-56; dir. hosp. inspection and licensure Md. Dept. Mental Hygiene, 1961-62; supt. Eastern Shore State Hosp., Cambridge, Md., 1962-84; regional mental health dir. State of Md., 1965-84; instr. psychiatry Johns Hopkins Sch. Medicine, Balt., 1961-84. With USNR, 1944-45; lt. comdr. MC, USNR, 1950-60. Recipient Gov. Md. citation for service to handicapped, 1965. Fellow Am. Psychiat. Assn. Home: Easton Md. Died Sept. 13, 1984.

ENNIS, THOMAS ELMER, JR., accounting educator; b. Salisbury, N.C., Jan. 1, 1930; s. Thomas Elmer and Annie (Williams) E.; m. Loraine May Van Dam, Aug. 1, 1959. BS in Bus. Adminstrn., U. N.C., 1952, MBA, 1955; PhD, U. Mich., 1964. Mem. faculty Washington and Lee U., Lexington, Va., 1955-84, instr., 1955-57, asst. prof. accounting, 1957-64, assoc. prof., 1964-68, prof., 1968-84. With AUS, 1952-54. Mem. Am. Acctg. Assn., Nat. Assn. Accts., Phi Beta Kappa, Beta Gamma Sigma, Omicron Delta Epsilon. Home: Lexington Va. Died July 29, 1984; cremated.

ENSLIN, MORTON SCOTT, theology educator; b. Somerville, Mass., Mar. 8, 1897; s. Theodore Vernon and Ada Eudora (Scott) E.; m. Ruth May Tuttle, June 1, 1922; children: Theodore Vernon, Priscilla. AB, Harvard U., 1919, ThD, 1924; BD, Newton Theol. Instn., 1922; DD, Colby Coll., 1945; DHL (hon.), Hebrew Union Coll., 1964. Prof. N.T. lit. and exegesis, head dept. Crozer Theol. Sem., Chester, Pa., 1924-54; lectr. textual criticism Phila. Div. Sch., 1924-25; lectr. patristics U. Pa. Grad. Sch., 1926-54; Craig prof. bibl. langs. and lit. St. Lawrence U. Theol. Sch., 1955-65, prof. emeritus, 1965-80; vis. lectr. history of religion Bryn Mawr Coll., 1965-68; prof. Dropsie Coll., 1968-80; vis. prof. Chgo. Theol. Sem., summer 1929, Drew Theol. Seminary, 1953-54, Iliff Sch. Theology, summer 1956, Hebrew Union Coll.-Jewish Inst. Religion, 1977; mem. Am. Sch. Classical Studies mng. com., Athens. Author several books including: The Ethics of Paul, 1930, rev. 1962, Christian Beginnings, 1938, The Prophet from Nazareth, 1961, Letters to the Churches, 1963, From Jesus to Christianity, 1964, Reapproaching Paul, 1972, Judith, 1972; editor Crozer Quar., 1941-52, Jour. Bibl. Lit., 1960-69. Ensign USNRF, 1918-22, active duty 1918-19. Mem. Am. Theol. Soc. (treas. 1927-55, pres. 1952), Soc. Bibl. Lit. (pres. 1945), Am. Oriental Soc., Phila. Oriental Club (pres. 1938-39), Masons, K.T., Shriners, Phi Beta Kappa, Pi Gamma Mu. Home: Wynnewood Pa. Died Dec. 14, 1980.

EPPELSHEIMER, DANIEL SNELL, educator; b. Chgo., Mar. 17, 1909; s. Daniel and Florence Irvina (Snell) E.; m. Marion Elizabeth Vaughn, Apr. 11, 1936; children: Daniel Snell, David Vaughn. BS cum laude in Mining and Metallurgy, Harvard, 1932, DSc in Phys. Metallurgy, 1935. Research asst. Harvard, 1929-35; research metallurgist Union Carbide & Carbon Research Lab., Niagara Falls, N.Y., 1935-38; prof., head engr. Exptl. Sta. U. N.H., 1938-45; chief. physics metallurgist, sales mgr. Metal Hydrides, Inc., Beverly, Mass., 1945-46; prof. nuclear and metall. engring. U. Mo. at Rolla, 1947-88, chmn. dept. metallurgy, 1957-58, 63-64; pres. Eppelsheimer Enterprises, Rolla, 1980-88; cons. in field. Mem. Mo. AEC, 1959-88; Mo. rep. So. Interstate Nuclear Bd., Atlanta, 1965-88, chmn., 1970-88; sci. adviser Gov. Mo., 1970-88. Contbr. articles to profl. jours. Dir. Mo. IncuTech Found., Rolla, 1984-88. Mem. AIME, Am. Soc. Metals, Am. Chem. Soc., Am. Crystallographic Assn., Am. Foundrymens Soc., Am. Soc. Engring. Edn., Brit. Inst. Physics, Brit. Inst. Metals, Brit. Iron and Steel Inst., Verein Deutscher Eisenhutten Leute, Franklin Inst., Sigma Xi, Pi Kappa Alpha. Clubs: Rotarian. (Boston), Harvard (Boston); Missouri Athletic (St. Louis). Home: Rolla Mo. Died Jan. 1, 1988; buried Rolla Cemetery, Rolla, Mo.

EPPENBERGER, FRED ARNOLD, lawyer; b. Chgo., Oct. 30, 1906; s. Arnold A. and Laura (Doerr) E.; m. Emily V. Hurd, Nov. 26, 1937; children: Katherine C., Frederick H. Student, St. Louis U., 1923; LLB, Washington U., 1928. Bar: Mo. 1928. Assoc. Husch, Eppenberger, Donohue, Elson & Cornfield (and predecessors), St. Louis, 1928-85, mem., 1936-85; active drafting of adoption law, juvenile court code; chmn. St. Lous County Commn. on Human Relations, 1964-70; vice chmn. joint adminstrv. com. St. Louis Constrn. Manpower Corp. (St. Louis Plan), 1968-74; vice chmn. St. Louis County Civil Service Commn., 1974, chmn. 1975-76. Bd. dirs. Mid-County YMCA, St. Louis; bd. dirs. Family and Children's Service of Greater St. Louis, v.p., 1955-58; mem. citizens adv. bd. Juvenile Ct. of St. Louis, chmn. 1963; adv. bd. St. Louis County Children's Treatment Ctr. Recipient Alumni citation Washington U., 1962, Disting. Alumni award Washington U. Law Sch., 1981. Fellow Am. Bar Found., Am. Coll. Probate Counsel; mem. ABA (ho. dels. 1961-68), Am. Judicature Soc. (dir. 1962-65), Bar Assn. St. Louis (chmn. juvenile laws com., exec. com. 1944-50), Mo. Bar Assn. (chmn. juvenile laws com., bd. govs. 1955-85, pres. 1960, pres. Found. 1962-65), Nat. Assn. Coll. and Univ. Attys., Order of Coif, Phi Delta Phi, Mo. Athletic Club. Congregationalist. Home: Saint Louis Mo. Died May 25, 1985; buried Bellefontaine Cemetery, St. Louis.

EPPERT, RAY R., business executive; b. Carbon, Ind., July 5, 1902; s. Russell and Effie (Webster) E.; m. Helen Marie Chaffee, Dec. 30, 1923. LHD, Hillsdale Coll., 1956; LLD, Western Mich. U., 1961, Mich. State U., 1962; DSc, BA, Detroit Inst. of Tech., 1961; DSc, U. Detroit, 1967. With Burroughs Corp., Detroit, 1921-67, beginning as shipping clk. and advancing to v.p. mktg., 1946-51, exec. v.p., 1951-58, pres., 1958-66, chmn. bd., chief exec. officer, 1966-67, dir., 1948-67; dir. Mich. Bell Telephone Co., Mich. Consol. Gas Co., Cunningham Drug Stores, Inc.; vice chmn. Internat. Exec. Service Corps. Mem. adv. bd. on hosp. effectiveness HEW; adv. com. on internat. bus. problems Dept. State; bd. dirs., mem. exec. com. United Found. Met. Detroit; dir., mem. exec. com. Mich. United Fund; dir. Mich. Soc. Mental Health; mem. exec. com. Met. Detroit Bldg. Fund; pres. Detroit Med. Ctr. Devel. Corp.; adv. com. Internat. Mktg. Inst., Harvard U. Grad. Sch., Mich. State U. Sch. Bus. Adminstrn.; chmn. bd. trustees Harper Hosp.; trustee Hillsdale Coll.; lay trustee U. Detroit; dir. Cranbrook Sch. Decorated chevalier Legion of Honor (France); comdr. Order Brit. Empire. Mem. US C. of C., NAM, Nat. Planning Assn., Detroit Club, Detroit Athletic Club, Economic Club of Detroit, Bloomfield Hills Country Club, Pine Lake Country Club, Capitol Hill Club of Washington, Harbor View Club of NY. Home: Bloomfield Hills Mich. Died July 17, 1986, interred Woodlawn Cemetery Mausoleum, Detroit.

EPSTEIN, RICHARD LEWIS, lawyer, association executive; b. N.Y.C., Apr. 26, 1930; s. Harry Browdy and Sarah (Bussell) E.; m. Diana Triplett, June 7, 1986; children: Elizabeth Bussell, Sarah Denonn. BA cum laude, Amherst Coll., 1951; LLB, Yale U., 1954. Bar: U.S. Supreme Ct. 1961, Ill. 1973, N.Y 1973. Assoc. firm Harris, Beach & Wilcox, Rochester, N.Y., 1954-63; partner Harris, Beach & Wilcox, 1963-72; partner firm Sonnenschein Carlin Nath and Rosenthal, Chgo., 1973-77; group v.p. law Am. Hosp. Assn., Chgo., 1977-80, sr. v.p., gen. counsel, 1981-86; mem. Fed. Services Impasses Panel, 1970-78; cons. labor relations Dept. State, 1972-78; mgmt. rep. Health Industry Wage Adv. Panel Cost of Living Council, 1973-75. Contbr. articles on health law and labor law to profl. jours.; mem. editorial bd.: Employee Relations Law Jour, 1975-86. Mem. Ill. Gov.'s Employee Relations Council, 1974-86; mem. nat. panel on edn. Am. Arbitration Assn., 1974-86; Bd. advisors Rochester St. Mary's Hosp., 1967-72; pres. Planned Parenthood of Rochester and Monroe County, 1971. Recipient Leroy Snyder Meml. award Rochester Jaycees, 1965; named to Outstanding Young Men in Am. U.S. Jaycees, 1965. Mem. ABA, Am. Acad. Hosp. Attys. (pres. 1975-76), Rochester C. of C. (trustee 1969-73). Clubs: Metropolitan (Chgo.), Carlton (Chgo.); Genesee Valley (Rochester), Rochester Yacht (Rochester), Tennis of Rochester (Rochester). Home: Chicago Ill. Died Oct. 28, 1986.

EPTING, LAWRENCE, advertising agency executive; b. Wyomissing, Pa., Oct. 3, 1934; s. Charles Walter and Leah (Yoder) E.; m. Louise Margaret Gallo, Apr. 25, 1959 (div. 1977); children—Margaret S., Christian C., Lee E. B.A., Muhlenberg Coll., 1958; M.B.A., CCNY, 1960. Vice-pres. Compton Advt., N.Y.C., 1960-67; sr. v.p. Ted Bates Advt., N.Y.C., 1968-72, exec. v.p., 1979—; pres. Norton Simon Communications, N.Y.C., 1973-77; exec. v.p. SSC&B, N.Y.C., 1978; dir. Ted Bates Worldwide; cons. Industry Labor Council, Lake Success, N.Y., 1983—, Dept. Transp., Washington. Served with U.S. Army, 1954-56. Mem. Am. Assn. Advt. Agys. Republican. Lutheran. Clubs: Board Room, West Side Tennis (N.Y.C.). Home: New York N.Y. Died June 5, 1988.

EPTON, BERNARD EDWARD, lawyer; b. Chgo., Aug. 25, 1921; s. Arthur I. and Rose (Goldstein) E.; m. Audrey Issett, June 8, 1945; children: Teri Lynn, Jeffrey David, Mark Richard, Dale Susan. Student, U. Chgo., 1938-39, Northwestern U., 1939-40, DePaul U., 1947. Bar: Ill. 1947. Since practiced in Chgo.; ptnr. firm A.I. Epton & Sons, 1941-47, Epton, Mullin & Druth, Ltd., 1947-87; mem. Ill. Gen. Assembly from 24th Dist., 1969-82; chmn. ins. com.; dir. Pemcor, Inc.; mem. Ill. Ins. Exchange, 1982-87, sec., 1985-87, chmn., 1986-87. Mem. South Shore O'Keefe Conservation Community Council, 1960-66; mem. Jewish Bd. Edn., 1965-70; past pres. Nat. Conf. Ins. Legislators; chmn. Ill. Ins. Study Commn., 1972-82; mem. Lloyds of London; v.p. Jane Dent Home Aged Negros, 1961-87, also bd. dirs.; bd. dirs. Jewish Community Ctrs. Chgo.; trustee Coll. Jewish Studies; mem. pres.'s council St. Xavier Coll.; mem. estate planning council DePaul U., Republican candidate for mayor, Chgo., 1983. Served to capt. USAAF, 1942-45, ETO. Decorated D.F.C. with oak leaf cluster, Air medal with three oak leaf clusters. Mem. Ill. Bar Assn., Chgo. Bar Assn., Decalogue Soc. Lawyers (bd. dirs. 1949, pres. 1961-62), Fedn. Ins. Counsel, Trial Lawyers Club, Am. Legion, Air Force Assn. (bd. dirs. 1947-50), South Shore C. of C. (dir., counsel 1953-87, pres. 1959-61), Mil. Order World Wars (vice comdr.), Chgo. Hist. Soc. (life), U. Chgo. Alumni Assn. (life). Clubs: Standard (Chgo.); Idlewild Country (Flossmoor, Ill.) (dir. 1964-67, dir., v.p. 1986-87). Home: Chicago Ill. Died Dec. 13, 1987; buried Oakwood Cemetery, Chgo.

ERICKSON, GEORGE ABRAHAM, advertising executive; b. Chgo., Mar. 23, 1904; s. Erick and Juliana (Helsing) E.; m. Nellie Knight, June 24, 1930; children: Pamela June (Mrs. Edward F. Hudson III), George Knight. Student, Knox Coll., 1924-25. Salesman Met. Newspaper Feature Syndicate, 1926-29, Stone, Webster & Blodget, investment bankers, 1930-33; with Doremus & Co., advt. and pub. relations, N.Y.C., 1934-86, account exec., v.p., exec. v.p., 1953-62, vice chmn., 1962-67, chmn. bd., 1967-86, mem. fin. com., 1962-68, chmn., chief exec. officer, 1968-73, dir., 1953-86. County committeeman Rep. Party, 1950-51; trustee Knox Coll.; mem. Pelham Sch. Bd., 1953-59, pres., 1958-59. Mem. City Midday Club, Pequot Yacht Club, Pelham Country Club, Pelham Men's Club (pres. 1946-47), Fairfield County Hunt Club, Tau Kappa Epsilon. Home: Fairfield Conn. Died Aug. 3, 1986; buried Oaklawn Cemetery, Fairfield, Conn.

ERICKSON, STATIE ESTELLE, educational administrator; b. Ouray, Colo., 1891; d. John and Lizzie (Wahl) E. AB, Colo. Coll., 1915; student, U. Minn., 1918-20; PhD, U. Calif., Berkeley, 1930. Tchr. elem. sch. Ouray, Colo., 1909-11; tchr. high sch. Ouray, 1915-18; county supt. Ouray County Schs., 1920-23; tchr., rrsch. nutrition dept. home econs. U. Ky., 1925-29, head dept. home econs., 1929-53, dir. Sch. Home Econs., 1953-56, disting. prof., rsch. home economist, from 1956. Recipient Sullivan award, 1957. Mem. AAUP, Am. Home Econs. Assn., Am. Dietetic Assn., Sigma Xi, Iota Sigma Pi, Phi Upsilon Omicron. Home: Lexington Ky. †

ERNST, HANS, engineer, educator; b. Melbourne, Australia, Oct. 22, 1892; came to U.S., 1915, naturalized, 1933; s. Julius T. and Olga (Straubel) E.; m. Adele Nicolet, Aug. 23, 1922; children: Marjorie Nicolet, Phyllis Adele (Mrs. William Crittenden Pierce). Diploma mech. and elec. engring., Melbourne Tech. Coll., 1911. Draftsman, designer Edmiston & O'Neill, 1912, Mephan Ferguson Prop. Ltd., 1912-13; instr. engring. Sunshine Tech. Coll., 1913-15; draftsman Pullman Car Co., Richmond, Calif., 1916-17; machine designer Western Cartridge Co., 1917, mech. engr., 1919-26; dir. rsch. The Cin. Milling Machine Co., 1926-57; Herman Schneider rsch. prof. engring., dir. grad. coop. program U. Cin., 1958-63, prof. emeritus, from 1963; State Dept. tech. cons. Govt. Israel, 1961. Author tech. articles; holder patents machine and tool fields. With RAF, 1918-19. Recipient outstanding engr. award Cin. Coun. Tech. and Social Scis., 1950. Fellow ASME; mem. N.Y. Acad. Scis., AAAS, Am. Soc. Tool and Mfg. Engrs. (nat. rsch. medal 1957), Engring.Soc. Cin., Aircraft Owners and Pilots Assn., Sigma Xi, Tau Beta Pi. Baptist. Home: Clearwater Fla. †

ERNST, JIMMY, artist; b. Cologne, Fed. Republic Germany, June 24, 1920; naturalized, 1951; s. Max and Louise Amalia (Straus) E. Student, Lindenthal Real-Gymnasium, Cologne, 1932-36, Sch. Arts and Crafts, Altona, Germany, 1938; hon. doctorate, Southampton Coll., L.I. U., 1982. Prof. dept. art Bklyn. Coll., 1951-82; represented by CDS Gallery, N.Y.C.; Am. specialist Dept. State's Cultural Exchange Program to, Russia and Poland, 1961; vis. artist Norton Galleries, Palm Beach, Fla. One-man shows Milw. Art Ctr., Grace Borgenicht Gallery, N.Y.C., Venice Biennial, Brussels World Fair, Kunstverein Cologne Mus., Arts Club, Chgo., 1968, Lucei Weil Gallery, Paris, 1972, Yares Gallery, Scottsdale, Ariz., 1974, Harmon Gallery, Naples, Fla., 1981, Armstrong Gallery, 1984, Guild Hall, East Hampton, N.Y., 1985, Century Club, N.Y.C., 1986, Wight Gallery, UCLA, Modern Mus. of New Delhi, India, 1987, Hofstra Mus., Hofstra U., N.Y., 1988, U. Wis. Mus., 1988, other nat. and internat. shows; work represented permanent collections Mus. Modern Art, Met. Mus. Art, Corcoran Gallery, Washington, Guggenheim Mus., Chgo. Art Inst., Albright Art Gallery, Buffalo, Whitney

Mus., others; meml. exhibit Acad. Arts and Letters, 1985; mural commns. include, exec. dining room Gen. Motors Tech. Center, Am. President Lines, S.S. Adams, Continental Nat. Bank, Lincoln, Nebr.; lectr., various mus. in U.S.; exhbns. in, Cologne, Bielefeld Mus., Germany, Am. House, Berlin; author: A Not-So-Still Life, 1984 (Germany, France, 1985). Recipient Brandeis Creative Arts award, 1957, Guggenheim grantee, 1961. Mem. AAAL. Home: East Hampton N.Y. Died Feb. 6, 1984; buried Green River Cemetary, East Hampton.

ERPF, CARL K., investment banker; b. Woodmere, N.Y., 1925. Ptnr. Ladenburg, Thalmann & Co., N.Y.C.; dir. Atlantic Industries, Broad Alliance Corp., Petro-Lewis Corp.; pres., dir. 960 Park Corp. Sec.-treas. Walter and Lucie Rosen Found., Inc.; pres. bd. trustees Columbia Grammar Sch.; trustee Arkville ERPF Fund, Inc. Home: New York N.Y. Deceased.

ESCAMILLA, ROBERTO FRANCISCO, physican, educator; b. Guadalajara, Mex., Oct. 9, 1905; came to U.S., 1906; s. Roberto Gregorio and Ida Eva (Vollers) E.; m. Orrie Montgomery, Aug. 12, 1938 (div. 1960); children: Elisa Katherine (Mrs. Edwin Schwartz), Roberta Frances (Mrs. James Garrison), Victoria Jean (Mrs. David Fleishhacker), William Gregory; m. Elizabeth Scoville Russo, July 20, 1960. AB, U. Calif., Berkeley, 1927; MD, Harvard U., 1931. Diplomate Am. Bd. Internal Medicine. Med. house officer Peter Bent Brigham Hosp., Boston, 1931-33; asst. vis. pathologist San Francisco Hosp., 1933; asst. resident physician U. Calif. Hosp., San Francisco, 1933-34, mem. staff, 1934-80; pvt. practice San Francisco, 1934-80; mem. staff Franklin Hosp., St. Francis Hosp.; civilian cons. to surgeon gen. U.S. Army, Letterman Gen. Hosp., San Francisco, 1945-76, emeritus; asst. in medicine U. Calif. Sch. Medicine, 1933-36, instr. 1936-40, asst. clin. prof. 1940-47, assoc. clin. prof. 1947-56, clin. prof. 1950-80; dir. Pituitary Bank, 1959-76; pres. Pituitary Bank Found., San Francisco, 1962-76. Author: Laboratory Aids in Endocrine Diagnosis, 1953, (with H. Lisser) Atlas of Clinical Endocrinology, 1957, 62, The Pacific Interurban Clinical Club-50 Year History, 1974; editor: Laboratory Tests in Diagnosis and Investigation of Endocrine Functions, 1962, 71; contbr. chpts. in books, numerous articles to profl. publs. Maj. to lt. col. MC, US Army, 1942-45. Fellow ACP (gov. No. Calif. and Nev., regent); mem. AMA, Calif. Med. Assn., San Francisco Med. Soc., Calif. Acad. Medicine, Assn. for Study Internal Secretions, Endocrine Soc., Am. Soc. Internal Medicine, Calif. Soc. Internal Medicine, San Francisco Soc. Internal Medicine, Pacific Interurban Clin. Club, Phi Beta Kappa, Phi Sigma Kappa, Nu Sigma Nu, Bohemian Club, Family Club (Knight of Appreciation 1971). Home: San Francisco Calif. Died 1980.

ESTERLY, JOHN ROOSEVELT, pathologist, educator; b. Friedensburg, Pa., Mar. 13, 1933; s. John E. and Della (Nein) E.; m. Nancy Burton, June 15, 1957; children: Sarah, Anne, John, Henry. BS, Yale U., 1955; MD, Johns Hopkins U., 1959. Intern Johns Hopkins Hosp., Balt., 1959-60, resident, 1960-63; asst. prof. dept pathology U. Chgo., 1968-72, assoc. prof., 1972-75, prof., 1975-87. Contbr. articles to profl. jours. Served with U.S. Army, 1966-68. Mem. Internat. Acad. Pathology, Am. Assn. Pathologists, Histochem. Soc., Teratology Soc., Pediatric Path. Soc., Am. Thoracic Soc. Home: Chicago Ill. Died Sept. 25, 1987.

ESTES, ELEANOR, author; b. West Haven, Conn., May 9, 1906; d. Louis and Caroline (Gewecke) Rosenfeld; m. Rice Estes, Dec. 8, 1932; 1 child, Helena Estes Sileo. Grad., Pratt Inst. Sch. Library Sci. (Caroline M. Hewins scholar), 1932. Children's librarian Free Pub. Library, New Haven, 1924-31, N.Y. Pub. Library, 1932-40. Author: The Moffats, 1941, The Middle Moffat, 1942, The Sun and the Wind and Mr. Todd, 1943, Rufus M, 1943, The Hundred Dresses, 1944, The Echoing Green, 1947, The Sleeping Giant, 1948, Ginger Pye, 1951 (winner Herald Tribune Spring Book Festival award), A Little Oven, 1955, Pinky Pye, 1958, The Witch Family, 1960, The Alley, 1964, Miranda The Great, 1967, The Lollipop Princess, 1967, The Tunnel of Hugsy Goode, 1972, The Coat-Hanger Christmas Tree, 1973, The Lost Umbrella of Kim Chu, 1978, The Moffat Museum, 1983, The Curious Adventures of Jimmy McGee, 1987. Recipient Newbery medal for distinguished contbn. to Am. lit. for children, 1951; ann. Alumni award Pratt Inst., 1967; N.Y. State assn. Supervision and Curriculum Devel. award for outstanding contbn. to childrens lit., 1961. Mem. PEN, Authors Guild. Episcopalian. Home: New Haven Conn. Died July 15, 1988, buried Oak Grove Cemetery, West Haven, Conn.

ESTES, ELLIOTT M., automotive executive; b. Mendon, Mich., Jan. 7, 1916. Student, Gen. Motors Inst., 1932-36; MME, U. Cin., 1940, DSc (hon.), 1971; LLD (hon.), Kalamazoo Coll., 1975, No. Mich. U., 1976. Chief engr. Pontiac Motor div. Gen. Motors Corp., 1956-61, gen. mgr., corp. v.p., 1961-65, v.p., gen. mgr. Chevrolet Motor Div., 1965-79, group exec. car and truck group, 1969-70, group v.p. overseas ops., 1970-72, exec. v.p. ops., staff dir., 1972-74; pres., chief operating officer, dir. Gen. Motors Corp., Detroit, 1974-81; dir. Owens-Ill. Inc., Kellogg Co., McDonnell Douglass Corp., COMSAT. Mem. Sigma Chi. Home: Saint Clair Mich. Died Mar. 25, 1988.

ESTEY, GEORGE FISHER, rhetoric educator, author; b. Cody's, N.B., Can., Jan. 21, 1924; s. Clarence A. and Eileen (Fisher) E.; m. Barbara Alice Brown, Aug. 25, 1951; children: Roger Scott, Gregory Alan. BA magna cum laude, Tufts Coll., 1952; MA, U. Conn., 1954; PhD, U. Ill., 1960. Instr. U. Conn., 1952-54, U. Ill., 1954-59; mem. faculty Boston U., 1959-84, assoc. prof., 1964-68, prof. rhetoric, 1968-84. Author: (with Harry H. Crosby) College Writing, 1968, 2d edit. 1975, Just Rhetoric, 1972; editor: (with Doris Hunter) Non-Violence, 1971, Violence, 1971, Interdisciplinary Perspectives, 1976-82. With USAAF, 1942-47. Mem. Nat. Council Tchrs. English, Conf. Coll. Composition and Communication, Assn. for Gen. and Liberal Studies, Phi Beta Kappa. Home: Lexington Mass. Died July 31, 1984; buried Lexington, Mass.

ETNIER, STEPHEN MORGAN, artist; b. York, Pa., Sept. 11, 1903; s. Carey and Susan Ellen (Smith) E.; m. Mathilde Gray, June 1926 (div. 1932); m. Elizabeth Jay, June 1933 (div. 1948); m. Jane Pearce, Sept. 1948 (dec. June 1949); m. Samuella Rose, Apr. 5, 1950; children—Suzanne Etnier Collins, Penelope Etnier Dinsmore, Stephanie Etnier Doane, Victoria Etnier Villamil, John, David. Student, Yale, 1926, Haverford Coll., 1928, Pa. Acad. Fine Arts, 1925-29; A.F.D., Bates Coll., 1969, Bowdoin Coll., 1969. One-man shows include: PS Galleries, Dallas, 1982, 83; represented in permanent collections, Met. Mus., N.Y.C., Boston Mus., Avery Meml., Hartford, Conn., Toledo Mus., New Britain Mus., Phillips Meml. Mus., Washington, Farnsworth Mus., Rockland, Maine, Vassar Coll., Pa. Acad. Fine Arts, Bowdoin Coll., Brunswick, Maine, Fairleigh Dickinson Coll., Rutherford, N.J., Buck Hill Art Assn., Buck Hill Falls, Pa., IBM, Dallas, Los Angeles, Springfield (Mass.) museums, Marine Mus., Searsport, Maine, Brooks Meml. Mus., Memphis, Parrish Art Mus., Southampton, L.I., others, murals, Everett (Mass.), Spring Valley (N.Y.) post offices. Served as lt. USNRF, World War II. Recipient Hon. mention Chgo. Art Inst., 1932; Saltus gold medal N.A.D., 1955; 2d Altman prize, 1956; Samuel F.B. Morse medal, 1964; purchase prize Butler Art Inst., Youngstown, Ohio. Academician N.A.D. Died October 7, 1984; buried Hillcrest Cemetery, S. Harpswell, Maine.

ETTER, PHILIPP, Swiss federal councillor; b. Menzingen, Zug, Switzerland, Dec. 21, 1891; s. Josef Anton and Jkobea (Stocker) E.; m. MAria Hegglin, 1918; 5 sons, 5 daus. Student, Gymnasium Einsiedeln; advocate, U. Zurich, 1917; Dr. honoris causa, Univ. Neuchatel, Fed. Poly. Sch., Zurich. Began as advocate 1917; dep. Grand Council, 1918; Councillor of State 1922, pres., 1927-28; mem. Council of States, 1930; Fed. Councillor from 1934; pres. Swiss Confedn., 1939, 42, 47, 53; chief Fed. Dept. of Interior. Author: Reden an das Schweiservolk, 1939, Sens et Mission de la Suisse, 1942, Stimmrecht der Geschichte, 1953. Maj. Swiss Infantry. Home: Berne Switzerland. †

EUBANK, GERALD A., insurance executive; b. Navasota, Tex., July 28, 1892; s. John Abner and Julia Alice (Robertson) E.; m. Harriet Purvis, June 24, 1913; children: Gerald Abner, Alice Purvis, Hugh Allen. Student, U.S. Naval Acad. (prep.), 1913. Mgr. Prudential Ins. Co. Am., N.Y.C., from 1927, also spl. asst. to pres., from 1949. Served to rear admiral USNR, 1917-52. Mem. Metropolitan Club (Washington), Army-Navy Club (Washington), Downtown Athletic Club (N.Y.C.), Downtown Assn. (N.Y.C.), Essex County Country Club (West Orange, N.J.), Los Angeles Country Club, Seaview Country Club (Absecon, N.J.). Home: East Orange N.J. †

EURICH, ALVIN CHRISTIAN, educator; b. Bay City, Mich., June 14, 1902; s. Christian H. and Hulda (Steinke) E.; m. Nell P. Hutchinson, Mar. 15, 1953; children: Juliet Ann, Donald Alan. BA, North Central Coll., 1924, LittD, 1949; MA, U. Maine, 1926, LLD, 1965; PhD, U. Minn., 1929; LLD, Hamline U., 1944, Clark U., Alfred U., Miami U., Yeshiva U., Redlands U.; LittD, New Sch. Social Research, 1952; LHD, U. Fla., 1953, U. Miami, Fla., 1968, Albion Coll., 1965, Fairfield U., 1971, W.Va. U., 1985; ScD, Akron U., 1960. Instr. U. Maine, 1924-26; served from asst. in ednl. psychology to prof., also asst. to pres. U. Minn., 1926-37; prof. edn. Northwestern U., 1937-38; prof. edn. Stanford U., 1938-48, v.p., 1944-48, acting pres., 1948; chmn. Stanford Research Inst.; 1st chancellor State U. N.Y., 1949-51; v.p. Ford Fund Advancement Edn., 1951-64, mem. bd. dirs., 1952-67; exec. dir. edn. div. Ford Found, 1958-64; pres. Aspen Inst. Humanistic Studies, 1963-67; founder, pres. Acad. Ednl. Devel., 1962-87, chmn., 1987; former pres. The Am. Lang. Acad.; former trustee Internat. Council for Ednl. Devel., Center for Public Resources; cons. U.S. govt. agys. during and following war years; supr. various ednl. surveys; served as mem. or cons. various commns. including Hoover Commn., Pres. Truman's Commn. Higher Edn., Pres. Kennedy's Task Force Edn.; chmn. Surgeon Gen.'s Commn. Nurses; cons. NASA, AID, Peace Corps; chmn. U.S. nat. commn. UNESCO, chmn. U.S. del. to gen. conf., Paris, 1968; chmn. adv. com. Haile Selassie U.; planning adviser U. Patras, Greece; ednl. adviser, Libya; mem. Nat. Commn. Libraries; vis.
prof. various univs.; vis. fellow Clare Coll., U. Can
bridge, Eng., 1967; mem. U.S. Council for Wor
Communications Yr., 1983. Author, co-author book
and studies in education; also psychol. and achieveme
tests, including Time Mag.'s Current Affairs Test
contbr. articles to profl. jours.; author: Reformin
American Education, 1969; co-author: Education
Psychology, 1935; editor: Campus, 1980, 1968, Hig
School, 1980, 1970, Major Transitions in the Huma
Life Cycle, 1981. Bd. dirs. Lovelace Found. Serve
from lt. comdr. to comdr. USNR, 1942-44; di
standards and curriculum div. Naval Personnel.
Recipient Outstanding Achievement award U. Minn
1951; Times Sq. Club's 4th Ann. award, 1953; An
award N.Y. Acad. Pub. Edn., 1963. Fellow AAA
(council 1941-45), Am. Psychol. Assn., Aspen Ins
mem. Sigma Xi, Phi Delta Kappa. Clubs: Universit
Century (N.Y.C.), Cosmos (Washington), Athenaeu
(London). Home: New York N.Y. Died May 27, 1987.

EUSTIS, WARREN PENHALL, lawyer, educator;
Fairmont, Minn., Nov. 30, 1927; s. Irving Nelson an
Florence (Penhall) E.; m. Doris Anne Grieser, Ma
1951 (div. Nov. 1968); children: Lillian, Paul; m. Nanc
N. Anderson, Jan. 15, 1971; 1 child, Soren. B.A
Carleton Coll., 1950; J.D., U. Chgo., 1953; M.A., U
Ark., 1956. Bar: Minn. 1953. Practice law Rochest
and Mpls., 1953—; prof. law U. Minn., 1974—; chm
Granville, Ctrs., Inc.; counsel Upper Midwest Researc
and Devel. Council; dir. Twin Cities Health Projec
1972—; orgnl. cons. in health and ednl. delivery sy
tems. Mem. Rochester Charter Commn., 1960-7
Minn. Higher Edn. Commn., 1965-67; pres. Rochest
Council Chs., 1966; pres. emeritus Minn. Chen
Dependency Assn.; chmn. 1st Congl. Dist. Min
Democratic-Farmer Labor Party, 1959-66; state fi
chmn. 1962-67; chmn. Granville Ctr., Inc. Served wi
Sci. and Profl. Corps, AUS, 1954-56. Mem. Minn. Tri
Lawyers Assn. (gov.), Olmsted County Bar Assn. (pa
pres.), Delta Upsilon, Phi Alpha Theta. Home: Mi
neapolis Minn. Died Sept. 22, 1988.

EVANS, DAVID R(ANNEY), banker; b. Akron, Ohi
Jan. 24, 1892; s. William H. and Carrie (Ranney) E
m.Myrtle Caves, July 1, 1938 (dec. Dec. 13, 1959
children: Phyllis (Mrs. J. R. Dannemiller), Davi
Crane. Student pub. schs., Akron. Pres. Evans Sav
Assn., 1940-50, later bd. dirs.; pres. The Dime Ban
Akron, 1950-60, chmn. bd. consolidated bank followin
merger with Bank of Akron; treas. Evans Agy. Co
from 1923; bd. dirs. Trent Realty Co., 2d Nat. Bldg. C
Mem. Akron C. of C., Portgage Club (dir.), City Clu
(dir.), Union Country Club (Cleve.). Home: Akro
Ohio. †

EVANS, GIL, musician, composer, arranger;
Toronto, Ont., Can., May 13, 1912; m. Ani
Evans. Formerly mus. arranger for bands lead b
Claude Thornhill, Miles Davis, then pianist and lead
of own band; compositions include (with M. Davis
Sketches of Spain (Grammy award 1960); albums in
clude Big Stuff, Blues in Orbit, Into the Hot, Littl
Wing, Out of the Cool, Gil Evans/Plays Hendrix, Pr
estess, The British Orchestra, 1983, Live at Sweet Bas
(with The Monday Night Orchestra) Bud and Bir
(Grammy award, 1989); musical score for film Absolut
Beginners. Winner Down Beat Readers Poll as Be
Arranger, 1966, 74-77, 84, 85. Died Mar. 20, 1988.

EVANS, JAMES CARMICHAEL, government officia
educator; b. Gallatin, Tenn., July 1, 1900; s. Jame
Royal and Lillie (Carmichael) E.; m. Rosallin
McGoodwin, Aug. 28, 1928; children: Jame
Carmichael, Rose Evangeline Wells. BS, MIT, 192
MS, 1926; LLD, Va. State Coll., 1955, Cen. State Coll
1956; LHD, N.C. A&T Coll., 1961. Engaged in ele
engring. constrn. Miami, Fla., 1926-28; tchr. Booker T
Washington High Sch., Miami, 1927; prof. tech. indus
tries, dir. trade and tech. div. W.Va. State Coll., 192
37, adminstrv. asst. to pres., 1937-42; asst. civilian aid
to sec. war 1943-47, civilian aide, 1947-48, adviser t
sec. def., 1947-49, asst., 1947, counsellor mil. an
civilian affairs, 1964-70; v.p. Afro-Am. Life Ins. Co
1954-88; adj. prof. elec. engring. Howard U., 1946-7
dir. Indsl. Bank Washington; vocat. tng. dir. asso
Council Nat. Def., War Manpower Commn., Wash
ington, 1941-43; mil. instr. World War I; coordinato
tng. programs for civilian, mil. pilots, 1939-43. Write
monographs tng. and placement in tech. fields; patente
utilization of exhaust gases to prevent icing on aircraft
Trustee Fla. Meml. Coll., Miami; regent Marymour
Coll. Va. Recipient Harmon award in sci. research i
electronics, 1926, Dorie Miller Meml. Found. awar
1953, Career Service award Nat. Civil Service Leagu
1959, Sec. Def. Meritorius Civilian Service medal, 1970
Mem. Nat. Tech. Assn. (exec. sec. 1932-57), Nat. Ins
Sci., IEEE, AAUP, NEA, Adelphian Club, Cosmo
Club, Tau Beta Pi, Epsilon Pi Tau, Alpha Kappa M
Alpha Phi Alpha, Sigma Pi Phi. Baptist. Home: Wash
ington D.C. Died Apr. 14, 1988.

EVANS, JOSEPH PATRICK, neurological surgeon
educator; b. La Crosse, Wis., Nov. 29, 1904; s. Edwar
and Sarah (Thompson) E.; m. Hermene Eisenman, Jun
24, 1929; children: Mary Frances Bapst, Edward
Frederick Nicholas, Caroline de Villa, Anne W. Lancto
Hermene Wolfe, John Fisher, Thomas More. Studen
Notre Dame U., 1921-23; AB, Harvard U., 1925, M

cum laude, 1929; MSc, McGill U., 1930, PhD, 1937; postgrad., U. Chgo. U. Minn., Yale U., Cambridge U., London U., Nat. Hosp., Queen Sq., London, Breslau; DSc (hon.), Loyola U., Chgo., 1964. Diplomate Am. Bd. Neurol. Surgery (mem. 1944-50), Am. Bd. Psychiatry and Neurology. Assoc. prof. surgery charge neurol. surgery U. Cin., 1937-54; prof. emeritus neurol. surgery U. Chgo., 1970; dir. div. neurol. surgery U. Chgo. Clinics, 1954-67; research assoc. physiology Yale U., 1948; med. mission Austria, 1947; dir. Internat. Office, 1979-82; cons. Pan. Am. Fedn. Assns. Med. Schs., 1971-76; Washington area rep. Internat. Physicians for Prevention of Nuclear War, 1982-85. Contbr. articles to profl. jours. Dir. N.Am. Liturgical Conf., 1960-66; mem. investigating commn. Dissent and Disorder, 1968-69. Fellow Adlai Stevenson Inst. Internat. Affairs, 1967-69, hon. fellow, 1969; Rockefeller fellow, 1935-36; recipient Condecoracion de Salud y Merito Asistencial Republic of Colombia. Fellow ACS (Latin Am. liaison rep. 1971-76, asst. dir. 1974-79, Disting. Service award 1981), Academia Medicina, Instituto Chile (hon.); mem. Am. Acad. Neurol. Surgery (pres. 1940-41), AMA, Assn. Research Nervous and Mental Diseases, Am. Assn. Neurol. Surgeons (v.p. 1961-62), Soc. Neurol. Surgeons (v.p. 1963-64, Disting. Service award 1980), Am. Neurol. Assn. (v.p. 1966-67), Quadrangel Club, Sigma Xi, Alpha Omega Alpha, numerous hon. fgn. socs. Roman Catholic. Home: Kensington Md. Died May 8, 1985.

EVANS, LOUIS HADLEY, clergyman; b. Goshen, Ind., May 31, 1897; s. William and Laura (Togerson) E.; m. Dec. 22, 1921; children: Lauralil Evans Deats, Louis Hadley, Marily Evans Demarest, William O. AB, Occidental Coll., DD, 1944; BD, McCormick Theol. Sem.; DD, Jamestown Coll., 1932, Washington-Jefferson Coll., 1932, Ill. Coll., 1953; LLD, J. Brown U., 1943, Baylor U., 1958; DLitt, Sterling Coll., 1963; LHD, Calif. Coll. Medicine, 1950, Lafayette Coll., 1954. Ordained to ministry Presbyn. Ch. Pastor 1st Presbyn. Ch., Westhope, N.D., 1922-25, Calvary Presbyn. Ch., Wilmington, Calif., 1925-28, 1st Presbyn. Ch., Pomona, Calif., 1928-31, 3d Presbyn. Ch., Pitts., 1931-41, 1st Presbyn. Ch., Hollywood, Calif., 1941-43; minister-at-large United Presbyn. Ch. Nat. Bd., 1953-62; lectr., preacher U.S., fgn. countries; pres. Presbyn. Bd. Nat. Missions; chmn. Com. Jewish Relief, 1940; active Urban League Los Angeles, 1951; founder, pres. Fellowship Christian Athletes, 1955-58. Author: This is America's Hour, The Kingdom is Yours, Youth Seeks a Master, Make Your Faith Work, Life's Hidden Power, Your Marriage-Duel or Duet?. Bd. govs. Occidental Coll., 1950; trustee Western Theol. Sem., Pitts., 1935-41, San Francisco Theol. Sem., 1945-53. With USN, World War I. Named Speaker of Yr. in Field of Religion, 1951, Churchman of Yr. Washington Pilgrimage Found., 1957; recipient award of merit USAF, 1953-54. Mem. Rotary. Home: Pasadena Calif. Died Sept. 21, 1981, buried Forest Lawn, Glendale, Calif.

EVANS, ORRIN BRYAN, law educator, academic administrator; b. Baraboo, Wis., Oct. 6, 1910; s. Alfred and Mary (Roundtree) E.; m. Margaret Louise Searle, Feb. 18, 1933; children: Margaret Aspinwall, Evan George, David Roundtree. AB, U. Wis., 1931, LLB, 1935; JD, Yale U., 1940. Asst. prof. law U. Idaho, 1937-38; from asst. prof. to prof. U. Mo., 1938-47, atty. for univ., 1940-47; prof. U. So. Calif., 1947-52, Henry W. Bruce law prof., 1952-79, George Phleger prof. law, 1979-85, assoc. dean law sch., 1952-63, dean, 1963-67, dean and Phleger prof. emeritus, 1980-85; vis. prof. law Yale U., U. Wis., Northwestern U., U. Calif., others. Commr. Los Angeles CSC, 1961-65; state inheritance tax referee, 1967-73; pub. trustee Food and Drug Law Inst. Mem. ABA, Mo. Bar Assn., Wis. Bar Assn., Los Angeles County Bar Assn., Assn. Am. Law Schs. (exec. com. 1955), Order of the Coif, Selden Soc., Phi Kappa Sigma, Phi Alpha Delta, Phi Kappa Phi. Episcopalian. Home: Laguna Hills Calif. Died Sept. 9, 1985.

EVANS, WILLIAM WADSWORTH, lawyer; b. Paterson, N.J., Oct. 5, 1886; s. John W. and Emily (Wadsworth) E.; m. Isabel Blauvelt, Apr. 23, 1913; children: Barbara (Mrs. Norman Boe), William W.; m. Josephine Koodray, Dec. 21, 1947; m. Ruth F. Werner, July 22, 1957. Grad., N.Y. Law Sch., 1908. Bar: N.Y. 1909, N.Y. 1911. Mem. House Assembly N.J., 1919-24, majority leader, 1922, speaker House, 1923; former mem. commn. studying forms mcpl. govt. N.J.; past mem. Supreme Ct. com. of character and fitness; former chmn. Mcpl. Magistrates Com., N.J. Commn. Jud. Adminstrn. Chmn. Paterson chpt. ARC, 1947-49; past pres. Philharm. Soc. Greater Paterson. Mem. ABA (past. bd. govs.), N.J. State Bar Assn. (pres. 1936-37), Passaic County Bar Assn., Am. Judicature Soc., Am. Law Inst., N.Y. County Lawyers Assn., Internat. Assn. Ins. Counsel, Paterson C. of C., Hamilton Club (past pres.), Rotary Club (past. pres. Paterson). Home: Glen Rock N.J. †

EVELETH, DWIGHT EDWARD, insurance executive; b. San Francisco, Apr. 17, 1891; s. William S. and Sarah E (Galagher) E.; m. Irene Dailey, Sept. 8, 1924; children: Mary, Alice Eveleth Osterman. BS, U. Calif., Berkeley, 1916. Salesman S.W. Strauss & Co., San Francisco, 1916; clk. Comml. Union Assurance Co., Ltd., San Francisco, 1922-25; dept. mgr. Calif. Ins. Co., San Francisco, 1925-30, Pacific Nat. Fire Ins. Co., San Francisco, 1931-41; v.p., gen. mgr. Premier Ins. Co., San Francisco, 1941-50, pres., 1950-56, chmn. bd., 1956-65. With U.S. Army, 1917-19. Mem. Am. Legion, KC. Republican. Roman Catholic. Home: Oakland Calif. †

EVERETT, GEORGE DUDLEY, banker; b. Ft. Fairfield, Maine, Sept. 6, 1892; s. Elden J. and Annie M. (Clark) E.; m. Gladys Collins, Feb. 20, 1915. Grad., Aroostook (Maine) Cen. Inst., 1912, Shaw Bus. Coll., 1913; LLD (hon.), U. Maine, 1962. With Merrill Trust Co., Bangor, Maine, from 1914, v.p., treas., 1942-44, pres., 1944-59, chmn. bd., from 1959; bd. dirs. Hannaford Bros. Co. Home: Bangor Maine. †

EVINRUDE, RALPH, outboard motors manufacturing executive; b. Milw., Sept. 27, 1907; s. Ole and Bessie (Cary) E.; m. Marion Armitage, Jan. 3, 1931 (dec.); m. Frances Langford, Oct. 6, 1955. Student, U. Wis. Testing mgr. Elto Outboard Motor Co., 1927-30; export sales mgr. Outboard Motor Corp., 1930-32, prodn. mgr., 1932-34, pres., 1934-36; chmn. bd., chmn. exec. com. Outboard Marine Corp. (formerly Outboard Marine & Mfg. Co.), 1936-86. Mem. Phi Gamma Delta, Univ. Club, Yacht Club, Milw. Athletic Club, Eldorado Country Club, Crown Colony Club. Home: Jensen Beach Fla. Died May 21, 1986, buried Fernhill Cemetery, Stuart, Fla.

EWEN, DAVID, musician, educator, author; b. Lemberg, Austria, Nov. 26, 1907; s. Isaac and Helen (Kramer) E.; m. Hannah Weinstein, Sept. 10, 1936; 1 son, Robert. Student, CCNY; mus. edn. with pvt. tutors; also spl. courses, Columbia U.; MusD (hon.), U. Miami, Fla., 1975. Dir. Allen, Towne & Heath, Inc., 1946-49; adj. prof. music U. Miami, 1965-72; music editor Cue, 1937-38; serious music critic Stage, 1938-39; editor Mus. Facts, 1940-41; mem. bd. Greater Miami Philharm. Orch., Fla. Philharm., Community Concerts Miami; hon. mem. Miami Beach Music and Arts League. Author many books on music and musicians, 1933-46; author: Haydn: A Good Life, 1946, Songs of America, 1947, American Composers Today, 1949, The Story of Irving Berlin, 1950, The Story of Arturo Toscanini, 1951, The Story of Jerome Kern, 1953, European Composers Today, 1953; (with Milton Cross) including The Milton Cross Encyclopedia of Great Composers, rev. edit. 1969, The Home Book of Musical Knowledge, 1954, Encyclopedia of the Opera, completely rewritten, 1969, A Journey to Greatness: The Life and Music of George Gershwin, completely rewritten, 1970, Panorama of American Popular Music, 1957, Richard Rodgers, 1957, The Complete Book of the American Musical Theater, 1961, David Ewen Introduces Modern Music, 1962, The Book of European Light Opera, 1962, With A Song in His Heart (a young people's biography of Richard Rodgers), 1963, The Life and Death of Tin Pan Alley, 1964, The Complete Book of Classical Music, 1965, The Cole Porter Story, 1965, Great Composers: 1300-1900, 1966, American Popular Songs: From The Revolutionary War to the Present, 1966, Famous Modern Conductors, 1967, The World of Twentieth Century Music, 1968, Composers for the American Musical Theatre, 1968, Composers Since 1900, 1969, 1st supplement, 1981, Great Men of American Popular Song, 1970, New Complete Book of the American Musical Theater, 1970, Composers of Tomorrow's Music, 1971, Opera, 1972, Orchestral Music, 1973, Solo Instrumental and Chamber Music, 1974, Vocal Music, 1975, All the Years of American Popular Music, 1977, Musicians Since 1900: Performers in Opera and Concert, 1978, American Composers: A Biographical Dictionary, 1982, American Songwriters, 1987; contbr. articles to periodicals, encycs. With AUS, 1944-45. Home: Miami Fla. Died Dec. 28, 1985.

EWEN, FREDERIC, language educator, author; b. Lemberg, Austria, Oct. 11, 1899; came to U.S., 1912; naturalized, 1912; s. Isaac and Helen (Kramer) E.; m. Miriam Gideon, Dec. 16, 1949; 1 son, Joel. BA, CCNY, 1921; MA, Columbia U., 1925, PhD, 1932. Instr. CCNY, 1923-30; asst. prof. Bklyn. Coll., 1930-52; lectr. Grad. Sch. Yeshiva U., Master Inst. N.Y.C., Bklyn. Acad., The Juilliard Sch., N.Y.C. Author: The Prestige of Schiller in England, 1932, Bibliography of 18 Century English Literature, 1935, The Poetry and Prose of Heinrich Heine, 1948, The Poetry of Heinrich Heine, 1969, Bertolt Brecht: His Life, His Art, and His Times, 1967, Heroic Imagination: The Creative Genius of Europe from Waterloo (1815) to the Revolution of 1848, 1984, The Collected Short Stories of Maxim Gorky, 1988; co-author: Musical Vienna, 1939; dramatic adaptations of James Joyce's A Portrait of the Artist, 1962-63, Thomas Mann's The Magic Mountain; dramatic adaptation of The Unknown Chekhov, CBS, Camera 3, 1968. Mem. Modern Lang. Assn., Am. Assn. U. Profs. Home: Manhattan N.Y. Died Oct. 18, 1988; buried Mt. Hebron Cemetery, Queens, N.Y.

EWING, FRANK, business executive; b. Louisville, Feb. 3, 1930; s. Frank D. and Inez A. (Gordon) E.; children: Stephen F., Jane E. BA, Pace Coll., 1957. Asst. controller Gimbel Bros. Corp., 1953-59; treas., controller H. Scheft Co., Boston, 1959-67; treas., dir. Freeman Shoe Co., Beloit, Wis., 1967-69; treas. Crown Auto Stores, Inc., Mpls., 1969-71; v.p. fin., treas. Hughes Supply, Inc., Orlando, Fla., from 1971. With USN, 1947-51. Roman Catholic. Home: Altamonte Springs Fla. Deceased.

EWING, LENA ULLRICH (MRS. SPENCER EWING), rural women's welfare volunteer; b. Decatur, Ill., Dec. 3, 1873; d. John and Elizabeth Wilhelmina (Litterer) Ullrich; m. Spencer Ewing, Dec. 27, 1901. BL, Smith Coll., 1896. Tchr. high sch. Decatur, 1896-97; pres. Day Nursery Assn., Bloomington, Ill., 1916-17; mem. Ill. speakers bur. Women's Council Def., 1917-19. Chmn. McLean County Food Conservation Dept., mem. Nat. and Ill. food conservation coms.; organizer, 1st pres. Ill. Home Bur. Fedn., 1925-27, state chmn. recreation com., 1927-41; del. Internat. Coun. Women, Vienna, 1930; chmn. Country Women's Coun. (U.S. br. Assoc. Country Women of World), 1944-50; mem. exec. com. McLean County chpt. ARC, 1917-32; v.p. Sambel-Captiva Audubon Soc., from 1959. Mem. Federated Women's Insts. Can. (hon.), Assoc. Country Women World (del. Triennial Conf. Washington 1936, London 1939, Amsterdam 1947), Smith Coll. Alumnae Assn., AAUW, Am. Assn. UN, Smith Coll. Club (Lakewood, Ohio). Home: Aspen Colo. †

EWING, SAMUEL EVANS, manufacturing company executive, lawyer; b. Bryn Mawr, Pa., July 27, 1906; s. Samuel E. and Fanny Badger (Neff) E.; m. Mrs. Harriet Corning Sinkler, Mar. 22, 1947 (dec. Feb. 1966); children: Samuel Evans, Steven; stepchildren: Wharton III, Edwin, Peter; m. Mary Alice Markell, July 23, 1966. Student, Haverford Sch., 1914-23; AB, Princeton U., 1927; LLB, U. Pa., 1930. Bar: Pa. 1931, D.C. 1970. Assoc. Saul, Ewing, Remick & Saul, Esquires, Phila., 1930-41, ptnr., 1946-47; of counsel engring. products dept. RCA Victor div. RCA, 1947-48, gen. atty. div., 1948-53, with mfg. and service divs., 1954-60, staff v.p., gen. atty. mfg. and service divs., 1960-67; v.p. RCA, Washington, 1967-73. Commr. for testimony Met. Washington Area Transit Authority, 1973-74; bd. commrs. Lower Merion Twp., Pa., 1939-42, 48-60, v.p., 1952-56, pres., 1956-60; trustee Temple U., 1963-79, hon. trustee, 1979-81; past trustee, mem. exec. com. Fed. City Council. Pvt. to maj. AUS, 1941-45. Mem. ABA, Pa. Bar Assn., Phila. Bar Assn., Electronic Industries Assn. (law com. 1949-67), Bus.-Govt. Relations Council (emeritus), Assn. Gen. Council. Home: Delray Beach Fla. Died Apr. 6, 1981.

EXTON, WILLIAM (PHILIP), JR., management consultant, business executive; b. N.Y.C., Mar. 15, 1907; s. William Gustav and Florence Nightingale Augusta (Phillips) E.; 1 son, William Exton III. BA, Harvard U., 1926; MA in Ednl. Psychology, Columbia U., 1953. Prin. William Exton, Jr. and Assocs., N.Y.C., from 1948; dir. Negotiation Inst., N.Y.C.; v.p., dir. Cole Gold Mines Ltd., 1935-41; cons. in field; fin. and indsl. clients include Citibank, Chem. Bank, Mellon Bank , Continental Ins., Merrill Lynch, IBM, Gen. Electric, Conoco, Mobil, British Ford, others; owner, operator dairy farm, Millbrook, N.Y. Author: Dynamics of Management, 1960, Clerical Errors: Their Cost and Cure, 1970, The Art of Motivating, 1972, Motivational Leverage: A New Approach to Managing People, 1975, Situation Management, 1986; author/editor: Audiovisual Aids to Instruction, 1947; Employee Benefits: Asset or Liability?, The Age of Systems, 1972; Selling Leverage, 1984; contbr. articles to profl. jours.; patentee employee attention chart, 1958. Chmn. city planning com. U.S. Jaycees, 1937-39; trustee, treas. Mcpl. Art Soc., 1927-41; trustee Am. Scenic and Hist. Soc., 1928-41; trustee, treas. Roadside Council, 1946-49, others. Served to capt. USNR, 1941-47. Fellow Internat. Acad. Mgmt., Soc. Profl. Mgmt. Cons. (past pres.); mem. Inst. Mgmt. Cons., Colloquium of Cons. Strategy Mgmt., N.Am. Mgmt. Council (bd. dirs.), Inst. Gen. Semantics (chmn.), Council of Mgmt. Cons. Orgns. Democrat. Clubs: Harvard, Overseas Press, Explorers. Died Dec. 26, 1988. Home: Dover Plains N.Y.

EYMAN, RALPH LEE, university dean; b. Golden, Ill., Aug. 5, 1885; s. Daniel F. and Sarah Emily (Shank) E.; m. Esther Allen Kern, Aug. 20, 1914; children: David Russell, Ruth Louise (Mrs. William Clyatt), Mary Jeanne (Mrs. L.A. Smith), Robert Lee. Student, Western Ill. State Tchrs. Coll., 1908-10; BS in Agr., U. Ill., 1914; EdD, U. Calif., 1928. Tchr. one room sch. 1904-07; prin. John Swaney Consol. Sch., McNabb, Ill., 1910-12; prof. chemistry, physics Kent (Ohio) State Tchrs. Coll., 1914-18; prof. agr. Ill. State Normal U., 1918-20; county agrl. agt. Jerseyville, Ill., 1920-26; prof. edn. Fla. State U., 1928-37, dean Sch. Edn., 1937-86; cons. Point IV Program, Thailand, 1951-53. Mem. Alpha Zeta, Kappa Delta Pi, Phi Delta Kappa, Phi Delta Phi, Zeta Psi, Masons. Democrat. Presbyterian. Home: Tallahassee Fla. Died Apr. 27, 1986.

EYTAN, RACHEL, novelist, educator; b. Israel, May 4, 1932; came to U.S., 1967, naturalized, 1979; d. Yaacov Litai and Sara (Zweig); m. Jerry H. Fishman, Oct. 1967; children: Omri, Hamutal, Yonatan. BA, Hakibutzim Tchrs. Coll., Israel, 1950, NYU, 1973; MA, NYU, 1975, doctoral student, 1976-79. Tchr. Israeli Kibbutz, Tel Aviv, 1950-53; prof. Israeli lit. Gratz Coll., Phila., 1967-68; prof. Israeli, Hebrew and Yiddish lit. Hofstra U., 1968-87; lectr. Am., European and Israeli univs., TV and radio. Novelist: The Fifth Heaven, 1963, English trans., 1985, Shida Veshidot, 1973; contbr. short stories and articles to Am. lit. mags.; editor, contbr. to Israel and Am. Lit. mags. and newspapers. Active Israeli-Arab Peace Movement; active NOW, Coalition of Am.-Israel Civil Liberties, Women Ink W Writers, Union of Concerned Scientists. Recipient Brenner prize for Lit. Israel, 1966; recipient Founders Day award NYU, 1973. Mem. MLA, AAUP, Israeli PEN Club, Am. PEN Club, Israeli Writers Assn. Home: New York N.Y. Died June 17, 1987; buried Tel Aviv, Israel.

FABREGAT, ENRIQUE RODRIQUEZ, diplomat; b. San José, Uruguay, 1898. Degree in humanities, U. Montevideo. Prof. history U. Montevideo; elected mem. Ho. of Deputies, later v.p.; minister of edn. 1929-32, as a result of polit. differences with Govt., resigned official positions and left country, 1933; prof. U. Rio de Janeiro, Brazil; apptd. minister plenipotentiary, permanent rep. of Uruguay U.N., 1947; vis. prof. Coll. of Liberal Arts and Scis. of U. Ill., Mills Coll., Oakland City, Calif.; rsch. in U.S. nat. archives for material for books. Author: The Life of Abraham Lincoln, The Life of Artigas, others. †

FABRIKANT, BENJAMIN, psychologist, educator; b. N.Y.C., Jan. 4, 1924; s. Samuel and Marcia (Fabryk) F.; m. Laurine Merriam Zucker, Aug. 28, 1949; children: Craig S., Gary K., Gail L. Student, Va. Mil. Inst., 1944-45, Shriveham Am. U., 1945; BA, Bklyn. Coll., 1948; MA, Temple U., 1950; PhD, U. Buffalo, 1953; postgrad., Am. U., 1958, L.I. U., 1962. Diplomate Am. Bd. Profl. Psychology, Am. Bd. Profl. Hypnosis, Am. Bd. Family Practice. Psychologist Topeka State Hosp., 1952-53; psychologist, then asst. chief, then chief psychol. research VA Hosp., Buffalo, 1953-59; chief psychologist Psychol. Service Ctr., Teaneck, N.J., 1959-62; mem. faculty Fairleigh Dickinson U., Teaneck, from 1962, prof., dir. clin. programs, from 1971; lectr. Grad. Sch. Orthodontics, from 1964; cons. in field. Author: (with J. Barron and J. Krasner) Psychotherapy, 1971, (with M. Protell and J. Krasner) Psychodynamics of Dental Practice, (with J. Barrow and J. Krasner) To Live is to Enjoy: A Primer of Psychotherapy; assoc. editor Psychotherapy Bull., 1976-80, editor from 1980; cons. editor N.J. Psychologist, Jour. Psychotherapy; editor The Relationship, 1978-81; contbr. articles to profl. jours. Bd. trustees North Bergen County YMHA, 1969-70; pres. Frabrikant Family Found. Served with AUS, 1942-45. Fellow Soc. Personality Projective Assessment, Am. Psychol. Assn. (adminstrv. coordinator div. psychotherapy from 1980, chmn. subcom. on profl. edn. and tng. bd. profl. affairs 1980-81); mem. Bergen County Psychol. Assn. (past pres.), N.J. Psychol. Assn., N.J. Group Psychotherapy Assn. (past pres.), Am. Acad. Psychotherapists, Soc. Clin. Exptl. Hypnosis, Sigma Xi. Home: Westwood N.J. Died May 11, 1985.

FACTOR, TED H., advertising agency executive; b. St. Louis, June 15, 1914; s. Nathan and Rose (Heiman) F.; m. Margot Kadel, Oct. 19, 1946; m. Barbara Currey Wood, July 11, 1965. Student, U. Calif., 1931-33, U. So. Calif., 1933-34. Internat. publicity dir. Max Factor & Co., 1934-36; pres. Ted. H. Factor Agy., named changed to Factor-Breyer, Inc., 1951, merged with Doyle Dane Bernbach, Inc., 1954, 1936-54; sr. v.p. charge West Coast ops. Doyle Dane Bernbach, Inc., 1954, exec. v.p. West Coast ops., 1969-79; vice chmn. Doyle Dane Bernbach Internat., also dir., mem. exec. com., 1974-79; founder DDB/West; ret. 1985; bd. dirs. Milici/Valenti Advt. Agy., Honolulu, Doyle Dane Bernbach Hong Kong Ltd. Mem. exec. bd. Art Center Coll. Design; adv. com. on Communications Los Angeles County Mus. Art; founding mem. Center Study Democratic Instns. Named Man of Yr. Western States Advt. Agys., 1970. Mem. Am. Assn. Advt. Agys., Tau Delta Phi. Clubs: Beverly Hills Tennis (past v.p.); Palm Springs Racquet, World Trade. Home: Beverly Hills Calif. Died Feb. 28, 1987.

FAIRWEATHER, OWEN, lawyer; b. Chgo., Aug. 18, 1913; s. George O. and Nellie (Dieter) F.; m. Sally Hallberg, May 4, 1940; children—Ellen Vail, Peter Gustav. A.B., Dartmouth, 1935; J.D., U. Chgo., 1938. Bar: Ill. 1938. Pvt. practice Chgo.; ptnr. Seyfarth, Shaw, Fairweather & Geraldson, 1945-87. Author: also internat. comparative labor law texts. Practice and Procedure in Labor Arbitration; Contbr. to legal jours. Mem. ABA (council sect. labor and employment law), Ill. Bar Assn., Chgo. Bar Assn. Home: Barrington Ill. Died Feb. 26, 1987; buried Graceland Cemetery, Chgo.

FALKENBERG, PAUL VICTOR, documentary filmmaker; b. Berlin, Germany, Oct. 26, 1903; came to U.S., 1938, naturalized, 1944; s. Hermann and Bertha F. (Ginsberg) F.; m. Alice H. Hirsekorn, Mar. 26, 1931 (dec. 1964); m. Lotte Hanemann, 1965. Asst. dir. with G.W. Pabst Germany, 1928-30; film editor with Fritz Lang, Carl T. Dreyer, A. Granovsky, G. Pascal, Otto Preminger and Fedor Ozep Berlin, Paris, London, Vienna, Rome, 1930-38; tech. and dialogue dir. 20th Century Fox Film Co., Hollywood, Calif., 1940-41; writer-editor for coordinator inter-Am. affairs Mus. Modern Art Film Library, 1941-45; producer-dir. UN, Viking Fund, United Jewish Appeal, others, from 1945; assoc. producer Guy Lombardo series, 1956; editor, adviser community edn. P.R. Govt., 1955-56; lectr. Columbia U., Einstein Coll., New Sch. Social Research, Phila. Mus. Coll. Art, Film Inst. of CCNY, Inst. for Advanced Study in Aesthetic Edn., Ill. State U.; vis. prof. Columbia Coll., Chgo. Producer-dir.: A Time for Bach, 1949; (with Lewis Jacobs) Lincoln Speaks at Gettysburg (Freedom Found. award 1950), 1950; (with Hans Namuth) Jackson Pollock, 1951; producer, author: Duerer and Renaissance, 1961; Caravaggio and Baroque, 1961; editor: (TV series) Valiant Years, 1960-61; F.D.R., 1962, Leukemia Soc. film, Gold Medal winner N.Y. Internat. Film and TV Festival, 1965; 2 films on humanities, McGraw-Hill, 1968-70; co-founder, producer, dir. Mus. at Large Ltd. films on Brancusi, Matisse exhibits, 1969, 70, Jackson Pollock, deKooning, Louis Kahn, John Little-Image from the Sea, 1956, Josef Albers-Homage to the Square, 1969, Calder's Universe at the Whitney, 1977, Alfred Stieglitz, Photographer (Red Ribbon Am. Film Festival 1983), Balthus at the Pompidou, 1984, 2 ind. films for NDR Hamburg, Peacock Island, 1977, Essay on Schinkel, 1981; contbr. articles to profl. jours. Mem. Dirs. Guild Am., Cinematologists (charter 1st v.p.). Died Jan. 13, 1986.

FANCHER, JAMES KENNETH, physician; b. Union Springs, N.Y., July 24, 1892; s. Henry Rufus and Minnie (Knollin) F.; m. Margaret Ennis, June 29, 1920 (dec.); children: James Kenneth, Margaret; m. Margaret Van Devanter, June 1946. AB, Coll. Mont., 1914; MD, Emory U., 1922. Diplomate Am. Bd. Internal Medicine. Tchr. high sch. Indiana Harbor, Ind., 1915-16; tchr., athletics coach Batavia, Ill., 1916-17; instr. physics Boys High Sch., Atlanta, Ga., 1917; instr. chemistry Tech. High Sch., Atlanta, 1919-20; began practice Atlanta, 1922; emeritus med. dir. Good Samaritan Clinic; mem. staff Spaulding Meml. Pavilion; endocrinologist Fulton County Juvenile Ct.; past lectr. endocrinology Emory U. Sch. Dentistry. Contbr. articles on endocrinology to med. jours. Served with Med. enlisted Rec. Corps, 1918-19. Fellow ACP; mem. AMA, So. Med. Assn., Am. Therapeutic Soc. (v.p. 1944), Med. Assn. Ga., Fulton County Med. Soc., Caduceous, Alumni Coun. Emory U., Chanter Club (pres. 1945-46), Masons, Shriners, Alpha Kappa Kappa. Home: Atlanta Ga. †

FANSHIER, CHESTER, manufacturing executive; b. Wilson County, Kans., Mar. 2, 1897; s. Thomas J. and Nora Bell (Maxwell) F.; m. Ina Muriel Goens, Apr. 12, 1918; 1 child, Norma Elaine (Mrs. Robert B. Rice). Registered profl. engr., Okla. Gen. mgr. Bart Products Co., 1932-39; pres., gen. mgr. Metal Goods Mfg. Co., Bartlesville, Okla., 1939-88. Patentee in field. Commr. from Tulsa Presbytery to 156th Gen. Assembly, Presbyn. Ch. U.S.A., 1944; pres. Sunday Eve. Fedn. chs., 1937-38. Recipient Wisdom award Honor, 1970, Gutenberg Bible award; named to Ring Order of Engrs. Mem. NSPE, Okla. Soc. Profl. Engrs. (charter Bartlesville chpt.), ASTM, ASME (life), Profl. Photographers Am., Nat. Rifle Assn. (life), Okla. Rifle Assn., Am. Def. Preparedness Assn. (life), Bartlesville C. of C., SAR. Presbyterian. Club: Engr. (bd. dirs. 1948-49, 54-55). Lodge: Rotary (pres. 1956-57, Paul Harris fellow). Home: Bartlesville, Okla. Died Oct. 16, 1988.

FARLEY, ARTHUR J(AMES), horticulturist; b. Waltham, Mass., Sept. 2, 1885; s. Frederick W. and M. Wheatie (MacDonald) F.; m. Edith McLaury, June 3, 1914; children: Margaret (Mrs. Stanley Page), Charles M.; m. 2d Mildred B. Murphy, Apr. 5, 1947. Grad., Mass. Agrl. Coll., 1908. With N.J. Coll. of Agriculture and Expt. Sta., 1908-55; later prof. pomology emeritus Rutgers U.; sec.-treas. N.J. Peach Coun., from 1928; sec. N.J. Apple Inst., until 1957; judge annual fruit exhibits. Recipient citation by N.J. Fruit Cool. Assn. Inc., 1953, Rutgers U. award, 1954. Mem. N.J. Hort. Soc. (life, sec.-treas. from 1927, awarded citation 1948), Union Club. Presbyterian. Home: New Brunswick N.J. †

FARMER, RICHARD NEIL, business educator; b. Alameda, Calif., Aug. 19, 1928; s. George Albert and Alice (Mellin) F.; m. Barbara Jean Flaherty, Sept. 18, 1951; children-Christine, Geoffrey, Sarah, Daniel. B.A., U. Calif. at Berkeley, 1950, M.A., 1951, Ph.D., 1957. Asst. prof. Am. U. Beirut, 1957-59; gen. mgr. Gen. Contracting Co., Al Khobar, Saudi Arabia, 1959-61; lectr. U. Calif., Davis, 1961-62; asst. prof. U. Calif., Los Angeles, 1962-64; prof. bus. Ind. U., Bloomington, 1964-87; also adviser Black Entrepreneurial Program. Author: (with B. Richman) Comparative Management and Economic Progress, 1964, International Business, 1965, Management in the Future, 1967, International Management, 1968, New Directions in Management Information Transfer, 1968, Benevolent Aggression, 1972, (with W.D. Hogue) Corporate Social Responsibility, 1973, The Real World of 1984, 1974, (with B. Richman) Leadership, Goals and Power in Higher Education, 1975, Management and Organizations, 1975, Why Nothing Seems to Work Any More, 1977; Islandia Revisited, 1984, Business: A Novel Approach, 1984, Advances in International Comparative Management, 1984. Served with AUS, 1951-53. Fellow Acad. Mgmt., Acad. Internat. Bus. (pres. 1977-78); mem. Soc. Internat. Devel. Home: Bloomington Ind. Died Feb. 28, 1987; cremated.

FARNSWORTH, DANA LYDA, physician; b. Troy, W.Va., Apr. 7, 1905; s. Henry Lyda and Isabell (Waggoner) F.; m. Elma Morris, Mar. 18, 1931. AB, BS, W.Va. U.; MD, Harvard U., 1933; DSc, Salem Coll., W.Va., 1959, Williams Coll., 1961, W.Va. U., 1965, Fairfield U., 1969, Rockford Coll., 1972; LHD, Lesley Coll., 1962, Roosevelt U., 1970; LLD, U. Notre Dame, 1964, Harvard U., 1971, Allegheny Coll., 1973. Diplomate Am. Bd. Psychiatry and Neurology. Instr. chemistry and physics Barrackville (W.Va.) High Sch., 1927-29; intern Mass. Gen. Hosp., Boston, 1933-35; asst. resident Boston City Hosp., 1935; asst. dir. health Williams Coll., 1935-41, dir. health, 1945-46; prof., med. dir. MIT, 1946-54, acting dean students, 1950-51; lectr. medicine Harvard U. Med. Sch., 1952-54, Henry K. Oliver prof. hygiene, dir. Univ. Health Services, 1954-71; mem. faculty pub. health, 1954-71, Henry K. Oliver prof. hygiene emeritus, 1971-86; Salmon lectr. psychiatry N.Y. Acad. Medicine, 1964; cons. neuropsychiatry U.S. Naval Hosp., Chelsea, Mass., 1947-54; assoc. physician Children's Med. Ctr., 1954-71; asst. physician, then physician Mass. Gen. Hosp., 1946-66, bd. consoltation 1966-76, hon. physician, 1977-86; cons. in medicine Peter Bent Brigham Hosp., 1954-71; vice chmn. Nat. Commn. on Marijuana and Drug Abuse, 1971-73; chmn. bd. Medicine in the Pub. Interest, 1973-86. Author: Mental Health in College and University, 1957, (with Fred Hein) Living, 1959, 6th rev. edit., 1975, (with Jack R. Ewalt) Textbook of Psychiatry, 1963, Psychiatry, Education and the Young Adult, 1966, (with others) Dimensions in Health, 1965; editor, contbr. College Health Adminstrn., 1964, (with Francis J. Braceland) Psychiatry, The Clergy and Pastoral Counseling, 1969, (with Graham B. Blaine Jr.) Counseling and the College Student, 1970; assoc. editor Am. Jour. Psychiatry, 1965-73; editorial dir. Psychiat. Annals, 1971-86; mem. editorial bd. New Eng. Jour. Medicine, 1970-73. Served with M.C., USN, World War II, PTO. Recipient Menninger award ACP, 1970, Pax Christi award St. John's U., 1971, Wm. A. Schonfield Disting. Service award Am. Soc. for Adolescent Psychiatry, 1971; John and Mary R. Markle fellow Austen Riggs Found., 1936-37. Fellow Am. Acad. Arts and Scis., Am. Psychiat. Assn. (mem. coun. 1958-61, chmn. com. on ethics 1965-67, mem. coun. med. edn. and career devel. 1967-69, disting. service award 1971), Am. Sch. Health Assn. (hon.); mem. AMA (mem. coun. on mental health 1963-72, chmn. 1967-70, mem. coun. health manpower 1968-70), Group for the Advancement of Psychiatry (pres. 1957-59), Am. Coll. Health Assn. (pres. 1953-54, Edward Hitchcock award 1968), No. New Eng. Br. Am. Psychiat. Assn., Mass. Med. Soc., Brit. Student Health Assn. (hon.). Home: Belmont Mass. Died Aug. 2, 1986.

FARNSWORTH, RAYMOND BARTLETT, agronomist, educator; b. Enterprise, Utah, May 21, 1915; s. Bartlett Canfield and Lillie Parthena (Holt) F.; m. Maurine Winsor, Dec. 31, 1943; children: Dennis Ray, Diane, Kevin, Karalie. BS, Brigham Young U., 1937; MS, Mass. State Coll., 1938; PhD, Ohio State U., 1941; postgrad., U. Ariz., Harvard U., U. Calif. at Berkeley. Agronomist Paulding (Ohio) Sugar Co., 1941; asst. agronomist Ohio Agrl. Expt. Sta., 1941-43; mem. faculty Brigham Young U., Provo, Utah, 1946-87, prof. agronomy, 1950-87, chmn. dept., 1950-55, 61-67, chmn. dept. agronomy and horticulture, 1967-87; acting dean Coll. Applied Sci., 1952, Coll. Biol. and Agrl. Scis., 1955-59; agrl. dir. Indian assistance program in agr. and home mgmt. 1970-87; soil scientist Oreg. State Coll. 1958-59; soil sci. adviser coll. agr. U. Teheran, Iran 1959-61; assoc. dir. advanced sci. edn. program, dir. grad. fellowship program NSF, 1965-66. Contbr. articles to profl. jours.; discoverer nitrogen fixation in six new plant families of nonlegumes. Bishop, Provo 8th ward Ch. of Jesus Christ of Latter-Day Saints, 1956-58. Served with USNR, 1943-46. Recipient Achievement award Coll. Biol. and Agrl. Scis., 1975, Karl G. Maeser Disting. Teaching award Brigham Young U. Fellow Am. Soc. Agronomy, Soil Sci. Soc. Am.; mem. Western Soc. Soil Sci. (chmn. soil fetility sect. 1957), Utah Acad. Sci., Arts and Letters (chmn. biol. sect. 1949), Sigma Xi. Home: Provo Utah. Died Oct. 31, 1987; buried Provo (Utah) City Cemetery.

FARRALL, ARTHUR W., author, educator, engineer, inventor; b. Harvard, Nebr., Feb. 23, 1899; s. John W. and Olive A. (Frazell) F.; m. E. Luella Buck, June 20, 1923; children: Margaret Longnecker, Robert Arthur. B.S., U. Nebr., 1921, M.S., 1922, D.Eng. (hon.), 1955; postgrad., U. Calif., 1926. Tchr. U. Calif., 1922-29; research dir. Douthitt Engring. Co., Chgo., 1929-33; research engr., dir. research Creamery Package Mfg. Co., 1933-45; prof. agrl. engring., chmn. dept. Mich. State U., 1945-64, prof., 1965-68, prof., chmn. emeritus, 1968-86, chmn. food tech., 1959-60; U.S. del. Internat. Dairy Congress, Stockholm, 1949; cons. U.S. Dept. Agr., 1964-65, Ford Found., Punjab Agr. U., India, 1968-69; cons. to industry in dairy and agrl. engring.; cons. food engring., Brazil, 1970; mem. research adv. com. Food Industry Research Center, Nat. Restaurant Assn., 1958-61; gen. chmn. Centennial Farm Mechanization, 1955. Author: Dairy Engineering, 1942, Engineering for Dairy and Food Products, 1963, History of the Farrall and Frazell Families, 1970; also bulls., tech. papers; co-author: Ency. Food Engineering, 1971; editor: dairy engring. sect. Am. Jour. Dairy Sci., 1945-52; asso. editor, co-author: Dairy Handbook and Dictionary, 1958; editor-in-chief, co-author: Agriculture Engineering-A Dictionary and Handbook, 1965; contbr.: Refrigeration Handbook, 1937; author: Food Engineering Systems 1, Operations, 1975; contbr.: Food Engineering Systems 2, Utilities, 1979; editor: Hall of Fame, Food Engineering, 1978, Dictionary of Agricultural and Food Engineering, 2d edit., 1979. Sponsor Arthur and Luella Farrall fellowship Mich. State U., 1979-86, A.W. Farrall Engring. Faculty award, 1979-86; pres. East Lansing Sr. Citizens, 1980-81; gen. chmn.

Mich. State U. Retirees Service Corps. Recipient Gold Medal award Dairy and Food Equipment Assn.-Am. Soc. Agrl. Engrs., 1972; A.W. Farrall Agrl. Engring. Hall named in his honor Mich. State U., 1985. Fellow Am. Soc. Agrl. Engring. (pres. 1962-63, chmn. food engring. com. 1965-66, editor Food Engring. newsletter 1966-68, Massey Ferguson Ednl. Gold Medal award 1971, sponsor ann. award to young educator 1972-86); mem. Am. Soc. Engring. Edn. (chmn. agr. engring. div. 1949, 60), AAUP, Am. Dairy Sci. Assn., Inst. Food Tech., AAAS, Mid-Mich. Geneal. Soc. (pres. 1971-73), Am. Legion, Phi Kappa Phi (exec. sec. Mich. State U. chpt. 1968-86), Sigma Xi, Alpha Gamma Rho, Alpha Zeta, Tau Beta Pi, Pi Tau Sigma, Alpha Epsilon. Congregationalist. Club: Mich. State Univ. Home: East Lansing Mich. Died June 18, 1986; buried Evergreen Cemetery, Lansing, Mich.

FARRAR, FREDERICK M., banker; b. Ft. Collins, Colo., Sept. 10, 1912; s. Fred and Mary H. (McMenemy) F.; m. Katherine E. Thatcher, June 20, 1941; children: Katherine Farrar Spahn, Logan, Elizabeth, Janet Farrar Timmerman. Student, Colo. Sch. Mines, 1931-33; BS in Bus., U. Colo., 1936; LLB, U. Denver, 1941. Bar: Colo. 1945. Practice in Denver, 1945-58; ptnr. Farrar and Martin; chmn. bd. First Nat. Bank, Pueblo, Colo., 1963-74, Colo. Comml. Bank, Colorado Springs, 1967-72, Exchange Nat. Bank, 1970-74; founder, chmn. Mountain Banks, Ltd., Colorado Springs, 1971-74; chmn. Citadel Bank, Colorado Springs, 1975-80, Garden of the Gods Bank, from 1977. Mem. bd. edn. Air Acad. Sch. Dist., 1963-69; chmn. Western Mus. Mining and Industry, from 1971; trustee Colo. Coll. With USAAF, 1942-45. Mem. Cheyenne Mountain (Colorado Springs), El Paso (Colorado Springs), Cactus (Denver) clubs. Episcopalian. Home: Black Forest Colo. Died July 17, 1985.

FARRELL, JAMES PATRICK, lawyer, foundation executive; b. Montclair, N.J., Jan. 22, 1903; s. Patrick J. and Martha (Farrell) F.; m. Kathryn Fischer, Oct. 24, 1929; children: James P., Mary Patricia Farrell Russell, Kathryn Anne Farrell Noumair, Hazel Claire Farrell Murray, Jr. LL.B., Fordham U., 1926, LL.D., 1976; LL.D., U. R.I., 1973, Trinity Coll., 1982. Bar: N.Y. 1932. Mem. firm Frueauff, Farrell, Sullivan & Bryan, N.Y.C., 1926-74, ptnr., 1936-80; former dir. Wigton-Abbott Corp., Cities Service Co., Tiffany & Co.; sec./treas. W. Alton Jones Found., Inc., 1944-71, pres., 1971-82; v.p. Charles A. Frueauff Found., Inc. Trustee Trinity Coll., Washington, Madison Sq. Boys Club, N.Y.C. Decorated Assn. Master Knights Sovereign Mil. Order Malta U.S.A., 1958, Knights and Ladies Equestrian Order Holy Sepulchre Jerusalem, 1962. Mem. Assn. of Bar of City of N.Y., N.Y. State Bar Assn., ABA, Gamma Eta Gamma. Home: Montclair N.J. Died July 27, 1988.

FARRELL, JOHN JOSEPH, surgeon, educator; b. Seneca, Wis., Sept. 6, 1917; s. Thomas Emmett and Caroline Mae (Nugent) F.; children: Mary Eileen, John Joseph, Patricia Ann. AB, Loras Coll., 1938; MD, Harvard U., 1942. Diplomate Am. Bd. Surgery. Intern St. Joseph's Hosp., Lexington, Ky., 1942-43; resident surgery Albany (N.Y.) Hosp. and Albany Med. Coll., 1946-50; instr. then asst. prof. surgery Albany Med. Coll.; prof. surgery, chmn. dept. Miami (Fla.) Sch. Medicine, 1954-61, clin. prof. surgery, 1962-65; surgeon-in-chief Jackson Meml. Hosp., Miami, 1954-61; dir. surgery Coral Gables (Fla.) VA Hosp., 1956-61, Kendall Hosp., Miami, 1958-63; bd. dirs. John Elliott Blood Bank, Dade County, 1956-65, Dade County chpt. Am. Cance Soc., 1958-65, Palm Beach County chpt. Am. Cancer Soc., 1966-83. Capt. M.C., AUS, 1943-46, ETO. Fellow exptl. surgery Dazian Found., ACS (bd. govs. 1960-63); mem. Pan. Am. Med. Assn., AMA, Southeastern Surg. Congress, Soc. Surgery Alimentary Tract, AAAS, N.Y. Acad. Scis., Fla. Assn. Gen. Surgeons (pres. 1972-74), Alpha Omega Alpha. Home: Palm Beach Gardens Fla. Died Apr. 4, 1983; interred Queen of Peace Cemetery, West Palm Beach, Fla.

FARRIS, JOHN LAUCHLAN, judge; b. Vancouver, B.C., Can., Sept. 5, 1911; s. John Wallace de Beque and Evlyn Fenwick (Keirstead) F.; m. Dorothy Beatrice Colledge, Sept. 13, 1933; children, Ann, John Haig de Beque, Katherine Colledge. B.A., U. B.C., 1931; LL.B., Harvard U., 1934. Bar: B.C. 1935. Past ptnr. Farris, Vaughan, Wills & Murphy, Vancouver; chief justice B.C., 1973-78; lectr. comml. law U. B.C., 1945-50; past dir. Kelly, Douglas Co. Ltd., Sun Pub. Co. Ltd., Loomis Armored Car Service Ltd., Pacific Petroleums Ltd., Toronto-Dominion Bank, B.C. Telephone Co. Chmn., bd. govs. Crofton House Sch., 1959-63. Fellow Am. Coll. Trial Lawyers; mem. Can. (council 1955-58, vice chmn. 1960-61, v.p. for B.C. 1962-64, pres. 1971-72, exec. com. 1966-86), Vancouver (exec. council 1954-62, pres. 1959-60), Am. (hon.) bar assns., Law Soc. B.C., Vancouver Club, Royal Vancouver Yacht Club, West Vancouver Yacht Club, Union Club. Mem. Liberal Party. Home: Vancouver B.C., Can. Died Oct. 14, 1986.

FARWELL, LYNDON JAMES, clergyman, administrator; b. Los Gatos, Calif., Oct. 29, 1940; s. Lyndon James and Louise Catherine (Bacigalupi) F. B.A., Gonzaga U., 1964; M.A. in History, UCLA, 1968; S.T.M. in Theology, Jesuit Sch. of Theology, Berkeley, 1972; Ph.D. in Religion, Claremont Grad. Sch., 1976. Joined Soc. of Jesus, 1958; ordained priest 1971; instr. Loyola High Sch., Los Angeles, 1965-68; parish asst. Our Lady of Assumption Ch., Claremont, Calif., 1971-73; asst. prof. theology U. San Francisco, 1976-78; exec. asst. to provincial Calif. Province of Soc. of Jesus, Los Gatos, 1978-81; pres. Jesuit Sch. of Theology, Berkeley, Calif., 1981-86; asst. to provincial Calif. Province, S.J., Los Gatos, 1986-88. Mem. editorial bd. Company, 1981-88. Trustee U. Santa Clara, 1977-84; bd. dirs. Cath. Charities, Diocese of San Francisco, 1979-81; trustee U. San Francisco, 1981-88 , Grad. Theol. Union, 1981-86, mem. edn. com. Oakland Diocesan Pastoral Council, Calif., 1985-86. Mem. Am. Acad. Religion, Am. Hist. Assn., Internat. Assn. History of Religions, N.Am. Acad. Liturgy, Soc. Calif. Pioneers. Democrat. Roman Catholic. Home: Los Gatos Calif. Deceased.

FAULHABER, ROBERT WILLIAM, economist, educator; b. Cleve., July 28, 1920; s. Frank F. and Agnes J. (Youkel) F.; m. Martha L. Finke, June, 17, 1950; children: Roberta, Peter, Christina, Elizabeth. Cert., Am. Inst. Banking, 1942; A.B., Cath. U. Am., 1948; M.A., U. Chgo., 1950; Doctorate, U. Paris, 1952. Messenger-teller Cleve. Trust Co., 1939-42; instr. econs. Loyola U., Chgo., 1949-50; mem. faculty DePaul U., Chgo., 1952-86; prof. econs. DePaul U., 1964-86, chmn. dept. econs., 1972-77; vis. tutor Grad. Inst., St. John's Coll., Santa Fe, N.Mex., summers 1973-74. Asso. editor: Rev. Social Economy. Mem. long-range planning com. Cath. Interracial Council Chgo., 1959; treas. Greater Ill. Faculty Com. on Vietnam, 1965-74; Chmn. legis. com. Ind. Voters Ill., 1954; mem. steering com. Com. Nuclear Overkill Moratorium, 1976-86. Served with USAAF, 1942-45, PTO. Mem. Am. Econs. Assn., Assn. for Social Econs. (1st v.p. 1978-79, pres. 1980, exec. council 1981-83), AAUP, Phi Beta Kappa, Pi Gamma Mu. Roman Catholic. Home: Chicago Ill. Died Aug. 17, 1986; buried St. Mary Cemetery and Mausoleums, Evergreen Park, Ill.

FAULKNER, DWIGHT FOSTER, investment banker; b. New Rochelle, N.Y., July 10, 1926; s. Dwight F. and Jeanne (Belvoir) F.; m. Katherine Snow, June 6, 1950 (div. June 1967); children—John C., William F., Sally S., Elizabeth; m. Susan Hunziker, July 26, 1969; 1 child, Alden C. B.A., Yale U., 1949. Analyst Ernst & Co., N.Y.C., 1950-53; salesman Laurence Marks & Co., N.Y.C., 1953-59; chmn., chief exec. officer Faulkner, Dawkins & Sullivan, N.Y.C., 1959-77; vice chmn. Shearson, Lehman Bros., N.Y.C., 1977-86. Bd. dirs. Ryan Homes Inc., Pitts. Treas., Big Sisters. With USAAF, 1944-45. Mem. Assn. Stock Exchange Firms (gov. 1965-72), Manursing Island Club, Apawamis Club, DTA, Mill Reef Club. Home: New York N.Y. Died Aug. 5, 1986.

FAULKNER, ELIZABETH COONLEY, civic worker; b. Chgo., Dec. 3, 1902; d. Avery and Queene (Ferry) Coonley; m. Waldron Faulkner, Nov. 18, 1926; children: Avery Coonley, Winthrop Waldron, Celia Ferry Faulkner Cleveger. AB, Vassar Coll., 1924. Bd. dirs. Madeira Sch. Alumnae Assn., 1943-68; trustee Vassar Coll., 1958-66, Potomac Sch., 1948-51; pres. bd. D.C. YMCA, 1951-53; chmn. women's activities centennial conv. AIA, 1957; mem. vestry St. Margaret's Episcopal Ch., 1953-55; bd. dirs. Episcopal Ctr. Children, 1962-68. Mem. Cosmopolitan Club, Sulgrave Club, City Tavern Club. Home: Washington D.C. Died Aug. 20, 1985.

FEATHER, WILLIAM, author, publisher; b. Jamestown, N.Y., Aug. 25, 1889; s. George E. and Henrietta (Hodgson) F.; m. Ruth Presley, Oct. 30, 1912; children: William Jr., Judith. AB, Adelbert Coll. (Western Reserve U.), 1910. Reporter Cleve. Press, 1910-15; with publicity dept. Nat. Cash Register Co., Dayton, Ohio, 1915-16; organizer William Feather Co., printers and pubs., Cleve., 1916; pres. William Feather Co., printers and pubs. Author: As We Were Saying, 1921, Haystacks and Smokestacks, 1923, Ideals and Follies of Business, 1927, Business of Life, 1949, Talk About Women, 1960; editor and pub. The William Feather Magazine, and group of house mags. for indsl. cos.; also articles under title A Business Man's Philosophy, in newspapers, etc. Home: Cleveland Ohio Died Jan. 7, 1981, cremated.

FEDIN, KONSTANTIN ALEXANDROVICH, novelist; b. 1892. Interned in Germany 1914-18; returned to USSR, 1918; with Commissariat of Edn., later journalist and war corr.; mem. Secretariat Union Soviet Writers, from 1953; chmn. Moscow Union Soviet Writers, 1955-59; chmn. Soviet-German Cultural and Friendship Soc., from 1958; 1st sec. Writers Union USSR, from 1959. Author: Anna Timofecvna, 1922, The Waste Lane, 1923, Cities and Years, 1924, Transvaal, 1926, Brothers, 1928, Rape of Europe, 1934, I Was an Actor, 1937, Sanatorium Arklur, 1940, Gorky Among Us, 1943-44, Return to Leningrad, 1945, Early Joys, 1945, No Ordinary Summer, 1948, Dichter, Kunst, Zeit, 1957, Die Flamme, 1962; (play) Bakunin in Dresden, 1922. Decorated Order of Lenin. Mem. USSR Acad. Scis., Deutsche Aka. der Künste. Home: Moscow USSR. †

FEEZOR, FORREST CHALMERS, clergyman; b. Lexington, N.C., July 1, 1892; s. Jacob David and Nancy (Lee) F.; m. Jessica Rae Fuller, Sept. 15, 1927; children: Ann Joy, Forrestine Fuller. Student, Churchland Acad., 1915, U. Chgo., 1925, Wake Forest Coll., 1920; DD, Wake Forest Coll., 1934; ThM, So. Baptist Theol. Sem., 1923. Ordained to ministry Baptist Ch., 1917. Tchr. William Jewell Coll., 1923-26; pastor 2d Bapt. Ch., Liberty, Mo., 1926-31, Tabernacle Bapt. Ch., Raleigh, N.C., 1931-42, Broadway Bapt. Ch., Ft. Worth, 1942-46, 1st Bapt. Ch., Waco, Tex., 1946; then exec. bd. Bapt. Gen. Conv. Tex.; radio speaker So. Baptist Hour, 1949, Religious Internat. Broadcast radio sta. WRUL, 1950-52. Pres. N.C. Bapt. Conv., 1941; 1st v.p. So. Bapt. Conv., 1951-52; mem. fgn. mission bd., Richmond, Va., 1933-52; pres. Tex. Bapt. Gen. Conv., 1951-53; trustee Meredith Coll., Raleigh, N.C., 1933-42, Baylor U. and Hillcrest Meml. Hosp., Waco, Tex., from 1946, So. Bapt. Theol. Sem., Louisville, 1934. Mem. Masons (32d deg.), Rotary. Home: Dallas Tex. †

FEHSENFELD, JOHN DIEDRICH, association executive; b. Troy, Mo., Feb. 25, 1892; s. J. Frederick and Dorothee S. (Wiemann) F.; m. Daisie H. Haenisch, June 11, 1919. BS in Agr., U. Mo., 1916. Engaged in farming from 1916; with soil survey Dept. Agr., 1917; mgr. Farmers Coop. Supply, Troy, 1932-49; agy. mgr. Farm Bur. Ins. Co., Troy, 1946-52; bd. dirs. St. Louis Live Stock Producers Mktg. Assn., from 1938, pres., from 1956; v.p. Nat. Live Stock and Meat Bd., Nat. Coun. Farmer Coops.; dir. Central Bank for Coops., St. Louis & Troy R.R. Co. Mem. appeal bd. Mo. SSS; mem. adv. com. Coll. Agr., U. Mo. With U.S. Navy, 1917-19. Recipient award of merit Gamma Sigma Delta, 1959, cert. of merit in agr. U. Mo., 1959. Mem. Farm House, Alpha Zeta. Home: Troy Mo. †

FEIN, A. EDWIN, management company executive; b. N.Y.C., Apr. 9, 1898; s. Samuel and Anne (Fein) F. Student, NYU, 1919-25, Columbia U., 1925-26. Mktg.-tech. cons. Walter Kidde & Co., Bloomfield, N.J., 1934-35; dir. sales DCA Food Industries, N.Y.C., 1936-38; chmn. Research Co. Am., N.Y.C., 1939-73; v.p., sec., dir. United Indsl. Corp., N.Y.C., 1959-86; sec., dir. Affiliated Hosp. Products Inc.; bd. dirs. Detroit Stoker Co., Neo Products Co. Author: This Is My Life; also ann. edits. Brewing Industry Survey (Ann. Advt. award), Basic Marketing Chart of U.S.; contbr. articles to profl. jours. With U.S. Army, 1918-19. Fellow Soc. Advancement Mgmt.; mem. Four Freedoms Found, Internat. Platform Assn., Assn. Corporate Growth, Am. Soc. Corporate Secs., N.Y. Zool. Soc. (chmn. industry com.), N.Y. C. of C., Am. Legion (comdr. 1931), City Club, Explorers Club (N.Y.C.). Home: New York N.Y. Deceased.

FELD, IRVIN, circus owner and producer; b. Hagerstown, Md., May 9, 1918; s. Isaac and Jennie (Mansh) F.; grad. high sch.; D.H.L. (hon.), Lehigh U., 1976; m. Adele Schwartz, Mar. 5, 1946 (dec.); children—Karen, Kenneth. Pres., Super Music City, 1940-56; pres., producer Super Attractions, Inc., Washington, 1954-67; producer Carter Barron Amphitheatre Summer Series for Dept. Interior, Washington, 1954-74; personal mgr. Paul Anka, 1957-64; pres., producer, chief exec. officer Ringling Brothers-Barnum & Bailey Combined Shows, Inc., Washington, 1968-82; chmn., producer, chief exec. officer Ice Follies, Holiday On Ice, Inc., 1979-84 ; assoc. producer Broadway musical Barnum, 1980; producer Beyond Belief show, Las Vegas, 1981-84, Walt Disney Prodns. World on Ice, 1981-84 ; owner Ringling Bros. and Barnum & Bailey Circus, Beyond Belief, Ice Follies and Holiday on Ice, Walt Disney Prodns. World on Ice, Walt Disney's Great Ice Odyssey, 1982-84 , Walt Disney's Magic Kingdom, 1983-84 ; producer One of a Kind, Las Vegas, 1984, Broadway musical Three Musketeers, 1984; chmn., producer, chief exec. officer Ringling Bros. and Barnum & Bailey Circus, 1982-84; hon. dir. Barnett Bank of Winter Haven N.A.; mem. Met. Washington Bd. Trade. Pres., Amity Club of Washington, 1951. Founder, Ringling Brothers and Barnum & Bailey Clown Coll., 1968; mem. endowment com. Circus World Mus.; mem. adv. council Wilmer Ophthal. Inst., Johns Hopkins U. Sch. Medicine. Recipient Champion of Liberty award Anti-Defamation League, B'nai B'rith, 1984. Mem. Nat. Press Club, Variety Club, Friars Club, Circus Saints and Sinners. Club: Woodmont Country. Contbr. to The Language of Show Biz, 1973; Variety newspaper. Died Sept. 6, 1984.

FELDMAN, ALVIN LINDBERGH, airline executive; b. N.Y.C., Dec. 14, 1927; s. Harry and Rose (Lefkowitz) F.; m. Rosemily Petrison, Feb. 15, 1952 (dec. July 1980); children—David, John, Susan. B.S. in Mech. Engring, Cornell U., 1949; S.E.P., Stanford U. Grad. Sch. Bus., 1966. With Cornell Aeros. Lab., 1949-52; engr. Convair div. Gen. Dynamics Corp., San Diego, 1952-54; asst. gen. mgr. Liquid Rocket Co.; pres. Aerojet Nuclear Systems Co., Aerojet-Gen. Corp., Sacramento, 1954-71; pres., chief exec. officer Frontier Airlines, Inc., Denver, 1971-80, Continental Airlines, Inc.,

Los Angeles, 1980-81; chmn. bd., dir. Denver br. Fed. Res. Bank of Kansas City, 1977-79; dir. Pub. Service Co. Colo.; pub. mem. Nat. Transp. Policy Study Commn., 1976-81. Asso. fellow AIAA; mem. Assn. Local Transport Airlines (dir.), Air Transport Assn. (dir.), Denver C. of C. (dir. 1975-76), LaJolla Country Club, Hiwan Golf Club, Aero Club of Washington. Home: Denver Colo. Died Aug. 9, 1981.

FELDMEIR, DARYLE MATTHEW, editor; b. Froid, Mont., Jan. 28, 1923; s. Frank X. and Clara B. (Rhoda) F.; m. Jeanne Elizabeth Meyer, Sept. 24, 1949 (dec. Apr. 1973); children: Ann Laurie, Matthew Joel, Todd Martin, Susan Jeanne; m. Joan Hicks de Romeo, Aug. 25, 1979. BA, St. Olaf Coll., 1948; MA, Harvard, 1949; postgrad. in Am. History, U. Minn., 1951-52. Staff writer, columnist Mpls. Tribune, 1949-55, news editor, 1955-56, mng. editor, 1956-68; mng. editor Chgo. Daily News, 1968-70, exec. editor, 1970-71, editor, 1971-77; edit. cons. Field newspapers, Chgo., 1977-78; ret. 1978. Master sgt. USAAF, World War II. led Chgo. Daily News to three Pulitzer Prizes. Mem. Phi Beta Kappa. Lutheran. Home: San Miguel Allende Mexico. Died May 19, 1987.

FELSON, BENJAMIN, radiologist, educator; b. Newport, Ky., Oct. 21, 1913; s. Solomon and Esther (Bussell) F.; m. Virginia Raphaelson, Mar. 18, 1936; children: Stephen, Nancy Felson-Rubin, Marcus, Richard, Edward. BS, U. Cin., 1933, MD, 1935. Diplomate Am. Bd. Radiology. Intern Cin. Gen. Hosp., 1935-36, resident in pathology, 1936-37, resident radiology, 1937-40; fellow in cancer therapy Indpls. City Hosp., 1940-41; pvt. practice radiology Tulsa, 1941-42; asst. prof. radiology U. Cin., 1945-48, assoc. prof., 1948-51, prof. radiology, 1951-83, prof. emeritus, 1983-88; radiologist Cin. Gen. Hosp., 1945-48, assoc. dir. radiology, 1948-51, dir., 1951-73; cons. Wright-Patterson AFB Hosp., Dayton and Cin. VA hosps., USPHS, VA Central Office, U.S. Army M.C., U.S. Navy Med. Dept., Walter Reed Hosp., Armed Forces Inst. Pathology; Felson lectr. Tel Aviv U., 1985. Author: Fundamentals of Chest Roentgenology, 1960, (with A. Weinstein, H.B. Spitz) Principles of Chest Roentgenology, 1965 (Gold Book award), Chest Roentgenology, 1973, (with M.M. Reeder) Gamuts in Radiology, 1974, 2d edit., 1987; editor: Index for Roentgen Diagnoses, 1961, jour. Seminars in Roentgenology, 1966—; mem. editorial bd.: jour. Chest, 1962-72, JAMA, 1974-79, Rev. Interamericana de Radiologia; contbr. numerous articles to sci. jours. Nat. bd. dirs. Friends of Hebrew U., Israel, U. Negev. Served to maj. M.C. U.S. Army, 1942-45. Felson lectureship U. Cin. inaugurated, 1973; recipient Daniel Drake award U. Cin., 1984, Living Legend in Radiology award, 1985; Ben Felson chair in radiology established U. Cin., 1987—. Fellow Am. Coll. Chest Physicians, Am. Coll. Radiology (chmn. commn. on edn. and chancellor 1966-69, Gold medal 1977), Royal Coll. Radiology (hon.) (Gt. Britain), Royal Coll. Radiology Australia (hon.), Royal Coll. Surgeons in Ireland (hon.); mem. Cin. Acad. Medicine, Am. Roentgen Ray Soc. (1st v.p. 1972, Cert. appreciation 1982, Caldwell lectr. 1986), Roentgen Soc. Chgo. (Gold medal), Ohio Med. Assn., Radiol. Soc. N.Am. (1st v.p. 1959, Gold medal 1979), Ohio Radiol. Soc. (spl. award 1981), Greater Cin. Radiol. Soc., Fleischner Chest Radiol. Soc. (pres. 1975), Alpha Omega Alpha, Pi Kappa Epsilon; hon. mem. Cuban, Brazilian, Colombian, Peruvian, Central Am., Costa Rican, Spanish, Japanese, South African, Canadian radiol. socs., Nat. Acad. Medicine Colombia, Venezuelan Thoracic Soc., Med. Soc. Okinawa, Chinese Med. Soc. Home: Cincinnati Ohio. Died Oct. 22, 1988.

FELTS, WAYNE MOORE, geologist, consultant; b. Oakland, Calif., Aug. 5, 1912; s. Isaac Thomas and Josephine Veva (Moore) F.; m. Bettie Lou Snoddy, June 25, 1942; children—Wayne Moore Jr., Thomas Arnon. B.S., Oreg. State Coll., 1934, M.S., 1936; Ph.D., U. Cin., 1938. Geologist Phillips Petroleum Co., Amarillo Tex. and Bartlesville, Okla., 1943-47, The Tex. Co. subs. Texaco Inc., numerous locations, 1947-58; div. geologist Texaco Inc., Los Angeles, 1958-62, asst. to div. mgr., Anchorage, 1962-66, mgr. hard mineral exploration, Denver, 1966-73; ret., 1973; pvt. investigator in field, Nev., Wash., Alaska, 1973-79; prin. W.M. Felts Geol. Services, Boulder City, Nev., 1979-88; vice chmn. Alaska com. Western Oil and Gas Assn., Anchorage, 1962-63; mem. ocean ops. com. Am. Petroleum Inst., Houston and Washington, 1968-71; assoc. prof. Pa. State U., 1949-50. Ohio Acad. sci. grantee, 1937. Fellow Geol. Soc. Am., AAAS; mem. Am. Assn. Petroleum Geologists (research com. 1954-57), Am. Inst. Profl. Geologists (cert. profl. geologist), SAR (pres. Las Vegas club 1975-76), Sigma Xi. Republican. Current work: Consulting petroleum geologist; petrology of cement clinker; concrete and ceramic materials. Subspecialties: Geology; Petrology. Home: Boulder City, Nev. Died Oct. 27, 1988, buried Boulder city.

FENNER, GOODRICH ROBERT, bishop; b. Beeville, Tex., Aug. 2, 1891; s. Robert Willis and Kate Elliott (Fenner) F.; m. Julia Hogan, Dec. 19, 1930. BSCE, Tex. A&M Coll., 1913; STB, Gen. Theol. Sem., N.Y.C., 1916, STM, 1934, STD, 1938. Ordained priest Episcopal Ch., 1916. Rector St. Philip's Ch., Uvalde, Tex., 1916-24, Christ Ch., Dallas, Tex., 1924-32; sec. Rural div. Nat. Coun. Episcopal Ch., 1932-35; rector St. Andrew's Ch., Kansas City, Mo., 1935-37; bishop co-adjutor Diocese of Kans., 1937-39; bishop from 1939. Author: The Episcopal Church in Town and Country, 1935; contbr. articles to religious jours. Served as chaplain U.S. Army, 1918. Home: Topeka Kans. †

FENNER, MILDRED SANDISON (MRS. ERNEST G. REID), editor, circus executive; b. Huntsville, Mo., July 9, 1910; d. John Forte and Minnielee (Holliday) Sandison; m. H. Wolcott Fenner, Feb. 1, 1940 (dec. Oct. 1972); m. Ernest G. Reid, Aug. 30, 1975. BS, N.W. Mo. State Tchrs. Coll., 1931; MA, George Washington U., 1938, EdD, 1942; LittD, Glassboro State Coll., 1962. With NEA Jour. (now Today's Education), 1931-75, successively mem. staff, asst. editor, mng. editor, 1931-54, editor, 1954-75; dir. dept. ednl. svcs. Ringling Bros.-Barnum & Bailey Combined Shows, from 1975. Author: (with Eleanor Fishburn) Pioneer American Educators, 1944, NEA History, 1945, (with H.W. Fenner) The Circus: Lure and Legend, 1970; also articles in field. Mem. Am. Assn. U. Women, Edn. Press Assn. Am. (sec.-treas. 1951-60, rep. internat. ednl. editors' workshop, Manila summer 1956, Amsterdam 1961), Horace Mann League (1st woman mem., pres. 1971-72), Woman's Nat. Dem. Club, Common Cause, Smithsonian Assocs., Pi Lambda Theta, Sigma Sigma Sigma. Methodist. Home: Washington D.C. Died Nov. 8, 1985.

FENSTERBUSCH, JACK ALVIN, insurance company executive; b. Rock Island, Ill., June 28, 1916; s. Alvin B. and Matilda (Klingebiel) F.; m. Jeanette Henchon, Aug. 10, 1940; children: Alan Kent, Susan Kay Fensterbusch Thomas. Student higher accountancy, LaSalle Extension U., 1935-38. With Bituminous Casualty Corp., Rock Island, Ill., 1935-86, pres., 1967-71, chmn. bd., chief exec. officer, 1971-81, chmn. bd., dir., 1981; chmn. bd., chief exec. officer, dir. Bituminous Fire and Marine Ins. Co., Rock Island, Ill., 1973-81, chmn. bd., 1981-86; chmn. bd., chief exec. officer, dir. Bitco Corp. Pres. Rock Island County United Way, 1971-72; chmn. bd. United Appeal Rock Island County, 1969; co-chmn. Rock Island Family Y Bldg. Fund, 1974. With AUS, World War II. Mem. Adminstrv. Mgmt. Soc. (past chpt. pres.), Rock Island C. of C. (past pres.), Rock Island Arsenal Golf Club, Union League Club, Masons. Lutheran. Home: Rock Island Ill. Deceased.

FENTON, BEATRICE, sculptor; b. Phila., July 12, 1887; d. Thomas Hanover and Lizzie Spear (Remak) F. Student, Sch. Indsl. Art, Phila., 1903-04, Pa. Acad. Fine Arts, 1904-11; AFD, Moore Inst. Art, 1954. Mem. faculty Moore Inst. Art. Prin. works include Seaweed Fountain, Fairmount Park, Phila., Fairy Fountain, Wister Woods, Phila., bronze meml. tablet to Charles M. Schmitz, Acad. Music, Phila., Eyre gold medal design Phila. Water Color Club, Nereid Fountain and Boy and Starfish Fountain, pvt. estates; bust of Peter Moran, bust of Thomas H. Fenton, statuette of John F. Huneker, Phila. Art Club; bust of William Penn, Penn Club, Phila.; bust of Marjorie D. Martinet, Martinet Sch. Art, Balt.; bust of I. P. Strittmater, M.D., Phila.; Wood-Music, Danby Park, Wilmington, Del.; gatepost figure Children's Hosp., Phila.; bust of Felix E. Schelling, U. Pa., bust of Joseph Moore; garden sculpture Baacchanale and Leaping Dolphin Fountain; Turner Meml. tablet, Johns Hopkins U.; Ariel Sun-Dial, Shakespeare Garden, U. Pa.; fountain figure Brookgreen Gardens, S.C.; Lizette Woodworth Reese meml. tablet, Pratt Library, Balt.; meml. drinking fountain, Hahnemann Med. Coll., Phila.; meml. sun-dial, Rittenhouse Sq., Phila.; two fish fountains, Fairmount Park, Phila.; Gill meml. tablet Muskingum Coll., new Concord, Ohio. Recipient hon. mention Panama-Pacific Internat. Expn., 1915, Plastic Club, 1916, silver medal Plastic Club, 1922, bronze medal Sesquicentennial Internat. Expn., Phila., 1926, hon. mention Woodmere Art Gallery, Chestnut Hill, Pa., 1951, DaVinci Alliance Bronze medal, 1954, Violet oakley Meml. prize Woodmere Art Gallery, 1962, Percy M. Owens Meml award, 1967; winning design for Congl. medal awarded by Albin W. Barkley, 1950; Cresson European scholar, 1909, 10. Fellow Nat. Sculpture Soc., Pa. Acad. Fine Arts (McCellan anatomy prize 1907, Edmund Stewardson prize 1908, gold medal 1922, Fellowship prize 1922); mem.Art Alliance. Home: Philadelphia Pa. †

FENTON, FREDERICK CHARLES, educator, engineer; b. Waterloo, Iowa, June 30, 1891; s. Agustus Clair and Jane (Craig) F.; m. Doris Maria Hays, June 8, 1922; children: Franklin Hays, Ruth Ellen, Jane Spencer. Student, Waterloo Coll. Commerce, 1909-10; BS, Iowa State Coll., 1914, MS, 1930; grad. study, Oxford U., 1919. Extension engr. Iowa State Coll., 1914-16, U. Mo., 1916-17; assoc. prof. Iowa State Coll., 1919-27; prof., head dept. agrl. engring. Kans. State Coll., Manhattan, from 1928, also agrl. engr. Kans. State Agrl. Expt. and Engr. Sta., dir. rsch. rural electrification; agrl. engring. advisor to govt. of India, 1956-58. Author coll. bulls. 1st lt. C.A.C., arty. tng., U.S. Army, Europe, 1917-19. Mem. Engring. Coun. Profl. Devel. (mem. accrediting com.), Am. Soc. Engring. Edn., Kans. Engring. Soc., Sigma Xi, Theta Delta Chi, Sigma Tau, Phi Kappa Phi, Alpha Zeta, Gamma Sigma Delta. Congregationalist. Home: Manhattan Kans. †

FERBER, ROBERT, statistician, market analys economist, educator; b. N.Y.C., Feb. 13, 1922; s. Samue and Dinah (Rosenthal) F.; m. Marianne Abeles, Aug 18, 1946; children: Don Richard, Ellen J. BS, City Coll N.Y, 1942; MA, U. Chgo., 1945, PhD, 1951; postgrad Columbia U., 1946-47. Chief statistician Indsl. Survey Co., Chgo., 1943-45; economist, statistician I. Deveg Co., N.Y.C., 1945-47; research assoc. prof., bur. econ and bus. research, dept. econs. U. Ill., 1948-57, researc prof. bur. econ. and bus. research and prof. dept. econs 1957-81, prof. dept. bus. adminstrn., dir. survey researc lab., 1965-81. Author: Statistical Techniques in Marke Researh, 1949, A Study of Aggregate Consumptio Functions, The Railroad Shippers' Forecasts, Factor Influencing Durable Food Purchases: A Basic Bibliography on Market Research (with H.G. Wales), Collecting Financial Data by Consumer Panel Techniques (with P.J. Verdoorn) Research Methods in Economic and Business, 1962, Handbook of Marketing Research 1974; also articles in research jours.; editor: Marketing Research: Selected Literature (with H.G. Wales), 1951 Jour. Mktg. Research, 1964-69, applications sect. Jour Am. Statis. Assn., 1968-76, coordinating editor, 1969-76; chmn. policy bd. Research on Consumer Behavior 1973-76; editor: Jour. Consumer Research, 1977-81. Recipient award for yr.'s outstanding contbn. to field o mktg. Am. Mktg. Assn., 1950, Parlin award for disting contbns. to mktg., 1972; named to Hall of Fame in Distbn., 1964. Mem. Am. Statis. Assn., Am. Econ Assn., Am. Mktg. Assn. (pres. 1969-70), Am. Winc Energy Assn., Assn. for Consumer Research, Econ metric Soc., Latin Am. Studies Assn. Home Champaign Ill. Died Sept. 8, 1981.

FERGUSON, CHARLES W., editor, author; b Quanah, Tex., Aug. 23, 1901; s. Charles Nathanie Newton and Jennie (Wright) F.; m. Victoria Wallace June 28, 1923 (div.); children: Charles Wallace, Hugh McGinnis. AB, So. Meth. U., 1923, LittD, 1966; postgrad., Union Theol. Sem., New Sch. for Social Research N.Y.C.; LittD, Hillsdale Coll., 1952. Minister Meth Ch., 1923-25; assoc. editor The Bookman, 1926-30; religious editor Doubleday, Doran & Co., 1926-30; sec Ray Long & Richard R. Smith Inc., 1930-32; pres Round Table Press, 1932-34; assoc. editor Readers Digest, 1934-40, sr. editor, 1940-68; cultural relations officer U.S. Embassy, London, 1946; vis. lectr. U. Tex. 1969, So. Meth. U., 1972. Author: The Confusion of Tongues: A Review of Modern Isms, 1927, Pigskin (novel), 1928, Fifty Million Brothers: A Panorama of American Lodges and Clubs, 1937, A Little Democracy is a Dangerous Thing, 1948, Naked to Mine Enemies The Life of Cardinal Wolsey, 1958, Say It With Words 1959, Getting to Know the U.S.A., 1963, The Abecedarian Book, 1964, The Male Attitude, 1966, A is for Advent, 1968, Organizing to Beat the Devil Methodists and the Making of America, 1971. Mem Nat. Council Boy Scouts Am.; v.p. pub. info. Nat Safety Council, 1960-67. Recipient Christopher award 1958. Mem. Sigma Alpha Epsilon. Methodist. Home Mount Kisco N.Y. Died Dec. 11, 1987; interred Fair Ridge Cemetery, Chappaqua, N.Y.

FERGUSON, JOHN A(LEXANDER), lawyer, trade association executive; b. Caruthersville, Mo., Oct. 26, 1892; s. Frank L. and Martha M. (Ward) F.; m. Doris Stubblefield, July 1, 1917; 1 child, John Alexander. Student, St. Vincent's Coll., 1908-11, St. Mary's Coll., 1911-12. Bar: Mo. 1930. Gen. mgr. Matthews-Stubblefield Farm & Devel. Co., Malden, Mo., 1920-26; U.S. commr. Ea. dist. Mo. and clk. U.S. Ct., Cape Girardeau, 1927-32; spl. dep. Mo. Fin. Dept.; also pvt. practice law 1932-35; exec. dir. Independent Natural Gas Assn. Am., Washington, from 1945. Mem. Mo Pub. Svc. Commn., from 1945. Mem. Mo. Athletic Club (St. Louis), Met. Club, Burning Tree Club, Nat Press Club, Congl. Country Club. Home: Bethesda Md. †

FERGUSON, LEONARD WILTON, psychologist; b Turlock, Calif., Mar. 2, 1912; s. William Ward and Sara Minium (Kaufman) F.; m. Edith Beverly Phemister, July 1, 1939; children: Barbara Ferguson Needham, Margaret Ferguson Gibson, Kathryn Ferguson McCarthy. A.B., Stanford U., 1933, M.A., 1935, Ph.D., 1942. Diplomate: in indsl. psychology Am. Bd. Examiners in Profl. Psychology. Instr. to asst. prof. psychology U. Conn., Storrs, 1939-43; asst. staff supr. Met. Life Ins. Co., 1943-51; research asst. Aetna Life Affiliated Cos., 1951-53; research asso. Life Ins. Agy. Mgmt. Assn., Hartford, Conn., 1953-55; program dir. Life Ins. Agy. Mgmt. Assn., 1955-63; prof. psychology Ohio U., Athens, 1966-77; sec. com. on tests Life Office Mgmt. Assn., 1940-47, sec. clerical salary study com., 1943-44, chmn., 1944-49; lectr. NYU, summer 1949, U. Conn. extension div., 1953-54, 54-55; treas. Joint Council Psychologists for Legis. in N.Y. State, 1951; mem. adv. com. on job evaluation Nat. Mgmt. Council, 1950. Editor: Clerical Salary Administration, 1947, The Journal Press, Provincetown, Mass., 1964-65; author: Personality Measurement, 1952, The Heritage of Industrial Psychology (series), Cape Cod Collection, a series, (with Edith P. Ferguson) A Leonard-Reference Series, parts I, II, 1985; numerous articles in profl. jours. Selectman Town of Provincetown, Mass., 1980-81. Home: Salt Lake City Utah. Died July 9, 1988; interred Turlock Meml. Park, Turlock, Calif.

FERGUSON, PHIL MOSS, engineer; b. Bartlett, Tex., Nov. 10, 1899; s. William Simpson and Annie Leonora (Moss) F.; m. Marion Hicks, Feb. 23, 1939 (div. 1940); 1 son, Yale Hicks. B.S. in Civil Engring, U. Tex., 1922, C.E., 1923; M.S., U. Wis., 1924. Registered profl. engr., Tex. Tutor in physics U. Tex. at Austin, 1922-23, asso. prof. civil engring., 1928-39, prof., 1939-76, prof. emeritus, from 1976, chmn. dept. civil engring., 1943-57, Dean T.U. Taylor prof. civil engring., 1968-72; structural engr. Dwight P. Robinson & Co., N.Y.C., 1924-28, summer 1930; field insp., designer R.O. Jameson, Dallas, summer 1929; designer bridge div. Tex. Hwy. Dept., summers 1931, 32, 35, 39; designer on Buchanan Dam, S.W. Engring. Co., Austin, Tex., summer 1936. Author: Plate Girder Theory, rev, 1935, Reinforced Concrete Fundamentals, 1958, 4th edit., 1979, also numerous papers on reinforced concrete and frame analysis. Chmn. bd. U. Coop. Soc., 1952-54. Recipient research award ASCE, 1961; Distinguished Service citation U. Wis., 1970; named Distinguished Engring. Grad. U. Tex. at Austin, 1972; Honor award Concrete Reinforcing Steel Inst., 1977; Balcones Structural Lab. renamed Phil M. Ferguson Structural Engring. Lab. in his honor, 1979. Mem. Nat. Acad. Engring., Am. Concrete Inst. (Wason medal for research 1954, 58, 68, pres. 1959, hon. mem. 1968, Lindau award 1972, Raymond C. Reese research medal 1973, Turner medal 1976, Kelly award 1977, Charles S. Whitney award 1979), ASCE (pres. Tex. sect. 1967, hon. mem. 1971), Reinforced Concrete Research Council, Comité Européen du Béton, Internat. Assn. Bridge and Structural Engring. (U.S. alt. dir. 1966-70), Nat. Soc. Profl. Engrs. (dir. 1966-70, S.W. regional vice chmn. Profl. Engrs. in Edn. 1968-71), Tex. Soc. Profl. Engrs. (pres. 1962), Sigma Xi, Tau Beta Pi, Phi Kappa Phi, Chi Epsilon. Methodist. Home: Austin Tex. Died Aug. 28, 1986, buried Austin Meml. Park.

FERGUSSON, FRANCIS, literary critic; b. Albuquerque, Feb. 21, 1904; s. Harvey Butler and Clara Mary (Huning) F.; m. Marion Crowne, Jan. 16, 1931 (dec. 1959); children—Harvey, Honora; m. Peggy Kaiser, July 26, 1962. Student, Harvard, 1921-23; B.A. (Rhodes scholar), Oxford U., 1926. Asso. dir. Am. Lab. Theatre, N.Y., 1926-30; drama critic The Bookman mag., N.Y., 1930-32; lectr., exec. sec. New Sch. for Social Research, N.Y.C., 1932-34; prof. humanities and drama Bennington (Vt.) Coll., 1934-47; mem. Inst. for Advanced Study, Princeton, N.J., 1948-49; dir. Princeton Seminars in lit. criticism 1949-52; adv. bd. humanities program Princeton, 1952-58; vis. prof. English Ind. U., 1952-53; prof. comparative lit. Rutgers U., 1953-68, Princeton, 1973-86. Author: books including The Idea of a Theatre, 1949, Plays of Moliere, Critical Introduction, 1950, Dante's Drama of the Mind (Christian Gauss award 1953), Aristotle's Poetics, Critical Introduction, 1961, Poems, 1962, Dante, 1966, Shakespeare: The Pattern in His Carpet, 1970, Literary Landmarks, 1976; also contbr.: poems to Critical Essays; The Human Image, 1957; Gen. editor: poems to Laurel Shakespeare, 1957-86; mem. editorial bd.: poems to Comparative Lit, 1952-60. Recipient award for lit. Nat. Inst. Arts and Letters, 1953. Mem. Nat. Inst. Arts and Letters. Home: Kingston N.J. Died Nov. 19, 1986.

FERRARA, RUTH REIORDAN, association executive; b. Ducktown, Tenn., Nov. 8, 1924; d. Robert Harrison and Lillian (Fralix) Reiordan; student public schs.; grad. Jones Bus. Coll.; m. Joseph James Ferrara, Oct. 10, 1946; children—James Michael, John Richard. Machinist, Jacksonville (Fla.) Naval Air Sta., 1942-44; with Greyhound Bus Co., Jacksonville, 1944-45; head cashier womens apparel Mangels Ladies Wear, Jacksonville, 1945-46; owner, operator restaurant, Jacksonville, 1946-47, Copperhill, Tenn., 1946-48; bookkeeper Henley & Beckwith, Inc., Jacksonville, 1949-50; mem. purchasing dept. Am. Hardware Corp., New Britain, Conn., 1948-49; sec.-mgr. Greater Jacksonville Fair Assn., 1966-69, dir., 1959-69, exec. sec., 1965-70; pres. Fla. Fedn. Fairs and Livestock Shows, 1969-70, also dir. public relations; exec. sec. Fla. Fedn. Fairs, 1970-85, S.C. State Fair, Greenville, 1972-77; exec. sec., mgr. North Fla. Fair, Tallahassee, from 1977. Mem. Fla. Council for Aged, 1966-70; mem. aging com. Community Planning Council, 1966-70. Bd. dirs. Jacksonville Fair, 1959-68, State and Provincial Assn. Fairs, from 1976; sec. Venetia Boys Club, 1958-62; bd. advisers Cathedral Towers, 1966-70. Democrat. Methodist. Clubs: Jacksonville Garden (dir. 1960-68), Order Eastern Star, Venetia Manor Garden Circle (pres. 1960-62). Home: Tallahassee, Fla. Deceased.

FERTIG, LAWRENCE, economist; b. N.Y.C., Mar. 19, 1898; m. Bertha Alexander, Aug. 1932. AB, NYU, 1919; AM, Columbia U., 1920. Founder Lawrence Fertig & Co., Inc., 1923, pres., 1923-60; syndicated econ. columnist 1944-86. Author: Prosperity Through Freedom, 1961. Trustee NYU, 1954-86; pres. Alumni Fedn., 1950-52; chmn. bd. trustees Found. Econ. Edn. Mem. Mont Pelerin Soc., Phi Beta Kappa. Home: New York N.Y. Died Oct. 26, 1986.

FESTINGER, LEON, psychologist, educator; b. N.Y.C., May 8, 1919; s. Alex and Sarah (Solomon) F.; m. Mary Oliver Ballou, Oct. 23, 1943; children: Catherine, Richard, Kurt; m. Trudy Bradley, Sept. 7, 1968. B.S., CCNY, 1939; M.A., State U. Iowa, 1940, Ph.D., 1942. Research assoc. State U. Iowa, 1941-43; instr. U. Rochester, 1943-45; assoc. prof. M.I.T., 1945-48, U. Mich., 1948-51; prof. psychology U. Minn., 1951-55, Stanford U., 1955-68; Else and Hans Staudinger prof. psychology, grad. faculty New Sch. for Social Research, N.Y.C., 1968-89. Author: A Theory of Cognitive Dissonance, 1957, Conflict, Decision and Dissonance, 1964, The Human Legacy, 1983. Fellow Am. Psychol. Assn. (pres. div. 8, 1963, Disting. Scientist award 1959), Am. Acad. Arts and Scis., Nat. Acad. Scis. Home: New York N.Y. Died Feb. 11, 1989.

FEYNMAN, RICHARD PHILLIPS, physicist; b. N.Y.C., May 11, 1918; s. Melville Arthur and Lucille (Phillips) F.; m. Gweneth Feynman; children: Carl, Michelle. B.S., Mass. Inst. Tech., 1939; Ph.D., Princeton, 1942. Staff atomic bomb project Princeton, 1942-43, Los Alamos, 1943-45; assoc. prof. theoretical physics Cornell U., 1945-50; prof. theoretical physics Calif. Inst. Tech., 1950-88; mem. Presdl. Commn. on Space Shuttle Challenger, 1986. Author: Quantum Electrodynamics, Theory of Fundamental Processes, Character of Physical Law, Statistical Mechanics, QED: The Strange Theory of Light and Matter, 1985, Surely You're Joking, Mr. Feynman -- Adventures of a Curious Character, 1985, What Do You Care What Other People Think? -- Futher Adventures of a Curious Character, 1988; contbr. theory of quantum electrodynamics, beta decay and liquid helium. Recipient Einstein award, 1954; Nobel prize in physics, 1965; Oersted medal, 1972; Niels Bohr Internat. Gold medal, 1973. Mem. Am. Phys. Soc., AAAS, Royal Soc. (fgn. mem.), Pi Lambda Phi. Died Feb. 15, 1988.

FIELD, FRANK MCCOY, clergyman, author, lecturer; b. Mason, Mich., May 4, 1887; s. Isaac H. and Eva C. L. G. (Brewer) F.; m. Rose Mildred Jenkins, Sept. 21, 1909 (dec. Nov. 1962); children: Doris Isabel (Mrs. Arthur H. Falter), Esther Evelyn (Mrs. Carl Forsberg), Marjorie Rose (Mrs. Charles Hall). AB, Albion Coll., 1909, DD, 1936; postgrad., Am. Sch. Oriental Rsch., Jerusalem, 1930, Am. Univ. Seminar, 1930. Ordained to ministry M.E. Ch., 1909. Organizer, pastor Oak Park Ch., Flint., Mich., 1909-13, pastor, 1924-31; pastor (successively at) Gladstone, Plymouth and Holmes Meml. chs., Detroit, 1913-24; dist. supt. Port Huron Dist., 1931-37; pastor East Grand Blvd. Meth. Ch., Detroit, 1937-43; dist. supt. Saginaw Bay Dist. Meth. Ch., 1943-49; pastor Mt. Clemens, Mich., 1949-53; pres. Holy Land Christian Mission Bd., 1953-72, pres. emeritus, from 1972; condr. Holy Land Tour, 1953-64; chmn. Baney Dead Sea Expdn. Bd., 1962-68; mem. bd. mgrs. Bd. Missions and Ch. Extension meth. Ch., 1941-53; past pres. conf. Bd. Missions and Ch. Extension; lectr. on Europeans scenes and Bible lands. Author: Bible Lands, 1949, Where Jesus Walked, 1951, The New Where Jesus Walked, 1959, rev. edit., 1975; assoc. editor Holy Land Pictorial News; contbr. articles to jours. Mem. Gen. Conf. M.E. Ch., 1936, Jurisdictional Conf. meth. Ch., 1948. Mem. Internat. Mark Twain Soc., Masons, Kiwanis, Exchange Club (past pres.), Delta Sigma Rho, Theta Phi. Republican. Home: Saint Petersburg Fla. †

FIELD, HENRY, anthropologist; b. Chgo., Dec. 15, 1902; m. Julia Rand Allen, Feb. 6, 1963; 1 dau., Juliana Lathrop; 1 dau. by previous marriage, Mariana Field Hoppin. Student, Eton Coll., Eng., 1916-21, New Coll., Oxford, 1921-26; BA, Oxford U., 1926, Diploma in Anthropology, 1926, MA, 1929, DSc, 1937. Researcher U. Heidelberg, 1926, Peabody Mus., Harvard U., 1936-37; anthropologist Field Mus. Natural History, Chgo., 1926-41, asst. curator phys. anthropology, 1926-36, curator, 1937-41; researcher for F.D. Roosevelt and H.S. Truman Library of Congress, Washington, 1941-45; mem. archeol. expdn., Europe, Africa, Southwestern Asia, 1927-55, Mongolia, 1973; leader Marshall Field Archael. Expdns. and others, Europe, N. Arabian Desert, Iraq, Jordan and Saudi Arabia; research fellow phys. anthropology Harvard U., 1950-69; hon. assoc. in phys. anthropology, 1969-86; adj. prof. U. Miami, 1966-86; Forbes Hawkes lectr. U. Miami, Lowell Inst., Boston, 1952; U.S. del. to internat. congresses and sci. confs. Author: (with David Hooper) books on different geog. areas, including Useful Plants and Drugs of Iran and Iraq, 1937, The Anthropology of Iraq, 1939, 40, 48, 51, 52, Contributions to the Anthropology of the Caucasus, 1953, The Track of Man, 1953, Los Indios de Tepoztlan Morelos, Mexico, 1954, Ancient and Modern Man in S.W. Asia, I, 1956, II, 1961, Bibliographies on S.W. Asia I-VII, 1953-61, Supplements I-VII, 1963-73, Anthropological Reconnaissance in West Pakistan, 1959, North Arabian Desert Arhaeological Survey, 1925-50, 1960, "M" Project for F.D.R.: Studies on Migration and Settlement, 1962, Physical Anthropology of India, 1970, Anthropology of Saudi Arabia, 1971, Arabian Desert Tales, 1976, Mongolia Tour. Mongolia Today, 1978, Trail Blazers, 1980; editor: Peabody Mus. Russian Translation Series, 1960-70, Field Research Projects, 1963-86. Mem. U.S. mission to Moscow and Leningrad for 220th anniversary of Acad. Scis. USSR, 1954, Internat. Congress, Moscow, 1964, Internat. Geog. Congress, London, 1964. Fellow AAAS, Royal Geog. Soc., Royal Cen. Asian Soc., Asiatic Soc. Bengal (Gold medal), Royal Anthrop. Inst., Zool Soc., Prehistoric Soc.; mem. Acad. Arts and Scis. Ams. (pres. 1964-75), Glasgow Archeol. Soc. (hon.), several fgn. sci. socs. (corr.), U.S. and fgn. profl. and sci. socs. and assns., anthropol., archael. and other spl. orgns., Explorers Club (N.Y.C.) (pres. S. Fla. chpt.). Home: Miami Fla. Died Jan. 4, 1986; buried York Harbor, Maine.

FIELD, RON, theatrical director, choreographer. s. Harry Field and Meta Adolf. Grad., High Sch. Performing Arts. Profl. debut at age 8 in Lady in the Dark; appeared in Broadway play The Boy Friend; mem. Jack Cole Dancers; choreographer Broadway plays Zorba (Tony nomination), Rags (Tony nomination); choreographer TV shows Ben Vereen...His Roots (Emmy award), America Salutes Richard Rogers (Emmy award), Baryishnikov on Broadway (Emmy award); choreographer nat. touring co. Cabaret starring Joel Grey, 1988; dir., choreographer Broadway plays On The Town, 1971, 5-6-7-8....Dance!, 1983, Applause starring Lauren Bacall (Tony awards); staged nightclub acts for Liza Minnelli, Carol Lawrence, Chita Rivera, TV dances for Fred Astaire and Angela Lansbury; staged and choreographed King of Hearts, 1978, also Acad. Awards shows, 5 years, Tony Awards shows, 3 years, Emmy Awards shows, 3 years; produced and staged prodns. for venues ranging from Casino de Paris to 1984 World's Fair in New Orleans, opening ceremonies for Olympic Games, L.A., 1984. Home: New York N.Y. Died Feb. 6, 1989.

FIELDING, GABRIEL (ALAN GABRIEL BARNSLEY), novelist, English language educator; b. Hexham, Northumberland, Eng., Mar. 25, 1916; s. George and Katherine Mary (Fielding-Smith) Barnsley; m. Edwina Eleanora Cook, Oct. 31, 1943; children: Michael Fielding, Jonathan Milne, Mario Simon George Gabriel, Felicity Ann, Mary Gabriel Elizabeth. B.A., Trinity Coll., Dublin, Ireland, 1940; mem., Royal Coll. Surgeons; licentiate, Royal Coll. Physicians, St. Georges Hosp., London, 1942; D.Litt. (hon.), Gonzaga U., 1967. Physician in gen. practice Maidstone, Eng., 1948-86; part-time med. officer Her Majesty's Tng. Establishment, Maidstone, 1952-86; occasional broadcaster BBC, 1961-86; author in residence Wash. State U., Pullman, 1966-67; prof. English Wash. State U., 1966-86. Author: (poetry) The Frog Prince and Other Poems, 1952; novel Brotherly Love, 1954, In the Time of Greenbloom, 1956, 2d edit., 1984, Eight Days, 1959, Through Streets Broad and Narrow, 1961, XXVIII Poems, 1955, The Birthday King, 1963, 2d edit., 1985 (W. H. Smith prize 1963, St. Thomas More Soc. gold medal, Chgo.), Gentlemen in Their Season, 1966, New Queens for Old, 1972, Pretty Doll Houses, 1979; (poems) Songs without Music, 1979, (novel) The Women of Guinea Lane, 1986. Served to capt. Royal Army Med. Corps, 1943-46. Hon. librarian Univ. Philos. Soc., Trinity Coll., 1938; recipient Anatomy prize, 1937, Silver medal for oratory, 1938; Journalism award Cath. Press Assn., 1965. Roman Catholic. Home: Addiscombe England. Died Nov. 27, 1986.

FIELDS, CLARENCE, savings and loan association executive; b. Nacogdoches, Tex., July 27, 1892; s. Thomas J. and Mary Jane (Garrett) F.; m. Frankie Lee Robertson, Oct. 7, 1923; 1 son, Frank R. BS, Langston U., 1936; MA, Colo. State Tchrs. Coll., Greeley, 1939. Tchr. indsl. arts Sand Springs High Sch., 1920-36, tchr. music, 1936-42; tchr. instrumental music Tulsa Pub. Schs., 1942-58; engaged in real estate bus. Tulsa, from 1958; with North Tulsa Savs. & Loan Assn., from 1968, pres., from 1969. With inf. U.S. Army, World War I. Mem. Masons, Kappa Alpha Psi. Home: Tulsa Okla. †

FIELDS, HARRY, physician; b. Bklyn., Aug. 6, 1911; s. Jacob and Rose (Goldstein) Rosenfeld; m. Ruth Dolfman, June 20, 1937; childrn: Gary, Jacqueline. BS, Haverford Coll., 1932; MD, U. Pa., 1936. Diplomate Am. Bd. Ob-Gyn. Intern Hosp. of Pa., Phila., 1936-38; resident in ob-gyn Hosp. U. Pa., Phila., 1938-41; pvt. practice Phila., 1941-86; mem. faculty U. Pa. Sch. Medicine, Phila., 1936-86, prof. ob-gyn, 1965-86. Author: Induction of Labor; also articles. Recipient Pioneer award Frankford High Sch., 1975, Alumni award Haverford Coll., 1976, Alumni award of merit U. Pa., 1979. Mem. Am. Coll. Ob-Gyn, A.C.S., A.C.P., Phila. County Med. Soc., Phila. Obstetrical Soc., Golden Square Club, Masons, B'nai B'rith. Home: Philadelphia Pa. Died Oct. 19, 1986.

FIFE, AUSTIN EDWIN, educator, author; b. Lincoln, Idaho, Dec. 18, 1909; s. Robert H. and Mary Elizabeth (Stocks) F.; m. Alta Stevens, Mar. 27, 1934; children: Carolyn (Mrs. Harry McDaniel), Marian Baldwin. BA, Stanford U., 1934, PhD, 1939; MA, Harvard U., 1937. Prof. French lang. Occidental Coll., Los Angeles, 1946-58; specialist for langs. U.S. Office Edn., 1959-60; prof. French, head dept. langs. Utah State U., Logan, 1960-75. Author: (with Mrs. Fife) Saints of Sage and Saddle, 1956, 81, Borzoi Book of French Folk Tales, 1956, Songs of the Cowboys, 1966, Cowboy and Western Songs, 1968, Ballads of the Great West, 1970, Forms upon the Frontier, 1969, Heaven on Horseback, 1970, Exploring Western Americana, 1988; contbr. articles to profl. jours. Lt. col. USAF, 1942-45, 51-53. Recipient Disting. Service award Utah State U., 1976; Fulbright exchange prof. French Nat. Museums, 1950-51; Guggenheim fellow, 1958-59, sr. fellow NEH, 1971-72. Fellow Am. Folklore Soc., Utah Hist. Soc., Utah Heritage Found., Utah Acad. Sci., Arts and Letters; mem. MLA, Rocky Mountain Modern Lang. Assn. Home: Logan Utah. Died Feb. 7, 1986; interred Logan, Utah.

FIFIELD, GARY MORTON, opera producer; b. L.A., May 1, 1939; s. Howard C. and Esther S. Fifield. Student, Jr. Coll. Kansas City, 1957-59, U. Mo., 1960-61. Bus. mgr. Kansas City Lyric Theater, 1962-65; asst. to gen. dir. San Francisco Opera Assn., 1965-69; exec. dir. Opportunity Resources for Arts, 1971-76; mng. dir. Washington Opera, 1976-85; guest lectr. in arts mgmt. Wharton Sch. U. Pa., SUNY, Bklyn. Coll., George Washington U. Mem. Opera Am. (bd. dirs.), Cultural Alliance Greater Washington (bd. dirs.). Died May 10, 1985.

FIFIELSKI, EDWIN PETER, lawyer; b. Chgo., Oct. 4, 1916; s. Walter A. and Bessie (Dombrowski) F.; m. Jewel Weglarz, June 18, 1944. LLB, John Marshall Law Sch., 1940, JD, 1950. Bar: Ill. 1940. Practiced in Chgo.; chmn. bd. Jefferson State Bank; pres. Spring Realty & Mortgage Co., Emancipator Ins. Agy. Inc. Alderman 45th ward, Chgo.1963-79; mem. com. Chgo. council Boy Scouts Am., 1958-85. Capt. AUS, 1940-46. Mem. AMVETS (state comdr. 1959-61, nat. comdr. 1961-62), Jefferson Park C. of C. (pres. 1959-61), Ill. Bar. Assn., Am. Judicature Soc., Nat. Advocates Soc., Am. Legion, VFW, Chgo. Soc. (pres. 1971), K.C., Jefferson Park Lions (pres. 1966-67). Home: Chicago Ill. Died June 2, 1985; interred St. Joseph Cemetery, Chgo.

FILIATRAULT, ALFRED CHARLES, JR., association executive; b. Duluth, Minn., Jan. 2, 1921; s. Alfred Charles and Alice (Shebetsky) F.; m. Mary Jane Smith, Sept. 13, 1952. B.S., U.S. Naval Acad., 1943. Commd. ensign U.S. Navy, 1943, advanced through grades to comdr., 1958; served in destroyers SW Pacific, World War II; exec. officer, then comdg. officer destroyer escort Pacific, 1946-48; comdg. officer mine location ship Fla., 1948-49; aide to comdr. 7th Fleet Korea, 1950-51; instr. NROTC, U. Minn., 1951-52; comdg. officer, then div. comdr. minesweep ships Pacific, 1953-56; mil. asst. adv. group Germany, 1957-59; comdg. officer two destroyers Pacific, 1959-61; assigned Navy staff, The Pentagon, 1961-65; ret. 1965; exec. sec. Propeller Club U.S., 1965-84. Trustee United Seaman's Service, 1965-87, Nat. River Acad., 1972-87. Decorated Bronze Star. Mem. Council Am. Master Mariners, Ret. Officers Assn., Navy League, U.S. Naval Acad. Alumni Assn. Club: Mason. Home: McLean Va. Died Apr. 15, 1987; interred Arlington (Va.) Nat. Cemetery.

FILLEY, FRANK H., hardware company executive; b. St. Louis, Nov. 12, 1874; s. Frank B. and Martha G. (Frederick) F.; m. Mary E. Colt, June 1914; children: Giles F., Joan D. Ed. pub. schs. Began as office boy Broderick and Bascom Rope Co., St. Louis, 1891; with Kans. & Tex. Coal Co., 1895-1900, Norvell Shapleigh Hardware Co., 1900-05, St. Louis Cordage Mills, 1905-09; pres. Am. Mfg. Co., Bklyn., 1929-53, chmn. bd. dirs., from 1953; trustee Greenpoint Savs. Bank. Mem. Round Hill Club. Republican. Episcopalian. Home: Greenwich Conn. †

FILLMORE, GEORGE BENJAMIN, business executive; b. Taylor, Pa., July 8, 1888; s. Harry Atherton and Emma (Sands) F.; m. Naomi Elizabeth Allen, Oct. 2, 1913; children: George Benjamin, Robert Allen. Student, Wyo. Sem., 1904-08; E.E., Lafayette Coll., Easton, Pa., 1912. Mine forman West End Coal Co., Mocanagua, 1913-18; chief insp. Hudson Coal Co., Scranton, Pa., 1919-21; asst. gen. sales agt. Hudson Coal Co., Scranton, 1921-29, gen. sales agt., 1929-37, v.p. sales, 1937-46, sr. v.p., 1947-49, pres., 1950-60, also bd. dirs.; pres. Quackenbush Assocs., from 1961; bd. dirs. Northeastern Pa. Nat. Bank, Scranton, Anthracite Inst., Wilkes-Barre, Pa. Mem. Scranton C. of C., Wilkes Barre C. of C., Scranton Club, Westmoreland Club, Sky Top Club, Scranton Country Club, Delta Kappa Epsilon. Home: Scranton Pa. †

FINCH, CHARLES CLIFTON, lawyer, governor of Mississippi; b. Pope, Miss., Apr. 4, 1927; s. Carl Bedford and Ruth Christine (McMinn) F.; m. Zelma Lois Smith, Dec. 12, 1952; children: Janet Herrington, Virginia Anne, Charles Clifton, Stephen Nicholas. BA, LLB, U. Miss., 1958. Bar: Miss. 1958. Pvt. practice Batesville, Miss., 1958-59; mem. Miss. Ho. of eps., 1959-63; dist. atty. 17th Jud. Dist., Miss., 1964-72; gov. State of Miss., Jackson, 1976-80. With U.S. Army, 1945. Mem. Am., Miss., Panola County (past pres.) bar assns., Am. (past assoc. editor Jour.), Miss. (pres. elect 1969)) Trial Lawyers Assns., Farm Bur., Am. Legion, VFW, Masons, Shriners, Lions, Civitan, Moose. Democrat. Baptist. Home: Batesville Miss. Died Apr. 22, 1986.

FINCH, JAMES AUSTIN, JR., judge; b. St. Louis, Nov. 13, 1907; s. James Austin and Carrie (Lehman) F.; m. Helen E. Carroll, Aug. 28, 1937; children: Gail Carroll, James Austin III, John David. Student, S.E. Mo. State Coll., 1925-27; A.B., U. Mo., 1930, J.D., 1932, LL.D., 1966. Bar: Mo. bar 1931. Asst. atty. gen. Mo., 1932; mem. firm Finch, Finch & Knehans (formerly Finch & Finch), Cape Girardeau, 1933-65; judge Supreme Ct. Mo., 1965-78, chief justice, 1971-73; pros. atty. Cape Girardeau County, 1941-42; Bd. dirs. Nat. Center for State Cts., 1971-78, pres., 1975-77; mem. exec. council Appellate Judges Conf., 1972-77, sec., 1974-77; pres. Mo. Press-Bar Commn., 1979-80; chmn. Mo. Supreme Ct. Com. on Rules, 1980-82; Mem. Mo. Citizens Adv. Com. on Higher Edn., 1956-57; Gov.'s Com. on Edn. Beyond High Sch., 1958-60; chmn. Gov.'s Council Higher Edn., 1959-63, Adv. Council Mo. Commn. Higher Edn., 1963-64. Mem. bd. curators U. Mo., 1951-65, pres. bd., 1954-64; bd. dirs. Mo. Law Sch. Found., 1952-64, pres., 1958-59; chmn. Jefferson City Commn. on Environ. Quality, 1981-87. Served as maj. USAAF, 1942-45. Recipient award for contbn. to Mo. edn. Phi Delta Kappa, 1964; Alumni Disting. Service award U. Mo., 1965; President's Disting. Service award U. Mo., 1982; Ann. Law Day award Law Sch., U. Mo. at Kansas City, 1968; Alumni Merit citation Sch. Law, U. Mo. at Columbia, 1970; Award of Merit Am. Judges Assn., 1976; Mo. Bar Found. Spurgeon Smithson award for service to justice in soc., 1977. Fellow Am. Bar Found.; mem. Am. Law Inst., Am. Judicature Soc. (dir. 1970-74), Am., Mo., Cole County, St. Louis bar assns., Mo. Hist. Soc., Supreme Ct. of Mo. Hist. Soc. (pres. 1984-88), Am. Legion, Order of Coif, Inst. Jud. Adminstrn., Acad. Mo. Squires, Phi Beta Kappa Assos., Phi Beta Kappa, Phi Delta Phi, Omicron Delta Kappa, Delta Sigma Rho, Phi Gamma Delta. Republican. Methodist. Clubs: Jefferson City (Mo.); Country, Rotary. Home: Jefferson City Mo. Died Apr. 1, 1988; buried Riverview Cemetery, Jefferson City, Mo.

FINCH, THOMAS AUSTIN, JR., furniture manufacturing company executive; b. Thomasville, N.C., Aug. 12, 1922; s. Thomas Austin and Ernestine (Lambeth) F.; m. Meredith Clark Slane, June 4, 1949; children: Thomas Austin III, John Lambeth, David Slane, Sumner Slane, Meredith Kempton. Grad., Woodberry Forest Sch., 1940; BS in Engring, Princeton U., 1943. With Thomasville Furniture Industries Inc., 1946-84, chmn. bd. dirs., 1979-84; group v.p. parent co. Armstrong Cork Co., Lancaster, Pa., 1979-84, also dir.; dir. Wachovia Bank and Trust Co., Winston-Salem, N.C., Norfolk So. R.R., Washington. Trustee Duke U., 1963-81, Woodberry Forest Sch., 1967-72, Community Gen. Hosp., Thomasville, 1964-71, 74-80, Davidson County Pub. Libr. System, 1974-84, Madeira Sch., 1981-84. Lt. (j.g.) USNR, World War II. Named Furniture Man of Yr. Am. Furniture Mart Corp., 1963, Industrialist of Yr. Thomasville Family YMCA, 1975. Mem. Furniture Factories Mktg. Assn., Rotary Club (pres. Thomasville 1958), Phi Beta Kappa. Methodist (ofcl. bd.). Died Mar. 26, 1984.

FINDLAY, JOHN NIEMEYER, philosopher, educator; b. Pretoria, South Africa, Nov. 25, 1903; came to U.S., 1966; s. John Judson L. and Elizabeth (Niemeyer) F.; m. Aileen May Davidson, Aug. 15, 1941; children: Paul H.D., Rachel Clare. BA, Transvaal U. Coll., 1922, MA, 1924; B.A., Balliol Col. Oxford U., Eng., 1926; M.A., Balliol Col. Oxford U., 1930; PhD, U. Graz, Austria, 1933. Prof. philosophy U. Otago, New Zealand, 1934-44, U. Natal, South Africa, 1946-48, King's Coll., Newcastle-upon-Tyne, Eng., 1948-51, King's Coll., U. London, 1951-66, U. Tex., 1966-67; Clark prof. moral philosophy and metaphysics Yale U., 1967-72; U. prof., Bowne prof. philosophy Boston U., 1972-87; Gifford lectr. U. St. Andrews (Scotland), 1964-66. Author: Meinong's Theory of Objects and Values, 2d edit., 1963, Hegel: A Re-Examination, 1958, Values and Intentions, 1961, Language, Mind and Value, 1963, The Discipline of the Cave, 1966, The Transcendence of the Cave, 1967, Axiological Ethics, 1970, Ascent to the Absolute, 1970, Plato: The Written and Unwrittn Doctrines, 1974, Plato and Platonism, 1978, Kant and the Transcendental Object, 1981, Wittenstein: A Critique, 1984, Studies in the Philosophy of J.N. Findlay, 1985; translator Logische Untersuchungen (Husserl). Fellow Brit. Acad., Am. Acad. Arts and Scis.; mem. Aristotelian Soc. (v.p. 1956-87). Home: Boston Mass. Died Sept. 27, 1987; cremated.

FINE, PERLE, artist; b. Boston, May 1, 1908; d. Simon and Sarah (Fine) F.; m. Maurice Berezov. Studied with, Hans Hofmann, Atelier 17. assoc. prof. fine art Hofstra U.; vis. prof. art Cornell U., 1961; tchr., lectr. Provincetown Art Assn., pvt. groups. Contbr. articles on art to profl. jours.; one-man shows include Marian Willard, 1945, DeYoung Mus., 1947, Nierendorf, 1946, 47, Tanager, 1955, Betty Parsons Galleries, 1949, 51, 52, 53, Graham Gallery, N.Y.C., 1961, 63, 64, 67, Bykert Gallery, Springs, N.Y., Andre Zarre Gallery, 1976, 77, Ingber Gallery, N.Y.C., 1982-86, Benson Gallery, Bridgehampton, N.Y.; also exhibited nat. group annuals, U.S. and abroad; retrospective exhbn., Guild Hall; works in permanent collections including Whitney Mus., Smith Coll. Mus., Rutgers U., Los Angeles County Mus., Parrish Mus., Brandeis U., Bklyn. Mus., Mus. Non-Objective Art, Munson-Williams-Proctor Inst., N.Y. U., U. Calif. at Berkeley, Hofstra U., Mus. Modern Art, Guild Hall, Easthampton, Ind. U., also pvt. collections. Recipient Guggenheim scholarship; purchase award for color woodcut Bklyn. Mus., 1956; 1st prize for oil paintings Silvermine Art Guild, 1961; 1st prize, collage, 1963; award for wood collage, 1967; 1st prize for wood collage Guild Hall, Easthampton, 1970; Nat. Endowment for Arts grantee, 1979; Am. Acad. Arts and Letters grantee, 1974. Mem. Am. Abstract Artists, Fedn. Modern Painters and Sculptors, Guild Hall. Home: Springs N.Y. Died May 31, 1988; buried Green River Cemetery, East Hampton, N.Y.

FINGESTEN, PETER, sculptor, educator; b. Berlin, Germany, Mar. 20, 1916; came to U.S., 1939; naturalized, 1943.; s. Michel and Bianca (Schiek) F.; married; 1 dau., Alexandra. BFA, Fine Arts Coll., Berlin, 1934; MFA, Fine Arts Coll., 1935; student, Pa. Acad. Fine Arts, 1940-43. Mem. faculty Coll. Liberal Arts, Manhattan Coll., N.Y.C., 1946-50; assoc. in arts Pace Coll., N.Y.C., 1950, assoc. prof., chmn. art dept., prof.; lectr. Asia Inst., summer 1950; vis. prof. Grad. Sch. Music Edn., N.Y. U. Held one man shows in Berlin, Milan, Paris, Phila., Woodstock, N.Y.C., 1935-87; represented in permanent collections Galerie Denise René, Paris, Gallery Bolaffio, Milan; author: Dr. F. Paronelli, Catalogo Delle 0pere Di Peter Fingesten (monograph), 1938, Ex Libris by Michel Fingesten (illustrated monograph), 1954, East is East, 1956, The Eclipse of Symbolism, 1970; contbr. articles to art jours. Served overseas with C.E., Tech. Intelligence, AUS, 1943-45. Recipient first prize Woodmere Art Gallery, Phila., 1942; Internat. Exhbn., Black and White, Milan, 1937; Louis Comfort Tiffany Found. grant for sculpture, 1948; Commn.. for Art of Democratic Living and Am. Fedn. of Art Nat. Traveling Exhbn., 1951. Mem. Coll. Art Assn., AAUP, Am. Soc. for Aesthetics., Soc. of Friends. Home: New York N.Y. Died Sept. 9, 1987.

FINLINSON, BURNS LYMAN, college president; b. Oak City, Utah, Nov. 24, 1904; s. Joseph Trimble and Edith Elzina (Lyman) F.; m. Lydia Jennings, Sept. 1, 1937; children: Edith Zoe, David Burns, Harriett Ann. BS, Brigham Young U., 1927, MS, 1929; postgrad., U. Calif., Berkeley, 1933-34, 42-43, Columbia U., 1937-38. Instr. social scis. Delta (Utah) High Sch., 1927-28; instr. Latter Day Saints Sem., Kanab, Utah, 1929-33; instr. history Br. Agrl. Coll., Cedar City, Utah, 1934-46, dept. chmn., 1944-46, dean of men, 1945-46; dir. Vets.' Guidance Ctr. Bakersfield (Calif.) Coll., 1946-49, dean admissions and records, 1949-56, dean ednl. services, 1956-58, v.p., 1958-68, pres., 1968-72, pres. emeritus, 1972-84. Councilman Cedar City, 1944-46. Mem. Kern County (Calif.) Mus. Assn. (pres. 1960-61), Phi Delta Kappa. Home: Bakersfield Calif. Died July 8, 1984.

FINNEGAN, MARCUS BARTLETT, lawyer; b. Morristown, N.J., Sept. 15, 1927; s. George Bernard and Elisabeth (Morgan) F.; m. Betsy Neil Hammer, June 3, 1950; children: Nancy Lee, Susan Bartlett, Katharine Elisabeth. BS, U.S. Mil. Acad., 1949; JD, U. Va., 1955; LLM, George Washington U., 1957. Bar: Va. 1955, D.C. 1955, N.Y. 1960, U.S. Supreme Ct. 1960. U.S. Patent adviser to Japan Tokyo, 1957-59; atty. Morgan, Finnegan, Durham & Pine, N.Y.C., 1959-63, Irons, Birch, Swindler & McKie, Washington, 1963-65; ptnr. Finnegan, Henderson, Farabow & Garrett, Washington, 1965-79; professorial lectr. law George Washington U., 1971-79; lectr. in field; cons. UN Indsl. Devel. Orgn., Vienna, Austria, 1971-79, on antitrust and licensing to UN, 1972-79; cons. and adviser on licensing and tech. transfer to Govt. Mexico, 1973-79; cons. UN Conf. Trade and Devel., Geneva, 1974-79; del. U.S. Dept State, 1974-75; cons. U.S.-USSR Joint Working Group on Intellectual Property, 1974-79; advisor White House Council Internat. Econ. Policy, 1975-77; mem. panel six experts to study patent policy ERDA, 1975-76; del. numerous internat. confs. Author: (with Richard W. Pogue) Federal Employee Invention Rights--Time to Legislate, 1957; co-author: Patent-Antitrust: Compliance and Confrontation, 1972; editor and author: The Law and Business of Patent and Know-How Licensing, 3d edit., 1975; co-editor and author: The Law and Business of Licensing, 1975; editorial adv. bd. Patent Trademark and Copyright Jour., 1972-79; contbg. editor Les Nouvelles Internat. Licensing Jour., 1972-79; contbr. articles to profl. jours. Capt. AUS, 1949-59. Hon. fellow Harry S. Truman Library; mem. Raven Soc., U.S. C. of C. (patent system adv. panel, antitrust and trade regulations com.), Am. (chmn. patent law com., adminstrv. law sect. 1974), Fed., D.C., Va., Inter-Am., Internat. bar assns., Am. Patent Law Assn. (bd. mgrs. 1974-79), Inst. Mil. Law, Internat. Legal Soc. Japan, D.C.-Va. State Bar, Am. Judicature Soc., Assn. Grads. U.S. Mil. Acad., N.Y., N.J. Patent Law assns., Licensing Execs. Soc. U.S.A. (trustee, v.p., pres.), Licensing Execs. Soc. Internat. (pres., Internat. Gold medal 1977), Am. Mgmt. Assn., Patent and Trademark Inst. Can., Internat. Platform Assn., Internat. Patent and Trademark Assn., Inter-Am. Assn. Indsl. Property, World Peace Through Law Ctr., World Assn. Lawyers, Am. Soc. Internat Law, Internat. Common Law Exchange Soc., Internat. Studies Assn., Supreme Ct. Hist. Soc., World Assn. Law Profs., Assn. Trial Lawyers Am., Md. Golf Assn., UN Assn. U.S.A., Corcoran Gallery Art, Nat. Assocs. Smithsonian, Alumni Assn. St. John's Coll., George Washigton U. Law Assn., Soc. Am. Law Tchrs., Fedn. Internationale des Conseils en Propriete Industrielle, Ligue Internat. Contre La Concurrence Deloyale, Army Athletic Assn., Assn. Bar City N.Y., N.Y. County Lawyer's Assn., West Point Soc. D.C., Am. Soc. for Metals, U. Va. Law Sch. Found., West Point Alumni Found., Congressional Country Club, Kenwood Country Club, Cosmos Club, Metropolitan Club, Touchdown, Army and Navy, Nat. Lawyers, Patents Lawyers, George Washington University, Internat. Club, Tokyo Am. Club, Washington Golf and Country Club, Army and Navy Country Club, Tamboo Club, Tabusintac Club, Mt. Kenya Safari Club, Marco Polo Club, Clermont Club of London, Order of Coif, Phi Delta Phi, Omicron Delta Kappa. Home: Bethesda Md. Died Apr. 15, 1979; buried West Point, N.Y.

FINNEGAN, RICHARD ALLEN, chemist, educator; b. Mpls., Feb. 5, 1932; s. James Clair and Grace Margaret (Mullin) F.; m. Marchand M. Hall, Aug. 4, 1956(div. Feb. 1970); children: Catherine Marie, Sarah Grace, Elizabeth Hope; m. 2d, Adria M. Rossman Campbell, Feb. 3, 1974 (div. June 1980). BA, U. Minn., 1953; PhD, MIT, 1957. Postdoctoral fellow U. Chgo., 1957-58, Wayne State U., Detroit, 1958-59; asst. prof. chemistry Ohio State U., 1959-63; assoc. prof. medicinal chemistry SUNY, Buffalo, 1963-66, prof., 1966-86. Contbr. articles to profl. jours. Del. Nat. Conv. Socialist Party U.S.A., 1966. Rsch. grantee The Rsch. Corp., Petroleum Rsch. Fund, NIH, NSF. Fellow Am. Inst. Chemists; mem. Am. Chem. Soc., Chem. Soc. (London), AAAS, Organic Chemists Club Western N.Y. (chmn. 1964-65), Am. Pharm. Assn., Acad. Pharm. Scis, N.Y. Acad. Scis., AAUP, Am. Soc. Pharmacognosy, Bison City Yacht Club, Sigma Xi, Phi Lambda Upsilon, Alpha Chi Sigma. Home: Buffalo N.Y. Died Mar. 8, 1986; cremated.

FINUCANE, BERNARD EMMET, banker; b. Rochester, N.Y., June 16, 1889; s. Thomas W. and Mary (Downing) F.; m. Freda Zimmer, Jan. 29, 1913; children: Frederick T., Mrs. Charles J. Symington Jr. Student, Phillips Acad., Andover, Mass.; LLD (hon.), Niagara U. Began as founder, operator elec. distbg. fir; chmn. bd., dir. Thomas W. Finucane Corp.; dir. Security Trust Co., Rochester, from 1930, pres., 1940-60, chmn. bd., from 1960, then hon. chmn.; chmn. bd. Security N.Y. State Corp., then hon. chmn.; dir. Rochester Telephone Corp., Sybron Corp., Bausch & Lomb Optical Co., Gen. Dynamics Corp., Assn. Dry Goods Corp. Trustee U. Rochester, chmn. fin. com., then emeritus. Decorated Knight of Malta; recipient Silver Antelope award Boy Scouts Am., civic achievement award Rotary. Mem. N.Y. State Bankers Assn. (pres.). Home: Rochester N.Y. Deceased.

FIRTH, RODERICK, emeritus philosophy educator; b. Orange, N.J., Jan. 30, 1917; s. Leo Earl and Ida (Lake) F.; m. Maria Lee Goodwin, June 10, 1943; 1 son, Roderick. B.S., Haverford Coll., 1938; M.A., Harvard, 1940, Ph.D., 1943. Instr. philosophy and psychology Coll. William and Mary, 1943-45; instr. to assoc. prof. philosophy Swarthmore Coll., 1945-53; assoc. prof. philosophy Harvard U., 1953-58, prof., 1958-87; prof. emeritus Harvard, 1987; Alford prof. Harvard U., 1962-87, chmn. dept., 1957-63; lectr. Summer Inst. Epistemology, 1972, 75; Cowling prof. Carleton Coll., 1974; Disting. Philosopher lectr. U. Ariz., 1978. Guggenheim fellow, 1952- 53; fellow Am. Council Learned Socs., 1959-60; fellow Center for Advanced Studies Behavioral Scis., 1964-65, 67-68. Mem. Am. Philos. Assn. (pres. Eastern div. 1980), Am. Acad. Arts and Scis., Council for Philos. Studies, Phi Beta Kappa, Soc. of Friends. Home: Lexington Mass. Died Dec. 22, 1987.

FISCHBACH, ALLEN DANIEL, business executive; b. N.Y.C., July 26, 1917; s. Henry and Beatrice (Adelman) F.; m. Patricia Cute (div.); 5 children; m. Sheila Gilmore (div.); 1 child. Student, Rensselaer Polytechnic Inst. With Fischbach Corp., N.Y.C., 1939-87; vice chmn., chief exec. officer Fischbach Corp., 1966-82, cons., 1982. Trustee Manhattan Coll. Served with USAAF, 1942-45. Decorated Air Medal. Club: Banyon Golf (West Palm Beach, Fla.). Died July 23, 1987.

FISCHER, CHESTER OWEN, insurance executive; b. St. Louis, July 25, 1891; s. Charles Owen and Emmeline (Raub) F.; m. Catherine Faber, Oct. 15, 1915 (died Dec. 1918); children: Catherine Meyers (Mrs. George Mason Parker), Elizabeth Faber (Mrs. Ernest Alfred Johnson Jr.); m. Grace Lucile Nelson, Apr. 14, 1923; children: Virginia (Mrs. Gordon N. Farquhar), Chester, Louis. LLB, U. Ill., 1912. Bar: Ill. 1912. Practice law Peoria, Ill., 1912-14; with Mass. Mut. Life Ins. Co., Springfield, Mass., from 1914, gen. agt. Peoria agy., 1914-26, gen. agt. St. Louis, 1926-36, v.p., 1936-56, also bd. dirs., mem. exec. com., from 1954; bd. dirs. Northeastern Life Ins. Co. of N.Y., N.Y.V., Baker Extract Co., Springfield, Mo. Rolling Mill Corp., St. Louis; mem. sr. adv. coun. McCormick & Co. Inc., Balt.; corporator Hampden Savs. Bank, Springfield. Mem. U. Ill. Found.; trustee Wesson Meml. Hosp.; chmn bd. trustees Springfield (Mass.) Coll.; trustee Springfield United Fund. Mem. Ill. Assn. Life Underwriters (1st pres.), Mo. Assn. Life Underwriters (1st pres.), Life Ins. Agy. Mgmt. Assn. (chmn. exec. com. 1944-45), Am. Coll. Life Underwriters (trustee, mem. exec. budget and investment coms.), Nat. Assn. Life Underwriters (v.p. 1925-27, trustee 1934-36), Assn. Life Agy. Officers (chmn. com. agy. practices), Springfield C. of C. (past pres.), Jr. C. of C. (hon.), U.S. C. of C. (dir. 1941-47, past chmn. annual meeting, nominating and ins. dept. coms., past mem. exec. com.), Newcomen Soc. Eng., Colony Club, University Club, Longmeadow Country Club, Masons, Kappa Sigma, Sigma Delta Chi, Phi Delta Phi. Congregationalist. Home: Weekapaug R.I. †

FISH, MARIE POLAND (MRS. CHARLES JOHN FISH), oceanographer; b. Paterson, N.J., May 22, 1900; d. Addison Brown and Mary (Dennis) F.; m. Charles John Fish, Feb. 10, 1923; 1 dau., Marilyn (Mrs. J. Barnes Munro Jr.). BA cum laude, Smith Coll., 1921; ScD, U. R.I., 1966. Hydrobiologist U.S. Bur. Fisheries, 1922-27; curator ichthyology Buffalo Mus. Sci., 1928-31; ichthyologist Arcturus Oceanographic Expdn., 1925, Pacific Oceanic biology project, Woods Hole Oceanographic Instn., 1946-50; rsch. assoc. Internat. Passamaquoddy Investigations, 1931-33, U.S. Nat. Mus., 1944-46, Narragansett Marine Lab., U. R.I., Kingston, 1937-39; biol. oceanographer charge Office Naval Rsch. Project Underwater Sound Biol. Origin, 1948-89, instr., 1942-43; ichthyoloist State of R.I., 1942-43; rsch. oceanographer U. R.I.; chmn. Kingfish com. USN, 1954-64; dir. USN Reference Libr. Underwater Sounds, 1954-70, USN Simultaneous Data Sta. Program, 1963-67, R/V TRIDENT Bioacoustics Program, 1962-66; rep. various cons. USN; cons. USN Atlantic Fleet Tng. Ctr., Newport, R.I., 1960, Submarine Forces Pacific Fleet, Hawaii and Calif., 1960. Author: Sonic Fishes of the Pacific, 1948, Marine Mammals of the Pacific with Particular Reference to the Production of Underwater Sound, 1949, Sounds of Western North Atlantic Fishes, 1970; also films and taped recordings of marine animal sound prodn., articles. Mem. Kingston Improvement Assn., instr. first aid ARC, Narragansett, 1942-46, chmn. Servicemen's Ctr., 1943-44; pres. Am. Youth Hostel, Wyoming, R.I., 1942-48, bd. dirs. R.I., 1939-48; pres. Kingston Players, 1936-38. Recipient Women's Centennial Congress award, 1940, Stamford Mus. Disting. Sci. award, 1863, Sophia Smith Disting. Alumna award Smith Coll., 1964, Disting. Pub. Svc. award USN, 1965. Mem. Am. Inst. Biol. Scis., AAAS, Am. Soc. Ichthyologists and Herpetologists, Soc. Woman Geographers, N.Y. Zool. Soc. (rsch. assoc.), Jr. League Providence, League Women Voters, Cocumscussoc, Pettaquamscutt hist. assns., South County Art Assn., Smith Coll. Alumnae Assn., Nat. Fedn. Bus. and Profl. Women's Club (Woman of Yr. award 1966-67), Am. Soc. Limnology and Oceanography, Triangle Club (Kingston, R.I.), South County Art Club (South Kingston, R.I.), Dunes Club (Narranganset, R.I.), Phi Beta Kappa, Sigma Xi, Phi Sigma. Republican. Presbyterian. Home: Kingston R.I. Died Feb. 1, 1989; buried Oak Grove Cemetery, Fall River, Mass.

FISHER, BENJAMIN COLEMAN, minister, religion executive, educator; b. Webster, N.C., May 27, 1915; s. Ben Franklin and Amy (Long) F.; m. Sara Gehman, Dec. 27, 1940; children: David Lincoln, Hugh Robert. AB, Wake Forest Coll., 1938, DD, 1971; MDiv, Andover Newton Theol. Sch., 1942; postgrad., U. N.C., 1946; LLD, Campbell Coll., 1968; DLitt, Mercer U., 1980, Grand Canyon Coll., 1980; DD, Stetson U., 1984. Ordained to ministry Bapt. Ch., 1938. Pastor Castalia-Peachtree Bapt. Ch., 1938-39; pastor First Bapt. Ch., Nashville, N.C., 1942-45, Newton, N.C., 1945-47; tchr. Gardner-Webb Coll., 1947-48, asst. to pres., dir. pub. rels., 1948-52; assoc. sec. Edn. Commn. So. Bapt. Conv., 1952-54, exec. sec., treas. edn. com., 1970, exec. dir., 1970-78; asst. to pres. Southeastern Sem., 1954-62; exec. sec. N.C. Edn. Com., 1962-70; adj. prof. religion Campbell U., 1978-85; chmn. bd. dirs. Bibl. Recorder, 1960-63. Author: A Public Relations Manual for Church-Related Colleges, 1954, An Orientation Manual for Trustees of Church Related Colleges, 4th edit., 1980; editor: New Pathways: A Dialogue in Christian Higher Education, 1980, The Idea of a Christian University in Today's World, 1989, Laughter Among the Trumpets: Mountain Preacher Stories, 1989. Advisor Chowan Coll. Mem. Am. Assn. Pres. of Ind. Colls. and Univs. (exec. sec.-treas. 1981). Home: Murfreesboro N.C. Died Nov. 3, 1985; buried Southeastern Bapt. Theol. Sem. Cemetery, Wake Forest, N.C.

FISHER, BENJAMIN REEVES, manufacturing company executive; b. Pitts., Apr. 5, 1916; s. Chester G. and Margaret (Aiken) F.; m. Lilian C. Hall, Apr. 10, 1939; children: Margaret Aiken Fisher McKean, Coburn Hall (dec.), Benjamin Reeves Jr., Christine Chase Fisher Allen. B.S., Yale U., 1938. With Fisher Sci. Co., Pitts., 1938-81, pres., chief exec. officer, 1965-75; chmn. bd. Fisher Sci. Co., Pitts, 1975-81. Trustee Children's Hosp. Pitts.; trustee Carnegie Hero Fund Commn., Pitts. Mem. Sci. Apparatus Makers Am. (bd. dirs. 1957-64), Am. Chem. Soc., Sigma Xi (assoc.). Home: Pittsburgh Pa. Died Mar. 26, 1987; buried Homewood Cemetery, Pitts.

FISHER, DAVID KIRKPATRICK ESTE, architect; b. Balt., Feb. 2, 1892; s. D.K. Esté and Sally Jones Milligan (McLane) F.; m. Jean Bellingham (Small), Feb. 18, 1933 (dec. July 1969); stepsons: Samuel Small (dec.), George Latimer Small. LittB, Princeton U., 1913; BS in Architecture, MIT, 1916. Archtl. draftsman N.Y., 1916-17, Balt., 1919-24; ptnr. Parker, Thomas & Rice, Balt., 1924-27, Taylor & Fisher, successors, Balt., 1927-73, Taylor, Fisher, Bowersock & Martin, Inc., Balt., from 1973. Served as 1st lt., 6th F.A., 1st div., A.E.F., later instr. Saumur F.A. Sch., 1917-19, and capt. F.A. Res., 1919-29. Fellow AIA (pres. chpt. 1937-38); mem. Am. Mus. Natural History (life), Balt. Mus. Art (life), Soc. of Cin. in N.J. (life), Maryland Club, Elkridge Club, Gibson Island Club. Democrat. Episcopalian (chmn. diocesan dept. religious art 1960-65). Home: Baltimore Md. Deceased.

FISHER, GORDON N(EIL), publisher; b. Montreal, Que., Can., Dec. 9, 1928; s. Philip Sydney and Margaret Linton (Southam) F.; student Lower Can. Coll., Montreal, Trinity Coll. Sch., Port Hope, Ont.; B.Eng. in Mech. Engring., McGill U., Montreal, 1950; m. Alison Nora Arbuckle, June 17, 1955; children—Derek Arbuckle, Philip Neil, Duncan Southam. With Southam Co. Ltd. (name changed to Southam Inc. 1978), Toronto, Ont., Can., 1958-85, mng. dir. head office, 1969-75, pres., 1975-85; dir. Southam Communications, Ltd., Southam Printing Ltd., Kitchener-Waterloo Record, Selkirk Communications Ltd., Pacific Press Ltd., TV Guide Inc., Coles Book Stores Ltd. Mem. bd. trustees Toronto Gen. Hosp. Mem. Can. Daily Newspaper Pubs. Assn., Can. Press, Am. Newspaper Pubs. Assn., Newspaper Advt. Bur. (dir.), Kappa Alpha. Clubs: Mt. Royal (Montreal); Toronto, York, Royal Can. Yacht. Badminton & Racquet. Died Aug. 8, 1985.

FISHER, PETER ROWE, lawyer; b. N.Y.C., May 24, 1933; s. Frank Cyril and Julia Anne (Potter) F.; m. Cary Randolph Fox, June 28, 1957; children: Diane R., Julian P., Elizabeth C. AB cum laude, Harvard U., 1954; LLB, U. Va., 1960. Bar: N.Y. 1960. Assoc. atty. Sullivan & Cromwell, N.Y.C., 1960-66; assoc. atty. Rogers & Wells, N.Y.C., 1967-69, ptnr., from 1969; adj. prof. law N.Y. Law Sch., N.Y.C., from 1980; village justice Village of Oyster Bay Cove, N.Y., from 1981. Mem. Town of Oyster Bay Landmarks Commn., 1978; trustee, v.p., treas. Theodore Roosevelt Assn., Oyster Bay, from 1975; trustee Oyster Bay Hist. Soc., from 1973,pres. 1977-81, treas. 1981-83, chmn. from 1983; trustee Soc. for Preservation o f L.I. Antiquities, Setauket, N.Y., 1977. Mem. ABA, Seawanhaka Corinthian Yacht Club (trustee), Harvard Club (N.Y.C.). Republican. Episcopalian. Home: Oyster Bay N.Y. Died June 20, 1985; buried St. John's Meml. Cemetary, Laurel Hollow, N.Y.

FISHER, SYDNEY NETTLETON, history educator; b. Warsaw, N.Y., Aug. 8, 1906; s. Addison Washburn and Pearl Ellen (Nettleton) F.; m. Elizabeth Evelyn Scipio, Sept. 3, 1938; children—Alan Washburn, Robert Lynn, Margaret Ellen Fisher McCarthy. A.B., Oberlin Coll., 1928, M.A., 1932; Ph.D., U. Ill., 1935; postdoctoral work, Princeton, 1935, U. Brussels, 1938. Tutor math. Robert Coll., Istanbul, Turkey, 1928-31; tutor English Robert Coll., 1936-37; instr. history Denison U., 1935-36; instr. history Ohio State U., 1937-42, asst. prof., 1942-47, assoc. prof., 1947-54, prof., 1954-72, prof. emeritus, 1972-87; coordinator (Grad. Inst. World Affairs), 1961-65; asso. chief econ. analysis Bd. Econ. Warfare, 1943, Fgn. Econ. Adminstrn., 1943-44; country specialist comml. policy div. Dept. State, 1944-46; lectr. Chautauqua Inst., 1940-42; vis. prof. Stetson U., 1949, U. So. Calif., 1954, 61; Dir. publs. Middle East Inst., 1952-53. Author: The Foreign Relations of Turkey, 1481-1512, 1948, Evolution in the Middle East: Revolt, Reform and Change, 1953, Social Forces in the Middle East, 1955, 68, 77, The Middle East: A History, 1959, 69, rev. edition, 1979, The Military in the Middle East, 1962, France and European Community, 1965; New Horizons for the United States in World Affairs, 1966; Editor: Middle East Jour, 1952-53. Grantee Am. Council Learned Soc., 1935, 38; Grantee Social Sci. Research Council, 1958-59. Fellow Royal Hist. Soc. (London), Ordinario, Accademia del Mediterraneo (Rome, Italy); mem. Middle East Studies Assn., Ohio Acad. History, Phi Beta Kappa, Phi Alpha Theta, Phi Kappa Phi. Presbyn. Home: Worthington Ohio Died Dec. 10, 1987.

FISHER, WILLIAM ROY, JR., investment banking executive; b. Wilson, Va., June 7, 1936; s. William Roy and Virginia Elizabeth (Lewis) F.; m. Lyle Marie Rea, Oct. 6, 1962; children: William, Richard, Carol. BSEE, Va. Poly. Inst., 1957; MBA, U. Va., 1968. Project engr. Sperry Rand Corp., Chralottesville, Va., 1957-66; security analyst Donaldson, Lufkin & Jenrette, N.Y.C., 1968-70, v.p., 1970-78, sr. v.p., 1978-81, exec. v.p., 1981-83. Trustee Cen. Presbyn. Ch., Summit, N.J., 1983. Samuel Forest Hyde scholar U. Pa., 1968. Mem. India House Club (N.Y.C.), Noe Pond Club (Chatham, N.J., Summit Tennis Club. Home: Summit N.J. Died Nov. 12, 1983; buried Fairmount Cemetery, Chatham, N.J.

FISHMAN, MEYER H., business executive; b. Russia, 1892; married. With M.H. Fishman Co., Inc., N.Y.C., from 1917, chmn. bd. Mem. Masons, Shriners. Home: New York N.Y. †

FITTS, OSMER C., lawyer; b. Brattleboro, Vt., Oct. 21, 1905; s. Clarke Cushing and Maud (Emerson) F.; m. Dorothy D. Moore, June 28, 1930. BS, Dartmouth Coll., 1926; JD, Harvard U., 1929; JD (hon.), Suffolk U., 1960. Bar: Vt., Mass. 1930. Ptnr. Sargent, Chase & Fitts, Ludlow, Vt., 1930-39; pvt. practice Brattleboro, Vt., 1939-54; ptnr. Fitts & Olson, Brattleboro, Vt., 1954-75, of counsel, 1975-85; reporter of decisions Supreme Ct. Vt., 1940-42; bd. dirs., chmn. exec. com. Vt. Nat. Bank; chmmn. Vt. Library Bd., 1970-85; exec. com. New Eng. Law Inst., 1955-73. Bd. govs. Springfield Shriners Hosp. Crippled Children, 1963-73; chmn. Vt. State Bd. Libraries. Lt. col. AUS, 1942-46. Mem. Am. (gov. 1954-57, chmn. ho. of dels. 1960-62), Vt. (pres. 1949) bar assns., Am. Coll. Trial Lawyers (regent 1954), Am. Coll. Probate Counsel (regent 1963-71), Assn. Ins. Attys. (pres. 1973), Judge Advs. Assn. (dir. 1943-44, 47-85, pres. 1970-71). Congregationalist. Home: Brattleboro Vt. Died July 8, 1985; interred Brattleboro, Vt.

FITZER, JOSEPH B., banker; b. Chgo., 1906. Sr. v.p., cashier Continental Ill. Bank & Trust Co., Chgo., 1925-71; v.p., dir. Continental Ill. Safe deposit Co., Chgo., 1960-71; dir. Continental Internat. Fin. Corp., Continental Bank Internat. Chmn. bd. trustees, Nazareth Hosp., Chgo. Mem. South Shore Country Club (Chgo.) (pres.). Home: Chicago Ill. Died Jan. 25, 1986.

FITZGERALD, CLIFFORD LLEWELYN, advertising agency executive; b. St. Louis, Oct. 10, 1903; m. Isabel Hanway, Dec. 31, 1924; children—Shirley Hanway Gately, Joan Hughes Schaffer, Clifford Llewelyn. Grad., The Principia, St. Louis, 1923; student, Dartmouth Coll., 1923-24. Advt. writer 1924; founder chmn. Dancer Fitzgerald Sample, Inc., N.Y.C., 1961-87; dir. Advt. Council Inc. N.Y. Exec. v.p. Fitzgerald Found. Mem. U.S. Sr. Golf Assn., Alpha Delta Phi. Clubs: Round Hill (Greenwich, Conn.); Clove Valley Rod and Gun (Legrangeville, N.Y.); Anglers (N.Y.C.); Dragon (Dartmouth). Home: Thomasville Ga. Died Apr. 9, 1987.

FITZGERALD, EDMUND, insurance company executive; b. Milw., Mar. 1, 1895; s. William Edmund and Jessie Lennox (Blackburn) F.; m. Elizabeth Bacon, Oct. 26, 1921; children: Elizabeth Fitzgerald Cutler, Edmund Bacon. PhB, Yale U., 1916; LLD (hon.), Marquette U., 1953, U. Wis., Madison, 1960. Sec. Northwestern Malleable Iron Co., Milw., 1920-27, Combined Locks Paper Co., Appleton, Wis., 1928; v.p. Second Wis. Nat. Bank, Milw., 1928-30, Nat. Bank of Commerce, Milw., 1930-31, First Wis. Nat. Bank, Milw., 1932-33; v.p. Northwestern Mutual Life Ins. Co., Milw., 1933-47, pres., 1947-58, chmn., 1958-60, trustee, 1943-69; former bd. dirs. Cutler Hammer Inc., Wis. Telephone Co., Will Ross Inc., Nat. Indsl. Conf. Bd., Gartland Steamship Co., Manpower, Inc., Green Bay Packaging, Inc. Bd. trustees Com. Econ. Devel; mem. Nat. Adv. Health Council, Mayo Found.,; trustee Milw. Downer Coll.; bd. dirs. Cutler-Hammer Found., 1951-76, The Johnson Found., Inc., Racine, Wis.; founder Wis. Marine Hist. Soc.; elder, trustee Immanuel Presbyn. Ch. Capt. U.S. Army. Recipient certificate for distinctive civic service Marquette U., 1932, Centennial Celebration award Northwestern, 1951. Mem. Milw. Club, University, Milw. Country Club, Colony Club, Berzelius Soc., Phi Beta Kappa. Republican. Home: Milwaukee Wis. Died Jan. 9, 1986, buried Forest Home Cemetery.

FITZGERALD, FRANCIS JOHN, chemical company executive; b. Springfield, Ill, Oct. 25, 1927; s. Francis John and Mayme (MacGrangh) F.; m. Patricia Ann Sullivan, June 10, 1950; children: Micky, John, Terry, Tim, Moira, Kerry, Megan. B.S., U. Notre Dame, 1950. Sales rep. Gerity Mich. Corp., Adrian, 1950-51; with Monsanto Co., 1951-86; group v.p., mng. dir. Monsanto Europe-Africa, Brussels, 1978-86; exec v.p., mng. dir. internat. Monsanto, St. Louis, 1981-86. Bd. dirs. Jr. Achievement, 1975-79; active Boy Scouts Am. Mem. Soap and Detergent Assn. (bd. dirs. 1972-75). Roman Catholic. Club: Bellerive Country. Home: Pleasant Plains Ill. Died Apr. 26, 1986.

FITZGERALD, JAMES AUGUSTINE, educator; b. Harpers Ferry, Iowa, Dec. 26, 1892; s. Maurice A. and Helena Gertrude (Farrell) F.; m. Patricia Geoghegan, June 12, 1935. AB, U. S.D., 1915, AM, 1924; PhD, U. Ia., 1931. Sch. prin. Erwin, S.D., 1915-17; salesman automobiles and ins. 1919-21; prin. Dell Rapids (S.D.) High Sch., 1921-24; supt. schs. Custer, S.D., 1924-25; assoc. prof. edn. So. State Tchrs. Coll., Springfield, S.D., 1925-28, 29-30; rsch. asst. and grad. student U. Ia., 1928-29, 1930-31; asst. prof., assoc. prof., asst. dean Loyola U., Chgo., 1931-39; prof. edn., chmn. div. elem. edn. Fordham U., N.Y.C., 1939-58; prof. edn. U. Scranton, from 1958. Author books including: The Teaching of Spelling, 1951, A Basic Life Spelling Vocabulary, 1951; (with Patricia G. Fitzgerald) Methods and Curricula in Elementary Education, 1955, Learning Words, 1956. 1st lt., F.A., U.S. Army, 1917-19; capt. Res., 1921-35. Mem. Am. Assn. Sch. Adminstrs., Am. Edn. Rsch. Assn., AAUP, NEA, Nat. Soc. Study Edn., Nat. Coun. Tchrs. English, Nat. Conf. Rsch. English, Assn. Supervision and Curriculum Study, Nat. Elem. Prins., Soc. Advancement Edn., Am. Legion, K.C., Phi Delta Kappa. Home: Scranton Pa. †

FITZGERALD, NUGENT EDMUND, college dean; b. Gerald, Mo., Apr. 18, 1891; s. William P. and Lizzie Emily (Henneke) F.; m. Julia Richardson, Oct. 10, 1918. B in Pedagogy, State Tchrs. Coll., Cape Girardeau, Mo., 1912; BS in Edn., U. Mo., 1915; BS in Agr., 1917; MS in Rural Edn., Cornell U., 1926; student, Columbia U., summer 1930, Ohio State U., summers 1931-38. Tchr. rural sch. 1909-10; tchr. history and English High School, Potosi, also prin.; instr. agr. State Tchr.'s Coll., Springfield, Mo., summers 1915, 17; instr. agr. for tchrs. U. Tex., 1915-18; assoc. prof. agrl. edn. Tex. A&M Coll., 1918-19; prof., head dept. agrl. edn. U. Tenn., 1919-43, dean Coll. Edn., 1943-61, retired. Co-author: Farm Practice Accounts, 1931; editor agrl. edn. sect., Vocational Edn. Mag., 1923-25, Am. Vocat. Assn. Jour., 1938-42. Mem. Tenn. adv. commn. on Conservation; chmn. com. on aims and objectives Tenn. State Ednl. Commn., 1933-35. 2d lt. F.A., U.S. Army, World War I. Recipient disting. service citations So. Regional Conf. Agrl. Edn., Future Farmers Am., Distributive Edn. Clubs of Am.. Mem. Soc. Advancement Edn., NEA, Am. Vocat. Assn., Am. Assn. Sch. Adminstrs., Masons, Acacia, Phi Kappa Phi, Phi Delta Kappa, Alpha Tau Alpha. Home: Knoxville Tenn. †

FITZ-GIBBON, BERNICE (MRS. HERMAN BLOCK), advertising executive; b. Waunakee, Wis.; s. William and Nora (Bowles) F.-G.; m. Herman Block, July 6, 1925; children: Peter, Elizabeth Bowles. BA, U. Wis., 1918. Tchr. English Chippewa Falls, Wis., 1918-19; mem. staff Rockford (Ill.) Register-Gazette, 1920; with Marshall Field & Co., Chgo., 1921, R.H. Macy, N.Y.C., 1923-35; advt. dir. Wanamaker's, 1936-40, Gimbel Bros., 1940-54; pres. Bernice Fitz-Gibbon, Inc., from 1954. Named Woman of Yr. in bus. AP Editors, 1955; named one of Top 7 Bus. Women Fortune mag., 1956. †

FITZGIBBONS, DAVID JOHN, drug company executive; b. Paterson, N.J., Jan. 18, 1906; s. David John and Elizabeth (Hynes) F.; m. Eleanor Corry Kelly, Feb. 22, 1941; children—Robert Anton, David James. Grad., Drake Bus. Coll., Paterson, 1925, Pace Inst., 1928. Office mgr., sec. Standard Plumbing & Heating, Inc., 1928-35; with Price, Waterhouse & Co. (C.P.A.'s), 1935-37; chief accountant Am. Ferment Co., 1937-39; v.p., treas. Sterling Products Internat., Inc., 1939-88, Sydney Ross Co., 1939-88, Winthrop Products, Inc., 1949-88; v.p. Sterling Drug, Inc., 1960-61, exec. v.p., 1961-63, pres., 1963-74, chmn. fin. com., 1974-88, also mem. exec. com., dir. Former bd. dirs. Nat. Fgn. Trade Council. Clubs: Essex Country (W. Orange, N.J.); Country of Fla. (Fla.), Delray Beach (Fla.). Home: Delray Beach Fla. Died May 27, 1988; buried Restland Meml. Pk., E. Hanover, N.J.

FITZPATRICK, EDWIN J., investor; b. N.Y.C., Apr. 15, 1910; s. James E. and Anna (Gallagher) F.; m. Betty C. Roney, July 5, 1940; children—Edwin J., Anne Roney. A.B., Cornell U., 1932. Asst. instr. econs. Cornell U., 1932-33; v.p. charge sales Clapp's Baby Foods, Inc., 1933-41; asst. chief food div. W.P.B., 1941-42; pres. Chef Boy-ar-dee Foods, Inc., Milton, Pa., 1946-49; also dir., v.p. Am. Home Foods, Inc., N.Y.C., 1946-49; pres. Permacel Tape Corp., New Brunswick, N.J., 1949-55; gen. partner Orvis Bros. & Co., N.Y.C., 1955-63; pvt. investor from 1963; pres. Roney-Fitzpatrick Found., Craigielea Ednl. Fund Inc.; Cons. bus. and def. service adminstrn. Dept. Commerce, 1954-55. Trustee Muhlenberg Hosp., Plainfield, N.J., Wardlaw Country Day Sch.; pres. Alumni Inter-frat. Council Cornell U. Maj. to col. Q.M.C. U.S. Army, 1942-46. Decorated Legion of Merit, Bronze Star. Mem. Phi Beta Kappa, Chi Phi, Quill and Dagger. Clubs: Genesee Valley (Rochester, N.Y.); Plainfield (N.J.); Country; University (N.Y.C.); Bath (Miami Beach), Indian Creek Country (Miami Beach). Home: Plainfield N.J. Died May 10, 1988; buried Hillside Cemetery, Plainfield, New Jersey.

FITZPATRICK, THOMAS EDWARD, JR., army officer; b. Boston, Nov. 19, 1920; s. Thomas Edward and Helena (Barry) F.; m. Gabrielle Antoinette Herman, Jan. 10, 1948; children: Anne, Kevin, Joan, Kathleen, John, Brian. BS, U.S. Mil. Acad., 1945; MS, U. So. Calif., 1956. Commd. 2d lt. U.S. Army, 1945, advanced through grades to maj. gen., 1972; service in Japan, Korea, Hawaii and Vietna; comdr. U.S. Army Air Def., NATO, 1973-75; dep. comdr.-in-chief Aerospace Def. Command, Colorado Springs, 1975-78, ret., 1978. Decorated Legion of Merit, Air medal, Bronze Star, Vietnam Cross of Gallantry with Palm. Mem. Assn. U.S. Army, Assn. Grads. U.S. Mil. Acad. Roman Catholic. Home: El Paso Tex. Died Oct. 12, 1987.

FJELDE, PAUL, sculptor; b. Mpls., Aug. 12, 1892; s. Jacob H. G. and Margarethe Veronica (Madsen) F.; m. Amy Nordstrom, 1918, 1 son, Rolf Gerhard. Student, Mpls. Sch. of Fine Arts, 1908-10, State Normal Sch., Valley City, N.D., 1912, Studio of Lorado Taft, 1913-16, Beaux Art Inst. of Design, N.Y., 1922-23, Art Students League, N.Y., 1923-24, Royal Acad., Copenhagen, 1924-25, Acad. de la Grande Chaumiere, Paris, 1925-26. Began as sculptor 1912; tchr. sculpture Carnegie Inst. Tech., 1928-29; prof. figure, design and sculpture Pratt Inst., 1929-59, emeritus. Principal works include: Lincoln Monument, Oslo, Norway; Col. Heg. Monument, Lier, Norway and Madison, Wis.; panels Westinghouse Monument, Pitts.; Lindbergh bronze, San Diego; numerous meml. tablets, busts, reliefs and medals; also archtl. sculpture in Eastern cities. Fellow Am. Scandinavian Found., Nat. Sculpture Soc.; mem. Allied Artists Am., Am. Artists Profl. League, Grand Central Art Galleries, Nat. Acad. Design. †

FLAVIN, JOSEPH B., manufacturing company executive; b. St. Louis, Oct. 16, 1928; s. Joseph B. and Mary E. (Toomey) F.; m. Melisande Barillon, 1946; children: Patrick Brian, Shawn Elaine. M.S., Columbia U. Grad. Sch. Bus., 1957; LL.D. (hon.), U. Mass., 1978. Acct. Cawley Aircraft Supply Co., 1953; with IBM World Trade Corp., 1953-67, controller, 1965-67; group v.p. Xerox Corp., 1968-70, exec. v.p., 1970-75, pres. internat. ops., 1972-75; chmn. chief exec. officer The Singer Co., Stamford, Conn., 1975-87, bd. dirs.; mem. Industry Policy Adv. Com. for Trade Policy Matters, Washington; trustee Northwestern Mut. Life Ins. Co., Milw.; dir. Pfizer, Inc.; mem. Bus. Council; dir. N.Y. Stock Exchange. Trustee Com. Econ. Devel., U.S. Council f Internat. Bus., Am. Bus. Found. for Cancer Researc Inc.; bd. dirs. United Way of Tri-State; vice chm Chancellor's Exec. Com. U. Mass./Amherst; mer Emergency Com. for Am. Trade. Served with USMC Recipient Nat. Brotherhood award NCCJ, 1978. mer Bus. Roundtable, Conf. Bd. (mem. corp.). Home: Ne Canaan Conn. Died Oct. 7, 1987; buried New Canaa Ct.

FLEETE, WILLIAM ALFRED, labor official; b. Nile Ohio, Jan. 21, 1892; s. William and Lucy (Jewkes) F m. Bertha Fogel, June 19, 1916; 1 child, Wi liam. Student pub. schs. Yard conductor N.Y. Centr R.R., Cleve., 1916-53; with Switchmen's Union N.A from 1916, local chmn., 1927-37, gen. chmn. N.Y. R.R. Lines West, 1937-52, internat. v.p., 1945-47, i ternat. pres., from 1953. Mem. Ry. Labor Execs. Assn Home: Buffalo N.Y. †

FLEISCHAKER, JOSEPH, retail electric applian executive; b. Louisville, Jan. 9, 1910; s. Siegfried ar Sophie (Lippold) F.; m. Marie Sales, June 14, 1937 (de June 1973); children—Carol R. (Mrs. Alvin G. We terman), Susan (Mrs. Eliot Lee Silbar), Joan (Mr Henry T. Evers III) (dec.); m. Nancy Ashley Smit Feb. 9, 1974. B.S. in Bus. Adminstrn, U. Miami, Fla 1932; extension courses, N.Y. U. Dist. sales mg Orbon Stove Co., Delaware, Ohio; v.p. Leppart Bros Inc., St. Louis. Columnist: Jerusalem Post. Mem. trea com. Jefferson County Republican Campaign Fund; b dirs. Jewish Hosp. Louisville, Hebrew Home for Age Old Peoples Home, St. Louis, Annie Maloney Hom asso. Jewish Hosp.; trustee Children's Hosp., St. Loui Served from lt. (j.g.) to comdr. USNR, 1941-46. Mer Nat. Appliance Radio-TV Dealers (pres. 1958- 59), K Retail Appliance Dealers (pres. 1954-56), Urban Leagu Am. Jewish Com., Jewish Hosp. Assn. (asso.), NCC Am. Legion, Brandeis U. (asso. fellow and life mem. Phi Epsilon Pi, Rho Beta Omicron. Jewish (temple pre 1952-55). Clubs: Kiwanian. (Louisville), Standar Country (Louisville) (v.p., chmn. house com. 1954-58 Deceased.

FLEISCHMANN, WOLFGANG BERNARD, ed cator; b. Vienna, Austria, July 10, 1928; came to U.S 1940, naturalized, 1950; s. Walter and Gertrude (Furt F. B.A., St. John's Coll., 1950; A.M., U. N.C., 195 Ph.D., 1954. Instr. English U. N.C., 1957-59; asst. pro comparative lit. U. Okla., 1959-61; asst. prof., asso. pro Emory U., 1961-63; faculty U. Wis., Milw., 1963-6 prof., chmn. comparative lit. dept. U. Wis., 1964-66; vi prof. Romance langs. Princeton, 1966-67; prof., chm comparative lit. dept. U. Mass., Amherst, 1967-70; pro comparative lit. Montclair State Coll., Upper Montclai N.J., 1970-87; dean Montclair State Coll. (Sc Humanities), 1970-80; vis. prof. comparative lit. N.Y U., 1972, 73-86; also lectr., critic. Mem. bd. visitors an govs. St. John's Coll., Annapolis, Md. and; Santa F 1967-79. Author: Lucretius and English Literatu 1680-1740, 1964; gen. editor: Ency. of World Lit. in th 20th Century, vol. 1, 1967, vol. 2, 1969, vol. 3, 197 mem. editorial bds.: Books Abroad (now World Li Today), 1959-87, James Joyce Quar, 1964-87. Serve with U.S. Army, 1953-55. Inst. Research in Humaniti fellow U. Wis., 1965-66. Mem. MLA (chmn. 1965, 67 Am. Comparative Lit. Assn. (editor Newsletter 196 72). Home: New York N.Y. Died Mar. 8, 1987.

FLEMING, DONALD METHUEN, government o ficial; b. Exeter, Ont., Can., May 23, 1905; s. Lou Charles and Maud Margaret (Wright) F.; m. Alice Mi dred Watson, 1933; children: David, Mar Donald. BA, U. Toronto, 1925, LLB, 1930; DCI Bishop's U., 1960. Bar: Ont. 1928. Pvt. practic Toronto, Ont.; counsel Blake, Cassels and Grayso Toronto; created King's Counsel, 1944; rep. Toront Eglinton constituency to Parliament, 1945-63; mem Privy Council for Can., minister fin., receiver-gen. c Can., 1957-62; min. justice, atty. gen. Can., 1962-6 gov. Internat. Bank and Internat. Monetary Fund, 195 63; chmn. Commonwealth Parliamentary Confs., 194 52, 54; chmn. Commonwealth Trade and Econ. Conf 1958; del. NATO confs., 1957-61; dir. Can. Na Exhbn., 1941. Contbr. articles legal publs. Decorate Red Cross medal (Greece). Mem. Can. Polit. Sci. Assn Can. Bar Assn., Canadian Club, Empire Club, Nat. A bany Club, Rideau Country Club, Masons, Independen Order Foresters. Home: Toronto Ont., Canada. Die Dec. 31, 1986.

FLESCH, RUDOLF, author; b. Vienna, Austria, Ma 8, 1911; came to U.S., 1938, naturalized, 1944; s. Hug and Helene (Basch) F.; m. Elizabeth Terpenning, Sep 6, 1941 (dec. 1975); children: Anne Sutherland Flesc Wares, Hugo Walter, Gillian Ruth, Katrina Woodbur Flesch Portillo, Abigail Allan Flesch Connors, Jane Amalia Flesch Sepasi-Tehrani. Dr.Jur., U. Vienna 1933; Ph.D., Columbia U., 1943. cons. FTC, 1976-82. Author: The Art of Plain Talk, 1946, The Way to Write (with A.H. Lass), 1947, The Art of Readable Writing 1949, rev. edit., 1974, The Art of Clear Thinking, 195 How to Make Sense, 1954, Why Johnny Can't Read 1955, The Book of Unusual Quotations, 1957, A Nev Way to Better English, 1958, How to Write, Speak an Think More Effectively, 1960, How to Be Brief, 1962 The ABC of Style, 1965, The Book of Surprises, 196 The New Book of Unusual Quotations, 1966, Say Wha

You Mean, 1972, Look It Up: A Deskbook of American Spelling and Style, 1977, How to Write Plain English: A Book for Lawyers and Consumers, 1979, Why Johnny Still Can't Read: A New Look at the Scandal of Our Schools, 1981, LITE English: Some Popular Words that Are OK to Use, 1983. Home: Dobbs Ferry N.Y. Died Oct. 5, 1986, buried Ferncliff, Hartsdale, N.Y.

FLETCHER, HARRIS FRANCIS, educator; b. Ypsilanti, Mich., Oct. 23, 1892; s. Azro and Elizabeth (Lambie) F.; m. Dorothy Bacon; children: Mary Elizabeth, Dorothy Priscilla, Charlotte Anne. B Pedagogy, Mich. State Normal Coll., 1912; AB, U. Mich., 1914, AM, 1923, PhD, 1926; LittD, U. Ill., 1961, Olivet Coll., 1962; LHD, Ea. Mich. U., 1962. Tchr. high sch. Wyandotte, Mich., 1912-13; supt. schs. Algonac, Mich., 1914-18; instr. rhetoric U. Mich., 1923-26; asst. prof. English U. Ill., 1926-31, assoc. prof., assoc. dean Coll. Liberal Arts and Scis., 1931-38, prof., from 1938. Author: studies on Milton's works; facsimile and critical text edit. of Milton's Poetical Works, Vol. 1, 1943, Vol. II, 1945, Vols. III, IV, 1948, The Intellectual Development of John Milton, Vol. I, 1956, Vol. II, 1961; contbr. Jour. English and Germanic Philology, Studies in Philology, Modern Lang. Notes, others. Fellow AAAS. Presbyterian. Home: Urbana Ill. †

FLETCHER, ROBERT DAWSON, meteorologist; b. Lampacitos, Mexico, Feb. 11, 1912; s. Edmond McC. and Grace (Dawson) F.; m. Elsie Walser, June 1, 1935; children—Robert Dawson, John E. B.S. in Mech. Engring, Calif. Inst. Tech., 1933, M.S. in M.E. (Aero), 1934, M.S. in Meteorology, 1935; D.Sc. in Meteorology, Mass. Inst. Tech., 1941. Meteorologist Am. Airlines, Inc., 1935-39; instr. meteorology U. Calif. at Los Angeles, 1940-42; meteorologist U.S. Weather Bur., 1940-50, supervising forecaster, 1941-46, chief hydrometeorol. sect., 1946-50; with USAF Air Weather Service, 1950-85, cons., 1950-52, dir. sci. services, 1952-64, dir. aerospace scis., 1964-71, chief scientist, 1971-72; sci. adviser Weather Cons., Inc. 1977-85; Tech. cons. OSRD, 1944, USAAF in, CBI and Caribbean, 1944-45; U.S. del. World Meteorological Orgn. (UN), 1952-85; USAF and NRC del., Manila, 1952, Bangkok, 1957; USAF and NRC del. NASA adv. group aero. research and devel. NATO Conf. Polar Meteorology, Oslo, Norway, 1956, Australian Conf. Tropical Storms, Brisbane, 1956; mem. meteorology panel U.S. Nat. Com. on Internat. Geophys. Year, 1955-64; liaison rep. com. on high altitude rocket and balloon research Nat. Acad. Scis., 1963-85, mem. panel on edn., 1963-85. Contbr. articles to profl. jours. Pres. Bannockburn (Md.) Citizens Assn., 1951-52. Recipient USAF decoration for exceptional civilian service, 1962, 72; Robert M. Losey award Am. Inst. Aeros. and Astronautics, 1969; Charles Franklin Brooks award Am. Meteorol. Soc., 1970. Fellow Am. Meteorol. Soc. (pres. 1956-57, councillor 1972-85); asso. fellow Am. Inst. Aeros. and Astronautics (chmn. tech. com. on atmospheric environment 1964-65); mem. Am. Geophys. Union, Royal Meteorol. Soc., Sigma Xi. Home: Tubac Ariz. Died Oct. 27, 1985; buried Valhalla Meml. Park, North Hollywood, Calif.

FLEUELLING, LEWIS EDWARD, automobile equipment manufacturing company executive; b. St. Thomas, Ont., Can., Aug. 24, 1920; (parents Am. citizens); s. James Arthur and Elsie (Bate) F.; m. Joyce Corbeille, Aug. 31, 1944; children: Anne, Paul, Nancy. BS in Engring., U. Mich., 1947. Project engr. Monroe (Mich.) Auto Equipment Co., 1947-49, asst. to sales mgr. mfrs. sales, 1949-51, sales mgr. mfrs. sales, 1951-64, v.p., gen. mgr., dir., 1964-78, sr. v.p., 1978-83. Pres. Monroe County United Fund, 1956. With USAAF, 1942-45. Decorated D.F.C., Air medal with three oak leaf clusters. Mem. Soc. Automotive Engrs. (pres. 1979), Engring. Soc. Detroit, Monroe Golf and Country Club (pres. 1961). Home: Monroe Mich. Died Nov. 12, 1983; buried St. Joseph's Cemetery, Monroe, Mich.

FLIEGEL, FREDERICK CHRISTIAN, sociology educator; b. Edmonton, Alta., Can., Apr. 3, 1925; came to U.S., 1928, naturalized, 1935; s. John Carl and Ruth Friedeborg (Aastrup) F.; m. Thellyn Ruth Haller, Aug. 25, 1955; children: Frederick M., Ruth E., David C., Johanna C. Student, Moravian Coll., 1942-43; B.A., U. Wis., 1949, M.A., 1952, Ph.D., 1955. Asst. prof. to assoc. prof. Pa. State U., 1955-65; assoc. prof. Mich. State U., 1966-67; prof. sociology U. Ill., 1968-87, head dept., 1970-73; vis. prof. U. Wis., summer 1963, Tamil Nadu Agrl. U., Coimbatore, India, spring 1977; Fulbright sr. research scholar CEPEC/CEPLAC, Brazil, spring 1985. Author: (with Roy, Sen and Kivlin) Agricultural Innovations in Indian Villages, 1968, Agricultural Innovation Among Indian Farmers, 1968, Communication in India: Experiments in Introducing Change, 1968; Editor: Rural Sociology, 1970-72. Served with USMC, 1943-46. Fellow Am. Sociol. Assn.; mem. Rural Sociol. Soc. (pres. 1975-76), Midwest Sociol. Soc., AAAS, AAUP. Died Sept. 11, 1987.

FLOCK, EUNICE VERNA, biochemist; b. Kellogg, Idaho, Aug. 20, 1904; d. Abraham Lincoln and Florence Louise (Ashby) Flock. BS, U. Wash., 1926; MS, U. Chgo., 1931; PhD, U. Minn., 1935. Fellow physiol. chemistry Mayo Found., 1933-36; cons. biochemistry Mayo Clinic, 1936; faculty Mayo Found., Grad. Sch. U. Minn., 1936-69, prof. biochemistry, 1957-69, emeritus prof. biochemistry, 1969-87; vis. scientist Nat. Inst. Arthritis and Metabolic Diseases, NIH, Phoenix Indian Med. Ctr., 1971-80. Spl. research amino acids of brain, metabolism thyroid hormones, diabetes. Fellow AAAS; mem. Am. Chem. Soc., Am. Diabetes Assn., Am. Soc. Biol. Chemists, N.Y. Acad. Sci., Alumni Assn. Mayo Found., Am. Thyroid Assn., Sigma Xi, Iota Sigma Pi, Sigma Delta Epsilon. Home: Phoenix Ariz. Died Mar. 17, 1987, buried Greenwood Cemetery, Kellogg, Idaho.

FLUKE, JOHN MAURICE, SR., electronic test equipment manufacturing company executive; b. Tacoma, Dec. 14, 1911; s. Lee and Lynda Pearl (Epley) F.; m. Lyla Adair Schram, June 5, 1937; children: Virginia Lee Fluke Gabelein, John Maurice Jr., David L. B.E.E., U. Wash., 1935; M.S., MIT, 1936; LL.D., Gonzaga U., 1982. Registered profl. engr., Wash. Engr. Gen. Electric Co., 1936-40; founder, pres. John Fluke Mfg. Co. Inc., Seattle, 1948-71; chmn. bd., chief exec. officer John Fluke Mfg. Co. Inc., 1971-87, John Fluke Internat. Co., 1966-83; dir. Peoples Nat. Bank Wash., Gen. Telephone Co. N.W.; leader Wash. Trade Mission to Orient, 1965; mem. exec. com. Assn. Wash. Bus., 1966-78; mem. President's blue ribbon panel Dept. Def., 1969-70, chmn. electronic test equipment task force, 1974-78; mem. trade mission to Eng. and Scotland, 1964; civilian aide to sec. Army, 1974. Patentee in field. Pres. Wash. Research Council, 1961-84; mem. exec. bd. Seattle-King County Safety Council, 1962-63; chmn. bd., hon. life mem. Seattle Area Indsl. Council, 1962-66; mem. Snohomish County Econ. Devel. Council, 1972-73; chmn. Wash. State Export Council, 1982-84; bd. dirs. Doctors Hosp., Seattle, 1969-73, Seattle Hist. Soc., 1974-79, Econ. Devel. Council Puget Sound, 1976-82, Seattle Found., 1970-84; v.p., bd. dirs. Seattle Symphony, 1969-84; chmn. vis. com. U. Wash. Coll. Elec. Engring., 1976-84; trustee Pacific Sci. Ctr., Seattle, 1971-78; chmn. personnel dir. selection com. City of Seattle, 1969; chmn. endowment fund Seattle Symphony, 1967, 77-79; mem. corp. vis. com. dept. elec. engring. and computer sci. MIT, 1976; pres., chmn. bd. Seattle Jr. Achievement, 1973-78, nat. dir., regional chmn., 1975-78, mem. field adv. commn., 1977-78, chmn. emeritus, 1976-78; mem. planning and devel. com. Salvation Army, 1976; mem. ann. fund bd. U. Wash., 1975-78; trustee Mus. Flight Found., from 1983. Served with USNR, 1940-46. Decorated Legion of Merit; recipient Man of Yr. award Mountlake Terrace C. of C.-State Adv. Council, 1966; Howard Vollum Sci. and Tech. award Reed Coll., 1976; Corp. Leadership award MIT, 1976; Gold Leadership award Jr. Achievement, 1981, Pub. Service award Jr. Achievement, 1967; Wildhack award Nat. Conf. Standards Labs., 1983; recognition award U. Wash., 1984; nat. community svc. award Am. Electronics Assn., 1988; donor Fluke Disting. Chair in Elec. Engring. U. Wash., 1982, chair in elec. engring. Stanford U., 1984; named pme pf 100 outstanding men for Wash. State Centennial as Pioneer of Electronics, 1988; high tech. bldg. on campus of U. Wash. to be named John M. Fluke Hall; medal struck in his honor by electronics industry. Fellow IEEE (engring. edn. and accreditation com. 1971-72, Industrialist of Yr. award 1966, Regional Pub. Service award 1967); mem. Am. Electronics Assn. (chmn. Wash. council tech. advancement 1983—), Am. Security Council, Instrument Soc. Am. (hon.), Seattle C. of C. (life mem.; pres. 1965-66), Tau Beta Pi. Republican. Lutheran. Clubs: Rainier, Seattle Golf (Seattle). Lodge: Rotary (Vocat. Service award Seattle). Home: Seattle Wash. Died Feb. 11, 1984; buried on pvt. island Vendovi, San Juan Islands , Puget Sound.

FLYNN, STREETER B(LANTON), lawyer; b. Guthrie, Okla., Nov. 2, 1892; s. Dennis Thomas and Adeline (Blanton) F.; m. Margaret Tuttle, Oct. 18, 1919; children: Margaret Tuttle, Adelaide (Mrs. J. Hawley Wilson Jr.), Streeter Blanton. AB, Yale, 1915; LLB, Columbia, 1917. Bar: Okla. 1919. Practice Oklahoma City, from 1919; ptnr. Rainey, Flynn & Welch, and predecessor, from 1925; dir., gen. counsel Okla. Gas & Electric Co., Oklahoma City; dir., v.p. Flynn Oil Co.; dir. A., T. & S.F. Ry., First Nat. Bank & Trust Co., Am. First Title and Trust Co., Oklahoma City, Oklahoma Hardware Co. Lt. (j.g.) USN, 1917-19. Mem. ABA, Okla. State Bar Assn., Chgo. Club, Yale Club (N.Y.C.), Oklahoma City Golf and Country Club, Beacon Club, Alpha Delta Phi. Home: Oklahoma City Okla. †

FOCKE, ALFRED BOSWORTH, physicist, educator; b. Cleve., Sept. 30, 1906; s. Theodore Moses and Anne (Bosworth) F.; m. Alice Beatrice Cook, Sept. 17, 1928; 1 son, Alfred Bosworth; m. 2d, Katherine Crawford, Aug. 12, 1944; children: Alice Anne, Theodore William, Francis George, Karl Crawford, Louis Ross. BS, Case Western Res. U., 1928; PhD, Calif. Inst. Tech., 1932. Instr. surveying Case Sch. Applied Sci., 1928; inst. fellow Calif. Inst. Tech., 1932-33; NRC fellow Yale U., 1933-34; instr. physics Brown U., 1934-38, asst. prof., 1938-45; physicist U.S. Dept. Navy, 1940-45, USN Electronics Lab., San Diego, 1945-53; dir. U. Calif. Marine Phys. Lab., 1954-58; tech. dir. Pacific Missile Range, Point Mugu, Calif., 1958-59; prof., chmn. dept. physics Harvey Mudd Coll., Claremont, Calif., 1959-71, emeritus, 1971-86; sci. dir. Operation Wigwam, USN, 1954-56; cons. naval applications to industry and AEC, Naval Ordnance Lab., Lawrence Radiation Lab. Bd. dirs. San Miquel Sch., San Diego, Bloy Episcopal Sch. Theology, Claremont. Fellow AAAS, Acoustical Soc. Am., Am. Phys. Soc.; mem. Am. Inst. Physics, Am. Assn. Physics Tchrs., Seismol. Soc. Am., Am. Geophys. Union, Coll. Fed. Council So. Calif. Home: Claremont Calif. Died June 8, 1986; interred Mountain View Mausoleum, Altadena, Calif.

FOCKE, THEODORE BROWN, tire sales company executive; b. Cleve., Sept. 16, 1904; s. Theodore Moses and Anne (Bosworth) F.; m. Mary duPont; children—William B., H. Elizabeth, Mary L. B.S., Case Inst. Tech., 1926; D.Sc., U. Nancy, France, 1928. Engr. Perfection Stove Co., 1929-42; factory mgr., gen. mgr. Curtiss-Wright Corp., 1946-49; v.p., gen. mgr. Wright Aero. Corp., 1949-52; pres., dir. Nat. Radiator Co., 1952-55, Nat.-U.S. Radiator Corp., 1955-60; v.p., gen. mgr. plumbing, heating, air conditioning group Crane Co., 1960; v.p. fin. and adminstrn. The Mitre Corp., Bedford, Mass., 1961-63; pres., dir. The Better Tire Sales Co., Johnstown, Pa., 1963-84, Wm. K. Stamets Co., Pitts., 1964-74. Served with Bur. Aeros. USN, 1942-46. Mem. Am. Soc. Metals. Home: Johnstown Pa. Died June 5, 1986.

FOELLINGER, HELENE R., newspaper publisher; b. Ft. Wayne, Ind., Dec. 12, 1910; d. Oscar G. and Esther Anna (Deuter) F. AB, U. Ill., 1932; LittD (hon.), Tri-State Coll.; LLD (hon.), Ind. U. With editorial dept. News Pub. Co., pubs. of News-Sentinel, Ft. Wayne, 1932-36, pres., 1936-87; pres. News-Sentinel Broadcasting Co., Inc.; dir. Lincoln Nat. Bank & Trust Co. Mem. Ft. Wayne Tennis Commn.; bd. dirs. Ft. Wayne Better Bus. Bur., Conv. Bur., Ft. Wayne-Allen County United Community Services, Ft. Wayne Horse Show Assn., Ft. Wayne Light Opera Festival, Allen County Tuberculosis Assn., Allen County chpt. Nat. Found. Infantile Paralysis, Allen County unit Ind. Cancer Soc., Ft. Wayne chpt. ARC, Jr. Achievement, Ft. Wayne Art Sch., Ft. Wayne Philharmonic Orch., Fine Arts Found., Legal Aid Soc., Ft. Wayne Zool. Soc., Ft. Wayne Found., Taxpayers Research Assn., U. Ill. Found., Ind.-Purdue Found. at Ft. Wayne; trustee Tri-State U., Allen County War Meml. Coliseum. Mem. Am. Newspaper Assn., Ft. Wayne Exec. Club, Ft. Wayne C. of C. (dir.), Altrusa, Ft. Wayne Country Club, Phi Beta Kappa, Pi Beta Phi, Pi Mu Epsilon, Mortar Bd., Psi Iota Xi. Republican. Lutheran. Home: Fort Wayne Ind. Died Mar. 25, 1987.

FOERY, WALTER A., bishop; b. Rochester, N.Y., July 6, 1890. Student, St. Andrews Prep. Sem., St. Bernards Sem., Rochester. Ordained priest Roman Cath. Ch., 1916. Curate 1916-22; pastor Mt. Carmel Ch., Rochester, 1922-32, Holy Rosary Ch., Rochester, 1932-37; consecrated bishop of Syracuse N.Y., 1937. Dir. Rochester Cath. Charities, 1930-37; Nat. Cath. Welfare Conf. rep. Internat. Conf. on Social Welfare, London, 1936. Home: Syracuse N.Y. †

FOGELMAN, LAZAR, editor; b. Newish, Russia, May 27, 1891; came to U.S., 1921, naturalized, 1927; s. Simha and Adele (Sacker) f.; m. Sarah Belle Damesek, Nov. 23, 1920 (dec. Dec. 1963); 1 child, Edwin; m. Elsie Botwinik, Dec. 27, 1965. JD, Imperial U., Warsaw, Poland, 1912; postgrad., Psychoneurol. Inst., Petrograd, Russia, 1913-15; LLD, Fordham U., 1927. Editorial and feature writer Jewish Daily Forward, N.Y.C., from 1921, editor, from 1962; dir. Jewish Tchrs. Sem., N.Y.C., 1924-27; editor Zukunft, 1939-41. Author: Paul Axelrod, 1928, Booker T. Washington, 1930, Workmen's Circle, 1931. Mem. World Meml. Jewish Martyrs, Jewish Labor Com., Jewish Culture Congress. Mem. Jewish Writers Union (pres. 1933-35), Workmen's Circle (treas. 1943-46). Home: Brooklyn N.Y. †

FOGLAR-DEINHARDSTEIN, HEINRICH, lawyer; b. Mostar, Austria, May 14, 1889; s. Friedrich von and Bianca (von Curinaldi) von Foglar-D.; m. Annerose Putzler, Mar. 25, 1932; children: Harald, Gabriele (Mrs. Karl Hoffman), Christa (Mrs. Friedrich Frölichsthal), Elisabeth (Mrs. Friedrich Gleissner). Student law and sci., U. Lausanne, U. Vienna. Bar: Austria 1920. Mem. staff Austrian cts., 1912-13, Finanzprokuratur, Austrian govtl. legal agy., 1913-20; pvt. practice law specializing in pvt. cos. and taxation Vienna, from 1920; ptnr. Viktor Kienbock, until 1954, Harald Foglar-Deinhardstein, from 1954; judge, examiner faculty laws U. Vienna, from 1955. Mem. Internat. Bar Assn. (past pres.). Home: Vienna Austria. †

FOGLER, RAYMOND HENRY, corporation executive; b. South Hope, Maine, Feb. 29, 1892; s. Henry Harrison and Mary Aurelia (Andrews) F.; m. Mabel Peabody, Jan. 23, 1920; children: Henry Harrison, Mary Aurelia (Mrs. Sumner A. Claverie), Ann Peabody (dec.), John Payson, Ruth Peabody (Mrs. Merle F. Goff), Martha (Mrs. Donald E. Hobbs), William Andrews, Thomas Knight. BS, U. Maine, 1915, LLD, 1939; MS, Princeton, 1917; LLD, Colby Coll., 1958; DSc, Nasson Coll., 1962. Exec. sec. Agrl. Estension Svc., U. Maine, 1917-19; with W. T. Grant Co., 1919-32, advancing through various positions to dir. pers. and real estate; with Montgomery Ward & Co., Chgo., 1932-40, successively retail oper. mgr., v.p., gen. oper. mgr., dir., 1932-38; pres. Montgomery Ward & Co., 1938-40; pres., gen. mgr. W. T. Grant Co., 1940-50, pres., 1950-52, also bd. dirs.; assoc. sec. of the Navy 1953-57; bd. dirs. Centennial Ins. Co., Grand Union Co.; trustee Atlantic Mut. Ins. Co. Trustee The Grant Found. Mem. Commercial Club (Chgo.), Nat. Republican Club, Union League (N.Y.C.), Masons, Sigma Chi, Phi Kappa Phi, Alpha Zeta, Eta Mu Pi. Republican. Baptist. Home: Hastings-on-Hudson N.Y. †

FOLLIN, JAMES WIGHTMAN, engineer; b. Washington, May 19, 1892; s. John Madison and Georgia (Dorsey) F.; m. Maud Mills, June 23, 1917; children: James Wightman, Katherine (Mrs. Peter G. Sulzer), Elizabeth Ann (Mrs. F. R. Jones). Student, Harvard U., 1909-10; BCE, U. Mich., 1913, MSE, 1916. Asst. san. engr. State of Mich., 1915-16; various engring positions; mng. dir. Producers' Coun., 1939-46; dep. adminstr. Fed. Works Agy., 1946-49; spl. asst. to adminstr. Gen. Svcs. Adminstrn., 1949-51, dir. office of contract settlement; chmn. subcom. on constrn., conservation div. ODM, 1951-53; dir. div. slum clearance and urban devel. HHFA, 1953-54, commr. urban renewal adminstrn., 1954-56; urban renewal cons., cons. engr. from 1957. Mgr. Renovize Phila. and Renovize R.I. campaigns, 1933. With AUS, 1917-19. Fellow ASCE (pres. Phila. 1932); mem. AIA (hon.), U. Mich. Alumni Assn. (bd. dirs. 1935), Columbia Country Club, Sigma Xi, Chi Phi, Tau Beta Pi. Home: Chevy Chase Md. †

FOLSOM, JAMES, former governor; b. Coffee County, Ala., Oct. 9, 1908; s. Joshua Marion and Eulala Cornelia (Dunnavant) F.; m. Sarah Albert Carnley, Dec. 25, 1936 (dec. July. 1944); children: Rachel, Melissa; m. 2d, Jamelle Moore, May 5, 1948; children: James E., Andrew, Jamelle, Thelma, Joshua, Eulala Cornelia. Student, U. Ala., 1928, Howard Coll., Birmingham, 1929, George Washington U., 1935. Dist. agt. Emergency & Aid Ins. Co., Elba, Ala., 1937-40, state mgr., 1940-46; gov. of Ala. 1947-51, 55-59; state del. at large, Nat. Dem. Conv., 1944. Mem. Masons, Elks. Baptist. Home: Cullman Ala. Died Nov. 21, 1987.

FONG, BENSON, actor, business executive; b. Sacramento, Oct. 10, 1916; s. Toon and Shee (Yee) F.; m. Gloria Chin, Nov. 11, 1946; children: Cynthia, Preston, Lori, Pamela, Lisa. Student, Lingnan U., Canton, China. Owner, operator A.H. Fong's Restaurants, Los Angeles, from 1946; pres. Maylia Corp., Cinlopamlis, Prescorp of Calif.; v.p. Landsberg, Ltd., Hong Kong. Appeared in over 200 theatrical and television films; appeared in Charlie Chan series as the Hon. Son. Recipient Public Service and Achievement awards from Hollywood Canteen, Public Service and Achievement awards from Los Angeles Chinese Community, Public Service and Achievement awards from AFL-CIO Council, Public Service and Achievement awards from Los Angeles chpt. WAIF, Public Service and Achievement awards from So. Calif. Chinese Hist. Soc., Public Service and Achievement awards from Sacramento Chinese Soc. Mem. Screen Actors Guild, AFTRA. Republican. Roman Catholic. Clubs: Los Angeles Chinese Golf, El Caballero Country, Hollywood Lakeside Golf. Home: Hollywood Calif. Died Aug. 8, 1987.

FONTENROSE, JOSEPH, educator; b. Sutter Creek, Calif., June 17, 1903; s. Antone and Alice Laura (Eddy) F.; m. Marie Holmes, June 22, 1942; children: Jane Fontenrose Cajina, Robert, Anne. AB, U. Calif., Berkeley, 1925, MA, 1928, PhD, 1933. Instr. classics Cornell U., 1931-33; asst. prof. Greek and Latin U. Oreg., 1934; mem. faculty U. Calif., Berkeley, 1934-86, prof. classics, 1955-70, emeritus, 1970-86, chmn. dept., 1962-66; vis. prof. classics Brandeis U., 1971. Author: Python: A Study of Delphic Myth and Its Origins, 1959, The Cult and Myth of Pyrros at Delphi, 1960, John Steinbeck: An Introduction and Interpretation, 1963, The Ritual Theory of Myth, 1966, The Delphic Oracle, 1978, Steinbeck's Unhappy Valley: A Study of the Pastures of Heaven, 1981, Orion: The Myth of the Hunter and the Huntress, 1981, Classics at Berkeley, 1981, Didyma - Apollo's Oracle, Cult, and Companions, 1988; contbr. numerous articles to profl. jours. Am. Council Learned Socs. fellow, 1935-36; Am. Acad. Rome sr. classics fellow951-52; Guggenheim fellow, 1958-59. Mem. Am. Philol. Assn., Philol. Assn. Pacific Coast (pres. 1974), Modern Lang. Assn., Am. Folklore Soc., Archaeol. Inst. Am., Am. Fedn. Tchrs., Dickens Fellowship, William Morris Soc., John Steinbeck Soc., Fabian Soc. (London, Eng.), U. Calif. Faculty Club, Sierra Club. Socialist. Home: Berkeley Calif. Died July 7, 1986; cremated.

FOOTE, JAMES HAROLD, engineer; b. Jackson, Mich., Nov. 21, 1891; s. James Berry and Rebecca Elilza (Tuttle) F.; m. Marie D. Dinius, Oct. 12, 1915; children: James Harold, Barbara Marie (Mrs. Joseph A. Crain). BSCE, Mich. State U., 1914; DSc in Engring. (hon.), Wayne State U., 1958. Registered profl. engr., Mich. Surveyor, engr., constrn. engr. Fargo Engring. Co., Consumers Power Co. and associated cos., Jackson, 1914-23; elec. engr. charge sta. and transmission line engring. Commonwealth Power Corp. Mich. and successors, 1924-31; supervising engr. charge elec. engring. no. div. Commonwealth & So. Corp. N.Y., 1932-36, in charge engring., 1936-49; v.p., bd. dirs. Commonwealth Svcs., Inc. N.Y., 1949-61, dir. engring., 1958-61; pres., bd. dirs. Commonwealth Assocs., Inc., Jackson, 1949-58, chief engr., 1958-61, bd. dirs., 1958-60; pres., bd. dirs. Commonwealth Bldgs., Inc., Jackson, 1955-61; pvt. practice from 1962; pres., bd. dirs. Waupakisco Realty Co., Battle Creek, Mich., 1937-43; v.p., bd. dirs. Miller Plating Corp., Jackson, 1963-69; mem. Internat. Conf. Large Elec. High Tension Systems; tech. adviser U.S. nat. com. Internat. Electrotech. Commn., 1955-70, del. tech. coms., 1955-58; mem. Mich. Bd. Registration Architects, Profl. Engrs. and Land Surveyors, 1943-50, chmn., 1950. Author in field. V.p. Mich. Coun. Chs. and Religious Edn., 1949; trustee Olivet (Mich.) Coll., 1943-50, Adrain (Mich.) Coll., 1956-59. Recipient Centennial award Mich. State U., 1955, Disting. Alumni award, 1961; named Mich. Engr. of Yr. Mich. Soc. Profl. Engrs., 1960. Fellow AAAS, IEEE (pres. 1959-60, Edison and John Fritz medal coms. 1960-63); mem. ASTM (chmn. com. elec. conductors 1938-50, adminstrv. com. standards 1953-60, hon. 1962), U.S.A. Standards Inst. (bd. dirs. 1956-63, elec. and electronics standards bd. 1952-70, Howard Coonley medal 1960), NSPE, Mich. Socs. Profl. Engrs. (bd. dirs. 1950-53), Mich. Engring. Soc. (pres. 1944-45, hon.), Am. Forestry Assn., Am. Inst. Cons. Engrs., Am. Soc. Engring. Edn., Tau Beta Pi, Eta kappa Nu, Pi Tau Sigma. Republican. Methodist. Home: Brethren Mich. †

FORBES, JOHN GEORGE, lawyer; b. N.Y.C., Oct. 19, 1919; s. George and Hazel (Mavricos) F.; m. Demetra Ramos, May 6, 1950; 1 son, John George. BSS, CCNY, 1940; LLB, Harvard U., 1943. Bar: N.Y. 1943. Pvt. practice N.Y.C., 1943; ptnr. Forbes & Sommers, 1975-85; lectr. Practising Law Inst., 1959-85; instr. Tax Workshop Sch., 1954-56. Editor Harvard Law Rev., 1942-43; contbr. articles to legal jours. Trustee, sec.-treas. Inst. Mus. Art City N.Y.; v.p., trustee Christian A. Johnson Endeavor Found.; mem. N.Y. N.G., 1944-47. Mem. ABA, Assn. of Bar of City of N.Y. Home: New York N.Y. Died Jan. 14, 1985; buried Woodlawn Cemetery, N.Y.C.

FORD, FREDERICK WAYNE, lawyer; b. Bluefield, W.Va., Sept. 17, 1909; s. George Michael and Annie Laurie (Linn) F.; m. Virginia Lee Carter, Aug. 12, 1933 (dec. Feb. 1958); 1 dau., Mary Carter; m. Mary Margaret Mahony, Oct. 11, 1959 (div. Aug. 1981); 1 son, Frederick Wayne. A.B., W.Va. U., 1931, J.D., 1934. Bar: W.Va. 1934, D.C. 1968. Jr. partner Stathers & Cantrall, Clarksburg, 1934-39; atty. FSA, 1939-42, OPA, 1942, 46-47; atty. FCC, 1947-53, mem., 1957-65, chmn., 1960; 1st asst. to asst. atty. gen. Office Legal Counsel Dept. Justice, 1953-56; acting asst. atty. gen. Office Legal Counsel, 1956-57; asst. dept. atty. gen. U.S., 1957; pres. Nat. Community TV Assn., 1965-69; sr. ptnr. firm Lovett, Ford, & Hennessey and predecessor, 1970-81; ptnr. Pepper & Corazzini, 1981-86. Editorial staff: W.Va. U. Law Quar, 1932-33. Mem. Harrison County Republican Exec. Com., 1936. Served as maj. USAAF, 1942-46. Mem. Am., Fed. Communications bar assns., W.Va. State Bar, Am. Law Inst., Alexandria Assn. (pres. 1950-53), Scabbard and Blade, Phi Delta Phi, Sigma Chi. Episcopalian. Clubs: Young Republican of Harrison County (pres. 1939), Congressional Country, Belle Haven Country. Home: Alexandria Va. Died July 26, 1986.

FORD, HENRY, II, automobile manufacturing executive; b. Detroit, Sept. 4, 1917; s. Edsel B. and Eleanor (Clay) F.; m. Anne McDonnell, July 13, 1940 (div.); children: Charlotte, Anne, Edsel Bryant II; m. Maria Cristina Vettore Austin, Feb. 19, 1965 (div.); m. Kathleen DuRoss, Oct. 1980. Grad., Hotchkiss Sch., 1936; student, Yale U., 1936-40. Dir. Ford Motor Co., 1938-87, with co., 1940-82, v.p., 1943, exec. v.p., 1944, pres., 1945, chmn., 1960-80, chief exec. officer, 1960-79; dir. Sotheby's Holdings, Inc.; trustee, chmn. Henry Ford Health Corp. Trustee The Ford Found., 1943-76, Edison Inst.; grad. mem. Bus. Council. Home: Detroit Mich. Died Sept. 29, 1987.

FORMAN, JONATHAN, internist, editor, author; b. Austinburg, Ohio, Sept. 30, 1887; s. Cassius Clay and Alice Florence (Coup) F.; m. Doris Marie Andrews, Nov. 1, 1923; children: Alice Ann, Cynthia Louise, Jonathan. AB, Ohio State U., 1910; postgrad., Harvard U., summers 1912-16; MD, Starling-Ohio Med. Coll., 1913. Diplomate Am. Bd. Internal medicine. Asst. in anatomy and physiology Ohio State U., 1910-11; asst. in pathology Coll. Medicine, Ohio State U., 1913-14, instr., 1914-16, asst. prof., 1916-19; spl. lectr. allergy 1933-34, lectr. medicine, from 1934, prof. history of medicine, from 1945, prof. emeritus; asst. in pathology Starling-Ohio Med. Coll., 1911-13; Austin teaching fellow Harvard U., 1919-20; pvt. practice Columbus, Ohio, from 1920; pathologist and gastroenterologist several hosps. and clinics; dir. lab. div. U.S. Naval Hosp., Naval Oper. Base, Hampton Roads, 1917-19. Author: History of the First Hundred Years of the College of Medicine of Ohio State University, 1934; editor or co-editor bulls., jours. and proc. various orgns., from 1916, including Ohio State Med. Jour., 1953-57; editor in chief Clin. Physiology, 1956-65; mem. editorial bd. World-Wide Abstracts, Vox Medica, Rev. Allergy and Applied Immunology; editor Archives Clin. Ecology; contbr. numerous articles to med. jours. Chmn. Friends of the Land, 1952-60. Recipient Louis Bromfield gold medal, 1961, Clemens von Pirquet gold medal, 1964. Fellow Am. Coll. Allergy (pres. 1949-50), Am. Acad. Allergy, Internat. Assn. Allergists, Soc. Tech. Editors and Pubs., Internat. Coll. Applied Nutrition; Mem. AMA, Argentine Soc. for Study of Allergy, Internat. Corr. Soc. Allergists (dir.-gen.), Alpha Omega Alpha, Sigma Del Chi, Phi Rho Sigma (Ainsley Griffin gold medal), Sigm Tau Delta. Home: Columbus Ohio. †

FORRESTAL, MICHAEL VINCENT, lawyer; b N.Y.C., Nov. 26, 1927; s. James Vincent and Josephir (Ogden) F. Student, Princeton U., 1949; LLB, Harvar U., 1953. Bar: N.Y. 1954. Practiced in N.Y.C.; ptnr then sr. ptnr. Shearman & Sterling, 1960-89; spl. asst. t Averell Harriman (dir. Marshall Plan), 1948-50; se Tripartite Naval Commn., Berlin, 1946; asst. U.S. nava attache, Moscow, USSR, 1946-47; dep. dir. East-Wes Trade Div. U.S. European Cooperation Adminstrn 1948-50; sr. staff mem. Nat. Security Council, 1962-6 pres. U.S.-USSR Trade and Econ. Council, 1978-8 promoter devel. Am. Trade Consortium. Chmn. Me Opera Guild, 1965-70; bd. dirs., treas. Met. Oper Assn., from 1967, Nat. Opera Inst., 1971-80; exec. se adv. com. Kennedy Inst. Politics, Harvard U., 1967-8 trustee Inst. Advanced Study, Princeton, N.J., fror 1970; trustee Phillips Exeter Acad., from 1979, pres. bc trustees, from 1981. Mem. ABA, Assn. Bar City N.Y Am. Arbitration Assn. (dir. 1980-83), Council Fgn. Re lations. Episcopalian. Clubs: Racquet and Tenni (N.Y.C.), Links (N.Y.C.); Metropolitan (Washington Travellers (Paris, France). Home: New York N.Y. Die Jan. 11, 1989.

FORRESTER, ALVIN THEODORE, physicist; b Bklyn., Apr. 13, 1918; s. Joseph D. and Rose (Kissen F.; m. Joy Levin, 1948 (dec. 1956); children—Bruce H Cheri J.; m. June Doris Berg, Oct. 5, 1956 (div. 1972 children—William C., Susan J. A.B., Cornell U., 193 A.M., 1939, Ph.D., 1942. Research asso. U. Calif. a Berkeley, 1942-45; physicist RCA Labs., Princetor N.J., 1945-46; asst. prof. physics U. So. Calif., Lo Angeles, 1946-51; asso. prof. U. So. Calif., 1951-54; vis asso. prof. physics U. Pitts., 1954-55; physicist Wes tinghouse Research Labs., Pitts., 1955-58; nuclear sp Atomics Internat., Los Angeles, 1958-59; dept. mg Electro-Optical Systems, Pasadena, Calif., 1959-65; pro U. Calif.- (Irvine), 1965-67, U. Calif.- (Los Angeles 1967-87; Vis. prof. astronomy U. Utrecht, Netherlands 1971; asso. Culham Lab., Eng., spring 1974; vis. pro physics Technion, Haifa, Israel, fall 1977. Fellow Am Phys. Soc., IEEE; mem. AIAA (Research award 1962 chmn. electrostatic propulsion panel 1960-61), AAAS AAUP, Am. Assn. Physics Tchrs., Sigma Xi, Phi Kapp Phi. Home: Culver City Calif. Died Mar. 28, 1987.

FORSBERG, EDWARD CARL ALBIN, SR., financ company executive; b. Bklyn., Dec. 2, 1920; s. Gunna A. and Martha E. (Boehme) F.; m. Byrne E. Johnson July 13, 1946; children: Edward Carl Albin, Cassandra Gayle. B.S., U.S. Mcht. Marine Acad., 1944. With First Family Fin. Services, Inc., 1958-86; pres., chie exec. officer First Family Fin. Services, Inc., Atlanta 1969-86; bd. dirs. Delta Life Ins. Co., Delta Fire & Casualty Ins. Co., Rhodes, Inc.; mem. consumer adv council Fed. Res. Bd., 1982-85. Mem. exec. com. credi mgmt. program Columbia U. Grad. Sch., 1975-86. Served as officer USN, 1943-46. Mem. Am. Fin. Svcs Assn. (chmn., exec. com. bd.), Georgia Consumer Fin Assn. (chmn., dir. exec. com.). Lutheran. Home Atlanta Ga. Died July 3, 1988; buried Arlington Meml Pk., Atlanta.

FORSEE, AYLESA, author; b. Kirksville, Mo.; d. Edward W. and Lena (Moore) F. BS, S.D. State U., MusB, MacPhail Coll. Music, Mpls., 1938; MA, U. Colo., 1939. Instr. history and music Rochester, Minn., 1939-45, U. Iowa, 1945-46, U. Denver, 1946-49; mem. staff writers conf. Temple Buell Coll., 1967, 68; mem. adv. bd. Nat. Writers Club. Author: The Whirly Bird, 1955, Miracle for Mingo, 1956, Too Much Dog, 1957, American Women Who Scored Firsts, 1958, Louis Agassiz: Pied Piper of Science, 1958, Frank Lloyd Wright: Rebel in Concrete, 1959, Women Who Reached for Tomorrow, 1960, My Love and I Together, 1961, Beneath Land and Sea, 1962, Albert Einstein, 1963, William Henry Jackson, 1964, Pablo Casals: Cellist for Freedom, 1965, Men of Modern Architecture, 1966, Headliners, 1967, Famous Photographers, 1968, Artur Rubenstein: King of the Keyboard, 1969, They Trusted God, 1980; contbr. articles to adult and juvenile periodicals. Recipient: Helen Fish award, 1955. Mem. Colo. Author's League (Tophand award 1966, 69). Christian Science practitioner. Home: Boulder Colo. Died Mar. 26, 1986.

FORSTALL, WALTON, mechanical engineer, educator; b. Rosemont, Pa., June 26, 1909; s. Walton Sr. and Ednah (Logan) F.; m. Jean Elizabeth Riegel, Jan. 15, 1942; children—Douglas Walton, Keith William. B.S., Lehigh U., 1931, M.S., 1943, M.E., 1951; Sc.D., MIT, 1949. Registered profl. engr., Pa. Asst. test engr. Delaware sta. Phila. Elec. Co., 1930; mem. sci. staff Franklin Inst., Phila., 1932-34; engring. asst. Phila. Gas Works Co., 1934-40; instr. then asst. prof. mech. engring. Lehigh U., 1940-44; project engr. Tenn-Eastman Corp., Manhattan Dist. Project, Oak Ridge, 1944-45; research assoc. MIT, Cambridge, 1946-49; assoc. prof. mech. engring. Carnegie-Mellon U., Pitts., 1949-57; asst. dean engring. and sci. Carnegie-Mellon U., 1955-57, George Tallman Ladd prof. mech. engring., 1957-74, prof. emeritus, 1974-88, assoc. head dept. mech. engring., 1963-77; sec. Beaumaris Land Co., Ltd.; mem. Indsl. Standards Bd. Cons. Pa., 1964-69; dir.

Beaumaris Land Co., Ltd., 1962-88, sec., 1962-79. Mem. sch. bd. West Jefferson Hills Sch. Dist., 1961-63, 65-71, pres., 1961-63, 69-71. Mem. ASME (chmn. Pitts. sect. 1958-59, regional sec. 1962-66, v.p. 1966-70), Franklin Inst., Am. Soc. Engring. Edn. (nat. council 1957-59), Am. Phys. Soc., Phi Beta Kappa, Sigma Xi, Tau Beta Pi, Pi Tau Sigma, Psi Upsilon. Presbyterian. Home: Pittsburgh Pa. Died July 15, 1988.

FORSYTH, VOLNEY KING, corporate executive; b. Edgewater, N.Y., Nov. 2, 1892; s. Enoch Avard and Susan Duffus (Smith) F.; m. Mary O'Neill, Sept. 8, 1921; children: Martha Joan (Mrs. W. B. Harmon Jr.), Mary (Mrs. Philip C. Reville), Anne (Mrs. R. W. Christensen), Frances Volney (Mrs. John Wayne Dawson). Grad., King's Collegiate Sch., Windsor, Can., 1908. With Bank of N.S., 1908-15, 19-27; reporter Halifax Herald, 1918-19; with N.Am. Solvay, Inc., N.Y.C., from 1927, v.p., treas., 1945-59, pres., from 1959, also bd. dirs.; bd. dirs. Libbey-Owens-Ford Glass Co., Toledo. lt. Can. Machine Gun Corps, 1915-18. Mem. Can. Soc. N.Y. (bd. dirs.), Can. Club. N.Y., Inc. (past pres.), City Midday Club, Scarsdale Golf Club. Home: Scarsdale N.Y. †

FORSYTHE, DONALD TAYLOR, newspaper publisher, editor; b. Conway, Pa., May 30, 1903; s. George Blazier and Mattie (Hendrickson) F.; m. Katherine L. Marshall, June 26, 1929; 1 son, James Howard. Grad., Thiel Coll., Greenville, Pa., 1924; DHL (hon.), McMurray Coll., 1954. Newspaper reporter 1917-24; mng. editor Hancock County Jour., Carthage, Ill., 1926-34, pub., 1934-70; owner, gen. mgr. Jour. Printing Co., Carthage, 1934-73; v.p. Marine Trust Co.; organizer, supr. dept. journalism Carthage Coll., 1929-38. Sec. bd. trustees Carthage Coll.; chmn. Am. Hearing Research Found.; mem. citizen's com. Western Ill. U.; mem. Profession of Journalism Ill. Press Assn., 1932. Mem. Greater Weeklies Assn. (past pres., chmn. bd.), Ill. Press Assn. (past pres.), C. of C., Masons, Kiwanis Internat. (pres. 1953-54), Keokuk Country, Chgo. Press. Home: Carthage Ill. Died Jan. 25, 1986.

FORTENBAUGH, SAMUEL BYROD, JR., lawyer, business executive; b. London, Mar. 2, 1902; s. Samuel Byrod and Florence (Cowden) F.; m. Katherine F. Wall, Dec. 29, 1926; children—Samuel Byrod III, William Wall. B.S., Union Coll., 1923; LL.B., Harvard, 1926. Bar: Pa. bar 1926. Since practiced Phila.; ptnr. Clark, Ladner, Fortenbaugh & Young; chmn. bd., dir. Devonshire Industries, Inc.; chmn. bd., treas., dir. Wall Industries, Inc., NYHM Transp. Co., Wall Rope Works, Beverly, N.J.; dir. Pub. Fin. Service, Inc., Phila., Phillips Petroleum Co. Past chmn. bd. trustees Union Coll., Schenectady; dir. ednl. fund Patroni Scholastic, Phila. Mem. Am., Pa., Phila. bar assns., Phila. Maritime Soc. (past pres.), Phi Beta Kappa, Beta Theta Pi. Clubs: Harvard (N.Y.C.); Racquet (Phila.); Merion Golf (Ardmore, Pa.); Bay Head (N.J.) Yacht. Home: Radnor Pa. Died July 25, 1985; buried Radnor, Pa.

FORTIER, DONALD ROBERT, government official; b. Columbus, Ohio, Jan. 9, 1947; s. Robert Erley and Stella Alice (Montgomery) F.; m. Alison Leslie Brenner, June 30, 1979; 1 child, Graham Donald. B.A., Miami U., Oxford, Ohio, 1969; M.A., U. Chgo. Mem. profl. staff U.S. Congress, Washington, 1975-79; dep. dir. policy planning Dept. State, Washington, 1981-82; dir. Western European affairs NSC, Washington, 1982-83, dep. nat. security advisor, 1983-86; cons. Rand Corp., Los Angeles, 1973-75. Republican. Club: Congl. Country (Bethesda, Md.). Home: Bethesda Md. Died Aug. 30, 1986.

FOSSE, BOB, director, choreographer; b. Chgo., June 23, 1927; s. Cyril K. and Sarah (Stanton) F. Choreographer, dir. musical plays, 1956-87, Pajama Game, 1956, Damn Yankees, 1957, Bells Are Ringing, 1958, New Girl in Town, 1958; play Redhead, 1959, Sweet Charity, 1966, also 1986 remake; film version, 1968, Pippin; stage, 1972, Chicago, 1975, Dancin', 1978; mus. staging How To Succeed in Business Without Really Trying, 1961; dir., film star, 1980-83; choreographer, co-dir. musical staging Little Me, 1962; actor musical staging Pal Joey, 1961, 63; actor, choreographer: film The Little Prince, 1974; choreographer, dir. films Cabaret, 1972, All That Jazz, 1979; dir. film Lenny, 1974; writer, dir., choreographer Broadway play Big Deal, 1986. Recipient Tony award for Pajama Game 1956, Damn Yankees 1957, Redhead 1959, Sweet Charity 1966, Pippin (2) 1972, Dancin 1978, Donaldson award for Pajama Game 1956, Dance Mag. and Tony award for Little Me 1963, Oscar award for Cabaret 1972, 3 Emmy awards for spl. Liza with a Z, Drama Desk award for Pippin 1972. Mem. Soc. Stage Dirs. and Choreographers (treas.). Home: New York N.Y. Died Sept. 23, 1987.

FOSTER, GEORGE BUCHANAN, lawyer; b. Montreal, Que., Can., Aug. 19, 1897; s. George G. and Mary Maud (Buchanan) F.; children: Hilda Margot, Joan Elizabeth. BCL, McGill U., 1921. Bar: Que. 1921. Sr. ptnr. Foster, Hannen, Watt, Leggat & Colby, Montreal, from 1940; dir., pres. Dominion Wire Rope & Cable Co. Ltd., Mount Royal Metal Co. Ltd.; dir. Travelers Ins. Co., Montreal Trust Co., Superheater Co. Ltd. Mem. Legis. Coun. Que., from 1946. Home: Westmount Que., Canada †

FOSTER, HARVEY GOODSON, airline executive; b. Indpls., Oct. 11, 1912; s. E.V. and Blanch Louise (Dodge) F.; m. Mable Louise Mahler, Aug. 3, 1936; children: John D., Daniel G. Student, U. Ky., 1932-33; LLB, U. Notre Dame, 1939. Bar: Ind. 1939, N.Y. 1962, U.S. Supreme Ct. With FBI, 1939-62; spl. agt. in charge. FBI, Indpls., 1957-58, N.Y.C., 1958-62; v.p., gen. mgr. Dallas Smith Transp. Corp., Phoenix, 1962-63; dir. security Gen. Telephone & Electronix Corp., 1963-64; v.p. audits and security Am. Airlines, Inc., N.Y.C., 1964-66; v.p. Am. Airlines, Inc., Chgo., 1966-73; v.p. Eastern div. Am. Airlines, Inc., N.Y.C., 1973-74; v.p. Cen. div. Am. Airlines, Inc., Chgo., 1974-77; cons. Real Estate Research, Inc., Chgo., 1978; dir. Merc. Nat. Bank, acting. chmn., 1978-79. Mem. N.y. State Mcpl. Police Tng. Council, 1959-62; mem. exec. bd. Greater N.Y. councils Boy Scouts Am., 1959-62, v.p., 1973-74, also chmn. health and safety com., adv. bd. Theodore Roosevelt council, Phoenix, 1962-63, exec. bd., commr. Greater N.Y. council, 1963-66, mem. exec. bd. Chgo. Area council, 1966-73. Named Notre Dame Man of Yr. in Indpls., 1952, in Chgo., 1977, N.Y. State Pistol Champion, 1959, Hoosier of Yr. in N.Y., Sons of Ind. of N.Y., 1961. Mem. ABA, Notre Dame Nat. Alumni Assn. (pres. 1952), Nat. Rifle Assn. (life), Internat., N.J. State Assn. Chiefs Police, N.Y. State Assn. Chiefs Police, Soc. Former Agts. FBI, Calif. Peace Officers Assn., Tex. Peace Officers Assn., Fed. Bus. Assn. (v.p. Greater N.Y. area 1959-60), Chgo. Assn. Commerce and Industry (bd. dirs.), Chgo. Conv. and Tourism Bur. (chmn. 1975), Am. Soc. Travel Agts., Notre Dame Club (gov. 1964-65), Nat. Monogram Club (pres. 1979-80). Home: Rancho Santa Fe Calif. Died Nov. 29, 1981.

FOULET, ALFRED LUCIEN, educator; b. Haverford, Pa., Dec. 5, 1900; s. Lucien and Elisabeth (Schmeling) F.; m. Margaret McMahon, Aug. 14, 1947 (dec. 1970). Licencié ès Lettres, U. Paris, 1921; Archiviste-Paléographe, Ecole des Chartes, 1924; PhD, Princeton U., 1927. Instr. French Princeton U., 1927-30, asst. prof., 1930-42, lectr., 1942-45, assoc. prof., 1945-53, prof., 1953-66, prof. emeritus, 1966-87; lectr. Bryn Mawr Coll., 1930, Johns Hopkins U., 1934-36; editorial com. Publs. Modern Lang. Assn. Am., 1952-62. Editor: La Lettre de Jean Sarrasin a Nicolas Arrode, 1924, Le Couronnement de Renard, 1929, (with Edward C. Armstrong, vols. 1-5, 7) The Medieval French Romand 'Alexandre, 1937, 42, 49, 55; contbr. articles on French lit. Named an officer in l'ordre des Palmes Académiques (France), 1982. Mem. Modern Lang. Assn. (sec. com. on research activities, 1944-48), Medieval Acad. Am., Renaissance Soc. Am., Société de l'Ecole des Chartes. Home: Princeton N.J. Died Apr. 15, 1987.

FOULKES, HOWARD TALLMADGE, lawyer; b. Fond du Lac, Wis., Oct. 14, 1888; s. Edward and Virginia (Tallmadge) F.; m. Helen Esther Joerns, Oct. 4, 1919 (dec. Aug. 1946); children: Elisabeth Wood (Mrs. Richard E. Phillipson), Cornelia (Mrs. Donald A. Austin). Grad., Phillip's Acad., Andover, Mass., 1907; BA, Yale U., 1911; LLB, U. Wis., 1913; LLD, Nashotah House, 1946. Bar: Wis. 1913. Ptnr. Borgelt, Powell, Paterson & Frauen (and predecessors), Milw., 1913-73. Chmn. group work div. Milw. Community Fund, 1945-46; chancellor Episcopal Diocese Milw., 1945-65, dep. to gen. conv. from diocese, 1943-69; sec. mem. chpt. All Saints Cathedral, Milw., from 1930, canon chancellor, from 1965; mem. Unity Commn. Episcopal Ch., 1943-61; bd. dirs. St. Luke's Hosp., Milw., 1954-73, pres. Medically Indigent Found.; trustee Nashotah House, 1943-73; sec. bd. dirs. Stark Hosp., Milw., from 1932. 1st lt. Q.M.C., U.S. Army, 1918-19. Mem. ABA, Wis., Milw (past chmn. real estate div.) bar assns., Order of Coif, University Club, Beta Theta Pi, Phi Alpha Delta. Republican. Home: Milwaukee Wis. †

FOULKROD, RAYMOND, consulting engineer; b. Phila., July 9, 1891; s. Harry and Clara C. (Vardy) F.; m. Cornelia Smith; children: Raymond, Nancy Foulkrod Schwarz, Glen. Student engr. Bell Tel. Co., Pa., 1914-16, 1919-20; engr. AT&T, 1920-27; transmission and protection engr. Mich. Bell. Tel. Co., Detroit, 1927-29, plant extension engr., 1929-51, chief engr., 1951-56; then cons. engr. With C.E., U.S. Army, 1916-19. Fellow AIEE; mem. Engring. Soc. Detroit (pres.). Home: Nantucket Mass. †

FOUSEK, PETER, banker; b. Prague, Czechoslovakia, Nov. 13, 1923; came to U.S., 1948; s. Frantisek and Helena F.; m. Adrienne Albee, Jan. 27, 1948; children: Elizabeth Kendall, John Howard, Christopher Albee. B.A., Cambridge U., (Eng.), 1946; M.A., Columbia U., 1949, Ph.D., 1959. With Fed. Res. Bank N.Y., N.Y.C., 1950-87, v.p. personnel, 1968-73, equal opportunity officer, 1971-73, econ. adviser, 1973-76, v.p., 1977-78, dir. research, 1977-87, sr. v.p., 1979-82, exec. v.p., 1983-87; staff economist Council of Econ. Advisers, Washington, 1960-61; adj. prof. Columbia U. Grad. Sch. Bus., N.Y.C., 1974-75; lectr. in field. Author: Foreign Central Banking: The Instruments of Monetary Policy, 1957; contbr. articles to profl. jours. Mem. adv. com. N.Y. State Health Care Capital Adv. Com.; mem. Mamaroneck Human Rights Commn., (N.Y.), 1970-87, chmn., 1974-79; mem.tax adv. com. Mamaroneck Sch. Bd., 1970-75; coach Larchmont Little League, (N.Y.), 1968-75. Served with Czechoslovak Army, 1942-45, Western Europe. Mem. Council on Fgn. Relations, Am. Econ. Assn. Club: Larchmont Shore. Home: Larchmont N.Y. Died Dec. 28, 1987.

FOUST, ALAN SHIVERS, chemical engineering educator; b. Dublin, Tex., June 26, 1908; s. Charles George and Carrie E. (Lattimore) F.; m. H. Elizabeth Aigler, Nov. 29, 1939 (dec. Aug. 1980); children: H. Patricia Foust Hoppe, Alan S., Carolyn E. Foust Klebe, Charles William. BS, U. Tex., 1928, MS, 1930; PhD, U. Mich., 1938. Chemist Magnolia Petroleum Co., Beaumont, Tex., 1930-32; devel. engr. Tex. Pacific Coal & Oil Co., 1932; assoc. prof. chemistry Tex. Coll. Mines (now U. Tex.), El Paso, 1935-36; instr. chem. engring. U. Mich., 1937-39, asst. prof., 1939-46, assoc. prof., 1946-48, prof. chem. engring., 1948-52; prof. chem. engring. Lehigh U., Bethlehem, Pa., from 1952, head. dept., 1952-62, dean, 1962-65, McCann prof. chem. engring., 1965-77, prof. emeritus, from 1977. Author: (with G.G. Brown and others) Unit Operations, 1950, Evaporization and Crystallization, 1955, (with others) Principles of Unit Operations, 1960, 2d edit., 1980; contbr. articles to profl. jours. Lt. col. Chem. Corps AUS, 1942-46. Decorated Legion of Merit. Fellow Am. Inst. Chem. Engrs.; mem. Masons, Shriners, Sigma Xi, Delta Kappa Epsilon, Tau Beta Pi, Phi Lambda Upsilon, Phi Kappa Phi. Home: Bethlehem Pa. Died Mar. 20, 1986, buried Meml. Park Cemetery, Bethlehem.

FOWLER, CHARLES A(RMAN), educator; b. Salt Lake City, Apr. 23, 1912; s. Charles A. and Beatice (Buckle) F.; m. Inez Hanson, Aug. 4, 1934; children: Scott Wellington, Craig Huntington. AB, U. Utah, 1933, MS, 1934; PhD, U. Calif., 1940. Instr. physics U. Calif., Berkeley, 1940-42, asst. prof., 1943-46; assoc. prof. Pomona Coll., 1947-49, prof., chmn. dept. physics, from 1950. Contbr. to sci. publs. Recipient NSF sr. postdoctorial fellowship for rsch. at Fourier Inst., U. Grenoble, France, 1960-61. Mem. Am. Physical Soc., Am. Assn. Physics Tchrs., AAAS, AAUP, Phi Beta Kappa, Sigma Xi. Home: Claremont Calif. †

FOWLER, FRANCIS E., JR., corporation executive; b. St. Louis, Sept. 24, 1891; s. Francis E. and mary A. (Harig) F.; m. Emily Robins Riddle, Apr. 29, 1916; children: Francis E., Truman Riddle, Philip Fouke. Student, St. Louis U., 1904-11. Organized Caligrapo Co., 1918, owner, 1918-37; organizer, pres. Midland Distilleries, Inc., So. Comfort Corp., from 1937. Pres. Francis E. Fowler Jr. Found. and mus. Mem. University Club. Home: Los Angeles Calif. †

FOWLER, JAMES ALEXANDER, JR., lawyer; b. Clinton, Tenn., Feb. 27, 1897; s. James Alexander and Lucy Ellen (Hornsby) F.; m. Helleda Thoams, July 17, 1920; children: James Alexander III, Ann A. Fowler Walters. AB, U. Tenn., 1916; LLB, Harvard U., 1919. Bar: N.Y. 1920. Assoc. Cahill, Gordon & Reindel, N.Y.C., 1921-27, ptnr., 1927-70; counsel Bur. Naval Personnel, 1942-44. Nat. chmn. Harvard Law Sch. Fund, 1955-57. Fellow Am. Coll. Trial Lawyers, Am. Bar Found.; mem. N.Y. Practicing Law Inst. (trustee emeritus), Am. Law Inst., ABA, N.Y. Bar Assn., Assn. Bar of City of N.Y., N.Y. County Lawyers Assn., Harvard Law Sch. Alumni Assn. (pres. 1961-63) University Club, Down Town Assn. Home: Setauket N.Y. Died Nov. 19, 1985; buried Caroline Ch., Setauket.

FOWLER, MEL, marble sculptor, retired U.S. Air Force officer; b. San Antonio, Nov. 25, 1921; s. Walter James Fowler and Thelma Anne (Hays) Gregory; m. Catherine Oeland Childs, May 9, 1981; by previous marriage—James Everett, Robert Michael, William Wade. Student Southwestern U., U. Tex., U. Md., Norfolk Sch. Art. One man shows include Tex. Luth. Coll., 1975, McCann-Wood Gallery, Lexington, Ky., 1975, Southwestern U., Georgetown, Tex., 1976, Art League, Galveston, Tex., 1976, Congl. Exhibition, U.S. House Reps., Washington, 1976, Art Council, Port Washington, N.Y., 1976, Galerie im Savoy, Kaiserslauten, Fed. Republic Germany, 1977, State Capitol Rotunda, Austin, Tex., 1977, Galerie Beck, Homburg, Fed. Republic Germany, 1977, Abilene Fine Arts Mus., Tex., 1977, Galerie Beck, Homburg, 1978, Art Mus., Abilene, Tex.; 1977, Internat. Art Mus., McAllen, Tex., 1983, Art Mus., Wichita Falls, Tex., 1985; exhibited in 14th internat. exhbns. in Europe, 15 nat. and regional exhbns., 1974-86. Served to lt. col. USAF, 1941-71; ETO, Vietnam. Decorated DFC with two silver oak leaf clusters, Bronze star, 13 air medals, Purple Heart, British Air medal, Vietnam medal of gallantry. Mem. Accademia Internazionale di Lettere, Scienze and Arte (Florence, Italy). Home: Liberty Hill, Tex. Deceased.

FOX, DANIEL W(AYNE), consumer products company executive; b. Johnstown, Pa., May 14, 1923; s. Daniel Francis and Marie Alma (Hill) F.; m. Martha Joyce Schmidt, June 6, 1948; children—Barbara Ann, Daniel S. B.S., Lebanon Valley Coll., 1948; M.S., U. Okla., 1951, Ph.D., 1953. Insulation specialist Gen. Elec. Co., Schenectady, 1953-55; plastic research mgr. Gen. Elec. Co., Pittsfield, Mass., 1955-89. Author: (with others) Aromatic Polycarbonates, 1962; contbr. articles and chpts. to profl. publs.; patentee in field. Trustee, Lebanon Valley Coll., Annville, Pa., 1975-83; bd. dirs. Pittsfield Anti-Tb Assn., 1980-89, Pittsfield Coop. Bank, 1985. Served to 1st lt. USAF, 1942-45, PTO. Fellow Am. Inst. Chemists; mem. Am. Chem.

Soc., Soc. Plastic Engrs. (inducted into Plastic Hall of Fame 1976, internat. award 1985), Nat. Acad. Egnrs., Pittsfield Country Club, Sigma Xi, Phi Lambda Upsilon. Home: Pittsfield Mass. Died Feb. 15, 1989.

FOX, EDWARD JACKSON, marketing educator; b. St. Thomas, Ont., Can., Sept. 9, 1913; came to U.S., 1935; naturalized, 1963.; s. Jay and Anne (Jackson) F.; m. Ruth Chesler, Sept. 9, 1959 (dec.); children: Brenda Steinman Fox Weissman, Gary Devenow, Sanford Lee Steinman, Lisa Terry. BA in Econs. and Polit. Sci. with honors, U. Western Ont., 1935; MS in Econs., London Sch. Econs., 1937; PhD in Econs., U. Calif., Berkeley, 1950. With Office of Price Adminstrn., 1940-41; Washington rep., then Can. textiles adminstr. Wartime Prices and Trade Bd. Can., 1941-47; prof. bus. adminstrn. U. Western Ont., 1949-54; dir. Bur. Bus. Research, 1950-53; prof. mktg. U. Miami, Fla., 1954-81, chmn. dept., 1956-69, assoc. dean grad. programs Sch. Bus. Adminstrn., 1973-74, dean, 1974-81, dean emeritus, 1981-87, disting. prof. mktg., 1981-82; mktg. and econs. cons., 1948-87; lectr. mktg., Calif. State U. Long Beach, 1982-87; prof. mktg. IMEDE Mgmt. Devel. Inst., Lausanne, Switzerland, 1967-69, Mktg. Execs. Program, 1970-72; mktg. adviser Miami-Israel C. of C., 1972-87. Author: (with E. Wheatley) Modern Marketing, 1978; editor (with David Leighton) Marketing in Canada, 1958; edit. bd. So. Jour. Bus., 1969-73. V.p. Jewish Vocat. Service, Dade County, Fla., 1964-67; mem. adv. bd. Fla. Anti-Defamation League, 1963-65; bd. dirs. Miami chpt. Am. Jewish Com., 1965-69; pres. Miami Beach chpt. UN Assn., 1956-57, Coral Gables chpt., 1962-63; bd. govs. Am. Histadrut Cultural Exchange Inst., 1965-66, bus. adv. com., 1967; tech. adv. com. Nat. Jewish Population Study, 1965-67; bd. govs. Hillel Found. U. Miami, 1971-76; bd. dirs. Jewish temple 1963-65, trustee 1966. Recipient Mktg. Educators award Acad. Mktg. Sci., 1979; Brookings Instn. fellow, 1940, U. Calif.-Ford Found. workshop fellow, 1964. Mem. Am. Mktg. Assn. (pres. Miami chpt. 1965-67), Alpha Kappa Psi, Alpha Delta Sigma, Beta Gamma Sigma, Omicron Delta Kappa, Order Artus. Home: Los Alamitos Calif. Died Jan. 14, 1987.

FOX, JOSEPH P., business executive; b. Rochester, N.Y., 1914. Grad., U. Notre Dame, 1936, Harvard Bus. Sch., 1938. chmn., dir. Champion Products, Inc., Rochester; dir. Cent. Trust. Co., Rochester, Sybron Corp., Rochester, Voplex Corp., Rochester. Home: Rochester N.Y. Died Aug. 30, 1988.

FOX, NOEL P(ETER), judge; b. Kalamazoo, Mich., Aug. 30, 1910; s. Charles and Caroline (Kokx) F.; m. Dorothy A. McCormick, Aug. 1, 1934; children—Maureen, Noel, Virginia. Ph.B., Marquette U., 1933, J.D. cum laude, 1935. Bar: Wis. 1935, Mich. 1935, U.S. Dist. Ct. (we. dist.) Wis. 1935, U.S. Dist. Ct. (we. dist.) Mich. 1936, U.S. Supreme Ct. 1959. Assoc. Bunker, Rogoski & Dunn, Muskegon, Mich., 1935-37; ptnr. Fox & Beers, Muskegon, 1946-48; assoc. Robert Cavanaugh, Paul Sorensen and Harry Knudsen, Muskegon, Mich., 1948-51; judge Mich. Cir. Ct. (14th jud. cir.), 1951-62; judge U.S. Dist. Ct. (we. dist.) Mich., 1962-71, chief judge, 1971-79, sr. judge, 1979-85, ret., 1985; mem. Mich. Labor Mediation Bd., 1941-44, chmn., 1949-51; pub. mem. for Office Econ. Mgmt. of Detroit Regional War Labor Bd., 1942-43; spl. asst. to dir. United Conciliation Service, 1946-47; mem. Mich. Youth Commn., 1949-58; vol. vets. reemployment rights committeeman Dept. Labor, 1948; mem. Mich. Gov.'s Constl. Planning Commn., 1961-62, chmn. Mich. Gov.'s Constl. Commn. for Study Jud. Articles Sect., 1961-62; chmn. spl. pub. rev. panel of hearing officers' salaries for 3 agys., 1963; panel mem. Seminar for Newly Appointed Dist. Judges, 1971-72. Bd. dirs. Muskegon Community Chest, 1955-56, Muskegon County (Mich.) Tb Assn., 1955-62; pres., mem. exec. bd. Timber Trails council Boy Scouts Am., 1955-62; chmn. Muskegon County Christmas Seal Dr., 1956; lay trustee Aquinas Coll. Recipient award for disting. service Am. Heritage Found., 1951, Civic Service award Fraternal Order Eagles, 1956, Community Service citation United Red feather Campaign Muskegon County, 1956. Mem. ABA, Fed. Bar Assn., Mich. State Bar Assn. (chmn. ct. adminstrn. com. 1960-62), Am. Judicature Soc., Muskegon County Bar Assn., Grand Rapids Bar Assn., Dist. Judges Assn. (pres. 6th Cir. 1976), Alpha Sigma Nu. Died June 3, 1987. Home: Grand Rapids Mich.

FOX, RUSSELL V., banker; b. West Milton, Ohio, 1891. Ed., Miami-Comml. Coll., 1911. Dir. emeritus 1st Nat. Bank Dayton, Ohio; bd. dirs. Anchor-Rubber Co. Trustee Ashland Coll. Mem. Msaons, Shriners. Home: Dayton Ohio. †

FOY, FRED CALVERT, chemical executive; b. San Francisco, Jan. 28, 1905; s. John M. and Emma (Squires) F.; m. Elizabeth Hamilton, Sept. 28, 1929; children: Ann Foy Gunn, Sara Foy Dixon, Fred Calvert. AB, U. Calif., 1928. Asst. mgr. pub. relations San Joaquin Light & Power Corp., Fresno, Calif., 1928-30; account rep. J. Walter Thompson Co., San Francisco, 1930-31; mgr. J. Walter Thompson Co., Los Angeles, 1932-33; v.p. J. Walter Thompson Co., Detroit, 1945-48; asst. gen. mgr. Seattle Gas Co., 1931-32; advt. mgr. Shell Oil Co., San Francisco, N.Y.C., 1933-38; v.p. Wilding Pictures, N.Y.C., 1938-40; account rep. Young & Rubicam, 1940-42; v.p. sales Koppers Co., Inc., Pitts., 1948-50, v.p., gen. mgr. tar products div., 1950-55, also bd. dirs., pres., chief exec. officer, 1955-58, chmn., pres., 1958-60, chmn., chief exec. officer, 1960-67, chmn., 1968-70, ret., 1970; bd. dirs. H.K. Porter Co., Inc. Chmn. bd. trustees Carnegie-Mellon U.; trustee Carnegie Inst.; bd. dirs. Episcopal Ch. Found. Lt. col. AUS, 1942-45. Decorated Legion of Merit. Fellow Internat. Acad. Mgmt.; mem. Bus. Council, Nat. Indsl. Conf. Bd. (sr.), Duquesne Cluv, Laurel Valley Golf Club, Rolling Rock Club, Bohemian Club. Republican. Episcopalian. Home: Rector Pa. Died Aug. 4, 1986.

FRAKER, ELMER L., association official; b. Hazelton, Kans., Nov. 18, 1892; s. John C. and Sarah Frances (Smith) F.; m. Edna M. Stuerke, June 5, 1923; children: Carolyn Fraker Atkinson, Robert Vincent. BA, U. Okla., 1920, MA, 1938. Head English dept. Cherokee High Sch., 1921-25; prin. high sch. Chickasha, Okla., 1926-39; pres. Mangum Jr. Coll., 1939-45; state adj. bus. mgr. Am. Legion Okla., 1945-55; adminstrv. sec. Okla. Hist. Soc., 1955-72, field dep., 1972-73; mem. coun. Am. Assn. State and Local History, 1960-68; v.p. N.Am. Historic Sites Commns. Assn., 1957-58; founder, 1st chmn. State History Adminstrs., 1968-69. Author workbooks: U.S. History, 1931, World History, 1933, Tall Tales, 1976; editor Okla. Legionnaire, 1945-55; mem. publ. bd. Chronicles of Okla., 1955-71. Mem. State Pardon and Parole Bd., 1942-45, Okla. City Schs. Policy Com., 1953, Oklahoma City adv. com. Salvation Army; dir. Civil Def., Southwestern Okla., State Salvage Com. World War II; mem. State Edn. Adv. Com., 4th Corps Army Area Civilian Adv. Com., State Vets. Employment Adv. Com.; candidate Dem. nomination U.S. Senate, 1944. Mem. Am. Legion (state comdr. 1935-36), U. Okla Alumni Assn. (pres. 1942), Mil. Order World Wars, Internat. Platform Assn., Oklahoma City Men's Dinner Club, Masons, Rotary, Odd Fellows, Sigma Nu. Methodist. Home: Oklahoma City Okla. Deceased.

FRANCIONI, J(OHN) B(APTISTE), JR., animal husbandry educator; b. Labdaieville, La., May 13, 1891; s. John Baptiste and Ptholama (Landry) F.; m. May A. Brown, June 16, 1915; children: Marjorie (Mrs. Charles F. Duchein), John III. BS, LA. State U. and A&M Coll., 1914, MS, 1925; postgrad., Iowa State Coll., 1923, 30-31. Technician and field-man La. State Sanitary Bd., 1914-16; with agrl. div. La. State U, 1917-19, asst. prof. animal husbandry dept., 1920-30, assoc. prof., 1930-31, prof., head animal industry dept., husbandman Agrl. Experiment Sta., 1931-61, prof. emeritus, from 1961, in charge all animal industry rsch. and teaching, 1950-55. Co-designer of steam blancher, lye peeler and continuos exhaust for use in Sch. Community Preservation Ctrs.; also developed cattle skinning cradle; author numerous articles and bulls. on livestock prodn., farm meats and food preservation. Mem. Inter-Civic Club Baton Rouge; bd. dirs. Camp Fire Girls, Salvation Army, Red Cross, Boy Scouts Am., Community Chest, Baton Rouge. Commended by U.S. Army for assisting in developing an over-seas butchering and slaughtering unit and training key personnel to man units; cited for outstanding work in edn. and rsch. on meat Nat. Livestock and Meat Bd., 1950; honors from food producing and processing agys. and orgns. Mem. AAAS (assoc.), Am. Genetic Assn., Am. Soc. Animal Prodn., Southern Agrl. Workers Assn., Future Farmers of Am., Kiwanis (past. pres., past lt. gov. La.-Miss.-W.Tenn. dist.), K.C., Block and Bridle Club, Civic Club, Alpha Zeta, Phi Kappa Phi, Omicron Delta Kappa, Theta Xi. Democrat. Roman Catholic. Home: Baton Rouge La. †

FRANCIS, CLARENCE, corporate executive; b. Port Richmond, S.I., N.Y., Dec. 1, 1888; s. Clarence Southar and Helen Annett (Hawes) F.; m. Grace Abbott Berry, May 5, 1914; children: Richard Hawes (dec.), John Berry, Barbara. BS, Amherst Coll., 1910; LLD (hon.), Trinity Coll., 1955, L.I. U. With sales dept. Corn Products Refining Co., N.Y.C., 1910-19; nat. sales mgr. cereal div. Ralston Purina Co., St. Louis, 1919-24; domestic sales mgr. Postum Co., N.Y.C., 1924; v.p., dir. Post Products, N.Y.C., 1924-27, pres., 1927-29; v.p. in charge sales Gen. Foods Corp., 1929-31, exec. v.p., 1931-35, pres., 1934-43, chmn., 1943-54, dir., mem. exec. com., 1954-58; chmn., chief exec. officer Studebaker-Packard Corp, 1961-63; chmn. Lillard Syndications, Inc., 1964-65, Francis-Lillard Assocs., Inc., from 1968; bd. dirs. Lehman Corp., Mead Corp., Air Reduction Co., Inc., N.P. Ry., Gen. Foods Corp., Mut. Life Ins. Co., Smith Corona Marchant, Inc.; bd. govs. Fed. Res. Bank of N.Y.; pub. gov. N.Y. Stock Exchange. Author: A History of Food and Its Preservation, 1937. Chmn. bd. dirs., mem. exec. com. Fund for Adult Edn. The Ford Found.; trustee Nutrition Found., Lawrence Hosp., Bronxville, N.Y., Eisenhower Exchange Fellowships, Inc.; fin. chmn., dir., chmn. devel. com. Lincoln Ctr. for Performing Arts; chmn. adv. com. Inst. Nutritional Sci. Columbia; Am. rep. European Productivity Agy.; pres., dir. Econ. Devel. Com., N.Y.C.; chmn. Citizens Com. for Hoover Report; trustee Com. Econ. Devel.; mem. planning group Moffett Program in agr. and bus. Harvard U., also numerous fed., state and local govtl. adv. bodies.; dep. sheriff Westchester County, N.Y. Lt. col. N.Y. State Guard, 1913-14. Decorated Order of Cruzeiro do Sul (Brazil), 1954; named Man of Yr., NAM, 1953; recipient U.S. C. of C. award, 1954, Gold Brotherhood Disting. Service award NCCJ, 1953, Henry Laurence Gantt gold medal award, 1954, Advt. award for public service, 1955, Clarence Francis cha for sociology established in his honor Amherst Coll 1968; inducted Hall of Fame, Boston Conf. on Distbn 1950. Mem. Am. Assembly (chmn. policy com.), Am Assn. for UN (pres. UN Week), Am. Korean Foun (dir.), Sales Execs. Club, U.S. C. of C. (dir.), Unio League, Sky Club, Bronxville Derby Club, Siwanc Country Club, Blind Brook Club, Am. Yacht Club Delta Upsilon. Republican. Mem. Dutch Ref. Ch. Home: Bronxville N.Y. Died Dec. 22, 1985.

FRANCIS, MARION SMITH, lawyer; b. Slater, Mo July 17, 1905; s. Marion L. and Annie Marian (Smith F.; m. Jewel M. Brandenberger, May 26, 1943; 1 son James Ashby. Student, Kemper Mil. Sch., 1923-24 A.B., U. Mo., 1927, J.D., 1929. Bar: Mo. bar 1928. Practice of law Mexico, Mo., 1929-38; pub. adminstr Audrain Co., Mo., 1931-33; mem. Pub. Service Commn Mo., Jefferson City, 1938-41; asso. Bryan, Cave McPheeters & McRoberts, St. Louis, 1942-50; partner Bryan, Cave, McPheeters & McRoberts, 1951-77 counsel, from 1978; Past trustee Mo. U. Law Sch Found. Served from 2d lt. to maj., judge adv. gen. dep AUS, 1943-46; served with 70th inf. div. 7th army ETO Mem. St. Louis, Mo. State, Am. bar assns., S.A.R Judge Advocates Assn., Phi Gamma Delta, Phi Delt Phi. Clubs: Mo. Athletic (St. Louis), Bellerive Countr (St. Louis). Home: Saint Louis Mo. Deceased.

FRANCIS, ROBERT, author; b. Upland, Pa., Aug. 12 1901; s. Ebenezer Fisher and Ida May (Allen) F. A.B Harvard U., 1923, Ed.M., 1926; L.H.D., U. Mass 1970. Author: poetry Stand With Me Here, 1936 Valhalla and Other Poems, 1938, The Sound I Listene For, 1944, The Face Against the Glass, 1950, The Or Weaver, 1960, Come Out Into the Sun, 1965, Lik Ghosts of Eagles, 1974, Robert Francis: Collecte Poems, 1936-76, 1976, Butter Hill and Other Poems 1984; fiction We Fly Away, 1948; essays The Satirica Rogue on Poetry, 1968, Pot Shots at Poetry, 1980, Th Satrical Rogue on All Fronts, 1984; prose sketches an poems A Certain Distance, 1976; autobiography Th Trouble With Francis, 1971, Frost: A Time to Talk Conversations and Indiscretions Recorded by Rober Francis, 1972; interview Francis on the Spot, 1976 Travelling In Amherst, 1986, The Trouble With God 1986; rec. Robert Francis Reads His Poems, 1975. Co recipient Shelley Meml. award, 1938; recipient Golde Rose award New Eng. Poetry Club, 1942, Jennie Tan Poetry award Mass. Rev., 1962; Brandeis U. Creativ Arts award in poetry, 1974; Phi Beta Kappa poet Tuft U., 1955; Phi Beta Kappa poet Harvard, 1960; Rom fellow Am. Acad. Arts and Letters, 1957-58; fellowshi, award Acad. Am. Poets, 1984; Amy Lowell poetr travelling scholar, 1967-68. Fellow Acad. Am. Poets hon. mem. Phi Beta Kappa. Home: Amherst Mass Died July 14, 1987; cremated.

FRANCO, JOHAN (HENRI GUSTAVE), composer b. Zaandam, Netherlands, July 12, 1908; came to U.S 1934, naturalized, 1942; s. S. Franco and Margaretha J.E.C. (Gosschalk) F.; m. Eloise Lavrischeff, Mar. 28 1948. Grad., First Coll., The Hague; studied composition with, Willem Pijper, Amsterdam, 4 yrs. Entire program of his compositions was presented at Town Hall, N.Y., 1938; commd. to write opening music a Centennial of his college, 1938; collaborated with Osca Thompson on sect. on Contemporary Dutch composer in the Cyclopedia of Music and Musicians, 1938; prin works include 5 symphonies, 6 concerti lirici, Divertimento for Flute and Strings, 1946, many songs, 2 cello sonatas, 1 viola sonata, 6 partitas for piano, 16 partita and other compositions for carillon, As the Prophet Foretold (cantata), The Stars Look Down (oratorio) The Prodigal, Songs of the Spirit (for soprano and woodwind quintet), The Song of Life (for mixed chorus a cappella), Seven Biblical Sketches (for carillon and narrator), Twelve Preludes (for piano); recs. Fantasy for Cello and Orch, The Virgin Queen's Dream (for soprano and orch.), Symphony V " The Cosmos", As the Prophets Foretold (for soloists, mixed chorus, brass, and carillon), Theater Music, Seven Biblical Sketches (for carillon and narrator); incidental music for 5 prodns The Tempest, The Book of Job, Romans By St. Paul Electra, The Pilgrim's Progress. Served in U.S. Army Mar. 1942-Sept. 1943. Mem. Am. Composers Alliance (B.M.I.). Home: Virginia Beach Va. Died Apr. 14 1988; cremated.

FRANCOIS-PONCET, ANDRE, diplomat; b. Provins France, June 13, 1887; m. Mlle Dillais; children: Louis Henri, Bernard, Jean, Geneviéve. Laureat at gen. exams., l'Ecole Normale Suérieure, 1907. Collaborator l'Opinion, 1911; lectr. l'Ecole Poly., 1913; with French Embassy, Bern, Switzerland, 1917-18; mem. Internat Econ. Mission to U.S.; del. of French govt. to confs Genoa and Ruhr, 1919; founder The Buelletin, 1920 mem. dirs. com. Rep. Dem. Alliance; elected dep. from 17th Arrondissement of Paris 1924, 28; mem. Commn of Fins.; under-sec. of state for Beaux-Art, participant numerous internat. confs., until 1931; ambass. to Germany Berlin, 1931-38; ambass. to The Quirinal 1938 returned to France, 1940, deported and interned by Gestapo, 1943; diplomatic councilor Frech Govt., 1948 High Commr. of French Republic in Germany 1949-55. Pub. 1st work on Les affinitiés électives (Goethe), 1910 author Ce que pense la jeunesse allemande, a study 1913, Souvenirs d'une Ambassade à Berlin, 1946, De

Versailles à Potsdam, 1946. Pres. French Red Cross, permanent commn. Internat. Red Cross, 1949. Lt. inf. French Army, 1914-16. Received 1st standing in exam. for German fellowship, 1910. Mem. Académie francaise, 1952 (elected). Roman Catholic. Home: Paris France. †

FRANK, AARON M., merchant; b. Portland, Oreg., Feb. 24, 1891; s. Sigmund and Fanny (Meier) F.; m. Ruth Rosenfeld, OCt. 26, 1916 (dec.); children: Richard (dec.), Gerald W.; m. Carrie Latz, Feb. 22, 1948. LLB, U. Oreg., 1913; LLD (hon.), Portland U., 1951. Bar: Oreg. 1913. Assoc. with Meier & Frank Co. (dept. store founded by grandfather 1857), from 1914, pres., gen. mgr., 1937, also bd. dirs. Elected Portland's first citizen, 1930. Home: Garden Home Oreg. †

FRANK, JEROME J., manufacturing company executive; b. Detroit, Oct. 31, 1912; s. Samuel and Kate (Jacob) F.; m. Barbara, June 1938 (dec. 1958); children: Keith H., Susan Frank Schwartz; m. 2d, Charlotte M. Meier, Apr. 27, 1973. BA in Math., U. Mich., 1934. Foundryman, engr., purchasing and corp. sec. D.A.B. Industries, Troy, Mich., 1934-48, v.p., 1948-56, exec. v.p., from 1956, pres., 1957-72, chmn. bd., from 1972; trustee, v.p. fin., chmn. fin., exec., nominating, long range coms. Sinai Hosp., Detroit. Mem. adv. staff War Prodn. Bd., 1940-46. Mem. Engring. Soc. Detroit, Soc. Automotive Engrs., Econ. Club Detroit, Detroit Hist. Soc., Founders Soc.-Detroit Inst. Arts., U. Mich. Alumni Assn. Republican. Jewish. Home: Troy Mich. Deceased.

FRANKHAUSER, GERHARD, biologist, educator; b. Burgdorf, Switzerland, Mar. 11, 1901; s. Max and Anna (Hermann) F.; m. Erna Koestler, Aug. 28, 1931; children: David, Andreas, Anne and Marguerite (twins). Student, U. Geneva, U. Zurich; PhD, U. Berne, 1924. Instr. zoology U. Berne, Switzerland, 1925-29; Rockefeller Found. fellow U. Chgo. and Yale U., 1929-31; asst. prof. biology Princeton (N.J.) U., 1931-39, assoc. prof., 1939-46, prof., from 1946, Edwin Grant Conklin prof. biology, 1956-69, prof. emeritus, from 1969. Contbr. articles to profl. jours. Mem. AAAS, Am. Soc. Zoologists, Am. Assn. Anatomists, Am. Genetics Soc., Am. Soc. Naturalists, Soc. Study Growth, Internat. Inst. Embryology, Internat. Soc. Cell Biology, Sigma Xi. Home: Princeton N.J. Died Oct. 1, 1981.

FRANTZ, HARRY WARNER, reporter; b. Cerro Gordo, Ill., Nov. 5, 1891; s. John S. and Ada (Carver) F.; m. Kathleen Hargrave, Feb. 15, 1924; 1 child, Jean (Mrs. Eric A. Blackall). Student, Stanford U., 1913-19. Internat. corr. from 1917; mem. staff fgn. dept. UPI, from 1920; dir. publicity Yellowstone Nat. Park, 1923; press. dir. Office Inter-Am. Affairs, 1941-44; info. officer with asst sec. state for Am. Republics 1944-45; mem. info. staff Chapultepec confs., San Francisco, 1945; explored Mountain Province, Luzon, 1916; ambulance driver French Army, Orient, 1917; sec., insp., historian Commn. to Serbia, ARC, 1917-19. Contbr. articles to news mags., jours. Decorated svc. medal with group citation French Army; Red Cross medal (Serbia); Order of White Eagle (Yugoslavia); Order So. Cross (Brazil); Order of Merit Eloy Colon Alfaro medal (Ecuador); recipient Maria Moors Cabot gold medal Columbia U., 1957, cert. of merit Internat. House, gold medal U.S. Antarctic Svc. Mem. Nat. Geog. Soc. (Jane N. Smith life mem., citation), Am. Geophys. Union, Antarctican Soc. Washington, Overseas Writers' Club. Episcopalian. Home: Ithaca N.Y. †

FRASER, PETER MACGREGOR, life insurance executive; b. East Orange, N.J., Mar. 10, 1891; s. Peter MacGregor and Martha (Morrison) F.; m. Mable Wark, May 3, 1915; children: Aileen Macgregor (Mrs. Frank Balbirne Alberts), Peter MacGregor. Student, pub. schs. Newark and Bklyn., Queens Park Sch., Scotland. Supr. Ives & Myrick Agy., Mut. Life Ins. Co. N.Y., 1914-18; gen. agt. Conn. Mut. Life Ins. Co., N.Y.C., 1918-30; v.p., dir. Conn. Mut. Life Ins. Co., Hartford, 1930-44, pres., 1944-55, chmn., 1955-57, chmn., exec. com., 1957-59, dir., mem. exec. com., from 1959; mem. adv. bd. Conn. Bank & Trust Co., Phoenix Ins. Co., Conn. Fire Ins. Co.; bd. dirs. The Hartford Courant, Conn. Light & Power Co., Hartford, Mohasco Industries Inc., Amsterdam, N.Y. Trustee Hartford Hosp. Mem. Island Club (Hobe Sound, Fla.), Hartford Club, Hartford Golf Club, St. Andrews Soc., Links Club (N.Y.C.), Seminole Club (Palm Beach, Fla.). Republican. Congregationalist. Home: West Hartford Conn. †

FRASURE, CARL MAYNARD, educator, consultant; b. Oakland, Ohio, Jan. 15, 1903; s. Nelson and Minnie (Valentine) F.; m. Louise Durham, Dec. 26, 1930; children: Carl Maynard, Robert Conway. BA, Ohio State U., 1924, MA, 1925, PhD, 1928; student, U. Chgo., 1925, 26, Cambridge (Eng.) U., 1929-30; LLD (hon.), Morris Harvey Coll., Charleston, 1966. Instr. polit. sci. and history W.Va. U., 1927-29, asst. prof. polit. sci., 1930-35, assoc. prof., 1935-40, prof., 1940-72, chmn. dept., 1935-61, dir. bur. Govt. Research, 1949-61, dean Coll. Arts and Scis., 1961-69; cons. exec. and legislative depts. W.Va., 1933-69, Council Govts. Disaster Project, Washington, 1972-76; dir. W.Va. Merit System, 1940-41, OPA for W.Va., 1942-43; chmn. W.Va. Commn. Interstate Coop., 1944-66; dir. OPS for W.Va., 1951; spl. asst. to regional, nat. dirs. OEP, 1958; chmn. com. on state ofcls. on drafting suggested state legislation Council State Govts., Chgo., 1965-73. Author: British Policy on War Debts and Reparations, 1940, (with others) West Virginia State and Local Government, 1963; editor State Papers of Governor Arch A. Moore, from 1976. Mem. Am. Polit. Sci. Assn., So. Polit. Sci. Assn., AAUP, Kappa Delta Rho. Democrat. Episcopalian. Home: Morgantown W.V. Died Apr. 10, 1986; buried Oak Grove Cemetery, Morgantown, W.Va.

FRAZIER, JOHN EARL, chemical engineer; b. Houseville, Pa., July 4, 1902; s. Chauncey E. and Mary Ellen (Gibson) F.; m. Frances Sprague Lang, June 23, 1936 (dec.); children: John Earl II, Thomas Gibson. BS, Washington and Jefferson Coll., 1922; postgrad., MIT, 1922-24, SM, 1924; ScD, U. Brazil, 1938. Chemist and engr. Berney Bond Glass Co. (now Owens-Ill. Inc.), 1924-26; fuel engr. Simplex Engring. Co., 1926-28, asst. sec., asst. treas., 1928-30, sec., treas., 1930-38; v.p., treas. Frazier-Simplex, Inc., 1938-45, pres., sec., 1945-67, pres., treas., from 1967; mem. adv. bd. Pitts. Nat. Bank (Washington County br.); pres., dir. Washington Union Trust Co., Washington County Motor Club; pres. adv. bd. dept. ceramic engring. U. Ill. Contbr. papers for trade and sci. publs. Pres. bd. trustees Western State Sch. and Hosp., Canonsburg; trustee, sec., treas., chmn. property com. Washington Hosp.; life trustee, v.p., asst. sec. bd. Washinton and Jefferson Coll.; chmn. Pa. Economy League (Washington County br.); pres. Washington C. of C., Nat. Soc. Am. Comp. Shooters. Recipient Achievement Citation award Washington and Jefferson Coll., 1953, Disting. Citizen award Washington City Council, 1960; named Kappa Sigma Frat. Man of Yr., 1964; named to Bus. and Profl. Hall of Fame, 1966. Fellow Royal Soc. Arts Eng. (Benjamin Franklin fellow), Am. Inst. Chemists, AAAS, Am. Ceramic Soc. (Albert V. Bleininger Meml. award 1969, John Jeppson award 1976, v.p. 1967-68, treas. 1968-69, pres. 1970-71, hon. life mem. 1978, chmn. Orton Meml. lecture com. 1968), Nat. Acad. Engring. U.S.A. (life), Intercontinental Biog. Assn. (life), Soc. Glass Tech. of Eng.; mem. Pa. Ceramic Assn. (pres., dir.), Ind. Heating Equipment Assn. (pres.), Am. Chem. Soc., Am. Soc. Mil. Engrs., NSPE, ASHRAE, ASTM, Nat. Inst. Ceramic Engrs. (PACE award judge 1962), Pa. Soc. of N.Y.C., Nat. Rifle Assn. Am., Pictorial Photographers Am., Royal Photog. Soc. of Eng., Photog. Soc. Am., Am. Legion., Pa. Atomic Scientists, N.Y. Acad. Scis., Pa. Acad. Sci., Keramos (Greaves-Walker roll of honor), Fortnightly Club, Univ. Pitts. Club, Masons, Shriners, Lions (Lion of Yr. 1970), Elks, Phi Beta Kappa, Sigma Xi, Phi Chi Mu, Kappa Sigma. Republican. Presbyterian. Home: Washington Pa. Died Jan. 1, 1985; buried Washington Cemetery, Pa.

FREDERICK, JULIAN ROSS, educator; b. Sioux Falls, S.D., June 10, 1913; s. Wellington Grey and Mabel Anne (Beebe) F.; m. Merian Ruth Brown, Feb. 27, 1944; children: James R., Richard D., Constance L., Linda S., Carol L. BS, Iowa State U., 1935, MS, 1936; PhD, U. Mich., 1948. Certified mfg. engr. Researcher assoc. U. Mich., Ann Arbor, 1939-46, researcher physicist, lectr. physics, 1950-57, asst. prof. mech. engring., 1957-64, assoc. prof., 1964-70, prof., from 1970; asst. prof. physics Brown U., Providence, 1947-50; v.p. Arborsonics Co. Author: Ultrasonic Engineering, 1965; guest editor Materials Evaluation, 1978. Mem. Ann Arbor City Council, 1945-47. Fellow Acoustical Soc. Am., Am. Soc. for Nondestructive Testing; mem. ASME, ASTM, European Acoustic Emission Working Group, U.S. Acoustic Emission Working Group, Am. Soc. for Metals, IEEE. Home: Ann Arbor Mich. Died Feb. 28, 1983; cremated.

FREDERICK, J(USTUS) GEORGE, author; b. Reading, Pa., Jan. 14, 1882; s. Frank B. and Rosa (Mansfield) F.; m. Christine McGaffey, June 29, 1907; children: David Mansfield, Jean Olive, Phyllis, Carol. Ed. high sch. Editor Judicious Advertising Mag., Chgo., 1905-07, Business World, 1907-08; mng. editor Printers' Ink, 1908-11; editor Advertising and Selling Mag., 1911-15; founder, then pres. Business Bourse International, a rsch. and publishing firm, N.Y.C.; public speaker, U.S. and Europe. Author numerous books including: Forecast of Business Changes to Come in Atomic Age, Introduction to Office Management, 1950, Introduction to Motivation Research, 1957, 1000 Pleasure Spots in Beautiful America, 1957, Brilliant Sales Promotion, 1959; co-editor, complier The technique of Marketing Research, 1937; staff contbr. Ency. Britannica and Belson Loose Leaf Ency.; contbr. articles to mags. Treas. original Vigilance Com., N.Y., out of which grew Better Bus. Burs. Mem. Soc. Arts and Scis., Comml. Standards Coun., Lotos Club, N.Y. Nat. Rep. Club, N.Y. Salesmanager's Club (founder), Asterisk Club, Writer's Club (pres.), Gourmet Club (pres.). Home: New York N.Y. †

FREDERICKS, CARLTON, nutritionist, researcher, author, educator; b. N.Y.C., Oct. 23, 1910; s. David Charles Caplan and Blanche Goldsmith; m. Betty Shachter, Oct. 26, 1946; children: Alice, April, Dana, Spencer, Rhonda. BA, U. Ala., 1931; MA, NYU, 1949, PhD, 1955. Dir. edn. Casimir Funk Lab., N.Y.C., 1939-44; nat. broadcaster local and network radio N.Y.C., 1941-83; dir. nutrition services Atkins Med. Ctr., N.Y.C., 1982-87; nutrition cons. Dr. Paul Rosch, Yonkers, N.Y., 1983-87; vis. prof. edn. Fairleigh Dickinson U., Rutherford, N.J., 1974-82; bd. dirs. Am. Inst. Stress, Yonkers, N.Y., 1982-87; founding fellow Internat. Coll. Applied Nutrition, La Habra, Calif., from 1955. Author: Low Blood Sugar and You, 1969 (ABA award 1970), Nutrition Guide, 1982, Program for Living Longer, 1983. Recipient Rachel Carson Found. award, 1982; recipient citations Huxley Inst., N.Y.C., 1980, citations Internat. Acad. Metabology, Los Angeles, 1980, Disting. Achievement award Fairleigh Dickinson U., 1984. Fellow Internat. Acad. Preventive Medicine (hon. pres.), Internat. Acad. Metabology (hon. pres.), Royal Soc. Health, Price-Pottenger Found., Internat. Acad. Orthomolecular Medicine (hon. mem.); mem. Phi Beta Kappa. Home: New York N.Y. Died July 28, 1987.

FREDERICKSON, EVAN LLOYD, physician, educator; b. Spring Green, Wis., Mar. 1, 1922; s. Edward and Rebecca Lloyd (Jones) F.; m. Ruth Evans Murphey, Sept. 17, 1946; children—Mary Evans, Helen Lloyd, Edward Dent. B.S., U. Wis., 1947, M.D., 1950; M.S., U. Iowa, 1953. Diplomate: Am. Bd. Anesthesiology. Intern Walter Reed Army Hosp., Washington, 1950-51; resident State U. Iowa Hosps., 1951-53; practice medicine, specializing in anesthesiology Atlanta, 1965-86; instr., asst. prof. U. Kans. Med. Sch., 1953-56, prof., 1959-65; asst. prof., then asso. prof. U. Wash. Sch. Medicine, 1956-59; prof., dir. anesthesia research Emory U. Sch. Medicine, Atlanta, 1965-86; dir. Computer Dynamics, Inc.; mem. anesthesiology tng. com. NIH, 1969-73; mem. adv. com. FDA, 1971-75; appointed faculty emeritus, Dept. Anesthesiology, Sch. Medicine Emory U., 1986. Asso. editor: Surveys of Anesthesiology, 1964-73, Clin. Anesthesia, 1967-70; Contbr. articles to profl. jours. Bd. dirs. Immunologic Cancer Research Fund; trustee Wood Library and Mus., Crawford W. Long Mus. Served with AUS, 1943-46, 50-51. Fellow Am. Coll. Anesthesiologists; mem. Am. Soc. Anesthesiologists, AMA, AAAS, Assn. U. Anesthesiologists, Sigma Xi, Alpha Omega Alpha. Home: Atlanta Ga. Died Nov. 17, 1986; buried Decatur (Ga.) Cemetery.

FREEDMAN, MRS. ISIDOR, organization executive; b. N.Y.C., Feb. 9, 1888; d. Max I. and Lina (Klein) Lefkowitz; m. Isidor Freedman, Mar. 27, 1906; children: Milton, Linore (Mrs. Jess Ward), Harriett (Mrs. Carl Marcus), David. Ed. pub. schs., N.Y.C. Charter mem., a founder Women's br., Union Orthodox Jewish Congregations Am. Can., nat. v.p., 1924-38, pres., 1938-46, hon. nat. pres., from 1946; a founder Hebrew Tchrs. Tng. Sch. for Girls, 1928, rec. sec., from 1928; mem. Nat. Jewish Welfare Bd., from 1941, chmn. religious activities com. Greater N.Y. Army and Navy com., from 1941; vice chmn. Jewish Coun. for Russian War Relief, 1942-47; mem. nat. steering com., nat. exec. bd. Supplies for Overseas Survivors Collection, mem. nat. coun. joint distbn. com., from 1946; del. 1st World Congress for Hebrew Lit. and Culture, Jerusalem, 1950; v.p. Fedn. Jewish Women's Orgns., Inc., Sisterhood of Congregation of Path of Life, from 1936; rec. sec. Jewish Braille Inst. Am.; founder Internat. Synagogue at idlewild Airport; mem. NCCJ, Nat. Coun. Jewish Women. Permanent del. to Am.-Jewish Conf., from 1944; del. 1st World Conf. Ashkenasi and Sephardic Synagogue Jews, Jerusalem, Jan. 1968; mem. organizing com. USO Canteen, Temple Emanu-El, World War II; fin. sec. League for Safeguarding the Fixity of the Sabbath, from 1930. Recipient citations Nat. Jewish Welfare Bd., U.S. Treasury Dept., Hebrew Tchrs. Tng. Sch. for Girls, Coun. for Russian War Relief. Home: New York N.Y. †

FREEHAFER, EDWARD GEIER, librarian; b. Reading, Pa., Feb. 11, 1909; s. Edward Franklin and Martha Frances (Weitzel) F.; m. E. Isabel Houck, July 7, 1934; 1 son, John Geier. AB, Brown U., 1930, LHD (hon.), 1955; BS, Columbia Sch. Library Service, 1932; LHD (hon.), Hamilton Coll., 1970. Student asst. Columbia Sch. Bus. Library, 1931-32; reference asst. main reading room and econs. div. N.Y. Pub. Library, 1932-36, gen. asst., 1936-41, chief Am. history and genealogy div., 1941-44, acting chief acquisition div., 1942-44, exec. asst., 1945-47, chief personnel office, 1947-53, chief reference dept., 1954, dir., 1954-70, ret., 1971; asst. librarian Brown U. Library, 1944-45. Mem. ALA, N.Y. Library Assn., Century Assn., Kappa Sigma. Home: Pelham N.Y. Died Dec. 16, 1985.

FREEHAFER, LYTLE JUSTIN, university administrator; b. Texhoma, Okla., Feb. 9, 1910; s. Franklin E. and Bertha (Krieg) F.; m. Ruth V. Ward, Oct. 14, 1933; children: Ann Freehafer Andersen, Luby Freehafer Wold, John (dec.). BA cum laude, De Pauw U., 1931. Auditor fiscal adminstrv. offices State of Ind., 1933-39, 47-48, dir. budget, 1949-52; asst. comptroller Purdue U., 1953, comptroller, asst. bus. mgr., 1954, bus. mgr., asst. treas., 1955-60, v.p. treas., 1961-74; dir. Lafayette Life Ins. Co. Contbr. articles to profl. jours. Col. AUS, 1940-46. Recipient Good Govt. award Ind. Jr. C. of C., 1950. Mem. Blue Key, Rotary, Sigma Delta Chi, Lambda Chi Alpha, Omicron Delta Kappa. Methodist. Home: West Lafayette Ind. Died Nov. 1, 1987.

FREEHOF, SOLOMON BENNETT, rabbi; b. London, Aug. 9, 1892; naturalized, 1916; s. Isaac and Golda (Blonstein) F.; m. Lillian Simon, Oct. 29, 1934. AB, U. Cin., 1914; rabbi, DD, Hebrew Union

Coll., Cin., 1916, DHL, 1944; DHL, Jewish Inst. Religion, 1945. Prof. rabbinics Hebrew Union Coll., 1915-24; rabbi K.A.M. Temple, Chgo., 1924-35, Rodef Shalom Temple, Pitts., from 1934; past pres. Cen. Conf. Am. Rabbis. Author: Preface to Scripture, 1950, Reform Jewish Practice, Vol. 2, 1952, The Book of Job: A Commentary, Responsa Literature, 1955, Reform Responsa, 1960. Chmn. Commn. on Jewish Edn.; former chmn. div. religious activites Nat. Jewish Welfare Bd.; hon. life pres. World Union Progressive Judaism. 1st lt. Am. Expeditionary Force, World War I. Home: Pittsburgh Pa. †

FREELAND, T. PAUL, lawyer; b. Princeton, Ind., Sept. 26, 1916; s. Leander Theodore and Leona B. (Tryon) F.; m. Caroline Van Dyke Ransom, July 7, 1941; 1 child, Caroline Carr (Mrs. Torrance C. Raymond). A.B., DePauw U., 1937; LL.B., Columbia U., 1940. Bar: N.Y., D.C., Mass. Assoc. firms Cravath, de Gersdorff, Swaine & Wood, N.Y.C., summer 1939, Dunnington, Bartholow & Miller, 1940-42; atty. office chief counsel IRS, 1945-48; ptnr. firms Wenchel, Schulman & Manning, Washington, 1948-62, Sharp & Bogan, Washington, 1962-65, Bogan & Freeland, Washington, 1965-83, Sutherland, Asbill & Brennan, Washington, 1983-88; lectr. various tax insts. Trustee Embry-Riddle Aero. U., 1972-82. Served as lt. USCGR, 1942-45, ETO. Fellow Am. Bar Found.; mem. Am., Inter-Am., Fed., D.C. bar assns., Internat. Fiscal Assn., U.S. C. of C. (task force on internat. tax policy), Phi Delta Phi. Clubs: Met. (D.C.), Chevy Chase (Md.). Home: Bethesda Md. Died Aug. 28, 1988.

FREEMAN, ALWYN VERNON, lawyer; b. Detroit, Dec. 11, 1910; s. Alexander and Sadie (Jacobs) F.; m. Grenna Sloan, Nov. 7, 1948; 1 child, Janne Sloan. AB cum laude, U. Mich., 1930; LLB, Harvard U., 1933; postgrad. (Carnegie fellow), Hague Acad. Internat. Law, 1934-35; diplome, Inst. U. Hautes Etudes Internationales, 1938; D es Sci. Politiques cum laude, U. Geneva, 1938. Bar: Mich. 1934. With AP Bur., Geneva, 1935; counsel U.S. sect. U.S.-Mex. Agrarian Claims Commn., 1939-40; with U.S. Maritime Commn., 1941-42; asst. legal adviser Dept. State, 1946-47, legal counsel, 1951-53; cons. U.S. Senate Fgn. Relations Com., 1953-58; dep. rep. IAEA at UN Hdqrs., 1958-62; U.S. agt. Jones Arbitration between Norway and U.S., 1952; lectr. internat. law Am. U., Washington, 1946-47; lectr. Acad. de Droit Internat., The Hague, 1955; assoc. prof. law Ohio State U., 1947-49; vis. prof. internat. law UCLA Law Sch., 1960, U. Mich. Law Sch., 1963, Johns Hopkins Sch. Advanced Internat. Studies, 1965-68; Stockton prof. internat. law Naval War Coll., 1972-74; del. ABA to 4th Inter-Am. Bar Conf., Santiago, Chile, 1945; mem. Am. del. Far Eastern Commn., 1946-47; Am. del. Conf. Govt. Experts for Revision Geneva Convs. on Prisoners of War, 1947; apptd. by Pres. as U.S. mem. Inter-Am. Juridical Com., 1949-50; U.S. del. 1st meeting Inter-Am. Council Jurists, Rio de Janeiro, 1950; U.S. rep., chief del. 4th Inter-Am. Council Jurists, Santiago, 1959; IAEA rep. 9th meeting Econ. Commn. for Latin Am., Santiago, 1960; mem. adv. bd. Am. Law Inst. Restatement Fgn. Relations Law; mem. Harvard Law Sch. adv. com. for draft codification on responsibility of states; mem. U.S. del. Xth Gen. Assembly UN, North Atlantic Treaty Assembly, 1976, 78-80; IAEA del. to UN Prep. Commn. Spl. Fund, to 13th to 16th Gen. Assemblies; dir. Research Ctr., Hague Acad. Internat. Law, 1957-58; U.S. mem. Canadian-Am. Lake Ontario Claims Arbitration Tribunal, 1966-68; adv. com. U.S. fgn. relations Dept. State, 1971-74, chmn., 1974; dir. Bank of the Commonwealth Detroit, vice chmn. bd., 1964-65; dir. 1st Charter Fin. Corp., Beverly Hills, Calif., Internat. Inst., Los Angeles. Author: The International Responsibility of States for Denial of Justice, 1938; Responsibility of States for Unlawful Acts of Their Armed Forces, 1956; editor-in-chief: Internat. Lawyer, 1975-78, editor emeritus, 1979—; bd. editors Am. Jour. Internat. Law, 1955-72, hon. editor, 1976—; contbr. articles to internat. law jours. Served to capt. JAGC, U.S. Army, 1942-46. Named hon. fellow Cedars-Sinai Med. Ctr. Mem. ABA (council sect. internat. law), Mich. Bar Assn., Am. Soc. Internat. Law (exec. council 1949-52, 56-59), Internat. Law Assn., Internat. Assn. Space Law, Soc. Comparative Legis. Internat. Law, Order of Coif. Clubs: Masons; Bahia de Santiago Golf and Country; Racquet (Palm Springs, Calif.); Harvard (Detroit and N.Y.C.); Cosmos (Washington); Anthony Wayne Soc. (Detroit). Home: Detroit Mich. Died Mar. 3, 1983; buried Machpelah Cemetery, Ferndale, Mich.

FREEMAN, CYNTHIA (BEA FEINBERG), author; b. N.Y.C.; d. Albert C. and Sylvia Jeannette (Hack) F.; married; 2 children. Student public schs. Interior designer; author: A World Full of Strangers, 1974, Fairytales, 1978, Days of Winter, 1977, Portraits, 1979, Come Pour the Wine, 1980, No Time for Tears, 1981, Catch the Gentle Dawn, 1983, Illusions of Love, 1985, Seasons of the Heart, 1986, The Last Princess, 1988. Home: San Francisco Calif. Deceased.

FREEMAN, PAUL LAMAR, JR., former army officer, business executive; b. Manila, The Philippines, June 29, 1907; s. Paul Lamar and Emma Rosenbaum F.; m. Mary Anne Fishburn, Aug. 18, 1932; 1 child, Anne Sewell (Mrs. Roy G. McLeod). Commd. 2d lt., inf. U.S. Army, 1929, advanced through grades to gen., 1962, served in CBI, 1941-43; in Philippine liberation campaign; participant Combines Chiefs of Staff Confs., London and Quebec, 1944; mem. Joint Brazil-U.S. Mil. Commn. in Brazil, 1945-47; chief Latin Am. br., plans and ops. div. Army Gen. Staff and U.S. Army div.,; mem. Joint Brazil-U.S. Def. Commn., Washington, 1948-50; comdr. 23d Inf. Reg. 2d Div., Korea, Aug. 1950, until wounded, Feb. 1951; dep. dir. Plans and Ops., U.S. European Command; comdr. 2d Inf. Div., 1955-57; sr. army mem. Weapons System Evaluation Group, Sec. of Def., Washington, 1957-58; comdt. Inf. Sch., comdg. gen. Inf. Ctr., Ft. Benning, Ga., 1958-60; dep. comdg. gen. for res. forces Ft. Monroe, Va., 1960-62; comdr. Joint Task Force Four, Ft. Monroe, 1961-62; comdr.-in-chief U.S. Army, Europe, also comdr. Cen. Army Group (NATO), 1962-65; comdg. gen. U.S. Continental Army Command, comdr.-in-chief U.S. Army Strike Command and U.S. Army Atlantic, Ft. Monroe, Va., 1965-67, ret., 1967; v.p. ops. planning Mellonics div. Litton Industries, 1968-70; spl. cons. Litton Industries, 1971-88. Decorated D.S.C., D.S.M., Legion of Merit, Silver Star with oak leaf cluster, Bronze Star with 3 oak leaf clusters, Air medal, Purple Heart, comdr. Legion of Honor, Croix de Guerre with Palm (France); Ordem do Merito (Brazil); Grand Cross Order of Merit (Germany); Grand Cross Order Mil. Merit (Spain), Gen. Staff insignia (Argentina). Clubs: Presidio Golf (San Francisco); Monterey Peninsula Country (Pebble Beach, Calif.). Home: Carmel Calif. Died Apr. 17, 1988, buried Arlington, Va.

FREESE, CARL GATES, banker; b. Framingham, Mass., Dec. 23, 1892; s. John Perley and Grace Eva (Gates) G.; m. Dorothy H. Clapp, May 3, 1924; children: Carl Gates, Nancy Jackson (Mrs. Boardman Brown). AB, Harvard, 1915. Rep. So. Ry., Argentina and Uruguay, 1914; joined R.L. Day & Co., investment bankers, Boston and N.Y.C., 1919, ptnr., 1928-43; v.p. Conn. Savs. Bank, New Haven, 1944, pres. and treas., 1948-62, chmn., 1962-67, vice chmn. and trustee, 1967-70, hon. trustee, from 1970; hon. trustee Conn. Med. Service (Blue Shield), So. Conn. Gas Co.; former dir. U.S. Casualty Co., New Amsterdam Casualty Co., Security Ins. Co., Francestown, N.H. Water Co., New Haven Gas Co.; mem. Savs. Bank R.R. Bond com. Author banking articles in trade mags.; speeches in N.Y. Times and other papers. Mem. investment mgmt. com. Monadnock Community Hosp.; former mem. fin. com. New Haven Hosp.; chmn. war fin. com. World WarII; chmn. Citizens Action Commn., 1954-57; past bd. dirs. New Haven Boys Club. Sgt. U.S. Army A.S. with French Army, 1917-18; attached to Peace Commn., Paris, 1918. Decorated Croix de Guerre (France). Mem. Savs. Bank Assn. Conn. (pres. 1947-48), Nat. Assn. Mut. Savs. Banks (pres. 1951-52), New Haven C. of C. (pres. 1947-49), Francestown Improvement and Hist. Soc. (past pres.), Harvard Club (Conn. and N.Y.C.), Mory's Assn., Lawn Club, Graduates Club, Kiwanis Club (New Haven). Congregationalist. Home: Francestown N.H. †

FREI, HANS WILHELM, religious studies educator, minister; b. Breslau, Germany, Apr. 29, 1922; came to U.S., 1938; s. Wilhelm Sigmund and Magda (Frankfurther) F.; m. Geraldine Frost Nye, Oct. 9, 1948; children—Thomas W., Jonathan G., Emily E. B.S., N.C. State U., 1942; B.D., Yale U., 1945, Ph.D., 1956; D.D. (hon.), Wabash Coll., 1979. Minister First Bapt. Ch., North Stratford, N.H., 1945-47; asst. prof. religion Wabash Coll., Crawfordsville, Ind., 1950-53; assoc. prof. theology Episcopal Theol. Sem. of SW, Austin, Tex., 1953-56; prof. Episcopal Theol. Sem. of SW, 1956-57; asst. prof. religious studies Yale U., New Haven, 1957-63; assoc. prof. Yale U., 1963-74, prof., 1974—, chmn. dept. religious studies, 1983-86; master Ezra Stiles Coll., Yale U., 1972-80. Author: The Eclipse of Biblical Narrative, 1974, The Identity of Jesus Christ, 1975; (with others) Faith and Ethics, 1957. Mem. editorial bd. Modern Theology. Fellow John Simon Guggenheim Meml. Found., 1980-81; Fulbright research scholar Goettingen, Federal Republic Germany, 1959-60. Fellow Am. Assn. Theol. Schs.; mem. Am. Acad. Religion (pres. New England sect. 1982-83), Duodecim Theol. Soc., The Biblical Theologians. Democrat. Home: North Haven Conn. Died Aug. 12, 1988.

FREIFELDER, DAVID MICHAEL, biochemist, author; b. Phila., July 19, 1935; s. Morris Leon and Florence (Levenson) F.; children: Rachel, Joshua. B.S. in Physics, U. Chgo., 1957, Ph.D. in Biophysics, 1959. Research asso. M.I.T., 1960-62, U. Copenhagen, 1962; asst. prof. med. physics U. Calif., Berkeley, 1963-66; mem. faculty Brandeis U., Waltham, Mass., 1966-83; prof. biochemistry Brandeis U., 1976-82; vis. prof. U. Calif.-San Diego. Author textbooks, articles in field. Grantee NSF, AEC, USPHS, 1967-85. Jewish. Home: San Diego Calif. Died Mar. 1987.

FRENCH, A. JAMES, physician; b. Van Houten, N.Mex., Sept. 3, 1912; s. A.P. and Elizabeth (Williams) F.; m. Genevieve Fetter, July 19, 1937; 1 child, Patricia Sue. AB, U. Colo., 1933, MA, 1936, MD, 1936; DSc (hon.), 1985. Diplomate Am. Bd. Pathology (trustee 1962-74, sec.-treas. 1964-74, exec. dir. 1974-78, cons. 1978-80). Intern Kansas City (Mo.) Gen. Hosp., 1936-37; resident pediatrics Children's Hosp., Denver, 1937-38; resident pathology St. Louis City Hosp., 1938-40; resident, instr. pathology U. Mich. Hosp., 1940-41, chief clin. labs., 1952-85; asst. prof. pathology Mich. Med Sch., 1946-47, assoc. prof., 1947-53, prof., 1953-80 chmn. dept., 1956-80; also editor Med. Bull., 1955-57 pathologist Surgeon Gen.'s Office, Washington and Fa East, 1941-46; cons. 1947-50; cons., mem. patholog adv. council VA Hosp., Ann Arbor; also Wayne Count Gen. Hosp., 1959-85; dir. Mich. Maternal Tissue Re gistry, 1957-85; mem. sci. adv. bd. Armed Forces Ins Pathology, 1965-70, chmn., 1968-70; mem. etiolog com. Am. Cancer Soc., 1962-65. Contbr. to med. jours. Col. AUS Res. Fellow ACP; mem. Mich. Pathol. Soc (pres. 1953, 73), Internat. Acad. Pathology (counc 1957-60, pres. 1966), Am. Soc. Clin. Pathology, Am Assn. Pathologists and Bacteriologists (mem. counc 1970, sec.-treas. 1971-74, pres. 1975), Coll. Am Pathologists (chmn. acad. sect. 1960-61, gov. 1964-70 sec.-treas. 1969-70), Am. Acad. Oral Pathology (hon mem.; vice chmn. 1974-76, chmn. 1976-85), AMA (sec sect. council on pathology 1972-85), Frederick A. Colle Surg. Soc. (hon.). Home: Ann Arbor Mich. Died Ma 15, 1985; buried St. Thomas Cemetery, Ann Arbo Mich.

FRENCH, JOHN DOUGLAS, neurosurgeon, educato b. L.A., Apr. 11, 1911; s. John Rollin and Effi (Douglas) F.; m. Dorothy Kirsten, July 18, 1955. AB UCLA, 1933; MD, U. So. Calif., 1937. Diplomate Am Bd. Surgery, Am. Bd. Neurol. Surgery. Intern interna medicine U. Calif. Hosp., San Francisco, 1937-38; inter surgery Strong Meml. Hosp. and U. Rochester Sch Medicine, 1938-39; from asst. resident surgery, assoc resident neurosurgery to chief resident surgery Stron Meml. Hosp., 1939-43, asst. surgeon, 1943-46; ass prof. neurol surgery U. Rochester Sch. Medicine an Dentistry, 1943-46; chief neurosurgery VA Hosp., Lon Beach, Calif., 1948-58, assoc. dir. profl. services fo rsch., 1950-58, chief cons. neurosurgery, 1958-76; clin prof. surgery-neurosurgery Coll. Medicine, UCLA, fron 1949, prof. anatomy, 1960-78, prof. emeritus, 1978-89 dir. Brain Rsch. Inst. UCLA, 1960-80; mem. biosci. tng com. NIH, 1958-63, biosci. subcom. Office Space Sci and Application NASA, 1960-66, com. bioastronautic Nat. Acad. Scis.-Armed Forces-NRC, 1958-62; mem Eviron. Policy Inst.-HAB L.A. Author, editor Frontiers in Brain Research, 1962; editor: (with R.W Porter) Basic Research in Paraplegia, 1962; contbr. ar ticles to profl. jours. and books. U. Ill. Neuropsychiat fellow, 1946-47. Mem. Am. Neurol. Assn., Am. Acad Neurol. Surgery, AMA, Calif. Med. Soc., L.A. Soc Neurology and Psychiatry, Pacific Coast Surg. Assn. Soc. Neurol. Surgeons, Soc. Univ. Surgeons, So. Calif Neurosurg. Soc. (pres. 1957-58), Western Neurosurg Soc. (pres. 1969), Sigma Xi, Alpha Omega Alpha. Home: Los Angeles Calif. Died Jan. 25, 1989.

FRENCH, ROBERT HOUSTON, lawyer; b. Dayton Ohio, Dec. 12, 1904; s. Edward Houston and Moile B (Nevin) F.; m. Dorothy M. Duff, July 22, 1933; chil dren—Mary F. Sweet, Nancy F. Pickard, Robert Hous ton. A.B. with honors, Ohio State U., 1927, J.D summa cum laude, 1927. Bar: Ohio bar 1927. Sinc practiced in Cin.; asst. U.S. atty. So. Dist. Ohio, 1928 31; spl. counsel to Atty. Gen., Ohio, 1938; mem. firn Pogue, Hoffheimer & Pogue, 1931-37, Pogue, Helmholz Culbertson & French, 1937-72, French, Short, Valleau & Bratton, 1972-79, French, Marks, Short, Weiner & Val leau, from 1979; spl. counsel City of Piqua, 1948-68. Pres. Ohio Valley chpt. Arthritis Found., 1957-60, 65 66, 78; bd. govs. Nat. Arthritis Found., mem. exec com., 1962-73, v.p., 1965-68, sec., 1970-73; budget rev com. United Appeal, Cin. Recipient Distinguished Ser vice award Nat. Arthritis Found., 1960, 66. Fellow Ohio, Am. bar assn. founds.; mem. Jud. Conf. U.S. Ct Appeals 6th Circuit (life), ABA, Fed. Bar Assn., Ohio Bar Assn. (exec. com. 1964-66), Cin. Bar Assn. (v.p 1959-63, pres. 1963-64), Legal Aid Soc. (trustee Cin 1963-64), Am. Coll. Probate Counsel, Phi Beta Kappa Order Coif, Phi Delta Phi. Republican. Clubs: Mason (Cin.), University (Cin.), Lawyers (Cin.). Home Cincinnati Ohio. Died Jan. 22, 1987.

FRENSDORFF, WESLEY, bishop; b. Hanover Germany, July 22, 1926; s. Rudolph August and Erma Margarete (Asch) F.; m. Dolores C. Stoker, Nov. 1 1953; 5 children. B.A., Columbia U., 1948; S.T.B. Gen. Theol. Sem., N.Y.C., 1951. Ordained deacon Episcopal Ch., 1951, priest, 1951; vicar St. Mary Virgin Ch., Winnemucca, Nev., St. Andrew's Ch., Battle Mountain, Nev., St. Anne's Ch., McDermitt, Nev. 1951-54; rector St. Paul's Ch., Elko, Nev. and; vicar St Barnabas and St. Luke Ch., Wells, Nev., and; St. Martin's Ch., Upper Skagit Valley, Nev. and, Community Ch., Newhalem, Wash., 1959-62; dean St. Mark's Canthedral, Salt Lake City, 1962-72; bishop Diocese of Nev., Reno, from 1972; dir. North Pacific and Western parish tng. program Episcopal Ch., 1959-64; interim bishop Navaho Land Area Mission, 1983; asst. bishop Ariz., from 1985; trustee Gen. Theol. Sem., 1965-74 priest in charge St. Francis Ch., Managua, Nicaragua 1968-69. Died May 17, 1988.

FREUND, ARTHUR J., lawyer; b. St. Louis, Apr. 17 1891; s. Fred S. and Fannie (Wurzel) F.; m. Margaret Drey, Jan. 24, 1925; children: Emily Freund Ullman Edith Freund Binder. AB, Washington U., St. Louis 1914, LLB, 1916. Bar: Mo. 1916. Practiced in St Louis, from 1916; spl. asst. atty. gen. Mo. 1920-24 mem. adv. com. civil rules Supreme Ct. U.S. Mem. bd police commrs. St. Louis, 1925-29, election commrs., 1936-37; past pres. St. Louis USO Council; pres. YMHA and YWHA, 1941-47, exec. com., from 1938; mem. exec. com. Nat. Jewish Welfare Bd.; past mem. exec. com. Am. Council Judaism; trustee John Burroughs Sch., St. Louis, 1947. Named Hon. Col. Staff Gov. Baker of Mo., 1925-29; recipient award for extraordinary pub. service City of St. Louis, 1927, citation for disting. service Washington U., citation for extraordinary service USO. Fellow Am. Bar Found.; mem. ABA (mem. ho. of dels., council criminal law sect., sect. individual rights and responsibilities, spl. com. minimum standards for adminstrn. criminal jusitce), Mo. Bar Assn. (past chmn. criminal law com.), St. Louis Bar Assn. (past v.p., past chmn. criminal law com.), Nat. Assn. Better Radio and TV (bd. dirs.), Am. Law Inst. (adv. com. pre-arraignment procedures), Inst. Jud. Adminstrn., Bar Assn. of City of N.Y., Mo. Atheltic Club (St. Louis.). Republican. Home: Saint Louis Mo. †

FREY, RICHARD LINCOLN, author, editor; b. N.Y.C., Feb. 12, 1905; s. Louis Joseph and Bessie Alice (Butzel) F.; m. Mabel Amy Planco, July 10, 1935; children: Steven Lewis (dec.), Stephanie Constance Frey-Secor. Extension student, Columbia U. With Fed. Advt. Agy., 1921-25; v.p., account exec. Herald Advt. Agy., N.Y.C., 1925-27; advt. mgr. for clothing mfrs. 1928-34; propr. Triangle Bridge Club, 1933-34; nat. sales mgr. Kem Playing Cards; also assoc. editor Bridge World mag., 1935-37; pres. Morehead, Frey & Whitman Advt., N.Y.C., 1938-39; freelance author 1940-60; editor, pub. rels. dir. Am. Contract Bridge League, 1959-70; editor-in-chief Ofcl. Ency. Bridge, from 1964; pres. Internat. Bridge Press Assn., 1969-80, chmn., from 1980; chmn. Goren Editorial Bd., from 1970. Author: According to Hoyle, How to Win at Contract Bridge in 10 Easy Lessons. Named Leading Am. Bridge Player, 1934, Life Master, 1936. Mem. Am. Soc. Journalists and Authors. Home: New York N.Y. Died Oct. 17, 1988; cremated.

FRIDE, EDWARD THEODORE, lawyer; b. Duluth, Minn., Jan. 8, 1927; s. Edward T. and Lina (Wick) F.; m. Patricia Ann; children: Edward O., Nancy E., Mark R., Timothy S., Scott D., Gail E., William A. AA, Duluth Jr. Coll., 1947; BS in Law, U. Minn., 1949, JD, 1951. Bar: Minn. 1951; diplomate Am. Bd. Trial Advocates. Pres. Hanft, Fride, O'Brien & Harries (P.A.), Duluth, Arco Bldg. Corp.; bd. dirs. First Bank Duluth, Man. RR Co., Mid-Continent Warehouse Co., Andresen-Ryan Coffee Co; instr. bus. law U. Minn., 1951-53, then lectr. V.p. Duluth Bd. Edn., 1964-68; pres. Duluth Rehab. Ctr., 1958-60. With U.S. Merchant Marine, 1944-46; with USNR, 1944-46. Fellow Internat. Soc. Barristers, Am. Coll. Trial Lawyers, Internat. Acad. Trial Lawyers; mem. ABA, Minn. Bar Assn., Duluth Bar Assn., Nat. Assn. Rd. Trial Counsel, Internat. Assn. Ins. Counsel, Maritime Law Assn. U.S., Fedn. Ins. Counsel. Home: Duluth Minn. Died Feb. 24, 1985; buried Duluth.

FRIDELL, ELMER ALFRED, religious educator, missionary executive; b. Minden, Nebr., Apr. 30, 1892; s. John Alfred and Petra (Finwall) F.; m. Bess Doudna, Oct. 18, 1917; children: Lee Doudna, Wilbur Medbury. AB, Des Moines Coll., 1917; BD, Berkeley Bapt. Div. Ch., 1922, DD, 1929; student, U. Calif., 1921, Pacific Sch. of Religion, 1924; DD (hon.), Sioux Falls Coll., 1940. Ordained to ministry Bapt. Ch. Bus. mgr. State YMCA of Iowa, 1919; pastor First Bapt. Ch., Fresno, Calif., 1924-29, First Bapt. Ch. Seattle, 1929-37; prof. homiletics and practical theology Berkely (Calif.) Bapt. Div. Sch., 1937-43; pres. Calif. Protestant State Council of Social Work, 1941-43; home sec. Am. Bapt. Fgn. Missionary Soc., 1955, later dir. promotion; mem. gen. council No. Bapt. Conv.; pres. No. Bapt. Conv.; v.p. Bapt. World Alliance. Author: The Christian Faces the World, The Church Faces the World, You Too May Go, Baptists at Work in Thailand and The Phillipines. With U.S. Army, 1918. Mem. City Commons Club (Berkeley), Masons. Home: Santa Barbara Calif. †

FRIED, ALEXANDER, music and art critic; b. N.Y.C., May 21, 1902; s. Henry and Sarah (Perlis) F.; m. Edith Trumpler, Jan. 28, 1949; children: Madelyn Natalie, Harriet. MusB, Masters in Music, Columbia U. Mng. editor Musical Digest, N.Y., 1924-25; music editor, then art editor San Francisco Chronicle, 1926-34; music and art editor San Francisco Examiner, 1934-77, ret., 1977. Jewish. Home: San Francisco Calif. Died May 9, 1988.

FRIED, MORTON HERBERT, anthropologist, educator; b. N.Y.C., Mar. 21, 1923; s. Norton and Sally (Solomon) F.; m. Martha Nemes, June 22, 1945; children: Nancy, Elman Steven. Mem. faculty Columbia U., 1949-86, prof. anthropology, 1961-86, chmn. dept., 1966-69; vis. prof. U. Mich., 1960-61, Nat. Taiwan U., 1963-64, Yale U., 1965-66, Fla. Atlantic U., 1970, U. B.C., 1973, U. Colo., 1974; mem. rev. com. div. anthropology NSF, 1970-72; mem. social scis. research rev. com. NIMH, 1973-86; cons., seminar dir. Nat. Endowment for Humanities, 1975-76. Author: The Fabric of Chinese Society, 1953; Readings in Anthropology, 1959; The Evolution of Political Society, 1967; The Study of Anthropology, 1972; Explorations in Anthropology, 1973; The Notion of the Tribe, 1975; others. Bd. dirs. Social Sci. Research Council, 1965-68. Served with AUS, 1943-46. Guggenheim fellow, 1963-64; NSF grantee, 1964-66, 73-86. Mem. Am. Anthrop. Assn. (mem. exec. bd. 1970-73), Asian Studies Assn., Am. Ethnol. Soc. (pres.-elect 1977-78), AAAS. Home: Leonia N.J. Died Dec. 18, 1986; cremated.

FRIEDBERG, SIDNEY MYER, leisure industry executive; b. Norfolk, Va., Aug. 8, 1907; s. Solomon and Jennie (Graff) F.; m. Charlton Gillet, Mar. 7, 1983; 1 child, Laura Friedberg Burrows. BA, Johns Hopkins U., 1971; LHD, Western Md. Coll., 1983. With Fair Lanes Inc. (and predecessor), Balt., 1926-85, chmn. bd., chief exec. officer, 1958-85; chmn. exec. com., dir. BTR Realty Inc. Trustee Peabody Inst., Balt.; bd. dirs. Balt. Symphony Orch., Balt. Opera Co. Mem. Johns Hopkins U. Alumni Assn. Jewish. Clubs: Va. Mil. Inst. Alumni, Johns Hopkins, Center, Suburban. Home: Baltimore Md. Died Feb. 9, 1985.

FRIEDEN, EDWARD HIRSCH, biochemist, educator; b. Norfolk, Va., Jan. 4, 1918; s. Simon and Sarah (Bluestein) F.; m. Betty Barnett, June 29, 1941; children: Ray Allan, Jeanne E., Robert E., Roger S., Joyce S. A.B., UCLA, 1939, M.A., 1941, Ph.D., 1942. Lalor Found. fellow U. Tex., 1942-43, instr., research asso. Med. Sch., 1943-46; research fellow Harvard U., 1946-52; instr. Med. Sch. Harvard, 1948-52; faculty Tufts U. Med. Sch., 1952-64, asso. prof. biochemistry, 1962-64; research coordinator, dir. Rotch Lab., Boston Dispensary, 1957-64; prof. chemistry Kent (Ohio) State U., 1964-84, research prof., 1985-87; research prof. molecular pathology Northeastern Ohio Univs. Coll. Medicine, 1980-87; vis. scientist H. Florey Inst., U. Melbourne, 1981; biochem. cons. Hynson, Westcott & Dunning, Balt., 1950-70. Contbr. articles to profl. jours. Guggenheim fellow, 1953-54. Mem. Am. Chem. Soc., Am. Soc. Biol. Chemists, Endocrine Soc., Soc. Exptl. Biology and Medicine, AAAS, Sigma Xi. Home: Kent Ohio. Died Dec. 18, 1987; buried Homeland, Rootstown, Ohio.

FRIEDMANN, HERBERT, educator, museum director, ornithologist; b. Bklyn., Apr. 22, 1900; s. Uriah M. and Mary (Behrmann) F.; m. Karen Juul Vejlo, 1937; 1 dau., Karen Alice (Mrs. J.N. Beall). B.Sc., Coll. City N.Y., 1920; Ph.D., Cornell U., 1923. Instr. in zoology Cornell U., summer, 1922, U. Va., summer 1923; NRC research fellow in zoology Harvard, 1923-26; instr. biology Brown U., 1926-27, Amherst Coll., 1927-29; curator of birds U.S. Nat. Museum, 1929-57, head curator zoology, 1957-61; dir. Los Angeles County Mus. Natural History, 1961-70; asst. prof. exptl. embryology Grad. Sch., Howard, 1931-33; Lida Scott Brown lectr. U. Calif., Los Angeles, 1957; adj. prof. biology U. So. Calif., 1962-87; research asso. zoology U. Calif. at Los Angeles, 1962, prof.-in-residence zoology, 1963-70, prof.-in-residence history of art, 1968. Author: books including The Cowbirds, 1929, Birds of North and Middle America, Part IX, 1941, Part X, 1946, Part XI, 1950, the Parasitic Cuckoos of Africa, 1948, The Symbolic Goldfinch, 1946, Birds of Mexico, Part I, 1950. Part II 1957, The Honeyguides, 1955, The Parasitic Weaverbirds, 1960, Host Relations of Parasitic Cowbirds, 1963, A Bestiary for St. Jerome, 1980; Contbr. on sci. and art subjects. Guggenheim research fellow, 1950-51; recipient Leidy medal Acad. Nat. Sci. Phila., 1955, Elliot medal Nat. Acad. Sci., 1959; Brewster medal Am. Ornith. Union, 1964. Fellow AAAS (sect. pres. 1939), Am. Ornithologists Union (pres. 1937-39); mem. Am. Soc. Zoologists, Am. Soc. Naturalists, Washington Acad. Sci. (hon. diploma in biology 1940, v.p. 1957), Biol. Soc. Washington (pres. 1957-58), Cooper Ornith. Soc. (div. pres. 1967), Nat. Acad. Sci., Paleobiol. Soc. Washington (pres. 1938), Deutsche Ornith. Gesellschaft (hon.), S. African Ornith. Union (hon.). Home: Laguna Hills Calif. Died May 14, 1987, buried Oak Hill Cemetery, Washington.

FRIEDRICK, JACOB FRANK, labor union official; b. Perjanios, Hungary, Jan. 31, 1892; came to U.S., 1904, naturalized, 1916; s. Frank and Barbara (Wolf) F.; m. Agnes Piechowiak, June 21, 1914; children: Maxine (Mrs. Philip La Porte), Frederick, Frank. Ed. pub. schs., Milw.; LLD, U. Wis., 1955. Mem. Lodge 66 Internat. Assn. Machinists, Milw., from 1913; bus. rep. Machinists Dist. Lodge 10, Milw., 1919-29; labor editor Milw. Leader, 1929-35; gen. organizer Milw. Federated Trades Coun., 1935-45, sec.-treas., 1952-59; regional dir. AFL, 1945-52; pres. Milw. County Labor Coun. AFL-CIO, from 1959. Mem. Wis. Coordinating Com. for Higher Edn., 1961-64; mem. Milw. Sewerage Commn., from 1923, chmn. com., from 1932; mem. Met. Sewage Commn., County of Milw., from 1932; mem. Wis. Continuing Revenue Survey Commn., 1959-60; pres. regents U. Wis., 1962-64; bd. dirs. United Community Svcs. of Greater Milw. Home: Milw. Wis. †

FRIEND, CHARLOTTE, microbiologist; b. N.Y.C., Mar. 11, 1921. BA, Hunter Coll., 1944; PhD, Yale U., 1950. Assoc. mem. Sloan-Kettering Inst., 1949-66; assoc. prof. microbiology Sloan-Kettering div. Med. Coll., Cornell U., 1952-66; prof., dir. Ctr. for Exptl. Biology, Mt. Sinai Sch. Medicine, CUNY, 1966-87. Recipient Alfred P. Sloan award, 1954, 57, 62; Am. Cancer Soc. award, 1962; Presdl. Medal Centennial award Hunter Coll., 1970. Fellow N.Y. Acad. Acis. (past chmn. sect. on microbiology, pres. 1978-87); mem. Nat. Acad. Scis., Tissue Culture Assn., Am. Soc. Hematology, Am. Assn. Cancer Research, Am. Assn. Immunology. Home: New York N.Y. Died Jan. 13, 1987; buried New Montifiore Cemetery, Farmingdale, N.Y.

FRIEND, IRWIN, economics educator; b. Schenectady, July 10, 1915; s. Solomon and Dina (Ryzowy) F.; m. Corinne Vernon, Nov. 5, 1941; children: Peter Sayre, Leslie Andrea. B.S., CCNY, 1935; Ph.D., Am. U., 1953. Asst. dir. trading and exchange div. SEC, 1937-47; chief bus. structure div. Dept. Commerce, 1947-53; Richard K. Mellon and Edward J. Hopkinson prof. finance and econs. U. Pa., Phila., 1953-87; vis. Frederick R. Kappel Prof. govt. and bus. U. Minn., 1970; cons. U.S. govt. agys., congressional coms., Portugal, India, Turkey, Greece, Italy, China, Argentina, Brazil, Japan, Israel, UN and bus. orgns.; mem. exec. com. Conf. on Income and Wealth, 1960-63; former dir. Rodney L. White Center for Financial Research; dir. or trustee Dean Witter/Sears Intercapital Funds and Trusts. Author: Impediments to Capital Formation, 1981, The Changing Role of the Individual Investor, 1978, Financial Effects of Capital Tax Reforms, 1978, The Consequences of Competitive Commissions on the New York Stock Exchange, 1972, Study of the Savings and Loan Industry, 1970, Mutual Funds and Other Institutional Investors: A New Perspective, 1970, Investment Banking and The New Issues Market, 1967, Private Capital Markets, 1964; A Study of Mutual Funds, 1962, Consumption and Saving, 1960, The Over-The-Counter Securities Market, 1958, Consumer Expenditures, Inc. and Savings, 1957, Individual Savings: Volume and Composition, 1954, The Structure and Reform of the U.S. Tax System, 1985; editorial bd. Am. Econ. Rev, 1968-71. Recipient research fellowship, research grants Ford Found. and NSF. Fellow Econometric Soc., Am. Statis. Assn. (chmn. bus. and econ. statis. sect. 1961-62, bd. editors jour. 1968-71); mem. Am. Econ. Assn., Am. Fin. Assn. (pres. 1972), Phi Beta Kappa. Home: Bryn Mawr Pa. Died Aug. 16, 1987; buried Haym Solomon Meml. Park, Frazer, Pa.

FRIENDLY, HENRY JACOB, judge; b. Elmira, N.Y., July 3, 1903; s. Myer H. Leah and Hallo (Friendly); m. Sophie M. Stern, Sept. 4, 1930 (dec. 1985); children: David, Joan, Ellen Simon. AB, Harvard U., 1923, LLB, 1927; DHL, Hebrew Union Coll.; LLD, Syracuse U., Bklyn. Law Sch., Jewish Theol. Sem., Western Res. U., Brandeis U., U. Cin., U. Chgo., Harvard U., Columbia U., Northwestern U., N.Y. U. Bar: N.Y. 1928, D.C. 1947. Law clk. to Mr. Justice Brandeis, Washington, 1927-28; assoc. law firm Root, Clark, Buckner & Ballantine, N.Y.C., 1928-36, ptnr., 1937-45; own firm Cleary, Gottlieb, Friendly & Hamilton, N.Y.C., 1946-59; dir., v.p., gen. counsel Pan Am. World Airways System, 1946-59; U.S. judge Ct. Appeals 2d Cir., 1959-86, chief judge, 1971-73; presiding judge spl. ct. under Rail Reorgn. Act. 1974-86. Author: The Need for Better Definition of Standards, 1962, Benchmarks, 1967, Federal Jurisdiction: A General View, 1973; contbr. articles to law periodicals. Overseer Harvard U., 1964-69. Recipient Louis Stein award Fordham Law Sch., Presdl. medal of Freedom, 1977, Thomas Jefferson Meml. award in law, 1978. Mem. Am., N.Y. State, N.Y.C. bar assns., Assn. Bar City of N.Y. (hon., Am. Law Inst., Coun., mem. exec. com.), Harvard alumni assn. (pres. 1960-51), Harmonie Club, Century Club, Mchts. Club. Home: Scarsdale N.Y. Died Mar. 11, 1986.

FRIER, SID, architect; b. Baton Rouge, Aug. 10, 1925; s. James L. and Elizabeth (Newell) F.; m. Margaret Stuck, June 21, 1946; 1 child, Jane F. B.S.M.E., La. State U., 1949. Draftsman E. A. Stuck, Architect, Jonesboro, Ark., 1949-55; ptnr. Stuck/Frier/Lane/Scott, Jonesboro, 1955-61, Little Rock, 1961-83; ptnr. Stuck Assocs., Inc., Little Rock, from 1983, pres., from 1984; dir. Union Nat. Bank, Little Rock. Bd. dirs. Ark. Arts Ctr., Little Rock, from 1982, Ark. Symphony, from 1983. Served as sgt. U.S. Army, 1941-46. Fellow AIA (pres. Ark. chpt. 1975); mem. Ark. State Bd. Architects, Nat. Council Architects (pres. registration bd. from 1983, Presdl. medal 1983). Democrat. Episcopalian. Died Aug. 15, 1985.

FRIES, VOLLMER WALTER, manufacturing executive; b. Pleasant Valley, N.Y., July 17, 1902; s. William Christian and Lona A. (Vollmer) F.; m. Ruth Dudley Wick, July 17, 1928; children: William Vollmer, Carole Wick. E.E., Rensselaer Poly. Inst., 1924; D.Eng. (hon.), Fenn Coll., 1965. With The White Motor Co., Cleve., 1924-56; v.p., dir., then exec. v.p., dir. The White Motor Co., 1944-55; chmn. bd., chief exec. officer White Consol. Industries, Inc. (formerly White Sewing Machine Corp.), Cleve., 1955-69; chmn. exec. com. White Consol. Industries, Inc. (formerly White Sewing Machine Corp.), 1969-70, dir., 1954-85; With conservation div. WPB, 1940-41; mem. W. Averell Harriman mission, Am. embassy, London, 1942-43. Trustee Fenn Ednl. Found., Rensselaer Poly. Inst., Troy, N.Y. Clubs: Union (Cleve.), Fifty (Cleve.); Ocean Reef (Key Largo, Fla.), Ocean Reef Yacht (Key Largo, Fla.), Card Sound Golf (Key Largo, Fla.), Key Largo Anglers (Key Largo, Fla.). Home: Key Largo Fla. Died Jan. 10, 1985; buried South Bristol, Maine.

FRINK, ORRIN, mathematician, educator; b. Bklyn., May 31, 1901; s. Orrin and Elizabeth Blauvelt (Romeyn)

F.; m. Aline Huke, June 3, 1931; children: Orrin III, Peter Hill, John Allen, Elizabeth. AB (Pulitzer scholar), Columbia U., 1922, AM, 1923, PhD (Univ. fellow), 1926. NRC postdoctoral fellow U. Chgo., 1926-27; NRC postdoctoral fellow Princeton U., 1927-28, instr., 1925-26; asst. prof. math. Pa. State U., 1982, assoc. prof., 1929-33, prof., 1933-88, head math. dept., 1949-60; Fulbright lectr. math. Univ. Coll., Dublin, 1960-61, 65-66; asst. chief engr. Spl. Projects Lab., Wright Field AFB, 1944-45. Assoc. editor Am. Math. monthly, 1935-45; contbr. articles to profl. jours. Mem. Math. Assn. Am. (chmn. Allegheny Mountain sect. 1948-50), Am. Math. Assn., Soc. Indsl. and Applied Logic, Phi Beta Kappa, Sigma Xi, Pi Mu Epsilon. Home: Kennebunkport Maine. Died Mar. 4, 1988.

FRITCHMAN, HARRY VERNON, coal company executive; b. McDonald, Pa., Nov. 27, 1907; s. Frank Markle and Margaret (Crilley) F.; m. Ethel Rendleman, Oct. 14, 1933; 1 son, Vernon N. A.B., Pa. State U., 1929; postgrad., U. Pa. Law Sch., 1929-30; LL.B., U. Pitts., 1932. Bar: Pa. bar 1933. Practice in Indiana, Pa., 1933-37; with Rochester & Pitts. Coal Co., Indiana, 1937-87; gen. counsel Rochester & Pitts. Coal Co., 1948-87, exec. v.p., 1959-70, pres., dir., 1970-73, dir., 1973-87. Mem. Nat. Coal Assn. (dir.), Beta Theta Pi, Phi Delta Phi, Pi Lambda Sigma. Presbyterian. Clubs: Elk (U. Pa.), Mason. (U. Pa.), Hare Law (U. Pa.); Indiana Country. Home: Indiana Pa. Died July 12, 1987; buried Greenwood Cemetery, Indiana, Pa.

FROESSEL, CHARLES W(ILLIAM), judge, educator; b. Bklyn., Nov. 8, 1892; s. Theodore and Barbara (Hoffman) F.; m. Elsie Stier, June 1, 1927 (dec.). LLB, N.Y. Law Sch., 1913, LLM, 1914, LLD, 1955; LLD, Adelphi Coll., 1954, Pace Coll., 1968; LHD, Wagner Coll., 1976. Bar: N.Y. 1915. Libr. N.Y. Law Sch., 1913-14; counsel to sheriff Queens County, 1916-20, asst. dist. atty. in charge of appeals, 1924-26, sr. trial asst., 1926-30; spl. asst. U.S. atty. gen. in charge slum clearance projects, N.Y., 1935-37; justice City of N.Y., Queens County, 1937, of Supreme Ct., 2d jud. dist. N.Y., 1937-49; assoc. judge Ct. Appeals of N.Y. State, 1950-62; dean N.Y. Law Sch., 1968-69, prof. from 1969, chmn. bd. trustees, 1957-72, hon. chmn. bd. trustees, from 1972; trustee Ridgewood (N.Y.) Savs. Bank. Chmn. N.Y. Gov.'s Commn. to Rev. N.Y. Abortion Law, 1968; mem. N.Y. State Ct. Appeals Reapportionment Commn., 1966; v.p. Queensborough C. of C., 1934-37; dir. Ridgewood C. of C. from 1932; pres. Queens Coun. Boy Scouts Am., 1930-49, also mem. exec. bd. for N.Y.C., regional chmn., 1951-56, exec. bd., nat. coun.; del. N.Y. State Constl. Conv., 1967; sponsor Queens Fedn. Chs.; mem. adv. bd. Big Brother movement, exec. com. N.Y. World's Fair Corp., 1964-65. With USNRF, World War I. Recipient Silver Buffalo award Boy Scouts Am., award NCCJ, 1955, Spl. Social Svcs. award, 1954, God and Country award St. George's Assn. Mem. ABA, N.Y. State Bar Assn. (chmn. jud. sect. 1945-46, Disting. 50-Yr. Lawyer award 1981), Queens County Bar Assn. (pres.), Am. Legion, Ret. Officers Assn., Brooklyn Club, Club at World Trade Ctr., Masons (past grand master, N.Y., chmn. conf. grand masters U.S. 1946-47, Disting. Achievement award N.Y.), Elks. Presbyterian (hon. pres. bd. trustees, elder). Home: Forest Hills N.Y. Deceased.

FROMM, PAUL, foundation executive; b. Kitzingen, Germany, Sept. 28, 1906; came to U.S., 1938, naturalized, 1944; s. Max and Matilde (Maier) F.; m. Erika Oppenheimer, July 20, 1938; 1 child, Joan. Ed. high sch.; Dr.Music (hon.), New Eng. Conservatory Music, Boston, Mass.; Mus.D. (hon.), U. Cin. Established Great Lakes Wine Co., Chgo., 1940; founder Fromm Music Found., Harvard U., 1952, since dir.; pres. Fromm Mgmt. Corp., Chgo., Kenwood Corp., Chgo.; dir. Am. Music Center. Mem. citizens com. U. Ill.; adv. council Princeton U.; vis. com. humanities and music U. Chgo.; bd. overseers Boston Symphony Orch.; bd. visitors Boston U. Recipient Ill. Gov.'s award for the Arts, 1978, Peabody medal Peabody Conservatory, 1983, Golden Baton award Am. Symphony Orchestral League, 1986. Home: Chicago Ill. Died July 4, 1987; buried Oak Woods Cemetery, Chgo.

FROMME, ALEX M., state supreme court justice; b. Hoxie, Kans., Mar. 11, 1915; s. Joseph H. and Frances (Morgan) F.; m. Ruth Marie Kesler, Sept. 16, 1939. AB, LLB, Washburn U. Bar: Kans. 1939. Since practiced in Hoxie; pvt. practice Sheridan County, 1941-48; justice Kans. Supreme Ct., 1966-82; ptnr. Fromme Ins. Agy., Hoxie; dir. First Nat. Bank Hoxie. Contbr. articles to legal jours. Instl. rep. local council Boy Scouts Am., 1948-49; home service chmn. Sheridan County chpt. ARC, 1941-47; pres. Sheridan County Community Fund, 1964-65. Mem. Am., Kans. (pres. 1961-62), N.W. Kans. (past mem. council) bar assns., Nat. Conf. Bar Presidents. Club: Rotary (local pres. 1947-48). Home: Topeka Kans. Died Oct. 22, 1982; buried Mt. Calvary Cemetery, Hoxie, Kans.

FROMMELT, HORACE ALOYSIUS, engineering company executive; b. Dubuque, Iowa, Oct. 6, 1891; s. Ludwig and Mary (Nesler) F.; m. Katherine Foley, Nov. 20, 1923. BSEE, Iowa State Coll., 1912, degree in EE, 1919; postgrad., Campion Coll., 1913-14; MA, St. Louis U., 1918. Supt. power plant Tipton, Iowa, 1912-14; asst. prof. mech. engring. Marquette U., 1916-20, prof., head dept., 1928-38; asst. works mgr. Falk Corp., Milw., 1920-25; dir. indsl. rsch. Kearney-Trecker Corp., Milw., 1938-44, dir. milling rsch., 1944-46; pres. H.A. Frommelt Assocs., from 1946; exec. v.p., chief engr. Ultra Products Corp., 1952; v.p., sales mgr. U.S. Engring. & Mfg. Co., from 1953. Author: Church Property and Its Administration, 1935; translator numerous German works; contbr. articles to profl. jours. Dir. Spring Garden Inst., Phila. Mem. ASME, Milw. Engrs. Soc., Am. Soc. Testing Engrs., KC, Tau Beta Pi, Sigma Omicron. †

FRUMKIN, PAUL, TV producer; b. Omaha, Aug. 20, 1914; s. Louis and Anna (Dubnoff) F. Student, Omaha U., 1932-34. Advt. mgr. M.L. Rothschild, Chgo., 1936-42; v.p. W.H. Altice Advt. Agy., 1947-51; producer Mike Douglas Hi Ladies, WGN-TV, 1952-55; producer-writer At Random, Susie's Show, CBS-TV, Chgo., 1956-62; producer Kup's Show, ABC-TV, Chgo., 1962-68, Kup's Show, NBC-TV, Chgo., 1968-77, PBS-WTTW-TV, 1977-79; creative cons. The Mike Douglas Show, Los Angeles, 1979-84. Mem. Chgo. Unltd., 1960-84, Council Fgn. Relations, 1958-84; adviser Am. Vets. from Vietnam; bd. dirs. Clarence Darrow Ctr. Served with AUS, 1942-46, ETO. Recipient Emmy award for best producer, 1966, 68, Peabody award, 1967. Mem. Nat. TV Hall of Fame, Acad. TV Arts and Scis. (life, pres. Chgo.), Press Club, Broadcast Advt. Club, Broadcast Pioneers, Hollywood Radio/TV Soc., Sigma Delta Chi. Club: Headline. Home: Los Angeles Calif. Died Aug. 18, 1984.

FRY, THORNTON CARL, mathematician; b. Findlay, Ohio, Jan. 7, 1892; s. William Watson and Elizabeth Hanna (Dingle) F. AB, Findlay Coll., 1912, DSc, 1958; AM, U. Wis., 1913, PhD, 1920. Instr. U. Wis., 1912-16; mathematician Western Electric Co., 1916-24; mathematician Bell Telephone Labs., 1924-56, dir. math. rsch., 1940-44, dir. switching rsch., 1944-47, dir. switching rsch. and engring., 1947-49, asst. to exec. v.p., 1949-51, asst. to pres., 1951-56; cons. communications Internat. Tel.&Tel. Co., 1956-57; sr. cons. Univac div. Sperry-Rand Corp., 1956-57; v.p., dir. Univac engring. Remington Rand div., 1957-60, v.p. rsch. and engring., 1960-61; cons. to dir. Nat. Ctr. for Atmospheric Rsch., 1961-67; cons., bd. dirs. Granville-Phillips Co., 1964-75; lectr. elec. engring. MIT, 1927; lectr. math. Princeton U., 1929-30; mem. div. 7, Nat. Def. Rsch. Com., 1940-44, chief sect. 7.2, 1942-44, dep. chief applied math. panel, 1942-45. Author: Elementary Differential Equation, 1929, Probability and Its Engineering Uses, 1928; contbr. articles to profl. jours. Recipient Presdl. Cert. of Merit, 1948. Fellow AAAS, IEEE, Am. Phys. Soc., Inst. Math. Stats.; mem. Am. Math. Soc., Math. Assn. Am., Am. Astron. Soc., Soc. for Promotion of Engring. Edn., Econometric Soc., Canadian Club, Metropolitan Club, University Club, Sigma Xi. Home: Carmel Calif. †

FULLER, C(HARLES) KENNETH, banker; b. Lynn, Mass., July 14, 1891; s. Charles S. and Addie G. (Usher) F.; m. Verna Sutton, June 13, 1931; children: Joan Cleveland, Martha Usher. BS, Dartmouth Coll., 1914; postgrad., Stanford U., 1919; MBA, Harvard U., 1927. Investment officer Old Colony Trust Co., Boston, 1931-34; v.p., trust officer Agrl. Nat. Bank, Pittsfield, Mass., 1934-38; v.p. Paterson Savs. Inst., 1938-43; bd. dirs. Union Securities Co., 1939-45, Peoples Bank & Trust Co., Passaic, N.J., 1948-51; pres., bd. dirs. County Bank & Trust Co., 1943-56, chmn. bd., 1956-58; chmn. bd. N.J. Bank & Trust Co., from 1958. Contbr. articles in field to profl. jours. Trustee N.J. Citizens Hwy. Com.; mem. exec. com. Greater Paterson Econ. Devel. Coun.; chmn. Paterson ARC, 1942-43; pres. United Community Chest, 1945-46. Mem. Am. Inst. Banking, Paterson Clearing House (Pres. 1953-54), Hamilton Club (bd. govs. 1943-49, pres. 1948-49), Arcola Club, Pennington Club, Economic Club. Republican. Unitarian. Home: Ridgewood N.J. †

FULLER, EDWARD C., chemist, educator; b. Helena, Mont., Aug. 8, 1907; s. George N. and Claudia E. (Tinker) F.; m. Dorothy B. Edsall, June 26, 1937; children: David Edsall, Carol Margaret. BS, Mont. State Coll., 1928; PhD, Columbia U., 1941. Asst. in chem. engring. Mont. State Coll., 1928-31; asst. in chemistry Columbia U., 1931-34, univ. fellow, 1934-35; instr., asst. prof., assoc. prof., prof. chemistry Bard Coll., 1935-43, pres., 1946-50; prof. chemistry, dir. area natural scis. and math. SUNY, Champlaign Coll., 1950-53; prof. chemistry Beloit Coll., 1953-73, chmn. dept., 1953-73. Author: Discussion Guide and Laboratory Manual for Basic Natural Science, Chemistry and Man's Environment, 1974; contbr. chpts. and papers to publs. Served as adminstrv. aide Manhattan Project, U.S. Army Engr. Corps, 1944-45. Fellow AAAS, Am. Inst. Chemists; mem. Am. Chem. Soc. (div. chem. edn., chmn. div. chem. edn. 1963), AAUP, Sigma Xi, Phi Lambda Upsilon, Alpha Chi Sigma, Phi Kappa Phi. Home: Beloit Wis. Died May 9, 1986, buried Beloit.

FULLER, LEONARD FRANKLIN, electrical engineer; b. Portland, Oreg., Aug. 21, 1890; s. Franklin Ide and Anna Jessie (Parrish) F.; m. Lucretia Robinson Strong, June 22, 1912 (dec. 1943); children: Franklin Ide, Leonard Franklin, Mary Esther; m. Eleanor Pearl Rideout, Sept. 15, 1944. Began as elec. engr. with Nat. Electric Signaling Co., Bklyn., 1912; chief elec. engr. Fed. Telegraph Co., 1913-1919; designed, superintended mfg. and installation high power transoceanic radio telegraph transmitters for USN, various parts of the world, 1914-19; mem. anti-submarine group NRC, 1917-1919; cons. practice 1919-22; designed carrier current telephone equipment installed on 165 kilovolt lines, Great Western Power Co., 1921, and 220 kilovolt lines Pacific Gas and Electric Co., 1922; elec. engr. Gen. Electric Co., 1923-24; cons. practice, 1924-26; elec. engr. Gen. Electric Co., 1926-28; exec. v.p. and chief engr. Fed. Telegraph Co., 1928-32; prof. elec. engring. and chmn. dept. U. Calif., and in cons. practice, 1930-43; cons. on carrier current installations Hoover Dam power lines, City of Los Angeles, 1936, cons. engr. Joshua Hendy Iron Works, 1943, chief engr., 1944-45; acting prof. elec. engring. and coordinator of Contract Research Stanford U., 1946-54; engaged in pvt. cons. practice, 1954-87. Patentee radio telegraph apparatus; contbr. tech. papers. Recipient Morris Liebmann prize Inst. Radio Engrs., 1919. Fellow Am. Inst. Elec. Engrs., Inst. Radio Engrs., AAAS; mem. Sierra Club, Sigma Xi, Eta Kappa Nu, Tau Beta Pi. Home: Palo Alto Calif. Died Apr. 23, 1987; buried Alta Mesa Meml. Pk., Palo Alto, Calif.

FULLER, MAURICE DELANO, lawyer; b. Eveleth, Minn., Oct. 3, 1898. A.B., U. Calif.-Berkeley, 1921, J.D., 1923. Bar: Calif. 1923. Assoc. firm Pillsbury, Madison & Sutro, San Francisco, 1923-40, ptnr., 1940-79; chmn. Com. Bar Examiners of Calif., 1950. Mem. Calif. State Bar Assn., San Francisco Bar Assn. Home: San Francisco Calif. Died Jan. 5, 1979.

FULLER, PARRISH, lumber manufacturer; b. Madison, Wis., May 21, 1892; s. William Wilson and Minnie Lora (Parrish) F.; student Wabash Coll. 1910-11, M.A., 1949, LL.D. (hon.), 1954; m. Hester Porter, Oct. 18, 1919; children—Mary Margaret (Mrs. James D. Voorhees), William Porter. Gen. mgr. J.O. Parrish Lumber Co., Shelbyville, Ind., 1914-18; asst. to pres. Hillyer Deutsch Edwards, Inc., Oakdale, La., 1919-20, v.p., gen. mgr., 1920-68; v.p. Hillyer Edwards Fuller, Inc., Glenmore, La., 1923-40; gen. partner King-Edwards-Fuller Co., St. Francisville, La., 1940-47, Avoyelles Timber Co., Bordelonville, La., 1940-64, Edwards & Fuller, Oakdale, La., 1938-70, Fuller Farms, 1930-72, Shelbyville, Ind.; v.p. King Lumber Industries, Canton, Miss., 1946-50, Canton & Carthage R.R. Co., 1946-53; gen. partner Heflands Timber Co., 1961-68; pres. J.O. Parrish Lumber Co.; v.p. Porter Steel Spltys., Inc., Shelbyville, Ind., 1946-51; dir., chmn. forest lands and products com. Celotex Corp., Chgo.; dir. Canton (Miss.) & Carthage R.R. Co., 1946-53; dir. South Shore Oil & Devel. Co., New Orleans, 1946-66, Nat. Bank of Commerce, New Orleans, 1946-66, New Orleans and Lower Coast R.R., 1951-70, J.O. Parrish Lumber Co. Chmn., La. State Salvage, 1942-45, United War Fund, 1943-45; mem. La. State Bd. Edn., pres., 1952; vice chmn. La. Commn. Higher Edn., 1955-56; chmn. Citizens Adv. Com. on La. Edn., 1964; mem. coordinating council La. State Colls. and La. State U., 1948-52. Bd. visitors Tulane U.; trustee Wabash Coll.; bd. govs. Ochsner Med. Found., New Orleans; chmn. bd. dirs. St. Francis Cabrini Hosp., Alexandria, La. Decorated Benemerenti medal (Pope John Paul II); recipient Citizenship Citation, La. div. V.F.W., Distinguished Pub. Service Citation, So. U., 1952, Pub. Service Citation, La. Council Coll. Pres.'s, 1953, award of merit Wabash Coll., 1960; Silver Beaver award Boy Scouts Am., 1974; named Humanitarian of Year, Abbeville Festival, 1960. Mem. Sigma Chi. Frat. Presbyterian. Clubs: Chicago; Boston, Internat. House, Country, Plimsoll (New Orleans); Woodstock (Indpls.); Pioneer (Lake Charles, La.), Pres. Pub. Affairs Research Council of La., Inc. 1958. Home: Oakdale, La. Deceased.

FULTON, CHARLES DARBY, educator; b. Kobe, Japan, Sept. 5, 1892; parents Am. citizens; s. Samuel Peter and Rachel Hoge (Peck) F.; m. Nannie Paul Ravenel, Oct. 10, 1917; children: Charles Darby, Margaret Adger (Mrs. John N. Walker), Samuel Ravenel. AB, Presbyn. Coll. of S.C., Clinton, 1911, DD, 1924; AM, U. S.C., 1914; BD, Columbia (S.C.) Theol. Sem., 1915; STB, Princeton Theol. Sem., 1916; LLD, King Coll., Bristol, Va., 1952. Ordained to ministry Presbyn. Ch., 1915. Pastor Bunker Hill and Glassboro, N.J., 1916-17; missionary Japan, 1917-25; field sec. Exec. Com. Fgn. Missions (now Bd. World Missions) Presbyn. Ch. U.S., 1925-31, field and candidate sec., 1931-32, exec. sec., 1932-61; prof. missions Columbia Theol. Sem., from 1962; moderator Gen. Asembly Presbyn. Ch. in U.S., 1948-49. Author: Star in the East, 1938, Now is the Time, 1946. Trustee Hangchow Christian Coll.; mem. bd. founders Nanking Theol. Sem.; exec. com. Com. on Cooperation in Latin Am.; mem. com. of reference and counsel, Fgn. Missions Conf. N.Am. (Fgn. Missions div. Nat. Coun. Chs. Christ U.S.A.), chmn., 1939-40. Mem. Friar Club (Princeton). †

FUOSS, RAYMOND MATTHEW, chemist, educator; b. Bellwood, Pa., Sept. 28, 1905; s. Jacob Zachariah and Bertha May (Zimmerman) F.; m. Rose E. Harrington, July 25, 1926; 1 dau., Patricia Rose; m. Ann M. Stein, Mar. 1, 1947. Sc.B., Harvard U., 1925; Ph.D., Brown U., 1932; M.A. (Hon.), Yale U., 1945. Sheldon research fellow Munich, 1925-26; Austin teaching fellow Harvard U., 1926-27; cons. Skinner, Sherman & Esselen, Boston, 1927-30; student with C.A. Kraus, Brown U., 1930-32;

research instr. Brown U., 1932-33, asst. prof., 1933-36; Internat. research fellow (on leave from Brown U.) Leipzig, Jena and Cambridge univs., 1934-35; research chemist Gen. Electric Co., Schenectady, 1936-45; Sterling prof. chemistry Yale U., 1945-74, emeritus, from 1974; Priestley lectr. Pa. State Co., 1948. Contbr. about 300 articles on electrolytes, polymers and dielectrics in various sci. jours. Mem. Am. Chem. Soc. (award in pure chemistry 1935), Nat., N.Y., Conn. acads. sci., Am. Acad. Arts and Scis., Sigma Xi, Alpha Chi Sigma, Phi Beta Kappa. Home: Hamden Conn. Deceased.

FURER, SAMUEL HENRY, lawyer; b. Louisville, Jan. 4, 1915; s. Abe and Alice (Barnett) F.; m. Gertrude Gooten, Oct. 12, 1947; children—Jerald A., Barbara A. B.A., Ohio State U., 1937; J.D., U. Cin., 1939; M.B.A., U. Wash., 1944. Bar: Ohio bar 1939. Practice law Cin., 1939-86; ptnr. firm O'Brien and Furer, 1951-63; sr. ptnr. firm Furer, Moskowitz, Siegel and Mezibov, 1979-86; pres. Findlay Market Assn., Cin., 1963-64; instr. U. Wash., 1943. Pres. Federated Civic Assns., Hamilton County, Ohio, 1963-64, exec. sec., 1965-66. Served with JAGC U.S. Army, 1943-46. Mem. ABA, Ohio State Bar Assn., Cin. Bar Assn., Alpha Epsilon Pi. Club: Lawyers (Cin.). Home: Cincinnati Ohio. Died July 25, 1986; buried Cincinnati.

FUREY, FRANCIS JAMES, bishop; b. Summit Hill, Pa., Feb. 22, 1905; s. John and Anna (O'Donnell) F. Student, St. Charles Sem., Overbrook, Pa., 1920-24; PhD, Pontificio Seminario Romano, Rome, 1926, STD, 1930; LLD, La Salle Coll., Phila., 1944, St. John's U., Bklyn., 1946, Villanova U., 1947, St. Joseph's Coll., Phila., 1949. Ordained priest Roman Cath. Ch., 1930, consecrated bishop, 1960. Pvt. sec. to Cardinal Dougherty 1930-36; pres. Immaculata (Pa.) Coll., 1936-46; rector St. Charles Sem., 1946-58, St. Helena's Parish, Phila., 1958-63; aux. bishop, Phila., titular bishop, Temnus, 1960-63, bishop of San Diego, 1963-69, archbishop of San Antonio, from 1969. Dir. Cath. Charities Appeal, Phila., 1958; bd. dirs. Misericordia Hosp., Phila., St. Joseph Hosp., Ravenhill Acad., Germantown, Pa.; trustee Roman Cath. High Sch., Phila. Named Domestic Prelate by Pope Pius XII, 1947; knight comdr. Legion Cedars Lebanon. Mem. Nat. Ednl. Assn., Pa. Cath. Ednl. Assn., Assn. Coll. Pres.'s Pa., John Henry Newman Soc. Home: San Antonio Tex. Died Apr. 23, 1979; buried Holy Cross Cemetery, San Antonio.

FURLONG, PHILIP JOSEPH, bishop; b. N.Y.C., Dec. 8, 1892; s. Peter A. and Marie E. (Cosgrove) F. AB, Cathedral Coll., 1914; grad., St. Joseph's Sem., 1918; PhD, Fordham U., 1922, LLD, 1956; LLD, Manhattan Coll., 1946, Iona Coll., 1956. Ordained priest Roman Cath. Ch., 1918. Curate St. Dennis Ch., Yonkers, N.Y., 1918-20; prof. history, dean, pres. Cathedral Coll., 1920-41; prin. Cardinal Hayes High Sch., N.Y.C., 1941-45; sec. edn. Archdiocese N.Y., 1945-46; 1st pastor St. Thomas More Ch., N.Y.C., 1950-69; aux. bishop Mil. Ordinariate, from 1955. Nat. Cath. chaplain Girl Scouts U.S., 1948-55. Decorated Al Merito, Govt. of Peru, Govt. of Ecuador. Mem. Am., Am. Cath. hist. assns., U.S. Cath. Hist. Soc., Am. Acad. Polit. and Social Sci., N.Y. Acad. Pub. Edn. Home: New York N.Y. †

FURST, MILTON, physicist, educator; b. N.Y.C., Sept. 10, 1921; s. Louis and Fannie (Smith) F.; m. Edna Hedy Gordon, June 9, 1945; children: David Arthur, Mitchell Leslie. Physicist N.Y. Naval Shipyard, 1947-50; from research asst. to research scientist NYU, 1950-67; mem. faculty Hunter Coll., 1955-83, prof. physics, 1967-83; sabbatical at Centre d'Etude Nucleaire De Saclay, France, 1961-62, Oakland U., Mich., 1974; cons. in field. Author, patentee in field. Served with USAAF, 1942-46. Mem. Am. Phys. Soc., AAAS, ACLU, Sigma Xi, Sigma Phi Sigma. Jewish. Home: Bronx N.Y. Died Mar. 4, 1983.

GABEL, ARTHUR BERTRAM, dental educator; b. Mt. Joy, Pa., Apr. 26, 1890; s. Clayton Grant and Annie Agusta (Hoffer) G.; m. Lenore Dorsey, Sept. 8, 1923; 1 child, Ann Dorsey (dec.). AB, Franklin and Marshall Coll., 1910; student, Worcester Poly. Inst., 1912-13; AM, Columbia U., 1917; student, Ecole Superieure d'Electricite, 1919, Sorbonne, Paris, 1919; DDS, U. Pa., 1925. Instr. physics, chemistry and math. Princeton Prep. Sch., 1914-16; asst. in physics Columbia U., 1916-17; ednl. dir. Vet. Bur., Pocono Pines, Pa., 1921; instr. physics Dental Sch., U. Pa., 1922-25; gen. dental practice Seattle, 1925-31; asst. prof. operative dentistry Sch. Dentistry, U. Pa., 1931-33, prof., 1933-37, Edwin. T. Darby prof. operative dentistry, from 1937, head dept., from 1933; vis. prof. dental sch. U. São Paulo, Brazil, 1951-53. Editor: American Textbook of Operative Dentistry; contbr articles to profl. publs. 1st lt. U.S. Army, World War I, France. Fellow AAAS; mem. Internat. Assn. Dental Rsch., Physics Club (past pres.), Masons, Psi Omega, Omega Kappa Upsilon, Sigma Xi. Home: Wynnewood Pa. †

GABRIEL, RALPH HENRY, history educator; b. Watkins Glen, N.Y., Apr. 29, 1890; s. Er Cleveland and Alta (Monroe) G.; m. Christine Davis, Aug. 18, 1917; children: Robert Todd, John Cleveland, Susan. BA, Yale U., 1913, MA, 1915, PhD, 1919; LittD (hon.), Bucknell U., 1952, Williams Coll., 1958; DHL (hon.), Colgate U., 1963. With Yale U., 1915-58, assoc. prof. history, 1925-28, prof., 1928-58, Sterling prof. emeritus of history, fellow Trumbull Coll., 1933-58; prof. Am. civilization Sch. Internat. Service, Am. U., Washington, 1958-64; vis. prof. NYU, summer 1933, U. Colo., summers 1941, 42, U. Sydney, Australia, 1946, Stanford U., 1949, Cambridge U., 1951-52, Tokyo U., spring 1964, George Washington U., summer 1965; acting prof. Leland Stanford U., summer 1934; Gina Speranza lectr. Columbia U., 1955; U.S. del. to 10th SCO Conf. Paris, 1958; mem. U.S. nat. commn. UNESCO; collaborator ednl. program 2d Army, 1942; mem. faculty War Dept. Sch. Mil. Govt., Charlottesville, Va., 1943-46. Author: The Course of American Democratic Thought, rev. edit., 1956, Traditional Values in American Life, 1952, Religion and Learning at Yale, 1958, (with Mabel D. Casner) The Story of American Democracy, (co-author) The School of the Citizen Soldier, 1942; gen. editor Library of Congress Series in Am. Civilization, Pageant of America, 15 vols.; dveleoper pioneering course in Am. thought and civilization. Trustee Colls. of Yale (China). Served to lt. inf. U.S. Army, World War I. Mem. Am. Hist. Soc., Newcomen Soc., Grad. Club., Aurelist Soc., Am. Studies Assn. (pres. 1962-63), Cosmos Club, Berzelius, Phi Beta Kappa, Sigma Xi, Beta Theta Pi. Home: Hamden Conn. Died Apr. 21, 1987; buried Watkins Glen, N.Y.

GAINES, FRANCIS PENDLETON, JR., university dean; b. State College, Miss., Sept. 7, 1918; s. Francis Pendleton and Sadie (Robert) G.; m. Dorothy Ruth Bloomhardt, Oct. 10, 1942; children—Francis Pendleton III, Paul Randolph, Sallie du Vergne; m. Marjorie Anne Hurt, Mar. 25, 1975. Grad., Woodberry Forest Prep. Sch., 1935; student, Washington and Lee U., 1935-37; A.B. summa cum laude, U. Ariz., 1942; M.A., U. Va., 1946, Ph.D. (DuPont fellow), 1950; L.H.D., Coll. Artesia, 1968. Engr. on Miss. River, War Dept., 1937-39; dean of men, asst. to pres. Birmingham So Coll., 1946-48; supt. Gulf Coast Mil. Acad., 1948; dir. pub. relations and devel. U. Houston, 1950; dean of students So. Meth. U., 1951-52; pres. Wofford Coll., 1952-57; v.p. Piedmont Nat. Bank, Spartanburg, S.C., 1957-58; dir. research study Fund for Advancement Edn., 1958-59; dean continuing edn. and summer session U. Ariz., Tucson, 1959-73; dean adminstrn. U. Ariz., 1973-86, also prof. ednl. adminstrn.; sec. Assn. Summer Session Deans and Dirs., 1961-62. Author: Presidents and Deans, 1987; editorialist: Spartanburg Herald-Jour; Contbr. profl. publs. Pres. Conf. Ch.-related Colls. South, 1956-57; ofcl. del. to jurisdictional, gen. and world confs. of Meth. Ch., 1956; mem. Council for Basic Edn, Woodrow Wilson Regional Selection com.; treas. S.C. Found. Ind. Colls.; citizens adv. council U.S. Senate Com. to P.O. and Civil Service; adv. com. Robert A. Taft Inst. Govt.; mem. Ariz. Civil War Centennial Commn. Served as capt. AUS, War Dept., Gen. Staff, M.I., 1942-45. Named S.C. Young Man of Year Jr. C. of C., 1954; Outstanding Faculty Mem. U. Ariz., 1971; recipient Ariz. Civil Def. award, 1971. Fellow Nat. Univ. Extension Assn.; mem. U. Ariz. Alumni Assn. (dir. 1967-87), Washington and Lee U. Alumni Assn. (pres. Tucson chpt. 1981-87), Newcomen Soc., Phi Beta Kappa, Omicron Delta Kappa, Phi Kappa Phi, Pi Delta Epsilon, Phi Kappa Sigma, Raven Soc. Methodist (mem adminstrv. bd.). Clubs: Davis-Monthan Officers; Old Pueblo (Tucson); Country (Spartanburg). Home: Tucson Ariz. Died June 11, 1987.

GALBRAITH, FRANCIS JOSEPH, foreign service officer, consultant; b. Timber Lake, S.D., Dec. 9, 1913; s. Fred J. and Clara Belle (Stearns) G.; m. Martha Townsley Fisher, July 18, 1948; children: Susan Kathleen, Kelly Francis. BA in History, Coll. Puget Sound, 1939; BA in Librarianship, U. Wash., 1940; postgrad. Indonesian lang. and area tng., Yale U., 1948-49. Reference libr. U. Wash., 1940-41; with Dept. State, 1946-74; vice counsul Hamburg, Fed. Republic Germany, 1946-48; polit. officer Am. Embassy, Djakarta, Indonesia, 1949-51, Indonesian desk officer, 1951-55; counselor, dep. chief of mission Am. Embassy, Djakarta, 1963-65; consul Medan, Sumatra, 1955; 1st sec., polit. officer Gt. Britain, 1958-62; fgn. service inspector 1965-66, ambassador to Singapore, 1966-69, ambassador to Indonesia, 1969-74; cons. internat. affairs Bechtel Corp., Freeport Indonesia, Weyerhauser Co., Intermaritime Mgmt.mo, 1974-86. Served to capt. F.A., AUS, 1941-46., PTO. Mem. Am. Fgn. Service Assn., Cosmos Club, Yale Club of Washington, Army Navy CountryClub, Columbia Country Club, Am. Club Singapore, Jakarta Golf Club, Dacor, Sigma Zeta Epsilon. Home: Washington D.C. Died June 25, 1986, buried Rock Creek Cemetery, Washingotn.

GALBREATH, JOHN WILMER, real estate developer, baseball club executive, horseman; b. Derby, Ohio, Aug. 10, 1897; s. Francis Hill and Belle (Mitchell) G.; m. Helen Mauck, Sept. 14, 1921 (dec. 1946); children: Joan Hill, Daniel Mauck; m. Dorothy Bryan Firestone, Feb. 17, 1955 (dec. 1985). BA, Ohio U., 1920, LLD (hon.), 1956; LLD (hon.), Athens Coll., 1956, Ohio State U., 1971; DBA (hon.), Ohio No. U., 1960. Founder, owner John W. Galbreath & Co., Columbus, Ohio, 1924-88; owner, chmn. Pitts. Pirates Baseball Team, 1946-85; world champions Pitts. Pirates baseball team, 1960, 71, 79; owner Darby Dan Farm; horses winners 2 Ky. Derbys, Preakness Race, Belmont Stakes; bd. dirs. Buckeye Fed. Bldg. and Loan Assn., Buckeye Internat. Inc., City Nat. Bank & Trust Co. Served to 2d lt. F.A., U.S. Army, World War I. Mem. Columbus Real Estate Bd. (pres.), Ohio Real Estate Assn. (pres.) Nat. Assn. Real Estate Bds. (pres.), Am. Inst. Real Estate Appraisers, Soc. Indsl. Realtors, Jockey Club, Masons, Delta Tau Delta. Home: Galloway Ohio. Died July 20, 1988.

GALLUP, GEORGE HORACE, public opinion statistician; b. Jefferson, Iowa, Nov. 18, 1901; s. George Henry and Nettie (Davenport) G.; m. Ophelia Smith Miller, Dec. 27, 1925; children: Alec Miller, George Horace, Jr., Julia Gallup Laughlin. B.A., State U. Iowa, 1923, M.A., 1925, Ph.D., 1928, LL.D., 1967; LL.D., Northwestern U., Drake U., Boston U., Chattanooga U.; D.Sc., Tufts Coll.; H.H.D., Colgate U.; D.C.L., Rider Coll., 1966, Pepperdine Coll., Okla. Christian Coll., Georgian Ct. Coll., Beaver Coll., Coe Coll. Head dept. journalism Drake U., 1929-31; prof. journalism and advt. Northwestern U., 1931-32; dir. research Young & Rubicam Advt. Agy., N.Y.C., 1932-47; prof. Pulitzer Sch. Journalism, Columbia U., 1935-37; pres. Market Research Council, 1934, 35, Nat. Municipal League, 1954-56, Internat. Insts. Pub. Opinion, 1947-84; chmn. emeritus Gallup and Robinson, Inc. (advt. and mktg. research); chmn. bd. Gallup Orgn., Inc. (mktg. and attitude research); made editorial surveys of many newspapers, also many editorial and advt. surveys of Liberty, Sat. Eve. Post, Ladies Home Jour. and Colliers; Founder Am. Inst., 1935, Brit. Inst. Pub. Opinion, 1936; founder and pres. Audience Research Inst., Inc., 1939; founder Quill and Scroll (internat. honor soc. for high sch. journalists), chmn. bd. trustees. Author: The Pulse of Democracy, 1940, The Miracle Ahead, 1964, The Sophisticated Poll Watcher's Guide, 1972, 2d edit., 1976, America Wants To Know, 1983, also numerous articles on pub. opinion. Recipient ann. advt. award, 1935, award for distinguished achievement Syracuse U., 1950; Distinguished Citizen award Nat. Municipal League, 1962; Parlin award Am. Mktg. Assn., 1965; Christopher Columbus Internat. prize for outstanding achievement in communications, 1968; Distinguished Achievement award N.J. chpt. Am. Mktg. Assn., 1975; award Nat. Assn. Secondary Sch. Prins., 1975, Iowa award, 1984; named to Hall of Fame in Distbn., 1962; elected to Advt. Hall of Fame, 1977; Market Research Hall of Fame, 1978, N.J. Advt. Hall of Fame, 1983. Mem. World Assn. Pub. Opinion Research, Am. Assn. Pub. Opinion Research (advt. Gold medal 1964, pres. 1954-55), Am. Acad. Arts and Scis., Council Fgn. Relations, Sigma Alpha Epsilon, Sigma Delta Chi, Sigma Xi, Nat. Press Club. Episcopalian. Home: Princeton N.J. Died July 27, 1984; buried Princeton.

GAMBLE, PHILIP LYLE, economist; b. Amesbury, Mass., Sept. 25, 1905; s. Fred Keightley and Sarah Olive (Lord) G.; m. Elisabeth Davis Scales, Aug. 7, 1939; children—Ruth Scales, Philip Lyle, Richard Andrew. B.S. cum laude, Wesleyan U., 1928; A.M. (Rich fellow in econs.), 1929; Ph.D. (N.Y. State Tax Commn. fellow), Cornell U., 1935. Instr. in econs. Cornell U., 1929-32, Wesleyan U., 1932-35; vis. instr. econs. Mt. Holyoke Coll., 1934-36; asst. prof. econs. Mass. State Coll., 1935-42; assoc. prof. Tulane U., summer 1939; vis. prof. Amherst Coll., 1942, Clark U., 1960, 61; prof., head dept. econs., govt. U. Mass., 1942-50, acting chmn. dept. bus. adminstrn., 1947, acting dean sch. bus. adminstrn., 1947-52, prof. econs., 1942-71, head dept., 1942-64; Theodore Roosevelt prof. econs. Naval War Coll., 1968-70, 71-74; prof. Sweetbriar Coll., 1977; Fulbright lectr. Tunghai U. China, 1964, 65. Author: The Taxation of Insurance Companies, 1937; State corr. and contbr. to: The Municipal Yearbook, 1937-40, 43-50. Pub. panel mem. War Labor Bd., 1943-44; mem. consumers council Atty.-Gen.'s Office. Mem. Consumers Union (mem. nat. ednl. adv. council), Am. Arbitration Assn., AAUP, Pioneer Valley Assn. (pres. 1962-64), Am. Econ. Assn., Tax Research Found., Phi Kappa Phi, Sigma Chi. Home: Newport R.I. Died Aug. 29, 1987, buried Wildewood Cemetery, Amherst, Mass.

GANTNER, GEORGE EUGENE, JR., pathologist; b. St. Louis, June 7, 1927; s. George Eugene and Dorothy (Andrews) G.; m. Genevieve Timm, June 16, 1951; children: George Eugene III, Christine, Jeanne Marie, Thomas, Robert, Michael, Stephen. BS, St. Louis U., 1949, MD, 1953. Diplomate: Am. Bd. Pathology. Intern in surgery St. Mary's Group of Hosps., St. Louis, 1953-54; fellow pathology St. Louis U. Sch. Medicine, 1954-57; pvt. practice pathology St. Louis, 1957-88; asst. pathologist St. Mary's Group Hosps., 1957-58; patholoist, dir. labs. St. Louis U. Hosps., 1958-88; assoc. prof. pathology St. Louis U. Sch. Medicine, 1962-88, acting chmn. dept. pathology, 1965-66, prof., 1969-88; coroner's pathologist St. Louis County, 1958-68; chief med. examiner from 1969. Author: A Practical Manual of Clinical Chemistry, vols. 1-6, 1966, Data Processing Methods for Diagnostic Codes: Systemized Nomenclature of Pathology, 1969, also articles. Served with USNR, 1945-46. Fellow Am. Acad. Forensic Scis. (gov. 1975-88, pres. 1983-84), Coll. Am. Pathologists; mem. Nat. Assn. Med. Examiners (sec.-treas.), Mo. Med. Assn., St. Louis Med. Soc., Mo. Soc. Pathologists, St. Louis Path. Soc. (pres. 1962), Internat. Assn. Coroners and Med. Examiners. Home: Saint Louis Mo. Died Nov. 15, 1988.

GANTZ, DAVID MARTIN, motor freight company executive; b. Wilkes-Barre, Pa., Nov. 29, 1907; s. Louis and Anna (Katz) G.; m. Lila Tashman, Sept. 15, 1951; children: Laura Ann, Joseph S., Harry M. BA, U. Wis., 1929. Ptnr. Joseph M. Gantz Agy., Cin., 1929-88; chmn. bd. Wilson Frieght Co., Cin., 1939-88. Served to lt. col. AUS, World War II, CBI. Mem. Common Carrier Conf. (bd. govs.), Am. Trucking Assn., Ohio Trucking Assn. (elected to Hall of Fame 1968), Eastern Cen. Motor Carries Assn. (pres.), Greater Cin. C. of C. (pres.), Kenwood Country Club, Losantiville Country Club, Bankers Club Cin., Pi Sigma Alpha. Home: Cincinnati Ohio. Died Jan. 14, 1988; buried United Jewish Cemeteries, Cin.

GARCEAU, OLIVER, educator; b. Boston, Nov. 22, 1911; s. Dr. Edgar and Sally Holmes (Morse) G.; m. Iris Virginia Thistle, Aug. 18, 1934; 1 son, Laurence. A.B., Harvard, 1933, M.B.A., 1935, A.M., 1939, Ph.D., 1940; student, Oxford (Eng.) U., 1933, U. Chgo., 1943-44. Instr., asst. prof. Harvard, 1935-41, 45-46; asso. prof. U. Maine, 1946-47; staff asso. Social Sci. Research Council, 1947-48; prof. govt. Bennington (Vt.) Coll., 1948-59; research prof. govt. Harvard, 1959-60, research cons. polit. economy and polit. behavior, 1960-87; exec. asso., cons. Ford Found., 1955-58; exec. bd. Inter-univ. Case Program, 1952-58. Author: Political Life of American Medical Association, 1941, Public Library in the Political Process, 1949; author, editor: Political Research and Political Theory, 1968; asso. editor: Human Organization, 1956-66. Mem. Gov.'s Task Force on State Govt. Reorgn., 1967-69. Served to lt. comdr. USNR, 1941-45. Fellow Social Sci. Research Council (mem. com. on polit. behavior 1950-64); mem. Am. Polit. Sci. Assn. (exec. council 1951-53), Phi Beta Kappa. Home: Sedgwick Maine. Died Jan. 23, 1987; cremated.

GARDNER, REECE ALEXANDER, lawyer; b. Columbia, Mo., Oct. 6, 1911; s. Glenn Warner and Hazel (Straight) G.; m. Jean Clare McKeen, July 15, 1939; 1 dau., Ann Morton. AB, Harvard U., 1933, JD, 1936. Bar: Mo. 1936, Kans. 1941. Ptnr. Stinson, Mag & Fizzell, Kansas City, Mo., 1939-83. Author, lectr. in field. City clk. Mission Hills, Kans., 1959-70; pres. Andrew Drumm Inst., 1955-78, treas. from 1978; trustee The Villages Inc., Mag Found., Park Found., H.O. Peet Found., Stinson, Mag, Thomson, McEvers & Fizzell Found.; hon. bd. dirs. Rockhurst Coll. Capt. AUS, 1942-46. Mem. Am., Fed., Kansas City bar assns., Am. Law Inst., Am. Judicature Soc., Ju ge Advocates Assn., Lawyers Assn. Kansas City, Mil. Order World Wars., Kansas City (Kans.) Country Club; Nat. Lawyers Club (Washington), University Club (Kansas City). Home: Kansas City Mo. Died June 24, 1984.

GARNETT, DAVID, author; b. Brighton, Sussex, Eng., Mar. 9, 1892; s. Edward and Constance (Black) G.; m. Rachel Alice Marshall, Mar. 1921 (dec. 1940); children: Richard Duncan Carey, William Tomlin Kasper; m. angelica Vanessa Bell, May 1942; children: Amaryliis Virginia, Henrietta Catherine Vanessa, Frances Olivia, Nerissa Stephen. A, Imperial Coll. Sci. and Tech., London, 1913, diploma of mem., 1915. Bookseller Francis Birrell, 1920. Author: Lady Into Fox, 1922 (Hawthornden prize, James Tait Black prize 1923), A Man in the Zoo, 1923, The Sailor's Return, 1924, Go She Must, 1927, No Love, 1929, The Grasshoppers Come, 1931, A Rabbit in the Air, 1932, Pocahontas, 1933, Beaney-Eye, 1935, War in the Air, 1941, The Golden Echo, 1953, Flowers of the Forest, 1955, Aspects of Love, 1955, A Shot in the Dark, 1958, A Net for Venus, 1959, The Familiar Faces, 1962, Two By Two, 1963, Ulterior Motives, 1967. With Dept. Fgn. Office, 1941-46. Flight lt. RAF, 1939-40. Decorated comdr. Order Brit. Empire. Fellow Royal Soc. Lit., Imperial Coll. Sci. and Tech. Home: Huntington England. †

GARRELS, ROBERT MINARD, geology educator; b. Detroit, Aug. 24, 1916; s. John C. and Margaret A. (Gibney) G.; m. Jane M. Tinen, Dec. 21, 1940 (div. 1969); children: Joan F., James C., Katherine G.; m. Cynthia A. Hunt, 1970. B.S., U. Mich., 1937, Sc.D. (hon.), 1980; M.S., Northwestern U., 1939, Ph.D., 1941; M.A. (hon.), Harvard U., 1955; Sc.D. (hon.), U. Brussels, 1969, U. Louis Pasteur, Strasbourg, France, 1976. From instr. to assoc. prof. geology Northwestern U., Evanston, Ill., 1941-52, prof. geology, 1965-69, 72-80; prof. geology Scripps Instn. Oceanography, 1969-71; prof. U. South Fla., 1980-88; geologist U.S. Geol. Survey, 1952-55; assoc. prof. geology Harvard U., 1955-57, prof., 1957-65, chmn. dept. geol. scis., 1963-65; Henri Speciael prof. sci. U. Brussels, Belgium, 1962-63; Capt. James Cook prof. oceanography U. Hawaii, Honolulu, 1972-74. Author: Textbook of Geology, 1951, Mineral Equilibria, 1959, (with C.L. Christ) Solutions, Minerals and Equilibria, 1965, (with F.T. Mackenzie) Evolution of Sedimentary Rocks, 1971, (with C.A. Hunt) Water, The Web of Life, 1972, (with F.T. Mackenzie, C. Hunt) Chemical Cycles and the Global Environment, 1975; (with T.L. Woods) Thermodynamic Values at Low Temperature for Natural Inorganic Materials—An Uncritical Survey, 1987. Recipient Wollaston medal Geol. Soc. London, 1981; Fla. Scientist of Yr. award Mus. Sci. and Industry, Tampa, 1985. Fellow AAAS, Geol. Soc. Am. (Arthur L. Day medal 1966, Penrose medal 1978), Mineral. Soc. Am. (Roebling medal 1981), mem. Geochem. Soc. (pres. 1962, V.M. Goldschmidt award 1973), Nat. Acad. Scis., Soc. Econ. Geologists, Am. Acad. Arts and Sci., Am. Chem. Soc., Sigma Xi. Home: Saint Petersburg Fla. Died Mar. 8, 1988; cremated.

GARRETT, ETHEL SHIELDS, civic worker; b. Pitts., May 7, 1896; d. Peter and Cora (Lewis) Shields; m. Harry Darlington, Jr., Jan. 31, 1917 (dec. Jan. 1931); children: Harry III, McCullough, Elaine Darlington (Mrs. Anderson Fowler); m. George Angus Garrett, Apr. 11, 1935. Grad., Miss Spence Sch., N.Y.C., 1915. Mem. exec. com. Nat. Symphony Orch.; nat. council Met. Opera; mem.-at-large Garden Club Am.; mem. Nat. Cathedral Assn.; Hon. trustee John F. Kennedy Centre for Performing Arts. Episcopalian. Home: Washington D.C. Died Mar. 15, 1986.

GARRETT, JAMES HAROLD, JR., editor; b. N.Y.C., July 2, 1940; s. James H. and Mary G.; m. Frances Gery, Sept. 5, 1964; children: Caroline, Jay. Student, St. John's U., N.Y.C., 1963-65. Staff photographer New York News, 1965-79, asst. night picture editor, 1979-80, picture editor, from 1980. Mem. N.Y. Press Photographers Assn. (sec. 1973-75, v.p. 1975-77), Nat. Press Photographers Assn. Club: N.Y. Press. Home: Scotch Plains N.J. Died Mar. 28, 1987.

GARRETT, PAUL, public relations counsel; b. Lincoln, Kans., Nov. 27, 1891; s. Sidney L. and Ida I. (Holcomb) G.; m. Lillian Riggs, July 19, 1939. BS, Whitman Coll., 1913, LLD, 1947; AM, Columbia U., 1914. With Bur. Mcpl. Rsch., N.Y.C., 1915; with bur. state rsch. N.J. C. of C., 1916-17; with War Industries Bd., Washington, 1918-19, Am. Internat. Corp., N.Y.C., 1919-20; fin. columnist The Investor, N.Y. Evening Post, 1920-25, fin. editor, 1925-31; dir. pub. relations GM, 1931-56, v.p., 1940-56; mem. exec. com., bd. dirs. TelePrompter Corp.; bd. dirs., chmn. fin. com. Nylok corp.; bd. dirs. G.T. Schieldahl Co., Celebrity Register, Ltd., Unimed, Inc.; pub. relations counsel Xerox Corp. Author: If I Had Your Chance, 1947, A New Dimension for Public Relations, 1956, numerous others. Bd. dirs. Automotive Safety Found., 1937-46, Nat. Indsl. Conf. Bd., 1947-56; bd. overseers Whitman Coll. Recipient Ann. award Nat. Assn. Pub. Relations Counsel, 1944, citation extraordinary N.Y. chpt. Pub. Relations Soc. Am., 1957. Mem. Automobile Mfrs. Assn. (chmn. pub. relations com. 1938-48), Advt. Fedn. Am. (chmn. bd. 1940-41), Everglades Club, Bath and Tennis Club, University Club, Recess Club, Detroit Athletic Club, Surf Club, Nat. Press Club, Bel-Air Country Club, Phi Beta Kappa, Phi Delta Theta. Republican. Home: New York N.Y. †

GARRETT, ROBERT YOUNG, JR., insurance executive; b. Balt., May 24, 1903; s. Robert Young and Anne (Hanson) G.; m. Margaret S. Ruff, Oct. 24, 1925 (dec. June 1970); 1 child, Robert Young III; m. Vivian M. Brown, Oct. 6, 1973. Student, Am. Inst. Banking; grad., Rutgers U. Grad. Sch. Banking, 1945. With Cen. Nat. Bank, Phila., 1921-35; with Farmers Bank and Trust Co., Lancaster, Pa., 1935-63, pres., 1961-63; pres. merged bank Lancaster County Farmers Nat. Bank, 1963-70; vice chmn. Nat. Cen. Bank, Lancaster, 1970-73; pres. Donegal Mut. Ins. Co., from 1972, chmn. bd., from 1974; bd. dirs. Watt & Shand, Lancaster; mem. adv. com. banking policies and practices 3d Nat. Bank Region, 1965-68. Treas. Lancaster Gen. Hosp., from 1952, vice chmn. bd., 1972, chmn. bd., 1973-77; pres. bd. Lancaster br. Pa. Assn. for Blind, 1963-80, N. Milton Woods Home for Ret. Presbyn. Ministers of Donegal Presbytery, from 1958; elderPresbyn. Ch., mem. bd. nat. missions, 1955-61; mem. distbn. com. Lancaster County Found. Recipient Benjamin Rush award Lancaster County Med. Assn., 1979. Mem. Pa. Soc., Lancaster C. of C., Lancaster Country Club, Hamilton Club (dir., treas. from 1976), Univ. Club Lancaster, Lions (pres. Lancaster 1949-50). Home: Lancaster Pa. Died Jan. 22, 1985; buried Arlington Cemetery, Phila.

GARRIS, EDWARD WALTER, university professor; b. Round O, S.C., Jan. 17, 1892; s. William Franklin and Janie (Black) G.; m. Erma Altha Westbury, Mar. 22, 1919; children: Minnie Reta, Erma Mardie (Mrs. E.W. Biggers), Edward Walter. BS, Clemson Coll., S.C., 1915; DSC (hon.), Clemson Coll., 1937; AM (Gen. Edn. Bd. scholarship, 1924), U. S.C., 1924; PhD, Peabody Coll., 1926. High sch. prin. Swanquarter, N.C., 1915-16, Williams, S.C., 1916-17; tchr. of agr. Estill, S.C., 1917-20; asst. state supr. of agrl. edn. Columbia, S.C., 1920-24; state supr. agrl. edn. Tallahassee, Fla., 1925-27; head dept. agrl. edn. U. Fla., from 1927. Author several books including Southern Horticultural Management, 1949, Teaching Vocational Agriculture, 1954. Trustee Masonic Home of Fla. With N.G., 1911-14. Mem. Am. and Fla. (past pres.) Vocational Assn., NEA, Fla. Edn. Assn., Nat. Geographic Soc., So. Assn. Secondary Schs. and Colls. (rsch. com.), Masons (32 degree, Shriner, past grand orator of Fla.), Order of Eastern Star (past grand patron of Fla.), Woodmen of the World, Tall Cedars of Lebanon Club, Alpha Zeta, Alpha Tau Alpha, Theta Chi, Phi Kappa Phi, Phi Delta Kappa, Kappa Delta Pi. Democrat. Baptist. Home: Gainesville Fla. †

GARRISON, LEMUEL ALONZO, conservation and environment educator; b. Pella, Iowa, Oct. 1, 1903; s. Lemuel Addison and Mary (Firth) G.; m. Inger Wilhelmine Larsen, Mar. 21, 1930; children: Lars A. Erik (dec.), Mary K. Garrison Reyer. Sch. tchr., also with U.S. Forest Service Alaska, 1929-31; ranger Sequoia and Yosemite Nat. Pk., 1932-39; supt. Hopewell Village Nat. Hist. Site, 1939-41; asst. chief info. Nat Park Service, Washington, 1941-42, chief conservation and protection, chmn. steering com. Mission 66 study and devel. program., 1955-56; Midwest region dir. Nat Park Service, Omaha, 1964-66; Northeast region dir. Nat. Park Service, Phila., 1966-70; asst. supt. Glacier and Grand Canyon nat. parks, 1942-53; supt. Big Bend Nat. Park, 1953-55, Yellowstone Nat. Park, 1955-63; dir. Horace M. Albright Tng. Acad., Grand Canyon, Ariz., 1970-73; prof. recreation and parks dept. Tex. A&M U., Colleg Station., 1973-84; free lance writer, 1935-84; del. Vatican-Italian Govt. Conf. on Spiritual Values in Tourism, 1967, spl. park study site of ancient Olympic Games, Govt. of Greece, 1969. Recipient Disting. Service award Dept. Interior, 1962, Pugsley Gold award, 1969, Meritorious Service award Nat. Park Resources, 1975. Mem. Nat. Recreation and Park Assn., Nat. Conf. State Parks (former pres.), Western History Assn., Internat. Union Conservation Nature, Wilderness Soc., Izaak Walton League, Sierra Club, Ducks Unltd., Trout Unltd, Nat. Geog. Soc., Outdoor Writers Am., Masons (32 deg.), Shriners, Rotary. Home: College Station Tex. Died Feb. 13, 1984.

GARVY, GEORGE, economist; b. Riga, Latvia, May 30, 1913; came to U.S., 1940, naturalized, 1948; s. Peter and Sophie (Fichman) G; m. Juliette Francoise Blanc, Oct. 17, 1940; 1 child, Helen Sylvie Garvy Arlette. Student, U. Berlin, 1931-33; licence-es-lettres, U. Paris, 1937; diploma, Inst. Stats., 1935; PhD, Columbia U., 1951. With Nat. Bur. Econ. Research, Inc., N.Y.C., 1941-43; with Fed. Res. Bank N.Y., from 1943, appointed officer, 1953, v.p., sr. adviser, 1974; vis. prof. Columbia U., 1959-60, NYU, Sch. Bus. Stanford U.; lectr. Econ. Devel. Inst., Washington, from 1957; mem. rev. com. balance of payments stats. Bur. Budget, 1963-64; chmn. com. internat. travel grants Social Sci. Research Council, from 1964; mem. fgn. missions Internat. Bank Reconstrn. and Devel., 1951-56; mem. selection com. W.S. Woytinsky Lectureship award U. Mich., from 1963. Author books and articles in field. Served with French Army, World War II. Fellow Am. Stats. Assn.; mem. Am. Econ. Assn., Am. Fin. Assn. (pres. 1965). Home: Manhasset N.Y. Died Oct. 6, 1987, cremated.

GARWOOD, WILMER ST. JOHN, lawyer, former judge; b. Bastrop, Tex., Dec. 15, 1896; s. Hiram M. and Hettie (Page) G.; m. Ellen Clayton, July 11, 1927; children—Wilmer St. John, William Lockhart. A.B., Georgetown U., 1917; postgrad., U. Tex., 1919; LL.B., Harvard, 1922. Bar: Tex. bar 1919, N.Y. bar 1923. Atty. legal dept. Texas Co., N.Y.C., 1922-23, Baker, Botts, Parker & Garwood, Houston, 1924-28; resident Am. counsel Standard Oil Co. (N.J.), Buenos Aires, 1929-33; mem. law firm Andrews, Kelley, Kurth & Campbell, Houston, 1934-41; pvt. practice Houston, 1945-47; vice chmn. Houston Civil Service Commn., 1945-46; apptd. to Supreme Ct. of Tex., 1948, assoc. justice, 1948-58; of counsel firm Graves, Dougherty, Hearon, Moody & Garwood (and predecessor), Austin, from 1958; prof. law U. Tex., 1961; dir. Austin Nat. Bank. Mem. U.S. delegation to Atlantic Congress, London, 1959; pres. Tex. Civil Jud. Council, 1964-71; A founder St. John's Sch., Houston, 1945; trustee U. Tex. Law Sch. Found. Served as 1st lt. Cav. 1918-23, Tex. N.G.; from lt. to lt. comdr., naval intelligence USNR, 1942-45. Decorated Orden al Merito Chile; hon. consul Poland for Tex., 1937-39. Fellow Am. Bar Found.; Mem. ABA, Am. Law Inst., Austin C. of C., Philos. Soc. Tex. (pres. 1960), English Speaking Union, Am. Judicature Soc. (dir. 1963-68), Order of Coif (hon.), Phi Delta Phi (hon.), Phi Delta Theta. Republican. Episcopalian (vestryman). Clubs: Kiwanis, Headliners. Home: Austin Tex. Died Jan. 15, 1987.

GASCON, JEAN, theatre director; b. Montreal, Que., Can, Dec. 21, 1921; s. Charles-Auguste and Rose (Dubuc) G.; m. Marilyn Gardner, Aug. 15, 1971; children: Marie, Helene, Isabelle, Nathalie, Olivier. BA, Coll. Ste. Marie, Montreal, 1940; MD, U. Montreal, 1945, LLA (hon.), 1974; hon. degrees, Bishop's U., 1969, Guelph U., U. Western Ont., Queen's U., 1972; LLD (hon.), McGill U., 1970. Artistic dir. Theatre du Nouveau Monde, Montreal, 1951-66, Stratford (Ont., Can.) Festival, 1967-74; dir. gen. Nat. Theatre Sch., Montreal, 1960-65; dir. theatre Nat. Arts Ctr. Ottawa, Ont., 1977-88; adminstr. La Presse, Montreal,. Decorated Order of Can.; recipient Molson award, 1967, Royal Bank award, 1974, Wrangler award Cowboy Hall of Fame; named best actor for A Man Called Horse, 1970. Mem. Union des Artistes, Actor's Equity, Can. Conf. of Arts, Royal Soc. Can. Home: Westmont Que., Canada. Died Apr. 20, 1988; buried Notre Dame des Niegos, Montreal.

GASSER, HENRY MARTIN, artist; b. Newark, Oct. 31, 1909; s. William Henry and Mary Teresa (Jansus) G.; m. Joane Rone, May 27, 1930. Student, Fawcett Art Sch., 1924-25, Newark Sch. Fine and Indsl. Art, 1928-34, Grand Cen. Art Sch., 1935, Art Students League, 1938-41. Dir. Newark Sch. Fine and Indsl. Art, 1946-54; former pres. N.J. Art Council; lectr. Nat.

Acad. Audubon Artists, Allied Artists Am., Mobile Art League, Shreveport Art Club, Art Assn. Guild New Orleans. Represented in collections numerous mus. and galleries throughout U.S. including Nat. Collection Fine Art Smithsonian Instn., Met. Mus., Phila. Mus. Boston Mus., Newark Mus.; author: (motion picture) Exploring Casein, 1962, (books) Casein Painting Methods and Demonstrations, Oil Painting Methods and Demonstrations, Water Color-How To Do It, Techniques of Painting, Techniques of Painting the Waterfront, Techniques of Picture Making, How to Draw and Paint. Served with inf., AUS, 1944-45. Recipient many honors and awards. Mem. NAD, Nat. Arts Club (life, most recent award 1981), Am. Water Color Soc. (v.p., lectr., most recent award 1980), N.J. Water Color Soc. (former pres.), Calif. Water Color Soc., Allied Artists Am., Conn. Acad. Audubon Artists, Artists and Craftsmen Assocs., Acad. Artists Assn., Am. Artists Profl. League, Royal Soc. Art London, Phila. Water Color Club, Balt. Water Color Club, New Haven Paint and Clay Club. Home: South Orange N.J. Please give date of death and place of burial or interment.

GASTON, EDWARD F., business executive; b. N.Y.C., 1891. Pres., dir. Am. Dist. Telegraph Co.; chmn. bd. Dominion Electric Protection Co., Toronto, Can. Home: Tenafly N.J. †

GATES, WILLIAM FRED, JR., bishop; b. Lexington, Va., Mar. 29, 1912; s. William Fred and Edna (Brundige) G; m. Jane Gregory Dillard, Apr. 25, 1938; children: Anne Gregory Gates, Susan Wenrick Gates. Student, Hobart Coll., 1931-32; BA, U. Chattanooga, 1934; BD, Va. Theol. Sem., 1937, DD (hon.), 1967; DD (hon.), U. of South, 1967. Ordained priest Episcopal Ch., 1938. Asst. minister Calvary Episc. Ch., Memphis, 1937-38; priest-in-charge St. John's Ch., Old Hickory, Tenn., 1938-42; rector St. Peter's Ch., Columbia, Tenn., 1943-66; suffragan bishop Episc. Diocese Tenn., Memphis, 1966-82, also. mem. bishop and council standing com., bd. exam. chaplains. Chmn. Maury County chpt. ARC, 1947-49; pres. Maury County United Givers Fund, 1965-66. Mem. No. Kappa Alpha, Memphis Country Club. Home: Memphis Tenn. Died Dec. 29, 1987; buried Ashwood Cemetery, nr. Columbia, Tenn.

GATZKE, HANS WILHELM, history educator; b. Duelken, Germany, Dec. 10, 1915; came to U.S., 1937, naturalized, 1944; s. Wilhelm and Else (Schwab) G. Student, U. Munich, Germany, 1935, U. Bonn, 1936; A.B., Williams Coll., 1938; M.A., Harvard U., 1939, Ph.D., 1947; M.A. (hon.), Yale U., 1964. Teaching fellow, tutor history Harvard U., 1939-41, 42-44, 46-47; Sheldon traveling fellow 1941-42; asst. sr. tutor Eliot House, 1942-43; instr. history Williams Coll., 1942; asst. prof. history Johns Hopkins U., 1947-51, assoc. prof., 1951-56, prof., 1956-64; prof. history Yale U., 1964-86, prof. emeritus, 1986-87; fellow Timothy Dwight Coll., 1964-87; mem. Inst. Advanced Study, Princeton U., 1951-52. Editor, translator: (Carl von Clausewitz) Principles of War, 1942, Germany's Drive to the West, 1950, Stresemann and the Rearmament of Germany, 1954, The Present in Perspective, 1957, European Diplomacy between Two Wars, 1972, Germany and the U.S.: A "Special Relationship", 1980, The Mainstream of Civilization, 1984, A History of the World, 1986; editorial bd.: Jour. Modern History, 1954-57, Current History; U.S. editor in chief: Documents on German Foreign Policy, 1969-87. Served as 2d lt. AUS, 1944-46. Guggenheim fellow, 1956-57; Rockefeller grantee, 1962-63. Mem. Am. Hist. Assn. (Herbert Baxter Adams prize 1950), Phi Beta Kappa, Delta Kappa Epsilon. Home: Weston Conn. Died Oct. 11, 1987.

GAULT, HARRY G., lawyer; b. Mt. Morris Twp., Mich., Jan. 25, 1892; s. William Henry and Nora (Ryan) G.; m. Alice Margaret Wiard, June 30, 1917 (dec. 1949); children: Barbara, James Lane; m. Hilda Reava Draws, Sept. 16, 1950. AB, U. Mich., 1915, JD, 1917, LLD, 1959. Bar: U.S. Supreme Ct. 1932. Pros. atty. Genesee County, Mich., 1921-24; mem. Gaulty & Parker, 1925-28, Carton, Gault & Parker, 1929-31, Carton & Gault, 1932-34, Carton, Gault & Davison, 1935-47, Gault & Davison, 1947-52, Gaulty, DDavison & Bowers, from 1952. Vice chmn. Charter Revision Commn., Flint, Mich., 1928-29; mem. Mich. State Crime Commn., 1929-43; mem. bd. commrs. Mich. State Bar, 1939-48, pres., 1947-48; trustee Women's Hosp. Assn. Mem. ABA (ho. of dels. 1948-54), Mich. State, Genesee County bar assns., Am. Judicature Soc. (bd. dirs. 1958-61), Order of Coif, Masons, Elks, Kiwanis, Flint Golf Club, Flint City Club, Flint Univ. Club, Detroit Club, Theta Chi, Phi Delta Phi. Home: Flint Mich. †

GAVIN, JOHN ANTHONY, water treatment company executive; b. Chgo., Sept. 25, 1916; s. John H. and Margaret A. (Regan) G.;m. Mary A. O'Donnell, Nov. 22, 1945; children: John N., Lawrence M., Marguerite Gavin Robson, Patricia Gavin Binder; m. 2d Eileen Gavin. BS, De Paul U. With Culligan Internat. Co., Northbrook, Ill., 1945-85, acct., purchasing agt., prodn. mgr. worldwide, 1960, pres., 1973-77, chmn., chief exec. officer, 1977-82, chmn. emeritus, 1985. Trustee De Paul U.; bd. dirs. Evanston Hosp, Am. Cancer Soc., Peacock Camp for Crippled Children. Recipient Disting. Alumnus award De Paul U., 1985. Mem. Am. Mgmt. Assn., Conf. Bd. Roman Caths., Exec. Club, N. Shore Country Club. Home: Wilmette Ill. Died Oct. 11, 1985.

GAW, WILLIAM A., artist, educator; b. San Francisco, Calif., Nov. 26, 1891; s. Hugh and Mary Anna (McCullough) G.; m. Helen Trexler Baer, Nov. 19, 1922; children: Patricia Elizabeth, Robert Baer. Student, Mark Hopkins Inst., San Francisco and N.Y. Prof. art, head art dept. Mills Coll., 1940-57, prof. emeritus, from 1957; John Hay Whitney vis. prof. Earlham Coll., 1957-58; tchr. fine arts Calif. Sch. Fine Arts, San Francisco, 1937-55; acting dir., 1940-44; mem. jury of awards Golden Gate Internat. Exhbn., 1939, for Paintings of the Year, N.Y.C., 1947. One-man show Calif. Palace of Legion of Honor, 1961; group exhibitions include: Modern Mus., N.Y.C., Chgo. Art Inst., Whitney Mus., Met. Mus., N.Y.C., Corcoran Gallery, Washington, and many others throughout U.S. and Japan; rep. in traveling shows of Western Mus. Dirs., Chgo. Art Ins., Am. Fedn. Fine Art, Colorado Springs Fine Arts Ctr.; rep. in collections Modern Mus., N.Y., others, and pvt. vollections. Recipient many prizes including first award Decorative Art State Fair, Sacramento, Calif., 1939, first award State Fair, Sacramento, Calif., 1940. Mem. San Francisco Art Assn. Home: Berkeley Calif. †

GAY, EUSTACE, SR., newspaper executive; b. Barbados, W.I., May 2, 1892; m. Cleoria Gay; 1 son, Eustace Jr. LHD, Pillar of Fire Coll. and Pentecostal Sem., York, Eng., 1970. With Phila. Tribune, from 1926, was successively sec. to editor, mng. editor, editor, treas., dir., v.p. and sec. to bd., then pres. and gen. mgr. Asst. chmn. bd. dirs. Office of Industry and Commerce, Phila.; has served as officer and dir. of several civic and religious orgns. Recipient Silver Beaver award Boy Scouts Am., 1964, Citation of Merit for outstanding performance in journalism in recognition of 39 yrs. with Phila Tribune, Lincoln U., 1965, Carter G. Woodson award of honor Phila. chpt. Assn. Study of Negro Life and History, 1968, City of Phila. citation, 1969. Baptist (chmn. com. fin.). Home: Philadelphia Pa. Deceased.

GEBHARD, BRUNO FREDERIC, health consultant; b. Rostock, Germany, Feb. 1, 1901; came to U.S., 1937, naturalized, 1944; s. Frederic William and Meta Louise Mary (Ross) G.; m. Gertrude Juliane Adolph, Apr. 8, 1927 (dec.); children: Suzanna Gebhard Goodman, Christine Gebhard McCabe (dec.), Ruth Gebhard Fink. Ed. Arbiturium, Realgymnasium, Rostock, 1919; student, U. Munich, Germany, 1921-22, U. Berlin, 1922-23; MD, U. Rostock, 1924. Diplomate Am. Bd. Preventive Medicine and Pub. Health. Resident physician Children's Hosp., Dortmund, Germany, 1926; curator German Hygiene Mus., Dresden, 1927-37; sci. dir. Office Expns., Berlin, 1932-37, dir. exhbns. Woman, Wonder of Life; cons. for med. and pub. health exhibits N.Y. World's Fair, 1937-40; dir. Cleve. Health Mus., 1940-65; assoc. in health edn. Western Res. U., 1940-65; cons. Army Med. Mus., Washington, 1951; del. Internat. Council Museums UNESCO, Paris, 1948. Author: From Medicine Show to Health Museum, 1947, (autobiography) Im Strom und Gegenstrom, 1919-1937, 1976. Recipient Austrian Red Cross award, 1930, Olympic Games award, 1936, Elisabeth S. Prentiss award, 1965, Outstanding Service award Cleve. Welfare Fedn., 1965, Golden Door award Nationality Services Ctr., 1968. Fellow AMA, Am. Pub. Health Assn., Rochester Mus. Arts and Scis. (hon.); mem. Am. Assn. History Medicine, Cleve. Acad. Medicine (Disting. Mem. award), Am. Assn. Mus., Midwest Mus. Assn. (v.p.) Internat. Coll. Dentists (hon. U.S. sect.), Hertzler Research Found. (hon life.), German Soc. History Medicine, Swedish Acad. Medicine (hon.), Rowfant Club, Rotary. Home: Carmel Calif. Died Jan. 11, 1985.

GEHRING, BENJAMIN ROBERT, management consultant; b. Chillicothe, Ohio, Feb. 26, 1915; s. Louis C. and Jennie (Rector) G.; m. Ellen R. Payne, Nov. 6, 1937; children: Julie, Barbara Lee, Susan Jane. Student, Ohio State U., 1936. CPA, Ohio. With Kent & Rector, 1940-49; pres. Andre Wood Products, Inc., 1949-59; pres., dir. Kilgore, Inc., Westerville, Ohio, 1951-56; pres. Am. Gen. Corp., Columbus, 1961-84; dir., sec. Timmons Metal Products Co., Stardust Lanes, Inc., Eastern Enterprises Corp., Columbus, Ohio, Zip Lock Co.; mgmt. cons. Mem. Am. Inst. CPAs, Am. Acctg. Assn., Am. Mgmt. Assn., Ohio Soc. CPAs. Clubs: Scioto Country, Athletic. Lodges: Masons, Rotary. Home: Columbus Ohio. Died Mar. 6, 1988; buried Greenlawn Abbey, Columbus, Ohio.

GEILING, EUGENE MAXIMILIAN KARL, pharmacologist; b. Orange Free State, Republic of South Africa, May 13, 1891; s. Alexander W.H. and Theresa (Keller) G. AB, U. S. Africa, 1911; MSc, U. Ill., 1917, PhD, 1917; student, U. Capetown, 1919-20, Yale U., 1920-21; MD, Johns Hopkins U., 1923; DSc (hon.), St. John's U., 1958. Lectr. in chemistry Coll. of Agr., Republic of South Africa, 1918; lectr. in physiol. chemistry Coll. of Medicine, U. Cape Town, 1918-19; Seessel fellow Yale U., 1920; Govt. Union of S. Africa fellow 1921; asst. in pharmacology Johns Hopkins Med. Sch., 1921-23, assoc., 1923-25, assoc. prof., 1925-35; prof. of pharmacology and chmn. of dept. of pharmacology U. Chgo., 1936-56, Frank P. Hixon disting. svc. prof. pharmacology, 1941; chief pharmacodynamics br., div. pharmacology FDA, Washington. Mem. editorial bd. Archaeol. Inst. of Pharmacodynamics; contbr. to mags. and textbooks. Recipient Mendel medal Villanova Coll., 1942, Oscar B. Hunter award Am. Therapeutic Soc., 1956. Mem. AAAS, Am. Soc. for Pharmacology and Exptl. Therapeutics (pres. 1939-40), Soc. for Exptl. Biology and Medicine (pres. 1948-49), Am. Physiol. Soc., Am. Soc. Biol. Chemists, AMA, Med. And Chirurg. Soc. of Md., German Pharmacol. Soc., Assn. Am. Physicians, Sigma Xi. Roman Catholic. Home: Washington D.C. †

GEIRINGER, KARL, musicologist, educator; b. Vienna, Austria, Apr. 26, 1899; came to U.S., 1940, naturalized, 1945; s. Ludwig and Martha (Wertheimer) G.; m. Irene Steckel, Apr. 19, 1928; children—Martin Frederick, George Karl; m. Bernice Abrams Shapiro. Student, U. Berlin, 1920-21; PhD, U. Vienna, 1923; MusD (hon.), Wooster Coll., 1984. Curator archives Soc. of Friends of Music, Vienna, 1930-38; vis. prof. Royal Conservatory Music, London, 1938-39; broadcaster BBC, London, 1938-39; vis. prof. Hamilton Coll., Clinton, N.Y., 1940-41; prof. music Boston U. Sch. Fine Arts, 1941-62, chmn. dept. history and theory of music. and div. grad. studies; prof. music charge grad. studies in music U. Calif. at Santa Barbara, 1962-70, prof. emeritus, from 1971. Author: Musical Instruments, 1943, rev. edit, Instruments in the History of Western Music, 1978, (with Irene Geiringer) Haydn: A Creative Life, 1946, 3d edit., 1982, Brahms, 3d edit, 1981, The Bach Family: Seven Generations of Creative Genius, 1954, reprinted, 1981, Music of the Bach Family, 1955, 80; Symbolism in the Music of Bach, 1956; P. Peuerl and I. Posch: Instrumental and Vocal Works, 1929, The Small Sacred Works by Haydn; The Structure of Beethoven's Diabelli Variations, 1964, reprinted, (with Irene Geiringer) Johann Sebastian Bach: The Culmination of an Era, 1966; Editor: J. Haydn: 100 Scottish Songs, 1961, J. Haydn-Orlando Paladino (opera), 1971, Chr. W. Gluck: Telemaco (opera), 1971, Isaac Posch: Harmonia Concertans (cantiones sacrae), 1972; Gen. editor: U. Calif. at Santa Barbara Series of Early Music, from 1970, The Harbrace History of Musical Forms, from 1973; contbr. to Grove's Dictionary Music and Musicians, Ency. Brit. Recipient Austrian Medal of Arts and Sci., 1969, Cross of Honor 1st class, 1982; Studies in 18th Century Music, a tribute to Karl Geiringer on his 70th birthday, edited by H.C.R. Landon and R. Chapman, 1970. Fellow Am. Acad. Arts and Scis.; mem. Am. Musicological Soc. (hon. mem., pres. 1955-56, exec. bd. 1954, exec. bd. 57-58, exec. bd. 64, exec. bd. 68-69), Internat. Musicological Soc., Austrian Musicological Soc. (hon. mem.), New Bach Soc. (hon. mem. Am. chpt.), Am. Brahms Soc (dir. 1983), Coll. Music Soc. (exec. bd. 1965-67), Music Library Assn., Handel and Haydn Soc. (hon. mem.), Riemenschneider Bach-Inst. (hon. mem.), Internat. Gluck Soc. (hon.). Home: Santa Barbara Calif. Died Jan. 10, 1989.

GEISINGER, WILLIAM ROBERT, economist-business forecaster, management consultant; b. Fredricksburg, Va., Oct. 21, 1908; s. William Morris and Glada Belinda (Hawthorne) G.; m. Verna E. Cragg, June 20, 1931 (div. 1946); children: Harry Clifford, William Robert. A.B. in Econs., Dartmouth Coll., 1930; post-grad., Cin. Art Acad., 1950-51; Ph.D. in Bus. Adminstrn., Hamilton State U., 1973; cert. stats., George Washington U. Credit analyst trust dept. Central Trust Bank, Cin., 1930-40; economist budgets Montgomery Ward Co., Chgo., 1940-49; forecast exec. Kroger Co., Cin., 1949-54; mktg. and distbn. specialist State Dept., Hicog, Germany, 1955; mgmt. cons. Geisinger Indicator, Troy, Ohio, 1965-87; lectr. fin. U. Miami, Oxford, Ohio, 1939-40, Northwestern U., Evanston, Ill., 1948, others; tchr. investments and analyzing fin. statements U. Cin., 1937-40, Am. Inst. Banking, 1938-40. Author: Pub. Forecasting Bus. Letter for Geisinger Indicator, 1963-83. Examiner for RFC, Cleve., 1938-39; chief of food and rest Office Price Stabilization, Washington, 1952; organizer Am. Coalition Patriotic Socs. Seminar, 1954; mem. Transatlantic council Boy Scouts Am. in Germany for Europe, N. Africa and Near East, 1955. Mem. Am. Econ. Assn., Am. Mgmt. Assn., Am. Statis. Assn., Found. for Study of Cycles, AAAS, Waco Hist. Soc. (founder). Lodges: Kiwanis, Masons. Home: Troy Ohio. Died May 16, 1987; buried Troy, Ohio.

GEISLER, RICHARD MARCUS, manufacturing company executive; b. Abilene, Kans., May 14, 1925; s. Augustus E. and Clare E. (Taylor) G.; m. Barbara J. Bernas, Aug. 4, 1972; children: Deborah, Michael, Michelle. BS in Acctg., Kans. State Tchrs. Coll., 1951; MBA, Tex. Christian U., 1964. Pres. Am. LaFrance div. A.T.O., Elmira, N.Y., 1969-71, Spalding div. Questor, Chicopee, Mass., 1971-79; pres., chief exec. officer Champion Products, Inc., Rochester, N.Y., 1979-81, chmn. bd., chief exec. officer, 1981-84. Trustee Springfield Coll.; bd. dirs. Jr. Achievement, 1974-79, Basketball Hall of Fame. With U.S. Army, 1946-48. Mem. Sporting Goods Mfg. Assn., Athletic Inst. Nat. Sporting Goods Assn., Nat. Knitwear Mfrs. Assn. (dir. 1981-84), Rochester Area C. of C. (dir. 1981-84). Home: Rochester N.Y. Died June 9, 1984; buried White Haven Meml. Pk. Cemetery, Rochester.

GELB, IGNACE JAY, Assyriologist, linguist, educator; b. Tarnow, Poland, Oct. 14, 1907; came to U.S., 1929, naturalized, 1939; s. Salo and Regina (Issler) G.; m. Hester Mokstad, May 13, 1938; children: Walter, Alexander, John Vincent. Student, U. Florence, Italy, 1925-26; PhD, U. Rome, 1929. Travelling fellow, research assoc. U. Chgo., 1929-41, asst. prof. Assyriology, 1941-43, assoc. prof., 1943-47, prof., 1947-65, Frank P. Hixon Disting. Service prof., 1965-78; vis. prof. U. Mich., 1956-67; mem. archaeol. expdns. to Nr. East, 1932, 35, 47, 65, 66; sci. collaborator Polish Acad. Scis., Cracow. Author: Hurrians and Subarians, 1944, Study of Writing, 1952, Sargonic Texts From the Diyala Region, 1952, Old Akkadian Writing and Grammar, 1952, Glossary of Old Akkadian, 1955, Sequential Reconstruction of Proto-Akkadian, 1968, Computer-Aided Analysis of Amorite, 1980, others; contbr. articles to profl. jours.; editor: Chicago Assyrian Dictionary, 1947-85. Served with AUS, 1943-45. Fellow Am. Acad. Arts and Scis., Brit. Acad.; mem. Am. Philos. Soc., Accademia Nazionale dei Lincei (Italy), Am. Oriental Soc. (br. pres. 1959-60, nat. pres. 1965-66) Am. Schs. Oriental Research and Linguistic Soc. Am., Internat. Linguistic Assn., Am. Name Soc. (pres. 1963-64), Archeol. Inst. Am., Soc. Hittiete (Paris), Inst. Assn. Studies (hon.), Soc. Asiatique (hon.), Nr. East Club Chgo. (pres. 1942-43), Quadrangle Club. Home: Chicago Ill. Died Dec. 21, 1985.

GELMAN, FRANK HERMAN, lawyer; b. Phila., May 11, 1912; s. Samuel and Fannie (Perchin) G.; m. Rivie Perlmutter, Mar. 17, 1940; children: Norris E., Marcia. BA, Temple U., 1932; JD, U. Pa., 1935. Bar: Pa. 1935. Practice in Phila., from 1935; ptnr. Mesirow, Gelman, Jaffe, Cramer & Jamieson, Phila., 1959-85; lectr. Am. Law Inst., Pa. Law Inst.; counsel, chief negotiator in collective bargaining Phila. Sch. Bd., 1966-69; pub. employer collective bargaining cons. to Northampton Sch. Dist. Author: The Real Estate Transaction, 1964, Pennsylvania Mortgages and Their Enforcement, 1965, also course materials Pennsylvania Leases, 1958. Served with USNR, 1943-46. Mem. ABA, Pa. Bar Assn., Union League Club, Phila. Lawyers Club. Home: Philadelphia Pa. Died Jan. 5, 1985; buried Roosevelt Meml. Park, Phila.

GEMMILL, CHALMERS LAUGHLIN, pharmacologist; b. Cresson, Pa., Nov. 24, 1901; s. Benjamin KcKee and Clara Marie (Genso) G.; m. Vivienne Angeline Warry, Jan. 10, 1938; 1 child, Daphne DeJersey. BS, Lafayette Coll., 1922; postgrad., U. Chgo., 1923; MD, Johns Hopkins U., 1926; postgrad., Kaiser Wilhelm Inst., Heidelberg, Germany, 1931, Physiol. Inst., Lund, Sweden, 1933, Biochem. Inst., Cambridge, Eng., 1934. Asst. in physiology Johns Hopkins Med. Sch., 1926-27, instr., 1927-28, asst. prof., 1928-41, assoc. prof., 1941-45; prof. pharmacology U. Va. Med. Sch., 1945-76, prof. emeritus, 1976-82. Author: Physiology in Aviation, 1943; contbr. numerous articles to profl. jouts. Served to lt. comdr., M.C., USNR, 1941-45; capt. from 1945. Commonwealth Fund fellow history of medicine, London, 1965. Mem. Am. Physiol. Soc., Cons. Armed Forces of Am., Am. Soc. Biology, Am. Soc. Pharm. Exptl. Therapy, Va. Acad. Sci., Endocrine Soc., Phi Beta Kappa, Sigma Xi, Alpha Omega Alpha, Nu Sigma Nu. Home: Charlottesville Va. Died June, 1982.

GENET, JEAN, playwright; b. Paris, Dec. 19, 1910; s. Gabrielle Genet; abandoned as a child. Author: (plays) The Maids, 1947, Deathwatch, 1949, The Balcony, 1956, The Blacks, 1959, The Screens, 1961, (novels) Our Lady of the Flowers, 1942, The Thief's Journal, 1949, The Miracle of the Rose, 1966, Querelle of Brest, 1966, A Prisoner of Love, 1986; also poems and prose poems. Recipient Literary Grand Prix, France, 1983; considered one of the most controversial French writers of the 20th Century; sentenced to life imprisonment following several petty crimes, such as vagrancy, he was officially pardoned in 1949 and thus permitted to follow up his artistic achievements. Home: Paris France. Died Apr. 14, 1986. buried Maroc-Larrache, France.

GENTZKOW, CLEON JOSEPH, physician, army officer; b. Minneiska, Minn., Jan. 1, 1891; s. William and Clara (Schneider) G.; m. Marguerite Hampton, Nov. 29, 1917. Student, Minn. State Tchrs. Coll., Winona, 1905-09; MD with distinction, George Washington U., 1915; PhD in Biology and Pub. Health, MIT, 1929; grad. advanced course, Med. Field Service Sch., Carlisle, Pa., 1935. Diplomate Am. Bd. Pathology. Tchr. pub. schs., Gilbert, Minn., Sept. 1909-Feb. 1910; assoc. with Census Bur., Washington, 1910-12; lab. undergrad. intern Garfield Meml. Hosp., Washington, 1912-15; resident Columbia Hosp. for Women, Washington, 1915-17; commd. 1st lt. Med. Sec., O.R.C., July 10, 1917; called to active duty July 20, 1917; advanced through grades to col. AUS, 1942; col. R.A., 1943; surgeon 5th Ammunition Train, 5th Div., AEF, France and Army of Occupation, Luxembourg, 1918-19; chief lab. service Base Hosp., Camp Pontenezon, Brest, France, 1919; stationed at Sta. Hosp. and 3d Army Lab., Coblenz, Germany, 1919-21, Sta. Hosp., Camp Grant, Ill., 1921; comdg. officer 5th Corps Area Lab., Ft. Benjamin Harrison, Ind., and Columbus, Ohio, 1921-24; on duty with 8th Corps Area Lab.; chief Lab. Service Sta. Hosp., Ft. Sam Houston, Tex., 1924-27, Fitzsimons Gen. Hosp., Denver, 1929-31; chief div. chemistry and physics Army Med. Sch., Washington, 1932-36, Med. Field Service Sch., Carlisle, Pa., 1935; guest worker Rockefeller Inst. for Med. Rsch., Feb.-July 1936; mem. Army Med. Rsch. Bd., Ancon, C.Z., 1936-38, pres., 1938-39; chief div. chemistry and physics Army Med. Sch., 1939-42, dir. dept. preventive medicine and clin. pathology, 1942; comdg. officer Deshon Gen. Hosp., Butler, Pa., 1942-46, Valley Forge Gen. Hosp., 1946-48; ret. U.S. Army, 1948; dir. bur. labs. Pa. Dept. Health, from 1949. Co-editor and contbr. Medical and Public Health Laboratory Methods, 6th edit., successor to lab. methods of U.S. Army; also contbr. to med. and sci. books and jours. Fellow ACP; mem. AMA, Am. Pub. Health Assn., Am. Assn. Pub. Health Physicians (charter mem.), Assn. State and Territorial Pub. Health Lab. Dirs. (pres. 1954-56), Pa. Assn. Clin. Pathologists, Comité International de la Lysotpie de Bactéries Entériques, Rotary, Phi Chi, Delta Omega, Sigma Xi. Republican. Roman Catholic. Home: Wynnewood Pa. †

GEORGEN, W. DONALD, accountant; b. Chgo., June 1, 1929; s. Michael A. and Lauretta M. G.; m. Eleanor J. Hays, Sept. 15, 1956; children: Susan M., Lauretta M., Catherine J., Sarah A., William D. B.S. in Acctg., U. Notre Dame, 1951; J.D., Northwestern U., 1953. Bar: Ill. 1953. With Touche Ross & Co., 1953-87; ptnr. Touche Ross & Co., Chgo., 1966-69; dir. audit ops. Touche Ross & Co., 1969-72, nat. dir. acctg. and auditing, 1972-79; ptnr.-in-charge Touche Ross & Co. (N.J. offices), 1979-84, vice chmn. bd. dirs., 1979-87, sr. ptnr., 1984-87. Served with AUS, 1954-56. Mem. Am. Inst. CPAs, Ill. Soc. CPAs, N.Y. Soc. CPAs, N.J. Soc. CPAs, Beta Alpha Psi. Roman Catholic. Clubs: Spring Brook Country, Baltusrol Golf. Home: Morristown N.J. Died Aug. 21, 1987.

GEORGI, CARL EDUARD, microbiologist, educator; b. Milw., Feb. 18, 1906; s. Herman Emil and Ottilie (Memmler) G.; m. Marjorie Clare Womelsdorff, Aug. 20, 1936 (dec. Sept. 1980); children: Liesl Andrea Turnus, Todd Anthony. BS, U. Wis., 1930, MS, 1932, PhD (Frasch Found. fellow), 1934; Fulbright scholar, U. Paris, 1951-52; student, Inst. Nuclear Studies, Oak Ridge, summer 1950, Cornell U., summer 1960. Diplomate Am. Bd. Microbiology. Chemist Pfister & Vogel Leather Co., Milw., 1924-26; asst. instr. chemistry U. Wis., 1934-35; mem. faculty U. Nebr., 1935-74, prof. bacteriology, 1947-74, chmn. dept., 1953-71, Regents prof. microbiology, 1964-71; mem. staff dept. biochemistry , nutrition; rsch. microbiologist Nebr. Agrl. Expt. Sta., 1949-64; lectr., cons. Author: (with G.L. Peltier and L.F. Lindgren) Laboratory Manual for General Microbiology; editorial bd.: Applied Microbiology, 1953-58; contbr. articles to profl. jours. Mem. numerous internat. sci. congresses; trustee Lincoln Gen. Hosp., 1962-75. Recipient Seaman award N.Y. Acad. Medicine, 1951; Sterling fellow Yale U., 1935. Charter fellow Am. Acad. Microbiology; fellow AAAS; mem. Am. Inst. Biol. Scis. (vis. coll. lectr. 1960-70), Am. Soc. Microbiology (pres. Mo. Valley br. 1942-43, chmn. nat. div. gen. microbiology 1966), Nebr. Acad. Sci. (past pres), Electron Microscope Soc. Am., Am. Soc. Cell Biology, Soc. Exptl. Biology and Medicine, Soc. Gen. Microbiology of Gr. Britain, AAUP (pres. Nebr. chpt. 1968-69), Am. Soc. Biol. Chemists, Sigma Xi (pres. Nebr. 1948-49), Phi Beta Kappa (hon. chpt. pres. 1972-73) Alpha Chi Sigma, Phi Lambda Upsilon, Gamma Alpha. Episcopalian. Home: Crete Nebr. Died Nov. 1, 1985; buried St. Matthews Cemetery, Lincoln, Nebr.

GERAGHTY, HELEN TIEKEN, theatrical producer, director; b. Chgo., Nov. 16, 1902; d. Theodore and Bessie (Chapman) Tieken; m. Maurice Patrick Geraghty, Apr. 15, 1933 (dec. 1918); children: Betsy Geraghty Fryberger, Helen, Molly. BS, U. Chgo., 1924, MA, 1928; student, Sorbonne U., France, 1926, Oxford U., Eng., summer 1926, Goodman Theatre, Chgo., 1927. Dir. Children's Theater, Chgo. Jr. League, 1930-32; producer, dir. Wings of a Century and Hispana shows, Century of Progress Exposition, Chgo., 1933-34; dir. dramatics Francis W. Parker Sch., Chgo., 1943-57; producer, dir. Wheels-a-Rolling, Chgo. R.R. Fair, 1948-49, Mile Posts, CB&Q R.R. Centennial, 1949, Frontiers of Freedom, Chgo. R.R. Fair, 1950, Song of Mid-Am., I.C. R.R. Centennial, 1951, Adam to Atom, Mus. Sci. and Industry Centennial of Engring., 1952, numerous other indsl. shows, 1951-59; dir. Seventeenth Star, symphonic drama, Ohio State Sesquicentennial, Columbus, 1953; dir. entertainment Chicagoland Fair, Chgo. Internat. Fair, 1957; dir. Galavante, Chgo. Lyric Opera Co., 1959; producer, dir. Galerie Vivante Ravinia Park Festival, Highland Pk., Ill., 1957, gen. mgr., 1963-64; chief arts program Ill. Sesquicentennial Commn., 1966-69; cons. Chgo. chpt. AIA; tech. dir. Passavant Hosp. Cotillion, 1950-70, St. Luke's Hosp. Fashion Show, 1948-60, Hull House Theater, 1937-40; producer, dir. Rotary Internat. Anniversary Album, 1955, Banner High for 75th Anniversary ARC, 1956, other charity benefit shows. Women's bd. dirs. Art Inst. Chgo., Presbyn.-St. Luke's Hosp., U. Chgo., Field Mus. Natural History. Mem. Chgo. Arts Club, Chgo. Jr. League, Phi Beta Kappa. Home: Palo Alto Calif. Died Aug. 26, 1987.

GERBODE, FRANK LEVEN ALBERT, surgeon, research executive; b. Placerville, Calif., Feb. 3, 1907; s. Frank A. and Anna Mary (Leven) G.; children: Maryanna Gerbode Shaw, Frank Albert, Penelope Ann, John Philip. BA cum laude in Physiology, Stanford U., 1932, MD, 1936; MD (hon.), U. Thessaloniki, Greece, 1964, U. Uppsala, Sweden, 1965; M Surgery (hon.), Nat. U. Ireland, 1961. Diplomate: Am. Bd. Surgery, Am. Bd. Thoracic Surgery (founding mem. 1951). Intern High land Hosp., Oakland, Calif., 1935-36; asst. in patholog U. Munich, Fed. Rep. Germany, 1936-37; asst. resider in surgery Stanford U. Hosps., 1937-38, 38-39, asst. i surg. research, 1938, resident in surgery, 1939-40; pv practice San Francisco, 1945-84; instr. surgery Stanfor U., 1940-42, asst. clin. prof. surgery, 1947-50, asso clin. prof., 1950-54, assoc. prof., 1954-59, clin. prof 1959-71, clin. prof. emeritus, 1971-84; chief dept. card ovascular surgery Heart Research Inst., Med. Researc Inst., Pacific Med. Ctr., San Francisco, 1959-84, dir 1959-84; chief dept. cardiovascular surgery Inst. Me Scis., 1959-79; mem. staffs Children's Hosp., Presby Hosp., San Francisco; cons. Letterman Army Hosp San Francisco; guest prof. surgery to univs., hosps 1953-74; clin. prof. U. Calif., San Francisco, 1964-7 mem. surgery tng. com. USPHS NIH, 1960-67. Editorial bd.: Annals of Surgery. Mem.-at-large Sa Francisco Bay Area council Boy Scouts Am., 1971-84 Served to lt. col. M.C. U.S. Army, World War II, ETC Africa. Decorated knight Brit. Order St. John Jerusalem; hon. perpetual student St. Bartholomew Hosp., London; recipient Disting. Civilian Service awa U.S. Army, 1978. Fellow Royal Coll. Surgeons (Eng (hon.), Royal Coll. Surgeons (Edinburgh) (hon.); mer Am. Coll. Cardiology, ACS, Am. Heart Assn., Cal Heart Assn., San Francisco Heart Assn., AMA, Cal Med. Assn., San Francisco Med. Assn., Pan Am. Me Assn., Am. Surg. Assn., Pacific Coast Surg. Assn., Pa Pacific Surg. Assn. (pres. 1966-69), Western Surg. Assn Argentine Surg. Assn., Am. Thoracic Soc., Cal Thoracic Soc., Calif. Acad. Medicine, Hollywood Aca Medicine, Calif. Acad. Sci., Excelsior Surg. Soc., S Surg. Soc., Halsted Soc., James IV Assn. Surgery, I ternat. Soc. Cardiovascular Surgery (pres. N.Am. chp 1961-62), Internat. Soc. Surgery (pres. N.Am. chp 1971-74, pres. congress 1973-75, pres. 1975-77), A Assn. Thoracic Surgery (pres. 1972-73), Sams Thoracic Surg. Soc., Soc. Thoracic Surgeons, Soc. Uni Surgeons, Soc. Vascular Surgery (pres. 1958-59), Sc Clin. Surgery, AAAS, Deutsche Gesselschaft fü Chirurgie, Soc. Thoracic and Cardiovascular Surgeo Gt. Britain and Ireland, Assn. Thoracic and Cardiova cular Surgeons Asia, Panhellenic Surg. Soc., La Socied Mexicana de Cardiologia, Societa Italiana di Chirurg Socié té de Chirurgie Thoracique de Lange Francais 38th Parallel Med. Soc. (Korea), St. Francis Yac Club, Stanford Club, Pacific-Union Club, Bohemi Club, Chit Chat Club San Francisco, Univ. Cl N.Y.C., Sigma Xi, Alpha Omega Alpha. Home: S Francisco Calif. Died Dec. 6, 1984.

GERDES, ROBERT H., foundation executive; b. Oa land, Calif., July 4, 1904; s. Robert Anton and An (Banks) G.; m. Narenda Blair, June 1, 1935; childr Sally Gerdes Wray, Anne Gerdes Vietmeyer, Barba Gerdes Brandes. BS, U. Calif., 1926, JD, 1928. B Calif. 1928. Assoc. Hugh Goodfellow, Atty., 1928- atty. law dept. Pacific Gas & Electric Co., 1929-35, as gen. counsel, 1943-45, gen. counsel, 1945-53, v.p., g counsel, bd. dirs., 1953-55, exec. v.p., bd. dirs., 1955- pres., 1963-65, chmn. bd., chief exec. officer, 1965- chmn. exec. com., 1969-77; ptnr. Earl, Hall and Gerd 1935-43; v.p., trustee James Irvine Found., S Francisco; pres. Edison Electric Inst., 1968-69. Me San Francisco Bar Assn., Pacific Coast Elec. As (former pres.), Bohemian Club, Pacific-Union Cl Claremont Country Club, Kappa Alpha, Phi Delta P Home: Piedmont Calif. Died Sept. 1, 1985; buri Mountain View Cemetery, Oakland, Calif.

GERHARD, DIETRICH, history educator; 1897. Found. prof. history Washington U., St. Lo prof. emeritus, until 1985. Died July 31, 1985.

GERHOLZ, ROBERT PAUL, home builder; b. M rill, Wis., June 25, 1896; s. Robert and Bertha (Degen G.; m. Freda Clark, Sept. 15, 1923; children: Rob Charles, Barbara Lee, Janyce Allyn. Grad., Ferris In Big Rapids, Mich., 1916, LLD (hon.), 1957; student, Wis., 1919-21; D in Adminstrn. (hon.), Limestone Co 1979. Founder Robert P. Gerholz Co., homebuild realtors, Flint, Mich., 1922; pres. Gerholz Ins. Serv 1940-59, Gerholz Community Homes, Inc., 1947- Gerholz Supply Co., 1949-85, Robert P. Gerholz Org 1952-85, Gerholz Realty, Inc., 1954-85, Gerholz Ag Inc., 1959-68; chmn. Gerholz Enterprises; tre Gerholz-Healy Co., 1941-47, Bassett Park Homes, In 1943-47; bd. dirs. Mich. Nat Bank of Flint, M Trucks, Inc., Mich. Nat. Corp. Active YMCA, Scouts Am.; mem. Mich. Gov.'s Exec. Com. St Unemployment Compensation, 1932, Civil Serv Commn., 1944-49; mem. industry adv. com. FHA, 19 61; mem. Gov.'s Commn. on Higher Edn., 1973- mem. Genessee County Real Estate Bd., sec.-tre 1927, pres., 1928; pres. Citizen's Civic League, 19 treas. Flint Light Opera Co., 1944; dir. Am. R Property Fedn., 1956; mem. adv. com. U. Wis. S Bus., 1966-68; mem. bd. control Ferris State Coll., 19 85, vice chmn., 1969-71, chmn. bd., 1972-79; exec. c Religious Heritage Am., 1969-85, chmn. bd. 1976- exec. com. Campus Crusade for Christ Internat.-He Life; mem. nat. exec. com. Horatio Alger awards, 19 85; gen. chmn. capital fund campaign Auto W Found., Flint, 1981 Served to lt. F.A., U.S. Ar 1917-19. Named Flint Realtor of Yr., 1966, M Realtor of Yr., 1966, Bus. Man of Yr. Religious H itage Am., Inc., 1971; recipient Mich. Minuter award, 1972, George Washington award Freedoms Found., 1975, Horatio Alger award, 1977, C.S. Mott Citizen of Yr. award, 1977, Realtor Emeritus award, 1977; named to Housing Hall of Fame, 1977; Robert P. Gerholz Inst. Life-Long Learning named in his honor, Ferris State Coll., 1983. Mem. Nat. Assn, Home Builders (pres. 1944, chmn. Research Inst. 1961, bd. dirs.), Mich. Real Estate Assn. (pres. 1931), U.S. C. of C. (dir.-at-large 1960-65, chmn. Can.-U.S. com. U.S. sect. 1963-64, pres. 1965-66, chmn. bd. 1966-67, chmn. exec. com. 1967-68, F. Stuart Fitzpatrick Meml. award 1968), Mich. C. of C. (bd. dirs. 1968-85, chmn. bd. 1972-73), Urban Land Inst. Am. (trustee 1946-69, 1st v.p. 1953-54), Nat. Assn. Real Estate Bds. (bd. dirs., pres. 1950), Flint Fedn. Chs. (pres. 1932), Rotary (pres. local chpt. 1932), Beta Gamma Sigma (hon. Alpha chpt.), Omicron Delta Kappa. Presbyterian (elder). Home: Flint Mich. Died Apr. 18, 1985.

GERMAN, DONALD ROBERT, author; b. Phila., Feb. 11, 1931; s. Samuel Edward and Reba Logan (Trimble) G.; m. Joan Alice Wolfe, Sept. 4, 1954; 1 child, Donald Robert. B.S., Temple U., 1955; M.A., Columbia Pacific U., 1984. Mgmt. trainee Central Penn Nat. Bank, Phila., 1956-60; bus. devel. dir. Indsl. Valley Bank, Phila., 1960-61; creative dir. First Fin. Advt. Group, Boston, 1962; dir. pub. relations Savs. Banks Assn. Mass., Boston, 1963; editor Warren, Gorham & Lamont, Inc., N.Y.C., 1964-86. Author: The Banker's Complete Guide to Advertising, 1966; Money & Banks, 1979; Mattie's Money Tree, 1984; (with Joan W. German) The Bank Teller's Handbook, 1970, rev. edit. 1981, The Bank Employee's Security Handbook, 1972, rev. edit. 1982; Successful Job Hunting for Executives, 1974; Bank Employees' Marketing Handbook, 1975; Tested Techniques in Bank Marketing, Vol. I, 1977, Vol. II, 1978; Make Your Own Convenience Foods, 1979; How to Find a Job When Jobs Are Hard to Find, 1981; Checklists for Profitability, 1983; The Only Money Book for the Middle Class, 1983; Money A to Z: A Consumer's Guide to the Language of Personal Finance, 1984; Ninety Days to Financial Fitness, 1985. Co-editor: Branch Banker's Report, 1968-86, Bank Teller's Report, 1969-86. Contbr. to books: Investment Guide, 1980-85; The Complete Guide to Writing Nonfiction, 1984. Contbg. editor Bank Mktg. Report, 1967-86, Money Maker mag., 1979-86. Contbr. articles to major mags. and profl. jours. Mem. exec. com. North Berkshire United Way, 1980-83; chmn. Friends of Berkshire Athaneaum, Pittsfield, Mass., 1981-82; fin. com. Town of Cheshire, Mass., 1981-85, mem. Democratic com., Town of Cheshire, 1981-86; bd. corporators City Savs. Bank, 1981-86. Served to 1st lt. U.S. Army, 1954-56. Recipient Cert. of Merit, Leukemia Soc., 1958; United Fund of Phila. award of Merit, 1959; Muscular Dystrophy Assn. Am. citation of Merit, 1960. Mem. Am. Soc. Journalists and Authors (dir.-at-large 1979-81), Authors Guild, Boston Authors Club, Berkshire Poets Workshop. Unitarian. Home: Cheshire Mass. Died June 25, 1986; buried Cheshire Cemetery.

GEROLD, NICHOLAS JOHN, biology educator; b. N.Y.C., Jan. 1, 1919; s. Nicolas Jean and Cecilia (Schwarz) G.; m. Patricia Kenyon, June 25, 1949; children: Nicolas John, Allison Louise. BA, Brown U., 1942, MA, 1948; PhD, Cornell U., 1951. Asst. prof. biology Hamilton Coll., Clinton, N.Y., 1951-58, assoc. prof., 1958-64, prof., 1964-81, chmn. dept. biology, 1966-72. Mem. Am. Inst. Biol. Scis., Am. Soc. Zoologists, AAAS, Nat. Assn. Biology Tchrs., Am. Assn. Med. Colls., N.Y. Acad. Scis., Sigma Xi. Home: Clinton N.Y. Died Apr. 9, 1986.

GERSON, NOEL BERTRAM, writer; b. Chgo., Nov. 6, 1914; s. Samuel Philip and Rose Anna (Noel) G.; children: Noel Anne Gerson Brennan, Michele Gerson Schechter, Margot Gerson Burgett, Paul; m. Marilyn A. Hammond. A.B., U. Chgo., 1934, M.A., 1935. Reporter, rewriteman Chgo. Herald-Examiner, 1931-36; exec. Sta. WGN, Chgo., 1936-41. Radio and TV scriptwriter over 10,000 scripts for nat. networks, 1936-51; Author numerous fiction and non-fiction books under own name and various pseudyonyms; books include The Golden Lyre, 1961, The Land is Bright, 1961, The Naked Maja, 1962, Queen of Caprice, 1963, The Slender Reed, 1964, Old Hickory, 1963, Sex and the Mature Man, 1964, Kit Carson, 1964, Lady of France, 1965, Yankee Doodle Dandy, 1965, Give Me Liberty, 1966, Sex and the Adult Woman, 1965, Light-Horse Harry Lee, 1966, The Swamp Fox, The Anthem, 1967, Sam Houston, 1968, Jefferson Square, 1968, The Golden Ghetto, 1969, P.J., My Friend, 1969, TR, 1969, Mirror, Mirror, 1970, Warhead, 1970, The Divine Mistress, 1970, Because I Loved Him, 1971, Island in the Wind, 1971, Victor Hugo, 1971, Double Vision, 1972, The Prodigal Genius, 1972, George Sand, 1972, Daughter of Earth and Water, 1973, State Trooper, 1973, Peter Paul Rubens, 1973, Rebel-Thomas Paine, 1974, The Exploiters, 1974, All That Glitters, 1975, The Caves of Guernica, 1975, Special Agent, 1976, Harriet Beecher Stowe, 1976, Liner, 1977, The Vidocq Dossier, 1977, The Smugglers, 1977, Trelawny's World, 1977, Wagons West, 1979, White Indian, 1980; also numerous articles. Fellow Internat. Inst. Arts and Letters; mem. Authors Guild Am., Mystery Writers Am., Am., Miss. Valley hist. assns., Am. Acad. Polit. and Social Sci., Centro Studi E Scambi Internat., Phi Beta Kappa, Kappa Alpha. Clubs: Boca Del Mar Country, Bankers. Home: Boca Raton Fla. Died Nov. 20, 1988, buried Boca Raton.

GESCHICKTER, CHARLES FREEBORN, physician, educator; b. Washington, Jan. 8, 1901; s. Leo and Rose (Zirkin) G.; m. Mildred Clark, May 21, 1927; children: Charles Freeborn, Edmund Harrison, Jacqueline. BA, George Washington U., 1920, MA, 1922; MD, Johns Hopkins U., 1927. Diplomate Am. Bd. Pathology. Intern in medicine Balt. City Hosp., 1927-28; fellow in surgery Mayo Clinic, Rochester, Minn., 1982; dir. surg. pathology lab. Johns Hopkins U., 1929-40; also assoc. in surgery, dir. cancer research lab. Med. Sch. 1929-40; dir. Garvan Cancer Research Fund, 1940-46; prof. pathology Georgetown U. Med. Sch., Washington, from 1946, chmn. dept. pathology, 1946-62, chmn. dept. research pathology, from 1962, chmn. com. devel. and planning, from 1960; spl. cons. pathology NIH, from 1946, Walter Reed Army Med. Hosp., from 1962; cons. Dept. Health, Edn., Welfare, Social Security Adminstrn., from 1961. Author: (with M.M. Copeland) Tumors of the Bone, 3d edit., 1949, Disease of the Breast, 3d. edit., 1948, (with N.J. White) Diagnosis in Daily Practice, 1947; editor: Color Atlas of Pathology, vols. I and II, 1954-56, vol. I rev., 1959; contbr. numerous articles to profl. jours., also chpts. to books. Served to comdr. USNR, 1942-46. Decorated Legion of Merit. Mem. AMA, Am. Geriatrics Soc., Coll. Am. Pathologists, Am. Soc. Clin. Pathologists, AAAS, Army-Navy Club Washington, Johns Hopkins Univ. Club. Home: Lorton Va.

GETTE, WARREN ANDREWS, physician, former hospital administrator; b. Phillipsburg, Pa., Apr. 17, 1910; s. Claude Anthony and Anna Margaret (Hamer) G.; m. Doris Fitzgibbon, July 8, 1944; 1 dau., Gladys Ruth. A.B., U. Pa., 1932, M.D., 1943. Intern U. Pa. Hosp., 1944; resident Dixon Hosp., South Mountain, Pa., 1944-45; Tb physician Dixon Hosp., 1945-51, chief med. staff, 1951-59, med. dir., 1959, clin. dir., until 1970. Pres. corp. South Mountain Ch. of God, 1960-87. Fellow Am. Coll. Chest Physicians; mem. AMA, Franklin County (pres. 1962), Pa. med. socs., Pa. Assn. Chest Physicians, Am. Thoracic Soc., Am. Assn. Tb Physicians. Lutheran. Home: Venice Fla. Died Sept. 7, 1987; buried Venice Meml. Gardens.

GETTYS, WARNER ENSIGN, sociologist; b. Ravenna, Ohio, Apr. 24, 1891; s. Charles William McHenry and Zoe (Humphrey) G.; m. Estelle Katherine Seger, Dec. 27, 1926; 1 dau., Nancy Lee. AB, Hiram (Ohio) Coll., 1913; AM, Ohio State U., 1916, PhD, 1924; student, U. Wis., summer 1915, U. Chgo., summers 1920, 21, 22. Instr. history Culver-Stockton Coll., Canton, Mo., 1913-15; asst. prof. sociology McGill U., Montreal, 1924-26; prof. sociology U. Tex., 1926-61, emeritus, from 1961, chmn. dept. sociology, 1928-58. Past pres. Tex. Soc. Welfare Assn. With M.C., AUS, 1917-19. Fellow Am. Sociol. Soc.; mem. S.W. Social Sci. Assn. (past pres.), Town and Gown Club, Acholia, Phi Beta Kappa, Alpha Kappa Delta, Pi Gamma Mu. Home: Austin Tex. †

GIBSON, ARRELL MORGAN, history educator; b. Pleasanton, Kans., Dec. 1, 1921; s. Arrell Morgan and Vina Lorene (Davis) G.; m. Dorothy Deitz, Dec. 24, 1942 (div. Apr. 1971); children: Patricia Gibson, Michael Morgan, Kathleen Camille; m. Shirley J. Black, Nov. 1971 (div. Nov. 1972); m. Rosemary P. Newell, July 1973. B.A., U. Okla., 1947, M.A., 1948, Ph.D., 1954; L.H.D., Coll. Idaho. Prof. history Phillips U., Enid, 1949-57; prof. history U. Okla., Norman, 1957-87, chmn. dept., 1964, 70-87, George Lynn Cross Research prof., 1972-87; curator history Stovall Mus., U. Okla., 1959-87; vis. prof. Ariz. State U., Tempe, 1973, U. N.Mex., Albuquerque, 1975; Montgomery lectr. U. Nebr., Lincoln, 1978; Goldwater Disting. prof. Am. instns. Ariz. State U., 1986, hon. disting. prof. U. South China; lectr. art of western Am. Rockwell Mus., Corning, N.Y., Denver Art Mus., 1987; conductor Pacific Basin Seminars, Australian and New Zealand Parliament, 1987. Author: The Kickapoos, 1963, Life and Death of Colonel Albert Jennings Fountain, 1965, Oklahoma: A History of Five Centuries, 1965, Fort Smith: Little Gibraltar on the Arkansas, 1969, The Chickasaws, 1971, Wilderness Bonanza, 1972, Edward Everett Dale: Frontier Historian, 1975, The West in the Life of the Nation, 1976, The Oklahoma Story, 1978, The American Indian: Prehistory to the Present, 1979, Will Rogers: A Centennial Tribute, 1979, Rudyard Kipling's West, 1981, Santa Fe and Taos: Age of the Muses, 1900-1942, 1983, The West Wind Blows, 1984, Between Two Worlds: The Survival of Twentieth Century Indians. Mem. adv. bd. Mus. Gt. Plains, Lawton, Okla., 1962-87. Served with USNR, 1942-45. Recipient Rockefeller Found. U. Okla. Press award, 1961, Am. Ind. Historian award, 1985; Am. Philos. Soc. Research grantee, 1963, 69; Duke Found. Research grantee, 1968, 69; U. Okla. Faculty Research grantee, 1957-71; named Okla. Writer of Yr., 1972; Outstanding Alumnus Mo. So. State Coll., 1972; inducted into Okla. Hall of Fame, 1985, Okla. Inst. Letters, 1987. Mem. Am. Hist. Assn., So. History Assn., Western History Assn. (Ray Billington award), Orgn. Am. Historians, Southwestern Social Sci. Assn., Okla. Hist. Soc. (bd. dirs., Muriel H. Wright award), Phi Beta Kappa, Phi Alpha Theta. Home: Norman Okla. Died Nov. 30, 1987; buried Osborne Cemetery, Joplin, Mo.

GIBSON, CHARLES, history educator; b. Buffalo, Aug. 12, 1920; s. William Walker and Helen (Jones) G. BA, Yale U., 1941, PhD, 1950; MA, U. Tex., 1947. Faculty mem. history dept. U. Iowa, 1949-65, assoc. prof., 1952-59, prof., 1959-65; prof. history U. Mich., Ann Arbor, 1965-85; vis. lectr. Harvard U., 1955-56. Author: Tlaxcala in the Sixteenth Century, 1952, The Aztecs Under Spanish Rule, 1964, Spain in America, 1966; editor: (with George Kubler) The Tovar Calendar, 1951, (with E.V. Niemeyer Jr.) Guide to the Hispanic Historical Review, 1958, Cartas de Relacion de la Conquista de la Nueva Espana, 1960, The Spanish Tradition in American, 1968, The Black Legend, 1971; bd. editors Hispanic Am. Hist. Rev., 1955-61, 66-85, Comparative Studies in Society and History, 1968-85, Am. Hist. Rev., 1973-85; contbg. editor Handbook Latin Am. Studies, 1950-70. Served with AUS, 1942-45. Social Sci. Research Council fellow, 1948, Guggenheim fellow, 1952-53, Rockefeller Found. fellow, 1961. Mem. Am. Hist. Assn., Conf. Latin Am. History, Hispanic Soc. Am., Am. Acad. Franciscan History. Home: Plattsburg N.Y. Died Aug. 22, 1985.

GIBSON, COLIN WILLIAM GEORGE, judge; b. Hamilton, Ont., Can., Feb. 16, 1891; s. Sir John Morison and Elizabeth (Malloch) G.; m. Florence Kerr, Aug. 21, 1916; children: Desmond Hope, Colin David, James Kerr, John Gordon. Student, Royal Mil. Coll., 1908-11, Osgoode Hall, 1912-15. Bar: Ont., 1915; qualified land surveyor, Ont. Pvt. practice Hamilton, 1919-40; apptd. King's Counsel 1935, M.P. from Hamilton West dist., 1940, 45, 49; apptd. minister nat. revenue Govt. of Can., 1940, minister Nat. Def. Air, 1945, sec. of state, 1946, minister of mines, resources, 1949; apptd. appelate Div. Supreme Ct. Ont. from 1950. Capt. Royal Fusiliers, 1914-19, col. inf. Can. Army, 1935-38. Decorated Mil. Cross (U.K.); Order of Leopold, Croix de Guerre (Belgium); Polonia Restituta (Poland). Mem. Can. Rifle Teams (comdr. 1951), Dom. Can. Rifle Assn. (chmn. coun. 1928-48, pres. 1952-54), Nat. Rifle Assn. Gt. Britain (v.p. from 1951), Masons, Alpha Delta Phi (internat. pres. 1948-49). Home: Toronto Ont., Canada. †

GIBSON, FREDERIC EVERETT, manufacturing executive; b. Bellingham, Wash., Apr. 11, 1895; s. John and Susan Edith (Everett) G. Student, U. Wash., 1916-17, 19-20. Joined Graybar Electric Co., N.Y.C., 1920, treas., dir., mem. exec. com., from 1951. 2d lt. A.S., 1917-19. Mem. Masons, Seattle Golf Club, Siwanoy Golf Club (Bronxville, N.Y.), Alpha Tau Omega. Home: Bronxville N.Y. †

GIBSON, JAMES ROBERT, business executive; b. 1892. Chmn., dir. Gibson Art Co. Home: Cincinnati Ohio. †

GIBSON, WILLIAM MERRIAM, educator; b. Wilmette, Ill., Jan. 16, 1912; s. Thomas Benton and Mary Gertrude (Stanbery) G.; m. Barbara Chadwick Crane, Oct. 21, 1943; children: Julia Stanbery Gibson Kant, Thomas Crane. A.B. cum laude, Princeton U., 1933; M.A., U. Chgo., 1934, Ph.D., 1940. Mem. faculty dept. English U. Chgo., 1937-41, Williams Coll., 1941-42, 46-49; mem. faculty dept. English N.Y. U., 1949-73, prof., 1951-73; prof. English U. Wis.-Madison, 1973-87; Fulbright lectr. U. Turin, Italy, 1960-61, U. Aix-Marseilles, summer 1961, U. Delhi, Mussoorie, India, 1963; Peking Lang. Inst./Com. on Scholarly Communication lectr., Peking, 1980. Author, editor: books in field, including Mark Twain-Howells Letters, 1960, (with Henry Nash Smith) The Art of Mark Twain, 1976, Three Humorists on Theodore Roosevelt, 1980. Served with AUS, 1942-46. Ford fellow, 1954-55; Guggenheim fellow, 1963-64, 76-77; NEH fellow, 1973. Mem. MLA (dir. Center for editions of Am. authors 1963-69), Am. Council Learned Socs. (mem. adv. com. in Am. studies 1966-69), Am. Studies Assn., AAUP, Internat. Assn. Univ. Profs. English. Home: Madison Wis. Died Jan. 22, 1987; cremated.

GIESE, HENRY, agricultural engineer, educator; b. Danville, Iowa, Dec. 23, 1890; s. George Fredric and Ella Elvira (Catlin) G.; m. Dollie Frances Kelly, June 7, 1913; children: Barbara R. Giese Graves, William Henry, Mary Joan Giese Herber. BS in Archtl. Engring., Iowa State Coll., 1919, MS in Agrl. Engring., 1927; MS in Archtl. Engring., 1930. Registered profl. engr. Iowa. Instr. Howe's Acad., Mt. Pleasant, Iowa, 1911-12; dir. manual tng. Ames (Iowa) Pub. Schs., 1912-16; instr. manual tng. tchrs. Iowa State Coll., summers, 1914-18, in charge instr., 1917-18, with engring. extension service, 1916-19, instr. in engring. math., 1923; with agrl. engring. dept. Iowa State U., 1923-81; with U.S. Vets. Bur., 1919-22; sr. engr. Farm Structures Research Survey for USDA, 1919-30. Author 300 publs. including books, latest book Of Mutuals and Men, fed. and state bulletins, tech. and popular jour. articles. Mem. fire prevention edn. com. Pres. Truman's Conf. on Fire Prevention. Served with U.S. Army, 1918. Recipient Cyrus Hall McCormick Gold medal for engring. achievemnt in agr., 1947, faculty citation Iowa State Coll. Alumni Assn., 1957, Merit award 1958. Fellow Iowa Acad. Sci., Am. Soc. Agrl. Engrs. (life); mem. Nat. Assn. Mut. Ins. Cos. (hon.), Iowa Engring. Soc.,

Masons (32 deg.), Shriners, Sigma Xi, Phi Kappa Phi, Tau Beta Pi, Gamma Sigma Delta, Phi Mu Alpha, Pi Kappa Pi. Republican. Presbyterian (elder). Home: Ames Iowa. Died Nov. 25, 1981.

GIFFORD, GEORGE HUSSEY, educator; b. New Bedford, Mass., May 3, 1892; s. Nathaniel William and Elizabeth Colden (Murray) G.; m. Frederica Harrison Gilbert, Aug. 29, 1922; children: Nathaniel Harrison, Augusta Todd (Mrs. John Stirling Getchell), George Hussey. AB, Harvard U., 1913, AM, 1920, PhD, 1927; student, Balliol Coll., Oxford U., 1913-16. Instr. Harvard U., 1916-17, 20-22, 23-24, U.S. Naval Acad., 1917-20; Am. reader U. Paris, 1922-23; asst. prof. Romance langs. U. Buffalo, 1924-28, Wade prof. modern langs., from 1931, head dept. Romance langs., 1940-58. Author: La France a travers les Siècles, 1936; contbr. articles to scholarly jours. Mem. MLA, AAUP, Dante Soc. Am. (pres. from 1959). Home: Cambridge Mass. †

GIGNOUX, EDWARD THAXTER, federal judge; b. Portland, Maine, June 28, 1916; s. Frederick Evelyn and Katherine (Denison) G.; m. Hildegarde Schuyler Thaxter, June 30, 1938; children: Marie Andrée (Mrs. James F. Grisé), Edward Thaxter. A.B. cum laude, Harvard U., 1937, LL.B. magna cum laude, 1940; LL.D. (hon.), Bowdoin Coll., 1962, U. Maine, 1966, Colby Coll., 1974, Nasson Coll., 1974, Bates Coll., 1977, Husson Coll., 1983, St. Joseph's Coll., 1984. Bar: D.C. bar 1941, Maine bar 1946. Assoc. Slee, O'Brian, Hellings & Ulsh, Buffalo, 1940-41, Covington, Burling, Rublee, Acheson & Shorb, Washington, 1941-42; ptnr. Verrill, Dana, Walker, Philbrick & Whitehouse, Portland, 1946-57; U.S. dist. judge Portland, 1957—; judge U.S. Temp. Emergency Ct. Appeals, 1980-87; former corporator Maine Savs. Bank; former mem. adv. com. bankruptcy rules U.S. Supreme Ct.; former mem. council and vis. com. Harvard Law Sch.; also chmn. vis. com.; past mem. adv. panel internat. law U.S. State Dept.; faculty Salzburg Seminar for Am. Studies, 1972; asst. corp. counsel, City of Portland, 1947-48, mem. city council, 1949-55, chmn., 1952; mem. U.S. Jud. Conf. (chmn. subcom. on supporting personnel 1968-70, chmn. standing com. on rules of practice and procedure 1980-87). Editor: Harvard Law Rev, 1939-40. Pres., bd. dirs. Greater Portland Community Chest, 1955-56, United Fund, 1956-57; former corporator, trustee Maine Med. Center; former trustee Maine Eye and Ear Infirmary, Portland Symphony Orch.; former bd. overseers Harvard Coll. Served as maj. AUS, 1942-46. Decorated Bronze Star, Legion of Merit; recipient Learned Hand medal, 1984, Edward J. Devitt Disting. Svc. to Justice award, 1986. Mem. ABA (former mem. spl. com. on jud. conduct), Maine Bar Assn., Cumberland County Bar Assn., Inst. Jud. Adminstrn., Jud. Conf. U.S. (chmn. standing com. on rules of practice and procedure 1980-87, former mem. jud. ethics com.), Am. Judicature Soc. (past bd. dirs.), Am. Law Inst. (council, 1st v.p. 1987). Episcopalian. Clubs: Harvard (pres. Maine 1957); Portland Country. Home: Foreside Maine. Died Nov. 4, 1988; buried Portland, Maine.

GIGUÈRE, PAUL ANTOINE, chemist; b. Quebec City, Can., Jan. 13, 1910; s. Joseph-Emile and Diana (Poitras) G.; m. Magdeleine Lippens, July 21, 1937. B.A., U. Laval, 1930, B.Sc., 1934; Ph.D., McGill U., 1937; D.Sc. (hon.), U. Sherbrooke, 1970. With Canadian Industries, Ltd., 1937-38; research fellow Calif. Inst. Tech., 1939-41; asst. prof. U. Laval, Que., 1941-43; asso. prof. U. Laval, 1943-47, prof., 1947-76, emeritus prof., 1978-87, dir. chemistry dept., 1957-68, mem. exec. council, 1969-72. Contbr. numerous articles to profl. jours. Decorated Companion Order of Can.; Guggenheim Found. fellow, 1946-47. Mem. Royal Soc. Can., Chem. Inst. Can. (v.p., pres. 1965-67), N.Y. Acad. Sci., AAAS, Can. Soc. for Chemistry (hon.), Compagnon de Lavoisier—Ordre des Chimistes du Que., Am. Chem. Soc. (emeritus), Association Canadienne Française Avancement des Sciences (pres.). Home: Quebec Que., Canada. Died Dec. 25, 1987, buried Columbarium St. Charles, Que. City.

GILDER, ROSAMOND, writer, drama critic; b. Marion, Mass., 1892; d. Richard Watson and Helena (deKay) G. Ed. pub. schs.; LHD (hon.), U. Denver, 1969. Staff mem. Theatre Arts mag., 1924-48, drama critic, assoc. editor, editor-in-chief, 1938-48; editorial sec. Nat. Theatre Conf., 1932-35; dir. Playwrights' Bur., Fed. Theatre, 1935-36; founder Internat. Theatre Inst., pres., 1947-75, hon. pres., 1975-86, also dir. U.S. Ctr., 1948-86; lectr. Barnard Coll., 1948-55; chmn. U.S. delegation 1st World Conf. on Theatre, Bombay, India, 1956, U.S. delegations Internat. Theatre Inst. Cong., 1948-86; former v.p. Am. Nat. Theater and Acad. Author: Letters of Richard Watson Gilder, 1916, John Giegud's Hamlet: A Record of Performance, 1937, Enter the Actress: The First Women in the Theater, 1960; translator: My Life (Emma Calvé), 1922; editor: A Theater Library: A Bibliography of 100 Books Relating to the Theater; co-editor: (with George Freedley) Theater Collections in Libraries and Museums; contbr. articles to profl. jours. Vol. worker with ARC, 1917-19, France, with Children's Bur. ARC, 1917-20. Decorated médalle d'Epidemie, médaille de Reconnaissance, France; officer l"Ordre des Arts et des Lettres, France, 1964; recipient Tony award Am. Theater Wing, 1948; Fulbright fellow Paris, 1955-56. Mem. N.Y. Drama Critics Circle, London Drama Critics Circle (hon.), Cosmopolitan Club N.Y.C. Home: Tyringham Mass. Died Sept. 5, 1986.

GILELS, EMIL, pianist; b. Odessa, Russia, Oct. 19, 1916; s. Grigory and Esphir (Zamoshina) G.; m. Farizet Hucistova, Jan. 19, 1947; 1 dau., Elena. Grad., Odessa Conservatory, 1935, Sch. of Mastership of Moscow Conservatory, 1938. Prof. Moscow Conservatory, USSR, 1954-85. First concert, 1929, concerts through, USSR, 1933-85, Europe, 1945-85, U.S.A., 1955-85, Mex., 1955, Japan, 1957, Can., 1958-85; debut in N.Y. at Carnegie Hall, 1969. Recipient 1st prize All Union Contest Musicians, Moscow, 1933, 2d prize Vienna Contest, 1936, 1st prize Internat. Contest Pianists, Brussels, 1938, State prize, 1946, Lenin prize, 1962; decorated Order Labor Red Banner, Order of Lenin, 1961, 2d Order of Lenin, 1966, Order de Commandeur Merite Culturel et Artisque de Paris, 1967, comdr. Order Leopold I., Brussels, 1964, Medaille de Vermeil de la Ville de Paris, 1967, Hero of Socialist Labor, 1976. Mem. Cen. Home Art WWirkers, Royal Acad. Music London (hon.). Home: Moscow USSR.

GILL, ROBERT SUTHERLAND, publisher; b. near Sault Ste. Marie, Mich., Nov. 5, 1886; s. Andrew Braden and Mary Jane (Stanton) G.; m. Marielle Walz, Sept. 15, 1909 (dec. 1939); children: Mary Alice (Mrs. John A. MacIsaac Jr.), Robert Stanton; m. 2d, Margaret M. Frampton, Jan. 18, 1940. Student, Seabury Divinity Sch., Fairibault, Minn., 1905-07; STB, Western Theol. Sem., Chgo., 1909. Clergyman filling various cures and offices P.E. Ch., 1909-18; dean St. Stephen's Pro-Cathedral, Portland, Oreg.; editor Loyal Legion Loggers and Lumbermen, Portland, Oreg., 1919-21; exec. sec. Am. Guild Printing Industry, 1921-23; in charge sales and advt. Williams & Wilkins Co., pubs. of sci. and med. material, Balt., 1923, sec.-treas., 1927, pres., 1942-53, chmn. bd., from 1953; pres. Passano Found. Inc., from 1944; bd. dirs. Waverly Press Inc. Author: (with Knight Dunlap) Dramatic Personality of Jesus, 1933, Author-Printer-Publisher Complex, 1949. 1st lt. A.S. Aircraft Production, 1918-19. Mem. Soc. Am. Bacteriologists. Home: Baltimore Md. †

GILLEN, RALPH LEONARD, business executive, government official; b. N.Y.C., May 3, 1928; s. Benjamin and Rose G.; m. Ruth Irene Sperling, Apr. 29, 1956; children: Gerald Roy, Jay Michael. B.A. magna cum laude, Queen's Coll., 1949; M.A., Fletcher Sch. Law and Diplomacy, Tufts and Harvard univs., 1950; postgrad. Fulbright fellow, U. Liverpool, Eng., 1950-51. Instr. econs. Tufts U., 1950-51; with Internat. Div. RCA, 1950; securities analyst E.F. Hutton, N.Y.C., 1951; mgmt. cons. McKinsey & Co., Washington, 1954-63, Cleve., 1963-68; ptnr. McKinsey & Co., 1961-68; v.p. mktg. pulp and paper group MacMillan Bloedel Ltd., Vancouver, B.C., 1969-70; group v.p. MacMillan Bloedel Ltd., 1970-71, v.p. strategic planning and devel., 1971-78; vice-chmn. bd. Ins. Corp. B.C., 1976-78, chmn., 1978-80; pres., chief exec. officer Can. Comml. Corp., Ottawa, Ont., 1978-82; chmn. Petroleum Monitoring Agy., 1982-86; Mem. regional export expansion council Dept. Commerce, 1965-66; bd. dirs. community services div. Cleve. Welfare Fedn., 1965-68; mem. Citizens League Candidate Eval. Com., Cleve., 1967; mem. exec. com. Nat. Mktg. Adv. Bd. to U.S. sec. commerce, 1967-68; sec.-treas., trustee Fed. Stats. Users Conf., 1957-64. Author: (with Paul W. Cherington) The Business Representative in Washington. Trustee, chmn. fin. com. Cleve. Inst. Music, 1965-69, mem. adv. council, 1969-86; vice-chmn., trustee Vancouver Acad. Music, 1970-79; chmn. com. Univs. Council B.C., 1976-79; adv. council Multiple Sclerosis Soc. B.C., 1976-80; trustee Hudson Inst. Can., 1975-86. Served to lt. USN, 1951-53. Mem. Am. Mktg. Assn. (pres. Washington 1963). Clubs: Nat. Economists (Washington); St. James (Montreal). Home: Ottawa Ont., Can. Died Sept. 22, 1986.

GILLETTE, EDWARD SCRANTON, publisher; b. Phila., Feb. 3, 1898; s. Halbert Powers and Julia Washburn (Scranton) G.; m. Claribel Reed Thornton, July 14, 1921; 1 son, Halbert Scranton. Grad., Sheffield Sci. Sch., Yale, 1919; B.S. in Civil Engring, U. Pa., 1921; postgrad., Germantown Friends Sch., Exeter Acad. Bank clk. 1918; acct. in charge Municipal Water Works Co., South Bellingham, Wash., 1921-22; bus. mgr. Gillette Pub. Co. (publs. Roads and Streets, Water and Sewerage Works, Caminos y Calles, Heavy Constrn., Cat. County and Township Roads, mag. Tech. bo, 1924-88, gen. mgr., v.p., sec., 1937-88; gen. mgr., v.p. Gillette Co., pub., pres., 1952; pres. Scranton Pub. Co., Inc. (now merged into Scranton Gillette Communications); pub. Water Engring. and Mgmt., Indls. Wastes, Water and Wastes Digest, Rural and Urban Roads; chmn. bd. Scranton Gillette Communications (with additional publs. Seed World, The Diapason, Piano Trade), 1978-88; past dir. Asso. Bus. Publs., Constrn. Industry. Chmn. bd. Cathedral Shelter.; past pres. Chgo. Bus. Papers Assn.; trustee Episcopal Charities. Mem. Constrn. Industry Mfrs. Assn., Am. Soc. C.E. (life mem.), Am. Legion, Delta Kappa Epsilon. Republican. Episcopalian. Clubs: Rotary, Lahaina Yacht, Maui Country; Villa Monterey (Scottsdale, Ariz.). Home: Lake Forest Ill. Died Aug. 3, 1988.

GILLHAM, MARY MEWBORN, librarian, educator; b. Atlanta, July 12, 1899; d. Clarence Edwin and Salie Atha (Matthews) Mewborn; m. Richard E. Gillham, May 27, 1922. BA, U. Toledo, 1927, MA, 1931; BA in Library Sci., U. Mich., 1941. Librarian U. Toledo, 1921-86, assoc. prof. library sci., 1944-50, prof. to prof. emerita, 1950-86, chmn. dept. library sci. Coll. Edn., 1933-69. Exec. sec. Friends of U. Library, 1938-69, U. Toledo Ann. Endowment Fund drives, 1943-47, chmn. library bldg. com., 1948-69; mem. adv. bd. WPA projects City of Toledo, 1938-41; mem. Ohio Sesquicentennial Commn., 1951-53; treas. Toledo Mcpl. League, 1957-69, also bd. dirs. Mary M. Gillham Hall U. Toledo Library bldg. named in her honor, 1971. Mem. ALA (com. Friends of Libraries), Ohio Library Assn. (chmn. coll. and univ. div. 1957-60), U. Mich. Library Sci. Alumni (pres. 1943-45), Orgn. for Study of Peace (bibliog. com. 1943-45), Ohio Coll. Assn. (pres. library div. 1958-59) AAUW (Toledo br.), Faculty Dames, Samagama, U. Toledo Alumni Assn. (mem. Tower Club 1965-86), Toledo Mus. Art, Clements Library Assn., Univ. Womens Club Toledo, Zonta, Alpha Omicron Pi (faculty alumni adviser Theta Psi chpt. 1940-51), Delta Kappa Gamma (chpt. pres. 1956-58), Phi Kappa Phi (pres. chpt. 1957-58), Beta Phi Mu, Chi Omega (chmn. Toledo alumnae chpt. recognition award com. 1954-86, Recognition award 1967). Republican. Methodist. Home: Toledo Ohio. Died Feb. 17, 1986.

GILLIAM, JAMES RICHARD, JR., banker; b. Lynchburg, Va., Jan. 11, 1891; s. James R. and Jackie B. (Johnson) G.; m. Nelle C. McCluer, Feb. 2, 1915 (dec. July 1935); children: Bates McCluer, Ellen C. Perry. BS, Va. Mil. Inst., 1910. With Lynchburg Trust & Savs. Bank, 1911, pres., 1943-54, chmn. bd., 1954-55; chmn. First Nat. Trust & Savs. Bank, 1955-59, hon. chmn. trust com., from 1959; bd. dirs. Chesapeake & Potomac Telephone Co. of Va., First Nat. Bank Danville, Lane Co., Altavista, Va., Va. Hot Springs Inc. V.p., dir. Jones Meml. Library; bd. dirs. Community House, Hot Springs, Va. Presbyterian. Home: Lynchburg Va. †

GILLICK, FREDERICK GEORGE, physician; b. Vallejo, Calif., May 14, 1911; s. John Chrysotom and Florence Louise (Fearon) G.; m. Elizabeth Ann Schiller, Oct. 24, 1939; children: Joseph George, John Schiller, Mary Beth, Michael F., Paul. Student, U. Sanat Clara, 1928-30; BS, St. Louis U., 1933, MD, 1935, M in Internal Medicine, 1939; MPH, Harvard U., 1941. Diplomate Am. Bd. Preventive Medicine and Pub. Health. Intern St. Mary's Group Hosp., St. Louis, 1935-36, resident fellow internal medicine, 1936-39; venereal disease control officer City of St. Louis, 1939-42, State Miss., 1942, D.C., 1942-45; commd. med. officer USPHS, 1942, advanced through grades to sr. surgeon; mem. heart sect., asst. clin. devel. Electrokymograph USPHS, Temple U., 1945-46; chief heart disease control br. USPHS, Washington, 1949-50, mem. research br. Nat. Heart Inst., 1950-51, med. dir., 1956; adj. clin. prof. medicine Georgetown U., 1951; prof. preventive medicine, dean Sch. Medicine Creighton U., Omaha, 1951-59; chief staff Creighton Meml.-St. Joseph's Hosp., Omaha, 1951-59; also pvt. practice internal medicine and cardiolog; dir. med. instns. Santa Clara County,, Calif., 1959-62; coordinator Med. Dist. 28 VA, Los Angeles, 1972-76; coodinator physician patient evaluation ctr. Wadsworth VA Hosp. Ctr., Los Angeles; isntr. internal medicine St. Louis U., 1940-47; lectr. Cath. U. Am., 1944-45; research assoc. medicine U. Calif., 1946-49. Editor: Proc. Conf. Electrokymography, 1951; contbr. articles to profl. jours. Bd. dirs. Omaha United Community Services, ARC Douglas County; chmn. bd. Cath. Social Service Santa Clara County; vice chmn. Archdiocesan Bd. Cath. Social Service San Francisco; pres., bd. dirs. St. Elizabeth's Day Home, San Jose, Calif. Fellow Am. Coll. Preventive Medicine, ACP, Am. Coll. Cardiology; mem. AMA, Am. Soc. Internal Medicine, Assn. Am. Med. Colls., Am. Heart Assn., Nebr. Heart Assn. (pres.), Apha Omega Alpha, Alpha Sigma Nu. Roman Catholic. Home: Los Angeles Calif. Died Aug. 6, 1981.

GILMAN, GLENDELL WILLIAM (GLENN GILMAN), management educator, consultant; b. Waupaca County, Wis., Aug. 9, 1911; s. Francis Clarence and Izola Jane (Pray) G.; m. Elvira Katherine Czeskleba, June 10, 1938 (dec.); 1 dau., Katherine Annette Gilman Upshaw; m. Charlotte Anne Ripley, Jan. 17, 1974. B.S. in Am. History, Central State Coll., Stevens Point, Wis., 1940; M.S. in Mgmt., Ga. Inst. Tech., 1947; Ph.D. in Sociology, U. Chgo., 1955. Tchr. Antigo High Sch., Wis., 1940-41; prof. Coll. Mgmt., Ga. Inst. Tech., Atlanta, 1945-81, prof. emeritus, 1981-85; Regents prof. Univ. System of Ga., Atlanta, 1968-81; personnel cons. Lockheed Aircraft, Marietta, Ga., 1955-60; cons. Ga. Cotton Mfg. Assn., Atlanta, 1960-63; dir., corp. sec. Scidata, Inc., Atlanta, 1965-69. Author: Human Relations in the Industrial Southeast, 1956, 78, Causes of Industrial Peace under Col. Bldg.: Case Studies, 1953. Mem. adv. council Ga. State Employment Security Agy., 1960-72; mem. legis. subcom. Ga. State Employment Security Agy., 1968-72. Served to capt. USMC, 1942-45; to col. USMCR, 1945-60. Mem. Am. Sociol. Assn. Episcopalian. Clubs: Commerce, Ansley Golf. Home: Atlanta Ga. Died Jan. 6, 1985.

GILMAN, HENRY, chemistry educator; b. Boston, May 9, 1893; s. David and Jane (Gordon) G.; m. Ruth V. Shaw, July 20, 1929; children: Jane Gordon, Henry Shaw. BS, Harvard U., 1915, MA, 1917, PhD, 1918; postgrad., Zurich Polytechnikum, 1916, Oxford U., 1916. Instr. in chemistry Harvard U., Boston, 1918-19; assoc. in chemistry U. Ill., 1919; prof. organic chemistry Iowa State U., Ames, 1919-86; cons. AEC; research dir. USAF; plenary lectr. Internat. Symposium Organometallic and Organometalloidal Chemistry; invited lectr. internat. confs. Bordeaux, France, 1970, Moscow, 1971, Madison, Wis., 1972; researcher Manhattan Project Dept. Def. Author: (with C.J. West) Organomagnesium Compounds in Synthetic Chemistry, 1922, (with R.J. Jones) Organo-lithium Compounds in Organic Reactions, (with J.W. Morton Jr.) Metalation in Organic Reactions, (with D. Wittenberg) Silylmetallic Compounds, (with F.K. Cartledge) Characterization of Organometallics, 1968, More Than One-half Century of Organometallic Chemistry, 1968; editor: Organic Syntheses, Vol. VI and Collective Vol. I, Organic Chemistry, Vol. I, II, III, IV, (with Benkeser) Organometallic Compounds in Ency. of Chem. Tech., (with R.K. Ingham) Organopolymers of Silicon, Germanium, Tin and Lead, (with W.H. Atwell and F.K. Cartledge) Catenated Organic Compounds of Group IV-B, (with G.L. Schwebke) Organic Substituted Cyclosilanes, (with H.J.S. Winkler) Organosilylmetallic Chemistry, Synthesis of Some Perflouro-organometallic Types, 1975; mem. editorial bd. Advances in Organo-metallic Chemistry, Acta Chimica Inorganica, Current Contents-Chemical Sciences; contg. editor ann. Survey of Am. Chemistry, 1928, 29-30, Organometallic Syntheses, Sci. Citation Index, Organometallic Reactions; assoc. editor Chem. Revs., 1936, Jour. Organometallic Chemistry, Organic Preparations and Procedures Internat., Acta Chimica Inorganica; exec. com. editorial bd. Jour. Organic Chemistry; assoc. editor Jour. Am. Chem. Soc.; contbr. to encys.; co-author monographs; contbr. articles in field to sci. periodicals. Served with Chem. Warfare Service, World War I. Recipient First Firestone Internat. Lecture award in organometallic chemistry, Initial Merit award Iowa Acad. Scis., 1973; named Disting. Prof. in Sci. and Humanities Iowa State U., 1962; chemistry bldg. named in his honor Iowa State U., 1973. Fellow AAAS (v.p. chem. sect., chmn. 1931), Chem. Soc. London (hon.), Am. Chem. Soc. (councillor at large 1939-41, 42-44, chmn. organic div., Frederick Stanley Kipping award, Priestly medal, Mid-West Gold medal Iowa chpt.), Nat. Acad. Scis. (ofcl. del., lectr. in USSR, 1963), Iowa Acad. Scis. (initial Merit award 1973, 100th Annv. Disting. fellow award 1975), Royal Soc. London; mem. N.Y. Acad. Scis. (hon. life), Phi Beta Kappa, Sigma Xi, Phi Kappa Phi, Phi Lambda Upsilon (hon.). Home: Ames Iowa. Died Nov. 7, 1986.

GILMAN, LEONARD RAYMOND, U.S. attorney; b. Detroit, Jan. 7, 1942; s. Hyman Norman and Alice (Weiner) G.; m. Donna Marie Rachunok, Mar. 15, 1970; 1 dau., Kelly Ann. B.S., Wayne State U., 1963, J.D. with distinction, 1967. Bar: Mich. 1967, U.S. Dist. Ct. (ea. dist.) Mich. 1967, U.S. Ct. Appeals (6th cir.) 1978, U.S. Supreme Ct. 1980. Field att. NLRB, Detroit, 1966-68; asst. pros. atty. Wayne County Prosecutor's Office, Detroit, 1968-73; sr. trail lawyer Oakland County Prosecutor's Office, Pontiac, Mich., 1973-78; chief Criminal div. U.S. Atty.'s Office, Detroit, 1978-81, U.S. atty., from 1981; instr. Harvard Law Sch., 1973, U. Mich. Law Sch., Ann Arbor, from 1978. Recipient U.S. Dept. Justice Dir.'s award, 1980; recipient Meritorious Service award Drug Enforcement Adminstrn., 1981. Mem. State Bar Mich., Oakland County Bar Assn., Legal Aid Found. Detroit. Republican. Jewish. Home: Detroit Mich. Died Feb. 1985.

GILMAN, STANLEY FRANCIS, engineering educator; b. Portland, Maine, Mar. 31, 1921; s. Frank William and Elotia Ann (Noyes) G.; m. Jean Elizabeth Murphy, Feb. 4, 1943; children: Susan, Michael, Kathleen, Steven, Christine. B.S. in Mech. Engring, U. Me., 1943; M.S., U. Ill., 1948, Ph.D., 1953. Registered profl. engr., N.Y., Pa. Co-owner Gilman Furnace Co., Portland, 1945-47; asst. prof. mech. engring. U. Ill., 1949-53; research and engring. mgmt. Carrier Corp., 1953-70; v.p. engring. Climatrol Industries, Milw., 1970-71; mgr. mktg. internat. group Am. Air Filter Co., Louisville, 1971-73; prof. archtl. engring. Pa. State U., University Park, from 1973. Contbr. articles to profl. jours. Served to lt. USNR, 1943-46. Mem. Am. Soc. Heating. Refrigrating and Air Conditioning Engrs. (dir., treas., v.p. 1964-72, pres. 1971-72), Nat. Soc. Prof. Engrs., Sigma Xi, Tau Beta Pi, Pi Tau Sigma, Sigma Alpha Epsilon. Republican. Roman Catholic. Deceased.

GIMBEL, PETER ROBIN, film producer-director; b. N.Y.C., Feb. 14, 1928; s. Bernard Feustman and Alva Belle (Bernheimer) G.; children—Peter Bailey, Leslie Laird. B.A., Yale U., 1951. Exec. trainee Gimbel Bros., Inc., N.Y.C., 1951; research analyst White, Weld & Co. (investment bankers), N.Y.C., 1952-60; pres. Blue Gander, Inc. Producer, dir.: film Blue Water, White Death, 1971, The Mystery of the Andrea Doria; TV spl., 1976, Andrea Doria: The Final Chapter, 1984. Trustee N.Y. Zool. Soc., 1957-78, bd. advisers, 1978-87; trustee Am. Mus. Natural History, 1958-63. Served to 2d lt. inf. AUS, 1946-47. Mem. Dirs. Guild Am. Home: New York N.Y. Died July 12, 1987.

GINGOLD, HERMIONE FERDINANDA, actress; b. London, 1897; d. Jame and Kate (Walter) G.; m. Michael Joseph; children: Leslie, Stephen. Student pvt. schs., London, governesses, Paris. Actress: Shakespeare at Stratford on Avon, also Paris; film appearances include: Gigi, 1958, Naked Edge, 1961, Gay Paree, 1962, Harvey Middleman-Fireman, 1965, Promise Her Anything, 1966, Garbo Talks, 1984; mem. cast Broadway shows: Side by Side by Sondheim, A Little Night Music; TV appearances on The Girl from U.N.C.L.E., Ed Sullivan Show, Omnibus, Matinee Theatre, Jack Paar, Alfred Hitchcock Presents, Merv Griffin Show, Mike Douglas Show; author: Sirens Should be Seen and Not Heard, 1963; recordings Peter and the Wolf (Grammy award), Carnival of Animals, Chitty Chitty Bang Bang, Lysistrata. Recipient Donaldson award; decorated dame Knights of Malta. Home: New York N.Y. Died May 24, 1987.

GISLASON, SIDNEY PAYSON, lawyer; b. Minn., May 22, 1908; s. Bjorn B. and Joan (Peterson) G.; m. Marjorie L. Fleck, Sept. 17, 1938; children: James H., Daniel A., Marion F. LLB, U. Minn., 1935. Bar: Minn. 1935. Asst. county atty. Brown County, Minn., 1936-42, county atty., 1942; city atty. New Ulm, Minn., 1946-50; dist. judge 9th Minn. Dist., 1950-51; lectr. legal trial techniques; govt. appeal agt. SSS, 1941-67; chmn. 85th Dist. War Finance, 1946-85; mem. faculty Law Sci. Inst.; chancellor Law-Sci. Found., 1957-58. Chmn. Little Crow dist. Boy Scouts Am., 1950-54; mem. Minn. Coll. Bd., 1967-73, Minn. Higher Edn. Coordinating Com., 1969-73; bd. dirs. Courage Found., 1973-85. Fellow Am. Bar Found.; mem. ABA (ho. dels. 1954-57), Minn. Bar Assn. (chmn. ct. rules com., bd. govs. 1951-72, v.p. 1953, pres. 1954-55), Am. Coll. Trial Lawyers, Internat. Acad. Trial Lawyers (dir. 1956-85, pres. 1959), Masons, Shriners. Lodges: Masons; Shriners. Home: New Ulm Minn. Died Sept. 25, 1985; buried New Ulm, Minn.

GIST, NOEL PITTS, sociologist; b. Hermitage, Mo., June 17, 1899; s. Ruzan and Lucy Josephine (Pitts) G.; m. Mabel Wilks, Dec. 24, 1923; children: Ronald Ralph, Patricia Jane. BS, Kans. State Tchrs. Coll., 1923; MA, U. Kans., 1929; PhD, Northwestern U., 1935; postgrad., Geneva (Switzerland) Sch. Internat. Studies, summer 1925, U. Chgo., summer 1929. Instr., asst. prof. sociology U. Kans., 1929-31, 32-37; asst. prof., assoc. prof. then prof. sociology U. Mo., Columbia, 1937-44, prof. emeritus, 1969-83; vis. lectr. U. Wis., 1944-45; vis. prof. summers various univs. and colls.; researcher in sociology with U.S. Endl. Found. in India, 1951-52, lectr. U. Calcutta, 1963-64; lectr. Sociologische Inst. The Netherlands, 1958-59; sr. specialist Inst. Advanced Projects East-West Ctr., Honolulu, 1968-69. Author: Secret Societies: A Cultural Study of Fraternalism in the United States, 1940; co-author: Urban Society, 1974, Selective Factors in Migration and Occupation, 1943, The Blending of Races: Marginality and Identity in World Perspective, 1972, Marginality and Identity: The Anglo-Indian Minority in India, 1973. Served with USNRF, 1981-19. Mem. Am. Sociolog. Soc. (exec. com. 1945-48) Mid-West Sociolog. Soc. (pres. 1938-39), AAUP, University Club Columbia, Alpha Pi Zeta, Alpha Kappa Delta, Kappa Delta Pi. Home: Columbia Mo. Died Oct. 21, 1983.

GITHENS, SHERWOOD, JR., physicist; b. Phila., Oct. 31, 1908; s. Sherwood and Charlotte (Fretz) G.; m. Nancy Elizabeth Coates, 1939 (dec. 1968); children: Sherwood, Nancy L. Githens Washburn, Janet, John Dexter; m. Elizabeth Majors Smith, 1969; stepchildren: Sarah Randles, Ellen Dunlap. BA, Bucknell U., 1931; MA, U. N.C., 1933, PhD, 1936; postgrad., Princeton U., 1933-34. Teaching fellow in physics U. N.C., 1931-33, 34-36; instr. Wake Forest Coll., 1936-37, asst. prof., 1937-41; instr. aircraft elec. systems Air Corps Tech. Sch., Chanute Field, Ill., 1941; asst. chief instr. Air Corps Tech. Sch., Sheppard Field, Tex., 1941-42; lectr. electronics Harvard U., 1942-45, instr. communication engring., 1945-46; physicist Applied Physics Lab. Johns Hopkins U., Silver Spring, Md., 1946-49; chmn. dept. physics Baylor U., Tex., 1949-52; dir. phys. scis. div. U.S. Army Office Ordnance Research, Duke U., Durham, N.C., 1952-58, dir. internal research div., 1958-59, dep. chief scientist, 1959-62; prof. sci. edn. Duke U., Durham, 1962-76, prof. emeritus, 1976-80; spl. lectr. N.C. State U., 1955, 56-57, NSF Summer Inst., Baylor U., 1957, Duke U., 1958-59. Author: (with others) Electronic Circuits and Tubes, 1947; contbr. articles to profl. jours. Councilman City of Takoma Pk., Md., 1947-49; trustee Durham Tech. Inst., 1961-80; program dir. U.S. Army Jr. Sci. and Humanities Program, 1963-80. Recipient Outstanding Civilian Service medal Dept. Army. Mem. Am. Phys. Soc., Am. Assn. Physics Tchrs., Rotary, Sigma Xi, Pi Mu Epsilon, Tau Kappa Epsilon. Home: Durham N.C. Died Aug. 16, 1980.

GLADMAN, MAURICE, association executive; b. Winnipeg, Man., Can., Mar. 19, 1919; came to U.S., 1934, naturalized, 1943; s. Jack Gladman; m. Rosabelle St. Clair, Oct. 22, 1943; children: Dennis, Patricia Ann. Gen. mgr. Roger S. Marshall Tire Co., Santa Monica, Calif., 1939-54; co-owner, then pres. Gladman & Wallace Tire Co., Santa Ana, Fullerton and Garden Grove, Calif., 1954-73; exec. dir. So. Calif. Tire Dealers and Retreaders Assn., Anaheim, 1973-87; chmn. bd. Am. State Bank, Newport Beach, Calif., 1973-79; internat. pres. Kiwanis, 1977-78. Pres. Santa Ana C. of C., 1963; chmn. bd. Salvation Army, Santa Ana, 1969-71; pres. Santa Ana-Tustin YMCA, 1961-62, Children's Hosp. Padrinos, 1981, Kiwanis Internat. Found., 1983-84; chmn. bd. St. Joseph Hosp. Found., Orange, Calif., 1974-75; vice chmn. Goodwill Industries Orange County, 1981, chmn., 1982; bd. dirs. Goodwill Industries Am., 1983-84. Served to col. AUS, 1942-46, 50-52, Korea. Decorated Bronze Star, Legion of Merit; Disting. Order Aux. Service Salvation Army; recipient Spirit of Life award City of Hope. Mem. Nat. Tire Dealers and Retreaders Assn. (past pres.), Am. Soc. Assn. Execs., So. Calif. Soc. Assn. Execs. (pres. 1985-86). Republican. Presbyterian. Home: Tustin Calif. Died Mar. 1, 1987; buried Valhalla Meml. Pk., North Holywood, Calif.

GLAVES, DONALD WILLIAM, lawyer; b. Chgo., Mar. 1, 1935. BA, Ill. Coll., 1956; JD, U. Chgo., 1962. Bar: Ill. 1962. Assoc. Ross & Hardies, O'Keefe, Babcock & Parsons, Chgo., from 1962; clk. to judge U.S. Ct. Appeals (D.C. cir.), 1963. Mem. Am. Law Inst., ABA. Deceased.

GLEASON, JACKIE, actor; b. Bklyn., Feb. 26, 1916; s. Herbert and Mae G.; m. Genevieve Halford, 1936 (div. 1971); children: Geraldine, Linda; m. Beverly McKittrick, July 4, 1971 (div. 1974); m. Marylin Taylor, 1975. Appeared in Follow the Girls on Broadway, 1945; TV series Life of Riley, 1949-50, Cavalcade of Stars, 1950-52, The Honeymooners, 1955-56; then in TV series Jackie Gleason Show, 1952-55, 57-59, 66-70, star, writer; condr. mus. score The Million Dollar Incident; 38 recorded albums with Jackie Gleason Orch.; motion picture appearances include Navy Blues, 1941, Springtime in the Rockies, 1942, The Desert Hawk, 1950, The Hustler, 1961, Gigot, 1962, Requiem for a Heavyweight, 1962, Soldier in the Rain, 1963, The Time of Your Life, Papa's Delicate Condition, 1963, Skidoo, 1968, How to Commit a Marriage, 1969, Don't Drink the Water, 1969, How Do I Love Thee?, 1970, Smokey and the Bandit, 1977, Smokey and the Bandit II, 1980, The Toy, 1982, Sting II, 1983, Smokey and the Bandit III, 1983, Nothing In Common, 1986; appeared on stage in Sly Fox, 1978. Recipient Antoinette Perry Award for best Broadway actor in Take Me Along 1959; elected to Television Hall of Fame, 1985. Home: Miami Beach Fla. Died June 24, 1987; buried St. Mary's Cathedral, Miami, Fla.

GLICK, WALTER R., college executive; b. Lakewood, Ill., May 7, 1892; s. Charles Walter and Sophronia Alice (Brownlee) G.; m. Nellie B. Sunwall, Oct. 1, 1915; children: Annelle (Mrs. Lewis Jordan), Claris; m. 2d Marie Elizabeth Moser, Nov. 10, 1938. Diploma, Southwest Tex. Tchr.'s Coll., 1925; BS, U. Tex., 1931, AM, 1932, PhD, 1949. Supt. of schs. Wharton, Jackson, and Atascosa Counties, Tex., 1913-29; dean, pres. Tex. Wesleyan Coll. (acad.), Austin, 1929-36; dean Tex. Wesleyan Coll., Ft. Worth, 1936-48, v.p., from 1948; supt. Dependents Schs., Munich, Germany, 1946-47. Mem. Tex. State Tchrs. Assn., Kiwanis Club, Phi Delta Kappa. Home: Fort Worth Tex. †

GLOVER, SHELDON LATTA, geologist; b. Tacoma, Dec. 24, 1891; s. Eli Sheldon and Sarah (Latta) G.;m. Edith Erika Johnson, Feb.28, 1920; children: Donald, Barbara Jean (Mrs. William W. Turner). BS, U. Wash., 1919, MS, 1921. Asst. mgr. Mullins Electric Co., Tacoma, 1910-13; aide Washington Geol. Survey, 1917; geologist 1919-21; assoc. in geology U. Wash., 1921, 24, 25; mem. Landes & Glover, cons. geologists, 1921-28; geologist, resident engr. Shenandoah Mining Co., B.C., Can., 1928-34; asst. supr. Div. Mines & Mining, 1941-45, Div. Mines & Geology, 1945-57; state supr. oil and gas 1954-57, pvt. practice cons. geologist, from 1957. Author numerous publs. Wash., Div. Geology, others. Enlisted as pvt., 4th Engrs., U.S. Army, 1917; commd. 2d lt., C.A., 1917; disch. 1st lt., 1919. Mem. Assn. Am. State Geologists, Geol. Soc. Am., Masons (32 degree, Shriner), Sigma Xi, Sigma Alpha Epsilon, Sigma Gamma Epsilon. Congregationalist. Home: Olympia Wash. †

GMEINER, HERMANN, social service association executive; b. Alberschwende, Austria, June 23, 1919; s. Hermann and Angelike (Eberle) G. Student in medicine and psychology, U. Innsbruck, Austria, 1946-49, Excellentis in Litteris (hon.), 1957; LHD (hon.), U. Fordham, 1963, LaSalle Coll., 1964. Pres., founder SOS-Kinderdorf (home villages for abandoned children), Innsbruck, also numerous villages worldwide, 1949-86. Author: Hermann Gmeiner: Die SOS-Kinderdorfer, 1953, Impressions, Reflections, Convictions, 1978. Served to lt. Austrian Army, 1942-45. Decorated Grand Cross Pontifical Order Gregory the Gt., Most Noble Order of Crown Thailand, 1964; recipient Silver Merit of Austrian Govt., 1956, Richard Meister medal U. Vienna, 1968, Prize for Humanity Variety Clubs Internat., 1979, Sonning prize, 1979; Wateler Peace prize, 1983; Aristotelis prize Alexander S. Onassis Found., 1985; twice nominated for Nobel Peace Prize. Mem. Austrian Acad. Scis. (hon.), Rotary. Home: Innsbruck, Austria. Died Apr. 26, 1986. Home: Innsbruck Austria.

GODBER, FREDERICK (LORD 1ST BARON GODBER OF MAYFIELD), business executive; b.

London, Nov. 6, 1888; s. Edward and Marion Louise (Peach) G.; m. Violet Ethel Beatrice Lovesy, Aug. 29, 1914; children: Joyce (Mrs. Andrew Agnew), Daphne (Mrs. Ian Debenham). With Asiatic Petroleum Co., 1904-19; pres. Roxana Petroleum Corp., St. Louis, 1919-29; dir. Shell Union Oil Corp.; mng. dir. Royal Dutch Shell Group, 1929-46; chmn. The Anglo-Saxon Petroleum Co. and The Shell Petroleum Co. Ltd., 1946-61; chmn. Commonwealth Devel. Fin. Co. Ltd., 1953. Chmn. overseas supply com. Petroleum Bd. World War II; chmn. exec. com. Help Holland Coun.; trustee Churchill Coll. Trust Fund, Cambridge, 1958. Decorated grand officer Order of Orange' Nassau, 1947; knighted, 1942; created baron, 1956; named hon. bencher Middle Temple, 1954, hon. liveryman Leathersellers Co., 1963;. Fellow Inst. Petroleum (hon.). Home: Mayfield Sussex, England. †

GODIN, EDGAR, bishop; b. Negauc, N.B., Can., May 31, 1911; s. Joseph Albanie and Marguerite (Breau) G. BA, Bethurst Coll., 1935; Lic. in Cannon Law, Laval U., 1947, Gregorian U., Rome, 1948; PhD, U. Moncton; LLD (hon.), St. Thomas U., 1970. Ordained priest Roman Catholic Ch., 1941. Dir. Retreat House Bathurst, N.B., 1942-46; vice-chancellor Diocese of Bathurst, 1948-51, chancellor, 1951-69; bishop of Bathurst 1969-85. Author: Hospital Ethics, 1959. Mem. Can. Assn. Cath. Hosps. (pres. 1967-69). Home: Bathurst N.B., Canada Died Apr. 6, 1985, buried Sacred Heart Cathedral, Bathurst.

GODSON, JOSEPH, foreign service officer; b. Poland, Jan. 15, 1913; s. Aaron and Clara (Drach) G.; m. Ruth Perlmann, Jan. 10, 1958; children—Roy, Carla. B.S.S., CCNY, 1937; LL.B., N.Y. U., 1940. Pub. relations dir. labor, charity orgns. 1940-50; joined U.S. fgn. service; attache Am. embassy, Ottawa, 1950-52; labor attache Am. embassy, London, 1953-59; 1st sec. Am. embassy, Belgrade, Yugoslavia, 1959-61; Am. consul. gen. Zagreb, Yugoslavia, 1962-64; labor, UN adviser European Bur., Dept State, 1964-68; Am. consul gen. Edinburgh, Scotland, 1968-71; coordinator Europe-Am. Conf., 1971-73; dir. Labour Com. for Transatlantic Understanding, 1974-86; European cons. Bd. for Internat. Broadcasting of U.S., 1976-81; European coordinator Center for Strategic and Internat. Studies, Georgetown U., 1976-86; cons. Adv. Com. European Democracy and Security, 1982-86. European editor: The Washington Quar., A Rev. of Strategic and Internat. Issues, 1977-86; author, editor: Transatlantic Crisis: Europe and America in the '70s; author, co-editor: The Soviet Worker—Illusions and Realities, 1981, The Soviet Worker—From Lenin Andropov, 1984; editor: Labour and Trades Union Press Service, 1975-86; editor: Challenges to the Western Alliance, 1984, 35 Years of NATO, 1985. Clubs: Hurlingham, Reform (London). Home: London England. Died Sept. 5, 1986.

GOETZENBERGER, RALPH L(EON), business executive; b. Mpls., Dec. 4, 1891; s. Edward and Emma Louise (Gatzman) G.; m. Edna Olive Cooper, Sept. 20, 1921; children: Louise Maude (Mrs. Warren H. Howard), Ralph Leon, Edward Basil. BS, U. Minn., 1913, EE, 1914. Mem. testing dept. GE, Schenectady, N.Y., 1914-15, with power and mining engr. dept., 1915-17; with engring. dept. Leeds and Northrop Co., Phila., 1926-28; mgr. indsl. regulator div. Mpls.-Honeywell Regulator Co., 1928-35; with Brown Instrument Co., Phila., 1935-39, became v.p., dir. Phila. co. when purchased by Mpls.-Honeywell Regulator Co., 1939-45, v.p. both cos., dir. Govt. Projects Office, then cons. engr.; pres. Equipment Co., Rockville, Md., from 1964; cons. engr. Franford Arsenal, Phila., 1921-26; chmn. Fire Control Engring Adv. Com., Ordnance Dept., U.S. Army, World War II, also chmn. Tank Fire Control Instrument Prodn. Integrating Com. Author tech. treatise on anti-aircraft gunnery and indsl. instrumentation and automatic controls; holder patents on anti-aircraft gun sighting systems and fuze setters. Chmn. Citizens Fed. Com. on Edn.; mem. edn. com. Washington Bd. of Trade; mem. Am. Coun. Edn.; del. Engrs. Joint Coun., U.S. Nat. Commn. for UNESCO. With Ordnance Dept., A.E.F., U.S. Army, 1917-21; maj. Ordnance Dept., U.S. Army, World War II. Decorated Legion D'Honneur (Black Star) of France. Fellow AIEE, ASME (dir. at large); mem. AAAS, Am. Acad. Polit. and Social Sci., D.C. Engring. and Archtl. Socs. (chmn.), Engrs. Joint Coun., Engrs. Coun. Profl. Devel. (exec. com.), Am. Soc. Engring. Edn. (rels. with industry com.), Instrument Soc. Am., Am. Ordnance Assn., Soc. Am. Military Engrs., Philos. Soc. Washington, Washington Soc. Engrs., NRC (mem. com. on UNESCO div. internat. rels.), Engrs. Club, Fenwood Golf and Country Club (Bethesda, Md.), Sigma Tau, Psi Upsilon, Theta Tau. Episcopalian. Home: Chevy Chase Md. †

GOFF, JAMES MATTHEW, transportation corporation executive; b. Memphis, June 20, 1927; s. Volney Barlow and Marguerite (Moreland) G.; m. Jennifer Joan Anderson, Aug. 25, 1973. B.A., Yale U., 1950; LL.B., U. Mich., 1953. Bar: Ill. 1953. Assoc. firm Sonnenschein, Carlin, Nath & Rosenthal, Chgo., 1953-59; ptnr. Sonnenschein, Carlin, Nath & Rosenthal, 1959-77; sr. v.p. GATX Corp., Chgo., 1977-79, asst. to chmn., 1987—; pres., chief exec. officer Gen. Am. Transp. Corp., Chgo., 1979-87; dir. 1st Nat. Bank of East Chicago (Ind.). Served with USN, 1945-46. Mem. Chgo. Bar Assn., Ill. State Bar Assn., Am. Coll. Trial Lawyers, Am. Bar Found. Clubs: Chgo.; Glenview (Ill.); Country of N.C. Home: Pinehurst N.C. Died Apr. 3, 1988, buried Pinelawn, Pinehurst.

GOH, CHOO SAN, choreographer; b. Singapore, Sept. 14, 1948; s. Kim Tak and Siew Han (Ch'ng) G. B.S., U. Singapore, 1970. tchr. Boston Sch. Ballet, Joffrey Ballet Sch., Jacob's Pillow, Mass. Tchr. Berlin Ballet, Boston Sch. of Ballet, Royal Danish Ballet, Jacob's Pillow Dance Festival, Joffrey Ballet Sch., Ballet de Santiago, Wash. Ballet; dancer Dutch Nat. Ballet, 1971-76, resident choreographer Washington Ballet, 1976-79, asst. artistic dir., 1979-84, assoc. artistic dir., 1984-87; ballets created include Helena, 1980, Birds of Paradise, Fives, 1978, Variaciones Concertantes, 1979, Leitmotiv, 1980, Celestial Images, 1980, Configurations, 1981, Due Pezzi Sacri, 1981, Configurations, 1981, In the Glow of the Night, 1982, Scenic Invitations, 1983, Romeo and Juliet, 1984, Schubert Symphony, 1985, Unknown Territory, 1986. Grantee Nat. Endowments Arts, 1978; Award for Excellence in Dance Met. Dance Assn., 1981, Award for Best Choreography Varna, Bulgaria Ballet Competition, 1983, Mayors Arts Award for Excellence in an Artistic Discipline, 1986. Home: Washington D.C. Died Nov. 29, 1987.

GOLDBERG, LEO, author, astronomer; b. Bklyn., Jan. 26, 1913; s. Harry and Rose (Ambush) G.; m. Charlotte B. Wyman, July 9, 1943 (div. Apr. 1986); children: Suzanne, David Henry, Edward Wyman; m. Beverley T. Lynds, Jan. 2, 1987. S.B., Harvard u., 1934; A.M., Harvard U., 1937, Ph.D., 1938; Sc.D. (hon.), U. Mass., 1970, U. Mich., 1974, U. Ariz., 1977. Asst. dept. astronomy Harvard U., 1934-37, Agassiz research fellow, 1937-38, spl. research fellow, 1938-41; research assoc. McMath-Hulbert Obs. U. Mich., 1941-46, asst. prof. astronomy, 1945-46, assoc. prof., chmn. astronomy, dir. obs., 1946-60, prof., 1948-60; Higgins prof. astronomy Harvard U., 1960-73, Higgins prof. emeritus, 1973-87, chmn. dept. astronomy, 1966-71, dir. Coll. Obs., 1966-71, assoc. Coll. Obs., 1984-87; dir. Kitt Peak Nat. Obs., Tucson, 1971-77, dir. emeritus, disting. research scientist, 1977-87; Martin Marietta chair Nat. Air and Space Mus., Smithsonian Instn., 1985-86; chmn. Astronomy Missions Bd., NASA, 1967-70; mem. U.S. nat. com. Internat. Astron. Union, 1954-66, 73-79, chmn., 1956-61, 84-86, chmn. U.S. del. to X Gen. Assembly, Moscow, 1958; mem. sci. adv. bd. USAF, 1959-62; mem. def. sci. bd. Dept. Def., 1962-64; mem. solar pshysics subcom. NASA, 1962-65, mem. sci. and tech. adv. com. manned space flight, 1964-71; chmn. adv. group on sci. programs NSF, 1974-76; mem. panel on health of sci. and tech. enterprise Office. Tech. Assessment, U.S. Congress, 1976-80. Contbr. articles to profl. jours.; collaborating editor Astrophys. Jour., 1949-51, chmn. editorial bd., 1954; editor Ann. Revs. Astronomy and Astrophysics, 1961-73. Trustee Assoc. Univs., Inc., 1957-66; bd. overseers Harvard U., 1976-82. Recipient Bowdoin Essay prize Harvard U., 1938; USN award for exceptional service to naval ordnance devel. in connection with devel. fire control devices for navy and NDRC, 1946; Russell lectr. AAS, 1973, Hale prize, 1985. George Darwin lectr. Royal Astron. Soc., London, 1978; Disting. Pub. Service medal NASA, 1973. Fellow Am. Acad. Arts and Scis.; mem. Nat. Acad. Scis. (mem. space sci. bd. 1958-64, chmn. astronomy sect. 1977-80), Internat. Astron. Union (v.p. 1958-64, pres. 1973-76, pres. Commn. 12, 1958-61, pres. Commn. 44, 1961-67), Am. Philos. Soc., Am. Astron. Soc. (pres. 1964-66), Assn. Univs. for Research in Astronomy, Inc. (dir. 1966-71), Royal Astron. Soc. (fgn. assoc.), Royal Astron. Soc. Can. (hon.), Societe Royale des Sciences, de Liège. Home: Tucson Ariz. Died Oct. 31, 1987.

GOLDEN, HAWKINS, lawyer; b. Morton, Miss., June 24, 1905; s. John J. and Mary Elizabeth (Hawkins) G.; m. Margaret Jackson, Feb. 25, 1939; children—Margaret, Hawkins. B.A., Vanderbilt U., 1926; M.A., Harvard, 1927; J.D., So. Methodist, U., 1930. Bar: Aditted to Tex. bar 1930. Practiced in Dallas, from 1930; mem. firm Leake, Henry, Young & Golden, 1932-47; sr. partner Leake, Henry, Golden & Burrow, 1947-59, Leake, Henry, Golden, Burrow & Potts, 1959-66, Golden, Potts, Boeckman & Wilson, from 1966. Mem. Dallas Hosp. Found.; research fellow Southwestern Legal Found.; Organizing dir. Dallas Crime Commn.; bd. rev. Judge Adv. Gen. Dept., World War II; Bd. devel. So. Meth. U. Mem. SAR, ABA, Tex. Bar Assn., Dallas Bar Assn. (pres. 1950, chmn. 1952), Phi Beta Kappa, Sigma Chi, Delta Theta Phi. Methodist (chmn. ofcl. bd. 1955). Clubs: Mason (Dallas) (Shriner, Jester, 32), Dallas Country (Dallas), Salesmanship (Dallas), Idlewild (Dallas), Terpsichorean (Dallas), Calyx (Dallas), Rotary (Dallas) (pres. 1955-56), Knife and Fork (Dallas) (pres. 1958-60), Press (Dallas). Home: Dallas Tex. Deceased.

GOLDENBERG, LOUIS, art dealer; b. New Brunswick, N.J., May 16, 1913; s. Max and Sadie (Grief) G.; m. Helen Domblatt, Aug. 20, 1944; children: Myra J., Barbara A. Grad., Pace Inst. Acct. Frederick William Greenfield Co., CPAs, N.Y.C., 1938-42; dir. govt. contracts Bulova Watch Co., N.Y.C., 1938-42, supt. internal acctg., 1942-46; ptnr. Goldenberg & Goldenberg, CPAs, N.Y.C., 1946-65; with Wildenstein & Co., Inc., art dealers, N.Y.C., 1946-81, v.p., 1958-68, pres., operating head, 1968-81. Councillor French C. of C. in U.S.; treas., trustee Wildenstein Found.; dir. v.p. Internat. Art Found. Art Research. Mem. N.Y. Soc. CPAs, Am. Inst. Accts. Home: Larchmont N.Y. Died Sept. 30, 1981.

GOLDER, BOYD E., university administrator; b. Allenwood, Pa., June 18, 1892; s. James D. and Laura (Dietterich) G.; children: boyd Edgar, Walter Edward, Arthur James, Harriet (Mrs. William R. Foxenberg). Student, Palmer Coll., Herrmanns Phys. Tng. Inst. Tchr. math., phys. edn. various pvt. schs., colls., pvt. instns.; assessor City of Utica, N.Y., 1938-46, mayor, 1946-55, also commr. parks, commr. pub. safety. V.p., bd. dirs. Utica Coll. found.; trustee SUNY; mem. com. representing U.S. Conf. Mayors, Internat. Conf. Municipalities, Vienna, Austria, 1953. Mem. Am. Mcpl. Assn. (past trustee), N.Y. State Conf. Mayors (past pres.), Kiwanis (past pres., lt. gov.). †

GOLDMAN, ERIC FREDERICK, historian, writer; b. Washington, June 17, 1915; s. Harry Eric and Bessie (Chapman) G.; m. Joanna R. Jackson, Mar. 7, 1952 (dec. 1980). MA, Johns Hopkins U., 1935, PhD, 1938; SCL, LittD, LHD, LLD. Instr. history Johns Hopkins, 1938-41; writer Time Mag., 1941-43, 45-47; assoc. prof. history Princeton U., 1947-55, prof., 1955-62, Rollins prof. history, 1962-85; spl. cons. to Pres. of U.S., 1963-66; State Dept. lectr., Europe, 1953-54, India, 1957; 1st U.S. rep. U.S.-Can. intellectual exchange program, 1975-76. Author: Charles J. Bonaparte, 1943, John Bach McMaster, American Historian, 1943, reprinted, 1971, (with F.C. Lane) The World's History, 1947, Rendezvous With Destiny, A History of Modern American Reform, 1952 (Bancroft prize for disting. Am. history 1952), 25th anniversary edit., 1977, The Crucial Decade, America 1945-55, 1956 (Nat. Book award nominee), The Crucial Decade—And After, America 1945-60, 1961, Tragedy of Lyndon Johnson, 1969; contbr. articles to popular and scholarly mags.; editor: Historiography and Urbanization, 1941, 2d edit., 1968; moderator NBC TV panel The Open Mind, 1959-68 (Emmy award 1962, 66); essayist CBS Morning News, 1975-76. Sr. fellow Coun. of Humanities, 1955-56; Guggenheim fellow, 1956-57; Libr. of Congress fellow, 1947; McCosh fellow, 1963-64. Mem. Am. Soc. Historians (pres. 1962-69), Century Club (N.Y.C.), Phi Beta Kappa. Home: Princeton N.J. Died Feb. 19, 1989.

GOLDSMITH, CLARENCE EARL, investment banker; b. South Orange, N.J., June 29, 1891; s. Clarence Arthur and Emily (DeLacey) G. Grad., Bordentown Mil. Inst., 1910; LittB, Princeton, 1914. With White Weld & Co., N.Y.C., from 1930, gen. ptnr., 1940-56, ltd. ptnr., from 1956; bd. dirs. Monarch Ins. Co. of Ohio. Mem. Racquet and Tennis Club, Links Club, River Club, India House Club. Home: Ringoes N.J. †

GOLDSMITH, EDWARD IRA, surgeon, educator; b. Far Rockaway, N.Y., Nov. 13, 1927; s. Abraham J. and Gertrude (Epstein) G.; m. Gene Louise French, Aug. 29, 1952; children: David Joshua (dec.), Joel Andrew (dec.), Jeremy Adam, William Glenn, Daniel French. AB, Cornell U., 1947, MD, 1950. Diplomate Am. Bd. Surgery. Intern N.Y. Hosp., 1950-51, resident, 1954-57, attending surgeon, from 1972; resident Boston Childrens Hosp., 1952, U. Colo. Med. Ctr., Denver, 1957-58; pvt. practice N.Y.C., from 1958; faculty dept. surgery Cornell U. Med. Coll., N.Y.C., from 1954, clin. assoc. prof., 1966-72, prof. from 1972; mem. adv. com. Joint Legis. Com. Mental Retardation, Physically Handicapped, N.Y. Legislature, from 1960; chmn. Com. Scientists for Use of Primates in Med. Rsch., from 1966; mem. com. on primates NRC; mem. N.Y. State Mental Hygiene Med. Rev. Bd. Editor: Medical Primatology, 1970-72, Jour. Med. Primatology, 1972; contbr. articles to profl. jours. Bd. dirs. Nassau Ctr. for Emotionally Disturbed Children, Woodbury, N.Y.; bd. visitors Rockland Childrens Psychiat. Ctr.; mem. adv. council to N.Y. State Commn. on Quality of Care for Mentally Disabled. 1st lt. M.C., AUS, 1952-54. Recipient Presdl. Merit medal, Phillipines, 1968, Trumpeldor medal, State of Israel, 1971. Fellow ACS; mem. AMA, Med. Soc. County N.Y., Am. Heart Assn., N.Y. Soc. Cardiovascular Surgery, N.Y. Surg. Soc., AAAS, N.Y. Acad. Scis., N.Y. Acad. Medicine, Am. Soc. Artificial Internal Organs, Transplantation Soc., Internat. Primatological Soc., Am. Soc. Tropical Medicine and Hygiene, Royal Soc. Tropical Medicine and Hygiene, N.Y. Cardiol. Soc., N.Y. Soc. Nephrology, Harvey Soc., N.Y. Gastroenterology Assn., N.Y. State Soc. Med. Rsch. (v.p.), Explorers Club, B'nai B'rith, Phi Sigma Delta Phi Delta Epsilon. Home: Katonah N.Y. Died June 11, 1985, buried Farmingdale, N.Y.

GOLDSMITH, RAYMOND WILLIAM, economist, educator; b. Brussels, Dec. 23, 1904; came to U.S., 1930, naturalized, 1939; s. Alfred and Camilla (Marcus) G.; m. Selma E. Fine, May 19, 1939 (dec. 1962); children: Jane, Donald, Paul. PhD, U. Berlin, 1927. Economist SEC, 1934-42, chief rsch. sect., asst. dirs. trading and exchange div., 1939-42; mem. staff War Prodn. Bd., 1942-46; various positions State Dept., 1945-48; mem. staff Nat. Bur. Econ. Rsch., 1952-70; prof. econs. NYU, 1958-59, Yale U., 1960-73; v.p. OECD Devel. Ctr., Paris, 1963-64. Author: Kapitalpolitik, 1933, The Changing Structure of American Banking, 1933, A

Study of Saving in the United States, 1955, Financial Intermediaries in the American Economy, 1958, The National Wealth of the United States in the Postwar Period, 1962, Studies in the National Balance Sheet of the United States, 1963, Flow of Capital Funds in the Postwar Economy, 1965, Financial Structure and Development, 1969, Capital Market Analysis and the Financial Accounts of the Nation, 1972, Comparative National Balance Sheets: A Study of 20 Countries, 1688-1978, 1985; editor: Institutional Investor and Corporate Stock, 1973. Home: Hamden Conn. Died July 12, 1988.

GOLDSTEIN, HAROLD, librarian, educator; b. Norfolk, Va., Oct. 3, 1917; s. Samuel and Jennie (Michelson) G.; m. Julia S. Deutsch, Nov. 4, 1943; children: William M., Richard H. B.S., U. Md., 1942; B.L.S., Columbia U., 1947, M.A., 1948, Ed.D., 1949. Asst. librarian Enoch Pratt Free Library, Balt., 1938-42; asst. prof. U. Minn., 1949-51; dir. library services USIS, Ceylon, 1951- 53; dir. Davenport Pub. Library, Iowa, 1955-59; prof. U. Ill., 1959-67; dean Sch. Library and Info. Studies, Fla. State U., Tallahassee, 1967-85; prof. Sch. Library and Info. Studies, Fla. State U., 1985-86; cons. N.Y. State LIbrary, Md. State Library, Pa. State Library, N.J. State Library, various community libraries; former pres. Ill. Library Assn., Iowa Library Assn. Author: (with others) State Library Policy, 1971; editor: Milestones to the Present: Library History Seminar V, 1976. Served with USAAF, 1942-46. Mem. AAUP, Am. Library Assn., Fla. Library Assn., S.E. Library Assn., NEA, Nat. Conf. Audiovisual Uses in Library Edn. (editor 1963), Conf. Evaluation of Library Edn. (editor 1967). Home: Tallahassee Fla. Died Dec. 8, 1986, Roselawn Cemetery, Tallahassee.

GOLDSTEIN, ISRAEL, rabbi; b. Phila., June 18, 1896; s. David L. and Fannie (Silver) G.; m. Bert Markowitz, July 21, 1918; children: Avram, Vivian Olum. BA, U. Pa., 1914; MA, Columbia U., 1917; grad., Jewish Theol. Sem. Am., 1918, DHL, 1927, DD (hon.), 1945; LHD, Brandeis U., 1958; LLD (hon.), NYU, 1961, U. Pa., 1976; DHL (hon.), Chgo. Coll. Jewish Studies, 1961, Dropsie U., 1971, Gratz Coll., 1973; PhD (hon.), Hebrew U., Jerusalem, 1971. Ordained rabbi, 1918. Rabbi Congregation B'nai Jeshurun, N.Y.C., 1918-60, rabbi emeritus, 1960-86; founder Brandeis U., 1946; pres. World Confedn. Gen. Zionists, 1947-56, co-chmn., 1956-72, hon. pres., 1972-86; pres. Jewish Conciliation Bd. Am., 1930-68, hon. pres., 1969-86; v.p. Conf. Jewish Orgns. on Material Claims against Germany, Austria, 1953-61; lectr. Homilectics Jewish Theol. Sem. Am., 1938; prof. Jewish history U. Judaism, 1954; served as leader in many Jewish orgns., pres. or chmn. of parent orgns. or of coms. including pres. Zionist Orgn. Am., 1943-45; chmn. World Jewish Congress, Western Hemisphere Exec., 1950-59; hon. v.p. World Jewish Congress, 1951-58, then hon. pres.; mem. Jewish Agy. Exec., 1948-86, treas., 1950-59; 1st chmn. Amidar Israel Nat. Housing Co., 1950; chmn. Israel's 10th Anniversary Celebration in U.S., 1958; del. World Zionist Congresses, 1935-61; world chmn. Keren Hayesed United Israel Appeal, 1961-71; hon. pres. Israel Interfaith Com., 1970-86; chmn. World Bible Ctr., Jerusalem, 1973-86; mem. NLRB, 1935; chmn. Brit. War Relief Commn., 1940-44. Author books and monographs including: American Jewry Comes of Age, 1955, Jewish Justice and Conciliation, 1981, My World as a Jew, 1984; contbr. to Universal Jewish Ency., Ency. Hebraica, articles to jours. Hon. vice chmn. Liberal Party N.Y., 1950-60; pres. Albert Einstein Found. Higher Learning Inc., 1946; bd. govs. Hebrew U. Jerusalem, Weizmann Inst. Sci., Rehovot, Israel, Haifa U.; mem. presidium of governing council World Zionist Orgn.; chmn. Jerusalem Artists House, 1965-70; pres. World Assn. Hebrew Culture, 1963-73. Israel Goldstein chair in practical theology Jewish Theol. Sem. Am. established in his name, 1958; chair in history of Zionism and modern Israel, Hebrew U., Jerusalem established in his name, 1967; Israel Goldstein Hebrew U. Synagogue, Jerusalem established in his name, 1967; Israel Goldstein Jerusalem Youth Village established in his name, 1950; recipient Israel Goldstein prize United Jewish Appeal, 1976, N.Y.C. medal, 1971; named Disting. Citizen of Jerusalem, 1976, hon. citizen of Eilat, 1966, of Carmiel, Israel, 1971. Home: Jerusalem Israel. Died Apr. 11. 1986; buried Jerusalem, Israel.

GOLDSTEIN, JEROME, contracting company executive; b. Chgo., Oct. 11, 1902; s. Asher and Mary (Adelsohn) G.; m. Mary Rose Greenstone, Jan. 7, 1931; children: Gerald N., Nancy Judith (Mrs. Alvin L. Gorman). BS, Armour Inst. Tech. (now Ill. Inst. Tech.), Chgo., 1923. An organizer Power Engring. Co., Chgo., 1926, ptnr., 1926-34; organizer, pres. Power Constrn. Inc., engrs. and gen. contractors, Elmhurst, Ill., 1935-86. Co-chmn. bldg. div. Combined Jewish Appeal, Chgo., 1951-52, vice chmn., 1953; mem. bldg. com. Desert Hosp., Palm Springs, Calif.; trustee Ill. Inst. Tech., 1962-86. Recipient Alumni medal Ill. Inst. Tech., 1975. Mem. Builders Assn. Chgo., Standard Club (Chgo.), Northmoor Country Club (Highland Park, Ill.), Tamarisk Country Club (Palm Springs, Calif.). Home: Wilmette Ill. Died May 14, 1986.

GOLDSTEIN, ROBERT V(ERNON), advertising executive; b. Omaha, Jan. 1, 1937; s. Arthur Harold and Ruth Marie (Cohen) G.; m. Nancy Sue Barron, June 29, 1958; children: Lawrence, Blaine, Jeffrey. BA, Harvard Coll., 1959; MBA, U. Chgo., 1961. With Procter & Gamble Co., Cin., 1961-87, brand asst., 1961-62, asst. brand mgr., 1962-64, brand mgr., 1964-69, assoc. advt. mgr., 1969-73, advt. mgr. toilet goods, 1973-75, advt. mgr. packaged soap and detergent div., 1975-77, project mgr. spl. products, 1977-79, gen. advt. mgr., 1979, v.p. advt., 1979-87; bd. dirs. Advt. Council, N.Y.C., 1979-87; mem. council of judges Advt. Hall of Fame, Washington, 1983-87; mem. Nat. Advt. Rev. Bd., N.Y.C., 1981-83; mem. com. on advt. edn. Advt. Ednl. Found. V.p. Jewish Fedn. Cin., chmn. pub. rels. com., strategy planning bd.; past pres. No. Hills Synagogue; bd. dirs. Cin. Jewish Community Rels. Council; mem. nat. pub. rels. com. United Jewish Appeal. Recipient Silver medal Cin. Advt. Club, 1982. Mem. Assn. Nat. Advertisers (chmn. 1983-84, bd. dirs. 1979-87), Harvard Alumni Assn., U. Chgo. Alumni Assn., Queen City Club. Republican. Home: Cincinnati Ohio. Died Aug. 1, 1987; buried, Omaha.

GOLDSTEIN, SIDNEY, lawyer; b. Bklyn., Oct. 13, 1906; s. Joseph and Esther (Mutchnick) G.; m. Olga Stein, Jan. 7, 1945 (dec.); 1 dau., Helena (Mrs. Peter Leslie). LL.B., St. John's Coll., 1930; M.A. in Polit. Sci, Columbia U., 1977. Bar: N.Y. 1931. Since practiced in N.Y.C.; atty. Port of N.Y. Authority, 1934-72, asst. gen. counsel, 1942-52, gen. counsel, 1952-72, cons. port and airport matters, 1972-86; Dir. 1172 Corp.; Panel mem. on noise abatement, commerce tech. adv. bd. Office Asst. Sec. Commerce, 1968-86. Contbr. articles to profl. jours. Served with Signal Corps AUS, World War II. Recipient Distinguished Pub. Service award Nat. Inst. Municipal Law Officers, 1956, Distinguished Service medal Port of N.Y. Authority, 1959, Distinguished Contbns. to Am. Aerospace Power award Met. Squadron Air Force Assn., 1961. Mem. ABA (com. chmn.), Assn. Bar City N.Y., N.Y. County Lawyers Assn. Airport Operators Council Internat. (gen. counsel), Am. Arbitration Assn. Home: New York N.Y. Died Nov. 24, 1986.

GOLENBOCK, JUSTIN MERTON, lawyer; b. N.Y.C., May 31, 1919; s. Philip Leo and Lillian (Barnett) G.; m. Hazel Bernice Taylor, Feb. 11, 1945; children: Susan Ann, Jeffrey Taylor, Douglas. A.B. cum laude, Univ. Heights Coll., N.Y. U., 1940; LL.B. cum laude, Yale, 1946. Bar: N.Y. 1947. Assoc. firm Milbank, Tweed, Hope, Hadley & McCloy, N.Y.C., 1946-48; ptnr. Lans, Goldstein, Golenbock & Abrams, N.Y.C., 1948-49, Goldstein & Golenbock, N.Y.C., 1949-51, Goldstein, Golenbock & Barell, N.Y.C., 1951-60, Golenbock & Barell, N.Y.C., 1960—; Dir. Fab Industries, Inc., Williams Electronics, Inc., Xcor Internat. Inc., Movielab Inc., Internat. Citrus Corp.; Vis. lectr. Yale Law Sch., 1973, 78, 79, 83—. Editor: Yale Law Jour, 1942; comment editor, 1946. Mem. Scarsdale (N.Y.) Non-Partisan Nominating Coms., 1967-73; Mem. Scarsdale Planning Bd., 1976—, chmn., 1981-83; bd. govs. Yale Law Sch. Fund, 1974-80, 81—, Com. for Modern Cts., 1978—, N.Y. chpt. Multiple Sclerosis Soc., 1978—, N.Y. Fedn. Jewish Philanthropies. Served to capt. USAAF, 1941-46. Mem. Am. Bar Found., Am. Judicature Soc., Assn. Bar City N.Y. (mem. corp. law sect. 1968-71, com. profl. responsibility 1972-78, chmn. com. 1978-81, com. on sports and entertainment 1981—), Am. Bar Assn., N.Y. State Bar Assn. (spl. com. on pre-paid legal services plan 1981—), Order of Coif, Phi Beta Kappa. Clubs: Yale (N.Y.C.); Beach Point (Mamaroneck, N.Y.) (bd. govs.); Quaker Ridge (Scarsdale) (gov. 1981—); Scarsdale Town (bd. govs. 1975-78). Home: Scarsdale N.Y. Deceased.

GOMBERG, WILLIAM, management educator; b. Bklyn., Sept. 6, 1911; s. Alexander and Marie (Shuloff) G.; m. Adeline Wishengrad, Sept. 24, 1939; 1 child, Paula. BS, CCNY, 1933; MS, NYU, 1941; PhD, Columbia U., 1947. Dir. mgmt. engring. dept. Internat. Ladies Garment Workers Union, AFL, N.Y.C., 1941-56; prof. indsl. engring. Washington U., St. Louis, 1956-58; prof. mgmt. and indsl. rels. Wharton Sch., U. Pa., 1959-85; vis. prof. Columbia U., 1958-59, Stanford, 1958-65; cons. transp. labor sec. of commerce, Nat. Acad. Sci.; indsl. engring. cons. UAW-CIO, Internat. Assn. Machinists, United Textile Workers, AFL, Comml. Telegraphers Union. Author: Trade Union Analysis of Time Study, 1948, Labor Union Manual on Job Evaluation, 1948, (with Shostak) Blue Collar World, New Perspectives in Poverty, 1965; also contbr. articles to profl. jours. Mem. Nat. Acad. Arbitrators, ASME, AAAS, Am. Arbitration Assn., Am. Inst. Indsl. Engrs., Am. Econ. Assn. Home: Wynnewood Pa. Died Dec. 8, 1985.

GOMEZ, FORTINO, clergyman; b. Celaya, Gto, Mex., Aug. 11, 1890; s. Felipe and Dolores (León) G. Student, Coll. Pio Marieno of Querétaro, Sem. of Monterrey; PhD, Coll. Pio Latino Americano, Rome, 1910, ThD, 1914, LLD, 1916. Ordained priest Roman Cath. Ch., 1913. Rector Sem. of Monterrey, 1934; gen. vicar Archdiocese of Monterrey, 1935, dean, 1937; archbishop of Antequera 1942-67, consecrated, 1943, archbishop of Ceramo, from 1967, asst. pontifical throne, 1955. Home: Celaya Mexico. †

GONDA, THOMAS ANDREW, physician, educator; b. Vienna, Austria, Aug. 24, 1921; came to U.S., 1924, naturalized, 1929; s. Victor E. and Ossy (Kopp) G.; m. Elizabeth Marie Chandler, July 3, 1944; children—Paul Chandler, William Stuart, Lynn. Student, U. Chgo., 1939-40; A.B., Stanford, 1942, M.D., 1945. Intern San Francisco Hosp., 1944-45; resident Langley Porter Clinic, San Francisco, 1948-51; clin. dir. psychiatry San Francisco Hosp., 1949-51; chief neurology and psychiatry VA Hosp., San Francisco, 1951-53; instr. psychiatry Stanford U. Sch. Medicine, 1954-55, asst. prof., 1955-58, assoc. prof., 1958-65, prof., 1965-87, Howard C. Robbins prof., 1986-87, acting exec., 1955-56, 58-61, assoc. dean, 1967-75; dir. Stanford U. Hosp., 1968-74; med. dir. Stanford U. Med. Center, 1974-75; chmn. dept. psychiatry and behavioral scis. Stanford U., 1975-87; vis. prof. Inst. Exptl. Psychology and spl. NIMH research fellow Oxford U., Eng., 1961-62; cons. VA, Calif. Dept. Mental Hygiene, 1956-87; chmn. Nat. Psychiat. Residency Adv. Bd., 1968. Mem. profl. adv. bd. Found. Thanatology, 1968-87. Served to capt., M.C. AUS, 1946-48. Fellow Am. Psychiat. Assn. (life), Am. Coll. Psychiatrists; mem. AMA, Calif. Med. Assn. Home: Stanford Calif. Died Aug. 12, 1987.

GOOD, CLARENCE ALLEN, physician, radiologist; b. St. Joseph, Mo., Sept. 20, 1907; s. Clarence Allen and Sophie Love (Evans) G.; m. Virginia McClure, Sept. 6, 1930; children: Clarence Allen III, John McClure, Andrew Evans, Stephen Conrad. AB, Williams Coll., 1929; MD, Washington U., 1933; MS in Radiology, U. Minn., 1938. Diplomate: Am. Bd. Radiology (asst. sec., asst. treas.). Asst. radiology Mallinkrodt Inst. Radiology, Washington U., 1933-34; intern medicine Barnes Hosp., St. Louis, 1934-35; fellow in radiology Grad. Sch. Mayo Found., U. Minn., 1935; from instr. to prof. radiology, head sect. diagnostic roentgenology Mayo Clinic, Rochester, Minn., sr. cons. diagnostic roentgenology, 1967-73, emeritus, 1973-84. Fellow Am. Coll. Radiology (emeritus); mem. AMA, Am. Roentgen Ray Soc., Radiol. Soc. N.Am., Minn. Radiol. Soc., Phi Beta Kappa, Sigma Xi, Alpha Omega Alpha, Theta Delta Chi, Nu Sigma Nu. Home: Rochester Minn. Died May 16, 1984.

GOOD, ROBERT CROCKER, college president; b. Mt. Vernon, N.Y., Apr. 7, 1924; s. Alfred and Josephine (Crocker) G.; m. Nancy Louise Cunningham, Aug. 21, 1946; children: Stephen L., Karen L., Kathleen J. B.A., Haverford (Pa.) Coll., 1945; B.D., Yale U., 1951, Ph.D. in Internat. Relations, 1956. Instr., then asst. prof. internat. relations Social Sci. Found., U. Denver, 1953-58; research asso. Washington Ctr. Fgn. Policy Research, 1958-61; dir. Carnegie Endowment Seminars Diplomacy, Washington, 1960-61, Pres.-Elect Kennedy's Task Force Africa, 1960, Office Research and Analysis Africa, Bur. Intelligence and Research, Dept. State, 1961; U.S. ambassador to Zambia, 1965-69; dean Grad. Sch. Internat. Studies, U. Denver, 1970-76; pres. Denison U., Granville, Ohio, 1976-83; cons. and/or mem. bd. Ctr. Global Perspectives, 1974-84, Global Perspectives in Edn., 1975-84, Council Religion in Internat. Affairs, 1975-81, Patterson Sch. Internat. Diplomacy and Commerce, U. Ky., 1975-77; external bd. govs. Nat. U. Lesotho, Roma, 1977-84. Author: Congo Crisis: The Role of the New States, 1961, U.D.I.: The International Politics of the Rhodesian Rebellion, 1973; co-author: Alliance Policy in the Cold War, 1959, Neutralism and Non-alignment: The New States in World Affairs, 1962, The Mission of the Christian Church in the Modern World, 1962, Foreign Policy in the Sixties: Issues and Instrumentalities, 1965, South Africa: Time Running Out, 1981; co-editor: Reinhold Niebuhr on Politics, 1960. Pres. Neighbors, Inc., Washington, 1961-65; mem. Study Commn. on U.S. Policy toward So. Africa, 1979-84. Kent fellow, 1951; recipient Superior Honor award Dept. State, 1964. Mem. Am. Polit. Sci. Assn., Ohio Coll. Assn. (pres. 1983-84), Internat., African studies assns., Soc. Values in Higher Edn., Phi Beta Kappa. Democrat. Unitarian. Home: Granville Ohio. Died Sept. 16, 1984.

GOODBODY, HAROLD P., business executive; b. Toledo, 1905; m. Mary Blair; children: Sarah Norris, James, Harold, William. Grad., Williams Coll., 1927. Mng. ptnr. Goodbody & Co., N.Y.C., until 1970; chmn. bd. dirs. Dalgood Instl. Service Corp., N.Y.C., 1971-88. Trustee Pingry Sch., Elizabeth, N.J. Home: Williamstown Mass. Died July 17, 1988.

GOODELL, CHARLES ELLSWORTH, lawyer, former U.S. Senator; b. Jamestown, N.Y., Mar. 16, 1926; s. Charles Ellsworth and Francesca (Bartlett) G.; m. Jean Rice, Aug. 28, 1954 (div. 1978); children: William Rice, Timothy Bartlett, Roger Stokoe, Michael Charles Ellsworth, Jeffrey Harris; m. Patricia Goldman. A.B., Williams Coll., 1948; LL.B., Yale U., 1951, M.A. (Ford Found. faculty fellow), 1952; hon. degree, Houghton (N.Y.) Coll., Alfred U., N.Y., St. Bonaventure U., N.Y. Bar: N.Y. 1954, Conn. 1951. Instr. Quinnipiac Coll., New Haven, 1950-51; congl. liaison asst. Dept. Justice, 1954-55; partner Van Vlack, Goodell & McKee, Jamestown, N.Y., 1955-59, Roth, Carlson, Kwit, Spengler & Goodell, N.Y.C., 1971-72, Hydena, Mason & Goodell, N.Y.C., 1973-87; mem. 86th-87th Congresses from 43d Dist. N.Y., 88th-90th Congresses from 38th Dist. N.Y., chmn. Planning and Research Com.; mem. U.S. Senate from N.Y. 1968-71; of counsel King & Spalding, Washington; chmn. bd. DGA Internat., Inc., Washington. Author: Political Prisoners in America, 1973. Chmn. Republican Com. Chautauqua County, 1958-59; chmn. Presdl. Clemency

Bd., 1974-75. Served as seaman USNR, World War II, 1st lt. USAAF, Korea. Mem. Jamestown Jaycees, Jamestown C. of C. (chmn. govtl. affairs com. 1956-58), ABA, Jamestown Bar Assn., Phi Beta Kappa, Gamma Sigma Chi. Episcopalian. Clubs: Capitol Hill (Washington), 86th Congress (Washington); New Yorker. Home: Washington D.C. Died. Jan. 21, 1987; buried Lakeview Cemetery, Jamestown, N.Y.

GOODFRIEND, JAMES HERMAN, lawyer; b. N.Y.C., Dec. 8, 1933; s. Arthur and Phyllis (LeVine) G.; m. Phyllis Poresky, Jan. 3, 1960 (div.); children—Lisa Ruth, David Peter. A.B., U. Chgo., 1953; J.D., Columbia U., 1956. Bar: N.Y. 1956, Fla. 1975, U.S. Supreme Ct. 1967. Ptnr. Tenzer, Greenblatt, Fallon & Kaplan, N.Y.C., 1959-87. Served with AUS, 1957-59. Fellow Am. Acad. Matrimonial Lawyers; mem. Assn. of Bar of City of N.Y. (matrimonial law com. 1986—). Club: K.P. Home: Jamaica N.Y. Died Mar. 12, 1987.

GOODMAN, BENNY, orchestra conductor, clarinetist; b. Chgo., May 30, 1909; m. Alice Hammond Duckworth, Mar. 1942 (dec. 1979); children: Rachel, Benjie. Student, Lewis Inst., Chgo.; studied clarinet with, Franz Schoepp of Chgo. Symphony Orch.; LLD, Ill. Inst. Tech., 1968; MusD (hon.), Harvard U., 1984, Columbia U., 1986. Began in orch. Lake Mich. excursion boats; played in theatre orchs. in N.Y.C.; organized own orch., 1933; began popular radio program Let's Dance, 1934; conducted swing concerts at Carnegie Hall, N.Y.C., Symphony Hall, Boston, Ravinia (Ill.) Park, Hollywood Bowl; clarinet soloist with Budapest String Quartet, N.Y. Philharmonic Symphony, Phila. Symphony, Rochester Symphony, others, also concerts with various artists; radio programs including Camel Caravan, 1937-40, Old Gold, 1941, Victor Borge-Benny Goodman Show, 1946-47; appeared in motion pictures A Song is Born, others; commentator on serious music WNEW; TV show Star Time; recorded for Columbia, Capitol, Chess, Command, Decca, Philips, RCA Victor records; life story filmed The Benny Goodman Story, 1956; re-formed big band, 1955 for engagements U.S. and abroad; organized new band, 1958, Brussels World's Fair; toured Europe, 1959; appeared with London Philharmonic, 1961, State Dept. Cultural Exchange Program tour of Russia, 1962; toured Europe with Brit. musicians, 1970-71; mus. good-will ambassador on tour Far East, under auspices Dept. State and ANTA exchange program; commissioned works by Bartok, Copland, Hindemith; author: (with Irving Kolodin) Kingdom of Swing. Recipient Apollo award, 1956, Kennedy Ctr. Honor , 1982, Grammy Lifetime Achievement award Am. Acad. Rec. Arts and Scis.; winner Internat. Jazz Critics Poll (clarinet), 1986; named to Playboy Hall of Fame, Downbeat Hall of Fame. Home: Stamford Conn. Died June 13, 1986; buried Stamford, Conn.

GOODMAN, HERMAN EDWARD, business executive; b. N.Y.C., Feb. 16, 1902; s. Abe and Anna (Smith) G.; m. Estelle Weinstein, June 15, 1933; children: Adam, Paul. Student, Columbia U., 1920-22, Sch. Bus. Adminstrn., 1924. Pres. Hego Fabrics Inc., N.Y.C., 1933-52; chmn. bd. dirs. Robbins Mills Inc., N.Y.C., 1952-53; v.p. Amerotron Corp., N.Y.C., 1954-55; v.p. Textron Inc., N.Y.C., 1955-60, also bd. dirs.; pres. The Franklin Corp., N.Y.C., 1960-86, also bd. dirs.; bd. dirs. Astrex Inc., Cylinders Inc., Indusl. Plywood Co. Inc.; dir. Postgrad. Ctr. Psychotherapy Inc., 1961. Mem. Nat. Cerebral Palsy Com.; bd. dirs. Home and Hosp. for Daus. of Jacob, Bronx, N.Y. Home: New York N.Y. Died Jan. 31, 1986.

GOODMAN, LEO MAGILL, foreign service officer, judge; b. Dec. 7, 1909; s. Tobias and Emma (Magill) G.; m. Thea M. Goodman. BSS, CCNY, 1931; student, Columbia U., 1931, JD, 1934; postgrad., Hunter Coll., 1942, Practicing Law Inst., N.Y.C., 1952, Indsl. Coll. Armed Forces, 1958-59, George Washington U., 1959; student, Nat. War Coll., 1962; LLD (hon.), U. Munich, 1972. Bar: N.Y. 1934. Practiced in N.Y.C., until 1941; atty., examiner Dept. Justice, 1941-42; chief trial div. U.S. War Crimes Group, Germany, 1946-47; chief adminstrn German justice div. Office Mil. Govt. Bavaria, 1948; chief presiding judge for Bavaria U.S. Cts. of Allied High Commn. for Germany, 1948-54; justice Ct. of Appeals, 1954-55; legal advisor Am. Embassy, Vienna, Austria, 1955-57, 1st sec., consul, 1956-57; assigned Dept. State, 1957-62; consul gen. Am. Consulate Gen., Bremen, Fed. Republic Germany, 1962-70; spl. advisor for Europe to Tobacco Assocs., Washington, 1970-72, for Bavaria to Am. C. of C., Fed. Republic Germany, 1970-85; U.S. justice Supreme Restitution Ct., Fed. Republic Germany, 1977-85; judge U.S. Ct. for Berlin, 1978-85; mem. U.S. Adoption Rev. Bd. for Bavaria, 1948; U.S. mem. 4 power reparations, deliveries and restitution directorate Allied Council for Austria, 1955-56, Joint Property Control and Restitution Commn. for Vienna, 1955-56, Fulbright Scholarship Selection Com. for Bavaria, 1953-54. Author: Selected Opinions of Leo M. Goodman, 3 vols., 1954, Bavarian Digest of Current Legal Opinions, 1949; contbr. to Erwartungen, 1980. Founder, hon. pres. Leo Goodman Internat. Law Library, U. Munich, 1954; mem. adv. bd. Munich Internat. Sch., European law internship program McGeorge Sch. Law, U. Pacific, Max Planck Inst. for Internat. Patent and Copyright Laws, Munich. With AUS, 1942-46, ETO; col. USAF Res. Decorated Bronze Star; Grand Cross with star Order Merit; Order Merit Bavaria (Fed. Republic Germany); recipient award City of Aachen, Germany, 1953. Mem. ABA, Am. Soc. Internat. Law, Am. Judicature Soc., Am. Assn. Comparative Study Law, Am. Fgn. Service Assn., Air Force Assn., Res. Officers Assn., German Am. Lawyers Assn. (adv. bd.), Alumni Fedn. Columbia U., Diplomat and Consular Officers Ret., Am. C. of C. in Germany (hon.), Fed. Bar Assn., Verein von Freunde des Fockemuseums Bremen, Fedn. German-Am. Clubs (v.p., bd. dirs. 1970-72), Columbus Soc. Munich (curatorium), Gesellschaft für Auslandskunde (Munich), Peutinger Kollegium Munich, Smithsonian Assocs. Clubs, zu Bremen Club, zur Vahr Club, Munich Herrenklub, Columbia U. Club (N.Y.C.), Internat. Lawyers Club, Nat. Lawyers Ckub, Dacor House (Washington), Kiwanis (hon.). Home: Munich Federal Republic of Germany. Died Dec. 17, 1985; buried Straubing, Fed. Republic Germany.

GOODMAN, OSCAR R., economist, educator; b. Chgo., July 25, 1922; s. Benjamin and Anna (Faber) G.; B.S., Northwestern U., 1943; M.S., U. Wis., 1948, Ph.D., 1952, J.D., 1960. CLU; chartered fin. analyst. Mdse. control mgr. Alden's, Inc., Chgo., 1943-45; sr. market analyst Spiegel's, Inc., Chgo., 1945-46; instr. U. Wis., 1948-52; assoc. prof. fin. State U. Wash., 1953-56, U. Calif., Berkeley, 1956-58; vis. prof. U. Geneva, 1963, U. Mich., 1966; assoc. prof. fin. Northwestern U., 1958-65; prof. fin. and econs. Roosevelt U., Chgo., 1966-85, chmn. fin. dept., 1968-76; atty., econ. cons. U.S. Dept. Justice Antitrust Div., U.S. House Banking and Currency Com.; expert witness U.S. Senate Com. on Antitrust and Monopoly; cons. fin. instns. and industry; lectr. Nat. Trust Sch., Am. Bankers Assn., Mortgage Banking Sch., Conf. State Bank Suprs. Trustee, Roosevelt U. Mem. Am. Econs. Assn., Nat. Assn. Bus. Economists, Fin. Mgmt. Assn., Royal Econ. Soc., Am. Fin. Assn., Midwest Fin. Assn. (pres. 1978-79, editor jour. 1977-85), Am. Risk and Ins. Assn., Inst. Chartered Fin. Analysts, ABA, Ill. Bar Assn., AAUP, Investment Analysts Soc. Chgo., Acad. Internat. Bus., Beta Gamma Sigma, Phi Delta Kappa, Phi Delta Phi. Author: Sales Forecasting, 1953; contbr. articles to Ency. Brittanica and profl. jours. Home: Chicago, Ill. Died Dec. 23, 1985; buried Chgo.

GOODNIGHT, CLARENCE JAMES, educator; b. Gillespie, Ill., May 30, 1914; s. Charles A. and Phoebe (Personeus) G.; m. Marie Louise Ostendorf, Aug. 25, 1940; children—Ann Marie, Charles James. Student, Ill. Coll., 1932-33; A.A., Blackburn Coll., 1934; A.B., U. Ill., 1936, M.A., 1937, Ph.D., 1939. Instr. zoology U. Ill., 1936-39, 42-44, research asso., 1939-40; instr. biology Bklyn. Coll., 1940-42, N.J. State Tchrs. Coll., 1944-46; asst. prof. biology Purdue U., 1946-49, asso. prof., 1949-55, prof., 1955-65; prof. biology Western Mich. U., 1965-87, head dept., 1965-75; cons. Sch. Sci. Curriculum Project U. Ill.; mem. com. Grad. Record Exam. Biology, Ednl. Testing Service, Princeton, N.J. Author: (with M. L. Goodnight) Zoology, 1954, (with M.L. Goodnight and R.R. Armacost) Biology: An Introduction to the Science of Life, 1962, (with M. L. Goodnight and P. Gray) General Zoology, 1964; also articles. Fellow A.A.A.S. (council); mem. A.A.U.P., Ecol. Soc. Am., Am. Micros. Soc. (pres. 1971), Am. Soc. Limnologists and Oceanographers, Soc. Systematic Zoology, N. Am. Benthological Soc. (sec.), Am. Inst. Biol. Scis. (governing bd.), Am. Soc. Zoologists (sec. 1973-76), Am. Arachnological Soc., Nature Conservancy, Am. Mus. Natural History (research asso.), Phi Beta Kappa, Sigma Xi. Democrat. Unitarian. Home: Kalamazoo Mich. Died Aug. 9, 1987; cremated.

GOONETILLEKE, OLIVER ERNEST, governor general; b. Ceylon, 1892; s. A.E. and Emily (Jayasekera) G.; m. Esther Jayawardena, 1920; children: Joyce (Mrs. Wijesinghe), Sheila (Mrs. Dodanwela), Oliver Ernest. Student, Wesley Coll., Colombo, Ceylon; BA, U. London; LLD, U. Ceylon. 1942 auditor gen., Ceylon, 1931-42; civil def. and food commr. Ceylon, mem. war coun., 1942-45, fin. sec., 1945-47, minister home affairs and rural devel., 1947-48, 51-52; Ceylon high commr. to London 1948-51; minister agr. and food Ceylon, 1952-53, leader Senate, minister fin., 1953-54, gov.-gen., from 1954. Ceylon govt. del. Internat. Ry. Congress, Cairo, 1933; chmn. Retrenchment Commn., 1938, Salaries Commn., 1945. Decorated Knight Commr. Order Brit. Empire, 1944, Knight Grand Cross, Order St. Michael and St. George, Knight Comdr. Royal Victorian Order, Knight Order St. John of Jerusalem, 1954. Fellow Royal Soc. Arts, Royal Empire Soc. Home: Colombo Sri Lanka. †

GORAN, MORRIS, science educator; b. Chgo., Sept. 4, 1916; s. David and Sara (Klein) G.; m. Cymia Walen, June 3, 1951; children: Marjorie, Ruth. B.S., U. Chgo., 1936, M.S., 1939, Ph.D., 1957. Chemist Dearborn Chem. Co., 1941-42; asst. prof. physics Ind. U., 1942-43; scientist Manhattan Dist. Corps of Engrs., Oak Ridge, 1943-45; prof., chmn. dept. phys. sci. Roosevelt U., 1945-86; cons. Plastofilm, Croft Ednl. Services; lectr. George Williams Coll., Elmhurst Coll.; Pres. Lincolnwood Bd. Edn., 1959-68. Author: Story of Fritz Haber, 1967, The Future of Science, 1971, Science and Anti-Science, 1974, The Modern Myth: Ancient Astronauts and UFOs, 1978, Fact, Fraud and Fantasy: The Occult and Pseudosciences, 1979, Ten Lessons of the Energy Crisis, 1980, Conquest of Pollution, 1981,
Can Science Be Saved?, 1981, (with Marjorie Go
The Myth of Longevity, 1984, The Past of Wes
Science, 1984, A Guide to the Perplexed At
Pseudoscience, 1985, A Treasury of Science Jokes, 1
contbr. articles to profl. jours. Fellow Am. I
Chemists; mem. Am. Chem. Soc., Am. Phys. S
AAAS, AAUP, History of Sci. Soc. Ho
Lincolnwood Ill. Died Sept. 6, 1987.

GORDON, AMBROSE, educator; b. Savannah,
May 23, 1920; s. Ambrose and Lenore (Hunter) G.;
Mary Spainhour, Sept. 1, 1960; children—Ma
Robertson, Ambrose. B.A., Yale U., 1942, M.A., 1
Ph.D., 1952. Lectr. Hunter Coll., 1946-48; instr. Y
U., 1951-54; mem. faculty Sarah Lawrence Coll., 19
58, U. Tex., Austin, 1958-87; prof. English U. T
1972-87; Fulbright lectr., 1966, 69. Author: The
visible Tent: The War Novels of Ford Madox F
1964; mem. editorial bd.: Furioso, 1946-50; con
poems, essays and revs. to various publs. Served
USNR, 1942-46. Mem. AAUP, Chi Delta Theta. C
Elizabethan of Yale U. Home: Austin Tex. Died M
7, 1987; buried Savannah.

GORDON, BURGESS LEE, physician, editor;
Spokane, Wash., Apr. 10, 1982; s. Burgess Lee
Ralphaleta (Simpson) G.; m. Margaret Huston; 1 s
Burgess Lee. AB, Gonzaga U., 1912, LLD, 1953; M
Jefferson Med. Coll., 1919; DSc, Pa. Med. Coll., 19
Intern Jefferson Hosp., Phila., 1919-21; resid
physician Peter Bent Brigham Hosp., Boston, 1921
teaching fellow in medicine Harvard Med. Sch., 1923
pvt. practice Phila., 1926-84; dir., physician-in-c
Barton Meml. and White Haven divs. Jefferson Ho
Pa. Kosp., 1946-51; clin. prof. medicine Jefferson M
Coll., 1941-51, vis. prof. medicine, 1961-84; dir. he
and welfare fund for study of anthracosilicosis Jeffe
Med. Coll. Hosp., 1941-51; pres., Mullen prof. medi
Pa. Med. Coll., 1951-57; dir. edn., mem. med. bd. L
lace Found. and Clinic, Albuquerque, 1957-60, c
med. edn., 1959-84; assoc. editor Jour. AMA, 1960-
editor Current Med. Info. and Terminology, 1966-
Current Procedural Terminology, 1974-84; dir. o
current terminology AMA, 1961-74, cons., 1974-
mem. physician in residence program VA, 1960-
Author textbooks; contbr. articles to med. jours.; edi
Clinical Cardiopulmonary Physiology (textbook), S
plified Medical Records System, 1975; co-editor Oxf
Medicine, 1946-58, Advances in Cardiopulmonary I
eases, 1962-84. Trustee Mercy-Douglass Hosp., 19
57, Phila Tb. and Health Assn., 1938-57, Am. C
Sports Medicine Fellowship Commn., Phila., 1952-
Col. M.C., U.S. Army, 1942-46. Recipient Recogni
award Am. Soc. Internal Medicine, Alumni Merit aw
in Arts and Scis. Gonzaga U., 1977. Fellow ACP, A
Coll. Chest Physicians (Gold medal for contbns. in c
diseases 1962, past pres.); mem. N.Mex. Med. S
(hon.), Phila. County Med. Soc., Pa. Med. Soc., A
Trudeau Soc., Am. Assn. Hist. Medicine, N.Mex. S
Biol. and Med. Research, Assn. Am. Physicians, A
Soc. Clin. Investigation, Soc. for Advances Med. S
tems (bd. dirs.), Coll. Physicians Phila. (mem. cour
award for meritorious service 1978), Council Inter
Orgns. Med. Scis., Com. Internat. Med. Nomenclat
Union League, Alpha Omega Alpha, Phi Chi. Ho
Philadelphia Pa. Died Nov. 16, 1984.

GORDON, HARRY HASKIN, physician, educator,
Bklyn., Aug. 4, 1906; s. Samuel and Ida (Haskin) G.;
Lois Chasins (dec. 1943); m. Fayga Halpern, June
1948; children: Charles, Deborah. B.A., Cornell
1926, M.D., 1929; D.Sc., Yeshiva U., 1969. Int
Montefiore Hosp., N.Y.C., then; New Haven Ho
1929-31; resident New Haven Hosp., then N.Y. Ho
1931-33; assoc. attending pediatrician N.Y. Hosp., 19
46; pediatrician-in-chief Colo. and Denver Gen. hos
1946-52, Sinai Hosp., Balt., 1952-62; attending pe
trician Johns Hopkins Hosp., 1952-62; attending pe
trician Bronx Mcpl. Hosp. Ctr., 1962-88, med. c
patient relations office, 1976-85; cons. pediatric
Montefiore Hosp. and Med. Center, 1964-88; dir. R
Fitzgerald Kennedy Center for Research in Me
Retardation and Human Devel., 1965-72, dir. emeri
1972-88; asst. prof. Cornell U. Med. Coll., 1933-
prof. pediatrics U. Colo., 1946-52; assoc. prof. pediat
Johns Hopkins U., 1952-62; prof. pediatrics Albert E
stein Coll. Medicine, 1962-77, prof. emeritus, 1977-
assoc. dean, 1966-67, dean, 1967-70; cons. in pediat
Surgeon Gen. U.S. Army, 1947-62, U.S. Childrens E
for Maternal and Child Health and Crippled Childr
Services, 1948-51; cons. Surgeon Gen. USPHS, and
NIH, 1949-78; mem. food and nutrition bd. NRC, 19
59, mem. adv. com. on child devel., 1971-73, mem.
on maternal, child and family health research, 1975-
mem. Health Task Force, N.Y. Urban Coalition, 19
73; cons. Kennedy Center for Bioethics, Georgetown
1974-85; Career scientist Health Research Council C
N.Y., 1962-67. Contbr. articles to profl. jours. Ser
from capt. to lt. col. M.C., AUS, 1942-46. Recipi
Borden award for nutritional research Am. Acad. Pe
atrics, 1944; Grover F. Powers Disting. prof. Nat. As
for Retarded Children, 1963-88. Fellow AAAS; me
Am. Pediatric Soc. (John Howland award 1975, p
pres.), Soc. Pediatric Research (past pres.), Am. Ac
Pediatrics (First Borden Rsch. award 1944, C. Ander
Aldrich award 1976), Am. Soc. Clin. Investigation, A
Assn. Mental Deficiency (Disting. Service award 197

Sigma Xi, Alpha Omega Alpha. Home: Rye N.Y. Died July 20, 1988, buried Hasting-on-Hudson, N.Y.

GORDON, JOHN BOYLE, vegetable oil expert; b. Columbia, Mo.; s. Wellington and Laura (Amonett) G.; m. Bertha Oshei, June 17, 1915; children: Laura Amonett (Mrs. F.R.W. Worth), Margaret Fleetwood (Mrs. Andrew H. Brown). BS, U. Mo., 1909; postgrad., U. Wis., 1909. Mem. faculty Iowa State Coll., 1909-11; tech. expert in milk plants, etc. N.Y., 1911-17; mgr. Kellogg Products Co., Buffalo, 1917-18; sales mgr. ea. region Rogers, Brown & Co., Seattle, 1918-20; gen. mgr. Capitol Refining Co., South Washington, Va., 1920-21; Washington rep. Bur. Raw Materials for Am. Vegetable Oils and Fats Industries, Washington, from 1921, sec., from 1923; mem. ofcl. U.S. vegetable oil mission to Brazil, 1942; sec. Copra Export Mgmt. Co., Inc., 1945; procurement agt. U.S. Comml. Co., 1945. Contbr. Ency. Britannica; articles in field to profl. jours. 2d lt. inf. U.S. Army, 1912-16. Mem. Am. Econ. Assn., U.S. C. of C., N.Y. Oil Trades Assn., S.C.W., S.R. (registrar gen.), Mo. Soc. Washington, Nat. Press Club, Jefferson Islands Club, Chevy Chase Country Club, Masons (32 degree), Shriners, Phi Sigma Kappa. Democrat. Presbyterian. Home: Washington D.C. †

GORDON, JOHN EVERETT, epidemiologist; b. Austin, Minn., June 18, 1890; s. Newton Smith and Fanny King (Ricketson) G.; m. Miriam Lapham, Dec. 24, 1921; children: Kathleen Louise, Donald Lapham. PhG, Northwestern U., 1913, PhC, 1914; SB, U. Chgo., 1916, PhD, 1921, MD, 1926; AM, Harvard U., 1943. Instr. in bacteriology U. Chgo., 1919; field dir. Rockefeller Found., N.Y.C., 1933; prof. preventive medicine and epidemiology Harvard U., 1938-58, prof. emeritus, from 1958; cons. preventive medicine Office of Surgeon Gen., Dept. Army, Mass. Gen. Hosp., Mass. Eye and Ear Infirmary; hon. civilian cons. to surgeon gen. Dept. Navy; vis. prof. MIT, 1962-63; cons. USPHS, WHO, Joint Commn. on Mental Illness; mem. tech. adv. com. Inst. nutrition Cen. Am. and Panama. Author: Virus and Rickettsial Diseases, 1940; co-author: The History of American Epidemiology, 1952; mem. editorial adv. bd. Med. History World War II; contbr. articles to profl. jours. Dir. ARC-Harvard Field Hosp. Unit, Salisbury, Eng., 1940; cons. Allied Forces in the Pacific, 1945-46. 1st lt. San. Corps, U.S. Army, 1918, col. M.C. U.S. Army, 1942-45, ETO. Decorated D.S.M., Legion of Merit, Bronze Star, medal U.S.A. Typhus Commn., Order de la Sante Publique, Croix de Guerre with palm; Liberty Cross (Norway); Order of Brit. Empire. Fellow AMA, ACP, AAAS, Royal Coll. Physicians, Royal Soc. Health, Am. Acad. Pediatrics, Am. Pub. Health Assn., Roumanian Soc. Biology; mem. Ecol. Soc. Am., Am. Epidemiol. Soc., Assn. Mil. Surgeons U.S., Am. Soc. Tropical Medicine, Harvard Club, Sigma Xi, Phi Beta Pi, Gamma Alpha, Alpha Omega Alpha. Home: Wellesley Mass. †

GORDON, ROBERT SIRKOSKY, JR., physician; b. N.Y.C., Mar. 26, 1926; s. Robert Sirkosky and Dorothy (Dodson) G.; m. Elizabeth Wilkins Brown, June 30, 1951; children: Hilary Ruth, Andrew Sirkosky, Peter Taylor, Dana Elizabeth. AB, MD, Harvard U., 1949; MHS, Johns Hopkins U., 1976. Intern, then resident Presbyn. Hosp., N.Y.C., 1949-53; investigator Nat. Heart Inst., 1953-64; chief clin. rsch. Pakistan-SEATO Cholera Lab., 1961-64, tech. cons., 1964-69; clin. dir. Nat. Inst. Arthritis, Metabolism and Digestive Diseases, NIH, Bethesda, Md., 1964-73, dir. Clin. Ctr., 1974-75; vis. prof. U. Md. Med. Sch., 1975-76; spl. asst. to dir. NIH, Bethesda, Md., from 1976. Editorial bd.: Jour. Lipid Rsch., 1965-68, Controlled Clin. Trials, from 1980. Mem. Am. Physiol. Soc., Am. Soc. Clin. Investigation, Am. Fedn. Clin. Rsch., Assn. Am. Physicians, Am. Gastroenterol. Assn., Soc. Epidemiol. Rsch., Am. Geriatrics Soc., Soc. Clin. Trials (v.p. 1979-81, pres. 1981-83). Republican. Episcopalian. Home: Kensington Md. Died Aug. 2, 1985.

GORDON, WALTER LOCKHART, Canadian government official; b. Toronto, Ont., Can., Jan. 27, 1906; s. Harry D.L. and Kathleen H. (Cassels) G.; m. Elizabeth Marjorie Leith Counsell, 1932; children: Kyra (Mrs. Jean Montagu), Jane (Mrs. William Glassco), John Counsell Lockhart. Ed., Upper Can. Coll. With Clarkson, Gordon & Co. (chartered accts.), 1927-63, ptnr., 1935-63; ptnr. Woods & Gordon (mgmt. cons.), 1940-63; M.P. from Toronto-Davenport Ho. of Commons, 1962-63; minister fin. Can. Govt., Ottawa, 1963-65; mem. Can. Govt., 1967-87, pres., 1967-68; chmn. bd. dirs., past pres. Can. Corp. Mgmt. Co. Ltd., 1968-87; assisted with orgn. Fgn. Exchange Control Bd., 1939; spl. asst. to dep. minister fin., 1940-42; pres. Toronto Bd. Trade, 1947; chmn. nat. exec. com. Can. Inst. Internat. Affairs, 1951-56; chmn. Royal Commn. Adminstrv. Classification in Pub. Service, 1946, Royal Commn. Can.'s Econ. Prospects, 1955, Com. Orgn. Govt. Ont., 1958. Author: Troubled Canada—The Need for New Domestic Policies, 1961, A Choice for Canada—Independence or Colonial Status, 1966. Chmn. nat. campaign Liberal Party, 1962, 63; bd. govs. U. Toronto, 1945-63. Died Mar. 21, 1987.

GORDY, WALTER, physics educator; b. Miss., Apr. 20, 1909; s. Walter Kalin and Gertrude (Jones) G.; m. Vida Brown Miller, June 19, 1935; children: Eileen, Walter Terrell. A.B., Miss. Coll., 1932, LL.D., 1959; M.A., U. N.C., 1933, Ph.D., 1935; Dr. honoris causa, U. Lille, France, 1955; D.Sc. hon., Emory U., 1983. Assoc. prof. math. and physics Mary Hardin-Baylor Coll., 1935-41; NRC fellow Calif. Inst. Tech., 1941-42; staff radiation lab. Mass. Inst. Tech., 1942-46; assoc. prof. physics Duke, Durham, N.C., 1946-48; prof. Duke, 1948-79, James B. Duke prof., 1958-79, James B. Duke prof. emeritus, 1979-85; Vis. prof. U. Tex., 1958; Mem. NRC, 1954-57, 68-74. Author: (with W.V. Smith, R.F. Trambarulo) Microwave Spectroscopy, 1953, (with Robert L. Cook) Microwave Molecular Spectra, 1970, 3d edit., 1984, Theory and Applications of Electron Spin Resonance, 1980; assoc. editor: Jour. Chem. Physics, 1954-58, Spectrochimia Acta, 1957-60; editorial bd.: Radiation Research, 1969-72. Recipient Sci. research award Oak Ridge Inst. Nuclear Studies, 1949, Disting. Alumnus award U. N.C., 1976, N.C. award for sci., 1979; 50th Anniversary award Miss. Acad. Scis., 1980. Fellow Am. Phys. Soc. (chmn. S.E. sect. 1953-54, mem. council 1967-71, 73-77, recipient Jesse W. Beams award Southeastern sect. 1974, Earle K. Plyler prize 1980), AAAS (council 1955); mem. Radiation Research Soc. (mem. council 1961-64), Nat. Acad. Scis., Sigma Xi. Home: Durham N.C. Died Oct. 6, 1985; cremated.

GORMAN, JOHN LEONARD, newspaper executive; b. Palmyra, N.Y., May 8, 1906; s. Walter J. and Margaret E. (Hickey) G.; m. Mary Elizabeth Edwards, Aug. 23, 1934 (dec. Dec. 1955); children: Jane (dec.), John, Ann (Mrs. Timothy T. Schenk); m. Mary Lighthall Verbeck, Dec. 30, 1957 (dec. Aug. 1977); stepchildren: K. Channing, Pieter L.; m. Iva A. Holzwarth, June 10, 1983; stepchildren: Bruce, Paul F., Anne E. Holzwarth Hutchins. Grad., Syracuse U., 1929. Reporter Syracuse (N.Y.) Herald, 1929; with pub. rels. dept. Syracuse U., 1930-32; copy reader Syracuse Post-Standard, 1933-41, editorial writer, 1941-47, city editor, 1947-53, mng. editor, 1953-59, exec. editor, 1959-60, 66-83, editor, 1960-66, exec. editor emeritus, 1983-85. Mem. N.Y. State Fair adv. com.; bd. dirs. Syracuse Cerebral Palsy Clinic, N.Y. State div. Am. Cancer Soc., Onondaga chpt. ARC; trustee Syracuse and Onondaga County Pub. Library. Mem. Syracuse C. of C. (bd. dirs.), AP Mng. Editors Assn., N.Y. AP Assn. (pres. 1956), Am. Soc. Newspaper Editors, N.Y. Soc. Newspaper Editors (pres. 1960-61), Syracuse U. Library Assocs., Rotary, Syracuse Press Club, University Club, Pi Delta Epsilon, Sigma Delta Chi, Phi Kappa. Republican. Roman Catholic. Home: Syracuse N.Y. Died Sept. 19, 1985; buried Oakwood Cemetery, Syracuse, N.Y.

GORODNITZKI, SASCHA, pianist, educator; b. Kiev, Russia, May 24, 1906; s. Ossip Borisovitch and Eugenia Samilovna (Von Stein) G.; m. Virginia Waite Henderson, Oct. 2, 1942; 1 dau., Diane Sue. Student, Inst. Mus. Art, N.Y.C., 1919-24; grad., Juilliard Sch. Music, 1932. Tchr. master classes Summer Sch. Juilliard Sch. Music., N.Y.C., 1932-42, mem. maj. piano faculty, 1948-86; tchr. master classes Temple U. Music Festival and Inst., 1968-70; recordings for Columbia, Capital, Pickwick Records; mem. jury internat. piano competitions. Soloist debut N.Y. Philharm., 1930; ann. recitals Carnegie Hall, 1931-53; ann. concert tour N.Am., 1931-86; appeared with U.S. symphony orchs., Phila., Chgo., Cleve., Cin., Pitts., Rochester, Balt., St. Louis, Detroit, Denver, Dallas, Houston, Nat. Symphony Orch., Washington, many others. Mem. The Bohemians. Home: New York N.Y. Died Apr. 4, 1986.

GORSLINE, GEORGE WILLIAM, computer science educator; b. Battle Creek, Mich., Dec. 19, 1923; s. James M. and Lora (Gates) G.; m. Anne Bonner, Aug. 9, 1947; children: George William, Gary B., C. Suzanne. Student, Mich. Coll. Mining and Tech., 1942-43; B.S. in Agronomy, Va. Poly. Inst., 1948; M.S., Pa. State U., 1957, Ph.D., 1959. Asst. prof. agronomy Pa. State U., 1956-63; dir. consultation, applied programming, customer relations Computer Center, Inst. Sci. and Engring., 1963-65; dir. computer center Ohio U., 1965-67; also lectr. math.; prof. computer sci. dept. Va. Poly. Inst. and State U., 1967-87. Author: Computer Organization: Hardware/Software, 1980, 2d edit., 1985, Modern Microcomputers: The INTEL I8086 Family, 1984, Assembly and Assemblers: the Motorola MC 68000 Family, 1988; contbr. articles to profl. jours. Served with AUS, 1943-45. Fellow AAAS; mem. AAUP, Assn. Computing Machinery (lectr., chmn., editor notes ACM/Sigsmall conf. and symposium), Sigma Xi, Phi Epsilon Phi, Gamma Sigma Delta, Upsilon Pi Epsilon. Home: Blacksburg Va. Died Apr. 14, 1987.

GORSUCH, JOHN ELLIOTT, lawyer; b. Denver, Sept. 2, 1899; s. John C. and Nancy (Johnson) G.; m. Freda H. Munz, Aug. 21, 1930 (dec. Sept. 1985); children: John Philip, Diane B. Kepner, David Ronald, Keith Edward. A.B., U. Denver, 1921, LL.B., 1925. Bar: Colo. 1925. Since practiced in Denver; of counsel firm Gorsuch, Kirgis, Campbell, Walker and Grover.; Lectr. U. Denver, U. Colo. Law Sch., Southwestern Legal Found. Life trustee Legal Aid Soc. Denver; vice chmn. Non-Ferrous Metals Commn., Nat. War Labor Bd.; Mem. adv. bd. Denver YWCA.; Bd. dirs. Denver Community Chest; life trustee U. Denver, Florence Crittendon Home; bd. govs. Presbyn. Hosp.; mem. adv. bd. Mt. Airy Hosp. Recipient Distinguished Law Alumni award U. Denver, 1962, Evans award, 1973, award Grad. Sch. Social Work, 1980; Distinguished Service award Denver Jaycees. Mem. Assn. Life Ins. Counsel, ABA (mem. labor law com.), Denver Bar Assn. (past pres., Award of Merit 1971), Colo. Bar Assn. (mem. bd. govs. 1947-48), Denver Symphony Soc. (past trustee), Colo. Conf. Social Workers (past pres.), Am. Arbitration Assn. (labor law com.), Nat. Acad. Arbitrators (past mem. bd. govs.), Phi Beta Kappa, Beta Theta Pi, Phi Delta Phi. Clubs: Mason, Mile High, Denver Athletic, Press, Denver Country, Kiwanis (internat. v.p.). Home: Denver Colo. Died 1987.

GORTNER, ROSS AIKEN, JR., biochemist, educator; b. Cold Spring Harbor, L.I., N.Y., June 2, 1912; s. Ross Aiken and Catherine (Willis) G.; m. Mary Priscilla Cahill, Dec. 20, 1938; children: Katherine Gortner Hood, Douglas Ross. Student (Alumni scholar), Oberlin Coll., 1929-30; A.B. magna cum laude, U. Minn., 1933, M.S., 1934; Ph.D., U. Mich., 1937; M.A. (hon.), Wesleyan U., Middletown, Conn., 1948. Faculty fellow, grad. teaching asst. U. Mich., 1934-37; faculty Wesleyan U., Middletown, Conn., 1937-80; prof. biochemistry Wesleyan U., 1948-80, prof. emeritus, 1980—; dir. Sci. Center, 1967-80; Fulbright lectr., Copenhagen, Denmark, 1954-55; vis. research prof. U. Giessen, Max Planck Inst. Biochemistry, Munich, Germany, 1961-62; asso. exec. sec. food and nutrition bd. NAS/NRC, 1943-44; dir. coll. sci. curriculum improvement program NSF, 1966-67; mem. bd. control Conn. Agrl. Expt. Sta., 1963-79, sec., 1967-79. Author: (with W. A. Gortner) Outlines of Biochemistry, 1949, (with P. E. Marsh) Federal Aid to Science Education: Two Programs, 1963; also articles. Mem. council Middlesex Meml. Hosp. Sch. Nursing, 1948-54; corporator Middlesex Meml. Hosp., 1967-75, corporator emeritus, 1975—. Served to lt. USNR, 1944-46. Fellow AAAS; mem. Am. Chem. Soc., Am. Inst. Nutrition, Conn. Acad. Sci. and Engring., Conn. Nutrition Council (chmn. 1952-54), Phi Beta Kappa, Sigma Xi, Phi Lambda Upsilon, Gamma Alpha, Alpha Chi Sigma. Club: Faculty (Middletown). Died Oct. 29, 1988.

GOSS, JAMES HASSELL, business executive; b. Paris, Ark., Sept. 22, 1907; s. Samuel and Mary Angeline (Berry) G.; m. Doris Almira Bunce, June 18, 1930; children: James Herbert, Cynthia Bunce. BSME, U. Ark., 1930; grad. advanced mgmt. program, Harvard U. Design engr. GE, West Lynn, Mass., 1931-47; asst. mgr., mgr. engring. indsl. control GE, Schenectady, N.Y., 1947-51; asst. to div. gen. mgr. small apparatus div. GE, Lynn, Mass., 1951; mgr. mfg. maj. appliance dept. GE, Louisville, 1951-53, dept. gen. mgr. home laundry dept., 1953-55; pres. Can. GE Ltd., Toronto, Ont., Can., 1955-57; v.p., group exec. GE, N.Y.C., 1957-68; pres. Automatic Sprinkler Co. of Am., 1968-71, also bd. dirs.; chmn. fin. com., vice chmn. bd. dirs. Pentasote Inc., 1972-73, chmn. bd. dirs., from 1973; bd. dirs. Internat. Nickel Co. of Can. Ltd., Tyco Labs. Inc., Am. Precision Industries. Mem. Assn. Profl. Engrs. Ont., IEEE. Home: Westbrook Conn. Deceased.

GOSS, WESLEY PERRY, mining company executive; b. Garland, Kans., Nov. 4, 1899; s. Frank Bailey and Lola May (Perry); m. Nellie F. McIntosh, Apr. 5, 1923; children: John Wesley, Patricia Caroline. BS, U. Calif., 1922. Asst. supt. United Verde Copper Co., Jerome, Ariz., 1933-34; gen. supt. Park City (Utah) Consol. Mines Co., 1934-37; mine supt. O'Kiep Copper Co., Namaqualand, Republic of South Africa, 1937-41; asst. gen. mgr. Gray Eagle Copper Co., Happay Camp, Calif., 1942-44; v.p., gen. mgr., dir. Magma Copper, 1944-53, pres., gen. mgr., dir., 1954-71, chmn. bd., dir., 1972-82, chmn. emeritus, 1983-85; v.p., gen. mgr. Magma Ariz. R.R., 1944-71, dir. from 1944, Ariz. Bd. Regents, 1963-70. Mem. Ariz. Copper Tariff Bd., AIME, Am. Mining Congress, Mining and Metall. Soc. Am., Am. Legion. Home: Tucson Ariz. Died July 13, 1985.

GOSSELIN, EDWARD N., manufacturing executive; b. Rutland, Vt., Sept. 19, 1892; s. N. and Rosalie (Abare) G.; m. Florilla Helena Webb, June 3, 1916; children: Edward Webb (dec.), Rosalie Webb (Mrs. William H. Mellick), James Webb (dec.), John Webb, Marjorie Webb (Mrs. Gerry F. Fitzgerald). PhB, Yale, 1915, ME, 1916. Pres. Gosselin Engring. Corp., New Haven, Pitts., Chgo., 1921-27; pres., gen. mgr. Phoenix Mfg. Co., Joliet, Ill., 1929-57, also bd. dirs.; chmn. bd. dirs. from 1957; pres. Graver Tank & Mfg. Co. Inc., East Chicago, Ind., 1933-56, chmn. bd. dirs., from 1957; bd. dirs. Union Nat. Bank & Trust Co., Joliet, Citizens Nat. Bank & Trust Co., Waukegan, Nat. Bank of North Chicago, North Shore Nat. Bank, Chgo. Lay trustee DePaul U., Chgo. Mem. Yale Club (N.Y.C., Chgo.), Chicago Club, Execs. Club, South Shore Country Club, Union League, Joliet Country Club, Chicago Golf Club (Wheaton, Ill.), Rolling Rock club (ligonier, Pa.). Home: Joliet Ill. †

GOTT, EDWIN HAYS, steel company executive; b. Pitts., Feb. 22, 1908; s. Leonard Hays and Isabel (Dalzell) G.; m. Mary Louise Carr, Oct. 6, 1934; children: Elizabeth C. Gott Byerly, Edwin H., Barbara D. Gott Martha. B.S. in Indsl. Engring., Lehigh U., 1929. With U.S. Steel Corp., 1937—, successively indsl. engr. Ohio Works, indsl. engr. Clairton Works, indsl. engr. Gary Steel Works, asst. div. supt. maintenance Gary Steel Works, asst. div. supt. Central Mills; asst. gen. supt. service depts., asst. gen. supt. South Works U.S.

Steel Corp., Chgo.; gen. supt. Youngstown Dist. Works U.S. Steel Corp., gen. mgr. operations-steel Youngstown Dist. Works, 1937-56, v.p. ops.-steel, 1956-58, v.p. prodn., steel producing divs., 1958-59, adminstrv. v.p. central operations, 1959, exec. v.p. prodn., 1959-67, pres., chief adminstrv. officer, 1967-68, chmn., chief exec. officer, 1969-73, dir., mem. exec., orgn. coms., 1973-80; dir. Internat. Husky, Inc.; past dir. Pitts. Baseball Club. Trustee Children's Hosp. Pitts., Lehigh U., Carnegie-Mellon U.; mem. adv. bd. Nat. Boy Scouts Am.; mem. exec. bd. Allegheny Trails council; chmn. Nat. Flag Founc.; past bd. dirs. Internat. Wilderness Leadership Found. Mem. Am. Iron and Steel Inst., Assn. Iron and Steel Engrs., Pa. Soc., Eastern States Blast Furnace and Coke Oven Assn., Western Pa. Engrs. Soc., Business Council. Clubs: Fox Chapel Golf, Duquesne (Pitts.); Longue Vue Country (Verona, Pa.); Royal Poinciana Golf, Rolling Rock, Pine Valley Golf, Naples Yacht. Home: Pittsburgh Pa. Died August 27, 1986; interred St. James Church, Lothian, Md.

GOTTLIEB, BERTRAM, industrial engineer, labor arbitrator; b. N.Y.C., Feb. 9, 1921; s. Samuel and Bessie (Halpern) G.; m. Phyllis Virginia Jacobson, Mar. 24, 1940; children—Richard Allan, Deborah Ann, Lisa Susan. B.S., Ill. Inst. Tech., 1949, M.S., 1950; post-grad., U. Wis., 1950-54. Registered profl. engr. Instr. econs. Ill. Inst. Tech., 1948-50; instr. indsl. engring. and labor relations U. Wis., 1950-54, 56-57; research prof. assigned to U. Philippines, U. Conn., 1954-56; indsl. engr. AFL-CIO, 1957-66, asst. dir. research, 1967-68; prof. bus. adminstrn. U. Iowa, 1966-67; dir. research Transp. Inst., Washington, 1968-74; Indsl. engring. cons. 1950-54, 56-57, 68-86; Labor arbitrator Fed. Mediation and Conciliation Service and Am. Arbitration Assn.; mem. tech. adv. bd. U.S. Dept. Commerce, 1957-68; mem. prodn., tech. and growth com., wages and indsl. relations com. Dept. Labor, 1957-74; mem. central com. to standardize indsl. engring. terminology Am. Nat. Standards Inst., 1964-86; investigator sex and race discrimination complaints in pvt. and govt. employment; expert witness fed. and state cts. and agys.; speaker, lectr. various univs., profl. socs., radio, TV. Contbr. articles to profl. jours., textbooks. Served with USAAF, 1943-46. Fellow Am. Inst. Indsl. Engrs. (editorial bd. 1960-72, nat. dir. div. indsl. and labor relations 1968-70, chpt. dir., mem. various coms.), Nat. Acad. Sci., Indsl. Relations Research Assn. (gov. 1966-68), Sigma Iota Epsilon. Home: Silver Spring Md. Died Jan. 2, 1986; buried Arlington (Va.) Nat. Cemetery.

GOUIN, LEON MERCIER, Canadian senator; b. Montreal, Que., Can., Dec. 24, 1891; s. Lomer and Eliza (Mercier) G.; m. Yvette Ollivier, Nov. 20, 1917; children: Elise (Mrs. Claude Fortier), Lomer (dec.), Therese (Mrs. Vianney Decarie), Ollivier. Student, St. Mary's Coll., Montreal, 1903-09; BA, Loyola Coll., Montreal, 1911; LLL, Laval U., Montreal, 1915; LLD, U. Montreal, 1920. Bar: Que. 1915; created King's counsel, 1925. Prof. law U. Montreal, 1919-63, U. Ottawa, from 1960; mem. Can. Senate from Que. Province, from 1940; bd. dirs. Credit Foncier Franco Canadien, Excelsior Life Ins. Co., Montreal City & Dist. Savs. Bank. Author: Cours de Droit Industriel, 1937, Droit d'Auteur, 1950. Capt. Can. Army, 1942-45. Decorated Legion of Honor, Instrn. Publique (France); comdr. Order St. John Jerusalem. Fellow Royal Soc. Can. Home: Montreal Que., Canada. †

GOULD, BENJAMIN Z., lawyer; b. Chgo., July 27, 1913; s. Samuel and Fanny (Tendrich) G.; m. Shirley Handleman, Nov. 22, 1942; children: Fredrick G. (dec.), Edward S., Barbara F. A.B., U. Chgo., 1935, J.D. cum laude, 1937. Bar: Ill. 1937. Practiced in Chgo.; asso. firm Gould & Ratner (and predecessors), 1937-49, sr. ptnr., 1949-86; sec., gen. counsel, dir. Henry Crown and Co., Univ. Exchange Corp., Century-Am. Corp., CHF Industries, Producers Supply Co., Stickney Terminal Corp., Monticello Realty Corp., Froning's Towing, Inc., Crown Point Envelope Co., Kratex of Troy, Inc., Kratex Products, SCNO Terminal, Inc., SCNO Barge Lines, Inc., Henderson Comp Products; sec., gen. counsel Material Service Corp. (subs. Gen. Dynamics Corp.), Marblehead Lime Co., Utah Marblehead Lime Co., Freeman United Coal Mining Co-div. Material Service Corp., Arie and Ida Crown Meml., Aberdeen Mfg. Corp., Finkel Outdoor Products, Inc., Werner-Finkel, Inc., Univ. Village Golf Course div. Univ. Exchange Corp., Thomas B. Bishop Co. div., Univ. Village Plaza div. Univ. Exchange Corp., Mills-Am. Envelope Co., Lemont Shipbldg. & Repair Co. div., Powell & Minnock Brick Works, Inc., Nu-Art, Inc., Exchange Bldg. Corp., J.S. Lock Co., Jefferson Lock Co., El Paso Sand Products, Inc., El Paso Rock Quarries, Inc., Valley Concrete Co., MLRT, Inc., Vowell Constrn. Co., Inc.; v.p., gen. counsel Standard Forgings Corp. Bd. dirs. Hebrew Theol. Coll. Chgo., Columbia Coll., North Light Repertory, Chgo. Loop Synagogue. Served with USCGR, World War II. Mem. Am. Arbitration Assn. (mem. nat. panel), Chgo. Council Fgn. Relations, Am. Soc. Corporate Secs., AIM (asso.), Internat., Am., Ill., Chgo. bar assns., Am. Soc. Internat. Law, Navy League U.S., Am. Judicature Soc., Phi Beta Kappa. Jewish (dir. Chgo. congregations). Clubs: Executive (Chgo.), Standard (Chgo.), One Hundred of Cook County (Chgo.). Home: Wilmette Ill. Died May 14, 1986, buried Shalom Cemetery, Palatine, Ill.

GOULD, CHARLES LESSINGTON, foundation executive; b. Youngstown, Ohio, Aug. 17, 1909; s. Fred Jay and Kathleen Helen (Murphy) G.; m. Peggy Ann Shannon, Mar. 30, 1951; children—Charles Lessington, Michael Edward. Spl. student, Northwestern U.; LL.D. (hon.), Golden Gate U., 1963, Western States U., 1975. Machinist Steel & Tubes, Inc., Cleve., 1927-28; engr. Am. Tel. & Tel., Cleve., 1928-29; reporter, writer, promotion mgr. Cleve. News, 1930-34; sales promotion mgr. Universal Match Corp., Chgo., 1934-35; writer, radio announcer, promotion dir. Chgo. American, 1935-42; plans dir. N.Y. Jour.-American, 1946-50, asst. pub., 1951-61; pub. San Francisco Examiner, 1961-75; San Francisco News Call Bull., 1962-65; v.p. William Randolph Hearst Found. and Hearst Found., 1975-86. Bd. govs. San Francisco Bay Area Council, United Bay Area Crusade, San Francisco Symphony Assn.; bd. dirs. San Francisco Boys' Club, Fine Arts Mus., San Francisco Conv. and Visitors Bur., Bay Area U.S.O., Ft. Point Museum Assn., Calif. Jockey Club Found., Louis R. Lurie Found.; bd. regents St. Mary's Coll., St. Ignatius Coll. Prep.; trustee Golden Gate U., U. San Francisco. Served from lt. (j.g.) to capt. USNR, 1942-46; dir. combat photography U.S. Navy, 1950-51, Korea; capt. Res. ret. Decorated D.S.M., Bronze Star, Air medal; recipient gold medal award Freedoms Found., 1964, 65, 70, 71, 72, 73. Mem. Navy League (nat. dir.), Knights Malta. Clubs: Commonwealth (San Francisco), Bohemian (San Francisco); N.Y. Athletic. Home: Hillsborough Calif. Died Nov. 23, 1986.

GOVAN, GILBERT EATON, librarian, editor; b. Atlanta, Apr. 28, 1892; s. William J. and Kate (Eaton) G.; m. Mary Christine Noble, June 10, 1918; children: Emmy Payne (Mrs. James G. West), Mary Quintard (Mrs. William O. Steele), James F. Student, Ga. Inst. Tech., 1908-11; DLitt, Tenn. Wesleyan Coll., 1959. Bookseller 1918-34; book rev. editor Chattanooga Times, from 1931; libr. U. Chattanooga, from 1934; assoc. editor Sewanee Rev., 1941-46. Author: (with James W. Livingood) University of Chattanooga, 60 Years, 1947, Chattanooga Country, 1540-1951, From Tomahawks to TVA, 1952, A Different Valor, General Joseph E. Johnston, C.S.A., 1956; co-editor: The Haskell Memoirs, 1969; contbr. to profl. jours. Adv. coun. U.S. Civil War Centennial Commn., Tenn. Hist. Commn., Tenn. Civil War Centennial Commn. Mem. ALA, Music., Southeastern, Tenn. libr. assns., Am. Anthrop. Assn., Nat. Assn. Secondary Sch. Prins., Soc. Am. Historians, So. Hist. Assn., Southeaster Modern Lang. Assn., Tenn. (past v.p.), East Tenn. (past v.p.), Chattanooga Area (past pres.) hist. socs. Democrat. Episcopalian. Home: Lookout Mountain Tenn. †

GOVAN, MARY CHRISTINE NOBLE, author; b. N.Y.C., Dec. 12, 1898; d. Stephen Edward and Mary Helen (Quintard) Noble; m. Gilbert Eaton Govan, June 10, 1918; children: Emily P. Govan West, Mary Q. Govan Steele, James Fauntleroy. writer, from 1928; author: Those Plummer Children, 1934, Murder on the Mountain, 1937, Plantation Murder, 1938, The Shadow and the Web (as Mary Allerton), 1939, Murder in the House With the Blue Eyes (as J.N. Darby), 1939, Jennifer's House, 1945, Finnish transl., 1946, The Pink Maple House, 1950, The Surprising Summer, 1951, Tilly's Strange Secret, 1953, The Superduper Car, 1953, Rachel Jackson , 1955, Mystery at Shingle Rock, 1955, The Year the River Froze, 1960, Mystery at the Mountain Face, 1956, Mystery at Mocassin Bend, 1957, Mystery at the Indian Hide-Out, 1957, Mystery at the Deserted Mill, 1958, Mystery of the Vanishing Stamp, 1958, Mystery at the Haunted House, 1959, Mystery at Plum Nelly, 1959, Mystery at Fearsom Lake, 1960, Mystery at Rock City, 1960, Mystery at the Wierd Ruins, 1964 (all with Emmy Govan West); author: Mystery of the Dancing Skeleton, 1960, Mystery of the Snowed-in Cabin, 1961, Willow Landing, 1961, The Delectable Mountain, 1962, Number 5 Hackberry Street, 1964, Mystery at the Echoing Cave, 1965, Return to Hackberry Street, 1967, Curious Clubhouse, 1967, Phinny's Fine Summer World, 1968, Mr. Alexander and the Witch, 1969, The Trash-Pile Treasure, 1970, Danger Down River, 1975; short stories: Miss Winters and the Wind in anthologies O. Henry Prize Collection, 1947, Timeless Stories for Today and Tomorrow in Stories Not for the Nervous, 1965, I Had Known Carrie for Years in Writing Books for Boys and Girls, 1952; book reviewer Chattanooga Times; contbr. to newspapers and mags; lectr. Home: Lookout Mountain Tenn. Deceased.

GRAD, HAROLD, applied mathematician; b. N.Y.C., Jan. 14, 1923; s. Herman and Helen (Selinger) G.; m. Betty Jane Miller, Jan. 23, 1949; children: Hilary Lynn Grad Goldberg, Michael Jonathan. BEE, Cooper Union, 1943; MS, NYU, 1945, PhD, 1948. Research asst. NYU, 1944-48, faculty, 1948-86, founder, dir. magneto-fluid dynamics div. Courant Inst., 1956-80, prof. math., 1957-86; mem. adv. com. fusion energy Oak Ridge Nat. Lab., 1964-67, 73-76; dir. Space Scis., Inc., 1966-71; vis. disting. prof. Faculty Sci., Nagoya U., Japan, 1981; cons. to industry and U.S. govt. Contbr. monographs to profl. jours.; mem. editorial bd. Physics of Fluids, 1968-71, Jour. Statis. Physics, 1969-75, Internat. Jour. Engring. Sci., 1963-86. Guggenheim fellow, 1981-82. Fellow AAAS, Am. Phys. Soc. (chmn. fluid dynamics div. 1963, chmn. plasma physics div. 1968, James Clerk Maxwell prize 1986); mem. NAS, Soc. Engring. Scis. (bd. dirs. 1963-74, Eringem medal 1982), N.Y. Acad. Scis. (bd. govs. 1979-86, Pregel award 1970), Am. Math. Soc., Soc. Indsl. and Applied Math., Soc. Natural Philosophy. Home: New Rochelle N.Y. Died Nov. 17, 1986; buried Sharon Gardens, Valhalla, N.Y.

GRADWOHL, BERNARD SAM, lawyer; b. St. Joseph, Mo., Apr. 5, 1905; s. Ben W. and Hattie (Hilpp) G.; m. Elaine Mayer, June 21, 1928; children: John Mayer, David Mayer. AB, U. Nebr., 1923, JD cum laude, 1924; LLM, Columbia U., 1925. Bar: Nebr. 1926. Pvt. practice Lincoln, Nebr., from 1926; nat. exec. sec. Am. Interprofl. Inst., editor quar., 1942-66, pres., 1966-67, pres. Lincoln chpt., 1948-49. Nat. adv. bd. Am. Council Judaismn 1944-68, co-chmn. nat. com. religious programs, 1949-58, mem. exec. com., 1954-58; bd. dirs. Lincoln Social Welfare Soc., 1944-45; exec. council Nebr. Welfare Assn., 1947-49; past pres. Open Forum Club; past chmn. bd. Lincoln NCCJ; chmn. Nebraskans Say America is Beuatiful Com., from 1970. Mem. ABA, Nebr. Bar Assn., Lincoln Bar Assn. (past treas.), Nebr. Fire Fighters (hon.), Lincoln C. of C., Izaak Walton League, Hillcrest Country Club (past pres.), Masons, Shriners, Phi Beta Kappa, Order of Coif, Delta Sigma Rho. Home: Lincoln Nebr. Died Aug. 24, 1985; buried Lincoln, Nebr.

GRADY, JOHN HENRY, computer company executive; b. San Mateo, Calif., Jan. 10, 1928; s. John H. and Monica (Klatt) G.; m. Alexandra Diepenbrock, Dec. 29, 1956; children: Kathleen, John Henry, Carolyn, James. A.A., Coll. San Mateo, 1949; B.S., U. Calif. at Berkeley, 1951. With Am. President Lines, 1951-52; with IBM, Armonk, N.Y., 1952-87, dir. stockholder relations, 1963-65, asst. sec., 1965-70, sec., 1970-85; v.p., sec. IBM, Armonk, 1985-87. Served with AUS, 1945-47. Mem. Am. Soc. Corp. Secs., Stockholder Relations Soc. N.Y. Died May 31, 1987; buried Putnam Cemetery, Greenwich, Conn.

GRADY, PAUL DAVIS, insurance executive; b. Seven Springs, N.C., Sept. 5, 1891; s. James Calhoun and Ella Smith (Outlaw) G.; m. Lelia Grace Swink, June 10, 1909; children: Eloise (Mrs. Elbert S. Eskridge), Elsie, Paul Davis, James C., Fred. Student, Tenn. Mil. Inst., 1907-08, Wake Forest Coll., 1910-11; grad., Washington and Lee U., 1910. Bar: N.C. 1911. Pres. N.C. Warehouse Corp., 1925-32; v.p. N.C. Cotoon Growers Corp., 1944-49; state consul Modern Woodmen Am.; chmn. Nationwide Mutual Fire Ins. Co., Columbus, Ohio; bd. dirs. N.C. Farmers Coop. Exchange, Farm Bur. Ins. Co., Tectum Corp., Newark, Ohio, Peoples Broadcasting Co., Worthington, Ohio, Peoples Devel. Co., Columbus, Alliance Mfg. Co., Coop. League of U.S., Chgo. Chmn. bd. edn., Kenly, N.C.; mem. N.C. Senate, 1923-25, 33-35, pres. Senate, 1935; county atty., 1935; candidate for gov., 1940; mem. Presdl. Electoral Coll., 1944. Home: Kenly N.C. †

GRADY, ROY ISRAEL, chemistry professor; b. East Union, Ohio, Dec. 18, 1890; s. Josiah Milburn and Carrie Augusta (Mackey) G.; m. Mary Jane Hair, July 19, 1916; children: Dorothy Jane, Harold Roy. BS, Coll. of Wooster, 1916; MS, Ohio State U., 1923, PhD, 1923. With Coll. of Wooster, Ohio, from 1918, instr. in chemistry, 1918-20, asst. prof., 1923-23, prof. and head of dept., from 1923, acting dean, 1954-55. Recipient award for excellence in chemistry teaching Mfg. Chemists Assn., 1959. Fellow AAAS, Ohio Acad. Sci.; mem. Am. Chem. Soc. (councillor) (pres. Wooster sect. 1941-43), Ohio Chemistry Tchrs. Assn. (pres. 1932-35), N.E. Assn. Chemistry Tchrs., Nat. Farm Chemurgic Coun., Wayne County Hist. Soc. (pres. from 1959), Kiwanis (past pres.), Phi Beta Kappa, Sigma Xi, Theta Chi Delta. Republican. Presbyterian. Home: Wooster Ohio. †

GRAEFE, JAMES ARTHUR, clergyman; b. Rajamundry, India, Mar. 20, 1924; came to U.S., 1937; s. John E. and Wilhelmina (Beyer) G.; m. Eleanor M. Stroehmann, June 9, 1946; children: John, David, Thomas, Stephen. B.A., Gettysburg Coll., Pa., 1947; M Div., Lutheran Theol. Sem., Phila., 1950; D.D. hon., Upsala Coll., East Orange, N.J., 1974. Ordained to ministry Luth. Ch. Am., 1950; pastor Ascension Luth. Ch., Lancaster, Pa., 1950-53, Salem Luth. Ch., Phila., 1953-59, Resurrection Luth. Ch., Mt. Kisco, N.Y., 1959-69; bishop Met. N.Y. Synod Luth. Ch. Am., N.Y.C., 1969-88; mem. council Theol. Edn. in the N.E. Bd., 1969-88. Bd. dirs. Wagner Coll., S.I., N.Y., 1969-88; bd. dirs. Phila. Sem., 1969-88. Served with U.S. Army, 1943-46. Named Man of Yr. Mt. Kisco Village Bd., 1969. Lodge: Lions (Mt. Kisco). Home: Dobbs Ferry N.Y. Died June 18, 1988.

GRAF, JULIUS EICHER, engineer; b. Pitts., Aug. 23, 1891; s. Henry and Elizabeth (Theis) G.; m. Mabelle E. Bliss, Oct. 2, 1912; children: Florence Elizabeth (Mrs. James E. Robinson), Norman Theron. Student, Carnegie Inst. Tech., 1910-14, Caton Tech. Sch., 1915-16. File clk. advancing to chief engr. Am. Sheet & Tin Plate Co., 1910-36; asst. chief engr. Carnegie-Ill. Steel Corp., 1936-39; v.p. Treadwell Engring. Co., Easton, Pa., 1939-40, from 1954, dir., from 1939; asst. chief engr. Jones & Laughlin Steel Corp., Pitts., 1940-47, chief engr., 1947-54. Vice chmn. Ally County San. Authority, from 1955; civilian chief engr. metals secst, Milt. Govt., German, 1945-46. Decorated Medal of Freedom. Mem.

Engr. Soc. Western Pa. (past pres.), ASME, Am. Iron and Steel Inst., Assn. Iron and Steel Engrs., Pitts. C. of C., Am. Ordnance Assn., Masons, Ashourne Hill Club (Warwickshire, Eng.); Duquesne Club (Pitts.), Delta Sigma Phi. Home: Pittsburgh Pa. †

GRAF, PAUL LUTHER, clergyman; b. North Lima, Ohio, Oct. 22, 1914; s. John Henry and Henrietta Augusta Louisa (Tiemann) G.; m. Ruth Esther Baer, Oct. 30, 1933; children: Paul, James, Karen, Kristin, Ruth Anne, Jon. AB, Thiel Coll., 1936, DD, 1954; BD, Northwestern Luth. Theol. Sem., Mpls., 1940, M.Div., 1971. Ordained to ministry Luth. Ch., 1940. Pastor Faith Luth. Ch., Walters, Minn., 1940-42, Trinity Luth. Ch., Kenosha, Wis., 1942-48; sterwardship dir. Evang. Luth. Synod of NW, 1948-50; pastor Holy Trinity Luth. Ch., Mpls., 1950-69; dir. Luth. Social Service Minn. Found., from 1969; pres. bd. world missions Luth. Ch. Am., 1958-64, mem. bd. Am. missions, 1966-72, mem. div. for mission in N.Am.; pres. bd. social ministry Minn. Synod, 1963-69; chmn. directing com. Luth. Evangelism Mission U.S. and Can., 1956-57; del. Constituting Conv., Luth. Ch. Am.; v.p. Luth Social Services of Minn., 1960-69. Mem. Alcoholic Task Force Hennepin County; pres. Day Activity and Tng. Ctr. Council Hennepin County, 1965-70, Minn. Synod Housing Corp.; chmn. Twin City Met. Strategy com.; pres. bd. dirs. Minn. Vols. Am.; bd. dirs. Martin Luther Manor, Mpls., Bethesda Hosp., St. Paul, 1967-69. Home: Minneapolis Minn. Deceased.

GRAHAM, JAMES ARTHUR, manufacturing executive; b. McComas, W.Va., Feb. 3, 1925; s. John Arthur and Ethel (Purdy) G.; m. Elizabeth Adele Wiegand, May 30, 1948. BSMechE, W.Va. U., 1949. Corp. mgr. prodn. SKF Industries, Phila., 1949-60; gen. mgr. bearings Bearings Co. Am., Lancaster, Pa., 1960-65; v.p., group gen. mgr. Standard Pressed Steel, Southfield, Mich., 1965-66; v.p., dir. mktg. tech. devel. Standard Pressed Steel, Jenkintown, Pa., 1966-71; pres. indsl. and automotive groups Gulf & Western, Southfield, 1972-80; pres., chief operating officer Sheller-Globe Corp., Toledo, from 1980, also bd. dirs. Lt. USAAF, 1943-46. Mem. Tau Beta Pi, Pi Tau Sigma. Republican. Presbyterian. Clubs: Detroit Athletic; Plum Hollow Country (Southfield, Mich.); Farmington Country (Charlottesville, Va.). Died Apr. 18, 1987.

GRAHAM, ROBERT, animal pathologist; b. Ames, Iowa, July 16, 1888; s. Thomas and Myra Louise (Hoover) G.; m. Lucy Keller Hutchcraft, Aug. 30, 1917; children: Robert Donald, Mary Gordon. DVM, Iowa State Coll., 1910; BS, U. Ky., 1912. Prof. vet. sci. U. Ky., 1911-17; veterinarian Ky. State Bd. of Health, 1912-15; pathologist Ky. State Live Stock Sanitary Bd., 1915-17; prof. animal pathology and hygiene U. Ill., 1917-45; dean Coll. Vet. Medicine, U. Ill., 1946-56; cons. FDA from 1948; spl. investigations in animal diseases, Haiti, 1924-25. Author various expt. sta. bulls. and scientific papers. Capt. Vet. Corps, U.S. Army, World War; maj. Res., ret. Mem. AAAS, Am. Pub. Health Assn., Ill. Acad. Sci., Am. Vet. Med. Assn., U.S. Live Stock Sanitary Assn., Masons, Shriners, Beta Theta Pi, Alpha Zeta, Sigma Xi, Phi Zeta. Episcopalian. Home: Urbana Ill. †

GRAHAM, WILLIAM ROGER, history educator; b. Montreal, Que., Can., Mar. 10, 1919; s. William Crieghton and Ella Gertrude (Cook) G.; m. Kathleen Winnifred McGirr, Oct. 21, 1942; children: David, Nancy. BA, U. Man., 1941; MA, U.Toronto, 1945, PhD, 1950; LLD (hon.), U. Winnipeg, 1969. Instr. to prof. U. Sask., Regina, Can., 1947-58, Saskatoon, Can., 1958-68; Douglas prof. Can. history Queens U., Kingston, Ont., Can., from 1968. Author: Arthur Meighan, A Biography, 3 vols., 1960, 63, 65, The King-Byng Affair: A Question of Responsible Government, 1968. Guggenheim Found. fellow, 1961-62, Can. Council sr. fellow, 1966-67. Mem. Can. Hist. Assn. (pres. 1970-71). Home: Kingston Ont., Canada. Died Nov. 17, 1988; buried Glenburnie, Ont., Can.

GRALTON, RICHARD T., diversified company executive; b. 1930. BA, Holy Cross Coll., 1954; MBA, Harvard U., 1956. Pres., chief oper. officer, dir. Lenox Inc., 1974-75; gen. mgr. audio elec. products dept. Gen. Electric Co., 1971-74, gen. mgr. home laundry product dept., 1975-77, v.p., gen. mgr. major appliance product mgmt. div., 1977-78, v.p., gen. mgr. major appliance sales and distbn. ops., 1978-79, v.p., gen. mgr. major appliance mktg. ops., 1979-82; pres., dir. Savin Corp., Valhalla, N.Y., from 1982. Home: Stamford Conn. Died Dec. 6, 1985.

GRAM, MOLTKE STEFANUS, philosophy educator; b. Waterloo, Iowa, Apr. 23, 1938; s. Moltke Stefanus and Dorothy (Foreman) G. Student, U. Kiel, Fed. Republic Germany, 1959-60; B.A. summa cum laude, Ind. U., Bloomington, 1960, Ph.D., 1966; postgrad., U. Heidelberg, Fed. Republic Germany, 1963-64. Instr. Ind. U., Bloomington, 1964-65; asst. prof. philosophy Northwestern U., Evanston, Ill., 1965-69; assoc. prof. U. Iowa, Iowa City, 1969-75, prof., from 1975; cons. NEH, 1977-79. Author: Direct Realism, 1983, The Transcendental Turn, 1984, Kant, Ontology and the Apriori, (Choice award one of best acad. books of yr. 1970), 1968; editor: Interpreting Kant, 1981, Kant: Disputed Questions, 1984, The Ontological Turn, 1974; exec. editor series in analytical philosophy, Northwestern U. Press, 1969-73. Fulbright fellow, 1963-64; Guggenheim fellow, 1970-71. Mem. Am. Philos. Assn. Home: Iowa City Iowa. Deceased.

GRAMBSCH, PAUL VICTOR, business management educator; b. Dayton, Ohio, Mar. 14, 1919; s. Rinold Herman and Victoria Catherine (Danecker) G.; m. Ada Elizabeth Branch, June 20, 1945; children: E. Donald, Paul Victor, Kathryn, Nancy, Richard, William, Anne, Mary. BA, North Cen. Coll., 1941; MA, U. Miss., 1947; DBA, Ind. U., 1955. Instr. Equality (Ill.) Twp. High Sch., 1940-42; asst. prof., acting chmn. dept. econs. U. Miss., 1948-50; assoc. prof. mgmt. Tulane U. Sch. Bus. Adminstrn., 1952-60, dean, 1956-60; dean Sch. Bus. Adminstrn., U. Minn., 1960-70, prof mgmt., 1970-84; mgmt. cons., educator cons. U.S. GAO; dir. rsch. project on univ. goals Ford Found., 1970-71; pub. interest dir. Fed. Home Loan Bank, Des Moines, 1971-78, chmn., 1972-78; bd. dirs. DTL-Tech. Inc., Midwest Fed. Savs. & Loan, Mpls., McQuay-Perfex Inc. Author: (with E. Gross) University Goals and Academic Power, Changes in University Organization, 1964-71. Mem. Gov.'s Adv. Commn. to Dept. Bus. Devel., 1961-63, Upper Midwest Regional Export Expansion Council; chmn. Gov.'s Tax Study Com., 1962; trustee Seabury Press. Lt. USNR, 1942-46. Fellow Acad. Mgmt.; mem. Inst. Mgmt. Scis., Fin. Execs. Inst., Strategic Mgmt. Soc., Mpls. C. of C., Rotary, Campus Club, Beta Gamma Sigma, Delta Sigma Pi. Episcopalian. Home: Minneapolis Minn. Died Nov. 12, 1984; inurned Cathedral Ch. of St. Mark Columbarium, Mpls.

GRAMSTORFF, EMIL ANTON, civil engineer; b. Everett, Mass., Apr. 23, 1892; s. Johann Christian Emil and Christine Agnes (Schroth) G.; m. Grace Mae Cribby, Nov. 11, 1916 (dec. Mar. 1931); children: Catherine MacGregor (Mrs. Howard Perkins Munday), Jane (Mrs. Gerald McLain Hargraves), Ann; m. 2d, Apphia Pauline Manning, June 27, 1934. BS, MIT, 1917, MS, 1936. Registered engr. Commonwealth of Mass., 1942. Contractor J.C.E. Gramstorff & Son, Boston, 1920-21; instr. in civil engring. Northeastern U., 1921-23, asst. pof., 1923-26, assoc. prof., 1926-39, prof. and chmn. dept. civil engring., from May 1939, dean of grad. sch. engring., from 1954. lt. (j.g.) constrn. corps, USN, Nov. 1917-July 1918; lt., July 1918, Apr. 1920. Chmn. tech. adv. com. Mass. Com. on Pub. Safety and chief bomb reconnaissance officer, State of Mass, during World War II.; chmn. tech. com. City of Boston, com on pub. safety, 1943-45; mem. city planning bd., City of Boston, 1940-46. Mem. ASCE, (pres. Northeastern sect., 1947, chmn. com. student chpts., 1947), Am. Soc. for Testing Materials (chmn. N.E. Coun. 1956-57), Am. Concrete Inst., Am. Soc. Engring. Edn. (past chmn. evening edn. div.), Boston Soc. C.E (past pres.), Masons, Tau Beta Pi. Republican. Congregationalist. Home: Boston Mass. †

GRANT, BENJAMIN WILLIAM, investment economist; b. Lawrence, Mass., Aug. 21, 1888; s. David Stuart and Mary Jane (Nice) G.; m. Violet England Rowell, Oct. 28, 1920; children: Benjamin W., Robert E., Richard W. BS, Wesleyan U., 1912; BCS, NYU, 1917. Instr. Gunnery Sch., Washington, Conn., 1912-14, Brunswick Sch., Greenwich, Conn., 1914-17; Albany rep. Lee, Higginson Co., 1918-32; cons. Albany office Kidder, Peabody & Co., from 1932. Trustee Wesleyan U., Middletown, Conn. 2d lt. USCG, 1918. Mem. C. of C., St. Andrew's Soc., Albany, Albany Country Club, University Club (Albany), Rotary, Delta Tau Delta. Home: Albany N.Y. †

GRANT, CARY, actor; b. Bristol, Eng., Jan. 18, 1904; came to U.S., 1921, naturalized, 1942; s. Elias and Elsie (Kingdom) Leach; m. Virginia Cherill, Feb. 1934 (div. Sept. 1934); m. Barbara Hutton, July 8, 1942 (div. Aug. 1945); m. Betsy Drake; m. Dyan Cannon, July 22, 1965 (div.); 1 dau., Jennifer; m. Barbara Harris, 1981. Student, Fairfield Acad., Somerset, Eng., 1914-19. dir. Faberge, Inc., Hollywood Park, Inc., Metro-Goldwyn-Mayer, Inc.; dir. emeritus Western Airlines. Began as actor in New York, 1921; played in: Street Singer, Nikki, Golden Dawn, Polly Boom Boom, Wonderful Night; starred in motion pictures: Walk, Don't Run, Mr. Lucky, Arsenic and Old Lace, Destination Tokyo, None But the Lonely Heart, The Bishop's Wife, I Was a Male War Bride, The Bachelor and the Bobby Soxer, Every Girl Should Be Married, Crisis, People Will Talk, Room for One More, Monkey Business, Dream Wife, To Catch a Thief, An Affair to Remember, Indiscreet, Houseboat, North By Northwest, Suspicion, Notorious, The Philadelphia Story, The Grass is Greener, Operation Petticoat, That Touch of Mink, Charade, Father Goose. Bd. govs. USO. Recipient Spl. Academy award for contbns. to film industry Acad. Motion Picture Arts and Scis., 1969, Kennedy Center honors medal, 1981. Mem. Ch. of Eng. Home: Beverly Hills Calif. Died Nov. 29, 1986.

GRANT, EDWARD DONALD, chemical manufacturing executive; b. Glasgow, Scotland, June 18, 1897; came to U.S., 1909, naturalized, 1922; s. Charles and Jemina (McDonald) G.; m. Georgia Voyles, July 14, 1921; 1 child, Edward Donald. AB, Austin Coll., Sherman, Tex., 1920, LittD, 1933; postgrad., YMCA Grad. Sch., 1924-25; MA, George Peabody Coll. for Tchrs., 1929; LHD (hon.), Southwestern U. at Memphis, 1954. Profl. fund raiser 1920-21; sec. edn. and promotion Fgn. Mission Bd., Presbyn. Ch. in U.S., 1921-34; also acting sec. Com. on Stewardship and Fin., 1931-35; exec. sec. Bd. Edn., Richmond, Va., 1934-52; mem. personnel bd. City of Richmond, 1950-52; dir. instns. State of La., 1952-58; pres. Grant Chem. Co., 1958-69; chmn. bd. dirs. Grant-Lehr Corp., 1962-65; sec.-treas. Gramor Chems Inc., 1965-68; chmn. bd. dirs., pres. Roadways Internat. Corp.; treas. Plasticos Y Estabalizadores (S.A.) Mex. Author: The Ambassador Supreme, 1933. Pres. Baton Rouge YMCA, 1969, 70; past pres. Am. Leprosy Missions Inc.; moderator Presbyn. Ch. in U.S., 1962-63, dir. bd. ch. extension, 1959-67; del. Internat. Missionary Council, Madras, India, 1938, World Council of Christian Edn., Birmingham, Eng., 1947. 2d lt. U.S. Army, 1918. Recipient Pub. Service award La. Coll., 1954, La. Mental Health award, 1955, La. Brotherhood medal, 1976, Kiwanis Dist. Layman's award, 1976, Austin Coll. Founders award, 1976, Americanism award DAR, 1978, Golden Deeds award, 1978; named La. Outstanding Naturalized Citizen, 1978. Mem. Phi Delta Kappa, Masons. Democrat. Home: Baton Rouge La. Died Nov. 13, 1985; buried Baton Rouge, La.

GRANT, JOHN BENJAMIN, lawyer; b. Willimantic, Conn., May 1, 1908; s. Frederick Benjamin and Ida (Lincoln) G.; m. Eleanor Quin, July 14, 1934; children: John Benjamin, Frances Grant Moore, Judith Grant McMeekin, Eleanor Grant Grave. B.A., Yale U., 1930, LL.B., 1932. Bar: Conn. 1933, R.I. 1975. Practiced in New Haven from 1933; mem. firm Tyler, Cooper, Grant, Bowerman & Keefe, 1944-81; of counsel Tyler, Cooper & Alcorn, from 1981; instr. law New Haven Coll., 1942-46; dir. F.D. Grave & Son Inc.; sec., dir. Conn. Radio Found. Inc., 1944-67. U.S. concilliation commr. in farm bankruptcies, 1942-46; judge Orange Town Ct., 1939-43; mem. bd., sec. Orange Zoning Commn., 1941-51. Mem. Am., Conn., R.I., New Haven bar assns., Newcomen Soc. N.Am., Phi Alpha Delta. Episcopalian (past vestry). Clubs: Point Judith Country (Narragansett, R.I.); Quinnipiack (New Haven); Port Malabar Country (Palm Bay, Fla.). Home: New Haven Conn. Deceased.

GRANT, M. EARL, savings and loan association executive; b. Parkersburg, W.Va., May 23, 1891; s. Jerry William and Mamie (Brock) G.; m. Flora Cathryn Davis, Sept. 1, 1935; 1 son, Donald David. Ed., Sumner Sch. Various positions Rock Island R.R., 1913-23; owner refuse collection firm Pasadena, Calif., 1923-60; founder, chmn. bd., pres. Broadway Fed. Savs. and Loan, L.A., from 1947, Watts Savs. and Loan, L.A., from 1949, Family Savs. and Loan Assn., L.A., from 1954; hog rancher Calif., 1925-52. Organizer So. Area Boys Club, L.A., 1956. Recipient Silver Beaver award Boy Scouts Am., Achievement award L.A. chpt. Nat. Assn. Market Developers, citation Am. Savs. and Loan League, citation L.A. Brotherhood Crusade. Mem. NAACP (life), Cal. Secondary Sch. Adminstrs. (hon.). Home: Pasadena Calif. Deceased.

GRAVES, MARIE LEONTINE See BULLOCK, MARIE LEONTINE

GRAVES, ROBERT (VON RANKE), author; b. London, 1895; s. Alfred Perceval and Amy G.; ed. Charterhouse Sch. and St. John's Coll., Oxford; m. twice, 8 children. Capt., Royal Welch Fusiliers, 1915; became prof. English lit. Egyptian U., 1926; prof. poetry Oxford U., 1961-66; Little lectr. MIT, 1963. Author numerous books, 1916-85, latest publs. being: Goodby to All That, 1929, rev. edit., 1957; I Claudius, 1934; Claudius the God, 1934; Collected Poems, 1939; Sergeant Lamb's Am., 1940; Proceed, Sergeant Lamb, 1941; (with Alan Hodge) Long Week-End, 1941; Story of Marie Powell, wife to Mr. Milton, 1942; (with A. Hodge) Reader Over Your Shoulder, 1943; Golden Fleece, 1944 (U.S., Hercules My Shipmate); King Jesus, 1946; The White Goddess, 1947; Watch the North Wind Rise, 1948; The Isles of Unwisdom, 1949; The Golden Ass, 1951; Greek Myths, 1954; (with Joshua Podro) The Nazarene Gospel Restored, 1953; Homer's Daughter, 1955; Collected Poems, 1955; Crowning Privilege, 1956; They Hanged My Saintly Billy, 1957; Five Pens in Hand, 1958; The Anger of Archilles, 1959; Collected Poems, 1961; The Penny Fiddle, 1961; (with Raphael Patai) Hebrew Myths, 1963; New Poems, 1963; Collected Short Stories; Man Does, Woman Is, 1964; Love Respelt, 1965; Poetic Craft and Principles, 1967; Poems 1965-68, 1969; On Poetry; Collected Talks and Essays, 1969; Poems about Love, 1969; The Crane Bag, 1969; Poems, 1970-72; Poems, 1973; Difficult Questions - Easy Answers. 1972; Collected Poems, 1975; An Ancient Castle, 1980; 90 others; works, manuscripts permanent exhbn. Lockwood Meml. Library, Buffalo, Recipient Russell Loines award for poetry Am. Acad. and Nat. Inst. Arts and Letters, 1958; gold medal award Nat. Poetry Soc. Am. 1960; Gold medal for poetry Mexican Cultural Olympics, 1968; Queen's Gold medal for poetry, 1968; Sol de Oro medal Madrid, 1973. Died Dec. 7, 1985; buried Deya, Majorca, Balearic Islands, Spain.

GRAY, BOWMAN, III, investment banker; b. Winston-Salem, N.C., Mar. 31, 1938; s. Bowman, Jr. and Elizabeth Palmer (Christian) C.; divorced; children: Elizabeth, Alice, Bowman, IV. Student, U. Va., U.

N.C. Salesman, then mktg. mgr. R.J.R. Archer Co. (div. R.J. Reynolds Industries), Winston-Salem, 1965-70; dir. internat. affairs Gen. Occidentale, Paris, 1971-72; pres. Gen. Occidental, Inc., N.Y.C., from 1972, Cavenham Holdings, Inc., from 1980; chmn. bd. Grand Union Co., 1980-81, Cavenham U.S.A., Inc., 1980—; dir. Diamond Internat. Corp. Trustee Woodberry Forest (Va.) Sch., Pasquaney Trust, Bristol, N.H. With AUS, 1957-60. Republican. Episcopalian. Clubs: Brook (N.Y.C.), Links (N.Y.C.); Metropolitan (Washington); Capital City (Atlanta). Deceased.

GRAY, EARL QUINCY, lawyer; b. Higgins, Tex., Jan. 24, 1891; s. Eli Clark and Nancy Adelaide (Patton) G.; m. Lucile D. Roberts, July 2, 1921; children: Roger K., Nancy L. (Mrs. Nancy Cheek). AB, U. Okla., 1910; SB, U. Chgo., 1911, JD cum laude, 1913. Bar: Okla. 1913. Practice Pauls Valley, Okla., 1913-14, Ardmore, Okla., from 1914; mem. Gray & Poindexter and predecessor firms, Ardmore, 1914-50; pvt. practice Ardmore, from 1950; cattle rancher Johnston and Murray counties; owner oil operations Carter, Stephens, Garvin & Marshall counties; oil royalty; other investment interests; mem. Okla. Securities Commn., 1958-59. Pres. Chickasaw council Boy Scouts Am., 1935-36; chmn. Community Chest campaign, Ardmore, 1955; chmn. com. bldg. campaign Okla. Bar Ctr., 1960-61; bd. dirs. Okla. Soc. for Crippled Children, 1950-70, pres., 1970. Fellow Am. Bar Found. (Fifty-Yr. award 1974); mem. Am. (Okla. state del. 1963-75, bd. govs. Dist. 11 1974-76), Okla. (pres. 1957, chmn. com. adminstrn. justice which submitted constl. amendment creating spl. ct. for removal of judges for cause, mem. 3-man com. to investigate corruption in Okla. Supreme Ct. 1964-65, resulting in removal and disbarment of 2 mems. of ct.), Carter County (past pres.) bar assns., Nat. Conf. Bar Presidents (mem. council, from 1961, treas. 1963-70, vice chmn. 1970-71, chmn. 1971-72), Ind. Producers Assn., Am. Judicature Soc. (dir. 1959-63), Okla Bar Found. (trustee from 1957, pres. 1963-65), Okla. Cattlemen's Assn., Rotary (local pres. 1933-34, dist. gov. 1953-54, mem. constn. and by-laws com. 1955-57, chmn. 1957-58, parliamentarian 1970 internat conv.), Order of Coif, Phi Beta Kappa. Home: Ardmore Okla. Died Jan. 27, 1979; buried Ardmore, Okla.

GRAY, EDWARD, publisher; b. Bucharest, Romania, 1915; came to U.S., 1961, naturalized, 1965; m. Carol Nader, 1955. M.A., U. Lille, France, 1934; D. Econs., U. Nancy, France, 1936. V.p. Maxwell Sci. Internat., Inc., N.Y.C. and Elmsford, N.Y., 1966-68; pres., dir. Maxwell Sci. Internat., Inc., 1968-87, Microforms Internat. Mktg. Corp., Elmsford, 1971-87; dir. micropublishing Pergamon Press, Inc., Elmsford, 1974-87; pres. Pergamon Press, Inc., 1975-77, sr. v.p. and micropub. dir., 1978-83; pres. Brit. Book Centre, N.Y.C. and Elmsford, 1972-83. Author papers microfiche alternative for current subscriptions and microfilm pub.; Editor: Micropub. of Current Periodicals, 1977-82, History of Economic Series in Microfiche; editor: Internat. Jour. Micrographics and Video Technology, 1982—; Editor: Malthus Library Catalogue, 1983; co-pub.: Bibliotheca Shakesperiana in Microfiche. Recipient Best Thesis award U. Nancy, 1936. Mem. N.Y. Acad. Scis., Soc. for Scholarly Pub., Nat. Micrographics Assn., Internat. Micrographics Congress, Antique Booksellers Assn. Home: Hartsdale N.Y. Died Mar 1, 1987; buried Sheron Gardens, Valhalla, N.Y.

GRAY, HENRY, writer, publisher; b. N.Y.C., June 20, 1892; s. Benjamin G. and Fannie (Kuhn) G.; m. Ann Bertha McLeod, Apr. 24, 1935. Student pub. schs., N.Y.C. Founder Ednl. Rsch. Bur., 1936, articles syndicated by Scripps-Howard Newspaper Info. Svc., 1937, incorporated entire group Newspaper Info. Svc. publs. with Ednl. Rsch. Bur., 1942; editor syndicated newspaper features How's Your I.Q., Question and Answers Ednl. Publs. Svc. Pub. World Atlas of Base Maps, 1955; contbr. articles to profl. jours. Mem. Am. Hist. Assn., Inter-Am. Bibliog. and Library Assn., Pan-Am. Found., Pi Gamma Mu. Home: West Palm Beach Fla. †

GREELEY, DANA MCLEAN, clergyman; b. Lexington, Mass., July 5, 1908; s. William Roger and Morjory Ellen (Houghton) G.; m. Deborah Webster, Dec. 27, 1931; children: Faith Scovel, Rosamond Hamlin, Cynthia McElwain, Penelope Elwell. BS, Harvard U., 1931, STB, 1933; DD, Meadville Theol. Sch., 1951, Tufts U., Emerson Coll., Calvin Coolidge Coll. Ordained to ministry Unitarian Ch., 1932. Minister Lincoln, Mass., 1932-34, Concord, N.H., 1934-35; minister Arlington St. Ch., Boston, 1935-58; sec. Am. Unitarian Assn., 1945-53, pres., 1958-61; pres. Unitarian Universalist Assn. N.Am., 1961-69, Internat. Assn. for Liberal Christianity and Religious Freedom, 1969-72; minister 1st Parish, Concord, 1970-86; vis. prof. Meadville Theol. Sch., U. Chgo.; co-chmn. World Conf. on Religion for Peace, Nat. Inter-Religious Peace Com. Author: Toward Larger Living, 1945, A Message to Atheists, 1948, 25 Beacon Street and Other Recollections, 1971, These Concordians, 1975, Toward Through the Ages, 1986. His library and papers—correspondence and writings are in Archives of Harvard Div. Sch., Cambridge, Mass. Hon. pres. Citizens Crime Com. New Eng.; past pres. Unitarian Service com., Mass. Council Chs.; pres. Benevolent Fraternity; bd. dirs. Isles of Shoals Assn., Home for Aged Women, Boston Urban League; trustee St. Laurence Theol. Sch., Emerson Coll.; past mem. vis. coms., mem. bd. overseas Harvard U. The Dana McLean Greeley Found. for Peace and Justice established in his honor, Concord, Mass., Apr. 1986. Mem. Unitarian Universalist Ministerial Union, Mass. Bible Soc. (v.p.), Harvard Musical Assn., Appalachian Mountain Club, Harvard Club, Rotary, Delta Upsilon. Home: Concord Mass. Died June 13, 1986; interred Monroe Cemetery, Lexington, Mass.

GREELEY, PAUL WEBB, plastic surgeon; b. Waterman, Ill., July 10, 1902; s. Paul Eber Norman and Maud Nancy (Webb) G.; m. Eunice Cooksy Goebel, June 12, 1927 (dec. 1978); 1 child, Paul Julius Goebel; m. Vivian Anderson, Aug. 1, 1981. AB, U. Ill., 1923; MD, Northwestern U., 1928. Diplomate Am. Bd. Plastic Surgery. Rotating intern Evanston (Ill.) Hosp., 1927-28, in gen. surgery tng., 1928-31; clin. asst. gen. surgery Northwestern U. Med. Sch. Chgo., 1930-34; pvt. practice Chgo., 1931-85; vol. asst. plastic surgery to Sir Harold Gillies and Sir. Archibald McIndoe London; in additional tng. in plastic surgery Freiburg and Munich, Germany, Vienna, Austria, 1934-35; clin. prof. surgery, head dept. plastic surgery U. Ill. Coll. Medicine, Chgo., 1937-70; prof. Rush Presbyn.-St. Luke's Med. Ctr., Chgo., 1971-85; attending plastic surgeon, chief plastic surgery service U. Ill. Hosp., Presbyn.-St. Luke's Hosp.; cons. plastic surgeon West Side VA Hosp., Mcpl. Tb Sanitarium, Chgo., U.S. Naval hosps., Great Lakes, Ill., San Diego. Contbr. numerous monographs to profl. lit. With M.C., USNR, 1943-46, rear adm. Res. Mem. AMA, ACS, Am. Soc. Plastic and Reconstructive Surgery (pres. 1950-51), Am. Assn. Surgery Trauma, Am. Assn. Plastic Surgeons, Am., Western, Cen. surg. assns., Internat. Fedn. Plastic Surgeons, Am. Assn. Ry. Surgeons, Ill. Med. Soc., Inst. Medicine Chgo., Chgo. Surg. Soc. (v.p. 1960), Argentine Soc. Plastic Surgeons (hon.), Internat. Soc. Surgeons, Warren H. Cole Surg. Soc., University Club, Indian Hill Club, Kappa Delta Rho, Omega Beta Pi, Nu Sigma Nu. Home: La Jolla Calif. Died Sept. 22, 1985.

GREEN, EDITH, former congresswoman; b. Trent, S.D., Jan. 17, 1910; d. James Vaughn and Julia (Hunt) Starrett; children: James S., Richard A. Student, Willamette U., 1927-29; B.S., U. Oreg., 1939; postgrad., Stanford U., 1944; 33 hon. degrees including, Linfield Coll., Boston Coll., Reed Coll., Oberlin Coll., Georgetown U., Yale U., Williamette U., U. Portland, Tex. Christian U. Tchr. sch. Salem, Oreg., 1930-41; comml. radio work KALE, Portland, 1944-45; free-lance KALE, 1943-47; dir. pub. relations Oreg. Edn. Assn.; mem. of 84th-93d congresses from 3d Oreg. Dist., mem. appropriations com., edn. and labor com.; Congl. del. NATO Conf., London, 1959, WHO, 1973, World Population Conf., 1974; mem. U.S. Commn. UNESCO., Pres.' Commn. on Status of Women. Del. Democratic Nat. Conv., 1956, 60, 64, 68, 72, chmn. state delegation, 1960-68. Recipient Brotherhood award B'nai B'rith, 1956; Women of Year award Amvets, 1958; Community service award Nat. Assn. Colored Womens Clubs, 1962; Edn. Service award Am. Coll. Pub. Relations Assn., 1964; Top Hat award Bus. and Profl. Women's Clubs Am., 1965; President's award Nat. Rehab. Assn., 1967; Disting. Service award U. Oreg., 1967; Disting. Service award Oreg. State U., 1972; AAUW Woman of Achievement award, 1974; 1st Citizen award Portland, 1978; others. Died Apr. 21, 1987; buried Mt. View Cemetery, Corbett, Oreg.

GREEN, HARRY EDWARD, lawyer; b. Coshocton, Ohio, Sept. 19, 1911; s. William and Jenny (Mobley) B.; m. Molly Morse Leachman, June 1, 1946; children: William Strother, Sara McLaurin, Nancy M. B.S. summa cum laude, Princeton, 1933; LL.B. cum laude, Harvard, 1936. Bar: Ohio bar 1936, N.Y. bar 1947, Ill. bar 1958. Asso. firm Squire, Sanders & Dempsey, Cleve., 1936-42, Armstrong & Keith, N.Y.C., 1946-47; gen. counsel, dir. W.I. Sugar Corp., 1947-52, v.p., sec., gen. counsel, dir., 1952-58; practiced in N.Y.C., 1946-58; dir., gen. counsel Melchior, Armstrong, Dessau Co., Ridgefield, N.J., 1948-59; gen. counsel Container Corp. Am., Chgo., 1958-59; v.p., gen. counsel Container Corp. Am., 1960-63, sr. v.p., 1963-76. Bd. dirs. Nat. Found./March on Dimes, 1972-85, chmn., 1977-83; bd. dirs., pres. Windham Children's Svc., 1955-58. Lt. col. USAAF, 1942-46; col. Res. Decorated Legion of Merit. Mem. Am., Ill. bar assns., Bar Assn. City N.Y., Am. Arbitration Assn. (dir., chmn. Chgo. adv. council). Clubs: Mid-Day (Chgo.); Indian Hill (Winnetka, Ill.). Home: Winnetka Ill. Died Apr. 6, 1987; buried Old Leeds Ch., Markham, Va.

GREEN, ROBERT HOLT, physician, educator; b. Charleston, S.C., Oct. 31, 1911; s. Walter Guerry and Daisie (Holt) G.; m. Audrey Greet Johnston, Apr. 29, 1943; children: Robert Holt, Barbara Johnston, William Guerry. BA, U. of the South, 1933; postgrad., U. N.C., 1933-34; MD, Johns Hopkins U., 1938; MA (hon.), Yale U., 1967. Diplomate Am. Bd. Internal Medicine. Intern Strong Meml. Hosp., Rochester, N.Y., 1938-39; fellow in medicine, asst. resident Lakeside Hosp., Cleve., 1939-41; asst. resident physician Rockefeller Inst. Hosp., N.Y.C., 1941-42, NRC fellow med. scis., 1941-42, 46-47; faculty Yale U. Sch. Medicine, 1947-60, 67-81, prof. medicine, 1967-69, prof. pathology and medicine, 1970-74, clin. prof., 1974-81; pvt. practice Madison, Conn., 1953-57; assoc. sci. dir. Health Research Council N.Y.C., 1960-64; assoc. prof., then prof. NYU Sch. Medicine, 1960-67; chief med. service VA Hosp., N.Y.C., 1964-67; vis. physician 3d and 4th med. divs. Bellevue Hosp. Ctr., N.Y.C., 1965-67; attending physician Univ. Hosp., N.Y.C., 1965-67; cons. physician internal medicine Willowbrook State Sch., S.I., N.Y., 1961-67; assoc. chief staff rsch. VA Hosp., West Haven, Conn., 1967-74; prof., also dean Coll. Medicine, Med. U. S.C., 1969-70; chmn. dept. medicine Middlesex Meml. Hosp., Middletown, Conn., 1974-81; prof. Sch. Medicine, U. Conn., 1974-81. Editor: Yale Jours. Biology and Medicine, 1952-53; co-editor Sect. H., Virology and Rickettsiology, CRC Handbook Series in Clinical Laboratory Science, 1979; contbr. numerous articles to profl. jours. Lt. comdr. USNR, 1942-46. Commonwealth Fund fellow, summer 1961. Mem. AMA, Am. Assn. Immunologists, Am. Fedn. Clin. Research, Am. Soc. Clin. Investigation, Harvey Soc., Conn. Med. Soc., Middlesex County Med. Soc., Soc. Exptl. Biology and Medicine, Phi Beta Kappa, Sigma Xi. Home: Madison Conn. Died Dec. 25, 1981.

GREEN, ROBERT MORRIS, insurance executive; b. Cin., Feb. 12, 1892; s. James Albert and Louise (Coy) G.; m. Ellen Burchenal, Nov. 15, 1916 (dec. Sept. 1949); children: Robert Morris, James Albert, John Burchenal, Ellen Burchenal, Charles Harrington, David Lonsdale, Louise, William Jackson; m. Dorothy Booth Wight, May 5, 1960. AB, Princeton, 1913. With Procter & Gamble Co., Cin., 1914-17; in the coal and iron bus. 1919-24; with Union Cen. Life Ins. Co., Cin., 1924-32, treas., 1928-32; asst. sec. Prudential Ins. Co., Newark, 1932-33, treas., 1934-37, v.p., 1937-47, v.p. and treas., 1947-49, v.p. in charge Can. ops., 1949-60, ret.; dir., assoc. mng. dir. Brit.-Am. Life Ins. Co. Ltd., Nassau, 1960-63, dir., asst. to pres., from 1963. Pres. West Essex Community Fund, 1935-40; chmn. Newark chpt. ARC, 1947-49; trustee Princeton, 1930-34, chmn. Grad. Coun. and Nat. Alumni Assn., 1941-45; mem. bd. govs. Appleby Coll. 1st lt. F.A., U.S. Army, 1917-19; with A.E.F. in France. Mem. Princeton Club (N.Y.C.), Nassau Club (Princeton), Toronto Club, Lyford Cay Club. Home: Princeton N.J. †

GREEN, ROY MELVIN, engineer; b. Red Willow County, Nebr., May 6, 1892; s. Richard Allan and Mary Jane (Wagy) G.; m. Norma J. Kidd, Aug. 14, 1919; children: Mary Elizabeth (Mrs. Gregory C. Meyer), Nancy Josephine (Mrs. Verner S. Johnson), William Earl (dec. 1945), Thomas Franklin. BSCE, U. Nebr., 1914; MS, Columbia, 1916. Asst. prof. hwy. engring. Tex. A&M Coll., 1916-18, assoc. prof., 1918-19, prof., 1919-20; prof. civil engring. U. Nebr., 1943-44, asst. dean engring., 1944-45, dean, 1945-57; pres., mgr. Western Labs, Lincoln, Nebr., 1920-43; cons. engr.; trustee Banker's Life Nebr. Ins. Co., Dempster Mill Manufacturing Co., Beatrice, Nebr.; sec., past chmn. State Bd. Examiners for Profl. Engrs. and Architects, 1937-62; disting. vis. prof. agrl. engring. Mich. State U., fall, 1958. Contbr. numerous articles on engring. to U.S. and fgn. jours. Recipient Service award Nat. Coun. State Bd. Engring Examiners, co-recipient with wife Disting. Service award U. Nebr. Alumni, 1960. Mem. Engrs. Coun. Profl. Devel. (mem. com. on accreditment, 1939-47, on student selection and guidance, 1946-47), Am. Soc. Engring Edn., Assn. Land Grant Colls. and Univs. (chmn. engring. div. 1948-49), Engr. Coll. Rsch. Assn. (dir.), ASCE (dir., Disting. Service award Nebr. sect. 1963), Am. Soc. Testing Materials, Assn. Asphalt Paving Techs., Nebr. Engring. Soc. (past pres.), Lincoln Engrs. Club, Sigma Xi, Sigma Tau, Chi Epsilon. Republican. Home: Lincoln Nebr. †

GREENBAUM, DOROTHEA SCHWARCZ, sculptor; b. Bklyn., June 17, 1893; d. Max and Emma (Indig) Schwarcz; m. Edward S. Greenbaum, Oct. 21, 1920 children: David S., Daniel W. One-woman shows, N.Y.C., N.J., Mass., Calif., Washington, San Francisco, others; sculpture represented in permanent collections Whitney, Moscow, Newark, Balt., Ogunquit, Maine, Trenton, N.J. state museums, Pa. Acad. of Arts, also many univ. museums including Princeton U., Brandeis U., Williams Coll., Oberlin Coll., U. Minn., U. Tex., Smithsonian Instn., others, also pvt. collections. Author: Friends & Foes from A-Z. U.S. del. 1st Internat. Conf. Arts, UNESCO, Venice, 1952; mem. adv. com. to combat artists U.S. War Dept., 1943-45. Recipient Widener Meml. medal Pa. Acad., 1941, medal of honor Nat. Assn. Women Artists, 1953, Cybis purchase prize N.J. State Mus., Blumenthal purchase prize N.J. State Mus., Ford Found. purchase prize Pa. Acad. Arts, others; grantee AAAL, 1947. Mem. Artists Equity (founding mem.), Sculptors Guild (founding mem.), Nat. Inst. Arts and Letters, N.J. Council Arts. Home: Princeton N.J. Died Apr. 6, 1986.

GREENBERG, CHARLES, psychiatrist; b. N.Y.C., Mar. 18, 1906; s. Enoch and Rachel Greenburg; m. Ruth Ostroff, Apr. 21, 1940; children: Ellen Ann (Mrs Allwyn Levine), Nina Jean (Mrs. Joseph Malkevitch). Student, Fordham U., 1923-25; BS, NYU 1927; postgrad., Dartmouth Coll., 1927-29; MD, U Chgo., 1931. Diplomate Am. Bd. Psychiatry and Neurology. Intern City Hosp., N.Y.C., 1931-33; resident in psychiatry Grasslands Hosp., Valhalla, N.Y. 1933-34, Syracuse (N.Y.) Psychiat. Hosp., 1934-35; pvt practice Wingdale, N.Y., 1935-52, Sonyea, N.Y., 1952

7, Rome, N.Y., 1957-86; asst. dir. Harlem Valley State osp., 1935-52; dir. Craig Colony Sch. and Hosp., 952-57, Rome State Sch., 1957-72; guest lectr. Upstate led. Ctr., Syracuse. Bd. dirs. United Fund, Rome. Lt. mdr. USNR, 1943-46. Recipient Stuckart Meml. ward. Fellow Am. Psychiat. Assn. (past br. pres.), m. Assn. on Mental Deficiency; mem. AMA, Livingon County (past sec.-treas.), Oneida County med. cs., Masons, Rotary. Home: New Hartford N.Y. ied July 20, 1986.

REENBLATT, ROBERT BENJAMIN, ndocrinologist; b. Montreal, Que., Can., Oct. 12, 1906; Louis and Hanna (Rabinovitch) G.; came to U.S., 933, naturalized, 1939; B.A., McGill U., 1928, M.D., .M., 1932; Docteur honoris causa, U. Bordeaux France), 1971; m. Gwen Lande, June 23, 1932; chilren—Nathaniel, Edward, Deborah. Intern, Englewood N.J.) Hosp., 1934-35; resident Univ. Hosp., Augusta, a., 1935-37; practice medicine, specializing in endocriology, Augusta, 1940-87; prof. endocrinology Med. oll. Ga., 1946-74. Cons. to surgeon gen. U.S. Army, 946-87; nat. cons. in endocrinology USAF, 1970-72. erved as comdr. USCGR, 1943-45. Recipient Crawford . Long Gold medal, 1941, Barren Gold medal, 1971; edallion Internat. Coll. Surgeons, 1972; decorated evalier French Legion of Honor. Mem. Am. Geriatric oc. (pres., Edward Henderson Gold medal, 1979), Am. hysicians Fellowship (pres.), Internat. Soc. Reproducve Medicine (pres.), Internat. Menopause Soc. (hon. es.), AMA (Billings Silver medal). Club: Rotary. uthor: Search The Scriptures, 1964; Ovulation, 1966; enopause, 1974; Love Lives of the Famous, 1978; hers. Developer sequential birth control pill, fertility ll. Home: Augusta, Ga. Died Sept. 27, 1987.

REENE, SIR HUGH CARLETON, publishing comany executive, brewer; b. Berkhamsted, Eng., Nov. 15, 910; s. Charles and Marion Greene; m. Helga Guiness, 1934; 2 children; m. 2d, Elaine Shaplen, 1951; 2 iildren; m. 3d, Tatjana Sais, 1970 (dec. 1981); m. 4th, rah Grahame, 1984. Ed. Merton Coll., Oxford U. ng.); D.C.L. (hon.), U. East Anglia, 1969; Dr. (hon.), pen U. and York U., 1973. Newspaper corr., ermany, 1934-39; expelled from Germany, 1939; corr., oland, 1939; head German Service, BBC, 1940-46; ontroller broadcasting Brit. Zone, Germany, 1946-48; ead East European Service, BBC, 1949-50; head mergency Info. Service, Malaya, 1950-51; asst. conoller Overseas Service, BBC, 1952-55, controller, 1955-, dir. adminstrn. BBC, 1956-58; dir. News and Curnt Affairs, 1958-59; dir.-gen. BBC, 1960-69; bd. govs., 969-71; chmn. The Bodley Head, 1969-81, hon. pres., 981-87; chmn. Greene King Brewery, 1971-78; v.p. uropean Broadcasting Union, 1963-68. Author: The y's Bedside Book, 1957; The Third Floor Front, 1969; e Future of Broadcasting in Britain, 1972; editor: The ivals of Sherlock Holmes, 1970; More Rivals of erlock Holmes, 1971; The Crooked Counties, 1973; e American Rivals of Sherlock Holmes, 1976; The rate of the Round Pond and Other Strange Adventure ories, 1977. Served with RAF, 1940. Decorated knight mdr. St. Michael and St. George, Order Brit. Empire U.K.), Grand Cross, Order of Merit (W.Ger.). Home: ondon. Died Feb. 19, 1987. Home: London England.

REENE, LAURENCE FRANCIS, urologist, edutor; b. Chgo., Nov. 11, 1912; s. Morris and Rose iedler) G.; m. Rosalyn R. Ravits, June 24, 1951; iildren: Edith, Richard, Nancy, James. BS, U. Chgo., 932; MD, Harvard U., 1936; PhD in Urology, U. inn., 1942. Diplomate: Am. Bd. Urology. Intern St. uke's Hosp., Chgo., 1936-38; fellow Mayo Found., 938-42; cons. urology Mayo Clinic, Rochester, Minn., 942-78; mem. faculty Mayo Grad. Sch. Medicine, U. inn., 1943-73, prof. urology, 1963-73; prof. urology ayo Med. Sch., 1973-74, Anson L. Clark prof. ology, 1974-78, prof. emeritus, 1978-84, mem. adv. bd. r continuing edn., 1973-84; prof. clin. surgery/urology Calif. Sch. Medicine, San Diego; urologic cons. Univ. osp., VA Hosp.; vis. prof. U. Okla., 1968, U. S.C., 76, U. So. Calif., 1979, Stanford U., 1980; mem. adv. l. Am. Family Physician GP. Author: Transurethral rgery, 1979; contbr. articles to profl. jours. Chmn. ochester com., 1965-71; pianist, mgr. Notochords ch., Rochester, 1958-84; bd. dirs. Minn. Orch. Assn., 66-84, Rochester Festival Music, 1965-66. Fellow MA; mem. Am. Urol. Assn., Am. Fertility Soc., Minn. rg. Soc., Am. Soc. Nephrology, Soc. Univ. Urologists, ternat. Soc. Urologists, Univ. Urologic Forum, Sigma ; corr. mem. La Soc. Mexicana de Urologia, Soc. edico-Quirurgica del Guayas. Home: Solana Beach, alif. Died Mar. 3, 1984; buried San Diego.

REENE, LEE SEIFERT, political scientist, educator; Esbon, Kans., May 31, 1905; s. Eugene C. and Marret E. (Cline) G.; m. Dorothy H. Kuersteiner, Dec. , 1932; children: Harriet Lee, Robert Everist. B.M., Kans., 1927, A.B., 1930; postgrad. (German-Am. change fellow), U. Leipzig, 1930-31; A.M., U. Wis., 32, Ph.D., 1934; postgrad., Brookings Instn., 1933-34, Mich., summer 1935. Social Sci. Research Council st-doctoral fellow 1937-38; instr. music U. Kans., 26-30; instr. U. Wis., 1934-36; research asso. and pr. pub. adminstrn. TVA, 1936-37, 1938-41; lectr. U. nn., Knoxville, 1937; asst. prof. polit. sci. U. Tenn., 38-39, asso. prof., 1939-45, prof., 1945-86, Distguished prof., 1965-75, prof. emeritus, 1975-86, acting head dept. polit. sci., 1942-46, head, 1946-71; dir. Bur. Pub. Adminstrn., 1945-71; exec. dir. Harris County (Houston) Home Rule Commn., 1956-57; exec. sec., Knoxville, Knox County Met. Charter Commn., 1957-59; cons. Knoxville Met. Planning Commn., 1960; vis. prof. U. Ala., summer 1948, U. Calif. at Los Angeles, summer 1949, Duke, summer 1950, Syracuse U., 1950-51, U. Ga., 1961, 65; mem. civil service bd., Knoxville, 1941-47, chmn., 1945-47; Cons. TVA, 1941-42, So. Regional Edn. Bd., 1952-53, FOA, 1954; Chmn. research com. Constl. Conv., Tenn., 1953; cons. ICA, 1955, Memphis Charter Com., 1966, Shelby County Structure Com., 1969; Public panel mem. and labor arbitrator Nat. War Labor Bd., Nat. Wage Stblzn. Bd., U.S. Conciliation Service, Fed. Mediation and Conciliation Service; arbitrator TVA; mem. nat. panel arbitrators Am. Arbitration Assn. Author: (with V.H. Brown and Evan A. Iverson) Administration of Natural Resources in Tennessee, 1948, (with D.R. Grant) A Future for Nashville, 1952, Metropolitan Harris County, 1957, (with R.S. Avery) Government in Tennessee, 1962, 2d edit., 1966, (with D. Grubbs, V. Hobday), 3d edit., 1975, 4th edit., 1982, (with George Parthemos) American Government: Policies and Functions, 1967, (with M.E. Jewell, D.R. Grant) The States and the Metropolis, (with Dye and Parthemos) American Government: Theory, Structure and Process, 1969, 2d edit., 1972, Governing the American Democracy, 1980, Lead Me On: Frank Goad Clement and Tennessee Politics, 1982, (with Montgomery and Folmsbee) History of U. of Tenn., 1984; editor: (with R. deV. Williamson) Five Years of British Labour, 1945-50, 1950, Resources and Policy, 1951, Jour. of Politics, 1953-57, assoc. editor (with R. deV. Williamson), 1949-52; spl. editor: Conservatism, Liberalism, and Natl. Issues (Annals Am. Acad.), 1962, City Bosses and Political Machines, 1964; Contbr. articles to profl. jours. Mem. Am. Polit. Sci. Assn., So. Polit. Sci. Assn. (pres. 1957-58), Nat. Mcpl. League, Am. Soc. Pub. Adminstrn., Nat. Inst. Pub. Affairs (trustee 1961-71), Phi Beta Kappa, Phi Kappa Phi, Pi Kappa Lambda, Beta Theta Pi, Phi Mu Alpha. Lodge: Masons. Home: Knoxville Tenn. Died Oct. 18, 1986; buried Mankato, Kans.

GREENE, LORNE, actor; b. Ottawa, Ont., Can., Feb. 12, 1915; s. Daniel and Dora G.; m. Rita Hands, 1940 (div. 1960); children: Belinda and Charles (twins); m. Nancy Anne Deale, Dec. 1961; 1 child. Ed., Queen's U., Neighborhood Playhouse Sch. of Theatre, N.Y.C. Am. debut in: The Prescott Proposals, N.Y.C., 1953; starred in, Stratford (Ont.) Shakespeare Festival, 1955; Broadway appearances include Speaking of Murder, 1956, Edwin Booth, 1958; appeared with, New Play Soc., Earl Grey Players, Toronto, Ont., founder, dir., actor, Jupiter Theater, Toronto; commentator documentary film: Churchill's Island; acted: in motion pictures including The Silver Chalice, 1954, Tight Spot, 1955, Autumn Leaves, 1956, Peyton Place, 1957, The Hard Man, 1957, Gift of Love, 1958, The Buccaneer, 1958, The Trap, 1959, Earthquake, 1974, Tidal Wave, 1975; regular on: TV series Bonanza, 1959-73, Griff, 1973-74, Lorne Greene's Last of the Wild, 1974-79, Battlestar Gallactica, 1978-79, Galactica, 1980, Code Red, 1981-82; TV movies include Man on the Outside, 1975, Nevada Smith, 1975; regular on: TV movies include SST-Death Flight, 1977; played in: mini-series The Moneychangers, 1976, Roots, 1977, The Bastard, 1978; spls. Swing Out, Sweet Land, 1971, The Great American Music Celebration, 1976; animated feature Heidi's Song; appearances various other TV shows. Former chmn. Nat. Wildlife Found.; bd. dirs. Am. Horse Protection Assn.; chmn. Am. Freedom from Hunger Found.; spl. civilian adv. Office Tech. Assessment. Served with RCAF. Mem. Actors Equity Assn., Screen Actors Guild, AFTRA. Died Sept. 11, 1987; interred Hillside Cemetery, L.A.

GREENE, SHERMAN LAWRENCE, clergyman, church official; b. Vicksburg, Miss., June 16, 1886; s. Henry and Delia (Wilson) G.; m. Pinkie Beatrice Spencer, June 21, 1905; children: Sherman Lawrence, Lillian V. Student, Alcorn (Miss.) Coll., 1900-02; AB, Campbell (Miss.) Coll., 1916; BD, Shorter Coll., Little Rock, Ark., 1912; DD, Allen U., Columbia, S.C., 1923; LLD, Wilberforce (Ohio) U., 1932. Ordained deacon A.M.E. Ch., 1908, elder, 1910, consecrated bishop, 1928. Pastor St. James Ch., New Orleans, 1915-16, Bethel Ch., Litle Rock, 1917-19; pres. Shorter Coll., Little Rock, 1918-24; presiding elder Pinbe Bluff and Little Rock dists., 1924-28; bishop Tenn. and West Indies, 1928-32, Miss. and La., 1932-48, Ala., 1948-51, Ga., from 1951; elected pres. Coun. of Bishops, 1952; del. Ecumenical Meth. Conf., London, Eng., 1921, Atlanta, 1932, Springfield, Mass., 1946, Oxford, Eng., 1951; pres. Nat. Conf. Ch. Leaders, 1936-40; state chmn. Gen. Commn. Rural Edn. and Inter-church Relations, 1940-44; mem. exec. bd. Nat. Coun. of Chs., U.S.A., 1950-54; v.p. Ga. Coun. of Chs., from 1953. Del. Nat. Rep. Conv., Phila., 1944; trustee Wilberforce U., from 1924, Atlanta U., from 1953. Mem. Am. Acad. Polit. and Social Sci., Masons, Elks, K.P, Kappa Alpha Psi. Home: Atlanta Ga. †

GREGORY, ROBERT TODD, mathematics educator; b. Owensboro, Ky., Mar. 19, 1920; s. Richeson Todd and Jennie (Howard) G.; m. Margaret Kathryn Bentzinger, Dec. 29, 1944; children: Rosalie Jane, Carl Richeson. Student, Georgetown Coll., Ky., 1937-38; BS, U.S. Naval Acad., 1942; MS, Iowa State U., 1948; PhD, U. Ill., 1955. Commd. ensign USN, 1942; instr. math. Fla. State U., 1949-50; rsch. asst. U. Ill., 1950-55; asst. prof. math. U. Calif., Santa Barbara, 1955-59; assoc. prof., prof. math. U. Tex., Austin, 1959-75; sr. rsch. mathematicianComputation Ctr. U. Tex., 1959-70, prof. math., 1963-75, prof. math. and computer sci., 1966-75, acting chmn. dept. computer sci., 1966-68, assoc. dir. Ctr. for Numerical Analysis, 1970-75; prof., head dept. computer sci., prof. math. U. Tenn., Knoxville, 1975-80; prof. computer sci. and math. U. Tenn., 1980-84. Author: Numeral Systems, 1963, Error-Free Computation, 1980; co-author: A Collection of Matrices for Testing Computational Algorithms, 2d edit., 1978, A Survey of Numerical Mathematics, 2 vols., 1972, Methods and Applications of Error-Free Computation, 1980; contbr. articles to profl. jours. With USN, 1942-46. Mem. Am. Math. Soc., Math Assn. Am., Soc. for Indsl. and Applied Math. (editorial bd. Journ. Applied Math.), Assn. for Computing Machinery, Sigma Xi. Home: Nashville Tenn. Died Nov. 14, 1984, buried Donnell Cemetery, Donnellson, Iowa.

GRESHAM, RUPERT N., lawyer; b. Luling, Tex., Apr. 7, 1892; s. Robert Hall and Jennie Lee (Robinson) G.; m. Gertrude negley, June 8, 1921; children: Rupert N., Susan (Mrs. James W. Crudgington). Legal student, U. Tex. Bar: Tex. 1916, U.S. Cir. Ct. 1918, U.S. Supreme Ct. 1945. Mem. Gresham, Davis, Gregory, Worthy & Moore. Contbr. articles to profl. jours. Fellow ABA (ho. of dels. from 1956, coun. tax sect. 1959-62); mem. San Antonio Bar Assn., State Bar Tex. (pres. 1954-55, chmn. com. real estate, trust and probate law, chmn. tax sect.), Am. Law Inst.,S.W. Legal Found., Order of Coif (hon.). Home: San Antonio Tex.†

GREY, JAMES DAVID, clergyman; b. Princeton, Ky., Dec. 18, 1906; s. George Lindsay and Lucy Ann (Keeney) G.; m. Lillian Gaines Tooke, Sept. 16, 1927; children: Martha Ann, Mary Beth. AB, Union U., Jackson, Tenn., 1929, DD, 1938; DD, Baylor U., 1953; ThM, Southwestern Bapt. Theol. Sem., 1932; LLD, La. Coll., 1952. Ordained to ministry Bapt. Ch., 1925. Pastor Tabernacle Ch., Ennis, Tex., 1931-34; pastor 1st Ch., Denton, Tex., 1934-37; pastor 1st Ch., New Orleans, 1937-72, pastor emeritus, 1972; minister radio program The Gospel Hour, New Orleans, 1941-72, Bapt. Hour, 1949, 52. Author: Epitaphs for Eager Preachers, 1972; religious booklets; contbr. to Bapt. periodicals. Bd. dirs. Met. Area Com., New Orleans, 1966-85, United Fund Greater New Orleans, Council for a Better La., Salvation Army, Gulf states area Info. Council of Ams., Pratt-Stanton Manor, Inc., So. Bapt. Hosps., Affiliated Bapt. Hosps., So. Bapt. Hosp. Found., Health Care Cons. and Mgmt. Services; bd. dirs. Met. New Orleans Crime Commn., pres., 1968-69; pres. La. Bapt. Conv., 1948-50, So. Bapt. Conv., 1951-53, New Orleans Fedn. Chs., 1957; organizer, bd. dirs. La. Moral and Civic Found., 1943-56, pres., 1953-56; pres. bd. trustees La. Coll., 1960-61; mem. Bold Missions Task Force, 1976-85, La. Commn. on Law Enforcement and Adminstrn. Justice, 1968-70, New Orleans Council on Naval Affairs, State Bd. Corrections, 1971-85; mem. exec. com. Bapt. World Alliance, 1950-70; mem. adv. bd. Big Bros., New Orleans. Recipient Times-Picayune Loving Cup, 1971; named to Hon. Order Ky. Col., 1950; named one of 10 Outstanding Persons New Orleans Inst. Human Understanding, 1976. Mem. Kiwanis (bd. dirs. local chpt. 1946-47), Alpha Tau Omega. Home: New Orleans La. Died July 26, 1985.

GRIBBLE, STEPHEN CHARLES, educator; b. Rico, Colo., Mar. 20, 1891; s. Samuel Stevens and Margaret Emma (Moeller) G.; m. Elizabeth Royce, July 23, 1921; 1 dau., Jane Elizabeth (Mrs. William H. Kretz Jr.). BS, U. Wis., 1917; MA, U. Iowa, 1924, PhD, 1925. Tchr. rural schs., 1909-10; high sch. prin. Hazel Green, Wis., 1912-14; asst. supt. Am. Tar Products Co., 1918-19; vice prin. High Sch., Waterloo, Iowa, 1919-21; supt. schs. Monona, Iowa, 1921-23; asst. prof. Colo. Coll. Edn., 1925-26; mem. faculty Washington U., 1926-57, assoc. prof., 1943-50, dir. summe sch., prof. edn., 1950-57, acting chmn. dept. edn., 1953-55, prof. emeritus, from 1957; lectr. in edn., summer tchr. U. W.Va., 1924, U. Iowa, 1928, U. Oreg., 1938, 39; vis. prof. edn. U. N.Mex., 1946-47. Mem. NEA, Nat. Soc. Study Edn., Nat. Conf. Profs. Sch. Adminstrn., Mo. State Tchrs. Assn., Tau Beta Pi, Kappa Delta Pi, Phi Delta Kappa, Alpha Sigma Phi. Congregationalist. Home: Saint Louis Mo. †

GRIFFIN, MARTIN I(GNATIUS) J(OSEPH), JR., historian, university dean; b. Phila., Nov. 13, 1933; s. Martin Ignatius Joseph and Constance Mary (Magee) G. A.B. (Benjamin Franklin scholar 1951-55), U. Pa., 1955; M.A. (Woodrow Wilson fellow), Yale U., 1956, Ph.D. (Jr. Sterling fellow), 1963; postgrad. (Fulbright fellow), U. London, 1958-59. Instr. history Yale U., New Haven, Conn., 1960-63; asst. prof. Yale U., 1963-68, Morse fellow, 1965-66, dir. undergrad. studies history, 1966-72, lectr. history, 1968-88, resident fellow Saybrook Coll., 1960-88, acting dean, 1966-67, dean, 1968-71, asst. dean Yale Coll., asso. dean undergrad. affairs, 1971-73, asso. dean Yale Coll., 1973-88, dean undergrad. studies, 1976-88. Mem. Am. Hist. Assn., Conf. Brit. Studies, Phi Beta Kappa (sec. Yale chpt.

1970-88, nominating com. United chpts. 1987-88), Sphinx Soc., Aurelian Soc. Clubs: Yale (N.Y.C.); Elizabethan. Home: New Haven Conn. Died Jan. 10, 1988.

GRIFFITH, JOHN EDWIN, JR., insurance company executive; b. Hartford, Conn., July 28, 1892; s. John Edwin and Elizabeth (Patterson) G. Grad., Worcester Acad., 1913; BA, Trinity Coll., 1917. With Aetna Life Ins. Co., from 1917; beginning as mem. staff group div., successively asst. sec. group div., sec., asst. v.p. 1917-52. Mem. Univ. Club (N.Y.C.), Sachems Head Club (Conn.) Yacht Club, Hartford Club, Hartford Golf Club (West Hartford, Conn.), Masons, Phi Gamma Delta. Home: West Hartford Conn. †

GRIGGS, MILTON WRIGHT, business executive; b. St. Paul, Nov. 15, 1888; s. C. Milton and Mary C. (Wells) G.; m. Arline Bayliss, Oct. 1, 1910; children: Arline (Mrs. George P. Mills), Chauncey Milton, Theodore Wright, Bayliss. Student, Phillips Andover Acad.; AB, Yale U., 1910. With Griggs, Cooper & Co. Inc., St. Paul, from 1910, pres., from 1931; dir. Griggs, Cooper & Co. Inc.; bd. dirs. Soo Line R.R., Zinsmaster Baking Co, First Nat. Bank, St. Paul; trustee Minn. Mutual Life. Ins. Co. Chmn. bd. dirs. Chas. T. Miller Hosp. Mem. U.S. C. of C., Nat., Am. Wholesale Grocers Assn. (past pres.), Nat. Assn. Mfrs., St. Paul Assn. Commerce (past pres.), Minnesota Club, Somerset Club (St. Paul). Republican. Episcopalian. Home: Saint Paul Minn. †

GRIGGS, RICHARD LESLIE, banker; b. Barclay, Pa., Dec. 8, 1886; s. Eli Zelotes and Anna (Kinney) G.; m. Neva Warner, Sept. 20, 1911; children: Leslie Elizabeth, Richard Clemson, Harold Warner. AB, U. Minn., 1907. With Bank of Virginia, Minn., 1899; treas. Virginia Electric Power & Water Co., 1910-14; engaged in real estate, ins. and automobile bus. Duluth, Minn., 1914-17; sec. No. Nat. Bank, Duluth, 1917-21, v.p., 1921-29, pres., 1929-46, chmn. bd., 1946-50; pres., bd. dirs. Kinney Coal Mining Corp., W.Va.; v.p., bd. dirs. Sterling Motor co., bd. dirs., mem. exec. com. Minn. Power & Light Co.; trustee Whitney Materials Co.; founder, bd. dirs. Greyhound Corp., 1927-63; bd. dirs. 1st Nat. Bank Hibbing, Minn., 1st Nat. Bank Virginia, 1st Nat. Bank Gilbert, Miners Nat. Bank Eveleth, Western Nat. Bank Duluth, Andresen Ryan Coffee Co., Merritt Chapman Scott Corp., N.Y. Bd. dirs. Duluth chpt. Infantile Paralysis Found.; mem. bd. regents U. Minn., 1939-63, regent emeritus, 1963-87, fellow Gov. John Sargent Pillsbury Found., 1975-87. Pvt. F.A., U.S. Army, 1918. Recipient Outstanding Achievement award U. Minn., Regents award U. Minn., Regents Award of Merit U. Minn., Hall of Fame award City of Duluth, Faculty and Staff Honor award U. Minn.-Duluth, Alumni Disting. Service award U. Minn.-Duluth, Student Commn. Recognition award U. Minn.-Duluth, Pub. Service citation Joint Session of Senate and Ho. of Reps. Minn. State Legislature, 1963, Pub. Service citation 8th Dist. Legislators Minn., Pres.'s award Kappa Sigma, citations Duluth Community Chest, Minn. Arrowhead Addn., Duluth chpt. Boy's Club Am., 1975, U. Minn. Bd. Regents, 1973-78, Klineburger Trophy award Game Conservation Internat., 1973, spl. citation City of Virginia, 1978; Legion of Merit award Govt. of Rhodesia, 1979. Mem. Newcomen Soc., Am. Legion (Honor award 1978), Trustees Soc. U. Minn., Masons (32 deg.), Shriners, Elks, Kitchi Gammi Club, Northland Country Club, Duluth Athletic Club, President's Club. Republican. Episcopalian. Home: Duluth Minn. Died May 16, 1987.

GRIMM, CARL HUGO, composer, conductor, organist; b. Zanesville, Ohio, Oct. 31, 1890; s. Carl William and Ida (Goetzinger) G.; m. Alberta Kumler, June 17, 1922; children: Carl Albert, Mary Carolyn. Ed. pub. schs., Cin.; studied, piano, organ and theory with his father, composition with Edgar Stillmon-Kelley, orchestration with Frank van der Stucken; largely self taught in composition and orchestration; Mus.D. (hon.), Cin. Cons. Music, 1930. Organist and choir dir. Immanuel Reformed Ch., Cin., 1907-12, Mt. Auburn Bapt. Ch., Cin., 1912-24, Mt. Auburn Presbyn. Ch., Cin., 1924-27, Knox Presbyn. Ch., Cin., 1938-52, Reading Rd. Temple, Cin., 1910-22, Isaac M. Wise Temple, Cin., 1922-70; pvt. tchr. piano, organ, music theory 1907-31; head composition dept. Cin. Cons. Music, 1931-52; condr. Cin. Cons. Music Symphony Orch., 1944-52. Compositions include: (for orchestra) Erotic Poem (tone poem), Thanatopsis (tone poem), Abraham Lincoln (tone poem), 116th Psalm (tone poem), Five Pictures for Peter and Wendy (suite), overture Pennsylvania for State U., Cantata for Whittier 150th anniversary yr., Scherzo Fantasie for piano and orch., Montana (two impressions), Victory Overture, Symphony in F minor, Byzantine Suite (for small orch.), String Quartet (chamber music), Serenade for Wind Instruments, Four Stencils for Flute, Cello, Piano, Song of Songs (chorus and orch.), Feast of Kol Folk (chorus and orch.), Concertino for Trumpet and Orch., Christmas Concerto, Five Designs for Brass Ensemble, Variations on Mooz Zur for chorus and organ, Dorian Suite for flute and string quartet, Miniature Concerto for flute and string orch., Capriccio Cromatico for flute and piano, Divertimento for 8 flutes, Five Etudes for 12 flutes, Rhapsody on Verses of an Unkown Prophet for chorus and orch., Communion Services for choir, organ and string orch., Gothic mass for choir, organ, string and brass instruments, also cantatas, anthems, services for synagogue, piano and organ pieces, etc.; compositions performed by Cin., Chgo., Rochester, L.A., Indpls., Huntington, Dayton and Fed. symphony orchs., Detroit Little Symphony, Ohio Sinfonietta. Sgt. U.S. Army, 1918. Recipient $1,000 prize for orchestral work Nat. Fedn. Music Clubs, 1927, $1,000 prize for choral and orchestral work MacDowell Club N.Y., 1930. Mem. Torch Club, Masons, Phi Mu Alpha, Pi Kappa Lambda. Presbyterian. Home: Cincinnati Ohio. Deceased.

GRIMSON, KEITH SANFORD, physician, surgeon, educator; b. Munich, N.D., Apr. 21, 1910; s. Judge Gudmundur and Ina (Sanford) G.; m. Ardyce Mozelle Johnson, Oct. 16, 1934; children—Roger Connell, Baird Sanford, Keith Sanford. B.A., U. N.D., 1930, B.S., 1931; M.D., U. Chgo., 1934. Intern Presbyn. Hosp., Chgo., 1934; fellow, resident surgery U. Chgo., 1935-39, instr. dept. surgery, 1940-42; Belgian Am. Ednl. Found. Research fellow with Prof. C. Heymans, Ghent, Belgium, 1939-40; asst. prof. surgery Duke U. Sch. Medicine, Durham, N.C., 1943-48; prof. Duke U. Sch. Medicine, 1948-88; prof. surgery Duke Hosp.; cons. AMA, HEW, Am. Heart Assn., surg. and med. socs. Assoc. editor: Ann. Revs. of Internal Medicine, 1952-88, The Am. Surg. Jour, 1953-88, Modern Medicine, 1955-88; contbr. artciles to profl. jours. Fellow A.C.S.; mem. Am. Surg. Assn., So. Surg. Assn., Am. Physiol. Soc., Am. Soc. Clin. Rsch., So. Soc. Clin. Rsch., Am. Heart Assn., Am. Soc. Pharmacology and Exptl. Therapeutics, Soc. U. Surgeons, Sigma Xi, Phi Delta Theta, Alpha Kappa Kappa. Presbyterian. Home: Chapel Hill N.C. Died Nov. 14, 1988.

GRISANTI, FRANK ANTHONY, management consultant; b. Buffalo, Oct. 21, 1920; s. Salvatore and Marian (Palermo) G.; m. Dorothy Louise Stolzenberg, July 14, 1951; children: Melanie Louise, Mari-Jo. B.S., Okla. A & M Coll., 1943. V.-p. Segal Lock and Hardware Co., N.Y.C., 1949-52; assoc. Robert Heller and Assos., Cleve., 1952-58; v.p. Young Spring and Wire Corp., Detroit, 1958-61, Mordy & Co. (Mgmt. Cons.), 1961-67; pres. Grisanti and Galef, Inc., Los Angeles, 1967-78; chmn. Spectrum Group Inc., 1978-87, Deutschman & Co., Los Angeles, 1987. Served with USNR, 1945-46. Mem. World Affairs Council., Town Hall of Calif. (life). Republican. Episcopalian. Clubs: Jonathan, Regency, Los Angeles Country, Congl. Country, The Springs. Home: Los Angeles Calif. Died Dec. 22, 1987.

GRISWOLD, JOHN CARROLL, business executive; b. Decatur, Ill., Oct. 3, 1901; s. Harry Ross and Edna Cantrell (Graves) G.; m. Marguerite Bessire, July 22, 1922 (dec. 1971); children: Jacqueline Louise Griswold Moore, David Ross; m. Anita Lihme de Lobokowicz, 1972 (dec. 1976). Student, Millikin U., 1919-21, LL.D., 1964; D.H.L., N.Y. Inst. Tech.; spl. courses, Chgo.-Kent Coll. Law, 1921-23. Clk., Continental Casualty Co., Chgo., 1922-25; resident v.p. in charge Continental Casualty Co., Chgo. office, 1931-36; with Rollins Burdick Hunter Co., 1925-31; dir., v.p. Fred. S. James & Co., Chgo., 1936; mgr. Fred. S. James & Co. (N.Y.C. office), 1939-45; founder, pres., dir. Griswold & Co., Inc., N.Y.C., 1945-62; exec. com., dir. Marsh & McLennan, Inc., 1962-69; v.p. W.R. Grace & Co., 1949-55, dir., 1950, exec. v.p., 1955-64; gen. partner Eastman Dillon, Union Securities & Co., 1964-72, sr. v.p., dir., 1971-72; dir., chmn. exec. com. Metromedia, Inc.; dir. Chemed, Inc., Safety First Shoes, Inc. Trustee Athens (Greece) Coll., Millikin U., Postgrad. Inst. Osteo. Medicine and Surgery; Trustee emeritus Brick Presbyn. Ch., N.Y.C.; co-chmn. bd. govs. N.Y. Coll. Osteo. Medicine. Mem. Griswold Family Assn. Am., U.S. Srs. Golf Assn., The Pilgrims, Sigma Alpha Epsilon, Phi Delta Phi. Presbyterian. Clubs: Links (N.Y.C.), Wall Street (N.Y.C.), River (N.Y.C.); Chicago; Bohemian (San Francisco), Pacific-Union (San Francisco). Home: New York N.Y. Died Mar. 24, 1987; buried Decatur.

GRONOWICZ, ANTONI, author; b. Rudnia, Poland, July 31, 1913; came to U.S., 1938, naturalized, 1962; s. Antoni and Paulina (Dorocinska) G.; m. Sophia Shymanska, June 8, 1940; children: Anthony Boleslaw, Gloria Andrea. PhD, U. Lwow, Poland, 1937. Author (poetry) Prosto w Oczy, 1936, Bunt Walki, 1937, Melodia Switow, 1939, The Quiet Vengeance of Words, 1968, Polish Poems, 1972; (essays) Byki Czystej Poezji, 1936, Pattern for Peace, 1951, Polish Profiles, 1976, Rocos, 1977, Shores of Pleasure, Shores of Pain, 1978 (1st prize Provincetown Acad. Arts competition 1979); (novels) I Chlopi Ida od Wschodu, 1937, Bolek, 1942, Hitler's Woman, 1942, Four From The Old Town, 1944, The Piasts, 1945, Gallant General, 1946, Virtue in Four Positions, 1965, An Orange Full of Dreams, 1972, The Hookmen, 1973, American Sextet, 1974; (art theory) Harmonizm, 1938; (plays) Niedroga Recepta, 1938, A Comedy of Angels, 1957, Chiseler's Paradise, 1958, Modjeska, 1962, Greta, 1967, The United Animals, 1967 (1st prize Internat. Competition, Geneva 1970), The Great Society, 1968, Forward Together, 1969, Colors of Conscience, 1979; (biog. novels) Paderewski, 1942, Chopin, 1943, Tchaikovsky, 1944, Rachmaninoff, 1946, Modjeska—Her Life and Loves, 1956; (biography) Béla Schick and the World of Children, 1954, God's Broker, 1984. Decorated Polonia Restituta Order (Poland); recipient Polish Nat. Lit. prize, 1938; Ford Found. grantee, 1959. Mem. PEN, Authors Leagu Am., Dramatists Guild, Cath. Poetry Soc. Am., Cat Press Assn. Home: New York N.Y. Died Oct. 16, 198 buried Warsaw, Poland.

GROSE, CLARENCE HERMAN, educator; b. Gilbo W.Va., Aug. 30, 1896; s. Walter Richmond and Mar (Scintilla Rader); m. Esther Mae Troeger, Aug. 2 1931; 1 child, Karen Jean. BS, W.Va. Wesleyan Col 1916, D Pedagogy (hon.), 1940; MA, U. Pitts., 192 PhD, 1940; LLD, Allegheny Coll., 1950. Tchr. hig sch. Buckhannon, W.Va., 1914-15, Salem, W.Va., 191 17, Huntington, W.Va., 1917-22; prin. Cammack J High Sch., Huntington, 1922-24; prin. jr. high sc Ambridge, Pa., 1924-30; supt. schs. City of Ambridg 1930-31, City of Mt. Lebanon, Pa., 1931-35, City Erie, Pa., 1935-49; dep. supt. Pa. Dept. Pub. Instr Harrisburg, 1949-52; pres. State Tchrs. Coll., Californi Pa., 1952-56; dep. supt. pub. instrn. Pa., 1956-58; asso sec., also sec. Pa. Council Edn., 1956-58; bd. pres. P State Tchrs. Colls., 1956-58; prof. ednl. adminstrn., di ednl. placement office Sch. Edn. U. Pitts., 1958-68, pro edn. emeritus, dir. ednl. placement, 1968-85. Contb articles to profl. jours. Dir. profl. edn. Am. Canc Soc., Allegheny County, Pa., 1971-76. Recipient Gov. citation, 1958, award Pa. Dept. Pub. Instrn., 196 Disting. Ednl. Leadership award Tri-State Area Sc Study Council, 1967, cert. of appreciation Con monwealth of Pa., 1970. Mem. Am. Assn. Sch. A minstrs. (adv. council 1945-51), Pa. Assn. Dist. Supt (pres. 1940), Pa. Edn. Assn. (pres. 1945), NEA (chm tax edn. and sch. fin. com. 1947-48), Pa. Assn. Healt Phys. Edn. and Recreation (Layman's Trophy 1947), P Instl. Tchr. Placement Assn. (pres. 1961), Mason SAR, Phi Delta Kappa (nat. commn. on support pu edn. in U.S. 1948-49), Delta Phi Epsilon, Alpha P Omega, Phi Sigma Phi. Republican. Presbyterian. Home: Pittsburgh Pa. Died. Jan. 22, 1985.

GROSECLOSE, ELGIN, economist, author; Waukomis, Okla., Nov. 25, 1899; s. M. Clarence an Della (Wishard) G.; m. Louise Elizabeth Williams, Ju 25, 1927; children: Sarah Jane (Mrs. Peter Theodorop lous), Nancy Margaret (Mrs. Herold Witherspoon Hildegarde Elsa (Mrs. Earl Bender), Suzy French (M Paul San Soucie). AB, U. Okla., 1920; MA, Am. U 1924, PhD, 1928. Tchr. Presbyn. Mission Sch., Tabri Persia (now Iran); spl. agt. U.S. Dept. Commerce, 192 26; with Guaranty Trust Co., N.Y.C., 1927-30; asso editor Fortune; lectr. CCNY, 1930-32; asst. prof. bu adminstrn. U. Okla., 1932-35; economist telephone i vestigation FCC, 1935-38; economist U.S. Dep Treasury, 1938-43; treas.-gen. Iran, 1943; prin. Elg Groseclose, Econ. Counsel, 1944-59; ptnr. Groseclo Williams and Broderick (fin. analysts and cons.), 195 83; founder, exec. dir. Inst. for Monetary Researc 1961-83. Author: Money: The Human Conflict, 193 rev. edit. pub. as Money and Man, 1976, The Persia Journey of the Rev. Ashley Wishard and his Serva Fathi, 1937, Ararat, 1939, 3d edit. 1977, The Firedrak 1942, Introduction to Iran, 1947, The Carmelite, 195 The Scimitar of Saladin, 1956, Fifty Years of Manage Money, the Story of the Federal Reserve, 198 Olympia, 1980, Comanche Country, 1982, al monographs. Founder Welfare of Blind Inc., 195 pres., 1956-66, 78-83. Recipient Nat. Book awar 1939, Found. for Lit. award, 1940, gold medalli Christian Book Pubs., 1978. Mem. Okla. Soc. Was ington (pres. 1945-46), Washington City Bible So (pres. 1966-72, bd. dirs. 1950-83), Nat. Economis Club, Cosmos Club, Kenwood Country Club, Phi Be Kappa, Phi Delta Phi, Alpha Kappa Psi, Delta Sigm Rho, Delta Tau Delta. Episcopalian. Home: Was ington D.C. Died Apr. 4, 1983; buried Rock Cre Cemetery, Washington.

GROSHANS, WERNER, artist; b. Eutingen, German July 6, 1913; came to U.S., 1927; s. Emil and Ann (Jung) G.; m. Yetta Abramowitz, June 3, 1944. Grad Newark Sch. Fine and Indsl. Arts, 1934. Chmn. fi arts dept. Jersey City Mus., 1966-69. Exhibited grou shows: Whitney Mus., 1948-50, 52-53, Carnegie Ins 1949, Met. Mus., 1950, 52, Butler Inst., NAD, Mon clair Mus. Art, Parrish Art Mus., Newark Mus Audubon Artists, Silvermine Guild, AFA Traveli Exhbn., Hirschl-Adler Gallery, Springfield (Mass.) Mu Fine Arts, Kennedy Gallery, Wadsworth Atheneum, Md., 1966-67, Quinata Gallery, Nantucket, Mass., 196 Centenary Coll., 2-man exhbn., Hackettstown, N. 1969, Okla. Mus. Art, 1969, New Britain Mus. A Art, retrospective, 1973, Babcock Galleries, one-m show, N.Y.C., 1973, Canton (Ohio) Art Inst., 4-m show, 1971, Nat. Inst. Arts and Letters Exhbn., 197 80, 82, Montclair (N.J.) Art Mus., retrospective, 197 Mus. Art, Industry and Sci., Bridgeport, Conn., 197 Rutgers U., Newark, 1980, Mus. Fine Art, Rosly N.Y., 1980, U. Del., 1980, retrospectives Butler In Am. Art, Youngstown, Ohio, 1986, N.J. State Mu Trenton, 1987, Jersey City Mus., 1987, othe represented permanent collections: Davenport (Iow Municipal Art Gallery, Ct. Gen. Sessions, Washingto Newark Mus., Newark Pub. Library, NAD Collectio Ency. Brit. collection, New Britain (Conn.) Mus. A Art, William Benton Mus., U. Conn., Storrs, Cant Art Inst., Dresden (E. Ger.) Mus. State Collectio Montclair Art Mus., N.J. State Mus., Trenton, Jers City Mus., also pvt. collections. Subject of exhbn. cat logues including: Werner Groshans: The Man and H

Work, Montclair Art Mus. Retrospective, 1976 (by Victor Alper), Werner Groshans and His Art, Butler Inst., Ohio, 1986 (by William H. Gerdts). Recipient Thomas B. Clarke award NAD, 1960; recipient Henry Ward Ranger Fund purchase prize, 1961-74, 1st prize Montclair Art Mus., 1961, Pauline Wick award, 1961, Painters and Sculptors award, 1964, Silver medallion N.J. Tercentenary Exhbn., 1964, Famous Artists Sch. award, 1965, Margaret C. Cooper award, 1966, Gold medal. Ligonier, Pa., 1966, N.J. Artist of Year award, 1966, Edward C. Roberts Meml. award New Britain Mus. Am. Art, 1969, N.J. State Council on Arts fellow, 1980-81, Hassam and Speicher Purchase award Nat. Inst. Arts and Letters, 1980; the Groshan papers are in the Archives of Am. Art, Smithsonian Institution. Nat. academician N.A.D. (council 1970-73); Mem. Audubon Artists, Conn. Acad. Fine Arts, Allied Artists, Artists Equity, Greene County Council on Arts. Home: Catskill N.Y. Died July 31, 1986; buried Catskill Rural Cemetary, Catskill, N.Y.

GROSS, CALVIN EDWARD, superintendent of schools; b. Los Angeles, Apr. 8, 1919; s. Harry Edward and Telah May (Calvin) G.; m. Bernice Marjorie Hayman, Mar. 29, 1946; children: Georgette Louise, Gary, Glenn. AB, UCLA, 1940; MS, U. So. Calif., 1947; EdD, Harvard U., 1955; LHD (hon.), Carnegie-Mellon U., 1963; D Pedagogy (hon.), Manhattan Coll., 1963; LLD, Ripon Coll., 1963, U. Akron, 1963. Grad. asst. math. Oreg. State U., 1940-41; tchr. math. dept., chmn., registrar, vice prin. Los Angeles City Schs., 1946-50; supt. schs. City of Weston, Mass., 1951-56, Niskayuna Cen. Sch. Dist., Schenectady, N.Y., 1956-58, City of Pitts., 1958-63, City of N.Y.C., 1963-65; dean Sch. Edn. U. Mo., Kansas City, 1965-72; pres. Nat. Coll. Edn., Evanston, Ill., 1972-78; supt. schs. Alamo Heights, San Antonio, Tex., 1978-87; mem. adv. com. on new ednl. media HEW; chmn. Nat. Council for Accreditation of Tchr. Edn.; chmn. study com. Gov.'s Conf. on Edn., 1968; mem. Council for Internat. Exchange of Scholars (Sr. Fulbright-Hays Program); mem. adv. council Associated Orgns. for Tchr. Edn.; mem. ednl. adv. bd. Sci. Research Assocs.; mem. governing bd. Nat. Com. for Citizens in Edn. Co-author: Research for Tomorrow's Schools: Disciplined Inquiry for Education, 1969. Chmn. exec. com., pres. bd. trustees Mid-Continent Regional Ednl. Lab; trustee Ednl. Testing Service, Carnegie-Mellon U., NCCJ; mem. vis. com. Harvard U. Summer Sch.; mem. adv. com. Kamehameha Schs.; mem. nat. adv. bd. Mott Found. Capt. AUS, 1941-46. Mem. Am. Assn. Sch. Adminstrs., Am. Assn. Colls. for Tchr. Edn. (com. on govt. relations, chmn.), Nat. Assn. State Univs. and Land-Grant Colls. (chmn. commn. on edn. for teaching), Joint Council Econ. Edn. (trustee), Cleve. Conf. Am. Assn. Pres. of Ind. Colls. and Univs. (bd. dirs.), Internat. Platform Assn., Harvard Club, University Club, Economic, Phi Beta Kappa. Home: San Antonio Tex. Died Mar. 14, 1987; cremated.

GROSS, ERIC TARAS BENJAMIN, electrical engineer; b. Vienna, Austria, May 24, 1901; came to U.S., 1939, naturalized, 1943; s. Berthold and Sophie (Gerstman) G.; m. Catharine B. Rohrer, Aug. 14, 1942; children—Patrick Walter Elizabeth Sophia, Margaret Joan. E.E., Tech. U., Vienna, 1923, D.Sc., 1932. Registered profl. engr., Ill., N.Y., Vt. Chartered engr., U.K. Elec. engr. in industry with emphasis on heavy electric power engring. 1923-42; asst. prof. elec. engring. Cornell U., 1942-45; prof. elec. engring. Ill. Inst. Tech., 1945-62; chmn. electric power engring. 1962-73; Philip Sporn prof. engring. Rensselaer Poly. Inst., Troy, N.Y., 1962-88; cons. War Dept., 1942-45; Vis. scholar Va. Polytech. Inst. and State U., 1972. Contbr. numerous articles to profl. jours. Recipient citation Am. Power Conf., 1972; Distinguished Faculty award Rensselaer Poly. Inst., 1972; Western Electric Fund award Am. Soc. for Engring. Edn., 1972; spl. citation Edison Electric Inst., 1976; Austrian Cross of Honor in Sci. and Arts 1st class, 1980. Fellow N.Y. Acad. Scis., IEEE (citation and silver plaque Brazil Council 1974, Northeastern Region award 1976, Power Generation Com. award 1977, Edn. Com. award 1978), AAAS, Inst. Elec. Engrs. (London); mem. Nat. Acad. Engring., Am. Arbitration Assn. (mem. nat. panel), Am. Soc. Engring. Edn., Panamerican Congress on Engring. (v.p. for U.S. 1970-78), Sigma Xi, Tau Beta Pi, Eta Kappa Nu (nat. pres. 1953-54, eminent mem. award 1975). Home: Schenectady N.Y. Died June 27, 1988.

GROSS, FRANZ BRUNO, political science educator; b. Vienna, Austria, July 29, 1919; came to U.S., 1940, naturalized, 1944; s. Max and Alice (Koref) G.; m. Margaret M. Chappell, Dec. 5, 1952; 1 child, Christopher John. Diploma, U. Rome, Italy, 1938; M.A., Harvard, 1943, Ph.D., 1952; postgrad., Grad. Inst. Internat. Relations, Geneva, Switzerland, 1947-50, Acad. Internat. Law, The Hague, Netherlands, 1958. Lectr. Grinnell (Ia.) Coll., 1943-44; with UN Secretariat, 1950-; vis. prof. Babson Coll., Mass., 1951-52, CCNY, 1953-54; acting chmn. Bradford Coll., 1954-59; mem. faculty, head polit. sci. dept. Widener Coll., Chester, Pa., 1959-71; chmn. liberal arts div. Widener Coll., 1962-67, also chmn. polit. sci. dept., Disting. prof., coordinator internat. affairs program, 1967-71; prof. internat. affairs and African studies Duquesne U., Pitts., 1971-78; dean Grad. Sch. Duquesne U., 1971-76; prof. polit. sci. U. New Haven, 1978-88, dean arts and scis., 1978-80; vis. prof. U. Pa. Grad. Sch., 1961-63, U. Dakar, Senegal, W. Africa, 1966-67, Free U. Berlin, Spring 1977; guest lectr. univs. in, Western and Eastern Europe, North and West Africa, Madagascar, India, Mexico; mem. acad. deans com. Pitts. Council Higher Edn., 1971-76; cons. on UN U. Pa. Fgn. Policy Inst., 1962-67. Editor, contbg. author: The United States and the United Nations, 1964; editor-writer: Des Moines Register and Tribune, 1944, UN Bulletin, 1950-51, N.Y. Sunday Times, 1960; editorial bd.: Polity, 1976-79. Pub. rep. Regional Mental Health Bd. II, State of Conn.; mem. rev. and eval. com., 1983-88; Mayor's New Haven Sister Cities Com., 1986-88. Served with M.I. AUS, 1944-46; press officer U.S. Mil. Govt. 1946-47, Germany. Recipient Outstanding Teaching award Widener Coll., 1965; Fulbright fellow Summer Inst. Indian Civilization, India, 1965; Fulbright Ednl. expert Germany, 1975. Fellow African Studies Assn.; mem. Internat. Studies Assn. (exec. com. Middle Atlantic region 1968-70, 74-78, pres. Phila. area 1971-72), Pa. Polit. Sci. Assn. (exec. com. 1972-74, v.p. 1974-75, pres. 1975-77), North Eastern Polit. Sci. Assn. (exec. com. 1970-72, exec. com. 74-76, v.p. 1976-78, pres. 1978-79), Am. Polit. Sci. Assn., Am. Assn. U. Adminstrs., AAUP, Pa. Assn. Grad. Schs. (pres. 1975-76), Am. Soc. Internat. Law, Profs. for Peace in Middle East (exec. com. 1970-73, v.p. 1973-88), Internat. Soc. for Ednl., Cultural and Sci. Interchanges (exec. sec. 1974-77), Nat. Com. on Fgn. Policy, World Federalists (mem. bd. Pitts. area council). Club: Harvard-Yale-Princeton (Pitts.); Harvard (N.Y.C.). Home: New Haven Conn. Died Mar. 13, 1988; cremated.

GROSS, H. R., congressman; b. Arispe, Iowa, June 30, 1899; m. Hazel E. Webster, June 29, 1929; children: Phil, Alan. Student, U. Mo. Newspaper reporter, editor 1921-35, radio news commentator, 1935-48; mem. 81st-94th Congresses from 3d Iowa dist. Served in Mex. border campaign, 1916; with A.E.F., World War I. Decorated Purple Heart. Mem. Masons, Elks. Republican. Presbyterian. Home: Waterloo Iowa. Died Sept. 22, 1987; buried Arlington Nat. Cemetery, Washington.

GROSS, IRMA HANNAH, educator; b. Omaha, July 21, 1892; d. David and Addie (Gladstone) G. BS, U. Chgo., 1915, AM, 1924, PhD, 1931. Tchr. foods Central High Sch., Omaha, 1915-21; mem. faculty Mich. State U., 1921-59; vis. prof. SND Thackersey U., Bombay, 1959-61; regional supervisor, consumer purchases study U.S. Bur. Human Nutrition and Home Econs., 1936; field supervisor Study of Family Spending and Saving in Wartime, 1942; conducted European Study Tour on Stnadards of Living, 1928. Author: (with Mary E. Lewis) Home Management, 1938; (with Elizabeth W. Crandall) Home Management in Theory and Practice, 1947, Management for Modern Families, 1954; contbr. articles to tech. bulls. and profl. jours. Sec. Mich. Youth Commn., 1949-51. Mem. Nat. Coun. on Family Rels., AAUW, Am. (Ellen H. Richards fellow 1929-30), Mich. (pres. 1939-40) home econs. assns., AAUP, Am. Sociol. Soc., Acad. Polit. and Social Sci., Soc. for Applied Anthropology, Phi Beta Kappa, Phi Kappa Phi, Omicron Nu (pres. 1949-51). Jewish. †

GROSS, PAUL MAGNUS, chemistry educator; b. N.Y.C., Sept. 15, 1895; s. Magnus and Ellen (Sullivan) G.; m. Gladys Cobb Petersen, Aug. 4, 1918; children: Paul Magnus, Beatrix Cobb. BS, CCNY, 1916; MS, Columbia U., 1917, PhD, 1919; postgrad., U. Leipzig. Instr. chemistry CCNY, 1916-18; asst. prof. Trinity Coll. (name now Duke U.), Durham, N.C., 1919-20, assoc. prof., 1920-25, prof., 1925-66, prof. emeritus, 1966-86, chmn. dept. chemistry, 1921-48, dean Grad. Sch., 1947-52, v.p., 1949-60, dean, 1952-58; pres. Oak Ridge Inst. Nuclear Studies, 1949-67, Oak Ridge Associated Univs., 1967-70; sci. advisor U.S. del. to 5th conf. UNESCO, Paris, 1949; cons. NASA, 1963-64, Council So. Univs.; cons. nat. adv. radiol. health council NIH, former bd. dirs. Am. Cancer Adv. Council; mem., vice chmn. N.C. bd. Sci. and Space Tech.; mem. N.C. Gov.'s Sci. Adv. Com., nat. adv. environ. health com. USPHS, Army adv. panel to Sec. of Army, panel toxicological info. Pres.'s Sci. Adv. Com.; chmn. munitions commd. adv. com. U.S. Army, 1968-86. Author: (with J.M. Bell) Elements of Physical Chemistry, 1929; contbr. articles to profl. jours. Bd. dirs. Research Triangle Inst., 1962-86; trustee Woodrow Wilson Nat. Fellowship Found., 1960-86. 2d lt. CWS, U.S. Army, 1918. Decorated comdr. Civil Order Brit. Empire; recipient Medal for Merit Pres. of U.S., 1948, medal So. Assn. Sci. & Industry, 1951, Townsend Harris award, 1953, Carnegie Manship award, 1954, citation SEC, 1969, Disting. Civilian Service award AUS, 1963. Fellow Am. Phys. Soc., N.Y. Acad. Sci.; mem. Am. Chem. Soc. (Herty medal Ga. sect. 1945, medal Fla. sect. 1952), AAAS (pres. 1962, chmn. bd. 1963), AAUP, Nat. Research Council, NSF (vice chmn. 1955-62), Phi Beta Kappa, Sigma Xi, Omicron Delta Kappa, Phi Lambda Upsilon. Home: Durham N.C. Died May, 4, 1986.

GROSS, ROBERT EDWARD, surgeon, educator; b. Balt., July 2, 1905; s. Charles Jacob and Emma (Houck) G.; m. Mary Louise Orr, June 11, 1931; children: Marcie Carol, Edith Orr. AB, Carleton Coll., 1927, ScD (hon.), 1951; MD, Harvard U., 1931. Diplomate Am. Bd. Surgery (founders group), Am. Bd. Thoracic Surgery (founders group). House officer pathology Children's Hosp., Boston, 1931, surgery, 1932-33, resident surgery, 1937-38, sr. mem. permanent staff, 1939-72, assoc. vis. surgeon, 1939-46, surgeon, 1936-46, surgeon-in-chief, 1947-72, chief cardiac program, 1966-72; house officer pathology Peter Bent Brigham Hosp., Boston, 1933-34, resident pathology, 1934-35, asst. resident surgery, 1935-37, George Gorham Peters Travelling fellow, 1937-38, resident surgeon, 1938-39, jr. assoc. surgery, 1939-40, assoc., 1940-46, sr. assoc., 1946-72; instr. pathology med. sch. Harvard, 1934-36, instr. surgery, 1937-39, assoc. surgery, 1939-42, asst. prof., 1942-47, Ladd prof. children's surgery, 1947-72; cons. pediatric surgery Boston Lying-In Hosp.; assoc. surg. staff N.E. Baptist Hosp.; courtesy staff Mass. Women's Hosp.; vis. surgeon, vis. surgeon to pediatric surg. service Mass. Meml. Hosp..; assoc. staff Faulkner Hosp., Jamaica Plain, Mass.; cons. to surg. staff Framingham (Mass.) Union Hosp.; cons. staff Woonsocket (R.I.) Hosp.; courtesy staff surgery Newton (Mass.)-Wellesley Hosp. Author: Abdominal Surgery of Infancy and Childhood (with William E. Ladd), 1941; contbr. numerous articles to med. jours.; mem. editorial bd. Am. Heart Assn., Circulation, Quarterly Rev. of Pediatrics, Jour. of Gen. Practice, Am. Heart Jour. Recipient Albert Lasker award Am. Heart Assn., 1954, 59. Fellow ACS, Am. Acad. Arts and Scis.; mem. Am. Acad. Pediatrics (exec. bd.), NRC, Am. (sci. council, founders group), N.E. heart assns., Am. Assn. Pathologists and Bacteriologists, Mass. Med. Soc., AMA, Boston Med. History Club, N.E. Pediatric Soc., Am. Assn. Thoracic Surgery, Am. Soc. Exptl. Pathology, Soc. U. Surgeons, Soc. Pediatric Rsch., N.E., Boston surg. socs., Soc. Clin. Surgery, Am. Cancer Soc., Am. Surg. Assn., Soc. Vascular Surgery (v.p.). Died Oct. 11, 1988.

GROSS, SIDNEY, public relations executive, journalism educator; b. Cleve., Sept. 7, 1923; s. Ernest and Katherine (Ney) G.; m. Zenith Henkin, Dec. 9, 1945; children: Kenneth, Lawrence, Kathy. B.A., Ohio State U., 1949, LL.B., 1950. Reporter Elyria (Ohio) Chronicle Telegram, 1938-41; reporter-deskman Press, Cleve., 1941-44; with AP, Columbus, Ohio, 1945-48; publicist, Ted Bates, N.Y.C., 1951-54; public relations exec. Vernon Pope Co., N.Y.C., 1955-70; founder Gross & Assocs., N.Y.C., 1971-82; chmn., prof. journalism and mass communications NYU, N.Y.C., 1983-86. Mem. Sch. Bd., Dumont and Tenafly, N.J., 1957-59, candidate for mayor, Tenafly, 1968. Mem. Public Relations Soc. Am. Home: New York N.Y. Died Nov. 26, 1986; buried Block Island, R.I.

GROSSE, ARISTID V., research chemist; b. Riga, Russia, Jan. 4, 1905; came to U.S., 1930, naturalized, 1937; s. Victor G. and Ella (Lieven) G.; m. Irene Lieven, Mar. 3, 1932; 1 child, Aristd. DEng, Technische Hochschule, Berlin-Charlottenburg, Germany, 1927. Research chemist Kaiser Wilhelm Inst. Chemistry, Berlin-Dahlem, 1927-28, Med. Analysis Labs., Shanghai, China, 1928-29; research assoc. Technische Hochschule, Berlin-Charlottenburg, 1929-32; research assoc. Universal Oil Products Co., Chgo., 1930-35, assoc. dir. research, 1935-40; vis. asst. prof. dept. .chemistry U. Chgo., 1931-40; Guggenheim research fellow dept. physics Columbia U., 1940-41, assoc. with H.C. Urey in war research labs. for Manhattan Project, 1942-43; cons. on synthetic rubber Houdry Process Corp., Phila., 1942-85, dir. research Houdry Labs., Houdry Process Corp. Pa., 1943-48; chief cons. on synthetic rubber WPB, Washington, 1942-43; mem. Am. rubber mission to USSR, 1942-43. Author: Chemie der Metallorganischen Verbindungen, 1937. Pres. Research Inst. Temple U. (name changed to Franklin Inst.), Phila., 1948-69, Germantown Labs., Inc. affiliate, 1969-85. Co-recipient award AEC, 1971. Mem. AAAS, Am. Chem. Soc., Am. Inst. Aeros. and Astronautics, Chem. Soc. (London), Am. Phys. Soc., Sigma Xi. Congregationalist. Home: Haverford Pa. Died July 21, 1985.

GROSSMAN, LOUIS I., dentistry educator; b. Phila., Dec. 16, 1901; s. Harry and Rachel (Musicant) G.; m. Emma May MacIntyre; children: Clara Grossman Reeves, Richard A. D.D.S., U. Pa., Phila., 1923; Dr.Med.Dentistry, U. Rostock, Germany, 1928; Sc.D. (hon.), U. Pa., Phila., 1978. Assoc. in oral medicine U. Pa., Phila., 1941-47, asst. prof. oral medicine, 1947-50, assoc. prof. oral medicine, 1950-54, prof. oral medicine, 1954-70, prof. emeritus oral medicine, 1970-88. Author: Endodontic Practice, 1st edit., 1940, 10th edit. 1980, transl. 7 languages; author, editor: Handbook on Dental Practice, 1948, 52, 60 (transl. into Spanish, Portuguese); Dental Formulas, 1952 (transl. into Spanish 1957); also articles; hon. editor Internat. Endodontic Jour. Fellow Royal Coll. Surgeons Eng. (hon.); mem. Am. Assn. Endodontists (pres. 1948-49), Am. Bd. Endodontics (pres. 1965-66), Internat. Assn. Dental Research, Acad. Stomatology, ADA, Fedn. Dentaire Internationale, Brit. Endodontic Soc., Sigma Xi. Home: Newtown Pa. Died Mar. 24, 1988.

GROTBERG, JOHN E., congressman; b. Winnebago, Minn., Mar. 21, 1925; s. Bernard Grotberg; m. Jean Oswalt; children—Sandra Mae, Karen Grotberg Weinberg, James Bernard; stepchildren—Melinda Oswalt, Benjamin M. Oswalt. B.S., George Williams Coll., 1961. Farmer N.D., 1942-44; theatrical and supper club entertainer and mgr. Fargo, St. Louis, Mpls., Chgo., 1944-47; mgr. YMCA Hotel Ship, 1948-49, 51, 59; dept. mgr. Montgomery Ward, Chgo., 1950;

resident mgr. Pheasant Run Lodge, St. Charles, Ill., 1964-65; dir. pub. relations YMCA Hotel, Chgo., 1966-71; corp. dir. fin. devel. YMCA Met. Chgo., 1966-71; mem. Ill. Ho. of Reps., Springfield, 1973-76, Ill. Senate, Springfield, 1976-85, 99th Congress from 14th Ill. dist., Washington, 1985-86; profl. singer and actor; cons. to mgmt. Hotel Baker Retirement Home for Sr. Citizens, 1972-86. Founder Fox Valley Hospice; former bd. dirs. St. Charles Community Chest; past pres., former mem. bd. dirs. Playmakers, Inc.; founder St. Charles YMCA Indian Guides, Ill.; Rep. precinct committeeman; past chmn. St. Charles Twp. Rep. Party, Ill.; chmn. Kane County Rep. Central Com., Ill.; chmn. bd., lay leader Baker Meml. United Methodist Ch. Mem. Assn. Profl. Dirs. YMCA, Kappa Delta Pi. Clubs: Geneva Golf, Tower (Chgo.). Lodge: Rotary. Home: Saint Charles Ill. Died Dec. 15, 1986.

GROTH, JOHN, artist, journalist; b. Chgo., Feb. 26, 1908; s. John and Ethel (Bragg) G. Student, Art Inst. Chgo., 1926-27, Art Student's League N.Y., 1937-38; D.Arts (hon.), Eastern Mich. U., 1976. Art dir. Esquire, 1933-36, Broun's Nutmeg, 1939; European war corr. Chgo. Sun, 1944, Am. Legion, 1945; lectr. 1945-46; art instr. Art Student's League N.Y., 1942-88; artist-war corr. Met. Group Syndicate Korea, French Indo-China, 1951; USAF corr. Congo-Central Africa, 1960; artist, war. corr. Dominican Republic, 1965, Vietnam, 1967; art instr. Pratt Inst., 1952-88, Parsons Sch. Design, 1954-55, N.A.D., 1962-88; corr. Sports Illustrated, Asia, 1954; artist in residence U. Tex., 1970. Illustrator: (by Kurt Sprague) The Promise Kept, 1975; Works represented, Mus. Modern Art, Library of Congress, Met. Mus. Art, Chgo. Art Inst., Bklyn. Mus., Butler Art Inst., Youngstown, Ohio, U. Tex. collection, U. Ga. collections, U.S. Army, Navy, Marines, Air Force; others, Surgeon Gen.'s Office; series of drawings of Jack Ruby trial, acquired Dallas Pub. Library, 1977; Illustrator: Grapes of Wrath (Steinbeck), 1947, Men Without Women (Hemingway), 1946, World of Wood, Field & Stream (Randolph), 1956, The Well Tempered Angler (Gingrich), 1959, War and Peace (Tolstoy), 1961, Exodus (Uris), 1962, Black Beauty, 1962, A Christmas Carol, 1963, The Stories of O'Henry (Ltd. Edits. Club), 1965, Gone With the Wind (Mitchell), 1967, War Prayer (Mark Twain), 1968, All Quiet on the Western Front (Erich Maria Remarque), 1969, John Groth's World of Sport, 1970, Life and Death of a Brave Bull, 1972, The Brave Men, 1972, Puddin' Head Wilson (Mark Twain), 1974, The Last Running (John Graves), 1974, The Fishing in Print (Arnold Gingrich), 1974, Biography of an American Reindeer (Alice Hopf), 1976, Journey to Pleasant Hill (Elijah Petty), 1982; illustrator-author: Studio: Europe, 1945, Studio: Asia, 1952; retrospective exhbn. Art Students League N.Y., 1987. Recipient Allied Artist award, 1961. Fellow Explorers Club; mem. Audubon Artists. (dir.); Mem. Soc. Illustrators, Am. Water Color Soc., N.A.D. (asso.). Clubs: Overseas Press (N.Y.C.), Illustrators (N.Y.C.), Lotos (N.Y.C.), Salmagundi (N.Y.C.). Home: New York N.Y. Died June 27, 1988.

GROVER, EARLE V., iron and steel contractor; b. Denver, Sept. 25, 1891; s. William Jonathan and Anna Louise (Taylor) G.; m. Ida Mae Spencer, Sept. 25, 1913; children: Dorothy Mae (Mrs. B. W. Thorne Jr.), Robert S. Pres. Apex Steel Corp. Ltd., also chmn. bd. dirs. Trustee Hollywood (Calif.) Presbyn. Hosp. Mem. Am. Inst. Steel Constrn. (pres. 1954-55), L.A. C. of C. (pres. 1949), Calif. Taxpayers Assn. (pres. 1954-55). Home: Los Angeles Calif. †

GROVES, ASA BIEHL, realtor; b. Viroqua, Wis., Dec. 21, 1891; s. John Wesley and Rachel Eunice (Biehl) G.; m. Frances Eugenia Moore, Oct. 12, 1938; 1 son, Asa Biehl. Student, U. Wis., 1908-10, 1911-13. Real estate developer 1913-33; with Home Owners' Loan Corp., from 1933; appraisal advisor Fed. Home Loan Bank Adminstrn.; v.p. Crawford Home Loan Corp. In 1939 organized and directed appraisal staff to assist Army, Navy and Dept. of Justice in acquisition of lands in connection with War Emergency; chief appraiser Vets. Adminstrn., 1946-58; exec. v.p. Desser Devel. Co., 1958, v.p., sec. Lefcourt Mortgage Co., from 1961. 1st lt. U.S. Army, 1917-1919. Mem. Phi Gamma Delta. Home: Miami Fla. †

GRUENTZIG, ANDREAS ROLAND, cardiologist, educator; b. Dresden, Germany, June 25, 1939; s. Wilmar and Charlotte G.; m. Margaret Anne Thornton, May 28, 1983; 1 dau., Sonja. Privat dozent U. Zurich, 1977-80; prof. medicine and radiology, dir. interventional cardiovascular medicine Emory U., Atlanta, 1980-85. Contbr. articles to med. jours. Recipient Goetz prize U. Zurich. Mem. Am. Heart Assn., Deutsche Gesellschaft fuer Herz und Kreislaufforschung, Schweizerische, Angliologische Gesellschaft. Home: Atlanta Ga. Died Oct. 27, 1985.

GRUPPE, KARL HEINRICK, sculptor; b. Rochester, N.Y., Mar. 18, 1893; s. Charles Paul and Helen Elizabeth (Mitchell) G.; m. Betty A. Clarke, Oct. 9, 1948; 1 child, Elizabeth Mitchell. Student, Royal Acad., Antwerp, Belgium, Art Student League, N.Y.C.; studied with, Karl Bitter, N.Y.C., 1912-15; chief sculptor monument restoration project, Dept. Parks, N.Y.C., 1934-37. With USMC, 1918-19. Recipient St. Gaudens prize Art Students League, 1912, Avery prize Archtl. League, 1920, Helen Foster Barnett prize, 1926, Saltus gold medal NAD, 1952, Dessie Greer prize 131st Ann. Exhbn. NAD, 1956, Lindsey Morris Meml. prize Nat. Sculpture Soc., 1968, Gold medal, 1975, Elizabeth Watrous gold medal for sculpture NAD, 1969, 76, Daniel Chester French award, 1974, Therese and Edwin H. Richard Meml. prize Nat. Sculpture Soc., 1977, medal of honor Nat. Arts Club, 1970, medal of honor Nat. Sculpture Soc., 1980. Mem. NAD (1st v.p. 1956-59), Art Commn. Assocs. (bd. dirs.), Nat. Sculpture Soc. (pres. 1950), Century Assn., Nat. Arts Club. Home: Southold N.Y. Died Sept. 1982; buried Southold, N.Y.

GUBBRUD, ARCHIE, agricultural company executive, former governor; b. Huron, S.D., Dec. 31, 1910; s. Marius Torwald and Ella Rachel (Rommeriem) G.; m. Florence Maxine Dexter, Aug. 15, 1939; children: John Dexter, Maxine (Mrs. Clair Freuik). Farmer Alcester, S.D., 1934-87; bd. dirs. State Bank Alcester, 1949-69; mem. S.D. Ho. of Reps., 1951-60, speaker, 1958-60; gov. State of S.D., 1961-64; Chmn. bd. Beefland Internat., Huron. Del. Rep. Nat. Conv., 1964, 68; bd. dirs. S.D. Farmers Home Adminstrn., 1969-87, Am. Beef, 1971-87; bd. regents Augustana Acad. Mem. Masons, Shriners. Home: Alcester S.D. Died Apr. 26, 1987; buried Lands Luth. Ch. Cemetery, Hudson, S.D.

GUERRANT, WILLIAM BARNETT, clergyman, educator; b. Danville, Ky., Feb. 2, 1892; s. Richard Putney and Anna (Davis) G.; m. Susie Gilmore Roberts, Sept. 25, 1917; children: William Barnett, John Summerfield. AB, Centre Coll., Danville, 1913, AM, 1914, LLD, 1950; BD, Louisville Theol. Sem., 1917; DD, King Coll., 1928; STD, Bibl. Sem. N.Y.C., 1930; LLD, Southwestern at Memphis, 1950. Ordained to ministry Presbyn. Ch., 1917. Pastor Guerrant, Ky., 1917-18; supt. Highland Inst., 1918-27; pres. Stonewall Jackson Coll., Abingdon, Va., 1927-30; coll. pastor, bible instr. Lincoln Meml. U., Harrogate, Tenn., 1930-35; supt. Bachman Meml. Sch. and Home, Farner, Tenn., 1935-39; prof. philosophy and religion Austin Coll., Sherman, Tex., 1939-43, pres., 1943-53; prof. Bible Hampden-Sidney Coll., 1953-54; minister ch. extension Presbytery of St. John, from 1955; moderator Synod of Tex., 1948-49. Mem. regional coun. Boy Scouts Am.; dir. Civic Forum, Sherman. Recipient Disting. Service award in field of Christian Edn., Austin Coll., 1956. Mem. Nat. Assn. Bibl. Instrs., Tex. State Tchrs. Assn., Presbyn. Ednl. Assn. south (pres. 1950), Dallas Presbytery, Rotary (dir. Sherman club), Phi Delta Theta. Home: Umatilla Fla. †

GUILDEN, IRA, finance corporation executive; b. N.Y.C.. Chmn. bd. Baldwin Securities Corp., John B. Stetson Co., Devel. Corp. for Israel; pres., treas. North Ocanic Securities Co., Inc. Home: New York N.Y. Died Nov. 11, 1984.

GUILFORD, JOY PAUL, psychologist; b. Marquette, Nebr., Mar. 7, 1897; s. Edwin Augustus and Arvilla (Monroe) G.; m. Ruth S. Burke, Sept. 8, 1927; 1 child, Joan S. AB, U. Nebr., 1922, AM, 1924, LLD (hon.), 1952; PhD, Cornell U., 1927; ScD, U. So. Calif., 1962. Instr. psychology U. Ill., 1926-27; asst. prof. psychology U. Kans., 1927-28; assoc. prof., then prof. U. Nebr., 1928-40; dir. Bur. Instructional Research, 1938-40; prof. psychology U. So. Calif., 1940-67, prof. emeritus, 1967-87. Author: Psychometric Methods, 1936, others. Col. USAAF, 1942-45. Decorated Legion of Merit. Fellow AAAS, Am. Psychol. Assn. (pres. 1949-50); mem. Psychometric Soc. (pres. 1938-39), Nat. Acad. Scis., Soc. Exptl. Psychologists, Midwestern Psychol. Assn. (pres. 1939-40), Western Psychol. Assn. (pres. 1946-47), So. Calif. Psychol. Assn., Calif. State Psychol. Assn., Soc. Multivariate Exptl. Psychologists, Calif. Color Soc. (pres. 1948-49), Blue Key, Phi Beta Kappa, Sigma Xi, Phi Sigma, Psi Chi, Phi Delta Kappa, Pi Kappa Alpha, Phi Kappa Phi. Democrat. Home: Beverly Hills Calif. Died Nov. 26, 1987.

GULICK, SIDNEY LEWIS, university official; b. Kobe, Japan, Aug. 17, 1902; s. Sidney L. and Cara May (Fisher) G.; m. Evelyn Mary Bade, July 31, 1931; children—Marian G. Wilson, Sidney Lewis III. A.B., Oberlin Coll., 1923, M.A., 1925; Ph.D., Yale U., 1931. Tchr. English, piano Doshisha U., Kyoto, Japan, 1923-24; asso. pub. speaking U. Calif. at Berkeley, 1927-30; instr. English U. Rochester, 1931-35; asst., then asso. prof. English, Mills Coll., 1935-45; asso. prof. English Calif. State U. at San Diego, 1945-49, prof. English, 1949-69, prof. emeritus, 1969-88, dean arts and scis., 1959-69, emeritus, 1969-88, adminstrv. adviser, 1969-88. Author: A Chesterfield Bibliography to 1800, 1935, rev. edit., 1979, Some Unpublished Letters of Lord Chesterfield, 1937, Gulick Vocabulary Survey, 1957, 61; Contbr. essays, articles to learned publs. Served as chief procurement and placement dist. postal censor San Francisco Office of Censorship, 1942-45. Mem. Modern Lang. Assn., AAUP, Philol. Assn. Pacific Coast, Phi Kappa Phi. Conglist. Club: Calif. Writers. Home: La Mesa Calif. Died Feb. 5, 1988; cremated.

GUMBART, WILLIAM BARNUM, lawyer; b. Norwalk, Conn., Feb. 14, 1892; s. Edward H. and Mary Frances (Barnum) G.; m. Lucy Adele Finch, Oct. 18, 1919; children: Mary (dec.), William B. AB, Dartmouth Coll., 1913; student law, Columbia; LLB, Yale U., 1915. Bar: Conn. 1916, Mass. 1916. Practic New Haven; counsel firm Tyler, Cooper, Gran Bowerman and Keefe; lectr. Conn. law Yale U. Sc LAw, New Haven, 1924-44; assoc. fellow Davenpo Coll. of Yale; sr. trustee Conn. Savs. Bank; hon. di New Haven Water Co., So. Conn. Gas Co. Trust emeritus Hopkins Grammar Sch.; past pres. New Hav Community Chest; former chmn. New Haven chp ARC. 1st lt. Q.M.C., U.S. Army, 1917-19; with An Expeditionary Force, France, 1918-19. Fellow Am. Ba Found.; mem. Am., Conn. (past pres.) bar assns Graduate Club, Quinnipiack (former pres.), Phi Be Kappa. Republican. Congregationalist. Home: Ne Haven Conn. Died Apr. 12, 1982; buried Riversid Cemetery, South Norwalk, Conn.

GUNN, GEORGE, JR., business executive; b. Tacom Apr. 10, 1891; s. George and Emma (Howe) G.; n Cleata Dyer, July 26, 1917; children: Cleata, Nanc Gloria, JoAnne. Student, U. Wash., 1912-14. Moto truck distbr. Tacoma, 1914; propr. Kelley-Springfie Truck Sales Co., Tacoma and Seattle, 1914-25; v.p sales mgr. White Motor Car Co., Cleve., 1925-30; v. Puget Sound Pulp & Timber Co., Everett, Wash., 193 37; pres. Am. Warehouse Co., 1936-46, Kirsten Pip Co., 1938-49, Pioneer Inc., Tacoma, 1940-44; pre Webster-Brinkley Co., 1941-44, v.p., 1945-49; pres. E gineered Products Co., 1944-48, Tote Engring. Inc from 1948, Westfield Oil and Gas Co., from 1956, Vo Oil Co., from 1959; owner Canteen Co. of Wash Seattle, 1938-48; dir. West Coast Airlines; pres. Great Seattle Inc., 1950-52. Chmn. new industries com. Was State Indsl. Devel. Com.; chmn. Seattle Centennia 1952; chmn. 13th Naval Dist. Citizens Com., Navy R lief Soc., 1942-43, Selective Service Bd. No. 7, Seattl 1941-46; mem. nat. distbn. coun. U.S. Dept. Commerc Mem. NAM (dir. 1944-48), Wash. Athletic Clu Seattle Golf Club, Rainier Club, Masons, Phi Gamm Delta (nat. archon 1956-60, nat. pres. 1962-64). Hom Seattle Wash. †

GUNN, HARTFORD NELSON, JR., broadcastir company executive; b. Port Washington, N.Y., Dec. 2 1926; s. Hartford N. and Edith (Arnold) G. BS, U. Mcht. Marine Acad., 1948; AB, Harvard U., 194 MBA, 1951; LHD, Northeastern U., 1957, Boston Col 1970; LLD, Cen. Mich. U., 1975. Dir. ops. Lowell Ins Coop. Broadcasting Council, Boston, 1951; asst. ge mgr. Sta. WGBH-FM, Boston, 1951-55; gen. mgr. Sta WGBH-FM, WGBH-TV, Boston, 1956-70, v.p., ge mgr., 1969-70; sr. v.p., gen. mgr. Sta. KCET-TV, 198 86; pres. Pub. Broadcasting Service, Washington, 197 76, vice chmn., 1976-86; bd. dirs. Boston Globe. Pre Ea. Ednl. Network, Cambridge, Mass., 1961-66; pa mem. nat. adv. com. Council for Pub. Schs.; past mer corp. Ednl. Devel. Ctr.; past vice chmn., mem. exe com. Mass. Ednl. Communications Commn.; past mer ednl. devel. commn. Mass Dept. Edn.; past mem. ad council Edward R. Murrow Ctr. Pub. Diplomacy, Tuf U.; assoc. in edn. Harvard Grad. Sch. Edn.; past dir. large Assn. Harvard Alumni; former trustee Wor Peace Found.; mem. exec. com. Internat. Music Counc With USNR, 1945-48; lt. comdr. Res. ret. Recipie Lamp of Knowledge award New Eng. chpt. Pub. Rel tions Soc. Am., 1964, Ralph Lowell medal, 1973, Ce Ednl. Networks award, 1977; named one of 11 Ou standing Men of Yr. award Boston Jr. C. of C., 1962 Fellow Am. Acad. Arts and Scis.; mem. Nat. Ass Ednl. Broadcasters (past dir., chmn. bd. ednl. TV sta div.), Soc. Motion Picture and TV Engrs., Interna Broadcast Inst., Harvard Club, Century Club, G orgetown Club, Cosmos Club, Tavern Club. Hom Washington D.C. Died Jan. 2, 1986.

GUNSON, LEO JOSEPH, business executive; Phila., July 5, 1896; s. John D. and Mary F. (Cahill) G m. Florence G. Cullen, June 29, 1922; children—Ma Elizabeth, Leo Joseph, Jr. Student, Notre Dame Acad Phila., 1902-08, St. Joseph's Coll., 1908- 12, U. Pa 1914-17. With Publicker Industries, Inc., 1924-7 treas., until 1976; pres., dir. Continental Distillin Corp., until 1976. Served to 1st lt. 312th Machine Gu Bn., World War I. Decorated knight grand cross Ord Holy Sepulchre. Club: Phila. Country. Home: Ph ladelphia Pa. Died May 16, 1988, buried Calva Cemetery, West Conshohocken, Pa.

GURDJIAN, ELISHA STEPHENS, neurologic surgeon; b. Smyrna, Turkey, Apr. 18, 1900; came U.S., 1920, naturalized, 1930; s. Stepan and Beru (Hagopian) G.; m. Dorothy Eileen Kratz, May 29, 193 children: Edwin, Joan, Ronald, Richard. MS, U. Mic 1924, MD, 1926, PhD, 1927. Diplomate Am. B Neurol. Surgery. Intern U. Mich. Hosp., 1925-27, 2 30, Rochester (N.Y.) Gen. Hosp., 1927-28; pvt. practi Detroit, 1930-85; head neurosurg. service Grace Hosp Detroit, 1938-70; prof. neurol. surgery Wayne State U 1949-56, chmn. dept. neurosurgery, 1956-70, di Bioengring. Research Ctr., 1966-70, prof. emerit 1970-85. Author: (with J.E. Webster) Operati Neurosurgery, 1952, (with Webster) Mechanism, D agnosis and Management of Head Injury, 1958, Oper tive Neurosurgery, 1964, Cranial and Intracranial Su peration, 1969; editor: (with L.M. Thomas) Operati Neurosurgery, 1970, Impact Injury and Crash Prote tion, 1970, Neckache and Backache, 1970, Head Inju from Antiquity to the Present, 1973, Impact Head I jury, 1975; contbr. articles to med. publs. Recipie

Bronze medal Roentgen Ray Soc., 1948, Gold medal Roentgen Ray Soc., 1960. Fellow ACS (chmn. adv. council neurol. surgery 1952); mem. AMA (chmn. sect. on nervous and mental diseases 1960, Silver Hektoen medal 1967), Am. Assn. Neurol. Surgeons, Cushing Soc., Congress Neurol. Surgeons (honored guest 1971), Am. Neurol. Assn. (v.p. 1969), Am. Assn. Anatomists, Am. Assn. Surgery Trauma, Cen. Surg. Assn., Cen. Neuropsychiat.Assn., Soc. Neurol. Surgeons, Sigma Xi, Phi Sigma, Alpha Omega Alpha. Home: Bloomfield Hills Mich. Died Nov. 30, 1985.

GURNHAM, C(HARLES) FRED(ERICK), chemical and sanitary engineer; b. Ludlow, Mass., Oct. 19, 1911; s. George Frederick and Ella Bertha (Hendrick) G.; m. Vivian Wikander, Aug. 25, 1934; children: Sandra J. (Mrs. Richard J. Barman) Diane W. (Mrs. Peter L. La Porte), Robert H., Roy F. BS, Yale U., 1932; MSChemE, NYU, 1940, DEng, 1942. Registered profl. engr., N.Y., Ind., Ill., Mich., Minn., Ohio, Tenn., Tex.; diplomate Am. Acad. Environ. Engrs. Chemist Smith Paper Co., Lee, Mass., 1932-34; chem. engr. Ludlow Mfg. Assocs., 1934-36, Naugatuck (Conn.) Chem. Co., 1936-38; asst. prof. chem. engring. Pratt Inst., 1938-41; chem. engr. Air Reduction Co., Stamford, Conn., 1942-44, Whitney Blake Co., Hamden, Conn., 1944-48; prof., head dept. chem. engring. Tufts U., 1949-52, Mich. State U., 1952-61; prof. environ. engring. and chem. engring. Ill. Inst. Tech., Chgo., 1962-68, chmn. dept. environ. engring., 1966-68; v.p., mgr. midwest ops. Cyrus William Rice & Co., Water Mgmt. Cons., Chgo., 1967-69; pres. Gurnham and Assocs. Inc., Chgo., later v.p., cons.; ind. cons. chem. and san. engring. from 1961; bd. dirs. Peter F. Loftus Corp., Chgo.; del. from electroplating industry to Nat. Tech. Task Com. on Indsl. Wastes USPHS, 1950-57, del. from mining industry, 1957-61, vice chmn., 1955, chmn., 1956. Author: Principles of Industrial Waste Treatment, 1955. Recipient Disting. Alumnus citation NYU, 1955; spl. recognition Am. Inst. Plant Engrs., 1970. Fellow ASCE, Am. Inst. Chem. Engrs., Am. Inst. Chemists; mem. Am. Chem. Soc., Water Pollution Control Fedn., Sigma Xi, Tau Beta Pi, Phi Lambda Upsilon, Alpha Chi Sigma, Sigma Pi Sigma. Home: Chicago Ill. Deceased.

GUSTAVE, HENRI See FRANCO, JOHAN

GUTMANN, JAMES, educator; b. N.Y.C., Apr. 11, 1897; s. Carl and Lilly (Liebmann) G.; m. Jeanette Mack, Feb. 3, 1920 (dec. 1960); children: Barbara Rosenkrantz, Carl Mack, Alice Brandfonbrener; m. 2d Ruth Adler Friess, Nov. 18, 1976 (dec.). AB, Columbia U., 1918, AM, 1919, PhD, 1936. Tchr. ethics Ethical Culture Sch., N.Y.C., 1918-28; assoc. leader Soc. Ethical Culture, 1927-30; with Columbia U., 1920-88, successively lectr. philosophy, instr., asst. prof., assoc. prof., 1920-48, prof. philosophy, 1948-62, prof. emeritus, 1962-88, chmn. dept., 1952-61, dir. univ. seminars, 1970-75; mem. exec. com. Com. to Abolish Capital Punishment; mem. East-West Philosophers Conf., U. Hawaii, 1969; rep. ACLU at UN. Author: Schelling: Of Human Freedom, 1936; co-author: Naturalism and Historical Understanding, 1967, Horizons of a Philosopher, 1963, Ethics and Social Justice, 1970, Dictionary of the History of Ideas, 1973, The Ency. of Bioethics, 1977, The Philosophy of Brand Blanshard, 1978; editor Marcus Aurelius' Meditations, 1963, Spinoza's Ethics, 1968, The University Seminars at Columbia, 1971, 75; mem. editorial bd. Studies in Romanticism (Boston U.). Bd. dirs. Encampment for Citizenship, chmn., 1973-75; bd. dirs. Conf. on Methods in Philosophy and Scis., Forum on Psychiatry and Humanities, Washington. Mem. AAUP, Am. Philos. Assn., Columbia Faculty Club, Phi Beta Kappa. Home: New York N.Y. Died Nov. 6, 1988.

GUY, WALTER C., business executive; b. Ind., Apr. 9, 1891; s. Charles F. and Rosa J. (Koontz) G.; m. Lura Leffel, Sept. 29, 1912; 1 son, Richard Leffel. Student, Winona Coll., 1909-14, U. Chgo., 1915-16; LLD, Ind. Tech. Coll. Chief adminstrv. div. U.S. Vets. Bur., St. Louis, 1923-26; dist. mgr. Remington Rand Inc., Little Rock, 1927-29; regional dir. Remington Rand Inc., Memphis, 1929-31; chmn. Ark. Printing & Lithographing Co., Ark. Stationery & Furniture Co., Internat. Bus. Forms Inc., Exec. Svcs. Inc. V.p. Ark. Live Stock Show Assn.; mem. bd. trustees Little Rock U. Found. Inc. Home: Little Rock Ark. †

GWATHMEY, ROBERT, artist; b. Richmond, Va., Jan. 24, 1903; s. Robert and Eva Mortimer (Harrison) G.; m. Rosalie Dean Hook, Nov. 2, 1935; 1 son, Charles. Student, N.C. State Coll., 1924-25, Md. Inst., 1925-26, Pa. Acad. Fine Arts, 1926-30. Represented permanent collections, Carnegie Mus., Pitts., Telfair Mus., Savannah, Ga., Boston Mus., Va. Mus., Richmond, Pa. Acad., Phila., San Diego Mus., Los Angeles Mus., Springfield Mus., Mass., IBM Corp., U. Tex., U. Okla., Ala. Poly. Inst., Butler Art Inst., Youngstown, Ohio, Rochester Meml. Gallery, N.Y., U. Ga., U. Ill., Whitney Mus., Mus. Modern Art, Sao Paulo, Brazil. Recipient First prize Contemporary Water Color Ann., San Diego Mus., 1941; recipient Second prize Carnegie Inst. ann., 1943, Second prize Pepsi-Cola Ann., 1946, Second prize Birmingham Mus., 1956, Fourth prize Corcoran Gallery, 1957; Nat. Acad. Arts and Letters grantee, 1946; Pa. Acad. Fine Arts fellow, 1958. Mem. Nat. Inst. Arts and Letters, NAD. Died Sept. 21, 1988.

HAAS, ROBERT GREEN, advertising executive; b. Chgo., Sept. 14, 1921; s. Adolph R. and Marie (Green) H.; m. Carolyn Buhai, June 29, 1947; children: Andrew Robert, Mari Beth, Betsy Ann, Thomas Michael, Karen Sue. Student, U. Ill., 1940-41, Westen Mich. U., 1944-45. Pres. Robert Haas Advt., Chgo., 1960-63, Bronner & Haas Advt., Chgo., 1963-67; exec. v.p. Grey-North Advt. Agy., Chgo., 1967-80; pres. CEE & H Co. Inc., Chgo., 1981-82, Haas & Assoc. Inc., Chgo., from 1983; pres. Maxwell's & Maxwell's Too Restaurants, Denver, The Vail Cookie Co.; mng. ptnr. JEB Leasing Co., from 1980. With USNR, 1942-46. Died June 30, 1984; cremated.

HABER, JACK N., editor; b. Bklyn., Feb. 26, 1939; s. Michael H. and Ada (Weiss) H. Attended, Bklyn. Coll., 1956-58. Assoc. editor Men's Wear mag., 1962-65; editor Scene mag., Esquire publ., 1965-68; sr. editor Clothes mag., 1968-69; editor Gentlemen's Quar. (acquired by Condé Nast Publs. 1979), N.Y.C., 1969-77; editor-in-chief Gentlemen's Quar. (acquired by Condé Nast Publs. 1979), from 1977; instr. exec. seminars in men's wear store mgmt. N.Y. U. Inst. Retail Mgmt., 1970-74; lectr. Field Studies Center N.Y., from 1980, Wharton Exec. Lifestyles lecture series Wharton Sch., 1980-81. Served with AUS, 1958-60. Recipient Lulu award for excellence in reporting men's fashion news Men's Fashion Assn.-Menswear Retailers Am., 1971, 72. Mem. Am. Soc. Mag. Editors. Home: New York N.Y. Deceased.

HABER, WILLIAM, educator, economist; b. Rumania, Mar. 6, 1899; came to U.S., 1909; s. Leon and Anna (Stern) B.; m. Fannie Gallas, Aug. 31, 1924; children—Ralph, Alan. B.A., U. Wis., 1923, M.A., 1926, Ph.D., 1927; postgrad., U. Wis. and Harvard, 1924-25; L.H.D. honoris causa, Hebrew Union Coll., 1961, Mich. State U., 1970; Ph.D. (hon.), Hebrew U., Jerusalem, 1971; LL.D., Brandeis U., 1974. Labor mgr. Hart, Schaffner & Marx, 1923; instr. econs. U. Wis., 1926-27; asso. prof. econs. Mich. State Coll., 1927-36; prof. econs. U. Mich., 1936-88, chmn. dept., 1962-63; dean Coll. Lit., Sci. and Arts, 1963-68, spl. adviser to exec. officers, 1968-88; dir. Oakland Housing, Inc., 1935-88, chmn., 1970-88; dir. Huron Valley Nat. Bank; impartial chmn. Kaiser UAW Retirement Fund, 1951-88; state emergency welfare relief adminstr., 1933-36; state dir. Nat. Youth Adminstrn. for Mich., 1935-36; dep. dir. WPA, 1934-36; chmn. Unemployment Ins. Study Commn., 1936; mem. Mich. Unemployment Compensation Commn., 1936-37; cons. Social Security Bd., 1939-45, Nat. Resources Planning Bd., 1940-44, chmn. com. long-range work and relief policy, 1941-44; spl. asst. to dir. Bur. Budget, 1942, mem. conf. post war relief readjustment of civilian and mil. personnel, 1943, chief planning div., 1942; dir. Bur. Program Requirement, War Manpower Commn., 1943, asst. exec. dir., 1944; adviser on manpower to dir. Office War Moblzn. and Reconversion, 1945, cons., 1945-46; mem. Am. Assn. Social Security (com. post-def. planning), 1941, U.S. Employment Service (tech. bd. on occupational research program), 1940; chmn. Fed. Adv. Council on Employment Security, 1948-88; mem. Manpower Cons. Com., Nat. Resources Security Bd., Nat. Def. Agy., 1947-48; mem. pub. adv. com. Area Redevel. Adminstrn., Dept. Commerce, 1962, mem. regional export expansion council, 1962; panel Am. Arbitration Assn.; mem. Nat. Acad. Arbitrators, Social Science Research Council (com. on econ. security), 1941-88; mem. indsl. com. (for paper products, rubber and textiles) Wage and Hour Adminstrn., 1941; mem. Adv. Council on Social Security, 1938-39; cons. on manpower to sec. of labor, and Def. Manpower Adminstrn.; Adviser on Jewish affairs to comdr.-in-chief U.S. Forces in Germany and Austria., 1948-49; mem. Pres.'s Task Force on Depressed Areas, 1961; Exec. com. Am.-Jewish Com., 1945-88; chmn. nat. Hillel commn. B'nai B'rith, 1949-64, hon. chmn., 1964-88; pres. Am. ORT Fedn. (rehab. through training), 1951; pres. central bd. World ORT Union, 1955-88. Author: Industrial Relations in the Building Industry, 1930, Unemployment Relief and Economic Security, 1936, The Cost of Financing Unemployment Insurance in Michigan, 1952, Labor Relations and Productivity in the Building Trades, (with H.L. Levinson), 1955; co-author: Post War Economic Reconstruction, 1945, The Michigan Economy: Its Potentials and Its Problems, 1960, (with Wilbur J. Cohen) Social Security Program Problems and Policies, 1961, (with others) Michigan in the 1970s, 1965, (with Merrill G. Murray) Unemployment Insurance in the American Economy, 1966; Editor: (with Merrill G. Murray) Readings in Social Security, 1948, Labor in a Changing America, 1966; co-editor: (with Merrill G. Murray) Manpower in the United States, 1954; contbr. to: (with Merrill G. Murray) others. Bd. dirs. United Service for New Americans, 1947-88; bd. govs. Hebrew U., Jerusalem, 1968-88; trustee Brandeis U., 1969-88. Recipient John Dewey award League Indsl. Democracy, 1960, John Lendrum Mitchell award indsl. relations U. Wis., 1924; Wertheim fellow for research indsl. relations Harvard, 1925. Mem. Am. Econ. Assn., Am. Pub. Welfare Assn., Soc. Pub. Adminstrn., Indsl. Relations Research Assn. (pres. 1960). Home: Ann Arbor Mich. Died Dec. 30, 1988.

HABICHT, FRANK, manufacturing executive; b. Buffalo, Oct. 18, 1887; s. George and Magdalena (Schuchman) H.; m. Winifred Morley, Nov. 3, 1913; children; Margaret Jane (Mrs. Peter Newton Todhunter), William Homer, Robert Frederick, Richard Charles. Ed. publ. schs., high sch. and tech. high schs, night tech. sch., Buffalo. Apprentice machine shop, 1899-1906; elec. engring. apprentice Westinghouse Electric and Mfg. Co., 1906-08; salesman, advancing to asst. to works mgr. Celfor Tool Co., 1908-1912, works mgr., 1913-16; gen. purchasing agt. Clark Equipment Co., 1916-35, v.p., 1925-53, dir., from 1925; gen. mgr. and v.p. Buchanan (Mich.) Land Co., 1918-53; bd. dirs. Buchanan Savs. and Loan Assn., from 1925. Mem. Buchanan Sch. Bd., 1921-41, Berrien County Rd. Commn., from 1939; v.p. southwestern area Boy Scouts Am., from 1935. Recipient Silver Beaver award from Boy Scouts Am. Mem. Masons (32 degree, Shriner), Elks Club. Home: Buchanan Mich. †

HACKER, LOUIS MORTON, educator, author, editor; b. N.Y.C., Mar. 17, 1899; s. Morris and Celia (Waxelbaum) H.; m. Lillian Lewis, June 26, 1921 (dec. 1952); children: Andrew, Betsy (Mrs. Roy Dexheimer); m. 2d, Beatrice Larson Brennan, June 17, 1953. Asst. editor New Internat. Ency., 1923-25, 28-29, Ency. of Social Scis., 1932-34; lectr. history and econs., summer sessions U. Wis., 1937, Ohio State U., 1939, Utah State Agrl. Coll., 1945, U. Hawaii, 1953, U. Puget Sound, 1970; lectr. econs. dept. Columbia U., 1935-42, asst. prof., 1942-44, assoc. prof., 1944-48, prof., 1948-67, prof. emeritus, 1967-87, dir. Sch. Gen. Studies, 1949-52, dean, 1952-58; mem. faculty New Sch., 1940, 43-48, Am. Inst. Banking, 1940-43; Harmsworth prof. Am. history, fellow Queens Coll., Oxford U., 1948-49; faculty Yeshiva U., 1958-59; lectr. Cambridge U., 1952, Army War Coll., from 1952, Nat. War Coll., 1953-54, 57; vis. disting. prof. Pa. State U., 1959-60; Bode Meml. lectr. Ohio State U., 1970; vis. disting. prof. Fairleigh Dickinson U., 1967-68; Relm Found. research fellow, 1967-68. Author: United States Since 1865 (with B.B. Kendrick), 1932; Farmer is Doomed, 1933; Short History of the New Deal, 1934; The United States: A Graphic History, 1937; American Problems of Today, 1938; Triumph of American Capitalism, 1940; Shaping of the American Tradition, 1947; New Industrial Relations (with others), 1948; England and America: The Ties That Bind, 1948; Government Assistance to Universities in Great Britain (with H.W. Dodds and L. Rogers), 1952; United States in the 20th Century (with H.S. Zahler), 1952; (with others) Capitalism and The Historians, 1954; Alexander Hamilton in the American Tradition, 1957; American Capitalism, 1957; Larger View of the University, 1961; The World of Andrew Carnegie, 1865-1901, 1968; The Coruse of American Economic Growth and Development, 1970; (with M.D. Hirsch) Joseph Mayer Proskauer, A Biography, 1976; editor: (and author with Allan Nevins) The United States and its Place in World Affairs, 1918-43; American Century Series: Major Documents in American Economic History, 2 Vols., 1961. Served S.A.T.C., 1918. Guggenheim fellow, 1948, 58-59; Benjamin Franklin fellow Royal Soc. Arts, Eng., 1963. Mem. Am. Assn. for Middle East Studies, Am. History Assn., Am. Econ. Assn., Econ. History Assn., PEN, Authors League, Mt. Pelerin Soc., Phi Beta Kappa. Republican. Clubs: Athenaeum (London); Pilgrims (N.Y.). Home: New York N.Y. Died Mar. 1987.

HACKETT, THOMAS PAUL, psychiatrist; b. Cin., July 6, 1928; m. Mary Ann Kamuf, 1951 (div. 1960); 1 dau., Melissa; m. Eleanor Mayher, 1961; children: Laura, Shelagh, Thomas. B.S., U. Cin., 1948, M.D., 1952. Diplomate: Am. Bd. Psychiatry and Neurology. Intern USPHS Hosp., San Francisco, 1952-53; clin. and research fellow in psychiatry Mass. Gen. Hosp., Boston, 1955-58; resident in psychiatry Boston Psychopathic Hosp., 1957-58; asst. in psychiatry Mass. Gen. Hosp., 1958-59, asst. psychiatrist, 1959-64, assoc. psychiatrist, 1964-72, chief psychiat. consultation service, 1968-76, psychiatrist, 1972—, acting chief psychiatry, 1974-76, chief psychiatry, 1976-88; clin. and research fellow Harvard Med. Sch., Boston, 1955-58, asst. in psychiatry, 1958-59, instr. psychiatry, 1959-67, clin. asso. in psychiatry, 1967-69, asst. prof. psychiatry, 1969-72, assoc. prof., 1972-76, prof., 1976-88, Eben S. Draper prof. psychiatry, 1977-88; cons. in psychiatry Div. of Legal Medicine, Commonwealth of Mass., 1955-74; spl. fellow in legal psychiatry Law-Medicine Inst., Boston U. Med. Sch., 1964-65, vis. prof., 1977-88; cons. Indsl. Accidents Bd., Commonwealth of Mass., 1970-88 , VA Hosp., Bedford, Mass., 1974-88; cons. internat. rehab. research program Social and Rehab. Service, HEW, 1974-88; cons. NIMH, NIH, 1975-88; cons. Nat. Heart, Lung & Blood Inst., 1977-88. Editor: (with N.H. Cassem) Massachusetts General Hospital Handbook of General Hospital Psychiatry, 1978; (with A.D. Weisman and A. Kucharski) Psychiatry in a General Hospital, The First Fifty Years, 1987; contbr. chpts. to books, articles to profl. jours.; assoc. editor: Psychosomatics, 1979-88; cons. editor: Psychiat. Medicine Update, 1978-88; mem. editorial bd.: Annals of Internal Medicine, 1977-83, Jour. of Affective Disorders, 1978-88; assoc. editor Jour. Psychosomatic Research, 1986-88; contbg. editor: Med. Econs, 1967-83; mem. rev. bd.: Jour. Cardiac Rehab, 1979-88. Fellow ACP, Am. Coll. Psychiatry, Am. Psychiat. Assn., Am. Acad. Psychosomatic Medicine; mem. Mass. Med. Soc., Am. Psychosomatic Soc., No.

New Eng. Psychiat. Soc., AAAS, Internat. Soc. and Fedn. Cardiology (mem. council on cardiac rehab.), Phi Eta Sigma. Home: Boston Mass. Died Jan. 23, 1988; buried Chilmark, Mass.

HADDAD, EUGENE, technical company executive; b. Tampa, Fla., Aug. 10, 1925; s. Simon Farrage and Mary (Lutz) H.; m. Barbara Eloise Brown, June 23, 1951; children—Mary Elizabeth, Thomas Eugene, Geoffrey Allen, Susan Eloise, Barbara Jane. A.A., U. Fla., Gainesville, 1947; B.S. in Engring. Physics, Ala. Poly. Inst. Tech., Auburn, 1948; M.S. in Physics, UCLA, 1951; Ph.D., U. Utah, 1959. Teaching asst. U. So. Calif., Los Angeles, 1949, UCLA, 1950-51; teaching fellow, research fellow U. Utah, 1953-55; mem. staff Los Alamos Sci. Lab., 1951-60; asst. group leader Gen. Dynamics Co., San Diego, 1960-66; instr. physics UCLA extension, San Diego, 1963-66; mem. staff AEC research div., 1966-68; vis. prof. physics Catholic U. Am., Washington, 1966-67; asst. to dep. dir. sci. and tech. U.S. Def. Atomic Support Agy., Washington, 1968-69; lectr. U. Tex. at Austin, 1969-71; exec. v.p. Columbia Sci. Research Inst., Austin, Tex., 1969-71; exec. v.p., dir. Columbia Sci. Industries Co., Austin, 1969-76; pres., chief exec. officer, dir. Columbia Sci. Industries Co., from 1976. Contbr. articles to profl. publs. Fellow Am. Phys. Soc.; mem. Am. Nuclear Soc., Sigma Xi, Sigma Pi Sigma, Phi Kappa Phi. Clubs: Cosmos (Washington); Balcones Country (Austin). Home: Austin Tex. Died Apr. 20, 1987.

HAEBERLIN, JOHN BENJAMIN, JR., physician, educator; b. Chgo., Sept. 25, 1909; s. John Benjamin and Carolyn (Parrott) H.; m. Clare Rogerson, Mar. 21, 1936; children—Susan, John. B.Sc., U. Chgo., 1930; M.D., C.M., McGill U., 1935. Diplomate: Am. Bd. Dermatology and Syphilology. Intern Ill. Research and Edn. Hosp., Chgo., 1936-37; practice of medicine 1937-88, specializing in dermatology, 1943-88; fellow dermatology U. Ill., 1946-49, clin. asst. prof. dermatology, 1948-88; chmn. dept. dermatology Presbyn. Hosp., 1953-59, Presbyn.-St. Lukes Hosp., Chgo., 1959-68; adj. prof. dermatology U. N.Mex., Albuquerque, 1972-82; hon. staff Bernalillo County Med. Center, 1973-82. Served from lt. to maj. AUS, 1942-46. Mem. A.M.A., Albuquerque, Bernallilo County med. assns., Chgo. Dermatol. Soc. (pres. 1967), N.Mex. Dermatol. Soc., Am. Acad. Dermatology, N.Mex. Med. Soc., Am. Dermatol. Assn., Psi Upsilon. Home: Scottsdale Ariz. Died Jan. 9, 1988.

HAGER, JOSEPH ARTHUR, chemical coatings manufacturing company executive; b. Chgo., Jan. 4, 1900; s. Adam and Wanda (Erdmann) H.; m. Margaret Mabel Walbaum, Jan. 5, 1929. Student, Northwestern U., 1919; LLB, Kent Coll. Law, 1920; DBA (hon.), Detroit Coll. Bus., 1976. Tchr. pub. sch. system, Chgo., 1920; purchasing agt. Great Atlantic & Pacific Tea Co., 1920-21, mfrs. rep., 1921-22; spl. agt. Bradley & Vrooman Co., Chgo., 1922-24; with Grand Rapids Varnish Corp. (now Guardsman Chems. Inc.), Mich., 1924-78; ret. Grand Rapids Varnish Corp. (now Guardsman Chems. Inc.), 1978, v.p., dir. sales, 1944-61, pres., chief exec. officer, 1961-66, chmn. bd., chief exec. officer, 1966-70; v.p. Grand Rapids Varnish Corp., N.C., 1952-61; pres., chief exec. officer Grand Rapids Varnish Corp., 1961-70; chmn. bd., chief exec. officer Lambert Corp., Houston, 1962-70, pres., 1965-70; chmn. bd. Lambert Corp., Fla., 1962-70; chmn. bd. Schaefer Varnish Co., 1964-70, pres., chief exec. officer, 1965-70; pres. Alma-Guard Ltd., 1963-69; cons. paint, varnish and lacquer, sect. chems. bur. WPB, 1942-43, Smaller War Plants, 1943-44. Emeritus chmn. bd. trustees Davenport Coll. Bus., Grand Rapids. Served with U.S. Army, 1917-19. Recipient George Baugh Heckel award of Paint Industry, 1954; named Ky. col., 1961; recipient Top Mgmt. award Sales and Mktg. Execs., Grand Rapids, 1964. Mem. Nat. Paint, Varnish and Lacquer Assn. (past dir., pres., chmn. bd., chmn. exec. com. 1964-66), Grand Rapids Assn. Furniture Designers, Sales and Mktg. Execs. Club Internat., Grand Rapids Sales and Mktg. Execs. Club (founder), Internat. Platform Assn. Clubs: Elks, Blythefield Country (bd. dirs. 1955-58), Peninsular (bd. dirs. 1933-48), Peninsular (Grand Rapids) (pres. 1937-41). Home: Grand Rapids Mich. Died 1986.

HAGERTY, HARRY C., insurance company executive; b. Rochester, N.Y., 1892. Fin. v.p., dir. Met. Life Ins. Co., vice chmn., 1959-62; bd. dirs. Comml. Solvents Corp., Nat. City Bank, N.Y.C., Radio Corp. Am., NBC, Erie R.R., Rochester Gas & Electric Co., Clupak Inc.; trustee East River Savs. Bank. Home: New York N.Y. †

HAGERTY, WILLIAM WALSH, university president; b. Holyoke, Minn., June 10, 1916; s. William Walsh and Alice Amanda (Lindberg) H.; m. Mary Elizabeth McKay, Sept. 30, 1939; children: William Walsh III, Catherine Mary (Mrs. Richard Garnett II), Michael McKay. BS in Mech. Engring., U. Minn., 1939; MS, U. Mich., 1943, PhD, 1947; DSc, Pa. Coll. Optometry, 1965; LLD, Phila. Coll. Textiles and Sci., 1968, Temple U., 1968. Registered profl. engr., Tex. With pumping sta. operation Gt. Lakes Pipe Line Co., St. Paul, 1935-39; jr. engr. U.S. Gypsum Co., St. Paul, 1939-40, Wright Field, Dayton, Ohio, 1940; instr. mech. engring. Villanova Coll., 1940-41, U. Cin., 1941-42; instr. engring. and mechanics U. Mich., 1942-47, asst. prof., 1947-49, assoc. prof., 1949-51, prof., 1951-55; dean U. Del. Sch. Engring., 1955-58; prof., dean Coll. Engring. U. Tex., 1958-63; pres., then pres. emeritus Drexel U., Phila., from 1963; bd. dirs. Communications Satellite Corp., Cen.-Pa. Nat. Bank, Drexel Bond Debenture Trading Fund, Phila. Electric Co., Selas Corp., Martin-Marietta Corp., Mut. Benefit Life Ins. Co., AAA; vice chmn. West Phila. Corp.; bd. mgrs. Germantown Savs. Bank, 1971-81; cons. to adminstr. NASA, 1964-70; mem. Nat. Sci. Bd., 1964-70, Phila. Commn. Higher Edn. Author: (with H.J. Plass Jr.) Engineering Mechanics, 1967; contbr. articles to profl. jours. Mem. Commn. Presdl. Scholars, 1964-69; chmn. Southeastern Pa. Devel. Fund, 1964-69; mem. Phila. coun. exec. bd., nat. coun. Boy Scouts Am.; trustee Jefferson Med. Coll., 1965-69; bd. visitors Air U., USAF, 1964-67; mem. adv. com. USCG Acad., 1964-74, chmn., 1968-74; mem. exec. com. Univ. City Sci. Ctr. Named Del. Engr. of the Yr., 1970; recipient Sesquicentennial award U. Mich., 1967, Outstanding Achievement award U. Minn. Alumni Assn., 1969. Mem. ASME, Am. Soc. Engring. Edn., Nat. Soc. Profl. Engrs., Tex. Soc. Profl. Engrs., Sigma Xi, Pi Tau Sigma, Phi Kappa Phi, Tau Beta Pi, Sigma Gamma Tau. Methodist. Clubs: Aronimink Golf, Mid-Ocean (Bermuda). Died Jan. 14, 1986.

HAGGARD, WILLIAM WADE, educator; b. Maryville, Tenn., Aug. 28, 1892; s. Christopher Columbus and Elizabeth (Wade) H.; m. Norma Swift, Aug. 6, 1921 (dec.); children: Margaret Jean, Wade Swift, Joan Elizabeth; m. 2d, Rachel Leona Peters, Feb. 26, 1946. AB, Maryville Coll., Tenn., 1917; EdD, Maryville Coll., 1939; AM, U. Mich., 1927; PhD, U. Chgo., 1937. Tchr. Ishpeming (Mich.) High Sch., 1917-1919; prin. Petoskey (Mich.) High Sch., 1919-21, Arthur Hill High Sch., Saginaw, Mich., 1921-24, Rockford (Ill.) High Sch., 1924-28; spt. Joliet (Ill.) High Sch. and Jr. Coll., 1928-39; pres. Western Washington Coll. of Edn., Bellingham, Wash., 1939-69; pres. emeritus Western Washington Coll. of Edn., from 1959; lectr. edn. U. Tenn., Knoxville, from 1960, summers U. Wis., 1930, Purdue U., 1938, 39. Contbr. to ednl. jours. 2d lt. F.A., Cen. Officers' Tng. Sch., Camp Taylor, Ky., 1918. Mem. Assn. Tchr. Edn. Instns. (dir. 1952-55), Nat. Assn. High Sch. Prins. (pres. 1932-33), Am. Assn. of Jr. Colls. (pres. 1936-37), N. Cen. Assn. Colls. and Secondary Schs. (sec. 1938-39), Wash. Edn. Assn., NEA, Am. Assn. of Sch. Adminstrs., Am. Assn. of Tchrs. Colls. (chmn. accrediting com., 1947-48), Masons, Rotary Club, Phi Delta Kappa, Kappa Delta Pi. Home: Knoxville Tenn. †

HAIDER, MICHAEL LAWRENCE, oil executive; b. Mandan, N.D., Oct. 1, 1904; s. Michael and Elizabeth (Milner) H. BS, Stanford U., 1927. Chem. engr. Richfield Oil Co., Los Angeles, 1927-29; chem. engr. Carter Oil Co., Tulsa, 1929-31, petroleum prodn. engr., 1931-35, chief engr., 1935-38; mgr. research and engring. dept. Standard Oil Devel. Co., N.Y.C., 1938-45; exec. asst. prodn. dept. Standard Oil Co. N.J., 1945-46, dep. coordinator producing activities, 1952-54, v.p., bd. dirs., exec. v.p., mem. exec. com., 1961-63, pres., vice chmn. exec. com., 1963-66; bd. dirs. 1st Nat. City Bank; gen. mgr. exploration and prodn. Imperial Oil Ltd. Toronto, Ont., Can., 1946-48, v.p., bd. dirs., 1948-52; pres. Internat. Petroleum Co. Ltd., 1954-59. Contbr. articles to profl. jours.; editor: Petroleum Reservoir Efficiency and Well Spacing, 1943. Mem. Am. Inst. Mining and Metall. Engrs. (pres. 1952), Am. Petroleum Inst., Can. Inst. Mining Engrs. Home: Atherton Calif. Died Aug. 14, 1986.

HAIGHT, GORDON SHERMAN, English educator; b. Muskegon, Mich., Feb. 6, 1901; s. Louis Pease and Grace (Carpenter) H.; m. Mary Treat Nettleton, June 24, 1937. AB, Yale U., 1923, PhD, 1933. Tchr. Kent Sch., 1924, Hotchkiss Sch., 1925-30; mem. faculty Yale U., New Haven, 1933-85, prof. English, 1950-66, Emily Sanford prof. English lit., 1966-69, prof. emeritus, 1969-85; fellow Calhoun Coll., 1933-49; master Pierson Coll., 1949-53; vis. prof. English Grad. Sch. Columbia U., 1945-46, U. Oreg., 1949. Author: Mrs. Sigourney, 1930, George Eliot and John Chapman, 1940, George Eliot: A Biography, 1968 (James Tait Black award, Van Wyck Brooks award, Heinemann award, Nat. Acad. Arts and Letters award); editor: Miss Ravenal (J.W. De Forest), 1939, 2d rev. edit., 1955, vols. Classics Club, 1941-42, Yale edit. The George Eliot Letters, 1954-55, 78, Adam Bede, 1948, Middlemarch, 1955, Mill on the Floss, 1961, 2d rev. edit., 1977, A Century of George Eliot Criticism, 1965, Portable Reader of Victorian Prose, 1971; gen. editor Clarendon edit. George Eliot's novels; contbr. articles to profl. jours. Recipient Wilbur Lucius Cross medal Yale U., 1977; Guggenheim fellow, 1946-47, 52-53, 60-61. Fellow Royal Soc. Lit., Brit. Acad. (corr.); mem. Berzelius, Elizabethan Club (New Haven), Century Club, Yale Club (N.Y.C.), Zeta Psi. Episcopalian. Home: Woodbridge Conn. Died Dec. 28, 1985; Grove Street Cemetery, New Haven.

HAINES, SAMUEL FAITOUTE, physician; b. Mantorville, Minn., Nov. 30, 1892; s. Fred Sumner and Carrie Woodruff (Faitoute) H.; m. Emily Williams, June 18, 1921; children: Caroline (Mrs. Thomas P. Anderson), Bertram Williams, Olivia (Mrs. Charles M. Blackburn), Sarah Faitoute (Mrs. John A. Jeffries Jr.). BS, Harvard U., 1915, MD, 1919; MS in Medicine, U. Minn., 1929. Intern Mass. Gen. Hosp., Boston, 1919-21; cons. in medicine Mayo Clinic, 1924-57, head sect. in div. medicine, 1932-48, chmn. sects. on metabolic diseases., 1948-55, sr. cons. metabolic diseases, 1955-57, mem. bd. govs., 1945-56, vice chmn. bd govs., 1947-53, chmn. bd. govs., 1953-57; vice chmn. Mayo Found. U. Minn., 1953-57, fellow in medicine Mayo Found., 1921-24, assoc. prof. medicine, 1940-46, prof., 1946-57, prof. medicine emeritus, from 1958. Mem. bd. dirs. Rochester Meth. Hosp., Rochester Art Ctr. Fellow ACP; mem. Am. Goiter Assn., Assn. Am. Physicians, Ctr. Soc. Clin. Rsch., Endocrine Soc., Am. So., Minn. med. assns, Mass., Minn., Miss. Valley, Zumbro Valley med. socs., Alumni Assn. Mayo Found., Aesculapians (Boston), University Club, Alpha Omega Alpha, Sigma Xi. Home: Rochester Minn. †

HALDEMAN, JACK CARROLL, hospital organization executive; b. Downey, Idaho, May 18, 1912; s. William O. and Bertie (Fields) H.; m. Lorena Spivey, Sept. 15, 1933; children: Jack Carroll, Joe William. AB, Phillips U., 1934; BS, U. Okla., 1935, MD, 1937; MPH, U. Mich., 1943. Diplomate Nat. Bd. Med. Examiners. Chief epidemiology Alaska Dept. Health, 1938-39; med. dir. Waso County (Oreg.) Health Dept., 1939-41; commd. USPHS, 1941; med. dir. county health dept. Hopkinsville, Ky., 1941-42; gen. med. cons. Puerto Rico, 1943-44, New Orleans, 1944-46; exec. officer div. hosp. facilities Washington, 1946-48; med. officer in charge, founder Arctic Health Research Ctr., Anchorage, 1948-51; chief div. state grants Washington, 1951-52; asst. chief bur. state services 1952-54, chief div. health services, 1954-57, asst. chief div. hosp. and med. facilities, 1957-58; chief, asst. surgeon gen. USPHS, 1958-63; pres. Health and Hosp. Planning Coun. So. N.Y., 1963-74. Fellow Am. Pub. Health Assn., N.Y. Acad. Medicine; mem. N.Y. Acad. Scis., Am. Assn. Hosp. Planning, Am. Hosp. Assn., Internat. Hosp. Fedn., N.Y. Acad. Preventive Medicine, Pub. Health Assn. N.Y.C., Am. Coll. Preventive Medicine, Am. Assn. Pub. Health Physicians, Phi Kappa Phi, Delta Omega. Home: Merritt Island Fla. Died July 17, 1985, cremated.

HALE, NANCY, author; b. Boston, May 6, 1908; d. Philip L. and Lilian (Westcott) H.; m. Fredson Bowers, Mar. 16, 1942; children (by former marriages)—Mark Hardin, William Wertenbaker. Grad., Winsor Sch., Boston, 1926; student, Sch. of Boston Mus. Fine Arts, 1927-28; studied in father's studio several years. Asst. editor Vogue, 1928-32, Vanity Fair, 1933-34; news reporter N.Y. Times, 1935; adv. capacity to advt. agy., 1930-35; lectr. short story Bread Loaf Writers Conf., 1957-65. Author: The Young Die Good, 1932, Never Any More, 1934, The Earliest Dreams, 1936, The Prodigal Women, 1942, Between the Dark and the Daylight, 1943, The Sign of Jonah, 1950, The Empress's Ring, 1955, Heaven and Hardpan Farm, 1957, A New England Girlhood, 1958, Dear Beast, 1959, The Pattern of Perfection, 1960; essays The Realities of Fiction, 1962, Black Summer, 1963, New England Discovery, anthology, 1963; The Life In The Studio, 1969, Secrets, 1971; biography Mary Cassatt, 1975, The Night of the Hurricane, juvenile, 1978; author: short stories which have appeared in over 40 anthologies, including the Foley and O. Henry collections. Recipient O. Henry prize for short-short story 1933, Benjamin Franklin spl. citation for short story 1958, Henry H. Bellaman award for lit. 1969; Sarah Josepha Hale award, 1974; Phi Beta Kappa vis. scholar, 1971-72. Club: Cosmopolitan (N.Y.C.). Died Sept. 29, 1988.

HALE, NEWTON JOHNSTON, merchant; b. San Francisco, Jan. 10, 1902; s. Reuben Brooks and May (Johnston) H.; m. Betty Caughey, July 29, 1922; children: Betty May Hale McLaughlin, Janet Hale Havard. Student, Hitchcock Mil. Acad., 1920, Stanford U., 1920-22, NYU Sch. Retailing, 1925-26. With Hale Bros., Inc., 1922, 26-48, dir., 1931, treas., 1934-43, chmn. bd., dir., 1943-48; v.p., dir. Hale Bros. Assocs., Inc. (now Hale Tech. Corp.); with R.H. Macy Co., Franklin Simon, 1925-26; sec., dir. O.C. Field Gasoline Corp., 1922-44; dir. Broadway-Hale Stores, Inc., 1948-72; hon. dir. Carter Hawley Hale Stores Inc. Mem. Retail Mchts. Assn. (pres., dir.), Retail Dry Goods Assn. (pres., dir.), Retail Credit Assn. San Francisco (pres., dir.), Pacific Union Club, Bohemian Club, Burlingame Country Club, Electric Club, Sigma Alpha Epsilon. Home: San Francisco Calif. Deceased.

HALE, ROBERT BEVERLY, art educator, curator; b. Boston, Jan. 29, 1901; s. Herbert Dudley and Margaret Curzon (Marqu) H.; m. Barbara Barnes, Nov. 11, 1941 (div.); m. Niké Mylonas, Dec. 8, 1962; children: Alexander Curzon, Evelyn Everett. AB, Columbia U., 1923; postgrad., Columbia Sch. Architecture, Fontainebleau, Art Students League. Assoc. editor Art News, N.Y.C., 1941-49; organizer dept. Am. art Met. Mus. of Art, N.Y.C., 1948, assoc. curator, head dept., 1949-57, curator Am. painting and sculpture, 1958-66, curator emeritus, 1968-85, mem. vis. com., 1973-85; lectr. artistic anatomy Pa. Acad. Fine Arts, 1968-85; instr. drawing, lectr. anatomy Art Students League, 1943-85; adj. prof. drawing Columbia U., 1946-67; lectr. artistic anatomy Cooper Union, 1973-85, prof. art, 1976-85; pres. Louis Comfort Tiffany Found., 1959-66, trustee, 1966-85; v.p. N.Y.C. Art Festival, 1961-85; mem. art com. Chase Manhattan Bank, 1960-85. Author: 100

merican Painters of the 20th Century,, 1950, Drawing essons from the Great Masters, 1964, Snowland, 1971, with Terry Coyle) Anatomy Lessons from the Great Masters, 1977, Albinus on Anatomy, 1979; editor, ranslator: Anatomie Artistique (Dr. Paul Richer), 1971, hys Caparn, 1972, (with Nik=248 Hale) Balcomb reen, 1977; contbr. to mags. of art, article Ency. Brit., 956; one-man shows, Stamford (Conn.) Mus., 1959, aempfli Gallery, N.Y.C., 1960; represented in ermanent collections, Whitney Mus., Met. Mus., U. riz., others, many pvt. collections; exhbn. Tribute to a urator: Robert Beverly Hale, Met. Mus., 1979. ecipient N.Y.C. Mayor's award honor for arts, 1977; enjamin Franklin fellow Royal Soc. Arts, 1969. Mem. rt Students League (v.p. 1941-43, hon. life mem.), Am. ine Arts Soc. (trustee), Am. Fedn. Arts (internat. om.), Am. Water Color Soc. (hon. mem., Dolphin gold edal 1981), Columbia U. Faculty Club, Century Club N.Y.C.). Home: Newburyport Mass. Died Nov. 14, 985.

HALL, ARTHUR ELDRIDGE, newspaper executive; Covington, Ky., Oct. 22, 1898; s. Ernest and Hettie nn (Arthur) H.; m. Evalyn Young, Sept. 19, 1919; 1 on, Richard Eldridge. Student, U.S. Naval Acad., 918-20. CPA, Ill. Pub. acct. 1920-29; auditor Chgo. aily News Inc., 1929-31, controller, asst. treas., 1931-, circulation dir., 1942-52, gen. mgr., v.p., treas., 1953-; gen. mgr. Chgo. Daily News, 1959-61; exec. v.p. ewspaper div., bd. dirs. Field Enterprises Inc. Former ayor of Sea Ranch Lakes, Fla. Mem. Chgo. Newspaper Pubs. Assn. (pres.), Internat. Circulation Mgrs. ssn., Am. Legion, Masons, Tower Club, Mid-Am. lub, Carlin Club. Republican. Home: Delray Beach a. Died Mar. 22, 1987.

HALL, CLARENCE E., lawyer; b. Kansas City, Mo., ug. 20, 1891; s. Clarence Hall and Laura Jane Murphy) H.; m. Dorothy Clements Kirk, Nov. 2, 1916; hildren: Janet (Mrs. John J. Boericke Jr.), Gordon ameron, Edward Cameron Kirk. BS, U. Pa., 1913, LB, 1915. Bar: Pa. 1915. Asst. trust officer Land itle Bank & Trust Co. Phila., 1916-20; pvt. practic; sr. tnr. Hall, Wainwright & Archer; mem. exec. com., bd. rs. Am. Electric Power Co.; bd. dirs. Welling and Voodward, Phillips & Jacobs, Inc. Contbr. numerous rticles in field to profl. jours. Mem. Phila. County Bd. aw Exams., 1937-59. Pvt. U.S. Army, 1918. Mem. BA, Am. Soc. Internat. Law, Internat., Pa., Phila. bar ssns., Am. Legion (past comdr.), Internat. Law Soc., ot. Soc. Lower Merion (pres.), Merion Community ssn. (v.p. 1926-40), Merion Civic Assn. (pres. 1930-7), Am. Judicature Soc., Midday Club, Lawyers' Club, onstitutional Club, Bar Harbor Club, Causeway Club, .E. Harbor Fleet Club. Republican. Episcopalian. Home: Merion Pa. †

HALL, E(UGENE) RAYMOND, zoologist, educator; Imes, Kans., May 11, 1902; s. Wilber Downs an usan Effie (Donovan) H.; m. Mary Frances Harkey, ug. 9, 1924; children: William Joel, Hubert Handel, enjamin Downs. AB, U. Kans., 1924; MA, U. Calif., erkeley, 1925, PhD, 1928. Field biologist U.S. Bur. iol. Survey, 1924-25; acting in charge Bur. Rsch., Calif. Dept. Fish and Game, 1926; curator mammals U. Calif. Mus. Vertebrate Zoology, 1927-44; asst. prof. vertebrate oology U. Calif., 1930-37, assoc. prof., 1937-44; prof. oology U. Kans., 1944-72, chmn. dept. zoology, 1944-; dir. mus. Natural History, 1944-67, editor mus. ubls., 1946-67, rsch. assoc., from 1967, Summerfield sting. prof. zoology, 1958-72; Fulbright rsch. prof., urkey, 1968; dir. Kans. Biol. Survey, 1946-67, sr. biologist, 1967-73; state zoologist, 1959-67; prin. investiator Office Naval Rsch., also NSF, from 1950; Maytag sting. prof. zoology Ariz. State U., 1972; mem. bd. ouncillors, bd. dirs. Save the Tallgrass Prairie, Inc., om 1972; mem. Nat. Pks. Adv. Bd., 1954-60, coun., om 1961. Author: The Mammals of North America, 959, 2d edit., 1981, others; contbr. articles to sci. jours. Recipient cert. of merit Nash Conservation Award, 956, Proud Kansan award Outdoor Writers Kans., 974; named Conservationist of Yr. Kans. Wildlife edn., 1972; Guggenheim fellow, 1942-43. Fellow AAS (v.p. and chmn. sect. zool. scis. 1956), Calif. cad. Sci., Wash. Acad. Sci.; mem. Am. Soc. Mammalogy (hon., pres. 1944-45), Am. Wildlife Soc., Am. om. for Internat. Wildlife Protection (exec. com. 1946-0), Prairie Nat. Pk. Natural History Assn. (pres. from 968), Am. Soc. Systematic Zoologists, Am. Assn. Museums, Defenders Wildlife (v.p. 1967-71), Am. rnithol. Union, Kans. Acad. Sci. (coun. 1968-72), Biol. oc. Washington, Soc. for Study Evolution, Cooper rnithol. Club, Sigma Xi (pres. Kans. chpt. 1959-61). Home: Lawrence Kans. Died Apr. 2, 1986.

HALL, JOHN FREDERICK, geologist, educator; b. Glassport, Pa., Mar. 11, 1923; s. George Arthur and athryn Elizabeth (Dressel) H.; m. Catherine Walker, ug. 22, 1957. B.S., W.Va. U., 1947; Ph.D., Ohio State ., 1951. Geologist Ohio Geol. Survey, 1951-52; asst. rof. geology Western Res. U., Cleve., 1952-63; assoc. rof. geology Case Western Res. U., Cleve., 1963-85; et. 1985; cons. various industries. Author: Geology of Hocking State Park, Ohio. Served with AUS, 1943-45. Decorated Bronze Star, Purple Heart; recipient Diekoff eaching award Case Western Res. U., 1982. Fellow Geol. Soc. Am.; mem. Am. Assn. Petroleum Geologists, Nat. Assn. Geology Tchrs., Am. Inst. Profl. Geology, No. Ohio Geol. Soc. (v.p. 1961, pres. 1962, treas. 1965-85). Republican. Home: Cleveland Ohio Died July 12, 1988.

HALL, JOHN MACFARLAND, lawyer; b. Dover, N.H., June 20, 1891; s. George E. and Elizabeth K. (MacFarland) H.; m. Genevieve M. Stehman, Nov. 11, 1925; 1 dau., Elizabeth Hall Daniels. AB, Oberlin Coll., 1913; LLB, Harvard U., 1916. Pvt. practice Los Angeles, from 1926; mem. McComb & Hall, Los Angeles, 1923-28, Lawler, Felix & Hall, Los Angeles, from 1938. Contbr. articles to law revs. Mem. Am., Los Angeles bar assns. Republican. Home: Pasadena Calif. †

HALLECK, CHARLES A., lawyer; b. De Motte, Ind., Aug. 22, 1900; s. Abraham and Lura I. (Luce) H.; m. Blanche A. White, June 15, 1927; children: Charles White, Patricia. AB cum laude, Ind. U., 1922, LLB, 1924. Bar: Ind. 1924. Pvt. practice Rensselaer, Ind.; pros. atty. 30th Jud. Cir., 1924-34; mem. 74th -90th Congresses from 2d Ind. Dist.; minority leader 86th to 88th Congresses. Permanent chmn., Republican nat. conv., 1960. With Inf., U.S. Army, World War I. Mem. Am. Letion, Columbia Club (Indpls.), Order of the Coif, Phi Beta Kappa, Beta Theta P, Phi Delta Phi. Home: Los Altos Calif. Died Mar. 4, 1986.

HALLENBECK, GEORGE AARON, surgeon, educator; b. Rochester, Minn., June 29, 1915; s. Dorr Foster and Bessie (Graham) H.; m. Marian Mansfield, Dec. 16, 1938 (div. 1979); children: John M., George A., Christopher G. (dec.), Linda; m. Nancy Peek Chamberlin, 1979. B.S., Northwestern U., 1936, M.D., 1940; Ph.D. in Physiology, Mayo Found., U. Minn., 1943. Diplomate: Am. Bd. Surgery. Intern Virginia Mason Hosp., Seattle, 1939-40; cons. surgeon Mayo Clinic, Rochester, Minn., 1949-60; sect. surg. research Mayo Clinic, 1961-66, chmn. gen. surgery sects., 1966-68; prof. surgery and physiology Mayo Found., U. Minn., 1960-68; prof. surgery U. Ala., Birmingham, 1969-75; chmn. dept. surgery Scripps Clinic, La Jolla, Calif., 1976-80; sr. cons. surgery Scripps Clinic, 1980-84; ret. 1984. Author numerous sci. publs. Served to maj., M.C. AUS, 1943-46. Fellow A.C.S.; mem. Am., Central, Western, So. surg. assns., Am. Gastroenterol. Assn., Soc. Clin Surgeons, Am. Physiol. Soc., Soc. Exptl. Biology and Medicine, So. Surgeons Club, Phi Beta Kappa, Alpha Omega Alpha, Phi Delta Theta, Phi Rho Sigma. Home: Rancho Santa Fe Calif. Died Jan. 19, 1988, buried Oakwood Cemetery, Rochester, N.Y.

HAMILTON, CLIFF STRUTHERS, chemistry educator; b. Blair, Nebr., Nov. 23, 1889; s. Samuel Leigh and Lillie Martha (Brownlee) H; m. Frances Howe, Aug. 4, 1921; children: Robert Wallis, Mary Frances (dec.), Martha Howe, Cliff Struthers. BS, Monmouth (Ill.) Coll., 1912, ScD (hon.), 1954; student, U. Ill., 1914-15, U. Minn., 1919-20; PhD, Northwestern U., 1922. Instr. in chemistry Ohio Wesleyan U., 1917-19; rsch. instr. in pharmacology U. Wis., 1922-23; asst. and assoc. prof. chemistry U. Nebr., 1923-27; assoc. prof. chemistry Northwestern U., 1927-29; prof. chem. U. Nebr., 1929-59, chmn. dept. chem., 1939-55; Mem. bd. editors Organic Syntheses; assoc. editor Chem. Rev., 1946-48; contbr. numerous rsch. articles on organic compounds containing arsenic, antimony and phosphorus, heterocyclic compounds to profl. jours. Cons. in Chemical Warfare Svc., World War I, 1917; mem. div. 9, N.D.R.C., World War II. Recipient Midwest Medal award St. Louis sect. Am. Chem. Soc., 1955. Mem. AAAS, Am. Chem. Soc. (chmn. organic div. 1940, chmn. divl. officers group, 1940-41), AAUP, Sigma Xi, Phi Lambda Upsilon, Alpha Chi Sigma. Home: Lincoln Nebr. †

HAMILTON, FAY W., insurance company executive; b. Rockford, Ill., Oct. 24, 1920; s. W.R. and J.G. Hamilton; married, 2 children. BS, U. Ill., 1942. With Allstate Ins. Co., Northbrook, Ill., from 1946, group v.p., from 1977. Served with USNR, 1942-46. Methodist. Home: Buffalo Grove Ill. Deceased.

HAMILTON, RAPHAEL NOTEWARE, educator; b. Omaha, Nebr., Nov. 5, 1892; s. Charles William and Maud (Noteware) H. Pvt. edn., Paris, 1907-08; AB, Creighton U., 1913; AM, St. Louis U., 1919, PhD, 1932. Ordained priest Roman Cath. Ch., 1926. Asst. prof. history Campion Coll., 1920-21, prof., head dept., 1921-23; instr. in history St. Louis U., 1928-29; asst. prof. Marquette U., Milw., 1930-32, prof., from 1932, head dept., 1932-56, acting dean of grad. sch., 1939-40, dean, 1940-44, univ. archivist, from 1961. Author: The Story of Marquette U. Sec., trustee Marquette U., 1940-48; alumni regent, 1948-49. Mem. Am., Am. Cath., Miss. Valley, Wis. State hist. assns., Jesuit Hist. Conf., Phi Alpha Theta. Home: Milwaukee Wis. †

HAMILTON, THOMAS JEFFERSON, newspaper correspondent; b. Augusta, Ga., Sept. 20, 1909; s. Thomas Jefferson and Daisy May (Ramsey) H.; m. Ethel Mathews, Nov. 3, 1934; children: Anne Elizabeth (Mrs. John K. Jessup, Jr.), Thomas Jefferson, William B.W. AB magna cum laude, U. Ga., 1928; MA (Rhodes scholar), Oxford U., 1930; student, Sch. English Lit., 1931. Reporter Atlanta Jour., 1931-34, Washington Bur. A.P., 1934-36, London bur., 1936-37, London bur. N.Y. Times, 1937-39; Madrid corr. 1939-41; staff Washington bur., 1941, 45-46; S.A., 1942; chief UN bur., 1945-65, Bonn bur., 1965-67, Geneva bur., 1967-87; UN corr. Freedom and Union, 1946-65. Author: Appeasement's Child: The France Regime in Spain, 1943. Lt. USNR, 1942-45. Decorated officer Legion of Honor (France); comdr. Order of Merit (Chile); recipient George Polk Meml. award for outstanding internat. reporting, 1955, 56; co-winner $500 Deadline Club awards for UN Coverage, 1962, 63. Mem. UN Corrs. Assn. (chmn. 1947-48, exec. 1948-50, 51-56, pres. 1950-51), Council Fgn. Relations, Soc. Silurians, Century Assn., Metropolitan Club, Phi Beta Kappa, Phi Delta Theta, Sigma Delta Chi. Home: Southbury Conn. Died 1987.

HAMLIN, OLIVER DEVETA, JR., judge; b. Oakland, Calif., Nov. 30, 1892; s. Mr. O. D. and Elizabeth C. (McMahon) H.; m. Mignon de Neuf, Mar. 25, 1916; children: Mignon H. (Rowe), Oliver Deveta III. BL, U. Calif., 1914. Dep. dist. atty. Alameda County, Calif., 1915-20; mem. Com. Bar Examiners, 1938-41; judge Superior Ct., Alameda County, 1947-53; U.S. dist. judge No. Dist., Calif., 1953-58; U.S. Cir. Ct. judge 9th Cir., from 1958. Mem. Alameda County Bar Assn. (pres. 1939), State Bar Calif. (pres. 1945-46, gov. 1943-46). Home: Lafayette Calif. †

HAMM, EDWARD FREDERICK, JR., traffic and transportation executive; b. Chgo., Mar. 27, 1908; s. Edward Frederick and Sarah (Meek) H.; m. Joy Elizabeth Fairman, June 23, 1934; children: Julie Hamm Finley, Thornton Edward, Martha Joy Hamm Spencer. Student, Dartmouth Coll., 1930. Pres., treas. Traffic Service Corp., from 1933; pub. Traffic World, Traffic Bull., Daily Traffic World, from 1944; pres. Coll. Advanced Traffic, Inc., from 1945; con. mag. sect. printing and pub. div. W.P.B., 1944-45; pres. Acad. Advanced Traffic; mem. distbn. council U.S. Commerce Dept.; mng. dir. ICC, 1953. Mem. Cho. Bus. Papers Assn. (pres. 1973), Assn. Bus. Papers (pres. 1948-49), Advt. Fedn. Am. (bd. dirs. 1948), Am. Soc. Traffic and Transp. (founder), Chgo. Club, Metropolitan Club (Washington), Burning Tree Country Club (Washington), Nat. Press Club. Republican. Episcopalian. Home: Washington D.C. Died Mar. 19, 1985; buried Lambert's Cove Cemetery, Vineyard Haven, Mass.

HAMMETT, LOUIS PLACK, chemist, educator; b. Wilmington, Del., Apr. 7, 1894; s. Philip Melancthon and Marie Louise (Plack) H.; m. Janet Thorpe Marriner, June 4, 1919; children: Philip Marriner, Jane. AB, Harvard U., 1916; postgrad., Tech. Hochshule, Zurich, 1916-17; PhD, Columbia U., 1923, ScD (hon.), 1962. Civilian chemist Bur. Aircraft Prodn. U.S. Army, 1917-19; comml. rsch. with E.C. Worden Millburn, N.J., 1919-20; with Columbia U., 1920-87, successively instr. chemistry, asst. prof., assoc. prof., 1935, prof., 1935-60, Mitchill prof. chemistry, 1960-61, prof. emeritus, 1961-87; on leave for work on explosives under Nat. Def. Rsch. Com., 1941-46; disting. vis. lectr. U. So. Calif., 1962; disting. vis. prof. Pa. State U., 1964, Purdue U., 1964; rsch. dir. Explosives Rsch. Lab., 1943-46; chmn. div. chemistry and chem. tech. NRC, 1946-47; chmn. bd. health Hampton Twp., N.J., 1964. Author: Solutions of Electrolytes, 1929, Physical Organic Chemistry, 1940, 2d edit., 1970, Introduction to the Study of Physical Chemistry, 1952; mem. editorial bd. Internat. Sci. and Tech., 1961-64. Recipient Wm. H. Nichols medal, 1957, James Flack Norris award in teaching, 1960, Priestly medal, 1961, Willard Gibbs medal, 1961, James Flack Norris award phys. organic chemistry, 1966, Gilbert Newton Lewis medal, 1967, Nat. Medal of Sci., 1968, Charles Frederick Chandler medal, 1968. Fellow Chem. Soc. London (hon.); mem. Am. Chem. Soc. (chmn. N.Y. sect. 1939, bd. dirs. 1956-61, chmn. bd. dirs. 1961), AAUP, Nat. Acad. Scis., Phi Beta Kappa, Sigma Xi, Phi Lambda Upsilon, Alpha Chi Sigma. Home: Newton N.J. Died Feb. 23, 1987.

HAMMOND, EDWARD CUYLER, epidemiologist; b. Balt., June 14, 1912; s. Edward and Agnes (Cuyler) H.; m. Marian E. Thomas, Jan. 3, 1948 (dec.); children: Thomas Cuyler, Richard Render, Jonathan Cuyler; m. Katharine S. Redmond, Sept. 23, 1972. BS, Yale U., 1935, MA, 1953; ScD, Johns Hopkins U., 1938; DMS (hon.), Johannesgutenberg U., Mainz-am-Rhein, Germany, 1969. Assoc. statistician, div. indsl. hygiene NIH USPHS, 1938-42; cons. med. rsch. sect. Bur. Aeros. USN, 1941-42; with civilian requirements br. Office of the Quartermaster Gen., 1942; dir. statis. rsch. sect. Am. Cancer Soc., 1946-66, v.p. for epidemiology and statistics, 1966-86; adj. prof. community medicine Mt. Sinai Hosp. Sch. Medicine, N.Y.C., 1966-86; prof. biometry, dir. grad studies Yale U., 1953-58, also chmn. univ. exec. com. statistics; lectr. preventive and environ. medicine Albert Einstein Coll. Medicine; cons. dept. biology Brookhaven Nat. Lab.; mem. Coal Mine Health adv. council HEW; mem. sci. adv. panel Rsch. to Prevent Blindness, Inc. Contbr. articles to profl. jours. Maj. USAAF, 1942-46. Recipient William R. Belknap award for excellence in biol. studies, 1935, Charles Evans Hughes award Riverside Ch., 1967, Edward W. Browning award, 1971. Fellow Am. Pub. Health Assn.; mem. Am. Statis. Assn., N.Y. Acad. Scis. (pres. 1974), AAAS (hon.), Royal Soc. Medicine London. Home: New York N.Y. Died Nov. 3, 1986; buried St. John's Cemetery, Ellicotte City, Md.

HAMMOND, HAROLD EARL, educator, author, historian, gerontologist; b. Albany, N.Y., Nov. 28, 1922; s. Walter Earl and Mae V. (McKeever) H.; m. Helen Stegmann, Oct. 6, 1942; children: Susan Jane (Mrs. Christopher John Wray), Bruce Martin, April Thorne (Mrs. Charles Weed), Melody Joy (Mrs. David Bedell), Russell James. B.A., Wagner Coll., 1942; postgrad. in elec. engring., Newark Coll. Engring., 1943; M.A., Columbia U., 1945, Ph.D., 1951; postgrad., St. Lawrence U., 1945-46, U. Conn., Boston U., U. N.H., 1978-79; Ed.D. candidate in gerontology, Boston U. History instr. Wagner Coll., Bergen Jr. Coll., 1946-48; asst. to pres. L.I. U.; asst. prof. history, dir. Eastern L.I. div. C.W. Post Coll., 1948-52; asst. prof. history, dir. pub. relations Union Coll., Schenectady, 1952-54; pres. Hammond, Beamish & Crannell, Inc. (accounts with Flight Engrs. Internat., 3d Luth. World Fedn. Assembly, Nat. Luth. Council, Nat. Geriat. Soc., N.Y. State Fair, N.Y. State Div. Safety, N.Y. State Homebuilders Assn.), 1954-60; asst. dean Grad. Sch., Yeshiva U., 1958-60; prof. history Univ. Coll., N.Y. U., 1960-66, assoc. dean, 1960-66; dean Inter-Am. U. P.R., 1966; prof. history, chmn. dept. Franklin Pierce Coll., Rindge, N.H., 1967-70; prof. social and polit. sci. N.H. Coll., Manchester, 1970-74; pres. Hammond Promotions, Inc., 1974-80; adj. prof. gerontology Antioch/New Eng. Grad. Sch., 1979-80; dir. N.H. Gerontology Center, 1978-80; Bd. dirs. Monodnock Adult Edn. Center, Inc., Peterborough, N.H., 1974-77; Leverhulme fellow, prof. history St. David's Univ. Coll. U. Wales, Lampeter, Dyfed, 1972-73; justice of peace, 1973—; nat. panel consumer arbitrators Better Bus. Bur.; comml. arbitrator Am. Arbitration Assn. Author: Pictorial Guidebook to Colleges and Universities in the Empire State, 1953, A Commoner's Judge, Life and Times of C. P. Daly, 1954, Diary of a Union Lady, 1962, We Hold These Truths, 1964, (with M.J. Belasko) A More Perfect Union, 1965, (with M.J. Belasko and E. Graff) The New Africa, 1966, (with E. Graff) Southeast Asia, 1967, (with M.J. Belasko) India-Pakistan, 1967, (with Rudolph Schwartz) China, Japan, and Korea, 1967, (with Thomas G. Kavunedus) The Middle East, 1968, (with M.J. Belasko) Soviet Russia, 1968; Contbr. articles to profl. jours. Recipient Great Scholars Am. award, 1971; mem. Exec. and Profl. Hall of Fame, 1970. Fellow Am. Geog. Soc.; mem. Am. Geriatrics Soc., Gerontol. Soc., Nat. Geriatrics Soc., Am. Hist. Assn., Polit. Sci. Acad., AAUP, New Eng. Assn., Soc. Aero. Flight Engrs., Am. Assn. Ret. Persons, Alpha Phi Omega, Phi Alpha Theta. Democrat. Lutheran (mem. laymen's movement stewardship). Lodges: Masons (32 deg.); Peterborough Lions. Home: Peterborough N.H. Died Dec. 4, 1986.

HAMMOND, JAMES WRIGHT, architect; b. Montclair, N.J., Apr. 12, 1918; s. Robert Stevens and Helen (Johnston) H.; m. Katrina Roy Boyden, Feb. 25, 1956 (div. June 1959); m. Helen Cheney Stuart Sloane, Nov. 27, 1976. BArch, Ill. Inst. Tech., 1942. Assoc. Perkins, Wheeler & Will & Eliel Saarinen, Assoc. Architects, Chgo., 1939-40; gen. ptnr. Skidmore, Owings & Merrill, Chgo., 1946-61; ptnr. Hammond and Roesch, Inc., Chgo., 1961-71, Hammond, Beeby and Assocs., Inc., Chgo., 1971-77, Hammond, Beeby & Babka, Inc., 1971-82; pvt. cons. 1982-86. Mem. facilities devel. com. Chgo. council Boy Scouts Am., from 1958; mem. Chgo. Crime Commn., from 1955; com. mem. Chgo. Welfare Council Met. Chgo.; bd. dirs. Chgo. Planetarium Soc., Chgo. Commons Assocs.; exec. bd. Auditorium Theatre Council Chgo.; trustee Thresholds, Chgo. With AUS, 1942-46. Fellow AIA; mem. University Club, Casino Club, Archtl. Club (pres.), Arts Club (Chgo.). Mem. Bahai Ch. Home: Glencoe Ill. Died Mar. 21, 1986; buried Traverse City, Mich.

HAMMOND, JOHN, recording executive; b. N.Y.C., Dec. 15, 1910; s. John Henry and Emily Vanderbilt (Sloane) H.; m. Jemison McBride, Mar. 13, 1941 (div. 1948); children: John Paul, Jason; m. Esmé O'Brien Sarnoff, Sept. 8, 1949 (dec. 1986). Am. rec. dir. English Columbia & Parlophone Co., Ltd., 1933-36; producer Little Old Boy, Playhouse Theatre, N.Y.C., 1933, Jayhawker, Cort Theatre, N.Y.C., 1935, From Spirituals to Swing, Carnegie Hall, N.Y.C., 1938-39; organizer Benny Goodman Band, 1933-35, Count Basie's Orch., 1936; assoc. rec. dir. Columbia Records, 1939-43, 46; co-editor, co-pub. Music and Rhythm, 1942-43; casting dir. Billy Rose prodn. Carmen Jones, 1943; rec. dir. Majestic Records, 1946-47; v.p. Mercury Record Corp., 1946-52; lectr. N.Y. U., 1953-56; pop record dir. Vanguard Record Soc., 1954-87; v.p., dir. Newport Jazz Festival Inst. of Jazz Studies, Horizon Press, N.Y.C., Crisis Publ. Co., N.Y.C.; columnist Down Beat, 1933-39; critic, columnist Bklyn. Eagle, 1934-36; record critic N.Y. Compass, 1950-52; columnist N.Y. Herald Tribune, 1953-55, Saturday Rev., 1958-59; dir. talent-acquisition Columbia Records, N.Y.C.; 2d v.p. Profl. Children's Sch., N.Y.C.; bd. dirs. Northside Ctr. Child Devel., N.Y.C., 1950-87. Home: New York N.Y. Died July 10, 1987.

HAN, YU-SHAN, history educator; b. Peking, China, May 18, 1899; came to U.S., 1941, naturalized, 1953; s. Tai-chong and Jui-lan (Liu) H.; m. Edna Nona Quick, Aug. 2, 1930. BA, Yenching U., 1924, BD, 1926; postgrad., Harvard U., 1927-28; PhD, Boston U., 1929. Del., speaker World Congress Edn., Geneva, 1929; assoc. dir. rural edn. Nat. Assn. of Mass Edn. Movement, 1929-31; sec. Nat. Christian Council, 1931-33; prof. history and govt. St. John's U., Shanghai, China, 1933-38; rsch. commr. Cen. Bank China, Chungking, 1940-41; lectr. history UCLA, 1941-47, assoc. prof. history, 1947-57, prof., 1957-66, prof. emeritus, 1966-83; dir. Art Council 1954-56; mem. panel for selection of history texts U.S. Armed Forces Inst., 1953-58. Author: Elements of Chinese Historiography, 1955, (with Carl Becker, Sidney Painter) The Past That Lives Today, 1952, rev. edit., 1961; bd. editors Pacific Hist. Rev., 1953-55. Mem. council internat. visitors and sister cities, Mayor's Office, City of L.A., 1962-73; charter mem. Hubert H. Humphrey Fund Found.; assoc. Nat. Archives, Simon Art Mus. Fellow Harry S. Truman Inst. Nat. and Internat. Affairs (hon.); mem. Am. Soc. for Legal History, UN Assn. L.A. (dir.), Am. Hist. Assn., Assn. for Asian Studies, AAUP, Soc. for Oriental Numismatics, Nat. Hist. Soc., Smithsonian Instn., Harvard Club of So. Calif. Home: Los Angeles Calif. Died Mar. 11, 1983.

HANCOCK, JAMES RALPH, farmer, association official; b. Jonesburg, Mo., Jan. 21, 1891; s. James Wilson and Nannie Price (Peery) H.; m. Mary E. Pettigrew, May 2, 1937. BSCE, U. Mo., 1913. Civil engr. 1913-21, contractor, 1921-38, farmer and livestock raiser, from 1938; pres. Am. Angus Assn., 1962-63. With U.S. Army, World War I. Mem. Am. Angus Assn. Home: New Franklin Mo. †

HANCOCK, RALPH LOWELL, author, specialist in Latin Am. affairs; b. Plainville, Ind., Nov. 23, 1903; s. John Hiram and Nancy (Cunningham) H.; m. Julia Ellen F. Ross, Dec. 25, 1924 (div.); 1 son, David Lowell (dec.); m. Frances Fenster Iversen, 1948; children—Nancy Lowell, Bret Hiram. Ed., Springfield (Mo.) Bus. Coll.; student, Washington U., St. Louis, 1924-27. Resident news corr. covering Latin America, 1936-40; organized publicity dept. Transportes Aereos Centro Americanos Airlines, 1940, dir., 1940-42; sr. economic analyst, specialist on Caribbean Area, Bd. Econ. Warfare, 1942-43; head of econ. mission to Latin Am., 1942-43; Latin Am. adviser on editorial staffs of 3 publishing houses 1943-49; Vice pres., dir. pub. relations in Latin Am. for Pan-Am. Found., Inc.; pres. Hemisphere Corp. Speaker 7th Ann. Conf. on Caribbean, U. of Fla., 1956. Author: Our Southern Neighbors, 1942, Mexico and Central Am, 1942, Latin America, 1943, Let's Look at Latin America, 1943, Opportunities in Latin America, 1946, Our Latin American Neighbors, 1946, The Rainbow Republics: Central America, 1947, The Magic Land: Mexico, 1948, Fabulous Boulevard, 1949, Caribbean Correspondent, 1951, Douglas Fairbanks: The Fourth Musketeer, 1953, Baja California, 1953, The Forest Lawn Story, 1955, Exploring American Neighbors, 1956, Laughter is a Wonderful Thing, 1956, Blondes, Brunettes and Bullets, 1957, Desert Living, 1958, Puerto Rico: A Success Story, 1960, The Lost Treasure of Cocos Island, 1960, Puerto Rico: A Travellers Guide, 1961, Mexico, 1964, The Compleat Swindler, 1968; authoritative articles on Book of Knowledge and Annual; Author and photographer of numerous ednl. films on Latin Am. and mag. and newpaper articles.; Latin Am. editor of: Invitation to Travel series; Editor-in-chief: Hemisphere Research. Lectr. Home: San Diego Calif. Died Sept. 19, 1987; cremated.

HAND, CHARLES CONNOR, lawyer; b. Shubuta, Miss., Dec. 6, 1890; s. Robert McLain and Annie Brevard (Case) H.; m. Irma Weems, Feb. 23, 1916; children: Charles Conner (dec.), John Weems, William Brevard, James Albert. AB, Millsaps Coll., 1909; student, U. Va., 1910-12. Bar: Miss. 1912, Ala. 1921. Practice Shubuta, to 1921, Mobile, Ala., from 1921; sr. mem. firm Hand, Arendall, Bedsole, Greaves & Johnston, 1940-76, of counsel, from 1977; officer, dir. various investment cos. Bd. dirs. Mitchell Found. Mem. Am., Ala., Mobile (past pres.) bar assns., Am. Counsel Assn., Am. Judicature Soc., Masons. Methodist. Home: Mobile Ala. Died Mar. 21, 1980; interred Mobile, Ala.

HAND, WAYLAND DEBS, folklorist; b. Auckland, N.Z., Mar. 19, 1907; s. Hyrum and Margaret (Wride) H.; m. Viola White, June 8, 1932 (div. 1956); children: Jacqueline, Winifred Hand Marsh; m. Celeste Gilford, Dec. 19, 1957; 1 child, Sidney Gilford. AB, U. Utah, 1933, MA, 1934; PhD, U. Chgo., 1936. Instr. German U. Minn., 1936-37; faculty UCLA, 1937-74, prof. German, folklore, 1952-74, prof. emeritus, 1974-86; trustee Am. Folklife Ctr., Library of Congress, 1976-86, chmn. bd., 1976-77; Fife Honor lectr., 1981; Katharine M. Briggs Meml. lectr., 1982. Author: books, monographs including A Dictionary of Words and Idioms Associated with Judas Iscariot-A Compilation Based Mainly on the Germanic Languages, 1942 (Chgo. Folklore Soc. prize), (with Gustave O. Arlt) Humaniora-Essays in Literature, Folklore and Bibliography Honoring Archer Taylor on His Seventieth Birthday, 1960, Popular Beliefs and Superstitions from North Carolina, 2 vols., 1961-64 (4th Internat. Folklore prize 1965), American Folk Legend-A Symposium, 1971, American Folk Medicine-A Symposium, 1976, Magical Medicine, 1980; editor: (with Anna Casetta and Sondra B. Thiederman) Popular Beliefs and Superstitions: A Compendium of American Folklore from the Ohio Collection of Newbell Niles Puckett, 3 vols., 1981, Dictionary of American Popular Beliefs and Superstitions, 1944-86; assoc. editor: Western Folklore, 1953-54, 54-66; adv. editor: Ethnomedizin, 1979; adv. editor Fc klore Studies, U. Calif. Publs., 1952-72; contt numerous articles, revs. to profl. jours. Studies in Hi tory Am. Civilization stipend LIbrary of Congres 1946; grantee-in-aid Am. Council Learned Socs., 194 46, 73, Am. Philos. Soc., 1951; John Simon Guggenhei Meml. Found. fellow, 1952-53, 60-61; research grant NEH, 1968-75, 80-82; NIH; Nat. Library of Medicir 1971-73; decorated knight 1st class Order of Lion Finland. Fellow Am. Folklore Soc. (pres. 1957-5 editor Jour. Memoirs 1947-51), So. Calif. Acad. Sc (v.p. 1973-74), Folklore Soc. London (hon.); mer MLA Am., Internat. Soc. for Folk-Narrative Rsch. (v. 1964-74), Deutsche Gesellschaft fuer Volkskunde (hon Am. Dialect Soc., Am. Name Soc., Calif. Folklore Sc (pres. 1969-70, rev. editor Quar. 1942-46, editor 195 66), MLA So. Calif. (pres. 1955-56), Tex. Folklore So N.Y. Folklore Soc. Home: Pompano Fla. Died Oct. 2 1986; buried Rose Hills, Whitier, Calif.

HANDLER, PHILIP, biological scientist, educator; N.Y.C., Aug. 13, 1917; s. Jacob and Lena (Heisen) H m. Lucille Marcus, Dec. 6, 1939; children: Mark, E Paul. BS, CCNY, 1936; PhD, U. Ill., 1939; DSc, Ca Western Res. U., Carnegie-Mellon U., Colo. State U U. N.C., Yeshiva U., Hahneman Med. Coll., Med. Co Wis., Temple U., N.Y. Med. Coll., George Washingt U., Mich. State U., Poly. Inst. N.Y., U. Alaska, Butl U., Southwestern at Memphis, U. Ill., U. Md., U. Fl PhD, Hebrew U., Jerusalem; LLD, CUNY, Emory U LittD, Nova U.; LHD, Fla. State U. Instr. Duke U 1939-40, assoc., 1940-41, asst. prof. physiology and n trition, 1942-45, assoc. prof. biochemistry, 1945-5 prof., chmn. dept., 1950-69, James B. Duke prof. ochemistry, 1961-69; dir. AEC fellowship tng. progra 1948-53; Disting. prof. sci. George Washington U 1970-81; pres. Nat. Acad. Scis., Washington, 1969-8 dir. Squibb-Beechnut, Inc., 1966-69; cons. USPH AEC, NRC, VA; chmn. biochem. study sect. NI 1956-58, nat. adv. com. rsch. facilities and resource 1963-67; mem. nat. adv. health council USPHS, 195 61; mem. biology and medicine rsch. facilities par NSF, 1958-60, mem. divisional com. for biology a medicine, 1960-62, mem. nat. sci. bd., 1962-74, chm 1966-70; chmn. com. radiation and aging NIH, al AEC, 1957-61; mem. Pres.'s Sci. Adv. Com., 1964-6 69-72, Pres.'s Commn. on Heart Disease, Cancer a Stroke, 1964-65; mem. adv. com. on environ. heal USPHS Surgeon Gen., 1966-67. Co-author: Princip of Biochemistry (textbook), Biology and the Future Man, The Life Sciences, also tech. publs.; mem. editor com. Jour. Theoretical Biology, 1961-68, Jour. Cor parative Biochemistry and Physiology, 1962-65, Jou Biol. Chemistry, 1964-70, Geriatrics, 1957-65. Trust Found. Advanced Edn. Med. Scis., 1964-72, Co Spring Harbor Lab. Quantitative Biology, 1963-6 Rockefeller U., 1969-81, Manpower Inst., 1971-81; b dirs. Multiple Sclerosis Soc., 1973-81, Nutrition Foun 1973-81, Hebrew U., 1972-81; bd. visitors Grad. Sc Yale U., Scripps Inst. Metabolic Disease; vis. com. l scis. U. Notre Dame, Johns Hopkins U.; mem. co Woods Hole Oceanographic Inst., 1974-81, Marine ology Lab., 1979-81; mem. Unitarian Service Con Med. Mission to Japan, 1951; mem. Com. on Na Medal of Sci., 1968-81. Decorated Great Medal Honor with silver star Austrian Govt.; comdr. Order Leoplod II (Belgium); comdr. Order of Merit (Polanc recipient N.C Award for sci., Stevens Honor awa Stevens Inst. Tech., Ann. award for Disting. Contbns. Med. Sci. AMA, Townsend Harris medal CCNY, Di ing. Alumnus award U. Ill., Copernicus medal Poli Acad. Scis., Pub. Service award Nat. Sci. Bd., NS 1979. Mem. Am. Soc. Biol. Chemists (sec. 1953-5 councilor 1958-61, pres. 1962-63), Fedn. Am. So Exptl. Biology (exec. com. 1959-65, chmn. bd. 1964-6 Nat. Acad. Scis. (pres. 1969-81, chmn. survey com. l scis. 1966-70, council 1968-81), Am. Inst. Nutritio AAAS, Soc. Exptl. Biology and Medicine (pres. S. sect. 1953-54), Am. Chem. Soc., Am. Acad. Arts a Scis., N.Y. Acad. Scis. (C.B. Mayer award), Am. Philc Soc., Royal Soc. Arts (hon.), Am. Inst. Chemists (hon Swiss Acad. Sci. (hon.), Mexican Acad. Medicine (hon Japanese Biochem. Soc. (hon.), German Acad. Natur Scis., Leopoldina (hon.), Cosmos Club, Phi Beta Kapp Sigma Xi, Alpha Omega Alpha. Home: Washingt D.C. Died Dec. 29, 1981.

HANES, JOHN WESLEY, finance company executiv b. Winston-Salem, N.C., Apr. 24, 1892; s. John W. a Anna (Hogdin) H.; m. Elizabeth Agnes Mitchel, No 21, 1916 (dec. 1935); m. Hope Yandell, Aug. 4, 193 children: John W., David G., June, Ormsby, Susan. S ptnr. Charles D. Barney & Co. (now Smith Barne Harris Upham & Co.); mem. SEC Jan.-July 1938, as sec. of Treasury, July-Nov. 1938, under sec., Nov. 193 Dec. 1939; mem. exec. com. and personal trust co Bankers Trust Corp.; mem. pension trust com., John Manville Corp.; dir., chmn. exec. com. U.S. Lines C dir. Olin-Mathieson Chem. Co. With USN, World W I. Mem. N.Y. Racing Assn. (chmn. 1960). Hom Millbrook N.Y. Died Dec. 24, 1987.

HANFMANN, GEORGE MAXIM ANOSSO archaeologist, curator, educator; b. St. Petersbu Russia, Nov. 20, 1911; came to U.S., 1934; naturalize 1940; Dr. Phil., U. Berlin, 1934; student, U. Je Munich U.; Ph.D., Johns Hopkins, 1935; MA, Harva U., 1949. Successively jr. prize fellow, instr., asst. pr

Harvard U., 1935-43, asst. prof., 1945-49, assoc. prof. fine arts, 1949-56, prof., 1956-86, John E. Hudson prof. archeology, 1971-86; curator classical art Fogg Art Mus., 1946-74; dir. archeol. exploration, Sardis, 1958-78; mem. Inst. Advanced Study, Princeton, 1947-48, 71-72; visitor classical dept. Mus. Fine Arts, Boston; mem. mng. com. Am. Sch. Classical Studies in Athens; U.S. editor OWI, 1943-44; chief German sect. ABSIE, 1943-45. Author: books, monographs, exhbn. catalogues, articles and revs. Fellow Am. Acad. Arts and Scis., Soc. Antiquaries London (Eng.), Brit. Acad. (corr.); mem. Instituto di Studi Etruschi Florence, German, Austrian archeol. insts., Archeol. Inst. Am. (gold medal for disting. archaeol. achievement 1979), Soc. Hellenic and Roman Studies, Am. Schs. Oriental Rsch., Am. Rsch. Ctr. Egypt, Acad. Mainz, Academie des Inscriptions et Belles Lettres France (corrs.), Am. Philos. Soc., Brit. Inst. Persian Studies, Phi Beta Kappa. Home: Watertown Mass. Died Mar. 13, 1986; interred Mt. Auburn Cemetery, Cambridge, Mass.

HANNA, PAUL ROBERT, emeritus teacher educator; b. Sioux City, Iowa, June 21, 1902; s. George Archibald and Regula (Figi) H.; m. Jean Shuman, Aug. 20, 1926 (dec.); children: Emily-Jean Hanna Johnson, John Paul, Robert Shuman; m. Aurella Klipper, Dec. 26, 1987. A.B., Hamline U., St. Paul, 1924, Ped.D., 1937; A.M., Columbia U., 1925, Ph.D., 1929. Asst. psychology Hamline U., 1923-24; supt. schs. West Winfield, N.Y., 1925-27; research assoc. Lincoln Sch., Columbia, 1928-35; asst. prof. Columbia Tchrs. Coll., 1930-35; assoc. prof. Stanford U., 1935-37, prof. edn., 1937-54, Lee L. Jacks prof. edn., 1954-67, emeritus, 1967-88; dir. Stanford U. (Stanford Internat. Devel. Edn. Center), 1954-68, emeritus, 1968-88; dir. Stanford Univ. Services Stanford U., 1941-44, founding chmn. Assoc. Libraries, 1973-75; sr. research fellow Hoover Instn., 1975-88; Cons. Office Edn., Mut. Security Agy., USAID; staff, cons. Nat. Resources Planning Bd., 1939-42; cons. Army Specialized Training Div. of War, 1942-44, War Relocation Authority, 1942-45, Sec. of War on German reedn., 1947, U.S. Govt. for Panama Canal Zone, 1947; mem. UNESCO consultative ednl. mission to, Philippines, 1949; coordinator Philippine Dept. Edn.-Stanford U. contract financed by USAID, 1953-60; cons. to coordinator Inter-Am. Affairs, assignments in, S.Am., 1940-41, C.Am., 1941-42; mem. staff ednl. policies commn. N.E.A., 1948; mem. internat. relations com. Am. Council on Edn., 1955-60; mem. com. on Atlantic studies Atlantic Council and Atlantic Inst., 1962-68; cons. Edn. and World Affairs, 1964-68; chmn. Yugoslavia team U.S. State Dept., 1966; Am. specialist assigned African nations on ednl. reform, 1967; dir. Stanford-Asia Found. seminar on higher edn. in nation bldg., Korea, 1968; chmn. Nat. Evaluation Com. Peace Corps/Univ. Relations, 1968-69; cons. coop. research br. U.S. Office Edn., 1963-69; mem. U.S. Nat. Commn. UNESCO, 1970-77; cons. numerous state and city bds. edn. Sr. author social sci. textbooks, Scott Foresman Co.; author numerous articles, profl. books, films for Ency. Britannica Films, World Book Ency. Bd. dirs. Internat. Bd. Atlantic Colls., 1966-69, Jessie V. and Clement W. Stone Found., 1969-72; trustee Castilleja Sch., 1957-88 , United World Colls., 1968-72; mem. W.K. Kellogg Found., 1944-58, Presdl. Task Force on Arts and Humanities, 1981-82. Fellow A.A.A.S.; mem. N.E.A. (life mem. several depts.), Nat. Soc. Study Edn., Soc. Internat. Devel., Asia Soc., Comparative Edn. Soc., Am. Acad. Polit. and Social Sci., Internat. House Japan, Nat. Planning Assn., Am. Forestry Assn., John Dewey Soc., Council Fgn. Relations, World Affairs Council, Sierra Club, Nat. Trust for Historic Preservation, Soc. Archtl. Historians, UN Assn. U.S., Redwood Region Conservation Council, Phi Beta Kappa, Theta Chi, Phi Gamma Mu, Phi Delta Kappa, Kappa Delta Pi. Republican. Clubs: Kiwanian. (Washington), Cosmos (Washington); Bohemian (San Francisco). Home: Palo Alto Calif. Died April 8, 1988.

HANNON, CLARENCE WILLIAM, business executive; b. Saginaw, Mich., 1889; s. William and Hannah (Ryan) H.; m. Nora Marie Murray; children: William, Nora Marie, Helen Hannon McVoy, Mary Hannon Dunigan. Grad., U. Mich., 1912. With Murray Ohio Mfg. Co., Cleve., from 1919, v.p., 1919-25, pres., 1925-62, chmn., from 1962. Home: Nashville Tenn. †

HANSEN, CONNOR THEODORE, state justice; b. Freeman, S.D., Nov. 1, 1913; s. William D. and Gladdus H. (Hall) H.; m. Annette Phillips Ferry, June 17, 1939; children: Annette (Mrs. Benjamin E. Olson), Peter C., David P., Jane (Mrs. Richard LaRonge). Grad., Wis. State Tchrs. Coll., Eau Claire, 1934; LLB, U. Wis., 1937. Bar: Wis. 1937. Dist. atty. Eau Claire County, 1938-43; spl. agt. FBI, 1943-44; pvt. practice Eau Claire, 1945-58; Eau Claire County judge 1958-67; justice Wis. Supreme Ct., 1967-87; pres. Wis. Bd. Juvenile Ct. Judges; commr. Circuit Ct. Eau Claire County, 1947-58; past county judge rep. Ct. Adminstrv. Com. for Wis.; past sec. Wis. Bd. County Judges; chmn. Eau Claire County Bd. Suprs., 1948-49, NCCJ, 1969-70. Past pres. Meml. High Sch. PTA, Eau Claire; bd. dirs. Wis. Welfare Council, 1968-71, Wis. State U. Eau Claire Found., Inc., Eau Claire Guidance Clinic, Eau Claire YMCA; mem. adv. bd. Eau Claire County Youth Camp; bd. visitors U. Wis. Law Sch. Recipient Disting. Service award Eau Claire Jr. C. of C., 1941, Crime Prevention award Eau Claire Exchange Club, 1963, Disting. Service award Alumni U. Wis., Eau Claire, 1967, Disting. Service award NCCJ, 1970. Mem. Am. Law Inst., State Bar Wis., Jefferson County Bar Assn., Eau Claire County Bar Assn. (past pres.), N.W. Peace Officers Assn. (past pres.), Wis. Dist. Attys. Assn. (past pres.), Alumni Assn. Wis. State U., Eau Claire (past pres.), Eau Claire Baseball Club (past pres.), Lions. Home: Lake Mills Wis. Died Aug. 21, 1987.

HANSEN, NIEL ESBURN, clergyman; b. Dayton, Ohio, Dec. 7, 1892; s. Hans Olsen and Josephine Catharine (Brandt) H.; m. Helen Sanders, Sept. 19, 1919; children: Mary Dagmar, Niel Sanders, Winifred Josephine. AB, Denison U., 1915; BD, Union Theol. Sem., 1920; DD, Chgo. Theol. Sem., 1936. Ordained to ministry Congl. Ch., 1920. Pastor Whitewater, Wis., 1920-26, Cen. Ch., Galesburg, Ill., 1926-36; assoc. dir. Chgo. City Missionary Soc. of Congl. Chs., 1936-42, gen. dir., from 1942. With French Army, 1917-19. Mem. Union League, Kappa Sigma. Home: Evanston Ill. †

HANSEN, WILLIAM CARL, college president; b. Neenah, Wis., July 4, 1891; s. Hans Christian and Anna (Hansen) H.; m. Esther Minnie Rintelman, Aug. 11, 1917; children: Helen Irene, Esther (Mrs. Peer A. Buck), Ruth (Mrs. Bruce Sanderson), Kathryn (Mrs. Robert W. Dean). Student, State Normal Sch., Stevens Point, Wis., 1909-11; BS in Agr., U. Wis., 1915, MS in Edn., 1925, grad. study, 1934-40. High sch. tchr. Menom, Menomonee Falls, Wis., 1911-13, St. Croix, Wis., 1915-17; princ. Milltown, Wis., 1917-22; supt. Niellsville, Wis., 1922-29, Oconto, Wis., 1929-32, Stoughton, 1932-40. Mem. NEA, Wis. Edn. Assn. (pres. 1943), Wis. Assn. Sch. Adminstrs., Wis. Alumni Assn., Masons (Consistory), Rotary Club, Phi Delta Kappa. Home: Stevens Point Wis. †

HANSON, HUGO HENRY, paper company executive; b. Sweden, Apr. 19, 1889; came to U.S., 1897; s. Anders and Cecelia (Henrikson) H.; m. Edith S. Plummer, Oct. 7, 1919; children: Holly (Mrs. Joseph Coors), John H., Hugh B. Student, MIT, 1912. Rsch. asst. MIT, 1912-13, assoc. prof. chem. engring., 1916-17; chief chemist Brown Corp., Latugue, Que., Can., 1913-16, Ea. Corp., Bangor, Maine, 1919-28; gen. mgr. Hamilton Paper Co. (formerly W.C. Hamilton & Sons), Miquon, Pa., 1928-36, pres., 1936-53, chmn. bd., from 1953, also bd. dirs.; bd. dirs. 1st Nat. Bank, Conshohocken, Pa. Episc. vestryman. With CWS, U.S. Army, 1917-19. Mem. Writing Paper Mfrs. Assn. (pres.), Am. Pulp and Paper Assn. (v.p., exec. com.), Union League, Merion Cricket Club. Home: Philadelphia Pa. †

HANSON, LESTER EUGENE, animal science educator; b. Willmar, Minn., Mar. 31, 1912; s. Edwin William and Esther Dorothea (Lundquist) H.; m. Gladys Diessner, Aug. 21, 1937; children: Bruce E., Ronald L., Karen. BS with distinction, U. Minn., 1936; MS, Cornell U., 1937, PhD, 1940. Fellow Am.-Scandinavian Found. study in Denmark, 1937-38; instr., then asst. prof., assoc. prof., prof. dept. animal husbandry U. Nebr., 1940-50; prof. dept. animal husbandry U. Minn., 1950-85, head dept., 1956-66, prof. dept. animal sci., 1966-85. Named Disting. Nutritionist, Distillers Rsch. Council, 1964; elected to U. Minn. Livestock Hall of Fame, 1972. Fellow Am. Soc. Animal Sci. (pres. 1962-63, dir. 1963-64, Am. Feed Mfrs. award for rsch. in swine nutrition and mgmt. 1955); mem. AAAS, AAUP, Am. Dairy Sci. Assn., Metric Assn., Am. Inst. Biol. Scis., Am. Inst. Nutrition, Farm-House, Sigma Xi, Phi Kappa Phi, Gamma Sigma Delta, Alpha Zeta, Phi Zeta. Lutheran. Home: Saint Paul Minn. Died Feb. 11, 1985; buried Lakewood Cemetery, Mpls.

HANSON, ROBERT WARREN, chemist, former educator; b. Bemidji, Minn., Aug. 7, 1923; s. Thomas T. and Clara M. (Severson) H.; m. Margaret Fern Allen, Jan. 1, 1947; children: Terrill Allen, Rebecca Lee (Mrs. Carroll E. Miller), Mark Robert. B.A., Bemidji State Coll., 1948; M.S., U. Minn., 1949; Ph.D., U. Iowa, 1961. Instr. chemistry Wis. State Coll., Platteville, 1949-51; research chemist 3M Co., St. Paul, 1951-52; instr. chemistry St. Cloud (Minn.) State Coll., 1952-59, assoc. prof., 1961-63; instr. sci. U. Iowa, 1959-60, research asst., 1960-61; assoc. prof. phys. sci. State Coll. Iowa, Cedar Falls, 1963-66; prof. chemistry and sci. edn. U. No. Iowa, Cedar Falls, 1966-85; sec.-treas. Nat. Assn. Acads. Sci., 1976-79, pres., 1980; liaison officer Iowa Gov.'s Sci. Adv. Council, 1977-81. Editor: Science and Creation, 1986. Editor Iowa Acad. Sci. Bull, 1967-83; mng. editor Procs. Iowa Acad. Sci. and Iowa Soc. Tchrs. Jour, 1976-84. Served with AUS, 1943-45. Fellow AAAS (Council 1982-85), Iowa Acad. Sci. (exec. dir. 1967-83); mem. Nat. Sci. Tchrs. Assn., Assn. Edn. Tchrs. Sci., Phi Delta Kappa, Phi Lambda Upsilon. Home: Eden Prairie Minn. Deceased.

HANSON, WESLEY TURNELL, JR., photography company executive; b. Carrollton, Ga., May 29, 1912; s. Wesley Turnell and Ruth (Gardner) H.; m. Marie McHatton, Nov. 12, 1936; children: Wesley Turnell, III, Eleonore (Mrs. E.H. Balbach), Thomas Hubbard, Marie Renee (Mrs. Page Newton). BS, U. Ga., 1930, MS, 1932; PhD, U. Calif., Berkeley, 1934; M Photography (hon.), Profl. Photographers Assn., 1958. Chemist photomicrography dept. rsch. labs. Eastman Kodak Co., Rochester, N.Y., 1934-36, color photography devel., 1936-43, with color process devel. dept., 1945-51, head color photography div., 1951-61, asst. dir. rsch. labs., 1961-72, dir. rsch., v.p., 1972-77, ret., 1977; with Manhattan Project, Oak Ridge, 1943-45; dir. Moog Inc., 1977-82. Author: (with R.M. Evans and W.L. Brewer) Principles of Color Photography, 1953; contbr. articles to mags., profl. jours. Trustee Monroe Community Coll., Allendale-Columbia Schs., U. Ga. Found., Internat. Mus. Photography. Recipient Progress medal Photog. Soc. Am., 1976, Progress medal Royal Photog. Soc. Eng., 1977, Jansen medal French Photog. Soc., 1977, Kulturpreis German Photog. Soc., 1977. Fellow Soc. Motion Picture and TV Engrs. (Herbert T. Kalmus Gold medal 1956, Progress Medal award 1966), Soc. Photog. Scientists and Engrs.; mem. Am. Chem. Soc., Optical Soc. Am., AAAS, Rochester Country Club, Cosmos Club, Hunt Hollow Ski Club. Home: Rochester N.Y. Died May 20, 1987; buried Athens, Ga.

HARBESON, JOHN FREDERICK, architect; b. Phila., July 30, 1888; s. James Page and Fredericka (Krauter) H.; m. Georgiana Newcomb Brown, Oct. 5, 1916 (div. 1929); children: John Frederick (dec.), Paul Cret. MS in Architecture, U. Pa., 1911. Began practice Phila., 1911; instr. i perspective PA. Acad. Fine Arts, 1916-55; assoc. prof. archtl. design Sch. Fine Arts, U. Pa., 1919-48, sometime chmn. dept. architecture; ptnr. of Paul P. Cret, 1919-45; then ptnr. Harbeson, Hough, Livingston & Larson, architects; cons. Am. Battle Monuments Commn., architect of U.S. Capitol, Nat. Monument Commn., Corregidor Bataan Meml. Commn. Prin. works include: Pioneer Mother Monument (with Charles Grafly, sculptor), San Francisco, 1916, Mallory Meml. Fountian, Phila., 1917, Whitfield MEml. (with R. Tait McKenzie, sculptor) U. Pa., restoration of Senate and House chambers U.S. Capitol, 1948, Normandy Am. War Meml., interior design Pa. R.R., Senator and Congl. trains; author: The Study of Architectural Design, 1926. Pres. Carpenters' Co. of Carpenters Hall, 1965. Recipient Arthur Spayde Brooke gold medal in design U. Pa., 1910, Walter Cope meml. prize Phila. chpt. AIA and T Suare Club, 1913, Henry Hering Meml. medal, 1960, John Howard Benson award Am. Inst. Commemorative Art, 1961, Medal of Honor NAt. Sculpture Soc., 1964, Phila. Art Alliance, 1974; named to Hall of Fame, Central High Sch., Phila., 1976; Benjamin Franklin fellow Royal Soc. Arts, 1960. Fellow AIA, NAD (pres. 1959-62); mem. Nat. Sculpture Soc. (v.p. 1964-65), Newcomen Soc. N.Am., Philomathean Soc. (hon.), Charleston Coun. Architects, Soc. Archtl. Historians, Nat. Trust Historic Preservation, Century Club (N.Y.C.), Salmagundi Club (N.Y.C.), Cosmos Club (Washington), Art Alliance, Franklin Chess Club, Sigma Xi. Presbyterian. Home: Philadelphia Pa. Deceased.

HARDEN, JOHN WILLIAM, publicist; b. Graham, N.C., Aug. 22, 1903; s. Peter Ray and Nettie Cayce (Abbott) H.; m. Josephine Holt, June 13, 1928 (dec. Dec. 1951); children: Glenn Abbott (Mrs. Fred Springer-Miller), John William; m. Sarah Plexico, Oct. 5, 1953; children: Holmes Plexico, Mark Michael, Jonathan Holder. AB, U. N.C., 1927. Circulation mgr., advt. mgr. Burlington (N.C.) Daily Times-News, 1922; also editor Graham news dept; classified advt. mgr. Raleigh News and Observer, 1923; with U. N.C. News Bur. 1923-28; reporter, columnist Charlotte (N.C.) News, 1928-37; news editor Salisbury Evening Post, 1937-44, Greensboro Daily News, 1944; pvt. sec. Gov. R. Gregg Cherry, 1945-48; campaign mgr. for U.S. Sen. William B. Umstead 1948; dir. pub. relations Burlington Industries, 1948-58, asst. v.p., 1948, v.p., 1949-58; pub. relations counsellor, cons. John Harden Assocs., Greensboro, from 1958; asst. to pres. Cannon Mills Co., Kannapolis, N.C.; v.p., dir. Rowan Corp. Author: Alamance County: Economic and Social, 1928, The Devil's Tramping Ground and Other North Carolina Mystery Stories, 1949, Tar Heel Ghosts, 1954, North Carolina Roads and Their Builders, 1966, Cannon, 1977; contbr. articles to trade publs. Mem.-at-large Greensboro council Boy Scouts Am.; mem. vis. com. Guilford Coll.; bd. dirs., mem. exec. com. Penick Meml. Hone; bd. dirs. N.C. Bus. Found., Carolina Regional Theatre; trustee Crossnore (N.C.) Sch. Mem. Greensboro C. of C. (dir., pres.), N.C. Hist. Preservation Soc., N.C. Press Assn., Gen. Alumni Assn. U. N.C. (pres. 1955), Pub. Relations Soc. Am., Greensboro City Club, Greensboro Country Club, Carolina Motor Club (pres., dir., mem. exec. com.), Grandfather Golf and Country Club (dir.), Grandfather Mountain Lake Club (pres.), Linville Golf Club, Rotary (dir., pres., dist. gov.). Democrat. Episc. (chmn. 1958 every mem. canvass, vestryman, sr. warden). Home: Greensboro N.C. Deceased.

HARDER, F. WILLIAM, investment banker; b. Delhi, N.Y., Aug. 16, 1904; s. William Henry and Alice L. (Every) H.; m. Myrtle P. Gerst, Feb. 28, 1925 (div.); children: Betty (Mrs. Donald M. McClellan), Phyllis Mae (Mrs. Richard Reininger), Alice Joanne (Mrs. Jay Woodward); m. Lois M. Chillingworth, May 16, 1952. Student, Del. Acad., 1921, Central City Bus. Sch., Syracuse, N.Y, 1922; LL.D. (hon.), Skidmore Coll., 1980; LHD (hon.), Russell Sage Coll., 1986. Security trader E.G. Childs & Co., Inc., Syracuse, 1922-30, Eshelman-Harder Co., Inc., 1930-32, Harder-Mengarelli, Inc., 1932-36, Harder & Co., Inc., N.Y.C., 1936-38; with Allen & Co., Inc., 1938-75, exec. asso., 1964-66, pres., dir., 1966-67, dir., chmn. exec. com., 1967-74, sr. cons., 1975-89; dir. emeritus Airborne Freight Corp., Seattle; dir., Arts-Way Mfg. Co., Armstrong, Iowa; dir. The Reading Co., Phila.; dir., Weigh-Tronix Inc., Fairmont, Minn. Trustee, v.p., chmn. fin. com. Nat. Mus. Racing, Saratoga Springs, N.Y.; trustee emeritus Skidmore Coll., Saratoga Springs; chmn. bd. govs. N.F.L. Alumni Assn. Clubs: Saratoga Golf and Polo (Saratoga Springs); Turf and Field (N.Y.C.), Cornell (N.Y.C.), Golf, Indian Creek Country (Indian Creek Village, Fla.), Surf (Surfside, Fla.). Home: Bal Harbour Fla. Office: 711 Fifth Ave New York NY 10022 Died Feb. 15, 1989.

HARDIN, HORD, trust company executive; b. Bardstown, Ky., Apr. 10, 1888; s. David C. and Hannah (Hord) H.; m. Edith Wilson, June 18, 1910; children: Hord Wilson, William Graham. Ed., St. Louis U. Asst. exec. officer Miss. Valley Trust Co., St. Louis, 1916, v.p., 1919, exec. v.p., 1934-51; exec. v.p. Merc. Trust Co., 1951-54, chmn. exec. com., 1954, also bd. dirs.; bd. dirs. Emerson Electric Mfg. Co., Laclede Gas Light Co., Stix, Baer & Fuller, A.P. Green Fire Brick Co. Author: Banking Laws of Missouri, Annotated, 1915. Mem. Racquet Club, Mo. Athletic Club, Bellerive Country Club. Home: Saint Louis Mo. †

HARDING, GEORGE TRYON, III, psychiatrist, educator; b. Columbus, Ohio, May 27, 1904; s. George Tryon, Jr. and Elsie (Weaver) H.; m. Mary Virginia Woolley, June 2, 1927; children: George T., Herndon P., Ann Elizabeth, Warren Gamaliel, Richard Kent. AB, Columbia Union Coll., 1923; MD, Loma Linda U., 1928. Intern Grant Hosp., Columbus, 1927-28; resident Harding Sanitarium, Worthington, Ohio, 1928-30; pres., med. dir. Harding Sanitarium, Worthington, 1934-48; resident Columbus State Hosp., 1930-31; practiced medicine with G.T. Harding, Jr. Columbus, 1931-34; mem. faculty Coll. Medicine Ohio State U., 1928-48, clin. prof. psychiatry, 1948; pres. Loma Linda U., 1948-51; med. dir. Harding Hosp., Worthington; clin. prof. psychiatry Ohio State U., 1951-85; mem. adv. bd. to dir. mental hygiene, State of Calif., 1949-51; mem. adv. com. to dir. mental hygiene, Ohio. Mem. Gov. Bricker's Welfare Survey for Ohio, 1944; mem. Ohio Postwar Planning Commn., 1945-46; pres. Ohio Citizens Council Health and Welfare, 1953-56; chmn. citizens com. Ohio Comprehensive Mental Health Planning, 1963-65. Fellow ACP, Am. Psychiat. Assn.; mem. AMA, Columbus Acad. Medicine (past pres.), Ohio State Med. Assn. (councillor), Torch Club, Kit Kat Club, University Club, Rotary. Mem. Seventh-Day Adventist Ch. Home: Worthington Ohio. Died Nov. 22, 1985.

HARDINGE, HARLOWE, manufacturing company executive; b. Denver, Mar. 17, 1894; s. Hal Williams and Bertha (Wilson) H.; m. Florence Donnelly, Mar. 23, 1929 (dec. Dec. 1978); children: Byron Cantine, Harlowe DeForest; m. Madeline Baumbach, Sept. 19, 1980. ME, Cornell U., 1916. Registered profl. engr., Pa. With Hardinge Conical Mill Co., N.Y.C., 1916-23; v.p., gen. mgr. Hardinge Co., Inc., York, Pa., 1923-39, pres., 1939-68, chmn., from 1964, also chief exec. officer; former dir. Nat. Cen. Bank Pa. Contbg. author: Zimmerman and Lavine Handbook of Engineering Costs. Trustee York Coll.; mem. council, former mem. admoinstrv. bd. Cornell U. Capt. Signal Corps AUS, 1917-19. Mem. AIME (Legion Honor, Richards award 1972, named Disting. Mem. Class 1975, Disting. Pensylvanian 1981), York Mfrs. Assn. (past pres.), Pa. C. of C. (bd. dirs.), Mining and Metall. Soc. Am., York Art Assn (life), Hist. Soc. York County, Laurel Fish and Game Assn., Rotary (fellow), Lafayette Club, York Country Club, Monterey Peninsula Country Club (Pebble Beach, Calif.), Sigma Xi, Phi Kappa Sigma. Republican. Home: York Pa. also: Carmel Calif. Died Nov. 17, 1984.

HARDRE, JACQUES, French language educator; b. Dinan, France, Jan. 10, 1915; came to U.S., 1945, naturalized, 1956; s. Rene S. and Berthe (Lefevre) H. BA, Guilford (N.C.) Coll., 1937; MA, U. N.C., 1942, PhD, 1948. Instr. French and German Guilford Coll., 1937-39; teaching fellow U. N.C., Chapel Hill, 1939, instr. French, 1941-42, 45-49, asst. prof., 1949-53, assoc. prof., 1953-57, prof., 1957-71, Kenan prof. French, 1971-77, prof. emeritus, 1978-83, chmn. dept. Romance langs., 1974-76, chmn. div. humanities, 1965-68; instr. Sewanee (Tenn.) French House, U. of the South, summers 1960-61, N.C. U., Durham, 1961. Author: Letters of Louvois, 1949, La France et sa Civilisation, 1969; editor: (with G.B. Daniel) Huis-Clos, 1962, Le Malentendu, 1963, Les Enfants Terribles, 1969; editor-in-chief The French Rev., 1968-74; contbr. articles to profl. jours. Lt. French Army, 1939-40, 42-45. Decorated Croix de Guerre, Mèdaille de la France Libre, Mèdaille des Combattants Volontaires, officier Ordre des Palmes Acadèmiques, chevalier Lègion d'Honneur, officier Ordre National Du Lion (Senegal), Mèdaille de Vermeil Socièté d'Encouragement Au Progrès. Mem. Am. Assn. Tchrs. French (past pres.), Modern Lang. Assn. (past chmn. nat. com.), South Atlantic Modern Lang. Assn. (past sect. chmn.), Modern Humanities Rsch. Assn., Fèdèration Internationale des Professeurs de Français (exec. council 1969-78, pres. 1972-76, hon. pres. 1976-78), Socièté des Professeurs Français en Amèique, Alliance Français Chapel Hill (hon. pres.). Home: Chapel Hill N.C. Died Nov. 19, 1983.

HARDY, EDWARD ROCHIE, clergyman, educator; b. N.Y., June 17, 1908; s. Edward R. and Sarah (Belcher) H.; m. Marion Dunlap, Sept. 14, 1939; 1 child, Stephen Minear. Grad., Friends Sem., N.Y.C., 1920; AB, Columbia U., 1923, MA, 1924, PhD, 1931; grad., Gen. Theol. Sem., N.Y.C., 1929, STB, 1933, STM, 1934, STD, 1956; STM, Union Theol. Sem., N.Y.C., 1932; MA, Cambridge U., 1969. Ordained to ministry P.E. Ch. as deacon, 1929, priest, 1932. Asst. pastor St. Paul's Ch., Spring Valley; also St. Stephen's Ch., Pearl River, N.Y., 1930-31; St. Andrew's Ch., Astoria, L.I., N.Y., 1932-36; fellow and tutor Gen. Theol. Sem., 1929-44, instr. Hebrew, 1940-44; assoc. prof. ch. history Berkeley Div. Sch., New Haven, Conn., 1945-47, prof., 1947-69; Univ. lectr. U. Cambridge, Eng., 1969-81, fellow, dean Jesus Coll., 1972-75; World Council of Chs. del. to Near East, 1947, 55; mem. Joint Commn. Ecumenical Relations (Episcopal Ch.), 1955-61, 64-70; mem. World Council Chs. Commn. on Faith and Order, 1961-75; mem. Joint Anglican-Orthodox Theol. Commn., 1965-81. Author: The Large Estates of Byzantine Egypt, 1931, Militant in Earth: Twenty Centuries of the Spread of Christianity, 1940, Christian Egypt: Church and People, 1952, Faithful Witnesses: Records of Early Christian Martyrs, 1959, (with Eugene Fairweather) The Voice of the Church: The Ecumenical Council, 1962, others; editor: Orthodox Statements on Anglican Orders, 1946, Christology of the Later Fathers, 1954, others. Home: Cambridge Eng. Died May 26, 1981; cremated, interred Swan Point Cemetery, Providence.

HARDY, JAMES DANIEL, physiologist, educator; b. Georgetown, Tex., Aug. 11, 1904; s. James Chappel and Lulu (Daniel) H.; m. Augusta Ewing Haugh, June 8, 1928; children: James Daniel, George Frederick. BA, U. Miss., 1924, MA, 1925; PhD, Johns Hopkins U., 1930; MA (hon.), Yale U., 1961; DSc, Kansas City Coll. Osteopathy and Surgery, 1966, Southwestern U., 1967; honoris causa, U. Lyon, France, 1970. Asst. prof. math, physics and astronomy U. Miss., 1925-27; NRC fellow physics U. Mich., 1930-32; rsch. fellow Russell Sage Inst. Cornell U., 1941-53, assoc. prof. physiology, 1941-53; prof. physiology U. Pa., 1953-61; prof. physiology, epidemiology, pub. health Yale Sch. Medicine, 1961-85; dir. John B. Pierce Found. Lab, New Haven, 1961-85; George Phillips Graves lectr., Ind. U., 1960; Rowe-Smith Meml. lectr., 1961; Kennon Meml. lectr. U. Miss. 1956; mem. man in space com., space sci. bd. NRC, 1958-60; chmn. Com. on Naval Med. Rsch., 1964-69. Editor: Temperature, Its Measurement and Control in Science and Industry, 3d edit., 1962, Pain Sensations and Reactions, 1952, Physiological Problems in Space Exploration, 1963, Thermal Problems in Aerospace Medicine, 1968, Physiological and Behavioral Temperature Regulation, 1970. Comdr. USNR, 1941-45; ETO; rear adm. Res. Decorated Legion of Merit, Purple Heart; recipient Meritorious Civilian Service award USN, 1961, William F. Peterson Found. award in biometeorology, 1972, Disting. Alumni award U. Miss., 1976. Fellow Am. Phys. Soc., Aerospace Med. Assn. (Eric Liljencrantz medal 1960), Nat. Acad. Scis., Am. Acad. Arts and Scis.; mem. Am. Physiol. Soc. (Ray Daggs award 1976), Harvey Soc., Soc. Exptl. Biology and Medicine, John Morgan Soc., Biophysics Soc., Am. Soc. Heating, Refrigeration and Air-Conditioning Engrs., Internat. Soc. Biometeorology, AAAS, Naval Res. Assn., Naval Hist. Assn., Yale Club of N.Y.C., Cosmos Club. Congregationalist. Home: Woodbridge Conn. Died Sept. 6, 1985.

HARE, FRANCIS HUTCHESON, lawyer; b. Lower Peach Tree, Ala., Aug. 13, 1904; s. Crosland C. and Sallie (Morrissette) H.; m. Isabelle Corr, Jan. 25, 1930; children: Lucille Hare Levin, Francis Hutcheson. Student, Auburn U., 1921-22, U.S. Naval Acad., 1922-23; LLB, U. Ala., 1927. Bar: Ala. 1927. Practiced in Birmingha; sr. mem. firm Hare, Wynn, Newell and Newton, 1944-83; assoc. justice Spl. Supreme Ct. Ala., 1967. Trial lawyer, lectr., author: My Learned Friends, 1976. Chmn. Jefferson County Civil Service Bd., 1951-52. Medalist Law Sci. Acad. Fellow Am. Bar Found., Am. Coll. Trial Lawyers; mem. ABA, Ala. Bar Assn. (pres. 1950), Birmingham Bar Assn. (pres. 1943), Internat. Acad. Trial Lawyers (dean, pres. 1967), Inner Circle Advs., Kappa Alpha, Phi Delta Phi. Methodist. Home: Birmingham Ala. Died 1983.

HARING, NIKOLAUS MARTIN, medieval historian, educator; b. Urmitz, Germany, June 6, 1909; came to Can., 1941, naturalized, 1947; s. Johann and Margarete (Erlemann) H. ThD, U. Rome, 1938; D History, Pontifical Inst. Medieval Studies, Toronto, 1947. Ordained priest Roman Catholic Ch., 1936. Prof. philosophy Theol. Coll., Limburg, Germany, 1939; prof. medieval history Pontifical Inst. Medieval Studies, 1947-66, Ctr. for Medieval Studies, Toronto U., 1966-76, Theologische Hochschule, Vallendar, Germany, 1976-82. Editor, author: Gerhoch of Reichersberg, 1964, Clarembald of Arras, 1965, Gilbert of Poitiers, 1966, Thierry of Chartres, 1971. Guggenheim fellow, 1962, 65; Can. Govt. grantee, 1966, 72. Fellow Royal Soc. Can. Home: Vallendar Germany. Died July 12, 1982; buried Limburg/Lahn, Germany.

HARKAVY, MINNA, sculptor, educator; b. Estonia, Nov. 13, 1887; d. Joel and Hannah Rothenberg; m. Louis Harkavy, 1910. BA, Hunter Coll.; student, Art Students League, N.Y.C.; studied with Antoine Bourdelle, Paris. Tchr. North Shore Community Art Ctr., Roslyn, N.Y.; privately N.Y.C. Exhibited: Met. Mus. Art, N.Y.C., Mus. Modern Art, N.Y.C., Whitney Mus. Am. Art, N.Y.C., Mus. Munie, St. Denis, France, Hermitage, St. Petersburg, USSR, Pushkin Mus., USSR, Mus. Western Art, USSR, Ain Herod Mus., Tel-Aviv, San Francisco Mus. Art, Art Inst. Chgo., Pa. Acad. Fine Arts, Albright-Knox Art Gallery, Buffalo, others; represented in permanent and pvt. collections, U.S., abroad. Recipient awards Met. Mus. Art, 1951, 64, 65; Nat. Assn. Women Artists, Audubon Artists, 1965. Mem. Artists Equity Assn., Fedn. Modern Painters and Sculptors, Sculptors Guild, Inst. Arts and Letters (assoc.). Home: New York N.Y. Died Aug. 8, 1987.

HARKNESS, HOPE KNIGHT HODGMAN (MRS. ALBERT HARKNESS), association executive; b. Buffalo, Nov. 2, 1889; d. William Lansing and Adelaide Maria (Knight) Hodgman; m. Thomas Ives Hare Powel, Oct. 27, 1923 (dec. Aug. 1939); children: Hope Hodgman (Mrs. Richard G. Alexander), Adelaide Hare (Mrs. Kenneth Hills Bitting Jr.), Thomas Ives Hare; m. Albert Harkness, Sept. 2, 1954. Regent Mt. Vernon Ladies Assn., from 1948; councilor Am. Assn. Mus. 1954-57. Mem. Nat. Soc. Colonial Dames State of R.I. (past pres.), Cosmopolitan Club. Home: Middletown R.I. †

HARKNESS, ROBERT DICKSON, industrialist; b. Osaka, Japan, Dec. 23, 1892; s. Robert and Isabel Jane (Wilson) H.; m. Frue Byden Leitch, Oct. 13, 1920; 1 child, Robert Hugh. BSEE, Queens U., Kingston, Ont. Can., 1913; LLD (hon.), Queens U., 1958. V.p., gen. mgr. No. Electric Co., Montreal, Que., Can., 1938, pres., 1948-61, chmn., 1961-62; dir., mem. exec. com. No. Electric Co. Ltd., Montreal Trust Co., Sun Life Assurance Co. Can.; dir. Dominion Bridge Co. Ltd. Dominion Tar & Chem. Co. Ltd., Consol. Mining & Smelting Co. of Can. Ltd., Royal Bank of Can.; mem. Def. Rsch. Bd., Can., 1947-50, 53-56. Mem. bd. mgmt. Montreal Gen. Hosp.' chmn. bd. trustees Queen's U., Kingston. With Can. Army, 1914-19. Decorated Disting. Service Order, Military Cross, 1914-15 Star, Knight of Grace, Venerable Order of St. John of Jerusalem. Mem. Engring. Inst. Can., Corp. Profl. Engrs. Que. University Club, St. James Club, Mount Royal Club, Seigniory Club, Mount Bruno Country Club, Forest and Stream Club, Cataraqui Golf Club. Home: Westmount Que., Canada. †

HARLAN, MABEL MARGARET, educator; b. Colorado Springs, Colo., July 16, 1892; d. James Lincoln and Bertha Adelia (Logan) H. AB cum laude, artist's diploma, Colo. Coll., 1914; AM, Ind. U., 1922, PhD, 1927; pvt. study, Madrid, 1920, 25-26, 36, 49. Instr. modern langs., violin Daniel Baker Coll., Brownwood, Tex., 1914-17, Colo. Coll., 1917-20; instr. Spanish Ind. U., 1920, asst. prof., 1922, assoc. prof., 1927, prof., from 1944. Editor: Lope de Vega's El desden vengado, The Relation of Moreto's El desdén con el desdén; (with J. M. Hill) Cuatro Comedias; contbr. articles on langs. and rsch. on German-Spanish cultural relationships to profl. jours. Mem. MLA, Nat. Coun. Women (triennial mem.), Renaissance Soc. Am., Am. Assn. Tchrs. Spanish, Internat. Inst. for Girls in Spain, Hispanic Inst. in U.S.A., Phi Beta Kappa. Democrat. Congregationalist. Home: Bloomington Ind. †

HARLOW, BRYCE NATHANIEL, manufacturing company executive; b. Oklahoma City, Aug. 11, 1916; s. Victor and Gertrude (Gindling) H.; m. Elizabeth Larimore, Sept. 25, 1940 (dec. 1982); children: Margery Gindling, Trudy Paxton, Bryce Larimore; m. Sarah Jane Studebaker, July, 1983. BA, U. Okla., 1936, MA, 1942; postgrad., U. Tex., 1936-37. Grad. asst. U. Tex., 1937; asst. librarian Ho. of Reps., 1938-40; profl. staff Com. Armed Services, 1947-49, chief clk., 1950-51; sec. to mem. Congress 1940-41; advt. mgr. Harlow Pub. Corp., Oklahoma City, 1946, v.p., 1951-52; spl. asst. to White House staff, adminstrv. asst., spl. asst., dep. asst. to Pres. 1952-61; dir. govtl. relations Procter and Gamble Mfg. Co., Washington, 1961-68, v.p., 1971-87; asst. to Pres. U.S., 1969, counsellor, 1969-70. Lt. col. U.S. Army, 1941-46. Decorated Legion of Merit. Mem. Okla. Hist. Assn., Oklahoma City Jr. C. of C., Capitol Hill Club, Army-Navy Country Club, Nat. Press Club, Carlton Club, Metropolitan Club, Nineteen Twenty-Five F Club, Phi Beta Kappa, Phi Delta Theta. Home: Arlington Va. Died Feb. 17, 1987.

HARLOW, REX FRANCIS, author, editor, publisher; b. Winfield, Mo., June 19, 1892; s. James and Mary Adeline (Davis) H.; m. Ruby Esther Wilson, Jan. 22, 1920; children: William (dec.), Esther Frances, Benjamin LeRoy (dec.). BS, Central State Tchrs. Coll., Edmond, Okla., 1934; AM, U. Tex., 1935; EdD, Stanford, 1937. Bus. mgr. Harlow's Weekly, 1912-15; sec.-treas. Harlow Pub. Co., 1915-24, v.p., 1924-36; instr. edn. Stanford, 1937-38, asst. prof. edn., 1938-40, assoc. prof. edn., social sci. and edn. rels., 1940-44; founder, pres. Pub. Rels. Inst. of West, from 1948; editor, pub. The Social Sci. Reporter, 1952-72, Pub. Rels. Rsch. Rev., 1958-60; pub. rels. cons. 1912-77; dir. Stanford School-Press Rels.

vestigation, 1938-39; organizer, pres. Am. Coun. Pub. els., 1939-47; del. World Conf. of Allied Ex-Service len of First World War, London, 1924. Author: klahoma Leaders, 1928, Public Relations in War and eace, 1942, The Daily Newspaper and Higher Education, 1939, The Minority Group Problem, 1954, Social cience in Public Relations, 1957, Years of Challenge, Autobiography, 1974, Building a Public Relations efinition, 1976, also 44 other books; co-author: Practical Public Relations, 1947, rev.edit., 1953; editor: arper Series of Public Relations Books, 1939-65; under, editor Public Relations Jour., 1945-47; contbr. ticles to nat. periodicals, Ency. Americana. Served ith 61st F.A. Brigade, 36th div., U.S. Army, 1918; .E.F.; maj., 45th Div., Okla. N.G. Named Distguished Ex-student, Central State U. and U. Tex.,)72; named to Okla. Journalism Hall of Fame, 1975. lem. Pub. Rels. Soc. Am. (co-founder 1947, bd. dirs.)47-52, Ann. Profl. award 1952, 69, named one of 12 ading pub. rels. profls. of century by U. Mich. 1970, t ann. medallion award No. Calif. chpts. 1976-77). ome: Palo Alto Calif. Deceased.

ARMON, NOLAN BAILEY, bishop; b. Meridian, liss., July 14, 1892; s. Nolan Bailey and Juliet (Howe) .; m. Rebecca Barry Lamar, June 20, 1923; children: olan Bailey III, George Lamar. AB, Millsaps Coll., ckson, Miss., 1914, DD, 1929; MA, Princeton, 1920; HL, Mt. Union Coll., 1946; DD, Duke, 1959; DLitt, m. U., 1946, Western Md. Coll., 1947, Hamline U.,)47; student, Emory U. Sch. Theology, 1916-17, DD,)58; LLD, Wofford Coll., Spartanburg, S.C., 1961. rdained to ministry M.E. Ch., South, 1918. Camp astor Walter Reed Gen. Hosp., Washington, 1918-19; astor chs. Md., Va., 1920-33; pastor Greene Meml. leth. Ch., Roanoke, Va., 1933-40; book editor Meth. h., 1940-56, bishop, from 1956; resident bishop Wesrn N.C. Conf., 1956-64; supt. bishop Ky. Conf., 1960, orth Ala. Conf., 1961-64; vis. prof. practical theology mory U., 1964, Candler Sch.; mem. book com. M.E. hs., 1930-40; mem. Joint Commn. on Meth. Hymnal,)30-34; mem. Hymnal Commn., 1960-64; mem. Meth. esquicentennial Commn., Commn. on Course of Studey r Conf. Undergrads, M.E. Chs., 1930-40; mem. gen. onf. M.E. Chs., 1930, 34, 38; mem. Uniting Conf. of lethodism, 1939; mem. gen. conf. Meth. Ch., 1940, 44, 3, 52, 56; mem. exec. com. Fed. Coun. Chs., 1944-48; em. curriculum com. Meth. Ch.; mem. Commn. on linisterial Tng., Commn. on Church Union, on Worip, 1940-56; mem. Bd. Edn., Meth. Ch., 1956-64; em. Bd. of Temperance. Author several books includg: Ministerial Ethics and Etiquette, 1928, The Famous ase of Myra Clark Gaines, 1946, The Organization of e Methodist Church, 1948; editor Abingdon-Cokesury Press, 1940-56, Methodist Book of Discipline,)40, 44, 48, 52, 56, Religion in Life (quar.), 1940-56, ncy. of World Methodism; contbr. articles to ch. publs. Dir. Save the Children Fedn., 1940-48; mem. United d. for Christian Colls. in China; trustee emeritus mory U., Ga.; trustee Drew U., N.J., 1940-56, High oint Coll., N.C., 1957-64, Wesley Theol. Sem., Am. U.,)64-68. 1st lt., chaplain O.R.C. Mem. Masons, appa Sigma. Home: Atlanta Ga. †

ARPER, CLAUDE, animal husbandman, educator; b. igonier, Ind., Sept. 29, 1891; s. Willis Leslie and Cisire Devault) H.; m. Mary Frances Vernon, June 30, 1915; hildren: Claude, Robert Vernon, Willis James. BS, urdue U., 1914; MS, U. Ill., 1918. Instr. animal husandry U. Ill., 1914-18; asst. sheep hunsbandry Purdue ., 1918-20, asst. animal husbandry, 1920-23, assoc.,)23-28, asst. chief, 1928-44, acting chief and head nimal husbandry, 1944-45, chief and prof., from 1945; ulbright rsch. scholar New Zealand, 1959. Dir. Inrnat. Livestock Expn., Chgo., 1960; cons. to Dept. gr., New Zealand, 1959; sec.-treas. Ind. Sheep reeders' Assn., 1919-39, Ind. Rambouillet Sheep reeders's Assn. Inc., 1931-46, Ind. Livestock Breeders' ssn. Inc., from 1935; chmn. 4-H Club Com., Lafayette otary Club, 1948-49. Fellow AAAS; mem. Am. Soc. nimal Prodn., Nat. Inst. Animal Agr. (treas.), Ind. oc. Chgo., Masons (32 degree), Nat. Block and Bridle, otary Internat., Sigma Xi, Epsilon Sigma Phi, Alpha amma Rho. Methodist. Home: West Lafayette Ind. †

ARPER, HORACE WILLIAM, labor representative; . Garland, Tex., Feb. 25, 1892; s. William A. and Oma McCullough) H.; m. Thelma LeMaster, Dec. 5,)36. Student, U. Tex., 1908-09. Clk. U.S. Ry. Mail ervice, El Paso, Tex., 1912-17, S.P. Co., 1918-23; gen. hmn. Brotherhood Ry. and S.S. Clks., S.P. Co., Tex., a., 1923-50, co-author death benefit system; mem. U.S. .R. Retirement Bd., Chgo., from 1950. Mem. Civil vc. Commn., Houston, 1931-34. 2d lt. inf., U.S. Army,)18. Mem. Am. Legion, Masons. Mem. Christian Ch. Home: Chicago Ill. †

ARRIMAN, WILLIAM AVERELL, former overnment official; b. Nov. 15, 1891; s. Edward Henry nd Mary (Averell) H.; m. Kitty Lanier Lawrence, Sept. 1, 1915; children: Mary (Mrs. Shirley C. Fisk), athleen (Mrs. Stanley G. Mortimer, Jr.); m. Mrs. larie Norton Whitney, Feb. 21, 1930 (dec. Sept. 1970); . Pamela Digby Churchill Hayward, Sept. 27,)71. B.A., Yale, 1913. Vice Pres. purchase and suplies Union Pacific R.R., 1915-17, chmn. bd., 1932-42; hmn. bd. Mcht. Shipbldg. Corp., 1917-25, W.A. Harman & Co., Inc., 1920-31; partner Brown Bros. Harriman & Co. (merger), 1931-46, ltd. partner, 1946-86; chmn. exec. com. Ill. Central R.R. Co., 1931-42, dir., 1915-46; Adminstr. Div. II, N.R.A., 1934, spl. asst. adminstr., 1934, adminstrv. officer, 1934-35; mem. bus. adv. council Dept. Commerce, 1933, chmn., 1937-39; chief materials br. prodn. div. O.P.M., 1940-41; spl. rep. of Pres. in Gt. Britain with rank of minister 1941, to USSR; chmn. mission), rank of ambassador 1941; apptd. rep. in London of Combined Shipping Adjustment Bd., 1942; apptd. mem. London Combined Prodn. and Resources Bd., 1942; U.S. ambassador to Russia, 1943-46, to Gt. Britain, 1946; sec. of commerce 1946-48, U.S. rep. in Europe under ECA of 1948, rank of A.E. and P., 1948-50, spl. asst. to Pres., 1950-51; Am. rep. on com. to study Western def. plans NATO, 1951; dir. Mut. Security Agy., 1951-53; gov. N.Y., 1955-59; ambassador-at-large 1961, 65-68, asst. sec. of state for Far Eastern affairs, 1961-63, under sec. of state polit. affairs, 1963-65; personal rep. of Pres. to conversations on Vietnam in Paris, 1968-69. Author: Peace with Russia?, 1959, America and Russia in a Changing World, 1971, Special Envoy: To Churchill and Stalin, 1941-46, 1975. Chmn. fgn. policy task force adv. council Democratic Nat. Com., 1974-86; del. Dem. Nat. Conv., 1976. Home: Washington D.C. Died July 26, 1986.

HARRIS, DAVID WILLIAM, petroleum executive, consultant; b. Machen, Ga., Sept. 7, 1891; s. Nathaniel Edwin and Fannie (Burke) H.; m. Mildred Stoutenborough, July 2, 1914; children: Walter Alexander, Holton Edwin. BS in Elec. Engring., Ga. Inst. Tech., 1912. Engr. Denver Gas & Electric Co., 1912-13; dir. budget, asst. treas. Cities Service Co., 1913-23; treas. Empire Gas & Fuel Co., 1923-27; v.p. Ind. Ty. Ill. Oil Co., 1927-28; v.p., gen. mgr. Ark. Natural Gas Corp. (and subs. cos.), pres., 1944-45; pres. Orange State Oil Co., 1939-45; v.p., dir. Cities Service Def. Corp., 1941-45; pres., chief exec. officer Universal Oil Products Co., 1945-60; chmn. David W. Harris & Assocs. (cons.), from 1962; dir. Harrel Inc. Recipient Alumni Distinguished Service award Ga. Inst. Tech., 1954. Mem. Mid-Continent Oil and Gas Assn. (exec. com., past pres. La.-Ark. div.), Am. Gas Assn. (dir. 1941-45), Bartlesville (Okla.) C. of C., Western Soc. Engrs., Newcomen Soc. N.Am., Masons (32d deg., K.T., Shriner), Chicago Club, Glenview Club, Westmoreland Club, McGraw Wildlife Found., Chi Phi. Home: Evanston Ill. Deceased.

HARRIS, FRED EARL, college president; b. Washington, June 8, 1917; s. James Riley and Elizabeth Annette (Schoolfield) H.; m. Frances Bandy, Dec. 24, 1938; children: Susan, Nancy. BS, Ind. State U., Terre Haute, 1940, MS, 1942; EdD, Ind. U., 1950. Dir. grad studies elem. edn., prof. edn. U. Ky., 1950-57; specialist fundamental edn. ICA, Egypt, 1954-55; cons. edn. Kabul, Afghanistan, 1959; dean coll. Baldwin-Wallace Coll., 1957-69; also v.p. acad. affairs 1964-69; v.p. acad. affairs U. Evansville, 1969-72; assoc. gen. sec. for higher edn. United Meth. Ch., 1972-77; pres. W.Va. Wesleyan Coll., Buckhannon, 1977-88; Mem. Nat. Edn. Study Team, Viet Nam, 1967, 70; cons. AID, Uganda, Tanzania, Kenya, 1969. Contbr. articles to profl. jours. Recipient Disting. Alumni award Ind. State U., 1965. Mem. Comparative Edn. Soc., Phi Delta Kappa. Methodist. Home: Bloomington Ind. Died Jan. 27, 1988; buried Bloomington, Ind.

HARRIS, GEORGE THOMAS, JR., lawyer; b. Henryetta, Okla., Sept. 12, 1922; s. George Thomas and Gertrude V. (Smith) H.; m. Martha J. Henry, Aug. 8, 1941; children: G. Thomas III, Ronald G., Debra Lyn. LLB, U. N.Mex., 1950. Bar: N.Mex. 1950. Assoc. firm Simms and Modrall, Albuquerque, 1950-56; ptnr. firm Modrall, Sperling, Roehl, Harris & Sisk, Albuquerque, 1956-85. 1st lt. USAAF, 1943-45; MTO. Fellow Am. Coll. Trial Lawyers; mem. Albuquerque Bar Assn. (past pres.), State Bar N.Mex. (past pres.), Am. Judicature Soc. Home: Albuquerque N.Mex. Died June 18, 1985; buried Sunset Meml. Park, Albuquerque.

HARRIS, JESSIE WOOTTEN, home economics educator; b. Washington, Ga., July 11, 1888; s. William Mercer and Jessie (Wootten) H. AB, U. Tenn., 1908; BS, Columbia U., 1912, AM, 1924. Tchr. San Marcos (Tex.) Bapt. Acad., 1908-11; head dept. econs. Sam Houston State Tchrs. Coll., 1912-18; state home demonstration agt. Tex. A&M Coll., 1917; assoc. prof. home econs. edn. U. Nebr., 1918-20; state dir. home econs. Tex. State Dept. Edn., 1920-26; dir. Sch. Home Econs. U. Tenn., 1925-47, vice dean Coll. Home Econs., 1947-57, dean, 1957-58, dean emeritus, from 1958, adminstrv. officer Inter-Univ. contract Home Econs., 1955-58; head home econs. dept. Winthrop Coll., Rock Hill, S.C., 1958-59; chief community nutrition div. Food Distbn. Adminstrn., USDA, 1943-44; chmn. Tenn. State Nutrition Com., 1940-41; vis. cons. Home Econs. Adminstrn., Exchange of PErsons Div., Dept. State, Germany, 1950; cons. on home econs. to India to F.O.A., U.S.A., 1954. Author: (with Ida A. Anders and Mildred T. Tate) Everyday Living, 1956, others. Mem. Am. Home Econ. Assn. (v.p. 1938-41, pres. 1942-44, mem. exec. com., chmn. com. on coms. 1939-40, chmn. com. on credentials 1940-42), Land Grant Coll. Assn. (mem. exec. com. 1948-51), Omicron Nu, Phi Kappa Phi, Pi Beta Phi (convention initiate 1939), Phi Upsilon Omicron. Democrat. Baptist. Home: Knoxville Tenn. †

HARRIS, ROBERT TAYLOR, philosophy educator; b. Joliet, Ill., Mar. 18, 1912; s. Eugene Nelson and Bess (Hutchinson) H.; m. Mary Margaret Simmons; children: Paul, Peter, Eugene, John. Ph.B. (Austin scholar), Northwestern U., 1937; M.A., Harvard, 1948, Ph.D., 1949. Mem. faculty U. Utah, 1949-52, So. Ill. U., 1952-55, Bradley U., 1955-58; prof. philosophy Miami U., Oxford, Ohio, 1958-70; chmn. dept. Miami U., 1958-69; vis. prof. philosophy Simmons Coll., 1970-71, Northeastern U., 1971; prof. philosophy Framingham (Mass.) State Coll., 1972-82, prof. emeritus, 1982-87. Author: (J. Jarrett) Language and Informal Logic, 1956, Social Ethics, 1962. Lt. col. ret. USMCR, 1942-45. Home: Brookline Mass. Died June 21, 1987.

HARRIS, RUFUS CARROLLTON, university chancellor; b. Monroe, Ga., 1897; s. Virgil Vascar and Jessie (Green) H.; m. Mary Louise Walker, June 23, 1918; children: Rufus Carrollton, Joseph Henry Walker, Louie Kontz. Grad., Gordon Inst., Barnesville, Ga., 1915; A.B., Mercer U., 1917, LL.D., 1931; LL.B., Yale U., 1923, J.D., 1924; LL.D., U. Ala., 1941, William Jewell Coll., 1943, U. Maine, 1953, U. Chattanooga, 1953, Northwestern U., 1958, La. State U., 1960, Tulane U., 1965; Litt.D., Birmingham So. U., 1950, U. Miami, 1958; D.C.L., U. Hawaii, 1952; prof. honoris causa, U. Pueblo, 1956; L.H.D., Samford U., 1961, Stetson U., 1962, Jacksonville U., 1964, Flagler Coll., 1975. Prof. law Mercer U. Law Sch., 1923-27, dean, 1925-27; dean, prof. law Tulane U., 1927-37, pres., 1937-60; pres. Mercer U., Macon, Ga., 1960-79; chancellor Mercer U., 1979-88; dir. U.S. Fed. Res. Bank, Atlanta, 1938-56, chmn. bd. dirs., 1954-56; Pres. So. Assn. Colls. and Secondary Schs., 1958; mem. Commn. on Colls., 1957-75; pres. Council So. Univs., 1956-57, So. U. Conf., 1941-43; mem. adv. com. VA, Washington, 1943-69, chmn., 1958-69; mem. U.S. Adv. Commn. on Internat. Ednl. and Cultural Affairs, 1965-69; chmn. So. Region Marshall Scholarship Com., 1956-73; mem. Ga. Higher Edn. Facilities Commn., 1964-74. Trustee Eisenhower Exchange Fellowships, Inc., 1953-88 , Inst. for Def. Analyses; mem. bd. Carnegie Found. for Advancement of Teaching, 1945-72, chmn., 1955. Served with inf. U.S. Army, 1917-19. Decorated chevalier French Legion of Honor, Confrerie des Chevaliers du Tastevin; Most Excellent Order Brit. Empire, 1970; Distinguished Civilian Service award Dept. Navy, World War II. Mem. Am., La., Ga., New Orleans bar assns., Nat. Planning Assn. (trustee, chmn. com. on So. devel.), Assn. Am. Law Schs. (sec. 1931-35, pres. 1935), Order of Coif, Phi Beta Kappa, Omicron Delta Kappa, Phi Delta Theta. Democrat. Baptist. Clubs: Boston (New Orleans); Round Table, Commerce (Atlanta); Century Assn. (N.Y.C.). Lodge: Masons. Home: Macon Ga. Died August 18, 1988, buried Rest Haven Cemetery, Monroe, Ga.

HARRIS, SHEARON, utility executive; b. Middleburg, N.C., Sept. 12, 1917; s. Joseph Pegues and Lucy (Shearon) H.; m. Helen Morgan, June 27, 1942; children: Sarah Helen, Jennie Grace, Susan Finch. AB, Wake Forest Coll., 1936, LLB, 1938, LLD (hon.), 1978. Bar: N.C. 1938. Practice in Albemarle, 1939-57, Charlotte, 1946-57; sr. ptnr. firm Harris & Coble, Albemarle, 1955-57; with Carolina Power & Light Co. Raleigh, from 1957; v.p. 1960-63, gen. counsel, 1962-63, pres., from 1963, chief exec. officer, from 1968, chmn. bd., from 1970, also dir.; dir. Durham Life Ins. Co., Wachovia Bank & Trust Co. N.A., Gen. Motors Corp., U.S. Steel Corp.; mem. listed cos. adv. com. N.Y. Stock Exchange; bd. dirs. Edison Electric Inst., from 1968, vice chmn., 1970, chmn., 1971; chmn. bd. dirs. Electric Power Research Inst., 1975-77. Parliamentarian, N.C. Bapt. Conv., 1957-62; prin. clk. N.C. Ho. of Reps., 1941-43; mem. N.C. Ho. of Reps. from Stanly County, 1955; chmn. exec. adv. commn. FPC, 1972-77; pres. N.C. Indsl. Council 1968; trustee Wake Forest Coll., 1955-59, Com. for Econ Devel.; bd. dirs. N.C. Found. Ch. Related Colls., from 1962, N.C. Bapt. Found., 1961-66, N.C. Citizens Assn., from 1966 (pres. 1970); chmn. bd. trustees Meredith Coll., from 1970. With AUS, 1943-45. Decorated Legion of Merit, Bronze Star medal; recipient Religious Heritage of Am. award. Mem. NAM (dir. 1972-75), C. of C. of U.S. (dir. from 1972, chmn. 1978-79), Bus. Council, Nat. Indsl. Energy Council, Nat. Assn. Electric Cos. (chmn. bd. dirs. 1969), Bus. Roundtable. Democrat. Home: Raleigh N.C. Died August 28, 1980; buried Raleigh Meml. Park.

HARRIS, SYDNEY JUSTIN, newspaper columnist; b. London, Sept. 14, 1917; m. Grace Miller (div. 1951); m. Patricia Roche, 1953; children: Carolyn (dec.), Michael, Barbara, David, Lindsay. Student, U. Chgo. and Central Coll., Chgo.; LL.D., Villa Maria Coll.; Litt.D., Schimer Coll.; D.H.L., Lenoir-Rhyne Coll. Employed in various positions Chgo. Herald and Examiner, 1934-35, Chgo. Daily Times, 1936; editor Beacon Mag., Chgo., 1937-38; with pub. relations dept. legal div. City of Chgo., 1939-41; with Chgo. Daily News, 1941-78; drama critic and writer column Strictly Personal (syndicated in U.S. and Can. by News Am. Syndicate), 1944-86; mem. faculty Univ. Coll., U. Chgo., 1946-86; vis. scholar Lenoir-Rhyne Coll., Hickory, N.C., 1980-82; dir. Hickory Humanities Forum, Wildacres, N.C., 1980—. Column appears in more than 200 newspapers; Author: Strictly Personal, 1953, A Majority of One, 1957, Last Things First, 1961, On the Contrary, 1964, Leaving the Surface, 1968, For the Time Being, 1972,

The Authentic Person, 1972, Winners and Losers, 1973, The Best of Harris, 1975, Would You Believe?, 1979, Pieces of Eight, 1982, Clearing the Ground, 1986; Mem. usage panel: Am. Heritage Dictionary. Trustee Francis W. Parker Sch., Chgo. Recipient Ferguson award Friends of Lit., 1958; Brotherhood award NCCJ, 1968; Press award ACLU, 1980. Mem. Sigma Delta Chi. Clubs: Arts, Headline, Press. Died Dec. 7, 1986.

HARRIS, VINCENT MADELEY, bishop; b. Conroe, Tex., Oct. 14, 1913; s. George Malcolm and Margaret (Madeley) H. Student, St. Mary's Sem., La Porte, Tex., 1934; S.T.B., N.Am. Coll., Rome, 1936, J.C.B., 1939; J.C.L., Cath. U. Am., 1940; L.H.D., St. Edward's U., Austin, Tex., 1982. Ordained priest Roman Catholic Ch., 1938; prof. St. Mary's Sem., 1940-51; chancellor Diocese Galveston-Houston, 1948-66, diocesan consultor, 1951-66; domestic prelate 1956, bishop of Beaumont (Tex.), 1966-71, coadjutor bishop of Austin (Tex.), 1971-88, bishop, 1971. Decorated knight grand cross Equestrian Order Holy Sepulchre Jerusalem. Mem. Sons Republic of Tex. Club: K.C. (chaplain Tex. 1967-69). Home: Austin Tex. Died Mar. 31, 1988; buried St. Anthony's Cathedral, Beaumont, Tex.

HARRIS, WILLIAM ROBERT, retail executive; b. Fayetteville, Ga., Aug. 16, 1914; s. Leonard A. and Millie L. (Boyd) H.; m. Gertrude Goss, Nov. 30, 1942; children: Sally Harris Alford, William Robert. Grad., Young Harris Coll., 1935. With F.W. Woolworth Co., 1935-42, 1945-79, v.p., N.Y.C., 1965-70, exec. v.p., 1970-77, dir., mem. exec. com., 1967-79, vice chmn. bd., 1976-79; pres. U.S. Woolworth-Woolco Operating div., 1975-79; bd. dirs. Kinney Shoe Corp., Richman Bros. Co., F.W. Woolworth Co., Ltd., Can. With Q.M.C. AUS, 1942-45. Mem. Nat. Retail Mchts. Assn. (bd. dirs.), Am. Retail Fedn., Newcomen Soc., Sales Execs. Club N.Y., Greenwich (Conn.) Country CLub, Seaview Country Club (Absecon, N.J.), John's Island Club (Vero Beach, Fla. Methodist. Home: Vero Beach Fla. Died Jan. 16, 1986.

HARRISON, EARL LEONARD, clergyman; b. Alto, Tex., Jan. 23, 1891; m. Eula Mae Anderson, Jan. 10, 1910 (dec. 1945); children: Earlene Jane (Mrs. Frederick George Sampson), Eldene Catherine (Mrs. Eugene W. James II), Earl Leonard; m. 2d, Ella B. Snell, June 13, 1948. Student, Butler Coll., 1912-13; BTh, Bishop Coll., 1915-19; student, Union Theol. Sem., 1935-37. Ordained to ministry Bapt. Ch., 1911. Pastor Tex., 1910-36; pres. Bishop Coll., Dallas, 1951-52; pastor Shiloh Bapt. Ch., Washington, from 1936; pres. Tex. Bapt. Fgn. Mission Conv., 1928-30, Bapt. Conv. D.C. and vicinity, 1943-44, Progressive Nat. Bapt. Conv. D.C., 1970-71; mem. Nat. Bapt. Conv. U.S.A. Inc., 1912-62; dir. Indsl. Bank, Washington. Pres. Nannie H. Burrough's Sch. Inc., Washington, 1968-69; chmn. bd. trustees Bapt. sem., Washington; trustee Bishop Coll., 1929-63; bd. dirs. Interdenominational Theol. Ctr., Atlanta; organizer, chmn. Washington Inst. Employment Tng., 1965-71. Home: Washington D.C. †

HARRISON, G. LAMAR, university president, education educator; b. Seward, Okla., June 3, 1900; s. General Price and Caroline (Dewberry) H.; m. Dorothy Marie Penman, June 20, 1932; children: Gerald (dec.), Richard B. (dec.). AB, Howard U., 1926; BE, U. Cin., 1927, AM, 1929; PhD, Ohio State U., 1936; DCL, U. Liberia, 1956. Acting head dept. edn. Va. Union U., Richmond, 1927-28; assoc. prof. edn., dir. elem. tchr. tng. W.Va. State Coll., Institute, 1928-31; prof. edn., dir. div. edn. Prairie View (Tex.) State Coll., 1932-39; pres. Langston (Okla.) U., 1939-86; guest prof. Va. State Coll., summer 1937; v.p., regional dir. Am. Tchrs. Assn., 1940-86; cons. tech. tng. Bur. of Tng., War Manpower Commn., 1943-45; pres. Assn. Pres. of Negro Land-Grant Colls., 1943; coordinator Commn. Tchr. Edn., Am. Council Edn.; mem. exec. com. Bd. Control, So. Regional Edn. Mem. bd. trustees Wilberforce U., 1932-37; guest of Pres. of Liberia, 1956; visitor to embassies in Rome, Paris, London, 1956. 1st lt. R.C., U.S.A. Knighted by Govt. of Liberia, 1955. Mem. NEA, Am. Soc. Sch. Adminstrs., Alpha Phi Alpha, Alpha Kappa Mu, Kappa Delta Pi, Sigma Pi Phi, Masons. Home: Chicago Ill. Died Jan. 18, 1986.

HARRISON, GUY FRASER, conductor, organist; b. Gildford, Surrey, Eng., Nov. 6, 1894; came to U.S, 1920; married; children: Basil, Myra. Scholar, Royal Coll. Music, London, from 1910. Formerly condr. Oklahoma City Symphony; then condr. Rochester (N.Y.) Civic Orch. and Rochester Civic Chorus, also assoc. condr. Rochester Philharmonic; guest condr. Mpls. Symphony Orch., St. Paul Opera Co. Recipient Alice M. Ditson award (twice). Home: San Miguel de Allende Mex. Died Feb. 20, 1986.

HARRISON, JOHN HARTWELL, urological surgeon, educator; b. Clarksville, Va., Feb. 16, 1909; s. Isaac Carrington and Rosalie (Smith) H.; m. Gertrude Chisholm, June 16, 1934 (dec. Feb. 1965); children: John Hartwell, Robert C. II, Cornelia Jeffrey; m. Mary Louise Harding, July 16, 1965. BS, U. Va., 1929, MD, 1932; MA (hon.), Harvard U., 1974; DSc (hon.), Roger Williams Coll., 1974. Diplomate Am. Bd. Surgery, Am. Bd. Urology (examiner from 1966, pres. 1973). Intern Lakeside Hosp., Cleve., 1932-33; intern, resident urology, then asst. resident surgery Peter Bent Bingham Hosp., Boston, 1933-38, Harvey Cushing fellow surgery, 1939, sr. assoc. urology, chief of service, 1945-75, acting surgeon in chief, 1967, urologic surgeon emeritus, from 1975; asst. genito-urinary surgery Harvard Med. Sch., 1935-37, instr. surgery, 1938-39, instr. genito-urinary surgery, 1939-41, assoc., 1941-46, asst. prof., 1946-48, assoc. clin. prof., 1948-54, clin. prof., 1954-65, Elliot Carr Cutler prof. surgery, 1965-75, prof. emeritus, from 1975; Edgar Burns vis. prof. urology Tulane U., 1961; Clyde Deming vis. prof. Yale Sch. Medicine, 1968; cons. urology Mass. Hosp. Sch. Crippled Children, Children's Med. Ctr., Boston Lying-In Hosp., VA Hosp., West Roxbury, Mass., Lemuel Shattuck Hosp., Jamaica Plain, Mass.; vis. prof. Ohio State U., 1964, UCLA, 1966, 67, Duke U., 1967, 77, U. Mo., 1968, Johns Hopkins U., 1969, U. Va., 1970, U. Calif. San Francisco, 1972, Med. Coll. Va., 1973, Northwestern U., 1976, Med. Coll. S.C., 1977, Albany Med. Coll, 1981, La. State U. Med. Ctr., Shreveport, 1981, Bishop John J. Russell Med. Coll. Va., 1981; Louis McDonald Orr vis. prof. Emory U., 1981; lectr. St. Mary's Hosp.; vis. faculty Mayo Clinic, 1965; cons. to surgeon gen. USAF. Author: Urology, 1970; mem. adv. bd. Jour. Surgery; editor: Campbell's Urology, 1978. Trustee Boston Med. Library; bd. visitors U. Va., 1966-74, chmn. med. com. Lt. col. M.C. AUS, 1942-45, PTO. Recipient Purkynje medal Czechoslovakian Med. Soc., 1971, Robert Cutler medal Peter Bent Brigham Trustees, 1973, Disting. Sci. Achievement award Mass. Kidney Found., 1979. Fellow ACS (gov. 1961-65), Royal Coll. Surgeons Ireland (hon.); mem. Am. Acad. Arts and Scis. (Amory prize), Am. Urol. Assn. (exec. com. 1961-62, Ramon Guiteras award 1965, pres. N.E. sect. 1953, Hon. mem. award), Boston Surgery Soc. (v.p. 1958, pres. 1972), N.E. Surgery Soc., Am. Surg. Assn. (1st v.p. 1970-71), Am. Assn. Genito-Urinary Surgeons (Barringer medal 1975, Edwin L. Keyes medal 1983, pres. 1976-77), Clin. Soc. Genito-Urinary Surgeons (pres. 1964-65), Urologic Forum Clin. Investigation, AMA, Roxbury Soc. for Med. Improvement, Tavern Club, Harvard Club, Brookline (Mass.) Country Club, Phi Beta Kappa, Alpha Omega Alpha,. Home: Dedham Mass. Died Jan., 1984; buried Brookline, Mass.

HARRISON, WARD DUNCAN, paper manufacturer; b. Blue Earth, Minn., Sept. 15, 1909; s. Charles H. and Grace (Putney) H.; m. Martha Jentz, Sept. 5, 1936; children—Frederick, Martha Ann, Lynn. B.S., Iowa State Coll., 1932; M.S., Inst. Paper Chemistry, Appleton, Wis., 1934, Ph.D., 1936. Registered engr., N.C. Chem. engr. Riegel Paper Corp., Milford, N.J., 1936-41; asst. to exec. v.p. Riegel Paper Corp., N.Y.C., 1948-49; v.p. Milford, 1949-55, N.Y.C., 1955-58; dir. 1950-58; pres. Allied Paper Corp. (now Allied Paper Inc. div. SCM Corp.), 1958-64, chmn. bd., 1964-70, chief exec. officer, 1964-70, also dir.; v.p., dir. SCM Corp., 1968-70, asst. to exec. v.p., 1971; chmn. bd. Howard Paper Mills, Inc., Dayton, Ohio, 1972-85; pres. Howard Paper Mills, Inc., 1972-84; past pres. chief exec. officer Maxwell Paper Corp., 1972-73; chmn. bd. Brazil Coal & Clay Corp., Ind., 1974-86; pres. Harrison Enterprises, 1978-86; chmn. bd. Watervliet Paper Co., Mich., 1981-84; asst. gen. mgr. Ecusta Paper Corp., Pisgah Forest, N.C., 1941-48. Contbr. articles to profl. publs. Mem. TAPPI (pres. 1957-58), Paper Industry Mgmt. Assn. Presbyterian. Home: Longboat Key Fla. Died Aug. 27, 1986; buried Dayton, Ohio.

HARRISS, JULIUS WELCH, apparel manufacturing executive; b. High Point, N.C., Oct. 26, 1905; s. Julius Ward and Florence (Welch) H. AB, Duke U., 1927. Pres. Harriss & Covington Hosiery Mills, Inc., High Point, 1928-73, chmn. bd., from 1974; pres., bd. dirs. Harco, Inc. Mem. Edenton (N.C.) Hist. Commn.; past mem. interstate com. YMCA's of Carolinas; past mem. internat. com. YMCA's of U.S. and Can.; past mem. nat. council Met. Opera, N.Y.C.; past bd. dirs. High Point Hist. Mus.; trustee Duke U., 1947-73, trustee emeritus, from 1973, also mem. bldg. com., bd. visitors Duke U. Library; mem. Meth. Coll. Found. N.C.; corp. mem. Rsch. Triangle Inst.; past trustee, treas., mem. exec. com. High Point Meml. Hosp., later trustee emeritus; past bd. dirs. High Point Community Concert Assn., Carolina United Community Service; former bd. dirs., mem. exec. com. N.C. Symphony; former trustee N.C. Cen. U., High Point Pub. Library. Lt. comdr. USNR, World War II. Mem. N.C. Art Soc. (life, former dir.), N.C. Lit. and Hist. Assn. (life), Emerywood Country Club (past sr. bd. dirs.), Quadrille Club, String and Splinter Club (High Point), Execs. Club (past dir.), Rotary (past pres.), Alpha Tau Omega. Home: High Point N.C. Died Dec. 20, 1984.

HARROWER, GORDON, textile manufacturer; b. Worcester, Mass., May 23, 1891; s. David and Mary Duncan (Struthers) H.; m. Elizabeth Lyman, Nov. 15, 1928 (div. July 1932); 1 child, Gordon; m. Helen Hopper, Oct. 25, 1933; 1 child, Helen Struthers. AB, Harvard U., 1914; postgrad., Ecole de Cavalrie, Saumur, France, 1917. Cotton textile apprenctice Nashawena Mills, New Bedford, Mass., 1914-16; sales clk. Clarence Whitman, N.Y.C., 1916-17; asst. sec., asst. treas. Wauregan Co., Quinebaug Co., 1919-32, also bd. dirs.; treas. Wauregan-Quinebaug Mills, 1932-43, also bd. dirs.; pres., treas. Wauregan Mills., Conn., 1943, chmn. bd.; v.p. charge R&D Hopper Paper Co.; bd. dirs. Am. Mut. Liability Ins. Co., Puget Sound Pulp & Timber Co., Am. Cotton Mfrs. Assn.; rep. to Internat. Textile Conf., Buxton, Eng., 1952. Pres. Day Kimball Hos Putnam, Conn. Lt. F.A., U.S. Army, 1917-19 Decorated Silver Star. Mem. Am. Cotton Mfrs. In Masons (32 degree), Harvard Club. Mem. Christ C (warden). Home: Pomfret Conn. †

HART, CHARLES R(ANDALL), language educator; Rochester, N.Y., Sept. 20, 1891; s. Henry and Marga Louise (McCoy) H.; m. Angie McCoy Harding, June 1939. AB, Williams Coll., 1913, MA, 1916; stude Am. Sch. Classical Studies, Athens, 1913-14; Ph Johns Hopkins, 1927. Head Latin dept. Greenfie (Mass.) High Sch., 1917; asst. prof. romance lan Lafayette Coll., 1919-26, Reed Coll., 1927-28; pr romance langs. Emory U., 1928-46, prof. Latin, 1946-(Author: (poetry) Master and Lackey, 1921, The Sie of New York, 1924; (plays) Coleridge, Nature Love Samuel Johnson, 1959. YMCA sec. with Foyer d Soldat, France, 1917-19. Mem. Classical Assn. Middle West and South, Phi Beta Kappa. Episcopali Home: Atlanta Ga. †

HART, DWIGHT HOWARD, JR., hotel executive; Los Angeles, Sept. 10, 1921; s. Dwight Howard a Mable Sophie (Runge) H.; m. Patt Bailey Cox, Dec. 1974; 1 child, Rosslyn Diane Whitaker. Stude Harvard Mil. Sch., 1932-38; B.S., A.B., U. So. Cal 1938-42. Former v.p. Allied Properties (owners Cl Hotels, San Francisco, Santa Barbara Biltmore Hote former v.p., mng. dir. Clift Hotel; supervising co Landmark Land Co.; dir. La Quinta Hotel, La Quin Calif. Mem. Am. Hotel Assn. (past dir.), Calif. Ho Assn. (past pres.), Pi Kappa Alpha. Clubs: Burlinga (Calif.) Country; Rancheros Vistadores (Santa Barba Calif.); Tavern (N.Y.C.). Lodge: Masons, Shriners Home: La Quinta Calif. Died Feb. 29, 1988; cremated.

HART, JAMES WIRTH, manufacturing company e ecutive; b. Trenton, N.J., Mar. 31, 1933; s. Earle Russ and Mildred (Barnes) H.; m. Joanne Weber, Mar. 1953; children: James Wirth, Steven Weber, Dougl Barnes, Jennifer Joanne Rife. BS, Drexel U., 19 MBA, U. Pitts., 1965; PhD, Harvard U., 1965. Sr. st and operating positions Westinghouse Electric Cor Pitts., 1955-66; exec. asst. to chmn., chief exec. offic Bendix Corp., Detroit, 1966-67; asst. office pres. IT N.Y.C., 1967-69; pres. Laird Enterprises, N.Y.C., 196 71; chief operating officer Weelabrator-Frye In N.Y.C., 1971-73; pres., chief exec. officer Mohawk Da Scis., 1974; pres., chmn. bd. Schick Inc., Westpo Conn., 1975-88. Clubs: Racquet and Tennis, Ox Rid Hunt, Boardroom, Landmark. Home: Darien Con Died July 17, 1988.

HART, LAURENCE COLLETT, association executiv b. Dayton, Ohio, May 8, 1891; s. Samuel F. and Cla (Burns) H.; m. Bernice Van Allen, Aug. 9, 1913; chi dren: Fred Van Allen, Bernice Virginia (Mrs. Robe Raymond Tompkins). Grad., Stivers Manual Tr High Sch., Dayton, Ohio, 1909; ScB, MIT, 1913. Salesman Bemis Bro. Bag. Co., St. Louis, Mo., 1913-1 acoustical engr. Johns-Manville Sales Corp., 1914, de mgr., 1916, sales mgr. western div., 1918, asst. gen. sal mgr. N.Y., 1923, gen. sales mgr. bldg. materials dep from 1935, v.p., from 1940, also bd. dirs.; v.p. John Manville Corp., 1947, ret., 1956; exec. v.p. Achievement Inc. Mem. Producers Coun. Inc. (pre dir. 1945-46), Engrs. Club, Masons, K.T., Shriner Sigma Alpha Epsilon. Home: Larchmont N.Y. †

HART, OLIVER JAMES, bishop; b. York, S.C., Ju 18, 1892; s. George Washington Seabrook and Elle Almene (Hackett) H.; m. mary McBee Mikell, July 2 1921; 1 child, Oliver James Jr. AB, Hobart Coll., 191 LLD, 1937; STB, Gen. Theol. Sem., 1916, STD, 194 BD, Union Theol. Sem., 1917; DD, U. Chattanoog 1926, U. of the South, 1935; LLD, U. Pa., 1942, Dic inson Coll., 1943; DCL, Temple U., 1952. Ordained ministry Episcopal Ch., 1917. Lay reader, deacon C of the Good Shepherd, Greenwood Lake, N.Y., 1915-1 curate St. Michael's Ch., Charleston, S.C., 1917-18, ass minister, 1919-20; rector Christ Ch., Macon, Ga., 192 26, St. Paul's Ch., Chattanooga, 1926-34, St. John's C Washington, 1934-40, Trinity Ch., Boston, 1940-4 bishop Diocese Cen. N.Y., 1937, Diocese Del., 193 bishop-coadjutor Diocese Pa., consecrated bishop in C of the Adv., Phila., 1942; active Dep. Gen. Conv., 192 37, chmn. Dept. religious edn., 1924-26, 28-29, e amining chaplain, 1932-33, mem. exec. coun., 1927-3 36-39; pres. Washington Diocese clericus, 1937; me Forward Movement Commn., 1935-38; dean Knoxvil Convocation, 1930-34. Author: History of Chr Church Parish of Macon, Georgia, 1825-1925. Trust Appleton Ch. Home, 1923-26; trustee Ch. Pensio Fund, from 1940, pres., 1958-63; warden St. John Orphanage, Washington, 1934-40; chmn. Army an Navy Commn., P.E. Ch., 1946-52. Capt. U.S. Arm 1918-19, 41-42. Mem. Masons, Rittenhouse Club, P Beta Kappa, Sigma Phi, Omicron, Delta Kappa. †

HART, ROY PUTMAN, railroad executive; Springfield, Mo., Feb. 14, 1892; s. Andrew Thomas an Nannie Clementine (Putman) H.; m. Clarissa A Rouse, Dec. 30, 1914; children: Margaret Helen (Mr Harry E. Nelson), Dorothy Clem (Mrs. Walter Thoma Petty), Roy Kenneth, Emily Jane (Mrs. James Bass). BS, U. Mo., 1913. Timekeeper bridge constr M.P.R.R., 1913, various positions, 1914-24, asst. brid gr., 1921-41, bridge engr., 1941-43, asst. chief engr., 943-45, chief engr., 1945-51, chief oper. officer, 1951-, v.p. ops., chief oper. officer, 1956-57, v.p. exec. dept. om 1957; bd. dirs. Mo.-Ill. R.R. Co., New Orleans & ower Coast R.R. Co., Am. Refrigerator Transit Co., ackers Car Line, Kansas City Terminal Ry. Co., lemphis Union Sta. Co., So. Ill. & Mo. Bridge Co., lo. Pacific Freight Transport Co. Mem. NSPE, ASCE, lo. Soc. Profl. Engrs., Am. Ry. Engring. Assn., Enneers Club, Noonday Club, Tau Beta Pi. Methodist. ome: Webster Groves Mo. †

ART, WILLIAM LEROY, educator, author; b. hgo., Oct. 12, 1892; s. Morris Philip and Martha lizabeth (Hoffmaan) H.; m. Elizabeth Moore Hughes, lar. 22, 1924 (dec. 1944); 1 dau., Helen Hughes; m. 2d, elen Margaret Johnston, June 22, 1946; 1 dau., Marie valyn. BS, U. Chgo., 1913, PhD in Math. and Astroomy, 1916. Instr. math. Harvard U., 1916-17; asst. rof. math. U. Minn., 1919-20, assoc. prof., 1920-25, rof., from 1925; chmn. curriculum com. for pre-meteor. tng. USAAF, 1943. Author: Trigonometry; Colge Algebra; Mathematics of Investment; Elements of nalytic Geometry; Calculus; Analytic Geometry and alculus; College Algebra and Trigonometry; Algebra, lementary Function, and Probability; contbr. articles tech., pedagog. jours. Served from 2d lt. to maj., AC, U.S. Army, 1917-19. Mem. AAAS, AAUP, Am. lath. Soc., Math. Assn. Am., Nat. Coun. Tchrs. Math., ni Beta Kappa, Sigma Xi. Presbyterian. Home: Saint aul Minn. †

ARTFIELD, DAVID, JR., lawyer; b. N.Y.C., May 5, 1919; s. David and Barbara Josie (Mayer) H.; m. reda Lustick Burling, Nov. 21, 1964. BA, U. Va., 941, LLB, 1943. Bar: N.Y. 1943, U.S. Supreme Ct. 949. Asst. U.S. atty. So. Dist. N.Y., 1943-45; assoc. rm White & Case, N.Y.C., 1945-55, ptnr., 1955-82, of unsel, 1982-83. Hon. bd. dirs. Kips Bay Boys Club, .Y.C. Mem. ABA, Am. Law Inst., Fed. Bar Assn., .Y. County Lawyers Assn., Am. Soc. Internat. Law, m. Judicature Soc., Order of Coif, Recess Club, Card und Golf Club, Farmington Country. Republican. ome: Key Largo Fla. Died July 1983.

ARTIG, HENRY EDWARD, electrical engineer; b. pls., Jan. 28, 1892; s. Henry C. W. and Emma (Ronr) H.; m. Dorothy Ashley Ellis, Aug. 20, 919. BSEE, U. Minn., 1918, PhD, 1924. Engr. R & D T&T, N.Y.C., 1919; instr. U. Minn., 1920-25, asst. of. elec. engring., 1925-31, assoc. prof., 1931-40, prof., om 1940, head dept. elec. engring., 1946-56. Author: with H. Dalaker) The Calculus, 1930. Pres. Robbindale (Minn.) Sch. Bd., 1930-39; asst. dir. lab., San iego, U. Calif. div. war rsch. on underwater warfare, .S.R.D., 1941-45. 2d lt. Signal Corp0s, U.S. Army, 918. Mem. AIEE (chmn. Twin City sect. 1946-47), ast. Radio Engrs. (chmn. Twin City sect. 1945-46), m. Phys. Soc., Sigma Xi, Tau Beta Pi. Presbyterian. ome: Robbinsdale Minn. †

ARTKE, GILBERT VINCENT, clergyman, educator; Chgo., Jan. 16, 1907; s. Emil and Lillian (Ward) . Grad., Loyola Acad., 1925; AB, Providence Coll., 929; AM, Cath. U. Am., 1938; postgrad., Northwesrn U., 1941; LLD (hon.), Notre Dame U., 1951; DFA, rovidence Coll., 1968; LHD, Georgetown U., 1971. lem. Order of Preachers since 1929; ordained priest oman Cath. Ch., 1936. Head grad. drama dept. Cath. Am., since 1937; trustee Players, Inc.; founder Chgo. oyola Community Theatre, 1927; mem. drama panel .S. Fine Arts Com., 1959-60; mem. nat. com. NESCO, 1959-60; nat. com. U.S.O., 1959-60; vice mn. Ford's Theatre Soc. Mem. Am. Ednl. Theatre ssn. (chmn. vets. com. 1950-52, mem. adv. council, ets. 1955), Am. Nat. Theatre and Acad. (corp.), Am. oc. Aesthetics, Am. Assn. U. Profs., Speech Assn. m., Catholic Theatre Conf. Appeared in Army Chaplain, KO series short subjects This Is America during /orld War II. Home: Washington D.C. Died Feb. 22, 986.

ARTLINE, HALDAN KEFFER, educator, physiogist; b. Bloomsburg, Pa., Dec. 22, 1903; s. Daniel chollenberger and Harriet Franklin (Keffer); m. Mary lizabeth Kraus, Apr. 11, 1936; children: Daniel Keffer, eter Haldan, Frederick Flanders. BS, Lafayette Coll., aston, Pa., 1923, DSc (hon.), 1959; MD, John opkins, 1927, LLD (hon.), 1969; ScD (hon.), U. Pa., 971; MD (hon.), U. Freiburg i/B, 1971; ScD (hon.), ockefeller U., 1976, U. Md., 1978, Syracuse U., 1979; dridge Johnson traveling rsch. scholar, U. Leipzig and unich, 1929-31. Nat. Rsch. fellow med. scis. John opkins U., 1927-29; fellow in med. physics Eldridge ohnson Rsch. Found. U. Pa., 1931-36, asst. prof. biophysics, 1936-40, 41-42, assoc. prof. biophysics, 1943-8, prof., 1948-49; assoc. prof. physiology Cornell U. led. Coll., N.Y.C., 1940-41; prof. biophysics, chmn. ept. Johns Hopkins U., Balt., 1949-53; prof. Rockeller U., N.Y.C., 1953-74, emeritus, 1974-83. ecipient William H. Howell award physiology, 1927, oward Crosby Warren medal exptl. psychology, 1948, .A. Michelson award Case Inst., 1964, Nobel prize in hysiology or medicine, 1967, Lighthouse award, .Y.C., 1969. Mem. NAS, Am. Physiol. Soc., Am. hilos. Soc., Am. Acad. Arts and Scis., Royal Soc. (fgn. n.), Biophys. Soc., Optical Soc. Am. (hon.), Physiol.

Soc. (U.K.) (hon.), Phi Beta Kappa, Sigma Xi. Home: New York N.Y. Died Mar. 17, 1983.

HARTMAN, DWIGHT DRYDEN, lawyer; b. Kearney, Nebr., Apr. 16, 1888; s. John Peter and Caroline Emily (Dryden) H.; m. Edna Thorne, July 3, 1935. BSME, U. Wash., 1912. Bar: Wash., 1915. Practice Seattle, from 1915; mem. Hartman & Hartman, 1915-37, Hartman, Hartman, Simon & Coles, 1937-42, Catlett, Hartman, Jarvis & Williams, from 1942; sec., dir. Spokane-Portland Cement Co. Capt. U.S. Army, 1918-19. Mem. ABA, Wash. Bar Assn., Seattle Bar Assn. Wash. Athletic Club, Rainier Club, Seattle Tennis Club, Masons (33 degree), Phi Gamma Delta. Republican. Presbyterian. Home: Seattle Wash. †

HARTMAN, ELIZABETH, actress; b. Youngstown, Ohio, 1943. Grad., Carnegie-Mellon U. Motion pictures include: Patch of Blue (nominated for Acad. award 1966), The Group, You're a Big Boy Now, The Fixer, The Beguiled. Home: Pittsburgh Pa. Died June 10, 1987.

HARTMAN, RALPH MAXWELL, government official; b. Tunnelton, W.Va., May 31, 1909; s. Lee Burtis and Mary Jane (Cummnings) H.; m. Mary Margaret Daingerfield, June 24, 1939; children: Carol Hartman Elden, Mary Jane Hartman Reber, Nancy Harman Farr, Judith Hartman Brewer. AB, U. Wva., 1931. Sec., adminstrv. officer W.Va. Workers' Compensation Fund, 1933-39; asst. mgr. Safety and Workmen's Compensation div. Bethlehem (Pa.) Steel Corp., 1940-73; mem. Benefits Rev. Bd. U.S. Dept. Labor, Washington, 1974-78, dir. Office Workers' Compensation Programs, from 1978; cons. state, fed. agys., coms., labor and industry coms., assns. Author safety, workers' compensation, casualty ins. manuals, papers, treatises, legis., from 1933. Mem. Internat. Assn. Indsl. Accident Bds. and Commns., Assn. Cert. Safety Profls. of Ams., Nat. Safety Council, Saucon Valley Country Club, Kenwood Golf Club, Country Washington Club. Republican. Presbyterian. Home: Washington D.C. Deceased.

HARTNETT, ROBERT CLINTON, clergyman, educator; b. Escanabe, Mich., Dec. 7, 1904; s. John M. and Mary Winifred (Killian) H. AB, Loyola U., Chgo., 1927; AM, St. Louis U., 1932; STL, Heythrop Coll., Eng., 1939; PhD, Fordham U., 1945. Entered Soc. of Jesus, 1927, ordained priest Roman Cath. Ch., 1938. Instr. English U. Detroit, 1932-35; instr. religion and sociology Xavier U., Cin., 1940-41; summer editor America 1943, 47; editor-in-chief America and Catholic Mind, pres. America Press., N.Y.C., 1948-55; assoc. prof., prof. polit. sci. U. Detroit, 1956; dean Coll. Arts and Scis. Loyola U., Chgo., 1956-58, prof. polit. sci., 1958-75, emeritus, 1975-87, lectr. Sch. Law, 1960-64; lectr. polit. philosophy Fordham U., 1945, polit. sci., fall 1948; dir. dept. polit. sci. U. Detroit, 1946-48; lectr. on current affairs affecting religion, from 1940. Author booklets: Equal Rights for Children, 1947, Federal Aid to Education, 1950, The State and Religious Education, 1952. Mem. Am. Polit. Sci. Assn. Home: Chicago Ill. Died Jan. 16, 1987.

HARTSHORNE, MARION HOLMES, clergyman, educator; b. Englewood, N.J., Jan. 11, 1910; s. Edward C. and Marian (Holmes) H.; m. Ruth Scotford, Jan. 13, 1939; children: Jonathan E., Richard A., Timothy S., Sarah M., William H. Becker. Student, MIT, 1928-30; BA, Williams Coll., 1933, MA, 1933; BD, Union Theol. Sem., N.Y.C., 1936, ThD, 1938. Ordained to ministry Presbyn. Ch., 1936. Pastor in Wilmington, Vt., 1938-40; at Olivet Coll., 1940-42, Doane Coll., 1942-46; mem. faculty Colgate U., 1946-75, prof. philosophy and religion, 1955-75, emeritus, from 1975, chmn. dept., 1963-70. Author: The Promise of Science and the Power of Faith, 1958, The Faith to Doubt, 1963. Mem. Soc. Religion in Higher Edn., Phi Beta Kappa, Phi Kappa Tau. Home: Hamilton N.Y. Died May 10, 1988; buried Colgate Cemetery, Hamilton, N.Y.

HARTSHORNE, RICHARD, judge; b. Newark, N.J., Feb. 29, 1888; s. William Sydney and Margaret Bentley (Harrison) H.; m. Ellen Sahlin, Mar. 15, 1919; children: Richard, Nancy, John Fritz, Penelope. Grad. Newark Acad., 1905; LittB, Princeton U., 1909; LLB, Columbia, 1912; LLD, Upsala Coll., 1952, Lincoln U., 1952. Bar: N.Y. 1912, N.J. 1912. Mem. Riker & Riker, Edward W. & Runyon Colie, Stewart & Hartshorne; spl. asst. U.S. atty. N.J., 1925; judge County Ct., Newark, 1931-51, U.S. Dist. Ct., from 1951; prof. constl. law and ins. law N.J. Law Sch.; pres. Interstate Commn. on Crime, 1935-43; chmn. N.J. Commn. on Interstate Cooperation; mem. bd. mgrs. Coun. State Govts.; chmn. N.J. Commn. for State Labor Dept. Survey; mem. joint conf. com. in charge Fed.-State Conf. on Law Enforcement Problems of Nat. Defense; del 8th Conf. Internat. pour l'Unification du Droit Penal, Copenhagen, Denmark, 1935. Contbr. articles to law jours. Pres. Jersey Boy's State. Lt. (j.g.) USNR, World War I; lt. col. N.J. State Guard. Mem. ABA (chmn. sect. jud. adminstrn.), N.J. Bar Assn., Essex County Bar Assn., Am. Legion (chmn. nat. law and order com. from 1937, comdr. N.J. Dept. 1930), SAR (nat. chancellor-gen. 1929-31, pres. N.J. Soc. 1928), Essex Club, East Orange Tennis Club, Masons. Republican. Presbyterian. Home: East Orange N.J. †

HARTSOOK, ARTHUR J., chemical engineering educator; b. Greenwood, Nebr., Nov. 17, 1891; s. William F. and Lizzie (Foster) H.; m. Gertrude Joy, June 20, 1914 (dec. Aug. 1953); 1 child, Edmund Arthur; m. Cecil S. Kemp, June 1, 1958. AB, Nebr. Wesleyan U., 1911; SB, MIT, 1920, MS in Chem. Engring., 1921. Profl. engr. Tex. Sci. tchr. Stromsberg, Nebr., 1912-13, Nebraska City, Nebr., 1913-15; supt. schs. Fairmont, Nebr., 1915-18; tchr. War Sch., U. Nebr., 1918; instr. indsl. chemistry Rice Inst., 1921-28, asst. prof. chem. engring, 1928-40, prof. chem. engring., from 1940, head dept. chem. engring. 1940-56. Mem. Am. Chem. Engrs., Am. Soc. Engring Edn., Sigma Xi, Tau Beta Pi. Home: Houston Tex. †

HARTWIG, CLEO, sculptor; b. Webberville, Mich., Oct. 30, 1911; d. Albert and Julia (Klunzinger) H.; m. Vincent Glinsky, 1951 (dec. Mar. 1975); 1 child, Albert. A.B., Western Mich. U., 1932, D.F.A. (hon.), 1973; student, Internat. Sch. Art, Europe, 1935. Tchr. pvt. schs. N.Y.C., 1935-42; instr. Cooper Union, 1945-46; sculpture instr. Montclair (N.J.) Art Mus., 1945-71. First one-man show, 1943; one-man show Montclair (N.J.) Art Mus., 1971, Benbow Gallery, Newport, R.I., 1979, Sculpture Ctr., N.Y.C., 1981, Cuny, Plattsburg, 1986, Harmon-Meek Gallery, Naples, Fla., 1987; group exhbns. include Nat. Acad., Pa. Acad., Detroit Inst. Arts, Art Inst. Chgo., Met. Mus., Phila. Mus., Whitney Mus., Newark Mus., Phila. Art Alliance, Denver Art Mus., Boston Mus. Sci., N.Y. Zool. Soc., Nebr. Art Assn., State U. Iowa, U. Ark., Des Moines Art Center, So. Vt. Art Center, U. Conn., Smithsonian Instn. Natural History, USIA in Europe, Nat. Inst. Arts and Letters, U. Minn., Canton Art Inst., N.Y. Bot. Garden, others, traveling one-man show, Can., U.S.; represented in permanent collections, Brookgreen Gardens, S.C., Newark Mus., Detroit Inst. Arts, Pa. Acad., Montclair Art Mus., Mt. Holyoke Coll., Western Mich. U., Oswego (N.Y.) Univ., Nat. Mus. Am. Art, Smithsonian Instn., Chrysler Mus., Norfolk, Va., NAD, So. Vt. Art Center, Gen. Electric Co., Mus. Internat. Art, Sofia, Bulgaria, Nat. Mus. Women in Arts, Washington. Recipient Kamperman Haass prize Mich. Artists Anu., 1943; Anna Hyatt Huntington prize for sculpture, 1945; L. Reusch & Co. prize N.Y. Soc. Ceramic Arts, 1946; Nat. Assn. Women Artists 1st prize for sculpture, 1951; medal of honor, 1967; Audubon Artists prize for sculpture, 1952; Pres.'s award, 1972; Today's Art award and medal of merit, 1975; award mural and sculpture competition Munson-Williams-Proctor Inst., 1958; Feist Meml. prize, 1968; Salomone prize, 1972; Jeffrey Childs Willis Meml. prize, 1975, 82, 86; Amelia Peabody award, 1976; Silver medal Nat. Sculpture Soc., 1969; Ellin P. Speyer prize NAD, 1979; L. J. Liskin Purchase prize Nat. Sculpture Soc., 1980; Edith H. and Richmond Proskauer prize, 1984; Chaim Gross Found., 1986; Audubon Artists medal of Honor, 1987. Fellow Nat. Sculpture Soc. (C. Percival Dietsch prize 1976, Leonard Meiselman prize 1978); mem. Audubon Artists, Sculptors Guild, Nat. Assn. Women Artists, Nat. Acad. Design (academician). Home: New York N.Y. Died June 18, 1988.

HARTZ, LOUIS, educator; b. Youngstown, Ohio, Apr. 7, 1919; s. Max and Fannie (Plotkin) H.; m. Stella Feinberg, July 3, 1943 (div. Dec. 1972); 1 son, Steven. BS summa cum laude, Harvard U., 1940, Sheldon traveling fellow, 1940-41, PhD, 1946. Writer Council for Democracy, 1941; instr. govt. Harvard U., 1945-47, asst. prof., 1947-50, assoc. prof., 1950-56, prof., 1956-74, chmn. com. Am. civilization, 1955-58; lectr. U. London, 1962; Walker-Ames vis. prof. U. Wash., 1963; Edward Douglass White lectr. La. State U., 1965; Centennial prof. U. Toronto, 1967. Author: Economic Policy and Democratic Thought, 1948, The Liberal Tradition in America, 1955, The Founding of New Societies, 1964; contbr. articles polit. sci., hist. periodicals. Mem. Am. Polit. Sci. Assn. (Woodrow Wilson prize 1956). Died Jan. 20, 1986.

HARVEY, THEODORE H., steel casting manufacturing executive; b. Austinburg, Ohio, Oct. 11, 1888; s. Horton L. and Frances J. (Ryder) H.; m. A. Mabel Sleep, Mar. 20, 1914; 1 child, Frances (Mrs. Sherwood R. Moran). Grad., Grand River Inst., 1905; AB, Oberlin Coll., 1910. Gen. mgr. Pelton Steel Casting Co., Milw., 1914-18; works mgr. Ohio Steel Foundry Co., Springfield, Ohio, 1918-26; v.p. in charge sales Ohio Steel Foundry Co., Lima, Ohio, from 1926, sr. v.p. Mem. Ohio Soc. Fin. Com., 1954-55. Mem. Steel Founders Soc. Am. (pres. 1932-33, Lorenze medal 1944). Home: Lima Ohio. †

HARVILL, HALBERT, college president; b. Hickman County, Tenn., Nov. 28, 1893; s. Young Fletcher and Fannie Madeira (Williams) H.; m. Catherine Evans, Apr. 21, 1925 (dec.); 1 son, Fletcher Evans; m. 2d, Mary Elizabeth Fortson, Mar. 31, 1955. BS, Middle Tenn. State Coll., 1927; AM, George Peabody Coll., Nashville, Tenn., 1938. Tchr. Hickman County rural schs. 1911-16; prin. Lascassas Sch., Rutherford County, Tenn., 1920-27, Englewood (Tenn.) Sch., 1927-29; instr. history Austin Peay State Coll., Clarksville, Tenn., 1929-30, dean, registrar, 1930-46, pres., from 1946. chmn. bd. dirs. First Trust & Savs. Bank, Clarksville. Commr. Edn., Tenn., 1938-39. With U.S. Army, 1917-18, 1943-46, lt. col. USAR. Mem. Am. Legion (Tenn. comdr. 1937-38, nat. exec. com. 1948-50), Vets. Fgn. Wars,

Clarksville C. of C., Tenn. Edn. Assn., Middle Tenn. Edn. Assn., NEA, Tenn. Coll. Assn. (pres. 1956-55), Clarksville Civitan Club, Kappa Delta Pi. Democrat. Methodist. Home: Clarksville Tenn. Died Dec. 1, 1986.

HARVILL, RICHARD ANDERSON, economist, former university president; b. Centerville, Tenn., Aug. 29, 1905; s. Young Fletcher and Fannie Madiera (Williams) H.; m. George Lee Garner, Aug. 12, 1936. SB with distinction, Miss. State Coll., 1926; AM in Econs., Duke, 1927, LLD, 1959; postgrad., U. Chgo., summers 1929, 33, 35; PhD in Econs., Northwestern U., 1932; Dr. honoris causa, Universidade Fed. do Ceará, 1966; LLD, U. Ariz., Ariz. State U., Bowling Green State U., 1971. Instr. history, econs. Miss. State Coll., 1927-28; instr. econs. Duke, 1928-30, 32-34; rsch. and teaching asst. Northwestern U., 1930-32; asst. prof. U. Ariz., 1934-39, assoc. prof., 1939-42, prof. econs., dean Grad. Coll., 1946-47, dean Coll. Liberal Arts, 1947-51, pres. univ., 1951-71, ret.; vis. asst. prof. econs. U. Buffalo, 1937-38; asst. dist. price exec. OPA, Phoenix, 1942-43, dist. proce exec., 1943-46; mem. Ariz. Bd. Edn., 1951-64, 70-71; vice chmn. Western Interstate Commn. on Higher Edn., 1958-59, chmn., 1959-60, sec. Ariz. commn., from 1956; council of pres.s Nat. Assn. State Univs. and Land-Grant Colls., 1951-71, exec. com., 1962-65, 69-71, pres., 1970. Contbr. to econ. and ednl. jours. Mem. adv. bd. Ariz.-Sonora Desert Mus., 1954-65, Tucson chpt. ARC, 1951-56; mem. Catalina coun. Boy Scouts Am., 1953-67; adv. bd. Inst. World Affairs, 1951-68; chmn. Ariz. com. Selection for Rhodes Scholarships, 1951-61, 65-66; hon. mem. Tucson Fine Arts Assn., 1960-69; bd. dirs. Devel. Authority for Tucson's Expansion, 1967-71; mem. Nat. Commn. Accrediting, 1956-61; cons. adv. com. econ. and manpower studies NSF, 1964-68; civilian liason group of comdg. gen. U.S. Army Electronic Proving Ground, Ft. Huachuca, from 1961; mem. Ariz. adv. bd. U.S. Bur. Land Mgmt., 1962-66; hon. bd. Phoenix Fine Arts Assn., from 1958; mem. acad. adv. com. Prescott Coll., 1962-65; lay adv. bd. St. Mary's Hosp., Tucson, 1959-67; nat. adv. coun. health rsch. facilities USPHS, 1963-66; bd. dirs. Def. Orientation Conf. Assn., 1960-62, 66-67; mem. higher edn. adv. com. Edn. Commn. States, 1966-67; bd. dirs. Hosp. Planning Coun. Greater Tucson Inc., 1964-67; mem. coun. presidents Western Athletic Conf., 1962-71; U.S. Army adv. panel ROTC affairs, 1964-67; nat. adv. gen. med. sci. council NIH, 1968-72; v.p. Baird Found., 1967-70, pres. from 1970; bd. visitors Air U., 1969-72. Fellow Royal Econ. Soc.; mem. Assn. Am. Colls. (commn. coll. adminstrn. 1966-69), U.S. (sect. Mexico-U.S. com. from 1961, mem. internat affairs com. from 1969), Tucson (dir. from 1951) chambers of commerce, Am., Western econ. assns., Western Coll. Assn., Can. Polit. Sci. Assn., Nat. Assn. State Univs. (exec. com. 1958-61, del. to Am. Council on Edn. 1958-60), Newcomen Soc., Ariz. Acad. Pub. Affairs (dir.), Kiwanis Club, Old Pueblo Club, Skyline Country Club, Blue Key, Phi Kappa Phi, Phi Eta Sigma, Alpha Kappa Psi, Beta Gamma Sigma, Kappa Kappa Psi, Pi Gamma Mu. Home: Tucson Ariz. Died Nov. 15, 1988.

HARVIN, LUCIUS HERMAN, JR., retail executive; b. Manning, S.C., July 27, 1914; s. Lucius Harman and Katharine (Susong) H.; m. Jessie Myrick Rose, Mar. 8, 1938; children: Lucius Herman III, Paul Rose (dec.), George Myrick, Jessie Rose, Emma Katharine. BS in Elec. Engring., Clemson (S.C.) U., 1934; MBA, Harvard U., 1939. Dist. mgr. Carolina Power & Light Co., 1934-37; exec. v.p., gen. mgr. Paul H. Rose Corp., 1949-53; exec. v.p., treas. Rose's Stores, Inc., Henderson, N.C., 1953-63, pres., chief exec. officer, 1963-79, chmn. exec. com., from 1979, also bd. dirs.; bd. dirs. Carolina Power & Light Co., Vachovia Bank, Durham Corp., Carlyle & Co. Stores. Chmn. Orange presbytery council First Presbyn. Ch., Henderson. 2d lt. AUS, 1941-43. Mem. Clemson U. Alumni Assn. (Disting. Service award 1972), Rotary, Shriners. Home: Henderson N.C. Deceased.

HASELHORST, DONALD DUANE, manufacturing company executive; b. Northville, S.D., May 21, 1930; m. Nancy G. Wilz, Aug. 29, 1953; children: Stephen, Linda, Lynn. BS in Elec. Engring., S.D. State U., Brookings, 1956. Engr. Univac div. Sperry Rand Corp., St. Paul, 1956-59; v.p. Fabri-Tek Inc., Amery, Wis., 1959-67; chmn., chief exec. officer Nicolet Instrument Corp., Madison, Wis., from 1967; dir. M & I Bank of Madison, Demco Inc., Viking Ins. Co., Realist Inc., Sigma-Aldrich Chem. Co., Union State Bank, Cen. Life Assurance Co. Pres. Madison Service Clubs Council, 1976-77; bd. dirs. Oakwood Luth. Homes, Madison, from 1976, Madison Gen. Hosp. With USAF, 1948-52. Recipient Disting. Engr. award S.D. State U., 1981, Disting. Alumni award S.D. State U., 1982. Mem. IEEE, Am. Mgmt. Assn. (president's council), Sales and Mktg. Assn. (Exec. of Yr. award 1981), West Kiwanis (pres.), Nakoma Golf Club, Madison Club. Lutheran. Home: Madison Wis. Died Nov. 22, 1984; buried Sunset Meml. Cemetery, Madison, Wis.

HASKELL, JOHN HENRY FARRELL, financial executive, army officer; b. Ft. Leavenworth, Kans., Dec. 5, 1903; s. Gen. William Nafew and Winifred (Farrell) H.; m. Paulette Heger, May 8, 1931; children: John H.F., Paul Heger. Student, Poly. Prep. Sch., Bklyn., 1917-19, Sainte-Croix, Paris, 1919-20; BS, U.S. Mil. Acad., 1925; grad., Army Command and Gen. Staff Sch., 1941. With Nat. City Co., N.Y.C., 1925-31; v.p. N.Y. Stock Exchange, 1939-55, ret.; def. adviser to NATO, U.S. rep. N. Atlantic and Mediterranean areas, 1955-60; rep. Bankers Trust Co., Paris, 1960-68, ret.; chief ECA mission to Sweden, 1948-49. Trustee Hoover Found., Brussels, 1971-75; bd. dirs. N.Y. chpt. ARC, 1949-55. 2d lt. C.E., U.S. Army, 1925; officer N.Y. N.G., 1925-40; chief of staff 27th div. in Pacific, 1942; acting fir. civil affairs div., gen. staff War Dept., 1942-43; with OSS in Middle East, Russia, Italy, France, 1943-44; comdg. officer T force, 12th army group, 1944-45; wounded in action Germany, 1945, ret. from army, 1946. Decorated Legion of Merit, Bronze Star, Purple Heart; chevalier Legion of Honor, Croix de Guerre (France); Czechoslovakian 1939 War Cross; Order Brit. Empire. Mem. clubs: American (Paris), Chevy-Chase, Army-Navy. Roman Catholic. Home: Grasse France. Died Nov. 10, 1987; interred West Point Acad.

HASS, HENRY BOHN, chemist, educator; b. Huntington, Ohio, Jan. 25, 1902; s. Rev. Frederick William and Alma Marie (Bohn) H.; m. Georgia Mae Herancourt, Sept. 20, 1921; children: Robert Henry, Charlotte Frances, Thomas William, Richard Frederick. Student, Heidelberg Coll., Tiffin, Ohio, 1917-18; BA, Ohio Wesleyan U., 1921, DSc, 1942; MA, Ohio State U., 1923, PhD, 1925; LLD, U. Chattanooga, 1945; DSc, L.I. U., 1965. Asst. in chemistry Ohio Wesleyan U., 1920-21, Ohio State U., 1921-25; rsch. dir. Balt. Gas Engring. Corp., 1925-28; asst. prof. chemistry Purdue U., 1928-33, assoc. prof., 1933-35, prof., 1935-49, rsch. dir., 1936, head dept., 1937, chem. cons., 1935-49; rsch. mgr. Gen. Aniline and Film Corp., 1949-52; pres. Sugar Rsch. Fund., 1952-61; dir. chem. rsch. M.W. Kellogg Co., from 1961; official investigator Nat. Def. Rsch. Com., 1940-42, Manhattan Project, 1942-46. Contbr. Ind. Engring Chemistry, Jour. Am. Chem. Soc., Chem. Edn., Ency. Brit., Ency. Chem. Industry. Patentee on chem. products and processes. Lt. comdr. USNR, 1937-41. Recipient Modern Pioneer award Nat. Assn. Mfrs., 1940, Perkins medal Soc. Chem. Industries, 1968; fellow Internat. Congress Anesthetists. Fellow Royal Soc. Arts; mem. Am. Inst. Chemists (pres. 1957-58, gold medal 1969), Société de Chemie Industrielle (pres. Am. br., hon.), Assn. Rsch. Dirs., Am. Chem. Soc. (councillor-at-large 1940-46), Chemists Club, Alpha Sigma Phi, Phi Beta Kappa, Phi Lambda Upsilon, Sigma Xi, Alpha Chi Sigma, Alpha Kappa Lambda. Home: Queens N.Y. Died Feb. 13, 1987; buried West Lafayette, Ind.

HASTIE, REID WILLIAM, art educator; b. Donora, Pa., Feb. 14, 1916; s. William and Ellen (Reid) H.; m. Olivia Kendrick, Aug. 8, 1941; children: Reid K., Bruce C. BS, State Tchrs. Coll., Edinboro, Pa., 1936; MA, U. W.Va., 1940; PhD, U. Pitts., 1953; student, Carnegie Inst. Tech., Harvard U., U. Minn. Art supr. Monongalie County Schs., W.Va., 1936-38; art tchr. Pitts. pub. schs., 1938-40; instr. dept. fine arts U. Pitts., 1940-41, 46-49; asst. prof., asso. prof., then prof. dept. art edn. U. Minn., 1949-87; mem. fine arts staff Carnegie Inst., Pitts., 1939-40, 46-49; prof. Tex. Tech U., Lubbock, 1969-87; Cons. Central Midwestern Regional Ednl. Lab., Inc. Exhibited paintings, Carnegie Inst., St. Paul Gallery, Mpls., Inst. Arts, Walker Art Center, U. Minn., water color exhibit, Minn. State Fair.; Author: (with Christian Schmidt) Encounter with Art, 1969; Editor: Art Education, 1965. Served to lt. USNR, 1941-46. Mem. Nat. Art Edn. Assn. (pres.), Western Arts Assn., Asso. Artists, St. Paul Painters and Sculpture Assn., NEA, Nat. Soc. Study Edn., Phi Delta Kappa, Delta Phi Delta, Omicron Delta Kappa. Home: Lubbock Tex. Died Aug. 31, 1987, buried Resthaven Meml. Park, Lubbock.

HASTINGS, ALBERT BAIRD, researcher; b. Dayton, Ky., Nov. 20, 1895; s. Otis Luther and Elizabeth (Henry) H.; m. Margaret Anne Johnson, 1918 (dec. 1979); 1 son, Alan Baird. B.S., U. Mich., 1917; Ph.D., Columbia U., 1921; Sc.D., U. Mich., 1941, Oxford, 1952, Boston U., 1956; M.A., Harvard, 1942, Sc.D., 1945; Sc.D., St. Louis U., 1965, Columbia, 1967, Ind. U., 1972. Chemist USPHS, 1917-21, Rockefeller Inst., 1921-26; prof. physiol. chemistry U. Chgo., 1926-28; prof. biochemistry Lasker Found. for Med. Research, 1928-35; Hamilton Kuhn prof. biol. chem. Harvard Med. Sch., 1935-59, emeritus, 1959-87; head lab. metabolic research Scripps Clinic and Research Found., La Jolla, Calif., 1959-66; mem. emeritus Scripps Clinic and Research Found., 1966-87; hon. prof. U. San Marcos, 1957; research assoc. U. Calif. at San Diego, 1960-87; Vis. prof. Pahlavi Univ., Shiraz, Iran, 1967; syndic Harvard Univ. Press; Fulbright lectr. Oxford U., 1952; mem. sr. common room Trinity Coll., 1953-87. Writer various articles; editor: Jour. Biol. Chemistry, 1941-54, 55-59, Am. Jour. Physiology, 1956-63, Endocrinology, 1963-67. Trustee Brookhaven Nat. Lab., Asso. Univs., 1948-51; cons. Com. on Biology and Medicine, U.S. AEC, 1947-63; mem. Nat. Adv. Health Council, 1947-48, USPHS Nat. Adv. Arthritis and Metabolic Diseases Council, 1956-60, Heart Council, 1960-64; cons. sci. adv. bd. Walter Reed Army Inst. Research, 1956-62; mem. vis. com. Brookhaven Nat. Lab., 1956-87 , chmn., 1962-63; nat. sci. adv. com. Okla. Med. Research Found. and Inst.; Mem. Com. on Med. Research, OSRD, 1941-46, Nat. Adv. Cancer Council, 1943-46; Research Bd. for Nat. Security, 1945; Mem. Sci. Adv. Com. The Nutrition Found., 1947-61; adv. bd. Biochem. Preparations, 1945-68; adv. council Life In Med. Research Fund, 1946-50; nat. adv. com. to Whi House Conf. on Aging, 1970-72. Recipient Presiden medal for Merit, 1948, Distinguished Service awa Med. Alumni Assn. U. Chgo., 1961; Banting medal Ar Diabetes Assn., 1962; A.C.P. award, 1964; USPH citation, 1964; Modern Medicine Distinguish Achievement award, 1965. Mem. Assn. Am. Physiciar Nat. Acad. Scis., AAAS, Royal Danish Acad. Sci. ar Letters, Am. Acad. Arts and Scis., Am. Chem. So Am. Soc. Biol. Chemists (pres. 1945-46), Am. Philc Soc., Am. Physiol. Soc., Soc. Exptl. Biol. Medici (pres. 1945-46), Assn. Clin. Chemists (hon.), Harv Soc., Sinfonia (Phi Mu Alpha), Alpha Chi Sigma, Sign Xi, Alpha Omega Alpha. Clubs: Century Ass (N.Y.C.), Harvard (N.Y.C.); Cosmos (Washingtor Chicago Literary. Home: La Jolla Calif. Died Sept. 2 1987.

HASTINGS, ELIZABETH THOMSON, academ administrator; b. Providence, Sept. 27, 1913; d. Willia Thomson and Hester Jane (Mercer) H. AB, Brown U 1934, AM, 1935; PhD, Yale U., 1939. Instr. Ill. Col 1939-42, asst. prof., 1942-44, prof. English, co-cha dept., 1994-51; prof. English, dean Flora Stone Math Coll., Case-Western Res. U. 1951-72. Mem. MLA, Ar Studies Assn., AAUP, AAUW, League Women Voter ACLU, Common Cause Sierra Club, Wilderness Soc Soc. Hist. Preservation, Phi Beta Kappa. Home: Clev land Ohio. Died Aug. 21, 1986; buried Swan Poir Providence.

HASWELL, ERNEST BRUCE, sculptor; b. Breck enridge County, Ky., July 25, 1889; s. Coleman E kridge and Emma (Board) H.; m. Leona Haldema May 31, 1917; 1 child, Evelyn Bruce. Ed., Art Acad Cin., 1906-16, Acadamie Royale des Beaux Arts, Bru sels, 1910-12. Assoc. prof. Coll. Applied Arts, Cin Prin. works include Northcott Meml., Springfield, Ill Moorman Meml., Louisville, Nippert Meml., Jacc Burnet meml., Holmes Meml., Mullen Meml. portrai bas refliefs on Times Star Bldg., Cin., Ohio State Bldg Columbus, MacDowell medal, Fine Arts Inst. meda Miami U. medal, Alms Portraits, Cin. Art Mus Proctor meml., Cin., McGuffey Meml., Miami U Verity Meml., Middletown, Ohio, shrine St. Xavier U medal and seal Village of Indian Hill, Dorl Meml. po trait, archtl. sculpture for chs., Dallas, LaCrosse, Wis Chgo., Yankton, S.D., Salina Cathedral, Kans., St. Pet Cathedral, Cin. Home: Cincinnati Ohio. †

HATCH, THEODORE FREDERICK, industri hygiene engineer, educator; b. Islesboro, Maine, Ma 23, 1901; s. William E. and Lena (Farnsworth) H.; m Jane D. Grimes, Sept. 16, 1933; children: Theodor Frederick, Ann Elizabeth. BS, U. Maine, 1924, Sc (hon.), 1966; SM, Harvard U., 1925. Instr. inds hygiene Harvard U., 1926-36; assoc. engr. div. inds hygiene N.Y. Labor Dept., N.Y.C., 1936-40; assoc. pro indsl. hygiene U. Pa., 1940-42; rsch. dir. Indsl. Hygien Found. Mellon Inst., Pitts., from 1945; prof. inds health engring. U. Pitts., 1949-66; U.S. del. Interna Conf. Pneumoconiosis, Sydney, Australia, 1950; men conf., Johannesburg, South Africa, 1959; men Permanent Internat. Commn. Indsl. Medicine; rsch exec. Armored Med. Rsch. Lab, Ft. Knox, Ky. Autho (with Philip Drinker) Industrial Dust, (with Paul Gross Pulmonary Deposition and Retention of Inhaled Ae osols. Decorated Legion of Merit; Fulbright sr. schola U. London Sch. Hygiene and Tropical Medicine, 1957 Mem. Am. Pub. Health Assn. (Bronfman prize 1962 Am. Indsl. Hygiene Assn. (pres. 1947, Cummings awar 1951), Am. Acad. Occupational Medicine (hon.), Sigm Xi, Phi Kappa Phi. Republican. Home: Concord N.H Died July 5, 1986; buried Fitzwilliam, N.H.

HATFIELD, WILLIAM DURELL, sanitary chemica engineer; b. Jacksonville, Ill., July 7, 1892; s. Elmer E and Jennie (Moffett) H.; m. Clarinda Wyne, Feb. 1 1919; children: Eleanor W. (Mrs. M. Homer Beatty Richard D., Walter L. BS, Ill. Coll., 1914; MS, U. Ill 1916, PhD, 1918. Registered profl. engr., Ill. Ass chemist and bacteriologist Ill. Water Survey, 1915-18 asst. prof. organic and phys. chemistry Mont. Stat Coll., 1919-20; supt. water filtration, Highland Park Mich., 1921-23; supt. san. dist. Decatur, Ill., 1924-58 cons. san. chem. engring. specializing in control, opera tion plants for treatment and purification sewage an indsl. wastes. from 1958. Contbr. articles to prof jours.; mem. editorial bd. Standard Methods of Wate Analysis, 8th, 9th, 10th edits. Chmn. Decatur City Pla Commn., 1947; pres. Decatur coun. Boy Scouts Am 1936. 2d lt., San. Corps, U.S. Army, 1918-19. Recipient Good Govt. award Decatur Jr. C. of C., 1958 Mem. ASCE (Rudolf Hering award 1931, Thoma Fitch Roland prize 1931), Water Pollution Contro Fedn. (Charles Alvin Emerson award 1953, pres. 1959) Am. Chem. Soc. (Disting. Service award water an sewage sect. 1957), Cen. State Sewage and Indsl. Waste Assn. (pres. 1945), Ill. Soc. Profl. Engrs. (pres. Cen. Ill 1946), Am. Water Works Assn., Rotary (pres. Decatu 1935). Home: Decatur Ill. †

HAUGE, GABRIEL, trust company executive; b Hawley, Minn., Mar. 7, 1914; s. Soren Gabrielson an Anna B. (Thompson) H.; m. Helen Lansdowne Resor Nov. 6, 1948; children: Ann Bayliss, Stephen Burnet an John Resor (twins), Barbara Thompson, Susan Lan sdowne, Elizabeth Larsen, Caroline Clark. AB, Concordia Coll., Moorhead, Minn., 1935, LLD, 1957; George Christian fellow, Harvard U., 1936-38, MA, 1938, Social Sci. Rsch. Coun. fellow, 1946, PhD, 1947; LLD, Bryant Coll., 1958, Muhlenberg Coll., 1959, Gettysburg Coll., 1960; LHD, Pace Coll., 1969; hon. degree, Hampden-Sydney Coll., Va., Yale U., 1978. Asst. dean men, coach forensics Concordia Coll., 1935-36; budget examiner Office Commr. Budget, State of Minn., 1938; instr. econs. Harvard U., 1938-40; sr. statistician Fed. Res. Bank N.Y., summer 1939; instr. econs. Princeton U., 1940-42; chief div. rsch. and statistics N.Y. State Banking Dept., 1947-50; editor Trend editorial Bus. Week Mag., asst. chmn. exec. com. McGraw-Hill Pub. Co., Inc., 1950-52; rsch. dir. Citizens for Eisenhower, 1951-52; rsch. dir. personal campaign staff Dwight D. Eisenhower, 1952; adminstrv. asst. for econ. affairs to Pres. of U.S., 1953-56, spl. asst., 1956-58; chmn. fin. com. Mfrs. Trust Co. (merged with Hanover Bank 1961), N.Y.C., 1958-61, also dir.; vice chmn. Mfrs. Hanover Trust Co., 1961-63, pres., 1963-71, chmn. bd., 1971-79, also dir.; bd. dirs. N.Y. Life Ins. Co., Amax Inc., N.Y. Telephone Co., Discount Corp. N.Y., Bklyn. Union Gas Co., Chrysler Corp., Royal Dutch Petroleum, SAS, Inc., Am. Home Products Corp. Mem. coun. Harvard Found. Advanced Study and Rsch., 1959-64; vis. com. Harvard Ctr. for Internat. Affairs, 1964-70; bd. dirs. Com. Econ. Devel.; trustee Juilliard Mus. Found., 1963-79; mem. pub. policy com. Advt. Coun., 1964-73. Served from ensign to lt. comdr. USNR, 1942-46; lt. comdr. Res. Recipient C. Walter Nichols award NYU, 1975. Mem. Coun. Fgn. Relations N.Y.C., Assn. Res. City Bankers, Pilgrims U.S., Am. Econs. Assn., Am. Bankers Assn. (econ. policy com.), U.S. Naval Inst., N.Y. Young Rep. Club, Econ. Club, Univ. Club, Links Club, Century Assn., N.Y. Athletic, Metropolitan Club. Lutheran. Home: New York N.Y. Died July 24, 1981; buried Woodlawn Cemetery, N.Y.

HAUGHTON, DANIEL JEREMIAH, aerospace manufacturing executive; b. nr. Dora, Ala., Sept. 7, 1911; s. Gayle Sr. and Mattie (Davis) H.; m. Martha Jean Oliver, Sept. 28, 1935. BS, U. Ala., 1933, also LLD; LLD (hon.), George Washington U., Pepperdine U., 1975; ScD (hon.), Clarkson Coll. Tech. Cost acct. Consol. Aircraft Corp., San Diego, 1936-39; with Lockheed Aircraft Corp., or its subsidiaries, from 1939, successively systems analyst, coordinator, asst. to v.p. Vega Airplane Co., asst. gen. works mgr. and asst. to v.p. Lockheed Aircraft Corp., pres. Airquipment Co. and Aerol Co., Inc., asst. gen. mgr. Ga. div. Lockheed Aircart Corp.; gen. mgr., v.p., Lockheed Ga. Co., 1952-56; exec. v.p. Lockheed Aircraft Corp., 1956-61, pres., 1961-67, chmn., 1967-76, dir. co. and subsidiaries; dir. United Calif. Bank, So. Calif. Edison Co. Chmn. Nat. Multiple Sclerosis Soc.; nat. chmn. Indsl. Payroll Savs. Campaign, Dept. Treasury, 1972; bd. govs. Am. Nat. Red Cross; trustee Nat. Space Club Found. Named Mgmt. Man of Yr. Nat. Mgmt. Assn., 1966, Salesman of Yr. Sales and Mktg. Assn., L.A., 1970, Employer of Yr. Nat. Indsl. Recreation Assn.; recipient Award of Achievement Nat. Aviation Club, 1969, Tony Jannus award Nat. Def Transp. Assn, 1970. Mem. AIAA, Nat. Aeros. Assn., Soc. Automotive Engrs., Armed Forces Mgmt. Assn., Assn. U.S. Army, Navy League U.S., Air Force Assn., Aviation Hall of Fame, Calif. Inst. Tech. Assocs., Nat. Def. Transp. Assn., Nat. Security Indsl. Assn. (trustee), Aerospace Industries Assn. (gov.), L.A. World Affairs Coun. (dir.), Harvard Advanced Mgmt. Assn. So. Calif., Calif. Club, Capital City Club. Home: Studio City Calif. Died July 5, 1987.

HAUROWITZ, FELIX, biochemist, educator; b. Prague, Czechoslovakia, Mar. 1, 1896; came to U.S., 1948, naturalized, 1952; s. Rudolf and Emilie (Russ) H.; m. Gina Perutz, June 23, 1925 (dec. June 1983). M.D., German U., Prague, 1922, Sc.D., 1923; M.D. (hon.), U. Istanbul, Turkey, 1973; Ph.D. (hon.), Ind. U., 1974. Asst. prof. physiol. chemistry Med. Sch. German U., Prague, 1922-30; assoc. prof. Med. Sch. German U., 1930-39; head dept. biol. chemistry, also prof. Med. Sch. U. Istanbul, Turkey, 1939-48; prof. chemistry Ind. U., 1948-87, Distinguished prof., 1958-87. Author: Biochemistry, 1953, Progress in Biochemistry, since 1949, 1959, Chemistry and Function of Proteins, 1963; Immunochemistry and the Biosynthesis of Antibodies, 1968. Recipient Paul Ehrlich prize and gold plaquette Paul Ehrlich Fund, Frankfurt, Germany, 1960. Fellow Am. Acad. Arts and Sci.; mem. Am. Chem. Soc. (chmn. div. biol. chemistry 1962-63), Leopoldina Acad. Scis., Am. Soc. Biol. Chemists, Am. Assn. Immunologists, Am. Soc. Microbiology (hon.), Societe de Chimie Biologique (hon.), Societe Immunologique (hon.). Home: Bloomington Ind. Died Dec. 2, 1987.

HAUSER, GAYELORD (HELMUT EUGENE BENJAMIN GELLERT HAUSER), author, nutritionist; b. Tubingen, Germany, May 17, 1895; came to U.S., 1912; naturalized, 1938; s. Christian and Agate (Rothe) H. D Naturopathy, Am. Sch. Naturopathy, N.Y.C., 1922; D Chiropractic, Am. Sch. Chiropractic; D Immutable Naturopathy, Naturopathic Health Sch., Chgo., 1923; hon. dr., U. Philotechnique, Brussels, 1932; BS, Am. U., L.A., 1942; hon. dr., Argentina Sch. Nutrition, Buenos Aires, 1954. Advisor on nutrition Republic of Argentina, 1954. Author books on nutrition: Eat and Grow Beautiful, 1936, Diet Does It, 1944, Look Younger, Live Longer, 1950, Gayelord Hauser's Treasury of Secrets, 1951, Be Happier, Be Mirror on the Wall, 1961; founder and editor Diet Digest, 1950. Books translated into 27 languages. Named one of makers of Twentieth Century, London (Eng.) Sunday Times, 1972; honored by statue, Kyoto, Japan, 1977. Home: Beverly Hills Calif. Died Dec. 26, 1984.

HAUSMANN, EMIL JOHN, securities broker; b. Bklyn., May 27, 1902; s. Henry and Sophia (Selig) H.; m. Edna Anna Maier, June 28, 1924; 1 son, Donald George. BS in Acctg., St. John's U., 1947, LLB, 1949. Bar: N.Y. 1955. Acct. Mfrs. Trust Co., N.Y.C., 1916-18, First Nat. City Bank N.Y., 1918-23; self employed Jamaica, N.Y., 1923-38; acct., controller Baker, Weeks & Co., N.Y.C., from 1929, gen. ptnr., 1957-69; mem. N.Y. Securities Panel arbitration com. N.Y. Stock Exchange; small claims ct. arbitrator Civil Ct. City N.Y.; bd. govs. acctg. sect. Assn. Stock Exchange Firms; gov. Am. Stock Exchange; mem. exec. com., chmn. Brokers and Dealers Taxation, N.Y.C. Adv. coun. St. John's U.; trustee Borough Queens, N.Y.C. Library System, 1946-52. Mem. ABA, Phi Delta Phi, Zeta Sigma Pi, Beta Gamma Sigma. Home: Merrick N.Y. Deceased.

HAVILAND, VIRGINIA, librarian, author; b. Rochester, N.Y., May 21, 1911; d. William J. and Bertha M. (Esten) Haviland. BA, Cornell U., 1933. With Boston Pub. Library, 1934-63, reader's adviser for children, 1952-63; dir. Children's Lit. Ctr., Library of Congress, from 1963; lectr. library services to children Simmons Coll. Sch. Library Service, 1957-63; profl. reviewer children's books, assoc. editor Horn Book Mag., from 1952; lectr. children's lit. Trinity Coll., from 1969; chmn. Newbery-Caldecott Award Com., 1953-54; judge N.Y. Herald Tribune Spring Book Festival awards, 1955, 57, Spring Book Festival, Book World, 1968, Nat. Book awards for children's books, 1969; mem. jury Hans Christian Andersen internat. children's book award, 1959-68, pres., 1971-74. Author: The Travelogue Storybook of the Nineteenth Century, 1950, William Penn, Founder and Friend, 1952, Favorite Fairy Tales Told in England, 1959, Favorite Fairy Tales Told in Germany, 1959, Favorite Fairy Tales Told in France, 1959, Favorite Fairy Tales Told in Russia, 1961, Favorite Fairy Tales Told in Norway, 1961, Favorite Fairy Tales Told in Ireland, 1961, Favorite Fairy Tales Told in Scotland, 1963, Favorite Fairy Tales told in Spain, 1963, Favorite Fairy Tales Told in Italy, 1965, Favorite Fairy Tales Told in Czechoslovakia, 1966, Favorite Fairy Tales Told in Sweden, 1966, Favorite Fairy Tales Told in Japan, 1967, Favorite Fairy Tales Told in Greece, 1969, Favorite Fairy Tales Told in Denmark, 1971, A Fairy Tale Treasury, 1972, Favorite Fairy Tales Told in India, 1973; compiler: 100 Best Books for Children, 1956; editor: Children's Literature: A Guide to Reference Sources, 1966, 1st Supplement, 1972, 2d supplement, 1977, Books in Search of Children, 1969, (with William J. Smith) Children and Poetry, 1969, The Wide World of Children's Books, 1972, Children's Books of International Interest, 1972, Children and Literature: Views and Reviews, 1973, (with Margaret N. Coughlan) Yankee Doodle's Literary Sampler of Prose, Poetry and Pictures, 1974, Legends of North America, 1979, The Openhearted Audience, 1980. Recipient Regina medal, 1976, Grolier award, 1976. Mem. Children's Library Assn. (chmn. 1954-55), Nat. Soc. Women Geographers, PEN, Authors Guild, Pi Lambda Theta. Home: Washington D.C. Died Jan. 6, 1988.

HAWKES, LESTER LITCHFIELD, editor, educator; b. Brimfield, Ill., Dec. 18, 1905; s. Arthur John and Mae (Litchfield) H.; m. Lydia Alvina Stindt, Feb. 24, 1932; children: Dennis L., Judith Hawkes Pagel and Jeanne Hawkes Hoffmann (twins). Student, Monmouth Coll., 1927, Carnegie Inst. Tech., summer 1934; BS, Stout State U., 1943; PhM, U. Wis., 1945. Co-editor Sheldon (Ill.) Jour., 1923-27; editor The Stoutonia, 1929-30; mgr. Campus Pub. Co., Madison, Wis., 1944-48; instr. U. Wis., Madison, 1944-48; prof. U. Wis., 1959-73, emeritus, from 1973, asst. dir. Journalism, 1967-73, exec. sec. student publs., 1952-73; tchr. Madison Adult Edn. Sch., 1930-44. Author: (with Carl Zielke) Your Front Page, 1949, Survey of Wisconsin House Publications, 1951, Seventeen Year Study of the Community Press of Wisconsin, 1972. Mem. Assn. for Edn. Journalism, Wis. Press Assn. (Disting. Service award 1962). Home: Madison Wis. Died June 24, 1988.

HAWKES, THOMAS FREDERICK, bank holding company executive; b. London, Jan. 8, 1903; s. William Thomas and Emily Janet (Norman) H.; m. Virginia Taylor Romney, June 5, 1929; children—Barbara, Julie, Robert. With First Security Corp., Salt Lake City, from 1923; v.p., treas. First Security Corp. Mem. Fin. Execs. Inst. Republican. Clubs: Alta, Hidden Valley Country. Died Apr. 27, 1988; buried Salt Lake City Cemetery.

HAWKINS, DAVID ROBERT, lawyer; b. Kansas City, Mo., Mar. 27, 1892; s. Robert Lewis and Clara (Miller) H.; m. Mary Margaret Landon, June 8, 1929; children: Anne Landon (Mrs. Joseph Gatti Jr.), John Landon, Elizabeth Mary. LittB, Princeton, 1914, AM, 1915; LLB, Harvard, 1921. Bar: N.Y. 1923. Practice N.Y.C., from 1923; ptnr. Sullican & Cromwell, 1927-64, of counsel, from 1964. Mem. mission to Poland, Am. Relief Asminstrn., 1919. Maj. inf. U.S. Army, 1918-19, A.E.F. Mem. ABA, N.Y. State Bar Assn., N.Y. County Bar Assn., Assn. Bar City N.Y., N.Y. Law Inst., Down Town Assn., University Club, New Canaan Country Club. Home: New Canaan Conn. †

HAWKINS, JOHN HAROLD, judge; b. nr. Cumming, Ga., May 22, 1892; s. Perry C. and Della (Bramblett) H.; m. Irene Northcutt, Apr. 22, 1914; children: Jane Northcutt (Mrs. C. W. Ramsey Jr.), Elizabeth Ann (Mrs. D. A. Dosser). Ed. pub. schs., Marietta Ga.; student, Dixie Bus. Coll., Atlanta. Ofcl. ct. reporter Blue Ridge Cir., 1915-17, judge, 1931-48; sec. Ga. Ct. Appeals, 1917-20; mem. Morris, Hawkins & Wallace, Marietta, 1920-31; assoc. justice Supreme Ct. Ga., from 1948. Pres. Marietta Bd. Edn., 1933-47. Mem. ABA, Ga. Bar Assn., Blue Ridge Cir. Bar Assn. Democrat. Baptist. Home: Marietta Ga. †

HAWKINS, ORWILL VAN WICKLE, lawyer; b. Freneau, N.J., Jan. 14, 1891; s. James Magee and Marion Eliza (Pullen) H.; m. Marian Katrina Harman, Sept. 17, 1917; children: Harman, Glenn Alan. PhB, Bucknell U., 1913, DCL (hon.), 1959; LLB, N.Y. Law Sch., 1917. Bar: N.Y. 1918. Formerly mem. Duer, Strong & Whitehead. Trustee Bucknell U. Mem. ABA, N.Y. County Lawyers Assn., Broad St. Club, University Club, Sigma Chi (v.p. Found.). Republican. Baptist. Home: Huntington N.Y. †

HAWKINS, ROBERT DAWSON, engineering educator; b. Lexington, Ky., Apr. 11, 1892; s. Edmund Decator and Willie Crutcher (Burton) H.; m. Martha Weakley, June 23, 1915; children: Willie Burton (Mrs. David M. Peetus), Martha (Mrs. W. H. Rush), Dorothy Dawson (Mrs. W. S. Coblin). BME, U. Ky., 1915, ME, 1921; ME, U. Pa., 1938; MS, U. Mich., 1939. Chief insp. Remington Arms Co., 1915-16; instr. mech. engring. U. Pa., 1916-18; mem. faculty U. Ky., from 1918, prof. engring., from 1924, head dept. gen. engring. Former chmn. city-county planning and zoning commn., Lexington, Fayette County, Ky., mem. bd. 1928-59. Mem. ASME, Am. Soc. Engring. Edn., Ky. Soc. Profl. Engrs., AAUP, Masons, K.T., Delta Tau Delta, Iota Alpha, Pi Tau Sigma, Tau Beta Pi. Home: Lexington Ky. †

HAWKINSON, JAMES R., marketing educator; b. Parkers Prairie, Minn., Feb. 10, 1895; s. John and Judith (Nelson) H. AB, Carleton Coll., 1917; MBA, Northwestern U., 1929. Sales supr. Wis. div. Proctor & Gamble Distbg. Co., 1919-24; instr. U. N.D., 1924-26; instr. Sch. Commerce Northwestern U., 1926-29, asst. dean, assoc. prof., acting dean, 1930-39, chmn. dept., 1947-50, prof. marketing emeritus, from 1963; vis. prof. U. Ariz., 1964, Syracuse U., 1965-66; taught Stanford U. Grad. Sch. Bus. summers 1949, 50, and exec. devel. program, 1952; exec. program U. Mich., summers 1954, 56; lectr. Cornell U., summer 1954; taught Inst. Grad. Study Bus. Adminstrn., Turin, Italy, 1955-56; exec. devel. program Stanford U., summer 1957, U. Tex., 1957, 58, 59, 60, 62, U. Colo., 1959; sales and mktg. cons., lectr. With U.S. Civil Service Commn. as sr. negotiations and review officer, later dir. Fed. Work Improvement Program, 1942-44; chief commerce sect., Shrivenham-Am. U., Eng., 1945; civilian adv., lecture bur., U.S. Army, Frankfort, Germany, 1946; mktg. cons. European Productivity Agy., Paris, 1956; cons. mgmt. devel. ENI, Milan, Italy, 1960-61. Mem. Am. Mgmt. Assn. (planning coun., mktg. div. 1948-58), Am. Econ. Assn., Am. Mktg. Assn., Am. Assn. Univ. Profs., Nat. Sales Execs. Assn. (chmn. commn. relations with univs. and colls.), University Club, Beta Gamma Sigma, Delta Sigma Pi, Sigma Chi. Home: Evanston Ill. Died Apr. 29, 1986.

HAWLEY, EDMUND SUMMERS, lawyer, investment executive; b. Bridgeport, Conn., Nov. 25, 1891; s. Charles Wilson and Katherine (Beardsley) H.; m. Dagmar Perkins, Sept. 12, 1922 (dec.); m. Marguerite Kalt Treadway, June 23, 1947; 1 child, Edmund Blair. Grad., Hotchkiss Sch., 1909; AB, Yale U., 1913; JD, Harvard U., 1916; postgrad., U. Sorbonne, Paris, 1919. Bar: Conn. 1916, N.Y. 1920. Assoc. Kirlin, Woolsey & Hickox, N.Y.C., 1916-17; atty. GM, N.Y.C., 1919-20, AT&T, N.Y.C., 1920-56; v.p. Inst. World Affairs, 1954-69, chmn. exec. com., 1962-67; mem. adv. com. Internat. Missionary Coun., 1952-55; mem.-at-large Protestant Coun., 1953-59; chmn. Labor Temple, 1956-57; bd. mgrs. Am. Bible Soc., 1946-66; adviser Inter-Am. Radio Conf., Mexico City, 1924, Internat. Radio Conf., Washington, 1941; industry rep. Internat. Telecommunicaitons Conf., Atlantic City, 1947. Bd. dirs. Samaritan Home for Aged, from 1959, v.p., from 1961; bd. elders local Presbyn. ch., 1955-61; bd. dirs., pres. Youth Found., from 1967. Lt. C.E., U.S. Army, 1918-19. Recipient Honor award Wisdom Soc., 1970. Mem. N.Y. Soc. Founders and Patriots Am. (gov. 1955-58), New Eng. Soc., Nat. Inst. Social Scis., N.Y. Hist. Soc., Assn. of Bar of City of N.Y., Mil. Order Fgn. Wars, N.Y. Soc. Mil. and Naval Officers World Wars, Soc. Colonial Wars, Huguenot Soc. (sec. 1957-59, pres. 1959-60), Pilgrims Soc., SAR, Revolution, St. Nicholas Soc., Union Club, Met. Opera Cluib, Everglades Cluib, Woodstock Country Club, Phi Beta Kappa, Sigma Xi. Presbyterian. Home: New York N.Y. †

HAWTHORNE, EDWARD WILLIAM, university dean, physiology educator; b. Port Gibson, Miss., Nov.

30, 1921; s. Edward William and Charlotte Bernice (Killian) H.; m. Eula Roberts, June 19, 1948; children: Coral, Dayle, Hilary, Leigh, Edward. B.S., Howard U., 1941, M.D., 1946; M.S., U. Ill., 1949, Ph.D., 1951. Asst. in physiology Howard U. Coll. Medicine, 1942-44; intern Freedmen's Hosp., Washington, 1946-47; asst. resident Freedmen's Hosp., 1947-48; asst. in physiology U. Ill., Chgo., 1948-49; Life Ins. Med. Research fellow in physiology Howard U. Coll. Medicine, Washington, 1949-51; asso. prof., head dept. physiology Howard U. Coll. Medicine, 1951-58, prof., head dept., 1958-69, asst. dean, 1962-67, asso. dean, 1967-70, research prof., chmn. dept. physiology and biophysics, 1969-74, research prof., 1969-86; dean Grad. Sch. Arts and Scis., Howard U., 1974-86; vis. prof. Sch. Vet. Medicine, Tuskegee (Ala.) Inst., 1966; vis. prof. dept. physiology U. Ala. Med. Center, Birmingham, 1968; med. advisor U.S. SSS, 1960-70; mem. medicine and osteopathy spl. improvement grants rev. com. Bur. Health Professions Edn. and Manpower, HEW, 1968-69; mem. cardiovascular rev. panel Space Sci. Bd., Nat. Acad. Sci., 1968-74; chmn. adv. com. for SCOR Hypertension, Nat. Heart, Lung and Blood Inst., 1972-75; mem. hypertension detection and follow up program policy adv. bd. NIH, 1972-73; mem. clin. applications and prevention adv. com. Nat. Heart, Lung and Blood Inst., 1975-78, mem. hypertension task force, 1975-78; mem.-at-large Space Programs Adv. Council, NASA, 1976-77; mem. NASA Adv. Com., Ames Research Center, Moffett Field, Calif., 1976; del.-at-large White House Conf. on Handicapped Individuals, 1977; cons. minority hypertension research devel. program Bowman Gray Sch. Medicine, Wake Forest U., 1977; mem. Md. State Planning Council on Devel. Disabilities, 1977, mem. council developmental disabilities tech. assistance system, 1977-86 ; mem. planning and adv. com. developmental disabilities councils consumer's tng. sessions Developmental Disabilities Tng. and Tech. Assiance Center, HEW, 1978; mem. Nat. Acad. Scis., 1980-81. Mem. editorial bd.: Am. Physiol. Soc, 1966-72, Jour. Med. Edn, 1969-72, New Directions, Howard U., from 1977; contbr. articles to profl. jours. Recipient Helen B. Taussig award Central Md. chpt. Am. Heart Assn., 1975; Percy L. Julian award Sigma Xi, 1980; numerous other awards, citations. Mem. Am. Heart Assn. (exec. com. council on basic sci. 1962-74, dir. 1964-73, policy com. from 1965, chmn. council on basic sci. 1966-68, mem. exec. com. 1966-73, v.p. 1969-72), Washington Heart Assn. (research com. 1963-67, dir. 1966-71), Assn. Former Interns and Residents Freedmen's Hosp. (exec. sec. 1957-69, pres. 1971-72), Am. Physiol. Soc. (co-chmn. Porter physiology devel. program from 1971), John Andrew Clin. Soc. (pres. 1965-66), Fedn. Am. Socs. Exptl. Biology, Am. Coll. Cardiology, Soc. Exptl. Biology and Medicine, Nat. Med. Assn., AMA, N.Y. Acad. Scis., Md. Acad. Scis., Physiol. Soc. Phila., Cardiac Muscle Soc., D.C. Med. Soc., AAUP, Medico-Chirurg. Soc., AAAS, Washington Soc. Pathologists, Am. Assn. Higher Edn., Orgn. Black Scientists, Sigma Xi, Alpha Omega Alpha, Alpha Phi Alpha. Home: Washington D.C. Died Oct. 7, 1986.

HAYDEN, STERLING, actor, author; b. Montclair, N.J., Mar. 26, 1916; s. George and Frances Walter; m. Madeleine Caroll, 1942 (div. 1946); m. Betty Ann De-Noon, 1947 (div. 1955); children: Gretchen, Matthew, Christian, Thor; m. Catherine McConnell, 1960; 2 children. Seaman sailing ships and fishing boats, became first mate, then capt. Author: Wanderer, 1963; novel Voyage, 1976; film debut in Virginia, 1941; other films include Asphalt Jungle, 1950, The Star, 1953, Johnny Guitar, 1954, Prince Valiant, 1954, The Killing, 1956, Dr. Strangelove, 1964, Loving, 1970, The Godfather, 1972, The Long Goodbye, 1973, 1900, 1977, Winter Kills, 1979, Nine to Five, 1980, Gas, 1981, Venom, 1982; appeared in TV plays including A Sound of Different Drummers, 1957, The Last Man, 1958, Old Man, 1958, Ethan Frome, 1960; TV miniseries The Blue and the Gray, 1982. Capt. USMC, World War II. Decorated Silver Star. Died May 23, 1986.

HAYES, ARTHUR HULL, broadcasting executive; b. Detroit, July 1, 1904; s. James J. Sr. and Helen (Hull) H.; m. Florence Gruber, Oct. 8, 1932; children: Arthur Hull, Joseph, Mary Ann, Florence Margaret. Student, U. Detroit, 1922-26, LLD (hon.), 1956; LLD (hon.), Loyola U., 1957; LHD, LeMoyne Coll., 1961. With nat. advt. dept. Detroit News, 1926; with media dept. Campbell-Ewald, 1928-30, asst. to v.p. charge media, asst. dir. radio, 1930-34; account exec. Columbia Broadcasting System radio spot sales, N.Y.C., 1934; ea. sales mgr. radio spot sales Columbia Broadcasting System radio spot sales, 1935-38; head WABC (now WCBS), 1938-40, gen. mgr., 1940-49; v.p. CBS, gen. mgr. KCBS (formerly KQW) 1949-55; pres. CBS Radio, 1955-67; dir. CBS, 1955-67. Mem. adv. bd. Vets. Hosp. Radio and TV; bd. dirs. Advt. Rsch. Found. Inc.; mem. lay bd. trustees Fordham U., Cath. Apostolate of Radio, TV and Advt.; trustee Nat. Newman Found. Decorated Knight Comdr. Equestrian Order Holy Sepulchre; Ursula Laurus citation New Rochelle Coll., 1957. Mem. Broadcast Pioneers, Radio Advt. Bur. (dir.), Nat. Assn. Broadcasters (bd. dirs.), Internat. Radio and TV Soc., Dutch Treat Club, Broadcasters Club. Home: Garrett Park Md. Died Apr. 14, 1986; interred St. Mary's Cemetery, Greenwich, Conn.

HAYES, JAMES MARTIN, archbishop; b. Halifax, N.S., Can., May 27, 1924; s. Leonard J. and Rita (Bates) H. Student, St. Mary's U., Halifax, 1939-43; B.A., Holy Heart Sem., Halifax, 1947; J.C.D., Angelicum, Rome, 1957; Litt. D. (hon.), St. Anne's U., Church Pt., N.S., 1966; S.T.D. (hon.), Kings Coll., Halifax, 1967. Ordained priest Roman Cath. Ch., 1947; chancellor Archdiocese of Halifax, 1957-63; rector St. Mary's Basilica, Halifax, 1963-66; aux. bishop Halifax, 1965-67, archbishop, from 1967; v.p. Can. Conf. Cath. Bishops. Home: Halifax N.S., Canada. Deceased.

HAYES, JOHN S., ambassador, communications executive; b. Phila., Aug. 21, 1910; m. Donna Gough; children: Jonathan S., Rhea Anne, Ellen Laurie, Peter Ogle. AB, U. Pa., 1931. Pres. Post-Newsweek Stas. and exec. v.p. Washington Post Co., 1947-66, also bd. dirs.; U.S. ambassador to Switzerland 1966-69; pres. United Way Am., 1962-64; mem. U.S. del. Internat. Conf. on Communication Satellite, 1969; mem. Fed. City Coun., Washington, 1963-66; chmn. Meridian House Internat., Washington, 1970-74, Radio Free Europe/Radio Liberty, from 1976. Author: (with Horace Gardiner) Both Sides of the Microphone, 1940. Trustee Springfield Coll., 1960-66, Nat. Urban League, Washington Performing Arts Soc., U. North Fla., from 1978; bd. dirs. USO, Nat. Symphony Orch.; mem. Carnegie Corp. Commn. on Ednl. TV, 1965, Washington Inst. Fgn. Affairs, 1972; chmn. United Arts Orgn., Washington, 1971. Lt. col. U.S. Army, 1941-46, comdg. officer Am. Forces Radio Network ETO. Decorated Bronze Star; Order of Brit. Empire; Croix de Guerre; recipient Washingtonian award Washington C. of C., 1953. Fellow Am. Acad. Polit. and Social Sci.; mem. Assn. Maximum Service Telecasters (dir.), Nat. Assn. Broadcasters (dir.), Federal City Club, Ponte Vedra Club, Players Club, Sawgrass Club, Pi Delta Epsilon (hon.). Home: Ponte Vedra Fla. Died Dec. 14, 1981; buried Arlington Nat. Cemetery, Va.

HAYES, L(UTHER) NEWTON, curator; b. Soochow, China, Apr. 19, 1883; (parents Am. citizens); s. John Newton and Mercie (Briggs) H.; m. Frances Gray, Apr. 10, 1923 (dec. 1924); 1 child, Francis Newton; m. Rhea Pumphrey, June 10, 1927. BS, Wooster Coll., 1905; AM, Princeton U., 1907. English tutor to Marquis Li Kuo Chieh (grandson of Prime Minister Li Hung Chang) Beijing, 1908-09; headmaster Putung Acad., Tientsin, China, 1909-11; sec. Internat. Com. for China YMCA, N.Y.C., 1911-32; gen. sec. YMCA, Nanking, China, 1911-14; exec. sec. YMCA, Chengtu, China, 1915-19; nat. exec. for tng. YMCA, Shanghai, China, 1921-26; ednl. and gen. sec. YMCA, Tientsin, 1927-32; ednl. dir. Providence ctr. YMCA, 1932-44; dir. Providence div. Northeastern U., Boston, 1933-42; dean men Bryant Coll., Providence, 1945-46; dir. admissions Associated Coll. Upper N.Y., 1946-49; dir. pub. relations Vellore (India) Christian Med. Coll.; curator Kent-DeLord House Mus., Plattsburgh. Author: The Great Wall of China, The Chinese Dragon; contbr. articles to mags. and jours. Mem. Episc. diocesan coun. R.I., 1943-46; chmn. China Friendship Week city-wide observance City of Providence, 1945. Decorated Order of Chia Ho. Fellow Royal Geog. Soc. London; mem. Royal Asiatic Soc. (N.C.B.), Soc. Mayflower Descendants (gov. R.I. soc. 1943-46, nat. bd. dirs. 1946-49), SAR (sec. R.I. soc. 1942-44, v.p. 1944-46), Nat. Red Cross China (hon. life mem.), Pilgrim John Howland Soc., R.I. Hist. Soc. (bd. dirs. 1944-46), R.I. Soc. Friends China (pres. 1940-46), Rotary (bd. dirs. local chpt.), Adirondack Mountain Club, Phi Beta Kappa. Home: Plattsburgh N.Y. †

HAYES, NEVIN WILLIAM, clergyman; b. Chgo., Feb. 17, 1922; s. James Timothy and Ella Mary (Williams) H. Ph.B., Mt. Carmel Coll., 1943; postgrad., Whitefriars Hall, Washington, 1943-47, Cath. U., 1944-50; LL.D. (hon.), Loyola U., Chgo., 1984. Joined Carmelite Order, 1939; ordained priest Roman Catholic Ch., 1946; instr. Romance langs. Carmelite Sem., Hamilton, Mass., 1947-51; pastor Lima, Peru, 1951-59; prelate nullius Sicuani, Peru, 1959-70; bishop Sicuani, 1965-70; aux. bishop Chgo., 1971-88; Episcopal vicar Hispanic Apostolate, Diocese of Chgo., 1979-83, vicar for sr. priests, from 1983; Episcopal vicar Western suburbs 1983-86; Co-founder Instituto Pastoral Andino, Cuzco, Peru, 1969, bd. dirs., 1969-71; pres. Comité Episcopal de Religiosos, Lima, 1967-70, Comité Episcopal para Laicos, Lima, 1970-71; chmn. com. for ch. in Latin Am. Nat. Council Bishops, 1976-79. Home: Chicago Ill.

HAYES, RALPH WESLEY, forestry educator; b. Albert Lea, Minn., Aug. 4, 1890; s. Edwin Foster and Eva Elizabeth (Hubbard) H.; m. Vera Beatrice Mather, Mar. 15, 1915; 1 child, Donna Yvonne (Mrs. William H. Clark). BS, Iowa State Coll., 1914, MF, 1924. With Indian forestry service U.S. Dept. Interior, 1914-24; asst. prof. forestry Colo. Agrl. Coll., 1924-26, La. State U., 1926-29, N.C. State Coll., 1929-34; prof. La. State U., from 1934, head. dept., 1934-48, dir. Sch. of Forestry, 1948-55. Mem. Soc. Am. Foresters, Masons, Phi Kappa Phi, Si Sigma Pi, Alpha Zeta, Lambda Chi Alpha. Presbyterian. Home: Baton Rouge La. †

HAYLES, ALVIN BEASLEY, pediatrician; b. Atmore, Ala., Oct. 18, 1915; s. Frederick Alvin and Sarah Vashti (Beasley) H.; m. Marilee A. Watson, Dec. 28, 1941; children: Mary Lee, Marjorie Jean, Marsha Kay. BS, Spring Hill Coll., 1937; student, U. Ala., Tuscaloosa, 1937-39; MD, Washington U., St. Louis, 1941; BS, U. Minn., Mpls., 1952. Lic. physician, Minn; diplomate Am. Bd. Pediatrics (chmn. sub-bd. pediatric endocrinology 1973-76). Rotating intern St. Louis City Hosp., 1941, U.S. Naval Hosp., Great Lakes, Minn., 1941-42; resident in pediatrics, fellow Mayo Clinic and Mayo Found., 1947-50, mem. staff, from 1952, cons. pediatric endocrinology; practice medicine specializing in pediatrics Lincoln, Nebr., 1950-52; prof. pediatrics and medicine Mayo Med. Sch.; vis. prof. U. Minn., 1965-78, U. Ala., 1970, 71, 75, U. South Ala., 1975, 78, Mass. Gen. Hosp., Boston, 1970-71, U. Rochester, 1979, U. Pitts., 1979, Hildren's Hosp., Boston, 1979; Ratchford lectr. U. Cin., 1975; med. adv. Human Growth Found., Inc., from 1964; v.p. VIII Internat. Thyroid Congress, 1979-80; advisor to growth hormone subcom. Nat. Pituitary Agy., 1972-75. Editor-in-chief Mayo Clinic Procs., 1969-76. Pres. Folwell PTA, 1953; bd. dirs. Rochester Figure Skating Club, 1954-58, pres. 1959-60; bd. dirs., pres. Rochester Art Ctr., 1966-68. Officer M.C. USNR, 1941-46. Recipient Book of Golden Deeds award Exchange Clubs, Rochester, 1979. Mem. So. Minn. Med. Soc., Zimbro Valley Med. Soc. (pres. 1962), Minn. Med. Assn. (Disting. Service award 1977), AMA, Northwestern Pediatric Soc. (pres. 1977), Endocrine Soc., Am. Thyroid Assn. (pres. 1978-79, Disting. Service award 1980), Am. Pediatric Soc., Am. Assn. Head and Neck Surgeons, Am. Soc. History of Medicine, Coun. Biology Editors, Lawson Wilkins Pediatric Endocrine Soc. (dir. 1973-76, pres. 1978-79). Home: Rochester Minn. Died Mar. 8, 1988; buried Sunset Hills Cemetery, Edwardsville, Ill.

HAYNES, EMERSON PAUL, Episcopal bishop; b. Marshfield, Ind., May 10, 1918; s. Ora Wilbur and Lydia Pearl (Walsh) H.; m. Helen Charlene Elledge, Nov. 15, 1935; children—Rosaline Elledge Haynes Triano, Emerson Paul II, Roland Lewis (dec.). A.B., Ind. Central U., 1942, LH.D., 1976; M.Div., United Theol. Sem., 1946; D.D., U. of South, 1975. Ordained as deacon Episcopal Ch., 1948, priest, 1949, bishop, 1974. Rector Holy Trinity Parish, Cin., 1948-53, All Saints Parish, Portsmouth, Ohio, 1953-57, Calvary Parish, Cin., 1957-59; canon chancellor St. Luke's Cathedral, Orlando, Fla., 1959-64; rector St. Luke's Parish, Ft. Myers, Fla., 1964-74; bishop coadjutor Diocese of S.W. Fla., St. Petersburg, 1974-88, mem. standing com., 1969-74, del. to provincial synod, 1969-74, dep. to Episcopal Gen. Conv., 1970, 73, chmn. Christian edn. of diocese, 1969-74. Mem. Ft. Myers City Planning Bd., 1968-73; trustee U. of South, Suncoast Manor, Bishop Gray Inn. Mem. County Ministerial Assn. (pres. 1956, 73). Died May 30, 1988; cremated, ashes interred at Cathedral Ch. of St. Peter, St. Petersburg, Fla.

HAYNES, HILDA MOCILE LASHLEY, actress; b. N.Y.C.; d. Charles C. and Leonora (Alkins) Lashley; 1 son, Christopher C. Diploma, Braithwaite Bus. Sch., 1934; postgrad., Am. Negro Theatre, 1941, Am. Theatre Wing, 1950, Am. Shakespeare Festival Acad., 1959. Appearances on Broadway include: Deep Are the Roots, 1946, Anna Lucasta, 1947, A Streetcar Named Desire, 1948, King of Hearts, 1954, Wisteria Trees, 1954, Lost in the Stars, 1956, The Long Dream, 1959, The Irregular Verb To Love, 1963, Blues for Mr. Charlie, 1964, The Great White Hope, 1968; appeared in off-Broadway prodns., summer stock; appeared in Blues for Mr. Charlie, World Theatre Festival, London, 1965, The Great White Hope, Washington, 1967, Golden Boy, Chgo., 1968, London, 1968, Seattle Repertory Theatre, 1971, Mourning in a Funny Hat; summer stock tour, 1972, Wedding Band, N.Y.C., 1972, The River Niger; nat. tour, 1973; numerous appearances on TV, including: The Rookies, Gimme a Break, Trapper John, M.D., Dynasty, Executive Suite, Sanford & Son, Starsky & Hutch, The Jeffersons, Good Times, Frontiers of Faith episode Light in the Southern Sky, 1958; appeared in TV movies including: Sarah T., Portrait of a Teenage Alcoholic, The Boy in the Plastic Bubble, Panic in Echo Park, The Miracle Worker; appeared in motion pictures including: Purlie Victorious, 1963, Home from the Hill, Keywitness, Taxi, A Face in the Crowd, Stage Struck, The Pawnbroker, Across 110th St, Diary of a Mad Housewife, River Niger, Let's Do It Again. Supr. Title II cultural enrichment program, Virgin Islands, 1966. Mem. NAACP, Negro Actors Guild, Actors Equity Assn. (councillor), Screen Actors Guild, AFTRA. Mem. Ch. Religious Sci. Home: New York N.Y. Died March 4, 1986; buried Woodlawn Cemetery, Bronx, N.Y.

HAYS, J(AMES) BYERS, architect; b. Sewickley, Pa., Feb. 11, 1891; s. Alden Farrelly and Augusta (Ulrich) H.; m. Charlotte Marie Hunker, Oct. 23, 1919; children: Elizabeth Augusta (Mrs. A. Raymond Schoenfeld), Alden Farrelly. Student, MIT, 1913. Registered architect, Ohio, Pa., N.C. With Henry Hornbostel, Pitts., 1915, Raymond Hood, N.C., 1916, Harrie Lindeberg, N.Y.C., 1917, Benno Janson, Pitts., 1919-20, Walker and Weeks, Cleve., 1920-30; mem., chief designer for various pub. and semi-pub. bldgs. 1924-30; ptnr. Hays, Simpson and Hunsicker, Cleve., 1930-41; assoc. Wilbur Watson and Assocs.; designer, prin. in charge war housing projects Fed. PHA, 1942-45; ptnr. Conrad, Hays, Simpson and Ruth, 1946-51, Hays and Ruth, 1952-62; archtl. cons. planning commns.

Brathenahl and Cleve., Ohio. Works include Cen. Nat. Bank, St. Paul's Episcopal Ch., Cleve. Mus. Art, Cleve. Zool. Park, Lakewood Civic Auditorium, Valley View Housing and Riverview Housing Projects for Cleve. Met. Housing Authority. Bd. govs. Western Res. U.; mem. archtl. adv. com. U. Circle Devel. Found. Lt. C.E., U.S. Army, 1917-19. Recipient award of merit Carnegie Inst. Tech. Fellow AIA (pres. Cleve. chpt. 1947, jury nat. honor awards 1955); mem. Regional Assn. Cleve., Am. Inst. Planners. Episcopalian. †

HAYS, WAYNE LEVERE, congressman; b. Bannock, Ohio, May 13, 1911; s. Walter Lee and Bertha Mae (Taylor) H.; m. Martha Judkins, June 3, 1937 (div. 1976); 1 child, Martha Brigitta; m. Pat Hays, 1976. BS, Ohio State U., 1933; postgrad., Duke U., 1935; LLD (hon.), Ohio U., 1966, Coll. Steubenville, 1968. Mayor Flushing, Ohio, 1939-45; mem. Ohio Senate, 1941-42; commr. Belmont County, Ohio, 1945-49; mem. 81st-94th congresses from 18th Ohio dist., chmn. com. house adminstrn., 1948-76; chmn. joint com. printin; mem. Ohio Ho. of Reps., 1978-80; chmn. Dem. Party, Belmont County, 1980; owner, Angus cattle and Tenn. walking horse breeder Red Gate Farm, Belmont, Ohio; pres. NATO Parliamentary Conf., Paris, 1956; pres. N. Atlantic Assembly, 1969-70, 74-75, permanent U.S. rep. to standing com.; chmn. Nat. Dem. Congl. Campaign Com.; bd. dirs. Citizens Nat. Bank, Flushing. Decorated Order of Merit (Italy, Grand Cross Order of Merit (Fed. Republic of Germany), 1975; recipient Caritas medal. Mem. Rotary. Presbyterian. Home: Flushing Ohio Died Feb. 10, 1989.

HAYWORTH, RITA (MARGARITA CARMAN CANSINO), actress; b. N.Y.C., Oct. 17, 1918; d. Eduardo and Volga (Haworth) Cansino; m. Edward C. Judson, 1936 (div. 1942); m. 2d, Orson Welles, Sept. 7, 1943 (div.); 1 dau., Rebecca; m. 3d, Ali Shah Khan, 1949 (div. 1953); 1 dau, Yasmin; m. 4th, Dick Haymes (div. 1955); m. 5th, James Hill, Feb. 2, 1958 (div. 1961). Ed. high sch., L.A. Stage debut in sch. play at age 11; profl. debut in stage prologue to motion picture Back Street, Carthay Circle Theatre, L.A.; with father as ptnr., appeared as dancer, night clubs and resorts; motion picture actress, from 1935, films include Loves of Carmen, 1948, Miss Sadie Thompson, 1954, Happy Thieves, 1962, Cover Girl, 1944, Tonight and Every Night, 1945, Gilda, 1946, Down to Earth, 1947, Lady from Shanghai, 1948, Affair in Trinidad, 1952, Salome, 1953, Fire Down Below, 1957, Pal Joey, 1957, Separate Tables, 1958, They Came to Cordura, 1959, Story on Page One, 1960, Money Trap, 1966, The Poppy is also a Flower, 1966, Road to Salina, 1971, The Wrath of God, 1972. Died May 14, 1987.

HAZELET, CRAIG POTTER, engineer; b. O'Neill, Nebr., Sept. 19, 1892; s. George C. and Harriet Sherman (Potter) H.; m. Frances Gillam, Nov. 12, 1920; children: Suzanne (Mrs. John H. Clark III), Sally Potter (Mrs. F. Weichel Drummond). BS, U. Wash., 1915; postgrad., MIT, 1918; DSc, U. Louisville, 1972. Surveyor Copper River and Northwestern Ry., Alaska, 1911; field engr. Kennecott (Alaska) Copper corp., 1912-14, designer mill contrn., 1915-17; designer B.&A., R.R., Fay, Spofford & Thorndyke, Boston, 1919, Smith Hinchman & Grylls, Ford Motor Co., Detroit, 1920, U. Ill., Urbana, 1920-22; chief engr., gen. mgr. Scherzer Rolling Lift Bridge Co., Chgo., 1922-31, pres., bd. dirs., 1931-36; mem. Hazelet & Erdal, from 1936; co-designer Interant. Bridge, Tientsin, China Chukiang Bridge, Canton, Peoples Republic of China, San Teimo Bridge, Seville, Spain, Ill. Waterway Bridges, Joliet, Queenston Rd. Bridge, Can., Miss. River Bridge, East St. Louis, Ill., Edsel Ford Expwy., Detroit, Columbia Expwy, Cin., Ohio Turnpike, Cleve.; sec. Ind. Toll Rd., Ky. Turnpike, Ohio River bridge, Parkersburg, W.Va., Bay St. Louis and Pascagoual Miss. bridges; designer Green River Ordnance Plant, 1942, static test lab. AC, Wright Field, Ohio, 1943; cons. design marine equipment Transp. Corps, U.S. Army, 1944. Mem. bd. overseers U. Louisville; bd. govs. J.B. Speed Art Mus. Lt. CE, U.S. Army, 1918. Recipient 1st prize internat. competition Am. Inst. Steel Constrn., 1938, Ann. award for design Am. Inst. Steel Constrn., 1938, award for design for bridges. Mem. Am. Inst. Cons. Engrs. (councilor), ASCE (bd. dirs. 1957-60, sec. ill. sect. 1940-41, pres. Ky. sect. 1951), Union League, Pendennis Club, Harmnoy Landing Country Club, Little Club, Phi Gamma Delta. Republican. Presbyterian. Home: Louisville Ky. †

HAZEN, EDWARD GATES, banker; b. Thomaston, Conn., June 8, 1906; s. Robert and Helen (Gates) H.; m. Virginia May Robert, Sept. 10, 1938; children: Edward Gates, Robert Dana. Student, Lawrence Acad., 1922-24; AB, Amherst Coll., 1928; LLB, U. Conn., 1938. Clk. Colonial Bank & Trust Co., 1933-46, trust officer, 1946-55, v.p., trust officer, 1955-65, sr. v.p., 1965-67, exec. v.p., 1967-69, exc. v.p., chmn. trust com., 1969-71; vice chmn. Thomaston Savs. Bank, 1971-80, chmn., 1980-81, also dir., corporator, ret., 1981; dir. Hallden Machine Co. Mem. Conn. Bankers Trust Com., 1966-71; mem. bd. finance, Town of Thomaston, 1946-48; trustee Waterbury Found., Inc., 1970-78, treas., 1968-70; mem. Watertown Sch. Bldg. Com., 1956-59, chmn. 1958-59; trustee Waterbury chpt. ARC, 1961-63. With USAAF, 1943-45. Mem. Litchfield County Univ. Club (treas. from 1975), Waterbury Club. Home: Watertown Conn. Died Oct. 31, 1986; buried Hillside Cemetery, Thomaston, Conn.

HEAD, HAYDEN WILSON, lawyer; b. Sherman, Tex., Feb. 6, 1915; s. Hayden Wilson and Ruth (Bulloch) H.; m. Marshall Elmore, July 2, 1938 (divorced); 1 child, Hayden W. Jr.; m. Annie Blake Morgan, June 15, 1950. B.A., Austin Coll., 1934; LL.B., U. Tex., 1937. Bar: Tex. 1937. Sr. ptnr. Head & Kendrick and predecessor firms, Corpus Christi, 1955-87; adv. dir. First City Bank, Corpus Christi, chmn. trust com., 1963-78. Pres. Nueces County chpt. ARC, 1948-49, United Community Services of Corpus Christi, 1962; chmn. Airport Adv. Bd. City Corpus Christi, 1956-86, chmn. Joint Airport Zoning Bd. City Corpus Christi and Nueces County, 1979-81; trustee Spohn Hosp., 1970-87 ; mem. exec. com. Coastal Bend Council Govts., 1970-87 , chmn., 1973. Served to capt. USSAF, 1941-45. Decorated D.F.C., Air medal with 9 oak leaf clusters; recipient Disting. Alumnus award Austin Coll., 1977, U. Tex. 1984, Disting. Alumnus award U. Tex. at Austin, 1984, Presdl. Citation U. Tex. at Austin, 1987. Fellow Tex. Bar Found., Am. Bar Found.; mem. ABA, Nueces County Bar Assn., State Bar of Tex. (chmn. mineral law sect. 1954-55), Corpus Christi C. of C. (chmn. area devel. com. 1982-87). Home: Corpus Christi Tex. Died July 24, 1987; buried Rose Hill Cemetery, Corpus Christi, Tex.

HEAPS, ALVIN EUGENE, labor union executive; b. Royalton, Ill., Dec. 4, 1919; s. John and Susie (Sprouse) H.; m. Evelyn M. Lassa, May 22, 1941 (div. Feb. 1968); 1 dau., Melody M.; m. Jo Anne C. Gibilaro, Mar. 10, 1968. Mem. Retail, Wholesale and Dept. Store Union, 1941—; pres. Retail, Wholesale and Dept. Store Union (Chgo. joint bd.), 1946-48, internat. sec.-treas., 1948-76, internat. pres., 1976-86, also chmn. bd. trustees union industry pension fund and union industry health and welfare fund; mem. exec. bd., indsl. union dept., until 1980; mem. exec. council AFL-CIO, 1977-86; Mem. Ill. Retail Industry Minimum Wage Bd., 1946-47; labor mem. Dept. Labor (com. fair labor standards to P.R.), 1963; mem. Labor Dept. (exchange program to Japan), 1964; mem. exec. com. Internat. Fedn. Comml., Clerical and Tech. Employees, Internat. Union Food and Allied Workers.; mem. Adv. Council on Social Security, 1982-86. Served with inf. AUS, 1943-45, ETO. Decorated Silver Star with oak leaf cluster, Purple Heart. Home: New York N.Y. Died Sept. 5, 1986; buried Evergreen Cemetery, Chgo.

HEARD, JOHN J., lawyer; b. Pitts., June 17, 1882. AB, Princeton, 1904; LLB, U. Pitts., 1907. Bar: Pa. 1907. Mem. Reed, Smith, Shaw & McClay, Pitts. †

HEARST, DAVID WHITMORE, publishing executive; b. N.Y.C., Dec. 2, 1915; s. William Randolph and Millicent (Willson) H.; m. Hope Chandler, Mar. 23, 1938; children: Millicent, David. Student, St. Bernard's, N.Y.C., 1927-30, St. George's, Newport, R.I., 1931-33, Princeton U., 1933-36. Reporter N.Y. Jour.-Am.; asst. advt. dir., then city editor Balt. News-Post; with classified and display advt. L.A. Evening Herald-Express, 1938-44, bus. mgr., 1944-45, gen. mgr., 1945-47, exec. pub., 1947-50, pub., 1950-60; v.p., bd. dirs. Hearst Corp. Mem. Calif. Club, Jonathan Club. Home: Los Angeles Calif. Died May 12, 1986.

HEATH, DONALD R., ambassador; b. Topeka, Aug. 12, 1894; s. Hubert A. and Estelle (Read) H.; m. Sue Louise Bell, Oct. 10, 1920; children: Sue Louise, Donald. Student, Washburn Coll., LLD; student, U. Montpellier, France. White House corr. United Press, 1920; vice consul Bucharest, Romania, 1921-23; consul Warsaw, Poland, 1923-25, Berne, Switzerland, 1925-29; chargé d'affaires ad interim Port-au-Prince, Haiti, 1929-30; consul and 2d sec. 1932-33; asst. chief Div. Latin-Am. Affairs, U.S. Dept. State, 1933-37, chief Div. North and West Coast Affairs, 1944; 1st sec. Am. embassy, Berlin, 1938-41; counselor Am. embassy, Santiago, Chile, 1941-44; counselor to U.S. polit. adviser for German; dir. polit. affairs Office of Mil. Gov. for Germany (U.S.), 1944; U.S. minister to Bulgaria 1947-50, U.S. minister to Associated States of Cambodia, Laos and Vietnam, 1st amb. to Cambodia and Vietnam, 1952, also minister plenipotentiary to Laos, amb. to Lebanon, 1955, to Saudi Arabia, 1958-61; v.p. Fgn. Bondholders Protective Council, 1961-67, pres., 1967-71, chmn. exec. com., 1972, cons., 1973-81; Regents prof. UCLA, 1962-63; lectr. on fgn. affairs. With U.S. Army, 1917-19, 1st lt. inf. Am. Expeditionary Force, 1918-19. Mem. Council Fgn. Relations, Metropolitan Club, University Club, Phi Delta Theta. Home: New York N.Y. Died Oct. 15, 1981.

HEATH, RICHARD NATHAN, advertising executive; b. Bay City, Mich., Apr. 17, 1901; s. Richard Phillip and Eliza Jane (McDonald) H.; m. Fern Elaine Anspach, May 31, 1924; children: Suzanne hedberg, Thomas Doran, Mary. Ed. pub. schs., Detroit. Writer Detroit Free Press, 1917-23; retail advt. exec. 1924-34; advt. rep. Curtis Pub. Co., 1934-37; with Leo Burnett Co., Inc., Chgo., 1939-61, exec. v.p., 1940-55, pres., 1955-58, chmn. exec. com., 1958-61, also bd. dirs. Mem. Chgo. Athletic Assn., Exmoor Country Club. Republican. Mem. Ch. of Christ, Scientist. Home: Highland Park Ill. Died Apr. 1, 1986.

HEAZEL, FRANCIS, lawyer; b. Shenandoah, Va., Dec. 10, 1891; s. James F. and Catherine (Morrisey) H.; m. Anna L. Flanagan, Apr. 28, 1914 (dec. Mar. 19720; children: Gertrude (Mrs. John J. Vogel Jr.), Francis James, CAtherine (Mrs. P. F. Clarke); m. Jane H. Rutland, May 16, 1972. Student, Mt. St. Mary's Coll., 1909-10; LLB, Washington and Lee U., 1912. Bar: Va. 1912, Tenn. 1916, N.C. 1922. City atty. Kingsport, Tenn., 1918-19; bd. dirs. Forman Realty Corp., Bismark Hotel Corp., Chgo.; dir. sec. Madison Sq. Garden Corp., N.Y.C., 1956-59. mem. Buncombe Co. Sinking Fund Com., 1933-54, N.C. Nat. Park, Pkwy. and Foerst Devel. com., 1947-53. mem. ABA, N.C., Buncombe Co. bar assns., C. of C. (pres. 1947), Ashville Indsl. Coun. (pres. 1947-48), KC (bd. dirs., past nat. treas.). Democrat. Roman Catholic. Home: Asheville N.C. †

HEBB, DONALD OLDING, psychologist; b. Chester, N.S., Can., July 22, 1904; s. Arthur Morrison and Mary Clara (Olding) H.; widower; children—Jane Nichols Hebb Paul, Mary Ellen Hebb Foley. B.A., Dalhousie U., Halifax, N.S., 1925; M.A., McGill U., Montreal, Que., Can., 1932; Ph.D., Harvard U., Cambridge, Mass., 1937. Research fellow Montreal Neurol. Inst., Ont., Can., 1937-39; lectr. psychology Queen's U., Kingston, Ont., Can., 1939-42; research fellow Yerkes Labs., Orange Park, Fla., 1942-47; prof. McGill U., Montreal, Que., Can., 1942-72, prof. emeritus, 1975-85. Author: Organization of Behavior, 1949, Essays on Mind, 1980. Fellow Can. Psychol. Assn., Am. Psychol. Assn., Royal Soc. London; fgn. assoc. mem. Nat. Acad. Scis. Home: Chester Basin N.S., Canada. Died Aug. 20, 1985.

HECKEL, CHARLES WILLARD, lawyer, church official; b. Bloomfield, N.J., May 1, 1913; s. Charles Otto and Edith Mae (Decker) H. AB, Dartmouth Coll., 1935; MA, Columbia U., 1936; LLB, U. Newark, 1940; LLD, Upsala Coll., Rutgers U., N.Y. Law Sch. Bar: N.J. 1941. Mem. law dept. City of Montclair, N.J., 1941-42; prof. law, dean faculty Rutgers U. Law Sch.; lectr. Princeton Theol. Sem. Chmn. Newark Citizens Com. Mcpl. Govt., 1952-54, commn. on human relations Mayor of Newark, 1955-56; pres. Newark chpt. Am. Assn. UN, 1961-63; hon. N.J. chmn. Am. Dem. Action, 1962-88; moderator Presbytery Newark United Presbyn. Ch. U.S.A., 1962-63, ruling elder, moderator 184th gen. assembly, 1972-88; bd. dirs. Bloomfield Coll., 1962-88. With USNR, World War II. Mem. ABA, AAUP. Home: Newark N.J. Died Apr. 6, 1988.

HECKMAN, WILLIAM ROBERT, aerospace executive; b. Greensburg, Pa., Jan. 16, 1921; s. Harry Leslie and Mary Cecilia (Coffman) H.; m. Jane Woods Lewis, July 8, 1943; children: William Robert, Harry Leslie. BSBA, U. Pitts., 1946; postgrad. exec. mgmt. program, Pa. State U., 1957. Spl. agt. FBI, 1947-52; various exec. positions ITT, Ft. Wayne (Ind.), Nutley (N.J.) and N.Y.C., 1952-69; dir. adminstrn. def.-space group ITT, 1966-69; v.p. adminstrn. Aerojet-Gen. Corp., La Jolla, Calif., 1969-87. 1st lt. USMCR, 1942-45. Mem. La Jolla Country Club, Rancho Bernardo (Calif.) Country Club, Delta Tau Delta. Home: San Diego Calif. Died July 31, 1987; buried San Diego.

HEDBERG, HOLLIS DOW, geologist, educator; b. Falun, Kans., May 29, 1903; s. Carl A. and Zada M. (Dow) H.; m. Helen F. Murray, Nov. 8, 1932; children: Ronald M., James D., William H., Franklin A., Mary F. A.B., U. Kans., 1925; M.S., Cornell U., 1926; Ph.D., Stanford, 1937; Hon. Doctorate, U. Uppsala, Sweden, 1977. Asst. Kans. Geol. Survey, 1924-25; petrographer Lago Petroleum Corp., Venezuela, 1926-28; stratigrapher, dir. geol. lab. Mene Grande Oil Co., Venezuela, 1928-39; asst. chief geologist Mene Grande Oil Co., 1939-46; chief geologist fgn. prodn. div. Gulf Oil Corp., 1946-51, exploration mgr., 1951-52; chief geologist Gulf Oil Corp., Pitts., 1952-53; exploration coordinator Gulf Oil Corp., 1953-57, v.p., 1957-64, exploration adviser, 1964-88; prof. geology Princeton, 1959-72, emeritus, 1972-88; exploration advisor Chevron Corp., 1983-86; mem. Am. Com. Stratigraphic Nomenclature, 1946-60, chmn., 1950-52; pres. Internat. Com. Stratigraphic Terminologyy, 1952-76; v.p. Internat. Commn. Stratigraphy, 1968-76; chmn. Consortium Exploration Adv. Group, Iran, 1965-72; chmn. tech. subcom. petroleum resources of ocean floor Nat. Petroleum Council, 1968-73; chmn. coordinating panel Internat. Geol. Correl. Program, 1969-72; chmn. JOIDES Panel Pollution Prevention and Safety, 1970-77; Bd. dirs. Cushman Found. Foraminiferal Research, 1951-63; mem. corp. Woods Hole Oceanographic Inst., 1972—. Editor: Internat. Stratigraphic Guide, 1975—; Contbr. articles profl. jours. Decorated Medalla de Honor de la Instruccion Publica, Venezuela).; Recipient Sidney Powers medal Am. Assn. Petroleum Geologists, 1963; Distinguished Service award U. Kans., 1963; Wollaston medal Geol. Soc. London, 1975; Distinguished Achievement award Offshore Tech. Conf., 1975; Energy award La. State U., 1983. Fellow Geol. Soc. Am. (pres. 1959-60, asso. editor bull. 1962-68, Penrose medal 1980, trustee Geol. Soc. Am. Found. 1980-84, hon. trustee 1984-88); mem. Nat. Acad. Sci. (Mary Clark Thompson award 1973), Am. Assn. Petroleum Geologists (asso. editor bull. 1937-83, pres. Eastern sect. 1948-49, Pres.'s award 1972, Human Needs award 1973), AAAS, Am. Geophys. Union, Paleontol. Soc. Am. (v.p. 1952), Soc. Econ. Paleontology and Mineralogy, Swiss Geol. Soc.,

Soc. Exploratory Geophys., Am. Inst. Mining, Metall. and Petroleum Engrs., Am. Geol. Inst. (pres. 1962-63, Ian Campbell medal 1983, Heroy award 1987), Internat. Union Geol. Scis. (chmn. U.S. nat. com. on geology 1965-66), Am. Inst. Profl. Geologists, Geol. Soc. Stockholm (hon. corr.), Soc. Geol. Venezolana (hon. plaque 1982), Geol. Soc. London (hon.), Danish Royal Acad. Sci., Phi Beta Kappa, Sigma Xi, Phi Kappa Phi, Sigma Gamma Epsilon. Clubs: Cosmos (Washington); Princeton (N.Y.C.), Mining (N.Y.C.). Died Aug. 14, 1988; buried Princeton Cemetery, Princeton, N.J.

HEFFELFINGER, WILLIAM STEWART, government official; b. Effingham, Kans., Jan. 31, 1925; s. William Stewart and Nora (Estell) H.; m. Dorothy M. Shockley, Sept. 24, 1944; children: William Stewart III, Sharon A., Lee S. With Sweet Hotel System, 1942-43; bus. mgr. Eleemosynary Instns., Kans., 1946-53; sec., trustee A. J. Rice Estates, 1948-86; dir. Olney facility FCDA, 1953-54, dir. adminstrv. operations office, 1955-56, asst. adminstr. for gen. adminstrn., 1956-58; mem. adv. com. GSA, 1956-62; dir. adminstrn. Exec. Office of Pres. U.S., 1958-62; reviewing officer Bd. of Surveys, 1956-62; chmn. bd. U.S. Civil Service Examiners, 1955-62; dir. program rev. Martin-Marietta Corp., 1962-69; spl. asst. to asst. sec. water and power devel. Dept. Interior, 1969; dep. asst. sec. Dept. Transp., Washington, 1969-70, asst. sec., 1970-77; asst. adminstr. for mgmt. and adminstrn. Fed. Energy Adminstrn., 1977; dir. adminstrn. Dept. Energy, 1977-81, asst. sec. energy for mgmt. and adminstrn., 1981-82, dir. adminstrn., 1982-86 ; mem. Joint Task Force Seven in Operation Redwing, 1956; vice chmn. ex-personnel bd. Dept. Transp.; vice chmn. Transp. System Acquisition Council; treas. U.S. Ry. Assn., 1974; mem. Fed. Adv. Council on Occupational Safety and Health, 1971-77. Served with AUS, 1943-46. Recipient Wm. A. Jump Meml. Found. Meritorious award, 1960. Mem. Am. Soc. Pub. Adminstrn., Am. Legion. Club: Mason. Home: McLean Va. Died Jan. 5, 1986, buried Arlington Nat. Cemetery, Va.

HEFFERNAN, JOSEPH VICTOR, lawyer, corporate executive; b. Washington, Ind., Dec. 23, 1905; s. William and Ellen (Sullivan) H.; m. Marion Cahill, 1942; 1 child, William C. AB, St. Louis U., 1928; JD, Ind. U., 1930; LLM, Columbia U., 1935. Bar: N.Y. 1936. With Cahill, Gordon & Reindel, N.Y.C., 1935-40; v.p., head law dept. RCA Corp., 1945-52; fin. v.p., bd. dirs. NBC, 1952-58; ptnr Hecht, hadfield, Farbach & McAlpin, N.Y.C., 1958-65; counsel, head law dept. Reynolds Metals Co., 1965-68; dep. chmn. Brit. Aluminium Co., Ltd., London, 1968-71; mem. panel arbitrators Am. Arbitration Assn., 1970-86. Contr. articles to profl. jours. Mem. bd. visitors Ind. U. Sch. Law, 1964-68; nat. chmn. Ind. U. Ann. Giving Campaign, 1964. Lt. USNR, World War II. Recipient Disting. Alumni award Ind. U., 1956. Mem. University Club. Home: Ardsley-on-Hudson N.Y. Died Mar. 2, 1986.

HEFFERNAN, PAUL MALCOLM, architect, educator; b. Decorah, Iowa, Jan. 23, 1909; s. Walter A. and Laura D. (Bethuram) H. B.S. in Archtl. Engring, Iowa State U., 1929, M.S. Archtl. Engring, 1931; M. Arch., Harvard, 1935; student, Ecole des Beaux Arts, Paris, France, 1935-38. Instr. Iowa State U., 1931-33; mem. faculty Coll. Architecture, Ga. Inst. Tech., Atlanta, 1938-87; Prof Coll. Architecture, Ga. Inst. Tech., 1944-76, dir. coll., 1956-76, dir. and prof. emeritus, 1976-87; adj. prof. study abroad program Coll. Architecture, Ga. Inst. Tech., Paris, 1976-77; designer Bush-Brown, Gailey and Heffernan (which conducted master plan and bldg. plans for Ga. Inst. Tech.), 1944-54; cons. archtl. edn. So. Regional Edn. Bd., 1953; cons. architect Ga. Inst. Tech., 1956-64, local firms; cons. design PHA, Washington; mem. archtl. award juries. Mem. Ga. Bd. Exam. and Registration of Architects, 1961-71, pres., 1967-69. Summer fellow Found. Architecture and Landscape Architecture, Lake Forest, Ill., 1929; Condé-Nast fellow Am. architecture, 1929-30; Sheldon fellow; also Appleton fellow Harvard, 1935; recipient Eugene Dodd medal Harvard, 1934; 28th Paris prize Soc. Beaux-Arts Architects; also certificate Beaux-Arts Inst. Design, N.Y.C., 1935; citation for effective teaching archtl. design Coll. Fellows AIA, 1955; hon. mention for West Stands Ga. Inst. Tech., Progressive Architecture mag., 1948; award for Price Gilbert Library AIA, 1952; citation Atlanta chpt. AIA, 1965; citation for profl. achievement Iowa State U., 1973; Bronze medal award Ga. Assn. AIA, 1982; Paris prize medal Soc. Beaux-Arts Architects, Nat. Inst. Archtl. Edn., 1983; Phillip Trammel Shutze medal Ga. Inst. Tech., 1984; award Atlanta Urban Design Commn., 1985. Fellow AIA (com. scholarships and awards 1956-58), Royal Soc. Arts (London); life fellow Internat. Inst. Arts and Letters, Lindau, Germany; mem. Theta Delta Chi, Tau Beta Pi, Phi Kappa Phi, Tau Sigma Delta, Sigma Upsilon. Home: Atlanta Ga. Died Apr. 9, 1987; buried Crest Lawn Cemetery, Atlanta, Ga.

HEFFNER, R(OE)-M(ERRILL) S(ECRIST), educator; b. Bellefontaine, Ohio, Aug. 25, 1892; s. Charles Wesley and Dora Ellen (Secrist) H.; m. Susan Thomas, Sept. 15, 1924. AB, Wittenberg Coll., 1913, AM, 1915, LittD (hon.), 1954; AM, Harvard U., 1916, PhD, 1925. Instr. Latin and German Wittenberg Coll., 1913-15; instr. German Worcester Poly. Inst., 1916-18; instr. German Harvard U., 1922-27, 28-36, asst. prof., 1936-38; assoc. prof. U. Wis., 1938-39, prof., from 1939, chmn. dept., 1946-62. Lt. Signal Corps, U.S. Army, 1918-19. Fellow AAAS; mem. MLA, Linguistic Soc. Am., Wis. Acad. Scis., Arts and Letters. Home: Madison Wis. †

HEFNER, ROBERT ARTHUR, educator; b. Lafayette, Ohio, Apr. 24, 1892; s. John and Flora (Growdon) H.; m. Rowena Ilo Hardin, May 21, 1921; children: Elinor Marcine (Mrs. J.E. James), Frank Willis (dec.), Anna Carolyn (Mrs. H.E. Veith), John Hardin, Robert Arthur Jr. BS, Ohio No. U., 1923; MS, Ohio State U., 1924, PhD, 1929. Engaged as tchr. in elementary schs. of Allen County, Ohio, 1912-16; high sch. sci. tchr., Lafayette, Ohio, 1921-23; instr. biology Heidelberg Coll., Tifflin, Ohio, 1924-25; asst. prof. zoology Miami U., 1925-29, assoc. prof., 1929-40, prof., from 1940, chmn. zoology dept., 1940-58, mus. curator, from 1958. Served as 1st lt. U.S. Army, 1917-19. Fellow AAAS, Ohio Acad. Sci. (v.p. 1939, pres. 1953); mem. Genetics Soc. Am., Am. Soc. Human Genetics, Sigma Xi, Phi Sigma, Gamma Alpha, Kiwanis (pres. 1950, lt. gov. 1952). Home: Oxford Ohio. †

HEIDT, LAWRENCE JOSEPH, physical chemist; b. Portage, Wis., Apr. 5, 1904; s. Frank and Barbara Cecilia (Ehr) H.; m. Agnes Grace Kiley, June 26, 1933; children: Marianne, David, Barbara. AB, U. Wis., 1927, MS, 1928, PhD, 1930. Teaching fellow U. Wis., 1927-29; rsch. fellow photochemistry Harvard U., 1930-35; instr. MIT, 1935-40, faculty with professorial rank, 1940-83, hon. lectr., 1969-83; Disting. Univ. prof. Emmanuel Coll., 1969-83; sci. adviser, lectr. Royal Inst. Tech., Sweden, 1959; Guggenheim fellow study, Japan, Australia, 1962-63; vis. prof. Tech. U. Berlin, 1969; vis. prof. Islamabad (Pakistan) U., 1970; cons. several orgns.; mem. several spl. phys. and inorganic chem. coms.; mem. com. photochem. storage energy NAS-NRC, 1956-61, mem. com. elec. insulation and dielectric phenomena, 1964, chmn., responsible officer Endicott House Symposium on Photochemistry Liquid-Solid States, 1957. Co-editor: Photochemistry of Liquid and Solid States, 1960; hon. editor Jour. Photochem. and Photobiology, 1961-83; contbr. profl. publs.; patentee invert sugar solutions intravenous feeding, voltage stabilized polyolefin dielectrics and thermally stabilized ozone. Dir. photochemistry and solar energy conversion for coll. tchrs. NSF, 1970; NSF mem. U.S.-Japan Coop. Sci. Program for Solar Energy Research on Cerium Catalyzed Photolysis of Water by Sun Light, Inst. Solid State Physics, Tokyo, 1975-76. Recipient Alfred P. Sloan Merit award MIT, 1956, cert. of appreciation U.S. Dept. Army, 1963; duPont fellow, 1929-30. Fellow Am. Acad. Arts and Sci. (Warren Fund Research award 1936), AAAS; mem. Am. Chem. Soc. (chmn. northeastern sect. 1964-65, councillor nat. soc. 1963-83), N.Y. Acad. Arts and Scis., AAUP, Sigma Xi (regional lectr. 1972), Phi Lambda Upsilon, Alpha Chi Sigma, Gamma Alpha. Roman Catholic. Home: Arlington Mass. Died Apr. 4, 1983; buried Mt. Auburn Cemetery, Cambridge, Mass.

HEIFETZ, JASCHA, violinist; b. Vilna, Russia, Feb. 2, 1901; naturalized, 1925; m. Florence Vidor, Aug. 20, 1928; children—Josepha, Robert; m. Frances Spiegelberg, Jan. 1947 (div.); 1 son, Joseph. Student at age 5, Royal Sch. of Music, Vilna, grad. at 9; pupil of, Prof. Leopold Auer, St. Petersburg; Mus.D. (hon.), Northwestern U., 1949. staff dept. music U. So. Calif. Appeared in: films They Shall Have Music, Carnegie Hall, Of Mice and Men; New York debut, Carnegie Hall, Oct. 27, 1917. Donor of concert hall at Tel-Aviv, Palestine, 1926. Decorated comdr. Legion of Honor, France, 1957; recipient Grammy award. Mem. Am. Guild Mus. Artists. Home: Beverly Hills Calif. Died Dec. 10, 1987.

HEILMAN, CHARLES GEORGE, engineer, manufacturing company executive; b. Catasauqua, Pa., Nov. 17, 1887; s. Richard Owen and Mary Martha (Schneller) H.; m. Della Webb, 1915; children: Ruth Phyllis Heilman Berndt, Kathryn Mary Heilman Weir. B.Chem.E., Lehigh U., 1910. Asst. supt. Bethlehem Steel Co., Pa., 1910-13; supt. heat treating dept. Northway Motor Co., Detroit, 1913-17; mem. U.S. Airplane Commn., 1917-18; chief metallurgist GM, Detroit, 1918-22; pres. Commonwealth Industries, Detroit, 1922-59, chmn., 1959-70; chmn. Commonwealth Industries div. Masco Corp., from 1970; treas., dir. Frank Bancroft Co. Fellow Am. Soc. Metals; mem. Metal Treating Inst., Am. Chem. Soc., Am. Soc. Mining and Metall. Engrs., Orchard Lake Country Club, Detroit Yacht Club, Econ. Club of Detroit, Masons. Republican. Episcopalian. Home: Bloomfield Hills Mich. Deceased.

HEINEMANN, MITCHELL, clothing executive; b. Hurley, Wis., 1892. Exec. v.p. Jantzen, Inc., Portland, Oreg., also bd. dirs. Mem. Multnomah Athletic Club (life). Home: Portland Oreg. †

HEINFELDEN, CURT H. G., insurance executive; b. Haverhill, Mass., Aug. 30, 1909; s. Curt H. G. and Edith (Prentiss) H.; m. Lois Gantert, Nov. 30, 1935; 1 child, Curt H. G. III. AB, Rutgers U., 1932; postgrad., U. Chgo. Law Sch., 1934; grad. advanced mgmt. program, Harvard U., 1950. Jud. examiner U.S. Fidelity & Guaranty Co., 1934-38; sales mgr. Am. Mut. Liability Ins. co., 1938-46; v.p. Employers Group Ins. Cos., 1946-58; dir. Balt. Life Ins. Co., 1959-85; mem bd. arbitration N.Y. Stock Exchange, 1971-85; bd. dirs Md. Nat. Bank. V.p. Balt. Area council Boy Scouts Am., 1960; bd. dirs. UN Md., 1963, Jr. Achievement Balt., 1963, Balt. United Appeal, 1964, Greater Balt Com., goodwill Industries, Balt. Indsl. Devel. Corp. pres. Greater Balt. YMCA, 1967; mem. Md. Fair Election Financing Commn., 1974-85, Balt. Police Retirement Bd., 1977-85, Balt. Contractors Pre-Qualification Com., 1977-85; mem. exec. com. Gov.'s Oper. Economy Survey Commn. With USNR, 1942-45, PTO. Mem Am. Mgmt. Assn., C. of C. Met. Balt. (pres. 1972-73) L'Hirondelle Club (pres. Ruxton, Md. chpt. 1977-78) Maryland Club, Country Club of Md., Center Club Rotary, Zeta Psi, Phi Delta Phi. Home: Baltimore Md Died Nov. 16, 1985; buried West Columbarium, Druid Ridge Cemetery, Balt.

HEINICKE, ARTHUR JOHN, pomologist; b. St Louis, Oct. 23, 1892; s. Martin Theodore and Magdalena (Beckert) H.; m. Marguerite Eva Riemann Sept. 15, 1917; 1 child, Arthur John. BSA, U. Mo. 1913, MA, 1914; PhD, Cornell U., 1916. Fellow in horticulture U. Mo., 1913-14; with Cornell U., from 1914, instr. pomology, 1914-17, asst. prof., 1917-20 prof., 1920-60, head dept., 1921-60, head div. pomology 1942, dir. N.Y. State (Geneva) Agrl. Expt. Sta., 1942-60, prof. emeritus, from 1960. Author various rsch bulls. issued by Cornell U.; contbr. articles to profl jours. Fellow AAAS,; mem. Am. soc. Hort. Sci. (pres 1937), Am. Bot. Soc., Am. Soc. Plant Physiologists Sigma Xi, Gamma Alpha, Phi Kappa Phi, Gamma Sigma Delta. Republican. Lutheran. Home: Ithaca N.Y. †

HEINLEIN, ROBERT ANSON, author; b. Butler, Mo., July 7, 1907; s. Rex Ivar and Bam (Lyle) H.; m. Virginia Doris Gerstenfeld, Oct. 21, 1948. Grad., U.S. Naval Acad., 1929; postgrad. physics and math. UCLA, 1934; L.H.D. (hon.), Eastern Mich. U., 1977. Commd. ensign U.S. Navy, 1929, advanced to lt. (j.g.) 1932; assignments at sea; disabled, retired 1934; aviation engr. U.S. Navy, 1942-45; owner silver mine Shively & Sophie Lodes, Silver Plume, Colo., 1934-35; James V. Forrestal Meml. lectr. U.S. Naval Acad., 1973. Author: 45 books including Beyond This Horizon, 1948, The Green Hills of Earth, 1951, Puppet Masters, 1951, Double Star, 1956 (Hugo award), The Door Into Summer, 1957, Citizen of the Galaxy, 1957, Methuselah's Children, 1958, Have Space Suit-Will Travel, 1958, Starship Troopers, 1959 (Hugo award), Stranger in a Strange Land, 1961 (Hugo award), Glory Road, 1963, The Moon is a Harsh Mistress, 1966 (Hugo award), I Will Fear No Evil, 1970, Time Enough for Love, 1973, Job: A Comedy of Justice, 1984, Farmer in the Sky, 1985, Rocketship Galileo, 1985, Glory Road, 1984, The Cat Who Walks Through Walls, 1985, To Sail Beyond the Sunset, 1987, others; films Destination Moon, 1950, Project Moonbase, 1954; works included in numerous anthologies and collections, stories have been sold or leased to TV and radio for various space series; guest commentator Apollo-11 1st lunar landing, 1969; author tech. books including Test Procedures for Plastic Materials Intended for Structural and Semi-Structural Aircraft Uses, 1944; also tech. and popular novels and lectures. Recipient Best Sci. Fiction Novel award World Sci. Fiction Conv., 1956, 59, 61, 66; Sequoyah award, 1961; Best Liked Book award Boys Clubs Am., 1959; Humanitarian of Year award Asso. Health Found. and Nat. Rare Blood Club, 1974; Nebula award Sci. Fiction Writers Am., 1975; also named Grand Master; Inkpot award, 1977; Humanitarian award Nat. Rare Blood Club, 1974; award Am. Assn. Blood Banks, 1977; award Council Community Blood Centers, 1977; Tomorrow Starts Here award Delta Vee Soc., Disting. Pub. Svc. medal NASA, 1988 (posthumously). Mem. Am. Inst. Aero. and Astronautics, Authors Guild Am., U.S. Naval Acad. Alumni Assn., Retired Officers Assn., Navy League, Assn. U.S. Army, Air Force Assn., World Future Soc., Nat. Rare Blood (donors) Club, U.S. Naval Inst., Calif. Arts Soc., Minutemen of U.S.S. Lexington, Am. Assn. Blood Banks. Home: New York N.Y. Died May 8, 1988; cremated.

HEINTZLEMAN, B. FRANK, former governor; b. Fayetteville, Pa., Dec. 3, 1888. BA in Forestry, Pa. State Coll., 1907; MF, Yale, 1910. With U.S. Forest Svc., Western States, 1910-18, Alaska br., 1918-34; coordinating officer in forest conservation to Forest Service, NRA, organizer timber-using industries of U.S. 1934-37; regional forester Alaska, 1937-53; commr. for Alaska Dept. Agr., 1937-53; gov. State of Alaska, 1953-57. Co-author: Regional Planning for Alaska—Its Resources and Development (Nat. Resources Com. report), 1938; contbr. articles to lumber and paper industry jours., also to tech. forestry jours. Dir. Alaska Spruce Log Program, World War II. Recipient Superior Service award Dept. Agr., 1952. Mem. Soc. Am. Foresters (William Schlich medal 1958), Cosmos Club, Masons, Elks. Republican. Lutheran. Home: Juneau Alaska. †

HEINZE, WALTER O., business executive; b. Chgo., Nov. 11, 1903; s. August and Daisy P. (Tuchband) H.; m. Louise Mendius, 1924; children: Don richard, Carol Louise, Dorothy Ann. Grad high sch., Chgo. Founder W.O. Heinze mgmt. cons., L.A., 1937; mem. Planning Bd. War Prodn. Bd., 1942; dir. ops. Smaller War Plants,

Inc., 1943; pres. Internat. Latex Corp., Dover, Del., 1943-68; chmn. bd. STP Corp., Ft. Lauderdale, Fla., 1968-72, chmn. exec. com., 1972-73; chmn. exec. com., bd. dirs. Benrus Corp., Ridgefield, Conn., 1968-77; pres. Internat. Water Savs. Systems, Inc., West Bridgewater, Mass., 1977-87. Bd. dirs. Child Welfare League Am., 1957-76, pres., 1971-72; bd. dirs. Am. Parents Com., 1960-87; chmn. bd. Deya Archaeol. Mus. Found., Inc., 1971-80. Mem. Archaeol. Inst. Am. (life), Asia Soc., African Wildlife Soc., Explorers Club. Home: Green Valley Ariz. Died June 29, 1987.

HEIRES, JOHN HOPKINS, international banker, lawyer; b. Sioux City, Iowa, Sept. 19, 1918; s. Arthur Francis and Frances (Hopkins) H.; m. Alice Rea Chamberlin, May 14, 1955; children: John Hopkins, David Chamberlin, Gregory Norris. B.A. magna cum laude, Yankton Coll., 1939; J.D., Yale, 1946; M.Litt (Rhodes scholar), Oxford (Eng.) U., 1948. Bar: D.C. 1950, also U.S. Supreme Ct. 1950. With Dept. Justice, 1941; legal asst. Pillsbury, Madison & Sutro, San Francisco, 1949-50; assoc. Covington & Burling, Washington, 1950-53; asst. to chief estimates staff and estimates officer Bd. Nat. Estimates, 1953-57; sec. intelligence adv. com. Nat. Security Council, 1957-58; exec. sec. U.S. Intelligence Bd., 1958-62; dep. legis. programs coordinator AID, 1962, officer charge Pakistan affairs, 1962-64; moderator Naval Acad. Fgn. Affairs Conf., 1964; regional legal counsel, attache for embassy and U.S. AID missions to India, Nepal and Ceylon, New Delhi 1964-69; v.p., sec. Pvt. Investment Co. for Asia (PICA), S.A., Tokyo, 1969-72, Singapore, 1972-73; v.p., internat. sec. Marine Midland Bank, N.Y.C.; corporate sec. Marine Midland Internat. Corp., Marine Midland Overseas Corp., Marine Midland, Inc., 1973-76; adviser Fed. Res. Bank N.Y., 1976-86; mem. Nat. Com. on U.S.-China Relations; mem. U.S. ofcl. del. to ann. Asian devel. bank meetings, 1977-85. Note editor: Yale Law Jour, 1942; case editor, 1946. Served to lt. USNR, 1942-46. Mem. ABA, Internat., D.C. Bar Assns., Am. Soc. Internat. Law, Assn. Am. Rhodes Scholars, Fgn. Policy Assn., Asia Soc., Japan Soc., Yale Law Assn., English Speaking Union, Pi Kappa Delta, Phi Delta Phi. Clubs: Chevy Chase (Washington), Internat. (Washington); Yale (N.Y.C.), Nat. Press. (Washington); Delhi Gymkhana (New Delhi); Fgn. Corrs. (Tokyo), American (Tokyo); Tokyo Lawn and Tennis; American (Singapore). Home: Chevy Chase Md. Died July 2, 1988, buried Gate of Heaven Cemetery, Silver Spring, Md.

HEISE, HERMAN ALFRED, physician; b. Milw., Oct. 20, 1891; s. Paul Edgar and Dora (Tyre) H.; m. Eugenia May Rothrock, June 28, 1919; children: Paul Henry, Eugenia Cleves. AB, U. Wis., 1913; MD, Rush Med. Sch., 1917. Instr. chemistry DePaul U., Chgo., 1913-17; intern Bridewell Hosp., Chgo., 1917; pathologist Uniontown Hosp., Pa., 1919-34, Columbia Hosp., Milw., 1934-35; pvt. practice specializing in allergy Milw., from 1934. Chmn. first aid Milwaukee County chpt. ARC, 1936-59. Capt. Med. Res. Corps., U.S. Army, 1918-19. Mem. AMA (past chmn. com. medicolegal problems), Wis., Milwaukee County med. socs., Am. Coll. Allergists, Am. Soc. Clin. Pathology, Wis. Soc. Internal Medicine, Am. Acad. Forensic Scis., Aerospace Med. Assn., Flying Physicians Assn., Am. Interprofl. Inst. Home: Milwaukee Wis. †

HELANDER, LINN, engineering educator; b. Chgo., Aug. 28, 1891; s. Henry and Oline (Bredsvold) H.; m. Harriet Rose Stein, Feb. 21, 1920. BS, U. Ill., 1915. Steam engr. Pitts. Crucible Steel Co., Midland, Pa., 1915-17; mem. editorial staff Iron Age, N.Y.C., 1917-18; asst. engr. tests ordnance dept. U.S. Army, 1918-19; gen. engr. Westinghouse Electric & Mfg. co., Pitts. and Phila., 1919-25; sr. engr. United Gas Improvement Contracting Co., 1925-29; cons. engr. Phila. and Canton (N.C.), 1929-31; asst. prof. mech. engring. U. Pitts., 1931-33; cons. engr. Chgo., 1933-35; prof. Kans. State Coll., from 1935, head dept., 1935-37; Del. 3d World Power Conf., 1936. Contbr. articles to profl. jours. Fellow ASME (v.p. 1945-48), AAAS; mem. Am. Soc. Elec. Engring. (pres. sect 1949-50), Sci. Rsch. Soc. Am., Am. Acad. Polit. and Social Sci., Newcomen Soc., Franklin Inst., Am. Soc. heating and Air conditioning Engrs. (chmn. coms. air distbn. and roof ventilators), Nat. Geog. Soc., Kans. Engring. Soc. (exec. com. 1936-38), Manhattan C. of C., Country Club, Sigma Xi, Pi Tau Sigma, Tau Beta Pi, Sigma Tau, Phi Kappa Phi, Theta Chi. Home: Manhattan Kans. †

HELFFERICH, DONALD LAWRENCE, college chancellor; b. Bath, Pa., Apr. 24, 1898; s. William Ursinus and Nora Helena (Shuler) H.; m. Anna Alverda Knauer, July 14, 1925; children: Ilse An (Mrs. karl Heinz Munzinger), William Ursinus. Student, Mercersburg Acad., 1914-17; AB, Ursinus Coll., 1921, LLD, 1952; LLB, Yale U., 1924; LLD, Temple U., 1959. With legal dept., asst. store mgr. Gimbel Bros., Inc., Phila., 1925-36; dir. Ursinus Coll., from 1927, exec. v.p., 1936-58, pres., 1958-71, chancellor, from 1971; dir. Upper Darby (Pa.) Nat. Bank, 1936-63, exec. v.p., 1936-58; sr. v.p. Girard Trust Corn Exchange Bank, Phila., 1958-63; chmn. bd. French Creek Granite Co., 1948-68; bd. dirs. Presbyn. Minister Fund for Life Ins. Mem. Pa. Council Edn., 1940-54, Bd. Vocat. Rehab., 1944-54; co-chmn. citizens com. Hoover Report; trustee Phila. Coll. Osteophathy, 1936-48; bd. regents Mercersburg (Pa.) Acad.; Elder, dir. bd. pensions and relief local United Ch. of Christ ch. 2d lt. A.C., U.S. Army, 1917-19. Mem. Nat. Council Chs. Christ in Am. (v.p.-at-large 1960-63), Pa. Soc. SAR, Pa. German Folklore Soc. (fin. sec. 1956), Am. Legion, Am. Acad. Polit. Sci., University Club, Yale Club, Phi Delta Phi. Republican. Home: Pottstown Pa. Died Jan. 23, 1984, buried St. Peter's Ch., Collegeville, Pa.

HELLER, ELINOR RAAS, college trustee; b. San Francisco, Oct. 3, 1904; d. Alfred E. and Ida B. (Fisher) Raas; m. Edward Hellman Heller, May 26, 1925 (dec. Dec. 1961); children: Clarence E., Alfred E., Elizabeth. BA, Mills Coll., 1925, LLD, 1952. Trustee Mills Coll., 1932-42, 46-56, 57-68, life trustee, 1975-87; mem. adv. com. San Francisco State Coll., 1950-61; bd. regents U. Calif., 1961-76, chmn. bd., 1975-76; chmn. edn. sec. Calif. and Mass. war fin. div. U.S. Treasury Dept., 1941-45; mem. council arthritis and metabolic diseases NIH, 1949-52; mem. accrediting commn. sr. colls. and univs. Western Assn. Schs. and Colls.; bd. dirs. Stanford Bank, Palo Alto, Calif. Author (with David Magee) Bibliography of Grabhorn Press, 1915-1940, 1940. Mem. Dem. Nat. Com., Calif., 1944-52, also past mem. exec. com.; del. Dem. Nat. Conv., 1944, 48, 56; bd. dirs. Childrens Health Council Mid-Peninsula; trustee Sta. KQED, Inc., 1968-76, Heller Charitable and Ednl. Fund; mem. bd. visitors Drew Postgrad. Med. Sch., Hastings Coll. Law. Fellow Am. Acad. Arts and Scis.; mem. LWV (past dir. Calif., San Francisco and Palo Alto), Phi Beta Kappa. Died Aug. 15, 1987.

HELLER, WALTER WOLFGANG, economist, educator; b. Buffalo, Aug. 27, 1915; s. Ernst and Gertrude (Warmburg) H.; m. Emily K. Johnson, Sept. 16, 1938; (dec.); children: Walter P., Eric J., Kaaren Louise. A.B., Oberlin Coll., 1935, LL.D., 1964; M.A., U. Wis., 1938, Ph.D., 1941, LL.D., 1969; Litt. D., Kenyon Coll., 1965; LL.D., Ripon Coll., 1967, L.I. U., 1968; L.H.D., Coe Coll., 1967, Loyola U., 1970, Roosevelt U., 1976. Fiscal economist U.S. Treasury, 1942-46, cons., 1946-53; assoc. prof. econs. U. Minn., Mpls., 1946-50; prof. U. Minn., 1950-66, Regents prof. econs., 1966-86, emeritus, 1986-87, chmn. dept. econs., 1957-61; vis. lectr. U. Wis., 1947, U. Wash., 1950, Harvard, 1951; mem. internat. adv. bd. Banca Natonale del Lavoro, Rome, 1984-87; bd. dirs. Nat. City Bancorp., Mpls., The Germany Fund; chief internal fin. U.S. Mil. Govt., Germany, 1947-48; chmn. Council Econ. Advisers to the Pres., 1961-64; cons. UN, 1952-60, Minn. Dept. Taxation, 1955-60, NEA, 1958, Exec. Office of Pres., 1965-69, 74-77; tax adviser Gov. of Minn., 1955-60; mem. OECD Group of Fiscal Experts, 1964-68, chmn., 1966-68; cons. Congl. Budget Office, 1975-87; mem. Trilateral Commn., 1978-84; mem. econ. adv. bd. Time mag.; mem. bd. contbrs. Wall St. Jour.; chmn. econ. study group Ctr. Nat. Policy. Author: (with Clara Penniman) State Income Tax Administration, 1959, New Dimensions of Political Economy, 1966, (with Richard Ruggles and others) Revenue Sharing and the City, 1968, (with Milton Friedman) Monetary and Fiscal Policy, 1968; (with Milton Friedman) Economic Growth and Environmental Quality: Collision or Coexistence?, 1973, What's Right with Economics, 1975, The Economy: Old Myths and New Realities, 1976, Economic Policy for Inflation (in Reflections of America), 1981, Activist Government (in Challenge), 1986. Mem. Carnegie Commn. on the Future of Pub. Broadcasting, 1977-78; trustee Oberlin Coll., 1966-78, 85-87, German Marshall Fund, Coll. Retirement Equities Fund, 1968-72, Lupus Found. Am., Inc., chmn. nat. campaign com. Disting. fellow Am. Econ. Assn. (v.p. 1967-68, pres. 1974); fellow Am. Philos. Soc., Am. Acad. Arts and Scis.; mem. Internat. Mgmt. and Devel. Inst. (asso.), Nat. Bur. Econ. Research (dir., chmn. 1971-74, 82-83), Phi Beta Kappa, Beta Gamma Sigma, Alpha Kappa Psi. Club: Skylight (Mpls.). Home: Leucadia Calif. Died June 15, 1987, buried Beachwold, Silverdale, Wash.

HELLERSON, CHARLES BENEDICT, accounting firm executive; b. N.Y.C., Oct. 1, 1912; s. Charles E. W. and Helen (Lumley) H.; m. Hildegard M. Pietzsch, June 22, 1940; children: Robert K., Douglas C. AB, Princeton U., 1933. Exec. ptnr. Main Hurdman, N.Y.C., 1953-81; bd. dirs. Century Sports, Inc., N.J. Trustee emeritus, treas. Wardlaw-Hartridge (N.J.) Sch. Lt. comdr. USNR, 1940-45. Mem. AICPA, N.Y. State Soc. CPA's, N.J. Soc. CPA's, Nat. Assn. Accts., Am. Acctg. Assn., Princeton Club, Nassau Club Princeton. Home: Princeton N.J. Died May 24, 1985; cremated.

HELLMAN, YEHUDA, organization executive; b. Riga, Latvia, Feb. 10, 1920; s. Jacob and Sulamith Hellman; B.A., Am. U., Beirut, 1945; came to U.S., 1946, naturalized, 1951; m. Aviva Weinberg, Sept. 26, 1948; children: Dorlee, Jonathon. Fgn. corr. Jerusalem Post, 1942-46; head Jewish Telegraphic Agy. and Overseas News Agy., Paris, 1949; exec. vice chmn. Conf. Presidents of Maj. Am. Jewish Orgns., N.Y.C., 1959-86; lectr. Middle Eastern affairs, cons. to orgns. dealing with Middle East, 1946-86; mem. internat. steering com. World Conf. on Soviet Jewry, 1971-86. Home: N.Y.C. Died May 18, 1986.

HELLMUTH, PAUL FRANCIS, lawyer; b. Springfield, Ohio, Dec. 7, 1918; s. Andrew Alfred and Clara Elizabeth (Link) H. A.B., U. Notre Dame, 1940; LL.B., Harvard U., 1947; spl. courses, MIT, Harvard Grad. Sch. Public Adminstrn. Bar: Ohio 1947, Mass. 1952. Mem. Hale and Dorr, Boston, 1947-76, ptnr., 1952-56, sr. mng. ptnr., 1956-76; dir. Bessemer Securities Corp., United Screw & Bolt Corp., Robbins & Myers, Inc., W.R. Grace & Co., Pioneer Western Corp.; gen. ptnr. M.H.M. & Co. Ltd., Cleve.; chmn., chief exec. officer, dir. Computer Systems Am., Inc., Figgie Internat.; trustee Travelers Real Estate Investment Trust, Travelers Realty Income Investors. Overseer Boys' Club of Boston, Inc.; trustee Univ. Hosp., Boston Ballet, Mus. of Science, Boston, Boston Mus. Fine Arts; trustee, vice chmn. Boston U. Med. Center; trustee, fellow U. Notre Dame; bd. govs. New Eng. Aquarium; bd. overseers Children's Hosp., Med. Center; mem. law sch. council U. Notre Dame; trustee, corporate mem. Retina Found.; fellow Brandeis U. Served from pvt. to 2d lt. AUS, 1941-42; advanced to lt. col. USAAF, 1945. Decorated Legion of Merit, Bronze Star medal; French Croix de Guerre. Mem. Harvard Law Sch. Assn. (treas.). Clubs: Union (Boston), Harvard (Boston), Comml. (Boston), Somerset (Boston); Country (Springfield). Home: Cambridge Mass. Died Aug. 3, 1986; buried Springfield, Ohio.

HELLYER, GEORGE MACLEAN, consultant; b. Riverside, Ill., Feb. 28, 1912; s. Harold J. and Dorothy A. (Maclean) H.; m. Margaret H. Dawson, July 2, 1953; children by previous marriage: Marion M. Hellyer King, Harold J., Robert T., David R. Cert., U. Lausanne, Switzerland, 1935. Tea mfr. Hellyer and Co., Shizuoka, Japan, 1932-34; lectr. Com. to Defend Am. by Aiding Allies, 1939; dir. Western div. Fed. Union, Inc., 1940-41; mgr. Robert Anderson and Co., Hong Kong, 1946; mgr. Taipei, Taiwan, 1947-48, ptnr., 1949-52; pub. affairs officer and attache USIA (and predecessors), Saigon, Phnom Penh and Vientiane, 1952-54; dep. asst. dir. Washington, 1954-55; asst. dir. charge Far Eastern programs 1955-58; counsellor for pub. affairs Am. embassy, Tokyo, 1958-60, Am. Mission to European Communities, Brussels, Kinshasa, Dem. Republic of Congo, 1967-69; mem. U.S. del. NATO, Brussels, 1969-70; cons. 1970-88. Served from pvt. to capt. AUS, 1942-45. Decorated Bronze Star, Air medal; Mil. Cross U.K. Clubs: Hong Kong, Royal Hong Kong Yacht, Orcas Island Yacht. Home: Eastsound Wash. Died Mar. 12, 1988; cremated.

HELM, (JOHN) BLAKEY, lawyer, judge; b. Auburn, Ky., Oct. 18, 1889; s. Thomas Oliver and Nellie (Blakey) H.; m. Catherine S. Burge, Sept. 17, 1925; children: (Mrs. T. V. Hartnett Jr.), John Blakey, Joseph B., Margie C. (Mrs. Robert H. Van Meter Jr.). Student, Cumberland U., 1905-07; AB, Princeton U., 1910; JD, U. Mich., 1914. Bar: Ky. 1913. Practice law Bowling Green, Ky., 1913-14, Louisville, from 1914; judge chancery br. Jefferson Cir. Ct., from 1960; mem. Statute Revision Commn. Ky., 1948-54, Nat. Conf. Commrs. on Uniform State Laws, 1947-56, and from 1958. Mem. Ky. Nat. Park Commn., 1936-43. 1st lt. inf. U.S. Army, World War I; lt. col. air transport command, U.S. Army, World War II. Mem. ABA (mem. ho. of dels. 1941-43, 50-53, mem. bd. govs. 1954-57), Ky. Bar Assn. (v.p. 1921), Louisville Bar Assn., Am. Legion, Louisville Com. Fgn. Rels., Kiwanis Club, Pendennis Club. Democrat. Presbyterian. Home: Louisville Ky. †

HELM, HAROLD HOLMES, banker; b. Auburn, Ky., Dec. 9, 1900; s. Thomas Oliver and Nellie (Blakey) H.; m. Mary Rodes, Feb. 14, 1925; children: Eleanor (Mrs. John C. Ketcham Jr.), John. BA, Princeton U., 1920; DCS (hon.), NYU, 1960; LLD, Hampden-Sydney Coll., 1962, Centre Coll., Ky., 1962, Bloomfield Coll., 1967; DCL, U. of the South, 1963. Clk. credit dept. Chem. Nat. Bank (name changed to Chem. Bank & Trust Co.), N.Y.C., 1920-26; asst. cashier Chem. Nat. Bank (name changed to Chem. Bank & Trust Co.), 1926-28, asst. v.p., 1928-29, v.p., 1929-46, 1st v.p., 1946-47, pres., 1947-55, also bd. dirs.; pres. Chem. Corn Exchange Bank (merger Chem. Bank & Trust Co. and Corn Exchange Bank), 1955, chmn. bd., 1955-59; chmn. bd. Chem. Bank N.Y. Trust Co. (merger Chem. Corn Exchange Bank and N.Y. Trust Co.), 1959-66, chmn. exec. com., 1966—; former chmn. and dir. Chem. Internat. Fin., Ltd.; former pres., bd. dirs. Chem. Internat. Banking Corp.; bd. dirs. Franklin Book Programs, Inc., Colgate Palmolive Co., F.W. Woolworth Co., Bethlehem Steel Corp., Cummins Engine Co., Inc., Equitable Life Assurance Soc. U.S., CPC Internat., Home Ins. Co., Western Elec. Co., Associated Dry Goods Corp., Lord and Taylor, The Home Indemnity Co., McDonnell-Douglas Corp., Uniroyal. Trustee Ky. Spindletop Research Ctr., Ida Cason Callaway Found., Hamilton, Ga., N.Y. Heart Assn., Presbyn. Hosp.-Columbia Presbyn. Med. Ctr., N.Y.C., Woodrow Wilson Found., Commn. on Ecumenical Mission and Relations, United Presbyn. Ch. U.S.A.; trustee, chmn. fin. com., mem. exec. com., curriculum, hon. degrees, ground and bldgs. coms. Princeton U.; mem. bd. govs. N.Y.C. Nat. Shrines Assns., Inc.; chmn. exec. com. Fed. Hall Meml. Assns., Inc.; mem. adv. bd. Hoover Instn. Decorated Royal Order St. Olav (Norway). Mem. N.Y. So. Soc., Nat. Indsl. Conf. Bd. (trustee, chmn.), Am. Inst. Banking (past chmn. adv. council N.Y. chpt.), Pilgrims Soc. U.S., Acad. Polit. Sci., U.S. Srs. Golf Assn., Campus Club, Economic Club, Filson Club, Links, Montclair Golf Club, Nat. Golf Links (trustee), University Club (past pres.), Princeton Club, Bond Club, Kentuckians Club. Presbyterian. Home: Montclair N.J. Died Nov. 19, 1985.

HELMS, CHARLES BRUMM, JR., manufacturing company executive; b. Phila., Nov. 5, 1922; s. Charles Brumm and Eva (Jagger) H.; m. Sarajane Fink, Dec. 20, 1947 (dec. June 1981); children: Jeffrey Charles, Janet Leslie; m. Mary-Anne Hehir, Dec. 11, 1982. Cert., Lafayette Coll., 1944; BS, U. Pa., 1950. CPA, Pa. Mem. audit staff Arthur Young & Co., Phila., 1950-52; asst. dir. fin. City of Phila., 1952-56; group controller Warner Lambert Pharm. Co., Morris Plains, N.J., 1956-61; v.p. fin., bd. dirs. Warner Co., Phila., 1961-64, Ultronic Systems Corp., Morristown (N.J.) and N.Y.C., 1964-67, Crompton & Knowles Corp., from 1967; bd. dirs. Crompton & Knowles Overseas Corp., Crompton & Knowles Can. Ltd., Kem Mfg. Corp., So. Mill Creek Products Corp. Bd. dirs. Crompton & Knowles Found. With U.S. Army, 1942-46, ETO. Mem. Fin. Execs. Inst., University Club. Republican. Presbyterian. Home: Princeton N.J. Deceased.

HEMEON, WESLEY C. L., environmental engineer; b. Leominster, Mass., Dec. 26, 1903; s. Chester Orlando and Edith (Kaiser) H.; m. Catherine Daunt, July 12, 1937. BSChemE, MIT, 1926, MSChemE, 1927; post-grad., Harvard U., 1936. Registered profl. engr., Pa. Design engr. Mass. Depts. Labor and Industry, Boston, 1936-43; Mellon Inst. sr. fellow, engring. dir. Indsl. Hygiene Found., Pitts., 1943-56; dir. Hemeon Assocs., Pitts., 1956-88; lectr. Harvard U. Grad. Sch. Engring., 1940-43; lectr. U. Pitts. Sch. Engring., 1945-50, adj. assoc. prof. Grad. Sch. Pub. Health, 1958-66. Author: Plant and Process Ventilation, 2d edit., 1963. Mem. ASME, Air Pollution Control Assn. (Frank A. Chambers award 1969), Am. Indsl. Hygiene Assn. (bd. dirs. 1944-48), Am. Inst. Chemists, Assn. Iron and Steel Engrs., Am. Acad. Environ. Engrs. (diplomate), University Club. Home: Pittsburgh Pa. Died Jan. 4, 1988; buried Indpls.

HENDEL, SAMUEL, educator; b. N.Y.C., July 6, 1909; s. Jodah and Leah (Gerber) H.; m. Clara Hoch, May 14, 1932; children: Linda Susan, Steven. BSS cum laude, CCNY, 1936; PhD, Columbia U., 1948. Bar: N.Y. 1931. Pvt. practice N.Y.C., 1931-41; legal cons. 1941-84; faculty CCNY, 1941-70, prof. polit. sci., 1957-70, chmn. dept., 1957-62, chmn. Russian Areas Grad. Program, 1960-70, ombudsman, 1969-70; prof. Trinity Coll., Hartford, Conn., 1970-78, chmn. dept., 1970-73; vis. prof. govt. grad. faculty Columbia U., 1958-60, 1962; vis. prof. comparative govt. and internat. relations claremont Grad. Sch., 1962; vis. prof. Grad. Ctr., U. City N.Y., 1975, U. Conn. Law Sch., 1975; adj. prof. NYU, 1979, 80; vis. prof. Barnard Coll., 1980, 81, 81-82. Author: Charles Evans Hughes and The Supreme Court, 1951; co-author, co-editor: The U.S.S.R. After 50 Years: Promise and Reality, 1967; editor: The Politics of Confrontation, 1971, The Soviet Crucible, 5th edit., 1980; co-editor: Basic Issues of American Democracy, 6th edit., 1970, editor 7th and 8th edits., 1973, 76. Chmn. acad. freedom com. ACLU, 1959-60, 66-73, bd. dirs., 1967-77, vice chmn., 1974-76; chmn. commn. on internat. affairs Am. Jewish Congress, 1959-61. Ford Faculty fellow, 1953-54; Inter-Univ. Com. Travel Grants grantee, 1957. Mem. Am. Polit. Sci. Assn. (council 1965-67), Am. Assn. Advancement Slavic Studies, Phi Beta Kappa (pres. Gamma chpt. 1960-61). Home: New York N.Y. Died Aug. 27, 1984.

HENDERSON, ALGO DONMYER, educator; b. Solomon, Kans., Apr. 26, 1897; s. Calvert Columbus and Ella Cora (Donmyer) H.; m. Anne G. Cristy, 1923 (dec.); children: Joanne E. (Mrs. James Reece Pratt III), Philip C.; m. 2d, Jean C. Glidden, 1963; 1 dau., Carol Rosenberg. Student, Kans. Wesleyan Coll. Commerce, 1914-15, Georgetown U., 1917-18; JD, U. Kans., 1921; postgrad., U. Chgo., 1923; MBA, Harvard U., 1928; LLD (hon.), Antioch Coll., 1948, Olivet Coll., 1959, Fenn Coll., 1963, Cleve. State U., 1968; LHD (hon.), Keuka Coll., 1950. CPA, Kans.; bar: Kans. 1922. Tchr. pub. schs., Kans., 1915-17, U. Kans., 1920-24; mem. faculty Antioch Coll., Yellow Springs, Ohio, 1925-48, assoc. prof., prof., bus. mgr., dean, exec. v.p., acting pres. and pres., 1935-48; assoc. dir. Temporary Commn. on Need for a State Univ. in N.Y. State, 1948-49; assoc. commr. of edn. charge higher, profl. edn. State of N.Y., 1948-50; prof. higher edn., dec. com. coll. rels. U. Mich., 1950-67, emeritus prof., 1967-88, founder, dir. Ctr. for Study of Higher Edn., 1957-66; rsch. educator Ctr. for R&D in Higher Edn., U. Calif., Berkeley, 1966-77; mem. Mich. Commn. Coll. Accreditation, 1950-64, Pres.'s Commn. Higher Edn., 1946-48, Exchange of Disting. Persons with Japan, 1956; mem. commn. ednl. orgns. NCCJ; cons. State of Conn., 1949-50, United Coll. Hong Kong, 1956, U. Ala. 1967-68, U. N.Mex., 1968, 70, UNESCO, 1969, Ford. Found. in Chile, 1970, Calif. Tchrs. Assn., 1974, Antioch Coll., 1974. Author books including: Utilizing Liberal Education, 1944, Policies and Practices in Higher Education, 1960, The Role of the Governing Board, 1967, La Educacion Superior en los Estados Unidos, 1968, Training University Administrators (English and French edits.), 1970, The Innovative Spirit, 1970, (with Jean G. Henderson) Higher Education in America, 1974, MS Goes to College, 1975; editor: Higher Education in Tomorrow's World, 1968; contbr. articles to jours. Mem. com. on selection scholars Kennedy-King Found.; bd. dirs., sec. bd. Internat. Hospitality Ctr., San Francisco; pres. Orinda-Moraga Dem. Club, 1976. 2d lt. U.S. Army, 1917-19. Recipient Disting. Alumnus award U. Kans., 1948, Sesquicentennial medal U. Mich., 1967, Honor award Colloquium on Higher Edn., 1971. Mem. ACLU, Assn. Higher Edn., Am. Soc. Pub. Adminstrn., Alpha Kappa Lambda. Unitarian. Home: Orinda Calif. Deceased.

HENDERSON, JAMES MICHAEL, electric utility executive; b. Detroit, Sept. 4, 1922; m. Joan Kuhns; children: Michael, Kathleen, John, Jan, Timothy. BSEE, U. Ill. Systems studies engr. Detroit Edison Co., 1947-53; electric utility application engr. GE Co., 1953-63; v.p. Middle West Services Co., 1963-68; dir. systems engring. div. Commonwealth Assocs., 1968-70; v.p. San Diego Gas & Electric Co., 1970-78; pres., chief exec. officer Central La. Electric Co., Pineville, from 1978; bd. dirs. Guaranty Bank & Trust Co., Alexandria, Va., La. Southeastern Electric Exchange. Author numerous tech. publs. Bd. dirs. St. Frances Cabrini Hosp., Alexandria; pres. Atakaspas council Boy Scouts Am., Alexandria. Ensign USN, 1943-46, PTO. Home: San Diego Calif. Died Nov. 8, 1985; cremated.

HENDERSON, LEON, economist; b. Millville, N.J., May 26, 1895; s. Chester Bowen and Lida C. (Beebe) H.; m. Myrlie Hamm, July 25, 1925; children: Myrlie Beebe, Lyn, Leon. AB, Swarthmore Coll., 1920; post-grad., U. Pa., 1920-22. Instr. Wharton Sch. U. Pa., 1919-22; asst. prof. econ. Carnegie Inst. Tech., 1922-23; dep. sec. Commonwealth of Pa., 1924-25; dir. consumer credit rsch. Russell Sage Found., N.Y.C., 1925-34; econ. adviser, dir. rsch. and planning div. NRA, 1934-35; mem. Nat. Indsl. Recovery Bd., 1934-35; econ. adviser U.S. Senate com. on mfrs. 1935; economist Dem. Nat. Campaign Com., 1936; cons. economist Works Progress Adminstrn., 1936-38; exec. sec. Temporary Nat. Econ. Com., 1938-39; commr. SEC, 1939-41; commr. Adv. Com., Council of Nat. Def., 1940; adminstr. Office Price Adminstrn. and Civilian Supply, 1941, Office Price Adminstrn.; mem. Supply Priorities and Allocation Bd., dir. Div. Civilian Supply O.P.M., 1941-42; apptd. dir. civilian supply div. War Prodn. Bd., 1942; pres. Am. Leduc Uranium Corp., 1956-57, Doeskin Products Inc., 1957-58; cons. economist 1959-86. Contbr. articles to mags. Capt. Ordnance Dept., U.S. Army, 1917-19. Mem. Am. Econ. Assn., Masons, Nat. Press Club, Delta Upsilon. Democrat. Home: New York N.Y. Died Oct. 19, 1986.

HENDERSON, LOY WESLEY, educator, foreign service officer; b. Rogers, Ark., June 28, 1892; s. George Milton and Mary May (Davis) H.; m. Elise Marie Heinrichson, Dec. 3, 1930. AB, Northwestern U., 1915, LLD, 1953; student, Denver U. Law Sch., 1917-18, D.Pub. Service, 1953; LLD, U. Ark., Bates Coll., 1957, Wayne U., 1962; D.Pub. Adminstrn., Southwestern Coll., 1959. Mem. Inter-Allied Commn. to Germany for repatriation of prisoners of war 1919; mem. ARC Commn. to Western Russia and Baltic States, 1919-20; in charge ARC, Germany, 1920-21; vice consul Dublin, 1922, Queenstown, 1923; with div. Eastern European Affairs Dept. of State, 1930; 3d sec. of ligation Riga, Kovno and Tallinn, 1927, 2d sec., 1929; with div. Eastern European Affairs Dept. of State, 1930; 2d sec. Am. Embassy, Moscow, 1934, 1st sec., 1935, 1st sec. and intermittently chargé d'affaires, 1935-38; asst. chief div. European Affairs Dept. of State, 1938; insp. diplomatic missions and consulate offices 1942-43; counselor of embassy and chargé d'affaires Moscow and Kuibyshev, 1942; E.E. and M.P. to Iraq 1943-45; dir. Near Eastern and African Affairs Dept. of State, 1945-48; A.E. and P. to India and E.E. and M.P. to Nepal 1948, became A.E. and P. to Iran, 1951, dep. under sec. of state for adminstrn., 1955; bd. cons. Nat. War Coll., 1957-60; chief of mission to arrange for opening new diplomatic and consular establishments in newly emerging countries in Africa 1960, ret.; prof. internat. rels., dir. Ctr. for Diplomacy and Fgn. Policy Am. U., 1961-68; appointed U.S. career ambassador, 1956; del. 17th Internat. Geol. Congress, Moscow, 1937, Baghdad Pact Conf., Iran, 1956; Am. mem. Suez Com., Cairo, Suez Canal Conf., London and Cairo, 1956; mem. U.S. del. 2d Suez Canal Conf., London, 1956; Am. observer Baghdad Pact Meeting, 1957. Bd. dirs. Am. Nat. Red Cross, 1957. Decorated Insignia of Imperial Order Homayoun, 1st class (Iran); Grand Cross Royal Order George I (Greece); comdr. de l'Ordre de la Republic of Tunisia; recipient award of merit Northwestern Alumni Assn., 1952, Disting. Service award Dept. of State, 1954, Pres.'s award for Disting. Fed. Civilian Service, 1958. Mem. Am. Fgn. Service Assn. (pres. 1956), Washington Inst. Fgn. affairs (pres. 1961-73, chmn. bd. from 1973), Coun. on Fgn. Affairs, Metropolitan Club, Cosmos Club, Delta Tau Delta, Phi Delta Phi. Home: Washington D.C. Deceased.

HENEMAN, HARLOW JAMES, management consultant; b. Minn.; s. Herman and Alice (Burfield) H.; m. Avis Louise Dayton; children: Joyce, Burfield. A.B., U. Minn.; M.A., U. Calif.; Ph.D., U. London. Assoc. prof. polit. sci. U. Mich.; editorial adviser Oxford U. Press; mgmt. analyst U.S. Bur. Budget; U.S. Mil Govt., Berlin; cons. U.S. rep. on U.N.A.E.C., Dept. State (and pvt. firms); spl. asst. to asst. sec. for occupied areas, dir. mgmt. staff Dept. State; formerly gen. partner firm Cresap, McCormick & Paget; pvt. cons.; Mem. bus. and arts com. N.Y. Bd. Trade, 1966-69; Pres. faculty rev. bd. U.S. Mil. Acad., 1967-68; pres. Cresap, McCormick and Paget Found., 1967-68; chmn. commn. on policies and operations Nat. Endowment for Arts, 1972-73; dir. Sci. Am., Inc.; cons. Mayo Clinic-Found., 1969-83. Author: (with others) Financing Higher Education, 1960-70, 1959, Professional Practices in Management Consulting, 1959, The Arts; A Central Element of a Good Society, 1965, The Arts: Planning for Change, 1966, Readings in Financial Analysis, 1970; Bd. editors: (with others) Financial Analysts Jour, 1964-67; Contbr. to (with others) profl. jours. in law, finance, health and edn. Bd. dirs. Salk Inst. Biology, 1960-61, Am. Symphony Orch. League, 1967-69; trustee Nat. Planning Assn., 1963-70, New Coll., 1966-69, Ringling State Mus. Art, 1971-80, Sarasota Meml. Hosp. Found., 1976-83, Mote Marine Lab., 1978-83 , Selby Bot. Gardens. Served with M.I. Service War Dept. Gen. Staff. Recipient Outstanding Citizen of Year award Fla. Library Assn., 1977, Disting. Layman of Yr. Fla. Med. Assn., 1982. Club: Field (Sarasota, Fla.). Home: Sarasota Fla. Died July 3, 1983.

HENKIN, DANIEL ZWIE, association executive; b. Washington, May 10, 1923; s. Zalmen and Sadie (Weinberg) H.; m. Hannah Ronen, May 19, 1957; children—Doron, Leora, Tamar. B.A., U. Calif. at Berkeley, 1948. Asst. editor, then editor Jour. Armed Forces, 1948-65; dir. ops. Office Asst. Sec. Def. Pub. Affairs, 1965-67; dep. asst. sec. def. 1967-69, asst. sec. def. for pub. affairs, 1969-73; v.p. for pub. information Air Transport Assn., Washington, 1973-87; lectr. Nat. War Coll., Indsl. Coll. Armed Forces. Served with USCGR, 1942-45. Recipient Meritorious Civilian Service medal sec. def.; Distinguished Pub. Service award Dept. Def. Club: Nat. Press (Washington). Home: Philadelphia Pa. Died Apr. 7, 1987; buried Arlington National Cemetery.

HENKIND, PAUL, ophthalmologist, educator; b. N.Y.C., Dec. 12, 1932; s. Samuel Joseph and Sadie (Weitzen) H.; m. Ellen G. Bogen, June 9, 1956; children: Steven Joseph, Karen Grace, Jennifer Faith; m. Janice V. Benjamin, May 22, 1977; 1 son, Aaron Samuel. B.A., Columbia U., 1955; M.D. (Fight for Sight student fellow), N.Y. U., 1959, M.S. in Ophthalmology, 1964; Ph.D. in Pathology, U. London, Eng., 1965. Diplomate: Am. Bd. Ophthalmology. Intern Henry Ford Hosp., Detroit, 1959-60; resident N.Y. U. (Bellevue Hosp.), N.Y.C., 1960-63; NIH spl. fellow Inst. Ophthalmology, London, 1963-65; asst. prof. ophthalmology N.Y. U., 1965-68, assoc. prof., 1968-70; prof., chmn. dept. ophthalmology Albert Einstein Coll. Medicine, Bronx, N.Y., 1970-86, Frances De Jur prof.; dir. ophthalmology Montefiore Hosp. and Med. Center, Bronx, from 1970; pres. Med. Dialogues, Inc., 1977-86 ; cons. N.Y. Zool. Soc., New Rochelle Hosp., Peninsula Gen. Hosp., Hackensack Hosp. Assn.; mem. sci. adv. bd. Fight for Sight, 1975-86 ; mem. vision research and tng. com. Nat. Eye Inst., NIH, 1972-76; cons., 1972-86 , Harvey Breslin Meml. lectr., 1975, Seymour Roberts Meml. lectr., 1975, G. Victor Simpson lectr., 1975, Royal Coll. Physicians and Surgeons (Can.) lectr., 1977, Alan Firman lectr., 1979; Paul Chandler lectr. Harvard U., 1979; A.A. Ticho lectr., Israel, 1979; Alex Krill lectr. Chgo Opthal. Soc., 1980; Mark Schoenberg lectr. N.Y. Soc. Clin. Ophthalmolo, 1983; R. Stein lectr. Tel Aviv U., 1983; other named Lectureships; vis. prof. Royal Soc. Medicine, London, 1981. Author: (with others) The Retinal Circulation, 1971, Manual for Eye Examination and Diagnosis, 1975, 2d edit., 1981, Diagnosis and Management of Open Angle Glaucoma, 1977, Compendium of Ophthalmology, 1983; editor: Physicians Desk Reference for Ophthalmology, 1972-86 , Ophthalmic Seminars, 1976-77, Ophthalmology; mem. editorial bd.: Investigative Ophthalmology, 1968-72, Survey Ophthalmology, 1970-86 , Am. Jour. Ophthalmology, 1974-79, Neuroradiology, 1976-86 , AMA Archives of Ophthalmology, 1976-79, Perspectives in Ophthalmology, 1978-81, Jour. Dermatol. Surgery and Oncology, 1978-86 , Ophthalmologica, 1983-86 ; sect. editor systemic ophthalmology: Duane's Clin. Ophthalmology, 1976-86 ; ophthalmic editor: Marcel Dekker, Inc, 1976-79; contbr. articles to profl. jours. USPHS grantee, 1968-80. Fellow A.C.S., N.Y. Acad. Sci.; mem. Assn. Research Vision and Ophthalmology (chmn. sect. pathology 1968, chmn. sect. anatomy and pathology 1969, sec.-treas. 1976-81), Am. Acad. Ophthalmology (asso. sec. continuing edn. 1974-79, chmn. com. ophthalmic pathology 1976-80, editor 1980-86), N.Y. Soc. Clin. Ophthalmology (chmn. program 1972-73, v.p. 1974-75, pres. 1975-76), Manhattan Ophthalmology Soc. (sec.-treas. 1972-74), AAAS, N.Y. Acad. Medicine, Ophthal. Soc. U.K., French Ophthal. Soc., Peruvian Ophthal. Soc. (hon.), Can. Ophthal Soc. (hon.), Colombian Ophthalmology Soc., Opthal Soc. N.Z. (hon.). Home: Bronx N.Y. Died June 1986.

HENNE, FRANCES ELIZABETH, library science educator; b. Springfield, Ill., Oct. 11, 1906; d. J.Z. and Laura (Taylor) H. AB, U. Ill., 1929, MA, 1934; BS, Columbia U., 1935; PhD, U. Chgo., 1949. Mem. libr. staff Springfield (Ill.) Pub. Libr., 1930-34, N.Y. Pub. Libr., 1935, N.Y. State Tchrs. Coll., Albany, 1935-38; libr. U. High Sch., U. Chgo., 1939-42; instr. N.Y. State Coll. for Tchrs., 1937-38, 39, U. Chgo. Grad. Libr. Sch.,

1939-46; asst. prof. Grad. Libr. Sch., U. Chgo., 1946-49, assoc. prof., 1949-54, assoc. dean, dean of students, 1947-50, acting dean, 1951-52; assoc. prof. Sch. Libr. Svc., Columbia U., N.Y.C., prof., prof. emeritus; vis. prof. U. Minn., summer 1950, Rutgers U., summer 1954. Author: Youth Communication and Libraries, 1949, Planning Guide for the High School Library Program, 1951; contbr. articles to profl. jours. Mem. N.Y. State Regents Adv. Coun. on Librs., 1964-74, com. on libr. devel. N.Y. State Commr. Edn., 1967-70. Recipient Carnegie fellowship, 1938, Lippincott award, 1963, Beta Phi Mu award, 1978. Mem. ALA (spl. centennial citation 1976, Pres.'s award 1979), Am. Assn. Sch. Librs. (nat. pres. 1948-49). Home: Springfield Ill. Died Dec. 21, 1985; buried Oak Ridge Cemetery, Springfield, Ill.

HENNELLY, MARK M., railroad company executive, lawyer. Bar: Mo. Pvt. practice St. Louis; judge St. Louis; with Mo. Pacific R.R. Co., subs. Mo. Pacific Corp., St. Louis, from 1957, gen. solicitor, 1960-62, v.p., gen. counsel, 1962-77, sr. v.p., gen. counsel, from 1977; bd. dirs., exec. v.p. parent co., v.p. law Tex. & Pacific Ry. Co.; bd. dirs. Chgo. & Eastern R.R. Co. Contbr. articles to various publs. in field; patentee. Recipient various awards Dept. Interior. Mem. Am. Inst. Mining, AIME (past chmn. Extractive Metallurgy, past v.p.), Metall. Soc. Am. (past pres.), AAAS, Soc. Mining Engrs., Sigma Xi. Mormon. Deceased.

HENNINGS, JOSEPHINE SILVA, government official; b. St. Louis; d. Francois P. and Mary Josephine (Barrick) Silva; m. Breen Halpin (dec.); children: Breen, Joan; m. Thomas C. Hennings Jr. (dec.). BA, Washington U., St. Louis; postgrad. in polit. sci., George Washington U. News reporter, editor Sta. KMOX, St. Louis, Sta. KGU, Honolulu; news analyst, dir. radio Civil Def., P.R. and the Virgin Islands; fgn. corr. St. Louis Globe-Democrat, CBS, Caribbean and Pacific; columnist, feature writer Honolulu Advertiser; feature editor St. Louis Star Times; editor Inter-Am. Affairs, USIA, State Dept.; sr. radio officer UN; news reporter, editor Sta. WINS, N.Y.C.; news reporter, editor, TV panelist ABC; dir. pub. relations V.I. Hotel, St. Thomas; editor U.S. Comptrollers Office, St. Thomas; fed. govt. liaison officer Dept. Def., Washington. Named Top Am. Woman Broadcaster in internat. field UN, Top Am. Woman Broadcaster in internat. field U.S. Dept. Labor. Mem. Am. Women in Radio and TV, Washington Press Club, Nat. Press Club, Overseas Press Club. Home: Washington D.C. Died Oct. 5, 1985.

HENRY, DONALD LEE, banker; b. Evansville, Ind., Jan. 25, 1918; s. Robert D. and Mary A. (Swope) H.; m. Mary Lou Hess, Dec. 24, 1941; children: Judith Ann, Don Richard. B.S., Purdue U., 1939, M.S., 1941, Ph.D., 1947; postgrad., U. Chgo., U. Chgo., 1946. Agrl. economist Fed. Res. Bank St. Louis, 1947-54; asst. cashier Fed. Res. Bank St. Louis (Louisville br.), 1954-56, cashier, 1957, mgr., 1957; v.p. Fed. Res. Bank St. Louis, 1957-68, sr. v.p., 1969-83. Past pres. Old Ky. Home council Boy Scouts Am., past pres. Ky.-Tenn. area, also mem. nat. exploring com. Served to lt. col. USAR. Mem. Sigma Xi, Alpha Zeta. Club:, (). Home: Louisville Ky. Died June 6, 1987, buried McCutchanville (Ind.) Cemetery.

HENRY, NELSON B(OLLINGER), professional society executive; b. Cape Girardeau, Mo., Feb. 22, 1883; s. Nelson B. and Lucretia (Thompson) H.; m. Nettie Winston, June 24, 1914; 1 child, Nelson Winston. PhB, Cen. Coll., 1901; AM, U. Okla., 1917; PhD, U. Chgo., 1923. Tchr. pub. schs. Mo., 1902-06; high sch. prin. Bloomfield, Mo., 1906-08, Poplar Bluff, 1908-14; supt. schs. Jenks, Okla., 1917-19; prof. edn. Lewis Inst., Chgo., 1923-24, 27-28; sec. com. on fin. Chgo. Bd. Edn., 1924-27; prof. edn. U. Chgo., 1928-48; sec., mem. editorial com. Elem. Sch. Jour., Sch. Rev., 1940-51; sec. Nat. Soc. for Study Edn., 1941-59, editor Yearbooks, from 1941. Mem. Am. Ednl. Rsch. Assn., Am. Assn. Sch. Adminstrs. Home: Chicago Ill. †

HEPBRON, JAMES M(ERRITT), criminologist; b. Chesterton, Md., Feb. 17, 1891; s. Archer Maxwell and Lida Pleasanton (Merritt) H.; m. Helen Lumianski, Dec. 23, 1940. Grad., Balt. City Coll., 1910; LLB, U. Md., 1913; studied penal and police methods and compilation of crime stats., Europe, 1927-28; LLD, Washington Coll., Chestertown, Md., 1930; DSc (hon.), Temple U., 1934; LHD, Md. Coll., 1939. Pub. law books 1913-17; mem. Fosdick commn. on tng. camps, 1917-19, U.S. Interdepartmental Bd., 1919-22; asst. dir. Balt. Criminal Justice Commn., 1922-24, mng. dir., 1924-53; instr. in criminology Johns Hopkins U., 1926-28; cons. Pa. State Crime Commn., 1928; mng. dir. Community Fund, Balt., 1929-54; chmn. parole bd. and dir. Dept. Parole and Probation, Balt.; police commr. City of Balt., 1955-61; cons., lectr. Redpath Bur.; mem. Md. Commn. on Prevention and Treatment Juvenile Deliquency, 1956; adminstrv. asst. U.S. Crime Com. (Kefauver Com.). Contbr. editorial page Balt. Evening Sun, articles and monographs including Probation and Penal Treatment in Baltimore, Crime Commissions, Their Origin, Purpose and Accomplishments. Mem. Gov.'s Adv. Com. on Unemployment Relief, Gov.'s Com. on Inferior Cts., 1939, com. on arrangements of Atty. Gen.'s Conf. on Crime, Md. Commn. on Inter-state Goodwill Industries; cons. dir. Phila. Criminal Justice Assn.; chmn. fin. com. Am. Prison Congress, 1931; cons. Washington Criminal Justice Assn.; pres. Nat. Assn. of Crime Commn. Execs., 1939; mem. Md. Youth Commn., Mayor's Com. on Recreation, Balt., bd. Balt. Coun. of Social Agys; chmn. Charities Endorsement Com., Balt. Coun. of Social Agys; dir. Community Placement Bur. of Balt.,; chmn. adv. com. Md. State Employment Svc.; chmn. Md. Commn. Juvenile Delinquency, 1941-43; chmn. Balt. Youth Commn.; mem. gen. staff Civilian Def. Protective Svcs., State Bd. of Welfare; Mayor's Jail Com.; trustee Morgan Coll.; past pres. Md. Conf. Social Work. Mem. Maryland Club. Democrat. Home: Baltimore Md. †

HEPP, MAYLON HAROLD, philosopher, educator; b. Mpls., Aug. 30, 1913; s. Maylon H. and Helen (Fink) H.; m. Anne Woodbury, June 9, 1936; children: Barbara (Mrs. Michael K. Tandy), Susanna (Mrs. Thomas A. Bullard), David Maylon. AB, Oberlin Coll., 1934, MA, 1936; PhD, Brown U., 1939; postgrad., Stanford U., 1959, U. Hawaii, 1964, Ohio State U., 1966. Instr. philosophy Brown U., 1939-41; instr., then asst. prof. Haverford Coll., 1941-45, asst. dir. grad. reconstrn. and relief tng., 1943-45; assoc. prof., chmn. dept. Park Coll., Parkville, Mo., 1945-46; faculty Denison U., 1946-86, prof., 1950-73, chmn. dept., 1954-57, 61-71, Maria Teresa Barney prof., 1965-73, prof. emeritus, 1973-86; vis. assoc. prof. Kent State U., 1948; Fulbright participant Inst. Chinese Civlization, Thughai U., Taiwan, 1962; participant 4th East-West Philosophers' Conf., U. Hawaii, 1964, 5th Conf., 1969; vice chmn. Western Conf. on Teaching Philosophy, 1964-66; rsch. assoc. U. Calif., Berkeley, vis. scholar San Francisco State Coll., 1966-67. Author: thinking Things Through, 1956; co-editor: The Range of Philosophy, 1964. Dir. Brasstown Vol. Work Camp Am. Friends Svc. Com., 1945, mem. adv. com. student work, 1945, regional com., 1951-56; pres. Granville (Ohio) Council Chs., 1958. Jubilee fellow Brown U., 1938-39, Gt. Lakes Colls. Assn. faculty fellow, 1966-67. Mem. Am. Philos. Assn., Ohio Philos. Assn. (sec.-treas. 1953-57), Assn. for Asian Studies, Am. Assn. for Chinese tudies (editor Newsletter 1967-75, 1st v.p. 1972-74, pres., chmn. bd. 1974-76, adv. council 1976—), Phi Beta Kappa. Home: Granville Ohio. Died Dec. 6, 1986.

HEPTING, GEORGE HENRY, plant pathologist, forester; b. Bklyn., Sept. 1, 1907; s. George and Lena (Schuler) H.; m. Anna Johnson Love, Mar. 17, 1934; children—George Carleton, John Bartram. B.S., Cornell U., 1929, Ph.D., 1933. Instr. plant pathology Cornell U., Ithaca, N.Y., 1929-30; forest pathologist USDA, various locations, 1931-61; prin. research scientist U.S. Forest Service, Asheville, N.C., 1962-71, chief plant pathologist, 1971; adj. prof. plant pathology and forestry N.C. State U., Raleigh, 1971-88. Author: Diseases of Forest and Shade Trees of the U.S., 1971. Recipient Superior Service award USDA, 1954, Merit award, 1967. Fellow Soc. Am. Foresters (Barrington Moore award 1963), Nat. Acad. Scis., Am. Phytopath. Soc.; mem. Forest History Soc. (Fred Weyerhauser award 1974). Clubs: Am. Bus., Country of Asheville. Home: Asheville N.C. Died Apr. 29, 1988; buried Lewis Meml. Pk., Ashville, N.C.

HERBERT, CHARLES JEROME, distilling executive; b. Balt., Oct. 4, 1926; s. Phillip Benjamin and Ann (Loughran) H.; m. Annalee Wells, Nov. 12, 1955; children—Charles, John, Robert, Elizabeth. B.S., U. Md., 1951; grad. Advanced Mgmt. Program, Harvard, 1971. With Heublein Co., various locations, from 1958; v.p., gen. sales mgr. Heublein Co. (Smirnoff Beverage and Import Co. div.), Hartford, Conn., 1971-72; pres. Theodore Hamm Co. div. Heublein Co., St. Paul, 1972-74; pres. Arrow Liquor Co. div. Heublein Inc., Hartford, from 1974, Heublein Spirit Sales Cos., from 1975. Served as sgt. AUS, 1945-46. Roman Catholic. Clubs: Wampanoag Country, Hartford Golf. Home: West Hartford Conn.

HERBERT, EDWARD, molecular neurobiologist, educator; b. Hartford, Conn., Jan. 28, 1926; s. Nathan and Celia (Katz) H.; m. Phyllis Sydney Torgan, June 8, 1946; 1 son, Edward A. B.S., U. Conn., 1948; Ph.D., U. Pa., 1953. Instr. biology MIT, Cambridge, 1955-57; asst. prof. biology MIT, 1957-61, assoc. prof., 1961-63; assoc. prof. chemistry U. Oreg., Eugene, 1963-66; prof. U. Oreg., 1966—, dir. cell biology program, 1982-83; dir. Inst. Advanced Biomed. Research Oreg. Health Scis. U., Portland, 1983-87; also Vollum prof. molecular biology, prof. biochemistry and cell biology Oreg. Health Scis. U.; mem. NIH study sect USPHS, Washington, 1981-87 ; mem. NIH adv. panel for tng. grant programs; mem. editorial bd. Addison Wesley Pub. Co., Reading, Mass., 1961-87. Contbr. over 120 articles in field to profl. jours.; author 35 book chpts. in field of neurobiology; mem. editorial bd. 7 sci. jours. and revs. Mem. adv. bd. State Legis. Com. on Trade and Econ. Devel., Salem, Oreg., 1982-83. Served with USN, 1943-45. Recipient Career Devel. award USPHS, 1964-74, Pfizer award and lectureship Clin. Research Inst., Montreal, 1978, Rosetta Briegal award U. Okla., 1981, Leslie Bennett award U. Calif., San Francisco, 1982, First Mark O. Hatfield award Oreg. Health Scis. U., 1983, Mentor award Oreg. Med. Rsch. Found., 1987; grantee NSF, NIH, Am. Heart Assn., Oreg. Heart Assn.; Murdock Trust grantee McKnight Found. Mem. AAAS, Internat. Soc. Biochem. Endocrinology, Am. Soc. Biol. Chemists, Endocrine Soc., NAS. Home: Portland Oreg. Died Feb. 19, 1987; buried Willamette National Cemetery, Portland, Oreg.

HERBERT, FRANK PATRICK, author; b. Tacoma, Oct. 8, 1920; s. Frank and Eileen M. (McCarthy) H.; m. Beverly Ann Stuart, June 23, 1946; children: Penny (Mrs. D. R. Merritt), Brian, Bruce. Student, U. Wash., 1946-47. Lectr. gen. and interdisciplinary studies U. Wash., Seattle, 1970-72; cons. social and ecol. studies Far East affairs Lincoln Found., Vietnam and Pakistan, 1971. Author: Under Pressure, 1955, Dune, 1965, Destination Void, 1965, Green Brain, 1966, Eyes of Heisenberg, 1966, Heaven Makers, 1967, Santaroga Barrier, 1968, Dune Messiah, 1969, Whipping Star, 1970, New World or No World, 1970, Worlds of Frank Herbert, 1970, Soul Catcher, 1971, God Makers, 1971, Book of Frank Herbert, 1972, Project 40, 1972, Threshold, 1973, Best of Frank Herbert, 1973, Children of Dune, 1976, The Dosadi Experiment, 1977, Priests of Psi, 1979, Direct Descent, 1980, God Emperor of Dune, 1981, The White Plague, 1982; (with B. Ransom) the Jesus Incident, 1979, Lazarus Effect, 1983; (with M. Barnard) Without Me You're Nothing: The Essential Guide to Home Computers, 1981; dir., writer, photographer (TV show) The Tillers, 1973. Mem. collegeum World Without War Council, 1970-73; bd. dirs. Seattle World Without War Council, 1972-86. Home: Port Townsend Wash. Died Feb. 11, 1986.

HERBSTER, BEN MOHR, clergyman, church official; b. Prospect, Ohio, Aug. 26, 1904; s. Richard W. and Mary E (Mohr) H.; m. Elizabeth Beam, June 25, 1929; children: Jane (Mrs. Marcus Buehrer), Anne (Mrs. Roger Liston). AB, Heidelberg Coll., 1926, DD; BD, Cen. Theol. Sem., 1929; DD, Franklin Marshall Coll., 1962, Lakeland Coll., 1963; STD, Talladega Coll., 1962; LLD, Elmhurst Coll. Ordained to ministry Reformed Ch. U.S., 1929. Pastor Corinth Blvd. Reformed Ch., Dayton, Ohio, 1929-31, Zion United Ch. of Christ, Norwood, Ohio, 1931-61; pres., mem. constn. commn., past co-chmn. exec. council United Ch. of Christ, 1961-69; past pres. S.W. Ohio Synod, Evang. and Reformed Ch.; accredited visitor 1st assembly World Council Chs., 1948, del. 2d assembly, 1954, 3d assembly, 1961, 4th assembly, 1968; former mem. cen. com. World Council Chs., 1968, former vice chmn. U.S. Conf.; former mem. exec. com. Reformed World Alliance, Internat. Congl. Council. Author: God Still Makes Sense, 1972. Trustee Heidelberg Coll., United Ch. Homes, Inc. Mem. Council Chs. Greater Cin. (past pres.), Masons. Home: Dayton Ohio. Died Dec. 16, 1984.

HERD, JOHN VICTOR, insurance executive; b. Milw., Apr. 12, 1902; s. John and Laura (Prescott) H.; m. Pauline May Hoffmann, Nov. 20, 1937; children: Pauline, Victoria. LLD, Pratt Inst., 1964. Hon. dir. IBM World Trade Europe/Mid. East/Africa Corp.; bd. dirs. Continental Reins. Corp. Ltd., Bermuda, Pan Am. Banks, Inc., London Guarantee & Reins. Corp., South Atlantic Fin. Corp; past pres. Assn. Casualty and Surety Cos., Nat. Bd. Fire Underwriters. Trustee Episcopal Ch. Found., Episcopal Found. for Edn. L.I. Diocese, Bklyn. Inst. Arts and Scis.; bd. dirs., vice chmn. bd. trustees Bklyn. Botanic Garden; bd. govs. Bklyn. Mus.; sr. warden Grace Ch., Brooklyn Heights, N.Y. Recipient Gold medal Gen. Ins. Brokers Assn., 1954, Fellow of the Coll. award Adelphi U., 1962. Mem. Am. Arbitration Assn. (bd. dirs.), Drug and Chem. Club (hon.), Arcola (N.J.) Country Club, Brooklyn Club, Heights Casino, Lawrence Beach Club, Links, Downtown Assn., Union League, Church Club (trustee). Home: Brooklyn N.Y. Died Mar. 27, 1987.

HERMAN, WOODROW CHARLES (WOODY HERMAN), orchestra leader; b. Milw., May 16, 1913; s. Otto C. and Myrtle (Barth) H.; m. Charlotte Neste, Sept. 27, 1936; 1 dau., Ingrid. Grad., St. John's Cathedral Prep. Sch., Milw., 1930; student, Marquette U., 1930-31. Appeared: vaudeville as Boy Wonder of the Clarinet, 1919; with vaudeville as, Tom Gerun Orch., 1931, Gus Arnheim, 1933, Harry Sesnick, 1933, Isham Jones, 1934-36; organized orch., Band t at Plays the Blues, 1936, later named First Herd, also Third Herd; now known as, Woody Herman and the Young Thundering Herd, toured, Europe for, State Dept., 1960, 67, appeared at, Newport, Monterey and Concord festivals, performer, Woody Herman's, New Orleans, 1981-87 ; Composer: songs including Goosey Gander, Apple Honey, Northwest Passage, Woocroppers Ball, Blowin' Up a Storm, Blues on Parade. Founder Woody Herman-Sister Fabian Scholarship Fund, 1975. Winner popularity poll Down Beat mag., 1945; Winner popularity poll Metronome mag., 1946, 53; recipient Billboard award, 1946; Silver award Esquire mag., 1946-47; Grammy award, 1963, 73, 74; named to Down Beat Mag. Hall of Fame. Mem. Am. Fedn. Musicians, ASCAP. Home: Hollywood Calif. Died Oct. 19, 1987.

HEROLD, DONALD GEORGE, museum director; b. Bklyn., June 8, 1927; s. Charles George and Emmy (Partheymuller) H.; m. Elaine A. Bluhm, Jan. 15, 1964; children: Jennifer Ann, Katherine Elaine Patricia. B.A., SUNY-Albany, 1948. Dir. Miami Jr. Mus., Fla., 1950-51; asst. dir. Mus. Village, Monroe, N.Y., 1953-56; dir. exhibits and interpretation Va. 350th Anniversary, Jamestown, 1956-57; dir. Davenport Pub. Mus., Iowa, 1958-68, Polk Pub. Mus., Lakeland, Fla., 1968-69, Mus. Arts and Scis., Daytona Beach, Fla., 1969-70,

Charleston Mus., S.C., 1971-82, Buffalo Mus. Sci., N.Y., 1982-84. Trustee Cypress Gardens of Charleston. Served with USMC, 1951-53. Recipient Elsie M.B. Naumburg award Natural Sci. for Youth Found., 1978. Mem. Am. Assn. Museums, S.E. Mus. Conf., Midwest Mus. Conf., Am. Assn. State and Local History, Sci. Museums Dirs. Assn., Assn. Systematics Collections, S.C. Fedn. Museums Collections (v.p.), N.Y. State Assn. Museums (pres. from 1983), N.E. Museums Conf., Am. Assn. for State and Local History. Home: Kenmore N.Y. Died July 11, 1984; buried Kenmore, N.Y.

HERON, ALEXANDER RICHARD, corporate executive, author; b. Flesherton, Ont., Can., Sept. 13, 1891; s. Albert Thomas and Mary (McIntyre) H.; m. Lulu Ross, Jan. 1, 1914 (dec.); m. Leah Cooper, Sept. 13, 1946. BS, Southwestern U., L.A., 1916; DBA (hon.), Coll. of Pacific, 1955. Began with credit reporting agy., credit mgr., pub. acct., auditor, CPA Calif., 1919; asst. supt. accounts State of Calif., 1919-21; dept. dir. edn., asst. supt. pub. instrn. 1921-25; dir. fin., chmn. State Bd. of Control, 1927-30; exec. Crown Zellerbach Corp., 1930-42, dir. indsl. pub. rels., v.p., from 1942, also bd. dirs.; cons. prof. indsl. rels. Stanford U., from 1940; lectr., conf. leader Indsl. REls. Confs., Princeton U., 1938, 40, Stanford U., 1939-42, U. Mich., 1940, Reed Coll., 1941, U. Vt., 1940, U. Oreg., U. Wash., U. Denver, U. Calif., Swarthmore Coll.; lectr. U. Calif. Author: Sharing Information with Employees, 1942, Why Men Work, 1948, Beyond Collective Bargaining, 1948, No Sale, No Job, 1954, Reasonable Goals in Industrial Relations, 1954. Pres. YMCA, Sacramento, dir. San Francisco, 1932-38, dir. Western area coun., pres. Calif., 1929; mem. gen. coun. Northern Bapt. Conv., 1931-38; mem. Nat. WSB, 1951-52; mem. bus. rsch. adv. com. U.S. Dept. Labor; dist. dir. for Tng. Within Industry, War Prodn. Bd. and War Manpower Commn., 1940-42; chief Civilian Pers., Army Service Forces, Sept. 1942-Mar. 1943; dir. Program Action Div., War Dept. Manpower Bd., from 1943; dir. postwar planning Calif., 1944-46; trustee Golden Gate Coll., U. of Redlands, Calif., Berkeley Bapt. Divinity Sch. Served as capt. Q.M.R., 1923-28, lt. col., 1928-35, col. U.S. Army, 1942. Recipient Human Rels. award Soc. Advancement of Mgmt., 1949. Mem. Calif. Soc. CPAs, Res. Officers Assn. of U.S. Army Ordnance Assn., Nat. Indsl. Conf. Bd. (adv. coun. Pers. Adminstrn.), Am. Mgmt. Assn. (pers. planning coun.), Indsl. Rels. Rsch. Assn., Am. Statis. Assn., Am. Arbitration Assn., Soc. Advancement Mgmt., Pub. Rels. Soc. Am., Am. Legion, Commonwealth Club, Sutter Club (bd. govs. 1942), Masons. Republican. Home: Berkeley Calif. †

HERRING, JOHN WOODBRIDGE, educator, clergyman; b. Winterset, Iowa, June 15, 1891; s. Hubert Clinton and Mary (Woodbridge) H.; m. Ruth Catherine Rhodes, Aug. 1, 1917; children: John Woodbridge, Thomas Hubert, Joan Elizabeth; m. Lorine Pruette, 1932; m. Helen M. Day, 1936; children: Howard Theodore, Peter James. Student, Oberlin Coll., 1910-12, AB, 1914; student, Columbia U., 1912-13, Oberlin Theol. Sem., 1914-15, Chgo. Theol. Sem., 1915-17. Ordained to ministry Congl. Ch., 1918. Organizer met. couns. adult edn. from 1924; coordinator emergency adult edn. program Works Progress Adminstrn., N.Y.C., 1934-35; supr. N.Y. State Adult Edn. Program, 1936-54; dir. Greater Kans. City Adult Edn. Assn., 1954-56; coord. Sardinian Community Devel. Project, European Productiivity Agy., 1957; minister Unitarian Soc. of Pomono Valley, 1958-61, San Bernadino Unitarian Soc., from 1961. Author: Adult Education and Social Planning, 1933, Trails to the New America, 1940. Dir. citizen unity program N.Y. State War Coun., 1942. Home: Claremont Calif. †

HERROLD, LLOYD DALLAS, advertising educator; b. Westville, Ind., May 24, 1892; s. Franklin Pierce and Charlotte (Norris) H.; m. Phoebe Mae Wilson, June 19, 1923; 1 child, Lloyd Wilson. AB, U. Wis., 1919; MBA, Northwestern U., 1925. Copy and account rep. Potts-Turnbull Advt. Co., Kansas City, Mo., 1919-20; dir. advt. Univ. Extension div. U. Wis., 1920-22; asst. prof. advt. Washington U., St. Louis, 1922-24; assoc. prof. advt. Northwestern U. Sch. Bus., 1924-47, prof., 1939-57, emeritus prof., from 1957, chmn. dept. advt., 1948-57; dir. rsch. Leo Burnett Advt. Co., Chgo., 1943-44; sr. ptnr. Lloyd Herrold, 1936-59, pres., from 1959. Author several publs. Lt. inf. U.S. Army, 1917-19. Mem. Beta Gamma Sigma, Alpha Delta Sigma, Alpha Kappa Psi. Methodist. Home: Pompano Beach Fla. †

HERSTEIN, ISRAEL NATHAN, mathematician, educator; b. Lublin, Poland, Mar. 28, 1923; came to U.S., 1946, naturalized, 1955; s. Jacob and Mary (Lichtenstein) H.; m. Marianne Deson, June 16, 1946 (div. Mar. 1973); m. Barbara, Mar. 20, 1980. B.Sc. with honors, U. Man., 1945; M.A., U. Toronto, 1946; Ph.D., Ind. U., 1948. Instr. U. Kans., 1948-50; lectr. Ohio State U., 1951; asst. prof. math. U. Chgo., 1951-53, prof., 1962-88; asst. prof. U. Pa., 1953-56, assoc. prof., 1956-57; assoc. prof. math. Cornell U., Ithaca, N.Y., 1957-58; prof. Cornell U., 1958-62; vis. prof. U. Rome, 1961-62, 63, 65, 66, 68, Stanford U., 1960, 64, U. Calif.-San Diego, 1979-80; Fulbright lectr., Rio de Janeiro, Brazil, 1967; joint prof. Weizmann Inst., 1971-73; vis. prof. U. Auckland, New Zealand, summer 1976; Fulbright lectr. Laguna U., 1976; vis. prof. Hebrew U., 1977-78; cons. Ramo Woodridge Co., 1956, Gen. Electric Co., 1958-6O, Lincoln Labs., 1958-59; editor Harper & Row, 1962-88. Author: Topics in Algebra, 1964, Non-Commutative Rings, 1967, Topics in Ring Theory, 1968, (with Sandler) Introduction To The Calculus, 1971, (with Kaplansky) Matters Mathematical, 1974, Rings with Involution, 1976, Abstract Algebra, 1986, (with D. Winter) A Primer on Linear Algebra, 1988, Matrix Theory and Linear Algebra, 1988; contbr. numerous articles to profl. jours. Dir. Comitato Internat. Matematico Estivo, Varenna, Italy, 1965. Guggenheim fellow, 1961-62, 68-69. Mem. Am. Math. Soc., Math. Assn. Am. Home: Chicago Ill. Died Feb. 9, 1988.

HERTWIG, CHARLES CHRISTIAN, textile executive; b. Macon, Ga., 1892; s. Herman and Emma (Schall) H.; m. Louise Bryant, Feb. 17, 1925; children: Charles Christian, Louise (Mrs. Henry Valery Hayes). BA, Mercer U., 1914. Clk. Firemans Fund Ins. Co., 1914-17; solicitor Macon, Dublin & Savannah R.R., 1920-21; with Bibb Mfg. Co., from 1921, successively paymaster, treas., v.p., pres., 1921-55, pres., chmn. bd., from 1955; bd. dirs. Citizens & So. Nat. Bank, Cen. of Ga. Ry. Co. Mem. Bd. Edn.; trustee Presbyn. Coll. 1st lt. U.S. Army, 1917-20. Mem. Nat. Cotton Coun., Cotton Mfrs. Assn. Ga. (past pres.), Am. Cotton Mfrs. Inst. (past pres.). Home: Macon Ga. †

HERTZBERG, HAZEL WHITMAN, history educator; b. Bklyn., Sept. 16, 1918; d. Charles Theodore and Grace Manross (Wood) Whitman; m. Sidney Hertzberg, Aug. 25, 1941 (dec.); children: Hendrik, Katrina. A.B., U. Chgo., 1958; M.A., Tchrs. Coll., Columbia U., 1961; Ph.D., Columbia U., 1968. Cert. tchr., N.Y. Exec. sec. Nat. Sharecroppers Fund, N.Y.C., 1947-49; social studies and English tchr. Ramapo Central Sch. Dist., Suffern, N.Y., 1957-62; instr. Tchrs. Coll., Columbia U., N.Y.C., 1963-68, asst. prof. history and edn., 1968-69, assoc. prof. history and edn., 1970-78, prof. history and edn., 1978—; prof. dept. history Grad. Sch. Arts and Sci. Columbia U., 1983—; cons. numerous sch. dists. and tchr. insts., 1974-88, Am. Indian Ctr., Newberry Library, Chgo., 1977-78, Nat. Inst. Edn., Washington, 1977, N.Y. Council for the Humanities, 1983-85; mem. adv. bd. Edn. for Democracy Project, 1986—; mem. Bradley Commn. on History in Schs., 1987—, Nat. Commn. on Social Studies, 1987—, Framework Com. of Civitas: A Framework for Civic Edn., 1988—. Author: The Great Tree and the Longhouse: The Culture of the Iroquois, 1966, The Search for an American Indian Identity: Modern Pan Indian Movements, 1970, Social Studies Reform, 1880-1980, 1981; dep. editor: Social Education, 1987—. Exec. sec. India Famine Emergency Com., N.Y.C., 1946; co-founder Ramapo LWV, 1952. Guggenheim fellow, 1983-84; NEH fellow, 1974-75; Woodrow Wilson Internat. Ctr. for Scholars fellow, 1975, 84. Mem. Social Sci. Edn. Consortium (bd. dirs. 1974-77), Conf. on Iroquois Research (planning com. 1978), Orgn. Am. Historians (planning com. 1981), Am. Hist. Assn., Nat. Council for Social Studies (archives com.). Democrat. Home: Palisades N.Y. Died Oct. 19, 1988.

HERZBRUN, HELENE MCKINSEY, artist, educator; b. Chgo.; d. Edward E. and Lillian (Smith) Eichenbaum; m. Philip Herzbrun, Nov. 11, 1961. BA, U. Chgo., 1945; postgrad., Am. U., 1951-55. Staff, then ptnr. Charles Elwyn Hayes Advt., Chgo., 1945-50; prof. art Am. U., Washington, from 1958, chmn. dept., 1964-66, 70-72, 76-78. Exhibited one-woman shows, from 1958; represented in permanent collections including Watkins Collection, Am. U., U. Va., Phillips Collection, Nat. Mus. Am. Art. Mem. Phi Beta Kappa. Home: Washington D.C. Died Mar. 15, 1983.

HERZOG, PAUL M., lawyer; b. N.Y.C., Aug. 21, 1906; s. Paul M. and Elsie (Lowenstein) H.; m. Madeleine Schafer, Apr. 11, 1929 (div.); children: John Paul, Andrea Elsie Herzog Chadwick; m. 2d, Julie Chamberlain Trowbridge d'Estournelles, 1959 (dec. May 1980); stepchildren: Julie T. Cullen, Alexander B. Trowbridge; m. 3d, Elizabeth Peterson Andrews, Dec. 19, 1981; stepchildren: Jean-Pierre Habicht, Margaret H. Robinson. S.B. magna cum laude, Harvard U., 1927; A.M., U. Wis., 1930; LL.B., Columbia U., 1936; LL.D., Hobart and William Smith Colls., 1959, Washington U., St. Louis, 1971. Bar: N.Y. 1936, U.S. Supreme Ct. 1950. Instr., U. Wis., 1928-30, Harvard U., 1930-31; asst. to sec. Nat. Labor Bd., Washington, 1933-35; practice, N.Y.C., 1936-37; apptd. one of original mems. N.Y. State Labor Relations Bd., 1937, chmn., 1942-44; chmn. NLRB, 1945-53; assoc. dean, grad. sch. pub. adminstrn. Harvard U., 1953-57, acting dean, 1957; exec. v.p. Am. Arbitration Assn., 1958-61, pres., 1961-63; pres. Salzburg Seminar in Am. Studies, 1965-71. Mem. Com. of experts on application of convs. ILO, 1956-67; trustee Colls. of Seneca (Hobart and William Smith), 1945-56. Served to lt. USNR, 1944-45. Decorated Grand Medal Order of Merit (Austria). Mem. Assn. of Bar of City of N.Y., ABA, Am. Soc. Pub. Adminstrn. (v.p. 1956-57), Am. Law Inst., Council on Fgn. Relations, Harvard Alumni Assn. (v.p. 1951-52), Phi Beta Kappa, Democrat. Presbyterian (elder). Clubs: Century, Harvard (N.Y.C.); Metropolitan (Washington); Harvard Faculty (Cambridge, Mass.); Mill Reef (Antigua, W.I.); Garrick (London). Home: N.Y.C. Died Nov. 23, 1986; cremated.

HESKETT, R(OLLAND) M(CCARTNEY), utilities executive; b. Baunville, Ohio, Feb. 3, 1881; s. Hartley and Sara (McCartney) H.; m. Mary C. Glynn, 1907; children: Jean, Mary, Robert, David. Degree in EE, Ill. Inst. Tech., 1902. V.p. Knox Heskett Engring. Co., from 1905, Minn. Utilities Co., 1913; with Mont. Dakota Utilities Co., Mpls., from 1924, pres., from 1943, chmn.; bd. dirs. Masonite Co. Home: Minneapolis Minn. †

HESS, ECKHARD HEINRICH, psychologist, ethologist, educator; b. Bochum, Germany, Sept. 27, 1916; came to U.S., 1927; naturalized, 1943; s. Heinrich Peter and Wilhelmina (Salewski) H.; m. Dorothea Burghard-Nawaisky, Sept. 29, 1942. AB, Blue Ridge Coll., New Windsor, Md., 1941; MA, Johns Hopkins U., 1947, PhD, 1948. Jr. instr. Johns Hopkins U., 1946-47; faculty U. Chgo., 1948-86, prof. psychology, 1959-86, chmn. dept., 1963-68; dir. W.C. Allee Lab. Animal Behavior, 1960-70; spring vis. assoc. prof. Swarthmore Coll., 1957, U. Calif., Berkeley, 1958; vis. prof. U. Md.-Balt. County, 1975; cons.-dir. Perception Lab., Interpublic, Inc., N.Y.C., 1960-67; mem. com. comparative devel. Social Sci. Rsch. Council, 1961-67. Author: The Tell-Tale Eye: How Your Eyes Reveal Hidden Thoughts and Emotions, Imprinting: Early Experience and the Developmental Psychobiology of Attachment, 1973; co-editor: Psychologische Forschung, 1967-74, Brain, Behavior, and Evolution, 1968-86; assoc. editor Animal Learning and Behavior, 1971-77; contbr. articles to sci. jours. With AUS, 1943-44. Ctr. Advanced Studies Behavioral Scis. fellow, 1955-56. Fellow AAAS (life), Soc. Exptl. Psychologists, Am. Psychol. Assn., Animal Behavior Soc.; mem. Internat. Brain Rsch. Orgn., Am. Mus. Natural History, Nat. Geog. Soc., Psychonomic Soc., Soc. Neurosci., Behavior Genetics Soc., Internat. Ehology Congress (internat. exec. com.), Quadrangle Club, Sigma Xi. Home: Cambridge Md. Died Feb. 21, 1986; buried Old Trinity Ch. Cemetery, Church Creek, Md.

HESTON, LILLA ANASTASIA, speech and interpretation educator; b. St. Helen, Mich., Oct. 1, 1927; d. Chester L. and Lilla (Charlton) H. B.S., Northwestern U., 1949, M.A., 1958, Ph.D., 1965. Instr. Vassar Coll., Poughkeepsie, N.Y., 1958-60; instr. Northwestern U., Evanston, Ill., 1961-65, asst. prof., 1965-68, assoc. prof. interpretation, 1968-73, prof. dept. interpretation, 1973-84, chmn. dept., 1979-84. Editor: Man in the Dramatic Mode, Books 1-6, 1970, Drama Lives!, Books 1-3, 1975; assoc. editor: Quar. Jour. Speech, 1977-80, Lit. in Performance, 1979-84 . Mem. Speech Communications Assn., AAUP, Ill. Speech and Theatre Assn., Central States Speech Assn. Home: Wilmette Ill. Died May 1984.

HETRICK, EMERY SYLVESTER, psychiatrist; b. Columbus, Ohio, Sept. 27, 1930; s. Emery S. and Laura Alice (Fields) H.; B.A., Ohio State U., 1953; M.D., Cornell U., 1957. Intern, Univ. Hosp., Columbus, 1957-58; resident Cin. Gen. Hosp., 1958-61; fellow div. social and community psychiatry dept. psychiatry Albert Einstein Coll. Medicine, 1963-66, instr., 1963-68; mem. staff Ackerman Family Inst., N.Y.C., 1965-68; head psychiatrist mobile crisis unit dept. psychiatry Gouverneur Hosp., N.Y.C., 1968-74, acting chief dept. psychiatry, 1974-76, coordinator acute psychiat. services, 1976; asst. chmn. Lower Eastside Mental Health Consortium, N.Y.C., 1974-76; chief psychiat. emergency and crisis treatment service Harlem Hosp. Center, N.Y.C., 1976-79; assoc. med. dir. Roerig div. Pfizer, Inc., 1979-84, sr. asso. med. dir. for clin. and sci. affairs, from 1984; asst. prof. clin. psychiatry Columbia U., 1976-82; clin. asst. prof. psychiatry NYU-Bellevue Med. Ctr., from 1982. Founding mem., bd. dirs. Sr. Action in a Gay Environment, Inc., 1977-81, chmn. bd., 1979-80; bd. dirs. N.Y. Polit. Action Council, 1980-84; founder, pres. Inst. Protection of Lesbian and Gay Youth, Inc.; mem. N.Y. State Task Force on Lesbian and Gay Issues, from 1983. Served with USNR, 1961-63. Diplomate Am. Bd. Psychiatry and Neurology. Fellow Am. Psychiat. Assn.; mem. AAAS, N.Y. Acad. Sci., N.Y. County Med. Soc., Gay Psychiatrists N.Y. (founder). Developed community-based outreach crisis intervention team; founder community orgns. Home: New York, N.Y. Died Feb. 3, 1987.

HETTINGER, ALBERT JOHN, JR., investment banker, economist; b. Strang, Nebr., Sept. 16, 1891; s. Albert John and Florence Lillian (Walker) H.; m. Catherine Zirpoli, Nov. 11, 1929; 1 son, Albert John III. AB, Stanford U., 1916, AM, 1917; PhD, Harvard U., 1920. Asst. prof. Grad. Sch. Bus. Adminstrn., Harvard, 1920-26; pres. Investment Rsch. Corp., Detroit, 1926-35; exec. sec. Durable Goods Industries Com., Washington, 1934-35; v.p., dir., mem. exec. com. Gen. Am. Investors Co. Inc., N.Y.C., 1935-43; ptnr. Lazard Freres & Co., N.Y.C., from 1944; chmn. Providentia Ltd., Instoria Inc.; dir. Gen. Reassurance Corp., Gen. Reins. Corp., Piedmont Adv. Corp., Gen. Reins. Life Corp., Harcourt Brace Jovanovich Inc., Nat. Fire Ins. Co., Transcontinental Ins. Co., Herbert Clough Inc., North Star Reins. Co., Olivetti Corp. Am., mem. exec. com.; hon. dir. Lincoln Nat. Life Ins. Co., Lincoln Nat. Corp.; emeritus dir. Owens-Ill. Inc. Trustee Salzburg Seminar in Am. Studies, Nat. Bur. Econ. Rsch.; ind. counsellor U.S. Steel and Carnegie Pension Fund. Mem. Rockefeller Ctr. Luncheon Club, Cosmos

Club (Washington), Phi Beta Kappa, Delta Kappa Epsilon. Presbyterian. Home: New York N.Y. Deceased.

HEWARD, BRIAN, stockbroker; b. Brockville, Ont., Can., July 15, 1900; s. Arthur Richard Graves and Sara Efa (Jones) H.; m. Anna Barbara Lauderdale Logie, Dec. 28, 1925; children: Barbara, Chilion F. G., Efa (Mrs Donald Greenwood), Faith (Mrs. William Berghuis). Grad., Lower Can. Coll., Montreal, Can., 1915; MA, St. John's Coll., Cambridge (Eng.) U., 1921. Acct. P.S. Ross & Sons, Montreal, 1921-22, Oswald & Drinkwater, Montreal, 1922-25; ptnr. Jones Heward & Co., Montreal, 1925-64, sr. ptnr., 1945-64; pres. Jones Heward & Co., Ltd., Montreal, 1965, chmn. bd., from 1966; chmn. bd. Consumers Glass Co., Ltd., Montreal, Toronto, Ont., Can. Midshipman Royal Can. Navy, 1918. Home: Westmount Can. Deceased.

HEWITT, WILLIAM PATRICK, manufacturing company executive; b. Syracuse, N.Y., Dec. 30, 1917; s. William Patrick and Hannah Rose (Renaud) H.; m. Zara Clara Sposato, Apr. 10, 1946; 1 child, William Joseph. BSBA, Syracuse U., 1940. With Carrier Corp., Syracuse, 1945-84, dir. budgets and fin. analysis, 1961-72, compt., 1973-84, asst. to fin. v.p., 1979-84. With AUS, 1941-45. Mem. Pastime Athletic. Home: Syracuse N.Y. Died Dec. 14, 1984, buried Wood Lawn Cemetery, Syracuse.

HEYMANN, WALTER, physician, educator; b. Brussels, Nov. 22, 1901; came to U.S., 1933, naturalized, 1939; s. Gustave and Selma (Kaufmann) H.; m. Marion Oberdorfer, Aug. 28, 1939; 1 child, Peter Walter. MD, U. Kiel, Fed. Republic Germany, 1923. Privat dozent pediatrics U. Freiburg Med. Sch., Fed. Republic Germany, 1931-33; mem. faculty Sch. Medicine, Case Western Res. U., 1936—, prof. pediatrics, 1962-73, emeritus, 1973—, dir. Renal Services Pediatrics, 1964-73. Charter mem. Kidney Found. Ohio, 1952, chmn., med. adv. bd., 1952-67; co-founder Cleve. Chamber Music Soc., 1950, pres., 1952, mem. exec. com., 1952—. Fellow AMA, Am. Acad. Pediatrics; mem. Am. Pediatric Soc., Soc. Exptl. Biology and Medicine, Am. Soc. Exptl. Pathology, AAAS, Am. Soc. for Pediatric Nephrology (pres. 1968-69), Am. Soc. Nephrology, Internat. Assn. Pediatric Nephrology, Sigma Xi. Home: Cleveland Ohio Died Jan. 24, 1985.

HIBBS, HENRY HORACE, JR., educator; b. Smithland, Ky., Nov. 25, 1887; s. Henry Horace and Susie (Adams) H.; m. Jessie Rowe Persinger, June 6, 1918; children: Jessie Persinger Hawke, Mary Sue Doss. AB, Brown U., 1910, AM, 1911; PhD, Columbia, 1916; LLD, U. Richmond (Va.), 1959. Fellow Boston Sch. Social Work, 1910-12; prof. history John Tarleton Coll., Stephenville, Tex., 1912-13; with dept. sociology U. Ill., 1914-15; with statistics bur. Met. Life Ins. co., N.Y.C., 1916-17; organizer Richmond Sch. Social Work and Pub. Health, 1917, Richmond div. Coll. Of William and Mary, 1925, Richmond Sch. Art, 1928, Richmond Sch. Distribution, 1937, Richmond Sch. Music, 1941, Sch. Occupational Therapy, 1942, other profl. schs. now organized as the Richmond Profl. Inst. of Coll. of William and Mary, Va. Polytechnic Inst. cooperating; provost Richmond Profl. Inst., Coll. William and Mary, until 1959, ret. Author: Infant Mortality, 1916. Mem. Phi Sigma Kappa. Episcopalian. Home: Lexington Va. †

HICKEN, PHILIP BURNHAM, artist; b. Lynn, Mass., June 27, 1910; s. Willis and Lena (Burnham) H.; m. Evangeline Chase, June 5, 1937; children: Tana Val, Theo Jo. Student, Mass. Sch. Art, 1928-32. Nat., internat. exhibits 1936-85; lectr. Sch. of Mus. of Fine Arts, Boston, Sch. Practical Arts, And Butera Sch. Fine Arts, 1947; instr. Grad. Sch. Design, Harvard, 1950-54; instr. drawing Boston U. Sch. Fine and Applied Arts, 1955-56; chmn. dept. design. Sch. Practical Art, Boston, from 1956; chmn. dept. fine arts Art Inst. Boston, from 1969. Represented in permanent collections, Met. Mus. Art, N.Y.C., Library of Congress, Phila. Mus. Fine Art, Nat. Bezalel Mus., Jerusalem, many others; mural Boston Five Cents Savs. Bank; combat art assignment Okinawa, U.S. Dept. Mil. History, 1970; easel and mural painter Fed. Art Project. Served as artist AUS, 1942-45. Recipient prizes Black Mountain (N.C.) Art Club, 1943, Springfield (Mass.) Soldier Art, 1944, New Eng. Soldier Art, 1944, Mint Mus., Charlotte, N.C., 1946; 1st Cambridge (Mass.) Art Assn. Ann., 1953; purchase award Bklyn. Mus. Print Ann., 1958; 1st award Nantucket Art Assn. Annual, 1958, 68; Directors award Nat. Soc. Casein Painters, 1963; 1st award Natick (Mass.) Art Festival, 1971, Copley Soc., Boston. Fellow Royal Soc. Arts London; mem. Nat. Serigraph Soc., Boston Printmakers, Boston Soc. Water Color Painters, Nantucket Artists Assn. Home: Nantucket Mass. Died Feb. 17, 1985; buried Nantucket, Mass.

HICKEY, DAVID FRANCIS, clergyman; b. St. Louis, Dec. 3, 1882; s. John and Catherine (Walsh) H. AB, St. Louis U., 1907, MA, 1909; LLD honoris causa, Marquette U., 1952. Joined S.J., 1902, ordained priest Roman Catholic Ch., 1917. Instr. math and chemistry Creighton U. High Sch., Omaha, Nebr., 1909-14, Loyola U., Chgo., 1918-20, Creighton U., 1921-26; missionary to British Honduras, 1926-42, superior of mission, 1942-48; consecrated bishop 1948; vicar apostolic Belize, British Honduras, 1948-56; bishop of Belize 1956-57; dir. retreats for workingmen and workingwomen St. Joseph Retreat House, St. Louis, from 1957. Home: Saint Louis Mo. †

HICKEY, EDWARD H., lawyer; b. Boston, July 22, 1912; s. James M. and Mary (Simpson) H.; m. Ragnhild Tait, Feb. 25, 1941; children: Shelagh (Mrs. George M. Covington), Karen, John. A.B. cum laude, Harvard U., 1933, LL.B., 1936. Bar: Mass. 1936, D.C. 1946, Ill. 1957. Practice in Boston, 1936-38, Washington, 1938-57, Chgo., from 1957; with Dept. Justice, 1938-42; spl. asst. to Atty. Gen., chief gen. litigation sect. 1945-57; counsel firm Bell, Boyd, Lloyd, Haddad & Burns, from 1957; dir. First Nat. Bank of Winnetka. Trustee Village of Winnetka, 1971-72, pres. village, 1972-74; Pres. Winnetka Community Chest, 1963-64; chmn. Winnetka Bicentennial Com., 1975-76; bd. dirs. Great Books Found. Served as lt. USNR, World War II. Decorated Presdl. citation. Fellow Am. Coll. Trial Lawyers; mem. Fed. Bar Assn., ABA, Ill. Bar Assn., Chgo. Bar Assn. (chmn. legal aid 1969, chmn. urban affairs 1970), 7th Fed. Circuit Bar Assn. (pres. 1974-75), Am. Law Inst., Jud. Conf. U.S. (com. on rules of practice and procedure), Harvard U. Alumni Assn. (dir. 1981-84), Law Club Chgo. Clubs: Attic (Chgo.), Harvard (Chgo.) (pres. 1973-75), University (Chgo.). Home: Winnetka Ill. Deceased.

HICKEY, EDWARD VINCENT, JR., federal commissioner; b. Dedham, Mass., July 15, 1935; s. Edward Vincent and Marion Rosaire (Caulfield) H.; m. Barbara Ann Burke, June 6, 1959; children: Edward V. III, Michael F., Joseph G., Paul V., John D., David T., Daniel J. B.S. in Bus. Adminstrn., Boston Coll., 1960; grad., Treasury Law Enforcemtn Officers Sch., 1964, U.S. Secret Service Spl. Agt. Sch., 1965. Juvenile officer Mass. Youth Authority, Boston, 1960-64; spl. agt. U.S. Secret Service, Boston, 1964-69; exec. dir. Calif. State Police, Sacramento, 1969-74; asst. dir. Office of Security, Dept. of State, Washington, 1974-78; sr. regional security officer Dept. of State, London, 1978-80; asst. to Pres., dir. spl. support services The White House, Washington, 1981; chmn. Fed. Maritime Commn. Regent Cath. U. Am. Served to cpl. U.S. Army, 1954-56. Recipient Dirs. Honor award U.S. Secret Service, 1974, Disting. Pub. Service medal Dept. Def., 1985; named Knight of St. Gregory, 1984. Mem. Internat. Assn. Chiefs of Police, Boston Coll. Alumni Assn., Friendly Sons of Saint Patrick (Washington chpt.). Republican. Roman Catholic. Home: Falls Church Va. Died Jan. 9, 1988.

HICKEY, WALTER B. D., retail men's clothing company executive; b. Rochester, N.Y., Mar. 19, 1906; s. Jeremiah G. and Constance (Duffy) H.; m. Elizabeth Flint, July 7, 1934; children: Margaret G. (Sister Mary Walter), Walter B.D., Jeremiah F., Elizabeth (Mrs. Connell Macken). BA, Georgetown U., 1927. With Hickey-Freeman Co., Rochester, 1927-80, pres., 1963-80, chmn. bd., 1976-80; hon. dir. Hart-Schaffner-Marx. Hon. bd. dirs. Highland Hosp., Rochester, St. John Fisher Coll., Rochester. Home: Rochester N.Y. Died July 24, 1988.

HICKMAN, WILLIAM HERBERT, economist, educator; b. Kirwin, Kans., Feb. 1, 1920; s. Isaac Herbert and Anna Myrtle (Powell) H.; m. Louise Weaver, Sept. 4, 1942. BS, Kans. State U., 1941; MA, Stanford U., 1949, PhD, 1952. Instr. Stanford U., 1946-49; asst. prof. Humboldt State Coll., 1949-51, Ford Found. faculty fellow, 1951-52; assoc. research technician State of Calif., 1952-53; asst. prof., assoc. prof. Sacramento State Coll., 1953-61, prof., 1961-87, head dept. econs., 1961-70; vis. assoc. prof. U. So. Calif., Pakistan, 1960-62; cons. AID, Brazil, 1959. Served to 1st lt. USAAF, 1942-46. Mem. Am., Western econ. assns., AAUP. Home: Sacramento Calif. Died Nov. 3, 1987; cremated.

HICKS, DAVID, opera producer, director; b. Phila., June 3, 1937; s. Paul W. and Mary (Ploucher) H. BS in Music, Temple U., 1959. Acting faculty Am. Opera Ctr., Juilliard Sch. Music, 1978-86. Appeared as singer with various opera cos., including N.Y.C. Opera and cos. in Phila., Cin., Balt., Hartford, Conn., until 1970; concert artist Community Concerts, throughout U.S., 1962-70; asst. dir. N.Y.C. Opera, 1967-73; free-lance dir., 1973-86 with opera cos. of Phila., Pitts., Balt., Charlotte, New Orleans, Western Opera of San Francisco, Memphis, Hawaii, Kansas City, Seattle and others; artistic dir. Florentine Opera, Milw., 1980-86; dir. opera prodns. Acad. Vocal Arts, Phila., 1973-77. Mem. Am. Guild Mus. Artists (bd. govs. 1965-75). Home: New York N.Y. Died Mar. 14, 1986.

HIGDON, EMERSON GRANVILLE, manufacturing company executive; b. Marshall, Mo., Jan. 6, 1909; s. Herbert Lovell and Sarah (Martin) H.; m. Alice Luverne Watt, June 8, 1930; children: Emerson Granville, Sherry Alice. BS in Bus., U. Kans., 1930; grad. advanced mgmt. program, Harvard U., 1958; DBA (hon.), Mo. Valley Coll., 1968. Pub. acct. Ernst & Ernst CPA's, Chgo., 1930-33; with Maytag Co., 1933-74, comptroller, 1941-60, v.p., 1956-60, exec. v.p., treas., dir., 1960-62, pres., treas., dir., 1962-72, chief exec. officer, 1966-74, chmn. bd., 1972-74; dir. Fed. Res. Bank Chgo., 1967-72, chmn., 1970-72. Mem. Fin. Execs. Inst., Newton C. of C., Alpha Kappa Psi. Republican. Presbyterian. Lodge: Elks. Home: Newton Iowa Died June 7, 1988; cremated.

HIGGINBOTHAM, WILLIAM HENRY, management consultant; b. Jefferson City, Mo., Apr. 19, 1909; s. William Barber and May (Pritchard) H.; m. Mildred Catherine Winsby, Mar. 4, 1944 (dec. Dec. 1959); children—Cynthia, Pamela (dec. Dec. 1974), Ronald; m. Suzanne Guge, Oct. 4, 1970. B.S., Washington U., St. Louis, 1953. Personnel dir. Rice-Stix Dry Goods Co., St. Louis, 1945-50; personnel mgr. White Rodgers Co., St. Louis, 1950-58; v.p. indsl. relations, dir. Century Electric Co., St. Louis, 1958-63; mgmt. cons. in pvt. practice St. Louis, 1963-88; mem. faculty St. Louis U., 1945-50, So. Ill. U., 1963-67; speaker; mem. faculty Creative Edn. Found., Buffalo, 1963-88; bd. dirs. Jr. Achievement of Miss. Valley, Inc. Weekly columnist St. Louis Bus. Jour.; author: Mirth in Management, 1988 (pub.Bearly Limited, Buffalo, N.Y.). Mem. Am. Soc. Tng. and Devel. (past officer St. Louis chpt.), Am. Soc. Personnel Adminstrn., Assn. Mgmt. Cons. (bd. trustees, nat. pres.), Creative Leadership Council of Creative Edn. Found., Indsl. Relations Assn. Greater St. Louis, Exec. Assn. Grad. Sch. Bus. Columbia U., Inst. Mgmt. Cons. (certified), Mgmt. Devel. Study Group, Nat. Speakers Assn. Republican. Christian Scientist. Club: Rotary (pres. Clayton, Mo. club, 1986-87). Home: Saint Louis Mo. Died Mar. 4, 1988; buried St. Louis.

HIGGINS, COLIN, writer, director; b. Noumea, New Caledonia, July 28, 1941; s. John Edward and Joy (Kelly) H. Student, St. Anthony's Coll., Robertson, N.S.W., Australia, 1958; B.A., Stanford U., 1967; M.F.A., UCLA, 1970. Author: stage plays Harold et Maude, Jean-Louis Barrault's Co., Paris, 1973, (with Denis Cannan) The IK, Peter Brook's Theater, Paris, 1974; screenplays Harold and Maude, 1971, Silver Streak, 1976, Foul Play (also dir.), 1978, (with Patricia Resnick) Nine to Five (also dir.), 1980, The Best Little Whorehouse in Texas (also dir.), 1982; co-scriptwriter, co-producer Out on a Limb., 1987. Served with U.S. Army, 1962-65. Mem. Writers Guild Am. West, Inc., Dirs. Guild Am., Acad. Motion Picture Arts and Scis. Democrat. Roman Catholic. Home: Los Angeles Calif. Died Aug. 5, 1988.

HIGGINS, FRANK H., grain merchant; b. Maniste, Mich., Dec. 12, 1892; s. John A. and Ellen (Barry) H.; m. Elisabeth Burrows, Sept. 2, 1919; 1 child, Elisabeth Ellen (Mrs. M.D. Vail, Jr.). Student night sch., U. Minn. Employed country grain elevators, N.D., 1912-16; mgr. Ely Salyards & Co., grain commn. mchts., Mpls., 1916-28; pres. Frank H. Higgins Co., Mpls., Duluth and Fargo, N.D., from 1928; with Regional Agr. Corp., Mpls., 1935-39; pres. Mpls. Grain Exchange, 1952-58, dir., 1943-52. Organizer, pres. Hennepin County chpt. Nat. Found. Infantile Paralysis; vice pres. Mpls. Rehab. Ctr., from 1956, Curative Workshop, 1953-55. Lt. F.A., U.S. Army, World War I. Mem. Nat. Fedn. Cash Grain Commn. Mchts. (v.p. 1952, pres. 1954-55), Mpls. Grain Commn. Mchts. Assn. (pres. 1927-28), Am. Legion (past comdr. local post). Home: Wayzata Minn. †

HIGHTOWER, JOHN MURMANN, journalist, educator, writer; b. Coal Creek, Tenn., Sept. 17, 1909; s. James Edward and Mary Elizabeth (Murmann) H.; m. Martha Nadine Joiner, Nov. 19, 1938; children—John Murmann, Leslie, James Edward. Student, U. Tenn., 1927-28. Assoc. editor Drug Topics mag., 1929-30; reporter Knoxville (Tenn.) News-Sentinel, 1931-87; reporter, editor Asso. Press, Nashville, 1933-36; assigned Assoc. Press (Washington Bur.), 1936-71, gen. reporting, news editing, 1936-40, Navy Dept. coverage, 1940-42, Dept. State and internat. affairs coverage, 1943-71, spl. corr., 1964-71; covered UN orgn. San Francisco, 1945; opening session UN, London, Eng., 1946, N.Y.C., 1946; European peace treaty sessions Council Fgn. Ministers, London, Moscow, USSR, N.Y.C., 1946-48; orgn. Marshall Plan, North Atlantic Treaty, Japanese Peace Conf., San Francisco, 1951, Bermuda Conf., 1953, Berlin Fgn. Ministers Conf., 1954, Big-Four Summit Conf., Four Power Fgn. Ministers Conf., Geneva, 1955, 2d Bermuda Conf., 1957, NATO Summit Conf., 1957, Berlin, Disarmament Negotiations, Paris Summit, 1960, Kennedy-Khrushchev Meeting, 1961, Manila Summit Conf. on Vietnam, 1966, Paris Peace Talks, 1968; assoc. prof. journalism U. N.Mex., Albuquerque, 1971-74. Recipient Pulitzer prize internat. reporting, 1951; Raymond Clapper Meml. award, 1951; Sigma Delta Chi award for nat. reporting, 1951; citation Overseas Press Club, 1955; Am. Acad. Achievement award for Washington corr., 1970; decorated Comdr.'s Cross Order Merit Fed. Republic Germany; chevalier Légion d'Honneur, Fance). Club: Gridiron (Washington). Home: Santa Fe N.Mex. Died Feb. 9, 1987.

HILDRED, SIR WILLIAM PERCIVAL, association executive; b. Hull, Yorkshire, Eng., July 13, 1893; s. William Kirk and Clare (Varley) H.; m. Constance Mary Chappell, July 20, 1920; children: Michael, Roderick, Barbara June, Anthony Clive. Student, Boulevard Sch., Hull, 1910; MA, Sheffield U., Eng., 1918, LLD, 1964. Entered Treas. Dept. United Kingdom, 1919, served as asst. prin., 1919-26; fin. officer Empire Mktg. Bd., 1926-34; head spl. measures br. Ministry of Agriculture and Fisheries, London, 1934-36; dep. gen. mgr. Exports Credits Guarantee Dept., 1936-38; dep. dir.-gen. civil aviation Air Ministry, London, 1938-39; prin. asst. sec. Ministry of Aircraft Prodn., 1939-40; assisted in formation RAF Ferry Command,

Montreal, 1941; dir.-gen. civil aviation Ministry of Civil Aviation, 194146; dir. gen. Internat. Air Transport Assn., Montreal, 1946-66. Served as 1st lt., 1st York and Lancaster Regiment, 1914-17; maj. Civil Service Bn., Home Guard. Decorated Knight, 1945, Companion of Bath, 1942, Officer Brit. Empire, 1936; Grand Officer, Order Orange Nassau, 1946, Order Crown of Belgium, 1948. Clubs: Reform, Athenaeum, Royal Aero (London). Home: Montreal, PQ Canada Died Nov. 21, 1987.

HILDRETH, HORACE A., ex-ambassador, broadcast executive, college president; b. Gardiner, Maine, Dec. 2, 1902; s. Guy and Florence T. (Lawrence) H.; m. Katherine C. Wing, Oct. 5, 1929; children: Josephine, Horace A., Anne L., Katherine G. AB, Bowdoin Coll., 1925; LLD, U. Maine, 1945, Temple U., 1950, Peshawar U., Pakistan, 1957; EdD, Suffolk U., 1950; Dr. Civil Laws, Bucknell U., 1954. Bar: Maine, Mass. 1928. With law firms Ropes, Gray, Best, Coolidge & Rugg, Boston, 1928-36, Hutchinson, Pierce, Connell, Scribner & Atwood, Portland, Maine, 1936-45; mem. Maine Ho. of Reps., 1940, Maine State Senate, 1941 (pres. 1943); gov. of Maine 1945-49; became pres. Bucknell U., 1949-53; ambassador to Pakistan 1953-57; then pres. Hildreth Network Radio and TV Sta. Home: Portland Maine. Died June 2, 1988.

HILL, DOUGLAS GREEN, musician; b. Tulsa, Oct. 7, 1930; s. Israel Phillip and Mabel (Turner) H.; m. Kathryn Thomas, Oct. 21, 1951 (dec.); children—Cynthia Ann, Barbara Diane, Lawrence Thomas. B.Music Edn., U. Tulsa, 1951, M.M., 1957; postgrad., U. N.M. Mem. string bass and tuba sect. Tulsa Symphony Orch., 1945-52, 54-57, New Orleans Symphony, 1949-50, El Paso Symphony, 1950, N.Mex. Symphony, 1961-78; string bassist Fred Waring Orch., 1950-51; tuba player N.Mex. Brass Ensemble, 1961-68, N.Mex. Symphony Brass Ensemble, 1968-78, Santa Fe Opera, 1962-72, Albuquerque Opera Theater, 1974-80; condr. Albuquerque Civic Light Opera, 1973-74; elementary band specialist Albuquerque Pub. Schs., 1960-86; instr. low brass and strings U. Albuquerque, 1967-70; Del. conf. on art in Ams. UNESCO, 1959, operating ptnr. Green Hill Prodns., from 1986. Served with AUS, 1952-54. Mem. Am. Fedn. Musicians, Music Educators Nat. Conf., N.Mex. Music Educators Assn., Phi Mu Alpha, Kappa Kappa Psi. Home: Albuquerque N.Mex. Died Jan. 9, 1987.

HILL, JAMES JULIAN, librarian; b. Vinita, Okla., Sept. 20, 1892; s. Davis and Frances E (Parks) H.; m. Katherine A. Barr, Aug. 12, 1919; children: John D., George M., Mary L. Hill Steele, Charles E. BA, MA, U. Okla., 1915; postgrad., Columbia U., 1916-17. Prin., librarian Okla. Mil. Acad., 1923-28; asst. librariam U. Okla., 1929-44, asst. prof. library sci., 1929-39, assoc. prof., 1939-44, bibliographer, from 1963; prof., dir. libraries U. Nev., 1944-61, emeritus, from 1962, cons. in bibliography, 1961-62. Mem. MLA, Calif. Library Assn., Nev. Library Assn. (pres. 1956-57), Okla. Library Assn. (pres. 1936-37), Assn. Coll. and Rsch. Libraries, Phi Beta Kappa, Phi Kappa Phi, Sigma Delta Chi, Sigma Nu. Democrat. Presbyterian. †

HILL, JOHN HUB, industrialist; b. Paris, Tex., Nov. 8, 1905; s. Joe Wilson and Tommie (Roberts) H.; m. Alstacheia Walker, June 6, 1953. Student, Paris. Bus. Coll., 1923-25. Classer-buyer McFadden Cotton Dallas Paper and Box Co., 1927-28, Acme Brick Co., Dallas, 1928-32; div. mgr. sales Acme Brick Co., 1932-51; propr. Hub Transp. Co., Dallas, 1933-40; pres. Houston-Harris Co., 1944-48, Hub Devel. Corp., 1944-48, Hub Improvement Corp., 1944-48, Denton Housing Corp., 1944-48, Sherman Housing Corp., 1944-48, Clearview Bldg. Corp., 1947-55, Clearview Park Inc., 1948-55, Dodd Corp., 1950-60, Hill-Elliott, Inc., Dallas, 1950—, Lakewood Terrace, Inc., 1950-70, Bergstrom Corp., 1951-58, Sill Corp., 1951-60, Hub Hill, Inc., Dallas, 1960-87, Hill-Elliott Investment Co., 1960-87, Tex.-Ariz. Motor Freight, Inc., 1964-65; ptnr. Sherman Bldg. and Supply Co., 1945-58, Jenkins Wholesale Lumber Co., 1946-50, Cavalier Lodge Motor Hotel, 1947-61, Hub Investment Co., 1948-65, Goodhue Bldg. Co., 1950-52, Lufkin Pine Lumber Co., 1950-54, Don Elliott Gen. Contractor, Dallas and Sherman, Tex., 1955-87, Rio Grande Valley farming interests, McAllen and Edinburg, Tex., 1961-87; pres., dir. Builders Loan Co., 1955-71; chmn. exec. com. Strickland Transp. Co., Inc., Dallas, 1967-78; pres., chmn. Tex. Bankers Investment Co., Dallas, 1968-87; pres. Wherry Mil. Housing Assn., 1958-61; chmn. bd., chmn. exec. com. Acme Brick Co., 1959-68; an organizer, mem. exec. com., dir. Park Cities Bank & Trust Co., 1959-62; developer, chmn. bd. Penn Towers, Inc., 1960-61; v.p., dir. L.M.S. Corp., 1961-65; dir. Transport Ins. Co., 1969-87, exec. com., investment com., 1971-87; dir. Transport Mgmt. Co., 1969-87; exec. com., investment com., 1971-87; dir. Transport Life Ins. Co., 1969-87, Am. Commonwealth Devel. Co., 1969-87. Mem. nat. adv. council Small Bus. Adminstrn., 1966-87, chmn. Tex. adv. council, 1962-67. Bd. dirs. Dallas Civic Opera, 1961-69, Children's Med. Ctr., Dallas, 1961-73, Tex. Council for Wildlife Protection, 1968-87, Dallas County Community Coll. Dist. Found., 1974-87; mem. adv. bd. Salvation Army, 1977-87; bd. visitors Tex. U.-M.D. Anderson Hosp. and Tumor Inst., Houston, 1968-87; mem. citizens council Scott and White Hosp., Temple, Tex., 1962-65; bd. dirs., mem. exec. com. Western Hwy. Inst., 1971-78; mem. chancellor's council U. Tex. System, 1973-87; mem. devel. council Baylor Coll. Dentistry, 1973-87; bd. devel. Dallas Bapt. Coll., 1970-87; mem. exec. com. S.W. Ctr. for Advanced Studies Devel., 1968-87; mem. adv. council Bishop Coll., Dallas, 1967-87, others. Mem. Dallas Council World Affairs, Tex. Bur. Econ. Understanding, Dallas C. of C., North Dallas C. of C., Dallas East C. of C., Oak Cliff C. of C., East Tex. C. of C., Lamar County C. of C. (hon. life mem.), U.S. C. of C., Tex. REsearch League, Newcomen Soc., N.Am., Internat. Platform Assn., Trinity Improvement Assn., Navy League U.S., Am. Trucking Assn. (bd. govs. common carrier conf. 1964-65, mem. Com. 100 1968—), Ind. Producers Assn., Am. Nat. Structural Clay Products Assn., Mid-Continent Oil and Gas Assn., Tex. Ind. Producers and Royalty Owners Assn., S.W. Clay Products Assn., Dallas Real Estate Bd., Tex. Real Estate Assn., Nat. Assn. Real Estate Bds., Dallas Execs. CLub, Dallas Petroleum Club, Ins. Club Dallas, Transp. Assn. Am., Admirals Club Am. Airlines. Methodist (past steward). Clubs: National Capital Democratic (Washington); Dallas Country, Dallas Athletic, Dallas Athletic Country, Imperial Lancers (Dallas); St. Anthony (San Antonio). Home: Dallas Tex. Died Mar. 19, 1987.

HILL, REUBEN LORENZO, JR., sociologist, educator; b. Logan, Utah, July 4, 1912; s. Reuben Lorenzo and Mary Theresa (Snow) h.; m. Marion Ensign, Sept. 9, 1935; children: Judith Ann Hill Wright, David Reuben, Susan Hill Oppegaard, Gladys Paulena Hill McBeth, George Richard. BS, Utah State U., 1935, HHD, 1977; PhM, U. Wis., 1936, PhD, 1938; postgrad., U. Chgo., 1941; Dr. honoris causa, U. Louvain, Belgium, 1970. From instr. to asst. prof. social edn. U. Wis., 1938-42; prof. sociology, head dept. U. S.D., 1942-44; assoc. prof. sociology Iowa State U., 1944-49; research prof. sociology U. N.C., 1949-53, 54-57, dir. Minn. Family Study Ctr., 1968-70, 71-73, Regents' prof. family sociology, 1973-83, Regents' prof. emeritus, 1983-85; fellow Ctr. for Advanced Study in Behavioral Scis., 1970-71; vis. prof. sociology Fla. State U., 1984; program cons. population Ford Found., 1964, 65-66; Fulbright sr. lectr. in family sociology Cath. U. Louvain, 1961-62; dir. family research, vis. prof. sociology U. P.R., 1953-54; dir. Groves' Conf. Marriage, 1950-57; cons. nat. orgns. Author: (with H. Becker) Marriage and Family, 1942, (with E.M. Duvall) when You Marry, 1945, rev. edit., 1967, Families Under Stress, 1949, (with W. Waller) The Family: A Dynamic Interpretation, 1951, (with J. Moss, C. Wirths) Eddyville's Families, 1953, (with Howard Becker) Family, Marriage and Parenthood, rev. edit., 1955, (with J.M. Stycos, K. Black) The Family and Population Control: A Puerto Rican Experiment in Social Change, 1959, (E.M. Duvall) Being Married, 1960, (with E. Driver and M. Nag) Needed Research in Population and Family Planning in India, 1968, (with Rene Konig) Families in East and West: Socialization Process and Kinship Ties, 1970, Family Development in Three Generations, 1970, (with others) Family Problem Solving, 1971, Family Economic Behavior: Problems and Prospects, 1973, (with W. Burr, Ivan Nye, I. Reiss) Contemporary Theories About the Family, 1979, (with T. Caplow and others) Middletown Families: Half a Century of Change and Continuity, 1981. Recipient Helen DeRoy award, 1956; Ernest Burgess award, 1963. Fellow Am. Sociol. Assn. (chmn. com. on internat. cooperation 1966-70); mem. Nat. Council Family Relations (dir.), Sociol. Research Assn., Internat. Sociol. Assn. (chmn. family research 1959-70, pres. 1970-74). Mormon. Home: Minneapolis Minn. Died Sept. 21, 1985; buried Ogden, Utah.

HILL, REY MARSHALL, government official; b. Beaver, Utah, Mar. 3, 1912; s. Charles Washington and Esther (Burgess) H.; m. Mary Howell, Aug. 9, 1935; 1 child, Lorna Rey (Mrs. Michael R. Anderberg). B.S., U. Utah, 1935. Staff statistician Utah Planning Bd., Salt Lake City, 1934-39; asst. economist U.S. Soil Conservation Service, Albuquerque, 1939-42; program officer Inst. Interam. Affairs, San Jose, Costa Rica, 1942-44; program officer Inst. Interam. Affairs, Washington, 1944-48, asst. dir. food supply div., 1948-50; dir. div. agr. and natural resources Inst. Interam. Affairs, 1950-52; asso. dir. for Latin Am. Fgn. Operations Adminstrn., Washington, 1952-54; asst. regional dir. for Near East of Ford Found., Beirut, Lebanon, 1954-58; dir. U.S. operations mission to Bolivia ICA, LaPaz, Bolivia, 1958-61; regional dir. for Latin Am. ICA, Washington, 1961; rep. for Iran of Ford Found., Tehran, 1961-64; dep. rep. Ford Found., New Delhi, India, 1964-68; dep. dir. U.S. AID mission to Thailand, Bangkok, 1968-69; dir. U.S. AID mission to Thailand, 1969-73; vis. lectr. AID, Calif. Poly. State U., 1973-75; internat. devel. cons. AID, from 1975; minister-counselor Am. embassy, Bangkok.; Chmn. bd. dirs. Calabrian Corp. Thailand, Ltd., Bangkok. Columnist, Valley Ctr. Roadrunner. Mem. adv. com. Musa Alami Found. of Jericho; bd. dirs. San Diego County Planning Group for Valley Center, Calif., 1980-83, Valley Center Community Recreation, Inc. Mem. Soc. Internat. Devel. (v.p. Thailand chpt. 1970-71), Escondido Country Club Community Assn. (bd. dirs. from 1984). Home: Escondido Calif. Died Oct. 10, 1986, buried Escondido.

HILL, ROBERT LELAND, economics educator; b. Coffeyville, Kans., July 12, 1922; s. Earl Winfred and Mary Greenshields (Latta) H.; m. Ann Elizabeth Rowe, 1977. BA in Econs., U. Mo., Kansas City, 1949, MA, 1951; PhD, Georgetown U., 1958. Economist Fed. Res. Bd., 1955-59; sr. assoc. Cresap, McCormick & Paget, N.Y.C., 1959-61; economist deptl. planning staff Dept. Commerce, 1961; dir. Office Emergency Readiness, 1962-65; prof. econs., chmn. econs. dept. Lynchburg (Va.) Coll., 1965-88, dir. program plans and research, 1965-68, William R. Perkins Jr. prof. econs., 1969-88, dir. Ctr. Econ. Edn., 1981-88. Contbr. articles, reports to profl. lit. Dir. Greater Lynchburg Transit Co., 1974-79, pres., 1976-79, Va. Assn. Pub. Transit Ofcls., 1977; mem. adv. bd. Va. Erosion and Sedimentation Control, 1974-76; bd. dirs. Robert E. Lee Water and Soil Conservation Dist., 1972-88. Served with AUS, 1942-45. Mem. Am. Econ. Assn., Va. Assn. Economists (pres. 1975-76), Order DeMolay, Gold Key Soc., Delta Xi, Masons. Home: Lynchburg Va. Died Apr. 15, 1988; buried York, Pa.

HILL, ROBERT MADDEN, judge; b. Dallas, Jan. 13, 1928; s. William Madden and Laila (Foster) H.; m. Patricia, Dec. 30, 1974; children by previous marriage—Alicia, Sally, John. B.B.A., U. Tex., 1948, LL.B., 1950. With R.T. Bailey, Dallas, 1950-52; with Caldwell, Baker & Jordan, 1952-59, Woodruff, Hill, Kendall & Smith, 1959-70; judge U.S. Dist. Ct., 1970-84, U.S. Ct. Appeals (5th cir.), Tex., from 1984. Mem. ABA, Am. Judicature Soc. Deceased.

HILLAIRE, MARCEL, actor; b. Cologne, Germany, Apr. 23, 1908; came to U.S., 1948, naturalized, 1954; s. Paul and Sofie (Lion) von Hiller. Grad. pub. schs., Cologne, Germany. Appeared numerous movies, TV, 1948-88 ; appeared as cooking prof. in: Sabrina, 1953; appeared as Insp. Bouchard in TV series Adventures in Paradise, 1959-61. Mem. Screen Actors Guild. Home: Los Angeles Calif. Died Jan. 1, 1988.

HILLENBRAND, HAROLD, dentist; b. Chgo., July 19, 1906; s. George Henry and Eleanor (Schmitt) H.; m. Marie Rose, Apr. 26, 1934; children: Keith Harold (dec. 1945), Gerald Bruce. Student, Loyola Acad., 1920-24, Sch. Arts Scis., Loyola U., Chgo., 1924-26; DDS, BSD, Loyola U., 1930, DSc, 1958; MDS, Nat. U. Ireland, 1952; DSc, U. Pa., 1953, Boston U., 1968, Coll. Holy Cross, 1970, U. P.R., 1970, U. Md., 1970; LLD, Temple U., 1963, Dalhousie U., 1972, Northwestern U., 1974; Dr. Pub. Service, U. Pacific, 1967. Pvt. practice dentistry, Chgo., 1930-45; sec. Am. Dental Assn., 1946-65, exec. dir., 1966-69, exec. dir. emeritus, 1970-86; assoc. prof. ethics and social relations Sch. Dentistry, Loyola U., 1942-52. Editor: Fortnightly Review of Chgo. Dental Soc., 1937-41, Desmos, 1938-44, Ill. Dental Jour., 1941-42; asst. editor Jour. Am. Dental Assn., 1942-45, editor, 1945-47; editor Jour. Dental Edn., 1970-72; contbr. numerous articles on various topics of dental practice to various jours. Recipient awards including Gold medal R.I. State Dental Soc., 1952; Fones medal Conn. State Dental Assn., 1954; Henry Spenadel award First Dist. Dental Soc., N.Y., 1954; Comdr. Order Duarte, Sanchez and Mella, Dominican Republic, 1956; hon. prof. U. de Santo Domingo, 1956; chevalier de l'Ordre de la Santé Publique (France); knight Order of Leopold II (Belgium); Officers Cross Order of Merit (German Fed. Republic); Silver medal City of Paris (France), 1961; Gold medal Pierre Fauchard Acad., 1966, John A. Callahan gold medal Ohio Dental Assn., 1969, Jarvie-Burkhart gold medal Dental Soc. State N.Y., 1970. Hon. diplomate Am. Bd. Dental Pub. Health. Fellow Royal Coll. Surgeons Eng. (dental surgery), Royal Soc. Health (hon.), Am., Internat. (hon.) colls. dentists, Royal Coll. Surgeons Ireland, Acad. Gen. Dentistry (hon.), Am. Pub. Health Assn., N.Y. Acad. Dentistry (hon.), Ill. Dental Soc. (hon.); hon mem. Internat. Assn. Dental Research, Swedish, Greek, Danish, Belgian, Brit., Finnish, Mexican, Dutch, Indian, Norwegian, Canadian, Philippine, French, German, Chilean, Argentinean, Italian, Peruvian, Swiss, Australian (Gold medal 1966) dental assns.; mem. Am. Dental Assn. (hon.), AAAS, Chgo. Dental Soc., Odontographic Soc. Chgo., Am. Hosp. Assn. (hon.), Med. Library Assn., Am. Assn. Dental Schs., Am. Assn. Dental Editors, World Med. Assn., Fedn. Dentaire Internat., Am. Acad. History Dentistry, Delta Sigma Delta, Omicron Kappa Upsilon. Roman Catholic. Club: Tavern. Home: Chicago Ill. Died June 1, 1986; buried Chgo.

HILLIER, WILLIAM HERBERT, lawyer; b. Chgo., Nov. 9, 1917; s. Harry Elias and Alice (Weed) H.; m. Frances Elizabeth Wynne, Feb. 9, 1946; children: David Richard, Herbert Spencer, Rebecca Alice, Robert Wynne. AB, Washington and Lee U., 1938; JD, U. Mich., 1941. Bar: Ill. 1941. Assoc. Lord, Bissell & Brook, Chgo., 1946-51, ptnr., 1952-81. Mem. Bd. Edn. Elementary Dist. 36, Wheaton, Ill., 1964-72, pres., 1966-72; mem. Community Sch. Dist. 200 Bd. Edn., Wheaton, 1972-74; bd. dirs. Beverly Farm Found., Godfrey, Ill., 1964-81, chmn., 1966-69, pres., 1973-81; bd. dirs. Cen. DuPage Hosp. Assn., Winfield, Ill., 1977-81, chmn., 1979-81; alumni dir. Washington and Lee U., 1969-73, chmn., 1972-73. Served with inf. AUS, WWII, ETO. Decorated Silver Star, Bronze Star, Purple Heart (2), Croix de Guerre (2) (France). Mem. ABA, Fedn. Ins. Council, Ill. Bar Assn., Chgo. Bar Assn., Chgo.

Law Club, Legal Club Chgo. Republican. Presbyterian. Club: University (Chgo.). Home: Chicago Ill. Died Mar. 12, 1981.

HILTNER, SEWARD, clergyman; b. Tyrone, Pa., Nov. 26, 1909; s. Clement S. and Charlotte (Porter) H.; m. Helen Margaret Johansen, May 29, 1936; children: James Seward (dec.), Anne Porter. AB, Lafayette Coll., 1931; Div. Sch., U. Chgo., 1931-35, PhD; DD, Lafayette Coll. Sec. Westminster Found., U. Chgo., 1933-35; exec. sec. Council for Clin. Tng. Theol. Students, 1935-38, Dept. Pastoral Services, Fed. Council Chs. of Christ in Am., 1938-50; assoc. prof. pastoral theology U. Chgo., 1950, then prof.; prof. theology and personality Princeton (N.J.) Theol. Sem., 1961-80, prof. emeritus, 1980-84; cons. profl. edn.; Alfred P. Sloan vis. prof. Menninger Sch. Psychiatry, 1957, hon. alumnus, 1970; Fulbright research scholar, New Zealand, 1958-59; vis. prof. U. Utrecht (Holland), 1970; cons. Trinity Counseling Service, Princeton; cons. The Menninger Found., 1957-72. Author: Religion and Health, 1943; Pastoral Counseling, 1949, Self-Understanding, 1951, The Counselor in Counseling, 1952, Sex Ethics and the Kinsey Reports, 1953, Sex and the Christian Life, 1957, Preface to Pastoral Theology, 1958, The Christian Shepherd, 1959; (with Lowell G. Colston) The Context of Pastoral Counseling, 1961; (with Karl Menninger) Constructive Aspects of Anxiety, 1963; Ferment in the Ministry, 1969; (with James L. Adams) Pastoral Care in the Liberal Churches, 1970; Theological Dynamics, 1972; editor: Christianity and Mental Hygiene, 1939, Clinical Pastoral Training, 1945, Toward a Theology of Aging, 1976; mem. editorial bd. Jour. Religion and Health, Theology Today, Am. Imago, Pastoral Psychology, Medical Aspects of Human Sexuality, Jour. Suicidology. Recipient Ann. award Acad. Religion and Mental Health, 1966; George Washington Kidd award Lafayette Coll., 1977; ann. award Am. Assn. Pastoral Counselors, 1980. Mem. Assn. Clin. Pastoral Edn. (disting. service award 1980), Phi Beta Kappa, Phi Gamma Delta. Presbyterian. Home: Princeton N.J. Died Nov. 19, 1984; buried Princeton Cemetery, Princeton, N.J.

HINCKLEY, ROBERT HENRY, business executive; b. Fillmore, Utah, June 8, 1891; s. Edwin S. and Adeline (Henry) H.; m. Abrella Seely, June 23, 1915; children: Robert Henry, Elizabeth, John Seely, Paul Ray. AB, Brigham Young U., 1916; LLD, Eton Coll., 1942. Instr. langs. Brigham Young U., 1914-16; in automobile bus. Mt. Pleasant, 1916-29; real estate and automobile bus; in aviation bus. Ogden, 1928-38; Mem. Utah State Ho. of Reps., 1918-20; mayor, Mt. Pleasant, 1924-25; asst. adminstr. WPA, 1935-36; mem. Civil Aeronautics Authority, 1938-40, chmn., 1939-40; asst. sec. of commerce, 1940-42; exec. Sperry Corp., N.Y.C., 1942-44; dir. Office of Contract Settlement, 1944-46; dir. First Security Corp., Salt Lake City; v.p., dir. Am. Paper & Supply Co., Salt Lake City; dir., mem. exec. com. Am. Broadcasting-Paramount Theaters Inc., from 1953; chmn. bd. Hinckeys Inc. Trustee Edward J. Noble Found.; regent U. Utah, 1928-41; Nat. Advisory Arthritis and Metabolic Diseases Council. Mem. University, Wings, Salmagundi, Nat. Press, Alta, Question clubs. Home: Salt Lake City Utah. †

HINE, JACK, educator, chemist; b. Coronado, Calif., July 2, 1923; s. Virgil Sylvester and Mildred Virginia (Wing) H.; m. Mildred Halacek, May 24, 1946; 1 child, Katherine; m. Myra Safley Baker, June 24, 1978. BS, U. Ark., 1944; PhD, U. Ill., 1948; LLD, Lewis Coll., 1965. Asst. research chemist Cities Service Oil Co., Okmulgee, Okla., 1943-45; research assoc. MIT, 1947-48; postdoctoral fellow Harvard U., 1948-49; asst. prof. chemistry Ga. Inst. Tech., 1949-51, assoc. prof., 1951-54, prof., 1954-58, Regents prof., 1958-65; prof. chemistry, then prof. emeritus Ohio State U., 1965-88; cons. NIH Medicinal and Organic Chemistry Fellowship Rev. Com., 1964-68. Author: Physical Organic Chemistry, 1956, 62, Divalent Carbon, 1964, Structural Effects on Equilibria in Organic Chemistry, 1975; mem. editorial adv. bd. Jour. Organic Chemistry, 1965-70. Alfred P. Sloan Research fellow, 1956-60. Mem. Am. Chem. Soc. (Fla. award 1962, Herty medal 1963, exec. com. div. organic chemistry 1963-65), Chem. Soc. London, Am. Phys. Soc., Société Chemique de France, AAAS, Faraday Soc., Phi Beta Kappa, Sigma Xi, Phi Kappa Phi, Alpha Chi Sigma, Phi Lambda Upsilon, Omicron Delta Kappa, Pi Mu Epsilon. Unitarian. Home: Upper Arlington Ohio Died July 6, 1988.

HINER, LOUIS CHASE, newspaperman; b. Astoria, Oreg., Apr. 19, 1919; s. Louis Chase and Rubye Marie (Isaac) H.; m. Phyllis Clark, Mar. 24, 1950; children: Gregory C., Bradley C.; 1 dau. by previous marriage, Mary Carolyn Hiner Koon. Student, Ind. U., 1938-39, 41-42. City editor Rushville (Ind.) Republican, 1942; editor Martinsville (Ind.) Reporter, 1946-47; with Indpls. News, 1947—, statehouse reporter, polit. and feature writer, 1947-52, aviation editor, 1949-52, Washington corr., columnist, from 1953, reporter presdl. campaigns, from 1948, reporter nat. polit. convs., from 1952; Washington corr. Gary (Ind.) Post-Tribune, 1956-67; Washington corr., columnist Phoenix Gazette, 1955-85, Muncie (Ind.) Eve. Press, from 1953. Served as pilot USAAF, 1943-46. Mem. White House Corrs. Assn., Ind. Hist. Soc., Ariz. Soc. of Washington, Am. Legion, Ind. Soc. of Washington, Sigma Delta Chi, Kappa Kappa Psi. Clubs: Nat. Press (Washington); Elks. Home: Falls Church Va. Died Feb. 7, 1987.

HINER, ROBERT L., transportation executive; b. Clinton County, Ind., Nov. 7, 1902; s. Ward Beecher and Vienna Susan (Fleming) H.; m. Margaret Stowers, Oct. 24, 1927; 1 child, Dan Stowers (dec. 1979). Student, Ind. U., 1923. Various positions leading to chmn. bd. Am. Red Ball Transit Co., Inc., Indpls., from 1925; lectr. traffic orgns. and lit. groups. Author: Songs of Life, 1971, On Wings of Words, 1976; contbr. articles to profl. jours. Named to Hon. Order Ky. Cols.; recipient Hanson H. Anderson award. Mem. Nat. Def. Transp. Assn. (life), Am. Truck Hist. Soc. (bd. govs., Spl. Citation 1980), Ind. Hist. Soc., Traffic Club N.Y.C., Ind. State, Indpls. chambers commerce, Indpls. Mus. Art. Clubs: Masons, Highland Golf and Country, Indpls. Athletic. Home: Indpls. Ind. Died May 28, 1987; buried Indpls.

HIROHITO, HIS MAJESTY, Emperor of Japan; b. Tokyo, Apr. 29, 1901; s. Emperor Yoshihito and Empress Sadako; ed. special tutors and The Peers' Sch.; m. Princess Nagako Kuni, Jan. 26, 1924; children: Shigeko (dec.), Kazuko, Atsuko, Akihito (Crown Prince), Masahito, Takako. Regent because of father's illness, 1921-26, became emperor, 1926; formally enthroned, 1928. Fellow Royal Soc. (U.K.). Author 9 books on marine biology. Home: Tokyo. Died Jan. 6, 1989.

HIRSCH, JAMES GERALD, physician, scientist, foundation executive; b. St. Louis, Oct. 31, 1922; s. Mack J. and Henrietta B. (Schiffman) H.; m. Marjorie Manne, June 6, 1943 (div. 1974); children: Ann I., Henry J.; m. Beate I. Fried, 1974; 1 dau., Rebecca A. B.S., Yale U., 1942; M.D., Columbia U., 1946. Intern, then asst. resident physician Barnes Hosp., St. Louis, 1946-48; NRC fellow Rockefeller U., N.Y.C., 1950-52; asst. prof. medicine and microbiology Rockefeller U., 1952-56, assoc. prof., 1956-60, prof., mem. inst., 1960-81, dean grad. studies, 1972-80; pres. Josiah Macy, Jr. Found., N.Y.C., 1981-87. Chmn. div. med. scis. Assembly Life Scis.; chmn. div. med. scis. NRC.; bd. dirs. Macy Found., Irvington House; chmn. bd. Trudeau Inst.; mem. corp. Yale U. Served to capt. USAF, 1948-50. Mem. Harvey Soc., Am. Assn. Immunologists, Soc. Am. Bacteriologists, Am. Acad. Microbiology, Soc. Exptl. Biology and Medicine, AAAS, Inst. Medicine, Am. Soc. Clin. Investigation, Assn. Am. Physicians, Nat. Acad. Sci., Alpha Omega Alpha. Home: New York N.Y. Died May 25, 1987, cremated.

HIRSCHFELD, TOMAS BENO, chemical engineer; b. Montevideo, Uruguay, Dec. 20, 1939; came to U.S., 1966, naturalized, 1974; s. Rudolf Georg Herman and Ruth (Nordon) H.; m. Judith Berggrun, Nov. 3, 1963; children: Noemi Brenda, Dinorah Jael, Susan Deborah. B.Sc., Vasquez Acevedo Coll., 1956; Ph.D., Nat. U. Uruguay, 1965. Asst. prof. spectrochemistry Nat. U. Uruguay, 1965-68; vis. scientist N.Am. Aviation Co., Thousand Oaks., Calif., 1966-67; staff scientist Block Engring. Co., Cambridge, Mass., 1969-71; chief scientist Block Engring. Co., 1971-79; scientist Lawrence Livermore (Calif.) Lab., from 1979; prof. Ind. U., Bloomington, 1977-83, U. Wash., Seattle, from 1983. Author; assoc. editor: Jour. Applied Spectroscopy; patentee in field. Trustee Temple Beth Sholom, Framingham, Mass., 1974-79, chmn. sch. com., 1975-76. Recipient IR-100 award Indsl. Research mag., 1975, 77, 81, 83, 85, 86. Fellow Optical Soc. Am. (editorial adv. bd. of jour.); sr. mem. IEEE; mem. Am. Chem. Soc., Coblentz Soc. (governing bd.), Soc. Applied Spectroscopy (hon. mem. 1987, Louis Straight award 1984, Pittsburgh award 1986, Meggers award 1987), Canadian Spectroscopic Assn., Soc. Photo-Instrumentations Engrs., Soc. Automated Cytology. Jewish. Club: B'nai B'rith. Home: Livermore Calif. Died Apr. 24, 1986; interred Eternal Home, Colnia, Calif.

HISCOCK, IRA VAUGHAN, educator; b. Farmington, Maine, May 7, 1892; s. Eugenie and S. Angie (Corbett) H.; m. Margaret McConway Scoville, Feb. 26, 1921; children: William McConway, Margaret Brooks (Weatherly). BA, Wesleyan U., 1914, MA, 1916, ScD, 1939; MPH, Yale U., 1921, MA, 1931; MD (hon.), Conn. Med. Soc., 1973. Bacteriologist Conn. Dept. Health, 1914-17, A.R.C., from 1917; served as 1st lt. A.E.F., 1918-19; col. U.S. Army, 1942; chief of pub. health Civil Affairs Div., War Dept., 1943-45; mem. faculty Yale U., 1920-60, prof. pub. health emeritus, 1960-86; sometime lectr. pub. health several univs. Author: Health and Welfare in Honolulu, Hawaii, 1929, Community Health Organization, 1929, Public Health in Hawaii, 1935, District Health Administration, 1936, Ways to Community Health Education, 1939, Practitioners' Library Preventive Medicine; contbr. reports of health surveys, articles to sci. mags. Mem. New Haven Bd. Health, from 1928, pres., 1942; pres. Conn. State Pub. Health League, 1951-52; vice chmn. health com. Nat. Boy Scouts Am.; mem. Conn. State Pub. Health Council, from 1952; health research cons. N.J. Health Dept., 1961-62; mem. Conn. State Pub. Welfare Adv. Com., 1962-69, Nat. Com. Community Health Action Studies, from 1962; pres. Nat. Health Council, 1938-40; exec. com. med. adv. bd. A.R.C., 1945-51; cons. pub. health Conn. Commn. on Reorgn. of State Dept.; mem. Conn. Commn. on Care and Prevention of Sickness, 1939-40; v.p. Nat. Social Welfare Assembly; active in direction of state and local health agys.; sometime officer severl nat. health affiliated agys.; pres. Accredited Schs. Pub. Health, 1957, Nat. Soc. Prevention Blindness, 1958; mem. health adminstrn. com. WHO, 1951-66; cons. to surgeon gen. AUS, from 1957. Decorated Legion of Merit; recipient Sedgwick medal Am. Pub. Health Assn.; medal Am. Cancer Soc., C.E.A. Winslow medal, Nat. Mental Health Bell; Helen Keller award Nat. Soc. Prevention Blindness; Conn. Bar Assn. Cup award. Fellow Am. Pub. Health Assn. (pres. 1955-56); mem. and sometime pres. several univ. and state health orgns., including Beaumont Club, Conn. Diabetes Assn., Assn. for Mental Health, mem. Soc. Am. Bacteriologists (pres. Conn. chpt.), Sigma Xi (former pres.), Delta Omega, Sigma Chi (former nat. pres.). Episcopalian. Mason. Clubs: Cosmos, Army-Navy (Washington); Graduate; Nat. Travel, Yale Club of N.Y.; N.H. Lawn; Randolph Mountain. Home: New Haven Conn. Died Apr. 4, 1986.

HISSONG, CLYDE, educator; b. West Milton, Ohio, June 29, 1892; s. Samuel and Edith (Pearson) H.; m. Clara Ethel Longanecker, 1913 (dec.); 1 child, Harriet; m. 2d, Mary Edra Champe, Aug. 30, 1929. Student, Earlham Coll., 1910-11; BS in Edn., Miami U., 1919, LLD, 1953; AM, Columbia U., 1924; PhD, Ohio State U., 1931. Tchr., pron. pub. schs., Ohio, 1911-28; dir. instruction, prof. edn. Bowling Green State U., 1928-29, dean, coll. of edn., 1929-45; state supt. pub. instrn., dir. edn. State of Ohio, 1945-54; prof. edn. Bowling Green State U., from 1954. Contbr. articles to profl. mags. Chmn. State Libr. Bd., 1945-54; exec. officer State Bd. for Vocat. Edn., 1945-54; mem. Ohio Tchrs and Pupils Reading Circle Bd., 1945-54. Mem. NEA, Ohio Edn. Assn., Northwest Ohio Tchrs. Assn. (pres. 1941-42), Kiwanis (lt. gov. Ohio dist. 1939-40, gov. 1942, chmn. internat. com. on vocat. guidance 1943, pres. Bowling Green Club 1934), Kappa Delta Pi, Phi Delta Kappa, Phi Beta Kappa. Methodist. Home: Bowling Green Ohio. †

HITCHCOCK, HENRY-RUSSELL, educator, architectural historian; b. Boston, June 3, 1903; s. Henry Russell and Alice Whitworth (Davis) H. Student, Middlesex Sch., 1917-20; A.B., Harvard U., 1924, M.A., 1927; student, Harvard Sch. of Architecture, 1923-24; D.F.A., N.Y. U., 1969; Litt.D., U. Glasgow, 1973; L.H.D., U. Pa., 1976; D.H.L., Wesleyan U., 1979. Asst. prof. art Vassar Coll., 1927-28; asst. prof. art Wesleyan U., Middletown, Conn., 1929-41; assoc. prof. Wesleyan U., 1941-47, prof., 1947-48; prof. art Smith Coll., 1948-61, Sophia Smith prof. art, 1961-68; prof. art U. Mass., Amherst, 1968; adj. prof. Inst. Fine Arts, N.Y.U., 1969-87; dir. Smith Coll. Museum Art, 1949-55; lectr. architecture MIT, 1946-48; vis. lectr. architecture Yale U., 1952-53, 59-60, 69, Cambridge (Eng.) U., 1962, Harvard, 1965; tchr. Conn. Coll., 1934-42; lectr. Inst. Fine Arts, N.Y.U., 1940, vis. lectr., 1951, 57; Mathews lectr. Columbia U., 1971; prin. investigator Am. Capitols Research Project, 1971; Civilian employee Navy Dept., 1942; tech. author Pratt & Whitney Aircraft, 1943-45. Prepared archtl. exhbns., Mus. Modern Art, N.Y.C., Springfield, Mass., Hartford, Conn., Worcester, Buffalo and Providence Mus.; circulated archtl. exhbns. from, Wesleyan; Author: Frank Lloyd Wright, 1928, Modern Architecture, 1929, J.J.P. Oud, 1931, Modern Architects, (with others), 1932, The International Style, (with Philip Johnson), 1932, The Architecture of H.H. Richardson, 1936, Modern Architecture in England, (with others), 1937, Rhode Island Architecture, 1939, In the Nature of Materials, the Buildings of Frank Lloyd Wright, 1942, American Architectural Books, 1946, Painting Toward Architecture, 1948, Early Victorian Architecture in Britain, 1954, Latin-American Architecture since 1945, 1955, Architecture: 19th and 20th Centuries, 1958, paperback edit., 1971, rev. edit., 1977, German Rococo: The Zimmermann Brothers, 1968, Rococo Architecture in Southern Germany, 1968, (with William Seale) Temples of Democracy, 1976, Netherlandish Scrolled Gables of the 16th and Early 17th Centuries, New York, 1978, German Renaissance Architecture, 1981, also articles U.S., foreign mags. Guggenheim fellow, 1945-46; recipient Am. Council Learned Socs. award, 1961, AIA award merit, 1978; Benjamin Franklin award Royal Soc. Arts, London, 1979; tribute by Helen Searing (editor) In Search of Modern Architecture, 1982. Fellow Pilgrim Soc., Royal Inst. Brit. Architects, London (hon.); mem. Coll. Art Assn., Soc. Archtl. Historians (dir., nat. pres., pres. N.Y. chpt. 1970-73), Royal Soc. Arts (London) (Franklin fellow), Victorian Soc. (London), Victorian Soc. Am. (pres. 1970-74), AAUP, Soc. Preservation N.E. Antiquities. Democrat. Unitarian. Club: Century (N.Y.C.). Home: New York N.Y. Died Feb. 19, 1987.

HITCHNER, ELMER REEVE, bacteriologist; b. Woodstown, N.J., Mar. 24, 1891; s. Wilbert Baker and Hannah (Reeve) H.; m. Barbara Dunn, June 18, 1927. BS, Pa. State Coll., 1915, MS, 1916; PhD, U. Wis., 1931. Instr. Pa. State Coll., 1916-17, N.Y. State Coll. Agriculture, St. Lawrence U., 1917-18; rsch. chemist E. I. Dupont Co., Deep Water, N.S., 1918-21; instr. U. Del., 1921-22; asst. prof. bacteriology U. Maine, 1922-24, assoc. prof., 1924-29, prof. bacteriology, from 1929, head dept. bacteriology, 1932-36, head dept. bacteriology and biochemistry, from 1936; dir. Pullorum Disease Control Program, Maine, from

1932. Contbr. articles dealing with bacterial taxonomy and physiology to scientific jours. Mem. Am. Acad. Microbiologists, Soc. Am. Bacteriologists, Inst. Food Technologists, Masons, Phi Kappa Phi, Sigma Xi, Alpha Zeta, Alpha Chi Sigma. Home: Orono Maine. †

HITESMAN, WALTER WOOD, publishing consultant; b. Baton Rouge, Aug. 9, 1918; s. Walter Wood and Anna (Allen) H.; m. Betty Parker, Oct. 9, 1948; 1 son, Jonathon. B.A., La. State U., 1939, postgrad., 1939-40. News editor Baton Rouge Advocate, 1939-40; bus. mgr. comml. printing div. McCall Corp., 1946-48; mng. dir. Reader's Digest, Can., 1948-60; v.p. Reader's Digest Assn., Inc., Pleasantville, N.Y., 1960-69; sr. v.p. Reader's Digest Assn., Inc., 1969-70, exec. v.p., 1970-71, 1st v.p., 1971-73, pres., 1973-74, dir., 1965-74; sr. v.p. Eastern Air Lines, N.Y.C., 1974-75; chmn. Am. Econ. Found., N.Y.C., 1976-77; publishing cons. 1977-86; Treas. Acad. Am. Poets. Bd. dirs. Marine Mil. Acad.; bd. dirs. Boscobel Restoration, Inc., Boys Clubs Am., Environ. Law Inst. Served to lt. col. USMCR, 1940-46. Named Direct Mail Mktg. Man of Year, 1969; Alumnus of Year, La. State U., 1974. Mem. Pilgrims of U.S., Sigma Pi, Sigma Delta Chi. Republican. Episcopalian. Clubs: Chappaquiddick Beach, Edgartown (Mass.) Yacht, Edgartown Golf (pres.). Home: Edgartown Mass. Died July 12, 1986; buried Edgartown, Mass.

HITSCHFELD, WALTER FRANCIS, educator; b. Vienna, Austria, Apr. 25, 1922; s. Alois and Amelie Hitschfeld; m. Irma Morissette, Sept. 6, 1947; children: Paul Alois, Charles Philip. Student, St. Francis Xavier U., Antigonish, N.S., 1942-43; B.A.Sc., U. Toronto, 1946; Ph.D., McGill U., 1950. Faculty Loyola Coll., Montreal, Que., Can., 1946-51; faculty McGill U., Montreal, 1950-86; vice prin. research McGill U., 1974-80, dean grad. studies, 1971-80; dir. McGill Internat., 1981-85. Contbr. articles to profl. jours. Recipient Patterson medal Atmospheric Environment Service. Fellow Am., Royal, Canadian meteorol. socs., Canadian Assn. Physicists, Royal Soc. Can. Home: Montreal Can. Died May 28, 1986.

HO, CHINN, investment banker; b. Waikiki, Honolulu, Feb. 26, 1904; s. Ti Yuen and Lan (Kam) H.; m. Betty Ching, Oct. 13, 1934; children—Stuart, Dean, Karen, John, Robin, Heather. Student, U. Hawaii Extension, 1925-26; LL.D. (hon.), U. Guam, 1980; H.H.D. (hon.), U. Hawaii, 1983. Various positions Bishop Bank, Duisenberg Wichman & Co., Swan Culbertson & Fitz, Philippines) and; Dean Witter & Co., Honolulu, 1924-43; chmn. bd., dir. Capital Investment of Hawaii, Inc., 1944-87; chmn. bd. Gannett Pacific Corp. (Honolulu Star-Bull., Inc., Guam Publs., Inc.); pres., dir. Makaha Valley, Inc.; internat. adv. bd. Sing Tao Newspapers, Hong Kong; dir. Host Internat., Inc., Victoria Ward, Ltd., Pacific Ins. Co.; mng. trustee Mark A. Robinson Trust, Mark A. Robinson Estate. Civilian aide to sec. of army, Hawaii, 1965-71. Named Optimist of Year Hawaii, 1956, Father of Year, 1961, Sportsman of Year, 1964, Salesman of Year Hawaii, 1966; recipient Golden Plate award Am. Acad. Achievement, 1968; Golden Eagle award, 1971; Nat. Jewish Hosp. honor award, 1972; Citizen of Year in Hawaii award, 1974; Golden Bear award Calif. Parks and Recreation Commn., 1981. Mem. Bishop Mus. Assn. (past pres.), Honolulu Stock Exchange (past pres.), Hawaii Visitors Bur. (past pres.), Honolulu Realty Bd. Club: Waialae Country. Home: Honolulu Hawaii. Died May 12, 1987; buried Makaha, Hawaii.

HOAGLAND, HUDSON, physiologist; b. Rockaway, N.J., Dec. 5, 1899; s. Mahlon Lounsbury and Ella (Baylis) H.; m. Anna Plummer, June 9, 1920; children: Mahlon Bush, Ann Holland, Peter, Joan. Student, Morris Acad., Morristown, N.J., 1913-17; AB, Columbia U., 1921; MS, MIT, 1924; PhD, Harvard U., 1927; DSc (hon.), Colby Coll., 1945, Wesleyan U., 1959, Clark U., 1962, Bates Coll., 1965, Boston U., 1966, Worcester Poly. Inst., 1966, Worcester Found. Exptl. Biology, 1979. Fellow NRC at Harvard U., 1927-28, instr. physiology, tutor biology, 1928-30; Parker fellow, spl. lectr. Cambridge (Eng.) U., 1930-31; prof. gen. physiology, dir. physiology labs. Clark U., Worcester, Mass., 1931-44; co-founder, exec. dir. Worcester Found. for Exptl. Biology, 1946-67, pres., 1967-68, pres. emeritus, 1969-82; rsch. assoc. physiology Harvard Med. Sch., tutor biochem. scis. Harvard Coll., 1940-41; cons. physiologist Worcester State Hosp., 1945-57; vis. lectr. physiol. psychology Harvard, 1945-46; rsch. prof. physiology Tufts Med. Sch., 1946-50, Boston U., 1950-68; cons. M.C., U.S. Army, 1948-54; bd. dirs. Guarantee Bank & Trust Co.; chmn. Macy Found. Conf. on Neuropharmacology, 1954-59; v.p. Conf. Sci., Philosophy and Religion, 1954. Author: Pacemakers in Relation to Aspects of Behavior, 1935, The Road to Yesterday, 1974, Reflections on Science and Human Affairs, 1974; editor: Hormones, Brain Function and Behavior, 1957; co-editor Exptl. Biology Monographs, Evolution of Man's Progress; mem. editorial bd. Ann. Rev. of Physiology; contbr. articles to profl. jours. Trustee George Washington Carver Found., 1960-68, Worcester Meml. Hosp., 1956-68, Woods Hole Oceanographic Instn., 1959-68; vis. com. Harvard Med. Sch. and Sch. Dental Medicine, 1959-64, dept. biology, 1965-71, dept. psychology and social rels., 1965-70. With U.S. Army, 1917-18. Recipient Humanist of Year award, 1965, Modern Medicine award, 1965, Worcester Engrin. Soc. award, 1969; Guggenheim fellow, 1944-45. Fellow AAAS (bd. dirs. 1966-70), Am. Acad. Arts and Scis. (pres. 1961-64); mem. Soc. Biol. Psychiatry (pres. 1967-68), Am. Physiol. Soc., Harvard Faculty Club, Worcester Club, St. Botolph Club, Century Assn. (N.Y.C.), Sigma Xi. Home: Southboro Mass. Died Mar. 4, 1982.

HOAGLUND, JAMES B., manufacturing company executive; b. Mpls., Sept. 15, 1924; s. Arthur William and Mary McCullough (Barron) H.; m. Mary Evans Lamb, Sept. 10, 1946; children: John Bjorn, Judith Ann, Nora Ellen. BEE, MIT, 1945, 1947. Chmn., chief exec. officer McQuay Inc., Mpls.; tech. dir. ITT, N.Y.C., 1969-72; v.p. corp. planning McQuay-Perfex Inc., Mpls., 1972-74, exec. v.p., 1979-82, pres., 1982; pres. McQuay Group, Mpls., 1974-79; chmn., chief exec. officer McQuay Inc., Mpls., 1983; bd. dirs. Pentair Inc., 1984. Patentee rooftop multizine air conditioning units. Bd. dirs. North Star Found., Mpls., 1983. Ensign USNR, 1943-46. Mem. ASHRAE, Air Conditioning and Refrigeration Inst. (bd. dirs. 1979-85), Mpls. Club, Interlachen Country Club (Edina, Minn.). Republican. Home: Edina Minn. Died Feb. 9, 1985.

HOBSON, HENRY WISE, clergyman; b. Denver, May 16, 1891; s. Henry Wise and Katherine Sophia (Thayer) H.; m. Edmonia Taylor Bryan, May 4, 1918; children: Katherine Bryan, Henry Wise, Anne Jennings, Margery Thayer. BA, Yale U., 1914; BD, Episcopal Theol. Sch., Cambridge, Mass., 1920; DD, Kenyon Coll., Gambier, Ohio, 1930, Yale U., 1937; LLD, Miami U., 1954, Ohio State U., 1955; LHD, Marietta Coll., 1959. Ordained deacon Protestant Episcopal Ch., 1919, priest, 1920, consecrated bishop, 1930. Asst. minister St. John's Ch., Waterbury, Conn., 1920-21; rector All Saints Ch., Worcester, 1921-30; bishop coadjutor Diocese So. Ohio, 1930-31, bishop, from 1931. Mem. nat. coun. Protestant Episcopal Ch., 1937-46, 50-55; trustee Kenyon Coll.; pres. bd. trustees Phillips Acad., Andover, Mass., from 1947; head Fight for Freedom Com. Capt. and adj. 356th Inf., 89th Div., U.S. Army, 1917; maj. in command 3d Bn. of same, 1917-18. Awarded D.S.C., 1918. Mem. Yale, Cin. Country, Hay Harbor, Fishers Island clubs, Skull and Bones, Psi Upsilon. Home: Cincinnati Ohio. Died Feb. 9, 1983, buried Spring Grove Cemetery, Cin.

HOBSON, LAURA ZAMETKIN, author; b. N.Y.C.; d. Michael and Adella (Kean) Zametkin; m. Thayer Hobson, July 23, 1930 (div. 1935); children: Michael, Christopher. A.B., Cornell U. Advt. writer to 1934; former reporter N.Y. Evening Post; promotion writer Time, Life and Fortune mags., 1934-40; became copy chief of all Time, Inc. mag. promotion, then dir. promotion for Time mag, full-time writer, fiction, newspaper columns, 1941-56; promotion cons. Time, Fortune, Sports Illus. mags., 1956-62; cons. editor Saturday Rev., from 1960; full-time novelist from 1963. Author: (juvenile) A Dog of His Own, 1941; The Trespassers, 1943, Gentleman's Agreement (Acad. award for Best Picture of 1947), 1947, The Other Father, 1950, The Celebrity, 1951, First Papers (Lit. Guild main selection), 1964; (juvenile) I'm Going to Have a Baby, 1967; The Tenth Month (also TV movie), 1971, Consenting Adult (alt. selection Lit. Guild, other book clubs), 1975, Over and Above, 1979, Untold Millions, 1982; Laura Z: The Early Years & Years of Fulfillment, 1987. Bd. overseers Coll. V.I. Mem. Authors League Am. (nat. council 1947-75), PEN, ACLU. Club: Regency Whist. Deceased.

HOCHWALT, CARROLL ALONZO, research chemist; b. Dayton, Ohio, Apr. 29, 1899; s. Albert Frederick and Adele (Butz) H.; m. Pauline Burkhardt, Sept. 27, 1922; children: Carroll A., Richard, Paula (Mrs. Robert E. Morie). BChemE, U. Dayton, 1920, DSc, 1935; DSc, Washington U., St. Louis, 1962, St. Louis U., 1964; LLD (hon.), Cath. U. Am., 1981. Research chemist Gen. Motors Corp., Dayton, 1920-24; prodn. mgr. Ethyl Gasoline Corp., Dayton, 1924-25; v.p. Thomas & Hochwalt Labs., Dayton, 1926-36; assoc. dir. central research dept. Monsanto Chem. Co., St. Louis, 1936-45; dir. Monsanto Chem. Co., 1945-48, coordinator research, devel. and engring., v.p., 1947-64, dir., 1949-64; pres. Chemstrand Corp., 1949-50, dir., 1949-64; dir. St. Louis Regional Commerce and Growth Assn., 1964-74; chmn. mgmt. com. Argus Chem. Corp. subs. Witco Chem. Co., Inc., N.Y.C., 1964-74; dir. Nat. Computer Service, Inc., Petrolite Corp., both St. Louis; cons. to policy com. Mallinckrodt Chem. Works, St. Louis, 1969-77; mem. tech. adv. com. Mallinckrodt Inc., St. Louis, 1981-87; mem. Manhattan Project on atomic bomb research; also mem. Div. 8., NDRC, World War II; mem. ordnance adv. com. research and devel. div. Dept. Army; ofcl. witness Operation Crossroads, Bikini Atoll, 1946; mem. Gov.'s adv. com. Mo. State Tech. Services Program, 1966-70, Greater St. Louis Arts and Edn. Council, 1963-69. Mem. lay bd. trustees St. Louis U., chmn., 1963-66, mem. pres.'s council, 1957-87; trustee Cath. U. Am., chmn. bd. trustees, 1968-70, U. Dayton, 1955-73, Charles F. Kettering Found., 1948-73; mem. Am. sponsors com. Am. Coll. in Paris, France, Cath. Commn. Intellectual and Cultural Affairs, 1952-87; adv. bd. Internat. Inst., 1964-87. Recipient Midwest award Am. Chem. Soc., 1956; Brotherhood citation NCCJ, 1969; Cardinal Gibbons award Cath. U. Am., 1970; Am. Sect. medal Soc. Chem. Industry, 1971. Mem. Am. Chem. Soc., Soc. Chem. Industry, Electrochem. Soc., Am. Inst. Chem. Engrs., AAAS, Am. Phys. Soc., Am. Ordnance Assn., Sigma Xi, Tau Beta Pi. Clubs: St. Louis, Bogey. Home: Saint Louis Mo. Died May 23, 1987; buried Calvery Cemetery, Dayton, Ohio.

HODGE, EDWIN, JR., manufacturing company executive; b. Henderson, Ky., Aug. 26, 1890; s. Edwin and Frances A. (Ditto) H.; m. Emma L. Clyde, June 10, 1915; children—Mrs. Margaret Dauler, Mrs. Frances Gordon, Mrs. Emma Sarosdy. B.S., Va. Mil. Inst., Lexington, 1910; LL.D., Thiel Coll., 1951, Washington and Jefferson Coll., 1962. Chmn., dir. Neville Chem. Co.; dir. Neville Cindu Chemie N.V., Uithoorn, Holland.; Mem. Greater Pitts. Airport Adv. Com.; Bd. dirs. emeritus Children's Hosp., Pitts.; emeritus mem. exec. com. Thiel Coll.; pres. Am. Ry. Car Inst., 1943-45, Drop Forging Assn., 1942-44. Episcopalian. Clubs: Mason. Clubs: Pitts. Athletic Assn. (Pitts.), Duquesne Fox Chapel Golf (Pitts.); Laurel Valley Golf Rolling Rock (Ligonier, Pa.); Port Royal Beach (Naples, Fla.), Hole-in-the-Wall Golf (Naples, Fla.). Home: Ligonier Pa. Died Apr. 1987.

HODGE, ELBERT J., lumber dealer; b. Carrollton, Ala., Mar. 6, 1892; s. James F. and Sallie (Lyles) H.; m. Emma Curry, Nov. 2, 1916; children: Kate (Mrs. William G. Lane), Elbert J., Ann. Student, Howard Coll., Birmingham, Ala., 1911-13. Engaged in lumber and agrl. enterprises 1919-32; with FCA, New Orleans, 1933-47; sole owner, mgr. retail and wholesale lumber bus., from 1947. Mem. Fed. Farm Credit Bd., FCA (Washington), Rotary. Home: Andalusia Ala. †

HODGES, ELMER BURKETT, lawyer; b. College View, Nebr., July 11, 1903; s. Charles Huntley and Mabel Gertrude (Blocher) H.; m. Maebelle Parsons, May 28, 1948; children: Deborah, Richard. Student, Jr. Coll. of Kansas City, Mo., 1921-23; LL.B., Kansas City Sch. Law, 1927. Bar: Mo. 1927, U.S. Supreme Ct 1940. Asst. county counselor Jackson County, Mo., 1929-35; mem. firm Gage, Hodges, Park & Kreamer, 1960-69; partner Gage and Tucker, Kansas City, 1970-79, of counsel, from 1980; sec. Parmelee Industries, Inc., U.S. Safety Service Co., Countryside Fund, Inc. Mem. Am., Mo. bar assns., Lawyer's Assn. Kansas City, SAR. Republican. Mem. Christian Ch. Clubs: Kansas City (Kansas City, Mo.), Mission Hills Country (Kansas City, Mo.), Owl (Kansas City, Mo.), Creek (Kansas City, Mo.); Westport Investors. Home: Kansas City Mo. Deceased.

HODGES, FRED MURCHISON, roentgenologist; b. Linden, N.C., Oct. 31, 1888; s. John Murchison and Sallie Worth (McNeill) H.; m. Louise M. Anderson, Sept. 3, 1929; children: Fred Murchison, Louise Meriwether. Student, U. Ga., 1903-06, Med. Coll. Va., 1906-08; MD, U. Pa., 1910; grad. work in radiology, Vienna, Austria, 1912-13. Gen. practice medicine Richmond, Va., 1910-12; specialist in radiology from 1914; clin. prof. radiology Med. Coll. Va., 1935-58, emeritus prof., from 1958. Maj., World War I; chief radiological group, Justis Hosp., Toule, France, 1918-19. Fellow Am. Roentgen Ray Soc. (former pres.), Am. Coll. Radiology (former pres.); mem. Richmond Acad. Medicine (former pres.), So. Med. Assn. (former pres.), AMA (chmn. sect. on radiology), Radiol. Soc. N.Am., Med. Soc. Va., Phi Chi, Commonwealth Club. Democrat. Presbyterian. Home: Richmond Va. †

HODGKINS, HENRY FOLLETT, manufacturing executive; b. Syracuse, N.Y., Feb. 2, 1892; s. Henry Clarence and Mary Ida (Follett) H.; m. Tuth Simmons, Oct. 6, 1917; 1 child, Henry Follett. ME, Cornell U., 1915. Registered profl. engr., N.Y. Prodn. engr. Savage Arms Corp., Utica, N.Y., 1916-19, Peters Mfg. Co., Ithaca, N.Y., 1919-21; dist. sales mgr. Wales Adding machine, Syracuse, 1921-23; gen. mgr. Jule Motors, 1923-26; with Lipe-Rollway Corp., 1926-29, gen. mgr., 1929-42, pres., 1929-58, chmn., 1958-68; pres. Rollway Bearing Co., 1936-58, chmn. bd., 1958-68; bd. dirs. 1st Trust & Deposit Co. Mem. bd. councilors Syracuse Meml. Hosp.; hon. chmn. Met. Devel. Corp., from 1959; mem. bd. govs. Syracuse U. Rsch. Inst. Mem. Anti-Friction Bearing Mfrs. Assn. (past chmn., bd. dirs.), Soc. Automotive Engrs., Nat. Mfrs. Assn. (past v.p., bd. dirs.), Mfrs. Assn. Syracuse (past pres., chmn. bd.), Citizens Found., Am. Ordnance Assn. (bd. dirs.), Navy Indsl. Assn. Inc., syracuse Home Assn. (bd. dirs.), Masons (32 degree), Onandage Golf and Country Club, Technology Club, Century Club, Rotary, University Club, Ft. Lakes Cruising Club, Cornell Club, Coral Harbour Yacht Club. Home: Syracuse N.Y. †

HODGKINSON, ROBERT, anesthesiologist, educator; b. Bolton, Eng., Feb. 2, 1922; came to U.S., 1952, naturalized, 1957; s. Robert and Mary (Shephard) H.; m. Ottillia Mathias, Aug. 7, 1974; children: Rima Stella, Sylvia Roxana. M.A., Cambridge U., 1944; M.D., 1946. Intern Plymouth, Eng., 1946-47; resident Townley Hosp., Eng., 1947-50; practice medicine specializing in anesthesiology; mem. staff Med. Center Hosp; faculty U. Tex., San Antonio, 1975-86; prof. anesthesiology U. Tex., 1981-86. Editor: Obstetric Anesthesia Digest. Served to capt. Brit. Army, 1950-52. Mem. AMA, Am. Soc. Anesthesiologists, Soc. Obstetric Anesthesia and Perinatology (pres.). Home: San Antonio Tex. Died Apr. 30, 1987.

HODGSON, CHARLES CLARK, lawyer; b. Kane, Pa., Oct. 24, 1906; s. J. Keene and Honora (Clark) H.; m. Helen G. Day, Jan. 6, 1937; children: Charles Clark, Helen (Mrs. Kerry L. Overlan), Stephen J., Richard J. A.B., Holy Cross Coll., 1927; LL.B., Temple U., 1939. Bar: Pa. bar 1931. Since practiced in Phila.; partner firm Stradley, Ronon, Stevens & Young, 1945-87; instr. bus. law U. Pa., 1940-52; Chmn. Phila. Parking Authority, 1953-55. Bd. dirs. Big Brother Assn., 1955-87. Mem. ABA, Pa. Bar Assn., Phila. Bar Assn. (bd. govs. 1954-55, com. censors 1960-62, chmn. com. specialization 1968-69). Democrat. Roman Catholic. Club: Phila. Cricket. Home: Philadelphia Pa. Died Nov. 12, 1987.

HOENECKE, KARL F., signal company executive; b. Ann Arbor, Mich., Apr. 1, 1930; s. Edgar Herman and Meta Amelia (Bunge) H.; m. Gretchen Riggs, Aug. 16, 1952; children: Meta, Sarah, Gretchen. B.A., U. Mich., 1954, M.B.A., 1955; A.M.P., Harvard U., 1968. Sales mgr. Univ. Microfilms Inc., Ann Arbor, 1955-57; pres. Graphic Systems Rockwell Internat., Chgo., 1957-75; chmn., pres. Fed. Signal Corp., Oak Brook, Ill., 1975-87; mem. N.Y. Stock Exchange Adv. Com.; dir. Am. Nat. Bank and Trust, Chgo., Puritan-Bennett Corp., Kansas City. Mem. com. Chgo. Symphony Orch., 1985; trustee Glenwood Sch. for Boys, Ill., 1974; bd. dirs. Community House Hinsdale, Ill., 1984-85. Mem. Chgo. Assn. Commerce and Industry (bd. dirs. 1984-87), Ill. Mfrs. Assn. (bd. dirs. 1974),. Clubs: Chicago, Mid Am. (bd. dirs., sec. 1981-84). (Chgo.); Hinsdale Golf. Home: Hinsdale Ill. Died Dec. 13, 1987.

HOFFMAN, CALVIN, poet; b. Phila., Nov. 1, 1916; s. Henry Michael and Rachel Elizabeth (Greentrees) H.; m. Rosemary Galowin, Nov. 15, 1941 (dec. Sept. 29, 1979). B.A., Columbia, 1937. Reporter UPI, N.Y.C., 1937-40; free lance book reviewer 1940-43; spl. lectr. Cambridge (Eng.) U., 1956-75, U. Birmingham, Eng., 1955-75, UCLA, 1960-65, numerous others in U.S. and Europe. Scenarist, Metro Goldwyn Mayer, Hollywood, Calif., 1943-46; drama critic Broadway (N.Y.) plays, 1946-60; poet, author, 1960-86; Author: Stigma, 1939, Science Isn't God, 1941, This Mad Peace, 1945, The Engulfing Tide, 1948, Condemned to Live, 1951, Of Love Enriched, 1954, The Murder of the Man Who Was Shakespeare, 1955, Maude Morgan, 1956, Sunset, 1958, Bondage, 1961, Expense of Spirit, 1965, Paid in Blood, 1968, Beaded With Roses, 1970, Time Must End, 1972, Of Pleasures Unknown, 1974, The Undying Quest: Was It Shakespeare or Marlowe?, 1975, The Warring Winds, 1976, Amber Waves, 1977, Man Hates Man, 1978, Wave of Doom, 1980. Mem. Marlowe Soc. Gt. Britain (named hon. chmn. 1958), Marlowe Clubs Am. (named hon. pres. 1959), Shakespeare Action Com. (dir. London 1958-66), Poetry Soc. Am., Elizabethan Soc., Dante Alighieri Soc., English Speaking Union, Renaissance Soc. Am. Home: Sarasota Fla. Died Feb. 4, 1986.

HOFFMAN, HARRY, lawyer; b. Ottawa, Ont., Can., Sept. 14, 1892; s. Edward and Sarah (Rosen) H.; m. Ethyle Miller, Mar. 26, 1917 (dec.); children: Edward Norman, Helen Grace (Mrs. Arthur Cranman), Ruth Paula (Mrs. Lee J. Sisisky), Flora Jean (Mrs. Fred F. A. Jacobsen). LLB, NYU, 1913. Bar: N.Y. 1915. Pvt. sec. Samuel Untermyer, 1908-16; pvt. practice law 1917-18; sec. to police commr. N.Y.C., 1917; assoc. Sutro Bros. & Co., 1920-22; sec.-treas. Fabrics Factors Corp., 1923-30; with Guggenheimer & Untermyer, N.Y.C., from 1932, ptnr., from 1944; ptnr. Guggenheimer, Untermyer, Goodrich & Amram, Washington, 1944-60, Guggenheimer, Untermyer & Goodrich, 1960-64; spl. asst. atty. gen. for elections, 1934-37. Bd. dirs., pres. Andrew Freedman Home; asst. sec. Dem. Nat. Conv., 1916. With AFC, U.S. Army, 1918-19. Mem. Am., N.Y. bar assns., Bar Assn. City N.Y., N.Y. County Lawyers Assn., Am. Soc. Internat. Law, Am. Judicature Soc., Am. Legion, Acad. Polit. Sci., Bankers Club Am., Nat. Dem. Club (N.Y.C.), Woodmere Country Club (past gov.), Masons. Home: Woodmere N.Y. †

HOFMANN, PHILIP B., pharmaceutical executive; b. Ottumwa, Iowa, May 25, 1909; s. Frank P. and Isabel (Matson) H.; m. Mary E. Kain, July 29, 1934; children: Judith, Carol I.; m. Georgia E. Fehlhaber, Feb. 8, 1968. Student, Wharton Sch. Fin. and Commerce, U. Pa., 1930. With Johnson & Johnson, New Brunswick, N.J., 1931-74; div. mgr. Johnson & Johnson, Boston, 1939; mgr. Ortho-Gynol div. Johnson & Johnson, 1940, bd. dirs., 1945-74, vice chmn. bd. dirs., 1949-63, chmn. exec. com., 1957-63, chmn. bd. dirs., chief exec. officer, 1963-74; pres. Ortho Pharm. Corp., 1941, chmn. bd. dirs., 1948-86; chmn. bd. dirs. , pres. Ethicon Inc., Ortho Pharm. (Can.) LTd., Ortho Pharm. Ltd., 1941-57; chmn. Johnson & Johnson Ethicon G.M.H., Germany, Chicopee Mfg. Corp., Chicopee Mills, LePage's Inc., Mass., Permacel Tape Corp., Johnson & Johnson-Ethicon A.B., Johnson & Johnson Internat., 1962-74, also chief exec. officer; bd. dirs. LePage's Inc., N.J.; commr. Port Authority N.Y. and N.J. from 1971; v.p. U.S. Equestrian Team Inc.; owner Wycombe House Stud thoroughbred horse farm, Reddick, Fla. V.p. Johnson & Johnson Rsch. Found.; mem. sch. bd. Branchburg Twp., 1944-86; trustee, chmn. joint conf. com. Somerset Hosp. Mem. N.Y. Bd. Trade (drug, chem. and allied trades sect.), Am. Cancer Soc. (pres. Somerset County chpt. N.J. div. Inc. 1946-49), Somerset County Community Forum (pres. 1948-49), Pharm. Mfrs. Assn. (bd. dirs. 1961-86), U.S. Combined Tng. Assn. (founder, past pres.), Thoroughbred Breeder's Assn. of N.J. (trustee), Capitol Hill Club, Essex Fox Hounds Club (Peapack, N.J.), Raritan Valley Country Club (N.J.). Home: Monmouth Beach N.J. also: Surfside Fla. Died Dec. 30, 1986; cremated.

HOFSTADTER, ALBERT, philosophy educator; b. N.Y.C., Mar. 28, 1910; s, Louis and Henrietta H.; m. Manya Huber, Feb. 12, 1936; 1 child, Marc. BS, CCNY, 1929; MA, Columbia U., 1934, PhD, 1935. Instr., asst. prof., then assoc. prof. NYU; assoc. prof. Columbia U., 1950-52, prof. philosophy, 1952-67, chmn. dept. fine arts and archeaology, 1955-57; prof. philosophy U. Calif., Santa Cruz, 1967-75, chmn. bd. studies in philosophy, 1967-68, 71-72, prof. humanities, 1975-76, prof. emeritus, from 1976; prof., chmn. dept. philosophy, grad. faculty New Sch. for Social Rsch., N.Y.C., 1976-78, prof. emeritus, from 1978. Author: Locke and Scepticism, 1936, (with Richard Kuhns) Philosophies of Art and Beauty, 1964, Truth and Art, 1965, Agony and Epitaph, 1970; translator, author intro. Poetry, Language, Thought by Martin Heidegger, 1971; contbr. articles to porfl. jours. Fellow Conf. on Sci., Philosophy and Religion in Relation to Democratic Way of Life; Guggenheim fellow, 1945, Ctr. Advanced Study Behavioral Scis. fellow Stanford U., 1966-67, NEH sr. fellow, 1974. Mem. Am. Philos. Assn. (v.p. Ea. div. 1968-69), N.Y. Philosophy Club (sec. 1950-54), Am. Soc. for Aesthetics (trustee from 1973), Am. Metaphys. Soc., Soc. for Phenomonology and Existential Philosophy (exec. com. from 1976), Heklegger Circle. Home: Santa Cruz Calif. Died Jan. 26, 1989.

HOGG, IRA D(WIGHT), educator; b. near Delphos, Kans., Dec. 31, 1892; s. William and Mary E. (Walmsley) H.; m. E. Leona Hotle, May 23, 1918; children: Ruth Irene, Warren D., Mervin E. Student, Miltonvale Wesleyan Coll., 1916-18; AB, U. Kans., 1921, AM, 1923, PhD, 1926. Asst. instr. anatomy U. Kans., 1921-23, instr., 1923-26; asst. prof. anatomy U. Pitts., 1926-46; prof. anatomy U. Miss., from 1946, chmn. dept., 1946-58. Contbr. articles to profl. jours. Dir. March of Dimes Nat. Found. Infantile Paralysis, Lafayette County, Miss., 1948-51. Mem. AAAS, Am. Assn. Anatomists, Miss. Am. Legion, Lions Club, Sigma Xi. Presbyterian. Home: Jackson Miss. †

HOGG, WILBUR, bishop; b. Balt., Aug. 28, 1916; s. Wilbur Emory and Ida May (Spath) H.; m. Lota Winchell Curtiss, Sept. 6, 1947. AB, Brown U., 1938; ThM, Phila. Div. Sch., 1941; DD, Gen. Theol. Sem., 1977. Ordained priest Episcopal Ch. Curate St. Mary's Ch., Burlington, N.J., 1941-43, rector, 1943-51; fellow, tutor Gen. Theol. Sem., N.Y.C., 1953-54; rector Ch. St. Mary the Virgin, Falmouth Foreside, Maine, 1954-68; dean St. Luke's Cathedral, Portland, Maine, 1968-73; bishop Diocese of Albany, N.Y., from 1974; chaplain, tchr. St. Mary's Hall, Burlington, N.J., 1943-51. With U.S. Army, 1945-46, 51-53. Fellow Coll. Preachers Washington; mem. Order Holy Cross (assoc.), Fort Orange Club. Home: Albany N.Y. Died May 10, 1986; interred Cathedral of All Saints, Albany.

HOHAUS, REINHARD A(RTHUR), insurance executive; b. N.Y.C., Aug. 29, 1896; s. Reinhard and Ursula (Hengstler) H.; m. Agnes Hyatt, May 12, 1933; children: Gretchen, Joanna, Reinhard A. AB, N.Y. State Tchrs. Coll., Albany, 1917. With Little Textile Corp., Am. Purchasing Corp., 1919-21; with actuarial div. Met. Life Ins. Co., N.Y.C., 1921-25, asst. actuary, 1925-40, assoc. actuary, 1940-46, actuary, 1946-52, v.p., actuary, 1952-53, v.p., chief actuary, 1953-59, sr. v.p., chief actuary, 1960-62, exec. v.p., 1962-63, also bd. dirs.; chmn. N.Y. State Commn. on Pensions, 1954-60, N.Y. State Adv. Coun. on Pensions, 1960-87; mem. Fed. Adv. Coun. on Social Security Financing, 1957-58. Contbr. articles to profl. and bus. publs. With USN, 1917-19. Fellow Soc. Actuaries; mem. Am. Inst. Actuaries (past pres.), Internat. Congress Actuaries, Health Ins. Assn. Am. (bd. dirs. 1956-60). Home: New York N.Y. Died Jan. 5, 1987.

HOHL, ELIZABETH MASON, physician, surgeon; b. Beaver City, Nebr., Aug. 8, 1890; d. William Henry and Nellie Lavina (Booth) Mason; m. Harrison L. Hohl, 1916 (div. 1934); 1 child, Mason. BS, U. Nebr., 1913, MD, 1915. Intern Nebr. Meth. Hosp., Omaha, 1915-16; pvt. practice McCook, Nebr., 1916-24, Hollywood, Calif., from 1924; cons. surgeon L.A. City Receiving Hosp.; chief Sunset Blvd. and Hollywood West hosps.; mem. staff Hollywood Presbyn., L.A. County Gen. hosps.; chief of staff Good Shepherd Convent Sch.; formerly mem. staff Plaza Community Ctr.; co-founder, chief of staff Cancer Prevention Soc. and Detection Clinic, from 1944, also adminstr. translator: Diseases of Women (Tortula 1170 of Salerno), 1940; contbr. to Ency. Brittanica, 1944. Founder, pres. L.A. Physicians Aid Assn., Career Women and Pan Am. Med. Women's Alliance; bd. dirs. Clark House for Girls, YWCA. Named Woman Physician of Yr., 1954, 55, L.A. Times Woman of Yr., 1956. Mem. Am. Med. Woman's Assn. (historian past pres.), AMA, Calif., L.A. County (coun.) med. assns., Internat., L.A. med. woman's assns., Hollywood Acad. Medicine, Pub. Health League, Am. Geriatrics Soc., Barlow Soc. History Medicine (past pres.). Republican. Home: Los Angeles Calif. †

HOLBROOK, GEORGE EDWARD, chemical engineer; b. St. Louis, Mar. 4, 1909; s. Edward M. and Doretta C. (Krentler) H.; m. Dorothy H. Williams, June 12, 1933; children: James E., Thomas E. B.S., U. Mich., 1931, M.S., 1932, Ph.D., 1933, D.Sc., 1967. With E.I. duPont de Nemours & Co., Inc., Wilmington, Del., 1933-76; asst. gen. mgr. organic chems. dept. E.I. duPont de Nemours & Co., Inc., 1955-56, gen. mgr. elastomer chems. dept., 1957-58, v.p., dir., mem. exec. com., 1958-69, dir., mem. finance, bonus and salary coms., 1970-76; Bd. dirs. Del. Research Found., Devel. Council U. Mich.; mem. adv. bd. residencies in engring. Ford Found.; mem. chem. engring. adv. bd. U. Rochester, U. Del.; adv. bd. Ford Found.; bd. overseers Newark Coll. Engring.; bd. engring. edn. U. Pa.; exec. com. Office Critical Tables, Nat. Acad. Scis.; governing bd. NRC, also exec. com. engring. div.; exec. com. engring. div.; exec. com. Hwy. Research Bd.; dir. Chem. Bur. Nat. Prodn. Authority, 1952. Contbr. articles to profl. jours. Vice-chmn. bd. trustees St. Francis Hosp. Fellow Am. Inst. Chem. Engrs. (pres. 1958, treas. 1963-69, Profl. Progress award 1953, Founders' award 1961, Van Antwerpen award 1980, Eminent Engr. 1983); mem. Engrs. Joint Council (v.p., dir., mem. exec. com. 1960-61), Mfg. Chemists Assn. (dir., mem. exec. com. 1960-61), Am. Chem. Soc. (com. on corp. assn. 1967-70), Soc. Chem. Industries, Am. Phys. Soc., AAAS, N.Y. Acad. Sci., Franklin Inst., Instn. Chem. Engrs. London (hon.), Nat. Acad. Engring. (charter; mem. exec. com. 1964), U.S. Power Squadron, Sigma Xi, Tau Beta Pi, Phi Lambda Upsilon, Phi Kappa Phi, Phi Eta Sigma, Iota Alpha. Clubs: Chemists; Univ. (Ann Arbor); Miles River Yacht, DuPont Country, Wilmington Country. Home: Hockessin Del. Died Feb. 26, 1987.

HOLBROOK, WILLARD AMES, army officer; b. Fort Grant, Ariz., May 31, 1898; s. William Ames Sr. and Anna Huntington (Stanley) H.; m. Helen Herr, June 7, 1930 (dec.); children: Joanne Stanley, Willard Ames III, Marion Herr. BS, U.S. Mil. Acad., 1918; student, Infantry Sch., Ft. Benning, Ga.; grad. tng. officer course, Cavalry Sch., 1924, grad. spl. advanced equitation course, 1925; grad., Command and Gen. Staff Sch., 1929, Army War Coll., 1940. Commd. 2d lt. U.S. Army, 1918, advanced through grades to brig. gen., 1944; served with 10th cav., Provisional Cav. Squadron, Am. Forces in Germany, 3d cav., Ft. Myers, Va., 2d cav., Ft. Riley, 14th cav., Ft. Sheridan, 10th cav., Huachuca, Ariz.; detailed to Gen. Staff G-2 (mil. intelligence), 1940-42; with 11th armored div., Camp Polk, La., Camp Barkeley, Tex., Camp Cooke, Calif., 1942-44; then stationed in German; pres., chief exec. Fed. Services Fin. Corp., also bd. dirs.; bd. dirs. Griffiths Consumers Co., Washington. Decorated Silver Star with oak leaf cluster, Legion of Merit, Bronze Star; Croix de Guerre (Belgium); Croix de Guerre, Legion d'Honneur (France). Mem. Army and Navy Club, Army and Navy Country Club (Washington), University Club (N.Y.C.). Home: Washington D.C. Died July 3, 1986.

HOLCOMB, RICHARD YOUNG, lawyer; b. Fayetteville, Ark., Jan. 28, 1915; s. Bruce and Daisy (Young) H.; m. Sylvia Wooster, Aug. 24, 1946; children: Bruce, Martha. AB, U. Ark., 1935; LLB, Columbia U., 1938. Bar: N.Y. 1938. Ptnr. Donovan Leisure Newton & Irvine, N.Y.C., 1938-86; village atty. Village of Ardsley, N.Y., 1957. Served to capt. U.S. Army, 1941-46, ETO. Mem. ABA, Assn. Bar City of New York, N.Y. State Bar Assn., Hemisphere Club. Democrat. Presbyterian. Home: Irvington N.Y. Died Mar. 10, 1986.

HOLDEN, ARTHUR CORT, architect; b. N.Y.C., Nov. 29, 1890; s. Edwin B. and Alice (Cort) H.; m. Miriam Young, Feb. 10, 1917 (dec.); children: Edwin Arthur (dec.), Jame (Mrs. Clay) (dec.), Richmond Young; m. 2d, Rose M. N. Barnes, 1977. Litt.B., Princeton U., 1912; B.Arch. and A.M. in Econs., Columbia, 1915. Began practice of architecture 1920; mem. Arthur C. Holden & Assocs., 1920-30, Holden, McLaughlin & Assocs., 1930-54, Holden, Egan, Wilson & Corser, 1954-68, Holden, Yang, Raemsch & Corser, 1968-77, Holden, Yang Raemsch, Terjesen, 1972; cons. on financing of constrn. and real estate, from 1977; cons. architect to N.Y. State Bd. Housing, 1926; spl. cons. to Temporary Commn. to Examine and REvise Tenement House LAw, 1927; mem. Pres.'s Conf. on Home Bldg. and Home Ownership, 1930; dir. Architect's Small House Service Bur. to 1931; mem. bd. architects exec. com. N.Y.C. Housing Authority, 1934; spl. advisor Div. of Econ. Rsch. and Planning NRA; mem. Mayor's Com. on City Planning, 1934-38, 20th Centruy Fund Housing Com., 1940-41; exec. bd. Citizens Housing Coun., 1936; chmn. Conf. Planning Men's Phys. Environ., Princeton Bicentennial, 1947. Author: Brick Architecture of the Colonial Period in Maryland and Virginia, 1919, Settlement Idea, 1922, Primer of Housing, 1927, Money in Motion, 1940, Sonnets for My City—An Essay on the Kinship of Art and Finance, 1965, At the Roots of the Urban Crisis, 1970, Credit Extending vs. Money Lending, 1976, Three Essays on the Inflation, 1979; also contbr. articles dealing with homebuilding and housing to leading mags., Britannica and Nat. encys.; designer: Garden Plan Apts. (5 projects); architect: Queensborough Community

Coll., housing projects in Jacksonville, Fla., Balt., Charleston, S.C., Dragerton, Utah, N.Y.C. (4 projects), Princeton, N.J. (3 projects), 1946; reconstructed Minetta Lane Slum, 1924. Mem. Com. Econ. Recovery; trustee Lenox Hill Hosp. Fellow AIA (dir., chmn. N.Y. com. omn apt. house awards, vice-chmn. com. postwar reconstrn., medal of honor N.Y. chpt. 1957, pioneer in housing 1972, pres. N.Y. chpt. 1944-45, exec. com. 1945-47, mem. N.Y. Bldg. Congress, v.p. 1936-43, chmn. land utilization com. 1933-38), N.Y. Urban League (pres. 1922-31, mem. exec. bd. to 1943), Univ. Club, Architectural League, Cosmos Club (Washington), Grolier Club, Players Club, Coffee House (N.Y.C.). Home: Washington Conn. Deceased.

HOLDEN, WILLIAM FRANKLIN, motion picture actor; b. O'Fallon, Ill., Apr. 17, 1918; s. William Franklin and Mary (Ball) Beedle; m. Ardis Ankerson (Brenda Marshall), July 13, 1941 (div.); children: Peter Westfield, Scott Porter. Student, Pasadena Jr. Coll., 1937-38. Former v.p. George W. Gooch Labs., L.A.; former pres. Toluca Prodns. Corp.; adviser to Hollywood Coordinating Com. Actor, starring in pictures: Golden Boy, 1939, Our Town, 1939, Arizona, I Wanted Wings, 1940, Dear Ruth, 1946, Apartment for Peggy, 1947, Sunset Boulevard, 1949, Born Yesterday, 1950, Stalag 17, 1952, The Moon is Blue, 1953, Executive Suite, 1953, Bridge at Toko-ri, 1954, Country Girl, 1954, Love is a Many Splendored Thing, 1955, Picnic, 1956, Proud and Profane, 1956, Toward the Unknown, 1956, Bridge on the River Kwai, 1957, The Key, 1957, Horse Soldiers, 1958, Counterfeit Traitor, 1962, World of Suzy Wong, Satan Never Sleeps, The Lion, The Longest Day, Alvarez Kelly, Casino Royal, 1967, The Devil's Brigade, 1968, The Wild Bunch, The Christmas Tree, Wild Rovers, 1971, The Revengers, 1972, Breezy, 1973, Open Season, Towering Inferno, 1974, Network (Acad. award nomination), 1976, Damien—Omen II, 1978, Fedora, 1979, S.O.B., 1981; TV miniseries The Blue Knight, 1973; TV movie 21 Hours at Munich, 1976. Recipient Best Actor award Look Mag., 1953, Acad. award for best actor, 1953, Internat. Film Exhibitor's award, 1954, Star of the Yr. award Theatre Owners of Am., 1956. Mem. Motion Picture Acad. Arts and Scis. (bd. dirs.), Motion Industry Coun. Home: Palm Springs Calif. Died Nov. 16, 1981.

HOLLAENDER, ALEXANDER, biophysicist; b. Samter, Germany, Dec. 19, 1898; came to U.S., 1921, naturalized, 1927; s. Heymann and Doris (Rotholz) H.; m. Henrietta Wahlert, Oct. 10, 1925. AB, U. Wis., 1929, MA, 1930, PhD, 1931, DSc honoris causa, 1969; DSc honoris causa, U. Vt., 1959, U. Leeds, Eng., 1962, Marquette U., 1967; MD honoris cause, U. Chile Med. Sch., 1970; Prof. honoris causa, Fed. U. Rio de Janeiro. Asst. phys. chemistry U. Wis., 1929-31; NRC fellow in biol. scis. 1931-33; investigator Rockefeller Found., 1934; investigator charge radiation work NRC project, Wis., 1934-37; asso. biophysicist Washington Biophysics Inst., NIH, USPHS, 1937-38, biophysicist, 1938-41, sr. biophysicist, 1941-45, prin. biophysicist, 1945-46, head biophysicist, 1946-50; dir. biol. div. Oak Ridge Nat. Lab., 1946-66, sr. research adviser, 1967-73; prof. radiation biology U. Tenn., 1957-66; prof. biomed. scis. U. Tenn.-Oak Ridge Grad. Sch. Biomed. Scis., 1966-86; dir. Archives Radiation Biology, U. Tenn., 1966-86; Messenger lectr. Cornell U., 1962; cons. Oak Ridge Nat. Lab., Brookhaven Nat. Lab., Nat. Inst. for Environ. Health Scis., Nat. Cancer Inst., Plenum Pub. Co.; cons. EPA; organizer fgn. and domestic workshops and tng. courses in environ. mutagenesis and carcinogenesis; civilian with AEC, OSRD, Office Surgeon Gen., USN; mem. com. radiation biology, mem. com. photobiology, div. biol. and agr., chmn. and mem. subcom. radiobiology, div. phys. scis. NRC; hon. pres. 9th Internat. Photobiology Congress. Editor: Radiation Biology (3 vols.), Vol. III, 1956, Radiation Protection and Recovery, 1960, Chemical Mutagens: Principles and Methods for their Detection, 7 vols, 1971-81, Genetic Engineering for Nitrogen Fixation, 1977, Limitations and Potentials for Biological Nitrogen Fixation in the Tropics, 1978, The Biosaline Concept: An Approach to the Utilization of Underexploited Resources, 1979, (with J.K. Setlow) Genetic Engineering: Principles and Methods, Vol. I, 1979, Vol. II, 1980, Vol. III, 1981, Vol. IV, 1982, Vol. V, 1983, Vol. VI, 1984, Vol. VII, 1985, Vol. VIII, 1986, (with Rains and Valentine) Genetic Engineering of Osmoregulation, 1980, (with others) Trends in the Biology of Fermentations for Fuels and Chemicals, 1981, Engineering of Microorganisms for Chemicals, 1981, (with R.A. Fleck) Genetic Toxicology: An Agricultural Perspective, 1982, (with others) Biological Basis of New Developments in Biotechnology, 1983, (with Kosuge and Meredith) Genetic Engineering of Plants: An Agricultural Perspective, 1983, (with D. Helinski et al) Plasmids in Bacteria, 1985, (with V. Dellarco et al) Aneuploidy: Etiology and Mechanisms, 1985, (with J. Warren) Genetic Engineering of Animals, 1986, (with M. Zaitlin and P. Day) Biotechnology in Plant Science: Relevance to Agriculture in the Eighties, 1986, (with D.M. Shankel et al) Antimutagenesis and Anticarcinogenesis: Mechanisms, 1986. Recipient AEC citation for outstanding service to atomic energy program, 1966, Finsen medal 5th Internat. Congress on Photobiology, 1968; E.M.S. award, 1975, Enrico Fermi award, 1983, disting. contbn. award Soc. for Risk Analysis, 1985; Outstanding Scientist and Engr. award Tenn. Technology Found., 1986; decorated Order Merit Republic Italy, 1961. Fellow AAAS, Am. Acad. Arts and Sci., Indian Nat. Sci. Acad. (fgn.), Brazilian Acad. Sci. (fgn.); mem. Solar Energy Soc., Am. Physiol. Soc., Radiation Research Soc. (pres. 1954-55), Am. Soc. Cell Biology, Internat. Assn. Radiation Research (pres. 1962-66), Nat. Assn. de Photobiologie (pres. 1954-60, hon. pres. 1964, exec. com. 1960-66), Genetics Soc. Am. (citation 1979), Am. Soc. Naturalists (v.p. 1952-53), Soc. Gen. Physiologists, U.S. Nat. Acad. Scis. (award for environ. quality 1979), Am. Soc. Microbiology, Am. Physiol. Soc., Environ. Mutagen Soc. (pres. 1969-71), Internat. Environmental Mutagens Soc. (pres. 1973-77), Knoxville Acad. Medicine (hon.). Died Dec. 6, 1986.

HOLLAND, EUGENE, business executive; b. Friend, Nebr., Oct. 29, 1891; s. Laurence and Mary Frances (Crowley) H.; m. Louise Bedwell, Oct. 21, 1916; children: Laurence B., Eugene Jr., Sara Louise Holland Alberts. Student, U. Nebr., 1913. Founder Holland Lumber Co., Lincoln, Nebr., Omaha and Sioux City, Iowa, 1917, pres., also bd. dirs., 1917-28, 1944-45; pres., also bd. dirs. Holland Lumber Co., Omaha, 1953-58, chmn. from 1958; pres., dir. Universal Gypsum & Lime Co., Chgo., 1928-36; bus. cons. Sanderson & Porter, N.Y.C., 1936-39; pres., dir. Florence Stove Co., Gardner, Mass, Marshall Stove Co., Lewisburg, Tenn., Am. Rock Wool Co., Chgo., 1940-46, Masonite Corp Am., 1946-52; v.p., dir. Masonite Corp. Can., Ltd., 1946-53; bus. cons. from 1953; v.p., dir. Standard Sandy Mix Co., Sioux City; bd. dirs. Parke Lumber & Coal Co., Hawkeye Bldg. Supply Co., Tri-State Cashway Lumber Co., Fairmont Foods Co., Thomas Hoist Co., Gulf, Mobile & Ohio R.R. Mem. Lincoln Assn. Commerce (life), Chgo. Club, Skokie Country Club, Old Elm Country Club, Delta Upsilon. Home: Glencoe Ill. †

HOLLEY, CLYDE EUGENE, lawyer; b. nr. Hillside, Mich., Mar. 17, 1891; s. Ephriam Eugene and Ella Francelia (Kies) H.; m. Elizabeth Ford Martin, Sept. 10, 1924; children: Nancy Elizabeth (Mrs. Edward McKenzie Hitchcock), Jeanne Louise (Mrs. Harold George Koos Jr.), Patricia Ann (Mrs. John Alan Karsten), Geraldine Frances (Mrs. John Luswig Christiansen). AB, Pomona Coll., 1913; student, Wharton Sch. Finance, U. Pa., 1919-20; LLB, Harvard, 1923. Bar: Calif. 1923. Promoter, organizer athletics in S.W. for A.G. Spalding & Bros., 1913-16; auditor Bur. Supplies and Accounts USN, 1919-21; assoc. Newin & Ashburn, Los Angeles, 1923-28, mem. firm, mng. ptnr., 1928-45; mng. ptnr. Newlin, Holley, Sandmeyer & Coleman, 1945-48, Newlin, Holley Sandmeyer & Tackabury, 1948-50, Newlin, Holley, Tackabury & Johnston, 1950-56, ptnr., Baird, Holley, Galen & Willard, 1957-74, Holley, Galen & Willard, from 1975. Chmn. San Marino Citizens Com. of 100, 1944-48; mem. San Marino Community Coun., from 1936, pres., 1944-46, 64-65; mem. San Marino Planning Commn., chmn., 1955-76; hon. life mem. Calif. PTA; alumni coun. Pomona Coll., 1933-40, 44-48, bd. overseers, 1926-33, sec., 1928-33. Served to lt. USNRF, World War I. Recipient Citizenship award for meritorious accomplishment for community San Marino Rotary, 1948. Mem. Am. Judicature Soc., Am. (Calif. mem. adv. com. on ethics and grievances 1953-58), Calif., Los Angeles (del. to ann. conv. Calif. 1956-73, chmn. membership com. 1962-68, mem. ethics com. 1935-45, 57-59) bar assns., Am. Legion, Masons (Shriner), Town Hall Club, Chancery Club, Kiwanis Club (Los Angeles), Harvard Club of So. Calif., Nat. Lawyers Club. Republican. Congregationalist. (chmn. bldg. com.). Home: San Marino Calif. Deceased.

HOLLYDAY, GUY T. O., title insurance company executive; b. Balt., Dec. 27, 1892; s. John Guy and Virginia May (Lannay) H.; m. Louise Este Fisher, Jan. 28, 1926; children: Louise Este, Guy Tilghman, Virginia Lannay, Este Fisher. Salesman M. & J. Brandt, Balt., 1914; asst. sec. Md. League for Nat. Defense, 1915; asst. to dir. indsl. bur. Balt. Bd. Trade, 1919-21; sales mgr. Mortgage Guarantee Co., 1921-26, The Roland Park Co., 1926-32; v.p. Key Realty Corp.; pres. Fiscal Mortgage Co. of Ala., 1932-35; former v.p. Permian Abstract Co., Midland, Tex.; former vice chmn. bd. Title Guarantee Co.; dir. James W. Rouse & Co., Inc., Loyola Fed. Savs. & Loan Assn., Savs. Bank Balt. Former mem. Build Am. Better Com.; former pres. Flight Blight Inc.; former mem. nat. adv. com. Fed. City Council, Washington; dir. ACTION, Inc.; trustee Boys' Latin Sch., Balt. Served with 11th U.S. Cavalry, WWI. Mem. Lambda Alpha. Home: Sparks Md. †

HOLM, RICHARD WILLIAM, educator, biologist; b. Dallas, June 2, 1925; s. Clyde William and Beryle (Joyce) H. A.B., Washington U., St. Louis, 1946, A.M., 1948, Ph.D., 1950. Instr. botany Washington U., 1948; herbarium botanist U. Calif. at Berkeley, 1948-49; mem. faculty Stanford, 1949-87, prof. biol. scis., 1965-87, dir. div. systematic biology, 1961-71, dir. undergrad. studies biol. scis., 1972-74; cons. editor McGraw Hill Book Co. Contbr. articles to profl. jours., books on evolution, population biology, and botany.; Editor: Evolution, 1964-66. Fellow AAAS; mem. Phi Beta Kappa, Sigma Xi. Home: Stanford Calif. Died Nov. 4, 1987.

HOLMAN, CLARENCE HUGH, educator, writer; b. Cross Anchor, S.C., Feb. 24, 1914; s. David Marion and Jessie Pearl (Davis) H.; m. Verna Virginia McLeod, Sept. 1, 1938 (dec.); children: Margaret McLeod Strowd, David Marion (dec.). Dir. pub. relations Presbyn. Coll., Clinton, S.C., 1936-39, dir. radio, 1939-41, instr. English, 1941-45, acad. dean, 1945-46; instr. English U. N.C., 1946-49, asst. prof., 1949-51, assoc. prof., 1951-56, prof., 1956-59, Kenan prof. English, 1959-81, chmn. div. humanities, 1959-62, chmn. dept. English, 1958-62, chmn. Coll. Arts and Scis., 1954-55, dean Grad. Sch., 1963-66, provost, 1966-68. Author 5 detective novels, 1942-47; (with others) The Development of American Criticism, 1955; (with W.F. Thrall and A. Hibbard) A Handbook to Literature, 4th edit., 1980; (with others) The Southerner as American, 1960, Southern Writers Appraisals in Our Time, 1964, Seven Modern American Novelists, 1964, Thomas Wolfe, 1960, John P. Marquand, 1965, The American Novel Through Henry James. A Bibliography, 1966, 2d edit., 1979, Three Modes of Modern Southern Fiction, 1966; (with others) Southern Fiction Today, 1969; Roots of Southern Writing, 1972, The Loneliness at the Core, 1975 (Mayflower Cup award, 1975, S.C. Excellence in Writing award 1976), The Immoderate Past, 1977, Windows on the World, 1979; editor: Short Novels of Thomas Wolfe, 1961, The Yemasse (W.G. Simms), 1961, The World of Thomas Wolfe, 1962, The Thomas Wolfe Reader, 1962, Simms's View and Reviews, 1962, Garretson Chronicle (G.W. Brace), 1964, Of Time and the River (Thomas Wolfe), 1965, Tucker's Partisan Leader, 1971; co-editor The Letters of Thomas Wolfe to His Mother, 1968, Southern Literary Jour., 1968-81, Southern Writing 1585-1920, 1970; (with L.D. Rubin) Southern Literary Study, 1975; contbr. articles to profl. jours. Publicity dir.. S.C. Coun. Nat. Def., 1942-44; trustee, chmn. exec. com. Triangle Univs. Ctr. for Advanced Study, 1975-81; trustee, v.p. Nat. Humanities Ctr., 1975-81. Acad. coord. 2199th BU, USAAF, 1943-45. Guggenheim fellow, 1967-68. Fellow Am. Acad. Arts and Scis.; mem. N.C. Univ. Press (chmn. bd. govs. 1957-73), Coll. English Assn., S. Atlantic MLA, MLA, (chmn. Am. Lit. sect. 1970), Am. Studies Assn., Nat. Coun. Tchrs. English, Phi Beta Kappa, Alpha Sigma Phi. Democrat. Presbyterian. Home: Chapel Hill N.C. Died Oct. 13, 1981; buried Chapel Hill Cemetery, Chapel Hill, N.C.

HOLMAN, M. CARL, urban organization executive; b. Minter City, Miss., June 27, 1919; s. Moses and Mamie (Durham) H.; m. Mariella Ama, Dec. 22, 1945; children: Kwasi, Kwame, Kinshasha. AB magna cum laude, Lincoln U., 1942; MA, U. Chgo., 1944; MFA, Yale U., 1954. Pres. Nat. Urban Coalition, Washington, 1971-88. Mem. Atlanta Coun. on Human Relations, 1958-6, Atlanta Student Adult Liaison Commn., 1960-62; press and publicity chmn. Atlanta NAACP, 1955-60; mem. exec. com. D.C. Bd. Higher Edn., 1968-72, Pres.'s Commn. on White House Fellows; exec. sec. Black Leadership Forum; co-convenor Nat. Com. on Concerns of Blacks and Hispanics; co-chmn. Nat. Com. for Urban Recreation; founder TransAfrica; bd. dirs., v.p. Field Found., Nat. Ctr. for Health Edn., Nat. Low Income Housing Coalition, Nat. Endowment for Humanities, Children's Hosp. Nat. Med. Ctr. Recipient Pub. Affairs Reporting award Am. Polit. Sci. Assn., 1962, Blevins Davis Playwriting award Yale U., 1954, Fiske Poetry prize U. Chgo., 1944, Outstanding Alumni award; Whitney fellow, 1952-54. Mem. Omega Psi Phi. Home: Washington D.C. Died Aug. 9, 1988, buried Rock Creek Cemetery, Washington.

HOLMES, J. LISTER, architect; b. Seattle, July 6, 1891; s. Samuel Judd and Alice (Lennox) H.; m. Jane Lambuth, Dec. 15, 1917; 1 son, Joseph L. Student engring., U. Wash., 1913; student architecture, U. Pa., 1915, Beaux Inst. Design, 1915-17. Various archtl. positions Phila., N.Y.C., 1917-22; practice architecture Seattle, from 1922; prin. J. Lister Holmes & Assocs., from 1939. Works include large scale group housing, Seattle, Vancouver, 1940-45; architect adminstrn. bldg. for pub. schs., other large structures, 1945-50, Pacific Coast bldgs. United Parcel Service, 1950-70; developer comprehensive plan for Ft. Lewis, 1950-55. Mem. Wash. State Architects Licensing Bd., 1944-47, Seattle Planning Commn., 1947-56; bd. dirs. Seattle Art Mus., 1929. Fellow AIA; mem. Am. Soc. Planning Ofcls. (nat. bd. 1951-53), PAcific N.W. Acad. Arts, Univ. Club. Home: Seattle Wash. †

HOLMES, JAMES MURRAY, educator, chemist; b. Doaktown, N.B., Can., Sept. 30, 1919; s. Akeley and Elsie (Murray) H.; m. Helen Hargrave Hill, Sept. 6, 1946; children—Janet (dec.), John, Jean. B.Sc., U. N.B., 1940; M.A., U. Western Ont., 1942; Ph.D., McGill U., 1944. Sessional lectr. McGill U., 1946-48; lectr. Carleton U., 1948-49, asst. prof., 1949-53, assoc. prof., 1953-61, prof. chemistry, 1961-84, adj. prof., 1984-86, chmn. dept., 1957-73. Mem. Ont. Com. Univ. Affairs, 1972-74; Bd. govs. Carleton U., 1972-81. Served with Can. Army, 1944-46. Beaverbook Scholar, 1936-40. Fellow Chem. Inst. Can. (Chem. Edn. award 1973); mem. Ont. Confedn. U. Faculty Assn. (chmn. exec. mem. 1966-69), Can. Assn. U. Tchrs. (exec. com. 1971-72), Am. Chem. Soc., Royal Chem. Soc. (Eng.), Sigma Xi. Club: Ottawa Hunt and Golf. Died Mar. 5, 1986.

HOLMES, JOHN CLELLON, author; b. Holyoke, Mass., Mar. 12, 1926; s. John McClellan and Elizabeth (Emmons) H.; m. Shirley Anise Allen, Sept. 9, 1953. Student, Columbia U., 1943, 45-46, New Sch. Social Research, 1949-50. Lectr. Yale U., 1959; vis. lectr. writers workshop State U. Iowa, 1963-64; writer in residence U. Ark., 1966; vis. prof. Bowling Green State U., 1968, Brown U., 1971-72; asso. prof. U. Ark., 1976-80, prof., 1980-87. Author: Go, 1952, The Horn, 1958, Get Home Free, 1964, Nothing More To Declare, 1967, The Bowling Green Poems, 1977, Death Drag: Selected Poems, 1979, Visitor, 1981, Gone in October, 1985, Displaced Person, 1987, Dire Coasts, 1987, Representative Men, 1988, Passionate Opinions, 1988, Elected Poems, 1989; contbr. to popular mags. Served with Hosp. Corps USNR, 1944-45. Recipient Playboy mag. award for best article, 1964, 71, 73, , John Clellon Holmes Collection award Boston U., 1966, Literary award Nat. Inst. Arts and Letters, 1988; Guggenheim fellow, 1976. Home: Old Saybrook Conn. Died Mar. 30, 1988, cremated.

HOLMES, JOHN WENDELL, institute executive; b. London, Ont., Can., June 18, 1910. B.A., U. Western Ont., London, 1932, LL.D., 1973; M.A., U. Toronto, Ont., 1933; postgrad., U. London, 1938-40; LL.D. (hon.), U. N.B., 1975, U. Waterloo, 1976, York U., 1981, St. Lawrence and Carleton U., 1983, St. Francis-Xavier U., 1986; D.C.L. (hon.), Acadia U., Wolfville, N.S., 1977, Trent U., 1985; D.Litt., U. Windsor, 1980. With Can. Inst. Internat. Affairs, Toronto, 1940-43, 60-88; with Can. Dept. External Affairs, 1943-53; served in Can. Dept. External Affairs, London, Moscow, N.Y.C.; under sec. state for external affairs 1953-60; prof. internat. relations U. Toronto, 1967-88, York U., 1971-81, U. Leeds, Eng., 1979, 85. Author: The Better Part of Valour, 1970, Canada: A Middle-Aged Power, 1976, The Shaping of Peace, Vol. 1, 1979 Vol. 2, 1982, Life with Uncle, 1984, No Other Way: Canada and International Security Institutions, 1986. Decorated Order Can.; Carnegie Endowment fellow, 1969. Fellow Royal Soc. Can. Home: Toronto Ont., Canada. Died Aug. 12, 1988.

HOLMES, P(ERCY) G(EORGE), railway executive; b. Park River, N.D., Jan. 27, 1892; s. George and Jessie (Smith) H.; m. Arlene Gibbons, July 14, 1920; 1 child, Kenneth D. Student bus. coll. Joined G.N. Ry., 1911, telegraph operator, agt., 1911-27; ticket agt. G.N. Ry., Grand Forks, N.D., 1927-28; traveling passenger agt. G.N. Ry., St. Paul, 1928-40; dist. passenger agt. G.N. Ry., 1940-47, asst. to passenger traffic mgr., 1948, passenger traffic mgr., from 1948; pres., dir. St. Paul Union Depot Co. Mem. Am. Assn. Passenger Traffic Officers, Army Transp. Assn., Union League (Chgo.), Athletic Club. Republican. Episcopalian. Home: Saint Paul Minn. †

HOLMQUIST, ALBERT MARTINIUS, biologist; b. Faribault, Minn., Oct. 7, 1891; s. Adam William and Mary (Groven) H.; m. Elsie Larimore Klovstad, July 8, 1929; 1 child, Mary Louise. AB, St. Olaf Coll., 1914; MS, U. Chgo., 1917, PhD, 1925. High sch. tchr. 1914-16, 19-20; instr. St. Olaf Coll., 1917-18, prof. biology, 1920-23, and from 1926, chmn. dept., 1949-53; vis. prof. U. N.M., 1951-52, and other summer professorships. Contbr. articles to biol. jours. With M.C., U.S. Army, World War I. Fellow AAAS; mem. Ecol. Soc. Am., AAUP, Am. Soc. Zoologists, Minn. Acad. Sci., Sigma Xi, Gamma Alpha, Phi Beta Kappa. Republican. Lutheran. Home: Northfield Minn. †

HOLMSTEDT, RALEIGH W(ARREN), college president; b. St. Edward, Nebr., Mar. 24, 1899; s. Oscar and Mary (Braman) H.; m. Mary S. Power, Aug. 16, 1930. AB cum laude, Hastings (Nebr.) Coll., 1924; AM, Columbia U., 1927, PhD, 1932; diploma, Sch. Mil. Govt., Charlottesville, Va., 1943. With Inst. of Math. Nebr. Sch. Agrl., 1924-26; asst. prof. edn. Ind. U., 1929-34, assoc. prof. edn., 1934-38, prof. edn., 1938-53, also asst. dean edn.; pres. Ind. State Coll., from 1953; cons. Survey of Adminstrn. and Fin., N.Y. City Sch. system, 1942; cons. on fin. Survey of D.C. Sch. System, 1948. Author: A Study of the Effects of the Teacher Tenure Law in New Jersey, 1932, State Control of School Finance, 1940, Factors Affecting the Organization of School Attendance Unit, 1934 (rsch. studies).; contbr. articles and survey reports dealing with sch. adminstrn. and fin. to profl. publs. Capt. U.S. Army, 1943-46; maj. O.R.C. from 1946. Mem. Am. Assn. Sch. Adminstrs., NEA, Rotary, Columbia Club (Inpls.), Country Club (Terre Haute, Ind.), Phi Delta Kappa. Republican. Home: Terre Haute Ind. Died Jan. 6, 1988.

HOLSTEIN, THEODORE DAVID, physics educator; b. N.Y.C., Sept. 18, 1915; s. Samuel and Ethel (Stein) H.; m. Beverlee Ruth Roth, Aug. 31, 1945; children: Lonna Beth Holstein Smith, Stuart Alexander. B.S. cum laude, N.Y. U., 1935; M.S., Columbia U., 1936; Ph.D., NYU, 1940. Instr. CCNY, 1940; research physicist Westinghouse Research Lab., Pitts., 1941-60; prof. U. Pitts., 1960-65, UCLA, 1965-85. Author articles on solid-state theory. Recipient Alexander von Humboldt sr. scientist prize. Fellow Am. Acad. Arts and Scis.; mem. Nat. Acad. Sci., Am. Phys. Soc. Jewish. Home: Santa Monica Calif. Died May 8, 1985; burial in Los Angeles.

HOLT, ALBERT CAMPBELL, clergyman; b. Kansas City, Mo., Dec. 27, 1882; s. Alonzo Teagraden and Lucy Bondurant (Cambell) H.; m. Mary Emma Ackerly, Dec. 23, 1908; children: Helen Jessie Holt Walter, Virginia Holt Entenza, Anna Ruth Holt Seay, Albert Ackerly, Duncan McKay, David Rice. AB, Park Coll., Parkville, Mo., 1905, AM, 1907; postgrad., U. Chgo., 1906-07; PhD, Peabody Coll., 1923; DD, Tusculum Coll., 1929; student, McCormick Theol. Sem., Chgo., 1914-15. Ordained to ministry Presbyterian Ch., 1915. Prof. Greek and history, also dean Tusculum Coll., 1905-21; asst. pastor 1st Ch., Nashville, 1922-27, Jakcsonville, Fla., 1927-52; dean Montreat (N.C.) Coll., 1952-58; pastor Keystone Heights (Fla.) Community Ch., from 1958. Author: Economic and Social Beginnings of Tennessee, 1923; contbr. to ch. papers. Mem. Kiwanis. Democrat. Home: Keystone Heights Fla. †

HOLT, ANDREW DAVID, educator; b. Milan, Tenn., Dec. 4, 1904; s. Andrew David and Mary E. (Brown) H.; m. Martha Chase, Nov. 25, 1938; children: Ann Elizabeth, Martha Frances, Andrew David. Student, West Tenn. State Coll., 1923, George Peabody Coll., 192; AB, Emory U., 1927; MS, Columbia U., 1929, PhD, 1933; LLD, Union U., 1950; LittD, Tusculum Coll., 1962; DSc (hon.), U. Chattanooga, 1965. Prin. Bluff Springs Elem. Sch., Milan, 1926; tchr., athletic coach Humboldt (Tenn.) High Sch., 1927-28; prin. tng. sch. West Tenn. State Coll., Memphis, 1929-30, prof. edn., 1930-37; high sch. supr. for West Tenn. 1930-37; exec. sec. Tenn. Edn. Assn., 1937-50; adminstrv. asst. to pres. U. Tenn., 1950-53, v.p., 1953-59, pres., 1959-70; bd. dirs. South Cen. Bell Tel. & Tel. Co., Birmingham, Ala., Hamilton Internat. Corp., Farmington, Mich., Provident Life & Accident Ins. Co., Chattanooga, Hamilton Nat. Bank, Knoxville; ednl. cons. Holiday Inns of Am., Am. Sch., Chgo.; mem. exec. com. So. Regional Edn. Bd.; chmn. White House Conf. Edn.; mem. Nat. Commn. to Promote Eradication of Adult Illiteracy; nat. chmn. sch. savs. com. U.S. Treasury Dept.; chmn. Am. del. World Orgn. Teaching Profession, Berne Switzerland; mem. council of advisors U.S. Commn. on Edn., N.A.M., Air Transport Assn.; advisor to Ednl. Policies commn. Author: Struggle for a State Sys. of Pub. Schs. in Tenn., 1937; editor The Tenn. Tcgr., 1937-50; contbr. articles to various ednl. publs. Mem. at large nat. coun. Boy Scouts Am.; trustee Am. Fund for Dental Edn. Maj. AUS, 1943-45. Mem. Nat. Congress Parents and Tchrs. (life), So. Assn. Colls. and Schs. (past pres.), NEA (pres. 1949-50, bd. dirs.), Am. Legion, Amateur Chefs of Am., So. Assn. Land-Grant Colls. and State Univs., Am. Council Edn. (com. taxation and fiscal reporting fed. govt.), Nat. Adv. Dental Rsch. Coun., Internat. Assn. Univ. Pres.s, Nat. Assn. State Univs. and Land-Grant Colls. (chmn. com. traffic safety rsch. and edn.), Masons (32d degree), Shriners, Rotary (bd. dirs.), Alpha Kappa Psi, Delta Tau Delta, Phi Kappa Phi, Iota Lambda Sigma, Phi Sigma Sigma, Phi Delta KAppa, Omicron Delta Kappa. Methodist (steward). Home: Knoxville Tenn. Died Aug. 7, 1987, cremated.

HOLT, JAMES SEABORN, judge; b. Harrison, Ark., Nov. 17, 1884; s. Joseph Rutherford and Paralee Elizabeth (Coffman) H.; m. Lucile Miles, Sept. 14, 1909. AB, U. Ark., 1907; student, U. Va. Law Sch., 1907-09. Bar: Ark. 1909. Practice Ft. Smith, Ark., 1911-38; asst. U.S. atty. Western Ark. Dist., 1917-20, U.S. atty., 1920-21; assoc. justice Ark. Supreme Ct., from 1938. Recipient Citation of Disting. Alumnus, U. Ark., 1944. Mem. Kappa Alpha. Democrat. Methodist. Home: Little Rock Ark. †

HOLT, VICTOR, JR., rubber company executive; b. Heavener, Okla., May 8, 1908; s. Victor and Ethel (Morrison) H.; m. Rowena Turner, Feb, 17, 1934 (dec.); children: Hanna Lu, Victoria Sue, Judith Carol. BS, U. Okla., 1928. With Goodyear Tire & Rubber Co., Akron, Ohio, 1929-72, pres., 1964-72. Recipient Helms Found. award as outstanding coll. basketball player, 1928. Mem. Rubber Mfrs. Assn. (bd. dirs.), Portage Country Club (Akron), Everglades Club. Home: Palm Beach Fla. Died Apr. 22, 1988; interred Hudson, Ohio.

HOMME, HERBERT GORDON, lawyer; b. Grafton, N.D., July 18, 1917; s. Herbert G. and Anna G. (Stokke) H.; children: Jeffrey S., Greggrey S. JD, U. N.D., 1948. Bar: N.D. 1948. Practice Grafton, 1948-54; U.S. atty. Guam, 1954-62; asst. counsel Senate Judiciary Com., 1965-68; atty. Office of Gen. Counsel ICC, Washington, 1971-75, asst. sec., 1975-78, sec., 1978-79. Mem. Univ. Club (Washington), Sigma Alpha Epsilon, Phi Delta Phi. Home: Rancho Mirage Calif. Deceased.

HOMRIGHAUSEN, ELMER GEORGE, seminary dean, clergyman, educator, author; b. Wheatland, Iowa, Apr. 11, 1900; s. Henry George (Keller) and Sophia Julia (Mordhorst Kuehl Ballien) H.; m. Ruth Willa Strassburger, Sept. 17, 1923; children: Richard James, Ruth Karolyn (Mrs. Taylor), Elmer Paul, David Karl, Mary Elizabeth (Mrs. Candland), John Frederick. Student, U. Chgo., Iowa U., U. Geneva, Rutgers U.; AB, Lakeland Coll., 1921, DD (hon.); ThB, Princeton Theol. Sem., 1924; ThM, U. Dubuque, 1927, ThD, 1930; AM, Butler U., 1931; DD, Union Theol. Sem., Tokyo, 1958; LHD, Bucknell U., 1963, Ursinus Coll., 1976. Pastor 1st English Ref. Ch., Freeport, Ill., 1924-29, Carrollton Ave. Evang. and Ref. Ch., Indpls., 1929-38; Thomas Synott prof. Christian edn. Princeton Sem., 1938-54, Charles R. Erdman chair pastoral theology, 1954-82, dean sem., 1955-65; lectr. univs. and colls. including Princeton U., Cornell U., Wellesley Coll.; travel lectr., Asia, 1948, 55, 58, 64, 66, Africa, 1958, 66, 68, Latin Am., 1960, 65, 71; del. Pan Presbyn. Conf., Belfast, Ireland, 1933, Universal Coun., Denmark, 1934, World Coun., Oxford and Edinburgh, 1937, World Coun. Christian Edn., Mexico City, 1941, Tokyo, 1958, Belfast, 1962, Lima, 1971; cons. World Coun. Chs. Assembly, Amsterdam, 1948, Evanston, Ill., 1954, Nairobi, 1975; mem. N.Am. World Coun. Christian Edn.; mem. div. overseas ministries and ministry to nat. parks Nat. Council Chs; mem. Acad. Religion and Mental Health; vice moderator United Presbyn. Ch., 1951-52, 70-71. Author books and articles including: Choose Ye This Day; I Believe in the Church; Christianity in America—A Crisis; Let the Church Be the Church; Current Theological Trends; Rethinking the Great Commission; Christian Education (in Indonesian); The Finality of Jesus Christ; co-translator: Barth's God in Action; Come Holy Spirit; God's Search for Man; contbg. editor Theology Today; contbr. Ency. Americana, Twentieth Century Ency. Religious Knowledge, Interpreters Bible, Dictionary Christian Education, Interseminary Series, Colliers Ency., Handbook World Christianity, Theological Education Book List (London); also contbr. to religious jours. Mem. bd. edn. Princeton Boro, 22 years; trustee Hood Coll., Frederick, Md.; mem. bd. founders Internat. Christian U., Tokyo; mem. internat. com. Nat. YMCA. Named Hon. Citizen of Seoul, Korea; Outstanding Educator, 1970; recipient Disting. Alumnus award Princeton Sem., 1970, LAkeland Coll., 1976. Mem. NEA, Religious Edn. Assn., Hugenot Soc., Ky. Cols., Nassau Club, Masons, Phi Kappa Phi. Home: Princeton N.J.

HOOD, CHARLES CARLISLE, publishing executive; b. Buffalo, Feb. 26, 1896; s. Robert Allen and Isabel (Burley) H.; m. Josephine Kuehmsted, Sept. 15, 1926; children: Charles Carlisle, Virginia Eloise (Mrs. Kenneth E. Stoltz), Elizabeth Ann. BS, Mich. State Coll., 1917. Free lance newspaper work Fed. Market News Service, Denver, 1917; with Curtis Pub. Co., from 1920; advt. salesman Country Gentleman, Chgo. and Sat. Evening Post, Detroit, 1925-45; Detroit mgr. Holiday, 1945-52; br. mgr. Curtis Pub. Co., Detroit, 1952, v.p., from 1954. Ensign, aviator USN, 1917-19. Recipient Centennial award Mich. State U., 1955. Mem. Bloomfield Hills Country Club, Orchard Lake Country Club (Bloomfield Hills, Mich.), Detroit Athletic Club, Recess Club, Econ. Club, Masons, Shriners, Phi Delta Theta. Home: Birmingham Mich. †

HOOD, FRANK GARDINER, corporation executive; b. Chgo., Nov. 1, 1887; s. Samuel E. and Nellie (Colestock) H.; 1 adopted child, Wayne Joris. Student, U. Wis., 1905-09, U. London, 1918-19. Bd. dirs. Trane Co., La Crosse, Wis., 1919-63, chmn., from 1953. Mem. University Club, California Club, L.A. Country Club, Beta Gamma Sigma. †

HOOD, JAMES MILTON, railroad executive; b. Beach City, Ohio, Oct. 30, 1891; s. Herbert E. and Ada (Shoemaker) H.; m. Le Nore Fulton, Oct. 30, 1941; children by previous marriage: Harry, Herbert, Dorothy, Robert, Barbara. Ed. pub. schs. Oper. officer, v.p. AC&Y Ry., Akron, Ohio, 1912-35; pres. Am. Short Line R.R. Assn., Washington, 1935-60. Mem. Am. Ry. Engrng. Assn., Nat. Def. Transp. Assn. Republican. Home: Washington D.C. †

HOOK, ALONZ LOHR, educator; b. Hanging Rock, W.Va., July 19, 1891; s. Robert Calvin and Sara (McDonald) H.; m. Jessie Dawson, Aug. 19, 1914; children: Sara Virginia (wife of Dr. H.W. Burton), Jessie Irene (wife of Dr. M.C. Covington), Mary Jeanne (wife of Dr. D.B. Harrell Jr.), Doris Patricia (Mrs. E.J. Neal Jr.). AB, Elon Coll., 1913, MA, 1914. Instr. math. and sci. Elon Coll., N.C., 1914-22; deam Elon Coll., 1922-35, prof. physics, from 1922, registrar, 1935-57, dir. placement bur., from 1957, chmn. dept. physics, from 1922. Mem. Am. Phys. Soc., Am. Assn. Physics Tchrs., N.C. Acad. Sci., Burlington Rotary (past pres.), Pi Gamma Mu. Democrat. Congregationalist. Home: Elon Coll. N.C. †

HOOKER, RICHARD JAMES, historian; b. Milw., Sept. 6, 1912; s. Harry A. and Edith (O'Donnell) H.; m. Nancy Harvison, Jan. 5, 1952. AB, U. Chgo., 1934, PhD, 1943. Rsch. asst. U. Chgo., 1936-40; instr. Cen. YMCA Coll., Chgo., 1941-44, asst. prof., acting chmn. dept. history, 1944-45; assoc. prof. Roosevelt U., Chgo., 1945-49, chmn. dept. history, 1945-49, 50-62, prof. Am. history, 1949-69, prof. emeritus, 1969-86. Author: The Carolina Backcountry on the Eve of the Revolution: The Journal and Other Writings of Charles Woodmason, Anglican Itinerant; The American Revolution: The Search for Meaning; The Book of Chowder; A History of Food and Drink in America; A Colonial Plantation Cookbook; contbr. articles to profl. jours. Trustee Roosevelt U., Chgo., 1952-55, 64-67. Mem. Am. Hist. Assn., Japan Am. Soc. (trustee 1961-68, v.p. 1964-68), AAUP, ACLU, Common Cause, Amnesty Internat., Alpha Delta Phi. Home: Lyndonville Vt. Died Sept. 14, 1986; cremated.

HOOSE, HARNED PETTUS, lawyer; b. Kuling, China, June 2, 1920; (parents Am. citizens); s. Earl and Saidee (Pettus) H.; m. Georgia Johnston; children: Winston, Lisa Windsor Hoose Lopez, Barbara Catherine Hoose Millburn, Theodore, Shelley, Georgia. AB, U. So. Calif., 1942, JD, 1949. Bar: Calif. 1949. Clk. Calif.

Supreme Ct., San Francisco, 1949-50; practice law L.A., 1950-81; assoc. firm O'Melveny & Meyers, 1950-54; sr. ptnr. firm Hoose Law Offices, 1954-81; govt. cons. to White House in preparation for Pres. Nixon's trip to China, 1972; entered China with first groiup Am. businessmen to open up trade with China and now represents Am. corps. in trade with China; assisted former Pres. Nixon in perparation for China trip, 1976; surrogate for Pres. Carter, 1976 election yr.; now cons. on China to White House; cons. prof. internat. bus. U. So. Calif.; speaker Nat. Coun. U.S.-China Trade, L.A. Rotary Club, Am. Soc. Newspaper editors, UPI ann. conv. Author: Peking Pigeons and Flutes, 1938, How to Negotiate with the Chinese, 1972, U.S.-China Joint Energy Coalition, 1974, China Proposes a Pacific Triumvirate, 1976, China under Hua Kuo-feng, 1976, The Taiwan Question, 1977, mem. editorial bd., asst. editor U. So. Calif. Sch. Law Rev.; contbr. articles to legal jours. Fellow, trustee L.S.B. Leakey Found.; mem. Bleitz Wildlife Found.; trustee Isotope Found.; chmn. bd. trustees United Meth. Ch. With USNR, World War II; comdr. spl. U.S. naval guerilla unit behind Japanese lines in China. Mem. Am., Calif., Los Angeles, Beverly Hills bar assns., Am. Judicature Soc., L.A. C. of C., L.A. Fgn. Affairs Coun., L.A. Philanthropic Found., World Peace Through Law Assn., Am. Legion, Calif. Yacht Club, Balboa Bay Club, Phi Alpha Delta. Home: Newport Beach Calif. Died Dec. 4, 1981.

HOOVER, CHARLES M., appliance corporation executive; b. Okla., 1920. Ed., Okla. State U., 1942. Gen. sales mgr. Marquette Corp., 1942-60; with Roper Corp., Kankakee, Ill., 1960-88; chmn. bd., chief exec. officer Roper Corp., 1967-88, also dir.; chmn. bd., pres., chief exec. officer Roper Sales Corp.; pres. Eastern Products Corp. Died July 26, 1988.

HOOVER, HELEN D. (MRS. ADRIAN E. HOOVER), author; b. Greenfield, Ohio, Jan. 20, 1910; d. Thomas Franklin and Hannah (Gomersall) Blackburn; m. Adrian Everett Hoover, Feb. 13, 1937. Student, Ohio U., 1927-29, DePaul U., U. Chgo., 1943-49. Addressograph operator D-J Novelties Co., Chgo., 1930; proofreader Audit Bur. Circulations, Chgo., 1931-42; chemist Pitts. Testing Lab., Chgo., 1943-45; prodn. metallurgist Ahlberg Bearing Co., Chgo., 1945-48; rsch. metallurgist Internat. Harvester Co., Chgo., 1948-54; free-lance writer gen., nature and juvenile mags. Minn., N.Mex. and Wyo., 1954-84. Author: The Long-Shadowed Forest, 1963, The Gift of the Deer, 1966, Animals at My Doorstep, 1966, Great Wolf and the Good Woodsman, 1967, A Place in the Woods, 1969, Animals Near and Far, 1970, The Years of the Forest, 1973. Patentee agrl. implement disks. Recipient Ann. Achievement award Metal Treating Inst., 1959, Blue Flame Ecology Salute, 1973, Zia award N.Mex. Press Women, 1973, Bklyn. Art Books for Children citation, 1976, 78, medal of merit Ohio Y. Alumni Assn., 1979. Mem. Authors Guild, MBLS, Sierra Found., Nat. Audobon Soc., Wilderness Soc., Defenders of Wildlife, Nat. Wildlife Fedn., Nature Conservancy, Friends of the Sea Otter, Com. Preservation of Tule Elk, Humane Soc. U.S., Soc. Animal Protective Legislation, Howl Inc., Jersey Wildlife Preservation Trust, Internat. Coun. Bird Preservation, Internat. Union for Conservation of Nature, Fauna Preservation Soc., Save the Redwoods League, World Wildlife Fund, Soc. Animal Rights, Cousteau Soc., North Shore Animal League. Home: Laramie Wyo. Died July 7, 1984.

HOOVER, LINN, geologist; b. Balt., Apr. 13, 1923; s. Z. Linn and Harriet (Beall) H.; m. Joan Patricia Williams, Jan. 31, 1953; children—Peter Linn, Hilary Joan. A.B., U. N.C., 1948; M.A., U. Mich., 1951; Ph.D., U. Calif. at Berkeley, 1959. Geologist U.S. Geol. Survey, 1948-60; exec. sec. div. earth scis. Nat. Acad. Sci., Washington, 1960-63; exec. dir. Am. Geol. Inst., Washington, 1963-74; dep. chief, office of energy resources U.S. Geol. Survey, Reston, Va., 1974-82, chief internat. sci. programs, 1982-85; mem., sec. U.S. Nat. Com. on Geology, 1976-85; del. Internat. Geol. Congress, Sydney, Australia, 1976, Paris, 1980. Served with AUS, 1943-45. Recipient Parker Meml. medal Am. Inst. Profl. Geologists, 1975. Fellow Geol. Soc. Am.; mem. Am. Assn. Petroleum Geologists, Am. Geophys. Union. Club: Cosmos (Washington). Home: Chevy Chase Md. Died Feb. 1985, buried Washington.

HOPKINS, ALBERT LAFAYETTE, lawyer; b. Hickory, Miss., Apr. 27, 1886; s. Oliver and Helen V. (Tucker) H.; m. Florence Odil, Apr. 19, 1922; children: Nancy Hopkins Gerson, Catharine Hopkins Ruml, Albert Lafayette. Student, Millsaps Coll., 1900-01, U. Miss., 1901-02; AB, U. Chgo., 1905, JD, 1908; LLB, Harvard, 1909. Bar: Ill. 1908. Asst. U.S. atty. No. dist. Ill., 1913-17; asst. counsel ICC, Washington, 1917-19; spl. atty. Internal Revenue Bur., 1919; mem. firm Hopkins, Sutter, Owen, Mulroy & Davis, Chgo. Author: Autobiography of a Lawyer; Save Our Country. Mem. Chgo. Club, Legal Club, Law Club, Mid-Day Club, Flossmoor Country Club, Mid-America Club. Democrat. Methodist. Home: Chicago Ill. †

HOPKINS, HENRY POWELL, architect; b. Annapolis, Md., Feb. 12, 1891; s. Harry Jump and Frances Elizabeth (Chattle) H.; m. Constance Medea Hummel, Jan. 12, 1915; 1 child, Henry Powell. Student, Cornell U., 1909-10; BArch, Columbia, 1914; postgrad., Eng., France, Italy, Spain, 1914-15; MA (hon.), St. Johns Coll., 1917; AFD, Washington Coll., Chestertown, Md., 1960. Instr. architecture Tex. A&M Coll., 1916; lectr. history architecture Columbia, 1919; practice architecture Balt., from 1919; adviser Md. State Code Commn., 1949; supervising architect for retoration of Md. State House; architect for devel. of Colonial Annapolis. Prin. works include: library U. Md.; Balt. Jr. Coll.; Woodlawn Sr. High Sch., Balt. county, Md.; sci. bldg. Washington Coll., Chestertown; Jr. Coll., Catonsville, Md.; Lansdowne and Dulaney High Schs., Balt. County; Fine Arts Bldg., U. Md.; library U. Balt.; dormitory and fine arts bldg. Hood Coll.; sr. and 2 jr. high schs., Frederick County, Md. Fellow AIA (pres. 1948-49); mem. SAR (v.p. 1951), Soc. Colonial Wars (gov.), Eastern Shore Soc. (pres. Balt. chpt.), S.R., Soc. of War of 1812, Maryland Club, Wine and Food Soc., Chester River Yacht and Country Club, Rotary (past pres.). Home: Baltimore Md. †

HOPPENOT, HENRI ETIENNE, government official; b. France, Oct. 25, 1891. Lit. and law; diploma, l'Ecole des Sciences Politiques. With French diplomatic svc., from 1914; diplomat French diplomatic svc., Berne, 1917, Tehran, 1919, Rio de Janeiro, 1924, Berlin, 1925, Peiping, 1933; sub-dir. Asiatic affairs French Fgn. Ministry, minister to Uruguay, 1940-42; mem. French Mil. Mission to U.S., 1943; rep. (until formal diplomatic relations between France and U.S. were resumed) French Com. of Nat. Liberation, Washington, 1943-44; ambassador Berne, 1945-52; permanent del. UN, 1952-55; high commr. Vietnam, 1955-56; councillor of state from 1957; pes. commn. supervision of referendum and legis. elections, Algeria, 1958, Cour arbitrale de la Communauté, 1959-61; mem. Haute-Tribunal militaire, 1961-62; pres. Commn. du plan pour l'equipment culture. Decorated grand officier Legion d'Honneur. Home: Paris France. †

HORAN, JAMES D., author; b. N.Y.C., July 27, 1914; s. Eugene and Elizabeth (Schaub) H.; m. Gertrude Dorrity, Sept. 4, 1938; children: Patricia, Brian, Gary, James C. Student, Drake Coll., Jersey City, Writing Ctr., NYU. Novelist, historia; ret. asst. mng. editor, Sunday editor, spl. events editor N.Y. Jour. Am., N.Y.C. Author: (with Gerold Frank) Out in the Boondocks, 1943, U.S. Seawolf, 1945; Action Tonight, 1945; Desperate Men, 1949; (with Howard Swiggett) The Pinkerton Story, 1951; Desperate Women, 1952; (novel) King's Rebel, 1953; Confederate Agent, 1954; (with Paul Sann) Pictorial History of the Wild West, 1954; Mathew Brady, Historian with a Camera, 1955; Across the Cimarron, 1956; The DA's Man, 1957; (novel) Seek Out and Destroy, 1958; The Mob's Man, 1959; The Great American West, 1959, rev. 1978; (novel) The Shadow Catcher (Western Heritage award), 1961; The Desperate Years, 1962; The Seat of Power, 1965 (novel of year N.J. Assn. Tchrs. English); America's Forgotten Photographer: Timothy O'Sullivan, 1966; (novel) The Right Image, 1967; The Pinkertons: The Detective Dynasty that Made History, 1968; The Life and Art of Charles Schrevogel: Painter-Historian of the Indian Fighting Army of the American West, 1969 (Westerners Buffalo award 1970, N.J. Tchrs. English award 1970); (novel) The Blue Messiah, 1970; The McKenney-Hall Portrait Gallery of American Indians, 1972; (novel) The New Vigilantes, 1975; The Authentic Wild West: The Gunfighters, 1976; The Authentic Wild West: The Outlaws, 1977; (novel) Ginerva, 1979; pub. (with Mrs. Horan) Jingle Bob Series; The Trial of Frank James for Murder, with Confessions of Dick Liddil and Clarence Hite; The Dalton Brothers; The Life of Tom Horn. Recipient award Mystery Writers of Am., 1957, Westerners Buffalo award, 1960, Gold Typewriter award N.Y. Press Club, 1960, hon. mention, 1962, award N.J. Tchrs. English, 1962, Page One citation Am. Newspaper Guild, 1961. Mem. Westerners (co-founder N.Y. Corral), N.Y. Civil War Round Table (past pres.), N.Y. Press club, Writers Guild Am., Am. Newspaper Guild. Died Oct. 13, 1981.

HORNBEAK, HAROLD LANCASTER, architect; b. Springfield, Mo., May 5, 1913; s. Harold Leslie and Flora Miller (Silsby) H.; m. Margaret Anne Getchell, Dec. 31, 1948. Student, DePauw U., 1931-34; BS, Washington U., St. Louis, 1948; MS, Tex. A&M U., 1955. Ops. agt. Eastern Airlines, Jacksonville, Fla., 1939-40, St. Louis, 1940-41; engr. McDonnell Aircraft Corp., St. Louis, 1941-43, 45-46, 48-49; asst. prof. architecture Tex. A&M U., 1949-55; assoc. prof. architecture U. Ill., Urbana, 1955-62, prof., from 1962; dir. architecture overseas program U. Ill., Versailles, France, 1969-72. With inf. U.S. Army, 1944-46. Decorated Purple Heart. Mem. Am. Soc. Engring. Edn. (chmn. div. archtl. engring. 1964-66), Am. Legion, SAR, Sigma Xi (assoc.), Tau Beta Pi Assn. Episcopalian. Home: Urbana Ill. Died Oct. 7, 1983.

HORNBLOWER, RALPH, JR., stockbroker, investment banker, real estate broker; b. Boston, Feb. 1, 1919; s. Ralph and Eleanor (Greenwood) H.; m. Priscilla Alder Blumer, Feb. 9, 1944 (dec. Feb. 1960); children: Rosalie (Mrs. Brian Catlin), Ralph III, Paul Skinner, Priscilla; m. Phoebe Mary Blumer, Oct. 12, 1960; children: John Greenwood, David Maitland, James Wainwright. Student, Milton Acad., 1934-37; B.S., Harvard U., 1941. Mem. N.Y. Stock Exchange. Bd. dirs. Greenwich Boys Club Assn., Henry Hornblower Fund, Inc. Clubs: Owl (Cambridge, Mass.); Round Hill (Greenwich); Edgartown Golf (Mass.); Squibnocket Assocs. (founder, gov.) (Chilmark, Mass.). Home: Greenwich Conn. Died Mar. 10, 1987, buried Christchurch, Greenwich.

HORNE, RALPH WARREN, consulting engineer; b. Malden, Mass., July 25, 1888; s. Charles K. and Mercie Emma (Knight) H.; m. Meta Wallis Cross, May 24, 1916; 1 dau., Muriel Elizabeth Horne Weldon. BCE, MIT, 1910. Registered profl. engr. Maine, N.H., Vt., Mass., R.I., N.Y. Asst. instr. MIT, Boston, 1910-11; designer Metcalf & Eddy Inc., Boston, 1911-15; with Fay, Spofford & Thorndike, Boston, from 1915, ptnr., 1922-56, pres., 1956-63, cons., dir., from 1963; v.p., dir. First Nat. Bank Malden, from 1953; trustee Malden Savs. Bank, 1947-68, hon. trustee, from 1968. Pres. Davenport Meml. Found., Malden, 1949-77; trustee Malden Hosp. Corp., 1961-71, hon. trustee, 1971; trustee Malden Pub. Libr., 1948-71, pres., 1971-72, hon. trustee, from 1971; mem. Malden City Council, 1930, Malden Plannning Bd., 1943-58; v.p. Malden Redevel. Authority, 1958-65. Recipient medal of Merit award City of Malden, 1965. Fellow Am. Inst. Cons. Engrs.; mem. Am. Cons. Engrs. Coun., ASCE, Boston Soc. Civil Engrs. (pres. 1932-33; hon. mem., Desmond Fitzgerald award 1944), Am., New Eng. water works assns., Am. Acad. Environ.Engrs., New Eng. Water Pollution Control Assn. (past pres.), Nat., Mass. socs. profl. engrs., Boston Engrs. Club (hon. from 1977), Shriners, Phi Sigma Kappa. Republican. Home: Malden Mass. Deceased.

HORSZOWSKI, MIECZYSLAW, pianist; b. Lwow, Poland, June 23, 1892; came to U.S., 1941, naturalized, 1948; s. Stanislaw and Rose Jeanne (Wagner) H. Studies with Theodore Leschetizky; MusD, Curtis Inst. Music, 1969. Faculty Curtis Inst. Music, Phila., from 1942. Concert pianist, from 1904; 1st recital, N.Y.C., 1906; frequent appearances withmaj. orchs. throughout world; soloist with Toscanini and NBC Orch., 1942, 53; participated annually Casals Festivals, Prades (France) and P.R. †

HORTON, CLIFFORD EMORY, athletic commissioner; b. Shelton, Wash., Dec. 31, 1892; s. Charles Edward and Annie Laurie (Reeves) H.; m. Garnette Elsie Scheid, June 15, 1921; children: Clifford Edward, Barbara Horton Theriault. BPE, Springfield Coll., 1919; MA, Clark U., 1923; EdD, Ind. U., 1942. Phys. dir. YWCA, Spokane, Wash., 1911-13; phys. dir. YWCA, Michigan City, Ind., 1913-19, part-time instr. phys. edn, 1917-18, 19-21; tchr. phys. edn. pub. schs., San Luis Obispo, Calif., 1921-22; instr. phys. edn., athletic coach Clark U., 1922-23; dir. health and phys. edn. Ill. State U., 1923-61; athletic commnr. Interstate Intercollegiate Athletic Commn., Normal, Ill., from 1945; dir. Camping for Handicapped Children, from 1950. Pres. Normal Community Coun., 1937; bd. dirs. Blooming coun. Boy Scouts Am., 1925-65 (recipient Silver Beaver award). Mem. Nat., Ill. (pres. 1950) assns., health, phys. edn. and recreation, Phi Delta Kappa, Phi Kappa Psi, Gamma Phi. Home: Normal Ill. †

HORTON, GILBERT ROBINSON, architect; b. St. Paul, Nov. 10, 1888; s. Gilbert Lafayette and Annie Burgess (Napier) H.; m. Evangelyn Mae Roberts, Nov. 10, 1913; children—Gilbert E., Kent H. U. Minn., 1909, U. Wash., 1910. Registered architect, N.D. Architect Gilbert R. Horton Architects, Jamestown, N.D., from 1913; v.p., then pres. N.D. State Bd. Architecture, 1941-55. Prin. works include 1st James River Nat. Bank., 1967 (honor award N.D. chpt. AIA). City engr. City of Jamestown, 1932-37; Alderman, 1920. Fellow AIA. Republican. Episcopalian. Lodges: Rotary, Masons. Home: Jamestown N.D. Died Nov. 2, 1985; buried Jamestown, N.D.

HORWITZ, ROBERT HENRY, political science educator; b. El Paso, Tex., Sept. 3, 1923; s. David and Louise (Mendelsohn) H.; m. Noreen Margaret Surti, Jan. 1948; children: Susheila Louise, David D. BA, Amherst Coll., 1949; MA, U. Hawaii, 1950; PhD, U. Chgo., 1954; LHD (hon.), Kenyon Coll., 1987. Asst. prof., researcher U. Hawaii, 1948-51; research asst. com. for study citizenship edn. U. Chgo., 1953-55; from asst. prof. to prof. polit. sci. Mich. State U., East Lansing, 1956-66; prof. polit. sci., chmn. dept. Kenyon Coll., Gambier, Ohio, from 1966, dir. Pub. Affairs Conf. Ctr., 1976-78. Co-author: John Locke's Questions Concerning the Law of Nature, 1986; editor: The Moral Foundations of the American Republic, 1977; contbr. articles to profl. jours. Served with AUS, 1942-46, ETO, PTO. Decorated Bronze Star; decorated Combat Inf. badge; fellow Emil Schwartzhaupt Found., 1953-55, Rockefeller Found., 1959, Ford Found., 1956-58; Earhard Found. fellow, 1972, NEH fellow, 1973-76. Mem. AAUP, Am. Polit. Sci. Assn., Am. Soc. Polit. and Legal Philosophy. Jewish. Home: Gambier Ohio Died May 27, 1987, buried Nashville, Tenn.

HOSEA, ADDISON, bishop; b. Pikeville, N.C., Sept. 11, 1914; s. Addison and Alma Eugenia (Bowden) H.; m. Jane Eubank Marston, June 24, 1944; children: Nancy Jane, Addison III, Anne-Cameron. AB, Atlantic Christian Coll., 1938; MDiv., U. South, 1949, DD,

970; postgrad., Union Theol. Sem., 1948, Duke U., 950-53; DD, Episcopal Theol. Sem., Ky., 1968. Ordained to ministry Episcopal Ch., as deacon, 1948, as priest, 1949. Tchr. pub. schs. Wayne County, N.C., 932-34, Currituck County, N.C., 1938-41; priest-in-charge St. Gabriel's, Faison, N.C., 1949-51; rector St. Paul's, Clinton, N.C., 1949-54, St. John's, Versailles, Ky., 1954-70; bishop coadjutor Diocese of Lexington, Ky., 1970; 4th bishop of Lexington 1971-85; prof. N.T. ang. and lit. Episcopal Theol. Sem., Ky., 1954-59, 65-0; mem. exec. coun. Diocese East Carolina, 1951-54, Diocese Lexington, 1954-70, examining chaplain, 1964-0, mem. standing com., 1957-58, 60-64; canon Cathedral St. George the Martyr, Crystal, Ky., 1964-0;dep. Gen. Conv., 1955, 58, 64, 67, 69. Trustee U. South, 1949-54, 70-85. Served to capt. AUS, 1941-46. Mem. Soc. Bibl. Lit. Home: Lexington Ky. Died Dec. 4, 1985, buried Lexington Cemetery.

HOUGH, HUGH FREDERICK, journalist; b. Sandwich, Ill., Apr. 15, 1924; s. Forrest Everett and Lila M. (Legner) H.; m. Ellen Marie Wesemann, Sept. 8, 948; children: Hollis Ann Hough Bahnsen, Heidi Ann Hough, Peter Clark, Christopher Hugh. BS, U. Ill., 951. Sports editor Dixon (Ill.) Evening Telegraph, 951-52; reporter, rewriteman Chgo. Sun-Times, 1952-6, columnist, 1974-86. Served with USAAF, 1943-45. Decorated Air medal; recipient Stick-o-Type awards Chgo. Newspaper Guild, 1960, 65, 66, award for prison reform stories John Howard Assn., 1961, Marshall Field award for outstanding editorial contbn. to Chgo. Sun-Times, 1969, Newswriting award Ill. Assoc. Press, 1974, Pulitzer prize for gen. local reporting, 1974. Home: La Grange Park Ill. Died Apr. 16, 1986; buried Parkholm Cemetery, LaGrange Park, Ill.

HOUGHTON, ROBERT BIGELOW, diplomat; b. Boston, Apr. 4, 1921; s. Robert B. and Helen Marion H.; m. Lois Chapman, Oct. 13, 1950; children: Worthington C., Robert B., Gill W., Richard H., Eleni. A.B., Harvard U., 1942. Commd. fgn. service officer Dept. State, 1945; served in Nairobi, Kenya, Jerusalem, Damascus, Syria, London; minister Am. embassy, Beirut; consul gen. U.S. Consulate, Istanbul; dir. Office Multinat. Force and Observer Affairs Dept. State, Washington D.C., until 1983; was mem. Fulbright Commn. Co-author: Peacekeeping in the Middle East. Bd. dirs. Adm. Bristol Hosp. Recipient Meritorious Service award Dept. State, 1977, John Jacob Rogers award, 1983. Mem. Middle East Inst. Club: Harvard Varsity, Cosmos. Died Feb. 9, 1987; cremated.

HOUGHTON, WILLIAM HENRY, business executive; b. Manitowoc, Wis., Sept. 15, 1891; s. William and Mary (Kaufman) H.; m. Ella May Perry, July 15, 1916. Ed. high sch.; ed., Wis. Bus. Coll. CPA, Mich. Auditor Ernst & Ernst, pub. accts., 1919-28; comptroller Bendix Aviation Corp., Detroit, 1928-42, v.p., treas. and dir., from 1942; bd. dirs. Bendix Eclipse Can. Ltd. Mem. AICPA, Masons, Economic Club, The Recess Club. Home: Detroit Mich. †

HOUSEHOLD, GEOFFREY EDWARD WEST, author; b. Bristol, Eng., Nov. 30, 1900; s. Horace W. and Beatrice (Noton) H.; m. Ilona Zsoldos-Gutmán; children: Geoffrey Andrew, Nicolette Ilona, Anna Cea. Student, Clifton Coll., Oxford U. Author: (novels) The Third Hour, 1937, Rogue Male, 1939 (adapted into movie Man Hunt), Arabesque, 1948, The High Place, 1950, A Rough Shoot, 1951, A Time to Kill, 1951, Fellow Passenger, 1955, Watcher in the Shadows, 1960, Thing To Love, 1963, Olura, 1965, The Courtesy of Death, 1968, Dance of the Dwarfs, 1968, (short stories) The Salvation of Pisco Gabar, 1938, Tales of Adventures, 1952, The Brides of Solomon, 1958, Sabres on the Sand, 1967, (autobiography) Against the Wind, 1958, also author romances, children's books, screenplays, radio plays for children for CBS. With Brit. M.I., World War II. Home: near Banbury England. Died Oct. 4, 1988.

HOUSEMAN, JOHN, producer, director, actor, author; b. Bucarest, Rumania, Sept. 22, 1902; s. Georges and May (Davies) H.; m. Joan Courtney, Dec. 1950; children: John Michael, Charles Sebastian. Student, Clifton Coll., Eng.; Dr.Arts (hon.), Temple U., 1973, Boston U., U. So. Calif., John-Hopkins U., 1985, Gettysburg U., 1985, Union Coll., Hofstra U., Pratt In-. Co-founder, pres. Mercury Theatre, 1937-39; v.p. David O. Selznick Prodns., 1941; chief overseas radio program bur. OWI, 1942-43; producer Paramount Pictures, 1943-46, RKO, 1947-49, Metro-Goldwyn-Mayer, 1950-56, CBS-TV, 1956-59; asso. prof. English drama Vassar Coll., 1937-38; lectr. New Sch. for Social Research, Barnard Coll., others; Regents lectr. U. Calif. Los Angeles, 1960; head drama div. Juilliard Sch., 1968-76; Cockefair chair U. Mo., Kansas City, 1971-72; s. prof. for performing arts U. S.C., 1977; pres. Martha Graham Center, 1972-73. Theatre dir.: plays Four Saints in Three Acts, 1934, Panic, 1935, Valley Forge, 1935, Hamlet, 1936, Liberty Jones, 1939, Lute Song, 1947, King Lear, 1951, Coriolanus, 1953, The Country Girl, 1972, Don Juan in Hell, 1973, Clarence Darrow, 1974, Richard III, 1985, The Cradle Will Rock, 1985; producer: plays Negro Macbeth, 1935, Dr. Faustus, 1937, The Cradle Will Rock, 1937, Julius Caesar, 1937, Shoemaker's Holiday, 1938, Native Son, 1940, Measure for Measure, 1955, King John, 1955, Much Ado About Nothing, 1956, Othello, 1957, King Lear, 1964; dir.: operas The Devil and Daniel Webster, 1939, Othello, 1963, 85, Tosca, 1965, 74, Pantagleize, 1967, The Mines of Sulphur, 1968, Chronicles of Hell, 1968, Antigone, 1970, The Losers, 1971, Byron, 1972, Macbeth, 1973, The Cradle Will Rock, 1983, 85, Richard III, 1985; artistic dir. Am. Shakespeare Festival, 1956-59, Profl. Theater Group of U. Calif. at Los Angeles Extension, 1959-63, City Center Acting Co., 1972-75, Acting Co., 1975—, producing dir., A.P.A. Repertory Co., 1967-69, Phoenix Theatre, 1969-70, dir. drama div., Juilliard Sch., N.Y.C., 1967-76, producer motion pictures, The Unseen, Miss Suzie Slagle's, 1944, The Blue Dahlia, 1945, They Live by Night, 1946, Letter from an Unknown Woman, 1947, The Bad and the Beautiful, 1952, Julius Caesar, 1953, Executive Suite, 1954, The Cobweb, 1955, Lust for Life, 1956, All Fall Down, 1961, Two Weeks in Another Town, 1962, The Dancer's World, Three by Martha Graham, also (for U.S. Govt.) Tuesday in November, 1944, Voyage to America, 1964; actor films including Seven Days in May, 1964, The Paper Chase, 1974, Rollerball, 1975, Three Days of the Condor, 1975, St. Ives, 1976, The Cheap Detective, 1977, Old Boyfriends, Ghost Story, 1981, Another Woman, 1988; TV shows Fear on Trial, 1975, Truman at Potsdam, 1976, Six Characters in Search of an Author, 1976, The Displaced Person, 1976, Washington, 1977, Aspen, 1977, The French Atlantic Affair, 1979, A.D., Winds of War, Christmas Without Snow, Marco Polo, Gideon's Trumpet, The Captains and the Kings; starred in: TV series Paper Chase, 1978; guest appearances TV series Silver Spoons; exec. producer: TV Seven Lively Arts, 1957, Playhouse 90, 1958-59, The Great Adventure, 1963, Gideon's Trumpet, 1980, Choices of the Heart, 1983; radio editor: TV Mercury Theatre of the Air; writer: TV Helen Hayes Theatre; (Recipient Acad. award best supporting actor The Paper Chase 1974); Author: Run-through, a memoir, 1972, Front and Center, 1979, Final Dress, 1983, Entertainers and the Entertained, 1986, Unfinished Business, 1986. Conservator of the Am. Arts, Am. Conservatory Theatre, San Francisco, 1984; recipient Algur Meadows award, So. Meth. U., 1984; Alley award, Alley Theatre, 1985, Congl. Arts Caucus award, 1986, Mayor's Liberty Medal, 1986; John Houseman Theatre Center named in his honor, N.Y.C., 1986. Mem. Author's League, Writers Guild, Screen Producers Guild, Actor's Equity, Screen Actors Guild, Nat. Theatre Conf. (pres. 1970-71), Internat. Theatre Inst. U.S. (v.p. 1968-70). Clubs: Century Assn. (N.Y.C.), Players (N.Y.C.). Died Oct. 31, 1988.

HOUSTON, LIVINGSTON W., educator; b. Wyoming, Ohio, Jan. 18, 1891; s. Archibald W. and Caroline (Evans) H.; m. Margery Caldwell, June 16, 1916 (dec. June 1959); children: Mrs. Christie H. Mahar, Nancy Evans, Mrs. Carol H. Maynard. ME, Renssalaer Poly. Inst., 1913; LLD, St. Lawrence U., Syracuse U.; J.U.D., Trinity Coll.; D.Eng., Stevens Inst. Tech., Poly. Inst. Bklyn.; DSc, Union Coll., Middlebury Coll. Asst. engr. Mobile Gas Co., 1913-14; asst. mgr. inspection Griffin Wheel Co., 1914-17; prodn. mgr. Ludlow Valve Mfg. Co., 1919-27; works mgr. Ludlow Valve Mfg. Co., 1927-32; pres. Ludlow Valve Mfg. Co., 1932-41, chmn. bd., 1941-60; trustee Troy (N.Y.)Savs. Bank; bd. dis. Mfrs. Nat. Bank, United Traction Co. Sec.-treas., exec. v.p., pres., chmn. bd., 1932-63, pres., chmn. bd. emeritus, from 1963, and trustee Rensselaer Poly. Inst.; trustee Troy Pub. Libr., Samaritan Hosp., Albany Acad. Fellow Am. Soc. M.E.; mem. SAR, Newcomen Soc., Troy Club, Engineers Club (N.Y.C.); Fort Orange Club (Albany); Delta Phi. Home: Troy N.Y. †

HOVEN, ARD, clergyman; b. Athena, Oreg., Oct. 21, 1906; s. Victor and Leona (Bodine) H.; B.A., Eugene Bible Coll., 1930, B.D., 1931; B.A., U. Oreg., 1933; M.A., Cin. Bible Sem., 1937; D.S.T., Milligan Coll., 1954; D.D., Ky. Christian Coll., 1954; m. Dorothy Lillian Harris, Sept. 30, 1938; children—Ardis Dee, Vicki Lee. Ordained to ministry Christian Ch., 1933; minister, Ceres, Calif., 1933-34, Cin., 1934-51, Broadway Christian Ch., Lexington, Ky., 1951-66, First Christian Ch., Columbus, Ind., 1966-78; head dept. Christian ministry Ky. Christian Coll., Grayson, from 1978. Speaker radio program Christians' Hour, from 1943; pres. N.Am. Christian Conv., 1950, mem. continuation com., from 1950; writer weekly Bible Sch. lesson The Lookout, Standard Pub. Co., Cin., 1958-85, mem. pub. com., from 1957. Republican. Mason, Rotarian. Author: Christ Is All, 1953; Meditations and Prayers for the Lord's Table, 1962. Died Apr. 16, 1987; buried Lexington Cemetery.

HOVEY, WALTER READ, educator, art critic; b. Springfield, Mass., July 21, 1895; s. Albert Henry and Sarah Elizabeth (Heywood) H. AB, Yale, 1918; MA, Harvard, 1926; AFD (hon.), Coll. of Wooster, Ohio, 1966. Asst. prof. fine arts U. Pitts., 1927-39, prof., head dept. fine arts, 1939-67, developed fine arts library and art gallery, Henry Clay Frick prof., dir. Henry Clay Frick Fine Arts Bldg., 1965-67; disting. prof. fine arts Point Park Coll., Pitts., from 1967; vis. lectr. Reading (Pa.) Mus. and Art Gallery, 1970-71; adviser Asiatic art Carnegie Inst., Pitts.; specialist U.S. Dept. State to Near East, Pakistan and Ceylon, 1954-55. Author: Potteries and Porcelains in the Frick Collection, 1955; lectr. series The Artsin Changing Societies, Frick Art Mus., Pitts., 1970-71; contbr. articles to profl. jours. and art publs. Bd. dirs. Westmoreland County Mus. Art, Greensburg, Pa. With mobile hosp. unit AEF, 1916-18. Named Man of Year in Art, Pitts. Jr. C. of C., 1964; Carnegie Found. Fellow, 1926. Mem. Coll. Art Assn., Assoc. Artists Pitts., Pitts. Bicentennial Assn., Cape Cod Art Assn. (hon. dir.), Univ. Club, Faculty Club, Pitts. Golf Club. Republican. Home: Pittsburgh Pa. Deceased.

HOVORKA, FRANK, educator; b. Cernikovice, Czechoslovakia, Aug. 5, 1897; came to U.S., 1913, naturalized, 1923; s. Frank and Anna (Pavlova) H.; m. Sophie Paul Nickel, June 12, 1926 (dec. 1979); m. Dorothy Humel, July 9, 1982. AB, Iowa State Tchrs. Coll., 1922; MS, U. Ill., 1923, PhD, 1925. Mem. faculty Case Western Res. U., Cleve., 1925-84, prof. chemistry, 1942-54, dir. chem. labs., 1942-58, chmn. dept. chemistry, 1950-58, 62-64, Hurlbut prof. chemistry, 1954-68, prof. emeritus, cons. dept., 1968-84, univ. fellow, 1973; rsch. assoc. Argonne Nat. Lab., 1954-62; Western Res. U. rep. coun. sponsoring instns. Assoc. Midwest Univs., 1947-58, dir. 1958-62. Contbr. articles phys. chemistry, electrochemistry, ultrasonics to profl. jours. Bd. dirs. Judson Park, Cleveland Heights, 1974. Recipient Disting. Tchrs. award Mfg. Chemists Assn., 1963, Alumni Achievement award State Coll. Iowa, 1964, Disting. Service award Cleve. Tech. Socs. Coun., 1969. Fellow AAAS, Electrochem. Soc., Soc. Chem. Industry (Gt. Britain), Chem. Soc. London; mem. U.S. Capitol Hist. Soc., Am. Chem. Soc., Faraday Soc. (Eng.), AAUP, NEA, Cleve. Mus. Arts Assn., Cleve. Coun. World Affairs, Cleve. Skating Club, Sigma Xi, Phi Lambda Upsilon, Pi Mu Epsilon, Epsilon Chi, Alpha Chi Sigma. Republican. Home: Shaker Heights Ohio. Died Apr. 9, 1984; buried Connersville, Ind.

HOWARD, JAMES J., congressman; b. Irvington, N.J., July 24, 1927; s. George P. and Bernice M. Howard; m. Marlene Vetrano; children: Kathleen Howard Tjunin, Lenore Howard Buchanan, Marie. BA, St. Bonaventure U., 1952; MEd, Rutgers U., 1958; LLD (hon.), Monmouth Coll., 1977, St. Bonaventure U., 1979, Georgian Court Coll., 1983. Tchr., acting prin. Wall Twp. (N.J.) Sch. System, 1954-64; mem. 89th-99th congresses 3d Dist. N.J., 1965-87; chmn. com. public works and transp; mem. Nat. Transp. Policy Study Commn., Nat. Adv. Council, Congl. award. Served with USN, World War II. Mem. NEA, N.J. Edn. Assn. (del. assembly), Monmouth County Edn. Assn. (past pres.). Democrat. Home: Washington D.C. Died Mar. 25, 1988.

HOWARD, ROBERT LORENZO, law educator; b. Millersville, Mo., July 25, 1891; s. James Bennett and Harriet Matilda (Miller) H.; m. Loreta Welty, Aug. 28, 1915; children: Frederick Lorenzo, Erma Loreta, Jane Eloise. B Pedagogy, S.E. Mo. State Normal Sch., 1915; AB, U. Mo., 1917, AM, 1918, LLB, 1925; postgrad., Colo. U. Law Sch., summer 1924; D Juridical Sci., Harvard U., 1933. Bar: Mo. 1925, U.S. Supreme Ct., 1939. Tchr. country schs. Cape Girardeau County, Mo., 1909-13; tchr. State Tchrs. Coll., Maryville, Mo., 1919-20; instr. polit. sci. U. Mo., 1920-22, mcpl. reference librarian, 1920-25, asst. prof. law, 1925-28, assoc. prof., 1928-29, prof., from 1929; pub. mem. 7th Regional War Labor Bd., Wage Stblzn. Bd., 1943-46, chmn. 9th Regional, 1951; mem. nat. panel Am. Arbitration Assn.; arbitrator labor disputes, Fed. Mediation and Conciliation Svc.; mem. permanent arbitration bd. Internat. Ladies Garment Workers, Kansas City Garment Mfrs. Assn. Co-editor: Labor Law Cases and Materials; contbr. to law revs. Chmn. Columbia Charter Commn.; elder Christian Ch. Lt. F.A., U.S. Army, World War I. Mem. ABA, Nat. Acad. Arbitrators, Indsl. Relations Rsch. Assn., Mo., Boone County bar assns., Mo. Nat. Conf. (commr.), Am. Law Inst. (commr. uniform state laws), Order of Coif, Phi Beta Kappa. Democrat. Home: Columbia Mo. †

HOWARD, TREVOR WALLACE, actor; b. Margate, Eng., Sept. 29, 1916; student Clifton Coll., Bristol, Eng., Royal Acad. Dramatic Art; m. Helen Cherry, 1944. Plays include: French Without Tears, The Recruiting Officer, 1944, Anna Christie, 1944, The Devil's General, 1953, The Cherry Orchard, 1954, Two Stars for Comfort, 1962, The Father, 1964, Table Number Seven, The Waltz of the Toreadors, 1974, Scenario, Toronto, 1977; films include: Brief Encounter, 1945, The Third Man, 1949, An Outcast of the Islands, 1951, The Heart of the Matter, 1953, Les amants du Tage, 1955, Cockleshell Heroes, 1955, The Key, 1958, Roots of Heaven, 1958, Sons and Lovers, 1960, Mutiny on the Bounty, 1962, Von Ryan's Express, 1966, The Charge of the Light Brigade, 1968, Ryan's Daughter, 1970, Mary Queen of Scots, 1972, The Offense, 1973, A Doll's House, 1973, II Harrowhouse, 1974, The Visitor, Hennessy, 1975, Conduct Unbecoming, 1976, Count of Monte Cristo, 1976, Eliza Fraser, 1977, The Last Remake of Beau Geste, 1977, Slavers, 1978, Meteor, 1978, Ludwig, Stevie, Hurricane, 1979, The Sea Wolves, 1980, Sir Henry at Rawlinson End, 1980, Windwalker, 1981, Light Years Away, 1982, The Missionary, 1983, Gandhi, 1983, Dust, 1986, White Mischief, 1987; TV plays include: Hedda Gabler, 1962, The Invincible Mr. Disraeli (Acad. award), 1963, Napoleon at St. Helena, 1966, Catholics, Night Flight, Staying On, 1980, And the Band Played On, 1981, No Country for Old Men, 1982, The Long Exile of Jonathan Swift, 1983, The Deadly Game, 1983, George Washington, 1984, Time After Time, 1985, This

Lightning Always Strikes Twice, 1985, Shaka Zulu, 1986, Sir Isaac Newton in Peter the Great, 1986; TV miniseries Peter the Great, 1986. Served with Royal Army, 1940-43. Home: Arkley Hertsfordshire, England. Died Jan. 7, 1988.

HOWE, DAVID WILLARD, newspaper publisher; b. Burlington, Vt., June 22, 1892; s. Willard B. and Annie (Bean) H.; m. Marjorie A. Roberts, Apr. 29, 1922; children: Leis Howe McClure, Nancy Howe Lieb, Barbara Howe Tucker. BA, U. Vt., 1914, LLD, 1952; LLD, Middlebury Coll., 1949. Mem. advt. dept. Charles Scribner's Sons, N.Y.C., 1915-17; advt. mgr. Syracuse Post Standard, 1919-21; asst. mgr. Burlington Free Press, 1921, bus. mgr., 1929-53, pub., 1953-60, co-pub., 1960-61, assoc. pub., 1961-67; pres. Vt. Broadcasting Corp., 1946; mem. Eastern adv. bd. Lumberman's Mut. Casualty Co.; trustee Burlington Savs. Bank from 1936; mem. bd. dirs. Fed. Mut. Fire Ins. Co. from 1941, Am. Newspaper Pubs. Assn., 1938, v.p., 1945-47, pres.,1947-49; v.p. Burlington C. of C., 1946; mem. advt. adv. com. to sec. of commerce, 1950. Mem. Rotary Club, Ethan Allen Club, Burlington Country Club, Phi Beta Kappa, Sigma Phi, Sigma Delta Chi. Republican. Congregationalist. Home: Burlington Vt. †

HOWE, ERNEST JOSEPH, utilities executive; b. Denver, July 4, 1900; s. Herbert Alonzo and Fannie (Shattuck) H.; m. Gladys Montgomery Sills, Sept. 3, 1927; 1 child, James Everett. AB, U. Denver, 1921; MS, Columbia U., 1923. Investment analyst Blyth & Co. Inc., N.Y.C., 1925-32; sec. Am. Brit. & Continental Corp., 1929-32; v.p. Pacific Western Oil Corp., 1929-32; investment counsellor 1932-34; fin. advisor FHA, 1934-35; investment supr. Lehman Bros., N.Y.C., 1936; v.p. James H. Causey & Co., 1937; chief fin. advisor ins. sect. Temp. Nat. Econ. Com. U.S. Senate, 1938-39; chief fin. officer for trusteeship Assoc. Gas and Electric System; dir., officer more than 25 cos., 1940-45; bd. dirs., mem. exec. com. Rochester (N.Y.) Gas & Electric Corp., 1940-83, v.p., 1945-57, comptroller, 1950-57, pres., 1957-65, chmn. exec. and fin. coms., 1974-80; v.p., dir. Canadea Power Corp., 1949-65. Author: Operating Results Investments of the 26th Largest Legal Reserve Life Insurance Companies Domiciled in the United States, 1940, (with Gerhard A. Gesell) Study of Legal Reserve Life Insurance Companies, 1941, (with J.R. Foster, H.J. Flagg, Malcom P. Davis) The New Jersey Rate Adjustment Plan, 1944; chpt. Free Trade as the Basis of International Cooperation (in Ways to Peace), 1924' contbr. articles to bus. mags. Mem. N.J. Water Policy Commn., 1943-45, N.J. Local Govt. Bd., 1943-44. Mem. Fin. Execs. Inst., Rochester Engring Soc., Internat. Conf. Large Electric High Tension Systems, Rochester Soc. Investment Analysts, Rochester Bur. Mcpl. Rsch., Am. Mgmt. Assn., AIM, Am. Gas Assn., Edison Electric Inst., Rochester C. of C., Newcomen Soc., George Eastman House Assocs., Univ. Club, Country Club of Rochester, Beta Theta Pi., Beta Gamma Sigma. Home: Rochester N.Y. Died Jan. 23, 1983; buried Brighton Cemetery, Rochester.

HOWE, OSCAR, artist, educator; b. Joe Creek, S.D., May 13, 1915; s. George T. and Ella Star (Not Afraid of Bear) H.; m. Heidi Hampel, July 29, 1947; 1 child, Inge Dawn. BA, Dakota Wesleyan U., Mitchell, S.D., 1952; MFA, U. Okla., 1954; HHD (hon.), S.D. State U., Hamline U., Dakota Wesleyan U. Tchr. Pierre (S.D.) Ind. Sch., 1939-40; tchr., dir. art Pierre High Sch., 1943-57; prof. fine arts, artist-in-residence U. S.D., Vermillion, 1957-80, prof. emeritus, 1980-83; artist-in-residence Dakota Wesleyan U., 1948-52; U.S. State Dept. lectr., Near East and S. Asia, 1971. One man shows of paintings include: U. S.D., Vermillion, 1959, 64, U. N.D., Grand Forks, 1959, S.D. State U., Brookings, 1960, Sioux City (Iowa) Art Ctr., 1960-61, U. Wis., Madison, 1961, Indian Arts and Crafts Ctr., Rapid City, S.D., 1962, Dakota Wesleyan U., 1963, Ill. State Mus., Springfield, 1963, U.S. Dept. Interior, Washington, 1963, Theodore Lyman Wright Art Ctr., Beloit, Wis., 1964, Eastern Wash. State Hist. Soc., Spokane, 1964, The Heard Mus., Phenix, 1964, Philbrook Art Ctr., Tulsa, 1964, Nobles County Art Ctr., Worthington, Minn., 1965, Albert Lea (Minn.) Art Ctr., 1965, Butler County Hist. Soc., Grand Island Nebr., 1965, Sioux Indian Mus., Rapid City, 1965, Evansville (Ind.) Coll., 1966, Baldwin Wallace Coll., Berea, Ohio, 1966, Joslyn Art Mus., Omaha, 1967, Am. Indian Arts Ctr., N.Y.C., 1967, Sioux Falls (S.D.) Coll., 1968, Mus. N.Mex., Santa Fe, 1957, Denver Art Mus., 1958; group shows in Paris, 1936, London, 1936, Philbrook Art Ctr., Chgo. Art Inst., Smithsonian Instn., Washington, Denver Art Mus., San Francisco Mus. Art, Gallery for Living Artists, Bklyn., Mus. Fine Arts, Stanford U., S.W. Mus., L.A., Mus. N.Mex., Mus. Modern Art, N.Y.C.; represented in permanent collections: Joslyn Art Mus., Gallup (N.Mex.) Art Gallery, Mus. N.Mex., Philbrook Art Ctr., Denver Art Mus., Montclair (N.J.) Art Mus.; murals in Mitchell (S.D.) Library, Mobridge Auditorium, S.D., Nebraska City, Nebr., Hinsdale, Ill.; book illustrator: Legends of the Mighty Sioux, 1941, The Little Lost Sioux (Martha Rabe), 1942, Bringer of the Mystery Dog (Ann Clark), 1943, North American Indian Costumes (O.B. Jacobson), 1952; retrospective exhbn. U. S.D. and Gilcrease Mus., Tulsa, 1982; works reproduced in numerous mags. and jours. Named S.D. Artist Laureate, 1960; recipient cert. appreciation Indian Arts and Crafts Bd., U.S. Dept. Interior, 1962, Recognition award Found. N.Am. Indian Culture, 1964, numerous awards for paintings. Fellow Internat. Inst. Arts and Letters. Home: Vermillion S.D. Died Oct. 7, 1983; buried Vermillion, S.D.

HOWELL, ALMONTE CHARLES, English educator; b. North Kingsville, Ohio, Sept. 9, 1895; s. Albert Benjamin and Clara Adela (Craytor) H.; m. Sara Barbour Holmes, Dec. 30, 1920; 1 child Almonte Charles. AB, Denison U., 1917; MA, Columbia U., 1920; PhD, U. N.C., 1924. Instr. English U. N.C., 1920, asst. prof, asst. to dean of grad. sch., 1924, assoc. prof., 1928, prof., since 1938, asst. dean Coll. Arts and Scis., 1939-45, adviser to transfer students Gen. Coll., 1940-45, sec. gen. faculty, from 1943, adviser to fgn. students, from 1958; in charge of English courses, Sch. of Engring., 1922-38; vis. prof. English, Grad. Sch. N.C. Coll. for Negroes, 1941-46 (summers); asst. dir. Wellesley Inst. Fgn. Students, 1946, 49, 50 (summers); vis. prof. English U. San Carlos de Guatemala, 1946-48, now hon. prof.; spl. lectr. English Inst. in San Salvador, 1946, and Tegucigalpa, Honduras, 1947; guest lectr. Instituto Guatemalteco-Americano, Guatemala, 1947; vis. prof. English, Seoul (Korea) Nat. U., 1955-56; Fulbright lectr. U. Asuncion, Paraguay, 1962-63. Author: Handbook of English in Engineering Usage, 1940; (with R.P. Baker) The Preparation of Reports, 1939; Mil. Correspondence and Reports, 1943; Ensayos sobre Literatura Norte Americana, 1948; The Kenan Professorships, 1956; contbr. articles to mags. and ednl. bulls. Mem. MLA, Engring. Edn. Soc., South Atlantic MLA, Phi Beta Kappa, Sigma Alpha Epsilon, Phi Mu Alpha (Sinfonia). Democrat. Home: Chapel Hill N.C. Died Sept. 30, 1986.

HOWELL, DAVID J., lawyer; b. Maryville, Mo., May 26, 1887; s. David J. and Elizabeth Elvira (Stewart) H.; m. Catherine Campbell, Oct. 21, 1933. Student, U. Kans., 1905-06; LLB, U. Mo., 1908. Bar: Wyo. 1908. Practiced in Cheyenne, Wyo; asst. pros. atty. Laramie County, Wyo., 1911-12; asst. U.S. atty. 1914-21, atty. gen. of State of Wyo., 1923-26; counsel Reconstrn. Fin. Corp., 1933-35. Pres. Wyo. Soc. S.A.R., 1925. Mem. Masons, (32 degree), Shriners. Democrat. Home: Santa Ana Calif. Deceased.

HOWELL, ELSWORTH SEAMAN, publisher; b. N.Y.C., Dec. 4, 1915; s. Clarence Seaman and Josephine Polhemus (Weller) H.; m. Elizabeth Roper, July 27, 1940; children—Jean Elizabeth Howell Salembier, Maureen Anne Howell Mawicke. Student, N.Y. U., 1935-36. Asst. editor Book of Knowledge, 1934-36; editor L'Encyclopedie de la Jeunesse, 1936- 37; mgr. mail order sales Grolier Soc., Inc., N.Y.C., 1939-46; v.p. Grolier Soc., Inc., 1947-59; pres., dir. Grolier Enterprises, Inc., N.Y.C., 1960-66; chmn. bd. Grolier Enterprises, Inc., 1967-68, House of Grolier Ltd., London, 1966-73; v.p. Grolier Internat., 1966-69, exec. v.p., 1969-73; pres., dir. Howell Book House, Inc., from 1961; dir. Grolier Ednl. Corp., Grolier Soc. Ltd., London, 1966-73; v.p., dir. Franklin Watts, Inc.; sec., dir. Americana Interstate Corp.; v.p., dir. Grolier, Inc., 1960-73, mem. exec. com., 1966-73; columnist Popular Dogs mag., 1955-66; editor Internat. Ency. of Dogs.; Pres. Allwood Homeowners Assn., Darien, Conn., 1963-65. Author: (with D.H. Tuck) The New Complete English Setter, 1964, 72, 82. Trustee Dog Writers Ednl. Trust. Recipient award Direct Mail Advt. Assn., 1954; Gaines' Dogdom's Man of Year award, 1970, 85. Mem. English Setter Assn. Am. (v.p., past pres.), Dog Writers Assn. Am. Clubs: Wee Burn Country (Darien); Am. Kennel (N.Y.C.) (del., judge); Dog Fanciers (judge best dog in show Westminster Kennel Club 1985, dir.), Westminster Kennel, Ox Ridge Kennel (gov., v.p.), Publishers Lunch. Home: Darien Conn. Died Mar. 19, 1987; interred Lakeview Cemetery, New Canaan, Conn.

HOWELL, HANNAH JOHNSON, librarian; b. Oskaloosa, Iowa, June 22, 1905; d. Irving Culver and Mary Hortense (Burnside) Johnson; m. Henry Wilson Howell Jr., June 5, 1947 (dec.). Student, Penn Coll., Oskaloosa, 1924-25; PhB, U. Chgo., 1927; BLS, Columbia U., 1928; student, NYU Inst. Fine Arts, also lectures N.Y. Hist. Soc., 1940-41. Reviser summer library sch. U. Ia., 1928; rsch. asst. Frick Art Reference Library, N.Y.C., 1928-34, head reference dept., 1935-47, asst. librarian, 1942-47, chief librarian, 1947-70, cons. librarian, 1970-88. Mem. hon. com. nat. capital sesquicentennial commn. exhbn., Am. Processional, Corcoran Gallery Art, 1950; patroness benefit exhbn. paintings for Smith Coll. Collection, Knoedler Galleries, N.Y.C., 1953. Mem. U. Chgo. Alumnae Assn. (pres. N.Y. chpt. 1932-37), Columbia U. Club (chmn. ladies com. 1942-44), Cosmopolitan Club (mem. library com. 1946-49). Presbyterian. Home: New York N.Y. Died May 21, 1988.

HOWLAND, HAROLD (JACOBS), writer; b. Chatham, N.Y., June 29, 1877; s. William Bailey and Ella May (Jacobs) H.; m. Madeline Sayles, Mar. 31, 1902; m. 2d, Lois Estabrook Sandison, Aug. 21, 1930. AB, Amherst Coll., 1898. With The Macmillan Co., N.Y.C., 1899-1900; asst. editor Town and Country, 1900-01; with J. Horace McFarland Co., Harrisburg, Pa., 1901-02; mem. editorial staff The Outlook, 1902-13; assoc. editor The Independent, 1913-20; mng. dir. Independent Corp., 1919-20; with Tamblyn & Brown Inc., N.Y.C., 1926-51, Ginn and Co., N.Y.C., from 1952 with Office of Censorship, N.Y. dist., 1943-45. Author Theodore Roosevelt and His Times (in Chronicles c America series); contbr. to Dictionary Nat. Biography Collier's, World's Work, Woman's Home Compnaion others. Publicity dir. St. Vincent Hosp. cmapaign, N.Y. 1925; regional dir. YMCA with Italian Army, Florence ITaly, 1918; Prog. candidate for Rep. congl. nomination 7th N.J. Dist., 1910; alt. del. Rep. Nat. Covention Chgo., 1912; mem. Prog. State Exec. Com., N.J., 1912 13. Mem. Nat. Arts Club (life), Chi Psi. Episcopalian. Home: New York N.Y. †

HOWORTH, M. BECKETT, orthopedic surgeon; b West Point, Miss.; s. Benjamin M. and Willie Cape (Beckett) H.; m. Marjorie Maye Meehan. B.S., U Miss., 1921; M.D., Washington U., 1925; Med.Sci.D Columbia U., 1933. Intern Presbyn. Hosp., N.Y.C 1925-27; attending surgeon fracture service Presbyn Hosp., 1933; resident N.Y. Orthopedic Hosp., 1927-29 asst. attending surgeon, 1934-51; asso. vis. orthopedi surgeon Bellevue, 1951-80; cons. orthopedist Vanderbi Clinic, N.Y.C., 1931-49, Roosevelt Hosp., 1935-80; assc clin. prof. orthopedic surgery Columbia Coll. Phys. an Surg., 1936-51, lectr. orthopedic phys. and occupationa therapy, 1944-50; lectr. nursing edn. Columbia Col Phys. and Surg. (Tchrs. Coll.), 1938-50; clin. pro orthopedics N.Y. U. Postgrad. Med. Sch., 1951-80; clir prof. orthopedic surgery U. Miss. Med. Center, Jacksor from 1981; lectr. orthopedic surgery Yale U., 1959-7 cons. orthopedic surgeon Greenwich (Conn.) Hosp 1949-52, chief orthopedic dept., 1952-76; cons orthopedic surgeon No. Westchester Hosp., Mt. Kisc N.Y., 1949-63, Stamford (Conn.) Hosp., 1959-80, New ington (Conn.) Children's Hosp.; Mem. adv. bd. Assn Aid Crippled Children, 1946-55, Rehab. Cente Stamford, Conn., 1950-70. Author: Textbook c Orthopedics, 1952, Examination and Diagnosis of th Spine and Extremities, 1962, Injuries of the Spine, 196 (with Fred Bender) Tennis Elbow, 1977, How to Cur Your Own Backache, 1984; Contbr. numerous articles t med. and nursing jours., consumer research publs., als articles on mountaineering. Fellow A.C.S.; mem. Assn Bone and Joint Surgeons, Pan Pacific Surg. Assn. (v.p orthopedics 1963-66), Internat. Orthopedic Assn. (se 1960—), Am. Orthopedic Assn. (v.p. 1962, pres. 196 Eastern Orthopedic Assn., Can. Orthopedic Assn., Swis Orthopedic Assn., New Zealand Orthopedic Assn Japanese Orthopedic Assn. (hon. mem.), Internat. So Orthopedics and Traumatology, Orthopedic Corr. Clul A.A.A.S., Am. Assn. Phys. Anthropology, A.M.A Orthopedic Research Soc., Am. Acad. Orthoped Surgeons, Interurban Orthopedic Club (sec. 1940-8 N.Y. Acad. Medicine, New Zealand Orthopedic Ass (corr.), Orthopaedic Corr. Club; hon. mem. Turkis Western Pacific, La., New Eng., South Africa orthopedic assns., Latin-Am., Chilean, Guatemala socs. orthopedics and traumatology, Alpha Omeg Alpha, Phi Rho Sigma. Methodist. Clubs: Rotaria (N.Y.C.), Am. Alpine (N.Y.C.); Appalachian Mounta (Boston); Alpine of Canada (Banff); Sierra (Sa Francisco); Rhino (South Africa); Spectators. Hom Jackson Miss. Died Apr. 16, 1986.

HOWSER, RICHARD ALTON, baseball manager; Miami, Fla., May 14, 1937. BS in Edn., Fla. State U Baseball player Kansas City Athletics, 1961-63, Clev Indians, 1963-66, N.Y. Yankees, 1967-68; mem. Am League All-Star team, 1961, 63; coach N.Y. Yankee 1969-78, mgr., 1980; baseball coach Fla. State U Talahassee, 1979; mgr. Kansas City Royals, 1981-87 Rookie of the Yr., Am. League, 1961; Managed Kans City Royals to World Series Championship, 1985. Die 1987.

HOWSON, LOUIS RICHARD, consulting engineer; Folletts, Iowa, Apr. 19, 1887; s. Thomas Henry an Anna Cora (Wessels) H.; m. Mabel Dunseth, Apr. 2 1913; children: Mary Mabel, Louise Ruth. BSCE, U Wis., 1908, CE, 1912. With Alvord & Burdick, 1908-2 mem. Alvord, Burdick & Howson, from 1921; served engr. on water supplies, sewerage and sewage disposa numerous locations throughout U.S. and Can.; expe for N.Y., Pa., Ohio, Wis., Mich. and Minn. in Lak Mich. Water Diversion Controversy; reported to U. sec. of war on requirements and costs of sewage trea ment for the Chgo. Dist.; expert testifying before IC and U.S. Stockyards Adminstrn. on cases on item "Going Value"; appraiser approx. 100 utilities and tes fied before numerous commns. and cts. regarding valu and rates; mem. several bds. arbitration fixing value utility properties for transfer or rates. Author tec papers on water supply, sewage treatment and pu utility valuation. Mem. Ill. State Bd. Conservation an Natural Resources. Mem. ASCE (pres. 1958), ASM Western Soc. Engrs. (former pres.), Am. Water Wor Assn. (former pres.), Ill. Soc. Engrs., Am. Inst. Con Engrs., Engrs. Club, University Club (Chgo.), Hinsda Golf Club. Republican. Methodist. Home: Hinsda Ill. †

HOYT, RALPH MELVIN, lawyer; b. Columbus, Wi Jan. 14, 1890; s. Judson E. and Edith (Evans) H.; Dorothy Louise Taylor, Apr. 14, 1917 (dec. 196 children: Hamilton Taylor, Stuart Evans. AB, U. Wi 1910, LLB, 1912. Bar: Wis. 1912. Asst. sec. R. Commn. Wis., 1912-14; practiced in Milw., 1914-20, 2 30, and from 1934; mem. law firm Hoyt, Greene

Meissner; dep. atty. gen. State of Wis., 1921-22; pres. Title Guaranty Co., Wis., 1930-34. Contbr. articles to profl. jours. Bd. dirs. Associated Hosp. Service (Wis. Blue Cross), 1946-74; chmn. bd. trustees Milw.-Downer Coll., 1949-62. Mem. ABA (com. on adminstrv. law 1936-37, 41-46, chmn. com. on adminstrv. agys. and tribunals in sect. jud. adminstrn. 1937-41, mem. council sect. adminstrv. law 1948-52), Wis. Bar Assn., Milw. Bar Assn. (pres. 1939-40), Milw. Club, Milw. Country Club, Masons, Order of Coif, Phi Beta Kappa, Sigma Nu, Phi Alpha Delta. Republican. Episcopalian. Home: Milwaukee Wis. Deceased.

HOYT, SAMUEL LESLIE, metallurgical consultant; b. Mpls., May 29, 1888; s. Alphonso Orlando and Hulda Lucretia (Hunt) H.; m. Jane Woodruff, Jan. 1, 1913; 4 children; m. Edyth S. Armstrong, Nov. 1946; m. Kay W. Dowd, Nov. 1966. EM, U. Minn., 1909; postgrad., Columbia U., 1909-11, PhD, 1914; postgrad., Royal Inst. Tech., Charlottenburg, Germany, 1911-13; ScD, S.D. Sch. Mines and Tech., 1955. Assoc. prof., founder dept. metallography U. Minn., 1913-19; metall. engr. GE, 1919-30; metallurgist A.O. Smith Corp., 1931-34, dir. metall. rsch., 1934-39, cons., 1939-41; tech. adviser Battelle Meml. Inst., Columbus, Ohio, 1939-53; metall. cons. indsl. rsch. to producing and fabricating cos., govt. agys. 1953-59; staff rep. rsch. and engring. div. U.S. Dept. Def., Frankfurt, Fed. Republic Germany, 1959-60; metall. cons. from 1960; staff cons. Anamet Labs., Berkeley, Calif., from 1968; Priestley lectr. Pa. State U., also ann. and meml. lectures; developer carboloy; initiated cemented carbide industry in U.S.; sci. cons. ALSOS Mission, 1945; mem. sci. adv. coun. Picatinny Arsenal; mem. NRC Commn. on Ship Steel. Author: Metal Data, 1952, other tech. books; inventor, developer Smith Alloy 10, developer low alloy steel otiscology, welding, metallurgy, steel procurement, failure analysis, gen. metall. rsch. Recipient Outstanding Achievement award U. Minn., medal U. Minn. Fellow Am. Soc. Metals (Metall. Milestone for 1928, trustee, hon.); mem. AIME (Legion of Honor, com. phys. chemistry steel making), AAAS, Am. Welding Soc., Inst. Medals, Welding Rsch. Coun., Am. Ordnance Assn., Iron and Steel Inst. Eng. (Metals Soc., Am. Soc. for Metals, Sigma, Delta Tau Delta. †

HSU, SHUHSI, diplomat; b. Swatow, China, Apr. 3, 1892; s. Wuju and Lanhsiang (Chang) H.; m. Grace Wenchuang Liu, July 7, 1921; childern: Yuanyo, Fucheng, Chichang. BA, Hongkong U., 1917; MA, Columbia, 1919, PhD, 1925. Prof. polit. sci. in charge internat. law and diplomacy Yenching U., Peiping, 1923-37, dean coll. pub. affairs, 1929-32; tech. adviser Chinese dels. to League of Nations Assembly and Coun., 1932-33; mem. nat. defense planning commn. NAt. Govt., 1933-36, mem. nat. resources com., 1936-38; adviser to Ministry of Fgn. Affairs, 1936-38, 40-49; tech. mem. Chinese del. to UN, 1945-47, min. plenipotentiary, 1947-52, amb., 1952-56; amb. to Peru and Bolivia from 1956; alternative rep. UN Security Coun., Gen. Assembly, Interim Com. of Gen. assembly, 1947-56, Peace Observatin Com., 1950-56; rep. com. on codification of internat. law, 1947, com. on definition of aggression, 1953; rep. UN Gen. Assembly, 1958, 60; mem. UN Internat. Law Commn., from 1948, Permanent Ct. of Arbitration, from 1958. Author: The Manchurian Question, 1929, The North China Problem, 1937, Chinese Foreign RElations, 1940; other works on Far Eastern internat. rels. †

HUBACHEK, FRANK BROOKES, lawyer; b. Mpls., Aug. 10, 1894; s. Frank R. and Nellie A. (Brookes) H.; m. Marjorie Mix, Dec. 15, 1917; children: Marjorie Ann Hubachek Watkins, Frank Brookes Jr. AB, U. Minn., 1915, LLB, 1922; student, Harvard Law Sch., 1915-17; LHD, Cornell Coll., 1962, Carlton Coll., 1972; LLD, Beloit Coll., 1970. Bar: Minn. 1922, Ill. 1929. Ptnr. Hubachek & Schall, Mpls., 1922-24; pvt. practice Mpls., 1924-34; mem. firm Hubachek, Kelly, Rauch & Kirby and predecessor firms, 1934-69; dir. Household Fin. Corp., 1925-67, chmn. exec. com., 1934-66; cons. OPA, Washington, alternate price adminstr.; cons. Com. under Presdl. order 8843, 1941-43. Author: Annotations on Small Loan Laws, Russell Sage Found., 1938; contbr. articles to law revs. Mem. Bd. Edn., Glencoe, Ill., 1932-36; pres., trustee Wilderness Rsch. Found., Lakeland Found.; v.p., trustee Art Inst. Chgo., life trustee, from 1970; hon. trustee Gads Hill Ctr. With ambulance corps, French Army, 1917; lt. (j.g.), pilot USN, 1918, USNR, 1919-22. Mem. Am. Forestry Assn. (Nat. award for service in conservation 1957), ABA, Ill. Bar Assn., Chgo. Bar Assn., Masons, Chicago, University, Mid-America, Skokie Country, Minneapolis clubs, Phi Delta Phi, Phi Kappa Psi. Republican. Baptist. Home: Glencoe Ill. Died Dec. 8, 1986.

HUBBARD, ALLEN SKINNER, lawyer; b. Auburn, N.Y., Jan. 31, 1891; s. William H. and Elizabeth Allen (Skinner) H.; m. Harriet E. Richardson, Dec. 24, 1913 (dec. Feb. 1977); children: Allen Skinner, David Richardson, Elizabeth Hubbard Stott, Charlotte Hubbard Fries, William Skinner (dec.). AB, Yale U., 1911; LLB, Harvard U., 1914. Bar: N.Y. 1915. With Stetson, Jennings & Russell, N.Y.C., 1914-17; assoc., then. ptnr. Hughes, Rounds, Schurman & Dwight, 1917-37; ptnr. Hughes, Hubbard & Reed and predecessors, from 1937. Mem., treas. Metro Rapid Transit Commn., 1954-59. Pvt. 41st Tng. Battery, U.S. Army, 1918. Mem. ABA, N.Y. State Bar Assn., Assn. of Bar of City of N.Y. (exec. com. 1951-55), N.Y. County Lawyers Assn., New Eng. Soc. City of N.Y. (pres. 1950), University Club, Downtown Assn. (N.Y.C.), Alpha Delta Phi. Home: New York N.Y. Deceased.

HUBBARD, L. RON, writer, explorer, philosopher, humanitarian; b. Tilden, Nebr., Mar. 13, 1911; s. Harry Ross and Ledora May (Waterbury) H.; m. Mary Sue Whipp; children: Diana Meredith de Wolf, Mary Suzette Rochelle, Arthur Ronald Conway. Student, George Washington U., 1932, Princeton Sch. Govt., 1945. Writer aviation and travel articles from 1930, explorer, from 1934; leader Caribbean Motion Picture Expdn., 1931, W.I. Minerals Survey Expdn., 1932, Alaskan Radio-Exptl. Expdn., 1940; organizer Hubbard Found. for pub. interests; founder Scientology, 1951; dir. internat. humanitarian orgns. including Dianetics and Scientology, 1952-66; resigned all directorships to devote full time to rsch., 1966, rsch. and tech. for improved edn., 1974-71, rsch. and internat. programs to resolve drug abuse, from 1966, exptl. works in music and photography, from 1974. Author: over 2000 works including Dianetics: The Modern Science of Mental Health, 1950, Science of Survival, 1951, The Fundamentals of Thought, 1956, Scientology: A New Slant on Life, 1966, Self Analysis, 1968, Dianetics Today, 1975, Battlefield Earth: A Saga of the Year 3000, 1982, The Way to Happiness, 1981; contbr. articles to various publs. Recipient community service awards in U.S. Internat. Inst. Community Service awards; over 75 awards for musical creations; internat. recognition for photog. creations, 1975; Internat. Social Reform award, 1976, Ingrams West award, 1977, Nat. Life Achievement award Ill. Soc. Psychic Rsch., 1978, Internat. Profl. Assn. award, 1978, Saturn award for spl. achievement Acad. Sci. Fiction, Fantasy and Horror Films for book Battlefield Earth, 1984; mumerous hon. citizenships and keys to cities in U.S. Home: Los Angeles Calif. Died Jan. 24, 1986.

HUBBARD, LESTER A(NDREWS), English educator; b. Willard, Utah, Mar. 8, 1892; s. Joseph and Sally Ann (Marsh) H.; m. Barbara Larsen, Sept. 24, 1919; children: Gene Beth (Mrs. Bryant H. Croft), Neva Elaine (Mrs. D.C. Bernson). Certificat Francais Superieur, Alliance Francaise, Paris, 1919; AB, U. Utah, 1920; AM, U. Chgo., 1925; PhD, U. Calif., 1933. Head dept. English Montpelier (Idaho) High Sch., 1920-22; tchr. Ogden (Utah) High Sch., 1922-24; mem. faculty U. Utah, from 1925, prof. English, from 1945. Author: (monographs) John Chinaman in the West, 1950, Traditional Ballads from Utah, 1951, others. With U.S. Army, 1917-19. Mem. Am. Folklore Soc., Rocky Mountain MLA, Utah Acad. Scis., Arts and Letters, AAUP, Phi Kappa Phi. Home: Salt Lake City Utah. †

HUBBARD, THOMAS BASSETT, consulting firm executive; b. Yonkers, N.Y., Dec. 4, 1921; s. Samuel Thomas and Margaret (Bassett) H.; m. Mary Elizabeth Bourne, Nov. 18, 1977; children by previous marriage: Richard B., Kerri B. Hubbard Hart, Amory A. Hubbard Millard. Student, Columbia U., 1940. Asst. advt. mgr. Cannon Mills, Inc., N.Y.C., 1940-52; v.p., dir. Oneita Knitting Mills, Inc., Utica, N.Y., 1952-54; v.p. Prince Matchabelli, Inc., N.Y.C., 1955; account mgmt. Young & Rubicam, Inc., N.Y.C., 1956-62; pres. T.B. Hubbard Assocs., Inc., Tampa, Fla., 1962-63, Wesley Advt., Inc., N.Y.C., 1963-68; chmn. bd., chief exec. officer THinc., Cons. Group Internat., Inc., N.Y.C., 1969-87, THinc. Cons. Group (UK) Ltd., THinc. Cons. Group (BDA) Ltd., THinc. Air Group, Inc. Bd. dirs., v.p., sec. Fire Found. of N.Y. Served to capt. USAF, 1941-45; CBI. Mem. Hump Pilots Assn., Def. Orientation Conf. Assn. Clubs: Union, Wings, St. Anthony, N.Y. Athletic Assn., Ex-Members of Squadron A (N.Y.C.); Army and Navy, Capitol Hill (Washington); Mid-Ocean, Royal Bermuda Yacht, Coral Beach (Bermuda). Home: New York N.Y. Died Sept. 5, 1987; buried Kensico Cemetary, Valhalla, N.Y.

HUBER, JOHN Y., JR., baking company executive; b. Phila., Dec. 16, 1886; s. John Y. and Anne Jackson (Willing) H.; m. Caroline Roberts Miller, Mar. 24, 1917; children: Anne Willing (Mrs. James J. Pocock Jr.), John Y. III, Richard Miller. Student, William Penn Charter Sch., 1905, Wharton Sch., U. Pa., 1909. Pres. Keebler Weyl Baking Co., 1922-29, Keebler Biscuit Co. div. United Biscuit Co. Am., Phila., from 1929; v.p., dir. United Biscuit Co. Am., from 1932. Mem. Phila. Art Alliance, Merion Cricket Club, Racquet Club, Rotary, Masons. Home: Haverford Pa. †

HUCK, JOHN WENZEL, retired association executive; b. Chgo., Nov. 1, 1916; s. Claude Alexander and Margaret Columbia (John) H.; m. Dorothy Elizabeth Montgomery, Oct. 10, 1942; children: Geoffrey James, Christopher Claude, Stuart Montgomery. Grad., Phillips Exeter Acad., 1934; A.B., Dartmouth Coll., 1938; M.A., Columbia U., 1940; postgrad., U. Chgo., 1940-41; L.H.D., Lincoln Coll., 1966. Dir. med. devel. U. Chgo., 1946-55; founder John W. Huck & Assocs., Chgo., 1955-60; exec. dir. Assoc. Colls. Ill., 1961-81. Sec. U. Chgo. Cancer Research Found., 1948-56; sec.-treas. Cancer Research Found., Inc., 1954-56; mem. citizens bd. Loyola U.; cons. v.p. Oscar Mayer Found., 1954-82; pres. Opera Theatre of Ill., 1979-84; dir. pub. relations St. Pauls House. Served as capt. Ordnance, AUS, 1941-46. Mem. Phi Sigma Kappa. Republican. Home: Hinsdale Ill. Died March 3, 1987; buried Montrose Cemetery, Chgo.

HUDSON, ARTHUR PALMER, educator; b. Palmer's Hall, Miss., May 14, 1892; s. William Arthur and Lou Garnett (Palmer) H.; m. Grace McNulty Noah, Sept. 12, 1916; children: William (dec.), Margaret Louise (Mrs. Almand R. Coleman), Ellen Noah (Mrs. Charles Graham). BS, U. Miss., 1913, AM, 1920; AM, U. Chgo., 1925; PhD, U. N.C., 1930. Prin. Gulfport (Miss.) High Sch., 1913-18; head English dept. Gulf Coast Mil. Acad., 1918-19; supt. schs. Oxford, Miss., 1919-20; asst. prof. English U. Miss., 1920-24, assoc. prof., 1924-27, prof., 1927-30; assoc. prof. English U. N.C., Chapel Hill, 1930-35, prof., 1935-51, Kenan disting. prof., 1951-63, Kenan disting. prof. emeritus, from 1963; prof. English U. Fla., summers 1938-39. Author, editor, from 1937; publs. include: Folklore and Folksongs in Dictionary of American History, 1940; Folklore, in a Literary History of the U.S. (editors: Robert Spiller, Willard Thorp, others), 1948; Am. Popular Literature in Chambers Ency.; (with H.M. Belden) vols. II, III of Frank C. Brown Collection of North Carolina Folklore, 1952; (with John T. Flanagan) Folklore in American Literature, 1958; Folklore Keeps the Past Alive, 1962; Songs of the Carolina Charter Colonists (1663-1763), 1962; editor: N.C. Folklore, 1954-64; contbr. folklore, articles to profl. jours. Recipient Smith research prize U. N.C., 1930; fellow in humanities Gen. Edn. Bd., Rockefeller Found., 1934-35. Fellow Am. Folklore Soc., Soc. Am. Historians; mem. Vanderbilt Conf. Humanities (exec. com.), N.C. Folklore Coun. (chmn.), N.C. (Brown-Hudson award 1970, v.p., sec.-treas.), Miss. (hon. life), Southeastern (exec. com.) folklore socs., South Atlantic Modern Lang. Assn., MLA, Am. Coll. English Assn., Nat. Coll. Folk Festival Assn., Phi Beta Kappa. Democrat. Episcopalian. Home: Chapel Hill N.C. †

HUDSON, ELLIS HERNDON, physician; b. Osaka, Japan, June 17, 1890; s. George Gary and Delia Ann (Herndon) H.; m. Mary Bruce Young, July 2, 1921; children: Bruce Herndon, Elspeth Gary. Ed., James Millikin U., 1911; MD, U. Pa., 1919; diploma in tropical medicine and hygiene, London Sch. Hygiene and Tropical Medicine, 1937. Instr. Am. U., Beirut, 1911-14, Blackburn Coll., Carlinville, Ill., 1914-15; founder Presbyn. Med. Ctr., Deir-ez-Zor, Syrian Arab Republic, 1924-36; mem. staff Clifton Springs (N.Y.) Sanitarium, 1937-39; community physician Norris, Tenn., 1939-40; dir. Health Svc., prof. hygiene Ohio U., Athens, 1940-55, prof. emeritus, from 1955; dir. bejelsyphillis project WHO, Iraq, 1950-51. Author: Treponematosis, 1946, Non-Venereal Syphillis, 1957; contbr. articles on tropical medicine to profl. jours. Pvt. armed forces, 1917-18, capt. M.C., USNR, 1942-46. Balfour scholar, 1937; Duncan medalist, 1937. Fellow ACP, AAAS, Am. Soc. Tropical Medicine; mem. Sigma Xi, Alpha Omega Alpha, Sigma Alpha Epsilon, Alpha Kappa Kappa. Presbyterian. Home: Cedar Grove Wis. †

HUDSON, ROCK (ROY FITZGERALD), motion picture actor, producer; b. Winnetka, Ill., Nov. 17, 1925; m. Phyllis Gates (div. 1958). Hon. Dr. Arts, Marrietta (Ohio) Coll., 1957; ed. high sch., Winnetka. Motion picture debut in Fighter Squadron; others include Giant (Acad. award nomination), Something of Value, A Farewell to Arms, This Earth is Mine, Pillow Talk, Come September, Lover Come Back, The Spiral Road, A Gathering of Eagles, Send Me No Flowers, Strange Bedfellows, Blindfold, Seconds, Tobruk, Ice Station Zebra, A Fine Pair, Darling Lill, The Hornet's Nest, Pretty Maids All in a Row, Showdown, Embryo, Avalanche, The Mirror Crack'd; star: TV series McMillan, 1971-76; mini-series Wheels, 1977-78; other TV appearances include The Starmaker, 1981, World War 3, 1981, The Devlin Connection, 1981; appeared in: plays I Do! I Do!, 1974-75, John Brown's Body, 1976, Camelot, 1977, On the Twentieth Century, 1979. Christmas Seal chmn., 1970. With USNR, 1941-46. Recipient Look mag. award, 1956, Exhibitor Laurel awards, 1958-66, Bambi awards, Germany, 1958-65, Golden Globe award as world favorite film actor Hollywood Fgn. Corrs. Assn., 1958, 60-62, King David award, 1970. Home: Beverly Hills Calif. Died Oct. 4, 1985.

HUESTIS, RALPH RUSKIN, biology educator; b. Bridgewater, N.S., Can., Jan. 14, 1892; s. Charles Herbert and Jessie Brown (Ackman) H.; m. Geraldine Lilley Parke, July 4, 1919; children: Gerald Ackman, Ralph Parke, Stephanie Monida Viola (Mrs. Frank A. McLean), Helen Michener (mrs. Robert L. Fisher). BSA, McGill U., 1914; MS, U. Calif., 1920, PhD, 1924. Rsch. asst. Scripps Instn., U. Calif., 1920-24; asst. prof. biology U. Oreg., 1924-30, prof., from 1930, head dept., 1952-56. Contbr. articles to profl. jours. lt. Can. Expeditionary Forces, 1914-19. Mem. Oreg. (pres. 1948), N.Y. acad. scis., Am. Soc. Mammalogists, Am. Soc. Zoologists, Genetics Soc. Am., Soc. Study Evolution, Sigma Xi. Home: Eugene Oreg. †

HUEY, STANTON ENNES, consulting civil engineer; b. Eureka, Mo., July 12, 1898; s. Frank S. and Carrie May (Markley) H.; m. Julia Frances Stubbs, June 26, 1929; children—Stanton Ennes, Palmer Stubbs, Francis

Markley. B.S. in Civil Engring. with honors, Washington U., St. Louis, 1924. Asst. to E.C. McGee (cons. engrs.), Monroe, La., 1924-26; civil engr. and surveyor Monroe, 1926-34; mem. La. Bd. State Engrs., New Orleans, 1934-40; chief state engr. La. Bd. State Engrs., 1940-41; chmn. S.E. Huey Co. (cons. engrs.), Monroe, 1941-88. Contbr. profl. jours. Mem. Monroe Utilities Commn., 1956-58. Fellow Am. Cons. Engrs. Council; mem. ASCE (life), Am. Concrete Inst., Am. Congress Surveying and Mapping, Am. Water Works Assn., Sigma Xi, Tau Beta Pi. Democrat. Presbyterian. Clubs: Lotus, Bayou DeSiard Country. Home: Monroe La. Died Aug. 9, 1988.

HUFF, BONNIE, civic leader, utilities executive; b. Salter, Ala., Dec. 11, 1889; s. Arthur Franklin and Laura Geroma (Harden) H.; m. Mary Emma Rouse, June 3, 1920; children: Frank Rouse, William DeKalb. Student, U. Ala., 1909-10. Tchr. rural sch. 1911; chief clk. Office of Probate Judge, Elmore County, Ala., 1912-16; tax adjuster Elmore County, 1919-23; land agt. Ala. Power Co., 1923-37; mgr. land and ins. dept. S.C. Power Co., Charleston, 1928-32, asst. sec., 1932-42, sec., 1943-50; asst. sec. S.C. Electric & Gas Co., from 1950. Mem. Boy Scouts Am.; past pres. Charleston Welfare Coun.; coord. Charleston County Civilian Def. Coun.; mem. exec. com., past chmn. Charleston chpt. ARC. Capt. inf. U.S. Army, World War I. Decorated citation for gallantry in action; recipient Silver Beaver award Boy Scouts Am. Mem. Charleston C. of C., Kiwanis, Country Club of Charleston, Sigma Nu. Democrat. Home: Charleston S.C. †

HUFF, GEORGE CHARLES, academic administrator, biology educator; b. Des Moines, Feb. 15, 1906; s. Charles Porter and Bertha Grace (Allen) H.; m. Ella Cecelia Sipple, Sept. 6, 1933 (dec. 1964); children: Marian Elaine, Dennis Karl; m. 2d, Ivadel T. Picht, Sept. 2, 1967. BS in Commerce, Drake U., 1928, ScD (hon.), 1973; MS, State Iowa U., 1929, PhD, 1935; student, Marine Biol. Lab., 1932, U. Chgo., 1935. Asst. dir. Mus. State U. Iowa, 1929-32; asst. prof. biology Drake U., Des Moines, 1933-34, prof. biology, from 1934, chmn. dept., 1935-55, dean Coll. Liberal Arts, 1949-51, 54-55, v.p. acad. adminstrn., 1955-67, v.p. spl. programs, 1967-71. Contbr. to sci. jours. Mem. AAAS, Am. Soc. Parasitology, Am. Micros. Soc., Iowa Acad. Sci., Prairie Club, Masons (33 deg.), Phi Beta Kappa, Sigma Xi, Gamma Alpha, Delta Sigma Pi. Republican. Methodist. Home: Des Moines Iowa. Died Mar. 19, 1985.

HUFF, ROBERT B., manufacturing company executive; b. Evanston, Ill., 1941. BBA, U. Hawaii, 1965; MBA, Harvard, 1968. With Bell & Howell Co., from 1965; v.p. Calhoun Co. subs. Bell & Howell Co., 1968-69, gen. mgr. video div., 1969-70; adminstrv. asst. to pres. Bell & Howell Co., 1970-72, asst. to pres., 1972-73, corporate v.p., dir. corporate planning, 1973-74, pres. consumer group, 1974-77, corporate v.p., pres. microimagery group, 1977-78, sr. v.p., 1978-80, exec. v.p., 1980-81, pres., chief operating officer, 1981-86. Died Nov. 1986; buried Polson, Mont.

HUGHES, EVERETT CHERRINGTON, sociologist, educator; b. Beaver, Ohio, Nov. 30, 1897; s. Charles Anderson and Jessamine Blanche (Roberts) h.; m. Helen Gregory MacGill, Aug. 28, 1927; children: Helen MacGill Cherrington, Elizabeth Gregory Roberts. AB, Ohio Wesleyan U., 1918; PhD, U. Chgo., 1928; LLD (hon.), Sir George Williams U., Boston Coll., Queen's U., McGill U.; LHD (hon.), Mich. State U., Ohio Wesleyan U.; D. ès Sciences Sociales, U. Laval, 1977; LittD, U. Montreal, 1978. Asst. prof. sociology McGill U., Montreal, Que., Can., 1927-38; Social Sci. Rsch. Coun. fellow, rsch. in Germany 1931-32; asst. prof. U. Chgo., 1938-43, assoc. prof., 1943-49, prof., 1949-61, chmn. dept. sociology, 1952-56; prof. sociology Brandeis U., Waltham, Mass., 1961-68, prof. emeritus, 1968-83; prof. sociology Boston Coll., Chestnut Hill, Mass., 1968-76, prof. emeritus, 1976-83; vis. prof. McGill U., U. Montreal, 1965. Author: (with others) Outlines of Sociology, 1940; French Canada in Transition, 1943, 63, (with J.C. Falardeau) Rencontre de deux mondes, 1945, 73, (with Helen Hughes) Where Peoples Meet: Racial and Ethnic Frontiers, 1952, Men and Their Work, 1958, (with Helen MacGill Hughes and Irwin Deutscher) Twenty Thousand Nurses Tell Their Story, 1958, (with Howard S. Becker and Blanche Geer) Boys in White: Student Culture in Medical School, 1961, Making the Grade, The Academic Side of College Life, 1968, The Sociological Eye, Collected Papers on Social Institutions, Race Relations, Work, and Sociological Method, 1971, (with others) Education for the Professions of Medicine, Law, Theology and Social Welfare, 1973; editor: (with E.T. Thompson) Race: Individual and Collective Behavior, 1958; editor Am. Jour. Sociology, 1952-60; also contbr. Fellow AAAS, Am. Sociol Assn. (pres. 1962-63), Am. Anthrop. Assn., Am. Acad. Arts and Scis.; mem. Soc. Applied Anthropology (pres. 1950-51), Can. Sociology and Anthropology Assn. (hon. pres.), Eastern Sociol. Soc. (pres. 1968-69), Alpha Sigma Phi. Democrat. Episcopalian. Home: Cambridge Mass. Died Jan. 5, 1983.

HUIE, WILLIAM BRADFORD, author; b. Hartselle, Ala., Nov. 13, 1910; s. John Bradford and Margaret Lois (Brindley) H.; m. Ruth Puckett, Oct. 27, 1934 (dec.); m. Martha Hunt Robertson, July 16, 1977. A.B., U. Ala., 1930. Author: Mud on the Stars, 1942, The Fight for Air Power, 1942, Can Do: The Story of the Seabees, 1944, From Omaha to Okinawa, 1945, The Case Against the Admirals, 1946, The Revolt of Mamie Stover, 1951, The Execution of Private Slovik, 1954, The Crime of Ruby McCollum, 1956, Wolf Whistle, 1959, The Americanization of Emily, 1959, The Hero of Iwo Jima, 1960, Hotel Mamie Stover, 1963, The Hiroshima Pilot, 1964, Three Lives for Mississippi, 1965, The Klansman, 1967, He Slew the Dreamer, 1969, In the Hours of Night, 1975, A New Life to Live, 1978, It's Me, O Lord!, 1979; also numerous mag. articles and stories. Mem. Phi Beta Kappa. Home: Scottsboro Ala. Died Nov. 20, 1986.

HUITT, RALPH KINSLOE, political science educator; b. Corsicana, Tex., Jan. 8, 1913; s. John Delloyd and Birdie (Wright) H.; m. Winnie Mavis Smith, Jan. 8, 1938; children: Frank Smith, Cynthia Beth. AB, Southwestern U., 1934, LLD, 1972; PhD, U. Tex., 1950. Boys work sec. Beaumont (Tex.) YMCA, 1934-42; asst. prof. Lamar Coll., Beaumont, 1942-46; asst. prof. polit. sci. U. Wis., 1949-54, assoc. prof., 1954-59, prof., 1959-65, 78-86; legis. asst. to Sen. William Proxmire, 1958; asst. sec. for legislation U.S. Dept. HEW, Washington, 1965-69; guest scholar Brookings Instn., 1969; exec. dir. Nat. Assn. State Univs. and Land Grant Colls., Washington, 1970-78; vis. prof. U. Okla. Author: (with Robert L. Peabody) Congress: Two Decades of Analysis, 1969; contbr. articles to profl. jours. Mem. commn. on adminstrv. rev. U.S. Ho. of Reps., 1975-76. With USNR, 1943-46. Named disting. alumnus Southwestern U., 1970; Fund for Advancement of Edn. fellow, 1953-54. Mem. Am. Polit. Sci. Assn. (exec. com. 1958-59, coun. 1957-59), Phi Delta Theta. Democrat. Methodist. Home: Madison Wis. Died Oct. 15, 1986; buried Forest Hill Cemetery, Madison.

HULBERT, MARSHALL BRANDT, college dean, liberal arts educator; b. Oshkosh, Wis., May 23, 1905; s. Chester Cephas and Anna (Brandt) H.; m. Ruth Logan, July 12, 1944; 1 child, Ann Logan. AB, Lawrence Coll., 1926, MusB, 1932; MA, Columbia U., 1939; PhD, Northwestern U., 1948; student voice, Frank La Forge, N.Y.C. Tchr. social sci. Wausau, Wis., 1926-30; sec. Lawrence Conservatory Music, Appleton, Wis., 1932-43; assoc. prof. music Lawrence U., Appleton, 1939, asst. dean, 1943-45, dir. admissions, 1945-58, dean adminstrn., 1948-54, dean coll., 1954-61, v.p., 1961-70, dir. fgn. studies, 1966-70, Mary Mortimer prof. liberal arts, 1965-80, emeritus, 1980-84; cons. Assoc. Colls. Midwest, 1970-74, dir. alumni relations, 1972-74. Bus. mgr. Lawrence European Tour, 1936; choral dir. First Presbyn. Ch., Neenah, Wis., 1938-60. Mem. AAUP, Assn. Coll. Admissions Counselors, Phi Beta Kappa, Phi Mu Alpha-Sinfonia, Pi Kappa Lambda, Phi Gamma Delta. Episcopalian. Home: Menasha Wis. Died Dec. 24, 1984.

HULBERT, WILLIAM GLEN, JR., electric utility executive; b. Everett, Wash., Jan. 22, 1917; s. William Glen and Mabel Katherine (Baker) H.; m. Jean Edwards, July 25, 1945; children: William Glen, III, Tanauan, David; m. Clare Mumford, Jan. 6, 1973. B.A., Stanford U., 1938; M.S., Inst. Paper Chemistry, Lawrece Coll., Appleton, Wis., 1940, Ph.D., 1942. With Champion Paper Co., 1942, William Hulbert Mill Co., 1946-86; with Public Utility Dist. 1 Snohomish County, Wash., Everett, 1962-84; mgr., chief exec. officer Public Utility Dist. 1 Snohomish County, 1966-84, commr., 1962. Campaign chmn. United Way Snohomish County, 1969. Served with USNR, World War II. Mem. Am. Public Power Assn. (pres. 1975, Disting. Service award 1977), Puget Sound Electric League (Elec. Man of Year award 1976). Episcopalian. Clubs: Cascade, Everett Golf and Country, Everett Yacht, Elks. Home: Lake Stevens Wash. Died Oct. 12, 1986; buried Trinity Episcopal Church, Everett, Wash.

HULBURT, HUGH MCKINNEY, university dean, chemical engineer; b. Nashua, N.H., Oct. 27, 1917; s. Clarence Hellings and Alice (McKinney) H.; m. Ann Podlucky, June 30, 1940; children: Susan Hulburt Wadelton, Margery Ann Hulburt Held; m. Pauline Podlucky, Dec. 1, 1956; 1 child, William Hugh. BA, Carroll Coll., Waukesha, Wis., 1938; MS, U. Wis., 1940, PhD, 1942. NRC fellow in chemistry Princeton U., 1943; sr. research chemist Shell Oil Co., 1943-44; instr. Hunter Coll., 1944-46; asst. prof., then asso. prof. chemistry and chem. engring. Cath. U. Am., 1946-51; supr. engr., then dir. research and devel. Chem. Constrn. Co., N.Y.C., 1951-56; with Am. Cyanamid Co., 1956-63, dir. phys. research, central research div., 1959-63; prof. chem. engring. Northwestern U., 1963-87, chmn. dept., 1964-70, asso. dean Grad. Sch., 1975-80, asso. dean Technol. Inst., 1980-83; Reilley lectr. U. Notre Dame, 1967; vis. prof. Swiss Fed. Tech. Inst., 1971; cons. in field. Editor: IEC Process Design and Development, 1962-87; contbr. articles to profl. jours. Mem. Am. Inst. Chem. Engrs. (inst. lectr. 1962), Am. Chem. Soc., Am. Phys. Soc., Royal Soc. Chemistry, Electrochem. Soc., Catalysis Club N.Y. (pres. 1962), Sigma Xi. Club: Economic (Chgo.). Home: Wilmette Ill. Died Mar. 22, 1987; buried Forrest Home Cemetery, Milw.

HULCY, DECHARD ANDERSON, petroleum products executive; b. Robertson County, Tex., Nov. 13, 1892; s. Joseph Clinton and Josephine Lilly (Anderson) H.; m. Elsie Lenore Bonner, Jan. 14, 1914; children: Louis Bonner, Mildred Hulcy Yeargan, Dechard Anderson, Mary Hulcy Pierce. Student, De Queen (Ark.) pub. schs. Messenger boy I. & G.N. R.R., Palestine, Tex., 1909-11; warehouse clk. Texas Co., Palestine, 1911-12; clk. Tex. State R.R., Palestine, 1912-17; auditor Rusk, Tex., 1917-19; clk. Lone Star Gas Co., Dallas, 1920-27, asst. comptroller and asst. to pres., 1927-35, v.p. and exec. v.p., 1935-40, pres., 1940-43; chmn. Lone Star Gas Co. and Lone Star Producing Co., Dallas, from 1957, Lone Star Gathering Co., Dallas, from 1961; bd. dirs. Employers Nat. Ins. Co., Dallas Ry. & Terminal Depot, Southwestern Life Ins. Co., Tex. Employer's Nat. Ins. Assn., Fed. Res. Bank of Dallas, llth Dist. Contbr. numerous articles to trade publs. Mem. exec. bd. State Fair Tex. Mem. Am. So. gas assns, Ind. Petroleum Assn., Ind. Natural Gas Assn., Tex. Mid-Continent Oil and Gas Assn., Am. Petroleum Inst., Dallas Country Club, Brook Hollow Golf Club, City Club, Dallas Petroleum Club, Dallas Athletic Club, Oak Cliff Country Club, Cipango Club (Dallas); Fort Worth Petroleum Club, Fort Worth Club (Fort Worth); Midland Petroleum Club (Midland); Austin Club. Methodist. Home: Dallas Tex. †

HULL, HARVARD LESLIE, corporate executive; b. Holstein, Nebr., Oct. 23, 1906; s. Joel Leslie and Caroline Evangeline (Larsen) H.; m. Alta Zera Jones, June 9, 1928; children: Gwen Alta Hull Quackenbush, Janet Barbara Hull Clark. A.B. with distinction, Nebr. Wesleyan U., 1927, D.Sci. (hon.), 1984; Ph.D. in Physics, Columbia U., 1933. Project engr. Sperry Gyroscope Co., Bklyn., 1933-35, research engr., 1935-40, dir. remote control devel., 1940-43; introduced new equipment Sperry Gyroscope Co., Ltd., Eng., 1934, 35-36; dir. process improvement electromagnetic process of separation Uranium 235 Tenn. Eastman Corp., Oak Ridge, 1943-46; asso. dir. Argonne Nat. Lab., Chgo., 1946-49; dir. remote control engring. devel. Argonne Nat. Lab., 1949-53; v.p. research and devel. div. Capehart-Farnsworth Co., Ft. Wayne, 1953-54; pres. Farnsworth Electronics Co., Co. (div. ITT), Ft. Wayne, 1954-56; v.p. Litton Industries, Beverly Hills, Calif., 1956-57; pres. Hull Assos., Chgo., 1957—; dir., pres. Chgo. Aerial Industries, Inc., Barrington, Ill., 1962-64, Internat. Tech. Corp., Western Springs, Ill.; dir. Central Research Labs., Inc.; Dir. research Aero-Space Inst., Chgo.; chmn. bd. Aero-Space Inst., 1973—. Fellow AIAA (assoc.); mem. IEEE (life), Am. Nuclear Soc. (cert. of appreciation 1978), AAAS, Am. Phys. Soc., Nat. Telemetering Conf. (chmn. 1956), Sigma Xi, Phi Kappa Phi, Theta Chi. Conglist. Club: Executives. Home: Lombard Ill. Died Oct. 1, 1988.

HULME, MILTON GEORGE, JR., manufacturing company executive; b. Pitts., Oct. 12, 1926; s. Milton George and Helen Beatrice (Clougherty) H.; m. Aura N. Raspaldo, Jan. 24, 1953; children: Milton George, Charles Alan, Leslie Caroline. BSEE, MIT, 1950; postgrad., Harvard U. Bus. Sch., 1957. With Mine Safety Appliances Co., Pitts., from 1950, asst. to pres., 1962-66, v.p. mktg., 1966-78, pres., chief exec. officer, 1978-85; dir. Pitts. br. Fed. Res. Bank, Cleve., 1980-85, chmn., 1981-85; v.p. Glover & MacGregor, Inc., Pitts., 1950-81, pres., 1981-85, dir., from 1950; chmn. bd. Thorofare Markets, Inc., 1975-80; dir. Pitts. Brewing Co., Reading & Bates Corp., Equitable Gas Co., Safety Equipment Inst., Koppers Co. Bd. dirs. United Way Allegheny County, 1979-85, Sta. WQED Public TV, 1971-85, Pitts. Symphony Soc., 1981-85; trustee Shadyside Hosp., 1966-85, chmn. bd. trustees, 1979-85; trustee Carnegie-Mellon U., Pitts., 1981-85; bd. dirs. Pitts. br ARC, Pitts. Assn. for Improvement of the Poor, Western Pa. Safety Coun., Indsl. Health Found., from 1973. With USNR, 1944-45. Mem. Indsl. Safety Equipment Assn. (dir. from 1975, v.p. 1975-77, pres. 1977-79), Duquesne Club (dir. 1980-85), Fox Chapel Golf Club, Laurel Valley Golf Club, Rolling Rock Club. Home: Pittsburgh Pa. Died Aug. 6, 1985; buried Pitts.

HUMELSINE, CARLISLE HUBBARD, foundation executive; b. Hagerstown, Md., Mar. 12, 1915; s. Charles Ellsworth and Anna Barbara (McNamee) H.; m. Mary Miller Speake, Aug. 16, 1941; children: Mary Carlisle Humelsine Norment, Barbara Anne Humelsine Harmon. A.B., U. Md., 1937, H.H.D. (hon.), 1974; LL.D. (hon.), Coll. William and Mary, 1963, Hampden-Sydney Coll., 1970; L.H.D. (hon.), Rutgers U., 1976. Editor publs., spl. asst. to pres. U. Md., 1937-41; exec. sec. U.S. Dept. State, 1947-50, asst. sec., dep. under-sec state, 1953; exec. v.p. Colonial Williamsburg Found., 1953-58, pres., chief exec. officer, 1958-77, chmn. bd., chief exec. officer, 1977-80, chmn. bd., 1980-85, chmn. emeritus, 1985-89; bd. dirs. N.Y. Life Ins. Co., Jackson Hole Preserve Inc., Historic Hudson Valley, Chesapeake & Potomac Telephone Co. Va.; chmn. emeritus Nat Trust for Hist. Preservation, 1980-89; bd. vis. Coll. William and Mary, Va., 1986-89; bd. dirs. B.F. Saul Real Estate Investment Trust. Former trustee, v.p. Nat Gallery Art; regent, chmn. exec. com. Smithsonian Instn.; bd. dirs. Nat. Geog. Soc.; trustee emeritus Mariners Mus.; former chmn. Va. Dept. Conservation, Am Revolution Bicentennial Commn.; former pres. Va. Mus Fine Arts. Col. U.S. Army, 1941-45. Decorated D.S.M., Bronze Star. Mem. Alpha Tau Omega

)micron Delta Kappa, Pi Delta Epsilon. Democrat. piscopalian. Clubs: Metropolitan (Washington); 'ommonwealth (Richmond); Gibson Island (Md.). Iome: Williamsburg Va. Died Jan. 26, 1989; cremated.

IUMES, JOHN P., lawyer, diplomat; b. N.Y.C., July 1, 1921; m. Jean Cooper Schmidlapp; 6 sons. Grad., t. Paul's Sch.; AB, Woodrow Wilson Sch. Pub. and nternat. Affairs, Princeton U., 1943; LLD, Fordham ., 1948, Marist Coll. Bar: N.Y. 1948. Assoc. firm hearman & Sterling, N.Y.C., 1948-55; ptnr. firm lumes, Andrews & Botzow, N.Y.C., 1956-69; ambasador to Austria, Vienna, 1969-75, ret., 1975. Author: xcerpts from the Vienna Diaries of Ambassador John ortner Humes. Vice chmn. founders coun. Inst. for tudy Diplomacy, Georgetown U.; exec. com. Nassau ounty coun. Boy Scouts Am.; hon. trustee Fay Sch., outhborough, Mass., Kips Bay Boys' Club; trustee lorth Shore Wildlife Preserve, Episcopal Found. Edn. iocese L.I., Nat. Art Mus. Sport, Salzburg (Austria) eminar in Am. Studies, Am. Inst. Mus. Studies, Graz, ustria, St. Luke's-Roosevelt Hosp. (hon.); hon. trustee ortledge Sch., Locust Valley, N.Y.; bd. visitors Ge-'getown Sch. Fgn. Service, Washington; bd. dirs. Coun. m. Ambassadors; founder, pres. Humes Found.; harter trustee Am.-Austrian Found.; treas. Reading eform Found. With AUS, 1943-46, ETO. Decorated reat Golden Medal of Honor with sash Republic of ustria; Merito Navali (Austria); grand officier hevaliers des Tastevins; N.Y. State squash racquets hampion, 1950. Mem. ABA, Assn. of Bar of City of .Y., N.Y. State Bar Assn., Internat. Law Assn., Enish Speaking Union, St. George's Soc., World Affairs oun. Phila. (adv. coun.), Soc. Colonial Wars, S.R.)isting. Patriot award), Alumni Assn. St. Paul's Sch. res. 1964-66), Pres.'s Coun., Am. Ditchley Found., .S. Squash Racquets Assn. (pres. 1954-56), Pilgrims .S., Brook Club, Down Town Assn. (trustee), N.Y. acht, Union Club, Piping Rock Club, Seawanahaka orinthian Yacht Club, Chevy Chase Club, Travellers lub (Paris), Royal Cornwall Yacht (Eng.), Royal orwegian Yacht, Masons, Jesters, Delta Theta Phi. ome: Mill Neck N.Y. Died Oct. 2, 1985.

UMMEL, MARTIN HENRY, JR., advertising gency executive; b. Glen Ridge, N.J., May 7, 1927; s. artin Henry and Florence (Lanken) H.; m. Evelyn ayer, Sept. 19, 1953; children: Martin Henry III, Pacia Katherine. AB, Cornell U., 1949. With Vick hem. Co., 1949-50, J. Walter Thompson, 1950-51, rowell-Collier Pub. Co., 1952-57; with Sullivan, auffer, Colwell and Bayles Inc., N.Y.C., 1957-84, exec. p., 1968-84, also bd. dirs.; vice chmn., mng. dir. SSC B-Lintas Internat. Ltd. With Stars and Stripes, orld War II. Mem. Am. Assn. Advt. Agys. (chmn. ternat. com.), Cornell Club, Pinnacle Club, Marco olo Club, Overseas Press Club, American Club ondon). Home: Montclair N.J. Died Dec. 18, 1984.

IUNGATE, JOSEPH IRVIN, JR., social worker; b. illarney, W.Va., Apr. 30, 1921; s. Joseph Irvin and ellie (Lickliter) H.; m. Betty Lou Hatzenbuehler, Sept. , 1948; children: Ann Elisabeth Hungate Clabough, seph Irvin, III, Sue Carol. A.B. cum laude, Concord oll., 1948; M.A., U. Chgo., 1950; Ph.D., U. Tex., 1963; ostgrad., St. Louis U., 1948-49. Disaster rep. Chgo. pt. ARC, 1950; chief psychiat. social work service alley Forge Army Hosp., Phoenixville, Pa., 1951; ychiat. caseworker Fitzsimons Army Hosp., Denver, 52-53; chief med. social work service Ft. Jackson, C., 1953-55; class dir., social work specialist program rmy Med. Sch., San Antonio, 1955-58; assoc. prof. cial work U. Tex., 1959-68; dean, prof. social work oll. Social Work, U. S.C., Columbia, 1968-79, dean oll. Allied Health Professions, 1973-75; clin. social orker S.C. Dept. Health, 1980-81; dir. social work unit C. State Hosp., Columbia, 1981-87; adj. prof. mgmt. mestone Coll., S.C., 1984-86; teaching cons. Austin ate Hosp., 1963-68, William S. Hall Psychiat. Inst., 72, Kans. Social and Rehab. Service, 1974; spl. cons. h. tng. div. Bur. Family Services, HEW, Washington, 62-65; mem. profl. adv. com. S.C. Mental Health ssn., 1970-79; chmn. S.C. Gov.'s Com. on Criminal stice, Crime and Delinquency, 1968-75; vice chmn., m. S.C. Health Care Adv. Bd., 1974-85, chmn., 1985-; mem. S.C. Gov.'s Health and Welfare Council, 1969-; chmn. S.C. Merit System Council, 1974-75; cons., culty mem. multiregional tng. in mgmt. Social Service lminstrn., HEW, 1974-75; mem. com. dependency and ate services S.C. State Planning Office, 1976-78. ithor: A Guide for Training Public Welfare Adminators, 1965; contbr. articles to profl. jours; sr. editor: ete, 1971-79. Mem. Columbia council USO, 1970-83; es. Arcadia Democratic Precinct, Columbia, 1974-76, ec. com., 1976-78. Served to 1st lt. USAAF, 1942-45; ot. M.S.C. U.S. Army, 1950-58. Decorated Air medal th 3 oak leaf clusters, Purple Heart. Home: Columbia C. Died July 16, 1988; buried Arlington Nat. Cemey.

JNSBERGER, ISAAC MOYER, chemist, author; b. akertown, Pa., Aug. 3, 1921; s. A.F. and Eliza oyer) H.; m. Elizabeth Rita Ochnich, Mar. 19, 1944; ldren: Donald Moyer, Elizabeth Anne, Gretchen, ark, Carol, Luke, Heidi. BS, Lehigh U., 1943, MS, 46, PhD, 1948; AEC postdoctoral fellow organic emistry, U. Ill., 1948-49. Asst., then assoc. prof. emistry Antioch Coll., 1949-55; assoc. prof. Fordham U., 1955-60; head dept. chemistry U. Mass., 1960-61, dean, rsch. prof. chemistry, 1961-69; program adviser edn. Ford Found., Pakistan, 1969-71; dean Coll. Arts and Scis., SUNY at Albany, 1971-73; provost U. Okla., Norman, 1973-75; free-lance writer, 1975-81; v.p. acad. affairs, dean of faculty Am. U. in Cairo, Egypt, from 1981; mem. com. modern methods handling chem. info. NRC, 1959-65. Author: (with others) Survey of Chemical Notation Systems, 1964, The Quintessential Dictionary, 1978; editor sect. 36: Chem. Abstracts, 1960-64; contbr. articles to profl. jours. With USAAF, 1943-45. Decorated D.F.C., Air medal with 5 oak clusters. Fellow AAAS, Am. Inst. Chemists; mem. Am. Chem. Soc., AAUP, Phi Beta Kappa, Pi Mu Epsilon, Phi Eta Sigma, Phi Lambda Upsilon. Home: Emmaus Pa. Died Feb. 1, 1987; buried Calvary Cemetery, Emmaus.

HUNT, WILLIAM ALVIN, psychologist, educator; b. Hartford, Conn., Nov. 10, 1903; s. Alvin Ashbell and Mabel Stetson (Hodges) H.; m. Edna Reeve Bossen, June 15, 1929 (dec. Apr. 1959); m. Diana Bengston Theobald, Dec. 19, 1960 (div. Sept. 1978); 1 dau., Margit. AB, Dartmouth Coll., 1928; AM, Harvard U., 1929, PhD, 1931. Instr. Dartmouth Coll., 1931-33; asst. prof. Conn. Coll. for Women, 1933-37; prof. Wheaton (Mass.) Coll., 1938-45; prof. psychology Northwestern U., Evanston, Ill., 1945-67, chmn. dept. psychology, 1951-67; prof. Loyola U., Chgo., 1967-74, prof. emeritus, 1974-86; research scientist Learning Ctr., Am. U., 1974; cons. clin. psychol. Surgeon Gen. Army, VA, 1946-86; cons. asst. sec. def., 1954-86, Army Sci. Adv. Panel, 1956-86; cons. clin. psychol. Surgeon Gen. Navy, 1958-86; cons. Nat. Security Agy., 1962-86, Nat. Heart, Lung and Blood Inst., 1975-86. Assoc. editor Jour. Clin. Psychology, 1945-86; contbr. articles to profl. jours. Mem. research adv. com. Nat. Coun. on Alcoholism, 1974-86. Served to comdr. USNR, World War II. Recipient Clin. Psychologist of the Yr. award Ill. Psychol. Assn., 1973, Psychologist of the Yr., 1978. Fellow Am. Psychol. Assn. (outstanding clin. award 1967, disting. contbns. award 1979, pres. div. clin. psychology 1954, pres. div. teaching 1951); mem. Soc. Exptl. Psychology, Phi Beta Kappa, Sigma Xi, Alpha Delta Phi. Home: Chicago Ill. Died Jan. 3, 1986.

HUNT, WILLIAM DUDLEY, JR., editor, architect; b. New Orleans, Mar. 23, 1922; s. William Dudley and Ruth (Lee) H.; m. Gwendolyn Pratt Munson, June 19, 1954; children: William Dudley III, Walter W., Ruth Lee, Stephen Clarendon Munson, Gwendolyn Munson, John Morgan. B.S., Jacksonville State U., 1949; B.Arch., Tulane U., 1957. Practice architecture William Dudley Hunt, Jr., New Orleans, Pensacola, Fla., N.Y.C., 1954-64; sr. editor Archtl. Record mag., N.Y.C., 1958-63; pub. A.I.A. Jour. mag., Washington, 1963-72; cons. editor archtl., related books McGraw-Hill, 1965-72; pub. dir. AIA, 1970-72, acting dep. exec. v.p., 1970-71; architecture editor John Wiley and Sons, Inc., 1972-82, cons. editor, 1983-86; archtl. cons. to bldg. industry firms and assns.; asst. prof. Jacksonville State U., 1948-53; instr. Tulane U., 1953-58; Dir. Prod. Systems for Architects and Engrs., Inc., 1970-71; Del., publs. chmn. XI Pan Am. Congress Architects, 1965; commr. Pan Am. Fedn. Architects, 1972-73; Mem. Archtl. Rev. Bd., Rye, N.Y., 1963. Author: Contemporary Curtain Wall, 1958, Total Design, 1972, Encyclopedia of American Architecture, 1980, American Architecture: A Field Guide, 1984; author, editor: Hotels, Motels, Restaurants and Bars, 1960, Hospitals, Health Centers and Clinics, 1961, Office Buildings, 1961, Comprehensive Architectural Services, 1965, Creative Control of Building Costs, 1967; contbr. to Contemporary Architects, 1980, Ency. Internat., 1982, Ency. Americana, 1984, 85, The New Book of Knowledge, 1984; Am. editor 2d internat. edit. Architects' Data, 1980; project dir. 7th edit. Architectural Graphic Standards, 1981; contbr. articles to profl. jours. Served with USAAF, 1942-45; lt. col. Res. ret. Recipient Dallas Mus. Fine Arts Furniture Design award, 1958; Merit award Am. Soc. Landscape Architects, 1980; Profl. and Scholarly Book award Assn. Am. Pubs., 1981; Outstanding Acad. Book award ALA, 1981. Fellow AIA; mem. Authors Guild, Authors League Am., Chi Phi, Tau Sigma Delta. Episcopalian. Home: Gloucester Va. Died Apr. 29, 1987, buried Ware Episc. Ch., Gloucester.

HUNTER, JAMES, III, federal judge; b. 1916; m. Jane Thierolf; children: Jane Hunter Wickes, Judith Ann, Janet Margaret. BA, Temple U., 1936; LLB, U. Pa., 1939. Pvt. practice Starr, Summerhill & Lloyd; ptnr. Vanderbuilt, Archer, Greiner, Hunter & Read; judge U.S. Ct. Appeals (3d cir.), N.J., from 1971. With USMC, 1942-46. Mem. ABA, N.J. Bar Assn. Home: Medford N.J. Died Feb. 10, 1989.

HUNTER, LEE, automotive equipment manufacturing company executive, inventor; b. St. Louis, Apr. 27, 1913; s. Lee and Ollie (Stark) H.; m. Jane Franklin Brauer, 1959; stepchildren: Arthur J. Brauer, Stephen F. Brauer. Ed., Westminster Coll., Fulton, Mo., Washington U., St. Louis; D.Sci. (hon.), Washington U., St. Louis, 1982, Westminster Coll., 1982. Draftsman, designer Herman Body Co., 1935-36; founder Lee Hunter Jr. Mfg. Co., 1936; pres. Hunter-Hartman Corp., 1937-42, Hunter Engring. Co., Bridgeton, Mo., 1947-55; chmn. bd., chief exec. officer Hunter Engring. Co., 1955-86; pres. Hunter Aviation Co., 1955-60; hon. consul of Belgium, St. Louis; adv. dir. St. Louis County Nat. Bank and County Nat. Bancorp. Trustee Washington U., St. Louis; bd. dirs. Jr. Achievement, West County YMCA; adv. trustee Westminster Coll., Fulton, Mo.; trustee Washington U., St. Louis; mem. St. Louis Consular Corps. Served to 1st lt. C.E. AUS, 1942-46. Recipient Alumni Achievement award Westminster Coll. Mem. Mo. C. of C., Phi Delta Theta. (Phi of Yr., Mo. chpt. 1980). Presbyterian (trustee). Clubs: St. Louis (St. Louis), Engineers (St. Louis); Bellerive Country, Racquet; Le Mirador (Switzerland). Home: Saint Louis Mo. Died Nov. 7, 1986; buried Bellefontaine Cemetery.

HUNTINGTON, SAMUEL, utility company executive; b. Apr. 24, 1939; married. AB, Harvard U., 1961; LLB, Columbia U., 1966. Law clk. to presiding justice U.S. Ct. Appeals, 1966-67; assoc. Hughes, Hubbuard & Reed, 1967-70; asst. to solicitor gen. U.S. Dept. Justice, 1970-73; assoc. prof. law Boston U., 1973-76; asst. gen. counsel New Eng. Electric System, Westboro, Mass., then gen. counsel, 1976-79, v.p., sec., gen. counsel, 1979-84, pres., chief exec. officer, 1984-85, also bd. dirs.; chmn., dir. New Eng. Power Co., Westboro, New Eng. Energy, Inc.; past pres., dir. New Eng. Power Service; bd. dirs. New Eng. Electric Transmission Corp., NEES Energy, Inc., Naragansett Electric Co., Mass. Electric Co., 1st Nat. Bank Boston. Home: Newton Mass. Died July 26, 1988.

HURD, PETER, artist; b. Roswell, N.Mex., Feb. 22, 1904; s. Harold and Lucy Chew (Knight) H.; m. Henriette Wyeth, June 29, 1929; children: Peter Wyeth, Carol (Mrs. Peter W. Rogers), Michael. Student, U.S. Mil. Acad., 1921-23, Haverford Coll., 1923-24, Pa. Acad. Fine Arts, and under N.C. Wyeth, 1924-26; D. Fine Arts, Technol. Coll.; LL.D., N.M. State U., 1968. Mem. Nat. Fine Arts Commn., 1959-63. Represented in collections, Met. Mus., N.Y.C., Nat. Gallery, Edinburgh, Rochester, N.Y., Wilmington, Del., Chgo., Andover, Mass., Kansas City, Bklyn., Honolulu, Roswell, Mpls., Dallas, Newark, museums, Ft. Worth Club, 16 fresco panels in mus., Tex. Technol. Coll., fresco murals in, U.S. P.O., Big Spring, Tex., Alamogordo, N.Mex., mural panel, Prudential Ins. Co. Bldg., Houston; retrospective show, Amon Carter Mus., Ft. Worth, Legion of Honor, San Francisco, 1964-65, Phoenix Art Mus., 1983, Denver Art Mus., 1983; Represented portrait, Pres. Johnson for White House Hist. Assn., now in permanent collection, Nat. Portrait Gallery, Washington; Book illustrator. With USAAF, 1942, Eng.; U.S. Air Transport Command S. Am., Africa, India, Arabia and Italy in 1944 as war corr. for Life mag. Winner competition for 3 mural panels in U.S. Terminal Annex P.O. Dallas, 1938; awarded 1st prize 16th Internat. Watercolor Exhbn. Chgo. Art Inst., 1937; Elected asso. Nat. Acad., 1941; N.A., 1942. Mem. Assn. Grads. U.S. Mil. Acad., Wilmington Soc. Fine Arts, Am. Watercolor Soc. Club: Century Assn. (N.Y.C.). Home: San Patricio N.Mex. Died July 9, 1984; buried on estate.

HUSKINS, WILLIAM EVERETT, JR., airline executive; b. Mpls., Feb. 10, 1925; s. William Everett and Bertha (Haukebo) H.; m. Shirley Eloise Larson, June 24, 1950; children: Deborah Lavonne, William Charles. B Aero. Engring., U. Minn., 1945. Registered profl. engr., Minn. With N.W. Airlines, Inc., 1946-80; ops. mgr. Orient region N.W. Airlines, Inc., Tokyo, 1955-59; asst. to pres. N.W. Airlines, Inc., 1959-61, v.p., 1961-67, v.p. communications and computer svcs., 1967-73, v.p. maintenance and engring., 1973-80; sr. v.p. engring. and maintenance Braniff Airways, Inc., 1980-81, exec. v.p. ops., 1981-83; sr. v.p. ops. svcs. Ea. Airlines, 1983-84. Mem. Masons, Order Easter Star, Beta Theta Pi, Tau Omega. Home: Chanhassen Minn. Died June 25, 1985; interred Endless Waters, No. Minn.

HUSTED, ELBERT ERVIN, manufacturing executive; b. Kansas City, Kans., June 8, 1892; s. James Delno and Jenny (Thorpe) H.; m. Ruth Blair, Jan. 5, 1918; 1 child, Elbert Ervin III. Student, Colo. State Coll., 1911-15. With Titeflex, Inc., Newark, from 1924, from salesman to pres., 1942-58, vice chmn. bd., from 1959; chmn. indsl. div. Newark Community Chest, 1943-44; chmn. com. econ. devel. Essex Co., 1943-44, North Jersey dist., 1945-46. Capt. U.S. Army, 1918, lt. col. Res. Mem. Soc. Automotive Engrs. (chmn. met. sect. 1943-44, councilor nat. orgn. 1948-49), C. of C. (pres. 1950-51, v.p. from 1956, bd. dirs.), Essex Club, Downtown Assn., Advertising Club, Colony Club, Beaverkill Trout Club. Home: Newark N.J. †

HUSTON, JOHN, writer, motion picture director; b. Nevada, Mo., Aug. 5, 1906; s. Walter and Rhea (Gore) H.; m. Evelyn Keyes, July 23, 1946; m. Enrica Soma, 1949 (dec. 1969); children: Walter Anthony, Anjelica; m. Celeste Shane, 1972 (div. 1975). L.H.D. (hon.), Monmouth Coll., West Long Branch, N.J., 1981. At various times during early career became reporter, editor to picture mag.; artist (painter), writer, actor, became writer, Warner Bros. Studios, 1938; collaborator: The Amazing Dr. Clitterhouse, 1938, Juarez, 1939, Dr. Ehrlich's Magic Bullet, 1940, High Sierra, Sergeant York, 1941; dir.: The Maltese Falcon, 1941, In This Our Life, 1942, Across the Pacific, 1942, Key Largo, 1948; writer and collaborator in: prodn. of screen play Three

Strangers, 1945; dir. The Treasure of Sierra Madre, 1949 (awards for dir., writer Acad. Motion Picture Arts and Sciences, also, New York Film Critics award for best direction of year), The African Queen, 1951, also Heaven Knows, Mr. Allison, Roots of Heaven, The Unforgiven, The Barbarian and the Geisha, The Misfits, Freud, The List of Adrian Messenger, Night of the Iguana, The Bible, Reflections in a Golden Eye, Casino Royale, Sinful Davey, A Walk with Love and Death, The Kremlin Letter, Fat City, The African Queen; Broadway play A Passenger to Bali, 1939, (collaborated in writing) In Time To Come (received N.Y. Drama Critics Circle award); Broadway prodn. of Jean Paul Sarte's play No Exit, 1945; opera The Mines of Sulphur, La Scala, 1966; producer-dir.: We Were Strangers, Horizon Films, which founded with S.P. Eagle; dir.: A Walk With Love and Death, 1969, The Kremlin Letter, 1970, Fat City, 1972, The Life and Times of Judge Roy Bean, 1972, The McIntosh Man, The Man Who Would Be King, 1975, Wise Blood, 1979, Escape to Victory, 1980, Annie, 1981, Lovesick, 1983, Prizzi's Honor, 1985, The Dead, 1988; actor in: Battle for the Planet of the Apes, 1973, Chinatown, 1974, The Wind and the Lion, 1975, Hollywood on Trial, 1977, Winterkills, 1977; writer, dir. Metro-Goldwyn-Mayer, from 1949; assigned filming: World War II documentaries The Battle of San Pietro Recipient One World award 1949, Screen Dirs. Guild award for the Asphalt Jungle 1950, named best dir. of the year for Moby Dick, New York Film Critics 1956, recipient award Nat. Bd. Rev. of Motion Pictures 1956, Silver Laurel award Screen Writers Guild 1963, Silver Dirs. Guild award for Night of the Iguana 1964, Martin Buber award, David di Donatello award for The Bible 1966, Motion Pictures Exhibitors' Internat. Laurel award for Reflections in a Golden Eye 1968; Author: autobiography John Huston—An Open Book, 1980. Served to maj. U.S. Army, 1942-45. Recipient Am. Film Inst. Lifetime Achievement award, 1983. Died Aug. 28, 1987; buried Hollywood Cemetery, L.A.

HUSTON, MCCREADY, writer, editor; b. Brownsville, Pa., Mar. 11, 1891; s. joseph Andrew and Elizabeth (Fishburn) H.; m. Daryl Greene, Sept. 22, 1913; children: Mrs. John E. Small, Mrs. Hollis M. Barron, James McCready (dec.). Ed. pub. schs. With Uniontown (Pa.) Morning Herald, Pitts. Gazette-Times, South Bend (Ind.) Tribune, South Bend News-Times, N.Y. World-Telegram, Phila. Pub. Ledger, Scranton (Pa.) Rep., Indpls. Times, Pitts. Sun-Telegraph, Phila. Inquirer; dir. pub. rels. Acad. Natural Scis. Phila., 1940-59. Author several books; editor Frontiers mag.; contbr. fiction to mags. Episcopalian. Home: Woodland Calif. †

HUTCHESON, THOMAS BARKSDALE, JR., agronomist, educator; b. Christiansburg, Va., Nov. 4, 1926; s. Thomas Barksdale and Rosilie (Stockard) H.; m. Francis Elizabeth McEver, Thomas Barksdale III, Joel Collier. BS, Va. Poly. Inst., 1950; MS, N.C. State U., 1952, PhD, 1956. Instr. agronomy N.C. State U., Raleigh, 1952-54; asst. prof. agronomy U. Ky., Lexington, 1956-59, assoc. prof., 1959-64; prof. Va. Poly. Inst., Blacksburg, 1964-67, prof., head dept. agronomy, 1967-85. Mem. editorial bd. Tobacco Sci., 1969-72, Agronomy Jour., 1970-73, Soil Sci. Soc. Am. Proc., 1970-73. Served with AUS, 1945-46. Fellow Am. Soc. Agronomy, Soil Sci. Soc. Am.; mem. Sigma Xi, Alpha Zeta, Phi Kappa Phi, Epsilon Sigma Phi, Phi Sigma, Gamma Sigma Delta. Presbyterian (elder). Home: Blacksburg Va. Died Oct. 23, 1985; buried Westview Cemetery, Blacksburg, Va.

HUTCHINS, CURTIS MARSHALL, business executive; b. Boston, Apr. 23, 1907; s. Charles P. and Lena (Curtis) H.; m. Ruth Rich, Feb. 128, 1931; children: Hilda, Christopher, Hope. Student, Country Day Schg., Newton, Mass.; AB, Williams Coll., 1928; forestry student, U. Maine, LLD, 1951; MS (hon.), Colby Coll., 1949; LHD, Husson Coll., 1971. Pres. Derad River Co., Bangor, Maine, 1935-57, chmn., from 1947; pres. Bangor and Aroostook R.R. Co., 1948-57, chmn., 1952-58, 65, dir., 1952-58, 64-65; pres. St. Croix Paper Co., 1959-63; dir. Scott Paper Co., 1954-77, State St. Bank &Trust Co., Boston, 1954-78, Guilford Industries Inc. (Maine), Bangor Punta Corp., 1964-79. Merrill Trust Co., Bangor, 1936-76. Mem. New Eng. Coun., pres., 1954; bd. dirs. Assn. Am. R.R.'s, 1951-54; mem. Maine Environ. Improvement Commn., 1969-72; mem. city coun., Bangor, 1941-43, chmn., 1943; mem. Maine Legislature, 1943. Mem. U.S. C. of C. (dir., chmn. natural resources com. 1961-69), Penobscot Valley Country Club, Tarratine Club (Bangor); Union Club (Boston); Pinnacle Club (N.Y.C.), Phi Beta Kappa. Home: Bangor Maine. Died Sept. 15, 1985.

HUTCHINSON, J. EDWARD, former congressman; b. Fennville, Mich., Oct. 13, 1914; s. Marc C. and Wilna (Leland) H.; m. Janice Eleanor Caton, Sept. 19, 1959. AB, U. Mich., 1936, JD, 1938. Bar: Mich. 1938. Mem. Mich. Ho. of Reps. from Allegan County, 1946-50, Senate from 8th Senatorial dist., 1951-60; del., v.p. Mich. Constl. Conv., 1961-62; mem. 88th-94th Congresses from 4th Mich. dist. With AUS, 1941-46. Republican. Home: Naples Fla. Died July 22, 1985.

HUTCHINSON, JOHN HARRISON, educator; b. Sumner, Ill., Sept. 2, 1892; s. William Albert and Caroline (Petty) H.; m. Martha C. Cooper, Aug. 8, 1922; children: Frances Ann (dec.), John Robert. B.E., Ill. State Normal U., 1923; A.M., U. Chgo., 1926, Ph.D., 1941. Tchr. rural schs., 1910-15; high sch. prin. 1915-17, 19-21, 23-24; asst. prof. edn. Drake U., 1926-28, prof., from 1928, chmn. exec. com. Coll. of Edn., 1942-46. With U.S. Army, 1918-19. Mem. NEA, Nat., Iowa adult edn. assns., Iowa State Tchrs. Assn., Frontier Club, Des Moines Schoolmasters Club, Univ. Club, Masons, Kappa Delta Pi, Phi Delta Kappa, Omicron Delta Kappa, Tau Kappa Epsilon. Home: Des Moines Iowa. †

HUTCHINSON, MAYNARD, government official; b. Allston, Mass., Sept. 18, 1885; s. George and Eliza Maynard (Clark) H.; m. Helen Sophia Knowlton, May 22, 1909 (dec.); children: Marion (Mrs. Harry S. Tschopik Jr.), George II, Andrew; m. Linda McLean Hawkridge, Dec. 31, 1956. AB, Harvard U., 1908. With W.H. McElwain Co., Internat. Shoe Co., 1908-24; treas., bd. dirs. Loomis Sayles & Co., Inc., 1928-54; collector of customs Dist. 4 Commonwealth of Mass., from 1954; bd. dirs. Loomis Sayles Mut. Fund, Inc., N.E. Mut. Life Ins. Co. Pres. Newton (Mass.) Community Chest, 1935-37; gen. chmn. Greater Boston United War Fund, 1942; dir. United Community Svcs. Met. Boston, 1942-53, Boston Better Bus. Bur., 1938-55, Boys and Girls Camps, Inc., from 1938; trustee Newton Wellesley Hosp., 1930-47, Northeastern U., 1939-54. Mem. Union Club, Harvard Club, Brae Burn Country Club. Republican. Home: Chestnut Hill Mass. †

HUTCHISON, JOSEPH CARSON, business executive; b. Cross Hill, S.C., Sept. 17, 1894; s. Joseph Carson and Bessie (Cauthen) H.; m. Annie Whitner, Oct. 7, 1919; children: Elise Whitner (Mrs. R. L. Cornell Jr.), Helen (Mrs. T. E. Tucker). AB, Wofford Coll., 1915. Tchr. high sch. Sanford, Fla., 1915-17; clk. Sanford Truck Growers, Inc., 1919, asst. sec.-treas., 1919-20, gen. mgr., sales mgr., 1920-35; propr. J.C. Hutchison & Co., Sanford, 1935-83; chmn. bd. Chase & Co., Sanford, 1963-69, adv. dir., 1969-83; chmn. exec. com. Fla. Celery Exchange, Orlando, 1961-74; chmn. adv. com. Fla. Celery Mktg. Order, Orlando, 1962-74; bd. dirs. Fla. Sweet Corn Exchange, Zellwood (Fla.) Sweet Corn Exchange, Sugar Cane Growers Coop. Fla. 2d lt. F.A., U.S. Army, 1917-19, brig. gen., 1940-46, lt. gen. Fla. N.G. ret. Decorated Silver Star, Legion of Merit, Bronze Star, Air medal, Fla. Cross. Mem. Fla. Fruit and Vegetable Assn. (bd. dirs. 1947-74), Masons, Elks, Kiwanis, Rotary (hon.). Democrat. Home: Sanford Fla. Died Dec. 7, 1983.

HUTCHISON, STUART NYE, JR., lawyer; b. Norfolk, Va., Aug. 19, 1910; s. Stuart Nye and Mary Jane (Hall) H.; m. Alberta McClure, Oct. 14, 1938; children: Barbara Ann, Stuart Nye III, Robert McClure. AB, Lafayette Coll., 1932; LLB, Harvard U., 1935. Bar: Pa. 1935. Assoc. Reed, Smith, Shaw & McClay, Pitts., 1935-44; ptnr. Kirkpatrick, Lockhart, Johnson & Hutchison, Pitts., from 1946; sec., bd. dirs. Kleinewefers Corp., Salem Corp., Fortune Nat. Life Ins. Co., Fortune Nat. Corp., Petroleum Pipe and Supply Co.; bd. dirs. Keystone Bank, Fourth Allegheny Corp. Trustee Clan Donald Ednl. and Charitable Trust. Served to lt. comdr. USNR, 1944-46. Mem. ABA, Pa. Bar Assn., Allegheny County Bar Assn., Phi Beta Kappa. Republican. Presbyn. Home: Pittsburgh Pa. Died Dec. 7, 1984; buried Homewood Cemetery, Pitts.

HUTH, DONALD EARL, foreign correspondent; b. Green Bay, Wis., May 28, 1915; s. Herman Albert and Ann (Klesges) H.; m. Anne Marie Kelly, Sept. 24, 1938; children—Dennis, Kathleen Marie. Ph.B., Marquette U. Reporter Milw. Sentinel, Milw. Jour., Waukesha (Wis.) Daily Freeman, Racine (Wis.) Jour.-Times, 1933-43; with A.P., 1943-78; editor A.P., Omaha; staff cable desk A.P., N.Y.C.; war corr. CBI Theater; corr. Calcutta, Bombay, New Delhi, 1945-48; world desk editor, chief bur. Manila, P.I.; war corr. Korea; chief bur. Manila, 1952-57, Singapore, 1958-59; chief Southeast Asian svcs., from 1959, exec. asst. world svc. div., until 1978; ret. 1978; Mem. publ. relations adv. com. Marquette U. Contbr.: chpt. on Nehru Men Who Make Your World. Recipient Byline award for outstanding reporting in Korea Marquette U., 1953; Alumni Merit award Marquette U. Alumni Assn., 1975. Mem. Fgn. Corrs. Assn. S.E. Asia (v.p. 1958-59). Clubs: Overseas Press of America, Overseas Press P.I. (v.p. 1952-55, pres. 1956-57), Tokyo Correspondents (sec. 1951-52). Died May 7, 1987; interred Holy Cross Cemetery, Milw.

HUTTON, JAMES FRANKLIN, food service executive; b. Harrisburg, Pa., June 10, 1916; s. James N. and Mabel (Bowers) H.; m. Shirley Roberts, Aug. 17, 1940; 1 dau., Jane. BA, Temple U., 1946. With Slater System Inc., 1935-61, v.p. ops., 1942-46, exec. v.p., 1946-60, pres., 1960-61; sr. v.p., bd. dirs., mem. exec. com. parent com. ARA Services Inc., Phila., 1961-65, exec. v.p., 1965-86. Mem. exec. bd. Valley Forge coun. Boy Scouts Am.; mem. Phila. Crime Commn.; pres. Cardiovascular Inst. Heart Research, Phila.; trustee Hahnemann Hosp., Harcum Jr. Coll. Mem. English-Speaking Union, Nat. Restaurant Assn., Pa. Restaurant Assn. (pres. 1952-53), Phila. Restaurant Assn. (1950-51), S.E. Pa. Heart Assn., Pa. Soc., Rotary Club, Union League, Overbrook Country Club, Porters Lake Club, Sigma Pi, Kappa Kappa Psi. Republican. Lutheran. Home: Gladwyn Pa. Died Dec. 21, 1986; buried St. Paul's Lutheran Ch Cemetery, Ardmore, Pa.

HUTZLER, ALBERT DAVID, JR., merchant; b. Ba timore County, Md., Mar. 1, 1916; s. Albert David an Gretchen (Hochschild) H.; m. Bernice Levy, Sept. 2 1937; children: Elizabeth Ann Hutzler Friedman, Albe David III, James Levy. Student, Friends Sch.; A Johns Hopkins U., 1937. Trainee R.H. Macy & Co N.Y.C., 1937-38; with Hutzler Bros. Co., 1938-78, pres gen. mgr., 1954-75, chmn. bd., 1975-78. Bd. dirs., pre Com. for Downtown Inc.; mem. exec. com. Greate Balt. Com. Inc.; mem. bd. dirs. United Fund Cen. M Inc.; bd. dirs. Assn. Jewish Charities and Welfare Fun pres., 1967-69; trustee Johns Hopkins U.; pres. Hutzle Fund Inc. Mem. Ctr. Club. Home: Boca Raton Fl Died May 31, 1985; buried Boca Raton, Fla.

HYATT, GERHARDT WILFRED, clergyman, colleg president; b. Melfort, Sask., Can., July 1, 1916; came t U.S., 1939, naturalized, 1945; s. Francis William an Mary Elizabeth (Faber) H.; m. Elda Rosa Mueller, Ma 8, 1946; children: Ruth (Mrs. Robert Cornelius Heffro Jr.), Matthew Leavenworth. Student, Concordia Coll Edmonton, Alta., Can., 1935-39, Concordia Sem., S Louis, 1939-44; D.D., Concordia Sem., St. Louis, 196 M.A., George Washington U., 1964; L.D.H., Tark Coll., Mo., 1974. Ordained to ministry Lutheran Ch 1944; pastor Our Savior Luth. Ch., Raleigh, N.C., 194 45; commd. 1st lt. U.S. Army, 1945; advanced throug grades to maj. gen.; with Office Dep. Chief of Sta Army Gen. Staff, 1960-63; div. chaplain 3d Armour Div. in Europe, dep. USAREUR chaplain, 1966-68; di personnel and ecclesiastical relations Office Chief Chaplains, Washington, 1968-69; command chapla U.S. Army Mil. Assistance Command, Vietnam, 196 70; dep. chief of chaplains U.S. Army, Washingto 1970-71; chief of chaplains U.S. Army, 1971-75; pre Concordia Coll., St. Paul, 1976-83; asst. to pres. Lut Ch.-Mo. Synod, 1983-85; established Grace Luth. Ch Woodbridge, Va., 1959; v.p. Luth. Ch.-Mo. Synod. Decorated D.S.M., Legion of Merit, Bronze Star, Joi Service Commendation medal, Army Commendati medal with oak leaf cluster, Civil Actions Honor med 1st class; Vietnam, Vietnamese Honor medal 1st clas recipient Four Chaplains award Alexander D. Good Ben Goldman Lodge, B'nai B'rith, 1969, Golden Ru award St. George Assn., N.Y.C. Police Dept., 1973 Mem. Mil. Order World Wars. Home: Saint Louis M Died Aug. 30, 1985.

HYDE, EDWIN, department store executive; Charleston, S.C., June 15, 1905; s. Tristram Tupper a Minnie (Black) H.; m. Camilla Price Alsop, Dec. 1930; 1 dau., Camilla (Mrs. Carlton P. Moffa Jr.). Student, Furman U., 1923-25; LLD, Washingt and Lee U. V.p. Bank Va., Richmond, 1931-44; exe v.p. Peoples Nat. Bank, Charlottesville, Va., 1944-4 v.p. Miller & Rhoads Inc., Richmond, 1946-47, exe v.p., 1947-53, pres., bd. dirs., 1953-68, chmn. bd. dir 1968-82; vice chmn., chmn. fin. com. Garfinckel, Broo Bros., Miller & Rhoades Inc., Washington, 1967-8 pres. Sixth St. Enterprises; bd. dirs., exec. com. V Indsl. Devel. Corp., bd. dirs. Cen. Va. Ednl. TV Cor Shenandoah Life Ins. Co., 1st and Mchts. Nat. Ban Woodward & Lothrop, Washington, United Va. Ban State-Planters, Frederick Atkins Inc. Mem. Adv. Cou on the Va. Economy, Citizens Adv. Com. of Communi Improvement, mchts. coun. NYU, Adv. Coun. Na Affairs, Nat. Citizens Com. for Community Relatio bd. dirs. United Givers Fund, Cen. Richmond Ass trustee, pres. Miller & Rhoads Found., Va. Mus. Fi Arts; bd. dirs. Richmond Meml. Hosp., Pub. Poli Research; trustee, mem. fin. com. retirement syste ARC; bd. dirs. Va. Found. for Ind. Colls. Me Richmond C. of C. (mem. civic progress com.), Va. of C. (bd. dirs.), soc. Colonial Wars in Va., SAR, Cecelia Soc., 55 Golf Assn., Va. Indsl. Grou Newcomen Soc. N.Am., Commonwealth Club, Count Club of Va., German Club (Richmond), Farmingt Country Club (Charlottesville). Home: Richmond V Died Apr. 24, 1982; buried Richmond.

HYDE, GORDON EUGENE, advertising executive; St. Paul, Aug. 8, 1898; s. Timothy D. Sheehan a Adah L. Hyde; m. Katharine Ridgley Thomas, Jan. 1925 (div. July 1948); children: Donald R., Barbara Hyde Crafford, Harriet Hyde Mauck; m. 2d, Loui Jane Hall, Sept. 18, 1948. AB, U. Minn., 1918. Salesman Packard Motor Car Co., 1919-23; advt. sol itor Curtis Pub. Co., 1923-28; v.p. sales, dir. Robeso Rochester Corp., 1928-31; account exec. N.W. Ayer C 1931-33; v.p., dir. J.M. Mattees Co., 1933-38, McCa Erickson Co., 1938-45; pres., dir. Fed. Advt. C N.Y.C., 1945-52; v.p., mem. adminstrv. bd. D'Ar Advt. Co. (merger Fed. Advt. Co.), N.Y.C., 1952-7 Bd. dirs. Am. Assn. Advt. Agys., 1945-47, Advt. Rs Found., 1946-51, 3d Ave. Assn., N.Y.C., from 1957; b dirs. Grand Jury Assn. N.Y. County, from 1947, pre from 1963. 1st lt. AC, U.S. Army, 1917-19. Me Metropolitan Club (bd. govs.), St. Nicholas Club (govs.), Chi Psi. Presbyterian. Home: North Salem N. Died Feb. 4, 1989.

HYDE, LAURANCE MASTICK, judge; b. Princet Mo., Feb. 2, 1892; s. Ira Barnes and Eliza Tomlins (Mastick) H.; m. Florence Fuller, June 15, 1922; c dren: Florence Hyde Frazier, Laurance Mastick. A

U. Mo., 1914, LLB, 1916, LLD, 1948. Bar: Mo. 1916. City atty. Princeton, Mo., 1916-17; mem. Hyde, Hyde & Fuller, Princeton, 1916-31; pres. Farmers State Bank, Princeton, 1922-31; mem. commn. of appeals Supreme Ct. of Mo., 1931, 35, 39, appt'd judge, Dec. 30, 1942, elected judge, 1945-55, 55-67, chief justice, 1949-51, 60-62. Contbr. articles to legal jours. Chmn. Conf. Chief Justices, 1949-50. 2d lt., Hdqrs. Co., 338th Inf., 85th Div., Camp Custer, Mich.; judge advocate, Spl. Tng. Camp, Indpls, 1917-18. Fellow Inst. Jud. Adminstrn. (pres. 1958-59); mem. Am. (coun. criminal law sect. 1954-67), Mo. bar assns. Scribes (pres. 1966-67), Am. Judicature Soc. (chmn. bd. 1951-55), Am. Law Inst. (coun. 1948), Alumni Assn. U. Mo. (pres. 1942-44), Nat. Conf. of Jud. Couns. (chmn. 1942-43), S.R., Masons (32 degree), Jefferson City Country Club, Rotary, Kansas City (Mo.) Club, Order of Coif, Phi Beta Kappa, Pi Kappa Alpha, Phi Delta Phi. Home: Jefferson City Mo. †

HYDE, ROBERT PAUL, telecommunications executive; b. Cambridge, Mass., Jan. 15, 1930; s. Lawrence Henry and Catherine Isabel (McMahon) H.; m. Zay Dunphy, June 6, 1953; children: Ellen, Robert, Alison, Anne, William. A.B., Harvard U., 1951, M.B.A., 1955. From asst. to pres. to sales mgr. Carling Brewing Co., Cleve., 1955-63; v.p. mktg. Stroh Brewery Co., Detroit, 1963-70; pres. Rheingold Breweries, Inc., N.Y.C., 1970-73, Onondaga Products Corp., Syracuse, N.Y., 1975-81; exec. v.p. Western Union Telegraph Co., Upper Saddle River, N.J., 1980-88. Served to capt. USMCR, 1951-53. Roman Catholic. Clubs: Harvard (Boston); Detroit Athletic, Country of Detroit, Cazenovia Country. Home: Cazenovia N.Y. Died Apr. 29, 1988.

HYMAN, HERBERT HIRAM, social psychologist, educator; b. N.Y.C., Mar. 3, 1918; s. David Elihu and Gisella (Mautner) H.; m. Helen Raphael Kandel, Sept. 30, 1945; children: Lisa D., David K., Alex R. AB with honors, Columbia U., 1939, AM, 1940, PhD, 1942. Social sci. analyst USDA, 1942; pub. opinion analyst Office War Info., 1942-44; dir. field surveys, morale div. U.S. Strategic Bomb Survey, 1944-45; asst. prof. Bklyn. Coll., 1946-47; prof. Columbia U., 1951-69, chmn. dept. sociology, 1965-68; fellow Ctr. Advanced Studies Wesleyan U., Middletown, Conn., 1968-69, prof. sociology, 1969-77, Cromwell univ. prof., from 1977; rsch. assoc. Nat. Opinion Rsch. Ctr., 1947-57; vis. prof. U. Calif., 1950, U. Oslo, 1950-51, U. Ankara, Turkey, 1957-58, U. Catania, Italy, 1976, MIT, 1976; program dir. Rsch. Inst. Social Devel., UN 1964-65. Author: Interviewing in Social Research, 1954, Survey Design and Analysis, 1955, Political Socialization, 1959, Applications of Methods of Evaluation, 1963, Readings in Reference Group Theory, 1968, Secondary Analysis of Sample Surveys, 1972, The Enduring Effects of Education, 1975, Education's Lasting Influence on Values, 1979. Recipient Fullbright award, Guggenheim award; spl. grantee Ford Found. Fellow Am. Psychol. Assn.; mem. Am. Assn. Pub. Opinion Rsch. (past pres., Julian Woodward Meml. award), Sociol. Rsch. Assn. (pres. 1974-75), Am. Sociol. Soc. (pres. methodology sect. 1962-63, social psychology sect. 1970-71), Soc. Psychol. Study Social Issues (exec. council), Sigma Xi. Home: Westport Conn. Died Dec. 18, 1985, buried Norwalk, Conn.

HYNEK, JOSEF ALLEN, astronomer, educator; b. Chgo., May 1, 1910; s. Josef and Bertha (Waska) H.; m. Martha Alexander, Dec. 25, 1932; m. Mriam Curtis, May 31, 1942; children: Scott, Roxane, Joel, Paul, Ross. BS, U. Chgo., 1931, PhD, 1935. Fellow Yerkes Obs., 1932-35; instr., asst. prof. Ohio State U., Columbus, 1935-41, assoc. prof., 1946-50, dir. McMillin Obs., 1946-53, asst. dean Grad. Sch., 1950-53, prof. astronomy, dir. astronomy teaching and research Perkins Obs.; supr. tech. reports Applied Physics Lab., Johns Hopkins U., Balt., 1942-45; assoc. dir. in charge satellite optical tracking program Smithsonian Astrophys. Obs., Cambridge, Mass.; research assoc. Harvard Coll. Obs.; prof. Northwestern U., Evanston, Ill., 1960-85, prof. emeritus, 1985-86, chmn dept. astronomy, dir. Dearborn Obs., dir. Lindheimer Astron. Research Ctr., 1964-75, dir. Ctr. for UFO Studies, 1973-85; sci. dir. USAF balloon astronomy project Stargazer. Author: The Challenge of the Universe, 1962, The UFO Experience, (with Vallee) The Edge of Reality, (with Apfel) Astronomy One; editor: Astrophysics, 1951. Mem. Internat. Astron. Union (sec. U.S. nat. com.), Am. Astron. Soc. (sec.), Astron. Soc. Pacific, Am. Mus. Natural History (corr.), Phi Beta Kappa, Sigma Xi. Home: Scottsdale Ariz. Died Apr. 27, 1986.

HYNES, JOHN FELIX, insurance executive; b. Avery, Iowa, June 26, 1891; s. Faley and Emma (Pettit) H.; m. Lena C. Herbold, Aug. 12, 1920; children: Mary Jo (Mrs. John Daly), Joan T. (wife lt. col. Joseph Salvo, USAF), John, Philip. BLitt, U. of Notre Dame, 1914, LLB, 1915. Bar: Iowa 1915. Pvt. practice Des Moines, 1915-18; claims atty. Employers Mut. Casualty Co., 1918-20, sec., 1920-40, v.p., 1940-47, pres., 1947-57, chmn., 1957-63, hon. chmn. bd., dir., from 1963; bd. dirs. Bankers Trust Co., Des Moines. Pres. Conf. Mut. Casualty Cos., 1950-51. Mem. Am., Iowa, Polk County bar assns., Am. Judicature Soc., Internat. Aassn. Ins. Counsels, Rotary. Home: Des Moines Iowa. †

IBRANYI, FRANCIS JOSEPH, philosophy educator; b. Budapest, Hungary, Apr. 30, 1901; s. Francis and Emilia (Pacsesz) I. BA, Piarist Coll., Budapest, 1919; STD, U. Pazmany, Budapest, 1925, DD Collegiatus, 1931; PhD, U. Angelicum, Rome, 1928. Ordained priest Roman Catholic Ch.; papal domestic prelate. Prof. ethics U. Pazmany, 1938-49, dean dept. theology, 1945-48; prof. ethics Laval U., Quebec, Que., Can, 1950-70; prof. philosophy Ursuline's Coll., Quebec, 1956-67; vis. prof. ethics Pontifical Coll. Josephinum, Worthington, Ohio, 1967-70; prof. philosophy and comparative religion Mt. St. Joseph Coll., Wakefield, R.I., 1970-76; vis. prof. Sem. of Our Lady of Providence, Warwick, R.I., 1970-71. Author" Theology of S. Gerard, 1938, Politics and Ethics, Principles of Ethics in Thomas Aquinas and Kant, Les principes premiers et secondaires de la loi naturelle, Les exigences de la morale chretienne, Violence and Morality, also articles. Mem. Hungarian Cath. Acad. Rome, Assn. des professeurs de philosophie de l'enseignement collegial au Canada francais. Died June 23, 1983; buried Mt. St. Mary's Cemetery.

IGL, RICHARD FRANKLIN, lawyer; b. Klamath Falls, Oreg., Feb. 15, 1923; s. Englebert Matthew and Rose Ann (Haas) I.; m. Frances Marie Pytleski, Mar. 15, 1980. B.A., U. Oreg., 1947, M.A. with honors, 1948; J.D., Yale U., 1950. Bar: Calif. 1951, U.S. Supreme Ct. 1975, U.S. Tax Ct. 1975. Instr. polit. sci. Yale U., 1949-50; law clk. to judge U.S. Ct. Apppeals, N.Y. Circuit, 1950-51; assoc. firm O'Melveny & Myers, Los Angeles, 1951-60, ptnr., 1960-63; pvt. practice Beverly Hills, Calif., 1963-86; judge pro tem Beverly Hills Mcpl. Ct., 1966; lectr. estate and tax planning course UCLA, 1963-64; lectr. Entertainment Law Inst., U. So. Calif., 1961; dir., sec.-treas. Crobsy Investment Corp., Los Angeles, 1960-86; gen. counsel, dir. Seven-Up Bottling Co. Los Angeles, Inc., 1967-68. Bd. dirs., sec. Western Inst. for Cancer and Leukemia Research, Beverly Hills, 1963-68. Served to capt. AUS, 1942-46. Mem. ABA (del. 1969-72), Calif. Bar Assn., Los Angeles Bar Assn. (trustee 1970-71), Beverly Hills Bar Assn. (bd. govs. 1960-71, pres. 1968), Copyright Soc. Los Angeles (dir. 1964-66), Beverly Hills C. of C. (dir. 1977-78), Phi Beta Kappa. Died Feb. 2, 1986; buried at sea.

ILLIG, MARJORIE BULLOCK, public health director, cranberry grower; b. Belchertown, Mass., Oct. 27, 1891; d. Lewis Edward and Susie A. (Butler) B.; m. Carl Weber Illig, Jr., Nov. 29, 1923; 1 dau., Barbara Weber. Grad., Sargent Coll., 1912; student, Bryant and Stratton Sch., 1912-15, Boston Sch. Phys. Edn., 1917. Phys. edn. dir. 1912; nat. chmn. div. health Gen. Fedn. Women's Clubs, 1932-38, 44-47; lay field rep. Am. Soc. for Control of Cancer, N.Y.C., 1935-36; nat. comdr. Women's Field Army, 1936-43; pres., owner The Bullock Cranberry Co. Inc., Wareham, Mass.; owner Marge Illig Flowers, N.Y.C.; assoc. Ruth Joyce Flowers, N.Y.C.; trustee Endicott Jr. Coll., Beverly, Mass., 1939-54. Chmn. Park dept, Town of Wareham, Mass., 1926-34; mem. Nat. Women's Adv. Com., Fed. Security Agy., Med. Dept., U.S.Army, World War I. Mem. Assn. of Women in Pub. Health, Am. Pub. Health Assn., Am. Legion (Wareham, Mass., Post 220), Internat. Fedn. Bus. and Profl. Women, Wareham Monday Club, State Presidents of Mass. Club, First Dist. President's Club (Cape Cod, Mass., pres. 1935-36). Republican. Episcopalian. Home: New York N.Y. †

IMLACH, GEORGE (PUNCH), professional hockey coach, business executive; b. Toronto, Ont., Can., Mar. 15, 1918. Profl. hockey player Toronto Marlboros, Toronto Goodyears; player, coach, gen. mgr. Que. (Can.) Aces, 1946-57, also co-owner; mgr., coach Springfield Indians, Am. Hockey League, 1957-69; coach, gen. mgr. Toronto Maple Leafs, Nat. Hockey League, 1959-69, coach, 1979-81; syndicated hockey columnist Toronto, 1969-70; coach, gen. mgr., v.p. Buffalo Sabres, 1970-79. Served with Canadian Army. Coach of 4 Stanley Cup championship teams. Died Feb. 1, 1987.

INGALLS, DAVID STINTON, lawyer; b. Cleve., Jan. 28, 1899; s. Albert Simson and Jane (Taft) I.; m. Louise Harkness, June 27, 1922 (dec. May 1978); children: Edith, Jane, Louise, Ann, David; m. 2d, Frances W. Wracc, Feb. 16, 1979. BA, Yale U., 1920; LLB, Harvard Coll., 1923. Bar: Ohio 1923. Assoc. Squire, Sanders & Dempsey, Cleve., 1923-29; mem. Ohio Ho. of Reps., 1927-29; asst. sec. of navy for aeronautics 1929-32; dir. Dept. Pub. Health and Welfare, Cleve., 1933-35; v.p., gen. mgr. Pan-Am. Air Ferries, Inc., 1941-42, mem. bd., 1949; practice law Cleve., from 1949; with Pan-Am. World Airways System, N.Y.C., 1945-49, also bd. dirs. With USN, World War I; capt. USNR, 1942. commodore, 1945. Decorated D.S.M., Legion of Honor (France), DFC (Gt. Britain). Mem. Union Club, Chagrin Valley Hunt Club. Republican. Episcopalian. Home: Chagrin Falls Ohio. Died Apr. 26, 1985; buried Warm Springs, Va.

INGBAR, SIDNEY HAROLD, physician, educator; b. Denver, Feb. 12, 1925; s. David Harry and Belle (Friedl) I.; m. Mary Lee Gimbel Mack, May 28, 1950; children: David Harry, Eric Edward, Jonathan Clarence. Student, UCLA, 1941-43; M.D. magna cum laude (fellow), Harvard U., 1947; D.Sc. (hon.), U. Mass., 1985. Practice medicine, specializing in endocrinology Boston, 1949-72; mem. faculty Harvard Med. Sch., 1955-72, William B. Castle prof. medicine, 1969-72; program dir. Harvard Clin. Research Center, Boston City Hosp., from 1962; physician-in-charge Harvard Clin. Research Center, Boston City Hosp. (Out-patient Endocrine Clinic), from 1963; assoc. dir. Thorndike Meml. Lab., 1963-72; prof. medicine, asso. dean U. Calif.-San Francisco, 1972-74; prof. medicine Harvard U., 1974—; also dir. Thorndike Labs, Beth Israel Hosp., Boston, 1974—; Cons. Newton-Wellesley Hosp., from 1957, Mass. Soldiers Home, Chelsea, from 1964; Mem. Surgeon Gen. Adv. Com. Gen. Medicine, chmn. subcom. endocrinology and metabolism, 1963-70; mem. medicine test com. Nat. Bd. Med. Examiners, 1967-70; mem. endocrinology study sect. NIH, 1966-70, chmn., 1971-73; mem. bd. sci. counselors Nat. Inst. Arthritis, Metabolism and Digestive Diseases, 1973-75, mem. advanced exam. com. endocrinology and metabolism, 1973-75, chmn., 1975-77; sr. med. investigator VA, 1973—; mem. med. adv. bd. Nat. Hormone and Pituitary Program, 1982—. Editor: Hormone and Metabolic Research; mem. editorial bd. Endocrinology, 1957-67, New Eng. Jour. Medicine, 1967-70, Jour. Clin. Investigation, 1968-72; editor-in-chief: Med. Grand Rounds, 1981—; mem. editorial adv. com. Jour. Endocrinologic Investigation, 1983—; contbr. articles to profl. jours. Recipient Maimonides award Boston Med. Soc., 1947; Hamburger prize Technion U., Haifa, 1980; scholar Howard Hughes Med. Inst., 1981. Fellow ACP; mem. Assn. Am. Physicians, Am. Fedn. Clin. Research, Am. Soc. Clin. Investigation (councillor 1967-70), Am. Thyroid Assn (pres. 1976-77, councillor 1972-75, Warner-Chilcott disting. lectr. 1978, Disting. Service award 1980), Endocrine Soc. (pres. 1985-86; Ernest Oppenheimer award 1965, councillor 1971-75, Disting. Leadership award 1979), Am. Physiol. Soc., Soc. Exptl. Biology and Medicine, Italian Endocrine Soc. (hon. fellow), Japan Endocrine Soc. (hon. mem.), Sigma Xi, Alpha Omega Alpha. Home: Brookline Mass. Died Oct. 6, 1988; buried Mt. Auburn Cemetery, Cambridge, Mass.

INGERSOLL, RALPH MCALLISTER, editor, author, publisher; b. New Haven, Dec. 8, 1900; s. Colin McRae and Theresa (McAllister) I.; m. Mary Elizabeth Carden, 1925 (div. 1935); m. Elaine Brown Keiffer, Aug, 9, 1945 (dec. 1948); children: Ralph McAllister II, Ian Macrae; m. Mary Hill Doolittle, Nov. 25, 1948 (div. 1963); 1 adopted son, Brooks; m. Thelma Bradford, 1964. Student, Hotchkiss Sch., Lakeville, Conn., 1917-18; BS, Yale, 1921; postgrad., Columbia, 1922. Mining engr; reporter New Yorker mag., 1925, mng. editor, 1925-30; assoc. editor Fortune, 1930, mng. editor, 1930-35; v.p., gen. mgr. Time Inc. (pub. Time, Life, Fortune and Aechtl. Forum, sponsoring radio and cinema prodns. "The March of Time"), 1935-38; pub. Time mag., 1937-39; organizer, financier co. to publish PM (N.Y. daily evening newspaper), 1939-40; pres. R.J. Co. Inc., 1948-59, Gen. Pubs. Inc. (newspaper mgmt.), 1959-75, Ingersolls Publs. Co., 1975-85. Author: In and Under Mexico, 1924, Report on England, 1940, America is Worth Fighting For, 1941, Action on all Fronts, 1941, The Battle is the Payoff, 1944, Top Secret, 1946, The Great Ones, 1948, Wine of Violence, 1951, Point of Departure, 1961. Served to lt. col. Gen. Staff Corps, AUS, 1943-45. Decorated Legion of Merit; officer Order of the Crown (Belgium). Mem. Brook Club (N.Y.C.). Home: Cornwall Bridge Conn Died Mar. 8, 1985.

INGLE, WILLIAM MARTELL, chemist; b. Bondurant, Iowa, July 12, 1941; s. Robert Thomas and Marie (Hayden) I. BS in Chemistry, San Diego State U., 1964, MS in Chemistry, 1966, PhD in Chemistry, 1973; cert. in exec. mgmt. devel., Ariz. State U., 1983. Staff scientist Motorola, Inc., Phoenix, 1973-78, prin. staff scientist, 1979-86, prin. investigator, 1975-78, chmn. sci. adv. bd. assn., 1985-86; guest lectr. Ariz. State U., Tempe. Contbr. articles to profl. jours.; patentee in field. Dan Nobel fellow Motorola, Inc., 1984; recipient Disting. Inventor award Motorola, iNc., 1984. Mem. Am. Chem. Soc., Writers Refinery. Club: Elite Bonzo Party (Phoenix) (pres.). Died Oct. 4, 1986; buried La Vista Meml., National City, Calif.

INGRAM, IRVINE SULLIVAN, educator; b. Tunnel Hill, Ga., Nov. 11, 1892; s. George Conley and Annie Lee (Irvine) I.; m. Martha Lewis Munro, June 11, 1921(dec. Apr. 1955); 1 dau., Anne Gayle. AB, U. Ga., 1928; MA, Emory U., 1933; EdD, Oglethorpe U., 1952. Supt. schs. Chipley, Ga., 1920; prin. 4th dist. A & M Sch., Carrollton, Ga., 1920-33; pres. West Ga. Coll., 1933-60, pres. emeritus, from 1960, interim pres., 1961; prof. edn. LaGrange (Ga.) Coll., from 1961; ednl. cons., lectr., newspaper columnist; bd. dirs. Carrollton Fed. Savs. and Loan Assn.; dir. expt. with staff on rural tchr. edn. at coll. under Rosenwald Grant, 1938-48; cons. Puerto Rico Jr. Coll., Rio Piedras, 1953; mem. bd. control rsch. expt. in elem. edn., U. Ga., Oglethorpe U., West Ga. Coll., 1955. Contbg. editor Wesleyan Christian Advocate, 1946-48. Mem. exec. com. Ga. Adult Edn. Coun. Inc., gen. conf. Methodist Ch., 1930, 34, 38, uniting conf., 1939, lay leader N. Ga. conf., 1934-38, mem. jurisdictional conf. S.E., 1948, mem. Conf. Bd. Edn., Ga. Meth. Commn. Higher Edn. Recipient Disting. Svc. award G.S.C.W., Milledgeville, 1956, Delbert Clark award adult edn., 1962. Mem. 4th Dist. High Sch. Assn. (pres. 1924), Ga. Assn. Colls. (pres. 1945-46),

So. Assn. Colls. and Secondary Schs. (exec. com. 1953-55), Ga. Soc. Hist. Rsch. (pres. 1949), So. Hist. Soc., Carrollton C. of C. (pres.), Rotary (state gov. 1945-46). Democrat. Home: Carrollton Ga. †

INNIS, DONALD QUAYLE, educator, geographer; b. Toronto, Can., Apr. 21, 1924; came to U.S., 1963; s. Harold Adams and Mary (Quayle) I.; m. Janet Marion Graham, 1949 (div. 1966); children: Mary Graham, John William; m. Winifred Norton Huggins, 1969; 1 dau., Katherine Anne. B.A. with honors, U. Toronto, 1947; Ph.D., U. Calif. at Berkeley, 1959. Instr. U. Chgo., 1948-50, U. Western Ont., 1952-53; instr., then asst. prof. Queen's U., Kingston, Ont., 1953-63; mem. faculty SUNY-Geneseo, 1963-88, prof. geography, chmn. dept., 1965-88, chmn. faculty senate, 1974-75; prof. emeritus 1988; exchange prof. soils dept. Moscow State U., 1984; chmn. Kingston br. African Students Found., 1962-63. Author: Canada: A Geographic Study, 1966, 21 Days on Spaceship Earth, 1983, Green Geopolitics, 1986. Recipient Chancellor's award SUNY, 1979. Mem. Canadian Assn. Geographers, Assn. Am. Geographers, Am. Geog. Soc., United Univ. Profs. (pres. chpt. 1976-77). Died Aug. 24, 1988.

INSTONE, FRANK DONALD, food company executive; b. Chgo., May 5, 1919; s. Joseph and Marion Inston; m. Margery Snyder, Jan., 1944; children: Diane Instone Bartels, Donald, Debra. Student, Washington U., St. Louis, 1937-40. Regional sales mgr. Richard Scale Co., Cin., 1946-55; sales mgr. Packing Equipment div. St. Regis Paper Co., Chgo., 1955-57; various managerial and officer positions Toledo Scale Co., 1957-68, v.p., gen. mgr., dir., 1966; v.p. corp. devel. Seaway Food Town, Inc., Maumee, Ohio, 1968-71, exec. v.p., 1971-86; bd. dirs. U.S. Berkel, Inc. Bd. dirs. Better Bus. Bur., Am. Cancer Soc., Goodwill Industries, Toledo Employers Assn., Toledo Area Govtl. Research Assn., Boys Club Am.; sec. Ohio Retail Council Mchts.; trustee Teamsters Health and Welfare Plan. With USAAF, 1940-45. Mem. Sylvania (Ohio) Country CLub, Toledo Club, Toledo Yacht Club. Catawba Island Club, Port Clinton, Ohio. Home: Oak Hills Fla. Died May, 1986.

INUMARU, TETSUZO, hotel executive; b. Ishikawa, Japan, June 8, 1887. Grad., Hitotsubashi Higher Comml. Sch. Pres., gen. mgr. Imperial Hotel, Tokyo. †

IRELAND, LESTER, corporation executive; b. Greenville, Oreg., Mar. 6, 1886; s. John Preston and Clarissa (Pierce) I.; m. Saidie Geroutte, Sept. 17, 1937; 1 child, Jessie Belle (Mrs. Kenneth Hanson). Student, Pacific U. Ptnr. Lester Ireland & Co., Hillsboro, Oreg.; bd. dirs. U.S. Nat. Bank Portland. Mem. C. of C. (pres. 1932-34). †

IRRGANG, WILLIAM, manufacturing company executive; b. Germany, Sept. 27, 1907; came to U.S., 1928, naturalized, 1933; s. Theodor and Hedwig (Preyer) I.; m. Mildred Klapka, Aug. 8, 1934 (dec.); children: Rosemary, Dorothy Louise. E.E., State Tech. Sch., Cologne, Germany, 1928; Dr. Sc. (hon.), Lake Erie Coll., 1967. With Lincoln Electric Co., Cleve., from 1929; successively supr., methods engr., plant engr., dir. plant engring., bd. dirs., exec. v.p. mfg., pres. and gen. mgr. Lincoln Electric Co., 1954-72, chmn. bd., chief exec. officer, from 1972; dir. Big 3 Industries, Houston. Trustee Euclid Gen. Hosp.; exec. com. Cleve. Council World Affairs. Mem. AIM, Am. welding Soc., Cleve. Engring. Soc., Nat. Elec. Mfrs. Assn. (bd. govs. James H. McGraw award). Baptist. Clubs: Fifty (Cleve.), University (Cleve.). Home: Cleveland Ohio Died July 18, 1988.

ISAACS, HAROLD ROBERT, writer; b. N.Y.C., Sept. 13, 1910; s. Robert and Sophie (Berlin) I.; m. Viola Robinson, Sept. 14, 1932; children: Arnold R., Deborah S. A.B., Columbia U., 1930. Reporter N.Y. Times, also Honolulu Advt., Shanghai Eve. Post and China Press, 1928-31; with Agence Havas, Shanghai and N.Y.C., 1931-40, CBS, N.Y.C. and Washington, 1940-43; war corr., CBI, assoc. editor Newsweek mag., Washington, also China, S.E. Asia and N.Y.C., 1943-50; research assoc. Center Internat. Studies, MIT, Cambridge, 1953-65; prof. polit. sci. Center Internat. Studies, MIT, 1965-76, prof. emeritus, from 1976. Author: The Tragedy of the Chinese Revolution, 1938, No Peace for Asia, 1947, Two-Thirds of the World, 1950, Scratches on Our Minds, American Images of China and India, 1958, Emergent Americans, a Report on Crossroads Africa, 1961, The New World of Negro Americans, 1963 (Anisfield-Wolf award 1964), India's Ex- Untouchables, 1965, American Jews in Israel, 1967, Idols of the Tribe: Group Identity and Political Change, 1975, reissued, 1989, Power and Identity: Tribalism in World Politics, 1979, Re-Encounters in China: Notes of a Journey in a Time Capsule, 1985. Editor: Straw Sandals, Chinese Stories, 1918-33, 1974. Guggenheim fellow, 1950. Fellow Am. Acad. Arts and Scis. Home: Newton Mass. Died July 9, 1986; buried First Unitarian Soc. of Schenectady Garden.

ISAACS, REGINALD RODERIC, city planning educator; b. Winnipeg, Can., July 20, 1911; came to U.S., 1922, naturalized, 1944; s. Mark and Sophia (Rai) I.; m. Charlotte Aldes, Mar. 24, 1937; children: Merry Aldes, Mark Aldes, Henry Aldes. B. Arch., U. Minn., 1935; M.Arch., Harvard U., 1939; student, U. Chgo., 1947-50. Lic. architect, Nat. Council Archtl. Registration Bds., D.C., Ill., Mass. Architect housing, city planner Washington, Mpls., Chgo., Phila., other cities, 1926-40; city planner Chgo. Plan Commn., Syracuse Plan Commn.; with various fed. agys. 1940-45; dir. planning staff Michael Reese Hosp., Chgo., 1945-53; cons. South Side Planning Bd., Chgo., 1946-53; Charles Dyer Norton prof. regional planning Harvard U., 1953-78, Norton prof. emeritus, 1978-86, chmn. dept. city and regional planning, 1953-64; cons. to P.R. Govt., 1956-75, UN, 1960-62, V.I. Gov., 1961-76, Gulf Regional Planning Comm., 1966-77, Ford Found.; specialist U.S. State Dept., 1959; chmn. cons. Am. Council to Improve Our Neighborhoods, 1954-55; dir. met. area planning study Met. Housing and Planning Council of Chgo., 1955-56. Author: (with John Dyckman) Capital Requirements for Urban Development and Renewal, 1960, Walter Gropius, Der Mensch und Sein Werk, Vol. I, 1983, Vol. II, 1984; contbr. articles profl. publs.; exhbns.: Mus. Modern Art, 1947, Chgo. Art Inst., 1936, 7th Pan-Am. Congress Architects, Havana, 1950. Mem. bd. overseers com. to visit Harvard Grad. Sch. Design, 1951-53. Fellow Royal Soc. Arts.; mem. Kuratorium, Bauhaus-Archiv (Berlin). Home: Cambridge, Mass. Died June 22, 1986.

ISBELL, MARION WILLIAM, restaurant and hotel executive; b. Whitehaven, Tenn., Aug. 12, 1905; s. Howard James and Mary (Mayfield) I.; student pub. schs.; m. Ingrid Lucida Helsing, Oct. 2, 1927; children: Marion William, Mary Elaine Isbell Cook, Robert James. Owner, pres., dir. Isbell's, chain of restaurants, Chgo., 1943-46; pres., chief exec. officer Ramada Inns, Inc., 1962-73, chmn. bd., 1962-79, hon. chmn. bd., 1979-81. Chief instl. users br. OPA, 1943-45, dir. Chgo. Met. Area, 1943-45; active ARC, Chgo. Community Fund. Mem. Nat. (past pres., dir.), Chgo. (past pres., dir.) restaurant assns. Clubs: Arizona (Phoenix); Paradise Valley Country (Scottsdale, Ariz.). Died Oct. 20, 1988. Home: Scottsdale Ariz.

ISHERWOOD, CHRISTOPHER, author; b. High Lane, Cheshire, Eng., Aug. 26, 1904; came to U.S., 1939; naturalized, 1946; s. Francis Edward and Kathleen (Machell-Smith) I. Student, Repton Sch., 1919-22, Corpus Christi Coll., Cambridge U., 1924-25; med. student, U. London, 1927-28. Sec. to Music Soc. String Quartet, London, 1926-27; pvt. tchr. English Berlin, 1928-33; travelled in Europe and China, 1934-38; guest prof. modern Eng. lit. L.A. State Coll. and U. Calif.-Santa Barbara, 1959-60; Regent's prof. UCLA, 1965, U. Calif.-Riverside, 1966. Scenario writer for MGM, Warner Bros. and other motion picture studios intermittently, 1939-86; author: 9 novels, 4 vols. autobiography, plays, travel books including Goodbye to Berlin, 1939 (basis for play I Am a Camera by John van Druten, Critics award 1951 and later film Cabaret, N.Y. Drama Critics award, best musical), Lions and Shadows, Prater Violet, 1945, The World in the Evening, 1954, Christopher and His Kind, 1976, (autobiography) My Guru and His Disciple, 1980; co-author: (with W.H. Auden) play On the Frontier, 1938; translator The Intimate Journals of Charles Baudelaire, 1947; translator (all with Swami Prabhavananda) The Bhagvad-Gita, 1944, The Crest Jewel of Discrimination, How To Know God, 1953; author: (travel) The Condor and the Cows, 1949, Down There On a Visit, 1962, A Single Man, 1964, Ramakrishna and His Disciples, 1965, Exhumations, 1966, A Meeting By The River, 1967 (play adapted from novel with Don Bachardy 1972), Kathleen and Frank, 1971; editor mag. Vedanta and the West, Hollywood, 1943-44, also introduction, several contbns. Vedanta for the Western World, 1945. Worked with Am. Friends Service Com. on refugee relief project, Haverford, Pa., 1941-42; mem. nat. adv. bd. trustees Inst. Study of Human Resources. Mem. ACLU, Wider Quaker Fellowship, Screenwriters Guild, Nat. Inst. Arts and Letters, Acad. Motion Picture Arts and Scis. Home: Santa Monica Calif. Died Jan. 4, 1986, body donated to UCLA Med. Ctr.

IVERSEN, ROBERT WILLIAM, public administration educator; b. Mpls., Apr. 22, 1920; s. Wilhelm Elpheim and Ruth Bonita (Judd) I.; m. Mary Patricia Drake, Nov. 25, 1942; children—Nicholas Drake, Frederick William. B.S., U. Minn., 1942; M.A., U. Iowa, 1948, Ph.D, 1951. Instr. history U. Iowa, Iowa City, 1946-49; prof. social sci. Drake U., Des Moines, 1949-58, Pa. State U., University Park, 1959-61; dep. dir. tng. Peace Corps, Washington, 1961-63; prof. pub. adminstrn. Maxwell Sch., Syracuse U., N.Y., 1963—, dir. midcareer program, 1970—; vis. prof. history Columbia U., 1952-53; instr. Dept. State, Washington, 1980—; dir. tng. programs AID, 1969-78. Author: Communists and Schools, 1959; contbr. articles to profl. jours. Served with U.S. Army, 1942-45. Mem. Am. Soc. Pub. Adminstrn. Democrat. Home: Syracuse N.Y. Died Sept. 28, 1988.

IVES, PHILIP, architect; b. N.Y.C., Aug. 8, 1904; s. Kenneth and Edith (Appleton) I.; m. Sarah Manning Holter, Nov. 10, 1928; children—Elizabeth Ives Clark, Sarah Ives Scully, Philip Appleton. Student, Yale U., 1927. Designer, assoc. Ewing & Allen and Leigh Hill French, Jr., 1927-32; practice architecture under firm name Philip Ives, N.Y.C., 1932-87; sr. project planner FPHA, World War II. Important works include St.
Barnabas Ch., Greenwich (award Ch. Archtl. Guil
Am.), Corp. Research Lab, Sterling Forest, N.Y. (ce
tificate of merit N.Y. State Assn. Architects), Quar
Knolls Housing, Greenwich (Honor award for desig
excellence Fed. Housing and Home Finance Agy.
Chapel of St. Jude, Georgetown, Washington (Honc
award Guild for Religious Architecture), First Presby
Ch., New Canaan, Conn., Visitors' Reception Ct
Gunston Hall Plantation, Lorton, Va., guest suite
Colonial Williamsburg (Va.) Found.; Author, edito
The Nativity in Stained Glass, 1977. Bd. dirs. Ya
Alumni Fund, 1950-55. Decorated Knight Order S
John of Jerusalem. Fellow AIA; assoc. NAD; men
Archtl. League N.Y., Guild for Religious Architectu
(dir. 1976-77), Century Assn., Pilgrims of U.S., Psi U
silon. Republican. Episcopalian (vestryman 1975-78
Club: Field (Greenwich, Conn.) (past pres.). Hom
Greenwich Conn. Died July 22, 1987.

JACKSON, CLARENCE EVERT, educator, enginee
consultant; b. Graceville, Minn., Sept. 4, 1906; s. Cale
Adin and Anna Emily (Johnson) J.; m. Anne Grac
Scott, June 25, 1936; children: Sue Anne Jackson Sloa
William Evert, Jane Scott Jackson Bruss. BA wi
honors, Carleton Coll., 1927; postgrad., George Was
ington U., 1932. Registered profl. engr., Ohio. Sc
instr. Hot Springs, S.D., 1927-30; jr. metallurgist Na
Bur. Standards, Washington, 1930-37; asst. metallurgi
U.S. Naval Gun Factory, Washington, 1937-38; hea
welding sect. Naval Research Lab., Washington, 193
46; research metallurgist, head welding sect. Meta
Research Labs. Union Carbide Corp., Niagara Fall
N.Y., 1946-57; assoc. mgr., electric welding devel. Linc
Div., Newark, 1957-64; assoc. prof. welding engrin
Ohio State U., Columbus, 1964-75, prof., 1975-77, pro
emeritus, 1977-87; guest lectr. Australian Welding Ins
Sydney, 1961, Chem. Soc., U. Leeds, Eng., 1977; de
Internat. Inst. Welding, 1960-87, also chmn. sever
coms.; conferee 1st and 2d World Metall. Congresse
Am. Soc. Metals. Editor: Arc Welding, 1958; contb
author: Modern Materials, 1960, Ency. American
1962, Weldability of Steels, 1971; contbr. over 70 tec
papers to profl. lit.; holder over 50 patents in field.
Recipient Disting. Civilian Service award Sec. Nav
MacQuigg Outstanding Tchr. award, Ohio State U
1971, Alumni Achievement award Carleton Coll., 198
Meritorious Service citation Ohio State U. Coll. Eng
ing., 1987. Fellow Brit. Instn. Metallurgists, Brit. Ins
Welding (hon.); mem. Am. Welding Soc. (nat. pre
1963-64, S.W. Miller gold medal, life, C.A. Adams lect
sci arc welding 1960, R.D. Thomas award 1976), An
Soc. Metals (life), Am. Inst. Mining and Metall. Engrs
French Soc. Welding, Tau Beta Pi. Presbyn. (elder).
Home: Worthington Ohio. Died May 2, 1987; burie
Walnut Grove Cemetery, Worthington.

JACKSON, ELMORE, political scientist; b. Mareng
Ohio, Apr. 9, 1910; s. John Wesley and Cora (Osborn
J.; m. Elisabeth Averill, Dec. 26, 1934; children: Kare
J. Williams, Gail Elisabeth. BA, George Fox Coll
Newberg, Oreg., 1931; MDiv, Yale U. (Tew prize 1932
1934; Univ. fellow in Govt., Yale U., 1935-36. Ass
sec. social-indsl. sect. Am. Friends Service Com., 193
40, personnel dir., 1941-46, asst. exec. sec., 1946-4
cons. Palestine refugees UN, 1948; dir. Quaker Progra
UN, 1948-52, 53-57, 58-61; personal asst. UN Re
India, Pakistan, 1952; personal asst., polit. officer U
Rep. India, 1952-53, cons., 1953-54, spl. adviser, 195
dir. Project Survey of Middle East, Am. Friends Servic
Com., 1957-58; lectr. internat. relations Haverford Coll
1951-53; spl. asst. policy planning to asst. sec. sta
internat. orgn. affairs Dept. State, 1961-64, spl. asst.
asst. sec. state for internat. orgn. affairs, 1964-66, cons
1966-69, mem. adv. com. on internat. orgns., 1972-7
adviser U.S. del. 16th-18th UN Gen. Assemblies; v.
policy studies UN Assn. U.S.A., 1966-73; full time con
Rockefeller Found., 1973-77; spl. adv. Aspen Ins
Humanistic Studies, 1978-81. Author: Meeting
Minds, 1952, Middle East Mission, 1983; contbr. a
ticles to profl. jours. Mem. corp. Haverford Coll.
Mem. Council Fgn. Relations. Clubs: Yale, Centur
Assn. Home: Newtown Pa. Died Jan. 17, 1989; burie
Wrightstown Friends Meeting, Wrightstown, Pa.

JACKSON, JOHN NELSON, lawyer; b. Brownwoo
Tex., Apr. 28, 1905; s. Charles Young and Kate Venab
(Wood) J.; m. Sallie Bell Gaston, May 17, 1935; chi
dren: Gertrude Gaston (Mrs. Robert Bush Smither, Jr.
Sallie Bell Flippen (Mrs. Nowell E. Loop). Studen
Howard Payne Coll., 1922-24; LL.B. with highe
honors, U. Tex., 1927. Bar: Tex. 1927. Practiced law
Ft. Worth, 1927-30; assoc., ptnr., of counsel Coke
Coke, Dallas, 1930-84; of counsel Carrington, Sloma
Slocam & Blumenthal, Dallas, 1985-86. Trustee Lelan
Fikes Found., Dallas Symphony Found., 1980-84. men
Dallas County Heritage Soc., chmn., 1978; hon. trust
Heard Mus.; trustee, past chmn. Friends of Dalla
Public Library; hon. trustee Goals for Dallas; trust
Univ. Med. Ctr. Inc. Recipient Founders Cup awa
Dallas County Heritage Soc., 1976; United Wa
Voluntarism award, 1979; Dallas Hist. Soc. awar
1984. Fellow Am. Bar Found., Tex. Bar Found., Ar
Coll. Probate Counsel; mem. Southwestern Leg
Found. (former vice chmn., now hon. trustee), Interna
Bar Assn., ABA, Dallas Bar Assn. (pres. 1959), Wor
Assn. Lawyers, State Bar Tex., Am. Soc. Internat. Lav
Am. Judicature Soc., Mexican Acad. Internat. Lav
Am. Law Inst., Internat. Acad. Estate and Trust Lav

SAR, S.C.V., Mil. Order Stars and Bars, Chancellors, Order of Coif, Phi Gamma Delta, Phi Delta Phi, Pi Kappa Delta. Episcopalian. Clubs: Northwood, City, Idlewild, Petroleum, Shakespeare (hon.), Codrington (hon.). Lodge: Mason. Home: Dallas Tex. Died Sept. 22, 1986; buried Greenwood Cemetery, Dallas.

JACKSON, LEE R., manufacturing executive; b. Akron, Ohio, 1891; s. Ralph D. and Emma (Daily) J.; m. Gladys Tuttle, May 3, 1919. Ed., U. Akron, 1912. With sales dept. Firestone Tire and Rubber Co., 1912; salesman Firestone Tire and Rubber Co., Detroit, 1913; dist. mgr. Firestone Tire and Rubber Co., Grand Rapids, Mich., 1916-18, Indpls., 1919; div. mgr. Pacific Coast Firestone Tire and Rubber Co., 1920, div. mgr. N.W., 1921; in charge mfrs.'s sales Firestone Tire and Rubber Co., Detroit, 1922; mgr. mfrs.'s sales Firestone Tire and Rubber Co., Akron, 1926; mgr. gen. sales Firestone Tire and Rubber Co., 1927, v.p., 1929-41, exec. v.p., 1941-48, pres., 1948-57, vice chmn. bd., from 1957. Chmn. bd. U. Akron, 1944-55. Mem. Masons, Shriners, Portage Country Club, University Club, Detroit Club, Detroit Athletic Club, Detroit Golf Club, Pepper Pike Country Club, Union Club, Bath Club, Surf Club, Rolling Rock Club. Republican. Methodist. Home: Akron Ohio. †

JACOB, FREDERICK MURRAY, dermatologist; b. Pitts., Mar. 6, 1892; s. William Henry and Mary Ann (Murray) J.; m. Regina Frauenheim, Apr. 14, 1921; children: Mary, Regina, Walter Lindsay, Edward Frauenheim, Frederick. MD, U. Pitts., 1913. Lab. resident Mercy Hosp., Pitts., 1914-15; Mellow fellow in pathology U. Pitts., 1915-16, instr. immunology, 1916-17; asst. in dermatology Washington U., St. Louis, 1919-20; from instr. to prof., chmn. dept. dermatology Washington U., from 1959. Lt. M.C., U.S. Army, World War I. Mem. AMA, Pa., Allegheny County med. assns., Am. Dermatol. Assn., University Club, Alpha Omega Alpha. Roman Catholic. †

JACOB, PHILIP ERNEST, political science educator; b. Istanbul, Turkey, July 12, 1914; s. Ernest Otto and Sarah Orilla (Conard) J.; m. Betty Muller, Dec. 24, 1935; children: Sarah Elizabeth, Albert Kirk, Stephen Philip. BA, Yale U., 1935; MA, U. Pa., 1939; PhD, Princeton U., 1941. Sec. Am. Friends Service Com., Phila., 1936-38, 41-45; tchr. polit. sci. Princeton, 1939-40, rsch. radio propaganda, 1940-41; mem. faculty internat. law and orgn., prof. polit. sci. U. Pa., Phila., 1945-71, dir. summer sch., also coll. collateral courses, 1950-57, dir. Internat Studies Values in Politics, 1964-71; prof. polit. sci. U. Hawaii, Honolulu, 1970-80, prof. emeritus, 1980-85; lectr. polit. sci. Swarthmore (Pa.) Coll., 1946-55; co-dir. Ford Found. grant rsch. on social values and pub. policy, 1960-65; sr. fellow East-West Ctr., 1969, 76-77, rsch. assoc., 1977-78; co-investigator, U.S. rep. Multi-Nat. study of Automation and Indsl. Workers, 1972-85; internat. coordinator Multi-nat. Comparative Studies of Leadership, Participation and Local Govt. Performance, 1979-85; dir. Stein Rokkan Internat. Comparative Archive. Author: (with Childs, Whitton) Propaganda by Short Wave, 1942, (with M. Sibley) Conscription of Conscience, 1952, Changing Values in College, 1957, (with J. Flink) Values and Their Function in Decision-Making, 1962, (with A. Atherton), The Dynamics of International Organization, 1965, 72, (with others) The Integration of Political Communities, 1964, Values and the Active Community, 1971, The City in Comparative Perspective, 1977, Cross-National Comparative Survey Research, 1977, Bonds Without Bondage: Cultural Relations of the Future, 1978, Automation and Industrial Workers, 3 vols., 1980-83. Recipient Franklin D. Roosevelt Found. award, 1953. Fellow Nat. Coun. on Religion in Higher Edn.; mem. Internat. Studies Assn., AAUP, Phi Beta Kappa. Mem. Soc. of Friends. Home: Kailia Hawaii. Died June 19, 1985; buried Salt Spring Island, B.C., Canada.

JACOBS, JAMES NAJEEB, school system administrator; b. Tonawanda, N.Y., Mar. 4, 1930; s. Leo and Sofea (Johns) J.; m. Suzanne A. Hetzel, July 26, 1969; children: Lance, Thor, Lars. BA in Psychology, Mich. State U., 1951, MA in Guidance and Counseling, 1952, EdD in Founds. of Edn., 1957. With Cin. Pub. Schs., 1954-85, examiner, 1954-61, assoc. dir. evaluation services, 1962-65, dir. program rsch. and design, 1965-73, asst. supt. rsch. and devel., 1973-76, supt. schs., 1976-85; mem. com. rsch. and devel. Cin. Coll. Bd.; tchr. Fletcher Elem. Sch., Tonawanda, 1951, Hughes Evening Sch., Cin., 1955; assoc. prof. coll. edn. U. Cin., 1960; vis. asst .prof. U. Md., 1960; adj. assoc. prof. Ohio State U., 1971; UNESCO cons. ednl.stats. Iraq Ministry of Edn., 1961-62; cons. U.S. Office Edn., Nat. Inst. Edn., Tex. Ednl. Renewal Ctr., Lansing (Mich.) Pub. Schs., Ohio State Evaluation Ctr., others; field agt. Mich. Dept. Vocat. Rehab., 1953; presenter/participant Urban Supts. Network, Nat. Inst. Edn., 1979-85. Editorial bd. Jour. Ednl. Measurement, 1972, Measurement and Evaluation in Guidance, 1969-76; editor Jour. Program Rsch. and Devel., Cin. Pub. Schs., 1972; contbr. numerous articles to profl. jours. Counselor Boys Reformatory Sch., N.Y., 1952; bd. dirs. Cin. Ednl. TV Found., Appalachia Ednl. Lab., Ctr. Econ. Edn., Jr. Achievement Greater Cin.; mem. community adv. bd. Paul I. Hoxworth Blood Ctr.; adv. council Miami U., Oxford, Ohio. Named Educator of Year award Ohio PTA, 1981, Dan Tehan award March of Dimes, 1978. Mem. Am. Personnel and Guidance Assn., Ohio Assn. Supervision and Curriculum Devel. (rsch. com.), Nat. Council Measurement in Edn., Am. Ednl. Rsch. Assn. , Am. Assn. Sch. Adminstrs, Cincinnatus Assn. Republican. Presbyterian. Home: Cincinnati Ohio. Died May 26, 1985; buried Cin.

JACOBS, MORRIS ELIAS, advertising executive; b. Omaha, Aug. 7, 1896; s. Nathaniel Elias and Gertrude (Shafton) J.; m. Rae Sara Iseman, Sept. 15, 1927; 1 dau., Susie. Student, U. Mo., 1914-16; LL.D., Creighton U., 1954, St. Joseph's Coll., 1960. Reporter Des Moines Register-Tribune, 1917-18; reporter, feature writer Omaha Daily Bee, Omaha Daily News, 1918-20; cons. Bozell & Jacobs Advt. and Pub. Relations Agy., Omaha, 1922-80; dir. Omaha Downtown Parking Assn. Mem. exec. com. Omaha Indsl. Found., 1953-87; pres. State Bd. Edn., 1955-57; active Boy Scouts Am.; chmn. Nat. Planning Com. for Coop. Electric Refrigeration Bur., 1931-33; mem. exec. com. Pub. Utilities Advt. Assn., 1932-36; co-chmn. initial gifts com. Jewish Philanthropies, 1939; mem., vice chmn. midwest region Am.-Jewish Joint Distbn. Com., 1940; mem. bd. electors Hall of Fame of Omaha U.; chmn. Jewish Philanthropies campaign for war relief and refugees, 1940; pres. W. Central States regional conf. Jewish Fedns. and Welfare Funds, 1941; del. Am. Jewish Conf., 1943; mem. nat. exec. com. Am. Jewish Com.; chmn. Com. of '52 Found.; Bd. dirs. Children's Meml. Hosp., Omaha Symphony Orch. Found.; nat. bd. dirs. United Service Orgn.; trustee Clarkson Hosp., St. Joseph Coll.; bd. dirs. Omaha YMCA, Nat. Conf. Christians and Jews; bd. regents Creighton U.; trustee chmn. 1954 Omaha Centennial Celebration, selected King Ak-Sar-Ben LX, 1954; nat. chmn. U. Mo. Sch. Journalism 50 year commemoration. Recipient B'nai B'rith Americanism citation, 1953; Beth Israel Synagogue, Neb. Wesleyan U., 1957. Mem. Am. Legion (life), Alpha Delta Sigma, Delta Sigma Chi, Zeta Beta Tau (asso.). Republican. Jewish (pres. temple 1940-41). Home: Coronado Calif. Died Feb. 22, 1987; cremated.

JACOBS, NATHAN ELLIS, advertising executive; b. Omaha, Dec. 21, 1901; s. Elias N. and Gertrude (Shafton) J.; m. Gladys Brandeis, Feb. 5, 1966; children: Anthony Smith, Linda (Mrs. Homer L. Bennett, Jr.). BJ, U. Mo., 1924. Reporter Omaha Daily News, 1924, comml. editor, 1925; v.p. Bozell & Jacobs Inc., advt. and pub. rels. agy., Omaha, 1925-34, v.p., mgr. Chgo. office, 1934-40, pres. Ill. corp., 1940-65; creator, mng. dir. Nat. Flower Week, 1945-50, Nat. Beauty Salon Week, 1950-79; creator Cosmetology Hall of Fame, 1964; pub. rels. counselor Nat. Hairdressers and Cosmetologists Assn. Chmn. Chgo. chpt. Am. Jewish com,; chmn. pub. rels. commn. of 50th Anniversary U. Mo. Sch. Journalism; bd. dirs. Jewish Welfare Bd.; pres., dir. Ill. Citizens for Eisenhower; bd. govs. United Rep. Fund Ill. Mem. Pub. Rels. Soc. Am., Def. Orientation Conf. Assn., Hai Resh (editor mag. 1926, nat. pres. 1927-28), Highland Country Club, Plaza Club, Capitol Hill Club (Washington), Nat. Press Club (Washington), Masons, B'nai B'rith, Kappa Beta Phi, Zeta Beta Tau (nat. v.p. 1940), Theta Nu Epsilon, Pi Tau Pi. Home: Omaha Nebr. Died May 12, 1988.

JACOBS, NATHAN L., judge; b. Feb. 28, 1905; m. Bernidine Rosenbaum; children: Ellen Coburn, Nancy Grossman. BS, U. Pa., 1925; LLB magna cum laude, Harvard U., 1928, SJD, 1931. Bar: N.J. 1928. Mem. firm Arthur T. Vanderbilt, 1928-34, Frazer, Stoffer & Jacobs, Newark, 1934-48; chief dep. commr., counsel D. Frederick Burnett, N.J. State commr. alcoholic beverage control, 1934-39; prof. adminstrv. law Rutgers U., 1929-48; chmn. state arbitration bd. Bell Telephone Co.-Telephone Workers Union of N.J., 1947; sr. judge Appellate Div. N.J. Superior Ct., 1948-52; assoc. justice N.J. Supreme Ct., 1948-52, 52-75. Del., vice chmn. jud. com. N.J. Constl. Conv., 1947; chmn. adv. coun. Inst. Mgmt. and Labor Relations, Rutgers U., 1947-48. Recipient Sears prize, 1927; Judah P. Benjamin fellowship, 1930-31. Mem. Am., N.J. State, Essex County bar assns. Home: Livingston N.J. Died Jan. 25, 1989.

JACOBSON, ROBERT, editor; b. Racine, Wis., July 28, 1940; s. Joseph and Frances (Barr) J. B.A. in English, U. Wis., 1962; postgrad. musicology, Columbia U., 2-63. Asst. editor Musical Am., 1963; freelance editor 1963-65; editor Lincoln Ctr. program Sat. Rev., 1965-73, Opera News, N.Y.C., from 1974, Ballet News, 1979-86; freelance music and dance critic Cue mag., 1973-76; freelance contbr. After Dark, 1969-79; contbg. editor L'Officiel, 1977-79, Ovation, from 1980. Author: Interviews with the World's Leading Musicians, 1974, Opera People, 1982, Magnificence, Onstage at the Met, 1985; also numerous articles, record liner notes; broadcaster: Met. Opera broadcasts Met. Opera Live, Live from Lincoln Center (PBS), also syndicated program First Hearing; lectr. in field. Home: New York N.Y. Died May 1987.

JACOBY, ROBERT BIRD, lawyer; b. Marion, Ohio, July 2, 1906; s. John Wilbur and Edna Leora (Bird) J.; m. Alice Helen Matthias, June 25, 1938; children—Robert Matthias, Richard Matthias. A.B., Ohio Wesleyan U., 1928; LL.B., Harvard, 1931. Bar: Ohio bar 1932, U.S. Dist. Ct. for D.C 1944, U.S. Supreme Ct 1945. Practiced law Jacoby and Jacoby, Marion, 1932; asso. Taft, Stettinius and Hollister, Cin., 1933-40; counsel Fed. Home Loan Bank of Cin., 1933-40; asso. gen. counsel Fed. Savs. and Loan Ins. Corp., Washington, 1941-46; dep. gov. Fed. Home Loan Bank System, 1946-47, became acting gov., Dec. 1947; with office chief counsel Bur. Internal Revenue, 1948-74; Lectr. Am. Savs. and Loan Inst., 1937-40. Co-author: Cyclopedia of Federal Savings and Loan Associations, 1939; Contbr. articles to savs. and loan pubs. Mem. ABA, Ohio State Bar Assn. (past pres.), Fed. Bar Assn., Washington Bar Assn., Phi Gamma Delta. Democrat. Methodist. Club: Harvard (Washington), Nat. Press, Cosmos, Internat. Home: Washington D.C. Died Apr. 20, 1987.

JACUZZI, ALDO JOSEPH, pump company executive; b. Berkeley, Calif., Apr. 26, 1921; s. Joseph and Rena (Beggio) J.; m. Granuccia Maria Amadei, Apr. 26, 1942; children—Roy Aldo, Victor Steven, Rita Carol. Student, Armstrong Bus. Coll., Berkeley. With Jacuzzi Bros. Inc., Berkeley, Calif., 1939-80, v.p. purchasing, 1965-70, chmn. bd., 1970-80, dir. Can. expansion project, 1951-54, cons., 1980-88; dir. Jacuzzi Mex. S.A., Jacuzzi Domestic Internat. Sales Corp. Active local Boy Scouts Am., Ark. Art Ctr., Salvation Army, Girl Scouts, United Way. With USNR, 1944-46. Mem. Ark. Hall of Fame. Mem. Ednl. Athletic Scholarship Assn., Ark. Auto Assn., Ark. Community Concert Assn., Little Rock C. of C., Leonardo da Vinci Soc., Sons of Italy, Serra Club, Little Rock Club, Capital Club. Democrat. Roman Catholic. Home: Little Rock Ark. Died Feb. 21, 1989.

JAFFRAY, CLIVE PALMER, investment banker; b. Mpls., Jan. 15, 1892; s. Clive Talbot and Madeleine (Palmer) J.; m. Harriet Turnham, June 22, 1925; children: Clive Palmer, James Freeman, Harriet Jaffray. Grad., Hotchkiss Sch., 1909; PhB, Yale U., 1912. Ptnr. Piper, Jaffray & Hopwood, Mpls., from 1932; bd. dirs. Green Giant Co., Marquette Corp., Twin City Fire Ins. Co. Mem. exec. com. Minn. Orchestral Assn. Mem. Minneapolis Club, Minikahda Club, Woodhill Country Club. Home: Minneapolis Minn. †

JAGENDORF, MORITZ ADOLPH, author; b. Czernowite, Austria, Aug. 24, 1888; came to U.S., 1903, naturalized, 1934; s. Samuel Getzel and Augusta (Fuss) J.; m. Sophie Sheba Sokolosky, Aug. 24, 1920; children: Merna Paula, André-Tridon. Student, Yale U., 19807, Columbia U., 1908-12, Columbia Dental Coll., 1916, Sorbonne U., 1922. Author: books for children including Noodlehead Stories, 1957, The Ghost of Peg-Leg Peter, 1965, Ghostly Folktales, 1967, Kwina the Eagle and Other Indian Tales, 1967, Folkstories of the South, 1972; adapted plays from French and Spanish including The Farce of Pierre Patelin, 1916, The Pie and the Tart, 1930, The Pastrybaker, 1931, The Cave of Salamanca, 1932, Jeppe of the Hills, 1932, Stories and Lore of the Zodiac; dir. Free Theatre, N.Y.C., 1920-24, Children's Palyhouse, N.Y.C., 1920. Deocrated Commandeur de Chevalier du Tastevin, Officier de Chain de Rotisseurs. Mem. N.Y. Story League (pres. 1967-76), Am. Folklore Soc., N.Y. Folklore Soc. (past pres.), Internat. Folklore Cong. (v.p. from 1967), Les Amis d' Escoffier Soc., Yale Club. Home: New York N.Y. Deceased.

JALBERT, EUGENE LOUIS, lawyer, judge; b. Arctic, R.I., Apr. 20, 1885; s. Joseph and Julie (Danis) J.; m. Nathalie H. Moreau, Nov. 28, 1912; children: Marie Heloise, Louis Eugene (dec.), Julienne Lillianne, Jean d'Arc, Eugene Oscar, Roland Arthur. BLitt, Laval U., 1904, LLD, 1942; B Jurisprudence magna cum laude, Boston U., 1910. Bar: R.I. 1909. Pvt. practice Woonsocket, R.I., from 1909; gen. counsel, bd. dirs. L'Union St. Jean-Baptiste d'Amerique, 1921-54; in mfg. bus. 1923-32; city solicitor City of Woonsocket, 1933; assoc. justice Superior Ct. R.I. Mem. ABA, R.I., Woonsocket bar assns., R.I. Club, Phi Delta Phi. Republican. Roman Catholic. Home: Woonsocket R.I. †

JAMES, CHARLES FRANKLIN, lawyer; b. Fayetteville, N.C., Oct. 11, 1919; s. Charles Fernando and Mary (Wellons) J.; m. Bette Conwill James, Apr. 2, 1943; children: Charles F., Jennifer. BA, Colo. Coll., 1948; LLB, U. Colo., 1951. Bar: Colo. 1951, Md. 1956, D.C. 1972. Pvt. practice Sterling, Colo. and Bethesda, Md., 1951-53, 57-59; atty-adv. Tax Ct. of U.S., 1960-61; with Fed. Nat. Mortgage Assn., Washington, 1961-87, asst. gen. counsel, 1969-71, assoc. gen. counsel, 1971-87, corp. sec., 1974-87. Lt. comdr. USNR, 1941-46, 53-57. Mem. ABA, Md. Bar Assn., D.C. Bar Assn., Am. Soc. Corp. Secs., Stock Transfer Assn., Nat. Assn. Corp. Dirs. Republican. Home: Potomac Md. Died Jan. 5, 1987; buried Arlington Nat. Cemetery, Washington.

JAMES, ERIC G., educator; b. Jamaica, Aug. 6, 1910; came to U.S., 1928, naturalized, 1928; s. Daniel Emanuel and Ella (Henry) J.; m. Beryl Theodore Clarke, Apr. 6, 1958; 1 child, Terri. BA, McGill U., 1941; MA, NYU, 1948, PhD, 1956. Dr. lectr. pub. adminstrn. U. W.I., Jamaica, 1949-52; adviser labor relations to Jamaic; mem. Jamaica Planning Bd., Ministry of Trade and Industry, 1952-56; instr. govt. Bklyn. Coll.; lectr. pub. adminstrn. NYU, 1956-59; UN sr adviser in adminstrn. to Republic of Sudan 1959-63; assoc. prof. internat. affairs U. Pitts., 1963-64; dean Manhattan Community Coll. CUNY, 1964-67, 71-73, prof. pub.

adminstrn. Baruch Coll., 1973-80; assoc. dir. U.S. AID Mission to Liberia, U.S. Dept. State, 1967-69, dep. dir., 1969-71. Mem. adv. coun. Internat. Study and Rsch. Inst., 1964-88. 2d lt. USAAF, 1942-44. Fulbright scholar, 1978-79. Fellow Am. Sociol. Assn.; mem. Am. Acad. Polit. and Social Sci., Am. Polit. Sci. Assn., Soc. Internat. Devel., Soc. Applied Anthropology, Brit. Inst. Pub. Adminstrn., Internat. Personnel Mgmt. Assn., Am. Soc. Pub. Adminstrn. Home: Melville N.Y. Died Sept. 22, 1988; buried Woodlawn Cemetery, N.Y.C.

JAMES, FLEMING, JR., law educator; b. Shanghai, China, Mar. 26, 1904; (parents Am. citizens); s. Fleming and Rebecca (Godwin) J.; m. Harriet Fairchild, June 26, 1930; children: Fleming, Sarah; m. 2d Ruth Kaubisch, Nov. 23, 1948. AB, Yale U., 1925, LLB, 1928; LLD (hon.), U. Lund, Sweden, 1968, U. Chgo., 1968. Bar: Conn. 1928. Mem. law dept. N.Y., N.H. & H. R.R. Co., 1929-33; assoc. prof. Yale U., New Haven, 1933-38, prof. law, 1938-41, Lafayette S. Foster prof. law, 1941-68, Sterling prof. law, 1968-72; acting dean U. Utah Sch. Law, 1939-40; dir. litigation div. OPA nat. office, 1943-45; vis. prof. law Harvard, 1957-58, univs. Stockholm, Uppsala, Lund (Sweden), 1968, U. London, 1971, U. Conn., 1972-80. Co-author: Cases on Trial Judments and Appeals, 1936, Cases and Materials on Torts, 1942, Law of Torts, 1956; author: Civil Procedure, 1964; advisor: Reporter, Torts Restatement; contbr. articles on torts and civil procedure to profl. jours. Mem. North Haven Bd. Edn., 1938-42, Zoning Commn., 1936-39, Town Plan Commn., 1946-47; chmn. conn. Bd. Labor Rels., 1955-81; Dem. candidate for state senator, 1938, 50; town chmn. North Haven, 1946-48. Mem. ABA, Conn. Bar Assn., New Haven County Bar Assn., Corbey Ct. Club, Phi Beta Kappa, Phi Delta Phi. Home: North Haven Conn. Died Aug. 23, 1981.

JAMES, JOSEPH B., political scientist, educator; b. Clearwater, Fla., July 17, 1912; s. L.P. and Ilah J. (Miles) J.; m. Jacquelyn McWhite, June 8, 1937; children: Glenn Joseph, William Bruce. B.A.E., U. Fla., 1934, M.A., 1935; Ph.D., U. Ill., 1939. Instr. gen. extension div. U. Fla., 1935-36; asst. and fellow U. Ill., 1936-39; head dept. history and polit. sci. Williamsport Dickinson Jr. Coll., 1939-40, Union Coll., Ky., 1940-43; dean of faculty William Woods Coll., 1943-45; head dept. social studies Miss. State Coll. for Women, 1945-58; dean of coll. Wesleyan Coll., Macon, Ga., 1958-71, Callaway prof. polit. sci., 1971-80, prof. emeritus, 1980-86; vis. prof. summer sessions U. Fla., U. Miss., Florence (Ala.) State Tchrs. Coll., Middle Tenn. State Coll. Author: The Framing of the Fourteenth Amendment, 1956, rev. edit., 1965, Ratification of the Fourteenth Amendment, 1984; contbr. to scholarly jours. and reference publs. Mem. So. Polit. Sci. Assn., Ga. Polit. Sci. Assn. (past mem. exec. council), Am. Acad. Polit. Sci., So. Hist. Assn., Assn. Coll. Honor Socs. (council), Phi Beta Kappa (past pres. Middle Ga. Grad. Assn.), Phi Kappa Phi (past pres. Wesleyan chpt.), Kappa Delta Pi, Kappa Phi Kappa, Pi Gamma Mu (nat. pres. emeritus, trustee). Methodist. Lodge: Rotary. Home: Macon Ga. Died Jan. 21, 1986; interred Riverside Cemetery, Macon, Ga.

JAMES, RICHARD VERNON, educator, engineer; b. Piatt County, Ill., June 20, 1892; s. Lewis Carpenter and Mary Belle (Tresenriter) J.; m. Ethel Henrietta Ernst, Oct. 15, 1919; children: Richard Ernst, Rhoda Jane (Mrs. Benjamin C. Singleton Jr.). BS, U. Okla., 1918; MS, U. Ill., 1928. Mem. faculty dept. mechanics U. Okla., from 1920, prof., chmn. dept. gen. engring., from 1937, prof. theoretical and applied mechanics; mem. Okla. State Bd. Registration for Profl. Engrs., 1942-52, chmn., 1946, 51. 2d lt. Am. Expeditionary Force, 1918-19. Mem. NSPE, Okla. Soc. Profl. Engrs., Am. Soc. Engring. Edn., Am. Assn. Engrs., Masons, Sigma Tau, Tau Beta Pi. Home: Norman Okla. †

JAMIESON, DONALD CAMPBELL, Canadian diplomat; b. St. John's, Nfld., Can., Apr. 20, 1921; s. Charles and Isabelle (Bennett) J.; m. Barbara Elizabeth Oakley, Dec. 20, 1946; children: Donna, Heather, Roger, Debbie. Student, Prince of Wales Coll., St. John's; LLD, Meml. U., 1970. Mem. Nfld. Legislature, 1979; leader Liberal Party in Nfld., 1979; leader of the opposition 1979-80; mem. Can. House of Commons, 1966-70, 72-76, minister of def. prodn., 1968, minister of transport, 1969, minister of regional econ. expansion, 1972-75, minister of indsl. trade and commn., 1975-76, minister of external affairs, 1976-79; Can. high commr. to Britain London, from 1983; mem. consultative com. on pvt. broadcasting Bd. Broadcast Govs.; mem. com. on broadcasting Troika Com., 1963; past. dir. broadcast news, past chmn. affiliates sect. network adv. com. CBC. Author: The Troubled Air, 1966. Past chmn. fin. com. Can. Cancer Soc. Mem. Can. Assn. Broadcasters (pres. 1961-64), City Club. Liberal. Presbyterian. Home: Saint John's Nfld., Canada. Died Nov. 19. 1986.

JANOWITZ, MORRIS, sociology educator; b. Paterson, N.J., Oct. 22, 1919; s. Samuel Louis and Rose (Myers) J.; m. Gayle Arlene Shulenberger, Dec. 22, 1951; children—Rebecca, Naomi. A.B., NYU, 1941; Ph.D.in Sociology, U. Chgo., 1948; Docteur Honoris Causus, U. Toulouse, 1977. Research asst. Library Congress, Washington, 1941; propaganda analyst Dept. Justice, Washington, 1941-43; instr. then asst. prof. The Coll. U. Chgo., 1947-51, vis. prof. Grad. Sch. Bus., 1961, prof. sociology, 1962-73, disting. service prof., 1973-87, prof. emeritus, 1987—, dir. Ctr. Social Organ Studies, 1962-73, chmn. dept. sociology, 1967-72; from asst. prof. to prof. sociology U. Mich., Ann Arbor, 1951-61; cons. to govt. and pvt. agys.; Pitt prof. Pet House U. Cambridge, 1972-73; mem. social sci. adv. bd. U.S. Arms Control and Disarmament Bd.; chmn. Inter-Univ. Seminar on Armed Forces and Soc. Author: The Professional Soldier, 1950, Social Change and Prejudice, 1964, Political Conflict, 1970, Institution Building in Urban Education, 1971, Black Sociologist, 1974, Social Conflict of the Welfare State, 1975, The Last Half-Century: Societal Change and Politics in America, 1978, The Reconstruction of Patriotism, 1983; editor: Heritage Sociology Series, U. Chgo., 1964-87, Armed Forces and Society: Interdisciplinary Jour., 1975-87; mem. editorial bd. Am. Jour. Sociology, 1962. Served to 2d lt. AUS, 1943-46. Decorated Purple Heart, Bronze Star; Fulbright research prof. U. Frankfurt, Germany, 1954-55; fellow Ctr. Advanced Study Behavioral Scis., Stanford, Calif., 1958-59; Guggenheim fellow, 1976. Fellow Am. Acad. Arts and Scis.; mem. Am. Sociol. Assn. (v.p. 1970-71, Career of Disting. Service award 1985), Am. Polit. Sci. Assn., Internat. Sociol. Assn. (research council), Phi Beta Kappa. Democrat. Home: Chicago Ill. Died Nov. 7, 1988; buried Ft. Sheridan Cemetery, Highland Park, Ill.

JARCHOW, CHRISTIAN E., corporation executive; b. Chgo., Jan. 24, 1891; m. Gladys Runyon, May 24, 1918; children: Willard R., Lawrence E. With Internat. Harvester Co., 1914-58, successively gen. auditor, asst. comptroller, comptroller, v.p. and comptroller, 1920-52, dir., 1947-58, exec. v.p., 1952-58; bd. dirs., chmn. bd. Wilmette State Bank (Ill.), Voi-Shan Industries, Los Angeles, Ill. Power Co., Decatur, Aladdin Industries, Nashville, Aladdin Industries Ltd., Greenford, Eng. Mem. task force budget and acctg., Hoover Commn., bd. trustees Village of Wilmette, 1937-41, bd. edn. New Trier Twp. High Sch., Winnetka, Ill., 1943-41, pres. bd., 1947-51; pres. bd. trustees Nat. Coll. Edn., Evanston, Ill. With Signal Corps, U.S. Army, World War I. Mem. Controllers Inst. Am. (pres. 1947-48, chmn. bd. 1948-49), Ill. Soc. CPAs, Chicago Athletic Club, Westmoreland Country Club, Michigan Shores Club (Wilmette); Three Lakes (Wis.) Rod and Gun Club, Beta Alpha Psi, Beta Gamma Sigma. Home: Wilmette Ill. †

JARVIS, HOWARD ARNOLD, association executive; b. Magna, Utah, Sept. 22, 1902; s. John Ransome J.; m. Estelle Jarvis. Formerly owner, pub. Magna Times and chain of 11 weekly newspapers, Utah; later with a chem. factior, an aluminum foundry and a noise-prevention pad mfg. factory, Oakland, Calif.; later owner Femco Corp.; ret. from bus. 1962; exec. dir. Apt. Assn. of Los Angeles County and United Orgns. of Taxpayers; founder Am. Tax Reduction Movement. Co-author: I'm Mad as Hell, 1979. Active in Rep. politics including Midwest regional campaign mgr. Eisenhower campaign, 1952, 56, Western states mgr. Richard Nixon campaign, 1960. Mem. Utah Press Assn. (past pres.). Home: Los Angeles Calif. Died Aug. 12, 1986.

JASPER, MARTIN THEOPHILUS, mechanical engineering educator; b. Hazlehurst, Miss., Mar. 19, 1934; s. Thomas Theophilus and Alice Maie (Norton) J.; m. Mary Altha Ledbetter, Nov. 2, 1963; children—Nellie Rebecca, Alice Hesta, Martin Theophilus, Mary Margaret, William Richard. B.S., Miss. State U., 1955, M.S., 1962; postgrad., Stevens Inst. Tech., 1963; Ph.D., U. Ala., 1967. Registered profl. engr., Miss. Engr. Am. Cast Iron Pipe Co., Birmingham, Ala., 1955-56; plant metallurigist Vickers, Inc., Jackson, Miss., 1957-59; sr. design engr. missile div. Chrysler Corp., Huntsville, Ala., 1959-60; instr. mech. engring. Miss. State U., 1960-63, asst. prof., 1966-68, assoc. prof., 1968-75, prof., 1975-88. Contbr. articles to profl. jours. Served to 2d lt., M.S.C. AUS, 1956-57. NSF fellow, 1963; NASA fellow, 1963-66. Mem. ASME (chmn. Miss. sect. 1971-72), Soc. Mfg. Engrs. (chpt. chmn. 1969-70, chmn. nat. research edn. grants com. 1974-75), Am. Soc. Engring. Edn., Miss. Acad. Sci., N.Y. Acad. Sci., Sigma Xi, Pi Mu Epsilon, Tau Beta Pi, Pi Tau Sigma. Democrat. Presbyterian. Lodges: Masons, K.T, Shriners, Kiwanis. Died Aug. 11, 1988; buried Odd Fellow's Cemetery, Starkville, Miss.

JASPERS, KARL, philosopher, psychiatrist; b. Oldenburg, Germany, Feb. 23, 1883; s. Karl and Henriette (Tantzen) J.; m. Gertrud Mayer, 1910. Ed., univs. of Heidelberg, Munich, Berlin and Göttingen; MD, 1909; D es lettres honoris causa, U. Paris, U. Lausanne, U. Geneva; MD honoris causa, U. Basel; PhD honoris causa, U. Heidelberg. Asst. Psychiat. Clinic, Heidelberg, Germany, 1910; lectr. in philosophy U. Heidelberg, 1913-16, asst. prof., 1916-21, prof., 1921-48, dismissed by Nazi govt., 1937, reinstated, 1945; prof. U. Basel, Switzerland, 1949-61, prof. emeritus, 1961-69; leader in existential thought. Author: General Psycholpathology, 1913, Man in the Modern Age, 1931, Philosophie, 3 vols., 1932, Max Weber, 1932, Reason and Existence, 1935, Nietzsche, 1936, Descartes, 1937, Existenzphilosophie, 1938, Nietzsche and Christianity, 1946, The Question of German Guilt, 1947, On the Origin and Goal of History, 1950, Reason and Anti-reason in Our Time, 1950, Way to Wisdom, 1950, Tragedy is Not Enough, 1952, Leonardo, 1953, Entmythologisierung, 1954, The Great Philosophers, 1957, Philosophy and the World, 1958, The Future of Mankind, 1958, Der philosophische Glaube angesichts der Offenbarung, 1962, Nicolaus Cusanus, 1964, Wohin Treibt die Bundesrepublik?, 1966. Recipient Goethe prize, 1947, Peace prize Deutsches Buchhandel, 1948. Mem. Netherlands Soc. for Psychiatry and Neurology (hon.), Soc. German Neurologists and Psychiatrists (hon.), Royal Medico-Psychol. Assn. (hon.), Acad. Scis (corr.). Died 1969.

JAVITS, JACOB KOPPEL, U.S. senator, lawyer; b. N.Y.C., May 18, 1904; s. Morris and Ida (Littman) J.; m. Marian Ann Borris, Nov. 30, 1947; children: Joy D., Joshua M., Carla I. LLB, NYU, 1926; 37 hon. degrees. Bar: N.Y. 1927. Pvt. practice N.Y.C., from 1927; mem. 80th-83d congresses 21st N.Y. Dist.; dist. atty. gen. New York, 1955-57; U.S. senator New York, 1957-80; ranking minority mem. Labor and Human Resources Com., Joint Econ. Com., mem. Fgn. Relations Com., Govt. Affairs Com; mem. firm Javits, Trubin, Sillcocks and Edelman, N.Y.C., 1958-71; of counsel Trubin Sillcocks, Edelman and Knapp, N.Y.C., from 1981; adj. prof. public affairs Columbia U., N.Y.C., from 1981; adj. prof. SUNY-StonyBrook, from 1982; chmn. No. Atlantic Assembly's Polit. Com., Com. of Nine, Parliamentarian's Com. for Less Developed Nations; U.S. del. to 25th anniversary UN Gen. Assembly, 1970; mem. Nat. Commn. Marijuana and Drug Abuse, 1971-73; lectr. on econ. and polit. subjects. Author: A Proposal to Amend the Anti-Trust Laws, 1939, Discrimination U.S.A., 1960, Order of Battle, A Republican's Call to Reason, 1964, Who Makes War, 1973, Javits: The Autobiobraphy of a Public Man, 1981; series of articles on polit. philosophy for Rep. party, 1946. Commd. maj. U.S. Army, 1942; asst. to chief of ops. in C.W.S.; served in ETO and PTO, 1942-45; discharged as lt. col.; col. chem. warfare N.Y.N.G. Decorated Legion of Merit; awarded Presdl. medal of Freedom, 1983. Mem. Am. Legion, VFW, Amvets, Jewish War Vets., Am. Vets. Com., City Athletic Club, Harmonie Club (N.Y.); Capitol Hill Club (Washington). Republican. Jewish. Home: New York N.Y. Died Mar. 7, 1986.

JEFFE, EPHRAIM F., engineer; b. St. Louis, Feb. 22, 1897; s. Maurice J. and Frieda Frances J.; married. BEE, Polytechnic Inst. of Bklyn., 1916. Elec. engr. Bklyn. Edison Co. Inc., 1916-17; pres. Nat. Electric Service Corp., 1923-32; asst. v.p. Consol. Edison Co. Inc., 1932-35; v.p. Consol. Edison System Cos., 1935-42; pres., dir. Kings County Lighting Co., N.Y., Richmond Gas Co., 1951-57; pres., chief exec. officer Mich. Gas Utilities Co., 1959-86; bd. dirs. Knapp-Monarch Co.; mem. N.Y.C. Transit Authority, 1953-86. Pres., dir. N.Y. Eye and Ear Infirmary, 1948-52; bd. dirs. Roosevelt Hosp.; campaign chmn. Greater N.Y. Red Cross, 1949, 50; dir. N.Y. chpt. ARC; mem. Army Adv. Com.; bd. dirs. N.Y. Women's League for Animals Ellin Prince Speyer Hosp. for Animals, 1948-86. 1st lt. to maj. Signal Corps, U.S. Army, 1917-20; maj. to brig. gen. U.S. Army, World War II. Mem. Tau Beta Pi. Home: Palm Beach Fla. Died Nov. 29, 1986; buried Arlington (Va.) Nat. Cemetery.

JEFFERSON, ELMER L., insurance broker; b. N.Y.C., 1901. Pres., bd. dirs. Willcox, Peck & Hughes Inc.; chmn., chief exec. officer Johnson & Higgins N.Y.C. Home: West Islip N.Y. †

JEFFERY, ALEXANDER HALEY, lawyer; b. London, Ont., Can., Jan. 29, 1909; s. James Edgar and Gertrude (Dumaresq) J.; m. Eulalie E. Murray, June 29, 1934; children: Alexander M., Judith E. (Nursey). Grad., U. Western Ont., 1931, Osgoode Hall, Toronto, 1934. Bar: Ont. 1934. Ind. practice law London, 1934-87; pres., dir. Forest City Investment Ltd.; dir. London Realty Mgmt. & Rentals Ltd., London Winery, Ltd. Mem. Parliament for Constituency City of London 1949-53. Mem. Am. Assn. Life Ins. Counsel, Can. Bar Assn. Anglican. Clubs: Mason (32 deg.), London Hunt and Country, London; Royal Canadian Yacht (Toronto); Windsor Yacht, Sarnia Yacht, Port Stanley Sailing Squadron, Great Lakes Cruising. Home: London England. Died May 11, 1987.

JELLIFFE, RUSSELL WESLEY, foundation administrator; b. Mansfield, Ohio, Nov. 19, 1891; s. Charles Wesley and Margaret (Ward) J.; m. Rowena Woodham, May 28, 1915; 1 child, Roger Woodham. AB, Oberlin Coll., 1914, LLD, 1944; AM, U. Chgo., 1915; HHD, Western Res. U., 1951; LHD, Cleve. State U., 1966. Founder, exec. dir. Karamu House, 1915-63, hon. life trustee, from 1963; founder, exec. dir. Karamu Found., from 1963; active in establishing Cleve. Urban League, 1916, Cleve. Met. Housing Authority, 1933, Cleve. Community Relations Bd. on Race Relations, 1945; del. 2d Pan-African Congress, Paris, 1921; pres. group work coun. Welfare Fedn. Cleve., 1938-40; foreman Cuyahoga County Grand Jury, 1960. Civic cons.; dir. Arts and Edn. Survey Boston, 1963, Cultural-Ednl. Survey St. Louis, 1967, Arts Survey Indpls., 1967, Arts and Cultural Survey Canton, Ohio, 1968; trustee Cleve. Coun. on Human Relations, 1960-65; trustee Oberlin Coll., 1960-67, hon. life trustee; trustee Cleve. Civil Liberties Union, from 1963/ mem. Cleve. Selective Svc. Bd. 20, 1960-68, Nat. Coun. Arts in Edn., 1960-63; life fellow Cleve. Mus. Art. Co-recipient (with Mrs. Jelliffe) Charles Eisenman Civic award ewish Welfare Assn., 1941, Human Race Relations ward NCCJ, 1944, Lane Bryant award, 1958, Cleve. Distinctive Svc. award United Appeal Cleve., 1961, Disting. Svc. award Nat. Fedn. Settlements, 1963, umerous others; named one of 10 Outstanding Citizens Cleve. Cleve. Press, 1950, 58. Mem. NAACP (exec. om. Cleve. br. from 1926), Gt. Lakes Shakespeare Assn. (1st v.p. 1962, trustee from 1962), Grand Jury Assn. (trustee from 1960), Jury Foremen's Coun. trustee from 1965), United World Federalists (trustee 962), Oberlin Coll. Alumni Assn. (trustee 1958-60), Citizens League Cleve., Men's City Club. Home: Cleveand Ohio. †

ENKINSON, EDWARD LEALAND, roentgenologist; . Rhinelander, Wis., Feb. 25, 1892; s. David Lealand and Lula Alma (Drewsen) J.; m. Margaret Parkinson, 919 (dec. 1945); 1 child, Margaret Carol; m. Helen W. napp, June 30, 1948. BS, St. Louis U., 1910, MD, 915. Intern Alexian Bros. and St. Luke's Hosp., St. Louis, 1914-15; roentgenologist St. Luke's Hosp., Chgo., rom 1916, St. Joseph's Hosp., 1923-39, Evanston Hosp., 1923-29; asst. prof. roentgenology Northwestern J. Med. Sch., 1919-24, assoc. prof. radiology, prof. hmn. dept. radiology; cons. roentgenologist C.&N.-W. y., C., R.I.&P. Ry., B.&O. R.R., C.M., St.P.&P Ry., Roseland Community Hosp., Presbyn.-St. Luke's Hosp.; ons. emeritus Rsch. Hosp. Contbr. articles on X-ray iagnosis and electrotherapeutics to profl. jours. Maj. M.C., AUS, 1917-19. Mem. AMA (chmn. radiology ect. 1935), Am. Bd. Radiology (pres. 1946-47), Ill. tate Med. Soc., Chgo. Roentgen Soc. (pres. 1922-25, 0-31), Am. Roentgen Ray Soc. (v.p. 1927, treas. 1932-6, chmn. fin. com. 1938, pres. 1940, gold medal 1954), Radiol. Soc. N.Am., Soc. Internal Medicine, Inst. Medicine, Chgo., Pasteur Meml., Masons, University Club, Am. Congress Radiology (sec. 1933), Am. Coll. Radiology (sec. 1933, bd. chancellors). Republican. Episcopalian. Home: Chicago Ill. †

ENKS, THOMAS ELIJAH, lawyer; b. Bronxville, N.Y., Apr. 5, 1910; s. Elijah and Anna (Robeson) J.; m. anet Shares, Sept. 19, 1936 (dec.); children: Linda Ann Mrs. Nils Swanson), Susan Shares (Mrs. Thomas J. Breen); m. Maurita Williams, Sept. 16, 1972. A.B., Williams Coll., 1931; LL.B. Columbia, 1934. Bar: N.Y. 934, D.C. 1936. With Office Spl. Adviser Fgn. Trade, 934-35; sec., asst. gen. counsel Export-Import Bank, 935-36; with firm Alvord & Alvord, Washington, 1936-1; partner Alvord & Alvord, 1942-50; partner firm Lee, Toomey & Kent, Washington, from 1950. Contbr. legal ours. Bd. dirs. Graydon Manor Psychiat. Ctr.; hon. rustee Miss Hall's Sch., Pittsfield, Mass. Mem. Am., D.C. bar assns., Internat. Fiscal Assn., Soc. Alumni Williams Coll. (planned giving com.). Phi Beta Kappa. Republican. Clubs: Chevy Chase (Md.); Nat. Lawyers Washington), International (Washington); Capitol Hill Washington); Congressional Country (Md.). Home: Washington D.C. Died Aug. 13, 1986; buried Nat. Meml. Pk., Falls Church, Va.

ENNER, ALBERT ERNEST, JR., lawyer; b. Chgo., une 20, 1907; s. Albert E. and Elizabeth (Owens) J.; m. adine N., Mar. 19, 1932; 1 dau., Cynthia Lee. J.D., . Ill., 1930, LL.D., 1979; LL.D. John Marshall Law ch., 1961, Columbia Coll., 1974, U. Notre Dame, 1975, Northwestern U., 1975, William Mitchell Law Sch., 976, U. Mich., 1976. Bar: Ill. 1930. Practiced in Chgo., from 1930; sr. partner firm Jenner & Block; ounsel, dir. Gen. Dynamics Corp.; spl. asst. atty gen. Il., 1956-68; counsel Ill. Budgetary Commn., 1956-57; rof. law Northwestern U., 1952-53; chmn. U.S. upreme Ct. Adv. Com. on Fed. Rules of Evidence, 965-75; Chmn. Ill. Commn. on Uniform State Laws, 950-80; mem. Nat. Conf. Commrs. Uniform State Laws, from 1952, pres., 1969-71; mem. Adv. Com. Fed. Rules of Civil Procedure, U.S. Supreme Court, 1960-70, Nat. Conf. Bar Assn. Pres.'s U.S., from 1950, pres., 952-53; mem. U.S. Loyalty Review Bd., 1952-53; mem. ouncil U. Ill. Law Forum, 1948-51; sr. counsel Presdl. Commn. to Investigate the Assassination of President Kennedy (Warren Commn.), 1963-64; chief spl. counsel o minority Ho. of Reps. Judiciary Com. that conducted npeachment inquiry regarding Pres. Richard M. Nix-n.; Law mem. Ill. Bd. Examiners Accountancy, 1948-1. Author and co-author: Illinois Civil Practice Act Annotated, 1933, Outline of Illinois Supreme Court and Appellate Court Procedure, 1935, Smith-Hurd Ill. Annotated Statutes, Volumes on Pleading, Evidence and Practice, 10 edits, 1933-87, also Vols. on Uniform Marriage and Dissolution of Marriage; Mem. permanent editorial bd.; Uniform Commercial Code, from 1961; Contbr. to law revs. and legal publs. on various phases f practice, pleading, evidence, procedure and other legal ubjects. Mem. Pres. Lyndon B. Johnson's Nat. Commn. on Causes and Prevention of Violence in U.S., 968-69; sec. U.S. Navy Meml. Found.; trustee Evan-ton-Glenbrook Hosp. Arthritis Found., Cerebral Palsey ound., Northwestern U. Library Bd.; mem. presdl. dv. bd. Mus. Sci. and Industry. Recipient Dist-nguished Service award for outstanding pub. service hgo. and Ill. Jr. C. of C., 1939, U. Ill. Disting. Alumni ward, 1962, Disting. Civic Achievement award Am. ewish Com., 1973, N.Y. U. Distinguished Citizen's ward, 1975; named Chicagoan of Year Chgo. Press lub, 1975; laureate Lincoln Acad. of Ill. Fellow Am. oll. Trial Lawyers (bd. regents, pres. 1958-59), In-rnat. Acad. Trial Lawyers; Am. Bar Found.; mem. Ill.

Soc. Trial Lawyers, Nat. Assn. Def. lawyers in Criminal Cases, Inter-Am. Bar Assn., Internat. Bar Assn., Am. Bar Assn. (ho. of dels. 1948—, fellow Young Lawyers Sect., state del. 1975-78, chmn. standing com. on fed. judiciary 1965-68, chmn. sect. individual rights and responsibilities 1973-74, mem. council sect. legal edn. 1967-75, bd. govs. 1977-80), Ill. Bar Assn. (pres. 1949-50), Chgo. Bar Assn. (bd. dirs. 1934-47, sec. 1947-49), Assn. Bar City N.Y., Am. Judicature Soc. (pres. 1958-60), Am. Inst. Jud. Adminstrn., Nat. Lawyers Com. for Civil Rights Under Law (dir., nat. co-chmn. 1975-77), Bar Assn. U.S. Ct. Appeals 7th Circuit (bd. govs. 1955-60, Robert Maynard Hutchins Distinguished Service award 1976), Am. Law Inst., Chgo. Council Lawyers, NAACP Legal Def. Fund, Center for Study Dem. Instns. (dir. 1975-79), Order of Coif, Alpha Chi Rho, Phi Delta Phi. Republican. Clubs: Tavern, Midday, Skokie Country, Law, Legal, Chicago. Home: Kenilworth Ill. Died Sept. 18, 1988.

JENNINGS, PAUL, labor union official; b. Bklyn., Mar. 19, 1918; m. Dorothy Jennings; children: Paul, Eileen. Ed., RCA Inst., Crown Heights Labor Sch. Electronic technician Sperry-Gryo, Bklyn.; successively mem. union organizing com., shop steward, grievance and shop chmn., acting pres. local union Internat. Union Elec. Radio and Machine Workers, AFL-CIO, mem. exec. bd., treas., local pres., from 1948, exec. sec. Dist. 4, from 1949, exec. sec. Dist. 3, internat. pres.; v.p. AFL-CIO; pres. Internat. Union Elec. Workers, 1965-76; v.p. non-proliferation, nuclear reactor safety; mem. adv. com. AEC, 1956-62, mem. adv. com. reactor safeguards, from 1962, N.Y.C. CIO Coun., chmn. merger com.; v.p. N.Y. State CIO Coun., co-chmn. merger com.; mem. exec. bd. N.Y. Central Labor Coun.; chmn. Internat. Fedn. Elec. and Electronics Co. Coun. Com.; chmn. Elec. and Electronics Industry Co. Coun. Internat. Metalworkers Fedn., 1968; mem. N.Y.C. Mayor's Com. on Exploitation; labor del. Econ. Econ. Cooperation and Development; mem. civil rights com. AFL-CIO. Mem. council Hofstra U.; trustee SUNY, Urban League. Died Sept. 7, 1987.

JENNINGS, WILLIAM MITCHELL, lawyer; b. N.Y.C., Dec. 14, 1920; s. Harry B. and Nettie I. (Mitchell) J.; m. Elizabeth Hite, Oct. 16, 1943; children: William Mitchell, Jeffrey H., Eunice M., Elizabeth B., Priscilla H. AB, Princeton U., 1941; JD, Yale U., 1943. Bar: N.Y. 1945. Law clk. to judge U.S. Circuit Ct. Appeals (2d cir.), N.Y.C., 1943-44; assoc. Simpson Thacher & Bartlett, N.Y.C., 1944-51, ptnr., 1952-81. Gen. chmn. Thunderbird Golf Classic, 1963-65; bd. dirs. World Golf Hall of Fame; founder, gen. chmn. Westchester Golf Classic, 1967-81; mem. nat. adv. com. Profl. Golfers' Assn. Am., Inst. Sports Medicine and Athletic Trauma; bd. govs. NHL, 1962-81, chmn. bd. govs. 1968-70; pres. United Hosp., Port Chester, N.Y., 1959-69, chmn. 1969-74, hon. chmn., 1974-81; trustee Rye (N.Y.) Presbyn. Ch. Recipient Lester Patrick trophy NHL, 1971, Disting. Service award Met. Golf Writers Assn., 1975, Gold Tee award, 1977; elected to Hockey Hall of Fame, Toronto, 1975, Westchester Sports Hall of Fame, 1979. Mem. N.Y. State Bar Assn., Bar Assn. of City of N.Y., Apawamis Club (Rye), Country Club N.C. (Pinehurst), Links Club, Downtown Assn., Madison Sq. Garden Club, Blind Brook Club (Port Chester). Home: Greenwich Conn. Died Aug. 17, 1981.

JESSUP, PHILIP C., judge, diplomat; b. N.Y.C., Jan. 5, 1897; s. Henry Wynans and Mary Hay (Stotesbury) J.; m. Lois Walcott Kellogg, July 23, 1921; 1 son, Philip C. AB, Hamilton Coll., 1919, LLD (hon.) 1937; LLB, Yale U., 1924, LLD (hon.), 1964; AM, Columbia U., 1924, PhD, 1927, LLD (hon.), 1970; LLD (hon.), Case Western Res. U., 1941, Rutgers U., 1950, Seoul Nat. U., 1950, Middlebury Coll., 1950, Brown U., 1949, St. Lawrence U., 1966, U. Mich., 1966, Johns Hopkins U., 1970, Brandeis U., 1971, Colby Coll., 1973; LCD (hon.), Colgate U., 1950, Union Coll., 1951; LittD (hon.), U. Hanoi, 1950; JD, Oslo U., 1946; Dr. honoris causa, U. Paris, 1948. Bar: D.C. 1925, N.Y. 1927. Mem. Parker & Duryea, 1927-43; lectr. internat. law Columbia U., N.Y.C., 1925-27, asst. prof., 1927-29, assoc. prof., 1929-35, prof., 1934-46, Hamilton Fish prof. internat. law and diplomacy, 1946-61, Jacob Blaustein lectr., 1970; judge Internat. Ct. of Justice, 1961-70; Whitney H. Shepardson sr. rsch. fellow in residence Coun. on Fgn. Rels., 1970-71; Barnette Miller lectr. Wellesley Coll., 1971; vis. prof. Harvard Law Sch., 1938-39; Storrs lectr. Yale Law Sch., 1956; Cooley lectr. Mich. U. Law Sch., 1958; Sibley lectr. U. Ga. Sch. Law, 1970; legal advisor to fed. govt. officers, dels., 1924-53, at internat confs., embassies and to U.S. dels. at UN; U.S. rep. to UN Gen. Assembly, 1948-52; apptd. ambassador at large, 1949, resigned, 1953; chmn. Chile-Norway Permanent Conciliation Commn.; hon. mem. governing coun. Internat. Inst. for Unification of Pvt. Law, 1967-86. Author: Elihu Root, 2 vols., 1938, A Modern Law of Nations, 1948; TRansnational Law, 1956, The Use of International Law, 1959, (with H.H. Taubenfeld) Controls for Outer Space & The Antarctic Analogy, 1959, The Price of International Justice, 1971, The Birth of Nations, 1974, others; supervising editor Columbia U. Studies in History, Economics and Public Law, 1929-33; hon. mem. bd. editors Am. Jour Internat. Law; former mem. bd. editors World Politics, Internat. Orgn. With Am. Expeditionary Force, World War I. Decorated Hungarian Cross of Merit, Class II; Oficial Ordem Na-

cional do Cruizeiro do Sul (Brazil); grand officer Nat. Order Cedars (Lebanon); recipient Hudson Gold medal Am. Soc. Internat. Law, Medal of Excellence Columbia Law Sch. Alumni Assn., 1977; Fowler Harper fellow Yale Law Sch., 1966. Mem. ABA, Am. Philos. Soc., Am. Acad. Arts and Scis., Institut de droit Internat. (1st v.p. 1973-75), Am. Soc. Internat. Law (hon. pres. 1969-73), Conn. Bar Assn. (Disting. Pub. Service award 1970), Coun. on Fgn. Rels., Round Table, Century Club, Cosmos Club (Washington), others. Home: Norfolk Conn. Died Jan. 31, 1986.

JEWELL, EDWARD OSWELL, government official; b. New Orleans, Feb. 17, 1891; s. Joseph Rand and Mollie (Godbold) J.; m. Sadie Bell Johnson, Apr. 30, 1920; children: Gertrude (Mrs. Albert A. Bowman), Edward J., Olive (Mrs. Edward Randle). Ed. pub. and night schs. Pres. E.O. Jewell & Co., 1932-40; gen. mgr. bd. commrs. Port of New Orleans, 1940-48, Norfolk (Va.) Port Authority, 1948-54; dir. world trade dept. Internat. House, New Orleans, 1954-55; gen. mgr. Toledo-Lucas County Port Authority. Mem. Gulf Ports Assn. (pres.), Am. (pres.), North Atlantic (pres.) port assns., Nat. Cotton Com. (bd. dirs.), Masons., Rotary. †

JEWETT, FRANK BALDWIN, JR., mechanical engineer; b. N.Y.C., Apr. 4, 1917; s. Frank B. and Fannie (Frisble) J.; m. Edar von L. Fleming, Sept. 5, 1942; children: Frank Baldwin III, Robert F., Rebecca L., Edar F. B.S., Calif. Inst. Tech., 1938; M.B.A. magna cum laude, Harvard U., 1940. Registered profl. engr., Minn. Research asst. Harvard Bus. Sch., 1940-41; with Nat. Research Corp., 1941-47, v.p., mgr. vacuum engring. div., 1944-47; with Gen. Mills, Inc., 1947-55, dir. devel. and bus. adminstrn. research labs., also dir. aero. research labs., 1947-52; mng. dir. engring. research and devel. Gen. Mills, Inc. (Mech. div.), 1952-55; v.p., dir. Vitro Corp. Am., N.Y.C., 1956-58; exec. v.p., dir. Vitro Corp. Am., 1959, pres., dir., 1959-69; pres. Tech. Audit Assos., Inc., 1969-86. Mem. U.S. Olympic Yacht Team, 1936, Edina (Minn.) Sch. Bd., 1953-55; trustee Tabor Acad., Marion, Mass., 1954-74; hon. Rockford Coll., Ill.; mem. corp. Woods Hole Oceanographic Instn.; adv. bd. Greenhouse Fund, 1983-86. Recipient certificate merit Crusade for Freedom, 1951; Time/Life Silver Anniversary All Am., 1963. Mem. ASME (hon. life), N.Y. Acad. Scis., Am. Nuclear, U.S. Yacht Racing Union (sr. judge). Clubs: Union League (N.Y.C.); Holmes Hole Sailing Assn., Vineyard Haven Yacht. Home: New Canaan Conn. Died June 28, 1986; buried Vineyard Haven, Mass.

JOANIS, JOHN WESTON, insurance company executive; b. Hopewell, Va., June 13, 1918; s. Edmund W. and Emma Elvira (Westen) J.; m. Marian G. Sinrud, Aug. 16, 1945; children: Susan Kay, Mary Ellen, William John. LL.B. U. Wis., 1942; grad. Advanced Mgmt. Program, Harvard, 1950. Bar: Wis. 1943. Pvt. practice Oshkosh, 1945-47; with Hardware Mut. Casualty Co. (now Sentry Ins. A Mut. Co.), Stevens Point, Wis., 1947-85; asst. sec. Hardware Mut. Casualty Co. (now Sentry Ins. A Mut. Co.), 1948-52, sec., gen. counsel, 1952-56, v.p., gen. counsel, 1956-62, exec. v.p., 1962-66, chief exec. officer, 1966-72, chmn. bd., chief exec. officer, 1972-85, dir., 1972-85; chmn. bd., chief exec. officer Sentry Life Ins. Co., 1967-85; chmn. bd., chief exec. officer Sentry Corp., 1973-85, dir., 1967-85; chmn. bd., dir. Sentry Indemnity Co., 1978-85, Dairyland Ins. Co., Scottsdale, Ariz., 1970-85, Gt. S.W. Fire Ins. Co., Scottsdale, 1972-85, Middlesex Ins. Co., Concord, Mass., 1974-85, Sentry Investors Ins. Co., Concord, 1974-85, Patriot Gen. Life Ins. Co., Concord, 1978-85, Australian Casualty Co. Ltd., Australia, 1978-85, Sentry Holdings Ltd., Australia, 1978-85, Sentry Fin. Mgmt., Ltd., Australia, 1978-85, Sentry Ins. (Australasia) Ltd., Australia, 1978-85, Sentry Life Assurance Ltd., Australia, 1978-85, Sentry Holdings (Antilles) N.V., 1978-85, Sentry (Hong Kong) Ltd., 1978-85, Sentry Holdings (PTE) Ltd., Singapore, 1978-85, City of Westminster Assurance Co. Ltd., Eng., 1978-85, City of Westminster Assurance Soc., Ltd., Eng., 1978-85, Sentry Fin. Ltd., Eng., 1978-85, Sentry Fin. Ltd. (numerous other affiliates); chmn. bd., pres. Sentry Assurance Internat. Ltd., Bermuda, 1979-85; dir. Sentry Investment Mgmt., Inc., Sentry Life Ins. Co. N.Y., Syracuse, A. E. Staley Mfg. Co., Decatur, Ill., 1st Nat. Bank, Stevens Point, Wis. Bd. dirs. Alliance Am. Insurers and Am. Insurers Hwy. Safety Alliance, 1966; bd. dirs. Wis. Found. Ind. Colls., Inc.; mem. exec. com. Wis. Clergy Econ. Edn. Conf.; trustee Stevens Point YMCA, 1969-85, past pres. bd. Served to capt. USAAF, 1942-45. Mem. Am., Wis., Portage County bar assns., Ins. Inst. Am. (trustee), Am. Inst. Property and Liability Underwriters (trustee), Internat. Assn. Ins. Counsel, Am. Legion,. Clubs: Elks, Rotary, Madison, Milw. Athletic, Marco Polo (N.Y.C.); Union League (Chgo.). Home: Stevens Point Wis. Died Nov. 18, 1985; cremated.

JOBUSCH, FREDERICK HENRY, architect; b. Collinsville, Ill., Feb. 24, 1916; s. Frederick August and Edna Emelia (Emig) J.; m. Josephine Buckley Cook, 1, May 20, 1939; children: Lizette Christine, Georgia Jean, Anthony Jack. B.S. in Archtl. Engring., U. Ill., 1937. Registered profl. engr., Ariz. registered architect, Ariz., N.Mex., Calif., C.Z. Structural designer Ind., Ill. and Ariz., 1937-45; archtl. engr. James Macmillan, Tucson, 1946-47, Place & Place (Architects), 1947-48, Terry

Atkinson, 1953-56; cons. structural engr. Tucson, 1948-53; prin., v.p. Friedman & Jobusch (Architects and Engrs., Inc.), Tucson, 1956-80; prin. Fred Henry Jobusch (Cons. Architect), 1980-87; dir. Great Am. Savs. Bank, FSB. Ariz.; chmn. Ariz. Bd. Tech. Registration for Architects and Engrs., 1955-56; mem. profl. adv. council Coll. Architecture, U. Ariz., 1958-87. Important works include Chris-Town Shopping Center Mall, Phoenix, City Hall Tower, Tucson, Health Scis. Center, U. Ariz., Chemistry Bldg., U. Ariz., New U. Library, Marana (Ariz.) High Sch., Ariz. Bank Plaza Bldg., Tucson, Kino Community Hosp., Pima County. Chmn. Old Pueblo Redevel. Com., Tucson Planning and Zoning Commn., 1963-64; pres. bd. dirs. United Way, Tucson, 1964; mem. exec. bd. Catalina council Boy Scouts Am., 1967-87, pres. bd., 1973-74; chmn. Catalina chpt. Nat. Eagle Scout Assn., 1975-87; mem. exec. bd. St. Lukes In The Desert, Inc., 1967-80, pres., 1976-80; active Pres.'s Club and U. Ariz. Found., 1968-87. Recipient Silver Beaver award Boy Scouts Am., 1975. Fellow AIA (pres. So. Ariz. chpt. 1956-57, 68, chmn. judiciary com. Western Mountain region 1966-69); mem. Ariz. Soc. Architects (pres. 1968), Ariz. Soc. Profl. Engrs. (pres. So. Ariz. chpt. 1952-53, Engr. of Year award 1964), Constrn. Specifications Inst. (pres. Tucson chpt. 1971), Structural Engrs. Assn. Ariz., Ariz. C. of C., Tucson C. of C. (chmn. Task Force for Old Town Devel. 1971-73), Am. Arbitration Assn. (arbitrator), U. Ill. Alumni Assn., Alpha Rho Chi. Clubs: Masons (32 deg.), KT, Shriners, Order Eastern Star, Downtown Tucson Sertoma, Old Pueblo. Home: Tucson, Ariz. Died Nov. 2, 1987.

JOCKERS, ERNST, educator; b. Sand, Germany, Jan. 7, 1887; came to U.S., 1924, naturalized, 1932; s. Jakob and Christina (Rieber) J.; m. Paula Annabert Buchler, May 18, 1925. MA, U. Strassburg, 1909, PhD, 1910. Prof. modern langs., dir. various colls., Europe, 1910-24; instr. German CCNY, 1925-26; asst. prof. U. Pitts., 1926-29; asst. prof. German lit. U. Pa., 1929-34, prof., 1934-57, prof. emeritus, from 1957; lectr. in field. Author several books including: Soziale Polarität in Gopethe's Klassik, 1942, J. Otto Schweizer: The Man and His Work, 1953, Die Akne, 1955, Mit Goethe, Gesammelte Aufsatze, 1957, Ludwig F. Barthel, Ein Lyriker in unser Zeit, 1960; contbr. numerous articles to profl. jours. Decorated Cross of Merit, Cross of Merit of Fed. Republic (Fed. Republic Germany). Mem. MLA, German Soc. Pa. (past pres.), Am. Assn. Tchrs. German, Art Alliance, Phi Beta Kappa. Home: Philadelpia Pa. †

JOCKMUS, LESLIE HARTER, manufacturing executive; b. Ilion, N.Y., Apr. 8, 1891; s. George and Maude (Harter) J.; m. Esther Marie Nordstrom, 1923; 1 child, Jane Marie (Mrs. Charles Thomas Sturgess). Grad., Peddie Sch., 1912. With Ansonia Mfg. Co., Conn., from 1917, sales mgr., 1919-30, gen. mgr., 1930-46, pres., treas., from 1946; bd. dirs. Plastic Wire & Cable Corp., Jewett City, Ansonia Savs. Bank, Birmingham Nat. Bank, Derby, Conn. Home: Pine Orchard Conn. †

JOFFREY, ROBERT (ABDULLAH JAFFA BEY KHAN), ballet company director, choreographer, dancer; b. Seattle, Dec. 24, 1930; s. Dolha and Marie (Galetti) J. Student, Mary Ann Wells Sch. of Dance, Seattle, 1944-48, Cornish Sch. Music, Seattle, 1945-48, Sch. Am. Ballet, 1948; pupil, Alexandra Federova; student modern dance with, May O'Donnell, Gertrude Shurr, 1949-52. Mem. faculty High Sch. Performing Arts, N.Y.C., 1950-55; also Am. Ballet Theatre Sch.; founder ballet sch. Am. Ballet Center, 1953, dir. faculty, 1953-65; Pres. Ballet Am. Found.; bd. dirs. Found. Am. Dance. Resident choreographer, N.Y. City Center Opera, 1955-61; founder, 1956, since artistic dir., choreographer, The Joffrey Ballet (formerly Robert Joffrey Ballet Co.), co. toured, Near East for, State Dept., 1962-63, toured, Russia, 1963, performed at, White House, 1963, 65, ann. U.S. tours, 1956-64; organizer dance dept., Chautauqua, N.Y., 1959, choreographer, NBC-TV Opera, 1955, 57, 58, made debut as soloist with Petit's Ballet de Paris; creator: ballets Remembrances, Astarte, 1967, The Nutcracker, 1987. Recipient ann. award Nat. Acad. Dance Masters, Chgo., 1962; Dance Mag. award, 1964; Dance Masters of Am. award, 1965; Disting. Service award Dance Notation Bur., 1985; Ford Found. grant Robert Joffrey Ballet, 1964; Geraldine Freund's Ballet Achievement award, 1987. Home: New York N.Y. Died Mar. 25, 1988.

JOHN, DEWITT, editor; b. Safford, Ariz., Aug. 1, 1915; s. Franklin Howard and Frances (DeWitt) J.; m. Morley Marshall, Feb. 14, 1942; children: DeWitt, Jennifer John Strom. BA, Principia Coll., Mo., 1936; MA, U. Chgo., 1937; MS, Columbia U., 1938. Editorial page editor St. Petersburg (Fla.) Times, 1938-39; mem. staff. Christian Sci. Monitor, Boston, 1939-42, editor, 1964-70, mgr. C.S. coms. on publ., 1962-64, bd. dirs., 1970-80; editor Christian Sci. Jour., Sentinel and Heralds, 1981-85. Author: The Christian Science Way of Life, 1962. With USNR, 1942-45. Decorated Bronze Star. Home: Lincoln Mass. Died Oct. 22, 1985.

JOHNSON, A. DEXTER, association executive; b. Manchester, Conn., Sept. 17, 1907; s. Aaron and Christine (Magnell) J.; m. Lois G. Stoller, July 15, 1957; children: Robert D., Dexter A. PhB, Brown U., 1930. With Eastman Kodak Co., 1934-72, advt. mgr., 1959-64, asst. v.p., 1960-72, dir. advt., 1964-72; dir. Eastman Savs. & Loan Assn.; mem. Assn. Nat. Advertisers, 1962-72, dir., 1968-71; mem. Nat. Advt. Rev. Bd., 1971-72; Nat. Advt. Coun. coordinator Prisoner of War campaign, 1971-72; pres. Rochester Advt. Coun., 1972-82; pub. rels. dir. new campus fund Rochester Inst. Tech., 1964-68; dir. Audit Bur. of Circulations, 1968-73. Bd. dirs. Point-of Purchase Inst., 1956-60; trustee Rochester Inst. Tech., 1965-78, Harley Sch., Rochester, 1953-54. Mem. Genesee Valley Club, Brown Univ. Club (Rochester). Home: Rochester N.Y. Died Sept. 3, 1984; buried Pittsford Cemetery, Pittsford, N.Y.

JOHNSON, ANDREW N., lawyer; b. Sparta, Wis., Nov. 10, 1887; s. Marcus M. and Susanne (Jensen) J.; m. Louise C. Weaver, Sept. 13, 1916 (dec. May 7, 1949); children: Douglas W., Alice J. (Mrs. Richard C. Keller), Gordon A. AB, Northwestern U., 1913, LLB, 1915; LLD, William Mitchell Coll. Law, 1971. Bar: Minn. 1916. Ptnr. Mercer & Jonson, Mpls., 1920-25, Sweet & Johnson, 1925-30, Sweet, Johnson & Sands, 1930-37, Johnson, Sands & Brumfield, 1937-47, Johnson, Sands, Brumfield & Maloney, 1947, Johnson & Sands; gen. counsel N.Am. Life & Casualty Co., 1946-62, bd. dirs., 1950-54; bd. dirs. Pure Milk Products Co., B.F. Griebenow. Author: Marcus and Susanne The Johnson (sen) Family, 1965, Enforceable World Peace: Thoughts of A Diplomat, Diplomatic Career for Denmark, 1927-27, 1973. Vice consul of Denmark, Minn., 1927-47, consul, 1947-58, consul gen. Minn., N.D., S.D., Mont., 1958-72; dean, trustee Mpls.-Minn. Coll. Law, 1940-56; pres. Mpls. coun. Camp Fire Girls, 1948-49, nat. bd. dirs., from 1962, chmn. nat. fin. com. exec. com. Camp Fire Girls, Inc., 1962-65; trustee William Mitchell Coll. Law, from 1956. Decorated knight Order Danish Flag, King Christian X Medal Liberation, knight 1st class Order of Danish Flag, Comdr. Cross Knighthood Danish Flag (Denmark); knight 1st class Order of Vasa (Sweden); recipient Disting. Svc. award Mayor of Mpls., 1972. Mem. ABA, Minn., Hennepin County bar assns., Mpls. Bus. Mens Assn. (past pres.), Order of Coif, Six O'Clock Club, Minneapolis Club, Mpls. Athletic Club, Skylight Club, Alpha Delta Phi, Delta Theta Phi. Home: Minneapolis Minn. Deceased.

JOHNSON, ARTHUR E., oil executive; b. Colorado Springs, Colo., Sept. 4, 1892; s. Nels and Laura Johnson; m. Helen Kennedy, Apr. 12, 1918; 1 child, Helen Barbara (Mrs. Gerald R. Hillyard). Ed., Colo. Springs High Sch.; hon. DSc. Engaged in oil bus. from 1913; dir. United Banks of Colo. Trustee Lovelace Found. Med. Edn. and Rsch., Denver Mus. Natural History; bd. dirs. USAF Acad. Found. 1st lt. U.S. Army, 1917-19. Mem. Denver Club, Cherry Hills Club, Colorado Springs Cooking Club, Denver Country Club, Wigwam Club, Garden of the Gods Club, Hiwan Country Club. Home: Denver Colo. †

JOHNSON, AXEL A., oil and steel company executive; b. Stockholm, 1910; married. Grad., Royal Inst. Tech., Stockholm, 1938. With Axel Johnson Group, from 1931; emeritus chmn., dir. A. Johnson and Co. Inc., N.Y.C.; chmn., dir. C.H. Sprague and Sons Inc. subs. A. Johnson and Co. Inc., Portsmouth, N.H. Deceased.

JOHNSON, CHARLES D., educator; b. Banner, Miss., May 27, 1888; s. Charles Albert and Evangeline (Howell) J.; m. Claude Jaudon Eager, 1913; 1 child, Charles Eager. AB, Miss. Coll., 1910, AM, 1916, LLD, 1950; postgrad., Johns Hopkins U., 1917, U. Mo., 1919; PhD, Iowa State U., 1921; LittD, Mercer U., 1953. Supt. pub. schs., coll., univ. faculties 1911-29; pres. Ouachita Coll., Arkadelphia, Ark., 1929-33; head dept. social sci. A&M Coll., Monticello, Ark., 1933-36, acting pres., 1935; dean Blue Mountain (Miss.) Coll., 1936-38; head dept. pub., editor Baylor Century Baylor U., 1938-39; organizer 1st Journalism Week in S.W., Southwestern Journalism Congress, Baylor U., 1927; founder So. Lit. Festival Assn., Blue Mountain Coll., 1937. Author: Higher Education of Southern Baptists, 1956; editor Coll. News and Views, from 1936, The So. Bapt. Educator, from 1947; assoc. editor Social Sci. Mem. So. Bapt. Edn. Commn., chmn., from 1932; mem. So. Bapt. Conv. Centennial Com. Mem. Tex. Inter-Racial Commn., So. Sociol. Congress, Am. Econ. Assn., Am. Inst. Banking (hon.), Nat. Assn. Wholesale Credit Men, Univ. Bd. Publs., Univ. Grad. Coun., Masons, Rotary, Pi Gamma Mu. Democrat. Baptist. Home: Clinton Miss. †

JOHNSON, DAVID LIVINGSTONE, electrical engineering educator; b. Gustavus, Ohio, Feb. 17, 1915; s. David Charles and Margaret (Delaney) J.; m. Eugenia Gibson McQuarie, Jan. 23, 1954. A.B., Berea Coll., 1936; M.A., State U. Iowa, 1938, B.S. in Elec. Engring, 1942; M.S., Okla. State U., 1950, Ph.D., 1957. Registered profl. engr., La., Okla. Instr. U.S. Naval Tng. Sch., Okla. State U., 1942-44; field engr. Airborne Coordinating Group, 1944-45; instr. Spartan Sch. Aeros., Tulsa, 1945-48; asst. prof. Okla. State U., 1948-55; prof., head dept. elec. engring. La. Tech. U., Ruston, 1955-80; prof. emeritus La. Tech. U., from 1980. Mem. A.A.A.S., I.E.E.E., Am. Soc. Engring. Edn., Assn. Computing Machinery, Nat. Soc. Profl. Engrs., Am. Assn. U. Profs., Instrument Soc. Am., Sigma Xi, Eta Kappa Nu, Phi Kappa Phi, Pi Mu Epsilon, Upsilon Pi Epsilon, Tau Beta Pi. Home: Ruston LA Oct. 18, 1983; buried Forest Lawn, Ruston.

JOHNSON, DONALD MILTON, insurance executive; b. Los Angeles, Feb. 15, 1920; s. Oscar E. and Maude F. (Philips) J.; m. Marguerite Glaze, Feb. 14, 1942; children: Stephen, Thomas, Andrew, Kenneth. B.S. UCLA, 1941. Field rep. Aetna Casualty & Surety Co. Los Angeles, 1946-50; supt. agy. dept. Aetna Casualty & Surety Co., 1950-55, mgr., 1956-60, gen. mgr., 1960-61; asst. v.p. exec. dept. Aetna Casualty & Surety Co. Hartford, 1960-65; v.p. corp. services Aetna Life & Casualty Co., 1965-66, v.p. exec. dept., 1966-67, sr. v.p., 1968, exec. v.p. ins. ops., 1968, pres., dir., mem. exec. com., 1970-76; chmn. bd., chief exec. officer Indsl. Indemnity Co., San Francisco, 1976-87; dir. Crum & Forster. Bd. dirs. Calif. Roundtable, St. Luke's Hosp.; trustee San Francisco Bay Area Council, City of Hope Pilot Med. Ctr., United Way of Bay Area; bd. dirs. Internat. Ins. Seminar, San Francisco Bay Area Council; bd. dirs., v.p. Calif. Workers' Compensation Inst. Served to maj. O.M.C. AUS, 1942-46. Mem. Am. Ins. Assn. (past chmn.), Health Ins. Assn. Am. (past chmn.), Nat. Assn. Casualty and Surety Execs. (past pres.), Ins. Inst. Am. (bd. govs.), Am. Inst. Property and Liability Underwriters (trustee), U.S. C. of C. (mem. policy com.), San Francisco C. of C. (dir., treas.). Congregationalist. Clubs: Pacific Union, Bankers (San Francisco); Menlo Country (Burlingame, Calif.). Died Apr. 16, 1987; cremated.

JOHNSON, EARL MORTIMER, hotel executive; b. Chgo., May 2, 1908; s. Francis Royal and Hilda Louise (Rapp) J.; m. Dolores Wetzel, Jan, 18, 1936; children—Dianne Marie, Dennis Dolan, Dolores Michelle, Valerie Ann, Bruce Anthony, Francis Jerome. B.S., Northwestern U., 1932. Pres. Johnson Land & Timber Co., 1936-86, Earl M. Johnson (realtors), 1945-86; owner Johnson's Rustic Resort, all Houghton Lake, Mich., 1936-86; Mem. exec. com. Mich. Indsl. Ambassadors. Pres. Mich. Tourist Council, 1953-54; Bd. dirs Mich. Accident Fund. Served to lt. USNR, 1943-45. Recipient Disting. Citizen award Mich. Ho. of Reps. 1978; named Mich. Ambassador of Tourism Gov. Millikan, 1980; named to Hospitality Mag. Hall of Fame, 1957. Mem. Hotel Assn. Redbook Directory Corp. (dir.), Am. Hotel Assn. (resort com., hon. mem.), Mich Hotel Assn. (past pres., hon. life dir.), Am. Hotel and Motel Assn. (cert. hotel adminstr., past pres., hon. life dir.), East Mich. Tourist Assn. (past pres.), Paul Bunyan Bd. Realtors (past pres.), Theta Xi. Clubs: Tavern (N.Y.C.); Chicago Culver (Chgo.), Executive (Chgo.). Home: Houghton Lake Mich. Died Oct. 20, 1986; buried Roscommon Twp. Cemetery, Houghton Lake.

JOHNSON, EARL SHEPARD, sociologist; b Stratford, Iowa, Sept. 14, 1894; s. Charles Frederick and Clara (Bridge) J.; m. Esther Charlotte Bailey, June 7, 1923 (dec.). AB, Baker U., 1918; MA, U. Chgo., 1932 PhD, 1941. Tchr., adminstr. pub. high schs., Kans. 1919-24; dir. field house activities South Park Commn. Chgo., 1925-30; fellow sociology U. Chgo., 1931, instr. sociology, 1932-36, asst. prof., 1936-41, asst. prof. social scis., 1941-46, assoc. prof., 1946-52, prof., 1952-59, prof. emeritus, 1959-86; chmn. com. divisional masters degree 1947-59; adviser to chancellor U. P.R., 1944; vis. prof. U. Mich., summers 1953, 54, Northwestern U., summers, 1956, 58; vis. prof. secondary edn. U. Wis., Milw., 1959-73; dir. Nat. Forum Found. Am. Edn., from 1958; cons. Ford Found. Fund for Advancement Edn., summer 1954, Indsl. Coll. Armed Forces, 1958. Author: Theory and Practice of the Social Studies, 1956 contbg, editor The Am. Behavioral Scientist, 1961-86 mem. exec. bd. Social Edn., 1960-86; mem. bd. advisers coun. for Mankind, 1960-86; contbr. articles to profl jours. 2d. lt., pursuit pilot U.S. Army, 1917-19. Mem Am. Sociol. Soc., Nat. Coun. Social Studies, Am. Assn Sch. Adminstrs. (mem. commn. 1948 yearbook), Delta Tau Delta. Democrat. Unitarian. Home: Milwaukee Wis. Died Jan. 8, 1986.

JOHNSON, GEORGE MARION, law educator, government official; b. Albuquerque, May 22, 1900; s. William Sloan and Ella (Alexander) J.; m. Evelyn Williams, July 23, 1954. AB, U. Calif., Berkeley, 1923, LLB, 1929, JSD, 1936. Bar: Calif. 1929. Pres. Student Inst. Pacific Rels., 1927; tax counsel Calif. Bd. Equalization, 1933-40; dep. chmn., acting gen. counsel Pres.'s Com. Fair Employment Practice, 1942-45; with Assn. Am. Law Schs., 1945-58, chmn. com. legal edn. and nat. def., 1953; prof. law Howard Law Sch., 1940-41, 45-58, dean, 1946-58; mem. U.S. Commn. Civil Rights, from 1958; mem. adv. com. D.C. Juvenile Ct., from 1958; guest lectr. Cath. U. of Rio de Janiero, 1959; seminar panelist U. Notre Dame, 1959; guest lectr. Douglass Coll., 1960; panelist 14th annual conf., div. social scis. Howard U., 1951. Contbr. articles to profl. jours. Bd dirs. D.C. Legal Aid Bur., 1955-87; mem. D.C. Auditorium Commn., 1956-67. Recipient D.C. Inspiration House achievement award, 1954; Sheffield-Sanborn scholar U. Calif., Berkeley, 1929-30. Mem. ABA, Nat Bar Assn., Am. Judicature Soc., Am. Assn. U. Profs. NAACP (legal com. 1950-87), Alpha Phi Alpha. Died Aug. 11, 1987.

JOHNSON, HAROLD T., congressman. m. Albra I. Manuel; 2 children. Mayor City of Roseville, Calif.; state senator Calif., 1948-58; mem. 86th -96th Congresses from 1st Calif. dist., 1959-81. Mem Brotherhood of Ry. Clks., Eagles, Moose, Elks, Lambda Chi Alpha. Home: Roseville Calif. Died Mar. 16, 1988.

JOHNSON, HOWARD J., banker. m. Mary Johnson; children: Mary Kay Johnson Frazier, Karen Johnson Vance, Rosemary Johnson Muchow, Diane Johnson Lolli, Robert, Terry. BA, DePaul U., JD, 1935; postgrad., Grad. Sch. Banking, Rutgers U. Fed. bank examiner 1935-37; with trust dept. Am. Nat. Bank, Chgo., 1937-73, v.p., 1952-66, exec. v.p., 1966-73, also sec. bd. dirs.; co-founder Water Tower Trust and Savs. Bank, 1974. Bd. dirs. St. Francis Hosp., Catholic charities; trustee Loyola U., DePaul U. Mem. Corp. Fiduciaries Assn. of Ill. (past pres.), Ill. Bankers Assn. (past pres. trust div.), Chgo. Bar Assn. (past treas.). Home: Evanston IL 60201 Died Feb. 22, 1987.

JOHNSON, HUGH, publishing company executive; b. N.Y.C., Nov. 27, 1919; s. C. Haldane and Sophie (Sanders) J.; m. Anne I. Marco Vecchio, Sept. 25, 1965; children by previous marriage—Marion S., Virginia W., Douglas H. Grad., Lawrenceville Sch., 1939. With A.S. Barnes & Co., N.Y.C., 1945-58; v.p. sales A.S. Barnes & Co., 1952-58; with Hammond, Inc., Maplewood, N.J., 1958-86, v.p., 1962-68, exec. v.p., 1968-86, dir., 1965-86; sr. v.p. Salem House, Inc., Boston, 1987. Pres. South Orange (N.J.) Rescue Squad, 1958-60; Trustee Arlington (N.J.) Cemetery, 1960-87. Served to 1st lt. inf. AUS, 1941-45, ETO. Mem. Assn. Am. Pubs. (program chmn. 1973), Pubs. Lunch Club (pres. 1974-75). Presbyn. Clubs: Seaview (Absecon, N.J.); Essex County Country (West Orange, N.J.); Coffee House (N.Y.C.). Home: Clifton N.J. Died Feb. 4, 1987, buried Arlington (N.J.) Cemetery.

JOHNSON, JESSE LEE, JR., banker; b. Pecos, Tex., 1891. Chmn., bd. dirs. 1st Nat. Bank Ft. Worth; chmn. Cicero Smith Lumber Co., W.T. Waggoner Bldg., Ft. Worth; bd. dirs. Ft. Worth & Denver City Ry.; mem. adv. com. Lumbermen's Underwriters, Houston. Home: Fort Worth Tex. †

JOHNSON, JOHN ARTHUR, livestock association executive; b. Mankato, Minn., Sept. 3, 1892; s. Swan Lundahl and Amanda Elizabeth (Johnson) J.; m. Esther Elvira Stark, Nov. 24, 1927. Student, U. Minn., 1911, Internat. Corr. Schs., 1916-17. Asst. supt. Widell Co., Mankato, 1914-20; ptnr., sec., treas. G.A. Lewis, Inc., Mankato, 1920-35; farmer 1935-51; dir. Cen. Livestock Assn., St. Paul, 1941-74, pres., 1954-73; mem. Cottonwood County Farm Bur., 1935—; bd. dirs. Farmers Elevator Co., Darfur, Minn., 1939-72, pres., 1944-72; chmn. Upper Watonwan River Watershed, 1964-73. Treas. Immanuel Hosp., Mankato, 1932-45. Mem. Masons, Shriners, Lions. Republican. Lutheran. Home: Darfur Minn. Deceased.

JOHNSON, JOHN HAROLD, sports association executive; b. S.I., N.Y., Sept. 26, 1921; s. John Walter and Alexandra (Niiles) J.; m. Lillian Alice Bauer, Nov. 1, 1947 (dec. Dec. 23, 1984); children: Barbara Ann Johnson Tornichia, Thomas Walter. Student public schs., S.I. Gen. mgr. Binghamton (N.Y.) Baseball Club, 1951-54; farm dir. N.Y. Yankees, 1956-64, v.p., 1965-69; adminstr. Office of Baseball Commr., N.Y.C., 1970-78; pres. Nat. Assn. Profl. Baseball Leagues, St. Petersburg, Fla., 1979-88; chmn. Ofcl. Baseball Rules Com. Served with USCG, 1942-46, MTO; ETO. Mem. Am. Legion. Lutheran. Home: Saint Petersburg Fla. Died Jan., 10, 1988; buried Ocean View Cemetery, Oakwood Heights, Staten Island, N.Y.

JOHNSON, KERMIT ALONZO, university president; b. Boaz, Ala., Dec. 16, 1911; s. John Arree and Eunice (Pruett) J.; m. Golda Watson, Mar. 21, 1932; 1 dau., Judith Kay. BS, U. Ala., 1938, MA, 1944; EdD, Columbia U., 1949. Tchr. Cullman (Ala.) County Schs., 1929-36; prin. Garden City (Ala.) Jr. High Sch., 1936-43, Kate Duncan Smith DAR High Sch., Grant, Ala., 1943-45; supt. Tuscaloosa (Ala.) County Schs., 1945-59; assoc. supt. Jefferson County (Ala.) Schs., Birmingham, 1959-61, supt., 1961-68; pres. U. Montevallo (Ala.), 1968-86; participant Fulbright Act, Italy, The Netherlands. Mem. Commn. of the States Compact; bd. dirs. Birmingham Civic Sumphony Assn., Community Chest; chmn. Shelby County March of Dimes; bd. dirs. Boy Scouts Am. Resipient Preeminent Ala. Educator award, 1971; named in honorKermit A. Johnson Field, U. Montevallo, Kermit A. Johnson Elem. Sch., Jefferson County, Ala., Kermit A. Johnson award for Outstanding Supt. of Schs. Mem. Am. Assn. Sch. Adminstrs. (life), Ala. Assn. Sch. Adminstrs. (pres. 1951-53), Ala. Hist. Commn., Coun. Univ. Pres.' Ala. (chmn. 1972-75), Ala. Edn. Assn. (pres. 1963-64), Ala. Congress Parents and Tchrs. (life, 2d v.p. 1958-61), NEA (life), Rotary (past pres. Tuscaloosa, dist. gov. internat. orgn. 1976-77, mem. U.S. Congl. Adv. Bd. 1984-86), Birmingham Execs. Club (past pres.), The Club, Vestavia Country Club, Phi Delta Kappa (past pres.), Kappa Phi Kappa (past pres.). Home: Birmingham Ala. Died Nov. 19, 1986; buried Southern Heritage, Birmingham.

JOHNSON, LELAND PARRISH, biologist, emeritus educator; b. Ponemah, Ill., Nov. 14, 1910; s. Carl W. and Dora M. (Parrish) J.; m. Marion E. Schiess, Aug. 25, 1940 (dec. 1976); children: Christine Ann, Don Alan; m. Carolyn Jones Eades, July 29, 1979. B.S., Monmouth Coll., 1932; M.S., State U. Iowa, 1937, Ph.D., 1942; Ford faculty fellow, Harvard U., 1955-56. Sci. tchr. Reynolds (Ill.) High Sch., 1933-36; mem. faculty Drake U., 1937-86, prof. biology, 1947-81, prof. emeritus, 1981-86, chmn. dept., 1956, coordinator sci. div., 1958; dean Drake U. (Coll. Liberal Arts), 1971-76, dir. cancer research, 1958-81; dir. insts. tchr. research participation programs NSF, 1959-81; cons. gen. edn. Iowa League Nursing, 1958-86 ; ednl. adv. bd. Iowa Meth. Hosp., 1952-86 ; chmn. Iowa Bd. Basic Sci. Examiners, 1957-86. Contbr. to lab. manuals, monographs, articles. Recipient Distinguished Alumni award Monmouth Coll., 1957. Mem. NEA, AAAS, Am. Micros. Soc., N. Y. Acad. Sci., Iowa Acad. Sci. (pres. 1965-66), Soc. Protozoologists, Am. Inst. Biol. Scis., Nat. Assn. Research Sci. Teaching, Nat. Assn. Biology Tchrs., Assn. Midwest Biology Tchrs. (pres. 1958), Soc. History Sci., Phi Beta Kappa, Sigma Xi. Home: Des Moines Iowa. Died Apr. 19, 1986.

JOHNSON, MARIAN WILLARD (MRS. DAN R. JOHNSON), art gallery executive; b. N.Y.C., Apr. 20, 1904; s. Eugene Sands and Ella (Guthrie) Willard; m. Dan R. Johnson, Sept. 7, 1944; children: Danna (Mrs. Daniel Schuyler Dunning), Marianne G. (Mrs. David Wirtz). Grad., Chapin Sch., 1922. Founder East River Gallery, N.Y.C., 1936-38; dir. Neumann Willard Gallery, N.Y.C., 1938-40; founder, prin. Willard Gallery, N.Y.C., from 1940. Chmn. adv. com., trustee Mus. Modern Art, N.Y.C., 1944-46; trustee, chmn. Asia House Gallery, N.Y.C., 1959-80; founding v.p. Mus. Am. Folk Art, N.Y.C., 1962-69, sec. 1971-73, hon. trustee, from 1975. Mem. Cosmopolitan Club. Home: New York N.Y. Deceased.

JOHNSON, NAPOLEON B(ONAPARTE), justice; b. Maysville, Okla., Jan. 17, 1891; s. John Wade and Sarah Jane (Mays) J.; m. Vera L. Cottingham, Feb. 1921 (div. 1922); 1 child, Betty Jean (Mrs. Marshal Alexander); m. Martha L. Weber, Aug. 24, 1927. Student, Henry Kendall Coll. (now Tulsa U., 1909-11, Okla. Mil. Acad., 1911-13; LLB, Cumberland U., 1921. Bar: Okla. 1921, U.S. Supreme Ct., 1946. Pvt. practice Claremore, Okla., 1921-23; asst. county atty. Rogers County, Okla., 1923-24, county atty., 1925-31; dist. judge 12th Jud. Dist., 1934-49; justice Supreme Ct. Okla., from 1948, vice chief justice, then chief justice, 1955-57; mem. adv. com. on Indian health Office of Surgeon Gen., 1956-59. Mem. arts commn. Thomas Gilcrease Inst. Am. History and Art, Inc.; mem. Crazy Horse Meml. Found. Commn., Cherokee Found.; past pres. Inter-Tribal Coun. 5 Civilized Tribes, Gov.'s Interstate Coun. on Indian Affairs, also Okla. rep., chmn. com. on law and order; pres. Nat. Hall of Fame Famous Am. Indians; bd. dirs., life mem. Okla. Hist. Soc. Recipient Freedoms Found. award, 1955. Mem. Nat. Congress Am. Indians U.S. and Alaska (past pres.), Okla. Bar Assn., Jud. Coun. Okla, Masons (32 degree), Elks, Rotary (hon.). Home: Claremore Okla. †

JOHNSON, NOYE MONROE, geology educator; b. Milw., Dec. 12, 1930; s. Oscar Monroe and Agnes (Seglar) J.; m. Dolores Ruth Adamson, June 9, 1953; children: Deborah Ann, Ann Therese. BS, Kans. U., 1953; MS, U. Wis., PhD, 1962. Mem. faculty dept. geology Dartmouth Coll., Hanover, N.H., 1961-87, prof., 1971-87, chmn. dept. earth scis., 1969-70; cons. geochemistry, water resources and geochronology; mem. U.S. nat. working group Internat. Geol. Correlation Program; cons. U.S. Com. on Lake Nutrient Cycling. Contbr. articles to profl. jours. Served as aviator USN, 1953-57. U.S. AEC grantee, 1962-68, NSF grantee, 1962-87. Fellow Geol. Soc. Am.; mem. Am. Geophys. Union. Home: Hanover N.H. Died Dec. 27, 1987; buried Hubbard Brook, Campton, N.H.

JOHNSON, PAUL SHELDON, clergyman; b. Na-Au-Say, Ill., July 15, 1891; s. Oliver C. and Anna Mary (French) J.; m. Franc Irene Dunning, Nov. 14 1918; children: Marian French, Paul Sheldon. AB, Carroll Coll., 1913, DD, 1928; grad., McCormick Theol. Sem., 1917; postgrad., U. Chgo., 1926-27, U. Wis., 1929-30. Ordained to ministry Presbyn. Ch. U.S.A., 1917. Pastor 1st Ch., Rapid City, S.D., 1919-20, Madison, S.D., 1920-24; synodical exec. Synod of S.D., 1924-26; pastor Christ Ch., Madison, Wis., 1926-30, 1st Ch., La Grange, Ill., 1930-36, Green Ridge Ch., Scranton, Pa., 1936-38; exec. sec., sput. Ch. Extension Bd. Presbytery of Chgo., 1938-56; parish minister Michillinda Ch., from 1957. Chaplain U.S. Army, 1918-19. Mem. Am. Legion, Masons, Elks, Tau Kappa Epsilon. Republican. Home: Pasadena Calif. †

JOHNSON, REDFORD K(OHLSAAT), physician; b. Chgo., Jan. 25, 1890; s. Joseph French and Caroline Temperance (Stolp) J.; m. Florence Virginia Dow, Apr. 20, 1927 (dec. 1951); m. Mildred Sohn Blancard, Feb. 24, 1953; 1 child, Joanne Johnson Eisenhardt. Student, Williams Coll.; MD, Columbia U., 1915. Intern Kings County Hosp., 1915-17; roentgenologist N.J. State Hosp., Trenton, St. Bartholomew's Hosp., N.Y.C., Midtown Hosp., 1920-40; bd. dirs. Andrew Todd McClintock Found. Bd. dirs. Alexander Hamilton Inst., from 1932, chmn. bd., from 1935. Mem. AMA, Radiol. Soc. N.Am. Unitarian. Home: New York N.Y. †

JOHNSON, STANLEY BRYCE, coal executive; b. Columbus, Ohio, Nov. 12, 1892; s. Edward and Helen (Musser) J.; m. Mary Landrum, Oct. 19, 1916; children: Stanley Bryce, Charlotte, Baylor (Mrs. William H. Barrett), Timothy L. Student, Ohio State U., 1915, Ecole Militaire, Saumur, France, 1918. Salesman The Lorain Coal & Dock Co., Columbus, 1919-24, sales mgr., 1924-32, pres., 1932-60, chmn. bd., from 1960; chmn. bd. Lorado Coal Mining Co.; founder Appalachian Coals, Inc.; mem. adv. coun. Eastman Kodak Co.; mem. Bituminous Coal Inst., Bituminous Coal Producers Bd. Dist. 4; mem. wage scale com. Bituminous Coal Div. Trustee Children's Hosp.; mem. adv. bd. Ohio State Safety Coun., Cleve.; mem. Mus. Natural History, Mus. Modern Art, N.Y.C. Lt. USAAF, 1918-19. Recipient 2d pl. award Freedoms Found., 4th pl. award Lorain-Lorado Jour., 1950. Fellow Am. Geog. Soc.; mem. Nat. Audubon Soc., Pictorial Photographers Am., Pictorial Soc. Am. (pictorial div. award of merit), Columbus Club, rocky Fork Hunt and Country Club, Castalia Club, Trout Club, Union Tavern Club. Home: Columbus Ohio. †

JOHNSON, WALLACE EDWARDS, motel chain executive and builder; b. Edinburg, Miss., Jan. 5, 1901; s. Felix A. and Josephine (Edwards) J.; m. Alma McCool, Aug. 10, 1924. Student, Moorehead (Miss.) Jr. Coll.; LLD, Gordon Coll., 1968, Harding Coll., 1970; hon. degree, Cal. Bapt. Coll., 1972. Co-founder, vice chmn. Holiday Inns Inc. (formerly Holiday Inns of Am. Inc.), Memphis, 1953-88; founder, chmn. Wallace E. Johnson Enterprises (formerly Wallace E. Johnson Inc.), builders, Memphis, 1941-88; pres. Service Mortgage & Investment Co., Memphis, 1945-88; co-founder, chmn. bd. dirs. Medicenters of Am. Inc., Memphis, 1966-88, Alodex Corp., Memphis, 1967-88. Mem. adv. bd. Bapt. Hosp., Memphis; chmn. exec. com. Religious Heritage Am. Inc., Washington; trustee Gordon Coll., Wenham, Mass., LeTourneau Coll., Lonview Tex. Named Layman of Yr., Religious Heritage Am. Inc., 1965; recipient Horatio Alger award, 1968, Outstanding Community Salesman award, Golden Plate award Am. Acad. Achievement, 1973; named to Hospitality Mag. Hall of Fame. Mem. So. Assn. Colls. and Schs. (adv. bd.), Nat. Assn. Home Builders (regional v.p. 1946-48), Memphis Home Builders Assn. (pres.), Kiwanis Club (life). Home: Memphis Tenn. Died Apr. 27, 1988; buried Memphis, Tenn.

JOHNSON, WENDELL EUGENE, civil engineer; b. Mpls., Sept. 23, 1910; s. Eugene Gustave and Lydia Magdalena (Jenson) J.; m. Margaret Selwyn Thomas, June 22, 1946; children: David Wendell, Tucker Eugene. BCE, U. Minn., 1931. Field office engr. Minn. Hwy. Dept., various cities, 1931-33; office engr., specifications writer C.E. U.S. Army, Conchas Dam, N.M. and Caddoa, Colo., 1938-40; chief div. engring. Omaha dist. C.E. U.S. Army, 1946-49; chief engring div. Missouri River div. C.E. U.S. Army, Omaha, 1949-61; chief engring. div. for civil works Office Chief of Engrs., Washington, 1961-70; chief sect. civil design Third Locks Panama Canal, Diablo Heights, C.Z., 1940-42, asst. constrn. chief to constrn. chief, 1942-43; internat. cons. engr. on dams, water resources, McLean, Va., 1970-82. Maj. C.E., AUS, 1943-45, ETO. Decorated Bronze Star with oak leaf cluster; recipient Outstanding Achievement award U. Minn., 1968. Mem. Nat. Acad. Engring, ASCE (hon.), Soc. Am. Mil. Engrs., Nat. Soc. Profl. Engrs., Cosmos Club, Washington Golf Club, Tau Beta Pi, Chi Epsilon. Home: McLean Va. Died Feb. 26, 1982; buried Arlington, Va.

JOHNSON, WILLARD LYON, organization executive; b. Sterling, Ill., Dec. 1, 1905; s. James William and Anna Laura (Lyon) J.; m. Marjorie Elta Hackenberg, Feb. 9, 1936; children—Willard Lyon, Miriam Ellen. A.B., Drake U., 1930, M.A., 1932; B.D., Colgate-Rochester Div. Sch., 1933. Ordained to ministry Disciples of Christ Ch., 1930; asso. minister Plymouth Congl. Ch., Des Moines, 1939-41; dean men, dir. personnel Drake U., 1934-38; regional dir. NCCJ, 1938-42, 58; dir. NCCJ, Chgo., 1955-58; asst. to pres. 1942-45, v.p., 1945-47, nat. program dir., 1947-51; European dir. World Brotherhood, 1951, sec.-gen., 1951-55; pres. Com. Internat. Econ. Growth, 1958-60; v.p. Am. Edn. Found., Geneva, Switzerland, sec. human rights com., 1947-49; chief mission CARE, Berlin, Germany, 1960-62; exec. dir. Unitarian Universalist Service Com., 1962-65, Am. Freedom from Hunger Found., Inc., FAO, 1965-66, Center for Research and Edn., 1966-67; dir. internat. devel. Calif. Western U., 1967-68; exec. dir. Planned Parenthood, San Diego, 1968-70; 1st v.p. Zero Population Growth, Inc., 1971, chmn., 1972-73; dir. Population Study Center, from 1974; Cons. State Dept., Germany, 1950; gen. sec. U.S. com. UN Genocide Conv., 1948; exec. com. Nat. Assn. Intergroup Relations Ofcls., from 1950; cons. nat. radio network programs Light of the World and Superman; religious news reporter sta. WHO, Des Moines, 1938-41, sta. KWK, St. Louis, 1941-42; asst. commentator Religion in the News, NBC, 1947-49; del. World Council Chs. Consultations, Salonika, Greece, 1959; mem. adv. bd. Integrated Planning Office County of San Diego, from 1975. Author: Population and Quality of Life, 1971, Better Organizations, 1974, Population Primer, 1974; Contbr. chpts., articles to various publs., also profl. jours. Trustee Bur. Intercultural Edn., Inst. Am. Democracy, World Alliance Internat. Friendship Through Religion, chmn. scholarship fund, Pleasantville, N.Y. Recipient Distinguished Service award Drake U., 1956. Mem. Religious Radio Assn. (pres. 1947-49), Soc. Psychol. Study Social Issues, Soc. Internat. Devel. (mem. council, pres. Boston chpt.), UN Assn. (pres. San Diego 1970-75), Phi

Beta Kappa, Omicron Delta Kappa, Psi Chi. Unitarian. Home: San Diego Calif. Deceased.

JOHNSTON, JAMES HUGO, JR., college administrator; b. Ettrick, Va., May 10, 1891; s. James Hugo and Anna (Burrell) J.; m. Bessie Adkins, Sept. 24, 1922; 1 child, James Hugo. Student, Va. State Coll., 1905-09; AB, Va. Union U., 1913; AM, U. Chgo., 1925, PhD, 1937. Mem. faculty Va. State Coll., from 1914, from instr. to prof. history, 1914-20, dean of coll., 1929-49, from 1950, acting pres., 1949-50, v.p., coll. historian. Author: Race Relations in the South, 1776-1860, 1837. Mem. Assn. Am. Colls. and Secondary Schs. for Negroes (pres. 1942), Am. Hist. Assn., Assn. for Study of Negro Life and History, Va. Social Sci. Assn. Address: Petersburg Va. †

JOHNSTON, PAUL ALEXANDER, business executive; b. Smithfield, N.C., May 17, 1916; s. Albert S. and Gayle (Makepeace) J.; m. Margaret McGirt, Aug. 31, 1949; 1 son, Paul A. AB, U. N.C., 1950, LLB, 1952. Bar: N.C. 1952. Assoc. Satterlee, Warfield and Stephens, N.Y.C., 1952; asst. dir. Inst. Govt., U. N.C., 1953; adminstrv. asst. to Gov. Luther H. Hodges 1954-57; dir. adminstrn. N.C., 1957-60; asst. to controller Burlington Industries, Greensboro, N.C., 1960; exec. asst. to sec. Dept. Commerce, 1961; v.p. contracts Martin Co. div. Martin Marietta Corp., 1961-63; pres. cement and lime div. Martin Co. div. Martin Marietta Corp., N.Y.C., 1963-65; v.p. Martin Marietta Corp., 1963-65; pres. Glen Alden Corp., 1965-72; chmn. bd., chief exec. officer Johnston Industries Inc. (acquired by GI Exports Corp., 1984), 1972-84, pres., chmn. bd., chief exec. officer Johnson Group subs., 1984-85; chmn. bd. dirs. Whitehead & Kales Inc., Detroit, 1977-85, Johnston Industries Ltd., London; bd. dirs. Beaufort Engring., Kirby-in-Ashfield, Eng. Editor-in -chief N.C. Law Rev., 1952. With AUS, 1944-46. Mem. N.C. State Bar, N.C. Bar Assn., Bar Eastern Dist. N.C., Order of Coif, Phi Delta Phi. Democrat. Presbyterian. Home: Chapel Hill N.C. Died Sept. 18, 1985, buried Chapel Hill.

JOHNSTON, PAUL WILLIAM, railroad executive; b. Transfer, Pa., July 5, 1892; s. William R. and Amelia (Nowlen) J.; m. Dorothea Abrams, Sept. 2, 1916; children: Paul W., Barbara T., Johnston Zarbock, James D., Dorothea R. AB, Allegheny Coll., 1914, LLD (hon.); postgrad., Boston U., 1916-17; ScD (hon.), Alfred U., 1951. With Erie R.R., from 1918, v.p., 1945-49, pres., 1949-56, chief exec. officer, 1956-57, chmn. bd., 1956-60, chmn. exec. com., from 1960. Trustee Allegheny Coll., Meadville, Pa. Brig. gen. AUS, 1944. Decorated DSM. Mem. Transp. Assn. Am., Phi Gamma Delta, Phi Beta Kappa, Delta Sigma Rho. Home: Shaker Heights Ohio. †

JOHNSTON, S(AMUEL) PAUL, museum executive; b. Pitts., Aug. 3, 1899; s. James Irvin and Bertha Wilson (Gill) J.; m. Virgina Thomas, 1956; children: Mrs. Thomas Ballard, James Irvin II. Student, Carnegie Inst. Tech., 1917-19; BSMechE, MIT, 1921; DSc (hon.), Adelphi Coll., 1957. With Aluminum Co. Am., 1921-29; writer, editor 1930-40; coordinator research NACA, 1940-42; with Curtiss-Wright Corp., 1942-43; dir., then exec. sec. Inst. Aero. Scis. (later merged with Am. Rocket Soc. to become AIAA), N.Y.C., 1946-64; dir. Nat. Air and Space Mus. Smithsonian Inst., Washington, 1964-69; dir. Chesapeake Bay Maritime Mus., 1969-70, mem. gov. bd., 1969-85; exec. dir. Pres.'s Air Policy Commn., 1948, Pres.'s Airport Commn., 1952; cons. MIT Lexington Project, 1948; mem. aero. com. on research and devel. Dept. Def., 1949-53; dir. Flight Safety Found., N.Y. Chmn. aero. engring. adv. com. Princeton U. With U.S. Army, 1918; capt. USNR, 1944-46, ETO, PTO. Decorated Legion of Merit. Fellow Inst. Aero. Scis., Royal Aero. Soc.; mem. Cosmos Club, Army and Navy Club, Army and Navy Country Club. Home: Sumner Md. Died Aug. 9, 1985.

JOLLEY, HAROLD DEAN, steel products company executive; b. St. Louis, Oct. 30, 1890; s. Edwin James and Emily (Dean) J.; m. Hazel Burch, Apr. 30, 1917. BS, Washington U., St. Louis, 1911, MCE, 1914. Structural engr. Brussell & Viterbo, St. Louis, 1911-16; chief engr. Ceco Steel Products Corp., Chgo., 1916-21, dist. mgr., Omaha, 1921-37, also bd. dirs., from 1924, v.p., 1927-51, sr. v.p., 1951-61, mem. exec. com., from 1961. Mem. Concrete Reinforcing Steel Inst. (pres. 1945-46), ASCE, Sigma Xi. Home: Oak Park Ill. †

JONAS, CHARLES RAPER, congressman; b. Lincolnton, N.C., Dec. 9, 1904; s. Charles A. and Rosa (Petrie) J.; m. Annie Elliott Lee, Aug. 14, 1928; children: Charles Raper, Richard Elliott. AB, U. N.C., 1925, JD, 1928. Bar: N.C. 1929. Asst. U.S. atty. western dist. N.C. 1931-33; mem. 83d-87th Congresses from 10th dist. N.C., 88th-91st Congresses from 8th dist. N.C., 91st-92d Congresses from 9th dist. N.C. Mem. N.C. Bd. Law Examiners, 1947-48. With U.S. Army, 1939-46; ret. col. N.C.N.G. Mem. Am., D.C., N.C. (pres. 1946-47), Lincoln County bar assns., Order of Coif, Rotary, Phi Delta Phi, Chi Phi. Republican. Methodist. Home: Lincolnton N.C. Died Sept. 28, 1988.

JONES, ALICE HANSON, economist; b. Seattle, Nov. 7, 1904; d. Olof and Agatha Marie (Tiegel) Hanson; m. Homer Jones, Apr. 21, 1930; children: Robert Hanson, Richard John, Douglas Coulthurst. A.B., U. Wash., 1925, M.A., 1928; Ph.D., U. Chgo., 1968. Teaching fellow U. Wash., 1927-28; fellow, research asst. econs. U. Chgo., 1928-29, 32-34; asst. editor Ency. Social Scis., N.Y.C., 1930; researcher, writer Pres.'s Com. Social Trends, N.Y.C., 1931; economist, asst. chief Cost of Living div. Bur. Labor Stats., Washington, 1934-44; economist div. statis. standards Bur. Budget, Washington, 1945-48; sec. com. nat. accounts Nat. Bur. Econ. Research, Washington, 1957; supervising economist, cons. Dept. Agr. Econ. Research, Washington, 1958-61; lectr. econs. Washington U., St. Louis, 1963-68, asst. prof., 1968-71, assoc. prof., 1971-73, adj. prof., 1973-77, prof. emeritus, 1977-86; prin. investigator Social Sci. Inst., 1969-86; adj. prof. econs. Claremont Men's Coll., 1973-74; econ. adviser Bank of Korea, 1967-68, AID, 1967-68. Author: American Colonial Wealth: Documents and Methods, 3 vols., rev. edit., 1978, Wealth of a Nation to Be: The American Colonies on the Eve of the Revolution, 1980. Named Woman of Achievement St. Louis Globe Democrat, 1980; research grantee NSF, 1969-75, NEH, 1970-76. Mem. Am. Econ. Assn., Econ. History Assn. (v.p. 1976-77, pres. 1982-83, trustee 1983-86), Orgn. Am. Historians, Internat. Assn. Reearch in Income and Wealth, Social Sci. History Assn., Mortar Board, Phi Beta Kappa, Delta Zeta (Nat. Woman of Yr. 1981), Beta Phi Alpha (nat. pres. 1932-32), Omicron Delta Epsilon. Congregationalist. Died Aug. 30, 1986.

JONES, EARL GARDNER, orthodontist; b. Granville, Ohio, June 13, 1891; s. Cyrus George and Anna (Gardner) J.; m. Anita C. Thomas, June 25, 1918; children: Joanne (Mrs. Ralph W. Howard), Barbara (Mrs.Thomas C. Taylor). DDS, Ohio State U., 1912; student, Coll. of Med., 1914-16. Pvt. practice Columbus, Ohio, 1912-14; pvt. practice limited to orthodontics from 1915; instr. in orthodontics (part-time) Coll. of Dentistry, Ohio State U., Columbus, 1916-25, asst. prof., 1925-34, assoc. prof., 1934-40, prof., from 1940, head dept., from 1916, head grad. and postgrad sch. of orthodontics, from 1940. Author: Chpt. 24, A Course of Study, 1935; contbr. articles to dental publs. Served as program chmn. 1st Pan-Am. Orthodontic Congress, 1942. Mem. ADA (past trustee), Ohio State Dental soc. (pres. 1937, treas. and sec.), Columbus Dental soc. (pres. 1929), Am. Dental Schs. Assn. (mem. com. on orthodontic curriculum survey, 1931-34), Great Lakes Orthodontic Soc., Am. Orthodontic Assn. (pres. 1947), Am. Bd. of Orthodontics, Mex. Assn. Orthodontists (hon. mem., Pierre Fauchard Acad. (hon.), Masons (Shriner, Scottish rite, 33 degree), Torch Club, Rotary Club, Xi Psi Phi, Alpha Kappa Kappa, Omicron Kappa Upsilon (pres. 1922). Republican. Mem. Methodist-Episcopal Ch. Home: Columbus Ohio. †

JONES, EDWIN HOWARD, JR., paper executive; b. Waterbury, Conn., July 21, 1917; s. Edwin Howard and Ruth (Angrave) J.; m. Evelyn Mae Rowe, Aug. 28, 1948; children: Edwin Howard, Stephen Rowe, Bruce Angrave, Sherrill Chapman. A.B., Yale U., 1939; M.B.A., Harvard U., 1941. With St. Regis Paper Co., N.Y.C., 1946-82, adminstrv. asst. to v.p., 1955-59, gen. sales mgr. Kraft div., 1960-61, exec. asst. to v.p., chief adminstrv. officer, 1962-68, v.p., gen. mgr. printing paper div., 1968-72, v.p. internat. div., 1972-74, exec. v.p. fin. and adminstrn., 1974-79, vice chmn., chief fin. officer, dir. internat. ops., 1979-82, chmn. exec. com., 1981-82, ret.; dir. Flakt, Inc., SC Mgmt. Corp. Mem. Rep. Town Meeting, Darien, Conn., 1957-64, chmn. fin. com., 1962-64; mem. Darien Bd. Edn., 1964-70, chmn., 1968-70; mem. Darien Bd. Fin., from 1985. Served with USNR, 1941-46, Atlantic, European, Far Eastern theatres; comdr. Res. ret. Methodist. Clubs: Masons, Wee Burn Country. Home: Darien Conn. Died Jan. 4, 1988.

JONES, ELMER RUTLEDGE, publishing executive; b. Balt., Aug. 18, 1921; s. Elmer O. and Elizabeth Virginia (Meyers) J.; m. Edith M. Averell, Feb. 8, 1948; 1 son, Christopher Warren. B.A. in Journalism, U. So. Cal., 1951. Circulation mgr. Annals of Internal Medicine; dir. bus. dept. Annals Internal Medicine, 1983-86; ret. 1986; publ. Am. Coll. Physicians, Phila., 1957-63; conv. mgr. for assn. Am. Coll. Physicians, 1963-73, publs. mgr. for assn., 1973-82; partner Sugarbush Antiques, Strasburg, Pa., 1972-88. Served with USAAF, 1942-45. Home: Phila. Pa. Died Aug. 10, 1988; buried Middle Octara Cemetery, Quarryville, Pa.

JONES, ERNEST CARL, finance educator; b. Atlanta, La., Feb. 17, 1921; s. Rufus T. and Nena (Franks) J.; m. Helen L. Worsham, Dec. 25, 1944; children: Kenneth Carl, Carol Annette. BS, Southwestern La. Inst., 1941; MA, La. State U., 1947, PhD (hon.), 1962. Faculty dept. econs. La. Tech. U., Ruston, 1947-74, prof. econs., 1962-74, head dept. econs. and fin., 1964-74; head dept. fin. Miss State U., 1974-85; cons. Gulf South Rsch. Inst., 1966, La. Revenue Dept., 1970-71. Author: Lincoln Parish, Louisiana, 1939-57, 1957, An Economic Appraisal of Public Revenues and Expenditures in Lincoln Parish, Louisiana, 1962, A Severance Damage Study on Interstate System, Louisiana, 1967, Louisiana's Agriculture: Some Observations, 1973, Contribution and Benefits from Louisiana's Fiscal Process, By Parish and Fiscal Year, 1969, Financing Agricultural Firms in Mississippi, 1976, Agricultural Agencies in Mississippi, 1976. With U.S. Army, 1942-45. Mem. So. Econs. Assn., Southwestern Fedn. Adminstrv. Disciplines, Fin. Mgmt. Assn., La. Tchrs. Assn. (unit pres. 1963-64), Lions (chmn. edn. com. 1967-68, 1st v.p. 1968, pres. 1969), Kiwanis, Nat. Block and Bridle Club (hon.), Beta Gamma Sigma, Delta Sigmal Pi, Omicron Delta Epsilon, Omicron Delta Kappa. Home: Starkville Miss. Died Dec. 1985.

JONES, FRED, automobile executive; b. LaFayette, Ga., Mar. 9, 1892; s. Thomas Jefferson and Jennie B. (Allison) J.; m. Mary Eddy Neal, Jan.25, 1923. Student pub. schs., LaFayette. Pres. Fred Jones Inc., Oklahoma City and Norman, Okla., from 1938, Fred Jones Co., Tulsa, from 1938, Fred Jones Mfg. Co., Oklahoma City, from 1946, Fred Jones Leasing Co., Tulsa, from 1961, Jones & Pellow Oil Co., Oklahoma City; v.p. Hall-Jones Oil Corp., Oklahoma City; bd. dirs 1st Nat. Bank & trust Co., Oklahoma City. Mem. advance com. Coun. Nat. Def., Washington; vice chmn. W.P.B., 1942; bd. dirs. Mills Coll., Simpson Coll. Mem. Orientation Conf. Assn., Oklahoma City Golf and Country Club (dir.). Home: Oklahoma City Okla. †

JONES, HOMER, economist, consultant; b. Ainsworth, Iowa, June 25, 1906; s. John Crawford and Nellie (Pearson) J.; m. Alice Cable Hanson, Apr. 21, 1930 (dec.); children: Robert Hanson, Richard John, Douglas Coulthurst. AB, State U. Iowa, 1927, MA, 1928; PhD, U. Chgo., 1949. Faculty mem. U. Pitts., 1929-30, Rutgers U., 1930-32; with Brookings Inst., Washington, 1934-35, FDIC, 1935-46, Com. Econ. Devel., 1946-49, Fed. Res. Bd., 1949-58; officer Fed. Res. Bank, St. Louis, 1958-71, sr. v.p., 1969-71, dir. econ. research, editor monthy rev., 1958-71; part-time vis. prof. Claremont Men's Coll., Washington U., St. Louis; regent's lectr. U. Calif. at L.A.; econ. advisor Republic of Korea. Author numerous articles in field. Fellow Royal Econ. Soc.; mem. Am Statis. Assn. (past. pres. Washington and St. Louis chpts.), Am. Fin. Assn., Am. Econ. Assn., Cosmos Club Washington, Phi Beta Kappa. Home: Webster Groves Mo. Died Mar. 14, 1986.

JONES, JOSEPH SEVERN, lawyer; b. Montpelier, Idaho, Mar. 23, 1905; s. John Joseph and Elizabeth (Severn) J.; m. Marjorie Allen, June 24, 1931; children: Allen Severn, John Samuel Roger, Joseph Stepehn Lowry. BA, U. Utah, 1927; JD, U. Chgo., 1930. Bar: Utah 1929, U.S. Dist. Ct. Utah, U.S. Tax Ct, U.S. Mil. Ct. Appeals, U.S. Ct. Appeals (10th cir.), U.S. Supreme Ct. Practiced in Salt Lake City, from 1930; of counsel Jones, Waldo, Holbrook & McDonough; Bd. dirs. Mountain Fuel Supply Co., Entrada Industries, Inc., Mountain Fuel Resources Inc., Wexpro Co., Celsius Energy Co. With UNSR, 1942-45.; comdr. ret. Mem. ABA, Utah Bar Assn. Democrat. Mem. Ch. of Jesus Christ of Latter Day Saints. Home: Salt Lake City Utah. Died Jan. 3, 1988; buried Salt Lake City Cemetery.

JONES, MARK MANDERVILLE, management consultant; b. Cedar Falls, Iowa, 1890; s. Fred Soule and Ada (Thompson) J.; m. May Irene Rinehart; 1 dau., Helen May Evatt. Student, East Waterloo (Iowa) High Sch.; LL.D., Bethany Coll., 1940. Successively chief clk. to gen. mgr. and traffic mgr. Waterloo, Cedar Falls and No. Ry.; traffic mgr. William Galloway Co., Waterloo, Iowa; indsl. sec. C. of C., Oakland, Calif.; dir. personnel Thomas A. Edison Industries, Orange, N.J., 1916-21; civilian rep. Sec. of War on devel. Army personnel system, 1917; dir. Div. Trade Tests of Army, 1917-18; dir. econ. staff Curtis, Fosdick and Belknap, N.Y.C.; on affairs of John D. Rockefeller, Jr. 1921-26; mgmt. cons. and cons. economist, N.Y.C. and Princeton, N.J., from 1926; cons. to pres. U.S. Steel Corp., 1953-59; pres. Akron Belting Co., 1934-54, Leadership Publs., Inc., 1948-54; editor Execs. Policy Letter, 1948-53; pres. Nat. Econ. Council, 1963-69; 1st sec. Nat. Assn. Employment Mgrs., 1916-21. Editor: Economic Council Letter, 1963-69. Republican. Presbyterian. Club: Union League (N.Y.C.). Home: Princeton N.J. Died June 8, 1986; buried Hudson, Ohio.

JONES, MARY COVER, psychology and education researcher, educator; b. Johnstown, Pa., Sept. 1, 1896; d. Charles Blair and Carrie Louise (Higson) Cover; m. Harold E. Jones (dec.); children: Barbara, Lesley. AB, Vassar Coll., 1919; MA, Columbia U., 1920, PhD, 1926. Diplomate Am. Bd. Profl. Psychology, Am. Bd. Counseling Psychology. Research assoc. U. Calif.-Berkeley, 1927-87, assoc. prof. to prof. edn., 1952-60; cons. intergenerational studies Inst. Human Devel. U. Calif.-Berkeley. Author: (with H.E. Jones) Adolescence, 1958, Developmental Psychology, rev. 1960; Growth and Behavior in Adolescence, 1957, 2d rev. (with L.J. Alexander), 1966; (with N. Bayley, M.P. Honzik and J.W. MacFarlane) The Course of Human Development, 1971; contbr. chpts. to numerous books. Contbr. numerous articles to profl. jours. and mags. Recipient G. Stanley Hall award child devel. div. Am. Psychol. Assn., 1968, Inst. Human Devel. award U. Calif.-Berkeley, 1969; Laura Spellman Rockefeller fellow, 1924-26. Fellow Am. Psychol. Assn., Gerontol. Soc.; mem. Soc. Research Child Devel., Western Psychol. Assn., Calif. State Psychol. Assn., Sigma Xi, Delta Kappa Gamma, Pi Lambda Theta. Died July 22, 1987.

JONES, ROBERT PARKE, railroad executive; b. Norfolk, Va., Apr. 20, 1892; s. John Ridley and Lally White (Burroughs) J.; m. Alpha Vane Holcombe, June 28, 1922; children: Robert Parke, Alpha Lee, Peter Ridley, Mary Parke. Student pub. schs., Portsmouth, Va. With various r.r.s 1907-10; various positions S.A.L. Ry. Co., 1910-58; chief fin. and acctg. officer for receivers S.A.L. Ry. Co., Norfolk, 1934-58, v.p., compt., 1938-58; v.p. Seaboard Air Line R.R. Co. S.A.L. Ry. Co., until 1958; bd. dirs. Nat. Bank Commerce, Norfolk, Ry. Express Agy., Inc., N.Y.C.; v.p. Balt. Steam Packet Co., from 1935, Macon, Dublin and Savannah R.R. Co. With ordnance Dept., U.S. Army, World War I. Mem. Norfolk Assn. Commerce, Transp. Assn. Am., Assn. Am. R.R.s (com. on gen. accounts 1929-34, adv. com. 1934-35, gen. com. from 1935), Va. Soc. SAR, Princess Anne Country Club, Virginia Club, Elks, German Club, Executives Club, Norfolk Yacht and Country Club. Home: Norfolk Va. †

JONES, THADDEUS JOSEPH, jazz musician; b. Pontiac, Mich., Mar. 28, 1923. Played trumpet, cornet and fluegelhorn with Count Basie, 1954-63, with Gerry Mulligan, 1964, George Russell, 1964, Thad Jones/Mel Lewis Orch., 1965-78; producer albums: The Magnificent Thad Jones, Brillance, Consumation, Potpourri, others; composer: Mean What You Say, Don't Git Sassy, Fingers, Tiptoe, Central Park North, others. Winner Downbeat mag. Reader's Poll, 1972-77, Downbeat Critics Poll, 1974-77. Home: Copenhagen Denmark. Died Aug. 20, 1986.

JONES, THOMAS ROY, business executive; b. Kingman, Kans., Apr. 26, 1890; s. Joseph Francis and Emma Laura (Miler) J.; m. Anna Margaret Seymour, Dec. 25, 1923 (dec.); children: Chalmer E., Margaret S. Jones Snow; m. Lura M. Forrest, Feb. 9, 1946; 1 child, Robert F. BS, U. Kans., 1913; postgrad., Harvard U., 1916-17; LLD (hon.), Lafayette Coll., 1952. Various positions as civil and mech. engr; works mgr. motor works Moline Plow Co., Rock Island, Ill.; asst. gen. mgr. Cin. Milling Machine Co.; v.p., gen. mgr. Harris-Seybold-Potter Co., Cleve.; pres., dir. Am. Type Founders, Inc. (changed to Daystrom, Inc. 1951), Elizabeth, N.J., 1932; pres. Daystrom, Inc., 1951-60, chmn. bd., 1960-62; merged with Schlumberger, Ltd., 1962, chmn. bd., from 1962; pres. Vickers-Armstrongs, Inc.; mem. Eastern adv. bd. Lumbermaen's Mut. Casualty Co.; chmn. Indsl. Relations Counselors; treas., trustee Com. on Econ. Devel.; former chmn. planning and devel. council N.J. Dept. Conservation and Econ. Devel.; past dir., chmn. exec. com. Am. Mgmt. Assn.; industry mem. Nat. War Labor Bd. and War Prodn. Bd. Past pres., dir. N.J. C. of C.; trustee, mem. exec. com. Jr. Achievement; past pres. N.J. State Safety Council; trustee, mem. fin. com/ N.J. Council Econ. Edn.; trustee Lafayette Coll.; chmn. bd. trustees Union Jr. Coll. Maj. U.S. Army, 1918-19. Recipient Laurence Gantt medal, 1951, citation for disting. service, U. Kan., 1956; named Outstanding Citizen of N.J. Advt. Club N.J., 1952, Bus. Statesman of Yr. Sales Execs Club No. N.J., 1953. Mem. NAM (bd. dirs.), Univ. Club, Union League Club, Pinnacle Club (N.Y.C.), Racquet Club (Chgo.), Essex Club (Newark), Adirondack League Club (Old Forge, N.Y.), Baltrusol Country Club (Summit, N.J.), Delta Sigma Pi, Beta Gamma Sigma. Home: Murray Hills N.J. †

JONSON, RAYMOND, artist; b. Charlton, Iowa, July 18, 1891; s. Gustav and Josephine (Abrahamson) J.; m. Vera White, Dec. 25, 1916. Student, Portland Art Sch., 1909-10, Chgo. Acad. Fine Arts, 1910-12. Executor settings and lighting effects Chgo. Little Theatre, 1913-19; tchr. Chgo. Acad. Fine Arts, 1918-21; prof. art emeritus U. N.Mex.; dir. Jonson Gallery. Works shown in leading Am. cities and collective exhibits in Europe; represented in permanent collection U. N.Mex.; two murals located at Ea. N.Mex. Coll., Portales; exhibited at Mus. Art, Norman, Okla. Recipient Englewood prize, Underwood prize, 1925; named a hon. fellow Sch. Am Rsch. and Mus. N.Mex., 1956. Home: Albuquerque N.Mex. †

JOPLING, R(AYMOND) C(ALVERT), oil executive; b. Italy, Tex., Apr. 28, 1891; s. Benjamin Lafayette and C. Lenora (Calvert) J.; m. Virginia Wiet, July 20, 1917; 1 child, Raymond Calvert. Joined Phillips Petroleum Co., Bartlesville, Okla., 1927, v.p., 1936-57; petroleum cons. from 1957. Mem. Am. Petroleum Inst., U.S. C. of C., Masons, Shriners, Press Club. Democrat. Baptist. †

JORDAN, ARTHUR MELVILLE, psychology educator; b. Somerton, Va., Oct. 9, 1888; s. Melville McConnell and Mary Florence (White) J.; m. Carrie Nicholson, June 15, 1914; children: Margaret Nicholson, Arthur Melville. AB, Randolph-Macon Coll., 1907; AM, Trinity Coll., N.C., 1909; PhD, Columbia U., 1919. Instr. psychology U. Ark., 1914, asst. prof., 1915-17, prof. edn., 1919-21, prof. psychology, 1921-23; prof. ednl. psychology U. N.C., from 1923; prof. ednl. psychology Northwestern U., summers 1927, 33, Columbia U., summers 1928, 30. Author: Measurement in Education, 1953, Educational Psychology, 4th edit., 1956, others; contbr. articles to mags. Mem. AAAS, Am. Psychol. Assn., Am. Ednl. Rsch. Assn., Phi Delta Kappa. Democrat. Methodist. Home: Chapel Hill N.C. †

JORDAN, HOWARD, JR., university chancellor; b. Beaufort, S.C., Dec. 28, 1916; s. Howard and Julia (Glover) J.; m. Ruth Menafee, Feb 14, 1943; 1 dau., Judith Louise. A.B., S.C. State Coll., 1938; spl. student, Howard U., 1938-39; Ed.D., N.Y. U., 1956. Faculty S.C. State Coll., Orangeburg, 1941-63; prof. edn. and psychology, chmn. dept. edn., dean S.C. State Coll. (Sch. Edn.), Orangeburg, 1950-60, dean faculty, 1960-63; pres. Savannah (Ga.) State Coll., 1963-71; vice chancellor for Services U. System Ga., 1971-86. Mem. Savannah-Chatham County Area Econ. Opportunity Authority; chmn. Orangeburg County Cancer dr., 1948-49, Orangeburg County Crippled Childrens Soc. dr., 1950; mem. State Adv. Com. for Adult Edn., State Adv. Council on Vocat. Edn.; bd. dirs. Greater Savannah Council, Interfaith Atlanta; bd. dels. United Way, Atlanta; bd. mgrs. SW YMCA; new bd. mentor Assn. Governing Bds.; mem. SE regional bd., Atlanta council exec. bd. Boy Scouts Am.; trustee Mather Sch. and Jr. Coll. Served with AUS, 1942-46, ETO. Mem. Am. Psychol. Assn., S.C. Psychol. Assn., Nat. Soc. Study Edn., Nat. (dept. higher edn.), Palmetto edn. assns., Ga. Planning Assn., Assn. U.S. Army, Phi Delta Kappa, Kappa Delta Pi, Alpha Kappa Mu, Alpha Phi Alpha, Sigma Pi Phi. Episcopalian (vestryman, sec.). Clubs: West End Rotary (pres.), Masons. Died Dec. 3, 1986; buried Westview Cemetery, Atlanta.

JORDAN, JOHN CLARK, English language educator; b. Varna, Ill., Nov. 3, 1883; s. George Clark and Mary (Downey) J.; m. Annabel Harrison, Aug. 2, 1911; children: Clark Harrison, Ann Fleming. AB, Knox Coll., 1908; AM, Columbia U., 1911, PhD, 1915. Instr. English U. Ill., 1912-14; prof. Drury Coll., Springfield, Mo., 1914-18; prof. U. Ark., from 1918, dean Coll. Arts and Scis., 1925-27, dean Grad. Sch., 1927-49; guest prof. U. Oslo, 1949-50, Defiance Coll. Author: Robert Green, 1915, A Grammar for Heretics, 1948. Mem. Blue Key (nat. pres. 1934-50), Phi Beta Kappa, Tau Kappa Alpha, Phi Mu Alpha Sinfonia, Phi Eta Sigma, Lambda Chi Alpha. Democrat. Presbyterian. Home: Defiance Ohio. †

JOYCE, JAMES AVERY, international law educator, economist, author; b. London, May 24, 1902; s. George Thomas Simeon and Mary Elizabeth (Leng) J. Student, Geneva Sch. Internat. Studies; Ph.D.; B.Sc. in Econs, London U.; grad., Inns. of Ct. law Sch.; LL.D., Morningside Coll., 1970. Bar: called to bar to practice common and criminal law on S.E. Circuit, also before High Ct. in London 1943. Lectr. London U.; popular law broadcasts BBC; faculty U. Denver Inst. Internat. Adminstrn., also Inst. Internal Affairs, Grinnell Coll., San Diego State Coll., NYU, Amherst Coll.; prof. Webster U. Coll. (Geneva (Switzerland) campus), from 1980; vis. lectr. other U.S. univs., colls., also New Delhi U.; speaker auspices Am. Friends Service Com., Midwest and N.E. communities, from 1948; Disting. prof. Lambuth Coll., 1969-70; sr. research asso. Fletcher Sch. Law and Diplomacy, 1970. Author: World Organization, 1944, Justice at Work, 1950, World in the Making, 1953, Revolution on East River, 1956, Red Cross International, 1959, Capital Punishment, A World View, 1960, Target for Tomorrow, 1962, Going One Way, 1963, Worker's Education Handbook, 1963, Education and Training, 1963, The Story of International Cooperation, 1964, World of Promise, 1965, Decade of Development, 1966, End of An Illusion, 1969, Story of the League of Nations, 1971, Which Way Europe, 1971, Jobs Versus People, 1974, New Politics of Human Rights, 1979, World Labour Rights and New Protection, 1980, The War Machine, 1980, One Increasing Purpose, 1981, Planning Disarmament, 1982, Animals Too Have Rights, 1986; Contbr. articles to profl. jours., nat. mags. Founder World Unity Movement (later became World Citizenship Movement), 1939, founder, 1929; nat. chmn. League of Nations Youth Movement; staff League of Nations Union; sec. Internat. Conf. Minorities of Lang., Race and Religion; Brit. sec. Internat. Assn. Labour Legislation; staff Internat. Labour Office, Geneva; cons. UNESCO and ECOSOC of UN.; Candidate for Parliament from, Oldham, 1951, Lambeth, 1955; Candidate for UN, 1971. Fellow Royal Geog. Soc., Royal Statis. Soc., Royal Econ. Soc.; mem. Royal Inst. Public Adminstrn., Internat. Law Assn., Howard League, World Calendar Assn. (UN rep.), Parliamentary Labour Assn., Brit. Inst. Internat. and Comparative Law, Internat. Lawyers Club, Internat. Center Criminological Studies (v.p.), Soc. Labour Lawyers, Internat. P.E.N., Translators Assn., AAUP, Am. Polit. Sci. Assn., UN Assn., World Federalists. Mem. Labour Party. Methodist. Home: London England. Deceased.

JOYNER, WILLIAM T., lawyer; b. Goldsboro, N.C., Apr. 11, 1891; s. James Yadkin and Effie E. (Rouse) J.; m. Sue Arrington Kitchin, Apr. 17, 1920 (dec. Aug. 1954); children: Sue Kitchin, William T., Walton Kitchin. AB, U. N.C., 1911; LLB, Harvard U., 1916. Instr. Woodberry Forest (Va.) Sch., 1911-13; pvt. practice Raleigh, N.C., 1916-17; asst. gen. solicitor So. Ry. Co., Washington, 1932-37, div. counsel, from 1937, counsel for all southeastern U.S. r.r.s in minimum wage case, 1940, counsel in nat. wage cases, 1941-43; mem. adv. com. on mil. justice U.S. War Dept., 1946-47, cons. on govt. operation of r.r.s, 1948; vice chmn. N.C. Adv. Com. on Edn., 1954-56; chmn. N.C. Hwy. Commn., 1957; chmn. steering com. for planning study for N.C. constn., 1967-68. Sec. N.C. Dem. Exec. Co., 1921-23; chmn. N.C. State Bd. Election, 1943-47. Maj. F.A., U.S. Army, 19171-18, col. N.C.N.G. Mem. ABA, Gen. Alumni Assn. U. N.C. (pres. 1945-46), Am. Legion (nat. exec. committeeman 1930-33), N.C., Wake County bar assns., Am. Coll. Trial Lawyers, Kiwanis, Phi Beta Kappa, Zeta Psi. Democrat. Baptist. Deceased.

JUDD, LEWIS COLEMAN, banker, real estate broker; b. Cleve., July 14, 1912; s. Harold Lewis and Juliette (Coleman) J.; m. Marion Louise Beeler, June 29, 1946; children: Donald Coleman, Barbara Louise, Richard Lewis, Elizabeth Garnett. Student, Dartmouth Coll., 1932-34, Cleve. Coll., 1934-36; BA, U. Fla., 1968. Sales rep. Lamson & Sessions, Cleve., 1935-37; with McTigue Real Estate and Ins., Ft. Lauderdale, Fla., 1938; ptnr. Combes & Judd Real Estate and Ins., Ft. Lauderdale, 1938-42, Taylor & Judd Real Estate, Ft. Lauderdale, 1946-47; prin. mgr., pres. L. C. Judd & Co. Inc., Ft. Lauderdale, 1947-85; chmn. bd. Landmark Banking Corp., Ft. Lauderdale, Landmark 1st Nat. Bank, Ft. Lauderdale. Served with USAAF, 1942-46. Mem. Ft. Lauderdale Bd. Realtors, Nat. Assn. Realtors, Fla. Assn. Realtors, Nat. Inst. Farm Brokers, Fla. Inst. Farm Brokers, Soc. Indsl. Realtors, Nat. Real Estate Flyers Assn., Lauderdale Yacht Club, Tower Club. Republican. Presbyn. Home: Fort Lauderdale Fla. Died Jan. 7, 1985.

JULIAN, LEO SEASE, lawyer; b. Prosperity, S.C., May 29, 1892; s. A. J. P. and Lilly Agnes (Sease) J.; m. dorothy Wellborn Johnson, Nov. 11, 1920; children: Eleanor (Mrs. Richard E. Cotton), William Alexander. BS, Va. Mil. Inst., 1912; grad., Saumur F.A. Sch., France, 1918; postgrad., U. Clearmont, France, 1919; LLB, U. va., 1920. Bar: Fla. 1915. Pvt. practice Miami, Fla., from 1920; trial counsel Shutts, Bowen, Simmons, Prevatt & Julian, 1930-57; lt. col. staff Gov. of Fla., 1949-52. Compiler: Florida Law Digest, Martindale Law Directory, 1924-30. Lt. F.A., U.S. Army, 1917-19. Mem. Internat. Bar Assn., ABA, Fla., Dade County (pres. 1944-45) bar assns., masons, Phi Sigma Kappa. Democrat. Episcopalian. Home: Coral Gables Fla. †

JULIAN, ORMAND CLINKINBEARD, surgeon; b. Omaha, May 6, 1913; s. William Harold and Ella (Clinkinbeard) J.; m. Rosemary Stirling Becker, Sept. 14, 1935; children—William H., Gail Elizabeth. B.S., U. Chgo., 1934, M.D., 1937, Ph.D., 1941. Intern St. Luke's Hosp., Chgo., 1937-38; resident U. Chgo. Clinics, 1938-42; practice medicine, specializing in cardiovascular surgery Chgo., from 1945; prof. surgery U. Ill. Coll. Medicine, 1947-71; chmn. div. surgery Presbyn.-St. Luke's Hosp., Chgo., 1965-72; chmn. dept. cardiovascular-thoracic surgery Presbyn.-St. Luke's Hosp., 1970-72; prof. Rush Med. Coll. Rush-Presbyn.-St. Luke's Med. Center, Chgo., from 1971; emeritus staff surgeon Eisenhower Med. Center, Rancho Mirage, Calif. Served to maj. M.C. AUS, 1942-45. Fellow A.C.S.; mem. Am. Surg. Assn., Soc. Clin. Surgery, Internat. Cardiovascular Soc., Soc. Vascular Surgery. Home: San Rafael Calif. Died Dec. 18, 1987; cremated.

JUNG, LEO, rabbi; b. Ung. Brod, Moravia, June 20, 1892; s. Maurice Tzevi and Ernestine (Silbermann) J.; m. Irma Rothschild, Feb. 28, 1922: children: Erna (Mrs. Miguel Villa), Rosalie (Mrs. Leonard Rosenfeld), Julie (Mrs. Michael Etra), Marcella (Mrs. E.D. Rosen). BA, London U., 1918, PhD, 1921; BA, Cambridge U., 1920, MA, 1926; DD, Yeshiva U., 1950; HLD, NYU, 1955; rabbinic diploma, Hildesheimer Sem., Berlin, 1920. Rabbi Congregation Knesset Israel, Cleve., 1920-22, Jewish Ctr., N.Y.C., from 1922; prof. ethics Yeshiva U., 1931-67, prof. emeritus, from 1968. Author numerous books on Jewish law and lore, comparative folklore; editor: The Jewish Library (8 vols.), from 1928. Pres. Rabbinical Coun., 1926-34, Jewish Acad. Arts and Scis., from 1950; chmn. N.Y. State Govt. Adv. Bd. for Kosher Law Enforcement, 1935-65, Cultural Religious commn., Joint Distbn. Com., from 1941; pres. Milah Bd. of N.Y.; chmn. bd. Womens Social Service of Israel. Recipient Congl. medal for work in World War II. Mem. AAUP, Rabbonim Aid Soc. (hon. pres.). Home: New York N.Y. †

JUST, CAROLYN ROYALL, lawyer; b. Shanghai, China, Sept. 15, 1907; d. Francis Martin and Mary Dunklin (Sullivan) Royall; m. Robert Just, Dec. 17, 1925 (dec. Nov. 1943). Ph.B., U. Chgo., 1934; J.D., DePaul U., 1938; LL.M., George Washington U., 1940; grad., Inter-Am. Acad. Comparative Internat. Law, Havana, Cuba, 1949, 50, 55, 57; cert., Hague Acad. Internat. Law, 31st Session, 1960, Escuela de Verano, San Carlos U., Guatemala City, 1965. Bar: D.C. 1938, Ill. 1940, U.S. Supreme Ct. 1941. Violin tchr. 1925-30; chief of staff concessions dept. Century of Progress Chgo. Expn., 1933; editorial asst., sec. to Dr. Forest Ray Moulton AAAS, 1930-38; practiced law Washington, 1938, 77-87; atty. Lands Div. U.S. Dept. Justice, 1938-43, atty. antitust div., 1943-50, atty. Tax Div., 1950-77; Mem. D.C. Citizenship (formerly I Am An American) Day Com., chmn. com. citizenship recognition, 1946, gen. sec., 1947-50; mem. Atty. Gen's. Adv. Com. on Citizenship and; del. representing Dept. Justice to nat. confs. on citizenship at, Phila., 1946, Washington, 1947, 48, 50-55, N.Y.C., 1949. Mem. Am. Bar Assn. (sects. of taxation, internat. law, chmn. com. on relations with internat. bar orgns. 1950-71, adv. com. on pub. relations 1962-65, mem. com. facilities Law Library Congress 1952-59), Fed. Bar Assn. (formerly asst. editor Fed. Bar Jour.), Nat. Assn. Women Lawyers, Bar Assn. D.C., Women's Bar Assn. D.C., Internat. Bar Assn. (charter patron, del. to confs. N.Y.C. 1947, London 1951, Madrid, 1952, Salzburg, 1960, Mexico City, 1964, Sydney, Australia, 1978, chmn. credentials com. Madrid 1952), Inter-Am. Bar Assn. (del. confs. Havana, Cuba 1941, Mexico City, 1944, Santiago, Chile, 1945, Lima, Peru, 1947, Detroit, 1949, Sao Paulo, Brazil, 1954, Dallas, 1956, Buenos Aires, 1957, Miami, 1959, Bogota, Colombia, 1961, San Jose, Costa Rica, 1967, 77, Caracas, Venezuela, 1969, Quito, Ecuador, 1972, Rio de Janeiro, 1973, Cartagena, Colombia, 1975, reporter gen. 1951-72, council 1951-72, Gold medal 1972, Vallance award found. 1979), Am. Law Inst., Am. Soc. Internat. Law, George Washington U. Alumni Assn., U. Chgo. Alumni Assn., Am. Judicature Soc., AAUW, Club de las Americas (pres. 1964-65), D.A.R., Internat. Law Assn. (Am. br.), Internat. Fiscal Assn., Am. Assn. for Internat. Commn. Jurists, English Speaking Union, Columbian Women of George Washington U., Georgetown Symphony Orch., Amateur Chamber Music Players, Friday Morning Music Club, Norwegian Chamber Music Soc. (Trondheim, Norway), Instituto Brasileiro de Direito Tributario (Sao Paulo, Brazil) (hon.), Pi Gamma Mu, Kappa Beta Pi, Phi Delta Gamma. Home: Washington D.C. Died Jan. 13, 1987, buried Woodlawn Meml. Park, Greenville, S.C.

JUSTEMENT, LOUIS, architect; b. N.Y.C., Nov. 20, 1891; s. Louis and Henriette (Jacob) J.; m. Jeanne Eger, Feb. 15, 1927; children: Marguerite, Louis. BS, George Washington U., 1911. Jr. ptnr. Sonnemann & Justement, 1919-24; pvt. practice 1924; sr. ptnr. Justement and Callmer and predecessor firms, from 1946. Prin. works include: Sibley Meml. Hosp., U.S. Courthouse, Washington, Howard U. Med. Sch.; author: New Cities for Old, 1946. Fellow AIA; mem. Washington Bldg. Congress (past pres.), Washington Bd. Trade, Cosmos Club. Home: Potomac Md. †

KAEBNICK, HERMANN WALTER, bishop; b. Brookston, Pa., Feb. 13, 1898; s. Julius Frederick and Caroline (Bloedow) K.; m. Gertrude Lillian Strehler, Aug. 4, 1927; children: Warren W., Winifred L. Student, Warren Conservatory Music, 1919-22; BA, Central U., 1926; postgrad., N.Y. Theol. Sem., 1925-26; Min.D, United Theol. Sem., 1927; postgrad., U. Pitts., 1927-28; S.T.M., Luth. Theol. Sem., 1933; postgrad., Yale U., 1948; LLD, Albright Coll., 1960; DD, Lycoming Coll., 1964; LHD, Lebanon Valley Coll., 1965. Ordained to ministry Evang. U. B. Ch., 1928. Oratorio singer 1922-28; pastor Evang. U.B. Ch., Forest Hills, L.I., N.Y., 1925-26, Freedom, Pa., 1927-28, Altoona, Pa., 1928-30, Somerset, Pa., 1930-39; supt. Pitts. Conf. Evang. Ch., 1939-50; gen. ch. treas. Evang. U.B. Ch., 1951-54; exec. sec. Gen. Coun. Adminstrn. Evang. U.B. Ch., Dayton, Ohio, 1954-58; bishop Eastern Area Evang. U.B. Ch., Harrisburg, Pa., 1959-67, United Meth. Ch., Harrisburg, 1968-72; tchr. Schuykill Coll., 1925-26; trustee Albright Coll., Lebanon Valley Coll., United Theol. Sem., Evang. Theol. Sem. Lt. (J.G.) USNRF, World War I. Mem. Masons, Kiwanis. Home: Hershey Pa. Died May 25, 1987.

KAFER, HOWARD GILMOUR, lawyer; b. Plainfield, N.J., Apr. 5, 1923; s. Lester Scott and Marie Paullin (Gilmour) K.; m. Nancy Kinnear, May 26, 1951; children: Karen, Peter Kinnear, Lynn. A.B., Princeton U., 1947; J.D., N.Y. U., 1951. Bar: N.Y. bar 1953. Since practiced in N.Y.C.; partner Chamberlin, Jube, Byrne & Kafer, 1963-70; partner firm Burns, Van Kirk, Greene & Kafer, 1970-79, Abberley, Kooiman, Marcellino & Clay, 1979-81, Byrne & Kafer, from 1982; pres., dir. Alamo Corp. Trustee Charles Edison Fund of East Orange, N.J., Sexauer Found., Short Hills (N.J.) Country Day Sch., 1964-73. Served with AUS, 1943-46. Mem. Am., N.Y. State bar assns. Congregationalist. Clubs: Short Hills; Princeton (N.Y.C.); Nantucket (Mass.) Yacht, Sankaty Head (Mass.) Golf. Home: Short Hills N.J. Died Oct. 12, 1985; cremated.

KAHAN, IRVING, editor; b. Passaic, N.J., Feb. 12, 1912; s. Harry R. and Sonia (Abbot) K.; m. Minna Richman, Sept. 11, 1941; children—Harriet R., Justine S. B.A., State U. Iowa, 1935, certificate in journalism, 1935. Editor Passaic Citizen, 1936-38, Paterson (N.J.) Sunday Chronicle, 1939-40, Textile Dyer, Paterson, 1940-48; mng. editor Textile Labor mag., N.Y.C., 1949-56; editor Textile Labor mag., 1957-69; pub. relations dir. Textile Workers Union Am., AFL-CIO, 1957-76, publs. dir., 1969-76. Author: Behind Taft-Hartley's Mumbo-Jumbo, 1949, The TWUA Story: They Said it Couldn't Be Done, 1964. Publicity dir. United Italian Appeal, Paterson, 1946. Served with inf. AUS, 1943-45. Sigma Delta Chi Scholar, 1935. Home: Lakewood N.J. Died Dec. 24, 1986; buried West Ridgelawn Cemetery, King Solomon Meml. Pk. Sect., Clifton, N.J.

KAHANE, MELANIE, interior and industrial designer; b. N.Y.C., Nov. 26, 1910; d. Morris and Rose (Roth) K.; m. Theodore Earl Ebenstein, Dec. 22, 1934 (div. 1945); 1 child, Joan Ebenstein Porter; m. Ben Grauer, Sept. 25, 1954 (dec. June 1977). Grad., Parsons Sch. Design, Paris, France, 1932; DFA (hon.), Parsons Sch. Design, N.Y.C., 1982. Illustrator Tobias Green Advt. Co., 1931-32; designer Lord & Taylor, 1933-34; founder, pres. Melanie Kahane, Inc., N.Y.C., 1935-52; pres. Melanie Kahane Assocs., 1952; designer for SBF Dept. and suburban stores, St. Louis, from 1958, Charles of Ritz, beauty salons, throughout U.S., from 1957, Playbill Restaurant, N.Y.C., 1958, Children's Mus., Ft. Worth, 1955, Ziegfield Theatre, N.Y.C., 1963, Gov. Shivers mansion, Austin, Tex., 1957, ofcl. residence of pres., Princeton U., 1958, Reid Hall, Paris, France, 1948, First Nat. Bank, Ft. Worth, 1962, Shubert Theaters, N.Y.C., Chgo., Phila., Boston, 1977-83, others; dir. styling and design Sprague & Carleton Furniture Co., Inc., 1962-70; lectr. Parsons Sch. Design, from 1950; design, color and fabric cons., from 1952. Author: There's a Decorator in Your Doll House, 1968; prod.: documentary film Decorating, A Way of Life, 1949; contbr. to books, encys. Mem. commn. to S.E. Asia for N.Y. World's Fair, 1964-65; mem. Nat. Panel Arbitrators, from 1963, NBC Monitor program mission to Russia, 1959, A.I.D. Design Team for NASA, 1972-73; mem. Parson's Sch. Design Bd. Overseers, 1984—; chmn. Greater N.Y. Fund, 1961. Named hon. citizen Knoxville, Tenn., Wichita, Kan. and Houston; recipient Decorator of Year award Carpet Assn. Am., 1953; Designer citation U.S. Commr. Gen. Cullman, 1958; award Brussels World Fair, 1958; Career Key award Girl's Club Am., 1961; chosen as one of 100 Am. Women of Accomplishment Harper's Bazaar mag., 1967; Eleanor Roosevelt humanities award, 1981; named to Interior Design Hall of Fame, 1985. Fellow Am. Inst. Interior Designers (hon. life mem., past nat. sec., dir., past pres. N.Y. chpt., nat. treas. 1971-75), Am. Soc. Interior Designers; mem. Municipal Art Soc., Decorator's Club N.Y.C. (pres. 1982-85), Archtl. League N.Y., Nat. Soc. Lit. and the Arts, Illuminating Engring. Soc., Inter-Soc. Color Council, Nat. Home Fashions League, Inst. Practising Designers (Eng.), Women's Forum, Am. Theatre Wing, Am. Mus. in Britain. Club: Cosmopolitan. Home: New York N.Y. Died Dec. 22, 1988.

KAHLE, RICHARD BENTON, oil executive; b. Lima, Ohio, Nov. 5, 1892; s. Albert Wesley and Clara Metheany (Lynch) K.; m. Ruth Dodd, June 27, 1916; children: Martha Ruth (Mrs. J. Newton Rodeheaver Jr.), Richard Benton, Myra May (Mrs. James Horsey Jr.). BSCE, Allegheny Coll., 1913. Civil engr. Pa. R.R., 1913-15; asst. city engr. Lima, Ohio, 1915; with Standard Oil Co. of N.J. and Imperial Oil Co., 1915-17; supt. ops., marine dept. Standard Oil Co. of N.J., 1919-23; pres. La. Oil Refining Corp., 1923-29, Beacon Oil Co., 1926-30; v.p. Standard Shipping Co., 193-32; pres. Eastern States Petroleum & Chem. Co., 1932-58, chmn. bd., chief exec. officer, 1958-60. Capt. Q.M.C., gasoline and oil br., U.S. Army, 1918-19. Mem. Masons (32 degree, KT), Phi Kappa Psi. Home: Houston Tex. †

KAHLER, WILLIAM V., telephone executive; b. Mendon, Mo., Sept. 30, 1898; s. William J. and Katherine (Schultz) K.; m. Virginia Tincher, Sept. 12, 1923. BS in Mech. Engring., U. Mo., 1922. Engr. asst. Bell Telephone Labs., N.Y.C., 1922-24; chief engr. Chgo. area Ill. Bell Telephone Co., 1938-40, asst. v.p., 1942-43, gen. mgr. state area, 1943-46, oper. v.p., 1946-50, pres., 1951-62, chmn. bd., 1962-87, bd. dir., 1946-87; bd. dirs. Marshall Field & Co., Union Tank Car Co., bur. constrn. WPB, Washing, 1940-43; hon. trustee Ill. Inst. Tech., MacMurry Coll., U. Chgo., Mus. Sci. and Industry. Fellow Am. Inst. E.E.; mem. Telephone Pioneers Am. (past internat. pres.), Western Soc. Engr. (former Pres.), Chgo. Club, Commercial Club. Home: Mendon Mo. Died Dec. 6, 1987.

KAHN, JACOB PHILIP, psychiatrist; b. Melitopol, Russia, May 16, 1914; s. Philip and Elizabeth (Kahn) K.; m. Doris Woodhouse, May 9, 1947; children—Philip, Victoria, Elizabeth (Mrs. Steven Davenport), Madeleine. M.D., U. Calif. at San Francisco, 1941. Diplomate: in psychiatry and child psychiatry Am. Bd. Psychiatry and Neurology. Rotating intern Franklin Hosp., San Francisco, 1940-41; asst. resident medicine Franklin Hosp., 1941-42; resident psychiatry Langley-Porter Clinic, San Francisco, 1946-49; research fellow child psychiatry James Jackson Putnam Children's Center, Boston, 1949-50; fellow child psychiatry James Jackson Putnam Children's Center, 1950-51, Judge Baker Guidance Center, Boston, 1950-51; faculty Stanford Sch. Medicine, from 1952, asso. clin. prof. psychiatry, from 1959; chief psychiatry Presbyn. Hosp., Pacific Med. Center, San Francisco, 1959-71; cons. Presbyn. Hosp., Pacific Med. Center, from 1971. Contbr. articles to profl. jours. and textbooks. Served to capt., M.C. AUS, 1942-46. Fellow Am. Psychiat. Assn. (life), Am. Acad. Child Psychiatry, Royal Soc. Medicine, Calif. Acad. Medicine, Am. Assn. Psychoanalytic Physicians; mem. Royal Coll. Psychiatrists (founding mem.), N.Y. Acad. Scis. Home: San Francisco Calif. Deceased.

KAHN, REUBEN LEON, educator, bacteriologist; b. Kovno, Lithuania, July 26, 1887; came to U.S., 1899; s. Lazarus and Lottie (Wolpert) K.; m. Dina Hope Weinstein, May 31, 1917 (dec. May 1967); children: Lyra Justine (Mrs. Frank S. Morgan), David Curry. AB, Valparaiso U., 1909, LLD, 1943; MS, Yale U., 1913; DSc, NYU, 1916; DSc (hon.), Institutum Divi Thomae, Cin., 1954; MD (hon.), Med. Sch. Nat. U., Athens, Greece, 1963; PhD (hon.), Far Ea. U., Manila, 1964. Rsch. chemist Harriman Rsch. Lab., N.Y.C., 1916-17; immunologist Mich. Dept. Health, Lansing, 1920-28; dir. labs. Univ. Hosp., asst. prof. bacteriology U. Mich., 1928-48, assoc. prof., 1948-51, prof. serology, 1952-57, prof. emeritus, from 1957, past chief serology lab. Univ. Hosp.; prof. microbiology (rsch.) Howard U. Coll Medicine, 1968-73, cons. in rsch., 1973—; vis. prof. immunology St. Thomas Inst., Cin. Author: Tissue Immunity, 1936, Serology with Lipid Antigen, 1950, An Itroduction to Universal Reaction in Health and Disease, 1951; contbr. articles to sci. and med. jours.; pub the standard Kahn Test, 1923. Capt. San. Corps, U.S Army, 1917-19. Recipient gold medal Phi Lambda Kappa, 1937, bronze medal for 25th anniversary of Kahn reaction, 1948. Fellow AAAS (11th ann. award 1933); mem. Am. Soc. Microbiology (hon.), Soc. Exptl. Biology and Medicine, Am. Assn. Immunologists, Am. Assn. Pathologists and Bacteriologists, Am. Pub. Health Assn., Mich. Acad. Scis., Dade County Med. Assn. (hon.), Research Club, Cosmos Club, numerous other med. socs., Sigma Xi, Phi Delta Epsilon. Home: Miami Fla. Deceased.

KAISER, EMIL THOMAS, chemistry educator; b. Budapest, Hungary, Feb. 15, 1938; s. Emil and Elizabeth (Timar) K.; m. Bonnie Lu Togias, Mar. 30, 1968; children: Elizabeth Ann, Charlotte Emily. B.S., U. Chgo., 1956; M.A., Harvard, 1957, Ph.D., 1959. Asst. prof. chemistry Washington U., St. Louis, 1961-63; mem. faculty dept. chemistry U. Chgo., 1963-84, asso. prof., 1967-70, prof., 1970-81, Louis Block prof., 1981-82; dir. Center Bioorganic and Bioinorganic Chemistry, 1981-82; prof. Rockefeller U., N.Y.C., 1982-88; Haggerty prof. Rockefeller U., 1984-88; vis. prof. U. Nice, France, 1976; Japan Soc. for Promotion Sci. prof., 1976; cons. Hoffmann-LaRoche, Wiley-Intersci. Co.Enricerche, Italy, Kureha Chem. Industry Ltd., Japan, Phillips Petroleum Co., Salk Inst. Biotech. Indsl. Assocs., Suntory Ltd., Japan; mem. medicinal chem. study sect. A NIH, 1973-77; vis. com. dept. chemistry Brookhaven Nat. Lab., 1978-81, chmn., 1981; vis. com. dept. chemistry Purdue U., 1979, NYU, 1985, U. Calif., Santa Barbara, 1986; mem. sci. adv. bd. Robert A. Welch Found., 1982-88, vis. com. dept applied biol. scis. MIT, 1986-88; adv. com. chemistry sect. NSF, 1984-86. Editor: Radical Ions, 1969, Progress in Bioorganic Chemistry, 1971, 73, 74, 76; editorial bd.: Jour. Am. Chem. Soc, 1973-82; mem. editorial adv. bd. Jour. Am. Chem. Soc., 1986—. NSF predoctoral fellow, 1956-58; NIH predoctoral fellow, 1958-59; NIH postdoctoral fellow, 1959-61; Alfred P. Sloan Found. fellow, 1968-70; Guggenheim Meml. Found. fellow, 1975-76. Fellow Am. Acad. Arts and Letters; mem. Nat. Acad. Scis., Phi Beta Kappa, Sigma Xi. Home: New York N.Y. Died July 18, 1988.

KAMENETZ, HERMAN LEO, physician; b. Kaunas, Russia, Sept. 1, 1907; came to U.S., 1953, naturalized, 1958; s. Leo I. and Flora (Bernstein) K.; m. Georgette Barbaix, Feb. 13, 1947. M.S., U. Paris, 1945, M.D., 1952. Diplomate: Am. Bd. Phys. Medicine and Rehab. Intern St. Anthony Hosp., Rockford, Ill., 1953-54; resident in phys. medicine State Vets. Hosp., Rocky Hill, Conn., 1954-56, Yale-New Haven Hosp., 1956-57; chief phys. medicine Woodruff Hosp., New Haven, 1957-59, State Vets. Hosp., Rocky Hill, 1959-75; chief profl. services State Vets. Hosp., 1960-66; chief rehab. medicine service VA Med. Center, Washington, 1975-83, cons. phys. medicine and rehab., 1983-87; physician out-patient dept. Yale-New Haven Hosp., 1960-75; cons. phys. medicine St. Francis Hosp., Hartford, Conn., 1964-75, Masonic Hosp., Wallingford, Conn., 1965-74, Waterbury (Conn.) Hosp., 1968-75, Manchester (Conn.) Meml. Hosp., 1969-70, Gaylord Rehab. Hosp., Wallingford, Conn., 1970-75; clin. instr. phys. medicine Yale U., 1958-64, asst. clin. prof. medicine, 1964-70; clin. prof. medicine George Washington U. Sch. Medicine and Health Scis., from 1975; professorial lectr. Dept. Phys. Medicine and Rehab., Georgetown U. Sch. Medicine, from 1976. Author: Physiatric Dictionary, 1965, The Wheelchair Book, 1969, (with Georgette Kamenetz) Dictionnaire de Medecine Physique, de Reeducation et Readaptation Fonctionnelles, 1972, English-French and French-English Dictionary of Physical Medicine and Rehabilitation, 1972, Dictionary of Rehabilitation Medicine, 1983; asst. editor: Medical Hydrology, 1963, Medical Climatology, 1964, Therapeutic Heat and Cold, 1965, Orthotics Etcetera, 1966, Rehabilitation and Medicine, 1968, Arthritis and Physical Medicine, 1969; editor for U.S.: Editorial Com. of Scandinavian-English Rehab. Terminology; contbr. articles in field to profl. books and jours. Mem. Am. Congress. Rehab. Medicine (emeritus), AAAS, Conn. Soc. Phys. Medicine (pres.), Am. Med. Writers Assn., Internat. Soc. History Medicine, Conn. Hosp. Assn., Am. Soc. Med. Hydrology, Yale Med. Assn., Internat. Rehab. Medicine Assn., Internat. Soc. Prosthetics and Orthotics. Home: Arlington Va. Died June 2, 1987; cremated.

KANANE, MARY CATHARINE, organization executive, judge; b. Kenilworth, N.J., Sept. 1; d. John Thomas and Jane Sara (Gillooly) K. Student, Fordham U., Seton Hall U. Surrogate 1963-78; lectr. Nat. regent Cath. Daus. Am. Author: Come Along with Me, 1959. Past pres. Union County Women's Republican club; bd. dirs. United Way. Recipient Pro Ecclesia et Pontifice citation, 1954. Mem. Bus. and Profl. Womens Club. Home: Union N.J. Died Dec. 16, 1978; buried St. Gertrude Cemetery.

KANTOR, JACOB ROBERT, psychologist; b. Harrisburg, Pa., Aug. 8, 1888; s. Julius and Mary (Slocum) K.; m. Helen Rich, Sept. 2, 1916 (dec.); 1 child, Helene Juliette. PhB, U. Chgo., 1914, PhD, 1917; DSc (hon.), Denison U., 1961; LittD, U. Akron, 1970. Instr. philosophy and psychology U. Minn., 1915-17; instr. psychology U. Chgo., 1917-20, vis. prof., 1925, rsch. assoc., from 1964; asst. prof. Ind. U., 1920-21, assoc. prof., 1921-23, prof., 1923-59, prof. emeritus, from 1959; vis. prof. Ohio State U., 1928, 38, NYU, 1962-63, U. Md., 1963-64. Author: Psychology and Logic, Vol. I, 1945, Vol. II, 1950, Problems of Physiological Psychology, 1947, The Logic of Modern Science, 1953, Interbehavioral Psychology, 1959, The Scientific Evolution of Psychology, Vol. I, 1963, Vol. II, 1969, The Aim and Progress of Psychology, 1971, The Science of Psychology: An Interbehavioral Survey, 1975, Psycho-logical Linguistics, 1977, others; editor Principia Press, from 1931; contbr. articles to sci. jours. Deceased.

KAPLAN, J(ACOB) GORDIN, biologist, educator; b. N.Y.C., Nov. 26, 1922; s. Michael and Nadia (Gordin) K.; m. Sylvia Mary Leadbeater, Aug. 31, 1949; children: Elizabeth, Michael Gordin. B.A., CCNY, 1943; M.A., Columbia U., 1948, Ph.D., 1950; D.Sc. (hon.), Concordia U., 1978. Mem. faculty Dalhousie U. Faculty Medicine, Halifax, N.S., Can., 1950-66; prof. biology U. Ottawa, Ont., Can., 1966-81; chmn. dept. U. Ottawa, 1975-81; prof. biochemistry, v.p. research U. Alta., Edmonton, Can., 1981-87, univ. prof., 1987-88; vice chmn. Tri Univs. Meson Facility; pres. XI Internat. Congress Biochemistry, Toronto, 1979; chmn. com. internat. sci. and tech. affairs Nat. Research Council Can., 1980—; bd. dirs. Alta. Research Council, Alta. Microelectronic Devel. and Application Centre, Centre Frontier Engring. Research, Edmonton Research and Devel. Park Authority; dir. Chembiomed Ltd., Majestic Laser Systems Ltd. Editor: Molecular Basis of Immune Cell Function, 1979, Can. Jour. Biochemistry, 1973-81. Served with AUS, 1942-46. Lalor Found. fellow; NSF sr. postdoctoral fellow; Can.-France Exchange fellow, 1973-74. Fellow Royal Soc. Can.; Mem. Can. Soc. Cell Biology (pres. 1969-70), Can. Soc. Biochemistry (pres. 1978-79), Can. Assn. Univ. Tchrs. (pres. 1970-71), Can. Fedn. Biol. Socs. (pres. 1975-76), Am. Soc. Biol. Chemists, Am. Soc. Cell Biology, Soc. Philomathique de Paris. Home: Edmonton Alta., Canada. Died July 6, 1988.

KAPLAN, JACOB MERRILL, merchant; b. Lowell, Mass., Dec. 23, 1891; s. David and Fanny K.; m. Alice M. Kaplan, June 30, 1925; 4 children. Organizer, pres., owner Welch Grape Juice Co., 1940-58; pres. Jemkap Inc., N.Y.C., from 1939. Founder, trustee J.M. Kaplan Fund, Inc., 1947-87. Home: East Hampton N.Y. Died July 18, 1987; buried Westchester Hills Cemetery, Hastings-on-Hudson, N.Y.

KAPLAN, NATHAN ORAM, biochemist, educator; b. N.Y.C., June 25, 1917; s. Philip and Rebecca (Uttef) K.; m. Goldie Levine, Feb. 9, 1947; 1 son, Jerold Laurence. AB, UCLA, 1939; PhD, U. Calif., Berkeley, 1943; DSc (hon.), Brandeis U., 1982. Rsch. assoc. Mass. Gen. Hosp., Boston, 1945-49; asst. prof. biochemistry U. Ill., 1949-50; asst. prof. biology Johns Hopkins U., Balt., 1950-52, assoc. prof., 1952-56, prof., 1956-57; prof. biochemistry, chmn. grad. dept. biochemistry Brandeis U., 1957-68; prof. chemistry U. Calif., San Diego, 1968-1986; assoc. dir. Cancer Ctr., La Jolla, Calif., 1980-86; adj. prof. dept. neoplastic diseases Mt. Sinai Sch. Medicine, CUNY, N.Y.C., 1976-86; Fogarty scholar-in-residence NIH, 1982. Adv. com. Oak Ridge Nat. Lab., Nat. Cancer Inst.; bd. dirs. Am. Cancer Soc. Recipient Sugar Rsch. awaard, 1946, Eli Lilly award in biochemistry, 1952, travel award NSF, 1952, award Am. Assn. Clin. Chemistry, 1976; Guggenheim fellow, 1965, 75. Fellow Harvey Soc. (hon.); mem. Am. Chem. Soc., Am. Soc. Biochemists, NAS, Am. Soc. Bacteriologists, AAAS, AAUP, Am. Cancer Soc. Coun. Rsch. and Clin. Investigation, Am. Acad. Arts and Scis., Internat. Union Biochemistry (U.S. nat. com.), Sigma Xi. Home: La Jolla Calif. Died Apr. 15, 1986.

KAPP, WILLIAM EDWARD, architect; b. Toledo, Aug. 20, 1891; s. John and Charlotte (Remmert) K.; m. Helen Ida Jochen, Sept. 23, 1916; children: Mary Louise (dec.), John William. Student, U. Pa., 1912-14. Registered architect, Mich. Pvt. practice Toledo, 1909-16, Detroit, from 1919; mem. Smith, Hinchman & Grylls, 1919-41; designer important religious, ednl., comml. and indsl. bldgs. Detroit area. Trustee Cranbrook Inst. Sci., from 1945. Lt. A.C., U.S. Army, 1917-18. Fellow AIA (pres. Detroit chpt. 1942-44); mem. Mich. Soc. Architects, Engring. Soc. Detroit, Detroit Hist. Soc., Detroit Astron. Soc., Cranbrook Inst. Sci. (trustee from 1945), Am. Legion, Masons, Players Club (pres. 1940). Home: Detroit Mich. †

KAPPE, STANLEY EDWARD, environmental engineer; b. Kingston, Pa., Aug. 11, 1908; s. Anthony and Pauline (Danelowicz) K.; BSCE, Pa. State U., 1930; m. Flora Syme Clarke, Nov. 10, 1935; 1 son, David S. Engring. asst. Pa. Health Dept., Phila., 1930-35; in charge of pollution abatement program on Del. River, U.S. Engrs., Phila., 1935-36; eastern mgr. Chicago Pump Co., Phila., 1936-46; chmn. bd. Kappe Assocs., Inc., Rockville, Md., 1946-85; spl. cons. to Hdqrs. USAF, 1952-70, USPHS, 1967-70. Recipient Ted Haseltine award Pa. Water Pollution Control Assn., 1973. Mem. ASCE, Am. Water Works Assn. (internat. dir. 1973-75, Fuller award Chesapeake sect. 1970, hon. mem. 1976-85), Am. Acad. Environ. Engrs. (exec. dir. 1971-81, editor Diplomate newsletter 1971-81; Fair award 1978, hon. diplomate 1981; award named in his honor 1980). Water Pollution Control Assn. (Arthur Sidney Bedell award 1980), Nat. Soc. Profl. Engrs., Am. Water Works Assn. (sec.-treas. sect. 1965-71, 75-78), Isaak Walton League Am., Pa. Water Works Operators Assn. (Harry S. Krum award 1972, pres. 1980). Clubs: Congl. Country. Kenwood Country; Engrs. (Phila.). Patentee, lectr. in field. Died Jan. 1985.

KARAGHEUZOFF, THEODORE, municipal official; b. Bklyn., Mar. 2, 1935; s. Sarkis and Anne (Papasian) K.; m. Odette Mary Chambart, May 23, 1964; children: Patricia, Nicole, Steven, Christopher. BCE, CCNY, 1955; MS, Northwestern U., 1956; LLB, Bklyn. Sch. Law, 1961. Bar: N.Y. 1961; registered profl. engr., N.Y. Traffic engr., asst. to dir. traffic signals N.Y.C. Traffic Dept., 1955-59, asst. dir. traffic signals, 1959-61, asst. to commr., 1961-63, dep. commr., chief engr., 1963-68, traffic commr., 1968-73, 74-78, commr. bldgs., 1973; asst. gen. supt. N.Y.C. Transit Authority, 1978-82, gen. supt., 1982-85; asst. prof. Ctr. for Safety Edn., NYU; cons. engr. traffic problems; mem. Nat. Com. for Uniform Traffic Laws. Recipient Outstanding Young Engr. award City Coll. Alumni Assn., 1969, Disting. Service award CCNY, 1973, Pub. Service award Fund for N.Y.C., 1976; named one of Outstanding Young Men of Year Bklyn. Jaycees, 1970. Mem. Inst. Transp. Engrs., Am. Soc. Mcpl. Engrs., N.Y. Soc. Mcpl. Engrs. (Mcpl. Engr. of Year award), ASCE, Queens County Bar Assn., Chi Epsilon, Tau Beta Pi. Home: Jamaica Estates N.Y. Died Apr. 21, 1985; buried Mt. St. Mary's Cemetery, Flushing, N.Y.

KARELSEN, FRANK EPHRAIM, lawyer; b. N.Y.C., Jan. 3, 1892; s. Frank E. and Emma (Williams) K.; m. Sophie Van Raalte, June, 1917; children: June (Mrs. Frank Goodman), Ellen (Mrs. Robert L. Solender), Frank Ephraim III. Bar: N.Y. 1916. Ptnr. Kurzman, Karelsen & Frank, N.Y.C.; past chmn. bd. State Bank Long Beach. Author: Human Relations-A Challenge to Our Public Schools, 1947, A Layman Looks at Academic Freedom, 1949; contbr. articles to profl. jours. Organizer, counsel Met. Ednl. TV Assn.; mem. N.Y. State com. White House Conf. on Edn., 1955, White House Conf. on Youth, 1960; chmn. adv. com. human relations N.Y.C. Bd. Edn., 1943-45; commr. Community Mental Health Bd., N.Y.C., 1952; past treas. Nat. Sch. Vol. Program, Inc.; mem. Jewish Bd. Family and Children's Services; mem. Nat. Adv. Council Edn. Disadvantaged Children under Title I, 1965-69; del. Dem. Nat. Conv., 1956, 60, 64; bd. dirs., sec. Irvington House Inst. for Rsch.; bd. dirs. Henry Ittelson Ctr. Child Rsch., Ramapo Anchorage Camp; life trustee N.Y. U. Med. Ctr.; mem. adv. bd. Dept. N.Y.C. Mental Health and Mental Retardation Services; hon. gov., past chmn. admissions com., hon. trustee Ethical Culture Sch. Lt. (j.g.) Anti-submarine Service USN, World War I. Decorated Navy Cross for disting. service. Mem. Assn. of Bar of City of N.Y., ABA, N.Y. State Bar Assn., N.Y. County Lawyers Assn., Ams. Dem. Action (v.p. nat. bd.), Am. Jewish Com. (hon. v.p. nat. exec. com., exec. com. N.Y. chpt., hon. chmn.), All Day Neighborhood Schs. (hon. pres.), Pub. Edn. Assn. (hon. v.p., past chmn. exec. com.), City Club, Harmonie Club, Nat. Dem. Club of N.Y.C. Home: New York N.Y. Died Oct. 6, 1983; cremated.

KARLEN, DELMAR, educator, author; b. Chgo., Jan. 6, 1912; s. Carl and Esther (Norman) K.; m. Alice Mary McGushon, July 12, 1940 (dec. 1984); children: Delmar, Karen Dunne, Elise; m. 2d, Adele. BA, U. Wis., 1934; LLB, Columbia U., 1937. Bar: N.Y. 1938, Wis. 1946, Va. 1981. With firm Simpson, Thacher & Bartlett, N.Y.C., 1937-46; mem. faculty U. Wis. Law Sch., 1946-52; prof. law NYU, 1952-77, prof. emeritus, 1977-88; prof. Marshall-Wythe Sch. Law, Coll. William and Mary, 1977-88; assoc. dir. Inst. Jud. adminstrn., N.Y.C., 1952-62, dir., 1962-71, v.p., 1969-76; vis. prof. U. Chgo., 1953, U. Sydney, 1972, U. So. Calif., 1975-76, U. Fla., 1977. Author: Primer of Procedure, 1950, Civil Litigation in Turkey, 1957, Cases and Materials on Pleading and Procedure before Trial, 1961, Cases and Materials on Trials and Appeals, 1961, Appellate Courts in the United States and England, 1963, Law in Action, 1964, The Citizen in Court, 1963, Anglo-American Criminal Justice, 1967, Judicial Administration, 1970, Procedure before Trial in a Nutshell, 1972, Cases and Materials on Civil Procedure, 1975, Civil Litigation, 1978; also monographs, articles. Am. co-dir. Legal Rsch. Inst., Ankara, Turkey, 1956-57; trustee Found. for Overseas LibRs. Am. Law, 1969-72; mem. sch. bd. Garrison, N.Y., 1955-56; Dem. candidate county judge, Putnam County, N.Y., 1958; bd. visitors Judge Adv. Gen. Sch., 1960-65. With AUS, 1942-46,. Mem. Am. Law Inst., Order of Coif (hon.), Middle Temple (hon.), Phi Beta Kappa. Home: Williamsburg Va. Died Dec. 30, 1988.

KARLSON, ALFRED GUSTAV, microbiologist, educator; b. Virginia, Minn., Apr. 26, 1910; s. Knute John and Pauline Henrietta (Johnson) K.; m. Janice Ruth Stillians, June 24, 1938; children: Alfred Lennart, Karl John, Kathy Jean, Trudy Ann, Julie Kay. BS, Iowa State U., 1934, DVM, 1935, MS, 1938; PhD, U. Minn., 1942. Diplomate: pub. health and med. microbiology Am. Bd. Microbiology, Am. Coll. Vet. Pathologists (pres. 1949). Instr. bacteriology Iowa State U., 1935-38; fellow exptl. medicine Mayo Grad. Sch., U. Minn., 1938-39, faculty, 1946-87, prof. comparative pathology, 1962-87, prof. med. microbiology, 1971; cons. exptl. medicine Mayo Clinic, 1946-53, cons. microbiology, 1953-87; sec. Conf. Rsch. Workers Animal Diseases, 1948-64; mem. Nat. Bd. Vet. Examiners, 1948-64. Sect. editor Biol. Abstracts, 1940-87; editorial bd. Jour. Bacteriology, 1950, 56, Am. Jour. Vet. Rsch., 1952-87, Applied Microbiology, 1967-87; contbr. articles to sci. jours. Lt. col. Vet. Corps AUS, 1941-45. Recipient Alumni Achievement award Iowa State U., 1965, Disting. Achievement citation, 1976. Fellow Am. Acad. Microbiology, Am. Vet. Med. Assn.; mem. Am. Thoracic Soc., Soc. Am. Bacteriologists, Soc. Exptl. Biology and Medicine, Sigma Xi. Mem. Unitarian-Univeralist Ch. Home: Rochester Minn. Died May 5, 1987; buried Rochester, Minn.

KARLSON, PHIL (PHILIP KARLSTEIN), film director; b. Chgo., July 2, 1908. Student, Loyola U., Chgo. and L.A. With May Co. Dept. Store, 1923-32. entered motion picture industry with Universal Studios in prop dept.; promoted to asst., then dir. Leatherneck series; mgr. Tryon Foy for one year; tech., assoc. dir. with Stuart Walker; asst. dir. Universal, then producer, 1940; dir. numerous films, 1945-85, including A Wave, A Wac, and a Marine, 1944, There Goes Kelly, 1945, G.I. Honeymoon, 1945, The Shanghai Cobra, 1945, Dark Alibi, 1945, Live Wires, 1946, The Missing Lady, 1946, Swing Parade of 1946, Behind the Mask, 1946, Bowery Bombshell, 1946, Wife Wanted, 1946, Black Gold, 1947, Kilroy Was Here, 1947, Louisiana, 1947, Adventures in Silverado, 1948, Rocky, 1948, Thunderhoof, 1948, The Ladies of the Chorus, 1948, Down Memory Lane, 1949, The Big Cat, 1949, The Iroquois, Trail, 1950, Lorna Doone, 1951, The Texas Rangers, 1951, Mask of the Avenger, 1951, Scandal Sheet, 1952, Kansas City Confidential, 1952, The Brigand, 1952, 99 River Street, 1953, They Rode West, 1954, Hell's Island, 1955, Tight Spot, 1955, Five Against the House, 1955, The Phoenix City Story, 1955, The Brothers Rico, 1957, Gunman's Walk, 1958, Hell to Eternity, 1960, Key Witness, 1960, The Secret Ways, 1961, The Young Doctors, 1961, The Scarface Mob, 1962, Kid Galahad, 1962, Rampage, 1963, The Silencers, 1966, A Time For Killing, 1967, The Wrecking Crew, 1968, Hornet's Nest, 1970, Ben, 1972, Walking Tall, 1973, Framed, 1974. Home: Los Angeles Calif. Died Dec. 12, 1985.

KARO, HENRY ARNOLD, government official; b. Lyons, Nebr., Dec. 24, 1903; s. Paul August and Hedwig Rosalie (Semler) K.; m. Ethel Leila Mitchell, June 26, 1926 (div. Apr. 1935); 1 child, Arnold M.; m. Elsie Cooper, Nov. 2, 1936; children: Douglas Paul, Kathryn Rosalie. BS, U. Nebr., 1923; grad., Indsl. Coll. of Armed Forces, Ft. McNair, Wash., 1955; DSc (hon.), Union Coll., 1958, U. Nebr. Registered profl. engr., D.C. Commd. ensign U.S. Coast and Geol. Survey, 1923; advanced through grades to vice adm. 1965, sea duty aboard ships surveying waters of Alaska, P.I., Atlantic, Pacific, Caribbean and Gulf coasts, 1923-41, Alaska and Aleutian Islands, 1946-50, duty with USAAF, 1942-45, chief Div. Charts, 1951-55; dir. Coast and Geol. Survey, Washington, 1955-65; dep. adminstr., vice adm. Environ. Sci. Services Adminstrn., Rockville, Md., 1965-67; pub. speaker Rep. Brit. Commonwealth Survey Officers Conf., London, 1951, 59, 63; mem. Inter-agy. com. on Oceanography; U.S. mem. Consultative com. to Intergovtl. Oceanographic Commn. UNESCO; headed U.S. del. to 2d UN Cartographic Conf. for Asia and Far E., Tokyo, 1958, 3d Conf., Bangkok, 1961, Nairobi, Kenya, 1963, Manila, Philippines, 1964; mem. U.S. del. UN Conf. Application Sci. and Tech. Less Developed Areas, Geneva, 1963; UNESCO Intergovtl. Conf. Oceanographic Rsch., Copenhagen, 1960, UNESCO Intergovtl. Oceanographic Commn., Paris, 1961, 62 (chmn. del. 1965); mem. Miss. River Commn. Author: World Mapping, 1955. Commdg. officer AF Aeronautical Chart Ctr., St. Louis, World War I. Recipient govtl. commendations, Philippines Legion of Honor for meritorious svcs., 1920's, 30's. Fellow ASCE; mem. Naval Inst., Soc. Am. Mil. Engrs. (pres.), Am. Soc. Photogrammetry, Am. Congress Surveying and Mapping (pres.), U.S. Power Squadron (govt. mem. governing bd.), Am. Geophys. Union, Explorer's Club, Cosmos Club, Sigma Xi, Sigma Tau, Masons. Home: Bethesda Md. Died May 23, 1986; inurned Arlington Nat. Cemetery, Washington.

KASELOW, JOSEPH, advertising executive; b. N.Y.C., Oct. 21, 1912; s. Frederick and Louise (Lehanka) K.; m. Alice Davidson, Jan. 12, 1940; children: Evelyn, Joseph Andrew, Frederick Lee. BA, Cornell Coll., Mt. Vernon, Iowa, 1934. With Cowan & Dengler Inc., Advt., 1934-36; mem. staff N.Y. Herald Tribune (briefly known as World Jour. Tribune), 1937-67, bus. news writer, 1939-52, columnist Along Madison Avenue with Kaselow, 1952-67; with Sullivan, Stauffer, Colwell & Bayless Inc. advt. agy., N.Y.C., 1967-68; v.p. corp. relations Cunningham & Walsh Inc., N.Y.C., 1968-72; pres. Kaselow Communications, N.Y.C., 1972-

73; sr. v.p. Grey & Davis Inc., N.Y.C., 1973-86; broadcaster radio sta. WOR, 1956, MBS, 1962, WINS, 1963-64; editor Ad World, sta. WOR-TV, 1958. Contbr. articles to nat. mags. Dir. N.Y. area Decade of Growth campaign Cornell Coll., 1963-64; bd. mgrs. Glen Rock (N.J.) Community Chest, 1959-62. With USNR, 1943-45, PTO. Recipient Alumni Achievement award Cornell Coll., 1962, annual award League Advt. Agys. 1962. Mem. N.Y. Fin. Writers Assn., Cornell Coll. Alumni Assn. (pres. N.Y. area 1957-59), Silurians, Kappa Tau Alpha, Alpha Delta Sigma, Sigma Delta Chi. Home: Glen Rock N.J. Died Apr. 9, 1986; cremated.

KASPER, WALTER FRANCIS, transportation executive; b. Owatonna, Minn., July 8, 1891; s. Frank J. and Anna F. (Renchin) K.; m. Laura G. Gorman, Apr. 10, 1918; children: Mary Ann, Frank Walter, Joe Gorman. ME, U. Minn., 1911. Automobile salesman 1911-13; with Fairmont Ry. Motors, Inc., from 1913, draftsman, 1913-15, chief engr., 1915-19, sales mgr., chief engr., 1919-28, v.p. in charge sales and engring., 1928-39, pres.; gen. mgr., 1939-57, chmn., 1957-59, also bd. dirs.; sec. Fairmont Ry. Motors Ltd., Can., 1928-39, pres., 1939-57, chmn. bd., 1957-59, also bd. dirs.; bd. dirs. Anchor Cas. Co., St. Paul. Pres. Water and Light Commn., Fairmont, Minn., 1920-50; trustee Coun. for Technol. Advancement, 1945-60. Mem. Minn. Employers Assn. (pres. 1949-59), Machinery and Allied Products Inst., Ry. Mfrs. Assn. (pres. 1934), Soc. Automotive Engrs., Am. Soc Testing Materials, Army Ordnance Assn., Rotary, Phi Gamma Delta, Theta Tau. Republican. Roman Catholic. †

KASS, IRVING, physician, educator; b. Topeka, July 15, 1917; s. David and Sophia R. (Sherr) K.; m. Edythe Blackberg, May 9, 1948; children: Mark David, Sharlene Rondi, Philip Alan. BA, U. Kans., 1939, MA in Bacteriology, 1944, MD, 1944. Diplomate Am. Bd. Internal Medicine. Intern Michael Reese Hosp., Chgo., 1944; resident Michael Reese Hosp., 1948-49, Nat. Jewish Hosp., Denver, 1947-48, New Eng. Med. Ctr., Boston, 1950-51; staff physician VA Ctr., Wadsworth, Kans., 1951-55; assoc. med. dir. Nat. Jewish Hosp., Denver, 1955-64; asst. prof. medicine U. Colo. Sch. Medicine, Denver, 1956-54; assoc. med. dir. Will Rogers Hosp., Saranac Lake, N.Y., 1964-66, dir. clin. rsch., 1964-66; assoc. prof. internal medicine U. Nebr. Coll. Medicine, Omaha, 1966-69, Margaret and Richard Larson prof. medicine, 1973-84; chmn. pulmonary medicine U. Nebr. Med. Ctr., Omaha, 1966-80; dir. rsch. pulmonary div. U. Nebr. Med. Ctr., 1980-84; mem. nat. adv. coun. Tb., Ctr. for Disease Control, Atlanta. 1970-73; cons. WHO, 1976, 79, Pan Am. Sanitary Bur., 1977, 79; chmn. pulmonary seminar 3d and 4th World Congresses, Internat. Rehab. Med. Assn., 1978, 82. Contbg. author text on lung disease, 1979; contbr. numerous articles on pulmonary disease to profl. jours., to chemotherapy of asthma. Leader Denver coun. Boy Scouts Am., 1955-64; chmn. winter carnival, Saranac Lake, N.Y., 1966. With M.C. U.S Army, 1945-47. Named Admiral Great Navy of State Nebr., 1968. Fellow A.C.P.; Am. Coll. Chest Physicians (gov. Nebr. 1972-82); mem. Am. Lung Assn. (nat. bd. rep. dir. 1969-81, chmn. com. disability criteria com. 1978-82), Am. Lung Assn. Nebr. (pres. 1977-78, dir. 1980-84), exec. com. 1966-80), AMA (co-chmn. respiratory com. 1980-84), Rotary, B'Nai B'rith, Sigma Xi, Phi Beta Kappa, Alpha Omega Alpha, Delta Sigma Rho. Jewish. Home: Omaha Nebr. Died Aug. 28, 1984.

KATONA, GEORGE, social scientist; b. Budapest, Hungary, Nov. 6, 1901; came to U.S. 1933; naturalized, 1939; s. Sigmund and Olga (Wittman) K.; m. Marian Beck, Nov. 2, 1929. PhD, U. Goettingen, Germany, 1921; Dr. honoris Causa, U. Amsterdam, 1977. Assoc. editor Der Deutsche Volkswirt, Berlin, 1926-33; investment counsel N.Y.C., 1933-36; lectr. New Sch. Social Rsch., N.Y.C., 1936-42; rsch. dir. com. on price control, Cowles Commn. U. Chgo., 1943-45; sr. study dir. div. program surveys Dept. Agr., Washington, 1945-46; program dir. survey rsch. ctr., prof. econs. and psychology U. Mich., Ann Arbor, 1946-71; vis. prof. MIT, 1961, NYU, 1964. Author: Organizing and Memorizing, 1940, War without Inflation, 1942, Price Control and Business, 1945, Psychological Analysis of Economic Behavior, 1951, Consumer Attitudes and Demand, 2953, Consumer Expectations, 1956, Business Looks at Banks, 1957, The Powerful Consumer, 1960, The Mass Consumption Society, 1964, Private Pensions and Individuals Saving, 1965, Consumer Response to Income Increases, 1968, Aspirations and Affluence, 1971, Psychological Economics, 1975; (with Burkhard Strumpel) A New Economic Era, 1978. Carnegie Found. grantee, 1938-40; fellow Guggenheim Meml. Found., 1940-42; winner lst Dr. Hegemann prize, Dusseldorf, Federal Republica of Germany, 1963. Mem. Am. Psychol. Assn. (Disting. Profl. Contbn. award 1977), Am. Econ. Assn., Am. Statis. Assn. Home: Ann Arbor Mich. Died June 18, 1981.

KATZ, LOUIS NELSON, physiologist, educator, researcher; b. Pinsk, Poland, Aug. 25, 1897; came to U.S., 1900; naturalized, 1904; s. Harry J. and Sarah (Rosenberg) Kates; m. Aline Grossner, June 15, 1928; 1 son, Arnold Martin. AB, Western Reserve U., 1918, MD, 1921, MA, 1923, DSc honoris causa, 1965. Intern and asst. resident medicine Cleve. City Hosp., 1921-23; dir. Cardiovascular Inst. Michael Reese Hosp. and Med.

Ctr., Chgo., 1930-67, emeritus, 1967, dir. dept. cardiovascular disease div. medicine, 1962-67, emeritus, 1967; asst. prof. physiology, U. Chgo., 1930-41, professorial lectr. physiology, 1941-67, emeritus, 1967; vis. prof. physiology, 1967; attending physician Michael Reese Hosp. from 1947. Author books; co-author publs. including: Experimental Atherosclerosis, 1953, Clinical Electrocardiography, 1965, Nutrition and Atherosclerosis, 1958; mem. editorial bd. Acta Cardiologica; editor sect. cardiovascular system Biol. Abstracts, Phila.; bd. editors Circulation, from 1958; contbr. to nat., internat. med. jours. Pvt. S.A.T.C., 1918. Recipient Lasker award Am. Heart Assn., 1956; served as pres. Ill. Inter-Am. Cardiol. Congress, 1948; permanent hon. pres. Inter-Am. Cardiol. Soc. Fellow A.C.P., AAAS; mem. Am. (pres. 1951-52, chmn. sci. coun. 1952-53), Chgo. (pres. 1954-57, chmn. sci. coun. 1952-53) heart assns., Am. Soc. Clin. Investigation, Cen. Soc. Clin. Rsch., Am. Soc. Study Arteriosclerosis (pres. 1954-55), Internat. Cardiol. Soc., A.M.A., Am. Physiol. Soc. (pres. 1956-57), Phi Beta Kappa, Sigma Xi, Alpha Omega Alpha. Jewish. Home: Chicago Ill. Deceased.

KATZ, WILBER GRIFFITH, educator, lawyer; b. Milw., June 7, 1902; s. George H. and Jessie (Griffith) K.; m. Ruth Weaver, Dec. 30, 1926; 1 dau., Elisabeth Harris. AB, U. Wis., 1923; LLB, Harvard U., 1926, SJD, 1930. Bar: N.Y. 1927, Ill. 1935. With firm Root, Clark, Buckner & Ballantine, N.Y.C., 1927-29; asst. prof. Law U. Chgo. Law Sch., 1930-33, assoc. prof., 1933-36, prof., 1936-62, dean Law Sch., 1939-50; prof. law U. Wis., Madison, 1962-70. Episcopalian. Home: Corning Iowa. Died May 17, 1979; buried Milwaukee, Wis.

KAUFMAN, ROBERT GARNEL, poet; b. New Orleans, Apr. 18, 1925; s. Joseph and Lillian (Vigne) K.; m. Eileen Singhe, June, 1958; 1 son, Parker. Student, New Sch. Social Rsch., N.Y.C., 1950. Author: (poetry) Solitudes Crowded with Loneliness, 1965, The Golden Sardine, 1966, The Ancient Rain; (anthologies of poetry) 185; Alix, 1973, The Poetry of the Negro, 1970, Soul Script; 1970, Three Authors: Kaufman, Burroughs, Pelieu, L'Herne, 1967; The Poetry of Black America, 1973, Mark in Time, Christa Fleischman, 1971, The Voice That Is Great Within Us, 1970; Making It New, 1973; (films) Dissent in The Arts, 1959, The Flower Thief, 1960, Coming From Bob Kaufman, Poet, 1972; founder (with Allen Ginsberg, John Kelly, William Margolis) Beatitude mag., 1959. Nominated for Guinness Poetry award, 1960-61. Home: Fairfax Calif. Died Jan. 12, 1986.

KAUFMAN, SEYMOUR ALVIN, radiologist; b. Boston, Apr. 5, 1926; s. Frank S. and Ida (Ganick) K.; m. Charlotte F. Rothberg, Feb. 10, 1951; children: Lisa Nan, John Andrew, Peter Ross. MD, Boston U., 1948. Intern Boston City Hosp., 1948-49, resident, 1949-50; resident Mass. Meml. Hosp., Boston, 1952-54; pvt. practice specializing in radiology Boston, 1963-84; mem. staff Boston U. Hosp., Boston City Hosp., Northeastern U.; clin. prof. radiology Boston U. Contbr. numerous articles to profl. jours. Active in fund raising United Fund, Mus. Fine Arts, Boston, Alumni funds, Combined Jewish Philanthropies; trustee New Eng. Sch. Keyboard Tech. Capt. M.C. USAF, 1950-52. Fellow Am. Coll. Radiology; mem. Radiol. Soc. N.Am., Am. Roentgen Ray Soc., New Eng. Roentgen Ray Soc., Mass. Radiologic Soc., AMA, Mass. Med. Soc., St. Botolph Club, Wightman Club. Home: Newton Center Mass. Died May 28, 1984, buried Sharon, Mass.

KAVINOKY, NADINA RINSTEIN (MRS. NAHUM KAVINOKY), physician, educator; b. Zurich, Switzerland, Jan. 5, 1888; came to U.S., 1891, naturalized, 1985; d. Boris and Anna (Mogilova) Reinstein; m. Nahum Kavinoky, 1907; children: Vita (Mrs. Herman Schott), Elsa (Mrs. Jules Kievits), Robert. MD, U. Buffalo, 1910; postgrad., Charite Hosp., Berlin, 1913. Pvt. practice L.A., from 1928; dir. mothers' clinics L.A. County Health Dept., 1929; instr. dept. gynecology Coll. Med. Evangelists, 1929; instr. sch. nursing Meth. Hosp., L.A.; vis. lectr. U. So. Calif., U. Calif., 1949-50. Contbr. articles to profl. jours. Del. Internat. Birth Control. Conf., Zurich, 1930, Centennial Celebration Am. Women, 1940, Internat. Congress Med. Women, Amsterdam, 1947, White House Conf. Family Life, Washington, 1948, White House Conf. on Children and Youth, 1950. Mem. AMA, Am. Assn. Marriage Counselors, Nat. Coun. Family Relations (pres. 1950-51, Assn. Study Internal Secretions, Am. Med. Women's Assn. †

KAY, GRADY TALMAGE, insurance executive; b. Maud, Ala., Sept. 4, 1892; s. Joseph Marion and Minerva (Burns) K.; m. Ruth Searcy, Nov. 8, 1912. Student, Birmingham-So. Coll., 1910-11. Adminstrv. asst. Liberty Nat. Life Ins. Co., Birmingham, Ala., from 1951. Mem. Masons (past comdr., past master, past grand orator), KT, Civitan (internat. pres. 1950-52). Home: Birmingham Ala. †

KAY, HERSHY, composer-arranger; b. Phila., Nov. 17, 1919; s. Louis H. and Ida (Aisen) K.; m. Maria J. Lawrenz, 1973. Student cello, Curtis Inst., 1936-40. Composer-arranger scores for Broadway shows including On the Town, 1944, A Flag Is Born, 1947, Peter Pan, 1950, Golden Apple, 1954, Sand Hog, 1955,

Candide, 1956, 73, Once Upon a Mattress, 1958, Juno, 1958, Livin' the Life, 1959, Happiest Girl in the World, 1961, Milk and Honey, 1961, 110 in the Shade, 1963, Kelly, 1965, Coco, 1969, Chorus Line, 1975, American Musical Jubilee, 1600 Pennsylvania Avenue, 1976, Music Is, 1976, Twentieth Century Ltd., 1977; prepared ballet scores for Martha Graham Co., 1947, Thief Who Loved a Ghost, Ballet Theatre, 1950, Cakewalk, 1951, Western Symphony, 1954, Stars & Stripes, 1958, Who Cares?, 1970 (all for N.Y.C. Ballet), The Concert for Ballets USA, 1956, L'Inconnue for Am. Ballet Theatre 1965, The Clowns for Joffrey Ballet Co., 1968, Grand Tour for Royal Ballet, London, 1971, Meadowlark and Cortege Burlesque for Eliot Feld Co., 1969, Winters Court for Royal Danish Ballet, 1972, Union Jack for N.Y.C. Ballet, 1976; orchestrated film scores including Man With a Gun, 1955, King and Four Queens, 1956, Cinerama (South Seas), 1958, Girl of the Night, 1960, Such Good Friends, 1971, Bite the Bullet, 1975, orchestral plays Kelly, 1965, (with Clare Grundman) Drat, the Cat, 1965; TV scores include Valiant Years, 1962, FDR series, 1964, Twentieth Century, 1963, This Nation at War, Startime, 1959, spl. projects, 1963 (all NBC); composer original background music Cyril Ritchard's Mother Goose rec., 1958; completed opera Good Soldier Schweik for composer Robert Kurka (dec.), 1959; reconstructed, orchestrated Louis M. Gottschalk's Grande Tarantelle for piano and orch., 1957; musicals include Evita, London, 1978, Carmelina, N.Y.C., 2979; tchr. orchestration Columbia U., 1972. Home: Danbury Conn. Died Dec. 2, 1981.

KAYE, DANNY, actor, comedian, baseball executive; b. N.Y.C., Jan. 18, 1913; s. Jacob and Clara (Nemerovsky) Kaminski; m. Sylvia Fine, Jan. 3, 1940; 1 dau., Dena. L.H.D., Colgate U. Founder, mng. ltd. partner Seattle Mariners baseball team, from 1976. Appeared on stage in: Straw Hat Revue, Ambassador Theatre, N.Y.C., 1939, Lady in the Dark, 1940, Let's Face It, 1941; on screen with, Samuel Goldwyn, Inc., 1943-48; motion pictures include Up In Arms, 1943, Wonder Man, 1944, Kid from Brooklyn, 1945, Secret Life of Walter Mitty, 1946, A Song is Born, 1947, The Inspector General, 1948, On The Riviera, 1950, Hans Christian Anderson, 1952, Knock on Wood, 1954, White Christmas, 1954, The Court Jester, 1955, Merry Andrew, 1957, Me and the Colonel, 1958, The Five Pennies, 1959, On the Double, 1961, The Man from the Diner's Club, 1962, The Madwoman of Chaillot, 1969; star: TV show The Danny Kaye Show; other TV appearances include Look In at Met. Opera, 1975, Pinocchio, 1976, Skokie, 1981, Live from Lincoln Center, 1981; Broadway play Two by Two, 1970-71. Ofcl. permanent ambassador-at-large UNICEF. Recipient Spl. Acad. award, 1954; Emmy award for Danny Kaye Show, 1963; Best Children's Spl. 1975; George Foster Peabody award for Danny Kaye Show, 1963; award Internat. Distinguished Service UN Children's Fund; Scopus Laureate; Wateler Peace Prize Carnegie Found. 1981; Kennedy Ctr. honor for lifetime contbns. to the arts, 1984. Home: Beverly Hills Calif. Deceased.

KAYE, NORA (NORA KOREFF), choreographer, dancer, ballet company artistic adminstrator; b. N.Y.C., Jan. 17, 1920; m. Herbert Ross, 1959. Studied with, Michael Fokine, Met. Opera Ballet Sch. Ballet debut with Met. Opera's children's ballet; joined Am. Ballet Theatre, N.Y.C., 1939; with N.Y.C. Ballet, 1951-54; returned to Am. Ballet Theatre, 1954-60, asso. artistic dir., 1977-87; co-founder, prima ballerina, Ballet of the Two Worlds, 1959-60; ret. as dancer, 1961; asst. to Herbert Ross on films, including The Sunshine Boys, prodn. asso.: film The Turning Point (Recipient Award of Distinction, Dance Mag. 1980). Died Feb. 28, 1987.

KAYE, SAMMY, orchestra leader, composer; b. Lakewood, Ohio, Mar. 13, 1913; s. Samuel and Mary (Zarnocay) K.; m. Ruth Knox Elden, Mar. 2, 1940 (div. 1956). BCE, Ohio U. Band leader 1933-87; performer on radio, TV and in movies; recording artist with Columbia Records. Composer of popular songs including Hawaiian Sunset, There Will Never Be Another You, Harbor Lights, Remember Pearl Harbor. Mem. Winter Golf League of Advt. Interests, Theta Chi. Home: New York N.Y. Died June 2, 1987.

KAZEN, ABRAHAM, JR., congressman; b. Laredo, Tex., Jan. 17, 1919; m. Consuelo Raymond; children: Abraham, Norma Kazen Dillman, Christina Kazen Attal, Catherine, Jo-Betsy. Student, U. Tex., 1937-40, Cumberland Law Sch., Lebonan, Tenn., 1941. Bar: Tex. 1942. Mem. firm Raymond, Alvaredo & Kazen, Laredo, 1946-55; mem. Tex. Ho. of Reps., 1947-52; mem. Tex. Senate, 1952-66, pres. pro tempore, 1959; acting gov. Tex., 1959; mem. 90th-98th congresses 23d Dist. Tex., mem. armed svcs. com., interior com. Capt. USAAF, World War II, ETO, CBI. Mem. Tex., Laredo bar assns., Am. Legion, VFW, Air Force Assn., U. Tex. Ex-Students Assn., K.C. Club. Home: Laredo Tex. Died Nov. 29, 1987.

KEADY, WILLIAM LEO, corporation executive; b. Rochester, N.Y., Jan. 5, 1894; s. M.B. and Anna (Duffy) K.; m. Margaret Jennings, Oct. 15, 1925 (dec. Oct. 1925); children: William L., Michael J., Peter, Thomas D. (dec.), Richard E.; m. Emily C. Novak, Feb. 27, 1965. Grad., U.S. Naval Acad., 1916; MS, Columbia U., 1923. Officer U.S. Navy, 1916-24; with

U.S. Gypsum Co., Chgo., 1924-49, v.p. ops., v.p. sales, dir., pres., 1942-49; pres., dir., gen. mgr. Marathon Corp., N.Y.C., 1950-51; pres., dir. Pabco Products Inc. (name changed to Fibreboard Paper Products Corp., 1956), San Francisco, 1952-56; pres. Fibreboard Paper Products Corp., San Francisco, 1956-60, dir., chmn., 1960-65; Brown Paper Corp. Portland, Maine, 1960-65; chmn. bd. Advalloy Corp., Palo Alto, Calif., 1965-86; bd. dirs. Brown Co., Berlin, N.H., Dyno Industries Inc., Berkeley, Calif., Phila. Steel & Iron Corp., Conshohocken, Pa., Ducommun Inc., Vernon, Calif. Bd. dirs. ARC. (San Francisco chpt.). Mem. Commercial Club (Chgo.), Chgo. Club, Burlingame Country Club, Hillsborough, Calif., Pacific Union Club (San Francisco). Home: Woodside Calif. Died May 25, 1986.

KEAN, BETTY WYNN, comedienne, television actress; b. Hartford, Conn., Dec. 15, 1918; d. Robert Samuel and Annette Helen (Hansen) K.; m. Lew Parker, Mar. 9, 1955; 1 dau., Deirdre Mahon. Featured dancer in George White's Scandals; starred in musicals Call Me Mister and Ankles Aweigh; appeared as part of Kean Sisters comedy team, 1950's; appeared on Ed Sullivan Show, on Broadway and in night clubs; guest star on TV shows Love Boat, Happy Days, The Odd Couple, The Bob Newhart Show, and Facts of Life. Home: Hollywood Calif. Died Sept. 29, 1986.

KEARINS, MICHAEL JOSEPH, JR., manufacturing executive; b. Chgo., Aug. 8, 1892; s. Michael J. and Elizabeth (Gannon) K.; m. Mildren Mary O'Neill, Sept. 29, 1923; children: Jean Anne (dec.), Patricia J., Barbara M. Ed. high sch., Chgo. Past pres. Whitman & Barnes Mfg. Co., Detroit; chmn. J.H. Williams Co., United Greenfield Corp. With U.S. Army, 1917-19. Mem. Chgo. Athletic Assn., Detroit Athletic Cluib, Oakland Hills Country Club. Home: Grosse Pointe Mich. †

KEATS, MARTIN MERRILL, dentist; b. Bklyn., Jan. 12, 1909; s. Samuel and Ida (Kaplan) K.; m. Judy Ida Stein, Sept. 24, 1931; children: Andrew Terry, Ronald Stuart. Student, Colby Coll., 1924-26; DMD, Harvard U., 1930. Pvt. practice N.Y.C., from 1930; practice devoted to rehab. prosthesis. Capt. AUS, 1944-46. Fellow Acad. Gen. Dentistry; mem. N.Y. Acad. Dentistry, Am. Acad. Periodontology, Am. Equilibration Soc., Am. Acad. Gnathologic Orthopedics, ADA, N.Y. State, 1st Dist. dental socs., Fedn. Dentaire Internat., Am. Prosthodontic Soc., N.Y. Acad. Scis., Internat. Acad. Gnathology, North Ea. Gnathological Soc., One Hundred Club, Harvard Club, Fenway Golf Club, Alpha Omega. Died Apr. 1, 1985; buried Mt. Pleasant Cemetery, Hawthorne, N.Y.

KEDDY, JOHN LEWIS, museum executive; b. London, Nov. 28, 1891; came to U.S., 1906, naturalized, 1916; s. Thomas William and Marian Eliza (Hardwick) K.; m. Kathryn Adelia Burks, June 27, 1921 (dec. June 1950); 1 child, Marian Burks (Mrs. Sterling Lee); m. Mildred Crews, May 31, 1952. AB, Hamilton Coll., 1915; AM, Columbia U., 1916, PhD, 1919. Rsch. asst. state budget systems N.Y. Bur. Mcpl. Rsch., 1915-17, 19-20; asst. chief investigator U.S. Bur. Efficiency, 1920-27; staff asst. Joint Congl. Commn. on Reorgn., 1921-23, staff mem. personnel classification bd., 1923, 25; field supr. Bur. Prohibition, Treasury Dept., 1927-30, asst. to dir. bur. of budget, 1934-38, spl. asst. to commr. Bur. Indsl. Alcohol,, 1930-33; asst to adminstr. Agrl. Adjustment Adminstrn., USDA, 1933-34; prin. budget examiner Bur. of Budget Exec. Office of Pres., 1938-46; budget adviser to gov. Panama Canal, 1945; asst. sec. Smithsonian Instn., from 1946. Lay leader Prisoner Sponsorship Movement, Washington; mem. com. on devel., alumni coun. Hamilton Coll., Clinton, N.Y., 1943-47; pres. D.C. Adult Edn Coun., 1947-52. Ensign USNR, 1917-19. Mem. Acad. Polit. Sci., Delta Upsilon. Mem. Soc. of Friends. Home: Alexandria Va. †

KEECH, RICHMOND B., judge; b. Washington, Nov. 28, 1896; s. Leigh R. and Anne L. (Contee) K.; m. Alice Cashell Berry, Sept. 24, 1957. LL.B., Georgetown U., 1922, LL.M., 1923. Practice law Washington, 1922-25; asst. corp. counsel D.C., 1925-30; people's counsel 1930-34; law mem. and vice chmn. Pub. Utilities Commn., 1934-40, corp. counsel, gen. counsel, 1940-45; adminstrv. asst. to Pres. U.S., 1945-46; judge U.S. Dist. Ct. D.C., 1946-66, chief judge, 1966, sr. dist. judge, from 1967. Served in transp. service USN, World War I; capt. J.A.G. Res. Mem. Bar Assn. D.C., Am. Legion, Barristers, Masters of Foxhounds Assn. Am., Phi Alpha Delta. Episcopalian (jr. warden emeritus). Clubs: Rotary (Washington), Lawyers (Washington), Nat. Press (Washington), Potomac Hunt (Washington), Lawyers (Washington), Metropolitan (Washington); Chevy Chase (Md.); American Foxhound, Virginia Foxhound. Home: Bethesda Md. Died Apr. 13, 1986.

KEELER, CHARLES BUTLER, artist; b. Cedar Rapids, Iowa, Apr. 2, 1882; s. Charles Butler and Ellen Calder (Rock) K.; m. Leila Love Brown, Sept. 27, 1920 (div.). AB, Harvard U., 1905; postgrad., Art Inst. Chgo., 1907-09; studies with John Johansen, summers 1910, 11, studies with Bertha E. Jaques. With Pond & Pond, Chgo., 1905; printer's devil Blakely Printing Co., Chgo., 1905. Landscape painter, etcher, pictorial photographer, designer of book plates, Christmas cards; represented in Fifty Prints of Year 1927, Fine Prints of Year 1929, L.A. Mus., Cedar Rapids Art Gallery, St. Paul Mus., Nat. Gallery Art, Washington, Library of Congress, others. Pvt. F.A., U.S. Army, 1918-19. Recipient hon. mention Panama Pacific Expn., 1913, silver medal St. Paul Inst., 1915, prize Wanamaker's, 1916. Mem. Wine and Food Soc., Gypsy Lore Soc. Home: Dana Point Calif. †

KEELER, WILLIAM W., petroleum company executive; b. Dalhart, Tex., Apr. 5, 1908; s. William and Sarah (Carr) K.; m. Sept. 15, 1933; children: William Robert, Bradford Roger, Kenneth Richard. Student, U. Kans., 1926-29; LLD, Coll. of Ozarks; ED, Colo. Sch. Mines. Asst. chemist Phillips Petroleum Co., Bartlesville, Okla., 1929-34, chemist, 1934, control chemist, 1934-37, engr., 1937-38, chief chemist, 1938-39, night supt., 1939-40, asst. mfg. supt., 1940-41, chief engring. div., 1941, processing engr., 1941, chief engr., 1941-43, tech. asst. to v.p., 1943-45, mgr., 1945-47, v.p., 1947-56, exec. v.p., 1956-62, chmn. exec. com., 1962-67, pres., chief. exec. officer, 1967-68, chief exec. officer, chmn. bd., 1968-73, dir., officer subs. cos., 1973-1987; bd. dirs. First Nat. Bank, Bartlesville; spl. cons. sec. interior, 1961; head del. U.S. Oil to USSR, 1960. Bd. dirs. Dwight Presbyn. Mission; mem. Commn. on Rights, Liberties and Responsibilities of Am. Indian; prin. chief Cherokee Nation, 1949. Mem Legion Honor; recipient Silver Beaver award Boy Scouts Am.; named to Okla. Hall of Fame. Mem. Am. Petroleum Inst., Mid-Continent Oil and Gas Assn., Ind. Nat. Gas Assn., Nat. Petroleum Assn. (trustee), Ind. Petroleum Assn. Am., Nat. Petroleum Coun., Def. Orientation Conf. Assn., C. of C., N.A.M. (chmn. 1969-70, exec. com. 1971-87), Masons (33 deg. Shriner), Order DeMolay, Hillcrest Country Club, Sigma Chi, Sigma Tau. Home: Bartlesville Okla. Died Aug. 24, 1987.

KEENAN, CHARLES WILLIAM, chemistry educator; b. Ft. Worth, Apr. 10, 1922; s. Charles Joseph and Mary Catherine (Markey) K.; m. Elizabeth Alden Pabody, Feb. 3, 1945; children: John Markey, Emily Spence. BS, Centenary Coll., La., 1943; PhD, U. Tex., 1949. Asst. prof. chemistry U. Tenn., Knoxville, 1949-54, assoc. prof., 1954-58, prof., 1958-83. Author: (with D.C. Kleinfelter and J.H. Wood) General College Chemistry, 1957, rev. edit., 1980, (with W.E. Bull and J.H. Wood) Fundamentals of College Chemistry, 1963, rev. edit., 1972. With USNR, 1945-46. NSF fellow Cambridge (Eng.) U., 1957-58, 64-65. Mem. Am. Chem. Soc., AAUP, AAAS, Sigma Xi, Phi Beta Kappa, Phi Kappa Phi. Unitarian. Home: Knoxville Tenn. Died Aug. 1, 1983; buried Knoxville, Tenn.

KEENAN, JOSEPH DANIEL, labor official; b. Chgo., Nov. 5, 1896; s. Edward and Mary (Curtin) K.; children: John E., Joseph D. Ed. high sch., Chgo. Cable splicer Chgo. Telephone Co., 1915-23; supt. elec. constrn. Fed. Electric Co., Chgo., 1921-30; elec. engr. in charge north side treatment plant Chgo., 1930-37; sec. Chgo. Fedn. Labor, from 1937; dir. WCFL, Chgo., 1937-40; labor advisor to assoc. dir. gen. O.P.M., 1940-41; assoc. dir. Labor Prodn. Bd., 1942; vice chmn. labor prodn. War Prodn. Bd., Washington, 1943-45; labor adviser to Gen. Clay Berlin, 1945-47; dir. Labor's League for Polit. Edn.; asst. to dir. O.D.M., from 1953; sec. Elec. Workers Union No. 134; sec.-treas. Bldg. and Constrn. Trades Dept., AFL, 1950-54; internat. sec. Internat. Brotherhood Elec. Workers, from 1954. Mem. Eagles, Irish Fellowship Club. Democrat. Roman Catholic. Home: Washington D.C. †

KEENY, SPURGEON MILTON, humanitarian relief worker, United Nations executive; b. Shrewsbury, Pa., July 16, 1893; s. Noah M. and Estelle M (Fife) K; m. Amelia Smith, July 1, 1921; 1 child, Spurgeon Milton. BA summa cum laude, Gettysburg Coll., 1914, MA, 1915, LHD (hon.), 1956. With Am. Relief Adminstrn. to USSR 1922-24; mem. staff Nat. Council YMCAs, 1924-42, dir. personnel, 1929-32, chief publs., 1932-43; exec. sec. N.Y.C. Pub. Affairs Com., 1935-42; with State Dept., 1943, mem. hdqrs. staff UNRRA, 1944, chief mission to Italy, 1944-47; chief Internat. Refugee Orgn, Italy, 1947; chief supply officer Europe UNICEF, 1948-50, dir. in Asia, 1950-63, ret., 1970; Asian rep. Population Council, Taiwan, 1970-83, cons. 1983-88; cons. World Bank, other orgns.; mem. Am. Relief Adminstrn., 1922-24. Author: Half The World's Children, 1957; contbr. articles to Atlantic Monthly, British Lancet. UN. Rev., UNESCO Courier. Vol. with Brit. Army before World War I. Rhodes Scholar in English Lit., Oxford U., 1920; recipient Outstanding Service to Children award Parents mag., 1957; decorated Star of Solidaity, Gold medal Italy, Cross of Knights Malta 1st class pro merito, Italy, medal City of Rome. Mem. Phi Beta Kappa, Rotary. Home: Washington D.C. Died Nov. 17, 1988.

KEGLEY, CHARLES WILLIAM, philosophy educator, clergyman; b. Chgo., Feb. 17, 1912; s. Charles R.W. and Orpha M. (Koch) K.; m. Elizabeth Meck, 1940; children: Charles William II and John Franklin (twins); m. Jacquelyn Ann Kovacevic, June 12, 1965. B.A., Northwestern U., 1933, M.A., 1937, Ph.D., 1943; B.D., Chgo. Luth. Sem., 1936. Ordained to ministry Luth. Ch., 1937; pastor St. Paul's Luth. Ch., Evanston, Ill., 1940-45; chmn. univ. bd. religion and dir. John Evans Religious Center, Northwestern U., 1944-46; lectr. philosophy Northwestern U., 1946-50; prof. philosophy religion and ethics, dean Grad. Sch., Chgo. Luth. Theol. Sem., Chgo., 1945-50; prof. philosophy Wagner Coll., N.Y.C., 1949-69; prof. philosophy, chmn. dept. philosophy and religious studies Calif. State U., Bakersfield, 1970-80; Rockefeller vis. prof. philosophy U. Philippines, 1965-67; condr. study tours, Europe, Far East, 1939-86; del. XIII Internat. Congress Aesthetics, 1964, XIV Congress, 1968; chmn. Am. Luth. delegation World Conf. Christian Youth, Amsterdam, 1939; lectr. Internat. Congress, Philosophy, Brussels, 1953, Venice, 1958, Athens, 1960, Mexico, 1963, Amsterdam, 1967, Uppsala, 1970. Author: Protestantism in Transition, 1965, Politics, Religion and Modern Man, 1968; coauthor: Religion in Modern Life, 1956, Existence Today, 1957, (with wife) Introduction to Logic, 1978; founder, editor: Library of Living Theology; editor: The Theology of Paul Tillich, 1952, enlarged edit., 1983, Reinhold Niebuhr—His Religious, Social and Political Thought, 1956, enlarged edit., 1984, The Theology of Henry Nelson Wieman, 1963, The Theology of Emil Brunner, 1966, The Theology of Rudolph Bultmann, 1970, The Philosophy and Theology of Anders Nygren, 1970; asso. editor: USA Today. Mem. Am. Philos. Assn., Am. Soc. Reformation Research, European Soc. Culture, Am. Soc. Ch. History, Omicron Delta Kappa. Clubs: Rich County Country (N.Y.C.); University (Chgo.); Bakersfield (Calif.); Racquet. Home: Bakersfield Calif. Died Sept. 1, 1986; buried St. John's Cemetery, Wytheville, Va.

KEITH, ROBERT TAYLOR SCOTT, naval officer; b. Washington, May 19, 1905; s. John A.C. and Mary Welby (Scott) K.; m. Eleanor Langhorne Hudgins, Feb. 22, 1936; children: Robert Taylor Scott, M. Langhorne. BS, U.S. Naval Acad., 1928; student, U.S. Naval Postgrad. Sch., 1936. Commd. ensign USN, 1928, advanced through grades to rear adm.; comdr. U.S.S. Nicholas, 1943-45, U.S.S. Missouri, 1954; comdt. midshipmen U.S. Naval Acad., 1954-56; comdr. Cruiser-Destroyer Force, U.S. Pacific Fleet, 1960-61, 1st Fleet, U.S. Pacific Fleet, from 1963. Sr. mem. UN Mil. Armistice Commn., Korea, 1961-62. Decorated Legion of Merit. Home: Falls Church Va. Died Feb. 12, 1989.

KELB, NORMAN ERNEST, industrial executive; b. Toledo, Apr. 2, 1893; s. Frank F. and Theresa (Himmelmann) K.; m. Carrie Bernice Schill, Aug. 15, 1917 (dec. 1948); 1 son, Edwin D.; m. Zelma Bird, 1952 (dec. 1975). Student, pub. schs. With France Stone Co., 1913-29; sec.-treas. Erie Stone Co., 1929-39; pres., dir. High Point Oil Co., Indpls., 1925-88, Cumberland Quarriers Inc., 1940-88. With U.S. Army, World War I. Mem. Nat. Coal Assn., Nat. Crushed Stone Assn. (pres. 1956-57), Ind., Indpls. C. of C., Columbia Club (Indpls.), Woodland Country Club, Masons, Shriners. Home: Indianapolis Ind. Died Feb. 23, 1988; buried Crown Hill Cemetery, Indianapolis.

KELLER, DAVID COE, department store executive; b. Warren, Ohio, Jan. 30, 1921; s. David Claude and Minnie Corlin (Furgerson) K.; m. Gladys Marie Carstens, Jan. 6, 1945; 1 dau., Anne Marie. B.B.A., Cleve. State U., 1943. Staff acct. Touche Ross & Co., Cleve., 1946-49; asst. controller M. O'Neil Co. (dept. store), Akron, Ohio, 1950-56; controller, treas., dir. F.N. Arbaugh Co. (dept. store), Lansing, Mich., 1956-59; v.p., treas., dir. Wurzburg Co. (dept. store), Grand Rapids, Mich., 1959-72; chief financial officer, v.p., treas. Wieboldt Stores Inc., Chgo., 1972-82, pres., chief exec. officer, 1982-86, chief operating officer, 1986; pres., owner Fasionfull, 1986-88. Bd. dirs. Jr. Achievement Grand Rapids, 1961-69; dir. Civic Fedn., Chgo., 1974-88. Served with USMCR, 1943-45. Named Grand Rapids Boss of Year Am. Woman's Clubs, 1969. Mem. Ill. Retails Mchts. Assn. (treas. 1977-88, bd. dirs., exec. com., chmn. bd. 1985-88), State St. Council (bd. dirs., exec. com.), Tau Kappa Epsilon. Club: Mason (Shriner). Home: Algonquin Ill. Died May 17, 1988; buried Windridge, Cary, Ill.

KELLER, IRA C., paper company executive; b. Portland, Maine, Feb. 2, 1899; s. Charles and Frances K.; m. Lauretta Brownson Taylor, Apr. 5, 1925; 1 son, Richard Brownson. ME, Rensselaer Poly. Inst., 1920. Apprentice Westinghouse Electric Co., 1920; with Union Carbide & Carbon Co., Nat. Acme Co. (Cleve.), Container Corp. Am. (Chgo.), 1926-53; exec. v.p. Container Corp. Am., Chgo., 1946-53; chmn. Western Sales Co., Portland, Oreg.; pres. Oreg. Grad. Ctr.; chmn. Found Oreg. Rsch. and Edn.; bd. dirs. Western Forestry Ctr.; chmn. adv. coun. U. Oreg. Health Scis. Ctr. With U.S. Army, World War I. Mem. Arlington Club, Waverley Country Club, University Club (Portland), Alpha Tau Omega. Unitarian. Home: Portland Oreg. Died Apr. 28, 1978; interred Portland, Oreg.

KELLOGG, ALFRED LATIMER, English educator; b. Cleve., Apr. 24, 1915; s. Alfred Noah and Clara Florence (Beck) K.; m. Ellen Carlisle Cushman, June 7, 1941 (dec. Dec. 1977); children—Marion Lewis Kellogg Fisher, Alfred Cushman. A.B., Western Res. U., 1937; Ph.D., Yale U., 1941. Instr. English Yale U., 1941-42, 45-47, Cornell U., 1942; asst. prof. English Rutgers U., New Brunswick, N.J., 1947-51; asso. prof. Rutgers U., 1951-61, prof., 1961-85, prof. emeritus, 1985-86; mem. Inst. for Advanced Study, Princeton U., 1951-52. Author: Chaucer, Langland, Arthur, 1972; contbr. articles to scholarly jours. Served with Signal Intelligence AUS, 1942-45, ETO. Am. Philos. Soc. Penrose Fund grantee, 1965, 77; Ford fellow, 1951-52; Guggenheim fellow, 1953-54; Rutgers Faculty fellow, 1976-77, 80-81. Mem. Medieval Acad. Am., MLA, Dante Soc., Modern Humanities Assn., Internat. Arthurian Soc., Internat. Assn. U. Profs. English, Phi Beta Kappa. Died June 22, 1986.

KELLOGG, JOHN HALL, lawyer; b. Topeka, Jan. 6, 1891; s. John Roswell and Charlotte (Hall) K.; m. Hannah Adelaide Witkop, Sept. 3, 1920; children: John Hall, Margaret Ann (Mrs. John E. Fries Jr), Willis Carl. AB, Oberlin Coll., 1912, AM, 1914; LLB, Western Res. U., 1917. Bar: Ohio 1917. Pvt. practice Cleve., from 1917; assoc., then ptnr. Hauxhurst, Sharp, Cull & Kellogg and predecessors, Cleve., from 1917. Mem. Jud. Counc. Ohio, from 1958; bd. commrs. grievances and discipline Supreme Ct. Ohio, from 1961, Citizens hosp. study com. Blue Cross N.E. Ohio, 1955-61, bd. edn. Shaker Heights City Sch. Dist., 1940-47, pres. 1943-47; gen. chmn. Shaker Heights 50th Anniversary Com., 1961; trustee Citizens League Cleve., 1959-65. Recipient citation Oberlin Coll., 1956. Mem. Am., Ohio (exec. com. 1953-56), Cleve. (pres. 1953-54) bar assns., Am. Law Inst., Am. Judicature Soc., Order founders and Patriots Am., SAR, Profl. Men's Club Cleve., Oberlin (pres. 1951-54), Western Res. U. Law Sch. (pres. 1929-30. 47-48) alumni assns., Masons (32 degree) Cheshire Cheese Club, Mid-Day Club (Cleve.), Order of Coif, Phi Beta Kappa, Phi Alpha Delta. Republican. Mem. United Ch. Christ. Home: Cleveland Ohio. †

KELLY, ARTHUR, judge; b. Toronto, Ont., Can., Dec. 28, 1900; s. Hugh T. and Mary (Hynes) K.; m. Aileen McDonagh, Oct. 24, 1928; children: Carol, Miriam, Hugh, Kevin. BA, U. Toronto, 1920; legal edn., Osgood Hall Law Sch., Toronto. Bar: Can. 1923; apptd. Queen's Counsel, 1944. With firm Day, Wilson, Kelly, Martin & Campbell and predecessors, Toronto, Ont., Can., 1928-60; justice Ct. of Appeals of Ont., Toronto, 1960-86; Gov. U. Toronto, 1944-70; chmn. insulin com., 1949-60; chmn. Connaught Med. Rsch. Labs., 1956-66. Chmn. Ont. Mental Health Found., 1962-69. Decorated knight comdr. Order St. Gregory. Mem. Can. Bar Assn. (pres. 1957-58), County of York Bar Assn. (pres. 1948), Theta Delta Chi. Home: Toronto Ont., Canada. Died May 30, 1986; interred Toronto, Can.

KELLY, CHARLES JAMES, lawyer; b. St. Johns, Nfld., Can., Aug. 22, 1892; s. Michael J. and Mary (Meehan) K.; m. Marjorie Fleming, Dec. 21, 1922; children: John Fleming, Mary Ellen Owen. Student, St. Bonaventures Coll., St. Johns, Nfld.; LLB, U. Colo., 1925. Bar: Colo. 1925. Mem. firm Lee, Shaw & McCreery, Denver, 1944-48, Lee, Bryans, Kelly & Stansfield, Denver, 1948-84. With U.S. Army, 1917-18. Fellow Am. Bar Found.; mem. Am. Colo. (pres. 1954-55), Denver bar assns., City, University, Denver Country clubs (Denver). Home: Denver Colo. Died Sept. 28, 1984; buried Fairmont Cemetery, Denver.

KELLY, CROSBY MOYER, business executive; b. Hinsdale, Ill., Mar. 23, 1918; s. Thomas Cowen and Mary Emma (Moyer) K.; m. Willah Mary Smith, Mar. 12, 1951. B.A., U. Ariz., 1939; postgrad., U. Mexico, 1939-40. With Ford Motor Co., 1941-48; dir. advt. and pub. relations Rapid Standard Co., Inc., Grand Rapids, Mich., 1949; exec. dir. Chgo. Fair of, 1950; sales rep. Central Services, Inc., Kansas City, Mo., 1951; owner-mgr. importing-distbg. co. Havana and Camaguey, Cuba, 1952-55; v.p., dir. advt. and pub. relations, asst. to chief exec. officer Litton Industries, Inc., Beverly Hills, Calif., 1955-65; chmn. bd. Crosby M. Kelly Assocs. Ltd., 1965-73, 78-86; chmn. Pres. Advt. Measurements, Inc., 1965-70; sr. v.p. Litton Industries, Inc., 1973-76; v.p. communications Rockwell Internat., 1976-78; pres. Sage Inst., Portland, Oreg., 1980-83; dir. Western World Ins. Co.; chmn. bd. Performance Measurements Co., Detroit, 1968-70; Cons., insp. gen. Fgn. Assistance, Dept. State, 1962; guest lectr. European Inst. Bus. Adminstrn. Fontainebleau, France, 1966; instr. U. Pitts. Grad. Sch. Bus., 1978. Head Am. delegation Internat. Congress Air Force Assns., Turin, Italy, 1964; del. UN Indsl. Devel. Orgn. 1st World Symposium, 1967; Trustee Albertus Magnus Coll., 1970-73, Mercy Hosp., Pitts., 1977-80, Found. Am. Communications, 1976-86. Decorated commendatore Order of Merit Republic Italy, 1969; recipient Roalman award Nat. Investor Relations Inst., 1985. Home: Litchfield Conn. Died Aug., 1986; interred Litchfield, Conn.

KELLY, E(VERETT) LOWELL, educator, psychologist; b. Kokomo, Ind., Nov. 15, 1905; s. Alva Elmont and Maude (Vickery) K.; m. Lillian Isaacs, Dec. 25, 1939; children: Patricia Ann Klinger, Paul Alan, Pamela Jane Scurry. BS, Purdue U., 1926, DSc (hon.), 1955; AM, Colo. Coll. Edn., 1928; PhD, Stanford U., 1930. High sch. prin., tchr. Taiban (N.Mex.) pub. schs., 1926-27; assoc. prof. psychology, dir. admissions U. Hawaii, 1930-32; Social Sci. Rsch. Coun. fellow Germany, Austria, 1932-33; chmn. dept. psychology U. Conn., 1933-39; asoc. prof. psychology, dir. psychol. clin Purdue U., 1939-42; br. chief clin. psychologist VA, 1946-47; prof. psychology U. Mich., Ann Arbor, 1946-75, prof. psychology emeritus, 1975-86, also chmn. dept. psychology, 1958-62; bd. dir. Bur. Psychol. Services, 1950-71, Inst. Human Adjustment, 1971-74; cons. USPHS, USN, VA. Adviser to dir. SSS, dir. selection Peace Corps, Washington, 1961-62. With USNR, 1942-46l comdr. Res. Recipient letter of commendation (with ribbon) sec. Navy, 1945. Mem. Am. Psychol. Assn. (pres. 1954-55), Mich. Psychol. Assn. (pres. 1948-49). Home: Ann Arbor Mich. Died Jan. 19, 1986.

KELLY, JAMES FRANCIS, university official; b. Washington, Aug. 5, 1915; s. James Francis and Mary (Carr) K.; m. Gloria Mary Soule, Mar. 21, 1941; children: Mary Carol, Joan Frances, James Francis, Laurel Ann, David Carr, Elizabeth Soule, John Quentin. Student bus. adminstrn., Columbus U., Washington; JD, Cath. U. Am., 1939; D. Polit. Sci., U. Pacific, 1969; DSc, N.Y. Med. Coll., 1970. Bar: N.Y. With Pub. Housing Adminstrn. and predecessor agys., 1934-54; with HEW, 1954-70, deptl. budget officer, 1954-61, deptl. comptroller, 1961-66, asst. sec. comptroller, 1966-70; exec. v.p. for adminstrv. affairs Georgetown U., Washington, 1970-73; exec. vice chancellor SUNY, 1973-81, acting chancellor, 1977-78; lectr. pub. adminstrn., 1955-81. Mem. Gov.'s Adv. Coun. on Health; chmn. Gov.'s Task Force on Health Manpower Policy, 1978-79, conf. biomed. scis., physicians for the future, Josiah Macy Jr. Found. Lt. USNR, 1943-46. Recipient Superior Service award Pub. Housing Adminstrn., 1954, Superior Service award HEW, 1958, Disting. Service award, 1960, Career Service award Nat. Civil Service League, 1968. Mem. Fed. Govt. Accts. Assn. (Leadership award 1966), Am. Soc. Pub. Adminstrn., Am. Acad. Polit. and Social Sci., Am. Pub. Health Assn., Nat. Acad. Sci. Inst. Medicine, Acad. Pub. Adminstrn. Home: Delmar N.Y. Deceased.

KELLY, JAMES FRANCIS, SR., physician; b. Boston, Feb. 1, 1891; s. John and Margaret T. (Meade) K.; m. Henriette Frances Wadsworth, July 2, 1917; children: Mary Francis, James Francis, Margaret Patricia, Alice Jane, Thomas Leo, Pauline Rita, Alvin Wadsworth, John Vincent, Gerard Joseph, Sara Rose. MD, Creighton U., 1915. Diplomate Am. Bd. Radiology. Intern St. Joseph's Hosp., Tacoma, 1915, Omaha, 1916; pvt. practice Omaha, from 1919; prof. radiology Sch. Medicine Creighton U., from 1933; chief radiol. svcs. St. Catherine's, Creighton Meml., St. Joseph's hosps., Omaha. Capt. M.C., U.S. Army, World War I. Fellow Am. Coll. Radiology; mem. AMA, Nebr. State (pres. 1953-54), Douglas County (pres. 1948) med. socs., Am. Roentgen Ray Soc., Am. Radium Soc., Radiol. Soc. N.Am., Midwest Clin. Soc. (pres. Omaha chpt. 1944), Am. Cancer Soc. †

KEMP, FRANK ALEXANDER, sugar manufacturing executive; b. Omaha, Nov. 9, 1891; s. Frank Alexander and Ida Loys (Bergman) K.; m. Estelle Kyle, June 12, 1917; Children: Frank Alexander, Philip Sperry; m. 2d, Katheryn M. McClure, Jan. 1, 1943. LLB, U. Colo., 1913. Bar: Colo. 1913. With Great Western Sugar Co., Denver, from 1923, pres., from 1936; bd. dirs. First Nat. Bank, Denver Tramway Corp., Denver; trustee Northwestern Mut. Life Ins. Co., Milw. Regent U. Colo.; trustee Loretto Heights Coll. Capt. AEF, World War I. Mem. U.S. C. of C. (dir.), Denver Club, Mile High Club, Beta Theta Pi. Episcopalian. Home: Denver Colo. †

KEMPER, MARK, insurance executive; b. Van Wert, Ohio, Oct. 7, 1901; s. Hathaway and Mary Jane (Scott) K.; m. Annabel Wagner, Jan. 4, 1934; children: John Scribner, Mary Ann Sowersby, Barbara Chalice. BS, Northwestern U., 1924; MBA, Harvard, 1927. With Lumbermen's Mut. Casualty Co., Chgo., 1919-68, mgr. investment dept., 1930-67, dir., 1936—, treas., 1941-55, sec., 1947-67, fin. v.p., 1955-67, chm. fin. com., 1968-85; Bd. dirs. Am. Mfrs. Mut. Ins. Co., Chgo., Fed. Mut. Ins. Co., Am. Motorists Ins. Co., Chgo.; mem., chmn. fin. com. all cos. Kemper Group; chmn., dir. Bank. Chgo.; dir., chmn. fin. com., mem. exec. com. Fidelity Life Assn., Fulton, Ill.; dir. Economy Fire & Casualty Co., Am. Protection Ins. Co., Blackhawk-Mercury Loan Cos., Empire State Mut. Life Ins. Co., Jamestown, N.Y., Richland Knox Mut. Ins. Co., Mansfield, O., Sequoia Ins. Co., Menlo Pk. Mem. adv. bd. Jr. Achievement, Boy Scouts Am.; v.p. James S. Kemper Found.; dir. McCormick Theol. Sem.; mem. citizens bd. U. Chgo. Mem. Am. Statis. Soc., Am. Fin. Assn., Investment Analysts, Chgo. Club, University Club, Mid-Day Econ. Club, Tower Club (Chgo.). Presbyterian (trustee). Home: Winnetka Ill. Died Oct. 26, 1985.

KENNA, F. REGIS, health industry consultant; b. Pitts., July 28, 1932; s. Walter Joseph and Wilma J. (Blattner) K.; m. Joanne Perner, Oct. 25, 1975; children: Regina, Regis, Richard, Kathleen, Matthew. BS, Duquesne U., 1954; MBA, U. Chgo., 1964. Asst. dir. U. Chgo. Hosps. and Clinics, 1967-69, dir., 1969-77; asst. prof. U. Chgo. Grad. Sch. Bus., 1971-77; pres. F. Regis kenna and Assocs., Addison, Ill., 1977-82. Mem. Am. Bd. Arbitrators. With U.S. Army, 1955-57. Mem. Chgo. Hosp. Coun. (chmn. bd. 1977), Am. Coll. Hosp. Adminstrs. Home: Tampa Fla. Died Sept. 4, 1988.

KENNEDY, FRANCES MIDLAM (MRS. JOSEPH CONRAD KENNEDY), advertising executive; b. Wilmington, Del., Feb. 26, 1913; d. Edward West and Annie (Bullen) Midlam; m. Joseph Conrad Kennedy, Sept. 4, 1937; children—Edward Carter, Stephen Dandridge, Katharine Conrad (Mrs. David C. Treadway). Student pub. schs. Writer Compton Advt., N.Y.C., 1939-47; v.p., copy chief Dancer-Fitzgerald-Sample, Inc., Chgo., 1947-62; v.p., creative group head, mem. creative rev. com. N.Y.C., 1962-69, sr. v.p., creative dir., chmn. creative/mgmt. rev. bd., 1969-81; exec. v.p., chmn. creative rev. bd. Saatchi and Saatchi DFS Advt. (formerly Dancer-Fitzgerald-Sample, Inc.), N.Y.C., 1981-87, chmn. creative strategy adv. bd., 1983-87. Recipient Emma Proetz award, 1954; Golden 30 award Chgo. Copywriters Club, 1958; named Chgo. Advt. Woman of Year, Advt. Women Chgo., 1960; YWCA Acad. women Achievers. Episcopalian. Club: Cosmopolitan, Fashion Group. Home: Weston Mass. Died July 16, 1988.

KENNEDY, G. DONALD, civil engineer; b. South Lyon, Mich., Jan. 25, 1900; s. John and Elizabeth (Bridson) K.; m. Ora L. Wood, June 2, 1928; children: David Donald, John T., Ann E. Kennedy Drucker, Patrick W., Michael J. B.S., U. Mich., 1921. Former registered profl. engr., Mich., Calif., Va., Oreg., Wash., Nebr., Kans., Ohio, Miss., Ill., D.C. Mem. survey party on housing project Dupont Engring. Co., Flint, Mich., 1919; asst. civil engr. Hoad and Decker; cons. engrs. Hoad and Decker, Ann Arbor, Mich., 1921-24; design engr. and city engr. Jackson, Mich., 1925-26; with City of Pontiac, Mich.; on spl. mcpl. problems, including water supply and airport devel. 1927-32; bus. mgr., cons. engr., dep. commr. and commr. Mich. State Hwy. Dept., 1933-42; past v.p. charge hwy. devel. Automotive Safety Found., Washington; with Portland Cement Assn., Chgo., 1950-67; successively cons. engr., asst. to pres., v.p., exec. v.p., pres. Portland Cement Assn., 1950-67; cons. post war planning com. U.S. Senate, 1943-44; cons. to legis. interim coms., Calif., Wash., Oreg., Kans., Nebr., Miss., Ohio, 1945-49; Bd. dirs. ACTION, Inc.; former bd. cons. The Eno Found.; former mem. adv. com. Transp. Center, Northwestern U.; State hwy. commr., Mich., 1940-42; ex officio mem. state adminstrv. bd., state bd. aeronautics, state planning commn.); chief Emergency Pub. Works Div.; mem. hwy. traffic adv. com. War Dept., 1942-45; vice chmn. Roosevelt interregional hwy. com. (interstate system plan), 1941-44; mem. adv. bd. Pub. Works Task Force; Commn. on Orgn. of Exec. Br. of U.S. Govt. (Hoover Commn.), 1948-49; mem. hwy. research bd. NRC, 1952-60, chmn., 1954-55; pres. Am. Assn. State Hwy. Ofcls., 1942; bd. govs. Met. Housing and Planning Council, Chgo., 1964-78; vice chmn., mem. exec. com. Automotive Safety Found., 1943-50; mem. Chgo. Citizens Traffic Safety Bd., 1955-62; Attended Internat. Concrete Road Congress, Rome, 1959, Symposium on Concrete Pavements, Buenos Aires, 1960, Internat. Road Fedn. Meeting, Madrid, 1962; mem. Tech. Mission to Japan, 1963. Recipient George S. Bartlett Award for outstanding contbn. to hwy. progress, 1948. Fellow ASCE (life; chmn. hwy. div. 1953), Inst. Transp. Engrs. (life mem.); mem. Am. Pub. Works Assn. (life), Am. Planning Assn. (life), Engring. Soc. Detroit (charter), Am. Road Builders Assn. (life). Club: Cosmos (Washington). Home: Wilmette Ill. Died Mar. 16, 1988.

KENNEDY, HARRY SHERBOURNE, bishop; b. Bklyn., Aug. 21, 1901; s. David K. and Ida (Hargreaves) K.; m. Katharine Kittle, July 27, 1927; children—Bruce H., David K., Paul S., Joel and Mark (twins). Student, Colo. State Coll., 1922-26; A.B., St. John's Theol. Sem., 1926; postgrad., U. So. Calif., 1931; D.D., Seabury-Western Theol. Sem., 1943; S.T.D., Ch. Div. Sch. Pacific, 1944; D.D., Trinity Coll., 1957; L.H.D., Colo. Coll., 1967. Ordained to ministry Episcopal Ch., 1926; clergyman P.E. Ch., 1926-44; bishop of P.E. Ch., Honolulu, from 1944. Served to capt. as chaplain AUS, 1942-43. Decorated comdr. Order Brit. Empire, 1964. Home: Honolulu Hawaii. Died Feb. 14, 1985; ashes in Chapel of Peace, St. Clements Church, Honolulu.

KENNEDY, J. LAWSON, oil company executive; b. Newburgh, N.Y., Feb. 7, 1921; s. Charles M. and Marion (Lawson) K.; m. Mary-Geraldine Groth, July 4, 1942 (dec. May 1981); children—Paul Lawson, Beth Kennedy Scaldini, David Dean; m. Brenda L. Harris, Feb. 5, 1983. B.A. in Econs., Colgate U., 1942. With Sonneborn Chem. & Refining Co. (merged to become Witco Corp. 1960), 1946-86; petroleum group v.p. Witco Chem. Corp., N.Y.C., 1967-75, dir., exec. v.p., 1975-84; sr. exec. v.p., dir. Witco Corp., N.Y.C., 1984-86; dir. Witco B.V. Netherlands. Active First Ch. of Christ, Scientist, Darien, Conn. Served as sgt. USAF, 1942-45; ETO. Mem. Nat. Petroleum Refiners Assn., Am. Petroleum Inst., Drug, Chem. and Allied Trades Assn. Republican. Club: WeeBurn Country (Darien). Home: Darien Conn. Died Apr. 15, 1986.

KENNEDY, JOHN LYON, psychologist; b. Saginaw, Mich., May 26, 1913; s. James Sheldon and Elizabeth (Lyon) K.; m. Nancy Elliott Kidd, Aug. 27, 1938; children: James Walden, Marianna Elliott, Katherine Ann. Cert., Sacramento Jr. Coll., 1932; AB, Stanford U., 1934; AM, Brown U., 1936, PhD, 1937. Rsch. asst. Yerkes Labs. Primate Biology Yale U., New Haven, Conn., 1936-37; Thomas Welton Stanford fellow psychical rsch. Stanford U., Calif., 1937-39; asst. prof. psychology Tufts U., Medford, Mass., 1939-42, assoc. prof., chmn. dept., 1945-46, prof., chmn. dept., 1946-51; also dir. Inst. Applied Exptl. Psychology, tech. asst. to exec. sec. com. on service personnel NRC, 1942-43; tech. aide OSRD, 1943-45; psychologist RAND Corp., 1951-57; Dorman T. Warren prof. psychology Princeton U.,

1955-67, chmn. dept. psychology, 1958-66, vis. prof., 1966-67; v.p. Inst. Ednl. Devel., 1966-69; vis. prof. U. So. Calif. Grad Sch. Bus. Adminstrn., 1969-71; lectr. mgmt. Sch. Bus. Adminstrn. and Econs. Calif. State U., Northridge, 1971-84, prof. mgmt., 1972-84; cons. psychologist govt. agys., bus. firms; Fulbright lectr. U. Vienna (Austria), 1975-76. Editor: Handbook of Human Engineering Data for Design Engineers, 1949; contbr. articles to profl. jours. Fellow Ctr. Advanced Study in Behavioral Scis., 1954-55. Mem. AAAS, Am. Psychol. Assn., AAUP, Soc. Exptl. Psychologists, Phi Beta Kappa, Sigma Xi. Home: Santa Monica Calif. Died July 14, 1984; interred Chebeague Island, Maine.

KENNEDY, ROBERT HAYWARD, surgeon; b. Southboro, Mass., Dec. 16, 1887; s. Samuel A. and Ilda M. (Hayward) K.; m. Nelle Moore Brooks, Mar. 19, 1926 (div. 1945); m. Florence Wallace, 1945. AB, Amherst Coll., 1908; MD, Columbia U., 1912. Diplomate Am. Bd. Surgery. Surg. dir. Beckman-Downtown Hosp., 1929-57; cons. surgeon Tuxedo Meml. Hosp., from 1930; attending surgeon Univ. Hosp., 1935-53, cons. surgeon, from 1953; vis. surgeon Bellevue Hosp., 1949-55, cons. surgeon, from 1955; assoc. clin. prof. surgery NYU Postgrad. Med. Sch., 1947-53, lectr., from 1953; cons. from 1953. Contbr. articles in field to med. jours. 1st lt. MRC, 1917-19, col. M.C., AUS, 1942-46. Decorated Legion of Merit. Fellow ACS (chmn. com. on trauma 1939- 52, gov. 1942-49, 1st v.p. 1952-53), Am. Surg. Assn.; mem. AMA, Am. Assn. for Surgery of Trauma (v.p. 1952-53, pres. 1954-55), Soc. U.S. Med. Cons. World War II, N.Y. Surg. Soc., N.Y. Acad. Medicine Internat. Soc. Surgeons, Masons, Amherst Club, Phi Beta Kappa, Phi Delta Theta, Nu Sigma Nu, Alpha Omega Alpha. Congregationalist. Home: New York N.Y. †

KENNEDY, RUTH LEE, Spanish language and literature educator; b. Centerville, Tex., Oct. 15, 1895; d. Oliver W. and Carrie Lee (McWaters) Kennedy. AB, U. Tex., 1916, AM, 1917; postgrad., U. Calif., 1924-25; PhD, U. Pa., 1931. Tchr. Spanish lang. San Benito (Tex.) High Sch., 1917-18, Temple High Sch., 1918-19; instr. English Okla. Coll. for Women, 1919-20; tchr. Spanish lang. Sam Houston State Normal Coll., 1920-21; instr. English U. P.R., 1921-22; head Spanish dept. S.W. Tex. State Tchrs. Coll., 1922-24, 1925-26, San Antonio Jr. Coll., 1926-28, 1929-30; asst. prof. Smith Coll., 1930-34, assoc. prof., 1935-44, prof. Spanish lang. and lit., 1944-61, prof. emeritus, 1961-88; prof. Romance langs. U. Ariz., 1961-70, prof. emeritus, 1970-88; dir. Smith Coll. Jrs. in Spain, 1956-58; vis. lectr. Oxford and Cambridge Univs., 1946, U. Mich., summer 1949, U. Ariz., 1950-51, U. Calif., summer 1951. Author: The Dramatic Art of Moreto, 1931-32, La prudencia en la mujer and the Ambient that Brought It Forth (Proceedings of MLA rated most influential article pub. by them in field of Spanish or Hispanic culture and lang. between 1885 and 1958), 1948, Studies in Tirso, I: The Dramatist and His Competitors, 1620-26; contbr. articles on Golden Age lit. culture of Spain to profl. jours. Fellow AAUW, 1937-38, 45-46, U. Pa., 1945-46; John S. Guggenheim fellow, 1950-51. Mem. Academia norteamericana de la lengua española (1st woman), MLA, Am. Assn. Tchrs. Spanish, Hispanic Soc. Am., Internat. Inst. for Girls in Spain, AAUW, Phi Beta Kappa. Republican. Home: Tucson Ariz. Died Feb. 4, 1988; buried Houston.

KENNEY, WILLIAM RICHARDSON, lawyer; b. Mineola, N.Y., Sept. 17, 1922; s. George Churchill and Alice Stewart (Maxey) K.; m. Rev. Marguerite Anne Shirley, Apr. 21, 1943; children: George, James, Charles, Anne, John, Thomas. Student, U. Cin., 1941-43; LL.B. cum laude, U. Balt., 1950; grad., Air Command and Staff Coll., 1951, Nat. Coll. State Trial Judges, 1970. Bar: Md. 1950, U.S. Supreme Ct. 1956. Enlisted in USAAF, 1943; advanced through grades to col.; combat navigator USAAF, S.W. Pacific, World War II; legal officer 1950-73; assigned Alaska, 1965-68, The Pentagon, 1968-73; ret. as chief judge 1973; v.p., mem. faculty Mil. Law Inst., 1970-86; dir. Retiree Activity Office, Bolling AFB, 1978-83; v.p. Retiree Activity Office, Langley AFB, Va., 1984-88, Mil. Law Inst., 1970-86; v.p., bd. dirs. "Beach House" (mental health facility), Virginia Beach, Va., 1985-88. Editor legal jours. Bd dirs. Friendly Citizens Assn., 1975-77, Potomac Sch. Law, 1975-82. Decorated Legion of Merit, Air medal, Joint Services Commendation medal, Air Force Commendation medal. Mem. ABA, Fed. Bar Assn. (pres. St. Louis chpt. 1958-59, The Pentagon 1964-65, Anchorage, Alaska 1965-66, nat. council 1962-88, nat. pres. 1975-76), Nat. Conf. Fed. Trial Judges (chmn. com. mil. judges 1971-72), Judge Adv. Assn. (dir. 1962-88, nat. pres. 1979-80), Air Force Assn. Episcopalian (vestryman 1967-68, chancellor 1968-88). Club: Nat. Lawyers (Washington). Home: Virginia Beach Va. Died Mar. 23, 1988, buried Arlington Nat. Cemetery.

KENT, CORITA, artist; b. Fort Dodge, Iowa, Nov. 20, 1918; d. Robert Vincent and Edith (Sanders) K. BA, Immaculate Heart Coll., 1941; MA, U. So. Calif., 1951. Mem. Immaculate Heart Sisters, 1936-68; elem. tchr. B.C., Can., 1941-46; prof. art Immaculate Heart Coll., L.A., 1946-68. artist specializing in serigraphy; numerous one-woman shows in museums, galleries, univs. in U.S., Can. and Spain including Cin. Art Mus., Munson Williams Proctor Inst., Brooks Meml. Art Gallery, Calif. Palace Legion of Honor, Balt. Mus., Morris Gallery, N.Y.C., The Contemporaries, Mus. N.Mex., Sala Gaspar, Barcelona, Sapin; represented in pub. collections: Met. Mus. Art, Mus. Modern Art, Library of Congress, Rosenwald Collection Nat. Gallery, Cin. Mus., Calif. Palace Legion of Honor, Los Angeles County Mus., Phila. Mus., N.Y.C. Pub. Library, Art Inst. Chgo., Victoria and Albert Mus., London, Bibliotheque Nationale, Paris; executed commns. for Internat. Graphic Arts Soc., Mus. Modern Art, Container Corp. Am., Los Angeles County Mus., Neiman Marcus Co., Reynolds Aluminim; author: Footnotes and Headlines: a Play-Pray Book, 1967, Sister Corita, 1968, (with Gerald Huckaby) City, Uncity, 1969, Damn Everything But The Circus, 1970, (with Joseph Piatauro) To Believe in God, 1968, To Believe in Man, 1970, To Believe in Things, 1971. Home: Boston Mass. Died Sept. 19, 1986; cremated.

KENT, EVERETT LEONARD, textile manufacturing executive; b. Delaware County, Pa., June 25, 1889; s. Henry Thomas and Louise (Leonard) K.; m. Helen Irwin, Apr. 24, 1915; children: William Irwin, Everett Leonard (dec.), Warren Thompson. Student, Cornell U., 1911; D Textiles (hon.), Phila. Textile Inst. Pres. The Kent Mfg. Co., 1918-1956, chmn., from 1956; pres. Clifton Heights Nat. Bank, 1934-54, Kent-Hampton Sales, Inc., N.Y.C., from 1936, Pa. Mfrs. Casualty & Fire Cos., from 1946; bd. dirs. Fidelity-Phila. Trust Co., from 1954. Republican. Home: Merion Pa. †

KENT, SHERMAN, government official; b. Chgo., Dec. 1, 1903; s. William and Elizabeth (Thacher) K.; m. Elizabeth Gregory, Dec. 20, 1934; children: Serafina, Sherman Tecumseh. PhB, Yale U., 1926, PhD, 1933. Instr. to assoc. prof. history Yale U., New Haven, 1928-47, prof., 1947-54; chief African sect., chief Europe-Africa div. Office Strategis Services, 1941-45; acting dir. Office Research and Intelligence, U.S. State Dept., Washington, 1946; mem. civilian staff Nat. War Coll., 1946, bd. cons., 1952-54; asst. dir. Office of Nat. Estimates, CIA, Washington, 1950-67. Author: Electoral Procedure under Louis Philippe, 1937, Writing History, 1941, Strategic Intelligence for American World Policy, 1948; mem. bd. editors Jour. Modern History, 1946-52. Recipient Nat. Civil Service League award, 1961, Pres.'s award for disting. fed. service, 1967. Mem. Am. Hist. Assn. Home: Washington D.C. Died Mar. 11, 1986.

KERTESZ, ANDRE (ANDOR KERTESZ), photographer; b. Budapest, Hungary, July 2, 1894; came to U.S., 1936, naturalized, 1944; s. Leopold and Ernestine (Hoffman) K.; m. Elizabeth Sali, June 17, 1933. Grad. Hungarian Acad. Commerce, Budapest, 1912; self-taught in photography. Photographer, 1912-85; accounts clk. Budapest Stock Exchange, 1912-14, 18-25; free-lance photographer, Paris, 1925-35, including for Frankfurt Illustrierte, Berliner Illustrierte, Uhu, Strasburger Illustrierte, Le Nazionale de Fiorenza, Vu, Sourire, The Times (London); contract photographer Keystone Studios, N.Y.C., 1936-37; free-lance mag. photographer, N.Y.C., 1937-49, including Harper's Bazaar, Vogue, Town and Country, Am. Mag., Collier's, Coronet, Look; contract photographer Conde Nast Publs., N.Y.C., 1949-62; free-lance photographer, N.Y.C., 1962-85; one-man shows: Galerie Le Sacre du Printemps, Paris, 1927, Art Inst. Chgo., 1946, L.I. U., N.Y.C., 1962, Bibliotheque Nationale, Paris, 1963, Modern Age Studio, N.Y.C., 1963, Mus. Modern Art, N.Y.C., 1964, Moderna Museet, Stockholm, 1971, Magyar Nemzeti Galeria, Budapest, 1971, Valokuvamuseum, Helsinki, Finland, 1972, Hallmark Gallery, N.Y.C., 1973, Light Gallery, N.Y.C., 1973, Wesleyan U., Middletown, Conn., 1976, French Cultural Inst., N.Y.C., 1976, Centre Beaubourg, Paris, 1977, Plains Art Mus., Moorehead, Minn., 1978, Serpentine Gallery, London, 1979, Kiva Gallery, Boston, 1979, Salford U. (Eng.), 1980, (two-man) Galerie Agathe Gaillard, Paris, 1980, Jane Corkin Gallery, Toronto, Ont., Can., 1981, E. Houk Gallery, Chgo., 1982, Chrysler Mus., Norfolk, Va., 1983; group shows include: Salon de l'Escalier, Paris, 1928, Deutscher Werkbund, Stuttgart, Germany, 1929, Julien Levy Gallery, N.Y.C., 1932, Salon Leleu, Paris, 1934, Galerie de la Pleiade, Paris, 1934, Mus. Modern Art, N.Y.C., 1937, Riverside Mus. and world tour, N.Y.C., 1967, Documenta 6, Kassel, W.Ger., 1977, Hayward Gallery, London, 1978, Galerie Zabriskie, Paris (and Zabriskie Gallery, N.Y.C.), 1979, Centre Culturel, Boulogne, Billancourt, France, 1981, Deja Vue Galleries, Toronto, Ont., 1981, Kestner-Gesellschaft, Hanover, W.Ger., 1982, Art Inst. Chgo., 1982; represented in permanent collections: Mus. Modern Art, N.Y.C.; Internat. Mus. Photographer, George Eastman House, Rochester, N.Y.; Smithsonian Instn., Washington; Carpenter Ctr., Harvard U., Cambridge, Mass.; Detroit Inst. Arts; art Inst. Chgo.; New Orleans Mus. Art; U. Nebr.-Lincoln; Ctr. Creative Photography, U. Ariz., Tucson; Musee d'Art Moderne, Paris; books: Paris Vu Par Andre Kertesz, 1934; Enfants, 1933; Nos Amies Les Betes, 1936; Les Cathedrales Du Vin, 1937; Day of Paris, 1945; Andre Kertesz, Photographer, 1964; On Reading, 1972; Sixty Years of Photography, 1973; J'Aime Paris, 1974; Washington Square, 1975; Of New York, 1976; Distortions, 1976; contbr. photographs to Am., European mags. Served with Austro-Hungarian Army, 1914-15; Poland, Albania, Rumania. Decorated comdr. Order Arts and Letters (France); recipient Photography Competition prize Borsszem Janko mag., 1916, Silver medal Exposition Coloniale, Paris, 1930, Gold medal 4th Mostra Biennale Internazionale della Fotografia, Venice, 1963, Gold medal Venice Biennale, 1976, Mayor's award N.Y.C., 1977, U. Salford award, 1980; Guggenheim fellow, 1974. Mem. Am. Soc. Mag. Photographers (mem. of honor 1965). Home: N.Y.C. Died Sept. 27, 1985.

KERTESZ, STEPHEN DENIS, educator, diplomat, author; b. Putnok, Hungary, Apr. 8, 1904; s. Lajos and Maria (Stolcz) K.; m. Margaret Cornelia de Fulop, Oct. 7, 1931; children: Marianne (Mrs. Endre Sipos), Agnes (Mrs. Peter Serenyi). LLD, U. Budapest, 1926, Ind. U., 1975; diploma internat. relations, U. Paris, 1928. With Hungarian Fgn. Ministry, 1931-47, head peace prep. div., 1945-46; sec.-gen. Hungarian Peace Del., 1946; Hungarian minister to Italy 1947; vis. assoc. prof. Yale Law Sch., 1948-50; prof. polit. sci. U. Notre Dame, 1950-75, prof. emeritus, 1975-86; cons. Fgn. Area Fellowship program, 1961-64, acting head dept. polit. sci., 1962-64, Franklin Miles prof., 1963, also dir. Soviet and East Cen. European Ctr., 1954-69, chmn. com. internat. relations, 1955-86, dir. Western European studies program, 1965-86, dir. Inst. on Internat. Studies, 1968-86, Cardinal O'Hara prof. govt. and internat. studies, 1969. Author: The International Responsibility of the State, Budapest, 1938, Diplomacy in a Whirlpool: Hungary Between Nazi Germany and Soviet Russia, 1953, Quest for Peace Through Diplomacy, 1967; editor, contbr.: The Fate of East Central Europe: Hopes and Failures of American Foreign Policy, 1956, American Diplomacy in a New Era, 1961, East Central Europe and the World: Developments in the Post-Stalin Era, 1962; Nuclear Non Proliferation in A World of Nuclear Powers, 1967, The Task of Universities in a Changing World, 1971; (with M.A. Fitzsimons) Diplomacy in a Changing World, 1959, What America Stands For, 1959. Recipient Spl. Presdl. award U. Notre Dame, 1975; Rockefeller fellow, 1935-37, Guggenheim fellow, 1958-59; Rockefeller grantee, 1965-66. Mem. Am. Polit. Sci. Assn., Internat. Free Acad. Sci. and Letters, Am. Acad. Polit. and Social Sci., Am. Assn. Advancement Slavic Studies, Am. Soc. Internat. Law, Cath. Commn. Intellectual and Cultural Affairs, Internat. Studies Assn. Home: South Bend Ind. Died Jan. 26, 1986.

KESSEL, LAWRENCE REEFER, corporation executive; b. Kansas City, Mo., Nov. 1, 1903; s. Paul and Laura (Reefer) K.; m. Marie Adler, Mar. 25, 1933; 1 child, Laura. BS magna cum laude, Harvard U., 1925; postgrad., univs. Goettingen, Sorbonne, Munich, Berlin, Columbia U., Harvard Bus. Sch. Entrepreneur, cons. various mining, farming and retail bus., Kansas City, 1925-48; assoc. Graham-Newman Corp., N.Y.C., 1949-54; pres. Adam Hat Stores, Inc., also chmn. bd.; bd. dirs. Nathan Straus-Duparquet, Utica Knitting Co., Dean Phipps Stores, Inc, United Cities Realty Corp., Studio Apts. Co. Inc, Greater N.Y. Devel. Co., Sidney Blumenthal & Co., Inc., Wood Harmon Corp., Curtis Pub. Co., Thew Shovel Co., Ogdensburg Terminal Corp., C.K.P. Devels. Ltd.; mem. exec. com., bd. dirs. A.S. Beck Shoe Corp., Arrow Machinery Co., Brantford Coach & Body, Ltd., Rutland Corp.; v.p., bd. dirs. Landis Machine Co.; bd. dirs. Am. Type Founders Co. Inc., Saturday Evening Post Co., Norwich & Worcester R.R. Co., Pibly Fund, Inc., United Am. Life Ins. Co.; gen. ptnr. Lawrence Kessel & Assocs., Alden Industries; v.p., chmn. exec. com., bd. dirs. Cockshutt Farm Equipment, Ltd.; pres. Lawrence and Marie Kessel Found., Inc.; bd. dirs., mem. fin. com. Del. & Hudson Co., Champlain Nat. Securities, Inc.; mem. bd. mgrs. Champlain Nat. Corp. Trustee United Svc. for New Ams. Mem. Am. Fin. Assn., N.Y. Soc. Security Analysts, Harvard-Yale-Princeton '25 Assn. (sec.), Harvard Club, Execs. Internat. Club. Home: New York N.Y. Died June 24, 1987.

KESSLER, ROBERT CLARENCE, physician; b. Roscoe, N.Y., May 9, 1923; s. Clarence L. and Florence McCall (Eells) K.; m. Shirley Mason, Mar. 23, 1946; children—Karen M., Bruce P., William M., Barbara J. Student, Union Coll., Schenectady, 1940-43; M.D., Albany Med. Sch., 1947. Diplomate: Am. Bd. Preventive Medicine. Intern Nat. Naval Med. Center, Bethesda, Md., 1947-48; resident U.S. Naval Hosp., Portsmouth, Va., 1948-49, Chelsea, Mass., 1952-54; staff physician Eastman Kodak Co., Rochester, N.Y., 1954-72; asst. med. dir. Eastman Kodak Co., 1973-74, med. dir., from 1974; vice chmn. health services adv. com. U.S. CD Council, 1964-72. Served with M.C. USN, 1947-54. Mem. Am. Acad. Occupational Medicine, Am. Occupational Medicine Assn. (pres. 1983-84), Indsl. Med. Assn. Upstate N.Y. (pres. 1974). Republican. Presbyterian. Home: Rochester N.Y. Died Aug. 20, 1986; buried Brick Ch. Cemetery, Sodus Center, N.Y.

KETCHLEDGE, RAYMOND WAIBEL, electrical engineer; b. Harrisburg, Pa., Dec. 8, 1919; s. Raymond A. and Sophie (Waibel) K.; m. Janet M. Bell, Sept. 16, 1970; children: Raymond, Carol, Bruce, William Bell, Kevin Bell, David, Randy Bell, Richard, Robin. B.S., Mass. Inst. Tech., 1941, M.S., 1942. With Bell Telephone Labs., 1942-82; exec. dir. electronic switching div. Bell Telephone Labs., Naperville, Ill., 1966-75; exec. dir. mil. systems div. Bell Telephone Labs., 1975-82; dir.

Naperville Bank & Trust Co., 1967-76. Fellow IEEE (Alexander Graham Bell medal 1976); mem. Nat. Acad. Engring. Home: Englewood Fla. Died Oct. 23, 1987, buried The Meml. Garden, Trinity Presbyn. Ch., Venice, Fal.

KETCHUM, MORRIS, JR., architect, writer; b. N.Y.C., May 5, 1904; s. Morris and Jane H. (Gillet) K.; m. Isabella Stiger, Apr. 28, 1934. BArch, Columbia U., 1928; diploma, Sch. Fine Arts, Fontainebleuau, France, 1928; chevalier, Chevalier des Arts et des Lettres, France, 1966. Prin. ptnr. Morris Ketchum, Jr. & Assocs., N.Y.C., 1928-74. Author: Blazing a Trial, 1982, Shops and Stores. Vice chmn. Landmarks Preservation Commn., N.Y.C., 1973-79. Recipient cert. N.Y. State Assn. Architects, 1963, Ann. Archtl. award N.Y. State Coun. on Arts, 1973, cert. of appreciation City of N.Y., 1979. Fellow AIA (nat. pres. 1965, 1st honor award 1950, Award of Merit 1950, 70, Medal of Honor N.Y. chpt. 1966), Century Assn. Home: Newton Pa. Died Nov. 22, 1984.

KEY, DAVID MCKENDREE, foreign service officer; b. Tokyo, Feb. 4, 1900; s. Albert Lenoir and Grace (Condit-Smith) K.; m. Marjorie Wright, Feb. 7, 1925; children—Albert Lenoir II, David McKendree, Marjorie. Student, The Groton Sch., Mass., 1912-18; A.B., Harvard, 1922; postgrad., Gonville and Caius Coll., Cambridge, Eng., 1922-23, Georgetown Sch. Fgn. Service, Washington, 1923-24. Detailed to Dept. State, 1925; vice consul of career at Antwerp, Belgium, 1926; 3d sec. embassy Berlin, 1927, London, Eng., 1929; attended Disarmament Conf., Geneva, Switzerland, 1932, London Econ. Conf., 1933; asst. chief Div. Current Info., 1934; consul, 2d sec. Ottawa, Ont., 1936; 1st sec. embassy Rome, 1940; asst. liaison officer Dept. State, 1941-44; consul gen. Barcelona, Spain, 1944-45; counselor of embassy Rome, 1945-46, Rio do Janeiro, Brazil, 1947-49; ambassador to Burma, 1950-52; Far Eastern adviser U.S. del. 6th, 7th, 8th gen. assemblies UN, 1952-53; asst. sec. state internat. orgn. affairs 1953-55; gen. mgr. Am. Fgn. Service Assn., 1957-61; pres. Diplomatic and Consular Officers Ret. Inc., 1957-58. Served with USMC, World War I. Clubs: Alibi (Washington), Dacor House (Washington). Home: Lake Wales Fla. Died July 15, 1988, buried Rock Creek Cemetery, Washington.

KEYNES, GEOFFREY LANGDON, surgeon, author; b. Cambridge, Eng., Mar. 25, 1887; s. John Neville and Florence (Brown) K.; m. Margaret Elizabeth Darwin, May 12, 1917; children: Richard Darwin, Quentin George, William Milo, Stephen John. Ed., Cambridge (Eng.) U., 1910, MD, 1918, DLitt (hon.), 1965; MA, St. Bartholomew's Hosp., London, 1913. Surgeon staff St. Bartholomew's Hosp., 1930-52; Wilkins lectr. Royal Soc., 1966. Author: Life of William Harvey, 1966, Bibliographies of Blake, 2d edit., 1969, Donne, 3d edit., 1958, Sir Thomas Browne, 2d edit., 1968, Evelyn, 2d edit., 1968; editor: Writings of William Blake, 1925-71, Sir. Thomas Browne, 1920-32, 1964. Trustee Nat. Portrait Gallery, 1942-66, chmn., 1958-66; founder, trustee William Blake Trust, 1949; trustee Rupert Brooke, 1933. With Brit. Expeditionary Force, 1914-19, RAF, 1939-45. Created knight bachelor, 1955; recipient James Tait Black award, 1966; hon. fellow Pembroke Coll., Cambridge U. Fellow Royal Coll. Surgeons (Cecil Joll prize 1953, Moynihan lectr. Royal Coll. Surgons 1963), Royal Coll. Surgeons Can., Royal Coll. Physicians (Harveian orator 1958, Osler orator, gold medal 1960), Royal Coll. Obstetricians and Gynecologists, Am. Surg. Assn. (hon.), Royal Soc. Medicine (hon.), MLA (hon.). Home: Brinkley England. †

KEYSERLING, LEON H., economist, lawyer; b. Charleston, S.C., Jan. 22, 1908; s. William and Jennie (Hyman) K.; m. Mary Dublin, Oct. 4, 1940. A.B., Columbia U., 1928, postgrad. in econs., 1931-33; LL.B., Harvard U., 1931; D.Bus. Sci. hon., Bryant Coll., 1965; L.H.D. hon., U. Mo., 1978. Bar: N.Y., D.C., U.S. Supreme Ct. Asst. dept. econs. Columbia U. (teaching), 1932-33; atty. AAA, 1933; sec., legis. asst. to Senator Robert F. Wagner, 1933-37; top expert Senate Com. Banking and Currency, 1935-37; gen. counsel U.S. Housing Authority, 1937-38, dep. adminstr. and gen. counsel, 1938-42, acting adminstr., 1941-42; acting commr. Fed. Pub. Housing Authority, 1942; gen. counsel Nat. Housing Agy., 1942-46; vice chmn. Pres.'s Council Econ. Advisers (Employment Act 1946), 1946-50, chmn., 1950-53, de facto mem. Cabinet and Nat. Security Council; cons., economist and pract. atty. working with var. nat. firms, orgns. and indiv. in U.S. and at times cons. to govts. of France, India, Israel & P.R. 1953-71, vol. pub. service U.S. econ. performance and nat. policies, 1971-88; hon. mem. faculty Indsl. Coll. Armed Forces, 1966-88; cons. to various mems. U.S. Senate and Ho. of Reps., 1942-46, 53-88; founder, pres. Conf. on Econ. Progress, 1954-88; pres. Nat. Com. for Labor Israel, 1969-73; dir. various cos. Author: (with Rexford G. Tugwell) Redirecting Education, 1934, Toward Full Employment and Full Production, 1954, The Gaps in our Prosperity, 1956, Consumption-Key to Full Prosperity, 1957, Inflation-Cause and Cure, 1959, The Federal Budget and the General Welfare, 1959, Key Policies for Full Employment, 1962, (with Benjamin A. Javits) The Peace by Investment Corporation, 1961, Poverty and Deprivation in the U.S., 1962, Taxes and the Public Interest, 1963, Two Top Priority Programs to Reduce Umemployment, 1963, The Toll of Rising Interest Rates, 1964, Progress or Poverty, 1964, Agriculture and the Public Interest, 1965, The Move toward Railroad Mergers, 1965, The Role of Wages in a Great Society, 1966, A Freedom Budget for All Americans, 1966, Goals for Teachers Salaries in Our Public Schools, 1967, Achieving Nationwide Educational Excellence, 1968, Israel's Economic Progress, 1968, Taxation of Whom and for What'9 , 1969, More Growth with Less Inflation or More Inflation without Growth'9 , 1970, Wages, Prices, and Profits, 1971, The Coming Crisis in Housing, 1972, The Scarcity School of Economics, 1973, Full Employment without Inflation, 1975, Liberal and Conservative National Economic Policies and Their Consequences, 1919-1979, 1979, Money, Credit, and Interest Rates: Their Gross Mismanagement by the Federal Reserve System, 1980, The Economics of Discrimination, 1981, How to Cut Unemployment to 4 Percent and End Inflation and Deficits by 1987, 1983, The Current Significance of the New Deal, 1984, Why Have Economists Learned So Little from U.S. Economic Experience, 1985; co-author: numerous pub. reports Council Econ. Advisers, 1946-53, also numerous articles. Winner $10,000 prize Pabst Postwar Employment Contest, 1944; recipient Congl. award Centennial of Fiorello H. LaGuardia, 1983; Spl. award Indsl. Coll. Armed Forces, 1983; award Nat. Ctr. Full Employment, 1986; named to Nat. Housing Hall of Fame, 1986; Man of Yr. awards Am. Jewish Congress, Washington and N.Y.C. Mem. Am. Econ. Assn., Am. Polit. Sci. Assn., Phi Beta Kappa. Clubs: Cosmos, Harvard, Columbia U. (Washington). Died Dec. 13, 1988.

KIDDER, JAMES HUGH, surgeon; b. N.Y.C., Jan. 7, 1902; s. Hugh and Ann Elizabeth (Jordan) K. Student, Columbia, 1919-20; A.B., Fordham U., 1924; M.D., Cornell U., 1928. Intern Peck Meml. Hosp., Bklyn., 1928, French Hosp., N.Y.C., 1929-30; cons. surgeon French Hosp., N.Y., Elmhurst Gen., St. Barnabas hosps.; clin. prof. surgery N.Y. Med. Coll.; dean Fordham U. Coll. Pharmacy, 1932, now emeritus. Pres. Interallied Confedn. Med. Res.-NATO, 1976-78. Ordered to active duty as Res. Officer, capt. M.C. U.S. Army, 1941; advanced to brig. gen. past exec. officer 7th Evacuation Hosp. So. Pacific; comdg. officer 134th Evacuation Hosp. ETO.; Cons. to Army Surgeon Gen. spl. asst. to Surgeon Gen. Fellow AAAS, AMA, A.C.S., Royal Soc. Health; mem. Am. Pharm. Assn., N.Y. State Pharm. Assn., N.Y. Acad. Medicine, N.Y. Acad. Pharmacy, N.Y. Acad. Sci., Assn., U.S. Army, Res. Officers Assn. (pres. D.C. Army chpt.), VFW, Am. Legion (comdr. Caduceus post), Mil. Order World Wars, Soc. Cons. to Armed Forces, Assn. Mil. Surgeons U.S. (nat. pres. 1967), Chi Gamma Iota, Phi Chi, Alpha Sigma Phi. Home: New York N.Y. Died Mar. 27, 1987; buried Arlington Nat. Cemetery.

KIDENEY, JAMES WILLIAMS, architect; b. Pitts., Apr. 25, 1899; s. William W. and Ada J. (Porter) K.; m. Isabel Houck, Aug. 15, 1930. B.S., U. Mich., 1921; student, Europe, 1922-23. Licensed architect, N.Y. certificate Nat. Council Archtl. Registration Bds. With archtl. offices Buffalo, 1921-26; entered practice 1926; partner Paul Hyde Harbach, 1929-42; pvt. practice, specializing in design schs., instnl. bldgs. and housing Buffalo, 1942-50; as James Wm. Kideney & Assocs., 1950-58, firm Kideney, Smith, Fitzgerald & Partners, 1958-74; cons. Community Planning Assistance Center, others. Architect: dormitory and student Union bldg, N.Y. State Tchrs. Coll., Buffalo, Lockport, Tonawanda and Syracuse office bldgs., N.Y. Telephone Co. (various design awards). Mem. adv. council on sch. bldgs., grounds N.Y. State Edn. Dept., 1941-43, panel community planning cons., 1945-47; cons. architect N.Y. Joint Legislative Com. on Investigating Sch. Costs, 1941; chmn. com. architects, engrs. and landscape architects of Buffalo for post war constrn.; mem. N.Y. Gov.'s vol. com. on housing and constrn.; mem. airport adv. bd., Buffalo, 1950-52; mem. N.Y. State Bd. Examiners for Architects, 1949-56, chmn., 1953. citation as outstanding citizen Buffalo Evening News, 1964; award for vol. services Community Planning Assistance Center, 1976. Fellow AIA (chmn. com. state and municipal pub. works 1942-46, chmn. com. local pub. bldgs. 1947-49), mem. C. of C., Buffalo Fine Arts Acad. (life), Buffalo Pub. Library (life), N.Y. State Assn. Architects (pres. 1938-42, Sidney L. Strauss award 1951, Award of Merit 1949, Award of Merit for N.Y. Telephone Co. offices), Alpha Rho Chi. Clubs: Buffalo, Rotary. Home: Buffalo N.Y. Died Nov. 10, 1987; buried Buffalo.

KIESS, CARL CLARENCE, physicist; b. Ft. Wayne, Ind., Oct. 18, 1887; s. John Frederick and Florence (Fordney) K.; m. Harriet Knudsen, June 21, 1919; children: Margaret Florence, John Anthony (dec.), Norman Halvor, Edward Marion. AB, Ind. U., 1910; PhD, U. Calif., 1913. Fellow Lick Obs., U. Calif., 1910-13; instr. astronomy U. Mo., 1913-15; asst. prof. Pomona Coll., 1915-16; instr. U. Mich., 1916-17; asst. physicist U.S. Bur. Standards, 1917-19, assoc. physicist, 1919-24, physicist, 1924-29, sr. physicist, 1929-46, prin. physicist, from 1946; rsch. assoc., lectr. in astrophysics Georgetown U.; mem. Nat. Geog. Soc. Solar Eclipse Expdns., Brazil, 1940-47, Mars Expdn., Mauna Loa, 1956. Contbr. articles to profl. jours. Decorated D.S.M.; recipient Exceptional Svc. medal U.S. Dept. Commerce, 1954. Fellow AAAS, Am. Phys. Soc.; mem. Am. Astron. Soc., Astron. Soc. Pacific (Donohoe medal 1911), Optical Soc. Am., Washington Acad. Scis., Phi Beta Kappa, Sigma Xi, Gamma Alpha. †

KILLENS, JOHN OLIVER, author; b. Macon, Ga.; married; 2 children. Student, Edward Waters Coll., Morris Brown Coll., Howard U., Terrell Law Sch., Columbia U., NYU. Founder, former chmn. Harlem Writers' Guild Workshop; writer-in-residence Fisk U., Howard U.; tchr. creative writing New Sch. Social Rsch.; former adj. prof., head Creative Writer's Workshop Columbia U. Author: Youngblood, 1954, And Then We Heard the Thunder, 'sippi, 1967, Slaves; (essays) Black Man's Burden, 1966; (screenplay) Odds Against Tomorrow; editor: the Trial Record of Denmark Vesey, 1970, The Cotillion, 1971, Great Gitting' Up Morning, 1972. writer-in-residence Creative Writer's Workshop and Black Culture Seminar; former mem. staff NLRB. With U.S. armed forces, World War II, PTO. Mem. Black Acad. Arts and Letters (v.p.), Author's Guild, Dramatists Guild, PEN. Home: Brooklyn N.Y. Died Oct. 27, 1987.

KILLIAN, JAMES R., JR., former college president; b. Blacksburg, S.C., July 24, 1904; s. James Robert and Jeannette (Rhyne) K.; m. Elizabeth Parks, Aug. 21, 1929 (dec. Nov. 1986); children: Carolyn (Mrs. Paul Staley), Rhyne Meredith. Student, Trinity Coll. Duke U., 1921-23, LL.D. (hon.), 1949; B.S., Mass. Inst. Tech., 1926; Sc.D. (hon.), Middlebury Coll., 1945; hon. degrees, Bates Coll., 1950, U. Havana, Cuba, 1953, Notre Dame U., 1954, Lowell Tech. Inst., 1954, Columbia, Coll. Wooster, Oberlin Coll., 1958, U. Akron, 1959, Worcester Poly. Inst., 1960, U. Me., 1963; LL.D., Union Coll., 1947, Bowdoin Coll., Northeastern U., 1949, Boston U., Harvard, 1950, Williams Coll., Lehigh U., U. Pa., 1951, U. Chattanooga, 1954, Tufts U., 1955, U. Cal., Amherst Coll., 1956, Coll. William and Mary, 1957, Brandeis U., 1958, Johns Hopkins, N.Y. U., 1959, Providence Coll., Temple U., 1960, U. S.C., 1961, Meadville Theol. Sch., 1962; D.Applied Sci., U. Montreal, 1958; D.Eng., Drexel Inst. Tech., 1948, U. Ill., 1960, U. Mass., 1961; Ed.D., R.I. Coll., 1962; H.H.D., Rollins Coll., 1964; D.P.S., Detroit Inst. Tech., 1972. Asst. mng. editor Technology Rev., 1926-27, mng. editor, 1927-30, editor, 1930-39; exec. asst. to pres. Mass. Inst. Tech., 1939-43, exec. v.p., 1943-45, v.p., 1945-48, pres., 1948-59, chmn. corp., 1959-71, hon. chmn., 1971-79; dir. Polaroid Corp., IBM, 1959-62, Gen. Motors Corp., 1959-75, Cabot Corp., 1963-75, AT & T, 1963-77, Ingersoll-Rand Co., 1971-76. Chmn. Carnegie Commn. on Ednl. TV, 1965-67; bd. dirs. Corp. for Pub. Broadcasting, 1968-75, chmn., 1973-74; mem. Pres. Communication Policy Bd., 1950-51, President's Com. on Mgmt., 1950-52; mem. sci. adv. com. ODM, 1951-57; chmn. Army Sci. Adv. Panel, 1951-56, Pres.'s Bd. Cons. on Fgn. Intelligence Activities, 1956-57; spl. asst. to Pres. U.S. for sci. and tech., 1957-59; chmn. Pres.'s Sci. Adv. Com., 1957-59, mem., 1957-61, cons., 1961-73; pres. Atoms for Peace Awards, 1955-58, 59-69; mem. Adv. Council on State Depts. Edn., U.S. Office Edn., 1965-68; chmn. President's Fgn. Intelligence Adv. Bd., 1961-63; mem. gen. adv. bd. U.S. Arms Control and Disarmament Agy., 1969-74; bd. visitors U.S. Naval Acad., 1953-55; moderator Am. Unitarian Assn., 1960-61; trustee Nutrition Found., 1954-70, Washington U., 1966-70, Mt. Holyoke Coll., 1962-72, Alfred P. Sloan Found., 1954-77, Boston Mus. Fine Arts, Mitre Corp.; chmn., 1967-69; bd. dirs. Nat. Merit Scholarship Corp., 1960-63, Winston Churchill Found. U.S. Ltd.; mem. Mass. Bd. Edn., 1962-65. Recipient President's Certificate of Merit, 1948, Certificate of Appreciation Dept. of Army, 1953; Exceptional Civilian Service award Dept. of Army; Pub. Welfare medal Nat. Acad. Scis., 1957; George Foster Peabody Broadcasting Spl. Edn. awards, 1968, 76; decorated Croix d'officer, Legion of Honor France, 1957; Hoover medal, 1963; Sylvanus Thayer award U.S. Mil. Acad., 1978; Vannevar Bush award Nat. Sci. Bd., 1980; others. Fellow Am. Acad. Arts and Scis.; mem. Nat. Acad. Engring., Am. Soc. Engring. Edn. (hon.), Sigma Chi, Phi Beta Kappa (hon.), Tau Beta Pi (hon.). Clubs: St. Botolph (Boston); Century (N.Y.C.). Home: Cambridge Mass. Died Jan. 29, 1988; cremated.

KILLOUGH, HUGH BAXTER, economist, educator; b. Waco, Tex., Dec. 30, 1892; s. Benjamin Terry and Martha Rowena (Lilley) K.; m. Lucy Burton Winsor, Oct. 27, 1923; 1 child, Ann Winsor Hehre. BS, Tex. A&M Coll., 1916; MS, U. Wis., 1920; PhD, Columbia U., 1925; MA (hon.), Brown U., 1943. Instr. econs. U. Minn., 1920-21; economist extension service Mich. State Coll., 1921-22; asst. economist U.S. Bur. Agrl. Econs., 1923-24; mem. faculty Brown U., 1924-59, prof., 1931-59; vis. prof. econs. Northeatern U., 1959-62, Interam. U., San German, P.R., from 1963; economist U.S. Bur. Labor Stats., 1943-46, ECA mission in China, 1950-51, J.G. White Engring. Corp. mission in Indonesia, 1952. Author: (with Lucy W. Killough) Raw Materials of Industrialism, 1929, (with Barrington Assocs. Inc.) The Economics of Marketing, 1933, International Trade, 1938, (with Lucy W. Killough) Economics of International Trade, 1948, International Economics, 1960, (with M. Margaret Ball) International Relations, 1956. 2d lt. U.S. Army, 1917-18. Mem. Am. Econ. Assn., local C. of C., Fgn. Trade Club (Providence). Home: Wellesley Mass. †

KIMBALL, SPENCER WOOLLEY, clergyman; b. Salt Lake City, Mar. 28, 1895; s. Andrew and Olive (Woolley) K.; m. Camilla Eyring, Nov. 17, 1917; children: Spencer LeVan, Olive Beth (Mrs. Grant M. Mack), Andrew Eyring, Edward Lawrence. Student, Gila Jr. Coll., 1910-14, Brigham Young U., 1917, U. Ariz., 1917; LL.D., Brigham Young U., 1969. Mem. Council of Twelve Apostles of the Ch. of Jesus Christ of Latter-day Saints, from 1943; now pres.; on mission Council of Twelve Apostles of the Ch. of Jesus Christ of Latter-day Saints, Mo., 1914-16; pres. Seventies Quorum, stake clk. Thatcher, Ariz., 1918-38; counselor St. Joseph Stake Presidency, 1924-36; pres. Mt. Graham Stake, 1938-43; teller, clk. later asst. cashier Ariz. Trust & Sav. Bank, Safford, 1918-23; Bank of Safford, 1923-26; pres., mgr. Kimball Greenhalgh Ins. & Realty Co., Safford, Ariz., 1927-43; sec. Gila Valley Irrigation Co., 1935-43; organizer, part owner Gila Broadcasting Co., Safford, 1935-85. Mem. Ariz. Assn. Tchrs. Retirement Bd., Thatcher and Safford (Ariz.) city councils; bd. dirs. A.R.C., Safford; chmn. war fund drives; trustee Gila Coll.; Mem. Boy Scouts Am. Clubs: Rotary Internat. (dist. gov.); Rotary (Safford) (pres.). Home: Chicago Ill. Died Nov. 5, 1985.

KIMBLER, OSCAR KAVANAH, petroleum engineering educator, consultant; b. Marengo County, Ala., Aug. 22, 1921; s. Nathaniel Omar and Effie Naomi (Surginer) K.; m. Sue Russell Toy, Dec. 28, 1945; children—Warren K., Karl L. B.E. in Chem. Engring., Vanderbilt U., 1948, M.S. in Chem. Engring., 1949; Ph.D., U. Tex., 1964. Registered petroleum engr., La. Asst. research engr. Atlantic Refining Co., Dallas, 1949-52, assoc., then sr. research engr., 1953-62; research engr. assoc. Tex. Petroleum Research Commn., Austin, 1962-64; from assoc. prof. to prof. petroleum engring. La. State U., Baton Rouge, 1964-78, Campanile prof. petroleum engring., 1978-82, prof. emeritus, 1982-87; cons. in field. Contbr. articles to profl. jours. Recipient teaching excellence award Halliburton Edn. Found., 1970; Mineral Industry Edn. award AIME, 1982. Mem. Soc. Petroleum Engrs. (sr.). Democrat. Methodist. Home: Baton Rouge La. Died MAr. 13, 1987; buried Fernwood Cemetery, Henderson, Ky.

KIMBROUGH, EMILY (EMILY KIMBROUGH WRENCH), writer; b. Muncie., Ind., Oct. 23, 1898; d. Hal Curry and Charlotte Emily (Wiles) K.; m. John Wrench, Dec. 31, 1926; children: Margaret Wrench Kuhn and Alis Wrench McCurdy (twins). BA, Bryn Mawr Coll., 1921; student, The Sorbonne, Paris, 1922. Editor Fashions of the Hour mag., Marshall Field & Co., Chgo., 1922-27; fashion editor Ladies' Home Jour., 1927, mng. editor, 1927-29, writer, from 1932; author: (with Cornelia Otis Skinner) Our Hearts Were Young and Gay, 1942, We Followed Our Hearts to Hollywood, 1943, How Dear to My Heart, 1944, It Gives Me Great Pleasure, 1948, The Innocents from Indiana, 1950, Through Charley's Door, 1952, Forty Plus and Fancy Free, 1954, So Near and Yet So Far, 1955, Water, Water Everywhere, 1956, And a Right Good Crew, 1958, Pleasure by the Busload, 1961, Forever Old, Forever New, 1964, Floating Island, 1968, Now and Then, 1972, Time Enough, 1974, Better Than Oceans, 1976. Home: New York N.Y. Died Feb. 10, 1989.

KIMBROUGH, EMORY CALLOWAY LANDON, JR., educator, sociologist; b. Clarksville, Tenn., Nov. 15, 1934; s. Emory Calloway Landon and Martha (Beaumont) K. A.B., Davidson Coll., 1957; M.A. (Nat. Woodrow Wilson fellow), U. N.C., 1959, Ph.D. (So. fellow), 1963. Teaching fellow U. N.C, 1960-62; instr. sociology Washington and Lee U., Lexington, Va., 1962-63; asst. prof. Washington and Lee U., 1963-66, asso. prof., 1966-69, prof., 1969-87, chmn. dept. sociology and anthropology, 1967-87. Fellow Am. Sociol. Assn.; mem. So. Sociol. Soc., Phi Beta Kappa, Beta Gamma Sigma, Alpha Tau Omega. Episcopalian. Home: Lexington Va. Died Jan. 8, 1987; buried Clarksville, Tenn.

KIME, EDWIN N(ICHOLAS), medical educator, physician; b. Jeffersonville, Ind., Feb. 23, 1891; s. John Huffman and Mary Ann (Durbin) K.; m. Lelah Belle Burns, Nov. 25, 1916; children: Charles Edwin, Margaret Mary (Mrs. William Richard Adams). AB, Ind. U., 1914, MD, 1916, MD cum laude, 1917. Asst. anatomy Ind. U., 1912-14, instr., 1914-18, instr. medicine Sch. Medicine, 1919-28, asst. prof. surgery, 1928-40; prof. postgrad. clin. anatomy Ind. U. Med. Ctr. from 1935; prof. anatomy, head dept. anatomy Ind. U., from 1940; prof. Normal Coll. N.Am. Gymnastic Union, 1920-40; dir. depts. phys. medicine Gen., Univ., and Meth. hosps., Indpls., 1925-40; tech. cons. Meth. Hosp., from 1940. Author: Head and Neck, 1940, Topographical and Appllied Anatomy, 1948; contbr. numerous articles to profl. jours. Civilian cons. Army A.S.T.P., Navy V-12, World War II. Lt. M.C., U.S. Army, 1918-19. Mem. AAAS, AAUP, NEA, AMA, Am. Congress Phys. Medicine, Coll. Internat. surgeons, Am. Physicians Med. Assn. (pres. 1932), Ind. State, Indpls. med. assns., Ind. U. Sch. Medicine Alumni Assn. (pres. from 1957), Am. Assn. Neoplastic Diseases, Am. Legion (charter), 40 and 8, Sigma Xi, Alpha Omega Alpha (charter, pres. 1916), Nu Sigma Nu (pres. 1916). Presbyterian. Home: Indpls. Ind. †

KIMMEL, JOE ROBERT, biochemist, educator; b. DuQuoin, Ill., May 3, 1922; s. Maurice Edward and Roberta (Pyatt) K.; m. Jean Howell, Apr. 3, 1947; children: Philip H., Lynn, Ellen, Bruce E. A.B., DePauw U., 1943; M.D., Johns Hopkins, 1947; Ph.D., U. Utah, 1954. Intern Salt Lake City Gen. Hosp., 1947-49; resident U.S. Naval Hosp., Oakland, Calif., 1950-52; research instr. biochemistry U. Utah Coll. Medicine, 1954-55, asst. research prof. biochemistry, 1955-59, asso. research prof. biochemistry, 1959-60, asso. prof. biochemistry, 1960-62, asso. prof. biochemistry and pediatrics, 1962-64; prof. biochemistry, dir. McIlvain Labs., Kans. U. Med. Center, 1964-85. Served with USNR, 1950-52. Recipient Career Devel. award USPHS, 1960; Henry Strong Denison scholar Johns Hopkins, 1946-47. Mem. Am. Soc. Biol. Chemists, Endocrine Soc., AAAS, AAUP, Alpha Omega Alpha. Deceased.

KINCHELOE, SAMUEL CLARENCE, writer, educator; b. Georgetown, Ohio, Nov. 20, 1890; s. Robert Stone and Elizabeth Olive (Kimball) K.; m. Alma Beulah Elifrits, June 16, 1916 (dec. Mar. 1949); children: Beulah Jean (Mrs. Fletcher Taylor), Robert Stone; m. Evah Irene Ostrander, Oct. 20, 1950. AB, Drake U., 1916, DD, 1959; AM, U. Chgo., 1919, PhD, 1929; LittD, Pacific U., 1949; DD, Chgo. Theol. Sem., 1957. Ordained to ministry Christian Ch., 1916. Pastor Lake City, Iowa, 1917-18; asst. dept. sociology U. Chgo., 1921-23, prof. Federated Theol. Faculty, 1943; head dept. George Williams Coll., 1923-28; rsch. assoc., lectr. sociology of religion Chgo. Theol. Sem., 1928-31, asst. prof., 1931-39, prof., 1939; pres. Tougaloo So. Christian Coll., 1956-60; prof. Interdenominational Theol. Ctr., Atlanta, 1960-64. Author: Religion in the Depression, 1937, The American City and Its Church, 1938; contbr. articles to religious publs. Chmn. Am. Missionary Assn. Bd. Home Missions, dean internat. seminar, 1949; mem. Coun. Chs. of Christ in U.S.A. Constituting Conv.; mem. Bd. Home Missions, Congl. Christian Chs., mem. exec. com., 1946-54; dir. rsch. and survey Chgo. Congl. Union, 1928-44, Ch. Fedn. of Greater Chgo., 1944-49; chmn. bd. U. Chgo. Settlement, 1946-49; trustee LeMoyne Coll. With U.S. Army, World War I. Mem. Quadrangle Club, Phi Beta Kappa. Home: Georgetown Ohio. Deceased.

KING, CECIL HARMSWORTH, newspaper publisher; b. London, Feb. 20, 1901; s. Sir Lucas and Geraldine (Harmsworth) K.; m. Margaret Cooke, June 23, 1923; children: Michael, Francis, Priscilla J., Colin; m. Ruth Railton, Nov. 1962. Student, Winchester, Eng., 1915-19; MA, Oxford (Eng.) U., 1922. Mem. staff London Times, 1919, Glasgow (Scotland) Record, 1923, London Daily Mail, 1923-26; dir. Empire Paper Mills, 1926-30, Daily Mirror Newspapers, Ltd., 1929-87, Sunday Pictorial, 1937-87; chmn., mng. dir. London Daily Mirror, 1951-63; chmn. Amalgamated Press, 1959-61; bd. dirs. Anglo-Can. Pulp & Paer Mills, Bank of Eng.; chmn. Overseas Newspapers, Internat. Pub. Corp., Reed Paper Group, Wall Paper Mfrs., Ltd. Mem. Nat. Parks Commn., Coun. Advt. Assn., 1940-49; chmn. Brit. Film Inst., 1948-52; part-time mem. Nat. Coal Bd., 1966. Mem. Newspaper Proprs. Assn. (chmn. 1961-87). Home: East Molesey England. Died Apr. 17, 1987.

KING, CHARLES GLEN, chemist; b. Entiat, Wash., Oct. 22, 1896; s. Charles Clement and Mary (Bookwalter) K.; m. Hilda Bainton, Sept. 11, 1919; children—Dorothy, Robert Bainton, Kendall Willard. B.S., Wash. State Coll., 1918; M.S., U. Pitts., 1920, Ph.D., 1923; postgrad., Columbia, 1926-27, Cambridge (Eng.) U., 1929-30; D.Sc., Wash. State Coll., 1950, U. Pitts., 1950, Drexel Inst., 1955; Dr. Pub. Service, Denison U., 1961. By-products specialist State of Wash., 1918-19; instr. chemistry U. Pitts., 1920-26, asst. prof., 1926-30, prof., 1930-43; research asst. Columbia, 1926-27, vis. prof. chem., 1942-46, prof., 1946-62, emeritus; asso. dir. Inst. Nutrition Sci., 1963-66; spl. lectr., 1967-73; dir. grants mgmt. St. Luke's Hosp. Center, 1966-67; sci. dir. Nutrition Found., 1942-55, exec. dir., 1955-61, pres., 1961-63, trustee, 1963-88; cons. Rockefeller Found., 1963-66; mem. sci. adv. bd. Robert A. Welch Found., 1954-63; Agrl. Research Policy Com. U.S. Dept. Agr., 1950-57; mem. exec. bd. U.S. com. UNICEF, 1968-69; Cons. Office of Surgeon Gen., AUS, 1940-66; NIH Study Sect. Chmn., 1946-51, Office Surg. Gen., USPHS, 1940-66. Trustee Boyce Thompson Inst., 1957-75, Food Law Inst., 1950-62; pres. 5th Internat. Congress on Nutrition, 1960; Mem. Food and Nutrition Bd., 1940-70. Served as pvt. 12th Inf. Machine Gun Co., 1918. Recipient Pa. Award of Merit, 1938, Pa. Pub. Health Assn. award, 1939, Pitts. award, 1943, G.M.A. award, 1944, John Scott award, 1949; Nicholas Appert award Inst. Food Technologists Chgo. sect., 1955; Charles Spencer award Am. Chem. Soc., 1963; Conrad A. Elvehjem award Am. Inst. Nutrition, 1966; Purkinje Gold medal Acad. Scis., Czechoslovakia, 1969. Mem. Internat. Union Nutritional Scis. (pres. 1966-69, hon. pres. 1972-88), N.Y. Acad. Medicine, Am. Chem. Soc., Am. Soc. Biol. Chemists (pres. 1954-55), Inst. Food Technologists, Nat. Acad. Scis. (exec. com. internat. council sci. unions 1966-69), Am. Forestry Assn., AAAS, Am. Inst. Nutrition (pres. 1949-50), Am. Pub. Health Assn. (treas. 1949-60, pres. 1961-62), Royal Soc. Health (Eng.), Harvey Soc., Nutrition Soc. (Eng.), Finland Soc. Biochemistry, Biophysics and Microbiology (hon.), Phi Beta Kappa, Sigma Xi, Omicron Delta Kappa. Quaker. Clubs: Century (N.Y.C.); Cosmos (Washington). Home: Kennett Square Pa. Died Jan. 23, 1988; cremated.

KING, HANFORD LANGDON, JR., bishop; b. Worcester, Mass., Sept. 18, 1921; s. Hanford Langdon and Hephizibah Vernon (Hopkins) K.; m. Helen R. Knospe, May 31, 1947; children—Deborah, Judith, Hanford Langdon. B.A., Clark U., 1943; S.T.B., Episcopal Theol. Sch., 1946; Ph.D., Columbia U., 1950; postgrad., Sch. of Prophets, San Francisco, 1952, 54; postgrad. (Coll. fellow), Coll. Preachers, Washington, 1958, Boston Theol. Inst., 1969, Grad. Theol. Union Calif., 1968, Aspen Inst. Humanistic Studies, 1964. Ordained deacon Episcopal Ch., 1946, priest, 1947; certified profl. ski instr., 1962. Lay vicar Episcopal chs. Mass., 1944-46; mem. staff St. James Ch., N.Y.C., 1946-47; rector chs. N.Y.C., 1947-50, Bozeman, Mont., 1951-60, Rapid City, S.D., 1960-72; consecrated bishop Episc. Ch., Idaho, 1972-81, ret.; dep. gen. conv. Episc. Ch., 1958, 61, 64, 67, 70; mem. com. evangelism 1970, bishop's com. evangelism, 1974, com. on ministry, 1974-76; mem. Nat. Joint Commn. on Ch. in Small Communities, 1974; mem. exec. council Diocese of Mont., 1951-53, 60, chmn. dept. youth, 1952-54, dept. promotion, 1953-55; chmn. budget dept. Diocese of S.D., 1962-68, chmn. resources and devel., 1966-68. Author: Doctrine of Conscience in Contemporary Anglo-Catholic Theology; contbr. articles to mags. Pres. Rapid City (S.D.) Bd. Edn., 1970; weightlifting commr. AAU, 1959-61; trustee St. Luke's Hosp., Boise, 1972-86, Mountain States Tumor Inst., 1972-86, Ch. Div. Sch. Pacific, 1978-86. Mem. Internat. Platform Assn. Home: Boise Idaho. Died Oct. 11, 1986, cremated.

KING, JOHN HARRY, JR., ophthalmologist; b. Washington, Sept. 28, 1910; s. John Harry and Mary (Ganley) K.; m. Helen Davis Tewksbury, Mar. 28, 1936; children: Suzanne Tewksbury (Mrs. William Doran Clark), John Harry III. BS, Georgetown U., 1932, MD, 1934. Diplomate Am. Bd. Ophthalmology. Intern Letterman Gen. Hosp., San Francisco, 1934-35; commd. U.S. Army, 1935, advanced through grades to col.; chief ophthalmology Tripler Gen Hosp., Honolulu, 1948-51; chief ophthalmology, dir. ocular rsch. Walter Reed Gen. Hosp., Washington, 1951-55; ret. 1955; pvt. practice Washington, 1955-86; sr. surgeon Washington Hosp. Ctr.; clin. prof. ophthalmology George Washington U. Med. Sch.; prof. emeritus Georgetown U.; med. dir., 1st pres. Internat. Eye Found.; nat. cons. emeritus to surgeon gen. USAF; cons. to surgeon gen. U.S. Army; organizer, 1st med. dir. Washington Eye Bank; organizer, bd. dirs. Eye Bank Assn. Am.; vis. prof. U. P.R. Author 4 textbooks on eye surgery; mem. editorial bd. Eye Digest Jours., Highlights Ophthalmology; contbr. numerous articles to sci. publs.; developer successful method of preserving human eye tissues, 1954; inventor eye surg. instruments; rsch. in eye preservation, surg. techniques, cornea transplantation. Decorated Air medal; assoc. comdr. Most Venerable Order Hosp. St. John of Jerusalem (Eng.); recipient citation, 1963. Fellow ACS, Am. Acad. Ophthalmology (cert. 1964, 65); mem. AMA, Am. Ophthal. Soc. (award 1958), Soc. Mil. Ophthalmology (past pres.), Pan Am. Assn. Ophthalmology (bd. dirs., Gradle medal 1968), Castroviejo Soc. (pres.), Mil. Order Caraboa; hon. mem. ohpthal. socs. Peru, Guatemala, El Salvador, Dominican Republic, Turkey, Greece, Barraquer Eye Bank Spain, Knight of Malta, Chevey Chase Country Club, Army-Navy Club. Home: Washington D.C. Died Mar. 16, 1986.

KING, JOSEPH LEONARD, JR., educator; b. Mappsville, Va., Aug. 12, 1892; s. Joseph Leonard and Annie (Hubbard) K.; m. Dora Evelyn Connor, Mar. 10, 1920; 1 child, William Connor. AB, U. Richmond, 1913, LLD, 1958; AM, Columbia, 1922, PhD, 1927. Asst., then assoc. prof. English Miss. Agrl. Coll., 1918-21; mem. faculty Denison U., from 1924, prof. English, from 1924, L.W. Burke prof., from 1938; prof. Howard Coll., from 1962; lectr. U. Ariz., summer 1962. Editor: Thoreau's Walden, 1929. 2d lt. U.S. Army, World War I, AEF in France. Mem. MLA, AAUP, Phi Beta Kappa, Phi Gamma Delta, Omicron Delta Kappa. Baptist. †

KING, KERRYN, corporation executive; b. Dallas, Oct. 15, 1917; s. Oswin Kerryn and Naiad Isobel (Keedy) K.; m. Carol Fritz, Nov. 11, 1939 (div.); children: Steven, Valerie King Steinhauer, Wyldon King Fishman, Zoe King Jacobie; m. Shirley L. Maytag, Dec. 16, 1967. BS, So. Meth. U., 1939, LLD (hon.), 1966. Asst. to v.p. Tex. Power & Light Co., 1939-42; publns. editor Consol. Vultee Aircraft Corp., 1942-43; with Hill & Knowlton Inc., 1943-52, v.p., 1947-52; dir. pub. rels. Texaco Inc., 1953-57, gen. mgr. pub. rels. and personnel, 1957-58, v.p., 1958-60, v.p., asst. to chmn. bd., 1960-63; v.p. charge ops. Texaco Inc., Latin Am., 1963-65; v.p. pub. rels. and personnel Texaco Inc., 1965-71, sr. v.p. World wide sales, pub. rels. and personnel, 1971-72, sr. v.p. pub. affairs, 1972-82, pub. affairs cons., 1983-86; chmn. civilian pub. rels. adv. com. U.S. Mil. Acad.; mem. Pub. Rels. News Editorial Adv. Bd., chmn., 1977-80. Trustee Found. Pub. Rels. Rsch. and Edn.; mem. adv. bd. Met. Opera Assn.; hon. trustee Horace Mann Sch.; bd. dirs. Allergy Found. Am., Eye-Bank for Sight Restoration Inc. Mem. Internat. Pub. Rels. Assn., Pub. Rels. Soc. Am. (pres. 1979), River Club, N.Y. Yacht Club, Am. Yacht Club (Rye, N.Y.), Sigma Delta Chi. Home: New York N.Y. Died May 23, 1986.

KING, LLOYD WENTWORTH, government official; b. Palmyra, Mo., June 18, 1892; s. John W. and Katherine (Vanlandingham) K.; m. Adaline Miles, Nov. 6, 1919; 1 child, Katherine. AB, William Jewell Coll., 1911; AM, U. Mo., 1932. Prin. high sch. Palmyra, Memphis and Shelbina, Mo., 1911-21; supt. schs. Monroe city, Mo., 1921-35; state supt. pub. schs. State of Mo., 1935-43; exec. sec. Am. Textbook Pubs. Inst., N.Y.C., 1943-58; cons. 1958; chief state plans and reports sect., aid to state and local schs. br. U.S. Office Edn., from 1958. With Am. Expeditionary Force, World War I. Mem. Mo. Tchrs. Assn. (past pres.), Masons, Advertsing Club, Kappa Delta Pi, Phi Delta Kappa. Democrat. Methodist. Home: Washington D.C. †

KING, MARIAN, author. d. Joseph and Jeanette (Michel) K. Student, Miss Maderia's Sch., Greenway, Va.; studied abroad. Author: ABC Game Book, 1928, The Mirror of Youth, 1928, ABC Game Cards, 1930, Kees, 1930 (Jr. Lit. Guild selection), The Story of Athletics, 1931, The Dutch Mother Goose, 1931, Amon, A Lad of Palestine, 1932, Skeeta, 1933, The Golden Cat Head, 1933, Kees and Kleintje, 1934 (Jr. Lit. Guild selection), A Boy of Poland, 1934, Sean and Sheela, 1937, It Happened in England, 1939, Piccolino, 1939, Elizabeth: The Tudor Princess, 1940, Young King David, 1948, The Coat of Many Colors, 1951, Life of Christ, 1953, Young Mary Stuart: Queen of Scots, 1954, Portraits of Children in the National Gallery of Art, 1954-55 (filmed and won 2 Emmy awards), A Gallery of Children, 1955, rev. edit., 1967, Portrait of Jesus (King James version abd Douay version, separate vols.), 1956, rev. edit., 1970, A Gallery of Mothers and their Children, 1958, What Would You Do?, 1962, Mary Baker Eddy Child of Promise, 1968, The Star of Bethlehem, 1968, The Ageless Story of Jesus, 1970, Mico and Piccolino, 1972, Adventures in Art: The National Gallery, Washington, 1978 (filmed for TV) (Cine Golden Eagle cert.); children's book editor The Nat. Observer; contbr. to Highlights mag. for children, 1972-86; selected Bible Text (King James version) for Paintings Depicting the Life of Christ for NAt. Gallery Art Folder No. 2; contbr. articles to periodicals; researcher TV film U.S. One. Served with Brit. Supply Missions, Washington, 1940-45; mem. White House Conf. Children, 1970; hist., book cons. Hospitality Information Services for Diplomats, Washington. Mem. Authors Guild, Nat. Coun. Women, Childrens Book Guild, Authors Book Guild Am., Am. Newspaper Women's Club. Home: Washington D.C. Died Mar. 12, 1986.

KINGSBURY, B(ERNARD) C(USSICK), dentist, educator; b. Susanville, Calif., Dec. 7, 1889; s. Fred Fillmore and Dora Amanda (Gray) K.; m. Florien D. Adair, July 1, 1915; children: Bernard Cussick, Kenneth Adair. DDS, Coll. Physicians and Surgeons, 1913. Gen. pvt. practice San Francisco, from 1913; clin. prof. prosthetic dentistry, trustee, treas. Coll. Physicians and Surgeons, from 1920. Contbr. articles to profl. jours. With Manpower Service, U.S. Procurement and Assignment Service, 1943-46. Fellow Am. Coll. Dentists (pres. San Francisco chpt.); mem. ADA (nat. pres. 1955-56), Calif. Dental Assn. (bd. dirs. 1927-51, pres. 1946), Calif. Acad. Periodontology, Am. Acad. Restorative Dentistry, Golden Gate Dental Congress (bd.dirs.), San Francisco Dental Soc. (bd. dirs. 1927-50, pres. 1927), Olympic Club, Presidio Golf Club (San Francisco), Masons, Shriners. Home: San Francisco Calif. †

KINGSLEY, ROBERT, judge; b. Cedar Falls, Iowa, Oct. 8, 1903; s. Frank Amos and Angeline (Van Niman) K.; m. Doris Field Forbes-Manson, June 12, 1937; m. Ninon Michelle Hogan, July 3, 1976. A.B., U. Minn., 1923, A.M., 1923, LL.B., 1926; S.J.D., Harvard, 1928; LL.D., U.S. Internat. U., San Diego, 1973. Bar: Minn. Bar 1926, Calif. bar 1934. Instr. law U. Minn., 1926-27; Thayer teaching fellow sch. law Harvard, 1927-28; asst. prof. law U. So. Calif., 1928-30, prof. law, 1930-63, vice dean sch. law, 1947-51, asso. dean, 1951-52, dean, 1952-63; vis. prof. law U. Chgo., 1930, U. N.C., 1955, Hastings Coll. Law, 1956; vis. lectr. U. Witwatersrand, Johannesburg, Republic of South Africa, 1958; judge Calif. Dist. Ct. Appeal, 2d Appellate Dist., Div. 4, 1963-87. Mem. Am. Bar Assn., Los Angeles County Bar Assn., Los Angeles Civic Light Opera Assn. (chmn.), Order of Coif, Phi Beta Kappa, Delta Sigma Rho, Delta Theta Phi. Home: Los Angeles Calif. Died Dec. 25, 1988; cremated.

KINNAIRD, LAWRENCE, educator; b. Williamstown, W.Va., July 9, 1893; s. John Asher and Virginia May (Hall) K.; A.B., U. Mich., 1915; postgrad. U. Grenoble, France, 1919; M.A., U. Calif., 1927, Ph.D., 1928; m. Lucia Fuller Burk, Aug. 3, 1929. Asst. and asso. prof. history San Francisco State Coll., 1932-36; asst. prof. U. Calif., Coll. Agr., 1936-37; asst. and asso. prof. history U. Calif., 1937-48, prof. history, 1948-60; vis. prof. Chatham Coll., 1962-63, U. Calif. at Santa Barbara, 1960-62, 63-66. Acting dir. Bancroft Library, 1954-55. Served as 1st lt., pilot U.S. Army, 1917-20 with Air Service. Cultural attaché , U.S. Embassy, Santiago, Chile, 1942-45; chmn. U.S. del. to 4th Inter-Am. Congress Tchrs., Santiago, 1943. Mem. Am. Hist. Assn., Orgn. Am. Historians, Western History Assn. (hon.), Calif. Hist. Soc., Alpha Sigma Phi. Editor and author: Spain in the Mississippi Valley, 3 vols., 1945; The Frontiers of New Spain, 1766-1768, 1958. Author: History of the Golden Gate (for Nat. Park Service), 1962; History of the Greater San Francisco Bay Region, 2 vols., 1966. Mem. bd. editors Pacific Hist. Rev., 1956-59. Contbr. to hist. pubs. †

KINNEY, SAMUEL MARKS, JR., lawyer, industrialist; b. Jenkintown, Pa., July 10, 1925; s. Samuel Marks and Margaret R. (Rennie) K.; m. Kathryn Clouser, Sept. 21, 1946; children: Lee K. Anthony, Samuel Marks III, Brian Scott. Grad., Lawrenceville Sch., 1942; student, Allegheny Coll., 1942-43; B.A., Pa. State U., 1946; J.D., Rutgers U., 1948. Bar: N.J. 1949, U.S. Supreme Ct. 1957. Assoc. atty. Martin & Reiley, Newark, 1949-51; counsel, mgr. army contracts Daystrom Instrument div. Daystrom, Inc., Murray Hill, Pa., 1951-54; asst. sec., counsel Daystrom, Inc., 1954-57, sec., counsel, 1957-59, asst. v.p. finance, 1959-61, v.p., gen. counsel, 1961-62; sec. Union Camp Corp., 1962-72, v.p., 1962-65, sr. v.p., 1969-70, exec. v.p., 1970-72, pres., 1972-77, mem. exec. com., 1972-79, vice chmn. bd., 1977-79, also dir.; mem. Hannoch Weisman, 1979-83; of counsel 1984-87; dir. 1st Fidelity Bancorp., 1st Fidelity Bank N.A., Can. Cement Lafarge Ltd., Montreal, Que., 1979-83, Lafarge Corp., Dallas; mem. internat. adv. bd. Lafarge Coppée (S.A.), France. Contbr. papers to profl. jours. Chmn. Union County (N.J.) Young Republican Club, Inc., 1951-52; mem. Westfield Town Council, 1961-67, chmn. finance and laws and rules coms.; mem. bus. exec. research com. Bus. Execs. Research Center, Rutgers U., 1957-58; trustee Overlook Hosp., 1978-83, Overlook Hosp. Found., 1983-86, C. F. Mueller Scholarship Found., 1982-84; bd. overseers Rutgers U. Found., 1977-84; mem. Pa. State U. Alumni Council, 1977-83. Served with USMCR, 1943-45. Recipient Disting. Alumnus award Pa. State U., 1977. Mem. ABA. Episcopalian (vestryman). Clubs: Echo Lake Country (Westfield) (trustee); Baltusrol Golf (Springfield, N.J.); Union League, Economic (N.Y.C.). Home: Westfield N.J. Died June 13, 1987; buried Fairview Cemetery, Westfield.

KINZEL, AUGUSTUS BRAUN, technical executive; b. N.Y.C., July 26, 1900; s. Otto and Josephine (Braun) K.; 1927 divorced; children: Carol (Mrs. Charles Uht) (dec.), Doris (Mrs. Richard Campbell), Augustus F., Angela (Mrs. John W. Talbot), Helen (Mrs. William Murray Hawkins, Jr.); m. Marie MacClymont, May 3, 1945 (dec. Nov. 1973). A.B., Columbia U., 1919; B.S., M.I.T., 1921, D.Metall. Engring., 1922; D.Sc., U. Nancy, France, 1933, D.hon. caucsa, 1963; D.Eng., N.Y. U., 1955; D.Sc., Clarkson Coll. Tech., 1957; D.Engr., Rensselaer Inst., 1965, Worcester Poly. Inst., 1965, U. Mich., 1967; LL.D., Queens U., 1966; D.Sc., Northwestern U., 1969, Poly. Inst. N.Y., 1981. Metallurgist Gen. Electric Co., Pittsfield, Mass., 1919-20, 22-23, Henry Disston & Sons, Inc., Phila., 1923-26; lectr., inst. extension courses in advanced metallurgy Temple U., 1925-26; research metallurgist Union Carbide & Carbon Research Labs., Inc., N.Y.C., 1926-28; group leader Union Carbide & Carbon Research Labs., Inc., 1928-31, chief metallurgist, 1931-45, v.p., 1945-48, pres., 1948-65; v.p. Union Carbide & Carbon Research Labs., Inc. (Electro Metall. Co. div.), 1944-54; dir. research Union Carbide Corp., 1954-55, v.p., research, 1955-65; pres., chief exec. officer Salk Inst. Biol. Scis., La Jolla, Calif., 1965-67; trustee Systems Devel. Found., Palo Alto, Calif., from 1961; v.p. Systems Devel. Found., from 1979; past dir. Menasco Mfg. Co., Sprague Electric Co.; chief cons. in metallurgy Manhattan Dist. and AEC, 1943-65; chmn. Naval Research Adv. Com., 1954-55, mem., 1951-79; Regent's lectr. U. Calif., San Diego, 1971; chmn. adv. bd. The Energy Center, U. Calif., San Diego, from 1976; chmn. governing council Courant Inst. Math. Scis., N.Y. U.; trustee Calif. Inst. Tech.; chmn. Engring. Found. Bd., N.Y.C., 1945-48; bd. dirs. Scripps Meml. Hosp., 1971-77; v.p., dir. Berkshire Farm Research Inst., from 1950; Howe Meml. lectr. Am. Inst. Mining and Metall. Engrs., 1952; Sauveur lectr. Am. Soc. Metals, 1952. Sr. author: Alloys of Iron and Chromium, vols. 1 and 2, 1937, 40; mem. editorial adv. bd.: Energy mag, 1977-87; contbr. articles on metallurgy and engring. to tech. publs. Recipient Morehead medal Internat. Acetylene Assn., 1955; Stevens Inst. Tech. Powder Metallurgy medal award, 1959; Indsl. Research Inst. medal, 1960; James Douglas gold medal award AIME, 1960; Wisdom award of honor, 1973; Miller medal Am. Welding Soc., 1953. Fellow N.Y. Acad. Scis., Royal Soc. Arts, Am. Inst. Chemists, Metall. Soc., Am. Soc. Metals (Campbell lectr. 1947, Burgess Meml. lectr. 1956, past chmn. N.Y. sect.), Metall. Soc.; mem. Eurospace (hon.), Engrs. Joint Council (hon. pres. 1960-61), Am. Philos. Soc., Soc. Chem. Industry, Nat. Acad. Engring. (founding pres.), Nat. Acad. Scis., AIME (hon. mem., past pres.), Am. Welding Soc. (dir., Adams lectr. 1944), Internat. Inst. Med. Electronics and Biomed. Engring., ASTM, Soc. Automotive Engrs., Am. Iron and Steel Inst., Internat. Inst. Welding (v.p., elector Hall of Fame). Clubs: La Jolla (Calif.); Beach and Tennis; Cosmos (Washington); University Chemists (N.Y.C.). Home: La Jolla Calif. Died Oct. 23, 1987; buried San Diego.

KIPLINGER, RALPH ERNEST, academic administrator; b. Loomis, Nebr., Jan. 30, 1891; s. Frederick W. and Ida (Morgan) K.; m. Mabel Ann Roach, Feb. 26, 1913; children: Mildred E. Kiplinger Frankson, Robert O. BCE, U. Nebr., 1912. With Holdrege State Bank, 1912-16; automobile distbr. 1916-35; gen. agt. Guarantee Mut. Life Co., Omaha, 1935-38, pres., 1951-61; pres. bd. regents U. Omaha; bd. dirs. U.S. Nat. Bank, Omaha. Bd. dirs. Boys Clubs Omaha, Salvation Army; trustee Nebr. Meth. Hosp. Mem. Omaha C. of C. (v.p., chmn. exec. com.), Masons, Rotary. Presbyterian. Home: Omaha Nebr. †

KIPNIS, CLAUDE, pantomimist, artistic director; b. Paris, Apr. 22, 1938; came to U.S., 1966; s. Albert and Sonia (Drutman) K.; m. Edith Chustka, 1959; children: Joel, Eric. B in Philosophy, 1956; student, Sch. Oriental Langs., U. Sorbonne, 1957-58. Founder mime sch. Tel Aviv, 1961; tchr. U Tel Aviv, 1962-64, Acad. Dramatic Arts, Ramat Gan, Israel, 1962-64; toured Europe, with appearances at Festival of Theatre of Nations Paris; 1st U.S. appearance N.Y.C., 1966-67; dir.-in-residence Boston Opera Co., 1966-67; artist-in-residence U. Ill., Champaign-Urbana, 1968-71; founder, mgr. Claude Kipnis Mime Theatre; dir. mime sect. Am. Acad. Dramatic Arts, N.Y.C., 1971-73; founder, mgr. Claude Kipnis Mime Sch., N.Y.C., 1976-81. Author: The Mime Book, 1974; creator mime versions of classical music compositions including Miraculous Mandarin (Bartok), 1967, Histoire du Soldat (Stravinsky), 1971, Renard (Stravinsky), 1971, Pictures at an Exhibition (Moussorgsky), 1974, Eine Kleine Nachtmusik (Mozart), 1975. Fellow Ctr. for Advanced Studies, U. Ill., Nat. Endowment for Arts. Mem. AFTRA, SAG, Am. Guild Variety Artists. Home: Brooklyn N.Y. Died Feb. 8, 1981.

KIRBY, ALLAN PRICE, corporation executive; b. Wilkes-Barre, Pa., July 31, 1892; s. Fred Morgan and Jessie (Owen) K.; m. Marian G. Sutherland, Feb. 14, 1918; children: Grace Jessie, Fred Morgan II, Ann Sutherland, Allan P. Jr. Student, Wyo. Sem., 1906-08, Lawrenceville (N.J.) Sch., 1908-10, Lafayette Coll., 1910-13; DHL, Lafayette Coll., 1946; LLD (hon.), St. Joseph's Coll., Phila., 1964. Office mgr. Bathurst (N.B.) Lumber Co., 1914-15; treas. Jenkins-Kirby Packing Co., 1915-22; pres. Kirby-Davis Co., 1922-34; v.p. 2d Nat. Bank, Wilkes-Barre, 1924-34; pres. Imperial Motor Corp., 1934-46; pres. Alleghany Corp., 1939-61, chmn. bd., chief exec. officer, 1963-67, chmn. emeritus, 1967-73. Mem. Masons, Zeta Psi. Republican. Episcopalian. Home: Morristown N.J. Died May 2, 1973; buried Hollenback Cemetery, Wilkes-Barre, Pa.

KIRCHHOFER, ALFRED HENRY, newspaper editor; b. Buffalo, May 25, 1892; s. Robert and Elizabeth (Boldt) K.; m. Emma M. Schugardt, Jan. 27, 1914 (dec.); 1 child, Robert A. Ed. high sch., Buffalo; LittD (hon.), St. Bonaventure U., 1963, D'Youville Coll., 1964. Boys' work sec. Genesee YMCA, Buffalo, 1909-10; with Buffalo Com., Buffalo Times, Buffalo Courier, until 1913; editor Western N.Y. Post, 1913-14; with Buffalo Evening News, 1915-66, Washington corr., 1921-27, mng. editor, 1927-56, editor, 1956-66; exec. v.p. Buffalo Evening News, Inc., 1956-66, also bd. dirs.; v.p. Sta. WBEN, Inc., 1930-56, pres., 1956-67; vis. prof. U. Mo. Sch. Journalism, 1967-72; bd. dirs. Trico Products Corp.; pres. Nat. Press Club, Washington, 1927. Publicity dir. U. Buffalo $5,000,000 endowment fund campaign, 1920-29; bd. dirs. U. Mo. Sch. Writing Seminar; active campaigns Liberty Loan, ARC, World War I; assoc. dir. publicity Rep. Nat. Com., 1928, dir. publicity, 1936; past bd. dirs. Millard Filmore Hosp., Internat. Inst.; past mem. adv. bd. Am. Press Inst.; pres. Am. Coun. Edn. Journalism, 1950-52; mem. Syracuse U. Sch. Journalism coun. of editors and pubs., 1958-66; dir. Crippled Children Camps, Inc., 1946-66; sec. bd. visitors Rosell Park Meml. Inst.; past bd. dirs. Buffalo chpt. ANRC, Buffalo Philharm. Orch.; past mem. coun. U. Buffalo; trustee U. Buffalo Found., 1962-65; mem., chmn. journalism adv. coun. St. Bonaventure U., 1965-69; mem. adv. bd. Children's Hosp.; hon. bd. dirs. Buffalo Fine Arts Acad.; bd. dirs. Health Rsch., Inc., Fresh Air Mission, N.Y. Def. Coun.; mem. exec. NCCJ. Recipient Journalism award U. Home: Buffalo N.Y. Died Sept. 19, 1985, buried Forest Lawn Cemetery, Buffalo.

KIRK, ARTHUR SHERMAN, banker, realtor; b. Hiawatha, Kans., June 25, 1891; s. Sherman and Harriot (White) K.; m. Elizabeth Leland Chamberlain, Sept. 9, 1919 (dec. Apr. 1972); children: Joseph C., Catherine (Mrs. Edwin Tim Elliot). AB, Drake U., 1914, LLB, 1923; AM, Harvard, 1915. Bar: Iowa 1923. Propr Chamberlain, Kirk, & Cline, realtors, Des Moines, 1923-73; pres. Home Fed. Savs. & Loan Assn., Des Moines 1936-57, chmn. bd., 1957-73; mem. exec. com., dir Valley Bank & Trust Co., Des Moines, 1934-73. Mem Des Moines Planning and Zoning Com., 1935-45; chmn trustees Drake U., 1964-66, chmn. relay com., 1959. With U.S. Army, 1917-19. Mem. Des Moines Real Estate Bd. (pres. 1926, 39), Iowa Assn. Real Estate Bds (pres. 1934-35), Am. Inst. Real Estate Brokers (pres 1945), Am. Inst. Real Estate Counselors (gov. counci 1966-69), Des Moines Club, Wakonda Club, Masons Order of Coif, Phi Beta Kappa, Sigma Alpha Epsilon. Home: Des Moines Iowa. †

KIRK, HADDON S(PURGEON), agricultural products executive; b. Belleflower, Ill., Oct. 18, 1891; s. George and Naomi Alice (Godwin) K.; m. Hilah Jane Link July 3, 1917; children: Hilah Jane (Mrs. C. R. Wood) Haddon S., Robert Link. AB in History with honors U. Ill., 1915; JD cum laude, U. Mich., 1917. With R.J

Reynolds Tobacco Co., from 1919, asst. supt. mfg., 1938, supt. mfg., 1947-56, v.p., 1952-58, exec. v.p., from 1958, chmn. exec. com., from 1959, also bd. dirs. 1st lt. inf., U.S. Army, 1918. Mem. Twin City Club, Forsyth Country Club, Civitan (pres. 1931), Torch Club (pres. 1942), Order of Coif, Phi Beta Kappa, Zeta Psi, Phi Delta Phi. Democrat. Presbyterian. Home: Winston-Salem N.C. †

KIRKLAND, WILLIAM LENNOX, business executive; b. Camden, S.C., Nov. 22, 1892; s. Thomas Jefferson and Fredrica (Alexander) K.; m. Eliza Lucas Frampton, Feb., 1925; 1 child, Mary Louise. Student, The Citadel, U. S.C. Surveyor canal work State of Fla., 1912-13; surveying engr. C.C.& O. Ry., 1914-15; county engr. Kenshaw County, S.C., 1915-16, 19-21; engr. Warren Bros. Co., Cambridge, Mass., 1921-38, v.p., 1938-42, pres., 1942-58, chmn. bd., 1958-61. Mem. Algonquin Club (Boston). Republican. Episcopalian. Home: Charleston S.C. †

KIRKPATRICK, CHARLES COCHRAN, naval officer; b. San Angelo, Tex., June 20, 1907; s. Charles Cochran and Elizabeth (Snyder) K.; m. Lalla Branch, Oct. 24, 1932; children: Lalla Branch (Mrs. George W. Woerner Jr.), Shelley Snyder. BS, U.S. Naval Acad., 1931. Commd. ensign USN, 1931, advanced through grades to rear adm., 1956, assigned battleships, cruisers, destroyers, submarines, minecraft, qualified to command submarines, 1935, comdr. U.S.S. Triton, 1942-43, comdr. U.S.S. Shea, 1944-45, aide, flag lt. to Fleet Adm. Ernest J. King, 1943-44; chief info. Dept. Navy USN, Washington, 1957-60; comdr. Amphibious Group I, U.S. Pacific 1960-61, comdr. Tng. Command, U.S. Pacific Fleet, 1961-62; supt. U.S. Naval Acad., Annapolis, Md., 1962-64. Decorated Navy Cross, Army D.S.C., Silver Star, Legion of Merit. Mem. Army and Navy Club, Nat. Press Club. Episcopalian. Home: Kerrville Tex. Died Mar. 12, 1988.

KIRKPATRICK, RICHARD BOGUE, newspaperman, lawyer; b. Van Buren, Ind., Dec. 16, 1912; s. Otto L. and Magnolia (Bogue) K.; m. Carolyn Ann Hawkins, Dec. 12, 1943 (dec. Sept. 1960); 1 son, Thomas Hawkins; m. Kay Poch Lynch, Aug. 26, 1971; children—Kip Michael, Kimberly Lisa; 1 stepdau., Vicki Lynch Porter. J.D., U. Cin., 1952. Bar: Ohio bar 1952, Ky. bar 1952, U.S. Supreme Ct 1963, D.C. bar 1968. With editorial dept. Cin. Enquirer, 1934-68, polit. columnist, 1948-68; head bur. Cin. Enquirer, Frankfort, Ky., 1948-56, Columbus, Ohio, 1956-61; bur. chief Cin. Enquirer, Washington, 1961-68; partner Ansary, Kirkpatrick & Rosse, Washington, 1968-69; sec. dir. Campbell Music Co., Inc., 1968-69; asst. minority counsel U.S. House Ways and Means Com., 1969-70; aide U.S. senator Paul J. Fannin, 1970; staff asst. criminal div. Justice Dept., Washington, from 1970; Cons. NASA, 1968-69; mem. scholarships adv. com. Am. Polit. Sci. Assn. Served to lt. col. AUS, 1941-45, 46-47. Mem. Am., Ohio, Ky., D.C. bar assns., Sigma Delta Chi. Methodist (trustee 1953-55). Club: Nat. Press (Washington). Home: Chevy Chase Md. Died Dec. 21, 1987; buried Cin.

KIRST, HANS HELLMUT, author; b. Osterode, Dec. 5, 1914; s. Johannes and Gertrud (Golldack) K.; m. Ruth Mueller, Dec. 14, 1962. Ed., Volkschule/Gymnasium, Osterode. Author: Wir nannten ihn Galgenstrick, 1950, 08/15, 1954, Febrik der Offiziere, 1960, Kameraden, 1961, Die Nacht der Generale, 1962, Aufstand der Soldaten, 1965, Die Wölfe, 1967, Kein Vaterland, 1968. Mem. PEN, Bundesrepublic Deutschland, Authors Guild U.S. Home: San Michele Switzerland also: Munich Federal Republic of Germany

KIRSTEIN, GEORGE GARLAND, insurance company executive, author; b. Rochester, N.Y., Dec. 10, 1909; s. Louis E. and Rose (Stein) K.; m. Jane Stolle Cianfarra, Sept. 26, 1957 (dec.); m. Paulina Dean Steward, Dec. 27, 1972 (div. May 1976). Grad., Berkshire Sch., 1928; AB, Harvard U., 1932. Asst. dir. RKO Radio Pictures, Hollywood, Calif., 1932-33; v.p. Bloomingdale Bros., Inc., 1933-41; exec. sec. Nat. War Labor Bd., 1941-43; dir. Mgmt.-Employee Relations, Inc., 1946-50; exec. v.p. Health Ins. Plan Greater N.Y., 1950-55; pub. The Nation, 1955-65; exec. v.p. Montefiore Hosp. and Med. Ctr., 1966-69. Author: The Rich, Better Giving. Mem. vis. com. Harvard Sch. Pub. Health, 1968-73. Lt. USNR, 1943-45. Mem. Sheldrake Yacht Club. Home: Mamaroneck N.Y. Died Apr. 3, 1986.

KISSNER, FRANKLIN H., business executive; b. Pa., 1909. Grad., Harvard U., 1930. With U.S. Mil. Govt., Germany, 1945-46, Textron, Inc., 1946-49; contr. Lever Bros., 1949-57; exec. v.p. Dyson-Kissner Corp., 1957-61, pres., 1961-88, also adviser, bd. dirs.; pres. Wallace-Murray Corp., 1965-67, chmn., 1967-88; bd. dirs. Kearney-Nat., Inc. With U.S. Army, 1941-46. Home: Bethlehem Pa. Died Feb. 4, 1988; buried Mauch Chunk Cemetery Assn., Jim Thorpe, Pa.

KITCH, PAUL RICHARD, lawyer; b. Marion, Kans., June 18, 1911; s. Charles A. and Anna (Haun) K.; m. Josephine Pridmore, Jan. 25, 1936; children: Edmund, Paul Richard, Thomas, James, David; m. Diana Parlette, Apr. 1, 1974; 1 dau., Mary. A.B., Southwestern Coll., Winfield, Kans., 1932; J.D., U. Chgo., 1935. Bar: Kans. 1935. Assoc. Brooks, Brooks & Fleeson, Witchita, Kans., 1935-42; mem. Brooks, Brooks & Fleeson, 1942; with Fleeson, Gooing, Coulson & Kitch, Wichita, 1942-88; sr. ptnr. Fleeson, Gooing, Coulson & Kitch, 1957-88; dir. Kans. State Bank & Trust Co., Wichita. Pres. Wichita Bd. Edn., 1947. Mem. Wichita Area C. of C. (pres. 1961). Home: Wichita Kans. Deceased.

KLAPPER, JOSEPH THOMAS, sociologist; b. N.Y.C., Jan. 11, 1917; s. Paul and Flora (Eydenberg) K.; m. Hope Lunin, July 15, 1949. BS cum laude, Harvard U., 1936; MA, U. Chgo., 1938; PhD in Sociology, Columbia U., 1960. Instr. English Bklyn. Poly. Inst., 1939-40; teaching tutor CCNY, 1939-41; rsch. asst., then rsch. assoc. Bur. Applied Social Rsch., Columbia U., 1946-49, rsch. assoc., project dir., 1954-58; acting asst. prof. sociology U. Wash., 1949-50; editor Wash. State Pub. Opinion Lab.; project dir., then chief media evaluation sect. Voice of Am., USIA, 1951-54; cons. communications rsch., behavioral rsch. svc. GE, 1958-62; dir. social rsch. CBS, N.Y.C., 1962-84; vis. asst. prof. sociology and anthropology Stanford U., summer 1950; cons. communications rsch. Am.-Jewish Com., also broadcasting and film commn. Nat. Coun. Chs. of Christ, 1957-64; assoc. Columbia Seminar on Pub. Communication, 1952-84, Columbia Seminar on Basic and Applied Rsch. Author: The Effects of Mass Communication, 1960; mem. editorial bd. Pub. Opinion Quar., Jour. Applied Communication Rsch.; contbr. numerous articles to profl. jours. mem. Pres.'s Commn. on Obscenity and Pornography, 1968-70, Surgeon Gen.'s Sci. Adv. Com., 1969-71; plenary speaker on mass communication World Congress World Fedn. Mental Health, 1973. Capt AUS, 1941-46. Rockefeller fellow, 1946-47. Mem. Am. Sociol. Assn., Am. Assn. Pub. Opinion Rsch. (exec. coun. 1954-69, counsellor-at-large 1956-57, 69-84, sec.-treas. 1957-61, pres. 1962-63, Exceptionally Disting. Achievement award 1976), World Assn. Pub. Opinion Rsch., Radio-TV Rsch. Coun. Home: New York N.Y. Died May 14, 1984; buried Mt. Hope, N.Y.

KLATSKIN, GERALD, medical educator; b. N.Y.C., May 14, 1910; s. Archibald and Celia (Golubowski) K.; m. Ethelyn Henry, Dec. 10, 1949; children: Jane, Robert P., Ann Henry. AB, Cornell U., 1929, MD, 1933; MA (hon.), Yale U., 1957. Diplomate Am Bd. Internal Medicine. Intern, asst. resident medicine New Haven Hosp., 1933-35, resident medicine, 1937-38; intern surgery Strong Meml. Hosp., Rochester, N.Y., 1935-36, assoc. resident, 1936-37; instr. medicine U. Rochester, 1936-37; from instr. to prof. Yale Sch. Medicine, 1937-64, David Paige Smith prof., 1964-86; assoc. physician Yale-New Haven Med. Ctr.; cons. West Haven VA Hosp. Contbr. articles to profl. jours. Capt. to lt. col. M.C., U.S. Army, 1942-46. Master ACP; mem. Assn. Am. Physicians, Interurban Clin. Club, Soc. Exptl. Biology and Medicine, Am. Assn. Study Liver Diseases (pres. 1957), Phi Beta Kappa, Sigma Xi, Alpha Omega Alpha. Home: Hamden Conn. Died Mar. 27, 1986.

KLEIN, EDWARD ELKAN, rabbi; b. Newark, May 25, 1913; s. Benjamin and Elsa (Elkan) K.; m. Ruth Anne Strauss, Sept. 11, 1940; children: Barbara Anne Klein Hillman, Stephen Alan. BA magna cum laude, NYU, 1934; MHL, Hebrew Union Coll.-Jewish Inst. Religion, 1940, DD, 1965. Ordained rabbi, 1940. Asst. rabbi Stephen Wise Free Synagogue, N.Y.C., 1940-42, rabbi, 1943-81, rabbi emeritus, 1981-85; dir. Hillel Found., U. Calif., Berkeley, 1942-43; vis. lectr. homiletics Hebrew Union Coll.-Jewish Inst. Religion, N.Y.C., 1966-85. Co-chmn. League of West Side Orngs., 1952-85; mem. N.Y.C. Mayor's Appeal Bd. for Fair Housing Practices, 1958-62, N.Y.C. Mayor's Adv. Com. on Higher Edn., 1966-68; mem. nat. adv. com. Religious Action Ctr., Washington; mem. social action commn. Union Am. Hebrew Conregations, 1960-85; past chmn. ch. and state com. Cen. Conf. Am. Rabbis; chmn. bd. Lincoln Sq. Community Coun.; bd. dirs. Am. Found. on Nonviolence. Nat. Coun. on Religion in Higher Edn. fellow. Mem. Phi Beta Kappa. Home: New York N.Y. Died July 14, 1985.

KLEIN, OTTO G(EORGE), government official; b. Walsenburg, Colo., Nov. 2, 1891; s. George C. and Minnie L. (Frye) K.; m. Alma Pope Samples, Jan. 12, 1915; 1 child, Otto George Jr. Student, U. Colo., 1911-12. Miner Huerfano Co., Colo., 1912-23; automobile dealer Walsenburg and Trinidad, Colo., 1923-43; sr. analyst War Prodn. Bd., 1943-46; asst. dept. regional dir. disposal U.S. War Assets Adminstrn., Denver, 1946; regional dir. U.S. War Assets Adminstrn., St. Louis, 1947, Chgo., 1947-50; regional commr. GSA, Denver, from 1950; mem. nat. field advisers SBA. Pres. Jefferson County Community Chest; chmn. Tri-County Mile High United Fund; alderman City of Walsenburg, 1922-23. Decorated Congl. Selective Svc. medal. Mem. Elks, Masons, Shriners. Home: Golden Colo. †

KLEIN, SEYMOUR MILLER, lawyer, business executive; b. N.Y.C., Mar. 14, 1909; s. Emanuel and Sadie (Miller) K.; m. Ruth Liberman, Oct. 29, 1939; children: Jeffrey Peter, Donald Stuart. BSS cum laude, CCNY, 1929; JD cum laude, Harvard U., 1932. Bar: N.Y. 1933, U.S. Supreme Ct. Asst. U.S. atty. So. Dist. N.Y., 1932-39; spl. asst. to atty. gen. U.S. 1934-36; ptnr. Shea & Gould (merged Lynton, Klein, Opton & Saslow and predecessors), N.Y.C., 1939-88; lectr. Practising Law Inst., 1946-88. Bd. editors Harvard Law Rev., 1932. Former pres. 100 Park Ave., Inc., Louis Adler Realty Co., Inc.; bd. dirs. Midtown Realty Owners Assn., Inc.; referee appellate div. N.Y. State Supreme Ct., 1963-88; mem. Gov.'s Jud. Nominating Com. for 1st Jud. Dept., 1975-88, Mayor's Com. Judiciary, 1974-78; mem. departmental com. for ct. adminstrn. 1st Jud. Dept., 1966-88; mem. N.Y. Jud. Nominating Com., 1976-88; mem. jud. relations com. appellate div. Supreme Ct. N.Y., 1968-76, chmn. exec. com. ct. administrn., 1969-88; hon. commr. Pub. Events City N.Y., 1969-73; mem. N.Y.C. Cultural Coun., 1969-73; pres. Louis and Bessie Adler Found., Ruth and Seymour Klein Found.; former pres. and chmn. bd. 92d St. YM-YWHA; bd. dirs. Citizens Tax Coun.; trustee Fedn. Jewish Philanthropies N.Y.; bd. dirs., mem. exec. com. Mus. Collaborative; trustee N.Y. Pub. Libr., 1985-88; hon. trustee Met. Mus. Art, 1983-88; mem. trustee painting and sculpture com. Mus. Modern Art. Recipient Friend of Lehigh award Lehigh U. Alumni Assn., 1970. Mem. ABA, N.Y. State Bar Assn. (com. on jud. selection 1974-88, spl. com. on requirements of cts. 1973-75), Assn. of Bar of City of N.Y. (past mem. exec. grievance and judiciary com., chmn. jud. com.), Am. Arbitration Assn. (nat. panel arbitrators), N.Y. County Lawyers Assn., Harmonie Club (bd. govs., exec. com. N.Y.C. chpt.), Sunningdale Country Club (pres. 1964-67, former exec. com., bd. govs.), Phi Beta Kappa, Zeta Beta Tau. Home: New York N.Y. Died July 31, 1988.

KLEINPELL, ROBERT MINSSEN, educator, paleontologist, geologist; b. Chgo., Sept. 13, 1905; s. William Ernst and Alma Louise (Wilke) K.; m. Dariel Shively, Dec. 29, 1934 (dec.); m. Mildred Knapp, Aug. 4, 1972. A.B., Occidental Coll., Los Angeles, 1926; A.M., Stanford, 1928, Ph.D., 1934. Field geologist Richfield Oil Co., 1928-31; asst. geologist U.S. Geol. Survey, 1931-33; cons. geologist and paleontologist Cal. petroleum industry, 1933-39; stratigrapher petroleum survey Nat. Devel. Co., P.I., 1939-45; instr. systematic biology and hist. geology, coll. curriculum Santo Tomas and Los Banos Internment Camps, P.I., 1942-45; mem. faculty U. Calif. at Berkeley, 1946-73, prof. paleontology, 1947-73, emeritus, 1973-86; cons. paleontologist, geologist, from 1945; vis. prof. micropaleontology Calif. Inst. Tech., 1939-41; acting dir. Mus. Paleontology, U. Calif., Berkeley, 1958-60; mem. bd. adv. editors geol. sci. U. Calif. Press, 1964-73. Editor: Cushman Found. for Foraminiferal Research, 1962-65; asst. editor, 1965-70. Author: Miocene Stratigraphy of California, 1955, The Miocene Stratigraphy of California Revisited, 1981. Contbr. articles to profl. jours. Fellow Geol. Soc. Am., Am. Geog. Soc., AAAS, Calif. Acad. Sci., Paleontol. Soc. (chmn. Pacific Coast sect., councilor 1963-64, nat. v.p., councilor 1964-65); mem. Am. Assn. Petroleum Geologists (Distinguished lectr. 1960, hon. life mem. Pacific sect. and nat.), Soc. Econ. Paleontologists and Mineralogists (hon. life mem. Pacific sect., nat. v.p., councilor 1961-62, councilor for paleontology 1967-68), Am. Mus. Natural History (bd. adviser dept. micropaleontology 1945-48), Am. Acad. Polit. Scis., Far Eastern Assn., Biosystematists, LeConte Soc., Phi Beta Kappa, Sigma Xi, Theta Tau, Alpha Tau Omega. Mem. Am. Party. Lutheran. Home: Goleta Calif. Died March 13, 1986.

KLOPFER, DONALD SIMON, book publisher; b. N.Y.C., Jan. 23, 1902; s. Simon Klopfer and Stella (Danziger) Jacobson; m. Marion Ansbacher, Sept. 14, 1925 (div. 1933); 1 child, Lois; m. Kathleen Scofield, July 19, 1981. Student, Williams Coll., 1918-20, LLD, 1975. Treas. United Diamond Works, Inc., 1921-25; v.p. Random House, Inc., N.Y.C., 1925-80; sec., treas. Random House, Inc., 1927, vice chmn. bd., 1965-70, chmn. bd., 1970-75, chmn. bd. emeritus, 1975-86, also chmn. exec. com., bd. dirs.; chmn. bd. Grossett Dunlap, Inc., 1956-57. Served to maj. USAF, 1942-45, ETO. Mem. Am. Inst. Graphic Arts (past pres.), Book Pubs. Council (past pres.). Democrat. Jewish. Club: Harmonie (N.Y.C.). Home: New York N.Y. Died May 30, 1986.

KLOPSTEG, PAUL ERNEST, educational and research consultant; b. Henderson, Minn., May 30, 1889; s. Julius and Magdalene (Kuesthardt) K.; m. Amanda Marie Toedt, June 11, 1914; children: Marie, Irma Louise (dec.), Ruth Helen. BSEE, U. Minn., 1911, MA, 1913, PhD, 1916; ScD, Northwestern U., 1942, Wesleyan U., 1948. Asst. in physics U. Minn., 1911-13, instr., 1913-17, asst. prof., 1917; devel. engr. Ordnance Dept. U.S. Army, 1917-18; in charge tech. advt. Leeds & Northrup Co., Phila., 1918-21; in charge devel. and mfg. Cen. Sci. Co., 1921-30, dir., 1922-55, pres., 1930-44; prof. applied sci. Northwestern U., adminstr. rsch. Tech. Inst., 1944-54, prof. emeritus, from 1954, spl. cons. to Univ. pres., 1961-63; spl. rsch. cons. nat. rsch. orgns.; bd. govs. Argonne Nat. Lab., 1947-50, chmn., 1949-50; assoc. dir. NSF, 1951-58, spl. cons., 1958-62; mem. com. atmospheric scis. NAS-NRC, 1957-64, chmn., 1958-60; trustee, mem. exec. com. U. Corp. Atmospheric Rsch., 1963-66; chmn. vis. com. John Crerar Library, 1963-66. Author books on archery; contbr. to Ency. Brittanica, sci. jours. and archery mags.; inventor numerous sci. instruments. Mem. Personnel Security Rev. Bd., AEC, 1953-62. Recipient Modern Pioneers' award NAM, 1939, medal for merit with Presdl. citation, 1948, Outstanding Achievement medal U. Minn., 1950, Maurice Thompson medal of honor Nat. Archery Assn., Compton Medal of Honor Nat. Field Archery Assn., Whiffen Meml. award Archery Inst.; named to Archery Hall of Fame Archery Assn. U.S. Fellow AAAS (bd. dirs. 1948-69, pres. 1959, chmn. 1960, treas. 1961-69, bd. govs.), Am. Phys. Soc., Am. Optical Soc.; mem. Am. Meteorol. Soc. (hon.), Am. Assn. Physics Tchrs. (founder, past pres.), Am. Inst. Physics (past chmn. bd.), University Club, Cosmos Club, Rotary. Home: Laguna Hills Calif. Deceased.

KLOTS, ALLEN TRAFFORD, publishing company executive; b. N.Y.C., Mar. 31, 1921; s. Allen Trafford and Mary (FitzBrown) K. B.A., Yale, 1943. Editor Dodd, Mead & Co., Inc., N.Y.C., 1948-66; sec., exec. editor Dodd, Mead & Co., Inc., 1966-82, sr. editor, 1982-87. Chmn. Young Friends of City Center, 1968-72; bd. dirs. City Center of Music and Drama, 1962-75; co-chmn. 30th anniversary com., 1973-74; bd. dirs. Contemporary Music Soc., 1975-79; bd. dirs., sec. Friends of French Opera, 1978-81. Served to lt. USNR, 1943-46. Clubs: Century, Dutch Treat. Died July 7, 1987.

KLUSS, WILFRED MARTIN, shipping company executive; b. Waterloo, Iowa, June 19, 1921; s. Fred John and Harriet Maude Kluss; m. Mary Monro Crandon; children: Stewart Radford, Annette Elizabeth, Suzanne Caroline. SB, Harvard U., 1942; BA, New Coll., Oxford (Eng.) U., 1949, MA, 1949. Specialist in overseas devel. ECA, Paris, 1949-50; statistician Morgan Stanley & Co., N.Y.C., 1950-51; asst. loan officer IBRD, Washington, 1951-54; with Mid. East affairs and marine depts. Mobil Oil Co., N.Y.C., 1954-71; chmn. Mobil Shiiping Co., London, 1966-69; mgr. internat. ops. Mobil Shipping Co., London, 1969-71; with Conoco, Inc., Stamford, Conn., 1971-79; with Conoco, Inc., Houston, 1979-81, v.p., 1975-81; vice chmn., bd. dirs. Robert E. Derecktor RI Inc.; with Shaarup Tankers, Inc., Greenwich, Conn. Mem. exec. com. European Rep. Com., London, 1968; bd. govs. New Rochelle (N.Y.) Hosp. Med. Ctr., 1977-78, treas., 1978; active ELISSA Restoration Galveston Hist. Found. Lt. comdr. USNR, 1943-46. Decorated Bronze Star; Rhodes scholar, 1947-49. Mem. Soc. Naval Architects and Marine Engrs., Am. Bur. Shipping, Oil Cos. Internat. Marine Forum (exec. com. 1977-81), Fedn. Am. Controlled Shipping, Am. Petroleum Inst., Larchmont Yacht Club (commodore 1973-76), Storm Trysail Club, Cruising Am. Club, Royal Ocean Racing Club, N.Y. Yacht Club, Circumnavigators. Episcopalian. Home: Stamford Conn. Died July 17, 1984; buried Union Cemetery, Little Compton, R.I.

KNAPP, DAVID WILLIAM, banker; b. Vinton, Iowa, June 15, 1936; s. Crawford E. and Beulah G (Wooderson) K.; m. Diana E. Erickson, Dec. 11, 1959; children: David, William, Stephen Crawford. BS in Engring., S.D. Sch. Mines and Tech., 1958; JD, U. Denver, 1962. Bar: Ill. Pres., chief exec. officer Am. Nat. Bank & Trust Co., Rockford, Ill. Served with U.S. Army, 1958-59. Mem. Ill. Bar Assn., Am. Bankers Assn., Rotary,. Lutheran. Home: Rockford Ill. Died Dec. 4, 1985.; buried Rockford.

KNAPP, SHERMAN RICHMOND, utility executive; b. Danbury, Conn., June 17, 1905; s. Frederick Abijah and Julia (Richmond) K.; m. Eleanor Tracy, June 23, 1928; children: Sherman R., Barbara, Duncan Tracy. BEE, Cornell U., 1928. With Conn. Light & Power Co., Berlin, 1928-81, cadet engr., 1928-31, sales engr., 1931-37, mgr. New Milford dist., 1937-41, asst. to sales v.p., 1941-48, asst. to pres., 1948-50, exec. v.p., 1950-52, pres., bd. dirs., 1952-64, chmn., bd. dirs., 1964-70; pres., chief exec. officer N.E. Utilities, Wethersfield, Conn., 1966-67, chief exec. officer, chmn. bd., 1967-69, chmn. exec. com., 1970-73; energy cons. 1973-81; bd. dirs. Conn. Bank & Trust Co., Emhart Mfg. Co., NUS Corp., Scovill Mfg. Co. Chmn. Conn. Flood Recovery Com., 1955; past pres. Edison Elec. Inst., Elec. Coun. New Eng., Atomic Indsl. Forum; past chmn. N.E. Power Coordinating Coun.; trustee emeritus Conn. Coll. Mem. The Hartford Club, Shuttle Meadow Country Club, Metropolitan Club, Lambda Chi Alpha. Home: Simons Island Ga. Died Oct. 5, 1981.

KNATCHBULL-HUGESSEN, ADRIAN, lawyer; b. Kent, Eng., July 5, 1891; s. Lord Brabourne and Ethel Walker; m. Margaret Duggan, Sept. 7, 1922; children: Edward, Kenneth, Andrew, Mary Knatchbull-Hugessen Keynes, James. Student, Eton Coll., 1905-07; BA, McGill U., 1912, BCL, 1914, LLD (hon.), 1960. Bar: P.Q. 1914; King's Counsel, 1931. Head firm Hugessen, Macklaier, Chisholm, Smith & Davis, Montreal, Que., Can., 1952-60; bd. dirs. Can. Marconi Co., Internat. Paints Ltd., Can. Apptd. Liberal Party senator Dominion of Can., 1937, dep. leader of senate, 1950-52; gov. McGill U.; chancellor Anglican Diocese Montreal. With Can. Army, 1916-18. Home: Montreal Can. †

KNEIP, RICHARD FRANCIS, former governor, former ambassador; b. Tyler, Minn., Jan. 7, 1933; s. Frank J. and Bernice D. (Pederson) K.; m. Nancy Pankey, Apr. 19, 1957; 8 children. Student, S.D. State U., 1955, St. John's U., Collegeville, Minn., 1956. Owner, operator Kneip Sales, Salem, S.D., 1962-87; mem. S.D. Senate, 1965-71; gov. State of S.D., 1971-78; amb. to Singapore 1978-80; co-chmn. Old West Regional Commn.; chmn. Dem. Govs.' Conf.; mem. Adv. Commn. on Intergovtl. Relations, 1971-87. Mem. S.D. Constl. Revision Commn., 1969-71. With USAAF, 1951-55. Mem. Elks. Roman Catholic. Home: Sioux Falls S.D. Died Mar. 9, 1987.

KNIGHT, BRUCE WINTON, economics educator; b. Colfax, Ill., June 27, 1892; s. Winton Cyrus and Julia Ann (Hyneman) K.; m. Myrtle Mary Eickelberg, June 25, 1925; children: Susan Gretchen, Bruce Winton Tucker. Student, Tex. Christian U., 1912-15; BS, U. Utah, 1921; postgrad., U. Chgo., summer 1921; AM, U. Mich., 1923; postgrad., U. Wis., 1923-24; AM (hon.), Dartmouth Coll., 1935. Prin. Stratford (Tex.) High Sch., 1915-16; sec., registrar S.E. Stte Normal Sch., Okla., 1916-17; instr. English U. Utah, 1920-21; instr. econs. U. Mich., 1921-23; asst. in econs. U. Wis., 1923-24; instr. Dartmouth Coll., 1924-25, asst. prof., 1925-35, prof., from 1935. Author: (with N. L. Smith) Economics, 1930, How to Run a War, 1936, Economic Principles in Practice, 1939, (with L. G. Hines) Economics, 1952; contbr. articles to profl. jours. With U.S. Army, 1917-19. Home: Hanover N.H. †

KNIGHT, CLIFFORD (REYNOLDS), author; b. Fulton, Kans., Dec. 7, 1886; s. Wesley C. and Flora Belle (Reynolds) K.; m. Louise Read Heath, Aug. 29, 1917 (dec. 1918); m. Jessamine Paret, Oct. 1, 1928. Student, Washburn Coll., 1907-09, U. Mich., 1910-11. With ry. co; asst. prof. Yale U.; mem. editorial staff Kansas City (Mo.) Star, 1920-30; free-lance writer from 1930. Author: Tommy of the Voices, 1918, The Affair of the Scarlet Crab, 1937 (prize Dodd Mead Forum Mag.), The Affair of the Heavenly Voice, 1937, The Affair of the Ginger Lei, 1938, The Affair at Palm Springs, 1938, The Affair of the Black Sombrero, 1939, The Affair on the Painted Desert, 1939, The Affair of the Circus Queen, 1940, The Affair in Death Valley, 1940, The Affair of the Crimson Gull, 1941, The Affair of the Skiing Clown, 1941, The Affair of the Limping Sailor, 1942, The Affair of the Splintered Heart, 1942, The Affair of the Jade Monkey, 1943, The Affair of the Fainting Butler, 1943, The Affair of the Dead Stranger, 1944, The Affair of the Corpse Escort, 1946, The Affair of the Sixth Button, 1947, Dark Abyss, 1949, Hangman's Choice, 1949, The Yellow Cat, 1950, Death of a Big Shot, 1951, The Dark Road, 1951, Death and Little Brother, 1952. Mem. Calif. Writers Guild (bd. dirs.), Authors Club. Republican. Presbyterian. Home: Los Angeles Calif. †

KNIGHT, LESTER LLOYD, railroad executive; b. Mascotte, Fla., Nov. 5, 1891; s. Elbert Montgomery and Lucinda (Lee) K.; m. Nancy Caroline Roper, Apr. 9, 1918; children: Caroline Lee (Mrs. David D. Green), Cynthia Elbert (Mrs. T. Sanford Cooke Jr.), Lester Lloyd. Student pub. schs., Fla. From clk. to auditor Tampa No. R.R. (name now S.A.L. Ry.), 1909-14; auditor, freight claim agt. Macon, Dublin & Savannah R.R. Co. (name now S.A.L. Ry.), 1914-18; from asst. auditor disbursements to chmn. budget com. S.A.L. Ry., 1918-46; compt. S.A.L. Ry., Portsmouth, Va., 1946-58; v.p. fin., acctg. S.A.L. Ry., from 1958; v.p. Athens Terminal Co., Tampa Union Sta. Co.; v.p., mem. exec. com., bd. dirs. Balt. Steam Packet Co.; v.p. Gainesville Midland R.R. Co. Ga., Fla. & Ala. R.R.; v.p., bd. dirs. Southeastern Investment Co., Tampa & Gulf Coast R.R. Co.; v.p. fin., acctg. Tavares & Gulf R.R. Co.; bd. dirs. Ry. Express Agy., Inc., Richmond Terminal Ry. Co., Duval Connecting R.R. Co.; mem. adv. bd. Cen. Nat. Bank, Richmond. Mem. Assn. Am. R.R.'s, Rotunda Club, Executives Club. Baptist. Home: Richmond Va. †

KNIGHT, SAMUEL BRADLEY, educator, chemist; b. Bowman, S.C., Dec. 25, 1913; s. Daniel Emory and Sarah Roberta (Bradley) K.; m. Frances Elizabeth Austin, June 16, 1937; children: Anne Bradley, Elizabeth Haston. BS, Clemson U., 1934; MS, U. N.C., 1937, PhD, 1938. Asst. prof., then assoc. prof. Davidson (N.C.) Coll., 1938-41; mem. faculty U. N.C., Chapel Hill, 1941-88, prof. chemistry, 1949-88; sr. vis. chemist Oak Ridge Lab., summer 1949. Author: Physical Chemistry for Premedical Students, 1950, Fundamentals of Physical Chemistry, 2d edit., 1964. Recipient Tanner award, 1959; grantee AEC, 1950-53, Office ordnance Rsch., 1953-55, NSF, 1960-68. Mem. Am. Chem. Soc. (chmn. N.C. sect. 1949-50), N.C. Acad. Sci., Sigma Xi, Phi Kappa Phi. Home: Chapel Hill N.C. Died Sept. 14, 1988.

KNIGHT, SAMUEL HOWELL, geology educator; b. Laramie, Wyo., July 31, 1892; s. Wilber Clinton and Emma (Howell) K.; m. Edwina Gazzam Hall, Dec. 23, 1916; children: Wilbur Hall, Eleanor Audrey Knight Keefer. AB, U. Wyo., 1913; PhD, Columbia U., 1929. Asst. prof. U. Wyo., 1916-17, prof. geology, from 1918, head dept., from 1928, curator univ. mus., from 1916, dir. sci. camp, from 1946; state geologist, dir. geol. survey Wyo. 1932-40. 1st lt. U.S. Army, 1917-18. Fellow Geol. Soc. Am.; mem. Am. Assn. Petroleum Geologists, AAAS, Paleontol. Soc., Vertebrate Paleontologists, Colo. Wyo. Acad. Sci., Wyo. Geol. Assn (past pres.), Phi Beta Kappa, Sigma Xi, Phi Kappa Phi, Lions. Home: Laramie Wyo. †

KNIGHT, TED (TADEUS WLADYSLAW KONOPKA), actor; b. Terryville, Conn., Dec. 7, 1923; s. Charles Walter and Sophia (Kovaleski) Konopka; m. Dorothy May Clarke, Sept. 14, 1948; children—Ted, Elyse, Eric. Student, Randall Sch. Dramatic Arts, Hartford, Conn. With various radio stas. N.Y.C.; formed Kono Prodns., Inc., 1976. Master of ceremonies, newsman; host late-night movies for various TV stas.; supporting actor Hollywood films, from 1957; actor radio and TV commls., also cartoon voices; played leading roles in legitimate theatre prodns. at Player's Ring Theatre, Omnibus Theatre, Pasadena Playhouse, others; played Ted Baxter in: (1970-77) Mary Tyler Moore Show; star The Ted Knight Show, 1977, TV series Too Close for Comfort, 1980-84; appeared in film Caddy Shack, 1980; producer Ted Knight Musical-Comedy Variety Special Special, CBS; made Broadway theatre debut with starring role in Some of My Best Friends, 1977; recorded album Hi Guys, 1975. Recipient award as best supporting actor in a comedy Nat. Acad. TV Arts and Scis. 1972-73, 75-76. Served with U.S. Army, 1942-44. Named TV Father of Yr., Nat. Fathers Day Com., 1975. Mem. Screen Actors Guild, AFTRA, Equity. Died Aug. 26, 1986; buried Forest Lawn Meml., Glendale, Calif.

KNIGHT, THOMAS A., lawyer; b. Dallas, June 11, 1891; s. Robert Edward Lee and Ann (Armstrong) K.; m. Marian Ralston, Jan. 31, 1921; Children: Ann (Mrs. J.R. Bower Jr.), Marian (Mrs. F.E. Rowe); m. 2d, Elma Weichsel, Jan. 3, 1942. AB, U. Tex., 1912; LLB, Harvard U., 1915. Bar: Tex. 1915. Pvt. practice Dallas, from 1915; mem. firm Thompson, Knight, Wright & Simmons, Dallas, from 1915; bd. dis. Producing Properties Inc. Capt. A.G.D., N.A., Fifth Div., 1917-19. Mem. Am., Tex. and Dallas bar assns., Phi Beta Kappa, Beta Theta Pi. Home: Dallas Tex. †

KNIGHT, WILLIAM WINDUS, manufacturing executive; b. Indpls., Feb. 10, 1878; s. Milton and Marina (Windus) K.; m. Edna Ford, Feb. 10, 1904; children: William Windus, Milton, Edward Ford, Samuel Bradford, Elizabeth Ross. PhB, Uale U., 1899; LLD, U. Toledo, 1938. Clk. Reynolds Bros., grain merchants, , Toledo, 1899; sec. The Bostwick-Braun Co, wholesale hardware, Toledo, 1904-08, v.p., from 1908, chmn. bd., from 1940; treas. The W. Biongham Co., wholesale hardware, Cleve., from 1911; formerly dir. Fed. Res. Bank of Cleve.; dir. Toledo Scale Co. from 1925, Libbey-Owens Ford Co. and Owens-Ill. Glass Co. (Toledo) from 1932; dir. Wyandotte Chemicals Co. from 1941, Hettrick Mfg. Co. from 1942, Toledo Trust Co., 1939, chmn. bd. 1940; pres. bd. trustees Toledo Hosp. from 1924; pres Toledo Met. Pk. Bd. from 1930. Del. to Republican Nat. Convention, 1920. Mem. Toledo Club, Union Club (Cleve.), Yale Club (N.Y.C.). Congregationalist. †

KNOBLAUCH, ARTHUR LEWIS, university president, political science educator; b. Riga, Mich., Nov 17, 1906; s. Ferdinand and Wilhelmina (Kolz) K.; m. Muriel Marguerite Clemes, Aug. 12, 1929; children: Jane Harriet (Mrs. Mann), Nancy Carolyn (Mrs. Sonnenberg), Muriel Ann (Mrs. Fanning). B.S., Mich State U., 1929; M.A., U. Mich., 1933; Ed.D. (McGregor scholar), Harvard U., 1942; LL.B., LaSalle U., 1979. Tchr. high sch. Buchanan, Mich., 1929-31; dir. athletics prin. 1931-35; supt. schs. Cassopolis, Mich., 1935-39 exec. sec. Conn. Edn. Assn., 1940-41; asso. prof. edn. U Conn., 1941-43, prof. edn., dir. div. univ. extension summer session and continuing edn., 1943-55; vis. prof U. Mich., 1950; pres. State U., Moorhead, Minn., 1955 58; pres. Western Ill. U., 1958-68, pres. emeritus, 1968 88; prof. emeritus polit. sci., pres. Univ. Found., Western Ill. U., 1960-68; pres. Kankakee (Ill.) Community Coll., 1976; prof.-in-residence U. Ariz., 1971-88; cons Saga Foods; dir. Community Bank, Galesburg, Ill. Contbr. articles to profl. jours. Pres. Eastern Conn council Boy Scouts Am., 1955; Pres. Prairie council 1960-65, mem. regional council, 1964-88, mem. nat council, 1960-88; mem. exec. bd. Catalina Council, 1977 pres. United Fund, 1960-62; mem. Gov's Adv. Counc Ill., 1968-72; Dir. Positive Attitude, Inc., Galesburg Regent Lincoln Acad. Ill., Ill. State U., Regency Univs Ill., 1969-88; mem. Ill. Bd. Higher Edn., 1973-88; pres Alpha Gamma Rho Nat. Ednl. Found., 1976-88; interin sec. Ill. Community Coll. Trustees Assn., 1970-7 trustee Univs. Retirement System, 1972-88; hon. lif trustee Ill. Jr. Colls. Recipient Silver Beaver award Bo Scouts Am., 1955, Silver Antelope award, 1964; Ful bright lectr. Burma, 1952-53; Fulbright lectr. Russia 1959; Fulbright lectr. Peru, 1968; Fulbright lectr Europe, 1952, 59, 69, 74, 77; Danforth grant seminar i higher edn. Wash., 1960; Distinguished Alumni awar Mich. State U., 1960; Patriarch award, 1979; Legion c Honor award Internat. Order of DeMolay, 1961; name Man of Yr. Chgo. Alumni Club Alpha Gamma Rhc 1976. Mem. Am. Soc. for Pub. Adminstrn. (pres. Conr chpt. 1946-47, 49-50), Conn. Schoolmasters Assn N.E.A., Sch. Pub. Relations Assn., A.A.A.S., So Adult Edn. (internat. understanding com. 1956-61), So for Acad. Achievement (pres. 1962-74), Alpha Gamm Rho, Alpha Zeta, Pi Kappa Delta, Phi Delta Kapp Alpha Phi Omega, Phi Sigma. Presbyterian. Club Mason (32 degree), Shriner, Rotarian. Home: Tucso Ariz. Died Nov. 27, 1988; interred East Lawn Cemeter Tucson.

KNOPF, ALFRED A., publisher; b. N.Y.C., Sept. 1 1892; s. Samuel and Ida (Japhe) K.; m. Blanche Wol

1916 (dec. June 1966); 1 son, Alfred; m. Helen Norcross Hedrick, 1967. A.B., Columbia U., 1912; L.H.D., Yale U., 1958, Columbia U., 1959, Bucknell U., 1959, Lehigh U., 1960, Coll. William and Mary, 1969, U. Mich., 1969, Bates Coll., 1971, U. Ariz., 1979; LL.D., Brandeis U., 1963; D.Litt., Adelphi U., 1966, U. Chattanooga, 1966, C.W. Post Center, L.I. U., 1973. Founded pub. firm 1915; pres. Alfred A. Knopf Inc., N.Y.C., 1918-57; chmn. bd. Alfred A. Knopf Inc., 1957-72, chmn. bd. emeritus, 1972—. Decorated comendador Ordem Nacional do Cruzeiro do Sul, Brazil; recipient Cornelius Amory Pugsley gold medal for conservation and preservation, 1960; Alexander Hamilton medal Assn. Alumni Columbia U., 1966; Outstanding Service award Nat. Parks Centennial Commn., 1972; Francis Parkman Silver medal Soc. Am. Historians, 1974; Distinguished Service award Assn. Am. Univ. Presses, 1975; Distinguished Achievement award Drexel U. Library Sch. Alumni Assn., 1975; Notable Achievement award Brandeis U., 1977; Machado de Assis medal Brazilian Acad. Letters, 1978. Clubs: Cosmos (Washington); Century Country (Harrison, N.Y.); Lotos (N.Y.C.). Home: Purchase N.Y. Died Aug. 11, 1984.

KNOTT, RICHARD GILLMORE, publisher; b. Louisville, Sept. 21, 1892; s. Richard Wilson and Jennie Amelia (Gillmore) K.; m. Ruth Willard Jones (professional name Ruth Breton), May 17, 1919; 1 dau., Ruth Gillmore. AB, Princeton U., 1912. Reporter Louisville Evening Post, 1912, Washington corr., 1917; pres. Evening Post Co., 1917; editor Evening Post, 1917; pub. Herald Post Co., 1923-24; with Goldman Sachs and Co., from 1933, cons., from 1966. Contbr. on polit. and social topics to mags. Mem. Arts Club (Louisville); Century Club (N.Y.C.). Democrat. Home: Georgetown Conn. †

KNOWLES, GLADYS ELLSWORTH HEINRICH (MRS. AUBREY KNOWLES), political worker; b. Rockville, Nebr., Oct. 25, 1892; d. Arthur Clarke and Ida (Thomas) Ellsworth; m. William Heinrich, Jan. 21, 1919; m. Aubrey Knowles, Dec. 27, 1937. Grad., Boyles Coll. Bus., Omaha, 1912. Various positions as tchr, office worker 1912, operator, owner live stock ranch, from 1933; Rep. committeewoman, state vice chmn. State of Mont., 1932-36; Rep. nat. committeewoman from 1940; mem. arrangement com. Rep. Nat. Conv., 1948, sec. conv., 1956; sec. Rep. Nat. Com, 1952-56. Mem. adv. com. Mont. Tb Assn.; bd. dirs. Mont. Field Army for Control Cancer. Recipient citation for war fund work nat. ARC, honor for outstanding ARC work Matrix Honor Table of Mont. State U.; named Woman of Yr. Mont. U., 1955. Mem. Missoula Bus. and Profl. Woman's Club (state legis. chmn. 1955), Mont. Fedn. Woman's Clubs (state scholarship chmn., pres. 1936-38, v.p. 1932-36), Gen. Fedn. Woman's Clubs (bd. dirs. 1938-40), Missoula Woman's Club (civic chmn.), Colonial Dames of 17th Century, DAR, PEO, Zonta. Home: Billings Mont. †

KNOWLES, HARVEY COLES, business executive; b. N.Y.C., Mar. 11, 1891; s. Andrew A. and Anna (Coles) K.; m. Adele Fitzpatrick, 1914; children: Harvey Coles, Jean Knowles Goodman. PhB, Yale U., 1912. Gen. supt. charge factories and mills Procter and Gamble Co., 1921, gen. mfg. mgr., 1930, v.p., dir., from 1942; v.p. Procter & Gamble Def. Corp. oper. Wolf Creek Ordnance Plant and Gulf Ordnance Plant, World War II; bd. dirs. Armco Steel Corp., Cin. Milling Machine Co.; chmn. high explosive loading adv. com. Safety and Secutiry Br., War Dept.; chmn. civilian adv. panel to Chief of Ordnance. Dir. Herman Schneider Found. Recipient Rice Gold Medal for prodn. arty. ammunition World War II, Gold medal ASME, 1950. Mem. Am. Ordnance Assn. (v.p., dir.), Yale Engring. Assn. (v.p., Ohio placement com.), Queen City Club, Commercial Club, Commonwealth Club, Optimist Club, Yale Club, St. Anthony Club, University Club, Vineyard Haven Yacht Club, Cin. Country Club, Seawanhaka-Corinthian Yacht Club. Home: Cincinnati Ohio. †

KNOWLES, HUGH SHALER, engineering executive; b. Hynes, Iowa, Sept. 23, 1904; s. Harry Holmes and Margaret (Heacock) K.; m. Josephine Knotts, Aug. 5, 1928; children: James, Margaret (Mrs. Schink), Katherine (Mrs. Strasberg). Student, Ala. Poly. Inst., 1920-21; AB, Columbia U., 1928; postgrad., U. Chgo., 1930-34. Dept. editor Popular Radio, N.Y.C., 1924-25; assoc. radio editor N.Y. Herald Tribune, 1927-28; engr. Hammarlund Mfg. Co., N.Y.C., 1927-28; gen. mgr. parts div. Silver Marshall, Inc., Chgo., 1928-30; chief engr. Jensen Mfg. Co., Chgo., 1931-50, v.p., 1940-50; lectr. in grad. physics U. Chgo., 1935-36; pvt. practice 1936-88; pres., dir. rsch. Indsl. Rsch. Products, Inc., Elk Grove Village, Ill., 1946-88, Knowles Electronics, Inc., Franklin Park, Ill., 1954-88; chmn. bd. Knowles Electronics, Ltd., Burgess Hill, Eng.; pres. Knotts Edward Corp., Franklin Park, 1965-88, Synchro-Start Products, Inc., 1968-88, Fin. Corp. Ill., 1969-88; mem. U.S. del. Electrotech. Commn. TC29, 1953, 54, head del., 1955, 57; head del U.S. Internat. Orgn. for Standardization TC43, 1955. Author: Acoustics, Loudspeakers, Telephone Recievers and Microphones, Wiley Engineering Handbook Series, 1936, 50, Loudspeakers and Room Acoustics, Henney's Radio Engineering Handbook, 1941, 50, 59; contbr. numerous tech. articles to profl. jours.; inventor in field of acoustics and electronics. Chmn. acoustics panel R & D Bd., U.S. Dept. Def., 1948-50; mem. Acoustical Standards Bd., 1958-60. Fellow IEEE (nat. chmn. PGA 1960-61, chmn. standards com. on electroacoustics 1938-41), Acoustical Soc. Am. (exec. coun. 1942-44, pres. 1945-47), Chgo. Radio Engrs. (past pres.), Radio Mfrs. Assn. (chmn. standards com. on sound equipment 1931-41, chmn. sound equipment sect. 1945-47), NRC (exec. com. sci. div. 1950-51), Am. Inst. Physics (gov. bd. 1951-58, exec. com. 1954-58), Nat. Acad. Engrs., Audio Engring. Soc. (pres. 1965-66), River Forest Tennis Club. Congregationalist. Home: Elgin Ill. Died Apr. 21, 1988.

KNUTSON, HERBERT CLAUS, entomologist, zoologist, educator; b. Crawfordsville, Iowa, Sept. 6, 1915; s. Frank John and Alta Pearl (Hough) K.; m. Helen Lambley, Sept. 14, 1939; 1 child, Kevin Thomas. AB, Iowa Wesleyan Coll., 1936; MS, So. Meth. U., 1937; PhD, U. Minn., 1941. Instr. biology So. Meth. U., 1939-40; instr. zoology U. R.I., 1942-43, asst. prof., 1946-48, assoc. prof., head dept. zoology, 1948-51, prof., head dept., 1951-53; adminstr. R.I. Div. Entomology and Plant Industry, 1946-48; prof., head dept. entomology, chief entomologist Kans. Agrl. Expt. Sta., Kans. State U., 1953-76, profl. entomologist, 1976-86; entomologist Kans. Entomol. Commn., 1953-63; mem. Nat. Plant Bd., 1956-59; spl. cons. USPHS; examiner Ednl. Testing Svc., Coll. Entrance Exam. Bd., Princeton, N.J., 1949-54; del. Internat. Congress Entomology, Canberra, Australia, 1972, Symposium de Acridiologia, St. Martin de los Angeles, Argentina, 1976; participant Insect-Hostplant Symposium, Slough, Eng., 1978, III Simposio Internacional de Acridiologia, Maracay, Venezuela, 1981. Contbr. articles to tech. jours. Lt. comdr. USPHS, 1943-46. Recipient Alumni Merit award Iowa Wesleyan Coll., 1961. Mem. Entomol. Soc. Am. (governing bd. 1962-65, pres. North Cen. br. 1970-71), kans. Entomol. Soc. (pres.), Assn. d'Acridologia, Masons, Shriners, Rotary, Sigma Xi, Lambda Chi Alpha, Phi Kappa Phi, Phi Sigma, Gamma Sigma Delta. Home: Manhattan Kans. Died Jan. 24, 1986.

KOCH, HARLAN CLIFFORD, education educator, university dean; b. Barrs Mills, Ohio, July 9, 1891; s. George and Cora (Penrod) K.; m. Cora M. Bechtol, 1912 (dec.); m. Leola Royce MvKinley, 1948. AB, Ohio U., 1919; AM, Ohio State U., 1923, PhD, 1926; LHD (hon.), No. Mich. Coll., 1960. Tchr. Ohio schs., 1909-14; prin. Mt. Vernon (Ohio) High Sch., 1919-24; rsch. assoc. Bur. Ednl. Rsch. Ohio State U., 1924-26; assoc. prof. secondary edn. U. Nebr., 1926-28, prof., 1928-34, chmn. dept. secondary edn., 1933-34; asst. dir. Bur. Cooperation with Edn. Insts. U. Mich., 1934-44, prof. edn., 1939-61, asst. dean grad. sch., 1949-58, assoc. dean., 1958-61, emeritus, from 1961; ednl. advisor Western Res. Acad., Hudson, Ohio, 1948-61. Recipient Disting. Alumni award Ohio U., 1960. Fellow AAAS; mem. AAUP (pres. Mich. chpt. 1948-49), Am. Ednl. Rsch. Assn., Am. Assn. Advancement Edn., Nat. Soc. Study Edn., Nat. Vocat. Guidance Assn., Nat. Soc. Coll. Tchrs. Edn., Mich. Acad. Arts and Scis, Mich. Psychol. Assn., N. Central Assn. Colls. and Secondary Schs. (exec. com., chmn. pub. relations 1954-60, Membership award 1959, editor N. Central Quar., 1941-60, mem. Mich. state com., chmn. 1935-40), Mich. Coll. Assn. (v.p. 1942-44), Rotary, University Club, Phi Beta Kappa, Phi Kappa Phi, Phi Delta Kappa (Service award 1961), Tau Kappa Alpha, Lambda Chi Alpha. Home: Ann Arbor Mich. †

KOCH, RICHARD, architect; b. New Orleans, June 9, 1889; s. Julius and Anna (Frotscher) K. BA, Tulane U., 1910; student, Atelier Bernier, Paris, 1911-12. Architect, mem. Armstrong & Koch, New Orleans, 1916-35; pvt. practice 1935-55; ptnr. Richard Koch and Samuel Wilson, Jr., New Orleans, from 1955; dist. officer Historic Am. Bldgs. Survey of La.; pres. La. State Bd. Archtl. Examiners; pres. Nat. Archtl. Accrediting Bd. Chmn. Zoning Bd. Appeals and Adjustment, New Orleans; past 2d v.p. Isaac Delgado Mus. Art. 1st lt. USAAF, 1916-18. Recipient Silver medal Archtl. League N.Y., 1938. Fellow AIA (past dir. Gulf States dist.; mem. NAD. Home: New Orleans La. †

KOCHENDORFER, FRED DANIEL, government space agency manager, engineer; b. Hoboken, N.J., Nov. 9, 1921; s. August Fred and Freda (Buettner) K.; m. Anna Mary Myers, Feb. 12, 1977; children: David Alan, Robert Brian, Jill Nadine. M.E., Stevens Inst. Tech., 1943; M.S.M.E., M.I.T., 1949. With NACA (later NASA), 1943-63, 70-85; mgr. Initial Def. Communications Satellite Program at Philco Ford Co., 1963-70; mgr. Pioneer and Helios Programs Hdqrs. NASA, Washington, 1970-85; advanced studies mgr. Office of Space Flight Hdqrs. NASA, 1970-80. Author numerous profl. reports. Recipient Exceptional Service award NASA. Fellow AIAA (assoc.). Died Sept. 14, 1988, buried Davidsonville, Mo.

KOCUREK, LOUIS JOE, investment company executive; b. Dime Box, Tex., Dec. 31, 1906; s. Joe L. and Adela (Bordovsky) K.; m. Millie Matcek, Nov. 19, 1932; children: Louis Joe, David Carl, Richard John, Mary Ann, Thomas Michael. BBA, U. Tex., 1929. With Mercantile Securities Co., Dallas, 1929-31; with Rauscher, Pierce Securities Corp., Dallas, from 1931, v.p., mgr., San Antonio, 1934-70, vice chmn., 1969-75, vice chmn. emeritus, from 1975; bd. dirs. Allegheny Corp., 1961-63. Pres. San Antonio Symphony, 1957-59, mem. bd. dirs., chmn. bd., 1961-62; bd. dirs. Santa Rosa Children's Hosp., Cancer Therapy Rsch. Ctr. Decorated Knight of Malta, 1966. Mem. San Antonio Country Club, San Antonio Club, St. Anthony's Club, Oak Hils Country Club. Home: San Antonio Tex. Died Apr. 18, 1982, buried Holy Cross Cemetery, San Antonio.

KOEPPEL, DONALD ALLEN, business executive; b. Chgo., Oct. 17, 1917; s. Joseph John and Ethel Mae (Cowley) K.; m. Gloria Lorraine Allan, Mar. 20, 1948; children—Bruce Allan, John Paul, Robert James. B.S., Northwestern U., 1949; J.D., Chgo. Kent Coll. Law, 1954. Bar: Ill. bar 1955. Mgmt. trainee Swift & Co., Chgo., 1937-42; gen. counsel, sec. Belnap & Thompson Co., Chgo., 1947-56; pres., dir. Blue Chip Stamps, Los Angeles, 1956-87; past dir. Buffalo Evening News, Precision Steel Warehouse; Inc. Past chmn. Los Angeles Regional Purchasing Council; bd. dirs., past pres. Cancer Research Assocs., U. So. Calif. Med. Center.; past trustee, mem. exec. com. U. Redlands; past bd. dirs. Hispanic Urban Center, Los Angeles; past pres. Los Angeles Urban Coalition. Served with U.S. Army, 1943-46. Decorated Bronze Star medal. Mem. Ill., Chgo. bar assns., Los Angeles C. of C. (past dir.), Walnut Elephant. Congregationalist. Club: Rotary (Los Angeles) (past pres.). Home: Arcadia Calif. Died Feb. 14, 1987.

KOHLBERG, LAWRENCE, psychology and human development educator; b. Bronxville, N.Y., Oct. 25, 1927; s. Alfred and Charlotte (Albrecht) K.; m. Lucille Stigberg, June 12, 1955; children: David E., Steven A. AB, U. Chgo., 1948, PhD, 1958. Asst. prof. psychology Yale U., 1956-61; fellow Ctr. Advanced Study of Behavioral Sci., 1961-62; asst. prof. to assoc. prof. psychology and human development U. Chgo., 1962-67; prof. edn. and social psychology Harvard U., 1967-87. Author: Moral Development and Moral Education, 1973. Fellow Am. Psychol. Assn.; mem. Soc. Rsch. in Child Devel. Home: Brookline Mass. Died Jan. 1987.

KOHN, HANS, history educator; b. Prague, Czechoslovakia, Sept. 15, 1891; came to U.S., 1933; s. Solomon E. and Berta (Fischer) K.; m. Yetty Wahl, Apr. 16, 1921; 1 child, Immanuel. JD, German U. Praha, 1923; DHL (hon.), Colby Coll., 1958; LLD (hon.), Am. Internat. Coll., 1962, U. Denver, 1963. Lectr. New Sch. Social Rsch., N.Y.C., from 1933; prof. history Smith Coll., 1934-41, Sydenham Clark Parsons prof. history, 1941-49; prof. history CCNY, 1949-62, emeritus, from 1962; prof. history St. Joseph's Coll., Phila., 1965-66; mem. Fgn. Policy Rsch. Inst., U. Pa., 1955-66; vis. prof., lectr. numerous univs. including Harvard U., U. Tex., from, 1935; Harris Found. lectr., U. Chgo., 1935; Moore Found. lectr., Dartmouth Coll., 1940; Fenton Found. lectr., U. Buffalo, 1943; Merrick lectr., Ohio Wesleyan U., 1944, Harris Found. lectr., Northwestern U., 1945-56; 1st Mabell Smith Douglas lectr., N.J. Coll. for Women, 1947; John Hay Whitney vis. prof., U. Denver, 1962-63. Author numerous books including: Nationalism and Liberty, 1956, American Nationalism, 1957, Basic History of Modern Russia, 1957, West Germany, New Era for German People, 1958, Mind of Germany, 1960, The Age of Nationalism, The First Era of Global History, 9162, Reflections on Modern History, The Historian and Human Responsibility, 1963, Ideas and Institutions in Europe, 1848-1960, 1963, Living in a World Revolution, 1964, Absolutism and Democracy, 1965, Prelude to Nation-States, 1967, Nationalism and Realism, 1967, Europe in Crisis, 1850-1914, : State, Class, Faith, 1969; mem. editorial bd. Jour. History of Ideas; contbr. articles to Ency. Britannica, Ency. Social Scis., Internat. Ency. Social Scis. Guggenheim fellow, 1940, Ctr. Advanced Study fellow, Wesleyan U., 1963-64; Fulbright prof. Free Univ., Berlin, 1968-69. Mem. Coun. Fgn. Relations, Internat. Soc. History Ideas (hon. pres.), Phi Beta Kappa, Phi Alpha Theta. Home: Philadelphia Pa. †

KOHN, ROBERT ROTHENBERG, medical educator; b. Cleve., June 14, 1925; s. Jacob Bertholdt and Carrie (Rothenberg) K.; m. Vilma Lavetti, July 27, 1952; children: Deborah D., Justin M., Steven M., Peter Lavetti. BS, U. Wis., 1949; PHD, U. Mich., 1953; MD, Western Res. U., 1957. Diplomate Am. Bd. Pathology. NSF fellow 1952-53, resident, USPHS fellow pathology, 1957-60; assoc. prof. pathology Case Western Res. U. Sch. Medicine, Cleve., 1964-70, prof. pathology, 1970-84, prin. adminstr. program aging rsch. and tng., 1962-77; Bd. sci. counselors Nat. Inst. Aging, 1977-78. Author numerous articles in field. With USNR, 1943-46. Mem. AAAS, Am. Assn., Pathologists, Gerontol. Soc., Sigma Xi, Alpha Omega Alpha. Home: Cleveland Ohio. Died March 28, 1984.

KOHNLE, EDWARD LEROY, corporate executive; b. Dayton, Ohio, Feb. 26, 1892; s. Frederick and Laura Ophelia (Hildabolt) K.; m. Esther Bridge, June 21, 1916; children: John Edward, Phyllis Ann (Mrs. Richard C. Castor). Student, U. Pa., 1911-13. With Monarch Marking System, from 1912, sec.-treas., bd. dirs., 1920-51, pres., 1951-63, chmn. bd., 1963-67, chmn. emeritus, from 1967; dir. emeritus Dayton Power & Light Co., 1st Nat. Bank; bd. dirs. State Fidelity, Fed. Savs. & Loan Assn. Pres. Dayton YMCA, 1936-40; mem. world's com. YMCA, 1937-42; mem. nat. exec. bd. Boy Scouts Am., from 1953, pres. Miami Valley coun., 1953-55, 64-65; bd. dirs. Jr. Achievement, pres., 1965; trustee Miami Valley Hosp., Wilmington Coll., 1957-60. 1st lt. CAC, U.S. Army, 1918-25. Recipient Silver Beaver award Boy Scouts Am., 1938, Silver Antelope award Boy Scouts Am., 1946, Silver Buffalo award Boy Scouts Am., 1958; Dayton YMCA leaders fellow, 1953. Mem. C. of C. (pres. 1935-36), Ohio Soc. N.Y., Ch. Fedn. Dayton (v.p.), Dayton Philharm. Assn. (bd. dirs.), Masons (33 degree), Rotary (past pres.), Engineers Cluib, Kappa Sigma. Baptist. Home: Kettering Ohio. Deceased.

KOKOSCHKA, OSKAR, artist, writer; b. Pochlarn, Austria, Mar. 1, 1886. Student, Vienna Sch. Arts and Crafts; DLitt, Oxford U. Designer decorative cards and fans Wiener Werkstatte; prof. Dresden Acad., 1920; went to Switzerland, 1909, then to Berlin; influenced by Expressionist movement; traveled in Eng., Switzerland, France, Spain, Italy, North Africa, Near East, 1924-31, then returned to Vienna, Prague, Czechoslovakia; went to Eng., 1938-58; vis. prof. Boston U., 1948; established Internat. Summer Sch., Salzburg, Austria, 1953. Exhibited painting, drawings and lithographs, also sculpture 1st Vienna Art Exhbn., 1908, leading European cities, N.Y.C., London, 1963; represented in permanent collections Albright Art Gallery, Buffalo Mus. Modern Art, Phillips Meml. Gallery, Washington, numerous others; author: (plays) Mörder, Hoffnung der Franen, 1907, Der brennende Dornbusch, 1911, Hiob, 1911, Orpheus and Eurydice, 1916, A Sea Ringed with Visions, 1962. Home: Villeuve Vaud Switzerland. †

KOLBE, FRANK FREDERICK, coal company executive; b. Ann Arbor, Mich., Dec. 4, 1892; s. Charles Frederick and Henrietta Amalia K.; m. Marjorie Heartt, 1922; children: Frederick, Elizabeth. AB, U. Mich., 1914, AM, 1917. Instr. econs. U. Mich., 1914-17, Nat. City Co., 1917, War Credits Bd., Washington, 1918; asst. treas. Gen. Motors Corp., 1922-29; pres. Aldebaran Corp., 1929-36, Pathe Film Corp., 1935-37; ptnr. Young, Kolbe & Co, 1932-37; pres. United Elect. Coal Cos., 1939-59, chmn., 1959-62, dir., 1935-63; bd. dirs. Clark Equipment Co. Hon. dir. Nat. Coal Assn.; sr. coun. Chgo. Assn. Commerce and Industry. Mem. Am. Inst. Mining and Metall. Engrs., Am. Econ. Assn., Chicago Club, Indian Hill Club, Adventurers Club. Home: Winnetka Ill. †

KOLLER, HERBERT RICHARD, information scientist; b. Cleve., Sept. 5, 1921; s. Daniel D. and Frieda A. (Wiener) K.; m. Shirley Ann Leavitt, Mar. 7, 1943; children: Donald Lee, Susan Lizbeth (Mrs. Willard C. VanHorne), Laura Frances. B.S. cum laude in Chemistry, Case-Western Res. U., 1942; J.D., Am. U., 1952. Chemist Indsl. Rayon Co., 1942-43; patent examiner, information systems research and devel. U.S. Patent Office, 1943-66; dir. client services EBS Mgmt. Cons., Washington, 1966-68; prin. info. scientist Leasco Systems & Research Corp., Bethesda, Md., 1968-69; exec. dir. Am. Soc. Information Sci., Washington, 1969-73; prin. asso. Moshman Assos., Inc., Bethesda, 1973-74; legal editor Bur. Nat. Affairs, Washington, 1975-76; with chem. documentation group U.S. Patent and Trademark Office, 1977-88; Research asso. Patent, Trademark and Copyright Research Inst., George Washington U., 1968-72; cons., lectr. in field. Contbr. articles to profl. jours. Sci. and tech. fellow Dept. Commerce, 1964-65. Fellow AAAS; Mem. Am. Chem. Soc., Assn. Computing Machinery, Am. Soc. Information Sci., Zeta Beta Tau. Home: Washington D.C. Died June 6, 1988; cremated.

KOLODIN, IRVING, music critic, educator; b. N.Y.C., Feb. 22, 1908; s. Benjamin and Leah (Geller) K.; m. Irma Levy, June 19, 1935 (div. 1970); stepchildren: Susan Zeckendorf, William Zeckendorf, Jr. Ed. grammar and high sch., Newark; student, Inst. Mus. Art, N.Y.C., 1927-31. Instr. harmony and theory Inst. Mus. Art, 1930-31; with N.Y. Sun, 1932-50; assoc. music critic and condr. New Records Column, 1936-50; lectr. on music criticism Juilliard Summer Sch., 1938, 39; mem. faculty Juilliard Sch. Music, 1968-88; program annotator N.Y. Philharm. Orch., 1953-58; music editor and critic to Sun, 1945-50; editor Recordings supplement of Saturday Rev. Lit., 1947-88; music editor Saturday Rev. Lit., 1950-52; assoc. editor Saturday Rev., 1952-88; contbr. Sunday edit. Newsday, Garden City, N.Y., 1978-88; v.p., editor Nat. Arts Group, Ltd., N.Y.C. Author: Metropolitan Opera, 1936, rev. edit., 1939, (with Benny Goodman) The Kingdom of Swing, 1939, The Critical Composer, 1940, Guide to Recorded Music, 1941, rev. edit., 1946, 49, 55, Story of the Metropolitan Opera, 1953, Composer as Listener, 1958, The Musical Life, 1958, Metropolitan Opera 1883-1966, 1966, The Continuity of Music, 1969, Interior Beethoven: A Biography of Music, 1974, The Opera Omnibus: Four Centuries of Critical Give and Take, 1976, In Quest of Music: Met. Opera Centennial Edit., 1966-84; contbg. author various mags. Entered mil. service, 1943; mem. staff Official Guide to AAF and Air Force mag., 1943-45. Home: New York N.Y. Died Apr. 29, 1988.

KOONTZ, ELIZABETH DUNCAN (MRS. HARRY LEE KOONTZ), government official, educator; b. Salisbury, N.C., June 3, 1919; d. Samuel Edward and Lena (Jordan) Duncan; m. Harry Lee Koontz, Nov. 26, 1947 (dec. 1986). AB, Linvingstone Coll., 1938, LHD (hon.), 1967; MA, Atlanta U., 1941, LittD (hon.); PhD (hon.), Pacific U., Bryant Coll.; EdD (hon.), Howard U.; LLD (hon.), Am. U.; LHD (hon.), Coppin State Coll.; HHD (hon.), Ea. Mich. U.; ScD in Edn. (hon.), Northeastern U. Tchr. Harnett County Tng. Sch., Dunn, N.C., 1938-40, Aggrev Meml. Sch., Landis, N.C., 1940-41, 14th St. Sch., Winston-Salem, N.C., 1941-45, Price High Sch., Salisbury, 1945-49, Monroe High Sch., 1949-65; tchr. spl. edn. Price Jr.-Sr. High Sch., 1965-68; pres. NEA, 1968-69; dir. Women's Bur., Dept. Labor, Washington, 1969-73; U.S. del. to UN Commn. Status of Woemn, Dept. Labor, 1975; coordinator nutrition programs N.C. Dept. Human Resources, 1973-75; asst. state supt. schs. N.C., 1975-82; mem. Youth Commn., Rowan County. N.C., 1955-57. Recipient Disting. Alumni medallion for achievement Livingstone Coll., Disting. Tchr. award Civitan Club, Salisbury, Disting. Citizenship award N.C. Dist. Civitan Internat. Mem. Rowan County Negro Civic League, N.C. Tchrs. Assn., Salisbury Tchrs. Assn., N.C. Classroom Tchrs. (pres. 1958-62), NEA (pres. dept. classroom tchrs. 1965-66), Zeta Phi Beta. Home: Salisbury N.C. Died Jan. 6, 1989.

KOOP, THEODORE FREDERICK, broadcasting executive; b. Monticello, Iowa, Mar. 9, 1907; s. Frederick William and Laura Abby (Hicks) K. A.B., Iowa U., 1928; L.H.D. (hon.), Iowa Wesleyan U., 1970. Reporter, editor AP, Des Moines, New Haven, N.Y.C. and Washington, 1928-41; mem. editorial staff Nat. Geog. Soc., Washington, 1941, 46-47; spl. asst. to U.S. Dir. Censorship, 1942-45, asst. dir. censorship, dept. dir., 1945; dir. news and pub. affairs CBS, Washington, 1948-61; v.p. CBS, 1961-71; Washington dir. Radio-TV News Dirs. Assn., 1972-76; chmn. Washington Journalism Center, 1973-78. Author: Weapon of Silence, 1946; Contbr. to: Dateline: Washington, 1949, Ethics, Morality and the Media, 1980. Served to lt. USNR, 1942-45. Mem. Phi Beta Kappa, Delta Upsilon, Sigma Delta Chi. Clubs: Gridiron (Washington), Nat. Press (Washington) (pres. 1953). Home: Washington D.C. Died July 7, 1988.

KORTH, EUGENE HENRY, history educator, priest; b. Mankato, Minn., Nov. 23, 1917; s. Simon G. and Anna (Deglman) K. AB in Classics, St. Louis U., 1941, PhL in Philosophy, 1943, MA in History, 1946, STL in Theology, 1950; PhD in History, U. Tex., 1956. Ordained priest Roman Catholic Ch., 1949. Joined Soc. of Jesus 1936; mem. faculty St. Louis U. High Sch., 1943-46; Doherty Found. fellow for rsch. in Latin Am. 1953-54; mem. faculty Marquette U., 1956-68, chmn. dept. history, 1958-60, assoc. prof., 1962-68, asst. univ. archivist, 1983-87; prof. history U. Detroit, 1969-83, chmn. dept. history, 1973-77; ednl. asst. Cath. U., Salta, Argentina, 1964-87, acting dean, 1967-69. Mem. Am. Assn. Higher Edn., Assn. Am. Colls., North Cen. Assn., NEA, Nat. Cath. Ednl. Assn., Jesuit Ednl. Assn., Am., Cath., Jesuit hist. assns., Conf. Latin Am. Hist., Mich. Hist. Soc., Phi Alpha Theta, Pi Gamma Mu, Sigma Delta Pi. Home: Milwaukee Wis. Died July 28, 1987; buried Calvary Cemetery, Milw.

KOSANKE, WILLIAM HENRY, farmer, rancher, cooperative administrator; b. Lone Wolf, Okla., Dec. 2, 1906; s. Herman and Minnie (Schaufele) K.; m. Emma Dunn, Aug. 6, 1930; 1 child, Bill Kent. BS, Okla. State U., 1930. Farmer, rancher Lone Wolf, 1930-86; mgr. Wrights Poultry Hatchery, Hobart, Okla., 1930-32; instr. Vet.'s Tng. Program, Lone Wolf, 1947-48; mgr. Planters' Coop. Assn. and Peoples' Coop. Funeral Home, Lone Wolf, 1956-73; pres. Producers Coop. Oil Mill, Oklahoma City, 1946-78, Union Equity Coop. Exchange, Enid, Okla., 1965-79; dir. Nat. Council Farmer Coops., Washington, 1977-78. Bd. dirs. Kiowa County Bd. Health, 1970-86, Kiowa County FHA, 1974-77; trustee Midwest Christian Coll., Oklahoma City, 1960-66; Kiowa County commr. (appointee Gov. Geo. Nigh), interim term, 1981-82. Recipient citation Okla. State U., 1969. Mem. Lions, Masons, Eastern Star. Democrat. Mem. Christian Ch. Home: Lone Wolf Okla. Died Aug. 27, 1986; buried Lone Wolf (Okla.) Cemetery.

KOSTER, HENRY, motion picture director; b. Berlin, May 1, 1905; came to U.S., 1936, naturalized, 1944.; s. Albert and Emma (Salomon) Kosterlitz; m. Cathrin Kiraly, 1935; 1 child, Robert;; m. Peggy Moran, Oct. 30, 1942; children: Nicolas, Peter. Student art schs., Berlin and Vienna (Austria), 1921-23. Author screenplays, dir. in Europe for Ufa, Terra, Aafa, European Universal, also Sascha-Tobis; dir. for Universal Pictures, 1936-42, Goldwyn, Warner Bros., 1946-47, 20th Century Fox, 1947-65, Metro-Goldwyn-Mayer, 1943-45, 65-88; dir. motion pictures including 100 Men and a Girl, Rage of Paris, It Started with Eve, Spring Parade, Music for Millions, Two Sisters from Boston, The Bishop's Wife, Come to the Stable, Inspector General, Belvedere Rings the Bell, Elopement, O. Henry's Full House, Stars and Stripes Forever, My Cousin Rachel, The Robe, Desiree, A Man Called Peter, Good Morning Miss Dove, Power and the Prize, My Man Godfrey, Flower Drum Song, Mr. Hobbs Takes a Vacation, Take Her, She's Mine, Dear Brigitte, The Singing Nun. Mem. Dirs. Guild Am. Home: Pacific Palisades Calif. Died Sept. 21, 1988.

KOTSHER, BENJAMIN JOHN, publisher; b. N.Y.C., Oct. 19, 1922; s. Jakob J. and Anne Deborah (Schwartz) K.; m. Helen, May 14, 1950; children—Paul Scott, Carol Lyn Kotsher Marden. B.A., NYU, 1943. Vice pres. Palmerton Pub. Co., NYC, 1960-72, pres., 1972-81; exec. v.p. Communication Channels, Inc., NYC, 1972-81, pres., 1981-87, dir., 1981-87; bd. dirs. Argus Press Holdings, Inc., Atlanta, Bus. Publs. Audit of Circulation Inc., N.Y.C., Premier Communications Inc., Atlanta, Second Communications Inc., Atlanta. Contbr. articles to profl. jours. Served to 1st lt. U.S. Army, 1942-46. Democrat. Jewish. Home: Atlanta Ga. Died July 21, 1987; buried Atlanta.

KOZELKA, RICHARD L., educator, academic administrator; b. Chgo., Aug. 19, 1899; s. Frank J. and Barbara (Cizek) K.; m. Winifred Bradley, Aug. 15, 1923; children: Richard Bradley, Robert Marvin. AB, Beloit Coll., 1921, LLD, 1950; MA, U. Chgo., 1926; PhD, U. Minn., 1931. Instr. econs. U. Minn., 1923-31, asst. prof., 1931-37, assoc. prof., 1937-44, acting dean Sch. Bus. Adminstrn., prof. econs. and statistics, 1944-45, dean, 1945-60, prof. bus. adminstrn. Author: Business Fluctuations in the Northwest, 1932, Industrial Trends in Minnesota, 1899-1937, 1938, A Procedure for Community Postwar Planning-Jobs and Production at War's End-Albert Lea, Minnesota, Charts a Course, 1943, Professional Education for Business Administration, 1953. 2d lt. U.S. Army, 1918. Recipient Social Sci. Rsch. Council Fellowship for Fgn. Study, 1934-45; Disting. Service Citation Beloit Coll., 1946. Mem. Am. Statis. Assn., Am. Assn. Collegiate Schs. of Bus. (pres. 1952), Am. Econ. Assn., Am. Mktg. Assn., Econometric Soc., Soc. Advancement of Mgmt., Royal Econ. Soc., Nat. Bur. Econ. Rsch., Campus Club, Rotary, Tau Kappa Epsilon, Beta Gamma Sigma (pres. 1955-58). Home: Minneapolis Minn. Died Nov. 12, 1985.

KRAEMER, CHARLES EDGAR STANBERRY, clergyman, academic administrator; b. Bonham, Tex., Apr. 25, 1909; s. Frederick Adolphus and Harriet (Phillips) K.; m. Beryl Birdsong, Sept. 9, 1932; children: Fred B., Jane Scott, Charles Phillips. AB, Davidson Coll., 1931, DD, 1947; BD, Louisville Presbyn. Theol. Sem., 1934; STM, Andover-Newton Theol. Sch., 1939. Ordained to ministry Presbyn. Ch. USA, 1934. Pastor chs. Hawesville, Ky., 1934-35, North Kansas City, Mo., 1935-41, Leland, Miss., 1941-45; pastor chs. 1st Ch., Charlotte, N.C., 1945-54; pres. Presbyn. Sch. Christian Edn., Richmond, Va., 1954-74; vis. prof. religion, Taiwan, 1964, Brazil, 1958, Mexico, 1961, Russia, 1969, Britain, 1969; moderator Gen. Assembly Presbyn. Ch. US, 1973-74, chmn. bd. ,1974-75; dir. ch. relations Davidson Coll., also Assn. US Presbyn. Colls; mem. pastoral, ednl. commns. Nat. Council Chs.; chmn. design com. Covenant Life Curriculum, 1957. Trustee Peace Coll., Montreat Coll., Christian Children's Fund. Earhart fellow clin. pastoral study Andover-Newton (Mass.) Gen. Boston Psychopathic hosps., 1939-39. Mem. Am. Assn. Schs. Religious Edn. (pres. 1958), Charlotte Mental Health Assn., Kiwanis (v.p. Richmond 1974), Rotary. Home: Charlotte N.C. Died June 23, 1988.

KRAFT, CHARLES HALL, statistics educator, researcher; b. Chgo., Mar. 20, 1924; s. Robert Hollo and Fanny Elizabeth (Hall) K.; m. Constance van Eeden, Dec. 8, 1960; children: Kathleen, Sally, Harry, Penny, Kari. Student, Hamilton Coll., 1943-44; BA, Mich. State U., 1948, MA, 1949; PhD, U. Calif., Berkeley, 1954. Acting asst. math. U. Calif., Berkeley, 1954-56; assoc. prof. Mich. State U., 1956-61, U. Minn., 1961-65; prof. U. Montreal, 1965-85. Author: (with C. van Eeden) Nonparametric Introduction to Statistics, 1968; assoc. editor: Ann. Math. Statistics, 1974-77; contbr. articles to statis. jours., 1955-85. Served wtih USAAF, 1942-45. Fellow AAAS, Inst. Math. Stats.; mem. Am. Statis. Assn., Can. Statis. Soc., Can. Math. Soc. Died Mar. 17, 1985; buried Hudson, Mich.

KRAFT, JOSEPH, journalist; b. South Orange, N.J., Sept. 4, 1924; s. David Harry and Sophie (Surasky) K.; m. Polly Winton, Jan. 6, 1960. AB, Columbia U., 1947; postgrad., Princeton U., 1948-49, Inst. Advanced Study, 1950-51; LLD (hon.), Claremont Grad Sch., 1973. Editorial writer Washington Post, 1951-52; staff writer NY Times, 1953-57; Washington corr; with Harper's mag., 1962-65; syndicated columnist Washington Post, L.A. Times, 1963-86. Author: The Struggle for Algeria, 1961, The Grand Design, 1962, Profiles in Power, 1966, The Chinese Difference, 1973; contbr. to New Yorker, others. Mem. panel Presdl. Debates, 1976. With AUS, 1943-46. Decorated chevalier French Legion of Honor. Mem. Council Fgn. Relations, Met. Gridiron Club, Century Club, Phi Beta Kappa. Home: Washington D.C. Died Jan. 10, 1986.

KRAMER, AMIHUD, horticulturist; b. Austria-Hungary, May 7, 1913; came to U.S., 1921; naturalized, 1926; s. Nathan and Sabina (Puder) K.; m. Diana Stevan, June 3, 1939; children: John B., Marc S. BS, U. Md., 1938, MS, 1939, PhD, 1942. Coop agt. Soil Conservation Service, Washington, 1938-40; food chemist Nat. Canners Assn., Washington, 1941-43; mem. Food and Nutrition Bd., Nat. Acad. Scis., NRC, 1943-45; mem. faculty U. Md., 1945-81, prof. horticulture and food sci., 1948-81; co-founder, dir. Internat. Foods Cons., 1962; sci. adviser, lab. dir. Refrigeration Rsch.

Found.; mem. coms. Nat. Acad. Scis.-NRC; cons., lectr. in field. Author: Quality Control for the Food Industry, 3d edit., 1970, Vol. 2-Applications, 1972, Food and the Consumer, 1973, Texture Measurements, 1974, Systems Analysis for the Food Industry, 1976, also jour. articles and book chpts.; editor Jour. Food Quality, 1977. Bd. dirs. Hillel Found. With Aus, 1943-45. Recipient Woodbury award Am. Assn. Hort. Sci., 1952, 54, Nicholas Appert award Inst. Food Tech., 1976; NSF fellow, 1958; grantee nat., internat. orgns. Fellow AAAS, Am. Soc. Quality Control, Am. Inst. Chemists, Am. Soc. Hort. Sci.; mem. Inst. Food Technologists, ASHRAE, ASTM, Inter Soc. Color Council, Internat. Inst. Refrigeration (v.p. comm. C2), AAUP, Cosmos Club, Cabin John Club, Seven Locks Tennis Club, Sigma Xi, Alpha Zeta, Phi Tau Sigma. Home: Bethesda Md. Died Dec. 8, 1981.

KRAMLICH, BENJAMIN PAUL, supermarket executive; b. Mound City, S.D., July 1, 1891; 1 child, Bernard Peter. Dist. mgr. Safeway Stoers, 1920-31; organizer Piggly Wiggly Super Markets (merged with Consol. Foods Corp., 1956), 1931-56, v.p., dir.; pres., dir. Piggly Wiggly Midwest, from 1938, also several subs.; bd. dirs. Kleins Super Markets, Mays Drug Stores, 1st Nat. Bank Rockford. Home: Rockford Ill. †

KRAUS, HANS PETER, rare book dealer, publisher; b. Vienna, Austria, Oct. 12, 1907; came to U.S., 1939, naturalized, 1945; s. Emil and Hilda (Rix) K.; m. Hanni Zucker Hale, Aug. 28, 1940; children: Mary Ann (Mrs. Mitchell), Barbara (Mrs. Gstalder), Evelyn (Mrs. Rauber), Susan (Mrs. Nakamura), Hans Peter. Student, Acad. Commerce, Vienna; LittD (hon.), U. Bridgeport. Ptnr. H.P. Kraus Co., N.Y.C., 1940-88; pres. Kraus Periodicals, Inc., N.Y.C., 1948-68, Back Issues Corp., 1962-69, Kraus Reprint Corp., 1962-68; chmn. bd. Kraus Thomson Orgn. Ltd., 1968-88. Author: A Pictorial Biography of Sir Francis Drake, 1970, A Rare Book Saga, The Autobiography of H. P. Kraus, 1978. Trustee Yale Library Assn. Decorated chevalier Legion of Honor (France). Mem. bibliog. socs. Am., London, Gutenberg Soc., Grolier Cluib, Goldens Bridge Hounds Club (bd. dirs. North Salem, N.Y. chpt.). Home: Ridgefield Conn. Died Nov. 1, 1988.

KRAUS, LILI, pianist, educator; b. Budapest, Mar. 4, 1908; d. Victor and Irene (Bak) Kraus; student of Zoltan Kodaly, Bela Bartok; student Royal Acad. Music, Budapest, 1915-22, tchrs. diploma, 1925; student of Steuermann, New Acad., Vienna, Austria, 1925-27, M.A., 1927; student Artur Schnabel, Berlin, 1930-34; Mus.D. (hon.), Chgo. Mus. Coll., Roosevelt U., 1969, Williams Coll., 1975; D.H.L. (hon.), Tex. Christian U., 1980; m. Otto Mandl, Oct. 31, 1930 (dec. Aug. 1956); children—Ruth Maria (Mrs. Fergus Pope), Michael Otto Patrick. Pianist with orchs. in Europe, 1926-86, Dutch East Indies, 1940; formed Kraus-Goldberg duo with violinist Szymon Goldberg, 1930's; Japanese prisoner-of-war, 1941-45; pianist in Australia and N.Z., 1945-86, Europe, N. and S. Am., Asia, 1949-86; world tours, appearances with major orchs. and all major European music festivals, 1925-86; gave concert in Eng.'s Canterbury Cathedral, 1st concert ever performed in Brasilia (Brazil); appeared with Salzburg Chamber Orch., Royal Moroccan Mozart Festival, orchestral concert honoring Bertrand Russell's 90th birthday, Royal Festival Hall, London; first to play all 25 Mozart piano concerti in N.Y., 1966-67; premiered newly-discovered Schubert Grazer Fantasy, CBS-TV, 1969; recorded all 25 Mozart piano concerti and complete Mozart piano sonatas for CBS; now recording complete Schubert piano repertoire; lectr. various univs., U.S. and Europe; head piano dept. Cape Town U., South Africa, 1949-50; artist-in-residence Tex. Christian U., 1967-83; adjudicator Van Cliburn Internat. Piano Competition, Tex. Named hon. citizen N.Z., late 1940's; decorated Cross of Honor for Sci. and Art (Austria). Hon. mem. Music Tchrs. Assn. Calif., Sigma Alpha Iota. Author: The Complete Original Cadenzas by W.A. Mozart for His Solo Piano Concertos. Died Nov. 6, 1986; cremated. Home: Celo Farm, nr. Burnsville, N.C. Died Nov. 6, 1986.

KRAUSMAN, ARTHUR HENRY, hardware chain executive; b. Chgo., 1913; grad. Northwestern U., 1936; m. Jean Appelgren, Sept. 21, 1945; children—Jeff, Andrea Buck. Formerly v.p., gen. mgr. Ace Hardware Corp., Chgo., chmn. bd., chief exec. officer. Past pres. Am. Field Services (Park Ridge chpt.); spl. gifts chmn. DuPage unit Am. Cancer Soc. Clubs: Regis, Housewares of Chgo., Central States Hardware. Died Mar. 8, 1987. Home: Kildeer Ill.

KRAUSS, EDWARD CAMPBELL, editorial writer; b. Ottawa, Ohio, Sept. 16, 1883; s. William Charles Glauner and Rebecca Jane (Gordon) K.; m. Myrtle Zopf, Dec. 1, 1909. Student, Ohio State U., 1900-02; AB, U. Mich., 1906. Telegraph editor Toledo Blade, 1906-07; reporter N.Y.C. News Assn., 1907-10; pub. Saranac Lake (N.Y.) News and Daily Item, 1910-19; reporter N.Y. Herald, 1919-21; mem. staff L.A. Times, 1922-58, editorial writer, 1928-58, ret. Mem. SAR, L.A. Athletic Club, Peter Pan Club (Big Bear City, Calif.), Masons. Presbyterian. Home: Los Angeles Calif. †

KREGER, WILLIAM CASTLES, newspaper editor; b. Albia, Iowa, Dec. 18, 1924; s. Don Castles and Mary (Marr) K.; m. Anita Jean Sackrison, Feb. 25, 1950; children: Thomas Castles, Laurie Ann. Reporter Dubuque (Iowa) Telegraph-Herald, 1948-51; with Wall Street Journal, N.Y.C., 1952-81, news editor, 1960-65, asst. mng. editor, 1965-81. With AUS, 1943-45. Mem. Spc. Profl. Journalists, Sigma Delta Chi. Died Aug. 1, 1981.

KREMER, FRANK S(IDNEY), lawyer, insurance executive; b. Estelline, S.D., Oct. 19, 1892; s. F(rank) M. and Sarah (Cliff) K.; m. Helen Robinson, June 26, 1921; 1 child, Hugh Robinson. BS, S.D. State Coll., 1915; LLB, U. Mich., 1918. Bar: S.D. 1918, Minn. 1934. Pvt. practice Watertown, S.D., 1919-31; mem. McFarland & Kremer; sr. atty. USDA, 1931-32; counsel FCA, Mpls., 1932-35; atty. Northwestern Nat. Life Ins. Co., Mpls., 1935-49, asst. counsel, 1949-50, asst. counsel, sec., 1950-52, v.p., sec., from 1952. Lt. U.S. Army, World War I. Mem. Assn. Life Ins. Counsel, Minn., S.D. bar assns., Masons, Shriners, Elks, Kappa Sigma, Phi Delta Phi. Republican. Presbyterian. Home: Minneapolis Minn. †

KREUTZ, OSCAR R., savings and loan association executive; b. Sioux City, Iowa; s. John and Jennie (Pehrson) K.; student schs., Sioux City, Cambridge, Mass.; m. Marion Benton, 1926 (dec. Apr. 1972); m. 2d, Virginia F. Skelton, Oct. 20, 1973; children—Mary Ann Kreutz Dodson, Barbara Jane Kreutz Barrett. Organizer, 1st Fed. Savs. & Loan Assn., Sioux City, 1923, mgr. officer, 1923-33; sec. Iowa Bldg. and Loan League, 1925-33; v.p. Fed. Home Loan Bank Chgo., 1934; chmn. rev. com. Fed. Home Loan Bank Bd., 1934-41; gen. mgr. Fed. Savs. and Loan Ins. Corp., Washington, 1941-44; exec. mgr. Nat. League Insured Savs. Assn., Washington, 1944-53, exec. cons., 1953-54, mem. exec. com., 1953-54; exec. v.p. Fla. Fed. Savs. and Loan Assn. (formerly First Fed. Savs. and Loan Assn.), St. Petersburg, 1953-54, pres., chmn. bd., 1954-68, chmn. bd., 1968-75, chmn. emeritus and cons., 1975-87; hon. v.p. Internat. Union Bldg. Socs. and Savs. Assn. Pres. bd. dirs. United Fund, St. Petersburg, 1956-57; pres. Com. 100, St. Petersburg, 1958-59; pres. St. Petersburg Improvement Found., 1961-62; mem. adv. bd. Abilities Inc. Fla.; hon. bd. dirs. Sci. Center, St. Petersburg, St. Petersburg Symphony Soc.; trustee Eckerd Coll. Named Mr. Sun, Producers of Sunshine Festival of States, 1962. Mem. Fla. Savs. and Loan League (pres. 1961), Nat. Savs. and Loan League (pres. 1960), Suncoasters of St. Petersburg, Inc. (pres.), Navy League U.S., Am. Legion. Clubs: Masons, Rotary, St. Petersburg Yacht, Golden Triangle Civic. Presbyterian. Author: The Way It Happened, 1972. Home: St. Petersburg. Deceased Feb. 15, 1987.

KRIEGER, DOROTHY TERRACE, internist; b. N.Y.C., Feb. 17, 1927; d. Morris Abraham and Esther (Marsh) Terrace; m. C. Wayne Bardin, Aug. 11, 1978; children by previous marriage: James, Nancy. AB summa cum laude, Barnard Coll., 1945; MD, Columbia U., 1949. Diplomate Nat. Bd. Med. Examiners, Am. Bd. Internal Medicine. Intern Mt. Sinai Hosp., N.Y.C., 1949-50, asst. resident in surgery, 1950-52, asst. resident in medicine, 1952-53, chief resident in medicine, 1954-55, mem. staff, 1954-55; pvt. practice specializing in endocrinology N.Y.C.; mem. faculty Mt. Sinai Sch. Medicine, N.Y.C., 1966-85, prof. medicine, 1972-85; dir. div. endocrinology Mt. Sinai Hosp. Endocrinology Lab., N.Y.C., 1973-85; chmn. endocrinology study sect. NIH, Washington, 1980-85; coun. mem. Nat. Inst. on Aging, 1982-85; prin. investigator USPHS grants, 1972-85. Author: Cushing's Disease, 1973-85; editor: Peptide Hormone Assay and Action, 1973-85, ACTH and Related Peptides, 1977, Circadian Rhythms, 1979, Neuroendocrinology, 1980; editor endocrinology sect. Ann. Rev. Physiology, 1980-84; editorial bd.: Jour. Clin. Endocrinology and Metabolism; contbr. over 200 articles to profl. Jours. Fellow ACP; mem. Am. Soc. Clin. Investigation, Assn. Am. Physicians, Endocrine Soc. (v.p. 1974-75). Home: New York N.Y. Died Apr. 2, 1985.

KRISHNAMURTI, JIDDU, religious educator, author, philosopher; b. Madanapalle, S. India, 1895. Ed. privately, Eng. Founder Krishnamurti Found., Ojai, Calif., 1969, Oak Grove Sch., Ojai. Author: Education and the Significance of Life, 1953, The First and Last Freedom, 1954, Commentaries on Living: 1st series, 1956, 2d series, 1958, 3d series, 1960, Life Ahead, 1963, Think on These Things, 1964, Freedom from the Known, 1969, The Only Revolution, 1970, The Urgency of Change, 1971, The Impossible Question, 1973, Beyong Violence, 1973, Flight of the Eagle, 1972, The Awakening of Intelligence, 1973, Beginnings of Learning, 1975, Krishnamurti's Notebook, 1976, Truth and Actuality, 1977, The Wholeness of Life, 1978, Meditations, 1979, Letters to the Schools, 1980, Krishnamurti's Journal, 1981, Questions & Answers, 1982, The Network of Thought, 1983. Home: Ojai Calif. Deceased.

KROEPSCH, ROBERT HAYDEN, education administrator, educator; b. Cambridge, Mass., Oct. 21, 1912; s. Robert Karl and Laura Melissa (Ringer) K.; m. Ruth Catherine Maurice, Aug. 13, 1945. AB, Bates Coll., 1933, LLD, 1971; EdM, Harvard U., 1938, EdD, 1951; student, Oxford U., summer 1939. Instr. English high sch., Melrose, Mass., 1933-37, Glens Falls, N.Y., 1938-41; demonstration tchr., instr. Harvard U., summer 1941; prin. high sch. Pembroke, Mass., 1941-42; instr. English U. Vt., 1946, registrar, 1946-48, dean adminstrn., 1948-65 (on leave 1949-50); exec. sec. N.E. Bd. Higher Edn., Boulder, Colo., 1960-86; lectr. Salzburg Seminar in Am. Studies, summer 1964; mem. rsch. adv. com. Western office Coll. Entrance Exam. Bd., 1965-67; mem. commn. on adminstrv. affairs Am. Council on Edn., 1966-70, dir. 1970-71, mem. commn. on acad. affairs, 1970-86; mem. commn. of scholars Bd. of Higher Edn., State Ill., 1966-86; mem. steering com. Colloquium on Higher Edn., 1966-86, chmn., 1967-68. Mem. spl. edn. adv. com. United Cerebal Palsy Assn., 1966-69; bd. govs. Ednl. Change Inc. Capt. USAAF, 1942-46. Mem. NEA, N.E. Assn. Collegiate Registrars (v.p. 1948-50), Council Social Work Edn. (del.-at-large 1958-60), Council State Govts. (chmn. nat. conf. interstate compact 1964-65), Am. Assn. Higher Edn. (mem. Mountain-Plains regional council 1970-86), Nat. League Nursing (dir. 1963-71, mem. com. on perspectives 1967-86), Nat. Commn. Community Health Service (task force on manpower 1963-65), Phi Delta Kappa, Tau Kappa Alpha. Home: Boulder Colo. Died Fed. 27, 1986.

KROGMAN, WILTON MARION, anatomy and physical anthropology educator, researcher; b. Oak Park, Ill., June 28, 1903; s. Wilhelm Claus and Lydia Magdelena (Wriedt) K.; m. Virginia Madge Lane, Jan. 22, 1931 (div. Feb. 1944); children—Marian Krogman Baur, William Lane; m. Mary Helen Winkley, Apr. 18, 1945; children—John W., Mark Austin. Ph.B., U. Chgo., 1925, M.A., 1927, Ph.D., 1929; LL.D. (hon.), Baylor U., 1955; D.Sc. (hon.), U. Mich., 1969, U. Pa., 1973. Assoc. prof. Western Res. U., Cleve., 1931-38; assoc. prof. U. Chgo., 1938-47; prof. Sch. Medicine, U. Pa., Phila., 1947-71; dir. research Lancaster Cleft Palate Clinic, Pa., 1971-82; emeritus dir. research Lancaster Cleft Palate Clinic, 1982-87; phys. growth and devel. cons.; expert to identify human skeletal remains for law enforcement personnel. Author: Growth of Man, 1941, The Human Skeleton in Forensic Medicine, 1962, 2d edit., 1986, Child Growth, 1972; contbr. articles to profl. jours. Research grantee Nat. Inst. Dental Research, 1947-68. Fellow Royal Coll. Surgeons. Democrat. Baptist. Home: Lititz Pa. Died Nov. 4, 1987, buried Sargentville, Maine.

KROHN, ALBERTINE, chemistry educator; b. Toledo, Nov. 28, 1924; d. Albert Herman and Bertha Marie (Rath) K. BS summa cum laude, U. Toledo, 1946, MS, 1949; MS, U. Mich., 1951, PhD, 1956. Instr. math. and chemistry U. Toledo, 1947-51, asst. prof. chemistry, 1951-57, prof., from 1963; cons. Delos M. Palmer & Assocs., Toledo, Lewis Rsch Ctr. of NASA, Cleve. Contbr. articles to profl. jours. Trustee St. Paul's Luth. Ch., Toledo, 1980-83; sec. St. Paul's Luth. Ch. Found., Toledo, from 1983. Recipient Gold "T" award Alumni Assn. U. Toledo, 1973. Fellow Ohio Acad. Sci.; mem. Am. Chem. Soc. (nat. councilor 1967-75, alt. counselor from 1976), Electrochem. Soc., Am. Electroplaters Soc., Sigma Xi, Phi Kappa Phi (pres. 1972-77, chmn. bd. 1972-77, Disting. Mem. award 1977, trustee found. 1969-80), Pi Mu Epsilon, Delta Kappa Gamma. Home: Sylvania Ohio. Died Dec. 30, 1985; buried Toledo, Ohio.

KROL, EDWARD JOSEPH, surgeon; b. Chgo., Apr. 3, 1913; s. Alexander and Mary (Madalinski) K.; m. Anne Estelle Shirvin, Feb. 1, 1942; children: Edwina Ann, Cynthia Lee, Edward Joseph, Gerald John. BS, Cen. YMCA, Chgo., 1936; MD, Loyola U., Chgo., 1939; postgrad. surg. tng., Cook County Postgrad. Sch., Tufts U., U. Ill., Bunt's Inst. Crile Clinic, Cleve., U. Minn., U. Kans. Diplomate Internat. Bd. Surgery, Am. Bd. Abdominal Surgery, Internat. Bd. Applied Nutrition. Extern Holy Cross Hosp., Chgo., 1938-39, sr. attending surg. staff, 1948-83, pres., chief of staff, 1957-59, chmn. dept. surgery, 1959-60, chmn. exec. bd., 1958-61, co-chmn. dept. surgery, 1961-62, sec. bd., 1961-62, mem. exec. bd.; intern St. Elizabeth's Hosp., Chgo., 1939-40; pvt. practice Chgo., 1940-42, 45-83; clin. asst. surgery Rush Med. Sch., 1940-42, Stritch Sch. Medicine, 1945-50, clin. instr. surgery, 1950-83. Mem. editorial staff Am. Jour. Abdominal Surgery, 1962; assoc. editor Internat. Jour. Applied Nutrition, 1961; contbg. editor surg. sect. Am. Jour. Proctology, 1952-83, Modern Nutrition Jour., 1961-83; contbr. numerous articles to profl. jours. Mem. Adv. Coun. to Gov. Ill.; chmn. adv. bd. Immaculata Coll., Chgo., 1955-83; trustee Intestinal Rsch. Inst., 1955-83; mem. pres.'s coun. St. Xavier's Coll., Chgo., 1956-82; chmn. bd. advisers Shelbourne Ctr., Valparaiso, Ind., 1960-83. Capt. M.C., USAAF, 1942-45. Recipient cert. of merit Internat. Acad. proctology, award of merit Dept. Calilf. Mil. Order Purple Heart, Meritorious Svc. award Clin. Congress Abdominal Surgeons, Gold Medal of Achievement Clin. Congress Abdominal Surgeons, 1962. Fellow Internat. Coll. Surgeons, Am. Soc. Abdominal Surgery (pres. 1965-66, 77-83), Internat. Acad. Proctology (trustee 1950-55, pres. 1953), Am. Coll. Gastroenterology (trustee 1950-64, pres. 1962-63), Am. Coll. Nutrtion, Royal Soc. Medicine, N.Y. Acad. Scis., AAAS, Am. Geriatric Soc., Miss. Valley Med. Soc., AMA (chmn. gen. surg. sect. 1962-63, exec. com. 1962-64, ho. of dels. 1977), Acad. Psychosomatic Medicine, Internat. Coll. Applied Nutrition (v.p., bd. govs. 1961-83), Soc. Acad. Achievement, Internat., Am. colls. angiology; mem. Am. Coll. Chest Physicians, World Med. Assn., Ill. Med. Soc. (del.), Chgo. Med. Soc. (counsellor), Chgo. Path.

Soc., Ill. Acad. Sci., Ill. Soc. med. Rsch., Am. Nutrition Soc., Assn. Mil. Surgeons, Am. Thoracic Soc., Assn. Am. Med. Colls., Fedn. Am. Scis., Cath. Physicians Guild, Assn. Am. Physicians and Surgeons, Inst. Medicine Chgo., Am. Sportsmens Club, Union League. Died July 4, 1983.

KROLL, FRED J., labor union executive; b. Phila., Oct. 29, 1935; s. Fred. C. and Catherine (Sweeney) K.; m. Hildegarde Franken, June 9, 1956; children: Karen, Anita, Michele. Student parochial schs. Rail clk. Pa. R.R., Phila., 1953-59; local chmn. Brotherhood of Railway Airline and Steamship Clks., Freight Handlers, Express and Sta. Employees Lodge 587, 1961-69; internat. v.p. Brotherhood of Railway Airline and Steamship Clks., Freight Handlers, Express and Sta. Employees Lodge 587, Phila., 1975-76, internat. pres., 1976-81; div. chmn. PennCentral Systems Bd., Phila., 1964-69, gen. sec.-treas., 1970-71, gen. chmn., 1971-75. Mem. K.C. Democrat. Roman Catholic. Home: Meadowbrook Pa. Died July 30, 1981.

KROLL, JOHN LEON, athletic equipment manufacturing company executive; b. Buffalo, Sept. 5, 1925; s. Hammond and Sylvia (Heimberger) K.; m. Evelyn Maher, Dec. 29, 1966; 1 dau., Sharon; stepchildren: John Brennan, James Brennan. B.S. in Phys. Edn. and Recreation, N.Y. U., 1948, M.A. in Health Edn, 1949; postgrad. in sch. adminstrn., U. Conn., 1953-55. Tchr. phys. edn. N.Y.C. Bd. Edn., 1948-49; dir. phys. edn. Waterford (Conn.) Public Schs., 1949-51; founder, chmn. bd. Jayfro Corp., Waterford, 1953-86; pub. Jayfro Periscope nat. newsletter, 1973-81; co-founder Nat. Athletic Mfrs. Catalog Distbg. Corp., Harbor City, Calif., 1973-77; co-founder (with wife) Kroll Press and Publ. & Advt. Waterford, Co., 1978; bd. advs., cons. Gymnastic Athletic Supply Co., Inc., San Pedro, Calif., 1975-86; dir. of adv. bd. Southeastern Conn. area Conn. Bank and Trust Co., New London, 1980; mem. adv. bd. Nat. Sports Mgmt. Studies Found., U. Mass., Amherst, 1980. Author: (with wife) It Doesn't Pay To Work Too Hard, 1979; contbr. (with wife) articles to profl. and trade jours., also mags. Chmn. promotional programs com. U.S. com. Sports for Israel, Inc., N.Y.C., 1975-79; bd. dirs. Tennis Found. N.Am., 1973-79, YMCA, Boca Raton, Fla., 1977-80, Waterford Day Sch. New Bldg. Assn., 1982-86, Conn. Jr. Achievement, 1982-86, S.E. Conn. Ostomy Com., 1980-86, Cath. Charities Corp. Fund Raising Bd., Norwich Diocese, 1981-86; mem. membership com. Ice Skating Inst. Am., 1975-81; hon. bd. dirs. Flatbush Boys Club, Bklyn., 1975-80. Served with USN, 1943-46; Served with USNR, 1946-51; Served with U.S. Army, 1951-53. Recipient Honor award Pres.'s Council Phys. Fitness and Sports, 1977, Disting. Service award City and County Adminstrs. of Health and Phys. Edn., AAHPER, 1978; honored at 25th ann. industry testimonial dinner, 1977. Mem. Athletic Inst. (dir. 1975-76), Am. Council Internat. Sports (dir. 1977-86), Edn. Industries Assn. (dir. 1972-76), Exhibitors Assn. AAHPER and Dance (exec. bd. dirs. 1970-76, pres. 1973-74), Nat. Intramural-Recreational Sports Assn. (hon. life; exhibitors com. 1974-78), Nat. Sporting Goods Assn., Sporting Goods Mfrs. Assn. (tennis and racquet sports com. 1973-80, phys. edn. and athletic com. 1972-76, internat. sporting goods show steering com. 1973-79, chmn. membership com. 1975-78), Nat. Sch. Supply and Equipment Assn. (dir., exec. com. 1973-75, chmn. conv. and exhbns. com. 1975-78), U.S. Tennis Ct. and Track Builders Assn., Booster Club Assn. Am. (contbg. industry co-founder). Clubs: 2001 (Dallas); Lambs (N.Y.C.); Delray Beach (Fla.); Rotary (Waterford); N.Y. U. (N.Y.C.). Home: New London Conn. also: Highland Beach Fla. Died Mar. 2, 1986; buried Cedar Grove Cemetery, New London, Conn.

KROOK, MAX, mathematics and astrophysics educator. Gordon McKay prof. applied math., prof. astrophysics Harvard U., Cambridge, Mass. Home: Arlington Mass. Died Aug. 4, 1985.

KROPOTKIN, IGOR NICHOLAS, publishing executive; b. Russia, May 2, 1918; came to U.S., 1927, naturalized, 1932; s. Nicholas and Tamara (Maximovitch) K.; m. Marjorie Albohn, Feb. 16, 1947; children—Valerie, Michael. Student, Columbia, N.Y. U. With Scribner Book Cos., N.Y.C., 1941-85; dir. Scribner Book Cos., 1957-85, v.p., 1960-67, sr. v.p., 1967-85; pres. Scribner Book Stores, Inc., 1970-85; treas. Am. Bookseller Pub. Co., Give-A-Book Certificate, Inc.; Pres. Am. Booksellers Assn., 1962-64, chmn. bd., from 1964; adv. com. internat. book programs State Dept., from 1962; steering com. Nat. Library Week, 1962-87; mem. Nat. Book Com., 1970-87. Trustee Princeton Store. Mem. Booksellers League N.Y. (pres.). Club: Cornell (N.Y.C.). Home: Fair Lawn N.J. Died Mar. 4, 1987.

KRUEGER, RAYMOND LESLIE, mathematics educator; b. Chgo., July 1, 1902; s. Fred Ralph and Rose Lois (Smith) K.; m. Adelaide Ruth McClenen, June 3, 1940; 1 son, Ross Tremaine. Student, Northern Ill. State Tchrs. Coll., DeKalb, 1923-25; AB, U. Ill., 1927, AM, 1928; PhD, Marquette U., 1934. Instr. math. Marquette U., 1928-33, Lake Forest (Ill.) Acad., 1933-37; asst. prof. math., dir. Elgar Weaver Obs., Wittenberg U., Springfield, Ohio, 1937-38, asst. prof. math., 1938-40, assoc. prof., 1942-46, Andrew W. Weikert prof. math., from 1946, head dept., 1940-61, coord. natural sci. div., 1945-48. Co-author: College Algebra, 1956, Mathematics of Finance, 1958, College Business Mathematics, 1960, College Algebra and Basic Set Theory, 2d edit., 1963. Mem. Masons, Phi Beta Kappa, Sigma Xi, Pi Mu Epsilon, Phi Delta Kappa, Tau Kappa Alpha, Kappa Phi Kappa, Psi Chi, Lambda Chi Alpha. Methodist. Home: Springfield Ohio Died Jan. 8, 1989.

KRUMHOLZ, LOUIS AUGUSTUS, biologist, educator; b. Harrington, Wash., Dec. 1, 1909; s. Frank Charles and Elizabeth (Griffin) K.; m. Edna Lorene Langhoff, Apr. 15, 1939. Student, St. Mary's Coll., Winona, Minn., 1927-29, 30-31; BS, Coll. St. Thomas, St. Paul, 1932; MS, U. Ill., 1938; PhD, U. Mich., 1945. Asst. zoologist and draftsman Ill. Natural History Survey, Urbana, 1937-40; aquatic biologist Mich. Inst. Fisheries Rsch., Ann Arbor, 1940-45; instr. zoology Ind. U.; also rsch. assoc. Ind. Lake and Stream Survey Bloomington, 1945-50; aquatic biologist TVA, Oak Ridge, 1950-54; resident biologist Lerner Marine Lab., Bimini, Bahamas, 1954-57; mem. faculty U. Louisville, 1957-81, prof. biology, 1963-76, Disting. prof. emeritus biology and water resources, 1976-81, dir. Water Resources Lab., 1967-76, asst. v.p. acad. affairs, 1976-81. Mem. Am. Soc. Ichthyologists and Herpetologists (Best Student Paper award 1939, mng. editor Copeia 1963-65), Wildlife Soc. (Best Fisheries Paper award 1958, editor Wildlife Monographs 1958-81), Ecol. Soc. Am., Am. Fisheries Soc., Brit. Ecol. Soc., Am. Soc. Zoologists, Am. Inst. Biol. Scis., AAAS, Am. Soc. Fishery Rsch. Biologists, Am. Soc. Limnology and Oceanography, Am. Water Resources Assn., AAUP (pres. U. Louisville chpt. 1968-69), Ind., Ky. (pres. 1971-72, Disting. Scientist 1976, editor Transactions 1974-81) acads. sci., Sigma Xi. Home: Louisville Ky. Died Jan. 23, 1981.

KRUMRINE, CHARLES SIDNEY, banker; b. Bellefonte, Pa., June 29, 1897; s. Sidney and Mary Jane (Bubb) K.; m. Jane Brown Gilfillan, Spet. 20, 1924; 1 child, Jane. Grad., Pa. State U., 1918. With Liberty Real Estate Bank & Trust Co., Phila., 1923-57, v.p., dir., pres., 1940-56, chmn. exec. com., 1956-57; pres., dir. Cen. Pa. Gas Co., 1958-66; dir. investment com. Phila. Life Ins. Co., 1940-77; mem. exec. com. Med. Service Assn. Pa. (Blue Shield), 1965-76, mem. fin. com., 1965-76. Chmn. U.S. Savs. Bond Com. for Pa., 1956-74, chmn. emeritus, from 1974; adv. bd. Holy Redeemer Hosp., Meadowbrook, Pa. With AC, USN, World War I. Decorated Star of Solidarity, Italy, 1956; recipient Merit award U.S. Treas. Dept., 1974; named hon. mem. Japan Def. Soc., 1973. Mem. Pa. Soc. S.R., Pa. Bankers Assn. (chmn. group 1 1956), Navy League, Def. Orientation Conf. Assn. (regional dir. 1974-76), Newcomen Soc., N.Am. Hist. Soc. Pa., Am. Legion, Bank Officers Club (past pres.), Sunday Breakfast Club, Union League Club, Phila. Country Club, Merion Cricket Club (Phila.), Right Angle Club, Seaview Country Club (Absecon, N.J.), Explorers Club (N.Y.C.), Sigma Alpha Epsilon. Republican. Episcopalian. Home: Merion Station Pa. Died Oct. 23, 1985; buried West Laurel Hill Cemetery, Phila.

KRUSEN, LESLIE CONARD, lawyer; b. Phila., May 7, 1897; s. George Cornell and Lavinia (Conard) K.; m. Kathryn Malan, Jan. 27, 1923 (dec.); children: Leslie C., Gordon M.; m. Leatha Davis, Nov. 25, 1949. B.S., U. Pa., 1918, LL.B., 1922. Bar: Pa. 1922. Asso. Biddle, Paul, Dawson & Yocum, Phila., 1922-30; ptnr. Krusen, Evans & Byrne (specializing in maritime and corporate law), Phila., from 1930; counsel various s.s., oil, ins. cos. Served as ensign USN, 1917-19. Mem. ABA, Pa., Phila. bar assns., Maritime Law Assn. U.S., Lambda Chi Alpha. Clubs: Riverton Country, Riomar Country, Downtown. Home: Delanco N.J. Died Sept. 12, 1987; buried Lakeview Meml. Pk., Cinnaminson, Burlington County, N.J.

KUBIK, GAIL, composer, conductor, educator; b. South Coffeyville, Okla., Sept. 5, 1914; s. Henry H. and Eva O. (Thompson) K.; m. Jesse Louise Maver, Apr. 5, 1938; m. 2d, Joyce Mary Scott-Paine, Dec. 21, 1946; m. 3d, Mary Gibbs Tyler, Apr. 9, 1952; m. 4th, Joan Allred Sanders, Sept. 1, 1970 (div. Oct. 1972). MusB with distinction, Eastman Sch., U. Rochester, 1934; MusM cum laude, Am. Conservatory, Chgo., 1935; postgrad., Harvard U., 1937-38; studied piano under Ida Smith, violin under Scott Willets, Samuel Belov, Robert Reed, Alexander Baird, composition under Edward Royce, Bernard Rogers, Leo Sowerby, Walter Piston, Nadia Boulanger, conducting under Harold Byrns, Igor Markevitch; MusD (hon.), Monmouth Coll., 1955. Composer music 1930-84; violin soloist Kubik Ensemble (Evalyn, Howard, Gail, Henry K.), 1930-37, N.Y. Civic Orch., 1937, Chgo. Civic Orch., 1938, Rochester Civic Orch., 1939; tchr. Monmouth (Ill.) Coll., 1934-36, Dakota Wesleyan U., 1936-37, Columbia Tchrs. Coll., 1938-40; staff composer, music program advisor NBC, 1940-41; concert, functional-music commns. 1940-82; dir. mus. OWI Bur. Motion Pictures, 1942-43; composer-condr. film, radio units USAAF, 1943-46; prof. music U. So. Calif., summer 1946; guest lectr. Accademia di Santa Cecilia, Rome, 1952, Oxford U., 1966; vis. prof. Kans. State U., 1969, Gettysburg (Pa.) Coll., 1970, Calif. State U., Fullerton, 1975-76, Mt. San Antonio Jr. Coll., 1978; prof. music, composer-in-residence Scripps Coll. and Claremont (Calif.) Grad. Sch., 1970-84; lectr. tours U.S., 1968-70, Morocco, 1978; recorded works RCA Victor, Columbia, Desto, Capitol, Orion and Contemporary; lectr., contbr. to profl. publs. Appeared guest condr. NBC, CLS, Denver, Columbus (Ohio) symphonies, Orch. Radio Italiana, Rome, Orch. Sinfonica Siciliana, Palermo, Orchestre Radio Symphonique, Paris, London Philharm. Orch., Dublin Symphony, BBC Concert Orch.; works include: Variations on a 13th Century Troubadour Song (orch.), 1935; In Praise of Johnny Appleseed (orch., chorus, soloist), rev. 1961; Stewball Variations (band), 1943; Memphis Belle: A War-time Episode (orch., narration), 1944; Litany and Prayer (men's chorus, brass, percussion), 1943-45; Folk Song Suite (orch.), 1945; A Mirror for the Sky (folk opera), 1946; Piano Sonata, 1947; Bachata Cuban Dance Pieve, 1947; Symphony in E Flat, 1947-49; Am. Profiles, Folk-Song Sketches (chorus) (commd. by Robert Shaw Chorale), 1949; Boston Baked Beans (opera Piccola), 1950; Celebrations and Epilogue (piano), 1938-50; Symphony Concertante (commd. by Little Orch. Soc.), 1951, rev., 1953; Thunderbolt Overture, 1953; Symphony No. 2 in F, 1955; Symphony No. 3 (commd. by Dimitri Mitropolous and N.Y. Philharm. Orch.), 1956; Scenario for Orchestra, 1957; Sonatinas for Piano, 1941; Violin and Piano, 1941; Clarinet and Piano, 1959; Two Divertimenti (small orch.), 1959; Scenes for Orch., 1964; A Christmas Set (chamber chorus, small orch.), 1968; Prayer and Toccata (organ, small orch.), 1969, (organ and two pianos), 1980; Fables in Song, Song Cycle (Theodore Roethke), 1969; A Record of Our Time (cantata for chorus, narrator and orch.), 1970; Five Theatrical Sketches (Divertimento No. 3) for violin, cello, piano, 1971; Scholastica: Five Medieval Poems (chorus), 1972; Five Birthday Pieces for Two Recorders (also for flute and clarinet), 1974; Magic, Magic, Magic; Three Incantations for Chamber Chorus and Small Orch. (Tex. Bicentennial Commn.), 1976; Symphony for Two Pianos (based on Symphony 1), 1980; film scores include: The World at War, 1942; Memphis Belle, 1943 (NY Film Critics award 1944); C-Man, 1949; Gerald McBoing Boing, 1950 (Acad. award 1951); Two Gals and a Guy, 1951; Transatlantic, 1952; The Desperate Hours, 1955; Hiroshima, The Silent Sentinel (TV), 1957-58; Down to Earth, 1959; Pastorale and Spring Valley Overture (for Delta Omicron), 1972; Household Magic (for U. Tex.), 1973. Recipient Golden Jubilee award (Scherzo for large orch.), Chgo. Symphony, 1941; 1st prize (Violin Concerto No. 2), Jascha Heifetz competition, 1941; Publ. award (Sonatina for violin, piano), Soc. Pub. Am. Music, 1943; Sinfonia Nat. Composition award for Trio for Piano, Violin and Cello, 1934; citation for documentary film score (World at War), Nat. Assn. Am. Composers and Condrs., 1943; Guggenheim fellow, 1944, 65; Prix de Rome award for Symphony in E Flat, 1950, 51; Pulitzer prize (Symphony Concertante), 1952; Am. del. Venice Film Festival, Internat. Conf. Music in Films, 1959; ASCAP del. UNESCO Internat. Conf., Denver, 1959; Am. del. UNESCO, Paris 1966, Budapest, 1966; fellow Villa Serbaloni, Rockefeller Found., 1976; Norlin Found. fellow MacDowell Colony 1979. Mem. ASCAP, Am. Music Ctr., Century Club, Phi Mu Alpha Sinfonia (hon. life), Delta Omicron (hon. life). Home: Claremont Calif. Died July 20, 1984.

KUEHNER, RICHARD LOUIS, environmental scientist; b. Plumville, Pa., Nov. 21, 1917; s. Harry S. and Mae Margaret (Van Horn) K.; m. Dorothy Caroline Johnson, Sept. 5, 1942; 1 child, Carol Louise (dec.). AB cum laude, Allegheny Coll., 1940; PhD, Yale U., 1943. Rsch. engr. York Corp. (Pa.), 1943-57; group leader Borg Warner Rsch. Ctr., Des Plaines, Ill., 1957-61, sect. mgr., 1961-73, staff scientist, 1973-77, cons., 1977-87. Contbr. numerous articles to profl. jours. Fellow ASHRAE, Royal Soc. Health Gt. Britain; mem. Am. Pub. Health Assn., Am. Soc. Microbiologists, Am. Chem. Soc., Inst. Environ. Sci., AAAS, NY Acad. Scis. Internat. Soc. Solar Energy. Home: Mount Prospect Ill. Died Nov. 30, 1987; cremated.

KUEKES, EDWARD DANIEL, cartoonist; b. Pitts., Feb. 2, 1901; s. Otto and Elizabeth (Lapp) K.; m. Clara Gray, Apr. 23, 1922; children—Edward Grayson, George Clive. Student, Baldwin-Wallace Coll., L.H.D. (hon.), 1957; student, Cleve. Inst. Art, Chgo. Acad. Fine Art. Artist, cartoonist Cleve. Plain Dealer, 1922-49, chief editorial cartoonist, 1949-66, cartoonist emeritus, 1966-87; cartoonist Metro Newspapers, Inc., Cleve., 1968-87. Creator of: The Kernel; collaborated with Olive Ray Scott in: prodn. cartoon features Knurl the Gnome, United Features Syndicate and Funny Fables. Author: five thousand original cartoons in collection at Syracuse U., Syracuse, N.Y., four hundred and fifty original cartoons in collection at, Baldwin-Wallace Coll., Berea, Ohio. Mem. Pres. Eisenhower's People to People Com. Recipient Newspaper Guild award, 1947, cert. of honor Nat. Safety Council, 1949, C.I.T. Found. award, 1949, DAV award, 1949, 1st prize Freedoms Found., 1949, 58, 2d prize, 1950, Disting. Service award, 1951, 59-61, 63, 66, 67, Disting. Service scrolls, 1952-57, Pulitzer prize for cartoons, 1953, Alumni merit award Baldwin-Wallace Coll., 1953, Silver T Square Nat. Cartoonists Soc., 1953, Gov.'s award, 1953, Presdl. Prayer citation U.S. Treasury Dept., 1954, Meritorious award Cleve. Dental Soc., 1954, Christopher award, 1955, cert. recognition NCCJ, 1955, Pres. Eisenhower's People to People Program cartoon div. award, 1956, George M. Humphrey U.S. Treasury citation, 1957, hon. mention Guild Award, 1957, 1st prize Guild Award,

1958, 1st prize Polit. Cartoon award Wayne State U., 1960, U.S. Treasury award, 1962, 64, Freedoms Found. award, 1963-69; named to Ohio State Sr. Citizens Hall of Fame. Mem. Assn. Am. Editorial Cartoonists, Cleve. C. of C., Newcomen Soc. Eng., Baldwin-Wallace Coll. Alumni Assn. (pres.), Am. Airlines Flagship Fleet (adm.), Nat. Cartoonists Soc., Lambda Chi Alpha, Sigma Delta Chi (Disting. Service award 1975). Methodist. Clubs: Kiwanis (pres. Berea), Masons (50 year pin); Mid Day (Cleve.), Cleve. Farmers (Cleve.). Home: Oklahoma City Okla. Died Jan. 13, 1987; buried Woodvale Cemetery, Middleburg Heights, Ohio.

KUGEL, KENNETH, consultant; b. Sheboygan, Wis., May 5, 1921; s. Herman Kenneth and Rebecca (von Kaas) K.; m. Sarajane Moore, Aug. 12, 1944 (div. May 1971); children—Kenneth Kaas, Melanie, Candace, Thomas Hans, Carol; m. Joanne S. Baker, Dec. 30, 1971 (div. Oct. 1978). B.A., Reed Coll., 1947; M.A., U. Mich., 1948; postgrad., George Washington U., 1949. Research asst. Republican Nat. Com., 1948; with Library Congress, Bur. Fed. Supply, 1948-49; various assignments natural resources Bur. Budget, 1949-62; dir. Office Thai Regional Affairs, AID, 1962; asst. dir. for program mission to Office Thai Regional Affairs, AID, Thailand, 1962-64; dep. dir. mission to Office Thai Regional Affairs, AID, Panama, 1964-66; asso. asst. adminstr. Vietnam bur. Office Thai Regional Affairs, AID, Washington, 1966-68; dir. operational coordination staff U.S. Budget Bur., Washington, 1968-72; dep. asst. dir. field activities Office Mgmt. and Budget, 1972-73, cons., 1973-78; also cons. Overseas Devel. Council, 1973-81, Congl. Budget Office, 1976-77, Pres.'s Reorgn. Project, 1977. Served to maj. USMCR, 1941-46. Mem. Theta Delta Chi. Unitarian (trustee). Home: Biglerville Pa. Died Feb. 1, 1988, buried Biglerville.

KUGLER, ARTHUR NOBLE, mechanical engineer; b. N.Y.C., July 13, 1902; s. Otto E. and Isabella J. (Noble) K.; m. Anna M. Nelson, Oct. 10, 1925; 1 dau., Florence M. (Mrs. Robert B. McCune). M.E., Stevens Inst. Tech., 1925. Registered profl. engr., N.Y., N.J. Field engr. Barker & Wheeler (cons. engr.), 1925-28; installation engr. RCA Photophone-Sound (motion pictures), 1928-29; chief welding engr. Airco Welding products div. Airco Inc., 1929-67; cons. mech. and welding engr. Bricktown, N.J., 1967-84; instr. Pratt Inst., eves., 1940-45; cons. U.S. Army Chem. Warfare Service, 1941-43; U.S. del. Internat. Inst. Welding commn. V111 (safety and hygiene), 1957-68. Author 18 texts on welding engring. for Internat. Corr. Schs.; contbr. to handbooks. Recipient James T. Moorehead medal Internat. Acetylene Assn., 1961. Fellow Soc. Mfg. Engrs. (life, Gold medal 1985); mem. Am. Welding Soc. (hon., Samuel W. Miller Meml. medal 1962), ASME (life), Nat. Soc. Profl. Engrs., Alpha Sigma Phi. Methodist. Club: Bear Mountain Figure Skating (Palisades Interstate Park, N.Y.) (a founder, pres. 1946-62). Home: Bricktown N.J. Died Aug. 26, 1984.

KUH, EDWIN, educator; b. Chgo., Apr. 13, 1925; s. Edwin J. Jr. and Charlotte (Greenebaum) K.; m. Anne Barry, June 11, 1947 (div. Apr. 1970); children, Joanna M., Elizabeth N., Thomas, Sarah, Daniel; m. Barbara Kapp, Jan. 1974 (div.); m. Simoni Zatiropoulos. BA, Williams Coll., 1949; PhD, Harvard U., 1955. Lectr. Johns Hopkins U., Balt., 1953-55; asst. prof. Sloan Sch. Mgmt., MIT, 1954-62, prof. mgmt. and econs., 1962-86; cons. U.S. Treasury, 1959-60; mem. adv. rsch. com. Brookings-SSRC Econometric Model, 1964-86; exec. dir NBER Computer Rsch. Ctr., 1971-78; dir. MIT Ctr. Computational Rsch., 1978-86; mem. staff President's Materials Policy Commn., 1951. Author: (with J.R. Meyer) The Investment Decision: An Empirical Study, 1957, Capital Stock Growth: A Micro-Econometric Approach, 1963; editor: (with others) Brookings Quar. Econometric Model of the U.S, Chgo. and Amsterdam, 1965, (with R.L. Schmalensee) Introduction to Applied Macroeconomics, 1973, (with David Belsley and Roy E. Welsch) Regression Diagnostics: Identifying Influential Data and Sources of Collinearity, 1980. With AUS, 1943-46. Fellow Econometric Soc., Am. Acad. Arts and Scis.; mem. Am. Econ. Assn., Am. Statis. Assn. Home: Cambridge Mass. Died June 9, 1986.

KUHLENBECK, HARTWIG, neurobiologist; b. Jena, Germany, May 2, 1897; came to U.S., 1934, naturalized, 1938; s. Ludwig and Helene (Ayrer) K.; m. Ozelia Marguerite Proteau, Jan. 30, 1924. BA, Dom-Gymnasium Naumburg, Germany, 1914; PhD, U. Jena, 1920, MD, 1922; MSc (hon.), Women's Med. Coll. Pa., 1965. Ship's surgeon 1922-23; pvt. practice Mexico City, 1923-24; lectr. anatomy and neurology Tokyo Imperial U. Med. Sch., 1924-27; asst., privatdozent anatomy U. Breslau, Germany, 1927-33; vis. fellow anatomy U. Pa. Med. Sch., 1934-35; prof. anatomy, chmn. dept. Women's Med. Coll. Pa. (now Med. Coll. Pa.), 1935-63, rsch. prof. anatomy, 1963-66, rsch. prof. neurology and neuropathology, 1966-71, emeritus prof. anatomy, 1971-84; cons. Armed Forces Inst. Pathology, 1947-55. Lt. German Army, 1914-18, maj. MC, AUS, 1944-46. Author: Lectures on the Central Nervous System of Vertebrates, 1927, The Human Diencephalon, 1954, Brain and Consciousness, 1957 (transl. into German 1973), Mind and Matter, 1961, The Central Nervous System of Vertebrates, 7 vols., 1967-78. Fellow AAAS, Coll. Physicians Phila.; mem. Am. Assn. Anatomists, Am. Assn. Neuropathologists, Assn. Mil. Surgeons US, NY Acad. Scis., Schopenhauer Gesellschaft, Japanese Assn. Anatomists (hon.), Max-Planck Soc. Advancement Sci. (fgn. sci. mem.), Inst. for Brain Rsch. (fgn. sci. mem.), Sigma Xi. Home: Philadelphia Pa. Died Dec. 14, 1984, buried West Laurel Hill Cemetery, Bala Cynwyd, Pa.

KUHSE, HAROLD H., lawyer; b. Sac County, Iowa, Dec. 7, 1921; s. Henry E. and Freida (Ackerman) K.; m. Jeanne M. Bendick, May 22, 1954; children: Theresa M., Melinda J., Mark B., Craig A., Mary C. BS in Engring, Iowa State U., 1949; JD, U. Iowa, 1951. Bar: Iowa 1951, Ariz. 1954. With Oliver Corp., 1951-52, State of Wash., 1952-53, City of Mesa (Ariz.), 1953-66; mem. firm Kuhse, Petrie & Reynolds, Mesa, 1958-82; sec., dir. Tribune Pub. Co., Phil Bramsen Distbg. Co. (both Mesa). Bd. dirs. Mesa Aqua Boosters. With USAAF, 1941-45. Decorated D.F.C. with cluster, Air medal with clusters; breat Order Yun Hui (China). Mem. Am. Assn. Trial Lawyers, State Bar Ariz., Mesa C. of C. (dir.), Masons (Shriner), Lions (pres. Mesa 1961-62). Republican. Methodist (trustee, chmn. bldg. com.). Home: Mesa Ariz. Died Nov. 3, 1982; buried Greenacres Meml. Gardens, Mesa, Ariz.

KULLMAN, CHARLES, tenor, educator; b. New Haven, Conn.; s. Charles and Frances (Danhauser) K.; m. Lisa Demander, Feb. 14, 1928; 1 child, Elise Kullman Burke. BS, Yale U., 1924; student, Juilliard Music Found.; also, Am. Conservatory, Fontainebleau, France. N.Y.C. concert debut 1924; soloist Yale Glee Club European tour, 1928; asst. prof. music Smith Coll., 1928-29; mem. Am. Opera Co. and Chgo. Civic Light Opera Co., 1930; debut with Met. Opera Co. 1935, since a leading tenor; appearances with operas in Berlin, Vienna, Salzburg, San Francisco; debut Teatro Colon, Buenos Aires, 1941, Teatro Municipale, Rio de Janeiro, 1942; radio, TV and concert artist; debut in motion pictures as star Song of Scheherazade, 1941; prof. voice Ind. U., 1957. Mem. Met. Opera Assn., Bohemian Club, Dutch Treat Club, Madison Beach Club, Madison Winter Club, Yale Club, Alpha Sigma Phi. Episcopalian. Home: Madison Conn. Died Feb. 8, 1983.

KUNSTMANN, JOHN GOTTHOLD, German language educator; b. Murtoa, Victoria, Australia, Oct. 25, 1894; came to U.S., 1913, naturalized, 1924; s. John Fuerchtegott and Maria Sophie Elisabeth (Martin) K; m. Hulda Johanna Kobs, June 30, 1918; children: Lois E. Kunstmann Huston, John William. Student, U. Leipzig, 1913; grad., Concordia Theol. Sem., St. Louis, 1916; PhD, U. Chgo., 1938. Tutor Latin and Greek Dresden, Saxony, 1910-13; asst. in Latin, French, history St. Paul's Coll., Concordia, Mo., 1916-18; in charge dept. German Concordia Coll., Ft. Wayne, 1918-27; also lectr. German Ind. U. extension div., 1924-25, 26-27; asst. prof., assoc. prof., then prof. German U. Chgo., 1927-54; vis. prof. German U. N.C., Chapel Hill, 1954-55, chmn. dept. Germanic langs., 1955-65, prof. German, 1965-67, prof. emeritus, 1967-88; vis. prof. German, Columbia U., 1947, Duke U., 1965; scholar-in-residence Valpairaso U., 1967; sr. fellow Southeastern Inst. Medieval and Renaissance Studies, Duke U., 1968. Contbr.: Studies in Philology, 1939-88; mem. editorial bd. Modern Philology, 1952-55, Studies in Germanic Langs. and Lits., 1955-67, Annuale Mediaevale, 1960-67, publs. of MLA, 1962-67. Sec. bd parish edn. Luth. Ch., Mo. Synod, 1951-54; founder Luth. Reformation Fesitval, U. Chgo., 1946. Recipient Emperor's prize for Festschrift: Middle Ages-Reformation Volkskunde August-Buerger Stiftung, 1959; decorated Gt. Cross of Merit of Order of Merit Fed. Republic Germany, 1961. Mem. MLA, Am. Assn. Tchrs. German (nat. pres. 1960-63), Chgo. Assn. Tchrs. German, S. Atlantic Modern Lang. Assn., Soc. for Advancement Scandinavian Studies, Am. Soc. for Reformation Research, Luth. Acad. fdor Scholarship (dir. reserach 1949-57), Renaissance Soc. Am., Medieval Acad. Am., Concordia Hist. Inst. Home: Chapel Hill N.C. Died Oct. 29, 1988; cremated.

KYNES, JAMES W., lawyer, business executive, state official; b. Mariana, Fla., Aug. 31, 1928; s. James Walter and Grace (Rowell) K.; m. Marjorie Ann Hiatt, July 1, 1950; children: James H., William L., John F. BS, U. Fla., 1950, LLB, 1955. Bar: Fla. 1955. Exec. asst. to gov. State of Fla., 1960-63, atty. gen., 1964-65; v.p. Jim Walter Corp., from 1965; exec. v.p., sec., gen. counsel sucessor cos. Hillsborough Holding Corp. and Walter Industries, from 1965. Mem. Fla. Bd. Edn., Fla. Securities Commn., Fla. Jud. Council, Fla. Pardon Bd., Fla. Budget Commn., Fla. Revenue Commn.; chmn. Fla. Cancer Crusade, 1963; coordinator Fla. Democratic candidates, 1960; del. Dem. Nat. Conv., 1964; chmn. bd. trustees Cen. Fla. Jr. Coll., 1957-61; active U. Fla. Devel. Corp. 1st lt. USAF, 1951-53, Korea. Named one of Fla.'s 5 Outstanding Young Men, 1960; recipient Disting. Service award , Ocala, Fla, 1958; named to Fla. Hall of Fame. Mem. Nat. Assn. Attys. Gen., U. Fla. Alumni Assn. (pres. 1960), Blue Key (past pres. Fla.), Kiwanis (pres. Ocala 1960), Kappa Alpha, Phi Delta Phi. Methodist (pres. Men's Club, Sun. sch. tchr.). Home: Tampa Fla. Died Oct. 13, 1988.

LABATUT, JEAN, architect, educator; b. Martres-Tolosane, Haute-Garonne, France, May 10, 1899; came to U.S., 1928, naturalized, 1939; s. Dominique and Gabrielle (Clarac) L.; m. Mercedes Terradell, June 10, 1929. Ed., Ecole St. Stanislas, Ecole du Caousou, Lycee Nat., Ecole des Beaux Arts et des Scis. Industrielles, Toulouse, France, Ecole Nat. Superieure des Beaux Arts, Paris; Laureat, Inst. de France; HHD (hon.), Princeton U., 1975. Pvt. practice France, 1924, urban planner, landscape architect, 1926; architect, assoc. landscape architect for town, ch., residence and gardens of Castillega de Gusman nr. Seville, Spain, 1926-31; prof. architecture Am. Summer Sch. Fine Arts, Palais de Fountainbleau, France, 1927-38, dir. sch., 1945-48, also trustee; prof. Princeton (N.J.) U., 1928-67, prof. emeritus, 1967-86, past dir. grad. studies Sch. Architecture, mem. adv. coun. Sch. Architecture and Urban Planning, founder Bur. Urban Rsch. and Archtl. Lab.; architect-in-residence Am. Acad. Rome, 1953, 59, 64, 68; cons. Bd. Design, N.Y. World's Fair, 1937-50, designer fountains for water, light and sound displays, 1937-40; architect José Marti Monument, Plaza and Park, Havana, Cuba; cons. on various planning and archtl. devels. Author: The Universities' Position with Regards to the Visual Arts; contbr. articles on architecture to profl. jours. With Engring. Corps, French Army, 1918-19. Decorated officer Legion of Honor; recipient medal and professorship in architecture Thomas Jefferson Meml. Found., 1973, joint award AIA-Assn. Collegiate Schs. Architecture, 1976, numerous others. Fellow AIA; mem. Am. Soc. Planning Ofcls., Academie d'Architecture, Ordre des Architectes, NAD (academician), Acad. Languedoc, Nassau Club, Princeton Club. Home: Princeton N.J. Died Nov. 26, 1986; buried Ewing (N.J.) Cemetery.

LABOUISSE, HENRY RICHARDSON, consultant, former organization executive, former U.S. ambassador; b. New Orleans, Feb. 11, 1904; s. Henry Richardson and Frances Devereux (Huger) L.; m. Elizabeth Scriven Clark, June 29, 1935 (dec. 1945); 1 dau., Anne (Mrs. Martin Peretz); m. Eve Curie, Nov. 19, 1954. A.B., Princeton U., 1926, LL.D.; LL.B., Harvard U., 1929; LL.D., U. Bridgeport, Lafayette Coll., Tulane U.; L.H.D., Hartwick Coll., Brandeis U. Bar: N.Y. 1930. Practice with firm of Taylor, Blanc, Capron and Marsh (and successor), N.Y.C., 1929-40; mem. firm Mitchell, Taylor, Capron and Marsh, 1940-41; with State Dept., 1941-51, chief div. def. materials, 1943, chief Eastern Hemisphere div., 1944; minister econ. affairs Am. embassy, Paris, 1944-45; spl. rep. in France FEA, 1944-45; spl. asst. to under sec. for econ. affairs Washington, 1945-46; spl. asst. and econ. advisor to dir. Office European Affairs, 1946-48; head U.S. del. Econ. Commn. Europe, 1948; coordinator fgn. aid and assistance 1948-49; dir. Office Brit. Commonwealth and No. European Affairs, 1949-51; chief ECA (Marshall Plan) mission to France 1951-52, chief MSA spl. mission to France, 1953-54; dir. UN Relief and Works Agy. for Palestine Refugees, 1954-58; cons. IBRD., 1959-61; dir. ICA, 1961; U.S. ambassador to Greece 1962-65; exec. dir. UNICEF (orgn. won Nobel Peace prize 1965), 1965-79. Bd. dirs. Farmers' Museum, Bassett Hosp., Cooperstown, N.Y., Internat. Inst. for Environment and Devel., Washington; trustee Clark Found., N.Y.; chmn. Am. Farm Sch., Thessoloniki, Greece. Mem. N.Y. State Hist. Assn. (dir.), Council Fgn. Relations. Episcopalian. Clubs: Metropolitan (Washington), Chevy Chase (Washington); Century Assn. (N.Y.C.). Home: New York N.Y. Died May 25, 1987; interred New Orleans, La.

LACEY, WILLIAM NOBLE, chemical engineer; b. San Diego, July 25, 1890; s. David Sherman and Charlotte (Noble) L.; m. Ruth Elder, Aug. 11, 1917; children: Margaret (Mrs. Paul V. Laylander), David Sherman II. AB, Stanford U., 1911, Chem. Engr., 1912; MS, U. Claif., 1913, PhD, 1915. Asst. in chemistry Stanford U., 1911-12, U. Calif., 1912-15; rsch. chemist Giant Power Co., San Francisco, 1915; rsch. assoc. in chemistry MIT, 1916; instr. Calif. Inst. Tech., 1916-17, asst. prof., 1917-19, assoc. prof., 1919-31, prof. chem. engring., from 1931, dean grad. studies, 1946-56, dean of faculty, from 1961. Author: Instrumental Methods of Chemical Analysis, 1924; (with Bruce H. Sage) Volumetric and Phase Behaviour of Hydrocarbons, 1939, Thermodynamic Properties of Hydrocarbons, 1950, Some Properties of Light Hydrocarbons, 1954; (with W. H. Corcoran) Introduction to Chemical Engineering Problems; contbr. articles to tech. jours. 1st lt. Ordnance Corps, U.S. Army, 1917-19; capt. res. Recipient Hanlon award NGAA, 1946, Anthony F. Lucas medal AIME, 1947, Presdl. Cert. of Merit, 1948. Mem. Am. Chem. Soc., Am. Inst. Chem. Engrs., Athenaeum Club (Pasadena), Sigma Xi, Tau Beta Pi, Phi Lambda Upsilon, Alpha Tau Omega. Republican. Presbyterian. Home: Altadena Calif. †

LADENSON, ALEX, librarian; b. Kiev, Russia, Sept. 25, 1907; came to U.S., 1913, naturalized, 1922; s. Nathan and Bertha (Schonheit) L.; m. Inez Sher, Aug. 14, 1938; children: Mark Lawrence, Robert Franklin. B.S. in Law, Northwestern U., 1929, J.D., 1932; M.A., U. Chgo., 1935, Ph.D., 1938; Litt.D., Rosary Coll., 1968. Bar: Ill. bar 1931. Project supr. WPA Library Omnibus Project, Chgo., 1938-43; asst. librarian Chgo. Pub. Library, 1943-67, acting librarian, 1967-70, chief librarian, 1970-74, spl. exec. asst. to bd. dirs., 1975-78, cons., from 1978; asst. dean Schurz Eve. Jr. Coll., Chgo., 1938-48; lectr. grad. dept. library sci. Rosary Coll., River Forest, Ill., 1965-69; exec. dir., legal counsel Urban Libraries Council, from 1978. Editor:

American Library Laws, 1964, American Library laws, supplements 1-4, 1965-71, 4th edit., 1973, Supplements 1-3 to 4th edit., 1974-79, 5th edit., 1983, Library Law and Legislation in the United States, 1982. Pres. Northtown Civic League, Chgo., 1958-60. Mem. Am. Library Assn., Ill. Library Assn. (pres. 1959-60, Librarian Citation award 1965). Club: Chicago Literary. Home: Chicago Ill. Died Aug. 6, 1987.

LAERI, JOHN HOWARD, corporation executive; b. Youngstown, Ohio, Mar. 22, 1906; s. Anton John and Lillian (Resch) L.; m. Betty Cochrane, Dec. 7, 1929; children: Suzanne (Mrs. Lee Plein), John Howard. Vice chmn. Citicorp, Citibank N.A.; bd. dirs. F&M Schaeffer Corp., St. Regis Paper Co., 1st Boston Corp., Firemans Fund Ins. Co. Mem. Am. Bankers Assn. (pres. 1967), Augusta Club, Nat. Golf Club, Blind Brook Club,. Methodist. Home: Greenwich Conn. Died June 27, 1986.

LAFONTAINE, JEAN-MARIE, clergyman; b. Montreal, Que., Can., Apr. 4, 1923; s. Georges Albert and Emmeline (Martel) L. Licence in theology, U. Montreal, 1948; D in Social, Polit. and Econ. Scis., U. Lille, France, 1951. Ordained priest Roman Cath. Ch., 1948. Adviser Confedn. Nat. Trades Union, Can., 1951-66; prof. social scis. U. Montreal, 1953-67; exec. sec. Que. Conf. Cath. Bishops, 1966-68; vicar gen. Cath. Diocese Montreal, 1968-79; aux. bishop 1979-81. V.p. United Coun. for Human Rights, 1965-68. Mem. Theologians Assn. Am. Home: Montreal Que., Canada. Died June 13, 1981.

LAFORE, LAURENCE DAVIS, history educator, author; b. Narberth, Pa., Sept. 15, 1917; s. John Armand and Anne (Shearer) L. BA, Swarthmore Coll., 1938; MA, Fletcher Sch. Law and Diplomacy, 1939, PhD, 1950. Mem. faculty Trinity Coll., Hartford, Conn., 1940-42; with Dept. State, 1942-43, OWI, 1943-44; asst. press attache Am. embassy, Paris, 1944-46; rsch. assoc. ECA, 1948; mem. faculty Swarthmore Coll., 1946-67, prof. history, 1960-67; vis. prof. U. Iowa, 1967-68, prof. history, 1969-85, chmn. dept., 1974-77; mem. Iowa State History Bd., 1979-82. Author: (with Paul Beik) Modern Europe, 1958, Learner's Permit, 1962, The Devil's Chapel, 1964, The Long Fuse, 1965, (with Sarah L. Lippincott) Philadelphia, The Unexpected City, 1965, Stephen's Bridge, 1968, Nine Seven Juliet, 1969, The End of Glory, 1970, The Days of Emperor and Clown, 1973, American Classic, 1975. Mem. Am. Hist. Soc., Conf. Brit. Studies, Phi Beta Kappa, Delta Upsilon. Home: Iowa City Iowa. Died Nov. 24, 1985; buried Bala Cynwyd, Pa.

LAGRONE, CYRUS WILSON, JR., psychologist, educator; b. Paint Rock, Tex., Jan. 8, 1911; s. Cyrus Wilson and Truda (Gough) LaG.; m. Bessie Frances Shipley, July 29, 1968. BA, East Tex. State U., 1930; MA, U. Tex., 1932, PhD, 1942; Ford fellow, vis. scholar, Columbia U., 1954-55. Certified in clin. psychology Am. Bd. Examiners Profl. Psychology. Instr. psychology Lee Jr. Coll., Baytown, Tex., 1934-40, U. Tex., 1940-42; asst. prof. U. So. Calif., 1946-47; prof. psychology Tex. Christian U., 1947-75, chmn. dept., 1950-66, inaugurated doctoral program. Contbr. articles to profl. jours. Served to lt. col. AUS, 1942-46. Fellow Am. Psychol. Assn.; mem. Southwestern Psychol. Assn., Tex. Psychol. Assn. (past pres.), AAUP, Sigma Xi, Alpha Chi, Phi Delta Kappa. Mem. Christian Ch. (Disciples of Christ). Home: Fort Worth Tex. Died Nov. 28, 1987; buried Greenwood Meml. Park, Ft. Worth, Tex.

LAHEE, FREDERIC HENRY, geologist; b. Hingham, Mass., July 27, 1884; s. Henry Charles and Selina Ida Mary (Long) L.; m. Louie Karr hodge, Dec. 23, 1912; children: Genevieve, Henry, Ruth Holden, John Aspinwall. AB, Harvard U., 1907, AM, 1908, PhD in Geology, 1911. Asst. instr. geology Harvard U., Radcliffe Coll., 1906-09, instr., 1909-12; instr. MIT, 1912-15, asst. prof., 1915-18; geologic aide U.S. Geol. Survey, 1915; with Sun Oil Co., 1918-55, chief geologist, in charge geol., paleontol. chem. and geophys. work, 1920-47, geol. and rsch. counselor, 1947-55; cons. geologist from 1955; instr. Wellesley Coll., 1910-18; cons. geologist White River Natural Gas Co., from 1959; adviser to Petroleum Info., Inc., Denver; expert witness on gas-rate cases. Author: Field Geology, 1916; contbr. articles to profl. jours. Chmn. Dist. III com. on exploration Petroleum Adminstrn. for War, 1942-45. Mem. AIME, Geol. Soc. Am., Geog. Soc. Am., Am. Assn. Petroleum Geologists (editor 1929-32, pres. 1932-33, chmn. com. on stats. of exploratory drilling 1935-55, rep. on NRC 1936-40, chmn. adv. com. on radioactive mineral exploration 1952), Soc. Econ. Geologists, Am. Petroleum Inst. (chmn. com. on oil res. 1946-55), Mid Continent Oil and Gas Assn., Harvard Club, Petroleum Club, Broohaven Country Club, Phi Beta Kappa. Unitarian. Home: Dallas Tex. †

LAING, PETER MARSHALL, lawyer; b. Montreal, Que., Can., Mar. 24, 1916; s. Campbell and Hazel (Marshall) L.; m. Kathleen McConnell, May 12, 1945; children: Murdoch, David. BA, McGill U., 1935, LLD, 1981; MA, Oxford (Eng.) U., 1945. Bar: Eng. 1939, Que. 1944; created Queen's counsel, Que. 1959. Mem. Clarkson & Tetrault; Chmn. Comtrust Holdings Ltd.; bd. dirs. Starlaw Investments. Emeritus mem. bd. govs. McGill U. With 9th Queen's Royal Lancers, 1939-43. Mem. Am. Coll. Trial Lawyers, Mt. Royal Club, University Club. Home: Montreal Que., Canada. Died July 26, 1986; buried Montreal.

LAKE, RICHARD HARRINGTON, international trade and public affairs consultant; b. Carlisle, Pa., Oct. 15; s. William Harrington and Diana C. (Strube) L.; m. Blair Moody, July 17, 1954; children: Richard Moody, Mary Anne (dec.), William Moody, Sara Blair. Grad., Strategic Intelligence Sch., 1951, Command and Gen. Staff Coll., 1954; B.S. in Commerce, Roosevelt U., 1958, M.A. in Econs. and Bus., 1961; postgrad., Fgn. Service Inst., 1965, Indsl. Coll. Armed Forces, 1972. Free-lance writer 1937-38; underwriter's asst. Guardian Life Ins. Co., 1938-40; mktg. exec. fgn. motion pictures in U.S., 1940; commd. 2d lt. U.S. Army, 1940, advanced through grades to lt. col., 1956; comdr. inf. and mil. police units U.S. and overseas 1941-46; chief agt. (Criminal Investigations Div.), Europe, 1947; chief U.S. liaison to USSR Forces Berlin, 1947-48; pub. relations and protocol officer to Mil. Gov. and High Commr. for Germany 1948-50; staff officer (2d Army Hdqrs.), Ft. Meade, Md., (5th Army Hdqrs.), Chgo., 1951-53; provost marshal 10th Inf. Div., 1954; sr. adviser to Royal Thai Army, Bangkok, 1954-56; dir. indsl. security, law enforcement and criminal investigations U.S. Army, 1957-61; mem. faculty Roosevelt U. Coll. Bus. Adminstrn., Chgo., 1958-60; cons. internat. affairs, alternate for sec. commerce to 1st White House Food for Peace Conf., Dept. Commerce, 1961; exec. sec. Fgn. Trade Zones Bd. U.S., 1961-69; dir. fgn. trade zones staff Bur. Internat. Bus. Operations, 1961-62, Bur. Internat. Commerce, 1963-69; owner Richard H. Lake Assos., 1970-87; assoc. Buckley Engring., Inc., Port-au-Prince, Haiti, 1979-81; mem. Bangkok-Sattahip port study group, Thailand, 1972; chief econ. devel. mission UN Indsl. Devel. Orgn., Belize, Brit. Honduras, 1973, Port-of-Spain, Trinidad and Tobago, 1974. Contbr. articles to govt. and bus. publs. Mem. Res. Officers Assn., Ret. Officers Assn., D.A.V., Ill. Assn. Chiefs Police, Marquis Biog. Library Soc., Policiá Secreta Nacional de Panamá (hon.). Episcopalian. Died May 18, 1987.

LALLY, FRANCIS JOSEPH, clergyman, editor; b. Swampscott, Mass., June 11, 1918; s. Frank and Catherine (Farragher) L. AB, Boston Coll., 1940; grad., St. John's Sem., 1944; licentiate of social sci., Laval U., 1948; LLD, Stonehill Coll., 1958, Marquette U., 1960, Manhattan Coll., 1961, Boston Coll., 1962, Northeastern U., 1966, Rivier Coll., Nashua, N.H., 1969. Ordained priest Roman Cath. Ch., 1944. Assoc. editor The Pilot, Boston, 1948-52, editor, 1952-72; spiritual dir. League Cath. Women, Boston, 1950-75; privy chamberlain to Pope Pius XII 1952, named domestic prelate, 1959; parish priest Sacred Heart Parish, Roslindale, 1971-75. Author: The Catholic Church in a Changing America, 1962. Bd. dirs. Tufts Civic Edn. Found., 1958-87, Religion and Labor Conf., 1982-87; mem. U.S. nat. commn. for UNESCO, 1957-62; mem. exec. com. Action for Boston Community Devel., 1962-69, v.p., 1964-66; mem. U.S. com. for UNICEF, Boston Redevel. Authority, 1957-70; chmn. Boston Redevel. Authority, 1961-70; dir. Archbishop's Stewardship Appeal, 1971-75; sec. dept. social devel. and world peace U.S. Cath. Conf., 1975-87; trustee Opera Co. Boston, mem. com. for permanent charity fund, 1970-87; bd. dirs. Boston Coun. for Internat. Visitors, 1962-87, Fund for Republic, 1957-77, Urban league Greater Boston; trustee Ednl. Devel. Centre, 1967-73, St. Elizabeth Hosp., Brighton, French Library, Boston, 1956-69, Boston Athenaeum, 1972-87; bd. consultors Archdiocese Boston, 1968-70; mem. vis. com. Harvard-Radcliffe Coll., 1973-79; mem. corp. Retina Found., 1972-87; chmn. Cath. com. White House Conf. on Families, 1978-81; mem. exec. com. Leadership Conf. on Civil Rights, 1981-87, sec., 1982-87. Decorated chevalier Legion of Honor, 1955; recipient Boston Coll. medal, 1953. Fellow Am. Acad. Arts and Scis. (v.p. 1964-66); mem. Internat. Friendship League (dir. 1958-87), Cath. Press Assn., Boston Com. Fgn. Relations, Tavern Club, Examiner Club, Fed. City Club. Home: Swampscott Mass. Died Sept. 2, 1987; buried Swampscott Cemetery.

LALLY, JOHN PETER, mining company executive; b. Pitts., Mar. 29, 1892; s. P. J. and Jane (McMahon) L.; m. Helen Mangan, Nov. 23, 1920; children: Jean A. (Mrs. M. C. O'Donnell), John R., Joan G. (Mrs. John A. Hillenbrand II). Treas. C. G. Hussey & Co., 1920-31, pres., 1931-59; v.p. Copper Range Co., Boston, 1936-55, pres., 1955-59, mem. exec. com., from 1955, chmn., from 1960, also bd. dirs.; pres. White Pine Copper Co., 1955-59, also bd. dirs.; pres. Copper Range R.R. Co., 1955-59, also bd. dirs., chmn. bd., from 1959; v.p., chmn. bd. dirs. Copper & Brass Rsch., from 1959. Dir. DePaul Inst., Pitts.; mem. adv. com. Duquesne U. Mem. Pitts. C. of C., St. Clair Country Club, Duquesne Club, Downtown Club)Boston). Home: Pittsburgh Pa.†

LAMB, EDWARD, lawyer, business executive; b. Toledo, Apr. 23, 1901; s. Clarence M. and Mary (Gross) L.; m. Prudence Hutchinson, June 15, 1930; children: Edward Hutchinson, Priscilla Prudence. AB, Dartmouth Coll., 1924; LLB, Case Western Res. U., 1927. Bar: Ohio 1927. Asst. law dir. City of Toledo, 1928; pvt. practice Toledo, 1928-87; Pres., chmn. bd. Lamb Enterprises, Inc.; pres. Bancorp. Leasing Co.; chmn. bd., chmn. exec. com. Seilon; chmn. bd. Thomson Internat. Co., Nev. Nat. Bancorp; chmn., chmn. exec. com., bd. dirs. Nev. Nat. Bank, Reno; treas., bd. dirs. Gt. Lakes Communications, Inc.; licensee Sta. WICU-TV, Erie, Pa.; bd. dirs. Wyneco, Inc., Cheyenne, Wyo. Author: Trial by Battle, No Lamb for Slaughter, The Sharing Society, Planned Economy in Soviet Russia. Mem. Nat. Emergency Civil Liberties Com.; bd. dirs. Ctr. Study Dem. Instns., Santa Barbara; trustee Wilberforce U.; former gov. UN Assn.-U.S.A. Mem. ABA, Ohio, Toledo, FCC bar assns., Am. Newspaper Pubs. Assn., Toledo Club, Kahkwa Club, Nat. Press Club, Overseas Press Club. Episcopalian. Home: Maumee Ohio. Died Mar. 23, 1987, buried Riverside Cemetery, Maumee.

LAMBERTON, JAMES WILSON, lawyer; b. Winona, Minn., Jan. 26, 1925; s. Henry M. and Gretchen (Leicht) L.; m. Barbara Ann Fox; children: Melissa, Hilary, Peter, Katherine, Abigail, John. A.B. magna cum laude, Carleton Coll., 1949; J.D., Yale U., 1952. Bar: D.C. 1953, N.Y. 1960, U.S. Supreme Ct. 1963. Assoc. firm Cleary, Gottlieb, Steen & Hamilton, N.Y.C., 1953-62, ptnr., 1963-82, ret. ptnr., 1982-86; dir. Western Union Corp., Western Union Telegraph Co., 1982-86. Bd. dirs. S.I. Mental Health Soc., 1965-73; bd. dirs. Community Action for Legal Services, N.Y.C., 1968-74; bd. dirs. Carleton Coll. Alumni Bd., 1981-86, pres., 1984-86. Fellow Am. Bar Found.; mem. ABA, N.Y. County Lawyers Assn. (dir. 1973-82, pres. 1981-82). Clubs: Yale (N.Y.C.); Nantucket Yacht. Home: Santa Fe N.Mex. Died July 22, 1986.

LAMEY, CARL ARTHUR, educator, geologist; b. St. Louis, Oct. 28, 1892; s. Frank W. and Otillia (Kittredge) L.; m. Mary Lucile Seaman, Aug. 16, 1924; 1 child, Howard Arthur. BS, EM, Mich. Coll. Mines, 1925; MS, Northwestern U., 1927, PhD, 1933. Asst. Mich. Coll. Mines, 1921-25; instr. Ind. U., 1927-30, Northwestern U., 1930-33, Mundelein Coll., 1934; instr. Ohio State U., 1935-40, asst. prof., 1940-45, assoc. prof., 1945-46, prof., 1946-85, chmn. dept., 1952-60; geologist U.S. Geol. Survey, Washington, 1942-45, summers 1945-54. Contbr. articles to profl. jours. Mem. AAAS, AIME, Am. Geophys. Union, Ohio Acad. Sci.,Soc. Econ. Geologists, Geol. Soc. Am., Masons, Phi Beta Kappa, Sigma Xi, Tau Beta Pi. Home: Columbus Ohio. Died Dec. 24, 1985.

L'AMOUR, LOUIS DEARBORN, author; b. Jamestown, N.D., 1908; s. Louis Charles and Emily (Dearborn) LaMoore; m. Katherine Elizabeth Adams, Feb. 19, 1956; children: Beau Dearborn, Angelique Gabrielle. Self ed.; LLD (hon.), Jamestown Coll., 1972, N.D. State U., 1981, U. LaVerne, 1981, Pepperdine U., 1984. Appearances on: Great Tchrs. TV program; Author: poems Smoke From This Altar, 1939, Hondo, 1953, The Burning Hills, 1956, Sitka, 1957, The Daybreakers, 1960, Kid Rodelo, Mustang Man, Kilrone, 1966, The Sky-Liners, 1967, The Broken Gun; Matagorda, 1967, Brionne, 1968, Chancy, 1968, Down the Long Hills, 1968 (Golden Spur awards Western Writers Assn.), The Empty Land, 1969, The Lonely Men, 1969, Conagher, 1969, A Man Called Noon, 1970, Reilly's Luck, 1970, Galloway, 1970, North to the Rails, 1971, Under the Sweet-Water Rim, 1971, Tucker, 1971, Callaghen, 1972, Ride the Dark Trail, 1972, Treasure Mountain, 1972, The Ferguson Rifle, 1973, The Man from Skibbereen, 1973, The Quick and the Dead, 1973, The Californios, 1974, Sackett's Land, 1974, War Party, 1975, Rivers West, 1975, Over on the Dry Side, 1975, Rider of Lost Creek, 1976, Where the Long Grass Blows, 1976, To the Far Blue Mountains, 1976, Borden Chantry, 1977, Fair Blows the Wind, 1978, Showdown at Yellow Butte, 1978, The Mountain Valley War, 1978, Bendigo Shafter, 1979, The Proving Trail, 1979, The Iron Marshal, 1979 (Golden Plate award), Shalako, 1980, The Strong Shall Live, 1980, Yondering, 1980, The Warrior's Path, 1980, The Comstock Lode, 1981, Buckskin Run, 1981, The Shadow Riders, 1982, The Lonesome Gods, 1983, The Walking Drum, 1984, Son of a Wanted Man, 1984, Louis L'Amour's Frontier, 1984, Jubal Sackett, 1985, Passin' Through, 1985, Last of the Breed, 1986, The Haunted Mesa, 1987. Served to 1st lt. AUS, 1942-46. Named Theodore Roosevelt Rough Rider by N.D., 1972, his portrait hangs in state capitol; recipient Congl. Golld Medal of Honor, 1983, Presdl. Medal of Freedom, 1984; Am. Book award, 1980, Buffalo Bill award, 1981, Disting. Newsboy award, 1981, Nat. Geneal. Soc. award, 1981. Mem. Acad. Motion Picture Arts and Scis., Calif. Acad. Scis., Nat. Acad. Scis. Died June 10, 1988.

LAMPE, JOHN HAROLD, university dean; b. Balt., Dec. 1, 1896; s. Julius Gerhard and Florence Mae (Thompson) L.; m. Rose Erich Diggs, June 23, 1923; children: Ruth Diggs, John Gerhard, Ross Warren. BS in Engring., Johns Hopkins U., 1918, ME, 1925, DEE, 1931; DE (hon.), Clarkson Coll. Tech., 1953; HHD, N.C. State U., 1965. Registered profl. engr., Conn., N.C. Rsch. engr. Winchester Repeating Arms Co., 1919-20; instr. elec. engring. Johns Hopkins U., 1920-25, assoc., 1925-31, assoc. prof., 1931-38; prof., head dept. elec. engring. U. Conn., 1938-40, dean engring., prof., 1940-45; dean engring N.C. State Coll., 1945-62; dean Sch. Engring. Old Dominion Coll., Norfolk, Va., 1962-86; cons. Consol. Gas, Elec. Light & Power Co., Balt.,

Pa. Water & Power Co., Chesapeake & Potomac Telephone Co., Homewood Elec. Co., Westinghouse Elec. & Mfg. Co., Gen. Elec. Co., Westcott & Mapes, Inc.; mem. Conn. State Bd. Registration for Profl. Engrs. and Land Surveyors, Conn. State Bd. Engring. Examiners, 1942-45; mem. adv. panel to congl. subcom. on mil. application of atomic energy, 1958-60; bd. dirs. Shallcross Mfg. Co., Selma, N.C. Contbg. editor Internat. Critical Tables; contbr. articles to profl. jours. Mem. exec. com. Night Sch. Tech., Johns Hopkins U., 1922-38, sec., 1923-38. 2d lt. Air Svc., U.S. Army, 1918-19. Fellow AIEE (Balt. sect. 1934-38, Conn. sect. program com. chmn. 1939-42, exec. com. 1941-42, chmn. elec. welding com. 1942-44, chmn. membership com. 1943-44, chmn. Fortescue fellowship com. 1956-57), Am. Soc. for Testing Materials, Conn. Soc. Civil Engrs., AAUP; mem. AAAS, NSPE, Assn. Land Grant Colls. and Univs. (sec. engr. div. 1944-46, chmn. 1948, exec. com. 1956-86), Am. Soc. Engring. Edn. (chmn. mil. affairs com. 1956-58), Am. Soc. Tool Engrs., N.C. Soc. Profl. Engrs., Masons, Am. Legion, Kiwanis, Hartford Engrs. Club (v.p. 1944-45), Johns Hopkins Club, Graduate Club, Raleigh Engrs. Club, N.C. Engrs. Soc., Sigma Xi, Tau Beta Pi, Sigma Alpha Epsilon, Eta Kappa Nu. Presbyterian. Home: Norfolk Va. Died Dec. 7, 1986.

LAMSA, GEORGE MAMISHISHO, author; b. Mar Bishoo, Kurdistan, Aug. 5, 1892; came to U.S., 1916; naturalized, 1923; s. Jando Peshah and Sarah (Y-okhanan) L. AB, Archbishop of Canterbury's Coll., Urmiah, Persia, 1907; student, English Sch., Van, Turkey, 1907-08, Va. Theol. Sem., 1918-21; spl. courses, Dropsie Coll., 1942-44. Field sec. Archbishop Canterbury's Assyrian Mission in Am., 1925-31; translator scriptures from Aramaic; founder Christian Jewish Mohammedan Soc., 1923, Aramaic Bible Soc., 1943. Author: The Secret of the Near East, 1924, The Oldest Christian People, 1926, Key to the Original Gospels, 1931, My Neighbor Jesus, 1932, (from Aramaic) The Four Gospels, 1933, Gospel Light, 1936, (from Aramaic) Modern Wisdom, The Shepherd of All Psalms, 1939, (from Aramaic) New Testament, 1940, New Testament Commentary, 1945, New Testament Origin, 1947, Short Koran, Designed for Easy Reading, 1949, (from Aramaic) The Holy Bible, 1957, Old Testament Light, 1964, The Kingdom on Earth, 1966, And the Scroll Opened, 1067, The Hidden Years of Jesus, 1968, More Light on the Gospel, 1968, The Man from Galilee, 1970, Idioms of the Bible Explained, 1971, Roses of Gulistan, 1973; translator The Holy Bible from Aramaic, 1957. Fellow Royal Soc. Arts (London), Am. Oriental Soc., Am. Geog. Soc.; mem. Author's League Am. Home: San Antonio Tex. †

LANCASTER, LANE W., political science educator; b. Bellaire, Ohio, Dec. 9, 1892; s. Charles Warren and Josephine (Crow) L.; m. Mary Alice Brown, Sept. 11, 1917 (dec. Dec. 1948); children: Mary, Susan; m. Margaret Farley, July 18, 1949 (dec. Sept. 1958); m. Mrs. Charles M. Littlefield, Sept. 12, 1959. AB, Ohio Wesleyan U., 1915; AM, U. ill., 1918; PhD, U. Pa., 1923. Instr. polit. sci. U. Pa., 1920-23; asst. prof. govt. and history Wesleyan U., Middletown, Conn., 1923-26; assoc. prof. Wesleyan U., 1926-30; prof. polit. sci. U. Nebr., 1930-60, prof. emeritus, from 1960, head dept., 1939-53, 55-57; vis. prof. polit. sci. Northwestern U., 1940-41; vis. Cowles prof. govt. Yale, 1948-49; vis. prof. U. Calif., Berkeley, 1949-50; mem. Grants in Aid com., Soc. Sci. Rsch. Coun., 1935-41. Author: State Supervision of Municipal Indebtedness, 1924, Government in Rural America, 1937, 2d edit., 1952, Masters of Political Thought: Hegel to Dewey, 1959; contbr. articles to profl. jours. With U.S. Army, 1918. Mem. Am. Polit. Sci. Assn. (v.p. 1951-52), Phi Beta Kappa, Delta Tau Delta. Democrat. Home: Berkeley Calif. †

LANCHESTER, ELSA, actress; b. London, Oct. 28, 1902; came to U.S., naturalized, 1950; d. James and Edith (Lanchester) Sullivan; m. Charles Laughton, Feb. 10, 1929. Ed. pvt. sch., studied dancing with Raymond Duncan, Chelsea and Isadora Duncan. Condr. free class (became Children's Theatre) London, 1918. Made stage debut in Thirty Minutes in a Street, 1922; appeared in: The Way of the World and The Duenna, 1924, Riverside Nights, 1926, also engagements as singer, screen debut in The Constant Nymph; 1st appearance on N.Y. stage in Payment Deferred, 1931; motion picture role Anne of Cleves in: the Private Life of Henry VIII, Eng., 1933; in repertory Old Vic-Sadler's Wells Co., 1933; various stage roles, Eng., 1935-37; role of Martha Jones in: The Beachcomber, 1937; on N.Y. Stage in They Walk Alone, 1941; starred with Turnabout Theatre, Los Angeles, 1941-56; film appearances include David Copperfield, Ladies in Retirement, 1941, Son of Fury, 1942, Tales of Manhattan, 1942, Forever and a Day, 1943, Lassie Come Home, 1943, Passport to Adventure, 1944, The Sprial Staircase, 1946, The Razor's Edge, 1946, Northwest Outpost, 1947, The Bishop's Wife, 1947, The Secret Garden, 1949, Come to the Stable, 1949 (Acad. award nominee 1949), The Inspector General, 1949, Mystery Street, 1950, Witness for the Prosecution, 1958 (Acad. award nominee 1958), Bell, Book and Candle, 1958, Mary Poppins, Honeymoon Hotel, 1963, The Darn Cat, 1964, Blackbeard's Ghost, 1966, Murder By Death, 1976, others; author: Charles Laughton and I, 1938. Died Dec. 26, 1986.

LANDEEN, WILLIAM MARTIN, college president; b. Sundsvall, Sweden, May 7, 1891; came to U.S., 1915; naturalized, 1923; s. Otto and Hedda (Haakanson) L.; m. Elizabeth L. Jenson, Sept. 9, 1917. BA, Walla Walla Coll., 1921, LLD (hon.), 1954; student, U. Wash., 1922, 29, U. Pa., 1929-30; PhD, U. Mich., 1939. Instr. history Walla Walla Coll., 1921-24, prof., 1931-38, pres., 1933-38; instr. history U. Pa., 1929-30; instr. U. Mich., 1930-31; from asst. prof. to prof. history Wash. State Coll., 1939-56, prof. emeritus, from 1956; prof. history La Sierra (Calif.) Coll., 1958-60, pres., from 1960. Author: E.O. Holland and The State College of Washington, 1916-1944, 1958; also articles. Served to maj. AUS, 1943-46. Mem. Am. Ch. History Soc., Am. Soc. Reformation Rsch., Phi Kappa Phi, Phi Alpha Theta. Home: La Sierra Calif. †

LANDGREBE, EARL FREDERICK, business executive, former congressman; b. nr. Valparaiso, Ind., Jan. 21, 1916; s. Edward William and Benna Marie (Broderman) L.; m. Helen Lucille Field, July 12, 1936; children: Ronald, Roger. Grad. high sch. Owner Landgrebe Motor Transport, Inc., Valparaiso, 1943-86; mem. Ind. Senate, 1959-68; owner Landgrebe & Son, Inc., 1967-86; mem. 91st-93d Congresses from 2d dist. Ind.; mem. com. edn. and labor, D.C. com., select subcom. edn., gen. subcom. labor. Past bd. dirs. Porter (Ind.) County Guidance Clinic; bd. dirs. N.W. Ind. United Cerebral Palsy. Mem. Valparaiso C. of C. (past pres.), Mental Health Orgn., Rotary, House 91st Club (sec.). Republican. Lutheran. Home: Valparaiso Ind. Died June 29, 1986.

LANDON, ALFRED MOSSMAN, former governor; b. West Middlesex, Pa., Sept. 9, 1887; s. John Manuel and Anne (Mossman) L.; m. Margaret Fleming, Jan. 9, 1915 (dec.); 1 child, Margaret Anne; m. Theo Cobb, Jan 15, 1930; children: Nancy Josephine, John Cobb. Ed., Marietta (Ohio) Acad.; LLB, U. Kans., 1908; LLD, Washburn Coll., 1933, Marietta Coll., 1934, Boston U., 1939, Coll. Emporia, 1969. Bookkeeper Independence, Kans., 1912; oil producer 1912-87; gov. State of Kans., 1933-37; operator radio stas. 1950-87; Disting. prof. Kans. State U., 1968-87. Chmn. Kans. Rep. Cen. Com., 1928; Rep. nominee for Pres. of U.S., 1936; mem. Pan-Am. Conf., Lima, Peru, 1938; del.-at-large Rep. Nat. Conv., 1940-44, 48. 1st lt. CWS, U.S. Army, World War I. Recipient Brotherhood award NCCJ, 1971. Mem. Blue Key, Masons., Odd Fellows, Elks, Phi Gamma Delta, Phi Delta Phi. Home: Topeka Kans. Died Oct. 12, 1987.

LANDON, CHAUNCEY LOUIS, advertising executive; b. Marysville, Ohio, Sept. 30, 1891; s. Hal D. and Edith Gail (Fairlamb) L.; m. Jane Gardner, Oct. 12, 1915; children: Gardner F., Jane Grey Landon Fairchild, Betty Wilmor Landon Dietz. Student, Georgetown U., 1910, 12, George Washington U., 1911-12. Jr. ptnr. patent law firm Noyes & Harriman, Boston, 1914-15; head patent dept. Goodyear Tire & Rubber Co., 1915-20; v.p. Dunlop Tire Co., 1920-23, Can. Dry Ginger Ale Co., 1924-33; with advt. firm Ellington & Co., Inc., N.Y.C., from 1933, pres., 1954-60, co-chmn., from 1960. Trustee N.Y. Med. Coll., Flower and Fifth Ave. Hosps. Mem. Sigma Chi. Home: Bronxville N.Y.†

LANDON, EDWARD AUGUST, artist; b. Hartford, Conn., Mar. 13, 1911; s. Per August and Hannah Matilda (Anderson) L.; m. Rachel Meltzer, Feb. 29, 1948. Student, Hartford Art Sch., 1928-29, Art Students League, 1930-31, U. Fine Arts, 1939. Painter, 1931-39; printmaker, from 1940, numerous one-man shows including Boston Printmakers, 1955, Paul Schuster Gallery, Cambridge, Mass., Meltzer Gallery, N.Y.C., 1956, U. Maine, 1970, Glass Gallery, N.Y.C., 1973, Gallery 2, Woodstock, Vt., 1974, So. Vt. Artists, Manchester, 1977, Duxbury (Mass.) Art Complex, 1981, Mary Ryan Gallery, N.Y.C., 1984; numerous group shows including Springfield Art League, 1945, Oakland (Calif.) Art Assn., 1952, Phila. Print Club, 1960, Boston Printmakers, 1960; represented in numerous permanent collections including Princeton Print Club, N.Y. Pub. Libr., Pa. Acad., San Francisco Mus., Sao Paulo, Brazil, Seattle Art Mus., Tel Aviv Mus. , Turkee Mus., Finland, Nat. Mus. Am. Art, Washington, Victoria and Albert Mus., London; author: Picture Framing, 1960; author: film Serigraphy, 1947; contbr. articles to profl. jours., 1950-70. Recipient prize N.W. Printmakers, 1944, 46, Bklyn. Mus., 1947, San Francisco Art Assn., 1949, Boston Printmakers, 1979, Nat. Serigraph Soc. purchase awards, 1952, 54, 57, 59, others; Solomon R. Guggenheim grantee, 1939-41; Fulbright rsch. fellow, 1950-51. Mem. Nat. Serigraph Soc. (founder 1942, editor Serigraph quar. 1945-50, pres. 1952), World Print Soc., Am. Color Print Soc., Print Coun. Am., Boston Printmakers Soc., Phila. Print Club, So. Vt. Art Assn. Home: Weston Vt. Died 1984.

LANDRITH, HAROLD FOCHONE, university dean; b. Seneca, S.C., Dec. 23, 1919; s. Walter Louis and Ethel (Powell) L. BS, Clemson U., 1948; MA, Vanderbilt U., 1949; EdD, U. Houston, 1960. Ednl. specialist, instr. tng. dept. Keesler AFB, Miss., 1951-55; head social sci. dept. South Tex. Coll., Houston, 1955-61; assoc. prof. history and edn. Clemson U., 1961-65, dean Coll. Edn., 1965-84; cons. Internat. Tel.&Tel. Co., Fed. Labs., Modern Optics, Inc., Jr. Coll. Edn. Author: Introduction to The Community Junior College, 1971. Chmn. com. deans edn., pres. dept. higher edn. S.C. State-Supported Colls. With USAAF, 1939-45. Recipient Disting. Svc. award S.C. Recreation and Park Soc., Disting. Svc. award Jr. C. of C., 1954. Mem. S.C. Edn. Assn. (v.p.). Home: Seneca S.C. Died Feb. 13, 1984; buried Return Bapt. Ch. Cemetery, Seneca.

LANDSBERG, HELMUT E(RICH), meteorologist; b. Frankfurt am Main, Germany, Feb. 9, 1906; came to U.S. 1934, naturalized, 1938; s. Georg Julius and Klara (Zedner) L.; m. A. Frances Simpson; 1 child, Bruce S.; Ph.D., U. Frankfurt, 1930; Supr., Taunus Obs., 1931-34; asst. prof. geophysics Pa. State U., 1934-41; asso. prof. meteorology U. Chgo., 1941-43; exec. dir. com. geophysics Research and Devel. Bd., 1946-51; dir. geophys. research Air Force Cambridge Research Center, 1951-54; dir. Office Climatology, U.S. Weather Bur., Washington, 1954-65; dir. Environ. Data Service, Environ. Sci. Services Adminstrn., 1965-66; vis. prof. Inst. for Fluid Dynamics and Applied Math., U. Md., College Park, 1964-67, research prof., 1967-76, acting dir. Inst. for Fluid Dynamics and Applied Math., 1974-76, prof. emeritus, 1976-84; ops. analyst, cons. USAAF, 1942-45; mem. Nat. Adv. Com. on Oceans and Atmosphere, 1975-77. Trustee Univ. Corp. for Atmospheric research, 1968-72. Fellow AAAS (v.p. sect. E 1972), Am. Acad. Arts and Scis. Am. Geophys. Union (pres. meteorology sect. 1956-59, v.p. 1966-68, pres. 1968-70), Am. Meteorol. Soc. (councilor 1952-60, v.p. 1962-63), Washington Acad. Sci.; mem. Am. Inst. for Med. Climatology (pres. 1967-81, dir. 1981-84), N.Y. Acad. Scis. (hon.), World Meteorol. Orgn. (pres. commn. for climatology 1969-78), Am. Assn. State Climatologists (hon. life), Nat. Acad. Engring., Explorers Club, Sigma Xi, Phi Beta Kappa, Sigma Pi Sigma, Sigma Gamma Epsilon. Club: Cosmos (Washington). Author: Physical Climatology, 1941; Weather and Health, 1969; The Urban Climate, 1981; (with others) The History of Geophysics and Meteorology, 1985; editor: Advances in Geophysics, 1951-76; editor-in-chief World Survey of Climatology; author articles in field. Died Dec. 6, 1984, buried Suitland, Md. Home: Temple Hills Md.

LANDSHOFF, FRITZ HELMUT, publishing company executive; b. Berlin, July 29, 1901; came to U.S., 1941; s. Siegfried and Anna (Kirchheim) L.; m. Sara Catherina Otte; children: Beatrice, Karen, Andrea, Andreas, Peter. PhD, U. Frankfurt, Germany, 1923. Pres. George Kiepenheur Verlag, Cologne, Germany, 1923-33, Querido Verlag, Amsterdam, Netherlands, 1933-40; v.p., co-founder L.B. Fischer Co., N.Y.C., 1940-46; pres. Excerpta Medica, Amsterdam, 1946-50; European rep. to exec. v.p. Harry N. Abrams, Inc., N.Y.C., 1952-85. Home: New York N.Y. also: Amsterdam The Netherlands. Died Mar. 30, 1988.

LANE, RICHARD KELVIN, utility consultant; b. Dodgeville, Wis., Apr. 18, 1891; s. Henry Richard and Adele Cecilia (Ranger) L.; m. Ruth Sowers, June 28, 1924. Student mech. and electrical engring., U. Wis., 1912-17. Asst. oper. engr. So. Ill. Light & Power Co., 1919-21; gen. supt. So. Okla. Power Co. and Consumers Light & Power Co., 1921-23; power plant design engr. Ill. Power & Light Co., 1923-27; v.p. in charge of op. and constrn., dir. Pub. Svc. Co. of Okla., 1927-39, pres. and dir., 1939-56, chmn. bd., 1956-61, cons., dir., from 1961; bd. dirs. First Nat. Bank and Trust Co. of Tulsa; mem. and former dir. U.S. C. of C. (past chmn. labor relations com., nat. resources com.); pres., dir. YMCA, 1951-53; mem. indsl. adv. bd. Okla. State U., Stillwater; chmn. bd. trustees U. Tulsa, 1958-64; past pres., dir. C. of C., Tulsa, Community Fund of Tulsa. Capt., U.S. Army, 1917-19. Fellow Am. Inst. Elec. Engrs., Masons (Scottish Rite, Shriner), Southern Hills Country Club (pres. 1951), Tulsa Club, Rotary. Home: Tulsa Okla. †

LANEY, LYNN MEADE, lawyer; b. Camp Floyd, Utah, Nov. 4, 1883; s. Joseph Samuel and Eliza Jane (Smith) L.; m. Orpha Mae Putney, June 30, 1915; children: Jack H., Orpha Lucille (Mrs. Cornelius M. Deasy), Marilyn Jane (Mrs. Roger W. Perry), Lynn Meade. BS, U. Calif., Berkeley, 1909; JD, Stanford, 1911. Bar: Ariz. 1912. Practice Phoenix, from 1912; ptnr. firm Laney & Laney, 1930; then ptnr. Laney, Randolph, Warner & Angle; county atty. Maricopa County, 1917-21. Mem. bd. edn. Ariz. State Coll., Tempe, 1941-45; bd. regents Univs. and State Coll. Ariz., 1945-62, pres., 1952, 61. Mem. Am., Ariz., Maricopa County bar assns., Arizona Club, Lions Club. Home: Phoenix Ariz. †

LANG, DANIEL, writer; b. N.Y.C., May 30, 1915; s. Nathan and Fanny (Cohen) L.; m. Margaret Altschul, July 19, 1942; children: Frances Altschul, Helen Goodhart, Cecily. BA, U. Wis., 1936. Reporter N.Y. Post, 1939-42; war corr. New Yorker mag., MTO, World War II; then, staff writer New Yorker mag. Author: Early Tales of the Atomic Age, 1948, The Man in the Thick Lead Suit, 1954, From Hiroshima to the Moon, 1959, (juvenile) A Summer's Duckling, 1963, An Inquiry into Enoughness, 1965, Casualties of War, 1969, Patriotism Without Flags, 1974, A Backward Look, 1979; contbr. Story mag, New Republic, Sat. Rev., others. Mem. Greater N.Y. com. United Negro Coll. Fund. Recipient Soc. Mag. Writers award for excellence best articles internat. relations, Sidney Hillman Found. award, Nat.

Mag. award for reporting excellence, George Polk award for mag. reporting. Mem. Century Assn., Skating Club (N.Y.C.). Home: Mamaronek N.Y. Died Nov. 17, 1981.

LANG, EMIL HENRY, metals processing company executive; b. Erie, Pa., June 29, 1885; s. George and Caroline (Doehrel) L.; m. Louise M. Uhdey, Apr. 20, 1911; 1 child, Carolyn. Student pub. schs. With various depts. Erie (Pa.) Forge Co., 1902-10, salesman, 1910-24, gen. sales mgr., 1924-46, pres., from 1946; pres. Erie Forge and Steel Corp., 1946-57, chmn. bd., from 1957; bd. dirs. First Nat. Bank, Erie. Mem. Soc. Naval Architects and Marine Engrs., Am. Soc. Naval Engrs., Am. Iron and Steel Inst., Erie Kahkwa Club, Shriners. Republican. Lutheran. Home: Erie Pa. †

LANG, SYLVAN, lawyer; b. Des Moines, June 7, 1891; s. Isaac and Henrietta (Wallerstein) L.; m. Mary Reinhardt, Dec. 27, 1922; children: Jeanne (Mrs. Irving Mathews), Sylvan Stephen. BS, U. Pa., 1912; LLM, U. Tex., 1914; LLD, St. Mary's U., 1964. Bar: Tex. 1914. Began practice San Antonio, 1914; sr. mem. firm Lang, Cross, LAndon, Oppenheimer & Rosenberg; gen. counsel Southland Greyhound Lines, Gt. Am. Life Ins. Co. (now FRanklin Life Ins. CO.), 1925-35; pres. Med. Arts Bldg. Co., 1937-60; v.p. San Antonio Transit Co., 1942-59; later v.p. San Antonio Bldg. Servicing Co.; pres. Milam Mgmt. Co., Lamawell Realty Co., Austin, Tex.; chmn. bd. Frost Bros. Inc., San Antonio; dir. Straus-Frank Co. Contbr. to Tex. Law Rev., 1952; chmn. publ. com. History of 90th Division. Chmn. bd. govs. St. Mary's Law Sch.; bd. dirs. S.W. Rsch. Ctr., S.W. Rsch. Inst., S.W. Found. Rsch. and Edn.; chmn., life trustee U. Tex. Law Sch. Found.; bd. dirs. San Antonio Art Inst.; past regional vice chmn. U.A. Com. for UN; nat. vice chmn. Joint Def. Appeal; pres. St. Mary's Edn. Found.; trustee St. Mary's U.; past mem. nat. exec. com. Union Am. Hebrew Congregations; mem. nat. bd. Am. Jewish Com., chmn. S.W. regional council; Col. staff Gov. Moody, 1927; declined appointment dist. judge, 1929; Rep. presdl. elector, 1948. Maj. inf. U.S. Army, 1917-19; col. inf. World War II. Decorated Silver Star, Purple Heart, Victory medal with 3 bars (U.S.); Croix de Guerre (France); recipient Brotherhood award NCCJ, 1959; Law Day honoree U. Tex., 1960. Mem. San Antonio Bar Assn. (chmn. courts bldg. com.), ABA, Am. Acad. Social nad Polit. Sci., U. Tex. Law Sch. Assn., Am. Fedn. Arts, Archives Am. Art, U. Pa. Alumni Assn. (pres. San Antonio), San Antonio C. of C. (chmn. pub. health com.), Oak Hills Country Club, Argyle Club, St. Charles Bay Hunting and Fishing Club (Rockport, Tex.), Tamarisk Country Club (Palm Springs, Calif.), Masons (33 deg.), Shriners, Sigma Pi, Delta Sigma Rho, Phi Delta Phi. Home: San Antonio Tex. †

LANGE, CARL JOHN, food distributing company executive; b. Chgo., May 11, 1930; s. Carl August and Frances Elenor (Bruski) L.; m. Arlene M. Wulff, Sept. 13, 1958 (dec. Oct. 1978); children—Lauren, LeAnne, Matthew; m. Edna Faye Moody Dicks. B.S. in Bus. Adminstrn., North Central Coll., Naperville, Ill., 1955; M.B.A., DePaul U., 1960. Plant mgr. Glidden SCM, Bethlehem, Pa., 1962-66; product mgr. Glidden SCM, Cleve., 1966-70; div. controller Sysco Corp., Albany, N.Y., 1970-74; v.p., controller, then sr. v.p., controller Sysco Corp., Houston, 1974-88. Mem. adv. com. Houston Community Coll., 1981-83. Served with USAF, 1950-54, PTO. Home: Houston Tex. Died Feb. 14, 1988; buried Meml. Oaks, Houston.

LANGER, SUZANNE KATHERINA, philosophy educator; b. N.Y.C., Dec. 20, 1895; d. Antonio and Elsie M. (Ulrich) Knauth; m. William L. Langer, Sept. 3, 1921 (div. 1942); children: Leonard C.R., Bertrand. AB, Radcliffe Coll., 1920, AM, 1924, PhD, 1926; student, U. Vienna, 1921-22; DLitt (hon.), Wilson Coll., 1954; Western Coll., Wheaton Coll., Mt. Holyoke Coll., 1962; LLD (hon.), Columbia U., 1964; DFA (hon.), Phila. Coll. Fine Arts, 1966; LHD (hon.), Clark U., 1968. Tutor philosphy Radcliffe Coll., 1927-42; asst. prof. philosphy U. Del., 1943; lectr. philosophy Columbia U., 1945-50; vis. prof. NYU, 1945, New Sch. Scoial Research, Northwestern U., Ohio U., U. Wash, U. Mich.; prof. philosophy Conn. Coll., 1954-62, prof. emeritus, research scholar, from 1962. Author: The Practice of Philosophy, 1930, Philosophy in a New Key: A Study in the Symbolism of Reason, Rite and Art, 1942, An Introduction to Symbolic Logic, 1953, Feeling and Form, 1953, Problems of Art, 1957, Philosophical Sketches, 1962, Mind: An Essay on Human Feeling, 3 vols., 1967-82; co-editor: Structure, Method and Meaning-Essays in Honor of Henry M. Sheffer, 1951; editor: Reflections on Art, 1958. Recipient Radcliffe Alumnae Achievement medal, 1950; Rockefeller Found. grantee , 1946-49, Edgar Kaufmann Found. research grantee, 1956-58, 58-63, 63-65. Mem. Am. Acad. Arts and Scis., Phi Beta Kappa. Home: Old Lyme Conn. Died July 17, 1985.

LANGFORD, ERNEST, architect; b. Ballinger, Tex., May 30, 1891; s. Marcus Lafayette and Maude Clarence (Fewell) L.; m. Lela Davidson, Dec. 24, 1913; 1 child, Keith. BArch, Tex. A&M Coll., 1913; MS, U. Ill., 1924. Architect A.O. Watson, Architect, Austin, Tex., 1913-15; instr. engring. drawing Tex. A&M Coll., 1915-19, prof., 1925-29, head Coll. Architecture, 1929-56, univ. archivist, 1957-71; instr. architecture U. Ill., 1920-25. Councilman City of College Station, Tex., 1938-42, mayor, 1942-66. Fellow AIA, Tex. Soc. Architects, Kiwanis, Phi Kappa Phi, Tau Beta Phi. Home: College Station Tex. Died Oct. 5, 1981.

LANGSTON, JOHN DALLAS, lawyer; b. Aurora, N.C., Mar. 22, 1881; s. George Dallas and Sallie Anne (Gibbs) L.; m. Mary Williams Williamson, Dec. 23, 1903; children: John Dallas, William Dortch, Mary Williamson, Dorothy, Elizabeth Carolyn. AB, Trinity Coll. (now Duke U.), 1903; student law dept., U. N.C., 1904. Bar: N.C. 1905. Began practice Mt. Olive, N.C.; mem. Langston and Langston, Goldsboro, N.C. Chmn. State Bd. Elections, 1927-28; chmn. Dist. Exemption Bd. for Ea. N.C., 1917; chmn. Planning Coun., mem. exec. oun., mem. interdept. com. legal affairs; chmn. Presdl. Appeal Bd.; asst. sir. pres. appeals and advisory bd. SSS. Lt. col. JAG Dept., U.S. Army, 1917-19; col. res.; col. U.S. Army, 1940-46. Decorated D.S.M. with bronze oak leaf cluster, Selective Service medal, Citation for Army Commendation Ribbon. Mem. Duke U. Alumni Assn. (pres. 1926-27), Masons, Shriners, Omicron Delta KAppa, Pi Kappa Alpha. Democrat. Methodist. Home: Goldsboro N.C. †

LANK, HERBERT HAYMAN, business executive; b. Seaford, Del., Jan. 7, 1904; s. Albert J. and Elizabeth E (Hayman) L.; m. Oriana Bailey, Mar. 19, 1927; children: Raymond, Alden, David. BA, U. Del., 1925, LHD (hon.), 1959; LLD (hon.), U. Montreal, 1956; DCL (hon.), Bishop's U., 1965. With E.I. DuPont de Nemours & Co., Inc., 1925-26, 28-31, La Societé Franç Duco, 1927-28; comml. dir. Industrias Quimicas Duperial, Buenos Aires, 1931-42; v.p. Can. Industries, Ltd., Montreal, Que., 1943-54, dir., 1949-54; founder, pres., dir. DuPont of Can., Ltd., Montreal, 1954-65, chmn. bd., 1965-69, dir., from 1965; chmn. bd. Crédit Foncier Franco-Canadien, Can. Enterprise Devel. Corp.; dir. Consol-Bathurst Ltd., No. Electric Co. Ltd., Pratt & Whitney Aircraft Can. Ltd., Hudson Bay Oil & Gas Co. Ltd, Dominion Bridge Co. Ltd., No. Electric Co. Ltd., Ireland, No. Telecom Inc., Bell Can., The Sun Life Assurance Co. Can., Dominion Glass Co., Ltd., Bathurst Paper Ltd., AMCA Internat. Corp, Nevron Industries Co. Ltd. Dir. Expo 67; exec. mem. bldg. com. Place des Arts; adviser to McGill U. Sch. Commerce, also dept. bus. adminstrn. Bishop's U., Lennoxville, Que. Home: Westmount Que., Canada.

LANKFORD, WILLIAM THOMAS, JR., steel company executive; b. Rockwood, Tenn., Nov. 1, 1919; s. William Thomas and Pearl (Chastain) L.; m. Gretchen Goldsmith, July 29, 1944; children: William T. III (dec.), Andrew James, John Robert, Kathleen. BS in Metall. Engring., Carnegie-Mellon U., 1941, ScD in Metall. Engring., 1945. Registered profl. engr., Pa. Devel. engr. Carnegie-Ill. Steel Corp., 1945; chief research engring. splty. products U.S. Steel Corp., 1954-60, div. chief sheet products, 1960-63, asst. dir. steel products devel., 1963-67, mgr. steel processing, 1967-75; assoc. dir. Research Lab., Monroeville, Pa., 1975-81, dir. research planning, from 1980. Contbr. articles to profl. jours. Trustee Carnegie-Mellon U., from 1980. Recipient Charles B. Dudley medal, Richard L. Templin award ASTM. Fellow ASME, Am. Soc. Metals, Metall. Soc. of AIME (Howe Meml. lectr.); mem. Iron and Steel Soc. of AIME, Am. Iron and Steel Inst., AAAS, University Club (Pitts.). Republican. Home: Pittsburgh Pa. Died Aug. 9, 1986, buried Allegheny Cemetery, Pittsburgh.

LANSDALE, ROBERT TUCKER, social welfare consultant; b. Elmira, N.Y., Jan. 22, 1900; s. Herbert Parker and Lida Rachel (Eppley) L.; m. Evelyn Gross, Dec. 31, 1925 (div. 1956); m. Carol Mary Standish, Jan. 28, 1956. AB, Oberlin Coll., 1921; diploma, N.Y. Sch. Social Work, 1924; MA, Columbia U., 1925; postgrad. sociology, U. Mich., 1925-27; LLD (hon.), St. Lawrence U., 1953. Chr. English and social Sci. East High Sch., Rochester, N.Y., 1921-23; instr. sociology U. Mich., 1925-27; exec. sec. Council Social Agys., Montclair, N.J., 1927-30; asst. to commr. U.S. Office Indian Affairs, 1930-34; adminstrv. asst. Fed. Emergency Relief Adminstrn., 1934-35; dir. state and local orgn. Gov.'s Commn. Unemployemnt Relief, 1935-36; in charge nat. study old age assistance adminstrn., com. pub. adminstrn. Social Sci. Research Council, 1936-37; mem. faculty N.Y. Sch. Social Work, 1937-43; dir. Inst. Welfare Research, Community Service Soc., N.Y.C., 1941-43; commr. N.Y. State Dept. Social Welfare, 1943-53; con. N.Y. State Commn. Fiscal Affairs State Govt., 1953-55; prof. Sch. Social Welfare, Fla. State U., 1955-63; vis. prof. Sch. Social Work, U. Md., Balt., 1964-66, prof. social work, 1966-70; cons. Md. Commn. on Aging, 1970-72, Gov. Md. Commn. to Study Problems in Nursing Homes, 1972-73; research assoc. Balt. Commn. on Aging and Retirement Edn., 1973-78; exec. sec. Mich. Conf. Social Work, 1925-27; cons. research div. Welfare Adminstrn., Dept. Health, Edn. and Welfare, Washington, 1964-66, Inst. Govtl. Research, Fla. State U., 1966-68; cons., lectr. numerous orgns., univs. Author: The Florida Suitable Home Law, 1962, Inadequacies of Statewide Programs of Public Assistance in Urban Areas, 1967, Supplemental Security Income: State Variations, 1977; co-author: Administration of Old Age Assistance, 1938, County Welfare in Florida, 1968, Maryland's Older Citizens: An Assessment of Needs and Services, 1972, also articles and reports. Chmn. N.Y. State Youth Commn., 1949-53, N.Y. State Joint Hosp. Survey and Planning Commn., 1947-53; sec. Fla. Citizens Adv. Com. on Aged, 1959-61; v.p. Met. Sr. Citizens Ctr., Balt., 1969-70. With U.S. Army, 1918. Mem. Nat. Assn. Social Workers, Acad. Cert. Social Workers, Am. Pub. Welfare Assn., Nat. Conf. Social Welfare, Md. Conf. Social Welfare. Home: Saint Petersburg Fla. Died Nov. 29, 1980; buried Green Mt. Cemetery, Balt.

LANTZ, MICHAEL, sculptor; b. New Rochelle, N.Y.; s. Frank and Mary (Jarvis) L. Student, NAD, 1924-26; student Beaux Arts Inst. Design, 1926-31. Asst. Lee Lawrie, 1925-35; art instr. Adult Edn. Ctr., New Sochelle, 1935-38; instr. Nat. Acad. Sch. Fine Arts, 1964-80, Old Lyme Acad. Fine Arts, 1977-80. Works include: sculptural bronze history of oil Sinclair Oil Bldg., N.Y.C.; sculptural panel Cement Industry, Lone Star Cement Corp., N.Y.C.; 2 sculptural panels Architects Bldg., Albany, N.Y.; scuptural panels lobby Celanese Corp. Bldg., Charlotte , N.C.; dining room DuPont Plaza Hotel, N.G. Meml. Bldg., Washington, Howard Trust Co., Burlington Vt., S.S. U.S. Ct. House, Lynchburg Va.; sculpture U.S. Battle Monument, St. Avold, France, City Hall, Milw.; 2 chapels Cathedral of Mary our Queen, Balt.; sculpture Temple, Mobile, Ala., Ct. Houe, Mobile; exhbns. piece Christmas Font for Steuben Glass; 29 seals Pan Am. World Health Ctr.; Thomas Bicentennial medal U.S. Mint; New Rochelle Bicentennial medal; 4 foot bronze eagle People's Bank for Savs., New Rochelle; Brookgreen Gardens Medallian Soc. Medallists; sculpture Edenton (N.C.) Courthouse; exhibited Nat. Acad., Archtl. League, Phila. Art Alliance, Pa. Acad.; editor Nat. Sculpture Rev. Recipient bronze silver medals Beaux Arts Inst. Design, 1st prize nat. competition Golden Anniversary medal City N.Y., 1948, Linday Morris Meml. award, 1950, silver medal Internat. Exhbn., Madrid, Spain, Hall of Fame medal NYU, Oliver Wendell Homes Sr. medal, John Paul Jones medal, Saitus award for medallic, 1969, Elizabeth Watrous gold medal, 1970, 1st prize nat. competition pair equestrian group Fed. Trade Bldg., Washington, 1988. Fellow Nat. Sculpture Soc. (exec. council, pres., Gold medal of Honor 1986), Find Arts Fedn. N.Y. (v.p. 1970); mem. Allied Artists Am. (silver medal), Acad. Artists Assn. (Springfield), Hudson Valley Artists Assn., Am. Artists Profl. League, Am. Numismatic Soc. Club: N.Y. Athletic. Home: Old Saybrook Conn. Deceased.

LAPAZ, LINCOLN, mathematics and astronomy educator, researcher; b. Wichita, Kans., Feb. 12, 1897; s. Charles Melchior and Emma Josephine (Strode) LaP.; m. Leota Rae Butler, June 18, 1922; children: Leota Jean, Mary Strode. AB, Fairmount Coll., 1920; MA, Harvard U., 1922; PhD, U. Chgo., 1928. Instr. math. Fairmount Coll., Wichita, 1917-20, Harvard U., Boston, 1921-22, Dartmouth Coll., 1922-25; NRC fellow U. Chgo., 1928-29, instr. math., 1929-30; asst. prof. math. Ohio State U., 1930-35, assoc. prof., 1935-42, prof., 1942-45; research mathematician Office f Sci. Rsch. and Devel., 1943-44; prof., head dept. math. and astronomy, dir. Inst. Meteoritics U. N.M., 1945-53, dir. div. astronomy, 1953-62, dir. Inst. Meteoritics, 1953-66; tech. dir. ops. analysis sect. Hdqrs. 2d Air Force, 1944-45; cons. Research and Devel. Bd. Air Material Command, O.S.I. (IG) USAF.; dir. Inst. Meteoritics surveys of meteoritic shower, Feb. 18, 1948, Furnas County, Nebr. and Norton County, Kans. resulting in discovery and excavation of largest aerolite of either witnessed or unwitnessed fall found in world at that time. Author: (with R.D. Carmichael and J.H. Weaver) The Calculus, 1938; co-author: Physics and Medicine of the Upper Atmosphere, a Study of the Aeropause, 1952, Advances in Geophysics, vol. 4, 1958, Space-Nomads: Meteorites in Sky, Field and Laboratory, 1961; contbr. The Book of Popular Science, 1963, 72, catalog of collections Inst. Meteoritics, 1965, Topics in Meteoritics, 1969; co-author: catalog of the meteorite collection of Inst. of Meteoritics at U. N.Mex., 1980; contbr. math. and astron. articles to profl. jours., also author classified reports; editor U. N.M. publs. in meteoritics, 1944-70; assoc. editor: Meteoritics, 1955-56. Recipient letters of commendation from Sec. of War Patterson, Gen. H.H. Arnold, Maj. Gen. R. Williams, Brig. Gen. J.K. Lacey, Col. W.B. Leach. Fellow Meteoritical Soc. (pres. 1941-46, rep. to AAAS); mem. Am. Math. Soc., Math Assn. Am., Brit. Math. Assn. (life), Internat. Astron Union (commn 22 1950-58), Am. Astron. Soc., Royal Astron. Soc. Can., British Astron. Assn. (life), Astron. Soc. of the Pacific, Am. Meteor Soc., N.Mex. Acad. Scis., Sigma Xi. Home: Albuquerque N.Mex. Died Oct. 19, 1985.

LA PIERE, RICHARD TRACY, sociology educator, author; b. Beloit, Wis., Sept. 15, 1899; s. Ernest and Ella (Brown) La P.; m. Helen Halderman, Dec. 31, 1934. A.B. magna cum laude, Stanford, 1926, A.M., 1927, Ph.D. in Sociology, 1930; student, London Sch. Econs. and Polit. Sci., 1927-28. Asst. econs. Stanford, 1928-29, instr., 1929-33, asst. prof. sociology, 1932-38, assoc. prof., 1938-40, prof., 1940-65, prof. emeritus, from 1965; prof. sociology U. Mich., 1938-39. Author: (with P. R. Farnsworth) textbook Social Psychology, 3d edit., 1947; (novels) Son of Han, 1937, When the Living Strive, 1941; Collective Behavior, 1938, Sociology, 1946, A Theory of Social Control, 1954, The Freudian Ethic,

1959, Social Change, 1965; cons. editor McGraw-Hill series Sociology and Anthropology, 1947-67; contbr. sci. jours. With air svc. U.S. Army, 1917-19; with Am. Expeditionary Force, France. Mem. Am. Sociol. Soc., Pacific Sociol. Soc. (pres. 1948), Sociol. Research Assn., Social Sci. Conf. Pacific Coast, Phi Beta Kappa. Home: Stanford Calif. Died Feb. 2, 1986, buried at sea.

LAPIN, RAYMOND HAROLD, mortgage banker; b. Inglewood, Calif., Feb. 13, 1919; s. Morris and Sarah (Goldberg) L.; m. Mary Elizabeth Woodcock, Jan. 3, 1950; 1 son, John Grattan. MBA in Fin., U. Chgo., 1954. Asst. mgr. rsch. dept. Fed. Res. Bank, Chgo., 1949-54; founding pres., chief. exec. officer Bankers Mortgage Co. Calif. (now Transam. Mortgage Co.), 1954-66; cons. Transam. Corp., 1966-67; pres. Fed. Nat. Mortgage Assn., Washington, 1967-68, dir., 1976-80; pres., chmn. bd. pvt. owned corp. Fed. Nat. Mortgage Assn., 1968-70; mem. current reporting series com. Fed. Res. Bd., 1951-54; founding pres. Govt. Nat. Mortgage Assn., 1968; pres., chmn. bd. R.H. Lapin & Co. Inc., from 1970; bd. dirs. San Francisco Devel. Fund, Securities Groups Money Fund, N.Y.C.; pres. San Francisco Mcpl. Ry. Improvement Corp., 1970-74, Am. Savs. & Loan Assn. Fla., L.B. Nelson Corp., C.L. Assets (CNA); hon. life mem. adv. com. FNMA. Commr. Art Commn. City and County San Francisco, 1964-65, Pub. Utilities Commn. City and County San Francisco, 1965-66; bd. dirs. Econ. Devel. Agy. Calif, 1966; bd. dirs., pres. San Francisco Housing Fin. and Devel. Corp., from 1980; pres. real estate adv. com. U. Calif., from 1980; mem. White House Task Force Mortgage Fin., 1967-68; bd. dirs. Coun. for Civic Unity, 1962-65, Mt. Zion Hosp., San Francisco, 1964-67, 70-76, San Francisco Planning and Urban Renewal Assn., 1974-77, Nat. Housing Conf., from 1975; pres. San Francisco Devel. Fund, 1970-74. Capt. AUS, 1942-46, PTO. Recipient Outstanding Alumnus award U. Chgo., 1968, award for better communities and decent homes Nat. Housing Conf., 1977; numerous awards from nat. mortgage banking, savs. and loan, realtor and home builder assns. for initiating maj. changes in nat. secondary mrotgage market. Mem. Fed. City Club, Georgetown Club (Washington), Stock Exchange Club, St. Francis Yacht Club (San Francisco), Lambda Alpha. Home: San Francisco Calif. Died Apr. 2, 1986; buried Daphne Fernwood Cemetery, Mill Valley, Calif.

LAPWING, LEO JOHN, metal tool manufacturing executive; b. Detroit, July 1, 1917; s. Leon and Sarah Czajka; m. Mary Kathryn Lepkojous; children: Carol, John, Janet. With Valeron Corp., Oak Park, Mich., from 1942, pres., chmn. bd., from 1944, also dir. Mem. KC. Roman Catholic. Home: Bloomfield Hills Mich. Deceased.

LARGE, JOHN WILLARD, research musician, educator; b. Appalachia, Va., Nov. 29, 1929; s. John Willard and Elma Elizabeth (Blankenship) L. B.F.A., U. N.Mex., 1954, M.Mus., 1955; D.Mus., Ind. U., 1962; Licence de Concert, Ecole Normale de Musique, Paris, France, 1963; Ph.D. (NIH fellow), Stanford, 1971. Prof. music N.Y. State U. Coll., Potsdam, 1965-66, San Francisco State U., 1966-69, U. So. Calif., 1969-72, Santa Clara U., 1973-74, U. Calif. at San Diego, 1974-78, N. Tex. State U., Denton, 1978-85, Tex. Christian U., 1985-87. Performing artist bass-baritone, Eastman Boomer Concert Mgmt., N.Y.C., 1965-68. Served with USNR, 1955-59. Recipient Fulbright award 1962-63. Mem. Nat. Assn. Tchrs. Singing, Acoustical Soc. Am. (dir. Internat. Conf. on Research in Singing 1975), Internat. Assn. Rsch. in Singing (formerly Internat. Assn. Exptl. Research in Singing; founder 1971, gen. sec. 1971-87; editor Jour. Rsch. Singing and Applied Vocal Pedagogy, 1977-87). Died Oct. 22, 1987; cremated, interred N.Mex.

LARIAR, LAWRENCE, cartoonist, editor, author; b. Bklyn., Dec. 25, 1908; s. Marcy and Ella (Poll) L.; m. Susan Meyer, Oct. 19, 1935; children: Linda, Stephen. Student, N.Y. Sch. Fine and Applied Arts, 1926-29, Academie Juliena, Paris, Art Students League, N.Y.C. Comml. advt. artist 1930-33, free-lance illustrator and polit. cartoonist, from 1933. Work has appeared in Sat. Evening Post, Collier's, Am. Mag., Judge, New Yorker, Coll. Humor, Country Gentleman, N.Y. daily newspapers; cartoon editor Liberty mag., 1941-48, Parade, 1957-81; dir. Profl. Sch. Cartooning, N.Y. Sch. Fine and Applied Arts (fellow 1927); author: Andrew the Ant, Cartooning for Everybody, 1941, Death Paints the Picture, 1943, Army Fun Book, 1943, He Died Laughing, 1943, The Man with the Lumpy Nose, 1944, Oh, Dr. Kinsey, 1953, Yankee Yiddish, 1953, Fish and Be Damned, 1953, Naked and Alone, 1953, Kiss and Kill, 1954, Golf and Be Damned, 1954, You've Got Me in Stitches, 1954, You've Got Me on the Hook, 1954, You've Got Me and How, 1955, Best Cartoons from Abroad, 1955, You've Got Me from 9 to 5, 1956, You've Got Me On the Rocks, 1956, The Real Lowdown, 1956, Hunt and Be Damned, 1956, Girl Running, 1956, Boat and Be Damned, 1957; editor: Bed and Bored, 1945, The Girl with the Frightened Eyes, 1945, (with Col. Stoopnagle) Father Stoopnagle, 1945, Run for Your Life, 1946, CBS TV Happy Headlines, 1947, Careers in Cartooning, 1949, Friday for Death, 1949, Easy Way to Cartooning, 1950, Stone Cold Blonde, 1951, American Saleman, 1951, Bantam Prince (N.Y. Herald-Tribune Syndicate), Murder for Madame, 1951, Knife at My Back, 1952, The Sunburned Corpse, 1952, The Day I Died, 1952, Don't Follow Me, 1953, How Green Was My Sex Life, 1955, You've Got Me in a Hole, 1955, The Salesman, 1955, Fix It and Be Damned, 1955; editor: Best Cartoons of the Year, 1942-81. Home: Freeport N.Y. Died Dec. 12, 1981.

LARKIN, ARTHUR EDWARD, JR., food company executive; b. Mpls., Mar. 7, 1917; s. Arthur Edward and Lou (McCabe) L.; m. Margaret Davis, Sept. 17, 1941 (div. 1962); children: Wendy, Barbara, Margaret; m. Ellen Keenan, Jan. 23, 1963; stepchildren: Michael, Timothy, Peter, Annabel. V.p., dir. George Hormel & Co., 1946-58; with Gen. Foods Corp., 1958-72, mktg. mgr. Maxwell House div., 1958-59, gen. mgr., 1959-62, v.p. corp., 1960-62, exec. v.p., 1962-66, pres., chief operating officer, 1966-72; pres., chief exec. officer Keebler Co., Elmhurst, Ill., 1972-81, chief exec. officer, 1976-78, chmn. bd., 1976-81; chmn. fin. com. United Biscuits U.S., 1979-81; bd. dirs. United Biscuits (Holdings) Ltd., Gt. Brit., Kemper Corp, H.P. Hood Co., Inc., Hercules, Inc. Trustee Elmhurst Coll. Lt. comdr. USNR, 1940-45. Mem. Mgmt. Execs. Soc., Grocery Mfrs. Am. (bd. dirs.), Council Fgn. Relations, Economic Club, President's Club (N.Y.C.). Home: Elmhurst Ill. Died Oct. 17, 1981.

LARMON, SIGURD STANTON, advertising executive; b. Stanton, Iowa, July 21, 1891; s. Peter and Sophia (Peterson) L.; m. Katherine Steen, June 14, 1916; children: Helen V. Larmon Benizger, Jay Stanton. BS, Dartmouth Coll., 1914, MA (hon.), 1948. Salesman Western Clock Co., 1914-21, mgr. for U.K., London, 1915-16, sales mgr., 1917-21; dist. mgr. Columbia Phonograph Co., 1921-24; account exec. N.W. Ayer and Son, 1924-28; assoc. Young and Rubicam, Inc., from 1929, pres., chmn. bd., 1942-58, chmn. bd., from 1958. Co-author: Primer for Americans. Mem. U.S. Adv. Commn. on Information; dir. N.Y. Conv. and Visitors Bur.; v.p., trustee. Nat Council on Crime and Delinquency; trustee Com. Econ. Devel.; mem. adv. council Columbia Grad Sch. Bus.; exec. com. Bus. Council for Internat. Understanding; trustee Dartmouth Coll.; nat. vice chmn. Citizens for Eisenhower, 1952, 56. Recipient Printers Ink Advt. Gold medal, 1962. Mem. Am. Assn. Advertising Agys. (past chmn.), Council Fgn. Relations, Internat. C. of C. (trustee U.S. council), Mex. C. of C. (bd. dirs.), Nat. Inst. Social Scis., Pinnacle Club, Dartmouth Club, Augusta Nat. Golf Club, Blind Brook Club, Economic Club, Union League Club, Links Club, Wianno Club. Home: New York N.Y. Died Jan. 1, 1987, buried Stanton, Iowa.

LARO, ARTHUR EMMETT, editor; b. Brownsville, Tex., Feb. 19, 1912; s. Arthur Elmo and Anna Maude (Hale) L.; m. Dorothy Vernon Jones, June 5, 1937 (dec.); 1 child, Mary Ann; m. Kay Dalton, Aug. 25, 1973. Ed., San Antonio pub. schs. Reporter San Antonio Light, 1929-36, Houston Press, 1936-37; real estate editor, spl. editor Houston Post, 1937-45, city editor, 1945-46, mng. editor, 1946, past exec. editor, v.p.; dir. Houston Post Co. 1949-60; exec. editor L.A. Mirror, 1960, editor, pub., 1960-62; editor Newhouse Nat. News Service, 1962-64; exec. v.p., editor Chgo. Tribune-N.Y. News Syndicate, Inc., 1964-66, pres., editor, 1966-74, cons., 1974-81; ptnr. Laro/Donahue Ltd., Houston, 1974-76; gen. mgr. Booke and Co., Inc., 1977-81. Dir. Energy Research and Edn. Found. Mem. Nat. Press Club, Houston Club, Sigma Delta Chi. Methodist. Home: Houston Tex. Died Dec. 23, 1981, buried Forest Park Lawndale, Houston.

LARSEN, JACK KIRBY, oil company executive, geologist; b. Fauna, Tex., July 8, 1919; s. Martin E. and Marion (Kirby) L.; m. Betty Jean Gill, July 31, 1945; children: Linda, Martin, Kirby, Janet. BA, U. Tex.-Austin, 1940. Div. mgr. Shell Oil Co., Baton Rouge and Lafayette, La., 1954-64; chief ops. Shell Oil Co., New Orleans, 1964; mgr. exploration So. Natural Gas, Houston, 1964-69; exec. v.p. Mesa Petroleum Co., Amarillo, Tex., from 1969, also bd. dirs. Capt. USAF, 1942-45. Republican. Presbyterian. Home: Amarillo Tex. Died Mar. 25, 1986, buried Eagle Lake, Tex.

LARSEN, ROY WILLIAM, savings and loan association executive; b. Grand Forks, N.D., June 15, 1891; s. Lawrence William and Christine (Anderson) L.; m. Meta Holmes, Nov. 5, 1929; m. 2d, Eleanor Farrington, Aug. 20, 1937; 1 dau., Christine Kay. BA, U. Minn., 1913; LLB, George Washington U., 1918. Sec., v.p. Twin City Fed. Savs. and Loan Assn., Mpls., 1929-43, pes., 1943-66, chmn. bd., from 1966; bd. dirs. Title Ins. Co., Mpls. Pres. Mpls. Taxpayers Assn.; treas., dir. Mpls. Jr. Achievement, Hennepin County Hist. Soc.; bd. dirs., exec. com. Minn. Hist. Soc.; bd. dirs. Minn. Zool. Soc.; chmn. Savs. and Loan Found. Recipient Alumni Svc. award U. Minn., 1962. Mem. Mpls. C. of C. (dir.), Minn. Hist. Soc. (dir.), Minneapolis Club, MinikahdaClub, Minneapolis Athletic (Mpls.); Hartford Club (Conn.), Phi Kappa Sigma, Phi Delta Phi. Home: Minneapolis Minn. †

LARSEN, WESLEY BERNARD, physician, osteopathic surgeon; b. Aurora, Ill., Sept. 5, 1908; s. Thomas Ludwig and Amalie (Anjou) L.; m. Lila Caroline Anderson, June 2, 1936; 1 child, Linda Sue. Student, Northwestern U., 1927-30; grad., Chgo. Coll. Osteopathy, 1945. Diplomate Am. Osteo. Bd. Gen. Practice. Intern Chgo. Osteo. Hosp., 1945-46, mem. staff, 1946-78, hon. staff, from 1978; pvt. practice Chgo., from 1946, Hinsdale, Ill., from 1957; asst. prof. dept. practice Chgo. Coll. Osteopathy, 1947-55, trustee coll., 1954-57; pres. Am. Osteo. Found., 1960-65; vice chmn. corp. Nat. Osteo. Found, 1962-65, bd. dirs. 1962-65, 74-79, mem. corp. from 1976; v.p. A.T. Still Osteo. Found. and Research Inst., 1962-65; mem. White Ho. Conf. on Health, 1966; pres. Ill. Inter-Profl. Council, 1973-74, 3d v.p., 1975-76, 2d v.p., 1976-77. Columnist Osteo. Annals. Named Hon. Chieftain Acoma Indian Tribe Okla., 1966, Hon. Citizen Tex., Gov. Tex., 1966, Hon. Citizen City of Corpus Christi, 1966, Ambassador Goodwill, Mayor of Louisville, Ky., 1966. Fellow Am. Coll. Gen. Practice in Osteo. Medicine and Surgery (pres. Ill. chpt. 1974-78, congress del., 1975-80, splty. cert.); mem. Internat. Acad. Preventive Medicine (hon. citation, trustee), Am. Osteo. Assn. (exec. com. from 1959, numerous com. chairmanships and other offices, 1st v.p. 1959-62, trustee 1962-65, pres. 1965-66, cons. adviser to aux.), Ill. Osteo. Assn. (pres. 1955-57, trustee, past dist. pres.), Ill. Assn. Osteo. Physicians and Surgeons (hon. life, trustee 1953-59 and from 1979, parliamentarian from 1976), Am. Acad. Osteopathy (bd. govs., chmn. coll. assistance com. 1968-71), Nat. Assn. Parliamentarians, Ill. Assn. Parliamentarians, Atlas Club, Masons (32 degree), Shriners. Home: Hinsdale Ill. Died Nov. 13, 1986, cremated.

LARSON, CARL THEODORE, architect, educator; b. Kansas City, Mo., Jan. 6, 1903; s. Peter and Bengta (Swenson) L.; m. Marjorie W. MacNaught, Apr. 24, 1930 (dec. Dec. 1963); children: Ronal W., Dana W.; m. Myra Ann Gulick, July 2, 1970. A.B. magna cum laude, Harvard, 1925, M.Arch., 1929, Nelson Robinson Traveling fellowship, 1929-30. Reporter Kansas City Star, summers 1922-25; Asso. editor Archtl. Record, 1930-36; research cons. F.W. Dodge Corp., N.Y.C., 1937; architect, project planner U.S. Housing Authority, 1938; tech. editor Archtl. Forum, 1939-42, 48; field rep. adminstrator's office Nat. Housing Agy., 1942-43; tech. cons. mil. affairs sub-com. U.S. Senate, 1944-45; asst. tech. dir. Nat. Housing Agy, 1946; tech. dir. Gen. Homes, Inc., Columbus, Ohio, 1947; prof. architecture U. Mich., 1948-73, prof. emeritus, 1973-88, dir. archtl. research lab., 1948-73; pvt. practice research and planning cons. 1973-88; dir. research project facilities early childhood devel. Ednl. Facilities Labs., Inc., 1969-72; sr. cons. social econs. UN Tech. Assistance Adminstrn. regional housing centre, Indonesia, 1956; archtl. cons. ICA, Ethiopia and Tunisia, 1960; cons. archtl. research USPHS, 1965. Author: (with K. Lonberg-Holm) Planning for Productivity, 1940, Plan Europe 2000: Role of Mass Media of Information and Communication, 1972, Development Index, 1953, (with K. Lonberg-Holm) Environmental Analysis, vol. 3 in School Environment Research series; also dir. series project; mem. editorial bd.: Human Systems Mgmt; also author articles. Mem. bldg. research adv. bd. Nat. Acad. Scis.-NRC, 1966-68, Fed. Constrn. Council, 1967-68. Fellow AIA (profl. devel. com., architecture for justice com.); mem. Am. Soc. Info. Sci., World Future Soc., Soc. for Internat. Devel., Architects for Social Responsibility, Phi Beta Kappa. Home: Ann Arbor Mich. Died Feb. 20, 1988.

LARSON, CHARLES PHILIP, pathologist; b. Eleva, Wis., Aug. 15, 1910; s. Clarence P. and Louise (Steig) L.; m. Margaret I. Kobervig, Dec. 10, 1944; children: C. Philip, Lillian L., Charles P., Christine, Elizabeth, Paul, Lawrence. BA, Gonzaga U., 1931, JD (hon.), 1980; MD, CM, McGill U., 1936; postgrad. neuropathology, U. Mich., 1939. Diploamte Am. Pathology, Am. Bd. Legal Medicine. Intern Pierce County Hosp., Tacoma, 1936-37; instr. U. Oreg. Med. Sch., 1939-41; pathologist, dir. labs. Tacoma Gen. Hosp., Tacoma Med. Labs, others, from 1946, later, dir. emeritus; sr. ptnr. Drs. Larson, Apa, Kapilowitz & Eggen, Lakewood Clin. Lab.; assoc. clin. prof. pathology U. Wash.; vis. prof. forensic pathology, U. Ted., 1960; criminologist, med.-legal crime investigator, lectr. crime detection; dir. Tacoma Polic Lab. Author: Manual of Neuropathology, 1940; contrb. articles to profl. jours. Dir. Nat. Careers Com. for Med. Tech.; trustee Pierce County Blood Bank. Lt. col. AUS, 1942-45. Fellow Am. Soc. Clin. Pathologists (dir. 1966, chmn. forensic pathology council), Am. Psychiat. Assn., Internat. Assn. Identification, Am. Acad. Forensic Scis.; mem. Nat. Assn. Med. Examiners (pres. 1972), Internat. Soc. Clin. Pathology (v.p.), AMA, Coll. Am. Pathologists (pres.), Am. Cancer Soc. (pres. Wash. div.), Nat. Mental Assn., N. Pacific Soc. Neurology and Psychiatry, Pacific N.W. Soc. Pathologists, Wash. Soc. Pathologists, Pierce County Med. Soc. (pres. 1967), Wash. Med. Assn. (v.p. 1967), McGill Grads. Soc. (past pres.), Nat. Boxing Assn. (pres. 1963), World Boxing Assn. (pres. 1963), Elks. Rotary. Home: Tacoma, Wash. Died Oct. 4, 1984, buried Haven of Rest, Tacoma.

LARSON, JENS FREDRICK, architect; b. Boston, Aug. 10, 1891; s. Leonard Ludwig and Andresigne (Andersen) L.; m. Elisabeth Goodale Frost, Oct. 12, 1920; children: Nils Frederick, Sara. Student, Boston Archtl. Club, 1907-10, Harvard U., 1910-12; MA, Dartmouth Coll., 1928; LHD, Washington and Jefferson Coll., 1940, Colby Coll., 1964; LLD, Upsala Coll., 1956, Bucknell U., 1959; DSc, St. Francis Xavier U., 1957. Resident architect Dartmouth Coll., Hanover, N.H., 1919-20, lectr. architecture, 1926-31, devel. plan, 1919-

52; mem. firm Larson & Wells, 1920-26; pvt. practice 1926-55; ptnr. Larson & Larson, 1955-69; adv. architect Assn. Am. Colls., 1928-50. Archtl. works include Baker Libr., Tuck Sch. Bus Aminstrn., Colby Coll. campus, Waterville, Maine, Internat. House U. Paris (France), Fuld Hall, Princeton U. Inst. for Advanced Study, Meml. U., Northfield, St. John's, gen. devel. plans and bldgs. Am. U., Cairo, Egypt, Bucknell (Pa.) U., Norwich U., St. Francis Xavier U., N.S., U. Louisville, Allegheny, Hanover, Hood, Marietta, St. Mary's, Washington and Jefferson, Coe colls., Lehigh U., Wake Forest U., Wells. Coll., Abbott, Clark and Holderness schs., Foxcroft and St. Johnsbury acads., Culver Mil. Acad., Upsala Coll., Briarcliff Jr. Coll., Kimball Union Acad., Pfeiffer Coll., N.B., Can., Wesley Coll., Bowman Gray Sch. Medicine, Winston-Salem Community Ctr., W.Va. Wesleyan Coll., St. Thomas U., N.B., Beaverbrook Auditorium, Fredericton, N.B.; author: Architectural Planning of the American College, 1933. With Can. F.A., France, 1914-16, capt. attached to Royal Flying Corps, 1916-19. Decorated Legion of Honor (France), Star, Victory and Brit. War medals. Mem. Assn. Am. Colls. (art commn.), AIA, Boston Soc. Architects, Harvard Engring. Soc., Boston Archtl. Club, Century Club (N.Y.C.). Home: Winston-Salem N.C. †

LARSON, JESS, lawyer; b. Mill Creek, Indian Terr., June 22, 1904; s. Leonard and Bessie (Downard) L.; m. Germaine Moreau, Dec. 25, 1929 (dec. May 1964); m. Mrs. Zdenka Sokitch, Apr. 18, 1967. Student, U. Okla., 1922-26, 33, Emerson Coll. Oratory, Boston, 1926-27; LL.D., Duquesne U., 1950. Bar: Okla. bar 1935, D.C. bar 1955, also U.S. Supreme Ct 1955. Rancher, engaged in dairy bus. Okla., 1927-28; mayor Chickasha, Okla., 1929-33; practice in Oklahoma City, 1934-35, 39-40, Washington, 1954-87; ptnr. firm Alvord & Alvord, Washington, 1965-85, Stoel, Rives, Boley, Fraser & Wyse, Washington, 1985-87; exec. dir. Okla. Sch. Land Commn., 1935-39; asst. gen. counsel War Assets Adminstrn., 1946, gen. counsel, 1946-47, assoc. adminstr., 1947, adminstr., 1947-49; adminstr. Fed. Works Agy., 1949, GSA, 1949-53, Def. Materials Procurement Agy., 1951-53. Chmn. bd. Nat. Patent Devel. Corp., N.Y.C., 1959-87. Entered Okla. N.G. as pvt., 1923; commd. 2d lt. 1923; advanced through grades to col. 1944; served in Mediterranean, Italian theatres 1942-43; dir. tactics F.A. Sch., 1944-45, Ft. Sill, Okla.; assigned War Dept. Gen. Staff, 1945; transferred to USAF Res., 1952, maj. gen., ret. Decorated Legion of Merit, Purple Heart. Mem. Am., Okla. bar assns., Bar Assn. D.C., Air Force Assn. (pres. 1964-67), Delta Tau Delta. Clubs: Mason (Washington and N.Y.C.) (32 deg.), Metropolitan (Washington and N.Y.C.); Army and Navy (Washington). Died Feb. 25, 1987.

LASER, MARVIN, English educator; b. Chgo., Nov. 2, 1914; s. Harry and Ida (Preskill) L.; m. Dorothy Kort, Feb. 8, 1948; children: Harvey R., Steven A. PhB, U. Chgo., 1935, MA, 1937; PhD, Northwestern U., 1948. Instr. English Wilson Jr. Coll., Chgo., 1938-42, 46-53; lectr. English Northwestern U., Chgo., 1947-49; prof. English Chgo. Tchrs. Coll., 1953-56; prof. English Calif. State U., L.A., 1956-65, chmn. div. lang. arts, 1956-63; prof. English, dean Sch. Humanities and Fine Arts Calif. State U., Dominguez Hills, 1965-80, emeritus, 1980-85. Co-author: Language in Your Life, 4 vols., 1965-70; co-editor: Television for the California State Colleges, 1962, Ideas and Issues, 1963, Studies in J.D. Salinger, 1963, Student, School and Society, 1964, Channel One, 1970; co-editor, joint author Harper & Row Scope series, 1965-67. Capt. USAAF, 1942-46. Mem. MLA, Phi Beta Kappa. Home: Palos Verdes Estates Calif. Died Feb. 5, 1985, buried at sea.

LASH, JOSEPH P., author; b. N.Y.C., Dec. 2, 1909; s. Samuel and Mary (Avchin) L.; m. Trude Wenzel, Nov. 8, 1944; 1 child, Jonathan. A.B., Coll. City N.Y., 1931; A.M., Columbia, 1932. Editor Student Outlook, 1933-35; nat. sec. Am. Student Union, 1936-39; gen. sec. Internat. Student Service, 1940-42; N.Y. sec. Ams. for Democratic Action, 1946-48; asst. to Elliott Roosevelt, 1948-50; UN corr. N.Y. Post, 1950-61, asst. editor editorial page, 1961-66. Author: Dag Hammarskjold: Custodian of the Brushfire Peace, 1962, Eleanor Roosevelt: A Friend's Memoir, 1964, 2 Vol. biography Eleanor and Franklin, 1971 (Pulitzer prize 1972, Nat. Book award 1972, Francis Parkman prize 1972) and Eleanor: The Years Alone, 1972, From the Diaries of Felix Frankfurter, 1975, Helen and Teacher: The Story of Helen Keller and Anne Sullivan Macy, 1980, Love, Eleanor: Letters to Friends, 1982; A World of Love: Letters to Friends 1943-62, 1984, Life Was Meant To Be Lived: A Contemporary Portrait, 1984. asst. editor: F.D.R., His Personal Letters, Vols. III-IV, 1950, Roosevelt and Churchill: 1939-41, 1976. Served to 2d lt. USAAF, 1942-45. Decorated Air Medal.; Recipient first Samuel E. Morison award, 1976. Home: Key West Fla. Died Aug. 22, 1987.

LASHLY, JOHN HENDERSON, lawyer; b. St. Louis, Aug. 20, 1916; s. Jacob Mark and Bessie (Henderson) L.; m. Jean McCrory, 1942; children: Mark, James, Patrick, Bonnie Jean; m. Claire Louise Lashly, 1973. A.B., Swarthmore Coll., 1938; J.D., Washington U., 1941. Bar: Mo. 1941. Practice law St. Louis, 1941-87; ptnr. Lashly, Baer & Hamel, P.C., 1950-87, chmn. bd., 1973-87. Pres. St. Louis Mcpl. Opera Bd., 1973-74, dir., 1955-87; pres. St. Lukes Hosp., 1964-66, St. Louis Mercantile Library, 1962-64. Served with USAAF, World War II. Recpient Disting. Law Alumni award Washington U. Sch. Law, St. Louis, 1987. Mem. ABA (ho. of dels. 1966-70, bd. govs. 1970-73), Mo. Bar (bd. govs., pres. 1966-67), Bar Assn. St. Louis (pres. 1960-62), St. Louis C. of C. (dir. 1957-61), Phi Delta Theta (Phi of Yr. 1978), Phi Delta Phi. Clubs: Media, Noonday, Bellerive, Stadium. Home: Saint Louis Mo. Died May 31, 1987, body donated to Washington U. Med. Sch.

LASKE, ARTHUR CHARLES, petroleum company executive, foundation executive; b. Bridgeport, Conn., Oct. 3, 1899; s. August A. and Mary (Miller) L; m. Evelyn R. Strasburger, Oct. 12, 1921; children: Marilyn F. Laske Chisnall, Arthur Charles. Grad. pub. schs., Bridgeport. Pres., dir. Sormir Petroleum Corp., from 1937, William T. Morris Found., Inc., N.Y.C., from 1939, Circle Petroleum Corp., from 1960. Mem. Algonquin Club. Home: Trumbull Conn. Deceased.

LASTER, HOWARD JOSEPH, physics educator; b. Jersey City, Mar. 13, 1930; s. Harry and Yetta (Adelman) L.; m. Miriam Sargeant, Apr. 26, 1952; children: Elizabeth, Jonathan, Jane, Sarah. A.B., Harvard U., 1951; Ph.D., Cornell U., Ithaca, N.Y., 1957. Mem. faculty U. Md., College Park, 1956-77; prof. physics U. Md., 1965-77, chmn. dept. physics and astronomy, 1965-75; dean Coll. Liberal Arts U. Iowa, Iowa City, 1977-84, prof. physics and astronomy, 1977-86; Mem. Md. Gov.'s Sci. Resources Adv. Bd., 1965-70; mem. Md. Gov.'s Sci. Adv. Council, 1970-77, chmn., 1973-75; mem. Iowa Gov.'s Sci. Adv. Council, 1980-83; vis. fellow Clare Hall, Cambridge (Eng.) U., 1970-71, 84; vis. program assoc. NSF, 1975-76; dir. Atlantic Research Corp., 1972-86. Research and publs. in cosmic ray theory, astrophysics, energy and science policy. Fellow Am. Phys. Soc., Royal Astron. Soc., Washington Acad. Scis.; mem. AAAS, Am. Astron. Soc., Am. Assn. Physic Tchrs., Soc. Internat. Devel., ACLU, AAUP, Washington Philos. Soc., Md. Acad. Sci., Iowa Acad. Sci., Phi Beta Kappa, Sigma Xi. Democrat. Home: Iowa City Iowa. Died Dec. 31, 1986.

LATANE, JAMES WILSON, farm cooperative executive; b. Washington, Nov. 12, 1918; s. James and Martchen Lindenkohl (Flemer) L.; m. Margaret DeRoulhac Hill, July 18, 1947; children: James Wilson, William Catesby III, Martha Ellen. BS, Va. Poly. Inst., 1938. Fiedl surveyor Rural Electrification Coops., Palmyra, Va., 1938-39; supr. field office Fed. Land Bank, Tappahannock, Va., 1940-41; farmer Oak Grove, Va., from 1947; pres. No. Neck Grain Coop., Inc., Nomini Grove, Va., 1958-60; bd. dirs. So. States Coop., Inc., Richmond, Va., 1968-78, pres., 1977-78. Mem. Westmoreland County, Va. Selective Service Bd., 1955-75; mem. Westmoreland County Planning Commn., 1970-77; lay reader St. Peter's Episc. Ch., Oak Grove. With C.E. U.S. Army, 1942-46. Decorated Bronze Star with oak leaf cluster. Mem. Va. Agribus. Council, Va. Beef Cattle Assn. (pres. 1967-70), Fredericks-Feeder Cattle Assn. Home: Oak Grove Va. Died Apr. 22, 1987, buried Oak Grove, Va.

LATHROP, DOROTHY PULIS, illustrator, writer; b. Albany, N.Y., Apr. 14, 1891; d. Cyrus Clark and I. (Pulis) Lathrop. Student, Columbia Tchrs. Coll.; art edn., Pa. Acad. Fine Arts under Henry McCarter, Art Students League under F. Luis Mora, N.Y.C. Illustrator: The Three Mulla-Mulgars, 1919, A Little Boy Lost, 1920, Down-Adown-Derry, 1922, Crossings, 1923, The Grateful Elephant, 1923, Silverhorn, 1924, Made-to-Order Stories, 1925, The Light Princess, 1926, Tales from the Enchanted Isles, 1926, The Princess and Curdie, 1927, Mopsa the Fairy, 1927, Treasure of Carcassonne, 1928, The Long Bright Land, 1929, Hitty-Her First Hundred Years, 1929, Stars Tonight, 1930, The Dutch Cheese, 1931, Fierce Face, 1936, Animals of the Bible, 1937 (Caldecott medal 1938), The Little Mermaid, 1939; author and illustrator: The Fairy Circus, 1931, The Little White Goat, 1933, The Lost Merry-go-round, 1934, Who Goes There?, 1935, Bouncing Betsy, 1936, Hide and Go Seek, 1938, Presents for Lupe, 1940, The Colt from Moon Mountain, 1941; editor and illustrator: Happy Flute (by Sant Ram Mandel), 1939. Recipient Eyre medal Phila. Water Color and Print Exhbn. for Pixie, a Flying Squirrel (wood engraving); fellowships Pa. Acad. Fine Arts, Albany Inst. History and Art. A.N.A. mem. Nat. Assn. Women Painters and Sculptors. Home: Falls Village Conn. †

LA TOZA, CHARLES ANTON, chemical company executive; b. Chgo., Feb. 2, 1928; s. Charles Joseph and Mildred Roberta (Anton) La T.; m. June Anderson, Aug. 20, 1949; children: Kenneth, Dennis, Gregory, Patricia, Judy, Sandra. PhB, Northwestern U., 1949; JD, DePaul U., 1956. Chemist Nalco Chem. Co., Oak Brook, Ill., 1949-55, mem. staff legal dept., 1955-68, asst. sec., 1968-74, sec., from 1974; pres. Nalco Found. Patentee in Italy. Exec. officer Luth. Ch. of the Good Shepherd; mem. pres.'s adv. council and council on univ. priorities and planning Valparaiso U., 1979-83; trustee, mem. exec. com. Associated Colls. Ill. Mem. Am. Soc. Corp. Secs., Am. Mgmt. Assn. (condr. seminars on corp. sec.'s function), ABA, Ill Bar Assn., Chgo. Bar Assn., Am. Chem Soc. Died Nov. 30, 1984.

LATTY, ELVIN REMUS, lawyer, educator, academic administrator; b. Hopkinton, Mass., May 12, 1903; s. Francis and Rosalind (Shaw) L.; m. Ruth Kenyon Wagner, Jan.25, 1932; 1 child, Joan Sabin Latty. BS, Bowdoin Coll., 1923, LLD (hon.), 1975; JD, U. Mich., 1930; JSD, Columbia U., 1936. Bar: N.Y. 1930. Instr. Romance langs., track coach U. Vt., 1923-28; assoc. Sullivan and Cromwell, N.Y.C., 1930-33; prof. law U. Kan., 1934-35, U. Mo., 1935-37, Duke U., Durham, N.C., 1937; acting dean, then dean Law Sch. Duke U., 1957-66; vis. prof. law George Washington U., 1937, Stanford U., 1938, U. N.C., 1941, 47, 49, 56, U. Tex., 1951, U. P.R., 1968, U. Fla., 1970; Fulbright lectr. law U. Pavia (Italy), 1954; spl. asst. to Am. ambassador, Caracas, Venezuela, 1942; asst. chief fgn. funds control div. U.S. Dept. State, 1943. Author: Subsidiaries and Affliated Corporations, 1936, Introduction to Business Associations, 1951, (with others) Basic Business Associations, 1963; editor: Law and Contemporary Problems, 1943-46; contbr. artciles to profl. jours. Mem. ABA, N.C. Bar Assn., Order of Coif, Phi Beta Kappa, SIgma Nu., Phi Delta Phi. Episcopalian. Home: Durham N.C. Died July 4, 1987, buried Durham N.C.

LAUCK, GEROLD MCKEE, merchandising and advertising consultant; b. Chgo., May 27, 1892; s. Henry Clarence and Alice Virginia (Gerold) L.; m. Ruby Noblit, June 8, 1911; children: Gerold M. Jr., Peter III, Sidney Carol. Ed. pub. schs., Chgo. and Tarpon Springs, Fla. Salesman United Pubs. Corp., 1911-13; sec. to compt. Chgo. Tribune, June 1913; advt. mgr. Welch Grape Juice Co., Westfield, N.Y., 1913-16, Am. Sugar Refining Co., N.Y.C., 1916-19; sucessively rep., ptnr., exec. v.p., dir. N.W. Ayers & Son, Inc., Phila., 1919-52. Decorated Officer Order of Artistic Merit (France). Mem. S.R., Racquet and Tennis Club (N.Y.C.), Nassau Club (Princeton, N.J.), Racquet Club (Phila.). Episcopalian. Home: Princeton N.J. also: Paris France. †

LAUFMAN, SIDNEY, artist; b. Cleve., Oct. 29, 1891; s. George and Bertha (Toffler) L.; m. Beatrice Ratner, Aug. 27, 1916. Student, Cleve. Sch. Art, 1911-12, Chgo. Art Inst., 1913-18, Art Students' League N.Y., 1919-20. Lived and worked in France 1920-30; instr. Art Students' League, N.Y.C., 1938-50; vis. lectr. fine arts Brandeis U., 1959-60. Represented in permanent collections major mus. throughout U.S. Recipient numerous prizes and awards. Mem. NAD (council 1947-50), Artists Equity Assn. (nat. sec., pres. N.Y. chpt. 1950-52), Woodstock Artists Assn., Woodstock Art Conf. (chmn. 1950). Died May 9, 1985.

LAUGHLIN, HENRY ALEXANDER, publisher; b. Pitts., Mar. 18, 1892; s. James B. and Clara B. (Young) L.; m.Rebecca Greenleaf Lord, June 3, 1916; children: Rebecca Ledlie (Mrs. John M. Woolsey Jr.), Henry A. Jr. Student, St. Paul's Sch., Concord, N.H., 1905-10; LittB, Princeton U., 1914. In employ Houghton Mifflin Co., The Riverside Press, book pubs. and mfrs., Boston, from 1914, mem. bd. dirs., from 1924, pres., 1939-57, chmn. bd., 1957-63; pres. Princeton U. Press, 1951-57; chmn. bd. dirs. Franklin Publs. Inc., 1960-61; trustee Middlesex Instn. Savs. Trustee Boston Symphony Orch., Boston Arts Festival, Boston Mus. Contemporary Art, Children's Hosp., Boston, Concord Free Pub. Libr.; mem. corp. Mass. Gen. HHosp; gen. chmn. Greater Boston United War Fund for 1945. Pvt. Bn. A, 1st Mass. F.A. on Mex. border, 1916; 2d lt. 301st F.A., U.S. Army, 1917, 41st F.A., 1918-19. Mem. Tavern Club, Union Club, Somerset Club (Boston); Century Club, Brook Club (N.Y.C.); Ivy Club (Princeton). Republican. Episcopalian. Home: Concord Mass. †

LAUPP, HUGO E., business executive; b. Wheeling, W.Va., 1891. Chmn., dir. Wheeling Dollar Savs. & Trust Co.; bd. dirs. Wheeling Tire Co., Centre Foundry & Machine Co. Mem. W.Va. C. of C. (bd. dirs.), Wheeling Automobile Club (v.p.). Home: Wheeling W.Va. †

LAURENCE, MARGARET, author; b. Neepawa, Man., Can., July 18, 1926; d. Robert Harrison and Margaret Campbell (Simpson) Wemyss; m. John Fergus Laurence, 1947 (div. 1969); children: Jocelyn, David. B.A., United Coll. now U. Man., 1947; D. Litt., McMaster U., 1971; D. Litt. hon., Trent U., 1971, U. Toronto, 1971, Carleton U., 1974, U. Brandon, 1974, Mt. Allison, 1976, U. York, 1980; LLD. hon., Dalhousie U., 1971. Writer in residence U. Toronto, 1969-70, U. Western Ont., 1973; chancellor Trent U., Peterborough, Ont., Can., 1981-83. Author: books A Tree for Poverty, 1960, This Side Jordan, 1960, The Prophet's Camel Bell, 1963, The Tomorrow-Tamer, 1963, The Stone Angel, 1964, A Jest of God, 1966 (Gov. Gen. award for Fiction), Long Drums and Cannons (essays on Nigerian lit.), 1968, The Fire Dwellers, 1969, Jason's Quest (children's fiction), 1969, A Bird in the House, 1970, The Diviners, 1974, Heart of a Stranger (essays), 1976, The Olden Days Coat (children's), 1979, The Christmas Birthday Story (children's), 1980, Six Darn Cows (children's), 1980. Contbr. short stories: Prism, Tamarack Rev., Saturday Evening Post, Ladies Home Journal, Chatelaine, Atlantic Monthly, Argosy, Winter's Tales; articles Holiday mag. Decorated Companion Order of Can., 1971; recipient Beta Sigma Phi award for Best First Novel by a Canadian, 1960, Pres. Medal for Best

Canadian Short Story U. Western Ont., 1961, 62, 64, Gov. Gen. award for fiction, 1966, 74, Molson award, 1975, Periodical Distributor's award, 1977, B'nai B'rith Woman of the Yr. award, 1976, award of Merit City of Toronto, 1978. Died Jan. 5, 1987.

LAUSE, CHARLES JOSEPH, oil company executive; b. Lawrence, Kans., Aug. 22, 1921; s. Charles Joseph and Dorothea Katherina (Kipp) L.; m. Patricia Ann Kelly, July 2, 1954; children: christopher Allen, Elizabeth Ann. BS, U. Dayton, 1943; MBA, Harvard U., 1947. Asst. controller J&L Steel Corp., Pitts., 1947-60; v.p. planning Mobil Internat. Oil Co., 1960-69; exec. v.p. Mobil Europe, London, 1969-73; controller Mobil Corp., N.Y.C., 1973-86, v.p., 1979-86; bd. dirs. Philip A. Hunt Chem. Corp. 1st lt. inf., AUS, 1943-46. Decorated Purple Heart with oak leaf cluster. Died Dec. 24, 1986.

LAVAN, PETER ICHABOD BAER, lawyer; b. Bklyn., Nov. 10, 1898; s. Samuel and Sara (Mundel) L.; m. Faye Collen, May 4, 1935; children: Spencer, Lawrence. AB, Columbia U., 1915, LLB, 1918. Bar: N.Y. 1919. Assoc. Strook & Strook, N.Y.C., 1919-41, ptnr., 1924-41; sr. ptnr. Strook, Strook & Lavan, N.Y.C., from 1941, later, counsel; bd. dirs. Mchts. & Mfrs., Inc., Winter & Co. and affiliated cos., United Factors Corp., Am. Securities Corp., Aeolian Am. Corp., Pianola Inc., Hardman Peck & Co., Fla. Growth Corp., Reihold Engring. & Plastics Co., Inc., Am. Super-Temperature Wires, Inc., Am. Super-Temperature Wires of P.R., Inc., Intercontinental Hotels Corp., Hemisphere Products Corp., Am. Machine & Metals Co., Molybdenum Corp. Am., Haveg Industries, Inc.; spl. cons. ICA. Author: Origins and Interesting Aspects of the Bible, 1949, Bombs and Basic Religion: The United Nation at Fifteen. Nat. chmn. U.S. Com. for UN, 1956; bd. dirs. Columbia Law Sch.; bd. dirs. Simon's Rock of Bard Coll., where ann. award is presented in his name; founder Pidly Fund (halfway houses for mentally disabled); bd. dirs. Berkshire Theater Festival, founder Lavan Ednl. Ctr. for Performing Arts at the theater; former mem. adv. bd. N.Y.C. Nat. Shrines; pres. Delavan Found., from 1941. Lt. Signal Corps, U.S. Army, World War I; personal counsel to chief War Prodn. Bd., World War II. Mem. Am. Acad. Polit. Sci. (life), N.Y. County Lawyers Assn., Fgn. Policy Assn., United Service for New Ams. (bd. dirs.), Peoples League for World Order (bd. dirs.), Kings Crown Columbia, Salvation Army Assn., N.Y. C. of C., Economic Club, Bankers Club, Overseas Press Club, Palm Beach Country Club, National Club, Republican Club, Phi Beta Kappa. Unitarian (former bd. dirs. service com., nat. campaign chmn., lectr. Isle of Shoals Unitarian Assn., Star Island, N.J., from 1949). Home: Palm Beach Fla. Died July 19, 1988.

LAVERY, CHARLES JOSEPH, college chancellor; b. Toronto, Ont., Can., May 1, 1915; s. Charles James and Eleanor (Bradley) L. BA, U. Toronto, 1937, MA, 1940; PhD, U. Chgo., 1950; DD (hon.), Hofstra U., 1968; LLD, Hobart and William Smith Coll., 1975, Nazareth Coll., 1978, U. Rochester, 1979. Joined Congregation of St. Basil, 1937; ordained priest Roman Cath. Ch., 1942. Instr. Aquinas Inst., Rochester, N.Y., 1940-41; dir. devel. U. St. Thomas, Houston, 1948; registrar, v.p. St. Michaels Coll., U. Toronto, 1949-58; pres. St. John Fisher Coll., Rochester, 1958-80, chancellor, 1980-85; mem. exec. com. Rochester Ares Colls., 1965-85; mem. Gov.'s Task Force on Higher Edn., 1975-85; chmn. pub. affairs com. Commn. Ind. Colls. and Univs. Chmn. Rochester Clean City Com.; mem. Inter-Faith Com. for Israel; mem. adv. bd. Jr. League; bd. dirs. Ednl. TV Assn., Rochester/Monroe County Athletes Hall of Fame, United Community Chest. Recipient County Civic medal, 1972, Monroe County Citizens Civic award, 1972; named Kiwanis of Yr., 1971. Mem. Rochester C. of C. (dir.), Fortnightly Club, Oak Hill Country Club, University Club, Genesee Valley Club. Home: Rochester N.Y. Died Dec. 3, 1985.

LAVERY, EMMET GODFREY, writer; b. Poughkeepsie, N.Y., Nov. 8, 1902; s. James A. and Katharine T. (Gilmartin) L. LL.B., Fordham U., 1924; L.H.D., Mt. St. Paul Coll., 1968; m. Genevieve E. Drislane, Nov. 3, 1925; children—Emmet, Elizabeth. Bar: N.Y. 1925; city editor Poughkeepsie Sunday Courier, 1925-35; vis. lectr. drama Fordham U., 1939; research grant drama from Rockefeller Found. at Vassar, 1940, heading research staff for Hallie Flanagan's history of Fed. Theatre, Arena; resident playwright at Smith Coll. on grant from Rockefeller Found., 1942; writer for stage and screen, 1935-85; stage plays include The First Legion (trans. into 14 langs., now sole propr. film and stage rights), 1934, Monsignor's Hour, 1935, Second Spring (life of Cardinal Newman), 1938, The Magnificent Yankee, 1946, on tour, 1947, Tarquin, 1950, Fenelon (stage play, Basle), 1956, Hail to the Chief, 1958, American Portrait, 1958, Dawn's Early Light, 1959, Ladies of Soissons, 1964; screen plays include Hitler's Children (dramatization of Gregor Ziemer's Education for Death), 1942, Behind the Rising Sun (dramatization of book by James R. Young), 1943, Guilty of Treason, 1950, The First Legion, 1951, The Magnificent Yankee, 1951, Bright Road, 1953 (adaptation See How They Run), The Court Martial of Billy Mitchell (collaboration) (Oscar nomination), 1955, Williamsburg, 1957; writer TV script Prairie Lawyer, NBC-TV, 1975; published plays: Brother Petroc's Return (from English novel by S.M.C.), 1940; Kamiano (Damien) (with Grace Murphy) in trilogy Theatre for Tomorrow, 1940; Murder in a Nunnery (based on novel by Eric Shepherd), 1944; Brief Music, 1940; The Gentleman from Athens, 1948; Song at the Scaffold (adaptation from novel by Gertrud von le Fort), 1949; Yankee Doodles (ballet), 1964; writer, producer El Dorado (folk ballet), 1968. War Dept. made arrangements, 1947, 48, for special prodn. The First Legion and the Magnificent Yankee in Austria as part of re-edn. program; co-licensor opera Dialogues des Carmelites (Poulenc); a founder Nat. Cath. Theatre Conf., 1937; dir. Nat. Service Bur. Fed. Theater, 1937-39; chmn. Hollywood Writers Mobilization, 1944-45. Pres. bd. aldermen, Poughkeepsie, 1929-33; mem. Joint Commn. Fair Judicial Election Practices Calif., 1976. Mem. Screen Writers Guild (pres. 1945-47), Motion Picture Acad. Arts and Scis. (v.p. 1946), Authors League, Dramatists Guild (N.Y.), Am. Bar Assn. (Gavel award for Magnificent Yankee TV prodn. 1965), Soc. Authors and Dramatists (Paris). Democrat. Roman Catholic. Clubs: The Players (N.Y.C.); Poughkeepsie Tennis; Newman (Los Angeles). Died Dec. 25, 1985, buried San Fernando Mission, L.A. Home: Encino Calif.

LAVINE, HAROLD, editor, writer; b. N.Y.C., Feb. 19, 1915; s. Elias and Pauline (Bershadsky) L.; m. Violet Edwards, Dec. 24, 1936; 1 dau., Cammie Caroline Edwards. Student, Townsend Harris Hall, 1927-30. Reporter N.Y. Am., 1932-33, N.Y. Evening Jour., 1933-34, N.Y. Evening Post, 1934-36; asst. mng. editor PM, 1941-44; with U.S. Army News Service, 1944-46; sr. editor Newsweek mag., 1946-63, Forbes mag., 1963-74; editorial writer, columnist Ariz. Republic, 1974-84. Author: Fifth Column in America, 1940, (with James A. Wechsler) War Propaganda and the United States, 1940, Central America, 1964, Smoke-Filled Rooms, 1970. Recipient Page One award, 1961; Ariz. Press Club award, 1979, 81, 83. Club: The Lotos (N.Y.C.). Died July 15, 1984; buried Forest Lawn Cemetery, Los Angeles.

LAW, MRS. MARC A., association executive; b. St. Paul, Feb. 2, 1892; d. John L. and Ann Cora (Jenkins) Townley; m. Marc A. Law, June 12, 1915; children: John Townley, Marc A., Mary L. Student, U. Wis., 1910-11, St. Agatha's Conservatory of Music, St. Paul, 1911-12, New Eng. Conservatory of Music, Boston, 1912-14. Mem. Highland Park (Ill.) Zoning Commn.; pres. Highland Park (Ill.) LWV, dir., v.p., from 1937; v.p. LWV of U.S., from 1944. First rep. of Carrie Chapman Catt Meml. Fund to be sent abroad (Italy), 1948-49, 1952-53, 58-59; del. UNESCO Conf. on Illiteracy, Rome, 1962; past mem. bd. edn., Northfield Twp. High Sch. Mem. Great Books reading group, Great Books Found. (exec. com.). Home: Northbrook Ill. †

LAWRENCE, CHARLES RADFORD, II, sociology educator; b. Boston, May 2, 1915; s. Charles Radford, Sr. and Lettia Bernette (Harris) L.; m. Margaret Morgan, June 5, 1938; children—Charles R., III, Sara Lawrence Lightfoot, Paula-Jean Lawrence Wehmiller. B.A., Morehouse Coll., 1936; M.A., Atlanta U., 1938; Ph.D., Columbia U., 1952; D. Div. (hons.), Gen. Theol. Sem., 1972, Berkeley Div. Sch., 1985; D. H.L. (hons.), Morehouse U., 1977, St. Paul's Coll., 1982, Va. Theol. Sem., 1985; D.C.L., Seaburg-Western Theol. Sem., 1978. Cert. secondary tchr., Ga. Tchr. Atlanta Pub. Schs., 1936-39; student YMCA Nat. Student YMCA, Southeastern Region, 1941-42; instr. sociology Fisk U., Nashville, 1943-47; instr. to prof. sociology CUNY, Bklyn., 1948-77, prof. emeritus, from 1977; nat. chmn. Fellowship of Reconciliation, Nyack, N.Y., 1954-63. Pres. House of Deps. The Episcopal Ch., 1976-85; v.p. East Ramapo Bd. Edn., Spring Valley, N.Y., 1957-64. Democrat. Club: Ch. of N.Y. Home: Pomona N.Y. Died Apr. 3, 1986.

LAWRENCE, FRANK DUDLEY, banker; b. Portsmouth, Va., Mar. 15, 1891; s. John and Virginia (Cherry) L.; m. Margarette C. Peed, Jan. 31, 1928. Student, Portsmouth pub. schs. Runner Mchts. and Farmers Bank, Portsmouth, 1907; organizer Am. Nat. Bank, Portsmouth, 1919, cashier, 1919-29, v.p., 1929-43, pres., from 1943; pres., dir. Portsmouth Hotel Corp.; owner Hotel Governor Dinwiddie; bd. dirs. Citizens Trust Co., Portsmouth; operator profl. baseball Va. and Piedmont Leagues, Portsmouth, 1914-15. Home: Portsmouth Va. †

LAWRENCE, NATHANIEL MORRIS, philosophy educator; b. Okmulgee, Okla., June 28, 1917; s. Nathaniel Morris and Anna (Trask) L.; m. Mary Elizabeth Wood, Oct. 9, 1939; children: Mary Ellen, Nathaniel Spencer Wood, Roger Trask Wood. A.B., Stanford U., 1938; S.T.B., Harvard U., 1942, M.A. in Philosophy, 1946, Ph.D., 1949. Instr. philosophy Wellesley Coll., 1945-47, U. Ill., 1947-50; asst. prof. La. State U., 1950-52; lectr. Harvard U., 1952-53; asst. prof. U. Calif. at Los Angeles, 1953-55; vis. lectr. Yale, 1955-56; assoc. prof. Yale U., 1956-60; prof. philosophy Williams Coll., from 1960, Mass. prof. philosophy, from 1976. Author: Whitehead's Philosophical Development, 1956, Alfred North Whitehead, 1974, (with R. Brumbaugh) Six Philosophers on Education, 1963, Philosophical Themes in Modern Education, 1973; Editor: (with Daniel O'Connor) Readings in Existential Phenomenology, 1967, (with J.T. Fraser) The Study of Time II, 1975, (with J.T. Fraser and D. Park) The Study of Time III, 1978, The Study of Time IV, 1981, (with J.T. Fraser and F.C. Haber) The Study of Time V, 1986; Contbr. articles to profl. jours. Mem. Metaphys. Soc. Am., Internat. Soc. for Study Time, Soc. for Phenomenology and Existential Philosophy. Home: Williamstown Mass. Died Mar. 12, 1986.

LAWRENCE, RICHARD ELMER, educator; b. St. Paul, Aug. 10, 1920; s. Arthur E. and Gladys (Steele) L.; children: Arthur Michael, Patti Jean (Mrs. Stephen Teague), Cheryl Marion; m. Joy Lynn Rotton, Aug. 15, 1975. BS, U. Minn., 1942; MA, Columbia U., 1948, EdD, 1953. Tchr. jr. and sr. high sch. N.Y., 1946-53; asst. prof. edn. No. Ill. State Tchrs. Coll., 1953-55; assoc. sec. Am. Assn. Colls. for Tchr. Edn., Washington, 1955-57, assoc. exec. sec., 1961-68; assoc. prof., assoc. dean summer sessions Syracuse U., 1957-61; dean Coll. of Edn. U. N.Mex., 1969-73, prof. ednl. adminstrn., 1973-87; dir. NDEA Nat. Inst. Advanced Study in Teaching Disadvantaged Youth, 1966-68; mem. Commn. on Edn. for the Teaching Professions, 1969-71; mem. exec. com. Assn. Colls. and Schs. of Edn. in State Univ. and Land Grant Colls., 1969-73. Cons. Albuquerque Goals Program, 1969. With USNR, 1942-45. Mem. AAAS, NEA, Am. Ednl. Rsch. Assn., Assn. Tchr. Educatros, Assn. Supervision and Curriculum Devel., Nat. Soc. Study of Edn., Phi Delta Kappa. Unitarian. Home: Albuquerque N.Mex. Died Oct. 16, 1987.

LAWRENCE, ROBERT, conductor, music critic; b. N.Y.C., Mar. 18, 1912; s. Robert Julian and Isabelle Lawrence. BA, CCNY, 1931; fellow in conducting, Juilliard Grad. Sch., 1933-36; MA, Colubia U., 1934. With music staff N.Y. Herald Tribune, 1939, apptd. dance critic, 1942; condr. N.Y.C. WPA Symphony Orch., 1940; made recs. of Wagner's Ring of the Nibelung (speech and piano) RCA Victor, 1940; ofcl. lectr. N.Y. season Phila. Orch., 1940-41; guest condr. Ill., R.I., N.Y.C. symphonies, Wallenstein Sinfonietta, Radio City Music Hall Broadcasting Symphony, 1941-42; condr. Thais with Met. Opera Co. singers, Montreal, Can., 1942, Trojans with Am. Opera Soc., 1960; quiz expert for weekly nat. broadcast of Met. Opera Saturday matinee, 1941-42, permanent quizmaster, 1952-57; noted as authority on music of Hector Berlioz; guest condr., opera and symphony, Italy, May to June 1944; dir. Tosca, Royal Opera, Rome, 1944-45; symphony concerts, 1945; Rome Radio Orch., 1944; guest condr. St. Cecilia Acad. Orch., Rome, 1945; dir. Maggio Mus. Orch., Florence, Italy, 1945; debut as condr. N.Y. Philharm.-Symphony, 1948; condr., music dir. Phoenix Symphony Orch., 1949-52; guest condr. NBC Symphony, 1953, Orquesta Sinfonica Nacional, Mex., 1953, Royal Philharm., London, 1955, Presdl. Philharm., Ankara, Turkey, 1955, Symphony of the Air, N.Y., 1955; conducted Damnation of Faust, Carnegie Hall, with Schola Cantorum, N.Y. Philharm., 1954; condr., music dir. Presdl. Symphony Orch. Turkey, Ankara, 1957-59; artistic dir., condr. Friends of French Opera, 1962-81; featured music commentator Sta. WQXR, 1963-68; dir. dept. opera Peabody Inst., Balt., 1968-73; lectr. opera N.Y. State U., Purchase, 1971-72; adj. prof. opera Temple U., Phila., 1976-81. Author adaptations Carmen, Aida, Lohengrin, Hansel and Gretel, 1937, The Ring of the Nibelung, 4 vols., 1938, Pinafore, The Mikado, The Gondoliers, 1939, Petrouchka, The Three Cornered Hat, 1940, Boris Godounoff, Bartered Bride, Magic Flute, 1942; (in collaboration) Metropolitan Opera Guide, 1939, Victor Book of Ballets and Ballet Music, 1950, The World of Opera, 1955; author: A Rage for Opera, 1971. Home: New York N.Y. Died Aug. 9, 1981.

LAWRENCE, SAMUEL EUGENE, river and harbor engineer; b. Ft. Smith, Ark., Oct. 26, 1882; s. Samuel and Katharine O. (Clark) L.; m. Odile M. Schaefer, Apr. 15, 1913 (dec.); children: Samuel Eugene Jr., Marion K., Dorothy (Mrs. J. B. Stubbs). BSME, Purdue U., 1907, ME, 1927. Registered profl. engr. and land surveyor, Fla., civil and med. engr., La. Spl. field tng. on dredging fleet Corps of Engrs., Galveston, Tex., 1907-10; jr. mech. engr. (civil svc.), operation and maintenance of dredges, lock and dam constrn. Corps of Engrs., Brazoa River, Tex., 1910-13; supt. machinery and floating plant, Ohio River Corps of Engrs., 1913-16, supt. rock removal, Delaware River, 1916; capt. 57th engrs. oper. French Rivers and Harbors and the Rhine U.S. Army, 1917-19, rebuilding Chesapeake and Del. Canal, in charge dredges, Atlantic City, Port of Wilmington, Del., 1920-24, supr. rock removal East River and Hell Gate, N.Y. Harbor, 1924-25, chief marine design div. C.E.; cons. engr., pres. East Coast Stone & Constrn. Co., Ft. Lauderdale, Fla., pres., gen. mgr., 1925-33; harbor engr., drainage engr. Port Everglades, Fla., 1931-32; flood control engr. Miss. River 1933-40; spl. assignment svc. tng. plan for coll. grads. Office Chief of Engrs., Washington and Phila., 1941; prof. hydraulic engring, asst. in orgn. of spl. course in river and harbor engring. La. State U., from 1946, acting. dir. sch. hydraulic engring., 1949-50; cons. engr. La. Dept. Pub. Works, from 1955; mem. rsch. com. on floating derricks, water jet-propelled boats, tugs etc. Transp. Corps, U.S. Army. Author textbook, also articles on dredging and marine constrn.; contbr. short stories to svc. publs.; patentee mech. lubricator, scale conversion instrument, precast sea wall. Commr. pub. safety, Ft. Lauderdale; Fla. state harbor commr. Col. engr. corps U.S. Army, 1942-47. Named to U.S. Engrs. Dept. Hall of Fame. Mem. SAR, Am. Legion (dist. comdr.), Union Nat. Des Combatants, Mil. Order World Wars, VFW, ASME, La. State Engring Soc., Soc. Am. Mil. Engrs., Knife and Fork club, Engineer Club (Phila.), Faculty Club (La. State U.), Kiwanis Club (Baton Rouge), Masons, Shriners, Scabbard and Blade, Sigma Pi, Acacia, Tau Beta Pi, Pi Tau Sigma, Phi Kappa Phi. Democrat. Presbyterian. Home: Baton Rouge La. †

LAWS, ROBERT HARRY, economist, engineering and consulting company executive; b. Mountain City, Tenn., Apr. 17, 1917; s. William R. and Charlotte (Seehorn) L. A.B., Carson-Newman Coll., 1940, LL.D. (hon.), 1974; M.A., U. Tenn., 1942; postgrad., U. Tex., 1948-50. Economist TVA, 1941-42; asst. prof. econs. U. Tenn., 1947-50, assoc. prof., 1950-53; teaching fellow in econs. U. Tex., 1948-50; dir. econ. research Soc. Advancement Mgmt., 1953-56; with Commonwealth Services, Inc., N.Y.C., 1956-74; v.p. Commonwealth Services, Inc., 1960-64, exec. v.p., 1965-67, pres., chief exec. officer, 1967-74, dir., from 1960; sr. v.p., dir. Gilbert/Commonwealth, Reading, Pa., from 1973; also dir. Gilbert/Commonwealth Internat. Inc., Reading, from 1973; sr. v.p., chief adminstrv. officer, dir. Gilbert Assos., Inc., Reading, Pa., from 1979; dir. APC Graphics, Inc., Gai-tronics, Inc.; dir., mem. exec. com. Peoples Gas System, Fla., 1962-76. Author: Labor Relations in the Motor Freight Industry, 1953; contbg. editor: Advanced Mgmt, 1953-56. Served with USN, 1942-47. Recipient Disting. Alumni award Carson-Newman Coll., 1972. Mem. Am. Econ. Assn., Am. Acad. Mgmt., Indsl. Relations Research Assn., Am. Arbitration Assn., Am. Acad. Polit. and Social Sci., Newcomen Soc. N. Am., Delta Sigma Pi, Pi Gamma Mu, Delta Nu Alpha. Clubs: Bd. Room (N.Y.C.), N.Y. (N.Y.C.), Pinnacle (N.Y.C.), Lawyers (N.Y.C.); City (Knoxville). Home: Vero Beach Fla. Died Oct. 9, 1986.

LAWSON, ALFRED HENRY, banker; b. Bethel, Conn., Apr. 19, 1891; s. Alfred and Elizabeth Alice (Whitely) L.; m. Katherine Gay, Sept. 3, 1925. LLB, Georgetown U., 1916, LLD, 1956. With Washington Loan & Trust Co., 1923-54, real estate officer, 1923-31, v.p., 1931-48, pres., 1948-54; pres. co. merged with Riggs Nat. Bank, 1954, asst. dir. profl. svcs. for rsch., from 1954; bd. dirs. Nat. Union Ins. Co.; v.p. Tremont Water & Gas Co.; bd. dirs. Equitable Savs. & Loan Assn., Dist. Title Ins. Co., Fidelity Storage Co. Trustee George Washington U. Republican. Episcopalian. Home: Washington D.C. †

LAWTON, BEN REDMOND, surgeon; b. Hillsboro, Wis., July 17, 1922; s. John Cliff and Cora (Wheeler) L.; m. Ruth Mathilda Klahn, Sept. 1, 1941; children: Richard, Margaret, Daniel, Ben. B.A., U. Wis., 1943, M.D., 1946. Diplomate: Am. Bd. Surgery, Am. Thoracic Surgery. Intern U. Colo., Denver, 1946-47; resident in gen. surgery U. Wis., Madison, 1947-48, resident in gen. and thoracic surgery, 1948-52; staff surgeon Marshfield Clinic, Wis., 1954-87, pres., 1969-71, 75-77, 79-80; mem. Gov.'s Health Policy Council, State of Wis., from 1971, vice chmn., 1971-72; vice chmn. Gov.'s Health Planning and Policy Task Force, 1971-72; mem. Inst. Medicine of Nat. Acad. Scis., Washington, 1976-87. Mem. bd. regents U. Wis., from 1976. Served with U.S. Army, 1952-54. Recipient Med. Alumni Citation award U. Wis., 1978; recipient Max Fox Preceptorship award, 1981. Fellow ACS; mem. AMA, Wis. Surg. Soc. (pres. 1971-72), Am. Thoracic Soc., Milw. Acad. Surgery, Wis. Thoracic Soc., State Med. Soc. Wis. (Council award 1978), Wood County Med. Soc. Democrat. Home: Marshfield Wis. Died May 18, 1987.

LAY, JAMES SELDEN, JR., government official; b. Washington, Aug. 24, 1911; s. James Selden and Lillian Lee (Lockhart) L.; m. Emily Graham Miller, Feb. 27, 1937; children: Carolyn Miller (Mrs. William J. Dowd), Patricia Lockhart (Mrs. Edward C. Dorsey), Emily Graham (Mrs. Paul I. O'Connell). BS, Va. Mil. Inst., 1933; MBA, Harvard U., 1935. Asst. to gen. sales mgr. Va. Electric & Power Co., Richmond, 1935-37; asst. to v.p. Stone & Webster Svc. Corp., N.Y.C., 1937-39; sales mgr. Hagerstown (Md.) Gas Co., 1939-41; mgmt. analyst U.S. Dept. State, Washington, 1945; sec. Nat. Intelligence Authority, 1946; div. chief Cen. Intelligence Group, 1947; asst. exec. sec. NSC, 1947-50, exec. sec., 1950-61, dep. asst. to dir., 1962-71; cons. Pres.'s Fgn. Intelligence Adv. Bd., 1971-87. Sec. joint intelligence com. Joint Chiefs of Staff, Washington, 1943-45; mem. sch. bd., Falls Church, Va., 1949-51, 61-64. Officer AUS, 1941-45. Decorated Legion of Merit; Order Brit. Empire; recipient Career Svc. award Nat. Civil Svc. League, 1964, Disting. Intelligence medal CIA. Roman Catholic. Home: Falls Church Va. Died June 28, 1987; buried Arlington (Va.) Nat. Cemetery.

LAYTHE, LEO L., government official; b. Kinbrae, Minn., Mar. 26, 1892; s. Silas Winfield and Ella (Swarthout) L.; m. Mary Eloise Large, Nov. 19, 1932. BS, Oreg. State Coll., 1916. Rancher 1916; county agrl. agt. Cody, Wyo., 1917, Tucson, 1918, Casa Grande, Ariz., 1919; supt. ranch Casa Grande, 1919-20; fieldman U.S. Biol. Survey, 1921; in charge of sta. U.S. Biol. Survey, Sacramento, Calif., 1923-24; in charge of sta. U.S. Biol. Survey, Denver, 1924-29, regional supr., 1930-34, regional dir., 1934-40; regional dir. U.S. Fish and Wildlife Service, Portland, Oreg., 1940-57, Bur. Sports, Fisheries and Wildlife, Portland, from 1957. Mem. Am. Fisheries Soc., Gamma Sigma Delta, Masons. Home: Portland Oreg. †

LAZARUS, HERMAN, lawyer; b. Phila., Apr. 21, 1910; s. Samuel and Fannie (Levin) L.; m. Sarah Edith Goldstein, Oct. 14, 1933; 1 dau., Ruth Helen Holmes. B.S. in Edn, Temple U., 1933, LL.B., 1937; LL.M., U. Pa., 1941. Bar: Pa. bar 1938, D.C. bar 1951. Atty. N.L.R.B., 1942-46, asst. to gen. counsel, 1946-47; head labor-mgmt. sect. Pub. Affairs Inst., 1947-49; counsel U.S. Senate Com. on Labor and Pub. Welfare, 1949-51; pub. mem. rev. and appeals com. W.S.B., 1951-52, also pub. mem. and vice chmn., 1952-53; practice law in Phila., 1953-86; ptnr. firm Cohen, Shapiro, Polisher, Shiekman & Cohen, 1972-81, counsel, 1981-86. Former pres. Jewish Employment and Vocational Soc. Mem. Am., Pa., Phila. bar assns. Home: Philadelphia Pa. Died Sept. 9, 1986; buried King David Cemetery, Phila.

LAZARUS, RALPH, retail stores executive; b. Columbus, Ohio, Jan. 30, 1914; s. Fred and Meta (Marx) L.; m. Gladys Kleeman, June 24, 1939; children: Mary (dec.), Richard (dec.), John, James. B. A., Dartmouth Coll., 1935, LL.D., 1965; LL.D., U. Miami, 1961; D.C.S., Suffolk U., 1962; LL.D., Xavier U., 1965. Vice pres., gen. mdse. mgr. F. & R. Lazarus & Co., 1935-51; with OPA, WPB, 1941-43; exec. v.p. Federated Dept. Stores, Inc., Cin., 1951-57, pres., 1957-67, chief exec. officer, 1966-81, chmn. bd., 1967-82, chmn. exec. com., 1982-84, chmn. emeritus, 1984-88; bd. dirs. GE, Gillette Co. Mem. steering com. Cin. Bicentennial Commn.; Cin. Bus. Com.; trustee Com. Econ. Devel.; nat. adv. com. Peace Corps. Served to lt. USAAF, World War II. Recipient Gold Medal award Nat. Retail Mchts. Assn., 1974; Brotherhood award NCCJ, 1975. Mem. Council on Fgn. Relations, Bus. Council. Clubs: Winding Hollow Country (Columbus); Harmonie, Sky (N.Y.C.); Blind Brook Country (White Plains, N.Y.); Losantiville Country (Cin.), Camargo (Cin.), Commonwealth (Cin.), Comml. (Cin.), Dartmouth (Cin.), Queen City (Cin.), Vintage Country (Calif.). Home: Cincinnati Ohio. Died June 19, 1988; buried Greenlawn Cemetery, Columbus, Ohio.

LEA, WILLIAM SENTELLE, clergyman; b. Easton, Wash., Nov. 24, 1911; s. Joseph Marshall and Kitty May (Sentelle) L.; m. Jean Emert, July 10, 1940; children: Anne (Mrs. John Tuohy), Jean (Mrs. Dennis Scully). B.S., Davidson Coll., 1932; B.D., U. of South, 1935, D.D., 1952, M.Div., 1965; postgrad., Oxford (Eng.) U., 1968, St. Andrews U., 1970. Ordained to ministry Episcopal Ch., 1935; rector St. Paul's Ch., Kingsport, Tenn., 1937-40, Ch. of Advent, Spartanburg, S.C., 1940-44, Christ Ch., Raleigh, N.C., 1944-46, St. Andrew's Ch., Maryville, Tenn., 1946-47, St. Johns Ch., Knoxville, Tenn., 1947-56; editor Episcopal Churchnews, 1956-57; dean St. John's Cathedral, Denver, 1957-62; rector Christ Ch., Winnetka, Ill., 1962-78; now free lance write; pres. Nat. Acad. Families, N.Y.C., 1978-84; instr. Maryville (Tenn.) Coll., 1945-46, Seabury-Western Theol. Sem., Evanston, Ill., 1964-66; pres. Denver Council Chs., 1960-61. Author: Is God Dead?, 1968, This We Can Believe, 1972, Life and Work of Theodore Wedel, 1972, Faith and Science— Mutual Responsibility for a Human Future, 1979, What is Man-Human Identity in an Age of Science?, 1981; assoc. editor: Anglican Theol. Rev, 1972-84, Living Church, 1957-74. Chmn. Mayor's Commn. on Human Relations, Denver, 1960-62; Bd. dirs. Episcopalian mag., 1957-84; mem. selection com. Rockefeller Fund for Theol. Edn., 1968-76. Mem. Phi Gamma Delta. Clubs: Indian Hill (Winnetka); Glenview Golf; University (Chgo.); Mission Valley (Nokomis, Fla.). Home: Sarasota Fla. Died Nov. 1, 1984, buried Christ Ch., Winnetka, Ill.

LEACH, WILFORD, playwright, director; b. Petersburg, Va., Aug. 26, 1932; s. Carson W. and Louise (Shupin) L. AB, Coll. William and Mary, 1950; MA, U. Ill., 1955, PhD, 1957. Prof. theatre and film Sarah Lawrence Coll., 1958-81; mem. faculty Yale U. Sch. Drama, 1978-79. Dir. film The Wedding Party, 1967, The Pirates of Penzance, 1982; co-dir. ETC Company of LaMama, N.Y.C., 1969-73, playwright, artistic dir. LaMama Theatre, N.Y.C., 1970-78, prin. dir. N.Y. Shakespeare Festival, 1978-88;, dir. Taming of the Shrew, 1978, Marie and Bruce, 1978, The Mandrake, 1979, Pirates of Penzance, 1980, Henry J., 1984, La Boheme, 1984, The Human Comedy, 1984, The Mystery of Edwin Drood, 1985 (Tony award Best Musical, Best Dir. of a Musical, 1986); author: plays Gertrude, 1960, In 3 Zones, 1965, Carmilla, 1970, Demon, 1971, Corfax (Don't Ask), 1974, Undine, 1975, Road House, 1976. Recipient Obie award for direction, 1972, 81; Tony award for direction, 1981; Drama Desk award for direction, 1981; nominated for Drama Desk award for design, 1978, 81; Guggenheim fellow, 1972-73; Nat. Endowment for Arts grantee, 1975. Died June 18, 1988; interred Rocky Point, N.Y.

LEARY, ROBERT MICHAEL, investment counsellor; b. Omaha, Oct. 9, 1913; s. Henry Shellington and Nell (Swift) L.; m. Alyce Rita Popp, Sept. 21, 1939; children: Sharon Leary Reichert, Sheila Leary Daly, Michele Leary Alexander, Kathleen Leary Lee, Suzanne. BSC, Creighton U., 1934; MBA, Northwestern U., 1936. With 7-Up Bottling Co., 1939-52; pres. 7-Up Bottling Co., Hastings, Nebr., 1946-52; zone mgr. Investors Diversified Services, Inc., Hays, Kans., 1953-55; div. mgr. King Merritt & Co., Hays, 1956-60; exec. v.p. Westamerica Securities Inc., Denver, 1960-68; pres. R.M. Leary & Co., Denver, 1968-84; pres., dir. Meridian Capital Corp., San Francisco, 1969-70; pres. Excalibur, Ltd., Denver, 1970-72; v.p., dir. Mountain Haus Devel. Co., Vail, Colo., 1970-75; chmn. Refinery Corp., Denver, 1970-72; v.p. Petro-Silver, Inc., Denver, 1971-84; v.p., dir. Carr Mason & Leary Inc., Beverly Hills, Calif., 1972-78; former dir. Carr, Mason & Leary, Beverly Hills, Calif., Prairie Drilling Co., Casper, Wyo., EGC Realty Corp., Denver. Trustee First Gen. Resources Co., N.Y.C., 1970-73, Soc. Fin. Counseling Ethics, Denver, 1969-71, Internat. Assn. Fin. Planners, 1969-73. Served to lt. (j.g.) USNR, 1944-45. Mem. Am. Legion, VFW, 40 and 8, Delta Sigma Pi. Republican. Roman Catholic. Clubs: Elks, K.C, Mt. Vernon Country, 26; Optimists (St. Joseph, Mo.) (past pres.); Colo. Harvard Bus. Sch; La Costa Country (Calif.). Home: Denver Colo. Died Oct. 24, 1984; buried Ft. Logan Nat. Cemetery, Denver.

LEBARON, ROBERT, scientist; b. Binghamton, N.Y., Oct. 31, 1891; s. James Robert and Katherine (Featherston) LeB.; m. Peggy Bancroft, Oct. 14, 1926. BS, Union Coll., Schenectady, N.Y., 1913, DSc (hon.), 1955; MS, Princeton U., 1917; grad., Ecole Superiere Nat. des Mines, U. Sorbonne, France, 1919; DSc (hon.), Thiel Coll., 1955. Rsch. chemist Arthur D. Little, Inc., Cambridge, Mass., 1919-21, with rsch. sales, 1921-23, asst. to pres., 1924-25, coord. sci. and tech. activities, petroleum rsch., 1923-25; tech. v.p. Petroleum Chem. Corp., N.Y., 1926-32; v.p. Nat. Distillers Products Corp., N.Y.C., 1926-32; sales dir. Va. Smelting Co., Norfolk, 1937-41, mem. planning com., 1938-41, dir. R&D, 1945-48, mem. exec. com., 1945-49, dir., 1948-49; tech. cons. Oronite Chem. Co., San Francisco, 1945-49; mem. chem. rsch. com. Calif. Rsch. Corp., San Francisco, 1945-49; chmn. mil. liaison com. AEC, 1949-54, cons. to chmn., 1954-59; dep. to sec. def. Atomic Energy, Washington, 1949-53; chmn. com. Atomic Energy R&D Bd., 1949-52; alt. mem. Combined Policy Com., U.S. Govt., 1949-54; indsl. cons. on atomic energy, 1954; mng. dir. LeBaron Assocs., Washington, 1956-72. Mem. vis. com. fine arts dept. NYU, 1942; vis. com. Brookhaven Nat. Lab., 1955-57; pres. LeBaron Found. Lt. F.A., U.S. Army, 1917-19. Mem. Am. Legion, Am. Chem. Soc., Inst. Fgn. Affairs, Nat. Inst. Social Scis., UN Assn. U.S.A., Princeton Club, Metropolitan Club, Columbia Country Club, 1925 F St. Club, International Club, Cosmos Club, Sigma Xi, Delta Upsilon. Home: Washington D.C. †

LE BLANC, MORELAND PAUL, JR., public accountant; b. Baton Rouge, Aug. 9, 1921; s. Moreland Paul and Carmen Marie (Haydel) Le B.; m. Lillian Frances Lanford, Sept. 16, 1946; children: Sharon Frances, Julie Ann, Paul Lanford, Mary Martha. BS, La. State U., 1948, MBA, 1949. CPA, N.Y. With Arthur Andersen & Co., 1949-85, ptnr., 1956-85, ptnr. charge New Orleans office, 1958-66, mng. ptnr. N.Y.C. office, 1966-78, vice chmn., 1972-75, co-chmn., 1975-80, regional mng. ptnr., chmn. bd. ptnrs., 1980-85. Nat. bd. dirs. Jr. Achievement, Achievement Found.; mem. adv. coun. Tulane U. Sch. Bus.; mem. bd. visitors Duke U. Lt. (j.g.) USN, 1943-46. Mem. AICPA, N.Y. State Soc. CPA's, University Club, Union League, Recess Club, Racquet and Tennis Club, Conn. Golf Club, Brook Club, Blind Brook Club, Wee Burn Country Club, Landmark Club, Chicago Club. Home: Darien Conn. Died Oct. 27, 1985; buried Darien, Conn.

LEBRA, WILLIAM PHILIP, anthropology educator; b. St. Paul, Sept. 2, 1922; s. William Charles and Stella Bertha (Welker) L.; m. Takie Sugiyama, Apr. 25, 1963. B.A., U. Minn., 1948, M.A., 1949; Ph.D., Harvard, 1958. Field asso. in anthropology NRC, 1953-54; teaching fellow in anthropology Harvard, 1954-55; instr. anthropology Pitts. U., 1957-58, asst. prof., 1958-61; vis. scholar East-West Center, Honolulu, 1961-62; assoc. prof. anthropology and Asian studies U. Hawaii, 1962-64, prof., 1964-86; dir. Social Sci. Research Inst., 1962-70, dir. culture and mental health program, 1967-77; vis. research fellow Japan. Soc. Promotion Sci., 1981-82. Author: Okinawan Religion, 1966, rev. edit., 1985, (with F.R. Pitts and W.P. Suttles) Post-war Okinawa, 1955, Okinawa no shukyo to shakai kozo, 1974; Editor: Transcultural Research in Mental Health, 1972, Youth, Socialization and Mental Health, 1974, (with T.S. Lebra) Japanese Culture and Behavior, 1974, Culture-Bound Syndromes, Ethnopsychiatry, and Alternate Therapies, 1976. Served with AUS, 1943-46. Prin. investigator NIMH grant, 1959-62, 67-77. Fellow Am. Anthrop. Assn., Royal Anthrop. Inst. Gt. Britain; mem. Japanese Soc. Ethnology, Asiatic Soc. Japan, Assn. Asian Studies, Soc. Applied Anthropology, Am Ethnol. Soc. Home: Honolulu Hawaii. Died Jan. 1 1986; buried Nat. Meml. Cemetery of the Pacific.

LE CORBEILLER, PHILIPPE, educator; b. Paris Jan. 11, 1891; came to U.S., 1941, naturalized, 1944; s Maurice and Marguerite (Dreux) Le C.; m. Dorothy

Leeming, Apr. 3, 1924; 1 son, Jean; m. Pietronetta Posthuma, May 7, 1964. Grad., Polytechnic Sch., Paris, 1913; Dr. Math., Sorbonne, 1926, lic. phil., 1938; MA (hon.), Harvard, 1949. With French Ministry of Communications, 1920-39, French Govt. Broadcasting, 1939-40; mem. faculty Harvard, 1941-60, emeritus prof. applied physics and gen. edn., from 1960; prof. New Sch. Social Rsch., N.Y.C.; W.A. Neilson rsch. prof. Smith Coll., 1960. Author: Self-Maintained Oscillations, 1931, Electro-Acoustics, 1934, Dimensional Analysis, 1966; author (with others) Electronic Tubes and Circuits, 1947, Science and Civilization, 1949, Matrix Analysis of Electric Networks, 1950, The Languages of Science, 1963. Am. Acad. Arts and Scis., Acoustical Soc. Am., AAAS. Home: Wassenaar The Netherlands. †

LEE, PERCY MERCER, judge; b. Ludlow, Miss., Nov. 14, 1892; s. Thomas Hugh and Alethia Jane (Denson) L.; m. Hattie Mae Nutt, Dec. 27, 1912 (dec. Nov. 1937); children: Percy M., Roy Noble, Annie Laurie (Mrs. W. J. James), James Walter, Robert Edward, Charles David; m. Claudia Stewart, Dec. 25, 1938; children: Elizabeth Jane, James Walter. AB, Miss. Coll., 1911; studied law under tutors and Judge A. H. Whitfield, 1915. Bar: Miss. 1916. Tchr. Ridgeland Sch., near Jackson, 1916-18; practiced with Huff & Lee, Forest, 1920-27; pvt. practice 1929-38; spl. asst. to atty. gen. State of Miss., 1918-19; atty. City of Forest, Town of Morton, and supervisors of Scott County, Miss., 1921-31; dist. atty. 8th Dist., 1929-38, cir. judge, 1939-50; assoc. justice Miss. Supreme Ct., Jackson, 1950-61, presiding justice, 1961-63, chief justice, 1964-65. Mayor City of Forest, 1922-26; pres. bd. trustees Forest Separate Sch. Dist., 1945-48. Mem. Miss. State Bar Assn., Masons (32 degree, past grand master Miss. 1937), K.T., Shriners, Eastern Star (past worthy patron), Woodman. Democrat. Baptist. †

LEE, RENSSELAER WRIGHT, art historian; b. Phila., June 15, 1898; s. Francis Herbert and Helen (Stavers) L.; m. Stella Wentworth Garrett, May 27, 1925; children: Julia Rensselaer, Mary Josephine Garrett (Mrs. Cyril Muromcew), Rensselaer Wright. AB, Princeton U., 1920, PhD, 1926, LHD, 1982; LHD, Northwestern U., 1971. Instr. English Princeton U., 1922-23, 25-28, vis. prof., 1948, 68-69, chmn. dept. art and archaeology, 1961-66, Marquand prof., 1961-66, prof. emeritus, 1966-84, chmn. adv. coun. dept. classics, 1942-55; assoc. prof. history of art, chmn. dept. Northwestern U., 1931-34, prof., 1934-40, Harris lectr., 1966; prof. art Smith Coll., 1941-48, Columbia U., 1948-54, NYU Inst. Fine Arts, 1954-55; mem. vis. com. dept. fine arts Fogg Mus., Harvard U., 1957-63; mem. Inst. Advanced Study, 1939, 42-44, 46-47; mem. adv. coun. Inst. Fine Arts, NYU; v.p. Internat. Fedn. Renaissance Socs. and Insts., 1961-70, Internat. Coun. Philosophy and Humane Scis., 1965-71; chmn. presdl. adv. com. on Yale Ctr. for Brit. Art and Brit. Studies, 1972-84. Author: Ut pitura poesis, The Humanistic Theory of Painting, 2d edit., 1967, Names on Trees: Ariosto into Art, 1977; editor in chief Art Bull., 1942-44, mem. editorial bd., 1945-84; contbr. articles and revs. to profl. jours. Fellow Am. Coun. Learned Socs., 1930-31, chmn. com. rsch. and publ. fine arts, 1942-44, exec. sec. com. protection cultural treasures in war areas, 1944-45, dir., 1953-61; trustee Am. Acad. in Rome, 1958-84, pres., 1968-71. Fellow Am. Acad. Arts and Scis.; mem. Am. Philos. Soc. (Henry Allen Moe prize 1982), Archeol. Inst. Am., Coll. Art Assn. Am. (sec. 1939-42, 49-50, pres. 1945-46, hon. dir. 1974-84), Mediaeval Acad. Am. (councilor 1961-64), Union Académique Internationale (pres. 1962-65), Renaissance Soc. Am. (exec. bd. 1960-70, pres. 1977-78), Grolier Club, Princeton Club, Century Club, Cosmos Club, Athenaeum. Episcopalian. Home: Princeton N.J. Died Dec. 4, 1984; buried Princeton.

LEE, ROBERT BARTLETT, lawyer; b. South Bend, Ind., Nov. 16, 1912; s. Clarence Eugnene and Mary Lillian (Jennings) L.; m. Ruth Elisabeth Wade, Sept. 27, 1941; children: Nancy Lee Shavill, Edward Bartlett, William Patton, Judith Ann Lee-Hockett. AB, DePauw U., 1935; LLB magna cum laude, U. Notre Dame, 1940. Bar: Ind. 1940, Colo. 1941. Ptnr. Simon, Lee & Shivers, Englewood, Colo., 1945-49, Lee, Shivers & Banta, Englewood, 1958-61; judge Colo. 18th Jud. Dist. Ct., 1960-69; assoc. justice Colo. Supreme Ct., 1969-83; of counsel Medsker & Lee, P.C., Englewood, 1983-87; dep. dist. atty. Arapahoe County, 1943-49; mem. adv. coms. to legis. council, 1963, 68, civil jury instructions com. Supreme Ct. Colo. 1969, commn. jud. qualifactions, 1967-69, commn. Calif. Rural Legal Assistance Inc., 1971; vis. lectr. practice moot ct. program U. Colo. Law Sch. Recipient Alumni citation DePauw U., 1985. Mem. ABA, Colo. Bar Assn., 18th Jud. Dist. Bar Assn. (pres.), Am. Judicature Soc., Nat. Coll. State Trial Judges, Order of Coif, Blue Key, Phi Kappa Psi. Methodist. Home: Aurora Colo. Died June 16, 1988.

LEEDS, WILLIAM LATHAM, lawyer; b. Dallas, July 24, 1910; s. William Latham and Kathleen (Francis) L.; m. Geneva Freeman, Mar. 27, 1959; children: Patricia Ann, Cheryl Francis. BBA, So. Meth. U., 1932; LLB with highest honors, U. Tex., 1936. Bar: Tex. 1936. Ptnr. Johnson, Bromberg & Leeds (and predecessors), 1945-84; sec. Temco Aircraft Corp., 1952-60, United Nuclear Corp., 1955-57; bd. dirs. emeritus UNC Resources, Inc. (formerly United Nuclear Corp.); bd. dirs. Channel 6, Inc., Bell Pub. Co., County Developers, Inc., Killeen Pub. Co., Temtex Industries, Inc. Student editor Tex. Law Rev. With USNR, 1942-44. Mem. Am., Tex., Dallas bar assns., Order of Coif, Dallas Country Club, Terpsichorean, Idlewild Club, Phi Delta Phi, Alpha Kappa Psi, Kappa Sigma. Methodist (steward). Home: Dallas Tex. Died Sept. 26, 1984.

LEEDY, HAROLD GAVIN, banker; b. Benton, Mo., Dec. 6, 1892; s. Charles Alvin and Laura (Gray) L.; m. Elva Liter, June 5, 1926. Student, William Jewell Coll., 1911-15; LLB, Kansas City Sch. Law, 1920. Bar: Mo. 1920. Practice specializing in corp., railroad and banking law Kansas City, 1920-38; retired from gen. practice 1938; counsel Fed. Res. Bank of Kansas City, 1924-38, v.p., gen. counsel, 1938-41, pres., 1941-61; cons. City Nat. Bank & Trust Co., from 1961; mem. bd. dirs. Starlight Theatre. Former chmn. Kans. City United Funds Bd. Served in AUS, 1917-19, France. Named hon. alumnus Mo. U. Mem. Am. Royal Live Stock and Horseshow Assn. (mem. bd. govs.), Saddle and Sirloin Club, Rotary, Mission Hills Club, Masons (32 degree), Kappa Sigma, Phi Alpha Delta. Democrat. Episcopalian. Home: Kansas City Mo. †

LEES, LESTER, aeronautical engineering educator; b. N.Y.C., Nov. 8, 1920; s. Harry and Dorothy (Innenberg) L.; m. Constance Louise Morton, Aug. 30, 1941; 1 son, David Grayson. B.S., M.I.T., 1940, M.S., 1941. Research fellow, instr. math. Calif. Inst. Tech., 1942-44, asso. prof. aeros., 1953-55, prof., 1955-74, dir. environ. quality lab., 1970-74, prof. environ. engring. and aeronautics, mem. sr. staff environ. quality lab., 1974-85, emeritus prof. environ. engring. and aeronautics, 1985-86; aero. engr. Nat. Adv. Com for Aeros., Langley Field, Va., 1944-46; asst. prof. aero. engring. Princeton U., 1946-48, assoc. prof., 1948-53; cons. TRW, from 1953, Aerospace Corp., 1960-65. Contbr. articles to profl. jours. Fellow Am. Acad. Arts and Scis., AIAA (hon.); mem. Nat. Acad. Engring. Democrat. Jewish. Home: Altadena Calif. Died Nov. 10, 1986, cremated.

LEESE, CHESTER ELWOOD, physiology educator; b. Clinton, Iowa, Aug. 15, 1899; s. Fred A. and Georgina (Thompson) L.; m. Katherine Louise Thompson, Aug. 30, 1922 (dec. 1961); children: Shirley Mae (Mrs. Jesse L. Starkey), Marilyn Louise (Mrs. Joseph L. Des Roches). AB, State U. Iowa, 1922, MA, 1925, PhD, 1930. Instr. physiology State U. Iowa Coll. Medicine, 1922-30; NRC fellow physiology Harvard Coll. Medicine, 1930-32; mem. faculty George Washington U. Sch. Medicine, 1932-86, prof. physiology, 1948-86, chmn. dept., 1951-58, Fry prof., 1958-86. Contbr. numerous articles in field to profl. jours. Mem. Washington Civic Orch., 1934-45, pres., 1936-45; mem. Drs. Symphonetta Washington, 1960-86. Mem. AAAS, Am. Physiol. Soc., Soc. Exptl. Biology and Medicine (sec., treas. 1940-41, chmn. D.C. chpt. 1942-43), George Washington U. Med. Soc., Washington Acad. Medicine, Am. Soc. Cybernetics, Smith Reed Russel Med. Soc., Sigma Xi (sec. George Washington U. chpt. 1941-43, chmn. 1943-44), Alpha Chi Sigma, Gamma Alpha, Nu Sigma Nu, Sigma Pi. Home: Washington D.C. Died Sept. 21, 1986.

LEFFINGWELL, HAROLD RANDALL, physician; b. Hartford, Ohio, Jan. 13, 1899; s. Wallace Cecil and Cora Irene (Randall) L.; m. Mary Louise Bachman, June 14, 1930; 1 child, Laurens William. BS, Allegheny Coll., 1923; MD, U. Pa., 1927. Intern Allegheny Gen. Hosp., Pitts., 1927-28; med dir. Paul Revere Life Ins. Co., Worcester, Mass., Mass. Protective Assn., from 1949. Mem. Med. Dirs. Assn. Am., Am. Life Conv. (med. sect.), AMA, Mass. Med. Soc., Assn. Mil. Surgeons, Am. Physicians Art Assn. Home: Holden Mass. †

LEFTWICH, JAMES ADOLF, writer, publisher, public relations executive; b. Newport News, Va., July 23, 1902; s. David and Eugenia L.; m. Ilka Renwick, Sept. 2, 1947; 1 child, Jean Renwick Leftwich Bushnell; m. Merry Ann Ottosen, Mar. 12, 1963. Student, Augusta Mil. Acad., 1920; student archtl. course, U. Va., 1921-25; hon. alumnus U. Calif. at San Diego, 1964. Feature writer Miami (Fla.) Tab, 1926; editorial dept. Sun, N.Y.C., 1926-29; with book rev. sect. N.Y. Am., 1930-31; feature editor Nat. Radio Press Syndicate, 1932-35; columnist Newport News Times Herald, 1934-36; feature writer, editor various publs. from 1936; dir. art, pub. relations Art Assocs., N.Y.C., 1939-42; pub. relations dir. Congl. Com. for Investigation FCC, 1943; pub. relations assoc. Com. Internat. Econ. Policy, Reciprocal Trade Agreements Act., 1944, Com. Internat. Econ. Policy for Loan Agreement to Gt. Britain, 1946; pub. relations counsel N.Y. Bd. Trade, 1943-50, vice chmn. aviation sect., 1947; mem. Leftwich & Barkley (pub. relations cons.), N.Y.C., 1951-56; pub. relations Ryan Aero. Co., 1957; pub. relations dir. Sorrento Valley Indsl. Park, Indsl. Developers, Ltd., San Diego; advt. dir., pub. relations counsel La Jolla Fed. Savs. & Loan Assn.; established La Jolla Press, 1968, pub./editor, 1971-86. Author: Frank Forester, 1930, O'Malley Loves Josephine, 1951, Meet Sir George Carteret, 1953, La Jolla Federal Story, 1962, Legend of Aztec Calendar, 1966, Duel of the Ironclads', 1969, Profile of Baron de Coubertin, 1977, La Jolla's House of Many Legends, 1978, Den of Agreeable Iniquity, 1983, La Jolla Life, 1984; also articles in gun publs.; editor: A Pathology Laboratory Can Be Attractive As Well As Efficient; editor mag. Am. Soc. Swedish Engrs, 1945-48; contbr., research dir. mag. Duel of the Ironclads, 1969; contbr. to Virginian. Advt. dir., pub. relations counsel La Jolla Town Council, La Jolla Decent Lit. Com.; pub. relations dir. La Jolla br. Am. Cancer Soc., 1959-60; Served as athletic officer 111th F.A., 1926, Va. N.G. Named col. Ky. Gov's. staff, 1952. Mem. John Erisson Soc., U.S. Olympians (v.p. 1954-55, exec. com.), San Diego Arms Collectors, Co. Mil. Historians, Thomas Jefferson Soc. of Alumni of U. Va., U. Va. Club So. Calif. (founder, pres.), Sigma Delta Chi. Episcopalian. Clubs: Nat. Press (Washington); Advertising (N.Y.C.); Country; Racquet (La Jolla) (pub. relations and advt. dir.), La Jolla Gun (La Jolla), Sportsmens (La Jolla), Beach and Tennis (La Jolla); Sportsmen (New Hope, Pa.); New Jersey Gun Collectors; Navesink River (N.J.); Rod and Gun, Maine Biggest Bucks, Mt. Desert Isle (Maine) Game Assn, San Diego Duck and Skeet (pub. relations dir.); Press and Union League (San Francisco). Home: La Jolla Calif. Died Apr. 15, 1987; buried Newport News, Va.

LEGORRETA, LUIS G., utility company executive, banker; b. Zamora, Mex., Jan. 30, 1898; s. Juan de Dios Legorreta and Guadalup Garcia de Legorreta; m. Guadalupe Vilchis, Dec 2, 1926; children: Xavier, Isabel, Ricardo, Fernando. Student, Instituto Cientifico de Mexico City, 1911. With Banco Nacional de Mex. S.A., Mexico City, 1913-86, pres., 1933-52, vice chmn., dir. dels., 1952-58, chmn. bd., dir. dels., 1958-70, hon. chmn., 1970-86; chmn. bd. Industria Electric de Mex., Mexico City; bd. dirs. Banco de Mex., Cia Fundidora de Fierro y Acero de Monterrey, Celanese Mexicana. Chmn. bd. trustees Fundacian Mier y Pesado, 1940-86. Mem. Bankers Club, Univ. of Mex. Club, Campestre de la Ciudad de Mex., Jockey Mexicano Club. Home: Mexico City Mexico. Died Sept. 2, 1986; buried Panteōn Francé de San Joaquín.

LEHMAN, JOHN HOWARD, lawyer; b. nr. Abilene, Kans., Nov. 19, 1905; s. Henry L. and Anna (Burkholder) L.; m. Vivian Canary, Dec. 21, 1935; children—Stanley, Carolyn, Patricia, Virginia. A.B., McPherson Coll., 1931; LL.B., U. Kans., 1935. Bar: Kans. 1935. Practice law Abilene; county atty. Dickinson County, Kans., 1937-41; sr. ptnr. Lehman, Guilfoyle & Hinkle (and predecessor), 1948-87; dir. Citizens Bank, Abilene. 1950-86. Mem. Abilene Bd. Edn., 1941-56, pres., 1955-56; spl. counsel Eisenhower Library Commn. Kans., 1961-68; incorporator Dwight D. Eisenhower Library Assocs., Inc., 1963; mem. Kans. Ho. of Reps., 1941-43, Kans. Senate, 1945-49; trustee Brown Meml. Found., 1949-84, Kans. Scottish Rite Found.; incorporator, trustee Eisenhower Found. Mem. ABA, Bar Assn. State Kans., Am. Judicature Soc., Order of Coif, Phi Alpha Delta. Mem. Ch. of Brethren. Club: Mason (33 deg., Shriner). Home: Abilene Kans. Died Feb. 12, 1987.

LEHNINGER, ALBERT LESTER, educator, biochemist; b. Bridgeport, Conn., Feb. 17, 1917; s. Albert O. and Wally Selma (Heymer) L.; m. Janet Wilson, Mar. 12, 1942. BA, Wesleyan U., 1939, DSc (hon.), 1954; MS, U. Wis., 1940, PhD, 1942; DSc (hon.), U. Notre dame, 1968, Acadia U., 1972, Meml. U., Nfld., 1973, U. Paris, 1977, U. Louvain, 1978; MD, U. Padua, Italy, 1966. Instr. physiology, chemistry U. Wis., 1942-45; asst. prof. biochemistry U. Chgo., 1945-49, assoc. prof., 1949-52; DeLamar prof. physiol. chem., dir. dept. Sch. Medicine, Johns Hopkins U., 1952-78, Univ. prof. med. sci., 1978-86; vis. prof. U. Frankfurt, Federal Republic of Germany, 1951. Author: The Mitochondrion, 1964, Bioenergetics, 2d edit. 1971, Biochemistry, 1970, 2d edit., 1975, Short Course in Biochemistry, 1973, Principles of Biochemistry, 1982; also articles in field; editorial bd. Jour. Mem. Pres.'s Panel on Biomed. Rsch., 1975-76. Recipient Paul Lewis award enzyme chemistry Am. Chem. Soc., 1948, Remsen award, 1969; Guggenheim fellow, 1951-52, 64. Mem. Am. Chem. Soc., AAAS, NAS (councilor 1976-86), Am. Soc. Biol. Chemists (pres. 1972-73), Am. Philos. Soc. (v.p. 1975-86), Am. Acad. Arts and Scis., Inst. Medicine (councilor 1976-86), Biochem. Soc. (London), 14 West Hamilton St. Club, Johns Hopkins Club (Balt.); Green Spring Valley Hunt Club, Gibson Island Yacht Squadron Club, Phi Beta Kappa, Sigma Xi, Phi Nu Theta. Home: Sparks Md. Died March 3, 1986.

LEIGHLY, JOHN BARGER, geography educator; b. Locust Grove, Okla., Nov. 6, 1895; s. Philip T. and Margaret (Reed) L.; m. Katherine Edmonds, Jan. 4, 1929. Student, Cen. Mich. Coll. Edn., 1919-20; AB, U. Mich., 1922; PhD, U. Calif., 1927. Instr. geography U. Calif., Berkeley, 1927, asst. prof., 1928, assoc. prof., 1935-43, prof., 1943-86; appointments with U.S. Soil Conservation Svc., 1934, 41, 42; with Weather Bur., 1940; instr. Army Air Forces Tech. Tng. Command, 1943-44; meteorologist Army Air Forces Weather Svc., 1944-46. Contbr. numerous articles in field to profl. jours. Fellow Am.-Scandinavian Found., 1925-26, Social Sci. Rsch. Coun., 1929-30. Fellow AAAS; mem. Assn. Am. Geographers (v.p. 1946), Am. Meteorol. Soc. (councilor 1937-39), Am. Geophys. Union, Phi Beta Kappa, Sigma Xi. Home: Berkeley Calif. Died July 9, 1986.

LEIGHTON, MARGARET CARVER, author, lecturer; b. Oberlin, Ohio, Dec. 20, 1896; d. Thomas Nixon and Flora Frazee (Kirkendall) Carver; student pub. schs., Cambridge, Mass., Lycée Fenelon, Paris, France, Villa Rogivue, Switzerland; A.B., Radcliffe Coll.; m. James Herbert Leighton, May 5, 1921 (dec. Feb. 1935); children—James Herbert, Mary (Mrs. Carson F. Thomson), Thomas Carver, Sylvia (Mrs. Douglas Wikle). Former mem. bd. edn., Westfield, N.J.; past mem. Santa Monica Library Bd., Calif. Served in Army Sch. of Nursing, World War I. Named Honored Grad., Radcliffe Coll., 1968. Mem. Writers' Guild (Calif.), Authors League Am., PEN. Republican. Author: Junior High School Plays, 1938, The Secret of the Old House, 1941, Twelve Bright Trumpets (pub. in Eng. as The Conqueror), 1942; The Secret of the Closed Gate, 1944; The Singing Cave, 1945 (Jr. Lit. Guild selection, also received silver medal Commonwealth Club Calif.), 1946; Judith of France, 1948; Sword and the Compass, 1951; The Secret of Bucky Moran, 1952; The Story of Florence Nightingale, 1952; The Story of General Custer, 1954; Who Rides By, 1955; Comanche of the Seventh, 1957; The Secret of Smuggler's Cove, 1959; Journey for a Princess, 1960; Bride of Glory (Dorothy Canfield Fisher award, Dorothy C. McKenzie award), 1962; Voyage to Coromandel, 1965; The Canyon Castaways, 1966; A Hole in the Hedge, 1968; Cleopatra, 1969; The Other Island, 1971; Shelley's Mary, 1973. Contbr. to Child Life, American Girl, Portal, Target, Classmate, Girls Today, Boys Today, also anthologies and sch. readers. Deceased.

LEISENRING, EDWARD B., JR., mining company executive; b. 1926; married. B.A., Yale U., 1949. With Westmoreland Coal Co., Phila., v.p., 1957-59, pres., 1959-87, chmn., chief exec. officer, dir.; dir. Norfolk So. Corp., SKF Industries Inc.; chmn., chief exec. officer Penn Va. Corp. Served with A.C., USN, 1944-46. Died May 16, 1987, buried Mauch Chunk, Pa.

LEKACHMAN, ROBERT, economist, educator; b. N.Y.C., May 12, 1920; s. Samuel and Jennie (Kominsky) L.; m. Eva Leona Woodbrey, June 11, 1948. AB, Columbia U., 1942, PhD, 1954. Mem. faculty Barnard Coll., 1947-65; prof. econs., chmn. dept. SUNY, Stony Brook, 1965-68; disting. prof. econs Lehman Coll., CUNY, 1973-89; cons. Fund for the Republic, Rockefeller Found., 20th Century Found.; adviser to Com. on Econ. Devel. Author: A Beginner's Guide to Capitalism; A History of Economic Ideas, 1959, The Age of Keynes, 1966, National Income and the Public Welfare, 1972, Inflation-The Permanent Problem of Boom and Bust, 1973, Economists at Bay, 1976, Greed is Not Enough, 1982, Visions and Nightmares: America after Reagan, 1987; some books translated into several langs. and used extensively as texts; columnist for Dissent mag.; mem. editorial bd. Challenge, New Leader, Civil Liberties Rev., Christianity and Crisis; contbr. articles to Annals od Acad. Polit. Sci., Polit. Sci. Quar., Am. Econ. Rev., others; contbr., book reviewer N.Y. Times, Washington Post and other periodicals; frequent speaker and appearances on radio and TV. Bd. dirs. Suffolk County ACLU, 1966-89, mem. nat. ch,-state and acad. freedom coms., 1963-65, mem. equality com., from 1972; founding mem. Riverside (N.Y.) Democrats, 1956. With AUS, 1942-45, PTO. Rockefeller fellow, 1962, Liberal Arts fellow Harvard Law Sch., 1968-69, Guggenheim fellow, 1972-73; recipient Blue Bear award Barnard Coll. student body, 1965, numerous other teaching career awards; named one of 50 faculty mems. in U.S. for major contbns. to undergrad. edn. Change mag., 1986. Mem. Am. Econ. Assn., AAUP, NAACP, League Indsl. Democracy, Phi Beta Kappa. Home: New York N.Y. Died Jan. 14, 1989.

LEKAKIS, MICHAEL NICHOLAS, sculptor; b. N.Y.C., Mar. 1, 1907; s. Nicholas and Sophia (Ritsos) L. One-man shows Whitney Mus. Am. Art, 1973, Dayton Art Mus., Ohio, 1968, Nat. Pinakothiki of Athens, 1980-81, Kouros Gallery, N.Y.C., 1983-84, N.Y Retrospective, 1987; exhibited in group shows Whitney Mus., 5 anns. and The Third Dimension show, 1984-85, Parrish Art Mus., Southampton, N.Y., 1985, Phila. Art Alliance, 1985, Robert Schoelkopf Gallery, N.Y.C., 1985, Kouros Meml. Exbn., 1988, also others; represented in permanent collections Mus. Modern Art, Whitney Mus., Guggenheim Mus., Phila. Mus. Fine Art, Vassar Coll. Mus., Portland (Oreg.) Mus., Dayton (Ohio) Mus., Hartford (Conn.) Mus., Mus. Israel, Pinakothiki Mus., Athens, Greece, U. Nebr. Art Mus., Lincoln, Weatherspoon Art Gallery, U. N.C. at, Greensboro, MIT, Guild Hall Mus., East Hampton, N.Y., Parrish Mus. Art, Southampton, N.Y., Met. Mus., N.Y., Whitney Mus. (Vital Signs), 1988, drawing Parrish Art. Mus., 1988, 2 drawings Guild Hall Mus., Easthampton, N.Y., Pinakothiki, Athens Meml. Exhbn., 1988, 1 sculpture, Met. Mus., N.Y., 1988; also in numerous pvt. collections; retrospective at Dayton Art Inst., 1968; author long poem Eros Psyche, 1973, others.. Served with USAAF, 1942-45. Home: New York N.Y. Died Nov. 17, 1987; cremated.

LEMNITZER, LYMAN L., army officer; b. Honesdale, Pa., Aug. 29, 1899; s. William L. and Hannah (Blockberger) L.; m. Katherine Mead Tryon, Nov. 6, 1923; children: Lois Katherine, William Lyman. BS, U.S. Mil. Acad., 1920; grad. basic course, Coast Arty. Sch., 1921, grad. battery officers course, 1931; postgrad., Command and Gen. Staff Sch., 1936, Army War Coll., 1940; D Mil. Sci. (hon.), U. Md., Norwich U.; HHD (hon.), U. Ryukyus; LLD, U. Scranton, Gettysburg Coll., Williams Coll., George Washington U., 1967; DSc, Carthage Coll. Commd. 2d lt. U.S. Army, 1920, advanced through grades to gen., 1955, instr. U.S. Mil. Acad., 1926-30, 34-35, instr. tactics C.A. Sch., 1936-39, mem. Gen. Staff Corps,, 1941-42; with war plans div. War Dept., asst. G-3, Hdqrs. and chief plans div. Army Ground Force; comdg. gen. 34th A.A. Brig. Norfolk (Va.) and Eng., 1942; asst. chief of staff, G-3 to Gen. Eisenhower Allied Force Hdqrs., London and Algiers, 1942; dep. chief of staff to Gen. M.W. Clark 5th Army, 1943; comdg. gen. 34th A.A. Brig., Tunisian campaign 1943; dep. chief gen. staff to Gen. Sir Harold Alexander 15th Army Group, Sicily and Italy, 1943-44; dep. chief of staff Allied Force Hdqrs. to Field Marshal Alexander 1945, Army mem. Joint Strategic Survey Com., Joint Chiefs of Staff, 1946-47; dep. comdt. Nat. War Coll., 1947-49; dir. fgn. mil. assistance Dept. Def., 1949-50; comdg. gen. 11th Airborne Div., 1951, 7th Inf. Div., Korea, 1951-52; dep. chief of staff plans and rsch. Dept. Army, 1952-55; comdg. gen. Army Forces Far East and 8th U.S. Army in Japan and Korea, 1955; comdr. in chief Far East Command; comdr. in chief UN Command, gov. Ryukyu Islands 1955-57, army vice chief of staff, 1957-59, army chief of staff, 1959-60, chmn. Joint Chiefs of Staff, 1960-62; comdr. in chief European Command, 1962-69; supreme allied comdr. Europe, 1963-69. Decorated D.S.M. with 3 oak leaf clusters, Silver Star, Legion of Merit, Legion of Merit (officer's degree), D.S.M. (USN), D.S.M. (USAF); companion of Bath, comdr. Brit. Empire; chevalier gt. cross Royal Crown of Italy, Mil. Order of Merit, knight grand cross Mil. Order Republic of Italy; Medalha de Guerra, Grande ofcl. Order Mil. Merit (Brazil); Gold Cross of Merit with swords (Poland); grand cross Legion of Honor, Croix de Guerre with palm (France); grand star Mil. Merit (Chile); Royal Order of White Eagle (Yugoslavia); Medal of Mil. Merit (Czechoslovakia); Order Mil. Merit Taeguk with gold star, order Mil. Merit, Taeguk, Order Svc. merit, 1st Class (Korea); Order Melnik (Ethiopia); citation and medal of Cloud and Banner (Taiwan); grand officer Order of Boyaca (Colombia); Most Exalted Order White Elephant (Thailand); grand cordon Order Leopold (Belgium); grand cordon Order Rising Sun (Japan); grand cross Order Disting. Svc. (Fed. Republic Germany); Grand Cross of George I (Greece); grand cross Grand-Ducal Order Crown of Oak (Luxembourg); grand cross Order Orange nassau (The Netherlands); grand cross Order Avis (Portugal), numerous others; recipient Medal of Freedom, White House, 1987. Mem. Masons (33 degree), KT, Shriners. Died Nov. 12, 1988; buried Arlington Cemetery, Washington.

LENS, SIDNEY, writer, activist; b. Newark, Jan. 28, 1912; m. Shirley Ruben, 1946. Ed. pub. schs., N.Y.C. Dir. local 329 United Service Employees Union, AFL-CIO, 1941-66; lectr. fgn. affairs and labor U. Chgo., Roosevelt U., De Paul U., U. Ill, numerous others; columnist Nat. Cath. Reporter. Author: Left, Right and Center, 1949, The Counterfeit Revolution, 1952, A World in Revolution, 1956, The Crisis of American Labor, 1959, Working Men, 1960, Africa Awakening Giant, 1962, The Futile Crusade, 1964, A Country Is Born, 1964, Radicalism in America, 1966, What Unions Do, 1968, Poverty: America's Enduring Paradox, 1969, The Military Industrial Complex, 1970, The Forging of the American Empire, 1972, The Labor Wars, 1973, Poverty: Yesterday and Today, 1973, The Promise and Pitfalls of Revolution, 1974, The Day Before Doomsday, 1977, Unrepentant Radical, 1980, The Bomb, 1982, The Maginot Line Syndrome, 1983, Strikemakers and Strikebreakers, 1985, The Militarization of War, 1987; editor: Liberation mag.; sr. editor: The Progressive; contbr. articles to mags., newspapers, newspaper syndicates. Candidate for Congress, 2d Ill. Dist., 1962, Ill. Legislature, 1964, U.S. Senate, Ill., 1980; bd. dirs. Chgo. Coun. Fgn. Rels.; co-chmn. Nat. Com. to End War in Vietnam, New Mblzn. Com. to End War in Vietnam; chmn. Justice, Action and Peace in Latin Am., Impeach Nixon Com., 1973., Inst. Social Studies; founder Moblzn. for Survival; co-chmn. Coalition against Mil. Escalation. Recipient Patron Saints award Midland Authors, 1970. Fellow Inst. for Policy Studies (assoc.). Home: Chicago Ill. Died June 18, 1986.

LENZEN, KENNETH, engineering educator; b. Evanston, Ill., Sept. 18, 1921; s. John Frederick and Edna Mathilda (Ketz) L.; m. Evelyn E. Koeppel, June 3, 1944; 1 child, Karen Jean. BSCE, Northwestern U., 1943, MS in Structural Engring., 1947; PhD in Engring. Scis., Purdue U., 1957. Registered profl. engr., Mo., Kans., Ill., N.J., Ind. Rsch. engr. Portland Cement Assn., Chgo., 1946-47; rsch. assoc. Northwestern U., Evanston, 1947-49; instr. in engring., rsch. assoc. Purdue U., West Lafayette, Ind., 1949-55; assoc. prof. mechanics and aerospace engring. U. Kans., Lawrence, 1955-60, prof., 1960-85, chmn. dept., 1965-67, dir. mechanics div. dept. civil engring., 1967-74, assoc. dean engring. for grad. studies and rsch., 1974-80; advisor univ. affairs NASA, Washington, 1980-81; v.p. Cadre Corp., Lawrence, 1967-85; cons. in field. Contbr. articles to profl. jours., chpts. to books. Patentee in field. With USAAF, 1945-46. Danforth assoc., 1961; Fulbright grantee, 1962-63, OAS grantee, Peru, 1974. Fellow ASCE (James R. Croes medal 1956); mem. Rsch. Council Riveted and Bolted Structural Joints, Am. Ry. Engring. Assn., AAUP, Am. Soc. Engring. Edn., Triangle, NSPE, AAAS, Sigma Xi, Sigma Tau, Tau Beta Pi. Home: Lawrence Kans. Died Mar. 18, 1985.

LERNER, ALAN JAY, playwright, lyricist; b. N.Y.C., Aug. 31, 1918; m. Liz Robertson, 1981. BS, Harvard U., 1940. Playwright: (with Frederick Loewe) Broadway mus. plays including What's Up?, 1943, The Day Before Spring, 1945, Brigadoon, 1947 (N.Y. Drama Critic's Circle award), Paint Your Wagon, 1951, My Fair Lady, 1956 (N.Y. Drama Critic's Cirlce award, Donaldson award, Antoinette Perry award), Camelot, 1960, (with Kurt Weill) Love Life, 1948, (with Burton Lane) On a Clear Day You Can See Forever, 1965 (Grammy award), (with Andre Previn) Coco, 1969, (with Frederick Loewe) Gigi, 1973 (Antoinette Perry award for best score), (with Leonard Bernstein) 1600 Pennsylvania Avenue, 1976, (with Burton Lane) Carmelina, 1979; screenplays include Royal Wedding, 1951, An American in Paris, 1951 (Best screenplay Oscar, Screenwriters Guild award), My Fair Lady, 1964, Camelot, 1968; producer Paint Your Wagon, 1969, On a Clear Day You Can See Forever, 1970, The Little Prince, 1974. Bd. govs. Nat. Hosp. for Speech Disorders, N.Y. Osteo. Hosp. Mem. Dramatists Guild Am. (pres. 1958-63), Shaw Soc., Players Club, Lambs Club. Died June 14, 1986.

LEROY, MERVYN, motion picture producer; b. San Francisco, Oct. 15, 1900; s. Harry and Edna (Armer) Le Roy; m. Doris Warner, Jan. 2, 1933; children: Warner Lewis, Linda Mervyn; m. Kathryn Spiegel, 1946. Ed. pub. schs. Began career as actor, 1912, asst. cameraman, 1919-20; directed motion pictures Little Ceasar, I Am a Fugutive from a Chain Gang, Tugboast Annie, Anthony Adverse, others; producer, dir., Warner Bros. Studios, 1936-38, Metro-Goldwyn-Mayer Studios, from 1938, organized own prodn. co., Arrowhead Prodns., Burbank, Calif., 1944; produced Stand Up and Fight, 1939, The Wizard of Oz, 1939, Blossoms in the Dust, 1941, Random Harvest, 1942 (Oscar best dir.), The House I Live In, 1945 (hon. Oscar short subject film), Madame Curie, Thirty Seconds Over Tokyo, Without Reservations, Little Women, Any Number Can Play, 1949, East Side, West Side, 1950, Quo Vadis, 1951, Lovely to Look At, Million Dollar Mermaid, 1952; produced, directed: No Time for Sergeants, 1958, The FBI Story, 1959, Wake Me When It's Over, 1960, Gypsy, 1962, Mary-Mary, 1964, Moment to Moment, 1965. author: It Takes More Than Talent, 1953, Mervyn Le Roy: Take One, 1974. Recipient Victoire du Cinema Francais award, 1954, Irving Thalberg award, 1975. Club: Hollywood Turf. Home: Beverly Hills Calif. Died Sept. 13, 1987; buried Forest Lawn Cemetery, Glendale, Calif.

LESER, TINA, designer; b. Phila., Sept. 12, 1910; d. Charles Shillard and Georgene (Wetherill) Smith; m. Curtin Arnold Leser, Nov. 11, 1931 (div. Mar. 1936); m. James J. Howley, Nov. 5, 1948; 1 child, Georgine Wetherill. Student, Agnes Irwin Sch. Girls, Bishop Sch., Acad. Fine Arts, Shipley Sch., Indsl. Art Sch., U. Sorbonne; DFA, Moore Coll., 1964. Opened retail store Honolulu, 1935; ind. designer 1936, mfr. in Honolulu for N.Y.C., 1939-40; owner, operator mfg. bus. N.Y.C., 1941-42; assoc. Edwin H. Foreman, Inc., 1942-52; designer, pres. Tina Leser, Inc., 1952-64; owner Tina Leser Internat., 1966-86; designer men's ties Signet, 1949-86, men's sportswear Stafford Wear, 1950-86; fashion corrdinator Fashions for Industry, fall 1952; lectr. fashion schs. and colls.; radio speaker fashion influences; sponsor charity shows; judge fashion contests. Pres., bd. dirs. Fla. Gulf Coast Art Ctr., 1951-86. Recipient Fashion Critics award, 1944, Nieman-Marcus award, Fashion award Phila. Festival Arts, 1962; nominated as one of 10 top designers Sports Illus., 1956, 57. Mem. DAR, Magna Charta Dames, Colonial Dames, Phila. Art Alliance, Mus. Modern Art, Nat. Soc. Arts and Letters. Mem. Free Quaker Soc. Phila. Home: Sands Point N.Y. Died Jan. 23, 1986.

LESLIE, JOHN C., aviation consultant; b. July 21, 1905; s. John and Bessie May (McAfee) L.; m. Jean Savage, May 23, 1929; children: Pauline Leslie Lange, John, Peter, Susan Leslie Abu-Haidar. BS, Princeton U., 1926, MIT, 1928; MS, MIT, 1943. Assoc. Fokker Aircraft corp., 1928-29; asst. to chief engr. Pan Am. Airways, Inc., 1929, asst. to div. engr., 1930-34, div. engr. Pacific div. developing engring. technique transocean flight, 1935-38, ops. mgr. Pacific div., 1938-41, mgr. Atlantic div., 1941-45, v.p. Atlantic div., 1945-46, v.p., 1946, adminstrv. v.p., 1950-59, v.p., also asst. to pres., 1959-64, v.p., asst. to chmn., 1964-68, sr. v.p. internat. affairs, 1968-70, dir., 1950-70; sr. assoc. R. Dixon Speas Assocs., 1970-76. Mem. exec. com. Internat. Air Transp. Assn., 1947-70. Lt. comdr. USNR. Decorated comdr. Order Orange-Nassau; comdr. Order Ivory Coast. Fellow Am. Inst. Aeros. and Astronautics, Roya. Aero. Soc.; mem. Am. Yacht. Club, Mill Reef Club. Home: Saint John's Antigua Died Jan. 19, 1982.

L'ESPERANCE, WILFORD LOUIS, economist, educator; b. N.Y.C., Dec. 9, 1930; m. Barbara Manochio, May 4, 1957; children: Annette, Suzanne, Claire, Wilford. AB, Columbia Coll., 1951; MS, Columbia U., 1952; PhD, U. Mich., 1963. Mktg. rsch. analyst GE,

N.Y.C. and Ft. Wayne (Ind.), 1952-53, 55-60; cons. GE, 1965; math. analyst Ordnance Corp, U.S. Army Guided Missile Devel. Div., Huntsville, Ala., 1953-55; lectr. Ind. U., 1956-60; rsch. asst. dept. econs. U. Mich., 1961-63; economist Bur. Comml. Fisheries, Dept. Interior, Ann Arbor, Mich., 1962-63; cons. Bur. Comml. Fisheries, Dept. Interior, Sandusky, Ohio, 1963-65; asst. prof. econs. Ohio State U., 1963-66, assoc. prof., 1966-70, prof., 1970-82, instr. exec. devel. program div. continuing edn., 1970-75; pres. M.W. Econometrics, Inc., Columbus, Ohio, 1973-79; cons. in field; mem. Ohio Gov.'s Task Force on Lake Erie Fisher, 1973-74, Population Study Group, Environ. Health Com., Office Comprehensive Health Planning, Ohio Dept. Health, 1973-76; mem. panel econ. adviser for John Glenn's U.S. Senate campaign, 1974; mem. tech. adv. group Columbus Mayor's Econ. Devel. Coun., 1975. Author (with others): Columbus Area Economy—Structure and Growth, 1950-85, 1966, Modern Statistics for Business and Economics, 1971, The Structure and Control of a State Economy, 1979; assoc. editor Jour. Regional Sci., 1978-82; contbr. articles on econs. to profl. jours. Grantee Dept. Interior Bur. Comml. Fisheries, 1963-64, Coll. Rsch. Com., Coll. Commerce and Adminstrn., 1965-66, Ohio Dept. Devel., 1967-68, Coll. Rsch. Com., Coll. Social and Behavioral Scis., 1969, 76. Mem. AAUP, Am. Econ. Assn., Am. Statis. Assn. (pres. Columbus chpt. 1968), Econometric Soc., Regional Sci. Assn., Ohio Acad. Sci., N.Y. State Soc. Cin., Ohio, Worthington hist. socs., Hoover Yacht Club. Home: Columbus Ohio. Died Jan. 27, 1982.

LEVENSON, SEYMOUR, educator; b. N.Y.C., Nov. 12, 1919; s. Samuel Falk and Lena (Miller) L.; m. Marilyn Carroll Greenspoon, May 2, 1953; children: Gail Catherine, Jenifer Falk. BBA, CCNY, 1942; grad., Indsl. Coll. Armed Forces, 1966. With pvt. bus. 1939-40, as acct., 1940-42; with U.S. Fgn. Svc., 1945-61; assigned Marseille, France, 1945-47, Nanking, China, 1947-49, Athens, Greece, 1950-52; assigned Dept. State 1952-54; assigned Brussels, 1954-59, Monrovia, Liberia, 1959-61; exec. dir. Bur. Security and Consular Affairs Dept. State, 1962-66, with Bur. Latin Am. Affairs, 1966-67; counselor embassy for adminstrn. Dept. State, Caracas, Venezuela, 1967-71; with Dept. State 1971-76; assoc. prof. Capitol Inst. Tech., 1976-86. With AUS, 1942-45, ETO. Mem. Am. Fgn. Svc. Assn., City Coll. Alumni Assn., Am. Soc. Pub. Adminstrn., Washington Performing Arts Soc., Alumni Assn. Indsl. Coll. Armed Forces. Home: Bethesda Md. Died Apr. 7, 1986; buried Farmingdale, N.Y.

LÉVESQUE, CHARLES-HENRI, bishop; b. St-André de Kamouraska, Que., Can., Dec. 29, 1921; s. Alexis and Atala (Garneau) L. BA, Ste-Anne-de-la Pocatière, 1944; PhB, Laval U., 1945, licentiate in theology, 1949; DDC, Angelicum, Rome, 1955. Ordained priest Roman Cath. Ch., 1948. Head discipline, tchr. history and letters Coll. Ste-Anne-de-la-Pocatière, 1949-51; sec., master of ceremonies Bishopric St. Anne, 1951; chancellor Diocese St. Anne, 1956, hon. canon, 1956, titular canon, 1957, secret chamberlain, 1960; aux. bishop Ste-Anne-de-la-Pocatière, 1965-68, bishop, 1968-84; mem. episcopal com. Office Catéchèse du Que.; mem. com. des priorités Assembleé des Eveques du Que.; pres. Com. to Broadcast Liturg. Celebrations; co-pres. episcopal com. liturgy Conf. des Eveques catholiques du Can. Decorated chevalier l'Order équestre du St. Sépulcre. Mem. Internat. Francophone Com. for Liturg. Transls., KC (4 degree). Died Nov. 24, 1984; buried Cathedral of Ste-Anne-de-la-Pocatière.

LEVESQUE, RENE, prime minister of Quebec; b. New Carlisle, Que., Can., Aug. 24, 1922; s. Dominique and Diane Dionne-Pineault L.; m. Corinne Côté; children: Pierre, Claude, Suzanne. Student, Laval U.; hon. doctorate, U. Sorbonne, Paris, 1980. Formerly radio announcer, war. corr. Am. Forces, Europe, 1944-45, Am. Forces, CBC, Korea, 1952; chief French Network News, 1952-56; former freelance radio and TV commentator Quebec; mem. Qué. Legislature for Montreal-Laurier, 1960-70; minister pub. works and hydraulic works Province of Qué., Québec City, 1960-61; minister natural resources Province of Qué., 1961-66, minister family and social welfare, 1965-66; mem. Qué. Legislature from Taillon Riding, from 1976; prime minister Qué., 1976-85; scenarist and animator TV program La Francophonie en question, 1987; journalist, radio commentator 1987; Founder Que. Sovereignty Assn., 1967; former pres. Parti Québecois. Author: Option Québec, 1968, La Passion du Québec, 1978, OUI, 1980, Attendez que je me rappelle, 1986. Decorated grand officer Légion d' Honneur; recipient Medal, City of Paris, 1977. Home: Montreal, Ont. Canada. Died Nov. 1, 1987, buried Quebec City.

LEVEY, GERRIT, chemist, educator; b. Friesland, Wis., Jan. 9, 1924; s. John G. and Bessie (Alsum) L.; m. Mary Ryland Belt, Dec. 27, 1952; children—Christopher Gerrit, Douglas John, Bryan Osborn. A.B., Hope Coll., Holland, Mich., 1946; Ph.D., U. Wis., 1949. Mem. faculty Berea (Ky.) Coll., 1949-87, prof. chemistry, 1958-87; also chmn. dept.; sabbatical leaves for study and research at Mass. Inst. Tech., U. Leeds (Eng.), Argonne Nat. Lab., Notre Dame U.; summer research appointments Brown U., U. Wis. Contbr. articles to profl. jours. Served with AUS, 1943-44. Recipient Seabury award for excellence in teaching Berea Coll., 1962. Mem. Am. Chem. Soc., Ky. Acad. Sci. (sec. 1957-64), South Central Assn. Chemists, Sigma Xi, Phi Lambda Upsilon. Home: Berea Ky. Died Nov. 3, 1987.

LEVICH, BENJAMIN GREGORY, physicist; b. Charkov, USSR, Mar. 30, 1917; s. Gregory and Evgeny (Atlasnez) L.; m. Tanya Rubinstein, Nov. 4, 1943; children: Alexander, Evgeny. M Physics, Kharkov U., USSR, 1937; PhD, Moscow Pedagogical Inst., 1940; DSc (hon.), Hebrew U., Jerusalem, Boston U., Carnegie-Mellow U. Sr. researcher, head theoretical dept. Inst. Elctrochemistry USSR Acad. Scis., 1940-58; prof. phys. chemistry Kazan U., 1943-54; prof. theoretical physics, head dept. Moscow Inst. Physics and Engring., 1954-65; head dept. chem. mechanics Moscow U., 1964-72; prof. Tel-Aviv U., 1978-79; Albert Einstein prof. sci. CUNY, 1979-87; dep. of sec. gen. Com. on Atomic Energy, USSR, 1946-50. Author: Physico-Chemical Hydrodynamics, 19562, Statistical Physics, 1949, Theoretical Physics. An Advanced Texst, 2 vols., 1962, rev. edit., 1971, English rev. edit., 4 vols., 1972-73, Spanish rev. edit., 4 vols., 1975-78; mem. editorial bd. Energy Conversion, Physico-Chem. Hydrodynamics; contbr. articles to profl. jours. Recipient Mendeleev prize, 1960, Palladium medal Am. Electrochem. Soc., 1973, medal Brit. Chem. Soc., 1981; named a hon. mem. Imperial Coll., London. Mem. Acad. Scis. USSR (corr., expelled 1979), Norwegian Acad. Scis. and Letters (fgn.), N.Y. Acad. Scis. (hon.). Died Jan. 19, 1987.

LEVIN, HAROLD ARTHUR, economic educator, consultant; b. N.Y.C., Oct. 9, 1918; s. Milton H. and Rachel (Cooperman) L.; m. Toby Poizner, Apr. 30, 1942; children: Jordan R., Erica. A.B., NYU, 1940, U. Denver, 1940-42; M.S., U. Denver, 1947; postgrad., Georgetown U., 1946-48, George Washington U., 1951-52. Personnel officer Office Emergency Mgmt., 1942-43; fgn. affairs officer Dept. State, 1946-49; requirements cons. ECA, Mission to Korea, 1949-50; internat. economist ECA, 1950-51; fgn. requirements specialist Def. Prodn. Adminstrn., 1951-53; control programs dir. East-West trade ICA, 1953-57; staff State Dept., U.S. mission to NATO and European Regional Orgns., Paris, 1957-61; dep. U.S. rep. to European Regional Trade Com., 1957-58; chief U.S. del. Internat. East-West trade coms.; also dir. Office Security Trade Controls, 1958-61; chief internat. bus. practices div. Dept. State, 1961-67, AID ofcl., 1967-74, chief internat. trade div., 1967-68; acting dir. Office Commodity Import Programs, 1968-69, Bur. for Vietnam, chief Laos desk, 1969-72; dir. Office Laos Affairs, 1972-74; asst. v.p. for internat. affairs, research and planning div. Pharm. Mfrs. Assn., 1974-75; lectr. bus. adminstrn. and econs. Montgomery Coll. (Md.), 1975-81, adj. prof., 1981-86; coordinator grad. programs Columbia Campus, Loyola Coll., 1976-79; econ. cons. internat. affairs, 1980-87; cons. Russel Sage Found., 1955; vis. scholar Georgetown U., 1973-74. Author articles on internat. subjects. Served to lt. USNR, 1943-46. Alfred P. Sloan Found. fellow, 1940-42. Mem. Am. Fgn. Service Assn., Govtl. Research Assn., Suburban Md. Internat. Trade Assn. (pres.-elect 1985-86), Phi Beta Kappa. Club: International (Washington). Home: Silver Spring Md. Died Feb. 10, 1986.

LEVIN, MEYER, writer; b. Chgo., Oct. 8, 1905; s. Joseph and Goldie (Levin) L.; m. Mable Schamp Foy (div. 1944); 1 child, Eli; m. Tereska Szwarc, Mar. 25, 1948; children: Gabriel, Mikael, Dominique. PhB, U. Chgo., 1924. Asst. editor Esquire and Coronet mags., 1934-38; film critic, writer-dir. OWI, 1942-43; war corr. Overseas News Agy., Europe, 1946; tchr. marionette theatre prodn. New Sch. for Social Rsch., N.Y.C., 1932. Author: Reporter, 1929, Frankie and Johnny, 1930, Yehuda, 1931, The New Bridge, 1933, The Golden Mountain, 1934 (republished as Classic Hassidic Tales, 1975), The Old Bunch, 1936, Citizens, 1940, My Father's House, 1946, In Search, 1950, Compulsion, 19567, Eva, 1959, The Fanatic, 1964, The Stronghold, 1965, Gore and Igor, 1968, Israel Haggadah for Passover, 1970, The Spell of Time, 1971, The Story of Israel, 1972, Beginnings in Jewish Philosphy, 1974, The Obsession, 1974, The Harvest, 1978, The Architect, 1981; (with T.K. Kurzband) Story of the Jewish Way of Life, 1959, Story of the Synagogue, The Settlers, 1972. Home: New York N.Y. Died July 9, 1981, buried Jerusalem.

LEVIN, NATHAN WILLIS, investment consultant; b. Joliet, Ill., Oct. 10, 1904; s. Ben and Ida (Grossman) L.; m. Ethel Gordon, Mar. 16, 1928 (dec. Aug. 1935); children: Joan Levin Kirsch, Marion Levin Gottfried (dec.); m. 2d, Pam Schorr, Apr. 2, 1941; children: Nina Levin Jalladeau, Robert N. PhB, U. Chgo., 1926; LLD, New Sch. Social Rsch., 1964. C.P.A., Ill. With Union Trust Co., Chgo., 1926-27; instr. econs. and acctg. State Coll. Wash., 1928; fellow econs. U. Chgo., 1929; fin. asst. to Julius Rosenwald 1929-32, asst. to Lessing J. Rosenwald in adminstrn. estate Julius Rosenwald, 1932-37, comptroller Julius Rosenwald Fund, 1929-48; investment cons., mgr., from 1937; pres., treas., dir. Fortnightly Corp., 1948-70, Internat. Devel. Svcs., Inc., 1955-69; pres. Reporter Mag., 1948-68; pres., dir. Clarksburg & Fairmont (W.Va.) TV Cable Corp., 1955-67, No. W.Va. Broadcasting Co., 1963-76; chmn. Pantheon Books, Inc., 1948-62; chmn., dir. Oil Shale Corp. (now Tosco Corp.), 1957-70, vice chmn., 1970-78; chmn., dir. Starwood Corp., 1959-60; vice chmn., dir. Pavelle Corp., 1967-72; v.p., dir. Chek-Chart Corp., 1955-70, Technol. Investors Corp., 1960-63; chmn. fin. com., dir. Sci. Am. Inc., from 1946; dir. Exmet Corp., Liberia Corp. Mem. investment com. Mus. Modern Art, from 1946; treas. N.Y. Fund for Children, 1948-70; mem. adv. com. on mgmt. Dept. State, 1965; pub. mem. Fgn. Svc. Inspection Corp., Dept. State, Africa, 1965; mem. Internat. Exec. Svc. Corp., Ethiopia, 1973; trustee New Sch. Social Rsch., from 1942, chmn. bd. trustees, 1960-63, acting pres., 1960-61, chmn. exec. com. from 1964; trustee Mus. Sci. and Industry, Chgo., from 1930, Adele R. Levy Fund, 1960-68, Hall of Sci., N.Y.C., 1969-78; trustee, chmn. exec. com. Internat. Inst. Rural Reconstrn., from 1967. Mem. Am. Inst. C.P.A.'s, Pub. Mem.'s Assn. of Dept. State (v.p., dir. 1965), Tavern, Quadrangle (Chgo.), Century clubs, Phi Beta Kappa. Home: Mount Kisco N.Y. Died Oct. 21, 1988.

LEVINE, ESTHER SARAH, librarian; b. Boston, Nov. 10, 1908; d. Edward I. and Mamie (Winer) L. Student, U. Chgo., 1927; BS, Simmons Coll., 1930; MLS, Columbia U., 1951. Gen. asst. Pawtucket Pub. Library, 1936-42; cataloging asst. Providence Pub. Library, 1936-42; librarian Harbor Defs. L.I. Sound, 1942-44, New Sch. for Social Rsch., 1944-86. Mem. ALA, N.Y. Library Assn., Sol. Libraries Assn. Died Feb. 1, 1986.

LEVINE, JOSEPH EDWARD, motion picture producer; b. Boston, Sept. 9, 1905; m. Rosalie Harrison, 1939; 2 children. L.H.D. (hon.), Emerson Coll., 1968. Owner theater New Haven, Conn., 1938; in movie distbn. bus. from 1943; owner Embassy Pictures distbn. co.; chmn. Joseph E. Levine Presents, Inc. Producer, motion pictures include Jack the Ripper, 1960, Hercules, 1959, Hercules Unchained, 1960, Bocaccio '70, 1962, The Sky Above-The Mud Below, 1960, Two Women, 1961, The Conjugal Bed, 1963, 8 1/2, 1963, Divorce-Italian Style, 1962, Marriage Italian Style, 1964, The Easy Life, Yesterday, Today and Tomorrow, 1964, The Carpetbaggers, 1964, Harlow, 1965, Zulu, 1964, Casanova '70, 1965, Darling, 1965, Woman Times Seven, 1967, The Graduate, 1967, The Producers, 1968, The Lion in Winter, 1968, Arruza, 1972, Thumb Tripping, 1972, They Call me Trinity, 1972, The Ruling Class, 1972, Carnal Knowledge, 1971, Day of the Dolphin, 1973, A Bridge Too Far, 1977, Magic, 1978, Tattoo, 1981. Home: Greenwich Conn. Died July 31, 1987.

LEVINE, LEWIS, brokerage house executive; b. N.Y.C., Sept. 22, 1889; s. William and Dora (Wrenn) L.; m. Mabel Shutkind, May 29, 1909; children: Milton, Charles B. Student pub. schs., N.Y.C. Sr. ptnr. Sartorius & Co., N.Y.C., from 1925; mem. N.Y. Stock Exchange, mem. bd. arbitration. Mem. Detectives Endowment Assn. N.Y.C. Police Dept. (hon.), Masons. Home: New York N.Y. †

LEVINE, PHILIP, immunohematologist, geneticist, biomedical scientist; b. Russia, Aug. 10, 1900; came to U.S., 1908, naturalized, 1917; s. Morris and Fay (Zirulick) L.; B.S., CCNY, 1919; M.D., Cornell U., 1923, M.A., 1925; Sc.D., Mich. State U., 1967; Sc.D., U. Wis.; m. Hilda Lillian Perlmutter, May 1, 1938 (dec.); children—Phyllis Ann Levine, Klein Mark Armin, Paul Karl (dec.), Victor Raphael. Asst., later assoc. Rockefeller Inst. Med. Research, 1925-32; mem. faculty U. Wis. Med. Sch., 1932-35; bacteriologist/serologist Newark Beth Israel Hosp., 1935-44; dir. immunohematology div. Ortho Research Found., Raritan, N.J., 1944, now cons. Ortho Diagnostics, Ortho Pharm.; vis. investigator Meml. Sloan Kettering Inst. Cancer Research, 1976-82; vis. fellow Faculty of Medicine, Cornell U., 1978; cons. Nassau Hosp., Mineola, N.Y.; hon. life mem. profl. staff Center for Immunology, SUNY, Buffalo, 1974-87; Gehrman lectr. U. Ill. Coll. Medicine, 1975-87; McNeal lectr., 1979. Recipient Passano Found. award, 1951, 1st Franz Oehlecker award and gold medal German Soc. Blood Transfusion, 1964, Joseph P. Kennedy Jr. Internat. award, 1965, Edward J. III award Acad. Medicine, N.J., 1966, Clement von Pirquet gold medal VII Forum on Allergy, 1966, Mead Johnson award, 1942, Ward Burdick award, 1946, Lasker award, 1946, Phi Lambda Kappa Grand award, 1947, Karl Landsteiner award, 1956, Townsend Harris award, 1956, award of merit Netherlands Red Cross, 1959, Gold medal award Norwegian Soc. Immunohematologists, Allan award Am. Soc. Human Genetics, Melvyn H. Motolinsky Research Found. award Rutgers Med. Sch., McNeill award N.J. Hosp. Assn., 1979; 80th birthday honoree Internat. Soc. Hematology and Blood Transfusion, Montreal, Que., Can., 1980; recipient Landsteiner gold medal Netherlands Red Cross; bronze medal Israel Red Cross Transfusion Service; lapel pin Bavarian Red Cross, all 1980. Fellow ACP, Royal Coll. Physicians, Explorers Club; mem. Nat. Acad. Sci., N.Y. Acad. Medicine, Am. Genetic Assn., Am. Assn. Immunologists, Soc. Exptl. Biology and Medicine, Med. Soc. State N.J., Am. Assn. Human Genetics (pres. 1969-70), Immunohematology (hon.), Sigma Xi. Jewish. Clubs: Lotos, Cosmos. Author numerous publs., original exptl. work on human blood groups, transfusions; author of laws in N.J. and Wis. on blood tests in paternity disputes; discovered (with Dr. Landsteiner) Blood factors M, N and P (M and N useful in paternity and bastardy cases); elaborated methods of studying bacteriophage; described causes of diseases of newborn (erythroblastosis fetalis); discovered human Rh blood factor and phenomenon of isoimmunization through pregnancy; described several other new blood antigens; discovered cause of anemia in Rh null individual; showed associated blood group antigens in malignancies and that high-titer antibodies specific for these antigens specifically cytotoxic for such malignant tissues; described a normal antibody in normal human sera, the Forssman antibody as related to aging, cancer and other immune complex diseases; mem. adv. bd. Vox Sanguinis; editorial bd. Transfusion. Home: N.Y.C. Died Oct. 18, 1987.

LEVINSON, JACOB, financial executive; b. Tel Aviv, 1932; s. Gershom and Dvorah L.; m. Nurit Zelnik, 1960; children—Gershom, Asaf, Iddo, Dan. Student, Hebrew U. of Jerusalem, 1958-61. Head dept. econs. Hevrat Ovdim, Israel, 1963-68; chmn. bd. mgmt. Bank Hapoalim B.M., Israel, 1968-73; mem. adv. com. adv. council Bank of Israel, 1959-81; chmn. bd. dirs. Bank Hapoalim B.M. and subs., 1973-81, Ampal Am. Israel Corp., N.Y.C., from 1975; and overseas banking subs. of Bank Hapoalim B.M., 1973-84. Contbr. articles to profl. jours. Died Feb.22, 1984.

LEVINSON, RICHARD LEIGHTON, writer, producer; b. Phila., Aug. 7, 1934; s. William and Georgia Francis (Harbert) L.; m. Rosanna Huffman, Apr. 20, 1968; 1 dau., Christine Leighton. B.S. in Econs., U. Pa., 1956. Co-pres. Richard Levinson/William Link Prodns., Los Angeles, 1978-87; chmn. playwrights com. Actors' Studio West, 1965-68. collaborator, free-lance writer with William Link: (play) Chain of Command, 1959, (play) Prescription: Murder, 1962, (novel) Fineman, 1972, (TV movie) The Certain Summer, 1972, (TV movie) My Sweet Charlie, TV movie (The Execution of Private Sloik), (TV series) Columbo (Emmy award), 1969, (TV series) Ellery Queen, 1975, Stay Tuned: An Inside Look at Prime-Time Television, 1981, (Broadway musical) Merlin, 1983 (Tony nominee), also numerous short stories, TV and film scripts, book revs.; author: (with William Link and Peter S. Fischer) TV series Murder, She Wrote; writer, producer Universal Studios, Universal City, Calif., 1966-77. Served with U.S. Army, 1957-58. Recipient Image award NAACP, 1970; recipient Golden Globe award, 1972, Edgar Allan Poe award Mystery Writers Am., 1979, 80, 83 (total of 4). Mem. Acad. TV Arts and Scis. (Emmy award 1970, 72), Caucus for Writers, Producers and Dirs. (steering com. 1976-77), Writers Guild Am. (award 1972). Home: Los Angeles Calif. Died Mar. 12, 1987.

LEVY, CHARLES, JR., business executive; b. Chgo., Apr. 27, 1913; s. Charles and Bertha (Friend) L.; m. Ruth Doctoroff, Oct. 15, 1939; 1 dau., Barbara. Student, Wharton Sch., U. Pa., 1931-35. Chmn. bd. dirs. Charles Levy Circulating Co., Chgo., 1961-86; bd. dirs. Jewish Fedn. Chgo., Michael Reese Hosp., Chgo., Park View Home, Temple sholom, Mt. Sinai Med. Rsch., Lincoln Park Zool. Soc. Bd. dirs. Jewish Fedn. Chgo., Michael Reese Hosp., Chgo., Park View Home, Temple Sholom, Mt. Sinai Med. Rsch., Lincoln Park Zool. Soc. With AUS, 1942-46. Decorated Bronze Star. Mem. Periodical Inst., Mid-Am. Periodical Assn., Coun. Periodical Distbrs., Standard Club, Bryn Mawr Country Club, Carleton Club, Mid-Am. Club. Home: Chicago Ill. Died July 20, 1986.

LEWENTHAL, RAYMOND, pianist, editor, author; b. San Antonio, Aug. 29, 1926; s. Edward A. and Renee (Katz) L. Student, Long's Profl. Sch., Hollywood, Calif., Juilliard Sch. Music, N.Y.C., 1946-48, Accademia Chigiana, Siena, Italy, 1957-60; student of Lydia Cherkassky, Olga Samaroff-Stokowski, Alfred Cortot, Guido Agosti. Debut with Phila. Orch., 1948, N.Y.C. debut at Town Hall, 1948; tours throughout U.S., Europe, S.Am.; rsch. on life and music of Charles-Valentin Alkan, also editor of his piano music and recording for RCA Victor; other recording for Westminster Records, EMI, Romantic Revival series Columbia Records; performed Liszt cycle Town Hall, 1965-66, London, 1967; contbr. numerous articles on mus. subjects. Decorated chevalier de l'Ordre des Arts et des Lettres (France); recipient Gainsborough award San Francisco, Harriet Cohen award, London, Eng.; winner Young Artist contest U. Calif. at L.A., also Occidental Coll. Home: Hudson N.Y. Died Nov. 21, 1988.

LEWENTHAL, REEVES, oil and gas executive; b. Rockford, Ill., June 17, 1909; s. Harry Reeves and Bella Broad (Petigorski) L.; m. Elinor Davidson, Feb. 17, 1932 (div.); 1 dau., Lana; m. 2d, Concetta Marie Citrano, May 14, 1971; 1 son, Reeves. Student, Slade Sch., London, Eng., 1928; extension course, U. Mich., 1926-27. Newspaper reporter 1928; dir. pub. relations Nat. Acad., 1929-34, Beaux Arts Inst., 1930-31, Mcpl. Art Soc., N.Y.C., 1930-33, Soc. Am. Etchers, 1929-34, Allied Artists Am., 1929-34; pres. Assoc. Am. Artists, 1934-44, chmn. bd., 1944-58; pres. United Printers and Pub. Inc. 1958-60; pres. Apollo Petroleum Corp., N.Y.C.; chmn. bd. Ray Resources Corp., Allegeheny and Western Energy Corp. Author: Work for Artists. Mem. N.Y.C. Com. Adult Edn., 1935-37, art adv. com. War Dept., 1942; expert cons. for art to chief of engrs. U.S. Army, 1942. Recipient Gold medal for contbn. to Am. art Nat. Commn. to Advance Am. Art, 1932, Gold medal and Diplome de Merite, Union Francaise des Inventeurs, 1954, de la Croix de Lorraine, L'Ordre Chevalier (France), 1954, de Republique Francaise, 1954, Croix d'Honneur, 2d Class (France), 1954. Mem. Crystal Collectors' Soc. (sec.), Am. Inst. Graphic Art, Acad. Polit. Sci., Republique Francaise Nationale Artistique et Litteraire. Home: Fort Lauderdale Fla. Died Apr. 19, 1987.

LEWIS, CHARLES W., lawyer; b. Danville, Va., Aug. 19, 1904; s. William Baskerville and Maggie (Watkins) L.; m. Ida Maria Bonzi, Dec. 8, 1937; children: Charles W., Maria Lewis Phillips. AB, Va. Mil. Inst., 1924; student, Washington and Lee U. Law Sch., 1924-26; LLB, Yale U., 1927. Bar: Va. 1926, N.Y. 1928. Capt., instr.English and mil. sci. Va. Mil. Inst., 1924-26; pvt. practice N.Y.C., 1927-85; mng. ptnr. Townsend & Lewis, N.Y.C., 1935-52, sr. ptnr., 1952-73; a mng. ptnr. Thacher, Proffitt & Wood, N.Y.C., 1973-76, counsel, 1977-85; bd. dirs. Gen. Am. Oil Co. of Tex., 1959-79, dir. emeritus, 1979-85. Bd. visitors Va. Mil. Inst., 1960-64; trustee VMI Found., 1955-79; trustee Brick Presbyn. Ch., N.Y.C., 1973-79, pres. bd. trustees, 1976-79, trustee emeritus, 1982-85. Recipient Disting. Svc. award Va. Mil. Inst. Found., 1980. Mem. Am., N.Y. State bar assn., Assn. Bar City N.Y., The Virginians (N.Y.) (gov. 1963-64), Va. Mil. Inst. Alumni Assn. (pres. N.Y. chpt. 1951-52), S.R., Soc. Colonial Wars, University Club, Fairfield County Hunt Club (Conn.), Masons, Hillsboro Club, Ponte Vedra Club (Fla.), Downtown Assn., Pilgrims U.S., Kappa Alpha (pres. alumni chpt. N.Y. 1934-35), Phi Delta Phi. Home: Fairfield Conn. Died Sept. 4, 1985; buried Oak Lawn Cemetery, Fairfield, Conn.

LEWIS, DANIEL CURTIS, JR., paper company executive; b. Suffolk, Va., Aug. 26, 1918; s. Daniel Curtis and Frances (Rawls) L.; m. Elizabeth Shirley Baer, June 5, 1948; children: Lawrence S., Clifford R., Robert D. A.B. cum laude, Washington and Lee U., 1942; M.B.A. with distinction, Harvard U., 1948, D.C.S., 1954. Jr. staff accountant Lybrand Ross Bros. & Montgomery, Boston, 1948-49; asst. prof. commerce Washington and Lee U., 1949-52; research assoc. bus. adminstrn. Grad. Sch. Bus. Adminstrn., Harvard, 1952-54; asst. to pres. Lynchburg Foundry Co., Va., 1954-56; controller Lynchburg Foundry Co., 1956-60, sec., asst. treas., 1960-63; asst. sec. Woodward Iron Co., Birmingham and Lynchburg, 1961-63; asst. to pres. Chesapeake Corp., West Point, Va., 1963-66, v.p. adminstrn., 1966-87, also dir.; pres., dir. Chesapeake Bay Plywood Corp., 1967-87; sec., dir. Greenlife Products Co., 1969-82; dir. York River Oyster Research Corp., Cands Lumber Co. Chmn. Lynchburg Citizens Sch. Study Commn., 1960-61; mem. Va. Commn. State and Local Revenues, Expenditures and Related Matters, 1962-63, Va. Commn. Higher Edn., 1964-65; mem. West Point Sch. Bd., 1964-76, chmn., 1965-76; mem. Va. Bd. Community Colls., 1966-76, vice chmn., 1970-71, chmn., 1971-76; mem. West Point Bi-racial Com., 1968-87, Va. Pub. Telecommunications Council, 1972-76; Bd. dirs. Lynchburg chpt. ARC, 1956-59, West Point Improvement Assn., 1964-67; bd. dirs. Lynchburg Guidance Center, 1956-59, pres., 1958-59; bd. dirs. United Fund Lynchburg, 1959-61; v.p. 1960-61; treas. Va. Found. Ind. Colls., 1957-63, trustee, 1966-87; trustee Va. Episcopal Sch., 1960-66, Williamsburg Community Hosp., 1967-70; pres. bd. dirs. Ednl. Found. for Community Colls., Va., 1968-76; dir. sponsors Sch. Bus. Adminstrn., Coll. William and Mary, 1970-87; bd. dirs. Va. Found. Humanities and Pub. Policy, 1978-84. Served with USNR, 1942-46. Mem. Financial Execs. Inst., Newcomen Soc. N.Am., So. Forest Inst. (pres. 1971), Alpha Circle of Omicron Delta Kappa. Episcopalian. (vestryman, layreader). Clubs: Harvard of Va.; West Point Country (dir.); Va. Yacht. Home: Williamsburg Va. Died Aug. 6, 1987, buried Williamsburg, Va.

LEWIS, DUDLEY CUSHMAN, lawyer, fiduciary; b. Honolulu, Mar. 26, 1909; s. Abraham and Alice Hall (Jones) L.; m. Elizabeth Sullivan Seymour, June 28, 1932; children: Peter Cushman, Leilani. AB, Harvard U., 1930, LLB, 1934. Bar: Hawaii 1935. Ptnr. Lewis, Buck & Saunders, Honolulu, 1946-66, Lewis, Saunders & Sharpless, Honolulu, 1966-68, Lewis, Saunders & Key, Honolulu, 1969-71; of counsel Damon, Key, Char & Blocken, Honolulu, 1971; bd. dirs. Mid Pacific Air, Japan Hawaii Fin., First Hawaiian Bank, 1st Hawaiian Inc., Hawaii Thrift & Loan; trustee S.M. Damon Estate; dep. atty. Gen. Hawaii, 1935-36, 45-46. Lt. (j.g.) to comdr., USNR, 1941-46. Mem. Internat. Game Fish Assn. (trustee, v.p.), ABA, Bar Assn. Hawaii (past pres.), Oahu Country Club, Pacific Club (Honolulu); Pacific Union Club (San Francisco); Butte Lodge Outing Club (Colusa, Calif.). Home: Honolulu Hawaii. Died August 26, 1985; buried Ohau Cemetery, Honolulu.

LEWIS, EDWARD SHAKESPEAR, educator, social work administrator; b. Platte City, Mo., Aug. 17, 1901; s. William Talifero and Belle Zora (Caldwell) L.; m. Mary Cecil Miller, June 5, 1926; children: Raphael, Carol (Mrs. Thomas Matthew). PhB, U. Chgo., 1925; AM, U. Pa., 1939; PhD, NYU, 1961; LLD (hon.), U. Cin., 1970. Prof. history Fla. A & M Coll., Talahassee, 1925-27; exec. dir. Kans. City (Mo.) Urban League, 1927-31; dir. Balt. Urban League, 1931-42; exec. dir. N.Y.C. Urban League, 1942-63; prof. coop. edn. Borough of Manhattan Community Coll., N.Y.C., from 1964, dir. coop. edn. programs, 1964-70, dean coop. edn., 1971-78, dean emeritus, from 1978; mem. Pres.'s Consumer Adv. Coun., 1963-64. Contbr. articles to profl. jours. Mem. adv. bd. on social welfare, N.Y.C from 1968; bd. dirs. Consumer-Farmer Found., Fedn. o Protestant Welfare Agys.; life mem., bd. dirs. Fresh Ai Fund, from 1960. Named Man of Yr. Balt. Afro-Am Newspapers, 1941; recipient merit award Com monwealth of P.R., 1954, Bronze medal City of N.Y 1963. Mem. Nat. Coop. Edn. Assn. (pres. 1971-72) Frontiers Club (Balt.), Kappa Alpha Psi. Home: Nev York N.Y. Died Mar. 12, 1986; interred Riverside Ch Columbarium, N.Y.C.

LEWIS, EMANUEL P., banker; b. Balt., May 3, 190 s. Joseph and Bertha (Westheimer) L.; m. France Donner, Feb. 14, 1934; children: Richard Arthur, Susa Donner. Student, pub. schs. Credit mgr. James Talcot Inc., N.Y.C., 1929, dir., 1936, v.p., 1938-56, exec. v.p. 1956-58; pres., dir. Shapiro Bros. Factors Corp., 1958 69; pres. Shapiro Factors div. Chase Manhattan Bank N.A., 1954-71; mng. dir. Slavenburg Corp. subsidiar N.V. Slavenburgs Bank, 1972-82; bd. dirs. 1200 Corp. former dir. Interstate Dept. Stores, Inc. Mem. N.Y Credit Men's Assn., Nat. Fedn. Textiles, Am. Arbitra tion Assn., Harmonie Club, The 475 Club, City Club Athletic Club (N.Y.C.). Home: New York N.Y. Die Nov. 11, 1986.

LEWIS, HOWARD PHELPS, physician; b. Sa Francisco, Feb. 18, 1902; s. Edmund P. and Mary Edit (Howard) L.; m. Wava Irene Brown, July 2, 1927; chil dren: Richard Phelps, Thomas Howard. BS, Orego State Coll., 1924; MD, U. Oreg., 1930. Diplomate Am Bd. Internal Medicine (dir. , chmn. 1959-61), Am. Bd Family Practice (dir. 1969-85); master ACP (Alfre Stengel award 1966, ex-gov. Oreg., regent, pres. 1959 60). Intern, resident in medicine Multnomah Hosp. Portland, Oreg., 1930-32; pvt. practice and part tim teaching 1932-42; assoc. prof. medicine U. Oreg. Med Sch., 1946-47, prof., head dept. medicine, 1947-71; prof emeritus 1971-85; former chief medicine Multnoma Hosp., U. Oreg. Med. Sch. Hosp.; hon. staff Goo Samaritan Hosp., Providence Hosp., Emanuel Hosp., St Vincent Hosp., Portland; mem. adv. coun. Nat. Hear Inst., 1956-60. Editor: Modern Concepts of Cardiovas cular Disease, Am. Heart Assn., 1956-61; editorial bd Archives of Internal Medicine, 1961-68, Circulation 1961-65, 66-71, Am. Heart Jour., 1969-76. Col. M.C. U.S. Army; served at William Beaumont, Halloran an Rhoads Gen. hosps.; cons. med. 2d Svc. Command 1942-46. Recipient Award of Merit Am. Heart Assn. 1960. Fellow Am. Coll. Cardiology; mem. Am. Hear Assn. (hon. fellow coun. clin. Cardiology 1963), Wester Assn. Physicians, Assn. Am. Physicians, Oreg. Multnomah County med. socs., AMA (chmn. sect. in ternal medicine 1954-55), Am. Clin. and Climatol. Assn (pres. 1958), Pacific Interurban Clin. Club, Nort Pacific Soc. Internal Medicine, Am. Fedn. Clin. Rsch. Western Soc. Clin. Rsch., AAAS, Waverley Countr Club, University Club. Home: Portland Oreg. Die Apr. 24, 1985.

LEWIS, JOHN REECE, banker; b. Whitford, Pa., Jul 6, 1891; s. George Davis and Hannah (Andrews) L.; m Margaret Louise Cruse, Nov. 14, 1914; children: Joh Reece Jr., George Davis II, Russell Cruse. Ed. Friend's Sch., Phila. With Brown Bros. Co., Phila. 1908-20, W.H. Newbold's Son Co., 1920-23; wit Elkins, Morris, Stokest Co., securities and brokerage from 1923, ptnr., from 1936; bd. dirs. Link Belt Co. Chgo. Bd. dirs. Jeanes Hosp., Phila., Phila. Boardin Home for Friends, Germantown, Pa. Mem. Welsh Soc of Pa., Colonial Soc. of Pa., Union League. Mem. Soc of Friends. Home: Phila. Pa. †

LEWIS, MEAD A(LLYN), investment banker; b Phoenix, Sept. 8, 1889; s. R. Allyn and Lactiti (McDermott) L.; m. Estelle Savin, Dec. 7, 1927. AB Princeton U., 1911. Office mgr. Dick & Merle-Smith N.Y.C., 1934-36, ptnr., from 1936. Mem. Downtow Club, Regency Club, Wee Burn Country Club. Home Darien Conn. †

LEWIS, OREN RITTER, judge; b. Seymour, Ind., Oct 7, 1902; s. Jno M. and Emma A. (Crabb) L.; m. Grac M. Wells, Aug. 12, 1925; children: Oren Ritter, Rober Wells. Student, Hanover Coll., 1924; LLB, Georg Washington U., 1939. Bar: Va. 1939. Circulation mgr Washington Times Herald, 1926-33; with various Hears newspapers, 1933-39; owner, pub. Alexandria-Arlington Fairfax Jours., 1940-61; pvt. practice Arlington County 1939-60; judge U.S. Dist. Ct., Eastern Dist. Va., Alex andria, 1960-, sr. status judge, 1973-83. County an dist. chmn. Republican Party, 1932-58. With USN World War I. Mem. ABA, Va. Bar Assn., Arlingto County Bar Assn. (pres.), Jud. Coun. U.S., Nat Lawyers Club, Masons (32 deg.), Shriners, Kiwanis (pres., lt. gov.), Washington Golf and Country. Home Arlington Va. Died June 12, 1983, buried Columbi Gardens, Arlington.

LEWIS, ROBERT JAMES, investment banker; b Macomb, Ill., Feb. 23, 1899; s. Robert E. and Addi (Applegate) L.; m. Ellen James Evans, Dec. 5, 192 (dec); children: Ellen Lewis Parisot, Robert E., Pete (dec.); m. Helen Hoyt Stookey, Aug. 5, 1971. A.B. Yale U., 1921. Supr. credit investigations Bankers Trus Co., 1921-24; sales mgr. Graham, Parsons & Co., 1924-31; partner Estabrook & Co., 1931-68; ltd. partner Clark, Dodge & Co., Inc., 1968-74; Bd. govs. N.Y.

Stock Exchange, 1960-66. Bd. dirs. Third St. Music Sch. Settlement. Served as seaman USN, World War I; to lt. comdr. USNR, World War II. Mem. Assn. Stock Exchange Firms (pres. 1958), Concern for Dying (dir.), New Eng. Soc. Presbyterian. Clubs: Bond (pres. 1956), Links, University, Pilgrims. Home: New York N.Y. Died May 17, 1988.

LEWIS, ROGER, transportation company executive; b. Los Angeles, Jan. 11, 1912; s. Clarence V. and Charlotte (Gibbons) L.; m. Elly Thummler, Mar. 8, 1938; children: Ronald, Gail Lewis Tobin, Pamela Lewis Casey. AB, Stanford U., 1934. Dir. materiel, later asst. sales mgr. Lockheed Aircraft Corp., 1934-47; v.p. Canadair Ltd., Montreal, Can., 1947-50, Curtiss-Wright Corp, 1950-53; asst. sec. USAF, 1953-55; exec. v.p. Pan Am World Airways, 1955-62; chmn., pres. Gen. Dynamics Corp., 1962-70, pres., 1970-71; pres., chmn. Nat. Railroad Passenger Corp., 1971-75; sr. v.p. corp. fin. Hornblower, Weeks, Noyes & Trask Inc., 1975-78, dir.; cons. Loeb Rhoades Hornblower; bd. dirs. Bunker-Ramo Corp., Granger Assocs., Nat. Alliance Businessmen, Nat. Indsl. Conf. Bd.; trustee Stanford U. Recipient Medal of Freedom, 1955. Fellow AIAA; mem. Links Club, University (N.Y.C.); Metropolitan (Washington); Bohemian (San Francisco), Sigma Nu. Home: Washington D.C. Died Nov. 12, 1987.

LEWY, HANS, emeritus mathematics educator; b. Breslau, Germany, Oct. 20, 1904; came to U.S., 1933; s. Max and Margaret (Rosel) L.; m. Helen Crosby, June 9, 1947; 1 child, Michael R. Ph.D., U. Gottingen, 1926. Privatdozent U. Gottingen, Germany, 1927-33; lectr. math. Brown U., R.I., 1933-35; lectr. math. U. Calif., Berkeley, 1935-37, asst. prof. math., 1937-41, assoc. prof. math., 1941-45, prof. math., 1945-72, prof. emeritus, 1972-88. Died Aug. 23, 1988.

LI, CHOH HAO, biochemist, endocrinologist; b. Canton, China, Apr. 21, 1913; came to U.S., 1935, naturalized, 1955; s. Kan-chi Li and Mewching Tsui; m. Annie Lu, Oct. 1, 1938; children: Wei-i Li, Ann-si Li, Eva Li. B.S., U. Nanking, 1933; Ph.D., U. Calif.-Berkeley, 1938; M.D. (hon.), Cath. U. Chile, 1962; LL.D., Chinese U., Hong Kong, 1970; D.Sc., U. Pacific, 1971, Marquette U., 1971, St. Peter's Coll., 1971; hon. doctor, Uppsala U., 1977; D.Sc., U. San Francisco, 1978, L.I. U., 1981, U. Colo., 1981, Med. Coll. Pa., 1982. Instr. chemistry U. Nanking, 1933-35; research asso. U. Calif.-Berkeley, 1938-44, asst. prof. exptl. biology, 1944-47, asso. prof., 1947-49; prof. biochemistry, prof. exptl. endocrinology dir. Hormone Research Lab., Berkeley and San Francisco, 1950-83; prof., dir. Lab. Molecular Endocrinology U. Calif.-San Francisco, 1983-87; mem. acad. adv. bd. Chinese U., Hong Kong, 1963-87; adv. bd. Chem. Research Center, Nat. Taiwan U., 1964-87; vis. scientist Children's Cancer Research Found., Boston, 1955, 63-73; co-chmn. Internat. Symposium on Growth Hormone, Milan, Italy, 1967, Internat. Symposium on Protein and Polypeptide Hormones, Leige, Belgium, 1968; hon. pres. Internat. Symposium on Gonadotropins, Bangalore, India, 1973; chmn. Internat. Symposium on Proteins, Taipei, 1978, Internat. Symposium Growth Hormones and other Biologically Active Peptides, Milan, Italy, 1979; vis. prof. U. Montreal, 1948, Nat. Taiwan U., 1958, Chinese U. Hong Kong, 1967, Marquette U., 1973. Co-editor: Perspectives in the Biochemistry of Large Molecules, Supplement 1, 1962; sect; editor: Chem. Abstracts, 1960-63; co-assoc. editor: Internat. Jour. Peptide and Protein Research, 1969-76, editor-in-chief, 1976-87; mem. editorial adv. bd.: Family Health, 1969-81, Biopolymers, 1979-87; editorial bd.: Current Topics in Exptl. Endocrinology, 1969-87, Archives Biochem. Biophysics, 1979-87; editor: Hormonal Proteins and Peptides, 1973-87, Versatility of Proteins, 1979. Recipient numerous honors, including Ciba award in endocrinology, 1947, Amory prize Am. Acad. Arts and Scis., 1955, Albert Lasker award for basic med. research, 1962, Golden Plate award Am. Acad. Achievement, 1964, Univ. medal Liege, Belgium, 1968; Sci. Achievement award AMA, 1970; Nat. award Am. Cancer Soc., 1971; Nicholas Andry award Assn. Bone and Joint Surgeons, 1972; Lewis prize Am. Philos. Soc., 1977; Nichols medal Am. Chem. Soc., 1979; Sci. award Academia Santa Chicra, Genoa, 1979; Koch award Endocrine Soc., 1981; Heyrovsky Gold medal Czech Acad. Sci., 1982; Luft award Swedish Soc. Endocrinology, Stockholm, 1985; Alan E. Pierce award 10th Am. Peptide Symposium, 1987; Harvey lectr., 1951; Faculty Research lectr. U. Calif., San Francisco, 1962-63; Evans lectr., 1976; Pres. Marcos lectr. Manila, 1967; Lasker award lectr. Salk Inst., 1969; Nord lectr. Fordham U., 1972; Geschwind lectr. U. Calif., Davis, 1980; Grattarola lectr. U. Milan, 1981; Guggenheim fellow, 1948. Fellow Am. Acad. Arts and Scis., AAAS, N.Y. Acad. Sci., Am. Inst. Chemists; mem. Am. Chem. Soc. (Calif. sect. award 1951), Am. Soc. Biol. Chemists, Endocrine Soc., Biochem. Soc. London, Soc. Exptl. Biol. Medicine; hon. mem. Harvey Soc., Argentina Soc., Endocrinol. Metabolism Biol. Soc. Chile, Academia Sinica (Republic of China; Hu Shih meml. lectr. 1967), Nat. Acad. Scis.; fgn. mem. Chilean Acad. Scis., Israel Biochem. Soc., Indian Nat. Scis. Acad. Home: Berkeley Calif. Died Nov. 28, 1987.

LIBERACE (WLADZIU VALENTINO LIBERACE), pianist, concert artist, composer; b. West Allis, Wis., May 16, 1919; s. Salvatore and Frances L. Student, Wis. Coll. Music. Soloist Chgo. Symphony Orch. in Milw., entertainer, Milw., 1940-45, TV debut, Sta. KLAC, Los Angeles, 1952, weekly TV show on film after 1952, concert tours, 1953; appeared Carnegie Hall, 1953, Madison Square Garden, 1954, recorded for Columbia Records, Coral Records; starred in: motion picture Sincerely Yours, 1955; appeared: in film The Loved One, 1965 Recipient Emmy awards (2), named Entertainer of Year 1973; Author: Liberace Cooks, 1970, Liberace, 1973. Mem. ASCAP, Nat. Acad. Rec. Arts and Scis. Died Feb. 4, 1987.

LICHT, FRANK, lawyer, governor, senator; b. Providence, Mar. 3, 1916; s. Jacob and Rose (Kassed) L.; m. Dorothy Shirley Krauss, June 16, 1946; children: Beth Ellen Licht Laramee, Carol Ann Licht Kanin, Judith Joan. AB, Brown U., 1938; LLB, Harvard U., 1941; LLD, St. Francis Coll., 1969, Yeshiva U., 1970, R.I. Coll., 1971, U. R.I., 1971; LHD, Hebrew Union Coll., 1971, Suffolk U., 1971; LLH, Our Lady of Providence Sem., 1973; LLD, Brown U., 1975. Bar: U.S. Supreme Ct. 1942, R.I. 1952. Law clk. to presiding justice U.S. Ct. Appeals (1st cir.), Boston, 1942-43; ptnr. Letts & Quinn, Providence, 1943-56, Letts, Quinn & Licht, Providence, 1973-87; assoc. justice R.I. Superior Ct., 1956-68; mem. R.I. Senate from Providence, 1949-56; gov. R.I., 1969-73; lectr. Bryant Coll., Providence, 1958-64, Nat. Conf. Trial Ct. Judges Coll., Reno, 1967; teaching fellow Kennedy Inst. of Politics, 1972-73. Contbr. articles to profl. jours. Vice pres. bd. Gen. Jewish Com. Providence, 1960-66, Gen. Jewish Com. R.I., 1967-68; co-chmn. So. New Eng. Conf. Christians and Jews, 1959-68; chmn. Chapin Hosp. Commn., Providence, 1967; v.p. Temple Emanuel, 1968; pres., bd. dirs. R.I. council Community Services; trustee, bd. dirs. Butler Hosp., Providence, Jewish Home for Aged; bd. dirs. Providence Human Relations Commn.; exec. com. Nat. Govs. Conf., 1971; trustee Brown U., 1981-87; pres. R.I. Philharmonic, 1981-84. Recipient Lehman award for R.I., 1965, Herbert H. Lehman Ethics award Jewish Theol. Sem. Am., 1969, Herbert H. Lehman citation Nat. Info. Bur. for Jewish Life, Inc., 1970; named Man of Yr. Providence Sunday Jour., 1969; hon fellow Hebrew U., Jerusalem, 1969; Ford found. grantee; naming of courthouse Frank Licht Jud. Complex Providence County, 1986. Mem. ABA, R.I. Bar Assn., Nat. Conf. Trial Ct. Judges (exec. com.), Phi Beta Kappa, Delta Sigma Rho. Jewish (v.p. temple). Home: Providence R.I. Died May 30, 1987.

LIDSTONE, HERRICK KENLEY, lawyer; b. Bellingham, Wash., Apr. 2, 1921; s. Herrick K. and Jean (Richardson) L.; m. Marcia E. Drake, Dec. 17, 1942; children: Herrick Kenley, Rosalind Grace, Christopher Drake. Student, State U. Iowa, 1938-39; A.B., Harvard U., 1942, LL.B., 1948. Bar: N.Y. 1949, Colo. bar 1978. Practiced in N.Y.C., 1949-77, Denver, 1978-86; partner Battle, Fowler, Lidstone, Jaffin, Pierce & Kheel, 1960-77, of counsel, 1978-86; cons. to Ireland, Stapleton & Pryor, from 1980; prof. law N.Y. Law Sch., 1950-53; vis. prof. law U. Colo. Law Sch., Boulder, 1978-83; asst. dir. Harvard Law Sch. Internat. Program Taxation, 1953-57; instr. law U. Va., 1957-58; lectr. Practising Law Inst., 1949-83, also various law insts. and panels; UN adviser taxation, Chile, 1954-57, pvt. adviser, 1957-61; U.S. Point 4 adviser taxation, El Salvador, 1955; panelist tax reform Ho. Reps. Ways and Means Com., 1973. Author: The Federal Estate Tax, 1952, Tax Administration in Underdeveloped Countries, 1956, Taxation in Chile, 1954, Taxation in El Salvador, 1955, Federal Income Taxation of Corporations, 1983, International Business Tax Planning, 1982; also articles; co-author: Taxation of Farmers, 1979, supplement, 1983; gen. editor, co-author: Tax Guide for Artists and Art Organizations, 1979. Chmn. adv. com. Pelham (N.Y.) Recreation Commn., 1965-67; trustee Sapelo Island Research Found., 1967-77. Served to capt. AUS, 1942-45. Mem. ABA (chmn. sect. taxation coms. legis. drafting 1959-62), Assn. Bar City N.Y., Tax Club N.Y.C., Greater Denver Tax Counsel Assn., Beta Theta Pi. Episcopalian. Club: Harvard (N.Y.C.). Home: Broomfield Colo. Died July 26, 1986; buried Slater, Colo.

LIEBMAN, WILLIAM LEWIS, investment banker; b. Milw., Aug. 19, 1919; s. Julius and Ethel (Lewis) L.; m. Eileen Liebman. Student, Kenyon Coll., 1942. With Blunt, Ellis and Loewi (and predecessor firm), Milw., 1946-82, v.p. gen. mgr., 1957-62; pres. Blunt, Ellis and Loewi (and predecessor firm), from 1963, chmn. bd., until 1982. Bd. dirs. Unicare Health Services Inc.; donor 18th Century porcelain to U. Wis., Milw. Art Ctr., Milw. Pub. Mus., The White Ho., the State Dept. Mem. Investment Banking Assn., Cen. States Investment Banking Assn., University Club, Wisconsin Club, Milw. Athletic Club, The Milw. Club., Psi Upsilon. Home: Milwaukee Wis. also: Boca Raton Fla. Died Apr. 1, 1986, buried Forest Home Cemetery, Milw.

LIGUTTI, LUIGI GINO, clergyman, religious organization administrator; b. Romans, Udine, Italy, Mar. 21, 1895; came to U.S., 1912, naturalized, 1918; s. Spiridione and Theresa (Ciriani) L. AB, St. Ambrose Coll., Davenport, Iowa, 1914, LLD (hon.), 1938; STB, St. Mary's Sem., Balt., 1917; AM, Cath. U. Am., 1918, LLD (hon.), 1968; LLD (hon.), Loyola U., New Orleans, 1947, St. Francis Xavier U., Antigonish, N.S., 1957, Drake U., 1964, Drew U., 1972. Ordained priest, Roman Catholic Ch., 1919. Tchr. Dowling Coll., Des Moines, 1918-20; pastor Woodbine, Iowa, 1920-26, Granger, Iowa, 1926-41; exec. sec. Nat. Cath. Rural Life Conf., Des Moines, 1941-49, exec. dir., 1949-58; dir. internat. affairs of conf. Vatican City, 1958-84; cons. 2d Vatican Counc. Commn. Lay Appostolate, mem. Pontifical Commn. for Justice of Peace; pres. Agrimission, 1971-84; apptd. ofcl. Permanent Observer for the Holy See with FAO, UN, 1949-81; apptd. Domestic Prelate; canon St. Mary Major's Basilica in Rome; protonotary apostolic. Author: (with Reverend John C. Rawe) Rural Roads to Security, 1939; contbr. to Commonweal, America, other mags. Recipient Nat. Peace award Cath Assn. Internat. Peace; subject FAO-UN Agricola medal, 1978. Mem. Am. Acad. Polit. and Social Sci., Cath. Sociol. Soc., Friends of the Land, KC. Home: Des Moines Iowa. Died Dec. 28, 1984.

LIKERT, RENSIS, social scientist, educator; b. Cheyenne, Wyo., Aug. 5, 1903; s. George Herbert and Cornelia A. (Zonne) L.; m. Jane Gibson, Aug. 31, 1928; children: Elizabeth J. Likert David, Patricia A. Likert Pohlman. AB, U. Mich., 1926; PhD, Columbia U., 1932; D honoris causa, U. Tilburg, Netherlands, 1967. Instr., later asst. prof. NYU; head research dept. Life Ins. Sales Research Bur.; head div. program surveys Bur. Agrl. Econs. Dept. Agr.; dir. morale div. U.S. Strategic Bombing Survey; dir. Survey Research Ctr. U. Mich., 1946-49, dir. Inst. for Social Research, 1949-70, dir. emeritus, 1971-81, prof. psychology and sociology emeritus; chmn. bd. Rensis Likert Assocs., Inc., from 1971. Author: (with Gardner Murphy) Public Opinion and the Individual, 1938, Morale and Agency Management, 1940, New Patterns of Management, 1961, The Human Organization: Its Management and Value, 1967, (with Jane Gibson Likert) New Ways of Managing Conflict, 1976; editor: (with S.P. Hayes) Some Applications of Behavorial Research, 1957; contbr. articles to jours. Recipient Medal of Freedom, 1946, Paul D. Converse award Mktg. Symposium, U. Ill., 1955, James A. Hamilton award Hosp. Adminstrs. Assn., 1961, Publs. award Orgn. Devel. Coun., 1962, Warner W. Stockberger award Soc. Personnel Adminstrn., 1963, Disting. Faculty Achievement award U. Mich., 1963, Human Relations award Soc. for Advancement Mgmt., 1967, Profl. Achievement award Am. Bd. Examiners in Profl. Psychology, 1968, Ouststanding Achievement award Am. Soc. Tng. and Devel., 1969, Exceptionally Disting. Achievement award Am. Assn. for Pub. Opinion Research, 1973. Fellow Am. Psychol. Assn. (dir. 1950-53); mem. Am. Stats. Assn. (v.p. 1953-55, pres. 1958), Am. Acad. Mgmt. (McKinsey Found. Book award 1962), Am. Sociol. Assn., Internat. Soc. Polit. Psychology, Am. Soc. Pub. Adminstrn., AAAS, Nat. Acad. Pub. Adminstrn., Inst. Mgmt. Scis., Sigma Xi, Phi Kappa Phi, Tau Beta Pi. Home: Kailua Hawaii. Died Sept. 2, 1981.

LIKOFF, WILLIAM, cardiologist, university chancellor; b. Phila., Feb. 5, 1912; s. Morris Aaron and Goldie (Sklaroff) L.; m. Mariell Jessup Moore, Oct. 22, 1978; children—Jane Ellen Likoff Yudis, Joy Likoff Kantor. B.A., Darmouth Coll., 1933; M.D., Hahnemann Med. Coll., 1938; D.Sc. (hon.), Phila. Coll. Pharmacy and Sci., 1980; LL.D. (hon.), Gannan U., 1982. Intern Mt. Sinai Hosp., Phila., 1938-39, resident in pathology, 1939-40, in internal medicine, 1940-42; resident in cardiology Peter Bent Brigham Hosp., Boston, 1942-43; practice medicine specializing in cardiology Phila., 1947-87; asst. prof. medicine Hahnemann Med. Coll. and Hosp., to 1946, asso. prof., 1946-51, prof., 1951-64, pres., chief exec. officer, 1977-82; chancellor Hahnemann U., 1982-87; Wilson-Myers lectr. Mich. Heart Assn., 1977; Ann. lectr. Am. Heart Assn./Southeastern Pa., 1978; Bernard B. Rotko lectr., 1980. Author: books, most recent being (with others) Your Heart, 1972, Protegez Votre Coeur Elsevier Sequola, 1975; mem. editorial bd. Am. Heart Jour, 1970-74; cons. editor Clin. Trends in Cardiology, 1977-87. Served with U.S. Army, 1943-46. Recipient Ann. Gold medal Phi Lambda Kappa, 1979, Father Clarence E. Shaffrey, S.D. award St. Joseph U., 1979; Strittmatter award, 1980; Disting. Am. award, 1980; William Likoff Alumni Lectureship established by Alumni Assn. Hahnemann Med. Coll. and Hosp., 1978; Achievement award in health and sports medicine Golden Slipper Club, 1981. Fellow Am. Coll. Cardiology (Disting.; pres. 1967-68, editor-in-chief extended learning program 1977-87), Am. Coll. Chest Physicians; mem. Pa. Heart Assn., Am. Acad. Scis., Pa. Med. Soc., Heart Assn. Southeastern Pa. (pres. 1965-66), Phila. Acad. Cardiology (founding physician 1978). Jewish. Clubs: Locust, Hahnemann. Home: Philadelphia Pa. Died July 3, 1987.

LILIENFELD, ABRAHAM MORRIS, epidemiologist, educator; b. N.Y.C., Nov. 13, 1920; s. Joel and Eugenia (Kugler) L.; m. Lorraine Zemil, July 18, 1943; children: Julia, Saul, David. BA, Johns Hopkins U., 1941, MPH, 1949; MD, U. Md., 1944, ScD (hon.), 1975. Intern, resident in obstetrics Luth. Hosp., Balt., 1944-46; assoc. pub. health physician N.Y. Dept. Health, 1949-50; dir. So. health dist. Balt. Dept. Health, 1949-52; asst. prof. epidemiology Johns Hopkins U., 1952-54, prof. chronic diseases, chmn. dept., 1958-70, prof. epidemiology, 1970-75, Univ. Disting. Service prof., 1975-84, temp. head dept. behavioral scis., dir. MPH program, 1980-84; dir. Gamma Globulin Ctr. USPHS, 1952; chief dept.

stats. and epidemiology Roswell Park Meml. Inst., 1954-58; Health Clark lectr and vis. prof. London Sch. Hygiene, 1979; mem. Nat. Adv. Heart Coun., 1962-66; chmn. joint coun. subcom. on cerebrovascular disease NIH, 1966-68; rsch. adv. coun. Am. Cancer Soc., 1965-70; staff dir. Pres.'s Commn. Heart Disease, Cancer and Stroke, 1964-67; chmn. adv. coun. preventive medicine Md. Dept. Health, 1964-68. Bd. editors Postgrad. Medicine, Preventive Medicine , Bull. History Medicine, Athersclerosis jour. Trustee Md. Heart Assn.; exec. bd. Md. div. Am. Cancer Soc., 1964-70; trustee Balt. Hebrew Coll., 1973-84, chmn., 1974-77. Recipient John Snow award for contbns. to epidemiology, 1975, Rsch. Career award NIH, 1962. Fellow Am. Pub. Health Assn. (Bronfman award pub. health achievement 1968), Am. Coll. Preventive Medicine, Am. Stats. Assn., Am. Coll. Epidemiology; mem. Am. Epidemiology Soc. (pres. 1970-71), AAAS, Soc. Epidemiol. Rsch., Inst. Medicine of Nat. Acad. Scis., Am. Assn. History of Medicine. Died Aug. 6, 1984.

LILLEY, ROBERT DODD, communications company executive; b. N.Y.C., Aug. 16, 1912; s. Alexander Park and Julia Ann (Dodd) L.; m. Helen Mary McGregor, May 25, 1944; children: Robert McGregor, Jane Park, Margaret Mary. AB, Columbia U., 1933, BS, 1934, M Engring., 1935; D Engring. (hon.), Newark Coll. Engring., 1968, Stevens Inst. Tech., 1975; LHD (hon.), Rutgers U., 1970. With Western Electric Co., 1937-65, asst. engr. mfg., 1956-57, asst. mgr. Balt. works, 1957-60, personnel dir., 1960, v.p. personnel and pub. relations, 1960-62, v.p. service, 1962-65, group v.p., 1965; pres., dir. N.J. Bell Telephone Co., 1965-69; with Am. Tel.& Tel. Co., N.Y.C., 1970-76, pres., 1972-76; bd. dirs. Pacific N.W. Bell Telephone Co., Pacific Tel. & Tel. Co., Bell Telephone Labs., Continental Corp., Chase Manhattan Bank, N.A., Chase Manhattan Corp., I.H. Macy & Co., Inc., Mut. Benefit Life Ins. Co. Chmn. Gov.'s Select Commn. to Study Civil Disorder, N.J., 1967; mem. Nat. Com. Support for Pub. Schs., Nat. Com. for Citizens in Edn., Urban Affairs Coun. N.J., 1969-71; mem. OIC Nat. Indsl. Adv. Coun.; exec. com. N.J. region NCCJ, 1966-69; chmn. fund raising campaign Spellman Coll., from 1972; steering com. Nat. Urbann Coalition, from 1972; adv. com. bus. programs Brookings Instn.; trustee Newark Mus., 1965-70, Greater Newark Urban Coalition, 1968-69, United Hosps. Newark, 1965-70, N.J. Coll. Fund Assn., 1967-70, Newark Coll. Engring., 1965-71, Columbia U., Victoria Found., Inc., Com. for Econ. Devel., United Student Aid Fund; bd. dirs. Internat. Exec. Service Corps, 1970-74; bd. advisers Seton Hall U., 1965-69, Grad. Bus. Sch. Rutgers U., 1965-69; vis. com. social scis Drew U., 1969-71; bd. overseers Found. at N.J. Inst. Tech.. from 1965. Recipient Alumni medal Columbia U., 1947, medal of merit U.S. Sec. Treasury, 1966, Lion award Columbia U. Club of Essex County, 1966, Americanism award N.J. regional adv. counc. Anti-Defamation League B'nai B'rith, 1967, 72, Brotherhood award NCCJ, 1968, Egleston medal Alumni Assn. Sch. Engring. ColumbiaU., 1969, Citizen award N.J. Soc. Profl. Engrs., 1969, Good Citizenship award Two Hundred Club Newark, 1970, Man of Yr. award Robert Treat counc. Boy Scouts Am., 1970, Dean's award Columbia Coll., 1970, Communications award Speech Rehab. Inst., 1972, Internat. Businessman of Yr. award Coll. Bus. Brigham Young U., 1974, Nat. Golden Key award OIC Am., 1975, Inst. HUman Relations award Am. Jewish Com., 1975. Mem. Telephone Pioneers Am. (pres. 1970-71), Columbia Engring. Coun., Columbia U. Engring. Alumni Assn. (pres. 1962-64), Columbia U. Alumni Fedn. (pres. 1966-68), University Glee Club, Economic Club (N.Y.C.), Baltusrol Golf Club (Springfield, N.J.), Blooming Grove Hunting and Fishing Club (Hawley, Pa.), Delta Kappa Epsilon, Beta Gamma Sigma. Home: Short Hills N.J. Died Oct. 16, 1986, cremated.

LILLIE, BEATRICE (LADY PEEL), actress; b. Toronto, Ont., Can., May 29, 1894; d. John and Lucie (Shaw) Lillie; m. Sir Robert Peel (dec. 1934); 1 child, Robert (dec. 1942). Student, St. Agnes Coll., Belleville, Ont. Made first stage appearance in Not Likely, London, 1914, subsequently numerous other London appearances including Auntie Mame, 1958; made American debute N.Y.C. in Andre's Charlots' Revue, N.Y.C., 1924; plays in N.Y.C. include Carlot's Revue of 1926, Oh, Please, 1926, She's My Baby, 1928, This Year of Grace (Noel Coward), 1928, The Third Little Show, 1931, Too True To Be Good (Bernard Shaw), 1932, Walk a Little Faster, 1932, At Home Abroad, 1935, The Show is On, 1936, Set to Music, 1939, Seven Lively Arts, 1944, Inside U.S.A., 1948-49, Golden Jubilee Ziegfield Follies, 1957, High Spirits, 1963-65; motion pictures include Exit Smiling, 1926, Doctor Rhythm, 1938, On Approval, 1943, Around The World in Eighty Days, 1955, Thoroughly Modern Millie, 1967, many others; numerous radio and TV appearances during World War II, entertained allied troops in Eng., Europe, Middle East and N. Africa; toured worldwide in one-woman act An Evening with Beatrice Lillie, 1952-56 (Tony award 1953); author: (autobiography) Every Other Inch a Lady, 1973. Decorated by Gen. Charles de Gaulle (France); recipient African Star , other war service citations, Donaldson award 1944-45, citation NCCJ, citation as Greatest Comedienne of All Time Am. Fedn. Women's Philanthropies, 1953, Spl. Antoinette Perry award for disting. contbn. to theatre, 1953, Sarah Siddons award, 1954, Outer Circle award, 1964. Home: Henley-on-Thames England. Died Jan. 20, 1989.

LINDAHL, MARTIN LEROY, economist, educator; b. Winton, Minn., Apr. 29, 1903; s. August and Jennie (Lindo) L.; m. Berta Russell Divet, June 14, 1929; children: Martia Alice, Elizabeth Russell. AB, Carleton Coll., 1924; AM, U. Wash., 1927; PhD, U. Mich., 1933. Instr. history and govt. Moorhead (Minn.) High Sch., 1924-26; teaching fellow econs. U. Wash., 1927-28; instr. econs. U. Mich., 1928-30, lectr. econs., summer 1937, vis. prof. econs., summer 1947, 59, 60; instr. econs. Dartmouth Coll., 1931-36, asst .prof., 1936-40, Prof., 1940-68, emeritus, 1968-87, chmn. dept. econs., 1953-57, 62-63; prin. transp. economist Bd. Investigation and Rsch. Transp. Act of 1940, Washington, 1943; cons. pub. utility R.R. regulatory cases, from 1949; mem. New Eng. Gov.'s Com. Pub. Transp., 1955-57; rsch. adv. com., transp. rsch. bd. New Eng. Coun., from 1961, chmn. com., 1966; subcom. chmn. Citizen's Task Force to Study Effectivness N.H. State Govt., 1969; vis. prof. Brown U., summers 1962, 63, New Coll., .Sarasota, Fla., 1972; fin. adviser Montshire Mus. Sci., from 1975. Author: (with Harry Purdy and William A. Carter) Corporate Concentration and Public Policy, 1942, also govt. reports, monographs, articles on polit. economy. Precinct commr., Hanover, N.H., 1946-58; bd. dirs. N.H.-Vt. Devel. Coun., Inc, McDonough Caddie Scholarship Found.; trustee Steamtown Found. Mem. Am. Econ. Assn. (chmn. transp. pub. utilities group 1962), Service Corps Ret. Execs. (chpt. pres. 1974-75), Phi Beta Kappa, Beta Gamma Sigma, Sigma Chi. Congregationalist. Home: Hanover N.H. Died Nov. 26, 1987; buried Pine Knoll Cemetery, Hanover, N.H.

LINDEN, JAMES VINCENT, legal jurisprudence educator; b. Milw., Oct. 28, 1891; s. Frank and Johanna (Connell) L. AB, Marquette U., 1912; MA, Mt. St. Michaels Scholasticate, 1921; postgrad., Ore Place, Eng., 1923-25, St. Louis U., 1925-27; PhD (hon.), Gregorian U., 1931. Joined S.J. Prof. philosophy Gonzaga U., Spokane, Wash., 1929-32, prof. jurisprudence, regent of law, chmn. dept. law, from 1932. Author: Fundamental Religion, 1927, On the Way Back Home, 1947, Come With Me O Mass, My Rosary. Home: Spokane Wash. †

LINDER, HAROLD F., financial consultant; b. Bklyn., Sept. 13, 1900; s. William and Florence (Strauss) L.; m. Bertha Rubin, Oct. 5, 1920; children: Prudence Linder Steiner, Susan. Mfg. positions 191-25; co-founder Cornell, Linder & Co., indsl. mgmt. and reorgns., 1925-33; ptnr. Carl M. Loeb, Rhoades & Co., security and commodity brokerage, banking, 1933-38; pres. Gen. Am. Investors Co., Inc., 1948-55; dep. asst. sec. of state for econ. affairs Dept. State, Washington, 1951, asst. sec., 1952-53; pres., chmn. Export-Import Bank, Washington, 1961-68; U.S. ambassador to Can. Ottawa, 1968-69; bd. dirs. various corps., 1938-61; cons. Internat. Fin. Corp., World Bank Group, 1970-76. Extensively engaged in philanthropic work, 1938-42, 45-48; trustee Inst. Advanced Study, Princeton, N.J., 1949-81, chmn. bd., 1969-72, emeritus, 1972-81; mem. bd. overseers faculty arts and scis., U. Pa.; mem. adv. coun. faculty internat. affairs, Columbia U.; mem. Coun. Sch. Advanced Internat. Studies Johns Hopkins U., Washington; mem. fin. com. Smithsonian Instn. Comdr. USNR, 1942-45. Benjamin Franklin fellow Royal Soc. Arts. Mem. Coun. Fgn. Relations, AAAS (fin. com.), Cosmos Club (Washington), Recess Club (N.Y.C.), Century Assn., White's Club (London). Home: New York N.Y. Died June 22, 1981.

LINDHORST, FRANK ATKINSON, clergyman, educator; b. Ramsey, Ill., Aug. 7, 1892; s. Henry Alexander and Lizzie Bell (Atkinson) L.; m. Alice Jenkins, 1916 (dec. 1917); m. Alice Miller, June 25, 1919; children: Frances Atkinson (Mrs. James E. Griffith), Alice Margaret (Mrs. Arthur C. LeClert). Tchrs. cert., Ill. State Tchrs. Coll., Charleston, 1912; AB, DePauw U., 1914; STB, Boston U. Sch. Theology, 1924; student, U. Chgo., 1929, 30; DD, Coll. Idaho, 1952. Exec. Boy Scouts Am., Prescott, Ariz., 1917-19; Meth. pastor Nebr., 1920-24; exec. sec. Meth. Ch. Bd. Edn., Del. and Ea. Shore of Md., 1924-29; mem. staff nat. office Meth. Ch. Bd. Edn., Chgo., 1929-39; exec. sec. Meth. Ch. Bd. Edn., Iowa, 1939-45; dir. Christian community asminstrn., prof. religious edn. Coll. of the Pacific, from 1945, chmn. dept. Bible and religious edn., 1957. Author: The Minister Teaches Religion, 1945, Teaching Adults, 1951; study units for youth camps and adults; producer motion picture In Wisdom and in Stature, also slide sets. Chaplain arty. U.S. Army, World War I. Mem. Fellowship of Reconciliation, Masons, Beta Theta Pi. Home: Stockton Calif. †

LINDLEY, DENTON RAY, clergyman, college administrator; b. May, Tex., May 27, 1905; s. Calvin Denton and Maud (Brown) L.; m. Maybon Marie Torrey, Mar. 17, 1926; children: Gene Ray, Neil Everett. Student, Johnson Bbile Coll., 1922-23; AB, Phillips U., 1926; BD, Tex. Christian U., 1941, DLitt (hon.), 1967; BD magna cum laude, Yale U., 1944, MA, 1945, PhD, 1947; LLD (hon.), Atlantic Christian Coll., 1956; LHD (hon.), William Woods Coll., 1972; DD (hon.), Culver-Stockton Coll., 1974; D en Humanidades (hon.), U. Ams., 1980. Pastor Cen. Christian Ch., Weatherford, Tex., 1928-30, First Christian Ch., Big Spring, Tex., 1930-33, St. Charles Ave. Christian Ch., New Orleans, 1933-37, Cen. Christian Ch., San Antonio, 1937-40; head dept. Christian ministries Brite Coll. of Bible, Tex. Christian U., 1941-47, dean, 1947-50, v.p., 1953-58, pres., 1959-62; pres. Atlantic Christian Coll., Wilson, N.C., 1950-53; pres. U. Ams., 1962-71, chancellor, from 1971; pres. La. Christian Missionary Soc., 1934-36, Tex. Christian Ministers' Inst., 1938; dean Young Peoples Summer Confs. of Disciples of Christ, 1935-46; v.p. internat. conv. Disciples of Christ, 1950-52; chmn. bd. higher edn. Disciples of Christ, 1952-53; del. World Conf. on Faith and Order, Lund, Sweden, 1952; mem. panel of scholars Disciples of Christ, 1955-87; bd. dirs. Sem. State Bank, Ft. Worth. Author: Alexander Campbell-Herald of Religious Liberty, 1948, Calling a Minister, 1950, Apostle of Freedom, 1957, (with others) The Faith of Tradition, 1963, also articles; editor Louisian Christian, 1933-37. Mem. Religious Edn. Assn., S.W. Bibl. Inst., Intersem. Assn., Tex. Coun. Ch. Related Colls. (pres. 1961-62), Am. C. of C. (bd. dirs.), Am. Soc. Mex. (bd. dirs.), Mexican-N.Am. Cultural Inst. (bd. dirs.), So. Assn. Colls. (commn. on Latin Am. relations), Masons, Rotary, University Club. Home: Columbia Tex. Died Jan. 30, 1987.

LINDQUIST, CLARENCE BERNHART, mathematics educator, consultant; b. Superior, Wis., Dec. 21, 1913; s. Gust and Hannah (Berentson) L.; m. Helen Jane Conroy, Dec. 29, 1941; children: Clarence Conroy, Thomas Ward, James Raymond, Robert Michael, Mary Lenore. BE, U. Wis., 1937, M Philospohy, 1939, PhD, 1941. Instr. U.S. Naval Acad., Annapolis, Md., 1941-42, asst. prof., 1945-46; mem. faculty U. Minn., Duluth, 1946-57, adminstrv. asst. to provost, 1949-51, prof., head. math. and engring., 1951-57; program and rsch. specialist U.S. Office Edn., Washington, 1957-78, chief higher edn. personnel tng. programs, Bur. Secondary Edn., 1974-76, program mgr. domestic mining and mineral fuel conservation fellowship program, 1976-78; cons. Conf. Bd. Math. Scis., NSF. Author: Mathematics in Colleges and Universities, 1965, Recent Trends in Soviet Scientific and Technical Education, 1964, Soviet Education Programs, 1960, Aspects of Undergraduate Training in the Mathematical Sciences, 1969; contbr. articles to profl. jours. Lt. comdr. USNR, 1942-45. U. Wis. Alumni fellow. Mem. NEA, Am. Math. Soc., Math. Assn. Am., Ret. Officers Assn., Sigma Xi. Lutheran. Home: Washington D.C. Died Feb. 2, 1987, Arlington Nat. Cemetery, Va.

LINDQUIST, ROBERT, banker; b. Grand Rapids, Mich., Sept. 6, 1902; s. Peter and Anna (Nelson) L.; m. Mildred Schuppert, Apr. 5, 1930 (dec.); children: Gloria Linquist Daily, Nancy Lindquist Temple; m. Muriel Lindquist. BA, U. Mich., 1923; grad., Rutgers U. Sch. Banking, 1945, Northwestern U. Sch. Fin. Pub. Relations, 1949. Advt. mgr. Grand Rapids Nat. Bank, 1923-28; v.p. T. Harris Smith & Assocs., Phila., 1928-37; asst. v.p. Am. Nat. Bank & Trust Co., Chgo., 1937-47; v.p. LaSalle Nat. Bank, Chgo., 1947-52; v.p., head mktg. Harris Trust & Savs. Bank, Chgo., 1952-65; first. dir., lectr. Sch. Fin. Pub. Relations Northwestern U. Author: Planning abd Budgeting a Bank's Advertising Program, 1945, The Bank and its Publics, 1956; contbr. Public Relations Handbook; developer Hubert the Harris Lion premiums for Harris Bank. Treas., dir. Jr. Achievement, Chgo., 1960's. Mem. Bank Pub. Relations and Mktg. Assn. (pres. 1947-48), Pi Kappa Alpha, Economic Club, University Club, Bankers Club (Chgo.). Home: Green Valley Ariz. Died Oct. 25, 1987.

LINDSAY, ROBERT BRUCE, physicist, educator, editor; b. New Bedford, Mass., Jan. 1, 1900; s. Robert and Eleanora Elizabeth (Leuchsenring) L.; m. Rachel Tupper Easterbrooks, July 29, 1922; children: Robert, Evelyn Tupper Lindsay Roberts. AB, Brown U., 1920, MS, 1920, DSc (hon.), 1978; PhD, MIT, 1924; EdD (hon.), R.I. Coll. Edn., 1959; ScD (hon.), Southeastern Mass. Technol. Inst., 1968. Instr. physics MIT, 1920-22; fellow Am.-Scandinavian Found., Copenhagen, 1922-23; instr. physics Yale U., 1923-27, asst. prof., 1927-30; assoc. prof. theoretical physics Brown U., 1930-36, Hazard prof. physics, from 1936, prof. emeritus physics, from 1971, chmn. dept., 1934-54, dean grad. sch., 1954-66, dir. ultrasonics lab., 1946-63; vis. prof. physics Poly. Inst. Bklyn., 1932-41; dir. phys. rsch. Div. Phys. War Rsch., Duke U., 1942-43; lectr. U.S. Navy Electronics Lab., San Diego, summers 1946, 49; cons. Bur. Ships, U.S. Navy Dept., 1944-47; chmn. governing bd. New Eng. Sch. Sci. Coun., 1947-50; dir. Rsch. Analysis group at Brown U. for rsch. in underwater sound, 1948-54; sci. advisor U.S. Naval War Coll., 1952-54; mem. div. phys. scis. NRC, 1953-57; chmn. phys. adv. com. Nat. Bur. Standards, 1957-60; regional counselor for R.I., Am. Inst. Physics Program, 1961-62; exec. com. governing bd. Am. Inst. Physics, 1959-71, mem. vis. scientists program; cons. rsch. and devel. Asst. Sec. Def., 1954-57; U.S. mem. Internat. Commn. Acoustics, 1963-69; cons. on physics instrn. U.S. Naval Acad., 1969-70. Author: (with G.W. Stewart) Acoustics, 1930, Physical Mechanics, 1933, (with H. Margenau) Foundations of Physics, 1936, Physical Statistics, 1941, Concepts and Methods of Theoretical Physics, 1951, Mechanical Radiation, 1960, The Role of Science in Civilization, 1963, The Nature of Physics, 1968, Lard Rayleigh—The Man and His Work, 1970, Basic Concepts of Physics, 1971, Julius Robert Mayer—Prophet of Energy, 1973, Acoustics, Its Historical and Philosophical Development, 1973, Physical Acoustics, 1974, Energy-Early Historical Development of the Concept, 1975, Applications of Energy: Nineteenth Century, 1976, The Control of Energy, 1977, Energy in Atomic Physics 1925-60, 1983; also articles in field; contbr.: Dictionary of Sci. Biography, 1970, Ency. Brit., 1974; editor-in-chief Acoustical Soc. Am., from 1957; editor: Sound, Its Uses and Control, 1962-63; gen. editor Benchmark Series in Acoustics, from 1971; co-editor Bendchmark Series on Energy, from 1974; cons. editor for acoustics McGraw-Hill Ency. Sci. and Tech., from 1978; assoc. editor: Am. Inst. Physics Handbook, 1980-81; editorial bd. Founds. of Physics, from 1970. Pres. Assn. Grad. Schs. in Assn. Am. Univs., 1965-66. With USNR, World War I. Fellow Brit. Inst. Acoustics (hon.), AAAS (v.p., chmn. sect. B 1959, sect. L 1968), Am. Phys. Soc. (chmn. New Eng. sect. 1935-36, mem. coun. 1943-46), Am. Acad. Arts. and Scis. (v.p. 1957-59), Acoustical Soc. Am. (v.p. 1951-52, pres. 1956-57, gold medal 1963, disting. svc. citation 1981); mem. Am. Inst. Physics (gov. bd. 1956-71), Am. Assn. Phys. Tchrs. (exec. com. 1945-47, disting svc. award 1963), Am. Math. Soc., History Sci. Soc., New Eng. Conf. Grad. Edn. (pres. 1961-62), Faculty Club, Phi Beta Kappa, Sigma Xi (nat. lectr. 1967-68, bicentennial lectr. 1975-77). Home: Portsmouth R.I. Died Mar. 2, 1985; buried Newport Meml. Park, Middletown, R.I.

LINEN, JAMES ALEXANDER, publishing company executive; b. Waverly, Pa., June 20, 1912; s. James Alexander Jr. and Genevieve (Tuthill) L.; m. Sara Scranton, Sept. 1, 1934; children: Ellen S. Linen Conway, James Alexander IV, Marion M. Linen Dawson, Jonathan, Christopher, Worthington Warren. Grad., Hotchkiss Sch., 1930; AB, Williams Coll., 1934; student acctg., Internat. Corr. Sch., 1930. Advt. salesman Time mag., 1934-37, pub., 1945-60, pres., 1960-69; pres., also bd. dirs. Time, Inc., 1960-69, chmn. exec. com., 1969-1973; advt. salesman Life mag., Detroit, 1937-38; advt. mgr. Life mag., N.Y.C., 1938-42; with Office of War Information, 1942-45. Past nat. fund chmn. ARC; past pres. United Community Funds and Couns. Am., Inc.; hon. trustee The Hotchkiss Sch., Alephi U.; trustee Williams Coll., Asian Inst. Tech.; chmn. coun., trustee Rockefeller U.; chmn. bd. exec. com. Athens (Greece) Coll.; vice-chmn. Iran-U.S. Bus. Coun.; mem. adv. coun. Japan-U.S. Econ. Relations; mem. Emergency Com. Am. Trade; mem. adv. com. Japan Found., U.S. Japan Commn., U.S. Japan Conf. on Cultural and Ednl. Interchange. Mem. Bus. Coun., Coun. Fgn. Relations, Internat. C. of C. (sr. trustee U.S. coun.), Nat. Urban League (past pres.), Blind Brook Club (N.Y.C., Round Hill Country Club (Greenwich, Conn.), Mid-Ocean (Bermuda), Seminole Club (West Palm Beach, Fla., Stanwich Club. Home: Greenwich Conn. Died Feb. 1, 1988.

LININGTON, BARBARA ELIZABETH, novelist; b. Aurora, Ill., Mar. 11, 1921; d. Byron Gerald and Ruth Cleveland (Biggam) Linington. A.B., Glendale Coll., 1942. Author: The Proud Man, 1955; The Long Watch, 1956; Monsieur Janvier, 1957; The Kingbreaker, 1958; Forging an Empire: Elizabeth I (juvenile), 1961, No Evil Angel, 1964, Come to Think of It, 1965, Date with Death, 1966, Something Wrong, 1967, Policeman's Lot, 1968, Practice to Deceive, 1911, Perchance of Death, 1977, No Villain Need Be, 1979; (as Egan O'Neill) The Anglophile (in U.K. as The Pretender), 1957; detective novels as Lesley Egan) A Case for Appeal, 1961; Against the Evidence, 1962, The Borrowed Alibi, 1962; Run to Evil, 1963; My Name Is Death, 1965; Detective's Due, 1965; Some Avenger, Rise!, 1966; The Nameless Ones, 1967; A Serious Investigation, 1968; The Wine of Violence, 1969; In the Death of a Man, 1970; Malicious Mischief, 1971; Paper Chase, 1972; Scenes of Crime, 1976; The Blind Search, 1977; A Dream Apart, 1978; Look Back on Death, 1978; The Hunters and the Hunted, 1979; Motive in Shadow, 1981; Consequence of Crime, 1981; The Miser, 1982; Skeletons in the Closet, 1982; Random Death, 1982; Little Boy Lost, 1983; Crime for Christmas, 1984; (detective novels as Dell Shannon) Case Pending, 1960; The Ace of Spades, 1961; Extra Kill, 1962; Knave of Hearts, 1962; Death of A Busybody, 1963; Double Bluff, 1963; Root of All Evil, 1963; Greenmask!, 1964; Mark of Murder, 1964; Root of All Evil, 1964; The Death-Bringers, 1965; Death by Inches, 1965; Coffin Corner, 1966; With A Vengeance, 1966; Chance to Kill, 1967; Rain with Violence, 1967; Kill With Kindness, 1968; Schooled to Kill, 1969; Crime on Their Hands, 1969; Unexpected Death, 1970; Whim To Kill, 1971; The Ringer, 1971; Murder with Love, 1972; With Intent to Kill, 1972; Crime by Chance, 1973; No Holiday for Crime, 1973; Spring of Violence, 1973; Crime File, 1974; Deuces Wild, 1975; Streets of Death, 1976; Appearances of Death, 1977; Cold Trail, 1978; Felony at Random, 1979; Felony File, 1980; Murder Most Strange, 1981; The Motive on Record, 1982; Exploit of Death, 1983; Destiny of Death, 1984; Felony Report, 1984; Chaos of Crime, 1987; Blood Count, 1987; The Scapel and the Sword, 1987, Alter Ego, 1988, The Dispossessed, 1988. Home: Arroyo Grande Calif. Died Apr. 5, 1988.

LINK, EDWIN ALBERT, aviation executive, inventor; b. Huntington, Ind., July 26, 1904; s. Edwin A. and Katherine (Martin) L.; m. Marion Clayton, June 6, 1931; children: William Martin, Edwin Clayton (dec.). Student, Lindsley Inst.; DE (hon.), Coll. Osteo. Medicine and Surgery, 1964; LLD (hon.), Hamilton Coll., 1964; DSc (hon.), Syracuse U., 1966, Fla. Inst. Tech., 1970. Aviator 1927-81; pres., founder Link Aviation, Inc., Binghamton, N.Y., 1935-53; pres. Gen. Precision Equipment Corp., 1958-59, also bd. dirs.; pres. Marine Sci. Ctr., Ft. Pierce, Fla.; bd. dirs., cons. Link div. Singer Co.; dir. emeritus U.S. Air, Inc.; gov. Flight Safety Found., 1953-61; mem. naval research adv. com. Lab. Adv. Bd. for Undersea Warfare, 1968-76; mem. Presdl. Task Force on Oceanography, 1969. Author: (with P.V.H. Weems) Simplified Celestial Navigation, 1940. Inventor Link Aviation Trainers; developer diver lock out small submarines, other underwater ocean engring. products. Founder Link Found., 1953; trustee Woods Hole Oceanographic Instn.; bd. dirs., trustee Harbor Br. Found., Inc. Recipient Potts medal Franklin Inst., 1945, Wakefield medal Royal Aero. Soc., 1947, Exceptional Service medal USAF, Frank G. Brewer trophy, 1957, Aviation Week award Flight Safety Found., 1958, Achievement award Nat. Aviation Club, 1963, Elisha Kent Kane Gold medal Geog. Soc. Phila., 1965, NOGI award for sci. Underwater Soc. Am., 1965, Centennial medal Syracuse U., 1970, Matthew Fontaine Maury medal for oceanographic achievement Smithsonian Instn., 1971, Gold medal Internat. Oceanographic Found., 1974; named to Ox 5 Club Aviation Hall of Fame, 1972, Aviation Hall of Fame, Dayton, Ohio, 1976. Fellow AIAA (de Flores award 1967); mem. Acad. Aero. (trustee emeritus), Inst. Nav. (past pres.), Nat. Geog. Soc., Binghamton Club, Wings (N.Y.C.), Nat. Aviation Club (Washington), Riomar Yacht Club (Vero Beach, Fla.). Home: Fort Pierce Fla. Died Sept. 8, 1981; buried Binghamton, N.Y.

LINK, RICHARD MEBOLDT, investment banker; b. Bklyn., July 27, 1913; s. Charles Christian and Anna (Meboldt) L.; m. Clara Cornell Tomlin, Dec. 26, 1936; children: Charles David, Laura Ann Link Graney. Student, Columbia, 1930-35; B.S., U. So. Cal., 1936. Security analyst William R. Staats & Co., Los Angeles, 1936-40; mgr. security analysis Bankamerica Co., San Francisco, 1940-42; regional rationing statistician OPA, San Francisco, 1942-43; analyst U.S. Navy Price Adjustment Bd., San Francisco, 1943-45; with Blyth & Co., Inc., Los Angeles, 1945-72; v.p. Blyth & Co., Inc., 1955-72, dir., 1959-72, sr. v.p., mem. exec. com., 1962-72; former dir. 8 corps.; Lectr. finance extension div. UCLA, 1946-51. Clubs: California (Los Angeles); Annandale Golf (Pasadena). Home: Pasadena Calif. Died Jan. 18, 1988.

LINK, S. GORDDEN, English language educator, poet; b. Chgo., Apr. 9, 1907; s. Joseph S. and Florence (Tannenholtz) L.; m. Mae Mills, Jan. 11, 1936. B.S., NYU, 1929, A.M., 1930; M.Ed., Harvard U., 1932; Ph.D., George Peabody Coll. for Tchrs., Vanderbilt U., 1938; postgrad., Yale, 1931, Columbia, 1935, George Washington U., 1956, Washington Sch. of Psychiatry, 1958. Faculty Limestone Coll., 1930-34; vis. prof. Northeastern U., 1932-33; lectr. George Peabody Coll. for Tchrs., 1934-38; asst. pastor McKendree Meth. Ch., Nashville, 1937-38; prof., chaplain Oglethorpe U., 1938-39; vis. prof. St. Lawrence U., 1939-40; dir. tng., personnel Microstat Corp., 1941-42; cons. tng. within industry programs WPB, 1941-42; dir. writing workshop McCoy Coll., Johns Hopkins, 1947-51; cons. office Chief of Staff, U.S. Army, 1948-49; chmn. div. humanities Anne Arundel Community Coll., Severna Park, Md., 1962-64; prof. English, poet in residence Anne Arundel Community Coll., 1962-66; writer-in-residence, dir. liberal arts Southeastern U., Washington, 1966-71; emeritus dir. liberal arts, writer in residence 1971-86; professorial lectr. grad. div. Loyola Coll., Balt., 1962-64; cons. various fed. agys., 1950-54, lectr. univs., Calcutta, New Delhi, Nanking, Shanghai, others, 1942-47; exec. dir. Orgn. for Advancement Coll. Teaching, 1964-73, pres., 1973—; pres. Center for Advanced Studies, Amos R. Koontz Meml. Found., Dellbrook campus, Riverton, Va.; dir. Dellbrook-Shenandoah Coll. Writers' Conf., 1969-84; Mem. nat. adv. bd. Am. Security Council.; spl. adviser U.S. Congl. Adv. Bd.; mem. Republican Presdl. Task Force. Writer in residence, Shenandoah Coll. and Conservatory Music, 1971-84; Author: One Small Unwilling Captain —A Study of the Japanese Mind, 1937, The German Prisoner of War, 1944, The Engineers in the Pacific, 1947, Pocket Guide to Germany, 1951, Three Poems for Now, 1953, 58, 72, Personal Journal for Yesterday, Now and Tomorrow Maybe: Poems 1943-1978, 1982, The Bakers Dozen You Asked For, 1982; Contbr. to poetry anthologies.; Poetry recorded Permanent Collection Modern Poetry, Library of Congress, 1961, 73. Chmn. bd. trustees Amos R. Koontz Meml. Found.; chmn. bd. govs. Shenandoah Valley Acad. Lit., 1976-86. Served from 2d lt. to col. M.I. U.S. Army, 1942-47, 48-53; served to lt. col. USAR, 1953-63. Decorated Army Commendation medal with oak leaf cluster, Bronze Star, Army-Navy Air Force medal 1st class China; Spl. Breast Order Yun Hui with rosette; Breast Order Pau Tang with rosette China; Order of Imperial Lion Nepal. Fellow Am. Assn. Social Psychiatry (Merrill Moore award 1960); mem. Latin Am. Inst. Washington (past pres.), Poetry Soc. Am. (Lola Ridge award 1948, James Joyce award 1971, Christopher Morley Meml. award 1976, v.p. 1978-81, nat. chmn. program com. 1978-81), Poetry Soc. Ga., New Eng. Poetry Club, Baker St. Irregulars, Mil. Order World Wars, The Ret. Officers Assn. (life), Shelley Soc. N.Y. (hon.), Am. Legion (chaplain No. zone Va. 1981-84). Republican. Methodist. Club: Army and Navy (Washington). Home: Riverton Va. Died June 21, 1986; buried Arlington Nat. Cemetery.

LINTHICUM, JESSE A(LLISON), newspaper editor; b. Balt., Oct. 27, 1891; s. Jesse Hayden and Annie Roberta (Clark) L.; m. Edna Lynn Foster, Aug. 12, 1914; 1 child, Edna M. Linthicum Chairs. Student, Balt. pub. schs. Staff mem. Balt. news, Balt. Star, 1910-11; asst. sports editor Evening Sun, Balt., 1912-17; night editor, makeup editor Morning Sun, Balt., 1917-22, city editor, 1922-24, sports editor, from 1924. Sports dir. Balt. chpt. ARC. Methodist. Home: Baltimore Md. †

LINTON, DONALD LOWRY, advertising agency executive; b. Bronxville, N.Y., Mar. 6, 1934; s. Walter Lyman and Jessie (Castle) L.; m. Marilyn Borst, June 22, 1974; children by previous marriage—Donald, David, Bonnie. B.A., Amherst Coll., 1959. Account exec. BBD&O Inc., N.Y.C., 1959-62, Fuller, Smith & Ross, N.Y.C., 1963-65; with SSC&B Inc., N.Y.C., 1965-72, 74-86, sr. v.p., mgmt. supr., 1978-86; pres. Advt. Projections, Inc., 1972-74. Vice pres. N.E. Greenwich (Conn.) Assn., 1968-70; bd. dirs. Tokeneke Assn., Darien, Conn., 1981-86. Served with AUS, 1953-55. Republican. Episcopalian. Home: Darien Conn. Died Sept. 28, 1986; buried St. Luke's Episc. Ch., Darien, Conn.

LIPETZ, MILTON EDWARD, psychology educator; b. Bklyn., Mar. 10, 1930; s. Samuel Phillip and Goldie Rebecca (Lipetz) L.; m. Marilyn Altman, Apr. 6, 1952; children: Bruce David, Valerie Ellin. B.A., NYU, 1951; M.A., Bklyn. Coll., 1953; Ph.D., Ohio State U., 1958. Diplomate Am. Bd. Profl. Psychology. Research assoc. Ohio State U., Columbus, 1958; asst. prof. psychology U. Colo., Boulder, 1958-63; assoc. prof. U. Colo., 1963-67, prof., 1967-87, dean Grad Sch., 1973-79, vice chancellor for research, 1974-79, vice chancellor for acad. affairs, dean of faculties, 1979-85, acting chancellor, 1981-82. Cons. editor Jour. Personality and Social Psychology, 1973-76; contbr. articles to profl. jours. Mem. Am., Colo. psychol. assns. Home: Boulder Colo. Died Nov. 29, 1987.

LIPINSKY DE ORLOV, LINO SIGISMONDO, artist, museum curator; b. Rome, Italy, Jan. 14, 1908; came to U.S., 1940, naturalized, 1945; s. Sigismondo and Elinita K. (Burgess) Lipinsky de O.; m. Leah S. Penner, Oct. 1, 1943; children: Lino S., Lucian C. Ed., Rome and Munich, 1914-19; studied under father at Brit. Acad. Arts, Rome, 1922-25; grad., Royal Acad. Arts, Rome, 1937. Dir. Garibaldi-Meucci Meml. Mus., S.I., N.Y., 1956—; dir. ann. Winter Antiques Show, N.Y., 1957-60; head exhibits design dept. Mus. City N.Y., 1959-67; mem. art admissions com. Huntington Hartford Found., 1962-65; curator history John Jay Homestead, N.Y. State Parks and Recreation Div. for Hist. Preservation, Katonah, 1967—; mem. Washington-Rochambeau Nat. Historic Route Com., Yorktown, N.Y., Bedford (N.Y.) Tricentennial Commn., 1980; art cons. Italian embassy, Washington; also consulate gen. Italy in N.Y.C. Painter, etcher, mus. curator, historian; Author: Pocket Anatomy in Color for Artists, 1947, Giovanni Da Verrazzano, The Discoverer of New York Bay, 1524, 1958, The Jay Family Genealogy, 1984; contbg. author numerous art and hist. books.; contbr. articles to profl. jours.; works exhibited fgn. countries, N.A.D., Art Inst. Chgo., Met. Mus. Art, Albright Art Gallery, Cleve. Mus. Art, Detroit Mus. Art, many other cities and mus.; one-man shows include Palazzetto Venezia, Rome, 1928, Boston Symphony Hall, 1941, Jr. League Gallery, Boston, 1941, Knoedler Gallery, N.Y.C., 1945, Avery Hall, Columbia U., 1955, Cosmos Club, Washington, 1955, Smithsonian Inst., U.S. Nat. Mus., 1955, Galleria Costa, Palma de Mallorca, Spain, 1955, numerous pvt. galleries; represented permanent collections Mus. City N.Y., Library Congress, Met. Mus., N.Y. Pub. Library, Columbia, Detroit Inst. Arts, Gabinetto delle Stampe, Rome, Galleria Nazionale d'Arte Moderna, Rome, numerous other museums and pvt. collections; executed mural for the banquet hall, Palace of Maharaja of Indore, 1947; several ch. murals, 1942-48; Diorama: Verrazzano's Discovery of New York Bay in 1524, 1955; circular mural View of New Amsterdam in 1660, Mus. City. N.Y., 1965; designed mus. exhibit, N.Y. World's Fair, 1964-65, Bedford Hist. Soc. Mus., 1970. Served with Italian Army, 1936; Served with U.S. intelligence div. 6th Service Command, OSS, World War II. Awarded numerous prizes, including Silver medal of Ministero dell'Educazione Nazionale, Rome, 1928, 31; diplome d'Honneur, silver medal Expn. de Budapest, 1936; Diplome de Grand Prix, gold medal, Diplome d'Honneur Paris Expn. Internationale, 1937; Chgo. Soc. Etchers, 1941, 50; Soc. Am. Etchers, 1942; Joseph Pennell prize Library of Congress, 1942; Detroit Inst. Arts, 1943; Guild Hall, Easthampton, N.Y., 1946; Kosciuszko Found., N.Y., 1948; decorated officer Order of Merit Rep. of Italy, 1958; recipient Gold medal and certificate of merit Order Sons of Italy in Am., 1961; L.L. Huttleston Staff award State N.Y. Council on Parks and Recreation, 1974; Hist. Tomahawk award Westchester County Hist. Soc., 1979. Mem. Soc. Am. Graphic Artists, Audubon Artists (chmn. exhbn. com. 1952), Chgo. Soc. Etchers, United Scenic Artists, Am. Assn. Museums, Comitato Nazionale Per le Onoranze a

Giovanni Da Verrazzano, Gruppo Romano Incisori Artisti, Internat. Platform Assn., Nat. Soc. Lit. and Arts, Bedford Farmers' Club, N.Y. State Assn. Mus., Knights Mark Twain, N.Y. State Employees Assn., Bedford Hist. Soc. Home: Katonah N.Y. Died Aug. 11, 1988.

LIPMANN, FRITZ (ALBERT), biochemist, educator; b. Koenigsberg, Germany, June 12, 1899; came to U.S., 1939, naturalized, 1944; s. Leopold and Gertrud (Lachmanski) L.; m. Elfreda M. Hall, June 23, 1931; 1 son, Stephen. Student, U. Koenigsberg, 1917-22, U. Munich, 1919; M.D., U. Berlin, 1924, Ph.D., 1928; M.D. (hon.), U. Marseilles, 1947, U. Copenhagen, 1972; M.A. (hon.), Harvard, 1949; D.Sc. (hon.), U. Chgo., 1953, U. Paris, 1966, Harvard U., 1967, Rockefeller U., 1971; L.H.D. (hon.), Brandeis U., 1959, Yeshiva U., 1964. Research asst. Prof. Meyerhof's Lab., Kaiser Wilhelm Inst., Berlin and Heidelberg, 1927-30; Dr. A Fischer's Lab., Berlin, 1930-31; Rockefeller fellow Rockefeller Inst. Med. Research, N.Y.C., 1931-32; research asso. Biol. Inst. Carlsberg Found., Copenhagen, Denmark, 1932-39; dept. biochemistry Med. Sch. Cornell U., 1939-41; research chemist, head biochem. research lab. Mass. Gen. Hosp., Boston, 1941-57; prof. biol. chemistry Harvard Med. Sch., 1949-57; prof. Rockefeller U., 1957-70, prof. emeritus, researcher, 1970-86. Author: Wanderings of a Biochemist, 1971; sci. papers. Recipient Carl Neuberg medal, 1948; Mead Johnson & Co. award for outstanding work on Vitamin B-complex, 1948; Nobel prize in medicine and physiology for discovery of coenzyme A, 1953; Nat. Medal Sci., 1966. Fellow N.Y. Acad. Sci., Danish Royal Acad. Scis.; fgn. mem. Royal Soc.; mem. Nat. Acad. Scis., Am. Chem. Soc., Am. Soc. Microbiology, Biochem. Soc., AAAS, Am. Soc. Biol. Chemists, Harvey Soc., Am. Philos. Soc. Home: Rhinebeck N.Y. Died July 24, 1986, cremated.

LIPPINCOTT, BENJAMIN EVANS, political scientist; b. Alexandria, Ind., Nov. 26, 1902; s. Jason Evans and Laura (d'Isay) L.; m. Gertrude Lawton, June 22, 1934. BS, Yale U., 1925; student, Brasemose, Oxford, Eng., 1926; PhD, London Sch. Econs. and Polit. Sci., U. London, 1930. Instr. polit. sci. U. Minn., 1929-32, asst. prof., 1932-39, assoc. prof., 1939-42, prof., 1946-71; vis. prof. Stanford, 1953; guest lectr. U. Mich., 1958, Yale Law Sch., 1966; lectr. Johns Hopkins U., 1957, vis. prof., 1966-68; Chmn. tng. guidance staff 2655th A.R.C., Mpls., 1955-59, adviser to comdr., 1960; mem. nat. ednl. adv. com. Consumer's Union.; Liaison officer USAF Acad., 1959-62, coordinator, Minn., 1961-62; mem. ROTC Panel, Res. Forces Policy Bd., Dept. Def., 1961-68. Author: Victorian Critics of Democracy, 1938, From Fiji Through the Philippines with the Thirteenth Air Force, 1947, Democracy's Dilemma, The Totalitarian Party in Free Socciety, 1965; Editor, contbr.: Govt. Control of the Economic Order, 1935, Lange and Taylor, On the Economic Theory of Socialism, 1938 (trans. into 7 langs), History Thirteenth Air Force (AAF Archives), 1944-45; Contbr.: Contemporary Political Science, 1950, Soviet Total War, 1956; articles to profl. jours. Trustee Walker Art Ctr., 1939-41. Commd. 1st lt. AC AUS, 1942; lt. col. 1946; col. USAF Res., 1952; historian 13th Air Force 1944-45, S. and S.W. Pacific. Decorated Legion of Merit.; recipient Cert. of Merit U. Minn., 1971. Mem. Royal Inst. Philosophy, AAUP (pres. U. Minn. chpt. 1960-61), Internat. Polit. Sci. Assn. (rep. Am. assn. at internat. congress Rome 1958), Am. Soc. Polit. and Legal Philosophy (first v.p. 1960-61), Midwest Polit. Sci. Assn., Am. Polit. Sci. Assn. (chmn. research com. on polit. theory 1941-42, established APSA polit. theory award 1975), Am. Acad. Polit. and Social Sci., Social Sci. Research Council (civil liberties com. 1941-43), St. Elmo Soc., Aurelian Honor Soc., Am. Fedn. Tchrs. (pres. U. Minn. chpt. 1938-39), Minn. Civil Liberties Union (chmn. acad. freedom com. 1965-67), Am. Peace Soc. (dir. from 1972), Center for Study of Presidency (bd. editors from 1974). Clubs: 39ers (U. Minn.); Skylight (Mpls.); Eastward Ho (Cape Cod). Home: Minneapolis Minn. Died Nov. 10, 1988.

LIPPITT, GORDON LESLIE, behavioral sciences educator; b. Fergus Falls, Minn., Aug. 20, 1920; s. Walter Otis and Lois (Garvey) L.; m. Phyllis Eleanor Parker, June 6, 1942; children: Anne Lippitt Rarich, Mary Lippitt Burner, Constance Lippitt Ridgway. BS, Springfield Coll., 1942, Litt (hon.), 1971; BD, Yale U., 1945; MA, U. Nebr., 1947; PhD, Am. U., 1959. Diplomate Am. Bd. Profl. Psychology. Dir. Indsl. Fedn., New Haven, Conn., 1942-46; exec. dir. YMCA, U. Nebr., 1946-49; asst. prof. psychology Union Coll., 1949-50; program dir. Midcentury White Ho. Conf. on Children and Youth, 1950; dir. edn. and tng. European productivity program Mut. Security Agy., 1951-52; program dir. Nat. Tng. Labs, NEA, 1952-59; dir. Ctr. Behavioral Scis. George Washington U., 1959-65, prof. behavioral scis., 1960-85; vis. scholar UCLA, 1967; pres. Leadership Resources, Inc., 1960-67, chmn. bd., 1967-69; pres. Project Assocs., Inc.; chmn. bd. Glenwood Manor Farms, Orgn. Renewal, Inc., Internat. Cons. Found.; bd. dirs. Petroleum Exploration & Devel. Funds, Inc. Author: Leader Looks at Group Effectiveness, 1962, Quest for Dialogue, 1966, Organization Renewal, 1969, rev. edit., 1982, Systems Thinking, 1981; co-author: Optimizing Human Resource Development, 1971, Visualizing Change, 1973, Consulting Process in Action, 1978; editor: New Trends in Political Education, 1959, Leadership in Action, 1955; co-editor: Handbook on Management Development and Training, 1975, Helping Across Cultures, 1978; monthly guest columnist mag. Nation's Cities, 1967, Tng. Dirs. Jour., 1969; contbr. articles to profl. jours. Mem. nat. community affairs com., nat. bd. dirs. YMCA, 1965-70; chmn. Nat. Youth Gov.'s Com., 1966-68; mem. organizational adv. com. Dem. Nat. Com., 1958-60; bd. dirs. Washington YMCA; trustee Nat. Rsch. Fund. Recipient Outstanding Civilian Service medal Dept. Army, 1962, Leadership award Hillsdale Coll., 1970, Century Club award YMCA, 1974-76, Wilbur McFeely award Internat. Mgmt. Councils, 1982; Rufus Jones lectr., 1966. Fellow Inst. Applied Behavioral Scis.; mem. Am. Psychol. Assn., Am. Soc. Pub. Adminstn., AAUP, NEA, Acad. Mgmt., Soc. Study Social Issues, Soc. Personnel Adminstrn. (exec. com. 1966-67, chmn. div. 1976), Am. Soc. Tng. and Devel. (bd. dirs. 1965-67, regional v.p. 1968, pres. 1969, Torch award 1975, Gordon M. Bliss award 1981), Pi Gamma Mu, Phi Delta Kappa, Psi Chi. Methodist. Home: Bethesda Md. Died Nov. 26, 1985.

LIPSETT, MORTIMER BROADWIN, physician, research center administrator; b. N.Y.C., Feb. 20, 1921; s. Theodore and Gertrude (Broadwin) L.; m. Lois Friedman, Mar. 10, 1974; children from previous marriage: Roger, Edward. AB, U. Calif., Berkeley, 1943; MS, U. So. Calif., 1947, MD, 1951. Diplomate Am. Bd. Internal Medicine. Research assoc. U. So. Calif., 1947; intern L.A. County Hosp., 1951-52; resident in internal medicine Sawtelle VA Hosp., L.A., 1952-54; commd. officer USPHS; USPHS fellow, asst. mem. Sloan-Kettering Inst., N.Y.C., 1954-57; mem. staff NIH, Bethesda, Md., 1957-74, 76-85; assoc. sci. dir. intramural research, chief reprodn. research br. NIH, 1970-74, assoc. dir. clin. care, dir. Clin. Ctr., 1976-82, dir. Nat. Inst. Child Health and Human Devel., 1982-85, dir. Nat. Inst. Arthritis, Diabetes and Kidney Diseases, Jan.-Nov., 1985; dir. Cancer Ctr. N.W. Ohio., Cleve.; prof. medicine Case-Western Res. U. Med. Sch., 1974-76; organizer, fin. chmn. Breast Cancer Task Force. Author or co-author over 275 sci. papers. With AUS, 1944-46. Decorated Bronze Star with oak leaf cluster; recipient Alfred P. Sloan award cancer research, Sloan-Kettering Inst., 1955, Superior Service Honor award Dept. Health, Edn. and Welfare, 1969, Disting. Service award Dept. Health and Human Services, 1981, Presdl. Meritorious Rank award, 1982. Fellow ACP; mem. Endocrine Soc. (sec.-treas 1974-78, pres. 1979-80, Disting. Leadership award 1976), Internat. Soc. Endocrinology (sec.-gen. 1976-85), AAAS, Am. Assn. Cancer Research, Am. Fedn. Clin. Research, Am. Soc. Andrology (named Disting. Andrologist 1984), Am. Soc. Clin. Investigation, Assn. Am. Physicians, Harvey Soc., Soc. Study Reprodn., German Endocrine Soc. (corr.), Japan Endoicrine Soc. (hon.). Home: Bethesda Md. Died Nov. 10, 1985.

LIPSHY, BEN ALLEN, retail jewelry corporation executive; b. Ft. Worth, Oct. 3, 1910; s. Julius and Ethel (Korman) L.; m. Udys Weinstein, Sept. 7, 1931; children: Joy Lipshy Burk, Barbara Lipshy Marcus, Bruce Arlen. Grad. high sch. With Zale Corp., Dallas, 1926-80, store mgr., Amarillo, Tex., 1934-40, supr. group stores, 1940-51, treas., 1951-57, pres., 1957-71, chmn. bd., 1971-80, chmn. emeritus, 1980-85; bd. dirs. RepublicBank Corp., Dallas. Mem. Dallas Crime Commn., Dallas Citizens Coun.; mem. Jewish Welfare Fedn. Dallas; mem. retail adv. group U. Tex.; chmn. bd. Univ. Med. Ctr., Inc.; bd. dirs. Dallas Community Coll. Dist. Found., World Trade Ctr., Dallas, Dallas chpt. ARC; trustee Nat. Jewish Hosp. Denver; nat. bd. dirs. NCCJ. Mem. Columbian Country Club, Masons, Shriners. Jewish. Home: Dallas Tex. Died Nov. 21, 1985.

LIPTON, SEYMOUR, sculptor; b. N.Y.C., Nov. 6, 1903; s. Simon and Gussie (Choen) L.; m. Lilliam Franzblau, Nov. 16, 1930; children—Michael Alan. Student, CCNY, 1921-22, Columbia U., 1923-27. Tchr. sculpture Cooper Union, N.Y.C., 1942-44; tchr. N.Y. State Tchrs. Coll., 1944-45, New Sch. Soc. Research, N.Y.C., 1945-86; vis. art critc Yale U., 1956; mem. curriculum adv. com. NYU. One-man shows include ACA Gallery, 1938, St. Etienne Gallery, 1943, Watkins Gallery, Washington, 1948, Betty Parsons Gallery, 1948, 50, 52, 54, Mus. Modern Art, N.Y.C. 1956, Venice Biennial, 1958, Rensselaer U. Mus., 1961, Philips Collection, Washington, 1964, Marlborough Gerson Gallery, N.Y.C., 1965, 71, Milw. Art Ctr., 1969, MIT, 1971, Va. Mus. Art, Richmond, 1972, Johnson Mus. Art, Ithaca, N.Y., 1973, Syracuse Mus. Art, N.Y., 1973, Jewish Mus., 1980; commns. include Dulles Internat. Airport, Washington, Inland Steel Bldg., Chgo., Lincoln Ctr., N.Y.C., Golden Gate Project, San Francisco, Watson Research Ctr., Kichawan, N.Y., Ctr. Performing Arts, Milw., MIT, 1971; works exhibited numerous museums and galleries throughout world; represented in permanent collections Mus. Modern Art, Yale U., Whitney Mus., Munson-William Proctor Inst., Santa Barbara Mus., Calif., Toronto Art Gallery, Tel Aviv Mus., Temple Israel, Detroit Inst. Fine Arts, Balt. Mus., Cornell U. Mus., Mass. U. Mus., Albright Art Gallery, Buffalo, Des Moines Art Ctr., U. Mich. Mus., Wadsworth Atheneum, Albany State Bldg., N.Y., Didrichsen Found., Helsinki, Finland, Phillips Collection, Washington, Mus. R.I. Sch. Design, Penn Ctr., Phila., U. Pa. Theatre, Smithsonian Instn., Verlane Found., N.Y.C., Flint Inst. Fine Arts, Mich., others; also pvt. and pub. collections. Sculptor chmn. Ar Commn. N.Y.C., 1967. Recipient 1st prize Chgo. Ar Inst., 1957, 1st prize Logan award, 1957, maj. acquisi tion prize Sao Paulo, Brazil, 1957, award Ford Found 1960, gold and silver medals Archtl. League, 1962 Widener Gold medal Pa. Acad. Arts, 1968, name honoree Internat. Sculpture Conf., New Orleans, 1976 grantee AAAL, 1958, Guggenheim fellow, 1960. Mem Nat. Inst. Arts and Letters, Nat. Soc. Lit. and Arts. Home: New York N.Y. Died Dec. 5, 1986.

LIST, ALBERT A., business executive; b. Fall River Mass., May 18, 1901; s. Alter and Ethel (Hymervitch L.; m. Vera Glaser, Dec. 31, 1929; children: Joann Lis Levenson, Olga List Mack, Carol List Schwartz, Vick Laura. Pres. Glen Alden Corp. and subs., 1959-65 Hudson Coal Co.; chmn. Glen Alden Corp. and subs from 1965; pres. Gt. Universal Devel. Corp.; owne Crescent Corp.; owner, chmn. Strahl & Pitsch, Babylon L.I., N.Y., until 1987; chmn. fin. com., bd. dirs McCrory Corp.; bd. dirs. Avnet Electronics Corp. Founder Albert A. List Found.; dir. Jewish Theol. Sem Am.; trustee Met. Opera, Mt. Sinai Hosp; mem. exec com. Citizens Budget Commn.; trustee Fgn. Policy Assn.; one of original fin. supporters New Sch. fo Social Research; supporter art ctrs. at Kirkland Coll Clinton, N.Y., Brown U., MIT.; endowed 1st chair fo Jewish studies Harvard U., 1982. 2 bldgs. at New Sch for Social Research named in his honor. Home: Byram Conn. Died June 22, 1987.

LITCHFIELD, URSULA See NORDSTROM, UR SULA

LITTLE, JAMES MAXWELL, pharmacologist, edu cator; b. Commerce, Ga., Dec. 16, 1910; s. Claude an Cora (Quillian) L.; m. Louise Toepel, Aug. 20, 193 (dec. Mar. 1978); children: Paul G., Nancy C., John M. m. Emily Angell, Mar. 30, 1979. AB, Emory U., 1932 MS, 1933; PhD, Vanderbilt U., 1941. Asst. in physi ology Emory U. Med. Sch., 1933-35; instr. biochemisty Vanderbilt U., 1936-41; mem. faculty Bowman Grey Sch. Medicine, Wake Forest U., Winston-Salem, N.C. from 1941, asst. dean, 1957-60, prof. pharmacology, as soc. physiology, 1963-81, emeritus, 1981-82, chmn dept., 1963-73. Author: An Introduction to the Exper imental Method, 1961; contbr. articles to profl. jours. Charter mem., pres. Piedmont Craftsmen, Inc., 1963-71 bd. dirs. N.C. League Creative Arts and Crafts, 1975-79 Fellow AAAS; mem. Am. Physiol. Soc., Soc. Exptl Biology and Medicine, Am. Soc. Pharmacology and Exptl. Therapeutics, Am. Heart Assn., N.C. Hear Assn. (Bronze and Silver medallion 1970), Forsyth County Heart Assn., Phi Beta Kappa, Sigma Xi. Presbyterian. Home: Winston-Salem N.C. Died Oct. 1 1982, buried Salem Cemetery, Winston-Salem, N.C.

LITTLE, JOHN RUSSELL, university administrator b. Aberdeen, Wash., May 29, 1904; s. Harry Drew and Grace (Garfield) L.; m. Lois Alberta Powell, June 5 1928; children—John Russell, Jean (Mrs. Raymond El liott). B.S., Colo. State U., 1928, M.S., 1934; Ed.D., U Colo., 1948. Elementary tchr. Akron, Colo., 1924-26 prin. Center (Colo.) Sch., 1928-33, supt., 1934-41; supt schs. Arvada, Colo., 1941-47; asst. prof., student coun sellor U. Colo., 1947-48, asst. dir. admissions, 1949-50 asso. prof., dir. admissions and records, 1950-55, prof. dean summer sessions, 1955-65, prof., asso. dean facul ties, 1965-72; acting dean U. Colo. (Coll. Arts and Scis.), 1959-61, sec. univ., sec. bd. regents, 1967-70 editor U. Colo. (Sch. and U. Rev.), 1970-72, dean, prof emeritus, 1972-87, pres. ret. faculty, 1979; cons. on scholarships Boettcher Found., 1952-87; cons. summer session studies U.S. Office Edn., 1959-65; dir. studies fo establishment univ. br. centers in, Colo., 1961-87. Author: State Responsibility for Public Education and Application to Colorado, 1948; Co-author, editor University of Colorado Report on Expansion of Higher Education in Colorado, 1961; prin. co-author, editor Year Around Operation in American Universities, 1963 Revision of the Laws of the Regents of the University o Colorado, 1968, Little by Little, a Biographical Narra tive, 1986. Contbr. articles to profl. jours. Mem. Am Assn. Jr. Colls., Higher Edn. Assn., Am. Assn. Col legiate Registrars and Admissions Officers (chmn. com on internat. scholarships 1952-56, chmn. nat. conventior com. 1955), Boulder C. of C., Colo.-Wyo. Assn. Col legiate Registrars and Adminstrn. Officers (past pres.) Assn. Deans U. Summer Sessions (pres. 1959, sec 1960), Rocky Mountain Assn. Summer Session Dirs (chmn. 1958), Nat., Colo. edn. assns., Am., Colo. assns sch. adminstrs., AAUP, Am. Assn. U. Summer Sch Adminstrs. (recorder 1964-69, pres. 1968), North Cen tral Conf. of Summer Schs. (pres. 1963-64, pres. emer itus), Phi Delta Kappa, Kappa Kappa Psi, Alpha Gamma Rho. Republican. Presbyterian. Clubs University Lodges: Masons (32 deg.), Rotary. Home Boulder Colo. Died Dec. 1, 1987; buried Mountain View Meml. Park, Boulder.

LITTLE, ROBERT NARVAEZ, JR., physics educator experimental nuclear physicist; b. Houston, Mar. 11 1913; s. Robert Narvaez and Lillian Forrest (Kinney) L.; m. Betty Jo Browning, June 1, 1942; children—Scot Robert, Emily Browning. Student, U. Tex.-Austin 1929-32; B.A. with honors in Math., Rice U., 1935 M.A. in Physics, 1942, Ph.D. in Physics, 1943. Seis mologist Shell Oil Co., Houston, 1936-40; mem. faculty dept. physics U. Oreg., Eugene, 1943-44, U. Tex., 1946-86, Universidad del Valle, Guatemale, 1977, Universidad Nacional de Education a Distancia, Madrid, 1981; chief nuclear physics Gen. Dynamics, Ft. Worth, 1953-55, cons., 1955-60. Author: Motion and Matter, 4th edit., 1984. Contbr. articles to profl. publs. Recipient Dedication of R.N. Little Lab. Physics, Universidad Nacional Autonoma de Honduras, 1981, Diploma de Reconocimiento, Universidad de el Salvador, 1984. Fellow Am. Phys. Soc., Tex. Acad. Sci.; mem. Am. Assn. Physics Tchrs. (Disting. Service award 1973, Outstanding Contbns. to Higher Edn. Tex. award 1978), Sociedad Centro-Americano de Fisica, Groupe Internat. des Recherches sur L'Enseignement de la Physique. Died May 21, 1986, buried Austin, Tex. Home: Austin Tex.

LITTLE, ROYAL, business executive; b. Wakefield, Mass., Mar. 1, 1896; m. Augusta Willoughby Ellis, Sept. 10, 1932 (div. 1959); children: Augusta Willoughby, Arthur Dehon. Student, Harvard, 1919. Chmn. bd. Lonsdale Enterprises, Inc. (fin. cons.); ret. chmn., dir. Amtel, Inc.; cons., past chmn. bd. Indian Head Mills, Inc.; founder, past chmn. bd. Textron Inc.; bd. dirs. Burro Crane Corp., Western-Cullen-Hayes; founder Am. TV and Communication, All Am. Beverages, Realty Income Trust, Narragansett Capital, Bevis, Sam Snead All Am. Golf. Author: How To Lose $100,000,000 and Other Valuable Advice. Trustee, v.p. Mus. Sci., Boston; trustee Lyford Cay Found., The Little Family Found. Home: Narragansett R.I. Died Jan. 12, 1989.

LITTLE, WINSTON WOODARD, university dean; b. Wesson, Miss., Apr. 14, 1892; s. Otto and Manerva (Davis) L.; m. Anna Stallings Humber, Aug. 8, 1936; children: Jo Anne, Winston Woodard, Marilyn Humber. BS, Miss. Coll., 1914; MA, U. Chgo., 1924. Prin. High Sch., Arcadia, Fla., 1914-17, St. Petersburg High Sch., 1920-31; co-founder, 1st dean St. Petersburg Jr. Coll., 1927; asst. prof. edn. U. Fla., 1931-34, assoc. dean gen. coll., 1934-37, dean, from 1937. Capt. U.S. Army, 1917-20; maj. A.M.G., 1943. Mem. So. Assn. Colls. and Secondary Schs. (chmn. Fla. Com., chmn. cen. rev. com. of secondary commn. 1937-40). Democrat. Methodist. Home: Gainesville Fla. †

LITTON, WILLARD WARREN, manufacturing company executive; b. Cambridge, Ill., Sept. 14, 1920; s. Merle Wells and Natalia (Zatterberg) L.; m. Betty Jean Ewing, May 24, 1947; children: Vicki Jo, Wendy Gay. BS in Indsl. Engring., Washington U., St. Louis, 1951; MBA, U. So. Calif., 1962. Registered profl. engr., Calif. Div. acct. Interpace Co., L.A., 1954-56; with Whittaker Corp., L.A., 1956-68, 72-81, div. contr., 1960-68, adminstr., 1972-75, div. v.p., 1975-81; treas. Tasker Industries, L.A., 1968-72. Dir., sec. Valencia Highlands, Inc., 1965-81. Lt. USAAF, 1943-47. Mem. Am. Inst. Indsl. Engrs., Disabled Officers Assn., Sigma Xi. Tau Beta Pi, Pi Mu Epsilon, Alpha Pi Mu, Sigma Phi Epsilon. Home: Northridge Calif. Died May 30, 1981.

LIU, JAMES JO-YÜ, educator; b. Peking, China, Apr. 14, 1926; came to U.S., 1961, naturalized, 1974; s. Yu-hsin and Pao-ling (Yen) L.; m. Claire Magdalen Morris, Nov. 30, 1957 (div. 1974); 1 dau., Sarah Meiwen. B.A., Fu Jen U., China, 1948; postgrad., Tsing Hua U., China, 1948, Oxford U., Eng., 1950-51; M.A., U. Bristol, Eng., 1952. Lectr. Chinese, London U., 1951-56; lectr. Hong Kong U., 1956-59; assoc. prof. English, New Asia Coll., Hong Kong, 1959-61; asst. prof. Chinese, U. Hawaii, Honolulu, 1961-64; vis. assoc. prof. U. Pitts., 1964-65; assoc. prof. U. Chgo., 1965-67; prof. Chinese, Stanford U., 1967-86, courtesy prof. comparative lit., 1977-86, chmn. dept. Asian langs., 1969-75; external examiner U. Bristol, 1953, U. London, 1958, Chinese U. Hong Kong, 1968-69, Australian Nat. U., 1983; Disting. vis. prof. Rutgers U., 1984; cons. NEH, 1973-86; dir. Summer Seminar Coll. Tchrs., 1976, 80, 85; mem. adv. screening com. in Chinese studies Council Internat. Exchange of Scholars, 1974-77. Author: The Art of Chinese Poetry, 1962, The Chinese Knight Errant, 1967, The Poetry of Li Shang-yin, 1969, Major Lyricists of the Northern Sung, 1974, Chinese Theories of Literature, 1975, Essentials of Chinese Literary Art, 1979, The Interlingual Critic, 1982, others. Editor: Jour. Hong Kong br. Royal Asiatic Soc, 1960-61. Guggenheim fellow, 1971; Am. Council Learned Socs. grantee, 1972, 82; NEH fellow, 1978-79. Mem. Chinese Lang. Tchrs. Assn., Assn. Asian Studies, Am. Comparative Lit. Assn. Home: Stanford Calif. Died May, 1986.

LIVERNASH, EDWARD ROBERT, economist, educator; b. Ft. Collins, Colo., Jan. 23, 1910; s. Edward Francis and Jeanette (Gillis) L.; m. Virginia Hall, June 7, 1936; children: Stephen E., Robert T. AB summa cum laude, U. Colo., 1932; MA, Tufts Coll., 1934; PhD, Harvard U., 1941. Teaching fellow Tufts Coll., 1932-35, asst. prof., 1940-42; instr. MIT, 1935-39; successively wage stablzn. dir., vice chmn., chmn. Nat War Labor Bd., Boston, 1943-45; dir. rsch. J.F. McElwain Co., Nashua, N.H., 1946-53; assoc. prof. bus. adminstrn. Grad. Sch. Bus. Adminstrn. Harvard U., 1953-57, prof., from 1957, Albert J. Weatherhead Jr. prof. bus. adminstrn., from 1965; on leave of absence, 1972-75; pres. Iran Ctr. for Mgmt. Studies, 1972-75. Contbr. articles to various publs. Mem. N.H. Pers. Commn., 1948-53. Mem. Indsl. Rels. Rsch. Assn., Phi Beta Kappa. Unitarian. Home: Arlington Mass. Died Feb. 2, 1987.

LIVINGSTON, FRANCIS DAVID, coal company executive; b. Charlottesville, Va., Sept. 29, 1914; s. James Draper and Permele Crawford (Elliott) F.; m. Janine Martin, Nov. 27, 1976; children: Kathy Anne, Anna Barbour. BA, Yale U., 1937; MBA, Harvard U., 1939; student mining, W.Va. U., 1937; LLD (hon.), Davis and Elkins Coll., 1961, Marshall U., 1963. V.p., gen. mgr. Princess Elkhorn Coal Co., David, Ky., 1940-42, pres., 1946-59; pres. Princess Coals, Inc. (merger Princess Elkhorn, Powellton, Sycamore and Cinderella coal cos.), 1959-63, chmn. bd., from 1963; pres. Princess Coal Sales Co., 1946-68, chmn. bd., from 1968; pres. Mallory Stores, Inc., Huntington, W.Va., 1946-63, Sycamore Coal Co., from 1968, Kathy's Farm, Inc., from 1978; pres. Princess Coals, Inc. (merger Kathy's Farm), 1975-78, chmn. bd., from 1979; dir. Appalachian Coals, Inc. Dir. So. States Indsl. Council, from 1950; chmn. W.Va. adv. com. Manpower Utilization; mem. W.Va. Rehab. Adv. Council, from 1961; mem. adv. council Outdoor Recreation Resources Rev. Commn., Washington, 1962; chmn. Cancer, United Fund-ARC campaigns; pres. Tri-State area council Boy Scouts Am.; chmn. W.Va. Citizens for Constl. Conv., 1967; vice chmn. Citizens Adv. Commn. on W.Va. Legislature, 1967-70; councilman City of Huntington, 1956-61; trustee, pres. Huntington Clin. Found.; trustee, mem. research com. Com. Econ. Devel. N.Y.C., from 1958; trustee Davis and Elkins Coll.; bd. dirs. W.Va. Found. Ind. Colls. Lt. comdr. USNR, 1942-45. Mem. U.S. C. of C. (dir. 1956-64, chmn. natural resources 1957-64, v.p. 1961-64), Nat. Coal Assn. (dir. from 1958, treas. 1960-61), So. Coal Producers Assn. (dir. from 1958, exec com.), AIME, NAM, Engrs. Club, Masons, Chi Psi. Presbyterian (elder). Home: Frankford W.Va. Died Mar. 18, 1985.

LIVINGSTON, MILTON STANLEY, nuclear physicist, educator, researcher; b. Brodhead, Wis., May 25, 1905; s. Milton McWhorter Livingston and Sarah Jane Ten Eyck; m. Lois Robinson, Aug. 7, 1930; children—Diane, Stephen. A.B., Pomona Coll., 1926; M.A., Dartmouth Coll., 1928; Ph.D., U. Calif.-Berkeley, 1931; D.Sc. (hon.), Dartmouth Coll., 1964, U. Hamburg, 1967, Pomona Coll., 1971. Asst. prof. Cornell U., Ithaca, N.Y., 1934-38; prof. MIT, Cambridge, 1938-70; chmn. accelerator program Brookhaven Nat. Lab., Upton, N.Y., 1946-48; dir. Cambridge electron accelerator Harvard U., Cambridge, Mass., 1956-67; assoc. dir. Fermi Nat. Accelerator Lab., Batavia, N.Y., 1967-70; cons. Los Alamos Sci. Lab., 1950-86, Nuclear Reg. Commn., Washington, 1971-83. Author: High Energy Accelerators, 1959, Particle Physics, 1968; co-author: Particle Accelerators, 1962. Home: Santa Fe N.Mex. Died Aug. 25, 1986.

LLOYD, R. MCALLISTER, foundation administrator, banker; b. N.Y.C., Jan. 12, 1898; s. Robert McAllister and Jennet Maitland (Belknap) L.; m. Isabel Goodwin, Oct. 8, 1921; children: Mary Remsen (Mrs. Frederic L. Steele), Robert McAllister, Eleanor (Mrs. William L. Helm Jr.). AB, Harvard U., 1919; LLD, Lawrence Coll., 1960, Juniata Coll., 1961, Yale U., 1963, NYU, 1963. Clk. Nat. City Bank N.Y., 1919-20; asst. trust officer N.Y. Trust Co., 1920-30; asst. v.p. Bank N.Y., 1930-36, v.p., 1936-45; pres., chmn. Tchrs. Ins. & Annuity Assn. Am., 1945-57, chmn., 1957-62, trustee, 1952-68; trustee William T. Grant Found., 1946-85, chmn., 1946-80. One-man shows included Lyman Allyn Mus., New London, Conn., 1974, Harkness House Gallery, N.Y.C., 1977, Artomation House Gallery, 1980. Mem. investments com. UN, 1952-72, chmn., 1962-72; mem. N.Y. State Commn. on Pensions, 1954-56, N.Y. State Commn. on Ednl. Fins., 1954-55, Royal Commn. on Freeport, The Bahamas, 1969-70; mem. adv. coun. Fed. Social Security Financing, 1957-58; trustee N.Y. Hist. Soc., 1947-85; active Ambulance Corps, ARC, 1917. Lt. inf. U.S. Army, 1918. Mem. Soc. Cin. in N.J., St. David's Soc., St. Andrews Soc., Loyal Legion, Am. Geog. Soc., Century Assn., Harvard Club. Republican. Presbyterian. Home: New Canaan Conn. Died June 21, 1985; buried Chocorua, N.H.

LLOYD, RALPH WALDO, college president emeritus; b. Friendsville, Tenn., Oct. 6, 1892; s. Henry Baldwin and Maud (Jones) L.; m. Margaret Anderson Bell, June 21, 1917; children: John Vernon, Hal Baldwin, Ruth Bell (Mrs. Frank A. Kramer), Louise Margaret (Mrs. James E. Palm). B.A., Maryville (Tenn.) Coll., 1915, D.D., 1929; B.D., McCormick Theol. Sem., 1924; LL.D., Centre Coll., 1940, U. Chattanooga, 1953; Litt.D., Lake Forest Coll., 1954, Westminster Coll., 1955; L.H.D., Lincoln Meml. U., 1955; S.T.D., Blackburn Coll., 1955; Pd.D., Monmouth Coll., 1961. Instr., athletic coach Westminster Coll., Salt Lake City, 1915-17; asst. to pres. Westminster Coll., 1918-19; with Fulton Sylphon Mfg. Co., Knoxville, Tenn., 1920-21; ordained to ministry Presbyn. Ch., U.S.A., 1923; supply First Presbyn. Ch., Ossian, Ind., 1922-23; pastor First Ch., Murphysboro, Ill., 1924-26, Edgewood Ch., Pitts., 1926-30; pres. Maryville Coll., 1930-61, pres. emeritus, from 1961; moderator Presbytery of Cairo, Ill., 1926, Presbytery of Union, 1932-33, Synod of Mid-South, 1944-46; gen. council Presbyn. Synod Tenn., 1931-40, chmn., 1940-42; Mem. permanent commn. inter ch. relations Presbyn. Ch. U.S.A., 1938-58, chmn., 1941-58, moderator gen. assembly, 1954-55; mem. Presbyn. Ch. U.S.A. deputation to China, 1946; chmn. com. lay edn. Presbyn. Council on Theol. Edn., 1943-48; mem. commn. on ecumenical mission and relations United Presbyn. Ch. U.S.A., 1958-60; mem. So. area bd. YMCA, 1939-54; Nat. Council Commn. Student Work., 1939-42, chmn. So. area, 1942-45, pres. So. area council, 1946-48; Am. sec. World Alliance Presbyn. and Ref. Chs., 1951-59, pres., 1959- 64; mem. central com. World Council Chs., 1951-61; gen. bd. Nat. Council Chs., 1950-60; Pres. Affiliated Ind. Colls. Tenn., Inc., 1958-61; mem. Nat. Conf. Ch. Related Colls., 1937-45, v.p., 1937, pres., 1938; pres. Pan-Presbyn. Coll. Union, Presbyn. Coll. Union, 1943, Tenn. Coll. Assn., 1942-43; mem. commn. insts. higher edn. So. Assn. Colls. and Secondary Schs., 1940-47; del. Presbyn. Ch. in U.S.A., World Council Chs., Amsterdam, 1948, Evanston, 1954, New Delhi, 1961. Author: The Presbyterian Colleges Today, 1948, The Christian College in America, 1951, The World Alliance of Reformed Churches, 1956, Maryville College-A History of 150 Years, 1969, Westminster United Presbyterian Church (Bradenton, Fla.)—A History of 50 Years, 1974; articles and addresses pub. in various ednl. and religious jours. Served as 1st lt. U.S. Army, 1917-18. Recipient Presbyn. Outlook award for significant contbn. to church unity, 1985. Died July 7, 1986.

LOBEL, ARNOLD STARK, author, illustrator; b. Los Angeles, May 22, 1933; s. Joseph and Lucille Harriet (Stark) L.; m. Anita, Apr. 16, 1955; children: Adrianne, Adam. B.F.A., Pratt Inst., 1955. Author, illustrator: children's books Zoo for Mister Muster, 1962, Prince Bertram the Red, 1963, Holiday for Mister Muster, 1963, Giant John, 1964, Lucille, 1964, Martha the Movie Mouse, 1966, Great Blueness and Other Predicaments, 1968, Small Pig, 1969, Frog and Toad Are Friends, 1970, Ice-Cream Cone Coot and Other Rare Birds, 1971, On the Day Peter Stuyvesant Sailed into Town, 1971, Mouse Tales, 1972, Frog and Toad Together, 1972, The Man Who Took the Indoors Out, 1974, Owl at Home, 1975, Frog and Toad All Year, 1976, Mouse Soup, 1977, How the Rooster Saved the Day, 1977, Gregory Griggs and the Nursery Rhyme People, 1978, Days With Frog and Toad, 1979, Fables, 1980 (Recipient Caldecott Honor award 1970-71, Newberry Honor award 1972, Christopher award 1971-76, Nat. Book awards finalist 1970, 71, 75), On Market Street, 1981, Uncle Elephant, 1981, Ming Lo Moves the Mountain, 1982, The Book of Pigericks, 1983. Mem. Authors Guild. Died Dec. 4, 1987.

LOCKE, HERBERT EDSON, lawyer; b. Augusta, Maine, Apr. 6, 1891; s. Edson and Ida May (Stevens) L.; m. Marguerite Grosvenor Lowell, May 24, 1916; 1 child, Nancy Locke Johnson. AB, Bowdoin Coll., 1912; LLB, Boston U., 1915. Bar: Maine 1915. Practiced in Augusta from 1915; ptnr. Locke, Campbell, Reid & Herbert; corp. counsel City of Augusta; commr. uniformity legislation, spl. tax counsel for Maine. Contbr. articles to profl. jours. Mem. ABA, Maine Bar Assn. (pres.), Country Club Augusta, Masons, Rotary; hon. life mem. Maine Med. Assn., Maine Hosp. Assn., N.E. Hosp. Assn. Home: Augusta Maine. †

LOCKHART, CARL FORD, professional football player; b. Dallas, June 4, 1943; s. Gertrude and Mable (Battle) L; m. Erma Jean Havis, Aug. 25, 1963; 1 child, Carl Ford. Student, N. Tex. State U., 1961-65. Defensive back N.Y. Giants, 1965-76; played in Pro Bowl 1966, 68. Mem. community adv. bd. Harlem Hosp., N.Y.C., 1968-71. Named to Sporting News All Eastern Conf. Team, 1970, UPI All Pro Team, 1970; named AP Def. Player of Week, 1970; recipient Gold Helmut award for Player of Week, Sept., 1968, Football Angel award Angel Guardian Home, 1968, Ann. Brotherhood award Men's Club Westchester Reform Temple, 1969, Most Popular Player award Cath. Youth Orgn., 1969, Chris Schenkel Medallion award, 1970. Home: Bronx N.Y. Died July 8, 1986.

LOCKHART, CARROLL HERBERT, Republican national committeeman, banker; b. Fall River, Wis., Nov. 5, 1892; s. Robert S. and Jessie (Grout) L.; m. Olive F. Walrath, Apr. 17, 1915; children: Robert H., Frances (Mrs. Eugene E. Hustad). Grad. high sch., Watertown, S.D. With First Citizens Nat. Bank, Watertown, from 1911, chmn. bd. dirs., from 1957; mem. Rep. Nat. Com., from 1958. Past mem. Watertown City Coun., Watertown Ind. Sch. bd.; bd. dirs. S.D. Crippled Children's Home and Sch. With inf. U.S. Army, World War I. Mem. Watertown C. of C. (past pres., dir.), Am. Legion (past state comdr.), S.D. Bankers Assn. (past pres.), Masons, K.T., Shriners, Elks, Rotary, Watertown Country Club. Home: Watertown S.D. †

LOCKHART, JACK HERBERT, publishing executive; b. Pitts., Oct. 12, 1909; s. John Clark and Ethel Gordon (Powell) L.; m. Nina Doris Tall, Sept. 28, 1935 (dec. June 1973); children: Doris J. Lockhart Saatchi, Richard Anthony, Jeffrey Herbert. Student, Pa. State Coll., 1927-29. With pub. relation staff Memphis Engring. Dist., Corps Engrs., War Dept., 1929; reporter, rewrite man, drama editor, night city editor, city editor The Comml. Appeal, Memphis, 1931-38, mng. editor, 1939-42; mng. editor Okla. News, Oklahoma City, 1938-39; in charge night ops. press div. Office of Censorship, Washington, 1942-43, asst. dir. censorship, head press div., 1943-45; asst. gen. editorial mgr. Scripps Howard Newspapers, N.Y.C., 1945-75. 2d lt. M.I. Res. Corps AUS, 1930-40. Mem. Chi Phi. Home: Scarsdale N.Y. Died Aug. 3, 1985.

LODGE, GEORGE TOWNSEND, clinical psychologist; b. Kent, Ohio, Nov. 2, 1907; s. Edward Ballard and Martha (Townsend) L.; m. Edith Pardee Bennett, June 18, 1929; children: Ann, David Townsend. BA, Oberlin Coll., 1929; MA, Ohio State U., 1932; PhD, Case Western Res. U., 1940. Diplomate Am. Bd. Profl. Psychology. Chief clin. psychology tng. unit VA, San Francisco, 1946-48; chief psychologist Letterman Gen. Hosp., San Francisco, 1948-51; chief clin. psychologist VA Hosp., Lebanon, Pa., 1951-53, Durham, N.C., 1953-57; staff psychologist VA Hosp., Tuskegee, Ala., 1957, Roanoke, Va., 1957-60; head human factors div. USN Aviation Safety Ctr., Norfolk, Va., 1960-67; prof. psychology, dir. Student Clin. Psychology Ctr. Old Dominion U., Norfolk, 1967-74; prof. psychiatry and behavioral sci. Eastern Va. Med. Sch., 1975-83; mem. state mental health and mental retardation profl. adv. bd., 1970-78. Contbr. articles to profl. jours. Fellow Am. Psychol. Assn., AAS; mem. Internat. Assn. Applied Psychology, Va. Acad. Clin. Psychologists, Va. Psychol. Assn., Southeastern Psychol. Assn., Sigma Xi. Home: Virginia Beach Va. Died Apr. 26, 1983, buried at sea.

LODGE, JOHN DAVIS, ambassador, lawyer, congressman, governor; b. Washington, Oct. 20, 1903; s. George Cabot and Matilda Elizabeth (Frelinghuysen) Lodge; m. Francesca Braggiotti, July 6, 1929; children: Lily, Beatrice. BA, Harvard U., 1925, JD, 1929; postgrad. Ecole de Droit, Paris, 1926; DS. (hon.), Worcester Poly., 1952; LLD (hon.), Trinity Coll., 1951. Assoc. Cravath, de Gersdorff, Swaine and Wood, N.Y.C., 1929-31; pvt. practice law, N.Y.C., 1931-32; with Am. Econ. Found., N.Y.C., 1946-50; mem. Congress from 4th Conn. Dist., 1946-50, mem. fgn. affairs com.; gov. State of Conn., 1950-54; ambassador to Spain, 1955-61, to Argentina, 1969-74, to Switzerland, 1983-85; ambassador on spl. presdl. missions to Panama, Costa Rica and P.R., 1953; mem. Gov. Reagan's Adv. Group on Fgn. and Def. Policies; del. rep. 37th session Gen. Assembly UN, 1983; former mem. Rep. Task Force on Fgn. Policy; exec. com. Nat. Govs. Conf. Speaker, writer, Westport, Conn., 1974-82; motion picture actor U.S., Eng., France, Italy, 1932-42; appeared in N.Y. theater prodns.; contbr. numerous articles on fgn. affairs. Nat. pres.Jr. Achievement, 1963-64; chmn. com. Fgn. Policy Rsch. Inst., U. Pa., 1964-69. Served with USN, 1942-46, to capt. USNR. Decorated Legion d'Honneur, Croix de Guerre with Palm (France); Grand officer, Order of Merit (Italy); Grand Cross, Noble Order of Charles III, Gold medal of Madrid, Gold Medal, Spanish Inst., Grand Cross, Orden de Mayo; Order Polonia Restituta. Mem. Assn. Former Intelligence Officers, Navy League, Res. Officers Assn., Western Conn. Ret. Officers Assn., Am. Legion, V.F.W., Conn. Republican Labor League, Harvard Alumni Assn., Former Mems. of Congress, Fgn. Service Assn., Mexican Acad. Internat. Law, N.Y. Bar Assn., Inter-Am. Bar Assn., Explorers Club, French Legion of Honor, Phi Beta Kappa. Clubs: Chowder and Marching (founder mem.), Grange, Harvard, Fairfield County Hunt, Dutch Treat, Nat. Press, DACOR House, Army and Navy. Died Oct. 29, 1985; buried Arlington Nat. Cemetery, Washington.

LOEB, CARL M., JR., metallurgist; b. St. Louis, Aug. 10, 1904; s. Carl M. and Adeline (Moses) L.; m. Lucille H. S. Schamberg, Jan. 30, 1929; children: Constance Margaret (Mrs. Cohn), Carl M. III, Peter Kenneth. B.S., Princeton, 1926; M.S., Mass. Inst. Tech., 1928. Metall. work Central Alloy Steel Corp., Canton, O., 1928-29, Anaconda Copper Mining Co., Mont., 1929-32; with AMAX Inc. (formerly Climax Molybdenum Co.), Detroit, 1932-85; dist. metallurgist AMAX Inc. (formerly Climax Molybdenum Co.), N.Y.C., 1933-37; v.p. in charge devel., publicity AMAX Inc. (formerly Climax Molybdenum Co.), 1937-54, dir., 1948-85, mem. exec. com., 1960-85, chmn., 1975-77; ltd. partner Loeb, Rhoades & Co., 1955-76. Chmn. com. on correctional and protectional care; also mem. exec. com. N.Y. State com. 1960 White House Conf. Children and Youth; mem. tech. assistance com. White House Conf., 1970; pres. Community Council Greater N.Y., 1953-60, chmn., 1960-62; trustee Nat. Council on Crime and Delinquency, 1963-82, v.p., 1966-67, pres., 1967-72, vice chmn., 1972-81, hon. chmn., 1981-82; chmn. N.Y.C. Bd. Correction, 1957-61; past v.p. Nat. Jewish Welfare Bd.; mem. commn. on correctional facilities and services Am. Bar Assn., 1970-76; cons. Commn. on Rev. of Nat. Policy toward Gambling, 1975-76; Bd. dirs. Day Care and Child Devel. Council Am., 1962-70; Mem. corp. devel. com. Mass. Inst. Tech., 1966—; pres. Nat. Crime Prevention Council, 1982-85 . Mem. S.A.R. Republican. Clubs: LaQuinta (Calif.) Country; Engineers (N.Y.C.), Princeton (N.Y.C.); Century Country (White Plains, N.Y.); Tower (Princeton). Home: New York N.Y. Died Apr. 13, 1985.

LOEHR, MAX JOHANNES JOSEPH, curator, art historian, educator; b. Chemnitz, Germany, Dec. 4, 1903; came to U.S., 1951; naturalized, 1957; s. Valentin and Minna (Lange) L.; m.Irmgard Kistenfeger, Aug. 31, 1928; children: Klaus Friedrich, Thomas Michael. Student, Berlin (Germany) U., 1933-34; Dr.phil., Munich (Germany) U., 1936; MA (hon.), Harvard U. Asst. curator Museum für Völkerkunde, Munich, 1936-40; dir. Sino-German Inst., Peking, China, 1941-45; assoc. prof. Tsingjua U., Peking, 1947-48; curator Museum Für Völkerkunde, Munich, 1950-51; lectr. Far Eastern art U. Munich, 1950-51; prof. Far Eastern art U. Mich., 1951-60; Abby Aldrich Rockefeller prof. Oriental art Harvard U., 1960-74. Editor: Sinologische Arbeiten, Peking, 1943-45; Far Eastern editor: Arts Orientalis, 1954-60; author: Chinese Art: Symbols and Images, 1967, Chinese Landscape Woodcuts, 1968, Ritual Vessels of Bronze Age China, 1968; also articles on Chinese art and archaeology; co-editor Harvard Jour. Asian Studies. Hon. rsch. assoc. Freer Gallery Art, Washington, 1952-60; Guggenheim fellow, 1957-58. Home: Lexington Mass. Died Sept. 15, 1988.

LOEW, MICHAEL, artist; b. N.Y.C., May 8, 1907; s. Samuel Jacob and Judith (Fass) L.; m. Mildred Clare Rodman, Oct. 15, 1940; 1 son, Jonathan. Student, Art Students League, N.Y.C., 1926-29, Academie Scadinave, Paris, 1930; with, Orthon Friesze, Hans Hoffmann Sch. Fine Arts, N.Y.C., 1946-49, Atelier Leger, Paris, 1950. Artist-in-residence Mus. Art Sch., Portland, Oreg., 1956-57; instr. in fine arts Sch. Visual Arts, N.Y.C., from 1958; co-chmn. dept. fine arts Sch. Visual Arts, 1961-68; vis. prof. U. Calif., Berkeley, 1961; guest lectr. U. Calif., 1966. Contbr. articles to art jours.; One-man shows, Artists Gallery, N.Y.C., 1949, Rose Fried Gallery, N.Y.C., 1953, 55, 57, 59, Portland (Oreg.) Art Mus., 1956, T.K. Gallery, Provincetown, Mass., 1959, Holland Goldowsky Gallery, Chgo., 1960, U. Calif., Berkeley, 1960, 66, Stable Gallery, N.Y.C., 1961, 62, 65, Landmark Gallery, N.Y.C., 1973, 76, Marilyn Pearl Gallery, N.Y.C., 1977, 79, 81, 82, 84, group shows include, Whitney Mus. Am. Art, N.Y.C., 1949, 61, 75, 77, Met. Mus. Art, N.Y.C., 1952, Mus. Modern art touring exhibit, N.Y.C., 1963, Art Inst. Chgo., 1964, Am. Abstract Artists, Europe, U.S., 1950-79, Newark Mus., 1978-79, Queens Mus., N.Y., 1980, Inst. Arts and Letters, N.Y.C., 1982, Portland (Maine) Mus., 1984, Montreal Mus. Fine Arts, 1984; represented in permanent collections, including, Whitney Mus. Art, Phila. Mus. Fine Arts, Joseph Hirshhorn Mus., Washington, Birla Acad. Art and Culture, Calcutta, India, Sheldon Meml. Mus., Lincoln, Nebr., Knox-Albright Mus., Buffalo, Portland (Maine) Mus., also other public collections and numerous pvt. collections; commd. to paint murals (with William De Kooning) Hall of Pharmacy, N.Y. World's Fair, 1939; Post Offices Amherst, Ohio and Belle Vernon, Pa, 1942. Served with USN, 1943-45. Recipient Ford Found. award 67th Ann. Am. Exhbn., Chgo. Art Inst., 1964, 1st Ann. Artist-Tchr. award Sch. Visual Arts, N.Y.C., 1982; Sadie A. May fellow, 1929; Nat. Endowment Arts fellowship grantee, 1976-77; Guggenheim Meml. Found. fellowship grantee, 1979-80. Mem. Am. Abstract Artists, Fedn. Modern Painters and Sculptors. Home: New York N.Y. Died Nov. 13, 1985.

LOEWE, FREDERICK, composer; b. Vienna, Austria, June 10, 1901; came to U.S., 1924; s. Edmund and Rose L.; m. Ernestine Zwerline (div.). Student piano with, Ferruccio Busoni and Eugene d'Albert; composition and orchestration with, Nicholas Reznicek; D. Mus. (hon.), U. Redlands; D.F.A. (hon.), NYU. Debut as concert pianist, Berlin, 1914, Carnegie Hall, 1942; writer music for Broadway musicals; collaborator with Alan Jay Lerner, music for My Fair Lady, 1956, The Day Before Spring, 1945, Brigadoon, 1947, Camelot, also producer, 1960, Gigi, 1973, Paint Your Wagon, 1951, What's Up, 1943; The Little Prince, 1974; composer, musical comedies, Salute to Spring, 1937, Great Lady, 1938, Life of the Party, 1942, Petticoat Fever, 1935; score for movie Gigi, 1959; wrote music for TV prodns. Salute to Lerner and Loewe, 1961, The Lerner and Loewe Songbook, 1962. Recipient Hollander medal Berlin, 1923, Tony award for music, My Fair Lady, 1957, for musical score, Gigi, 1974, Motion Picture Acad. award for song Gigi, 1958, Kennedy Ctr. honor, 1986. Home: Palm Springs Calif. Died Feb. 14, 1988.

LOEWY, RAYMOND, industrial designer; b. Paris, Nov. 5, 1893; naturalized, 1938; s. Maximilian and Marie (Labalme) L.; m. Viola Erickson, 1948; 1 dau., Laurence. Student, Paris U., 1910; grad. engring., Ecole de Lanneau, 1918; D.F.A., U. Cin., 1956, Art Center Coll. Design, 1970. Art dir. Westinghouse Electric Co., 1929; started pvt. orgn. of indsl. design 1929; founder Raymond Loewy Internat. (cons. designers U.S. and fgn. corps., in fields of product design, transp., package, retail specialized bldg. design, corpora; cons. to NASA on Skylab sta., recuperable earth shuttle orbiter, Saturn-Apollo applications, from 1967; indsl. design cons. to USSR Com. for Sci. and Tech., 1974-86; Raymond Loewy expn. Smithsonian Instn., Washington, 1975; mem. Superior Council Indsl. Design, France, from 1975; lectr. Mass. Inst. Tech., N.Y. U., Harvard Grad. Sch. Bus. Adminstrn., Columbia U., Pratt Inst., Royal Soc. Arts, London, Leningrad Inst. Arts, Moscow Com. Sci. and Tech., Indsl. Design and Ergonometry.; Bd. dirs. Art Center Coll. Design, French Inst. Am. Author: The Locomotive-Its Aesthetics, 1937, Never Leave Well Enough Alone, 1951, Industrial Design Album, 1979. Mem. Adv. Bd. Vocat. Edn., N.Y.C. Bd. Edn.; mem. exec. bd. Art Center Coll., Los Angeles; mem. adv. com. indsl. designers Coll. Architecture, U Calif. at Los Angeles. Served as capt. C.E., attached t Gen. Staff 5th Army, 1914-18, France; liaison officer A.E.F. Decorated grand officier French Legion o Honor, Croix de Guerre (4 citations), Interallied Medal Award Hon. Designer to Industry Brit. Royal Soc. Arts London, 1937, award Pres. of France, 1980; grand priz Internat Conv., ICSID, 1981; named One of 10(Makers of the 20th Century London Times, 1969, On of 100 Who Shaped Am. Life mag., 1979. Fellow Am Soc. Indsl. Engrs. (past pres.), Royal Soc. Arts London mem. French C. of C. of U.S. (v.p. 1958), Soc Automotive Engrs., ASME, Am. Acad. Achievement Soc. Naval Architects and Marine Engrs., Am. Soc Space Medicine, Am. Hist. R.R. Assn. (hon. life mem.). Club: Racquet (Palm Springs, Calif.). Home: Wes Palm Beach Fla. Died 1986.

LOFTSGARD, LAUREL DUANE, university pre sident; b. Hoople, N.D., Sept. 4, 1926; s. Theodore G and Dora (Jore) L.; m. Carol June Evenson, Dec. 27 1951; children: Bradley Trent, Cynthia Sue. B.S., N.D State U., 1954; Ph.D., Ia. State U., 1958. With N.D State U., 1958-87, prof. agrl. econs., 1963-87; dir. N.D Water Resources Research Inst., 1965-66, v.p. acad. affairs, 1966-68, acting pres., 1968, pres., 1968-87; dir Met. Fed. Savs. and Loan Assn., Fargo. Contbr. articles to mags. and bulls. Civilian aide to sec. Army for N.D., 1975-77. Served with inf. AUS, 1946-47; with Corps of Engrs. 1950-51. Mem. Am. Farm Econ. Assn. Western Farm Econ. Assn. (certificate of merit 1964) Neuropsychiatric Inst. (bd. dirs.), Fargo C. of C., Am Legion, Sigma Xi, Alpha Zeta, Gamma Sigma Delta Phi Delta Kappa, Phi Kappa Phi. Lodges: Elks Kiwanis, Eagles. Home: Fargo N.D. Died Oct. 1, 1987 buried Riverside Cemetery, Fargo.

LOGAN, ALBERT BOYD, lawyer; b. Colorad Springs, Colo., Jan. 27, 1909; s. Glen Hayes and Mar garet (McGee) L.; m. Martha Elizabeth Hutchison, Sept 28, 1934; children: Marla Lee Logan Hollingsworth Glenda Sue Logan Harrison. A.B., U. Colo., 1930 J.D., 1932. Bar: Colo. 1932. Sole practice Colorad Springs, 1932-56; with Office Solicitor, Dept. Interior Denver, 1956-66; counsel Indian Claims Commn. Washington, 1966-70, Office Gen. Counsel, VA, 1970-78; pres. Nat. Inst. Jud. Dynamics, Washington and Colorado Springs.; lectr. jud. problems; exec. dir N.Am. Judges Assn., 1960-67; sec., trustee Jud. Research Found., Washington, 1960-68; cons. Am. Judicature Soc., Nat. Council Alcoholism, U. Colo. Sch Alcohol Studies, Colo. Commn. Alcoholism, Inst. Law and Psychiatry, Mil.-Jud. Conf. Hwy. Safety, Nat Council Indian Opportunity, Internat. Acad. Metabology, (Nat. Center Alcoholic Studies), 1975; chmn. com. on criminal justice Nat. Coalition for Adequate Alcoholism Programs; founder Concerned Lawyers, Inc. Author: Struggle For Equal Justice, 1968, Justice in Jeopardy, 1973, With Liberty and Justice for All, 1972; editor: Municipal Ct. Rev., 1960-67, Municipal Ct. Briefs, 1960-67; contbr. to legal periodicals. Trustee, bd. dirs. Harmony Found., Inc.; bd. dirs. Youth Recognition, Ltd., Riegel Ctr. of Penrose Hosp., Colorado Springs. Served with USMC, 1944-45. Recipient Beyond Call of Duty award Nat. Assn. Mcpl. Judges, 1961; Disting. Service award Nat. Council on Alcoholism, 1979, Reed McDougall award, 1985; Disting. Service award Harmony Found., 1985. Mem. Fed. Bar Assn., ABA (chmn. com. alcohol and drug abuse 1975-78), Colo. Bar Assn., Am. Legion, Am. Judicature Soc., U.S. Jaycees (nat. dir.), N.Am. Judges Assn. (founder, exec. dir., hon. life mem., Amicus Curiae award 1964), Internat. Platform Assn., Order Ky. Cols., Phi Alpha Delta, Sigma Delta Chi, Alpha Tau Omega. Clubs: Colorado Springs Press (Colorado Springs), El Paso (Colorado Springs), Exchange (Colorado Springs) (pres.); Nat. Lawyers, Nat. Press. Home: Colorado Springs Colo. Died March 19, 1987.

LOGAN, JOHN A., retail management counseling executive; b. Athens, Ohio, Feb. 4, 1896; s. Earl C. and Elizabeth (Spaulding) L.; m. Rebecca Pollard Guggenheim, Apr. 1962; children by previous marriage—John A., Jerome H. (dec.). Ph.B., U. Chgo., 1921; LL.D., N.M. State U., 1957. Salesman, mgr. Canadian dept., H.M. Byllesby & Co., Chgo., 1921-27; sales mgr. Blair & Co., Chgo., 1927-29; partner Ames, Emerich & Co., Chgo., 1929-31; asso. James O. McKinsey (mgmt. counsel), Chgo., 1931-34; lectr. Sch. Bus., U. Chgo., 1931-32; exec. v.p. Food and Grocery Chain Stores of Am.; founder, pres., dir. successor orgn. Nat. Assn. Food Chains, Washington, 1934-61; founder, vice chmn., dir. Internat. Assn. Chain Stores, 1953-86; pres. John A. Logan Assos. (mgmt. counsel), 1961-76; dir. Drug Fair, Inc., Washington Channel Waterfront Inc.; spl. adviser Office Internat. Trade Fairs, U.S. Dept. Commerce; adviser Dept. of Agr., Dept. of Treasury; mem. Pres.'s Citizens Food Com., 1948; assisted devel. Market Center Operation procurement of perishables for mil., Food Stamp Plan and; Surplus Food Mktg. Program; sponsor, planner, supr. industry Dept. State visitor study groups from Germany, Japan, Poland, Mex., Eng., Italy, Spain, others, 1950-59; ofcl. coordinator joint govt.-food industries projects, Italy, Yugoslavia, Spain, Germany, Belgium, India, others, 1956-59; mem. panel Fed. Aid to Agr.; mem. exec. com. Greater Nat. Capitol Com.; trustee trust funds. Contbr. articles to profl. jours. Mem. inaugural ball com. for

Pres. Truman, Eisenhower (2), Johnson, Nixon; chmn. Cherry Blossom Ball, 1949-64, Inaugural Ball for Johnson-Humphrey.; Sec.-treas. Overseas Citizens for Johnson-Humphrey, 1964; alternate U.S. rep. to UNESCO Gen. Conf., Paris, 1968; Trustee Ramiose Found., 2 Marjorie Merriweather Post Founds.; mem. profl. adv. com. D.C. Assn. Mental Health; trustee Nat. Council for Community Improvement, Menninger Found., Arthritis Inst. Enlisted U.S. Army, 1917; served with 258th Aero Squadron, A.E.F. discharged as 1st lt., Air Service U.S. Army, 1919; dir. World War I overseas flyers. Decorated Purple Heart U.S.A.; ufficille Order of Merit Italy; Queen Isabella Sword Spain; comdr. Order of Merit Fed. Republic Germany; named to Hall of Fame in Distribution, Pioneer in Agrl. Mktg.; spl. tribute for lifetime contribution to Am. food industry Food Mkgt. Inst. 1985. Mem. S.A.R., Disabled Officers Assn., Mil. Order World War, Am. Legion (past comdr.), Order Ky. Cols., Fgn. Policy Assn. (dir.), English Speaking Union (dir.), Beta Theta Pi. Episcopalian (vestry, chmn. Canvass 1965). Clubs: Mason. (Washington), Metropolitan (Washington), Nat. Press (Washington), City Tavern (Washington), 1925 F Street (Washington), Burning Tree (Washington), Chevy Chase (Washington); University (Chgo.); Metropolitan (N.Y.C.); Ha' Penny Bay Beach (St. Croix), Yacht (St. Croix), Tennis (St. Croix). Home: Washington D.C. Died Sept. 21, 1986.

LOGAN, JOSHUA, playwright, director, producer; b. Texarkana, Tex., Oct. 5, 1908; s. Joshua Lockwood and Sue (Nabors) L.; m. Nedda Harrigan, 1945; children: Thomas Heggen, Harrigan Lockwood. Student, Culver (Ind.) Mil. Acad., 1922-27, Princeton, 1927-31. Dir., actor, Univ. Players, 1931-35; dir.: stage prodns. On Borrowed Time, 1938, I Married An Angel, 1938, Knickerbocker Holiday, 1938, Two for the Show, 1938, Stars in Your Eyes, 1939, Mornings at Seven, 1939, Charlie's Aunt, 1940, By Jupiter, 1942, This is the Army, 1942, Annie Get Your Gun, 1946, Happy Birthday, 1946, Wish You Were Here, 1952, Picnic, 1953 (Antoinette Perry award for best dir. 1953), Blue Denim, 1958, There Was A Little Girl, 1960, Ready When You Are, C.B, 1964; producer, dir.: stage prodns. John Loves Mary, 1947, Kind Sir, 1953, Middle of the Night, 1956, World of Suzie Wong, 1958, Horowitz and Mrs. Washington, 1980; co-author, dir.: stage prodns. Mister Roberts, 1948 (co-recipient Antoinette Perry awards for best play and best author 1948); co-author, dir., producer: stage prodns. South Pacific, 1949 (Antoinette Perry award for best dir. 1950, co-recipient for best author 1950), Fanny, 1954, author, dir., producer, Wisteria Trees, 1950; dir.: motion pictures I Met My Love Again, 1938, Picnic, 1955, Bus Stop, 1956, Sayonara, 1957, South Pacific, 1957, Camelot, 1967, Paint Your Wagon, 1969, Look to the Lilies, 1970; dir., producer: motion pictures Tall Story, 1959, Fanny, 1961; dir., co-producer: motion pictures All American, 1961, Mr. President, 1962, Tiger Tiger Burning Bright, 1962; dir., producer, co-author: motion pictures Ensign Pulver, 1964 (Recipient Pulitzer prize for South Pacific 1950); Author: autobiography Josh: My Up and Down, In and Out Life, 1976; Movie Stars, Real People, and Me, 1978. Served to capt. USAAF, 1942-46. Club: Triangle (pres. 1930-31). Home: New York N.Y. Died July 12, 1988; buried St. Mathews Ch., Bedford Village, N.Y.

LOGAN, MAURICE, artist; b. San Francisco, Feb. 21, 1886; s. George William and Elizabeth Ann (Robinson) L; m. Bertha Dorothy Kipke, July 12, 1915; children: Richard Maurice, Jean Elizabeth Logan Rees. Student, Partington Art Sch., Mark Hopkins Inst. Art,, San Francisco, 1907-13; MFA, Coll. Arts and Crafts, Oakland, Calif. Painter backgrounds for exhibits Acad. Scis., Golden Gate Park, San Francisco, backgrounds in Africa with Leslie Simpson for exhbn. Exposition Park, L.A.; dir. Coll. Arts and Crafts, Oakland. Mem. Nat. Acad. Art, N.Y.C., Bohemian Club (San Francisco) (bd. dirs.). Home: Oakland Calif. †

LOMBARDY, ROSS DAVID, food company executive; b. Cleve., Mar. 20, 1920; s. David Ross and Minnie (Roberto) L.; m. Louise Adelaide McMahon, Oct. 28, 1940; children: Louise, Ross Daivd, David J., Kathleen L., Mary A., Thomas J. Student pub. schs. Pres. David Lombardy Co., Cleve., 1942-57; v.p., sec. Seaway Foods Inc., Bedford Heights, Ohio, 1957-59, exec. v.p., 1979-88. Recipient Grocery Man of Yr. award, 1973. Mem. Internat. Order Alhambra (grand comdr.). Roman Catholic (pres. Holy Name Soc., 1955). Lodge: K.C. (trustee). Home: Lyndhurst Ohio. Died Oct. 21, 1988, interred All Souls Cememtery, Chardon, Ohio.

LOMEDICO, THOMAS GAETANO, sculptor; b. N.Y.C., July 11, 1904; s. Philip and Angelina (Cimino) LoM.; m. Leonora Lisciandra, Feb. 23, 1952. Student, Beaux Arts Inst. Design, N.Y.C., evenings 1920-30. Sculptor pvt. studio N.Y.C., from 1935; lectr. Sch. Indsl. Arts, N.Y.C., Students Craft Inst., N.Y.C.; instr., lectr. Nat. Acad. Sch. Fine Arts. Designer archtl. sculpture, 1920-35; works include eight life size sculptures for Wilmington (N.C.) P.O. and Courthouse, 1936, Am. Family group for Met. Life Ins. Co. exhibit N.Y. World's Fair, 1938, ceramic sculpture for Crookville (Ohio) P.O., 1941, Aviator sculpture, Artists Victory, 1942, Herbert Adams Meml. award medal Nat. Sculpture Soc., 1946 (J. Sandoed award 1956), 38th issue Soc. of Medalists, 1948, medal for 2d assembly World Council Chs., Evanston, Ill., 1954, portrait plaque Charles W. Goodyear A. Conger Goodyear, Lasker award Albert and Mary Lasker Found., Walter W. Moyer Meml., Walter E. Otto trophy Medallic Art Co., Cincuentenario medal for U. P.R., portraits of Jack Baar Met. Life Ins. Co., cellist Carlo Pitello, Met. Opera Assn., Nicholas Papalcure, Woodhaven, L.I., Peter Cimino, Bklyn. Pub. Service award Inst. Life Ins., N.Y.C., Samuel Musman Meml. fountain, Woodbury, Conn., 6 statues Nat. Shrine Immaculate Conception, Washington, meml. portrait Charles H. Mayo medal Freemasons, Capt. Cook medal Brit. Commemorative Soc., Madame Marie Curie medal Franklin Mint, Patrick Henry medal Hall of Fame Gt. Ams., NYU, sculptures for N.Y.C. pub. schs., 6 10-foot sculptures for Ch. of Immaculate Conception, Washington, 1956; collaborator statuary for Lansdowne Room Met. Mus. Art; works represented in Met. Mus. Art, Mus. Natural History, Whitney Mus. Am. Art, Pa. Acad. Fine Arts, Nat. Acad., Salmagundi Club, Archtl. League, Rockland Found. Recipient citation for medals submitted in competition Golden Anniversary N.Y.C., 1948, Mrs. Louis Bennet award, 1952, hon. mention sculpture exhbn. Archtl. League, 1953, Alice Freeman Palmer award, Herbert Adam medal for contbrn. to sculpture, 1987. Fellow Nat. Sculpture Soc. (Lindsay Morris Meml. award 1952, Herbert Adams Meml. medal for advancement of sculpture 1987 which he designed), Am. Numis. Soc. (J. Stanford Saltus award medal), Tappantown Hist. Soc. (pres.), Le Club de la Medaille (Paris), Sculptors Guild, Allied Arts Am., Rockland Found., NAD. Home: Tappan N.Y. Died Nov. 29, 1985, buried Tappan, N.Y.

LONDON, KURT LUDWIG, political scientist, author; b. Berlin, Sept. 12, 1900; s. Maurice and Betty L.; ed. univs. Berlin, Heidelberg, Wuerzburg, Paris, London; Ph.D., U. Wuerzburg, 1928; m. Jean Louise Fraser, May 12, 1951. Mem. faculty CCNY, 1938-42, Bklyn. Coll., 1940-43; with OWI, 1943-45; sr. regional specialist Dept. State, Washington, 1945-47, Dept. Def., Washington, 1947-62; prof. internat. affairs George Washington U., Washington, 1962-70, prof. emeritus, 1970-85, founder, dir. Inst. Sino-Soviet Studies, 1962-70; author: Backgrounds of Conflict, 1945; How Foreign Policy is Made, 1949; The Seven Soviet Arts, 1938; The Permanent Crisis, 1962; The Making of Foreign Policy-East and West, 1965; editor: Unity and Contradiction, 1962; Eastern Europe in Transition, 1966; The Soviet Impact on World Politics, 1974; The Soviet Union in World Politics, 1980. Served to lt. col. USAFR, 1950-58. Recipient Cert. of Merit with distinction U.S. Govt., 1962. Mem. Am. Polit. Sci. Assn., Am. Assn. Advancement Slavic Studies, Internat. Studies Assn., Washington Inst. Fgn. Affairs. Unitarian. Club: Cosmos (Washington). Died July 25, 1985; cremated.

LONG, HOWARD RUSK, journalism educator, editor; b. Columbia, Mo., July 30, 1906; s. Connor Melbourne and Carrie (Bramblett) L.; m. Margaret Helen Carney, May 3, 1931; children: Nancy Long Bearss, Joseph Carney. BJ, AB, U. Mo., 1930, MA, 1941, PhD, 1948. Pub. Crane (Mo.) Chronicle, 1934-40; prof. U. Mo., 1940-50; mgr. Mo. Press Assn., 1941-49, Long Ranch. livestock farm, Rochester, Ind., 1950-53; chmn. dept. journalism So. Ill. U., 1953-70, dir. Sch. Journalism, 1970-74; vis. prof. Grad. Sch. Journalism, Nat. Chengchi U., Taipei, Taiwan, 1947-48; guest editor China Post, Taipei, 1947-48. Author: (with Leilyn M. Young) Fifty Years fo Community Service, 1954, The People of Mushan, Life in a Taiwanese Village, 1960, (with H.R. Pratt Boorman) Recalling the Battle of Britain, 1965, Mainstreet Militants, 1977; editor Grassroots Editor, 1960-74, New Horizons in Journalism series, from 1964. Founder, sec. Internat. Soc. Weekly Newspapers Editors, 1955-74. Grantee State Dept., 1957, 64. Mem. Am. Soc. Journalism Sch. Adminstrs. (pres. 1960), Assn. Edn. Journalism, Inst. Journalists (Brit.), Royal Photog. Soc. Gt. Britain, Internat. Press Inst., China Acad. (academician), Nat. Inst. Journalists (Eng.), U. Mo. Journalism Alumni Assn. (pres. 1940), Mo. Hist. Soc. (life), Rotary, Kappa Alpha Mu, Kappa Tau Alpha, Alpha Delta Sigma, Sigma Delta Chi. Home: Carbondale Ill. Deceased.

LONG, J. EMERY, lawyer, banker; b. N.Y.C., June 13, 1919; s. Frank R. and Ruby (Smith) L.; m. Beverly Glenn, May 6, 1950. AB, Columbia U., 1941, JD, 1946. Bar: N.Y. 1946. With trust dept. Chem. Bank, N.Y.C., 1946-48; v.p. Union Trust Co., Providence, 1948-51; sr. v.p. trust dept. Indsl. Nat. Bank R.I., 1951-82. Trustee U. R.I. Found.; chmn. of R.I. Gov.'s Commn. on Mental Health, 1963-65; bd. dirs. Hospice Care of R.I., Hearing and Speech Svcs. of R.I., Am. Bankers Assn. Trust Coun.; trustee of U. R.I. Found.; mem. R.I. Estate Planning Coun.; deacon Cen. Congregational Ch.; active United Way of Southeastern New Eng. Capt. USAAF, 1942-46, ETO, MTO. Mem. Univ. Club, Turk's Head Club, Phi Delta Phi. Congregationalist (deacon 1970-74). Home: Providence R.I. Died Dec. 28, 1987; entombed Swan Point Cemetery, Providence.

LONG, KENNETH C., public utilities executive; b. Chgo., Jan. 13, 1892; s. Sumner C. and Frances (Cook) L.; m. Dorothy V. Law, Sept. 11, 1925; 1 child, Nancy Delores. Ed., Dayton-Steele High Sch.; M in Industry (hon.), Purdue U., 1942. Successively electrician's helper, meter test asst., meter reader, meter tester, power salesman, power engr., comml. mgr. Dayton (Ohio) Power & Light Co., 1913-31, acting gen. mgr., 1934, v.p., assoc. gen. mgr., 1937, pres., gen. mgr., 1946-58, chmn. bd., from 1958; bd. dirs. Peoples Bank & Trust Co. Assoc. bd. lay trustees U. Dayton. With U.S. Army, 1918-19. Mem. Newcomen Soc., Ky. Cols., Dayton C. of C., Ohio C. of C., Community Chest, Ohio Safety Coun., Dayton Art Inst., Dayton Dist. Devel. Com., Coun. World Affairs, Am. Gas Assn., Edison Electric Inst., Edison Pioneers Inc., Am. Legion, Dayton Bicycle Club, Dayton Country club, Engineers Club, Theta Xi. Home: Dayton Ohio. †

LONGMAN, WILLIAM, publishing executive; b. London, Nov. 14, 1882; s. Charles James and Harriet Anne (Evans) L.; m. Katherine Elizabeth Stuart, Dec. 31, 1930. Student, Harrow Sch., Oxford U. Dir. Longmans Green & Co., 1909; chmn. Longmans Green & Co., Ltd., 1936-63, also bd. dirs. Author: Tokens of the Eighteenth Century, 1916. Mem. Book Trade Employers Fedn. (chmn. 1923-24), Pub. Assn. Gt. Britain and Ireland (pres. 1929-30), Croquet Assn. (chmn. 1924-26), Booksellers Provident Assn. (pres. 1925-46, Worshipful Co. Stationers and Newspaper Makers (liveryman), United Univ. Club, Hurlingham Club, Roehampton Club. Home: London Eng. †

LONGSHORE, WILLIAM LEVI, lawyer; b. Columbiana, Ala., Jan. 31, 1892; s. Adolphus P. and Fannie Terrell (Jennings) L.; m. Jatie Lawrence, Aug. 30, 1924; children: William Levi, Thomas L. Student, Howard Coll., 1907-10; LLB, U. Ala., 1913. Bar: Ala. 1913. Pvt. practice Birmingham, Ala.; judge 18th Jud. Cir. Ala., 1920-22; asst. U.S. atty. No. Dist. Ala., 1931-33, U.S. atty., from 1956. Vice chmn. Rep. State Exec. Com. Ala., 1954-56; del. Rep. Nat. Conv., 1940, 48, alt. del., 1944, 52. Lt. U.S. Army, World War I. Mem. Ala. Bar Assn., Birmingham Bar Assn., Sigma Nu. Baptist. Home: Birmingham Ala. †

LONGSWORTH, LEWIS GIBSON, chemist; b. Somerset, Ky., Nov. 16, 1904; s. Lawrence Roscoe and Sarah Elizabeth (Nichols) L.; m. Helen Frances Cady, June 24, 1929; children: Anne Louise, Ralph Cady, Stella Caroline. AB, Southwestern Coll., Winfield, Kans., 1925; AM, Kans. U., 1927, PhD, 1928; hon. deg., Rockefeller U., 1978. NRC fellow chemistry Rockefeller Inst. Med. Rsch. (now Rockefeller U.), 1928-30; asst. Rockefeller Inst. Med. Rsch. (now Rockefeller U.), N.Y.C., 1930-39, assoc., 1939-45, mem., 1949-70; prof. emeritus Rockefeller Inst. Med. Rsch. (now Rockefeller U.), 1970-81. Contbr. numerous articles on chemistry to sci. jours. Mem. NAS, Am. Chem. Soc. (award 1973), N.Y. Acad. Scis., Harvey Soc., Phi Beta KAppa, Sigma Xi, Alpha Chi Sigma. Republican. Congregationalist. Home: Flushing N.Y. Died Aug. 9, 1981.

LOOMIS, JOHN EDWARD, lawyer; b. Wichita, Kans., May 9, 1921; s. Frederick Herbert and Claudine Marguerite (Rathman) L.; m. Dorothy Rudolph Culver, Feb. 14, 1959; children: John, Jamie. B.S.C., U. N.D., 1943; postgrad., U. Mich. Law Sch., 1946-47; J.D., Yale, 1949. Bar: Wis. 1949, D.C. 1962, U.S. Supreme Ct. 1970. Assoc. firm Miller, Mack & Fairchild, Milw., 1949-57; assoc. dir. div. trading and exchanges SEC, 1957-58, assoc. dir. div. corp. regulation, 1958-59; gen. counsel Devel. Loan Fund, 1959-61; ptnr. firm Loomis, Owen, Fellman & Howe, Washington, from 1962, sr. ptnr., from 1971. Author: Public Money Sources for Overseas Trade and Investment, 1963, International Finance: Official Agencies and U.S. Business, 1970; mem. adv. bd. Securities REgulation and Law Report, from 1970. 1st lt. USAAF, World War II, PTO. Mem. Am., Fed., Wis., D.C. bar assns., Internat. Club, Capitol Hill Club, Yale Club, Sigma Alpha Epsilon, Delta Sigma Pi. Episcopalian. Home: McLean Va. Died Mar. 15, 1984; buried Nat. Meml. Park, Va.

LOOS, ANITA (MRS. JOHN EMERSON), author; b. Sisson, Calif., Apr. 26, 1893; d. Richard Beers and Minnie Ella (Smith) L.; m. John Emerson, 1919. Ed. high sch., San Diego. Scenario writer with D. W. Griffith 5 yrs., Douglas Fairbanks 3 yrs., Constance Talmadge 2 yrs. (all in collaboration with John Emerson); author: Gentlemen Prefer Blondes, 1925 (also producer of play); But Gentlemen Marry Brunettes, 1928; (with John Emerson) The Whole Town's Talking, The Fall of Eve, Cherries Are Ripe, The Social Register; also (motion pictures) Red Headed Woman, Hold Your Man, Girl From Missouri, San Francisco, Saratoga, Great Canadian, Alaska, The Women, Blossoms in the Dust, I Married an Angel, The Pirate (scenario for M.G.M.), Happy Birthday (play, starring Helen Hayes), 1946, Gentlemen Prefer Blondes (stage play with music), 1949, A Mouse is Born, 1950, This Brunette Prefers Work, 1956, Gentlemen Still Prefer Blondes, No Mother to Guide Her, 1961, Mama Steps Out, They Met in Bombay, A Girl Like I, 1966, Kiss Hollywood Good-by, 1974, The Talmadge Girls, 1978. Died Aug. 18, 1981.

LOPEZ, ROBERT SABATINO, history educator; b. Genoa, Italy, Oct. 8, 1910; s. Sabatino and Sisa (Tabet) L.; m. Claudia Kirschen, Aug. 27, 1946; children—Michael S., Lawrence C. Litt.D., U. Milan, Italy, 1932; Ph.D., U. Wis., 1942; H.L.D. (hon.), Hebrew Union Coll., U. Rome, U. Montpellier. Asst. prof. Tchrs. Colls. of, Cagliari, 1933-34, Pavia, 1934-35, Genoa, 1935-36; asst. prof. U. Genoa, 1936-38; research asst. U. Wis., 1939-42; script editor Italian sect. OWI, N.Y.C., 1942-43; lectr. history Bklyn. Coll., 1943-44; fgn. news editor CBS, N.Y.C., 1944-45; lectr. history Columbia, 1945-46; asst. prof. history Yale U., 1946-50, assoc. prof., 1950-55, prof. history, 1955-62, Durfee prof. history, 1962-70, Sterling prof. history, 1970-81, chmn. medieval studies, 1964-75; vis. prof. Wesleyan U., 1947-48, 49-50, Middlebury Coll., 1955, 59, Coll. de France, 1977, Tel Aviv U., 1981-82. Author: Medieval Trade in the Mediterranean World, 1955, The Tenth Century: How Dark the Dark Ages?, 1959, The Birth of Europe, 1962, The Three Ages of the Italian Renaissance, 1970, The Commercial Revolution of the Middle Ages, 1971, Byzantium and the World Around It, 1978, La Città Medievale, 1984; mem. editorial bd.: UNESCO Com. Urban History; contbr. articles to profl. publs. Guggenheim fellow, 1948- 49, 54; Fulbright fellow in Italy, 1957-58; Lauro De Bosis lectr. Italian history Harvard, 1960-61; Nat. Found. Humanities sr. fellow, 1967-68; Rockefeller Found. resident fellow Villa Serbelloni, 1972, 74. Fellow Mediaeval Acad. Am., Am. Acad. Arts and Scis., Società Ligure di Storia Patria; corr. fellow Brit. Acad., Académie des Inscriptions, Institut Belgian Acad., Accademia dei Lincei, Israel Acad. Arts and Scis.; mem. Soc. for Italian Hist. Studies (pres. 1966-68), New Eng. Medieval Conf. (pres. 1974-75), Am. Hist. Assn., Econ. Hist. Soc. Home: New Haven Conn. Died July 6, 1986.

LORD, D. W., heavy equipment company executive. With Finning Ltd., Vancouver, B.C., Can., 1960, several sr. sales mgmt. positions, v.p. br. ops., 1976-84, exec. v.p., 1984-88, pres., 1988, also bd. dirs. Died Nov. 19, 1988.

LORD, SAMUEL, banker; b. Steele County, Minn., Sept. 24, 1929; s. Samuel and Mary-Louise (Lyon) L.; m. Jette Jacobsen, Dec. 31, 1966; children: Samuel, Anne-Marie. AB cum laude, Amherst (Mass.) Coll., 1951; JD, U. N.Mex., 1954; grad., Stonier Grad. Sch. Banking, Rutgers U., 1962; grad. Advanced Mgmt. Program, Harvard U., 1965. Bar: Minn. 1954, N.Y. 1957, Wash. 1977. V.p. Citibank N.A., Citicorp., N.Y.C., 1954-76; sr. v.p., sec. Rainier Bancorp., Rainier Nat. Bank, Seattle, 1976-86; bd. dirs. Lord Corp., Erie, Pa.; mem. thesis panel examiners Stonier Grad. Sch. Banking; mem. adv. com. corp. debt financing project Am. Bar Found. Trustee Am.-Scandinavian Found., N.Y.C., 1971-86. Mem. ABA, Wash. Bar Assn., Assn. Bar City N.Y., Am. Soc. Corp. Secs., Rainier Club, Wing Point Golf and Country Club. Home: Bainbridge Island Wash. Died Feb. 14, 1986.

LORENTZEN, EDEN CHRISTIAN, business management educator; b. Nephi, Utah, Jan. 24, 1892; s. Godtfred and Christina (Smith) L.; m. Ruth Blake, June 6, 1917; children: Bertha, Keith, E. Karl, Robert Vern (dec.). BS in Commerce, Utah State Agrl. Coll., 1921; AM in Econs., U. Calif., 1923; PhD in Mktg., Northwestern U., 1943. Prin., tchr. sch. in Deweyville, Utah, 1916-17; tchr. social scis. Wasatch High Sch., Heber City, Utah, 1919-21; part-time tchr. Armstrong Schs. Bus., Berkeley, Calif., 1922-23; instr. U. Utah, Salt Lake City, 1923-25, asst. prof., 1925-29, assoc. prof., 1933-41, prof., from 1942, head dept., from 1946; vis. prof. Northwestern U., summer 1939; dir. rsch. tire div. Goodrich Silvertown, Inc., 1929-31, B.F. Goodrich Co., Akron, Ohio, 1931-32; reasercher A.C. Nelson Co., Chgo., summer 1933. Mem. AAUP, Acad. Mgmt., Am. Inst. Mgmt., Utah Edn. Assn., Pacific Econ. Conf., Aztec Club, Men's Faculty Club U. Utah, Delta Sigma Pi, Phi Kappa Phi, Beta Gamma Sigma. †

LORENZ, KONRAD ZACHARIAS, zoologist; b. Vienna, Austria, Nov. 7, 1903; s. Adolf and Emma (Lecher) L.; student medicine, N.Y.C., Vienna, MD, 1928; PhD in Zoology, Vienna, 1933; PhD (hon.), U. Leeds, Eng., 1962; MD (hon.), U. Basel, 1966, Yale U., 1967; ScD (hon.), U. Oxford, 1968, Loyola U., Chgo., 1970, Durham, 1972, U. Birmingham, 1974, Vet. U., Vienna, 1980; m. Margarethe Gebhardt, June 24, 1927; children—Thomas, Dagmar, Agnes Lorenz von Cranach. Asst. 2d, Anat. Inst., Vienna, 1928-35; lectr. comparative anatomy, psychology U. Vienna, 1937-38, asst. prof., 1938-40; prof. psychology, head dept. U. Konigsberg (Germany), 1940-42; head Inst. Comparative Ethology, Altenberg, Austria, 1949-51; head rsch. dept. comparative ethology Max-Planck Found., Buldern, Germany, 1951-54, vice dir. inst., 1954-61, Seewiesen, dir., 1961-73; dir. dept. for animal sociology Austrian Acad. Sci., 1973-82; dir. Konrad-Lorenz Inst. Austrian Acad. Sci., 1982—; lectr., U. Vienna; hon. prof. U. Munster, U. Munich; vis. prof. U. Colo., Denver. Recipient Golden medal Zool. Soc. N.Y., Preis der Stadt Wien, Goldene Wilhelm Bolsche Medaille, Osterreichisches Ehrenzeichen für Wissenschaft and Kunst, Ehrenmedaille der Bundeshauptstadt Wien in Gold, Prix Mondial Cino del Duca, Jean Delacour Medaille, Ordre Pour Le Mérite, Grosses Verdienstkreuz mit Stern der Bundesrepublik Deutschland, Nobel prize in physiology and medicine, 1973, Bayerischer Verdienstorden, Cervia Ambiente Naturschutzpreis, Ehrenmedaille d. Katholischen Univ. Mailand, Bayer. Maximiliansorden. Mem. Austrian Acad. Sci., Bavarian Acad. Sci., Nat. Acad. Scis. (fgn. assoc.), N.Y. Zool. Soc., Royal Soc., Am. Acad. Arts and Scis., numerous others. Author: King Solomon's Ring, 1952, Man Meets Dog, 1954, On Agression, 1966, Evolution and Modification of Behavior, 1966, Civilized Man's Eight Deadly Sins, 1973, Behind the Mirror, 1977, The Year of the Greylag Goose, 1980, The Foundations of Ethology, 1981, The Waning of Humaneness, 1987, The Eight Deadly Sins of Civilized Humanity, The Decay of the Humane. Pioneer in modern ethology; formulated school of study based on concept that an animal's behavior is a product of adaptive evolution. Home: Altenburg, Austria. Died Feb. 27, 1989.

LORING, AUGUSTUS PEABODY, professional trustee; b. Beverly, Mass., Aug. 24, 1915; s. Augustus P. and Rosamond (Bowditch) L.; m. Elisabeth Blake, Sept. 2, 1944; children—Peter Blake, Ellen Gardner, Christopher Blake, Jonathan Blake. A.B., Harvard, 1938, M.B.A., 1940. Dir. Emhart Corp., Hollingsworth & Vose; chmn. bd. Haverhill Gas Co., Bank of New Eng. Bd. dirs. Community Workshop; trustee Peabody Mus., Woods Hole Oceanographic Instn., Conn. Coll.; bd. overseers Harvard Coll.; trustee Boston Althenaeum. Mem. Trustees of Reservations. Republican. Unitarian. Club: Mason. Home: Prides Crossing Mass. Died Nov. 27, 1986.

LOSER, JOSEPH CARLTON, lawyer, former congressman; b. Nashville, Oct. 1, 1892; s. Henry J. and Willie M. (McConnico) L.; m. Pearl D. Gupton, Jan. 25, 1915; children: Dorothy D. (Mrs. Paul Storey), Margy A. (Mrs. Don Gass), Joseph Carlton. LLB, Cumberland U., 1923. Bar: Tenn. 1922. Sec. to mayor Nashville, 1917-20; asst. city atty. Nashville, 1923-29, asst. dist. atty., 1929-34, dist. atty., 1934-57; mem. 85th-87th Congresses from 5th Dist. Tenn., 1956-62; then practiced law Nashville. Del. Dem. Nat. Conv., 1944-52, 60; sec. Tenn. Dem. Exec. Com. Mem. Tenn. N.G., 1910, USCGR (T), 1944. Mem. Internat. Typog. Union, Sigma Alpha Epsilon, Masons (32 deg., K.T., Shriner). Baptist. Home: Nashville Tenn. Died July 31, 1984.

LOUCKS, CHARLES ERNEST, army officer; b. Mayfield, Calif., June 29, 1895; s. Menzo Samuel and Maria Letitia (Sherman) L.; m. Pearl Reyburn, Jan. 13, 1921 (dec. 1967); children: Charles Sherman, Lois Reyburn (Mrs. William Allen Nixon); m. Barbara Wilson Haupt, Oct. 8, 1973. A.B., Stanford U., 1921; M.Sc., MIT, 1931; grad., Army Chem. Warfare Sch., 1926, Field Officers Course, Chem. Warfare Sch., 1938, Army Indsl. Coll., 1940. Commd. 2d lt. U.S. Army, 1917; advanced through grades to maj. gen.; asst. mil. attache U.S. Arny, Paris, London, 1940, 41; comdr. Rocky Mountain Arsenal Denver, 1942-44; chief chem. officer Army Occupation Japan, 1945; chief research and devel. div. Chem. Corps 1945-48, chief chem. officer European Command, 1948-51, comdg. gen. Army Chem. Center, 1951; dep. chief chem. officer U.S. Army., 1951-55; tech. dir. Nat. Paint, Varnish and Lacquer Assn., Inc., 1956-62. Decorated D.S.M., Legion of Merit. Mem. Am. Chem. Soc., AAAS, Am. Def. Preparedness Assn., Am. Legion, Soc. Mayflower Descs., Descs. Colonial Govs., Old Plymouth Colony Descs., SAR, Huguenot Soc., Descs. Colonial Clergy, Pilgrims, S.R., Soc. Colonial Wars, Mil. Order Loyal Legion (registrar), Ancient and Hon. Arty. Co. Mass. (Right of Descent), Ams Armorial Ancestry, Loyalists and Patriots (historian gen.), Order Founders and Patriots Am. (councillor gen., nat. exec. com.), Soc. of War of 1812, Mil. Order World Wars, Mil. Order of Carabao, St. Andrew's Soc., Clan Fraser, Order of First Families of Mass., Sons Colonial New Eng., Soule Kindred, Alpha Chi Sigma. Presbyn. Clubs: Mason, Odd Fellow, Army and Navy (Washington). Home: Arlington Va. Died Dec. 16, 1987; buried Arlington Nat. Cemetery.

LOUIS, JEAN FRANCOIS, engineer, educator; b. Ixelles, Brussels, Mar. 31, 1932; m. Marigold Ann Beck, Nov. 15, 1958; children—Claudine, Paul, Daniel. Ingeniéur Civil Mecanicien et Electricien, Free U. Brussels, Belgium, 1954; Ph.D., Cambridge (Eng.) U., 1957. Prin. research scientist AVCO, Everett, Mass., 1960-69; assoc. prof. MIT, 1969-72, prof. aeros. and astronautics, from 1972, dir. fossil fuels program Energy Lab., 1974-81, assoc. dir., 1976-81, assoc. dir. Center for Health Effects of Fossil Fuels Utilization, 1978; asso. dir. Center for Health Effects of Fossil Fuels Utilization Univ. Coal Research Consortium of N.E., 1979-80; cons. to engring. firms, labs.; vis. prof. Stanford, 1968-69; Henri Spaciael chair Free U. Brussels, 1970-71. Contbr. articles to profl. jours. Recipient diploma for sci. achievement High Temperature Inst. USSR Acad Scis. Fellow AIAA (asso.). Home: Brookline Mass. Died June 21, 1988; buried West Baldwin, Maine.

LOURIE, REGINALD SPENCER, physician; b. Bklyn., Sept. 10, 1908; s. Inte and Elsie (Horowitz) L.; m. Lucille Radin, Feb. 26, 1931; children: Seth H., Ira S., Benjamin D. BS, Cornell U., 1930; MD, L.I. Coll. of Medicine, 1936; Med.Sci.D., Columbia U., 1942. Pediatric intern L.I. Coll. Hosp., 1936-37, resident pediatrics, 1937-38; resident psychiatry N.Y. State Psychiat. Inst., 1938-39, Bellevue Hosp., N.Y.C., 1939-40; resident child psychiatry. Markle Fellow Babies Hosp., N.Y.C., 1940-43; pediatric psychiatrist U. Rochester (N.Y.), 1946-48; dir. psychiatry Children's Hosp. Nat. Med. Ctr., Washington, 1948-74, dir. emeritus, 1974-88; prof. child health and devl., psychiatry George Washington U. Coll. Medicine, 1948-74, prof. emeritus, 1974-88; mem. Pres.'s Panel Mental Retardation, 1961-64, Nat. Adv. Mental Health Council, 1964-68; pres., also chmn. Joint Commn. Mental Health Children, 1965-73; chmn. Human Services Inst. For Children and Families, 1973-74; med. dir. emeritus Hillcrest Children's Ctr.; sr. research scientist NIMH; sr. cons. Psychiat. Inst. Washington, 1974-85; pres. Nat. Ctr. for Clin. Infant Programs, 1977-88; cons. Nat. Naval Med. Ctr., Walter Reed Army Med. Ctr., NIH, NIMH, Nat. Burs. Standards, Children's Bur.; med. dirs. Regional Ctr. for Infants, Rockville, Md., 1985-88. Co-editor books, anns.; contbr. articles to med. jours., chpts. to books. Mem. adv. council, bd. mem. to nat., lcoal philanthropic and sci. assns. Served to lt. comdr. M.C., USNR, 1943-46. Recipient award for disting. service to Am. Medicine SUNY Downstate Med. Ctr, 1964; named comdr. Royal Order Phoenix (Greece). Mem. Am. Orthopsychiat. Assn. (past pres.), Am. Acad. Child Psychiatry (past pres., Simon Wile award), Am. Child Guidance Found. (past. pres.), Am. Acad. Pediatrics (editorial bd.), Internat. Study Group Child Psychiatry (treas.), World, Am. (council McGavin award), psychiat. assns., Am. Internat. Psychoanalytic Assn., World Soc. Ekistics (exec. com.), Internat. Assn. Child Psychiatry and Allied Professions (past treas.), Interam. Council Psychiat. Assns. (pres. 1978-79, hon. pres. 1986), Alpha Omega Alpha. Club: Cosmos (Washington). Home: Chevy Chase Md. Died Mar. 20, 1988.

LOVE, CHARLES MARION, JR., lawyer; b. Huntington, W.Va., Jan. 10, 1902; s. Charles Marion and Minnie Elizabeth (Moore) L.; m. Naomi Nale, Feb. 3, 1927; children: Naomi (Mrs. E.G. Jefferson), Lucy Temple (Mrs. W.R. Skinner), Charles Marion III. AB, W.Va. U., 1924, JD, 1926. Bar: W.Va. 1926. Ptnr. firm Love, Wise, Robinson & Woodroe, Charleston, W.Va., from 1926; atty. Kanawha County Ct., 1932; asst. U.S. atty. 1934-43; referee in bankruptcy So. Dist. W.Va., 1944-45, conscientious objector hearing officer, 1956-68; mem. W.Va. Senate, 1946-54. Chmn. W.Va. Tax Study Commn., 1958-60, chmn. exec. com., 1959-60; chmn. W.Va. Citizen Action Coun. Crime and Delinquency, from 1957; chmn. Charleston Dem. Exec. Com., 1952-60; del. at large Dem. Nat. Conv., 1956, 60; chmn. bd. visitors Coll. Law, W.Va. U., 1956-87. Mem. Am., W.Va., Kanawha County (past pres.) bar assns., W.Va. State Bar, Edgewood Country Club, Duquesne Club (Pitts.). Home: Charleston W.Va. Died Apr. 18, 1987; buried Charleston.

LOVE, HAROLD OREN, lawyer; b. Indpls., May 27, 1909; s. Roscoe A. and Clara (Evans) L.; m. Sara Elizabeth Scherling, June 12, 1937; children: Robert Evans, Barbara Lynn. AB magna cum laude, Butler U., 1933; JD, U. Mich., 1936. Bar: Ind. 1930, Mich. 1936. Practiced in Detroit; mem. Love & Kipp, 1937-40, Love & Miel, 1943-46, Love & Snyder, 1946-50, Love, Snyder & Lewis, 1950-84; dir., officer numerous corps.; pres., pub. Tombstone Epitaph; pres. Crystal Palace; owner O.K. Corral; pres. Historic Tombstone Adventures. Author: Business as Usual, 1951, Tax Free Profits for your Family, 1954, More for your Money, 1957; contbr. articles to mags., periodicals. Former exec. v.p., then hon. trustee Archives Am. Art; bd. dirs. Tucson Mus. Art; past mem. Detroit Art Commn.; former chmn., treas. 14th Congl. Rep. Com.; former mem. Wayne County Rep. Com.; v.p. Detroit City Plan Commn., 1940, pres., 1941-42; mem. Regional Planning Com.; mem., pres. Grosse Pointe Woods Planning Commn., Grosse Pointe Woods Charter Com.; mem. Wayne County Bd. Suprs.; bd. dirs. Detroit Symphony Orch., Inc.; bd. govs. Players; trustee Detroit Adventure. Lt. USNR, 1943-45. Mem. ABA (past chmn. retirement and security sect.), Mich. Bar Assn., Detroit Bar Assn., Fine Arts Soc., Soc. Contbrs. to Detroit Symphony Orch. (pres.), Detroit Hist. Soc., Friends Grosse Pointe Library, Detroit Inst. Arts Founders Soc., Greater Detroit Bd. Commerce, Phi Delta Theta, Tau Kappa Alpha, Phi Kappa Phi, Kappa Delta Rho. Presbyterian. Clubs: Lawyers (U. Mich.), Mich, Indian Village (bd. govs.), University, Country of Detroit; Skyline Country (Tucson). Home: Tucson Ariz. Died Mar. 21, 1986; buried Tombstone, Ariz.

LOVE, JAMES LOWREY, wood products company executive; b. Hackley, La., Mar. 20, 1913; s. Robert Davis and Loulie (Harris) L.; m. Mary Evelyn Modisette, Mar. 14, 1941; children—James H., Margaret (Mrs. H. Warren Taylor III), Elisabeth (Mrs. Cyril D. Stapleton, Jr.). Mus.B., La. State U., 1936, postgrad., 1937. Pres. Love Wood Products Co., Inc., Hammond, La., 1947-56, Diboll, Tex., 1951-75; chmn. bd. Love Wood Products Co., Inc., 1975-85; pres. Miracle Bark, Inc., Diboll, 1960-74, Moldwood Plastic Products Corp., Diboll, 1964-68; dir. So. Asphalt Roofing Corp., Little Rock, 1959-74, Lufkin Fed. Savs. and Loan, Tex. Vice pres. East Tex. Boy Scout Found., Inc., 1968-85; pres. Friends of Tex. Libraries, 1961-63; Chmn. bd.

commrs. La. State Library, 1953-57; chmn. bd. Houston Area Library System, 1975-85; bd. dirs. East Tex. Area council Boy Scouts Am., 1965-85, v.p., 1972-73, pres., 1975-76; mem. Hall of Fame, 1979, also mem. exec. com.; bd. dirs. Lufkin Hist. and Creative Arts Center, 1979-85; mem. steering com. First Tex. Govs.' Conf. on Libraries, Austin, 1965-66; chmn. Tex. Library Assn. Awards Com., 1975; chmn. bd. T.L.L. Temple Meml. Library, 1961-81, bd. dirs., 1981-85; mem. award com. J. Frank Dobie Library Trust, 1975-85. Recipient Silver Beaver award Boy Scouts Am., 1971, Nat. Trustee citation Am. Library Assn., 1967. Mem. Forest Products Research Soc. (dir. 1959-62, 70-71, v.p. 1971-72, pres. elect 1972-73, internat. pres. 1973-74, Fred Gottschalk Meml. award 1971), Tex. Forestry Assn. (pres. 1967-68), La. Forestry Assn., Tex. Library Trustee Assn. (pres. 1963-64, named Tex. Library Trustee of Yr. 1964), Sigma Chi. Presbyterian (elder 1949-85, trustee 1958-85). Clubs: Rotarian (Lufkin) (pres. Hammond 1951, dir. Diboll 1972-74), Lukfin (Lufkin), Lukfin Country (Lufkin), Crown Colony Country (Lufkin). Home: Lufkin Tex. Died Aug. 25, 1985; buried Garden of Memories, Lufkin, Tex.

LOVE, STEPHEN, lawyer; b. Lemberg, Austria, July 26, 1891; came to U.S., 1900; s. Thaddeus and Helen (Stroynowska) Love-Szydlowski; m. Helen Higginbotham, June 26, 1915; 1 child, Helen Constance. Student, Cen. YMCA Inst., 1906-08, Northwestern U. Law Sch., 1908-11. Bar: Ill. 1912. Mem. Wolf & Love, Chgo., 1912-45; pvt. practice Chgo., from 1945; prof. law Northwestern U., from 1925; formerly assoc. prof. DePaul U. and Loyola U.; mem., former chmn. com. on character and fitness Ill. Supreme Ct.; chmn. com. which completed Standardized Jury Instrns. Ill. Author: Mechanics' Liens in Ill.; numerous legal articles. Recipient Immigrants' Svc. League award for Person of Fgn. Birth Pre-eminent in the Professions. Mem. Ill. Bar Assn. (gen. chmn. com. on grievances), Chgo. bar Assn. (chmn. com. on grievances, bd. mgrs.), Polish Lawyers Assn. (pres.), Order of Coif, Delta Theta Phi. Catholic. Home: Chicago Ill. †

LOVEJOY, ROBERT CARR, lawyer; b. Janesville, Wis., Jan. 20, 1917; s. Allen Perry and Isabel (Thomas) L.; m. Margaret Bissell Thom, June 28, 1941; children—Julia (Mrs. Lawrence A. Weiser), Mary (Mrs. Elmer B. Sweet, Jr.), Alexandra, (Mrs. W. James Waefler), Allen Perry IV, Katharine (Mrs. Fernando Villa-Alvarez). Grad., Deerfield (Mass.) Acad., 1935; A.B., Yale, 1939; J.D., U. Mich., 1942. Bar: Wis. 1942. Practiced in Janesville, 1945-88; ptnr. firm Nowlan & Mouat, 1948-88; former chmn. bd. Marine First Nat. Bank Janesville; lectr. U. Wis. Law Sch., 1977-82. City councilman, Janesville, 1969-73; Bd. dirs. Janesville YMCA, 1958-79, pres., 1965-68; bd. dirs. Cedar Crest. Served with USNR, 1942-45. Mem. State Bar Wis. (bd. govs. 1948-50, 61-63, 68-71). Republican. Congregationalist. Clubs: Rotary, Madison, Janesville Country; Timber Ridge Country (Minocqua, Wis.). Home: Janesville Wis. Died July 27, 1988.

LOVELL, ENDICOTT REMINGTON, business executive; b. Chihuahua, Mexico, July 20, 1892; s. Wallace D. and Caroline Newhall (Whitten) L.; m. Martha L. MacNaughton, Dec. 20, 1917; children: Endicott R. (dec.), James MacNaughton (dec.), Robert Gray. BS, Mich. Coll. Mining and Tech., Houghton, 1922, EM, 1922. Asst. supt. smelting and refining dept. Calumet & Hecla Consol. Copper Co. (later named Calumet-Hecla Inc.), 1922-33, supt., 1933-40, gen. supt., 1940-41, gen. mgr., 1941, dir., v.p., 1942-44, pres., 1944-57, chmn. bd., 1957-61, dir., from 1961; bd. dirs. Stanray Corp., Sno Line R.R. Co., Detroit and No. Savs. & Loan Assn., Harshaw Chem. Co. Capt. F.A., U.S. Army, World War I, France. Mem. AIME, Mining and Metall. Soc. Am., Chicago Club, Miscowaubik Club (Calumet, Mich.), Glen View Club, (Golf, Ill.), Paradise Valley country Club (Scottsdale, Ariz.). Home: Scottsdale Ariz. †

LOVELL, RALPH MARSTON, state senator, pharmacist; b. Waldoboro, Maine, Dec. 19, 1910; s. John Harvey and Lottie E. (Magune) L.; m. Lillian Margaret Moriarty, Oct. 30, 1930; children: Marilyn (Mrs. Leo Burke), Maxine C. (Mrs. Burton Faulkner); m. 2d, Rita Margarite Ferron, Sept. 15, 1940; children: Susan Marston, Ross, Dean, Barbara. Ph.G., Mass. Coll. Pharmacy, 1933. Pharmacist Lovell's Pharmacy, Sanford, Maine, 1933-73; owner Lovell's Wholesale Ice Creams, 1936-72, Lovell's Ambulance Service, 1950-70; mgr. Rexair Co., 1946-52; mem. Maine Senate, 1960-66, 76-86, chmn. com. on aging, retirement and vets., mem. co,. on labor; mem. Maine Ho. of Reps., 1974-76; field adviser Small Bus. Adminstrn., 1953-61, adv. coun., 1975-77; indsl. devel. cons., 1954-86; tourist and indsl. devel. specialist in Central Africa, U.S. Dept. Commerce, 1960; pres., dir. York County Bus. Devel. Corp., 1963-73; organizer Medicare Prescription Program for Maine and New Eng. Pres. United Fund, Sanford, 1953, campaign chmn., 1955, sec. 1956-60, dir. 1950-68; mem. Pine Tree coun. Boy Scouts Am.; asst. dir. Civil Def., 1956-59; founder Maine Sight Conservation Assn., 1955, treas., 1955-60, bd. dirs., 1955-62; mem. Maine Gov.'s com. for Nat. Legislative Conf., 1965-66; chmn. Maine Legis. Com. on Indsl. Devel. and Tourism, 1960-65; mem. Maine Legis. Com. Health and Instnl. Services, 1974-80; grand marshall Sanford Meml. Day Parade, 1976; chmn. Rep. City Commn., 1952-62, 72. Recipient plaque as outstanding pharmacist in Maine; award for indsl. work in Africa, Dept. Fgn. Commerce; citations as outstanding citizen VFW, Lions, Rotary, Kiwanis. Mem. Maine (dir. exec. com. 1958—), York County pharm. assns., Newcomen Soc., Sanford C. of C. (pres. 1959, indsl. devel. com., chmn. 1958-59, plaque for outstanding work), Sanford Fish and Game Assn., Red Men, Grange, Masons, Shriners, Lions (dist. gov. 1955, internat. counsellor 1956-86, pres.'s medal). Congregationalist. Home: Sanford Maine. Died Dec. 15, 1986; buried Sanford, Maine.

LOVETT, ROBERT ABERCROMBIE, banker; b. Huntsville, Tex., Sept. 14, 1895; s. Robert Scott and Lavinia Chilton (Abercrombie) L.; m. Adele Quartley Brown, Apr. 19, 1919; children: Evelyn (dec. 1967), Robert Scott 2d. BA, Yale, 1918, MA, LLD; postgrad. law, Harvard, 1919-20, postgrad. bus. adminstrn., 1920-21; LLD, Amherst, Brown U., Columbia U., Harvard U., L.I. U., Princeton U., Sam Houston State Tchrs. Coll., Williams Coll. Clk. Nat. Bank Commerce, N.Y.C., 1921; ptnr. Brown Bros. Harriman & Co., 1926, resigned, Dec. 1940, readmitted, 1946-47, 49-50, gen. ptnr., from 1953; spl. asst. to sec. war 1940-41, asst. sec. war for air, 1941-45, undersec. state, 1947-49, dep. sec. def., 1950-51, sec. def., 1951-53. Life mem. emeritus corp. MIT. Served as pilot, lt. comdr. AS, USN, 1917-18. Decorated 1919 Navy Cross, D.S.M.; Grand Cross Order Leopold II (Belgium); Presdl. Medal of Freedom, 1963. Mem. Century Assn., Yale Club, Creek Club (Locust Valley), Met. Club (Washington), Links Club (N.Y.C.). Home: Locust Valley N.Y. Died May 7, 1986.

LOW, GEORGE MICHAEL, college president; b. Vienna, Austria, June 10, 1926; s. Arthur and Gertrude (Burger) L.; m. Mary R. McNamara, Sept. 3, 1949; children: Mark S., Diane E., G. David, John M., Nancy A. BS in Aero. Engring., Rennelaer Poly. Inst., 1948, MS in Aero. Engring., 1950, Eng.D. (hon.), 1969; ScD, U. Fla., 1969; Eng.D. (hon.), Lehigh U., 1979. With NASA and predecessor, 1949-76, dept. assoc. adminstr. manned space flight, 1963-64; dept. dir. Manned Spacecraft Ctr. NASA and predecessor, Houston, 1964-67; mgr. Apollo Spacecraft program NASA and predecessor, 1967-69; dep. adminstr. NASA and predecessor, Washington, 1969-76; pres. Rensselaer Poly. Inst., Troy, N.Y., 1976-84; bd. dirs. GE. Trustee Com. Econ. Devel., Hartford Grad. Ctr., Commn. Ind. Colls. and Univs. Decorated Cross of Honor Sci. and Art 1st class (Austria), 1980; recipient Outstanding Leadership medal NASA, 1962, 2 Disting. Service medals, 1969, Arthur S. Flemming award U.S. Jr. C. of C., 1963, Space Flight award Am. Astronautical Soc., 1968, Paul T. Johns trophy Arnold Air Soc., 1969, Astronautics Engr. award Nat. Space Club, 1970, Robert H. Goddard Meml. trophy, 1973, Nat. Civil Service League Career Service award, 1973, Rockefeller Pub. Service award for adminstrn., 1974. Fellow AIAA (hon. fellow; Louis W. Hill Space TRansp. award 1969); mem. Nat. Acad. Engring. (Founders award 1978, council). Home: Troy N.Y. Died July 17, 1984.

LOWE, MILDRED, librarian; b. N.Y.C., Apr. 4, 1927; d. Kalman and Frieda (Fuchs) Rabinowitz; m. Rubin Lowe, June 16, 1946; children: Carl, Stefanie, Allen. B.A., Bklyn. Coll., 1960; M.L.S., Pratt Inst., 1965; D.L.S. (Higher Edn. Act Title 11B fellow 1968-71), Columbia U., 1972. Musical dir. Community Theatre, Messapequa, N.Y., 1950-65; govt. documents and serials librarian SUNY, Farmingdale, 1965-68; mem. faculty St. John's U., Jamaica, N.Y., 1969—, assoc. prof. library sci., 1978—, acting dir. div. library and info. sci., 1979-82, dir. div. library and info. sci., 1982-87; trustee Woodstock (N.Y.) Library, 1987-88, Mid Hudson Library System, N.Y., 1988; mem. N.Y. State Govt. Documents Task Force, 1975-78. Democratic committeewoman Nassau County, N.Y., 1969-73. Mem. ALA, N.Y. State Library Assn. (chmn. legis. com., library educators sect. 1972-74, founder Govt. Documents Roundtable 1978, pres. 1978-80, council 1987-88), Nassau County Library Assn. (pres. coll. and univ. library div. 1977-78), N.Y. Library Club (exec. council 1970-71), Am. Printing History Assn., Council Library and Info. Sci. Assn. (sec./treas. council 1985-88), Beta Phi Mu. Home: Willow N.Y. Died Aug. 22, 1988.

LOWE, VICTOR (AUGUSTUS), philosophy educator; b. Cleve., Aug. 29, 1907; s. Henry Albert and Katherine (Heiser) L.; B.S., Case Sch. Applied Sci., 1928; M.A., Harvard U., 1931, Ph.D., 1935; m. Victoria Lincoln, Apr. 3, 1934 (dec. June, 1981); children—Thomas Cobb, Louise Lincoln Lowe Kittredge; 1 stepdau., Penelope Thayer Lowe Williams; m. Alice D. Gray, June 30, 1984. Asst. philosophy Harvard U., 1937-39; instr. philosophy Syracuse (N.Y.) U., 1941-42; instr. Ohio State U., 1942-45, asst. prof., 1945-47; assoc. prof. Johns Hopkins U., Balt., 1947-62, prof., 1962-73, prof. philosophy emeritus, 1973-88; vis. prof. McGill U., 1963-64, Nixon prof. Whittier (Calif.) Coll., 1977. Nat. Endowment Humanities sr. fellow, 1968-69; hon. research fellow U. Coll. London, 1967, 68, 70, 72. Mem. Am. Philos. Assn., Soc. Advancement Am. Philosophy, Metaphys. Soc. Am., Center Process Studies. Author: Understanding Whitehead, 1962; The Life of Alfred North Whitehead, Vol. I, 1985; editor: (with others) Classic American Philosophers, 1951; contbr. articles in field to profl. jours. Home: Baltimore, Md. Died. Nov. 16, 1988; buried Newton, Mass. Address: for estate of Victor Lowe Mrs Alice G Lowe 3930 Cloverhill Rd Balt MD 21218.

LOWE, WILLIAM HENRY, SR., steel company executive; b. Windsor, Ont., Can., Aug. 12, 1917; came to U.S., 1938, naturalized, 1944; s. William D. and Jean (Newcomb) L.; m. Jeannette R. Kennedy, June 4, 1943; children: William Henry, Glenda J., Bonnie Beth. B.A., Assumption Coll. of U. Western Ont., 1938; M.B.A., Harvard U., 1940; LL.D., Pikeville Coll., 1960. With Inland Steel Co., Chgo., 1940-81, asst. sec., 1948-50, asst. treas., 1950-54, treas., 1954-63, v.p., treas., 1963-68, v.p. finance, 1968-81, dir., chmn. finance com., 1967-81; chmn. Ft. Dearborn Income Securities, Inc.; bd. dirs. First Ill. Bank of Wilmette, First Nat. Bank East Chgo. Fin. v.p. Nat. Safety Council, 1954-60, chmn. bd., 1960-63; chmn. bd. mgrs. YMCA Met. Chgo., 1972-73; pres. New Trier Twp. High Sch. Bd. Edn., 1966-67; treas. bd. Evanston Hosp., 1969-78; bd. dirs. McCormick Theol. Sem., 1973-82, chmn., 1979-82; budget chmn. 198th Gen. Assembly United Presby. Ch.; past chmn. Wilmette Fire and Police Commn.; former pres. Taxpayers Fedn. Ill.; dir. North Shore Sr. Ctr. Served from pvt. to 1st lt. C.E. AUS, 1943-46. Mem. Am. Iron and Steel Inst., Fin. Execs. Inst. Club: Mid-Day (Chgo.). Home: Wilmette Ill. Died June 14, 1988.

LOWINSKY, EDWARD ELIAS, educator, musicologist; b. Stuttgart, Germany, Jan. 12, 1908; came to U.S., 1940, naturalized, 1947; s. Leopold and Clara (Rosenfeld) L.; m. Gretel J. Hoffmann, Aug. 10, 1938; children: Naomi Ruth, Simon Leo, Benjamin David, Joshua Michael; m. 2d Bonnie J. Blackburn, Sept. 10, 1971. Grad., Hochschule für Musik, Stuttgart, 1928; PhD, U. Heidelberg, 1933. Asst. prof. Black Mountain Coll., 1942-47; assoc. prof. Queens Coll., 1949-56; prof. U. Calif., Berkeley, 1956-61; Ferdinand Schevill disting. service prof. U. Chgo., 1961-76, emeritus, 1976-85, Colvin rsch. prof., 1964-65; founder, chmn. Renaissance Seminar, 1963-76; dir. Internat. Josquin Festival Conf., Lincoln Ctr., N.Y.C., 1971; hon. mem. Com. for Preparation of New Josquin Edit. Author: Orlando di Lasso's Antwerp Motetbook, 1937, Secret Chromatic Art in the Netherlands Motet, 1946, reprint, 1967, Tonality and Atonality in Ideology in Sixteenth-Century Music, 1961, reprint, 1962, 89, The Medici Codex, 3 vols., 1968 (Otto Kinkeldey award Am. Musicological Soc. 1969), Cipriano de Rore's Venus Motet: Its Poetic and Pictorial Sources, 1986, Music in the Culture of the Renaissance and Other Essays, 2 vol. edit., 1989; also numerous articles; editor: (N. Vicentino) L'antica musica ridotta alla moderna prattica, 1959; procs. Internat. Josquin Festival conf. of 1971, 76; gen. editor: Monuments of Renaissance Music, 1964-76. Guggenheim fellow, 1947-48, 76-77; fellow Inst. Advanced Study, 1952-54; Bollingen fellow, 1952-54, 56-58. Fellow Am. Acad. Arts and Scis.; fgn. mem. Royal Netherlands Acad.; mem. Soc. Ethnomusicology, Am. (hon.), Internat., Belgian, Dutch musicol. socs., Music Library Assn., Renaissance Soc. Am. Home: Chicago Ill. Died Oct. 11, 1985; buried Chgo.

LUBALIN, HERBERT FREDERICK, graphic designer; b. N.Y.C., Mar. 17, 1918; s. Joseph and Rose J. L.; m. Sylvia Kushner, Oct. 5, 1940; children: Peter J., Robert H., David O.; m. Rhoda Sparber, Feb. 14, 1981 (dec. May 24, 1981). B.F.A., Cooper Union, 1976. Designer Display Guild, 1939; art dir. Deutsch & Shea Advt., Inc., 1940, Men's Wear mag. Fairchild Publs., 1942, Reiss Advt., Inc., 1943; v.p., creative dir. Sudler & Hennessey, 1945-64; pres. Herb Lubalin, Inc., 1964-68, LSC, Inc., 1968-76, LSC&P Design Group, Inc., N.Y.C., from 1976; exec. v.p. Lubalin Burns, from 1970, Lubalin, Delpire et Cie, Paris, 1971, Lubalin Maxwell Ltd., London, 1971, Internat. Typeface Corp., 1971; v.p. D.P.I. Inc., N.Y.C., 1977; tchr. graphics Cornell U., 1973; prof. design Cooper Union, 1974-81; lectr. numerous univs.; lectr., juror numerous art dirs. clubs, throughout U.S., Can. and Europe. Contbr. articles to mags. and newspapers.; one-man shows, Overseas Press Club, 1964, Gallery 303, 1968, TGI Gallery, 1975, Ryder Gallery, Chgo., 1975, Hampshire Coll., Mass., 1976, Centre Georges Pompidou, 1979, group shows include, Am. Inst. Graphic Arts, 1952-81, New York Art Dirs. Club, 1952-81, C.A. Mag., 1958-81 , Soc. Publ. Designers, 1962-81, Type Dirs. Club, 1952-81, Whitney Mus., 1974; represented in permanent collections Smithsonian Instn., Library of Congress, Nat. Gallery, Washington. Mem. adv. bd. Hampshire Coll., Kean Coll., N.J. Recipient Cleo award for best TV comml. Am. TV Festival, 1963, Lotus Club award, 1973, Cooper Union Profl. Achievement citation, 1972, U.S. Govt. citation for design of airmail stamps, 1963, Augustus St. Gaudens medal for profl. achievement, Cooper Union Alumni Assn., 1973; named to Art Dirs. Club Hall of Fame, 1977. Mem. Am. Inst. Graphic Arts (dir., medal award 1981), N.Y. Art Dirs. Club (past pres., 7 Gold medals, 3 Silver medals), N.Y. Type Dirs. Club, Soc. Publ. Designers, Soc. Illustrators, Nat. Soc. Art Dirs. (Art Dir. of Year award 1962), Scandinavian Soc. Designers (hon.), Soc. Typographic Artists Chgo. (hon.), Alliance Graphique Internat. (internat. v.p.). Home: Amenia N.Y. Died 1981.

LUBELL, SAMUEL, writer; b. Poland, Nov. 3, 1911; came to U.S., 1913; s. Louis and Mollie (Reitkop) L.; m. Helen Sopot, Mar. 22, 1941; children: Bernard, Walter. Evening student, CCNY, 1927-31; BS, Sch. Journalism, Columbia, 1933. Reporter, rewrite man L.I. DAily Press, 1935-36; reporter, Army and Navy editor, and writer "Federal Diary" column Washington Post, 1936-37; copy desk, labor editor Richmond (Va.) Times-Dispatch, 1937; reporter, rewrite man Washington Herald, 1937-38; free lance writer nat. mags., chiefly Sat. Evening Post, 1938-41; writer Office of Facts and Figures, later OWI, 1941; gen. sec. Rubber Survey Com. (Baruch Com.), 1942; asst. to James F. Byrnes, dir. Office Econ. Stblzn., 1942; asst. to Bernard M. BAruch, adv. unit on war and post-war adjustment policies Office War Moblzn.; CBI war corr. Sat. Evening Post; European corr. Providence Jour., 1946; dir. Opinion Reporting Workshop Sch. Journalism, Columbia U., 1958-68; Harvard fellow Kennedy Inst. Politics, 1974; vis. prof. U. Conn., 1975. Author: The Future of American Politics, 1952, Revolution in World Trade, 1954, Revolt of the Moderates, 1956, White and Black, 1964, The Hidden Crisis in American Politics, 1970, The Future While it Happened, 1973, syndicated column The People Speak; commentator CBS and NBC TV and radio, 1952-60; polit. analyst, commentator RKO Gen. TV & Radio, 1964, Voter Speak Reports, 1952-72. Recipient Pulitzer traveling scholarship Columbia U., 1934, Woodrow Wilson Found. award Am. Poli. Sci. Assn., 1952, Columbia U. Journalism award, 1976; Guggenheim fellow, 1951, 54; Kennedy fellow Inst. Politics, Harvard, 1973-74. Democrat. Home: Los Angeles Calif. Died Aug. 16, 1987.

LUBIN, CHARLES W., food products company executive. Founder, chmn. bd. Kitchens of Sara Lee, Deerfield, Ill.; v.p., dir. Consol. Foods. Corp. (now Sara Lee Corp.), Chgo. Home: Chicago Ill. Died July 15, 1988.

LUBOFF, NORMAN, composer, conductor; b. Chgo., May 14, 1917; m. Gunilla Luboff; children: Peter, Bettina. Student, U. Chgo.; BA, Chgo. Central Coll.; postgrad., Am. Conservatory, Chgo. Former tchr. music theory Central Coll. Singer, arranger, coach various radio shows, Chgo. and N.Y.C.; arranger, conductor Railroad Hour radio show; composer movie scores, Warner Bros., Hollywood, Calif., from 1948; leader Norman Luboff Choir in concerts and records; rec. artist, Columbia, RCA Victor; co-editor, arranger: Songs of Man. With Signal Corps, AUS, World War II. Mem. ASCAP. Home: Bynum N.C. Died Sept. 22, 1987.

LUCE, CLARE BOOTHE, playwright, congresswoman, ambassador; b. N.Y.C., Mar. 10, 1903; d. William F. and Ann (Snyder) Boothe; m. George Tuttle Brokaw, Aug. 10, 1923 (div. 1929); m. Henry R. Luce, Nov. 23, 1935. Ed., St. Mary's, Garden City, L.I., N.Y., 1915-17, The Castle, Tarrytown, N.Y., 1917-19; Litt.D. (hon.), Colby Coll., Fordham U., Hamilton Coll., Mundelein Coll.; LL.D. (hon.), Temple U., Creighton U., Georgetown U., Seton Hall Coll., Mt. Holyoke Coll., Boston U., Westminster Coll.; D.H.L. (hon.), U.S.C. Med. Sch.; A.F.D. (hon.), St. John's U. Assoc. editor Vogue, 1930; assoc. editor Vanity Fair, 1931-32, mng. editor, 1933-34; newspaper columnist 1934, playwright, from 1935; mem. 78th-79th Congresses from 4th Conn. Dist., 1943-47; U.S. ambassador to Italy, 1953-57; mem. Pres.'s Fgn. Intelligence Adv. Bd., 1973-77, 82-87; cons. in field. Author: Stuffed Shirts, 1933, Europe in the Spring, 1940; plays Abide with Me, 1937, The Women, 1937,(Old Vic Co. prodn. 1986), Kiss the Boys Goodbye, 1938, Margin for Error, 1939, Child of The Morning, 1951, Slam the Door Softly, 1970, Saints for Now, 1952; movie Come to the Stable, 1947; contbr. articles and fiction to mags. Decorated knight Order of Grand Cross, Order of Lafayette, Dame of Malta; recipient Dag Hammarskjold medal, Laetare medal, Am. Statesman medal, Trinity award, Fourth Estate award, Internat. Achievement award, Sylvanus Thayer award, Disting. Service to Congress award, Am. Eagle award., Presdl. Medal of Freedom. Mem. Acad. Polit. Sci., Am. Inst. Fgn. Trade, Am. Security Council (dir.), Am. Soc. Oceanography (dir.), Honolulu Acad. Arts (dir.), U.S. Capitol Hist. Soc. (dir.), Nat. Inst. Social Sci., Hawaii Found. Am. Freedoms, Former Members Congress, Nat. Fedn. Press Women, Assn. Former Intelligence Officers, Center for The Book, Com. on Present Danger, Nat. Com. U.S.-China Relations, U.S. Strategic Inst., Council Am. Ambassador; Hillsdale Assocs.; Mem. Nat. Soc. Lit. and Arts., DAR. Republican. Roman Catholic. Club: Overseas Press. Home: Washington D.C. Died Oct. 9, 1987.

LUCIA, SALVATORE PABLO, physician, educator; b. San Francisco, Mar. 9, 1901; s. David and Julia (Cassino) L.; m. Marilyn Matys, 1959; children: Salvatore Pablo, Darryl. AB, U. Calif., 1926, MD, 1930, DSc, 1948. Diplomate Nat. Bd. Med. Examiners, Am. Bd. Internal Medicine. Mem. teaching staff dept. medicine U. Calif. Med Sch., 1931-84, prof. medicine, 1947-84, chmn. dept. preventive medicine, 1938-64, also prof. preventive medicine; cons. internal medicine, San Francisco, 1931-84; dir. med. rsch. wine adv. bd. Calif. Dept. Agr. Author: The Hemorrhagic Diseases, 1948, Wine as Food and Medicine, 1954, A History of Wine as Therapy, 1963, Alohol and Civilization, 1963, Wine and Health, 1969, Wine and the Digestive System, 1970, Wine and Your Wellbeing, 1971, Wine Diet Cook Book, 1974; contbr. numerous articles to sci. jours. Recipient Rsch. award Soc. Med. Friends of Wine, 1964; NRC fellow, Naples, Italy and London, 1930-31. Fellow ACP; mem. Pan-Am. Med. Assn., Med. Friends of Wine (pres. 1947), Wine and Food Soc., Internat. Soc. Hematology, Am. Pub. Health Assn., Am. Geriatric Soc., Assn. Tchrs. Preventive Medicine, Am. Soc. Hematology, Phi Beta Kappa, Sigma Xi, Alpha Omega Alpha. Died Mar. 31, 1984.

LUCIONI, LUIGI, artist; b. Malnate, Italy, Nov. 4, 1900; came to U.S., 1911, naturalized, 1922; s. Angelo and Maria (Beati) L. Student, Cooper Union Art Sch., 1916-20, Nat. Acad. Design, 1920-25. Represented Met. Mus. Art, Whitney Mus. Am. Art, Denver Art Mus., Nelson Gallery Art, Pa. Acad. Fine Arts, Neb. State Capitol, Canajoharie (N.Y.) Mus., Phillips Meml. Gallery, Andover, Mass., Library of Congress (3 etchings), Victoria and Albert Mus., London (1 etching), Williams Coll. (3 etchings, 1 painting), N.Y. Pub. Library (2 etchings), Carnegie Inst., Seattle Mus., Zanesville (Ohio) Mus., Raywood Art Gallery (1 etching, 1 watercolor), Dartmouth, Hamilton Coll., High Mus., Atlanta. Recipient Tiffany medal 1928, Allied Artists medal of honor 1929, Nat. Arts Club prize for flower painting 1939, 1st popular prize Carnegie Internat. 1939, 1st popular prize Corcoran Biennial, Washington 1939, 41, 47, 49, Purchase prize Library of Congress 1946, 1st $1000 prize 2d Nat. Print Exhb., N.Y.C. 1947, Purchase prize N.A.D. 1959, Purchase prize Albany Print Club 1970. Roman Catholic. Club: Lotos (N.Y.C.). Home: New York N.Y. Died July 22, 1988, buried Fairview (N.J.) Cemetery.

LUCKETT, HUBERT PEARSON, editor; b. Cameron, Tex., Nov. 18, 1916; s. Henry Lee and Matilda Adelia (Pearson) L.; m. Nancy Frazer, Jan. 16, 1982; children—Daniel, Arleigh, James. Student, U. Tex., Austin, 1935-42. Photographer Christianson-Leibermann Studios, Austin, Tex., 1942-44; photographer Popular Sci. Mag., N.Y.C., 1945-57; tech. editor Popular Sci. Mag., 1957-64, exec. editor, 1965-70, editor-in-chief, 1971-84; editorial dir. Times Mirror Mags., Inc., 1977-84, also v.p. Writer, dir., performer TV series for, NET. Mem. Bd. Edn. Union Free Sch. Dist. 3, Dobbs Ferry, N.Y., 1961-66, pres., 1965-66; trustee Village Dobbs Ferry, 1967-70; mem. Dobbs Ferry Zoning Bd., 1988. Mem. Am. Soc. Mag. Editors. Clubs: Overseas Press (N.Y.C.), Dutch Treat (N.Y.C.), Overseas Yacht (N.Y.C.); Tarrytown (N.Y.); Boat. Home: Dobbs Ferry N.Y. Died July 10, 1988, buried Tarrytown, N.Y.

LUCKEY, GEORGE P(AUL), manufacturing executive; b. Ontario, Calif., Apr. 4, 1891; s. G. W. A. and Bertha (Musson) L.; m. Olive Lehmer, July 12, 1922; children: George William, Helen. AB, U. Nebr., 1910, AM, 1912; postgrad., U. Goettingen, 1912-14; D.Eng. (hon.), U. Nebr., 1952. Mem. staff Mt. Wilson Obs., Pasadena, Calif., Carnegie Inst., 1915-16; Charles E. Brush fellow Nela Rsch. lab. GE, Cleve., 1916-17; rsch. engr. lab. Westinghouse Elec. & Mfg. Co., East Pittsburgh, 1917, 19; experimenter Naval Exptl. Sta., New London, Conn., 1918; physicist engring. div. A.S. McCook Field, Dayton, Ohio, 1920-26; head tachometer dept. Hamilton Watch Co., 1927-30, dir. rsch., asst. gen. supt., 1930-33, factory mgr., 1933-40, v.p. in charge mfg., 1940-52, pres., 1952-54, chmn. bd., 1952-54; bd. dirs. Nuclear Rsch. Chems. Inc., Orlando. Contbr. articles to profl. jours.; holder 22 U.S. patents. Mem. long range planning bd. Winter Park. With AC, 1919. Mem. Armed Forces Communications and Electronics Assn., AAAS, Am. Phys. Soc., Horol. Inst. Am. (hon.), Am. Ordnance Assn., University Club, Cen. Fla. Dinner Club, Sigma Xi. Home: Winter Park Fla. †

LUDLAM, CHARLES, playwright, actor, theatrical company artistic director; b. FLoral PArk, N.Y., Apr. 12, 1943; s. Joseph William and Marjorie (Braun) L. BA, Hofstra U., 1965. Actor, dir., artistic dir. The Ridiculous Theatrical Co., N.Y.C., 1967-87; assoc. adj. prof. and playwright in residence Yale U., New Haven, 1982-83. Author: plays Bluebeard, 1970, Stage Blood, 1975, Reverse Psychology, 1980, Galas, 1983, The Mystery of Irma Vep, 1984 and 24 other plays. Playwrighting fellow John Simon Guggenheim Found., 1971, Rockefeller Found., 1976, Nat. Endowment for Arts, 1981, 84; recipient Drama Desk award to Ridiculous Theatrical Co., 1982. Mem. Internat. Betta Congress. Home: New York N.Y. Died May 28, 1987.

LUDLUM, ROBERT PHILLIPS, college president emeritus; b. Bklyn., Jan. 13, 1909; s. Walter Denton and Irene (Daniell) L.; m. Ruth Althea Smith, Sept. 20, 1930 (dec. Dec. 1975); children: Susan (Mrs. Richard King), Margaret; m. Joyce I. Hall, Nov. 27, 1976. A.B., Cornell U., 1930, M.A., 1932, Ph.D., 1935. Mng. editor LeRoy (N.Y.) Gazette-News, 1930-31; instr. history, polit. sci. Tex. A&M U. (30), 1935-37; asst. prof. Tex. A&M U., 1937-39; research assoc. Gen. Edn. Bd., Cornell U., 1939-40; asst. prof. history, polit. sci. Hofstra Coll., 1940-42; assoc. social sci. analyst OWI, 1942; assoc. sec. AAUP, 1942-47; v.p. Antioch Coll., 1947-49; pres. Blackburn Coll., 1949-65; dean Coll. Arts and Scis., Adelphi U., 1965-68; pres. Anne Arundel Community Coll., 1968-76, pres. emeritus, 1976-87. Author: (with Howard B. Wilder, Harriett M. Brown) This Is America's Story, (with others) American Government, 1964; also articles. Mem. Ill. Tchr. Certification Bd., 1952-62; Mem. bd. Christian edn. United Presbyn. Ch. in U.S.A., 1959-62. Hon. fellow Consular Law Soc., 1953. Mem. Fedn. Ill. Colls. (exec. com. 1956-58, pres. 1960-62), Asso. Coll. Ill., Presbyn. Coll. Union (pres. 1957-58), Orgn. Am. Historians, Am. Assn. U. Profs., Zeta Psi. Club: Cornell (N.Y.C.). Home: Arnold Md. Died Mar. 23, 1987.

LUEPKE, GORDON MAAS, architect; b. Randolph, Wis., July 27, 1913; s. Otto Frederick and Lillian Elizabeth (Maas) L.; m. Janice Campbell, June 4, 1938; children: Gretchen, Kristin Luepke Coleman, John. BFA, U. Ariz., 1939. Owner Gordon Maas Luepke (architect), Tucson, 1945-84; ptnr. Luepke & Marum Assocs., 1950-55; mem. profl. council Coll. Arch., U. Ariz., 1959-67; mem. Ariz. Bd. Tech. Registration, 1949-56, chmn., 1955. Prin. works include: Palo Verde High Sch., 1961, U. Ariz. bldgs. Coll. Edn., 1963, Modern Lang., 1966, Computer Ctr., 1968, Pima County Superior Cts. Bldg., 1975. Chmn. Pima County Planning and Zoning Commn., 1949-58, Pima County Air Pollution Control Adv. Council, 1966-75. Mem. AIA (pres. 1951, Ariz. Architects medal 1975). Home: Tucson Ariz. Died Nov. 25, 1984; cremated.

LUHRS, ALBERT WEIGAND, association executive; b. N.Y.C., Jan. 17, 1898; s. Ernst A. and Magdalena (Weig) L.; m. Ethel Adelaide Voss, June 3, 1926 (dec. 1946); 1 dau., Caro Elise; m. Kathryn Cecelia Shulkcum, Nov. 27, 1948. B.C.E., Cooper Union, 1921. With Erie R.R., U.S. R.R. Adminstrn., C.B.&Q. R.R., Bur. Explosives and Freight Container Bur., Am. Ry. Assn., 1915-23; organized Container Testing Labs., Inc., 1923; since cons. mfrs. all types containers, accessories; mem. adv. bd. transp. div. Dept. Commerce, 1926; organizer Foreningen Container Lab., Stockholm, 1930; established Lab. Gen. pour Emballages, Paris, 1931; chief cons. containers OPM, 1940-42; chmn. U.S. Army container coordinating com., 1941-42; chmn. WPB, 1941-43, chief packing and packaging br., 1942; mem. Munitions Bd. Industry Adv. Com.; tech. cons. Weatherproof Fibre Box Group, Solid Fibre Box Group, 1943-66; exec. mgr. Nat. Paperboard Assn. and Fibre Box Assn., 1948-68; exec. v.p., sec. Pulp, Paper and Paperboard Inst., Inc., 1963-68; organizer, life dir. Internat. Corrugated Case Assn., 1962-87; partner Luhrs Research, 1976-87. Contbr. papers to publs. Served as 2d lt. Q.M.C. Res., 1929-34. Mem. Am. Nat. Cattlemen's Assn., ASCE, Am. Mgmt. Assn. (exec. com. 1933-36), ASTM, TAPPI, 100 Mile Endurance Ride. Lutheran. Clubs: Traffic (N.Y.C.), Canadian (N.Y.C.), Metropolitan (N.Y.C.); Traffic (Chgo.); Loudoun County Golf and Country (Purcellville); International (Washington). Home: Purcellville Va. Died Oct. 25, 1987, buried Purcellville.

LUJAN, EUGENE DAVID, state justice; b. Mora, N.Mex., Apr. 25, 1887; s. Mateo and Ambrose (Vaur) L.; m. Rita Pino, Apr. 1, 1927; children: Eileen Lujan Mead, Llewellyn. LLB, Nat. U., Washington, 1923, LLM, 1924. Bar: N.Mex. 1925. Asst. dist. atty. 2d Judicial Dist., Albuquerque, 1927-28, dist. atty., 1929-32; pvt. practice 1933-36, 43-44; dist. judge 7th Judicial Dist., Socorro, N.Mex., 1937-42; justice N.Mex. Supreme Ct., Santa Fe, from 1945, occasional chief justice. Mem. ABA, N.Mex. Bar Assn., Am. Law Inst., Am. Judicare Soc., Elks. Democrat. Home: Santa Fe N.Mex. †

LUKOWSKY, ROBERT OWEN, state supreme court justice; b. Covington, Ky., Aug. 23, 1927; s. Robert Owen and Esther Agnes (Cole) L.; m. Rosemary Domaschko, Dec. 30, 1969. JD, U. Cin., 1949; LLD (hon.), No. Ky. U., 1978. Bar: Ky. 1949. Practice Covington, 1949-52, 55-62; judge pro tem Kenton County (Ky.) Ct., 1952-55; judge 3d div. 16th Jud. Cir. Ky., Covington, 1962-75, Ky. Ct. of Appeals, Frankfort, 1975-76; assoc. justice Ky. Supreme Ct., Frankfort, 1976-81; adj. prof. law Salmon P. Chase Coll. Law, No. Ky. U., 1973-81; mem. faculty Nat. Jud. Coll., 1970-81; mem. Ky. Crime Commn., 1967-74, Joint Com. Revision Substantive Criminal Law of Ky., 1969-73. Contbr. articles to profl. publs. Bd. dirs. Ky. Assn. Mental Health, 1962-65, No. Ky. Mental Health Assn., 1959-62, Boys Club Kenton County, 1965-68. Lt. col. USAF Res. (ret.). Mem. Am. (chmn. bd. elections 1977-78, mem. bd. elections 1978-81), Fed. (pres. Cin. 1976-77), Ky., Kenton County (v.p. 1962) bar assns., Judge Advocates Assn., Appellate Judges' Conf., Alpha Psi Omega, Sigma Delta Psi, Phi Alpha Delta. Home: Fort Mitchell Ky. Died Dec. 5, 1981.

LUMIANSKY, ROBERT MAYER, author, scholar, English educator and association executive; b. Darlington, S.C., Dec. 27, 1913; s. Maurice Saul and Miriam (Witcover) L.; m. Janet Schneider, Apr. 18, 1946. B.A., The Citadel, 1933; M.A., U. S.C., 1935, H.L.D. (hon.), 1965; Ph.D., U. N.C., 1942; LL.D. (hon.), U. So. Calif., 1974; LL.D., U. N.C., Chapel Hill, 1979; L.H.D. (hon.), City U. N.Y., 1977, Tulane U., 1982, Ohio State U., 1982, Clemson U., 1985, Duke U., 1986. Tchr. English Walhalla (S.C.) High Sch., 1934-38; instr. English U. N.C., 1938-42, vis. asst. prof., summers 1946-47; asst. prof. English Tulane U., 1946-47, assoc.

prof., 1947-48, prof., head dept., 1949-54; dean Tulane U. (Grad. Sch.), 1954-63, provost univ., 1960-63; vis. prof. English U. Wash., summer 1962, U. Ill., 1963; prof. English Duke U., 1963-65; prof., chmn. English dept. U. Pa., 1965-73, Avalon Found. prof. humanities, 1967-74; pres. Am. Council Learned Socs., N.Y.C., 1974-82; pres. pro tem Am. Council Learned Socs., 1985-86; prof. English NYU, 1975-83; Mem. nat. selection com. Woodrow Wilson Fellowship Corp., 1958-65; mem. council Nat. Endowment for the Humanities, 1965-67. Author: Chaucer's Canterbury Tales in Modern English, rev. edit, 1960, Chaucer's Troilus and Criseyde in Modern English, 1952, Of Sondry Folk: the Dramatic Principle in the Canterbury Tales, 1955, 80; Editor, contbr.: Malory's Originality: A Critical Study of Le Morte Darthur, 1964; Co-editor: Critical Approaches to Six Major English Works: Beowulf through Paradise Lost, 1968, A Facsimile Edition of Ms Bodley 175 of the Chester Mystery Cycle, 1973, Edition of the Chester Mystery Cycle, Vol. 1, 1974, Vol. II, 1985, A Reduced Facsimile Edition of Huntington Library MS2 of the Chester Mystery Cycle, 1980, Malory's Le Morte d'Arthur, 1982, The Chester Mystery Cycle: Essays and Documents, 1983; contbr. articles, revs. to profl. jours. Bd. visitors Tulane U., 1975-82, chmn., 1979-80; trustee Coll. Retirement Equities Fund., 1966-74, Nat. Bd. Grad. Edn., 1971-75, Nat. Humanities Center, 1976-87, Duke U., 1979-87, Presdl. Task Force on Arts and Humanities, 1981. Served from 1st lt. to maj. AUS, 1942-45. Decorated Bronze Star U.S.; Croix de Guerre; chevalier Legion of Honor; Palmes Academiques France; Stella della Solidarieta Italiana; recipient Distinguished Alumnus award U. N.C., 1971; Ford faculty fellow, 1951; Guggenheim fellow, 1968-69. Fellow Medieval Acad. Am., Am. Acad. Arts and Scis.; mem. Am. Philos. Soc., Council So. Univs. (v.p. 1958), Am. Council Learned Socs. (chmn. bd. dirs. 1959-74), Modern Lang. Assn. Am. (v.p. 1960), S. Central Modern Lang. Assn. (v.p. 1952), Internat. Arthurian Soc., New Chaucer Soc. (trustee 1977-80), Medieval Acad. Am. (v.p. 1980-81, pres. 1981-82), Conf. Deans So. Grad. Schs. (pres. 1962), Phi Beta Kappa (v.p. 1973-76, pres. 1976-79). Club: Century. Home: New York N.Y. Died Apr. 3, 1987, buried Chapel Hill, N.C.

LUMSDEN, ARTHUR JAMES, business and association executive; b. Lorain, Ohio, July 18, 1919; s. James and Annie (Jackson) L.; m. Ruth Julia Pandy, Apr. 3, 1946; 1 dau., Lynne Anne. B.S., Case Inst. Applied Sci., 1941. Student engr. Nat. Tube Co., Lorain, 1937-41; exec. v.p. East Moline Silas Assn. Commerce, 1948-50, Joliet (Ill.) Assn. Commerce, 1950-56; pres. Greater Hartford (Conn.) C. of C., 1956-83; vice chmn. Greater Hartford Corp., 1969-88; pres. Arthur Lumsden Assos. Inc., 1981-88; chmn. Dodd Mead Co., Inc., 1986-88. Author: Community Leadership and Group Influences, 1965, Riding the Circuit, 1981. Bd. dirs. Hartford Hosp., Wadsworth Atheneum, Caribbean/Central Am. Action Group; founder Community Renewal Team (anti-poverty agy.). Served to capt. USAAF, 1941-48. Decorated Purple Heart, Air medal; recipient Pres. Leadership citation Rensselaer Poly Inst., 1971; commendation Pres. Nixon for advancing edn., improving housing and employment opportunities, 1970. Mem. Nat. Inst. Orgn. Mgmt., Am. C. of C. Execs. (past pres.), Conn. C. of C. Execs. Assn. (past pres.). Clubs: Wampanong Country, Hartford Golf, Hartford; Delray Dunes (Fla.); International Golf (Bolton, Mass.); Economic (N.Y.C.). Home: West Hartford Conn. Died Jan. 13, 1988; interred West Hartford, Conn.

LUNDBERG, DAN, publisher; b. New Britain, Conn., Oct. 24, 1912; s. Daniel and Frieda (Hallberg) L.; LL.D., Los Angeles Coll. Law, 1957; m. Mesa Vernell Dobson, Nov. 7, 1948; children—Guy, Dana, Trilby, Jan, Darius. Chmn. bd. Lundberg Survey, Inc., North Hollywood, Calif., also pub. Lundberg Letter, bi-lingual Energy Detente; commentator Public Service Network TV. Recipient Resolution for TV Talk Program, Los Angeles City Council, 1958. Mem. Public Relations Soc. Am. (accredited), Writers Guild Am., West. Clubs: Greater Los Angeles Press, Calif. Yacht, Petroleum of Los Angeles. Author: River Rat, 1941; Getting Into Serve Yourself, 1949. Home: Los Angeles, Calif. Died Aug. 3, 1986; cremated.

LUONGO, ALFRED L., judge; b. Phila., Aug. 17, 1920; s. Daniel A. and Innocenza (Godio) L.; m. Dorothy West, Mar. 2, 1946; children: Stephen, Cecilia. B.S. in Econs, U. Pa., 1941, LL.B., 1947. Bar: Pa. 1948. Law clk. Ct. Common Pleas, Philadelphia County, 1948-49, U.S. Dist. Ct. Eastern Dist. Pa., 1949-52, 53; asst. U.S. atty. (Eastern Dist. Pa.), 1952-53; with firm Blank, Rudenko, Klaus & Rome, Phila., 1953; partner Blank, Rudenko, Klaus & Rome, 1954-61; judge U.S. Dist. Ct., Eastern Dist. Pa., from 1961, now chief judge. Trustee Community Coll. Phila., 1964-70. Served with AUS, 1942-46. Decorated Bronze Star. Mem. Am., Pa., Phila. bar assns., Justinian Soc., St. Thomas More Soc., Am. Legion, VFW, Order Sons of Italy in Am. Died July 19, 1986.

LUSH, JAY LAURENCE, research worker; b. Shambaugh, Iowa, Jan. 3, 1896; s. Henry and Mary Eliza (Pritchard) L.; m. Adaline Lincoln, Dec. 20, 1923; children: Mary Elizabeth, David Alan. BS, Kans. State Agrl. Coll., Manhattan, Kans., 1916, MS, 1918; PhD, U. Wis., 1921; Dr. Agr., Agrl. Coll. Sweden, U. Giessen, 1957, Royal Danish Vet. and Agrl. Coll., 1958; LLD, Mich. State U., 1964; DSc, U. Ill., 1969, Kans. State U., 1970, U. Wis., 1970, Swiss Fed. Inst. Tech., 1971, Agrl. U. Norway, 1975. Researcher in animal genetics Tex. Agrl. Exptl. Sta., 1921-29; prof. animal breeding Iowa State Coll., from 1930; temp. duty U.S. Dept. State in Gt. Britain and with Coun. for Sci. and Indsl. Rsch. in Australia, 199948; guest lectr. Advanced Sch. Agr. and Vet. Medicine, Vicosa, Brazil, 1941, FAO Ctr., New Delhi, India, 1954; lectr. INTA, Argentina, 1966-67; NRC fellow in Denmark, 1934. Author: Animal Breeding Plans, 1945. 2d lt. U.S. Army, 1919. Recipient 1st Morrison award Am. Soc. Animal Prodn., 1946, Borden award for rsch. dairy prodn., 1958, von Nathusius medal, 1960, U.S. Nat. Medal Sci., 1968, prize for agr. Wolf Found., 1979. Fellow Royal Soc. Edinburgh (hon.); mem. NAS, Am. Soc. Naturalists, Genetics Soc. Am., Am. Soc. Animal Sci., Masons, Sigma Xi. Presbyterian. Home: Ames Iowa. Died May 2, 1982.

LYNCH, FRANCIS WATSON, physician; b. Winona, Minn., June 21, 1906; s. John Francis and Eva (Watson) L.; m. Viola E. White, Aug. 3, 1931; children: Peter, Thomas, Mary. BS, U. Minn., 1928, MB with distinction, 1929, MD, 1930, MS in Dermatology, 1933. Diplomate Am. Bd. Dermatology (pres. 1959). Intern U. Hosps., Mpls.; mem. faculty div. dermatology U. Minn. Med. Sch., from 1930, beginning as fellow, successively instr., asst. prof., clin. asst. prof., clin. assoc. prof., clin. prof., 1930-57, prof., 1957-74, prof. emeritus, 1974-88, head dept. dermatology, 1957-71; chief staff St. Joseph's Hosp., Ancker Hosp., 1959. V.p., trustee Minn. Med. Found.; mem. Am. Com. XII Internat. Congress Dermatology, 1962; dir. manpower unit Nat. Program Dermatology, 1972-75. Recipient Disting. Svc. award Archbishop St. Paul, 1961, Clark W. Finnerud award Dermatology Found., 1972. Mem. Am. Acad. Dermatology (pres. 1960, hon. mem. 1974-88), Am. Dermatol. Assn. (dir., pres. 1964), Assn. Profs. Dermatology (pres. 1963), AMA (chmn. sect. dermatology 1952), Soc. Investigative Dermatology (dir., v.p.), Chgo (pres. 1947), Minn. (pres.) dermatol. socs., Ramsey County Med. Soc. (pres. 1958), Am. Cancer Soc. (dir.), Pacific Dermatol. Assn. (hon.), Danish Dermatol. Soc. (hon.), Colombian Soc. Dermatology and Syphilology (corr.), Sigma Xi, Alpha Omega Alpha, Phi Rho Sigma. Home: Saint Paul Minn. Died Oct. 4, 1988.

LYNCH, THOMAS CONNOR, state attorney general; b. San Francisco, May 20, 1904; s. Patrick and Mary (O'Connor) L.; m. Virginia Lee Summers, Jan. 23, 1932; children: Michael, Kevin. Ed., Santa Clara (Calif.) U.; JD, U. San Francisco. Bar: Calif. Asst. dist. atty. No. Dist. Calif., 1933-43; chief asst. dist. atty. San Francisco, 1942-51, dist. atty., 1951-64; atty. gen. State of California, 1964-70; tchr. Insts. Continuing Legal Edn.; mem. President's Nat. Crime Commn.; del. White House Conf. Narcotics. Chmn. for No. Calif. Brown for Gov. of Calif., 1962, Kennedy for President, 1960. Recipient Man of Yr. award City of Hope. Fellow Am. Coll. Trial Lawyers; mem. Am. Law Inst., Phi Alpha Delta. Democrat. Home: San Francisco Calif. Died May 29, 1986.

LYNDE, PAUL EDWARD, actor, comedian; b. Mt. Vernon, Ohio, June 13, 1926; s. Hoy C. and Sylvia (Bell) L. BS, Northwestern U., 1948. Appeared night clubs, 1950-82; theatre debut Happy Birthday, Corning (N.Y.) Summer Theatre, 1951; Broadway debut New Faces of '56; other theatre appearances include: Anything Goes, Dream Girl, Show Boat, A Streetcar Named Desire, Irene, Panama Hattie, Visit to a Small Planet, Desk Set, Season in the Sun, Dig We Must, Once More With Feeling, Bye Bye Birdie; film appearances include: New Faces, 1954, Bye Bye Birdie, 1963, Under the Yum-Yum Tree, 1963, Son of Flubber, 1963, For Those Who Think Young, 1964, Send Me No Flowers, 1964, The Glass Bottom Boat, 1965, Beach Blanket Bingo, 1965, How Sweet It Is, 1968, Hugo the Hippo, 1978, Rabbit Test, 1978, The Villain, 1979; appeared in TV series: Bewitched, Hollywood Squares, 1966-82, The Paul Lynde Show, 1972-73, Temperatures Rising, 1974; TV movies: Gidget Grows Up, 1969, Gidget Gets Married, 1972; host TV variety hour Paul Lynde Comedy Hour, 1975; numerous other TV appearances. Mem. AFTRA, Acad. Motion Picture Arts and Scis., SAG, Actors Equity Assn., Deru frat., Phi Kappa Sigma. Died Jan. 11, 1982.

LYNHAM, JOHN MARMADUKE, lawyer; b. Washington, Feb. 19, 1908; s. Edgar Hardwick and Mera Elsie (Marmaduke) L.; m. Adele Randolph Pugh, May 22, 1947; children: Adele Lynham Brey, John M. Jr., Mary Lynham Anderson, Gale Lynham Davis. B.S. in Govt., Am. U., 1935; J.D., George Washington U., 1931, LL.M., 1932. Bar: D.C. 1931, U.S. Supreme Ct. 1936, Md. 1953. Ptnr. Minor, Gatley & Drury, Washington, 1939-51; ptnr. Drury, Lynham & Powell, Washington, 1951-69; v.p., trust officer NS&T Bank, Washington, 1969-81, cons., from 1981; of counsel Ross, Marsh & Foster, Washington, from 1981. Author: The Chevy Chase Club, A History, 1958. Bd. mgrs. Chevy Chase Village, 1963-73, vice chmn., 1965-73; trustee Nat. Ballet Soc., 1969-72, Nat. U., 1947-54, TRS Landon Sch., 1966-74, chmn. bd. dirs., 1967-74; bd. dirs. Gunston Hall Sch., 1941-46. Served to comdr. USNR, 1941-45. Fellow Am. Bar Found.; mem. ABA, Am. Judicature Soc., Inst. Jud. Adminstrn., D.C. Bar Assn., Md. Bar Assn. Episcopalian. Clubs: Chevy Chase (gov. 1949-55, 59-65, pres. 1955); Metropolitan (gov. 1968-73, pres. 1973), Lawyers (pres. 1981), Barristers (pres. 1960) (Washington). Home: Chevy Chase Village Md.

LYONS, HAROLD ALOYSIUS, physician, educator; b. Bklyn., Sept. 14, 1913; s. Harry A. and Louise (de Tourreil) L.; m. Rita M. Wood, Mar. 9, 1940; children: Harold Aloysius, Frances Louis, Gail Jean, Robert Louis, Margaret Alida Marie, George Christopher, J. Lawrence, Anne Marie. BS cum laude, St. John's U., 1935; MD, L.I. Coll. Medicine, 1940. Diplomate Am. Bd. Internal Medicine (ofcl. examiner), Pan Am. Med. Assn. Intern L.I. Coll. Hosp., 1939-40, Bklyn. Hosp., 1940-41; resident U.S. Naval Hosp., St. Albans, 1945-48; instr. internal medicine Downstate Med. Ctr., SUNY, Bklyn., 1948-49; dir. pulmonary disease div. King County Hosp. Ctr. and Downstate Med. Ctr. Univ. Hosp., Brooklyn, 1953-83; chmn. medicine St. Clare's Hosp., N.Y.C., 1983-84; instr. L.I. Coll. Medicine, 1948-49, asst. prof., 1949-50; asst. prof. Georgetown U. Coll. Medicine, Washington, 1950-51; assoc prof. SUNY Coll. Medicine, 1953-59, prof., 1959-84; vis. prof. Cath. U. Chile, Santiago, 1967, Nat. Def. Ctr. and Nat. U. Sch. Medicine, Taipei, Taiwan, 1965, U.S. Army Hosp., El PAso, 1971, Brown U. Sch. Medicine, 1974; cons. Bklyn Hosp., 1953-84, U.S. Naval Hosp., St. Albans, N.Y., 1958-73, Mercy Hosp., Rockville Center, N.Y., 1957-84, VA Hosp., Bklyn., Brookdale Med. Ctr.; sr. cons. USPHS Hosp., S.I.; med. examiner FAA; med. adv. cons. U.S. Pub. Health Social Welfare, 1964-84. Editor: Vascular Diseases of Lung. Former chmn. com. pulmonary diseases regional med. program Nassau and Suffolk counties; mem. com. pulmonary disease regional med. program met. N.Y.; mem. internat. adv. com. Aspen Lung Conf. Served to comdr. M.C., USNR, 1941-53. Decorated Air medal; recipient Achievements award Am. Acad. Angiology, 1966. Fellow Am. Coll. Chest Physicians (mem. gov.'s com., com. postgrad. courses), ACP, N.Y. Acad. Medicine, N.Y. Acad. Scis., Chilean Tb Soc. (hon.); mem. Med. Rsch. Soc. (Gt. Britain), Harvey Soc., Am. Nuclear Soc., AMA, N.Y. Med. Soc., Kings County Med. Soc., Am. Heart Assn. (exec. com., chmn. nominating com., mem. cardiopulmonary coun.), N.Y. Heart Assn., Am. Thoracic Soc., N.Y. Thoracic Soc. (past pres.), Internat. Soc. Cardiovascular Diseases, Am. Fedn. Clin. Rsch., Am. Assn. Med. Colls., Bklyn. Soc. Internal Medicine (past pres.), Bklyn. Thoracic Soc. (past pres.), Bklyn. Lung Assn. (v.p.), Am. Physiol. Soc., AAAS, Aerospace Med. Assn., IEEE, Soc. Biomed. Engring (charter), Sigma Xi, Alpha Omega Alpha. Home: Sands Point N.Y. Died Aug. 26, 1984.

LYONS, JOHN H., union official; b. Cleve., Oct. 29, 1919; s. John H. and Elizabeth M. (Sexton) L.; m. Dorothy Ann Boyen, Apr. 15, 1944; children: Cheryl Ann Lyons Lawbaugh, Joanne. B.S. in Mech. Engring., Mo. Sch. Mines, 1942, D.Eng. (hon.), 1982. With Gen. Bronze Corp., N.Y.C., 1946-54; mem. Internat. Assn. Bridge, Structural and Ornamental Iron Workers, 1937-86, rep., 1954-86, gen. organizer, 1954-58, gen. v.p., 1958-61, gen. pres., from 1961, pres. emeritus; v.p., mem. exec. council bldg. and constrn. trades dept. AFL-CIO, 1962-86, v.p., mem. exec. council metal trades dept., 1962-86, v.p., mem. exec. council, 1967-86, mem. internal disputes panel, 1961-86; mem. adv. com. White House Conf. on Balanced Nat. Growth and Econ. Devel., 1978; mem. citizens adv. council Pres.'s Com. Juvenile Delinquency, 1962-66, Bur. Employment Security, from 1962; mem. Taft-Hartley Labor-Mgmt. Panel, 1963-67; chmn. labor adv. com. Pres.'s Com. Equal Employment Opportunity, 1964-65; mem. Nat. Manpower Adv. Com., 1965-74, Nat. Commn. Urban Problems, 1967-69, Labor Policy Com. for Multilateral Trade Negotiations, 1975, Adv. Com. on Reform of Internat. Monetary System, 1977, Constrn. Industry Collective Bargaining Commn., 1969-71, Nat. Commn. on Productivity, 1970-74, Constrn. Industry Stblzn. Com., 1971-74, Commn. on Exec. Legis. and Jud. Salaries, 1973, Nat. Commn. for Manpower Policy, 1974, Collective Bargaining Com. in Constrn., 1975-76, Nat. Commn. on Productivity and Work Quality, 1975-76, Pay Adv. Com., 1979, President's Commn. on Pension Policy, 1979; chmn. labor adv. com. for trade negotiations and trade policy U.S. Dept. Labor, 1980-86; mem. President's Commn. on Strategic Forces, 1983-86. Bd. dirs. Boys Town Mo., 1966-86; trustee Connelly Sch. of Holy Child, 1979-86 . Served with USAAF, 1943-46. Home: Potomac Md. Died Oct. 26, 1986.

LYONS, M. ARNOLD, lawyer, educator; b. Mpls., June 3, 1911; s. Simon Harry and Sarah (Schoenberger) Labovitz; m. Vera Nissenson Dec. 22, 1935; children: David, Barbara Gates, Lisa. BA, U. Minn., 1932, JD, 1934. Bar: Minn. 1934, U.S. Dist. Ct. Minn. 1935, U.S. Ct. Appeals (8th cir.) 1938, U.S. Tax Ct. 1941, U.S. Supreme Ct. 1948. Ptnr. Robins, Zelle, Larson & Kaplan and predecessor firm Robins, Davis & Lyons, Mpls., 1938-88; prof. law U. Minn., Mpls., 1974-76, Hamline U., St. Paul, 1975-85. Co-author: Stein on Probate, 1986. Mem. ABA, Minn. Bar Assn., Hennepin County Bar Assn, Am. Judicature Soc., Am. Arbitration Assn. (nat. panel). Lodges: Masons, Shriners. Home:

Minneapolis Minn. Died Jan. 29, 1988; buried Mpls. Jewish Cemetery.

LYONS, THOMAS WILLIAM, clergyman; b. Washington, Sept. 26, 1923; s. Thomas William and Nora (Bagley) L. Student, St. Charles Coll., 1937-43; A.B., St. Mary's Sem., Balt., 1945, S.T.B., 1946, postgrad., 1946-48. Ordained priest Roman Catholic Ch., 1948; served at St. John the Evangelist Ch., Silver Spring, Md., 1948-49, St. Matthew's Cathedral, Washington, 1949-53; dir. Mackin High Sch., Washington, 1953-57; asst. dir. edn. archdiocese Washington, 1954-64; dir. 1964-73; sec. for Christian edn., 1973-75; pastor St. Francis de Sales Ch., Washington, 1963-66, St. Thomas Apostle Ch., Washington, 1966-76; consecrated bishop; aux. bishop Washington, 1974-88; Chmn. Archdiocesan Commn. on Sacred Music, 1966-70. Mem. Nat. Cath. Ednl. Assn. (v.p. 1965-69), Assn. Cath. Sch. Supts. (chmn. 1968-70). Home: Waldorf Md. Died Mar. 25, 1988; buried Gate Of Heaven Cemetery, Md.

MABRY, EDWARD L., business executive; b. Norlina, N.C., 1897; m. Carol S. Mabry; children: Edward L., D. Shelton. With Vick Chem. Co. (later Richardson-Vicks), 1916-64, pres., 1948, chmn., 1957-64; chmn. exec. com., dir. Richardson-Merrell Inc., N.Y.C.; chmn. bd. Reinsurance Corp. N.Y. Vice chmn. bd. trustees Richardson Found., N.Y.C., Greensboro, N.C. Mem. Pinnacle Club, Economic Club (N.Y.C.). Home: Litchfield Conn. Died Feb. 1, 1989.

MABRY, GIDDINGS ELDON, lawyer; b. Tupelo, Miss., Oct. 8, 1877; s. Milton Harvey and Ella Dale (Bramlitt) M.; m. Mabel Robey, Nov. 1, 1906; 1 child, Mabel. Student, W. Fla. Sem., Tallahassee, 1894-96, Richmond (Va.) Coll., 1896-98; LLB, Cumberland U., 1901. Bar: Fla. 1901. Sr. ptnr. Mabry, Reaves, Carlton, Fields & Ward, Tampa; city atty. Tampa, 1910-13; Hillsborough (Fla.) county atty. 1917-23. Trustee Tampa Old Peoples Home, Fla. Bapt. Children's Home, Lakeland, YMCA, Tampa. Me. ABA, Fla. Bar Assn., Hillsborough County Bar Assn., Tampa Bar Assn., Masons, Phi Gamma Delta. Home: Tampa Fla. †

MABRY, HARRY COOPER, lawyer; b. Carlisle County, Ky., Feb. 16, 1895; s. Jesse J. and Onie (Nance) M.; m. LaVerne Dages, June 30, 1930; children: Dorothy Mabry Chambers, Marjorie Mabry Howard, Elizabeth Mabry Rhodes. Grad. summa cum laude, Southwestern Coll., 1916; LLB, Yale U., 1923, JD, 1971. Bar: Calif. 1924. Practiced in L.A., from 1924; counsel Boulder Dam project, Boulder Dam power line, Mono Basin Water Devel.; local counsel Mfrs. Trust Co., N.Y.C.; spl. counsel Supt. Banks of Calif.; atty. for heirs of Lady Mendl, Don Kosloff, William Cornell Greene, Mary Greene Wiswall, Michael O'Donnell, Frank Wilkins, others; supt. Moorewood pub. schs., 1913-15. Author: (with others) Disputing Indisputable Presumptions, Revoking Irrevocable Trusts, Breaking Unbreakable Wills and Enforcing Unenforceable Agreements; lyricist, composer: Lyrics and music adaptation Hail Southwestern Hail, others. Regional rep. Yale Law Sch., 1928-36; chmn. Yale Class Reunion, 1938, 63, 68, 73; mem. Yale U. Alumn Bd., 1968-83, Yale Law Sch. Grad. Bd., 1957-83, Yale class sec., 1962-83; bd. govs. Yale Pub. Assn., 1933-38. 1st lt. U.S. Army, World War I, aviator. Named hon. Indian chief Shooting Star Pacific Internat. Expn., San Diego, 1936; hon. col. staff Gov. of N.Mex., 1950. Mem. ABA (resolutions com. 22 yrs., chmn. 1963-64), L.A. County Bar Assn., Am. Coll. Probate Counsel (founder, pres. 1949), Am. Judicature Soc., Chancery Club Am. (pres. 1929-30), Am. Legion (comdr. L.A. post 1938-39), SAR (pres. L.A. 1942-50), Calif. Jr. C. of C. (pres. 1929-30), ASCAP, Soc. Authors and Composers Mexico, L.A. World Affairs Coun., Book and Gavel (Yale), Masons, Shriners, Scottish Rite, Yale of Southern Calif. (pres. 1934-36), L.A. Athletic, Greater L.A. Press clubs, Phi Alpha Delta, Pi Kappa Delta, Tau Kappa Epsilon. Home: Los Angeles Calif. Died May 15, 1983; buried at sea.

MACCONOCHIE, ARTHUR F(RANCIS), engineer, educator; b. Edinburgh, Scotland, Nov. 8, 1891; came to U.S., 1923, naturalized, 1930; s. Arthur and Elizabeth Taylor (Gibson) MacC.; m. Agnes M. Oliphant, Dec. 24, 1921 (dec. Mar. 26, 1956); children: Arthur Alastair, Ian Oliphant, Francis Montgomery, Sheila Margaret; m. Mary Florine Dana Kopper, Apr. 5, 1958. Student, U. Edinburgh, 1911-14; BS in Engring., U. London, 1916. With Barr & Stroud, Glasgow, Scotland, 1915-16, Royal Ordnance Factories, Woolwich Arsenal, London, 1916-19; trainer wounded soldiers Eng., 1919-23; prof., head dept. mech. engring. U. Va., mem. grad. engring. sch. com.; in charge evening engring. edn. in Va. from 1929; engring. cons., Charlottesville, Va., from 1927; cons. U.S. Ordnance Corps; rsch. engr., nat. def. rsch. com., World War II; with shell forging rsch. com. Army Ordnance. Author: Thermodynamics Applied to Engineering, 1927, Kinematics of Machines, 1948; contbr. numerous articles in field to profl. jours. Mem. ASME, Am. Ordnance Assn. (adv. bd. Washington chpt.), Newcomen Soc., Raven, Farmington Country Club, Tau Beta Pi. Home: Charlottesville Va. †

MACCREA, JOHN LIVINGSTONE, naval officer, life insurance company executive; b. Marlette, Mich., May 29, 1891; s. Henry and Lillie (Livingstone) McC.; m. Estelle Murphy, Nov. 30, 1925 (dec.); children: Meredith McCrea Coyne, Anne Lambert McCrea Falvey; m. 2d, Martha Houser Tobey, Jan. 2, 1965. BS, U.S. Naval Acad., 1915, U.S. Naval War Coll. (jr. course), 1924; LLB, George Washington U., 1929, LLM, 1934. Bar: D.C., Mass., U.S. Supreme Ct. Commd. ensign 1915, and advanced to vice admiral, 1946; assigned to U.S.S. New York, 1915-19; stationed in North Sea with British Grand Fleet 1917-18; aide to Adm. Hugh Rodman, comdr. in chief, U.S. Pacific Fleet, 1919-21, various ship and shore assignments, 1921-40; aide to Adm. H.R. Stark, chief naval ops., 1940-41; naval aide to Pres. Roosevelt, 1942; detached to sea duty, 1943, to command U.S.S. Iowa; command Cruiser Division in Pacific Fleet, 1944; assigned as dep. chief naval ops., 1946; dep. comdr.-in-chief U.S. Pacific Fleet, 1948; with office of Sec. Def., 1949-52; ret. from active naval svc., 1953; 2d v.p. John Hancock Mut. Life Ins. Co., 1953, v.p., 1956-66; dir. Franklin Mgmt. Corp., Four Square Fund, Inc., Boston. Mem. adv. com. Mass. Dept. Correction, Mass. Coun. on Crime and Delinquency, 1961; bd. dirs. Boston Ctr. for Adult Edn.; mem. nat. coun. USO. Decorated Legion of Merit, gold star in lieu of 2d Legion of Merit (combat); Order of Leopold (Belgium); Order of Merit (Chile); Order of George I (Greece); Order of Ouissam Alaouite Cherifien (Morocco); Legion d'Honneur (France). Mem. ABA, Boston Bar Assn., New York Yacht Club, Army and Navy Club, Army and Navy Country Club (Washington), Somerset Club, Thursday Evening Club, Algonquin Club (Boston), The Country Club (Brookline), Delta Theta Phi. Episcopalian. Home: Chestnut Hill Mass. †

MACDIARMID, HUGH (CHRISTOPHER MURRAY GRIEVE), writer; b. 1892. Ed., Edinburgh U., also LLD. Founder Scottish P.E.N. Club; hon. pres. Glasgow Unity Theatre; dir. Theatre Workshop Ltd.; chmn. Scottish Renaissance Soc. Author: Annals of the Five Senses; Contemporary Scottish Studies; Albyn, or the Future of Scotland; The Present Conditions of Scottish Arts and Affairs; Scottish Scene; At the Sign of the Thistle; Scottish Eccentrics; Robert Burns: Today and Tomorrow; (translation from Spanish) The Handmaid of the Lord; The Scottish Islands; (poems) Sangschaw, Penny Wheep, A Drunk Man Looks at the Thistle, To Circumjack Cencraslus, Stony Limits, First Hymn to Lenin, Second Hymn to Lenin, Cornish Heroic Song for Valda Trevlyn, (from Gaelic) The Birlinn of Clanranald, Direadh, Golden Treasury of Scottish Poetry; (autobiography) Lucky Poet; Speaking for Scotland; A Kiss of Whistles; R. B. Cunninghame Graham; In memoriam of James Joyce; Stony Limits and Scots Unbound; (Translation from Swedish with E. H. Schubert) Aniara; The Battle Continues; (with M. Lindsay and T. S. Eliot) John Davidson: A Selection of His Poems; David Hume; More Collected Poems; A Lab of Honours; Chyach Sheaf; editor: The Voice of Scotland. A founder Scottish Nationalist Party. Home: Lanarkshire Scotland. †

MACDONALD, JOHN DANN, author; b. Sharon, Pa., July 24, 1916; s. Eugene Andrew and Marguerite Grace (Dann) MacD.; m. Dorothy Mary Prentiss, July 3, 1937; 1 son, Maynard John Prentiss. Student, U. Pa., 1934-36; B.S., Syracuse U., 1938; M.B.A., Harvard Grad. Sch. Bus. Adminstrn., 1939; D.H.L. (hon.), Hobart and William Smith Colls., 1978, U. S. Fla., 1980. Author over 500 pieces of fiction, novels, 1946-86 including The Executioners, 1958, Please Write for Details, 1959, The End of the Night, 1960, A Flash of Green, 1962, A Key to the Suite, 1964 (Grand prix de litterateur policiere), The House Guests, 1965, The Last One Left, 1967, No Deadly Drug, 1968, The Turquoise Lament, 1973, The Dreadful Lemon Sky, 1975, Condominium, 1977, The Empty Copper Sea, 1978, The Green Ripper, 1979 (Am. Book Award as best hard-cover mystery 1980), Free Fall in Crimson, 1981; (Recipient Benjamin Franklin award for the best Am. short story 1955); Cinnamon Skin, 1982, One More Sunday, 1984, The Lonely Silver Rain, 1985, Barrier Island, 1986. Served with OSS, World War II and to lt. col. AUS, 1940-46. Recipient Pioneer medal Syracuse U., 1971, Edgar Grand Master award Mystery Writers Am., 1972. Mem. Mystery Writers Am. (pres. 1962), Authors Guild, P.E.N. Club.; mem. Explorers Club. Home: Sarasota Fla. Died Dec. 28, 1986.

MACDONNELL, JAMES MACKERRAS, member of Canadian parliament; b. Kingston, Ont., Can., Dec. 15, 1884; s. Georges Milnes and Mary Louise (Philips) M.; m. Christine Marjorie Parkin, July 23, 1915; children: Peter, Anne (Mrs. Peter Clarke), Katharine. MA, Queens U., 1905, LLD; BA, Oxford U., 1908; student, Osgoode Hall Law Sch., Toronto, 1911. With Nat. Trust Co., 1911-44, successively trust officer, br. mgr., asst. gen. mgr., gen. mgr., 1911-39, pres., 1939-44; mem. Canadian Parliament, 1944-47, opposition mem., from 1945; minister without portfolio, mem. Canadian cabinet 1957-60; mem. Canadian Privy Coun.; created Queens counsel, 1931. Trustee Queen's U. Maj., CEF, Canadian Army, 1914-19. Decorated Mil. Cross; Croix de Guerre (France). Mem. Can. Inst. Internat. Affairs, Can. Polit. Sci. Assn. Home: Toronto Ont., Canada. †

MACDOUGALL, CURTIS DANIEL, journalist, educator; b. Fond du Lac, Wis., Feb. 11, 1903; s. Gilbert Thomas and Mae Isabella (McCollum) MacD.; m. Genevieve Rockwood; children: Gordon Pier, Allan Kent, Lois Mae West, Priscilla Ruth, Bonnie Maurine Cottrell. BA, Ripon Coll., 1923; MS, Northwestern U., 1926; PhD, U. Wis., 1933; LittD, Columbia Coll., Chgo., 1965. Reporter Daily Commonwealth, Fond du Lac, 1918-23; spl. writer Two Rivers (Wis.) Chronicle, 1923-25; staff corr. Chgo. bur. U.P., 1926-27; head courses in journalism Lehigh U., Bethlehem, Pa., 1927-31; reporter St. Louis Star-Times, 1933-34; editor Evanston (Ill.) Daily News-Index, 1934-37, Nat. Almanac and Yr. Book, 1937-40, News Map of Week, 1938-39; state supr. Ill. Writers Project, 1939-42; editorial writer Chgo. Sun, 1942; prof. journalism Northwestern U., Evanston, Ill., 1942-71; commentator Matters of Opinion WBBM-CBS, Chgo., 1972-75; columnist Chgo. Skyline, 1978-80; editorial adviser Suburban Press Found., 1959-63. Author: Brown and White Manual, 1930, Reporting for Beginners, 1932, Teachers Manual, 1932, Interpretative Reporting, 1938, rev., 1948, 57, 63, 68, 72, 77, Hoaxes, 1940, rev., 1957, Newsroom Problems and Policies, 1941, rev., 1963, Covering the Courts, 1946, Understanding Public Opinion, 1952, rev., 1966, Greater Dead Than Alive, 1963, The Press and its Problems, 1964, Gideon's Army, 1965, Reporters Report Reporters, 1968, News Pictures Fit to Print, 1971, Principles of Editorial Writing, 1973, Superstition and The Press, 1983; contbr. to mags. Bd. dirs. Chgo. Area Project; chmn., commr. Cook County Housing Authority, 1946-56; nat. adv. com. on acad. freedom ACLU. Recipient Ball State U. Disting. Service in Journalism award, 1964, alumni citaion U. Wis., 1971, citation Ripon Coll., 1951, citation of merit Journalism Sch. Adminstrs., 1983. Fellow Am. Sociol. Assn.; mem. Am. Assn. Tchrs. Journalism (pres.), Am. Assn. Pub. Opinion Rsch., Assn. Edn. Journalism, Nat. Conf. Editorial Writers (life), Soc. Midland Authors, Phi Beta Kappa (disting. service award Chgo. assn. 1983), Sigma Delta Chi (awards 1946, 53, 68, outstanding journalism edn. award So. Ill. U. 1972), Alpha Kappa Delta, Tau Kappa Alpha, Pi Delta Epsilon, Pi Kappa Delta, Acacia. Home: Evanston Ill. Died Nov. 10, 1985; buried Fond du Lac.

MACDOUGALL, RODERICK MARTIN, college financial official, business executive; b. N.Y.C., Mar. 27, 1926; s. Albert Edward and Ira (Brown) MacD.; m. Barbara Park, Oct. 31, 1953; children—Douglas, Gordon, Susan, Harriett. A.B., Harvard Coll., 1951; LL.D.(hon.), U. Mass., 1984. Vice pres. Morgan Guaranty Trust, N.Y.C., 1951-68; pres. Marine-Midland Bank, Rochester, N.Y., 1968-74; chmn. Bank of New Eng., Boston, 1974-84; treas. Harvard Coll., Cambridge, Mass., 1984-86; dir. Bank of New Eng. Corp., Boston, E.G.& G., Inc., Boston, New Eng. Mut. Life, Boston, Arkwright Boston Ins., Stop & Shop Cos., Inc., Boston. Served with USN, 1943-46. Democrat. Episcopalian. Home: Weston Mass. Died Nov. 1986.

MACDOWELL, ELMER GEORGE, business executive; b. Pavilion, N.Y., Sept. 13, 1891; s. Robert and Margaret (McEwen) MacD.; m. Mary E. Ball, May 22, 1929. PhB, Brown U., 1914, LLD, 1959. Various positions aluminum industr; with Aluminum Co. Am., 1914-28; pres. Aluminum Union, Ltd., since 1928; v.p., bd. dirs. Aluminum, Ltd., since 1939; bd. dirs. Aluminum Fiduciaries, Ltd., Aluminum Labs., Ltd., Aluminum Secretariat, Ltd., Aluminum Securities, Ltd., Aluminum Co. Can., Ltd., Aluminium Ltd. Sales, Inc., Internat. Aluminium Co., Ltd., Saguenay Power Co., Ltd. Trustee Brown U. Mem. English-Speaking Union, Brook Club, University Club, Dunes Club, Point Judity Country Club, Alpha Delta Phi. Home: Saunderstown R.I. †

MACFEE, WILLIAM FRANK, surgeon; b. Concord, Tenn., Aug. 14, 1890; s. William Thomas and Laura Caroline (Misemer) MacF.; m. Mary Virginia Stoddard, Dec. 26, 1926. AB, U. Tenn., 1914; MD, Johns Hopkins, 1918; postgrad., U. Nancy, France, spring 1919. Pvt. practice N.Y.C., from 1919; asst. attending surgeon St. Luke's Hosp., N.Y.C., 1925-29, assoc., 1929-35, attending surgeon, 1935-52, dir. surgery, 1938-52; cons. surgeon North Country Community Hosp., Glen Cove, N.Y., Nyack (N.Y.) Hosp.; assoc. attending surgeon N.Y. Postgrad. Hosp., 1935-40, N.Y. Hosp., 1936-38, attending surgeon, 1938-58, cons. surgeon, from 1958; assoc. prof. clin. surgery Cornell Med. Sch., 1936-52, prof. clin. surgery, 1952-58, emeritus prof. from 1958; clin. prof. surgery Coll. Physicians & Surgeons, Columbia, 1947-52; cons. surgeon Lawrence Hosp., Bronxville, N.Y., N.Y. Hosp., St. Luke's Hosp., N.Y., Stamford (Conn.P Hosp.; chief surg. svc. N.Y. VA Hosp., 1954-56. With M.C., AUS, 1917-18; 1st lt., 1918-19; with AEF 25 mos.; col. M.C., AUS, comd. 2d Evacuation Hosp. (St. Luke's Hosp. Unit), 1944-45; cons. surgeon, 15th Army 1945; served overseas, 1942-45. Decorated Croix de Guerre (France), AEF citation, Silver Star (World War I), Legion of Merit for meritorious svc., 1943-45; recipient Exceptional Svc. medal VA, 1961. Fellow ACS; mem. Am. Surg. Assn., Internat. Soc. Surgery, Soc. Clin. Surgery, N.Y. Surg. Soc., So. Surg. Assn., Soc. Plastic and Reconstructive Surgery, Pan Pacfic Surg. Assn., Eastern Surg. Soc., Pilgrims of U.S., Union Club, Century Assn. Presbyterian. Home: New York N.Y. †

MACGREGOR, LAWRENCE JOHN, banker; b. Itasca, Ill., Dec. 9, 1892; s. John Hope and Mary E. (Sherer) MacG.; m. Mary Elizabeth Childs, Oct. 6, 1923 (dec. Oct. 1955); children: Lois Alward Messner, Samuel Childs, John Duncan (dec.). PhB, U. Chgo., 1916; postgrad., Edinburgh U., 1919. Sales rep. Halsey Stuart & Co., N.Y.C., 1919-25; statistician Bank Am., 1925-29; investment advisor N.Y. Trust Co., 1929-33; pres., dir. Summit Trust Co., 1933-58, chmn., 1958-63; bd. dirs., mem. fin. com. Mut. Benefit Life Ins. Co.; dir. Jersey Cen. Power & Light Co., N.J. Power and Light Co. Pres. Soc. Fgn. Mission Welfare, from 1954; del. Am. Friends Svc. Com., Portugal, 1945; chmn. Atlanta U., from 1949, Spelman Coll., from 1954; trustee, mem. fin. com. Morehouse Coll., from 1946. With U.S. Army, 1918-19. Mem. St. Andrews Soc., Phi Beta Kappa, Beta Theta Pi. Congregationalist. Home: Chatham N.J. †

MAC INNES, HELEN (MRS. GILBERT HIGHET), author; b. Glasgow, Scotland, Oct. 7, 1907; d. Donald and Jessica (McDiarmid) MacI.; M.A., Glasgow U., 1928; student U. Coll., London, 1930-31; m. Gilbert Highet, Sept. 22, 1932 (dec. 1978); 1 son, Gilbert Keith MacInnes. Came to U.S., 1937, naturalized, 1951. Author: Above Suspicion, 1941; Assignment in Brittany, 1942; While Still We Live, 1944; Horizon, 1946; Friends and Lovers, 1947; Rest and Be Thankful, 1949; Neither Five Nor Three, 1951; I and My True Love, 1953; Pray For A Brave Heart, 1955; North from Rome, 1958; Decision at Delphi, 1960; Assignment: Suspense, 1961; The Venetian Affair, 1963; Home is the Hunter, 1964; The Double Image, 1966; The Salzburg Connection, 1968; Message from Malaga, 1971; The Snare of the Hunter, 1974; Agent in Place, 1976; Prelude to Terror, 1978; The Hidden Target, 1980; Cloak of Darkness, 1982; Ride a Pale Horse, 1984. Recipient Wallace award Am.-Scottish Found., 1973. Presbyterian. Home: East Hampton, N.Y. Died Oct. 1, 1985.

MACINTYRE, CHRISTINE MELBA, magazine editor, publisher; b. Los Angeles, June 13, 1939; d. George Lewis and Grayce (Parker) Shehady; m. Donald MacIntyre; children—Jeff, Megan. B.S., UCLA, 1962, M.S., 1965, postgrad. Prof. health Pasadena (Calif.) City Coll., 1969-80, weight control therapist, 1972-80; lectr. kinesiology UCLA, 1964-69; editor-in-chief Shape Mag., Woodland Hills, Calif., 1980-87; cons. Pres.'s Council on Phys. Fitness, Washington, Weider Health Fitness, Woodland Hills, Calif., Jack LaLanne Spas, Greater L.A. Nutrition Council, Calif. Dept. Health Recreation and Phys. Fitness. Author: Fitness: Teacher's Guide; Body Conturing/Conditioning, 1970, 77; contbr. articles to profl. jours. Mem. Soc. Bariatric Physicians, Am. Coll. Sports Medicine. Republican. Club: Malibu Women's. Home: Malibu Calif. Died Sept. 16, 1987.

MACK, PETER FRANCIS, JR., congressman; b. Carlinville, Ill., Nov. 1, 1916; s. Peter F. and Catherine (Kelly) M.; m. Romona North; children: Mona Catherine, Romona Melanie. Student, Blackburn Coll., St. Louis U.; aviation courses, Springfield Jr. Coll., St. Louis U., Springfield Aviation Sch., Brayton Flying Sch. Propr. own bus, comml. pilot; sponsor Mack Ednl. Tours; pilot Friendship Flame, flight in interest of peace; mem. 81st-87th Congresses, 21st Ill. Dist.; asst. to pres. So. Ry. System, 1963-75. Aviator Naval Air Force, World War II; comdr. Res. Recipient Air Trophy, 1952. Democrat. Roman Catholic. Home: Potomac Md. Died July 4, 1986; buried Arlington National Cemetery.

MACKAY, ALBERT CALDER, lawyer; b. Salt Lake City, Feb. 11, 1891; s. John Calder and Catherine Jane (Moses) M.; m. Leah Hortense Newton, Sept. 23, 1915; children: John Calder, Richard Newton, Leah Louise. AB, U. Utah, 1915; LLB, George Washington U., 1917. Bar: Utah, 1917, Calif., 1926. Gen. law practice Salt Lake City, 1919-22; spl. atty., rep. U.S. govt. in 1st case tried before Bd. Tax Appeals Bur. Internal Revenue, Washington, 1922-26; law practice specializing in taxation law Los Angeles, from 1926; sr. ptnr. firm Mackay, McGregor and Bennion, from 1940; bd. dirs. Am. Hosp. Supply Corp., Don Baxter Inc., E & J Mfg. Co., Plomb Tool Co.; occasional adv. Stanford, U. So. Calif. and other ednl. and religious instns. Sec. Italian War Damages Bd. of Am. Peace Commn., Paris and Rome, 1918-19. With U.S. Army, World War I. Mem. ABA, Calif. State Bar Assn., Los Angeles Bar Assn., Stanford Assocs., Friends of Colls. at Claremont, Masons, Bel-Air Bay Club (Santa Monica, Calif.), Los Angeles Country Club, Calif. Club, Lincoln Club. Home: Beverly Hills Calif. †

MACKAY, JOHN ALEXANDER, philosopher, clergyman, educator; b. Inverness, Scotland, May 17, 1889; came to U.S., 1932; naturalized, 1941; s. Duncan and Isabelle (Macdonald) M.; m. Jane Logan Wells, Aug. 16, 1916; children: Isobel Elizabeth Mackay Metzger, Duncan Alexander Duff, Elena Florence Mackay Reisner, Ruth Mackay Russell. MA with 1st class honor in philosophy, U. Aberdeen, Scotland, 1912; BD, Princeton Theol. Sem., 1915; postgrad., U. Madrid, 1915-16; DLitt, U. Lima, Peru, 1918, U. Bonn, Germany, 1930; DD, Princeton; LLD, Ohio Wesleyan U., 1937, Albright Coll., 1938, Coll. Wooster, 1952; DD, Aberdeen U., 1939, Debrecen U., Hungary, 1939, Presbyn. Coll., Montreal, 1942, Serampore Coll., India, 1953; LHD, Boston U., 1939, Lafayette Coll., 1939; hon. fellow, Stanford U., 1941. Prin. Anglo-Peruvian Coll., Lima, 1916-25; prof. philosophy Nat. U. Peru, 1925; lectr., writer under S.Am. Fedn. YMCA's, 1926-32; named lectr. numerous colls., sems., univs., from 1932; sec. Presbyn. Bd. Fgn. Missions, 1932-36; pres. Princeton Theol. Sem., prof. ecumenics, 1936-59, pres. emeritus; adj. prof. Hispanic thought Am. U., Washington, 1961-64; Joseph Cooke lectr. in Asia, 1961. Author numerous books in Spanish, English, 1927-83, including Mas Yo OS Digo, 1927, El Sentido de la vida, 1931, The Other Spanish Christ, 1932, A Preface to Christian Theology, 1942, Christianity on the Frontier, 1950, Gods Order: The Ephesian Letter and this Present Time, 1953, The Presbyterian Way of Life, 1960, His Life and Our Life, 1964, Ecumenics: The Science of the Church Universal, 1964, Christian Reality and Appearance, 1969, Realidad e Idolatria, 1970; editor: Theology Today, 1944-51; chmn. editorial coun., 1951-59. Mem. adv. coun., dept. philosophy Princeton, 1941-62; pres. Am. Assn. Theol. Schs., 1948-50; mem. cen. com. World Coun. Chs., 1948-54; chmn. Internat. Missionary Coun., 1947-59, hon. chmn., 1959-61; chmn. joint com. Internat. Missionary Coun. and World Coun. Chs., 1948-54, pres. Presbyn Bd. Fgn. Missions, 1945-51; chmn. Commn. Universal Ch. and World Nations, Oxford Conf. on Ch., Community and State, 1937; moderator Gen. Assembly Presbyn. Ch. in U.S.A., 1953-54. Decorated comdr. Palmas Magisteriales (Peru); recipient Upper Room citation, 1954. Mem. Cosmos, Nassau clubs. Home: Hightstown N.J. Died June 9, 1983.

MACKEEN, HENRY POOLE, government official; b. Glace Bay, N.S., Can., June 17, 1892; s. David and Jane (Crerar) MacK.; m. Alice Richardson Tilley, Oct. 6, 1928; children: Judith Tilley MacKeen Moreira, David. BA, McGill U., 1914, BCL, 1920, LLD, 1964; LLB, St. Mary's U., 1966; DCL, U. King's Coll., Halifax, N.S., 1966. Bar: N.S. 1921; created King's counsel, 1932. Read law with Henry Rogers, Harris & Stewart, Halifax, 1919-21; ptnr. Stewart, Smith & MacKeen, Halifax, 1921-63; lt. gov. N.S., from 1963; bd. dirs. N.S. Trust Co., Atlantic Bldg. Materials Ltd. Conservative candidate for Parliament, 1945; bd. dirs. Point Pleasant Pk. With Can. Army, 1914-19. Decorated knight Order St. John of Jerusalem. Mem. N.S. Barrister's Soc. (pres. 1942-44, hon. pres. 1960-62, hon. life), Internat. Soc. Barristers, University Club (Montreal), Halifax Club, Royal N.S. Yacht Squadron Club, Saraguay Club, Masons, Zeta Psi. Presbyterian. Home: Halifax N.S., Canada. †

MACKENDRICK, LILIAN, artist; b. Bklyn., July 14, 1906; d. Joseph and Rebecca (Keila) Block; m. David MacKendrick, Aug. 16, 1936. BS, NYU, 1928. Exhibited in one-man shows at Mortimer Levitt Gallery, N.Y.C., 1949, 51, Galeria d'Arte Contemporanea, Bordighera, Italy, 1955, Ga. Mus. Art, Athens, 1955, Galerie Benezit, Paris, 1957, 56, 59, 65, Hirschl and Adler Galleries, N.Y.C., 1958, 60, 62, 64, 67, Main St. Gallery, Chgo., 1959, Galaxy Gallery, Phoenix, 1963, Volta Pl. Gallery, Washington, 1964, Hammer Galleries, N.Y.C., 1970, Jacob Guttmann Gallery, N.Y.C., 1976, Hurlburt Gallery, Greenwich, Conn., 1976, Palm Beach (Fla.) Galleries, 1978, retrospective, 1946-81, Wally Findlay Galleries, N.Y.C., 1981, Windjammer Gallery, Hamilton, Bermuda, 1983, others; exhibited in group shows Audubon Artists, N.Y.C., 1951, 53, Witte Mus. Art, San Antonio, 1952, N.Y. City Ctr., 1954, 55, Galerie 65, Cannes, France, 1959, others; represented in permanent collections at Mus. Fine Arts, Houston, Wadsworth Atheneum, Hartford, Conn., Walker Art Ctr., Mpls., Hirshhorn Mus. Art, Washington, Met. Mus. Art, N.Y.C., Brandeis U., Waltham, Mass., Israel Mus., Jerusalem, Museo de Arte de Ponce (P.R.), Radcliffe Inst. at Harvard, also pvt. collections. Recipient Gold medal Third Biennial of Am. Painting, Italy, 1955. Subject of numerous mag. articles. Home: New York N.Y. Died Oct. 6, 1987; cremated.

MACKENZIE, CHALMERS JACK, academic administrator, engineer; b. St. Stephen, N.B., Can., July 10, 1888; s. James and Janet (Campbell) M.; m. Claire Rees, 1916 (dec. 1922); 1 child, Peter; m. Geraldine Gallon, 1924; children: Sylvia, Eleanor. BE, Dalhousie U., 1909, LLD (hon.), 1941; MCE, Harvard U., 1915; DEng (hon.), U. Toronto, 1944, N.S. Tech. Coll., 1950; DSc (hon.), McGill U., 1941, Laval U., 1946, McMaster U., 1951, Cambridge U., 1946, U. B.C., 1947, Princeton U., 1949, U. Man., 1953, U. Montreal, 1953, U. N.B., 1953, U. Ottawa, 1958; LLD (hon.), Western Ont. U., 1943, Queen's U., 1944, Algiers U., 1944, Sask. U., 1945; DCL (hon.), Bishop's U., 1952, Carleton U., 1968. With Maxwell and Mackenzie, engr., Edmonston, Can., 1912-16; prof. civil engring. U. Sask., 1918-39, dean Engring. Coll., 1921-39; pres. Can. NRC, Ottawa, 1939-52; dir. Can. Patents and Devel., Ltd.; mem. Def. Rsch. Bd., 1947-59; pres. bd. AEC, Can., 1948-61; pres. Atomic Energy of Can., Ltd., 1952-53; chancellor Carleton U., Ottawa, 1954-68. Officer Can. Expeditionary Force, 1916-18, ETO. Decorated Mil. Cross, comdr. Order St. Michael and St. George, 1943, chevalier Legion of Honor (France), 1947, companion Order of Can., 1967; recipient U.S. Medal for Merit, 1947, Kelvin medal, 1953, R.B. Bennett Empire prize, 1954, Royal Bank prize, 1968. Fellow Royal Soc. Can., Royal Coll. Physicians (hon.), Royal Coll. Sci. (hon.); mem. Engring. Inst. Can. (pres. 1941, Plummer medal, Sir John Kennedy medal 1943), Can. Geog. Soc. (past dirs.). Home: Ottawa Ont., Canada. †

MACKENZIE, NORMAN ARCHIBALD MACRAE, senator, university president; b. Pugwash, N.S., Jan. 5, 1894; s. James Arthur and Elizabeth J.C. (MacRae) MacK.; m. Margaret R. Thomas, Dec. 19, 1928; children: Susan Elizabeth, Patrick Thomas, Shelia Janet MacRae. BA, Dalhousie U., 1921, LLB, 1923; LLM, Harvard U., 1924; grad. student, St. John's Coll., Cambridge, 1925, Gray's Inn, London, 1924-27; LLD, Mt. Allison U., 1941, U. N.B., 1941, U. Toronto, 1945, U. Ottawa, 1947, U. Bristol, 1948, U. Alberta, 1950, Glasgow U., 1951, St. Francis Xavier, 1953, Dalhousie U., 1953, McGill U., 1954, U. Sydney, 1955, U. Rochester, 1956, U. Alaska, 1957, U. Calif., 1958; DCL, Whitman Coll., 1946; D Commercial Law, U. Saskatchewan; DSc, Laval U., 1952. Bar: Nova Scotia 1926. Queen's counsel 1942; legal advisor Internat. Labor Office, Geneva, 1925-27; M.P. from B.C. Senate, 1966-69; assoc. prof. law, U. Toronto, 1927-33, prof. internat. and Can. constl. law, 1933-40; pres. U. N.B., 1940-44; pres. U. B.C., 1944-62; chmn. consultative com. on Doukhobor problems, from 1950; mem. adv. com. U. Training Vets., Dept. Vets. Affairs, numerous govtl. commns. and coms. on various items. Author several books, 1937-41; contbr. to law jours. and other publs. Chmn., hon. pres. Save the Children Fund, Can.; chmn. Can. Del. to 10th gen. conf. UNESCO; trustee Carnegie Found. for Advancement Teaching (chmn. bd. trustees 1958-59), Tchrs. Ins. and Annuity Assn. With Can. Inf., France and Belgium, 1914-19. Awarded Mil. medal and bar; recipient John E. Reid medal Can. Coun. Internat. Law; Decorated Companion of St. Michael and St. George, 1946. Fellow Royal Soc. Encouragement Arts, Mfrs. and Commerce, Royal Soc. Can.; mem. several profl. assns., Vancouver and Canadian clubs. Mem. United Ch. of Can. Died Jan. 26, 1986.

MACKERSY, L(INDSAY) STUART, banker; b. Edinburgh, Scotland, Apr. 21, 1891; s. William Robert and Mary Luke (Callum) M.; m. Gladys Kyle Osborn, Sept. 10, 1918; children: Monica Mackersy Boynton, Joan Mackersy Grills, Anne Mackersy Hull. Student, George Watson's Coll., Edinburgh. With Imperial Bank Can., from 1911; mem. staff Nelson, B.C.; asst. mgr. Edmonton; asst. Western supt., later mgr. Winnipeg; gen. supr. Toronto, asst. gen. mgr., gen. mgr. then pres., 1911-56, chmn. bd., from 1956; bd. dirs. N.Am. Life Assurance Co., Gt. Lakes Paper Co., Ltd. Maj. arty. Royal Army, 1914-19. Decorated Mil. Cross. Home: Toronto Ont., Canada. †

MACKILLOP, MALCOLM ANDREW, utilities executive; b. San Francisco, Aug. 1, 1922; s. Andrew Peter and Linda Ruth MacK.; children—Scott, Suzanne. A.B., Stanford U., 1943, J.D., 1949. Mem. firm Leon Warmke, Stockton, Calif., 1950-53, Warmke, Arbios, Woodward and MacKillop, Stockton, 1953-55; atty. Pacific Gas & Electric Co., San Francisco, 1955-61; sr. atty. Pacific Gas & Electric Co., 1961-69, asst. gen. counsel, 1969-76, v.p. govtl. relations, 1976-81, sr. v.p. corp. relations, 1981-87. Pres. Calif. Tax Found., 1980, bd. trustees, 1981-85; bd. trustees Jr. Statesmen Found., 1982-86; bd. dirs. Public Affairs Council, 1978-86, vice chmn., dir., 1981-82, chmn., 1986-87; alt. del. Republican Conv., 1984; pres.'s adv. com. Women's Bus. Ownership, 1984; del. White House Conf. on Aging, 1981, co-chmn. pvt. sect. com.; Presdl. bd. advisors on Pvt. Sector Initiatives, 1986-87. Served with U.S. Army, 1943-46. Mem. Am. Gas Assn., Am. Nuclear Energy Council (dir.), Calif. Roundtable (dep.), Calif. Taxpayers Assn. (pres., dir. 1981-82), Edison Electric Inst. (chmn. exec. adv. com. on planning 1982), Pacific Coast Elec. Assn., Pacific Coast Gas Assn., Calif. Bar Assn., San Francisco Bar Assn., San Francisco Planning and Urban Research Assn. (dir. 1981). Clubs: Commonwealth, World Trade, Sutter, Georgetown. Died Feb. 5, 1987.

MACLEAN, ALISTAIR, author; b. Scotland, 1922. Ed., Glasgow U. Former tchr. jr. secondary sch. Rutherglen, Glasgow, Scotland; author, screenwriter 1955-87. Books include HMS Ulysses, 1955, The Guns of Navarone, 1957, South By Java Head, 1958, The Last Frontier, 1959, Night Without End, 1960, The Dark Crusader, 1961, Fear is the Key, 1961, The Golden Rendezvous, 1962, The Satan Bug, 1962, All About Lawrence of Arabia, 1962, Ice Station Zebra, 1963, When Eight Bells Toll, 1966, Where Eagles Dare, 1967, Force 10 from Navarone, 1968, Puppet on a Chain, 1969, Caravan to Vaccares, 1970, Bear Island, 1971, Captain Cook, 1972, The Way to Dusty Death, 1973, Breakheart Pass, 1974, Circus, 1975, The Golden Gate, 1976, Seawitch, 1977, Goodbye California, 1978, Athabasca, 1980, River of Death, 1981, Partisans, 1982, Floodgate, 1983, San Andreas, 1985, The Lonely Sea, 1986, Santorini, 1986; screenplays include Breakheart Pass; also wrote under pseudonymIan Stuart. Served with Royal Navy, World War II. Died Feb. 2, 1987.

MACLEAN, ANGUS HECTOR, educator, clergyman; b. N.S., Can., May 9, 1892; came to U.S., 1923, naturalized, 1935.; s. Neil and Margarite (MacRae) MacL.; m. Ruth Rogers, May 29, 1922; children: Colin Duart, Susanne. BA, McGill U., 1920; BD, Presbyn. Theol. Coll., 1923; MA, Columbia U., 1924, PhD, 1930; DD, Tufts U., 1955, Meadville Theol. Sch., 1957. Ordained to ministry Universalist Ch. Am., 1945. Instr. tchrs. coll. Columbia U., 1924-28; prof. religious edn. theol. sch. St. Lawrence U., Canton, N.Y., 1928-51, dean, from 1951. Author: The Idea of God in Protestant Religious Education, 1930, The New Era in Religious Education, 1936; contbr. articles to profl. jours. Trustee Clinton Liberal Inst. With Can. Armed Forces, 1917-19, France, 1917-19. Intercollegiate traveling fellow, 1924. Mem. NEA, Religious Edn. Assn., Am. Edn. Fellowship, Alpha Kappa Delta. Home: Canton N.Y. †

MACMILLAN, HUGH ALEXANDER, clergyman, educator; b. Lucknow, Ont., Can., July 24, 1892; s. John and Mary (Ross) MacM.; m. Donalda MacIntosh, Aug. 2, 1924; children: Ruth Mary (Mrs. James R. Lewis), Alexander Donald. BA, Univ. Coll., Toronto, Can., 1921; BD, Knox Coll., Toronto, 1924, DD (hon.), 1962; MA, U. Toronto, 1932; PhD, U. Edinburgh (Scotland), 1949. Ordained to ministry Presbyn. Ch. in Can., 1924. Sec. student YMCA, U. Toronto, 1920-22; sec. for Can. Student Vol. Movement Fgn. Missions, 1922-24; missionary to Formosa 1924-63; nat. sec. Student Christian Movement Can., 1931-32, 40-42; moderator Presbyn. Ch. in Can., 1964-65. Bd. dirs. Mackay Meml. Hosp., Formosa, 1949-61, Tunghai U., Formosa, 1953-61; mem. Sino-British Fellowship Trust, Formosa, 1953-60. Served with Can. and British forces, Wirld War I and II. Recipient citation Presbyn. Ch. Can., 1962. Home: Toronto Ont., Canada. †

MACPHERSON, CRAWFORD BROUGH, political scientist; b. Toronto, Ont., Can., Nov. 18, 1911; s. Walter Ernest and Elsie Margaret (Adams) M.; m. Kathleen Margaret Walker, Sept. 25, 1943; children: Susan Margaret, Stephen Denis, Sheila Jane. BA, U. Toronto, 1933; MSc, U. London, 1935, DSc, 1955; DLitt (hon.), Meml. U. Nfld., 1970; LLD (hon.), Queen's U., 1970, U. Western Ont., 1973, U. Guelph, 1980. Lectr. polit. economy U. Toronto, 1935-42, 44-45, faculty, from 1945, assoc. prof. polit. economy, 1951-56, prof. polit. sci., from 1956, Univ. prof., from 1975; acting prof. econ., polit. sci. U. N.B., 1942-43; exec. officer Wartime Info. Bd., Ottawa, Ont., 1943-44; vis. prof. Hebrew U., Jerusalem, 1972, Inst. Philosophy, Aarhus (Denmark) U., 1975. Author: Democracy in Alberta - The Theory and Practice of a Quasi-Party System, 1953, 2d edit., 1962; The Political Theory of Possessive Individualism, Hobbes to Locke, 1962, transls.: German, 1967, Spanish, 1970, French, 1971, Italian, 1973, Portuguese, 1979, Japanese, 1980; The Real World of Democracy (The Massey Lectures, 4th Series), 1965, English edit., 1966, U.S. edit., 1972, transls.: Japanese, 1967, German, 1967, Spanish, Swedish, 1968, Danish, 1970, French, 1976; Democratic Theory - Essays in Retrieval, 1973, transls.: German, 1977, Japanese, 1978; The Life and Times of Liberal Democracy, 1977, transls.: Italian, Japanese, Portuguese, 1978; Burke, 1980; editor: (with P.-A. Crepeau) The Future of Canadian Federalism, 1965, Thomas Hobbes' Leviathan (with an Introduction and a Note on the Text), 1968, Property, Mainstream and Critical Positions (with chpts. 1, 12), 1978, John Locke's Second Treatise of Government, 1980, Can. Govt. Series, 1961-75. Nuffield Found. fellow, 1952-53, Can. Coun. sr. fellow, 1959-60, Churchill Coll., Cambridge U. fellow, 1967-68, Inst. Advanced Studies, Australian Nat. U. fellow, 1973; Commonwealth U. interchange scholar, 1965; decorated officer Order of Can. Fellow Royal Soc. Can., Royal Hist. Soc. (Eng.); mem. Internat. Polit. Sci. Assn. (exec. mem. 1950-58), Can. Polit. Sci. Assn. (pres. 1963-64), Conf. for Study Polit. Thought (chmn. 1972-74, 76-77), Can. Assn. U. Tchrs. (pres. 1968-69). Home: Toronto Ont., Canada. Died July 21, 1987.

MACQUIDDY, ERNEST LYNN, physician; b. Hanford, Calif., Mar. 27, 1889; s. John Talbert and Pauline Sarah (Smith) MacQ.; m. Edna O. Jefson, May 17, 1918; 1 child, Ernest Lynn. AB, Park Coll., Mo., 1914; MD, U. Nebr., 1921; student, U. Edinburgh, Scotland, 1919. Practice specializing in internal medicine from 1922; physician Armour & Co., Omaha, 1922-28; med. advisor to Nebr. state labor commr. 1928-33; assoc. prof. internal medicine U. Nebr. Coll. Medicine, prof. emeritus; mem. faculty Grad. Coll., U. Nebr. Contbr. to Am. Jour. Allergy, Jour. Indsl. Hygiene and Toxicology, Jour. Am. Hosp. Assn., Archives of Otolaryngology, Nebr. State Med. Jour. Bd. dirs. Omaha Masonic Home for Boys, past pres.; bd. dirs. C.W.M. Poynter Found. Nebr., Nebr. State Blue Cross; former dir. Nebr. Blue Shield. Fellow ACP, Am. Acad. Allergy; mem. AMA, Omaha-Douglas County Med. Soc. (p.p.), Omaha Midwest Clin. Soc., Nebr. State Med. Soc., Omaha Club, Rotary Club, Masons, Phi Chi. Presbyterian. Home: Omaha Nebr. †

MACRAE, EMMA FORDYCE (MRS. HOMER SWIFT), artist; b. Vienna, Austria (parents American citizens), Apr. 27, 1887; d. John Addison and Alice Dean (Smith) Fordyce; m. Thomas MacRae, Jan. 18, 1910; 1 dau., Alice; m. 2d, Homer F. Swift, Apr. 22, 1922. work on exhbns. various pvt. collection, ANA, 1930, NA, 1950. Awarded hon. mention Nat. Assn. Women Painters and Sculptors, 1924-27, Kingdon Gould prize, same, 1928, Nat. Arts Club medal, 1930, Hon. mention on Foxgloves, Allied Artists of Am., 1932; Edith Penman meml. prize Nat. Assn. of Women Painters and Sculptors, Lucille Douglas Meml. prize, Am. Woman's Assn., 1941, Hans Hinrich prize, Allied Artists Am., 1942, medal of Merit Royal Acad. Arts, Eng., 1963., Celine Bakeland prize for landscape, Nat. Assn. Women Artists, 1945, 1st prize Pen and Brush Club, 1946, 2d prize, 1950, prize, 1955; elected Nat. Academician., 1951. Mem. Nat. Assoc. Women Artists, Allied Artists of Am., Grand Cen. Art Gallery, North Shore Art Assn., N.Y. Soc. Painters, Mural Painters, The Ten, Cosmopolitan Club, Pen and Brush Club. Home: New York N.Y. †

MAC RAE, GEORGE WINSOR, clergyman, educator; b. Lynn, Mass., July 27, 1928; s. George Roy and Katherine (MacDonald) M. BA, Boston Coll., 1953; MA, Johns Hopkins U., 1957; STL, Weston Coll., 1961; PhD, Cambridge U., 1966. Joined Soc. of Jesus, 1948; ordained priest Roman Cath. Ch., 1960. Instr. Fairfield (Conn.) Prep. Sch., 1954-56; prof. Weston Sch. Theology, Cambridge, Mass., 1965-73; Stillman prof. Roman Cath. studies Harvard Div. Sch., from 1973. Editor: New Testament Abstracts, 1967-72; several books. trustee Fordham U., 1968-71, Coll. of Holy Cross, from 1978. Am. Coun. Learned Socs. fellow, 1972-73. Mem. Soc. Bibl. Lit. (exec. sec. 1973-76), Coun. on Study Religion (vice-chmn. 1969-74, chmn. 1977-82), Internat. Soc. New Testament Studies (mem. editorial bd. 1973-77), Cath. Bibl. Assn. (editorial bd.), Boston Ministers Club. Home: Cambridge Mass. Died Sept. 6, 1985; buried Jesuit Cemetary, Weston, Mass.

MACRAE, GORDON, singer, actor; b. East Orange, N.J., Feb. 12, 1921; m. Sheila Stephens, May 21, 1941; children: Meredith, Heather, W. Gordon, Bruce; m. Elizabeth Lambert Schrafft, Sept. 25, 1967; 1 dau., Amanda. Child actor radio, stock, stage appearances: Three to Make Ready; juvenile soloist: Ray Bolger Revue; appeared in Millpond Playhouse, Roslyn, L.I.; motion pictures include Big Punch, 1948, Look for the Silver Lining, 1949, Backfire, 1949, Return of the Frontiersmen, 1950, Tea for Two, 1950, West Point Story, 1951, On Moonlight Bay, 1951, About Face, 1952, Desert Song, 1952, Three Sailors and a Girl, 1953, Oklahoma, 1955, Carousel, 1956, The Best Things in Life Are Free, 1956; night club and TV appearances; rec. artist, Capitol Records. Recipient star of season award March of Dimes, 1968. Home: Beverly Hills Calif. Died Jan. 24, 1986.

MACY, JOHN WILLIAMS, JR., management consultant; b. Chgo., Apr. 6, 1917; s. John Williams and Juliette (Shaw) M.; m. Joyce Hagen, Feb. 12, 1944; children: Thomas L., Mary, Susan Macy Jarvinen, Richard H. B.A., Wesleyan U., 1938; LL.D., Cornell Coll., Mt. Vernon, Iowa, 1963, Colgate U., 1965, Allegheny Coll., 1965, Eastern Ky. Coll., 1966, Dartmouth Coll., 1966, Wesleyan U., 1967, U. Del., 1967, Ind. State U., 1968, Ithaca Coll., 1969, St. John's U., 1969, Austin Coll., 1972. Govt. intern Nat. Inst. Pub. Affairs, Washington, 1938-39; adminstrv. aide Social Security Bd., Washington, 1939-40; personnel specialist War Dept., Washington and Chgo., 1940-42; asst. dir. civilian personnel War Dept., Washington, 1942-43, 46-47; dir. orgn. and personnel AEC Los Alamos, 1947-51; spl. asst. under-sec. Army, Washington, 1951-53; exec. dir. CSC, Washington, 1953-58; chmn. CSC, 1961-69; exec. v.p. Wesleyan U., 1958-61, trustee, 1954-59, 61-74, vice chmn., 1969-74; pres. Corp. for Pub. Broadcasting, 1969-72, Council Better Bus. Burs. Inc., 1973-74, Devel. and Resources Corp., 1975-79; dir. Fed. Emergency Mgmt. Agy., Washington, 1979-81; v.p. Nat. Exec. Service Corps, 1981-86; chmn. Com. for Food and Shelter Inc.; mem. Internat. Civil Service Adv. Bd., 1964-70. Author: Public Service, 1971, (with W.R. Keast) Faculty Tenure, 1973, To Irrigate A Wasteland, 1974, (with others) America's Unelected Government, 1984. Bd. dirs. Inst. Ct. Mgmt., 1969-79; trustee Bennett Coll., 1970-73, Potomac Sch., Va., 1967-73, Expt. in Internat. Living, 1966-69, 82-86; trustee Am. Film Inst., 1971-75, treas., 1974-75; bd. visitors George Mason U., 1973-79; bd. govs. Am. Stock Exchange, 1972-77, ARC, 1979-81; bd. dirs. Cultural Resources, 1978-79, WETA, 1981-86; bd. certification U.S. Circuit Ct. Appeals Ct. Exec., 1982-86. Served as capt. USAAF, 1943-46. Mem. Nat. Planning Assn. (trustee 1978-79, 81-86), Nat. Acad. Pub. Adminstrn., Am. Soc. Pub. Adminstrn. (nat. pres. 1958-59), Inst. Pub. Adminstrn. (trustee 1982-86), Phi Beta Kappa, Phi Nu Theta. Clubs: Army and Navy (Washington), City Tavern (Washington); University (N.Y.), Century (N.Y.); Nantucket Yacht. Home: McLean Va. Died Dec. 22, 1986.

MACY-HOOBLER, ICIE G(ERTRUDE), chemist; b. Gallatin, Mo., July 23, 1892; d. Perry and Ollie (Critten) Macy; m. B. Raymond Hoobler, June 11, 1938 (dec. June 1943). BA, Cen. Coll. for Women, 1914; BS, U. Chgo., 1916; MS, U. Colo., 1918; PhD, Yale U., 1920; ScD (hon.), Wayne U., 1945. Instr. U. Calif., 1920-23; dir. Nutrition Rsch. Labs., Merrill Palmer Sch. and Children's Hosp. Mich., 1923-30; dir. Rsch. Lab., Children's Fund of Mich., 1930-54; cons. Merrill Palmer Sch., from 1954. Author: Nutrition and Chemical Growth in Childhood, I Evaluation, 1942, Nutrition and Chemical Growth in Childhood, II Original Data, 1946, Nutrition and Chemical Growth in Childhood, III Interpretation; (with H.H. Williams) Hidden Hunger, 1945, (with Harriet G. Kelly) Chemical Anthropology, 1957; also articles in sci. jours. Bd. dirs. Detroit Inst. Cancer Rsch., Woman's Hosp., Detroit; mem. bd. control Grand Valley State Coll. Recipient Norlin Achievement award U. Colo., 1938, Borden award Am. Econ. Assn., 1939, Modern Medicine award, 1954. Fellow Advancement Sci., Am. Public Health Assn., Am. Inst. Chemists; mem. Am. Chem. Soc. (Francis P. Garvan medal 1946), Am. Soc. Biol. Chemists, Am. Inst. Nutrition (Osborne and Mendel award 1952), Am. Dietetic Assn., Mich. Acad. Sci., Letters and Arts, Detroit Engring. Soc., Founders Soc. Detroit, Detroit Pediatric Soc., Inst. Art, Detroit Yacht Club, Detroit Athletic Club, Sigma Xi, Phi Beta Kappa, Kappa Delta Pi, Iota Sigma Pi, Pi Beta Phi. Democrat. Presbyterian. Home: Ann Arbor Mich. †

MADDEN, JOHN BECKWITH, banker; b. Bklyn., Jan. 22, 1919; s. John James and Rachel (Beckwith) M.; m. Mary Audrey Ritter, June 18, 1950; children: Nancy F. Madden-Gioia, John Beckwith, Peter Fiske. B.A., Yale U., 1941; M.B.A., NYU, 1949. With Brown Bros. Harriman & Co., N.Y.C., 1946-88; gen. partner Brown Bros. Harriman & Co., 1955-88, mng. partner, 1968-83; dir. CrossLand Savs. F.S.B., Freeport McMoRan, Inc., Bklyn. Union Gas Co.; trustee Mut. Life Ins. Co. N.Y. Hon. trustee Boys' Club of N.Y.; mem. distbn. com. N.Y. Community Trust; bd. dirs. James Found. Served as capt. AUS, 1941-45. Died Feb. 9, 1988.

MADDEN, RAY J(OHN), congressman; b. Waseca, Minn., Feb. 25, 1892; s. John and Mary Elizabeth (Burns) M. Ed., Sacred Heart Acad., Waseca; LLB, Creighton U., Omaha, 1913. Bar: Nebr. 1913. Mcpl. judge Omaha, 1916; city compt. Gary, Ind., 1935-38; county treas. Lake County, Ind., 1938-42; mem. 78th-94th congresses from 1st Ind. Dist., chmn. house rules com. Democrat. Home: Gary Ind. Died Sept. 28, 1987.

MADEIRA, PERCY CHILDS, JR., banker; b. Phila., Feb. 8, 1889; s. Percy Childs and Marie Virgine (Marié) M.; m. Margaret T. Carey, May 2, 1914 (dec.); children: Percy Childs 3d, Francis King Carey, Eleanor Irwin Carey; m. Eugenia Cassatt Davis, Feb. 21, 1952. Grad., DeLancey Sch., Phila., 1906; AB, Harvard U., 1910; LLB, U. Pa., 1913, MA, 1933. Bar: Pa. 1913. Assoc. Morgan, Lewis & Bockins, 1913-21; ptnr. Ballard, Spahr, Andrews & Madeira (now Ingersoll), 1921-27; v.p. Madeira, Hill & Co., 1927-34; v.p. in charge trust dept. Land Title Bank & Trust Co., 1934-39, pres., 1940-53; bd. dirs. electric Storage Battery Co., Home Ins. Co., Bellevue-Stratford Hotel Company, Benjamin Franklin Hotel Co. Contbr. articles to profl. jours. Pres., trustee Univ. Mus.; bd. dirs. Family Soc. 1st lt. inf. U.S. Army, World War I. Fellow Royal Geog. Soc., Am. Geog. Soc., Delta Psi; mem. English-Speaking Union (bd. dirs., treas.), Philadelphia Club, Gulph Mills Golf Club, Explorers Club. Republican. Home: Berwyn Pa. †

MADIGAN, MICHAEL J., consulting engineer; b. Danbury, Conn., Dec. 6, 1894; s. Richard Michael and Josephine (Canty) M.; m. Sybil Stearns (dec.); 1 dau., Mary Jane. Pres. firm Madigan-Hyland, S.A.; chmn. bd. dirs., pres. Madigan-Hyland Co., Ltd.; asst. to under sec. war, 1941-45; cons. engr. World Bank, 1947-49. With U.S. Army, World War I; overseas. Awarded Medal for Merit. Mem. ASCE (hon.), Inst. Cons. Engrs., Cosmos Club, Union League N.Y.C. Home: Hinsdale N.H. Died Oct. 24, 1981.

MADISON, CHARLES A(LLAN), author, editor; b. Kiev, Russia, Apr. 16, 1895; came to U.S., 1906, naturalized, 1916; s. David and Pessie (Burakowsky) M.; m. Edith Hellman, July 1, 1924; 1 child, Jeppy (Mrs. Leonard Yarensky). AB, U. Mich., 1921; AM, Harvard U., 1922. Mechanic in automobile factories Detroit, 1909-16; asst. book editor Am. Book Co., N.Y.C., 1922-24; coll. book editor Henry Holt and Co., 1924-50, mng. editor, 1950-62. Author: Critics and Crusaders, 1947, rev. edit., 1959, American Labor Leaders, 1950, rev. edit., 1962, Leaders and Liberals in 20th Century America, 1961, The Owl Among Colophons, 1966, Booking Publishing in America, 1966, Yiddish Literature: Its Scope and Major Writers, 1968, Eminent American Jews, 1970, Irving to Irving: Author-Publisher Relations, 1974, Jewish Publishing in America, 1976, The Automobile and American Culture, 1983; co-author: American Radicals, 1957; contbr. critical essays and revs. to periodicals. mem. Authors Guild, Phi Beta Kappa. Home: New York N.Y. Died Feb. 2, 1985; buried West Redding, Conn.

MAGILL, ROBERT NATHANIEL, political scientist, writer; b. Kirin, Manchuria, Oct. 6, 1916; s. Orrin Rankin and Ellen (Bell) M.; children: Gordon Langdon, Ellen Gordon, Robert Nathaniel. AB, U. N.C., 1938; fellow, Littauer Sch. Pub. Adminstrn., Harvard, 1941-42. Intern Nat. Inst. Pub. Affairs, Albuquerque, 1940; spl. asst. to dir. United China Relief Inc., N.Y.C., 1941; rsch. analyst Far East Div. OSS, 1942-45; economist office fin. and devel. affairs Dept. State, 1945-47; polit. economist Far Eastern Bur., Dept. State, 1945-47; dep. spl. asst. to ambassador for mut. dev. assistance program Am. Embassy, Oslo, Norway, 1951-52, chief polit. sect., 1953-54; polit. counselor Am. Embassy, Bangkok, Thailand, 1955-57; NATO advisor, also dep. dir. office European regional affairs Dept. State, 1958-61; dep. dir. office polit. affairs U.S. del. to NATO, Paris, France, 1962; chief Berlin and Eastern affairs sect. Am. Embassy, Bonn, Germany, 1963, chief Atlantic community and def. affairs sect., 1963-64; mem. policy planning coun. Dept. State, 1964-68, exec. sec. policy planning coun., 1967-68; v.p., treas. Salzburg Seminar in

Am. Studies, 1968-70; found. and govt. rels. officer Drew U., 1970-72; sr. staff Brookings Instn., 1972-73; exec. dir. Va. Found. for Humanities and Pub. Policy, 1973. Mem. United Bd. for Christian Higher Edn. in Asia, 1971-74. Mem. Soc. Cin., Order Golden Fleece, Phi Beta Kappa. Home: Charlottesville Va. Died Aug. 1983; buried New Dublin Presbyn. Ch. Cemetery, Dublin, Va.

MAGNIN, CYRIL, retail trade executive; b. San Francisco, July 6, 1899; s. Joseph and Charlotte (Davis) M.; m. Anna Smithline, Nov. 19, 1926 (dec. Nov. 1948); children: Donald, Ellen Magnin Newman, Jerry. Student, U. Calif., 1919-22; LLD, U. Pacific, 1967; PhD in Fine Arts (hon.), U. San Francisco, 1978; MFA (hon.), Acad. Art Coll., 1979, Am. Conservatory Theatre, 1977. Pres. Joseph Magnin Co., Inc., San Francisco, 1940-75, chmn. bd., chief exec. officer, 1952-75; gen. ptnr., chmn. Cyril Magnin Investments Ltd.; chmn. bd. Lilli Ann. Corp.; dir. Spectrum Foods, Inc. Chief protocol City and County San Francisco, from 1964; v.p. Calif. Mus. Found.; mem. Asian Arts Com., Blyth Zellerbach Com.; bd. dirs. March of Dimes Nat. Found.; mem. Nat. Coun. Fine Arts Museums San Francisco; mem. exec. com. Asian Art Mus. San Francisco; trustee Am. Cancer Soc., San Francisco Opera Assn., Boys Town Italy; pres. bd. advisors Calif. Culinary Acad. Decorated Star of Solidarity (Italy); officer Order Orange-Nessau (Netherland); Legion of Honor (France); 3d class Order Sacred Treasure (Japan); comdr. Brit. Empire; Cross of Order of Merit (Fed. Republic Germany); Order of Phoenix (Greece); comdr. Royal Order N. Star (Sweden); Order de Isabel La Catolica (Spain); recipient numerous awards including: Calif. Maritime award, 1959, Man of Yr. award NCCJ, 1962, Retailer of Yr. award, 1962, Booker T. Washington award, 1962, Honor award Nat. Jewish Hosp., 1965, Disting. Citizens award City and County L.A., 1965, San Franciscan award San Francisco Jr. C. of C., 1969, Bus. and Profl. award Nat. Asthma Ctr., 1978, Leadership award Fashion Inst. Design and Merchandising, 1978, Service to Youth award Cath. Youth Orgn., 1978, Public Affairs award Coro Found., 1980, Rodeo Dr. award, 1982. Mem. UN Assn. San Francisco (life dir.), Greater San Francisco C. of C. (pres., chmn., San Franciscan award 1968), Masons, Shriners, St. Francis Yacht Club, World Trade Club (dir.). Home: San Francisco Calif. Died June 9, 1988.

MAGOON, WALLACE HERBERT, foreign languages educator; b. Syracuse, N.Y., Nov. 19, 1907; s. Herbert Arthur and Marian (Waite) M.; m. Iris Eppens, Dec. 31, 1930; children: Dougald, Duncan, Mary Anne Magoon Haring, Roderick, Patricia. AB, U. Mich., 1930, MS, 1931, MA, 1934, PhD, 1940. Dean, instr. sci. and fgn. langs. Freshman Coll., So. Haven, Mich., 1934-36; head corr. study dept., instr. Latin, Greek and zoology U. Mich. extension div., 1936-38; from instr. English to assoc. prof. Latin and Greek East Mich. U., 1938-48; prof. classical langs., chmn. dept. fgn. lands. Ball State U., Muncie, Ind., from 1948; cons. devel. fgn. langs. programs; chmn. Regional High Sch. Achievement Program for Ind., 1949-61. Co-author: Unified English Compositions, 3 edits., 1942-62. Bd. dirs. Boys Club, Muncie, 1956-58. Lt. (s.g.) USNR, 1943-46. Mem. Am. Classical Assn. Midwest and South, Am. Assn. U. Profs., Ind. Coll. Classical Tchrs. Assn., Ind. Tchrs. Assn., Nat. Assn. Colls. Tchrs. Edn. Home: Albany Ind. Died Feb. 21, 1986.

MAGOWEN, ROBERT ANDERSON, business executive; b. Chester, Pa., Sept. 18, 1903; s. Edward Thomas and Estelle (Smith) M.; m. Doris Merrill, June 15, 1935; children: Robert Anderson, Merrill L., Peter A., Stephen C., Mark E. BS, Harvard U., 1927; LLD (hon.), Widener Coll., 1960, Trinity Coll., 1963. Mdse. mgr. R.H. Macy & Co., 1927-34; v.p. N.W. Ayer & Son, 1934-35; v.p. Safeway Stores, Inc., San Francisco, 1935-38, chmn. bd., from 1955, chmn. exec. com., from 1975; chief exec., chmn. bd. Can. Safeway Ltd.; v.p. Merrill Lynch & Co., Inc., 1938-40, ltd. ptnr., from 1955; former dir. R.H. Macy & Co., Bank of Calif., Fibreboard Paper Products Corp., Caterpillar Tractor Co., Del Monte Properties, Inc.; former mem. exec. com., dir. So. Pacific Co. Bd. dirs. Beekman Dowtown Hosp., N.Y.C., 1953, San Francisco Opera; trustee San Francisco Mus. Art, 1956; mem. exec. com. Bay Area Crusade. Lt. USNR, 1942-45. Decorated Knight Comdr. Order Brit. Empire, Knight Venerable Order Hosp. St. John of Jerusalem. Mem. Assn. Stock Exchange Firms (gov. 1948-55), Brook Club River Club, Harvard Club (N.Y.C.), Nat. Golf., Shinnecock Hills Golf Club, Meadow Club, Southampton (N.Y.) Club, Bohemian Club, Burlingame Country Club, Pacific Union Club, San Francisco Golf Club, Cypress Point Club (Pebble Beach, Calif.), Everglades Club, Bath and Tennis Club, Seminole Club (Palm Beach, Fla.). Episcopalian (trustee). Home: San Francisco Calif. Died Dec. 17, 1985, buried San Francisco, Calif.

MAHAN, ARCHIE IRVIN, research physicist; b. Portland, Maine, Sept. 1, 1909; s. A.E. and Harriett E. (Lockhart) M.; m. Frances Ford Beck, Apr. 7, 1941; 1 child, Archie Harvin; m. Lillie G. Mahan, 1980. AB, Friends U., 1931; student, U. Kan., 1932; PhD, Johns Hopkins U., 1940. Instr. physics Georgetown U., 1939-41; physicist, div. chief Naval Ordnance Lab., 1942-56; sr. and prin. physicist Applied Physics Lab., Johns Hopkins U., from 1956; grad. sch. lectr. Georgetown U., 1955, 56; spl. research phys. and geometrical optics; postdocotoral research program and rev. com. NRC. Contbr. numerous articles to profl. jours. Recipient merit award Navy Dept., 1943, 50. Fellow Am. Phys. Soc., Optical Soc. Am. (bd. dirs., treas. from 1962, assoc. editor jour. from 1955, Disting. Service award 1979), AAAS, Washington Acad. Sci.; mem. Am. Inst. Physics (bd. dirs. from 1962, exec. com. 1970), Washington Philos. Soc. (pres. 1953). Home: Silver Spring Md. Died Jan. 28, 1987, buried Ft. Lincoln Cemetery, Md.

MAHON, GEORGE HERMAN, congressman; b. Mahon, Claiborne Parish, La., Sept. 22, 1900; s. John Kirkpatrick and Lois Willis (Brown) M.; m. Helen Stevenson, Dec. 21, 1923; 1 child, Daphne. BA, Simmons U., 1924; LLB, U. Tex., 1925; postgrad., U. Minn., summer 1925; LLD (hon.), Waynesburg Coll., 1951, Wayland Coll., 1960, Tex. Tech U., 1962, Hardin-Simmons U., 1964, Pepperdine Coll., 1965. Bar: Tex. 1925. Pvt. practice Colorado City, Tex., 1925; county atty. Mitchell County, Tex., 1926; dist. atty. 32d Jud. Dist. Tex., 1927, 28, 30, 32; mem. 74th to 95th congresses, 19th Tex. Dist., mem. house def. appropriations com., 1949-78, author ann. def. appropriation bills, chmn. house appropriations com., 1964-78, sr. in continuous service in house, dean Congress, 1976-78. Regent Smithsonian Instn. Recipient Disting. Pub. Service award Am. Legion, 1973, Congl. award VFW, 1974, Minute Man award Res. Officers Assn., 1974, Guardian of Small Bus. award Nat. Fedn. Ind. Bus., 1976, Forrestal Meml. award Nat. Security Indsl. Assn., 1977; George Mahon Elem. Sch., Lubbock, Tex. named in his honor, 1973; George and Helen Mahon Library, Lubbock, named in his and wife's honor, 1974. Democrat. Methodist. Home: Colorado City Tex. Died Nov. 19, 1985.

MAHON, PAUL THOMAS, lawyer; b. Dunkirk, Ohio, July 14, 1889; s. Thomas C. and Maude (Alexander) M.; m. Mary O. Dobbins, Sept. 16, 1916; children: Marjorie Mahon Bowman, Patricia Mahon McCulloch. BA, Ohio Wesleyan U., 1911; postgrad., Harvard U.; JD, U. Cin., 1914. Bar: Ohio 1914. Pvt. practice Kenton, Ohio, from 1914; sr. mem. Mahon, Tudor, Van Dyne & Evans, Kenton, from 1967; chmn. bd. Kenton Nat. Bank, 1964-70, chmn. emeritus from 1970, dir. Chmn. Mcpl. Civil Svc. Commn., 1942-46; pres. lay adv. trustees San Antonio Hosp.; pres., trustee Hardin County Dist. Libr. Mem. Ohio, Hardin County (past pres.) bar assns., Masons (32 degree), Beta Theta Pi, Delta Phi. Home: Kenton Ohio. †

MAHONEY, JAMES OWEN, mural painter, art educator; b. Dallas, Oct. 16, 1907; s. James Owen and Lacy Edna (Braden) M. B.A., So. Meth. U., 1929; B.F.A., Yale U., 1932; fellow in painting, Am. Acad. Rome, 1932-35. Mem. faculty Cornell U., from 1939, prof. art, from 1954, chmn. art dept., 1963-68. Prin. mural commns. include Hall of State, Tex. Centennial Expn., Dallas, 1936, Hall of Judiciary, Fed. Bldg., Communications Bldg, all at N.Y. World's Fair, 1938, presdl. suite, Adolphus Hotel, Dallas, 1950, Shriver Hall at Johns Hopkins U., 1957, altar piece, All Saints Episcopal Ch., Chevy Chase, Md., 1958, Fairmont Hotel, Atlanta, 1974, Acad. of Medicine, Atlanta, 1983. Served to capt. USAAF, World War II, ETO. Recipient Prix de Rome, 1932. Mem. Nat. Soc. Mural Painters. Club: Century Assn. (N.Y.C.). Home: Ithaca N.Y. Died Oct. 18, 1987.

MAJERUS, RAYMOND EDWARD, union official; b. Campbellsport, Wis., Aug. 26, 1924; s. Joseph and Agnes Matilda (VanDerGrind) M.; m. Alyce Magdalen, Jan. 25, 1947; children—Rick, Jodi, Tracy. Student public and vocat. schs. Internat. rep. UAW, Detroit, 1953-72, regional dir., 1972-80, internat. sec.-treas., 1980-87; head UAW collective bargaining units including aerospace, Dana Corp., Champion Spark Plug. Contbr. articles to labor newspapers and house organs. Wis. rep. Democratic Nat. Com., 1976-80; bd. regents U. Wis., 1978-87; mem. Milw. Harbor Commn., 1975-80; bd. dirs. Wis. Med. Coll., 1974-78; chmn. Wis. Group Ins. Commn., 1974-79, United Way of Wis., 1974-80; mem. Nat. Adv. Council Vocat. Edn., 1981-87. Served to staff sgt., Q.M.C. AUS, 1943-46, PTO. Recipient awards State of Wis., awards Bd. Wis. Med. Coll., awards Adv. Com. Unemployment Compensation, awards City of Milw., awards United Way, awards ARC. Mem. Indsl. Relations Research Assn. Roman Catholic. Home: Detroit Mich. Died Dec. 18, 1987.

MALAMUD, BERNARD, writer; b. Bklyn., Apr. 26, 1914; s. Max and Bertha (Fidelman) M.; m. Ann de Chiara, Nov. 6, 1945; children: Paul, Janna. BA, Coll. City N.Y., 1936; MA, Columbia U., 1942. Tchr. English evening high schs., N.Y.C., 1940-49; instr. to assoc. prof. English Oreg. State U., 1949-61; mem. lang. and lit. div. Bennington (Vt.) Coll., from 1961; vis. lectr. Harvard, 1966-68; pres. PEN Am. Ctr., 1979-81; Partisan Review fellow fiction, 1956-57. Author: The Natural, 1952, The Assistant, 1957, The Magic Barrel, 1958 (Fiction prize Nat. Book award 1959), A New Life, 1961, Idiots First, 1963, The Fixer, 1967 (fiction prize Nat. Book award 1967, Pulitzer prize 1967), Pictures of Fidelman, 1969, The Tenants, 1971, Rembrandts Hat, 1973, Dubin's Lives, 1979, God's Grace, 1983, The Short Stories of Bernard Malamud; contbr. short stories, periodicals, collections. Recipient Rosenthal award Nat. Inst. Arts and Letters, 1958, Daroff Meml. award, 1958, Nat. Book award for fiction, 1959, 67; Ford fellow humanities and arts program, 1959-61, Jewish Heritage award B'nai B'rith, 1976, Gov.'s award Vt. Coun. on the Arts, 1979; creative arts award for fiction Brandeis U., 1981, Gold medal fiction Acad. Inst., 1983. Mem. Am. Acad. Arts and Scis. Home: New York N.Y. Died Mar. 18, 1986.

MALAVASI, RAY, professional football coach; b. Passaic, N.J., Nov. 8, 1930; s. Raymond and Maria Malarasi; m. Mary Fleming, July 31, 1955; children: Dennis, Maureen, Sheila, Bill, Bryce. Ed., West Point Mil. Acad. With Los Angeles Rams, def. coordinator, 1973-77, head coach, from 1977; now defensive coordinator Los Angeles Express. Chmn. Am. Diabetes Assn. Celebrity Golf Classic; active Heart Assn. Jog-a-thon. Served with AUS. Roman Catholic. Club: St. Simon Judes Men's. Home: Huntington Beach Calif. Died Dec. 15, 1987.

MALLEY, FRANCIS JOHN, advertising and public relations executive; b. Youngstown, Ohio, Aug. 23, 1923; s. John P. and Mary (Hunt) M.; m. Gloria T. Kane, Oct. 23, 1948; children: Francis, Joseph, Regina, Ethel, Stephen, Mary Theresa, Thomas J.V. BA, Manhattan Coll., 1947; postgrad., Fordham U., 1949-53. Mng. editor The Spectator, N.Y.C., 1947-53; with Doremus & Co., N.Y.C., 1952-84, dir. pub. relations dept., 1965-84, sr. v.p., 1966-73, exec. v.p., 1973-84, also bd. dirs., mem. exec. com. Mem. alumni adv. council Manhattan Coll., 1967-72; scoutmaster, mem. com. Nassau County council Boy Scouts Am., 1957-72. Cpl. USAAF, 1943-45, ETO. Mem. Pub. Relations Soc. Am. (chmn. counselors acad., chmn. investor relations soc.), Fin. Communications Soc. (past pres.), City Midday Club. Home: Port Washington N.Y. Died Apr. 21, 1984.

MALLORY, G. BARRON, lawyer; b. Port Chester, N.Y., Apr. 25, 1919; s. Philip Rogers Mallory and Dorothea (Barron) Lillie; m. Eleanor Moore Davis, July 14, 1941 (div.); children: Peter D., George B., Mary R., Elizabeth P. Grad. magna cum laude, Kent Sch., 1937; BA with honors, Yale U., 1941, LLB, 1947. Bar: Conn. 1947, N.Y. 1948, Ind. 1959. Assoc. Brown, Wood, Fuller, Caldwell & Ivey, N.Y.C., 1947-51, ptnr., 1951-58; dir. P.R. Mallory & Co., Inc., Indpls., from 1956, adminstrv. v.p., 1958-60, pres., 1960-68, chmn., 1968-71, dir., until 1978; counsel Jacobs Persinger & Parker, N.Y.C., 1971-81; bd. dirs. Am. Fletcher Corp, Sutton Pl South Corp. Author: Profit Sharing Plans. Trustee Mystic Seaport Mus.; trustee, mem. membership, edn., research and policy coms. Com. for Econ. Devel. Lt. comdr. USNR, 1941-45. Mem. Assn. of Bar of City N.Y., Electronics Industry Assn. (life), Downtown Assn., Union Club (N.Y.C.), Zeta Psi, Phi Delta Phi. Democrat. Episcopalian. Died Apr. 6, 1986, buried Little Rock, Ark.

MALLORY, GEORGE KENNETH, pathologist, educator; b. Boston, Feb. 14, 1900; s. Frank Burr and Persis McClain (Tracy) M.; m. Carol Fisher, Sept. 30, 1931; children: Margaret Persis, George Kenneth. BA, Harvard U., 1922, MD, 1926. Resident in pathology Boston City Hosp., 1928, 1st asst., 1920, asst. pathologist, 1933-51, pathologist-in-chief, 1951-56, physician-in-chief for pathology, 1956-66, dir. Mallory Inst., 1951-66; prof., chmn. dept. pathology Med. Sch., Boston U., 1948-66, prof. emeritus, from 1966; chief anatomic pathology Boston VA Hosp., 1966-76, sr. pathologist, from 1976. Contbr. articles to profl. jours. Lt. comdr. USNR, 1934-50. Fellow Coll. Am. Pathologists; mem. New Eng. Path. Soc. (v.p. 1945, pres. 1946), Am. Soc. Exptl. Pathology, Am. Assn. Pathologists and Bacteriologists, AMA. Deceased.

MALLORY, HENRY REED, mechanical engineer, business executive; b. San Antonio, Dec. 17, 1892; s. John S. and Sarah (Reed) M.; m. Margaret Beauchamp Ussher, Jan. 10, 1920; children: Joan Ussher Mallory Reeves, Margaret Louise Mallory Dominick, Sarah Anne Mallory Cheney. Grad., Culver Mil. Acad., 1910; BMechE, Cornell U., 1915. Indsl. mgmt. positions various firms Buffalo and Syracuse, N.Y., 1915-26; with Cheney Bros., Manchester, Conn., 1927-56, exec. v.p., dir., 1939-56; pres., co-founder subs. Pioneer Parachute Co., Manchester, 1938-50, chmn. bd., 1950-55; ret. 1956; bd. dirs. Conn. Power Co., Hartford, Hartford Fire Ins. Co., Hartford Gas Co.; hon. dir. Hartford Nat. Bank & Trust Co. Trustee Manchester Meml. Hosp., Gaylord Farm Sanatorium, Wallingford, Conn., prior 1956; trustee Mary Imogene Bassett Hosp., Cooperstown, N.Y., from 1956. Maj. inf. U.S. Army, World War I. Decorated Silver Star medal, Purple Heart. Home: Cooperstown N.Y. †

MALONE, DUMAS, historian, educator; b. Coldwater, Miss., Jan. 10, 1892; s. John W. and Lillian (Kemp) M.; m. Elisabeth Gifford, Oct. 17, 1925; children: Gifford Dumas, Pamela. A.B., Emory U., 1910, Litt.D., 1936; B.D., Yale U., 1916, A.M., 1921, Ph.D., 1923; LL.D., Northwestern U., 1935, Thomas Jefferson U., 1983; Litt.D., U. Rochester, 1936, Dartmouth Coll., 1937, Coll. William and Mary, 1977, Hampden-Sydney Coll., 1979, Dickinson Coll., 1982; L.H.D., U. Chattanooga,

1962. Instr. history Yale U., 1919-23, vis. prof. Am. history, 1926-27, sr. Sterling traveling fellow, 1927; assoc. prof. history U. Va., 1923-26, prof., 1926-29, Thomas Jefferson Found. prof. history, 1959-62, biographer-in-residence, 1962-86; an editor Dictionary Am. Biography, 1929-31, editor in chief, 1931-36; dir. Harvard U. Press, 1936-43; prof. history Columbia U., 1945-59; cons. Nat. Assn. Ednl. Broadcasters on The Jeffersonian Heritage, 1952. Author: The Public Life of Thomas Cooper, 1926, Saints in Action, 1939, Edwin A. Alderman, A Biography, 1940, Jefferson the Virginian (vol. I of 6 vol. work entitled Jefferson and His Time), 1948, Vol. II: Jefferson and the Rights of Man, 1951, Vol. III: Jefferson and the Ordeal of Liberty, 1962, Vol IV: Jefferson the President: First Term, 1970, Vol. V: Jefferson the President: Second Term, 1974 (5 vols. awarded Pulitzer prize in history 1975), Vol. VI: The Sage of Monticello, 1981, The Story of the Declaration of Independence, 1954, Thomas Jefferson as Political Leader, 1963, (with Basil Rauch) Empire for Liberty, 2 vols., 1960; joint author: The Interpretation of History, 1943; editor: Correspondence between Thomas Jefferson and P.S. du Pont de Nemours, 1930; contbr. to mags.; editor: (with Allen Johnson) Dictionary Am. Biography, vols. IV to VII, 1930-31; as editor in chief vols. VIII to XX, 1932-36, editor, Hist. Book club, 1948-86; mng. editor: Polit. Sci. Quar., 1953-58. Bd. dirs. Thomas Jefferson Meml. Found., 1956-69; mem. adv. coms. on publ. Papers of Jefferson and Madison. Served from pvt. to 2d lt. USMC, 1917-18. Recipient John Addison Porter prize Yale U., 1923, Wilbur L. Cross medal, 1972; Thomas Jefferson award U. Va., 1964; Presdl. medal of Freedom, 1983; award Miller Ctr., 1982; chmn.'s citation NEH, 1979; Guggenheim fellow, 1951-52, 58-59. Mem. Am. Hist. Assn., Am. Antiquarian Soc., Am. Acad. Arts and Scis., Mass. Hist. Soc. (Kennedy medal 1972), So. Hist. Assn. (pres. 1967-68), Soc. Am. Historians (Bruce Catton prize 1984), Va. Hist. Soc., Phi Beta Kappa (vis. scholar 1964-65, 60-67; medal for contbn. to humanities 1982), Omicron Delta Kappa, Raven Soc. Democrat. Clubs: Century (N.Y.C.), Virginians (N.Y.C.); Cosmos (Washington). Home: Charlottesville Va. Died Dec. 27, 1986.

MAMOULIAN, ROUBEN, stage and motion picture director; b. Tiflis, Caucasus, Russia, Oct. 8, 1897; came to U.S., 1923, naturalized, 1930; s. Zachary and Virginia (Kalantarian) M.; m. Azadia Newman, 1945. Ed., Lycee Montaigne, Paris, Tiflis Gymnasium; grad. in law, Moscow (Russia) U. Stage dir. 1918—; guest lectr. UCLA, U. So. Calif., U. Utah, Washington Club; Lectures, seminar and showing Mamoulian films U. Calif., Santa Barbara, Feb., 1975, Calif. State Coll. at Long Beach, 1976, Am. Film Inst., 1976, 77, N.C. State U., 1977, Filmex, Hollywood, 1977, U. So. Calif., 1977; pres. Internat. jury Internat. Film Festival, San Sebastian, Spain, 1973. (Recipient Rouben Mamoulin Award for best Australian Short Film established 1974, Award of Excellence Armenian Am. Bicentennial Commemoration 1976, Hall of Fame award Count Dracula Soc. 1977, named King Internat. Cat Film Festival 1976), Author (with Maxwell Anderson); mus. play The Devil's Hornpipe; made into: mus. film The Cat at the Manger, 1964, Shakespeare's Hamlet, A New Version, 1966; Contbr.: mus. film Reader's Digest, 1968, Ararat, 1969; Writer of short stories, verse and, articles in field.; first English prodn. Beating on the Door, St. James' Theatre, London, 1922; dir. prodn., Eastman Theatre, Rochester, N.Y., 1923-26, grand operas, operettas and musicals; organizer, Eastman Theatre Sch., 1925, dir., until 1926, Theatre Guild on Broadway, 1926-30; of plays Porgy and Bess; opera; motion pictures Rings on Her Fingers; musical prodn. Oklahoma, N.Y.C., 1943, in Rome, Paris, Naples, Milan, Venice, 1955, Sadie Thompson in New York, 1944, Carousel in New York, 1945, St. Louis Woman in New York, 1946; Summer Holiday musical film (Eugene O'Neill's Ah, Wilderness), 1947, Lost in the Stars, 1949, Arms and the Girl, 1950, Oklahoma and, Carousel, in Los Angeles and San Francisco, 1953, Adolph Zukor's Golden Film Jubilee Celebration, 1953, Silk Stockings, 1956; dir. films: Applause, 1929, City Streets, 1931, Dr. Jekyll and Mr. Hyde, 1932, Love Me Tonight, 1932, Song of Songs, 1933, Queen Christina, 1933, We Live Again, 1934, Becky Sharp, 1935, The Gay Desperado, 1936, High, Wide and Handsome, 1937, Golden Boy, 1939, The Mark of Zorro, 1940, Blood and Sand, 1941, Rings on Her Fingers, 1948, Summer Holiday, 1957; World premiere prodn. Shakespeare's Hamlet, A New Version, Lexington, Ky., 1966, Tribute to Rouben Mamoulian, retrospective; appeared World premiere prodn., U.S., lCan., Eng., 1967-71, guest of honor, Internat. Film Festivals, Moscow, 1971, Sydney Australia, Tehran, Iran, Republics Armenia and Georgia, 1971, Ispahan, Shiraz and Persipolis, 1974; numerous TV, radio and personal appearances including Swiss TV, 1977. Home: Beverly Hills Calif. Died Dec. 4, 1987.

MANDANICI, JOHN C., mayor; b. Bridgeport, Conn., Jan. 1, 1918; s. Virgil and Mary (Guardina) M.; m. Mary Grace Mullins, Aug. 31, 1940; children: Mary Louise, John C., Francis V., Cecelia E. Grad. high sch. Various positions to store mgr. A&P Tea Co., Bridgeport, from 1938; mem. Bridgeport Zoning Commn., 1965-68; city clk. City of Bridgeport, after 1969, then, mayor. Trustee council, pres. adv. bd. treas. Bridgeport Roman Cath. Diocese. Mem. Unico Club. Democrat. Died Jan. 7, 1986.

MANDELBAUM, DAVID GOODMAN, anthropologist, educator; b. Chgo., Aug. 22, 1911; s. Samuel and Lena (Goodman) M.; m. Ruth Weiss, May 23, 1943; children—Michael E., Susan F., Jonathan E. (dec.). B.A., Northwestern U., 1932; Ph.D., Yale, 1936. Instr., asst. prof. U. Minn., 1938-46; research analyst U.S. Govt. agys. 1942-43; chief Indian-Cylon sect. Office Research and Intelligence, Dept. of State, 1946; asso. prof. anthropology U. Calif. at Berkeley, 1946-48, prof., 1948-87, chmn. dept., 1955-57; chmn. Center South Asia Studies, 1965-68; vis. Fulbright prof. U. Cambridge, Eng., 1953; dir. Ednl. Resources in Anthropology Project, 1959-61. Author: The Plains Cree, 1940, 2d edit., 1978, Soldier Groups and Negro Soldiers, 1952, Society in India, 1970, Human Fertility in India, 1974, Women's Seclusion and Men's Honor, 1988; Editor: Selected Writings of Edward Sapir, 1949; co-editor: The Teaching of Anthropology, 1963; festschrift: Dimensions of Social Life: Essays in Honor of David G. Mandelbaum, 1987. Mem. U.S. Nat. Commn. for UNESCO, 1957-62, 75. Served from 1st lt. to maj. AUS, 1943-46. Fellow NRC, 1937-38; Fellow Carnegie Corp., 1941-42; Guggenheim fellow, 1949-50; fellow Center Advanced Studies Behavioral Scis., 1957-58; sr. fellow Am. Inst. Indian Studies, 1963-64, 75; recipient citation of merit U. Calif., 1979. Mem. Am. Anthrop. Assn., Am. Oriental Soc., Soc. Applied Anthropology, Am. Ethnol. Soc., Assn. Asian Studies, Soc. South India Studies (pres. 1980—), AAAS (chmn. anthropology sect. 1976), Sigma Xi. Home: Berkeley Calif. Died Apr. 19, 1987; buried Rolling Hills Cemetery, El Sobrante, Calif.

MANDELBAUM, MAURICE H., philosophy educator; b. Chgo., Dec. 9, 1908; s. Maurice H. and Ida (Mandel) M.; m. Gwendolyn Norton, Oct. 1, 1932; children: Ann, John D.; m. Alice L. Moran, Mar. 21, 1949; m. Leland B. Hill, 1981. A.B., Dartmouth Coll., 1929, M.A., 1932, D.H.L., 1979; Ph.D., Yale U., 1936; D.H.L., Johns Hopkins U., 1981. Asst. instr. biography and comparative lit. Dartmouth, 1931-32; from instr. to assoc. prof. philosophy Swarthmore Coll., 1934-47; prof. philosophy Dartmouth Coll., 1947-57; prof. philosophy Johns Hopkins U., 1957-67, Andrew W. Mellon prof. philosopy, 1967-78, prof. Humanities Center, 1974-78; adj. prof. philosophy Dartmouth Coll., 1979-87; vis. prof. Harvard, Haverford Coll., U. Mich.; mem. Council Philos. Studies, 1969-72. Author: The Problem of Historical Knowledge, 1938, The Phenomenology of Moral Experience, 1955, Philosophy, Science, and Sense Perception, 1964, History, Man, and Reason, 1971, The Anatomy of Historical Knowledge, 1977, Philosophy, History, and the Sciences, 1984, Purpose and Necessity in Social Theory, 1987; Am. collaborator: Bibliographie de la Philosophie, 1937-40; Editor: Art, Perception, and Reality, 1972; Co-editor: Philosophic Problems, rev, 1967, Phenomenology and Existentialism, 1967, Spinoza: Essays in Interpretation, 1975. Mem. Nat. Bd. Grad. Edn., 1971-75; mem. Md. Commn. Humanities and Pub. Policy, 1974-77. Recipient Wilbur L. Cross medal Yale U. Grad. Sch., 1980; Guggenheim fellow, 1946; fellow Center Advanced Study Behavioral Scis., 1967-68; Mellon sr. fellow Nat. Humanities Ctr., 1986. Mem. Am. Philos. Assn. (pres. 1962, chmn. bd. officers 1968-74), Am. Acad. Arts and Scis., Phi Beta Kappa. Home: Hanover N.H. Died Jan., 1987.

MANGES, HORACE S., lawyer; b. N.Y.C., July 20, 1898; s. Samuel F. and Alice (Bamberger) M.; m. Natalie Bloch, June 24, 1924 (dec. Sept. 1983): children: James H., Gerard H. (dec.). AB, Columbia U., 1917, AM, LLB, 1919. Bar: N.Y. 1920, D.C 1953. Ptnr. firm Gleason, McLanahan, Merritt & Ingraham, N.Y.C., 1924-26, Weil, Coursen & Manges, N.Y.C., 1926-31; ptnr. firm Weil, Gotshal & Manges, N.Y.C., 1931-76, of counsel, 1976-86; spl. asst. to atty. gen. U.S., 1953-55; cons. to Librarian of Congress on Gen. Revision of U.S. Copyright Law; counsel Am. Book Pubs. Coun. Inc.; former trustee, v.p. Copyright Soc. U.S.A. Govt. appeal agt. SSS, 1940-47; trustee Mt. Sinai Hosp., N.Y.C., 1942-63. Fellow Am. Coll. Trial Lawyers; mem. ABS, Assn. Bar City N.Y. (exec. com. 1949-53, com. on grievances 1954-57, vice chmn. 1956-57, com. on judiciary 1943-48, 61-64), N.Y. County Lawyers Assn., Am. Arbitration Assn. (arbitrator, past dir.), Delta Sigma Rho, Pi Lambda Phi. Died Feb. 11, 1986; buried Hastings-on-Hudson, N.Y.

MANIER, MILLER, lawyer; b. Nashville, Jan. 15, 1897; s. Will Rucker and Mary (Owsley) M.; m. Ada Childers, Mar. 8, 1956. B.S., Vanderbilt U., 1917, LL.B., 1920; grad., U.S. Army Sch. Mil. Aeros., U. Tex., 1918. Bar: Tenn. 1919. Assoc., later ptnr. Manier & Crouch, Nashville, 1919-48; ptnr. Manier, White, Herod, Hollabaugh & Smith, and predecessors, 1948-86; instr. Nashville YMCA Night Law Sch., 1924-53; Mem. Davidson County bd. Tenn. War Price and Rationing Bd., 1941-42, Uniform Law Commn. Tenn., 1940-60. Assoc. editor: Ins. Counsel Jour, 1947-57. Served as pfc. (flying cadet) A.S. Aeronautics U.S. Army, 1917-18; from lt. to lt. comdr. USNR, 1942-52; active duty 1944-45, PTO. Recipient Presdl. certificate, Tenn. certificate for services Registration Day, 1940; H. Laird Smith Alumni award Nashville chpt. Phi Delta Theta Alumni Club, 1972. Fellow Internat. Acad. Trial Lawyers; mem. ABA, Tenn. Bar Assn. (chmn. ins. sec. 1957-58), Nashville Bar Assn. (50-Yr. award 1970), Inter-Am. Bar Assn., Internat. Ins. Counsel Assn., Am. Judicature Soc., Vets. World War I of U.S.A., Assn. Ins. Attys. (gov. Tenn., exec. com 1953-58, pres. 1956-57), Probate Attys. Assn. (pres. 1956-57, exec. com. 1955-58, chmn. bd. 1958), Comml. Law League Am. (life), Law Sci. Acad. (diplomate), Am. Coll. Trial Lawyers, C. of C., Nat. Conf. Uniform Law Commrs. (life), SAR, VFW, Retreads, Inc., Am. Coll. Probate Counsel (pres. 1957-59, bd. regents 1960-67), Am. Legion (adj. Davidson County post 1919-22, Golden certificate 1973, life mem.), 40 and 8, Scribes, Phi Delta Phi (internat. pres. 1927-29, mem. ct. appeals 1929-39), Phi Delta Theta (past pres. Gamma province, mem. survey commn.). Methodist (chmn. bd. stewards 1946-48, mem. ofcl. bd. 1924—, now trustee). Lodges: Rotary (50 yr. button, Paul Harris fellow), Elks (Nashville). Home: Nashville Tenn. Died Dec. 17, 1986, buried Mt. Olivet Cemetery, Nashville.

MANLEY, MARIAN CATHERINE, librarian; b. Atchison, Kans., June 17, 1892; d. Reuben and Harriet (Stringfellow) M.; m. Gerald Haldane Winser, Oct. 18, 1924. MA (hon.), Rutgers U., 1950. Adminstrv. asst. Newark Pub. Library, 1915-20, head fiction dept., 1923-25, bus. br. librarian, 1926-54; head adult dept. Sioux City (Iowa) Pub. Library, 1920-23; library cons.; lectr. Rutgers U. Sch. Bus. Adminstrn., Grad. Sch. Library Svc., 1956. Author: Business Information and Its Sources, 1931, supplement, 1939, Business Magazines—Classified by Subject, 1933, Business Directories—A Key to Their Use, 1934, Business Book Shelf, 1935, Public Library Service to Business, 1942, Business Information: How to Find and Use It, 1955; editor: Special Library Profession and What It Offers, 1938, Business and the Public Library, 1940, Library Service to Business, 1946, Handbook for Library Trustees, 1955; editor Spl. Libraries, 1934-39; contbr. articles to profl. jours. Chmn., mem. com. econ. devel. Library Svc.. from 1944; mem. Summit (N.J.) Library Bd., 1947-59. Recipient Lippincott award, 1953. Mem. Spl. Libraries Assn. (chmn. comml. tech. group, chmn. membership com., 1932-34, exec. bd., 1935-39, pres. N.J. chpt. 1937-39, chmn. tng. and recruiting com. 1937-39, elected Hall of Fame 1959), ALA (activities com. 1937-39, candidate for exec. bd. 1940, nominating com. 1942, editorial com. 1942-44, chmn. com. on relations with local groups), N.J. Library Assn. (v.p. 1945-46, pres. 1946-47). Democrat. Episcopalian. Home: Summit N.J. †

MANN, FREDRIC RAND, corrugated products company executive; b. Gomel, Russia, Sept. 13, 1903; came to U.S., 1904, naturalized, 1914; s. Oscar and Fannie (Fradkin) M. BS, U. Pa., 1924; MusD (hon.), Combs COll. Music, 1958, Phila. Mus. Acad., 1959. Pres. Mannkraft Corp., from 1959; bd. dirs. Bankers Bond & Mortgage Guaranty Corp., Loft Candy Co., St. Joe Paper Co. U.S. ambassador to Barbados and spl. rep. to Antigua, Dominica, Granada and St. Kitts-Nevus, 1968-69; commr. Fairmont Park, Phila,, from 1951; treas. Hebrew and Gognate Learning Dropsie Coll., from 1953; founder, v.p. Phila. Indsl. Devel. Corp., from 1957; dir. Phila. Port Corp., from 1965; mem. U.S. Mint Assay Commn., from 1943, Nat. Ind. Hist. Park Commn., from 1960; treas. Phila. Orch. Pension Found., from 1948; pres. Robin Hood Dell Concerts, Inc., from 1949. Decorated cavaliere ufficil le del Ordine al Merito Republica Italiana, 1949, Nat. Order So. Cross (Brazil), 1965. Deceased.

MANN, JAMES HAROLD, lawyer; b. Edmonton, Ky., Nov. 23, 1913; s. James Harbert and Margaret Bell (Walker) M.; m. Margaret Ellis Blackwell, Aug. 31, 1940; children: Margaret B., Judith W. AB with honors, Centre Coll., 1935; LLB with distinction, Cornell U., 1938. Bar: Ky. 1938, U.S. Supreme Ct., 1962. Atty. U.S. Treas. Dept., Washington, 1938-40, 41-42; asst. prof. law U. Ark., 1940-41; spl. asst. to Am. ambassador to Buenos Aires, 1942-44, London, 1944-45; Am. mem. Joint Commn., U.S., U.K., France, Switzerland, 1945-47; ptnr. Lucas, Friedman & Mann (and predecessor firms), Washington, 1948-85. Exec. vice chmn. Dem. Cen. Com., Montgomery County, Md., 1954-58, mem. resolutions com. Md. Dem. Conv., 1956, candidate for nomination U.S. Congress, 1958; del. Dem. Nat. Conv., 1960. Named Disting. Alumnus Centre Coll., 1980. Mem. D.C. Bar Assn., Cornell Law Assn. (exec. com. 1957-60) Am. Judicare Soc., Cornell Club, Dacor House (Washington), Delta Theta Phi, Delta Kappa Epsilon. Home: Poolesville Md.

MANN, STELLA IRENE (MRS. GEORGE DOUGLAS MANN), newspaper executive; b. Buxton, N.D., Feb. 2, 1892; d. Ole S. and Maria Charlotte (Olson) Hilleboe; m. George Douglas Mann, Mar. 20, 1929 (died Mar. 26, 1936). Student, Mayville Tchrs. Coll., 1909-11; BA, U. N.D., 1915; MA, U. Iowa, 1927. Tchr. city sch. Grand Forks, N.D., 1915-16, Mayville, N.D., 1916-17, Mpls., 1918-21, Duluth, Minn., 1922-24; instr. Minn. State Tchrs. Coll., Bemidji, 1924-26, N.D. State Tchrs. Coll., Ellendale, 1926-28; pres. and treas. Bismarck Tribune Co., from 1936, also bd. dirs. Bd. dirs. Red Cross. Recipient Pulitzer Gold medal in journalism Bismarck Tribune, 1938. Mem. Fortnightly Club, Alpha Phi, Pi Lambda Theta, Delta Kappa Gamma. Republican. Lutheran. Home: Bismarck N.D. †

MANNING, MERRILL MILE, lawyer; b. Crawford, Nebr., June 22, 1891. BS, Iowa State Coll., 1914; LLB, Harvard U., 1917. Bar: N.Y. 1918. Mem. firm.

Cadwalader, Wickersham & Taft, N.Y.C. Mem. ABA, N.Y. State Bar Assn., Assn. Bar City N.Y. †

MANNING, REGINALD, (Reg) West, cartoonist, copper wheel crystal designer and engraver; b. Kansas City, Mo., Apr. 8, 1905; s. Charles Augustus and Mildred Ann (Joslin) M.; student pub. schs., Kansas City, Phoenix; m. Ruth Elizabeth Littlefield, Oct. 1, 1926; 1 son, David Clark. Free lance cartoonist, 1924-26; cartoonist Ariz. Republic Phoenix, 1926-86; editorial cartoonist McNaught Syndicate, Inc., N.Y.C., 1948-71; owner Reganson Cartoon Books; lectr. illus. polit. satire; exhibited one-man show crystal engravings at Phoenix Art Mus., 1973-74. Bd. dirs. Pioneer Ariz. Found. Recipient Pulitzer prize for cartooning, 1951, Freedoms Found. Cartoon Awards, 1950, 51, 52, 55, 59, 61, 63, 67, 68, 69, 73, 74, 75, Nat. Safety Council award, 1957, Abraham Lincoln award Freedom's Found., 1971, 72. Mem. Assn. Am. Editorial Cartoonists, Nat. Cartoonists Soc., S.A.R., Ariz. Srs. Golf Assn. (pres. 1966), S.W. Parks and Monuments Assn. (chmn. bd. 1967-68), Ariz. Hist. Soc., Syracuse U. Library Assos. (life), Ariz. State U. Library Assos. (chmn. bd. 1974-75). Clubs: Prescott Country, Ariz. Press (life), Phoenix Press. Author: Cartoon Guide of Arizona, 1938; What Kinda Cactus izzat?, 1941; From Tee to Cup, 1954; What is Arizona Really Like?, 1968; Desert in Crystal, 1973; creator more than 15,000 editorial cartoons. Died Mar. 11, 1986; buried Green Acres Meml. Gardens, Scottsdale, Ariz. Home: Scottsdale Ariz.

MANSELL, IRVING LAWSON, newspaper editor; b. McKeesport, Pa., June 4, 1908; s. Irving Van Voorhis and Cordelia Wheeler (Smith) M.; m. Agnes Lucille McConaghy, June 30, 1931; children: John Lawson, Jane Lucille. BA, Westminster (Pa.) Coll., 1929, DLitt (hon.), 1954. Reporter Youngstown Vindicator, 1929-38, copy reader, make-up editor, fin. editor, telegraph editor, 1938-44, asst. city editor, 1946-49, mng. editor, 1949-76; editor New Wilmington (Pa.) Globe, 1935-36. Trustee Westminster Coll.; pres. bd. dirs. Shenango United Presbyn. Home. Lt. armed guard USNR, 1944-46. Mem. Westminster Coll. Alumni Assn. (nat. pres. 1950-52), Pi Delta Epsilon, Alpha Sigma Phi. Home: New Wilmington Pa. Died July 26, 1983.

MANSFIELD, DONALD BRUCE, lawyer, utility executive; b. Hamilton, Ohio, Jan. 31, 1910; s. Paul Chandler and Katharine Simon (Marr) M.; m. Louise Elliott Littehale, Dec. 23, 1939; children: Alexander, Jane, Louise, Muriel. AB, Kenyon Coll., 1930, LLD (hon.), 1971; LLB, Duke U., 1933; JSD, Yale U., 1935; LHD (hon.), U. Akron, 1968. Bar: Ohio 1933. Prof. law Temple U., 1934-38; sr. atty. SEC, 1938-40; assoc. prof. law U. Calif., 1940-41; ptnr. Amerman Mills, Mills, Jones & Mansfield, Canton, Ohio, 1941-48; gen. counsel Ohio Edison Co., Akron, 1948-60, exec. v.p., 1959-64, pres., 1964-75; also bd. dirs. Ohio Edison Co., from 1960; chmn. Pa. Power Co., New Castle, 1964-75. Trustee Kenyon Coll. Mem. Ohio C. of C., Akron C. of C., City Club, Portage Club, Congress Lake Club, Masons, Order of Coif, Phi Beta Kappa. Home: Akron Ohio. Died Mar. 7, 1985, buried Rose Hill Cemetery, Akron.

MANSFIELD, HARVEY CLAFLIN, SR., political science educator; b. Cambridge, Mass., Mar. 3, 1905; s. George Rogers and Adelaide (Claflin) M; m. Grace Winans Yarrow, Sept. 6, 1930; children: Harvey C., Charles Y., John T., Margaret Ann Mansfield Barnes. Student, Deep Springs Coll., 1921-25; BA, Cornell U., 1927, MA, 1928; PhD, Columbia U., 1932. Instr. govt. Yale U., 1929-33, asst. prof., 1933-42; acting asst. prof. Stanford U., 1939-40; vis. prof. Oreg. State Sch. System, Portland, summer, 1940; adminstrv. officer Consumer Goods div. Office Price Adminstrn., Washington, 1942, assoc. price exec., 1942-44, asst. div. dir., 1945, agy. historian, 1946-47; prof. polit. sci. Ohio State U., 1947-65, chmn. dept., 1947-59; prof. dept. pub. law and govt. Columbia U., 1965-72, Ruggles prof. pub. law., 1972-73, prof. emeritus, 1973-88, spl. lectr., 1973-75; vis. prof. Columbia U., summer, 1956, Yale U., 1947-58, LBJ Sch. Pub. Affiats, U. Tex., 1972, 76, U. B.C., summer, 1972, Harvard U., summers, 1973-74, Deep Springs Coll., 1976, 77, 79, U. Tenn., winter, 1979; sr. cons. Pres.' Com. on Adminstrv. Mgmt., 1936; vis. expert OMGUS, Germany, 1949; project dir., writer Conn. Commn. State Govt. Orgn., 1949-50; cons. Com. Pub. Adminstrn. Cases, 1950, Econ. Stabzn. Agy., 1951, mcpl. fin. study Mayor's Com. on Mgmt. Survery, N.Y.C., 1951, Govtl. Affairs Inst., 1952-53, Commn. on Intergovtl. Relations, 1954-55; mem. staff Commn. on Money and Credit, 1960-61; cons. House Banking and Currency Com., 1963. Author: The Lake Cargo Coal Rate Controversy, 1932, The General Accounting Office, 1937, The Comptroller General, 1939, A Short History of OPA, 1949 (with Mills and Stein) Arms and the State, 1958; editor, contbr.: Congress Against the President, 1975, (OPA series) Historical Reports on the War Administration, 1947-49; mng. editor Am. Polit. Sci. Rev., 1956-65; contbr. chpts. to books, articles to porfl. jours. Pres. Terruride Assn. (endowed ednl. fund), Ithaca, N.Y., 1931-33, 43, custodian, 1929-37, 41-45; chmn. bd. trustees Inter-Univ. Case Program, from 1956. Mem. Am. Polit. Sci. Assn. (sec. 1953-55, v.p. 1967-68), Nat. Acad. Pub. Adminstrn. (trustee 1973-76), Cosmos Club (Washington), Phi Beta Kappa, Delta Sigma Rho. Democrat. Home: New York N.Y. Died May 3, 1988.

MANSFIELD, THOMAS ROBERT, insurance executive; b. Dallas, July 31, 1891; s. William Halleck and Anna (Blessing) M.; m. Nancy Morrison, Sept. 23, 1916. Student, Dallas High Sch., 1904-07. With I. Reinhardt & Son, ins. gen. agy., Dallas, 1907-18; 1st asst. sec. Republic Ins. Co., Dallas, 1918-21, sec., 1921-25; organized Gulf Ins. Co., 1925, 1st sec., 1925-31, v.p., 1931-45, pres., 1945-59, chmn. bd., from 1959; chmn. bd. Atlantic Ins. Co., Select Ins. Co., Western Security Life Ins. Co.; bd. dirs. Southwestern Life Ins. Co. Mem. Tex. Ins. Advisors Assn. (gov. com.), Assn. Tex. Fire and Casualty Execs. Blue-Goose. Home: University Park Tex. †

MANSFIELD, WALTER ROE, judge; b. Boston, July 1, 1911; s. Frederick W. and Helena E. (Roe) M.; m. Gertrude Rient, Jan. 27, 1947; m. Elizabeth Palmer Bergfeld, July 20, 1979; children: Matthew, Trina; 1 stepchild, Peter Rient. AB, Harvard U., 1932, LLB, 1935. Bar: Mass. 1935, N.Y. 1936, U.S. Dist. Ct. (so. dist.) N.Y. 1938, U.S. Ct. Appeals (2d cir.) 1952, U.S. Supreme Ct. 1964. Assoc. Donovan, Leisure, Newton & Irvine, 1935-38, 41-42, 46-49, ptnr., 1949-66; asst. U.S. atty., 1938-41; judge U.S. Dist. Ct., so. dist. N.Y., 1966-71; U.S. cir. judge U.S. Ct. Appeals (2d cir.), 1971-87; chmn. adv. com. on fed. civil rules, U.S. Jud. Conf., 1978-85, mem. Standing Com. on Rules and Practice, 1985-87. Trustee New Canaan Country Sch., 1950-66, pres. bd., 1954-57. Served to maj. USMC, 1943-45. Decorated Bronze Star, Legion of Merit; Recipient Learned Hand award Fed. Bar Council, 1981, award Riot Relief Fund, 1984. Mem. ABA, Am. Judicature Soc., Am. Coll. Trial Lawyers, Bar Assn. City N.Y. Republican. Presbyterian. Clubs: Century Assn.; Country (New Canaan). Died Jan. 7, 1987. Home: Stamford Conn.

MAPES, RUSSELL WESLEY, pediatrician, educator; b. Fairfax, Mo., Feb. 11, 1905; s. Ora Prentiss and Clara Belle (Dragoo) M.; m. Barbara Stephens, May 24, 1941; children: Claire Stephens, John Russell. Student, Washburn Coll., 1924-27; MD, U. Kans., 1931. Diplomate Am. Bd. Pediatrics. Intern St. Francis Hosp., Wichita, Kans., 1931-32; mem. staff Children's Hosp., L.A., 1932-36, from 1968, dir. clin. services, 1968-71, dep. chmn. dept. medicine, from 1971; pvt. practice Beverly Hills, Calif., 1936-68; prof. pediatrics U. So. Calif., Beverly Hills, from 1958; cons. Shriner's Crippled Childrens Hosp. Mem. med. adv. bd. L.A. chpt. Cerebral Palsy Assn., 1950-64; bd. dirs. Children's Home Soc. Calif., 1958-68. Lt. col. USAAF, 1942-46. Mem. Am. Acad. Pediatrics (pres. 1969-70), S.W. Pediatric Soc. (pres. 1950), L.A. Acad. Medicine (pres. 1962-63). Home: Los Angeles Calif. Died Mar. 3, 1985.

MAPLE, CLAIR GEORGE, educator; b. Glennwood, Ind., Mar. 17, 1916; s. Clair Albert and Ora Edna (Dunn) M.; m. Mary Louise Catron, Sept. 20, 1942. BA, Earlham Coll., 1939; MEd, U. Cin., 1940; DSc, Carnegie Inst. Tech., 1948. Instr. math. W.Va. Inst. Tech., Montgomery, 1940-41, Ohio State U., Columbus, 1941-44; rsch. assoc. Carnegie Inst. Tech., 1946-48; assoc. prof. math. North Tex. State U., Denton, 1948-49; mem. faculty Iowa State U., from 1949, prof. math., from 1956; dir. computation ctr. from 1963; div. chief math. and computer sci. div. Ames Lab., Dept. Energy, 1966-78; cons. Nat. Security Agy., 1953-60, Zenith Radio Corp., 1954-66, Land Air Corp., 1960-61, United Electro-Dynamics, 1961, Collins Radio Co., 1959-60; mem. Gov. Iowa Sci. Adv. Com., 1966-69. Author: (with Holl and Vinograde) Introduction to the Laplace Transform, 1959; also articles. Treas. YMCA Iowa State U., 1960-68. With USN, 1944-46, 50-52. Mem. IEEE (midwest area com. 1968-85), Am. Math. Soc., Math. Assn. Am., Assn. Computing Machinery, AAUP, AAAS, Iowa Acad. Sci., Soc. Indsl. and Applied Math. (chmn. Iowa 1964-65, nat. coun. 1970), Sigma Xi, Phi Kappa Phi, Pi Mu Epsilon. Mem. IEEE (midwest area com. 1968-85), Am. Math. Soc., Math. Assn. Am., Assn. Computing Machinery, AAUP, AAAS, Iowa Acad. Sci., Soc. Indsl. and applied Math. (chmn. Iowa 1964-65, nat. coun. 1970), Sigma Xi, Phi Kappa Phi, Pi Mu Epsilon. Methodist. Home: Ames Iowa. Died Aug. 13, 1985; buried Iowa State U. Cemetery, Ames.

MARAVICH, PETE (PETER PRESS), basketball player; b. Aliquippa, Pa., June 22, 1948; m. Jackie Maravich; children: Joshua, Jaeson. Grad., La. State U., 1970. With Atlanta Hawks, 1970-74, New Orleans Jazz, 1974-80, Boston Celtics, from 1980; played Nat. Basketball Assn. All-Star Game, 1973, 74, 77; former broadcaster USA Cable Network. Named Coll. Basketball Player of Yr., 1970; inducted Basketball Hall of Fame, 1987. Home: Covington La. Died Jan. 6, 1988.

MARBURY, WILLIAM LUKE, lawyer; b. Baltimore County, Md., Sept. 12, 1901; s. William Luke and Silvine von Dorsner (Slingluff) M.; m. Natalie Jewett Wheeler, Dec. 3, 1935; children: Luke, Anne Jewett, Susan Fendall. Student, Va. Mil. Inst., 1918-19; A.B., U. Va., 1921; LL.B., Harvard, 1924, LL.D., 1970; D.M.A., Peabody Inst., 1967. Bar: Md. bar 1925. Practiced in Balt.; mem. firm Piper & Marbury (and predecessor firms), Balt., 1931-88; gen. counsel Md. Port Authority, 1956-67; trustee Peabody Inst. of Balt., 1935-67, pres., 1948-57, chmn. bd. trustees, 1957-67; asst. atty. gen. State of Md., 1930-31; chief counsel procurement program War dept., 1942-45; expert cons. procurement to Sec. War 1940-41; mem. Md. Commn. on Judicial Disabilities, 1971-83; Mem. U.S. del. to 2d session Signatories of GATT, Geneva, 1948. Fellow Harvard Coll., 1948-70; chmn. Md. Commn. on Higher Edn., 1946- 47; chancellor Episcopal Diocese of Md., 1962-71; adv. bd. Center for Advanced Studies, U. Va., 1971-78. Recipient Presdl. medal for Merit, 1945. Fellow Am. Bar Found. (50-Yr. award 1984), Md. Bar Found. (chmn. 1973-75), Am. Coll. Trial Lawyers; mem. Am. Acad. Arts and Scis., Nat. Inst. of Trial Advocacy (dir. 1971-76), Am. Law Inst. (mem. council 1946-80), Md. Inst. for Continuing Profl. Edn. Lawyers (pres. 1976-78, trustee 1976-81), Am. Judicature Soc. (dir. 1939-41, Herbert Harley award 1981), ABA (mem. com. jud. conduct 1969), Md. Bar Assn. (pres. 1965-66), Balt. Bar Assn., Order of Coif, Phi Beta Kappa. Episcopalian. Clubs: Elkridge (Balt.), 14 West Hamilton St (Balt.). Home: Baltimore Md. Died Mar. 5, 1988.

MARCHAND, JEAN, goverment official; b. Champlain, Que., Can., Dec. 20, 1918; s. Gustave and Laura (Cousineau) M.; m. Georgette Guertin; 1 child, Marie-Eve. Ed., Sch. Social Scis, Laval U., D in Social Scis. (hon.); D in Indsl. Relations (hon.), U. Montreal. Pres., sec. gen. Gen. Confedn. Nat. Trade Unions, 1942065; mem. Can. Ho. of Commons, from 1965, minister citizenship and immigration, 1965-66, minister manpower and immigration, Can., 1966-68, minister forestry and rural devel., 1968-69, minister regional econ. expansion, 1969-72, minister transport, 1972-75, minister without portfolio, 1975-76, minister of environment, 1976; mem. Can. Senate, from 1977, speaker, from 1980; mem. Royal Commn. of Enquiry on Bilingualism and Biculturalism, 1963-65; former mem. Econ. Council Que.; mem. nat. adv. com. Unemployemnt Ins. Commn., No. Am. Internat. Bur. Christian Trade Unionists. Home: Quebec Que., Canada. Died Aug. 28, 1988.

MARCUS, MIAH, rubber company executive; b. Latvia, 1884. Hon. chmn. Am. Biltrite Rubber Co., from 1969. Home: Brookline Mass. †

MARDEN, VIRGINIA MCAVOY (MRS. ORISON SWETT MARDEN), civic worker; b. N.Y.C., Mar. 1, 1906; d. John Vincent and Marian (Newcomb) McAvoy; m. Orison Swett Marden, Mar. 1, 1930; children—Orison Swett III, John Newcomb. B.A., Barnard Coll., 1927. Asst. to supt. West Side Hosp., 1927-29; sec. to bd. Friends of Music, 1929-30; dir., pres. Family Service of Scarsdale, N.Y., 1955-57; 1st vice chmn. Westchester County Council Social Agys., 1955-65; dir. Family Service Assn. Am., 1959, sec., 1961-66; dir. Westchester Legal Aid Soc., 1963-87, sec., 1964-87; exec. com. Plays for Living, 1965-70, women's div. N.Y. Legal Aid Soc., 1960-87; bd. Nat. Study Service, Inc., 1960. Club: Scarsdale Golf. Home: Scarsdale N.Y. Died Feb. 26, 1987; buried Hartsdale, N.Y.

MAREK, GEORGE RICHARD, manufacturing executive, author; b. Vienna, Austria, July 13, 1902; came to U.S., 1920, naturalized, 1925; s. Martin and Emily (Weissberger) M.; m. Muriel Hepner, Aug. 19, 1926; 1 son, Richard. Student, Vienna U., 1918-20. Vice pres. J. D. Tarcher Advt. Agy., 1930-50; music editor Good Housekeeping mag., 1941-57; v.p. Radio Corp. of Am., N.Y.C., 1950-87. Author: A Front Seat at the Opera, 1948, Good Housekeeping Guide to Musical Enjoyment, 1949, Puccini, 1950, The World Treasury of Grand Opera, 1957, Opera as Theater, 1962, Richard Strauss: The Life of a Non-Hero, 1967, Beethoven: Biography of A Genius, 1969, Mendelssohn: Gentle Genius, 1971, The Eagles Die: Franz Joseph and Elisabeth of Austria, 1974, Toscanini: a biography, 1975, The Bed and the Throne: Isabella d'Este, 1976, Chopin: a biography, 1978, Cosima Wagner, a biography, 1981. Mem. panel radio program Met. Opera Quiz. Clubs: Players (N.Y.C.), Dutch Treat (N.Y.C.). Home: New York N.Y. Died Jan. 1987.

MARGULIES, WALTER PIERRE, industrial designer; b. Paris, France, May 31, 1914; m. Harriett Browne, 1946; children: Linda, Marianne Margulies Roberts. Studied in, Rome, Vienna; student, Ecole des Beaux Arts, Paris. Jr. architect Paris Expn., 1937; with design staff for bldgs. N.Y. World's Fair Walter Dorwin Teague, 1939, charge interiors Statler Hotels; founding ptnr. Lippincott & Margulies, Inc., mktg. cons. and designers indsl. packaging and trademarks, N.Y.C., 1945, later, pres., then chmn. emeritus, until 1982; also pres. Lippincott & Margulies, Ltd.; chmn. bd., treas. Package Research Inst., Image Research, Inc., Names, Inc., Mktg. Systems, Inc. Author: Packaging Power, 1970. Mem. Sky Club (N.Y.C.), Westhampton Mallet Club (chmn. bd.). Home: Scardale N.Y. Died Apr. 28, 1986.

MARIE, JEAN HENRI THEOPHILE, maritime official; b. Honfleur, France, Jan. 8, 1891; s. Paul and Blanche (Quesnel) Marie; m. Madeleine Villard; children: Francoise (Mme. Pierre Calvet), Micheline (Mme. Marie Pedinielli). Student, Honfleur Coll., Rouen Lyceum, Ecole Polytechnique; Dr. honoris causa, Temple U., 1954. Arty. officer, battery comdr., arty. staff officer 1914-19; with Engr. Corps, naval constrn.,

Admiralty, 1921; mgr. Compagnie Generale Transatlantique, 1933, mng. pres., 1939, chmn., 1944-61; hon. pres. Compagnie Generale d'Armements Maritimes; mgr. mercantile fleet and maritime employment 1938-40, employed as state counsellor, 1938; gen. engr. Naval constrn., 1940; mgr. Maritime Transports, Merc. Admiralty, 1939-40. Mem. Marine Acad.; past pres. com. France-Am., mem. bd. French Patronage Com. Am. Field Service. Decorated Grand Cross of Legion of Honor, Comdr. Maritime Merit Military Cross. Mem. Central Com. Ship Owners of France. Home: Paris France. †

MARIL, HERMAN, artist, educator; b. Balt., Oct. 13, 1908; s. Isaac H. and Celia (Maril) Becker; m. Esta C. Maril, June 8, 1948; 2 children. Student, Balt. Poly. Inst.; grad., Md. Inst. Fine Arts, 1928. Instr. painting Cummings Art Sch.,, Mass., 1935-40, King-Smith Sch., Washington, 1945-46; asst. prof. fine arts U. Md., 1947-64, prof., 1964-79, prof. emeritus, 1979-86. Exhibited one-man shows in galleries and mus. in U.S., 1935-87; represented in pub. and pvt. collections including Santa Barbara (Calif.) Mus., N.Y. U. Gallery, Walter's Art Gallery, Balt., Whitney Mus. Am. Art; commd. by fed. govt. to paint murals for Alta Vista (Va.) P.O. and West Scranton (Pa.) P.O.; Awarded Municipal Art Soc. Prize for best work in All-Md. Exhbn. 1935, Municipal Art Soc. Purchase Prize, Balt. 1939, Balt. Mus. Art Purchase Prize 1940, first prize for best painting, Peale Museum, Balt. 1947, and several other prizes including Berney Meml. Prize, Balt. Mus. Art 1952, Stefan Hirsch Meml. award Audubon Soc. Artists, Nat. Acad., N.Y.C. 1972, award Hoschild-Kohn Dept. Store, Balt. 1972, Pres.'s award, ann. exhbn. Soc. Audubon Artists, NAD 1975, award for painting Am. Acad./Inst. Arts and Letters 1978. Hon. trustee Balt. Mus. Art. Served with spl. service AUS, 1942-45. Mem. Coll. Art Assn., Artists Equity Assn., Provincetown Art Assn., AAUP. Home: Provincetown Mass. Died Sept. 6, 1986.

MARIS, ALBERT BRANSON, judge; b. Phila., Dec. 19, 1893; s. Robert Wood and Elma (Branson) M.; m. Edith M. Robinson, July 3, 1917 (dec. Oct. 1967); children: William Robinson, Robert Wood; m. Mildred C. Butler, Oct. 24, 1968 (dec. Sept. 1984). Grad., Westtown (Pa.) Sch., 1911, Drexel U., 1926; LLD (hon.), Drexel U., 1946; LLB, Temple U., 1918, LLD (hon.), 1940; LLD (hon.), Haverford Coll., 1957, Swarthmore Coll., 1968; DCL (hon.), Villanova U., 1974. Bar: Pa. 1918. Practiced in Chester, Pa., 1918, Phila., 1919-36; mem. firm White, Maris and Clapp; judge U.S. Dist. Ct. (ea. dist. Pa.), 1936, U.S. Ct. of Appeals. (3d cir.), 1938; judge U.S. Emergency Ct. of Appeals, 1942, chief judge, 1943-62; sr. cir. judge (ret.) 3d Circuit, 1959-89; spl. master to Supreme Ct. on Lake Mich. water diversion cases, 1959-67, Atlantic continental shelf case, 1970-74; adj. prof. law Temple U. Law Sch., 1941-55; chmn. com. revision laws Jud. Conf. U.S., 1944-67, chmn. com. rules practice and procedure, 1959-73; mem. adv. com. on codification laws of V.I., 1955-57, mem. U.S. adv. com. internat. rules jud. procedure, 1959-63; adv. com. pvt. internat. law State Dept., 1964-69. Editor: The Legal Intelligencer, Phila., 1933-36; pres. Assoc. Ct. and Comml. Newspapers U.S., 1936. Democratic county chmn., Delaware County, Pa., 1924-30; mem. Pa. Dem. State Com., 1930-34; auditor Borough of Lansdowne, Pa., 1928-34; pres. People's Assn. of Delaware County, 1935-36; mem. council Borough of Yeadon, Pa., 1935-36; bd. dirs. Elwyn Inst., 1929-65, pres., 1951-65. Served as 2d lt. coast arty. U.S. Army, 1918. Recipient V.I. Medal of Honor, 1956, Edward J. Devitt disting. service to justice award, 1983. Fellow Am. Bar Found. (hon.); mem. Am., Fed., Pa., Phila., Delaware County, Montgomery County, City of N.Y. bar assns., Am. Law Inst., Inst. Jud. Adminstrn., Am. Judicature Soc., Lawyers Club, Order of Coif. Mem. Religious Soc. of Friends (presiding clk. Phila. yearly meeting 1966-67). Club: Lawyers. Home: Gwynedd Pa. Died Feb. 7, 1989.

MARKELIUS, SVEN GOTTFRID, architect; b. Stockholm, Oct. 10, 1889; s. Oscar and Hilma (Lundin) Jonsson; m. Ka Simon, Nov. 22, 1938; children: Jan, Anita (Mrs. Rolf Akesson), Katrin, Stefan, Bo. Grad., Stockholm Inst. Tech., 1913, Royal Acad. Fine Arts, Stockholm, 1915. Town planning dir. Stockholm, 1944-54, architect, from 1954; Mem. adv. com. UN Hdqrs., Manhattan, 1947, UNESCO Hdqrs., Paris, 1952-58, mem. art com., 1954; vis. prof. Yale, 1949, MIT, 1962, U. Calif., 1962; prof. Royal Inst. Brit. Architects, 1959. Works include Halsingborg Concert Hall, U. Tech. Students Corp. Bldg., Collective House, structure for Stockholm Bldg. Assn., Swedish Pavilion at N.Y. World's Fair, interior of ECOSOC chamber UN hdqrs., Trade Union Ctr. (Linkoping and Stockholm), Burgerhaus (Giessen), Park Hotel and Sweden House. Recipient Howland meml. prize Yale, 1949. Mem. Royal Inst. Brit. Architects (gold medal 1962), AIA, Town Planning Inst. (London), Internat. Inst. Arts and Letters, World Acad. Arts and Scis., Akademie Arkitektforening (Copenhagen), Swedish Royal Acad. Fine Arts, Fedn. Swedish Architects Soc. (pres. 1953-56). Home: Danderyd Sweden. †

MARKELL, ISABELLA BANKS, artist; b. Superior, Wis., Dec. 27, 1891; d. William and Marion (Lewis) Banks; m. John Markell, Mar. 31, 1914 (dec.); children: Isabella Markell Powel, John, Marion Markell McAdoo; m. 2d, H. Craig Cooper, 1960. One woman exhbns. include Bodley Gallery, Yolos Gallery, N.Y.C., Memphis Art Mus., Milw. Art Mus., Mus. City New York, Cornell Coll., Great Hist. Mus., others; works exhibited Met. Mus. Art, Pa. Mus. Art, Ringling Mus. Art, Sarasota Mus., Archtl. League, Nat. Acad. of Design, Boston Mus. of Art, Smithsonian Institution, many others, also Brussels, Antwerp, Belgium; traveling shows Am. Graphic Artists, Libr. Congress, Nat. Assn. Women Artists, Studio Guild; represented permanent collections Rockefeller Bros. Found., Museum of City of N.Y., Grinnell Pub. Libr., First Nat. Bank, Superior Libr., N.Y. Hist. Soc., Wilmington Mus. Art, Phila. Libr., Portsmouth Mus. of Art; also in pvt. collections. Recipient etching prize So. States Art League, 1943, 1st prize Portsmouth Art Mus., 1953, award N.J. Painters and Sculptors, 1957, Wilmington Soc. Fine Arts, 1958; Boston Mus. Art, 1958, Nat. Assn. Women Artists, 1958, 61, Knickerbocker Artists, Pen and Brush, 2 gold medals Am. Artists Profl. League, 1961, Grumbacher award, 1961. Mem. Soc. Am. Etchers, Pen and Brush, Fountainbleau Soc., Wilmington Soc. Fine Arts, New Haven Paint and Clay, Phila. Print Club, Allied Artis Am., Nat. Assn. Women Artists (past pres.), Am. Artists Profl. League (3d v.p.), Painters and Sculptors Assn. (pres., mem. bd.), Miami Art League, Artists Profl. League (v.p. charge chpts.), Portland Soc. Fine Arts, Springfield Soc. Arts, N.J. Sculptors and Painters, Am. Graphic Artists, Boston Printmakers, Washington Printmakers, Colonial Dames Am. Republican. Episcopalian. Home: Gibson Island Md. †

MARKEY, D(AVID) JOHN, business consultant; b. Frederick, Md., Oct. 7, 1882; s. J. Hanshew and Ida (Williard) M.; m. Mary Edna Mullenix, June 13, 1907 (dec. 1935); children: D. John, Mary E. Markey Hooper; m. Carlotta Kinnamon, June 20, 1941. Student, Western Md. Coll., 1900-01, Md. Agrl. Coll., 1902-04. Pres. Frederick Bd. Trade (1st comml. orgn. to join U.S. C. of C.), 1912-13; pres. Frederick C. of C., 1921-24; organizer W. Md. C. of C., 1921-24; pres. Frederick YMCA; bd. visitors Md. Sch. for Deaf, from 1914; Rep. nominee U.S. Senate, 1946. With Md. NG, 1898-1916, 1919-47, Spanish Am. War, maj. gen. ret., 1947; brig. gen. U.S. Army, 1917-19, Am. Expeditionary Force. Decorated D.S.M., Officer Legion of Honor (France), Office Order of the Crown (Belgium). Mem. Am. Legion (past dept. comdr., mem. nat. com.), Army and Navy Club (Washington), Masons. Mem. Reformed Ch. U.S. Home: Frederick Md. †

MARKLE, DONALD, coal operator; b. Hazleton, Pa., Aug. 29, 1892; s. Alvan and Mary (Dryfoos) M.; m. Mary Orme, Feb. 19, 1917; children: Mary Orme, Donald, Gordon Orme, Eckley Coxe, Joan, Dorothy, Isabel Parham. Student, Hill Sch., Pottstown, Pa., 1906-11; PhB, Yale, 1914; student, Lehigh U., 1914-16. Began as inside coal mine foreman and worked successively in various depts. of the mining industr; pres. Jeddo-Highland Coal Co., ret.; pres. Raven Run Coal Co. and the Jeddo Tunnel Co.; bd. dirs. Va. Coal and Iron Co., Gen. Coal Co., Stonega Coke & Coal Co., Northeastern Pa. Bank & Trust Co., Anthracite Inst. Maj. World War I, A.E.F. Decorated Verdun medal; awarded citation for exceptional meritorious and conspicious service as comdg. officer by Gen. Pershing. Mem. AIME (Erskine Ramsey gold medal), St. Anthony Club, University Club, Midday Club, Racquet Club, Boston Club, Louisiana Club, Masons. Republican. Presbyterian. Home: Hazleton Pa. also: Pass Christian Miss. †

MARKLEY, FRANK RANCK, petroleum executive; b. Warfordsburg, Pa., Dec. 4, 1891; s. Judge Hiram K. and Lesley (Ranck) M.; m. Winona Baker, July 16, 1921; 1 child, Adele (Mrs. Harry G. Smith). Student, Shippensburg State Tchrs. Coll., 1910-12, Pratt Inst., 1913-14. With Westinghouse Electric & Mfg. Co., Pitts., 1914-17; with Sun Oil Co., Phila., from 1920, v.p., bd. dirs., from 1950. Mem. AIEE, Am. Petroleum Inst., Nat. Petroleum Assn., Aronimink Goilf Club, Union League, Racquet Club, Seaview Country Club, Rolling Green Golf Club. Home: Swarthmore Pa. †

MARKLEY, RODNEY WEIR, automobile manufacturing company executive; b. Denver, Nov. 18, 1912; s. Rodney Weir and Hazel M. (Hayes) m.; m. 2d, Annabel Pugh, Dec. 21, 1968; children: Judith Cornick, Mary Helen. Student, Occidental Coll., 1931-35. Indsl. paint sales rep. Andrew Brown Co., Sherwin Williams Co.,, L.A., 1935-42; contract termination mgr. Douglas Aircraft, Santa Monica, Calif., 1942-49; account exec. Aircraft Industries Assn., Washington, 1949-51; assoc. Ford Motor Co., Washington, 1951-54, mgr., 1954-64, mng. dir., 1964-66, v.p. Washington staff, 1966-67, v.p. govtl. rels. staff, from 1976. Trustee Sidwell Friends Sch., Washington, 1962-67; mem. Fed. City Coun., Washington, Bus-Govt. Rels. Coun., Inc. Mem. Carlton, Burning Tree, 1925 F St., Internat. (gov.) clubs, Kappa Sigma. Home: Washington D.C. Died Oct. 12, 1988.

MARKS, JOHNNY (JOHN D.), songwriter; b. Mt. Vernon, N.Y., Nov. 10, 1909; s. Louis B. and Sadie (Van Praag) M.; B.S., Colgate U., 1931; m. Margaret Hope May, Oct. 25, 1947 (dec.); children—Michael, Laura, David. Composer popular songs including: Rudolph The Red-Nosed Reindeer, Address Unknown, She'll Always Remember, Night Before Christmas Song, I Heard the Bells on Christmas Day, Rockin' Around the Christmas Tree, A Holly Jolly Christmas, Anyone Can Move a Mountain, Silver and Gold, When Santa Claus Gets Your Letter, A Caroling We Go, Joyous Christmas, Don't Cross Your Fingers, Cross Your Heart, Everything I've Always Wanted (ASCAP award), She'll Always Remember, Who Calls; editor and arranger two carol books; originator of melody and harmony method of easy piano arrangements; composer 1-hr. ann. Christmas TV color spectacular Rudolph the Red-Nosed Reindeer with 8 songs for NBC, from 1964, TV spectacular Ballad of Smokey the Bear, with 8 songs for NBC, 1965, 67, 68, TV spl. The Tiny Tree with eight songs, 1975, 76, 77, 78, 79, TV spectacular Rudolph's Shiny New Year (Emmy nominee), with 8 songs for ABC, 1976, 77, 78, 79, 80, 81, 82, 11 songs motion picture with Ethyl Merman, Rudolph and Frosty; also commls. Gen. Electric Corp.; pres., St. Nicholas Music, Inc.; tour with U.S.O.-ASCAP, Far East, 1968. Trustee Colgate U., chmn. Pres.' Club; judge Stephen Foster Singing Contest, Fla. Served to capt. U.S. Army, 1942-46. Decorated Bronze Star with 4 battle stars; named Songwriter of Year by Songhits mag., 1949; Gold award Comml. Film and TV Festival of N.Y., 1967, Internat. Soc. Santa Claus award, World Achievement award McBurney Sch.; named to Songwriter's Hall of Fame. Mem. ASCAP (dir. from 1957, bd. rev., advisory com.), TV Acad. N.Y. (gov.), Marshall Chess Club (dir.), Phi Beta Kappa, Kappa Phi Kappa, Mu Pi Delta. Died Sept. 3, 1985. Address: 117 W. 11th St., New York, NY, 10011.

MARKS, LAWRENCE, pharmaceutical company executive; b. Jersey City, Oct. 26, 1926; s. David Maxwell and Bess (Harris) M.; m. Elinor Kleiner, July 29, 1951; children: Anthony and David (twins). BS, Rutgers U., 1948; JD, NYU, 1952, MD, 1959. Bar: N.J. 1953. Mem. firm Kleiner & Marks, Paterson, N.J., 1953-55; intern USPHS Hosp., S.I., N.Y., 1959-60; resident VA Hosp., East Orange, N.J., 1960-61; pvt. practice New Brunswick, N.J., from 1961; with E.R. Squibb and Sons, Inc., New Brunswick, 1961-82; pres. Mfg. Enterprises, Inc., Humacao, P.R., from 1969, Squibb Chem. Co., Humacao, from 1969; dir., v.p. Squibb Corp., from 1974; also dir., chmn. Squibb Inst. Med. Research, from 1974, then exec. v.p.; mem. drug research bd. Nat. Acad. Scis.-NRC, 1971-73. With U.S. Army, 1945-46. Fellow Am. Coll. Legal Medicine. Home: Summit N.J. Died June 11, 1982.

MARLEY, FRANCIS MATTHIAS, lawyer; b. Muncie, Ind., June 9, 1910; s. William B. and Emma (Haney) M.; m. Barbara O. Reinhard, Aug. 30, 1939; children: William Edmund, Francis Matthias, Susan Ann, Michael Joseph, Barbara Louise. BA cum laude, U. Notre Dame, 1932, JD, 1934. Bar: Ohio 1934. Pvt. practice Fostoria, Ohio, 1934-85; asst. pros. atty. Seneca County, Ohio, 1934-36; bd. dirs. Midwest Plant Foods, Inc., Napoleon, Ohio, 1950-72. Chmn. Fostoria Planning Commn., 1954-58, Fostoria Civil Service Commn., 1959-63; pres. Fostoria Dem. Club, 1950-58, treas., 1959-60; Dem. state cen. committeeman, 1958-68, Seneca County Dem. chmn., 1970-72. Mem. ABA, Ohio Bar Assn. (exec. com. 1972-75), Seneca County Bar Assn. (pres. 1942-45), Law-Sci. Acad. Am., Notre Dame Law Assn., Acad. Internat. Lex et Scienta, Am. Judicare Soc., Ohio Acad. Trial Lawyers, Am. Title Assn., Ohio Title Assn., Fostoria United Sportsmen (sec. 1935), Elks (presiding justice 1953-62), Eagles (pres. 1939-41), KC (4th degree grand knight 1938-40). Home: Fostoria Ohio. Died Jan. 6, 1985; buried St. Wendelin Cemetery.

MARQUETTE, BLEECKER, housing and health administrator; b. Whitehall, N.Y., Sept. 7, 1892; s. Edward Franklin and Catherine (Heysette) M.; m. Frances Colter Stuart, Aug. 14, 1941; 1 child from previous marriage, Marjorie. AB, Cornell, 1915; student spl. courses, Sorbonne, Paris, summer 1912. Head. dept. French Schenectady (N.Y.) High Sch., 1912-13; asst. sec. N.Y. Tenement House Com., 1915-18; cons. dept. psychiatry Coll. Medicine, U. Cin., from 1960; cons. Better Housing League of Cin., Cin. Met. Housing Authority; mem. exec. com. on study vol. health agys., Am. Heart Assn., Nat. Health Coun.; past chmn. Nat. Conf. for Health Coun. Work.; studied England's health ins. plan, 1927, housing in Europe, 1935. Co-author: A Housing Manual For Teachers; Postwar Housing in the U.S.; Health Survey of Detroit, 1948; author reports and articles on housing and public health. Mem. Gov.'s Com. on Mental Health PRogram for Ohio; chmn. Cin. Com. on Health Svcs. to Medically Indigent; pres. bd. dirs. Cen. Mental Hygiene Clinic, Social Hygiene Soc., Shoemaker Ctr.; mem. com. on prevention Ohio Mental Health Project; bd. dris. Child Guidance Home. Recipient award for disting. svc. to cause of pub. health in greater Cin., 1947, citation Ohio Mental Health Assn., 1955. Fellow Am. Pub. Health Assn. (mem. com. on hygiene of housing); mem. Nat. Com. Housing Assns., Nat. Housing Conf. (hon. v.p.), Ohio Housing Coun. (past pres.), Ohio Mental Hygiene Assn. (past pres.), Ohio Welfare Conf. (past pres.), Am. Assn. Social Workers (past pres. Cin. chpt.), Nat. Assn. Housing Ofcls (past. pres., chmn. com. postwar housing, past chmn. joint com. health and housing with Am. Pub. Health Assn.), Nat. Assn. Housing and Renewal Ofcls. (life), Am. Inst. City Planners, Cin. Acad. Medicine (hon.), Cin. Dental Soc. (hon.), Royal Soc. Health, England, Glendale Literary Club (past pres.), Phi Beta Kappa. †

MARSDEN, RALPH WALTER, geologist, educator; b. Jefferson County, Wis., Apr. 11, 1911; s. Walter and Inger (Evenson) M.; m. Ellen E. Pletcher, Aug. 31, 1957; children: Jean Inger, Katherine Ellen. Ph.B., U. Wis., 1932, Ph.M., 1933, Ph.D., 1939. Asst. instr. U. Wis., 1936-39; geologist Wis. Geol. Survey, summers 1936, 38-39, Jones & Laughlin Steel Corp., Pitts., summer 1937, 45-46, 47-51; geologist Philippine Geol. Survey, Philippine Bur. Mines, 1939-40, chief geol. survey div., 1940-45; intern, Cebu City, Philippines, also Santo Tomas Los Banos, 1942-45; assoc. prof. geology U. Okla., 1946-47; geologist U.S. Steel Corp., Duluth, Minn., 1951-53; mgr. geol. investigations iron ore U.S. Steel Corp., 1953-67; dir. explorations Cartier Mining Co., Ltd., Duluth, 1954-57, Quebec Cartier Mining Co., 1957-59; prof. geology U. Minn., Duluth, 1967-80, prof. emeritus, 1980-86, head dept., 1967-74; treas. Econ. Geology Pub. Co., 1976-86; lectr. UN, Moscow, 1979; mem. adv. bd., cons. Natural Resources Research Inst., Duluth, 1983-86; mem. steering com. Earth Sci. Curriculum Project. Mem. editorial bd. Econ. Geology, 1968-73; editorial adv. bd. Mining Engineering Handbook; mem. adv. com., contbr. to Ore Deposits of the United States, 1933-1967. Fellow Geol. Soc. Am.; mem. Soc. Econ. Geologists (treas. 1976—, past councilor), AIME (past v.p.), AAAS, Mining and Metall. Soc. Am. (councilor 1981-86), Am. Inst. Profl. Geologists, Soc. Econ. Geologists (treas., treas. found. 1976—). Home: Duluth Minn. Died Nov. 10, 1986, buried St. Andrews by the Lake Episc. Ch., Duluth.

MARSH, BURTON WALLACE, traffic and transportation engineer; b. Worcester, Mass., Jan. 9, 1898; s. Luman Wallace and Florence Duncan (Wells) M.; m. Mary Elizabeth Allison, Oct. 8, 1927; children: Jean Allison Marsh Adams, Mary Elizabeth Marsh McCartor, Alan Burton. B.S. in Civil Engring., Worcester Poly. Inst., 1920, D.Engring. (hon.), 1961; postgrad., Yale U., 1920-21. Engaged in work on housing projects, city planning, zoning, traffic planning various cities, including Worcester, Norfolk, Va., Dayton, Ohio, 1921-24; city traffic engr. Pitts., 1924-30, Phila., 1930-33; dir. traffic engring. and safety dept. Am. Automobile Assn., Washington, 1933-64; exec. dir. AAA Found. for Traffic Safety, 1964-66, Inst. Traffic Engrs., 1967-70; cons. engr. 1970-82; lectr., instr., dean in traffic courses and schs. including Traffic Engring. and Traffic Officer Tng. Schs. at Yale, Harvard, Northwestern U., Pa. State U., U. Md.; pioneer municipal traffic engr. Past mem., past chmn. exec. com. Transp. Research Bd. of Nat. Acad. Scis.-Nat. Acad. Engring.; mem., past chmn. Nat. Com. Uniform Traffic Laws and Ordinances; affiliate mem., past chmn. Nat. Com. on Uniform Traffic Control Devices; mem. U.S. del. Pan Am. Hwy. Congresses, Panama City, Panama, 1957, Bogota, Colombia, 1960, Washington, 1963, Montevideo, Uruguay, 1967, Quito, Ecuador, 1971, San Jose, Costa Rica, 1975. Trustee Worcester Poly. Inst., 1953-67, emeritus from 1967; pres. Theodore M. Matson Meml. Fund, Inc., 1978. Recipient Roy W. Crum award Hwy. Research Bd., 1954; Paul Gray Hoffman award, 1959; Theodore M. Matson Meml. award, 1960; Arthur Williams Meml. medal, 1970; first recipient ann. Burton W. Marsh award Inst. Traffic Engrs., 1970; citation for distinguished service to safety Nat. Safety Council, 1974; named hon. life chmn. tech. com. on hwy. ops. Pan Am. Hwy. Congresses, OAS, 1975; life hon. trustee AAA Found. for Traffic Safety, 1974; hon. mem. Inst. Transp., Am. Pub. Works Assn., 1975; recipient P.D. McLean Meml. award for contbns. to better hwy. transp. in the public interest, 1979. Fellow ASCE, Inst. Transp. Engrs. (past pres., a founder, hon. mem.); mem. Sigma Xi, Tau Beta Pi. Presbyterian. Club: Cosmos (Washington). Home: Washington D.C. Deceased.

MARSHALL, DOROTHY NEPPER, academic administrator, educator; b. Brighton, Mass., Aug. 26, 1913; d. Christian V. and Anna C. (Jacobsen) Nepper; m. J. Nathaniel Marshall, Sept. 3, 1948; children: Nicholas Nepper, Emily Rachel. AB, Smith Coll., 1935, MA, 1937, LLD (hon.), 1972; PhD, Bryn Mawr Coll., 1944; LLD (hon.), Regis Coll., 1972, Worcester Poly. Inst., 1975. Mem. faculty Bryn Mawr (Pa.) Coll., 1942-69, dean, 1948-69; dir. spl. studies Holy Cross Coll., Worcester, Mass., 1970-71; vice chancellor for academic affairs, dean of faculty U. Mass., Boston, 1971-74; Commonwealth prof., dir. Latin Am. studies U. Mass., from 1973, emeritus, 1973-86; bd. dirs. Charlestown Savs. Bank, Boston; past pres. Internat. Inst. in Spain; mem. nat. bd. cons. NEH, 1974. Trustee Smith Coll., 1959-69, 73-86, chmn. bd., 1976-79; trustee, sec. Bryn Mawr Coll., 1971-86; trustee Ford Found., 1970-86, Coll. Holy Cross, 1971-86. Dorothy Marshall Chair in Hispanic Studies established Bryn Mawr Coll. Mem. MLA, Am. Acad. Polit. Sci., Alumnae Assn. Bryn Mawr Coll., Alumnae Assn. Smith Coll., Phi Beta Kappa. Home: Boston Mass. Died Feb. 24, 1986.

MARSHALL, JAMES, lawyer; b. N.Y.C., May 12, 1896; s. Louis and Florence (Lowenstein) M.; m. Lenore K. Guinzburg, Aug. 20, 1919 (dec. 1971); children: Ellen F. Scholle, Jonathan; m. Eva Garson Levy, May 6, 1974. Student, Columbia Sch. Journalism, 1913-16; LL.B., Columbia U., 1920. Bar: N.Y. bar 1921, bar U.S. Supreme Ct 1924. Asso. Guggenheimer, Untermyer & Marshall, N.Y.C., 1920-29; mem. Guggenheimer, Untermyer & Marshall, 1929-30; pvt. practice law 1930-34; mem. Marshall, Bratter, Greene, Allison & Tucker, and predecessors, 1934-47, counsel, 1947-82; counsel Burns Summit Rovins & Feldesman, 1982-86; sole practice N.Y.C., 1986; lectr. pub. adminstrn. NYU, 1953-59, adj. prof. pub. adminstrn., 1959-65; tng. asso. Human Relations Center, Boston U., 1966-70. Author: Ordeal by Glory, 1927, Swords and Symbols; The Technique of Sovereignty, 1939, rev. edit., 1969, The Freedom to Be Free, 1943, Law and Psychology in Conflict, 1966, rev. edit., 1980, Intention in Law and Society, 1968; The Devil in The Classroom: Hostility in American Education, 1985. Contbr. articles to publs. Bd. dirs. N.Y. State Tng. Sch. for Boys, 1933, pres., 1934-35; mem. N.Y.C. Charter Commn., 1934; mem. N.Y.C. Bd. Edn., 1935-52, pres., 1938-42; mem. U.S. Nat. Commn. for UNESCO, 1946-51; adv. U.S. del. UNESCO Conf., Paris, 1946, Mexico City, 1947, cons., Florence, Italy, 1950; ednl. cons. on prejudice and discrimination ECOSOC Conf. Non-Govt. Orgns., Geneva, 1959; v.p. Am. Jewish Com., 1959-62, hon. v.p., 1962—; mem. exec. com. Am. Jewish Joint Distbn. Com.; hon. gov. Hebrew U.; v.p. Natural Resources Def. Council, 1970-86 ; hon. v.p. Citizens' Com. Children; bd. dirs. Martha Graham Found. Contemporary Dance, Adirondack Council, 1977-86. Enlisted June, 1917; and served as 2d lt. San. Corps, A.E.F. U.S. Army, 1918-19. Recipient Butler Silver medal for contbn. to polit. philosophy and edn. Columbia U., 1941; Disting. Pub. Service award Educators lodge B'nai B'rith, 1946; Gold medal for distinguished service to N.Y.C. pub. schs. Public Edn. Assn., 1952; Publ. Service award N.Y. region Am. Vets. Commn., 1952; named hon. fellow Hebrew U., 1983. Fellow Fellows Am. Bar Found.; mem. ABA Inst. Internat. Edn. (hon. trustee), Am. Friends of Hebrew U. (hon. v.p., past chmn. bd.), Jewish Publ. Soc. (hon. v.p.), Am. Assn. for Internat. Office Edn. (v.p. 1943-47), NAACP (past dir., counsel), Assn. Bar City N.Y. Wilderness Soc. (governing council), P.E.N. (dir. Am. chpt. 1972-78). Clubs: Cosmos (Washington); Lotos. Home: New York N.Y. Died Aug. 11, 1986.

MARSHALL, WHITFIELD HUFF, lawyer; b. Washington, Sept. 14, 1910; s. Thomas Worth and Kathleen (Huff) M.; m. Mary Jane Walne, Aug. 1, 1940 (dec. 1977); 1 dau., Diana Marshall Joor; m. Coletta Lake Ray, Apr. 13, 1978. AB magna cum laude, Duke U., 1931; JD with highest honors, George Washington U., 1936. Bar: D.C. 1936, Tex. 1937. Assoc. Fulbright & Jaworksi, Houston, 1936-47, ptnr., 1947-67, sr. ptnr., 1967-86. Trustee Houston Mus. Fine Arts, 1957-80, Houston Ballet Found., 1955-86, St. Luke's Episcopal Hosp., Houston, 1978-81, Episcopal Theol. Sem. Southwest, Austin, Tex., 1974-77. Served to lt. comdr. USNR, 1942-45. Mem. ABA, State Bar Tex. Home: Houston Tex. Died May 16, 1986.

MARSTELLER, WILLIAM A., advertising and public relations executive; b. Champaign, Ill., Feb. 23, 1914; s. P. L. and Minnie (Finder) M.; m. Gloria Crawford, Apr. 22, 1938; children: Elizabeth M. Gordon, Julie V. B.S., U. Ill., 1937. Reporter Champaign News-Gazette, 1932-37; group supr. Mass. Mut. Life Ins. Co., Chgo., 1937-41; advt. and sales promotion mgr. Edward Valves, Inc., East Chicago, Ind., 1941-43; sec. Edward Valves, Inc., 1943-45, v.p., dir., 1945-51; mgr. advt., pub. relations and market research Rockwell Internat. Corp., Pitts., 1945-49; v.p. Rockwell Internat. Corp., 1949-51; pres. Marsteller Research, Chgo., 1951-80; pres., chmn., chief exec. officer Marsteller Inc., 1951-80, chmn., 1980-87; co-founder Burson-Marsteller, 1953. Author: The Wonderful World of Words, 1972, Creative Management, 1981; contbr. articles to marketing and advt. publs. Trustee, dir. or officer Barnard Coll., Whitney Mus. Am. Art, Marsteller Found., U. Ill. Found., James Webb Young Fund; founder mem. Whitney Circle, U. Ill. Pres.'s Assn. Recipient Achievement award U. Ill., 1973, Pres.'s award, 1976; Barnard medal of distinction, 1979; G.D. Crain award, 1979; named to Advt. Hall of Fame, 1979, Ill. Bus. Hall of Fame, 1986; Service award Am. Acad. Advt., 1981. Mem. Am. Mgmt. Assn. (trustee), Am. Assn. Advt. Agys., Chgo. Indsl. Advertisers Assn. (pres. 1945-46), Nat. Indsl. Advertisers Assn. (pres. 1947-49), Football Writers Assn. Am., Art Inst. Chgo. (life), AAUP, Sigma Chi. Home: Palm Beach Fla. Died Aug. 3, 1987.

MARSTON, ROLAND F., insurance company executive; b. Rock Island, Ill., July 13, 1924; s. Frank and Mildred (Wainwright) M.; m. Margaret Ann Fuller, Nov. 23, 1944; children: Roland Michael, William Frank, Gertrude Ann, Rebecca Kay. Student, DePauw U., 1942-44; B.A. in Bus. Adminstrn, Ill. Wesleyan U., 1947. Salesman, sales mgr. Corn Belt Motor Co., Bloomington, Ill., 1947-50; owner Marston Buick Co., Kewanee, Ill., 1950-55; with State Farm Ins. Cos., 1956-87; dep. regional v.p. State Farm Ins. Cos., Winter Haven, Fla., 1962-65; regional v.p. State Farm Ins. Cos., St. Paul, 1965-72; v.p. State Farm Mut. Automobile Ins. Co., Bloomington, 1972-77; exec. v.p. State Farm Mut. Automobile Ins. Co., 1977-83, vice chmn. bd., 1983-85, chmn. bd., 1985-87. Mem. allocations com. United Fund, St. Paul, 1968-70; trustee Ill. Wesleyan U., Bloomington, 1975. Served as ensign USNR, 1944-46. Mem. Phi Delta Theta. Clubs: Rotary, Masons. Home: Babson Park Fla. Died July 29, 1987.

MARTIN, ARMOUR EMERSON, lawyer; b. N.Y.C., May 11, 1917; s. Emile F. and Alice (Sadowich) M.; m. Mary Sirman, July 6, 1946; children: Mary Alison, Armour Emerson II. AB, Columbia U., 1938, JD, 1940. Bar: N.Y. 1942, U.S. Supreme Ct. 1970. Exec. sec. stock trust certificate holders com. So. Ry., Mobile, Ala. and Ohio, 1940-42; pvt. practice N.Y.C., 1946-61, 69-85; assoc. Appleton, Rice and Perrin, 1961-63; ptnr. Emmet, Marvin and Martin, 1963-68; pres., dir. Amrail, Inc., 1973-85, LIFO Internat., Inc., 1983-85; lectr. Columbia Law Sch., N.Y.C., 1952; mem. policy planning staff internat. security affairs Office Sec. Def., 1961-62. Commr. Nassau County council Boy Scouts Am., 1958; campaign chmn. Community Chest, Port Washington, N.Y., 1953-54, mem. exec. com., 1953-59, pres., 1955-56; trustee Bie Family Found., 1966-85. Capt. AUS, 1942-46; lt. col. Res. ret. Mem. N.Y. State Bar Assn., Mil. Order Fgn. Wars (judge adv. mem. council 1975-85), Sands Point Club (N.Y.), Bath and Racquet Club (dir..1963-70, treas. 1964-70, v.p. 1965-70), Princeton Club of N.Y., Delta Phi. Home: Port Washington N.Y. Died Aug. 26, 1985, buried Nassau Knolls Cemetery, Port Washington, N.Y.

MARTIN, CECIL RAYMOND, cereal manufacturer; b. Pittsville, Mo., Aug. 6, 1892; s. Isaac Raymond and Donah Mary (Smith) M.; m. Annabel Groom, Oct. 28, 1915 (dec.); children: Jack Raymond, Mary Louise; m. Elizabeth Cottier, Jan. 7, 1948. AB, William Jewel Coll., Liberty, Mo., 1914. Div. sales mgr. Aunt Jemima Mills, St. Joseph, Mo., 1920-26; sales mgr. Quaker Oats Co., St. Joseph, 1926-37, mgr. St. Joseph plant, from 1937; past v.p., dir. The Tootle Empire Nat. Bank & Trust Co.; dir. Union Terminal Ry., St. Joseph; past pres. Associated Industries Mo. Former mem. St. Joseph City Coun. Recipient citation as number 1 boss of year St. Joseph Jr. C. of C., 1958, citation of achievement William Jewell Coll., 1958. Mem. Am. Corn Millers Fedn. (pres. 1927, dir.), C. of C. (dir.), Kappa Alpha, St. Joseph Country Club, Moila Country Club, Masons, Shriners, Jesters. Republican. Baptist. †

MARTIN, EDWARD WILLIAM, architect; b. Inverarnan, Scotland, Nov. 2, 1891; s. Edward and Sarah Ann Martin: m. La Reine Kennard, Oct. 19, 1927; children: Edith Frances (Mrs. Charles H. Grady), Alice Kennard (Mrs. Malcolm R. Mansfield), Dorothy Hewitt. Student, U. Pa., 1912-13; BS, U. Del., 1913-16; B.Arch., U. Liverpool, Eng., 1920-22; MA (hon.), U. Del., 1936. Began career in architect's office Wilmington, Del., 1910; began independent practice Phila., 1922; pvt. practice Wilmington, from 1926; past pres. Del. State Bd. of Examiners and Registration of Architects. Works include: State Legislature Bldg., State Hall of Records and State Hwys. Testing Lab., Dover, Del.; bldgs. for U. Del.; Post Office, Customs and Court House, Wilmington, Del.; state armories at Georgetown and Milford, Del.; sch. bldgs., Del., Pa. and Md.; many other pub. and pvt. bldgs. Bd. dirs. Wilmington Symphony Orchestra; trustee Newark Acad.; past pres. Wilmington Music Sch. Fellow AIA (past pres. Del. chpt.); mem. Sigma Phi Epsilon, Phi Kappa Phi, Tau Sigma Delta. Home: Newark Del. †

MARTIN, FRANCIS LINTON, lawyer; b. Chattanooga, Jan. 6, 1891; s. Francis and Lydia (Linton) M.; m. Emily T. Kelley, Aug. 17, 1933 (dec.); 1 child, Caroline T. (Mrs. Erwin Brady Bartusch). PhB, Yale, 1912; LLB, Columbia, 1915. Bar: Tenn. 1916. Practice Chattanooga; mem. firm Miller, Martin, Hitching, Tipton, Lenihan and Waterhouse, and predecessor firms, 1923-72. Pres. bd. Tonya Meml. Found.; sec. bd. Frye Inst.; bd. dirs. Boys Club Chattanooga. 1st lt. F.A., U.S. Army, 1917-19, AEF in France. Decorated Silver Star; Fourragere of Croix de Guerre (France). Mem. ABA, Assn. Life Ins. Counsel, Chattanooga Golf and Country Club, Mountain City Club. Home: Memphis Tenn. †

MARTIN, HAYES, surgeon; b. Dayton, Iowa, June 24, 1892; s. John O. and Christina (Nelson) M.; m. Madeleine Senyi, Aug. 25, 1939; 1 son, Hayes Senyi. Student, U. Iowa, 1909-10, 11-12; MD, State U. Iowa, 1917. Diplomate Am. Bd. Surgery (founder), Am. Bd. Radiology (founder), Am. Bd. Plastic Surgery (founder). Intern 4th surg. div. Bellevue Hosp., N.Y.C., 1920-21, resident surgeon 2d surg. div., 1923-25, adj. asst. attending surgeon 2d surg. div., 1926-28; intern Polyclinic Hosp., N.Y.C., 1921-22; intern, resident surgeon Meml. Hosp., N.Y.C., 1922-23, clin. asst. attending surgeon, asst. attending, assoc. attending surgeon, 1925-31, attending surgeon, 1933-57, emeritus, from 1957, chief head and neck svc.; practiced, N.Y.C., from 1925; cons. surgeon N.Y. Infirmary for Women and Children, Speech Rehab. Inst., St. Clare Hosp. (all N.Y.C.), White Plains (N.Y.) Hosp., Lawrence Hosp., Jersey City Med. Ctr.; assoc. prof. clin. surgery Cornell Med. Coll., 1945-57. Author: Surgery of Head and Neck Tumors; contbr. over 125 articles to profl. jours. Gov. Speech Rehab. Inst. Served from lt. (j.g.) to lt. (s.g.) USN, 1917-19. Decorated Chevalier Legion of Honor (France). Fellow ACS, Kansas City Acad. Medicine; mem. Am. Coll. Radiology, Am. Acad. Dental Medicine (assoc.), AMA, N.Y. Med. Soc., N.Y. County Med. Soc., Am. Cancer Soc., Am. Radium Soc.

(pres.), Soc. Head and Neck Surgeons (founder, pres.), Am. Soc. Cancer Rsch., Bellevue Alumni Assn., James Ewing Soc., N.Y. Acad. Medicine, N.Y. Surg. Soc., N.Y. Acad. Scis., Radiol. Soc. N.Am., Internat. Surg. Group, Am. Soc. Plastic and Reconstructive Surgery, Tacoma Surg. Club, also numerous fgn. med. socs, University Club. Home: New York N.Y. †

MARTIN, JOHN BARTLOW, author; b. Hamilton, Ohio, Aug. 4, 1915; s. John Williamson and Laura (Bartlow) M.; m. Frances Rose Smethurst, Aug. 17, 1940; children: Cynthia Ann Martin Coleman, Daniel Bartlow, John Frederick. BA, DePauw U., 1937; LLD (hon.), Ind. U., 1971; LHD (hon.), Knox Coll., 1975. Reporter Indpls. Times, 1937-38; freelance writer 1938-87; mem. campaign staff Adlai Steveson, 1952, 56, John F. Kennedy, 1960; ambassador to Dominican Republic, 1962-64; mem. campaign staff Lyndon B. Johnson, 1964; sr. fellow Ctr. for Advanced Studies, Weslyan U., Middletown, Conn., 1964-65; vis. fellow pub. affairs Princeton U., 1966-67; vis. disting. prof. Grad Ctr., CUNY, 1968; mem. campaign staffs Robert F. Kennedy, Hubert H. Humphrey, 1968; prof. journalism, Medill Sch. Journalism Northwestern U., 1970-80, emeritus, 1980-87. Author 16 books including: Why Did They Kill, 1953, Break Down the Walls, 1954, The Deep South Says Never, 1957, The Pane of Glass, 1959, Overtaken By Events, 1966, The Life of Adlai Stevenson, 1976, 77, U.S. Policy in the Caribbean, 1978, (novel) The Televising of Heller, 1980, It Seems Like Only Yesterday, Memoirs of Writing, Presidential Politics and the Diplomatic Life, 1986; also numerous articles. Recipient Benjamin Franklin Mag. award, 1953, 56, 57. Mem. Sigma Delta Chi (Mag. award 1950, 57), Century Club (N.Y.C.), Arts Club (Chgo.). Democrat. Home: Highland Park Ill. Died Jan. 3, 1987, buried Mt. Emblem Cemetery, Elmhurst, Ill.

MARTIN, JOHN GILBERT, beverage company executive; b. Coventry, Eng., Dec. 27, 1905; (parents U.S. citizens); s. Percy and Alice (Heublein) M.; m. Jane Weeks, Oct. 17, 1948. Salesman Heublein, Inc., Farmington, Conn., 1928-32, v.p., 1932-37, pres., 1937-61, chmn., chief exec. officer, 1961-66, chmn. bd., 1964-66, mem. exec. com., 1966-75, chmn. exec. com., 1966-75, cons., 1975-86. Mem. Hartford Club, Hartford Golf Club. Home: Naples Fla. Died May 29, 1986.

MARTIN, MARION ELIZABETH, state official; b. Kingman, Maine, Jan. 14, 1900; d. William Henry and Florence Marie (MacLaughlin) M. AB, U. Maine, 1935, LLD (hon.), 1972; law student, Yale U., 1935-36, Northwestern U., summer 1937; MA (hon.), Bates Coll., 1938; LLD (hon.), Nasson Coll., 1953. Mem. Maine Ho. of Reps., 1931-32, 33-34, Maine Senate, 1935-36, 37-38; mem. Rep. Nat. Com. from Maine 1936-47, asst. chmn. Rep. Nat. Com., 1937-47; commr. labor and industry State of Maine, 1947-72; govt. adviser ILO 42d and 43d sessions, Geneva, Switzerland. Founder Nat. Fedn. Rep. Women's Clubs; pres. Bradford Jr. Coll. Alumnae Assn., 1949-52; trustee Bradford Jr. Coll., 1952-64; mem. lay com. Nat. Council Chs. of Christ in U.S.A., 1952-55, mem. gen. bd., 1954-55; dir. Nat. Safety Council from 1950, exec. bd., 1952-60, and from 1961, v.p. women's activities, 1952-60, chmn. women's conf., 1955-58, vice chmn. bd. dirs. from 1972; rep. Nat. Tb Assn., 1955-72, exec. com., 1964-65; sec. Nat. Tb and Respiration Disease Assn., 1969-70; chmn. adv. com. on occupational health U.S. Bur. Pub. Health, 1956, mem. 1954-59; bd. dirs. Maine Tb Assn., from 1950; mem. Pres.' Task Force on Safety, 1970; adv. com. Bur. Labor Standards, from 1970; mem. tech. com. on transp. of aging White Ho. Conf. Aging, 1971; mem. Nat. Commn. on State Workmens' Compensation Laws, 1971-72; project vol. cons. state planning com. ARC, 1973-75; mem. Maine Apprenticeship Council, from 1972, Maine Adv. Council Vocat. Edn., from 1974. Recipient award of acheivement New Eng. region Soroptomists, 1959, Deborah Morton award Westbrook Jr. Coll., 1964, Roselle W. Huddilston award Maine Tb Assn., 1966. Mem. Internat. Assn. Govtl. Labor Ofcls. (pres. 1949-50, exec. com. 1969-72), Assn. Labor Mediation Agys. (exec. bd. 1964-71), Am. Arbitration Assn. (panel labor mgmt. mediators), AAUW, Vets. of Safety, Bricklayers, Masons, Plasterers Union (hon.), Alpha Omicron Pi, Phi Beta Kappa, Sigma Mu Sigma, Delta Kappa Gamma. Episcopalian. Home: Hallowell Maine. Died Jan. 8, 1987; buried Mt. Hope, Bangor, Maine.

MARTIN, MELISSA MARGARET, educator; b. Michigan City, N.D., 1892; d. James Prater and Sarah Elizabeth (Wilson) M.; m. C. Marshall Dawes, Jan. 2, 1953. AB, U. Oreg., 1912; BS, Oreg. State Coll., 1915; AM, Columbia U., 1920; postgrad., U. Calif., U. Madrid, Centro de Estudios Historicos, U. Sorbonne, U. Mex., Middlebury Spanish Sch., Middlebury German Sch. Mem. faculty Oreg. State Coll., from 1915, prof. head dept. modern langs., from 1937; dir., broadcaster Spanish courses Sta. KOAC, Corvallis, Oreg., 1933-36. Assoc. editor Oreg. Modern Lang. Jours., 1932-38; editorial cons. Brit. World Lang. Dictionary, 1953-55; contbr. articles in profl. jours. Recipient 1st prize for original poem Middlebury Spanish Soc., 1934; chosen Theta Sigma Phi Woman of Achievement, 1959. Mem. MLA, AAUW, AAUP, DAR, Am. Assn. Tchrs. German, Am. Assn. Tchrs. Spanish, Mortar Bd., Altrusa Internat. (local v.p. 1959-60), sigma Delta Pi, Alpha Phi, Alpha Lambda Delta, Delta Kappa Gamma (state chmn. on grad. scholarships 1958-60), Pi Delta Phi. Republican. Presbyterian. Home: Corvallis Oreg. †

MARTIN, OTIS ORVAL, financial management consultant; b. Gadsden, Ala., Aug. 10, 1906; s. Walter and Clara (Pickett) M.; m. Jean Mildred Zeiders, June 25, 1930; 1 dau., Carol Lee. Student, U. Calif. at Los Angeles, 1926, Tex. Tech. Coll., 1926-27; B.C.S., Benjamin Franklin U., Washington, 1936, M.C.S., 1937; postgrad., Am. U. C.P.A., Md. With Clovis Nat. Bank, N.Mex., 1924, Los Angeles First Nat. Bank, 1925, FHA, 1934-38; bank examiner Treasury Dept., 1938-46; treas., comptroller, dir. Paul Stone, Inc. (realtors, builders and developers), Washington, 1946-56; internal auditor HHFA, 1956-59; mem. staff Smithsonian Instn., 1959-66, treas., 1959-66, financial mgmt. adviser, 1966-70; financial mgmt. cons. 1970-77. Served with AUS, 1944-45. Mem. Men's Forum (treas.), Fed. Govt. Accountants Assn., Rho Epsilon. Christian Scientist. Club: Mason. Home: Longwood Fla. Deceased.

MARTIN, PARK HUSSEY, engineer, community planning executive; b. Bellevue, Pa., Dec. 5, 1887; s. David Herron and Angeline (Starr) M.; m. Ina Burry, May 26, 1909 (dec.); 1 child, Mary A. Martin Palmer; m. Eleanor Eckels, Apr., 1950. DEng (hon.), Carnegie Inst. Tech., 1949. Draftsman, engr. Pitts. & Lake Erie R.R., 1904-06; resident engr. Pitts.-Butler Interurban Ry., 1906-07; pvt. practice Pitts., 1910-33; chief engr., planning dir. Allegheny County, Pa., 1933-45, chmn. Met. Study Commn.; exec. dir. Allegheny Conf. Community Devel., from 1945, vice chmn. state adv. com. on recreation; exec. dir. Pitts. Regional Planning Assn., from 1952. Contbr. articles to profl. jours. Trustee Carnegie Inst., Carnegie Inst. Tech.; bd. dirs., past pres. St. John's Hosp.; exec. sec. civil def., Allegheny County, World War II. Mem. ASCE (past pres. Pitts. chpt.), Am. Soc. Planning Ofcls. (pres.), Am. Planning and Civic Assn., Bellvue C. of C. (pres. 1922-26), Pitts. Motor Club (pres.), University Club. Home: Pittsburgh Pa. †

MARTIN, QUINN, film and TV producer; b. N.Y.C., May 22, 1922; m. Marianne Martin, Mar. 28, 1961; children—Jill, Cliff, Michael. B.A., U. Calif., Berkeley, 1949. Head post prodn. for ind. cos. Universal Studios, 1950-54; chief exec. officer, pres. QM Prodns., 1960-79; chmn. bd., chief exec. officer Quinn Martin Films; pres. Quinn Martin Communications Group, 1982-87; cons. Taft Broadcasting; adj. prof. drama Warren Coll., U. Calif.-San Diego, LaJolla, 1983-87. Producer: TV show Jane Wyman Theater, 1957; exec. producer: TV show Untouchables, Westinghouse Playhouse, 1958-59; producer: numerous TV series including The Streets of San Francisco, Canon, Barnaby Jones; movies including Face of Fear. Trustee Buckley Sch., North Hollywood, Calif.; pres. Del Mar Fair Bd., 1983-84; pres. LaJolla Playhouse, Calif., 1985-86 Served with U.S. Army, 1940-45. Endowed chair of drama Warren Coll., U. Calif.-San Diego, 1983. Clubs: Bel Air Country; Fairbanks Ranch Country (founding). Home: Rancho Santa Fe Calif. Died Sept. 5, 1987.

MARTIN, RICHARD MILTON, philosopher, author; b. Cleve., Jan. 12, 1916; s. Frank Wade and Lena Beatrice (Bieder) M.; m. Marianne von Winter, Oct. 23, 1948. A.B., Harvard U., 1938; M.A., Columbia U., 1939; Ph.D., Yale U., 1941. Instr. math. Princeton U., 1942-44; instr. math. U. Chgo., 1944-46; asst. prof. philosophy Bryn Mawr Coll., 1946-48; asst. prof., asso. prof. philosophy U. Pa., 1948-59; prof. philosophy U. Tex., 1959-63, N.Y. U., 1963-73, Northwestern U., 1973-84; guest prof. U. Bonn, 1960-61, U. Hamburg, 1970-71; vis. prof. Yale U., 1964-65, New Sch. for Social Research, 1972, Temple U., 1973, U. Conn., 1980; cons. Alderson & Sessions (mktg. cons.), Phila., 1950-55; chmn. exec. com. Conf. on Method in Philosophy and the Scis., N.Y., 1970; mem. East-West Philosophers Conf., U. Hawaii, 1973, Workshop on Kinship Relations sponsored by Maths. Social Sci. Bd., NSF at Center for Advanced Study in Behavioral Scis., Stanford U., 1974, Inst. for Advanced Study, Princeton, N.J., 1975-76; mem. adv. bd. Peirce Edit. Project, NSF and Nat. Endowment for Humanities, 1976-82; research assoc. Boston U. Center for Philosophy and History of Sci., 1977-85. Author: Truth and Denotation, A Study in Semantical Theory, 1958, The Notion of Analytic Truth, 1959, Towards A Systematic Pragmatics, 1959, Intension and Decision, A Philosophical Study, 1963, Belief, Existence and Meaning, 1969, Logic, Language and Metaphysics, 1971, Whitehead's Categoreal Scheme and Other Papers, 1974, Events, Reference and Logical Form, 1978, Semiotics and Linguistic Structure, 1978, Peirce's Logic of Relations and Other Studies, 1979, Pragmatics, Truth, and Language, 1979, Primordiality, Science, and Value, 1980, Logico-Linguistic Papers, 1981, Mind, Modality, Meaning and Method, 1983, Metaphysical Foundations: Mereology and Metalogic, 1985; Editor: (with Alan Anderson and Ruth Marcus) The Logical Enterprise, 1975, Studies in the Scientific and Mathematical Philosophy of Charles S. Peirce (Essays by Carolyn Eisele), 1979; mem. editorial bd.: The Monist, 1961-85, (with Alan Anderson and Ruth Marcus) Philosophy and Phenomenological Research, 1966-85, The Ency. of Philosophy, 1967, Transactions of the Charles S. Peirce Soc, 1969-85, Philosophia, 1969-85, Kant-Studien, 1971-85, Philosophical Studies, 1971-76, The Philosophy Research Archives, 1974-85, Eidos, 1976-85, The Southern Jour. of Philosophy, 1978-85; Contbr. articles to profl. jours. John Simon Guggenheim Meml. Found. fellow, 1951-52; Fund for Advancement Edn. fellow, 1955-56; Am. Council Learned Socs. fellow, 1961; asso. fellow Clare Hall, Cambridge U., 1971-85; research grantee NSF, 1958-74; research grantee Vaughn Found., 1970, 77. Mem. Assn. for Symbolic Logic (exec. com. and council 1950-53), Am. Philos. Assn. (exec. com. Eastern div. 1964-67), N.Y. Philosophy Club (chmn. 1971-74), Charles S. Peirce Soc. (pres. 1981), Metaphys. Soc. Am. (chmn. program com. 1978-84), Internat. Soc. Metaphysics. Home: Milton Mass. Died Nov. 22, 1985.

MARTIN, W(ALTER) REID, investment banker; b. Madison, N.C., Mar. 3, 1891; s. Luther W. and Cora (Reid) M.; m. Katherine Hampton, June 16, 1916 (dec. Apr. 1962); children: Katherine Martin Levine, Margaret Martin Davidson. Grad., Kings Bus. Coll., Raleigh, N.C. Store mgr., acct. Barber & Towler, Raleigh, 1910-13, Garland (N.C.) Lumber Co., 1914-17; v.p., cashier Raleigh Savs. Bank and N.C. Bank & Trust Co., 1917-30, Page Trust Co., 1930-33; sr. v.p., Raleigh br. mgr. R.S. Dickson & Co., from 1933, also bd. dirs.; bd. dirs. Ruddick Corp., Charlotte, N.C. Investment counselor Wake Forest Coll. Endowment Assn. Mem. Raleigh Execs. Club, Kiwanis. Home: Raleigh N.C. †

MARTIN, WILLIAM HARRIS, government official; b. Dothan, Ala., June 15, 1908; s. Cody A. and Lenore (Harris) M.; m. Gladys Odell Drake, Dec. 24, 1934; 1 child, Joyce Lenore. BS, Wilberforce (Ohio) U., 1930, EdB, 1932, LHD (hon.), 1964; MA, Ohio State U., 1933, PhD, 1944. Prof. edn. Shorter Coll., North Little Rock, Ark., 1933-34, Tex. Coll., Tyler, 1934-39; dean Dunbar Jr. Coll., Little Rock, 1939-45; prof., dir. div. tcnr. edn. Langston U., 1945-53; prof. edn. Hampton Inst., 1953-55, dean faculty, 1955-65, acting pres., 1959-60, dir. self study under grant Fund for Advancement Edn., 1954-55, campus coordinator AID project Hampton Inst./Sierra Leone, 1961-63; edn. adv. Bur. African Affairs Dept. State, Washington, 1963-66, regional edn. officer for Africa, Office Overseas Schs., 1966-69, br. chief Inst. Internat. Studies fellowships and overseas projects, 1969-74, br. chief Ethnic Heritage Studies Program, 1974-84; cons. Intercultural Workshop Mich. Dept. Edn., Bur. Intercultural Edn., Western Mich. Coll., summer 1946. Contbg. author Negro Education in America. Trustee Wilberforce U.; bd. dirs. Met. Washington chpt. Africare. Fellow Okla. Acad. Sci., John Dewey Soc. for Study Edn. and Cluture; mem. Assn. Overseas Educators (adv. council), Internat. Assn. Community Educators (dir.), African Studies Assn., Fed. Schoolmen's Club, NEA, Assn. Higher Edn., Kappa Delta Pi, Phi Delta Kappa, Kappa Alpha Psi. Mem. A.M.E. Ch. (bd. stewards). Home: Washington D.C. Died June 10, 1984.

MARVEL, CARL SHIPP, research chemist, educator; b. Waynesville, Ill., Sept. 11, 1894; s. John Thomas and Mary Lucy (Wasson) M.; m. Nelle Beggs, June 1918 (div. 1933); m. Alberta Hughes, Dec. 16, 1933; children: Mary Catharine, John Thomas. AB, MS, Ill. Wesleyan U., 1915, DSc (hon.), 1946; AM, U. Ill., 1916, PhD, 1920, DSc (hon.), 1963; DSc (hon.), Poly. Inst. N.Y., 1983, U. Louvain, Belgium, 1970. Instr. chemistry U. Ill., Urbana, 1920-21, assoc., 1921-23, asst. prof., 1923-27, assoc. prof., 1927-30, prof. organic chemistry, 1930-53, research prof. organic chemistry, 1953-61, emeritus, from 1961; prof. chemistry U. Ariz., Tucson, 1961-87; cons. E.I. DuPont Co., Wilmington, Del., from 1928. Author: An Introduction to the Organic Chemistry of High Polymers, 1959. Recipient Plastic Sci. Engring. award Soc. Plastic Engrs. Internat., 1964, Perkin medal Am Sect. Soc. Chem. Industry, 1965, Achievement award U. Ill. Alumni Assn., 1976, Creative Sci. award U. Ariz. Found., 1978, Nat. Medal of Sci., U.S. Govt., 1986; chemistry bldg. U. Ariz. rededicated as the Carl S. Marvel Labs. of Chemistry, 1984; inducted into Plastics Hall of Fame, 1986. Mem. Am. Chem. Soc. (pres. 1945-46, Nichols medal N.Y. sect. 1944, Willard Gibbs medal Chgo. sect. 1950, Priestly medal 1956, Polymer Chemistry award 1964, Madison Marshall award North Ala. sect. 1966, Chemistry of Plastics and Coatings award 1973, 40 Yrs. Service Council Mem. award 1980, Chem. Edn. award 1984, 45 Yrs. Service Council Mem. award 1985), Am. Acad. Arts and Scis., Nat. Acad. Scis., Am. Inst. Chemists (Gold medal 1955), Am. Philos. Soc., Alpha Chi Sigma (John R. Kuebler award 1970). Club: Cosmos. Home: Tucson Ariz. Died Jan. 4, 1988; buried nr. Tucson.

MARVEL, RICHARD DOUGLAS, state senator; b. Hastings, Nebr., Dec. 8, 1917; s. Archie Douglas and Ruth (Capps) M.; m. Oline Ida Lindemann, May, 17, 1941; children: Douglas James, Anne Elizabeth. Student, U. Leipzig, U. Freiburg, Germany, 1938-39; BA, Hastings Coll., 1940; MA, U. Nebr., 1960, PhD, 1966. With Gen. Credit Corp., Hastings, 1946-55, Peoples Loan Co., Hastings, 1955-58; faculty Omaha U., 1962-68; assoc. prof. polit. sci. Nebr. Wesleyan U., Lincoln, 1968-83, chmn. dept., 1973-83; mem. Nebr. Senate, 1959-83, chmn. appropriations com., 1961-76, chnm. exec. bd. unicameral, 1976-78, speaker of legislature, 1979-83. Contbr. articles to profl. jours. Chmn.

Adams County Rep. Com., 1954-58. With USAAF, 1942-46. Mem. Am. Legion (comdr. Nebr. 1946-47). Home: Hastings Nebr. Died Dec. 2, 1986; buried Hastings.

MARVIN, LEE, actor; b. N.Y.C., Feb. 19, 1924; s. Lamont W. and Courtenay D. M.; m. Pamela Feeley, Oct. 18, 1970. Appeared with summer stock cos.; Broadway debut in Billy Budd; film debut You're in the Navy Now; other films include: Diplomatic Courier, We're Not Married, Down Among the Sheltering Palms, Eight Iron Men, The Stranger Wore a Gun, Big Heat, Gun Fury, The Wild One, The Caine Mutiny, Gorilla at Large, The Raid, Bad Day at Black Rock, Life in the Balance, Violent Saturday, Not as a Stranger, Pete Kelly's Blues, I Died a Thousand Times, The Rack, Shack Out on 101, Attack, Cat Ballou, The Professionals, The Dirty Dozen, Paint Your Wagon, Point Blank, Sergeant Ryer, Hell in the Pacific, Prime Cut, Pocket Money, Emperor of the North Pole, The Iceman Cometh, The Spikes Gang, The Klansman, The Great Scout and Cathouse Thursday, Shoot at the Devil, Avalanche Express, Death Hunt, Gorky Park, TV film The Dirty Dozen: The Next Mission, 1985. Served with USMC, World War II. Recipient Best Actor award Berlin Film Festival, Acad. award for Cat Ballou, 1965, Brit. Acad. award for best fgn. actor, 1965, Spanish Silver Film award, 1970. Died Aug. 29, 1987.

MARX, RUDOLF, surgeon; b. Bruchsal, Germany, Mar. 1, 1891; came to U.S., 1922; naturalized, 1929; s. Frederic and Elise (Weyl) M.; m. Agnes O'Malley, Mar. 31, 1926 (dec.); children: Gretel, Paul Frederic; m. 2d, Margot Gauss-Lindenberg, 1959. Grad., Bruchsal Gymnasium, 1908; student, U. Freiburg, 1909, U. Munich, 1910; MD, U. Heidelberg, 1914. Diplomate Am. Bd. Surgery. 1st resident surgeon Bethany Hosp., Dortmund, Germany, 1918-22; specialized in surgery in L.A. from 1923; mem. staff Cedars of Lebanon Hosp., Mt. Sinai Hosp. Author: The Health of the Presidents, 1960; contbr. med. and hist. jours. Fellow ACS; mem. AMA, L.A. County Med. Assn., L.A. Surg. Soc. Home: Beverly Hills Calif. †

MASER, EDWARD ANDREW, art history educator; b. Detroit, Dec. 23, 1923; s. Andrew J. and Bozena (Slezak) M.; m. Inge Besas, Mar. 31, 1956. Student, U. Mich., 1941-43; M.A., U. Chgo., 1948, Ph.D., 1957; postgrad., U. Frankfurt-am-Main, Germany, 1949-50, U. Florence, Italy, 1950-52. Instr. Northwestern U., Evanston, Ill., 1952-53; dir. U. Kans. Mus. Art, 1953-61, assoc. prof. history art, 1957-61; prof. art U. Chgo., 1961-88, prof. emeritus, 1988—, chmn. art dept., 1961-64; dir. D. and A. Smart Gallery, U. Chgo., 1972-83; Cons. S.H. Kress Found. Author: Catalog of Museo del Opificio delle Pietre Dure, 1952, Giovanni Domenico Ferretti, 1968, Iconologia of Cesare Ripa, 1971, Drawings of J.M. Rottmayr, 1971. Served with USAAF, 1943-45. Decorated Austrian Cross of Honor for Letters and Art 1st class, 1974; Fulbright Research scholar, 1965-66; Guggenheim fellow, 1969-70. Mem. Coll. Art Assn., Am. Assn. U. Profs., Phi Beta Kappa. Home: Chicago Ill. Died Oct. 7, 1988.

MASON, DAVID MALCOLM, chemical engineering educator; b. Los Angeles, Jan. 7, 1921; s. David Malcolm and Anna Pride (McKelvy) M.; m. Honora Elizabeth MacPherson, Sept. 12, 1953. BS in Applied Chem., Calif. Inst. Tech., 1943, MS in Chem. Engring., 1947, PhD in Chem. Engring., 1949. Registered profl. engr. Calif., 1949. Chem. engr. Standard Oil Calif., 1943; instr. chem. engring. Calif. Inst. Tech., Pasadena, 1949-52, research group supr. Jet Propulsion Lab., 1952-55; prof. chem. engring. Stanford (Calif.) U., 1955—, prof. chemistry and chem. engring., 1955-86, chmn. dept. chem. engring., 1960-72, assoc. dean undergrad. studies, 1974-76, assoc. dean Sch. Engring., 1980-83, prof. emeritus chem. engring. and chemistry, 1986—; liaison scientist Office of Naval Research, London, 1972-73. Author 100 papers in field. Served to lt. USN, 1943-46. Named to 1st group of Disting. Alumni, Calif. Inst. Tech, 1966; honored with endowed lectureship in his name, Chem. Engring. Dept., Stanford U., 1975—; NSF fellow Imperial Coll., London, 1964-65 . Fellow Am. Inst. Chem. Engrs. (Founders award 1984); mem. Am. Chem. Soc., Am. Electrochem. Soc., Sigma Xi, Tau Beta Pi. Republican. Home: Los Altos Calif. Died Aug. 10, 1988.

MASON, JAMES, actor; b. Huddersfield, Eng., May 15, 1909; s. John and Mabel Hattersley (Gaunt) M.; m. Pamela Kellino, Feb. 1941 (div.); children: Portland Allen, Alexander Morgan; m. Clarissa Kaye, 1971. Student, Marlborough Coll., 1923-28; BA, Cambridge (Eng.) U., 1931, MA, 1943. Began career in theater, 1931; screen debut in Late Extra, 1935; films include Lolita, 1961, Island in the Sun, Cry Terror, North by Northwest, Georgy Girl, 1966, The Deadly Affair, 1966, Age of Consent, 1968, Spring and Port Wine, 1969, Childs Play, 1971, The Last of Sheila, 1972, Dr. Frankenstin, 1973, The Marseilles Contract, 1974, Great Expectations, 1974, Mandingo, 1974, The Devil and the Schoolteacher, 1975, Autobiography of a Princess, 1975, The Voyage, 1975, Water Babies, 1976, Cross of Iron, Fear in the City, 1976, The Passage, Murder by Decree, Bloodline, 1978, Heaven Can Wait, Boys From Brazil, 1977, The Verdict, 1982, Dr. Fischer of Geneva or the Bomb Party, 1984, The Shooting Party, 1984; actor, producer: (film) Bigger than Life; producer 20th Century-Fox studio; actor (TV programs) Your Readers' Series, 1955, The Roots of the Mafia, 1975, Jesus of Nazareth, 1976; (Broadway play) Faith Healer, 1979; author: Before I Forget, 1981. Home: Vevey Switzerland Died July 27, 1984; buried Vevey, Switzerland.

MASSEY, HARRIS BENTON, automobile retail executive; b. Tennille, Ga., Oct. 18, 1900; s. Harris Benton and Jodie (Brown) M.; m. Doris Mae Jenkins, Apr. 18, 1926. Student, The Citadel, 1918-19. Pres. Dormont Buick Co., 1936-43, Massey Buick Co., Pitts., 1943—; bd. dirs. Dormont Tire Co., Massey Rental Co., Pure Air Muffler Co., Rockwell-Standard Corp., South Hill Co. Trustee Massey Buick Employees Retirement Fund. Mem. Masons, Shriners. Baptist. Home: Bethel Park Md. Deceased.

MASSON, ANDRE, artist; b. Jan. 4, 1896. Ed., Acad. Royale des Beaux-Arts, Brussels, Ecole des Beaux-Arts, Paris. Former mem. Cubist and Surrealist groups, Paris; illus. many books; designer ballet sets for Les Presages, 1933; retrospective exhbns., Paris, London, N.Y.C., Hanover, Fed. Republic Germany, Zurich, Switzerland, others; rep. Dunn Internat. Exhbn., London, 1963; commd. to paint ceiling Theatre de France, 1965; rep. prin. galleries contemporary art, Europe and U.S.; author: Anatomie de mon Univers, 1942, La Pieuvre, 1944, La Renconire de la Chimere, 1944, Memorandum, 1936-45, Bestiare, 1945, Metamorphoses, 1946. Decorated officer Legion of Honor, comdr. des Arts et des Lettres; recipient Grand Prix nat. des Arts, 1954, Sao Paulo Biennale prize, 1963. Home: Paris France. Died Oct. 28, 1987.

MAST, GERALD, film history educator; b. Los Angeles, May 13, 1940; s. George and Bess (Gorelnik) M. B.A., U. Chgo., 1961, M.A., 1962, Ph.D., 1967. Instr. NYU, N.Y.C., 1964-65; instr. Oberlin Coll., Ohio, 1965-67; from asst. to assoc. prof. Richmond Coll., CUNY, S.I., N.Y., 1967-78; prof. U. Chgo., 1978-88, est. Film Archive and Study Ctr.; chmn. Dept. English U. Chgo., 1987—. Author: A Short History of the Movies, 1971, The Comic Mind: Comedy and the Movies, 1973, Film/Cinema/Movie, 1977, Howard Hawks, Storyteller, 1982, Can't Help Singin': The American Musical On Stage and Screen, 1987. Mem. Soc. for Cinema Studies, MLA, Authors' Guild Am., PEN, Actors' Equity Assn. Home: Chicago Ill. Died Sept. 1, 1988.

MASTERS, DEXTER WRIGHT, author, editor; b. Springfield, Ill., June 15, 1908; s. Thomas Davis and Gertrude (Mettler) M.; m. Christina Malman, Mar. 8, 1941 (dec. Jan. 1959), m. 2d, Joan Brady, Sept. 23, 1963; 1 son, Alexander Wright. Grad., Choate Sch., 1926; Ph.B., U. Chgo., 1930. Editor Tide mag., 1930-36, Consumer Reports, 1937-42; editor Radar, mem. staff Radiation Lab. MIT, 1943-45; editorial cons. McGraw-Hill Pub. Co., N.Y.C., 1945-46; publs. dir. Consumers Union, 1947-51, dir., 1957-63, editorial cons., 1963-67. Author: (radio series) One World or None (Peabody award 1947), 1947; (novel) The Accident, 1955; (essays) The Intelligent Buyer and the Telltale Seller, 1966; (novel) The Cloud Chamber, 1971; editor: (with K. Way) One World or None: A Report on the Full Meaning of the Atomic Bomb, 1946; contbr. to nat. mags. Home: Totnes, Devon England. Died Jan. 5, 1989; buried Oakland Cemetary, Petersburg, Ill.

MASUR, ERNEST FRANK, civil engineering educator; b. Berlin, July 15, 1919; came to U.S., 1939, naturalized, 1944; s. Martin M. and Else (Brukstein) M.; m. Eva Henriette Magnus, Dec. 16, 1944; children—Robert Edward, Howard Alan, Sandra. B.S., U. Pitts., 1941; M.S., Ill. Inst. Tech., 1948, Ph.D., 1952. Instr., asst. prof., then asso. prof. civil engring. Ill. Inst. Tech., 1948-55; asso prof., prof. engring. mechanics U. Mich., 1955-64; head dept. materials engring. U. Ill., Chgo., 1964-82, prof. engring. mechanics, from 1982; Structural, aerospace engring. cons., from 1948; cons. NSF, from 1962, dir. div. civil and mech. engring., 1979-80; Nat. Acad. Scis. exchange scientist with Bulgaria, 1972, with Poland, 1977. Editor: Jour. Structural Mechanics, 1972-82; Contbr. articles to profl. jours. Served with AUS, 1943-46. Recipient Laurie award ASCE, 1960. Fellow ASCE (past chmn. engring. mechanics div., mem. mgmt. group B), Am. Acad. Mechanics; mem. ASME, AAUP, Sigma Xi, Chi Epsilon, Sigma Tau. Home: Evanston Ill. Died Oct. 4, 1986; buried Lincolnwood, Ill.

MATHESON, WALLACE ALEXANDER, publisher; b. Montreal, Que., Can., July 29, 1931; s. Alexander G. and Grace deF. (Wallace) M.; m. Martha Ann Driscoll, May 25, 1957; children—Heather Ann, Alexander James, Martha Jean. B.A., Acadia U., 1953. Canadian field rep. coll. div. Prentice-Hall, Inc., Englewood Cliffs, N.J., 1953-58; dir. Prentice-Hall, Inc., 1976-88, Can. dist. mgr., 1958-61; v.p. Prentice-Hall of Can., Ltd., 1961-65, pres., 1965-88, also dir.; Bd. govs. Canadian Copyright Inst., 1973-88; bd. dirs. Montreal Internat. Book Fair, 1973-88. Bd. dirs. Can. Scottish Heritage Found.; mem. pres. adv. com. Children's Aid Soc. Found. Mem. Canadian Book Pubs. Council (past v.p., pres. 1972-73), Canadian Library Exhibitors Assn. (pres. 1966-68, dir. 1968-70). Club: Mason. Home: Willowdale Ont., Canada. Died Jan., 1988.

MATHEWSON, J. ARTHUR, lawyer, business executive; b. Montreal, Que., Can., June 26, 1890; s. Samuel James and Carrie Louise (Smith) M.; m. Ruby Kathleen Tatlow, Jan. 15, 1918; 3 children. BA in Econs. and Polit. Sci. magna cum laude, McGill U., BCL, LLD (hon.); DCL (hon.), U. Montreal; student, The Sorbonne, Paris. Bar: Que. 1917; created King's counsel, 1926. Practiced in Montreal; counsel Lafleur & Brown; lectr. McGill U., 192532; chmn., dir. Franki of Can. Ltd., Ogilvie Flour Mills Co. Ltd., Montreal adv. com. Can. Permanent Toronto Gen. Trust Co.; bd. dirs. Can. Steamship Lines Ltd., Catelli Food Products, Consol. Bakeries Can. Ltd., Gillespie-Munro Ltd., Hall Engring. Ltd., Miller Bros. & Sons Ltd., Toronto-Dominion Bank. Mem. Legis. Assembly Que., 1939-48; treas. Province Que., 1939-44; chmn. Montreal Central Protestant Sch. Bd., 1930-34. Capt. Can. Army, 1914-19. Mem. Can. Bar Assn., Que. Bar Assn., University Club, Mt. Royal Club, Forest and Stream Club. Mem. Anglican Ch. Home: Montreal Que., Canada. †

MATHIS, HAROLD FLETCHER, educator; b. Wichita Falls, Tex., July 19, 1916; s. Henry Fletcher and Annie Martha (Petty) M.; m. Lois Reno, June 6, 1942; children: Robert, Betty. BS, U. Okla., 1939, EE, 1954; MS, Tex. A&M U., 1941, EE, 1952; PhD, Northwestern U., 1953, Case Western Res., 1961. Res. asoc. Northwestern U., 1946-49; assoc. prof. elec. engring. U. Okla., 1949-54; rsch. specialist Goodyear Co., Akron, Ohio, 1954-60; prof. elec. engring. Ohio State U., Columbus, from 1960; cons. N.Am. Rockwell Corp., 1962-70. Contbr. articles to profl. jours. With USNR, 1942-46, 51-53. Mem. IEEE, Am. Soc. Engring. Edn., Am. Bell Assn., Sigma Xi, Phi Eta Sigma, Sigma Tau, Eta Kappa Nu, Kappa Delta Pi. Home: Columbus Ohio. Died May 12, 1985; buried Union Cemetery, Columbus, Ohio.

MATHIS, PAUL CARL, educator; b. Dubuque, Iowa, May 26, 1917; s. Paul Carl and Alma (Petersen) M.; m. L. Edna Viken, June 4, 1941; children: Karen, Paul, William, John. BA cum laude, U. Dubuque; postgrad., U. Mich., 1938-39; MA, U. Iowa, 1940, PhD, 1946. Instr. McCook (Nebr.) Jr. Coll., 1941-42; asst. prof. Carleton Coll., Northfield, Minn., 1946-47; prof. U. S.D., 1947-62; prof. Cen. Mich. U., Mt. Pleasant, 1962-83, chmn. dept. econs., 1962-72; cons. in field. Contbr. articles to profl. jours. With AUS, 1942-46. Fellow GE Found., Found. Econ. Edn. Mem. AAAS, Am., Midwest econ. assns, Econs. Soc. Mich., Masons (32 degree), Omicron Delta Gamma. Home: Mount Pleasant Mich. Died July 27, 1986; buried Concord Cemetery, Garner, Iowa.

MATSON, RAY H(ENRY), banker; b. Chgo., June 18, 1901; s. Hans and Martha (Domke) M.; m. Caroline Miller Whitehead, Apr. 30, 1938; children: Patricia L., John W. BS, Northwestern U., 1923. With credit dept. Foreman Nat. Bank, Chgo., 1926; 2d cashier 1st Nat. Bank Chgo., 1931-40; asst. v.p. Foreman-State Nat. Bank, 1930, 1940-47, v.p., 1947-63, sr. v.p., 1963-67; bd. dirs. Walter E. Heller & Co., Household Fin. Corp. Mem. Robert Morn's Assocs., Union League, Bankers Club, Skokie Country Club, Pi Kappa Alpha, Beta Alpha Psi. Republican. Home: Glencoe Ill. Died Aug. 7, 1986.

MATSON, THEODORE EDWIN, clergyman; b. St. Ignace, Mich., Sept. 16, 1906; s. Emil and Mary G. (Lindberg) M.; m. Evelyn E. Larson, Sept. 19, 1931; children: Paul T., Mary E. AB, Augustana Coll., 1928, DD, 1952; BD, Augustana Luth. Theol. Sem., 1931. Ordained to ministry Evang. Luth. Ch., 1931. Pastor Ishpeming, Mich., 1931-40; regional dir. bd. Am. missions Augustana Luth Ch., 1940-45, exec. dir., 1955-63; pastor Chgo., 1945-55; pres. Wis.-Upper Mich. Synod Luth. Ch. Am., 1963-87; mem. gen. bd. Nat. Coun. Chs.; del. Luth World Assembly, Hanover, Germany, 1952; v.p. Nat. Coun. Chs. of Christ U.S.A., chmn. div. home missions, 1961-63; mem. commn. on worship Luth. Ch. Am., 1963-87, mem. bd. theol. edn., 1968-87; mem. commn. on evangelism and stewardship Luth. World Fedn. Author: Edge of the Edge, 1961. Sec. bd. dirs. Augustana Hosp., Chgo., 1950-55; bd. dirs. Luth. Sch. Theology, Carthage Coll., Suomi Coll. Home: Milwaukee Wis. Died Apr. 24, 1987.

MATTELL, ROSCOE ARNOLD, petroleum engineer; b. New Sharon, Iowa, Jan. 6, 1892. †

MATTHEWS, BURNITA SHELTON, judge; b. Burnell, Miss., Dec. 28, 1894; d. Burnell and Lora Drew (Barlow) Shelton; m. Percy Ashley Matthews, Apr. 28, 1917. LL.B., George Washington U. (formerly Nat. U.), 1919, LL.M., 1920, LL.D., 1950; LL.D., Am. U., 1966. Bar: D.C., Miss., U.S. Supreme Ct. bars. Practice in Washington, 1920; active in securing equal rights for women; formerly mem. faculty Washington Coll. Law; judge U.S. Dist. Ct., D.C., 1949-68; sr. judge U.S. Dist. Ct., 1968-83. Past mem. Com. Experts Women's Work ILO; formerly mem. research com. Inter-Am. Commn. Women; former mem. Nat. Woman's Party.; Mem., past 1st v.p. nat. bd. Med. Coll. Pa. (formerly Woman's Med. Coll. Pa.); nat. devel. com. Am. U. Recipient Alumni Achievement award George Washington U., 1968; Distinguished Service award Bar Assn. D.C., 1968. Mem. Am. Bar Assn., Nat. Assn. Women

Lawyers (past pres.). Home: Washington D.C. Died Apr. 25, 1988.

MATTHEWS, H. FREEMAN, U.S. ambassador; b. Balt., May 26, 1899; s. Henry Clay and Bertha (Freeman) M.; m. Elizabeth Luke, Sept. 15, 1925 (dec.); children: H. Freeman, Thomas Luke; m. Helen Skouland, Apr. 24, 1957 (dec.); m. Elizabeth H. Bluntshli, July 8, 1967. AB, Princeton U., 1921, AM, 1922, LLD, 1962; postgrad., Ecole Libre de Scis. Politiques, Paris, 1922-23. Apptd. to U.S. Diplomatic Svc., 1924; 3d sec. to Budapest, 1924-26, Bogota, 1926-30; 3d sec. to Dept. State, 1930-33, asst. chief Div. Latin-Am. Affairs; 1st sec. Dept. State, Havana, Cuba, 1933, Paris, 1937-39, Madrid, 1939, Vichy, France, 1940-41; counselor Dept. State, London, 1941, minister, 1942; chief Div. European affairs Dept. State, 1943; acting chief civil affairs officer staff to Gen. Eisenhower London and Algiers (Algeria), 1942; dep. dir. Office European Affairs, 1944, dir., 1944; mem. del. Crimea Conf., 1945, Berlin Conf., 1945; polit. adviser Coun. Fgn. Ministers, 1945-47, Paris Peace Conf., 1946; amb. to Sweden 1947-50, dep. under Sec. of State, 1950-53, amb. to The Netherlands, 1953-57, amb. to Austria, 1957-62; chmn. permanent joint bd. def. Can.-U.S., 1962-70. Mem. Chevy Chase Club, Metropolitan Club, Quadrangle Club, The Brook Club. Home: Washington D.C. Died Oct. 19, 1986; buried Friends Cemetery, Balt.

MATTHEWS, MARJORIE SWANK, clergywoman; b. Onaway, Mich., July 11, 1916; 1 son, William. B.A. summa cum laude, Central Mich. U., 1967; B.D., Colgate Rochester Div. Sch., 1970; M.A. in Religion, Fla. State U., 1971, Ph.D., 1976. Ordained to deacon United Methodist Ch., 1963. Sec. to pres., asst. treas. automotive parts mfg. corp. Mich., 1946-63; elder United Methodist Ch., 1965; minister chs. N.Y., Fla., Ga., Mich., 1959-75; dist. supt. Grand Travers Dist., Western Mich. Conf., 1975-80; bishop Wis. Area, 1980-84; chmn. Coll. and Campus Ministries div. Bd. Higher Edn. and Ministry, Area Commn. on Higher Edn.; mem. Commn. on Status and Role of Women Western Mich. Conf.; mem. North Central Jurisdiction Com. on Ordained Ministry Gen. Conf. Meth. Ch., 1974-75, mem. Com. to Study Episcopacy, 1972-76, del. chmn., 1980; former vice chmn. bd. Center for Parish Devel.; mem. faculty and staff Western Mich. Conf. Native Am. Pastors' Sch. Contbr. articles, meditations to publs. Trustee Garrett-Evang. Theol. Sem. Recipient Alumni Recognition awards Central Mich. U., 1976; recipient Alumni Recognition awards Fla. State U., 1980. Mem. Nat. Fedn. Bus. and Profl. Women (regional, state, local offices). Died July 2, 1986.

MATTHIAS, RUSSELL HOWARD, lawyer; b. Milw., Aug. 7, 1906; s. Charles G. and Lena (Martin) M.; m. Helene Seibold, Dec. 28, 1932; children: Russell Howard, William Warrens, Robert Charles. AB, Northwestern U., 1930, JD, 1932. Bar: Ill. 1933, D.C. 1947, Okla. 1947, Fla. 1979. Spl. asst. to atty. gen. U.S. R.R. Retirement Act, 1934-35; sec. Ill. Fraternal Congress, 1935-40, 45-60; ptnr. Meyers & Matthias, Chgo., 1951-78; pres., treas. Meyers & Matthias, P.C., 1978-80; ptnr. Matthias & Matthias, 1980-82; chmn. bd. Old Orchard Bank & Trust Co.; bd. dirs., gen. counsel United Founders Life Ins. Co. Ill., United Founders Life Ins. Co. Okla., Wesco Inc.; gen. counsel Nat. Ind. Statis. Svc. Chgo. Drafting Com., Ill. Ins. Code, 1938, annotating com., 1940; mem. drafting com. La. Ins. Code, 1948. Trustee Valparaiso U. Law Sch. Lt. col. AUS, 1942-46. Recipient Alumni award Northwestern U., 1973. Mem. Luth. Brotherhood (bd. dirs., gen. counsel), Internat. Assn. Life Ins. Counsel, Indian Hill Country Club, Mid-Day Club, University Club, Kenilworth Club, Minneapolis Club, Citrus Club, Country Club, Phi Delta Theta. Republican. Lutheran. Home: Wilmette Ill. Died Mar. 6, 1982; buried Kenilworth, Ill.

MATTINGLY, RICHARD FRANCIS, physician, educator; b. Zanesville, Ohio, Oct. 25, 1925; s. James Joseph and Frances Katherine (Shaw) M.; m. Mary Elizabeth Kohlamn, Sept. 19, 1948; children: Kevin, Kerry, Kent, Kathleen, Keith, Kelly, Kristen. BA, Ohio State U., 1949; MD, Cornell U., 1953. Diplomate Am. Bd. Ob-Gyn. Intern, then resident ob-gyn Johns Hopkins Hosp., 1953-58, instr., then asst. prof. ob-gyn, 1958-61; prof., chmn. dept. gynecology and obstetrics Med. Coll. Wis., Milw., from 1961; dir. dept. gynecology and obstetrics Milw. County Gen. Hosp., from 1961; mem. cons. staff Milw., St. Joseph's, St. Luke's, St. Mary's, Mt. Sinai, Columbia hosps. Editor in chief: Obstetrics and Gynecology. With M.C., AUS, 1944-46. Fellow AMA, Am. Coll. Ob-Gyn; mem. Am. Gynecol. and Obstet. Soc., Med. Soc. Milw. County, AAUP, Assn. Profs. Gynecology and Obstetrics, Cen. Assn. Obstetricians and Gynecologists, Wis. Med. Soc., Wis. Soc. Ob-Gyn, Am. Fertility Soc., Soc. Pelvic Surgeons (pres. 1980-81), Am. Soc. Cytology, N.Y. Acad. Sci., Am. Radium Soc., Soc. Gynecol. Oncology, Soc. Biol. Editors. Home: Milwaukee Wis. Died Jan. 1, 1986; buried Holy Cross Cemetery.

MATTSON, VERNON LINNAEUS, oil company consultant; b. Chgo., July 12, 1902; s. Axel Linnaeus and Stella (Buck) M; m. Carribelle Pitcher, Aug. 9, 1982 (div. 1975); 1 child, Joseph T.; m. Thelma Makeig (dec. 1977); m. Aliece Makeig, 1978. Student, Carnegie Inst. Tech., 1920-22; EM, Colo. Sch. Mines, 1926. Registered profl engr. Colo., N.Mex. Mine examiner Mazapil Copper Co. and Norrie Tower Co., 1926-30; v.p., gen. mgr. Celo Mines, Inc., Burnsville, N.C., 1930-44; chief engr. Consol. Feldspar Corp., 1944-49; mgr. mines and mills, v.p. and tech. adviser to the pres. Kerr-McGee Corp., v.p. research, 1968-69, v.p. spl. projects, 1969-71; cons. in mineral and petroleum bus. from 1971; Mem. Gov.'s Adv, Com. Sci. and Industry. Recipient Disting. Service Achievement award Colo. Sch. Mines, 1960. Mem. AIME (named to Legion of Merit 1973), Okla. Sci. Soc., Colo. Sci. Soc., N.Y. Acad. Sci., Okla. Acad. Sci., Colo. Soc. Engrs., Colo. Mining Assn., Am. Nuclear Soc., Geol. Soc. Am., Teknik Club Denver, Mt. Vernon Country Club, Denver, Petroleum Club Denver, Mining Club, N.Y.C. Home: Estes Park Colo. Died Nov. 18, 1984.

MAVIS, FREDERIC THEODORE, civil engineer; b. Crocketts Bluff, Ark., Feb. 7, 1901; s. Martin John and Hinda (Cassens) Mewes; m. Edith Frances Foley, June 7, 1930. BSCE, U. Ill., 1922, MS, 1926, CE degree, 1932, PhD, 1935; postgrad., Technische Hochschule Karlsruhe, Baden, Germany, 1927-28. From jr. engr. to asst. engr. Kelker, DeLeuw & Co., Chgo., 1922-25; office engr. in charge Kelker, DeLeuw & Co., 1926-27; rsch. asst. com. on concrete, reinforced concrete arches ASCE, 1925-26, Freeman traveling fellow, 1927-28; from asst. prof. mechs. and hydraulics to prof. and head dept. State U. Iowa; assoc. dir. in charge lab. to cons. engr. Iowa Inst. Hydraulic Rsch., 1928-39; prof., head dept. civil engring. Carnegie Inst. Tech., Pitts., 1944-57; prof., dean Coll. Engring. U. Md., 1957-65, prof. mech. engring., 1965-67, cons. engr., 1967-83; Chmn. panel R & D Bd., 1947-48; mem., mem.-at-large Div. Engring. and Indsl. Rsch. NRC, 1955-64. Author, editor monographs in field. Recipient Wason medal Am. Concrete Inst., 1959. Mem. ASCE, ASME, Am. Soc. for Engring. Edn., Soc. Am. Mil. Engrs., Am. Water Works Assn., Internat. Assn. Hydraulic Rsch., Rotary (Paul Harris fellow), Sigma Xi, Pi Kappa Phi, Theta Tau, Chi Epsilon, Gamma Alpha, Tau Beta Pi, Phi Kappa Phi, Pi Tau Sigma, Pi Mu Epsilon, Kappa Alpha Mu. Home: Macomb Ill. Died Nov. 2, 1983; buried Hillsgrove Cemetery, Macomb, Ill.

MAXON, GLEN W., construction engineer; b. Ft. Davis, Tex., Sept. 15, 1884; s. Mason M. and Grace (Fuller) M.; m. Blanche Estelle Smith; 1 child, Glen W. Student, U. S.D., 1900-01, U. Cin., 1904-05. Civilian staff C.E. U.S. Army, 1906-11; supt., prodn. mgr., mng. ptnr. Nat. Contract Co., Evansville, Ind., 1912-25; supervising engr. U.G.I. Contracting Co., Phila., 1925-28; pres. Maxon Constrn. Co., Inc., Dayton, Ohio, 1928-62, also bd. dirs., chmn. bd., from 1962; bd. dirs. Brown-Pacific-Maxon, San Francisco, Bailey-Jones, Inc., Greenburg, Ind.; mem. adv. com. Nat. Petroleum Authority, chmn. tech. com. to survey constrn. African air base for U.S. Army, 1952; mem. Co. for Econ. Devel.; mem. Export Expansion Council, 1962. Trustee Dayton Rotary Found. Mem. U.S. C.of C., Ohio C. of C., Dayton C. of C., Nat. Rsch. Devel. Assn., Soc. Am. Mil. Engrs., Am. Ordnance Assn., U.S. Naval Inst., Assn., Gen. Contractors Am. (exec. com.,, past pres., past chmn. heavy engring. div.), Cons. Constructors Council Am. (past chmn.), Moles (Outstanding Achievement in Constrn. award 1954), Newcomen Soc. N.Am., Dayton Club, Dayton Country Club, Dayton Engrs., Rotary, Masons, KT, Delta Tau Delta. Home: Dayton Ohio †

MAXWELL, DAVID F., lawyer; b. Phila., Nov. 7, 1900; s. Alexander and Rachel Sellers (Farrow) M.; m. Emily Ogden Nelson, Nov. 16, 1925 (dec.); children: Fairlie (Mrs. William H. Pasfield), David O.; m. Dorothy Wing Underhill, June 15, 1983. BS, U. Pa., 1921, LLB, 1924; LLB (hon.), Nat. U. Ireland, Dickinson Law Sch. Bar: Pa. 1924. Assoc. Edmonds, Obermayer & Rebmann (name now Obermayer, Rebmann, Maxwell & Hippel), Phila., 1924-29, ptnr., 1929-75, of counsel, 1975-85. Contbr. articles to profl. jours. Hon. bd. dirs. Crime Commn. Phila., pres., 1965-67; trustee Woods Schs.; trustee emeritus Dickinson Law Sch. Recipient Citizenship award SAR, award of merit U. Pa. Mem. ABA (pres. 1956-57, ho. of dels. 1944-85, chmn. ho. of dels. 1952-54), Pa. Bar Assn. (chmn. hol. of dels. 1966-68), Phila Bar Assn., Am. Bar Found. (pres. 1956-57), St. Andrew's Soc. Phila. (pres. 1958-59), Fellows of Am. Bar Found. (chmn. 1958-59), Am. Coll. Trial Lawyers (regent 1966-69), Internat. Acad. Astronautics (bd. dirs. 1959-60), Masons (past master), Kiwanis (pres. 1951), Penn Club, Sarasota Yacht Club (pres. 1981-85), Ivy League Club (bd. dirs. 1983-85). Home: Sarasota Fla. Died Oct. 8, 1985.

MAY, J. T., psychiatrist; b. Roland, Ark., Nov. 17, 1922; s. John Rye and Nona (Porter) M.; m. Helen Louise Hearn, Feb. 19, 1943; children: Susan May Milder, Stephen, Michael, Marilyn May Lawlor, Robin May Allen. Student, Hendrix Coll., 1939-41; MD, U. Ark., 1944. Intern Ark. Bapt. Hosp., Little Rock, 1944-45, resident in medicine, 1945-46; resident psychiatry VA Hosp., North Little Rock, 1952-55; staff mem. VA Hosp., Little Rock, 1955-58; clin. instr. dept. psychiatry Sch. Medicine, U. Ark., 1952-56, asst. clin. prof., 1956-58; chief of service Mental Health Inst., Cherokee, Iowa, 1958-61, clin. dir. impatient services, 1962-67, supt., 1969-73, cons., 1973-76; mem. staff VA Hosp., North Little Rock, 1976-78; supt. Mental Health Inst., Independence, Iowa, 1978-80; dir. profl. services for rsch. and edn. VA Hosp., Gulfport, Miss., 1961-62; asst. prof. Sch. Medicine SUNY, Buffalo, also chief psychiatry and neurology VA Hosp., Buffalo, 1967-69; acting dir. Bur. Mental Health, Iowa Dept. Social Services, 1972-73. Capt. M.C., AUS, 1946-48. Fellow Am. Psychiat. Assn.; mem. Iowa Psychiat. Assn. (past pres.). Home: Hot Springs Ark. Died July 1, 1985.

MAY, MARK ARTHUR, psychology educator; b. Jonesboro, Tenn., Aug. 12, 1891; s. Samuel and Mary Etta (Kyker) M.; m. Ruby Patton, Sept. 12, 1917; children: Samuel Cassamere, Martha Norwood. AB, Maryville (Tenn.) Coll., 1911; PhB, U. Chgo., 1912; student, Union Theol. Sem., N.Y.C., 1913-15; MA, Columbia, 1915, PhD, 1917; MA, Yale, 1927; LLD (hon.), Syracuse U., 1949; LHD, Maryville Coll., 1961. Instr. mil. psychology U.S. Army, Camp Greenleaf, Ga., 1917-18; statistician Surgeon General's Office, Washington, 1918-19; asst. prof. psychology Syracuse U., 1919-20, assoc. prof., 1920-21, prof., 1921-24, rsch. assoc., 1924-27; prof. ednl. psychology, dir. Inst. Human Rels. Yale, 1927-60, prof. emeritus of psychology, from 1960; sci. cons. War Dept., 1944-45; chmn. U.S. Adv. Commn. on Information, 1953-62, chmn. bd. dirs. Teaching Films Custodians Inc. Author: The Mechanism of Controlled Association, 1918, How to Study in College, 1924; co-author: (with Hugh Hartshorne) Studies in Deceit, 1928; Studies in Service and Self Control, 1929; Studies in the Organization of Character, 1930; Education of American Ministers (3 vols.), 1933; (with R. B. Stoeckel and R. S. Kirby) Safety on the Road, 1936; (with L. Doob) Competition and Coöperation, 1937; Educatio in the World of Fear, 1941; A social Psychology of War and Peace, 1943, Learning from Films, 1957. Recipient certificate of merit U.S. Army. Fellow AAAS; mem. Am. Psychol. Assn., Sigma Xi. Home: Hamden Conn. †

MAY, PHILIP REGINALD ALDRIDGE, psychiatrist, educator; b. Weymouth, Eng., May 30, 1920; m. Genevieve May. B.A., Cambridge U., Eng., 1941, M.B., B.Ch., 1944, M.A., 1946; M.D., Stanford U., Calif., 1944. Diplomate Royal Coll. Physicians and Surgeons, Am. Bd. Psychiatry and Neurology. Resident in medicine and neurology Guy's Hosp., London, 1945, resident psychiatrist, 1945-46; resident Bexley Hosp., 1946-47, U. Colo. Sch. Medicine, Boulder, 1949-50; from. instr. to asst. prof. psychiatry UCLA Med. Sch., 1950-53, from. asst. clin. prof. to assoc. clin. prof., 1956-68, clin. dir. Neuropsychiat. Inst., 1962-73, prof. psychiatry, 1969-83, Della Martin prof. psychiatry, 1983-86; chief health services R & D Lab. Brentwood Vet. Adminstrn. Hosp., Los Angeles, 1970-86; chief male inpatient service Colo. Psychopathic Hosp., 1950-51, asst. dir. Hosp., 1951-53: cons. Fitzsimmons Army Hosp., Denver and U.S. Armed Forces Epidemiology Bd., 1951-53, VA Hosps., Denver, 1951-53, Los Angeles, 1966-70; clin. dir. Camarillo State Hosp., Calif., 1955-59, chief research, 1959-62, now cons.; cons. Superior Ct., Santa Barbara and Ventura Counties and Probation Dept., Ventura, Calif., 1958-66. Served in Med. Corps Brit. Royal Army. Recipient Paul Hoch award Am. Psychopath. Assn., 1974. Fellow Am. Psychiat. Assn. (Bronze award 1963; Van Giesen award 1979; Stanley R. Dean award 1986), Am. Coll. Neuropsychopharmacology (pres. 1975); mem. AMA, Internat. Coll. Psychopharmacology, Royal Coll. Physicians. Died Dec. 9, 1986.

MAYER, AUGUSTUS KIEFER, wholesale druggist, rancher; b. Indpls., May 8, 1891; s. Charles and Josephine (Kiefer) M.; m. Marguerite Van Camp, Nov. 6, 1912; children: Marguerite Van Camp (dec.), Elizabeth (Mrs. John Thomas Trixler); m. 2d, Lucy Barnett, Apr. 17, 1950. Student, Phillips Exeter Acad., 1908, Wabash Coll., 1909-10, Indpls. Coll. Pharmacy, 1910; ScB (hon.), Sch. Pharmacy, Butler U., 1934. With A. Kiefer Drug. Co. and Kiefer-Stewart Co., 1910-60, 1st v.p., pres., 1915-55, pres., 1955-60, ret., 1960. Capt. S.C., U.S. Army, World War II, AEF. Mem. Nat Wholesale Druggist Assn., Indpls. Athletic Club, Univ. Club, M.O. Club, Tucson Country Club, Masons, Shriners, Sigma Chi. Republican. Presbyterian. Home: Indianapolis Ind. †

MAYER, JOHN ANTON, banker; b. Terre Haute, Ind., July 30, 1909; s. Herman and Antoinette (Brinkman) M.; m. Effie F. Disston, Oct. 1, 1937; children: John Anton, Christopher, Mark Disston. B.S., U. Pa., 1932, M.B.A., 1933; LL.D, Ind. State U., 1971. Asst. sec. Penn Mut. Life Ins. Co., 1936-39, asst. to pres., 1939-47, sec., 1947-49; pres., dir. Reliance Life Ins. Co. of Pitts., 1949-51; v.p. Mellon Nat. Bank & Trust Co. (now Mellon Bank, N.A.), 1951-57, exec. v.p., 1957-59, pres., 1959-67, chief exec. officer, 1963-74, chmn. bd., 1967-78; chmn. bd., chief exec. officer Mellon Nat. Corp., 1972-74, dir., 1972-78; dir. H.J. Heinz Co. 1959-84, Aluminum Co. of Am., Pitts., 1967-83 Norfolk & Western Ry. Co., 1974-82; former dir. Gen Motors Corp. Emeritus trustee Carnegie Mellon U. emeritus mem. bd. dirs. Western Pa. Hosp. Served as comdr. USNR, World War II. Decorated Legion of Merit. Mem. Assn. Res. City Bankers (pres. 1963-64 hon. mem.), Sigma Chi. Episcopalian. Clubs: Duquesne Laurel Valley Golf, Pittsburgh Golf (Pitts.); Rolling Rock (Ligonier, Pa.); St. Andrews, Gulf Stream Golf

(Fla.). Home: Ligonier Pa. Died July 28, 1987; buried St. Michael's of the Valley Cemetery, Ligonier, Pa.

MAYHER, LAURENCE THOMPSON, management consultant; b. Easthampton, Mass., Feb. 17, 1910; s. Philip and Katharine (Thompson) M.; m. Matilda Lawrence Dunham, Jan. 25, 1947; children: Madeleine C. Mayher, Eleanor J. Mayher Hackett, Margaret E. Mayher Ramsdell, Philip L., Katharine D. Mayher Kane, Gretchen. A.B., Amherst Coll., 1930. Salesman, sales supr. Socony-Vacum Oil Co., Inc., 1930-38; asso. Robert Heller & Assos., Inc., 1939-50, v.p., 1950-58, sr. v.p., 1958-63, dir., 1954-63; pres. Robert Heller Assos., Inc., 1963-68, dir., 1963-69; mgmt. cons. 1968-86; exec. dir. Commn. on Pub. Sch. Personnel Policies in Ohio, 1970-73. Exec. dir. Citizens' Council for Ohio Schs., 1974-78; Mem. Shaker Heights Bd. Edn., 1954-61, pres., 1957-60; Trustee Cleve. Inst. Music, Cleve. Inter-Faith Housing Corp.; former trustee Greater Cleve. Neighborhood Centers Assn. Episcopalian. Home: Cleveland Ohio. Died Feb. 5, 1986.

MAYO, CHARLES GEORGE, educational consultant; b. Long Beach, Calif., Aug. 1, 1931; s. Maurice Melvin and Irene Marie (Jost) M.; m. Iris Jean Cook, July 12, 1953; 1 child, Carolyn Ann. AB, Reed Coll., 1953; AM, U. So. Calif., 1960, PhD, 1963. Insp. Equitable Life Assurance Soc. U.S., 1956-57; teaching asst. U. So. Calif., 1958-62; asst. prof. San Francisco State Coll., 1963-66; assoc. dean Grad. Sch., asst. prof. polit. sci. U. So. Calif., 1966-68, assoc. prof. polit. sci., 1968-74, chmn. dept., 1968, dean Grad. Sch., 1968-74, interim dean Coll. Letters, Arts and Scis., 1968-69; pres., prof. polit. sci. West Chester (Pa.) State Coll., 1974-82; sr. cons. Am. Assn. State Colls. and Univs., from 1982; pres. Western Assn. Grad. Schs., 1972-73; mem. exec. com. Pa. Assn. Colls. and Univs., 1978-82; chmn. Commn. for Pa. State Colls. and Univ., 1981-82; mem. ednl. mission to Republic of China, 1978. Co-editor, contbr.; Dimensions of Political Analysis: An Introduction to Contemporary Study of Politics, 1966, American Political Parties: A Systemic Perspective, 1967; contbr. to profl. jours. Trustee Chadwick Sch., 1971-74. Served with AUS, 1954-56. Malcolm fellow, 1958-59. Mem. Am. Polit. Sci. Assn., AAUP, Blue Key, Phi Kappa Phi, Pi Sigma Alpha. Home: Alexandria Va.

MAZZOLA, VINCENT PONTORNO, physician; b. Italy, May 2, 1898; s. Paul and Antoinetta (Pontorno) M. BS, Fordham U., 1919, MS, 1926; MD, L.I. Coll. Hosp., 1923; DSc (hon.), Alfred U., 1938. Diplomate Am. Bd. Obstetrics and Gynecology. Intern, resident medicine and ob-gyn L.I. Coll. Hosp. and N.Y. Lying-In Hosp., 1927-28; attending obstetrician/gynecologist L.I. Coll. Hosp. and St. Peters Hosp., 1928-82; med. dir. St. Peters Hosp., 1963-82; asst. clin. prof., dir. ob-gyn L.I. Coll. Medicine; cons. ob-gyn L.I. Coll. Hosp.; ltd. ptnr. Coleman & Co.; v.p., bd. dirs. Green Acre Wood Lands, Inc., East Paterson, N.J.; mem. med. grievance com. N.Y. State Bd. Regents, 1938-43; mem. appeal bd. SSS, 1940-82; bd. dirs. Loon Mountain Recreation Corp., Lincoln, Lodi Trust Co. (N.J.). Mem. bd. contbg. editors Med. Times, 1940-82; contbr. articles to profl. jours. Mem. Mayor's Screening Panel for selection of mems. Bd. Higher Edn., 1964-82, Citizens Adv. Com. for Constl. Conv.; mem. Gov.'s Med. Adv. Com. for Health and Social Welfare; spl. asst. to Gov. Rockefeller, 1968-82; mem. Bishops Lay Com. for Charities, 1953-82; adviser to undersec. for adminstrn., 1968; bd. dirs. Assn. for Children with Retarded Mental Devel.; pres., life trustee Bklyn. Benevolent Soc., trustee USO; mem. bd. visitors Elmira Reformatory, 5 terms; mem. N.Y. State Hosp. Rev. and Planning Coun., 1972-82. With U.S. Army, World War II; brig surgeon N.Y. Guard. Recipient By-Line award N.Y. Newspaper Reporters Assn., 1950, Disting. Svc. award N.Y. Dept. State, 1972, Meritorious Svc. award SSS, 1972, citation of merit Am. Correctional Chaplains Assn., 1959; named hon. citizen State of N.H., 1968; Mediterranean Acad. fellow, 1950. Fellow N.Y. Acad. Medicine, N.Y. Obstet. Soc., Bklyn. Gynecol. Soc., Internat. Coll. Surgeons, Am. Coll. Obstetrics and Gynecology; mem. N.Y. Reporters Assn. (hon.), Soc. Silurians, Circus Sts. and Sinners, Bordeaux, Madrid, Rome, Brazil surg. socs. (hon.), Downtown Athletic Club, Turf and Field Club. Died June 8, 1982.

MAZZONELLI, RUDY WILLIAM, hotel executive; b. Mt. Carmel, Pa., Nov. 29, 1925; s. Anthony and Grace M.; m. Marianne Amstutz, Nov. 25, 1973; children: Joan Marie, Mark Anthony, Valerie Claire. Maitre d'hotel Copacabana, N.Y.C., 1957-66; dir. banquets Waldorf Astoria Hotel, N.Y.C., 1966-77; dir. food and beverage Hotel Pierre, N.Y.C., 1977-78; exec. v.p. food and beverage Resorts Internat. Hotel/Casino, Atlantic City, 1978-85; v.p. food and beverage Showboat, Atlantic City Casino Hotel, 1985-88. Bd. dirs. Atlantic Community Coll. Culinary Sch. Served with U.S. Army, 1942-46. Decorated cavaliere Italian Order of Merit. Mem. Am. Hotel/Motel Assn. (cert. food and beverage exec., culinary com.), Confrerie de la Chaines des Rotisseurs (chef de Table). Home: Somers Point N.J. Died Mar. 6, 1988; buried Calverton Nat. Cemetery, Calverton, N.Y.

MC AFEE, KENNETH EMBERRY, lawyer; b. Spadra, Ark., Aug. 27, 1903; s. Thomas W. and Corah M.B. (Dowell) McA.; m. Maxine Maples, Apr. 21, 1930; 1 child, Jacqulyn (Mrs. Gary Wayne Williams). B.S., LL.B., U. Okla., 1934. Bar: Okla. bar 1934. Since practiced in Oklahoma City; mem. firm McAfee & Taft (P.C.), 1934-86. Bd. dirs. U. Okla. Found. Served to lt. comdr. USNR, 1942-45. Mem. Am. Bar Assn., Am. Inst. C.P.A.'s, Order of Coif, Beta Gamma Sigma. Clubs: Lion, Sirloin, Economics, Mens Dinner. Home: Oklahoma City Okla. Died Sept. 9, 1986.

MCARTHUR, EDWIN, conductor, pianist; b. Denver, Sept. 24, 1907; s. William Wesley and Anna Louise (Price) McA.; m. Blanche Victoria Pope, Mar. 4, 1930. Studied under Henry Houseley, Charlton Harris, Rosina Lhevinne, Hermann Weigert. Began as choir boy Cathedral of Denver, 1917, became asst. to the musical dir.; accompanist for Richard Crooks tour of West at age 1; organist and musical dir. Broadway Tabernacle, N.Y.C., 1933-36; accompanist for Kirsten Flagstad, Elisabeth Rethberg, Ezio Pinza, Dusolina Giannini, John Charles Thomas, many others. Debut as condr. Sydney, Australia, 1938, followed by concert with Melbourne, Australia Symphony Orch.; Am. debut with San Francisco Orch., Aug., 1938; debut as operatic condr. with Chgo. Opera, Nov. 1938; condr. San Francisco Opera, 1939, Chgo. Opera, 1939-40, Met. Opera of N.Y., 1940, 41, 42; guest condr. numerous orchs. throughout 1940s; RCA-Victor recs. with the Phila. Orch., Victor Symphony Orch., San Francisco Opera and leading Met. Opera soloists. Mem. Beethoven Assn., Bohemian Club, Lotos Club N.Y.C. Episcopalian. Home: New York City N.Y. Died Feb. 24, 1987.

MCARTHUR, JAMES NEVILLE, dairyman; b. Preston, Miss., Oct. 13, 1892; s. John Wesley and Hattie (Henderson) McA.; m. Nellie Mosley, Aug. 18, 1918; children: James Neville, Jean McArthur Davis. BS in Sci., Miss. State Coll., 1916; BS in Edn., U. Fla., 1922. Rep. to study agr. and internat. relations in 8 European countries USDA. Fla. chmn. World's Fair in Dominican Republic, 1956; chmn. trade dels. to promote bus. and goodwill Latin Am. countries; past chmn. Dade County Nat. Com. to Employ Physically Handicapped, ann. fund drive Dade County Tb Assn., campaign Heart Assn. Dade County; dir. Dade County United Fund; trustee, past pres. citizen's bd. U. Miami; chmn. Rotary Found. Decorated Star of Solidarity (Italy); recipient award NCCJ; named Outstanding Citizen in Dade County, 1960. Mem. C. of C. of Ams. (past pres.), U.S. C. of C., Fla. C. of C. (chmn. Inter-Am. div.), Miami C. of C. (past pres.), Opera Guild Miami (bd. dirs.), Civitans (past pres.), Rotary (Miami Shores), Century Club, Surf Club, La Gorce Country Club (Miami). Home: Miami Fla. †

MCBRIDE, EARL DUWAIN, orthopedic surgeon; b. Severy, Kans., June 16, 1891; s. Aaron and Almedia Frances (Tucker) McB.; m. Pauline Mary Wahl, 1913; children: Pollyanna Almeda McBride Ishmael, Mary Frances McBride Tullius, Dorothy L. McBride Molloy. Student, Epworth U. (now Oklahoma City U.), 1907-10; BS, U. Okla., 1912; MD, Columbia U., 1914. Pvt. practice Hitchcock, Okla., 1914, Ralston, Okla., 1915-17, Oklahoma City, from 1919; dir., chief orthopedic surgeon Bone and Joint Hosp. and McBride Clinic; clin. prof. orthopedic surgery U. Okla. Sch. Medicine; cons. surgeon St. Anthony Hosp., Wesley Hosp., Mercy Hosp.; Diplomate Am. Bd. Orthopedic Surgery. Author: Disability Evaluation, 1936, 6th edit., 1960, Crippled Children - Their Nursing, Care and Treatment, 1937; assoc. editor: Clinical Orthopedics; contbr. articles to profl. jours. 1st lt. M.C. U.S. Army, ETO, 1917-19. Fellow Internat. Coll. Surgeons, ACS, Am. Acad. Orthopedic Surgeons; mem. Assn. Bone and Joint Surgeons (past pres.), Am. Orthopedic Assn., AMA, So. Med. Soc., Clin. Orthopedic Soc., Oklahoma City Golf and Country Club, Men's Dinner Club, Dr.'s Dinner Club, Masons, Shriners (32 deg.), Sigma Nu. Home: Oklahoma City Okla. †

MC CABE, CYNTHIA JAFFEE, museum curator, historian; b. N.Y.C., Feb. 8, 1943; d. Harry and Pauline (Techefsky) Jaffee; 1 child, Zachary. B.A., Cornell U., 1963; M.A., Columbia U., 1967. Organizer fine arts catalogue Lower East Side: Portal to American Life (1870-1924) Jewish Mus., N.Y.C.; Smithsonian Instn., Washington, 1966-67; research Nakian Retrospective Mus. Modern Art, N.Y.C., 1966; organizer fine arts sect. Erie Canal Sesquicentennial, N.Y. State Council Arts, 1967; research U.S. rep. Venice Biennale, 1968; curator painting and sculpture Hirshhorn Mus. and Sculpture Garden, Smithsonian Instn., 1967-76, curator exhbns., 1976-86; organizer The Golden Door: Artist-Immigrants of Am., 1876-1976 1976; asst. professorial lectr. George Washington U., 1975-76; lectr. Spoleto (S.C.) Festival, 1978; organizer Fernando Botero, Hirshhorn Mus. and tour, 1979-80, Hans Richter's Stalingrad (Victory in the East), Hirshhorn Mus., 1979-80, Nakian: The Hirshhorn Mus. Collection, 1980, Artistic Collaboration in the Twentieth Century, Hirshhorn Mus. and tour, 1984-85, Am. Experience/Contemporary Immigrant Artists, Ind. Curators Inc. tour, 1985-86; co-chmn. Smithsonian Colloquia-The Muses Flee Hitler, I & II, 1980; adj. prof. U. Md., 1981; guest curator Balch Inst. for Ethnic Studies, Phila., 1981-86; curator, U.S. del. UNESCO World Conf. on Cultural Policies, 1983. Author: Sculptors and Their Drawings: Selections from the Hirshhorn Museum Collection, 1974, Henry Moore at the Hirshhorn Museum and Sculpture Garden, 1974, The Golden Door: Artist-Immigrants of America, 1876-1976, 1976, Wanted by the Gestapo: Saved by America, Varian Fry and the Emergency Rescue Com., 1983; others; art historian, critic. John J. McCloy fellow Am. Council on Germany-Met. Mus. Art, 1982-83. Mem. Internat. Council Museums, Am. Assn. Museums (chmn. curators com. 1977-79), Coll. Art Assn., ArtTable, Internat. Assn. Art Critics. Died Nov. 5, 1986; buried King David Cemetery, Falls Church, Va.

MCCABE, FRANK WELLS, banker; b. Brewster, N.Y., Jan. 22, 1903; m. Mary Lee Borden, 1930; children: Pauline, Mary Lee, Martha. BA, Yale U., 1925; postgrad., Oxford U., 1925-26. Pres. Nat. Comml. Bank, Albany, N.Y., 1955-64, chmn. bd., 1964-73; pres. Wytex Corp., Albany, until 1985, Litchfield Corp., Albany, until 1985; past bd. dirs. CMP Industries, Inc., Matthew Bender & Co., Conroy, Inc. Past trustee Albany Med. Coll.; past hon. gov. Albany Med. Ctr. Hosp. Mem. Fort Orange Assn., Yale Club N.Y.C. Home: Salisbury Conn. Deceased.

MCCAFFREY, JOHN LAWRENCE, business executive; b. Fayetteville, Ohio, Sept. 23, 1892; s. John F. and Ida (Smith) McC; m. Florence Springmeier, Oct. 8, 1914; children: Robert L., James F. Ed. pub. schs.; DCS, Coll. of the Holy Cross, 1949; LLD, Northeastern U., 1954, DePaul U., 1956, Loyola U., Chgo., 1957. With Internat. Harvester Co., from 1909, v.p., 1940-41, sr. v.p., dir., 1941-45, 1st v.p., 1945-46, pres., 1946-56, chmn. bd. dirs., chief exec. officer, 1956-57; bd. dirs. Voi-Shan Industries (L.A.), AT&T, A.,T&S.F. Ry., Corn Products Co., Roper Corp., Stewart Warner Corp.; gov. Midwest Stock Exchange. Chmn. Chgo. Plan Com.; trustee U. Chgo., U. Chgo. Cancer Rsch. Found., Eisenhower Exch. Fellowships Inc., Midwest Rsch. Inst., Mus. Sci. and Industry, Chgo., Cath. Charities; lay trustee U. Notre Dame; bd. dirs. Chgo. Boys Clubs, Goodwill Industries, Citizens of Greater Chgo., Citizens Traffic Safety Bd. Met. Chgo., Nat. Com. on Boys and Girls Club Work; mem. adv. bd. Chgo. Youth Commn. Recipient Legion of Honor (France). Mem. Ill. Mfrs. Assn. (bd. dirs.), Am. Heritage Found. (vice chmn. bd. U.S. Inter-Am. Coun.), Internat. C. of C. (trustee U.S. Coun.), Commercial Club, Chicago Club, Westmoreland Country Club (Wilmette, Ill.). Republican. Roman Catholic. Home: Chicago Ill. †

MCCALLIE, JAMES PARK, educator, headmaster; b. James County, Tenn., Sept. 9, 1879; s. Thomas Hooke and Ellen Douglas (Jarnagin) McC.; m. Harriet P. Bibb, 1904; children: James Park (dec.), Anne Elizabeth, Robert Lewis. BA, MA, U. Va., 1900, PhD, 1903; LLD (hon.), Davidson (N.C.) Coll., 1933, King Coll., Bristol, Tenn., 1939. Instr. math. Culver (Ind.) Mil. Acad., 1903-05; sec., treas., headmaster McCallie Sch., Chattanooga, headmaster emeritus, treas., 1949, later pres. bd. trustees. Organizer Chattanooga plan of bible study used over 1000 pub. schs.; chmn. com. on bible study in pub. schs., Chattanooga; elder Presbyn. Ch. U.S., moderator Appalachia Synod, 1962-63, del. Consulate Conf. on World Missions, Montreat, N.C., 1962. Recipient Man of Year in Chattanooga award Kiwanis, 1948, Russell Colgate cotation for disitng. service in religious edn. Internat. Com. Religious Edn., Columbus, Ohio, 1949, silver cert. div. Christian Edn. Nat. Council Chs. of Christ in Am., 1951; Astronomy fellow Leander McCormick Obs., U. Va., 1900-1903. Mem. Nat. Assn. Evangs., Sigma Alpha Epsilon, Lambda Pi. Democrat. Home: Chattanooga Tenn. †

MCCALLION, HARRY JOHN, lawyer, educator; b. N.Y.C., July 29, 1914; s. John and Katherine (Meehan) McC.; m. Edna Johnson, May 24, 1941; children—Douglas, Kenneth, Donald, Peter. B.S. cum laude, CCNY, 1937; J.D., Fordham U., 1941. Bar: N.Y. 1941, U.S. Dist. Ct. (so. and ea. dists.) N.Y. 1954, U.S. Supreme Ct. 1959. Assoc. Debevoise, Stevenson, Plimpton and Page, N.Y.C., 1941-47; atty. N.Y. Life Ins. Co., N.Y.C., 1947-51, counsel, 1951-54, asst. gen. counsel, 1954-57, assoc. gen. counsel, 1957-65, v.p. and gen. counsel, 1965-72, sr. v.p., 1972-79; spl. counsel recodification N.Y. ins. law Life Ins. Council of N.Y., 1979-82; sole practice N.Y.C., 1941-83; adj. prof. law Fordham Law Sch., 1977-83; dir. Mut. of Am. Life Ins. Co. Treas., bd. dirs. Legal Aid Soc., N.Y.C., 1977-83. Served as lt. (j.g.) USNR, 1943-46. Fellow Am. Bar Found.; mem. ABA (past chmn. life ins. com. of ins. sect.), Fed. Bar Assn., Assn. Life Ins. Counsel (past pres.), N.Y. State Bar Assn. (past chmn. ins. sect.), Assn. Bar City N.Y. (past v.p., past chmn. exec. com., past chmn. admissions com., past chmn. ins. com., past mem. judiciary com.), Fordham Law Alumni Assn. (dir., past pres.; medal of achievement 1978), Fordham Law Rev. Assn. (past pres., dir.). Club: Pelham (N.Y.) Country. Contbd. articles to legal jours. Died Aug. 25, 1986; buried Cutchogue, N.Y. Home: Pelham Manor N.Y.

MCCANN, GLENN CROCKER, sociologist, educator; b. Sunnyside, Utah, Apr. 15, 1922; s. John Edward and Clara May (Harvey) McC.; m. Marjorie Maxine Neptune, Jan. 8, 1946 (dec.); 1 son, John Edward; m. Anne MacRae Perry Stephenson, Sept. 12, 1969; stepchildren: John Boddie Stephenson, Elizabeth Ann Stephenson Newton. B.A., U. Colo., 1947, M.A., 1949; Ph.D.,

Wash. State U., 1953. Research asst. prof. sociology U. Wash., Seattle, 1952-53; social psychologist Dept. Air Force, Maxwell AFB, Ala., 1953-54, Randolph AFB, Tex., 1954-57; asst. prof. sociology N.C. State U., Raleigh, 1957-60, assoc. prof., 1960-65, prof., 1965-86; vis. prof. sociology Agrarian U., Peru, 1963-65; vis. prof. Seoul Nat. U., Korea, 1967; cons. in field. Contbr. articles to profl. jours., chpts. to books. Bd. dirs. Raleigh-Wake County Symphony Devel. Assn., 1978-86; mem. Wake County Ext. Adv. Com., 1979-86; mem. exec. com. Raleigh Area Ministry, Unitarian Ch., 1978-86. Served with USAAF, 1943-45, ETO. Decorated Air medal with six oak leaf clusters; Ford-Rockefeller grantee, 1963-65; recipient grant Agrl. Devel. Found. and Asia Found., 1967. Mem. Rural Sociol. Soc., Am. Sociol. Assn., Am. Pub. Opinion Assn., AAUP, So. Pub. Opinion Assn., N.C. Sociol. Soc., Phi Kappa Phi, Pi Gamma Mu, Alpha Kappa Delta. Democrat. Unitarian. Home: Raleigh N.C. Died Feb. 12, 1986; buried Littleton, N.C.

MC CARROLL, JAMES RENWICK, physician, educator; b. N.Y.C., Nov. 14, 1921; s. Edward Loomis and Emma Sellers (Robertson) McC.; m. Eleanor Hall Thomas, Feb. 9, 1962. B.A., Colby Coll., 1942; M.D., Cornell U., 1946. Intern Bellevue Hosp., N.Y.C., 1946-47; asst. resident medicine Bellevue Hosp., 1947-48, psychiatry, 1950; sr. resident medicine Bklyn. VA Hosp., 1951; asso. prof., dir. epidemiology Cornell U. Med. Coll., 1954-66; prof., chmn. dept. environ. health U. Wash. Sch. Pub. Health, Seattle, 1966-73; asst. med. dir. City of Los Angeles, 1973-76; clin. prof. preventive medicine U. Calif.-Irvine, 1975-76, 84-88; program mgr. health effects Electric Power Research Inst., Palo Alto, Calif., 1976-82, sr. sci. adviser, 1982-84; clin. prof. dept. community and preventive medicine Stanford U. Med. Sch., 1977-84; mem. nat. air quality criteria com. and sci. adv. bd. EPA; coordinating research com. Am. Petroleum Inst. Author numerous articles on health effects of environment, especially air pollution. Bd. dirs. Tb and Respiratory Disease Assn. Served to capt. M.C. AUS, 1948-50. Recipient award for accident research Nat. Safety Council, 1964. Fellow Am. Pub. Health Assn., Am. Coll. Preventive Medicine, Am. Occupational Med. Assn., Am. Acad. Occupational Medicine; mem. Internat. Soc. Accident and Traffic Medicine (founding), Royal Soc. Medicine, AMA, Am., Internat. epidemiol. assns. Home: Palm Desert Calif. Died June 4, 1988; buried Green Wood Cemetery, Bklyn.

MC CARTHY, FRANK, motion picture producer; b. Richmond, Va., June 8, 1912; s. Frank J. and Lillian (Binford) McCarthy. A.B., Va. Mil. Inst., 1933; A.M., U. Va., 1940. Instr. and tactical officer Va. Mil. Inst., 1933-35, 36-37; reporter Richmond (Va.) News Leader, 1935-36; press agt. for theatrical prod. George Abbott, N.Y.C., 1937-39; mil. sec. to chief of staff War Dept., 1941-43, asst. sec. gen. staff, 1944-45; asst. sec. state U.S. Dept. State, 1945; rep. for Motion Picture Assn. Am. in Hollywood and Europe, 1946-49; alternate del. U.N. Conf. on Freedom of Information, Geneva, 1948; exec. and producer 20th Century-Fox Studios, 1949-62, 65-72; producer Universal Studios, 1963-65, 72-77. Films produced include Decision Before Dawn, Sailor of the King, A Guide for the Married Man, Patton (received Oscar for Best Picture 1970), Fireball Forward, MacArthur. Trustee George C. Marshall Research Found., Va. Mil. Inst. Found.; mem., v.p. bd. dirs. Norton Simon Mus. Art, Los Angeles Music Center Theatre Group, Motion Picture and Television Fund, Motion Picture Permanent Charities Com. Served as 2d lt. field arty., res. U.S. Army, 1933; advanced through grades to brig. gen. 1957. Decorated D.S.M., Legion of Merit; officer Most Excellent Order of Brit. Empire; selected one of America's 10 outstanding young men by U.S. Jr. C. of C. for distinguished contbn. to nation's welfare during 1945; named Virginian of Yr. Va. Press Assn., 1970. Mem. Acad. Motion Picture Arts and Scis., Va. Mil. Inst. Soc., Geo. C. Marshall Research Found., Va. Hist. Soc. Episcopalian. Home: Beverly Hills Calif. Died Dec. 1, 1986.

MCCARTHY, GLENN HERBERT, oil company executive; b. Beaumont, Tex., Dec. 25, 1907; s. William Peter and Leah (Townsend) McC.; m. Faustine Lee, June 18, 1930; children: Mary Margaret, Glennalee Satterfield, Leah McCurry, Faustine Gambrecht, Glenn H. Jr. Student, Allen Acad., Bryan, Tex., Tex. A. & M., Coll. Sta., Tulane U., 1929, Rice Inst., Houston, 1930. Operater cleaning and pressing plant and filling stas., 1932; discoverer, driller oil fields, 1933; organizer Beaumont Natural Gas Co., 1939, McCarthy Bldg. Co., 1943, Jefferson Pipe Line Corp., Neches Natural Gas Corp., Absorption Plant Inc., McCarthy Oil and Gas Corp. and McCarthy Ctr. Inc., 1945, Houston Export Co., Houston Fgn. Trade and Export Co., 1947, News Inc. (newspaper orgn. and pubs. suburban weeklies), 1947; constructer McCarthy Chem. Co. plant, 1948, Glenn McCarthy Prodns., 1948, Radio Sta. KXYZ, Houston, 1948, McCarthy-Internat. Tube Corp., Detroit, 1948; builder Shamrock Hotel, Houston, 1949; bd. dirs. Eastern Air Lines, 2d Nat. Bank, Houston (mem. adv. com.). Bd. dis. Independent Petroleum Assn. of Am. (mem. resolutions com.), Nat. Aeronautic Assn., Houston Anti-Tuberculosis League, Houston Fat Stock Show and Livestock Exposition; chmn. Airport Com. Trustees of Houston; trustee Meth. Hosp. of Houston; mem. Community Chest of Houston and Harris County (mem. campaign com.), Sister Elizabeth Kenny Found. (mem. exec. com. Tex. chpt.). Mem. East Tex. , Port Arthur, Houston (mem. Internat. Gateway Com., chmn. info. and edn. subcom.) Cs. of C., Houston Jr. C. of C. (hon. mem.), Tex. Independent Producers and Royalty Owners Assn. (v.p.), Mid-Continent Oil and Gas Assn., Tex. Mfrs. Assn. (mem. and chmn. legis. com.), Sheriffs' Assn. of Tex., Sons of the Republic of Tex., Houston Horse Show Assn. (dir.), Masons, The Lawyers' Club (N.Y.C.), Salesmanship Club (Houston), International House (New Orleans). Home: Houston Tex. Died Dec. 26, 1988.

MCCARTHY, JOHN JOSEPH, newspaper publishing executive; b. N.Y.C., June 24, 1920; s. Jerry and Helen (Duffy) McC.; m. Leona Mary Hart, May 25, 1947; children: John, Mary Ellen, Robert Emmett, Eileen, Doreen, Terrence, Kathleen, Daniel, Elizabeth Ann. BBA, St. John's U., Jamaica, N.Y., 1947; JD, St. John's U., 1951. Bar: N.Y. 1952. With Dow Jones & Co., Princeton, N.J., 1946-81, bus. mgr., 1963-65, treas., 1965-70, v.p. fin., 1970-77, v.p. adminstrn., 1977-81. Served with USAAF, 1941-45, ETO. Decorated Bronze Star. Mem. Delta Psi Upsilon. Home: Cranford N.J. Died Dec. 2, 1981.

MCCHESNEY, RUSSELL JAMES, art materials company executive; b. West Orange, N.J., Dec. 8, 1916; s. Russell Dudley and Margaret Clothilda (Monoghan) McC.; m. Marjorie Jane Miller, Sept. 6, 1947; children: R. Douglas, Susan L., Deborah L. Student, Bloomfield Coll., 1935-39, Rutgers U., 1951-54, NYU, 1965-66. With Binney & Smith, Inc., Easton, Pa., 1935-85, v.p. mktg., 1967-70, exec. v.p., 1970-71, chmn. bd., 1971-85, pres., 1973-85; past bd. dirs. Easton Nat. Bank and Trust Co. Served with AUS, 1940-45. Decorated Croix de Guerre (France). Mem. Nat. Art Edn. Assn. (life), Crayon, Water Color and Craft Inst. (past bd. dirs., past v.p., past pres.), Am. Assn. Sch. Adminstrs.-Ednl. Industries Assn. Joint Com., Chgo. Athletic Club, Upper Montclair (N.J.) Country Club, Pomfret Club, Northampton Country Club, Chemists' Club. Home: Kinnelon N.J. Died Jan. 14, 1986; cremated.

MC CLEMENT, JOHN HENRY, medical educator; b. Watertown, N.Y., May 6, 1918; s. Henry Grant and Florence Jeanette (Brenon) Mc C.; m. A. Mary Emery, Mar. 24, 1945 (div.); children: John H., Joanne M., Michael G., Christopher E.; m. Lynn Coleman Christianson, Dec. 20, 1961. Student, Syracuse U., 1935-38; MD, U. Rochester, 1943. Diplomate Am. Bd. Internal Medicine (chmn. subsplty. bd. pulmonary disease). Intern and asst. resident Peter Bent Brigham Hosp., Boston, 1943-44; resident and fellow in pulmonary physiology Bellevue Hosp., N.Y.C., 1944-47; instr. medicine Cornell U., 1948-49; assoc. medicine Columbia U., 1949-52; asst. prof. medicine U. Utah, 1952-55; assoc. prof. medicine Columbia U., 1955-68; prof. medicine NYU, from 1968; dir. chest svc. Bellevue Hosp., from 1955. Contbr. articles on pulmonary diseases to profl. jours. Fellow ACP, N.Y. Acad. Medicine; mem. N.Y. Lung Assn. (bd. dirs.), Am. Thoracic Soc. (pres. Eastern sect.), N.Y. Trudeau Soc., N.Y. Tb and Health Assn. (pres.), Better Bellevue Assn. (pres.). Home: New York N.Y. Died Apr. 8, 1986.

MCCLINTOCK, R. OTIS, banker; b. Cridersville, Ohio, Feb. 19, 1891; s. Frank Garfield and Gertrude (Redinbaugh) McC; m. Gladys Belle Stebbins, Nov. 4, 1913; 1 child, Frank Grant. Grad. high sch., Tulsa, 1909. Began as warehouseman Okla. oil fields, 1909; v.p. Gypsy Oil Co., 1923-26, Philmack Co., 1926-28; pres. First Nat. Bank & Trust Co., Tulsa, 1928-55; chmn., chief exec. officer First Nat. Bank & Trust Co., 1956-60, sr. chmn. bd., 1960-64, chmn. emeritus, from 1964; bd. dirs. N.M. & Ariz. Land Co. Mem. Tulsa Club, Southern Hills Country Club, Masons (32 degree). Home: Tulsa Okla. †

MC CLORY, ROBERT, former congressman, lawyer; b. Riverside, Ill., Jan. 31, 1908; s. Frederick Stevens and Catherine (Reilly) McClory; m. Audrey Vasey (dec. Sept. 1967); children: Beatrice McClory Etienne, Michael, Oliver; m. Doris S. Hibbard, Mar. 1969. Student, L'Institut Sillig, Vevey, Switzerland, 1925-26, Dartmouth Coll., 1926-28; LL.B., Chicago-Kent Coll. Law, 1932. Bar: Ill. 1932. Pvt. practice Chgo. and Waukegan, 1932-62; mem. Ill. Ho. of Reps., 1951-52, Ill. Senate, 1952-62; mem. 88th-97th congresses from 13th Ill. Dist., ranking Republican mem. Judiciary Com.; mem. House Select Com. on Intelligence, 1976; of counsel Baker & McKenzie, Washington, 1982-88; mem. congl. del. to Interparliamentary Union, 1964-82; participant Ditchley Conf., London, 1966; mem. congl. del. to Environ. Conf., Stockholm, 1972. Mem. Am., Ill., Lake County bar assns., Navy League, Waukegan-Lake County C. of C., Psi Upsilon, Phi Delta Phi. Republican. Christian Scientist. Clubs: Chgo. Law; Bath and Tennis (Lake Forest, Ill.); Capitol Hill (Washington). Home: Washington D.C. Died July 24, 1988; buried North Shore Garden of Memories, Chgo.

MCCLOSKEY, MARK A(LEXANDER), social agency administrator; b. N.Y.C., Oct. 21, 1891; s. John and Jane Ann (Bennett) McC.; m. Winifred Doherty, June 26, 1919; children: Barbara Jean McCloskey MacDonald, Janet Ann McCloskey Robbins, Winifred Doherty McCloskey Hackett. Grad., Princeton U., 1918, Columbia U. Sch. Social Work, 1922. With ARC, 1919; assoc. head worker Hudson Guild, 1920-36; mem. staff Fieldston Sch., 1926-36; dir. Nat. Youth Adminstrn., N.Y.C., 1936-38; dir. div. community edn. Bd. Edn., N.Y.C., 1938-55; chmn. N.Y. State Youth Commn., 1955-60; dir. recreation Fed. Security Agy., 1941-42; dir. Office War Community Svcs., 1943-45; dir. numerous orgns. in field of welfare and edn.; lectr. CCNY, NYU, Columbia U.; v.p. United Neighborhood Houses; bd. dirs. N.Y. Adult Edn. Coun., Pub. Edn. Assn., Nat. Fedn. Settlements; pres. United Seamens Svc.; mem. polit. adv. com. Princeton U., 1948; mem. Pres. Truman's Com. on Religious and Moral Welfare and Character Guidance in Armed Forces, 1948. Trustee Vassar Coll., from 1946. 1st lt. F.A., U.S. Army, World War I. Recipient Presdl. Medal for Merit, 1946, N.Y.C. Adult Edn. award, 1947. Democrat. Episcopalian. Home: New York N.Y. †

MCCOLLUM, JOHN ISAAC, JR., English educator; b. Conway, Ark., Oct. 13, 1919; s. John Isaac and Hazel (Schroeder) McC.; m. Bettie Lou Johnson, Dec. 19, 1947; children: John Isaac III, Mark Stephen. BA, U. Miami, Coral Gables, Fla., 1946; MA, U. Miami, 1949; PhD, Duke U., 1956. From instr. to assoc. prof. English U. Miami, 1949-63, prof. English, 1963-84, assoc. dean Univ. Coll., 1960-61, chmn. dept., 1961-73; past local rep. Fulbright Program and Danforth Found.; mem. regional selection com. Woodrow Wilson Nat. Fellowship Found., 1959-62, local rep., from 1955; mem. Fla. Certification Com., 1966-70. Author: Essentials of Grammar and Style, 1966; editor: The Age of Elizabeth, 1960, The Restoration Stage, 1961, Jonson's The Alchemist, 1965; contbd. articles to profl. jours., Ency. Americana. Pastor Goulds (Fla.) Bapt. Ch., 1944-46, Coral Bapt. Ch., Miami, 1950-52; trustee Coral Gables Congl. Ch., 1966-70, pres. council, 1974-83; trustee Conf. of the United Ch. of Christ, 1976-84, bd. dirs., 1978-84. Mem. MLA, Southeastern Renaissance Soc., Renaissance Soc. Am., South Atlantic MLA, Phi Kappa Phi, Omicron Delta Kappa, Phi Alpha Theta. Home: Coral Gables Fla. Died Jan. 22, 1985.

MC COLLUM, ROBERT STUART, business executive; b. Denver, Nov. 23, 1916; s. Stuart T. and Mary B. (Hadley) McC.; m. Lydia E. Nelson, May 2, 1947; children: Mary L., Patricia A., Robert Stuart, Bruce C. B.A., Amherst Coll., 1938. Tchr., Deerfield Acad., 1938-41; pres. Auto Equipment Co., Denver, 1946-57, McCollum-Law Corp., Denver, 1953-56; chmn. bd. McCollum-Law Corp., 1957-75; adminstr. refugee program bur. security and consular affairs Dept. State, 1957-60; vice chancellor U. Denver, 1960-69; pres. Robert McCollum Assos., 1969-74, Capps/McCollum Enterprises, 1982-87. Mem. Denver City Council, 1951-55, pres., 1955; mem. nat. bd. CARE; bd. dirs. Met. Denver YMCA, 1978-87; trustee Inst. Internat. Edn., 1954-57, Mills Coll., 1961-87, Loretto Heights Coll., 1976-87, Western States Coll. Found., 1982-87; pres. Colo. Council Econ. Edn., 1976-87; v.p. Luth. Med. Center, 1974-77, pres., 1977-82; elder Montview Presbyterian Ch., 1970-87; candidate for U.S. Congress, 1956. Served with USAAF, 1942-46. Decorated Order Orange Nassau Netherlands; Cavallieri Ufficiale (Govt. of Italy); recipient Outstanding Community Service award Nat. Council Chs., 1952. Mem. Am. Assn. UN (state pres.). Club: Rotary (1st v.p. 1955, dir.). Home: Englewood Colo. Died Jan. 2, 1987; buried Fairmount Cemetery, Denver.

MCCOMB, MARSHALL FRANCIS, judge; b. Denver, May 6, 1894; s. Harry and Estelle (Tredenick) McC. AB, Stanford U., 1917; JD cum laude, Yale U., 1919; LLD, Loyola U., Los Angeles, 1936; hon. degree, U. San Fernando Valley, 1969. Bar: Calif. 1920. Practiced in Los Angeles 1920-27; Superior Ct. judge Los Angeles, 1927-37; justice Dist. Ct. Appeals 1937-55; assoc. justice Calif. Supreme Ct., San Francisco, 1956-77. Ensign USN, World War I; served also as lt. comdr. Res. Mem. ABA, Calif. Bar Assn., Los Angeles Bar Assn., San Francisco Bar Assn., Delta Chi, Sigma Delta Kappa, Delta Theta Phi, California Club, Los Angeles Country Club, Bohemian Club, Los Angeles Athletic Sutter Club (Sacramento), Cuyamaca Resort Club (San Diego). Republican. Home: San Francisco Calif. Died Sept. 6, 1981.

MCCONNELL, JOHN PAUL, military officer; b. Booneville, Ark., Feb. 7, 1908; s. Samuel Paul and Dessau (Dorsey) McC.; m. Regine Yvonne Chauchoin Sept. 1940 (div. May 1946); m. Sally Dean, 1946; children: Bruce William, Dorsey Winter. BS magna cum laude, Henderson State Coll., 1927; BS, U.S. Mil. Acad. 1932. Commd. 2d lt. A.C. U.S. Army, 1932, advanced through grades to maj. gen., 1950; served 20th Pursuit Squadron 1933-37; with 5th Bombardment Group Hawaii, 1937-39; assigned to A.C. Tactical Sch. 1939-40, to S.E. A.C. Tng. Ctr., 1940-41, asst. exec. to Chief A.C., 1941-42; chief of staff Tech. Tng. Command U.S. Army, 1942-43; dep. comdr. 3d Tactical Air Force Un and dep. chief of staff Air Command Southeast Asia 1943-44; sr. air staff officer 1944-45, chief of staff China Theater, 1945-46; dir. Air Div. Army Adv. Group Nanking, Republic of China, 1946-47; chief component group hdqrs. USAF, Washington, 1947-50; air commander in London 1950-53; dir. Plans Hdqrs. SAC Offutt AFB, Nebr., 1953-57; comdr. 2d Air Force 1957-61 vice-comdr.-in-chief SAC, Offutt AFB, 1961-86.

Decorated D.S.M., Legion of Merit with 3 oak leaf clusters, D.F.C., Bronze Star, Air medal; Asiatic-Pacific Theater Ribbon with 4 Campaign Stars; Comdr. Order Brit. Empire; Pao-Ting Medal with Banner Ribbons, Gen. Citation Medal, Tas-hou Cloud Banner, Los-hou medal, Chinese Pilot's Wings (Republic China). Mem. Pi Kappa Delta (degree of spl. distinction). Home: Booneville Ark. Died Nov. 21, 1986.

MCCONNELL, PHILIP I., company executive; b. Houston, Sept. 2, 1935; s. Fred I. and Elizabeth (Ayers) McC.; m. Patricia R. Griffin, Sept. 6, 1958; children: Elizabeth, Susan. BA, U. Tex., 1958, JD, 1962. Bar: Tex. 1962, Mo. 1964, Kans. 1972, Ark. 1975. Gen. atty. Southwestern Bell Telephone Co., St. Louis, 1968-77; v.p., sec. Cen. and S.W. Corp., Dallas, from 1977. Mem. Am. Soc. Corp. Secs. (treas. 1981-82, sec. 1982-83, v.p. 1983-84), State Bar Tex., State Bar Assn. Mo., Kans. Bar Assn., Ark. Bar Assn., Edison Electric Inst. (legal com.), Northwood Club, Aerobics Activity Ctr. Home: Dallas Tex. Deceased.

MC CONNELL, THOMAS RAYMOND, educator; b. Mediapolis, Iowa, May 25, 1901; s. William John and Nell (Cox) McC.; m. Ruth Kegley, June 20, 1925; children: Robert Willis, Carol Ruth. AB, Cornell Coll., Mt. Vernon, Iowa, 1924, LLD (hon.), 1949; AM, U. Iowa, 1928, PhD, 1933; DHL (hon.), Syracuse U., 1952. Instr. English and journalism Cornell Coll., 1925-26, instr. and asst. prof. edn. and psychology, 1927-29, dean of coll., prof. edn. and psychology, 1932-36; instr. edn. U. Iowa, 1930-31, summers 1931-36; prof. ednl. psychology U. Minn., 1936-50, chmn. com. ednl. research, 1937-47, assoc. dean Coll. Sci., Lit. and Arts, 1940-44, acting dean Coll. Sci., Lit. and Arts, 1942-44, dean, 1944-50; chancellor U. Buffalo, 1950-54; prof. U. Calif., Berkeley, 1954-68; prof. emeritus U. Calif., from 1968; chmn. Center for Study of Higher Edn., 1957-66; rsch. educator Center Research and Devel. in Higher Edn., 1966-76, U. Calif., Berkeley; mem. Pres. Truman's Commn. on Higher Edn.; fellow Ctr.for Advanced Study of Behavioral Scis., 1959-60; mem. com. on devel. youth Social Sci. Rsch. Counc., 1957-68; chief cons. Restudy of Needs of Calif. in Higher Edn., 1954-56; mem. U.S. Pres.'s Com. on Pub. Higher Edn. in D.C., 1963-64; adviser to subcom. mgmt. and financing undergrad. edn. Com. on Econ. Devel.; chmn. Ill. Commn. Study Non-Pub. Higher Edn., 1968-69; adv. com. Inst. Coll. & U. Adminstrs., 1958-70. Author: (with others) Psychology in Everyday Living, 1938, Educational Psychology, 1948, (with T.C. Holy and H.H. Semans) A Restudy of the Needs of California in Higher Education, 1955, A General Pattern for Am. Public Higher Edn, 1962, (with others) Training for Educational Research, 1968, Omnibus Personality Inventory, 1968, Governments and the University: A Comparative Analysis, 1966, (with K.P. Mortimer) The Faculty in University Governance, 1971, The Redistribution of Power in Higher Education, 1971, (with B.R. Clark, P. Heist, M.A. Trow and G. Yonge) Students and Colleges: Interaction and Change, 1972, (with R.O. Berdahl and M.A. Fay) From Elite to Mass to Universal Higher Education: The British and American Transformations, 1973, (with Stewart Edelstein) Campus Government at Berkeley: A Study in Jurisdictions, 1977, (with Kenneth Mortimer) Sharing Authority Effectively: Participation, Interaction, and Discretion, 1978. Chmn. bd. editors: Ency. Ednl. Research, 1964-69. Contbr. to books and various publs. on edn. and psychology. Recipient 1966 award for disting. contbns. to ednl. rsch. Am. Ednl. Rsch. Assn.-Phi Delta Kappa, 1966; Disting. Service award U. Iowa, 1968; Centennial award U. Calif., Berkeley, 1968; 1st ann. award Colloquium in Higher Edn., 1970; award for contbns. Carnegie Commn. Higher Edn.-Assembly Univ. Goals and Governance-Center for R&D in Higher Edn., 1971; award for disting. rsch. on coll. students Am. Ednl. Rsch. Assn. and Am. Coll. Testing Program, 1977. Mem. Nat. Acad. Edn., Phi Beta Kappa. Methodist. Home: Oakland Calif. Died Jan. 16, 1989.

MCCORMICK, HENRY J., librarian; b. Watertown, N.Y., July 2, 1919; s. Henry J. and Anna (Yager) McC.; m. Marie Elizabeth Atwater, Oct. 1, 1949 (dec. Nov. 1954); children: John, Mary, Henry J., Martha; m. Mary Jane Heenan, Feb. 11, 1956; children: Anne, Margaret, Eileen. BA, Syracuse U., 1940, MLS, 1947. Reference librarian Grosvenor Library, Buffalo, 1947-48; exec. dir. Olean (N.Y.) Pub. Library, 1948-54; asst. dir. Syracuse (N.Y.) Pub. Library, 1954-61, dir., 1962-75; asst. dir. Onondaga County Pub. Library, 1976-78; instr. English, history and ROTC Fla. Mil. Acad., 1940-41, history St. Bonaventure (N.Y.) U., 1949-50, 52-54; past bd. dirs. Assn. N.Y. Libraries for Tech. Services. Capt. AUS, 1942-45, 51-52. Mem. ALA, N.Y. Library Assn., Beta Theta Pi, Beta Phi Mu (former bd. dirs.), Rotary. Home: Syracuse N.Y. Died Sept. 29, 1987; buried St. Mary's Cemetery, Syracuse.

MCCORMICK, WILLIAM WALLACE, physicist, educator; b. Marissa, Ill., Aug. 30, 1906; s. James Harvey and Bessie Mae (Cowden) McC.; m. Beulah Mae Ewing, Dec. 24, 1938. BS, Geneva Coll., 1927, DSc (hon.), 1969; MS, U. Mich., 1932, PhD, 1938. High sch. principal Darlington (Pa.) Schs., 1927-29; physics faculty Geneva Coll., Beaver Falls, Pa., 1929-43; research physicist U. Mich., Ann Arbor, 1943-45; chmn. dept. physics Coll. William and Mary, Williamsburg, Va., 1945-47; prof. physics U. Mich., 1947-80. Author: Fundamentals of College Physics, 1965, Laboratory Experiments in Physics, 1966; assoc. editor Am. Jour. Physics, 1951-53; contbd. many articles to profl. jours. Fellow Am. Phys. Soc., Optical Soc. Am.; mem. Am. Assn. Physics Tchrs. (pres. Western Pa. sect. 1941, Mich. sect. 1959-60), Sigma Xi, Rotary. Presbyterian. Home: Ann Arbor Mich. Died June 16, 1987.

MC CRACKEN, JAMES, tenor; b. Gary, Ind.; s. John A. and Doris (Hafey) McC.; m. Sandra Warfield; children: Ahna-Maureen, John. MusD (hon.), Ind. U. Appeared with maj. opera cos. including Met. Opera, Vienna Staatsoper, Covent Garden, Paris Opéra, Bayerische Staatsoper, Deutsche Oper Berlin, Saltzburg Festival, Hamburg Staatsoper, Arena di Verona, Zurich Opera, Rome Opera, Teatro Colón, San Francisco Opera, Seattle Opera, others; leading roles in: Otello, Tannhäuser, Le Prophete, Carmen, Il Trovatore, Pagliacci, Fidelio, Aida, Contes d'Hoffmann, Faust, Ariadne auf Naxos, Turandot, La Forza del Destino, La Bohème, Ballo in Maschera; soloist with maj. orchs. in Phila., Boston, Detroit, Dallas, San Francisco, Milw., others; recs. include The Meeting of the Waters, McCracken on Stage, Fidelio, Duets of Love and Passion, Otello (Grand Prix du Disques 1972), I Pagliacci, Le Prophète, Carmen, (Grammy award 1974), Gurrelieder; author: (with Sandra Warfield) A Star in the Family, 1971. Served with USN, World War II. Named Hoosier of Year Ind. Soc. N.Y., 1977. Club: Lotos. Died Apr. 30, 1988.

MCCRACKEN, ROBERT THOMPSON, lawyer; b. Phila., July 15, 1883; s. James and Josephine (Thompson) McC.; m. Anna Erdman, June 1, 1909 (dec. 1934); 1 child, Matilda. BS, U. Pa., 1905, LLB, 1908, LLD (hon.), 1953. Bar: Pa. 1908. Ptnr. Montgomery, McCracken, Walker & Rhoads, Phila.; Trustee Penn Mut. Life Ins. Co. Trustee U. Pa., chmn. bd., 1948-56. Mem. ABA (chmn. com. profl. ethics and grievances 1935-38), Pa. Bar Assn. (pres. 1938-39, chancellor 1945-46), Union League Club, Rittenhouse Club, Phila. Club, Century Assn. (N.Y.C.). Home: Philadelphia Pa. †

MC CREE, WADE HAMPTON, JR., law educator, former solicitor general U.S.; b. Des Moines, July 3, 1920; s. Wade Hampton and Lulu H. (Harper) McC.; m. Dores B. McCrary, July 29, 1946; children: Kathleen L. Mc Cree Lewis, Karen L., Wade H. A.B., Fisk U., 1941; LL.B., Harvard U., 1944, LL.D., 1969; LL.D., Wayne State U., 1964, Tuskegee Inst., 1965, Detroit Coll. Law, 1965, U. Detroit, 1968, Mich. State U., 1971, U. Mich., 1971, Oakland U., 1971, Lewis & Clark/ Northwestern U., 1976, Howard U., 1977, Atlanta U., 1977, Boston U., 1977, Chgo.-Kent Sch. Law, 1978, George Washington U., 1979, U. Pa., 1979, N.Y. Law Sch., 1979, Eastern Mich. U., 1979, U. Dayton, 1980, Brandeis U., 1980, Bowdoin Coll., 1980, Georgetown U., 1980, Harvard U., 1969, Suffolk U., 1985, U. Ariz., 1985, No. Mich. U., 1985; D.C.L., U. Toledo, 1979, Colgate U., 1985; L.H.D., DePaul U., 1980, Marygrove Coll., 1980, Hebrew Union Coll., 1982; Litt.D., Centre Coll., 1975. Bar: Mich. 1948. Practice law Detroit, 1948-52; commr. Mich. Workmen's Compensation Commn., 1952-54; circuit judge Wayne County (Mich.), 1954-61; judge U.S. Dist. Ct. Eastern Dist. Mich., 1961-66, U.S. Ct. Appeals 6th Circuit, 1966-77; solicitor gen. U.S. 1977-81; mem. faculty U. Mich. Law Sch., Ann Arbor, 1981-87, Salzburg Seminar Am. Studies, 1969; summer faculty Ind. U. Law Sch.; dir. Nat. Bank Detroit, Unisys Corp.; former mem. vis. com. Wayne State U. Law Sch., Case Western Res. Law Sch., Harvard Law Sch.; mem. liaison com. med. edn. AMA; U.S. del. 3d UN Congress Prevention of Crime, Stockholm, 1956. Adv. bd. United Found. Detroit; exec. bd. Detroit Area council Boy Scouts Am.; trustees Fisk U., Nashville; trustee Fisk U.; founding trustee Friends Sch., Detroit; bd. dirs. Met. Hosp., Henry Ford Hosp., Founders Soc. Detroit Inst. Arts, Nat. Jud. Coll. Served to capt., inf. AUS, 1942-46, ETO. Fellow Am. Coll. Trial Lawyers (hon.), Am. Bar Found.; mem. ABA. mem. commn. on standards jud. adminstrn., other commns.), Nat. Bar Assn., Detroit Bar Assn., State Bar Mich., Inst. Jud. Adminstrn., Am. Judicature Soc., Am. Law Inst. (council), Am. Assn. Law Schs. (exec. com.), Seminar Soc. (Detroit), Phi Beta Kappa Assos. Unitarian-Universalist. Died Aug. 30, 1987.

MCCUE, GOLDIE OPAL, religion educator; b. West Chester, Ohio, 1891; d. Philip Melvin and Martha (Harding) McC. BA, Ohio Wesleyan U., 1916; MRE, Boston U., 1921, STB, 1933. Instr. to assoc. prof. Ohio Wesleyan U., 1921-57, prof., 1958-59, Found. prof. religion, 1931-59, asst. dean women, 1932-41. Mem. women's planning com. Japan Internat. Christian U. Found., 1961; sec. Ohio Wesleyan YWCA, 1929-47. Mem. Nat. Assn. Bibl. Instrs., AAUP, Religious Edn. Assn., Delaware C. of C., Phi Beta Kappa, Mortar Bd. Methodist. Home: Delaware Ohio. †

MC CURDY, EVERETT DARLING, lawyer; b. Port Townsend, Wash., Feb. 15, 1905; s. William Horace and Ella (Darling) McC.; m. Eugenia J. Somma, Feb. 12, 1938. A.B., Western Res. U., 1926, LL.B., 1934; student, Harvard Law Sch., 1927-28. Bar: Ohio 1928. Since practiced in Cleve.; chmn. firm Spieth, Bell, McCurdy & Newell (and predecessor), 1952-86; lectr. in law Cleve. Coll., Western Res. U., 1945-64; Pres. Western Res. Residences, Inc.; pres., trustee Spieth & Co., 1963-80; sec. Yorktown Land Co.; dir. Bohme & Blinkmann, Inc. Republican candidate for chmn. Cuyahoga County, 1966. Mem. Am., Ohio, Cleve. bar assns., Ct. of Nisi Prius, SAR, Mass. Soc. Mayflower Descs., Phi Kappa Psi. Christian Scientist. Clubs: Mason (South Euclid, Ohio) (32 deg., Shriner), Mayfield Country (South Euclid, Ohio). Home: Cleveland Heights Ohio Died July 11, 1986.

MCCURDY, JOHN R., academic administrator; b. Princeton, Maine, Apr. 4, 1890; s. John and Augusta Evelyn (Heath) McC; m. Lucy G. Poter, Mar. 24, 1920 (dec. Oct. 1958); 1 child, Jean McCurdy Vanderwiel; m. Nancy M. Miner, June 14, 1959. AB, Clark U., 1912; postgrad., Wash. State Coll., 1913-16; AM, Columbia Tchrs. Coll., 1925, postgrad., 1936-38; LLD (hon.), Springfield Coll., 1953. Tchr. Suffield (Conn.) Sch. for Boys, 1912-13; with YMCA, 1916-52, grad. sec. intercollegiate br., N.Y.C., 1916-17, exec. sec., 1920-25, camp sec. Plattsburg Barracks and Camp Mills, 1917, exec. sec. Bronx Union br., 1925-38, chmn. com. secretarial tng., N.Y.C., 1925-35, gen. sec. New Haven br., 1938-45, met. gen. sec., Toronto, Ont., Can., 1946-53, chmn. com. phys. edn. nat. council, U.S. and Can., 1936, chmn. profl. edn. com., 1943-53, mem. nat. council, 1947-52; pres. George Williams Coll., Chgo., 1953-61, ret., vice chmn. bd. with spl. responsibility devel. program, from 1961. Editor New Phys. Edn., 1936-37. Chmn. Bronx Counc. Social Agys., 1933-35; chmn. com. regional orgn. social work Welfare Coun. N.Y.C.; bd. dirs. Bronx Big Bros.; bd. dirs. Welfare Coun., Toronto, chmn. div. recreation, 1950-52; bd. dirs. S.E. Chgo. Commn., from 1953; bd. dirs. Welfare Coun. Met. Chgo., from 1958, chmn. Div. III, 1956-58. 2d lt. Am. Expeditionary Force, 1918-1919; dir. 2d Army YMCA, France, 1919. Mem. YMCA of U.S. (mem. nat. coun. 1933), Quandrangle Club (Chgo.), University Club (Chgo.), New Haven Kiwanis, Rotary (Toronto), Kappa Delta Pi. Home: Chicago Ill. †

MCCURDY, JOSEPH PATRICK, labor organization executive; b. Balt., Mar. 20, 1892; s. John A. and Mary Ellen McC.; m. Genevieve Birrane, Feb. 24, 1938; children: Joseph Patrick, John Francis. Night courses, Balt. Bus. Coll. Pres. Balt. Fedn. of LAbor, 1933-41, Md. State and D.C. Fedn. of Labor; mem. exec. coun. AFL-CIO; assoc. dir. exec. com. Union Labor-Life-Ins. Co.; AFL del. to Trades and Labor Congress of Can., 1934, Brit. Trades Union Congress, 1950; pres. United Garment Workers of Am.; mem. Md. Unemployment Compensation Bd., 1937-51, Nat. Labor Rels. Regional Bd., 1939. Author: Reasons Why Labor Should Oppose Prohibition. Mem. Gov.'s com. to draft Md. Old Age Pension Law; mem. Gov.'s com. to amend Md. Workmen's Compensation Law; active in community and nat. welfare work. Mem. Elks, K.C. Roman Catholic. Home: Baltimore Md. †

MCCURDY, WALLACE M., investment banker; b. Phila., Oct. 23, 1892; s. Robert and Elizabeth (Boyd) McC.; m. Charlotte Goette, June 1, 1920; children: Emily M. McCurdy Sutton, Nancy McCurdy Schnebly. BS, U. Pa., 1914. With Thaver Baker & Co., Phila., from 1920, salesman, v.p., 1929-45, pres., 1945-60, chmn. bd., from 1960. Bd. dirs. Wellington Fund; mem. Swarthmore (Pa.) Borough Coun., 1932-38. Lt. (j.g.) USNRF, World War I. Mem. U. Pa. Gen. Alumni Soc. (v.p., award of merit), Union League Club (Phila.), Rolling Green Golf Club, Seaview Country Club, Alpha Chi Rho. Home: Wallingford Pa. †

MCCUSKEY, GEORGE, financial consultant; b. Cuyahoga Falls, Ohio, Dec. 25, 1914; s. Charles C. and Lottie (Wilcox) McC.; m. Phyllis Herzberg, 1939; children: Anne Carolyn, Margery Sue. BA, Denison U., 1936; JD, Cleve. Sch. Law, 1941. Investment analyst Boyd & Co., Cleve., 1937-43; assoc. wage stblzn. dir. War Labor Bd., 1943-44; gen. counsel, sec.-treas. Perfection Stove Co., 1944-52; asst. to pres. Youngstown (Ohio) Sheet and Tube Co., 1952-54, v.p., 1954-70, pres., 1970-71; exec. v.p. Lykes-Youngstown Corp., 1969-71; chmn. Arthur G. McKee Co., 1971-77, Liquid Capital Income Inc., 1977-78; chmn. exec. com. McKee Corp., 1977-78; fin. cons. Naples, Fla., 1978-87. Former trustee Western Res. Acad., Cleve. Home: Naples Fla. Died Aug. 12, 1987; buried Cuyahoga Falls, Ohio.

MCCUTCHEON, ROBERT HAYNES, military and government official; b. Damascus, Va., Oct. 11, 1917; s. Jesse R. and Effie C. (Rhea) McC.; m. Mary Elizabeth White, Aug. 6, 1943; children: Robert Haynes, Patrick John. AB, Berea (Ky.) Coll., 1939; MBA with high distinction, Harvard U., 1949; grad. Air Corps Flying Sch., Indsl. Coll. of the Armed Forces. Commd. 2d lt. USAAF, 1940, advanced through grades to maj. gen., 1965; assigned bombardment aircraft U.S. and PTO 1940-43; at Hdqrs. USAAF, 1943-47; logistics assignments Wright-Patterson AFB, Ohio, 1950-56, Seville, Spain and Wiesbaden, Fed. Republic Germany, 1955-58; at Office Sec. Def. 1959-65; dir. procurement and prodn. Air Force Logistics Command, Wright-Patterson AFB, 1965-67; comdr. Ogden (Utah) Air Material Area, 1967-70; dep. dir. DSA, Alexandria, Va., 1970-71; asst. Postmaster Gen. procurement and supply 1971-81; instr. indsl. mgmt. Georgetown U., 1963-64. Decorated D.S.M., Legion of Merit (3), Air medal. Mem. Order

Daedalians, Pi Gamma Mu, Delta Phi Alpha. Home: Springfield Va. Died July 15, 1981.

MCDANIEL, WILLIAM EARL, agriculture educator; b. Fresno, Calif., May 30, 1915; s. Jesse F. and Emma (Mischler) McD.; m. Frances M. Bissett, Dec. 26, 1946; children: William Earl II, Michael Anthony. BS in Agr., U. Mo., 1942; MS in Agrl. Econs., U. Ill., 1943; PhD, U. Minn., 1951. Instr. commerce U. Minn., 1947-48, instr. agr., 1948-51; from instr. to prof. U. Del., Newark, 1951-79, chmn. dept. agrl. econs., 1957-65, dean Coll. Agrl. Scis., 1965-77; dir. Del. Agr. Experiment Sta. Newark, 1965-77; sec. Del. Dept. Agr., 1977-79; chmn. Gov.'s Council on Natural Resources and Environ. Control, 1970-77. Contbd. articles to profl. jours. Former v.p., bd. dirs. Brookside Community Assn., Newark. Mem. Am. Agrl. Econs. Assn., Am. Soc. Farm Mgrs. and Rural Appraisers, Gamma Sigma Delta, Alpha Zeta. Home: Newark Del. Deceased.

MCDERMOTT, WALSH, physician, educator; b. New Haven, Oct. 24, 1909; s. Terence and Rosella (Walsh) McD.; m. Marian Anne MacPhail, Nov. 11, 1942. BA, Princeton U., 1930, DSc (hon.), 1974; MD, Columbia U., 1934; DSc (hon.), Dartmouth Coll., 1976; DMS (hon.), Med. Coll. Ohio. Intern, then asst. resident N.Y. Hosp., 1934-37; with Cornell U. Med. Coll., N.Y.C., 1937-81, Livingston Farrand prof., chmn. dept. pub. health, 1955-72, prof. pub. affairs in medicine, 1972-75; spl. advisor Robert Wood Johnson Found., Princeton, N.J., 1972-81. Co-editor Beeson-McDermott-Wyngaarden Textbook of Medicine. Trustee Columbia U., 1973-81. Recipient Lasker award, 1955, Trudeau Medal, 1963, James D. Bruce Meml. award ACP, 1968, Woodrow Wilson award Princeton U., 1969. Fellow Royal Coll. Physicians, Societas Medica Polonorum; mem. Nat. Acad. Scis., Nat. Acad. Scis. Inst. Medicine, Am. Acad. Arts and Scis., Am. Soc. Clin. Investigation, Assn. Am. Physicians, Council on Fgn. Relations, Interurban Clin. Club, Century Assn. (N.Y.C.), Cosmos Club (Washington). Home: Princeton N.J. Died Oct. 17, 1981.

MCDONALD, CHARLES BERT, investment banker; b. Cherokee, Iowa, May 16, 1892; s. John and Mary (Donald) McD.; m. Alice English, Mar. 11, 1952 (dec. Oct. 1971); 1 child, Joan Irene (Mrs. David Graham); m. 2d, Catherine H. Oppmann, June 7, 1973. Student, Iowa State Tchrs. Coll., 1908-15, U. Iowa, 1917-18. With McDonald & Co., Cleve., from 1922, sr. partner, from 1944. Mem. Investment Banking Assn. Am. Home: Shaker Heights Ohio. †

MCDONALD, HOWARD S., educational official; b. Salt Lake City, July 18, 1894; s. Francis and Rosella (Stevenson) McD.; m. Ella Gibbs, Sept. 26, 1917; children: Ruth McDonald Boyer, Melva McDonald Orgill. BS, Utah State Agrl. Coll., 1921; MA, U. Calif., Berkeley, 1925; EdD, U. Calif., 1949, HHD, 1952. Instr. Utah State Agrl. Coll., 1921-24; tchr. San Francisco Pub. Schs., 1924-29; vice-prin. Balboa High School, 1929-34; dir. teaching personnel San Francisco Schs., 1934-36, dep. supt. schs., 1936-44; supt. Salt Lake City Pub. Schs., 1944-45; pres. Brigham Young U., Salt Lake City, 1945-49, Los Angeles City Coll., 1949-58, L.A. State Coll. Applied Arts and Scis., 1949-62; regional rep. for U.S. Commr. Edn. HEW Region 9, 1962-64; pres. Salt Lake Mormon Temple, 1964-86. Former bd. dirs. Hollywood (Calif.) YMCA, Los Angeles County Mus. Art. Served with U.S. Army during World War I. Mem. Am. Assn. Sch. Adminstrs., Univ. Archeol. Soc., Phi Delta Kappa, Alpha Phi Omega, Schoolmasters Club (pres. 1943-44), Rotary, California Club. Mormon. Home: Salt Lake City Utah. Died Oct. 25, 1986.

MCDONALD, JOSEPH F(RANCIS), editor, publisher; b. Denver, Aug. 4, 1891; s. Willard F. and Cecilia (Kelligher) McD.; m. Leola Lewis, Nov. 13, 1915; children: Joseph Francis, Robert Lewis. BS, U. Nev., 1915, PhD in Journalism (hon.), 1956. Bus. mgr. U. Nev., Reno, 1914-15; reporter Nev. State Jour., 1915, bus. mgr., 1922-26, editor, mgr., from 1940, pub., from 1951; reporter Reno Evening Gazette, 1916-21, city editor, 1917-39; treas. Reno Newspapers, Inc., 1951, v.p., 9154-55, pres., 1956, ret. Pres. Reno-Sparks Community Chest, from 1957; chmn. Nev. Parole and Probation Bd.; del. Dem. Nat. Conv., 1948, 56. Mem. Nev.-Calif.-Lake Tahoe Assn. (pres. from 1957), Calif. Automobile Assn. (v.p. from 1959, Nev. bd. dirs. 1950), Reno C. of C. (bd. dirs.), U. Nev. Alumni Assn. (past pres.), Am. Soc. Newspaper Editors, Rotary, Sigma Delta Chi, Sigma Alpha Epsilon. Roman Catholic. Home: Reno Nev. †

MCDONALD, JOSEPH LEE, college dean; b. Coldwater, Ohio, Nov. 21, 1892; s. Kenneth J. and Anna (Dietrich) McD.; m. Edith B. Seibel, Aug. 18, 1927. AB, Ind. U., 1915; AM, Columbia U., 1926; AM (hon.), Dartmouth Coll., 1930, LHD, 1959. Instr. Coll. St. Thomas, St. Paul, 1915-17; instr. econs. U. Pa., 1917-18, U. Minn., 1919-23; instr. econs. Dartmouth Coll., 1923-24, asst. prof., 1924-31, prof., from 1931, prof. fgn. trade Amos Tuck Sch., 1937-49, dean coll., from 1952; prin. economist USDA. Pvt. U.S. Army, 1918. Mem. AAUP, Am. Econ. Assn., Royal Econ. Soc., Hanover Country Club, Graduate Club. †

MCDONALD, LYLE, utilities executive; b. N.Y.C., Nov. 28, 1891; s. Robert and Mary (Mulherron) McD.; m. Florence Broberg, June 15, 1918; 1 child, Elsa McDonald Ellmaker. BCS, NYU. Statistician Pub. Service Electric & Gas Co., Pub. Service Coordinated Transport and subs. cos., 1916-37, compt., 1937-44, v.p., compt., 1944-48, v.p. in charge fin., Newark, 1948, also bd. dirs., from 1941, later chmn. bd., mem. exec. com., from 1941; then bd. dirs. Pub. Service Electric & Gas Co. With USN, World War I. Mem. Am. Gas Assn., Edison Elec. Inst., Am. Transit Assn., Essex Club (Newark), Baltrusol Golf Club (Springfield, N.J.), Harvard Club (N.Y.C.). Republican. Home: Newark N.J. †

MCDONALD, THOMAS FRANCIS, lawyer; b. Buchanan County, Iowa, Oct. 7, 1890; s. Timothy and Honora (McCarthy) McD.; m. Marguerite Ely, July 6, 1925; children: Thomas Ely and Francis Ely (twins). Student, Valparaiso Coll., 1908-09, U.S. Mil. Acad., 1912-14; LLB, U. Mich., 1917, LLM (hon.), 1936. Bar: Mo. 1919. Ptnr. McDonald, Wright & Bryan. Mem. State Bd. Law Examiners, 1931-39, sec. 1932-49; mem. Appellate Jud. Commn. Mo., 1952-57; mem. spl. bd. for Survey of Legal Edn. and Admission to bar, State of Calif., 1947-49; co-chmn. St. Louis exec. bd. NCCJ, 1940-48, mem. nat. bd. 1945-47; candidate for judge Mo. Supreme Ct., 1938. Maj. U.S. Army, World War I. Selected by pres. U. Mich. to rep. legal profession at Univ. Centennial Celebration, 1937. Fellow Am. Bar. Found.; mem. ABA (ho. of dels. 1940-42, chmn. sect. on legal edn. and admissions to bar 1951-53), Mo. State Bar, Bar Assn. St. Louis (pres. 1935-36), Am. Judicature Soc. (dir. for Mo. 1937-40, 46-54, chmn. bd. 1940, 41, v.p. 1954-59), Am. Legion (past comdr. St. Louis post), U. Mo. Alumni Assn. (hon. mem. law chpt.), Mo. Athletic Club, Lawyers Club, Phi Alpha Delta. Home: Chesterfield Mo. †

MCDONALD, WILLIAM JOSEPH, auxiliary bishop; b. Kilkenny, Ireland, June 15, 1904; s. Patrick and Bridget (Foskin) McD. BA, St. Kieran's Coll., Kilkenny, 1924; MA, Cath. U. Am., 1937, PhD, 1939; LLD (hon.), Northwestern U., 1958, Mt. St. Mary's Coll., 1959; JUD (hon.), Nat. U. Ireland, 1959; ScD (hon.), St. John's U., Bklyn.; PaedD (hon.), La Salle Coll., Phila.; EdD (hon.), Providence Coll.; LittD (hon.), St. Francis Coll., Bklyn. Ordained priest Roman Catholic Ch., 1928, invested domestic prelate, 1948. Chaplain Newman Club, Stanford (Calif.) U., 1928-30; assoc. editor The Monitor, San Francisco, 1930-32; moderator Newman Club, San Francisco State Coll., 1934-36; curate St. Paul's Ch., San Francisco, 1934-36; prof. philosophy Cath. U. Am., 1940-67, vice rector, 1954-67, rector, 1957-67; aux. bishop of Washington, 1964-68, San Francisco, from 1968; titular bishop of Aquae Regiae; pres. Internat. Fedn. Cath. Univs., 1960-63; founder, mem. Cath. Culture Guild, from 1934. Editor-in-chief New Cath. Ency.; contbr. articles to various publs. Home: San Francisco Calif. Died Jan. 7, 1989.

MCDONOUGH, SARAH F. (MRS. JOHN D. BATTLE), association executive; b. Quincy, Mass., July 7, 1892; s. Benjamin and Sarah T. (Burke) Johnson; m. James H. McDonough, July 12, 1909 (dec. 1925); 1 child, Dorothy May; m. John D. Battle, July 20, 1936. Student, Woodward Inst., Quincy, Mass., 1906-09. Various secretarial positions Boston, Chgo., Washington, 1917-29; exec. sec. Assn. ICC Practitioners, Washington, 1929-57; mng. editor Interstate Commerce Commn. Practitioners' Jour., editorial supr. all documents released by orgn., 1929-57. Mem. Women's Nat. Press. Club, Am. Newspaper Women's Club, Kenwood Golf and Country Club. Republican. Congregationalist. Home: Washington D.C. †

MCDONOUGH, WALTER AUSTIN, utilities executive; b. Evanston, Ill., Oct. 6, 1891; s. James A. and Mary Ellen (Mulcahy) McD.; m. Lenora Shea, June 4, 1924; children: Mary Jane (Mrs. James NcNally), Thomas G., Diane (Mrs. Thomas Shaffer), Robert, John. Student, Ind. U. Extension, 1922. Acct. Pub. Svc. Co. No. Ill., 1912-18; auditor Peoples Gas, Light & Coke Co., 1919-21; auditor No. Ind. Pub. Svc. Co., Hammond, 1922-27, chief acct., 1927-34, asst. controller, 1934-39, controller, sec., 1939-49, v.p., controller, from 1949, also bd. dirs. Mem. Controllers Inst. Am., Am. Gas Assn., KC. †

MCDOWELL, WILLIAM RALSTON, lawyer, railway executive; b. Shreveport, La., Jan. 18, 1917; s. Miles R. and Mollie (Ayres) McD.; m. Fern Bronstad, Sept. 15, 1939; children: Rebecca Gail McDowell Craver, Mollye McDowell Bell. BBA, U. Tex., 1940, JD, 1940. Bar: Tex. 1940. Spl. agt. FBI, Washington, 1940-41, adminstrv. asst. to dir., 1941-45; assoc. McBride & Johnson, Dallas, 1945-47; asst. dist. atty. Dallas County, 1947-48; gen. counsel Tex. and Pacific R.R., Dallas, 1948-58, v.p., 1958-81; gen. counsel Missouri-Pacific R.R., Dallas, 1962-76, v.p., 1976-81; past bd. dirs. Weatherford Mineral Wells, Northwestern R.R. Co. Served on bd. dirs. Tex. Research League. Mem. ABA, Dallas Bar Assn., State Bar of Tex., Am. Judicature Soc., Assn. ICC Practitioners, Soc. Former Agts. of FBI. Lutheran. Home: Dallas Texas Died Aug. 3, 1982; buried Restland Meml. Park, Dallas.

MCELROY, GEORGE SPAHR, chemical company executive; b. Columbus, Ohio, July 8, 1915; s. Austin and Elizabeth (Spahr) McE.; m. Elvira Hazard Bullock, May 31, 1940; children: George Spahr, Candace McElroy Bahrenburg, Austin Chandler. Grad., Phillips Acad., Andover, Mass., 1933; BS in Engring., Princeton U., 1937. Engr. E.I. du Pont de Nemours Co., Leominster, Mass., 1937-38; foreman Rico Barton Corp., Worcester, Mass., 1938-45; mktg. mgr. Owens Corning Fiberglas Corp., N.Y.C., 1945-65; pres. Ironsides Co., Columbus, 1965-82, Columbus Gallery Fine Arts, 1967-73. Served with USNR, 1943-45. Mem. Wire Assn., Soc. Aerospace Materials and Process Engring., Am. Inst. Steel Engrs., Princeton Club of N.Y.C., Rocky Fork Golf Club, Castalia Trout Club, Little Sturgeon Trout Club, Columbus Country Club, Beach Club of Columbus, Columbus Club. Home: Columbus Ohio. Died 1982; buried Columbus.

MCEVILLA, JOSEPH DAVID, university dean; b. Aspinwall, Pa., Sept. 11, 1919; s. Joseph Edward and Christiana (Steffler) McE.; m. Avis Walter, Feb. 5, 1943; children—Arlene Avis, Joseph David. B.A., U. Fla., 1944; B.S. in Pharmacy, U. Pitts., 1949, M.S. (Geo. A. Kelly Sr. fellow), 1952, Ph.D., 1955. Asst. prof. U. Pitts., 1955-58, asso. prof., 1959-61, prof., 1962-74; prof. pharm. econs., dean Sch. Pharmacy, Temple U., Phila., 1974-85, prof. emeritus, 1985-88; cons. St. Clair, Armstrong County hosps., Task Force on Prescription Drugs, HEW, Colombian Govt., Inst. Social Security, Nat. Assn. Bds. Pharmacy Manpower Study, Nat. Pharmacy Ins. Council, drug studies br. Social Security Adminstrn.; Pitts. area cons. Hosp. Audit, Inc., Merck, Sharp and Dohme; mem. Allegheny adv. council Western Pa. Comprehensive Health Planning Assn.; co-chmn. Pharmacy Panel on Inter-relation of Secondary Schs., Colls. and Profl. Schs.; study dir. Am. Pharm. Assn. Found. Author: Remington's Practice of Pharmacy, 1961, Pharmacy Administration, 1965, Perspectives on Medicine in Society. Served with USMCR, 1943-45. Fellow Acad. Pharm. Scis.; mem. Am., Pa., Chester County pharm. assns., AMA, Am. Econ. Assn., Am. Pub. Health Assn., Soc. Pa. Economists, Am. Assn. Colls. of Pharmacy Conf. Tchrs. (chmn. 1964-65), Am. Acad. Pharm. Scis. (sect. chmn.), Rho Chi, Kappa Psi. Home: Berwyn Pa. Died July 4, 1988; buried Jefferson Meml. Pk., Pitts.

MCFARLAN, RONALD LYMAN, electronic engineer, manufacturing executive; b. Cin., Mar. 8, 1905; s. Frank Gressinger and Mary Ella (Henninger) McF.; m. Ethel Warren White, Sept. 6, 1933; children: Franklin Warren, Ethel Louise Bowen Hamann. BA, U. Cin., 1926; PhD, U. Chgo., 1930. Instr. physics Harvard U., 1932-35; chief physicist United Drug Co., 1935-40, B.B. Chem. Co., 1940-43; dir. research Bulova Watch Co., 1943-46; exec. asst. dir. engring. Raytheon Co., 1946-56; pres. Internat. Med. Tech., Inc., from 1975; past bd. dirs., cons. Slater Electric Inc.; past cons. Datamatic div. Honeywell Regulator Co., Mpls., Raytheon Corp., Boston Safe Deposit and Trust Co., Arthur D. Little, Inc., Searle Medidata Inc., AVCO Mfg. Co. (research-advanced devel. div.), Pickard & Burns div. Gorham Corp.; also consulted to pres. Polytech. Inst. Bklyn.; former advisor U. Rochester Sch. Engring. Fellow IEEE; mem. IRE (dir. 1957-62, pres. 1960, chmn. profl. group on edn. 1958-59), Inst. Aero. Scis., Am. Phys. Soc., Am. Chem. Soc., Am. Soc. Naval Engrs., Sigma Xi. Home: Belmont Mass. Died Nov. 7, 1987; buried Mt. Auburn Cemetery, Cambridge, Mass.

MCGAUGHEY, JANIE WOOD, church official; b. Atlanta, Jan. 6, 1891; d. George Burkhart and Mamie Buchanan (Wood) McG. AB, Agnes Scott Coll., 1913; student, Bible Sem., N.Y., 1921, MRE (hon.), 1957; DRE (hon.), Southwestern Bible Sem., Memphis, 1942. Tchr. North Ave. Presbyn. Ch., Atlanta, 1913-19; assoc. prof. Bible Assembly's Tng. Sch., Richmond, Va., 1921-22; dir. religious edn. First Presbyn. Ch., Knoxville, Tenn., 1922-26; prof. Bible Mary Baldwin Coll., Staunton, Va., 1926-27; dir. spiritual life dept. Dept. Woman's Work, Presbyn. Ch. in U.S., 1928, sec., from 1929, exec. sec., 1949-56; field Bible tchr.; visitor woman's work depts. chs. and missions, Mex., 1941, Brazil, 1949; head counselor Camp Greystone, Tuxedo, N.C., 1920-26. Author: Life Messages from Jesus, The Son of Man, 1928, Life Challenges from the Risen Christ, 1929, They Were Called Christians, 1958, History of Women's Work; Presbyterian Church, U.S., 1961; contbr. articles to newspapers. Mem. AAUW, Phi Beta Kappa. Home: Atlanta Ga. †

MCGIFFERT, ARTHUR CUSHMAN, JR., clergyman, educator; b. Cin., Nov. 27, 1892; s. Arthur Cushman and Gertrude Huntington (Boyce) McG.; m. Elisabeth Eliot, May 29, 1917; children: David Eliot, Michael, Ellen. AB, Harvard U., 1913; postgrad. Harvard Divinity Sch., 1919, Am. Sch. Archaeology, Athens, Greece, 1913-14; BD, Union Theol. Sem., 1917; MA, Columbia U., 1917; postgrad., U. Zurich, 1919-20; DD, Chgo. Theol. Sem., 1939; LLD, Coll. of the Pacific, 1945; LittD, Pacific Sch. Religion, 1945. Ordained to ministry Congl. Ch., 1917. Pastor All Souls Ch., Lowell, Mass., 1920-26; prof. Christian theology Chgo. Theol. Sem., 1926-39, pres., 1946-58, pres. emeritus from 1959; pres. Pacific Sch. Religion, 1939-45. Author: Jonathan Edwards, 1932; editor: Christianity as History and Faith, 1934, Young Emerson Speaks, 1938. Truste

Dillard U.; mem. ACLU. 1st lt. U.S. Army. Mem. Phi Beta Kappa, Delta Upsilon. Home: Mount Desert Maine. †

MC GINNIS, THOMAS CHARLES, psychotherapist, sports psychologist, marriage and family therapist, author, educator; b. Monroe, N.C., June 2, 1925; s. Robert Ashe and Mamie (Warlick) McG.; m. Mary Yorke Kluttz, Feb. 15, 1947; children: Thomas Charles Jr., Karen Yorke, John Richard. B.A., Catawba Coll., 1946, Lit.D., 1979; M.S. in Psychiat. Social Work, U. N.C., 1949; certificate, William A. White Inst. Psychiatry, Psychoanalysis and Psychology, 1957, Inst. for Research in Hypnosis, 1977; Ed.D., Columbia U. Tchrs. Coll., 1963. Diplomate Marital and Family Therapy. Supt. Carteret County (N.C.) Dept. Pub. Welfare, 1949-51; adj. and psychotherapist Mental Hygiene Cons. Service, Ft. Dix, N.J., 1951-53; dir. Clinic for Mental Health Service, Passaic County, N.J., 1953-59; pvt. practice Fair Lawn, N.J., 1952-87; dir., sponsor, pres. Counseling and Psychotherapy Center (P.A.), Fair Lawn, 1959-87; dir. Human Services Center for Edn. and Research, Fair Lawn, 1973-80; pres. Inst. Profl. Sports Psychology, 1982-87, Internat. Union Family Orgns. in U.S.A., 1978-87; non-govt. cons. UN, 1978-87; instr. Fairleigh Dickinson U., 1963-65; asso. prof. N.Y.U. Grad. Sch. Edn., 1965-73, co-dir. grad. program human sexuality, marriage and family, 1969-73; cons. Asims All Star Tennis Acad., 1985-87, N.Y. Mets Baseball Orgn., 1986-87; host weekly radio show haring Sta. WFDU-FM, 1981-84; roster of sports psychology U.S. Olympic com., 1985-87. Author: Your First Year of Marriage, 1967, A Girl's Guide to Dating and Going Steady, 1968, Sensitivity Training, 1970; co-author: Preparation for Marriage, 1971, Open Family and Marriage, A Guide to Personal Growth, 1976, Open Family Living, 1976, More Than Just A Friend, 1981; mem. editorial bd.: Sexual Behavior mag, 1971-73, Jour. of Divorce, 1976-87; contbr. numerous articles and papers in fields psychotherapy, sports psychology, marital and family therapy, sensitivity tng. Bd. dirs. N.J. League Emotionally Disturbed Children, 1955-56; sec. com. legislation for community mental health service N.J. Welfare Council, 1956-57; exec. com. Passaic County Health and Welfare Assn., 1957-58; sec. coordinating com. legislation for emotionally disturbed child N.J. Welfare Council, 1957-59; chmn. N.J. Community Mental Health Adv. Council, 1958-59; cons. Music Corp. Am., 1962-68, Major League baseball teams, 1965-87, U. N.C. Sch. Medicine, 1974; sec. U.S. nat. com. Internat. Union Family Orgns., N.Y., 1968-80, exec. bd., Paris, 1969-80; mem. N.J. Bd. Marriage Counselor Examiners, 1969-74, vice chmn., 1974-76; mem. grant rev. bd. NIMH, 1969-70; pres. Yorktown, Inc., 1970-73; cons. in USSR on invitation Soviet Women's Bur., 1966, Nat. Marriage Guidance Council Gt. Britain, 1970-73; mem. U.S. Olympic Com. Roster of Approved Sports Psychologists. Served with U.S. Mcht. Marine Cadet Corps, 1945-46; lt. (j.g.) USNR, 1946-47; 1st lt. AUS, 1948-51. Recipient Whitner medal Catawba Coll., 1946, citation for Service Clinic Mental Health Service Passaic County, 1959; O.B. Michael Outstanding Alumni award Catawba Coll., 1971; Distinguished Service award State of N.J., 1975. Fellow Am. Assn. Marriage Counselors; mem. N.J. Assn. Mental Hygiene Clinics (pres. elect 1959), N.J. Assn. Marriage Counselors (pres. 1966-69), Am. Assn. Sex Educators and Counselors (v.p. 1968-69), Am. Assn. Marriage and Family Counselors (pres. 1970-71), Am. Psychol. Assn., Sci. Soc. Study Sex, N.J. Psychol. Assn., Am. Acad. Psychotherapists, Nat. Assn. Social Workers (charter), Nat. Council Family Relations, N.J. Welfare Council, Author's Guild. Club: Rotarian. Home: Fair Lawn N.J. Died July 20, 1987.

MC GOWAN, CARL, judge; b. Hymera, Ind., May 7, 1911; m. Josephine V. Perry, Jan. 20, 1945; children: Mary, Rebecca, John, Hope. AB, Dartmouth U., 1932; LLB, Columbia U., 1936, LLD (hon.), 1988; LLD (hon.), Northwestern U., 1976, Vt. Law Sch., 1980, U. Mich., 1982, Georgetown U., 1984. Bar: N.Y. 1936, Ill. 1940, D.C. 1948. Counsel to gov. Ill., 1949-53; sr. mem. firm Ross, McGowan, Hardies & O'Keefe, Chgo., 1953-63; gen. counsel C. & N.-W. Ry., 1957-63; judge U.S. Ct. Appeals for D.C. Circuit, 1963—, chief judge, 1981. Mem. Am., Chgo., Ill., D.C. bar assns., Am. Law Inst., Phi Beta Kappa. Home: Washington D.C. Died Dec. 1, 1987.

MCGOWEN, NORRIS COCHRAN, gas corporation executive; b. Chgo., Dec. 1, 1890; s. Edward J. and Rose Mary (Phee) McG.; m. Nelle Quigles, Dec. 12, 1917; children: Charley Nelle McGowen Rives, Norris Cochran Jr. Grade and comml. sch. edn.; LLD, Centenary Coll. La. and Spring Hill Coll., Mobile, Ala. Acct. and yard man Chgo. and Northwestern R.R. local freight office, 1908-10; successively with Globe Commn. Co., David Palmer & Co., auditors and accts., then with Audit. Co. of N.Y., being assigned to properties in Shreveport, La., 1913-14; joined Atlas Oil Co., 1917, as acct., handling gen. purchases, leasing, in charge of field devel. and pipe line constrn. and operation, from 1918 in gen. charge of properties as v.p. and gen. mgr., and head of various cos. which merged into present orgn., pres., 1929-56; chmn. bd. dirs. United Gas Corp., Union Producing Co., United Gas Pipe Line Co., 1956-66, hon. chmn. bd., dir. emeritus, from 1966. Mem. Petroleum Industry War Coun., also chmn. Natural Gas and Natural Gasoline Com., Dist. 3, during World War II. Mem. Am. Gas Assn. (pres. 1938, bd. dirs.), Knights of Holy Sepulchre of Jerusalem, Knights of St. Gregory (papal), Boston Club (New Orleans), Shreveport Country Club, Shreveport Club, Ramada Club (Houston). Home: Shreveport La. †

MCGRATH, CHRISTOPHER C., congressman, judge; b. N.Y.C., May 15, 1902; s. Michael J. and Anna (Donohue) McG.; m. Helen Gaffney, June 29, 1929 (dec. 1963); children: Michael, Terence, Kevin Barry, Christopher, Mary Ann McGrath Collier, Kathleen McGrath Cunnion. BA, Columbia U., 1923; JD, Fordham U., 1924. Bar: N.Y. 1927. Practiced law N.Y.C., 1927-35; Justice Mcpl. Ct. N.Y.C., 1935-48; Rep. in Congress from N.Y. Washington, 1949-71; of counsel Shea & Gould, N.Y.C, 1972-78; mem. N.Y. State Assembly, 1928-35; adj. prof. Fordham U. Law Sch., 1957-61. Mem. Delta Theta Pi, KC. Democrat. Roman Catholic. Home: Bronx N.Y. Died July 7, 1986.

MCGRATH, RICHARD T., bishop; b. Oderin, Nfld., Can., June 17, 1912. Ordained priest Roman Cath. Ch., 1936. Bishop Archdiocese of St. George's, Nfld., Can., 1970-85. Home: Corner Brook Nfld., Canada. Died May 9, 1987; buried Belvedere, St. John's.

MC GRAW, ARTHUR GARFIELD, JR., university dean; b. Chgo., Dec. 9, 1918; s. Arthur Garfield and Justine (Caswell) McG.; m. Doris Helen Knudson, Nov. 28, 1952; children: Bruce Arthur, David Paul, Erik Steven. B.Ed., Whitewater State Tchrs. Coll., 1940; M.S. in Ednl. Adminstrn., U. Wis., 1948, Ph.D., 1958. Tchr. pub. high sch. Ft. Atkinson, 1940-42, Whitewater, Wis., 1946-48; prin. campus elem. sch., chmn. dept. elem. edn. U. Wis.-Whitewater, 1948-68, asso. dean Grad. Sch., 1968-71, dean, 1971-84; treas., mem. exec. bd. Whitewater Found., 1964-66. Author: Ready for the Teaching Team!?, 1961. Mem. adv. com. Park and Recreation Bd., Whitewater, 1973; pres. bd. edn. Whitewater Unified Sch. Dist., 1973-75. Served with M.C., AUS, 1942-46. Recipient Disting. Alumni Service award 0. of Wis., 1978, Community Svc. award Whitewater Rotary Club; Mc Graw Computing Ctr. named in his honor U. Wis., Whitewater. Mem. Wis. Elem. Sch. Prins. Assn. (life; exec. bd. 1961-69), Phi Kappa Phi, Kappa Delta Pi, Phi Delta Kappa. Episcopalian (sr. warden 1965-74, 77-79, jr. warden 1975-77, treas. 1980-88). Lodge: Rotary (25 Yr. Community Service award, Whitewater chpt. 1986). Home: Whitewater Wis. Died Mar. 25, 1988; buried Hillside Cemetery, Whitewater, Wis.

MCGREGOR, ARTHUR, lawyer; b. Ogden, Utah, Sept. 10, 1891; s. William and Charilla Emily (Browning) McG.; m. Mildred Arleen Pardoe, Nov. 15, 1919; children: Arthur Pardoe, Bruce Gordon, Jed Keith, Douglas Earl. BSC, Washington Sch. Bus. Adminstrn., 1925; LLB, George Washington U., 1924. Bar: D.C. 1924, Calif. 1931. Auditor Bur. Internal Revenue, 1919-25, atty. Gen. Counsel's Office, 1926-28; mem. Dempsey & Mackay, L.A., 1928-39; ptnr. Mackay, McGregor & Bennion, L.A., from 1939. Active Boy Scouts Am. Cadet U.S. A.S., World War I. Mem. Am., L.A. bar assns., State Bar Calif., Kiwanis Club (dir. 1954-55), The Debonairs Club, Univ. Club, Phi Alpha Delta. Mormon. Home: Los Angeles Calif. †

MC GUINNESS, AIMS CHAMBERLAIN, pediatrician, educator; b. Chester, N.Y., Mar. 10, 1905; s. J. Holmes and Amy Aims (Chamberlain) McG.; m. Margaret A. Hatfield, Sept. 2, 1933 (dec. July 14, 1975); children—Louise Hatfield (Mrs. G.C. Ludlow, Jr.), Margaret (Mrs. John Hinman Denny), Aims C. A.B., Princeton, 1927; M.D., Columbia, 1931. Intern U. Pa. Hosp., Phila., 1931-33; resident Children's Hosp., Phila., 1933-34; emeritus physician Children's Hosp., 1980-87; pvt. practice pediatrics Phila., 1934-48; faculty U. Pa. Sch. Medicine, 1934, asst. prof. pediatrics, 1946-50, asso. prof., 1951-57, adj. prof., 1968-80, prof. emeritus, 1980-87; dean U. Pa. Sch. Medicine (Grad. Sch. Medicine), 1951-54; clin. dir. Miners Meml. Hosp. Assn., United Mine Workers Am. Welfare and Retirement Fund, 1954-56, cons., 1956-57; Spl. asst. for health and med. affairs to sec. HEW, 1957-59; exec. sec. Com. on Med. Edn., N.Y. Acad. Medicine, 1959-66; asso. dir. Ednl. Council Fgn. Med. Grads., 1967-74, trustee, 1957-66, pres. bd. trustees, 1963-66; asst. vis. physician Children's Hosp., Phila., 1940-46, sr. vis. physician, 1947-54, dir. hosps., 1948-51, cons. staff, 1954-57, 68-79; dir. emeritus Phila. Serum Exchange, 1934-54; mem. subcom. on blood Health Resources Adv. Bd. ODM, 1953-57; asso. mem. commn. immunization Armed Forces Epidemiological Bd., 1954-58; examiner Am. Bd. Pediatrics, 1949-65, emeritus examiner, 1980-87; mem. Fed. Council Sci. and Tech., 1959. Contbd. articles to med. jours. Mem. U.S. del. WHO, 1957-59, City N.Y. Community Mental Health Bd., 1962-64, Health Research Council City N.Y., 1962-64, 74-79; past bd. dirs. Am. Council Emigrés in Professions; former trustee Keene Valley (N.Y.) Hosp., v.p., 1955-62; trustee Am. Nat. Council Health Edn. of Pub., 1962-68; v.p., 1959-63; trustee Princeton Hosp, 1962-68. Served as lt. col. M.C. AUS, World War II. Decorated Legion of Merit. Fellow N.Y. Acad. Medicine; mem. AMA, Assn. Am. Med. Coll., Am. Acad. Pediatrics, Am. Pediatric Soc. (past sec.), Council on Med. Adminstrn., Assn. Med. Consultants World War II, John Morgan Soc. (pres. 1942-46), Phila. Pediatric Soc. (pres. 1949), Philadelphia County Med. Soc., Soc. Pediatric Research. Episcopalian. Home: Princeton N.J. Died Apr. 19, 1988.

MCGUIRE, HAROLD FREDERICK, lawyer; b. N.Y.C., June 27, 1906; s. Frederick Francis and Lillian (Shaw) McG.; m. Lillian Virginia Jones, Dec. 28, 1933; children: Harold Frederick, Bartlett Hoyle. AB, Columbia U., 1927, LLB, 1929. Bar: N.Y. 1929. Assoc. Cravath, de Gersdorff, Swaine & Wood, N.Y.C., 1930-39; ptnr. Gardner, Morrison, Rogers & McGuire, Washington, 1939-41, Wickes, Riddell, Bloomer, Jacobi & McGuire, N.Y.C., 1942-79; of counsel Morgan, Lewis & Bockius, N.Y.C., 1979-81; past bd. dirs. Seaboard Surety Co. Chmn. gymnasium bldg. fund Columbia U., 1958-81, trustee, 1960-81, vice chmn. bd. trustees, 1968-77. Mem. Assn. Bar City N.Y., N.Y. County Lawyers Assn., Alumni Fedn. Columbia U. (pres. 1958-60), Phi Beta Kappa, Psi Upsilon, Downtown Assn. (N.Y.C.), Point O'Woods Country Club (Fire Island, N.Y.). Home: New York N.Y. Died Dec. 1, 1981.

MC GUIRE, JAMES T., corporate executive; b. Boston; m. Audrey McGuire; children: Carol Ann, James T. Grad., Boston Coll. Vice chmn. Canteen Corp., also dir.; dir. Nat. Automatic Merchandising Assn., 1962—, mem. exec. com., 1963—, sr. v.p., 1966, pres., 1967; trustee Nat. Inst. Foodservice Industry; dir. Katy Industries, Inc., Mdse. Nat. Bank, Skokie Fed. Savs. & Loan. Trustee Boston Coll., Mundelein Coll.; bd. dirs. Boys Hope, Chgo. Crime Commn. Mem. Nat. Restaurant Assn., Ill. Restaurant Assn., Chgo. Restaurant Assn., Chgo. Assn. Commerce and Industry (dir.), Ill. C. of C., Boston Coll. Alumni Assn., Northwestern U. Assocs. Clubs: Executives, Tavern, Mchts. and Mfrs. (pres. bd. govs.) (Chgo.); Evanston (Ill.) Golf (pres. 1979-80), Variety Internat. Lodge: K.C. Home: Skokie Ill. Deceased.

MCGURN, JOHN MARTIN, utility executive; b. El Paso, Tex., Oct. 25, 1931; s. Martin James and Margaret (McGovern) McG.; m. Catherine Elizabeth Pinner; children: John M., Katrina C., Arthur S., Teresa C., Christopher P., Monica N. B.E.E., N.Mex. State U., 1934. Engr. El Paso Electric Co., 1934-41; with Va. Electric and Power Co., Richmond, 1941-84, sr. v.p., 1966-67, pres., chief exec. officer, 1967-70, vice-chmn., 1970-71, chmn., chief exec. officer, 1971-84; past bd. dirs. Edison Electric Inst., Electric Power Research Inst., Southeastern Electric Exchange, Va. Trust Co., Bank of Va. Co., Robertshaw Controls Co. Past trustee Benedictine High Sch., Richmond; chmn. Gov.'s Adv. Bd. Indsl. Devel., 1970-84. Recipient Nat. Brotherhood award Richmond chpt. NCCJ, 1973. Roman Catholic. Home: Richmond Va. Died Aug. 14, 1984.

MCHAFFIE, ROBERT ERNEST, moving company executive; b. Putnam County, Ind., Jan. 8, 1917; s. Robert M. and Amy (Ruark) McH.; m. Mary Florence Miller, Aug. 1, 1945; children: Joan McHaffie Jackson, Thomas Robert, Amy Lee. JD, Ind. U., 1939. Bar: Ind. 1939. Chief clk. Ind. Boys Sch., 1935-38; assoc. atty. Chadd & McHaffie, Danville, Ind., 1939-40; various positions Mayflower Corp., Carmel, Ind., 1940-82, exec. v.p., sec., gen. counsel, 1977-79, sr. exec., v.p., gen. counsel, 1979-82. Served with AUS, 1942-45. Decorated Bronze Star. Mem. ABA, Ind. State Bar Assn., Indpls. Bar Assn., Am. Judicature Soc., Assn. ICC Practitioners, Sigma Delta Kappa, Masons, Kiwanis, Indpls. Athletic Club. Home: Indianapolis Ind. Deceased.

MCHOSE, ALLEN IRVINE, educator, musician; b. Lancaster, Pa., May 14, 1902; s. Clarence N. and A. Margaretta (Vollmer) McH.; m. Helen Elizabeth Kelley, Apr. 8, 1928 (dec. Dec. 1964); children: David I., Allen J.; m. Dorothy Hutcheon, June 11, 1966. B.S., Franklin and Marshall Coll., 1923, D.F.A., 1948; B.Mus., U. Rochester, 1927, Mus.M., 1929; Mus.D., Okla. City U., 1945. Instr. sci., math. Moravian Prep. Sch., Bethlehem, Pa., 1923-25; faculty Eastman Sch. Music, U. Rochester, N.Y., 1930-67; chmn. theory dept. Eastman Sch. Music, U. Rochester, 1931-62, dir. summer session, 1954-67, asso. dir. sch., 1962-67; music cons., lectr., author; Rose Morgan vis. prof. U. Kans., 1969-70; Organist, dir. music Brick Presbyn. Ch., Rochester, 1932-67. Author: (with Ruth N. Tibbs) Sight Singing Manual, 1944, (with Donald F. White) Keyboard and Dictation Manual, 1949, Contrapuntal Harmonic Technique of the 18th Century, 1947, Teachers Dictation Manual, 1948, Basic Principles of the Technique of 18th and 19th Century Composition, 1951, Musical Styles 1850-1920; Composer: Sonata for Violin and Piano, 1929, Concerto for Oboe and Orchestra, 1932, others. Trustee Hochstein Meml. Music Settlement Sch., Rochester, N.Y., 1970-78, trustee emeritus, 1978-86; trustee, v.p. Music Tchrs. Nat. Assn. Scholarship Found., 1971-81, pres., chmn. bd. trustees, 1981-86. Mem. Music Library Assn., Music Tchrs. Nat. Assn. (treas. 1959-79), Nat., Nat. Cath. music educators confs., Am. Mus. Soc., Phi Mu Alpha, Chi Phi. Clubs: University (Rochester); Cliff Dwellers (Chgo.). Lodge: Rotary. Home: Naples N.Y. Died Sept. 14, 1986.

MCILNAY, OLIN FOSTER, air force medical officer; b. Polo, Ill., Feb. 28, 1902; s. John William and Amy Viola (Slater) McI.; m. Mary Alba Guyer, June 9, 1927; 1 child, Martha D. BS, Cornell U., 1924; MD, U.

Iowa, 1928; grad. as flight surgeon, U.S. Air Corps Sch. of Aviation Medicine, 1935. Diplomate Am. Bd. Preventive Medicine. Commd. med. officer USAF, 1928, advanced through grades to Maj. Gen., 1956; active duty Letterman Gen. Hosp., San Francisco, 1928; commd. Regular Service 1929, assigned duty Army Air Corps, 1934; staff surgeon 8th Fighter Command and 2d Air Div., 1940-45; staff surgeon, then surgeon Hdqrs. USAF Tng. Command, 1945-52; dir. plans and hospitalization Office of Surgeon Gen. USAF, 1952-57; dep. surgeon gen. USAF, from 1957. Decorated Legion of Merit, Bronze Star; Croix de Guerre with palm. Mem. Aero Med. Assn., Assn. Mil. Surgeons. Home: Polo Ill. Died July 2, 1985.

MC ILWAINE, WILLIAM ANDREW, clergyman; b. Kochi, Japan, Apr. 24, 1893; s. William Beauregard and Harriet Meade (Jones) McI.; m. Georgia Elisabeth Gifford, May 19, 1919 (dec. 1929); m. Bess Martin Blakeney, Aug. 27, 1931 (dec. 1935); m. Frances Aurine Wilkins, Dec. 28, 1939 (dec. 1982); 1 child, Frances Ellen. AB, Davidson Coll., 1915, DD, 1940; BD, Union Theol. Sem., Va., 1919. Ordained to ministry Presbyn. Ch. in U.S., 1919. Tchr. English Mt. Hermon Sch., 1915-17; missionary to Japan 1919-63; prof. O.T. studies Cen. Theol. Sem., 1937-41; prof. O.T. Kobe Reformed Theol. Sem., 1947-63; moderator Gen. Assembly Presbyn. Ch. in Am., 1976; spl. lectr. Westminster Theol. Sem., 1964-65; guest prof. Ref. Theol. Sem., 1966-67, ministerial adv., 1966-85. Trustee Westminister Theol. Sem., 1945-71, Kinjo Gakuin U., 1947-63; chmn. bd. trustees Shikoku Christian Coll., 1951-58, 60-63; chmn. Japan Protestant Centennial, 1959, Japan Protestant Conf., 1960-63; dir. Japan Intervarsity Christian Fellowship, 1960-61. Chaplain AUS, 1943-46. Home: Pensacola Fla. Died Nov. 30, 1985; buried Bayview Cemetery, Pensacola, Fla.

MCINNES, S. RODERICK, brewery and oil exploration company executive; b. Toronto, Aug. 1, 1933; m. Gladys Macintyre, July 9, 1963; 1 child, Roderick. Student, Humberside Collegiate Inst., Toronto. Former chartered acct. Touche Ross; brand and mktg. services mgr., mktg. services mgr., mgr. methods and procedures, comptroller Carling Breweries Ltd., 1960-65; products mgr., asst. products mgr. Gen. Foods Ltd., 1966-68; mktg. mgr. Salada Foods Ltd., 1968; v.p., gen. mgr. Can. Food Products Ltd., 1969-72; former exec. v.p., dir. fin., then pres., chief exec. officer Conaught Labs. Ltd., 1972-76; pres., chief exec. officer Carling O'Keefe Breweries of Can. Ltd., 1976-79; chmn., pres., chief exec. officer Carling O'Keefe Ltd., Toronto, 1984-87. Bd. dirs. North York Gen. Hosp.; bd. govs. Olympic Trust of Can., Variety Village Sport Tng. and Fitness Ctr. Clubs: Donalda, York. Died Feb. 5, 1988.

MCINNIS, EDWIN, lawyer; b. Oakland, Calif., May 19, 1902; s. Michael A. and Margaret Anne (Mulgrew) McI.; m. Mary Frances Costello, Sept. 9, 1928; children—Mary F. McInnis Glass (dec.), Margaret A. McInnis Verge, Jeanne McInnis Flynn, George E., E. Catherine McInnis Yonke, Therese McInnis Pedemonte. A.B., St. Marys Coll., Oakland, 1924; LL.B., Oakland Coll. Law, 1934. Bar: Calif. bar 1936. Instr. St. Marys Coll., 1924-25; v.p. Bank of Am. N.T. and S.A., 1925-67; practicing atty. O'Gara & McGuire, 1967-87; sr. trust officer Calif. 1st Bank (formerly The Bank of Tokyo of Calif.), San Francisco, 1967-76. Author: legal and trust lit. including Trust Functions and Services, 1971. Ret. counsel Hanna Boys Center; past pres. bd. regents St. Marys Coll., past pres. internat. alumni. Decorated Knights of Malta. Mem. San Francisco Estate Planning Council (founding mem.), Calif. Bar Assn. Club: K.C. Home: Oakland Calif. Died Mar. 27, 1987.

MC KEE, JOSEPH VINCENT, JR., appliance company executive; b. N.Y.C., Jan. 1, 1921; s. Joseph Vincent and Cornelia (Kraft) McK.; m. Phyllis Feldmann, May 1, 1948; children—Charlotte Cornelia McKee Worcester, Catherine Barbara McKee Donovan, Joseph Vincent III, Charles Russell. Grad., Phillips Exeter Acad., 1938; A.B., Princeton U., 1942; LL.B., Columbia U., 1948. With N.Y. Supreme Ct., 1948-49, Henney Motor Co., Inc., N.Y.C., 1949-52; v.p. Oneida Products Corp., N.Y.C., 1952-53; v.p., treas., dir. Nat. Union Electric Corp., 1953-66, exec. v.p., dir., 1966-74, chmn. bd., pres., 1974-77, chmn., 1977-82; cons. AB Electro lux, Stockholm, 1983-85; dir. Lone Star Industries, Inc. Bd. dirs. Greenwich (Conn.) Boys' Club Assn.; trustee Woods Hole Oceanographic Inst. Served with F.A. AUS, 1942-45. Decorated Air medal, Bronze Star. Roman Catholic. Clubs: Indian Harbor Yacht (Greenwich), N.Y. Yacht (N.Y.C.), Clove Valley Rod and Gun (Lagrangeville, N.Y.), Lyford Cay (Bahamas). Died Sept. 24, 1988.

MCKEE, WILLIAM F., business executive, former air force officer; b. Va., Oct. 17, 1906; m. Gertrude S. McKee; children—Christopher Fulton, William St. John. B.S., U.S. Mil. Acad., 1929; grad., Coast Arty. Sch., 1936. Commd. 2d lt. U.S. Army, advanced through grades to gen., 1961; apptd. asst. vice chief of staff USAF, 1947; vice comdr. air material command Wright Patterson AFB, Ohio, 1953; comdr. (Air Force Logistics Command), 1961-62; vice chief of staff USAF, 1962-64; asst. adminstr. for mgmt. devel. NASA, 1964-65; adminstr. FAA, 1965-68; pres. Schriever-McKee Assos., Arlington, Va., 1968-70, Shriever & Mckee, Inc., Washington, 1971-87. Decorated D.S.M. with 2 oak leaf clusters. Home: Washington D.C. Died Feb. 28, 1987.

MCKEEFERY, WILLIAM J., philosophy educator; b. Phila., Dec. 29, 1918; s. William J. and Anna (Reichelt) McK.; m. Ruth Franklin, June 6, 1948; children—Virginia Lou, Carol Ann, William James, III. B.S., U. Pa., 1941; M.Div., Princeton U., 1945; Ph.D., Columbia U., 1949. Instr. engring. Princeton U., 1943-45; prof. philosophy Alma Coll., Mich., 1948-50; dean Alma Coll., 1950-58; v.p. Washburn U., Topeka, 1958-61; dean acad. affairs So. Ill. U., Carbondale, 1961-69; exec. v.p. Va. Poly. Inst., Blacksburg, 1969-73; pres. William Paterson Coll. of N.J., Wayne, 1973-76, prof. philosophy, 1973-87, chmn. dept., 1973-86; vis. prof. higher edn. Rutgers U., New Brunswick, N.J., 1976-77; dir. Nat. Study Interinstnl. Cooperation, Am. Assn. State Colls. and Univs., Washington, 1977-79; coordinator liberal arts study North Central Assn. Colls., 1951-58. Author: Parameters of Learning-Perspectives in Higher Education Today, 1970; contbr. articles to profl. publs. Moderator Presbytery of Saginaw, Presbyn. Ch. U.S.A., 1955-56. Served as chaplain USNR, 1945-46. Mem. Mich. Coll. Assn. (pres. 1955-57), Kappa Delta Pi, Tau Beta Pi. Club: Rotarian. Home: Cranbury N.J. Died July 30, 1987.

MCKEEN, HENRY EUGENE, business executive; b. Woodstock, N.B., Can., 1890. Grad., U. N.B., 1910. Past sr. v.p. Canron Ltd., Montreal, Que., Can., later hon dir. †

MCKELVEY, VINCENT ELLIS, geologist; b. Huntingdon, Pa., Apr. 6, 1916; s. Ellis Elmer and Eva Rupert (Faus) McK.; m. Genevieve Patricia Bowman, June 5, 1937; 1 son, Gregory Ellis. B.A. with honors, Syracuse U., 1937, D.Sc., 1975; M.A., U. Wis., 1939, Ph.D., 1947; D.Sc., S.D. Sch. Mines and Tech., 1976. Jr. geologist Soil Conservation Service, part time, 1938-40; asst. geologist Wis. Geol. and Natural History Survey, part time, 1939-40; geologist U.S. Geol. Survey, 1941-87; chief radioactive minerals investigations U.S. Geol. Survey, Washington, 1950-53; asst. chief geologist for econ. and fgn. geology U.S. Geol. Survey, 1960-65, sr. research geologist, 1969-71, 78-87, chief geologist, 1971, dir., 1971-78; adj. prof. Fla. Inst. Tech., 1982-84; McKinstry Meml. lectr., 1971, J. Seward Johnson Meml. lectr., 1976, Donnel Foster Hewett Meml. lectr., 1976, Ga. U. Center Disting. speaker, 1982; U.S. adv. OECD energy com., 1965-67; U.S. rep. seabed com. UN, 1968-73; sr. sci. adv. U.S. del. UN Conf. Law of Sea, 1978-81; mem. bd. mineral resources NRC, 1980-83. Contbr. articles to profl. jours. Bd. dirs. Resources for the Future, 1978-86. Recipient Distinguished Service award Interior Dept., 1963; award for sustained excellence Nat. Civil Service League, 1972; Rockefeller Pub. Service award, 1973; Alexander Winchell Distinguished Alumnus award Syracuse U., 1976; Distinguished Service award N.W. Mining Assn., 1977; Distinguished Service award Rocky Mountain Assn. Geologists, 1977; Mt. McKelvey, Antarctica, named in his honor, 1977; Ann. V.E. McKelvey Forum named in his honor, 1985. Fellow AAAS, Geol. Soc. Am. (mem. council 1969-72), Am. Geophys. Union; mem. Am. Geol. Inst. (bd. dirs. 1968-70), Soc. Econ. Geologists (council 1967-70), Econ. Geol. Pub. Co. (dir.), Soc. Econ. Paleontologists and Mineralogists, Am. Inst. Mining Engrs. (Henry Krumb lectr. 1968), Am. Assn. Petroleum Geologists (Spl. award for meritorious service 1977, Human Needs medal 1978), Soc. Exploration Geophysicists (hon.), Marine Tech. Soc., Sigma Xi. Club: Cosmos (Washington). Home: Saint Cloud Fla. Died Jan. 23, 1987.

MCKEON, RICHARD PETER, humanities educator; b. Union Hill, N.J., Apr. 26, 1900; s. Peter Thomas and Mathilda (Hirschfeld) McK.; m. Clarice Muriel Thirer, July 10, 1930 (dec. May 1964); children: Peter (dec.), Nora, Michael; m. Zahava Karl, Mar. 11, 1979. AB, AM, Columbia U., 1920; postgrad., U. Paris and Ecole des Hautes Etudes, 1922-25; PhD, Columbia U., 1928; LittD, Jewish Theol. Sem. Am., 1942; Dr honoris causa, U. Aix, Marseilles, France, 1951. Instr. philosophy Columbia U., N.Y.C., 1925-29, asst. prof., 1929-35, instr. Greek and Latin, summer 1926; vis. prof. history U. Chgo., 1934-35, prof. Greek, 1935-47, prof. philosophy, 1937-47, dean div. humanities, 1935-47, Disting. Service prof. Greek, philosophy, 1947-85, William H. Colvin research prof., 1965-66, then Charles F. Grey Disting. Service prof. emeritus; pres. Internat. Inst. Philosophy, 1953-57; v.p. Internat. Fedn. Philos. Socs., 1953-85. Author: The Philosophy of Spinoza, 1928, Freedom and History, 1952, Thought, Action and Passion, 1954, (with R. K. Merton, W. Gellhorn) The Freedom to Read, 1957, (with Blanche B. Boyer) Peter Abailard SIC ET NON A Critical Edition, 1977; co-author several books; editor: Introduction to Aristotle, Selections from Medieval Philosophers; editor, translator books; contbr. articles to profl. jours. Mem. U.S. del. Gen Conf. UNESCO, Paris, 1946, Mexico City, 1947, Beruit, 1948; U.S. counselor UNESCO affairs Am. embassy, Paris, 1947. Apprentice seaman USN, 1918. Fellow Medieval Acad. Am., Am. Acad. Arts and Scis., AAAS; mem. Am Philos. Assn. (pres. 1952), Am. Philol. Assn., History Sci. Soc., Inst. Internat. de Philosophie Politique, Am. Coun. Learned Socs. (vice chmn. 1939), Quadrangle Club, Phi Beta Kappa, Kappa Alpl Home: Chicago Ill. Died Mar. 31, 1985; cremat

MCKHANN, CHARLES FREMONT, pediatrician Cin., Dec. 21, 1898; s. Charles Fremont and M (Grassel) McK.; m. Emily Priest, June 23, 1928 (1932); children: Charles Fremont, Guy Mead; m. Il Semenenko, Sept. 20, 1933 (dec. 1977); 1 son, Se Nicholas; m. Laura Dane, Apr. 9, 1979. AB, Miami Ohio, 1918; BS, U. Cin., 1920, AM, 1921, MD, 19 Diplomate Am. Bd. Pediatrics (pres. 1947-50). In Cin. Gen. Hosp., 1922-23; asst., instr. pedia Harvard U. Med. Sch., Cambridge, Mass., 1923-28; prof. pediatrics and communicable diseases Med. Sch. Pub. Health, 1928-36, assoc. prof., 1936-40; prof. pediatrics Peiking Union Med. Coll., China, 36; prof., chmn. dept. pediatrics and communicable eases U. Mich. Med. Sch., 1940-43; asst. to pres charge of research and devel. Parke, Davis & Co., 45; prof. pediatrics Western Reserve U. Sch. Medi 1945-50, Jefferson Med. Coll. Phila., 1952-56; dir. atrics Univ. Hosps., Cleve., 1945-50; chmn. exec. Chemway Corp., 1954-71, chmn., pres., 1963-64; chmn. Cleve. Health Coun., 1947-49. Mem. AMA, Pediatric Soc., Am. Soc. Clin. Investigation (emeri Am. Soc. for Pediatric Research (emeritus), Phi Kappa, Sigma Xi, Alpha Omega Alpha, Delta Om Republican. Clubs: University (N.Y.C.), Wi (Mass.). Home: Osterville Mass. Died June 25, buried Wianno, Mass.

MCKIBBIN, CLIFFORD WORDEN, savings and association executive; b. Lansing, Mich., Nov. 11, s. Joseph Taylor and Emma Augusta (Barnes) McK Ruth Mead, Jan. 4, 1913; children: Clifford Wo John Mead, Elsie Holmes. BS, Mich. Agrl. Coll., MF, 1916. With U.S. Forest Service, 1910-16; al sec. Mich. Agrl. Coll., 1917-20; with real estate br office, 1921-30; realtor and broker Lansing, Mich., 1930; dir. Capitol Savs. & Loan Assn., from 1941, from 1945, pres., 1962-69, chmn. bd., from 19 Trustee Lansing YWCA; pres. trustee John Elizabeth Whiteley Found. Mem. Lansing Bd. Rea (pres. 1930-31, bd. dirs. from 1964), Mich. Real E Assn. (pres. 1933), Soc. Real Estate Appraisers, Inst. Real Estate Brokers. Home: East Lansing Mic

MCKILLOP, ALAN DUGALD, language educ author; b. Lynn, Mass., May 24, 1892; s. D McKenzie and Katherine Jane (McKinnon) McK Lorel Pruitt, Aug. 27, 1921 (dec. Aug. 1966). Harvard U., 1913, AM, 1914, PhD, 1920. Instr glish U. Ill., 1917-18; instr. English Rice Inst., Hou 1920-24, asst. prof., 1924-30, prof., 1930-62, tr disting. prof., from 1962; vis. prof. English summe Chgo., 1925-62, Northwestern U., 1926, U. Tex., 31, 48, John Hopkins U., 1932, 40, U. Minn., 193 49, Harvard U., 1941, 52, Ind. U., 1947, U. Colo., Columbia U., 1961. Author: Samuel Richar Printer and Novelist, 1936, The Background of T son's Seasons, 1942, English Literature from Dryd Burns, 1948, The Background of Thomson's Lit 1951, The Early Masters of English Fiction, editor: (with L.I. Bredvold and Lois Whitney) Century Poetry and Prose, 1939, James Thomson ters and Documents, 1958, James Thomson: The of Indolence and Other Poems, 1961; also artic learned jours. Guggenheim Meml. fellow, Englan France, 1928. Fellow Newberry Library; mem. M Language Assn. Am. (editorial com. 1949-53), Cen. Modern Language Assn. (pres. 1950-51), Tex. Letters, Houston Philos. Soc., Philos. Soc. Tex. Beta Kappa. Home: Houston Tex. †

MCKINNEY, JAMES WILLIAM, brokerage com executive; b. Pitts., July 19, 1913; s. James Barcla Elizabeth (Ringl) McK.; m. Winifred Shaffer, Ja 1938; 1 son, James Barclay II. Student, U. Pitts., 35, NYU, 1947-51. Asst. in corp. research, credi investment mgmt. J.P. Morgan & Co., N.Y.C., 19 head portfolio div. Thomson & McKinnon, N. 1952-56; v.p., trust investment officer Palmer 1st Bank and Trust Co., Sarasota, Fla., 1956-68, U Bancshares Fla., 1968-71, Miami Beach (Fla.) 1st Bank, 1968-71, Pan Am Bank, Miami, 1971-77; trust officer Pan Am. Bank Sarasota (Fla.), 19 account exec. Dean Witter Reynolds Inc., 19 portfolio dir. Kashner Securities Corp., Sarasota, 85; mem. faculty Fla. Bankers Assn. Trust Sch. U 1959-74; instr. Sarasota County Adult Evening Program, 1962-64. Treas., bd. dirs. Sarasota C Heart Assn., Sarasota-Manatee Assn. Me Retarded Children; bd. dirs. Sarasota County ARC. Served with Amphibious Corps USNR, 19 PTO. Mem. Fla. Bankers Assn. (com. chmn.), M Shriners. Home: Sarasota Fla. Died Aug. 1, buried Sarasota Meml. Park.

MC KINNEY, STEWART B., congressman; b. Jan. 30, 1931; m. Lucie Cunningham; children: S B., Lucie, Jean, Libby McKinney Gaeta, John. Kent Sch., 1949; student, Princeton U., 1949-51; B Am. History, Yale U., 1958. Mem. Conn. Ho. of 1966-70, minority leader, 1969-70; mem. 92th Congresses from 4th Conn. dist., 1971-87. Bd Bridgeport (Conn.) Hosp., Bridgeport Child Gu Clinic, Rehab. Center of Ea. Fairfield County.

USAF, 1951-55. Mem. Fairfield C. of C. (past v.p.). Republican. Club: Rotary.

MCKINNON, GEORGE EDMUND, journalist; b. Providence, Apr. 16, 1921; s. George Linus and Ann Marie (Sheridan) McK. AB, Boston Coll., 1943. With Boston Globe, 1943-85, movie and theater critic, 1964-73, theater/arts columnist Marquee,, 1973-85. Roman Catholic. Home: Boston Mass. Died Nov. 19, 1985; interred St. Joseph's Cemetery, West Roxbury.

MCKNIGHT, LYNN B(OYD), industrial company executive; b. Mishawaka, Ind., Mar. 7, 1891; s. Robert S. and Ella S. (Boyd) McK.; m. Pauline Light, Oct. 8, 1918; children: Marilyn McKnight Crump, Patricia McKnight Steck. BS, Purdue U., 1915. Dist. sales mgr. Dodge Mfg. Corp., Mishawaka, 1920-27; managerial positions Chain Belt Co., 1927-48, v.p., dir., 1948-51, exec. v.p., 1951-53, pres., 1953-59, chmn. exec. com., from 1958; trustee Northwestern Mut. Life Ins. Co.; bd. dirs. Sterling, Inc., Heil Co., Safway Steel Products, Pelton Steel Casting Co., Interstate Drop Forge Co., George J. Meyer Mfg. Co. Mem. Milwaukee, University, Milwaukee Country clubs. Home: Milwaukee Wis.†

MCKNIGHT, TIMOTHY IRLE, lawyer; b. Oblong, Ill., June 10, 1891; s. William Edward and Lucy Emily (Wilkin) McK.; m. Lucile Britton, Dec. 25, 1912; children: Richard Morgan (dec. 1952), William Britton. AB, McKendree Coll., Lebanon, Ill., 1912, LLD, 1955; LLB, U. Illinois, 1915. Bar: Ill. 1915. Practiced in Carrollton, 1915-25, city atty., 1915-20; state's atty. Greene County, 1920-24; ptnr. Wheeler, Ochmke & McKnight, East St. Louis, Ill., 1925-27; mem. Sims, Welch, Godman & Stransky, Chgo., 1927-38; ptnr. Sims, Handy, McKnight & Carey, 1938-41, McKnight, McLaughlin & Dunn, 1942-56; pvt. practice, Chgo., from 1956. Trustee McKendree Coll. Fellow Am. Bar Found., Am. Coll. Trial Lawyers; mem. ABA (ho. of dels. 1952-54),Ill. State Bar Assn. (pres. 1953-54), Chgo. Bar Assn., Law Union League, Westmoreland Country Club, Evanston University Club, Phi Alpha Delta. Methodist. Home: Evanston Ill. †

MCLAREN, NORMAN, film producer; b. Stirling, Scotland, Apr. 11, 1914; emigrated to Can., 1941, naturalized, 1952; s. William and Jean (Smith) McL. Student, Glasgow Sch. Art, 1931-36; D.Litt., Glendon Coll. York U., 1972. With Gen. Post Office Film Unit, 1937-39, Nat Film Bd. of Can., 1941-84. Dir.: The Obedient Flame, Film Centre, London, 1939; producer: NBC TV movie Greeting Card, 1939; abstract color films, Guggenheim Mus. of Non-Objective Art, 1939-40; films C'est L'Aviron, 1945, Keep Your Mouth Shut, 1945, Hoppity-Pop, 1946, La Haut sur es Montagues, 1946, A Little Phantasy of a 19th Century Painting, 1946, Poulette Grise, 1947, Fiddle-de-Dee, 1947, Begone Dull Care, 1949, Around is Around, 1950-51, Now is the Time, 1951, Neighbors, 1952 (Oscar 1953); film Two Bagetelles, 1952, Blinkety-Blank, 1955, Rythmetic, 1956, Chairy Tale, 1957, Le Merle, 1958, Short and Suite, 1959, Lines Vertical, 1960, Lines Horizontal, 1961, Mosaic, 1965, Pas de Deux, 1968, Spheres, 1969, Synchromy, 1971, Ballet Adagio, 1972, Animated Motion Parts 1, 2 and 3, 1977, Animated Motion Parts 4 and 5, 1978, Narcissus, 1983, UNESCO, 1949,-50, 52-53. Decorated Order of Can., Ordre National du Que.; recipient Medal of Royal Can. Acad. Arts, 1963; recipient Molson prize, 1971. Home: Hudson Que., Canada Died Jan. 26, 1987.

MCLAUGHLIN, FRANCIS, psychoanalyst, psychiatrist; b. Syracuse, N.Y., Oct. 2, 1914; s. Thomas Flynn and Lillian (Baeder) McL.; m. Louise Polly Porter, Aug. 23, 1959; children: Thomas, Carol (Mrs. Stuart Miller). Student, Johns Hopkins U., 1932-35; MD, U. Md., 1939. Intern Univ. Hosp., Balt., 1939-41; staff psychiatrist Sheppard-Enoch Pratt Hosp., Balt., 1941-46; supr., tng. analyst, mem. faculty Inst. for Psychoanalysis, Balt. and Washington, 1946-86; mem. staff, faculty Johns Hopkins U. Med. Sch. and Hosp., 1962-86. Fellow Am. Psychiat. Assn.; mem. Md. Psychiat. Assn. (pres. 1967-68), Internat. Psychoanalytic Assn. (1977-81, treas. 1981-86), Am. Psychoanalytic Assn. (chmn. bd. profl. standards 1970-73, pres. 1975-76), AAAS, Royal Soc. Health (Eng.). Home: Baltimore Md. Died Feb. 17, 1986; cremated.

MCLENDON, GORDON BARTON, radio station executive; b. Paris, Tex., June 8, 1921; s. Baron Robert and Jeannette (Eyster) McL.; married; children: Jan, Bart, Kristen, Anna Gray. AB, Yale U., 1943; student, Harvard Law Sch., 1946. Owner radio sta. KNET, Palestine, Tex., 1946; pres., owner Liberty Broadcasting System, Dallas, 1948-52, Sta. KOST, L.A., Sta. KNUS, Dallas; ptnr. McLendon Co., McLendon Pacific Corp., Sunshine Broadcasting Corp., Coronado, McLendon Theatres; spl. communications adviser Peace Corps, 1964-65. Author: The Old Scotchman's Scrapbook, Style in Use of English, How to Communicate More Effectively, The Way to a More Colorful Vocabulary. Selected Outstanding Football Announcer, Sporting News, 1950; named One of 10 Outstanding Young Men, U.S. Jr. C. of C., 1951; recipient Betty award Assn. Broadcasting Execs. Tex., 1967, Radio's Man of Yr. award, Pulse. Mem. City Brook Hollow Golf, Dallas Country, Broadcast Pioneers, Variety Internat. (chief barker), Cipango clubs, Chi Psi. Methodist. Home: Dallas Tex. Died Sept. 14, 1986.

MCLENNAN, CHARLES EVART, obstetrician, gynecologist; b. Duluth, Minn., Dec. 26, 1909; s. Archibald James and Grace Jane (McLean) McL.; m. Margaret Jane Thomas, June 26, 1937; children: James Edward, Nancy Ann, Jane, Thomas. AB, U. Minn., 1930, AM, 1932, MD, 1934, PhD, 1942. Diplomate Am. Bd. Obstetrics and Gynecology (bd. dirs.). Teaching fellow in medicine U. Minn., Mpls., 1936-38, instr. obstetrics and gynecology, 1938-40; Commonwealth Fund fellow dept. medicine U. Va., 1940-41; asst. prof. U. Minn., 1941-43, assoc. prof., 1943-44; prof., head dept. obstetrics and gynecology U. Utah Sch. Medicine, 1944-47; prof., head dept. obstetrics and gynecology Stanford U., 1947-75, prof. emeritus, 1975-86; chief obstet. and gynecol. service Stanford Hosp., until 1975; gynec. cons. Menlo Med. Clinic, Menlo Park, Calif., 1975-86. Author: Synopsis of Obstetrics, 9th rev. edit., 1974. Mem. Am. Coll. Obstetricians and Gynecologists, AMA, Am. Gynecol. Soc. (pres. 1972-73), AAAS, Am. Fedn. Clin. Research, Calif. Med. Assn., San Francisco Gynecol. Soc. (past pres.), Pacific Coast Obstet. and Gynecol. Soc. (pres. 1972-73), Soc. Gynecologic Investigation (past pres.), Phi Beta Kappa, Sigma Xi, Alpha Omega Alpha, Theta Chi, Nu Sigma Nu. Home: Palo Alto Calif. Died Mar. 8, 1986.

MC LEOD, DANIEL ROGERS, state attorney general; b. Sumter, S.C., Oct. 6, 1913; s. D. Melvin and Bertie (Guyton) McL.; m. Ellen D. LaBorde, May 20, 1941 (dec.); children: Daniel R., Elizabeth Ann; m. Virginia B. Hart, July 29, 1962. Student, Wofford Coll., 1931-32, LL.D. (hon.), 1983; LL.B., U. S.C., 1948. Bar: S.C. bar 1948. Asst. atty. gen. S.C., 1950-58; atty. gen. 1958-83. Mem. ABA, S.C. Bar Assn. Methodist (ofcl. bd.). Home: Columbia S.C. Deceased; buried Greenlawn, Columbia.

MCLEOD, JAMES CURRIE, clergyman, educator; b. Buffalo; s. Dugald and Mary Holmes (Currie) McL.; m. Emily Louise Johnson, Aug. 24, 1929; children: Mary Louise (Mrs. James S. Aagaard), Adrienne (Mrs. Craig Heatley), James Currie. BS, Middlebury Coll., 1926, DD, 1950; BD, Yale U., 1929; DD, Alfred U., 1941. Ordained to ministry Presbyn. Ch., 1929. Univ. chaplin Alfred (N.Y.) U., 1929-40; minister to students Ohio State U., Columbus, 1940-43; univ. chaplin, prof. history and lit. of religion Northwestern U., Evanston, Ill., 1946-50, prof., 1950-71, prof. emeritus, from 1971, dean students, 1952-67; research fellow Yale Div. Sch., 1963-64; vis. scholar Colgate-Rochester Div. Sch., 1967-68; guest preacher Presbytery of Glasgow, Scotland, 1950, also at Syracuse, N.Y., Chgo., Rutgers, Lake Forest, Middlebury, Stanford, Howard, others. Author: (symposium) Fruits of Faith; contbr. articles to profl. jours. Pres., trustee Evanston Pub. Library; bd. dirs. Vis. Nurses Assn., Evanston. Served as lt. comdr., chaplain USNR, 1943-46. Mem. Nat. Acad. Religion, Nat. Assn. Student Personnel Adminstrs. (pres. 1963-64), Religious Edn. Assn. (v.p. 1963-64), Presbytery Chgo., Delta Upsilon (internat. pres. 1972-73), Rotary Club (past pres.), St. Andrew Soc. (pres. 1973-74), Yale Club Chgo. Republican. Home: Wilmette Ill. Deceased.

MCLEOD, WILLIAM NORMAN, business executive; b. Owen Sound, Ont., Can., July 17, 1889; s. Alexander G. and Alexina (Reid) McL.; m. Maude Reyes, Apr., 1924; children: Margery McLeod Campbell, Bruce, Ian. BA, Queens U., Kingston, Ont., Can., 1912; DLittS (hon.), Victoria U., Toronto, Can., 1954. With Algoma Steel Corp., 1912-18; with Moore Corp., Ltd. and predecessor firms, from 1918, v.p., 1928-46, pres., from 1946, also bd. dirs.; v.p., dir. Bank of Nova Scotia. Mem. United Ch. Can. (chmn. bd. fin. from 1946). Home: Toronto Ont., Canada. †

MCMAHON, BERNARD JOHN, otolaryngologist; b. St. Louis, May 10, 1892; s. John F. and Margaret E. (Murphy) McM.; m. Alice Maloy, Feb. 7, 1918; children: Peggy McMahon McDonald, Polly McMahon Dozier, Patsy McMahon Rowan, Pamela McMahon Reese, Peter. AB, St. Louis U., 1913, MD, 1917; MS, U. Pa., 1926. Diplomate Am. Bd. Otolaryngology (pres. 1959-61). Intern St. Louis City Hosp., 1917-18; pvt. practice St. Louis, from 1917; asst. prof. dept. otolaryngology Wash. U., St. Louis, 1924-43, assoc. prof., 1943; dir. dept. otolaryngology sch. medicine St. Louis U., from 1945, prof. clin. otolaryngology, from 1950. Contbr. articles to profl. jours. Mem. Am. Laryngol., Rhinol. and Otol. Soc., Am. Otol. Soc. (v.p. 1946-47, pres. 1947-48, mem. coun. 1947-51), Am. Laryngol. Assn. (pres. 1956, mem. coun. 1956-60), Am. Acad. Ophthalmology and Otolaryngology, AMA, University Club (St. Louis), Sigma Xi, Alpha Omega Alpha. Home: Ladue Mo. †

MCMAHON, FRANCIS ELMER, writer, philosophy educator; b. Chgo., June 5, 1906; s. John Joseph and Anna (Purtell) McM.; m. Sarah Elizabeth McAninch, Nov. 27, 1948. Student, Loyola U., Chgo., 1923-24; PhB, De Paul U., 1927; MA, Cath. U. Am., 1929, PhD, 1931; postgrad., Louvain U., Belgium, 1931-32, Munich U., 1932-33. Instr. U. Notre Dame, 1933-36, asst. prof., 1936-39, assoc. prof. philosophy, 1939-43; assoc. prof. philosophy U. Chgo., 1944-46; columnist N.Y. Post, 1944-46, fgn. corr. in Spain and Latin Am., 1946-48; lectr. in philosophy Sheil Inst., Chgo.; prof. Roosevelt U., Chgo., 1961-73, prof. emeritus, 1973-87. Author: The Humanism of Irving Babbitt, A Catholic Looks at the World; contbr. articles to periodicals. Ams. for Dem. Action rep. to UN, 1950. Mem. Cath. Assn. for Internat. Peace (past pres.), Am. Cath. (past pres.), Am. Philos. Assn., Fight for Freedom (past Ind. chmn.), Am. Maritain Assn., KC. Home: Chicago Ill. Died Sept. 11, 1987; buried All Saints Cemetery, Des Plaines, Ill.

MCMAHON, FRANK MURRAY PATRICK, oil executive; b. Moyie, B.C., Can., Oct. 2, 1902; s. Francis Joseph and Stella Maud (Soper) McM.; m. Betty Betz; children: Francine Patricia, William George, Marion B., Bettina L. Student, Gonzaga U., Whitworth Coll. Chmn. bd. emeritus Westcoast Transmission Co. Ltd.; bd. dirs. Royal Bank Can. Clubs: Vancouver, Shaughnessy Golf and Country (Vancouver), Recess, Wall Street, Blind Brook Golf and Country (N.Y.C.), Bath and Tennis, Everglades, Seminole (Palm Beach). Home: Paget Bermuda. Died May 21, 1986; buried St. Paul's Epsicopal Ch., Paget, Bermuda.

MCMAHON, GERALD J., lawyer; b. N.Y.C., Dec. 24, 1907; s. Jeremiah M. and Delia B. (Clifford) McM.; m. Jane Morley Williams, Nov. 27, 1943; children: Kevin C., Richard T., Jane Scott, Thomas Morley. AB, CCNY, 1929; LLB, Columbia U., 1932. Bar: N.Y. 1933. Assoc. Peaslee & Brigham, N.Y.C., 1932-36; ptnr. Peaslee, Albrecht & McMahon, N.Y.C., 1963-73; assoc. counsel for Am. claimants against Germany in sabotage cases, 1933-39; asst. sec. gen. Internat. Bar Assn., 1947-53, acting sec. gen., 1953-56, sec. gen., 1956-76; bd. dirs. Can-Car Inc., Agy. Can. Car & Foundry Co. Ltd., Corinth Machinery Co., Tree Farmer Equipment Inc., Chip-n-Saw Inc., Dosco Corp. Author: Restraints of Trade at Common Law, 1932, International Associations in United States Law, 1956. Served as lt. col., staff judge adv. 9th Armored Div., AUS, 1943-46. Decorated Bronze Star. Fellow Am. Bar Found.; mem. Legal Aid Soc., Internat. Law Assn., Am.Judicature Soc., Assn. Bar City N.Y., ABA, Internat. Bar Assn., Inter-Am. Bar Assn., N.Y. Bar Assn., Am. Soc. Internat. Law, Nat. Legal Aid Assn., Selden Soc. Clubs: Assn. Ex-Mems. Squadron A, Town, Scarsdale Golf. Home: Scarsdale N.Y. Died July 25, 1984.

MCMAHON, JOSEPH HENRY, French language educator; b. N.Y.C., Oct. 21, 1930; s. Thomas A. and Catharine Loretto (Freeman) McM. B.A., Manhattan Coll., 1952; M.A., Stanford U., 1959, Ph.D., 1960; M.A. ad eundem gradum, Wesleyan U., 1973. From instr. to assoc. prof. Yale U., New Haven, 1960-68; dean Pierson Coll., Yale U., New Haven, 1963-66; editor Yale French Studies Yale U., New Haven, 1963-68; assoc. prof. Wesleyan U., Middletown, Conn., 1968-73, prof., 1973-82, Hollis prof.French, 1982-87, dean of coll., 1968-69. Author: (lit. criticism) Imagination of Jean Genet, 1963, Humans Being: The World of Jean-Paul Sartre, 1971; asst. editor: French Rev., 1977; contbr. articles to profl. jours. Mem. scholarship com. Heublein Found., Farmington, Conn., 1968-85. Served with U.S. Army, 1955-57. Fulbright fellow, 1952; Morse fellow, 1966; Guggenheim fellow, 1972. Mem. AAUP, Conn. Acad. Arts and Sci., Am. Assn. Tchrs. French. Democrat. Club: Twilight Park. Home: Middletown Conn. Died Nov. 12, 1987.

MCMASTER, ROBERT CHARLES, engineering educator; b. Wilkinsburg, Pa., May 13, 1913; s. Charles Royal and Pearl (Beaver) McM.; m. Laura Elizabeth Gerould, Sept. 7, 1937; children: Leonard Royal, James Albert, Lois McMaster Bujold. B.E.E., Carnegie Inst. Tech., 1936; M.S., Calif. Inst. Tech., 1938, Ph.D., 1944. Supr. dept. elec. engring. Battelle Meml. Inst., Columbus, Ohio, 1945-54; Regents prof. welding engring, elec. engring. and research supr. Engring. Experiment Sta. and Research Found., Ohio State U., Columbus, 1955-77; prof. emeritus Engring. Experiment Sta. and Research Found., Ohio State U., 1977-86; dir. F.W. Bell, Inc., 1965-69; cons. industry. Editor: Nondestructive Testing Handbook, 2 vols., 1959, 2d edit., 1970; contbr. articles to profl. jours. Recipient Nat. Reliability award, 1966. Fellow Am. Soc. Nondestructive Testing (Coolidge award 1957, also De Forest award, Gold medal 1977, delivered Mehl hon. lectr. 1950, life mem.; nat. pres. 1952-53); mem. Am. Welding Soc. (life; Adams lectr. 1965), ASTM (Marburg lectr. 1952), Nat. Acad. Engring., IEEE (life), Am. Soc. Metals (life). Home: Delaware Ohio Died July 7, 1986.

MC MILLAN, KENNETH, actor; b. Bklyn., July 2, 1932; m. Kathryn McDonald; 1 child, Alison. Mem. resident acting co., Studio Arena Theatre, Buffalo and Milw. Repertory Theatre; Broadway debut in Borstal Boy, 1970; also on Broadway in American Buffalo, Streamers; appeared off-Broadway in Little Mary Sunshine, Moonchildren, Weekends Like Other People (Obie award 1982), various roles for N.Y. Shakespeare Festival, Central Park including Falstaff in Henry IV; films include The Taking of Pelham, 1,2,3, 1974, Serpico, 1974, The Stepford Wives, 1975, Oliver's Story, 1978, Bloodbrothers, 1979, Chilly Scenes of Winter, 1979, Hide in Plain Sight, 1980, Little Miss Marker, 1980, Carny, 1980, Borderline, 1980, True Confessions, 1981, Heartbeeps, 1981, Ragtime, 1981, Whose Life is it Anyway?, 1981, Eyewitness, 1981, Partners, 1982, Blue

Skies Again, 1983, Protocol, 1984, Dune, 1984, Reckless, 1984, The Pope of Greenwich Village, 1984, Malone, 1986, Runaway Train, Armed and Dangerous, The Killing Hour, Three Fugitives, 1989; appeared on TV in Rhoda, Maggie Briggs, 1983, Family Honor, 1985; appeared in TV movies Salem's Lot, A Death in Caanan, King; nat. tour with The Last of the Red Hot Lovers; appeared at Lincoln Ctr. in Danger: Memory, Streamers, La Jolla, The Matchmaker; tchr. acting Debbie Reynolds Studio, Burbank, Calif. Home: Santa Monica Calif. Died Jan. 8, 1989.

MCMULLIN, THOMAS EDISON, education and psychology educator; b. nr. Sebree, Ky., May 12, 1904; s. Martin Luther and Nannie Belle (Denton) McM.; m. Mila Verne Drake, June 7, 1928; children: Carolyn Drake, James Martin, Robert Ogden, Nancy Drake. AA, Morton-Elliott Jr. Coll., 1924; AB, Ky. Wesleyan Coll., 1926; AM, Columbia U., 1929; PhD, U. Ky., 1941. From instr. to prof. edn. and psychology Ky. Wesleyan Coll., 1926-37, dean of men, 1932-36; asst. prof. edn. U. Pa., Phila., 1937-48, assoc. prof., 1948-54, prof., 1954-63, vice dean sch. edn., 1948-63, sec. personnel com., 1938-48; vis. lectr. edn. Dropsie Coll., from 1946; vis. lectr. ednl. psychology Bryn Mawr Coll., 1952-53; Fulbright lectr. edn. Am. U., Cairo, 1951-52; acting exec. sec., mem. commn. secondary sch. Middle Atlantic States Assn. Colls. and Secondary Schs., 1943-45; cons. summer workshops for tchrs. Mem. NEA, Pa. State Edn. Assn., Phi Delta Kappa, Kappa Phi Kappa, Pi Kappa Delta, Alpha Phi Omega. Died Apr. 30, 1986.

MC MURRAY, PAUL RAY, nuclear company executive; b. Emporia, Kans., July 23, 1923; s. Guy Ray and Clara Esther (Simcox) McM.; m. Betty Churchill, June 7, 1946; children: Philip Ray, David Ruel, Daniel Paul, Mary Ann, James Emmett, Julie Diane. B.S. in Engring, U.S. Naval Acad., 1946. Various supervisory and managerial positions in nuclear ops. Gen. Electric Co., Richland, Wash., 1947-58; mgr. Purex Chem. Separations Plant, 1958-63; corp. mgmt. devel. cons. Purex Chem. Separations Plant, W. Lynn, Mass., 1963-66; bus. sect. mgr. Purex Chem. Separations Plant, 1966-68; mgr. mfg. Aerospace Instruments, Wilmington, Mass., 1968-70; v.p., gen. mgr. fuel reprocessing dept. Exxon Nuclear Co., Inc., Bellevue, Wash., 1970-77; dir. Exxon Nuclear Co., Inc., 1977-80, exec. in charge mktg. and uranium ops., 1978-80, pres., chief exec. officer, chmn. bd. dirs., from 1981. Pres. Tri-City YMCA, Richland, 1956-57; v.p. Pacific N.W. Area Council YMCA, Seattle, 1960-62; chmn. Richland Jr. Achievement, 1954-56. Served with USN, 1943-47. Mem. Atomic Indsl. Forum (dir.), Am. Nuclear Soc. Methodist. Home: Kirkland Wash. Died May 2, 1986, buried Kirkland Cemetery.

MC MURRY, ROBERT NOLEMAN, management consultant; b. Chgo., Dec. 19, 1901; s. Oscar Lincoln and Sadie (Adelaide) McM.; m. Doris Baird, Oct. 3, 1936 (dec. Oct. 1965); children: Michael Baird, Sara Lou; m. Katherine Miller, Apr. 29, 1966. Ph.B., U. Chgo., 1925, M.S. in Psychology, 1932; Ph.D. (fellow Inst. Internat. Edn.), U. Vienna, 1934. Diplomate: Am. Bd. Examiners Profl. Psychology. With Fed. Electric Co., Chgo., 1925-27, Yellow Cab Co., 1927-28, Transit Mixers, Inc., Chgo., 1928-31; charge Chgo. office Psychol. Corp., 1935-43; cons. service personnel, indsl. relations, market research Robert N. McMurry & Co., Chgo., 1943-53, McMurry, Hamstra & Co., Chgo.; (name changed to McMurry Co., Oct. 1958), from 1943; chmn. John Wareham Internat., N.Y.C., 1978. Author: Handling Personality Adjustment in Industry, 1944, Tested Techniques of Personnel Selection, 1955, McMurry's Management Clinic, 1960, How to Recruit, Select and Place Salesmen, 1964, How to Build a Dynamic Sales Organization, 1968, 101 Business Problems and their Solutions, 1973, The Maverick Executive, 1974. Fellow Am. Psychol. Assn.; mem. Indsl. Relations Research Assn., Am. Mgmt. Assn., Am. Statis. Assn., Chgo. Psychoanalytic Assn., Am. Marketing Assn., Inst. Mgmt. Scis. Home: Chicago Ill. Died Mar. 219, 1985.

MCMURTRY, ROBERT GERALD, author, research historian; b. Elizabethtown, Ky., Feb. 17, 1906; s. Robert Terry and Nellie (Bridwell) M.; m. Florence Louise Koberly, Dec. 22, 1934; children: Joyce Ellen, Stephen Terry, Susan Bridwell, Linda Hoke, Jan Leslie. AB, Centre Coll., 1929, LittD, 1953; LLD, Iowa Wesleyan Coll., 1946; DHL, Lincoln (Ill.) Coll., 1962. Librarian, mem. rsch. staff Lincoln Nat. Life Found. sponsored by Lincoln Nat. Life Ins. Co., Ft. Wayne, Ind., 1931-35; dir. dept. Lincolniana, asst. prof. Am. history, adminstrv. sec. Lincoln Meml. U., Harrogate, Tenn., 1937-56; dir. Lincoln Nat. Life Found., Ft. Wayne, 1956-73; lectr. Internat. Ednl. Exchange Svc., State Dept., 1959. Lincoln historian; author over 25 books, more than 200 articles, brochures relating to Lincoln; editor The Lincoln Herald, 1947-56, editor-in-chief, from 1974; editor Lincoln Lore, 1956-73. Mem. Lincoln Meml. Hwy Commn. Ky., 1935; Ind. mem. Nat. Lincoln Sesquicentennial Commn., 1957. Mem. Soc. SAR, Filson Club (hist.), Civil War Round Table N.Y., Lincoln Fellowship So. Calif. (hon.), Phi Delta Theta, Kappa Phi Kappa. Presbyterian. Home: Fort Wayne Ind. Died Oct. 29, 1988; buried Lindenwood Cemetery, Ft. Wayne, Ind.

MCNAIR, MALCOM PERRINE, retailing educator; b. Dansville, N.Y., Oct. 6, 1894; s. Samuel Edwin and Harriet (Perrine) McN.; m. Mary Lowe Hemenway, June 25, 1918; children: Malcolm Perrine, Robert Edwin, John Lowe (dec.). AB, Harvard U., 1916, AM, 1920; LLD, Northwestern U., 1962. Asst. English and govt. Harvard U., Cambridge, Mass., 1917-20; instr. Harvard U. Grad. Sch. Bus. Adminstrn., 1920-24, asst. prof. mktg., 1924-27, assoc. prof., 1927-31, prof., 1931-50, Lincoln Filene prof. retailing, 1950-61, Lincoln Filene prof. retailing emeritus, 1961-85; asst. dir. Harvard U. Bur. Bus. Research, mng. dir., 1929-33; dir. Div. Research, 1933-36; lectr. London Sch. Econs., 1931; chmn. bd. Allerton, Berman & Dean; dir. emeritus Allied Stores Corp.; bd. dirs., trustee John Wanamaker, Phila.; hon. dir. Cambridge Trust. Author: (with others) Problems in Marketing, 1957, (with Anita Hersum, Elizabeth Burnham) Cases in Retail Management, 1957, (with Eleanor G. May) The American Department Store 1920-60, 1963, (with William Applebaum, Walter Salmon) Cases in Food Distribution, 1964, (with E.A. Helfert, E.G. May) Controllership in Department Stores, 1965; editor: The Case Method at the Harvard Business School, 1954. Mem. Am. Acad. Arts and Scis., Am. Mktg. Assn., Phi Beta Kappa, Sigma Alpha Epsilon. Unitarian. Home: Madison N.H. Died Sept. 9, 1985.

MCNAIR, RONALD ERWIN, astronaut, physicist; b. Lake City, S.C., Oct. 21, 1950; s. Carl Columbus and Pearl (Montgomery) McN.; m. Cheryl Moore, June 27, 1976; children: Reginald Ervin, Joy Cheray. BS in Physics magna cum laude, N.C. A&T State U., 1971, LLD (hon.), 1978; PhD in Physics, MIT, 1976; ScD (hon.), Morris Coll., Sumter, S.C., 1980, U. S.C., 1984. Staff physicist Hughes Research Labs., Malibu, Calif., 1976-78; astronaut NASA, Houston, 1978-86; lectr. physics Tex. So. U., Houston, 1983-86. Contbr. articles to profl. jours. Trustee N.C. Sch. Sci. and Math., Durham, 1981-86; mem. vis. com. MIT, 1984-86. Presdl. scholar, 1967-71; Ford Found. fellow, 1971-74; Nat. Fellowship Fund fellow, 1974-75; NATO fellow, 1975; named Omega Psi Phi Scholar of Yr., 1975, Disting. Nat. Scientist, Nat. Soc. Black Profl. Engrs., 1979; recipient commendation Los Angeles Pub. Sch. System, 1979; Friend of Freedom award, 1981, others. Mem. AAAS, Am. Optical Soc., Am. Phys. Soc. (com. minorities in physics 1980—), Omega Psi Phi. African Methodist Episcopal-Baptist. Died aboard Challenger Jan. 26, 1986.

MC NAMARA, PAUL JAMES, hotel executive; b. Elmira, N.Y., July 15, 1912; s. James P. and Harriet (Lynch) McN.; m. Betty Waters, Jan. 11, 1947; children—Susan, Joan, Paul James, William Burke. B.S., Cornell U., 1935. With Castleton Hotel, New Castle, Pa., 1935-38, Van Curier Hotel, Schenectady, 1938-40, Roosevelt Hotel, Pitts., 1940-42; gen. mgr. Warwick Hotel, Phila., 1950-62; pres. Independence Motor Inn, Prussia Motor Inn Corp., Kulpesville Motor Inn Corp. Bd. dirs. Eagleville Hosp., United Way, Nat. Council Alcoholism. Served as maj. AUS, World War II. Mem. Phila. C. of C. (past dir.), Am. Hotel Assn., Pa. Hotel Assn. (sec.), Phila. Hotel Assn., Friendly Sons St. Patrick, Phi Delta Theta. Clubs: Cornell, Racquet, Phila. Country (Phila.); Seaview Country (Absecon, N.J.); Quail Ridge Golf and Tennis (Delray Beach, Fla.); Merion Cricket (Haverford, Pa.). Home: Haverford Pa. Died Nov. 26, 1986.

MCNAMEE, FRANK A., lawyer; b. Albany, N.Y., Dec. 17, 1892; s. Frank A. and Mary (Prior) McN.; m. Margaret Walker Stuart, July 1, 1930 (dec. Jan. 28, 1936); m. Ellen Parker, May 10, 1941. AB, Williams Coll., 1915; student, Harvard, 1915-17, 1919-20. Bar: N.Y. 1921. Ptnr. Whalen, Murphy, McNamee & Creble, 1923, Whalen, McNAmee, Creble & Nichols, Albany, N.Y., from 1931, McNamee, Nichols, Lochner & Titus, from 1970; bd. dirs. State Bank of Albany, also chmn. exec. com., from 1951; adv. dir. Albany Internat. Corp., from 1969; cons. Dept. Def., 1947-48. Mem. Civil Service Commn., Albany, 1921-30; regional dir. 2d Region Office Civilian Def., 1943-44; dep. dir. Office Civil Def., 1944-45; mem. N.Y. State Def. Coun., from 1950; dir. U.S. Strategic Bombing Survey; trustee Albany Acad., Trinity Instn., Albany Med. Coll., v.p., Legal Aid Soc., v.p.; pres. Med. Ctr. Found., Inc., 1958-68; lay dep., gen. conv. Albany Diocese, Protestant Episcopal Ch., 1937, 40, 52, mem. standing com., chancellor, 1950-64, chancellor emeritus, from 1964. Capt., F.A., U.S. Army, World War I; col. F.A., U.S. Army. World War II; col. Arty. USAR. Decorated D.S.C., Silver Star, Legion of Merit with oak leaf cluster. Mem. Albany County (pres. 1938-39), N.Y. State, Am. bar assns., Ft. Orange Club (pres. 1932-34), Schuyler Meadows Club, Iroquois Club, Army and Navy Club, Alpha Delta Phi. Home: Loudonville N.Y.†

MC NICHOLS, RAY, federal judge; b. Bonners Ferry, Idaho, June 16, 1914; s. Michael T. and Kathleen (Clyne) McN.; m. Mary Katherine Riley, Aug. 1, 1938; children—Michael E., Kathleen (Mrs. John Dreps). LL.B., U. Idaho, 1950. Bar: Idaho 1950, U.S. Supreme Ct. 1950. Practice Orofino, Idaho, 1950-64; U.S. dist. judge Dist. Idaho, Boise, from 1964. Served as officer AC USNR, World War II. Mem. Phi Delta Theta, Phi Alpha Delta. Roman Catholic. Died Dec. 25, 1985.

MC NULTY, FREDERICK CHARLES, architect; b. Soochow, Kiangsu, China, Oct. 6, 1919; s. Henry Augustus and Edith (Piper) McN.; m. Sara Gene Farny, June 18, 1947; 1 dau., Margaret Piper. B.A. (Edwin Gould Found. scholar), Princeton U., 1942, M.F.A., 1949; grad., Kent Sch., 1938. Draftsman Robert Stanton, Carmel, Calif., 1949-52; designer Butner, Holm & Waterman, Salinas, Calif., 1952-57; assoc. Wallace Holm & Assocs., Monterey, Calif., 1957-64; sr. assoc. Wallace Holm & Assocs., 1964-72; v.p. Wallace Holm, Architects, Inc., Monterey, 1973-83; ret. 1984; instr. adult edn. program Monterey Peninsula Coll., 1958-59; owner Piper Paper and Plastics, Carmel, 1967-86. Designer adminstrn. bldg., library, creative arts center, engring.-physics bldg., Monterey Peninsula Coll., 1956-64; editor: Monterra, a Planned Residential Community General Development Plan Phase Environmental Reconnaissance. Mem. Mayor's Adv. Com. for Master Plan, Carmel-by-the Sea, 1955-56, mem. planning com., 1982-85; past bd. dirs. New Monterey Property Owners' Assn., Monterey County Citizens' Planning Assn. Served with AUS, 1942-45, ETO. Decorated Legion of Merit; recipient Alexander Guthrie McCosh prize, 1942. Mem. AIA (past chpt. bd. dirs.), White Pine Soc., Sigma Alpha. Republican. Episcopalian. Home: Carmel Calif. Died Nov. 12, 1986, buried at sea.

MCPHAIL, HARVEY FRANKLIN, electrical engineer; b. Santa Barbara, Calif., Jan. 12, 1892; s. Albert Franklin and Helen (Stevens) McP.; m. Ruth James, Apr. 26, 1912; children: Mildred McPhail Ralph, Harvey Franklin Jr. BSEE, U. Nev., 1914. Engr. Nev. Valleys Power Co., Lovelock, 1915-16; elec. contracting and other bus. activities Lovelock, 1916-18; powerhouse foreman U.S. Reclamation Svc., Lingle, Wyo., 1919-20, resident engr., powerplant and power system constrn., Cody, Wyo., 1921-23; elec. engr. U.S. Bur. Reclamation, Denver, 1923-28, asst. chief elec. engr. supervising elec. designs of Hoover, Grand Coulee, Parker, Shasta and other powerplants, 1928-43, dir. br. power utilization, Denver, 1943-46, Washington, 1946-52, asst. commr. supervising power utilization, project planning, mgmt. planning and personnel, 1952-53, asst. commr. supervising all irrigation and power activities, 1953-54; mgr. Hydroelectric div. Kuljian Corp., Phila., 1954-60; exec. dir. Colo. River Basin Consumers Power, Inc., 1960-65; cons. engr., from 1965. Mem. U.S. nat. com. Internat. Commn. on Irrigation and Drainage, U.S. nat. com. Internat. Commn. on Large Dams; chmn. U.S. del. to Internat. Conf. Large Electric Systems, Paris, 1948. With U.S. Army, 1918. Recipient Disting. Nevadan award U. Nev., 1959. Fellow AIEE; mem. Am. Legion, Masons. Home: Walnut Creek Calif. †

MC PHEETERS, THOMAS S., JR., lawyer; b. St. Louis, Jan. 2, 1912; s. Thomas S. and Madeleine (Taussig) McP.; m. Carroll W. Jones, Oct. 4, 1939; children: Thomas S. III, Hugh, John C., Peter G.; m. Martha B. Legg, Sept. 24, 1960 (dec. Nov. 1968); stepchildren: John C., Louisa O. Deland, Martha L. Reeve; m. Gladys McRee, Feb. 23, 1973. A.B., Princeton U., 1933; LL.B., Washington U., St. Louis, 1936. Bar: Mo. 1936. Since practiced in St. Loui; assoc. Bryan, Williams, Cave & McPheeters (and successor Bryan, Cave, McPheeters & McRoberts), 1936-87, ptnr., 1951-87. Mem. Ladue (Mo.) City Council, 1950-60; trustee David Ranken, Jr. Tech. Inst., Westminster Coll. Served with Am. Field Service, 1944-45, CBI. Democrat. Presbyterian. Clubs: St. Louis Country (St. Louis), Racquet (St. Louis), Noonday (St. Louis), Log Cabin (St. Louis). Home: Saint Louis Mo. Died Dec. 1, 1987; buried Bellefontaine Cemetery, St. Louis.

MCPHERSON, JOHN DALLAS, investment company executive; b. Inglewood, Calif., Sept. 18, 1922; s. John and Hazel (Mitchell) McP.; m. Ida Morgan, May 17, 1959; children: Dallas B., John Gordon; m. Ann Autry, Feb. 7, 1970; 1 dau., Jacqueline Dee. BS, U. Calif., Berkeley, 1941. With exec. tng. Gen. Electric Corp., Schenectady, N.Y., 1941-42; tng. officer VA, 1946; founder, pres. Airborne Freight Corp., San Francisco, 1946-69; founder, pres., bd. dirs. Ralston Investment Corp., 1969-87; pres. Am. Orient Travel Corp., Personal Security Life Ins. Co.; chmn. bd. Star Airline Catering Inc., Jack Carpentier Cos., Portal/Albertsen Travel Service Inc., Dipaco Inc., S&S Ice Vending Machine Co. Inc.; bd. dirs. Mediacast Inc.; mem. adv. bd. Bay View Fed. Savs. Bd. dirs. Med. Problem Welfare Assn. Inc., U. Calif. Internat. House, Meals for Millions Found.; bd. dirs. Medic Alert Found. Internat., pres., 1975-79. Served to lt. comdr. USNR, 1942-46. Mem. San Francisco C. of C., San Francisco Art Assn., World Bus. Coun. (pres. 1974-75, bd. dirs. 1975-87), Newcomen Soc. N.Am., Air Force Assn., Navy League, Confrerie de la Chaine des Rotisseurs, Sonoma County Trail Blazers, Bay Area Police Officers Assn. Presbyterian. Clubs: Commonwealth of Calif., The Hundred. Lodge: Masons. Home: Hillsborough Calif. Died May 23, 1987; buried Skylawn Meml. Park, San Mateo, Calif.

MEADOR, H(ENRY) GRADY, business executive; b. Murray, Ky., July 23, 1890; s. James M. and Fenna L. (Dugger) M.; m. Sara Boone Mattlingly, Dec. 24, 1909. Student, Harvard U., 1950. With Gulf Oil Corp.,

1910-57, v.p., later sr. v.p., 1949-57, ret., 1957; bd. dirs. several subs.; pres., bd. dirs. Propet Co., Ltd. Pres. Better Bus. Bur., New Orleans, 1943; pres. bd. commrs. Port of New Orleans, 1947; pres. New Orleans area Boy Scouts Am., 1938; col. Gov.'s staff Ky., La., Miss., Ga.; King Mardi Gras, 1939. Mem. Internat. House New Orleans (past bd. dirs.), New Orleans C. of C. (pres. 1940, SAR, New Orleans Country Club (pres. 1944), Boston Club (New Orleans), Pitts. Athletic Club, Duquesne Club, Rolling Rock Club, Fox Chapel Golf Club (Pitts.). Home: New Orleans La. †

MEADOW, WILLIAM KING, lawyer; b. Madison County, Ga., Dec. 7, 1891; s. David W. and Susie A. (Colbert) M.; m. Nan Ivey, June 18, 1932; children: David W., Suzanne. AB, U. Ga., 1912, LLB, 1914. Bar: Ga. 1914. Pvt. practice Atlanta, from 1932; asst. atty. gen. State of Ga., 1932-33; mem. Spalding, Sibley, Troutman, Meadow & Smith, 1945; later mem. King & Spalding. Mem. ABA, Ga. Bar Assn., Atlanta Bar Assn., Lawyer's Club of Atlanta. Home: Atlanta Ga. †

MEADOWS, PAUL, sociologist; b. Herrin, Ill., June 19, 1913; s. William C. and Mae (McCree) M.; m. Mary Nell Gouldin, Aug. 17, 1941; children: Michael, Peter. AB, McKendree Coll., 1935; MA, Washington U., St. Louis, 1936; PhD, Northwestern U., 1940. Instr. Western Mich. U., Kalamazoo, 1940-41, Northwestern U., 1941-44; asst. prof., research assoc. Mont. State U., 1944-47; assoc. prof., then prof. U. Nebr., 1947-59; prof. sociology, chmn. sociology dept. Syracuse (N.Y.) U., 1959-69; chmn. dept. sociology SUNY, Albany, 1969-72, research prof., from 1972; dir. research Diocese of Albany, 1970-73; sr. staff cons. Inst. on Man and Sci., Rensselaerville, N.Y. Author: The Culture of Industrial Man, 1950, (with Reinhardt and Gillette) Social Problems and Social Policy, 1951, John Wesley Powell: Fontersman of Science, 1949, Tecnologia y en Orden Social, 1947, El Proceso Social de la Revolucion, 1961, Marcos para el Estudio de los Movimentos Sociales, 1961, The Masks of Change, 1965, Industrial Man: Profiles of Developmental Society, 1965, The Rhetoric of Sociology, 1966, The Many Faces of Change: Explorations in the Theory of Social Changes, 1971; editor: Urbanization, Urbanism and Change, 1968, 2d rev. edit., 1976, Bibliographical Guide to the Literature on Recent Immigration, 1977, Policy and Practice: The Interface between the Social Sciences and Urban Planning, 1978; contbr. articles to profl. jours. Pres. bd. Family Welfare Assn. Lincoln, Nebr., 1951-53. Mem. Midwest Sociol. Soc. (pres. 1957-58, editor jour. 1953-56), Ea. Sociol. Soc., Phi Beta Kappa. Home: Schenectady N.Y. Deceased.

MEADOWS, ROBERT MERLE, communication, wire, cable and equipment company executive; b. Berwick, Ill., Feb. 5, 1917; s. Arlien Aden and Eva Lena (Byram) M.; m. Shirley Sue Hallman, June 18, 1949; children—Robert Byram, Joan Adele. Student, Brown's Bus. Coll., 1935, 46, Internat. Accountants Soc., 1949, Alexander Hamilton Inst., 1950. Order clk. Abingdon Potteries (Ill.), 1936-41; sec., asst. treas. Hyalyn Porcelain, Inc., Hickory, N.C., 1946-58; chief accountant Superior Continental Corp., Hickory, 1958-60; sec.-treas. Superior Continental Corp., 1961-75; v.p. finance Pepsi-Cola Bottling Co. of Hickory, Pepsi Cola Bottling Co. of Asheville (N.C.), Pepsi Cola Bottling Co. of Spruce Pine, N.C., 1975-87. Treas. Hickory Landmarks Soc., 1968-87. Served with USAAF, 1941-45. Mem. Am. Mgmt. Assn. Mem. Ch. of Christ (deacon 1964-70). Clubs: Moose, Lake Hickory Country. Home: Hickory N.C. Died July 27, 1987.

MEANS, GARDINER COIT, economist, author; b. Windham, Conn., June 8, 1896; s. Frederick Howard and Helen Chandler (Coit) M.; m. Caroline Farrar Ware, June 2, 1927. AB, Harvard U., 1918, AM, 1927, PhD, 1933. Assoc. in law Columbia U. Law Sch., N.Y.C., 1933-34; econ. adviser on fin. Sec. Agr., 1933-35; mem. consumers adv. bd. NRA, 1933-35; dir. indsl. sect. Nat. Resources Planning Bd., 1935-37, Nat. Resources Com., 1937-40; fiscal analyst Bur. Budget, 1940-41; research assoc. dir. Com. for Econ. Devel., 1943-49, econ. cons., 1949-58, mem. adv. bd., 1949-54; econ. cons. Fund for Republic, 1957-59, 1959-87; ptnr. Lawn Grass Devel. Co., from 1951. Author: (with J.C. Bonbright) The Holding Company -- Its Public Significance and Its Regulation, 1932, (with A.A. Berle) The Modern Corp. and Private Property, 1932, (with Caroline F. Ware) Modern Economy in Action, 1936, The Structure of the American Economy, 1939; co-author: Jobs and Markets, 1946, Pricing Power and the Public Interest, 1962, The Corporate Revolution in America, 1962; contbr. articles to profl. jours. Served to 2d lt., inf. U.S. Army, 1917, 2d lt. Signal Corps, aviator, 1918-19. Mem. Am. Econ. Assn., Royal Econ. Soc., Am. Statis. Assn. Home: Vienna Va. Died Feb. 15, 1988.

MEDAWAR, PETER BRIAN, biological scientist; b. Rio de Janeiro, Brazil, Feb. 28, 1915; s. Nicholas and Muriel (Dowling) M.; MA, Oxford (Eng.) U., 1939, DSc (hon.), 1945; hon. doctorates U. Alta., Cambridge (Eng.) U., Birmingham (Eng.) U., Liege (Belgium) U., U. Brazil, U. B.C., U. Brussels U. Chgo., U. Dalhousie, U. Exeter (Eng.), U. Hull (Eng.), U. Dundee, U. Glasgow (Scotland), U. Aston, U. Southhampton (Eng.), U. South Fla., Washington U., St. Louis, Harvard U., London U.; m. Jean Taylor, Feb. 27, 1937; children: Caroline Medawar Garland, Charles, Louise Medawar Harding, Alexander. Lectr., Oxford U., 1938-47; fellow Magdalen Coll., Oxford, 1938-47; head zoology dept. Birmingham U., 1947-51; head zoology dept. U. Coll., London, 1951-62; dir. Nat. Inst. for Med. Research, London, 1962-71; research Clin. Research Centre, 1971-87; prof. at large, Cornell U., Ithaca, N.Y., 1966-69. Recipient Nobel prize in medicine or physiology (with Burnet), 1960; Copley medal Royal Soc., 1969; Hamilton Fairley medal Royal Coll. Physicians, 1971. Fellow Royal Soc., Brit. Acad. (hon.), Royal Coll. Surgeons, Royal Can. Coll. Physicians and Surgeons, Nat. Acad. Sci. (fgn.), Am. Philos. Soc., Am. Acad. Arts and Scis., N.Y. Acad. Scis., ACP, Brit. Assn. Advancement Sci. (pres. 1968-69). Author: The Uniqueness of the Individual, 1956; The Future of Man, 1960; The Art of the Soluble, 1967; Induction and Intuition in Scientific Thought, 1969; The Hope of Progress, 1972; (with J.S. Medawar) The Life Science, 1977; Advice to a Young Scientist, 1979; Pluto's Republic, 1982; (with J.S. Medawar) Aristotle to Zoos: A Philosophical Dictionary of Biology; The Limits of Science, 1984; also articles; research on growth and aging, reactions to tissue transplantation especially immunity reactions prohibiting transplantation between individuals; discovered acquired immunological tolerance. Died Oct. 2, 1987. Home: London England.

MEE, JOHN F., business educator, consultant; b. Ada, Ohio, July 10, 1908; s. R. Kirk and Helen F. (Hickernell) M.; m. Muriel E. Collins, Apr. 5, 1941; children: Marcia Joan, Virginia Ann, Raymond Kirk. AB, Miami U., 1930, LLD, 1964; AM, U. Maine, 1932; PhD, Ohio State U., 1959. Lic. psychologist, Ind. Teaching fellow U. Maine, 1930-32; dean Beal Coll., Bangor, Maine, 1932-34; placement dir., instr. Ohio State U., Columbus, 1934-39; asst. prof., dir. placement Ind. U., Bloomington, 1939-41, 46-85, prof. mgmt., chmn. dept., 1946-62, Mead Johnson prof. mgmt., 1962-85, dean div. gen. and tech. studies, 1966-85; Ford disting. vis. prof. NYU, 1962; cons. Ford Found., 1956-59; cons. pers. mgmt. and indsl. relations; pres. Mee Farms Inc., 1965-85, Richard D. Irwin Found., 1975-85, bd. dirs. Richard D. Irwin Inc.; mem. arbitration panel Gov. of Ind.; staff dir. Ind. Study Commn. Intergovtl. Relations, 1954; arbitrator Fed. Mediation and Conciliation Service; chmn. Am. Mgmt. Team to France, 1952; chmn. avd. com. Ind. Exec. Devel. Program, 1951-70, Mead Johnson Inst., 1957-68. Author: Management Thought in a Dynamic Economy, 1963; editor Personnel Handbook, 1951, Irwin-Dorsey Series in Behavioral Sci.; cons. editor Advanced Management, 1951-52; chmn. editorial bd. Business Horizons, 1957-85; mem. adv. bd. Mgmt. Internat., 1964. Commr. Ind. Dept. Staff Revenue, 1948; cons. exec. office Pres. of the U.S., 1950; staff dir. Pres. Com. on Presdl. Appointments, 1950; mem. Sec. Navy's Adv. Bd. Edn. and Tng., 1972-73; exec. dir. Ind. Tax Study Commn.; bd. advisers Indsl. Coll. Armed Forces. Col. USAAF, 1941-46. Named Ind. Sagamore of Wabash, 1964, Ky. col., 1966. Fellow Internat. Acad. Mgmt.; mem. Acad. Mgmt. (pres. 1951, bd. govs.), Soc. Advancement Mgmt. (v.p. 1964, Taylor Key award 1972), Am. Inst. Mgmt., Am. Psychol. Assn., C. of C. (dir.), Coun. Profl. Edn. Bus. (pres. 1956-57), SAR, Beta Gamma Sigma (nat. pres. 1970-71), Phi Beta Kappa, Delta Sigma Pi, Phi Delta Theta. Presbyterian. Club: Explorer's. Home: Bloomington Ind. Died Nov. 17, 1985; buried Darrtown, Ohio.

MEEK, DEVON WALTER, chemistry educator; b. Johnson County, Ky., Feb. 24, 1936; s. Don C. and Willa M. (Walters) M.; m. Violet I. Imhof, Aug. 21, 1965; children: Brian Philip, Karen Anne. B.A., Berea Coll., 1958; M.S. in Chemistry, U. Ill., 1960, Ph.D. in Inorganic Chemistry, 1961. Asso. analytical chemist Oak Ridge Nat. Lab., summers 1957-59; teaching, research asst. U. Ill., Urbana, 1958-60; research fellow U. Ill., 1960-61; mem. faculty dept. chemistry Ohio State U., Columbus, 1961-88; assoc. prof. Ohio State U., 1966-69, prof., 1969-88, chmn. dept., 1977-81, 86-88; Vis. scholar Northwestern U., Evanston, Ill., 1967; cons. Argonne (Ill.) Nat. Lab., 1968-69, Shepherd Chem. Co., Ohio, 1975-80, Procter & Gamble Co., 1979-88; vis. sr. research fellow U. Sussex, Brighton, Eng., 1974; vis. scholar Cambridge U., 1981, U. Calif., Berkeley, 1982. Author: (with W.T. Lippincott and F.H. Verhoek) Experimental General Chemistry, 1970, 2d edit., 1974; (with others) Experimental General Chemistry, 1984. Gen. Electric Found. grad. fellow, 1960-61; John Simon Guggenheim fellow, 1981-82. Mem. Am. Chem. Soc., Royal Soc. (London), Sigma Xi. Home: Columbus Ohio. Died Dec. 7, 1988; buried Paintsville, Ky.

MEESKE, FRITZ L., business executive; b. Muskegon, Mich., 1892; s. Otto G. and Augusta (Heinemann) M.; m. Edna Thomasma, June 15, 1921; children: Philip F., Joan (Mrs. William Feick Jr.), Donn (dec.). Ed., U. Mich., 1914. V.p. Anaconda Wire & Cable Co., Muskegon, from 1929, also bd. dirs.; bd. dirs. Hackley Union Nat. Bank & Trust Co., Wis.-Mich. S.S. Co., Sand Products Corp., West Mich. Dock & Market Corp. Mem. Muskegon Country Club, Racquet Club, Chicago Club, Detroit Club, Elec. Mfrs. Club. †

MEHR, ROBERT IRWIN, finance educator, author; b. Phila., June 24, 1917; s. Charles Nathaniel and Elizabeth (Williams) M.; m. Margaret Louise Cochrun, Jan. 20, 1959; 1 son, James Lawrence. B.S., U. Ala., 1938, M.S., 1939; Ph.D., U. Pa., 1943. Instr. U. Ala., 1938-41; asst. prof. U. N.C., 1943-45; asso. prof. Butler U., Indpls., 1945-47; prof. finance U. Ill., Urbana, 1947-85, emeritus prof., from 1985. Author: Modern Life Insurance, 1949, 3d edit., 1961, Risk Management in the Business Enterprise, 1963, Principles of Insurance, 1952, 8th edit, 1985, Life Insurance Theory and Practice, 1970, 4th edit., 1985, Inflation, Technology and Growth: Long-Range Implications for Insurance, 1972, Principles of Insurance—Self Review, 1973, rev., 1977, Risk Management: Concepts and Applications, 1974, Life Insurance: Self Review, 1979, The Illinois System of Insurance Pricing: Practices and Attitudes of Selected Insurers, 1981, 2d edit., 1987, Insurance Capacity: Issues and Perspectives, 1981, Fundamentals of Insurance, 1983, rev. edit., 1986, Pension Assets and Insurance Reserves: A Corporate Resource, 1986; editor: Jour. Risk and Ins, 1974-80. Recipient Elizur Wright awards for outstanding original contbn. to lit. of ins., 1956, 64. Mem. Am. Risk and Ins. Assn. (past pres.), Am. Fin. Assn. (past dir.), Pacific Ins. Conf. (co-founder, past chmn., mem. exec. com.), InterAm. Ins. Forum (co-founder, mem. exec. com., founder Risk Theory seminar). Home: Urbana Ill. Died May 9, 1988.

MEHUS, OSCAR MYKING, educator, college dean; b. Brinsmade, N.D., May 15, 1894; s. Mikkel Knutson and Anne (Myking) M.; m. Emma Hille, Aug. 25, 1920 (dec. Jan. 1941); children: Dorothy Jeannette, Donald Vincent, Orion Myking; m. Jewell Ross Davis, Sept. 9, 1945; 1 stepchild, Elizabeth Lou Davis. AB, Augsburg Coll., Mpls., 1916; AM, U. N.C., 1920, PhD, 1931; postgrad., U. Chgo., summer 1917, U. Minn., 1924-26. Prin. high sch. Fessenden, N.D., 1916-17, supt., 1917-18; prin. Harvey, N.D., 1918-19; supt. schs. Spring Grove, Minn., 1920-21; prof. State Tchrs. Coll., Mayville, N.D., 1921-24; instr. sociology U. Minn., 1924-26; asst. prof. edn. Wittenberg Coll., Springfield, Ohio, 1926-28; prof. sociology and tchr. tng. State Tchrs. Coll., Maryville, Mo., 1928-39; pres. Winona (Minn.) State Tchrs. Coll., 1939-43; chief vocat. rehab. and edn. div. VA Regional Office, Kansas City, Mo., 1943-60, St. Louis, 1960-63; dean student work program Sch. Ozarks, Point Lookout, Mo., 1965-66. Co-author: Extra-Curricular Activities at the University of Minnesota, 1929; contbr. articles to profl. jours. Mem. Mayor's Com. on Juvenile Delinquency, Kansas City; dir. Unitarian Forum, kansas City, 1944-60. With U.S. Army, 1918. Decorated Medal of Liberation (Denmark); recipient spl. commendation award Adminstrn. Vets. Affairs, 1960, Disting. Alumnus citation Augsburg Coll., 1975. Mem. Am. Scandinavian Found., Urban League Kansas City, Mo. Assn. for Social Welfare, Kansas City Coun. on World Affairs (gov.), Nat. Rehab. Assn., Mo. Assn. Adult Edn., Westport-Roanoke Community Coun. (pres.), Mo., Kansas City assns. mental hygiene, Am. Humanist Assn., Soc. Advancement Scandinavian Study, League of norsemen, Am. Legion (comdr. 1974-76), Last Men's Club (pres.), Hallinglaget of Am. (pres. 1960-65), Am. War Dads, Masons, Rotary (chmn. pub. rels. com. local chpt., spl. award 1981), Kansas City Farmers Club, Scandinavian Club Greater Kansas City (pres., Norseman award 1977), Phi Delta Kappa, Pi Gamma Mu, Kappa Phi Kappa. Unitarian. Home: Branson Mo. Died Nov. 22, 1983; cremated.

MEIERS, RUTH LENORE, state government official; b. Parshall, N.D., Nov. 6, 1925; d. Axel and Grace (Williams) Olson; m. Glenn E. Meiers, June 28, 1950; children—David, Michael, Monte, Scott. B.A. in Social Work, U. N.D., 1946. Dir. Mountrail County Welfare Bd, Stanley, N.D., 1947-52; mem. N.D. Ho. of Reps., 1975-85, chmn. legis. social services and vets.' affairs com., 1983-85; lt. gov. State of N.D., Bismarck, 1985-87. Mem. jud. nominating com. State of N.D., 1979-80, adoption council, 1980-83; pres. Mountrail County Hist. Soc., 1984-87; bd. dirs. Upper Mo. Dist. Health Unit, 1957-84, N.D. Supreme Ct. Disciplinary Bd., 1979-84. Recipient Outstanding Service award N.D. Pub. Health Assn., 1984. Mem. Women Execs. in State Govt., Nat. Lt. Govs.' Assn. Democrat. Lutheran. Club: Homemakers (Stanley). Home: Ross N.D. Died Mar. 19, 1987.

MEIGS, JOE VINCENT, gynecologist, educator; b. Lowell, Mass., Oct. 24, 1892; s. Joe Vincent and Sarah (Parker) M.; m. Elizabeth Wallace, Apr. 2, 1921; children: Wallace, Sarah, Elizabeth. AB, Princeton U., 1915; MD, Harvard U., 1919; DSc (hon.), Northwestern U.. Lowell Tech. Inst.; MD (hon.), U. Turino, Italy. Intern Mass. Gen. Hosp., Boston, 1919-21; asst. resident, then resident The Free Hosp. for Women, Brookline, Mass., 1921; pvt. practice Boston; instr. surgery Harvard Med. Sch., 1932-42, clin. prof. gynecology, 1942-60, emeritus clin. prof., from 1960; cons. vis. surgeon Mass. Gen. Hosp.; chief gynecol. service Vincent Meml. Hosp., 1941, cons. vis. gynecologist, 1955; gynecologist Pondville Hosp., from 1927. Author: Tumors of the Female Pelvic Organs, 1934, (with Somers Sturgis) Progress in Gynecology, 1946, 2d edit., 1957; author and editor: The Surgical Treatment of Cancer of the Cervix, 1954. Fellow Royal Coll. Surgeons Edinbourgh (hon.), Royal Coll. Obstetricians and Gynecologists, Am. Acad. Arts and Scis.; mem. Am. Surg. Assn., So. Surg. Soc., Am. Assn. Obstetricians and Gynecologists, Am. Gynecol. Soc., Swedish

Obstet. and Gynecol. Soc. (hon.), Country Club Somerset, Tavern Club. Home: Boston Mass. †

MEILING, RICHARD LEWIS, physician, educator; b. Springfield, Ohio, Dec. 21, 1908; s. Lester L. and Matilda (Lobenherz) M.; m. Ann Elizabeth Lucas, June 21, 1940; 1 son, George. AB, Wittenberg U., 1930, DSc (hon.), 1950; MD, U. Munich, 1937; DHL (hon.), Ohio State U., 1977. Diplomate Am. Bd. Obstetrics and Gynecology, Am. Bd. Preventive Medicine. Prof. obsterics and gynecology Ohio State U., 1947-74, prof. emeritus, 1974-84, dean coll. medicine, 1961-70, v.p., 1970-74, dir., 1961-72; hon. staff Univ. Hosp., St. Ann's Hosp., Mt. Carmel Hosp., Riverside Hosp., Grant Hosp., all of Columbus; v.p. Nutrition Today Soc. Inc., Annapolis, Md.; dir. Pharmacy Systems Co.; dir. emeritus Medicor USA Inc., Columbus; dir. med. services Dept. Def., 1949-51; asst. to Sec. Def., 1949-51; chmn. Armed Forces Med. Poliy Coun., 1951. Contbr. articles to profl. jours. Trustee emeritus Children's Hosp., Columbus. Maj. gen. USAF, ret. Fellow Am. Coll. Obstetricians and Gynecologists, ACS, Aerospace Med. Assn., S.E. Surg. Congress; mem. AMA, Ohio Med. Assn. (pres. 1956-57), Cen. Assn. Obstetrics and Gynecology, Columbus Acad. Medicine. Episcopalian. Home: Columbus Ohio. Died Dec. 14, 1984.

MELBY, ERNEST OSCAR, educational consultant; b. Lake Park, Minn., Aug. 16, 1891; s. Ole Hanson and Ellen Caroline (Stakke) M.; Aurora Marie Herbert, Dec. 29, 1914; 1 child, Stanley Herbert. BA, St. Olaf Coll., 1913; MA, U. Minn., 1926, PhD, 1928; LLD, NYU, 1956; D Pedagogy, Elizabethtown Coll., 1956; LLD, Bowling Green State U., 1957, Newark State Coll., 1960. High sch. tchr. and prin. 1913-15; supt. schs. Brewster, Blackduck and Long Prarie, Minn., 1915-26; instr. edn., research asst. pub. schs. U. Minn., Mpls., 1926-27, asst. dir. Bur. Ednl. Research, 1927-28; asst. prof. edn. Northwestern U., Evanston, Ill., 1928-29, assoc. prof., 1929-31, prof., 1931-34, dean sch. edn., 1934-41; pres. Mont. State U., 1941-43, 44-45; chancellor U. Mont., 1943-44; dean sch. edn. NYU, 1945-56, prof. edn., 1945-56; disting. prof. edn. Mich. State U., 1956-75, disting. prof. emeritus, 1975-87; vis. prof. Fla. Atlantic U., 1964-67; cons. in community edn., 1967-87. Author and co-author several books including: Administering Community Education, 1955, Education of Free Men, 1956, Education for Renewed Faith in Freedom, 1959, The Teacher and Learning, 1962, (with V.M. Kerensky) Education II: A Social Imperative, 1971, 2d rev. edit., 1975. Sec. Am. Coun. on Edn., 1937-40; pres. State Citizens Coun. Mem. NEA, Nat. Soc. Study Edn. (bd. dirs. 1944-47), Am. Ednl. Research Assn., Nat. Soc. Coll. Tchrs. Edn., Am. Edn. Fellowships, Am. Assn. Sch. Adminstrs., N.Y. Acad. Pub. Edn., Nat. Child Labor Com., John Dewey Soc. (pres. 1947-48, award for disting. lifetime service 1970), Assn. for Supervision and Curriculum Devel., Nat. Community Sch. Edn. Assn. (hon. life), Phi Delta Kappa, Masons. Home: Boca Raton Fla. Died January 11, 1987; buried Boca Raton.

MELCHER, DANIEL, publishing consultant; b. Newton Center, Mass., July 10, 1912; s. Frederic Gershom and Marguerite (Fellows) M; m. Peggy Zimmerman, Feb. 19, 1937 (dec. Feb. 1967); 1 child, Frederic G. II; m. Margaret Saul, Oct. 3, 1967. AB, Harvard U., 1934. Publicity asst. George Allen & Unwin, pubs., London, 1934-35; student pub. methods London & Leipzig, 1935; with publicity, editorial work and sales Henry Holt & Co., 1936; advt. mgr. Oxford U. Press, 1937-39; gen. mgr. Alliance Book Corp., 1939-40; with sch., library, bookstore and mail-order sales promotion Viking Press, N.Y.C., 1940-42; publs. cons. War Finance div. U.S. Treasury Dept, Washington, 1942-43, nat. dir. Edn. Sect., 1943-45; dir. Nat. Com. on Atomic Info., Washington, 1946; gen. mgr., bd. dirs. R.R. Bowker Co., v.p., 1959-63, pres., 1963-68, chmn., 1968-69; pres. Jacques Cattell Press, 1961-67; chmn. bd. Gale Research Co., Detroit and N.Y.C., 1971-73. Author: The Printing and Promotion Handbook, 1949, 3d rev. edit., 1967, Melcher on Acquisition, 1971. Trustee Montclair Pub. Library, 1972-73; bd. dirs. Insts. for Achievement Human Potential, Phila., 1969-85. Mem. ALA (coun. 1972-74). Home: Charlottesville Va. Died July 29, 1985.

MELICK, DERMONT WILSON, surgeon; b. Williams, Ariz., Mar. 3, 1910; s. Prince Albert and Cora (Wilson) M.; m. Dorothy Helen Marvel, Jan. 1, 1943; children: Richard Wilson, John Wilson, Penelope Ann Wilson (dec.). BS, U. Ariz., 1931; MD, U. Pa., 1935, MSc, 1941, DSc, 1945. Intern Grad. Hosp., U. Pa., 1935-37; resident U. Wis., 1939-41, U. Mich., 1941-42; instr. surgery U. Wis., Madison, 1942-45; practice medicine, specializing in thoracic and cardiovascular surgery Phoenix, 1945-67, 77-85; prof. surgery, coord. regional med. program U. Ariz. Coll. Medicine, Tucson, 1967-77. Chmn. Western Interstate Commn. Higher Edn., 1964; chmn. bd. S.W. Blood Banks Inc., 1955-67; v.p. Sahuaro Med. Arts Found. 1st lt. M.C., AUS, 1941. Recipient Merit medallion U. Ariz., 1960, Disting. Service award Maricopa County Med. Soc., 1957, Disting. Citizen award U. Ariz., 1966, Joseph Bank medal, 1967; named (with father) Pioneer Family in Medicine in Ariz., Phoenix Hist. Soc., 1977. Fellow ACS; mem. AMA, Maricopa County Med. Asn. (pres. 1951), Ariz. Med. Assn. (pres. 1959), Masons (32 degree), Sigma Xi, Kappa Sigma, Alpha Kappa Kappa. Republican. Presbyterian. Home: Phoenix Ariz. Died July 20, 1985.

MELICK, JOHN VLIET, manufacturing executive; b. Oldwick, N.J., Sept. 15, 1889; s. Caius Cassius and Mary (Wilson) M.; m. Mabel Florence Huckle, June 21, 1924; children: Katherine E. (Mrs. Robert R. Sherlock), Alice M. (Mrs. Peter D. Hyde), John Vliet. DBA, Ohio No. U., 1951. With Dana Corp., from 1923, sec., from 1933, v.p., from 1948, also bd. dirs.; pres., bd. dirs. Atlas Drop Forge Co., Lansing, Mich., Gen. Drop Forge Corp., Buffalo. Trustee Flower Hosp., Toledo, Ohio No. U. Mem. A.I.M., Toledo Club, Sylvania Country Club. Methodist. Home: Toledo Ohio. †

MELICK, WILLIAM FRANK, urologist; b. St. Louis, Nov. 9, 1914; s. William Grant and Elizabeth (Tweedy) M.; m. Margaret Franklin Rhodes, June 7, 1939 (dec. Dec. 1976); children: Carolyn (Mrs. Burton W. Noll), Margaret (Mrs. Aaron P. Scholnik), Frances (Mrs. Robert M. Slusher Jr.), William Frank, Mary Katherine; m. Mary A. McElfresh, Mar. 17, 1979; stepchildren: Peter Duncan, Stuart, Bruce. MD, Washington U., St. Louis, 1939; M Urology, St. Louis U., 1943. Diplomate Am. Bd. Urology. Intern St. Lukes Hosp., St. Louis, 1939-40; resident St. Louis U. Hosp., 1940-43; mem. faculty St. Louis U. Sch. Medicine, 1943-84, chmn. dept. urology, 1959-71, clin. prof., 1962-84. Served with M.C. AUS, 1943-46. Fellow ACS; mem. AMA, Am. Urol. Assn. (exec. com. 1972-84, nat. pres. 1980-81, exec. com. cen. sect. 1964-67, sec. south cen. sect. 1967-70, pres. 1972, exec. com. 1974-75), Am. Acad. Pediatrics (sect. urology). Home: Webster Groves Mo. Died Dec. 15, 1984; buried Webster Groves.

MELLITZ, SAMUEL, judge; b. Bridgeport, Conn., May 6, 1891; s. Jacob and Peppie (Hausman) M.; m. Sadye L. Silverman, June 18, 1916; children: Jacob, Barbara Mellitz Krentzman, Beulah Mellitz Framson. LLB cum laude, Yale U., 1911; LLD (hon.), Yeshiva U., 1954. Bar: Conn. 1912. Practiced in Bridgeport, 1912-35; judge Ct. Common Pleas, Conn., 1936-42; judge Superior Ct., 1942-58, chief judge, 1957-58; assoc. justice Supreme Ct. of Errors, from 1958; chmn. Judicial Council of Conn., from 1960; state referee, from 1961; bd. dirs. West Side Bank, Bridgeport, 1927-33, chmn., 1934-37; bd. dirs. West End Savs. and Loan Assn., Bridgeport. Pres. Jewish Community Council, Bridgeport, 1936-38, hon. pres., from 1938; bd. dirs. St. Vincent's Hosp., Bridgeport; bd. dirs. Yeshiva U.; trustee Beardsley Meml. Scholarship Fund. Yale U; v.p. Union Orthodox Jewish Cong. Am. Mem. ABA, Conn. Bar Assn. Home: Bridgeport Conn. †

MELNITZ, WILLIAM WOLF, university dean; b. Cologne, Germany, Apr. 14, 1900; came to U.S., 1939; naturalized, 1945; s. Hans and Fancy (Elias) M.; m. Ruth Nathansohn, Apr. 29, 1939. Student univs., Cologne and Berlin, 1920-23; MA, UCLA, 1943, PhD, 1947. Stage dir. and producer, Europe, 1923-38; mem. faculty UCLA, from 1947, prof. theatre arts, then prof. emeritus, dean Coll. Fine Arts, from 1960. Author: (all with Kenneth Macgowan) Theater Pictorial, 1953, The Living Stage, 1955, Golden Ages of the Theatre, 1959. Mem. AAUP, Am. Ednl. Theatre Assn., Phi Beta Kappa. Home: Los Angeles Calif. Died Jan. 12, 1989.

MELOY, HARRY, lawyer; b. Hoopeston, Ill., Mar. 24, 1908; s. John Templeton and Sarah (Wilson) M.; m. Cordelia Buck, Sept. 4, 1937; children—Buck, Sarah (Mrs. R. Kent Landmark), Alex James. A.B., Monmouth Coll., 1931; J.D., DePaul U., 1935. Bar: Ill. bar 1935. Atty., asso. gen. counsel Ill. Agrl. Assn., Bloomington, 1935-61; gen. counsel, sec. CF Industries Inc., Chgo., 1961-73; ret. CF Industries Inc., 1973; of counsel McDermott Will & Emery, Chgo., 1973-80; ret. 1980; sec., counsel Cooperative Fertilizers Internat., 1966-73; counsel Nat. Livestock Producers Assn. Mem. Wilmette (Ill.) Village Bd., 1953-62; bd. dirs. Association House of Chgo. Mem. Am., Ill., Chgo. bar assns., Tau Kappa Epsilon. Presbyn. (elder 1949-52). Clubs: Tower, Sheridan Shore Yacht, Wilmette Rotary. Home: Wilmette Ill. Died Dec. 20, 1987.

MELTZER, ABRAHAM, lumber company executive; b. 1917; m. Florence Meltzer; children: Irving, Bruce, Robert, Gael Brudner. With Triangle Pacific Corp., Dallas, 1943-85, chmn. bd., chief exec officer, until 1985. Home: New York N.Y. Died Sept. 18, 1985.

MELTZER, LEON, lawyer; b. Phila., Apr. 30, 1903; s. Alexander and Minnie (Epstein) M.; m. Ruth Meyers, Dec. 20, 1936; children: Joan, Elaine. B.S., U. Pa., 1923, LL.B., 1926. Bar: Pa. bar 1926. Since practiced in Phila.; sr. ptnr. Meltzer & Schiffrin; Chmn. bd. Congl. Life Co.; dir. Simkins Industries, Cine-Tel Communications Corp.; chmn. bd. Sonitrol Sers. Inc.; sec.-treas., dir. Eagle Downs Racing, Keystone Race Track; pres. Silverside Developers, Inc. Trustee Pa. Coll. Podiatric Medicine. Mem. Am., Pa., Phila. bar assns., Am. Judicature Soc. Democrat. Clubs: Locust (Phila.); Philmont Country (Hungtington Valley, Pa.). Home: Meadowbrook Pa. Died July 31, 1985.

MELVIN, HAROLD WESLEY, English educator; b. Cambridge, Mass., Apr. 12, 1892; s. Albert Francis and Mary Helen (Burns) M.; m. Jessie Sumners Mullan, July 23, 1921; children: Harold Wesley, Willian Francis. AB, Boston U., 1915, AM, 1926. Began a tchr. 1915; prin. New Marlboro High Sch., Mill Rive Mass., 1915-16; instr. English Brewster Acad Wolfeboro, N.H., 1916-20; instr. English Northeaster U., 1920-21, asst. prof., 1921-22, prof., 1922-62, pro emeritus, from 1962, dean of students, 1929-57. Co author: Basic Principles of Writing, 1937, 43; contb poetry and children's stories to various publs. Mem Town Meeting, Milton, Mass., 1928-58; mem. Warran Com., Milton, 1934, 35. Mem. Am. Soc. Engring Edn MLA Am., New Eng. Poetry Club (Boston), Masons. Republican. Unitarian. Home: Milton Mass. †

MENARD, HENRY WILLIAM, geologist; b. Fresn Calif., Dec. 10, 1920; s. Henry William and Blanch (Hodges) M.; m. Gifford Merrill, Sept. 21, 1946; chi dren: Andrew O., Elizabeth M., Dorothy M. BS, Cali Inst. Tech., 1942, MS, 1947; PhD, Harvard U., 194 DSc (hon.), Old Dominion U., 1980. Geologis Amerada Petroleum Corp., 1947; from assoc. t supervisory oceanographer Navy Electronics Lab., 194 55; assoc. prof. marine geology Inst. Marine Resource U. Calif., 1955-61, prof., 1961-86, acting dir., 1967-6 prof. geology Scripps Inst. Oceanography, 1955-86; dir U.S. Geol. Survey, 1978-81; mem. panel underwate swimmers Nat. Acad. Scis.-NRC, 1955, mem. Pacifi sci. bd., 1956-62, panel on ocean resources, 1958; mem com. sci. and pub. policy, tech. asst. U.S. Office Sci. an Tech., 1965-66; mem. oceanographic expdns., Mi Pacific, 1949, Capricorn, 1952-53, Chinook, 195 Downwind, 1957-58, Nova, 1967, Ngendie, 1983; dir Geol. Diving Cons. Inc., 1953-58. Served from ensig to lt. comdr. USNR, 1942-46. Decorated Bronze Sta Guggeneim Meml. Found. fellow, 1962-63; Oversea fellow Churchill Coll., 1970-71; Woods Hole Ge ographic Inst. fellow, 1973. Fellow Geol. Soc. Am. Am. Geophys. Union, AAAS; mem. Nat. Acad. Scis. Am. Acad. Arts and Scis., Am. Assn. Petroleum Ge ologists, Royal Astron. Soc., Sigma Xi. Home: La Joll Calif. Died Feb. 9, 1986.

MENDELL, M(ORDECAI) LESTER, banking com pany director; b. N.Y., June 18, 1896; s. Abraham an Fannie (Weintraub) M.; m. Malvina Winifred Cohen June 15, 1919; children: Edward, Oliver, Olga Mendel Toll. Student, CCNY, 1916-17, Sheffield Sci. Sch., Yal U., 1918-19. Various positions mfg. and wholesal lumber firms 1920-35, with liquidating com. N.Y banks, 1933; dir., then chmn. Flushing Nat. Bank, 1940 50, merged into Bankers Turst Co. N.Y., 1950, v.p banking dept., 1950-61; dir., mem. exec. com. Gle Alden Corp.; dir. Interstate Dept. Stores, Nat. Equip ment Rental Corp., Palestine Econ. Corp., Bank Leumi N.Y.C., First Nat. Bank Palm Beach. Bd. dirs. ARC Palm Beach County (Fla.) Small Bus. Adminstrn., Nat Jewish Welfare Bd., Mental Health Hosp., Plam Beach Havilitaion Ctr., Fla. chpt. ARC, Civic Assn. Palm Beach; bd. govs. Good Samaritan Hosp.; bd. dirs., sec Community Fund Palm Beach; trustee, mem. exec. com United Jewish Appeal; trustee Fedn. Jewish Philan thropies N.Y.; founder L.I. Jewish Hosp.; chmn. lay bd Queens Gen. Hosp., Triboro Hosp., N.Y.C.; nat. co chmn. legacy com. Brandeis U. With USN, 1917-18. Mem. Flushing Interfaith Soc. (gov.), Harmonie, Lotos Palm Beach Country (dir., pres.) clubs. Home: Palm Beach Fla. Died Sept. 16, 1984.

MENDELSOHN, ROBERT SAUL, physician; b Chgo., July 13, 1926; s. Herman Martin and Rosamond (Kanter) M.; m. Rita Remer, Mar. 29, 1952; children—Ruth Mendelsohn Lockshin, Sally Mendelsohn Lowenfeld. Ph.B., U. Chgo., 1947, B.S., 1949, M.D. 1951. Diplomate Am. Bd. Pediatrics. Intern Cook County Hosp, Chgo., 1951-52; resident in pediatrics Michael Reese Hosp., Chgo., 1952-55; practice medicine specializing in pediatrics and family medicine Chgo. 1955-88; assoc. prof. dept. preventive medicine and community health U. Ill. Coll. Medicine, Chgo., 1969-80. Author: Confessions of a Medical Heretic, 1979, Male Practice, 1981, How to Raise a Healthy Child in Spite of Your Doctor, 1984. Syndicated newspaper columnist: The People's Doctor, 1976-88 . Served with USNR, 1944-45. Jewish. Home: Evanston Ill. Died Apr. 5, 1988; buried Chgo.

MENEELY, GEORGE RODNEY, physician; b. Hempstead, N.Y., Sept. 30, 1911; s. Charles D. and Emily F. (Gahn) M.; m. Mary Leslie Stewart, May 29, 1968; children by previous marriage: Judith, Denny Meneely Chapnick, George Rodney. BS, Princeton U. 1933; MD, Cornell U., 1937. Diplomate: Am. Bd. Internal Medicine. James Gleason fellow medicine U. Rochester Sch. Medicine and Dentistry, 1940-41, asst. resident medicine Strong Meml. Hosp., also asst. medicine, 1939-40, fellow medicine, 1938-39; intern medicine Strong Meml. Hosp., 1937-38; instr. medicine La. State U. Sch. Medicine, 1941-43; vis. physician Charity Hosp., New Orleans, 1941-43; dir. lung sta. Charity Hosp., 1942-43; mem. faculty Vanderbilt U. Sch. Medicine, 1943-62; vis. physician Vanderbilt U. Hosp., 1943-62, asso. prof. medicine, 1953-62; asso. prof. medicine Northwestern U. Med. Sch., also dir. dept. sci. assembly AMA, 1962-63; mem. staff U. Tex. M.D. Anderson Hosp. and Tumor Inst., 1963-66, acting head dept. biomath., 1964-65, internist, 1963-66, chief cardio-pulmonary function lab., 1963-66, cons., 1966-75; prof. nuclear medicine U. Tex. Grad. Sch. Biomed. Sci.

at Houston, 1963-66; prof. emeritus physiology, biophysics and medicine La. State U. Sch. Medicine, Shreveport, 1982-87; asso. dean La. State U. Sch. Medicine, 1966-73, dir. planning office, 1977-81, now dean spl. projects; vis. physician La. State U. Hosp., 1966-87; cons. in field, 1943-87; mem. sci. adv. com. United Health Founds., 1963-70, Grayson Found., 1965-75. Author numerous articles, chpts. in books. Master ACP; fellow Am. Coll. Cardiology (pres. 1957-58), Am. Coll. Nuclear Medicine (disting. fellow), Council Clin. Cardiology, Council Clin. Epidemiology, Am. Heart Assn.; mem. Am. Physiol. Soc., Nat. Assn. Disability Evaluating Physicians (charter), So. Soc. Clin. Investigation, Soc. Exptl. Biology and Medicine, Am. Fedn. Clin. Research, Am. Thoracic Soc., N.Y. Acad. Scis., Assn. Computing Machinery, AAUP, Pan Am. Med. Assns., Sigma Xi. Home: Shreveport La. Died Sept. 6, 1987.

MENEN, AUBREY (SALVATOR AUBREY CLARENCE MENON), author; b. London, Apr. 22, 1912; s. Kali Narain and Alice Violet (Everett) M. Student, U. Coll., London, 1930-32. Drama critic The Bookman, London, 1934; dir. Exptl. Theatre, London, 1935-36; with Personalities Press Svc., London, 1937-39; head English drama dept. (Allied war publicity) All India Radio, 1940-41; script editor info. films Govt. of India, 1943-45, staff polit. dept., 1946; head. motion picture dept. J. Walter Thompson Co. (Eastern Ltd.), 1947-48; free-lance writer from 1948. Author: The Prevalence of Witches, 1949, The Stumbling Stone, 1949, The Backward Bride, 1950, The Duke of Gallodoro, 1952, Dead Man in the Silver Market, 1953, The Ramayana, 1954, The Abode of Love, 1956, The Fig Tree, 1959, Rome for Ourselves, 1960, Speaking the Language Like a Native, 1962, Shela, 1962, A Conspiracy of Women, 1965, India, 1969, The Space Within the Heart, 1970, Upon This Rock, 1972, Cities in the Sand, 1973, Fonthill, 1974, (with Graham Hall) The Mystics, 1974, London, 1976, Venice, 1976, Four Days of Naples, 1979, Art and Money, 1980, also essays and criticism for N.Y. Times Book Rev., articles for The New Yorker, Harper's Bazaar, Holiday, N.Y. Times Mag. Home: Kerala India. Died Feb. 13, 1989.

MENG, JOHN JOSEPH, political science educator; b. Cleve., Dec. 12, 1906; s. George Edward and Marie Louise (Gott) M.; m. Marjorie F. Brunini, Aug. 18, 1937 (dec. Mar. 1988); children—Marie Louise, Marjorie Kathryn, John Joseph, George Edward, Alexander Brunini, Charles Frederick and Matthew Thomas (twins), Michael Richard. A.B., Catholic U. Am., 1928, A.M., 1929, Ph.D., 1932, LL.D., 1975; student, Ecole Libre des Sciences Politiques, Paris, 1930-31; LL.D., Manhattan Coll., 1960, Hunter Coll., CUNY, 1979; L.H.D., Canisius Coll., 1961; D.Litt., Siena Coll., 1966; Pd.D., St. John's U., 1966; L.H.D., Wilberforce U., 1967, Georgetown U., 1977. Asst. in politics Cath. U. Am., Washington, 1931; instr. Cath. U. Am., 1932-38, asst. prof., 1938; instr. polit sci. Queens Coll., Flushing, L.I., N.Y., 1938-41; asst. prof. Queens Coll., 1941-48, asso. prof., 1948, chmn. dept. polit. sci., 1941-44, 45-49, chmn. div. social scis., 1942-43, 47-48; lectr. Nazareth Coll., Rochester, N.Y., summer 1932; lectr. govt. Turner's Diplomatic Sch., Washington, 1937, 38; prof. history Hunter Coll., N.Y., 1949-52; prof. history, dean adminstrn. Hunter Coll., 1952-60, pres., 1960-67, emeritus, 1967-88; exec. v.p. Fordham U., 1966-69; pres. Marymount Coll., Tarrytown, N.Y., 1969-75, emeritus, 1975-88; exec. dir. Consortium Small Pvt. Colls., 1975-76, sr. staff adviser, 1976-78; pres. Meng Assoc. Consultants, Inc., 1978; engaged in hist. research Carnegie Instn. Washington, 1936-54; sec. Coll. Arts and Scis., Cath. U. Am., 1937-38. Author: The Comte de Vergennes: European Phases of His American Diplomacy, 1932; Co-author: Guide to Materials for American History in Libraries and Archives of Paris, Vol. II, 1944, Christianity and America, 1948; Editor: Despatches and Instructions of Conrad Alexandre Gerard, 1939. Chmn. bd. trustees Found. Ednl. Futures, Inc. Served with USMCR, 1929-30. Mem. Am. Cath. Hist. Assn. (exec. com.), Cath. Commn. on Intellectual and Cultural Affairs, U.S. Cath. Hist. Soc., Institut Francais de Washington (trustee). Home: Jackson Miss. Died Feb. 15, 1988.

MENK, LOUIS, architect; b. Newark, Sept. 23, 1908; s. Herman and Sarah (Rubin) M.; m. Olga Raskind, May 27, 1934; children: Frances, Doris Menk Patrick. BS, NYU, 1928, BArch, 1931. Instr. graphics dept. architecture NYU, 1929-31, asst. prof. architecture, 1931-42, exec. sec. Coll. Fine Arts, 1934-38, asst. dean Sch. Architecture and Allied Arts, 1938-42; project mgr. Albert Kahn Assocs., Inc., Architects and Engrs., Detroit, 1942-64, assoc. firm, 1947, corp. sec., 1961-62, treas. 1962-76, v.p., 1969-76, also bd. dirs. Archtl. works include: Fairchild Aircraft C-82 Assembly Plant, Hagerstown, Md., 1945, Sinai Hosp., Detroit, Med. Complex, from 1950, Chrysler Jet Engine Plant, Warren, Mich., 1954, Shaarey Zedek Synagogue, Southfield, Mich., 1963, Eastern Air Lines maj. overhaul base, Miami, 1966, Home for Aged, Detroit, 1966, Trane Co., adminstrn. bldg., LaCrosse, Wis., 1968; author monographs on archtl. topics. Fellow AIA (adminstrv. office practice com. 1969-71, dir. Detroit chpt. 1965-68, mem. com. on ins. 1968, mem. task force uniform fed. architect engr. contract 1968-69); mem. Mich. Soc. Architects (dir. 1966-69, treas. 1966-67, chmn. com. on firm membership 1966-69, mem. interprofl. com. on state registration 1970-71, Gold medal 1971), Engring. Soc. Detroit (mem. edn. com. 1970-71), Mich. Assn. Professions, Am. Soc. Technion (Detroit chpt.), N.Y. U. Alumni Assn. (cert. honor 1968), Founders' Soc. Detroit Inst. Art, Standard Club. Home: Southfield Mich. Died June 12, 1987; buried Montefiore Cemetery, N.Y.C.

MENON, SALVATOR AUBREY CLARENCE See **MENEN, AUBREY**

MENZEL, MARGARET YOUNG, biology educator; b. Kerville, Tex., June 21, 1924; d. Walter Patterson and Mary (Hightower) Young; m. Robert Winston Menzel, Apr. 9, 1949; children: Robert W., Gary Patterson, Mary Linda. B.A. magna cum laude, Southwestern U., 1944; Ph.D. (Blandy fellow 1945-49), U. Va., 1949. Instr. chemistry and bacteriology Lamar Coll., Beaumont, Tex., 1944-45; instr. agronomy Tex. Agrl. Expt. Sta., College Station, 1949-54; plant geneticist Agrl. Research Service, U.S. Dept. Agr., Tallahassee, 1956-62; research geneticist Agrl. Research Service, U.S. Dept. Agr., 1962-63; research assoc. dept. biol. scis. Fla. State U., Tallahassee, part-time, 1955-63; assoc. prof. Fla. State U., 1963-68, prof. biol. sci., 1968-86, assoc. chmn. grad. affairs, 1972-73, univ. service prof., 1986-87; vis. research scientist Tex. A&M U., College Station, 1974-75. Contbr. articles to various publs. Mem. Am. Genetic Assn., Am. Soc. Plant Taxonomists, Am. Soc. Cell Biology, Assn. Tropical Biology, Assn. Southeastern Biologists (v.p. 1967-68, Research prize 1950, Meritorious Teaching award 1985), Bot. Soc. Am., Genetics Soc. Am., Crop Sci. Soc. Am., Sigma Xi (chpt. pres. 1971-73), Soc. Study Evolution. Democrat. Methodist. Home: Tallahassee Fla. Died May 31, 1987, buried Georgetown, Tex.

MERCER, CHARLES, writer; b. Stouffville, Ont., Can., July 12, 1917; s. Alfred and Alma (Hoover) M.; m. Alma Sutton, Feb. 21, 1940. A.B., Brown U., 1939. Reporter Washington Post, 1939-42; reporter, feature writer, columnist A.P., N.Y.C., 1946-59; sr. editor G.P. Putnam's Sons, N.Y.C., 1966-79; v.p. G.P. Putnam's Sons, 1975-79. Author: novels The Narrow Ledge, 1951, There Comes A Time, 1955, Rachel Cade, 1956, The Drummond Tradition, 1957, Enough Good Men, 1960, Pilgrim Strangers, 1961, The Reckoning, 1962, Gift of Life, 1963, Beyond Bojador, 1965, Promise Morning, 1966, The Minister, 1969, Revolt in April, 1971, The Castle on the River, 1975, Witch Tide, 1976, Murray Hill, 1980, Pacific, 1981; nonfiction Alexander The Great, 1963, Legion of Strangers, 1964, Miracle at Midway, 1977, Monsters in the Earth: The Story of Earthquakes, 1978, Statue of Liberty, 1979; also numerous short stories, articles. Served to 1st lt. AUS, World War II, Korean War. Mem. Phi Beta Kappa, Alpha Delta Phi. Club: Overseas Press (N.Y.C.). Home: Edison N.J. Died Dec. 28, 1988, buried Rosedale Cemetery, Monclair, N.J.

MEREDITH, JAMES HARGROVE, federal judge; b. Wedderburn, Oreg., Aug. 25, 1914; s. Willis H. and Ollie (Hargrove) M.; m. Dorothy Doke, Sept. 7, 1937 (dec. Feb. 1972); 1 son, James Doke; m. Susan B. Fitzgibbon, 1977. A.B., Mo. U., 1935, LL.B., 1937. Bar: Mo. bar 1937. Pvt. practice New Madrid County, 1937-42, 46-49; spl. agt. FBI, 1942-44; ptnr. Stolar, Kuhlmann & Meredith, St. Louis, 1952-61; partner Cook, Meredith, Murphy & English, 1961-62; ptnr. Stuart & Meredith, Washington, 1961-62; judge U.S. Dist. Ct. (ea. dist.) Mo., 1962-88, chief judge, 1971-79; judge U.S. Fgn. Intelligence Surveillance Ct., 1979-80; chief counsel Mo. Ins. Dept., Jefferson City, 1949-52; Past dir. Bank St. Louis, Comml. Bank St. Louis County, Gen. Bancshares, Inc., Investment Securities Co., Northland Bank. Mem. Mental Health Commn. Mo., 1961-62; trustee Friends U. Mo. Library, U. Mo. Law Sch. Found. Served with USNR, 1944-46. Recipient Patriots award SR, 1974. Mem. Jud. Conf. U.S. (exec. com. 1976, subcom. on improvement judiciary 1971-81, com. to rev. circuit council conduct and disability orders, 1982-87, com. to celebrate Bicentennial of U.S. constn.), Mo., D.C., St. Louis, Am. bar assns., Lawyers Assn. St. Louis, Mo. Squires, VFW, Am. Legion, Order of Coif, Sigma Chi (Significant Sig award), Phi Delta Phi (Disting. Alumni award). Presbyterian. Clubs: Mason (St. Louis) (Shriner), Old Warson Country (St. Louis), Mo. Athletic (St. Louis). Home: Saint Louis Mo. Died Dec. 8, 1988.

MERLE, LAWRENCE J., corporate executive; b. Union, N.Y., July 7, 1891; s. Gustav John and Marie (Schopp) M.; m. Lola Isabelle Merle, Aug. 11, 1911. Student pub. schs. V.p. Endicott-Johnson Corp., also bd. dirs. †

MEROLA, MARIO, lawyer; b. Bronx, N.Y., Feb. 1, 1922; s. Michael and Lucia (Morano) M.; m. Tullia Palermo, Aug. 21, 1949; children—Michael, Marylou Merola Zappa, Elizabeth. B.A., NYU, 1947, LL.B., 1948; LL.D. (hon.), Coll. Mt. St. Vincent, 1980. Bar: N.Y. 1949, U.S. Ct. Appeals (2d cir.) 1982, U.S. Dist. Ct. (so. dist.) N.Y. 1982. Sole practice Bronx, N.Y., 1949-57; atty. Dept. of Investigations, N.Y.C., 1957-60; asst. dist. atty. Bronx Dist. Attys' Office, 1960-64, dist. atty., 1973-87; councilman City Council, N.Y.C., 1964-72. Served to lt. USAAF, 1942-45. Mem. N.Y. State Bar Assn., Bronx County Bar Assn., Bronx County Criminal Bar Assn. Democrat. Roman Catholic. Home: Bronx N.Y. Died Oct. 27, 1987.

MERRIAM, JOHN FRANCIS, gas company executive; b. Constableville, N.Y., July 1, 1904; s. Charles Edward and Hilda (Doyle) M.; m. Lucy Lamon, Aug. 28, 1940; 1 son, James Alexander. PhB, U. Chgo., 1925; LLB, Chgo. Kent Coll. Law, 1930. With U. Chgo. bus. office, 1925-27, Hathaway & Co., 1927-30; with No. Natural Gas Co. (now Enron), Omaha, 1930-75, dir., from 1946, pres., 1950-60, chmn. bd., 1960-66, chmn. exec. com., 1966-75; bd. dirs. Sperry Rand Corp., Container Corp. Am., Bankers Life Co., Des Moines. Trustee U. Chgo., 1956, life, from 1970; chmn. bd. trustees Josyln Art Mus., Omaha; trustee Com. Econ. Devel., Oakland (Calif.) Mus., from 1974, Aspen (Colo.) Inst. Humanistic Studies; bd. dirs. Mus. Soc. San Francisco. Home: San Francisco Calif. Died Aug. 23, 1988.

MERRIAM, ROBERT EDWARD, business executive; b. Chgo., Oct. 2, 1918; s. Charles and Elizabeth Hilda (Doyle) M.; m. Marguerite DeTernova, Feb. 4, 1950; children—Aimee, Oliver, Monique. M.A., U. Chgo., 1940. Dir. Met. Housing Council, Chgo., 1946-47; alderman City Chgo. 1947-55; asst. dir. U.S. Bur. Budget, Washington, 1955-58, dep. dir., 1958; dep. asst. to Pres. U.S., 1958-61; pres. Spaceonics, Inc., 1961-64, Univ. Patents, Inc. of Ill., Chgo., 1964-70; exec. v.p. Urban Investment and Devel. Co., Chgo., 1971-76; chmn. bd. MGA Tech., Inc., Chgo., 1971-87; ptnr. Alexander Proudfoot, 1977-87; chmn. Merriam/Zuba, Ltd., 1988; Co-chmn. Ill. Commn. Urban Area Govt., 1969-72; chmn. Adv. Commn. Intergovtl. Relations, 1969-78. Author: Dark December: The Full Account of the Battle of the Bulge, 1947 (paper edit. titled Battle of the Bulge), (with Charles E. Merriam) The American Government: Democracy in Action, 1954, (with Rachel Goetz) Going Into Politics: A Guide for Citizens, 1957; also numerous mag. articles. Republican candidate for mayor Chgo., 1955. Served from pvt. to capt. AUS, 1942-46. Mem. Am. Polit. Sci. Assn., Am. Soc. Pub. Adminstrn., Nat. Acad. Pub. Adminstrn. Clubs: Casino, Chgo., Tavern (Chgo.). Home: Chicago Ill. Died Aug. 25, 1988, buried Arlington Nat. Cemetery.

MERRILL, CHARLES BOUGHTON, investment banker; b. Schoharie, N.Y., Aug. 4, 1892; s. William Dietz and Ella (Widman) M.; m. Ruby Husband, Apr. 5, 1918; children: Barrant Vroman, Peter Dietz. AB, Cornell U., 1915. With Burke, Hord & Curtiss, 1915; then assoc. Guaranty Trust Co. N.Y.; founder Merrill & Co., Cleve., 1924; became Merrill, Hawley & Co., 1926; became Merrill, Turben & Co., 1936, pres., 1936-58, chmn. bd., 1959-62, chmn. exec. com., from 1963; dir. Gen. Corp. Ohio; mem. New York Stock Exchange. V.p., mem. exec. com. No. Ohio Opera Assn.; trustee Cleve. Symphony Orch. Mem. Am. Legion, SAR, Union Club, Pepper Pike Club, Chagrin Valley Hunt Club, Country Club, Bankers Club (N.Y.C.), Hole-in-the-Golf Club, Port Royal Beach Club (Fla.). Home: Cleveland Ohio. †

MERRILL, EZRA, non-profit corporation executive; b. Misswa, Minn., Jan. 3, 1909; s. Ezra Birdette and Mabel (Brown) M.; m. Eva L. Vandenbergh, Dec. 22, 1965. A.B., Kalamazoo Coll., 1930; LL.B., Harvard U., 1933, postgrad. econs., 1934-35. With H.P. Hood & Sons, Boston, 1934-85; treas. H.P. Hood & Sons, 1962-66, pres., 1966-71, vice chmn. bd., 1971-74; also asso. Agribus. Assos., Boston, 1974-77; cons. Agribus. Council, N.Y.C., 1977-81; founder, exec. dir. Careers for Later Years, Boston, 1982-85. Mem. corp. or bd. dirs. Boston Children's Service Assn., Mass. Correctional Assn., Mass. Half-way Houses; co-founder Flynn Houses Boston. Clubs: Harvard (Boston), Commercial (Boston). Home: Boston Mass. Died Mar. 9, 1985; buried Ch. of Advent, Boston.

MERRILL, OLIVER BOUTWELL, lawyer; b. Summit, N.J., Nov. 13, 1903; s. Oliver Boutwell and Kitty Earl (Lyall) M.; m. Laura Gardner Provost, Sept. 1, 1928 (dec. Feb., 1985); 1 child, Barbara Louise Merrill Huggins. Grad., Phillips Acad., Andover, Mass., 1921; BA, Amherst Coll., 1925, LLD (hon.), 1976; LLB, Columbia U., 1928. Bar: N.Y. 1930. Legal sec. to Supreme Ct. Justice Stone 1928-29; practiced in N.Y.C.; ptnr. Sullivan & Cromwell, 1937-74; counsel Nat. War Fund, 1941-46; govt. appeal agt. local SSS, 1942-45; bd. dirs. Am. Water Works Co., Inc., 1947-51. Bd. dirs. Peoples Symphony Concerts, 1951-85; trustee Beardsley Sch., 1943-53; trustee Amherst Coll., 1951-85, chmn. bd. trustees, 1969-73. Decorated comdr. Order Brit. Empire. Mem. ABA, Univ. Club., Century Assn. N.Y.C. Home: New York N.Y. Died Feb. 12, 1985; cremated.

MERRILL, REED MILLER, educator, psychologist; b. Salt Lake City, Oct. 25, 1919; s. Daniel R. and Nettie M.; m. Maurine Wright, Nov. 4, 1937; children: Robert W., Roger G., Lynne, Shelley. BA, U. Utah, 1941, MA, 1946; PhD, U. Wash., 1953. Clin. psychologist U.S. Army, 1941-46; dir. counseling ctr., prof. ednl. psychology U. Utah, from 1954, head dept., 1962-70. Contbr. articles to profl. jours. Mem. Am. Psychol. Assn., Western Psychol. Assn., Utah Psychol. Assn. (pres.), AAAS, AAUP (pres. local chpt.). Home: Salt Lake City Utah. Died Dec. 24, 1985.

MERRIMAN, HEMINWAY, lawyer, business executive; b. N.Y.C., Nov. 2, 1912; s. Merritt Heminway and Sally Mallory (Betts) M.; m. Natalie Smith Rowbottom, Feb. 3, 1945; children: Mallory Betts Merriman Constantine, M. Heminway, Natalie Smith. BA, Yale U., 1934, JD, 1937. Bar: Conn. Ptnr. firm Carmody & Torrance, Waterbury, Conn., 1938-42, 46-48; with Scovill Mfg. Co. (now Scovill Inc.), Waterbury, from 1948, sec., gen. counsel, treas., v.p.; dir. Banking Ctr., Waterbury. Bd. dirs. ARC; trustee Watertown Found., Woodward Fund, Evergreen Cemetery Assn.; mem. zoning bd. appeals Watertown Fire Dist. With USN, 1942-46. Mem. Watebury Bar Assn., Litchfield County Bar Assn., Conn. Bar Assn., Conn. State Srs. Golf Assn. (2d v.p.), Waterbury, Waterbury Country, Weekapang, Yacht, Univ. Litchfield County clubs, Phi Delta Phi, Alpha Delta Phi. Republican. Episcopalian. Home: Watertown Conn. Died Apr. 1987; buried Evergreen Cemetery, Watertown.

MERRITT, ARTHUR DONALD, educator, physician; b. Shawnee, Okla., June 11, 1925; s. Arthur B. and Frances (Harris) M.; m. Doris Honig, May 5, 1953; children—Kenneth Arthur, Christopher Ralph. Student, U. Md., 1946-47; A.B., George Washington U., 1949, M.D., 1952. Diplomate: Am. Bd. Internal Medicine. Rotating intern D.C. Gen. Hosp., 1952-53; asst. resident medicine George Washington U. Hosp., 1953-54, clin. instr., 1959-60; asst. resident medicine Duke Hosp., 1954-55, fellow medicine, 1955-56, chief resident, 1956-57, instr. medicine, 1956-57; clin. assoc. Nat. Inst. Arthritis and Metabolic Diseases, Bethesda, Md., 1957-58; chief med. investigation sect. Nat. Inst. Dental Research, Bethesda, 1958-60; asso. prof. medicine and biochemistry Ind. U. Sch. Medicine, 1961-65; chmn. med. genetics program Ind. U. Sch. Medicine (Grad. Sch.), 1962-66, chmn. dept. med. genetics, 1966-78, prof. medicine and med. genetics, 1966-79; chief health professions applications br. Lister Hill Nat. Center for Biomed. Communications, Nat. Library Medicine, NIH, Bethesda, Md., 1979-84; cons. Indpls. VA Hosp., 1961-79. Med. adviser, bd. dirs. Ind. Cystic Fibrosis Found., 1961-77. Served with AUS, 1943-46; Served with USPHS, 1957-60. Fellow ACP; mem. William Beaumont Med. Soc., Smith-Reed-Russell Med. Soc., George Washington U. Med. Soc., Duke Med. Alumni Soc., AMA, Ind. Med. Assn., Marion (Ind.) County Med. Soc., N.Y. Acad. Scis., Am. Fedn. Clin. Research, Central Soc. Clin. Research, Am. Soc. Human Genetics (treas. 1964-67, 67-70), Behavior Genetics Assn., Genetics Soc. Am., Sigma Xi, Nu Sigma Nu, Alpha Omega Alpha. Home: Bethesda Md. Died Nov. 25, 1986; cremated.

MESCON, HERBERT, physician, educator; b. Toronto, Ont., Can., Apr. 3, 1919; (parents Am. citizens); s. Morris and Bella (Paleschuck) M.; m. Barbara Jeanne McKenzie, Sept. 15, 1946; children: Susan Lee, Gary Lawrence, Robin Lenore, Stanley Richard. BS, Coll. City N.Y., 1938; MD, Boston U., 1942. Diplomate Am. Bd. Dermatology and Syphilology, Am. Bd. Skin Pathology. Resident pathology Mallory Inst. Pathology, Boston City Hosp., 1942-43; med. intern Tufts U. med. service, 1947-48; rotating intern Lebanon Hosp., Bronx, N.Y., 1946-47; fellow dept. dermatology Hosp. U. Pa., 1948-51, Damon Runyon cancer rsch. fellow, 1949-51; asst. instr. dermatology U. Pa. Med. Sch., 1948-50, instr., 1950-51, assoc., 1951-52, instr. dermatology Grad. Sch. Medicine, 1952; attending physician VA Hosp., Wilmington, Del., 1950-51, cons., 1951-52; cons. Skin and Cancer Hosp., Phila., 1951-52; prof. Boston U. Sch. Medicine, 1952-85, also head dept. dermatology, from 1952; dir. genito-infectious diseases clinic U. Hosps., 1958-74, asst. mem. Robert Dawson Evans Meml. dept. clin. rsch. and preventive medicine, 1952, assoc. mem., 1954-60, mem., from 1960; dir. dermatology Boston City Hosp., 1974-85; cons. dermato-pathology and dermatology VA Hosp., Boston, from 1955, area VA, 1960-66; sr. cons. dermatology Lemuel Shattuck Hosp., Boston, 1955-85. Mem. Am. Assn. Pathologists and Bacteriologists, Soc. Investigative Dermatology (pres.), Boston (pres.), New Eng. (pres.) dermatol. socs., Am. Acad. Dermatology and Syphilology (dir. 1972-74, v.p. 1974), AMA, Histochem. Soc., Am. Dermatol. Assn. Lt. col. M.C., AUS, 1943-46. Home: Newton Mass. Died Nov. 16, 1985; body donated to sci.

MESSINGER, WILLIAM HENRY, lawyer; b. Fulton, Ind., Sept. 9, 1897; s. Henry and Mary E. (Stingley) M.; m. Vera M. Felder, Oct. 1, 1923 (dec. Apr. 1980); children: Paul Raymond, Philip William, Mary Joan (Mrs. Chisato Kitagawa); m. Clara Seeler Vreeland, Jan. 9, 1985. A.B., U. Mich., 1921, J.D., 1923. Bar: Mich. 1923, Ariz. 1943. Practice law Grand Rapids, Mich., 1923-43, Phoenix, 1944-87; mem. firm Cunningham, Carson, Messinger & Carson, 1947-56, Cunningham, Carson & Messinger, 1956-62, Carson, Messinger, Elliott, Laughlin & Ragan, 1963-87. Mem. Bd. Edn. Scottsdale, Ariz., 1948-54. Mem. ABA, Mich. Bar Assn., Ariz. Bar Assn., Maricopa County Bar Assn., Grand Rapids Bar Assn. (pres. 1942). Republican. Congregationalist. Clubs: Mason (Phoenix) (32 deg.), Arizona (Phoenix); Kiwanis (pres. Scottsdale 1948). Home: Scottsdale Ariz. Died Mar. 15, 1987; buried Paradise Meml. Gardens, Scottsdale.

MESSMORE, FRED W(ILBER), judge; b. Boone, Iowa, July 11, 1889; s. Hiram Alfred and Calarinda Jane (Davidson) M.; m. Jennie Frances Saxe, Apr. 30, 1913; children: Hiram Allison, Frederick Boughn (dec.), John Colby. Student, Northwestern Normal and Bus. Sch., 1908-09; LLB, Creighton U., 1912. Bar: Nebr. 1912. Practiced in Beatrice, Nebr.; county atty. 1915-18, county judge, 1921-29, dist. judge, 1929-37; assoc. justice Supreme Ct. Nebr., from 1937; mem. Nat. R.R. Adjustment Bd., Nat. Emergency Bd. Pvt. AUS, 1918-19, lt. col., JAGC, Res. Mem. Nebr. Bar Assn., Am. Legion, Masons, Kiwanis, Delta Theta Phi. Home: Lincoln Nebr. †

METCALF, MICHAEL PIERCE, newspaper publishing executive; b. Providence, Sept. 1, 1933; s. George Pierce and Pauline Pumpelly (Cabot) M.; m. Charlotte L. Saville, Jan. 30, 1971; children: Hannah, Jesse, Lucy. B.A., Harvard U., 1955; M.B.A., Stanford U., 1959. Reporter Charlotte Observer, 1959-60; sales exec. Phila. Bull., 1960-61; asst. to pres. Providence Jour. Co., 1962-71, exec. v.p., 1971-74, pres., 1974-85, chmn., 1985-87, pub., 1979-87, chief exec. officer, 1983-87, also dir.; pres., dir. Providence Jour. Broadcasting Corp., 1978-87; dir. Colony Communications, Communications Properties, R.I. Hosp. Trust Nat. Banks. Trustee Providence Performing Arts Center, Providence Found., R.I. Sch. Design; bd. dirs. Newspaper Advt. Bur., Am. Press Inst., U. R.I. Found.; adv. council U. R.I. Marine Programs. Served to lt. (j.g.) USN, 1955-57. Mem. Inter-Am. Press Inst., Gravure Research Inst., Am. Newspaper Pubs. Assn. Clubs: Brook, Agawam Hunt and Hope. Died Sept. 20, 1987.

METHOD, HAROLD LAMBERT, educator, surgeon; b. Duluth, Minn., July 22, 1918; s. Harold S. and Irene (Lambert) M.; m. Margaret Elizabeth Nelson, May 3, 1943. B.S., Northwestern U., 1940, B.M., M.D., 1944, M.S., 1949. Diplomate: Am. Bd. Surgery. Intern Cook County Hosp., Chgo., 1944; resident Cook County Hosp., 1949-52; resident Passavant Meml. Hosp., Chgo., 1947-48, mem. attending staff, 1952-87; mem. attending staff Cook County Hosp., Chgo., 1950-52, VA Research Hosp., Chgo., 1953-87; faculty Northwestern U. Med. Sch., 1949-87, asso. prof. surgery, 1973-75, prof. surgery, 1975-87; pres. med. staff Passavant Meml. Hosp., 1965-67; med. dir. Chgo. Tribune, 1980-87. Contbr. articles to med. jours.; Asso. editor: Surgery, Gynecology and Obstetrics, 1970-87. Served to lt. M.C. USNR, 1944-46. Recipient Service award Northwestern U., 1959; All-Am. Football award Sports Illustrated 25th Anniversary, 1964. Mem. AMA., Ill.Med. Soc., Chgo. Med Soc. (award excellence and originality in research in art and sci. surgery 1947), Chgo. Surg. Soc., A.C.S., Western Surg. Assn., Soc. Surgery Alimentary Tract, James IV Surg. Assn., Am. Fedn. Clin. Research, Northwestern U. Alumni Assn. (council med. div. 1952-54, v.p. charge activities 1954-55, pres. 1957-59, bd. dirs. 1956-58). Clubs: Tavern of Chgo. (pres. 1974-76), Lake Zurich Golf (pres. 1976-77). Home: Chicago Ill. Died Feb. 16, 1987; buried All Saints Cemetery, Des Plaines, Ill.

METZ, CARL ALTGELD, structural engineer, architect; b. Tolono, Ill., Nov. 30, 1892; s. Philip William and Emma (Albrecht) M.; m. Adeline M. Albrecht, June 1, 1936. BSCE, U. Ill., 1915. Draftsman, engr. various firms 1915-25; ptnr. Dovell & Metz, structural engrs., 1925-30; owner C.A. Metz Engring. Co., 1930-47; ptnr. Shaw, Metz and Dolio, architects and engrs., Chgo., 1947-50, 1947-50; ptnr. Shaw, Metz and Assocs., 1959-66, Shaw, Metz, Train, Olsen & Youngblood, Inc., Chgo., from 1966. Mem. ASCE, Western Soc. Engrs., Ill. C. of C., Engrs. Club, Builders Club, Lake Shore Club, Medinah Country Club (Chgo.). Home: Chicago Ill. †

METZGER, LEON DANIEL, lawyer; b. Sinnemahoning, Pa., Apr. 23, 1891; s. William Howard and Ella Samantha (Berfield) M.; m. Josephine Adele Klopp, Feb. 23, 1921 (div. June 1952); children: JoAnn (Mrs. Robert McFadin), Mary Jane (Mrs. William Slike). AB, U. Mich., 1914, LLB, 1916. Bar: Mich. 1916, Pa. 1920. Practice law specializing in corp. taxes Harrisburg, Pa., from 1935; ptnr. Metzger, Hafer, Keefer, Thomas & Wood, and predecessors, from 1937; part-time prof. Dickinson Sch. Law, 1928-39; tchr. Extension Sch., U. Pa., 1928-41. Trustee, treas. Pa. Assn. for Blind, pres. 1955-56. 1st lt. inf. U.S. Army, World War I. Mem. Am., Pa., Dauphin County (pres. 1955) bar assns., West Shore Country Club (pres. 1935), Masons (32 deg.), Sigma Phi Epsilon, Phi Delta Phi. Republican. Methodist. Home: Camp Hill Pa. †

METZGER, SIDNEY M., bishop; b. Fredericksburg, Tex., July 11, 1902; s. Francis and Ida (Dietz) M. Student, St. Mary's Sch., Fredericksburg, 1910-15, St. John's Sem., San Antonio, 1915-22; ThD, N.Am. Coll., Rome, Italy, 1926; Dr. Canon Law, Pontifical Inst. Canon and Civil Law, Rome, 1928; LLD, St. Edwards U. Ordained priest St. John Lateran Basilica, Rome, 1926. Prof. St. John's Sem., San Antonio, 1928-33, rector, 1933-40; regent St. Mary's U. Law Sch., San Antonio, 1935-40; consecrated aux. bishop Santa Fe (titular bishop Birta), 1940; installed as coadjutor bishop of El Paso with right of succession, 1942; succeeded to See of El Paso, 1942; asst. to Papal Throne, 1965. Decorated knight comdr. Equestrian Order of Holy Sepulchre of Jerusalem, 1952; Grand Cross of King Alfonso X, The Wise (Spain), 1957; Doctor Mundunae Sapientias, Boswell Soc., 1963; recipient St. Joseph the Worker award Tex. AFL-CIO, 1973, John Casey Labor Man of Yr. award Cath. Labor Inst., 1973, award Amalgamated Clothing Workers Am., 1973. Home: El Paso Tex. Died Apr. 12, 1986.

MEYER, ADOLPHE ERICH, historian, educator, writer; b. N.Y.C., Oct. 15, 1897; s. Adolphe and Frieda (Schelker) M.; m. Margaret Holt McDonald, 1924 (dec.); children: Margaret Patricia (dec.), Adolph Erich (dec.); m. 2d, Jessie Bryant, 1942. BS, NYU, 1921, AM, 1922, PhD, 1926. Instr. German NYU, 1922-28, instr. edn., 1928-30, asst. prof., 1930-34, assoc. prof., 1934-48, prof. ednl. history, 1948-63, then emeritus; vis. prof. history edn. U. Ill. at Urbana, 1965-67; Disting. prof. history edn. Old Dominion U. , Norfolk, Va., 1967-68; ednl. cons. various publs. Author: Public Education in Modern Europe, 1927, Fundamentals of German, 1927, Education in Modern Times, 1931, John Dewey and Modern Education, 1932, Modern European Educators, 1934, A Student's Outline in the History of Education, 1935, Development of Education in the 20th Century (Book-of-Month and NEA choice), 1939, rev. edit., 1949, Japanese edit., 1961, Voltaire—Man of Justice (Book-of-Month alternate choice), 1945, An Educational History of the American People, 1958, rev. edit., 1967, An Educational History of the Western World, 1965, rev. edit., 1972, Grandmasters of Educational Thought, 1975; co-author: Becoming an Educator, 1963; author introduction: Centennial Offering, 1977; translator: Georg Kaiser, The Phantom Lover, 1928; contbr. to Ency. Brit., 1958-59, 1973. Mem. Authors League Am., Phi Delta Kappa, Kappa Delta Pi, Kappa Phi Kappa. Home: Champaign Ill. Died Sept. 30, 1988.

MEYER, ALVIN EARL, lawyer; b. New Albany, Ind., Apr. 1, 1923; s. Henry W. and Hallie (Leach) M.; m. Joanne Warvel, Feb. 12, 1949; 1 child, John C. BS, Ind. U., 1944, LLB with distinction, 1946. Bar: Ind. 1946. Pvt. practice New Albany, 1946-48, Indpls., 1948; prof. law U. Louisville, Ind. U., 1946-47; ptnr. Stewart, Irwin, Gilliom & Guthrie, Indpls., 1955-86. Home: Indianapolis Ind. Died Mar. 17, 1986.

MEYER, BERNARD S(ANDLER), botanist, educator; b. Nantucket, Mass., July 20, 1901; s. John Frederick and Florence Katherine (Hinkle) M.; m. Blanche Montgomery, 1931 (div.); m. 2d, Grace Townsend, 1948. BA, Ohio State U., 1921, MA, 1923, PhD, 1926; student, in Eng., Germany, 1930. Grad. asst. Ohio State U., 1921-23, instr., 1923-27; assoc. forest ecologist U.S. Forest Svc., 1927-28; asst. prof. botany Ohio State U., 1928-34, assoc. prof., 1934-40, prof., from 1940, chmn. dept. botany and plant pathology, from 1946, and Ohio Agr. Exptl. Sta., 1948-65; investigator, Desert Lab. Carnegie Inst., summer 1929; prof. plant physiology, Stone Biol. Lab. summers 1937, 38, 40, 41; assoc. physiologist, U.S. Dept. Agr., summer 1943, physiologist, summers 1944-45; bus. mgr. Ohio Jour. Sci., 1930-41; collaborator, rubber investigations, U.S. Dept. Agr., 1942-44; cons. Nat. Sci. Found., from 1958. Co-author: Plant Physiology, 1939, Laboratory Plant Physiology, 1943, Introduction to Plant Physiology, 1960; editor-in-chief Am. Jour. Botany, 1946-51; contbr. Ency. Britannica, tech. jours. Recipient Cert. of Merit Bot. Soc. Am., 1959. Fellow AAAS, Ohio Acad. Sci. (v.p. 1933); mem. Am. Inst. Biol. Scis. (governing bd. 1958-64, v.p. 1961), Bot. Soc. Am. (chmn. physiol. sect. 1941, v.p. 1952), Am. Phytopath. Soc., Ecol. Soc. Am., Am. Soc. Plant Physiols. (v.p. 1940, pres. 1943), Faculty Club, Phi Beta Kappa, Sigma Xi, Gamma Alpha. Home: Columbus Ohio. Died Sept. 25, 1987.

MEYER, HAROLD DIEDRICH, educator; b. Augusta, Ga., Nov. 20, 1892; s. John Henry and Mena (Sancken) M.; m. Helen Wright, Sept. 27, 1917; children: Harold Diedrich (dec.), George Wright. AB, U. Ga., 1912, AM, 1916; postgrad., Columbia, 1925-26; LLD, Fla. So. Coll., 1941; RSD, Salem Coll., W.Va.; LHD, Catawha Coll., 1951. Prin. high sch. Statesboro, Ga., 1912-13; supt. schs. Statesboro, 1913-15; prof. history State Normal Sch., Athens, Ga., 1916-18, prof. sociology, 1919-21; assoc. prof. sociology U. N.C., 1921-26, prof., from 1926, Taylor Grandy prof. art and philosophy of living, from 1962; instr. spl. courses U. Ga., 1916-21; summer sch. tchr. U. Fla., U. Wsah., Emory U., NYU, U. Colo.; chief bur. recreation, U. Extension div. U. N.C.; regional dir. edn. and recreation, Works Projects Adminstrn. region 4, 1935-38; ednl. cons. Nat. Congress of Parents and Tchrs., 1941; cons. Office of Edn. on Tng. of Recreation Leaders for Nat. Def., 1941, nat. def. recreation project Works Projects Adminstrn., 1941; U.S. del. and chmn. I.L.O. Internat. Recreation Conf., Geneva, 1949. Author: Handbook of Extra-Curricular Activities, 1926, Financing Extra-Curricular Activities, 1929, The School Club Program, 1932; co-author: American Democracy Anew (high sch. text), 1940, Community Recreation, 1949, State Recreation, 1950, Recreation Administration, 1955, others; editor: Extra-Curricular Library, 20 vols., 1929-35, N.C. Recreation Rev.; mem. editorial bd. Social Forces, Youth Leaders Digest; contbr. articles to jours. Ednl. chmn. region 6, mem. nat. coun. Boy Scouts Am., from 1930; mem nat. exec. bd. Camp Fire Girls, 1946-49; mem. regional com. Girl Scouts Inc., 1946; mem. state bd. mgrs. N.C. PTA, 1924-52; exec.

dir. N.C. Recreation Com., coordinator recreation State Office Civilian Def. in N.C., 1943-45; chmn. Ea. Conf. State Recreation Com., 1944; mem. Nat. Recreation Policies Com.; dir. N.C. Recreation Commn., 1945; mem. recreation com. VA. 1st lt. U.S. Army, 1917. Recipient Silver Beaver award Boy Scouts Am., 1940. Mem. Coll. Conf. Tng. Recreation Leaders (nat. chmn. 1939-40, 40-42), N.C. High Sch. Athletic Assn. (mem. exec. com., 1925-50), Am. Sociol. Soc., N.C. Conf. Social Service, Nat. Conf. Social Work, Am. Recreation Soc. (pres. 1946-48, nat. chmn. legis. com.), Am. Group Work Assn., So. Sociol. Soc., N.C. Recreation Soc., Alpha Kappa Delta, Phi Delta Kappa, Alphi Phi Omega, Omicron Delta Kappa, Delta Tau Delta. Democrat. Episcopalian. Home: Chapel Hill N.C. †

MEYER, HOWARD RAYMOND, architect; b. N.Y.C., Feb. 17, 1903; s. Emile and Estelle (Freund) M.; m. Schon Landman, Oct. 16, 1928; 1 son, Paul Emile. A.B., Columbia U., 1923, B.Arch., 1928. With office William Lescaze (architect), N.Y.C., 1926, Bertram G. Goodhue Assocs. (architects), N.Y.C., 1929-30; travel in Europe, 1930-31; supr. constrn. Albanian-Am. Inst. of Nr. East Found., Kavaja, Albania; for Thompson & Churchill (architects), N.Y.C., 1932; ptnr. Morris B. Sanders & Howard R. Meyer (architects), N.Y.C., 1933-34; pvt. practice architecture Dallas, 1935-42, 46-88; cons. to PHA; archtl. advisory panel Office Chief Engrs., Dept. Army; cons. architect student chapel Tex. A&M Coll., 1956; Chmn. architects adv. com. Dallas Hist. Monuments Commn., 1961. Prin. works include 13th Ch. of Christ Scientist, N.Y.C., 1934, Temple Beth El, Tyler, Tex., 1938, Hillel Found. at U. Tex, 1950, Red River Arsenal and Longhorn Ordnance Works, 1951-53; 2 pub. housing projects, Dallas, 1953; Burnet Elementary Sch, Dallas, 1955, 3525 Turtle Creek apt. bldg, Dallas, 1957, Temple Emanu El, Dallas, 1957, Dallas Rehab. Center, 1960, Turtle Creek Village, 1962, Dallas Home and Hosp. Jewish Aged, 1963, 1st Presbyn. Ch, Denton, Tex., 1966, Nogales Bldg, Vicksburg, Miss., 1966, McKinney (Tex.) Job Corps Center for Women, 1967, Aircraft Instrument Trainer Bldg, Ft. Wolters, Tex., 1968; bachelor officer's quarters, Ft. Hood, Tex., 1969, officer family housing, Bergstrom AFB, Tex., 1969; U.S. P.O. and Fed. Bldg, Rockwall, Tex., 1970, St. Paul Luth. Ch, Denton, 1972, Adminstrv. Tng. Bldg. for Big Brown Steam Electric Sta., Tex., 1972, Byer Sq. at Dallas Home for Jewish Aged, 1974, Dallas West Br. Library, 1974, Ruth W. and Milton P. Levy Bldg, Dallas, 1977, Denton Area Tchrs. Credit Union, 1978. Mem. design com. Greater Dallas Planning Council. Served to maj. C.E. AUS, 1942-46. Recipient grand prize Matico competition Mastic Tile Corp. Am., 1959. Fellow AIA (award merit 1959, chmn. com. on housing 1966); mem. Tex. Soc. Architects (medal merit 1950, award merit 1958), Guild Religious Archtecture, Zeta Beta Tau. Jewish. Home: Dallas Tex. Died Jan. 10, 1988.

MEYERHOFF, ARTHUR EDWARD, advertising agency executive; b. Chgo., Mar. 12, 1895; s. Emanuel and Jennie (Lewin) M.; m. Madelaine H. Goldman, 1921; m. Elaine Clemens, Jan. 27, 1945; children: Jane, Arthur E., Joanne, William, Judith Lynn. Student pub. schs. With Hood Rubber Co., 1914-22; classified advt., circulation mgr. Wis. News, Milw., 1922-29; with Neisser & Meyerhoff, advt. and merchandising, Chgo., 1929-41; pres. Arthur Meyerhoff Assos., Inc. (formerly Arthur Meyerhoff & Co.), Chgo., 1941-65; chmn. Arthur Meyerhoff Assos., Inc. (formerly Arthur Meyerhoff & Co.), 1965-80; founder chmn. bd. BBDO (formerly Arthur Meyerhoff Assos., Inc.), 1981-86; organized Gibraltar Industries, Inc., 1958; dir. Santa Catalina Island Co., Chgo. Nat. League Ball Club; organized Myzon, Inc., 1951; mem. adv. bd. KBIG-KBRT, Los Angeles. Author: Strategy of Persuasion, 1965. Bd. dirs. Nat. Horse Show Registry. Served with AEF, World War I. Received 1st prize Marshall Field candid div. 6th ann., 3d internat. competition and salon, 1939; George Washington Honor medal award Freedoms Found. Valley Forge, 1967. Mem. Am. Assn. Advt. Agys., C. of C. Died Aug. 29. 1986.

MEYERS, CHARLES JARVIS, lawyer, educator; b. Dallas, Aug. 7, 1925; s. Percy Avery and Katherine (Jarvis) M.; m. Pamela Adams, Aug. 4, 1954; children—George Frederick, Katherine. B.A., Rice U., 1945; LL.B., U. Tex., 1949; LL.M., Columbia, 1953, J.S.D., 1964. Bar: Tex. bar 1949, Colo. bar 1981. Asst. prof. law U. Tex., Austin, 1949-52; asso. prof. U. Tex., 1952-54; asso. prof. Columbia, 1954-57, prof., 1957-62; prof. law Stanford, 1962-81, Charles A. Beardsley prof., 1971-76, Richard E. Lang prof. and dean, 1976-81; partner Gibson, Dunn & Crutcher, Denver, 1981-88; dir. Pub. Advs., Inc., San Francisco, 1971-78; vis. prof. U. Minn., 1953-54, Cornell U., 1961, U. Mich., 1963, U. Utah, 1965, U. Chile, Santiago, 1968-69; sr. prof. Chile Law Program, Santiago, 1968-69; asst. gen. counsel Nat. Water Commn., 1970-73; pres. Assn. Am. Law Schs., 1975; vice chmn. Gov.'s Commn. to Study Calif. Water Rights Law, 1977-79; dir. S.W. Forest Industries; mem. Pres.'s Intelligence Oversight Bd., 1982-88. Author: (with H.R. Williams) Oil and Gas Law, 1959, 3d edit. 1985, Cases on Oil and Gas Law, 5th edit, 1986, Report to President's Task Force on Communications Policy, Market Exchange of Spectrum Rights, 1968, (with Tarlock) Water Resource Management, 2d edit, 1979, Legal-Economic Aspects of Environmental Protection, 1971. Served to lt. (j.g.) USNR, 1945-46, PTO. Mem. Am. Law Inst., Am., Tex., Colo. bar assns., Nat. Acad. Engring. (com. pub. policy 1970-73), Order of Coif, Phi Beta Kappa, Phi Delta Phi. Republican. Home: Denver Colo. Died July 17, 1988; interred Fairmount Cemetery, Denver.

MEYERS, WALLACE EDWIN, industrial consultant; b. N.Y.C., Aug. 13, 1892; s. Edwin L. and Frances E. (Oppenheimer) M.; m. Francis Genevieve Stoneman, June 4, 1939; 1 child, Peter W. Student, Phillips Exeter Acad.; LittB, Princeton, 1913; spl. student, Army Indsl. Coll., 1944. Sec. Quality Silks Mills Inc., Granville, N.Y., 1914-16; asst. gen. mgr. Louis Meyers & Son Inc., N.Y.C. and Gloversville, N.Y., 1920-22, sec.-treas., 1923-33, pres., 1934-40; sr. negotiator contracts Q.M.C., 1942-45; chief assets liquidation unit Gen. Hdqrs., Supreme Comdr. Allied Powers, Tokyo, 1946-48; mem. Far East Command Requirements Com., Tokyo, 1947, Econ. Coordinating Com., Tokyo, 1948; fgn. svc. res. officer ECA, ICA, Italy, Portugal, Costa Rica, Pakistan, 1949-61, ret., 1961; tech. cons. Ceylon, 1962; cons. Brit. Colour Coun., 1935-40. Capt. U.S. Army, 1917-19, AEF. Home: Sarasota Fla. †

MICHAELIS, JOHN HERSEY, army officer, management consultant; b. San Francisco, Aug. 21, 1912; s. Otho E. and Louise E. (Haas) M.; m. Mary Wadsworth, Dec. 28, 1937; children: Maurene L., Marie A. BS, U.S. Mil. Acad., 1936; grad., Command and Gen. Staff Sch., 1942, Armed Forces Staff Coll., 1944, 49; LLD, Franklin and Marshall Coll., 1964, Chungang U., 1970. Commd. 2d lt. U.S. Army, 1936, advanced through grades to gen., 1969; assigned U.S., P.I., C.Z., 1936-43; comdr. 502d Parachute Inf., 101st Airborne Div., 1944; chief of staff 101st Airborne Div., 1944-45; assigned Gen. Staff, War Dept., 1945; sr. aide to Gen. Eisenhower 1947-48; asst. chief of staff ops. 8th Army, 1949-50; comdg. officer 27th Inf. Regt., Korea, 1950; asst. div. comdr. 25th Inf. Div., 1950-51; dep. for tng. SHAPE, 1951-52; spl. rep. for Pres. Eisenhower's European Def. Conf; comdt. of cadets U.S. Mil. Acad., 1952-54; readiness officer Hdqrs. Allied Forces So. Europe, 1954-55; comdg. gen. So. European Task Force, 1955-56; chief legis. liaison Office Sec. Army, 1956-59; comdg. gen. U.S. Army, Alaska, 1959-62, U.S. Army V Corps, Fed. Republic Germany, 1962-63, Land-S.E., 1963-66, 5th U.S. Army, 1966-69; dep. comdg. gen. 8th U.S. Army, 1969; comdr. in chief UN Command; also comdr. U.S. Forces Korea, 8th U.S. Army, 1969-72; ret. 1972; mgmt. cons. Hanjin Internat. Inc., 1972-85. Decorated D.S.M. with 2 oak leaf clusters, Bronze Star with V device and 2 oak leaf clusters, Air medal, Purple Heart with oak leaf cluster: Croix de Guerre with palm (France); Croix de Guerre with palm (Belgium); Bronze Lion (The Netherlands); comdr. Order of Merit (Italy); Philippine Legion of Honor; Ulchi Disting. Mil. Svc. medal with gold star, Tong-Il medal 1st class Order Nat. Security Merit (Republic of Korea); Army Mil. medal 1st class (Chile); grand comdr. Royal Order King George I (Greece); 1st Knight grand cross Exalted Order White Elephant (Thailand). Home: Saint Petersburg Fla. Died Oct. 30, 1985.

MICKEL, CLARENCE E(UGENE), entomologist; b. Lincoln, Nebr., Feb. 29, 1892; s. Fred Walter and Carrie Aurilla (Brown) M.; m. Mae Electa Allen, Dec. 22, 1914; children: Virginia Ysobel (Mrs. James H. Littlefield), Stanley Allen, Thelma Mae (Mrs. Thomas Klick). BS, U. Nebr., 1917; MS, U. Minn., 1923, PhD, 1925. Extension entomologist U. Nebr., 1917-20; rsch. entomologist Am. Beet Sugar Co., Rocky Ford, Colo., 1920-22; extension entomologist U. Minn., 1922-27, asst. prof., 1925-31, assoc. prof., 1931-41, prof., from 1941, acting chief, div. entomology and economic zoology, 1944-45, chief, from 1945; adviser entomology Coll. Agr., Seoul Nat. U., Republic of Korea, 1957. Contbr. articles to profl. jours. Recipient award Elizabeth Thompson Sci. Fund, 1926; John Simon Guggenheim Meml. Found. fellow, 1930-31. Fellow AAAS, Entomol. Soc. Am. (pres. 1944, chmn. North Cen. br. 1956), Royal Entomol. Soc. London; mem. Internat. Gt. Plains Conf. Entomology (pres. 1946-55), Am. Assn. Econ. Entomology, Farm House, Sigma Xi, Gamma Sigma Delta, Alpha Zeta. Baptist. Home: Saint Paul Minn. †

MIDDLEBROOK, ROBERT WARD, pharmaceutical company executive; b. Pomona, Kans., July 8, 1916; s. Robert and Julia McPherson (Ward) M.; m. Georgianna Shephard Leslie, May 10, 1947; children: Leslie Deborah, Julia Anne. AB, Princeton U., 1937; LLB, Columbia U., 1940. Bar: N.Y. 1940. With Mudge, Stern, Williams & Tucker, N.Y.C., 1940-49; vice consul Calcutta, India, 1941-44; sec., gen. counsel Huylers, N.Y.C., 1949-51; v.p., dir. Pfizer Internat., 1951-63; v.p. Olin Mathieson Chem. Corp., N.Y.C., 1963-66; gen. mgr. Olin Internat., 1963-66; pres., dir. Squibb Internat. Co., 1963-67; sr. v.p. Richardson Merrell, Inc., 1967-81, ret.; past bd. dirs. Richardson Vick Inc., Piedmont Mgmt. Co., Inc., Reins. Corp. N.Y. Trustee Smith Richardson Found.; fin. chmn. Washington (Conn.) Art Assn.; past deacon, moderator, trustee First Congl. Ch., Washington. Served to lt (j.g.) USNR, 1944-46. Clubs: Knickerbocker (N.Y.C.); Washington (Conn.); Princeton. Home: Washington Conn. Died Feb. 4, 1989.

MIDER, GEORGE BURROUGHS, physician, educator; b. Windsor, N.Y., Aug. 9, 1907; s. Carrol A. and Elizabeth (Pawson) M.; m. Ruth Isabelle Lyman, Jan. 7, 1939; 1 dau., Ruth Elizabeth Mider Murdock. AB, Cornell U., 1930, MD, 1933. Diplomate Am. Bd. Pathology in Pathologic Anatomy. Intern, resident, asst. surgery Albany (N.Y.) Hosp., 1933-36; asst. surgery, instr. rsch. assoc. surgery, then prof. cancer rsch. U. Rochester Sch. Medicine and Dentistry, 1936-52; instr. pathology, asst. prof., asst. pathologist Cornell U., 1941-44; assoc. prof. pathology U. Va., 1944-45; assoc. dir. charge rsch. Nat. Cancer Inst., Bethesda, Md., 1952-60; dir. labs. and clinics NIH, 1960-68; spl. asst. to dir. Nat. Library Medicine, 1968-69, dep. dir., 1970-72; exec. officer Univs. Assoc. for Rsch. and Edn. in Pathology, 1972-75; adv. bd. biomed. div. Samuel Roberts Noble Found., 1958-65; mem. standing com., com. fed. labs. Fed Coun. Sci. and Tech., 1964-68; bd. dirs. Gorgas Meml. Inst.; trustee Leonard Wood Meml. Hosp. Recipient Disting. Service award HEW, 1960, James Ewing Soc. Lectureship, 1968, Nat. Library Medicine Dir.'s Honor award, 1972. Mem. AMA (chmn. com. occupational cancer, coun. indsl. health 1954-60), Am. Cancer Soc. (adv. com. instnl. rsch. grants 1956-58), Am. Assn. Cancer Rsch., Am. Assn. Pathologists and Bacteriologists, James Ewing Soc., Am. Soc. Exptl. Pathology (exec. officer), Washington Acad. Medicine, AAAS, Sigma Xi, Alpha Omega Alpha, Pi Kappa Alpha, Nu Sigma Nu. Home: Rockville Md. Died Dec. 13, 1985.

MILES, EUGENE L., banker; b. Balt., Oct. 15, 1889; s. Frank W. and Evaline (Langrall) M.; m. Helen E. Winter, Feb. 9, 1918; children: Helen M. (Mrs. William H. Fusting), Eugene L., Jerome F. Ed. pub. schs. 1st v.p. Fidelity-Balt. Nat. Bank, also bd. dirs.; bd. dirs. Fin. Co. Am., 1st Federated Life Ins. Co. Mem. Am., Md. bankers assns., Newcomen Soc., Maryland Club, Merchants Club, Balt. Country Club. Home: Baltimore Md. †

MILLARD, FRANK GURNEE, lawyer; b. Corunna, Mich., Mar. 1, 1892; s. Frank and Emma (Gurnee) M.; m. Dorothy E. McCorkell, Nov. 8, 1930. AB, U. Mich., 1914, JD, 1916; JD, Detroit Coll. Law, 1952. Bar: Mich. 1916. Practice Flint City, Mich.; atty. Flint, 1927-34; atty. gen. State of Mich., 1951-54; gen. counsel Dept. of Army, 1955-61. Mem. Flint Bd. of Edn., 1962-63; del. Mich. Constl. Conv., 1961; chmn. Genesee County Rep. Com., 1922-24, 40; mem. Rep. State Central Com., 1948-50; mem. exec. com. Friends of Mich. Hist. Collections, 1972-74. With U.S. Army, World Wars I and II; brig. gen. Mich. N.G., ret. Decorated Army Commendation medal; recipient Disting. Civilian Service award U.S. Army. Mem. Fed., Am., D.C., Mich., Genesee County bar assns., Am. Legion, V.F.W., Army and Navy Club (Washington), Flint Golf Club, City Club, Univ. Club (Ann Arbor, Mich.), Coral Ridge Yacht Club (Ft. Lauderdale, Fla.), Kiwanis Club, Elks, Masons (33 deg.), Delta Theta Phi, Phi Kappa Sigma. Home: Flint Mich. †

MILLER, ARTHUR LARUE, steel company executive; b. Kokomo, Ind., 1909; s. John E. and Emma (Coppock) M; m. Genevieve Elvin, Aug. 18, 1933; children: Eleanor Jane, Sarah Elizabeth, Marjorie Diane. BME, Purdue U., 1931. With Continental Steel corp., Kokomo, from 1933, mech. engr., machine shop supt., constrn. engr., asst. chief engr., asst. gen. supt., gen. supt., 1954-56, v.p. ops., 1956-64, exec. v.p., 1964-65, pres., 1965-71, cons., from 1971. Chmn. Ind. Statewide Health Coordinating Coun., 1977-78. Mem. Am. Iron and Steel Inst. (bd. dirs.), Assn. Iron and Steel Engrs., Rotary, Theta Chi. Home: Kokomo Ind. Died June 1985; buried Kokomo.

MILLER, C(HARLES) PHILLIP, JR., physician, educator; b. Oak Park, Ill., Aug. 29, 1894; s. Charles Phillip and Louise (Pebbles) M.; m. Florence Lowden, Oct. 20, 1931; children: Phillip Lowden, Warren Pullman. BS, U. Chgo., 1916; MS, Rush Med. Coll., 1919, U. Mich., 1920. Intern Presbyn. Hosp., Chgo., 1918-19; vol. rsch. asst. pathology U. Mich., 1919-20, asst. prof., 1920; asst. resident physician Hosp. of Rockefeller Inst. for Med. Rsch., 1920-24, asst. pathology and bacteriology, 1924-25; vol. rsch. asst. Institut für Infektionskrankheiten Robert Koch, Berlin, 1926; asst. prof. medicine U. Chgo., 1925-30, assoc. prof., 1930-41, prof., 1941-60, prof. emeritus, from 1960; cons. to Sec. of War, 1941-49; mem. Commn. Meningitis and Commn. on Air Borne Infection, Army Epidemiol. Bd., 1941-45; sr. sci. officer Office Sci. and Tech., Am. Embassy, London, 1948; mem. NRC, med. fellowship bd, 1947-53, exec. com. 1957-62, Streptococcal Commn., Armed Forces Epidemiology Bd., 1949-54, Commn. Radiation and infection, 1963-68, com. epidemiol. survey, from 1968, divisional com. Biol. and Med. Scis., NSF, 1955-60. Trustee Farm Found., 1943-64. Master ACP; fellow Am. Acad. Microbiology; mem. Internat. Assn. Microbiologists (neisseria subcom. nomenclature com.), Conf. Bd. Assoc. Rsch. Couns., Com. Internat. Exchange Persons, 1950-53, Radiation Rsch. Soc. (councillor 1957-60), Am. Forest Assn., Am. Clin. and Climatol. Assn. AMA, AAAS, Am. Assn. Immunologists, Am. Soc. Exptl. Pathology (sec.-treas. 1930-34, councillor 1934-36, v.p. 1936, pres. 1937), Am. Soc. Clin. Investn. (v.p. 1938), Assn. Am. Phys. (pres. 1956-57), Nat. Acad. Sci., Am. Soc. Exptl. Biology (sec.

1933), Chgo. Inst. Medicine, Am. Acad. Arts and Scis., Am. Soc. Microbiology, Soc. Exptl. Biology and Medicine (editorial bd. 1953-58), Soc. Gen. Microbiology (Gr. Britain), Soc. Mayflower Descs., Quadrangle, Wayfarers, Casino, Arts, Tavern, Cosmos clubs, Sigma Xi. Episcopalian. Home: Chicago Ill. Died Sept. 5, 1985; buried Graceland Cemetery, Chgo.

MILLER, CLAUDE RUE, lawyer; b. Bowie, Tex., Nov. 9, 1906; s. Irad O. and Katherine (Lively) M.; LL.B., So. Methodist U., 1931; m. Irene Elizabeth Risser, Dec. 19, 1931; children—Anna Carolyn Miller Cosby, Ralph Irad. Bar: Tex. 1930, Ill. 1941. Ptnr., Strasburger, Price, Kelton, Miller & Martin, and predecessor, Dallas, 1931-66; sole practice, Dallas, 1967-72; mem. firm Miller, Blankenship & Potts, Dallas, 1972-76; gen. counsel Mars, Inc., Chgo., 1943-49, Grant Advt. Inc., 1940-56; sec., dir. Morten Investment Co., 1934-63; chmn. bd. Comet Rice Mills, 1955-57; pres., chmn. bd. Comet Rice Mills, Inc. and subs., 1957-65; exec. v.p Gulfco Corp., 1961-65; owner So. Boat Co., 1949-65, Springwood Co., 1949-84; mem. faculty So. Meth. U., 1936-38; founding pres. Rice Council for Market Devel., 1957-60. Trustee, Menninger Found., 1962-84, Mangold Trusts. Mem. ABA, State Bar Tex., Dallas Bar Assn., Ill. Bar Assn., Chgo. Bar Assn., Pres. Profl. Assn. (founding), Dallas Country Club. Methodist. Author: Practice of Law, 1946; Living More Successfully, 1981. Home: Dallas Tex. Died Dec. 14, 1984.

MILLER, CLIFTON MCPHERSON, investment banker; b. Missoula, Mont., Aug. 7, 1892; s. Harvey H. and Rosa B. (McPherson) M.; m. Emily Thompson, Mar. 10, 1920; children: Clifton McPherson, Duncan; m. Caroline H. duPont, Jan. 11, 1935. LLB, Stanford, 1916. Bar: Calif. 1916. With bond dept. Lumbermen's Trust Co., Portland, Oreg., 1916-17; rep. William Salomon & Co., investment bankers, N.Y.C., 1917, 19-20; with Dillon Read & Co., investment bankers, San Francisco, 1920-24; with Dillon Read & Co., investment bankers, N.Y.C., 1924-30, ptnr., 1927-30; ptnr. White, Weld & Co., investment bankers, N.Y.C., 1930-35; farmer and cattle breeder Kent County, Md., 1935-55; bd. dirs. Canadiar. Chmn. bd. visitors and govs. Washington Coll.; del. Rep. Nat. Conv., 1944, 48. With A.C., AUS, 1917-18. Mem. Masters of Foxhounds Assn., Union Club (N.Y.C.), Maryland Club (Balt.), Delta Tau Delta, Phi Delta Phi. Home: Chestertown Md. †

MILLER, DAVID FRANKLIN, entomologist, educator; b. Greenfield, Ohio, Oct. 25, 1892; s. David H. and Caroline (Sheafer) M.; m. Edythe Herbert, Sept. 3, 1919; 1 child, David L. AB, Wittenberg Coll., 1917, DSc (hon.), 1952; MA, Ohio State U., 1924, PhD, 1928. Tchr. pub. schs. Ohio, 1917-19; instr. Wittenberg Coll., summer 1917; prof. natural sci. Kingfisher Coll., 1919-22; instr. Ohio State U., 1923-29, asst. prof., 1929-33, assoc. prof., 1933-42, prof. zoology and entomology, from 1942, chmn. dept., from 1947; chmn. dept. entomology Ohio Exptl. Sta.; from 1947; field asst. U.S. Bur. Entomology, summers 1928-30. Author: Biology For You, 1946, Methods and Materials for Teaching Biological Scienc, 1938, Biology Activities, 1942; contbr. articles to profl. jours. Mem. Nat. Assn. Biology Tchrs., AAAS, Am. Soc. Zoologists, Entomologists Soc. Am., Ohio Acad. Sci., Sigma Xi, Gamma Sigma Delta, KT. Home: Columbus Ohio. †

MILLER, DAVID LOUIS, philosophy educator; b. Lyndon, Kans., May 6, 1903; s. Reese P. Miller; m. Mary Evelyn Harsh, 1929. BA, Coll. Emporia, 1927; PhD, U. Chgo., 1932. Instr. U. Tex., Austin, 1934, assoc. prof., 1939, prof. philosophy, from 1945, chmn. dept. philosophy, 1952-59; vis. prof. U. Hamburg, Germany, 1960; disting. vis. prof. Kans. State U., 1967, U. Miami, 1970. Author: The Philosophy of A.N. Whitehead, 1938, Modern Science and Human Freedom, 1959, Individualism, Personal Achievement and the Open Society, 1967. Recipient Alexander von Humbolt award, Govt. West Germany, 1969. Mem. Southwestern Philos. Soc. (pres. 1947), Am. Philos. Assn., Philosophy Sci. Assn., Am. Assn. U. Profs. Home: Austin Tex. Died Jan. 8, 1986.

MILLER, DELMAS FERGUSON, college dean; b. McMechen, W.Va., Feb. 26, 1907; s. Francis B. and Sarah Ann (Wilson) M.; m. Myrtle Conner, June 7, 1932; children: Priscilla (Mrs. Charels Haden II), Bette Jo (Mrs. David Hobbs). AB, West Liberty State Coll., 1931; MA, W.Va. U., 1934; PhD, U. Pitts., 1943. Prin. Moundsville (W.Va.) Jr. High Sch., 1930-38, Moundsville (W.Va.) High Sch., 1938-50, University High Sch., Morgantown, W.Va., 1950-56; dir. tchr. edn. W.Va. U., 1957-68, dean, 1969-86; exec. dir. W.Va. Secondary Sch. Prins. Commn., 1978-86. Author: (with J. L. Trump) Secondary School Curriculum Improvement, 1969; contbg. author: The High School Curriculum, 1966, The Changing Secondary School Curriculum, 1967. Mem. W.Va. Edn. Assn. (pres. 1953-54), Nat. Assn. Secondary Sch. Prins. (pers. 1968-69), W.Va. Secondary Sch. Prins. Commn. (exec. sec. 1974-86, exec. dir. 1978-86), Masons, Rotary (pres. local chpt. 1945-46). Home: Morgantown W.Va. Died Jan. 6, 1986; buried Mt. Rose Cemetery, Moundsville, W.Va.

MILLER, EDWARD AUGUST, civil engineer; b. Bklyn., Aug. 28, 1915; s. August and Sophie (Van Axen) M.; m. Dorothy Shaver, Nov. 1, 1943; children: Edward August, Greta Katherine Miller Line, William Van Axen, Douglas MacRae. C.E., Cornell U., 1943, M.C.E., 1943. Registered profl. engr., N.Y., Mich. With Fenestra, Inc., Detroit, 1943-61; successively research engr. bldg. panel div., chief engr., mgr., v.p. bldg. products div. Fenestra, Inc., 1943-59, exec. v.p., 1959, pres., 1959-62; acting dir. Thyssen Bauelemente Gmbh, Dusseldorf, Germany, 1962; mgr. fabricated sheet products Am. Bridge div. U.S. Steel, 1962-63; sec.-treas. Metal Roof Deck Tech. Inst., 1945-55, pres., 1957-58; pres. Albert Pick Co. Inc., Chgo., also; Hobb Electric Supply Co., N.Y.C., Hobb Electric Supply Co. (subsidiaries Straus Duparquet, Inc.), N.Y.C., 1964-65; pres. Hill Electronics, Inc., Mechanicsburg, Pa., 1965-69, also dir.; gen. mgr. Erie Frequency Control, Carlisle, Pa., 1969-82. Chmn. Cumberland County Redevel. Authority. (past sec.), Carlisle Econ. Devel. Ctr.; Mem. bd. Sir Edward Coke Found. Mem. ASTM, ASCE, Engring. Soc. Detroit, Carlisle C. of C. (pres.), Harrisburg Civil War Round Table, Sigma Xi, Delta Chi, Tau Beta Pi, Chi Epsilon. Clubs: Detroit Athletic, Economic (Detroit); Ill. Athletic; Cornell (N.Y.C.); Chgo. Home: Camp Hill Pa. Died June 18, 1986; buried Rolling Green Cemetery, Camp Hill.

MILLER, ELIZABETH CAVERT, oncology educator, research laboratory administrator; b. Mpls., May 2, 1920; d. William Lane and Mary Elizabeth (Mead) Cavert; m. James Alexander Miller, Aug. 30, 1942; children: Linda Ann, Helen Louise. B.S., U. Minn., 1941; M.S., U. Wis., 1943, Ph.D, 1945; D.Sc. (hon.), Med. Coll. Wis., 1982. Instr. dept. oncology U. Wis. Med. Center, 1946-48, asst. prof., 1948-58, assoc. prof., 1958-69, prof., 1969-87; assoc. dir. McArdle Lab. for Cancer Research, U. Wis., Madison, 1973-87; Wis. Alumni Research Found. prof. oncology U. Wis., 1980-87, Van Rensselaer Potter prof. oncology, 1982-87. Assoc. editor: Cancer Research, 1957-62; contbr. numerous articles on chem. carcinogenesis and microsomal oxidations to profl. jours. Recipient (with J.A. Miller) Langer-Teplitz award for cancer research Ann Langer Cancer Research Found., 1962, Lucy Wortham James award for cancer research James Ewing Soc., 1965, Bertner award M.D. Anderson Hosp. and Tumor Inst., 1971, Wis. div. award Am. Cancer Soc., 1973, Outstanding Achievement award U. Minn., 1973, Papanicolau award for cancer research Papanicolaou Cancer Research Inst., Miami, 1975; Rosenstiel award for basic med. scis. Brandeis U., 1976; Nat. award Am. Cancer Soc., 1977; Bristol-Myers award in cancer research, 1978; Gairdner Found. Ann. award, 1978; Founders award Chem. Industry Inst. Toxicology, 1978; Prix Griffuel Assn. pour Developpement de Recherche sur Cancer, 1978; 3M Life Sci award Fedn. Am. Socs. Exptl. Biology, 1979; Freedman award N.Y. Acad. Sci., 1979; Mott award Gen. Motors Cancer Research Found., 1980, Noble Found. Research award, 1986. Fellow Am. Acad. Arts and Scis., Wis. Acad. Sci., Arts and Letters; mem. Nat. Acad. Sci., Am. Assn. for Cancer Research, Am. Soc. Biol. Chemists, Japanese Cancer Soc. (hon.). Home: Madison Wis. Died Oct. 14, 1987, cremated.

MILLER, FERN V., government official; b. Denver, Nov. 29, 1892; d. Howard V. and Eva (Hodgson) Cornell; m. Albert L. Miller, June 25, 1913; children: Roland C., Elton N., Allyn J. Ed. pub. schs., Denver. Tchr. rural schs. 1910-13; sec. Consol. Sch. Dist., Platteville, Colo., 1936-42, 47-50; supt. U.S. Mint, Denver, from 1961. Mem. Ft. Vasquez Improvement Com., Fed. Garden Club, 1957-61; vol. worker local ARC and relief coms.; sec.-treas. Colo. Dem. Sustaining Fund, 1959-60; Dem. precinct committeewomen, Platteville; vice chmn. Weld County Dem. Com., Colo. Dem. Com., 1948-61. Methodist. Home: Platteville Colo. †

MILLER, FLORA WHITNEY, museum administrator. Trustee, pres., chmn. Whitney Mus. Am. Art, N.Y.C., from 1936. Home: Old Westbury N.Y. Died July 18, 1986; buried Old Westbury, N.Y.

MILLER, FLORENCE LOWDEN (MRS. C. PHILLIP MILLER), civic worker; b. Chgo., May 4, 1898; d. Frank O. and Florence (Pullman) Lowden; m. Charles Phillip Miller, Oct. 20, 1931; children—Phillip Lowden, Warren Pullman. Student, Oriental Inst., U. Chgo., 1929-34. Owner and operator Upland Farms, Oregon, Ill., 1959-86; operator Sinnissippi Exptl. Forest, Oregon, 1943-73; owner Sinnissippi Exptl. Forest, 1959-73, partner, 1973-79. Trustee Florenden Plantation, Osceola, Ark., 1943-72; Mem. Ill. Nature Preserves Commn., 1968-74; Mem. bd. Southeast Chgo. Commn., 1955-70; mem. exec. com. Chgo. Community Trust, 1958-70; pres. George M. Pullman Ednl. Found., 1949-78; trustee Westover Sch., 1958-67, Shimer Coll., 1951-58; life trustee Chgo. Hort. Soc., 1979. Recipient Westover award, 1964, U. Chgo. medal for disting. service, 1976, Heritage Conservation and Recreation Service Cultural Achievement award U.S. Dept. Interior, 1979; award of merit Gamma Sigma Delta, 1966. Fellow Met. Mus.; mem. Ill. Hist. Soc., Chgo. Hist. Soc. (dir.), Chgo. Hearing Soc. (dir.), Soc. Mayflower Descs., Nat. Soc. Colonial Dames, Orchestral Assn. Chgo., Antiquarian Soc. of Art Inst. Chgo. (pres. 1939-45, 49-51), Art Inst. Chgo. (life trustee, past pres., mem. women's bd.),

Womens' Bd. U. Chgo. Republican. Episcopalian. Clubs: Casino (Chgo.) (past dir.), Friday (Chgo.), Fortnightly (Chgo.), Woman's Athletic (Chgo.), Arts (Chgo.); Colony (N.Y.C.). Home: Chicago Ill. Died Apr. 27, 1988; buried Graceland Cemetery, Chgo.

MILLER, FRANK, musician, conductor, composer; b. Balt., Mar. 5, 1912; s. Samuel and Leah (Rose) M.; m. Shirley Hauk Blichmann, 1971; children by previous marriage: David S., Paul. Cellist, Phila. Orch. under Stokowski, 1930-35; 1st cellist Mpls. Symphony Orch. under Ormandy and Mitropoulos, 1935-39, asst. condr 1936-38; 1st cellist NBC Symphony under Toscanini 1939-54; organizer, condr. Hempstead (N.Y.) Community Orch., 1951-53; condr. Great Neck (L.I., N.Y.) Symphony Orch., 1953-54, Fla. Symphony Orch., Orlando, 1955-59; prin. cellist Chgo. Symphony Orch. 1959-60, then from 1961; assoc. condr. Mpls. Symphon Orch., 1960-61; condr. Evanston (Ill.) Symphony Orch. from 1963; cello tchr. U. Minn., Mpls. Coll. Music Phila. Settlement Sch. Music, Ind. U., Nat. Music Cam at Interlochen, Mich.; performer U.S. and Can., with leading chamber music ensembles; rec. artist Columbia Mercury adn Decca records; condr. Gilbert and Sullivan operas; composer: (opera) Thespis, (children's narrative Charlie the Cello, Little Suite for Large Orchestra, Laz Mary Symphonic Suite, solo pieces for piano, three string quartets, suites from string quartet. Home: Skokia Ill. Died Jan. 6, 1986.

MILLER, GEORGE PAUL, congressman; b. Sa Francisco, Calif., Jan. 15, 1891; s. Joseph and Margare (Anson) M.; m. Esther M. Perkins, May 21, 1927; child, Ann (Mrs. Donald Muir). BSCE, St. Mary' Coll., Moraga, Calif., 1912; grad., Sch. of Fire, Ft. Sil Okla., 1918. Engaged in practice as civil engr. Calif from 1912; mem. assembly 52d and 53d sessions Calif Legislature; exec. sec. Calif. Div. Fish and Game, 1941 45; mem. 79th-82d Congresses from 6th Calif. Dist mem. 83d-92d Congresses from 8th Calif. Dist., chmn com. on sci. and astronautics; adviser to U.S. ambas sador to UN on peaceful uses outer space. Mem. Nat Hist. Publs. Commn. Lt. F.S., U.S. Army, 1917. Mem Am. Legion (past 1st vice comdr. Dept. of Calif. 1924 Lions, Eagles, Elks. Home: Alameda Calif. †

MILLER, GEORGE TYLER, college president; b Washington, Va., July 25, 1902; s. John J. and Evely M. (Tyler) M.; m. Kathryn G. Weaver, May 7, 191 (dec. 1935); children: G. Tyler, William W.; m. 2d, Elis Reaguer, July 25, 1947 (dec. 1956); 1 dau., Elise; m. 3d Elizabeth Mauzy, Aug. 18, 1968. Grad., Randolph Macon Acad., 1919; BS, Va. Mil. Inst., 1923; LLD Bridgewater (Va.) Coll., 1955; grad. student, U. Va 1931-48. Tchr., asst. prin. Washington (Va.) High Sch 1923-24, prin., 1924-25; real estate bus. Okeechobee an Miami, Fla. 1925-26; gen. ins. and farming, Washington Va., 1926-28; div. supt. schs., Warren and Rappahan nock Cos., Front Royal, Va., 1928-45; supt. city schs Charlottesville, Va., 1945-46; state supt. pub. instrn Richmond, Va., 1946-49; pres. Madison Coll., Ha risonburg, Va., 1949-70, pres. emeritus, from 1971; sec treas., mem. exec. com. Nat Commn. Accrediting, 1963 67; dir. Va. Nat. Bank, Harrisonburg; pres. Shenandoa Valley Ednl. TV Corp., from 1965; mem. exec. com. Va Pub. Telecommunications Coun., from 1972. Pres., bc dirs. Front Royal Recreation Ctr., 1939-45; chmn. dis aster com. Warren County chpt. ARC, 1942-45; dir coordinator Civilian Def., Front Royal and Warren Co 1941-45; bd. dirs. Va. Library Bd., 1945-49, Va. Stat Planning Bd., Adv. Coun. Va. Economy (ex-officio); ex officio mem. bd. visitors U. Va., Med. Coll. Va Richmond, Coll. William and Mary, Va. Poly. Inst., Va Mil. Inst., Va. Sch. Deaf and Blind, 1946-49; pres. bd trustees Rockingham Meml. Hosp. Contbr. articles t Va. ednl. pubs. Mem. Am. Assn. State Colls. an Univs. (dir. 1960-67), pres. 1968), Am. Assn. Va. Cools (pres. 1955-56), Am. Assn. Sch. Adminstrn., Chief Stat Sch. Ofcls. (nat. coun. 1946-49), Va. Acad. Sci., Va Edn. Assn. (dist. pres. 1944, pres. 1945-46), Rotary, Ph Delta Kappa. Episcopalian (vestrymen). Home: Ha risonburg Va. Died July 25, 1988.

MILLER, JOHN ELVIS, judge; b. nr. Aid, Mo., Ma 15, 1888; s. John Anderson and Mary K. (Harper) M m. Ethel Lucile Lindsey, Oct. 21, 1914 (dec.); children Mary Louise, John E.; m. 2d, Ethel L. Skinner, Dec. 27 1956. Student, S.E. Mo. State Tchrs. Coll., Cap Girardeau, Valparaiso (Ind.) U.; LLB, U. Ky., 1912 LLD (hon.), U. Ark., 1949, Harding Coll., Searcy, Ark Practiced law Searcy, from 1912; mem. firm Miller Yingling; pros. atty. 1st Jud. Circuit, Ark., 1919-22 mem. 72s to 75th congresses from 2d Ark. Dist.; U.S senator from Ark., 1937-41; judge U.S. Dist. Ct. (we dist.) Ark., from 1941, then sr. judge. Del. Ark. Const Conv., 1918. Recipient award Sebastian County Ba Assn., 1961, Internat. Acad. Trial Lawyers, 1977 Hatton W. Sumners award Southwestern Legal Found 1973; named to Hall of Disting. Alumni U. Ky.; judg John E. Miller Scholarship Fund established by Ark Bar Found. Mem. Ark. Bar Assn. (award 1966 Masons (32 deg.), Shriners. Democrat. Methodist Home: Fort Smith Ark. Died Jan. 30, 1981, Fores Lawn, Ft. Smith.

MILLER, JULIUS SUMNER, physicist, educator; b Billerica, Mass., May 17, 1909; s. Samuel and Sar (Newmark) M.; m. Alice Marion Brown, Apr. 2

1934. BS in Philosophy, Boston U., 1932, MA in Theoretical Physics, 1933; MS in Exptl. Physics, U. Idaho, 1940; postgrad., U. Okla., 1940-41. Prof. physics El Camino (Calif.) Coll., 1952-74, prof. emeritus, from 1974; vis. prof. physics Am., Can. univs.; lectr. physics U. Uppsala , Sweden, U. Oslo, Norway, U. Sydney, Australia; hon. tenure prof. USAF Acad.; cons. OECD on demonstrations in physics, Paris, 1962; internat. lectr. Museo Nazionale della Scienza della Tecnica Leonardo da Vinci, Milan, Italy, 1963; lectr. Found. for Edn., Sci. and Tech., South Africa, 1975. Appeared as Prof. Wonderful on Walt Disney Mickey Mouse programs, 1964-65; numerous TV appearances throughout world. Author: (with others) Time, 1965, Apollo and the Universe, 1967, Demonstrations in Physics (Australia), Millergrams, 2 vols. (Australia), The Kitchen Professor, (series) Why It Is So; contbr. over 300 articles to sci. jours. Civilian physicist Signal Corps, World War II. Named to Alumni Hall of Fame U. Idaho, Collegium Disting. Alumni Coll. Liberal Arts Boston U. Outstanding Educator in Am., 1971; recipient award TV Soc. Australia, 1966; Carnegie Found. grantee, 1950, Ford Found. grantee, 1952. Mem. Am. Assn. Physics Tchrs. (extraordinary service award 1984). Home: Torrance Calif. Died Apr. 14, 1987.

MILLER, LOYE WHEAT, newspaperman; b. Mt. Vernon, Ill., Jan. 18, 1899; s. Thomas Edward and Elsie (Wheat) M.; m. Sara Vance Davis, Apr. 3, 1929; children: Loye Wheat, Wayne Watson, Michael Van Hook. Grad. high sch., Evansville, Ind., 1916. Reporter Evansville Press., 1916-20, Cleve. Press., 1920-21; mng. editor Knoxville (Tenn.) News, 1921-26; mng. editor Knoxville News-Sentinel, 1926-41, editor, 1941-67. Author: Tennessee's Universal Registration Law, Enacted, 1951. Mem. Tenn. Great Smoky Mountain Pk. Commn., 1958-76, chmn., 1973-76. With U.S. Army, 1918-19. Mem. Am. Soc. Newspaper Editors, Tenn. Soc. S.R. (pres.), Tenn. Press Assn. (pres. 1953-54), Am. Judicature Soc., Nat. Press Club, Rotary, Sigma Delta Chi. Presbyterian. Home: Knoxville Tenn. Died Nov. 30, 1979.

MILLER, LYLE LESLIE, educator; b. Deer Lodge, Mont., Aug. 20, 1919; s. Birl O. and Anna (Oakley) M.; m. Grace Moore, Sept. 12, 1942; children: thomas Oakley, Patricia Ann Sebetka. BS, Mont. State Coll., 1940; MS, U. So. Calif., 1944; PhD, Ohio State U., 1949. Tchr. Gallatin County High Sch., Bozeman, Mont., 1940-42; indsl. personnel worker Walter Butler Assocs., Coeur d'Alene, Idaho, 1942-43, Douglas Aircraft & Calif. Flyers, L.A., 1943-44; guidance coordinator Flathead County High Sch., Kalispell, Mont., 1944-46; asst. jr. dean Coll. Edn., Ohio State U., 1946-49; supr. student employment and study skills ctr. U. Wyo., Laramie, 1949-53, prof. edn., chmn. guidance and spl. edn., 1953-65, prof., head dept. guidance and counselor edn., 1965-72, prof., 1972-85; coordinator N.W. Regional Ctr. Counselor Edn., 1969-71; dir. Reading Rsch. Ctr., 1955-85. Author: Increasing Reading Efficiency, 4th edit., 1977, Maintaining Reading Efficiency, 4th edit., 1978, Developing Reading Efficiency, 4th edit., 1980, Counseling Leads, 3d edit., 1980, The Guidance Wheel, 1962, The Time Budget Sheet, 1962, Teaching Reading Efficiency, 1963, Accelerating Growth in Reading Efficiency, 2d edit., 1981, Half Century of Guidance in Wyoming, 1981; videotape series on reading efficiency, 1974. Mem. exec. bd. Laramie United Fund, 1950-62; rep. nat. exec. bd. Boy Scouts Am., 1961-85. Recipient Nat. Disting. Svc. award, 1968. Mem. AAUP (chpt. pres. 1965-67), Am. Personnel and Guidance Assn. (nat. membership chmn. 1962-63), Am. Soc. Group Psycholtherapy and Psychodrama, NEA (life), Assn. Counselor Edn. and Supervision (nat. pres. 1963-64), Am. Psychol. Assn., Moreno Acad., Assn. Specialists in Group Work, Coll. Reading Assn. (life), Internat. Reading Assn., Phi Delta Kappa. Presbyterian. Home: Fort Myers Fla. Died Dec. 29, 1985; cremated.

MILLER, MERLE, author; b. Montour, Iowa, May 17, 1919; s. Monte M. and Dora B. (Winders) M. Student, State U. Iowa, 1935-38, 39-40, London Sch. Econs., 1938-39. Washington corr. Phila. Record, 1940-41; editor Yank mag., 1941-45; contbg. editor Time mag., 1945; editor Harpers mag., 1947-49. Author: Island 49, 1945, We Dropped the A-bomb, 1946, That Winter, 1948, The sure Thing, 1949, The Judges and the Judged, 1952, Reunion, 1954, A Gay and Melancholy Sound, 1961, A Day in Late September, 1963, Only You, Dick Daring, 1964, On Being Different, 1972, What Happened, 1973, Plain Speaking, An Oral Biography of Harry S. Truman, 1974, Lyndon, An Oral Biography of Lyndon Baines Johnson, 1980; contbr.: a treasury of Great Reporting, 1949, The Best from Yank, 1945, Yank the GI Story of the War, 1947, Women Today, 1953, Highlights from Yank, 1953; screenplays and TV plays. Mem. Authors guild, Authors League. Died June 10, 1986.

MILLER, O(RRIS) J(OSEPH), civil engineer, business executive; b. New Lyme, Ohio, Nov. 27, 1891; s. Maynard E. and Mary (Laird) M.; m. Blanche Lutenbur, July 12, 1916; children: Richard Dean, Mary Miller Crusoe. BS, Hiram Coll., 1914; BCE, Ohio State U., 1916, MCE, 1920. Engr. E.W. Clark & Co. (mgmt. corp.), Columbus, Ohio, 1916-20; civil and hydraulic engr. Tenn. Elec. Power Co., Chattanooga, 1920-24, prodn. supt., 1924-28, mgr. prodn. and transmission, 1928-39, mgr. transp., Nashville, 1939-40; asst. supervising engr. Commonwealth So. Corp., Jackson, Mich., 1940-43; supt. operation Duke Power Co., Charlotte, N.C., 1943-48, gen. mgr., 1948-49, v.p., 1949, exec. v.p., from 1956, also bd. dirs. Fellow AIEE; mem. ASCE, local engring. socs., Charlotte Country Club, Kiwanis. Presbyterian. Home: Charlotte N.C. †

MILLER, PARK HAYS, JR., educator, physicist; b. Phila., Jan. 22, 1916; s. Park Hays and Elizabeth (Crider) M.; m. Carolyn B. Anfinsen, June 6, 1942 (div. June 1972); children: Karen Elizabeth, Park Hays III, Christine Sophia. BS, Haverford Coll., 1936; PhD, Calif. Inst. Tech., 1940. Grad. asst. physics Calif. Inst. Tech., Pasadena, 1936-39; instr. physics U. Pa., Phila., 1939-42, asst. prof., 1942-46, assoc. prof., 1946-49, prof., 1949-56, acting chmn. dept. physics, 1945-46; rsch. OSRD, 1942-45; asst. dirs. rsch. Gulf Gen. Atomic Inc. (formerly know as Gen. Atomic), San Diego, Calif., 1956-59; prof., chmn. physics dept. U.S. Internat. U., Calif. Western Campus, San Diego, 1969-74; sr. physicist fusion, sci. and techs. dept. AC Techs. (formerly Gen. Atomic), 1974-81, cons., from 1981; owner cons. firm Extragalactic Enterprises Inc., from 1981; also in rsch. on Reagan adminstrn.'s Strategic Def. Initiative (Star Wars); cons. Naval Ordnance Lab., Dept. of Def. Materials Adv. Bd. NASA. Fellow Am. Phys. Soc.; mem. AAAS, Soc. Exploration Geophysicists, Am. Assn. Physics Tchrs., Am. Nuclear Soc., Am. Geophys. Union, Phi Beta Kappa, Sigma Xi. Home: La Jolla Calif. Died May 14, 1986.

MILLER, ROBERT JUSTIN, lawyer; b. Crescent City, Calif., Nov. 17, 1888; s. Robert Willis and Matilda (Morrison) M.; m. May Merrill, June 20, 1915; children: Jean Marian Miller Friedland, Merrill Justin. AB, Stanford U., 1911, JD, 1914; LLB, U. Mont., 1913, LLD, 1941; DCL, Yale U., 1934; LLD, Franklin and Marshall Coll., 1945, Boston U., 1948; U. Ariz., 1948. Bar: Mont. 1911, Calif. 1913, Minn. 1924, N.C. 1931. Pvt.practice Hanford, Fresno, San Francisco, Calif., 1914-21; dist. atty. Kings County, Calif., 1915-18; atty. and exec. officer Calif. State Commn. of Immigration and Housing, 1919-21; prof. of law 1921-27, successively at U. Ore., U. Minn., Stanford, U. Cal. Columbia, 1927-30; law sch. dean U. So. Calif., 1927-30, Duke U., 1930-35; spl. asst. to atty. gen. of U.S. 1934-36; mem. U.S. Bd. Tax Appeals, Washington, 1937; assoc. justice U.S. Ct. of Appeals, Washington, 1937-45; pres. Nat. Assn. Broadcasters, 1945-51; chmn. U.S. Salary Stblzn. Bd., 1951-53; chmn. bd., gen. counsel Nat. Assn. Radio and TV Broadcasters, 1951-54; cons. Broadcast Music Inc., Nat. Assn. of Broadcasters. Author: Miller on Criminal Law, Fair Trial and Freedom of Information: The Advocate before Adminstrative Agencies, History California Code of Civil Procedure; also articles in legal and other periodicals. Pres. Fed. Bar Assn., 1935, 36, Nat. Conf. of Citizenship, 1952-58; formerly mem. U.S. Adv. Commn. on Info.; vice chmn. U.S. nat. commn. on UNESCO; chmn. sect. criminal law, mem. house of dels., chmn. several coms. of ABA; mem. and/or officer several community, state and nat. civic prof., sci. socs. and orgns; mem. bd. of visitors Stanford U. Law Sch. Pvt Calif. NG on Mex. Border, 1916. Fellow Am. Bar Found.; mem. Legion Lex, Rotary, Phi Beta Kappa, Order of Coif, Delta Chi. Home: Pacific Palisades Calif.†

MILLER, ROSCOE EARL, radiologist, educator; b. Shelby County, Ind., Jan. 6, 1918; s. Herschel M. and Hazel Belle (Ross) M.; m. Dorothy J. Long, June 1, 1952; children: Andrew, Jeffrey, Douglas. BS, Ind. U., 1948, MD, 1951. Diplomate Am. Bd. Radiology. Intern U. Chgo. Clinics, 1951-52, resident in radiology, 1952-55; fellow U. Lund, Malmo, Sweden, 1964-65; practice medicine specializing in radiology Indpls., 1956-1984; instr. dept. radiology U. Chgo., 1955-56; asst. prof. dept. radiology Ind. U. Sch. Medicine, Indpls., 1956-61, assoc. prof., 1961-66, prof., 1966-76, Disting. prof. radiology, 1976-84; vis. lectr. and/or vis. prof. various med. schs. in U.S. and Can., 1956-84; Litchfield lectr. Oxford U., 1978, vis. prof., 1983-84; vis. lectr. Ind. U., Wishard Meml., VA hosps., all Indpls.; cons. to various pharm. cos., med. equipment cos., pubs., 1960-84, Cen. State Hosp., Indpls., 1956-70. Author: Radiographic Contrast Agents, 1977, Radiology of the Small Bowel: Modern Enteroclysis Technique and Atlas, 1982, The Radiological Examination of the Colon: Practical Diagnosis, 1983; mem. editorial bd. Jour. Radiology, 1976-84; assoc. editor Jour. Gastrointestinal Radiology, 1975-84; contbr. numerous articles on gastrointestinal radiology and radiographic techniques to profl. jours. Served from pvt. to maj. U.S. Army, 1941-46. Decorated Bronze Star, Belgium Fourra Guerre; recipient numerous awards and cert. of merits; named Sagamore of Wabash by Ind. gov., 1980; Eli Lilly & Co. grantee, 1971-76. Fellow Am. Coll. Radiology (com. on radiologic coding 1955-61, com. on cancer detection 1969-79); mem. Am. Roentgen Ray Soc. (cert. of merit 1973, 75, 81), Radiol. Soc. N.Am. (counselor for Ind. 1972-77, cert. of merit 1977, 81), Soc. Gastrointestinal Radiologists (Walter B. Cannon medal award 1980), Am. Gastroent. Assn., Ind. Roentgen Soc. (treas. 1972-75, pres. 1976-77), Am. Assn. Univ. Radiologists, Assn. Am. Med. Colls., AMA, Ind. Med. Soc., Marion County Med. Soc., Alpha Omega Alpha (sec.-treas. Ind. U. chpt. 1958-70, councillor 1971-84). Lutheran. Home: Indianapolis Ind. Died Dec. 14, 1984.

MILLER, VERNON XAVIER, legal educator; b. St. Paul, Mar. 27, 1902; s. Francis Xavier and Margaret Louise (Kelly) M.; m. Sara Margaret Singley, June 29, 1938; 1 son, Timothy Singley. BA, U. Minn., 1923, LLB, 1925; JSD, Yale U., 1929. Bar: Minn. 1925, Wis. 1933, D.C. 1955. Clk. asst. under Justice Butler of U.S. Supreme Ct., 1925-26; prof. law Loyola U., New Orleans, 1938-51, acting dean Sch. Law, 1940-41, 42-45, faculty editor Layola Law Rev., 1941-50, dean Sch. Law, 1945-51; dean Law Sch. U. San Francisco, 1951-54; prof. law Cath. U. Am., 1954-72, dean, 1954-68; vis. prof. law U. Pacific, 1972-73; sec., treas. Assn. Am. Law Schs., 1962-63, pres., 1965. Author, editor: Selected Essays on Torts, 1960; mem. editorial bd. Jour. Legal Edn., 1952-55. Recipient Oustanding Achievement award U. Minn., 1965, St. Thomas More award St. Mary's U., San Antonio, 1966. Mem. ABA (coun. sect. legal edn. 1970-73), Iron Wedge Soc. U. Minn., Order of Coif, Phi Beta Kappa, Delta Sigma Rho, Delta Theta Phi. Democrat. Roman Catholic. Home: Bethesda Md. Died Feb. 21, 1986.

MILLER, VICTOR CHARLES, geology consultant; b. Stamford, Conn., Mar. 17, 1922; s. Walter Strong and Mary Priscilla (Gortner) M.; children: Michelle, Denise, David. A.B., Columbia U., 1943, M.A., 1948, Ph.D., 1953. Photogeologist, Sinclair Oil Co., Denver, 1947-49; pres. Miller-McCulloch Ltd. (cons. photogeologists), Calgary, Can., 1952-55, V.C. Miller & Assos. Photogeologists Ltd. Calgary, 1955-57, Miller & Assos. (cons. photogeologists), Denver, 1957-62; chmn. dep. geology U. Libya, Tripoli, 1962-64; chmn. dept. geology C.W. Post Coll., Greenvale, N.Y., 1964-67; prof. dept. geography and geology Ind. State U., Terre Haute, Ind., 1967-83; cons. photogeology and remote sensing Mesa, Ariz., 1983-88. Author: Photogeology, 1961, Interpretation of Topographic Maps, 1988. Served with USAAF, 1943-45, ETO. Fellow Geol. Soc. Am.; mem. Am. Assn. Petroleum Geologists, Am. Soc. Photogrammetry, Assn. Am. Geographers. Home: Mesa Ariz. Died Apr. 1, 1988.

MILLER, WALTER H., retail supermarket executive; b. 1933; m. Mary Ann Cullen; children: Mary Kathleen, Kerry, Kelly, Michael, Matthew, Timothy, Patrick, Sean, Cullen. B.S.S., John Carroll U., 1955; B.S., Georgetown U., 1956; postgrad., NYU Sch. Fin., 1962. New bus. tng. Hemphill, Noyes & Co., 1961-63; trader Estabrook & Co.; supr. King Kullen Grocery Co., Inc., Westbury, N.Y., 1958-60, liaison Wall st. and fin. community, 1960-64, buyer, 1964-65, asst. v.p., 1965-68, v.p., 1968-69, exec. v.p., 1969-71, pres., 1971-86, chmn. bd., dir., 1974-86; pres. Richmond Hill Savs. Bank, 1986-88, chmn., 1987-88. Died May 3, 1988; buried Holy Rood Cemetery, Westbury, N.Y.

MILLIN, LUCINDA ALFREDA, political worker; b. St. John, V.I., Aug. 26, 1892; d. Philip Abraham and Albertha (Knevel) Sewer; m. Allan Alexander Millin, Sept. 6, 1922; children: Henry Allan, Dorothy E. Millin Penn, Agnes Althea. Tchrs. cert., Female Tchrs. Tng. Coll., St. Johns, Antigua, B.W.I., 1913. Tchr. U.S. Govt., St. Thomas, V.I., from 1951; mem.-at-large V.I. Senate, from 1955. Mem. Women's League, Bus. and Profl. Women's Club. Home: Charlotte Amalie St. Thomas, V.I. †

MILLONZI, ROBERT I., lawyer; b. Buffalo, July 12, 1910; s. Philip and Frances (Laduca) M.; m. Eleanor Verduin, Jan. 27, 1940; children: Mary (Mrs. C. Victor Raiser II), Elizabeth J. (Mrs. Richard A. Levinson). B.A., U. Buffalo, 1932, LL.B., 1935. Bar: N.Y. 1935, D.C. 1979. Counsel N.Y. State Dept. Agr., 1939-42; atty. Western N.Y. Savs. Bank, Buffalo, 1947-81; atty., dir. First Nat. Bank Buffalo, 1947-55; commr. SEC, Washington, 1951-52; cons. RFC, 1952-53; sr. ptnr. Diebold & Millonzi, 1947-81; gen. counsel First Empire State Corp., 1970-83; dir., mem. exec. com. Mfrs. & Traders Trust Co., 1956-81; now counsel Damon & Morey; Pub. mem. U.S. del. UN, 1967. Pres., bd. dirs., mem. exec. com. Buffalo Philharm. Soc.; bd. dirs. Buffalo Fine Arts Acad., Buffalo Council on World Affairs; trustee John F. Kennedy Ctr. for Performing Arts, Washington, 1966, 68-78, co-chmn. adv. com. on arts, 1979; chmn. governing com. Buffalo Found., 1976-77; trustee Power Authority State N.Y., 1977-82; mem. council of trustees SUNY-Buffalo, 1977-81, chmn., 1978-81, chmn. emeritus, 1981-86; mem. Com. for Preservation of White House, 1979; council mem. N.Y. State Council on Arts, 1985-87. Fellow ABA; mem. N.Y. State, Erie County, D.C. bar assns. Democrat. Clubs: Buffalo, Country, Saturn (Buffalo); Burning Tree (Washington); Metropolitan (N.Y.C.). Home: Buffalo N.Y. Died Sept. 27, 1986; buried Buffalo, N.Y.

MILLS, CLARENCE ALONZO, physician, experimental medicine educator; b. Miami, Ind., Oct. 9, 1891; s. Alonzo F. and Margaret Elizabeth (Winninger) M.; m. Edith Clarissa Parrett, June 22, 1915; children: Russell Clarence, Marjorie Ruth, Donald Harper. Student, Valparaiso U., 1914; AB, U. S.D., 1917, LLD, 1961; student, U. Kans., 1917-18, U. Chgo., 1918; PhD, U. Cin., 1920, MD, 1922. Tchr. pub. schs. S.D., 1910-12; instr. physiology U. Kans., 1917-18, Marquette U. Med. Sch., 1918; instr. biochemistry U. Cin. Med. Sch., 1919-22, instr. medicine, 1922-23, asst. prof. medicine, 1923-26, assoc. prof. medicine, 1928-30, Heady prof. exptl. medicine, 1930-62, prof. emeritus, from 1962; assoc.

prof. medicine Peking (China) Union Med. Coll., 1926-28; pres. Reflectotherm, Inc. Author: Living with the Weather, 1934, Medical Climatology, 1939, Climate Makes the Man, 1942, Reflective Radiant Conditioning, 1952, Air Pollution and Community Health, 1954, This Air We Breathe, 1962, World Power Amid Shifting Climates, 1963; also chpts. and articles in sci. publs. Mem. AMA, Am. Physiol. Soc., Am. Soc. Biochemists, Am. Assn. Phys. Anthropology, AAAS, Cen. Soc. Clin. Rsch., Rsch. Club. Cin., Sigma Xi, Alpha Omega Alpha, Alpha Kappa Kappa. Home: Cincinnati Ohio. †

MILNER, CLYDE ALONZO, philosophy educator; b. Unitia, Tenn., Aug. 2, 1899; s. Fremont Beverly and Ella Margaret (Walker) M.; m. Ernestine Cookson, July 5, 1928. AB, Wilmington (Ohio) Coll., 1921, LLD, 1950; AM, Haverford Coll., 1922, LLD, 1963; BD, Harford Theol. Sem., 1924, PhD, 1934; student, Woodbrooke Coll., Eng., 1919-20, U. Marburg, Germany, 1927-28, U. Geneva, Switzerland, 1928. Dean of men and prof. psychology Earlham Coll., 1924-30; dean coll., prof. philosophy Guilford Coll., 1930-34, pres., 1934-65, pres. emeritus, from 1965. Author: The Dean of the Small College, 1936, A Survey of Philosophical and Religious Thought in Western Civilizaion, 1937; co-author: Concerning Mysticism, 1939. Min. Soc. Friends, 1924; served as interim pastor East Main St. Friends, Richmond, Ind., May-Sept. 1929, Asbeboro St. Friends Meeting, Greensboro, N.C., Aug.-Dec. 1939; pres. N.C. Found. Ch. Related Colls., 1961-63; mayor town of Guilford Coll., 1939-61; chmn. bd. edn. Five Yrs. Meetings of Friends in Am., 1945-69; dir., mem. exec. com. Piedmont U. Ctr., 1963-64. In rehabilitation work in France under the Am. Friends' Service Com., 1919. Mem. So. Soc. for Philosophy and Psychology, Am. Psychol. Assn. (assoc), N.C. Philos. Soc., N.C. Coun. Chs. (pres. 1949-50, 50-51), Assn. Friends Colls. (chmn. 1942-48), Friars Club, Rotary. Home: Greensboro N.C. Died Mar. 6, 1988.

MILNES, HUMPREY NEWTON, language educator; b. Oneida, N.Y., Nov. 2, 1919; s. Paul and Adele (Noyes) M.; m. Lillian Brett, Oct. 4, 1941 (div. Jan. 1963); children: Paul, Beverly; m. 2d, Irma Laakso McDonough, Sept. 28, 1966. BA, U. Toronto, 1941, MA, 1947; PhD, Ohio State U., 1949. Instr. German Ohio State U., 1946-48; lect. German U. Coll., U. Toronto, 1948-52; asst. prof. U. Toronto, 1952-59, assoc. prof., 1959-64, prof., 1964-81, head dept., from 1967; vis. lectr. Marburg U., Germany, 1954; vis. prof. U. Coll., London, Eng., 1959-60. Contbr. articles to scholarly jours., U.S., Can., Eng. With Can. Army, 1943-46. Mem. Can. Assn. U. Tchrs., Can. Assn. U. Tchrs. German, Faculty Club U. Toronto. Home: Toronto Ont., Canada. Died Mar. 23, 1981.

MILTON, HUGH MEGLONE, undersecretary of army, university president; b. Lexington, Ky., Mar. 23, 1897; m. Josephine Baldwin Milton, Feb. 10, 1933; children: Hugh Meglone III, John Baldwin. BS, U. Ky., 1919, ME, 1922, LLD, 1953; student, Tex. A & M, 1919-22; grad., Chem. Warfare Sch., Edgewood, Md., 1931, Command and Gen. Staff Sch., Ft. Leavenworth, Kans., 1937, Engr. Sch., Ft. Belvoir, Va., 1943; DCL, U. Toledo, 1953; LHD, St. Bonaventure U., 1953; DMS, Pa. Mil. Coll.; Dr. Engring., Alfred U., Worcester Polytech. Inst.; LittD, Okla. Baptist U., 1960. Instr. and asst. prof. mech. engring. N.M. State U., 1924-35, dean engring., 1935-38, pres., 1938-47; pres. N.M. Mil. Inst., 1947-51; cons. engr., 1922-35; asst. sec. army, 1953-58, undersecretary army, 1958-61; then v.p. 1st Nat. Bank Dona Ana County, Las Cruces, N.M. 2d lt., U.S. Army, World War I; 1st lt. and capt., USAR, 1925-29; maj. and lt. col. Chem. Corps, N.M. N.G., 1929-41; col. Chem. Warfare Service (on leave from Univ.); advanced to brig. gen., June 1945, served as chief of staff, XIV Corps, in Pacific Area; maj. gen., 1951, serving as exec. for Res. and ROTC affairs, spl. staff Dept. Army. Participated in campaigns: No. Solomons, Bismarck Archipelago, So. Philippines, No. Philippines, Japanese Occupation. Author: Mechanical Engineering Laboratory Manual, 1925, Power Producing Qualities of Certain Petroleum Products, 1922, Heat Coefficient of Adodes, 1931. Decorated Legion of Merit, Silver Star, Bronze Star; recipient Asiatic-Pacific Service medal with 5 stars and 1 arrowhead, Philippine Liberation medal with 2 stars, Am. Def. and Campaign medals, World Wars I and II Victory medals, Japanese Occupation medal, War Dept. citation. Mem. Am. Legion (life), Res. Officers Assn., U.S. C. of C. (dir.), Newcomen Soc. London, Assn. U.S. Army (life), Masons, K.T., Shriners, Lions, Kiwanis (dist. gov. 1931), Tau Kappa Epsilon, Mu Phi Pi. Home: Las Cruces N.Mex. Died Jan. 27, 1987.

MINAR, EDWIN LEROY, JR., educator; b. Portland, Oreg., Apr. 17, 1915; s. Edwin LeRoy and Alma Inez (Jackson) M.; m. Louise Padberg, 1937; m. 2d Anne Marie Kelley, 1950 (div. 1962); children: Robert K., Jane E., Annette A.D. AB, Reed Coll., 1936; PhD, U. Wis., 1940. Asst. prof. fgn. langs. Dakota Wesleyan U., 1939-40; asst. to assoc. prof. classics Conn. Coll., New London, 1940-51; assoc. prof. classical langs. and lit., head dept. DePauw U., Greencastle, Ind., 1951-54, prof. classical langs., Greek, head dept., from 1954; Vis. prof. Ind. U., spring 1961, summer 1963; faculty fellow Fund for Advancement Edn., 1954-55. Author: Early Pythagorean Politics in PRactice and Theory, 1942; translator: Lore and Science in Ancient Pythagoreanism (Burkert), 1972; contbr. articles to classical jours. Mem. Soc. Ancient Greek Philosophy (pres. 1966-68), Am. Philol. Assn., Classical Assn. Middle West and South, AAUP. Democrat. Home: Greencastle Ind. Died Sept. 4, 1985.

MINARD, GUY MCRAE, pulp and paper company executive; b. Ottawa, Ont., Can., Dec. 19, 1906; s. Duncan McRae and Stella Lee (Allen) M.; m. Anne Marie Slingerland, Apr. 19, 1933; children: Sylvia Lee (Mrs. Murray), Anthony McRae. BS, Queens U., Kingston, Ont., 1928. Various positions Spruce Falls Pwer & PAper Co Ltd., Kapuskasing, Ont., 1928-40, asst. to mng. dir., 1945-47, mill mgr., 1948-50, v.p. mfg., 1951-61, sr. v.p., 1961-62, pres., 1962-67, 1967-72, chief exec. officer, 1968-72, chmn., 1970-72. Chmn. bd. Sensenbrenner Hosp., 1948-60; councillor Queen's U., 1958-85; town councilman Kapuskasing, 1947-51. Served with RCAF, 1940-45. Decorated officer Order of the British Empire. Mem. Tech. Assn. Pulp and Paper Industry, Profl. Engrs. Ont., Can. Pulp and Paper Assn. (exec. bd.), Newsprint Assn. Can. (exec. bd.). Died Aug. 13, 1985.

MINER, DOUGLAS FULLER, engineer; b. Hazardville, Conn., Sept. 13, 1892; s. Harry Willard and Helena Jane (Prickett) M.; m. Marion Louise Townsend, June 12, 1919; 1 child, Helen Louise. AB, Clark U., 1912; BS, Worcester Poly. Inst., 1915, degree in EE, 1917; DEng, U. Pitts., 1940. Lab. engr. Westinghouse Electric & Mfg. Co., 1919-27, mgr. material and process engring dept., 1927-36, mgr. engring. labs. and standards dept., 1936-38; pvt. practice cons. from 1938; George Westinghouse prof. engring. Carnegie Inst. Tech., 1938-47, dir. div. student personnel and welfare, 1947-56, asst. dir., 1945-47. Author: Insulation of Electrical Apparatus, 1941; co-editor: Handbook of Engineering Materials, 1955; contbr. articles to profl. jours. Mem. Forest Hills Sch. Bd., 1930-36; trustee East End Christian Ch. Lt. Col. AC, U.S. Army, 1942-45. Fellow AIEE; mem. Am. Soc. Engring. Edn., Sigma Xi, Tau Beta Pi, Phi Kappa Phi. Republican. Home: Sherwood Forest Md. †

MING, SAMUEL PATERSON, labor union executive; b. Atchison, Kans., Dec. 15, 1891; s. Harry P. and Willie Ann (Surry) M.; m. Gladys O. Sheffield, June 1, 1918; 1 child, Robert Sheffield. Grad. high sch., Atchison. Various positions flour milling industry 1910-38; v.p. West Coast dist. Am. Fedn. Grain Millers, AFL-CIO, 1938-40, internat. pres., from 1940, also bd. dirs. With F.A., U.S. Army, World War I. Mem. VFW. Home: Mpls. Minn. †

MINNELLI, VINCENTE, motion picture director; b. Chgo., Feb. 28, 1910; m. Judy Garland (div.); 1 dau., Liza May; m. Georgette Magnani (div.); 1 dau., Christiana Nina.; m. Denise Gigante (div.); m. Margaret Lee Anderson. Student, Art Inst. Chgo. art dir. Radio City Music Hall. Child actor Minnelli Bros. Dramatic Tent Show; asst. stage presentations, Balban & Katz, then, N.Y.C. Paramount Theatre, stage, Du-Barry, N.Y.; screen debut Very Warm for May, 1943; dir. motion pictures Cabin in the Sky, 1943, I Dood It, 1943, Ziegfeld Follies, 1944, Meet Me in St. Louis, 1944, The Clock, 1944, Madame Bovary, 1949, The Pirate, 1949, Father of the Bride, 1950, An American in Paris, 1951, The Bad and the Beautiful, 1952, The Bandwagon, 1953, The Long Long Trailer, 1954, Brigadoon, 1954, Kismet, 1955, Lust for Life, 1956, Tea and Sympathy, 1956, Gigi, 1958 (Oscar for Best Dir.), Reluctant Debutante, 1958, Some Came Running, 1958, Home from the Hill, 1959, Bells are Ringing, 1960, Four Horsemen of the Apocalypse, 1962, The Courtship of Eddie's Father, 1963, Goodbye Charlie, 1965, The Sandpiper, 1965, On a Clear Day You Can See Forever, 1970, A Matter of Time, 1976; dir. stage Ziegfeld Follies, Winter Garden theatre, N.Y.C., 1933, At Home Abroad, N.Y.C.; author: motion pictures I Remember It Well, 1974. Decorated Order Arts and Lettres, Command Nat. Légion D'Honneur (France); recipient City of Rome award, 1984. Died July 25, 1986; interred Forest Lawn, Glendale, Calif.

MINOR, STANLEY NELSON, corporate executive; b. Chillicothe, Mo., Sept. 10, 1891; s. James Carl and Mary (Bissett) M.; m. Gladys Waterhouse, Dec. 22, 1919; children: Mary Lou (Mrs. Donald A. MacMillan), Stanley Nelson Jr. Grad., Yale U., 1913. Chemist U.S. Steel Corp., South Chicago, 1913-14; ptnr. Zimmerman, Alderson, Carr & Co., 1914-22; with sales orgn. Blyth Witter & Co., Seattle, 1922-24; ptnr. Dean Witter & Co., 1924-37; pres. Ferris & Hardgrove, 1937-45; pres. Pacific N.W. Co. (merger Ferris & Hardgrove and Drumheller Ehrlichman Co.), Seattle, 1945-54, chmn. bd., 1954-59, chmn. exec. com., also bd. dirs.; pres., bd. dirs. United Pacific Corp.; chmn. fin. com., vice chmn. exec. com., bd. dirs. United Pacific Ins. Co.; bd. dirs. United Pacific Life Ins. Co., Cascade Ins. Co., v.p., bd. dirs. Equity Fund, Inc., from 1945. Mem. Seattle Golf club, Rainier Club, University Club. Republican. Presbyterian. Home: Seattle Wash. †

MINOT, JAMES JACKSON, stockbroker; b. Boston, Nov. 17, 1891; s. James Jackson and Elizabeth (Whitney) M.; m. Miriam Sears, Oct. 12, 1921 (dec.); children: Eleanor (Mrs. Guy H. Lewis), Louisa Minot Moseley, Constance (Mrs. Harry J. Crossan Jr.), Miriam (Mrs. Peter R. Cable). Grad., Noble and Greenough, 1909; AB, Harvard, 1913. Runner Jackson & Curtis, Boston, 1913-14, salesman, 1914-17, sales mgr., 1919-23, ptnr., 1923-38, sr. ptnr., 1938-42; sr. ptnr. Paine, Webber, Jackson & Curtis, 1942-61; dir. emeritus W.R. Grace & Co. Mem. fin. com. Mass. Soc. Prevention Cruelty to Children; formerly chmn. fin. com. div. and other positions Boston Community Fund. Maj. U.S. Army, 1917-19. Mem. Investment Bankers Assn. Am. (past v.p.), Boston Bond Club (pres. 1935-46), Boston Assn. Stock Exchange Firms (chmn. bd. govs. 1936-37), N.Y. Stock Exchange (gov. 1940-45), Boston C. of C. (gov. 1941-44), Somerset Club, Myopia Hunt Club, Tavern Club, Brook Club. Republican. Unitarian. Home: Beverly Mass. †

MINOTTO, JAMES, government official, rancher, cattle feeder, banker; b. Berlin, Germany, Feb. 17, 1891; came to U.S., 1914; naturalized, 1921; s. Count Demetrio and Agnes (Zaremba, also known as Agnes Sorma, German actress) M.; m. Idamay Swift, Jan. 15, 1916 (dec. Oct. 1943); children: Mitri, Idamay; m. 2d, Julia Franklin, Nov. 17, 1944; Children: James, Anina. Clk. Deutsche Bank, Berlin, London, 1909-13; mgr. S.A. dept. Guaranty Trust Co., N.Y.C., 1915-16, Equitable Trust Co., 1917-18; v.p. Nafra Co., Chgo., 1919-20, Boulevard Bridge Bank, 1921-24; chmn. bd. Mission Ranch Inc., Phoenix, from 1945; pres. Mission Dairy Inc., 1925-45, Mission Foods Inc., from 1945, Minotto Investment Co., from 1925; asst. to pres. Cudahay Packing Co., Chgo., 1947; pres., chmn. bd. Bank of Phoenix, 1958-61; dir. pub. relations Western Savs. Loan Assn., from 1971. Mem. Ariz. State Senate, 1933-34, 39-40, 43-44; asst. to chief ECA mission to Italy. 1950-51; Chief of Mission to Portugal of Mut. Security Agy., with rank of minister, 1951-55; spl. cons. to U.S. Senate; staff mem. Congl. Inaugural Com., 1964-65; cons. profl. staff mem. U.S. Senate com. on fgn. relaltions and appropriations, 1956, 57, 62, 64, 65, 67, 68; pub. relations cons. Ariz. Pub. Svc., 1966, 67, 68; profl. staff mem. U.S. Senate com. on appropriations doing surveys in Cen. and S.Am., 1968. Capt., pres. Maricopa County Mounted Sheriff Posse, 1938-48. Decorated Comdr. Order of Merit (Italian Republic). Mem. Elks, Kiva Club, Paradise Valley Country Club, Phoenix Club, Coronada (Calif.) Yacht Club. Home: Phoenix Ariz. †

MINTENER, JAMES BRADSHAW, lawyer; b. Trempealeau, Wis., July 6, 1902; s. John William and Anna Balfour (Bradshaw) M.; m. Eleanor Van Gilder White, Mar. 3, 1934; children: Anne Randolph Heegard, James Bradshaw, Susan Perine Northrop. AB, Yale U., 1923; student, Oxford U., Eng., 1923-26, Harvard Law Sch., 1926-27; JD, U. Minn., 1929; LLD, Macalester Coll., W.Va. Wesleyan U., Gallaudet Coll.; Dr. Pub. Svc., Ohio Wesleyan U. Bar: Minn. 1930. With firm Cobb, Hoke, Benson, Krause & Faegre, Mpls., 1929-33; instr. Minn. Coll. Law, 1929-35; assoc. Pillsbury Mills Inc. and predecessor cos., 1933-88; asst. gen. counsel Pillsbury Flour Mills. Co., Mpls., 1933-46, asst. sec., 1935-46, v.p. and gen. counsel, 1946-54; asst. sec. HEW, 1954; sr. ptnr. Mintener and Mitchell, 1962-75; cons. Chocolate Mfrs. U.S., Am. Cocoa Rsch. Inst.; gen. counsel Parenteral Drug assn.; former Washington counsel Govt. of U.S.V.I.; bd. dirs. Group Hospitalization Inc., Washington; past vice chmn., hon. mem. bd. trustees Am. U.; past pres, hon. mem. bd. trustees Wesley Theol. Sem.; vice chmn. bd. trustees Gallaudet Coll.; trustee, exec. com., v.p. Sibley Meml. Hosp.; assoc. trustee Hamline U.; bd. drs. mem. exc. com. Consortium of Univs., Washington; bd. dirs. Wesley Found., George Washington U..; bd. dirs., hon. mem. exec. com. Wolf Trap Found., Washington; chmn., mem. exec.com., hon. v.p. Methodist Bd. Publ.; mem. Folke Bernadotte Meml. Found., Gustavus Adolphus Coll., St. Peter, Minn. Contbr. Christian Century. Mem. several civic groups on edn., youth, govt., human relations; active in youth groups local, state, nat. race relations groups, related activities; pres., treas., exec. com. D.C. Hosp. Coun.; mem. Pres.'s Commn. on Registration and Voting; mem. 2d citizens adv. com. FDA; mem. Surgeon Gen.'s Adv.Coun. Hosp. Rsch. Facilities; lay del. World Meth. Conf., Meth. Gen. and Jurisdictional Conf.; mem. bd. Meth. World Coun., Meth. Commn. to Study Ministry. Recipient Jewish war vets. human relations award B'nai B'rith, nat. Jr. C. of C. good govt. award Mpls. Jr. C. of C.; outstanding achievement award U. Minn. Mem. many comml. and profl. assns. and orgns., exec. of several, including English Speaking Union (exec. com. nat. coun., pres. Washington br.), Chevy Chase Club, Capitol Hill Club, Cosmos Club (past dir., chmn. admissions and program com.), Metropolitan Club, Palaver Club (Washington). Home: Washington D.C. Died Dec. 31, 1988.

MISHOE, LUNA ISAAC, college president, mathematician; b. Bucksport, S.C., Jan. 5, 1917; s. Henry and Martha (Oliver) M. BS, Allen U., 1938; MS, U. Mich., 1942; PhD, N.Y. U., 1953; postgrad., Oxford (Eng.) U., 1955-56; MBA, U. Pa., 1985; DSc (hon.), Lincoln U., 1986. Prof. math. and physics Kittrell (N.C.) Coll., 1939-42; prof. math. and physics Del. State Coll., Dover, 1946-48, pres., from 1960; assoc. prof. physics Morgan State Coll., Balt., 1948-54; prof. Morgan State Coll., 1954-60, chmn. div. natural sci., 1956-60; rsch. mathematician Ballistics Rsrch. Lab., Aberdeen (Md.) Proving Ground, summers 1952-57, cons., 1957-60. Mem. Edn. Commn. of the States, from 1977; bd. dirs. Am. Council Edn., 1978; trustee U. Del., Del. State Coll., from 1977; bd. dirs. Univ. City Sci. Ctr., Phila. Mem. Am. Math. Soc., Math. Assn. Am., Del. Acad. Sci. (pres. 1967-68). Home: Dover Del. Died Jan. 16, 1989.

MITCHELL, BROADUS, economist, historian; b. Georgetown, Ky., Dec. 27, 1892; s. Samuel Chiles and Alice Virginia (Broadus) M.; m. Adelaide Hammond, Sept. 1, 1923 (div.); children: Barbara Sinclair, Sidney Hammond; m. Louise Pearson Blodget, Dec. 31, 1936 (dec. 1986); children: Theodora, Christopher. AB, U. S.C., 1913; fellow, Johns Hopkins, 1917-18, PhD, 1918; LHD, Hofstra U., 1967. Instr. in polit. economy Johns Hopkins, 1919-22, assoc., 1922-27, assoc. prof., 1927-39; vis. prof. Occidental Coll., L.A., 1939-40, prof., 1940-41; vis. lectr. econs. NYU, 1942-44; Speranza lectr. Columbia U., 1956-57; McBride lectr. Western Res. U.; mem. rsch. dept., later cons. economist Internat. Ladies Garment Workers Union, 1943-47; prof. econs. Rutgers U., 1949-58; Whitney vis. prof. Hofstra Coll., 1958-59; teaching fellow New Coll., Hofstra U., 1960-68; cons. to dir. NRA div. Rev., 1935-36; lectr. Howard U., 1935-36; vis. prof. U. P.R., 1961-62; mem. tech. adv. com. standard budget U.S. Dept. Labor. Author or co-author numerous books including: Alexander Hamilton, 1962, Postscripts to Economic History, 1967, Alexander Hamilton, The Revolutionar Years, 1970, The Road to Yorktown, 1971, The Price of Independence, 1974, Alexander Hamilton, a Concise Biography, 1976. former pre. Balt. Urban League; former trustee Christian Social Justice Fund; mem. bd. League for Indsl. Democracy, Inter-Union Inst.; chmn. N.J. Civil Liberties Com. Sgt. U.S. Army, 1918. Mem. Met. Econ. Assn. (past pres.), Phi Gamma Delta, Phi Beta Kappa. Home: Croton-on-Hudson N.Y. also: Wendell Mass. Died Apr. 28, 1988; buried Locks' Village Cemetery, Wendell, Mass.

MITCHELL, DAVID LESTER, investor; b. Kansas City, Mo., Sept. 15, 1919; s. Ralph Wallace and Esther (Clark) M.; m. Beatrice Alleen Sand, Dec. 20, 1941; children: David Clark, Karen Sandra (Mrs. Donald E. Gleash). BA, De PAuw U., 1940; MBA, U. Chgo., 1954. CPA, Ill. Controller, asst. treas. Am. Bakeries Co., Chgo., 1940-63, fin. v.p., 1969-70, exec. v.p., 1970-72; fin. v.p. Gold Bond Stamp Co., Mpls., 1963-65; pres. First Nat. Bank Barron, Wis., 1965-67; treas., dir. Jewels Internat., 1972-77. Capt. USMCR, 1941-46. Mem. Moon Valley Country Club (Phoenix), Masons, Phi Delta Theta. Republican. Presbyterian. Home: Scottsdale Ariz. Died Oct. 2, 1985; buried Scottsdale.

MITCHELL, HENRY VINCENT EDWARDS, III, lawyer; b. N.Y.C., Dec. 10, 1915; s. Henry Vincent Edwards and May (Matteson) M.; m. Paula Matilda von Gleske, Oct. 31, 1953; children: Margaret Ann Bliss, Debora H. McPEck, H.V.E. Vincent, PAmela Adams Andros, Hamilton Vaughan. AB, Williams Coll., 1938; JD, Yale U., 1941. Bar: Ohio. Ptnr. Bowman & Bailey, Springfield, Ohio, 1941-42; asst. atty. U.S. Dept. Interior, Bonneville Power Adminstrn., Oreg., 1942-43; ptnr. McAfee, Hanning, Newcomer, Hazlett & Wheeler, Ohio, 1943-67; sr. ptnr. Squire, Sanders & Dempsey, Cleve., 1967-83. Mem. investment com. First United Meth. Ch. of Cleve. Fellow Am. Judicature Soc.; mem. ABA, Am. Coll. Trial Lawyers, Bar Assn. Greater Cleve., Bar Assn. Dist. Columbia, Cleve. Def. Atty. Group, Oreg. State Bar Assn., Ohio State Bar Assn., Cuyahoga County Bar Assn., Inter-Am. Bar Assn., Bar Assn. Greater Cleve., Citizens League, Cleve. Colony of Mayflower Descs., SAR, Cleve. Athletic Club, Columbus Athletic Club, Masons, Shriners. Presbyterian. Died Sept. 12, 1983; buried Westlake Cemetery, Cleve.

MITCHELL, HOMER IRVING, lawyer; b. L.A., Dec. 9, 1899; s. Irving Jefferson and Susan (Bingham) M.; m. Katharine Reid, Oct. 18, 1927 (d. Aug. 6, 1977); m. Katharine Howard Robinson, Dec. 14, 1977. AB, Stanford, 1922, JD, 1923. Bar: Calif. 1923. Dep. dist. atty. L.A. County, 1924-26, dep. county counsel, 1926-28; with O'Melveny & Myers, L.A., 1928-82, ptnr., 1936-73, of counsel, 1974-82. Bd. visitors Stanford Law Sch., 1958-63, 78-80. Fellow Am. Coll. Trial Lawyers; mem. ABA, L.A. Bar Assn., Calif. Club, L.A. Yacht Club, Annandale Golf Club, Theta Delta Chi, Phi Delta Phi. Home: San Marino Calif. Died Mar. 1982.

MITCHELL, HOWARD, orchestra conductor; b. Lyons, Nebr., Mar. 11, 1911; s. George Cheever and Vera (Bundy) M.; m. Alma Metcalf, June 2, 1931; children: Lorraine, Glenn, Martha, Gerard, Andrew John. Student, Peabody Conservatory, 1928-30, Mus.D., 1966; honor grad., Curtis Inst. Music, 1935; Mus. D., Am. U., 1950, Georgetown U., 1960, Howard U., 1960, Western Md. Coll., 1966, Catholic U., 1969. First cellist Nat. Symphony Orch., Washington, 1933-46, assoc. condr., 1946-49, condr., music dir., 1949-70; music dir. nat. orch. Uruguay, from 1970. Mem. Nat. Cultural Ctr. Com., adv. com. arts. Recipient Alice M. Ditson award Nat. Cath. Music Educators and Nat. Music Coun., Nat. Assn. for Am. Composers and Condrs., 1957, Laurel Leaf, Am. Composers Alliance, 1959, Nat. Fedn. Music Clubs award, 1960, Nat. Music Coun. Condr. citation, 1951, 55, 57, 61, 64; citation and scroll of commendation Concert Artists Guildm 1959, Peabody Conservatory Disting. Alumni award, 1963, Jean Sibelius medal, Finland, 1965, Hadassah Myrtle Leaf award, 1968; decorated Nat. Order Condor of Andes (Bolivia); comdr.'s cross Order of Merit (Fed. Republic of Germany); Knight of ST. Gregory (Vatican). Home: Palm Coast Fla. Died June 22, 1988.

MITCHELL, JOHN NEWTON, lawyer, business consultant; b. Detroit, Sept. 5, 1913; s. Joseph Charles and Margaret Agnes (McMahon) M.; m. Martha Beall, 1957 (separated 1973) (dec. 1976); children: John Newton III, Jill Elizabeth Mitchell Reed, Martha. Student, Fordham U., 1932-34, LLB, 1938; postgrad. law, St. John's U., 1938-39. Bar: N.Y. 1938-75. Assoc. firm Caldwell & Raymond, N.Y.C., 1938-42; ptnr. Caldwell, Trimble & Mitchell, 1942-66, Nixon, Mudge, Rose, Guthrie, Alexander & Mitchell, 1967-68; atty. gen. U.S. 1969-72. Campaign mgr. for Richard M. Nixon, 1968; chmn. Com. to Re-elect Pres., 1972. With USNR, 1943-46. Mem. ABA (local govt. sect.). Died Nov. 9, 1988.

MITCHELL, ULYSS STANFORD, clergyman, sociologist; b. Marshfield, Mo., July 2, 1902; s. Robert Campbell and May (Edwards) M.; m. Viola Elizabeth Westlund, Sept. 16, 1924; children: Robert Louis, Marcia Ann, Ellen May. AB, U. So. Calif., 1931; AM, U. Philippines, 1932; ThB, Cen. Bapt. Theol. Sem., Kansas City, Mo., 1928, BD, 1931, ThD summa cum laude, 1934; Am. Rsch. student in Orient. Dir. youth work White Temple, San Diego, 1929-31; pastorates Atherton Bapt. Ch., L.A., 1932-34, First Bapt. Ch. (City Temple), Sioux Falls, S.D., 1934-36; dir. adult and social edn. Am. Bapt. Conv., Phila., 1939-43; nat. v.p. and Western exec. dir. NCCJ, Inc., 1943-47; Western exec. sec. Ch. World Svc., Inc., 1947-49; pres. U.S. Mitchell Assocs., Inc., Found. for Humanity, Inc., 1963-81; me. U.S. del. founding UN, 1945; del. World Conf. Freedom, Justice, and Responsibility, 1946; bd. dirs. No. Calif. Coun. Chs.; gen. coun. Am. Bapt. Conv.; pres. Am. Bapt. ministers coun.; chmn. social svc. com., chmn. world affairs com.; founder Coun. on Christian Social Progress; active Nat. Coun. Chs. of Christ in Am.; chmn. com. indsl. rels., coops., mem. com. Am. home; leader, lectr. world affairs, human rels.; lectr. for U.S. Army Office Info. and Edn., USA, Ala. and Aleutian Islands, World War II; chmn. edn. com. UNESCO; founder, pres. Found. for Humanity, Inc., 1963; chaplain-counselor Heart Warmers Visitation Agy. div., from 1972. Author: Manchurian Situation; contbr. publs. Recipient 1st awards Collegiate Internat. Forensics, Honolulu, Tokyo, 1931, Wisdom award od honor, 1970. Mem. Fedn. Am. Scientists, Am. Polit. Sci. Assn., Am. Sociol Assn., Acad. Polit. Sci., Am. Assn. for UN, United World Federalists, Kiwanis, Commonwealth Club, Phi Chi Phi, Delta Sigma Rho, Pi Kappa Delta. Home: Oakland Calif. Died Oct. 9, 1985; buried Skylawn Meml. Park, San Mateo, Calif.

MITHOEFER, JOHN CALDWELL, physician, educator; b. Cin., Feb. 12, 1920; s. William and Florence (Shanks) M.; m. Olivia Procter McCullough, June 20, 1942 (div.); children: Michael C., C. Keith, Olivia Procter; m. Mary Whitaker Hager, 1972. AB, Brown U., 1941; MD, Harvard, 1944. Rotating intern Cin. Gen. Hosp., 1944-45, asst. resident medicine, 1945-46, fellow cardiac lab., 1947-49; rsch. fellow MAry Imogene Bassett Hosp., Columbia, 1949-52, dir. cardiopulmonary lab., 1952-68, assoc. physician, 1957-68; rsch. assoc. physiology Faculte de Medecine, Paris, 1954; vis. colleague cardiology Hammersmith Hosp., London, 1963; asst. clin. prof. medecine Columbia Coll. Phys. and Surgeons, 1963-68; prof. medicine, chief cardiopulmonary div. Dartmouth Med. Sch., 1968-72; prof. medicine, dir. pulmonary div. Med. U. S.C., 1972-81. Contbr. articles to profl. jours. Bd. dirs. Otsego County Heart Assn., 1959-61, 65-67, pres., 1961; mem. rsch. com. N.Y. State Heart Assn., 1964-66, N.Y. State Tb and Respiratory Diseases Assn., 1965-68; chmn. Nat. Heart and Lung Inst. com. Nat. Rsch. and DemonstrationCtrs., 1973-75; mem. S.C. Health Care Adv. Bd., 1973-78. With M.C., AUS, 1946-47. Fellow Am. Coll. Cardiology (gov. 1970-72), Am. Coll. Chest Physicians (gov. 1971-72, 76-81, vice chmn. forum on pathophysiology, 1980-81, mem. sci. program com. 1973); mem. Am. Soc. Clin. Investigation, Am. Physiol. Soc., Am. Thoracic Soc., So. Soc. Clin. Investigation, Assn. U. Cardiologists, Am. Heart Assn. (fellow coun. clin. cardiology, mem. program com. coun. cardiology 1968-69, program com. cardiopulmonary coun. 1975). Home: Charleston S.C. Died Oct. 6, 1981.

MITIGUY, HARRY ROBERT, banker; b. Bethel, Vt., July 17, 1923; s. Andrew Jackson and Hazel (Whitney) M.; m. Harriet Stafford, May 19, 1945; children: Jane, Nancy, Mary. B.S., Cornell U., 1945; M.S., U. Vt., 1954. County agr. agt. U. Vt., Bennington, 1947-52, U. N.H., Milford, 1952-55; from agrl. economist to sr. v.p. Fed. Res. Bank, Boston, 1955-69; v.p. Keystone Custodial Funds, Boston, 1969-74; pres., chief exec. officer, dir. Howard Bank, N.A., Burlington, Vt., 1974-86, pres., chief exec. officer, bd. dirs., Howard Bancorp, 1985-87; bd. dirs. Fed. Res. Bank of Boston. Trustee U. Vt., 1979-85, Shelburne Mus., (Vt.), 1980-87. Served to 1st lt. USMCR, 1943-46. Mem. Am. Bankers Assn. (treas., dir.). Died 1987. Home: Shelburne Vt.

MIZENER, ARTHUR MOORE, educator; b. Erie, Pa., Sept. 3, 1907; s. Mason Price and Mabel (Moore) M.; m. Elizabeth Rosemary Paris, July 16, 1935; children: Rosemary Moore (Mrs. LEonard B. Colt Jr.), Arthur Paris (dec.). Grad. cum laude, The Hill Sch., Pottstown, Pa., 1926; BS with highest honors, Princeton, 1930, PhD, 1934; MA, Harvard, 1932. Instr. English Yale, 1934-40; asst. prof. Wells Coll., 1940-44, assoc prof., 1944-45; prof., chmn. English dept. Carleton Coll., Northfield, Minn., 1945-51; Mellon Found. prof. English Cornell U., Ithaca, N.Y., 1951-73, prof. emeritus, 1973-88. Author: The Far Side of Paradise: A Biography of F. Scott Fitzgerald, 1951, The Sense of Life in the Modern Novel, 1964, Twelve Great American Novels, 1967, The Saddest Story: A Critical Biography of Ford Madox Ford, 1970, Scott Fitzgerald and His World, 1973; editor: Afternoon of an Author, 1957, The Fitzgerald Reader, 1963, The Last Chronicle of Barset, 1964. Proctor fellow in English, Princeton, 1933-34; Fulbright lectr. Am. Studies, U. London, 1955-56; Guggenheim fellow, 1964-65; sr. fellow NEH, 1968. Mem. Tower Club, Phi Beta Kappa. Democrat. Presbyterian. Home: Bristol R.I. Died Feb. 11, 1988.

MODINE, ARTHUR BERNARD, manufacturing company executive; b. Chgo., Oct. 27, 1885; s. John A. and Amanda (Landberg) M.; m. Margaret J. Bartlett, June 12, 1915; children: Thomas B., Margaret Modine Gomez, Julie E. Modine Woodrow. BS, U. Mich., 1908. Founder, later chmn. Modine Mfg. Co., Racine, Wis., from 1916; founder, dir. Twin Disc Clutch Co., Racine, from 1918; bd. dirs., v.p. Am. Bank & Trust Co., Racine, from 1928. Trustee St. Luke's Hosp., Racine, Kemper Hall, Kenosha, Wis. Home: Racine Wis. †

MOE, JOHN HOWARD, orthopaedic surgeon, educator; b. Grafton, N.D., Aug. 14, 1905; s. Hans Jacob and Gunhild (Loseth) M.; m. Marguerite Elizabeth Clough, 1936 (dec. 1969); children: Elizabeth Ann, Lawrence Dexter; m. Mary Lou Kruger Wood, Aug. 1, 1976; Richard, Claudia, Kathleen, Nancy Wood. B.S., U. N.D., 1927; M.B., Northwestern U., 1929, M.D., 1930. Diplomate: Am. Bd. Orthopedic Surgery. Mem. staff Med. Sch. U. Minn., Mpls., 1933-88; prof., chmn. dept. orthopedic surgery Med. Sch. U. Minn., 1933-75, prof. emeritus dept. orthopedic surgery; former chief staff Gillette Children's Hosp. Co-author: The Milwaukee Brace in Scoliosis, 2d edit, 1980, Scoliosis and Other Spinal Deformities, 1978, Moe's Textbook of Scoliosis and Other Spinal Deformities, 1987; contbr. numerous articles to profl. jours. Founder Twin Cities Scoliosis Center, Mpls.; founder Scoliosis Service Santa Casa Hosp., Sao Paulo, Brazil, 1969, Twin Cities Scoliosis Fund, John Moe Scoliosis fellowship of U. Minn. Dept. Orthopedic Surgery, Mpls. Recipient Bernardo O'Higgins medal Chile, 1969, Sioux award U. N.D., 1968, Northwestern U. Alumni Merit award, 1987. Mem. ACS, Am. Acad. Orthopedic Surgery, Clin. Orthopedic Soc. (past pres.), Am. Orthopedic Assn. (pres. 1971-72), Hennepin County Med. Soc. (pres. 1958), Minn. Acad. Medicine Soc. Internat. Orthopedics and Surgery (U.S. del. 1971-75), Canadian Orthopedic Assn., Scoliosis Research Soc. (founder, pres.), Nat. Acad. Sci., Nat. Acad. Medicine (Brazil), Venezuelan Orthopedic Soc., Argentine Soc. Orthopedics and Traumatology (corr.), Brit. Orthopedic Assn. (corr.); hon. mem. Chilean, Brazilian, Colombian, Peruvian, Yugoslavian, Costa Rica orthopedic socs. Home: Bloomington Minn. Died Apr. 2, 1988.

MOFFETT, HARRY LEE, natural resources consultant; b. Cleve., June 27, 1912; s. Leon Wesley and Mildred (Hixson) M.; m. Annie Wright Parker, Apr. 7, 1934; 1 dau. Marianne Virginia Moffett Schul. AB, Am. U., 1933, LLB, 1951. Dist. mgr. Washington Post, 1933-34; dir. pub. rels. Planning and Coordinating Com. for Petroleum Industry, 1934-35; dir. pub. affairs Am. Mining Congress, 1935-66; asst. dir. pub. Land Law Rev. Commn., 1966-69; dir. office minerals and solid fuels, office asst. sec. for mineral resources Dept. Interior, 1969-71, dep. asst. sec. mineral resources, 1971-73; assoc. BKW and Assocs., Washington, from 1973; Washington mgr. Dunn Geosci. Corp., Latham, N.Y., from 1974; cons. interior and insular affairs com. Ho. of Reps., 1966; mem. U.S. del. on mineral resources to UN, 1971-73; v.p., dir. Francis Scott Key Hotel; dir., officer Spl. Indsl. Radio Services Assn. Assoc. editor Mining Congress Jour., 1935-66; contbr. articles to profl. jours. Pres. Woodrow Wilson High Sch. Home and Sch. Assn., 1946-47. Served to col. AUS, 1939-46, PTO. Decorated Legion of Merit; recipient Disting. Service awards Spl. Indsl. Radio Services Assn., 1964, 65, U.S. Dept. Interior, 1973. Mem. Mining and Metall. Soc., Nat. PRess Club, VFW, Masons (32d deg.), Shriners, Alpha Tau Omega. Home: Rockville Md. Died June 30, 1984; buried Arlington Nat. Cemetery.

MOFFITT, THOMAS EDWARD, chemical company executive; b. Wallace, Idaho, Feb. 22, 1898; s. Edward Hazelton and Jane (Colburn) M.; m. Sally Gyde, Sept. 22, 1926; children: Jane Moffitt Calderhead, Sally Moffitt Kennedy. AB, Cornell U., 1922. Draftsman Wash. Water Power Co., Spokane, 1922-23; chem. engr. Guy C. Howard Co., Seattle, 1924-27; sec./treas. Sunset Marine Engring. Corp., Seattle, 1927-30; asst. western sales mgt. Hooker Electrochem. Co. (name changed to Hooker Chem. Corp., 1958), Tacoma, Wash., 1930-45; works mgr., western mgr., then v.p. charge westrn ops. Hooker Electrochem. Co. (name changed to Hooker

Chem. Corp., 1958), Tacoma, 1950-56, exec. v.p., Niagara Falls, N.Y., 1956-57, pres., 1957-61, chmn. bd., from 1961; chem. engr. Wyerhaeuser Timber Co., 1945-46; sales mgr. Pa. Salt Mfg. Co., Tacoma, 1946-50; bd. dirs. Hooker Chems., Ltd., Vancouver. B.C., Solar Salt Co., Salt Lake City, Marine Trust Co. Western N.Y., Ranier Nat. Park Co., Tacoma. Mem. Ranier Club (Seattle), University Club, Chemists Club (N.Y.), Masons, Shriners, Phi Sigma Kappa. Republican. Presbyterian. Home: New York N.Y. †

MOHAMMED, REZA SHAH PAHLEVI, shah of Iran; b. Tehran, Iran, Oct. 26, 1919; s. Riza Shah Pahlevi and Tajomolouk Pahlevi; m. Princess Fawzia of Egypt, 1939 (dissolved 1948); 1 child, Shahnaz; m. soraya eshandiari, 1951 (div.); m. Farah Diba, Dec. 21, 1959; children: Reza Cyrus Ali, Ali Reza, Maasoumeh Farahnaz, Layla. Ed., Tehran and Switzerland; DCL (hon.), U. Mich., 1949; LLD, Harvard U., 1968. Succeeded to throne following father's abdication 1941, abdicated, 1979. Author: Mission for My Country, The White Revolution. Decorated Sovereign Order of Golden Spur (Vatican); Order of Pahlevi, Order of Crown (Iran); Order of Mohammed Ali the Great (Arab Republic of Egypt); Order of Rafeddin (Iraq); Order of Leopold (Belgium); Order of White Lion (Czechoslovakia); Legion of Honor (France); Order of St. Savior (Greece); Order of Cedar (Lebanon); Order of Almar Aali (Afghanistan); Order of Bath (U.K.); Order of Ommegah (Syrian Arab Republic); Order of propitious Cloud (Peoples Republic of China); Legion of Merit (U.S.). Died July 27, 1980.

MOHLER, HAROLD SHEAFFER, food company executive; b. Ephrata, Pa., Mar. 8, 1919; s. Milton Keller and Esther Landis (Sheaffer) M.; m. Melda Lorraine Artz, July 21, 1945; children: Jeffrey Lee, Susan Lorraine, Julie Lynn. B.S. in Indsl. Engring, Lehigh U., 1948, LL.D., 1975; LL.D., Elizabethtown Coll., 1979. Registered profl. engr., Pa. With Hershey Chocolate Corp. (Pa.) (name changed to Hershey Foods Corp. 1968), 1948-84, asst. to pres., 1957-62, v.p., 1962-65, pres., chief exec. officer, 1965-74, chmn. bd., pres., 1974-76, chmn. bd., chmn. exec. com., 1976-84; chmn. bd., dir. Hershey Bank; former chmn., bd.dirs. Hershey Trust Co., 1986; dir. Herco, Inc. (formerly Hershey Estates), Pa. Power & Light Co., Ashland Oil, Inc. Former bd. dirs., former mem. exec. com. Pa. Economy League; past chmn. Pennsylvanians for Effective Govt.; mem., past chmn. Bus.-Industry Polit. Action Com.; bd. mgrs. Milton Hershey Sch., until 1985, M.S. Hershey Found., until 1985; trustee Hershey Fund, until 1984; pres. bd. trustees Lehigh U., 1973-85, trustee for life. Served to 1st lt. navigator USAAF, 1943-45. Decorated Air medal with 2 oak leaf clusters, Purple Heart. Mem. ASME, Newcomen Soc., Am. Cocoa Research Inst. (past chmn. bd.), Chocolate Mfrs. Assn. U.S. (past chmn.), Pa. C. of C. (dir., past chmn.), Alpha Kappa Psi (hon.), Alpha Pi Mu. Republican. Presbyterian. (elder). Clubs: Mason, Rotarian, Hershey Country; Saucon Valley Country, Garden of the Gods. Home: Hershey Pa. Died Aug. 31, 1988.

MOLDENHAUER, HANS, musicologist; b. Mainz, Republic of West Germany, Dec. 13, 1906; came to U.S., 1938; s. Richard and Theckla (Weil) M.; m. Mary K. Hockett, Sept. 4, 1982: children by two previous marriages: Trude Ann Moldenhauer Donovan, Myra Ruth Moldenhauer Cathcart, Joseph, Margaret Moldenhauer Hutchingson. Grad., Humanistisches Gymnasium and Mcpl. Coll. Music, Mainz, 1925; BA, Whitworth Coll., 1945, DMus, 1986; MusD, Boguslawski Coll. Music, 1945; DFA, Roosevelt U., 1951. Founder, dir. Spokane (Wash.) Conservatory, 1942-55, pres., 1946-86; sr. lectr., adviser to grad. students U. Wash., Seattle, 1961-64; lectr. numerous coll. and univs. in U.S. and Europe; chmn. First Internat. Webern Festival, Seattle, 1962; organizer internat. Webern festivals, Seattle, 1962, Salzburg/Mittersill, 1965, Buffalo, 1966, Dartmouth Coll., 1968, Vienna, 1972, Baton Rouge, 1978; founder, dir. with Rosaleen Moldenhauer, Moldenhauer Archives, Spokane, with brs. Northwestern U., Evanston, Ill, Wash. State U., Pullman, Bavarian State Library, Munich, Zurich Cen. Library, Vienna City Library, Paul Sacher Found., Basel, Harvard U., Cambridge, Mass., Whitworth Coll., Spokane, Library of Congress. Performer piano concert, weekly 2 piano broadcasts, 1943-55; author: Duo-Pianism, 1950, The Death of Anton Webern-A Drama in Documents, 1961, Anton von Webern: Perspectives, 1966, Anton von Webern: Sketches, 1968, (with Rosaleen Moldenhauer) Anton von Webern: Chronicle of His Life and Work, 1978, 2d edit. 1979, German edit. 1980 (ASCAP Deems Taylor award); contbr. numerous articles to profl. jours. and various encys. Hon. curator of 20th Century Music in Harvard Coll. Library, Harvard U., Cambridge, 1984. Recipient Austrian Cross of Honor for Sci. and Art, 1st Class, 1970, Comdr.'s Cross of Order of Merit Federal Republic of Germany, 1980; Golden Order of Merit of the City of Vienna, 1981. Mem. Am. Musicological Soc. (Pacific Northwest chpt. chmn. 1958-60), Internat. Webern Soc. (pres. 1962-86). Club: Am. Alpine (life). Lodge: Rotary (hon.). Home: Spokane Wash. Died Oct. 19, 1987.

MOLOGNE, LEWIS ASPEY, army officer, surgeon, medical center administrator; b. Mt. Pleasant, Pa., Jan. 21, 1932; s. Lewis Aloysius and Kathryn (Fischer) M.; m. Rose Marie Galiardi, June 18, 1960; children—Lewis Alan, Timothy Scott, Michael John, Mary Kathryn, Amy Louise. B.S., U.S. Mil. Acad., West Point, 1954; M.D., U. Pitts., 1961. Diplomate Am. Bd. Surgery. Commd. 2d lt. U.S. Army, 1954, advanced through grades to maj. gen., 1984; chief dept. surgery Fitzsimons Army Med. Ctr., Aurora, Colo., 1978-80; comdr. USA Medcom-Korea, Seoul, Korea, 1980-81; dep. comdr. Fitzsimons Army Med. Ctr., Aurora, Colo., 1981-82; chief med. corps affairs Pentagon, Washington, 1982-83; comdg. gen. Walter Reed Army Med. Ctr., Washington, 1983-88; prof. clin. surgery Uniformed Services U. Health Scis., Bethesda, Md., 1984-88. Contbr. chpts. to books, articles to profl. publs. Decorated D.S.M., Legion of Merit, Meritorious Service medal with oak leaf clusters, Army Commendation medal. Fellow ACS; mem. Assn. Mil. Surgeons of U.S., Phi Kappa Phi, Alpha Omega Alpha. Republican. Roman Catholic. Died Aug. 22, 1988.

MOLOTOV, VYACHESLAV, government official USSR; b. Kirov dist., Russia, Mar. 9, 1890; s. Mikhail Scriabin. Student, Polytechnic Inst., St. Petersburg, 1911. Temp. head Bolshevist party, 1917; 2d sec. Bolshevist party under Stalin; premier and minister fgn. affair; chmn. People's Economy Coun., Northern Region, 1918, Nijegorodsky regional exec., 1919; sec. Donets Regional Party com., 1920; mem. and sec. Central Com. Community Party of Soviet Union; candidate mem. Polit. Bur., 1921; mem. Poli. Bur., C.P.S.U., 1926, Central Exec. Com. Russian Soviet Socialist Rep., 1927; sec. Moscow com. C.P.S.U., 1928; mem. Presidium Central Exec. Com., USSR, 1929, chmn., 1st v.p. Coun. People's Commissars, 1939-40; mem. Polit. Bur. C.P.S.U., State Defence Com., Supreme Soviet; USSR del. to UN Gen. Assembl, People's Commissar for Fgn. Affairs, 1939-46, minister fgn. affairs, 1946-49, 53-56, dep. prime minister, 1949-57, state control minister, 1957 (ministry abolished 1957), no longer mem. of the Presidium, from 1957, ambassador to Outer Mongolia, 1957-60; permanent rep. at hdqrs. Internat. Atomic Energy Agy., 1960-61; Head Soviet del. San Francisco meeting orgn. of UN, 1945. †

MONAGHAN, BERNARD MICHAEL, mining company executive; b. Nanaimo, B.C., Can., Apr. 26, 1925; s. Michael Joseph and Margaret Esther (McMurray) M.; m. Lise M. Vaillancourt, Dec. 11, 1954; children: Leslie, Odette, Nancy, Michael, Lise Anne. B.E., U. Sask., 1946; A.M.P., Harvard U., 1970. Chief engr. Iron Ore Co. of Can., Sept-Iles, Que., 1948-62, mgr., 1963-76, v.p., 1976-78; v.p. tech. services Hanna Mining Co. (now M.A. Hanna Co.), Cleve., 1979-80, sr. v.p. ops., from 1981, v.p., dir. subsidiaries. Mayor City of Sept-Iles, 1962-64. Roman Catholic. Club: Clevelander. Home: Lakewood Ohio. Died Mar. 16, 1988; buried Sept Iles, Quebec, Can.

MONCRIEF, WILLIAM ALVIN, oil producer; b. Sulphur Springs, Tex., Aug. 25, 1895; s. Lafayette Barto and Jennie (Smith) M.; m. Elizabeth Bright, May 28, 1918; children: William Alvin, Richard Barto. Student, Okla. U., 1916-18. Assoc. Marland Oil Co. (now Continental Oil Co.), Ponca City, Okla. and Ft. Worth, 1919-29; ind. oil and gas producer Tex., from 1929. Lt. U.S. Army, World War I, ETO. Mem. Ind. Petroleum Assn. Am. (dir.), Am. Petroleum Inst., Los Angeles Country Club, Rivercrest Country Club, Shady Oaks Country Club, Ft. Worth Club, Thunderbird Club, Raquet Club, Masons, Shriners. Episcopalian. Home: Fort Worth Tex. Died May 21, 1986.

MONK, IVAN, machinery company executive; b. Funston, Ga., Jan. 6, 1912; s. Jeremiah Bryant and Balma (Stephenson) M.; m. Eleanor Elizabeth Yarbro, Oct. 2, 1937 (dec. Aug. 1973); children—Juanita Elizabeth (Mrs. Bradley Hosmer), Ivan Stanley; m. Janet Roman, Feb. 2, 1974; 1 child, Robin Jennie Roman. B.S., Ga. Inst. Tech., 1934; postgrad., Harvard Bus. Sch., 1956. Registered profl. engr., D.C. Commd. ensign USN, 1934, advanced through grades to capt., 1956, ret., 1960; mem. process selection bd. Office Saline Water, Dept. Interior, 1957-60; dept. mgr. turbine div. De Laval Turbine Inc., 1961-64, asst. gen. mgr. turbine div., 1965, v.p., gen. mgr. turbine div., 1966-68, v.p., group mgr. heavy equipment group, 1969, group v.p., 1970-71, exec. v.p., 1972, pres., chief exec. officer, 1972-75, vice chmn. bd., 1976-78; also dir.; pres. PIMS Assocs., Strategic Planning Inst., 1978-81; Mem. Princeton Regional Planning Bd., N.J. Gov.'s Sci. Adv. Com., N.J. Gov.'s Mgmt. Improvement Panel. Contbr. articles to profl. publs. Decorated Legion of Merit, Bronze Star. Fellow ASME (chmn. Trenton sect.); mem. Soc. Naval Architects and Marine Engrs. (chmn. Phila. sect.), Am. Soc. Naval Engrs. (pres., mem. council), Newcomen Soc., Phi Sigma Kappa, Pi Tau Sigma. Presbyn. (mem. session). Clubs: N.Y. Yacht, Rotarian (Trenton, N.J.), Nassau (Princeton, N.J.), Harvard Bus. (Princeton, N.J.); Engineers (Trenton). Home: Princeton N.J. Deceased.

MONK, THELONIOUS SPHERE, composer, pianist; b. Rocky Mount, N.C., Oct. 10, 1918; s. Thelonious and Barbara (Batts) M.; m. Nellie Smith, Sept. 15, 1948; children: Thelonious, Barbara. Ed. high sch., N.Y.C. With Kenny Clarke, Charlie Christian, Dizzie Gillespie, Charlie Parker pioneered movement in jazz popularly known as bop music; recordings Blue Note, Prestige, Riverside Records; composer songs including Round Midnight, Ask Me Now, Pannonica, Off Minor, Brilliant Corners, Monk's Mood, Well You Needn't, Straight No Chaser, Work. Critic's award as outstanding jazz pianist, 1958, 59, 60; named to Down Beat Mag. Hall of Fame. Home: New York N.Y. Died Feb. 17, 1982.

MONSON, KAREN ANN, writer; b. New Haven, Mar. 25, 1945; d. Harold and Sarah Catherine (McBride) M. B.A., Radcliffe Coll., 1966. Music critic Los Angeles Herald-Examiner, 1969-73, Chgo. Daily News, 1973-78, Balt. Sun, 1984-85; fellow Rockefeller Found. project for tng. music critics U. So. Calif., 1967-69, mem. resident faculty, 1971-73; mem. summer faculty Ravinia (Ill.) Mus. Critics Assn., 1973; free-lance corr. Wall Street Jour., Ovation, Mus. Am.; commentator-co producer Stravinsky '75, WFMT, Chgo., 1975, The Music of Alban Berg, WFMT, Chgo., 1977, 20th Century Art Song, WFMT, 1979; mem. faculty U. Chgo. Extension; music columnist Chicago mag., 1978-80; dir. Music Critics Assn. Insts., Aspen, Colo., 1978, 80, Louise Lincoln Kerr Cultural Center, Scottsdale, Ariz., 1980-82. Author: Alban Berg, 1979, Alma Mahler, Muse to Genius, 1983; contbr. to newspapers, mags. Recipient Peabody award, 1975, Deems Taylor award for criticism ASCAP, 1977; Armstrong award, 1980; Fulbright fellow West Berlin, 1966-67. Mem. Music Critics Assn. (chmn. edn. com., treas.). Club: Radcliffe of Chgo. (dir. 1976, v.p. 1977). Home: Baltimore Md. Died Jan. 30, 1988.

MONTGOMERY, FRANCIS RHODES, utility executive; b. Meriwether County, Ga., Aug. 1, 1916; s. Simpson James and Sarah Hall (Sims) M.; m. Priscilla Anderson, May 14, 1966 (dec.); 1 son, Thomas R.; m. Margaret Lucas, Apr. 25, 1981. BSME, Ga. Inst. Tech., 1948. Registered profl. engr., Hawaii. Mech. engr. CAA, Honolulu, 1947-51; with Hawaiian Electric Co. Inc., Honolulu, 1951-79, mech. engr., prin. mech. engr., mgr. engring. design, 1951-68, exec. engr., 1969, v.p. engring., 1970-79, ret., 1979; pres. Montgomery & Assocs., mech. engring. cons., 1953-63; dir. Foster Equipment Co.; chmn. Hawaii Bd. Registration, 1962-71; mem. Com. Alt. Energy Sources for Hawaii, 1974-85, mem. Manganese Nodules Adv. Guoup, 1976. With USN, 1943-46. Recipient Disting. Service certificate NAt. Coun. State Bd. Engrin Examiners, 1967. Fellow ASME; mem. Nat. Soc. Profl. Engrs., Hawaii Soc. Profl. Engrs., Navy League U.S., Air Force Assn., Waialae Country Club, Pacific Club, Rotary Club. Home: Honolulu Hawaii. Died July 28, 1985; buried Honolulu.

MONTGOMERY, RICHARD MATTERN, foundation executive, former air force officer; b. Hollidaysburg, Pa., Dec. 15, 1911; s. Charles W. Sr. and Eva (Mattern) M.; m. Anne Johnson Young, Oct. 1, 1947; children: Nancy, Richard Mattern, Thomas. BS, U.S. Mil. Acad., 1933; student, Flying Tng. Ctr., San Antonio, 1933-34, AC Tng. Sch., 1937-38, Air War Coll., 1946-47. Commd. 2d lt. U.S. Army, 1933, advanced through grades to lt. gen., 1962; chief insp., test pilot Panama Air Depot, France Field, C.Z., 1935-37; assigned Chanute Field, Ill., 1937-38; flynig instr., flight and stage comdr. Randolph Field, Tex., 1938-42; dir. flying tng. Army Air Field, Enid, Okla., 1942; comdr. Army Air Field, Independence, Kans., 1943; chief individual tng. div. office asst. chief Air Staff Tng. Pentagon, Washington, 1943-44; comdr. 383d Bomb Wing, 1944-45; mem. joint strategic plans and ops. group Hdqrs. Far East Command, Tokyo, Japan, 1947-48; comdr. 51st Jet Fighter Wing, Naha Air Force Base, Okinawa, 1948-49; dep. comdr. 97th Bomb Wing, Biggs AFB, El Paso, Tex., 1949-51; dep. chief staff Hdqrs. Strategic Air Command, Omaha, 1951-52, chief of staff, 1952-56; dep. comdr. 2d Air Force Barksdale AFB, Shreveport, La., 1956-58; comdr. 3d Air Div. Anderson AFB, Guam, 1958-59; asst. vice chief of staff Hdqrs. USAF, Washington, 1959-62; vice comdr.-in-chief USAF, Europe, 1962-66, ret., 1966; exec. v.p. devel. Freedoms Found., Valley Forge, Pa., 1967-68; regional v.p. Freedoms Found., Valley Forge, 1968-76; bd. dirs. Gen. Services Life Ins. Co., Washington. Town commr. Longboat Key, Fla., 1971-78; mem. coun. trustees Freedoms Found at Valley Forge, 1976-87. Decorated D.S.M. with oak leaf cluster (Army and Air Force), Legion of Merit with oak leaf lcuster, Army Commendation Medal with 2 oak leaf clusters; recipient Silver Beaver award Boy Scouts Am., 1965, Silver Antelope award, 1966, Gold Medal Humanitarian award Pa. State U., 1968. Mem. Masons, Shriners, Order Daedalians, Army-Navy Club (Washington). Republican. Methodist. Home: Longboat Key Fla. Died Aug. 27, 1987.

MONTGOMERY, SPENCER BISHOP, lawyer; b. Dargent, N.D., Dec. 22, 1890; s. George Samuel and Mary (Bishop) M.; m. Eleanor Gilbert, Feb. 3, 1923; children: Marion (Mrs. William M. Flook Jr.), Jane (Mrs. A. Richard Brooks), Parker Gilbert, Sara (Mrs. Marc A. Rieffel). AB, Miami U., Oxford, Ohio, 1913; LLB, Harvard, 1916. Bar: Mass. 1916. With firm Roberts, Roberts, Cushman, patent attys., Boston, 1916-20; exec. Bird & Son Inc., East Walpole, Mass., 1920-30; ptnr. Powers & Hall, Boston, 1930-72. Editor: Harvard Law Rev., 1914-16. Treas., mem. bd. Pub. Welfare Boston, 1949-51; trustee Mabel Louise Riley Trusts; past sec. Harvard Law Sch. Class 1916; chmn. bd. advisers Harvard Law Sch., 1915-16. Capt. F.A.,

U.S. Army, World War I. Mem. Soc. Colonial Warriors, SAR, Union Club, Country Club (Brookline, Mass.), Phi Beta Kappa, Delta Kappa Epsilon. Episcopalian (past vestryman). Home: Boston Mass. †

MOORE, DAN KILLIAN, lawyer, former governor North Carolina; b. Asheville, N.C., Apr. 2, 1906; s. Fred and Lela (Enloe) M.; m. Jeanelle Coulter, May 4, 1933; children: Edith (Mrs. Edgar Blanton Hamilton), Dan K. B.S., U. N.C., 1927. Bar: N.C. 1928. Practiced in Sylva, 1928-46; solicitor Superior Ct., 20th Dist. N.C., Sylva, 1946-48; judge Superior Ct., 20th Dist. N.C., 1948-58; gov. N.C., 1965-69; assoc. justice Supreme Court of N.C., Raleigh, 1969-79; ret. 1979; mem. firm Moore, Ragsdale, Liggett, Ray & Foley P.A., Raleigh, 1979-86; asst. sec., counselor Champion Papers, Inc., Canton, N.C., 1958-63; bd. mgrs. Wachovla Bank & Trust Co., Asheville, N.C., 1969. Vice chmn. N.C. Bd. Water Resources, 1959-65; Mem. N.C. Ho. of Reps., 1941-43. Served with AUS, 1943-45. Mem. N.C. Bar Assn., Phi Beta Kappa, Pi Kappa Phi. Democrat. Methodist. Clubs: Civitan (Canton, N.C.); Mountain City (Asheville, N.C.), Mountain View (Waynesville, N.C.); Carolina Country (Raleigh). Lodges: Masons, Rotary. Home: Raleigh N.C. Died Sept. 7, 1986.

MOORE, DOUGLAS ROSS, college president; b. Paducah, Tex., Mar. 12, 1928; s. Shelly B. and Gladys Dora (Biddy) M.; m. Rebecca Elizabeth Zimmerman, Aug. 28, 1948; children: Sarah Elizabeth, Douglas Ross, Mark Allen. B.S., Tex. Wesleyan Coll., 1950; S.T.B., Boston U., 1957, Ph.D. (Danielson fellow), 1964. Ordained to ministry Methodist Ch., 1956; pastor Meth. Chs. in, Tex. and Mass., 1948-64; dean students, asst. prof. psychology Southwestern Coll., Winfield, Kans., 1964-67; provost, asso. prof. psychology Callison Coll., U. of Pacific, 1967-71; exec. v.p., prof. psychology Minn. Met. State Coll., St. Paul, 1971-74; pres. Mankato (Minn.) State U., 1974-78, U. Redlands, Calif., 1978-87; cons. Ednl. Testing Service, Danforth Found. Contbr. articles to profl. jours. Active Boy Scouts Am.; bd. dirs. Inland Action, Inc., Ind. Colls. So. Calif., Assn. Ind. Colls. and Univs. Mem. Am. Assn. Higher Edn., Am. Council on Edn., Am. Psychol. Assn., Los Angeles Philanthropic Soc., Redlands C. of C. Democrat. Club: Redlands Country; California (Los Angeles). Lodge: Rotary. Home: Redlands Calif. Died Mar. 21, 1987.

MOORE, DWIGHT MUNSON, botany educator; b. Zanesville, Ohio, Dec. 10, 1891; s. Newton Hoffman and Mary Adela (Munson) M.; m. Elizabeth Alice French, Sept. 5, 1922; 1 child, Dwight French. BS, Denison U., Granville, Ohio, 1914, MS, 1921; PhD, Ohio State U., 1924; student, U. Montpellier, France, spring 1919. Prin. Monroeville (Ohio) High Sch., 1914-17; instr. chemistry Zanesville (Ohio) High Sch., 1917, 19-20; instr. biology Denison U., 1920-23; instr. botany Ohio State U., 1923-24; asst. prof. botany U. Ark., 1924-26, prof., head dept., 1926-50, prof. botany, curator herbarium, 1950-57, emeritus prof. botany and bacteriology, from 1957; assoc. prof. forestry Ark. A&M Coll., 1957-59, prof. forestry, 1959-61; prof. biology, head dept. Ark. Poly. Coll., from 1961; prof. plant ecology Ohio Conservation Lab., summers 1940-42; regional supr. Milkweed Floss div. War Hemp Industries, 1944; Smith-Mundt appointee as prof. botany U. Saigon, Viet Nam, 1958-59. Contbr. articles to profl. jours. Sgt. U.S. Army, 1917-19. Fellow AAAS; mem. Bot. Soc. Am., Am. Hort. Soc., Plant Taxonomists, Am. Fern Soc., Ark. Acad. Sci. (pres. 1963-64; editor proc. 1941-51), Sigma Xi, Lambda Chi Alpha. †

MOORE, EARL VINCENT, educator; b. Lansing, Mich., Sept. 27, 1890; s. Frank W. and Clara Frances (Keith) M.; m. Blanche W. Anderson, Aug. 26, 1914; children: E. Vincent, Stanley Anderson, Mary (Mrs. William E. Huff). Artist diploma in organ, U. Mich. Sch. Music, 1910; AB, U. Mich., 1912, AM, 1915, MusD. (hon.), 1964; postgrad. organ and theory, under Widor, Paris, 1913; study in composition and conducting, under Holst and Boult, London, under Sepilli, Milan, Italy, under Heger, Vienna, 1924-25; Mus.D. (hon.), U. Rochester, 1929, Am. Cons. Music, Chgo., 1938; DFA (hon.), Drake U., 1945; LLD, Eastern Mich. U., 1959. Head organ dept. Sch. Music U. Mich., 1914, head theory dept., 1916, instr. music Coll. Lit. and Arts, 1916-19, asst. prof., 1919-23, prof., 1923-60, dir. Sch. Music, 1923-46, dean, 1946-60, dean emeritus, from 1961, univ. organist, 1913-23; M.D. Anderson prof. music, chmn. dept. U. Houston, 1960-70; condr., mus. dir. Ann Arbor MAy Music Festivals, 1923-39; nat. dir. WPA Music PRogram, 1939-40, cons., 1941-43; cons. Ward Dept. Sch. Spl. Service, 1942-46; mus. cons. ednl. surveys U. Fla., U. Ga., Fla. State U.; cons. dept. music Knox Coll., Galesburg, Ill, Stetson U., 1965-67; adviser for music adv. council Rice U., Houston, 1971-73. Author: The Symphony and Symphonic Poem, Introduction to Music Literature; composer: The Voyage of Arion, The Bird Man (cantatas for chilsren's voices); organ and choral music. Civilian mem. Elizabeth Sprague Coolidge Found. com Libr. of Congress, 1959-72; mem. adv. com. on arts Nat. Cultural Ctr., Washington, 1959-70; cons. in music Ednl. Radio and TV Ctr., Ann Arbor, Mich., 1958-59. Mem. Am. Guild Organists, Music Educators Nat. Conf. (contbr. Procs.), Music Tchrs. Nat. Assn. (pres., contbr. Procs.), Nat. Assn. Music Schs. (founder mem., pres. 1936-38, chmn. commn. curricula 1949-64, cons. 1964-70), Phi Delta Theta, Phi Mu Alpha, Pi Kappa Lambda (nat. pres. 1946-50, bd. regents from 1946), Kappa Kappa Psi. Episcopalian. Home: Omena Mich. †

MOORE, EMMETT BURRIS, consulting engineer; b. Gallatin County, nr. Bozeman, Mont., Dec. 10, 1900; s. William Enoch and Mary Elizabeth (Burris) M.; m. Iris Marie Brown, Jan. 15, 1925; 1 son, Emmett Burris. B.S., Mont. State U., 1924, C.E., 1928; M.S., Wash. State U., 1933. Registered profl. engr., Wash. Asst. comdt. cadets Western Mil. Acad., Alton, Ill., 1918-20; asst. county engr. Gallatin County, Bozeman, 1924-29; instr. civil engring. acting head dept. indsl. engring. Mont. State U., 1929; instr. asst. prof., asso. prof., prof., head dept. civil engring. Wash. State U., 1929-66, chmn. dept., 1945-66, asso. office of the pres., 1945-46; faculty rep. Pacific Coast Intercollegiate Athletic Conf., 1952-59, pres., 1954-57; cons. engr. 1966-87; mem. Wash. State Council on Hwy. Research, 1955-66. Author: A Manual of Structural Design in Steel, 1940, Sponsoring Committee, Effective Teaching, 1950. Bd. dirs. Levere Meml. Found., Evanston, Ill., 1940-51, pres. bd., 1949-51. Mem. Am. Soc. Engring. Edn., Sigma Alpha Epsilon (nat. pres. 1949-51), Phi Kappa Phi, Tau Beta Pi, Sigma Tau, Omicron Delta Kappa. Club: Rotarian. Home: Olympia Wash. Died Aug. 3, 1987, buried Pullman, Wash.

MOORE, FRANK STANLEY, fertilizer company executive; b. Prospect, Va., Sept. 10, 1905; s. James Stanley and Mary (Glenn) M.; m. Margaret Carolyn Morrison, June 27, 1934; children: Frank S., Mary McCulloch. Student, U. Va., summers 1925, 26; BS, Hampden-Sydney Coll., 1927. Mem. faculty Norfolk (Va.) Acad., 1927-29; with Royster Co., Norfolk, 1929-77, successively lab. technician, factory foreman, rsch. chemist, prodn. supr., purchasing asst., asst. v.p., 1939-50, v.p., 1950-61, exec. v.p., 1961-72, cons., 1972-77, also bd. dirs.; pres. Ill. Nitrogen Corp., Marseilles, Ill., 1963-77; dir. Edward W. Face Corp., 1979-81, sec. 1980-81. Chmn. exec. com. Fla. Phospate Coun., 1964-65, 74; trustee Tidewater Devel. Coun., 1959-62; life dir. Norfolk United Community Fund, v.p. 1964, pres., 1965; chmn. bd. United Communities Fund, 1975; bd. dirs. Norfolk Gen. Hosp., 1955-73, Norfolk Community Hosp., 1952-81, chmn. hosp. commn., 1956-77; mem. Com. to Select Outstanding Scholar in Area, 1976-82. Recipient citation for Outstanding Service Norfolk City Coun., 1963, 65. Fellow Am. Inst. Chemists; mem. Va. Mfrs. Assn. (pres. 1960-62, dir.), Am. Chem. Soc., C. of C. (chmn. law enforcement task force 1968), Omicron Delta Kappa, Chi Beta Phi. Presbyterian (elder, chmn. synod's com. on Christian higher edn. 1957, moderator presbytery 1962). Home: Norfolk Va. Died Sept. 16, 1986; buried Prospect, Va.

MOORE, FRED HOLMSLEY, oil executive; b. Comanche, Tex., Nov. 2, 1909; s. Robert Hartwell and Fannie (Holmsley) M.; m. Grace Hunter, July 26, 1929 (dec. 1940); m. Ella Mae Rudd, Apr. 11, 1941; children: Carla Moore Clark, Mary Moore Donaldson. BA, Tex. Tech. Coll., 1930; MA, U. Va., 1931; postgrad., Yale U., 1931-33; LLD, Middlebury Coll., 1963; DSc (hon.), Hartwick Coll., 1966; LHD, Marlboro Coll., 1967; DBA, Our Lady of Lake U., 1977. Geologist Magnolia Petroleum Co., 1935-50, asst. to pres., 1950-56, exec. v.p., 1959; exec. v.p. Mobil Oil Can., Ltd., 1956-57; mgr. worldwide producing dept. Socony Mobil Oil Co., Inc. (name now Mobil Oil Corp.), 1957-58, exec. v.p., bd. dirs., 1961-66, spl. asst. to pres., 1967-69, petroleum cons., 1969-85. Author: Marbles and Limestones of Connecticut, 1935. Bd. dirs. Tex. Tech Coll., 1952-56; trustee Our Lady of Lake Coll., 1973-76, Austin Coll., 1977-85; mem. adv. coun. U. Tex. Sch. Bus. Decorated knight Order of San Jacinto; recipient Presdl. citation U. Tex., 1984; named to Hall of Fame U. Tex. Coll. Bus., 1984. Fellow SAR, Geol. Soc. Am.; mem. Am. Assn. Petroleum Geologists, Am. Inst. Profl. Geologists, Tex. Hist. Assn. (exec. coun., hon. life pres.), Soc. Mayflower Descs., Sons Republic Tex., Sigma Xi, Gamma Alpha. Presbyterian. Home: Austin Tex. Died July 20, 1985.

MOORE, HENRY, sculptor; b. Castleford, Yorkshire, Eng., July 30, 1898; s. Raymond Spencer and Mary (Baker) M.; m. Irene Radetzyky; 1 child, Mary Spencer. Student Leeds Coll Art, 1919-21, Royal Coll. Art; hon. degrees; D.Litt., London, Reading, Oxford, York, Durham; D.Arts, Yale U., Harvard U.; LL.D., Cambridge U., St. Andrews, Sheffield, U. Toronto, Manchester; Litt.D., Sussex, Warwick, Leicester, Hull, York U., Toronto, Columbia U.; D.Eng., U. Berlin; Hon. Dr., RCA, 1967, others. Founder, Henry Moore Found., 1977; exhibited in London, 1928, 31, 33, 35, 36, 40, 45, 48, 51, 53, 55, 60, 61, 63, 65, 67, 68, 74, 75, 76, 78, Leeds, 1941, N.Y.C., 1946, 70, Chgo., 1947, San Francisco, 1947, Australian tour, 1947, Venice Biennale (1st prize for sculpture), 1948, European tour, 1949-51, 60-61, Cape Town, 1951, Scandinavian tour, 1952-53, 75-76, Rotterdam, 1953, Antwerp, 1953, Sao Paulo (1st prize in fgn. sculpture), 1953; German tour, 1953-54, Basle, 1955, Yugoslavian tour, 1955, Can., N.Z., Australian, U.S.A. tour, 1955-58, Paris, 1957, 71, 77, Arnhem, 1957, Japan tour, 1959, 69-70, Spain and Portugal tour, 1959, Poland tour, 1959, Edinburgh, Scotland, 1961, Latin Am. tour, 1964-65, U.S.A. tour, 1966-68, East European tour, 1966, Israel tour, 1966, Can. tour, 1967-68, East European tour, 1966, Israel tour, 1966, Holland and Germany tour, 1968, Iran tour, 1971, Munich, 1971, Florence, 1972, Luxembourg, 1973, Los Angeles, 1973, Toronto, 1974, Zurich, 1976, Bradford, 1978; represented in permanent collections Tate Gallery, London, Nat. Gallery, Washington, Mus. Modern Art, N.Y.C., Albright Knox Art Gallery, Buffalo, also other public galleries in U.K., U.S.A., Germany, Italy, Switzerland, Holland, Sweden, Denmark, Norway, France, Australia, Brazil, Israel, South Africa, Japan, others; hon. prof. emeritus sculpture Carrara Acad. Fine Arts, 1967. Trustee, Tate Gallery, 1941-48, 49-54, Nat. Gallery, 1955-63, 64-76; mem. Arts Council, 1963-67, Royal Fine Art Commn., 1947-71. Served with Brit. Army, 1917-19. Decorated Order of Merit (W. Ger.), Order of Merit (Italy); recipient Feltrinelli Found. Internat. Sculpture prize, 1963, Erasmus prize, 1968, Einstein prize, 1968, Biancamano prize, 1973, Goslar prize, 1975; hon. fellow Churchill Coll., Cambridge. Fellow British Acad., Royal Inst. British Architects (hon.); mem. Inst. Acad. des Beaux Arts (Paris), Serbian Acad. Scis. and Arts, Royal Scottish Acad. Painting, Sculpture and Architecture (hon.), Acad. Flamade des Sciences (fgn. corr.), Lettres et Beaux Arts de Beligique (fgn. corr.), Swedish Royal Acad. Fine Arts (fgn.), Am. Acad. Arts and Scis. (fgn. hon.). Club: Athenaeum. Author: Heads, Figures and Ideas, 1958; (with Philip James) Henry Moore on Sculpture, 1966; Catalogues Raisonne, Sculpture, 4 vols.; Graphics, 2 vols.; Henry Moore at the British Museum, 1981. Home: Much Hadham, Herts, England. Died Aug. 31, 1986.

MOORE, MAURICE EDWIN, transportation company executive; b. Jackson, Tenn., Nov. 7, 1910; s. Hal R. and Bessie (Fick) M.; m. Lillian Gautier, Nov. 11, 1937; 1 son, Maurice Edwin. Student pub. schs., Jackson. Passenger traffic mgr. southwestern Transp., Texarkana, Tex., 1930-36; v.p., gen. mgr. Ark. Motor Coaches, Little Rock, 1937-52; pres. Continental Bus System, 1943-65, Memco Corp., Dallas; chmn. bd. Eagle Internat. Inc. Mem. Petroleum Club (Dallas). Home: Carrollton Tex. Died June 5, 1986; buried Sportsman Hillcrest, Dallas.

MOORE, MAURICE THOMPSON, lawyer; b. Deport, Tex., Mar. 16, 1896; s. Dr. John H. and Ollie (Thompson) M.; m. Elisabeth Luce, Sept. 17, 1926; children—Maurice Thompson, Michael. B.A., Trinity U., 1915, LL.D., 1945; M.A., Columbia U., 1916, LL.B., 1920; LL.D., St. Lawrence U., 1955, Columbia U., 1968. Bar: N.Y. bar 1920. Mem. law firm Cravath, Swaine & Moore, N.Y.C., 1926-80; of counsel Cravath, Swaine & Moore, 1980-86; past chmn. Time, Inc., dir., 1939-70; spl. asst. to adminstr. ECA, 1948. Exec. com., past bd. dirs. YMCA Greater, N.Y.C., trustee, 1964-82; chmn. trustees Columbia U., 1955-67; trustee Trinity U., 1944-67. Served as 1st lt. Inf. U.S. Army, 1917-19. Mem. Philos. Soc. Tex., Beta Theta Pi. Presbyn. Clubs: Century Assn. (N.Y.C.), Racquet and Tennis (N.Y.C.), University. (N.Y.C.), Wall Street (N.Y.C.). Died June 22, 1986; interred Trinity Ch. Cemetery and Mausoleum, N.Y.C.

MOORE, ROBERT B(RYSON), film, stage and television director. s. Samuel R. and Forrest (Rash) M. Student, Cath. U. Am., 1946-48. Dir. films Murder By Death, 1976, The Cheap Detective, 1978, Chapter Two, 1980; dir. Broadway plays The Boys in the Band, 1968, Promises, Promises, 1968, Last of the Red Hot Lovers, 1969, The Gingerbread Lady, 1970, Lorelei, 1974, My Fat Friend, 1974, Death Trap, 1978, They're Playing Our Song, 1979, Woman of the Year, 1981. With USN, 1945-46. Died May 10, 1984.

MOORE, RUTH, author; b. St. Louis; d. William Dunn and Ethel (Sledd) M.; m. Raymond W. Garbe. AB, MA, Washington U., St. Louis; DLitt, McMurray Coll., 1955. Staff writer Chgo. Sun-Times newspaper, 1943-70, Washington corr., 1943-50. Author: Man, Time, and Fossils, 1953, Charles Darwin-A Great Life in Brief, 1955, The Earth We Live On, 1956, The Coil of Life: The Story of the Great Discoveries in the Life of Sciences, 1953, 2d edit., 1961, Evolution, 1962, Niels Bohr: His LIfe, His Science and the World They Changed, 1966, (with Sherwood L. Washburn) Ape Into Man, 1973, rev. edit, Ape Into Human, 1980, Man in the Environment, 1975. Chmn. Prarie Ave. Historic Dist., 1974-82; mem. Commn. on Chgo. Hist. and Archtl. Landmarks, 1974-86; pres. women's bd. U. Chgo., 1973-77; pres. Chgo. Architecture Found., 1978-80; trustee Washington U. Recipient ann. award Friends of Lit., 1955, Alumni citation, Washington U., 1963, Champion Fighter for a Better Chgo. award Met. Housing and Planning Council, $1 million endowment Ruth and Norman Moore Professorship in Architecture and Urban Design Washington U., St. Louis, 1986; $1 million endowment Ruth (Moore) and Raymond Garbe Professorship in Urban Design, Harvard U., 1987; named Chgo. Preservationist of Yr., 1981. Mem. AIA (hon.), AAAS (standing com. on pub. understanding sci.), Phi Beta Kappa. Clubs: Women's Nat. Press (Washington); Fortnightly (Chgo.). Home: San Francisco Calif. Died Jan. 2, 1989.

MOORE, WILBERT ELLIS, educator, sociologist; b. Elma, Wash., Oct. 26, 1914; s. Lavergne Walker and Bertha (Maffit) M.; m. Dorothy Mary Hewitt, June 15, 1936 (div. 1957); children: Dorothy Marjory, Flo Hewitt; m. Jeanne Brindle Bailey, July 12, 1957 (dec.

1959); m. Jeanne Ellen Yates, Mar. 12, 1960. B.A., Linfield Coll., 1935; M.A., U. Oreg., 1937; A.M., Harvard U., 1939, Ph.D., 1940; LL.D., Loretto Heights Coll., 1977. Instr. sociology Pa. State U., 1940-41, asst. prof., 1941-43; research asso. Office Population Research, Princeton, 1943-51, asst. prof., 1945-48, asso. prof., 1948-51, prof., 1951-64; sociologist Russell Sage Found., N.Y.C., 1964-70; prof. sociology and law U. Denver, 1970-83, prof. emeritus, 1983-87; dir. Social Sci. Research Council, 1960-63. Author: Economic Demography of Eastern and Southern Europe, 1945, Industrial Relations and the Social Order, rev. edit, 1951 (reprinted 1977), Industrialization and Labor, 1951, Economy and Society, 1955, The Conduct of the Corporation, 1962, Man, Time and Society, 1963, Social Change, rev. edit, 1974, The Impact of Industry, 1966, Order and Change: Essays in Comparative Sociology, 1967, Trusteeship and the Management of Foundations, 1969, The Professions, 1970, American Negro Slavery and Abolition, 1971, reprinted, 1980, World Modernization: The Limits of Convergence, 1979; editor: Technology and Social Change, 1972; co-editor: Twentieth Century Sociology, 1945, Economic Growth: Brazil, India, Japan, 1955, Labor Commitment and Social Change in Developing Areas, 1960, Industrialization and Society, 1963, Indicators of Social Change, 1968. Mem. Eastern Sociol. Assn. (pres. 1953), Western Social Sci. Assn., Law and Soc. Assn., Am. Philos. Soc., Am. Sociol. Assn. (pres. 1966, Career of Disting. Scholarship award 1987), Am. Acad. Arts and Scis., Sigma Xi, Phi Beta Kappa. Home: Littleton Colo. Died Dec. 29, 1987, cremated.

MOORHEAD, PAUL GRADY, classical languages educator; b. Gaffney, S.C., Nov. 23, 1891; s. James Longstreet and Mary Frances (Werts) M.; m. Helen Rebecca Snead, Sept. 20, 1916. Student, Limestone Coll., 1908-10; AB, U. S.C., 1913, MA, 1914; PhD, U. Chgo., 1923. Asst. in Latin Fork Union Mil. Acad., 1914-17; prof., head dept. ancient langs. Juniata Coll., 1917-20; fellow in Latin U. Chgo., 1920-23; prof., head dept. classical langs. Coll. Charleston, 1923-28; prof. classical langs. La. State U., from 1928. Author: (with Charles E. Smith) A Short History of the Ancient World, 1939. Mem. Am. Classical League, Classical Assn. Middle West and South (So. sect.), Am. Philol. Assn., Assn. Drs. Philosophy U. Chgo., Aeropagus Club, Masons (32 deg.), Phi Beta Kappa, Eta Sigma Phi. Democrat. Episcopalian. Home: Baton Rouge La. †

MOORHEAD, WILLIAM SINGER, lawyer, former congressman; b. Pitts., Apr. 8, 1923; s. William Singer and Constance (Barr) M.; m. Lucy Galpin, Dec. 23, 1946; children: William Singer III, Lucy Perrin Galpin Grayson, Stephen Galpin, James Barr. B.A., Yale U., 1944; J.D. cum laude, Harvard U., 1949; LL.D., Duquesne U., 1965. Bar: Pa. 1949, D.C. 1979, Va. 1983. Partner firm Moorhead & Knox, Pitts., 1952-70; mem. 86th-87th Congresses 28th Dist. Pa.; mem. com. on banking and currency, com. on govt. ops.; mem. 88th-96th Congresses, 14th Pa. Dist.; mem. com. on banking, fin. and urban affairs, com. govt. ops., joint econ. com., chmn. Ho.-Senate Conf. on Energy Security Act of 1980; ptnr. Coan, Couture, Lyons & Moorhead, Washington, 1981-87; Asst. city solicitor, Pitts., 1954-57; sec. Allegheny County Housing Authority, 1956-58. Past trustee Tb League Pitts., Park and Playground Soc. Pitts., Shadyside Hosp., Pitts., Western Pa. Conservancy. Served as lt. (j.g.) USNR, World War II. Mem. Am., D.C., Pa., Allegheny County, Va. bar assns. Democrat. Episcopalian. Clubs: Pittsburgh Golf, Chevy Chase. Home: Washington D.C. Died Aug. 3, 1987; buried Madison, Conn.

MORAN, DOUGLAS EDWARD, publishing company executive, corporate controller; b. Newton, Mass., Nov. 5, 1938; s. John Edward Moran and Edna (Stahl) Moran-Moore; 1 child, Deborah. BS, Boston U., 1960; MBA, Harvard U., 1970. CPA, Mass. Sr. audit mgr. Price Waterhouse, Boston; asst. corp. controller Pepsico, Purchase, N.Y., 1976-81; corp. controller Macmillan, Inc., N.Y.C., 1981-87, v.p., corp. controller, 1987-88. Mem. Am. Inst. CPA's, Mass. Soc. CPA's, Fin. Execs. Inst., Nat. Assn. Accts. Clubs: Harvard of Boston; Harvard Bus. Sch. (N.Y.C.). Home: New York N.Y. Died May 18, 1988.

MORAN, EDWIN BRYAN, association executive; b. Grand Rapids, Mich., Nov. 5, 1892; s. John and Verena (Keller) M.; m. Lenore L. Slorah, Jan. 11, 1919; children: Margaret J. Moran O'Donnell, Ruth E. Moran Kilby, Virginia M. Moran Lindley, Mary Ann Moran Gallagher, John Harry, William E., James B. Student, Grand Rapids Bus. Coll., 1910-12. Clk., credit investigator R.G. Dun and Co., Grand Rapids, 1912-14; br. mgr. Lyon Mercantile Agy., St. Louis, 1915-16; salesman Nat. Assn. Credit Men, 1916-17, exec. dept. mgr., 1919-25, br. mgr., 1925, divisional mgr., 1925-29, divisional mgr., sales dir., Chgo., 1933-51, sec., 1951-55, v.p., 1955-58, exec. v.p., 1958-60, cons., from 1960, also sec./treas. ins. adv. coun. N.Y. chpt.; exec. sales mgr. The Bradstreet Co., N.Y.C., 1929-33; mem. Grad. Sch. Sales Mgmt. and Mktg., Rutgers U., from 1958; mem. adv. com. mktg. U. Ill; mem. adv. bd. Sch. Bus. Adminstrn., Pace Inst. Author: The Credit Side of Selling, 1947; co-author: The Credit Side of Credit Correspondence, 1956; contbr. articles to profl. jours. 1st lt. U.S. Army, 1917-19. Mem. Nat. Sales Execs., Inc., Comml. Law League Am., Am. Soc. Assn. Execs. (Washington chpt.), Spl. Agts. Assn. Chgo., Am. Legion, Union League Club, Sales Execs. Club Chgo. (pres. 1943-44), Sales Execs. Club (N.Y.C.), Irish Fellowship Club (Chgo.), Advt. Club, Mktg. Club U. Ill., Rotary (pres. N.Y.C. 1935-36, Chgo. 1942-43). Republican. Roman Catholic. Home: Mount Prospect Ill. †

MORE, ROBERT E(LMER), lawyer; b. Denver, Mar. 11, 1892; s. E. Anson and Caroline A. (Bacon) M.; m. Alice Bancroft, June 16, 1916; 1 child, Jeremy. AB, Dartmouth Coll., 1913; LLB, Harvard U., 1916; postgrad., Denver U., U. Colo., 1940-42. Bar: Colo. 1916. Mem. Dines, Dines & Holme, successor firm Holme, Roberts, More & Owen, from 1925; prof. law Denver U., 1921-33. Author: Colorado Evergreens, rev. edit., 1949, Evergreens for the Rocky Mountains, 1958; contbr. articles to profl. jours. Founder, dir. Glenmore Arboretum; trustee Denver Mus. Natural History, from 1946, Denver Bot. Gardens, from 1951. Mem. ABA, Colo., Denver (pres. 1935) bar assns., Civic League (pres. 1936), Colo. Forestry and Horticulture Assn. (trustee 1944-54), Denver Athletic Club, Cacuts Club, Phi Delta Phi, Kappa Kappa Kappa. Home: Denver Colo. †

MOREAU, ARTHUR STANLEY, JR., naval officer; b. Mt. Ranier, Md., June 3, 1931; s. Arthur Stanley and Helen (O'Leary) M.; m. Katherine Ann Schindling, June 5, 1953; children: Arthur Stanley, Steven Matthew, Kathleen Elizabeth Moreau, Christopher Andrew, Katherine Johanna. Grad., U.S. Naval Acad.; M.S. in Internat. Affairs, George Washington U. Commd. ensign U.S. Navy, advanced through grades to adm., 1969-70; comdg. officer USS Roark 1970-72; sr. aide and exec. asst. to comdr. in chief U.S. Pacific Fleet Makalapa, Hawaii, 1972-75; comdg. officer U.S. Naval Sta. Subic Bay, 1975-77; dir. logistics-security assistance to comdr. in chief Pacific Staff 1977-79; dir. strategy, plans and policy div. Chief of Naval Ops. Washington, 1979-81; comdr. Cruiser-Destroyer Group 3, San Diego, 1981-82; dep. chief naval ops. Washington, 1982-83; asst. to chmn. Joint Chiefs of Staff, 1983-85; comdr.-in-chief U.S. Naval Forces Europe/comdr.-in-chief Allied Forces So. Europe, 1985-86. Decorated D.S.M., Legion of Merit, Bronze Star, Def. Superior Service medal, others. Mem. U.S. Naval Acad. Alumni Assn., U.S. Naval Inst. Methodist. Club: Masons. Home: Alexandria Va. Died Dec. 8, 1986, buried Arlington Nat. Cemetery.

MOREELL, BEN, naval officer, business executive; b. Salt Lake City, Sept. 14, 1892; s. Samuel and Sophia (Sossnitz) M.; m. Clara Klinksick, Oct. 19, 1923 (dec. 1958); children: Marion, Patricia; m. 2d, Mrs. Harry Anderson, Dec. 12, 1960 (dec. 1971): m. 3d, Jessie Grimm, July 14, 1971. BCE, Washington U., St. Louis, 1913; DEng, Washington U., 1942; student, Ecole Nationale des Ponts et Chaussees, Paris, 1932-33; DEng, Ill. Inst. Tech., 1944; other hon. degrees, latest being LLD, Grove City Coll., 1966. Designer resident, engring. construction projects St. Louis, 1913-17; apptd. lt. Civil Engr. Corps, USN, 1917; advanced through grades to adm. USN, 1946, chief Bur. Yards asnd Docks, chief civil engrs., 1937-45; chief material div. Navy Dept., 1945-46; retired 1946; pres. Jones & Laughlin Steel Corp., 1947-52, chief exec. officer, 1947-57, chmn. bd., 1947-58, dir., mem. exec. com., 1947-65. Author: Standards of Design for Concrete, 1929, Our Nation's Water Resources: Policies and Politics, 1956,The Admiral's Log, Vol. I: God, Man, Rights, Government, 1958, Vol. II: In Search of Freedom, 1960; also articles in engring. jours. Chmn. task force water resources and power 2d Hoover Commn., 1953-55; bd. visitors U.S. Naval Acad., 1953-55, chmn. bd., 1955, chmn. Spl. Adv. Commn. Future Devel. Acad. Facilities, from 1961; mem. nat. strategy com. Am. Security Coun.; chmn. bd. emeritus Americans for Constl. Action. Decorated World War I Medal with star, DSM with gold star, Legion of Merit (U.S.), Medal Honor and Merit (Haiti), Comdr. Order Brit. Empire; recipient numerous medals, awards from Am. Concrete Inst., Freedoms Found., others, from 1934; hon. v.p. Naval Hist. Found. Mem. Am. Iron and Steel Inst. (hon. v.p.), ASCE (hon.), Am. Concrete Inst. (hon., past pres.), Soc. Am. Mil. Engrs. (hon. mem., past pres.), Mil. Order World Wars (life), U.A. Naval Acad. Alumni Assn. (hon.), ASME (hon.), Newcomen Soc. Eng., Army-Navy Club (past pres.) (Washington); Army-Navy Country Club (Arlington, Va.); Duquesne Club (Pitts.); Sigma Xi, Tau Beta Pi. Home: Ventura Calif. †

MORGAN, ALFRED Y., beverage manufacturer; b. N.Y.C., Dec. 4, 1906; s. Alfred Y. and Annette (McDonnell) M.; m. Muriel Stafford, Sept. 15, 1934; children: Muriel, Alfred, Martha. Student, Fordham U. Pres. White Rock Corp., Bklyn., also bd. dirs.; trustee East N.Y. Savs. Bank. Mem. Knights of Malta. Home: New York N.Y. Died Feb. 24, 1988.

MORGAN, CHARLES STILLMAN, economist; b. Niles, Mich., Dec. 29, 1891; s. Leander James and Edith Amelia (Richardson) M.; m. Florence Mildred Gross, Jan. 6, 1917; children: Jeanne Noyes (Mrs. H. Richard Fox), Suzanne Elizabeth (Mrs. Ward O. Fearn). AB, U. Mich., 1914, postgrad., summers 1915, 16; PhD, Yale U., 1920. Instr. econs. and sociology Marietta Coll., 1914-16; asst. and assoc. economist Bur. Standards, Dept. Commerce, Washington, 1918-20; economist, valuation analyst Bur. Valuation, ICC, 1920-23; economist Inst. Econs., Washington, 1923-27; sr. economist ICC, 1927-28, prin. economist of commn., 1928-33, asst. dir. Bur. Motor Carriers, 1936-42, chief carrier rsch. analyst, 1942-57; transp. cons. from 1957; dir. rsch. Fed. Coordinator Transp., 1933-36; lectr. on transp. U. Md., 1924-25, Grad. Sch., Am. U., 1927-41. Author: Regulation and the Management of Public Utilities (Hart, Schaffner & Marx prize essay), 1923, (with H.G. Moulton and A.L. Lee) The St. Lawrence Navigation and Power Project (Inst. of Econ. Series), 1929; dir., joint author Comparative Labor Standards in Transportation, 4 parts, 1936-37, Public Aids to Transportain, 4 vols., 1940, other govtl. reports; contbr. articles to econ. and other jours. Mem. Am. Econ. Assn., Am. Statis. Assn., Cosmos Club, Pi Gamma Mu. Home: Washington D.C. †

MORGAN, CLYDE B., business executive; b. Seabrook, N.H., Aug. 16, 1889; s. Fred H. and Gusta (Wilcox) M.; m. Maud E. Goodrich, Nov. 10, 1910; children: Norma Benson (Mrs. James M. Tompkins), Edith Goodrich (Mrs. Chester R. Dolan), Gusta (Mrs. Fredrick H. Giddings). Student, Tilton Acad., Boston U. Pres., dir. Eastern Corp., Bangor, Maine, 1941-51; pres., dir. Rayonier Inc., N.Y.C., 1951-58, chmn. bd. dirs, from 1958; pres., dir. Royal Lace Paper Works, Bklyn., 1941-51; chmn., dir. Alaska Pine & Cellulose Ltd.; bd. dirs. Northwest Orient Airlines Inc., F.H. Giddings Inc. Mem. Pinnacle Club, Union League, Rainier Club (Seattle), Apawamis Club, Theta Delta Chi. Republican. Methodist. Home: Rye N.Y. †

MORGAN, D(AVID) W(ILLIAM) R(OWSEN), mechanical engineer, business executive; b. Martins Ferry, Ohio, Sept. 16, 1892; s. William E. and Sarah (Thomas) m.; m. Ethel Beatrice Hine, Sep. 2, 1916; children: Evelyn B. Morgan Olds, David W.R. ME, Ohio Northern U., 1913; ED, Drexel Inst. Tech., Clarkson Coll. Tech. Chief engr. condenser div. Westinghouse Elec. Corp., Phila., 1917-26, mgr. condenser and diesel engine div., 1926-40, asst. mgr. engring., steam div., 1940-41, works mgr., 1943-45, mgr. steam div., South Phila. works, 1945, gen. mgr., 1946, v.p. ops. steam and stoker div., 1948-53, v.p. staff, 1953-56; prof. engring., trustee Drexel Inst. Tech., from 1956; dir. Del. County Nat. Bank. Patentee power plant field. Mem. Borough Coun., Swarthmore, Pa., 1936-44, pres. 1942-43. With USN, World War II. Recipient Westinghouse Order of Merit, 1942, Cert. Commendation Sec. Navy for outstanding svc. during World War II, 1947. Mem. Am. Soc. Mech. Engrs. (pres. 1955, v.p.), Del. County C. of C. (dir.), Newcomen Soc. Eng., Engrs. Club, Aronimink Golf Club, Masons, Sigma Xi, Sigma Pi, Phi Kappa Phi, Pi Tau Sigma. Republican. Presbyterian. Home: Swarthmore Pa. †

MORGAN, LLOYD, architect; b. Jersey City, Pa., Dec. 14, 1892. Grad., Pratt Archtl. Sch.; student, MIT, U. Pa., Columbia, Ecole Nationale Superieure des Beaux Arts, Paris, Villa Medici, Rome. Registered architect Calif., Fla., N.J., N.Y., Tex., Va., Wis. With Howells & Stokes, Dennison & Hirons, and John Russell Pope, 1911-17; chief designer M. Laloux, M. Jacquet & Lamaresque, Paris, 1921-26; chief designer Schultz & Weaver, 1926-28, mem. firm, 1928-40; then prin. Lloyd Morgan, Architect, N.Y.C. Principal works include Waldorf-Astoria Hotel, N.Y.C., White Plains (N.Y.) Hosp., Met. Life Ins. Bldg., N.Y.C. Sgt. U.S. Army, World War I. Recipient 1st prize Masonic Temple, Washington, gold medal Swedish Archtl. Exhbn. Fellow AIA; mem. N.Y. State Assn. Architects, Archtl. League, Am. Inst. Decorators (nat. gov. 1945-47), Met. Mus. Art, NAS, Am. Mus. Nat. History, Am. Forestry Assn. Home: Tarrytown N.Y. †

MORGAN, ROY LEONARD, lawyer, government official; b. Morgantown, W.Va., Nov. 14, 1908; s. Henry Clay and Elizabeth (Aitken) M.; m. Rosamond Woodruff, Sept. 6, 1930; 1 child, Richard W. BS, U. Va., 1930, LLB, 1933, JD (hon.), 1971. Bar: Va. 1932, N.C. 1941, Japan 1951. Atty. USDA, 1933; spl. agt. FBI, 1934-45; pvt. practice Greensboro, N.C., 1945-47, 50; assoc. pros. atty. war criminals Internat. Tribunal, Tokyo, 1946; of counsel Ford Motor Co., Japan, 1950-54; Am. adviser Prime Minister Japan, 1955-56; chief justice U.S. Civil Adminstrn., Appellate Ct. for Far East, 1956-60; spl. asst. to sec. commerce U.S. Dept. Commerce, 1960-61, dir. Office Field Svcs., 1961-67; cons. U.S. govt., adviser on internat. trade with Japan; head U.S. govt. trade missions to Japan, 1962, 68. Author articles in field. Active Boy Scouts Am, United Givers; chmn. Am. Cancer Soc.; mem. Greensboro City Coun., 1948-50; bd. dirs., gen. counsel Elizabeth Saunders Home, Tokyo, 1951-53; founding mem. Mt. Sinai Med. Ctr., Miami Beach, Fla.; hon. v.p. Am. C. of C. in Tokyo, 1953. Mem. Explorers Club, Diplomatic and Consular Officers Ret., Masons, Rotary, Execs. Club (Greensboro pres.), Presidents Club, University Club (Washington), Sigma Chi, Phi Alpha Delta. Home: Lambsburg Va. Died Oct. 3, 1985; buried Low Gap, N.C.

MORGAN, RUSSELL HEDLEY, physician; b. London, Ont., Can., Oct. 9, 1911; came to U.S., 1937, naturalized, 1943; s. Alfred Hedley and Edith (Rowe)

M.; m. Mary Stella McManus, Jan. 25, 1938; children: Monica May, Mary Margaret. AB, U. Weatern Ont., 1934, MD, 1937, DSc (hon.), 1963; DSc (hon.), U. Chgo., 1969. Intern Harper Hosp., Detroit, 1937-39; resident in pathology St. Luke's Hosp., Chgo., 1938-40; resident in radiology U. Chgo. Clinics, 1940-42; instr. radiology U. Chgo. Med. Sch., 1942-43, asst. prof. radiology, 1943-44, assoc. prof., 1946-47; prof. radiology and radiol sci. Johns Hopkins Sch. Medicine, 1947-76, Univ. prof. medicine, 1975-76, Univ. prof. emeritus, 1976-86, prof. emeritus radiology and radiol. sci, also environ. health sci., 1976-86, dean, 1971-75, dean emeritus Med. Faculty, 1976-86; v.p. health div. Johns Hopkins U., 1973-75; radiologist-in-chief Johns Hopkins Hosp., 1947-72. Author: Mass Radiography of the Chest, 1945; Medical Physics (2 chpts.) edited by Otto Glasser, 1945, Handbook of Radiology, 1955, Physical Foundations of Radiology, 1970. Sr. surgeon (comdr.) USPHS, Washington, 1944-46. Fellow Am. Coll. Radiology; mem. AMA, Am. Roentgen Ray Soc., Radiol. Soc. N.Am. Home: Baltimore Md. Died Feb. 24, 1986.

MORGAN, THEODORE HARDING, electrical engineering educator; b. Fredricton Junction, N.B., Can., Sept. 23, 1892; came to U.S., 1918, naturalized, 1932; s. John Burtt and Margaret Belle (Porter) M.; m. Marion Gordon, Sept. 23, 1927. Student, U. B.C.; AB, Stanford U., 1920, BEE, 1929. Supt. Found. Co., Victoria, B.C., 1917-19; testing engr. Inspiration Consol. Copper Co., 1920-21; engr. Gt. Western Power Co., San Francisco, 1921-22, 23-26; instr. elec. engring. Stanford U., 1922-26, asst. prof., asst. exec. head dept., 1926-31; prof. elec. engring. Worcester (Mass.) Poly. Inst., from 1931, head dept., 1931-58; dep. dir. engring. sci. and mgmt. war tng. program, U.S. Office Edn., Washington, 1942-45. Contbr. articles to profl. jours. Fellow AIEE, AAAS; mem. Inst. Radio Engrs. (sr. mem.), Am. Soc. Engring. Edn., Worcester Engring. Soc., Fgn. Policy Assn., Worcester Econ. Club, Worcester Rotary, Sigma Xi, Tau Beta Pi, Eta Kappa Nu, Alpha Tau Omega. Home: Worcester Mass. †

MORIN, RICHARD WEDGE, librarian; b. Albert Lea, Minn., Dec. 11, 1902; s. William A. and Katherine (Trusdell) M.; m. Dolores Dilkes, July 3, 1928; children: Joan, Anne, Sarah; m. Pauline Morin. BS, Dartmouth, 1924, MA, 1952; LLB, Harvard U., 1928. Fgn. service officer U.S., 1929-35; practicing lawyer 1935-42, 45-48; with Dept. State, 1942-45; exec. officer Dartmouth Coll., 1948-50, librarian, 1950-68. Dem. nominee U.S. Ho. of Reps., 1st Congl. dist., Minn., 1936. Mem. ABA, ALA, Century Club, Grolier Club. Died May 29, 1988.

MORISON, ROBERT SWAIN, physiologist, educator; b. Milw., Nov. 25, 1906; s. George Abbot and Amelia Huntley (Elmore) M.; m. Beningna Rempel, Dec. 26, 1936; children-Christiana Leonard, John R. Grad., Phillips Exeter Acad., 1924; B.A., Harvard U., 1930, M.D., 1935; D.Sc., Loyola U., Chgo., 1970, U. Rochester, 1973. Resident physician Collis P. Huntington Meml. Hosp., Boston, 1934-35; Austin teaching fellow Harvard U. Med. Sch., 1935-36, instr. physiology, 1936-38, asso. anatomy, 1938-41, asst. prof. anatomy, 1941-44; asst. dir. med. scis. div. Rockefeller Found., 1944-48, asso. dir., 1949-51, asso. dir., div. medicine and pub. health, 1951-55; dir. biol. and med. research 1955-59, dir. for med. and natural scis., 1959-64; prof. biology, dir. div. biol. scis. Cornell U., Ithaca, N.Y., 1964-70; Richard J. Schwartz prof. sci. and soc. Cornell U., 1970-75; Class of 1949 vis. prof. Mass. Inst. Tech., Cambridge, 1975-86; Mem. NSF Nat. Sci. Bd., 1963-72, exec. com., 1966-71; mem. sci. adv. com. Gen. Motors Corp., 1971-79, Hitchiner Mfg. Co. Author: Scientist, 1964; Editor: The Contemporary University: USA, 1966; co-editor: Ethical and Scientific Issues Posed by Human Uses of Molecular Genetics, 1976, Limits of Scientific Inquiry, 1979. Bd. dirs. Grass Found., Quincy, Mass., Inst. Soc., Ethics and Life Scis., 1969-84; mem. overseers' coms. to visit Med. Sch., Sch. Dental Medicine and Biology and Related Research Facilities, Harvard; trustee Russell Sage Found., 1968-78, Bennington (Vt.) Coll. Recipient Henry Knowles Beecher award in med. ethics, 1984. Fellow Am. Acad. Arts and Scis. (v.p. 1969-72); mem. Harvey Soc. N.Y., AAAS, Am. Physiol. Soc. Am. Assn. Anatomists, Am. Acad. Neurology, Phi Beta Kappa, Alpha Omega Alpha. Home: Peterborough N.H. Died Dec. 2, 1986.

MORRILL, JAMES LEWIS, educator; b. Marion, Ohio, Sept. 24, 1891; s. Harrison Delmont and Mary (Lewis) M.; m. Freda Rhodes, June 22, 1915; children: John Rhodes, Mary (Mrs. William E. Knepper), Sylvia (Mrs. W.A. Todd). AB, Ohio State U., 1913; LLD, Miami U., 1936, Ohio State U., 1945, U. Wyo., 1946, U. Cin., 1948, Carleton Coll., 1950, Macalester Coll., 1951, Northwestern U., 1952, Mich. State U., 1955, U. Exeter (Eng.), 1956, U. Calif., L.A., 1957, Iowa State Coll., 1958, U. Wis., 1959, Hamline U., 1960, U. Minn., 1962; LHD, Muhlenberg Coll., 1949. Reporter, copy reader, editorial asst., polit. and legislative corr. 1913-17; city editor Cleve. Press, 1919; exec. sec. U.S. Food Adminstrn. in Ohio and Ohio br. Coun. Nat. Def., 1917-19; alumni sec., editor Ohio State U., Columbus, 1919-28, instr. journalism and edn., 1925-29; jr. dean Coll. Edn., 1928-32, v.p., 1932-41; pres. U. Wyo., Laramie, 1942-45, U. Minn., Mpls., 1945-60; cons. Ford Found., 1960-70; chmn. U.S. adv. com. ednl. exchange Dept. State, 1951-55; mem. Pres.'s com. problems edn. beyond high sch. HEW, 1956-57. Chmn. Am. Council Edn., 1950-51; trustee Eisenhower Exch. Fellowships, 1953-54, Inst. Internat. Edn., 1957-60. Decorated comdr. Royal Order North Star (Sweden), 1956. Mem. North Central Assn. Colls. and Secondary Schs. (mem. com. profl. edn. of commn. colls. and univs. 1953-57), Am. Assn. Land Grant Colls. and Univs. (pres. 1947-48), Assn. Am. Univs. (pres. 1954-56), Nat. Assn. State Univs. (pres. 1957-58), Ohio State U. Faculty Club, Rotary. Episcopalian. Home: Columbus Ohio. †

MORRILL, PHILIP EVERETT, manufacturing executive; b. Haverhill, Mass., June 27, 1892; s. William E. and Hattie (Davis) M. m. Helen D. White, Sept. 4, 1916; 1 child, Jean Lida. BSCE, MIT, 1914. Assoc. Bemis Bro. Bag Co., from 1914, v.p., also bd. dirs. Republican. Unitarian. Home: Boston Mass. †

MORRIS, JAMES JOSEPH, banker; b. Phila., Nov. 19, 1933; s. Daniel A. and Winifred (Barrett) M.; m. Shirley A. Vollrath, Jan. 26, 1957; children—Christopher, Patrick, Robert, John, Matthew, Juliet. B.A. in Fin., La Salle U., Phila., 1955. Exec. trainee Continental Bank, Phila., 1958-60, br. mgr., 1960-63, regional v.p., 1963-67, exec. v.p., 1968-74, vice chmn. bd., 1974-86. Bd. dirs. Southeastern Pa. Devel. Fund, 1975-86. Served with U.S. Army, 1956-58. Recipient Humanitarian award Am. Cancer Soc., Phila., 1977. Club: Squires Gap (bd. dirs.) (Ambler, Pa.). Home: Elkins Park Pa. Died May 7, 1986.

MORRIS, JOHN ALBERT, stockbroker; b. Phila., Mar. 27, 1891; s. Alfred Hennen and Jessie (Harding) M.; m. Edna Brokaw, May 27, 1942; children: John Albert, Alfred Hennen. Student, Pomfret Sch., Pomfret Center, Conn., 1904-09; AB, Harvard, 1913. Assoc. with Stone & Webster, 1913-17, Charles D. Barney & Co., N.Y.C., 1923-29; ptnr. Gude, Winmill & Co., N.Y.C., 1929-71; ltd. ptnr. in successor firm Prescott, Ball & Turben, N.Y.C., 1971-85; former chmn. bd. Cue Pub. Co. Bd. dirs. Seaman's Ch. Inst.; trustee Jockey Club Found.; bd. fgn. parishes Am. Protestant Episcopal Chs. in U.S.A. Capt. F.A., U.S. Army, 1917-19; AEF in France. Decorated Croix de Guerre. Mem. N.Y. Racing Assn. (trustee 1957-73), Thoroughbred Racing Assn. U.S. (pres. 1952-54, treas. 1954-78, asst. treas. 1978-85), New Eng. Soc. N.Y. (pres. 1976), Newcomen Soc. N.Am., Masons (32 deg., K.T., Shriner), Racquet and Tennis Club, Union Club (pres. 1962-67), Rockaway Hunting Club, City Midday Club (trustee), Recess Club, Turf and Field Club (past pres.), River Club, Harvard Club (N.Y.C.), Jockey Club, Bath and Indian Creek Club (Miami Beach, Fla.). Home: New York N.Y. Died Feb. 17, 1985.

MORRIS, ROBERT EARL, metalworking machinery distributing company executive; b. Westfield, Mass., Feb. 3, 1913; s. August and Christina (Hemke) M.; m. Dorothy Mathews, July 20, 1940; children: Robert Earl, Lee B., Anthony P. Student public schs., Westfield. Founder Robert E. Morris Co., Farmington, Conn., 1941; chmn. bd. Robert E. Morris Co., 1976-88; founder Rem Sales Inc., Farmington, 1957; chmn. bd. Rem Sales Inc., 1979-88; co-founder Nichols-Morris Corp., 1943-56, Universal Mktg. Corp., 1944-56; incorporator Contacts Inc., 1957-67, Four M Corp., 1957; dir. Diebel Mfg. Co., Morton Grove, Ill.; mem. asso. bd. West Hartford br. CBT Corp., 1968-88. Decorated officer Order Brit. Empire; named Ky. Colonel, 1973. Mem. Soc. Mfg. Engrs. (life), Am. Machine Tool Distbrs. Assn. Republican. Clubs: Avon (Conn.) Golf, Mariner Sands Country (Stuart, Fla.). Died Aug. 22, 1988.

MORRISON, ROBERT WENDELL, lawyer; b. Renovo, Pa., June 4, 1923; s. Thomas Cyril M. and Edith Louisa (Hall) Marshall; m. Charlotte Coyne, Dec. 28, 1960; children: Robert Wendell, Thomas Thayer. BA, U. Pa., 1943, MBA, 1947; JD, Columbia U., 1950. Bar: N.Y. 1950, Calif. 1951, U.S. Ct. Mil. Appeals 1956, U.S. Supreme Ct. 1956. Assoc. in law Columbia U., N.Y.C., 1950-51; law clk. U.S. Dist. Ct., Portland, Oreg., 1951-52; assoc. Pillsbury, Madison & Sutro, San Francisco, 1953-85. Bd. dirs. Laguna Honda Hosp. Vols., San Francisco, 1976-85; bd. dirs. Shriners Hosp. for Crippled Children, 1977-85, chmn., 1980-82. Col. JAGC, AUS, 1943-46, Res. ret. Decorated Legion of Merit. Mem. San Francisco Bar Assn., Calif. Bar Assn., Fed. Bar Assn., Nat. Lawyers Club, Res. Officers Assn., Judge Advs. Assn., Assn. U.S. Army, University Club, Tavern Club, Masons, Royal Order Scotland, Phi Beta Kappa. Home: Belvedere Calif. Died Sept. 18, 1985.

MORRISON, THEODORE, language educator, writer; b. Concord, N.H., Nov. 4, 1901; s. Henry Kent and Emma Marshall (Howard-Smith) M.; m. Florence Kathleen Johnston, Oct. 22, 1927; children: Robert Henry, Anne Guthrie. AB, Harvard U., 1923; LittD (hon.), Middlebury (Vt.) Coll., 1951. Asst. in English Harvard U., 1923-25, instr., tutor English, 1931-37, asst. prof., 1937-39, lectr. English, 1939-63, prof. English, from 1963, then emeritus; tchr. occasional seminar on writing for Nieman Fellows, from 1944; editorial staff Atlantic Monthly Press and Atlantic Monthly, 1925-30. Author: The Serpent in the Cloud, 1931, Notes of Death and Life, 1935, The Devious Way, 1944, The Portable Chaucer (transl., introduction and commentary), 1949, The Dream of Alcestis, 1950, The Stones of the House, 1953, To Make a World, 1957, The Whole Creation, 1962, Chautauqua: A Center for Education, Religion, and the Arts in America, 1974, Middlebury College Bread Loaf Writers' Conference: The First Thirty Years, 1976, Leave of Absence (novel), 1981; editor: (with others) Five Kinds of Writing, 1939. Joined staff Bread Loaf Writers Conf., Middlebury Coll., 1930, dir., 1932-55; cons. course in composition, speech and Am. History Army Air Forces Premeteorol. Tng. Program, 1943. Mem. Am. Acad. Arts and Scis. Home: Amherst Mass. Died Nov. 27, 1988; buried Middlebury, Vt.

MORROW, LOUIS LARAVOIRE, bishop; b. Weatherford, Tex., Dec. 24, 1892; s. Joseph LaRavoire and Elizabeth Morrow. STD, Pontifical U. of Palafox, Puebla, Mexico, 1921. Joined Salesian Soc. of St. John Bosco, 1912, ordained priest Roman Cath. Ch., 1921. Dir. Cath. Recreational Ctr., Puebla, 1921-22; sec. Apostolic Del., Manila, Philippines, 1922-39; bishop of Krishnagar West Bengal, India, from 1939. Author: A Short History of the Filipino People, 1937, My Catholic Faith, 1936, My Bible History (U.S., Philippines, India, China), 1936, My First Communion (40 edits. different langs.), Our Catholic Faith, 1969, 71; also booklets. Councilman, Town of Krishnagar, 1952-65. Home: Krishnagar India. †

MORSE, FREDERIC CLARKE, banker; b. Emporia, Kans., Jan. 16, 1887; s. Park L. and Mary Luella (Smith) M.; m. M. Estelle Klett, Jan. 22, 1913; 1 child, Frederic Clarke. AB, Coll. Emporia (Kans.), 1905, LLD, 1964; AM, U. Tex., 1906; student, U. Chgo., 1908; grad., Grad. Sch. of Banking, Rutgers U., 1940. Bar: Tex. 1910. Began as court reporter 1906; practice Austin, Tex., 1910-20; organized Mut. Savs. Instn., 1920, pres., later mem. exec. com., chmn. bd.; began Fidelity Trust Co., 1936; v.p., dir. Gracy Title Co. Author: The Mutual Savings Institution, Forty Million Dollars in Forty Years, The Romance of Business and The Fundamentals of Money Making, Going into Business for Yourself, Ex-Students History of the University of Texas—In Pictures; also articles in various jours. and newspaper column Personals Column, Austin Am. Statesman, 1951-71. Mem. Friends of the Libr., Austin, Friends Tex. A&M U. Libr.; dir. Heritage Soc., Capitol City area Boy Scouts Am. Recipient Silver Beaver award Boy Scouts Am., Freedom Found. medal, cert., cash prize. Mem. Tex. Bar Assn., Am. Judicature Soc., Tex. Fine Arts Assn. (v.p.) C. of C., SAR, Country Club, Masons, Rotary (hon. internat. fellow). Home: Austin Tex. †

MORSE, PHILIP MCCORD, research physicist; b. Shreveport, La., Aug. 6, 1903; s. Allen Craft and Edith (McCord) M.; m. Annabelle Hopkins, Apr. 26, 1929 (dec. Mar. 1985); children: Conrad Philip, Annabella. BS, Case Sch. Apllied Sci., 1926, ScD (hon.), 1940; AM, Princeton, 1927, PhD, 1929. Salesman, reporter, lectr. 1922-30; instr. in physics Princeton, 1929-30; Internat. Rsch. Fellow 1930-31; asst. prof. physics MIT, 1931-34, assoc. prof., 1934-37, prof., 1937-69, emeritus, 1969-85, dir. Computation Ctr., 1956-68, dir. Ops. Rsch. Ctr., 1958-69, chmn. faculty, 1958-60; dir. Brookhaven Nat. Lab., 1946-48; trustee Rand Corp., 1948-52, Analytical Svcs. Inc., 1962-73, Inst. for Def. Analysis, 1956-61; dir. Control Data Corp.; mem. NDRC Div. 6; asst. dir. Office Field Service OSRD, 1943-45; dir. rsch. Weapons Systems Evaluation Group, Office Sec. of Def., 1949-50; dir. Ops. Rsch. Group, U.S. Navy, 1942-46; mem. Ordnance Rsch. Adv. Com., 1950-56; chmn. NATO Adv. Panel Ops. Rsch., 1960-65, OECD Panel on Ops. Rsch., 1963-68. Author: (with E.U. Condon) Quantum Mechanics, 1929, Vibration and Sound, 1936, rev. edit. 1946, (with G.E. Kimball) Methods of Operations Research, 1950, (with H. Feshbach) Methods of Theoretical Physics, 1953, Queues, Inventories and Maintenance, 1958, Thermal Physics, (with K.U. Ingard) Theoretical Acoustics, 1967, Library Effectiveness, 1969, In At the Beginnings, a Physicist's Life, 1977; assoc. editor Tech. Rev., 1936-46; mem. editorial bd. Sci., Bull. Atomic Scientists; editor: Annals of Physics, 1957-77, Notes on Operations Research, 1959, Operations Research for Public Systems, 1967, Analysis of Public Systems, 1972; contbr. articles to profl. jours. and mags. Trustee Am. Inst. Physics, 1948-50, 1953-57, 73-75, chmn. bd. govs., 1975-80; chmn. bd. govs. Rsch. Soc. Am., 1950-58; chmn. Navajo Coop. Commn., NAS, 1980-85. Decorated Medal for Merit, U.S., 1946; recipient silver medal Operational Rsch. Soc. London, 1965, Gold medal Case Alumni Assn. Fellow Ops. Rsch. Soc. Am. (1st pres. 1952-53, Lanchester prize 1969, G.E. Kimball medal 1974), Am. Acad. Arts and Scis., Am. Phys. Soc. (mem. coun. 1935-40, 72-75, v.p. 1970-71, pres. 1971-72, chmn. panel on pub. affairs 1975-76), Acoustical Soc. Am. (pres. 1950-51, gold medal 1973); mem. Internat. Fedn. Ops. Rsch. Socs. (exec. sec. 1961-65), NAS, Cosmos Club (Washington), Sigma Xi, Tau Beta Pi. Democrat. Presbyterian. Home: Winchester Mass. Died Sept. 5, 1985; cremated.

MORSE, RICHARD STETSON, corporate executive; b. Abington, Mass., Aug. 19, 1911; s. Kenneth Lee and Mary (Skinner) M.; m. Marion Elsa Baitz, Nov. 27, 1935; children—Richard Stetson, Jr., Kenneth P. S.B., MIT, 1933; postgrad., Technische Hochschule Munich, Federal Republic Germany, 1933-35; D.Sc. (hon.), Clark U., 1958; D.Eng. (hon.), Bklyn. Poly. U., 1959. Mem.

sci. staff Eastman Kodak Co., Rochester, N.Y., 1935-40; pres. Nat. Research Corp., Cambridge, Mass., 1940-58; asst. sec. Army for Research and Devel., Washington, 1958-61; sr. lectr. Sloan Sch., MIT, Cambridge, 1961-77; pres. MIT Devel. Found., Cambridge, 1961-77; corp. mem. Boston Mus. Sci., 1950-88, Woods Hole Oceanographic Inst., Mass., 1955-88; chmn., dir. PMC-Beta Corp., Natick, Mass., 1970-88, dir. Tracer Tech. Inc., Newton, Mass., Boston Five Bank. Contbr. articles to profl. jours.; patentee in field. Named one of Ten Young Men Most Likely to Succeed, Nat. C. of C., N.Y.C., 1947; recipient Disting. Civilian Service medal Dept. Defense, 1959. Mem. Am. Chem. Soc., Nat. Acad. Engring. Republican. Clubs: St. Botolph, Commercial Merchants (Boston); Quissett Yacht (Falmouth, Mass.); St. Andrews (Delray Beach, Fla.). Home: Wellesley Mass. Died June 1, 1988.

MORTON, BEN L., foundation official; b. Zanesville, Ohio, Oct. 30, 1927; s. Edward R. and Katie (Lampton) M.; m. Ruthanne Coe, Apr. 17, 1950; children—Richard A., Julie E., Rebecca A. B.S. cum laude, Ohio U., 1952, M.S., 1953; Ph.D., U. Mich., 1963. Asst. in pub. relations Evansville (Ind.) Coll., 1953-54; dir. pub. relations Morris Harvey Coll., Charleston, W.Va., 1954-56; asst. exec. dir. Am. Coll. Pub. Relations Assn., Washington, 1956-57; asst. to pres., dir. devel. Inter-Am. U. of P.R., 1957-60; exec. dir. Kansas City (Mo.) Regional Council for Higher Edn., 1963-64; exec. sec. Mo. Commn. on Higher Edn., Jefferson City, 1964-70; exec. officer Ill. Bd. Govs. State Colls. and Univs., 1970-74; chancellor W.Va. Bd. Regents, 1974-80; v.p. Higher Edn. Assistance Found., 1980-87; Mem. Ednl. Commn. of States, 1965-70; chmn. Assn. Exec. Dirs. State Higher Edn. Facilities Commns., 1968-69, State Higher Edn. Exec. Officers Assn., 1969-70; bd. dirs. So. Regional Edn. Bd. Mem. Phi Kappa Phi, Kappa Tau Alpha. Presbyterian. Home: Charleston W.Va. Died May 5, 1987; buried Alexander Cemetery, Athens, Ohio.

MORTON, CHARLES BRUCE, II, surgeon; b. Tappahannock, Va., Jan. 10, 1900; s. William Jackson and Dorothy Ashby (Moncure) M.; m. Virginia Marshall, Jan. 30, 1925; children: Charles Bruce, Virginia Marshall, Caroline Bartlett. BS, U. Va., 1920, MD, 1922. Diplomate Am. Bd. Surgery (founders group). Lab. asst. biology U. Va., 1917-18, lab. asst. biochemistry, 1919-20; intern U. Va. Hosp., 1921-22; house officer St. Luke's Hosp., N.Y.C., 1922-24; fellow in surgery Mayo Found., 1924-27, 1st asst. in exptl. surgery, 1925-26; asst. prof. surgery and gynecology U. Va., 1927-36, prof., 1936-70, emeritus, 1970-85, chmn. dept. surgery, 1953-54, mem. exec. and blfg. coms., 1935-55; attending surgeon and gynecologist U. Va. Hosp., 1927-70; attending surgeon courtesy med. staff Martha Jefferson Hosp. Contbr. articles to med. jours. Recipient Hosley Meml. prize for rsch. in surgery U. Va., 1927, Pres. Bd. Visitor's Rsch. prize, 1928; Thomas Fortune Ryan scholar U. Va., 1918-21. Fellow Am., So. (v.p. 1946) surg. assns., ACS; mem. Société Internationale de Chirurgie, Alumni Assn. Mayo Found., Albermarle County Med. Soc. (pres. 1934), Med. Soc. Va., So. Soc. Clin. Surgeons (pres. 1946), Eastern Surg. Soc. (pres. 1957), Va. Surg. Soc. (pres. 1955), AMA, Southeastern Surg. Congress, N.Y., Minn., and Va. state bds. of med. exam. (licentiate), Farmington Country Club, Raven, Sigma Xi, Pi Kappa Alpha, Nu Sigma Nu, Alpha Omega Alpha, Iota Sigma. Home: Sarasota Fla. Died Dec. 26, 1985.

MORTON, LAWRENCE, musicologist, curator; b. Duluth, Minn., July 13, 1904. Student, U. Minn., 1921-31, also pvt. music tchrs. Curator music Los Angeles County Mus. of Art, Los Angeles, 1965-83. Theater organist, Mpls., N.Y.C., 1922-28, ch. organist, Chgo., Los Angeles, 1929-38; orchestrator films and radio, Hollywood, Calif., 1939-50; dir.: Monday Evening Concerts, Los Angeles, 1954-71; artistic dir., Ojai (Calif.) Festivals, 1954-59, 67-70, 82, 84; music reviewer: Notes, Modern Music, Hollywood Quar., Tempo. Served with Signal Corps U.S. Army, 1942-43. Recipient Stravinsky award ASCAP, 1962, citation, 1979; Laurel Leaf award Am. Composers Alliance, 1966; citation Mayor Los Angeles, 1971; letter of distinction Am. Music Center, 1979; Centennial award Sch. Music, U. So. Calif., 1984; Guggenheim fellow, 1959, 60. Home: Los Angeles Calif. Died May 8, 1987; buried May 8, 1987.

MORTON, WILLIAM HANSON, investment banker; b. New Rochelle, N.Y., Sept. 17, 1909; s. Charles and Rosina A. (Hanson) M.; m. Margaret Sparkman Dobbin, Oct. 26, 1934; children: Margaret Elizabeth, William H. AB, Dartmouth, 1932. With Chase Harris Forbes Corp., 1932-33; with Chase Nat. Bank, 1933-46, v.p., 1942-46; pres. W. H. Morton & Co. Inc., N.Y.C., 1946-66, chmn., 1966-68; chmn. Equitable Securities, Morton & Co. Inc., 1968-71; vice chmn., dir. Am. Express Co., 1966-68, pres., 1968-74, ret., 1974; bd. dirs. Crocker Nat. Bank, The Singer Co., Boise Cascade Corp., Rand McNally & Co., Deck House Inc.; trustee Greenwich Savs. Bank, N.Y.C. Bd. dirs. Nat. Football Found. and Hall of Fame; trustee Andrew W. Mellon Found., Dartmouth Coll. Mem. Investment Bankers Assn. (v.p. 1956-58, chmn. mcpl. securities div. 1948-49, gov. 1954-56), Mcpl. Bond Club of N.Y. (pres. 1949-50), Am. Yacht Club, Apawamis Club (Rye, N.Y.), Bond Club, Wall Street Club, Pilgrims Club, Links Club (N.Y.C.), Augusta (Ga.) Nat. Golf Club, Blind Brook Club (Port Chester, N.Y.), Country Club of Fla. (Delray Beach), Pacific Union (San Francisco). Home: Rye N.Y. Died Apr. 11, 1987; buried Hanover Center, N.H.

MORTON, W(OOLRIDGE) BROWN, lawyer; b. Farmville, Va., May 7, 1882; s. George B. and Emma W. (Brown) M.; m. Lucie C. Taylor, Oct. 14, 1909; children: W. Brown, Edward T., Lucie Morton Davis. Student, Va. Poly. Inst., 1898-1900. Bar: D.C. 1906, N.Y. 1918. Mem. Pennie, Edmonds, Morton, Taylor and Adams, N.Y.C., from 1920; bd. dirs. Vitamin Food Co., Inc., Wilbro Corp. Mem. Century Assn. (N.Y.C.), University Club (Washington). Home: King George Va. †

MOSELEY, ROBERT DAVID, JR., radiologist, educator; b. Minden, La., Feb. 29, 1924; s. Robert David and Lettie E. (Looney) M.; m. Janet C. Watson, Mar. 15, 1947; children: Robert David III, Richard Havard, Marianne Lee. M.D., La. State U., 1947. Diplomate Am. Bd. Radiology. Intern Highland Sanitarium and Clinic, Shreveport, La., 1947-48; asst. resident U. Chgo. Clinics, 1949-50; asst. resident Los Alamos spl. research project, dept. radiology U. Chgo., 1950-51; staff mem. U. Calif.-Los Alamos Sci. Lab., 1951-52, radiologist, assoc. chief staff med. ctr., 1951-52; mem. staff dept. radiology U. Chgo., 1954-71, prof., chmn. dept., 1958-71; prof., asst. chmn., dir. div. diagnostic radiology U. N.Mex. Sch. Medicine, Albuquerque, 1971-78; prof., chmn. dept. radiology U. N.Mex. Sch. Medicine, 1978-85, prof. emeritus, 1985-87; chief of staff Bernalillo County Med. Center, 1971-72, 78, 79; bd. dirs. Nat. Council Radiation Protection, 1973-80; mem. radiation study sect. USPHS, NIH, 1971-75; mem. radiology tng. com. NIH, 1966-70; chmn., 1969-70; U.S. rep. UN Sci. Com. on Effects Atomic Radiation, 1976-86; chmn. adv. com. on biology and medicine U.S. AEC, 1967-73; chmn. U.S. delegation Internat. Congresses of Radiology, Rio de Janeiro, 1977, Brussels, 1981; pres. XVI Internat. Congress Radiology, Hawaii, 1985. Pres. bd. dirs. James Picker Found., 1972-86. Served as lt. (s.g.) USNR, 1952-54. Fellow Chgo. Roentgen Soc. (past sec.-treas. bd. trustees, pres. 1966-67), Am. Coll. Radiology (pres. 1973-74, Gold medal 1980), Royal Coll. Radiologists (Eng.) (hon.), Swedish Soc. Med. Radiology (hon.); mem. Internat. Soc. Radiology (pres. 1985-87), N.Mex. Med. Soc., Assn. U. Radiologists (founding mem., past pres., Gold medal 1980), Am. Roentgen Ray Soc., Radiation Research Soc., Acad. Soc. Lund (Sweden) (corr.), Deutsche Röntgengesellshaft (corr.), Radiol. Soc. N.Am., Inter Am. Coll. Radiology, Royal Physiographic Soc. (fgn. mem., Lund, Sweden), N.Mex. Soc. Radiologists, Sigma Xi, Sigma Nu, Phi Chi. Club: Univ. (Chgo.). Home: Albuquerque N.Mex. Died Mar. 12, 1987, buried Santa Fe Nat. Cemetery, N.Mex.

MOSKOWITZ, CHARLES C., business executive; b. N.Y.C., Feb. 20, 1892; s. Louis and Anna (Rubenfeld) M. BCS, NYU, 1914. V.p. Loew's Inc., 1942-57, treas., 1945-57, dir., 1934-58; pres., treas., dir. Robbins Music Corp., Leo Feist Inc., Miller Music Corp., Lion Music Corp., Big Three Music Corp., Pine Ridge Music Corp., Variety Music Inc., Walter Jacobd Inc., Lion Record Corp.; v.p., treas., dir. Metro-Goldwyn-Mayer Studios Inc., Hearst Metronome News Inc.; treas., dir. Metro-Goldwyn-Mayer Pictures Can. Ltd. Mem. Mayor's Com.; hon. dep. police commr. N.Y.C.; chmn. N.Y. City Theatres com. 5th War Loan. Recipient Dean Madden Mem. Fund award NYU Sch. Commerce. Mem. NYU Sch. Commerce Alumni Assn. (dir.), Motion Picture Pioneers, Masons, Shriners, K.T., Glen Oakes Country Club (Great Neck, N.Y.), Variety Club, Univ. Club, Alpha Epsilon Pi. Home: Kew Gardens N.Y. †

MOSLEY, J(OHN) BROOKE, JR., bishop; b. Phila., Oct. 18, 1915; s. John Brooke and Bertha Alice (Urwiler) M.; m. Betty Mary Wall, June 6, 1942; children: Miriam Mosley Wood, Sarah Emma Sandor, Peter Brooke. B.A., Temple U., 1937, LL.D., 1971; M.Div., Episcopal Theol. Sch., 1940; postgrad., Grad. Sch. Applied Religion, 1941, Washington Sch. Psychiatry, 1948; D.D., Kenyon Coll., 1954, Colgate U., 1971; S.T.D., Hobart Coll., 1956, Dickinson Coll., 1973; Litt.D., Jewish Theol. Sem., 1971. Ordained to ministry P.E. Ch. as deacon 1940, priest, 1941; asst. minister St. Barnabas Ch., Cin., 1940-42; minister in charge St. Barnabas Ch., 1942-44; dir. dept. social relations Diocese of Washington, 1944-48; dean Cathedral Ch. of St. John, Wilmington, Del., 1948-53; bishop coadjutor Diocese of Del., 1953-55, bishop, 1955-68; dep. for overseas relations Episcopal Ch., 1968-70; bishop in charge, convocation Am. churches in Europe, 1968-70; pres. Union Theol. Sem., N.Y.C., 1970-74; asst. bishop Diocese Pa., Phila., 1974-82; rector St. Aidan's Ch., South Dartmouth, Mass., 1959-87. Home: Philadelphia Pa. Died Mar. 4, 1988, buried St. Aidan's Meml. Garden, S. Dartmouth.

MOSS, HOWARD, writer, editor; b. N.Y.C., Jan. 22, 1922; s. David L. and Sonya (Schrag) M. B.A., U. Wis., 1944; postgrad., Columbia U., Harvard U. Book reviewer Time mag., 1943; instr. English Vassar Coll., 1944-45; adj. prof. English Barnard Coll., 1975, Columbia U., 1977, 81, 83, U. Calif., Irvine, 1979, U. Houston, 1980, 83, 87; poetry editor New Yorker mag., 1948-87; chancellor Academy of American Poets, New York, 1987. Author: (poems) The Wound and The Weather, 1946, The Toy Fair, 1954, A Swimmer in the Air, 1957, A Winter Come, A Summer Gone, 1960, Finding Them Lost, 1965, Second Nature, 1968, Selected Poems, 1971, Buried City, 1975, A Swim Off the Rocks, 1976, Notes From the Castle, 1979, Rules of Sleep, 1984, New Selected Poems, 1985; (criticism) The Magic Lantern of Marcel Proust, 1962, Writing Against Time, 1969, Whatever Is Moving, 1981, Minor Monuments: Selected Essays, 1986; (plays) The Folding Green, 1958, The Palace at 4 A.M, 1972, Two Plays, 1981; (satire) Instant Lives, 1974, Instant Lives and More, 1985; (juvenile) Tigers and Other Lilies, 1977; (transl.) The Cemetery by the Sea (Paul Valéry), 1986; editor: (with introduction): Keats, 1959; The Nonsense Books of Edward Lear, 1964, The Poet's Story, 1973, New York: Poems, 1979. Judge Nat. Book awards, 1964, 57; judge Brandeis Creative award, 1962, Avery Hopwood award U. Mich., 1963. Recipient Janet Sewall David award Poetry mag., 1944; award creative writing Am. Acad. and Inst. Arts and Letters, 1968; Nat. Book award in Poetry, 1972; Brandeis Creative Awards citation in poetry, 1983; Nat. Endowment Arts award, 1984; Lenore Marshall/Nation Poetry prize, 1986. Fellow Acad. Am. Poets, 1986; mem. P.E.N., Authors Guild, Am. Acad. and Inst. Arts and Letters. Home: New York City N.Y. Died Sept. 16, 1987.

MOSS, JAMES MERCER, physician; b. Gray, Ga., Dec. 15, 1917; s. Fred August and Rosa (Mercer) M.; m. Rachel Scott Bybee, Sept. 6, 1941; children: James Marion, Fred Aubrey (dec.), William Wallace, Robert Edward. M.D., U. Va., 1941. Diplomate: Am. Bd. Internal Medicine. Intern U. Va. Hosp., 1941-42, resident medicine, 1947-49; fellow, instr. endocrinology Duke U., 1946-47; practice medicine specializing in internal medicine Alexandria, Va., 1949-87; instr. clin. medicine Georgetown U., 1949-51, clin. asst. prof., 1952-56, clin. asso. prof., 1956-62, clin. prof., 1962-87; dir. diabetic clinic Georgetown U. Hosp., 1949-75, D.C. Gen. Hosp., 1950-55; active staff Circle Terr. Hosp., 1956-86, pres., 1964-68; dir. City Bank & Trust, 1963-71, Circle Terr., Inc., 1965-75 (all Alexandria); mem. pub. adv. com. on endocrine drugs FDA, 1974-78; mem. Health Manpower Commn. Va., 1973-77. Author: Fundamentals of Diabetic Management, 1962, Mongraph on Diabetes, 1974; editorial bd.: Va. Med. Monthly, 1961-70; editorial cons.: Am. Acad. Family Practice, 1969-87; contbr. articles to profl. jours. Treas. No. Va. Med. Com. Good Govt., 1960-62; chmn. Va.-Med. Polit. Action Com., 1966-67, Va. Physicians for Reelection Pres., 1972; mem. Alexandria Republican Com., 1972-75. Served from lt. to maj. M.C., AUS, 1942-46. Recipient awards for sci. exhibits, Vicennial medal Georgetown U., 1970, med. staff award Louise Obici Meml. Hosp., 1981, Charles R. Fenwick Outstanding Alumnus award U. Va., 1987. Fellow ACP (gov. Va. 1979-83, laureate award Va. chpt. 1987, master, 1987), Am. Coll. Cardiology; mem. Am. Soc. Internal Medicine (chmn. pharms. com. 1974-78, Spl. Recognition award 1980), Va. Soc. Internal Medicine (pres. 1962-63, Disting. Internist award 1976), No. Va. Soc. Internal Medicine, Am. Heart Assn., Am. Diabetes Assn. (Pfizer award 1981), Va. Diabetes Assn. (pres. 1971-72), Endocrine Soc., So. Med. Assn. (asso. counselor 1975-80, counselor 1980-85, chmn. sect. medicine 1979-80, mem. com. sci. work 1976-87, Seale Harris award 1986), Med. Soc. Va. (pres. 1970-71), AMA (council continuing edn. 1971-77, chmn. exhibit com. 1975-76, chmn. audiovisual com. 1976-77, cert. of appreciation 1977), Diabetes Assn. D.C. (pres. 1956-57), Med. Council Washington Met. Area (pres. 1958-59), Heart Assn. No. Va. (pres. 1964-65), Am. Assn. Physicians and Surgeons (del. from Va. 1974-76), Am. Podiatry Assn. (hon., Gold medal 1964), Am. Med. Writers Assn., Alexandria Med. Soc. (pres. 1958-59), Med. Alumni Assn. U. Va. (pres. 1965-66), Phi Chi, Alpha Omega Alpha. Home: Alexandria Va. Died Sept. 16, 1987; buried Arlington Nat. Cemetery.

MOSS, LEONARD WALLACE, anthropologist, educator; b. Detroit, Sept. 7, 1923; s. Adolph and Minnie (Moskowitz) M.;. m. Beebe Gottesman, Dec. 2, 1945; 1 child, Amelia Moss Simms. BS, Wayne State U., 1947, MA, 1950; PhD, U. Mich., 1955. Mem. faculty Wayne State U., 1952-84, prof. anthropology, 1965-84, chmn. dept. sociology and anthropology, 1962-68, sec. Liberal Arts Coll. Faculty Coun., 1970-74, acting chmn. anthropology, 1982-83, mem.-at-large univ. coun., 1975-84; vis. lectr. U. Internazionale degli Scienzi Sociale, 1962, Scuola Italiana per Servizio Sociale, 1956; mem. faculty Rome campus Trinity Coll., summers 1970-76, Mead lectr., 1971, Barbieri lectr., 1974, 76. Author numerous articles in field. Vice chmn. citizen's adv. com., Oak Park (Mich.) Bd. Edn., 1960-61; mem. Mich. regional adv. bd. Anti-Defamation League, B'nai B'rith, 1961, 62-63, 64-69, 71-76; mem. adv. bd. Am.-Yuogslav Project Regional and Urban Planning Studies, 1968-72, Nat. Italian Am. Found.; founding mem., bd. dirs. Italian-Am. Cultural Soc. and Community Ctr., 1973-84 With USAAF, 1942-45. Decorated knight Order of Merit (Italy); recipient Faculty Merit award Wayne State U., 1975, 76, Faculty Service award Wayne State U. Alumni Assn., 1978, Merit award Italian-Am. Cultural Soc., 1977; Fulbright rsch. scholar U. Rome, 1955-56, Fulbright sr. lectr. anthropology, 1961-62, Fulbright-Hays sr. rsch. scholar, 1968-69;. Fellow Am. Anthrop. Assn., AAAS, Royal Anthrop. Soc.; mem.

Mich. Sociol. Soc. (pres. 1963-64), Cen. States Anthrop. Soc. (pres. 1969-70, Disting. lectr. 1980), Mich. Acad. Sci. Arts and Letters (exec. coun. 1960-61, 63-64), Centro Italiano di Antropologia Culturale (exec. bd. 1962-64), Am. Italian Hist. Assn. (founding mem., exec. bd. 1966-72), Assn. Italiana di Scienze Sociali, Am. Assn. Phys. Anthropologists, Sigma Xi, Alpha Kappa Delta, Omicron Delta Kappa. Home: Southfield Mich. Died Feb. 5, 1984; buried Clover Hill Pk. Cemetery, Royal Oak, Mich.

MOSSNER, ERNEST CAMPBELL, language professional, educator; b. N.Y.C., Oct. 22, 1907; s. Gustave and Lillian (Campbell) M.; m. Carolyn Walz, June 22, 1936; 1 son, David Campbell. B.A., City Coll. N.Y., 1929; M.A., Columbia, 1930, Ph.D., 1936; D.Litt. (hon.), Edinburgh, 1976. Fellow, tutor, instr. English City Coll. N.Y., 1929-37; asso. prof. English Syracuse U., 1937-43, prof., 1943-47; prof. English U. Tex., Austin, 1947-86; Ashbel Smith prof. English and philosophy U. Tex., 1970-86, emeritus, 1972-86; vis. prof. English Columbia U., summer 1947, U. Colo., summer 1960; editorial bd. Adam Smith bicentenary com. Glasgow U., 1965-86. Author: Bishop Butler and the Age of Reason, 1936, The Forgotten Hume, 1943, The Life of David Hume, 1954, rev. edit., 1980; Editor: Justa Edovardo King, 1938, Bishop Butler: The Analogy of Religion, 1960, David Hume: Philosophical Essays on Human Understanding and Other Essays, 1962, David Hume: A Treatise of Human Nature, 1969; co-editor: New Letters of David Hume, 1954, A Letter from a Gentleman to his Friend in Edinburgh; 1745: A Pamphlet Hitherto Unknown by David Hume, 1967, Texas Studies in Literature and Language, 1965-72, Correspondence of Adam Smith, 1977; adv. editor: Abstracts of English Studies, 1960-64; editorial bd.: Ency. Philosophy, 1963-67; Contbr. articles, chpts. to profl. jours., books, encys. Served with AUS, 1943-45. Guggenheim fellow, 1939-40, 45-46; Am. Council Learned Socs. grantee, 1965; Fulbright fellow, 1968-69. Mem. Internat. Assn. U. Profs. English, Modern Lang. Assn. Am., S.W. Modern Lang. Assn., Modern Humanities Research Assn., Tex. Inst. Letters (Best Biography award 1955), Phi Beta Kappa, Phi Kappa Phi. Home: Austin Tex. Died Aug. 5, 1986.

MOSZYNSKI, JERZY ROBERT, mechanical and aerospace engineer; b. Lwow, Poland, May 12, 1925; came to U.S., 1955; s. Stanislaw K. and Miroslawa (Sterzynska) M.; m. Barbara M. Trzasko-Durska, Dec. 16, 1950; children: Stanley K., Catherine I. Student, Polish Univ. Coll., London, Eng., 1946-47; B.Sc. with 1st class honours in Engring, U. London, 1949, M.Sc. in Engring, 1952, Ph.D., 1958. Asst. lectr. mech. engring. Woolwich Poly., U. London, 1949-52, lectr., 1952-54; sr. design engr. English Electric Co., Leicester, Eng., 1954-55; research asso. Brown U., Providence, 1955-58; asst. prof. mech. engring. Case Inst. Tech., Cleve., 1958-60; asso. prof. Case Inst. Tech., 1960-63, prof., 1963-66; prof. mech. and aerospace engring. U. Del., Newark, 1966-87; vis. prof. Polish Acad. Sci., 1972-73, 79, Warsaw Tech. U., 1980; cons. TRW, Inc., Babcock and Wilcox Co., Argonne Nat. Lab, Brookhaven Nat. Lab., others; lectr. in field. Contbr. articles to sci. and tech. jours. Served with Polish Underground Army, 1942-45. Humboldt Found. sr. fellow, 1974, 75. Fellow Instn. Mech. Engrs. (Gt. Britain); Mem. ASME (chmn. standing com. on thermophys. properties 1965-68, honors and awards com. heat transfer div. 1979-80, Max Jakob bd. of award 1983), Am. Soc. for Engring. Edn., AAUP, Polish Soc. for Theoretical and Applied Mechanics (fgn.), Polish Vets. in Exile (pres. Cleve. 1965), Sigma Xi, Tau Beta Pi. Home: Lake Park Fla. Died May 8, 1987; buried Our Lady of Czestohara Shrine, Doylestown, Pa.

MOTT, THOMAS HEZEKIAH, JR., computer science educator; b. Houston, Jan. 24, 1924; s. Thomas Hezekiah and Margaret M. (Suttles) M.; m. Ivarean Bryan, Aug. 7, 1948 (div. Feb. 1975). B.A., Rice Inst., 1948; Ph.D., Yale U., 1956; M.B.A., Rutgers U., 1984. Asst. instr. Yale U., 1954-55; research mathematician Univac Sperry Rand, 1956-58; mem. tech. staff RCA Labs, 1958-61; adj. prof. Villanova U., 1959-61; sr. mem. research staff Lockheed Electronics Co., 1961-62; co-founder 1962; dir., treas. Applied Logic Corp., 1962-73; mem. faculty Rutgers U., 1962-89, prof. computer sci., from 1963, chmn. dept., 1967-69, dir. univ. computer centers, 1966-69, dean Grad. Sch. Library and Info. Studies, 1969-83, prof. bus. and info. studies, 1984-89; vis. prof. Stevens Inst. Tech., 1964-67, U. Pitts., 1967; invited lectr. summers U. Mich., 1959, U. Pa., 1960-61; research asso. psychology and psychiatry Cath. U. Am., 1965; cons. RAND Corp., 1970-72. Author: (with D. Dimitry) Introduction to Fortran IV Programming, 1966, (with S. Artandi and L. Struminger) Introduction to PL/I Programming for Library and Information Science, 1971; contbg. author: Handbook of Engineering Sciences, Vol. I and II, 1967; contbg. editor: Advanced Technology/Libraries, 1974-78; editor: (with E. DeProspo) Internat. Series on Library and Info. Studies, 1978-80. Served to 1st lt. USAAF, 1944-46. Mem. Assn. Symbolic Logic, IEEE, AAUP, AAAS, Am. Philos. Assn., Assn. Computing Machinry, Am. Soc. Info. Sci., ALA (councilor 1981-84), Spl. Libraries Assn., N.J. Library Assn., Internat. Communication Assn., Phi Beta Kappa, Sigma Xi, Beta Gamma Sigma. Home: Rocky Hill N.J. Died Jan. 17, 1989; buried Houston, Tex.

MUDRICK, MARVIN, English educator; b. Phila., July 17, 1921; s. Jacob and Yetta (Minkus) M.; m. Jeanne I. Little, Nov. 1, 1946; children: Lee Arthur, Ann Elisabeth, Ellen Jeanne, Jane Harper. B.A., Temple U., 1942; M.A., U. Calif.-Berkeley, 1947, Ph.D., 1949. Mem. faculty dept. English U. Calif.-Santa Barbara, 1949-86, prof. English, 1963-86, provost Coll. Creative Studies, 1967-84; vis. prof. English Queens Coll., Flushing, N.Y., 1960-61. Author: Jane Austen, 1952, On Culture and Literature, 1970, The Man in the Machine, 1977, Books are Not Life but Then What Is?, 1979, Nobody Here But Us Chickens, 1981; editor: Conrad, 1966. Served with USAAF, 1942-45. Guggenheim fellow, 1959-60. Mem. P.E.N. Am. Home: Santa Barbara Calif. Died Oct. 1986.

MUHLBERG, WILLIAM, physician, medical administrator; b. Cin., Apr. 8, 1875; s. William and Celestine (Mueller) M.; m. Edna Zinke, Sept. 7, 1904; 1 child, Elizabeth. MD, U. Cin., 1897; postgrad., Austria and Switzerland, 1895-99. Intern Cin. Hosp., 1897-98; demonstrator in physiology Harvard U., 1899-1900; prof. physiology U. Cin., 1901-07; asst. med. dir. Union Cen. Life Ins. Co., 1907-16, med. dir., from 1916, med. dir., v.p., from 1932; pres. Pub. Health Fedn. Cin., 1930-32, Cin. Bd. Health, from 1938, Cin. Anti-Tb League, 1937. Author: Long Life, 1916, Heart Talks, 1916, The Medical Side of Field Work, 1920, Mental Adjustments, 1944; contbr. articles to profl. pubs. Recipient Award of Honor Cin. Pub., Health Fedn.; William Muhlberg Health Ctr. dedicated in his name and William Muhlberg lectr. established, 1955. Mem. AMA, Ohio State Med. Assn., Cin. Med. Soc., Assn. Life Ins. Med. Dirs. (pres. 1929-30), Am. Diabetes Assn. (treas., Banting medal), Cin. Country Club, Sigma Alpha Epsilon, Nu Sigma Nu. Episcopalian. Home: Cincinnati Ohio. †

MULHOLLAND, EDWARD J., manufacturing executive; b. Ottawa, Ill., Feb. 15, 1891; s. William and Rose (Doyle) M.; m. Sadie Mcnichols, June 10, 1914; children: Edward Joseph, Kenneth Leo, Lorraine Marie, John William, Thomas Francis. Student, Northwestern U., 1920-22. With Nat. City Bank, Ottawa, 1908; with Chgo. Carton Co., from 1908, pres., from 1949; prodn. mgr. Gas Def. Plant, Long Island City, N.Y., 1917-19; bd. dirs. United Biscuit Co. Am. Mem. KC, Tavern Club, Butterfield Country Club, Long Beach Country Club. Roman Catholic. Home: Oak Park Ill. †

MULLANEY, PATRICK J., railroad executive; b. Somerville, Mass., Dec. 30, 1892; s. Edward J. and Elizabeth (Walsh) M.; m. Elizabeth M. O'Keefe, May 4, 1935; children: Patrice, Elizabeth, Edward. Student pub. schs. Somerville. V.p. traffic B. & M. R.R., from 1951; pres., dir. Mystic Terminal Co.; bd. dirs. Trailer Train Co., Springfield Terminal Ry., Boston and Maine Transportation Co., Boston and Maine R.R. 1st lt. inf. U.S. Army, World War I. Mem. Am. Soc. Traffic and Transp. (founder), Nat. Freight Traffic Assn. (v.p.), Boston Traffic Assn., Boston Traffic Assn. (past pres.), Madison Square Garden (orignial mem., mem. bd. govs.), Algonquin Club, Winchester Country Club. Home: Winchester Mass. †

MULLEN, BUELL (MRS. J. BERNARD MULLEN), artist; b. Chgo., Sept. 10, 1900; d. Charles Clinton and Modrea (Hoyne) Buell; m. J. Bernard Mullen, Dec. 29, 1920; children: J. Bernard, Modrea Hoyne (Mrs. Rene Seiler), Clinton Buell. Grad., Univ. Sch. for Girls, Miss Spence's Sch.; student, Audubon Tyler Art Sch., Brit. Acad., Rome; studied with, Petrucci and Lipinsky, Rome, Cucquier, Belgium; D.F.A., Lake Erie Coll., 1970. Bd. dirs. N.Y. Fedn. Fine Arts, U.S. Nat. Cultural Commn. Muralist, portrait painter.; Author: movie short Painting on Metals; contbr. mag. articles.; Exhbns. include, Salon, Paris, Gruppo Moderno, Rome, Italy, Birmingham Mus. of Art, Dayton Art Inst., one-man shows, Findlay, Chgo., Feragil, N.Y.C., Nat. Collection of Fine Arts, Washington., Murals on stainless steel, Hispanic room Library of Congress (1st mural to be painted on steel), U.S. Naval Acad., Annapolis, Ross Hall, Gt. Lakes Naval Tng. Sta., Searle Lab., Chgo., Ministry of War, Buenos Aires, Volta Redonda Steel Mills, Brazil, Chase Manhattan Bank, Republic Steel Co., Case Western Res. U., Inland Steel, Dun & Bradstreet, Internat. Tel. & Tel., Gardner-Diamond Co., Internat. Nickel Co., Union Carbide & Carbon Co., No. Adams Hosp., Glennan Space Lab., Am. Chem. Soc., Western Electric, Fine Arts Bldg., Denver, Simon Fraser U., Vancouver, B.C., Life-Scis. Bldg., Ohio State U., Lab. Internat. Minerals & Chem., Life-Scis. Bldg., Lake Erie Coll., Paul Wolfe Chapel, Interam. U., P.R., Damavand Coll., Teheran, Human Potential Inst., mural, Calgary (Can.) Leprosarium; portraits on metal include Cardinal Cushing; hist. portrait Capt. James Lawrence for, Battleship N.J., Reaching for the Ball, for, Mrs. Lou Gehrig; latest portraits include others. Rep. Internat. Assn. Arts for U.S. Nat. Commn. of UNESCO; co-chmn. Muralists Nat. Bi-Centennial Com. Fellow Royal Soc. Arts, Inst. Arts and Letters (1st v.p.), Nat. Soc. Mural Painters (pres.); mem. Internat. Art Assn., Unity in Art (mem. bd.). Home: Chicago Ill. Died Aug. 31, 1986.

MULLEN, ROBERT RODOLF, writer, public relations executive; b. Alamogordo, N.Mex., Nov. 24, 1908; s. Robert Gordon and Madeline (Rodolf) M.; m. Edna Cummings, Mar. 13, 1936; children: Robert R., Jonathan, Christopher, Suzanne. Student, U. Wis., 1928-29, U. Denver, 1930-31. Reporter Rocky Mountain News, Denver, 1931-33; staff corr. Christian Sci. Monitor, Boston, 1934-42, U.S. mem. pub. rels. com. U.S.-U.K. Combined Bds., 1943-45; asst. editor, editorial writer Life mag., N.Y.C., 1946-48; dir. info. ECA, 1949-52; pub. rels. chief Citizens for Eisenhower, 1952; exec. dir. Nat. Citizens Com for Ednl. TV, 1953-55; chmn. Robert R. Mullen & Co., pub. rels., Washington and N.Y.C., 1956-72, ret., 1972; chmn. pub. rels. Nixon-Agnew campaign, 1968. Author books including The Latter Day Saints: The Mormons Yesterday and Today, 1966; contbr. to periodicals. Mem. Rotary, Met. Club (Washington), Overseas Press Club (N.Y.C.). Republican. Christian Scientist. Home: Frederick Md. Died Mar. 16, 1986; interred Rock Hall, Frederick.

MULLER, HILGARD, foreign minister; b. Transvaal, May 4, 1914; s. Cornelius J. and Martha (Dreyer) M.; m. Nita Dyason, 1943; 1 child, Cornelius. LLB, U. South Africa, 1946; BLitt (Rhodes scholar), Oxford U., 1940; DLitt, Pretoria U., 1942. Called to South African side bar, 1947. Sr. ptnr. firm Dyason, Douglas, Muller & Meyer, Pretoria, 1947-61; sr. lectr. Latin, Pretoria U., 1941-46, pres. convocation, from 1953, chancellor, from 1965; mayor of Pretoria 1953-55; mem. Parliament for Pretoria E., 1958-61, for Beaufort West, from 1964; South African High Commr. in U.K., 1961; ambassador to U.K., 1961-63; mem. South African delegation to UN, 1963; fgn. minister South Africa, 1964-77. Author books on ancient history. Decorated Gran Cruz Extraordinaria (Paraguay); Grand Cross Order of Christ (Portugal). Died July 10, 1985.

MULLIKEN, ROBERT SANDERSON, retired scientist, educator; b. Newburyport, Mass., June 7, 1896; s. Samuel Parsons and Katherine (Mulliken) M.; m. Mary Helen Noé, Dec. 24, 1929 (dec. Mar. 1975); children: Lucia Maria (Mrs. John P. Heard), Valerie Noé (dec.). B.S., MIT, 1917; Ph.D., U. Chgo., 1921; Sc.D. (hon.), Columbia U., 1939, Marquette U., 1967, Cambridge U., 1967, Gustavus Adolphus Coll., 1975; Ph.D. (hon.), Stockholm U., 1960. Research on war gases Washington, 1917-18; tech. research with N.J. Zinc Co., 1919; research on separation of isotopes 1920-22, research on molecular spectra and molecular structure, 1923-84; Nat. research fellow U. Chgo., 1921-23, Harvard, 1923-25; asst. prof. physics Washington Sq. Coll. (N.Y. U.), 1926-28; assoc. prof. physics U. Chgo., 1928-31, prof. physics, 1931-61, Ernest DeWitt Burton Disting. Service prof., 1956-61, Disting. Service prof. physics and chemistry, 1961-84; Disting. Research prof. chem. physics Fla. State U., 1965-71; Baker lectr. Cornell U., 1960; vis. prof., Bombay, 1962, Indian Inst. Tech., Kanpur, 1962; Silliman lectr. Yale, 1965; Jan Van Geuns vis. prof. Amsterdam U., 1965; J.S. Guggenheim fellow for European study, 1930, 32, leave of absence, 1942-45; as dir. information div. Plutonium Project at Chgo.; editor Plutonium Project Record in Nat. Nuclear Energy Series; Fulbright research fellow for research at Oxford, 1952-53; vis. fellow St. John's Coll., Oxford, 1952-53; sci. attaché Am. Embassy, London, 1955. Served with C.W.S. U.S. Army, 1918. Decorated Order of Rising Sun 2d class (Japan). Recipient medal U. Liege, 1948; Gilbert N. Lewis medal Calif. sect. Am. Chem. Soc., 1960; Theodore W. Richards medal Northeastern sect., 1960; Peter Debye award Am. Chem. Soc., 1963; J.G. Kirkwood medal New Haven sect., 1964; Willard Gibbs medal Chgo. sect., 1965; Baskerville medal CCNY Chemistry Alumni Assn., 1965; Nobel prize for chemistry, 1966. Fellow Am. Phys. Soc. (chmn. div. chem. physics 1951-52), AAAS, Royal Irish Acad. (hon.), Indian Nat. Acad. Sci. (hon.), London Chem. Soc. (hon.); mem. Nat. Acad. Scis., Am. Philos. Soc., Am. Chem. Soc. (Priestley medal 1983), Internat. Acad. Quantum Molecular Sci., Am. Acad. Arts and Scis., European Acad. Arts, Scis., and Humanities (titular mem.), Royal Soc. (fgn. mem.), French Chem. Soc. (hon.), Royal Soc. Sci. of Liège (corr.), Chem. Soc. Japan (hon.), Gamma Alpha, Phi Lambda Upsilon. Club: Cosmos (Washington). Home: Arlington Va. Died Oct. 31, 1986, buried Chgo.

MULLINS, DAVID WILEY, university president; b. Ash Flat, Ark., Aug. 11, 1906; s. Roscoe C. and Emma Matilda (Roberts) M.; m. Eula Elizabeth Harrell, Aug. 9, 1935; children: Carolyn Jeanne, David Wiley, Gary Eugene. BA cum laude, U. Ark., 1931; MA, U. Colo., 1934; EdD, Columbia U., 1941; LLD, Hendrix Coll., 1965. High sch. tchr. Williford (Ark.) Consol. Schs., 1931-32, supt., 1932-35; supt. schs., Lepanto, Ark., 1935-41; assoc. prof. Sch. Adminstrn. Ala. Poly. Inst., 1941-43, research prof. edn., 1946-47, acting dir. div. instrn., 1947-49, exec. v.p., 1949-60; pres. U. Ark., 1960-74, pres. emeritus, prof. higher edn., 1974-77; mem. Nat. Commn. on Accrediting, 1960-63; adv. com. Inst. Internat. Edn.; mem. So. regional panel for selection White House Fellows; vice chmn. So. Regional Edn. Bd. Served as lt. USNR, 1943-46. Mem. Internat. Assn. Univ. Presidents, Land Grant Assn. (former chmn. com. radio and TV), Ala. (pres. 1955-56), Ark. edn. assns., Nat. Planning Assn., NEA, Am. Assn. Sch. Adminstrs., Ark. C. of C. (bd. dirs. 1960-63), Nat. (pres. 1971-72, chmn. legislative com. 1968-70, exec. com. 1972-73), So.

(pres. 1962-63) assns. state univs. and land grant colls., So. Univ. Conf. (pres. 1968-69), Am. Council on Edn. (former dir., mem. commn. on fed. relations), Rotary (dist. gov. 1950-51), Phi Beta Kappa, Phi Kappa Phi, Phi Delta Kappa, Omicron Delta Kappa, Phi Eta Sigma, Kappa Delta Pi, Pi Mu Epsilon, Phi Alpha Theta, Alpha Kappa Psi. Democrat. Home: Fayetteville Ark. Died Sept. 22, 1987.

MULTER, ABRAHAM J., justice; b. N.Y.C., Dec. 24, 1900; s. Max and Emma (Rock) M.; m. Bertha Leff, June 14, 1925; children: Robert K., Howard C. Student night classes, CCNY; LLB, Bklyn. Law Sch., 1921, LLM, 1922; LLD, Yeshiva U., 1965. Gen. practice law 1923-86; spl. asst. atty. gen. N.Y. State; counsel, Dem. leader State Assembly; spl. counsel mayor City N.Y.; vice chmn. N.Y. State Dem. Law Com.; exec. com. N.Y. State Dem. Com.; practiced law with Congressman Leo F. Rayfiel, firm of Rayfiel and Multer, to 1947; sr. mem. firm Multer, Nova & Seymour, N.Y.C., to 1967; mem. 80th-82d Congresses, 14th N.Y. Dist., 83-90th Congresses, 13th N.Y. Dist.; justice Supreme Ct. N.Y. State, 1967-77, dir. Supreme Ct. Intern Program. Mem. pres.'s council Yeshiva U.; vice chmn. Albert Einstein Med. Coll. Com.; chmn. lawyers com. Jewish Nat. Fund; chmn. nat council Am. Israel Friendship League; hon. pres. Bklyn. Jewish Community Council, B'nai Zion, Temple Beth Emeth; adv. bd. East Midwood Jewish Ctr.; bd. dirs. Nottingham Civic Assn., YM and YWHA; trustee Union Am. Hebrew Congregations. Served with USCGR. Mem. Conf. Pres.'s of Maj. Am. Jewish Orgns., Inter-Am., Bklyn. bar assns., N.Y. Law Inst., Fed. Bar Assn., ABA, Am. Soc. Internat. Law, Am. Judicature Soc., Am. Zionist Fedn., Jewish Chatauqua Soc., Police Athletic League, N.Y. Vet. Police Assn., Internat. Assn. Jewish Judges and Lawyers, Former Mems. Congress Assn., Bklyn. Law Sch. Alumni Assn. (former pres., dir.), Assn. Supreme Ct. Justices (former dir.), Elks, Masons, K.P., B'nai B'rith, Richmond County Country Club. Home: Brooklyn N.Y. Died Nov. 4, 1986.

MUMAW, LLOYD GERBER, steel company executive; b. Canton, Ohio, June 1, 1895; s. Aaron and Margaret Anne (Gerber) M.; m. Anne Elizabeth Chamberlain, Nov. 16, 1929; children: Barbara Anne Mumaw Sullivan. C.E., U. Cin., 1921. With Elec. Power Co., Mt. Eaton, Ohio, 1920-21; mgr. Charlotte (N.C.) Office So. G-F Co., 1922-33; with Easterby & Mumaw, Inc., Charlotte, 1933-60; office mgr., cons. Fla. Steel Corp., Charlotte, 1960-81, chmn. exec. com., chmn. bd. dirs., 1960-83. Bd. mgrs. Thompson Episc. Orphanage. Served with U.S. Army, 1917-19. Republican. Clubs: Myers Park Country, Charlotte City. Lodges: Rotary, Masons, Shriners. Home: Charlotte N.C. Died July 6, 1983.

MUMFORD, WILLIAM WALDEN, SR., electronics consultant; b. Vancouver, Wash., June 17, 1905; s. Edgar Manley and Carrie Lucretia (Royal) M.; m. Elizabeth Neal Douglass, Feb. 20, 1931; children: William Walden, Joan (Mrs. Lloyd S. Sturtz). AB, Wilamette U., 1930. Registered profl. engr., N.J. Mem. tech. staff Bell Telephone Labs., Holmdel, N.J., 1930-53, Whippany N.J., 1953-70; cons. microwave radiation safety, microwave techniques 1970-85; adj. assoc. prof. environ. medicine NYU Med. Ctr., 1971-85; Mackay vis. prof. elec. engring. U. Calif. Berkeley, 1955; Ford Found. vis. prof. elec. engring. U. Wis., 1962; mem. electromagnetic radiation mgmt. adv. council Nat. Telecommunications and Info. Adminstrn., 1969-85. Author: (with E.H. Scheibe) Noise Performance Factors in Communication Systems, 1968, (with Bell Labs. tech. staff) Radar Systems and Components, 1949; contbr. numerous tech. articles to profl. jours.; patentee in field. Recipient Alumni citation Wilamette U., 1968; named Engr. of Distinction-Engring. Joint Council, 1969. Fellow IEEE; life mem. Soc. Microwave Theory and Techniques (adminstrv. com. 1952-85, Morris E. Leeds award 1966, Microwave Career award 1974); mem. Internat. Sci. Radio Union, Internat. Microwave Power Inst., Am. Nat. Standards Inst., Am. Radio Relay League, Telephone Pioneers (life), Quarter Century Wireless Assn. (life), Soc. Wireless Pioneers (profl. life), N.Y. Acad. Sci., Brass Pounders League. Republican. Methodist. Clubs: Rag Chewers, Old Old Timers (life), Mt. Diablo. Home: Morris Plains N.J. Died June 19, 1985; buried Somerset Hills, Basking Ridge, N.J.

MUNGER, PAUL FRANCIS, educator; b. Perrysburg, Ohio, Oct. 26, 1915; s. George John and Mary (Rossbach) M.; m. Arlene Lorraine mcFillen, May 7, 1942; children: Paul David, Peter George. BA, Ohio State U., 1938, MA, 1940; PhD, U. Mich., 1954. Counselor, then dir. counseling VA Ctrs. in Cleve. and Toledo, 1946-48, 53-57; asst. prof. psychology U. Toledo, 1948-53; mem. faculty U. N.D., 1957-63, prof. counseling and guidance, 1962-63; prof. counseling and guidance Ind. U., 1963-86, chmn. dept., 1963-71; cons. to govt., 1961-86. Author: (with others) Counseling and Guidance for Underachieving Fourth Grade Students, 1964, Guiding Human Growth, 1971; also articles; editor: Upgrading Guidance Practices, 1968. Served to 1st lt. USAAF, 1942-46. Mem. Am. Psychol. Assn. (fellow div. 17), Assn. Counselor Edn. and Supervision (pres. 1967-68), Am. Personnel and Guidance Assn. Home: Bloomington Ind. Died Dec. 3, 1986.

MUNN, JOHN CALVIN, marine corps officer; b. Prescott, Ark., Oct. 17, 1906; s. John Calvin and Cora (Hitt) M.; m. Ben Alice Day, Jan. 6, 1955. Commd. 2d lt. USMC, advanced through grades to lt. gen., asst. comdt.; comdg. gen. marine corps base Camp Pendleton, Calif., 1963-64; ret. 1964; v.p. Oceanside Nat. Bank (Calif.), from 1964. Decorate Silver Star, Legion of Merit (2). Died Apr. 20, 1986.

MUNN, ROBERT FERGUSON, librarian; b. Seattle, July 17, 1923; s. Ralph and Anne (Shepard) M. AB, Oberlin Coll., 1949; MA, U. Chgo., 1950; PhD, U. Mich., 1961. Rsch. asst. U. chgo., 1949-50; reference asst. Pa. State U., 1950-52; chief reference librarian W.Va. U., Morgantown, 1952-53, asst. librarian, 1953-56, librarian, 1956-59, dir. librs., 1959-76, dean libr. services, 1976-86, asst. provost, 1965-68, provost, 1968-71. Author: Coal Industry in America, 1977; contbr. articles to profl. jours. Mem. ALA, W.Va. Libr. Assn. Home: Morgantown W.Va. Died Mar. 13, 1986.

MUNSON, THOMAS LEWIS, lawyer; b. Friendship, N.Y., May 28, 1915; s. Frederick Ten Eyck and Floy (Tefft) M.; m. Barbara Talcott, Dec. 27, 1941; children: Thomas T., Kathryn T., Munson Nickle, David W., James R. BA, Duke U., 1936; JD, U. Mich., 1939. Bar: Mich. 1939. Practiced in Detroi; ptnr. Dykema, Gossett, Spencer, Goodnow & Trigg, 1951-83. Pres. Grosse Pointe War Meml. Assn., 1962. Served to maj. AUS, 1941-46, ETO. Mem. ABA (ho. of dels. 1966-71), Mich. Bar Assn., Detroit Bar Assn. (pres. 1966-67), Am. Judicature Soc., Thomas M. Cooley Club. Republican. Methodist. Home: Grosse Pointe Farms Mich. Died Sept. 17, 1983; buried Livingston, Mont.

MUNVES, WILLIAM, lawyer; b. Mt. Vernon, N.Y., Oct. 3, 1911; s. Sol and Bertha (Bakwin) M.; m. June Stella Kay, Nov. 7, 1942; children: Douglas Robert, Beverly Sue. BA, CCNY, 1932; JD, NYU, 1936; LLM, George Washington U., 1950. Bar: N.Y. 1936, D.C. 1972, U.S. Supreme Ct. 1972. Pvt. practice N.Y.C., 1939-42; atty., adviser Dept. Army, 1946-50; asst. gen. counsel Dept. Air Force, 1954-66, dep. gen. counsel, 1966-72; pvt. practice Washington, 1972-83; counsel Wilner & Scheiner, Washington, 1972-73, Chadbourne, Parke, Whiteside & Wolff, 1973-80; lectr. to assns., schs., symposiums; mem. Commn. on Govt. Procurement Study Program, 1971-72. Contbr. articles to profl. jours. With inf. AUS, 1942-45. Decorated Bronze Star; recipient Exceptional Civilian Svc. award Dept. Air Force, 1965, 72. Mem. ABA (chmn. R&D com. 1975-76, chmn. patents, tech. data and copyrights com. pub. contracts sect. 1976-77, code coord. model procurement code project for state and local govts. 1976-83), Fed. Bar Assn. (dep. chmn. govt. contracts com. for nat. programs 1973-74, vice chmn. 1972-73), Nat. Contract Mgmt. Assn., Theta Sigma Lambda. Home: Boca Raton Fla. Died Nov. 3, 1983.

MURCHISON, CHARLES HOLTON, lawyer; b. Greensboro, N.C., Jan. 13, 1899; s. John Colin and Lillian Louis (McDonald) M.; m. Helen Wadsworth Spratt, Oct. 15, 1921 (dec. Sept. 1982); children—Helen Spratt Murchison Lane, Margaret W. Murchison Corse; m. Althea M. Gould, June 15, 1985. A.B., U. Mich., 1921; LL.B., Harvard U., 1924. Bar: Fla. 1924. Ptnr. Stockton, Ulmer & Murchison, 1926-54, Adair, Ulmer, Murchison, Kent & Ashby, Washington, 1954-61, Ulmer, Murchison, Ashby, Taylor & Corrigan, Jacksonville, Fla., 1962-87; Chmn. exec. com., dir. Capital Airlines, Inc., 1947-61, vice chmn. bd., 1960-61, gen. counsel, 1944-61; chmn. tax amortization bd. War Dept., 1941; expert cons. to sec. war, 1941-46; regional dir. 4th Region Office Civilian Def., 1942-43. Pres. Traveler's Aid Soc., Jacksonville, 1926-39; chmn. Duval County Welfare Bd., 1932-37; mem. exec. com., bd. dirs. Community Chest, 1925-39; bd. overseers Sweet Briar Coll., 1948-64, Jacksonville Downtown Devel. Authority, 1972-80. Served with U.S. Army, 1918. Mem. ABA, Jacksonville, Fla. bar assns., Am. Judicature Soc., Am. Law Inst. (life), Nat. Symphony Orch. Assn. Washington (bd. dirs. 1954-60), Delta Kappa Epsilon. Democrat. Baptist. Clubs: Seminole, Florida Yacht, Timuquana Country, Ponte Vedra (Jacksonville); Burning Tree, Metropolitan, Chevy Chase (Washington). Home: Jacksonville Fla. Died Nov. 13, 1987, buried Evergreen Cemetery, Jacksonville.

MURCHISON, CLINTON W., JR., professional football team executive, businessman. Founded Dallas Cowboys, 1960, owner, until 1984. Home: Dallas Tex. Died Mar. 30, 1987; buried Hillcrest Meml. Park, Dallas.

MURDOCH, DONALD R., lawyer, pharmaceutical company executive; b. Chgo., May 29, 1942; s. Stuart M. and Olive K. Murdoch; m. Ellen Press, Aug. 14, 1971; 1 child, Catherine London. BA, U. Wis., Madison, 1964, JD, 1968. Bar: Wis. 1968, Pa. 1968. Spl. counsel to dir. OEO, Washington, 1969; spl. counsel to Pres. White House, Washington, 1969-71; dep. dir. bur. domestic commerce U.S. Dept. Commerce, Washington, 1971-72; asst. dir. Cost of Living Coun. for Program Devel., 1972-73; ptnr. firm DeWitt, Sundby, Huggett, Schumacher & Morgan, Madison, Wis., 1973-82; sr. v.p., gen. counsel G.D. Searle & Co., Skokie, Ill., 1982-88; cons. to White House, Washington, 1974-75; cons. to sec. def., Washington, 1981. Mem. adv. bd. Wis. Clin. Cancer Ctr., Madison, 1984-89; alderman common coun. City of Madison, 1975-77. Mem. ABA, State Bar Assn. Wis., Def. Adv. Com. on Women in Svc. Republican. Home: Evanston Ill. Died Feb. 22, 1989.

MURPHY, ARTHUR RICHARD, JR., publishing company executive; b. Boston, Aug. 26, 1915; s. Arthur Richard and Ann (Graham) M.; m. Gertrude Elliot, Mar. 31, 1940 (div. 1969); children: Arthur Richard III, Pamela G.; m. Hermine Pooré, Sept. 1, 1972. BS, Boston U., 1937. With Time Inc., N.Y.C., 1937-65, successively as bus. mgr. Fortune, gen. mgr. Life., pub. Sports Illus.; v.p., dir. prodn. McCall Corp., N.Y.C., 1965, pres., 1965-69, chmn. exec. com., 1967, former v.p. parent co.; pres. Curtis Pub. Co. Former trustee Boston U. Served with USAAF, 1943-46. Mem. Mag. Pubs. Assn. (former dir.). Died Aug. 29, 1987.

MURPHY, GEORGE EDWARD, pathologist, educator; b. Kansas City, Mo., Aug. 22, 1918; s. Franklin Edward and Cordelia (Brown) M.; m. Annette Forbes Cross, June 12, 1943. A.B., U. Kans., 1939; M.D., U. Pa., 1943. Intern U. Kans. Med. Center, 1943; asst. resident, resident in pathology Johns Hopkins Hosp., 1944-45; asst. pathologist Johns Hopkins Med. Sch., 1944-45; asst. physician Hosp. of Rockefeller Inst. for Med. Research, 1946-53; asso. prof. pathology Cornell U. Med. Coll., N.Y.C., 1954-68; prof. pathology Cornell U. Med. Coll., 1968-87; asst. attending pathologist N.Y. Hosp., 1954-60, asso. attending pathologist, 1961-67, attending pathologist, 1968-87. Contbr. exptl. and histologic studies on the nature of rheumatic fever, rheumatic heart disease, glomerulonephritis and arteriosclerosis. Chmn. bd. dirs. Asphalt Green Youth Center (Comprising George and Annette Murphy Ctr. for Sports and Arts and Fireboat House Environ. Ctr.), N.Y.C., 1974-87; bd. dirs. Cross Found., Burden Center for the Aging, N.Y.C., 1975-87. Served as lt. (j.g.), M.C. USNR, 1945-46. Recipient William Osler medal Am. Assn. Hist. Medicine, 1943; Lederle Med. Faculty award, 1954-57; Golden Doughnut award Salvation Army, 1974; award of distinction East Side Assn. N.Y.C., 1978; Citizen of Yr. award East Mid-Manhattan C. of C., 1982; Am. Legion N.Y. County Community Service award, 1984; Presdl. Pvt. Sector Initiative award, 1984; Mcpl. Art Soc. of N.Y. award, 1985; Jefferson award Am. Inst. for Pub. Service, 1986; 1st Ann. Leadership award Doctors Hosp., 1986; Pres.'s Citizenship award Med. Soc. State of N.Y., 1986; Fellow Life Ins. Med. Research Fund, 1946-49; Helen Hay Whitney Found. fellow, 1949-53. Mem. N.Y. Acad. Scis., N.Y. Acad. Medicine, Harvey Soc., Am. Assn. Pathologists, Am. Heart Assn. (council cardiovascular disease in young, council arteriosclerosis), Am. Rheumatism Assn., Sigma Xi, Beta Theta Pi, Nu Sigma Nu. Club: Century Assn. Home: New York N.Y. Died July 14, 1987, buried Kansas City, Mo.

MURPHY, JAMES EDWARD, state judge; b. Bridgeport, Conn., Aug. 13, 1896; s. Timothy J. and Catherine (Crowley) M.; m. Marion Josephine Hayes, May 31, 1927; children: James Timothy, Jerome Emmett. LLB, U. Notre Dame, 1922. Reporter Bridgeport Standard and Farmer, 1915-16; admitted to Conn. bar 1923; practiced in Bridgeport as mem. firm Delahaney, Murphy & Kotler, 1923-41; exec. sec. Gov. Robert A. Hurley, 1941-42; judge Superior Ct., 1942-57; assoc. justice Conn. Supreme Ct., 1957-66. Served as capt. U.S. Army, 1917-19. Mem. ABA, Am. Legion, VFW (past dept. judge adv. and post comdr.), Cath. War Vets., Cath. Charitable Bur. (past pres.), Elks, K.C. (past grand knight). Home: Bridgeport Conn. Died May 12, 1986.

MURPHY, JAMES PATRICK, engineer; b. Sanborn, N.D., Aug. 18, 1914; s. Willie and Anna Bertha (Riedman) M.; m. Blanche Rose, Oct. 30, 1936; 1 dau., Michelle Murphy Suggs; 1 stepson, Larry Spiller. B.S. in Civil Engring., U. N.D., 1937. Jr. engr. Chgo. Surface Lines, 1937-40; asso. engr. C.E. 1940-44; sr. asst. traffic engr. City of Detroit, 1944-45; co-founder, prin. Crawford, Murphy & Tilly, Inc. (Cons. Engrs.), Springfield, Ill., 1946-79; town engr. Town of Surprise (Ariz.), from 1981. Bd. dirs. Springfield (Ill.) Coll., 1976-79; mem. Recreation Adv. Bd. Sun City West (Ariz.), 1980-84; chmn. bd. Springfield Met. Expn. and Auditorium Authority, 1965-74. Mem. Ill. Soc. Profl. Engrs. (hon. past pres.), Ill. Registered Land Surveyors Assn., ASCE (life), Am. Cons. Engrs. Council (life), Inst. Transp. Engrs., Am. Public Works Assn. (life, past pres. Ill. chpt.), Nat. Soc. Profl. Engrs. Republican. Methodist. Club: Briarwood Country. Lodge: Elks (life). Home: Sun City West Ariz. Deceased.

MURPHY, JAMES RUSSELL, lawyer; b. Piedmont, Mo., Jan. 8, 1905; s. Leslie Wayne and Cora (Stevens) M.; m. Doris Thrift Haines, Nov. 15, 1930; children: Doris Jean (Mrs. Kingston Lee Howard), James Russell II. J.D., George Washington U., 1931. Bar: D.C. 1931, Va. 1933. Gen. practice law D.C., 1931-86; mem. firm Cross, Murphy & Smith, Washington, 1951-86; gen. counsel Nat. Milk Producers Fedn., Washington; Staff Coordinator of Information and OSS, 1941-46. Decorated Medal of Merit, Medal of Freedom U.S.; Legion of Honor; Croix de Guerre France; War Cross; Merito Di Guerra Italy). Mem. Am., D.C., Va. bar assns., Phi Delta Phi, Phi Sigma Kappa. Clubs:

Lawyers (Washington), Barristers (Washington); Washington Golf and Country (pres. 1958-59 Arlington). Home: Arlington Va. Died Oct. 7, 1986.

MURPHY, JOHN DAMIAN, naval officer, lawyer; b. Newton, Kans., Aug. 19, 1896; s. John Daniel and Honora (Burns) M.; m. Dorothy Regina Mannion, Dec. 13, 1930; children—Joan Dorothy, Honora Ann, John Damien, Dennis. Student, U. Kans., 1915-18; J.D., George Washington U., 1929; grad., Joint Army-Navy Staff Coll., 1945; B.S., Am. U., 1955. Bar: bars D.C, U.S. Supreme Ct. Enlisted apprentice seaman USNR, 1918, commd. ensign, 1919; commd. ensign USN, 1922, advanced through grades to rear adm.; served in USS Denver, 1919-22; student Torpedo Sch. USN, Newport, R.I., 1922-23; served on USS Beaver USN, 1923-25, USS Pa., 1925-27; with Navy Dept. and George Washington Law Sch., 1927-30; served on USS Wyo. 1930; aide, legal officer to comdt. 16th Naval Dist., Cavite, P.I., 1931-32; exec. officer USS Mindanao, Asiatic sta., 1932-33; with Navy Dept., U.S. Army Chem. Warfare Sch., 1933-36; aide, flag sec. to Rear Adm. Edward B. Fenner, 1936-37, Rear Adm. David Worth Bagley, 1937-38; comdr. USS Sicard, 1938-39; chief of divs. Office Judge Adv. Gen., 1939-42; comdr. USS Alcor, fleet repair and flagship, 1942-44, Joint Army Navy Units and Marine Corps Air groups; recapture Joint Army Navy Units and Marine Corps Air groups, Sulu Archipelago, 1945; planning officer 7th Amphibious Force Philippines, Korea, China, 1945; legal officer staffs fleet Adm. Chester W. Nimitz, comdr.-in-chief Pacific, U.S. Pacific Fleet and Vice Adm. George D. Murray, comdr. Marianas Area, 1945; naval aide Justice Frank Murphy, spl. U.S. rep. to Philippine Republic, 1946; dir. War Crimes, U.S. Pacific Fleet, 1946-49. Enlisted as apprentice seaman USNR, 1918; commd. ensign 1919; commd. ensign USN, 1922. Decorated Legion of Merit, Bronze Star medal (combat); Commendation ribbon; Am. Def. medal; Am. Area; Asiatic Pacific Area (3 stars); Philippine Liberation medal (2 stars); World War II Victory medal. Mem. Ret. Officers Assn. (comptroller, dir. 1950-68), U.S. Naval Acad. Alumni Assn. (asso.), Phi Kappa Theta, Delta Theta Phi. Roman Catholic. Club: Army-Navy Country (Washington). Home: Arlington Va. Deceased.

MURPHY, JOSEPH HAWLEY, lawyer; b. Syracuse, N.Y., Nov. 24, 1916; s. Joseph B. and Ruth M. M.; m. Helen E. McGuire, Jan. 25, 1947; children: Anne W., Joseph Hawley, Robert J., Sarah B., Nelson A. A.B., Syracuse U., 1937, M.A., 1939, LL.D., 1940; LL.D. (hon.), St. Johns U., 1976. Bar: N.Y. 1940, U.S. Dist. Ct. 1940, U.S. Supreme Ct. 1947. Atty. Dept. Treasury, 1940-44; asso. Murphy & Young, Syracuse, 1946-55; asst. atty. gen. State N.Y., 1955-56; ptnr. Hancock, Estabrook, Ryan, Shove & Hust, Syracuse, from 1946; commr. taxation and fin. N.Y. State, 1959-69; adj. prof. law Syracuse U., 1946-81. Author: Murphy's Will Clauses; editor N.Y. Tax Service; contbr. articles to legal jours. Trustee St. John's U.; regent Le Moyne Coll., 1976-84. Served with USNR, 1944-46. Recipient George Arents Pioneer medal Syracuse U., 1967, Disting. Service award Syracuse U. Coll. Law, 1973. Mem. ABA, N.Y. State Bar Assn. (pres. 1975-76, ho. of dels.), Onondaga Bar Assn., Albany Bar Assn., Fed. Bar Assn., Am. Law Inst. Republican. Roman Catholic. Home: Fayetteville N.Y. Deceased.

MURPHY, TURK (MELVIN EDWARD MURPHY), trombonist; b. Palermo, Calif., Dec. 16, 1915; s. Alton E. and Mildred G. (Pickering) M.; m. Geraldine Chick, Aug. 7, 1955 (div. Mar. 1959); m. 2d, Harriet Hafner, Apr. 7, 1960; 1 child, Carson Edward. Profl. trombonist, traveling with numerous mus. orgns. since 1933. An organizer Lu Watters Yerba Buena group, San Francisco, 1939; formed own group, known as Turk Murphy Jazz Band, 1948; arranger Turk Murphy Series for E.B. Marks Music Corp., N.Y.C., 1956; recorded for Columbia, Good Time Jazz, Verve, Roulette, RCA Victor, others; part owner McGoon's nightclub, San Francisco; music for pub. service film Nothing to Sneeze At. Served with USNR, WWII. Mem. ASCAP. Author introduction to Heart of Jazz, 1955; also articles on Am. jazz. Home: San Francisco Calif. Died May 30, 1987.

MURPHY, WILLIAM PARRY, physician; b. Stoughton, Wis., Feb. 6, 1892; s. Thomas Francis and Rose Anna (Parry) M.; m. Harriet Adams, Sept. 10, 1919; children—Priscilla Adams (dec.), William Parry. A.B., U. Oreg., 1914; M.D., Harvard, 1920; D.Sc., Gustavus Adolphus Coll., 1963. Diplomate: Am. Bd. Internal Medicine. Intern R.I. Hosp., Providence, 1920-22; asst. resident physician Peter Bent Bringham Hosp., Boston, 1922-23; jr. asso. Peter Bent Bringham Hosp., 1923-28, asso. in medicine, 1928-35, sr. asso., 1935-58, cons. hematology, 1958—; asst. in medicine Harvard, 1923-28, instr. medicine, 1928-35, asso. in medicine, 1935-48, lectr. medicine, 1948-58, lectr. emeritus, 1958—; pvt. practice medicine Brookline, 1923—; cons. internal medicine Melrose, Quincy hosps., Emerson Hosp., Concord, all Mass.; Del. State Hosp., Franhurst. Author: Anemia in Practice Pernicious Anemia, 1939; Contbr. sci. articles to med. jours., numerous papers. Dir. Cordis Corp. Served with M.C. U.S. Army, 1917-18. Recipient Cameron prize, 1930; Nobel prize in Medicine, 1934; comdr. Order of White Rose 1st rank Finland, 1934; gold medal Humane Soc. State Mass., 1935; Distinguished Achievement award City of Boston, 1965; Nat. Order of Merit Carlos J. Finlay, Cuba; Internat. Bicentennial Symposium award, 1972; Gold badge Mass. Med. Soc., 1973; 50-Year Service award Peter Bent Brigham Hosp., 1975. Mem. U. Oreg. Med. Alumni Assn. (hon.), AMA (Bronze medal for sci. exhibit 1934), Am. Soc. Clin. Investigation, Assn. Am. Physicians, AAAS, Internat. Soc. for Research on Civilization Diseases and Vital Substances (hon.), N.Y. Acad. Scis., Soc. Finnish Physicians for Internal Diseases (hon.), Nat. Inst. Social Scis., Kaiserlich Leopold Caroline deutsche Acad. der. Naturforscher, Sigma Xi, Alpha Kappa Kappa; hon. mem. Robert K. Duncan Club of Mellon Inst. Republican. Congregationalist. Clubs: Harvard, Aesculapian, Rotary (Paul Harris fellow award 1980). Died Oct. 9, 1987.

MURRAY, C. EDWARD, JR., manufacturing executive; b. Trenton, N.J., May 7, 1891; s. C. Edward and Floy (Cornell) M.; m. Louise Morrison, May 21, 1914 (dec. Aug. 1959); children: Louise Murray Harper, Helen Murray Dougherty, Gail Murray Putziger. Student, Mercersburg Acad., Cornell U., 1910-12. With Crescent Insulated Wire & Cable Co., Inc., 1914-66, v.p., 1930-43, pres., 1943-66. Home: Morrisville Pa. †

MURRAY, HARRY A., department store chain executive; b. Asbury Park, N.J.; m. Peggie Jo; children: Patricia Ann Sparrer, Peter. Student, NYU. With Lord & Taylor, N.Y.C., 1948-75, pres., 1972-75. Served with USN, WWII. Home: Spring Lake N.J. also: Longboat Key Fla. Died Sept. 17, 1985.

MURRAY, HOWARD LENFORD, manufacturing executive; b. Phila., Jan. 21, 1892; s. Ralph L. and Laura G. (Compton) M.; m. Catharine C. Cox, Jan. 4, 1927; children: Donald L., Kenneth S., Craig G. Student, U. Pa., 1910-14. With H. Belfield Co., Phila., 1914-25, sec., 1925-33, pres., 1933-49; merged with Mpls. Honeywell Regulator Corp., 1949, v.p., pres. valve div., from 1949; bd. dirs. Liquidating Co., Enterprising Mfg. Cos. Silex Corp. Mem. Old Guard Soc., Union League, Merion Golf Club, Everglades Golf Club, Pine Valley Club, Eastward Ho Country Club, Palm Beach Golfers Club, Rotary. Home: Villanova Pa. †

MURRAY, HUGH VINCENT, lawyer, banker; b. Carlyle, Ill., Jan. 19, 1908; s. Hugh Vincent and Mary Ellen (Hogan) M.; m. Jane Hassett, Oct. 30, 1940 (dec.); children: Hugh Vincent III, John H., Elizabeth A., Mark Hilary, Nicholas F.S.; m. Rosalind Cummings, May 27, 1967. AB, Holy Cross Coll., 1929; LLB, Harvard U., 1932. Bar: Ill. 1932. Practiced in Centralia, Ill.; chmn., pres. Old Nat. Bank, Centralia, 1959-80. Former trustee St. Mary's Hosp., Centralia Found. Served to lt. USNR, 1944-46. Fellow Am. Coll. Trial Lawyers; life mem. Am. Law Inst. Clubs: Palma Ceia Golf and Country (Tampa), Univ. Mo. Athletic (St. Louis), University (St. Louis). Home: Centralia Ill. Died Oct. 4, 1984; buried Cath. Cemetery, Carlyle, Ill.

MURRAY, PETER MARSHALL, gynecologist; b. Houma, La., June 9, 1888; s. John and Louvinia (Smith) M.; m. Charlotte Wallace, July 2, 1917; 1 child, John Wallace. AB, New Orleans U., 1910, DSc (hon.), 1935; MD, Howard U., 1914; DSc (hon.), Lincoln U., 1944; postgrad., N.Y. Post Grad. Sch. and Hosp., Columbia U., NYU, Bellevue Med. Sch. Diplomate Am. Bd. Ob-Gyn. Intern Freedmen's Hosp., Washington, 1914-15, asst. surgeon in chief, 1918-20; asst. to dean and prof. surgery Howard U. Med. Sch., 1915, clin. instr. surgery, 1915-20; med. insp. pub. schs. Washington, 1917-18; cons. gynecologist Harlem Hosp.; dir. ob-gyn Sydenham Hosp.; courtesy surgeon St. Clare's Hosp., N.Y.C. Contbr. articles to profl. jours. Trustee Howard U., SUNY. Fellow ACS, Internat. Coll. Surgeons; mem. AMA (ho. of dels.), Nat. Med. Assn. (pres. 1930-31), N.Y. Acad. Med., N.Y. County Med. Soc. (pres. 1954-55), Alpha Omega Alpha. Democrat. Methodist. Home: New York N.Y. †

MURRAY, ROBERT LINDLEY, chemical manufacturing executive; b. San Francisco, Nov. 3, 1892; s. Augustus T. and Nella (Howland) M.; m. Ramona McKendry, May 9, 1916 (dec. 1951); children: Robert Lindley, Augustus T.; m. Gertrude Wright Porter, Sept. 23, 1953. Grad. in ChemE, Stanford U., 1913, grad. in CE, 1914. Draftsman Western Sugar Refinery, San Francisco, 1914-15; chemist, asst. supt. Pacific Coast Borax Co., Alameda (Calif.) and Bayonne (N.J.), 1915-16; with Hooker Chem. Corp., Niagara Falls, N.Y., in charge sulphuric/nitric plants, 1918, supt., 1920-32, chief engr., 1932-36, dir. devel., 1937-40, v.p. charge devel. and rsch., 1941-49, exec. v.p., 1949-51, pres., 1951-55, chmn., chief exec. officer, 1955-58, chmn., from 1958, also bd. dirs.; pres., bd. dirs. Marble Nye Co., Inc.; tech. cons. C.W.S., Germany, 1945; bd. dirs. Marine Midland Corp. Univ. nat. tennis champion, 1917-18. Mem. AAAS, Am. Arbitration Assn. (panel arbitrators), Am. Chem. Soc., Am. Inst. Chem. Engrs. (bd. dirs. 1940-43), Soc. Chem. Industry, Elctrochem. Soc., Chem. Corps Assn., Niagara Club, Niagara Falls Country Club, Buffalo Tennis and Squash, Internat. Lawn Tennis Club, Chemist Club, Phi Beta Kappa, Sigma Xi, Kappa Alpha. Republican. Mem. Soc. of Friends. Home: Lewiston N.Y. †

MURRAY, WILLIAM HALLAM GILLIS, consulting engineer; b. Nutley, N.J., Sept. 15, 1891; s. David and Carol B. (Gillis) M.; m. Elisabeth Morss, June 29, 1918; children: Hallam Gillis, Dwight Morss, Kenneth Adams. ME, Cornell U., 1916. V.p. Smith-Murray Corp., 1925-35, pres., 1935-50; mgr. N.Y. region Johns-Manville Sales Corp., Syracuse, N.Y., 1953-55; cons. engr. from 1956; bd. dirs. Carrier Corp., Marine Midland Trust Co. of Cen. N.Y. Dir. Boys Club. Lt. U.S. Army, 1917-18. Mem. ASME, Nat. Soc. Profl. Engrs., Lake Placid Club (N.Y.C.), Century Club (Syracuse), Delta Kappa Epsilon. Home: Syracuse N.Y. †

MURREY, ENNIS E., mortgage banker; b. Caney Springs, Tenn., Mar. 2, 1883; s. James McCutcheon and Betty Gibson (Woodall) M.; m. Daisy Houston, Oct. 24, 1906; children: Dora Houston Murrey McBride, Catherine E. Murrey Daniel, Ennis E. Ed., Chapel Hill Prep. Sch. Salesman for clothing co. Ga., 1905-09; owner, operator clothing store Lewisburg, Tenn., 1905-16; organizer, exec. v.p. Union Bank and Trust Co., Lewisburg, 1916; rep. Fed. Land Bank of Ky., 1917; v.p. Am. Trust Co. and Nashville Trust Co., 1922-23; organizer, then pres. First Mortgage Co. of Nashville, from 1935; pres. Ga. Properties Co., Atlanta, Charles Loridans Bldg. Corp, Nashville,; bd. dirs. Hermitage Hotel, Am. Nat. Bank, Nashville. Trustee Scarritt Coll. for Christian Workers, Nashville; bd. dirs. YMCA, Boy Scouts Am.; col. on staff Gov. Tenn. Mem. Tenn. Banks Assn., Mortgage Bankers Assn. Am. (pres. 1928-29), Nashville C. of C., Masons (32 deg.), Rotary. Methodist (bd. stewards). Home: Nashville Tenn. also: New York N.Y. †

MURTAGH, JOHN ANTHONY, JR., physician, educator; b. Webster, Mass., June 12, 1905; s. John and Mary (Connolly) M.; m. Eleanor Jacot, Sept. 10, 1938; children—Jane, Mary. A.B., Brown U., 1930; M.D., U. Mich., 1934; M.A., Dartmouth, 1956. Intern Rochester (N.Y.) Gen. Hosp., 1934-35; intern otolaryngology New Haven Hosp., 1935-36, asst. resident, 1936-37; instr. Yale Med. Sch., 1937-38; faculty Dartmouth Med. Sch., 1938-86, prof. otolaryngology, 1956-86; head dept. otolaryngology Hitchcock Clinic, 1938-86; cons. communications scis. study sect. NIH, 1965-86. Contbr. papers to profl. lit. Fellow A.C.S.; mem. AMA, Am. Laryngol. Assn., Am. Triological Soc., Am. Bronch Esophacological Assn., Acad. Ophthalmology and Otolaryngology, New Eng. Otol. Soc. Home: Pompano Beach Fla. Died Jan. 15, 1986.

MUSGRAVE, CHARLES ROBERT, oil executive; b. Sedan, Kans., Aug. 15, 1892; s. John William and Margaret F. (Stears) M.; m. Alice G. Barris, June 21, 1911; 1 son, Charles Robert. Student, pub. schs.; extension work in bus. adminstrn. With oper. dept. Santa Fe R.R., 1910, terminal supt., 1922; asst. traffic mgr. Phillips Petroleum Co., Bartlesville, Okla., 1922-23, traffic mgr., 1923-27, gen. traffic mgr., 1927-30, v.p. transp., 1930-1957, mem. bd. dirs. and mem. exec. com., 1942-57, petroleum cons., from 1957. Chmn. Terminal and Storage Com. Mil. Petroleum Adv. Bd., Def. Dept. Mem. Transp. Assn. Am. (dir., hon. life mem.), Am. Soc. Traffic and Transp. Inc.(founder mem.), Assoc. Traffic Clubs of Am. (hon. life mem., trustee), Midcontinental Oil Gas Assn. (hon. life), Nat. Freight Traffic Assn. (life), Twenty-five Yr. Club of Petroleum Industry, Ind. Natural Gas Assn., ABA Practitioners before ICC, C. of C. Bartlesville, Trans. Club, Tulsa Club, Traffic Club (Tulsa); Traffic Club (hon. life) (St. Louis); Traffic Club (Wichita); Frank Phillips Mens Club, Petroleum Club. Home: Bartlesvill Okla. †

MUSSEHL, FRANK EDWARD, educator; b. Jefferson, Wis., Dec. 3, 1891; s. William and Freda (Mueller) M.; m. Inez Clough, June 20, 1917. BS, U. Wis., 1915, postgrad., 1916-17. Instr. Kans. State Coll., 1915-16, U. Wis., 1916-17; prof. agr. U. Nebr., 1917-57, prof. emeritus, from 1957. Assoc. editor Poultry Sci., 1934-38; contbr. articles to profl. jours. Fellow AAAS, Poultry Sci. Assn. (bbd. dirs. 1934-36); mem. Masons (32 degree), Sigma Xi, Gamma Sigma Delta. Congregationalist. Home: Lincoln Nebr. †

MYERS, BEVERLEE ANN REARDAN, public health educator; b. Berkeley, Calif., Oct. 14, 1930; d. Harmon Huntington and Helene Anna (Ouer) Reardan; m. Duane Sigurd Myers, Jr., Sept. 20, 1952. A.B., Washington U., St. Louis, 1951; M.P.H., U. Mich., 1962. Lab. research asst. various instns. 1952-57; program dir., local chpt. exec. N.Mex. Heart Assn., 1957-61; public health adviser USPHS, HEW, Rockville, Md., 1965-67; dep. dir. div. health care services Community Health Service, Health Services and Mental Health Adminstrn., 1968-69; dep. dir. panel on effectivness Sec.'s Task Force on Medicaid and Related Programs, 1969-70; asst. adminstr. for resource devel. Health Services and Mental Health Adminstrn., 1971-72, assoc. adminstr. program planning and evaluation, 1972-73; dep. commr. for med. assistance dept. social services State of N.Y., Albany, 1973-76; vis. lectr. Sch. Public Health, U. Mich., 1976-77; counsel U.S. Senate Anti-Trust and Monopoly Subcom., 1977; mem. health advisory com. Office Tech. Assessment U.S. Congress, 1978-82; dir. Calif. State Dept. Health Sers., Sacramento, 1978-83; prof., head div. health services Sch. Pub. Health, UCLA, 1983-86; cons. Rand Corp. Author: A Guide to Medical Care Administration, Vol. I: Concepts and Principles, 1965; contbr. numerous articles to profl. jours; mem. editorial bd.: Med. Care, 1966-69, 72-73, Am. Jour. Pub. Health, 1984-86, Jour. Health, Politics, Policy and Law, 1985-86; editorial advisory bd.: Who's Who in Health Care, 1979. Bd. dirs. Alan Guttmacher Inst. Recipient Superior Service award HEW, 1969; Nat. Merit award excellence in public health practice, 1978. Fellow Am. Public Health Assn. (speaker governing council 1975-84); mem. Inst. of Medicine of Nat. Acad. Scis., Western Consortium on the Health Professions (v.p. 1984-86), Am. Public Welfare Assn., Delta Omega, Phi Kappa Phi. Home: Los Angeles Calif. Died Dec. 24, 1986.

MYERS, CHARLES MASON, educator, philosopher; b. Dowagiac, Mich., Sept. 9, 1916; s. Charles McClellan and Gertrude (Mason) M.; m. Madeline G. Detwiler, Nov. 22, 1947. BS, Western Mich. U., 1941; MA, U. Mich., 1949, PhD, 1954. Jr. instr. U. Mich., 1953-55; asst. prof. L.I. U., 1955-59; assoc. prof. No. Ill. U., De Kalb, 1959-62, head dept. philosophy, 1959-65, prof., 1959-86; vis. prof. St. Marys U., Halifax, N.S., 1968-69, U. Mich., summers 1966. Home: De Kalb Ill. Died Dec. 3, 1986; buried Grandville, Mich.

MYERS, LOUIS MCCORRY, educator; b. Jackson, Tenn., Nov. 16, 1901; s. John Caldwell and Alice O'Neil (McCorry) M.; m. Cornelia Bowden Pipes, Dec. 13, 1930; 1 child, John Martin. AB, St. Stephen's Coll., N.Y., 1925; AM, Columbia U., 1929; PhD, U. Calif., 1935. Instr. French, U. Oreg., 1929-32; instr. English, Western Wash. Coll. Edn., 1935-36, U. Idaho, 1936-37; prof., head dept. English, Ariz. State U., Tempe, 1937-57; head div. lang. and lit. Ariz. State U., 1957-62, prof. English, 1962-72, prof. emeritus, 1972-88. Author: American English, 1952; Guide to American English, 1955, 5th edit., 1972; The Roots of Modern English, 1966; Companion to the Roots of Modern English, 1973; also articles. Served to lt. col. Signal Corps, AUS, 1942-46. Decorated Legion of Merit. Mem. Phi Beta Kappa. Home: Tempe Ariz. Died Jan. 21, 1988.

MYERS, MARCEAU CHEVALIER, music educator; b. Ottawa, Ill., Oct. 9, 1929; s. St. Clair and Marcella (Chevalier) M.; m. Judith May Kleine, Dec. 23, 1954; 1 dau., Daraugh Anne. B.S., Mansfield State Coll., 1954; M. Music Edn., Pa. State U., 1957; Ed.D., Columbia U., 1972; postgrad., Ind. U., 1954-55. Tchr. instrumental music Bronxville (N.Y.) pub. schs., 1957-60; asst. prof. music Western Conn. State Coll., Danbury, 1960-70, chmn. dept. music, 1965-69; dean Conservatory Music Capital U., Columbus, Ohio, 1970-74; dean Sch. Music North Tex. State U., Denton, 1974-87, Stephen Farish interim dean sch. of music. Contbr. articles to profl. jours. Mem. adv. bd. Music Found., 1976-87; mem. adv. bd. G.B. Dealey Awards, 1981-87; chmn. Cultural Commn., Danbury, Conn., 1965-70; bd. dirs. Fort Worth Symphony. Served with USMC, 1950-52. Mem. Nat. Assn. Schs. Music, Tex. Assn. Schs. Music, Tex. Council Arts in Edn., Music Tchrs. Nat. Assn., Coll. Music Soc., ASCAP (mem. standard awards panel), Phi Mu Alpha (Orpheus award 1974), Phi Kappa Lambda. Home: Denton Tex. Died July 26, 1987.

MYERS, WILLIAM IRVING, agricultural economics educator; b. Lowman, N.Y., Dec. 18, 1891; s. George B. McLellan and Florence (Lowman) M.; m. Marguerite Troxell, May 28, 1915; children: Elizabeth, William Irving (dec.), Marian, Ruth Margaret, Madeline. Student, Elmira (N.Y.) Free Acad., 1905-08; BS, Cornell U., 1914, PhD, 1918. Instr. farm mgmt. Cornell U., 1914-18, asst. prof., 1918-20, prof. farm fin., 1920-33, 38-59, head dept. agrl. econs., 1938-43, dean Coll. Agr., 1943-59, prof. farm fin. emeritus, from 1959; dep. gov., gov. Farm Credit Adminstrn., 1933-38; former dir., dep. chmn. Fed. Res. Bank N.Y.; bd. dirs. N.Y. State Electric & Gas Corp., Insular Lumber Co., Avco Mfg. Corp., Smith-Corona, Marchant, P and C Food Markets, Inc., Am. Agriculturist Inc., Marine Midland Corp., Grand Union Co., Marine Midland Trust Co. So. N.Y., also chmn. exec. com.; trustee Mut. Life Ins. Co. N.Y.; served as officer, dir., adv. group with numerous govt. agys. relating to agrl. problems, including Pres. Com. Farm Tenancy, 1937, Pres. Famine Emergency Com., 1946, Pres. Com. Fgn. aid, 1947, Citizen's Food Com., 1947, Nat. Agrl. Adv. Commn., chmn., 1952-59; mem. internat. devel. adv. bd. Internat. Coop. Adminstrn., 1953-58. Bd. dirs. N.Y. State Assn. Crippled Children; trustee Rockefeller Found., Gen. Edn. Bd., 1941-57, Carnegie Inst., Eisenhower Exch. Fellowships, Agrl. Devel. Coun., Cultural Affairs, Elmira Coll., 1949-52, Vassar Coll., 1955-63; dir. N.Y. State Sci. and Tech. Found. Recipient Am. Agr. Service awards Am. Farm Bur. Fedn., Am. Assn. Agrl. Editors. Fellow Am. Farm Econ. Assn. (pres. 1934); mem.. Agrl. Econ. Assn. of Eng., Internat. Conf. Agrl. Economists, Cornell Club, Century Assn. (N.Y.C.), Statler Club, Rotary, Sigma Xi, Phi Kappa Phi, Kappa Delta Rho, Epsilon Sigma Phi, Alpha Zeta. Presbyterian. Home: Ithaca N.Y. †

MYLONAS, GEORGE EMMANUEL, archeologist; b. Smyrna, Asia Minor, Dec. 9, 1898; came to U.S., 1928, naturalized, 1937; s. Emmanuel Basil and Maria (Tenekides) M.; m. Lella Papazoghlou, May 2, 1925; children: Alexander (dec.), Nike Maria, Ione Doris, Daphne Irene. BA, Internat. Coll., Smyrna, 1918; PhD, U. Athens, 1927, Johns Hopkins U., 1929; LLD, Ohio State U., 1958; LHD, Ohio Wesleyan U., So. Ill. U., 1960; PhD (hon.), U. Thessaloniki, 1970; LittD, Washington U., 1971; student various Am., European and Oriental museums. Prof. Greek Internat. Coll., 1922; with Am. Sch. Classical Studies, Athens, 1923-27; dir. Night Sch. Langs., U. Athens, 1925-27, assoc. in classics, 1923-27; assoc. in classics U. Ill., 1931-33; mem. faculty Washington U., St. Louis, from 1933; prof., head dept. art and archeology Washington U., 1938-39, 40-65; Rosa May disting. prof. humanities emeritus until 1988; summer instr. several colls. and univs.; mem. or dir. excavating crews, from 1928; officer permanent council Internat. Congress of Prehistoric and Proto Hist. Scis., Oslo, Norway, from 1936; mem. mng. com. Am. Sch. Classical Studies at Athens, 1937-39, 45-88, vice chmn., 1949-59; Fulbright sr. research scholar in Greece, 1951-52, Fulbirght prof. archeology U. Athens, 1954; prof. U. Athens (by Royal decree), 1955-88; annual prof. Am. Sch. Classical Studies, Athens, 1951-52, 63-64; mem. Inst. Advanced Study, Princeton, N.J., 1968-69; vice chmn. Soc. Byzantine Studies; chmn. Com. Restoration of the Acropolis of Athens; bd. dirs. Greek War Relief Assn., from 1940. Author numerous books; those since 1955 include Mycenae, the Capital City of Agamemnon, 1956, Aghios Kosmas, 1959, Eleusis and teh Eleusinian Mysteries, 1961, Mycenae and the Mycenaean Age, 1966, Grave Circle B of Mycenae, 1972, The Cult Center of Mycenae, 1972, The West Cemetery of Eleusis, 1975, Mycenaen Religion, 1977; also books pub. in Greece.; contbr. articles to Am. and Greek publs. Decorated by King Paul of Greece for archeol. discoveries, 1955; grand comdr. Order of Phoenix (Greece); recipient 1st Aeschylean Gold medal of Eleusis, 1980; Guggenheim fellow; Ford Found. grantee, 1970-72; mem. Inst. Advanced Study, 1955-56. Hon. fellow Soc. Antiquaries (London); me. several profl. assns. and orgns., including AIA (pres. 1956-60, gold medal 1970), Am. Acad. Arts and Scis., Acad. of Athens (pres. 1980), Archeol. Soc. Athens (v.p. 1978-80, gen. sec. 1980—). Home: Athens Greece. Died Apr. 15, 1988; buried Mycenae, Argolid, Greece.

NADEL, ELI MAURICE, pathologist, educator, medical center administrator; b. Bronx, N.Y., Oct. 9, 1918; s. Joseph P. and Rae (Gross) N.; m. Ruthe Galler, June 13, 1943; children: Robert Eric, James Oliver, Amy Elizabeth. BS, Coll. City N.Y., 1937, MS, 1939; MD, L.I. Coll. Medicine, 1945. Intern Mt. Sinai Hosp., N.Y.C., 1945; commd. officer USPHS, 1946-65, ret. as med. dir.; pathologist NIH, Bethesda, Md., 1948-56; DRG project rev. officer, exec. sec. pathology, gen. medicine and hematology study sect. NIH, 1956-58, asst. dir. to assoc. dir., 1960-62, chief diagnostic research, 1962-65; chief research in pathology, hematology and lab. medicine Research Career Devel. Program, VA Cen. Office, Washington, 1965-68; clin. prof. research pathology Georgetown U. Med. Ctr., Washington, 1966-68; assoc. dean, prof. pathology St. Louis U. Sch. Medicine, 1968-72, acting chmn. dept. pathology, 1968-69, 71-72, acting chmn. dept. physiology, 1969-70, prof. community medicine, 1970-72; med. staff St. Louis U. Hosps., 1968-72, 75-81; assoc. dean, prof. pathology Med. U. S.C., Charleston, 1972-75; chief of staff VA Hosp., Charleston, 1972-75, acting dir., 1974-75; asst. v.p. for med. research, prof. pathology, cancer coordinator St. Louis U. Med. Ctr., 1975-81; cons. research services VA Hosp., St. Louis, 1975-78; cons. research service VA Cen. Office, Washington, 1968-70, Jefferson Barracks VA Hosp., 1970-72. Served to 1st lt. M.C., AUS, 1945-46. Mem. Am. Soc. Exptl. Pathology, Soc. Health and Human Values, Am. Assn. Pathology and Bacteriology, Am. Soc. Clin. Pathologists, Acad. Clin. Lab. Physicians and Scientists, Endocrine Soc., Internat. Acad. Pathology, AMA, Montgomery County Tb Assn., AAAS, AAUP, Am. Assn. Cancer Research, Am. Soc. Cytology, St. Louis Pathology Soc. (pres. 1976-78), Am. Cancer Soc. (chmn. St. Louis profl. edn. com. 1977-80), Am. Assn. Oncology Tchrs., Washington, St. Louis ethical socs., Sigma Xi. Home: Saint Louis Mo. Died Mar. 9, 1981, interred Jefferson Barracks, Mo.

NAGEL, ERNEST, philosophy educator; b. Novemesto, Czechoslovakia, Nov. 16, 1901; came to U.S., 1911; naturalized, 1919; s. Isidor and Frida (Weisz) N.; m. Edith Haggstrom, Jan. 23, 1935; children—Alexander, Sidney. B.S. in Social Studies, CUNY, 1923, L.H.D., 1972; A.M., Columbia U., 1925, Ph.D., 1931, D. Litt, 1971; L.H.D., Bard Coll., 1964; D.Sc., Brandeis U., 1965; D.Litt., Rutgers U., 1967, Case Western Res. U., 1970. Tchr. pub. schs. N.Y.C., 1923-29; instr. philosophy CUNY, N.Y.C., 1930-31; instr. Columbia U., N.Y.C., 1931-37, asst. prof., 1937-39, assoc. prof., 1939-46, prof., 1946-55, John Dewey prof. philosophy, 1955-66, Univ. prof., 1967-70, emeritus prof., 1970-85. Author: On the Logic of Measurement, Sovereign Reason, 1954, Logic Without Metaphysics, 1957, (with J.R. Newman) Godel's Proof, 1958, The Structure of Science, 1961, Teleology Revisited, 1978; author or co-author several books; contbr. to publs.; editor: Jour. Philosophy, 1940-56, Philosophy of Sci., 1956-59, Jour. Symbolic Logic, 1939-45. Guggenheim fellow, 1934-35, 50-51; fellow Ctr. Advanced Study Behavioral Scis., Stanford, Calif., 1959-60. Fellow AAAS (v.p. sect. L 1951, 73), Am. Acad. Arts and Scis., Am. Philos. Soc., Brit. Acad. (corr. fellow); mem. Assn. Symbolic Logic (pres. 1947-49), Am. Philos. Assn. (pres. eastern div. 1954), Conf. Methods Philosophy Sci. (chmn. 1946-47), N.Y. Philos. Soc., Inst. Unity Sci. (v.p.), Internat. Union Philosophy and History of Sci., Philosophy of Sci. Assn., Phi Beta Kappa. Home: New York N.Y. Died Sept. 20, 1985.

NAGEL, FRITZ ANDREW, lawyer; b. Denver, Feb. 6, 1891; s. Henry Peter and Clara (Kaub) N.; m. Josephine R. Gaylord, Nov. 17, 1919 (dec. Nov. 1973); children: Fritz Gaylord, Jerome Kaub. AB, Cornell U., 1912; LLB, Harvard, 1915. Bar: Colo. 1915. Practice law 1915-16; trust officer Am. Nat. Bank Denver, 1920-33, dir., v.p., counsel, 1933-70; mem. firm Winters & Nagel, Denver, 1933-43, Pershing, Bosworth, Dick & Dawsen, and successor firm Dawson, Nagel, Sherman & Howard, Denver, 1943-71. Mem. bd. control State Home for Children, 1952-55. Mem. Colo. N.G. Mexican Border Campaign, 1916-17; capt. F.A., U.S. Army, World War I. Mem. Am., Colo. (treas. 1954-58), Denver (pres. 1950-51) bar assns., Newcomen Soc. N.Am., Judicature Soc., University Club. Home: Denver Colo. †

NAGLE, ALEXANDER COOPER, banker; b. Westchester, N.Y., Sept. 24, 1891; s. William and Charlotte (Alexander) N.; m. Marguerite Maxwell Greer, Jan. 14, 1920; children: Alexander Cooper, William Greer, Braxton Richardson. Student pub. schs., N.Y.C. With 1st Nat. Bank N.Y., from 1907, pres., 1945-55; chmn. exec. com. 1st Nat. City Bank, 1955-56; dir. Nat. Biscuit Co. Mem. Union League, Scarsdale Golf Club (Hartsdale, N.Y.), Am. Yacht Club (Rye, N.Y.), Knickerbocker Club, Nat. Golf Links Club (Southampton, L.I.). Republican. Episcopalian. Home: Scarsdale N.Y. †

NAGLER, FRED, artist; b. West Springfield, Mass., Feb. 27, 1891; s. Frederick August and Kate (Wild) N.; m. Edith Janet Kroger, Aug. 3, 1918; 1 child, Joe John. Student, Art Students League, N.Y.C., 1914-18. Artist numerous oil paintings on religious subjects; also wood carvings; works exhibited from 1930's at Midtown Galleries, N.Y.C., also at Valleyhouse Galleries, Dallas; numerous paintings and drawings in pvt. collectsions at Cathedral of St. John the Divine, N.Y.C., So. Meth. U., Vanderbilt U., Temple U. Recipient Hallgarten prize, Altman prize, Carnegie prize (all NAD); Corcoran prize, Washington; La Mont prize Farbry prize (both Audobon Artists). Home: Dallas Tex. Died Nov. 24, 1983.

NAKIAN, REUBEN, sculptor; b. College Point, N.Y., Aug. 10, 1897. Studied with Homes Boss, A.S. Baylinson, Robert Henri Sch.; student, Art Students League, 1912; apprenticed to Paul Manship, 1917-20, also Gaston LaChaise. Instr. Newark Fine Arts and Indsl. Arts Coll., Pratt Inst. One man shows include Downtown Gallery, 1933, 35, Charles Egan Gallery, 1949, 50, 52, 63, 64, Stewart-Marean Gallery, N.Y.C., 1958, Los Angeles County Mus. Art, 1962, São Paulo, 1961; exhibited in group shows at Salons of Am., N.Y.C., Whitney Studio Club, N.Y.C., Whitney Mus. Am. Art, Art Inst. Chgo., Pa. Acad. Fine Art; represented in permanent collections Mus. Modern Art, NYU. Guggenheim Found. fellow, 1930; Ford Found. grantee, 1959. Home: Stamford Conn. Died Dec. 4, 1986.

NANCE, JAMES J., management consultant; b. Ironton, Ohio, Feb. 19, 1900; s. George W. and Florence (Van Horn) N.; m. Larua Battelle, Aug. 8, 1925; children: James Battelle, Marcia Louanne (Mrs. M.N. Atcheson). AB, Ohio Wesleyan U., 1923; postgrad., Ohio State U.; LLD, Lawrence Coll., 1949, St. Lawrence U., 1957, Cleve. State U., 1975. With Nat. Cash Register Co., Dayton, Ohio, 1924-27, Frigidaire div. Gen. Motors Corp., 1927-40; v.p. Zenith Radio Corp., Chgo., 1940-45; pres., chief exec. officer Hotpoint, Inc., Chgo., 1945-52, Packard Motor Car Co., Detroit, 1952-54, Studebaker-Packard Corp., 1954-56; v.p. Ford Motor Co., Dearborn, Mich., 1957-59; pres., chief exec. Central Nat. Bank Cleve., 1960-62, chmn., chief exec., 1962-67, hon. chmn., 1967-71; chmn., chief exec. First Union Real Estate Investments, 1968-78; then owner James J. Nance Co. (mgmt. adv.); dir. Standard Oil Ohio, 1953-60; dir. Montgomery Ward & Co., 1962-70, chmn. exec. com., 1966-70; dir., mem. exec. com. Montgomery Ward Life Ins. Co., 1966-75, Oglebay Norton Co.; dir., chmn. exec. com. Globe Refractories, 1964-70; chmn. exec. com., dir. Pioneer Trust & Savs. Bank, Chgo., 1968-74. Life trustee Northwestern U.; 1st chmn. bd. trustees Cleve. State U., 1964-70; trustee Ohio Wesleyan U., 1940-64, Univ. Hosps. of Cleve. Recipient Horatio Alger award, 1951; Ohio Sesquicentennial award, 1953; Ohio Gov.'s award, 1957; Leadership award Appliance Mfrs. Industry, 1960; Man of Yr. Award, Cleve., 1966; award Am. Acad. Achievement, 1967; Cleve. Pub. Service medal Cleve. C. of C., 1969; named Finance Banker of Yr., 1966; named to Hall of Fame-Distbn., 1953. Mem. Automobile Mfrs. Assn. (pres. 1954-56), Phi Delta Theta, Beta Gamma Sigma, Omicron Delta Kappa. Republican. Clubs: Masons, Union (Cleve.); Piper's Landing (Stuart, Fla.); Chagrin Valley Hunt (Cleve.); Quail Ridge (Delray, Fla.); Univeristy (N.Y.C.); Commercial, Chicago. Home: Chagrin Falls Ohio. Deceased.

NAPIER, ALAN, actor; b. Birmingham, Eng., Jan. 7, 1903; came to U.S., 1939, naturalized, 1952; s. Claude

Gerald and Milicent Mary (Kenrick) Napier-Clavering; m. Emily Nancy Pethbridge, Aug. 14, 1930 (div. 1943); m. 2d, Aileen Dickens Hawksley, Dec. 16, 1944 (dec. Feb. 1961); 1 child, Jennifer Mary Bissell. Student, Birmingham U., 1921-22, Royal Acad. Dramatic Art, 1922-23. Joined Oxford Player Co., 1923; featured role Bitter Sweet, 1929, West End, Old Vic theatres, London, 1930-39; star Lady in Waiting, N.Y.C., 1940; appeared in films, TV; movies include The Uninvited, 1943, Across the Wide Missouri, 1947, Marnie, 1963; actor TV series Batman, 1966-67. Democrat. Deceased.

NAROLL, RAOUL, anthropologist, educator; b. Toronto, Ont., Can., Sept. 10, 1920; s. Albert and Tessa (Soskin) N.; m. Frada Kaufman, 1941; 1 child, Maud. AB, UCLA, 1950, MA, 1951, PhD, 1953. Rsch. assoc. Human Rels. Area Files, Washington, 1955-57; asst. prof., then assoc. prof. anthropology Calif. State U., Northridge, 1957-62; assoc. prof., then prof. anthropology, sociology and polit. sci. Northwestern U., 1962-67, acting chmn. dept. anthropology, 1964-65; dir. Inst. Cross Cultural Studies, 1962-85; prof. anthropology SUNY, Buffalo, 1967-79; Disting. prof. SUNY, 1979-85; pres. Human Rels. Area Files, 1973-81; field studies in Germany, 1945, Austria, 1956, Greece, 1965-66, Switzerland, 1966. Author: Data Quality Control, 1962, What Have We Learned from Cross-Cultural Surveys, 1970, The Moral Order, 1983; (with wife, Vern Bullough) Military Deterrence in History, 1974; editor: (with Ronald Cohen) Handbook of Method in Cultural Anthropology, 1970; (with wife) Main Currents in Cultural Anthropology, 1973; editor-in-chief: Behavior Science Research, 1973-81; editorial cons.: Jour. Conflict Resolution. Served with AUS, 1939-45. Fellow Ctr. Advanced Study Behavioral Scis., 1954-55. Fellow Am. Anthrop. Assn., AAAS; mem. Am. Ethnol. Soc., Soc. Cross Cultural Research. Home: Buffalo N.Y. Died June 25, 1985.

NARVER, DAVID LEE, engineer, construction company executive; b. Seattle, Dec. 27, 1889; s. David Cotner and Ida Lee (Turner) N.; m. Alice Vida Lovejoy, Nov. 7, 1919; children: David Lee, Richard Lovejoy; m. 2d, Virginia Woodland Heagney, Dec. 2, 1972. AB in Civil Engring, Stanford, 1914; LLD, Pepperdine Coll., 1962. Registered profl. engr., Calif., Ariz., Hawaii, Nev. Engr. Standard Oil Co., Calif., 1914; asst. mgr. Java and Straits settlements Standard Oil Co., N.Y., 1914-17; chief structural engr. Paul E. Jeffers, Los Angeles, 1919-29; profl. cons. structural engr. Los Angeles, 1929-33; co-founder, exec. v.p. Holmes & Narver Inc., Los Angeles, 1933-54, chmn. bd., 1954-71, bd. dirs., 1971-73, hon. chmn. bd. dirs., from 1973; bd. dirs. Hyperion Engrs., L.A., 1955-58. Contbr. articles to profl. jours. Mem. Los Angeles County Bd. Appeals for Bldg. and Safety, 1946-66, chmn. 1956-66; mem. Los Angeles City Adv. Bd. Pub. Works Contracts, 1953-54; mem. com. civil and san. engring. MIT, 1956-61; mem. engring. fund com. Stanford, 1959-65. 1st lt. C.E., U.S. Army, 1918. Fellow ASCE (pres. Los Angeles sect. 1949), Inst. for Advancement Engring.; hon. mem. Structural Engrs. Assn. So. Calif. (pres. 1937, bd. dirs. 1934-38), Am. Standards Assn., Los Angeles C. of C. (bd. dirs. 1956-61, Constrn. Man of Yr. award 1962), Emeritus Cons. Engrs. Assn. Calif., San Gabriel (Calif.) Country Club, Coral Ridge (Fla.) Country Club, Sigma Alpha Epsikon, Tau Beta Pi. Home: Duarte Calif. †

NASH, JAMES PHILIP, oil operator; b. Phila., Apr. 23, 1892; s. James and Catherine (Higgins) N.; m. Anne Thornton, Oct. 6, 1915; children: Catherine (Mrs. Robert Teten), Mary (Mrs. Frederick Scott), Beverly Anne (Mrs. Jerry Bell). Student, George Washington U., 1914; LLD, St. Edwards U. Testing engr. U. Tex., 1914-17; dep. oil and gas supr. Tex. R.R. Commn., 1920; oil and gas operator, ptnr. Nash & Windfohr; hon. chmn., dir. Capital Nat. Bank, Austin, Tex.; chmn. bd. Air Conditioning Inc.; dir. Telacom Co. Tex. Chmn. state adv. com. reduce flare gas, Tex.; alternate del. U.S. Mission to 9th Gen. Assembly UN. Decorated knight comdr. Order St. Gregory the Great, Knight of Malta. Mem. Kappa Sigma, K.C. Home: Austin Tex. †

NASH, PHILLEO, educator, anthropologist; b. Wisconsin Rapids, Oct. 25, 1909; s. Guy and Florence Belle (Philleo) N.; m. Edith Rosenfels, Nov. 2, 1935; children: Maggie (Mrs. E.C. Kast), Sally. Lectr. anthropology U. Toronto, 1937-41; spl. lectr. U. Wis., 1941-42; mgr. Biron Cranberry Co., 1941-42, pres., 1946-77; spl. asst. to dir. White House liaison Office of War Info., 1942-46; spl. asst. White House, 1946-52; adminstrv. asst. Pres. of U.S., 1952-53; lt. gov. State of Wis., 1959-61; asst. to sec. pub. land mgmt. Dept. Interior, Washington, 1961; U.S. commr. Indian Affairs 1961-66; adj. prof. Am. U., Washington, 1971-73, prof., 1973-87, cons. anthropologist, 1966-87; spl. cons. sec. war, 1943. Author numerous sci. articles and addresses. Chmn., Wis. Dem. Com., 1955-57. Mem. Assn. Am. Indian Affairs (bd. dirs. 1943-87), Am. Anthrop. Assn. (treas. 1968-70), AAAS (past sect. sec.), Soc. Applied Anthropology (pres. 1971), Anthrop. Soc. Washington (past pres.). Club: Cosmos (Washington). Home: Washington D.C. Died Oct. 12, 1987.

NASTUK, WILLIAM LEO, physiology educator; b. Passaic, N.J., June 17, 1917; s. William and Mary (Tulchak) N.; m. Ruth Alden Lester, Apr. 1, 1950; children: William Lester, John Andrew, Mary Alden. B.Sc., Rutgers U., 1939; Ph.D., 1945. Mem. faculty Columbia, 1945-86, prof. physiology, 1960-86, also dir. Bioengring. Inst., 1974-78; cons. USPHS, NIH, 1960-66. Editor: Physical Techniques in Biological Research, vols. 4, 5, 6; mem. editorial bd.: Physiol. Rev, 1960-66. Mem. sci. adv. bd. Myasthenia Gravis Found., 1963-86. Fellow N.Y. Acad. Sci.; mem. Am. Physiol. Soc. (travel award 1950), Soc. for Neurosci., Biophys. Soc., Assn. Research Nervous and Mental Diseases, Sigma Xi, Phi Lambda Upsilon, Alpha Zeta, Alpha Omega Alpha. Home: Tenafly N.J. Died Nov. 6, 1986, buried Brookside Cemetery, Englewood, N.J.

NATHAN, ADELE GUTMAN, writer, theatrical director; b. Balt.; d. Louis Kayton and Ida (Newburger) Gutman. A.B., Goucher Coll.; postgrad., John Hopkins U., Columbia U., Peabody Inst. Founder, dir. Vagabond Players, Balt., 1916; spl. lectr. East Carolina Tchrs. Tng. Coll.; columnist Balt. Post; dir. dramatics Balt. playgrounds; dir. Cellar Players, Cherry Lane Theatre and Jr. Theater Workshop, N.Y.; staged and directed Centenary Pageant, The Parade of the Iron Horse, B. & O. R.R., Balt., 1927, Centenary, Internat. Harvester Co., 1929, The Subway (for Elmer Rice); Hist. Communications Exhibit for AT&T, Museum City, N.Y.; dir. Rochester Centennial Pageant, N.Y., Parade of the Yrs., Great Lakes Expn., Cleve.; dir. short subjects Paramount Pictures; dir. N.J. Fed. Theater, 1937; Eastern editor Grand Nat. Pictures, 1938-39; dir. Attack, 1942, Will-to-Win, 1943, Weirton Steel Co., Time is Now (Army-Navy E), 1944; chief script writer Dept. Edn., 1941; dir. Columbia U. Bicentennial Pageant, 175th Anniversary of Declaration of Independence Bicentennial Pageant, also 300 Years Under Freedom; writer shorts and for radi; dramatized Wheels A'Rolling, Chgo. R.R. Fair, 1948-49; staged Hist. Spectacle for Piedmont Festival, Winston-Salem, N.C., 1949; dir. Operation Independence Phila. for Dept. Treasury, 1950-51, Island Story for Gen. Electric, 1941; co-authored, produced, staged (with Marc Connelly) Mr. Lincoln Goes to Gettysburg (Valley Forge Freedom Found. award 1953), 1952; installed hist. mus. Niagara Falls, N.Y., 1962; coordinator 100th Anniversary Battle of Gettysburg and Lincoln's Gettysburg Address, Commonwealth of Pa., 1963; dep. chmn. Edward R. Murrow Meml. Library, 1968. Author or co-author numerous books since 1931 including: Building the First Transcontinental Railroad, Wheat Won't Wait, 1952, Seven Brave Companions, 1953, Railroad Stations of the World, 1953, The Train that Went to Gettysburg, 1955, Lincoln's America (Barondess award Civil War Round Table of N.Y.), 1961, The First Transatlantic Cable (Jr. Book of Month Club choice), 1963, Churchill's England, 1964, John Andre Gentleman Spy, 1969, How to Plan and Conduct a Bicentennial Celebration, 1972; contbr. to numerous periodicals; lectr. Am. Theatre Wing Profl. Sch., others. Cited by the Vagabond Players, 1971; recipient Spl. Decoration U.S. Navy; Alumnae Assn. award Goucher Coll., 1981. Mem. Lincoln Circle, Am. Revolution Round Table (archivist 1941-50). Clubs: Woman Pays (pres. 1967-68, 77-83), Overseas Press (N.Y.C.). Home: New York N.Y. Died July 24, 1986.

NAUHEIM, FERDINAND ALAN, marketing and advertising consultant, writer; b. N.Y.C., Nov. 3, 1909; s. Elias and Sadie (Rosenberger) N.; m. Beatrice Strasburger, Aug. 23, 1934; children: Gail Nauheim Kaufmann, Stephen. Student pub. schs. Asst. advt. mgr. Continental Baking Co., N.Y.C., 1930-36; owner Plymouth Printing Co., 1936-49; direct mail and sales cons. Washington, 1949-56; gen. partner Kalb, Voorhis & Co. (mems. N.Y. Stock Exchange), Washington, 1956-77; fin. planning, mktg., sales tng. cons. from 1977, also writer; professorial lectr. Sch. Bus., Am. U., Montgomery Coll. Author: Business Letters That Turn Inquiries Into Sales, 1957, Saleman's Complete Model Letter Handbook, 1967, Ferd Nauheim's 9 Day Sales Clinic, 1964, Behold the Upright, 1971, Build Family Finances and Reduce Risks and Taxes, 1973, (with Art Linkletter) 200 Ways to Avoid the Financial Pit, 1977, Expanding Your Financial Planning Horizons, 1978, Move Your Assets to Beat Inflation, 1980, Letter Perfect, 1981, The Retirement Money Book, 1981. Mem. citizens adv. com. D.C. Bar Assn.; mem. adv. bd. Salvation Army, Washington; bd. regents Coll. Financial Planning, chmn., 1971-72; trustee Columbia Lighthouse for Blind, Washington. Served with AUS, 1944-45. Recipient award for best war novel Thomas Y. Crowell, Harrap of London, Columbia Pictures, 1946. Mem. Internat. Soc. Financial Planners (dir.), Sales and Mktg. Execs. Washington (pres. 1957-58), Direct Mktg. Assn. Washington, Direct Mail Advt. Assn. (nat. bd. govs. 1958-61). Home: Washington D.C. Died Jan. 12, 1986.

NEALE, J. HENRY, lawyer, banker; b. N.Y.C., July 25, 1904; s. J. Henry and Henrietta (Schmidt) N.; m. Laura Button, July 7, 1928; children: Edwin B., J. Henry Jr. AB, Amherst Coll., 1924, LLD (hon.), 1974; LLB, Harvard, 1927. Bar: N.Y. 1927, U.S. Supreme Ct. 1927. Assoc. Strang & Taylor, White Plains, N.Y., 1927-31; ptnr. Neale & Wilson, White Plains, 1931-36, Scarsdale, N.Y., 1936-89; counsel Bur. Supplies and Accounts Dept. Navy, 1944-45, gen. counsel, 1945-46; pres. Scarsdale Nat. Bank and Trust Co., 1946-68, chmn. bd., 1968-76. Mem. White Plains Bd. Edn., 1935-42; chmn. Amherst Coll. Alumni Fund, 1956-57; co-chmn. council ch. and race United Presbyn. Ch. U.S.A., 1968-74, trustee , past pres., elder Presbyn. Ch.; co-chmn., dir. Presbyn. Econ. Devel. Corp., 1968-77; trustee Scarsdale Found., 1958-78, treas., 1965-78; bd. dirs. Legal Aid Soc., Westchester County, from 1958, pres., 1961-62; bd. govs. White Plains Hosp., from 1947; trustee YWCA of White Plains and Central Westchester, 1960-67, pres., 1963-67. Lt. comdr. USNR, 1942-44. Decorated Legion of Merit; recipient Eminent Service medal Amherst Coll. , 1959; Scarsdale Bowl, 1976. Fellow Am. Bar Found., N.Y. State Bar Found.; mem. Am. Bankers Assn. (exec. council 1961-64, state v.p. 1967-69), N.Y. State Bankers Assn. (pres. 1959-60), Westchester County Bankers Assn. (pres. 1949-52), ABA (ho. of dels. 1972-78), N.Y. State Bar Assn. (pres. 1967-68), Westchester County Bar Assn. (pres. 1953-55)), Am. Law Inst., Am. Judicature Soc., Supreme Ct. Hist. Soc., Delta Kappa Epsilon. Democrat. Home: Scarsdale N.Y. Died Feb. 6, 1989.

NEBLETT, WILLIAM HAYNLE, lawyer; b. Lunenburg County, Va., Aug. 21, 1889; s. Norman and Lillian (Hite) N.; m. Leona Walton, Nov. 20, 1916 (div.); 1 child, Norman Henry; m. Ruby Briner, Nov. 24, 1930 (div.); children: Halo, Mary Jane; m. Lorraine Higuera DeLonge, May 26, 1956. AB, Coll. of William and Mary, 1912; LLB, Washington and Lee U., 1914. Bar: Calif., N.Mex., U.S. Ct. Appeals (D.C. cir.), U.S. Supreme Ct. Mem. Powel & Neblett, Silver City, N.Mex., 1915-16; practice L.A., 1919-41; mem. McAdoo & Neblett; chief counsel Record Pub. Co. (in free speech cases), 1931, for U.S. Spl. Com. investigating receivership and bankruptcy proceedings, and adminstrn. of justice in fed. cts., 1933-36. Author: Pentagon Politics, 1953, No Peace With the Regulars, 1957. Chmn. Los Angeles County Dem. Cen. Com., 1925-27; del. to Dem. Nat. Convs., 1932, 36. Capt. F.A., U.S. Army, World War I, France; col. Res.; col. USAF, 1941-47, PTO; col. Air Force Res., ret., 1949. Decorated Croix de Guerre with palm, Silver Star with oak leaf cluster. Mem. Res. Officers Assn. (nat. pres. 1947-48), Mil. Order World Wars, Am. Legion, Vets. Fgn. Wars, ABA, Calif. Bar Assn., Army and Navy Club (Washington), Phi Beta Kappa, Kappa Sigma, Phi Delta Phi. Episcopalian. Home: Los Angeles Calif. †

NEEDLESS, IRA GEORGE, rubber company executive; b. Bertram, Iowa, Sept. 1, 1893; s. Elson Reid and Joanna (Hunter) N.; m. Marian Marie Westover, Dec. 24, 1917; children: George William, Lauranna Marie (Mrs. G. A. Jones), Myron Westover. Student, Coe Coll., 1910-13; AB, Northwestern U., 1915. Fellow, in charge bur. employment Northwestern U., 1915-16; with B.F. Goodrich Co., 1916-60, charge personnel N.Y. office, 1919-20; with sales tng. Akron, Ohio, 1920-21; with sales promotion Phila. dist. 1921-25; asst. sales mgr. B.F. Goodrich Co. Can., Ltd., Kitchener, Ont., Can., 1925-30, gen. tire sales mgr., 1930-45, v.p., gen. sales mgr., 1945-51, pres., bd. dirs., 1951-58, chmn. bd., 1958-60; bd. dirs. Waterloo Mfg. Co., Ltd.; tech. adviser to rubber controller Ottawa, Can., 1942-44. Chmn. bd. govs. Waterloo Coll. and Assoc. Faculties, 1958-60. Mem. Can. Mfrs. Assn. (exec. coun.), Soc. Automotive Engrs., Westmount Golf and Country Club, Granite Club, National Cluib, Phi Kappa Sigma. Home: Kitchener Ont., Canada. Died Jan. 7, 1986.

NEF, JOHN ULRIC, historian, educator; b. Chgo., July 13, 1899; s. John Ulric and Louise Bates (Comstock) N.; m. Elinor Henry Castle, Nov. 19, 1921 (dec. Feb. 1953); m. Evelyn Stefansson, Apr. 21, 1964. BS, Harvard U., 1920; PhD, Robert Brookings Grad. Sch., Washington, 1927; Dr Honoris Causa, U. Paris, 1955, U. Strasbourg, 1968. Asst. prof. econs. Swartmore Coll., 1927-28; asst. prof. econs U. Chgo., 1929-31, assoc. prof., 1931-35, assoc. prof. econ. history, 1935-36, prof., 1936-50, founder interdisciplanary grad. dept. Com. on Social Thought, 1941, chmn., 1945-64, chmn. Ctr. Human Understanding, 1961-68, mem. vis. com. social scis., from 1977; vis. prof. Inst. d'Etudes Politiques, U. Paris, 1949, Coll. de France, 1953; Wiles Found. lectr. U. Belfast, 1956; Smith lectr. history U. St. Thomas, Houston, 1961. Author: The Rise of the British Coal Industry, 2 vols., 1932, 2d edit., 1966, Industry and Government in France and England, 1540-1640, 1940, The United States and Civilization, 1942, 2d edit., 1967, Works of the Mind, 1947, Universities Look for Unity, 1943, La Rouge de la guerre totale, 1949, War and Human Progress, 1950, Letters and Notes of Elinor Castle Nef, 1953, La Naissance de la civilisation industrielle et le monde contemporain, 1954, Cultural Foundations of Industrial Civilization, 1958, Search for Civilization, 1962, Bridges of Human Understanding, 1964, The Conquest of the Material World, 1964, Towards World Community, 1968, Search for Meaning: Autobiography of a Non-Conformist, 1973; contbr. articles to profl. jours. Pres. John and Evelyn Nef Found., from 1965. With U.S. Army, 1918. Decorated Order of Phoenix, Greece, Officier Legion of Honor, France; recipient Leonardo da Vinci medal Soc. History Tech., 1979, U. Chgo. medal, 1980. Fellow Royal Soc. Arts, Am. Acad. Arts and Scis.; mem. Econ. History Assn. (v.p. 1942-44), World Acad. Art and Sci., Royal Hist. Soc., Lit. Soc. Washington, Quadrangle Club (Chgo.), Cosmos Club (Washington). Home: Washington D.C. Died Dec. 25, 1988.

NELSON, EVERETT JOHN, philosophy educator; b. Castle Rock, Wash., Oct. 18, 1900; s. John C. and Annie (Raphaelson) N.; m. Cecilia Williamson, May 1, 1943; children: Robert John, Philip Nelson, Eliot Clark. AB, U. Wash., 1923; AM, Harvard U., 1928, PhD, 1929; postgrad., Göttingen, Freiburg, and Sorbonne, Paris. Asst. in philosophy U. Wash., summer, 1923, asst. prof., 1930-34, assoc. prof., 1934-43, prof. philosophy, 1941-52, exec. officer dept. philosophy, 1947-52; asst. in philosophy Harvard U., 1927; vis. prof. U. Chgo., winter 1949, Harvard U., summer 1949, Columbia U., summer 1951; prof. philosophy Ohio State U., from 1952, chmn. dept. philosophy, 1952-68; summer vis. prof. at various univs. Cons. editor Jour. Symbolic Logic, 1936-50; contbr. numerous articles to profl. jours. Lt. USNR, 1943-44. Shelden traveling fellow in Europe, 1929-30, Guggenheim fellow, 1939-40. Mem. AAUP, Assn. Symbolic Logic, Am. Philos. Assn. (pres. Pacific div. 1946, Western div. 1966-67), Phi Beta Kappa. Home: Seattle Wash. Died Sept. 29, 1988.

NELSON, MILTON NELS, economics educator; b. Chgo., July 7, 1891; s. Andrew and Augusta Nathalia (Larson) N.; m. Lorene Edith Mae Bigelow, Dec. 24, 1917; children: Dantzelle Marie, Patricia Lou. AB, U. Ill., 1915, AM, 1917, PhD, 1921. Instr. mktg. U. Minn., 1921-22; instr. econs. U. Ill., 1922-23, vis. prof., 1940-41; asst. prof. bus. orgn. Ohio State U., 1923-26; prof. econs. Oreg. State Coll., from 1926, head dept., 1926-58; econ. cons. Bonneville Power Adminstrn., 1945-46; rating prin. economist U.S. Civil Svc. Commn., 1942. Author: Open Price Associations, Social Sci. Series Publs., U. Ill., 1922, Readings in Corporate Finacne, 1926, The Economic Base for Power Markets in Benton County, Oregon, (with Carol Clover) The Economic Power Base for Power Markets in Linn County, Oregon, U.S. Dept. Interior, 1946, also book chpts., bulls.; contbr. articles to profl. jours. 2d lt. Q.M. Corps, AUS, 1917-19. Mem. AAUP, Western Econ. Assn., Corvallis C. of C., Country Club, Town Club, Triad Club, Delta Phi, Gamma Sigma Delta, Pi Gamma Mu, Alpha Kappa Psi, Artus. Home: Corvallis Oreg. †

NELSON, RALPH, producer-director, playwright; b. N.Y.C., Aug. 12, 1916; s. Carl Leo and Edith (Lagergreen) N.; children by previous marriage: Theodor, Ralph Bahnsen; m. Barbara Powers, Feb. 6, 1954 (dec.); children: Peter Powers, Meredith Liv. LHD, Columbia U., 1974. Profl. actor 1933; TV dir. NBC, 1948-49, CBS, 1949-52; free-lance dir. 1952-87; pres. Rainbow Prodns. Producer-dir.: Mama, 1949-55; theater dir.: The Troublemakers, 1952, Here's Mama, 1952, This Happy Breed, 1956, The Man in the Dog Suit; dir.: Nutcracker Suite, (films) Requiem for a Heavyweight, 1961, Lillies of the Field, 1962 (Golden Globes award 1964, award NCCJ, Oscar nominee), Soldier in the Rain, 1963, Fate is The Hunter, 1964, Father Goose, 1965, Counterpoint, 1967, Charly, 1969; dir., producer (films) Once A Thief, 1965, Duel at Diablo, 1966, Charly, 1967, Tick...Tick...Tick, 1968, Soldier Blue, 1969, Flight of the Doves, 1970, The Wrath of God, 1972, The Wilby Conspiracy, 1974, Embryo, 1975, A Hero Ain't Nothing But A Sandwich, 1976, Because He's My Friend, 1977, You Can't Go Home Again, 1978, Christmas Lilies of the Field, 1979; dir.: Playhouse Ninety, CBS-TV; author: (plays) Mail Call, 1943 (John Golden prize), Angels Weep, 1944 (1st prize Nat. Theatre Conf.), The Man in the Funny Suit, also screenplays. Capt. USAAF, 1941-45. Recipient Emmy award Acad. TV Arts and Scis., 1957, Roman Cath. award Luth. Rose, 1963, Bell ringer award (2). Fellow Nat. Theatre Conf.; mem. Authors League Am. (life), Dramatists Guild, Writers Guild Am., Actors Equity, SAG, AFTRA, Dirs. Guild Am., ASCAP, Dir. Guild Mex. (hon.), Players Club. Died Dec. 21, 1987.

NELSON, RAYMOND OTIS, research services executive; b. St. Paul, Apr. 9, 1928; s. Walter Irving and Mary (Slocomb) N.; m. Jacqueline Marjorie Wightman, May 1, 1954; children—Marilyn Ann, Craig Richard. B.S. in Stats, U. Wyo., 1952. Sampling statistician Nat. Analysts, Phila., 1952-59, assoc. dir. research, 1959-76; v.p., gen. mgr. Chilton Research Services, Radnor, Pa., 1976-79; regional mgr. Chilton Research Services, 1980-82; mgr. Ad Chart Chilton Co., Radnor, Pa., 1982-87; v.p. Burke Mktg. Research, Cin., 1979-80; bd. dirs. Chilton Co. Contbr. articles to profl. publs. and confs. Served with U.S. Army, 1946-48. Recipient Cert. of Appreciation Census Adv. Com., Dept. Commerce. Mem. Am. Statis. Assn., Am. Mktg. Assn., Advt. Research Found. Republican. Presbyterian. Home: Media Pa. Died Jan. 13, 1987.

NELSON, RICK (ERIC HILLIARD NELSON), actor, singer, songwriter; b. Teaneck, N.J., May 8, 1940; s. Ozzie and Harriet (Hilliard) N.; m. Kristin Harmon, Apr. 20, 1963; children: Tracy Kristine, Gunnar Eric and Matthew Gray (twins), Sam Hilliard. Ed. pub. schs., Hollywood, Calif. Rec. artists Capitol Records. Appeared on radio in Adventures of Ozzie and Harriet, 1949-54, on TV, 1952-66; films include Here Come the Nelsons, 1951, Story of Three Loves, 1953, Rio Bravo, 1958, Wackiest Ship in the Army, 1960, Love and Kisses, 1965. Died Dec. 31, 1985.

NERVI, PIER LUIGI, civil engineer; b. Sondrio, June 21, 1891; s. Antonio and Maria Luisa (Bartoli) N.; m. Irene Calosi, Apr. 27, 1924; children: Antonio, Mario, Carlo, Vittorio. Dr. Civil Engring., U. Bologne, 1913; Dr. Arch., U. Buenos Aires, 1950; LLD (hon.), U. of Edinburgh, 1960; hon. degrees, Technische Hochschule, Munich, 1960, Warsaw U., 1961, Harvard U., 1962, Dartmouth Coll., 1962. Designer tech. dept. Soc. Construzioni Cenetizie, Bologne, 1913-15; designer and works supt. Soc. Construzioni Cenetizie, Florence, Italy, 1918-22; chief designer, works supt. Soc. Ing. Nervi & Nebbiosi, Rome, Italy, 1922-32; chief designer, works supt. Soc. Ing. Nervi & Bartoli, Rome, from 1932, also pres., adminstr.; chief prof. charge dept. tech. and technique of constrn. Faculty Architecture, Rome U., 1946-61. Mem. superior coun. pub. works Ministry Pub. Works, Rome. Served as engring. officer, 1915-18. Recipient Brown medal Franklin Inst. of Phila., 1957, Exner medal Austrian Technicological Soc. of Vienna, 1958, Cavaliere di Gran Crocre al merito delia Repubblica Italiana, Gold medal Royal Inst. of Brit. Architects, 1964, Cavaliere Ordine Civile di Savoia, 1964. Mem. Am. Acad. Arts and Scis. (hon. fgn.), Internat. Union Architects (pres. Itlaian Sect.), Royal Acad. Fine Arts of Stockholm (fgn. sect.), Rotary; hon. mem. AIA, Am.acad. Arts, Sci. and Letters. Home: Rome Italy. †

NESBITT, RALPH BERYL, clergyman; b. Tunnelton, Pa., Dec. 15, 1890; s. Samuel Marshall and Martha Jane (Davis) N.; m. Agnes Torborg Swenson, July 8, 1920; children: Ralph (dec.), Agnes (Mrs. C.E. Williams), George, Lois (Mrs. Richard M. Flanagan). AB, Princeton, 1914; student, Theol. Sem., 1916-19; AM, Columbia U., 1927; DD, Coll. Wooster, 1961. Ordained to ministry Presbyn. Ch., 1919. Travelling sec. Student Vol. Movement, 1919-20; missionary in India 1920-31; asst. min. Cen. Presbyn. Ch., Summit, N.J., 1931-39; assoc. min. Fifth Ave. Presbyn. Ch., N.Y.C., 1939-62; min. of visitation Larchmont Ave. Ch., Larchmont, N.Y., from 1962. Author: A Protestant Believes, 1962. Mem. Phi Beta Kappa. Home: Larchmont N.Y. †

NESS, EVALINE (MRS. ARNOLD A. BAYARD), illustrator, writer; b. Union City, Ohio, Apr. 24, 1911; d. Albert and Myrtle Woods (Carter) Michelow; m. Arnold A. Bayard, Nov. 1959. Student, Muncie (Ind.) State Tchrs. Coll., 1931, Chgo. Art Inst., 1933, Corcoran Art Sch., 1945, Art Students League, N.Y.C., 1947, Accademia de Belle Arti, Rome, Italy, 1950. Tchr. children's art classes Corcoran Sch. Art, Washington, 1945-46, Parsons Sch. Design, N.Y.C., 1959-60; fashion illustrator Saks Fifth Ave., N.Y.C., 1946-49; mag. and advt. illustrator 1946-49, illustrator numerous books, from 1959. (Recipient 1st prize painting Corcoran Sch. Art 1945, Caldecott medal childrens books 1967); Author, illustrator: Josefina February, 1963, Gift for Sula Sula, 1963, Pavo and the Princess, 1964, Exactly Alike, 1964, A Double Discovery, 1965, Sam Bangs and Moonshine, 1966, The Girl and the Goatherd, 1969, Do You Have the Time, Lydia, 1971, Yeck Eck, 1973, Marcella's Guardian Angel; author, designer: Fierce: The Lion, 1980, American Colonial Paper House, Paper Palace, Four Rooms from the Metropolitan Museum, Victorian Paper House, Shaker Paper House. Home: Palm Beach Fla. Deceased.

NEUHAUS, VERNON FRANK, oil producer, banker; b. Schulenburg, Tex., Feb. 18, 1901; s. Frank H. and Adele (Boettcher) N.; m. Gertrude Morris, 1936; children: Grace Richards, Patricia Gift, Vernon Frank. Student, Rice U., U. Tex. With Gulf Oil, Tex., 1920-22; lease broker Tex. and La., from 1936, Gillring Oil, McAllen, Tex., from 1950; bd. dirs. Kirby Industries, Houston, Houston Natural Gas, McAllen State Bank, Tex. State Bank, Harlingen State Bank, 1st City Nat. Bank. Mem. Petroleum Club. Died Aug. 10, 1983; buried McAllen, Tex.

NEUMANN, AUGWILL WALTER, transportation company executive; b. Milw., June 26, 1914; s. Walter Frederick and Katherine M. (Heyer) N.; m. Ann Jo Woodward, Dec. 25, 1943; children: Barbara Neumann Simmonds, David, Stephen. Student architecture, U. Ill., 1938-42; M.B.A., Harvard U., 1943. Supt. constrn. W.F. Neumann & Sons., Milw., 1936-38; asst. to exec. v.p. Willett Co., Chgo., 1946-48; dir. maintenance and purchasing Willett Co., 1948-59, exec. v.p., dir., 1971-74; gen. mgr. Willet Truck Leasing Co., 1959-64, v.p., 1964-65, pres., 1965-77, dir., 1965-79; pres. Willett Nat. Lease Co., 1965-77, chmn. bd., 1977-79; exec. v.p., dir. Willett Transports, Inc., 1971-74; exec. v.p. corp. affairs parent co. Willett, Inc., 1974-79, dir., from 1979; pres., dir. Nat. Truck Leasing System, 1967-69; sec., dir. Nat. Lease Purchasing Corp., 1969-71; dir. Hooven & Allison Co., Xenia, Ohio, Jefferson Corp., Chgo.; farm agt. Homestead Farm, Xenia, from 1976; mem. Gov. Ill. Adv. Com. Fleet Vehicle Mgmt., 1969; designer bldgs. and homes, from 1942. Contbr. articles to profl. publs. Active local Boy Scouts Am.; adv. Chgo. Jr. Achievement; bd. dirs. Barbereux Sch., Evanston, Ill.; v.p., bd. dirs. Hilltop Sanitorium, Lake Bluff, Ill.; bd. dirs., v.p., treas. Howard L. Willett Found., from 1972. Served as capt. AUS, 1943-46. Mem. Am. Trucking Assn. (chmn. engring. equipment and policy com. 1960-64), Automotive Transp. Suprs. Assn., A.I.M., Nat. Def. Transp. Assn., Am. Ordnance Assn., Soc. Automotive Engrs., Soc. Advancement Mgmt., Pvt. Truck Council Am. (dir., chmn. equipment and maintenance com. 1960-67). Christian Scientist. Clubs: Univ. (Chgo.); Westmoreland Country (Wilmette), Mich. Shores (Wilmette); Rotary. Home: Wolfeboro N.H. Deceased.

NEUMEIER, KARL GLADE, lawyer; b. Stillwater Minn., Jan. 29, 1889; s. Frederick C. and Anna Catherine (Glade) N.; m. Pauline Hospes, June 2, 1915 children: Josephine Neumeier Langford, Catherine Neumeier Bell, Karl E. BA, U. Minn., 1911; LLB, St Paul Coll. Law, 1914. Bar: Minn. 1914. Pvt. practice Stillwater, from 1914; mem. Minn. Senate 43d Dist. 1935-51; spl. asst. to atty. gen. U.S., 1953-55; pres Stillwater Realty Co.; bd. dirs. First Nat. Bank Stillwater. Bd. regents U. Minn., 1953-59. Recipient Outstanding Achievement award U. Minn., 1961. Mem. ABA, Minn. Bar Assn., Washington County Bar Assn. Home: Stillwater Minn. †

NEVELSON, LOUISE, sculptor; b. Russia, Sept. 23, 1899; d. Isaac and Minna Sadie (Smolerank) Berliaswky; husband dec.; 1 son, Myron Nevelson. Ed., Mexico; studied with, Hans Hoffman, Germany, 1931; studied with hon. degrees, Hamlin U., Mpls. Sch. Art and Design, Bowdoin Coll., Hobart and William Smith Coll. One-woman shows: Janis Gallery, The Bienniel, Venice, Italy, 1963, also in Germany, London, Paris, Documenta III, 1964, Pace Galleries, N.Y.C., Columbus, 1969, 71, Museo Civico de Torino, 1969, Galerie Jeanne Bucher, Paris, 1969, Kroller-Muller Mus., Holland, 1969, Akron Art Inst., 1969, Mus. Fine Arts, Houston, 1969, U. Tex., 1970, Galerie de France, Rennes, 1981, Wildenstein Gallery, London, 1981, Fay Gold Gallery, Atlanta, 1982, Greenberg Gallery, St. Louis, 1983, Barbara Krakow Gallery, Boston, 1984; one-woman retrospective exhbn., Whitney Mus. Am. Art, 1970; represented permanent collections; Juilliard Sch., Princeton, Whitney Mus. Am. Art, Bklyn. Mus., Neward Mus., Carnegie Inst., Sara Robi Found., Brandeis U., Birmingham Mus., Houston Mus., Riverside Mus., Mus. Modern Art, Met. Mus. Art, N.Y. U Mus., Nebr. Mus., also numerous pvt. collections. Recipient 1st award United Soc. Artists, 1959; award Chgo. Inst., 1959; Ford Found. gift for Tamarind Workshop Norfolk Mus., 1963; Brandeis U. Creative Arts award sculpture; Skowhegan medal sculpture; N.Y. State Gov.'s Arts award, 1987. Mem. Am. Acad. and Inst. Arts and Letters, Fedn. Modern Painters and Sculptors (v.p.), Artists Equity (past pres.), Am. Abstract Artists, Sculptors Guild (exec. bd.). Home: New York N.Y. Died Apr. 17, 1988.

NEVILLE, ROBERT BREEN, lawyer; b. Akron, Ohio, July 9, 1917; s. Thomas George and Bessie (Breen) N.; m. Anne Henderson Love, Dec. 7, 1945; 1 child, Breen Anne. AB, Western Res. U., 1939, JD, 1941. Bar: Ohio 1941. Pvt. practice Willoughby, Ohio, 1941; commd. 2d lt. USMC, 1942, advanced through grades to col., 1962, inf. officer 1st Marine Div. Guadacanal, Solomons campaigns, 1942-44, legis. asst. to comdt., 1956-59, legal advisor, 1964-66; dep. chief staff USMC, Vietnam, 1966-67; asst. dir. personnel USMC, 1968; asst. Washington counsel Nat. Restaurant Assn., 1968-71, Washington counsel, 1971-79, acting exec. v.p., 1980-81, gen. counsel, 1981-82, exec. v.p., v.p., 1982-85. Decorated Legion of Merit with combat V; Ranney scholar, 1939-40. Mem. ABA, Am. Soc. Assn. Execs. Home: Arlington Va. Died Jan. 7, 1985; buried Arlington (Va.) Nat. Cemetery.

NEWBURY, GEORGE ADELBERT, lawyer; b. Ripley, N.Y., Nov. 7, 1895; s. Clarence Rollin and Mary Catharine (Moore) N.; m. Laura Hildred, Sept. 16, 1922 (dec. Jan. 1924); 1 child, George Hildred; m. Eleanor Louise Murray, Apr. 4, 1931 (dec. Nov. 1980). LLB, Cornell U., 1917; LLD, Keuka Coll., Lycoming Coll., Houghton Coll. Bar: N.Y. 1919. Pvt. practice Westfield, N.Y., 1919-24, Buffalo, 1924-46, 62-84; mem. Babcock Newbury & Russ, 1924-45; with Blue Cross Western N.Y., 1944-68, pres., 1944-55, chmn., 1955-67; exec. v.p. Mfrs. & Traders Trust Co., Buffalo, 1946-54, pres., 1954-63; counsel Hodgson, Russ, Andrews, Woods & Goodyear, 1962-75; v.p. Health Svc., Inc., Chgo., 1950-58, also bd. dirs. Dir. Legal Aid Soc., 1936-54, Nat. Health and Welfare Retirement Assn., 1960-68; pres. Children's Aid Soc., 1942-49; campaign chmn. Community Chest, Buffalo and Erie County, 1950-52; v.p., dir. Child Welfare League Am., 1950-52; mem. adv. bd. Rosary Hill Coll., Buffalo, 1955-65, SUNY Coll., Fredonia; trustee keuka Coll., Keuka Prk, N.Y., 1967-75, Buffalo Gen. Hosp., 1943-66; trustee Cornell U., 1959-69, trustee emeritus, presdl. counsellor, 1969-84; chmn. mem's adv. com. Children's Hosp. Buffalo; dir., 1st pres. WNED-TV. Recipient Silver Beaver award Boy Scouts Am., Disting Alumnus award Cornell U. Law Sch., 1980; honoree Cult of White Buffalo, 1976. Mem. Am. Hosp. Assn. (hon. life., Justin Ford Kimball award 1959), Buffalo C. of C. (pres. 1943-45), Buffalo Bd. Trade (pres. 1943-45), Am. (past v.p. N.Y. sect.), N.Y. State (chmn. legis. com.) bankers assns., ABA, N.Y. (chmn. banking law sect., pres. 1961-62), Erie County bar assns., Cornell Law Assn., Newcomen Soc., Masons (33 degree, pres. internat. conf. supreme coun. 1975-84), Buffalo Club, Cornell Club (past pres.), Thursday Club, Tau Kappa Epsilon. Presbyterian. Home: Buffalo N.Y. Died Mar. 5, 1984; buried Ripley, N.Y.

NEWCOMB, REXFORD, academic administrator; b. Independence, Kans., Apr. 24, 1886; s. Frederick and Margaret (Salathiel) N.; m. Ruth Howell Bergen, Oct. 23, 1911; children: Theodore F. (dec.), Rexford, Margaret Anna. Student, U. Kans., 1906-08; BArch, U. Ill., 1911, MArch, 1918; MA, U. So. Calif., 1915. Head.

dept. fine and applied arts Long Beach (Calif.) Poly. High Sch., 1912-17, also prin. evening sch., 1913-17; adj. prof. history of art and architecture U. So. Calif., 1916-17; asst. prof., later acting prof. architecture and archtl. engring., also coll. architect Agrl. and Mech. Coll. Tex., 1917-18; asst. prof. architecture U. Ill., 1918-19, asst .prof. archtl. history, 1919-21, prof. history architecture, 1921-54, dean Coll. Fine and Applied Arts, 1932-54, emeritus, from 1954; dir. Bur. Community Planning, 1934-54, emeritus; mem. Ill State Planning Commn., 1940-43. Author: Architecture of the Old Northwest Territory, 1950, Architecture in Old Kentucky, 1953, others; archtl. editor Western Architect, Chgo., 1923-30, editor-in-chief, 1930-31. Fellow AIA (past pres. Cen. Ill. chpt.), AAAS; mem. Am. Soc. Archtl. Historians (pres. 1943-45), Kan. Hist. Soc., Ky. State Hist. Soc., Ill. State Hist. Soc., Ill. Acad. Sci., Soc. Midland Authors, Quivera Soc., Gargoyle, University Club (Urbana, Ill.), Filson Club (Louisville), Sigma Xi, Alpha Rho Chi, Scarab, Phi Kappa Phi, Sigma Tau, Alpha Sigma Phi, Phi Beta Kappa. Home: Santa Ana Calif. †

NEWCOMER, MABEL, economic educator; b. Oregon, Ill., July 2, 1891; d. Alphonso Gerald and Carrie Mabel (Jackson) N. AB, Stanford U., 1913, AM, 1914; PhD, Columbia U., 1917; LLD (hon.), Smith Coll., N.J. Coll. for Women, Wellesley Coll., Wheaton Coll.; LHD (hon.), Russell Sage Coll.; DSc (hon.), U. Pa., 1957. With Vassar Coll., from 1917, instr. econs., 1917-18, asst. prof., 1918-20, assoc. prof., 1920-26, prof., 1926-57, prof. emeritus, from 1957, chmn. dept. econs., 1932-50; spl. investigator N.Y. State Joint Com. on Taxation and Retrenchment, 1921-22, 23-24, 25-26, N.Y. Commn. on Revision Tax Law, 1931-32, N.Y. State Commn. on State Aid, 1935-38; economist Ednl. Fin. Inquiry, 1922-23, Calif. Tax Commn., 1928-29, tax cons. Adv. Com. on Edn.. 1937, N.Y. State Joint Com. on Fiscal Policies, 1937, U.S. Treasury, 1941-42; vis. prof. econs. Columbia U., 1943-44; ofcl. Am. del. to UN Conf., Bretton Woods, N.H., July, 1944; mem. Gov.'s Commn. on Rural Homes, State of N.Y., 1932, Gov.'s Tax Adv. Com., 1943; chief cons. taxation and revenue Office Mil. Govt. U.S. in Berlin, 1946-47; mem. E.C.A. tech. assistance mission on German refugees, 1950. Author or co-author numerous books in field. Trustee Tchrs. Ins. & Annuity Assn. Coll. Retirement Equities Fund. Mem. Am. Econ. Assn., Nat. Tax Assn., Tax Inst. Home: Saratoga Calif. †

NEWELL, WILLIAM B., educator; b. Boston, Dec. 17, 1892; s. Louis B. and Louisa (Stumpf) N.; m. Celina Alexendra Kennedy, Aug. 22, 1921; children: William Albert David, Frederick Louis B., Dorothy (Mrs. Robert B. Wood. Jr.), Joyce (Mrs. Charles J. Stockford Jr.), Diane (Mrs. Howard Wilson). AB, Syracuse U., 1924; MA, U. Pa., 1934; postgrad. in edn., U. Fla., 1949-51. Licentiate L.I. Presbytery, 1940; certified tchr. Fla., 1950. Sci. rsch. asst. U. Mus., Phila., 1932-35; head dept. civic participation Haskell Inst., 1935-37; ethnologist and authority on primitive art Bklyn. Mus., 1937-38; regular lectr. on new world art and architecture Pratt Inst., Bklyn., 1937-48; dir. Am. Indian Mus. Arts and Scis., 1938-43; assoc. prof. sociology U. Fla., 1947, vis. assoc. prof., acting head dept. sociology, summer 1948; chmn. dept. sociology and anthropology Trumbull br. U. Conn., New London, 1946-49; mem. pub. sch. system, Hillsboro County, Fla., 1949-54; instr. Brandon (Fla.) High Sch., from 1954. Author: Crime and Justice Among the Iroquois Nations; editor: The Quipu, mus. publ.; The Six Nations, N.Y. State Indian Welfare Soc. publ.; Hillsborough County Teacher, 1959-60; contbr. articles to vaious publs. Leader in drive to secure adequate schs. for N.Y. State Indian reservations, 1920-24; founder Six Nations Assn. Indian Welfare Soc. of N.Y. State, 1926; missionary to the Seneca Indians, Cattaraugas Reservation, N.Y., 1924-28; founder Soc. Neighborhood Indians, Phila., 1933, Big Soldier Playgrounds, Mayetta, Kans., 1936; dir. ednl. projects, recreational coun., Delaware County, Pa., 1934-35; mem. city-county ednl. and cultural com. Youth Mus. Sci. and Natural History of Tampa, Fla.; bd. dirs. Mus. Sci. and Natural History, Tampa. Mem. Am. Acad. Polit. and Social Scis., Am. Anthropol. Assn., AAAS, NEA, Fla Edn. Assn., Am. Assn. Mus., Columbia Scholastic Press Advisers Assn. (hon. life), AAUP (sec. Trumbull chpt.), Soc. Colonial History, Nat. Coun. Social Studies, Nat. Assn. Journalism Dirs., Nat. Assn. R.C.E., Vets. Fgn. Wars, Caughnawaga Hist. Soc. (founder; pres. 1962), Vets. World War I, Am. Assn. State and Local History, Inst. Iroquoian Studies, River Grove Civic Club (Tampa), Masons, Phi Delta Kappa. Home: Caughnawaga Que., Canada †

NEWHOUSE, NORMAN NATHAN, editor; b. Bayonne, N.J., Mar. 31, 1906; m. Alice Gross, June 9, 1946; children: Robin A., Mark W., Peter C., Jonathon E., David. AB, NYU, 1925; LHD (hon.), St. John's U., 1960. Editor L.I. Daily Press, 1936; then exec. editor L.I. Press (name changed); exec. cons. New Orleans Times-Picayune, New Orleans States-Item, Cleve. Plain Dealer, Mobile Press Register, Birmingham News. Lt. col. AUS, 1943-45, MTO. Decorated Legion of Merit.; Conspicuous Svc. Cross (N.Y.); knight officer Order Saints Mauritzo y Lazaro (Italy). Mem. Zeta Beta Tau. Home: New Orleans La. Died Nov. 6, 1988.

NEWKIRK, GORDON ALLEN, JR., astrophysicist; b. Orange, N.J., June 12, 1928; s. Gordon Allen and Mildred (Fleming) N.; m. Nancy Buck, Apr. 11, 1956; children—Sally, Linda, Jennifer. B.A., Harvard U., 1950; M.A., U. Mich., 1952, Ph.D., 1953. Research asst. Observatory, U. Mich., 1950-53; astrophysicist Upper Air Research Observatory, 1953; sr. research staff High Altitude Observatory, Boulder, Colo., 1955-85; adj. prof. dept. astrogeophysics U. Colo., 1961-65, adj. prof. physics and astrophysics, 1965-76; dir. High Altitude Obs., 1968-79; cons. NASA, 1964-85; mem. geophysics research bd. Nat. Acad. Sci., 1976-80. Contbr. articles on solar-interplanetary physics to profl. jours. Served with U.S. Army, 1953-55. Mem. AAAS, Am. Astron. Soc. (chmn. solar physics div. 1972-73), Internat. Astron. Union (pres. com. 10 1975-79), Research Soc. Am., Commn. V Union Radio Sci. Internat., Am. Geophysical Union, Sigma Xi. Home: Boulder Colo. Died Dec. 1985.

NEWTON, LOUIE DE VOTIE, clergyman; b. Screven County, Ga., Apr. 27, 1892; s. William Moore and Dicie E. (Robbins) N.; m. Julia Carstarphen; children: Mrs. Eden N. Guerin, Mrs. Catherine N. Robertson. AB, Mercer U., 1913, DD (hon.), 1932; MA, Columbia U., 1915; DD (hon.), Oglethorpe U., 1929; LittD (hon.), Cumberland U., 1949; LLD (hon.), William Jewel Coll., 1951. Ordained to ministry Bapt. Ch., 1929. Prof. history Mercer U., 1913-17; editor, columnist Christian Index, 1920-29; pastor Druid Hills Bapt. Ch., Atlanta, 1929-68; pres. So. Bapt. Conv., 1946-47, Ga. Bapt. Sunday Sch. Conv., 1948-49, Ga. Bapt. Conv., 1950-51; mem. exec. com. Bapt. World Alliance, 1923-25, v.p., 1939-47. Author 4 books; daily and weekly columnist various publs. Active numerous civic orgns. Named Clergyman of Yr. Religious Heritage Am., 1953. Died June 3, 1986.

NEWTON, MICHAEL, physician; b. Malvern, Eng., June 4, 1920; came to U.S., 1941, naturalized, 1949; s. Frank Leslie and Alice (Henderson) N.; m. Niles Polk Rumely, Mar. 27, 1943; children: Elizabeth Willoughby (Mrs. Robert M. Reed), Frances Lees (Mrs. Stephen C. Stuntz), Edward Robson, Warren Polk. B.A., Cambridge (Eng.) U., 1942, M.B., B.Ch., 1944, M.A., 1946; M.D., U. Pa., 1943. Diplomate: Am. Bd. Surgery, Am. Bd. Ob-Gyn. House surgeon in English hosps. 1944-46; tng. physiology, surgery, ob-gyn U. Pa. Med. Sch., 1946-53; prof., chmn. dept. ob-gyn U. Miss. Med. Center, Jackson, 1955-66; dir. Am. Coll. Obstetricians and Gynecologists, Chgo., 1966-74; prof. ob-gyn Pritzker Sch. Medicine, U. Chgo., 1966-77, Northwestern U. Med. Sch., 1977-88; dir. Nat. Bd. Med. Examiners, 1966-69. Editor: (with E.E. Philipp and J. Barnes) Scientific Foundations of Obstetrics and Gynecology, 1970, 3d edit., 1986 mem. editorial bd.: Internat. Corr. Soc. Obstetricians and Gynecologists, Jour. Reproductive Medicine; mem. internat. bd. editors: Excerpta Medica; author: (with E.R. Newton) Complications of Gynecologic and Obstetric Management, 1988, Geriatric Gynecology, 1988; contbr. articles to profl. jours. and chpts. to books. Rockefeller student, 1941. Fellow Am. Gynecol. and Obstet. Soc., Am. Coll. Obstetricians and Gynecologists, A.C.S.; mem. Am. Fertility Soc., Central Assn. Obstetricians and Gynecologists (life), Assn. Profs. Gynecology and Obstetrics (hon.), Chgo. Gynecol. Soc. (v.p. 1975-76), Assn. Chgo. Gynecol. Oncologists (pres. 1979-81), Internat. Soc. Psychosomatic Obstetrics and Gynecology (exec. sec. 1980-83). Home: Chicago Ill. Died May 24, 1988.

NEY, JEROME M., department store executive; b. Ft. Smith, Ark., Aug. 23, 1906; s. Rudolph and Marie (Baer) N.; m. Ione Sternberg, Nov. 26, 1936; children: Randolph J., Jerome M. Grad., Culver Mil. Acad., 1924. Dept. store work 1924-88; stock boy Chgo.; salesman 1925-26, asst. dept. mgr., 1926-28, dept. mgr., 1928-30, divisional mdse. mgr., 1930-32, gen. mdse. mgr., 1932-36; pres., gen. mgr. Boston Store Dry Goods Co., Fort Smith and Fayetteville, Ark., 1936-73; chmn. bd. Boston Store Dry Goods Co., 1973-81, chmn. exec. com., 1981-88; on leave with OPA, Washington, 1942-46; chief program planning br. OPA, 1943, dir. miscellaneous products rationing div., 1944, asst. dept. adminstr. for rationing, 1944, dir. consumer goods price div., 1944-45, dep. adminstr. price, 1945-46; pres. Kerr's, Inc., Oklahoma City, 1953-61; v.p., dir. Daniels & Fisher Stores Co., Denver, 1954-57, Stix, Baer & Fuller, Inc., St. Louis, 1949-60; pres., dir. Lawrence Corp., Denver, 1957-61; pres. White House Dry Goods Co., Beaumont, Tex., 1950-61; chmn. bd. White House Dry Goods Co., 1961-81, chmn. exec. com., 1981-88; chmn. exec. com. Balliet's, Inc., Oklahoma City, 1967-88; trustee, exec. com. Am. Retail Fedn., 1945-60, chmn. bd., 1947-48; mem. Emergency Econ. Stablzn. Retailing Industry Adv. Com., 1968-70. Trustee Sparks Meml. Hosp., Ft. Smith, 1963-65; lay adv. bd. St. Edward Mercy Hosp., 1967-70; endowment trustee Old Fort Mus., Ft. Smith, Ark., 1985-88. Mem. Nat. Retail Mchts. Assn. (dir., v.p. 1960-61, 72-73, chmn. vendor relations com. 1959-70, silver plaque for service to retailing 1965, exec. com. 1966-69, dir. 1974-78). Home: Fort Smith Ark Died Jan. 26, 1988.

NEY, ROBERT LEO, physician, educator; b. Brno, Czechoslovakia, May 22, 1933; came to U.S., 1941, naturalized, 1946; s. Paul Ernst and Katherine Beatrice (Kroner) N.; m. Sally Sanford Burrage, June 24, 1956; children: Elizabeth Burrage, Sarah Alden, Peter Albert. B.A., Harvard U., 1954; M.D., Cornell U., 1958. Intern, Vanderbilt U., Nashville, 1958-59; resident in medicine Vanderbilt U., 1960-61, instr. medicine, 1961-63, asst. prof., 1965-67; resident in medicine Pa. Hosp., Phila., 1959-60; assoc. prof. U. N.C., Chapel Hill, 1967-70; prof. medicine and physiology U. N.C., 1970-80, chmn. dept. medicine, 1972-80; prof. medicine, dir. Div. Endocrinology and Metabolism, Johns Hopkins U. Sch. Medicine, Balt., 1981-86. Served with USPHS, 1963-65. Mem. Am. Soc. Clin. Investigation, Assn. Am. Physicians, Am. Fedn. Clin. Investigation, Am. Clin. and Climatol. Assn., ACP, Am. Physiol. Soc., Alpha Omega Alpha. Home: Baltimore Md. Died Aug. 27, 1986; Mt. Auburn Cemetery, Cambridge, Mass.

NICHOLLS, MERRILL EDGAR, clergyman; b. Highland Park, Mich., Aug. 27, 1913; s. Jack J. and Satie C. (Bell) N.; m. Vinita I. Wallin, Aug. 29, 1935; children: Merrilly K., Glenn Earl, Jeanette I. DD, L.I.F.E. Bible Coll., 1933. Ordained to ministry Foursquare Gospel Ch. With Lockheed Aircraft Co., 1929-33, Kinner Aircraft Co., 1933-34; pastor various chs. Colo. and Calif., 1935-59; supr. Gt. Lakes dist. Internat. Ch. Foursquare Gospel, 1959-74; gen. supr. L.A., 1974-81, v.p., 1979-81; also bd. dirs.; tchr. L.I.F.E. Bible Coll., 1951-59. Mem. Nat. Assn. Evangelicals (bd. dirs.), Pentecostal Fellowship N.Am. (pres., chmn. 1978). Republican. Home: Los Angeles Calif. Died Mar. 12, 1981; buried L.A.

NICHOLS, ALEXANDER LOWBER, lawyer; b. Tularosa, N.Mex., Feb. 28, 1906; s. Henry Dodge and Adele (Lowber) N.; m. Dorothy A. Ackart, Apr. 9, 1937; children: David A., Carolyn N. Cobb, Alan B. BA, Haverford Coll., 1928; LLB, U. Pa., 1931. Bar: Del. 1932. Assoc. Hugh M. Morris, 1932-40; ptnr. Morris, Nichols, Arsht & Tunnell, Wilmington, Del., 1940-76, of counsel, 1977-85. Mem. exec. com. United Community Fund No. Del., Inc., 1950-60; pres. Family Svc. No. Del., 1955-57; bd. dirs., past v.p. Wilmington YMCA. With Citizens Mil. Tng. Camps, 1924-25. Fellow Am. Bar Found.; mem. ABA (ho. dels. 1957-75, bd. govs. 1970-73), Del. Bar Assn., Rotary, Phi Delta Phi. Republican. Episcopalian. Home: Wilmington Del. Died July 16, 1985; buried Wilmington.

NICHOLS, BILL, congressman; b. Amory, Miss., Oct. 16, 1918; m. Carolyn Funderburk; children: Memorie (Mrs. Chris Mitchell), Margaret (Mrs. Christos Vlachos), Flynt. B.S. in Agr, Auburn U., 1939, M.A., 1941. V.p. Parker Fertilizer Co., Sylacauga, Ala., 1947-66; pres. Parker Gin Co., Sylacauga, 1947-60; mem. Ala. Senate, 1963-66; mem. 90th-92d Congresses from 4th dist. Ala., chmn. mil. affairs, fin. and taxation coms., mem. armed services com., agr. com., chmn. house flag day com., 1971-76; mem. 93d-100th Congresses from 3d dist. Ala., 1973-88, chmn. subcom. on mil. compensation, 1978-82, chmn. investigations subcom., 1983-88. Mem. Sylacauga Bd. Edn.; bd. govs. Nat. Hall of Fame; trustee Auburn U. Served to capt. AUS, 1942-47, ETO. Decorated Bronze Star, Purple Heart; named Outstanding Mem. Ala. Senate Capitol Press Corps, 1965, Man of Year in Agr. Progressive Farmer mag., 1965. Mem. Am. Legion, V.F.W., D.A.V., Ala. Cattlemens Assn., U. Auburn Alumni Assn., Ala. Farm Bur., Blue Key, Scabbard and Blade, Gamma Sigma Delta. Democrat. Methodist (steward). Home: Sylacauga Ala. Died Dec. 13, 1988.

NICHOLS, CHARLES WALTER, JR., engineering executive; b. Bklyn., Dec. 23, 1911; s. Charles Walter and Adelaide (Batterman) N.; m. Marjorie H. Jones, June 5, 1934 (dec.); children: Joan, Charles Walter III, David Huntington; m. Marguerite Prince Sykes, May 22, 1948. Student, Choate Sch., 1922-29, Williams Coll., 1929-32. Salesman Nichols Copper Co., Nichols Engring. and Rsch. Corp., N.Y.C., 1933-72, chmn. bd.; chmn. exec. com. Neptune Internat. Corp., 1972-79; bd. dirs. Allied Chem. Corp., Allegheny Power System, Inc., Allegheny Power Svc. Corp., Monongahela Power Co., Potomac Edison Co., West Penn Power Co. Vice chmn. bd. mgrs. Coop. Social Settlement Soc., N.Y.C.; bd. dirs. NYU, pres., bd. dirs. Nichols Found., 1953-87; v.p., chmn. exec. com. N.Y. Zool. Soc.; corporator Putnam Meml. Hosp.; trustee Animal Med. Ctr. Mem. River Club, Hemisphere Club, Links Golf Club, Pilgrims Soc., Lahinch Club, Ekwanok Club. Congregationalist. Home: New York N.Y. Died Sept. 20, 1987.

NICHOLS, LESLIE, lawyer; b. Portland, Oreg., July 13, 1892; s. Edmund Scott and Annie (Humphrey) N.; m. Marie Shuck, Aug. 20, 1917; children: Elizabeth Jane, Mary Carolyn. BA, Ohio State U., 1912, JD, 1915. Bar: Ohio 1915, U.S. Supreme Ct. 1927. Practiced in Cleve., from 1915; ptnr. Jones, Day, Cockley & Reavis and predecessor firms, from 1915. Capt. arty., U.S. Army World War I, ETO. Mem. ABA, Ohio Bar Assn., Cleve. Bar Assn., Am. Legion, Union Club, Cleve. Country Club, Mid-Day Club (Cleve.), Order of Coif, Kappa Sigma, Phi Delta Phi, Gamma Phi. Home: Cleveland Ohio. †

NICHOLS, SUMMER ELY, banker; b. Girard, Pa., May 30, 1891; s. Harry Hay and Jennie (Ely) N.; m. Bessey Hart, July 22, 1916; children: James, Robert, Richard H., Summer H. AB, Allegheny Coll., 1912, D. in Bus. Adminstrn., 1962; LLD, Gannon Coll., 1962. Teller Girard (Pa.) Nat. Bank, 1914-19; cashier 1st Nat. Bank, Albion, Pa., 1919-24; cashier, exec. v.p. Peoples

Bank & Trust Security-Peoples, Erie, Pa., 1924-29; v.p. Security-Peoples Trust Co., Erie, 1929-37, pres., 1937-64, chmn. bd., from 1964; dir. Earl E. Knox Co., Erie; pres. Erie Compressor Co. Trustee Allegheny Coll. Mem. Pa. Bd. Banking, Masons, Shriners, Phi Gamma Delta. Home: Erie Pa. †

NICHOLSON, GUNNAR WALFRID ENANDER, corporate director; b. nr. Växiö, Sweden, July 11, 1893; s. Alfred and Mathilda (Niklasson) N.; m. Lillian Greenough, Nov. 22, 1928 (dec.). Chem.E., Chalmers Inst. Tech., Gothenburg, Sweden, 1916; Chem.E. hon. Dr. Engring. Engr. various pulp and paper mills Sweden, 1916-21; engr., supt. various mills U.S. and Can., 1921-27; gen. supt. Bogalusa Paper Co., 1927-31; mgr. mills So. Kraft Corp., 1931-41; resident mgr. Union Bag and Paper Corp., Savannah, Ga., 1941-45; v.p. Union Bag and Paper Corp., N.Y.C., 1945-52; exec. v.p., dir. Union Bag and Paper Corp., 1952-56; pres., dir. Tenn. River Pulp & Paper Co., 1956-67. Trustee Norwich U., Am. Scandinavian Found.; appointed comdr. of royal Order of the Polar Star by His Majesty King Karl XVI Gustaf of Sweden, 1984. Decorated comdr. Order Wasa Sweden; recipient Gold medal Am. Scandinavian Found., Gustaf-Dalén Medal The Chalmer's Tech. Engring. Organisation, 1987. Mem. TAPPI (gold medal award 1954, v.p. 1944-45, pres. 1946), Newcomen Soc., Swedish Acad. Engring. Sci., Engring. Inst. Can. (life), Swedish Pulp and Paper Assn. (hon.). Episcopalian. Club: Union League (N.Y.C.). Home: New York N.Y. Died May 12, 1988.

NICHOLSON, JESSE THOMPSON, orthopaedic surgeon; b. Camden, N.J., Apr. 28, 1903; s. Joseph Lippincott and Elizabeth (Thompson) N.; m. Edith Rose, Apr. 8, 1942; children: Elizabeth Thompson, Edith Davis, Joseph Lippincott, Virginia. BS, U. Pa., 1925, MD, 1928. Diplomate am. Bd. Orthpaedic Surgery., Pan Am. Med. Assn. Intern Pa. Hosp., Phila., 1928-30; pvt. practice 1938-87; resident orthopaedic surgery Phila. Orthopaedic Hosp. and Infirmary for Nervous Diseases, 1930-32, Shriner's Hosp., Phila., 1932, Johns Hopkins Hosp., 1932, Mass. Gen. Hosp., 1933; orthopaedic surgeon Grad. Hosp., 1934-87, Phila. Children's Hosp., 1935-87, Lankenau Hosp., 1953-87; prof., chmn. dept. orthopaedic surgery U. Pa. Grad. Sch. Medicine, 1946-68, prof. emeritus, 1969-87; cons. Phila. Gen. Hosp., Naval Hosp., Phila., Atlantic City Seashore House. Co-editor: Bone as a Tissue, 1959; assoc. editor Jour. Bone and Joint Surgery, 1947-49, 57-60, 61-64; contbr. articles to profl. jours. Rsch. dir. N.Y. Cancer Rsch. Inst., Inc., 1952-57; mem. orthopedic sect. NRC, 1946-49; med. adviser Phila. chpt. Nat. Found. Poliomyelitis, 1935-55. Capt. M.C., USNR, 1942-46. Fellow ACS, Internat. Coll. Pediatrics; mem. Am. Rheumatism Assn., Phila. Acad. Surgeons, Aid Assn. Phila. County Med. Soc. (sec.-treas. 1947-57, v.p. 1958, pres. 1959-60), Phila. Coll. Physicians, Am. Acad. Orthopaedic Surgeons (treas. 1954-59), Am. Orthopaedic Assn. (pres. 1964-65), Am. Assn. Surgery Trauma, Internat. Soc. Orthopaedic Surgery and Traumatology, AMA (chmn. orthopedic sect. 1955), Argentina de Ortopedia y Traumatologia (corr. mem. extraordinary). Republican. Mem. Soc. of Friends. Home: Haverford Pa. Died Mar. 24, 1987; buried Haverford Friends Meeting Graveyard-Bucklane.

NICHOLSON, JOHN BURTON, JR., librarian; b. Chgo., Dec. 28, 1912; s. John Burton and Florence Love (Bridgman) N., Sr.; m. Mildred Vivian May Livsey, June 7, 1941; 1 son, John Burton. A.B., Washington and Lee U., 1935, A.M., 1936; B.S.L.S., Columbia, 1937; postgrad., U. Chgo., 1940, Western Res. U., from 1951. Reference asst. Duke Library, 1937-38; reference librarian Dickinson Coll., Carlisle, Pa., 1938-43; librarian Fenn Coll., Cleve., 1943-45; librarian Kent (Ohio) State U., 1945-64, dir. library, 1945-66, librarian and head dept. library sci., 1946-66; asso. prof., dir. dept. library tech. Catonsville (Maryland) Community College, 1966-68; chief librarian U. Balt., 1968-86; exec. dir. Congress Acad. Library Dirs.; founder, dir., treas. Episcopal Faculty Conf., 1979-86. Contbr. articles to prof. jours. Mem. Am., Md. library assns., Assn. Coll. and Reference Libraries (v.p. tri-state chpt. 1953-54, pres. 1954-55), Ohio Library Assn. (pres. coll. library div. 1947-48, pres. Kent Research group 1949), Phi Sigma Kappa. Republican. Episcopalian. Clubs: Wranglers Torch, Brotherhood of St. Andrew, Rowfant, Grolier, Balt. Bibliophiles. Home: Baltimore Md. Died Oct. 14, 1986.

NICHOLSON, ROBERT LAWRENCE, educator; b. Chgo., Oct. 17, 1908; s. Benjamin Franklin and Grace (Butters) N. AB, U. Chgo., 1930, AM, 1931, PhD, 1938. Mem. faculty Bucknell U., 1943-46; prof. history U. Ill., Chgo., 1946-85. Author: A History of Chicago's Industrial Development, 1833-1940, 1941, Joscelyn I, Prince of Edessa, 1954. Mem. English-Speaking Union, Chgo. Coun. Fgn. Relations, Fgn. Policy Assn., Atlantic Union Com., Phi Beta Kappa, Phi Delta Theta. Home: Chicago Ill. Died Oct. 22, 1985.

NICHT, FRANK JOSEPH, newspaper syndicate executive; b. Auburn, N.Y., Feb. 23, 1889; s. Joseph and Frances (Ellstner) N.; m. Anne Hammesfahr, Oct. 10, 1914. Student pub. schs., Poughkeepsie, N.Y. Comml. mgr. United Press, 1908-13; comml. rep. AT&T, 1914-16; svc. and bus. mgr. Internat. News Svc., 1917-19; sales mgr. King Features Syndicate, 1919-43; gen. sales mgr. King Features Syndicate, Internat. News Svc., Internat. News Photos, 1943-56; dir. Hearst Corp., from 1956. Mem. Masons. Mem. Reformed Ch. Home: North Tarrytown N.Y. †

NICKELL, VERNON LEWIS, school system administrator; b. Bellflower, Ill., Mar. 2, 1891; s. Elias D. and Ida Mae (Lewis) N.; m. Leta O. Nofzigger, 1916 (dec.); children: Geraldine N. Donald, Maxine N. Kettlewell. Student, Ill. Wesleyan U., 3 yrs., EdD (hon.); BE, Ill. State Normal U., 1929; MA, U. Ill., 1932. Rural sch. tchr. 1909; supt. schs. Champaign, Ill., 1930-43; supt schs. State of Ill., 1943-59; chm. bd. State Life of Ill., from 1959. Pres. County Tb Assn.; past pres. Arrowhead council Boy Scouts Am.; mem. Nursing Sch. com. Burnham City Hosp.; served on many local civic welfare coms. Recipient citations and commendations for outstanding record as supt. pub. instrn. by various univs., coll. and assns. Mem. NEA, Ill. Edn. Assn. (past pres.), East Cen. Dist. Edn. Assn., Chief State Sch. Officers of U.S. (past pres.), Exchange Club, Masons, Shriners, Elks, Kappa Phi Kappa, Phi Delta Kappa, Kappa Delta Pi. Republican. Methodist. Home: Champaign Ill. †

NICKSON, JAMES JOSEPH, physician, educator; b. Portland, Oreg., Dec. 31, 1915; s. Delbert Harry and Elvira W. (Wallin) N.; m. Margaret Jane Hofrichter, June 12, 1939 (div.); children: Robert Frazier, James Bridges; m. Elizabeth Gibson, Dec. 2, 1967; 1 child, Michael Andrew. BS, U. Wash., 1936; postgrad., Harvard U. Med. Sch., 1936-38; MD, Johns Hopkins U., 1940. Mem. metall. lab. U. Chgo., 1942-47; sr. fellow NRC, 1947-49, cons.; dir. dept. radiation therapy Meml. Hosp.; mem. Sloan-Kettering Inst., N.Y.C., 1950-65; prof. Sloan-Kettering div. Cornell Med. Sch., 1952-55, Cornell U. Med. Coll., 1955-65; chmn. dept. radiation therapy Michael Reese Hosp., Chgo., 1965-72; mem. Michael Reese Med. Research Inst., 1965-72; prof. radiology Pritzker Sch. Medicine, U. Chgo., 1969-72; prof. radiation oncology U. Tenn. Med. Sch., 1972-81; dir. Memphis Regional Cancer Ctr., 1974-79; cons. USPHS. Editor: Symposium on Radiobiology, 1952; contbr. articles to profl. jours. Fellow Am. Coll. Radiology; mem. Radiation Rsch. Soc., AAAS, AMA, Am. Soc. Therapeutic Radiologists (past pres.), Radiol. Soc. N.Am., N.Y. Acad. Scis., Am. Radium Soc., Chgo. Roentgen Soc., Chgo. Med. Soc., Am. Cancer Soc., Internat. Coll. Radiology, Pan Am. Med. Assn., Phi Beta Kappa, Sigma Xi. Home: Germantown Tenn. Died Nov. 22, 1985.

NIDECKER, JOHN E., religious community brother; b. Phila., Mar. 30, 1913; s. Arnold W. and Anne J. (Williams) N.; m. Jeanne Kara Brodhead, Apr. 12, 1958; children: Arnold W., Stephen A. Student, LaSalle U. extensions, 1948-49, Cranston U. Various positions in marketing Sun Oil Co., Phila., 1934-47; various mgmt. positions Cities Service Co., Inc., 1947-69, corp. mgr. bus. devel., 1967-69; dep. spl. asst. to President Nixon, 1969-73, spl. asst., 1973-74; spl. asst. to President Ford, 1974-75; pres., owner John E. Nidecker & Co., 1975-79; professed Brotherhood of St. Gregory, 1976, asst. superior, 1977; pastor St. Anne's Ch., 1979-81; curate Prince George's Parish-Christ Ch., 1981; staff St. Dunstan's Ch., McLean, Va., 1981-86; mem. advance staff Dwight D. Eisenhower and Richard M. Nixon, 1956, 60, 62, 68. Lay reader Episc. Ch., 1929-88. Served with USMCR, 1936-40. Mem. Order St. Luke. Club: Capitol Hill (Washington). Lodges: Shriners, Masons. Home: Rockville Md. Died June 20, 1988.

NIDEN, GEORGE, manufacturing company executive; b. Oshkosh, Wis., Apr. 7, 1917; s. Michael and Paraskeva (Krevchena) N.; m. Barbara C. Macdonald, Aug. 23, 1945; children: Martha C., George, Wilma Bates and Lucinda Hubbard (twins). B.S., U. Mass., 1938; postgrad., Northeastern U., 1941, Yale U., 1942, Boston U., 1950. With Am. Locker Co., Inc., 1939-85; successively trainee, staff asst., dist. mgr. Am. Locker Co., Inc. (West Coast), dir. sales, 1950, asst. v.p. sales-service, 1957-62, v.p., 1962-64, exec. v.p., 1964-73, pres., 1973-85; also dir; exec. v.p. Can. Locker Co., Ltd., 1966-73, pres., 1973-85; also dir; exec. v.p. Automatic Voting Machine Corp., 1973; ret. 1985. Served from pvt. to maj. U.S. Army and USAAF, 1941-45. Mem. Am. Legion, Adelphia (v.p.), Am. Assn. Airport Execs., Am. Bus Assn., Can. Motorcoach Assn., Hocksters Internat. (pres. 3 years), Am. Operators Councils Internat., U. Mass. Alumni Assn. (dir. 1981-86), Kappa Sigma (pres.). Republican. Presbyterian. Clubs: Livingston (dir.), Wellesley Country, Sportsmen of Western N.Y, Rod and Gun. Home: Auburndale N.Y. Died Feb. 1, 1986.

NIEMOELLER, MARTIN, clergyman; b. Lippstadt, Westphalia, Germany, Jan. 14, 1892; s. Heinrich and Paula (Mueller) N.; m. Else Bremer, Apr. 20, 1919 (dec. Aug. 1961); children: Brigitte (Mrs. Benno Johannesson), Hans Jochen (dec.), Heinz Hermann, Jan, Herta, Jutta (dec.), Martin. Ed. pub. schs., Lippstadt, 1898-1900; student, Gymnasium, Elberfeld, 1900-10; student theology, U. Muenster, 1920-23; DD, U. Göttingen, Germany, St. Louis U., U. Halifax, Bethany Bibl. Sem., Chgo., Budapest, Hungary, Bratislava, Czechoslovakia, U. London (Ont.), Inter-Am. U. P.R.; DLitt, U. New Delhi, India. Served in German Imperial Navy, 1910-20, submarine service, 1916-18; farm laborer 1919; dir. Home Mission for Province Westphalen, 1923-31; pastor Lutheran Parish, Berlin-Dahlem, 1931-45; founder Pastors Emergency League to Resist Hitlerism, 1933; confined in concentration camps of Sachenhausen and Dachau as Hitler's personal prisoner 1937-45; v.p. Evang. Ch. in Germany, 1945-49, pres. office fgn. affairs, 1945-56; pres. of ch. in Hesse and Nassau 1947-64; addressed biennial meeting Fed. Coun. Chs. of Christ, Seattle, Wash., 1946. Author books and articles on religious and political themes. Chmn. Fellowship of Christian Chs. in Germany, 1948-61; standing dep. exec. com. World Coun. Chs., 1948-61, pres. 1961-68. Recipient Lenin Peace prize Soviet Union, 1967; great cross Order Merit (Fed. Republic Germany), 1970. Home: Wiesbaden Federal Republic of Germany. †

NIESS, ROBERT JUDSON, educator; b. Mason City, Iowa, Aug. 25, 1911; s. George and Mary Anne (Thibodeau) N.; m. Martha Isabelle Laing, June 18, 1938; children: Martha (Mrs. H. Gene Moss), Barbara (Mrs. John W. Buys Jr.). AB magna cum laude, U. Minn., 1933, AM, 1934, PhD, 1937. Teaching fellow Romance langs. Washington U., St. Louis, 1936-37, instr., 1937-39; asst. prof. Mundelein Coll., Chgo., 1939-42; assoc. prof. U. Ky., 1946-47; asst. prof. French Harvard U., 1947-49; from assoc. prof. to prof. U. Mich., Ann Arbor, 1949-72; prof. Duke U., 1972-81. Author: Julien Benda, 1952, Zola, Cèzanne and Manet, 1968; contbr. articles to profl. jours. Dem. candidate for state senate, Mich., 1952. Maj. USAAF, 1942-46. Recipient U. Mich. Press prize, 1970; Am. Coun. Learned Socs. fellow, 1951-52; Am. Philos. Soc. grantee, 1956, 68, 74. Mem. AAUP, Modern Lang. Assn., South Atlantic Modern Lang. Assn., Am. Assn. Tchrs. French, Palmes Acadèmiques, Phi Beta Kappa, Theta Chi, Phi Sigma Iota. Home: Durham N.C. Died May 20, 1981.

NIMS, MARSHALL GRANT, physician; b. Bronxville, N.Y., July 11, 1908; s. Harry Dwight and Emma C. (Grant) N.; m. Mary Elizabeth Naugle, Aug. 23, 1933; children: Barbara Grant, Julie Boeck, Peter Dwight, Christopher Grant. MD, U. Colo., 1936. Diplomate Am. Bd. Internal Medicine. Intern Harper Hosp., Detroit, 1936-37; house physician Bellevue Hosp., N.Y.C., 1937-39; pvt. practice Denver, 1939-42, 45-84; attending physician Denver Gen. Hosp. Maj. AUS, 1942-45. Sigma Xi rsch. fellow, 1940-84. Fellow ACP; mem. Denver Country Club, Alpha Delta Phi, Nu Sigma Nu. Home: Denver Colo. Died Apr. 2, 1984.

NININGER, HARVEY HARLOW, meteoriticist; b. Conway Springs, Kans., Jan. 17, 1887; s. James Buchanan and Mary Ann (Bower) N.; m. Addie N. Delp, June 5, 1914; children: Robert D., Doris Elaine, Margaret Ann. Student, Northwestern State Tchrs. Coll., 1907-09; AB, McPherson Coll., 1914, DSc, 1937; AM, Pomono Coll., 1916, DSc (hon.), 1976; postgrad., U. Calif., 1915-18; LLD, Ariz. State U., 1961. Tchr. rural schs. 1909; substitute prof. biology Northwestern State Tchrs. Coll., Alva, Okla., 1912-13; prof. La Verne Coll., 1914-18, Southwestern Coll., Winfield, Kans., 1919-20, McPherson Coll., 1920-30; founder Nininger Lab. for Rsch. on Meteorities (name changed to Am. Meteorite Lab. 1937), Denver, dir., 1930-46; curator meteorites Colo. Mus. Natural History; cons. N.Am. Aviation Space Sci. Lab.; pres., founder Rocky Mountain Summer Sch., Palmer Lake, Colo.; established Am. Meteorite Mus., 1946; extensive rsch. Ariz. Meteorite Crater, 1946-56; expdn. Australia, study meteorite craters, 1958-59; explored and surveyed new meteorite crater Western Australia, 1959; studied meteorite collections, Europe, 1960; meteorite expn. B.C., Can., 1966. Author: Our Stone-Pelted Planet, 1933, A Comet Strikes the Earth, 1942, Chips From the Moon, 1947, Nininger Collection of Meteorites, 1950, Out of the Sky, 1952, Arizona's Meteorite Crater, 1956, Ask a Question About Meteorites, 1962, Field Guide to Birds of Central Kansas, Published Papers of H. H. Nininger, 1971, Find a Falling Star, 1972, A Photographic Study of Surface Features of Meteorites, 1977; contbr. numerous articles to sci. jours. Spl. field agt. food conservation program U.S. Bur. Entomology, 1918-19. Recipient Leonard medal on 80th birthday; established Nininger Meteorite award, 1961. Fellow AAAS, Soc. for Rsch. on Meteorites (co-founder, sec. 1933-37, pres. 1937-41), Kans. Acad. Sci. (pres. 1924-25); mem. Am. Astron. Union. Congregationalist. Home: Sedona Ariz. Died Mar. 1, 1986.

NIVOLA, COSTANTINO, sculptor; b. Sardegna, Italy, July 5, 1911; came to U.S., 1939; m. Ruth Guggenheim, Aug. 4, 1938; children—Pietro, Claire. M.A., Inst. Superiore d'Arte, Monza, Italy, 1936. Instr. Columbia U., N.Y.C., 1961-63; dir. design workshop Harvard U. Grad. Sch., Cambirdge, Mass., 1953-57; vis. prof. Carpenter Ctr. for Visual Arts, Harvard U., 1970, 73, U. Calif.-Berkeley, 1978, 81, Dartmouth Coll., 1978, Royal Acad. Fine Arts, The Hague, Netherlands, 1982; artist-in-residence Am. Acad., Rome, 1972; developed sand casting technique; executed numerous murals. One-man shows: Tibor de Nagy Gallery, N.Y.C., 1950, Harvard U., Cambridge, 1956, Architectural League N.Y., 158, Arts Club Chgo., 1960, Galleria dell'Ariete, Milan, Italy, 1962, Byron Gallery, N.Y.C., 1965, 66, 67, Marlborough Galleria d'Arte, Rome, 1973, Boston Inst. Contemporary Art, 1974, Dartmouth Coll., Hanover,

N.H., 1978, Washburn Gallery, N.Y.C., 1985, 87, Duchamp Gallery, Cagliari, Italy, 1982, San Quirico, Italy, 1987, D.E.A. Found., 1988; group shows include: Bklyn. Mus., 1947, Quadrienale, Rome, 1950, Riverside Mus., N.Y.C., 1955, Whitney Mus. Am. Art, N.Y.C., 1957, Inst. Contemporary Art, N.Y.C., 1957, Dallas Mus., 1958, Corcoran Art Gallery, Washington, 1958, Mus. Modern Art, N.Y.C., 1958, Sculptors Guild, N.Y.C., 1966, Peggi Guggenheim Collection Mus., Venice, Italy, 1988; designed war meml. dedicated to Four Chaplains, Washington, 1954; executed bas-reliefs and murals; works include commn. of 15 large sculptures in marbel for govtl. bldg. in Cagliari, Italy, 1986-87; represented in permanent collections: Hirshhorn Mus., Washington, Phila. Mus. Art, Mus. Modern Art, N.Y.C., Whitney Mus. Am. Art, N.Y.C., Kellogg's Hdqrs. Mem. Vietnam Vet. Meml. Jury, Washington, 1982. Recipient numerous awards, including cert. of excellence Am. Inst. Graphic Arts, 1956-57, Phila. Decorators Club award, 1959, Fine Arts gold medal AIA, 1967, award for excellence in design Art Commn. N.Y.C., 1985; hon. fellow Yale U., 1984. Fellow Royal Acad. Fine Arts (Netherlands) (hon.); mem. Nat. Inst. Arts and Letters, Am. Acad. in Rome, Archtl. League N.Y. (silver medal 1962, 65). Home: East Hampton N.Y. Died May 5, 1988; buried Green River Cemetery, East Hampton, N.Y.

NIX, ROBERT N. C., congressman; b. Orangeburg, S.C., Aug. 9, 1908; s. Nelson Cornelius and Sylvia (Benjamin) N.; m. Ethel Lanier (dec.); 1 child, Robert N. C. Jr. AB, Lincoln U., 1921; LLB, U. Pa., 1924. Bar: Pa., U.S. Dist. Ct. (ea. dist.) Pa. Pvt. practice 1925-87; spl. dep. atty. gen. Commonwealth of Pa., 1934-38; with escheats div. Dept. Revenue; mem. policy com., co-chmn. inter-relations com. Dem. Campaign Com., Phila., 1953-87; mem. 86th-95th Congresses from 2d dist. Pa., 1957-78; chmn. Post Office and Civil Svc. Com., ranking mem. Fgn. Affairs Com. del. Dem. Nat. Conv., Chgo., 1956; asst. treas. Dem. County Com., 1958; mem. Phila. Citizens' Com. Against Juvenile Delinquencies, NAACP, YMCA. Mem. Phila. Bar Assn., Am. Woodman, Pyramid Club, Elks, Omega Psi Phi. Baptist. Home: Philadelphia Pa. Died June 22, 1987.

NOBLE, JAMES VAN PETTEN, lawyer; b. Las Vegas, N.Mex., Apr. 4, 1922; s. Merrill Emmett and Martha (Van Petten) N.; m. Sara Jane Crail, Sept. 10, 1948; children—James Van Petten, Sara Ann, Charles Fulton. Student U. N.Mex., 1940-43; LL.B., U. Colo., 1949; Bar: N.Mex. 1949, Navajo Nation 1973. Assoc., Noble and Spiess, Las Vegas, 1949-51; ptnr. Noble, Spiess and Noble, 1951-55; ptnr. Noble and Noble, 1955-60; asst. chief counsel Las Vegas Savings Bank, 1949-59, chief counsel, 1959-63; asst. chief counsel Found. Res. Ins. Co., 1949-57, chief counsel, 1957-63; asst. chief counsel Lloyds N.Mex. Ins. Co., 1950-57, chief counsel, 1957-63; asst. city atty. city of Las Vegas, 1949-58, spl. asst. atty. gen., 1956-57; asst. dist. atty. 4th Jud. Dist., 1957-59; city atty. Las Vegas, 1958-60; asst. atty. gen. State of N.Mex., 1963-68, 1st asst. atty. gen., 1968-70; chief counsel Merc. Investment Corp., 1970-86, also dir.; spl. asst. atty. gen. State Hwy. Dept. N.Mex., 1970-82; dir. Las Vegas Portland Cement Co.; mem. Commn. on Uniform Rules of Criminal Procedure, Uniform Jury Instrns., Rules of Procedure in Children's Ct., N.Mex. supreme Ct.; mem. commn. real property, land titles, ins., legal retreat N.Mex. State Bar. Author: (student with Ben S. Galland) Re-statement of the laws of Corporations, Colorado, 1949. Mem. exec. com., bd. dirs., v.p. N.Mex. Soc. of Crippled Children; mem. Mayor's Santa Fe Action Airport com., 1972-86; bd. dirs. Las Vegas community TB, Inc., 1959-63, Las Vegas Devel. Corp. Served with AUS, 1942-43, to 2d lt. USAAF, 1941-57; maj. Res. ret. Mem. Jaycees (internat. senator 1967-86, pres. N.Mex. unit 1957-58), ABA (N.Mex. publications, Law Day, Adv. opinions, unauthorized practice of law, grievance), N.Mex. State Bar Assn., San Miguel County Bar Assn. (pres. 1954-63), World Peace Through Law Ctr., Am. Judicature Soc. Died Oct. 12, 1986. Home: Santa Fe N.Mex.

NOGUCHI, ISAMU, sculptor; b. Los Angeles, Nov. 17, 1904; s. Yonejiro and Leonie (Gilmour) N.; m. Yoshiko Yamaguchi, 1953 (div. 1955). Student, Columbia U., 1922-24, Leonardo da Vinci Art Sch., 1924; studied with, Constantin Brancusi, 1928; studied drawing, Peking, China. Author: A Sculptor's World, 1968, (catalogue of permanent collection) Isamu Noguchi Garden Museum, 1987; subject of: Isamu Noguchi (Sam Hunter), 1978, The Sculpture of Isamu Noguchi, 1924-79 (Nancy Grove and Diane Botnick), 1980; one-man shows include Eugene Shoen Gallery, N.Y.C., 1928, Marie Sterner Gallery, N.Y.C., 1929, Marie Harriman Gallery, N.Y.C., 1935, Arts Club, Chgo., 1929, 32, Becker Gallery, N.Y.C., 1931, 32, Demotte Gallery, N.Y.C., 1932, Mellon Galleries, Phila., 1933, San Francisco Mus. Art, 1942, Mitsukoshi Store, Tokyo, 1951, Mus. Modern Art, Kamakura, 1952, Stable Gallery, 1953, 55, 59, Cordier and Ekstrom Gallery, 1963, 65, 67, 70, 71, Claude Bernard Gallery, Paris, 1964, Whitney Mus. Modern Art, 1966, 68, 80, Gimpel Fils and Gimpel Hanover, 1972, Pace Gallery, 1975, 80, 83, 86, Emmerich Galleries, N.Y.C., 1980, Galerie Maeght, Paris, 1981, comprehensive traveling exhbn. including, Walker Art Center, 1978, Denver Art Mus., 1978, Cleve. Mus. Art, 1979, Detroit Inst. Arts, 1979, San Francisco Mus. Modern Art, 1979, George J. Doizaki Gallery, Los Angeles, 1983, Jacksonville Art Mus., 1983, Arnold Herstand Gallery, 1985, Venice Biennale, Italy, 1986; exhibited numerous group shows in U.S., fgn. countries; represented in permanent collections: Whitney Mus. Am. Art, Met. Mus. Art, Mus. Modern Art, N.Y.C., 140 Broadway, N.Y.C., Seattle Art Mus., Western Wash. State Coll., Bellingham, Bayerische Vereinsbank, Munich, Germany, Cleve. Mus., Art Inst. Chgo., Tokyo Mus. Modern Art, Art Gallery of Ontario, Toronto, Rijksmuseum Kroller-Muller, The Netherlands, Ulster Mus., Belfast, others; important works include mural in market, Rodriguez, Mexico, bas-relief, A.P. Bldg., N.Y.C., gardens, Keio (Japan) U., UNESCO Bldg., Paris, Beinecke Rare Book and Manuscript Library, Yale U., New Haven, Conn., sculpture and Sunken Garden in Chase Manhattan Bank Plaza, N.Y.C., Billy Rose Sculpture Garden, Israeli Mus., Jerusalem, Calif. Scenario, Costa Mesa, Little Tokyo, Los Angeles, fountains at Expo '70, Osaka, Japan, fountain and sculpture, John Hancock Bldg., Chgo., GSA, Seattle, IBM, Armonk, N.Y., Pepsi Co., Purchase, N.Y., Dodge Meml. Fountain, Detroit Civic Center Plaza, playground, Atlanta, sculpture, Storm King Art Ctr., interior garden and granite pylon, Sogetsu Sch. of Flower Arranging, Tokyo, 2 bridges for Peace Park, Hiroshima, Japan, Bayfront Pk., Miami, Fla., Moere Pk., Hokkaido, Japan; designed 20 sets for Martha Graham ballets Frontier, 1935, Herodiade, Appalachian Spring, 1945, Dark Meadow, 1946, Ballet Orpheus; designed: sets and costumes King Lear, London, 1955; designer Akari lamps. Recipient 1st prize Nat. Competition for relief at entrance to A.P. Bldg. 1938, Logan medal 63d Exhbn. Painting and Sculpture Art Inst. Chgo. 1959, Gold medal N.Y. Archtl. League 1966, Brandeis Creative Arts award 1966, 2d prize Soc. Four Arts Competition, Palm Beach, Fla. 1974,. Kyoto Prize, Inamori Found., 1986, Nat. Arts Medal, 1987; Guggenheim fellow, 1927-29, Bollingen fellow, 1950; recipient The Order of the Sacred Treasure, Gold Rays with Neck Ribbon Imperial decoration, 1988. Mem. Am. Inst. Art and Sci., Am. Acad. Art and Letters, N.Y. Soc. Architects. Home: L.I. City N.Y. Died Dec. 30, 1988.

NOLAN, LLOYD, actor; b. San Francisco, Aug. 11, 1902; s. James and Margaret Nolan; m. Mell Efird, 1933; children: Melinda Joyce, Jay. MA in Theatre, Coll. Theatre Arts of Pasadena Playhouse, 1958. Made Broadway debut in Cape Cod Follies, 1929, appeared in (plays) Sweet Stranger, 1931, Reunion in Vienna, 1931-32, The Third Americana Revue, 1932, One Sunday Afternoon, 1933, One More River, 1960; film appearances include Stolen Harmony, 1934, Texas Rangers, 1936, Big Brown Eyes, 1937, House Across the Bay, 1943, Bataan, 1943, Guadalcanal, 1943, The House on 92d St., 1945, Circumstantial Evidence, 1945, A Tree Grows in Brooklyn, 1945, Somewhere in the Night, 1946, Two Smart People, 1946, Lady in the Lake, 1946, Wild Harvest 1947, Green Grass of Wyoming, 1948, Street with No Name, 1948, Bay Boy, 1949, Easy Living, 1949, The Sun Comes Up, 1949, The Lemon Drop Kid, 1951, We Joined the Navy, 1952, Island in the Sky, 1953, The Last Hunt, 1956, Santiago, 1956, Abandon Ship, 1957, A Hatful of Rain, 1957, Peyton Place, 1957, Sergeant Ryker, 1958, Portrait in Black, 1960, Susan Slade, 1961, Circus, 1964, Never Too Late, 1965, The Double Man, 1968, Ice Station Zebra, 1969, Airport, 1970, Earthquake, 1974, Hannah and Her Sisters, 1985; (TV) Martin Kane, Private Eye, 1951-52, Julia, 1968-71; toured in The Silver Whistle, 1950; co-star in Island in the Sky, Crazylegs, All American, 1953; played role of Philip Queeg in The Caine Mutiny Court Martial, N.Y.C., 1953-54, London, 1955. Recipient Davidson award, Oustanding Actor award N.Y. Drama Critics, 1953-54, Emmy award, 1955. Died Sept. 27, 1985.

NOLAN, RAY D., state official; b. Hurley, Wis., Oct. 25, 1891; m. Violet Baker; 1 son, Terry. Mining engr. Minn. Dept. Lands and Minerals, 1933, chief engr., 1935, dir., from 1937; emergency coordinator mines, War Prodn. Bd., World War II. With U.S. Army World War I. Mem. AIME. Home: Saint Paul Minn. †

NOLEN, WILLIAM ANTHONY, surgeon, author; b. Holyoke, Mass., Mar. 20, 1928; s. James Robert and Katherine Margaret (Dillon) N.; m. Joan Helene Scheibel, Nov. 28, 1953; children: James, Joan, William, Anna, Julius, Mary. A.B., Holy Cross Coll., 1949; M.D., Tufts U., 1953. Diplomate: Am. Bd. Surgery. Intern Cornell surg. div. Bellevue Hosp., N.Y.C., 1953-54; resident in surgery Cornell surg. div. Bellevue Hosp., 1954-55, 57-60; surgeon Litchfield (Minn.) Clinic, 1960-86; mem. staff Meeker County Hosp., Litchfield, Minn.; chief dept. surgery Meeker County Hosp., 1960-79, 84-86; attending surgeon Hennepin County Hosp., U. Minn., Mpls., 1962-69. Author: The Making of a Surgeon, 1970, A Surgeon's World, 1972, Healing: A Doctor in Search of a Miracle, 1974, Surgeon Under The Knife, 1976, The Baby in The Bottle, 1978, A Surgeon's Book of Hope, 1980, Crisis Time! Love, Marriage and the Male at Midlife, 1984; columnist, McCall's Mag. Served as capt. M.C. USAR, 1955-57. Fellow A.C.S. Home: Litchfield Minn. Died Dec. 20, 1986, buried Litchfield, Mass.

NOLTMANN, ERNST AUGUST, biochemist, educator; b. Gotha, Germany, June 27, 1931; came to U.S., 1959, naturalized, 1971; s. Ernst Heinrich and Tela Adelheid (Hoecke) N.; m. Lisel Ruth Voss, June 2, 1956; children: Ingo, Udo. Student, U. Mônster, Germany, 1950-53, U. Freiburg, 1953-54; MD, U. Dôsseldorf, Germany, 1956. Asst. biochemist U. Dôsseldorf Med. Sch., 1956-59; postdoctoral fellow U. Wis. Inst. Enzyme Rsch., 1959-62; asst. prof. biochemistry U. Calif., Riverside, 1962-65, assoc. prof., 1965-69, prof. biochemistry, 1969-86, chmn. dept., 1971-72, 75-76, assoc. dean. biomed. scis., 1976-83, divisional dean biomed. scis., 1983-86. USPHS rsch. grantee, 1963-86; NSF grantee, 1964-66, 79-86. Mem. Am. Soc. Biol. Chemists, Am. Chem. Soc., Deutsche Gesellschaft fôr Biologische Chemi, Sigma Xi. Home: Riverside Calif. Died Feb. 26, 1986; interred Olivewood Cemetery, Riverside.

NORDHEIM, LOTHAR WOLFGANG, physicist; b. Munich, Nov. 7, 1899; came to U.S., 1935, naturalized, 1940; s. Moritz Maximilian and Anna Lore (Tandler) N.; m. Gertrud Poeschl, Jan. 12, 1935 (dec. 1949); 1 child, Erik Vincent. PhD, Goettingen U., 1923; ScD, Karlsruhe, 1951; DSc (hon.), Purdue U., 1962. Lectr. Goettingen U., 1928-33; rsch. assoc. Paris, 1933-34, Harlem, The Netherlands, 1934; prof. physics. Duke U., 1937-56; chief physicist, dir. physics div. Clinton Labs. (name now Oak Ridge Nat. Lab.), 1943-47; resident cons. Los Alamos Sci. Lab., 1950-52; rsch. physicist Gulf Gen. Atomic Inc., San Diego, 1956-59, sr. rsch. adviser, 1959-85, chmn. theoretical physics dept., 1960-65; vis. prof. Ohio State U., 1930, Moscow, 1932, Purdue U., 1935-37, Heidelberg, 1949; mem. adv. com. on reactor physics AEC, 1963-85. Mem. editorial coun. Annals of Physics; mem. editorial bd. Nuclear Sci. and Engring.; contbr. articles to sci. publs. Rockefeller fellow, 1927-28. Fellow Am. Phys. Soc., Am. Nuclear Soc. (past bd. dirs.); mem. AAAS, Fedn. Am. Scientists. Home: La Jolla Calif. Died Oct. 1, 1985.

NORDMEYER, HENRY W(ALDEMAR), German language educator; b. Magdeburg, Germany, July 2, 1891; came to U.S., 1913, naturalized, 1924; s. Ernst August and Mary Barker (Andrews) N.; m. Frieda Ida Zimmerman, June 18, 1932; 2 stepsons: Harry Wolfgang and Klaus Willy Altvater. Grad., Gymnasium, Braunschweig, Germany, 1910; student, U. Leipzig, 1910-13; PhD, U. Wis., 1914. Asst. in German U. Wis., 1913-14; instr. Ohio State U., 1914-15, U. Ill., 1915-18; with Open Ct. Pub. Co., Chgo., 1918-20, U. Chgo. Press, 1920-21; prof. modern langs. Grand Rapids (Mich.) Jr. Coll., 1921-24; asst. prof. Swarthmore Coll., 1924-25, Washington U., 1925-29; assoc. prof. German, chmn. dept. NYU, 1929-32, prof., chmn. dept., 1932-35; prof. German, chmn. dept. U. Mich., Ann Arbor, from 1935. Author: (with K.E. Richter) Introduction to Commercial German, 1931; translator into German verse: Rubaiyat des Omar Khayyam by Edward Fitzgerald, Letzte Fassung deutsch, 1926; contbr. articles to profl. jours. Mem. MLA (exec. coun. 1947-50, 2d v.p. 1952, pres. 1916, proc. editorial com. 1930-40), Soc. for Advancement Scandinavian Study, Am. Assn. Tchrs. German (exec. coun. 1941-44), Rsch. Club U. Mich., Phi Kappa Phi. Home: Ann Arbor Mich. †

NORDSTROM, URSULA (URSULA LITCHFIELD), book editor; b. N.Y.C.; d. William and Marie (Nordstrom) Litchfield. Student, Northfield Sch. for Girls, Scudder Prep. Sch. Asst. to children's book editor Harper & Bros., 1936-40, head children's book dept., from 1940, also sr. v.p., bd. dirs. Author: The Secret Language, 1960. Mem. ALA, Am. Assn. Sch. Librs., Children's Libr. Assn., Children's Book Coun. (pres. 1954), Cosmopolitan Club. Home: New York N.Y. Died Oct. 11, 1988.

NORRIS, LOUIS W(ILLIAM), college president; b. Columbus, Ohio, Feb. 3, 1906; s. Vernon Ward and Gertrude (Hamilton) N.; m. Florence Cronise Howard, June 4, 1931; children: Martha Ellen, Joanna May. AB, Otterbein Coll., 1928, LLD, 1953; BST magna cum laude, Boston U., 1931, PhD, 1937; postgrad., U. Berlin, 1931-32, Harvard U., 1936-37. Ordained to ministry Meth. Ch., 1934. Pastor Evang. Congl. Ch., Dunstable, Mass., 1930-31, 32-37; asst. prof. philosophy and religion Baldwin-Wallace Coll., Berea, Ohio, 1937-39, assoc. prof., v.p., 1939-46; vis. prof. Garrett Biblical Inst., Evanston, Ill., summer 1945, 50; prof. philosophy DePauw U., 1946-52, head dept. philosophy and religion, 1947-52, dean, 1950-52; pres. MacMurray Coll., Ill., 1952-86; mem. Conf. on Christian Bases of World Order, 1943; chmn. Ohio Conf. on Character Edn., 1946; participant 9th and 10th Confs. on Sci., Philosophy and Religion, 1948, 49. Author: Polarity: A Philosophy of Tensions Among Values, 1956, The Good New Days, 1956; contbr. articles to profl. jours. Chmn. Ohio area bd. student activities YMCA, 1942-45, mem. Nat. Coun., 1943-46; mem. Nat. Student Com., 1943-46, Nat. Commn. on Our Christian Purpose, YMCA-YWCA, 1942; mem. com. on exams. and advanced standing Ohio Coll. Assn., 1942-46; chmn. tech. cons. com. White House Conf. on Children and Youth, Ill. sect., 1960. Roswell R. Robinson fellow Boston U., Borden Parker Bowne fellow Boston U., Inst. Internat. Edn. fellow, 1931-32. Mem. Am. Philos. Assn., AAUP, Nat. Assn. Biblical Instrs. (treas. 1947-50), Ill. Conf. Meth. Chs., NEA, Nat. Assn. Advancement Sci., Delta Phi Alpha. Home: Jacksonville Ill. Died Apr. 14, 1986.

NORRIS, ROBERT REYNOLDS, newspaper executive; b. Columbus, Ga., Nov. 11, 1926; s. G. Rudolph and Eva Roberta (Reynolds) N.; m. Nita Adams, Aug. 8, 1947; children: Christopher Reynolds, Ann Allison. B.S., Auburn (Ala.) U., 1957. Formerly mech. supr. Columbus (Ga.) Enquirer, Oreg. Jour., St. Petersburg (Fla.) Times; formerly bus. mgr., gen. mgr. Augusta (Ga.) Chronicle-Herald; now v.p., gen. mgr. Lubbock (Tex.) Avalanche-Jour. Trustee Meth. Hosp., Lubbock, West Tex. Mus. Assn.; bd. dirs. Tex. Tech. Found., Red Raider Club, S. Plains Fair; exec. bd. Ranch Hdqrs.; mem. pres.'s bd. Lubbock Christian Coll.; fin. chmn. Goodfellows Club; past v.p. Lubbock Arthritis Found.; past pres., dir. Lubbock Symphony. Served with USN, 1943-46. Mem. Newspaper Enterprise Assn., Newspaper Advt. Bur., Tex. Daily Newspaper Assn. (dir.), Am. Press Inst., UPI Editors Assn., So. Newspapers Pubs. Assn., Am. Newspaper Pubs. Assn., Ducks Unlimited (past chpt. pres.). Presbyterian. Clubs: Lubbock, Lubbock Country, University City. Home: Lubbock Tex. Died Oct. 3, 1986.

NORSTAD, LAURIS, army officer, business executive; b. Mpls., Mar. 24, 1907; s. Martin and Marie (Johnson) N.; m. Isabelle Helen Jenkins, Apr. 27, 1935; 1 dau., Kristin Norstad Jaffe. BS, U.S. Mil. Acad., 1930; grad., AC Sch., 1931, AC Tactical Sch., 1939. Commd. 2d lt. cav. 1930, advanced through grades to gen., 1952; duty with Gen. Hdqrs. Air Force, 1940-42, 43; with N.W. African Air Force; dept. chief staff ops. Hdqrs. USAF; acting vice chief staff Air Forces, 1950; comdr. in chief U.S. and Allied Air Forces in Cen. Europe, 1951; air dep. SHAPE, 1953-56, supreme allied comdr. Europe, 1956-63; ret., 1964; pres. Owens-Corning Fiberglass Corp., 1964-67, chmn., 1967-72, ret., 1972, then chmn. emeritus; dir. emeritus United Air Lines. Hon. trustee Eisenhower Coll. Decorated D.S.M., Silver Star, Legion Merit, Air medal; hon. comdr. Order Brit. Empire; comdr. Legion Honor: Croix de Guerre avec Palme (French); grand officer l'Ordre Ouissam quissam Alaouite Cherifien (Morocco); grand cross Aviz (Portugal); grand cross Order of Merit (Germany); grand cross Royal Order of George I (Greece); knight grand cross Order on Merit of Italian Republic; grand cordon Order of Leopold (Belgium); grand cross Royal Norwegian Order of St. Olaf; grand cross Order of Orange-Nassau (The Netherlands); grand cross Order Crown of Chene (Luxembourg). Mem. English-Speaking Union U.S. (dir.), Army and Navy Club (Washington), Belmont Country Club (Toledo), Links. Home: Tubac Ariz. Died Sept. 12, 1988.

NORTH, CECIL JACKSON, insurance executive; b. Kansas City, Mo., Nov. 15, 1894; s. Cecil Barber and Elizabeth (Keating) N.; m. Adelaide E. Marler, Apr. 9, 1928; children: Cecil J., Mary A. (Mrs. Alan F. French), Sarah (Mrs. Peter N. Hillyer). BS, Harvard U., 1917, MBA, 1921. With Met. Life Ins. Co., N.Y.C., 1920-81, v.p., 1937-58, exec. v.p., bd. dirs., 1958-59, pres., bd. dirs., 1959-67; bd. dirs., mem. exec. com. Am. Coll. Life Underwriters, Life Ins. Sales Agy. Mgmt. Assn., Hartford, Conn., pres., 1946. Capt. F.A., U.S. Army, World War I. Republican. Presbyterian. Clubs: Seminole, Tequesta Country, Harvard (N.Y.C.). Home: Jupiter Fla. Died July 3, 1981.

NORTH, MONROE D., textile company executive; b. N.Y.C., July 19, 1910; s. Louis and Ray (Klein) N.; m. Viola Utstein, Jan. 23, 1933 (dec. 1979); children: Charles, Julie (Mrs. Kenneth Schwarz); m. Evelyn Leader Goldfarb. LLB, Bklyn. Law Sch., 1934, LLM, 1935. V.p. Albert H. Vandam Co., Inc., N.Y.C., 1944-46; v.p., sec. D.B. Fuller & Co., Inc., N.Y.C., 1946-61; v.p. Fruit of the Loom, Inc., N.Y.C., 1961-62, pres., 1962-75; pres. Converse & Co., Inc., 1962-88. Home: Atlantis Fla. Died May 24, 1988.

NORTH, WILLIAM STANLEY, manufacturing company executive; b. Chgo., May 1, 1911; s. Francis Stanley and Julia (Morgan) N.; m. Sarah Jackson, 1934; children: Sarah Randolph, Elizabeth Holmes; m. Patricia Cathcart Armstrong, Mar. 20, 1958 (dec. Nov. 1978); 1 stepson, James Cathcart Armstrong; m. Margo Reid Donald, Dec. 11, 1979; stepchildren—Alanson Donald, Sangwoo Ann, Mrs. James Leonard, Mrs. Gordon Wilson. B.M.E., Harvard U., 1934, postgrad., 1935. With Union Spl. Corp., Chgo., 1935-87; engr. and salesman, personnel dir. Union Spl. Corp., 1941-44, v.p., 1944-47, asst. gen. mgr., 1947-52, pres., gen. mgr., 1952-74, chmn., chief exec. officer, 1974-76, chmn., 1976-87. Bd. dirs. exec. fin. com., past chmn. Lawson YMCA, Chgo.; bd. dirs., v.p., past pres. Lyric Opera Chgo.; trustee, past pres. Allendale Sch. Boys; bd. dirs., v.p., treas. Lake Forest Open Lands Assn.; governing mem. Chgo. Symphony Orch.; mem. U.S. Srs. Golf Assn. Mem. Ill. Mfg. Assn. (past pres.), Midwest Indsl. Mgmt. Assn. (past pres.). Republican. Episcopalian (past sr. warden). Clubs: Univ. (Chgo.), Harvard (Chgo.), Campfire (Chgo.), Casino (Chgo.) (past gov.), Commonwealth (Chgo.) (past pres.), Comml. (Chgo.); Onwentsia (Lake Forest, Ill.) (past gov.), Old Elm (Lake Forest, Ill.) (past gov.), Winter (Lake Forest, Ill.) (past pres.); Tin Whistles (Pinehurst, N.C.); Pine Valley (N.J.) Golf, Gulf Stream Bath and Tennis, Gulf Stream Golf (bd. govs.); Three Score and Ten (Pinehurst, N.C.); Royal and Ancient Golf of St. Andrews (Fife, Scotland). Home: Delray Beach Fla. Died Mar. 23, 1987.

NORTHEN, MARY MOODY, business executive; b. Houston, Feb. 10, 1892; d. William Lewis Jr. and Libbie Rice (Shearn) Moody; m. Edwin Clyde Northen, Dec. 1, 1915. Student pvt. schs. Chmn. bd. Nat. Hotel Co.; past chmn. bd. Moody Nat. Bank; past pres. W.L. Moody & Co., bankers; dir. Am. Nat. Ins. Co. Bd. dirs. Med. Rsch. Found. Tex., Tex. Hist. Found., Sam Rayburn Found.; trustee Galveston Hist. Found., Moody Found.; mem. U. Tex. Com. Seventy-five; assoc. Rice U.; bd. trustees Hollins (Va.) Coll.; bd. trustees, hon. alumnus Va. Mil. Inst., Lexington. Recipient Boy Scouts Am. medallion, 1963. Mem. Galveston Civil League, Galveston Civic Music Assn., A.R.C., Nat. Soc. Colonial Dames Am., Daus. Am. Colonists, DAR, Nat. Soc. U.S. Daus. of 1812, Tex., Va. hist. socs., United Daus. Confederacy, Huguenot Soc. S.C., Order of Washington, Order First Crusade, Colonial Order of Crown, Plantagenet Soc., Nat. Soc. Magna Charta Dames, Soc. Descs. Most Noble Order of Garter, Sovereign Colonial Soc. Am. Royal Desc. Methodist. Home: Galveston Tex. †

NORTHROP, EUGENE STANLEY, banker; b. Kansas City, Mo., May 21, 1905; s. Eugene H. and Josephine (Cooper) N.; m. Elizabeth Lee Latimer, Apr. 11, 1931. AB, U. Pa., 1927; grad., Rutgers U. Grad. Sch. Banking, 1948. With Equitable Trust Co., N.Y.C., 1927-31; with Mfrs. Hanover Trust Co. (formerly Mfrs. Trust Co.), N.Y.C., 1931-84, v.p., 1948-57, sr. v.p., 1957-61, exec. v.p., 1961-70, vice chmn. bd., 1962-70, also bd. dirs. Author (with Arthur Stein): Mathematical Odds in Contract Bridge, 1933. Bd. dirs. Vis. Nurse Svc. N.Y. Comdr. USNR, 1942-45. Mem. University Club, Blind Brook Club, Pine Valley Golf Club, Woodway Country Club, Royal Poincian Golf Club, Phi Gamma Delta (past pres., bd. govs. N.Y. chpt.). Republican. Home: New Canaan Conn. Died Aug. 19, 1984.

NORTHROP, JOHN HOWARD, scientist; b. Yonkers, N.Y., July 5, 1891; s. John I. and Alice Belle (Rich) N.; m. Louise Walker, June 1918; children—Alice Havemeyer, John. W.B. B.S., Columbia U., 1912, M.A., 1913, Ph.D., 1915, D.Sc., 1937; D.Sc., Harvard U., 1936, Yale U., 1937, Princeton U., 1940, Rutgers U., 1941; LL.D., U. Calif., 1939. Cutting traveling fellow Columbia U., 1915; apptd. asst. Rockefeller Inst. for Med. Research, 1916, asso. mem., 1922, member of Inst., 1924-62, prof. of Inst. emeritus, 1962-87; Hitchcock prof. U. Calif., 1939; Thayer lectr. Johns Hopkins U., 1940, De Lamar lectr., 1937; Jesup lectr. Columbia, 1938; prof. bacteriology, biophysics, research biophysicist Donner Lab., U. Calif., 1958-59, prof. emeritus, 1959-87; mem. com. on proteins NRC cons. and official investigator to NDRC, 1942. Author: Crystalline Enzymes; Hon. editor, contbr.: Jour. Gen. Physiology; contbg. editor: Funk & Wagnalls Ency. Trustee Marine Biol. Lab., Woods Hole, Mass. Capt. C.W.S. U.S. Army, 1918-19. Recipient Stevens prize Coll. Phys. and Surg., Columbia, 1930; Chandler medal Columbia, 1937; Giraud medal Nat. Acad. Sci., 1944; shared Nobel prize in chemistry, 1946; certificate of merit, 1948; Columbia Lion Award Alumni Club of Essex County, 1949; Alexander Hamilton medal Columbia U., 1961; Hon. fellow Chem. Soc., London. Mem. Nat. Acad. Sci., S.A.R., Am. Soc. Biol. Chemistry, Soc. Gen. Physiologists, Soc. Philomathique (Paris), Am. Philos. Soc., Sigma Xi (research fellowship com.), Phi Lambda Upsilon, Kais. Deutch. Akad. der Naturforscher, Delta Kappa Epsilon. Club: Century Assn. Home: Wickenberg Ariz. Died May 27, 1987; cremated.

NOVIKOFF, ALEX BENJAMIN, cell biologist, educator; b. Russia, Feb. 28, 1913; came to U.S., 1913, naturalized, 1918; s. Jack and Anna (Tretyakoff) N.; m. Phyllis M. Iaciofano, Dec. 1, 1968; children—Kenneth, Lawrence. B.S., Columbia U., 1931, M.A., 1933, Ph.D., 1938; D.Sc. (hon.), U. Vt., 1983. Fellow biology dept. Bklyn. Coll., 1931-35, instr., 1936-47, asst. prof. biology, 1947-48; Am. Cancer Soc. research fellow U. Wis. Med. Sch., 1946-47; prof. exptl. pathology, assoc. prof. biochemistry U. Vt. Coll. Medicine, 1948-53; sr. investigator Waldemar Med. Research Found., Port Washington, N.Y., 1954-55; assoc. research prof. pathology Albert Einstein Coll. Medicine, 1955-57, prof. pathology, 1958-87; mem. pathology study sect. NIH, 1972-76. Author: (with Eric Holtzman) Cells and Organelles, 1970, 2d edit., 1976, 3d edit., 1984; author books on sci. for children, films on enzymes and carbohydrate metabolism for U.S. Army; contbr. 292 sci. articles to profl. publs. Recipient Disting. Service award Columbia U., 1960, E.B. Wilson award Am. Soc. Cell Biology, 1982; Nat. Cancer Inst. research career award, 1962-87. Mem. Am. Soc. Cell Biology, Am. Assn. Cancer Research, Am. Assn. Pathologists, N.Y. Soc. Electron Microscopists, Am. Soc. Biolog. Chemists, Nat. Acad. Scis., Japanese Soc. Cell Biology (hon.), Société Française de Microscopie Electronique (hon.), Japanese Histochem. Soc. (hon.), The Histochem. Soc. (hon.). Home: Bronx N.Y. Died Jan. 9, 1987; buried Mt. Pleasant Cemetery, Valhalla, N.Y.

NOVINS, LOUIS A., film company executive, lawyer; b. Boston, Feb. 22, 1909; s. A. S. and Bessie (Fisher) N.; m. Jane S. Wessel, Nov. 10, 1942; children: Susan W., Andrew S. LLB, Boston U., 1931. Bar: Mass. Pvt. practice Boston; asst. atty. gen. Commonwealth of Mass.; former gen. counsel, bd. dirs. S.W. region Anti-Defamation League of B'nai B'rith; asst. to pres. Paramount Pictures Corp., sec., then v.p., pres.; bd. dirs. Internat. Telemeter Corp.; chmn., bd. dirs. Telemeter Magnetics, Inc. Trustee, chmn. exec. com. Am. Heritage Found.; v.p. Jewish Community Relations Com. L.A. Home: Beverly Hills Calif. Died June 29, 1988.

NOWACZYNSKI, WOJCIECH JERZY, endocrinologist, educator; b. Nisko, Poland, Mar. 27, 1925; emigrated to Can., 1953, naturalized, 1959; s. Jan and Irena (Listowska) N.; m. Beverly Kathleen Cooke, Oct. 31, 1953; children—Maria, Barbara, Mark, Francis, Paula, Peter. B.Sc., Cyprian Norvid Polish Coll., Paris, France, 1942, Polish Coll., Zurich, Switzerland, 1944; Doctorandum, U. Fribourg, Switzerland, 1950; D.Sc. magna cum laude, U. Fribourg, 1952. With dept. clin. research Hotel-Dieu Hosp., Montreal, Que., Can., 1953; asst. prof. medicine U. Montreal, 1962-65, assoc. prof., 1965-70, prof., 1970-88; lectr. McGill U., Montreal, 1964-65; asst. prof. exptl. medicine McGill U., 1965, assoc. prof., 1966-70, prof., 1970-79; prof. medicine U. B.C., Vancouver, 1979-88; mem. div. endocrinology and metabolism, dept. medicine and pathology St. Paul's Hosp., Vancouver, 1979-88; mem. house staff St. Paul's Hosp., 1980-88, dir. steroid research lab., 1979-88; Research assoc. Med. Research Council Can., 1962-65, permanent research asso., 1965-88, prin. investigator research group on hypertension, 1972-79; dir. dept. steroid research Clin. Research Inst. of Montreal, 1967-79; career investigator Med. Research Council Can., 1979-88; mem. med. adv. bd. council for high blood pressure research Am. Heart Assn., 1968-80, fellow, 1980-88. Contbr. articles to profl. jours. Recipient Marcel Piché award for discovery of aldosterone-binding specific plasma globulin and its relationship to human hypertension. Mem. Internat. Soc. Hypertension, Inter-Am. Soc. Hypertension (mem. council 1978-80), Am. Endocrine Soc., Can. Soc. Clin. Investigation, N.Y. Acad. Scis. Club: Faculty of U. B.C. Home: Vancouver B.C., Canada. Died Feb. 6, 1988.

NUGENT, JOSEPH C., securities broker; b. N.Y.C., Sept. 25, 1903; s. Henry J. and Mary Henrietta (Clark) N.; m. Kathleen M. Dolan, Nov. 19, 1927 (dec.); children: Barbara (Mrs. Donald P. Bovers), Constance (Mrs. James R. McQuade), Joseph C. Jr.; m. Mrs. John V. Mara, Feb. 14, 1980. A.B. in Econs, Columbia, 1925; L.H.D., Marymount Manhattan Coll., 1970. With Whitney & Co. (stocks and bonds), 1925-38, Mabon & Co., N.Y.C., 1938-88; ptnr. Mabon & Co. (firm name changed to Mabon, Nugent & Co. 1965), 1941, now ltd. ptnr.; former mem. N.Y. State Banking Bd. Former v.p. Cardinal's Com. of Laity; former chmn. bd. trustees Marymount Manhattan Coll.; former chmn. Cath. Youth Orgn., N.Y.; trustee Cath. Charities, St. Patrick's Cathedral, N.Y.C.; past trustee N.Y. Med. Coll.; treas. Roman Cath. Orphan Asylum. Decorated knight comdr. Order of Holy Sepulchre of Jerusalem, Knight of Malta. Mem. Friendly Sons of St. Patrick (past pres.), John Jay Assos. of Columbia. Clubs: Bond (N.Y.C.); Spring Lake Golf, Winged Foot Golf, Spring Lake Bath and Tennis. Home: New York N.Y. Died Dec. 3, 1988; buried Spring Lake, N.J.

NUNGESTER, WALTER JAMES, educator, immunologist; b. Lima, Ohio, Feb. 22, 1901; s. William A. and Margery (Woodworth) N.; m. Lucille E. Roush, Sept. 21, 1924; children: Margery Patricia (Mrs. Peter S. Wright), Nancy Ann (Mrs. Robert E. Meader). Student, Oberlin Coll., 1919; BS, U. Mich., 1923, MS, 1924, ScD, 1938; MD, Northwestern U., 1934. Instr. Northwestern U. Med. Sch., Chgo., 1928-33, asst. prof., 1933-35, assoc. prof., 1935-47; prof. microbiology U. Mich. Med. Sch., Ann Arbor, 1947-85, chmn. dept.; cons. U.S. Army Test and Evaluation Command, other govt. agys. Contbr. articles on disinfectants, infection and resistance, etc. to profl. jours. Mem. AAAS, Soc. Exptl. Biology and Medicine, Am. Soc. Microbiology (pres. 1951). Home: Ann Arbor Mich. Died Sept. 18, 1985.

NUNNEMACHER, RUDOLPH FINK, educator, zoologist; b. Milw., Mar. 21, 1912; s. Henry Jacob and Gertrude Anita (Fink) N.; m. Sylvia Acken Hendricks, Dec. 29, 1938 (dec. Feb. 3, 1975); children: Robert, Sallie, Gretl, Dorothea; m. Doris C. Adams, Aug. 9, 1975. B.Sc., Kenyon Coll., 1934; M.A., Harvard U., 1936; Ph.D., Harvard, 1938; Sc.D. (hon.), Clark U., 1984. Instr. in histology Okla. U. Med. Sch., 1938-39; mem. faculty Clark U., Worcester, Mass., 1939-88; prof. zoology Clark U., 1956-83, prof. emeritus, 1983-88, chmn. dept. biology, 1958-76; trustee Bermuda Biol. Sta. for Research, Inc. Mem. Sutton Sch. Com., 1966-69, chmn., 1972-75; Trustee Bermuda Biol. Sta. Recipient Disting. Teaching award Clark U., 1983; CASE Silver award as Vol. of Year, 1985. Fellow AAAS; mem. Explorers Club, Am. Soc. Zoology, Electron Microscopy Soc. Am., Sigma Xi. Home: Sutton Mass. Died Mar. 1, 1988.

NYE, ERNEST LEWIS, banker; b. N.Y.C., May 25, 1888; s. Ernest Deal and Elizabeth (Spaulding) N.; m. Mary Leland, Apr. 4, 1918; children Jane Spaulding (Mrs. J.F. Burditt), Barbara Ward (Mrs. Norman de Planque). Student, Barringer Sch., 1901-05. With Guaranty Trust Co., 1905-09, Freeman Co., bankers, N.Y.C., from 1909; cons. in field. Author: Equipment-

Trust Securities, 1911, More about Equipment Trusts, 1913, Problems of Financing Equipment, 1924. Mem. Rumson Country Club, Sea Bright Beach Club. Home: Rumson N.J. †

NYE, JAMES GORDON, lawyer; b. Moorhead, Minn., Feb. 28, 1891; s. Carroll A. and Mary A. (Grodon) N.; m. Margaret H. Mason, June 20, 1928; children: James Gordon, Mason Whitney. LLB, U. Wis., 1914. Bar: Minn. 1915. Pvt. practice Duluth, Minn., from 1920; ptnr. Nye, Sullivan, McMillan, Hanft & Hastings and predecessor firms, from 1937. Pres. Duluth Symphony Assn., 1933-38, Duluth Community Chest, 1942-43. Capt. inf., U.S. Army, World War I. Decorated Order of Brit. Empire. Mem. ABA, Minn. Bar Assn. (pres. 1957-58), Duluth C. of C., Newcomen Soc., Am. Judicare Soc. (bd. dirs. from 1959), Kitchi Gammi Club, Duluth Athlectic Club, Masons, Shriners (3s degree), Rotary, Phi Delta Phi, Sigma Nu. †

NYQUIST, EWALD B(ERGER), college president; b. Rockford, Ill., Nov. 1, 1914; married; 3 children. BS, U. Chgo., 1936, postgrad., 1936-41; D Pedagogy, St. John's U., 1953; LLD, Hartwick Coll., 1953, Canisius Coll., 1957, St. Francis Coll., 1958, Juniata Coll., Alfred U., 1959, Manhattanvillle Coll., 1960, Gettysburg Coll., 1961, Ithaca Coll., St. John Fisher Coll., St. Lawrence U., Manhattan Coll., Elizabethtown Coll.; LHD, Fordham U., 1959, Yeshiva U., 1960; DCL, Pace Coll., 1961; DSc, George Washington U., other univs. Asst. dir. univ. admissions Columbia U., 1945-48, dir., 1948-51; asst. commr. higher edn. N.Y. State Dept. Edn., 1951-55, assoc. commr. higher edn. and profl. edn., 1955-57, dep. commr. edn., 1957-70, commr., 1970-77; pres. SUNY System; v.p. acad. devel. Pace U., 1977-87; sec. commn. insts. higher edn. Mid. States Assn. Colls. and Secondary Schs., 1948-53, chmn., 1953-59, hon. mem., 1960-87; mem. exec. com. accreditation policies Nat. League Nursing, 1953-55, mem. com. accreditation hosp. schs. nursing, 1959-87; mem. commn. accreditation Coun. Social Work Edn., 1954-57, 61087; mem. advance placement com. Coll. Entrance Exam. Bd., 1960-87. Bd. dirs. Nat. Scholarship Svc. Fund, 1961-87. Recipient Edn. award N.Y. State Assn. Fgn. Lang. Tchrs., 1973, AID award, 1975, award N.Y. State Assn. Jr. Colls., 1976, Nat. Humanities award, 1976. Mem. Am. Psychol. Assn., Psychometric Soc., Sigma Xi, Psi Chi. Died July 24, 1987.

OAKLAND, RALPH EDWARD, automotive company executive; b. Chgo., Jan. 12, 1899; s. Edward T. and Fannie (Darrow) O.; m. Ruth Turnquist, Oct. 20, 1922; children: David D., Barbara. Student, Northwestern U.; cert. acct., U. Ill., 1922. CPA. Bookkeeper Livestock Exchange Bank, 1915-16, Safe-Guard Account Co., 1916-17; controller Commonwealth Motors Co., 1919-20; acct. Price, Waterhouse & Co., 1920-21, 22-23, Nat. Tea Co., 1921-22, S.W. Straus & Co., 1923-24; with Checker Cab Mfg. Corp. (name changed to Checker Motors Corp.), Kalamazoo, 1924—, v.p. With U.S. Army, 1917-19. Mem. AICPA, Masons, Elks, Kalamozzo Country Club, Park Club. Home: Kalamazoo Mich. Deceased.

OATES, GORDON CEDRIC, aeronautical engineer, educator; b. Vancouver, B.C., Can., Feb. 28, 1932; came to U.S., 1959, naturalized, 1967; s. Arthur James Lawson and Kathleen Maude Alix (Binns) O.; m. Joan Euker, Aug. 23, 1961; children: Kenneth Marshall, Brian Cedric, Donald Lawson, Janine. B.A.Sc., U. B.C., 1954; M.Sc., U. Birmingham, Eng., 1956; Ph.D., Calif. Inst. Tech., 1959. Grad. apprentice Rolls Royce Co., Derby, Eng., 1954-55; asst. prof. dept. aeros. and astronautics M.I.T., 1959-64, assoc. prof., 1964-67; assoc. prof. U. Wash., 1967-70, prof., 1970-86; guest prof. Royal Inst. Tech., Stockholm, 1970; disting. vis. prof. U.S. Air Force Acad., 1975-76; vis. prof. Air Force Office of Sci. Research, 1983; cons. United Techs. Research Ctr., United Technologies Chem. Systems Div., Volvo Flygmotor. Author articles and books in field. Recipient disting. teaching award U. Wash., 1982, John Leland Atwood award AIAA-Am. Soc. Engring. Educators, 1985 ; Athlone fellow, 1954-56. Fellow AIAA (Air Breathing Propulsion award 1987, Pendray Aerospace Lit. award 1988); mem. ASME, Sigma Xi. Home: Seattle Wash. Died Nov. 1, 1986; buried Mt. Rainier, Wash.

OBER, FRANK BENEDICT, lawyer; b. Balt., Sept. 25, 1889; s. Albert G. and Rebecca G. (Hambleton) O.; m. Margaret DeLancey Rochester, Apr. 16, 1914; children: Richard F., DeLancey R., Frank Benedict, Rochester; m. Helen Montgomery, May 25, 1964. Grad., Gilman Sch., Balt., 1906; AB, Princeton U., 1910; LLB, Harvard U., 1913. Bar: Md. 1912. Mem. Ober, Grimes & Shriver, 1916-81. Author: Communism and the Supreme Court, 1956; contbr. articles to profl. jours. Mem. State Commn. on Interracial Relations, 1942-45, War Emergency Legislation, 1942-43; chmn. Med. Dems. for Dewey, 1944, Md. Commn. on Subversive Activities, 1948-49. Maj. F.A., U.S. Army, 1917-19, 4th American Expeditionary Force, France. Decorated Silver Star. Mem. ABA (adv. bd. Jour. 1955-58), Md. Bar Assn. (pres. 1950), Balt. Bar Assn., Law Assn., Maryland Club, Merchants Club, Elkridge Club. Home: Baltimore Md. Died Jan. 15, 1981, buried Druid Ridge Cemetery, Balt.

OBERHELMAN, HARRY ALVIN, surgeon; b. Randolph, Kans., Aug. 30, 1888; s. Henry and Christina (Schroer) O.; m. Beatrice W. Babel, June 14, 1922; children: Harry Alvin Jr., Robert Hugh, Barbara Jean Oberhelmen Uecker, John Heyworth. BS, N. Cen. Coll., 1916, DSc (hon.), 1954; MD, U. Chgo., 1920. Diplomate Am. Bd. Surgery (founder's group). Intern Presbyn. Hosp., Chgo., 1920-21, resident pathology, 1921-24, asst. attending surgeon, 1924-41; instr. to assoc. clin. prof. surgery Rush Med. Coll., Chgo., 1924-41; prof. Stritch Sch. Med., Loyola U., Chgo., from 1941, former chmn. dept. surgery; cons. surgeon Cook County (Ill.) Hosp.; attending surgeon West Suburban Hosp., Oak Park, Ill.; past chief surgeon Mercy Hosp., Chgo., later attending surgeon. Fellow ACS, Am. Coll. Gastroenterology, Internat. Acad. Proctology, Internat. Coll. Surgeons; mem. AMA, Ill. Med. Soc., Chgo. Med. Soc., Chgo. Path. Soc., Inst. Medicine Chgo., Ill. Surg. Soc., Cen. Ill. Surg. Soc., Chgo. Surg. Soc., University Club (Chgo.). Republican. Congregationalist. Home: Oak Park Ill. Died Sept. 13, 1977.

OBERMEYER, ERNEST DAVID, publishing executive; b. N.Y.C., Nov. 6, 1924; s. David Harris and Marguerite (Floersheimer) O.; m. Phyllis Horton, Oct. 12, 1951 (div. Nov. 1972); 1 child, David; m. Shirley Weber, Nov. 18, 1972. Grad., Phillips Acad., Andover, Mass., 1942; BA, Yale U., 1948. Salesman Gen. Foods Co., N.Y.C., 1948-50, Am. Molasses Co., 1950-52; salesman Supermarket News, Fairchild Publs., N.Y.C., 1952-71, advt. dir., 1971-72, advt. dir., pub., 1972-83, v.p., 1974-83. 1st lt. USAAF, 1943-46, PTO. Mem. Yale Club. Republican. Died Aug. 26, 1983.

OBOLER, ELI MARTIN, librarian; b. Chgo., Sept. 26, 1915; s. Leo and Clara (Obelr) O.; m. Marcia Lois Wolf, Dec. 25, 1938; children: Leon David, Carol Judy. BA, U. Chgo., 1941, postgrad. Sch. Library Scis., 1946-49; BS, Columbia U., 1942. Asst. chief Lend-Lease Expediting Bur., WPB, 1942-43; head reserved book room U. Chgo., 1946-49, librarian Univ. Coll., 1947-49; lectr. great books program U. Chgo., 1948-49; librarian Idaho State Coll., 1949-63; univ. librarian Idaho State U., 1963-81; summer sch. faculty Utah State U., 1960, 66, U. Wash., 1975; lectr. library schs., from 1981; condr. weekly radio program Books and You, 1949-76; mem. panel weekly TV program Idaho Looks at the World, 1973-76; columnist Intermountain and Alameda Enterprise, 1952-60, Idaho State Jour., 1960-65, 81-83, reviewer Library Jour., from 1953, Choice, from 1964, Intermountain Observer, 1967-73, Western Critic, 1973-75. Author: The Fear of the Word, 1974, Ideas and the University Library, 1977, Defending Intellectual Freedom, 1980; editor: College and University Library Accreditation Standards, 1957, Education and Censorship, 1981; editor Idaho Librarian, 1950-54, 57-58; asst. editor Library Periodicals Round Table Newsletter, 1953-54, editor, 1961-62; contbr. articles to jours. mem. Nat. Adv. Com. Library Rsch. and Tng. Projects, 1966-69, chmn., 1968-69; bd. dirs. Pocatello United Campaign Fund, 1961-66; mem. adv. coun. Pacific N.W. Regional Health Scis. Library, U. Wash., 1968-77; dir. for Idaho, Pacific N.W. Bibliog. Ctr., 1970-71; trustee, exec. com. Freedom to Read Found., 1971-75, 76-80, v.p., 1979-80. With U.S. Army, 1943-46. Recipient Robert Downs Intellectual Freedom award, 1976; Eli M. Oboler Library named in his honor Idaho State U., 1983. Mem. ALA (councilor representing Idaho 1950-58, chmn. library periodicals roundtable 1953, Idaho chmn. membership com. 1954-59, Intellectual Freedom com., 1964-70, councilor-at-large 1977-81, vice chmn. Intellectual Freedom Round Table 1979-80, chmn. 1980-81, H.W. periodical award 1964, post-mortem cash award Intellectual Freedom Round Table 1985), Pacific N.W. (chmn. legis. com. 1951-53, pres. 1955-56, chmn. publs. com. 1958-67), Idaho (pres. 1950-53, chmn. publs. com. 1950-54, chmn. library edn. com. 1961-63, chmn. Intellectual Freedom com. 1967-79, named Idaho Librarian of Yr. 1974) library assns., Assn. Coll. and Rsch. Libraries (mem. editorial bd. 1962-63, chmn. coll. sect. 1963-64), B'nai B'rith (local pres. 1951-53). Jewish. Home: Pocatello Idaho. Died June 15, 1983; buried Pocatello.

O'BOYLE, PATRICK ALOYSIUS CARDINAL, former archbishop of Washington; b. Scranton, Pa., July 18, 1896; s. Michael and Mary (Muldoon) O'B. Student, St. Thomas Coll. (now Scranton U.); grad., St. Joseph's Sem.,, Yonkers, N.Y., 1921, N.Y. Sch. Social Work, 1931. Ordained priest Roman Catholic Ch., 1921; Served St. Columba's Ch.,, 1921-26; tchr. Fordham U. Sch. Social Services; exec. dir. Nat. Cath. War Relief Services; became exec. dir. Cath. Charities N.Y., 1947; consecrated archbishop Diocese Washington Jan. 14, 1948, elevated to cardinal, June 26, 1967, ret., 1973. Home: Washington D.C. Died Aug. 10, 1987.

O'BRIEN, EUGENE LOUIS, paint manufacturing company executive; b. N.Y.C., Apr. 29, 1913; s. George Louis and Helen (Knott) O'B.; m. Mary Ellen Chrisman, Sept. 24, 1938 (div. 1956); children: George Dennis, Michael Francis, Eugene Louis, Frederick Joseph II, Christopher John, Mary Ellen, Ann Hilary; m. Laura Graflin Lee, Mar. 28, 1961. Grad., Lake Forest Acad., 1931; AB, U. Notre Dame, 1935. With O'Brien Paint Co., South Bend, Ind., 1935-63, exec. v.p., bd. dirs., 1950-63; pres., bd. dirs. Balt. Paint & Chem. Corp., 1963-69; v.p., bd. dirs. Thomas Mfg. Co., Parkton, Md., 1964-79. V.p. Balt. Opera Co., Inc., 1965-72; bd. dirs. South Bend chpt. Boy Scouts Am., 1946, South Bend YMCA, 1946, Tucson Opera Co., 1973-75; mem. Tucson Coun. for Arts and Culture, 1974-77. Named Outstanding Young Businessman of South Bend South Bend Jr. C. of C., 1948. Mem. Greater Balt. Com., Nat. Paint and Lacquer Assn., U. Notre Dame Alumni Assn. (pres. St. Joseph's Valley chpt. 1942), Tucson Country Club, Charles Ctr. Club, Skyline Country Club, Old Pueblo Club, Pima County Polo Club. Home: Tucson Ariz. Died Dec. 31, 1979.

O'BRIEN, GEORGE MILLER, congressman; b. Chgo., June 17, 1917; s. Matthew J. and Isabel (Hyde) O'B.; m. Mary Lou Peyla, Sept. 6, 1947; children: Caryl Isabel O'Brien Bloch, Mary Deborah O'Brien Pershey. A.B., Northwestern U., 1939; J.D., Yale U., 1947. Bar: Ill. 1947. Sr. partner O'Brien & Garrison, Joliet, 1966-78; mem. 93d-97th congresses from 17th Dist. Ill., 98th-99th Congresses from 4th Dist. Ill. Chmn. Will County chpt. ARC, 1957-58; pres. Joliet-Will County Community Chest Program.; mem. Will County Bd. Suprs., 1956-64; mem. Legislative Adv. Com. to Northeastern Ill. Planning Commn., 1971-72; mem. Ill. Ho. Reps., 1970-72, mem. exec. and judiciary II coms. Served to lt. col. USAAF, 1941-45. Recipient Distinguished Service award Joliet Boys Club. Mem. Am., Ill., Will County bar assns., Trial Lawyers Assn. Ill., Am. Legion, V.F.W., Phi Beta Kappa. Roman Catholic. Clubs: Elk (Chgo.), Rotarian. (Chgo.), Union League (Chgo.). Home: Joliet Ill. Died July 17, 1986.

O'BRIEN, WILLIAM L., printing company executive; b. Chgo., Sept. 1, 1887; s. William and Margaret (Cowdon) O'B.; m. Eleanor Coyle; children: Patricia Margaret, Eleanor Mary. Student, Christian Bros. Sch., De LaSalle U. Pres. The Fred J. Ringley Co., Chgo.; bd. dirs. C.,M.,St.P.&P. R.R. Lt. U.S. Army, World War I. Mem. Graphic Arts, Franklin Assn., Chgo. Athletic Assn. Club, South Shore Country Club. Home: Chicago Ill. †

OCKENGA, HAROLD JOHN, clergyman, theological seminary president ex-officio; b. Chgo., July 6, 1905; s. Herman and Angie (Tetzlaff) O.; m. Audrey L. Williamson, Aug. 6, 1935; children: Audrey Starr, Aldryth Sabra, Harold John. A.B., Taylor U., 1927, D.D., 1937; student, Princeton Sem., 1927-29; Th.B., Westminister Sem., Phila., 1930; A.M., U. Pitts., 1934, Ph.D., 1939; Litt.D., Suffolk U., 1939; Hum. D., Bob Jones Coll., 1944; LL.D., Houghton Coll., 1946; D.D., Wheaton Coll., 1960, Fuller Theol. Sem., 1963; Litt.D., Norwich U., Vt., 1962, Seattle Pacific Coll., 1963, Chungang U., Seoul, Korea, 1975; D.D., Gordon Coll., 1968, Internat. Christian Grad. U., 1982. Ordained ministry Presbyn. Ch., 1931; asst. minister First Ch., Pitts., 1930-31; minister Point Breeze Ch., Pitts., 1931-36, Park St. Ch., Boston, 1936-69; co-founder, 1st pres. Fuller Theol. Sem., Pasadena, Calif., 1947-54, 59-63; chmn. bd. Fuller Theol. Sem., 1961-69; pres. Gordon Coll. and Gordon-Conwell Theol. Sem., 1969-79; Mem. Pres. Truman's Clergymen's Mission to Europe, 1947; vis. lectr. to missionary confs. and colls. on two world tours to 35 countries; summer supply preacher Westminister Chapel, London, 1946, 48, 51, 53, 57, 64; Travelled in, Europe, Asia and, Africa, S.Am., Australia., Pres. u2Nat. Assn. Evangs. for United Action, 1942-44; v.p. World Evang. Fellowship, 1951-61. Author: These Religious Affections, 1937, Our Protestant Heritage, 1938, Have You Met These Women?, 1940, Everyone That Believeth, 1942, The Comfort of God, 1944, Our Evangelical Faith, 1946, The Spirit of the Living God, 1947, Faithful in Christ Jesus, 1948, The Church in God, 1955, Protestant Preaching in Lent, 1956, Power Through Pentecost, 1959, Women Who Made Bible History, 1961, Preaching in Thessalonians, 1963, Faith in a Troubled World, 1972; Chmn. bd.: Christianity Today mag., 1956-81; contbr. to religious jours. Trustee Gordon Coll., Boston; trustee Suffolk U., 1939-49; bd. dirs. Billy Graham Evang. Assn. Named Clergyman of Yr. Religious Heritage of Am. Assn., 1982; named in his honor Harold John Ockenga chair Fuller Theol. Sem., 1982; Recipient Legion of Honor Taylor U., 1977. Mem. Am. Acad. Polit. Sci. Club: Rotary. Home: Hamilton Mass. Died Feb. 8, 1985.

O'CONNELL, HAROLD P., banker; b. Chgo., Apr. 24, 1891; s. Patrick J. and Frances B.; m. Charlotte Anne Woodward, Jan. 16, 1932; 1 son, Harold P. Student, Northwestern U., 1909-10. With acctg. dept. Chgo. Rys. Co., 1910-16; with credit, sales depts. Lane Roloson & Co., Chgo., 1916-20; Chgo. credit rep. Nat. City Bank N.Y., 1920-23; with Continental & Comml. Nat. Bank, 1923-27; with credit dept. Continental Ill. Nat. Bank & Trust Co. Chgo. (formerly Continental Ill. Bank & Trust Co.), 1929-30, asst. cashier, 1930-32, 2d v.p., 1932-39, v.p., 1939-54, sr. v.p., 1954-58; v.p. Glore Fergan & Co., investment bankers, N.Y.C. and Chgo., from 1958; bd. dirs. Kroehler Mfg. Co., Naperville, Ill., Victor Adding Machine Co., Delaware Bldg. Corp., Chgo. With USN, 1917-19. Mem. Oak Park Country Club, Chicago Club, Everglades Club (Palm Beach, Fla.). Home: Chicago Ill. †

O'CONNOR, EUGENE J(OSEPH), clergyman, language educator; b. Augusta, Ga., Sept. 4, 1887; s. Michael Joseph and Johanna (Hartigan) O'C. Student,

Sacred Heart Coll., Augusta, 1901-04, St. Stanislaus Coll., Macon, Ga., 1905-10; AB, Woodstock Coll., 1911; MA, St. Louis U., 1918; PhD, Gregorian U., Rome, 1928. Ordained priest Roman Cath. Ch., 1921. High sch. tchr., Grand Coteau, La., 1913-14; instr. Spring Hill (Ala.) Coll., 1914-17; instr. Jesuit High Sch., New Orleans, 1917-18, 22-23, prin. Tampa, Fla., 1924-26; instr. English Loyola U., New Orleans, 1926, chmn. dept. English, 1938, then prof. Mem. MLA, Blue Key. Home: New Orleans La. †

O'CONNOR, HARVEY, writer; b. Mpls., Mar. 29, 1897; s. James and Jessie (Kenney) O'C.; m. Jessie Bross Lloyd, June 16, 1930; children: Stephen Lloyd, Kathleen Maverick. Ed. pub. schs. Labor editor Seattle Daily Union Record, 1919-24; asst. editor Locomotive Engrs. Jour., 1924-27; mgr. N.Y. bur. Federated Press, 1927-30; editor, publicity dir. Oil Workers Internat. Union, 1945-48. Author: Mellon's Millions, 1933, Steel-Dictator, 1935, The Guggenheims, 1937, The Astors, 1941, History of the Oil Workers International Union, 1950, The Empire of Oil, 1955, World Crisis in Oil, 1962, Revolution in Seattle, 1964. Chmn. Nat. Com. Against Repressive Legislation, 1964-76, chmn. emeritus, 1976-87; mem. Pitts. Civil Liberties Com., mem. exec. com., 1934-36; mem. Chgo. Civil Liberties Com., mem. exec. com., 1937-44; chmn. Emergency Civil Liberties Com., 1955-63, mem. nat. coun., 1966-86. Mem. Sakonnet (R.I.) Yacht Club. Unitarian. Home: Little Compton R.I. Died Aug. 29, 1987.

O'CONNOR, MARTIN F., college president; b. Cambridge, Mass., Feb. 24, 1891; s. William P. and Catherine E. (Murphy) O'C.; m. Alice M. Dillon, June 1917; children: Mary (Mrs. Thomas Patterson), Barbara (Mrs. Edward J. Acton). AB, Boston Coll., 1913; EdM, Harvard, 1927; EdD (hon.), R.I. Coll. Edn., 1947. Instr. Rindge Tech. Sch., Cambridge, 1914-21; head master Roberts Sch., —, 1921-36; dir. evening schs. —, 1929-36; lectr. Boston Coll., 1934-36; pres. Framingham State Tchrs. Coll., from 1936. Mem. NEA (life), Mass Tchrs. Fedn. (past pres.). Home: Framingham Mass. †

ODAWARA, DAIZO, iron company executive; b. Hiroshima, Japan, Nov. 10, 1892. Tchr.'s cert. in acctg., 1913, tchr.'s cert. in commerce, 1916. Clk., Amagasaki plant Kubota Iron & Machinery Works Ltd., from 1916, sr. mng. dir. Amagasaki plant, from 1945, pres., Osaka, from 1950. Awarded prime minister's Nat. Decoration for contbn. to devel. industry, 1959. Mem. Japan UN Assn. (pres. Kansai chpt.), Osaka C. of C. and Industry (pres. from 1960). Home: Osaka Japan. †

ODELL, ARTHUR GOULD, JR., architect; b. Concord, N.C., Nov. 22, 1913; s. Arthur Gould and Grace (Patterson) O.; m. Polly Robinson, Nov. 10, 1941 (div. 1950); children—William R., Alexandra; m. Mary Walker Ehringhaus, Oct. 30, 1951; 1 son Charles; stepchildren—Carroll Eringhaus Niles, Michael Ehringhaus. Student, Duke U., 1930-31; B.Arch., Cornell U., 1935; Atelier Debat-Ponsan, Ecole des Beaux Arts, Paris, France, 1935-36. Chmn. Odell Assos. Inc., Charlotte, N.C., Greensboro, N.C., Richmond, Va., Greenville, S.C., 1940-82; vis. critic Cornell U. Coll. Architecture, 1955-56; chmn. N.C. Bldg. Code Council, 1957-59; mem. various nat. archtl. award juries; chmn. Potomac planning task force; U.S. Dept. of Interior, 1965-67; pres. Mint Mus. Art, Charlotte, 1959-63. Works include Wachovia Bank & Trust, Raleigh, Greensboro and Salisbury, Duke U. Nuclear Lab, Burlington Industries Corp. Hdqrs, Greensboro, St. Andrews Coll, Laurinburg, Spl. Warfare Center, Ft. Bragg, R.J. Reynolds World Hdqrs, Winston-Salem, N.C., Blue Cross Blue Shield, Chapel Hill, Ciba Geigy Hdqrs. and Labs, Greensboro, Springs Mills offices and computer center, Lancaster, S.C., Meml. Hosp, Chattanooga, Balt. Civic Center, Hagerstown (Md.) Library, So. Ry. UPS System, Atlanta, Virginia Beach Conv. Center, Hampton (Va.) Coliseum, U.S. Army Logistic Center, Va., U.S. Army Arsenal Hdqrs, Va., Richmond Eye Hosp; schs., univ. bldgs. and health facilities in, Md., Va., N.C., S.C., plans of devel. for, Charlotte, Raleigh, N.C. State Govt. Center, Camp Lejeune, N.C., Camp Barrett, Quantico, Va. Mem. Cornell U. Council, 1960-62, 65; bd. dirs. N.C. Art Soc.; trustee N.C. Symphony. Served to lt. col. C.E. U.S. Army, 1941-45. Decorated grand ofcl. Orden del Sol de Peru; recipient N.C. award; Sch. Exec. design award; Progressive Architecture citation; Copper and Brass Research Assn. design award; Instns. Mag. award. Fellow AIA (nat. comm. sch. bldgs. 1955-58, pres. N.C. chpt. 1953-55, nat. dir. 1959-63, nat. pres. 1964-65, various design awards); mem. Soc. of Cincinnati, Alpha Tau Omega. Methodist. Clubs: Charlotte Country, Charlotte City, Charlotte Athletic, Quail Hollow Country (Charlotte). Home: Charlotte N.C. Died Apr. 21, 1988.

O'DONNELL, EDWARD JOSEPH, clergyman, university chancellor; b. Milw., May 11, 1909; s. Edward and Ella (Lloyd) O'D. AB, Marquette U., 1931; postgrad., St. Louis U., 1933-36, 39-43; LLD, U. Wis., 1956, St. Ambrose Coll., 1959. Joined S.J., 1942, ordained priest Roman Cath. Ch., 1942. Instr. St. John's Coll., Belize, 1946-47, prin., 1947-48; pres. Marquette U., Milw., 1948-62, chancellor, 1962-86; bd. dirs. Fed. Home Loan Bank Chgo. Mem. Naval Adv. Commn., Community Welfare Coun. Cited for meritorious pub. svc. USN, 1954. Mem. Wis. Found. Ind. Colls., Assn. Urban Univs., Nat. Cath. Edn. Assn., NEA, Assn. Higher Edn., Milw. Assn. Commerce, North Cen. Assn. Colls. and Secondary Schs., University Club. Died June 30, 1986.

O'DOWD, FRANK EDMUND, parish manager; b. Chgo., June 17, 1920; s. Frank Edmund and Loretto Marie (Reeve) O'D.; m. Margaret Frances Dempsey, July 11, 1945; children: Margaret M., Frank Edmund III, Thomas D., Kathleen L., John R., Maureen D., Gerald M., Patricia M., Michael J. Ph.B. in Commerce, U. Notre Dame, 1942; M.B.A., U. Chgo., 1953. With Edward Hines Lumber Co., Chgo., 1942-76; exec. mktg. dir. Edward Hines Lumber Co., 1971-76; exec. v.p. Nat. Bldg. Materials Distbrs. Assn., Glenview, Ill., 1976-85; parish mgr. St. Francis Xavier Ch., Wilmette, Ill., 1985-87. Trustee Village of Wilmette, Ill., 1973-81; precinct capt. New Trier Twp. Republican Orgn., 1962-87, area chmn., 1979-87; chmn. Bus. Mobilized for Loyola U., 1981-82. Served with USN, 1942-45. Decorated Bronze Star.; Named Father of Yr. Nat. Cath. Family of Yr., 1962. Roman Catholic. Clubs: Univ. (Chgo.); Wilmette Golf, Michigan Shores. Home: Wilmette Ill. Died Dec. 16, 1987.

OETTERSHAGEN, MARTIN WILLIAM, engineer; b. Chgo., Dec. 23, 1891; s. Martin and Marie (Holtz) O.; m. Amy Luella Lane, May 14, 1917. Student, Armour Inst. Tech., Northwestern U. Registered structural engr., Ill. Rodman, instrument man rolling mill, blast furnace plant, ore yard and open hearth constrn. 1909-13; rodman, asst. engr. Div. Surveys, City of Chgo., 1914-17; draftsman, bridge designing 1917, harbor engr., port mgr., 1917-54; dep. adminstr. St. Lawrence Seaway Devel. Corp., 1954-61, adminstr., from 1961; city del. to annual conv. Am. Assn. Port Authority, Miss. Valley Assn., Nat. River and Harbor Congress, others; adv. engr. com. on harbors, wharves and bridges Chgo. City Coun.; cons. engr. Chgo. Regional Port Dist., 1951-54. Mem. Am. Assn. Port Authorities (pres. 1930-31), Chgo. Assn. Commerce and Industry (mem. harbors and waterways com.), ASCE, Western Soc. Engrs., Chgo. Propeller Club (pres. 1953). Home: Massena N.Y. †

OGATA, THOMAS SHOICHI, state justice; b. Waiakoa, Hawaii, Jan. 8, 1917; s. Seisuke and Kiyo (Sato) O.; m. Dagmar Yaeko Morimoto, June 1971; children: Thomas Shoichi, Dennis K. BA, U. Hawaii, 1938; LLB, U. Mich., 1941. Bar: Hawaii 1945. Law clk., then dep. atty. City and County of Honolulu, 1945-49; dep. county atty. Maui County, 1949-57; spl. counsel for bd. suprs. 1957-58; mem. Hawaii Territorial Senate, 1958-59; 3d Dist. mem. Hawaii Senate, 1959-64; judge 1st Cir. Ct. Hawaii, 1966; justice Hawaii Supreme Ct., 1974-83. Mem. Maui County Dem. Com., 1955-57. Mem. ABA, Hawaii Bar Assn. Buddhist. Home: Honolulu Hawaii. Died Nov. 25, 1983.

OGGEL, MELVIN VERNE, clergyman; b. Holland, Mich., May 23, 1889; s. John Peter and Lillie (Bright) O.; m. Louise E. Warnshuis, June 30, 1914; 1 dau., Lillian Jean. Student, Hope Coll., 1907-09; AB in Lit. Law, U. Mich., 1911; student, N.B. Sem., 1914; DD, Wabash Coll., 1926; LHD, Cen. Coll., Pella, Iowa, 1963. Ordained to ministry Reformed Ch. Am., 1914. Pastor in New Paltz, N.Y., 1914-17, Chgo., 1919-24, Crawfordsville, Ind., 1924-38, Lincoln, Nebr., 1938-43, Glen Rock, N.J., 1943-65; pres. Gen. Synod, Reformed Ch. Am., 1963-64. Chaplain inf. U.S. Army, 1918-19. Home: Ramsey N.J. †

OGILVIE, RICHARD BUELL, lawyer, former governor; b. Kansas City, Mo., Feb. 22, 1923; s. Kenneth S. and Edna Mae (Buell) O.; m. Dorothy Louise Shriver, Feb. 11, 1950; 1 child, Elizabeth. B.A., Yale, 1947; J.D., LL.D. (hon.), Chgo.-Kent Coll. Law, 1949; LL.D. (hon.), Lincoln Coll., Millikin U., Ill. Wesleyan U., Lake Forest Coll., MacMurray Coll., Greenville Coll. Bar: Ill. 1950. Practiced in Chgo., 1950-54, 55-58, 61-62, 73-88; asst. U.S. atty., Chgo., 1954-55; spl. asst. to U.S. atty. gen., Chgo., 1958-61; sheriff Cook County, Ill., 1962-66; pres. Cook County Bd. Commrs., 1966-68; gov. of Ill. 1968-73; ptnr. firm Isham, Lincoln & Beale, 1973-88; dir. Continental Ill. Corp., Alberto Culver Corp., CNA Fin. Corp., Fansteel Corp., LaSalle St. Fund, Chgo., So. Pacific Transp. Co., R.R. Donnelly Co., Chgo. Chmn. Young Republican Orgn. Cook County, 1953-54; trustee Robert Wood Johnson Found. Served with AUS, 1942-45. Mem. Am., Ill., Chgo., Fed. bar assns., Phi Alpha Delta, Beta Theta Pi. Republican. Presbyterian. Clubs: Masons, Chicago, Glen View, Tavern, Old Elm, Casino, Sangamo. Home: Chicago Ill. Died May 10, 1988.

OGILVY, STEWART MARKS, editorial consultant; b. Winnipeg, Man., Can., Apr. 22, 1914; came to U.S., 1923, naturalized, 1943; s. Ralph Wardlaw and May (Marks) O.; m. Barbara C. Swift, Feb. 4, 1961 (div. 1964); m. Avis Bigelow Reynick, Nov. 14, 1964. Grad., Kent Sch., 1932; BS, Trinity Coll., Hartford, Conn., 1936. Instrn. asst. in English and fine arts Trinity Coll., 1936-37; promotion writer N.Y. Times, 1937-42; assoc. copy dir. Muir & Co., advt., 1942-44; copywriter McCann-Erickson, Inc., 1944-46; mng. editor World Govt. News, N.Y.C., 1946-52; promotion writer Fortune mag., N.Y.C., 1952-57, writer editorial dept., 1957-61, assoc. editor, 1961-69; exec. dir. Hugh Moore Fund N.Y.C., 1969-71; editor, exec. Population Inst., N.Y.C. 1972-79; editorial cons. from 1979. Editorial bd. World Peace News, from 1974; author articles, brochures contbr. to books and mags. Mem. N.Y. exec. bd. Fed Union, Inc., 1939-41; editor N.Y. Corr., 1939-41; bd dirs., sec., treas., publs. chmn. World Federalists, 1941-47; rep. World Federalists U.S.A. on U.S. Counci Movement World Fed. Govt., 1946-47; chmn. nat. pubs com. United World Federalists, acting exec. dir., 1947 bd. dirs. Am. Movement for World Govt., from 1970 v.p. Friends of the Earth, 1969-76, bd. dirs. 1969-78 hon. pres. from 1978; v.p. Friends of the Earth Found. 1972-78, dir. emeritus, from 1978; mem. adv. bd. Scenic Hudson Preservation Conf., 1970-80; v.p. Negative Population Growth, Inc., 1972-73; adv. council Zero Population Growth N.Y.C., 1973-80. Recipient Alumr medal for excellence Trinity Coll., 1963, Trinity Coll fellow, 1957-63. Mem. Sierra Club (editor Argonau pub. 1957-59, chmn. Atlantic chpt. 1960-61, Spl Achievement award 1966), Alpha Delta Phi. Home New Orleans La. Deceased.

O'HARA, ALMERIN C., state official; b. Hudson N.Y., Nov. 10, 1910; s. Michael J. and Anna Drew (Cartwright) O'H.; m. Marjorie Rushmore, June 15 1935; children: Edmund R., Almerin C. Grad., Command and Gen. Staff Coll., 1941. Commd. 2d lt N.Y.N.G., 1934; advanced through grades to maj. gen 1958; comdr. 27th Armored Div., 1958-60; chief of sta to Gov. of N.Y., spl. asst. to, 1974-75; comdg. gen. N.Y Army N.G., 1960-71; commr. N.Y. State Office Gen Svcs., 1971-75; dir. N.Y. State Emergency Fuel Office mem. secretariat to Com. on Pub. Access to Records 1975; with Universal Match Corp., 1945-60, sales dir N.Y. State, 1954-60; bd. dirs. Internat. Life Ins. Co Buffalo. Mem. Res. Forces Policy Bd.; Dem. candidat for N.Y. State Assembly, Columbia County, 1946; pres N.Y. Mil. Acad., Cornwall. Decorated Silver Star D.S.M. Mem. Soc. Mil. Engrs., Am. Legion, Buffalo Niagara Sales Execs. Club (hon.), N.Y. Gov.'s Club, Se View (N.J.) Country Club, Ft. Orange Club, Universit Club, Wolfert's Roost Club, Rotary. Episcopalian. Home: Albany N.Y. Died July 5, 1987.

O'KEEFE, RAYMOND THOMAS, banker. Exec. v.p Chase Manhattan Bank, N.Y.C.; trustee Chas Manhattan Mortgage & Realty Trust, Cen. Savs. Bank bd. dirs. Chgo. Title & Trust Co., Chgo. Title Ins. Co Pres. Lower Downtown Manhattan Assn.; bd. dirs Realty Found. N.Y. Mem. Mortgage Bankers Assn Am. (gov.), Plandome Country Club, Wall St. Club. Home: Manhasset N.Y. Died Feb. 9, 1986.

O'KEEFFE, GEORGIA, artist; b. Sun Prairie, Wis Nov. 15, 1887; d. Francis and Ida (Totto) O'K.; m Alfred Stieglitz, Dec. 11, 1924 (dec. 1946). Student, A Inst. Chgo., 1904-05, Art Students' League, N.Y.C 1907-08, U. Va., summer 1912, Columbia U., 1914-1 DHL, Columbia U., 1971; DFA (hon.), Coll. Willian and Mary, 1938, U. N.M., 1964, Brown U., 1971, Minn Coll. Art and Design, 1972; LittD, U. Wis., 1942, Mil Coll., 1951, Mt. Holyoke Coll., 1971; DArts, Harvar U., 1973. Illustrator for advt. cos. 1929; supr. art pub schs. Amarillo, Tex., 1912-14; instr. art U. Va., summer 1913-16; head art dept. West Tex. State Normal Coll Canyon, 1916-18. One of group sponsored by Alfre Stieglitz; paintings first exhibited by him at 291, N.Y.C 1916-17, Anderson Galleries, 1923, 24, 25; ann. one woman shows at Intimate Gallery, An Am. Plac N.Y.C., until 1946; retrospective exhbn. Art Inst. Chgo 1971, San Francisco Mus. Art; solo exhbn. at Joh Berggruen Gallery, San Francisco, 1982; group exhbn included Kennedy Galleries, N.Y.C., 1980, 81, Na Mus. Modern Art, Paris, Whitney Mus. Am. A N.Y.C., 1981, U. Ariz. Mus. Art, Tucson, 1981, 8 Terra Mus. Am. Art, Evanston, Ill., 1982, San Francisc Mus. Modern Art; represented in maj. mus. includin Amon Carter Mus., Ft. Worth, Bklyn Mus., Albrigh Knox Mus., Buffalo, Art Inst. Chgo., Met. Mus. A N.Y.C., Mus. Modern Art, N.Y.C., Nat. Galler London, Tate Gallery, London, Nat. Gallery Ar Washington, throughout U.S.; author: Georgia O'Keef Drawings, 1968, Georgia O'Keeffe, 1976. Recipie Creative Arts award Brandeis U., 1963, M. Car Thomas award Bryn Mawr Coll., 1971, Edwa MacDowell medal MacDowell Colony, 1973, awa Skowhegan Sch. Painting and Sculpture, 1973, Presd Medal of Honor, 1977, Nat. Medal of Arts, 1985. Mem. Nat. Inst. Arts and Letters (Gold medal f painting 1970), Am. Acad. Arts and Letters, Am. Aca Arts. and Scis. Home: Albuquerque N.Mex. Died Ma 6, 1986.

OKEY, RUTH, educator; b. Woodsfield, Ohio, 1893; Alfred and Mina (Reinherr) O. BS, Monmouth Col 1914; MS, U. Ill., 1915, PhD, 1918. Faculty U. Cali Berkeley, 1919-79, asst. prof., then assoc. prof., 1919-4 prof., 1944-79, chmn. dept. nutrition and home econ 1956-79. Home: Berkeley Calif. Died Dec. 9, 1987.

O'KONSKI, ALVIN E., former congressman; Kewaunee, Wis., May 26, 1904; s. Frank and Anton (Paska) O'K.; m. Veronica Hemming; Aug. 2 1935. B.S., State Teachers Coll., 1926; grad. student, Ia., 1927-28, U. Wis., 1932. Instr. high schs. 1926-2 instr. speech Ore. State Coll., 1928-31; supt. schs. P laski, Wis., 1932-35; instr. Jr. Coll., Coleraine, Min

1935-36; head speech dept. U. Detroit, 1936-38; pub. relations counsel state Republican orgns., 1938-40; mem. 78th-92d Congresses, 10th Wis. Dist.; mem. armed services com.; pres. Alvin E. O'Konski Enterprises, Inc.; engaged in television ownership and mgmt.; pres. Northland Television, Inc.; dir. Universal Telephone, Milw. Author: Speech Practice, 1937. Pres. Am. Anti-Communist Orgn., Inc., 1947; mem. Katyn Forest Massacre Com.; past dir. World League to Stop Communism. Decorated Polonia Restitucia medal Polish govt. in Exile, 1953. Mem. Pi Kappa Delta. Republican. Home: Winter Park Fla. Died July 8, 1987; buried St. Hedwig's Cemetery, Kewaunee, Wis.

OLDBERG, ERIC, surgeon; b. Evanston, Ill., Nov. 7, 1901; s. Arne and Mary Georgiana (Sloan) O.; m. Hilda Edwards, June 3, 1929 (dec.); 1 child, George Sloan (dec.); m. Mary Swissler, Jan. 2, 1971. B.S., Northwestern U., 1923, M.S., 1926, M.D., 1927, Ph.D., 1928, LL.D. (hon.), 1961; LL.D., Ill. Inst. Tech., 1968; D.Sc. (hon.), Chgo. Coll. Osteo. Medicine, 1970. Diplomate: Am. Bd. Neurol. Surgeons. Instr. in physiology Northwestern U. Med. Sch., 1925-28; Eliz. J. Ward fellowship in physiology 1927-28; surg. house officer Peter Bent Brigham Hosp., Boston, 1928; asst. resident surgeon Peter Bent Brigham Hosp., 1929; resident neurol. surgeon to Dr. Harvey Cushing, 1930; Guggenheim traveling fellow 1930 (resigned); George Gorham Peters traveling fellow Kaiser Wilhelm Inst., Berlin, Germany and Oxford (Eng.) U., 1930-31; asst. prof. surgery U. Ill. Coll. Medicine, 1931-34, assoc. prof. surgery, acting head dept., 1934-36, prof., head dept. neurology and neurol. surgery, 1936-71; dir. neurol. div. and neurol. surgeon Neuropsychiat. Inst., U. Ill.; sr. attending neurol. surgeon, chmn. dept. Presbyn.-St. Luke's Hosp., Chgo., until 1970; sr. attending neurol. surgeon U. Ill. Hosps., Chgo., until 1972; sr. neurol. surgeon Hines VA Hosp., until 1972; pres. Chgo. Bd. Health, 1960-79; chmn. Mayor's commn. Bd. Edn., 1953-68; pres. Chgo. Health Research Found.; chmn. Chgo. Regional Commn. Heart Disease, Cancer and Stroke. Assoc. editor: Jour. Neuropathology; author articles and revs. Life trustee Lake Forest Coll.; bd. dirs. Ednl. TV Channel 11, 1953-62, John Crerar Library; bd. dirs. Nat. Med. Fellowships, pres., 1964-65; gov., life mem. Art Inst. Chgo.; mem. Citizens Bd., U. Chgo.; life mem. Chgo. Natural History Mus.; dir. Chgo. Zool. Soc.; hon. chmn. Chgo. Hort. Soc.; advisory bd. YMCA Met. Chgo.; pres. Protestant Found. Greater Chgo. Recipient Hutchinson medal, 1975, Northwestern U. Alumni medal, 1953, Chgo. medal of merit, 1961, Loyola U. citation for civic leadership, 1966. Fellow A.C.S.; mem. AAAS, Am. Assn. Ry. Surgeons, Chgo. Surg. Soc., AMA, Am. Neurol. Assn., Am. Surg. Assn., Assn. Research in Nervous and Mental Diseases, Central Neuro-Psychiat. Assn., Chgo. Inst. Traumatic Surgery, Chgo. Med. Soc., Chgo. Neurol. Soc. (pres. 1948), Chgo. Path. Soc., Harvey Cushing Soc. (pres. 1943), Ill. Med. Soc., Inst. Medicine Chgo. (pres. 1957, George H. Coleman award 1966), Soc. Exptl. Biology and Medicine, Soc. Neurol. Surgeons, Western Surg. Assn., Chgo. Orch. Assn. (pres. 1952-63), Sigma Xi, Alpha Chi Sigma, Alpha Omega Alpha, Phi Rho Sigma (Irving Cutter award 1956). Episcopalian. Clubs: University, Cliff Dwellers Chicago, Commercial (pres. 1962-63), Lyric Opera (dir.), Casino, Literary, Wayfarers (Chgo.); Onwentsia (Lake Forest). Home: Lake Forest Ill. Died June 28, 1986.

O'LEARY, JOHN FRANCIS, utility executive; b. Reno, Nev., June 23, 1926; s. Francis Adrian and Mary Teresa (Fitzgerald) O'L.; m. Hazel Reid. BS, George Washington U., 1950. Economist U.S. Dept. Interior, Washington, 1950-61, dep. asst. sec., 1962-67, dir. U.S. Bur. Mines, 1968-70; chief U.S. Bur. Natural Gas Fed. Power Co., Washington, 1967-68; energy cons. Washington, 1970-72, 79-87; dir. licensing U.S. Atomic Energy Commn., Washington, 1972-74; adminstr. FEA, Washington, 1977-78; dep. sec. U.S. Dept. Energy, Washington, 1978-79; chmn. bd., chief exec. officer Gen. Pub. Utilities Corp., Parsippany, N.J., 1987. Home: Washington D.C. Died Dec. 19, 1987.

OLESEN, J. M., metal products company executive; b. Chgo., 1904. Grad., U. Ill., 1925. Chmn. bd. Lyon Metal Products, Inc., Aurora, Ill.; bd. dirs. Mchts. Nat. Bank, 1st Am. Bank. Mem. bd. govs. Copley Hosp.; bd. dirs. Aurora Coll. Mem. Union League, Elks, Moose. Home: Aurora Ill. Died Sept. 18, 1983; buried Aurora.

OLIFF, CHARLES, printing executive; b. Chgo., Jan. 3, 1891; s. Jacob and Bertha (Ochs) O.; m. Jeanette Dolnitzky, June 1, 1919; children: Hershel, Thelma L. (Mrs. Louis Klein), Jacquline (Mrs. Martin Rogin), Rochelle R. (Mrs. Arthur R. Weil). Student, Bryant & Stratton Bus. Coll., Chgo. With W. F. Hall Printing Co., Chgo., from 1905, sr. v.p., treas., dir.; sec., treas., dir. Chgo. Rotoprint Co., Central Typesetting & Electrotyping Co.; dir. Art Color Printing Co.; former sec. Nat. Code Authority for Gravure Printing Industry; former mem. appeals panel Chgo. Labor-Mgmt. Com., War Manpower Commn. Life mem. gov. bd. Nat. Coll. Edn., Evanston, Ill.; mem. bd. overseers Jewish Theol. Sem. of Am.; 1st pres. Midwest br. United Synagogue of Am., hon. pres. Chgo. Coun. Established Charles and Jeanette Oliff scholarship at Jewish Theol. Sem. Am. Mem. Graphic Arts Fedn. Ill. (former v.p.), Nat. Gravure Printers Assn. (sec., treas.), Izaak Walton League Am. (life), City Club, Covenant Club, Northwest Fellowship Club (founder), Twin Orchard Country Club, Masons, B'nai B'rith. Home: Chicago Ill. †

OLIVER, FRED NASH, lawyer; b. Waco, Tex., Sept. 3, 1890; s. Jefferson D. and Lina (Nash) O.; m. Juliette Casavant, Nov. 25, 1921; 1 dau., Marie Nash. AB, George Washington U., 1920, LLB, 1921. Bar: D.C. 1921. Atty. Interstate Commerce Commn., 1921-24, trial lawyer, 1924-28; pvt. practice, Washington, from 1928, N.Y.C., from 1933; rep. Va. R.R., T.&T. Ry., B&O. R.R., Chgo. Belt Line R.R., Postal Telegraph, Port Galveston, Tex., L.&N.E. Ry., others, 1928-32; gen. counsel, Nat. Assn. Mut. Savs. Banks and Savs. Banks Assn. of N.Y., from 1932; asst. mcpl. reorgns., including Akron, Atlantic City and Toledo, 1932-35; asst. R.R. reorgns., from 1935; chmn. bd. Casavant Freres (pipe organ builders), St. Hyacinthe, Que., Can.; bd. dirs., mem. exec. com. Cen. R.R. Co. N.J., N.Y.&Long Br. R.R.; spl. rep. U.S. and Can. Cable & Wireless, Ltd. Author case book on railroad valuation law. Maj. inf. U.S. Army, 1917-20. Decorated Purple Heart. Mem. Cosmos Club, Union League Club (N.Y.C.), Mt. Bruno Country Club (Montreal, Can.). Democrat. Home: Washington D.C. †

OLIVER, RALPH ADDISON, judge; b. Eddyville, Iowa, July 31, 1886; s. John Franklin and Fannie M. (Wilhermsdorfer) O.; m. Dorothy Williams, Aug. 11, 1917; children: Dorothy Crane, Frank Williams. AB, U. Iowa, 1907, LLB, 1909. Bar: Iowa 1909, S.D. 1910. Corp. counsel Sioux City, 1930-31; judge Dist. Ct. Iowa, 1931-32; justice Supreme Ct. Iowa, from 1938, chief justice, July-Dec., 1939, June-Dec., 1947, July-Dec., 1951, July-Dec., 1955. 1st lt. aero squadron U.S. Army, World War I. Mem. ABA, Iowa Bar Assn., Sioux City Bar Assn., Am. Legion, Phi Delta Phi, Sigma Chi. Republican. Congregationalist. Home: Sioux City Iowa. †

OLMSTEAD, RALPH W., business executive; b. Milner, Idaho, June 2, 1911; s. Fred Loomis and Lulu (Bates) O.; m. Jeanne Charrier, Aug. 29, 1937; children: Frederick Law, Carol Emilie. AB, U. Idaho, 1932; LLB, JD, George Washington U., 1935. Sec. U.S. senator, Washington, 1933-39; with Office Sec. Agr. (Office Personnel), Washington, 1940; asst. sec. agr., Washington, 1941; asst. to adminstr. Surplus Mktg. Adminstrn. (and its successors), Agrl. Mktg. Adminstrn., Food Distbn. Adminstrn. and Office Distbn., Washington, 1941-45; dir. supply CCC War Food Adminstrn., Washington, 1945; v.p., dir., pres. Fed. Surplus Commodities Corp. UNRRA, Washington, 1945; dir. Henningsen Produce Co., Shanghai, China, 1946, gen. mgr., gen. counsel, 1947-85; Gen. counsel Fed. Inc., Harkson Motors; pres., chmn. bd. H.K. Ferguson Co., Cleve., until 1971; v.p., dir. Morrison Knudson Co. Inc., Boise, Idaho. Mem. Nat. Pub. Adv. Com. Regional Econ. Devel., Washington; adviser to Premier of China; founding mayor Foxfire Village, N.C. 2d lt. O.R.C. AUS, 1932; lt. col. 1942-46. Decorated Legion of Merit. Mem. Am. Soc. Pub. Adminstrn., D.C. Bar, Masons, Elks, Shaker Heights Country Club (Cleve.), Fox Fire Country Club (Pinehurst, N.C.), Georgetown Club (Washington), Blue Key, Scabbard and Blade, Delta Sigma Rho, Kappa Sigma. Home: Jackson Springs N.C. Died Sept. 17, 1985.

O'LOUGHLIN, JOSEPH MARTIN, banker; b. Waltham, Mass., Oct. 12, 1924; s. Peter and Ellen (Tierney) O'L.; m. Jean Gallant, Aug. 26, 1950; children: Anne, Jean Noreen, Joellyn, Martin. BS, Coll. of Holy Cross, 1946; LLD, Fordham U., 1950. Bar: N.Y. 1951. Assoc. atty. Kissam & Halpin, 1950-58; pvt. practice N.Y.C., 1951-58; trust officer Fedn. Bank & Trust Co., N.Y.C., 1958-65; v.p., trust officer Sterling Nat. Bank & Trust Co., N.Y.C., 1965-84. With USNR, 1943-46. Home: Floral Park N.Y. Died Oct. 16, 1984.

OLSON, ARTHUR ANDREW, patent lawyer; b. Chgo., Jan. 9, 1888; s. Andrew and Augusta M. (Johnson) O.; m. Ruth Olive Carlson, June 28, 1916; children: Doris Ruth Olson Stephenson, Arthur Andrew Jr. LLB, Chgo. Kent Coll. Law, 1911. Bar: Ill. 1911. Practiced in Chgo., assoc. Jones, Addington, Ames & Seibold, 1919-21; mem. successor firms Ames, Theiss, Olson & Mecklenburger; Thiess, Olson & Mecklenburger; Thiess, Olson, Mecklenburger, von Hols & Coltman; Olson, Mecklenburger, von Hoslt, Pendleton & Neuman, from 1921; dir., chmn. exec. com. Republic Metals & Roofing Materials, Inc. Trustee Chgo. Kent Coll. Law. Mem. ABA, Am. Judicature Soc., Am. Patent Law Assn., Internat. Patent and Trade-Mark Assn., Chgo. 7th Fed. Cir. Bar Assn., Chgo. Patent Law Assn. (pres. 1949), Union League Club, Executives Club. Presbyterian. Home: Evanston Ill. †

OLSON, CARL AUGUSTUS, educator; b. Jamestown, N.Y., Sept. 29, 1891; s. John and Augusta (Johnson) O.; m. Mabel Helen Culbranson, Sept. 1, 1926. AB, Upsala Coll., 1917, DSc, 1953; MSc, NYU, 1926. Instr. chemistry Upsala Coll., 1920-22; instr. chemistry NYU, 1923-26, asst. prof., 1926-32; asst. prof. chemistry U. Newark, 1933-36, assoc. prof., 1936-46; prof. chemistry, dir. Div. Natural Scis. Newark Coll. Arts and Scis., Rutgers, State U. N.J., 1946-57, prof. emeritus, from 1957; assoc. prof. chemistry Ohio No. U., 1957-58; head chemistry Newark Acad., 1958-60. Trustee Upsala Coll., 1927-51. With. inf. U.S. Army, AEF, 1918-19. Mem. Am. Chem. Soc., AAAS. Lutheran. Home: Houtzdale Pa. †

OLSON, HARVEY S., travel agency executive; b. Chgo., Feb. 28, 1908; s. Nils and Hildur (Lind) O.; m. Paula C. Jonas, July 23, 1966. BS, Purdue U., 1929. Founder, past pres. Campus Tours, Inc., Chgo., 1930-85, Olson Travel Orgn., 1946-85, Olson's Royal Coach Tours, Inc., 1968-85; founder cons. Olson-Travelworld Orgn.; speaker on travel on radio and TV. Author: Aboard and Abroad, 13th edit., 1968, Olson's Orient Guide, 1962, Olson's Hotel, Restaurant and Shopping Guide to Europe, 1953, Olson's Complete Motoring Guide to the British Isles, 1967, Olson's Complete Motoring Guide to France, Switzerland and Italy, 1967, Olson's Complete Motoring Guide to Germany, Austria and The Benelux Countries, 1968. Lt. comdr. USNR, 1942-45. Decorated officer Tourist Order Merit (France); recipient Shalom award Israel Tourist Office, 1973; named to Travel Hall of Fame, 1980. Mem. Conf. Tour Operators (past chmn.), Am. Soc. Travel Agts., Soc. Midland Authors, Western Golf Assn. (bd. dirs. 1964-67), Executives Club (pres. 1964-65), International Club, Oak Hills Country Club, Sunset Ridge Country Club. Home: San Antonio Tex. Died Dec. 17, 1985.

OLSON, RAYMOND VERLIN, agronomist, educator; b. Cavalier, N.D., Oct. 4, 1919; s. Henry L. and Lean B. (Bobert) O.; m. Jean Schumacher, May 25, 1943; children: Nancy, Peter, Susan. Student, N.D. Sch. Forestry, 1937-39; BS, N.D. State Agrl. Coll., 1941; MS, U. Wis., 1942, PhD, 1947. Chemist Hercules Powder Co., Wilmington, Del., 1942-45; assoc. prof. soils Kans. State U., 1947-50, prof., 1950-85, head dept. agronomy, 1952-70, dir. Internat. Agrl. Programs, 1970-72; chief project Ahmadu Bello U. Kans. State U., Zaria, Nigeria, 1964-66, 72-74; dean faculty agr. Kans. State U., 1964-66, provost for agr. and vet. medicine, 1972-74; agrl. cons. I.R.I. Inst., N.Y. and Brazil, 1969; cons. AID, west Africa, 1976, USDA, Govt. Philippines, 1977. Contbr. articles to profl. jours. Chmn. Nat. Soil Rsch. Com., 1957-58; Internat. Exec. Svc. Corps vol. to Ministry Agr., Iran, 1968. Fellow Am. Soc. Agronomy; mem. AAAS, Soil Sci. Soc. Am. (chmn. com. chem. analysis, assoc. editor proc. 1954-56), Sigma Xi, Phi Kappa Phi, Gamma Sigma Delta (Internat. Svc. to Agr. award 1968), Alpha Zeta. Home: Manhattan Kans. Died Mar. 14, 1985; buried Sunrise Cemetery, Manhattan, Kans.

OLSON, ROBERT AUGUST, agronomy educator; b. Fullerton, Nebr., Apr. 14, 1917; s. Per August and Mary (Jacobson) O.; m. Jean Elizabeth Wade, Jan. 30, 1939; children: James Robert, Dianne Elizabeth, Patrick Eugene. B.S., U. Nebr., 1938, M.S., 1949. Cert. on nuclear methods, Oak Ridge Inst. Nuclear Studies, 1951. Soil technologist U.S. Dept. Agr., Okla., Nebr., 1938-42; ext. agronomist U. Nebr., Lincoln, 1946-48, instr. agronomy, 1948-50, asst. prof., 1950-53, assoc. prof., 1953-57, prof., 1957—; cons. Orgn. European Economic Coop., Paris, 1958; head soils sect. Internat. Atomic Energy Agy., Vienna, 1962; mgr. FFHC Fertilizer program Food & Agr. Orgn., Rome, 1967-68; acting dir. Joint FAO-IAEA Div. Agr., Food and Agr. Orgn., Vienna, 1974-75; mem. com. Nat. Acad. Sci., Tropical Soils, 1970-72; mem. wheat del. to, People's Rep. of China, 1976. Editor-in-chief: Fertilizer Technology and Use, 1971, Nutritional Quality of Cereal Grains, 1986; contbr. numerous articles to tech. jours., chpts. to books. Pres. Wesley Found., Lincoln, Nebr., 1961; mem. Nebr. Gov.'s Radiation Adv. Council, 1981—. Served with USNR, 1942-46. Recipient awards Am. Soc. Agronomy, 1971, 82; recipient awards U. Nebr., 1980, awards Soil Sci. Soc. Am., 1983. Fellow Am. Soc. Agronomy, Soil Sci. Soc. Am., AAAS; mem. Internat. Soc. Soil Sci., Phi Beta Kappa, Sigma Xi, Gamma Sigma Delta. Republican. Lutheran. Home: Walton Nebr. Deceased.

OMAN, CARL R., dental educator; b. Mpls., June 6, 1892; s. Nels P. and Emma Louise (Bergman) O.; m. Mildred Nicholson, May 18, 1918; children: Jane Louise, Carl Robert, Frederick Paul. DDS, U. Minn., 1914. Pvt. practice Seattle, 1914-18, 29-36, Mpls., 1919-29; mem. staff U. Minn. Coll. Dentistry, 1920-25; asst. prof. Columbia U. Sch. Dental and Oral Surgery, 1936-37, asosc. prof., 1937-45, prof., head operative div., from 1945. Lt. comdr. USNR. Fellow Am. Coll. Dentists; mem. ADA, N.Y. State Dental Assn. 1st Dist. Dental Soc, Omicron Kappa Upsilon, Delta Sigma Delta. Presbyterian. Home: Hastings-on-Hudson N.Y. †

OPPENHEIMER, JESS, producer; b. San Francisco, Nov. 11, 1913; s. James and Stella C. (Jessurun) O.; m. Estelle Weiss, Aug. 5, 1947; children: Joanne, Gregg. Student, Stanford U., 1931-33. Writer Fred Astaire Packard Program, 1936-38; head writer Screen Guild Program, 1938-40; writer Rudy Vallee Sealtest Program, 1940-41; writer, dir., producer Fanny Brice in Baby Snooks Program, 1942-47; producer, dir., head writer My Favorite Husband with Lucille Ball, 1948-51; creator, producer, head writer I Love Lucy, 1951-56; exec. producer, creator Angel, 1960-61; producer, creator Glynnis, 1963-64; producer, dir., writer Bob

Hope Chrysler Theater, 1965-66; producer, writer Get Smart, 1967-68; creator, exec. producer, writer Debbie Reynolds Show, 1968-69; exec., producer Gen. Motors 50th Anniversary Show NBC, 1956-88; pres. Rinkeed, Inc. Bd. govs. City of Hope; bd. dirs. Vista Del Mar Child Care Service. Served with USCGR, 1941-45. Recipient Sylvania Corp. award, 1952, Michael award Acad. Radio and TV Arts and Scis., 1953. Mem. Acad. TV Arts and Scis. (bd. govs. 1966-88, Emmy award 1952, 53, nominations 1954, 55, 57, 59, 62), Soc. Motion Picture and TV Engrs., Writers Guild Am., Dirs. Guild Am., TV Producers Guild. Home: Los Angeles Calif. Died Dec. 27, 1988.

O'QUIN, LEON, lawyer; b. Montgomery, Ala., Aug. 3, 1892; s. John Thomas nd Clara (Hicks) O'Q.;. Student, Washington and Lee U., 1910-12; LLB, La. State U., 1915. Bar: La. 1915. Pvt. practice Shreveport, La., from 1915; ptnr. firm Blanchard, Walker, O'Quin & Roberts and predecessor, Shreveport, from 1920. Capt. F.A., U.S. Army, World War I, AEF in France and Germany. Mem. Shreveport Club, Sigma Nu. †

ORBISON, ROY, rock and country western musician; b. Vernon, Tex., Apr. 23, 1936. Songs include Oooby Dooby, 1956, Only The Lonely, 1960, Running Scared, 1961 Dream Baby, 1962, In Dreams, 1963, Falling, 1963, Borne on The Wind, 1964, Oh Pretty Woman, 1964, Crawlin' Back to You, 1965, Too Soon to Know, 1966, There Won't Be Many Coming Home, 1966, That Lovin' Feeling Again, 1980 (Grammy award, featured in film Urban Cowboy); albums include All Time Greatest Hits, 1973, At the Rockhouse, 1980, Golden Days, 1981, The Big O Country, 1983, The Sun Years, Regeneration, Class of '55 (Sun reunion album with Jerry Lee Lewis, Johnny Cash, Carl Perkins), 1985, Traveling Wilburys, 1988, Mystery Girl, 1988,. Died Dec. 7, 1988.

ORDOVER, SONDRA T., publisher, editor; b. N.Y.C., Feb. 19, 1929; d. Emmanuel R. and Dorothy T. (Ginsburg) Hellman; m. Irwin Touster, 1949; children: Joshua, David; m. Alfred Ordover, Dec. 17, 1967; stepchildren: Sarah, Andrew. Grad., U. Iowa, 1950. With Fawcett Publs., N.Y.C., 1962-69, mng. editor, 1964-69; sr. editor Ballantine Books, N.Y.C., 1973-77; editor-in-chief Jove (paperback unit Harcourt, Brace Jovanovich, N.Y.C., from 1977; pub. Jove (paperback unit Harcourt, Brace Jovanovich), N.Y.C., from 1978; also corp. v.p. Harcourt, Brace Jovanovich, from 1978; pres., pub. Pinnacle Books, 1983-88. Home: New York N.Y. also: Woodstock N.Y. Died Dec. 12, 1988.

O'REAR, JAMES BIGSTAFF, corporate executive; b. Mt. Sterling, Ky., June 18, 1892; s. Edward C. and Virginia Lee (Hazelrigg) O'R.; m. Agnes Todd Saffell, June, 21, 1914; children: Agnes Saffell O'Rear Perry, Frances Taylor O'Rear Dunstall, Virginia Lee O'Rear Barnard. Student engring., U. Ky., 1911-14. Farmer, contractor, railroading until 1925; gen. mgr. F.&C. R.R., 1925-34; pres. Buffalo Springs Distillery, 1934-41; v.p. Schenley Industries, Inc., N.Y.C., from 1941. With U.S. Army, 1918-19. Home: Versailles Ky. †

O'REILLY, RICHARD THOMAS, marketing consultant; b. N.Y.C., Aug. 30, 1921; s. Edward John and Marie (Kiegler) O'R.; m. Mary Lou Burrichter, Aug. 24, 1946; children: Richard Thomas, Brian Francis. Student, Colo. Sch. Mines, 1943-44. Sr. v.p., dir. N.W. Ayer & Son, 1946-65; exec. v.p., dir. SSC & B, 1966-68; vice chmn. bd., dir. Wells, Rich, Greene, Inc., N.Y.C., 1969-76; pres. Richard T. O'Reilly, Inc., 1976-87, Campaign '80, Reagan presdl. campaign advt. agy., July-Nov. 1980; dir. Tudor Fund, Pacific Fund, WPG Fund, WPG Growth Fund, WPG Govt. Fund, CBA Money Fund, Sci-Tech Holdings, Inc., Internat. Holdings, Eagle Div. Holdings, Fed. Securities Trust, S.A., Hawaiian Tax-Free Trust, Hawaiian Cash Assets Trust, Fund for Tomorrow, Falcon Diversified Holdings, Merrill Lynch CMA Fund Merrill Lynch CMA Tax-Exempt Fund, Merrill Lynch CMA Govt. Securities Fund, Merrill Lynch Mcpl. Bond Fund, Merrill Lynch Corp. Bond Fund, Merrill Lynch Corp. IAP Fund, Merrill Lynch Mcpl. IAP Fund, Retirement Global Bond Fund, Multi-currency Bond Fund, Euro Fund, 1st Convertible Securities Fund, U.S.A. Income Fund; trustee Centennial Capital Cash Mgmt. Trust, Oxford Cash Mgmt. Trust, Merrill Lynch Mcpl. Series Trust, Tax Exempt Trust Oreg. Author: Newspaper Advertising, 1949. Nat. dir. Media Advt. Partnership for a Drug Free Am., 1986-87. Served with AUS, 1942-46. Clubs: Stanwich (Greenwich); N.Y. Athletic (N.Y.C.). Home: Greenwich Conn. Died August 1, 1987; buried St. Mary's Cemetery, Greenwich, Conn.

ORMES, ROBERT VERNER, editor; b. N.Y.C., Sept. 10, 1921; s. Ferguson Reddie and Mabrie (Verner) O.; m. Mary Ann Otto, Sept. 2, 1950; children: Julia C. Ormes Robinson, Carolyn V., Margaret F. AB, Wabash Coll., 1943; postgrad., Columbia U. Instr. Wabash Coll., Crawfordsville, Ind., 1947-49; tech. writer Cushing & Nevell, N.Y.C., 1954; editorial asst. Sci. jour. AAAS, Washington, 1954-57, asst. editor, 1957-60, mng. editor, 1961-81, assoc. pub., 1981-84. Lt. (j.g.) USNR, 1943-46. Mem. Coun. Biology Editor, Phi Beta Kappa, Beta Theta Pi. Democrat. Home: Alexandria Va. Died May 21, 1984; buried Alexandria, Va.

ORNSTEIN, LEO, pianist, composer; b. Krementchug, Russia, Dec. 2, 1892; came to U.S., 1907; s. Rev. Abram and Clara O.; m. Pauline Mallet-Prevost, Dec. 13, 1918. Began piano under father at 3; pupil, Imperial Conservatory of Music, Petrograd, 1901; student, Mrs. Bertha Fiering-Tapper, 1907; student lit., Friends Sem. formerly mem. faculty Phila. Musical Acad., dir., head piano dept. Ornstein Sch. Music; mem. spl. faculty Temple U. First pub. concert at New Amsterdam Theatre, N.Y., Mar. 9, 1933; appeared as soloist with N.Y. Symphony Orch., Boston Symphony Orch., Phila. Orch., Chgo. Symphony Orch., St. Louis Symphony Orch., Los Angeles Philharmonic Orch., and others and has concertized through U.S. and Can., also appeared in Norway, Sweden, Paris; composer: (orch.) Impressions of Chinatown, Marche Funèbre, sonatas for piano and violin, piano and cello, six preludes for cello and piano; (piano) 9 miniatures, poems of 1917; (piano and orch.) concerto, quintette for piano and string quartette, songs; 5 songs for voice and orch.; string quartette Op. 99; Pantomime, for orch.; Suite for orch., Lysistrata; Nocturne and Dance of Fates (orch.), 1936; Nocturne for Clarinet and Piano, Suite in Classic style for Flute and Clarinet; 6 Etudes, 10 Valses for Piano, Ballade for Saxaphone and Piano; Three Moods; Prelude and Intermezzo for Flute and Piano; Hebrigne Fantasy for Violin and Piano; numerous piano pieces. Recipient 1st prize Nat. Anthem Contest, 1930. †

ORTON, VREST, merchant, publicist, author; b. Hardwick, Vt., Sept. 3, 1897; s. Gardner Lyman and Lelia (Teachout) O.; m. Rosita Lefkov, 1926 (div. 1932); 1 child, Geoffrey Dean Conrad; m. Mildred Ellen Wilcox, Jan. 12, 1935; children: Lyman Kennerly, Jeremy Roderick (dec.). Student, Harvard U., 1923. Ptnr. Baccus & Orton, L.A.; mem. U.S. Consular Svc., Mex., 1924-25; mem. staff Am. Mercury Mag., N.Y.C., 1925-27; advt. mgr. Saturday Rev. of Lit., 1927-28; founder, editor The Colophon: Book Collectors' Quar., N.Y.C., 1930; with advt. and pub. relations Alfred A. Knopf, 1928-30; founder, gen. mgr., editor Stephen Daye Press, Brattleboro, Vt., 1931; founder, gen. mgr. Countryman Press, Weston, Vt., 1935; counsel pub. relations Mary Fletcher Hosp., Dartmouth Coll., Wesleyan Coll., others, 1935-41; a founder Vt. Guild Old-Time Crafts and Industries, Weston, 1936, sec.-treas., 1936-38; founder 1st restored country store in rural U.S. 1945; established Voice of the Mountains nat. mail order catalog for The Original Vt. Country Store Weston, 1945-85; cons. U.S. Dept. Def., Washington, Ford Motor Co., Dearborn, Mich. Author: Dreiserana, A Book About His Books, 1929, Proceedings of The Company of Amateur Brewers, 1932, A Line of Men 100 Years Long, 1936, Goudy: Master of Letters, 1939, Mary Fletcher Comes Back, 1939, The Army-Navy War Contractors Guide, 1943, Vermont Academy Way, 1945, Official Guide to Vermont's hiostoric Sites, 1958, Guide to Calvin Coolidge Home, 1959, Calvin Coolidge's Unique Vermont Inauguaration, 1960, The Famous John Rogers Groups, 1963; (with Mildred Orton) Cooking with Wholegrains, 1951, The Forgotten Art of Building a Fireplace, 1969, Vermont Afternoons with Robert Frost, 1969, The History of the Vermont Country Store, 1970, The Homemade Beer Book, 1973, The American Cider Book, 1973, A History of the Republic of Vermont, 1977, The Voice of the Green Moutains, 1979; editor: And So Goes Vermont, 1937; founder The Colophon: Book Collectors Quar., 1930; a founder of Vermont Life; contbr. articles to mags., newspapers, anthologies. Mem. bd. curators, v.p. Vt. Hist. Soc., 1929-54, chmn. Vt. Hist. Sites Commn., 1951-59; pub. relations officer Phila. Ordnance Dist., 1942-43; in charge pub. relations for contract termination and surplus property, staff War Dept., 1943-45; mem. Vt. Law Enforcement Coun.; dir. pub. relations Vt. for Eisenhower State Com., 1952; del. Rep. Nat. Conv., 1952, alt. del., 1956; mem. exec. com. Vt. for Reagan as Pres. of U.S., 1979-80. With U.S. Army, Army Expeditionary Force, 1918-19. Cited as Outstanding U.S. Retailer NYU Sch. Retailing, 1952. Mem. Assn. Hist. Sites Pub. Ofcls. (founder, pres. 1956), Brook Club, Harvard Club of Vt. (v.p. 1953), Bentley Drivers' Club. Home: Weston Vt. Died Dec. 1985; buried Weston.

OSBORN, PAUL, playwright; b. Evansville, Ind., Sept. 4, 1901; s. Edwin Faxon and Bertha (Judson) O.; m. Millicent Green, May 10, 1939; 1 child, Judith Judson. A.B., U. Mich., 1923, M.A., 1924; postgrad., Yale Dramatic Workshop, 1927. Instr. English U. Mich., 1925-26. Author: plays The Vinegar Tree, 1931, Oliver Oliver, 1933, revived 1985, On Borrowed Time, 1938, Morning's at Seven, 1939 (revived 1980, Tony award 1980, The Innocent Voyage, 1943, A Bell for Adano, 1944, Point of No Return, 1952, The World of Suzie Wong, 1948, Maiden Voyage, 1960, Hot September, 1965, Contessa, 1966, To-morrow's Monday, 1985; motion picture scripts The Yearling, 1947, Mme. Curie, 1944, The Young in Heart, 1938, East of Eden, 1955, Sayonara, 1957, South Pacific, 1958, Wild River, 1960, John Brown's Body, 1967, also numerous others. Home: New York N.Y. Died May 12, 1988, cremated.

OSBORN, PRIME FRANCIS, III, railroad executive, lawyer; b. Greensboro, Ala., July 31, 1915; s. Prime Francis and Anne (Fowlkes) O.; m. Grace Hambrick, Aug. 30, 1939; children: Prime Francis IV, Mary Anne. JD, U. Ala., 1939, LLD (hon.), 1970. Bar: Ala. 1939, Ky. 1952, N.C. 1959, U.S. Dist. Ct. Ala., 1959, U.S. Ct. Appeals Ala., 1959, U.S. Supreme Ct. Asst. atty. gen. Ala. 1939-41; atty. G.M.&O. R.R., 1946-51, commerce atty., 1950-51; gen. solictor L&N R.R., 1951-57; v.p., gen. counsel, dir. A.C.L. R.R., 1957-67; v.p., law dir. Seaboard Coast Line R.R. Co., 1967-69, pres., 1969-78, chief exec. officer, 1972-86, chmn. bd., 1978-86, also bd. dirs.; pres. SCL Industries, Inc., 1970-78, chmn., chief exec. officer, 1978-86; pres., chief exec. officer Louisville & Nashville R.R. Co., 1972-78, chmn., chief exec. officer, 1978-80; chmn. bd. CSX Corp., 1980-82; bd. dirs. Ethyl Corp. Mem. nat. council, regional exec. com., regional chmn. Boy Scouts Am., 1965-69; bd. overseers, bd. dirs. Jacksonville U., Jacksonville Epsic. High Sch.; chmn. nat. adv. bd. Salvation Army, 1979-83; chmn. exec. bd. St. Vincent's Hosp., from 1982; mem. ho. deps. gen. conv. Protestant Episc. Ch. Am.; provincial chmn. Episcopal Ch. Found. Lt. col., arty. AUS, 1941-46; with res. Office Emergency Transp. Dept. Transp. Decorated Bronze Star; named Man of Year Duval County, Fla., 1962, Outstanding Citizen Duval County, 1982; recipient Bicentennial Brotherhood award NCCJ, Nat. Religious Heritage of Am. Transp. award, 1975, George Washington Medal of Honor Freedoms Found., 1977, Boy Scouts Am. awards, Wiliam Booth award Salvation Army; named to Ala. Hall of Honor, 1982, Ala. Bus. Hall of Fame, 1983. Mem. ABA, Ala. Bar Assn. (award of merit 1976), Bar Assn. of City of N.Y., SCV, Mil. Order Stars and Bars, VFW, Am. Legion, Order Constantine, Mil. Order World Wars, SAR, Newcomen Soc. N.Am., Nat. Def. Transp. Assn. (Man of Year 1980), Episcopal Men. of Ky. (past pres.), Episcopal Men Ala. (past pres.), Jacksonville Area C. of C. (pres. from 1971, Com. of 100), Fla. Council 100 C. of C., Louisville Area C. of C. (bd. dirs. 1972-74), Jasons, Scabbard and Blade, Ponte Verde (Fla.) Beach Club, River Club, Fla. Yacht Club, Timuquana Country Club, Union League Club N.Y.C., Metropolitan Club (Washington), Country Club of Va., Pendennis Club, Louisville Country Club, Augusta Nat. Golf Club, Laurel Valley Country Club (Ligonier, Pa.), Tournament Players Club, Rotary, Sigma Alpha Epsilon, Omicron Delta Kappa, Tau Kappa Alpha, Alpha Kappa Psi (hon.), Beta Gamma Sigma (hon.). Home: Jacksonville Fla. Died Jan. 4, 1986.

OSBORN, RICHARD KENT, educator, physicist; b. Ft. Wayne, Ind., Mar. 12, 1919; s. George Burr and Florence (Stowell) O.; m. Elizabeth Rich, June 16, 1945; children—Mary R., D. Richard, David C., Ann S. B.S., Mich. State U., 1948, M.S., 1949; Ph.D., Case Inst. Tech., 1952. Physicist Oak Ridge Nat. Lab., 1951-57; mem. faculty U. Mich., Ann Arbor, 1957-87; prof. nuclear engring. U. Mich., 1959-87; lectr. U. Tenn., 1951-57; dir. reactor engring. design KMS-Fusion Corp., Ann Arbor, 1972. Author: (with S. Yip) Foundations of Neutron Transport Theory, 1969; also articles. Fellow Am. Phys. Soc., Am. Nuclear Soc.; mem. Sigma Xi, Phi Kappa Phi. Home: Ann Arbor Mich. Died Feb. 26, 1987.

OSBORN, STANLEY HART, government official; b. Peabody, Mass., May 3, 1891; s. Charles Lincoln and Alice Cornelia (Hart) O.; m. Gertrude Mellen Hooper, Sept. 16, 1921; children: Stanley Hart, Henry Hooper, William Charles. MD, Tufts Coll. Med. Sch., 1914, DSc (hon.), 1942; cert. in pub. health, Harvard U./MIT Sch. Health Officers, 1915; DrPH (hon.), Trinity Coll., 1945; MPH, Harvard U., 1947. Acting biologist Met. Water Bd., Boston, 1914; in charge field unit ARC Sanitary Commn. to Serbia, 1915-16; dist. health officer Mass. Dept. Pub. Health, 1916, epidemiologist, 1917, 19-20; dep. commr. health, dir. Bur. Preventable Diseases, Conn. Dept. Health, 1920-22, state commr. health, from 1922; lectr. in pub. health Yale Sch. Medicine, from 1924. Mem. New Eng. Water Pollution Commn., Milk Regulations Bd., Conn., from 1922, Interstate Sanitation Commn. (Conn., N.J., N.Y.), from 1931; rep. Conf. to Nat. health Coun., 1925-50; pres. Conf. State and Provincial Health Authorities N.Am., 1932-33. With U.S. Army, 1918-19, Res., 1919-34. Decorated Order of St. Sava, 3d class (Serbia); Cross Nat. Order Civil Merit Bulgaria, 2d class. Fellow AMA (del. sect. on preventive medicine, indsl. hygiene and pub. health 1929-52), AAAS, Am. Pub. Health Assn.; mem. Nat. Tb Assn., Conn., Hartford and hartford County med. socs., Conn. Pub. Health Assn., Conn. Soc. for Mental Hygiene, Am. Legion, Masons (32 degree), Rotary, Alpha Kappa Kappa, Delta Omega. Congregationalist. Home: West Hartford Conn. †

OSBORN, STELLANOVA (STELLA BRUNT), author, international organization executive; b. Hamilton, Ont., Can., July 31, 1894; d. Edward Brunt and Rosa Lee; m. Chase Salmon Osborn, Apr. 9, 1949 (dec. Apr. 1949). AB magna cum laude, U. Mich., 1922, AM, 1930, LittD, 1978. Staff editor New Internat. Yr. Book, 1923; contbg. editor sociology and econs. sects. New Internat. Ency. Supplement, 1924; asst. editor Good Health Mag., 1925; editor U. Mich. Ofcl. Publ., 1925-30; sec., collaborator with Gov. Osborn 1931-49; editor, pub. Atlantic Union Herald, Mich. and Ont., 1950-57; contbr. editor Freedom & Union, 1965-72; Disting. prof. humanities Abraham Baldwin Agrl. Coll., Tifton, Ga., 1972-88. Author: Eighty and On, 1941, Some Sidelights on the Battle of Tippecanoe, 1943, A Tale of Possum Poke in Possum Lane, 1946, Balsam Boughs, 1949, Jasmine Springs, 1953, Polly

Cadotte, 1955, Beside the Cabin, 1957, Iron and Arbutus, 1962, Summer Song on the St. Marys, 1981 (with Chase Osborn) The Conquest of a Continent, 939, Schoolcraft-Longfellow-Hiawatha, 1942, Hiawatha with Its Original Indian Legends, 1944, Errors in Official U.S. Area Figures, 1945; editor (with others): Whimsies, 1920-22, An Accolade for Chase S. Osborn, 1940, Northwoods Sketches, 1949; contbr. articles to various publs. mem. Mich. State-wide Com. for Mackinac Straits Bridge, 1938; mem. adv. panel on legal structure for fgn. relations N.Y. State Bar Assn.; mem. Citizens for Haig for U.S. Pres., 1979; benefactor mem. Chehaw coun. Boy Scouts Am.; mem. Chippewa County, Detroit, Tippecanoe County, Head-of-the-Lake, St. Lakes, Ga., Mich. hist socs. Recipient citation Phi Beta Kappa Assocs., 1949, award Atlantic Union Com., 951, 61, award Poulan (Ga.) Community Coun., 1954, award Upper Peninsula (Mich.) Writers, 1967, Outstanding Achievement award U. Mich., 1967, 1st Frank Cyril James award Internat. Assn. for Union Democracies, 1977. Mem. Friends U. Mich. Hist. Collections exec. bd. 1972-88), Poetry Soc., Inc., Poetry Soc. Mich., Acad. Am. Poets, Henry P. Tappan Soc. (Charter), Hamilton Assn. Advancement Edn., Sci. and Arts, Nat. Smithsonian Assocs., Adult Edn. Assn. U.S.A., Soc. for Continuing Edn. in World Affairs, Common Cause, Pu. Citizen, English-Speaking Union, Staffordshire Record Soc., Friends of Christ Ch. Cathedral, London Inst. World Affairs, Internat. Assn. for Fed. Union Democracies (one founder, hon. v.p. 1972, adv. bd. Youth for Fed. Union 1972-75), European-Atlantic Group, Grotius Found., Union Atlantischer Foederalisten (hon.), Atlantic Union Com. (nat. coun. 1950-61, d. dirs. 1951-61, exec. com., com. on liaison with other countries 1957-61, exec. dir. Mich. br. 1951-52, chmn. 952-61, exec. v.p. Ga. br. 1953-61, ofcl. del 2d Internat. tudy Conf. Atlantic Community 1953, spl. rep. Holand and West Germany 1955, Iceland 1956, spl. citations 1951, 61), Intrenat. Movement Atlantic Union founder, sec. N.Am. br. 1958-65, v.p. 1965-88, del. ongress 1961, 65, gen. meeting 1969, ofcl. observer tlantic Treaty Assn. Assemblies 1964-70, observer orth Atlantic Assembly 1959, 68, 69, 71), Fed. Union Am. (bd. dirs. 1961-88, corr. sec. 1961-72, del. to observe European elections 1979), Atlantic Coun. U.S. sponsor), AAUW, LWV, Bus. and Profl. Women (citaon Capital club D.C. 1971, D.C. Fedn. 1972), Mich. League, Presidents Club, Abraham Baldwin Agrl. Coll. a. Club, Phi Beta Kappa (hon. mem. exec. com. D.C. hpt. 1971-72, life mem. Assocs.). Presbyterian. Home: ault Sainte Marie Mich. also: Poulan Ga. Died Mar. 3, 988.

SBORNE, ARTHUR ELLSWORTH, JR., department store executive; b. Chgo., May 21, 1920; s. Arthur Ellsworth and Esther Irene (Harrison) O.; m. Barbara ne Rupp, May 21, 1943; children: Arthur Ellsworth, I., Richard Harrison, David Charles. Student, Grinell (Iowa) Coll., 1942. With Marshall Field & Co., hgo., 1945-85; v.p. women's apparel Marshall Field & o., 1966-71, v.p., gen. mgr., 1971-74, corp. v.p., 1974-5, sr. v.p., 1976, pres. Chgo. div., 1977-85, corp. exec. p., 1978-85, also dir.; dir., mem. exec. com. Upper ve. Nat. Bank, Chgo., 1972-85. Chmn. Chgo. crusade m. Cancer Soc., 1975, Ill. crusade, 1978, State St. ouncil, 1972-73, 78-79; bd. dirs. Evanston (Ill.) Hosp., 074-85, Chgo. Boys Clubs, 1979-85; chmn. Chgo. unit m. Cancer Soc., 1979, vice-chmn. 1977-78; vice chmn. ate Street Mall Commn., Chgo. Served to capt. SAAF, 1942-45. Decorated D.F.C., Purple Heart, Air edal, Presdl. citation. Mem. Nat. Retail Mchts. Assn. xec. com., dir. 1973-85), Chgo. Hist. Soc. (dir. 1977-). Episcopalian. Clubs: Chicago (Chgo.), Mid-Am. hgo.); Glen View, Country of Fla. Home: Glenview . Died Aug. 31, 1985.

SBORNE, HAROLD SMITH, electrical engineer; b. syetteville, N.Y., Aug. 1, 1887; s. Cyrus P. and Ella S. mith) O.; m. Mary Agnes Wilson, Aug. 14, 1918 ec. 1932); children: Margaret Ellen Osborne McLane, ary Agnes Wilson Osborne Smith; m. Dorothy Beckvay, Mar. 24, 1938. BS, MIT, 1908, DEng, 1910. ith Edison Electric Illuminating Co., Boston, summers 05-08, Turners Falls (Wis.) Power Co., summer 1909; th Am. Tel. & Tel. Co., 1910-52, successively engr. ansmission and protection dept., asst. to transmission d protection engr., transmission engr., operating sults engr., plant engr., asst. chief engr., 1910-43, chief gr., 1943-52; cons. engr. Brazilian Traction, Light & wer Co., also Brazilian Telephone Co., 1952-60; dir. eritus Rsch. Corp; cons. Internat. Bank for Reconn. and Devel., 1961-63; vis. lectr. MIT, 1953. ontbr. tech. articles. Mem. town planning bd., Montir, N.J., 1930-40, 52-56, 61-64, chmn., 1933-40; chmn. sex County Coun. Mcpl. Planning Bds., 1937-39; v.p. egional Plan Assn. N.Y. and Environs., 1942-52, pres., nn., 1953-59; v.p. Internat. Electrotech. Commn., eneva, 1949-52, pres., 1952-55, pres. U.S. nat. com. action, 55-58; mem. bd. commrs., dir. dept. pub. works, ontclair, N.J., 1952-56; mayor Town of Montclair, 61-64; spl. cons. Office Sec. War, World War II, mem. egraph com. War Communications Bd.; mem. instry adv. coun. Fed. Specifications Bd., industry adv. n. for supply cataloging Munitions Bd.; mem. adv. ternat. tech. assistance NRC, 1953-56, mem. RC, 1954-64. Decorated knight Royal Order of Vasa weden); recipient Howard Coonley medal Am. andards Assn., 1956, 75th anniversary medal ASME.

Fellow AIEE (chmn. tech. program com. 1936-39, pres. 1942-43, bd. dirs., mem. exec com. 1942-45, chmn. bd. trustees Volta Meml. Found 1949-59, Edison medal award), Acoustical Soc. Am., Am. Phys Soc., AAAS, Inst. Radio Engrs.; mem. Am. Planning and Civic Assn. (bd. dirs. 1948-51), Am. Soc.. Planning Ofcls. (pres., silver medal award), Am. Soc. Engring Edn. (chmn. com. engring. economy 1951-53), Am. Assn. UN (dir. Montclair br. from 1950), N.J. Fedn. Planning Bds. (bd. dirs. 1950), Engrs. Joint Coun. (chmn. com. on unity engring. profession 1949-53, chmn. com. on constitution and by-laws 1952-58), Montclair Soc. Engrs. (pres. 1928-30), Coun. Social Agys., Century Assn. Club, Downtown Athletic Club, University Club (N.Y.C.), Upper Montclair Country Club, Tau Beta Pi, Eta Kappa Nu. Home: Upper Montclair N.J. †

OSGOOD, ROBERT ENDICOTT, educator, author; b. St. Louis, Aug. 14, 1921; s. Harold A. and Harriet (Johnson) O.; m. Gretchen Anderson, Aug. 3, 1946. AB, Harvard U., 1943, PhD, 1952. With rsch. sect. U. Chgo., 1951-52, from asst. prof. to prof. polit. sci., 1956-61; rsch. assoc. Washington Ctr. Fgn. Policy Rsch., 1961-65, dir., 1965-87; prof. Johns Hopkins Sch. Advanced Internat. Studies, 1961-87, dean, 1973-87; NATO vis. prof. U. Manchester, Eng., 1959; lectr. Salzburg (Austria) Seminar in Am. Studies, 1957, 61; mem. sr. staff Gov. NSC, 1969-70. Author: Ideals and Self-Interest in America's Foreign Relations, 1953, Limited War, 1957, NATO: the Entangling Alliance, 1962; (with Robert W. Tucker) Force, Order and Justice, 1967, Alliances and American Foreign Policy, 1968; (with Robert W. Tucker, others) America and the World, 1970, Retreat from Empire?, 1973, The Weary and The Wary, 1972; (with Ann L. Hollick) New Era of Ocean Politics, 1974; (with George Packard III and John Badgley) Japan and the United States in Asia. Mem. bd. overseers Harvard U. With inf. AUS, 1943-46. Mem. Am. Polit. Sci. Assn., Coun. Fgn. Relations, Atlantic Coun. (bd. dirs.). Home: Chevy Chase Md. Died Dec. 28, 1987.

OSMENT, FRANK CARTER, oil company executive; b. Birmingham, Ala., July 20, 1918; s. Clarence Eugene and Mary (O'Keefe) O.; m. Josephine Finke, Dec. 16, 1942; children: Michael, Andrew, Mary Jenifer. BS, Birmingham-So. Coll., 1939; MS, U. Ill., 1941; grad. advanced mgmt. program, Harvard U., 1952. Field geologist Tenn. Geol. Survey, Nashville, 1941; dist. geologist Amoco Prodn. Co., Shreveport, La., 1945-51; div. geologist Amoco Prodn. Co., Houston, 1951-55; mgr. exploration Amoco Prodn. Co., Tulsa, 1955-59; v.p., div. mgr. Amoco Prodn. Co., Calgary, Alta., Can., 1959-64; exec. v.p. Amoco Prodn. Co., Tulsa, 1964-65; v.p Standard Oil Co. of Ind., Chgo., 1965-67, exec. v.p., 1974-87, also bd. dirs.; pres. Amoco Internat. Oil Co., Chgo., 1967-74. Lt. (s.g.) USNR, 1941-45. Mem. Am. Assn. Petroleum Geologists, Am. Petroleum Inst. Home: Winnetka Ill. Died May 12, 1987.

OSOL, ARTHUR, chemist, former college president; b. Riga, Latvia, Dec. 1, 1905; came to U.S., 1906, naturalized, 1915; s. Peter and Caroline (Irbit) O.; m. Amelia Virginia Lebo, Dec. 28, 1928 (dec. Aug. 1981). Ph.G., Phila. Coll. Pharmacy and Sci., 1925, B.S. in Chemistry, 1928; M.S. in Chemistry, U. Pa., 1931, Ph.D., 1933; LL.D., Eastern Bapt. Coll., 1964; Sc.D., Thomas Jefferson U., 1971. With Phila. Coll. Pharmacy and Sci. 1928-88, instr., 1930-33, asst. prof., 1933-34, assoc. prof., 1934-37, prof., 1937-75, prof. emeritus, 1975-88, dir. chem. labs., 1937-43, dir. chem. dept., 1943-63, dean sci., 1959-63, pres., 1963-75, pres. emeritus, from 1975; prescription editor Am. Druggist Mag., N.Y.C., 1933-45; editorial cons. Blakiston-McGraw-Hill, N.Y.C., 1944-73; dir. Univ. City Sci. Center Corp.; pres. West Phila. Corp.; chmn. com. phys. chemistry Nat. Conf. Pharm. Research, 1934-41; collaborating research worker League of Nations Health Com. (investigating methods of analysis of opium and coca), 1933-37; mem. sci. adv. com. Smaller War Plants Corp., World War II; mem. U.S. Pharmacopeia rev. com., 1950-70; chief chem. br. Phila. Tech. Def. Div. Assoc. editor: United States Dispensatory (2d edit., 1937, supplement, 1940; co-editor (with Horatio C. Wood, Jr. 23d edit.), 1943, supplement, 1944, editor-in-chief 24th to 27th edits., 1947-73; chmn. editorial bd.: Remington's Pharm. Scis., 14th edit., 1970, 15th edit., 1975, 16th edit., 1980; co-editor: Blakiston's New Gould Med. Dictionary, 1949, 2d edit., 1956, 3d edit., 1972, Blakiston's Illustrated Pocket Med. Dictionary, 1952, 2d edit., 1960, 3d edit., 1973, A Sesquicentennial of Service of Phila. Coll. Pharmacy and Sci.), 1971; contbr. to sci. jours. Trustee, Chapel of Four Chaplains. Recipient Procter gold medal for disting. service in pub. welfare Phila. Drug Exchange, 1975, Griffith Alumni Sci. award Phila. Coll. Pharmacy and Sci., 1987. Fellow Am. Inst. Chemists, AAAS; mem. Am. Chem. Soc. (chmn. Phila. sect. 1943-44, councilor, dir.), Am. Electrochem. Soc. (chmn. Phila. sect. 1949-51), Am. Pharm. Assn. (pres. Phila. sect. 1939-40), Franklin Inst., Am. Acad. Polit. and Social Sci., N.Y. Acad. Scis., Phila. Sci. Council (dir.), Sigma Xi, Phi Delta Chi, Rho Chi. Republican. Presbyterian. Clubs: Rotary (dir. Phila.), Metachemical. Home: Bala-Cynwyd Pa. Died Oct. 22, 1988.

OSTRANDER, GILMAN M., historian, educator; b. San Francisco, Aug. 2, 1923; s. Frank Sidney and Katherine (Burnham) O.; m. Katherine Hill, July 7,

1946; m. Jean Frappier, July 3, 1963; children: David, Robert, Sara. AB, Columbia U., 1946; PhD, U. Calif., Berkeley, 1954. Teaching intern Reed Coll., 1953-54; instr. Ohio State U., Columbus, 1954-57; asst. prof. U. Mo., 1957-59; assoc. prof., then prof. Mich. State U., 1959-67; prof. history U. Mo., St. Louis, 1968-71, U. Waterloo, Ont., Can., from 1971; Fulbright lectr., Tokyo, 1967-68. Author: Prohibition Movement in California, 1848-1933, 1957, Rights of Man in America, 1606-1861, 1960, Nevada, The Great Rotten Borough, 1859-1964, 1966, American Civilization in the First Machine Age, 1890-1940, 1970. Served with AUS, 1943-45. Deceased.

O'SULLIVAN, RICHARD CHARLES, steel company executive; b. Chgo., Nov. 2, 1927; s. Eugene Patrick and Leona (Schmitt) O'S.; m. Dorothy Mae Gallagher, Dec. 2, 1950; children—Mark, Deborah, Barbara, Patricia. B.Sc., DePaul U., 1950; M.B.A., U. Detroit, 1955; postgrad., N.Y.U., 1959-60. Cost accountant Signode Steel, Chgo., 1950-52; trainee Calif.-Tex. Oil Co. Ltd., N.Y.C., 1952-53; cost analyst Ford Motor Co., Highland Park, Mich., 1953-55; supr. spl. projects Chrysler Corp., Highland Park, 1955-56; asst. to chmn. bd. Curtiss-Wright Corp., Woodridge, N.J., 1956-62; dir. cost analysis Gen. Dynamics Corp., N.Y.C., 1962-64; comptroller Gen. Dynamics Corp. (Electric Boat div.), Groton, Conn., 1964-68; v.p., controller Textron Corp., Providence, 1968-71; controller Monsanto Co., St. Louis, 1971-88; treas. Monsanto Co., 1975-88, v.p., 1976-79, v.p. econ. and fin. analysis, 1979-81; chief fin. officer Allegheny Ludlum Corp., Pitts., 1981-88; Mem. Fin. Accounting Standards Adv. Council, 1975-76. Served with USMC, 1945-46; Served with USNR, 1946. Mem. Fin. Execs. Inst. (pres. St. Louis chpt. 1979, Pitts. chpt. 1986). Clubs: Duquesne, Pitts. Field. Home: Fox Chapel Pa. Died Feb. 20, 1988.

OTIS, ARTHUR N., business executive; b. Syracuse, N.Y., Jan. 7, 1892; s. Edgar F. and Addie (Talbot) O.; m. Ella Willaume, 1915; children: Louise (Mrs. O'Donnell), Ramona (Mrs. Cookman), Joanne (Mrs. Raiola), Arthur N.; m. 2d, Irene Anderson, June 18, 1943. Student, U. Pa., 1910-11. With Mchts. Bank, Daytona Beach, Fla., 1911-29, becoming v.p.; cashier; bank liquidator State Banking Dept., Tallahassee, 1929; asst. v.p. Irving Trust Co., N.Y.C., 1930-40; chmn., dir. Mchts. REfrigerating Co., 1961-70, ret., 1970; cons. Office Sec. War. Past pres. Refrigeration Rsch. Found. Mem. Nat. Assn. Refrigerated Warehouses (past pres.), Mchts. Club, Arkwright Club, Pinnacle Club. Home: Cos Cob Conn. †

OTTAVIANO, ALFREDO, cardinal; b. Rome, Italy, Oct. 29, 1890; s. Enrice and Palmira (Catalini) O. PhD, Pontilicia U. Lateranense, Rome, 1912, DD, 1916, JUD, 1918; LLD (hon.), U. Notre Dame, Cath. U. Am., Seton Hall U., Loras Coll., Creighton U. Ordained priest Roman Cath. Ch., 1916. Prof. philosophy Poltilicia U. Urbiana Dell Apollinare, 1919-20; prof. pub. ecclesiastical law Ateneo Giurdico, 1921-30; cofounder rev. Appollinairis; minutante Congregation de PRopagand Fide, 1919-21; minutante Della Segreatria di Stato-Extraordinary Ecclesiastical Affairs, 1921, undersec., 1927-29, sostituto, 1929-58, sec., 1958-66, proprefect, from 1966; assessor Supreme Sacred Congregation of the Holy OFfice, from 1935, cardinal, pro-sec., from 1953; mem. Concistorial Congregation, Religious Congregation, Propaganda Fide Congregation, Ceremonial Congregation, Extraordinary Ecclesiastical Congregation, Seminaries and Univs. Congregation, also mem. Tribunale Supremo Della Segnature Apostolica, Pontifical Bib. Commn., Pontifical Commn. for Revision Code Canon Law. Author: Institutiones Juris Publici Ecclesiastics, 2 vols., 4th edit., Compendium Juris Publici Ecclesiastici, 5th edit., Il Baluardo, others. Cofounder Potifical Oratory of St. Peter, 1964; founder orphanage Oasi di Sta. Rita Frascate, 1960. Decorated gran cross Dell'ordine di Cristo (Portugal); grand cross dei Ss. Maurizio E Lazzaro (Italy); grand cross Della Corona (Romania); grand ufficiale Della Legione D'onore; grand cross D'isabella (Spain). Home: Rome Italy. †

OTTESEN-JENSEN, ELLSE, association executive; b. Höjland, Norway, Jan. 2, 1886; d. Immanuel and Karen Ursula (Essendrop) Ottesen; m. Albert Jensen, Feb. 2, 1915 (dec. 1945). MD (hon.), Uppsala U., 1958. Journalist Norwegian Daily Mail, 1908-15; fgn. corr. in Denmark for Norwegian Newspapers, 1915-19; pres. The Swedish Assn. for Sex Edn., 1933-59; v.p. Europe region Internat. Planned Parenthood Fedn.., Stockholm, 1953-59, pres., 1959-63. Recipient Royal Medal Illisquorum, 1951, Lasker award, N.Y.C., 1954. Home: Stockholm Sweden. †

OTTO, ROBERT WILLIAM, lawyer, gas company executive; b. Washington, Mo., Dec. 25, 1892; s. Edmund H. and Mallita (Hoffman) O.; m. Katrine Ewing Dallmeyer, Oct. 12, 1922; children: Robert Ewing and William Hoffman (twins). Student, U. Mo.; LLB, Northwestern U., 1915. Bar: Mo. 1915. Practiced in Kansas City, Mo., from 1915; pros. atty. Franklin County, Mo., 1917-20; asst. atty. gen. State of Mo., 1921-25, atty. gen., 1925-26; assoc. justice Supreme Ct. Mo., from 1926; former pres., then chmn. bd. LaClede Gas Light Co., St. Louis. Author: Information and Indictments in Criminal Cases, 1925, Instructions in

Criminal Cases, 1925. Mem. Am. Gas Assn. (pres.). Home: Saint Louis Mo. †

OUIMET, ALPHONSE, communications engineer; b. Montreal, Que., Can., June 12, 1908; s. Alphonse and Blanche (Geoffrion) O.; m. Jeanne Prevost; 1 child, Denyse Ouimet Vincent. BA, Coll. Ste-Marie, Montreal, 1928; B in English, McGill U., Montreal, 1932, LLD (hon.), 1963; DASc. (hon.), U.Montreal, 1957; DCL (hon.), Acadia U., 1962; LLD (hon.), U. Sask., Can., 1962, Royal Mil. Coll. Can., 1974; DSc in Sociology (hon.), U. Ottawa, Ont., Can., 1967; DAdm (hon.), U. Sherbrooke, Que., 1967; D es Arts, Laval U., 1978. Research engr. Can. TV Ltd., 1932, Can. Electronics Ltd., 1933, Can. Radio Broadcasting Commn., 1934-36; with CBC, 1936-67; asst. gen. mgr. CBC, Montreal, 1952-53; gen. mgr. CBC, 1953-58; pres. CBC, Ottawa, 1958-67; cons. communications Ottawa, 1968-85; chmn. bd. Telesat Can., 1969-80, dir., 1980-84; chmn. CBC Corp. Olympics Com., 1973-76, Communications Research Adv. Bd., 1975-80; mem. Consultative Com. on Implications of Telecommunications for Can. sovereignty, 1978-79; pres. Conseil d'orientation Institut International de la Communication, 1975-77; bd. dirs. Can. Communications Research Info. Center, 1973-77. Internat. editorial bd.: Telecommunications Policy, 1977-82. Mem. exec. bd. UNESCO Can., 1969-74; gov. Lakeshore Gen. Hosp., Pointe Claire, Que., 1970-74. Decorated companion Order of Can.; recipient Archambault medal l'Association Canadienne francaise pour l'avancement des sciences, 1957, Spl. award Soc. Motion Picture and TV Engrs., 1974, Gold medal Can. Council Profl. Engrs., 1975, Internat. EMMY Directorate award, 1976, Public Service award Internat. Communications Soc., 1978, Gt. Montrealer award, 1978, Que. TV award, 1983; named to De L'Ordre des Francophones d'Amerique, 1986. Fellow Can. Acad. Engring., IEEE (life mem., McNaughton medal 1972); mem. Corp. Profl. Engrs. Que. (life), Engring. Inst. Can. (life, Ross medal 1948, Julian C. Smith medal 1959, Sir John Kennedy medal 1969), titulaire du Comité International de Television. Home: Montreal Que., Canada. Died Dec. 20, 1988.

OVERACKER, LOUISE, political science educator; b. Centerville, Calif., Nov. 18, 1891; d. Howard and Louise Eolia (Matthews) O. AB, Stanford U., AM, 1917; PhD, U. Chgo., 1924. Instr. polit. sci. Vassar Coll., 1920-22; prof. govt. Wilson Coll., Chambersburg, Pa., 1924-25; asst. prof. polit. sci. Wellesley Coll., 1925-31, assoc. prof., 1931-40, prof., 1941-57, prof. emeritus, from 1957; John Hay Whitney vis. prof. polit. sci. Bethany (W.Va.) Coll., 1957-58; Bacon lectr. Boston U., 1945; vis. prof. UCLA, 1960-61. Author: The Presidential Primary, 1926; (with C. E. Merriam) Primary Elections, 1928; Money in Elections, 1932, Presidential Campaign Funds, 1946, The Australian Party Sustem, 1952. Guggenheim fellow, 1951. Fellow Am. Acad. Arts and Sci.; mem. Am. Polit. Sci. Asn. (bd. editors Am. Polit. Sci. Rev.), Nat. Mcpl. League, AAUP. Home: Saratoga Calif. †

OVERBY, ANDREW NORRIS, banker; b. Cheyenne Agency, S.D., Mar. 27, 1909; s. Samuel O. and Anna Marie (Amundsen) O.; m. Annette Picus, Sept. 21, 1928 (dec. Aug. 1988). Student, U. Minn., 1926-28; BS, Columbia U., 1930, MS, 1940. With Irving Trust Co., N.Y.C., 1930-41, with fgn. banking sect., asst. to v.p. in charge portfolio investments, 1936-41; spl. asst. to v.p. Fed. Res. Bank, N.Y.C., 1942, asst. v.p., 1946, spl. asst. to sec. treasury in charge internat. fin., 1946-47; U.S. exec. dir. Internat. Monetary Fund, 1947-49, dep. mng. dir., 1949-52; asst. sec. U.S. Treasury, 1952-57; mem. NSC Planning Bd., 1952-57; U.S. exec. dir. Internat. Bank Reconstrn. and Devel., 1952-57, Internat. Fin. Corp., 1956-57; v.p. 1st Boston Corp., N.Y.C., 1957-64, mem. exec. com., 1963-76, vice chmn. bd., 1964-74; bd. dirs. 1st Boston Corp., 1st Boston, Inc., Internat. Exec. Svc. Corps.; mem. Internat. Monetary Relations Com., U.S. Coun., ICC, 1973-82. Trustee Citizen's Budget Commn., N.Y.C., 1973-84. With AUS, 1942-46. Decorated Legion of Merit, Army Commendation ribbon; Order of the Rising Sun (Japan); recipient Alexander Hamilton award U.S. Treasury, 1957. Mem. Coun. Fgn. Relations, Japan Soc. (pres. 1977-79, hon. dir. 1979-84), University Club, India House, Century Assn., Alfalfa Club, Army and Navy Club, Metropolitan Club, Psi Upsilon, Beta Gamma Sigma (alumni Nat. Honor award 1947). Home: New York N.Y. Died Apr. 28, 1984.

OVERSTREET, BONARO WILKINSON, author, lecturer; b. Geyersville, Calif., Oct. 30, 1902; d. Edward and Margaret Elizabeth (Bonar) Wilkinson; m. Harry Allen Overstreet, Aug. 23, 1932. AB, U. Calif., 1925, teacher's cert., 1926. Instr. U. Va. Continuation Ctr., Falls Church. Author: Poetic Way of Release, 1931, Footsteps on the Earth, 1934, Search for ta Self, 1938, Brave Enough for Life, 1941, Leaders for Adult Education, 1940, American Reasons, 1943, Courage for Crisis, 1943, Freedom's People, 1945, How to Think About Ourselves, 1948, Understanding Fear: In Ourselves and Others, 1951, The Mind Alive, 1954, Hands Laid Upon the Wind, 1956, The Mind Goes Forth, 1956, The War Called Peace: Khrushchev's Communism, 1961, The Iron Curtain, 1963, The Strange Tactics of Extremism, 1964, Signature: New and Selected Poems, 1978; (with H.A. Overstreet) Town Meeting Comes to Town, 1938, What We Must Know About Communism, 1958, The FBI in Our Open Society, 1969; contbr. articles to jours. Mem. Adult Edn. Assn. U.S.A., Nat. Press Club, International Club, Phi Beta Kappa, Sigma Delta Pi, Theta Sigma Phi. Home: Falls Church Va. Died Sept. 10, 1985.

OVERSTREET, JAMES WILLIAM, manufacturing company executive; b. Thaxton, Va., June 21, 1888; s. James Henry and Jenny (Quisenberry) O.; m. Rosel Killey, Apr. 29, 1916 (dec.); 1 dau., Emily Bissett Overstreet Kirk; m. Betty Krumm, Feb. 14, 1936. Student, Sunnyside Acad., Bedford, Va., 1893-1907; LLD, Roanoke Coll., 1961. With So. Express Co., Ry. Express Co., 1908-20; gen. mgr. Nat. Electric Coil Co. (merger McGraw-Edison Co. 1958), 1920-35, pres., 1935-58, also bd. dirs., pres. Nat. Electric Coil div. McGraw-Edison Co., 1958-64, then bd. dirs., mem. exec. com.; bd. dirs. McGraw-Edison Ltd., Can., 1st Nat. Bank, Bluefield, W.Va., Pa.-Reading Seashore Lines, 1st and 2d Ohio Capital Funds. Trustee Roanoke Coll. Mem. Am. Mining Congress (bd. govs. 1950-59, chmn. mfrs. div. 1955), Nat. Elec. Mfrs. Assn. (bd. govs. 1943-48), Ohio Soc. N.Y, Newcomen Soc. N.Am., Columbus Club, Columbus Athletic Club, Columbus Country Club, Ohio State Univ. Faculty and Presidents Club, Union League Club (Phila.), Duquesne Club (Pitts.). Episcopalian. Home: Columbus Ohio. †

OWEN, ROBERT EVERETT, school principal; b. Gardiner, Maine, May 19, 1892; s. Charles Edson and Nellie Eugenia (Nason) O.; m. Eva I. Pratt, June 24, 1914. BS, Colby Coll., 1914; EdM, Harvard U., 1927. Prin. Erskine Acad., S. China, Maine, 1914-18, Oak Grove Sch., Vassalboro, Maine, from 1918. Mem. Maine Ho. of Reps., 1930-31, Maine Senate, 1937-46. Mem. Masons, Rotary, Zeta Psi. Republican. Mem. Soc. of Friends. Home: Vassalboro Maine. †

OWEN, VAUX, lawyer, government official; b. Buford, Ga., June 23, 1890; s. John Wesley and Salyda C. (Whitbey) O.; m. Grace Edenfield Rather, Apr. 20, 1924; children: Mary Owen Cornett, Vaux Owen (dec.). Student, Howard Coll., 1913-16; LLB, Atlanta Law Sch., 1927, LLM, 1934, LLD, 1951. Bar: Ga. 1927. Tchr., Fackler, Ala., 1916-17; clk. USPHS, Atlanta, 1919-20, statistician, 1920, mgr. personnel and accounts div., 1920-21; asst. adminstrv. officer 5th Dist. Vets. Bur., Atlanta, 1921-23, adminstrv. officer, 1923-25, chief svc. div., regional office, 1925-27, asst. to regional mgr., 1927-30, asst. to mgr. VA combined facility, 1930-33, chief atty., 1933-45, mgr., 1945; asst. mgr. regional office VA, 1955-64. Pres. Fed. Employees Credit Union; state pres. Ga. Credit Union League; pres. Nat. Fedn. Fed. Employees, 1957-64. Mem. ABA, Am. Judicature Soc., Ga. Bar Assn., Atlanta Bar Assn., Am. Legion, Mil. Order World Wars, Ga. Writers Assn., Atlanta Writers Club, Masons, Delta Theta Phi. Home: Atlanta Ga. †

OWENS, ARTHUR NEAL, plastic surgeon; b. Helfin, Ala., Aug. 5, 1899; s. James Arthur and Laura (Neal) O.; m. Georgia May Little, Sept. 30, 1931; children: Laura (Mrs. George Lewis), Lucille (Mrs. John C. Pryor), Alice (Mrs. Lee McKay Johnson), Arthur Neal. BS, U. Ala., 1924; MD, Emory U., 1926. Diplomate Am. Bd. Plastic Surgery. Rotating intern Birmingham Bapt. Hosp.; resident St. Agnes Hosp., Balt.; tng. gen. surgery, plastic surgery 1928-33; studied plastic surgery London and Balt., 1933; prof. plastic surgery Tulane U. Sch. Medicine; surgeon charge dept. plastic surgery Eye, Ear, Nose and Throat Hosp., New Orleans; cons. staff Touro Infirmary, Ill. Cen. R.R. Hosp., USPHS Hosp., Crippled Children's Hosp.; mem. surg. staff Hotel Dieu, Mercy Hosp., Sara Mayo Hosp.; vis. surgeon Charity Hosp. Author: Year Book of Plastic Surgery; developer use of celluloid in correction defects of contour, surg. tub for treatment of burns and infected wounds, protective pressure dressing for wound treatment, surg. fabric, use of periosteal grafts. Pres., bd. dirs. Audubon Park Natatorium; mem. Audubon Park Commn. With USN, 1918. Recipient Honor award Am. Med. Writers Assn. Fellow ACS, Internat. Coll. Surgeons (exec. coun., v.p. U.S. sect., chmn. plastic surgery sect.); mem. AMA, Am. Assn. Plastic Surgeons (past pres., trustee), Am. Soc. Plastic and Reconstructive Surgeons (past pres.), So. Med. Assn., La. Med. Soc., Orleans Parish Med. Socs., Am. Cancer Soc. (bd. dirs.), C. of C. (bd. dirs., coun.), SAR, La. Soc., Internat. House, So. Surg. Assn., Southeastern Soc. Plastic Reconstructive Surgeons (founder, 1st pres.), Masons, New Orleans Country Club, Lotus Club, Little Lake Club (pres.), Bohemian Club, Sigma Xi, Sigma Chi, Phi Chi, Alpha Phi Omega. Home: Metairie La. Died Mar. 29, 1985.

OWENS, EDWARD JOSEPH, advertising executive; b. Chgo., June 29, 1891; s. John Francis and Margaret (Tracy) O.; m. Agnes Frances Harding, June 28, 1919. With Kudner Agy., Inc., 1916-57. Mem. Cath. Youth Orgn., Police Athletic League. Sgt. maj. U.S. Army, 1917-19. Home: New York N.Y. †

OWENS, JOHN, labor union official; b. Oct. 29, 1890; m. Bernice Cash; children: R.C., Willard P. Sec.-treas. United Mine Workers Am. Home: Cambridge Ohio. †

OWINGS, NATHANIEL ALEXANDER, architec engineer; b. Indpls., Feb. 5, 1903; s. Nathaniel Flemin and Cora Mima (Alexander) O.; m. Emily Otis, Sept. 1931 (div. 1953); children: Emily, Natalie, Jennife Nathaniel; m. Margaret Wentworth, Ja 1954. Student, U. Ill., 1921-22; BS, Cornell U., 192 LLD, Ball State U., 1970; LHD, Ind. U., 1973, Butl U., 1976. Registered architect. Founding ptn Skidmore, Owings & Merrill, 1936; architects for U. Govt. mil. installations, air bases, Oak Ridge, Air For Acad. Pvt. commns. include reflecting basin before U. Capitol Bldg., Washington, lever House, N.Y.C., Cha Manhattan Bank, N.Y.C., Norton Bldg., Crown Zell bach office bldg., Alcoa Bldg., Hartford Ins. Bldg., S Francisco, Equitable Life Bldg., Chgo., Oakland (Cali Coliseum, Mauna Kea hotel, Hawaii; S.O.M. firm sho Mus. Modern Art, N.Y.C., 1950; author: The Americ Aesthetic, 1968, The Spaces In Between: An Architec Journey, 1973. Chmn., Chgo. Plan Commn., 1948-5 Pres.'s Coun. on Design of Pa. Ave, 1964-73, me Permanent Commn., 1973-78; Calif. Hwy. Scenic Rd Commn., 1964-67; chmn. Bd. Control Urban Desi Concept team for Interstate Hwy. System Balt., 1967-7 mem. sec. interior adv. bd. on Nat. Parks, Hist. Sit Bldgs. and Monuments, Washington, 1966-70, chm 1970-72, mem. coun., 1972-84; mem. vis. com. Joint C for Urban Studies, MIT-Harvard U., 1965-70; trust Am. Acad. Rome. Recipient Conservation Svc. awa U.S. Dept. Interior, 1968, Gold medal honor awa AIA, 1983. Fellow AIA (co-chmn. exec. com. Hum Resources Coun. 1970-84); mem. Sierra Club (hon. lif Century Assn., Wayfarers Club, Sigma Chi. Home: P Sur Calif. Died June 13, 1984; buried Grimes Point, E Sur, Calif.

PACE, FRANK, JR., organization executive; b. Lit Rock, July 5, 1912; s. Frank and Flora (Layton) P.; Margaret Morris Janney, Nov. 22, 1940; children: Pa Layton (Mrs. Kent Smith), Priscilla Janney (Mrs. Ma von Matthiessen), Margaret Morris, (Mrs. Edwa Schott). A.B., Princeton U., 1933, M.A., 1950; LL. Harvard U., 1936; LL.D., U. Louisville, 19 Dartmouth Coll., Syracuse U., Temple U., U. Ar 1951, Northland Coll., 1956, Adelphi Coll., 1958, W. U., 1959, Columbia U., 1960, Norwich U., 1960; D.S Lafayette Coll., 1952, Clarkson Coll.; L.H.D., Wa Coll., 1955. Bar: Ark. 1936. Dist. atty. 12th Jud. Dis Ark., 1936-38; gen. atty. Revenue Dept. Ark., 1938- mem. firm Pace, Davis and Pace, 1941-42; spl. asst. atty. gen. U.S. taxation div., 1946; exec. asst. postmaster gen. U.S., 1946-48; asst. dir. Bur. of Budg 1948-49, dir., 1949-50; sec. of army 1950-53; past chm chief exec. officer, dir. Gen. Dynamics Corp.; past chm Canadair, Ltd.; pres., chief exec. officer Internat. Ex Service Corps, N.Y.C., 1964-82; chmn. bd. Nat. Ex Service Corps, 1977-88; chmn. bd. Corp. for P Broadcasting, 1968-72; past dir. Carriers and Gene Corp., Dividend Shares, Inc., Nation-Wide Securit Co., Bullock Fund; dir. First Am. Bank N.Y., Colg Palmolive Co.; former dir. Putnam Trust Co., C tinental Oil Co., Time, Inc., Alliance Capital; mem. a bd. Comml. Nat. Bank Ark. Chief U.S. del. Co Postal Experts, Paris, 1947; rep. Universal Postal Uni at UN, 1947-48; v.p. Paris conf.; chmn., mem. NA Def. Ministers Conf., Brussels, 1950, mem. conf., C and Italy, 1951; chmn. Am. council NATO, 1957- dir., 1960; vice chmn. President's Commn. Nat. Go 1959-60; mem. President's Council Youth Fitn Pres.'s Commn. for a Nat. Agenda for 1980's; past pr chmn. council NATO; mem. President's Fgn. In ligence Adv. Bd., 1961-73; mem. nat. policy panel U Assn. Exec. com. Greater N.Y. council Boy Scouts A mem. internat. council Am. Field Service; mem. commn. performance-based edn. Ednl. Testing Serv mem. Nat. Com. on Careers for Older Americans; m policy bd. Internat. Health Resource Consortium.; trustee George C. Marshall Research Found.; p trustee Calif. Inst. Tech.; bd. dirs. Inst. for Future; Internat. Mgmt. and Devel. Inst.; mem. adv. Stanford Research Inst. Strategic Studies Center; m adv. com. Edna McConnell Clark Found.; nat. bd. B Clubs' Am.; mem. corp. Greenwich Hosp. Assn.; ch bd. visitors USAF Systems Command; vice chmn. trustees Robert A. Taft Inst. Govt.; mem. founding Civilian Mil. Inst., 1976; chmn. com. on marshall human resources President's Task Force on Pvt. Se Initiatives, 1982-88 . Served to maj. USAAF, 1942- Decorated grand officer Order of Crown Belgiu recipient Internat. Leadership award N.Y. Pres.'s socs., 1987. Mem. Nat. Inst. Social Scis. (pres. 19 77), Nat. Acad. Public Adminstrn. (panel on mng. govt.-role of Pres.), Assn. U.S. Army (life mem., p 1968-71, recipient George Catlett Marshall med Brookings Instn. Episcopalian. Home: Greenw Conn. Died Jan. 8, 1988.

PACH, G. VINCENT, sugar refining company exe tive; b. Easton, Pa., July 10, 1891; s. A. L. and Joa (Stewart) P.; m. Mildred Heinekamp, 1919; children Warner, G. Vincent. Fin. dir. N.Y. World's Fair, 19 40; v.p. Bath Iron Works Co., 1941-45; v.p., treas. Sugar Refining Co., N.Y.C., from 1945; bd. Spreckels Sugar Co., San Francisco, U.S. Mut. Ins. Boston, Cen. Cunaqua S.A., Cuba. Mem. Mas Union League, Pacific Union. Home: Mount Ver N.Y. †

PACHT, ISAAC, lawyer; b. Austria, May 28, 1890; came to U.S., 1900, naturalized, 1919; s. Nathan and Belle R. (Hochstadt) P.; m. Rose Rudolph; children: Rudolph, Jerry, Lucy (Mrs. Arthur Kuriloff). LLB, St. Lawrence U., 1911. Bar: Calif. 1913. Judge Superior Ct. Calif., 1931-36; pvt. practice L.A., from 1936; mem. Pacht, Ross, Warne, Bernhard, Sears & Nutter. Mem. L.A. Jewish Community Coun., 1949-51; chmn. United Jewish Welfare Fund, 1934-35; pres. Jewish Orphans Home So. Calif., 1937-48; dir. Fedn. Jewish Welfare Orgns. L.A., 1936-56; dir. Calif. Fedn. Civic Unity, 1948-56, pres., 1947; dir. NCCJ, 1955-56; v.p. Nat. Community Relations Adv. Coun., 1954-62; pres. State Bd. Prison Dirs., Calif., 1940-50; chmn. Calif. Commn. Criminal Law and PRocedure, 1947; mem. Calif. Bd. Corrections, 1945-50. Mem. Am., Los Angeles County (past trustee), Beverly Hills bar assns., Hillcrest Country Club, Stock Exchange Club. Home: Malibu Calif. †

PACKEL, ISRAEL, lawyer, former judge, educator; b. Phila., Dec. 28, 1907; s. Hyman and Anna (Prevorotsky) P.; m. Reba Wesler, June 30, 1935; children—John, Edward, Richard. B.S., U. Pa., 1929, LL.B., 1932, LL.M., 1933. Bar: Pa. 1932, U.S. Supreme Ct. 1940. Atty. NRA, 1935, REA, 1935-37; state rationing atty. Phila., 1942-43; mem. firm Speiser, Satinsky, Gilliland & Packel, Phila., 1946-60, Fox, Rothschild, O'Brien & Frankel, Phila., 1960-70, 78-85; atty. gen. State of Pa., 1973-75; counsel to Pa. Gov., 1971; judge Pa. Superior Ct., 1972, Pa. Supreme Ct., 1977; vis. prof. Temple Law Sch., 1975-87. Editor: Law of Cooperatives, 4th edition, 1970. Served with USN, 1943-45. Gowen fellow, 1933. Mem. Am., Pa., Phila., Fed. bar assns., Am. Law Inst., Order of Coif. Club: Social-Legal. Home: Philadelphia Pa. Died July 1, 1987.

PACSU, EUGENE, chemistry educator; b. Budapest, Hungary, July 13, 1891; came to U.S., 1928, naturalized, 1936; s. George and Anna (Lahm) P.; m. Martha Gergely, June 5, 1926; children: Anne Gregory, Margaret Gregory. PhD, Royal Hungarian U., Budapest, 1914. Univ. asst. Royal Hungarian U., Budapest, 1919-20, adj. prof., 1920-30, pvt. docent (life), from 1926; Internat. Edn. Bd. fellow Bur. Standards/NIH, Washington, 1928-29; asst. prof. organic chemistry Princeton U., 1930-34, assoc. prof., 1934-37, prof., from 1947; rsch. assoc. Textile Rsch. Inst., Princeton, N.J., from 1945. Contbr. articles to profl. jours.; patentee in field. 1st lt. arty. Austro-Hungarian Army, 1914-18. Recipient 3 war decorations on Russian front, 1916-17. Mem. AAAS, AAUP, Am. Chem. Soc., Fiber Soc., Nassau Club, Sigma Xi, Phi Lambda Upsilon (assoc.). Republican. Roman Catholic. Home: Princeton N.J. †

PAGE, CHARLES GREENLEAF, lawyer; b. Fortress Monroe, Va., Mar. 30, 1902; s. Henry and Edith Longfellow (Greenleaf) P.; m. Jeannette Markell, Dec. 18, 1937. AB, Princeton U., 1922; LLB, Harvard U., 1925. Bar: Md. 1925. Pvt. practice 1925-28, 34-36; asst. supt. law dept. U.S. Fidelity and Guaranty Co., Balt., 1928-31; asst. U.S. atty. Balt., 1931-34; ptnr. White, Page & Lentz (and predecessor), 1954-85; lectr. U. Md. Law Sch., 1929-35. Contbr. articles to legal jours. Bd. dirs., counsel Md. Soc. Prevention of Blindness, 1935-85, Munsell Color Found., 1941-74; trustee, counsel, mgr. Middendorf Found., 1953-85. Fellow Md. Bar Found.; mem. ABA, Md. Bar Assn., Balt. Bar Assn., Am. Law Inst. (life), Maryland Club, Merchants Club, Balt. Country Club, Wranglers Club, Elkridge Club. Republican. Episcopalian. Home: Baltimore Md. Died Dec. 23, 1985.

PAGE, FREDERICK WEST, investment broker; b. East Orange, N.J., June 15, 1907; s. Robert W. and Florence (Welles) P.; m. Dorothy Donham, June 10, 1930; children: Frederick W. 3d, Joan D. (Mrs. Robert S. Hayes Jr.). BA, Dartmouth Coll., 1930; MBA, Harvard U., 1932. V.p., mem. exec. com., bd. dirs. Tri-Continental Corp., N.Y.C., 1948-71, Broad St. Investing Corp., 1950-71, Nat. Investors Corp., 1950-71, Whitehall Fund, 1950-71; ptnr. J&W Seligman & Co., N.Y.C., 1955-71, ltd. ptnr., 1971-80; bd. dirs., mem. exec. com. Bklyn. Union Gas Co., 1950-80; bd. dirs., mem. fin. com. Am. Express Internat. Banking Corp., Am. Express Co., 1961-73; bd. dirs. Cen. & South West Corp., 1968-80, Coca-Cola Bottling Co., Miami, Fla., 1971-76. Councilman Borough of Glen Ridge, N.J., 1949-54; trustee Mountainside Hosp., 1961-70, Conglist. ch. Mem. Towanda Country Club, Glen Ridge Country Club (pres. 1958-61). Home: Glen Ridge N.J. Died July 30, 1984; interred Glen Ridge Congl. Ch.

PAGE, GEORGE AUGUSTUS, JR., aircraft designer; b. Sewickley, Pa., Dec. 14, 1891; s. George Augustus and Martha (Bush) P.; m. Violet Louise Heinrich, Feb. 3, 1938. Student pub. schs., Bklyn. Became airplane pilot 1913; various engring. assignments involving design participation of over 90 types Curtis Wright Corp. and predecessor orgns., 1917-51; dir. rsch. and engring. Aeronca Mfg. Corp., Middletown, Ohio, 1951-54, v.p. rsch. and engring., 1954-59, asst. to dir. engring., from 1959; cons. Fellow Inst. Aero. Sci.; mem. Soc. Automotive Engrs., Am. Helicopter Soc., Am. Rocket Soc., Quite Birdmen, Early Birds, Aero Club of Am. (F.A.I., brevet 279), Ox-5 of Am., Masons. Home: Reynoldsburg Ohio. †

PAGE, GERALDINE, actress; b. Kirksville, Mo., Nov. 22, 1924; d. Leon and Pearl (Maize) P.; m. Rip Torn; children: Tony and John (twins), Angelica. Student, Goodman Theatre Dramatic Sch., Chgo., 1942-45; studied acting at, Herbert Berghof Sch., N.Y.C., also Theatre Wing; studied voice with, Alice Hermes. Played in stock at, Lake Zurich, Ill., Marengo, Ill., Woodstock, Ill., 1944-52; artist in residence Mirror Repertory Co., N.Y.C., appeared in: Summer and Smoke in, Greenwich Village, 1952; mem. cast, NBC Best Plays radio series, 1953, Summer and Smoke, Ethan Frome, Glass Menagerie; Broadway plays include: Mid-summer, 1953, The Immoralist, 1954, The Rainmaker, 1954-55, London, 1956-57, Separate Tables, 1957-58, Sweet Bird of Youth, 1959-60, Strange Interlude, 1963, The Three Sisters, 1964, P.S. I Love You, 1964, The Great Indoors, 1966, Black Comedy, 1967, Absurd Person Singular, 1974-75, Clothes for a Summer Hotel, 1980-81, Mixed Couples, 1980-81, Agnes of God, 1982-83; supporting actress: (motion picture) Hondo, 1953; appeared: (motion pictures) Summer and Smoke in, 1961, Sweet Bird of Youth, 1962, Toys in the Attic, 1963, Dear Heart, 1964, The Happiest Millionaire, 1966, You're a Big Boy Now, 1966, Monday's Child, 1966, Whatever Happened to Aunt Alice?, 1969, Beguiled, 1971, Pete and Tillie, 1972, Day of the Locust, 1974, Abbess of Crewe, 1976, Interiors, 1978, Honky Tonk Freeway, 1981, Harry's War, 1980, The Pope of Greenwich Village, 1984, White Nights, 1985, Flanagan, 1985,. Nominated for best performance by supporting actress, Hondo, Acad. Motion Picture Arts and Sci.; recipient Theatere World Award, season, 1952-53; New York Drama Critics award, season, 1952-53; Donaldson award, Theatre World award, 1952-53; Critics Circle award, Sweet Bird of Youth, 1960; Sarah Siddons award Chgo., 1960; Donatello best fgn. actress award for Sweet Bird of Youth, 1963; Emmy award as best actress, A Christmas Memory, TV Acad. of Arts and Scis., 1966; Emmy award for A Thanksgiving Visitor, 1969; Brit. Acad. Film and TV Arts award for Interiors, 1979; Acad. award for best actress The Trip to Bountiful, 1986. Mem. Actors Equity Assn., Screen Actors Guild, Am. Fedn. TV-Radio Artists, Phi Beta. Home: New York N.Y. Died June 13, 1987.

PAGE, HERMAN RIDDLE, bishop; b. Coeur d'Alene, Idaho, May 3, 1892; s. Herman and Mary Moorhead (Riddle) P.; m. Lois Dickinson, June 25, 1922 (dec. 1930); m. Gwendolyn Byllesby Cummins, June 26, 1933; 1 child, Herman. AB, Harvard U., 1913, postgrad., 1914; BD, Episc. Theol. Sem., 1917; DD (hon.), Kenyon Coll., 1943. Oradined to ministry Protestant Episcopal Ch. Minister in charge St. John's Ch., Okanogan, Wash., 1919-22, St. Luke's Ch., Wenatchee, Wash., 1922-23; rector St. Michael's Ch., Yakima, Wash., 1923-25; staff mem. St. Paul's Cathedral, Boston, 1925-27, St. Paul's Ch., Oakwood, Dayton, Ohio, 1927-42; bishop Diocese of No. Mich., from 1942. Mem. Mich. Civil Def. Council; chaplain Mich. State Police; pres. Province of Mid-West, 1951-57. Chaplain U.S. Army, 1917-19, 1941-42. Home: Menominee Mich. †

PAGE, JOHN PERCY, Canadian government official; b. Rochester, N.Y., May 14, 1887; s. Absalom Bell and Elizabeth (Thomas) P.; m. Maude Roche, Mar. 25, 1910; 1 dau., Helen Patricia Page Hollingsworth. BA, Queen's U., Kingston, Ont., 1913; BCS, Am. Inst. Bus., Des Moines, 1936; LLD, U. Alta., 1961. Instr. Rothesay (N.B.) Coll., 1908-09, St. Thomas (Ont.) Collegiate Inst., 1909-11; prin. McDougall and Victoria high schs., Edmonton, 1912-52; mem. Alta. Legislature from West Edmonton Dist., 1940-59; lt. gov. Province Alta., from 1959. Author: Practical Business Training, 1930. Decorated Knight of Grace, 1960. Mem. Rotary (hon.). Home: Edmonton Alta., Canada. †

PAGEL, RAY HERMAN, journalist, horticulture consultant; b. Green Bay, Wis., Apr. 30, 1913; s. Albert and Emma (Schneider) P.; m. Eleanora Minnie Gauger, Oct. 15, 1937 (dec. June, 1981); children: Sandra (Mrs. Richard Burg), John, Paul, Peter. Student, U. Wis., Northwestern U., N.E. Wis. Tech. Inst. Gen. assignment reporter, sports writer, sports editor, state editor. regional editor, farm editor Green Bay-Press Gazette, 1936-69, spl. assignments writer environ., sci., agrl. affairs, 1969-78; spokesman for agr. Wis. Agri-Bus. Council, 1976; Pres. agrl. adv. bd. Green Bay Schs., 1974-87; pub. relations cons. schs.; sec. Kellogg Pub. Library, 1959-68; mem. Fox River Study Group, 1973-77; chmn. Brown County Environ. Protection Com., 1969-75. Bd. dirs. Brown County Fair, 1972-87 . Recipient Forum award Atomic Indsl. Forum, 1974; hon. state farmer degree Wis. Future Farmers Am., 1972; hon. Am. farmer degree, 1976; U. Wis. Friends of Extension award, 1971; other awards. Mem. Newspaper Farm Editors Am. (pres. 1969), Gardeners Club Green Bay (pres. 1967-69, 72-73), Green Bay C. of C. Lutheran (pres. Wis. dist. brotherhood 1952-54). Home: Hartford Wis. Died Mar. 23, 1987; buried Nicolet Meml. Gardens, Green Bay, Wis.

PAGELS, HEINZ RUDOLF, science academy executive, theoretical physicist; b. Bklyn., Feb. 19, 1939; s. Heinz and Marie Christiane (Roesing) P.; m. Elaine L. Hiesey, June 7, 1969; children: Sarah Marie, David van Druten. B.S. in Physics magna cum laude, Princeton U., 1960; Ph.D. in Physics, Stanford U., 1965. Research assoc. U. N.C., Chapel Hill, 1965-66, Rockefeller U., N.Y.C., 1966-67; asst. prof. physics Rockefeller U., 1967-69, assoc. prof., 1969-82, adj. prof., 1982-88; research visitor Stanford Linear Accelerator Ctr., CERN, Fermi Nat. Accelerator Lab., Lawrence Radiation Lab.; mem. council for advancement of sci. writing. Author: The Cosmic Code, 1981, Perfect Symmetry, 1985, The Dreams of Reason, 1988; contbr. articles to profl. jours. Pres. Internat. League Human Rights, N.Y.C., 1983; bd. dirs. Helsinki Watch, 1984, N.Y. Hall of Sci., 1984. NSF fellow, 1962; A.P. Sloan Found. fellow, 1967-69. Fellow Am. Phys. Soc., N.Y. Acad. Scis. (gov. 1976-82, pres. 1981, bd. dirs. 1983). Home: New York N.Y. Died July 23, 1988, buried N.Y.C.

PAHLMANN, WILLIAM CARROLL, interior and industrial designer; b. Pleasant Mound, Ill.; s. Benjamin Otto and Iva Florence (Perkins) P. Grad., Parsons Sch. Design, N.Y.C. and Paris, 1930. Mem. theater cast Good news, also Follow Thru N.Y.C., 1927-30; with B. Altman & Co., 1933; head interior design, buyer antiques Lord & Taylor, N.Y.C., 1936-42; founder, pres. William Pahlmann Assocs., 1946-87; interior designer Bonwit Teller Stores, Rice U., Tex. A&M U., also restaurants, hotels, clubs, numerous pvt. houses, U.S., Venezuela, The Bahamas, Dominican Republic, Can., Switzerland, Hong Kong; lectr. in field. Author: The Pahlmann Book of Interior Design, 3d edit., 1968; columnist A Matter of Taste. Past pres., chmn. bd. Resources Coun. Lt. col. USAAF, 1942-46. Recipient Cavalier Mchts. award, 1942, Elsie De Wolfe award, 1964, numerous others. Fellow Am. Inst. Interior Designers (past chmn., past pres. N.Y. chpt.); mem. Am. Soc. Interior Design (Designer of Distinction 1979). Home: San Antonio Tex. Died Nov. 8, 1987; buried Sunset Park, San Antonio.

PALAMOUNTAIN, JOSEPH CORNWALL, JR., college president; b. West Newton, Mass., Nov. 26, 1920; s. Joseph Cornwall and Ellen (Coles) P.; m. Anne A. Tonnesen, Aug. 8, 1946; children—Bromley Coles, Bruce Kent. BA summa cum laude, Dartmouth Coll., 1942, LLD (hon.), 1976; MA, Harvard U., 1948, PhD, 1951; LHD (hon.), Wesleyan U., Middletown, Conn., 1968; LittD (hon.), Union Coll., 1986; LLD (hon.), Skidmore Coll., 1987; DSc (hon.), Albany Med. Coll., 1987. Teaching fellow, tutor in govt. Harvard, 1947-51, instr., 1951-52, asst. prof., 1952-55; also sr. tutor Adams House, 1951-55; assoc. prof. govt. Wesleyan U., 1955-59, prof., 1959-65, provost, 1961-65; pres. Skidmore Coll., Saratoga Springs, N.Y., 1965-87, pres. emeritus, 1987; cons. Brookings Instn., 1959-60; vis. lectr. Yale, 1964-65; dir. Value Line Mut. Funds, 1984-87 , mem. audit com., 1984-87 ; dir. Adirondack Trust Co., 1965-84, adv. dir., 1985-87 . Author: Politics of Distribution, 1956, Government and the American Economy, 1959, The Dolcin Case and the Federal Trade Commission, 1963, A Tangled Web of Law, Economics and Politics, 1965; co-author: American National Government, 1971, Such Growth Bespeaks the Work of Many Hands: The Story of Skidmore Coll., 1976; editor: Issues and Perspectives in American Government, 1971, American Government Reading Series; assoc. editor: Daedalus, 1955-59. Assoc. N.Y.U. Med. Center Bd., 1965-84; Chmn. Gov.'s Com. on Establishment Br. of U. Conn. in Middlesex County, 1964-65; mem. Nat. Citizens Com. for a Cabinet Dept. Edn., 1977-79; mem. adv. council State N.Y. Joint Legis. Com. on Higher Edn., 1970-74; mem. Commn. Ind. Colls. and Univs., chmn., 1969-70, exec. com., 1965-78, 84-87, bd. dirs., 1965-78, 84-87, treas., 1971-72, 74-78, 86-87, chmn. student fin. aid com., 1978-84, chmn. state legis. com. 1984-87, chmn. fin. & investment com., 1986-87; bd. dirs. N.Y. State Coalition for Ind. Colls. and Univs., 1986-87, treas., 1986-87; mem. Adv. Com. on Planning for Acad. Libraries N.Y. State, 1971-73; mem. exec. com. Ind. Coll. Funds Am., 1973-76; mem. adv. council Regionalism for Northeastern N.Y., 1972-78; mem. Commr's. Adv. Bd. on Regents External Degrees, State N.Y., 1971-86; commn.'s adv. council Higher Edn., N.Y., 1971-78; Mem. Middletown Democratic Town Com., 1961-65; chmn. Empire State Found. Ind. Liberal Arts Colls., 1968-69; bd. dirs. Wolf Trap Farm Performing Arts, Washington, 1968-82, Middletown Family Service Board, 1961-65; bd. dirs. Saratoga Performing Arts Center, 1965-87, chmn. edn. com., 1965-72, investment com., 1975-87, chmn. nominating com., 1986-87, membership steering com., 1986-87; vice chmn. bd. trustees Ind. Day Sch., 1962-65, Bennett Coll., Millbrook, N.Y., 1969-74, chmn. bd. dirs., 1984-87; bd. dirs. Corp of Yaddo, Saratoga Springs, 1970-87, exec. com., 1970-87, devel. com., 1987-87; bd. dirs. Harkness Ballet Found., 1980-85; bd. govs. Albany Med. Center Hosp., 1975-86; bd. dirs. Albany Med. Ctr., 1986-87, council for acad. health scis., 1986-87, pensions & investments com., 1986-87, planning com., 1986-87; trustee N.Y. State Higher Edn. Services Corp., 1980-87, mem. audit com., 1980-87, vice chmn., 1981-87; mem. Title IV state adv. council, State of N.Y., 1978-87; mem. com. on higher edn. Adv. Council to Dems. in N.Y. State Senate, 1980-82; mem. edn. com. Bus. Council of N.Y. State, 1981-84; mem. Empire Blue Cross & Blue Shield Albany Regional Adv. Body, 1985-87; hon. chmn. Saratoga Springs City Ctr. Authority, 1985-87; mem. adv. com. for Navy Coll. Courses at Sea Project, 1987. Served from ensign to lt. comdr. USNR, 1942-46. Recipient Social Sci. Research Council research grant, 1959-60, Corning Glass Works Higher Edn. Leadership award, 1983, Citation for Disting. Service N.Y. State Higher

Edn., Assn. Colls. & Univ. N.Y., 1984, Cert. Appreciation for Support on Behalf N.Y. State Higher Edn., 1986, Acad. Laureate award for Disting. Achievement & Leadership N.Y. State Higher Edn., 1986, Denis Kemball-Cook award Skidmore Coll., 1987; named Pillar for Outstanding Contns. to Community, City of Saratoga Springs, 1986; N.Y. State Legis. resolution passed in name of honoring many years in edn., 1987; Citation for Commitment to Higher Edn., Commn. on Ind. Colls. and Univs., 1987. Mem. Am. Polit. Sci. Assn., Am. Soc. Pub. Adminstrn., Dartmouth Coll. Alumni Assn., Univ. Club, Reading Room, Phi Beta Kappa, Alpha Delta Phi, Gamma Psi. Home: Saratoga Springs N.Y. Died Nov 23, 1987; buried Saratoga Springs, N.Y.

PALLETT, EARL MANLEY, education educator; b. Mt. Ida, Wis., Sept. 20, 1892; s. Thomas Manley and Isabel (Beadle) P.; m. Agnes Theresa Johnson, July 9, 1918; children: Jacquelyn Agnes, Earl Marshall. Student, Wis. State Normal Sch., Platteville, 1912-14, U. Toulouse (France), 1919; B.S. with high sr. honors, U. Wis., 1921, MS, 1922; student, U. Chgo., 1923; PhD, U. Oreg., 1931. Prin. Harlem Consol. Sch., Rockford, Ill., 1914-17; dir. extension Ea. State Tchrs. Coll., Madison, S.D., 1921-27; registrar U. Oreg., 1927-48, acting dean of men, 1929-30, exec. sec. and asst. to pres., 1930-49, prof. edn. Sch. Edn., also dir. tchr. placement svc., 1949-55. Author (monograph): Studies in Student Mortality at University of Oregon, 1933. Sec. Oreg. State Bd. Higher Edn., from 1955. Sgt. U.S. Army, 1917-19. Mem. Am. Assn. Basic Sci. Bds. (pres. 1961-62), Am. Legion, Am. Assn. CollegiateRegistrars, Nat. Instl. Tchr. Placement Assn., Pacific Coast Assn. Collegiate Registrars (pres. 1937-38), Northwest Assn. Coll. Placement Ofcls. (pres. 1950-51), Oreg. Assn. Instl. Placement Ofcls. (pres. 1950-51), Eugene Gleemen (pres. 1940-53), Lions Club (Eugene pres. 1950-51), Masons, Phi Delta Kappa, Alpha Zeta. Home: Eugene Oreg. †

PALMER, ARCHIE M(ACINNES), author, editor, research director; b. Hoboken, N.J., May 9, 1896; s. Robert Kelty Kennedy and Sarah Grace (MacInnes) P.; m. elizabeth Cheatham, June 24, 1930; children: Elizabeth Reynolds, Archie MacInnes. AB, Cornell U., 1920; AM, Columbia U., 1927; DCL, U. of the South, 1941. Sec., acting dean Coll. Arts and Sci., Cornell U., Ithaca, N.Y., 1920-23, exec. sec. Cornellian Coun., 1934-38; with sales and personnel rsch. Procter & Gamble Co., 1923-24; alumni sec., mag. editor Columbia U., 1925-27; asst. dir. Inst. Internat. Edn., 1927-29; assoc. sec. Assn. Am. Colls., 1929-34; pres. U. Tenn., Chattanooga, 1938-42; assoc. dir. food rationing OPA, 1942-43, War Prodn. Bd., 1943-44; with U.S. Dept. State, 1944-46; dir. patent policy survey NRC, 1946-66; chmn. Govt. Patents Bd., 1950-55; dir. Gale Rsch. Ctr., 1965-81; past pres. Tenn. Recreation Assn. and Southeastern Aviation Tng. Assn.; sec.-treas. So. U. Conf., 1941-42; mem. patent policy com. NRC, 1933-66. Author: (with J. Fredrick Larson) Architectural Planning of the American College, 1933; (with Grace Holton) College Instruction in Art, 1934, University Patent Policies, 1934, Survey of University Patent Policies, 1948, Medical Patents, 1948, University Research and Patent Problems, 1949, University Patent Policies and Practices, 1952, Nonprofit Research and Patent Management, 4 vols., 1955-64, Patents and Nonprofit Research, 1957, University Research and Patent Policies, Practices and Procedures, 1962; author, editor: The Liberal Arts College Movement, 1930; editor: Research Centers Directory, 1964, 68, 72, 75, 79; New Research Ctrs., 1965-81. Dir. Washington office Lasdon Found., 1957-60. 1st lt. inf., U.S. Army, 1917-20; with Am. Expeditionary Force, France and Germany. Decorated officer Order of White Lion (Czechoslovakia). Mem. AAAS, Am. Hist. Assn., Am. Legion, Mil. Order Fgn. Wars, Chattanooga Exec. (former pres.), Cornell Club, Half Century Club, Torch Club (pres. Washington chpt. 1946-47), The Inquirendo (pres. 1954-55), Masons, Rotary, Phi Beta Kappa, Phi Delta Kappa, Delta Sigma Rho, Pi Gamma Mu. Episcopalian. Home: Washington D.C. Died May 13, 1985.

PALMER, CHARLES DOUGLAS, transportation company executive; b. Erie, Pa., Mar. 27, 1900; s. Franklin A. and Anna M. (Bates) P.; m. Dorothy Snelbaugh, Jan. 10, 1929; 1 child, Gloria. Student, Carnegie Inst. Tech., 1919; BCE, Cornell U., 1922. Engr. Pa. R.R., 1922-23, Ala. Power Co., 1923; engr. Pitts. Rys. Co. (name now Pittway Corp.), 1924-26, rsch. engr., 1926-34, comml. mgr., 1934-50, pres., 1951-66, vice chmn. bd., from 1966, sr. v.p., from 1970; former bd. dirs. Port Authority Allegheny County. Mem. Pitts. Conv. Bur. (bd. dirs.), Duquesne Club, University Club, St. Clair Country Club, Masons, Rotary. Home: Pittsburgh Pa. Deceased.

PALMER, KYLE DULANEY, editor; b. Bristol, Tenn., Aug. 27, 1891; s. William Henry and Lannie May (Haynes) P.; m. Elizabeth Jane Halff, Jan. 16, 1941. Student, Staunton Mil. Acad., Throop Poly. Inst. Reporter L.A. Evening Express, 1912-19; polit. writer, Washington corr. L.A. Times, 1919-34, polit. writer, war corr., 1942-55, polit. editor, 1939-61, contbg. columnist, polit. cons., from 1961; pub. rels. counsel Motion Picture Prod. Assn., Hollywood, Calif., 1934-39; contbg. editor Honolulu Advertiser. Mem. Outrigger Canoe Club (Honolulu), Nat. Press. Club (Washington). Republican. †

PALMER, LILLI, actress, author; b. Posen, Germany, May 24, 1914; came to U.S, 1945; d. Alfred Peiser and Rose Lismann Palmer; m. Rex Harrison, Jan 25, 1943 (div. Feb. 6, 1957); 1 child, Carey; m. Carlos Thompson, 1957. Student, Hohenrollern Gymnasium, Berlin, 1932. Plays include Little Ladyship, 1939, No Time for Comedy, 1940, My Name is Aguilon, 1949, Cesar and Cleopatra, 1950, Bell, Book and Candle, 1951; motion pictures include Great Barrier, 1937, Thunderrock, 1942, Notorious Gentleman, 1944, Cloak and Dagger, 1946, Body and Soul, 1947, The Four Poster, 1951, Main Street to Broadway: Is Anna Anderson Anastasia?, 1956, But Not For Me, 1959, Conspiracy of Hearts, 1960, The Pleasure of His Company, 1961, Counterfeit Traitor, 1962, Adorable Julia, 1964, The Flight of the White Stallions, 1964, The Great Spy Mission, Murders in the Rue Morgue, 1971, The House That Screamed, 1971, Lotte in Weimer, 1977, The Boys from Brazil, 1978; appeared in (TV series) Zoo Gang, 1975; author: The Autobiography of Lilli Palmer, 1975, The Red Raven, 1978, A Time to Embrace, 1980, Night Music, 1983. Died Jan. 27, 1986.

PALMER, RICHARD EMERY, pathologist; b. Washington, Mar. 24, 1919; s. Maurice Emery and Mattie May (Mankin) P.; m. Mary Lou Nash, July 3, 1943; children: Richard N., Deborah E., Maurice R., Mary E. AB, George Washington U., 1941, MD, 1944; DLH, U. S.C., 1977. Diplomate Am. Bd. Pathology. Intern, then sr. resident pathology George Washington U., 1945-46, 48-49; teaching fellow, resident Med. Sch., 1945-46, assoc. prof. clin. pathology, 1963-75, clin. prof., 1975-86; pathologist Alexandria (Va.) Hosp., 1949-86, pres. med. staff, 1953; pathologist Office Chief Med. Examiner Va., 1949-86; pathologist Circle Terr. Hosp. Lab., Alexandria, 1955-86, pres. med. staff, 1958, bd. dirs., 1956-75; commr. Joint Commn. Accreditation Hosps., 1967-86, chmn., 1971-72; mem. spl. med. adv. group VA, 1975-86; bd. dirs. Peoples Bank and Trust Co., Fairfax, Va. Contbr. articles to med. jours. Mem. nat. com. med. exploring Boy Scouts Am., 1973-79; founder, coord. No. Va. Med. Com. for Good Govt., 1960-86; Va. del.-at-large, mem. platform com. Rep. Nat. Conv., 1972; mem. bd. govs. Hosp. Corp. Am., St. Stephens Sch. Boys, Alexandria, 1968-74. Capt. AUS, 1946-48. Recipient Alumni Achievement award George Washington U., 1971; named Outstanding Profl. of Yr. Va. Assn. Professions, 1978.tstanding Profl. of Yr. Va. Assn. Professions, 1978. Mem. AMA (coun. med. svcs. 1969-70, trustee 1970-75, sec. bd. trustees, sec.-treas. assn. 1972-86, pres.-elect 1975, pres. 1976), ACP, Alexandria Med. Soc. (pres. 1955), Am. Cancer Soc. (pres. Alexandria chpt. 1958-59), Am. Soc. Clin. Pathologists (pres. 1961-62, Disting. Svc. award 1974), Med. Soc. Va. (pres. 1964, Community Svc. award 1976), George Washington U. Med. Alumni Assn. (pres. 1965-66, award 1975), Pvt. Practitioners Pathology Found. (pres. 1966-67), Coll. Am. Pathologists (Disting. Svc. award 1974), Internat. Acad. Pathology (pres. 1974, pres. XI Congress 1976), Am. Assn. Blood Banks, Am. Soc. Nuclear Medicine, Washington Golf and Country Club, George Washington Univ. Club, Alpha Omega Alpha. Home: Alexandria Va. Died June 22, 1986.

PALMER, WILLIAM CHARLES, artist; b. Des Moines, Jan. 20, 1906; s. Orrin Karl and Frankie A. (Dyre) P.; m. Catherine Wechsler, Sept. 9, 1939. Student, Art Students' League N.Y., 1924-31, Ecole des Beaux Arts, Fontainbleau, France, 1927; D.F.A. (hon.), Hamilton Coll., 1974. Instr. Art Students' League, N.Y.C., 1936-41; dir. Munson-Williams-Proctor Inst., Sch. Art, Utica, N.Y., 1940-73; emeritus Munson-Williams-Proctor Inst., Sch. Art, 1973-87. Artist-in-residence Hamilton Coll., Clinton, N.Y., 1941-48; represented in permanent collections including, Nat. Collection of Fine Arts, large museums and galleries of U.S., one-man shows throughout U.S., 1932-87 , including Midtown Gallery, N.Y.C., 1957; retrospective exhbn. Wichita Art Mus., Kans., 1986, Munson-Williams Proctor Inst., 1986; executed mural for 1st Nat. City Bank N.Y., 1956, Homestead Savs. and Loan Assn., Utica; included in Am. Painting Exhbn. Worlds Fair, N.Y.C., 1964. Am. Acad. Arts and Letters and Nat. Inst. Arts and Letters, grantee, 1953. Mem. Nat. Soc. Mural Painters (sec. 1936-39), Midtown Galleries, Art Students' League N.Y., Am. Fedn. Arts, Audubon Soc., Nat. Acad. Design, Archtl. League N.Y., Nat. Assn. Museums. Home: Clinton N.Y. Died Aug. 24, 1987, buried Hamilton Coll. Cemetery, Clinton, N.Y.

PANOFF, ROBERT, nuclear engineer; b. N.Y.C., Aug. 16, 1921; s. Emanuel and Lillie P.; m. Kathleen D. Beck, Sept. 19, 1953; children—Kathleen Dorothy, Robert Michael, James Brian, Thomas Andrew, Stephen Edward, Timothy John. B.S. in Elec. Engring, Union Coll., Schnectady, 1942; D.Sc. (hon.), Allegheny Coll., 1959. Registered profl. engr., D.C. Engaged in design ships power systems, submarine propulsion systems Bur. Ships, Navy Dept., 1942-46, new design submarine propulsion systems, 1947-49; mem. staff comdr. Joint Task Force I for Atomic Weapons Test, Bikini, 1946-47; with Joint Bur. Ships/AEC Naval Reactor Group, 1949-64; head submarine nuclear propulsion plant, design group, also sr. submarine nuclear propulsion plant project officer and asst. mgr. naval reactors for s AEC, 1962-64; prin. officer, dir. MPR Assos., Inc. (engrs.), Washington, from 1964. Recipient Disting. Civilian Service award USN, 1959. Roman Catholic. Home: Washington D.C. Deceased.

PANOFSKY, HANS ARNOLD, educator, meteorologist; b. Kassel, Germany, Sept. 18, 1917; came to U.S., 1934, naturalized, 1944; s. Erwin and Dora (Mosse) P.; m. Margaret Ann Riker, July 24, 1943; children: Ruth Alice Morgan-Jones, Anne Davison. A.B., Princeton, 1938; Ph.D., U. Calif. at Berkeley, 1941. Mem. faculty Wilson Coll., Chambersburg, Pa., 1941-42, NYU, 1942-51; mem. faculty Pa. State U., 1951-82, Evan Pugh research prof. atmospheric scis., 1966-82; vis. prof. U. Minn., 1961, U. Wash., 1966, 73, U. Ariz., 1977, Post-grad. Sch. USN, 1980, Colo. State U., 1982; Erskine fellow U. Canterbury, N.Z., 1983; research assoc. Scripps Inst. Oceanography U. Calif.-San Diego, La Jolla, 1984-88; cons. to govt., 1953-88. Author: Introduction to Dynamic Meteorology, 1955, (with Glenn Brier) Some Applications of Statistics to Meteorology, 1958, (with John L. Lumley) Structure of Atmospheric Turbulence, 1964, (with John A. Dutton) Atmospheric Turbulence, 1984; also articles. Guggenheim fellow, 1960. Fellow Am. Meteorol. Soc. (Meisinger award 1965, Rossby Meml. medal 1976), Am. Geophys. Union, AAAS; mem. Royal Meterol. Soc. (hon.), Phi Beta Kappa, Sigma Xi. Home: San Diego Calif. Died Feb. 28, 1988; buried Centre County Meml. Pk., State Coll. Pa.

PAOLINO, THOMAS JOSEPH, state justice; b. Providence, Dec. 4, 1905; s. Joseph and Elvira (Cardarelli) P.; m. Florence Dolce, June 23, 1932; children: Loreen Ann, Thomas Joseph, Linda Vera. AB, Brown U., 1928; LLB, Harvard U., 1931; LLD, Bryant Coll., 1964, St. Francis Coll., Biddeford, Maine, 1971, Suffolk U., 1973, Salve Regina Coll., 1976. Bar: R.I. 1931. Mem. Fooley, Dunn & Paolino, 1940-87; assoc. justice R.I. Supreme Ct., 1956-87. Author: The Digest of Rhode Island Zoning Cases, 1960, Zoning—Its Growth and Development in Rhode Island, 1963, A Digest of R.I. Zoning Cases, 2d vol., 1987. Chmn. bd. trustees Roger Williams Coll.; mem. corp. Miriam Hosp., Providence, 1971-87. Decorated knight St. Gregory. Mem. ABA, R.I. Bar Assn., Am. Judicature Soc., Am. Soc. Legal History (br. v.p.), Harvard Law Sch. Assn. R.I. (v.p.), Assn. Master Knights Sovereign Mil. Order Malta in U.S., KC, Aurora Civic Assn., Harvard Club, Brown Club. Home: Cranston R.I. Died Apr. 18, 1987; buried St. Ann's Cemetery, Cranston, R.I.

PAPPER, SOLOMON, educator, physician; b. Bklyn., May 28, 1922; s. Max and Lillian (Weitzner) P.; m. Renee Wolfson, Oct. 2, 1943; children: Robert Allen, Margaret Anne, Ellen Martha. AB, Columbia U., 1942; MD, NYU, 1944. Diplomate Am. Bd. Internal Medicine. Intern Mt. Sinai Hosp., N.Y.C., 1944-45; resident Goldwater Meml. Hosp., N.Y.C., 1945-46, Cushing VA Hosp., Framingham, Mass., 1948-50; rsch. fellow Harvard and Thorndike Meml. Lab., 1950-52, May Inst. at Jewish Hosp., Cin., 1952-53; from chief metabolism sect. to asst. chief medicine Boston VA Hosp., 1953-60; from. clin. instr. to assoc. prof. medicine Tufts U. Med. Sch., 1953-60; instr. Harvard Med. Sch., 1953-60; prof. medicine, preventive medicine, chmn. dept. Med. Coll. Va., 1960-62; prof., chmn. dept. U. N.Mex. Med. Sch., 1962-68; prof., co-chmn. dept. medicine U. Miami (Fla.) Med. Sch., 1968-71; prof. U. Colo. Med. Sch., 1971-73; disting. prof. Health Sci. Ctr., U. Okla., 1973-84, head dept. medicine, 1977-84; chmn. dept. medicine Gen. Rose Meml. Hosp., Denver, 1971-73; disting. physician Oklahoma City VA Hosp., 1973-77; chief medicine Bernalillo County Med. Ctr., 1962-68; cons. Albuquerque VA Hosp., 1962-68; mem. study sect. gen. medicine NIH, 1963-65; chief med. svc. Miami VA Hosp., 1968-71. Author: Clinical Nephrology, 2d edit., 1978. Fellow ACP; mem. AMA, Assn. Am. Physicians, Am. Fedn. Clin. Rsch., Am. Soc. Clin. Investigation, Argentona Soc. Nephrology (hon.), Phi Beta Kappa, Alpha Omega Alpha. Home: Oklahoma City Okla. Died Aug. 19, 1984; buried Farmingdale, N.Y.

PARFREY, SYDNEY WOODROW, actor; b. N.Y.C., Oct. 5, 1922; s. Sydney and Hazel (James) P.; m. Rosa Ellovich, Feb. 18, 1950; children: Adam, Jonathan, Jessica, Juliet. Student, Erwin Piscator's Dramatic Workshop, New Sch. for Social Rsch., 1946-50, Am. Theatre Wing, 1950-52. Appeared on Broadway in The Rehearsal, 1952, Room Service, 1953, Cradle Song, 1955, Winesburg, Ohio, 1957, Oh Captain!, 1958, The Rivalry, 1959, Advise and Consent, 1961-62, Giant, Son of Giants, 1962, others; on tour in The Typists and The Tiger, 1969; appeared in films Carny, Bronco Billy, Hearts of the West, Stay Hungry, The Outlaw Josey Wales, Papillon, Charley Varrick, Oklahoma Crude, Dirty Harry, Cold Turkey, The Planet of the Apes, the Flim-Flam Man, How To Save A Marriage, The War Lord, others; appeared on numerous TV shows, 1948-84. With inf. AUS, 1942-45. Decorated Purple Heart, Silver Star; recipient Kemble award, 1962. Mem. Acad. Motion Pictures Arts and Scis. Home: Malibu Calif. Died July 29, 1984.

PARIS, GORDON DANIEL, savings and loan association executive; b. Boston, Mar. 11, 1908; s. William H. and Emma (Martin) P.; m. Isa B. Smith, Sept. 24, 1932;

children: James G. (dec.), Dorothy H. Sisler (dec.). Student pub. schs., Boston; LLD, U. Ariz., 1978. Store mgr. Atlantic & Pacific Tea Co., Boston, 1925-29; asst. mgr. City Mortgage div. John Hancock Mut. Life. Ins. Co., 1929-45; exec. v.p. Home Fed. Savs. & Loan Assn., Tucson, pres., 1964-74, chmn. bd., 1966-75, chmn., cons., 1975-80, chmn. emeritus, 1981-84; bd. dirs. Fed. Home Loan Bank San Francisco. Mem. Tucson Crime Commn., 1969-72; mem. bd. edn. Amphitheatre Pub. Schs., 1950-55; dir. Tucson Airport Authority, 1959-65, pres., 1964; bd. dirs. United Community Campaign, 1955-59, pres., 1958; mem. bd. regents Ariz. Univs., 1969-77, pres., 1975. With USCGR, 1943-45. Mem. U.S. Savs. and Loan League, Savs. and Loan League Ariz. (bd. dirs. 1956-64, pres. 1958-59), Soc. Residental Appraisers, Tucson C. of C. (past bd. dirs.), Skyline Country Club, Old Pueblo Club, Tucson Country Club, Masons, Shriners, Alpha Kappa Psi (hon.). Episcopalian. Home: Tucson Ariz. Died Apr. 5, 1984; buried Eastlawn Cemetery, Tucson.

PARISH, HOWARD WELLS, publishing executive; b. Alpena, Mich., Apr. 28, 1890; s. Charles and Anna (Callow) P.; m. Kathleen Grover, June 18, 1913; 1 child, Gloria Kathleen. Student pub. schs., Seattle. Mgr. circulation Seattle Star, 1907-12, pres., pub., 1942-48; dir. circulation Scripps N.W. League, 1912-28, pres., gen. mgr. of group, 1928-35; gen. mgr. Seattle Post-Intelligencer, 1935-36, Reading (Pa.) times, 1937-38; pub., gen. mgr. Jacksonville (Fla.) Jour., 1938-41; pres. Columbia Basin News, Pasco, Wash., Howard Parish and Assocs. Mem. Wash. Athletic Club, Rainier Club, The Highland Club. Home: Seattle Wash. †

PARISH, MARGARET CECILE (PEGGY), writer; b. Manning, S.C., July 14, 1927; d. Herman Stanley and Margaret Cecile (Rogers) P. B.A., U. S.C., 1948. Tchr. schs. in Ky., Okla. and N.Y., 1948-67; lectr. colls. and univs., tchr. workshops. Author books for juveniles, 1961—, latest being Mind Your Manners, 1978, Be Ready at Eight, 1979, Amelia Bedelia Helps Out, 1979, Beginning Mobiles, 1979, Amelia Bedelia and the Baby, 1981, No More Monsters for Me, 1981 (Recipient Garden State Children's Book award 1974, 80, Palmetto Writers Juvenile award 1977), Mr. Adam's Mistake, 1982, The Cats' Burglar, 1983, Amelia Bedelia Goes Camping, 1985, The Ghosts of Cougar Island, 1986, Merry Christmas Amelia Bedelia, 1986, Amelia Bedelia's Family Album, 1988, Scruffy, 1988, Good Hunting Blue Sky, 1988. Recipient Milner award City of Atlanta, 1984, Keystone State Children's Book award State of Pa., 1986, Garden State Children's Book award N.J., 1988. Mem. Author Guild Am., Delta Kappa Gamma. Died Nov. 18, 1988; buried Manning Cemetery, Manning S.C.

PARKER, ALFRED CHARLES, illustrator; b. St. Louis, Oct. 16, 1906; s. Alfred Bevan and Carlotta Marie (Bender) P.; m. Evelyn Buchroeder, Apr. 18, 1930; children: Jay Creighton, Susan, Kit. Student, St. Louis Sch. Fine Arts, Washington U., 1923-28; DFA (hon.), RISD, 1978; DFA, Calif. Coll. Arts and Crafts, 1979; MA, Acad. of Art, San Francisco, 1980. Founder, mem. faculty Famous Artists Schs., Westport, Conn., 1947-85. Illustrated 1st mag. cover, 1930, mag. illustration, 1933; contbr. illustrations to nat. mags., also advt. art for mags., newspapers, posters, other advt. media; work exhibited, U.S. and Can. Recipient numerous awards, gold medals including citation Washington U., 1953, award Phila. Art Dirs. Club, 1962; named to Hall of Fame Soc. Illustrators N.Y., 1965. Fellow Internat. Inst. Arts and Letters; mem. Soc. Illustrators L.A. (hon., Life Achievement award 1980), St. Louis Art Dirs. Club (hon.), Art Dirs. and Artists Club San Francisco, Westport Artists Group (founder, past pres.). Home: Carmel Valley Calif. Died Mar. 27, 1985.

PARKER, CLIFFORD STETSON, language educator; b. Woburn, Mass., Mar. 5, 1891; s. Henry Carlton and Clara Hathaway (Stetson) P.; m. Mary E. Landreth, Aug. 18, 1917; children: Richard Landreth, Margaret Stetson. AB, Harvard, 1912, AM, 1914; PhD, Columbia, 1925. Master and instr. prep. schs. and Union Coll., 1912-17; asst. prof. U. Nebr., 1919-20; instr. French Columbia, 1920-28; assoc. prof. French U. Maine, 1928-31; prof. langs. U. N.H., 1931-60, prof. emeritus, from 1960. Editor and author textbooks for study of French; translator biography from French and Italian; contbr. book revs. and articles to newspapers, mags. and lit. jours.; editor Foreign Language News and Views in N.H. 1st lt. U.S. Army, 1917-19, France. Recipient Palmes Académigues (France). Mem. MLA Am., AAUP, Am. Assn. Tchrs. French, Phi Kappa Phi. Republican. Unitarian. Home: Durham N.H. †

PARKER, HARRY D., lawyer; b. St. Paul, Nebr., Apr. 23, 1891. LLB, U. Mich. Bar: Ill. 1917, Calif. 1923. Practice law L.A.; of counsel firm Parker, Stanbury, McGee & Roberts. Mem. Am., Los Angeles bar assns., State Bar Calif. †

PARKER, HARRY M., lawyer; b. Orting, Wash., Oct. 22, 1891. AB, San Francisco Law Sch., 1912. Bar: Calif. 1931. Mem. firm Wyckoff, Parker, Boyle & Pope, Watsonville, Calif. Mem. Santa Cruz County Bar Assn. (pres. 1945), State Bar Calif. (gov. 1948-51). †

PARKER, JOSEPH E., banker; b. Gorham, Maine, 1891. Pres. Milliken, Tomlinson Co., Portland, Maine; pres., trustee Gorham Savs. Bank; hon. chmn. Casco Bank & Trust Co., Portland. Mem. Fed. Loan & Bldg. Assn. (v.p., dir.), Masons. Home: Gorham Maine †

PARKER, KARR, electrical engineer; b. Sebree, Ky., July 3, 1892; s. Sanford Ruby and Victoria (Wilson) P.; m. Enid Marie Sympson, Dec. 30, 1915 (dec. Feb. 1968); children—Karr, Marjorie; m. Mary Gallagher, Nov. 1968. Student, Carthage Coll.; B.S., U. Ill., 1913, M.S., 1914, D.Sc., 1929. Radio engr. Marconi Wireless Telegraph Co. Am., Cleve. and Milw., 1913-15; elec. engr. McCarthy Bros. & Ford (elec. engrs.), from 1930; chmn. Buffalo Electric Co.; mem. bd. dirs. Buffalo Savs. Bank. Exec. com. Buffalo War Council.; Mem. council, chmn. bldgs. and grounds com. U. Buffalo. Fellow ASME; mem. Buffalo C. of C. (past pres.), Electric League Niagara Frontier (past pres.), Asso. Electric Contractors of Buffalo (past pres.), Engring. Soc. Buffalo (past pres.), AIEE, Illuminating Engring. Soc., Sigma Xi. Republican. Episcopalian. Clubs: Yacht (Buffalo) (commodore), Buffalo (Buffalo), Country (Buffalo), Athletic (Buffalo), Twin Falls (Buffalo) (pres.); Engineers (N.Y.C.); Wianno (Cape Cod, Mass.). Home: Buffalo N.Y. also: Delray Beach Fla. Deceased.

PARKER, ROBERT PLEWES, college president, clergyman; b. Covington, Va., June 13, 1917; s. W. Carlton and Mabel (Plewes) P.; m. Frances Joye Brantley, June 28, 1945; children: John Brantley, Robert Plewes II, Dana Carlton, Christopher Stewart. AB, Randolph-Macon Coll., 1938, DD, 1960; MDiv magna cum laude, Yale U., 1942; MEd, U. Va., 1966. Ordained to ministry Meth. Ch., 1942. Instr. Randolph-Macon Coll., 1938-39, chaplain, 1948-52, asst. prof. Bible, 1949-51; pastor Middle Bedford and Bedford, Va., 1942-46, Danville, Va., 1946-48, Ashland, Va., 1948-52; pastor Westover Hills Meth. Ch., Richmond, Va., 1952-59; dir. Assn. Ednl. Instns., Richmond, 1959-65; pres. Randolph-Macon Acad., 1965-69, Shenandoah Coll. and Conservatory of Music, 1969-87. Author: How To Be a Dynamic Disciple, 1960, The Church on the Move, 1964; also weekly commentary sunday sch. lessons, Va. Meth. Adv., 1953-65. Dir. Va. Campaign for Higher Edn., 1961-65; dean Va. Meth. Conf. Pastors Sch., 1956-60. Mem. Winchester-Frederick County C. of C. (pres. 1975), Rotary, Phi Beta Kappa, Omicron Delta Kappa, Tau Kappa Alpha. Home: Winchester Va. Died Nov. 29, 1987.

PARKER, WILLIAM AMORY, banker; b. Boston, Dec. 31, 1892; s. Francis Stanley and Harriet Amory (Anderson) P.; m. Elise Ames, Aug. 17, 1917; children: Amory, Oliver Ames (dec. 1943). Student, Harvard U., 1911-14. Journalist, 1914-47; with Spencer Trask & Co., investment bankers, Boston, 1920-24; asst. treas. Inc. Investors, from 1925, then chmn. bd., dir.; chmn. bd., asst. treas., bd. dirs. Inc. Income Fund, Parker Corp.; chmn. exec. com. Rayonier, Inc.; bd. dirs. Metro-Goldwyn-Mayer, Putnam Mgmt. Corp., Inc., Easton land Co., Union Freight R.R. Co., Rayonier, Inc., Fiduciary Trust Co.; corporator North Easton Savs. Bank. Bd. mgrs. Mass. Eye and Ear Infirmary. 2d lt. field arty. U.S. Army, 1917-19. Mem. Somerset Club. Home: North Easton Mass. †

PARKIN, JOHN HAMILTON, mechanical engineer; b. Toronto, Ont., Can., Sept. 27, 1891; s. Frederick and Lily (Hamilton) P.; m. Margaret Gertrude Locke, May 19, 1916; 1 child, Margaret Lillian. BAS, U. Toronto, 1912, MME, 1919, LLD (hon.), 1961. Registered profl. engr., Ont. Initiator aerodyn. rsch., designer, installer 4-foot wind tunnel U. Toronto, 1917, initiator, planner 1st undergrad. course aero. engring. in Can., lectr., instr. all aero. courses, 1928, assoc. prof. mech. engring., 1926-29; mem. assoc. com. aero. rsch. NRC, Ottawa, Can., from 1920, asst. dir. div. physics, 1929-37, dir. div. mech. engring., 1937-57, sr. con. div. mech. engring., 1957-62; made wind tunnel tests for aircraft designers and builders in devel. Can. aircraft, 1917-29; 1st dir. Nat. Aero. Establishment, 1951-57; mem. tech. adv. com. aero. Dept. of Nat. Def., 1924; apptd. one of 3 mems. representing Can., Commonwealth Adv. Aero. Rsch. Council, 1947; incorporator, gov.-at-large Aviation League of Can., 1928. Contbr. articles to profl. jours. Recipient 1st prize Montreal Witness Model Aeroplane Meet, 1910, Czowski Medal of Engring. Inst. of Can., 1937, medal U. Toronto Engring. Alumni, 1951, McCurdy award Can. Aero. Inst., 1956. Fellow Royal Aero. Soc., Inst. Aero. Scis. (hon.), Royal Soc. Can.; mem. Soc. Automotive Engrs., ASME. Home: Ottawa Ont., Canada. †

PARKIN, WALTER H., business executive; b. Galva, Ill., Apr. 29, 1887; s. Walter H. and Mary D. (Harrah) P.; m. J. Blanche Millard, Jan. 18, 1913 (dec.); m. Gladys E. Eichele, 1959. AB, U. Ill., 1909. Apprentice foundry, machine shop, steam fitting, 1900-09; bookkeeper Nat. Wire Cloth Co., 1909-11; with Nat. Cable & Mfg. Co., Niles, Mich. (now Nat.-Standard Co.), from 1909, as bookkeeper, engr., sec., treas., v.p., gen. mgr., pres., 1933-52, chmn. bd., 1952-60, ret., 1960; pres., bd. dirs. Nat.-Standard Co., Guelph, Can.; bd. dirs. Nat.-Standard Co., Kidderminster, Eng., Clark Equipment Co., Buchanan, Mich. Mem. Niles bd. pub. works, 1915-31, 40-53. Mem. Union League Club (N.Y.C. and Chgo.), Chgo. Athletic Assn. Club, Sarasota Yacht Club, Field Club, Germantown Cricket Club (Phila.), Masons, Elks. Republican. Episcopalian. Home: Sarasota Fla. †

PARLEE, NORMAN ALLEN DEVINE, metallurgical engineer; b. South Farmington, N.S., Can., Mar. 23, 1915; came to U.S., 1953, naturalized, 1959; s. Allen Chipman and Margaret Lavinia (Foster) P.; m. Eileen Elliott, Sept. 22, 1938; children: Cherie Parlee Ball, Alan. BS, Dalhousie, Halifax, N.S., Can., 1935, MS, 1937; PhD, McGill U., Montreal, Can., 1939; postgrad., Cambridge (Eng.) U., 1959-60. Dir. r & d Dominion Steel & Coal Corp. Can., 1939-52; mem. faculty Purdue U., 1953-62; prof. extractive metallurgy Stanford U., 1962-85, chmn. metallurgy programs applied earth scis. dept., 1972-85. Co-author: Electric Furnace Steelmaking, 1962; co-editor: Metallurgy at High Temperatures and Pressures, 1963; contbr. articles to profl. jours.; patentee in field. Recipient Martin Murphy prize Engring. Inst. Can., 1948; NSF fellow, 1959-60. Fellow Chem. Inst. Can., Am. Inst. Chemists; mem. AIME, AAUP, Am. Soc. Metals, Can. Inst. Mining and Metallurgy, Am. Soc. Engring. Edn., N.S. Inst. Scis., Ductile Iron Soc., Sigma Xi. Presbyterian. Home: Los Altos Hills Calif. Died Jan. 22, 1985; buried Kingston, N.S., Can.

PARR, LELAND WILBUR, educator; b. Cooksville, Ill., Nov. 2, 1892; s. Marion Elmer and Edna May (Brigham) P.; m. Grace Belle Ghormley, June 16, 1915; children: Martha Grace (dec.), Patricia (Mrs. John Kibler Bash), Robert Ghormley. Student, Drake U., 1913-15; SB, U. Chgo., 1916, PhD, 1923; postgrad., Pasteur Inst., Paris, summer 1928. Instr. Assiut (Egypt) Coll., 1916-19; adj. prof. hygiene and bacteriology, then assoc. prof. Am. U. Beirut, 1923-30; assoc. prof. bacteriology U. Chgo., 1930; chief bacteriologist, with rsch. lab. Rockefeller Found., Andalusia, Ala., 1931-32; assoc. prof. dept. bacteriology, hygiene and preventive medicine George Washington U., 1932-37, prof., 1937-58, exec. officer, 1938-58, prof. emeritus in residence, from 1958; cons. infectious diseases Office Surgeon Gen. U.S. Army, 1942-44; mem. bacteriol. study sect. USPHS; cons. in bacteriology cen. office VA, Washington; cons. Clinl. Ctr., NIH; adviser to dir. Nat. Selective Svc., from 1948. Author: (with C. V. Ariens Kappers) An Introduction to the Anthropology of the Near East; contbr. articles to profl. jours. Recipient award Army Svc. Forces. Fellow Am. Acad. Microbiology; mem. Am. Soc. Exptl. Pathology, Soc. Am. Bacteriologists (sec.-treas. 1944-49), Am. Pub. Health Assn., Soc. Exptl. biology and Medicine, Am. Genetic Assn., Conf. Profs. of Preventive Medicine (chmn. 1949), Wash. Acad. Scis. (pres. 1943), Wash. Acad. Medicine, Cosmos Club, Phi Beta Kappa, Sigma Xi, Phi Delta Theta, Nu Sigma Nu. Republican. Home: Port Republic Md. †

PARRA, FRANCISCO JOSÉ, lawyer; b. Ponce, P.R., Nov. 18, 1904; s. Pedro Juan and Matilde (Toro) P.; m. Maria Isabel Sanchez, Aug. 24, 1931; children: Margarita, Maria Isabel. LL.B., U. P.R., 1927. Bar: P.R. 1927. Since practiced in Ponce; partner firm Parra, del Valle & Frau, 1968-85; dir. Banco de Ponce, 1951-75, vice chmn., 1971-75; mem. cons. com. P.R. Law Rev., Catholic U. P.R., 1961-67; mem. Jud. Council P.R., 1939-41, P.R. Bar Examiners Bd., 1947-48, P.R. Commn. Reputation for Admission to Bar, 1974-78. Municipal assembly-man, Ponce, 1932-36; mem. P.R. Municipal Complaints Commn., 1956-77; trustee U. P.R., 1934-41, Cath. U. P.R., 1958-61; trustee Damas Hosp., 1946-85, chmn. bd. trustees, 1976-85. Served to col. AUS, 1940-46; served to brig. gen. USNG (Ret.). Decorated Legion of Merit, Army Commendation medal; Knight Equestrian Order of St. Sylvester (Vatican). Mem. ABA, P.R. Bar Assn. (dir. 1932-33, chmn. Ponce 1954-56). Roman Catholic. Clubs: Rotary (Ponce) (past pres.), Deportivo (Ponce), Yacht and Fishing (Ponce). Home: Ponce P.R. Died Dec. 2, 1985.

PARROTT, ROBERT BELGROVE, agribusiness consultant, retired grain merchant; b. Fargo, N.D., Feb. 1, 1913; s. Alfred H. and Pearl (Canniff) P.; m. Paula C. Verne, June 14, 1938; children: Michael, Christopher, Stephen. B.S., N.D. State U., 1935, LL.D. (hon.), 1960. V.p. Northwest div. Cargill, Inc., Mpls., 1935-56; sr. exec. v.p. Central Soya Co., Inc., Ft. Wayne, Ind., 1956-78; also dir.; pres. Robert B. Parrott Inc. (Agribus. Cons.), 1978-87; dir. Early and Daniel Industries Inc., Zapata-Haynie Co., New Orleans, Gen. Grain Co., Tidewater Grain Co., Phila., Manna Pro Corp. Trustee N.D. State U.; bd. dirs. Chgo. Bd. Trade, Parkview Hosp., Ft. Wayne. Mem. Nat. Grain Trade Council (bd.), Grain and Feed Dealers Nat. Assn. (bd.), Mpls. Grain Exchange,, Chgo. Mercantile Exchange, Blue Key, Sigma Chi. Republican. Episcopalian. Clubs: Mason (Shriner), Quest, Fort Wayne Country; Union League (Chgo.). Home: Fort Wayne Ind. Died Feb. 19, 1987; buried Ft. Wayne, Ind.

PARSONS, EDWARD ERSKINE, JR., investment broker; b. Wilkinsburg, Pa., Dec. 3, 1905; s. Edward E. and Alice (Blake) P.; m. Myrtle Stebner, Aug. 17, 1929; children—Edward Erskine III. Robert. Student, Antioch Coll., 1923-24. Pres., dir. Parsons & Co., Inc., Cleve., 1951-86, Forest City Industries, Inc., Cleve., 1950-86; dir. Cleve. Mortgage Co. Mem. Nat. Security

Traders Assn. (past pres.). Home: Lakewood Ohio Died May 28, 1986.

PARSONS, ROBERT WADE, investment banker; b. Elizabeth, N.J., June 11, 1900; s. Elias W. and Lily (Barnard) P.; m. Irene Johnson, Nov. 11, 1931; children: Robert W., Roger B., Stanley G. (dec.). BS, Wesleyan U., 1922. With Bankers Trust Co., N.Y.C., 1922-60, from sales mgr. to asst. v.p., 1922-54, v.p., 1954-60; past. chmn., bd. dirs. Charles E. Pettinos Graphite Corp., former chmn. bd., Intercontinental Adv. Corp., Ltd.; former treas. Eurofund, Inc.; former cons. Continental Research Corp.; bd. dirs. Previews, Inc., Summit & Elizabeth Trust Co. Past pres. Mantoloking (N.J.) Borough Coun.; mem. N.J. Am. Revolution Bicentennial Celebration Commn.; chmn., dir. John Jay and Eliza Jane Watson Found., Charles E. and Joy C. Pettinos Found.; chmn., trustee Lillia Babbitt Hyde Found.; trustee emeritus Wesleyan U.; former trustee N.Y. Skin and Cancer Hosp., Stuyvesant Sq. Hosp., NYU Med. Ctr., Overlook Hosp.; past trustee, treas. Inst. for Sci. and Tech., N.J.; chmn. bd. trustees Pingry Sch.; pres., trustee Hist. Deerfield, Inc.; former pres., trustee Elizabethtown Hist. Found.; trustee Psi Upsilon Found., N.J. Coll. Medicine and Dentistry Found., N.J. Hist. Soc. Mem. SAR, Squadron A. Ex-mems. Assn., Skull and Serpent Soc., Bay Head Yacht Club, University Club, Baltusrol Golf Club, Spring Lake Golf Club, Nassau Club, Psi Upsilon (exec. coun.). Episcopalian. Home: Summit N.J. Died July 6, 1984.

PARSONS, ROSE PEABODY (MRS. WILLIAM BARCLAY PARSONS), civic worker; b. Groton, Mass., Oct. 11, 1891; d. Endicott and Fanny Peabody; m. William Barclay Parsons, Mar. 22, 1919; children: William Barclay, Rose Peabody (Mrs. Rose P. Lynch), Anne Barclay (Mrs. Anne P. Priest). Student, St. Timothy's Sch., Catonsville, Md., 1908-10. Adminstr. vol. svs. North Atlantic area ARC, 1942-45; founder Women United for UN, 1946, chmn., 1946-53, founder Com. Corr., chmn., 1952-55, vice chmn., 1961-64, mem. exec. com., 1963-70; liaison officer Internat. Coun. Women with the UN, 1963-70; v.p. Internat. Coun. Women, 1954-63, mem. exec. com., 1970-85; non-govt. rep. Nat. Coun. Women U.S., 1946-63, pres., 1956-59, hon. pres., 1959-62, mem. exec. com., 1970-85. Former chmn. women's group People-People Program; vice chmn. exec. com. Non-govt. Orgns. at UN, active devel. program UN, UN Spiritual Assembly; mem. women's adv. coun. N.Y. World's Fair Exec. Com.; nurse hosps. and orphanages ARC, France, 1916-17, U.S. Mobile Hosp., 1918-19. Decorated Croix de Guerre Militaire (France), 1918. Mem. Cosmopolitan Club. Home: New York N.Y. Died Mar. 28, 1985.

PARTCH, VIRGIL FRANKLIN, II, cartoonist; b. St. Paul Island, Alaska, Oct. 17, 1916; s. Paul C. and Anna (Pavaloff) P.; m. Helen Marie Aldridge, 1938; 2 sons, 1 dau. Ed., U. Ariz., Chouinard Art Inst., Calif., Disney Extra Curr. Art. Contbr.: cartoons to True; creator: newspaper comic strip Big George; Author: newspaper comic strip New Faces on the Barroom Floor, 1961, VIP's Ouios, 1975. Home: Laguna Beach Calif. Died Aug. 11, 1984.

PASLEY, VIRGINIA SCHMITZ (MRS. FRED PASLEY), journalist; b. Chgo., Oct. 19, 1905; d. Joseph A. and Winifred (Blackney) Schmitz; m. Fred Pasley (dec. May 1951). BA, Northwestern U., 1927. Reporter Chgo. Herald Examiner, 1927, Chgo. Tribune, 1928-30, Tower mags., 1930-34; free-lance writer 1934-41, 45-51; Washington corr. N.Y. Daily News, 1941-45; feature writer, book editor Newsday, Garden City, N.Y., 1951-86. Author: The Christmas Cookie Book, 1948, The Holiday Candy Book, 1952, 21 Stayed, 1955. Pres., co-founder Eleanor Roosevelt Newspaperwomen's Fellowship Fund, 1963. Recipient Community Svc. award Suffolk Civil Svc. Workers Assn., 1964; named L.I. Woman of Yr. Hempstead B'nai B'rith, 1964. Mem. N.Y. Newspaperwomen's Club (treas N.Y.C. chpt. 1964-65). Home: Mineola N.Y. Died May 21, 1986.

PASSMAN, OTTO ERNEST, congressman; b. Washington Parish nr. Franklington, La., June 27, 1900; s. Ed and Pheriby (Carrier) P.; m. Willie Bateman (dec. 1984); m. 2d, Martha P., 1985. Grad., Baton Rouge High Sch., Comml. Bus. Coll., Bogalusa, La. Owner Passman Investment Co.; mem. 80th-94th congresses form 5th La. Dist. State comdr. Am. Vets. World War II, Inc.; dir. Masonic Temple Comml. Bldg., New Orleans. Commd. lt. USN, 1942; materiel and procurement officer until 1944. Mem. Am. Legion, Masons (33 deg.), Shriners, K.T. Democrat. Baptist. Home: Monroe La. Died Aug. 13, 1988.

PASTORIUS, JACO, jazz-rock musician; b. Norristown, Pa., Dec. 1, 1951; m. Ingrid; children from previous marriage—Mary, John. Played bass in numerous bands including Wayne Cochran, Joni Mitchell, Pat Metheny, Albert Margellsdorf, Herbie Hancock; joined: jazz group Weather Report, 1976; recorded with (with Weather Report) albums include Word of Mouth (Winner Downbeat Reader's Poll best electric bassist 1978, 79, 80, 81), Jaco Pastorius, Heavy Weather, Black Market, Mr. Gone, 8:30, Night Passage. Died Sept. 21, 1987.

PATE, JOHN RALSTON, goverment official, organization executive; b. Scranton, S.C., Aug. 27, 1906; s. Charles H. and Nell (Singletary) P.; m. Alice Drew Chenoweth, Feb. 12, 1942; 1 child, John Ralston. AB in Edn., AM, U. S.C., 1927; BS, MD, Duke U., 1933; LLB, U. Louisville, 1945; MPH, Johns Hopkins U., 1948. Bar: U.S. Supreme Ct. 1969. Grad. instr. English U. S.C., 1926-27; tchr. Charleston (S.C.) High Sch., 1927-29; intern Strong Meml. Hosp., Rochester, N.Y.; mem. faculty George Washington U. Sch. Medicine, 1933-38, assoc. prof. community medicine and internat. health; mem. staff Ky. Dept. Health, 1938-47; with D.C. Dept. Pub. Health, 1948-85, dir. bur. disease control, 1953-64, chief bur. communicable disease control, 1964-85. Contbr. articles to profl. jours. Mem. nat. council Boy Scouts Am.; mem. bd. visitors Freedoms Found. at Valley Forge; mem. Pres.'s Com. for Handicapped, Gov. of Va. Com. for the Handicapped Employment; bd. dirs. Social Hygiene Soc. D.C.; mem. adv. bd. partridge Schs. and Rehab. Ctr., Gainesville, Va.; mem. Civitan Internat., 1955-85, gov. Chesapeake dist., 1961-62, v.p. zone 3, 1962-64, internat. pres.-elect, 1964-65, pres., 1965-66. Recipient 1st Albernon Sydney Sullivan medallion U. S.C., citation LWV D.C., 1952, Scroll of Honor Omega Psi Phi, 1957; named Mr. Civitan Chesapeake dist. Civitan Internat., 1962. Fellow Am. Pub. Health Assn., Am. Coll. Legal Medicine; mem. Am. Assn. Pub. Health Physicians (charter), Am. Venereal Disease Assn., AMA, Assn. Tchrs. Preventive Medicine, Royal Soc. Medicine Gt. Britain, Am. Assn. History of Medicine, D.C. Med. Soc., Clin. Club Washington, Ky. Bar Assn., Am. Geriatric Soc., World Med. Assn., Acad. Medicine, Masons (32 degree), Shriners, Phi Beta Pi, Alpha Tau Omega. Democrat. Episcopalian. Home: Arlington Va. Died Oct. 9, 1985.

PATTERSON, BOYD CRUMRINE, college president; b. McKeesport, Pa., Apr. 23, 1902; s. John Pollock and Louisa Celeste (Crumrine) P.; m. Eleanor Dennison, Aug. 3, 1927. AB, Washington and Jefferson Coll., 1923, LLD, 1970; postgrad., U. Chgo., 1923; AM, Johns Hopkins U., 1925, PhD, 1926; LLD, Waynesburg Coll., 1953; ScD, Duquesne U., 1965; LHD, Jefferson Med. Coll., 1967. Asst. prof. math. Washington and Jefferson Coll., 1926-27, pres., 1950-70; assoc. prof. Hamilton Coll., 1927-36, prof., 1936-50, chmn. dept., 1943-50. Author: Projective Geometry, 1937; contbr. articles to profl. jours. Mem. AAAS, Math. Assn. Am. (v.p. N.Y. sect. 1949-50, pres. 1950-51), Am. Math. Soc., Mid. States Assn. Colls. and Secondary Schs. (commn. on instns. of higher edn.), Pa. Assn. Colls. and Univs. (pres. 1956-57), Duquesne Club, Ft. Schuyler Club, Phi Beta Kappa, Sigma Xi, Phi Kappa Psi. Presbyterian. Home: Clinton N.Y. Died July 12, 1988, buried Hamilton Coll., Clinton.

PATTERSON, FREDERICK DOUGLASS, educator, institution president emeritus; b. Washington, Oct. 10, 1901; s. William Ross and Mamie Lucille (Brooks) P.; m. Catherine Elizabeth Moton, June 12, 1935; 1 son, Frederick Douglass. D.V.M., Iowa State Coll., 1923, M.S., 1927; Ph.D., Cornell U., Ithaca, N.Y., 1932; LL.D. (hon.), Va. State Coll., Ettrick, Shaw U., Tuskegee Inst., Ala., Atlanta U., John Marshall Coll.; H.H.D. (hon.), Wilberforce U., Xenia, Ohio, Va. Union U., Richmond, Bklyn. Coll., 1982; Sc.D. (hon.), Lincoln U., Pa.; D.Social Sci. (hon.), Xavier U.; D.H.L. (hon.), Morehouse Coll., N.Y. U., St. Augustine's Coll., 1977. Instr. vet. sci. Va. State Coll., 1923-26, dir. agr., 1927-28; head of vet. div. Tuskegee Inst., 1928-33, dir. Sch. Agr., 1933-35, pres., 1935-53, pres. emeritus, 1953-88; pres. Phelps-Stokes Fund, 1953-70; pres. Robert R. Moton Inst., 1969-73, chmn. bd., 1973-81, chmn. emeritus, 1981-88; Spl. asst. to sec. U.S. Dept. of Agr., 1944-53; cons. on higher edn., Republic of Liberia, 1954. Author: College Endowment Funding Plan; co-author: Economic Report of Economic Development of Nigeria of International Bank; Co-editor: Robert Russa Moton of Hampton and Tuskegee; Contbr. to: also sci. publs. The Campus View. Mem. Internat. Bank Mission to Nigeria, 1953; mem. Pres.'s Commn. on Higher Edn., 1947, Pres.'s Com. on Nat. Employment of Physically Handicapped, Fed. Def. Com., Com. on the South; founder, hon. pres. United Negro Coll. Fund.; Mem. Com. on So. Regional Studies in Edn.; chmn. bd. trustees Bennett Coll., 1965-72; trustee Phelps Stokes Fund, 1953-70, Tuskegee Inst. Commd. 2d lt. O.R.C., 1923. Decorated Star of Africa (Liberia). Recipient Wilson Fairbanks award for Disting. Service to Higher Edn., 1969, recipient Roy Wilkins award and citation Iowa State U, 1980, Pres. Reagan's White House citation for leadership in devel. coll. endowment funding plan, 1985, Nat. Leadership award Phelps-Stokes Fund, 1986, Presdl. medal of Freedom, 1987, Phelps Stokes Aggrey medal, 1987. Mem. Vet. Med. Soc. (Iowa chpt.), John A. Andrew Clin. Soc. (Tuskegee), Nat. Bus. League (former chmn. bd.), Phi Kappa Phi, Phi Delta Kappa, Alpha Phi Alpha. Methodist. Died Apr. 26, 1988, buried Tuskegee (Ala.) Univ.

PATTERSON, HANK CALVIN, actor; b. Birmingham, Ala., Oct. 9, 1888; s. Green Davis and Mollie Isabel (Newton) P.; m. Daisy Margaret Sheeler, May 8, 1915. Student, Bush-Temple Conservatory Music, Dallas, 1907-10. Pianist, 1910-12; played throughout Midwest with dramatic and mus. comedy shows, 1913-23; dir., actor Army show, Camp Kearney, San Diego until 1923; starred in road show Hello Good Times, 1922; appearances in numerous motion pictures, from 1940; host, narrator TV shows The Adventures of Kit Carson, 1952-56, Green Acres, from 1965; composer: Hopi Lullaby, 1950, Hank Patterson Album #1, 1962, Hank Patterson Album #2, 1962. Home: Northridge Calif. †

PATTERSON, HOWARD ALEXANDER, surgeon; b. Salem, N.C., Aug. 31, 1902; s. Andrew Henry and Eleanor Spurrier (Alexander) P.; m. Sarah Elizabeth Robertson, Nov. 22, 1930; children: Drew, Howard Alexander, Sarah Elizabeth. AB, U. N.C., 1921, postgrad., 1921-23; MD, Harvard U., 1925. Intern Roosevelt Hosp., N.Y.C., 1925-28, asst. surgeon, chief surg. clinic, 1929-37, assoc. surgeon, 1937-47, attending surgeon, 1947-52, chief surg. svc., 1952-68, cons. surgeon, 1968-85; asst. resident surgeon Peter Bent Brigham Hosp., Boston, 1928; cons. surgeon Southampton Hosp., Lawrence Hosp.; clin. prof. surgery Columbia U. Contbr. articles to surg. jours. Lt. col. AUS, 1942-45. Fellow ACS (pres. 1965-66), Am. Surg. Assn., So. Surg. Assn.; mem. N.Y. Acad. Medicine, N.Y. Gastroenterol. Soc. (pres. 1952), N.Y. Clin. Soc., N.Y. Surg. Soc., Am. Bd. Surgery, Century Assn., University Club, Pilgrims Club, St. Adnrew's Golf Club, Phi Beta Kappa, Sigma Alpha Epsilon, Phi Chi. Episcopalian. Home: Bronxville N.Y. Died Mar. 27, 1985.

PATTERSON, MARCEL, medical educator; b. Deleon, Tex., Apr. 4, 1919; s. L. Guy and Dora Lena (Miller) P.; m. Josephine Kelly, Dec. 25, 1947; children: Margaret, Guy, Robert. BA, U. Tex., 1939; MD, Tulane U., 1943. Intern San Francisco Hosp. U. Calif. Svc., 1943-44, resident, 1944-45; fellow Lahey Clinic, Boston, 1948, mem. staff gastroenterology div., 1949-53; instr. Med. Sch. U. Calif., San Francisco, 1954-55; mem. faculty Med. Sch. U. Tex., Galveston, 1955-84, chief div. gastroenterology, 1955-84, Piper prof., 1962, prof. medicine, 1965-84; cons. USPHS Hosp., Galveston, 1957-84, Wilford Hall. Book rev. editor Am. Jour. Digestive Diseases, 1969-84. Pres. Friends of Rosenberg Library, Galveston, 1960. With M.C., AUS, 1945-47. Fellow ACP, Am. Gastroent. Assn., Am. Assn. Study Liver Disease; mem. So. Med. Assn. (chmn. gastroenterology sect. 1964), Tex. Med. Assn. (chmn. digestive diseases sect. 1964), Am. Pancreatic Assn., Tex. Acad. Internal Medicine (v.p. 1970), Tex. Soc. Gastrointestinal Endoscopy (pres. 1983), Sigma Xi, Alpha Omega Alpha, Delta Xi, Phi Chi. Democrat. Episcopalian. Home: Galveston Tex. Died Aug. 18, 1984.

PATTERSON, WILLIAM DUDLEY, publisher, travel and tourism consultant; b. Kernville, Calif., July 25, 1910; s. Harold Lindsay and Louise (Dudley) P.; m. Ellen Day, Sept. 1, 1934; children: Gwen, Day, Philip. A.B., Yale U., 1932. Newspaperman specializing in pub. affairs 1932-39; domestic, fgn. assignments N.Y. dailies and A.P., 1939-42; asst. to Am. ambassador, Madrid, 1942; staff New Republic, 1946-48; v.p. Fred Smith & Co. (public relations), 1948-50; staff Sat. Rev., 1950—, assoc. pub., 1951-68, pub., 1968-72; v.p., sec. Sat. Rev., Inc., 1962-69, exec. v.p., 1970-72; v.p., pub., dir. Saturday Rev. Industries, Inc., 1972-73; cons. on travel and tourism 1973-86; chmn. bd. Travel & Tourism Cons. Internat., Inc., 1975-86; ofcl. rapporteur and spl. rep. UN, Internat. Union Ofcl. Travel Orgns.; asst. dir. OWI, London, ETO, 1943-44; transferred Psychol. Warfare Div., SHAEF, Germany, 1944-45; travel adv. com. Dept. Commerce, Dept. Interior; mem. U.S. del. UN Conf. Internat. Travel, Rome, 1963; del. White House Conf. Internat. Coop., 1965; chmn. ICY Sub-Com. on Internat. Travel; mem. Pres.'s Spl. Travel Task Force, 1967-68; co-chmn. Pres.'s Travel Commn., 1971-73; mem. U.S. travel mission to USSR, 1974; chmn. adv. com. grad. program travel studies New Sch. U., 1975-80. Author articles on current polit., internat. affairs, internat. travel and tourist industry; syndicated book column; creator, prin. writer: ann. Big Picture report on world travel and ann. World Tourism Overview (involved travel to 113 countries); editor: America Miracle at Work; supervising editor: Is the Common Man Too Common?. Recipient New Sch.'s Founder's medal for disting. service, 1980. Clubs: Century, Yale, Sky, Wings (N.Y.C.); Nat. Press (Washington). Home: Brooklyn N.Y. Died July 26, 1986.

PATTON, JOHN BARRATT, geologist; b. Marion, Ind., July 1, 1915; s. Barratt Marsh and Mary Frances (Kuntz) P.; m. Jean Glenn, 1941; children—Barratt Marsh II, Roger Craig, Frank Jamison Campbell, Ian Alastair. A.B. in Chemistry, Ind. U., 1938, A.M. in Geology, 1940, Ph.D. in Geology, 1954. Geologist Magnolia Petroleum Co., 1940-47; head indsl. minerals sect. Ind. Geol. Survey, 1947-53, prin. geologist, 1951-59, state geologist, dir., 1959-86, state geologist emeritus, 1986—; asst. prof. geology Ind. U., 1948-52, asso. prof. econ. geology, 1952-55, prof. economic geology, 1955-86, chmn. dept. geology, 1959-71, asso. dean research and advanced studies, 1973-75, prof. econ. geology emeritus, 1986—; commr. Am. Commn. Stratigraphic Nomenclature, 1960-63, 64-69, 75-78, vice chmn., sec., 1962-63; mem. earth scis. div. NRC, 1967-73. Contbr. articles to profl. jours., other publs. Fellow Geol. Soc. Am., Ind. Acad. Sci. (pres. 1975); mem. Am. Assn. Petroleum Geologists (pub. service award 1983), Soc. Econ. Geologists, Soc. Mining Engrs. (disting. mem.), Ind. Acad., Am. Inst. Mining, Metall. and Petroleum Engrs., Ind.-Ky. Geol. Soc., Assn. Am. State

Geologists (pres. 1966-67), ASTM, Interstate Oil Compact Commn., Phi Beta Kappa, Sigma Xi. Home: Bloomington Ind. Died Sept. 16, 1988, buried Clear Creek (Ind.) Cemetery.

PAUL, RODMAN WILSON, educator; b. Villa Nova, Pa., Nov. 6, 1912; s. Oglesby and Laura Little (Wilson) P.; m. Anne Catherine Thomson, July 21, 1951; children—Rodman Wilson, Deborah Anne (Mrs. Charles Philip Gibbs), Judith Thomson. A.B., Harvard, 1936, A.M., 1937, Ph.D., 1943. Asst. dean, instr. history Harvard, 1937-43; instr. history Yale, 1946-47; assoc. prof. history Calif. Inst. Tech., Pasadena, 1947-51; prof. Calif. Inst. Tech., 1951-72, Edward S. Harkness prof., 1972-81, Edward S. Harkness prof. emeritus, 1981-87; Mem. Nat. Archives Adv. Council, Washington, 1968-77, chmn., 1977; mem. hist. adv. com. NASA, Washington, 1970-73. Author: Abrogation of the Gentlemen's Agreement, 1936, California Gold, 1947, Mining Frontiers of the Far West, 1963, California Gold Discovery, 1966, A Victorian Gentlewoman in the Far West, 1972. Chmn. dept. coll. work Diocese of Los Angeles, 1962-65, mem. standing com., 1965-69; Trustee Calif. Hist. Soc. Served from lt. (j.g.) to lt. comdr. USNR, 1943-46. Huntington Library fellow, 1946, 61; Ford Fund for Advancement Edn. fellow, 1955-56; Guggenheim fellow, 1967-68; Soc. Am. Historians fellow, 1979; Calif. Hist. Soc. fellow, 1980; recipient Henry R. Wagner Meml. medal, 1984. Mem. Western History Assn. (pres. 1977-78), Am. Hist. Assn. (pres. Pacific Coast br. 1980-81), Orgn. Am. Historians, Am. Antiquarian Soc. Democrat. Episcopalian. Club: Valley Hunt (Pasadena). Home: Pasadena Calif. Died May 15, 1987, buried Santa Barbara (Calif.) Cemetery Assn.

PAYNE, HARRY DANIEL, architect, engineer; b. St. Louis, May 20, 1891; s. Alex Wesley and Mary Capen (Perks) P.; m. Margaret Frances deGarmo, May 15, 1918; children: Mary Payne May, Frances Payne Clark, Sarah Payne Thomas. BArch, Washington U., St. Louis, 1915; student, Army Svc. Sch., France, 1918-19; student engring., 1923-25; student, U. Tex., 1927-28; study in, Mex., 1938, 41. Assoc. William B. Ittner, St. Louis, 1915-25; pvt. practice Houston, from 1926. Prin. works include ednl. and ecclesiastical bldgs. and complexes, maj. site planning. Capt., inf., U.S. Army, 1917-19; AEF in France. Fellow AIA (Edward C. Kamper award 1962), ASCE, Tex. Soc. Architects (emeritus), Constrn. Specification Inst., Scarab, Masons (32 degree), Sigma Chi. Presbyterian (elder, past deacon, clk. of session and congregation, rep. Presbytery and synod, commr. gen. assembly). Home: Houston Tex. †

PAYNE, WILLIAM THOMAS, oil producer; b. Tecumseh, Nebr., Jan. 26, 1892; s. Thomas J. and Ellen (Meyer) P.; m. Katheryne Bond, June 17, 1935; 1 child, Stephen Bond. BS in Sci. and Lit., Okla. A&M Coll., 1915; LLD, Okla. Christian Coll., 1974. Grad. asst. microbiology Mass. State Coll., 1916; chemist Digestive Ferments Co., Detroit, 1916-17; bacteriologist City of Detroit, 1917-18; oil scout N.Am. Oil Co., 1919-21; supt. W.H. Helmerich Co., 1921-26; v.p. Helmerich & Payne, 1926-36; founder, pres. Big Chief Oil Co., Oklahoma City, 1936-58, chmn. bd., 1958-72; chmn. bd. Seneca Oil Co., 1961-75; pres. Payne Petroleum Corp., from 1945. Chmn. appeal bd. Western Fed. Jud. Dist. Okla., SSS, 1943-45, 48-67; bd. dirs. Oklahoma City United Fund; mem. exec. com. Okla. Med. Rsch. Found. 2d lt. San. Corps, U.S. Army, 1918-19. Recipient Horatio Alger award Am. Schs. and Colls. Assn., 1958, Outstanding Service award Mercy Hosp., Oklahoma City, 1958, Silver Beaver award Boy Scouts Am., 1958, Silver Antelope award, 1964, Alumni Hall of Fame award Okla. State U., 1959, Outstanding Citizen award Oklahoma City United Fund, 1960, Man With Heart award, 1960, Coll. Arts and Scis. award Okla. State U., 1962, Oil Man Yr. award Okla. Petroleum Coun., 1966; named to Okla. Hall of Fame, 1966. Mem. Ind. Petroleum Assn. Am. (dir.), Oklahoma City C. of C. (dir.), Am. Assn. Oilwell Drilling Contractors (pres. 1945), Mid-Continent Oil and Gas Assn. (pres. Kans.-Okla. div. 1947-49), Gen. Mid-Continent Oil and Gas Assn. (pres. 1950-51), Oklahoma City Golf and Country Club, Petroleum Club, Quail Creek Country Club, Beacon Club, Mens Dinner Club, Beta Theta Pi. Home: Oklahoma City Okla. †

PEABODY, STUYVESANT, JR., business executive; b. Chgo., Nov. 26, 1914; s. Stuyvesant and Anita M. (Healy) P.; m. Virginia Case Preston, May 15, 1937; children: Virginia Case, Anita May. Student, U. Chgol, 1933-34; grad., Chgo. Bus. Coll., 1936. Salesman Peabody Coal Co., 1936-41, pres., 1946-54, chmn. bd., 1954-55; bd. dirs. Exchange Nat. Bank Chgo., Ea. Airlines, Inc., Churchill Downs, Inc., Cen. Waxed Paper, Inc. 2d lt. U.S. Army, 1942-46. Mem. Ill. Mfrs. Assn. (bd. dirs.), Chicago Club, University Club, Chgo. Golf Club, Racquet Club, Onwentsia Club; Racket and Tennis Club (N.Y.C.). Home: West Palm Beach Fla. Died Jan. 20, 1986.

PEACH, WILLIAM NELSON, economist, educator; b. Granite, Md., Oct. 21, 1912; s. Frank and Mary Anna (Nelson) P.; m. Dorothy Jean Hausman, Sept. 1, 1939; children: Dorothy Jean, James Thomas, Joseph William. PhD, Johns Hopkins U., 1939. Instr. econs. U. Tex., 1938-42; asst. mgr. rsch. and stats. dept. Fed. Res. Bank, Dallas, 1942-44; asst. prof. U. Tex., 1946-47; assoc. prof. Syracuse U., 1947-49; prof. econs. U. Okla., Norman, 1949-65; then rsch. prof. econs. and George Lynn Cross prof. econs. U. Okla.; adviser in finance U. Pa. Agy. Internat. Devel. project, Karachi, Pakistan, 1956-58; spl. cons. select com. on small bus. U.S. Ho. of Reps., 1960; fiscal and fin. adviser AID, Washington, 1961. Author: Basic Data of the American Economy, 1948, Basic Data of the Economy of Pakistan, 1960, Principles of Economics, 1960, (with James A. Constantin) Zimmermann's World Resources and Industries, 3d edit., 1972, The Energy Outlook for the 1980's, 1973. Bd. dirs. Norman Mcpl. Hosp. With USNR, 1944-46. Mem. S.W. Social Sci. Assn., Am. Soc. for Pub. Adminstrn. Home: Norman Okla. Died Jan. 28, 1984; body donated to sci.

PEARSON, JAMES HURT, agricultural education consultant; b. Keytesville, Mo., Dec. 22, 1892; s. Edward Smith and Rebecca Leona (Hurt) P.; m. Louisa Ruby Terrill, Nov. 18, 1922; 1 son, Bruce Terrill; m. Edna Rose Mahoney, Dec. 27, 1941. Student, Mo. State Coll.; BS, U. Mo., 1920; grad., Colo. State Coll., U. Nebr., Am. U. Prin., tchr. Rural Consol. Sch., 1915; tchr., state supr. vocat. agr., 1921-29; specialist adult edn. in agr. U.S. Office Edn., 1929, successively regional agt., field rep., asst. dir., program coord. vocat. edn., 1935-55, asst. commr. edn., dir. div. vacat. edn., 1955-61; vis. prof. So. Ill. U., 1962. Govt. advisor ILO meeting at Geneva, 1956; edn. rep. Fed. Com. on Apprenticeship. With USN, World War I. Recipient Superior Svc. award Dept. Health, Edn. and Welfare; hon. Am. Farmer degree Future Farmers Am. Mem. NEA, Am. Vocat. Assn., Am. Legion, Alpha Tau Alpha, Iota Lambda Sigma, Phi Delta Kappa. Home: Arlington Va. †

PEARSON, LIONEL IGNATUS CUSACK, classicist, educator; b. London, Eng., Jan. 30, 1908; came to U.S., 1938; s. Arthur Anselm and Ellen (Cusack) P.; m. Doris Elliott Wilson, Dec. 12, 1946 (dec. 1964). BA, Trinity Coll., Oxford U., 1930; PhD, Yale U., 1939. Lectr. Greek Glasgow (Scotland) U., 1930-31; lectr. classics, then asst. prof. Dalhousie U., 1932-38; instr. classics Yale U., 1935-36; instr. Latin N.Y. State Coll. Tchrs., 1939-40; faculty Stanford U., 1940-73, prof. classics, 1952-73, emeritus, from 1973. Author: Early Ionian Historians, 1939, Local Historians of Attica, 1942, The Lost Histories of Alexander the Great, 1960, Popular Ethics in Ancient Greece, 1962, Plutarch: On the Malice of Herodotus, 1965, Demosthenes, Six Private Orations, 1972, The Art of Demosthenes, 1976, The Commentary of Didymus on Demosthenes, 1983, The Greek Historians of the West: Timaeus and His Predecessors, 1987. With Brit. Army, 1943-46. Guggenheim fellow, 1957-58. Mem. Am. Philol. Assn. (dir. 1971-74), Philol. Assn. Pacific Coast (pres. 1964), Archaeol. Inst. Am., Classical Assn. (Eng.), Soc. Hellenic Studies (Eng.). Home: Los Altos Hills Calif. Died Sept. 18, 1988.

PEARSON, VICTOR ROSENIUS, clergyman, religion educator; b. Wahoo, Nebr., Apr. 30, 1892; s. Nels and Betty (Trulson) P.; m. Ingeborg Olson, Feb. 18, 1928; children: Victory Gladys Pearson Deffenbaugh, Lois Ruth, Keith Lawrence, David Eugene, Donald Victor. Grad., Luther Bus. Coll., 1909, Luther Acad., 1911; AB, Augustana Coll., Rock Island, Ill., 1915; BD, Augustana Theol. Sem., Rock Island, 1917, ThD, 1924; grad. study, John Hopkins U. and U. Chgo. Ordained to ministry Luth. Ch., 1917. Pastor Immanuel Ch., Evanstorn, Ill., 1917-20, Messiah Ch., Lindsborg, Kans., 1920-22, 1st Gethsemane Luth. Ch., Chgo., 1922-35; prof. religion, Augustana Coll., 1935-63, prof. emeritus, from 1963, chmn. div. philosophy and religion, 1946-63; lectr. ch. history United Luth. Ch. Bible, Grand Forks, N.D., 1964; interim pastor St. Luke's Luth. Ch., 1965. Author: Life and Teachings of Christ, 1940, rev. edit., 1949, radio booklet My God and I; editor Bible Study Quarterly, 1939, 47; contbr. to Luth. Quar. and other religious publs.; speaker at young people's meetings, commencements, etc. Pres. Luth. Mins. Assn., Chgo., 1932-33; v.p. coun. religious edn. Chgo. Ch. Fedn., 1934-35, Am. Scandinavian Found., Ill. Conf. Parish Edn. Commn., 1940-49. 1st chaplain U.S. Army, 1918-19. Mem. AAAS, AAUP, Am. Acad. Polit. and Social Sci., Nat. Assn. Bibl. Instrs., Swedish Pioneer Hist. Soc. Inc., Ill. State Acad. Sci. Home: Grand Forks N.D. †

PECK, HUBERT RAYMOND, textile company executive; b. Newark, N.J., Feb. 23, 1923; s. Hubert Raymond and Helen (White) P.; m. Barbara Fleming Smith, Sept. 7, 1946; children—Hubert Raymond, Thomas Heyward, Laura, Sarah, Mary Tucker. B.A., U. Pa., 1947; B.S., N.C. State U., 1949. Salesman, L.P. Muller & Co. Inc., N.Y.C., 1948-50, mgr., 1957-64, ptnr., N.Y.C. and Phila., 1960-62, v.p., Phila., 1962-74, exec. v.p., Valley Forge, Pa., 1974-80, pres., Charlotte, N.C., 1981-86; chmn. Peck Mfg. Co., Warrenton, N.C., 1983-85. Served with USAF, 1943-45; Eng. Republican. Episcopalian. Club: Phila. Tennis Assn. (pres. 1978-80). Avocations: tennis; antiquarian books. Home: Radnor, Pa. Died Sept. 22, 1986.

PEETS, ELBERT, landscape architect; b. Cleve., May 5, 1886; s. Edward Orville and Mary (Houghton) P. AB, Western Res. U., 1912; MLA, Harvard U., 1915. Gen. practice landscape architecture and town plannin; assoc. planner Kohler, Wis., Washington Heights, Wis., Wyomissing Park, Reading, Pa., Greendale, Wis., Park Forest, Ill.; chief site planning sect. U.S. Housing Authority and Fed. Planning and Housing Authority; cons. town planning San Juan, P.R.; mem. Commn. on Fine Arts, 1950-58; lectr. city planning Yale U.; lectr. landscape architecture Harvard U. Author: (with W. Hegemann) Civic Art, 1922; contbr. articles in field to profl. jours. Served as civilian engr. in camp planning sect. War Dept., World War I. Home: Washington D.C. †

PELL, JOHN HOWLAND GIBBS, historian; b. Southampton, L.I., N.Y., Aug. 9, 1904; s. Stephen Hyatt Pelham and Sarah Gibbs (Thompson) P.; m. Pyrma Tilton, Sept. 3, 1929; children: Sarah Gibbs, John Bigelow. Student, Harvard U., 1922-24; LL.D., Adelphi Coll., 1963, Chung-ang U., 1963, Fairleigh Dickinson U., 1964; L.H.D., Russell Sage Coll., 1964, New Rochelle Coll., 1976, Hamilton Coll., 1976, St. Lawrence U., 1984, Norwich U., 1984. Engaged in hist. research Ft. Ticonderoga, 1925-29; in estate mgmt. 1930-32; organizer, partner John H.G. Pell & Co., 1932-84; dir. Macmillan, Inc.; trustee Dime Savs. Bank of N.Y., 1960-80; chancellor L.I. U., 1962-64. Author: Life of Ethan Allen, 1929; also articles in hist. and fin. fields; contbr. chpt.: General Washington's Generals, 1964. Mem. Commr. Edn.'s Com. on N.Y. State Mus., 1960-69; pres. Ft. Ticonderoga Assn., 1950-87 ; mem. Interstate Commn. on Lake Champlain Basin, 1955-65; mem. council SUNY-Plattsburgh, 1960-75; chmn. Fed. Hudson-Champlain Celebration Commn., 1958-59, N.Y. State Am. Bicentennial Commn., 1968-81; dir. N.Y.C. Am. Bicentennial Com., 1971-76; trustee N.Y. State Historic Trust, 1966-87 , Estate and Property Episcopal Diocesan Conv. N.Y., Juilliard Sch. Music.; bd. mgrs., lay v.p. Seaman's Ch. Inst., 1935-70. Served from lt. to comdr. USNR, 1941-45; enlisted personnel officer 3d Naval Dist.; duty in U.S.S. Ordroneaux, 1944. Decorated officer Order of Orange Nassau (Netherlands); chevalier Legion of Honor (France); recipient Chauncey Depew medal, citation and gold medal SAR, commendation Sec. Navy; fellow Churchill Meml. of Westminster Coll., 1986. Mem. N.Y. State Hist. Assn. (trustee, v.p.), Am. Scenic and Historic Preservation Soc. (trustee, pres. 1970-87), N.Y. Hist. Soc. (trustee), English Speaking Union, Soc. Colonial Wars (council), Pilgrims of U.S. (exec. com.), Colonial Lords of Manors (pres.), Theodore Roosevelt Assn. (pres.), Soc. of Cincinnati (hon.), France Amerique (dir.). Clubs: Knickerbocker, Century Assn., Metropolitan (Washington); Spouting Rock Beach Assn.; Newport Reading Room. Home: New York N.Y. Died Oct. 13, 1987; buried Newport, R.I.

PELT, ADRIAN, association executive; b. Koog Aan De Zaan, The Netherlands, May 8, 1892; s. Marimus Adrianus and Dorothea Johanna (Endt) P.; m. Andree Bernard, Feb. 3, 1919; children: Jeanne Pelt von Blankenstein, Marceline Pelt Amar, Dorothea, Andree. Degree diplomatic sect., Sch. Polit. Sci., Paris, 1919; D honoris causa, U. Amsterdam, 1956. Editor various Dutch newspapers Amsterdam, 1909-15; London corr. Dutch newspapers, 1915-16, Paris corr., 1916-19, fgn. sub-editor, 1919-20; mem. info. sect. League Nations Secretariat, Geneva, 1920-33, dir. 1934-40; head The Netherlands Govt. Info. Bur., London, 1940-45; The Netherlands del. to San Francisco Conf., to UN exec. com. and prep. commn., 1945, to 1st part of 1st session UN Assembly, 1946; asst. sec. gen., dept. conf. and gen. svcs. UN, N.Y.C., 1945-50; UN commr., Libya, 1950-52; dir. European Office UN, Geneva, 1952-58; sec. gen World Fedn. UN Assns., 1958-59; personnel rep. Sec. Gen. UN in Guinea, 1959-63; pres. World Fedn. UN Assns., 1963-66, hon. pres., from 1966. Decorated knight Oreder of Lion (The Netherlands); grand cross Order of Mohammed Ali el Senussi (Libya); hon. citizen N.Y.C. Mem. Dutch Reformed Ch. Home: Geneva Switzerland. †

PEN, RUDOLPH THEODORE, painter, lithographer; b. Chgo., Jan. 1, 1918; s. John and Agnes (Klemczak) P.; m. Yvonne Fillis, June 29, 1946; children: Ronald Allen, Yvonne Pauline. BFA, Art Inst. Chgo., 1943. Mem. faculty Art Inst. Chgo., 1948-63, North Shore Art League, Winnetka, Ill., 1948-87; founder, tchr., dir. Rudolph Pen Sch. Painting, Chgo., 1963-86; tchr. pvt. painting classes; dir. Oxbow, the Summer Sch. of Painting, Saugatuck, Mich. Numerous one-man shows including Carroll Carstairs Gallery, N.Y.C., 1944-45, Marshall Fields Gallery, Chgo., 1959, Frank Ochlschlaeger Gallery, Chgo., 1962, Vincent Price Gallery, Chgo., 1968, Art Inst. Chgo., 1977, 79, Joseph Welna Gallery, Chgo., 1972, Old Town Art Gallery, Chgo., 1977, North Shore Art League Gallery, Winnetka, Ill., 1984, Univ. Club Gallery, Chgo., 1985; numerous group shows include Carnegie Inst., Pitts., 1946, Art Inst. Chgo., 1966, Phila. Acad. Fine Arts, 1946, Corcoran Mus. Art, Washington, 1949, Marshall Field Art Gallery, Chgo., 1979; represented in permanent collections, Washington and Lee U., Va., Davenport (Iowa) Mus., Library of Congress, Washington, Art Inst. Chgo., also pvt. collections. Recipient prize NAD, 1946, prizes Union League Club, Chgo., 1957, 61, 65, 1st prize Ill. State Fair, 1954; Joseph Ryerson traveling fellow, 1943; Huntington Hartford Found. grantee, 1958. Mem. Am. Watercolor Soc., Alumni Assn. Art Inst. Chgo. (pres. 1960-62), Union League Civic and Arts Found. (hon.). Episcopalian.

Club: Arts of Chgo. Home: Chicago Ill. Died Jan. 8, 1989, buried Graceland Cemetery, Chgo.

PENDLETON, CLARENCE MCLANE, JR., business executive, political activist; b. Louisville, Nov. 10, 1930; s. Clarence McLane and Edna Marie (Ramsaur) P.; m. Margrit K.; children: George, Susan, Paula. B.S., Howard U., 1954, M. Ed., 1962. Chmn. San Diego Transit, 1974-86, San Diego Local Devel. Corp., 1978-86; dir. Great Am. First Savs. Bank, San Diego; past trustee Scripps Inst., San Diego; ptnr. Pendleton & Assocs., San Diego. Pres. San Diego Urban League, 1975-82; mem. Republican Nat. Com., 1980-88; mem. Citizens for the Republic, Los Angeles, 1981, Calif. Higher Edn. Loan Authority. Served with AUS, 1954-57. Home: San Diego Calif. Died June 5, 1988.

PENDRAY, GEORGE EDWARD, public relations counsel, author, foundation executive; b. Omaha, May 19, 1901; s. John Hall and Louisa (Wolfe) P.; m. Leatrice Gregory, June 27, 1927 (dec.); children: Guenever Pendray Knapp, Elaine Pendray Jennings, Lynette Pendray Wertsch; m. 2d, Annice D. Crema, Oct. 30, 1972. Student, Jireh Wyo. Coll., 1914-17; AB, U. Wyo., 1924, LLD, 1943; AM, Columbia U., 1925. Reporter Laramie (Wyo.) Rep. Boomerang, 1923-24; reporter N.Y. Herald-Tribune, 1925-30, picture editor, 1930-32, sci. editor, 1932-33; editorial dir. Milk Rsch. Coun., N.Y.C., 1932-36; sci. editor Literary Digest, 1933-36; asst. to pres. Westinghouse Electric & Mfg. Co., in charge of pub. relations, advt. and edn., 1936-45; head own pub. relations firm, 1945-47; sr. ptnr. Pendray & Co., pub. relations, 1948-70; former pub. relations counsel to over 100 corps. and orgns., including Gt. No. Paper Co., Westinghouse Elec., Am. Machine & Foundry Co., Guggenheim founds., Toronto-Dominion Bank (Can.), Can. Westinghouse, Internat. Bank for Reconstrn. and Devel., Am. Electric Power, Brookhaven Nat. Lab., Stanford Rsch. Inst., others; sec. Westinghouse Ednl. Found., 1944-45; co-founder Am. Rocket Soc. (later incorporated into AIAA), 1931, editor Astronautics, 1936-39; assisted in the devel. of liquid fuel rocket motor, also rsch. in tank design, rocket flight stblzn. and control. Author: (pen name Gawain Edwards) Earth Tube, 1929, Men, Mirrors and Stars, 1935, The Coming Age of Rocket Power, 1945; editor: Book of Record of the Time Capsule, 1938, City Noise, 1940, (with Mrs. Goddard) The Papers of Robert H. Goddard, 3 vols., 1970; also articles and fiction in many mags. Co-adminstr. Ann. Sci. Talent Search; mem. mng. com. George Westinghouse Sci. Writing Award; cons. Select Com. on Astronautics and Space Flight, accreditation bd. Pub. Relations Soc. Am.; bd. dirs. Harry F. Guggenheim Found., from 1965, Am. Jour. Nursing Co., 1972-76. Recipient Alumni award U. Wyo., 1964. Fellow AAAS, AIAA (bd. dirs.); mem. Pub. Relations Soc. Am. (exec. com. 1948, editor Jour. 1950-54, sec. 1952, chmn. accreditation bd. 1964-65, recipient citations 1953, 63, Disting. Service award 1963). Home: Jamesburg N.J. Died Sept. 15, 1987.

PERCIVAL, WALTER CLEMENT, forestry educator; b. Jericho, Vt., June 25, 1901; s. Charles Eugene and Sarah Jane (Nattress) P.; m. E. Phyllis Pennington, July 14, 1928; children: Charles Leigh, Phyllis Marcia, Lilian Margaret. BS, N.Y. State Coll. Forestry, 1923, MS, 1926, PhD, 1933. Silvicultural foreman U.S. Forest Service, 1933-34, dist. ranger, 1934; mem. faculty W.Va. U., from 1934, prof. forestry and forester, 1939-66, head div. forestry, 1937-66, founder W.Va. Forestry Sch. as div. forestry Coll. Agr. and Forestry, 1937, asst. dean Coll. Agr., Forestry and Home Econs., dir. div. forestry, forester W.Va. Agrl. Expt. Sta., 1959-66, prof. emeritus, from 1966; mem. W.Va. State Bd. Registration for Foresters. W.Va. Univ.'s new forestry bldg. named Percival Hall in his honor, 1973; named to W.Va. Agrl. Hall of Fame, 1977. Fellow Soc. Am. Foresters; mem. Morgantown Power Squadron (comdr.), Sigma Xi, Sigma Nu. Republican. Methodist. Home: Morgantown W.Va. Died Jan. 19, 1986; buried Macon Cemetery, Tecumseh, Mich.

PEREIRA, WILLIAM L., architect, city planner; b. Chgo., Apr. 25, 1909; m. Margaret McConnell, June 24, 1934; children: William L., Monica I.; m. Bronya Kester, 1976. BS, U. Ill., 1930, Otis Art Inst., 1964, Art Ctr. Coll. Design, 1971; LLD (hon.), Pepperdine U., 1974. Registered architect thirty-four states. Began as architect 1930; assoc. Holabird & Root, Chgo., 1930-32; then pvt. practice, Chgo., also, Los Angeles; prof. architecture U. So. Calif., 1949-57; partnership Pereira Assoc., from 1958; architect in residence Am. Acad. in Rome, 1971; mem. adv. com. to bd. dirs. Crocker-Citizens Nat.; mem. Pres.'s Nat. Coun. on Arts, 1965-68; adviser Aeros. and Space Engring. Bd., 1969; chmn. Calif. Gov.'s Transp. Task Force Com., 1967-68; bd. dirs. Urban Am., Inc. Designed or planned: African Riviera, Ivory Coast, Cape Canaveral, CBS Television City, Union Oil Ctr., L.A. Mus. Art, Houston Ctr., New Eng. Ctr. for Continuing Edn., Cen. Library, U. Calif., San Diego, Occidental Ctr., Crocker-Citizens Bldg., L.A., Transamerica Hdqrs., San Francisco, Marineland of the Pacific, Palos Verdes, Doha Hotel and Conf. Ctr., Qatar; master planner: Irvine Ranch, Mountain Pk., L.A. Internat. Airport, U. Calif. at Irvine, U. So. Calif.; others. Decorated comdr. Order of Ivory Coast; recipient Scarab medal, 1940, Humanitarian medal, 1942, citaion Mus. Modern Art, 1944, Phila. Art Alliance award, 1949, Man of Yr. award L.A. C. of C., 1967. Fellow AIA (honor and merit awards, 1951-69); mem. Gargoyle Soc., Soc. Am. Mil. Engrs., Acad. Motion Picture Arts and Scis. (Oscar 1942), Alpha Sigma Mu (hon.). Home: Los Angeles Calif. Died Nov. 1985.

PERKINS, DWIGHT GOSS, merchant; b. Ogunquit, Maine, Mar. 9, 1890; s. Jedediah Moses and Ava (Goss) P.; m. Anna Belle Clark, Dec. 25, 1913; children: Clark Goss, Gordon Dwight; m. Esther Marie Williams, 1936; children: David Dodd, Jane Carol. Student, U. Denver. Stock boy dept. store, salesman, savs. teller, 1908-16; buying exec. Daniels & Fisher Stores Co., 1916-24; with divisional mdse. mfg. Strawbridge & Clothier, Phila., 1924-44, gen. mdse. mgr., 1944-46, v.p., 1946, pres., 1947-55, chmn., from 1955, also bd. dirs.; bd. dirs., mem. exec. com., fgn. office com. Assoc. Merchandising Corp.; bd. dirs. John B. Stetson Hat. Co. Bd. dirs. Better Bus. Bur., Phila. Mem. Phila. Mchts. Assn. (pres.), Greater Phila. C. of C. (bd. dirs., exec. com.), Phila. Country Club, Racquet Club, Downtown Club (gov.). Home: Villanova Pa. †

PERKINS, R(ICHARD) MARLIN, zoo director; b. Carthage, Mo., Mar. 28, 1905; s. Joseph Dudley and Mynta Mae (Miller) P.; m. Elise More, Sept. 12, 1933 (div. Oct. 1953); 1 dau., Suzanne; m. 2d, Carol M. Cotsworth, Aug. 13, 1960. DsC, U. Mo., 1926, Rockhurst Co., Northland Coll.; D Pub. Svc., MacMurray Coll. Curator of reptiles St. Louis Zoo, 1926-38; curator Buffalo Zoo, 1938-44; dir. Lincoln Park Zoo, Chgo., 1944-62; dir. St. Louis Zoo, 1962-70, dir. emeritus, 1970-86. Author: Animal Faces, 1944, Marlin Perkins' Zooparade, 1954, (with Carol Perkins) I Saw You from Afar (The Bushmen of the Kalahari Desert), (autobiography) My Wild Kingdom, 1982; several sci. papers on herpetology, memmalogy; originator: TV program Zoo Parade, 1949-57 (winner of numerous awards including Peabody, Look, 4 Emmy awards); (with Don Meier) TV series Mut. of Omaha's Wild Kingdom, 1962-86 (winner 4 Emmy awards and numerous others). Mem. Am. Soc. Ichthyologists and Herpetologists, Internat. Union Dirs. of Zool. Gardens, Am. Assn. Zoo. Parks and Aquariums, Explorers Club, Adventurers Club (Chgo.); Mo. Athletic Club. Home: Saint Louis Mo. Died June 16, 1986.

PERKINS, WALTER FREDERICK, business executive; b. Balt., June 3, 1891; s. William and Ida (Frederick) P.; m. Lucinda M. Rawley, Nov. 24, 1914; children: Doris Perkins Schnieder, Suzanne Perkins Ross. Student, Balt. Poly. Inst., 1906-09; BCE, Lehigh U., 1913. Draftsman Chesapeake & Potomac Telephone Co., 1909; rodman B&O R.R., 1910-11; engr. Paving Commn. Balt., 1913-15; supt., later gen. supt. Bartlett Hayward Co., Balt., 1915-27, v.p., gen. mgr., 1932-34; pres. Bartlett Hayward Co. (absorbed by Koppers Co. 1936), Balt., 1934-36; v.p., gen. mgr. metal products div. Koppers Co., Balt., 1936-56, ret.; works mgr. Worthington Pump & Machinery Corp., Harrison, N.J., 1927-32; pres. Md. Hosp. Laundry Inc.; bd. dirs. Md. Dry Dock & Shipbldg. Co., Balt. Gas. and Electric Co., Mercantile Safe Deposit & Trust Co., Eutaw Savs. Bank. Chmn. Airport Bd. Balt., 1947-60; bd. trustees Johns Hopkins U.; pres. bd. trustees Johns Hopkins Hosp., 1955-63, chmn., from 1963; gen. chmn. Balt. Community Fund, 1938. Fellow ASME; mem. Balt. Country Club, Tau Beta Pi. Home: Baltimore Md. †

PERLSTEIN, HARRIS, business executive; b. N.Y.C., Aug. 18, 1892; s. Abram and Betsy (Cohen) P.; m. Anne Agazim, Mar. 11, 1929 (dec. Sept. 1956); children—Betsy Ann (Mrs. Kenneth R. Cowan) (dec.), Lawrence A.; m. Florence L. Weiss, Oct. 23, 1960 (dec. Sept. 1973). B.S. in Chem. Engring, Armour Inst. Tech., Chgo., 1914; LL.D., Ill. Inst. Tech., 1965. Chemist, engr. 1914-18; ptnr. Singer Perlstein Co. (cons. engrs.), Chgo., 1918-24; treas., dir. Premier Malt Products Co., Peoria, Ill., 1924-27; pres. Premier Malt Products Co., 1927-32, Premier Malt Products Co. (co. merged with Pabst Brewing Co.), 1932; pres., dir. Pabst Brewing Co., Chgo., 1932-54; chmn., pres., dir. Pabst Brewing Co., 1954-56, chmn., dir., 1956-72, chmn. exec. com., dir., 1972-79, chmn. emeritus, 1979-82; Mem. adv. hosp. council Ill. Dept. Pub. Health, 1961-71; bd. dirs. U.S. Brewers Assn., 1944-79, hon. dir., 1979-86 ; bd. dirs. Ill. Mfrs. Assn., 1945-55, 58-59; hon. chmn., life trustee, past chmn. bd. Ill. Inst. Tech. Pres., bd. dirs. Perlstein Found.; past pres., dir. Jewish Fedn. Met. Chgo.; mem. Ill. Bd. Pub. Welfare Commrs., 1949-53. Mem. Am. Chem. Soc., Pi Delta Epsilon. Clubs: Mason (Chgo.) (Shriner), Lake Shore Country (Chgo.), Northmoor Country (Chgo.), Standard (Chgo.); Chemist (N.Y.C.). Home: Chicago Ill. Died Aug. 16, 1986.

PERRIN, LESLIE N., business executive; b. Chgo., Aug. 22, 1886; s. Norman Harry and Marie C. (Casey) P.; m. Lydia Marie Anaheim, June 29, 1910 (dec. 1953); 1 child, Jean Leslie (Mrs. William J. Walton); m. Helen B. Perrin, 1954; m. Agnes P. Perrin, 1958. Ed. pub. schs. Acct. W. H. Laidley & Co., investments, Chgo., 1901-05; with Nye & Jenks Grain Co., 1906-11, v.p., dir., 1911-19, dir., 1919-21, pres., 1921; Chgo. dir. grain purchases Washburn Crosby Co., Chgo., 1922-28; Chgo. and Kansas City dir. grain purchases Gen. Mills Inc., Chgo., 1928-36; Mpls. grain purchases and v.p. Gen. Mills Inc., Mpls., 1936-42, exec. v.p., dir., 1942-48, pres., 1948-52, dir., mem. exec. com., from 1952; chmn bd. dirs. Toro Mfg. Corp., from 1959; bd. dirs Donaldson Inc., E. T. Longyear Co. Mem. Minneapolis Club, Minekahda Club, Everglades Club (Palm Beach Fla.), Bath and Tennis Club (Palm Beach), Seminole Club (Palm Beach), Union League (Chgo.). Home Minneapolis Minn. †

PERRY, BERNARD BERENSON, editor, consultant b. Boston, Dec. 16, 1910; s. Ralph Barton and Rachel (Berenson) P.; m. Marian Wynn, Oct. 10, 1941 (div 1947); m. 2d, Elizabeth B. Jennings, Nov. 22, 1947 children: Marjorie Elizabeth, David Jennings, Rachel Berenson. Student, U. N.C., 1932-33; AB, Harvard U. 1934. With W.W. Norton & Co., 1934-35; assoc. editor E.P. Dutton & Co., 1936-40; assoc. editor, sales mgr Vanguard Press, 1940-45; gen. mgr. A.A. Wyn, Inc. 1945-49; founder, dir. Ind. U. Press, Bloomington, 1950-76, cons. editor, from 1976; vis. prof. creative writing U N.Mex., summer 1950; cons. editor W.D. Howells Edit. panelist Nat. Endowment for Humanities, 1978 editorial cons. Univ. Press New Eng.; reader Book-of-the-Month Club. Contbr. chpts. How To Write for Pleasure and Profit, also to N.Y. Times Book Rev. Saturday Rev., Scholarly Pub. Mem. Assn. Am. Univ. Presses (v.p. 1973-74), Harvard clubs of N.Y.C. and Ind., Arts Club, Phi Kappa Sigma. Home: Bloomington Ind. Died Sept. 17, 1985.

PERRY, CHARNER MARQUIS, philosophy educator; b. Franklin, Tex., Mar. 15, 1902; s. William Charner and Ola (Cox) P.; m. Faith Adams, June 10, 1924 (dec.); 1 dau., Alison; m. 2d, Ruth Fuller Sergel, Aug. 5, 1966. BA, U. Tex., 1924, MA, 1925; PhD, U. Chgo. 1926. Instr. philosophy U. Minn., 1926-27; adj. prof philosophy U. Tex., 1927-33; asst. prof. philosophy U. Chgo., 1933-44, assoc. prof., 1944-51, prof., 1951-67, chmn. dept. philosophy, 1948-60; vis. prof. U. Kans., 1969. Editor: The Philosophy of American Democracy, 1943; editor internat. jour. Ethics, 1934-67. Fellow Social Sci. Rsch. Coun., 1931. Mem. Am. Philos. Assn., Quadrangle Club, Cliff Dwellers Club, Phi Beta Kappa. Democrat. Home: Montague Mich. Died Sept. 14, 1985.

PERRY, GEORGE MCDONALD, food company executive; b. Bury, Eng., Nov. 12, 1921; came to U.S., 1923, naturalized, 1929; s. Robert and Rose (McDonald) P.; m. Blenda Cheshire, May 13, 1943 (dec. 1976); children: Jordice, Beth, Robert.; m. Carolyn Varga, Apr. 1982. B.S. in Indsl. Mgmt., U. R.I., 1943; M.S. in Bus. Adminstrn., Columbia U., 1947. Engr. Western Electric Co., N.Y.C., 1947-49; with Gen. Foods Corp., 1949-70; v.p., gen. mgr. Birds Eye, 1966-67, group v.p. food services, 1967-70; pres. Dobbs Life Savers, Inc., N.Y.C., 1970-80; group v.p., dir. Squibb Corp., N.Y.C., 1970-80; gen. partner Kelley Partners Ltd., N.Y.C.; dir. Steak & Shake, Inc., Indpls., Fairmont Products, Inc. Served with USAAF, 1943-46. Mem. Tau Kappa Epsilon. Home: Naples Fla. Died Feb. 15, 1986.

PERRY, MARVIN BANKS, educational publisher; b. Machen, Ga., Apr. 2, 1891; s. Edwin Fletcher and Varina Davis (Banks) P.; m. Elizabeth Mosby Gray, Aug. 16, 1917 (dec. 1951); children: Marvin Banks, John Mosby; m. Nelle Alexander, Sept. 10, 1953. AB, U. Ga., 1912. Tchr. English Univ. Sch. for Boys, Stone Mountain, Ga., 1912-13; acting prin. High Sch., Athens, Ga., 1913-14; So. rep. Am. Book Co., Atlanta, Ga., 1914-19, D.C. Heath & Co., Atlanta, 1919-28; treas. D.C. Heath & Co., Boston, 1928-46, dir., 1936-67, pres., 1946-57, chmn. bd., 1957-60; trustee Newton Savs. Bank; pres. Am. Textbook Pubs. Inst. Trustee Athens Regional Libr., U. Ga. Found. Capt. F.A., U.S. Army, World War I. Mem. U. Ga. Alumni Soc. (pres. 1962-63), Masons, Brae Burn Club (Newton); Algonquin Club (Boston), Athens Country Club, Kappa Sigma. Home: Athens Ga. †

PERRY, ROBERT WILLIAM, educator, mechanical engineer; b. Niagara Falls, N.Y., Apr. 2, 1921; s. Robert William and Marie Elizabeth (Hirschle) P.; m. L. Esther Sheperdson, Apr. 21, 1945 (dec. Mar. 1965); 1 son, Robert William III. B.Mech. Engring., Cornell U., 1943, M.M.E., 1947, Ph.D., 1951. Registered profl. engr., N.Y., Tenn., Ky. Mgr. hypervelocity br. Gas Dynamics Facility, Arnold Engring. Devel. Center, Tullahoma, Tenn., 1953-59; chief hyperaerodynamic research Republic Aviation Corp., Farmingdale, N.Y., 1959-65; prof. aerospace engring. Poly. Inst. Bklyn., 1965-67; sr. staff cons. Liquid Metal Engring. Ctr., Canoga Park, Calif., 1968-70; Disting. prof. mech. engring. U. Louisville, 1971-87; Mem. NASA research adv. com. for fluid mechanics, 1959-60; cons. adv. group for aerospace research and devel. NATO, Brussels, 1966. Mem. ASME (life), Sigma Xi. Home: Louisville Ky. Died July 18, 1987, buried Meml. Park, Niagara Falls, N.Y.

PERRYMAN, RUFUS (SPECKLE RED), popular music piano player; b. Monroe, Va., Oct. 23, 1892; s. Henry Emmit and Ada-Jane (Westmoreland) P.; m. Lade Hunter. June, 1921. Ed. pub. schs., Hampton, Ga. An originator of barrelhouse boogie woogie; composer song Dirty Dozens, 1928, recorded for Bruswick Records, 1928, for RCA Victor, 1932; also recorded for Delmar Records, 1955-57, Storyville Records, 1959;

composer other songs including Right String But Wrong Yo-Yo, 1938; toured throughout country, also concert tour British Isles, 1959; played with St. Louis Jazz Club, 1955. Home: Saint Louis Mo. †

PERSICHETTI, VINCENT, composer; b. Phila., June 6, 1915; s. Vincent R. and Martha (Buch) P.; m. Dorothea Flanagan, June 3, 1941; children—Lauren, Garth. B.Mus., Combs Conservatory Music, 1936; diploma conducting, Curtis Inst., 1939; M.Mus., Phila. Conservatory, 1940, D.Mus., 1945; DH, Bucknell U., Millikin U., State U. Ariz., Combs Coll., Baldwin-Wallace Coll., Peabody Conservatory, Drake U., The New Sch. of Music. Head composition dept. Juilliard Sch. Music, 1947-87; dir. publs. Elkan-Vogel Co., Inc., 1952-87, Theodore Presser Co., Bryn Mawr, Pa., 1971-87; adv. Nat. Endowment for Arts, 1977. Sculptor in marble, granite and wood, 1926-87 ; Compositions include, 12 piano sonatas, 9 symphonies, 4 string quartets, 15 serenades for miscellaneous instruments, 12 band works, 65 songs, 19 choral works, 36 piano works; 27 chamber works Te Deum; The Creation for Chorus & Orch., The Pleiades, Celebrations for Chorus and Wind Ensemble; for chorus and orch. Hymns and Responses for the Church Year, 2 vols., Harmonium Cycle; for soprano and piano; author: 20th Century Harmony: Creative Aspects and Practice. Recipient Juilliard Pub. award, 1943, Blue Network award, 1945, Brandeis U. Creative Arts award, Pa. Gov.'s award, Columbia Records Chamber Music award, Julliard Publ. award; grantee Nat. Inst. Arts and Letters, 1948; medal Italian Govt., 1958; citation Am. Bandmasters Assn., 1964; commns. from Juilliard Music Found., 1948; commns. from Martha Graham Company, 1949; commns. from Louisville Orch., 1950; commns. from Samaroff Found., 1952; commns. from Koussevitzky Found., 1955; commns. from St. Louis Symphony, 1959; commns. from Naumburg Found., 1960; commns. from Lincoln Center, 1962; commns. from N.Y. Philharmonic, 1977; recipient First Kennedy Center Friedheim award, 1978; Medal of Honor Italian Govt.; Guggenheim fellow, 1959, 69, 73. Mem. ASCAP (dir.), Phila. Art Alliance (Medal for Disting. Achievement). Home: Philadelphia Pa. Died Aug. 14, 1987.

PETERKIN, DANIEL, JR., corporate executive; b. Chgo., Mar. 12, 1906; s. Daniel and Jeanette (Knights) P.; m. Bessie Shaw, June 15, 1929 (dec.); children: Joan Peterkin Foxwell, Ann Shaw Peterkin Snyder, Joy Peterkin Rasin; m. 2d, Dorothy P. BS, Princeton U., 1928. Salesman Morton Salt Co. (now div. Morton Thiokol Inc.), 1928, assoc. sales dept., 1928-41, dir., from 1937, v.p., 1938-41, pres., 1941-71; chmn. Can. Salt Co., Ltd., Morton-Norwich Products Inc. (now Morton Thiokol Inc.); pres. Turboflite Inc. subs. French firm Marcel Dissault and French co., SUD Aviation. Trustee Morton Arboretum, Mark Morton Meml. Fund. Mem. Athletic Assn., Mid-day, Tavern, Chicago, Lake Geneva, Country, Cap and Gown clubs. Home: Chicago Ill. Died May 9, 1988.

PETERS, FRANK C., university president; b. Russia, July 5, 1920; s. Cornelius C. and Mrs. (Hildebrandt) P.; m. Melita Krause, Aug. 15, 1943; children: Robert James, Edward Allen, Gerald Franklin, Marianne Joyce, John Wesley. BA, Tabor Coll., 1947; MSc, Kans. State U., 1948; BD, U. W.Ontario, 1950; MTh, Victoria U., 1952; ThD, Cen. Baptist Coll., Kansas City, 1956; PhD, U. Kans., 1959. Instr. psychology Waterloo Coll., 1949-53; pres. Tabor Coll., 1953-56; dean Mennonite Brethren Coll. Arts, 1957-65; prof. psychology Wilfrid Laurier U. (formerly Waterloo (Ont.) Luth. U.), 1965-68, pres., 1968-78, acting dean arts and sci., 1967-68, also vice chancellor. Co-author: History of the Mennonites, 1967, The Compassionate Community, 1969. Mem. Can. Psychol. Assn., Ont. Psychol. Assn., Rotary. Mennonite. Home: Kitchener Ont., Canada. Died Oct. 7, 1987.

PETERS, OLIVER FRANK, shoe manufacturing executive; b. St. Louis, Nov. 16, 1888; s. Henry William and Anna K. (Stoenner) P. LLB, Washington U., St. Louis, 1911; HHD (hon.), John Brown U., 1964. Bar: Mo. 1911. With Peters Shoe Co. (later unit Internat. Shoe Co.), St. Louis, 1907, mgr. collection dept., 1911-12, mgr. collection dept. Peters div. Internat. Shoe Co., 1912-13, asst. mgr. Peters div., 1920-31, bd. dirs., from 1928, v.p., 1931-62, mem. exec. com., 1931-47. With U.S. Army, World War I. Mem. St. Louis City C. of C., St. Louis County C. of C., St. Louis Symphony Soc., Zool. Soc. St. Louis, Mo. Hist. Soc., St. Louis YMCA, Century Club Washington U. Law Sch., Mo. Athletic Club (St. Louis), Kappa Sigma. Republican. Home: Clayton Mo. †

PETERS, RUDOLPH ALBERT, biochemist; b. London, Apr. 13, 1889; s. Albert Edward and Agnes Malvina (Watts) P.; m. Frances W. Vérel, 1917; children: Rudolph Vérel, Francis Raymond. Student, King's Coll., London; MA, Gonville and Caius Coll., Cambridge, Eng., 1914; MD, 1919; MA (by decree), Oxon Coll., 1923; MD (hon.), Liege U., 1950, U. Paris, 1952, U. Amsterdam, 1953; DSc (hon.), U. Cin., 1953, London U., 1954, Leeds U., 1959, Australian Nat. U., 1961; LLD (hon.), Glasgow U., 1963. Dunn lectr., sr. demonstrator biochemistry Cambridge U.; Whitley prof. biochemistry Oxford U., 1923-54, fellow Trinity Coll., 1925-54; past head biochemistry dept. agrl. rsch. council Inst. Animal Physiology, Babraham, Cambridge U.; Dunham lectr., Harvard U., 1946-47, Herman Leo Loeb lectr. St. Louis U., 1947, Christian Herter lectr. NYU, 1947, Croonian lectr. Royal Soc., 1952, Dohme lectr. Sch. Medicine, Johns Hopkins U., 1954; vis. prof. Dalhousie U., Halifax, Can., 1963; mem. Med. Rsch. Council, 1946-50; mem. sci.adv. council Mil. Coll. of Sci., 1947-50, Ministry of Supply, 1950-53. Hon. fellow Trinity Coll., Oxford U., Gonville and Caius Coll. Cambridge U.; recipient Thruston medal, 1918, Royal Soc. medal, 1949, Cameron prize Edinburgh U., 1949, Medal of Freedom with silver palm (U.S.0, 1947. Fellow Royal Soc. London, Royal Soc. Edinbrough, Royal Coll. Physicians, Royal Soc. Pathologists; hon. fellow Royal Soc. Medicine, British Nutrition Soc., Assn. Clin. Biochemists, Biochem. and Phsyiol. Socs., Soc. Philmathique of Paris, Royal Netherlands Acad. Sci. and Letters, Belgian Royal Acad., Accademia Nazionale del Lincei of Rome, Am. Acad. Arts and Scis., Soc. Biol. Chemists, Am. Inst. Nutrition; mem. Conseil Internat. des Unions Scientifiques (pres. 1958-61),. Home: Cambridge England. †

PETERSON, C(ARL) DONALD, state justice; b. Mpls., Feb. 2, 1918; s. Karl Emil and Emma Marie (Sellin) P.; m. Gretchen Elaine Palen, Dec. 6, 1952; children: Barbara Elaine Peterson Burwell, Craig Donald, Mark Bradley, Polly Suzanne Peterson Bowles, Todd Douglas, Scott Jeffrey. B.A. cum laude, U. Minn., 1939; J.D. with honors (mem. Law Rev.), U. Ill., 1941; grad., Appellate Judges Seminar, N.Y. U., 1967, Nat. Coll. State Trial Judges, 1969. Bar: Minn. 1941, U.S. Supreme Ct 1941. Practice in Mpls., 1941-66; partner firm Howard, Peterson, LeFevere, Lefler, Hamilton & Pearson, 1953-66; justice Supreme Ct. Minn., 1967-86; ret. 1986. Contbr. article to Am. Bar Assn. Jour. Co-chmn. task force study creating Nat. News Council, 20th Century Fund, 1972-73; bd. dirs. state youth in govt. project YMCA, 1968-78; Mem. Minn. Ho. Reps., 1959-62, minority whip, 1961-62, Republican nominee for lt. gov., Minn., 1962. Served to maj. USAAF, 1942-45; Served to maj. USAF, 1951-52. Decorated Bronze Star. Mem. ABA, Minn. Bar Assn., Inst. Jud. Adminstrn., Am. Law Inst., Am. Judicature Soc., Minn. News Council (chmn. 1971-81), Am.-Swedish Inst., Delta Sigma Rho. Presbyn. (elder 1963-87, pres. 1964, 79). Clubs: Minnesota (St. Paul); Torske Klubben (Mpls.). Home: Edina Minn. Died Dec. 19, 1987; buried Lakewood Cemetery, Mpls.

PETERSON, DARREL EMIL, textbook publishing company executive; b. Spokane, Feb. 19, 1911; s. Dan Emil and Sarah Ethel (Fenby) P.; m. Katherine Millar, June 5, 1933; children: Karen Peterson Falkner, Richard. BA, U. Wash., 1935. Elem. sch. prin. Naches, Wash., 1930-34; elem. sch. tchr. Spokane, 1934-36; with Scott, Foresman & Co., Chgo., from 1936, v.p., gen. sales mgr., 1959-60, exec. v.p., dir., 1960-64, pres., 1964-70, chmn. bd., chief exec. officer, 1970-76, ret., then dir., from 1976; dir. Madison Bank & Trust Co., Chgo; v.p. Am. Textbook Pubs. Inst., 1965, pres., 1966. Trustee MacMurray Coll., Jacksonville, Ill., 1970. Lt. (s.g.) USNR, World War II. Mem. Western Golf Assn. (dir.), Park Ridge Country Club, Masons. Mem. Community Ch. Home: Bermuda Dunes Calif. Died Mar. 16, 1986.

PETERSON, JOHN MARSHALL, economist, educator; b. Ft. Worth, Jan. 6, 1922; s. Walter Leonard and Elizabeth (Hudson) P.; m. LaVerne Gutteridge, Feb. 1, 1960; children by previous marriage: Wndy Peterson Negley, Rhonda. AB, U. Wash., 1942; MBA, Harvard U., 1947; MA, U. Chgo., 1950, PhD, 1956; economist, U.S. Bur. Labor Stats., 1951-53, TVA, 1953-55. assoc. dir. Indsl. Rsch. and Extension Ctr., U. Ark., Little Rock, 1955-62; prof. U. Ark., Fayetteville, 1962-67; adminstrv. asst. Office Gov. Ark., 1967-70; dean Coll. Bus. Adminstrn., Ohio U., Athens, 1970-79, prof. econs., from 1976. Author: (with Ralph Gray) Economic Development of the United States, 1969, 2d edit., 1974, (with Charles T. Stewart Jr.) Employment Effects of Wage Minimums, 1969, Minimum Wage Measures and Industry Effects, 1981. Mem. Am. Econ. Assn. With AUS, 1943-46. Home: Athens Ohio. Died Apr. 14, 1985.

PETERSON, P(ETER) VICTOR, college president; b. Hampton, Iowa, Feb. 11, 1892; s. Chris and Mary (Jensen) P.; m. Mary Short, June 18, 1919; children: Peter Victor, John Edward, Eleanor. AB, Iowa State Tchrs. Coll., 1917; AM, Stanford U., 1921, PhD, 1930. Supt. schs. Clarksville, Iowa, 1917-18; instr. chemistry Iowa State Tchrs. Coll., 1919-20; instr. chemistry Santa Maria High Sch. and Jr. Coll., 1921-22, prof. chemistry, chmn. natural sci. dept., 1922-47; dean profl. edn. San Jose State Coll., 1946-47; acting pres. L.A. State Coll., 1947-49; pres. Long Beach (Calif.) State Coll., 1949-59. Author: (with Corwin and Corwin) Jr. High Sch. Sci., 1939; various elem. sci. guides pub. by Calif. State Dept. Edn., contbg. staff mem. 1935-36, mem. adv. com., 1934-41. Dir. West Coast Sch. Nature Study; mem. Calif. State com. for study elem. and secondary sci. programs; mem. San Jose Planning Commn., 1936-48, Calif. State Scholarship Commn. With U.S. Army, 1918-19. Mem. Am. Chem. Soc., Long Beach C. of C., YMCA, Rotary, Sigma Xi, Phi Delta Kappa, Delta Sigma Rho, Phi Lambda Upsilon. Home: Long Beach Calif. †

PETERSON, VICTOR HERBERY, association executive; b. Rockford, Ill., Oct. 9, 1916; s. Herbert T. and Mary Olive (Lind) P.; m. Ruth-Elizabeth Colman, Dec. 30, 1939 (div. 1968); children: Sager Lynn, Harriett Vicki, Elizabeth Ann; m. 2d, Sonia d'Ancona, 1968. BA, Beloit Coll., 1938; MA, U. Chgo., 1939. Tchr. pub. schs. Rockford, 1939, Kingsport, Tenn., 1940-42; reporter-photographer Indpls. Times, 1943-50, city editor, 1950-52, asst. mng. editor, 1952-53, mng. editor, 1953-54; mem. pub. relations dept. Socony Mobil Oil Co., Inc., N.Y.C., 1954-57, asst. mgr., 1957-59; asst. mgr. pub. relations dept. Standard-Vacuum Oil Co., White Plains, N.Y., 1959-62; mgr. pub. relations Mobil Petroleum Co., Inc., also Mobil Oil Corp. (formerly Socony Mobil Oil Co., Inc.), 1962-74, mgr. information, 1964-67; dir. pub. relations Hooker Chem. Corp., 1967-69; v.p. pub. relations and edn. Chem. Mfrs. Assn., Washington, 1969-80, v.p. mem. services, from 1981; adj. prof. Am. U., Washington, from 1979; owner PR Counseling (pub. relations firm). Author: MCA 1872-1972, A Centennial History; co-author: Fifty Plus and Holding, The Exercise Prescription for Musculoskeletal Problems. Mem. Deadline, By-line, Circumnavigators, Overseas Press, Nat. Press clubs, Phi Beta Kappa, Sigma Delta Chi, Sigma Alpha Epsilon. Home: Washington D.C. Died June 23, 1986; buried Ferncliff Cemetery, Hartsdale, N.Y.

PETITT, CLIFFORD WALTER, religious organization executive; b. Concordia, Kans., Feb. 7, 1890; s. I.M. and Anna (Garner) P.; m. Ruth Randle, June 14, 1911; children: Clifford Walter, Richard Randle, Philip Emerson. Grad., Concordia Normal Coll., 1908, Salt City Coll. Bus., 1909; student, George Williams Coll., Peking Sch. Chinese Studies, 1918-19. Asst. sec. YMCA, Hutchinson, Kans., 1911-13, fin. sec., LaFayette, Ind., 1913-15, gen. sec., LaPorte, 1915-18; sec. internat. com. YMCA, assigned bus. mgmt., tng. nat. com. YMCA of China, 1918-24, personnel, mgmt., 1926-31; gen. sec. YMCA, Tsingtao, China, 1924-26; bus. sec. West Side YMCA, N.Y.C., 1931-34; exec. dir. Seamens House YMCA, 1934-36; gen. sec. Fgn. YMCA, Shanghai, China, 1936-39; bus. mgr. YMCA N.Y.C., 1939-48; exec. dir. Protestant Coun. N.Y.C., 1948-54; assoc. exec. Puerto Rico YMCA, 1954-55; assisted N.Y. Com. Billy Graham, 1957, Crusade in N.Y., 1956; exec. and sec.-treas. Alliance YMCA N.Am., from 1957. Pres. China Famine Relief, U.S.A., Inc., 1946-52; v.p. United Svc. to China; pres. Internat. Assn. Ret. Secs. YMCA; sec.-treas. Employed Officers Alliance YMCA; chmn. World Svc. Fellowship, Halifax Area Health, Welfare and Recreation Planning Coun.; mem. Overseas Rotary Fellowship; chmn. bd. deacons Riverside Ch., 1947-48. Mem. Shangai Tiffin Club (pres. 1946-46) (N.Y.C.), Rotary. Home: Port Orange Fla. †

PETTERSSON, HANS, oceanographer; b. Hessleröd, Sweden, Aug. 26, 1888; s. Otto and Agnes (Irgens) P.; m. Dagmar Wendel, July 31, 1917; children: Agnes, H. Rutger Irgens. Student, U. Uppsala; DSc, Stockholm U., 1914. Docent oceanography U. Götebörg, 1914-30, prof., 1930-56; dir. Oceanographic Inst., 1939-56; guest prof. U. Hawaii, 1957; leader Swedish Deep Sea Expdn. with the Albatross, 1947-48. Recipient Vega medal, Founder's medal Royal Geog. Soc. London, Joh's Schmidt medal City of Copenhagen, silver medals. Mem. Royal Soc. London (fgn.), Royal Soc. Edinburgh, Vienna Acad. Sci. (corr.). Home: Götebörg Sweden. †

PETTIT, JOSEPH MAYO, college president; b. Rochester, Minn., July 15, 1916; s. Joseph Asahel and Florence (Anderson) P.; m. Florence Rowell West, June 8, 1940; children: Marjorie Pettit Wilbur, Joseph Roy, Marilyn Pettit Backlund. B.S., U. Calif. at Berkeley, 1938; E.E., Stanford, 1940, Ph.D., 1942. Registered profl. engr., Calif. Instr. U. Calif. at Berkeley, 1940-42; spl. research assoc., asst. exec. engr. Radio Research Lab. Harvard U., 1942-45; tech. observer USAF, India-China, 1944; assoc. tech. dir. Am. Brit. Lab., ETO, 1945; supervising engr. Airborne Instruments Lab., Inc., N.Y.C., 1945-46; faculty Stanford U., 1947-72, prof. elec. engring., 1954-72, assoc. dean engring., 1955-58; Stanford U. (Sch. Engring.), 1958-72; pres. Ga. Inst. Tech., Atlanta, 1972-86; Dir. Varian Assocs., Sci. Atlanta, Inc., Ga. Motor Club, Inc.; Mem. Army Sci. Adv. Panel, 1957-63; mem. Nat. Sci. Bd., 1977-82. Author: Electronic Switching, Timing and Pulse Circuits, 1959, 2d edit, (with M.M. McWhorter), 1970, (with others) Very-High-Frequency Techniques, 1947, (with F.E. Terman) Electronic Measurements, 1952, (with McWhorter) Electronic Amplifiers, 1961. Recipient Presdl. Certificate of Merit; Electronics Achievement award IRE. Fellow IEEE (Founders medal 1983), AAAS; mem. Nat. Acad. Engring., Am. Soc. Engring. Edn. (pres. 1972-73), Ga. Acad. Scis. Congregationalist. Clubs: Rotary; University (N.Y.C.); Cosmos. Home: Atlanta Ga. Died Sept. 15, 1986.

PETTIT, KARL DRAVO, investment counsel; b. Pitts., Nov. 6, 1889; s. Clarence and Mary (Dravo) P.; m. Estelle Fitch, Feb. 14, 1914; children: Karl Dravo, Walter Fitch, Anne Elizabeth, William Dutton, Mary Estelle, Barbara Patricia, Samuel Leonard. ME, Cornell U., 1912. With Nat. Cash Register Co., 1912; treas. Thomson, Press & Mfg. Co., 1913-20; pres. Am. Cupter Corp., 1920-29; investment banker, counsel from 1929; sr. ptnr. Karl D. Pettit & Co., investment counsel, N.Y.C., from 1932; chmn. Knickerbocker Shares Inc.,

N.Y.C., from 1938; chmn. Knickerbocker Growth Fund, N.Y.C., from 1952, chmn. emeritus. Mem. Quill and Dagger Soc., University Club (N.Y.C.); Nassau Club (Princeton, N.J.), Chi Phi. Republican. Presbyterian. Home: Princeton N.J. †

PETTY, WILBERT CORNELIUS, foreign service officer; b. Asheville, N.C., Oct. 12, 1928; s. Herman Wakefield and Julia Hattie (Murray) P.; m. Irene Mae Powell, May 30, 1959. BA cum laude, Howard U., 1951; MFA, Cath. U., 1955; postgrad., Universite de Paris, 1955, Inst. Langs., Georgetown U., 1956, UCLA, 1968-69. Tchr. art pub. schs. Washington, 1954-59; with USIA, from 1959; asst. cultural affairs officer Tunis, Tunisia, 1959-60; asst. pub. affairs officer USIS, Conakry, Guinea, 1960-61; cultural affairs officer Dakar, Senegal, 1962-65, pub. affairs officer; 1st sec. Am. embassy, Abidjan, Ivory Coast, 1965-68; cultural affairs officer USIS; 1st sec. Am. embassy, Lagos, Nigeria, 1970-71, Stockholm, 1971-74; spl. asst. Office Pub. Info., USIA, Washington, 1974-76, program officer, Africa area, 1976-78; dir. EEO Office, ICA, Washington, 1978-80; pub. affairs officer ICA Am. embassy, Dakar, Senegal, from 1981; tchr. ceramic sculpture Ecole des Beaux Arts, Dakar, Senegal, Abidjan, Ivory Coast. Trustee, cons. Expt. in Internat. Living; trustee, chmn. bd. Fine Arts Chamber Orch., N.Y.C. With AUS, 1951-53. Decorated Purple Heart, Bronze Star medal; recipient Superior Service award USIA. Mem. NEA, Scabbard and Blade, Alpha Phi Omega. Home: Washington D.C. Died June 13, 1985; buried Washington.

PEYRE, HENRI MAURICE, educator; b. Paris, Feb. 21, 1901; came to U.S., 1925; s. Brice and Marie (Tuvien) P.; m. Diana Festa; 1 son, Brice; stepsons: Sergio McCormick, Marco McCormick, Carlo McCormick. Grad., Ecole Normale Superieure, Paris, 1920, The Sorbonne; doctorate, U. Paris; hon. degrees, Tufts U., Oberlin Coll., Rice U., Middlebury Coll., Rutgers U., others. Mem. faculty French univs., then Bryn Mawr Coll., 1925-28; prof. Yale U., 1928-33, Sterling prof. French, 1938-69, emeritus, from 1969, chmn. dept. romance langs., 1938-69; prof. French lit. Egyptian U., Cairo, 1933-38; disting. prof. French Grad. Center, CUNY, 1969-80; mem. Nat. Commn. on the Humanities, 1963; former bd. dirs. Lycée Français, N.Y.C. Author 14 books including: The Failures of Criticism, 1967, Historical and Critical Essays, 1968, French Novelists of Today, The Contemporary French Novel, Literature and Sincerity, Dostoevsky and French Literary Imagination, 1975, What is Romanticism, 1977; contbr. articles to profl. jours. Decorated Officer Légion d'Honneur, France. Mem. Am. Philos. Soc. Am. Acad. Arts and Scis., MLA (former pres.), Am. Assn. Tchrs. French, Am. Council Learned Socs. (former bd. dirs.). Home: Westport Conn. Died Dec. 9, 1988.

PEYTON, WILLIAM T., medical educator; b. Traverse County, Minn., Jan. 11, 1892; s. Michael and Katherine (Gallagher) P.; m. Clara Krapp, 1920. Student, St. John's U., Collegeville, Minn., 1908-14; BS, U. Minn., 1916, BM, 1918, MD, 1919, AM, 1924, PhD, 1926, PhD in Surgery, 1930. Pvt. practice 1919-22; instr. anatomy U. Minn., 1922-26, instr., fellow in surgery, 1929-30, asst. prof., 1930-34, assoc. prof., 1934-40, dir. div. neurosurgery dept. surgery, from 1937, prof., from 1940. Mem. AMA, Hennepin County Med. Soc., Western Surg. Assn., Minn., Mpls. and St. Paul surg. socs., Minn. Soc. Neurology and Psychiatry, Minn. Path. soc., Am. Bd. neurosurgery, Soc. Neurol. Surgeons, Am. Acad. Neurology, Harvey Cushing Soc. Home: Minneapolis Minn. †

PFEIFFER, CARL CURT, pharmacologist; b. Peoria, Ill., May 19, 1908; s. Curt Richard and Minnie D. (Meiers) P.; m. Lillian H. Twenhofel, June 13, 1930; children: Helen Nancy, Edward Carl. A.B., U. Wis., 1931, A.M., 1933, Ph.D., 1935; M.D., U. Chgo., 1937. Asst. instr. pharmacology U. Wis., 1930-35; instr. pharmacology U. Chgo., 1936-37, 38-40; intern Wis. Gen. Hosp., Madison, 1937-38; asso. prof. pharmacology Wayne U. Coll. Medicine, 1940-41; chief pharmacology Parke Davis & Co., Detroit, 1941-43; prof., head dept. pharmacology U. Ill. Coll. Medicine, Chgo., 1945-54; prof., chmn. dept. pharmacology Emory U., 1954-57, dir. div. basic health scis., 1956-60; head sect. psychopharmacology Bur. Research, N.J. Neuropsychiat. Inst., 1960-74; dir. Brain Bio Center, 1974—. Author articles in med. jours.; former editor: Internat. Rev. Neurobiology. Sec.-treas. N.J. Mental Health Research and Devel. Fund, Inc.; trustee Brain Research Found.; sci. adv. bd. Am. Schizophrenic Assn. Served as lt. USNR; charge pharmcology and toxicology Naval Med. Research Inst. 1943-45, Bethesda, Md. Mem. AMA, Am. Soc. Pharmacol. and Exptl. Therapeutics (pres. 1961-62), Am. Soc. Exptl. Biology and Medicine, AAAS, Am. Chem. Soc. (medinial div.), Acad. Neurology and Biol. Psychiatry, N.Y. Acad. Sci., Assn. Research Nervous and Mental Diseases, Sigma Xi. Office: Princeton N.J. Died Nov. 18, 1988.

PFEIFFER, RICHARD CLAIR, university president; b. Kenton, Ohio, Dec. 12, 1915; s. Henry Albert and Ruth (Borland) P.; m. Jean Elizabeth Homan, Oct. 4, 1941; children: Dan E., Marc A. (dec.), Amy Lou Pfeiffer Turner. BCS, Tiffin U., 1954; LLD, Heidelberg Coll., 1972. Registered pub. acct., Ohio. Jr. acct. W. Leslie King & Co., C.P.A.'s, Cleve., 1940-43; ptnr. Deinzer-Pfeiffer & Co., pub. accts., Tiffin, Ohio, 1946-67; pres. Tiffin U., 1953-81; dir. Tri-County Nat. Bank, Tiffin. Mem. Ohio Adv. Coun. Vocat. Edn., 1974-77. Capt. AUS, 1943-46, 51-52. Mem. Nat., Ohio pub. accts. socs., Ohio Bus. Tchrs. Assn., Am. Assn. Ind. Coll. and Univ. Pres.'s, Am. Legion, Tiffin U. Alumni Assn., Tiffin C. of C. (treas.)., Masons, Shriners, Rotary, Elks. Mem. United Ch. of Christ (moderator Gen. Synod, 1969-71, treas. N.W. Ohio Assn., from 1963). Home: Tiffin Ohio. Died July 14, 1985; buried Fairmont Cemetery, Tiffin.

PFRETZSCHNER, PAUL ALFRED, government educator; b. Pelham Manor, N.Y., Nov. 6, 1922; s. Alfred and Rheta (Isaacs) P.; m. Caroline Putnam, Sept. 3, 1948; children: Margaret B., Susan C., Ellen P. AB, U. Buffalo, 1947; MA, Yale U., 1948; PhD, State U. Iowa, 1953. Faculty govt. Lafayette Coll., Easton, Pa., from 1949, prof., from 1959, chmn. dept. govt. and law, 1960-63, 76-80; Fulbright lectr. U. Dublin, 1963-64; vis. lectr. U. Buffalo, 1948, 56, 60, U. Pa., 1955-56; cons. Pa. Dept. Commerce, 1958-70. Author: Procedural Guide for Planning Commissions, 1960, Capital Improvements Programming, 1961, Community Renewal, 1962, County and Regional Planning, 1963, The Dynamics of Irish Housing, 1965, Political Culture in Ireland, 1976; editor: Mid-Eastern Counties Boroughs Reporter, 1955-60. Impartial chmn. Pa. Blouse Industry, from 1959; commr. Easton Housing Authority, 1957-62, 65-71, Northampton County Park Bd., 1974-82; bd. dirs. Lehigh-Del. Devel. Coun., Easton, chmn., from 1972. With AUS, 1943-46. Mem. Am. Polit. Sci. Assn., Inst. Pub. Adminstrn. (Ireland), Am. Com. for Inst. Studies. Home: Easton Pa. Died Jan. 12, 1986; buried Easton.

PHAUP, BERNARD HUGO, clergyman; b. Farmville, Va., July 17, 1912; s. George Leroy and Minnie (Dunkum) P.; m. Dorothy Mae Foster, Oct. 16, 1935; 1 son, Gary Bernard. Student, Central S.C. Wesleyan Coll., 1930-32; D.D., Houghton Coll., 1961. Ordained to ministry Wesleyan Meth. Ch., 1936; pastor Radford, Va., 1932-35, Charlotte, N.C., 1935-38, 48-53, 81—, Altavista, Va., 1938-41, High Point, N.C., 1941-46, Thomasville, N.C., 1973-81; gen. evangelist, 1946-48; v.p. N.C. Conf. Wesleyan Meth. Ch., 1950-53, pres., 1953-59; gen. supt. Wesleyan Ch., 1959-73, mem. bd. adminstrn., 1955-73, 76-86, chmn. bd., 1959-69, 72-73, chmn. bd. trustees all corp., 1959-69, chmn. commn. world missions, 1959-68, 72-73, chmn. commn. extension and evangelism, 1968-72, supt. Eastern zone, 1959-63, supt. Western zone, 1963-68, 72-73, supt. So. zone, 1968-72; world-wide adminstrv. and preaching ministry, 1962. Chmn. bd. Hephzibah Children's Home, 1959-84; pres. Wesleyan Investment Found., 1968—; bd. dirs. Central Wesleyan Coll., 1976—, Houghton Coll., 1976-80, Kernersville Wesleyan Acad., 1976-80. Home: Charlotte N.C. Died July 18, 1986.

PHEIFFER, WILLIAM TOWNSEND, ambassador, congressman; b. Purcell, Okla., 1898; m. Frances Uihlein, Mar. 20, 1954. Grad., U. Okla., LL.B., 1919. Bar: Okla., Tex., N.Y. Mem. 77th Congress from 16th N.Y. Dist., 1941-43, 16th N.Y. Dist.; U.S. ambassador to Dominican Republic, 1953-57. Mem. Counsel for Petroleum Adminstrn. for War; exec. asst. to chmn. Republican Nat. Com. Served as capt. cav. U.S. Army Res. Corps, World War I, World War II. Recipient award of Merit, World War II. Mem. ABA, Assn. Bar City N.Y., Am. Legion (past post comdr.), Chi Phi, Phi Alpha Delta, Delta Sigma Rho. Unitarian. Clubs: Masons, Metropolitan (N.Y.C.); Everglades, Beach (Palm Beach, Fla.). †

PHELPS, PHELPS, ambassador; b. Bonn, Germany, May 4, 1897; came to U.S., 1899; naturalized, 1910; s. Franz von Rottenburg and Marian (Phelps) P. AB, Williams Coll., 1922; LLB, Fordham U., 1927; LLD, U. Santo Domingo, 1953, St. Peter's Coll., Jersey City, 1975. Dep. state commr. N.Y. State Vets. Relief Commn., 1922-23; mem. N.Y. Assembly, 1924-28, 37-38, N.Y. State Senate, 1939-42; news commentator radio stas. WMCA, WINS and WOVO, N.Y.C., 1935-42; gov. Samoa, 1951-52; ambassador to Dominican Republic, 1952-53. Author: Our Defenses Within and Without, 1932, America on Trial, 1933. Mem. Sch. Bd. Manhattan Borough, N.Y.C., 1949-50, Palisades Interstate Park Commn., N.J., 1956-70; chmn. Am. Com. for Liberation Greek Children, 1950-51; exec. editor Chelsea Clinton News; campaign chmn. Hudson County March Dimes, 1962; del. at large Nat. Urban League Conf., 1963, 64; dir. Chelsea Civic Assn.; appeared on radio and TV to aid Greater N.Y. Fund, United Hosps., Boy Scouts Am. drives; del. Dem. Nat. Conv., 1936, 56, 60, State Conv., 1950, 54,, N.J. State Constl. Conv., 1966. Served as cadet RAF (Can.), 1917-19; capt. AUS, 1942-47. Decorated Order Knight Comdr. of King George I (Greece); recipient George Washington Carver award, 1962, ann. award Urban League Essex County, N.J., 1966. Mem. NAACP, Soc. Colonial Wars, Am. Legion, VFW, Am. Assn. for UN (dir.), Union League Club, University Club, Army-Navy Club, National Capitol Club, Democratic Club, Ahepa Club, Elks (exalted ruler), KP, Eagles, Delta Theta Phi, Psi Upsilon. Home: Wildwood N.J. Died June 10, 1981.

PHILARET, GEORGE VOZNESENSKY, primate Russian Orthodox Church; b. Kursk, Russia, Mar. 22, 1903; came to U.S., 1964; s. Nicholas and Lydia (Vinogradova) Voznesensky. Elec. engr., Russian-Sino Politech. Inst., Harbin, China, 1929; grad. pastoral theol. sch., Harbin, 1931. Ordained priest Russian Orthodox Ch., 1931, took vows of monkhood, 1931, named archimandrite, 1937; consecrated Bishop of Brisbane, Australia, vicar bishop Australian Diocese Russian Orthodox Ch., 1963; elected metropolitan, primate of Russian Orthodox Ch. Outside Russia, 1964. Home: New York N.Y. Died Nov. 21, 1985; buried Holy Trinity Monastery, Jordanville.

PHILBRICK, DONALD WARD, lawyer; b. Skowhegan, Maine, Mar. 16, 1896; s. Samuel White and Mabel Emma (Ward) P.; m. Ruth Lockey, Apr. 17, 1922; children: Donald L., Jean Philbrick Strout, John W. AB, Bowdoin Coll., 1917; LLB, Harvard U., 1922. Bar: Maine 1922. Practiced in Portland from 1922; ptnr. firm Verrill, Dana, Philbrick, Putnam & Williamson, 1924-74; of counsel Verrill & Dana, 1974-84; corporator Maine Savs. Bank. Mem. local SSS Bd., 1940-46; moderator, mem. budget com., charter com,, adv. coun. Town Meeting, 1940-58; chmn. Cape Elizabeth Sch. Com., 1933-39; mem. Bowdoin Alumni Coun.; pres. Pine Tree coun. Boy Scouts Am.; bd. corporators Maine Med. Ctr.; mem. Maine Ho. of Reps. from Cape Elizabeth, 1935-40, speaker, 1939-40; chmn. Maine Office Bldg. Authority; del. Rep. Nat. Conv., 1944, 48, 52; col. gov. Maine staff, 1941-44; chmn. Cumberland County Rep. Com., 1940-46; trustee North Yarmouth Acad.; chmn. bd. dirs. Bowdoin Alumni Fund, Portland Salvation Army; bd. dirs. Assoc. Charities Portland. 1st lt. inf. U.S. Army, 1917-19. Mem. ABA, Maine Bar Assn., Cumberland County Bar Assn. (pres. 1958), Am. Legion, Masons, Lincoln Club (pres.), Exchange Club (pres.), Portland (v.p.), Bowdoin Club (pres.), Phi Beta Kappa, Delta Kappa Epsilon. Died Sept. 1, 1984; buried Southside Cemetery, Showhegan, Maine.

PHILIPS, EDITH, educator; b. Boston, Nov. 3, 1892; d. Jesse Evans and Mary (Durham) P. AB, Goucher Coll., 1913; D, U. Paris, 1922. Mem. faculty Goucher Coll., 1923-31; mem. faculty Swarthmore Coll., from 1931, assoc. prof., 1931-37, prof. French, from 1937, chmn. dept. modern langs., from 1949. Author: Les Refugiés Bonapartistes en Amerique, 1923, The French Legend of the Good Quaker, 1931. Guggenheim fellow, 1928-29. Home: Swarthmore Pa. †

PHILLIPS, ARIS, engineering educator; b. Smyrna, Asia Minoe, Nov. 30, 1915; came to U.S., 1947; naturalized, 1950; s. Herakles and Julia (Stamatiadis) Philppidis.; m. Bessie Barbikas, Nov. 20, 1949; children, John Aristotle, Dean Aris. Diploma in engring., Nat. Tech. U., Athens, Greece, 1937; Dr.Lng. Tech., U. Berlin, 1939; M.A. (hon.), Yale U., 1960. Asst. prof. engring. mechanics Stanford U., 1947-54; mem. faculty Yale U., 1954-85, prof. civil engring., 1960-63, prof. engring. and applied sci., 1963-79, dir. undergrad. studies sect. applied mechanics, 1971-85. Author: Introduction to Plasticity, 1956, Plasticity in Structural Engineering Fundamentals and Applications, 1979, also rsch. papers; editor: Acta Mechanica, 1965-85. Fellow ASME, Conn. Acad. Arts and Scis., Am. Acad. Mechanics, AAAS; mem. Soc. Engring Sci., Am. Soc. Engring. Edn., Sigma Xi. Home: North Haven Conn. Died Aug. 9, 1985.

PHILLIPS, ARTHUR, metallurgy educator; b. Troy, N.Y., Feb. 3, 1892; s. John and Emma (Powell) P.; m. Minnie L. Willis, June 16, 1917. PhB, Yale U., 1913, MS, 1915; DEng, Stevens Inst. Tech., 1944; D honoris causa, U. San Paulo, Brazil, 1944. Metallurgist Bridgeport (Conn.) Brass Co., 1915-19; mem. faculty Yale U., 1919-59, successively asst. prof., assoc. prof., 1919-34, prof. metallurgy, 1934-59, chmn. dept., 1950-59, prof. emeritus, from 1960; cons. metallurgist; bd. dirs. Henry G. Thompson & Son Co., New Haven. Contbr. articles to profl. jours. Home: New Haven Conn. †

PHILLIPS, BURR WENDELL, educator; b. Rock River, Wis., June 14, 1892; s. William Henry and Jessie (Wood) P. Student, U. Chgo., summer 1920; AB, U. Wis., 1921, AM, 1922. Prin. local grade sch., Bear Creek, Wis., 1912; tchr. history and Latin Ripon (Wis.) High Sch., 1913-17; asst. in history U. Wis., 1920-24, instr. history tchr. edn., 1924, asst. prof., 1926-38, assoc. prof., 1938-45, prof., 1945-46, prof. edn. and history, from 1946; mem. edn. study group Office Mil. Govt. for Germany, 1947; mem. social studies cons. U.S. Mil. Govt. in Greater Hesse, 1948, Bavaria, 1949; specialist history and edn. Univs. Greater Hesse, U.S. Dept. State, 1951. Co-editor The Social Studies Program in Wisconsin Schools, 1943; contbr. articles to profl. jours. Mem. NEA, Nat. Coun. for Social Studies (bd. dirs., pres. 19460, Wis. Coun. for Social Studies (bd. dirs.), Am. Hist. Assn., Miss. Valley Hist. Assn. (chmn. and editor tchrs. sect. 1939-42), State Hi.t. Soc. Wis., Phi Beta Kappa, Phi Delta Kappa. Episcopalian. Home: Madison Wis. †

PHILLIPS, BURRILL, composer, educator; b. Omaha, Nov. 9, 1907; s. LeRoy Grey and Anna (Burrill) P.; m. Alberta Mayfield, Nov. 17, 1928; children—Stephen, Ann (Mrs. Robert Basart). Student, Denver Coll.

Music, 1924-28; Mus.B., Eastman Sch. Music, 1932, M.Mus., 1933. Faculty Eastman Sch. Music, 1933-34, faculty theory and composition, 1933-49, vis. prof. composition, 1965-66; prof. music U. Ill., 1949-64, chmn. div. theory and composition, 1957-60; Fulbright lectr. U. Barcelona, Spain, 1960-61; vis. composer East West Center, U. Hawaii, 1965; vis. prof. Juilliard Sch. Music, 1968-69, Cornell U., 1972-73. Compositions include Selections from McGuffey's Reader; suite for orch. Courthouse Square; orch. Play Ball; ballet for stage, orch. American Dance; bassoon, strings String Quartet; Dance Overture; sch. orch. Tom Paine; overture Don't We All; opera buffa The Return of Odysseus; baritone solo, chorus and orch. Soleriana Concertante; Sonata in Two Movements; violin, harpsichord, 1966, That Time May Cease; men's voices, piano, 1966, La Piñata; for dance, commd. by José Limón, 1969, Canzona V; chorus, solo piano Yellowstone, Yates and Yosemite; tenor saxophone, concert band Eve Learns a Little; soprano, piano and 5 wind instruments Huntingdon 2's and 3's; flute, oboe, cello Intrada; for seven instruments Just a Minimal Bite, said Eve; 2 alto saxophones and actress If I Am Persephone; actress, alto saxophone, two pre-recorded tape tracks The Recesses of My House; soprano, clarinet, percussion, piano Scena da Camera; violin and cello Hernan y Marina; soprano and piano Song in a Winter Night, 1981; soprano, flute, clarinet, string quartet, piano Letters from Italy Hill, 1984; woodwind quintet Canzona VI, 1985, for string orch. Imaginary Boundaries, 1986; trio for cello, clarinet and piano; compositions performed by orchs. under Hanson, Stokowski, Thor Johnson, Kubelik, Wallenstein, Reiner, Ormandy, Fennell, Bales, Shaw, Sherman and Slonimsky, Barati, compositions performed by chamber ensembles, Paganini String Quartet, Walden String Quartet, Eastman Piano Quartet, Heritage Piano Quartet, Huntingdon Trio. Recipient Am. Acad. Arts and Letters award 1944, Nat. Endowment for Arts grantee 1976; Fromm Found. commn., 1956-57; Elizabeth Sprague Coolidge Found. commn., 1959; Guggenheim fellow, 1942-43, 61, 62. Mem. ASCAP. Home: Branchport N.Y. Died June 22, 1988; buried Italy Hill, Yates County, N.Y.

PHILLIPS, CHANNING EMERY, clergyman, university administrator; b. Bklyn., Mar. 23, 1928; s. Porter W. and Dorothy A. (Fletcher) P.; m. Jane Celeste Nabors, Dec. 22, 1956; children: Channing Durward, Sheilah Nahketah, Tracy Jane, Jill Celeste, John Emery. Student, U. Utah, 1945-46; A.B., Va. Union U., 1950; M.Div., Colgate Rochester Div. Sch., 1953; postgrad., Drew U., 1953-56. Ordained to ministry United Ch. of Christ 1952. Instr. Howard U., 1956-58; sr. minister Lincoln Temple, Washington, 1961-70; pres. Housing Devel. Corp., 1967-74; v.p. Va. Union U., 1974-75; congl. liaison officer Nat. Endowment for Humanities, Washington, 1978-82; minister planning and coordination Riverside Ch. of N.Y.C., 1982-87. Chmn., D.C. del. Nat. Democratic Conv., 1968; D.C. Dem. Nat. committeeman, 1968-72; Mem. adv. bd. ACLU. Served with USAAF, 1945-47. Mem. Alpha Phi Alpha. Home: New York N.Y. Died Nov. 11, 1987.

PHILLIPS, DAVID ATLEE, lecturer, author; b. Ft. Worth, Oct. 31, 1922; s. Edwin Thomas and Mary Louise (Young) P.; m. Helen Hausman Haasch, June 5, 1948 (div. Dec. 1967); children: Maria, David Atlee, Christopher, Atlee (dec.); m. Virginia Pederson Simmons, Mar. 28, 1969; 1 son, Todd Phillips; stepchildren: Deborah, Bryan, Wynne. Student, William and Mary Coll., 1940-41, Tex. Christian U., 1941-42, U. Chile, 1948-49. Lectr. on Latin Am. 1954-57; propr. David A. Phillips Assocs. (pub. relations), Havana, Cuba, 1958-61; joined U.S. Fgn. Service, 1961; assigned Mexico City, 1961-65, Santo Domingo, 1965-67, Washington, 1968-69; 1st sec. Am. embassy, Rio de Janeiro, Brazil, 1970-72, Caracas, Venezuela, 1972; mem. staff Dept. State, Washington, 1973-75; ret. Dept. State, 1975; lectr. Potomac Lecture Bur., 1975-88. Actor, writer, 1942-48; editor, pub.: South Pacific Mail, Santiago, Chile, 1949-54, Stone Trail Press, 1984-88 . Author, pub.: The Night Watch, 1977, The Carlos Contract, 1978, The Great Texas Murder Trials, 1979, Careers in Secret Operations, 1984, How to Write for Pleasure and Profit in Retirement, 1985, Counterterrorist, 1987; Washington editor Internat. Jour. Intelligence and Counterintelligence, 1986-88. Served with USAAF, 1943-45. Decorated Purple Heart, Air medal. Mem. Assn. Former Intelligence Officers (founder, chmn. bd. 1978-88). Democrat. Club: Tournament Players at Avenel. Home: Bethesda Md. Died July 7, 1988; buried Arlington (Va.) Nat. Cemetery.

PHILLIPS, GUY BERRYMAN, educator; b. Randolph County, N.C., Nov. 26, 1890; s. Jesse Lee and Fannie Polk (Waddell) P.; m. Annie Elizabeth Craig, June 27, 1917; children: Guy, Charles, Craig, Helen, Robert. AB, U. N.C., 1913; spl. student, U. Chgo., 1940; MA, Tchrs. Coll., Columbia U., 1942. Tchr. English Raleigh High Sch., 1913-16; supt. city schs. Oxford, N.C., 1916-20; prin. Greensboro (N.C.) High Sch., 1925-29; supt. city schs. Greensboro, 1924-36; prof. edn., dir. tchrs. placement bur. U. N.C., from 1936, dir. summer session, from 1937, exec. officer Coll. for War Tng., from 1942, dean Sch. Edn., 1948-55, prof. edn. adminstrn., from 1959. Mem., exec. sec. gov.'s com. to study problems Negro edn. in N.C., Gov.'s Commn. on Edn., 1938; dir. orgn. N.C. Sch. Bd. Assn., 1937, exec. sec., from 1937; mem. N.C. State Bd. Edn., from 1958; mem. nat. bd. advisors Boy Scouts Am. Mem. NEA (life), N.C. Edn. Assn. (pub. rels. program dir. 1932-33, pres. 1934-35), So. Assn. Secondary Schs. and Colls. (N.C. secondary commn.), N.C. Conf. for Social Service (chmn. edn. commn., mem. exec. bd.), Greensboro Civitan Club (past pres.), Salisbury Rotary Club (past pres.). Democrat. Methodist. Home: Chapel Hill N.C. †

PHILLIPS, HARRY, judge; b. Watertown, Tenn., July 28, 1909; s. Norman Cates and Bernice (Neal) P.; m. Virginia Major, Nov. 26, 1936; children: Harriet (Mrs. Robert E. Scott), Rachel (Mrs. Sidney S. Eagles, Jr.), Caroline (Mrs. Robert M. Ligon), Martha (Mrs. James M. Robinson). A.B., Cumberland U., 1932, LL.B., 1933, LL.D., 1951. Bar: Tenn. bar 1933. Practiced in Watertown, 1933-37; asst. atty. gen. Tenn., 1937-43, 46-50; mem. firm Phillips, Gullett & Steele (and predecessors), Nashville, 1950-63; exec. sec. Tenn. Code Commn., 1953-63; judge U.S. Ct. of Appeals, 6th Circuit, from 1963, chief judge, 1969-79, sr. judge, from 1979. Author: Phillips' Family History, 1935, Phillips' Prichard on Wills and Administration of Estates, 1955, co-author, rev. edit., 1983, History of Wilson County, Tennessee, 1962, History of the Sixth Circuit, 1976. Served to lt. comdr. USNR, 1943-46. Recipient award of merit Bar Assn. Tenn., 1960. Fellow Am. Bar Found. (hon.); mem. ABA (standing com. fed. jud. improvements from 1978), S.A.R., Order of Coif (hon.), Sigma Alpha Epsilon. Baptist. Clubs: Cumberland (Nashville), University (Cin.); Exchange. Home: Nashville Tenn. Died Aug. 3, 1985; buried Lebanon, Tenn.

PHILLIPS, JAMES PAUL, II, foreign service officer, international communications consultant; b. Jellico, Tenn., July 7, 1927; s. James Paul and Myrtle Edith (Harris) P.; m. Patricia Adelaide Neeld, July 12, 1952; 1 son, Mark Neeld. B.S., U. Tenn., 1948; postgrad. internat. relations, Georgetown U., 1950-51, Am. U., 1955-56. Copy editor Knoxville (Tenn.) News-Sentinel, 1947-48; textbook writer Dept. Navy, 1949-51; social scientist Internat. Info. Adminstrn., 1951-56; info. officer Am. embassy, Mexico, 1957-59, Republic China, 1960-61, Vietnam, 1961-63; spl. asst. to asst. sec. state for internat. orgn. affairs 1963-66; asst. regional dir. III Corps, Vietnam, 1967-69; program officer USIS, India, 1970-71; dir. Office Pub. Info., Dept. State Bur. Ednl. and Cultural Affairs, Washington, 1971-73; dep. dir. USIS, Manila, 1973-77; dir. USICA, Hong Kong, 1977-78; internat. communications cons. Bethesda, Md., 1978-86. Author: Electronic Aids to Navigation, 1949, Naval Search and Fighter-Director Radar, 1950, Electronics Technician, 1951. Bd. govs. Am. Internat. Sch., New Delhi, 1970-71. Served to lt. comdr. USNR, 1945-46. Decorated medal of Honor 1st class, Psychol. Ops. medal Vietnam; recipient Meritorious Honor award USIA, 1970. Mem. U.S. Naval Inst., Am. Fedn. Govt. Employees, Phi Delta Kappa. Unitarian. Home: Rockville Md. Died Oct. 4, 1986.

PHILLIPS, JAY A., business executive; b. Holland, Tex., Mar. 31, 1892; s. James Monroe and Carrie Frances (Williams) P.; m. Edna E. Gilmore, Nov. 26, 1911. Student pub. schs. Mng. ptnr. Phillips, Sheffield, Hopson, Lewis and Luther, Houston, from 1925; bd. dirs. North Tex. Advt. Co., North Tex. Realty Co., Houston Watch Co. Mem. Tex. State Securities Bd., from 1957; pres. Better Bus. Bur.; chmn. bd. trustees Scott & White Meml. Hosp. Temple; bd. dirs., v.p. South Tex. Coll. CPA, Tex., La. Mem. AICPA (pres., mem. coun., trial bd., v.p., chmn. com. on fed. taxation, state legis.), Nat. Conf. Lawyers and CPA's, Am. Acctg. Assn., Tex. Soc. CPA's (pres.), Soc. La. CPA's, Assn. CPA Examiners (pres.), Houston C. of C. (bd. dirs.), Houston Club (pres. 12 yrs.), Houston Country Club, Westwood Country Club, Romada Club, Petroleum Club, Austin Club, Downtown Club (Dallas), Kiwanis (pres.). Home: Houston Tex. †

PHILLIPS, RICHARD IDLER, government official; b. Artesia, N.Mex., Apr. 2, 1911; s. Edward F. and Florence (Idler) P.; m. Irene Shields, Feb. 7, 1942 (dec. July 1964); m. 2d, Katherine H. Mayberry, Apr. 23, 1965. Student, U. Nebr., 1928-29; AB, U. So. Calif., 1932, JD, 1934. Bar: Calif. 1934. Practiced in Los Angeles 1934-36; auditor Singer Sewing Machine Co., Buenos Aires, Argentina, 1936-38; ptnr. law firm Marval, Rodriguez, Larreta & O'Farrell, Buenos Aires, 1938-41; exec. sec. Coordination Com. of Uruguay, Montevideo, 1941-46; 2d sec. Am. embassy, Montevideo, 1946-48, Caracas, Venezuela, 1948-51; adviser U.S. del. to UN, 1951-52; consul, Nairobi, Kenya, 1952-54; adviser Bur. Inter-Am. Affairs, Dept. State, 1954-57, 58-61; consul, Guadalajara, Mexico, 1957-58; spl. asst. Bur. Pub. Affairs, 1962-63; dir. Office News, 1963-64, dep. asst. sec. state for pub. affairs, 1964-69, acting asst. sec. state for pub. affairs, 1969-70; consul gen., Monterrey, Mexico, 1970-71; indsl. community relations adviser Nat. Inst. on Alcohol Abuse and Alcoholism, Dept. Health, Edn. and Welfare, Washington, from 1972. Treas. Am. Theater, Buenos Aires. Recipient disting. honor award, 1969, Meritorious Service award, 1966. Mem. Calif. Bar Assn., Am. Fgn. Service Assn., Dacor, Rotarian, American (treas. Buenos Aires 1940-41) clubs, Phi Beta Kappa, Sigma Nu. Home: Washington D.C. Died June 28, 1985; body donated to sci.

PHILLIPS, SAMUEL J., corporation executive; b. North Vandergrift, Pa., Sept. 17, 1931; s. Samuel and Margaret (Solomon) P.; m. Matina Fidanis, Jan. 28, 1953; children: Diana M., Samuel T., Candice A., Tracy L., Daniel J. B.S., U. Md., 1953; M.B.A., Xavier U., 1960; LL.D. (hon.), Franconia Coll., 1978. With Procter & Gamble Co., Cin., 1956-67; mgr. cost acctg. dept., food products div. Procter & Gamble Co., 1964-65; controller, chief fin. officer Folger Coffee Co. div., Kansas City, Mo., 1965-67; controller film div. Polaroid Corp., Waltham, Mass., 1967-69; group controller Polaroid Corp., Cambridge, Mass., 1969-70; v.p. ops. Parkwood Laminates, Inc., Lowell, Mass., 1971-74; pres. Parkwood Laminates, Inc., 1972-74; pres., chmn. Acton Corp., Mass., 1975-82, chmn., 1975-85; pres., chmn. Beltran Corp., 1982-85, First Phillips Corp., 1980-85; chmn. The Robb Report, 1983-85; dir. Phillips Corp., College Park, Md. Trustee Cin. Summer Opera, 1964-65; chmn. exec. com., trustee Franconia (N.H.) Coll., 1976-78; trustee N.H. Coll., Manchester, 1979-85, Phillips Found., Annapolis, Md. Served to 1st. lt. U.S. Army, 1953-56. Recipient Kansas City Boy Scout award for community service, 1966, M.B.A. Exec. Achievement award Xavier U., 1981, medal for Top 100 Growth Cos. Commonwealth of Mass., 1980, 81. Died Nov. 17, 1985.

PHILLIPS, SEYMOUR, apparel manufacturing company executive; b. 1903; m. B.A., Columbia U., 1924. With Phillips Van Heusen Corp., from 1924, pres., chief exec. officer, 1938-68, chmn. bd., chief exec. officer, 1968-71, chmn. bd., dir., 1971-87. Home: Manhattan, N.Y. Died Jan. 16, 1987. Home: New York N.Y.

PHILLIPS, WAYNE, government official; b. Waltham, Mass., June 11, 1925; s. Arthur J. and Evalyn (Hill) P.; m. Sybil Marion Wittstein, Aug. 25, 1962; children: Patricia Jayne, Ruth Evalyn, Kathleen Mildred. AB, Harvard U., 1948; MS in Journalism, Columbia U., 1949; MA in History, cert., Russian Inst., 1953. Reporter Denver Post, 1949-51, N.Y. Times, 1951-61; spl. asst. to adminstr. HHFA, 1961-64; dir. news and info. Dem. Nat. Com., 1964-66; dir. pub. affairs HUD, 1966; pub. Sybilline mag., 1947-48; tchr. journalism U. Denver, 1950-61, Columbia U., 1954-61; pub. Sybilline mag., 1947-48. Contbr. articles to mags. 2d v.p. N.Y. Newspaper Guild, 1960-61. With USNR, 1943-45. Recipient Page One award, 1959. Mem. Am. Newspaper Guild, Capital Press Club. Home: Reston Va. Died Sept. 5, 1988.

PHLEGER, HERMAN, lawyer; b. Sacramento, Sept. 5, 1890; s. Charles W. and Mary (McCrory) P.; m. Mary Elena Macondray, Apr. 2, 1921; children: Mary Elena Phleger Goodan, Atherton Macondray, Anne Phleger Gates. BS, U. Calif., 1912; postgrad., Harvard Law Sch., 1913-14; LLD, Mills Coll., 1935, U. Calif., 1957. Ptnr. Brobeck, Phleger & Harrison, San Francisco; legal adv. Dept. State, 1953-57; dir. Moore Dry Dock Co., various other cos.; mem. U.S. del. Inter-Am. Conf., Caracas, 1954, Indo-China and China confs., 1954, Summit, Fgn. Ministers confs., Geneva, 1955, Suez Conf., London, 1956, Bermuda Conf., 1957; U.S. mem. Permanent Ct. Arbitration under Hague Treaties, 1957-63, 70-76; U.S. rep. 13th UN Gen. Assembly, 1958; chmn. U.S. del. with rank of ambassador, chmn. Antarctica Conf., Washington, 1959; mem. gen. adv. com. U.S. Arms Control and Disarmament Agy., 1960-68. Trustee Stanford U., 1944-64, emeritus, from 1964; trustee William G. Irwin Charity Found. (both San Francisco). Lt. USN, 1917-18; assoc. dir. legal div. Office Mil. Gov. (Germany), 1945. Fellow ABA; mem. Coun. Fgn. Relations, Am. Soc. Internat. Law, Internat. Law Soc., Pacific Union Club, Bohemian Club, Burlingame Country, Links, Metropolitan Club. Home: Redwood City Calif. Died Nov. 21, 1984; buried Cypress Lawn Cemetery, Colma, Calif.

PICARD, ROBERT (GEORGE), psychologist; b. Edmonton, Alta., Can., Mar. 27, 1905; s. Joseph Henri and Martine (Voyer) P. B.A., Xavier Coll., Edmonton; Ph.D., Immaculate-Conception Coll., Montreal, Que., Can., 1929; Ph.D. Diploma, Inst. Psychology, Sorbonne, U. Paris, 1940. Joined S.J., Roman, 1923; prof. psychology Immaculate-Conception Coll., 1940-70, rector, 1957-63; prof. U. Montreal (Ecole Normale), 1941-57, Institut de Psychologie, 1948-57; editor Education et Societe, Montreal, 1970-75; pres. Editions Bellarmin, Montreal, 1976-78; ret. 1978. Contbr. articles to profl. jours. Mem. Am. Psychol. Assn., Am. Anthropl. Assn. Home: Montreal Que., Canada. Died 4 Sept. 1987; buried Jesuit Cemetery, St. Jerome, Que.

PICCIONI, ATTILIO, diplomat; b. Italy, 1892. Ed. univs., Rome, Turin. Mcpl. councillor City of Turin, 1920-23; retired from pub. life during fascist regim; organizer Christian Dem. Party, Tuscany, 1943, later pres.; with Ministry of Justice; then Ministry for Fgn. Affairs; v.p. Council of Ministers, Rome, 1960-62; minister fgn. affairs Council of Ministers, 1962-63; minister of state without portfolio 1963. Home: Rome Italy. †

PICKRELL, KENNETH LEROY, plastic surgeon; b. Old Forge, Pa., June 6, 1910; s. Thomas and Anna May

(Williams) P.; m. Katharine Council, June 11, 1935; children: Judith, Katharine Lee, Anna May, Elizabeth. BS, Franklin and Marshall Coll., 1931; MD, Johns Hopkins, 1935. Diplomate Am. Bd. Plastic Surgery (chmn. 1962-63), Am. Bd. Surgery. Fellow surgery Johns Hopkins Hosp., 1935-36, instr. pathology, neurosurgery, plastic surgery, gen. surgery, assoc. surgery, 1936-44; asst. prof. plastic surgery Duke Sch. Medicine and Hosp., 1944-46, assoc. prof. plastic surgery, 1946-50, prof. plastic and reconstructive surgery, from 1950; cons. plastic surgeon Va. hosps., Durham, Fayetteville, N.C., Womack Army Hosp., Ft. Bragg, N.C. Contbr. sect. Sabiston's Textbook of Surgery, 1981; also numerous articles to surg. jours., chpts. to books. Fellow ACS, So. Surg. Assn.; mem. Soc. Univ. Surgeons, Soc. Univ. Profs., Am. Soc. Surgery Hand, Am. Soc. Plastic and Reconstructive Surgery (pres. 1960), Am. Assn. Plastic Surgeons, Am. Surg. Assn., Internat. Soc. Surgery, Japanese Soc. Plastic Surgeons. Home: Durham N.C. Died Aug. 20, 1987; body donated to Duke U. Med. Ctr.

PIECZENTKOWSKI, HERMAN ARNOLD, naval officer, engineering and construction company executive; b. Auburn, R.I., May 28, 1907; s. Albert George and Hulda (Sealander) P.; B.S., U.S. Naval Acad., 1930; M.S., MIT, 1940; postgrad. U.S. Naval War Coll., 1949-50; m. Helen Van Horn Herron, June 2, 1934; children—Peter Arnold, Marshall Albert. Commd. ensign USN, 1930, advanced through grades to rear adm., 1957; dir. torpedo research U.S. Naval Torpedo Sta., Newport, R.I., 1943-45; head ordnance dept. Naval Postgrad. Sch., 1950-52; comdg. officer USS Sturgeon, comdr. Sub Div. 72, Submarine Squadron 5; comdg. officer USS Hamul, comdr. Destroyer Squadron II, 1955-57, ret., 1957; staff asst. to v.p., mgr. bus. devel. Bechtel Power Corp., San Francisco, 1957-75; bus. cons., 1975-79. Decorated Silver Star, Bronze Star. Mem. U.S. Naval Acad., Mass. Inst. Tech. alumni assns., Submarine Vets World War II. Home: Coronado, Calif. Died July 31, 1985; cremated.

PIERCE, ANNE E(LISE), music educator; b. Saginaw, Mich., Mar. 14, 1892; s. Clifton J. and Minnie C. (Pierson) P. B.Mus., Am. Conservatory Music, 1926, M.Mus., 1928, MusD, 1960; BA, State U. Iowa, 1927; MA, Columbia, 1930; studied voice with Karlton Hackett, albert V. Jeannotte, Herbert Witherspoon, Frank La Forge, Estelle Liebling, studied musical theory with Peter C. Lutkin, Adolph Weidig, John Palmer. Profl. singer, voice tchr. 1914-26; prof. voice Cornell Coll. Conservatory Music, Mt. Vernon, Iowa, 1919-23; asst. prof. music, head music Univ. Schs. U. Iowa, 1926-39, prof. music, from 1939; vis. prof. music edn. Northwestern U., summers 1938-46; specialist music Nat. Survey Secondary Edn., 1932. Author: Discriminative Listening Lessons in Music Grades I-VI, 1927; (with Robert S. Hilton) Instruction in Music and Art, 1933; (with Sarah T. Barrows) The Voice: How to Use It, rev. edit., 1938; Class Lessons in Singing, 1937, Music of the United Nations, 1945, Collection of Choral Music, 1947, A Christmas Program for the Elementary School, Music for American Children, 1958, Teaching Music in the Elementary School, 1959; contbr. articles to yearbooks, mags., encys. Mem. AAUW, AAUP, Music Tchrs. Nat. Assn., Music Educators Nat. Conf. (sec. rsch. coun. 1934-48), Nat. Soc. Study Edn. (yearbook com.), Nat. Assn. Tchrs. Singing, Phi Beta Kappa, Pi Lambda Theta, Alpha Xi Delta. Episcopalian. Home: Iowa City Iowa. †

PIERCE, CLAYTON BAXTER, lawyer; b. Kansas City, Mo., Oct. 27, 1889; s. Charles Melvin and Maggie Ellen (Chalfant) P.; m. Gladys Fay Means, Jan, 11, 1918. Student, Baker U., 1907-12, LLB, 1914. Bar: Mo., 1914, Okla. 1922. Supt. schs. Merriam, Kans., 1912-14; practiced in Kansas City, 1914-17, Tulsa, 1922-25; sr. ptnr. Pierce, Duncan Couch & Hendrickson, Oklahoma City, from 1925; counsel Okla. Farm Bur., from 1948. Capt. F.A. U.S. Army, 1917-20, ETO. Mem. Internat. Assn. Ins. Counsel, ABA, Okla. Bar. Assn. (pres. 1938), ACLU (bd. dirs. 1965-68), Delta Theta Phi, Masons. Unitarian (pres. ch. 1949-56). Home: Oklahoma City Okla. †

PIERCE, DAREN LAINE, textile and interior designer; b. Lebanon, Oreg., May 23, 1922; s. Frederick Franklin and Frances Alice (Frum) P. Student, Wolfe Sch. Costume Design, Los Angeles, 1940-41, U. Oreg., 1941-42. Textile designer Dorothy Liebes Textiles, San Francisco, 1945-48; interior designer William Pahlmann Assocs., Inc., N.Y.C., 1948-64; pres., designer Woolworks, Inc., N.Y.C., from 1964; designer Edward Fields Carpets, N.Y.C., Philip Graf Wallpapers, N.Y.C., Eaglesham Fabrics, N.Y.C.; bd. dirs. Franciscan Fabrics, San Francisco. Author cookbooks and design publs. Fellow Am. Soc. Interior Designers; mem. Indian Inst. Interior Designers (hon.). Republican. Home: New York N.Y. Died Jan. 24, 1984; buried Sandridge Cemetery, Lebanon, Oreg.

PIERCE, TRUMAN MITCHELL, university dean; b. Equality, Ala., Apr. 25, 1906; s. Willie Mitchell and Martha Temple (Nolan) P.; m. Lucille Lawson, July 2, 1930; 1 child, Martha Jean Pierce Williams. PhB, Piedmont Coll., 1926; MA, U. Ala., 1938; PhD, Columbia U. Pub. sch. tchr., sch. adminstr. Ala., 1928-44; dean Troy State Coll., 1946-47; prof. edn. U. Tenn., 1947-50; prof. edn., dir. So. states program ednl. adminstrn. Peabody Coll., 1950-55; dir. assocs. programs ednl. adminstrn. Auburn U., 1955-60, dean Sch. Edn., from 1955, dean emeritus, pres. univ. council ednl. adminstrn., 1960-62; assoc. exec. sec. So. State Work Conf., 1952; exec. com. Am. Assn. State Univs. and Grant Colls., 1961-64; pres. bd. Southeastern Edn. Lab., 1966-86. Author: Federal, State and Local Government in Education; Controllable Community Characterisitics Related to the Quality of Education, 1946; co-author: Community Leadership for Public Education, 1955, White and Negro Schools in the South, 1955, Public School Administration, 2d edit., 1961, A Profession in Transition, 1960, Public Higher Education in Tennessee, 1957, The West Virginia Board of Education, 1961; mem. editorial bd. School Executive, 1953-58. Home: Auburn Ala. Died June 8., 1986.

PIEROTTI, JOHN, cartoonist; b. N.Y.C., July 26, 1911; s. Roger and Emily (Brucato) P.; m. Helen Mastrangelo, June 5, 1938 (dec.); children—Melba, John, Pamela; m. Orla Smith Pierotti. Student, Mechanics Art Inst., 1930, Cooper Union, 1931, Art Students League, 1932-33. Copy boy, illustrator, sports, news cartoons, portraits N.Y. Telegram, 1927; engaged in drawing for N.E.A. Syndicate, Sporting News, St. Louis; advt. for Gen. Foods; sports cartoonist Washington Post, 1933; sports editor 1943; sports cartoonist N.Y. Star (successor to PM), 1948-49; sports editor, cartoonist McClure Syndicate, 1949-51; sports, cartoonist N.Y. Post, from 1951. Artist: comic strip Hippo and Hookie, King Features Syndicate, 1939; staff cartoonist comic strip, N.Y. daily PM, 1940; syndicated own strip: Nutcracker U, 1950; illustrator children's, sports, polit. books. (Recipient nat. recognition for portrait Georges Clemenceau 1928, 2d prize award for best editorial cartoon Los Angeles Pub. Assn. 1955, Page One award for best sports cartoon Graphic Arts 1955, Silurian award for best editorial cartoon 1965, 67, 68, 71, 72, Page One award for best sports cartoon 1965, for best editorial cartoon 1967, 68, 70, 71, 72, 73, 75); Contbr. cartoons to popular mags., U.S., Can., Gt. Britain, France, S.Am.; movie animation work Popeye and Betty Boop, N.Y.C., 1936-37; joined movie animation work, United Features Syndicate, 1937. Mem. Nat. Cartoonists Soc. (pres. 1957-59, named Best Editorial cartoonist 1975), Baseball Writers Assn., Banshees Artists and Writers Assn., Newspaper Reporters Assn. N.Y.C., U.S. Harness Writers Assn. (pres. N.Y. chpt.). Home: Brigantine N.J. Died May 6, 1987.

PIGEON, LOUIS PHILLIPE, law educator, judge; b. Henryville, Que., Can, Feb. 8, 1905; s. Arthur and Maria (Demers) P.; m. Madeleine Gaudry, Aug. 29, 1936; children: Jacques, Madeleine, Louise, Francois, Yves, Michel. BA, Petit Seminaire de Que., 1925; LLB, Laval U., 1928, LLD; LLD, U. Ottawa. Bar: Que., 1928; created queen's counsel, 1940. Assoc. St. Laurent, Gagne, Devlin & Taschereau, 1928-37; ptnr. Hudon and Pigeon, 1938-40, Germain, Pigeon, Thibedeau & Lesage, 1946-67; law clk. Legis. of Que., 1940-44; justice Supreme Ct. Can., Ottawa, 1967-80; prof. constl. law Laval U., 9142-67; prof. civil law U. Ottawa, 1980-86; legal adviser prime minister Que., 1960-66; batonnier Dist. Que., 1960-61; chmn. Nat. Council Adminstrn. Justice, 1963-67; v.p Conf. Commrs. Uniformity Legis. in Can., 1966-67; chmn. Nat. Profl. Conduct Com., 1966-67. Mem. Can. Bar Assn. (v.p. Province Que. 1965-66), Rideau Club (Ottawa), Cercle Universitaire (Que.). Roman Catholic. Died Feb. 23, 1986.

PILAT, OLIVER, newspaperman; b. N.Y.C., Aug. 7, 1903; s. Oliver I. and Emma (Ramsay) P.; m. Avice Riddle, Apr. 11, 1930; children: Carl Jeffrey, Betsy. B.A., Amherst Coll., 1926. With Bklyn. Eagle, 1926-36, European corr., 1930-34; with New York Post, 1937-65, Washington corr., 1943-49; polit. reporter New York Post, N.Y.C., 1949-65; asst. to Mayor Lindsay, N.Y.C., 1966-67; asst. to council Pres. Garelik, N.Y.C., 1970-71; writer-in-residence New Sch. for Social Research, 1974-79. Author: Sea-Mary, 1936, The Mate Takes Her Home, 1939, (with Jo Ranson) Sodom by the Sea, 1942, The Atom Spies, 1952, Pegler: Angry Man of the Press, 1963, Lindsay's Campaign, 1968, Drew Pearson: An Unauthorized Biography, 1973. Vice chmn. N.Y. County Liberal party, 1974-78. Mem. Authors Guild, Inner Circle, P.E.N., N.Y. Newspaper Guild (pres. 1965), Silurians (pres. 1972), Phi Beta Kappa, Phi Gamma Delta. Home: New York N.Y. Died July 21, 1987.

PILCH, JUDAH, religion educator, author; b. Kiev, Ukraine, USSR, Sept. 8, 1902; came to U.S., 1923, naturalized, 1928.; s. Joesph H. and Batsheba (Milstein) P.; m. Bernice Shapery, June 24, 1933; children: Yosef Hayim, Ben-Zion. BS, Lewis Inst., Chgo., 1932; MA, Columbia U., 1946; PhD, Dropsie U., 1951; D Jewish Lit. (hon.), Jewish People's Sem. and People's U., 1978. Lectr. Coll. Jewish Studies, Chgo., 1929-39; ednl. dir. Jewish Edn. Assn., Rochester, N.Y., 1939-44; dist. cons. Jewish Edn. Com., N.Y., 1944-49; exec. dir. Am. Assn. Jewish Edn., 1949-60; lectr. edn. NYU, Dropsie Coll., 1959-64. Author: Jewish Life in Our Times, 1943, Teaching Modern Jewish Histry, 1948; editor: Jewish Educations Register and Directory, Vol. 1, 1951, Vol. 2, 1959, Vol. 3, 1965, Readings in Jewish Educational Philosophy, 1960, The Contemporary Jewish Scene, 2 vols., 1962, The Nazi Holocaust, 1967, A History of Jewish Education in the United States, 1969, The Weak Against the Strong, 1973, Between Two Generations, 1977, Yalkut, 1979; co-editor: Judaism and the Jewish School, 1966, The Jewish Catastrophe in Europe, 1968; mem. editorial bd. Jewish Edn. jour., The Reconstructionist mag. Pres. Nat. Council Jewish Edn., 1948-50, Nat. Conf. Jewish Social Service, 1954-55; v.p. Religious Edn. Assn. U.S. and Can., 1952-59, chmn. exec. com., 1959-62; chmn. Nat. Bible Contest Com., 1958-60. Recipient Alumni citation Dropsie Coll., 1957, 50 Yr. citation Hebrew Union Coll., 1978. Mem. Acad. Religion and Mental Health, Soc. Sci. Study of Religion, Histadrut Ivrit Am. Home: Los Angeles Calif. Died Jan. 29, 1986, buried Los Angeles.

PILLAI, K.C. SREEDHARAN, statistician, educator; b. Veliyanadu, Kerala, India, Feb. 24, 1920; came to U.S., 1962, naturalized, permanent resident, 1966; s. K. Padmanabhan and Kutti (Amma) P.; m. L. Kamalakshi Amma, Aug., 1941; children: Mohanan, Anandan, Sudha. BS, Kerala U., 1941, MS, 1945; postgrad., Princeton U., 1951-52; PhD, U. N.C., 1954. Research scholar, dept. stats. Kerala U., 1941-45, lectr., 1945-51; research asst. Princeton U., 1951-52; research assoc. U. N.C., 1952-53; asst. statistician UN, N.Y.C., 1954-55, statistician, 1960-62, later sr. stats. adviser; prof. depts. math. and stats. Purdue U., West Lafayette, Ind., 1962-85; vis. prof. stats. U. Philippines, Manila, 1956-59. Author 2 books, numerous research papers and articles. NSF grantee Aerospace Research Labs., USAF. Fellow Inst. Math. Stats., Am. Statis. Assn.; mem. Internat. Statis. Inst., Biometric Soc., Phillipine Statis. Assn. (life). Hindu. Home: West Lafayette Ind. Died June 5, 1985, cremated.

PILPEL, ROBERT, organization executive; b. N.Y.C., Mar. 27, 1905; s. Emanuel and Cècile (Meyer) P.; m. Harriet F. Fleischl, June 15, 1933; children—Judith E. Pilpel Appelbaum, Robert H. Student, Ethical Culture Schs., 1910-22, Reed Coll., 1922-23; A.B., Harvard, 1926; LL.B., N.Y. Law School, 1931. Bar: N.Y. bar 1932. Pvt. practice N.Y.C., 1932-39; exec. asst., gen. counsel Am. Jewish Joint Distbn. Com., Inc., 1939-52; exec. sec. Am. Booksellers Assn., 1952-53; v.p. Robert Joseph & Co., Inc. (indsl. real estate), 1953-63; asst. to exec. dir. Hudson Guild Neighborhood House, 1963-68; cons. div. on aging Fedn. Protestant Welfare Agys., 1968-71; asst. to pres. Nat. Assn. on Drug Abuse Problems, Inc., 1974-87. Bd. govs. Ethical Culture Schs., 1933-51; trustee Ednl. Alliance, N.Y.C., 1949-87 ; Vice pres. Central Bur. for Jewish Aged, Inc. Home: New York N.Y. Died July 7, 1987; buried Mt. Pleasant, Westchester County, N.Y.

PINAY, ANTOINE, government official; b. Saint-Symphorien-sur-Coise, Dec. 30, 1891. Hon. pres. Syndicat des Cuirs et Peaux du Rhone; mayor St.-Chamond, 1929; gen. counsel Canton of Loire, 1934, dep., 1936-38, from 1951, senator; v.p. Dem. Alliance, 1938-40; sec. of state for econ. affairs, Queuille cabinet Govt. of France, 1948, minister of pub. works and transp., Pleven cabinet, 1950, 51, Queuille cabinet, 1951, with Faure cabinet, 1952, pres. coun. of ministers, minister fin. and econ. affairs, 1952, minister fgn. affairs, Faure cabinet, 1955, minister of fin. and econ. affairs, 1958-60. Recipient Croix de l'Ordre Royal de Daneborg, Grand Cordon de l'Ordre de leopold, Grand Crox du Nissam Alaouite, Medaille Militaire, Croix de Guerre, 1914-18, grand croix d'Isabella Catholique, de Cruzeiro do Sul, de Mérite de l'Ordre du malta, de l'Ordre Royal du Cambridge, comdr. de Mérite Touristique, du Mérite Agricole, de l'Ordre de l'Economie Nat. Home: Paris France. †

PIPER, MARTHA KIME, academic administrator; b. Salem, Va., June 11, 1931; d. Robert Sagendorf and Katharine Walker Kime; m. Joseph Henry Piper, Apr. 26, 195 (div. 1963); children: Mark, Penna. BA, Elmhurst Coll., 1960; MS, U. Kans., 1969; PhD, U. Tex., 1973. Dir. elementary sci. project Shawnee Pub. Schs., Overland Park, Kans., 1968-72; prof. U. Houston, Univ. Park, Victoria, Tex., 1974-79; dir. acad. affairs U. Houston, 1979-80, chair faculty senate, 1980, spl. asst. to pres. for acad. affairs, 1981; chancellor U. Houston, Victoria, 1981-86; pres. Winthrop Coll., Rock Hill, S.C., from 1986; trustee Roanoke Coll., Salem, Va., 1980—. Author: Teaching Science: A Handbook for Elementary Teachers, 1976; editor, researcher: Attitudes Toward Science: Investigations, 1977; also 20 pub. articles. Trustee Roanoke Coll., Salem, Va., from 1980; bd. dirs. Bach Bd., Victoria, 1983-85, Mus. Bd., Victoria, 1983-85, Victoria Savs., 1983-85, Regional Med. Ctr., Victoria, 1983-85; v.p. Victoria C. of C., 1983-85. Recipient Leadership award Phi Delta Kappa, Houston, 1976, Outstanding Woman award YWCA, Houston, 1980. Mem. Am. Assn. Colls. and Univs., Am. Council on Edn., DAR (Catawba chpt.), Phi Kappa Phi. Home: Rock Hill S.C. Deceased.

PIPER, OTTO ALFRED, theologian, educator; b. Lichte, Germany, Nov. 29, 1891; came to U.S., 1937; naturalized, 1942; s. Moritz and Julie (Naveau); m. Elizabeth A. Salinger, Apr. 14, 1920 (dec. 1948); children: Ruth M. White, Manfred K., Gero K. (Dec. 1944); m. 2d, Elisabeth J. Rueger, Aug. 24, 1950. Th.D., U. Goettingen, Germany, 1920; D.D., Faculté Libre, Paris, France, 1928; LLD, Wittenberg U., 1949. Mem. faculty U. Goettingen, Germany, 1920-30, assoc. prof. systematic theology, 1928-30; prof. systematic theology U. Muenster, Germany, 1930-33; expelled by Hitler 1933; fellow Woodbrooke Coll., Eng., 1933-34; guest prof. U. Wales, Swansea Coll., 1934-36, U. Wales, Bangor Coll., 1936-37; vis. prof. Princeton Theol. Sem., 1937-41, Helen P. Manson prof. N.T. lit. and exegesis, 1941-62, prof. emeritus; vis. lect. U. Heidelberg, 1950, U. Sao Paulo (Brazil), 1953, Presbyn. Sem., Campinas, Brazil, 1957, Theol. faculty, Montpellier, France, U. Muenster, 1958, Union Coll., U. Vancouver (B.C.), 1960, Bibl. Sem., N.Y.C., 1962, 64, New Brunswick Theol. Sem., 1963; Croall lectr. U. Edinburgh, 1935; Stone lectr. Princeton Theol. Sem., 1938; Smyth lectr. Columbia Sem., Decatur, Ga., 1949; Sprunt lectr. Union Sem., Richmond, Va., 1959; with Luth. Theol. Sem., Phila., 1964, Gettysburg Luth. Sem., 1964-65, Bibl. Sem., N.Y.C., 1965-66, Western Theol. Sem., Holland, Mich., 1966, Duke U., Durham, N.C., 1967; ecumenical confs. at Lausanne, 1927, Oxford and Edinburgh, 1937; dir. Lilly Endowment bibliog. project for N.T. lit., 1961-68. Author: Das religiose Erlebnis, 1920, Grundlagen der evangelischen Ethik, 2 vols., 1929-31, Recent Developments in German Protestantism, 1934, God in History, 1939, Christian Interpretation of Sex, 1941, Biblical View of Sex and Marriage, 1960, Protestantism in the Ecumenical Age, 1965, The Christian Meaning of Money, 1965, Christian Ethics, 1970, New Testament Lexicography: An Unfinished Task chpt. in festschrift, 1972. V.p. Am. Relief Cen. Europe; pres. Emergency Com. German Protestantism, 1945-66. Decorated Order of Merit (Fed. Republic Germany). Mem. Am. Theol. Soc. (pres. 1958-59), Soc. Bibl. Lit. (hon. pres. 1970-71), Soc. Ch. History, Soc. Reformation Rsch., Am. Oriental Soc. Home: Princeton N.J. †

PIPES, SAMUEL WESLEY, III, lawyer; b. Mobile, Ala., Feb. 28, 1916; s. Samuel Wesley Jr. and Miriam (Larkin) P; m. Maude Breeland, June 19, 1940; children: S. Wesley, Prather Pipes Brooker. LLB, U. Ala., 1938. Bar: Ala. 1938. Practice law Mobile, 1938-82; ptnr. Lyons, Pipes & Cook, Mobile, 1940-82; lectr. seminar on oil and gas Fla. State U., 1974; bd. dirs. Comml. Guaranty Bank, Title Ins. Co.; spl. justice Supreme Ct. Ala., 1971, mem. standing com. on civil practice and procedure. Contbr. articles to profl. jours. Bd. dirs. U. Ala. Law Sch. Found., from 1964, pres., 1966-68; bd. visitors Ala. Law Inst.; chmn. bldg. fund Ala. Bar Found., 1966-82. Recipient Daniel J. Meador Oustanding Alumnus award U. Ala., 1973. Fellow Am. Coll. Trial Lawyers; mem. Ala. State Bar Assn. (pres. 1969), Mobile Bar Assn. (pres. 1959), Athelstan Club (Mobile) (pres. 1964-65). Episcopalian (vestryman, past ch. treas.). Home: Point Clear Ala. Died Oct. 28, 1982, buried Mobile, Ala.

PIRET, EDGAR LAMBERT, energy resources company executive; b. Winnipeg, Man., Can., July 1, 1910; came to U.S., 1922, naturalized, 1927; s. Hubert and Maria Celine (Dutileaux) P.; Alice Moeglein, Sept. 4, 1945; children: Mary Louise, Marguerite, Jacqueline, John, Robert, James. BChemE, U. Minn., 1932, PhD, 1937; D in Biochemistry, U. Lyon (France), 1936. Instr. chem. engring. U. Minn., 1937-41, asst. prof., 1941-43, prof., 1945-65, dir. chem. products from peat project, 1954-59; chief chem. engring. Minn. Mining & Mfg. Co., 1943-45, cons., 1937-65; dir. European ops. Energy Resources Co., Cambridge, Mass., 1977-87; sci. attaché Dept. State, Am. Embassy, Paris, 1959-67, then counselor sci. and technol. affairs.; asst. exec. dir. Am. Chem. Soc., Washington, 1975-77; adminstr. chem. catalysis program U.S.-USSR, 1976-87; guest and vis. prof. MIT, 1965-66; cons. U.S. Naval Research Lab., 1951-55. Author over 60 papers on continuous reactor theory and design, theory of crushing, leaching, heat and mass transfer, fluidized bed gasification and combustion, clean energy from forest and agrl. wastes; editorial bd. Jour. Am. Inst. Chem. Engrs., 1957-70, Chem. Engring. Progress, 1957-70, Jour. Internat. Chem. Engring., 1961-70.Patentee in field. Recipient Freidel medal U. Paris, 1951, medal U. Liege, Belgium, 1951, Palms Académiques, Officier d'Académie, France, 1951, Bronze medal Swedish Assn. Engr.s, 1954; named chevalier Legion of Honor, France, 1957; France-Am. fellow, 1935-36; Fulbright research prof. U. Nancy, U. Paris, France, 1950-51. Fellow AAAS, N.Y. Acad. Scis., Am. Inst. Chem. Engrs. (nat. program com. 1948, 49, 50, Walker award 1955, awards com. 1958-63), Am. Soc. Engring. Edn., Chemists Club, Am. Fgn. Service Assn., AAUP, Automobile Club de France, Cosmos Club, Alpha Chi Sigma, Sigma Xi, Phi Lambda Upsilon, Tau Beta Pi. Home: Lexington Mass. Died Sept. 24, 1987.

PIRIE, JOHN CHARLES, lawyer, airline executive; b. Denver, Aug. 26, 1907; s. Charles R. and Lena (Harms) P.; m. Edith F. Murdoch, Aug. 2, 1935. AB, U. Nebr., 1929, Oxford U., 1934; MA, Oxford U., 1964. Bar: N.Y. 1936, Md. 1973. With Root, Clark, Buckner & Ballantine, N.Y.C., 1936-43; with Pan. Am. World Airways, Inc., N.Y.C., 1943-71, asst. gen. counsel, 1946-56, assoc. gen. counsel, 1956-68, gen. counsel, 1968-71, v.p., 1958-70, sr. v.p., 1970-71; with Hartman & Crain, Annapolis, Md., from 1973. Mem. ABA, Assn. of Bar of City of N.Y., N.Y. State Bar Assn. Home: Annapolis Md. Died Oct. 5, 1988.

PIRNIE, MALCOLM, civil engineer; b. N.Y.C., Feb. 6, 1889; s. George and Florence Augusta (Pomeroy) P.; m. Gertrude Willard Knowlton, Mar. 25, 1916; children: Malcolm, Gertrude Knowlton Pirnie Taylor, Florence Anne. SB, Harvard U., 1910, MCE, 1911; DEng (hon.), Rensselaer Poly. Inst., 1945. Asst. engr. Hazen and Whipple, N.Y.C., 1911-16; ptnr. Hazen, Whipple & Fuller (later Hazen, Everett & Pirnie), 1916-29; pvt. cons. practice as civil engr., N.Y.C., 1929-46, Malcolm Pirnie Engrs. (4 ptnrs.), from 1946. Trustee Scardsdale, N.Y., 1931-32, mayor, 1933-34, chmn. bd. appeals for zoning, 1935-55; mem. task force on water resources and power Hoover Commn., 1953-55; mem. bd. cons.'s Water Project Authority State Calif., 1953-54; chmn. Harvard Found. for Advanced Study and Rsch., 1950; trustee White Plains Hosp., Vassar Coll. Asst. san. engr. ARC Mission to Russia, 1917; capt. Transp. Corps Engrs. Constrn., dir. gen. Transp. Am. Expeditionary Force, 1918-19; cons. to war dept. on groundwater and water supply related to ship canals, Fla., 1936, N.J., 1946; cons. comdg. gen. Army Svc. Forces and Fed. Works Agy., 1944-45; cons., mem. adv. coms. Army and Navy Munitions Bd., War Prodn. Bd. Recipient Pres.'s cert. of merit in recognition outstanding svc. in study and formulation specific proposals for postwar industrial control measures in Germany and Japan, 1946, Scarsdale Bowl, contbns. civil life, 1950. Fellow Am. Pub. Health Assn., Fla. Engring. Soc.; mem. ASCE (bd. dirs., v.p., pres., Hoover medal 1948), Am. Water Works Assn. (bd. dirs., chmn. water works practice com., pres., hon. mem.), Am. Inst. Cons. Engrs. (pres.), Soc. Am. Mil. Engrs., Am. Geophys. Union, Engrs. Joint Coun. (chmn. exec. com., nat. engrs. com., chmn. com. on internat. rels.), AIME (Hoover medal 1948), Santo Domingo Soc. Engrs. and Architects (hon.), Engring. Inst. Can. (hon.), Coll. Engrs. Puerto Rico, New Eng. Water Works Assn., Engineers Club (N.Y.C.), Harvard Club (N.Y.C.), Cosmos Club (Washington), Am. Yacht Club (Rye, N.Y.). Republican. Congregationalist. Home: Scarsdale N.Y. †

PIRRUNG, GILBERT ROBINSON, business executive; b. Columbus, Ohio, July 12, 1911; s. Henry Casper and Catherine Manley (Robinson) P.; m. Lila Marshall Childress, 1937 (div. 1941); m. Joan D. H. Burgess, July 9, 1947; children: Lynette R. H. Lillstrom, Clifford Mark, Henriette Christine, Timothy Burgess. BS, Yale U., 1934. Owner, mgr. Pirrung Racing Team, Indpls., 1934-36; with prodn., sales depts. Gaylord Container Corp., St. Louis, 1936-39, budget dir., asst. to treas., 1939-41, bd. dirs., 1950-56; owner, mgr. Aragon Farms, Bainbridge, Ga., 1950-86; chmn. bd. Vada Corp., Bainbridge; bd. dirs. Nat. Trans. Network, St. Louis. Trustee Aiken Prep. Sch., 1962-74, Ga. Conservancy, Inc., 1969-86; mem. nat. exec. bd. Boy Scouts Am., 196--73, internat. commr., 1968-72; pres. Interam. Scout Com., 1968-70, v.p., 1970-86, mem. adv. coun., 1973-77; v.p., sec. U.S. Found. for Internat. Scouting; chmn. Gen. Coun. Presbyn. Ch. U.S., 1962-71, Ga. Found. Ind. Colls., 1971-73; elder Presbyn. ch. Col. C.E., AUS, 1941-45. Decorated Silver Star, Bronze Star with two oak leaf clusters; Croix de Guerre; recipient Silver Beaver, Silver Antelope, Silver Buffalo award Boy Scouts Am., Scout decorations from Japan, Paraguay, Chile, Guatemala, Ecuador, Venezuela, Peru, Inter-Am. Region, World Conf. Mem. St. Louis Country Club, Racquet Club, St. Anthony Club, Yale Club, Capitol City Club. Home: Bainbridge Ga. Died Mar. 23, 1986.

PLANK, HARVEY H., utilities executive; b. Pamelia, N.Y., May 22, 1892; s. Frank D. and Anna (Lyng) P.; m. Marian Brown Rae, Oct. 23, 1920;. BS, Clarkson Coll., 1917, DEng, 1954. With Henry L. Doherty & Co., 1917, 19-20, Syracuse Lighting Co., 1920-22, United Gas Improvement Co., Phila., 1922-43, Del. Power & Light Co., Wilmington, from 1943; chmn. bd. Del. Power & Light Co. With U.S. Army, 1917-19. Mem. AIEE, Edison Electric Inst., Am. Gas Assn., Del. C. of C., Wilmington Country Club, Tau Beta Pi, Eta Kappa Nu. Home: Wilmington Del. †

PLATT, GEOFFREY, architect; b. Cornish, N.H., Aug. 6, 1905; s. Charles A. and Eleanor (Hardy) P.; m. Helen Choate, Dec. 20, 1932 (dec. June 1974); children: Penelope, Nicholas, Geoffrey; m. Alice Doubleday Holbrook, June 26, 1976. Grad., St. Mark's Sch., 1923; AB, Harvard U., 1927; MArch, Columbia U., 1930. Mem. firm William & Geoffrey Platt, N.Y.C., 1934-72, Platt, Wyckoff & Coles, N.Y.C., 1972-85. Works include bldgs. for Princeton U., Deerfield Acad., Smith Coll., Bennet Coll., Middlesex Sch., chapel at Am. Mil. Cemetery, France, Gen. Douglas MacArthur Meml., Norfolk, Va., Rye (N.Y.) City Hall, Garden Ctr., Cleve., addition to Pierpont Morgan Library, N.Y.C., houses throughout U.S. particularly N.Y. and N.E. area. Chmn. N.Y.C. Landmarks Preservation Commn., 1962-68; v.p. N.Y. Landmarks Conservancy. Maj. USAAF, 1942-45. Decorated Order Brit. Empire; recipient 1st prize for cen. bus. dist. plan Stockholm Internat. Competition, 1935, Gold medal N.Y. Mcpl. Art Soc., 1968, medal N.Y. Archtl. and Engring. Soc., 1972. Fellow AIA; assoc. NAD. Home: Bedford Hills N.Y. Died July 12, 1985, buried Stockbridge, Mass.

PLAZA, GALO, agricultural economist; b. N.Y.C., 1906; s. Lewonidas and Avelina Lasso d Plaza; m. Rosario Pallares Zaldumbide, Mar. 7, 1944; children: Elsa Plaza Crespo, Luz Plaza Polanco, Galo, Rosario Plaza Alvarez, Marcela Plaza Zambrano, Margarita Plaza Ponce. Mem. Mcpl. Council Quito, Ecuador, 1937-38; mayor of Quito 1938-39; minister nat. def. Ecuador, 1939-40, ambassador to U.S., 1944-45, 46; mem. Ecuador Senate 1947, pres. of Ecuador, 1948-52; sec. gen. OAS, 1968-75; chmn. spl. econ. com. Econ. Commn. Latin Am., 1958-59; chief UN observation group, Lebanaon, 1958; dir. Basic UN Com. to Study Problems of Evacuating Belgian Treaty Bases in Congo, 1960; spl. rep. then mediator for UN Sec. gen. in Turkey-Greece crisis over Cyprus, 1964-65. Co-author: The United Fruit Company in Latin America, 1958, Problems of Democracy in Latin America, 1955, Latin America Today and Tomorrow, 1971. Recipient decorations from govts. U.S., Mex., Columbia, Chile, Costa Rica, Bolivia, Guatemala, Venezuela, Paraguay, Peru, Found. of Americas award, 1969, Disting. Alumnus award U. Md., 1968, Elise and Walther Haas award U. Calif. Berkeley, 1967, Key Man of Americas award, 1969. Home: Quito Ecuador. Died Jan. 28, 1987.

PLITT, EDWIN AUGUST, foreign service officer; b. Balt., Oct. 2, 1891; s. Louis A. E. and Anna Katherine (Gessner) P.; m. Jeanne Riboulet, Aug. 26, 1919; 1 child, James Robert. Grad., Balt. Poly. Inst., 1910. Archtl. draftsman, quantity surveyor 1910-11; structural designer Balt. Sewerage Commn. and Bldg. Insp.'s Office, 1912-15; engr. U.S. Reclamation Svc., 1916-17, C.E., U.S. Army, 1917-19; office mgr. French-Am. Co., France, 1919-20; civil engr. Balt. City Hwys. Dept., 1920-21; apptd. vice consul of career U.S. Fgn. Svc., 1921, Sofia, Bulgaria, 1921, Constantinople, Turkey, 1922; consul U.S. Fgn. Svc., 1925, Athens, Greece, 1926, Paris, 1933; sec. of embassy Paris, 1937; with Dept. State, Washington, 1941; apptd. acting asst. chief, Spl. Div., then asst. chief 1942, chief Spl. War Problems Div., 1944; counselor Am. Legation, Bern, Switzerland, 1945-47; diplomatic agt., consul gen. with rank of minister Tangier, Morocco, 1947-49; career minister 1949; pres. com. Control Internat. Zone of Tangier, 1950-51; advisor on UN affairs, Bur. Near Ea., South Asian and African affairs Dept. State, 1951-60; mem. U.S. del. Japanese Peace Conf., San Francisco, 1951, 6th Gen. Assembly UN, Paris, 1951-52; Dept. State rep., chmn. Inteim Mixed Parole and Clemency Bd., Bonn, Germany, 1953; dep. insp. gen. Fgn. Svc. Inspection Corps, 1957. Mem. Chevy Chase Club. Home: Washington D.C. †

PLUMB, JOHN JAY, insurance consultant; b. Hackensack, N.J., Apr. 4, 1916; s. Carmen and Mary (Anthony) P.; children: Stephen J., David L. B.A., Duke U., 1938; M.B.A., NYU, 1948. Exec. dir. Prudential Life Ins. Co., Newark, 1938-55; sr. v.p. Paul Revere Life Ins. Co., Worcester, Mass., 1955-66; successively sr. v.p., pres. Channing Mut. Funds; pres. Variable Annuity Life Ins. Co. (subs. Am. Gen. Group); staff cons. to Am. Gen. Group, Houston, 1966-81. Served to lt. USCG, World War II. Mem. Am. Soc. C.L.U.s, Nat. Assn. Life Underwriters, Phi Beta Kappa. Deceased.

PLUMMER, FRANK ARTHUR, banker; b. Richland, N.Y., June 18, 1912; s. Charles Eugene and Nettie (Dwight) P.; m. Elizabeth Higgins, Sept. 10, 1938. BS, Syracuse U., 1932, MS, 1933; grad., Rutgers U. Grad. Sch. Banking. Exec. v.p., dir. Marine Bank & Trust Co., Tampa, Fla.; sr. v.p., dir. First Nat. Bank Montgomery (Ala.), 1953-58, pres., 1964-69, chmn. bd., pres., 1969-87, also chief exec. officer; pres., dir. Birmingham (Ala.) Trust Nat. Bank, 1959-61, chmn. bd., pres., 1961-64; pres., chmn. bd., chief exec. officer First Ala. Bancshares, Inc.; bd. dirs. Ala. Power Co., Maytag Corp.; former mem. fed. adv. council Fed. Res. Bd., Washington. Chmn. United Appeal, Montgomery, 1957; bd. visitors Berry Coll.; mem. adv. bd. U. Ala. Med. Ctr., 1979-80; past chmn. bd. regents Stonier Grad. Sch. Banking, Rutgers U.; bd. dirs. So. Research Inst., Jackson Hosp. Found. Lt. col. AUS, 1940-46. Mem. Montgomery C. of C. (past pres.), Beta Theta Phi, Delta Phi Sigma, Alpha Kappa Psi, Beta Gamma Sigma. Home: Montgomery Ala. Died Oct. 3, 1987, buried Cortland, N.Y.

PLUMMER, WILBUR CLAYTON, economist, educator; b. Hagerstown, Md., July 5, 1889; s. Charles William and Sarah Ellen (Eakle) P.; m. Florence Braastad, Aug. 30, 1920; 1 dau., Fredericka Plummer Appleton. AB, Lebanon Valley Coll., 1910, LLD, 1939; AM, U. Pa., 1922, PhD, 1924. Tchr. high schs., 1910-17, 19-20; instr. econs. Wharton Sch. Fin. and Commerce, U. Pa., 1921-27, asst. prof., 1927-31, prof., 1931-60, prof. emeritus, from 1960; lectr. econs. LaSalle Coll., from 1961; chief bus. specialist, U.S. Dept. Commerce, 1928-33; economist U.S. Agrl. Adjustment Adminstrn., 1933; dir. div. profl. projects Fed. Works Progress Adminstrn. for Pa., 1935, dep. adminstr., 1936; mem. rsch. staff mayor's adv. fin. commn., Phila., 1937-38; mem. staff Nat. Bur. Econ. Rsch., 1938-40; economist cons. Inst. Local and State Govt., U. Pa., 1942-43; economist U.S. War Manpower Commn. and U.S. Employment Svc., 1944-46. 1st sgt. U.S. Army Ambulance Svc. with French Army, 1917-19. Author: The Road Policy of Pennsylvania, 1925, Social and Economic Consequences of Buying on the Instalment Plan, 1927; co-author: Sales Finance Companies and Their Credit Practices, 1940, The Finances of the City of Philadelphia, 1943, also numerous articles and spl. rsch. studies in field of credit. Decorated Croix de Guerre (France), (twice). Mem. AAUP, Am. Econ. Assn., Hist. Soc. Pa. Home: Philadelphia Pa. †

PLUNKETT, ROBERT EDWARD, physician; b. Troy, N.Y., Aug. 2, 1889; s. John D. and Elizabeth (Purcell) p.; m. Rose A. Wilson, June 16, 1915; children: Marion Wilson (Mrs. Peter F. McCarthy), Robert Wilson. MD, Albany Med. Coll., 1913. Diplomate Am. Bd. Preventive Medicine and Pub. Health. Resident physician Lakeview Tb Sanatorium, Troy, 1913-15; pvt. practice Whitehall, N.Y., 1915-17, 20-23; coroner Washington County, N.Y., 1922-23; clinic physician in Tb N.Y. State Dept. Health, 1923-25, dir. div. Tb, 1925-35, gen. supt. Tb hosps., 1935-47, asst. commr. for Tb control, 1947-59; U.S. del. to Pan-Am. Tb Union, Cordoba, Argentina, 1928, to Internat. Tb Union, Lisbon, Portugal, 1936; adviser Tb, Dominican Republic, 1940, Colombia, 1941; cons. Calif. State Health Dept. Tb Control, 1937, Med. Tb Adminstrn. for Conn. Tb. Commn., 1949; cons. regarding state Tb hosps. State of Del., 1950; adviser regarding new state Tb hosps. Mich. State Legis. Com., 1951; mem. nat. rsch. sub-com. on Tb Med. Sci. Div., 1946-57; cons. Commn. on Orgn. of Exec. Br. Govt. (Hoover Commn.), 1948, Devel. Ariz. Statewide Tb Program, 1952, Cook County (Ill.) Commn. on Tb Control, 1952; European con. Tb quarantine div. USPHS, 1951; mem. tech. adv. com. Heart of Harlem Project, N.Y.C., 1952. Contbr. articles to profl. jours. Trustee Troy Country Day Sch., 1934-36, Russell Sage Coll., 1937-54, Potts Meml. Inst., Livingston, N.Y., 1938-48; pres. Lansingburgh Boys Club, North Troy, N.Y., 1938-51; bd. dirs. Troy Community Chest, 1939-44, pres., 1940; mem. Troy Planning Commn., 1944-50. Recipient Charles Evans Hughes award Am. Soc. Pub. Adminstrn., 1954. Mem. AMA, Internat. Tb Union, Nat. Tb Assn. (bd. dirs. Rensselaer County chpt. 1940-51), Am. Pub. Health Assn., N.Y. State Med. Soc., Am. Trudeau Soc., N.Y. State Assn. Supts. and Mgrs. Tb Sanatoria, N.Y. State Trudeau Soc., N.Y. State Pub. Health Assn., Troy Country Club. Home: North Troy N.Y. †

POAGE, WILLIAM ROBERT, former congressman; b. Waco, Tex., Dec. 28, 1899; s. William Allan and Helen Wheeler (Conger) P.; m. Frances Cotton, Feb. 14, 1938. Student, U. Tex., summer 1919, U. Colo., summer 1923; A.B., Baylor U., 1921, LL.B., 1924, LL.D., 1967; L.H.D., Mary Hardin-Baylor Coll., 1973. Bar: Tex. 1924. Farmer Throckmorton County, Tex., 1920-22; instr. geology Baylor U., 1922-24, instr. law, 1924-28; practiced in Waco; mem. firm Poage and Neff, 1928-35; mem. Tex. Ho. of Reps., 1924-28, Tex. Senate, 1930-36; mem. 75th-95th congresses from 11th Tex. Dist., chmn. com. on agr., 1967-74, vice chmn., 1953-66, 75-80; Am. del. Inter-Parliamentary Union, 1947-74. Served with USNRF, 1918. Mem. Am. Legion. Democrat. Presbyterian. Club: Mason. Home: Waco Tex. Died Jan. 3, 1987; buried Oakwood Cemetery, Waco.

PODELL, JACOB JOSEPH, lawyer; b. Odessa, Russia, Aug. 10, 1887; s. Mordecai and Minna (London) P.; m. Rose Soffer, Aug. 10, 1922; children: madeleine (Mrs. Marvin Michael), Robert Louis, Carol F. (Mrs. Myron L. Vinson). AB, Columbia U., 1912; LLB, JD, NYU, 1915. Bar: N.Y. 1916. Mem. govt. appeal agt. Selective Svc., 1940-45. Rep. candidate for presdl. elector, 1940. With USN, World War I. Mem. Am. Legion, N.Y. State Bar Assn., N.Y. County Lawyers' Assn. Home: New York N.Y. †

POHL, HERBERT ACKLAND, chemist, educator; b. Lisbon, Portugal, Feb. 17, 1916; came to U.S., 1916; s. Lucien Charles and Emily May (Williams) P.; m. Eleanor Kathleen Rich, Aug. 23, 1941; children—Douglas, Patricia (Mrs. Robert Langdon), Elaine (Mrs. Gene Roy Oltmans), Charles, William. A.B. magna cum laude, Duke, 1936, Ph.D., 1939. Rockefeller fellow in anatomy Johns Hopkins Med. Sch., 1939; Carnegie Instn. of Washington fellow 1940; NDRC fellow chem. engring. Johns Hopkins, 1941-42; sr. chemist Naval Research Lab., 1942-45; research assoc. E.I. duPont de Nemours & Co., 1945-57; sr. research assoc., lectr. plastics dept. Sch. Engring., Princeton, 1957-62; vis. prof. materials sci. Poly. Inst. Bklyn., 1962-63; vis. prof. quantum chemistry group Uppsala U., Sweden, 1963-64; prof. physics Okla. State U., Stillwater, 1964-86; regional dir. Okla. Cancer Research Lab., 1980-81; pres., dir. Pohl Cancer Research Lab. Inc., 1982-86 ; vis. prof. U. Calif., Riverside, 1970, Cavendish Lab., U. Cambridge, Eng., 1971; NATO sr. sci. fellow, 1971; Vice pres. Sci-Tech. Corp., N.Y.C. Author: Semiconduction in Molecular Solids, 1960, Quantum Mechanics, 1967, (with W.F. Pickard) Dielectrophoretic and Electrophoretic Deposition, 1969, How to Tell Atoms from People, 1970, Dielectrophoresis-The Behavior of Matter in Nonuniform Electric Fields, 1978; Editor: Jour. Biol. Physics, 1977-86 ; editorial bd.: Jour. Cell Biophysics; Contbr. articles to profl. jours. Pres. Princeton chpt. United World Federalists, 1959-61; v.p. Stillwater Unitarian Ch., 1978-79. Recipient Rensselaer award in sci., 1933, Soc. Plastics award, 1959; A. & K. Wallanberg fellow, 1963-64. Fellow Am. Inst. Chemists, Explorers Club; mem. Am. Phys. Soc., AAAS, Am. Assn. Physics Tchrs., AAUP, Am. Chem. Soc., Okla. Acad. Sci. (past chmn.), Philos. Soc. Home: Stillwater Okla. Died June 21, 1986, buried Franklin, Pa.

POLIER, JUSTINE WISE, lawyer, retired judge; b. Portland, Oreg., Apr. 12, 1903; d. Stephen S. and Louise (Waterman) Wise; m. Leon Arthur Tulin, June 14, 1927 (dec. Dec. 1932); 1 child, Stephen Wise; m. Shad Polier, Mar. 26, 1937 (dec. June 1976); children—Trudy H., Jonathon W., Michael W. (dec. Mar. 10, 1945). Student, Bryn Mawr Coll., 1920-22, Radcliffe Coll., 1922-23; A.B., Barnard Coll., 1924; LL.B., Yale U., 1928, LL.D., 1979; LL.D., Princeton U., 1976, Kenyon Coll., 1977, CUNY, 1978, Brandeis U., 1985. Bar: Conn. 1928, N.Y. 1929. Began practice in N.Y.; referee N.Y. State Dept. Labor, 1929-34; asst. corp. counsel N.Y.C., 1934-35; counsel and sec. Mayor's Com. on Relief, 1934-35; counsel Emergency Relief Bur., 1935; justice Domestic Relations Ct., N.Y., 1935-62; judge N.Y. State Family Ct., 1962-73; dir. program for juvenile justice Children's Def. Fund-Washington Research Project Fund, 1973-76; cons. Office Civilian Def., 1941-42. Author: Everyone's Children, Nobody's Child, 1941, Back to What Woodshed, 1956, Parental Rights, The Need for Law and Social Action, A View From the Bench, The Rule of Law and the Role of Psychiatry, 1968; Co-editor: Personal Letters of Stephen Wise, 1956; Contbr. to social and sci. jours. Mem. N.Y. Citizens Com. Foster Care Children; v.p. N.Y.C. Citizens Com. for Children; chairperson Eleanor Roosevelt Inst.; mem. Joint Commn. Inst. Juvenile Adminstrn.-Am. Bar Assn.; mem. adv. rev. bd. Human Resources Adminstrn.; mem. Commr.'s adv. council for children with handicapping conditions N.Y. State Dept. Edn., N.Y. State Task Force on Mental Health Services for Children and Youth.; Bd. dirs., pres. Wiltwyck Sch.; trustee N.Y. Sch. Nursery Years, Ch. Peace Union; v.p. Field Found.; bd. dirs. Marshall Field Awards, Inc., Research Center of Human Relations; pres. Louise Wise Services, Kenworthy-Swift Found.; hon. pres. women's div., chmn. exec. com. Am. Jewish Congress; mem. exec. com. World Jewish Congress.; N.Y. del. White House Conv. on Children, 1960; mem. White House Planning Conf. on Civil Rights, 1965; bd. visitors Antioch Sch. Law; bd. dirs. Children's Def. Fund. Named Woman of Month Dec., 1948, Woman of Month Dec. Am. Women's Assn.; recipient Isaac Ray award Am. Psychiat. Assn., 1964, Naomi Lehman award Fedn. Jewish Philanthropies, 1965, Distinguished Service award City N.Y., 1973; Human Services award N.Y. and Bronx Mental Health Assn., 1973; Human Services award N.Y. Assn. U. Women, 1973; Hannah G. Solomon award Nat. Council Jewish Women, 1975; Eleanor Roosevelt Humanitarian award bd. dirs. Wiltwyck Sch., 1975; Gertrude F. Zimand Meml. award Nat. Child Labor Com., 1976; Marion E. Kenworthy award Columbia U. Sch. Social Work, 1979; Josephine Shaw Lowell Meml. award Community Service Soc., 1986. Mem. Assn. Bar City N.Y., Am. Orthopsychiat. Assn. Jewish. Home: New York N.Y. Died July 31, 1987.

POLLARD, HARRY, mathematics educator; b. Boston, Feb. 28, 1919; s. David and Rebecca (Bell) P.; m. Helen May Rickard, May 13, 1943; children: Joel, Carl Jesse, Betsy Helen Pollard Fulton, Harry Seth, Amy Hester Pollard Ryan. Grad., Boston Latin Sch., 1935; AB, Harvard U., 1939, AM, 1940, PhD, 1942. Mem. faculty Cornell U., 1946-61, prof., 1956-61; prof. math. Purdue U., 1961-77, prof. math and edn., 1977-85; vis. prof. Harvard U., 1970-71, 73, So. Meth. U., 1978, Calif. State U.-Chico, 1980; lectr. Copernical Congress, Warsaw, Poland, 1973; lectr. in field; cons. projects applied math., space projects. Author: Theory of Algebraic Numbers, 1950, rev. edit., 1975, Introduction to Celestial Mechanics, 1966, Applied Mathematics, An Introduction, 1972, Celestial Mechanics, 1977; also numerous papers on classical analysis and celestial mechanics. Mem. Am. Math. Soc., Math. Assn. Am., Soc. for Indsl. and Applied Math. Home: West Lafayette Ind. Died Nov. 20, 1985; buried Grandview Cemetery, West Lafayette.

POLLOCK, LAWRENCE S., paper products company executive; b. Dallas, June 17, 1892; s. Ruben C. and Jeanne (Wollff) P.; m. Hortense Dreyfuss, Sept. 30, 1919; children: Lawrence S., Robert G. Pres., gen. mgr. Pollock Paper Corp., Dallas, from 1918; pres. Pollock Realty Co., Burkett Paper Co., Amarillo, Tex., Tex. Paper Co., Dallas; bd. dirs. Republic Nat. Bank, Gulf Envelope Co., Houston; mem. exec. com., dir. Southwestern Life Ins. Co., Amarillo, St. Regis Paper Co., N.Y. V.p. Dallas Community Chest; pres. Dallas Symphony Orch., Inc. 2d lt. U.S. Army, 1918. Mem. Nat. Paper Trades Assn. N.Y. (past pres.), Folding Paper Box Assn. Am. (bd. dirs., Dallas C. of C. (bd. dirs.), Mfrs. amd Wholesalers Assn. (past pres.), Southwestern Paper Mchts. Assn. (past pres.). Home: Dallas Tex. †

POLLOCK, THOMAS CLARK, English educator; b. Monmouth, Ill., Mar. 31, 1902; s. Thomas Cithcart and Mary (Heade) P.; m. Katherine Gantz, Oct. 23, 1930; m. Lillian S. Stevenson, July 19, 1975. AB, Muskingham Coll., 1922, LittD (hon.), 1948; MA, Ohio State U., 1927; PhD, U. Pa., 1930; D honoris causa, U. Brazil, U. Bahia, 1959. Prof. philosophy Gordon Coll., Punjab U., India, 1922-24; instr. pub. speaking Muskingum Coll., 1924-25; asst. in English Ohio State U., 1925-26, instr., 1926-28; asst. in English U. Pa., 1928-31, univ. fellow for research in English, 1931-32; chmn. humanities div. Mcpl. U., Omaha, 1932-33; asst. prof. English Ohio State U., 1933-36, assoc. prof., 1936-38; head dept. English N.J. State Tchrs. Coll., Monclair, 1938-41, dean instrn., 1943-44; chmn. dept. English edn. NYU, 1941-43, 44-47; prof. English Wash. Sq. Coll. Arts and Sci., NYU, 1947-70, prof. emeritus, 1970-88, dean, 1947-62, acting provost, 1951-52, acting dean grad. sch., 1958-59, v.p., sec. univ., 1962-67. Author: The Philadelphia Theatre in the Eighteenth Century, 1933, (with others) Democracy in Transition, 1937, The Teaching of English Grammar in the Secondary Schools of New Jersey, 1937-38, 1940, The Nature of Literature, 1942, A Theory of Meaning Analyzed, 1942, The English Language in American Education, 1945, Summary of Practical English, 1947, (with Oscar Cargill) Thomas Wolfe at Washington Square; co-editor: The Correspondence of Thomas Wolfe and Homer Andrew Watt, 1954; author recent textbooks. Trustee Council on Religion and Internat. Affairs. Mem. MLA (v.p. 1953, Phi Beta Kappa Assocs., Nat. Council Tchrs. English (1st v.p. 1947, pres. 1948), Metropolitan Club, Church Club, Century Club, Phi Beta Kappa. Home: Durham N.C. Died May 12, 1988.

POLYA, GEORGE, mathematics educator; b. Budapest, Hungary, Dec. 13, 1887; came to U.S., 1940; s. Jakob and Anne (Deutsch) P.; m. Stella Vera Weber, Aug. 1, 1918. Ph.D., U. Budapest, 1912. Asst. Swiss Inst. Tech., Zurich, 1914-28, prof. math., 1928-40; prof. math. Brown U., Providence, 1940-42, Stanford U., Calif., 1940-53. Author 10 books including How to Solve It (trans. into 17 langs.). Author over 250 articles on mathematics. Home: Palo Alto Calif. Died Sept. 7, 1985, buried Alta Mesa Cemetery, Palo Alto.

POMERANTZ, LOUIS, art conservator; b. Bklyn., Sept. 26, 1919; s. Jacob and Gussie (Watnick) P.; m. Elisabeth C. Picard, Oct. 5, 1951; children: Carrie Johanna, Lonnie Roberta. Student, Art Students League, N.Y.C., 1938-40, Academie Julian, Paris, 1949-50; apprenticeships with, T.G. Satinover, Paris, 1949-50, H.H. Mertens, chief restorer, Rijksmuseum, Amsterdam, 1950-51, G.L. Stout, dir. Worcester Art Mus., 1951, S&C Keck Bklyn. Mus., 1952-54, Inst. Royal du Patrimoine Artistque, Brussels, 1963, Central Lab. Belgium Mus., Brussels, summer 1954, 56, 58. Founder conservation studio N.Y.C., 1952; instr., lab. asst. Bklyn. Mus., 1954; founder dept. conservation, apptd. conservator dept. painting and sculpture Art Inst. Chgo., 1956-61; ind. art conservator Evanston, Ill., 1961-78, 1979-88; founder, pres., treas. Pomerantz Inst. for Advancement of Fine Art Conservation, Spring Grove, Ill., 1982-88; pres. Louis Pomerantz, Ltd., 1971-88; cons. Milw. Art Mus., 1958-88, Nat. Gallery Can., 1961, George F. Harding Mus., Chgo., 1965-68; UNESCO cons., 1968; cons. Smithsonian Instn. Travelling Exhbn. Services, Iowa Mus. Art; vis. lectr. in field. Author: Is Your Contemporary Painting More Temporary Than You Think?, 1962; assoc. editor: Jour. Am. Inst. Conservation, 1982-88. Mem. bd. advisors Urban Gateways, 1975-79; dir. Art Commn. City of Evanston, 1968-75, pres., 1975-76; bd. dirs. Campbell Ctr. Hist. Preservation Studies, 1983-88. Served with U.S. Army, 1941-45. Fellow Internat. Inst. Conservation of Historic and Artistic Works, Am. Inst. Conservation (hon., past chmn., dir. 1979-82). Unitarian. Home: Spring Grove Ill. Died May 19, 1988; cremated.

POMPA, GILBERT GUTIERREZ, lawyer, government official; b. Devine, Tex., Oct. 1, 1931; s. Alfred and Manuela (Gutierrez) P.; m. Hermelinda Bocanegra, Dec. 19, 1954; children—Janiece, Darlene, Russell. J.D., St. Mary's U., San Antonio, 1958. Bar: Tex. Pvt. practice law San Antonio, 1958-60; asst. city atty. San Antonio, 1960-62; asst. dist. atty. Bexar County, Tex., 1963-67; community relations specialist Bexar County, 1968-69; asst. dir. community relations service U.S. Dept. Justice, Washington, 1969-70; assoc. dir. U.S. Dept. Justice, 1970-76, dep. dir., 1976-78, dir., from 1978; lectr. Harvard U. Law Sch. Contbr. articles to profl. jours. Bd. govs. ARC, from 1984; mem. League United Latin Am. Citizens, Mexican-Am. Legal Def. and Edn. Fund, NAACP, Nat. Urban League, Am. G.I. Forum, Mexican-Am. Correctional Assn., Nat. Hispanic Law Enforcement Officers Assn. Served with USAF, 1950-52. Salzburg Seminar fellow, 1985. Mem. Tex. Bar Assn. Roman Catholic. Home: Fairfax Va.

POND, ALONZO WILLIAM, anthropologist; b. Janesville, Wis., June 18, 1894; s. William Samuel and Marie (Olson) P.; m. Dorothy Helen Long, July 20, 1926; children: Chomingwen Dorothy, Arthur Alonzo. B.S., Beloit (Wis.) Coll., 1920; studied, Am. Sch. in Europe for Prehistoric Research, 1921-22, Ecole d'Anthropologie, Paris, 1922; M.A., U. Chgo., 1928. Asst. curator Logan Museum, Beloit Coll., 1925-31; leader of Logan Sahara Expdn. of Beloit Coll., 1925-26; assoc. with Dr. George L. Collie; dir. Logan Mus. in excavation at Dordogne, France, 1926; asst. in charge paleolithic excavations Mechta el Arbi, Algeria, 1926-27; archaeologist for Dr. Roy Chapman Andrews on Central Asiatic Expdn. of Am. Museum Natural History, 1928; leader 2 Logan Museum Expdns. to Africa, 1929, 30; dir. eastern group Rainbow Bridge-Monument Valley Expdn., 1933; archaeologist Nat. Park Service, June-Sept. 1935; in charge excavation and study of desiccated body of prehistoric miner found in Mammoth Cave Nat. Park Service, Ky.; mgr. newly discovered Cave of the Mounds, Blue Mounds, Wis., 1940-45; owner-mgr. Wis. Gardens, scenic attraction, 1958-68; editorial research specialist USAF Arctic Desert Tropic Info. Center, also chief desert sect.; prof. desert geography Air U., 1949-58; with French Army and U.S. Ambulance Service, France, 1917-19. Author: bulletins Climate and Weather in Central Gobi of Mongolia; scenario (ednl. motion picture) Lime Stone Caverns; tech. adv.: A.F. tng. film Sun, Sand, and Survival; author: (with Nesbitt and Allen) The Survival Book, 1959, reprinted as A Pilot's Survival Manual, 1978, The Desert World, 1962, Deserts, Silent Lands, 1964, Caverns of the World, 1969, Survival in Sun and Sand, 1969; (with Lafferty and Eady) Desert Survival Problem, 1970; Andrews: Gobi Explorer, 1972; Dr. Kate & the Million Penny Parades, 1974; chief cons. (documentary) Reliving the Past, Beloit Coll., 1986. Recipient Disting. Service citation Beloit Coll., 1978, cert. of merit Raconteurs, 1982, Alumni Achievement award Wayland Acad., 1984. Mem. Explorers Club, Sigma Xi. Republican. Club: Raconteurs (Wis.). Home: Minocqua Wis. Died Dec. 25, 1986; buried Oak Hill Cemetery, Janesville, Wis.

PONTIUS, CLARENCE ISAIAH, banker, college president; b. Chicora, Pa., Dec. 1, 1892; s. Solomon Isaiah and Sarah Katherine (Summerville) P.; m. Ruth Elizabeth Birch, Oct. 7, 1922; children: Betty Jane Pontius Filley, Clarence Birch. Grad., Ohio State U., 1915; LLD, Oklahoma City U., 1936; LHD, U. Tulsa, 1960. Founder and pres. several fin. cos. in Ohio, 1916-30; associated with 1st Nat. Bank & Trust Co., Tulsa, from 1930; with gen. investment banking bus., 1931-35; pres. U. Tulsa, 1935-58, chancellor, 1958-63, pres. emeritus, from 1963, chmn. bd. trustees, 1935-52, life trustee. Pres., bd. dirs. Okla. Ind. Coll. Found. Inc.; mem. exec. coun. Thomas Gilcrease Inst. Am. History and Art; mem. adv. coun., trustee Okla. Presbyn. Found. Inc.; life mem. Internat. Sci. Found.; mem. 15th Joint Civilian Orientation Conf.; chmn. state community activities com. U.S. Savs. Bond Div.; vice moderator Presbyn. Synod Okla., 1956-57; chmn. Okla. Scottish Rite Fellowship Com.; v.p. Tulsa Scottish Rite Charitable and Edn. Found.; active other local and state civic orgns. Recipient Man of Yr. award Tulsa C. of C., 1949, citation by Gov. Phillips; inducted into Okla. Hall of Fame, 1951. Mem. Royal Order Jesters, Red Cross of Constantine, Okla. Hist. Soc., Okla. Meml. Assn., Tulsa Club, Rotary (pres.), Masons (33 deg., comdr.), Shriners, Delta Sigma Pi, Phi Delta Theta, Alpha Phi Omega, Pi Gamma Mu, Pi Delta Epsilon, Phi Eta Sigma, Omicron Delta Kappa. Home: Tulsa Okla. †

POOL, ITHIEL DESOLA, political science educator; b. N.Y.C., Oct. 26, 1917; s. David deSola and Tamar (Hirshenson) P.; m. Jean MacKenzie, Mar. 3, 1956; cildren: Jonathan, Jeremy, Adam. BA, U. Chgo., 1938, MA, 1939, PhD, 1952. Chmn. div. social scis. Hobart Coll., 1942-49; assoc. dir. RADIR project Hoover Inst., Stanford U., 1949-53; prof. polit. sci. MIT, 1953-84, founder, 1st chmn. dept. polit. sci., 1959-61, 65-69, fellow Ctr. Advanced Study in Behavioral Scis., 1957-58; vis. prof. Keio U., Tokyo, 1976; mem. sci. adv. bd. USAF, 1961-64; mem-at-large Def. Sci. Bd., 1968-71; fellow Churchill Coll., Cambridge U., Eng., 1977. Author: Symbols of Internationalsim, 1951, Symbols of Democracy, 1952, The Comparative Study of Symbols, 1952, The Prestige Press, 1952, 2d. edit., 1970, Satellite Generals, 1955, Trends in Content Analysis, 1959, American Business and Public Policy, 1963 (Woodrow Wilson award 1963), The People Look at Educational Television, 1963, Candidates Issues and Strategies, 1964, Contemporary Political Science, 1967, Talking Back, 1973, Handbook of Communication, 1973, The Social Impact of the Telephone, 1977, Forecasting the Telephone, 1983, Technologies of Freedom, 1983, Korean edition, 1984, Japanese edition, 1988 (Kammerer award Am. Polit. Sci. Assn. 1984), Communications Flows, 1984, The Collected Papers of Ithiel deSola Poll, 1989, The Social Impact of the Media, 1989. Recipient World Communication prize for Disitng. Svc. in Advancement of Communications The Japan Soc. for Info. and Communication, awarded posthumously. Fellow Am. Acad. Arts and Scis.; mem. Council Fgn. Relations, Am. Polit. Sci. Assn., Am. Assn. Pub. Opinion Research (posthumous award for Exceptionally Disting. Achievement, 1984), Cosmos Club. Home: Cambridge Mass. Died Mar. 11, 1984; buried Cambridge, Mass.

POOR, ALFRED EASTON, architect; b. Balt., May 24, 1899; s. Charles Lane and Anna Louise (Easton) P.; m. Janet Sheppard, Oct. 26, 1929; children: Charles Lane, John Sheppard, Anna Easton. Student, St. George's Sch., Newport, R.I., 1911-16; A.B., Harvard, 1920; B. Arch., U. Pa., 1923, M. Arch., 1924; Woodman travelling fellow architecture, 1925. Draftsman Peabody, Wilson & Brown, John Russell Pope, 1923-25; ind. practice architecture 1925-27; partner Rodgers & Poor, N.Y.C., 1927-32, Walker & Gillette and Alfred Easton Poor, N.Y.C., 1946-47, Walker & Poor, 1947-52, Walker & Poor (Office of Alfred Easton Poor), 1952, Poor and Swanke, 1972-75, Poor, Swanke, Hayden & Connell, 1975-88. Architect Army bldgs., labs., Ft. Monmouth, Ft. Jay, Lowry Field, 1932-40, Rio de Janeiro Airport, 1933; chief architect: Red Hook (N.Y.) Houses, 1938; architect: Army bldgs., labs. Rome (N.Y.) Air Depot, 1941; banks of Bank of Manhattan Co, 1946-88; Parke-Bernet Gallery, 1949; airfield and assembly plant for, U.S.N., L.I., two air bases in France for, U.S. A.F.E.; House and prison for, City of N.Y., 1953; alterations and addition to the, New House Office Building and Capitol of U.S., Washington, Washington; asso. architect: Queens County Courthouse and Prison, 1961, U.S. Customs Ct. and Fed. Office Bldg, N.Y.C., James Madison Meml, Library of Congress; architect: McGraw-Hill Home Office Bldg, N.Y.C.; restoration and extension, E. front U.S. Capitol, restoration old, Supreme Ct. Chamber and old Senate Chamber, 1975, adv. architect, Johns Hopkins, Balt.; architect: Annenberg Sch. Communications, U. Pa.; Author: Cape Cod, Martha's Vineyard and Nantucket, 1932. Trustee Met. Mus. Art, Burke Found. Ensign USN, 1918-19; flight instr. Air Sta. Key West, Fla.; comdr. USNR, 1942-46; Bur. Aeor. rep. 1943-45, Trenton, N.J. Fellow Morgan Library; Awarded Commendation ribbon.; Winner open competition award Meml. to Wright Bros., Kitty Hawk, N.C., 1928; hon. mention apt. house design N.Y. chpt. AIA, 1928; open competition low cost housing N.Y.C., 1933; Olympic medal for architecture, 1936; Archtl. award Fifth Ave. Assn., 1950, 52, 54, 63; 75th Anniversary medal Nat. Sculpture Soc., 1968; Herbert Adams Meml. medal Nat. Sculpture Soc., 1974.
N.A. Fellow AIA, Internat. Inst. Arts and Letters, Royal Soc. Arts; mem. Nat. Inst. Archtl. Edn., N.A.D. (pres.), Am. Water Color Soc., Fedn. Alliances Francaises (dir.), Delta Phi. Republican. Episcopalian. Clubs: Metropolitan (Washington), Knickerbocker (pres.), Century (N.Y.C.). Home: New York N.Y. Died Jan. 13, 1988.

POPE, GENEROSO PAUL, JR., publisher; b. N.Y.C., Jan. 13, 1927; s. Generoso Paul Sr. and Catherine (Richichi) P.; m. Lois Frances Berrodin, May 29, 1965; children: Generoso Paul III, Michele, Maria, Gina, Paul, Lorraine. B.S. in Gen. Engring, Mass. Inst. Tech., 1946. V.p. Forange, Inc., N.Y.C., 1945-51; v.p., treas. Colonial Sand and Stone Co., Inc., N.Y.C., 1946-51; v.p. Empire Sand and Stone Corp., N.Y.C., 1946-51; exec. v.p., gen. mgr. Sta. WHOM, N.Y.C., 1946-51; editor Il Progresso Italo-Americano, N.Y.C., 1947-51; v.p. Coastal Sales Corp., N.Y.C., 1947-51; sec.-treas., v.p. Progress Mdsg. Corp., N.Y.C., 1947-51; dir. Pope Found., Inc., N.Y.C., 1947—; v.p. Roslyn Sand and Gravel Corp., N.Y.C., 1948-51, Coastal Brokerage Co., Inc., N.Y.C., 1948-51, Colonial Blue Diamond Mortar Corp., N.Y.C., 1949-51; intelligence officer CIA, Washington, 1951; pub. Nat. Enquirer, Inc., Lantana, Fla., 1952—, chmn. bd., 1976-84; pres. Generoso Pope Jr. Found., Lantana, 1963—; chmn. bd. Distbn. Services, Inc., 1976-84; chmn. bd. holding co. GP Group, Inc. 1984— and subs., Nat. Enquirer Inc., Distbn. Services Inc., Weekly World News Inc.; pres. Fairview Real Estate, Inc., Fairview Printing, Inc. Mem. N.Y.C. Mayor's Com. Unity, 1949-52, N.Y.C. Mayor's Com. Mgmt. Survey, 1950, N.Y.C. Bd. Higher Edn., 1950-54, Grand St. Boys Assn., N.Y.C., 1948-51; co-chmn. spl. groups div. March of Dimes, 1949-50; chmn. N.Y.C. Mayor's Com. Police Dept. vs. Fire Dept. Baseball Championship, 1950; pres. Columbus Citizens Com., N.Y.C., 1950-51; trustee Library Presdl. Papers, 1965-70, Englewood (N.J.) Hosp., 1965-71, JFK Med. Ctr., Atlantis, Fla., 1972—; bd. dirs. Three Sch. Devel. Found., Englewood, 1965-71; bd. lay advisers St. Joseph's Village for Children, Rockleigh, N.J., 1965-71; chmn. bd. trustees JFK Med. Ctr., Atlantis, Fla., 1988—. Mem. Sachem, Soc. of Tammany, Columbia Assn. N.Y. Post Office (hon. pres.), Columbian Assn. Bd. Transp. City N.Y., Columbia Assn. Police Dept. City N.Y. Democrat. Roman Cath. Died Oct. 2, 1988.

POPENOE, FREDERICK WILSON, horticulturist, agricultural explorer; b. Topeka, Mar. 9, 1892; s. Fred O. and Marion (Bowman) P.; m. Dorothy Hughes, Nov. 17, 1923 (dec. Dec. 1932); m. 2d, Helen Barsaloux, Jan. 10, 1939 (Dec. Mar. 1961); m. 3d, Alice Weiss, Feb. 14, 1969. Student, Pomona Coll.; DSc, U. San Marcos, Lima, Peru, 1925, Pomona Coll., 1947, U. Fla., 1950. With Dept. Agr., 1913-25; explorer to obtain useful plants to introduce into U.S. Cen., S.Am.; investigator cultural problems of bananas and other tropical crops in Caribbean region United Fruit Co., 1925-41; founder Escuela Agricola Panamericana, Tegucigalpa, Honduras, 1941, dir., 1942-57, dir. emeritus, from 1957; hon. prof. Univ. de San Carlos de Guatemala. Author: Manual of Tropical and Subtropical Fruits, 1920; also many papers on avocados and other tropical and subtropical fruits. Decorated Orden al Merito (Chile and Ecuador), Medalla Agricola Interamericana, Orden de Vasco Nuñez de Balboa (Panama), Orden al Merito Agricola e Industrial (Cuba), comdr. Orden al Mérito Agricola (Ecuador), Orden de Ruben Dario (Nicaragua), Orden de Morazan (Hondura), Orden del Quetzal (Guatemala); recipient George Robert White medal Mass. Hort. Soc., 1950, Wilder medal Am. Pomological Soc. Mem. Calif. Avocado Soc. (hon.), Am. Soc. Foresters, Soc. Venezolana de Ciencias Naturales (corr. mem.), Washington Acad. Sci., Cosmos Club (Washington; Explorers Club (N.Y.C.). Home: Gainesville Fla. †

POPHAM, RICHARD ALLEN, botany educator; b. Charleston, Ill., Sept. 29, 1913; s. Frank and Charlotte (Kluge) P. BEd, Eastern Ill. U., 1936; MS, Ohio State U., 1937, PhD, 1940. Mem. faculty Ohio State U., Columbus, 1940-88, assoc. prof. botany, 1950-68, prof. botoany, 1968-82, prof. emeritus, 1982-88; chief ballistician Scioto Ordnance Plant, 1942-43; supt. atomic bomb mfg. plant, Los Alamos, 1943-45; cons. Batelle Meml. Inst., 1958-70; research collaborator Brookhaven Nat. Lab., 1964-88. Author: Developmental Plant Anatomy, 1952, Laboratory Manual for Plant Anatomy, 1966, also sci. papers. Recipient Alfred J. Wright award Ohio State U., 1966. Mem. Bot. Soc. Am. (bus. mgr. Am. Jour. Botany 1972-88), Internat. Soc. Plant Morphologists, Ohio Acad. Sci. (pres. 1965-66, patron 1971-88), Soc. Econ. Botany, Columbus Numis. Soc. (pres. 1973, treas. 1974-77), Sigma Xi, Gamma Alpha (nat. treas., pres. 1956-60, nat. editor 1968-73). Home: Columbus Ohio. Died Feb. 3, 1988.

POPP, HENRY WILLIAM, educator; b. Millvale, Pa., Nov. 19, 1892; s. William and Emelie (Trautvetter) P.; m. Margaret Patricia McElhaney, July 1, 1919; children: Mary Jean (Mrs. Frank P. Smeal), Margaret Kathryn (Mrs. Ross B. Lehman), Ruth Popp Mosch (dec.). Student, Carnegie Inst. Tech.; BS, Pa. State U., 1917, MS, 1922; PhD, U. Chgo., 1926. Analytical chemist Crucible Steel Co., Pitts., 1912-14; asst. zoology and entomology Pa. State U., 1916-17, instr. botany, 1920-23, asst. prof., 1925-30, assoc. prof., 1930-37, prof., 1937-58, head dept. botany and plant pathology, 1950-58, prof. emeritus, from 1958; head dept. biology Cen. State Tchrs. Coll., Lockhaven, Pa., 1917-20; asst. plant physiologist, plant biochemist Boyce Thompson Inst. Plant Rsch., 1923-25. Author: (with others) Biological Effects of Radiation, 1936, Agricultural Chemistry, 1950; (with Hill, Overholts) Botany, A Textbook for Colleges, rev. edit., 1961; contbr. sci. papers to profl. jours. Sgt. M.C., U.S. Army, 1918. Fellow AAAS; mem. Am. Soc. Plant Physiologists, Wild Life Soc., Torrey Bot. Club, Pa. Acad. Sci., Bot. Soc. Am. (chmn. N.E. sect. 1958), NRC, Masons, Sigma Xi, Gamma Sigma Delta, Phi Kappa Phi, Phi Epsilon. Home: State College Pa. †

POPPELE, JACOB R., radio and television executive, broadcasting consultant; b. Newark, Feb. 4, 1898; s. Jacob John and Katherine (Amendt) P.; m. Pauline Bacmeister, Oct. 30, 1925; children: Lorraine Poppele Flower, June, Virginia Poppele Endres. Student, Marconi Wireless Sch., N.Y.C., 1914-15. Sta. engr., chief engr., builder sta. first transmitter Sta. WOR, N.Y.C., 1922-52; v.p. in charge engring. Mut. Broadcasting System (parent co. Sta. WOR), 1947-52; also bd. dirs. Mut. Broadcasting System, N.Y.C., until 1986; v.p. in charge engring. Gen. Teleradio, Inc., N.Y.C., 1947-52; founder, pres. Tele-Measurements Electronics, N.Y.C., 1962-86; v.p., treas. Teleglobe Pay TV, N.Y.C., 1962-86; designer, dir. constrn. early TV sta., Washington, 1947; radio cons. N.J. State Police; assisted devel. sta. synchronization for deception enemy radio ranging, World War II; mem. broadcast adv. com. Voice of Am., dir., 1953-56; pres. Green Mountain Enterprises, Inc. (Vt.), Wace Broadcasting Co., Chicopee, Mass. Pres. Essex County chpt. Am. Cancer Soc.; dir. Newark council Boy Scouts Am.; council Orange (N.J.) chpt. ARC; chmn. communications sect. technical adv. com. N.J. Civil Def.
Served as radio operator Army Transport Service, World War I. Fellow Inst. Radio Engrs., Radio Club Am. (David Sarnoff award 1974, Pres.' award 1980, Allen B. DuMont award 1984); mem. TV Broadcasters Assn. (founder, dir., pres. 1945-51), FM Broadcasters Assn. (founder), Nat. Assn. Radio and TV Broadcasters (exec. mem. engring. com.), Am. TV Soc., Vet. Wireless Operators Assn. (pres., dir.), Acoustical Soc. Motion Picture Engrs., De Forest Pioneers (pres). Home: South Orange N.J. Died Oct. 7, 1986; buried Restland Meml. Park, East Hanover, N.J.

POPPER, HANS, pathologist; b. Vienna, Austria, Nov. 24, 1903; s. Carl and Emma (Gruenhaum) P.; m. Lina Billig, June 4, 1942; children—Frank, Charles. M.D., U. Vienna, 1928; M.S., U. Ill., 1941, Ph.D., 1944; M.D. (hon.), Catholic U. Louvain, 1965, U. Bologna, 1965, U. Hannover, 1974, U. Turin, 1975, U. Tuebingen, 1977, Cath. Coll., Seoul, Korea, U. Lisbon, 1981, U. Freiburg, 1984, U. Goettingen, Germany, 1987; Ph.D. (hon.), U. Vienna, 1965; D.Sc. (hon.), Mt. Sinai Med. Sch., 1979, Coll. Medicine and Dentistry, N.J., 1981. Resident, asst., dept. pathology and medicine U. Vienna, 1928-38; practice medicine, specializing in pathology Chgo., 1938-57, N.Y.C., 1957-88; research fellow Cook County Grad. Sch. Medicine, 1938-42; dir. labs. Cook County Hosp., 1944-46, dir. dept. pathology, 1946-57; sci. dir. Hektoen Inst. Med. Research, 1943-57; asst. prof., asso. prof., prof. pathology Med. Sch. Northwestern U., 1946-57; pathologist-in-chief Mt. Sinai Hosp., 1957-72, cons. pathologist, dir. emeritus dept., 1972-88; prof. pathology Columbia, 1957-67; dean acad. affairs, prof. pathology, chmn. dept. pathology Mt. Sinai Sch. Medicine, City U., N.Y., 1965-72; pres., dean Mt. Sinai Sch. Medicine, City U., 1972-73, pres. and dean emeritus, 1973-88, Gustave L. Levy disting. service prof., 1972-88; hon. prof. U. Arequipa, Peru, 1965; cons. VA Hosp., Bronx, USPHS Hosp., S.I., Communicable Disease Center, Atlanta, 1957-88. Author: Clinical Pathological Conferences of Cook County Hospital, 1948, Liver: Structure and Function, 1957; Editor: Progress in Liver Diseases, 1961, 65, 70, 73, 76, 79, 82, 86, Clinical Pathological Conferences of Mount Sinai Hospital, 1963, Trends in New Medical Schools, 1967, Collagen Metabolism in the Liver, 1975, Intrahepatic Cholestasis, 1975, Chronic

Hepatitis, 1976, Membane Alterations as Basis of Liver Injury, 1977, Primary Liver Tumors, 1978, Problems in Intrahepatic Cholestasis, 1979, Communications of Liver Cells, 1980, Liver, Biology and Pathobiology, 1982; Contbr. articles to med. jours. Served to maj. M.C. U.S. Army, 1944-46. Fellow Am. Acad. Arts and Scis.; mem. Nat. Acad. Scis., Internat. Assn. for Study of Liver (past pres.), Am. Assn. Study Liver Diseases (past pres.), Chgo. Pathol. Soc., N.Y. Pathol. Soc. (past pres.), Deutsche Akademie der Naturforscher Leopoldina. Home: New York N.Y. Deceased.

PORT, EDMUND, judge; b. Syracuse, N.Y., Feb. 6, 1906; s. Abraham M. and Clara (Alderman) P.; m. Barbara Streeter, Jan 2, 1945; children—Alan David, Linda Kay. LL.B., Syracuse U., 1929. Bar: N.Y. bar 1930. Asst. U.S. atty. No. Dist., N.Y., 1943-51; U.S. atty. No. Dist., 1951-53; U.S. judge No. Dist., N.Y., 1964-86. Home: Smyrna Beach Fla. Died Mar. 2, 1986.

PORTER, JOHN WESLEY, JR., lawyer, former judge; b. Eufaula, Okla., Nov. 7, 1911; s. John Wesley and Mary Elizabeth (Baskett) P.; m. Nanabel Blankenship, June 18, 1937; children: Janita (Mrs. George W. Emrick), John Wesley III, Mary Jane. LL.B., Cumberland U., 1935. Bar: Okla. 1935, U.S. Supreme Ct. 1948. Practice law Muskogee, Okla., 1935, 76-86; police judge Muskogee, 1948-53; asst. county atty. Muskogee County, 1953-61; county judge 1961-69, judge dist. ct., 1969-76. Contbr. articles to profl. jours. Leader Explorer Scouts, 1959-60; Adv. bd. dirs. Muskogee Salvation Army, 1967-69. Mem. Fed. Bar Assn., ABA, Okla. Bar Assn., Muskogee County Bar Assn. (sec. 1938), Am., Okla. trial lawyers assns., Am. Judicature Soc., Lambda Chi Alpha. Democrat. Baptist. Clubs: Muskogee Knife and Fork (dir.), Lions (dir.), Kiwanis, Elks, Order DeMolay. Home: Muskogee Okla. Died Dec., 1986; buried Meml. Pk. Cemetery, Muskogee, Okla.

PORTER, JOHN WILLARD, biochemist, educator; b. Mukwonago, Wis., June 12, 1915; s. George Willard and Josephine (Gunderson) P.; m. Helen Reynolds, June 12, 1941; children: John Willard, Mary Grace, Susan Ann, James Alvin. Asst. chemist Purdue U., 1942-45, asst .prof., 1945-49; asst. chemist Armed Services Med. Nutrition Lab., Chgo., 1945; sr. scientist GE, Hanford, Wash., 1949-54; Enzyme Inst. fellow U. Wis., Madison, 1954-56, assoc. prof. dept. physiol. chemistry, 1956-64, prof., 1964-84; asst. chief Radioisotope Service, VA Hosp., Madison, 1956-64, chief Lipid Metabolism Lab., 1964-84. Author: (with E.T. Mertz) Laboratory Experiments in Biochemistry, 1948, Plant and Animal Biochemistry, 1949; editor: (with S.L. Spurgeon) Biosynthesis of Isoprenoid Compounds, 1981, also numerous research publs. primarily in field of elucidation of pathways and mechanisms of control of biosynthesis of carotenes, cholesterol and fatty acids. Mem. Nat. Acad. Sci. (chmn. subcom.), Am. Soc. Biol. Chemists, Am. Chem. Soc., Am. Soc. Plant Physiologists, AAAS, Am. Inst. Chemists, Sigma Xi. Home: Madison Wis. Died June 27, 1984.

PORTER, LEWIS CASS, railroad executive; b. Temple, Tex., Aug. 9, 1891; s. Lewis Cass and Frances Elizabeth (Black) P.; m. Alyne J. Bush, Sept. 11, 1912; children: Jane Bush (Mrs. Harry F. Burns), Carolyn Frances (Mrs. Robert B. Martin). Student pub. schs., Rosebud and Knox City (Tex.). With oper. dept. Gulf, Tex. & Western R.R. Co., 1910-17; with claim and legal depts. T.&P. Ry., 1917-31, asst. to pres., 1938-48, v.p. operation, from 1948; gen. mgr. Tex. & Pacific Terminal Warehouse Co., Ft. Worth, 1931-38; v.p. Abilene & So. Ry. Co., Denison & Pacific Suburban Ry. co., Eagle Ford Land & Indsl. Co., Ft. Worth Belt Ry. Co., Mchts. Cold Storage Co., Tex. & Pacific Coaches, Inc., Tex. Short Line Ry. Co., Weatherford Mineral Wells & Northwestern Ry. Co., Tex. Pacific-Mo. Pacific Terminal R.R. New Orleans; v.p., bd. dirs. Tex.-N.Mex. Ry. Co., Tex. & Pacific Motor Transport Co.; bd. dirs. El Paso Union Passenger Depot Co., Union Terminal Co. Mem. bd. control Texarkana Union Sta. Trust. Mem. Dallas C. of C., Newcomen Soc. Eng. (N.Am. br.), Athletic Club, City Club, Downtown Club, Lions, Ft. Worth Club, Union League. †

PORTER, RODNEY ROBERT, biochemist, educator; b. Newton-le-Willows, Eng., Oct. 8, 1917; s. Joseph L. and Mae (Reese) P.; BS, Liverpool U., PhD, U. Cambridge , Eng., 1949, DSc. (hon.) Liverpool U., 1973, Vrije U., Brussels, 1974, Hull U., 1974, St. Andrews Coll., 1976, Manchester U., 1976, London U., 1983; m. Julia Frances New, Mar. 23, 1948; children: Susan Clare, Nigel Geoffrey, Ruth Wendy, Timothy Richard, Helen Jane. Mem. sci. staff Nat. Inst. for Med. Research, Mill Hill, Eng., 1949-60; Pfizer prof. immunology St. Mary's Hosp. Med. Sch., London U., 1960-67; Whitley prof. biochemistry U. Oxford, Eng., 1967-85. Mem. editorial bd. Biochem. Jour., 1961-67, Archives Biochemistry and Biophysics, 1962-85, Immunochemistry, 1964-85. With Brit. Army, 1940-46. Recipient award of merit Gairdner Found., 1966, CIBA medal Biochem. Soc., 1967, Karl Landsteiner Meml. award Am. Assn. Blood Banks, 1968, Nobel prize for medicine, 1972. Fellow Royal Soc. (Royal medal 1973, Copley medal 1983), Royal Coll. Physicians (hon.), Royal Soc. Edinburgh (hon.); mem. Am. Soc. Biol. Chemists (hon.), Am. Assn. Immunologists, Am. Acad. Arts and Scis. (hon. fgn.), Soc. Français d'Immunologie (hon.). Died Sept. 6, 1985, buried Oxford, Eng.

PORTER, WILLIAM J., diplomat; b. Cheshire, Eng., Sept. 1, 1914; naturalized, 1936; s. William and Sarah (day) P.; m. Eleanore Henry, Oct. 30, 1944; children: William, Eleanor. Grad. secretarial course, Thibodeau Coll. Bus. Adminstrn., 1933. Pvt. sec. to Am. Minister to Hungary 1936-37; joined Fgn. Service, 1937; clk. Am. Embassy, Bagdad, Iraq, 1937-41; vice counsul Beirut, Lebanon and Damascus,, Syria, 1941-46; legation attaché Damascus, 1945-46; Palestine desk officer Dept. State, June-Nov., 1946; vice-consul Jerusalem, 1946, consul, 1947; established U.S. consulate Nicosia, Cyprus, 1948-49; assigned to div. internat. broadcasting Dept. State, 1951, officer in charge Greek affairs, 1951; consul Rabat, French Morocco, 1953, consul gen., 1954; established U.S. Embassy Rabat, Morocco, 1956-57, 1956-57, dir. N. African affairs, 1957-60; assigned Fgn. Service Inst. Washington, 1960-61; consul gen. with rank of minister Algiers, 1961-62; ambassador to Algeria, 1962-65, Republic of Viet Nam, 1965-67, Republic of Korea, 1967-71; chief delegation, ambassador Paris meetings on Viet Nam 1971-73, Under Sec. of State for polit. affairs, 1973-74; ambassador to Can., 1974-76, Saudi Arabia, 1976-78. Recipient Disting. Honor award Dept. State, 1966, Pres.' award for disting. fed. civilan service, 1967, Viet Nam service medal, 1968. Home: Wesport Mass. Died Mar. 15, 1988.

POST, ALLEN, lawyer; b. Newnan, Ga., Dec. 3, 1906; s. William Glenn and Rosa Kate (Muse) P.; m. Mary Chastaine Cook, Dec. 27, 1934; 1 son, Allen W. A.B. summa cum laude, U. Ga., 1927; B.A. 1st honors, Oxford U.; Rhodes scholar, 1929, B.C.L. 2d honors, 1930, M.A., 1933. Bar: Ga. 1930. Spl. atty. gen. Ga., 1933, 1935; asst. atty. gen. assigned Ga. Pub. Service Commn., 1934; partner Moise, Post & Gardner, Atlanta, 1942-61, Moise, Post & Gardner (specializing in bus. and corp. law), Hansell, Post, Brandon & Dorsey, 1962-83, Hansell & Post; dir., exec. com. Atlanta Gas Light Co.; dir. Am. Cast Iron Pipe Co., Atlantic Am. Corp., Thomaston Mills, other corps.; hon. dir. 1st Nat. Bank Atlanta, 1st Atlanta Corp.; lectr., writer on legal subjects. Pres. Atlanta Estate Planning Council, 1960; trustee Ragan and King Charitable Found., W. N. Banks Found., The Howell Fund; mem. State Democratic Exec. Com., mem. com. to rewrite election laws and revise primary rules of Ga., 1956, Dem. presdl. elector.; Mem. Governor's Staff; mem. State Com. to Revise Income Tax Laws of Ga., 1956, Ga. Income Tax Study Commn.; Chmn. Northside Hosp. Served as lt. comdr. USNR, World War II. Mem. Atlanta Bar Assn. (exec. com., pres. 1956), ABA, Ga. Bar Assn., Am. Coll. Probate Counsel, Am. Coll. Trial Lawyers, Am. Judicature Soc., Atlanta Claims Assn., S.A.R., Navy League, Res. Officers Naval Services (1st pres. Atlanta chpt.), Mil. Order World Wars, Am. Legion (comdr.), Am. Assn. Rhodes Scholars, Sphinx, Gridiron, Phi Beta Kappa, Phi Kappa Phi, Phi Delta Phi, Kappa Alpha. Methodist (chmn. ofcl. bd., trustee). Clubs: Capital City (Atlanta), Piedmont Driving (Atlanta), Lawyers (Atlanta); Old War Horse Lawyers (pres. 1962), Commerce, Rotary. Home: Atlanta Ga. Died Jan. 11, 1986.

POST, CURTIS WALTER, editor, organization official; b. Oxford, N.Y., Jan. 22, 1888; s. Hubert and Martha (Turner) P.; m. Grace A. Proctor, Sept. 5, 1914; children: Martha Jane (Mrs. Roy E. Teele), Helen Edith, John Curtis. LLB, Chgo. Kent Coll. Law, 1914. Bar: Ill. 1915. Originator course in printed advt; instr. Chgo. Sch. Printing, 1925-34; editor Comml. Law Jour., from 1942. Author: (with Ben. C. Pittsford) Pittsford's Manual for Advertisers. Mem. ABA, Ill. Bar Assn., Comml. Law League Am. (exec. sec.), Am. Judicature Soc., Kiwanis Club (Chgo.). Republican. Methodist. Home: Evanston Ill. †

POST, GAINES, history educator; b. Haskell, Tex., Mar. 7, 1902; s. Henry S. and Rachel (Ballard) P.; m. Katherine Rike, July 5, 1935; children: John Fredric, Gaines. AB, U. Tex., 1924; AM, Harvard U., 1925, PhD, 1931; student, Ecole de Chartes, 1927-28. Instr., tutor Harvard U., Boston, 1929-35; asst. prof. history U. Wis., Madison, 1935-38, assoc. prof., 1938-41, prof., 1941-64; prof. history Princeton (N.J.) U., 1964-70, prof. emeritus, 1970-87; lectr. Riccobono Seminar, 1947, Medieval Inst. U. Notre Dame, 1949; fellow Inst. Advanced Study, Princeton U., 1959-60; chmn. Inst. of Research and Study in Medieval Canon Law. Author: Studies in Medieval Legal Thought, also articles on medieval univs. and intellectual history. Recipient Fulbright research award, France, 1951-52; Guggenheim fellow, 1939-40, 55-56. Fellow Medieval Acad. Am., Am. Acad. Arts and Scis., Am. Soc. for Legal History (hon.); mem. Am. Hist. Assn., Heidelberg Akademie der Wissenschaften, Philosophisch-historische Klasse (corr.). Home: Haskell Tex. Died Dec. 19, 1987; buried Haskell, Tex.

POSTLETHWAITE, KEITH THOMSON, clergyman; b. Millville, Ky., July 4, 1892; m. Anna May Penland, Feb. 28, 1929; children: Anna Frances, Shirley Rebecca. AB, Maryville Coll., 1916; BD, Presbyn. Theol. Sem., 1922; grad., Chaplain's Sch., Harvard U., 1943; MST, Princeton Theol. Sem., 1947. Ordained to ministry Presbyn. Ch., 1929; lic. engr., Tenn. Transitman Tenn. Electric Power Co., 1916-17, draftsman, engr., 1927-30; surveyor U.S. Engring. Dept., 1917-19; from insp. to jr. engr. Tenn. Hwy. Dept., summer 1919, 1922-24; draftsman Standard Iron and Wire Works, 1924-25, Converse Bridge and Steel Co., 1926-27; pastor South Pittsburg, Tenn., 1930-36, 1st Cumberland Ch., Birmingham, Ala., 1936-42, 1st Presbyn. Ch., Ocean City, Md., 1947-52, Eastminster Presbyn. Ch., Bladensburg, Md., 1952-64; supply pastor Riverread Ch. Wash., from 1964; moderator Birmingham Presbytery and Ala., Miss. Synod, East Tenn. synod and Chattanooga Presbyter; leader Washington City Presbytery's del. to Gen. Assembly, 1960; mem. jud. commn. Balt. Synod, 1960; mem. comity and evangelism coms. Washington Fedn. Chs.; vice-moderator, mem. examining com. Washington City Presbytery, 1955, chmn. com. on evangelism, 1960, also com. cooperation and ch. union; bd. dirs. Birmingham Sunday Sch. Coun., Gen. Assembly's Bd. Christian Edn.; mem. State Bd. Ala. Commn. on Evangelism for All Protestant Denominations, 1941-42. Chmn. Marion County chpt. ARC, 1935. Ensign USN, 1918-19, maj. U.S. Army, 1942-46. Mem. Am. Legion (chaplain 1934-35). Home: Arlington Va. †

POTOK, ANNA MAXIMILIAN, furrier; b. Warsaw, Poland, June 4, 1897; came to U.S., 1939, naturalized, 1945; d. Leon and Tyla (Glasswine) Apfelbaum; m. Leon Potok, July 12, 1930 (dec. 1965); 1 child, Andrew. With family fur business Warsaw, until 1939; designer Maximilian Furs, N.Y.C., 1939-72, pres., 1953-72, cons., 1972-87. Recipient Coty Fashion award, 1945, 65, Restituta Pologna (Poland), 1934. Mem. Fashion Group. Home: New York N.Y. Died Apr. 22, 1987.

POTTER, GEORGE FREDERICK, scientist; b. Madison, Wis., Aug. 7, 1891; s. George Frederick and Jane Leslie (Findlay) P.; m. Pearl Ada Schnackenberg, Sept. 20, 1917; children: Frances, George, Ada (Mrs. W.E. Snyder), Clarence. BS, U. Wis., 1913, MS, 1916. Instr. in horticulture U. Wis., 1913-18, asst. prof., 1918-20; prof. horticulture and horticulturist of expt. sta. U. N.H., 1920-38; prin. physiologist Hort. Crops Rsch. Br., Agr. Rsch. Svc., U.S. Dept. Agr., Bogalusa, La., from 1938. Contbr. author: Fruit Nutrition, 1954; author or joint author of about 60 scientific papers. Recipient Wilder medal Am. Pomol. Soc., 1953; named Man of the Yr. in Tung, Am. Tung Oil Assn., 1955. Fellow AAAS (N.H. rep. governing coun. 1937-38); mem. La. Acad. Scis., N.H. Acad. Scis., Am. Soc. Hort. Sci. (pres. 1946), Am. Soc. Plant Physiologists, AAUP (pres. N.H. chpt. 1938), Alpha Zeta, Sigma Xi, Phi Kappa Phi. Democrat. Presbyterian. Home: Bogalusa La. †

POTTER, ROBERT STURGIS, lawyer; b. Boston, Apr. 28, 1920; s. Robert S. and Dorothy (Tweedy) P.; m. Isabel Doolittle Russell, Nov. 1944; children: Louise Ross, Isabel Aldrich, Lorna Potter Walker, Linda Potter-Shriver, Robert Sturgis Jr. AB, Harvard U., 1942; LLB, U. Va., 1948; D Canon Law (hon.), Yale U. Bar: N.Y. Ptnr. firm Emmet, Marvin & Marvin, N.Y.C., 1948-51, 53-62; with Psychol. Strategy Bd., Washington, 1951-53; ptnr. firm Patterson, Belknap, Webb & Tyler, N.Y.C., from 1962; then sec., dir. Dow Jones & Co., Inc., N.Y.C.; dir. Fiduciary Trust Co. Trustee Community Svc. Soc. N.Y., 1965-79, Community Coun. Greater N.Y., from 1970, NAACP Legal Def. Fund, from 1974, Episcopal Theol. Sch., 1971-75, Investor Responsibility Rsch. Ctr., 1972-80; chancellor Episcopal Diocese N.Y., 1972-76. With USNR, 1942-45. Mem. Century, River clubs. Republican. Episcopalian. Home: New York N.Y. Died Aug. 20, 1988.

POTTER, WILLIAM EVERETT, corporate consultant; b. Oshkosh, Wis., July 17, 1905; s. William B. and Arlie Belle (Coulter) P.; m. Ruth Elizabeth Turner, July 21, 1936; children: Jo Ann (Mrs. George B. Hipp), Susan Ruth (Mrs. Gunner Schull). BS, U.S. Mil. Acad., 1928; BSCE, MIT, 1933; postgrad., Engr. Sch., 1936-37, Command and Gen. Staff Sch., 1941; DEng (hon.), Drexel U., 1960, Nat. War Coll., 1951-52. Commd. 2d lt. U.S. Army, 1928, advanced to maj. gen., 1956, company officer 1st Engrs., 1928-29, assigned Nicaragua Canal Survey, 1929-32, with Pitts. Engr. Dist., 1933-36; asst. prof. mil. sci. and tactics Ohio State U., 1937-40; comdg. officer 25th Armoired Engr. Bn., also 1138th Armored Engr. Group 1940-43; asst. G-4 for plans and ops. ETO and Communications Zone, 1943-45; dist. engr. Kansas City, Mo., 1945-48, Alaska, 1948-49; asst. chief Engrs. for Civil Works Dept. Army, Washington, 1949-51; with Engrs. for Spl. Projects 1951; div. engr. Mo. River Div. Omaha, 1952-56; gov. Canal Zone 1956-60; pres. Panama Canal Co., 1956-60; ret. 1960; exec. v.p. N.Y. World's Fair 1964-65 Corp., 1960-65; v.p., sr. v.p. Walt Disney World Co., 1965-73, cons., 1973-88; mem. bd. suprs. Reedy Creek Improvement Dist.; bd. dirs. Carlisle Corp., Fla. Gas Co., Fla. Shares, Inc., Am. Bankers Ins. Co. Fla., Trust Co. Fla. Bd. govs. Orange Meml. Hosp.; bd. dirs. Loch Haven Art Mus.; vice chair Orlando Airport Authority Bd. Decorated Legion of Merit, Bronze Star, D.S.M.; Croix de Guerre with palm (France). Fellow ASCE; mem. Soc. Am. Mil. Engrs., Army-Navy Club, Orlando Country Club, Citrus Club. Home: Orlando Fla. Died Dec. 5, 1988; buried Woodlawn Meml. Park, Orlando.

POTTHOFF, CARL JOHN, physician; b. Morgan, Minn., Jan. 14, 1904; s. Henry Anthony and Florence

Amelia (Baechtold) P.; m. Mercedes T. Gunn, May 28, 1975. B.S., Hamline U., 1926; M.D., U. Minn., 1933; M.P.H., 1941. Diplomate: Am. Bd. Preventive Medicine. High sch. prin. Slayton, Minn., 1926-28; supt. schs. Welcome, Minn., 1928-29; intern Asbury Hosp., Mpls., 1932-33; pvt. practice medicine Hallock, Minn., 1934-36; asst. prof. biol. sci. and pub. health U. Minn., 1937-41, assoc. prof., 1941-45; supr. emergency and admitting service Mpls. Gen. Hosp.; asso. med. dir. ARC, Washington, 1945-52; med. dir. Albuquerque Area Bur. Indian Affairs, 1952-53; prof. preventive medicine and pub. health U. Nebr., 1954-70, also former chmn.; asst. commr. health, Omaha, 1954-55. Author: American Red Cross First Aid Textbook, rev, 1957, American Red Cross First Aid Textbook for Juniors; columnist: Todays Health in Safety & First Aid, 1950-71, Am. Jour. Public Health, 1964-67, Sun City News-Sun, 1973-79; author articles on health. Fellow Am. Coll. Preventive Medicine, AAAS, Am. Pub. Health Assn. Home: Sun City Ariz. Died Aug. 18, 1987; cremated.

POTTLE, FREDERICK ALBERT, English educator; b. Lovell, Maine, Aug. 3, 1897; s. Fred LeRoy and Annette Wardwell (Kemp) P.; m. Marion Isabel Starbird, Sept. 9, 1920; children: Annette (dec.), Christopher, Samuel Heald. AB summa cum laude, Colby Coll., 1917, LittD (hon.), 1941; AM, Yale U., 1921, PhD, 1925; LLD (hon.), U. Glasgow, 1936; LittD (hon.), Rutgers U., 1951; LHD (hon.), Northwestern U., 1967. Asst. prof. English U. N.H., 1921-23; instr. in English Yale U., New Haven, Conn., 1925-26, asst. prof., 1926-30, prof., 1930-66, emeritus, 1966-87, Emily Sanford prof. English lit., 1942-44, Sterling prof. English, 1944-46, pub. orator, 1942, 46.; Former chancellor Acad. Am. Poets. Author 6 books including: Stretchers, the Story of a Hospital on the Western Front, 1929, The Idiom of Poetry, 1941, rev. edit., 1946, James Boswell, the Earlier Years, 1740-1769, 1966; editor 26 books including: Boswell's London Journal, 1762-1763, 1950, Boswell in Holland, 1763-1764, 1952, (with Frank Brady) Boswell in Search of a Wife, 1766-1769, 1956, (with W.K. Wimsatt) Boswell for the Defence, 1769-1774, 1959, (with Charles Ryskamp) Boswell, the Ominous Years, 1774-1776, 1963, (with C. Weis) Boswell in Extremes, 1776-1778, 1970; chmn. editorial com. Yale edits. of the Private Papers of James Boswell; contbr. to mags. Trustee Colby Coll., 1932-59, 66-87; former trustee Gen. Theol. Sem. Fellow Davenport Coll.; mem. Joint Commn. on Holy Matrimony Episc. Ch., 1940-46. Surg. asst. evacuation hosp. Am. Expeditionary Forces, 1917-19. Recipient John Addison Porter prize Yale U., 1925, Wilbur Lucius Cross medal, 1967, William Clyde DeVane medal, 1969; Guggenheim fellow, 1945-46. Fellow Internat. Inst. Arts and Letters; mem. Am. Acad. Arts and Scis., Conn. Acad. Arts and Scis. (pres. 1967-68), Am. Philos. Soc. (John F. Lewis prize 1974), Provincial Utrechtsch Genootschap van Kunsten en Wetenschnappen, Guild of Scholars, MLA, Medieval Acad., Johnson Soc. Lichfield, Eng. (pres. 1974), Grolier Club, Ends of the Earth Club (N.Y.C.), Elizabethan Club (New Haven), Johnson Club, Johnson Club of London, Phi Beta Kappa, Alpha Tau Omega. Home: New Haven Conn. Died May 16, 1987; buried Otisfield, Maine.

POWELL, PHILIP WAYNE, educator, author; b. Chino, Calif., Oct. 30, 1913; s. Robert Chester and Muriel June (Holcomb) P.; m. Mariá Luisa Vanegas Guarín, Jan. 22, 1942; children: Diana Linda (Mrs. Larry M. Fornas), Lilia Patricia (Mrs. James A. Rochester). Student, Occidental Coll., 1930-32; B.A., U. Calif. at Berkeley, 1936, Ph.D., 1941. With State Dept., 1941-43; vis. prof. history U. Pa., 1943-44; asst. prof. Northwestern U., 1944-48; prof. history U. Calif. at Santa Barbara, from 1948, chmn. dept., 1958, 62-64; dir. univ. study center at U. Madrid, Spain, 1964-66; Chmn. Nat. Conf. Latin Am. History, 1947; spl. adviser 9th Internat. Conf. Am. States, Bogota, 1948. Author: Soldiers, Indians and Silver: The Northward Advance of New Spain, 1550-1600, 1952, Ponzoña en Las Nieves, 1966, Tree of Hate: Propaganda and Prejudices Affecting United States Relations with the Hispanic World, 1971, Arbol de Odio, 1972, Mexico's Miguel Caldera: The Taming of America's First Frontier, 1548-1597, 1977, La Guerra Chichimeca, 1977, Capitán Mestizo: Miguel Caldera y la Frontera Norteña, 1548-1597, 1980; adv. editor: The Americas, from 1953. Served with USMCR, 1942-43. Decorated comdr. Order Isabel the Catholic (Spain). Mem. Instituto de Cultura Hispánica (Madrid) (hon.), Phi Beta Kappa, Phi Gamma Delta. Home: Santa Barbara Calif. Deceased.

POWELL, ROBERT LEE, clergyman, church official; b. Covington County, Miss., Jan. 22, 1888; s. John P. and Rosamond Francis (Chambers) P.; m. Altha Talbot, Sept. 4, 1919; children: Jurell (Mrs. Jerry McCrorie), Mary-Beth (Mrs. Peter J. Cran), Rosaltha. Student, South Miss. Coll., Miss. Coll.; DD (hon.), Howard-Payne Coll., 1930. Ordained to ministry Bapt. Ch., 1911. Pastor various So. cities, 1912-31, 1st Bapt. Ch., Tacoma, 1932-34, Temple Bapt. Ch., Tacoma, 1934-62; mem. exec. coun. Internat. Coun. Christian Ch., Am. Coun. Christian Chs. for Wash.; past chmn. Gen. Assn. Regular Bapt. Sch., mem. coun. of 14. Editor Temple Tidings. Past chmn. Glendawn Bapt. Bible Camp, Auburn, Wash.; past mem. coun. Bapt. Mid-Missions; trustee L.A. bapt. Coll. and Sem.; vol. chaplain War Dept., World War I. Home: Tacoma Wash. †

POWER, HARRY HARRISON, petroleum engineering educator; b. Chassel, Mich., July 7, 1892; s. Elmer Lambert and Ivy Belle (Spencer) P.; m. Gladys Katherine Drach. BSChemE, State Coll. Wash., 1919, degree in ChemE, 1936; MS in Petroleum Engring., U. Calif., 1928; PhD, U. Pitts., 1946. Jr. engr. Cities Svc. Co., Denver and Bartlesville (Okla.), 1919-22; asst engr. Bartlesville, 1922; valuation engr. U.S. Internal Revenue Bur., Washington, 1922-26; prodn. engr. Gulf Oil Corp., Tulsa, 1927-30, chief prodn. engr., 1930-36; prof. petroleum engring., chmn. dept. U. Tex., 1936-56, 57-62, prof. emeritus, from 1962; Fulbright prof. U. Cairo, 1962-63; Fulbright lectr. Tech. U. Delft, The Netherlands, 1956; cons. Office Petroleum Adminstr. for War, U.S. Dept. State, World War II; mem. Lucas Medal Com. Contbr. papers to profl. jours. Pvt. U.S. Army, World War I. Recipient medal Tech. U. Delft, 1956. Mem. AIME, So. Regional Edn. Bd. (chmn. petroleum bd.), Am. Soc. for Engring Edn., AIME (chmn. petroleum div. 1935, mineral industries ednl. div., Mineral Industry Edn. award 1964), Am. Assn. Petroleum Geologists, Am. Inst. Chem. Engrs. (s.w. sect.), Am. Petroleum Inst. (chmn. devel. and prodn. rsch.), Masons, Sigma Xi, Sigma Tau, Tau Beta Pi, Sigma Gamma Epsilon, Teta Theta Pi. Home: Austin Tex. †

POWER, JOSEPH THOMAS, labor organization executive; b. Chgo., Feb. 22, 1920; s. Joseph and Mary (Kelly) P; m. Mary Kathryn Powers, Oct. 12, 1943; children: John J., Kathryn E., Mary Ann, Joan, Joseph, Shiela. Grad. high sch. V.p. Plasterers' Local 5, Chgo., 1954-55, pres., 1955-56; internat. v.p. Operative Plasterers' and Cement Masons' Internat. Assn., Washington, 1956-59, exec. v.p., 1959-70, gen. pres., 1970-81; mem. Nat. Joint Bd. for Settlement of Jurisdictional Disputes, 1961-71, v.p., mem. exec. council bldg. and constrn. trades dept., 1970-81; del. Internat. Labor Orgn., Geneva, Switzerland, 1971, 72, Japanese Confedn. Labor, Tokyo, 1972, Japan/Korea, 1974, Washington, 1975; mem. Dept. State mission to S.Am., 1973. Pub. mem. Fgn. Service Selection Bd. III, Dept. State; bd. vis. U.S. Mil. Acad., 1977-81. With USCGR, 1941-46. Roman Catholic. Home: Falls Church Va. Died Apr. 27, 1981; buried Columbia Gardens, Falls Ch.

POWER, SARAH GODDARD, association executive; b. Detroit, June 19, 1935; d. Wendell Converse and Katharine Shearer (Russel) Goddard; m. Philip Harwick Power, July 5, 1971. B.A. in History, Vassar Coll., 1957; M.A., Grad. Sch. Politics and Internat. Relations, N.Y. U., 1965; A.A. (hon.), Schoolcraft Community Coll., Livonia, Mich., 1975. Adminstrv. asst. Gov. Nelson Rockefeller, 1959-63; exec. dir. N.Y.C. Commn. for UN and for Consular Corps (office of Mayor John Lindsay), 1966-69, U.S. UN/N.Y.C. Host Country adv. com., 1969-72; asst. chmn. U. Mich. Commn. for Women, Ann Arbor, 1973-74; vice chmn. U.S. Nat. Commn. for UNESCO, Washington, 1975-76; chmn. U.S. Nat. Commn. for UNESCO, 1976-79; dep. asst. sec. of state for human rights and social affairs Bur. Internat. Orgn. Affairs, U.S. Dept. State, Washington, 1980-81; dir. UN Assn. U.S.A., 1973-80, 82-87, mem. nat. council, 1980-82; dir. UN Assn. U.S.A. (Mich. chpt.), 1978-87; rep. U.S. Nat. Commn. for UNESCO, Mex., 1975; U.S. del. UNESCO confs., 1976-78, UN conf., 1980; mem.-at-large exec. com. Mich. Conf., Nat. Commn. Internat. Women's Year, 1975; chmn. task force on status of women U.S. Nat. Commn. for UNESCO, 1974-76. Dir. Nat. Women's Ednl. Fund, 1980-87; Regent U. Mich., 1975-87; mem. Mich. adv. bd. Project on Equal Edn. Rights, NOW Legal Defense and Edn. Fund, 1978-84; dir. U. Musical Soc., U. Mich., 1975-87; trustee Gerald R. Ford Found., 1983-87; mem. judicial conf. Com. for Bicentennial of U.S. Constitution, 1986-87. Recipient Mich. Internat. Council Major Internat. award, 1980, award Alpha Rho chpt. Delta Kappa Gamma, 1980, resolution of tribute Legislature State of Mich., 1980, Disting. Service award Mich. Edn. Assn., 1981. Mem. Am. Council on Edn., Automobile Assn. Mich. (dir. 1982-87), Commn. on Women in Higher Edn., Council on Fgn. Relations. Home: Ann Arbor Mich. Died Mar. 24, 1987.

POWER, THOMAS F., JR., diplomat, consultant; b. Worcester, Mass., May 15, 1916; s. Thomas F. and Mabel (Quinn) P.; m. Mina Waterman, Dec. 12, 1942 (div.); 1 dau., Margaret; m. Julia Minds Schimmel, Aug. 23, 1974. AB, Amherst Coll., 1938; AM, Columbia U., 1939, PhD, 1942. Rsch. specialist Dept. State, 1942-45, specialist dependent area affairs, 1945; asst. com. sec. Internat. Secretariat, UN Conf. on Internat. Orgn., San Francisco, 1945; mem. U.S. del. to UN, 1946; spl. asst. to sec.-gen., chief div. of reports and documentation, dep. sec.-gen., permanent mission and U.S. del. UN Gen. Assembly, 1946-50; pron. sec. UN Mission to Libya, 1950-52; personal rep. UN sec. gen., 1950-55; resident rep. UN Tech. Assistance Bd. in Libya, 1952-55; UN observer Libyan Pub. Devel. and Stblzn. Agy., 1952-55; UN adviser Libyan Finance Corp., 1953-55; spl. asst. to chmn. UN Tech. Assistance Bd., 1955, resident rep. in Iran, 1955-61; chief adminstrv. officer UN Emergency Force, Egypt, 1956-57; resident rep. UN Tech. Assistance Bd. and Spl. Fund, Pakistan, 1961-66; spl. adviser to adminstr. UN Devel. Programme, 1966-67; exec. sec. Fund of UN for Devel. of West IRian, 1967-70; regional rep. UN Devel. Programme, Thailand, 1971-76; cons. from 1976. Author: Jules Ferry and the Renaissance of French Imperialism, 1944. Decorated Order Hormoz (Iran). Mem. Am. Hist. Assn., Coun. Fgn. Rels. N.Y., Phi Beta Kappa. Home: Somers N.Y. Died Oct. 13, 1988, buried Augusta, Maine.

POWERS, ANNE, author; b. Cloquet, Minn., May 7, 1913; d. John Patrick and Maud (Lynch) P.; m. Harold A. Schwartz, Aug. 22, 1938; children: Weldon, Lynn. Student, U. Minn., 1932-33. Lectr., instr. writing Marquette U., Milw.; instr. creative writing Marquette U. (Coll. Journalism. Marquette U.). Author: The Gallant Years, 1946, Ride East, Ride West, 1947, No Wall So High, 1949, The Ironmaster, 1951, The Only Sin, 1953, The Thousand Fires, 1957, Ride With Danger, 1958, No King But Caesar, 1960, Rachel, 1973, The Four Queens, 1977, The Royal Consorts, 1978, The Young Empress, 1979, Possession, 1979, Eleanor, the Passionate Queen, 1981. Recipient ann. award best gen. book submitted Nat. Fedn. Press Women, 1946; matrix citation fiction writing Theta Sigma Phi, 1951; Headliner of Yr. award Wis. Women in Communication, 1983. Mem. Allied Authors, Fictioneers (Best Biog. Romantic Hist. Novel, Romantic Times Mag., 1986), Sigma Kappa. Roman Catholic. Club: Shorewood Woman's (Milw.). Home: Milwaukee Wis. Died July 26, 1987; buried St. Peter's Cemetery, East Troy, Wis.

POWERS, EDWARD MICHAEL, industrial consultant; b. LeRoy, Ill., Sept. 4, 1892. Grad., Air Corps Engr. Sch., 1931, Tactical Sch., 1936. Enlisted Signal Corps Res., 1917; commd. 2d lt. U.S. Army, 1920, advanced through grades to maj. gen., 1945; mil. observer Office of Mil. Attaché, London, 1941; Army Air Forces rep. aircraft scheduling unit Army Air Forces Materiel Ctr., Dayton, Ohio, 1942-43; Army mem. Joint Prodn. Survey Com. U.S. Joint Chiefs of Staff, Washington, 1943; asst. chief Air Staff for Materiel and Svcs., 1945; apptd. mem. Nat. Adv. Com. for Aero., 1945; chmn. ind. div. Air Coordinating Com., 1946; v.p., dir. engring. Curtiss-Wright Corp., Wood-Ridge, N.J.; gen. mgr. Wright Aero div.; owner E.M. Powers, Assocs.; bd. dirs. Chris-Craft Industries, Walter Kidde & Co., Inc. Fellow Inst. Aero. Scis. †

POWERS, JUSTIN LAWRENCE, publishing representative; b. Owensboro, Ky., Aug. 25, 1892; s. A.D. and Ethel (Bryant) P.; m. Susan Moore, 1937; children: Carolien, Joshua, Thomas M., Susan. Student, U. Tex., 1911-13. Mgr. United Press Assn., Buenos Aires, many yrs.; rep. La Prensa of Buenos Aires and other publs., N.Y.C., 1926-72; bd. dirs. Interam. Press Assn.; treas. Tinker Found. Decorated commendador Order Bernardo O'Higgins Cruzeiro Do Sul (Brazil); recipient Cabot award Columbia U., gold medal Pan. Am. Soc. Mem. Metropolitan Club. Republican. Home: New York N.Y. †

POWERS, PHILIP NATHAN, nuclear engineer, educator; b. Terre Haute, Ind., Aug. 17, 1912; s. Samuel Ralph and Eda (Olds) P.; m. Eleanor Ritchie, Apr. 25, 1936 (div.); 1 child, Cameron; m. Evelyne Schanze, May 22, 1959; stepchildren—Jacques le Sourd, Liliane Maginot. B.A., Columbia U., 1932, Ph.D., 1940; Gen. Edn. Bd. fellow, U. Chgo., 1940-41. Assoc. sci. New Coll. Tchrs. Coll., Columbia, 1932-35; assoc. New Coll. Community, 1937-38; instr. natural scis. Stephens Coll., 1939-42; physicist Naval Ordnance Lab., 1942-44, tng. dir., 1944-46; chief sci. edn. br. Office Naval Research, 1946; adviser sci. personnel Pres.' Sci. Research Bd., 1947, AEC, 1947-50; manpower specialist, sec. sci. manpower adv. com. NSRB, 1950-51, cons., 1953; dir. atomic project Monsanto Chem. Co., 1951-55; chmn. bd. Internuclear Co., Clayton, Mo., 1955-59; pres. Internuclear Co., 1955-60; prof. nuclear engring. Purdue U., 1960-78, head Sch. Nuclear Engring., 1960-73, dir. Energy Engring. Center, 1973-78, prof. emeritus, 1978-88, acting dir. Coal Research Lab., 1977-78, assoc. dir. engring. expt. sta., 1960-61, dir. engring. expt. sta., 1961-68, also v.p. Purdue Research Found., 1961-62; Chmn. council Assoc. Midwest Univs., 1964-65; chmn. nuclear engring. edn. com. Asso. Midwest Univs., 1964-65; trustee, exec. com. Argonne Univs. Assn., 1965-72, pres., 1966-72; dir. Atomic Indsl. Forum, 1968-74; chmn. Great Lakes-Great Plains advisory council, 1973-74; cons. com. on specialized personnel ODM, 1951-63, mem. com. manpower resources, 1953; cons. NSF, 1952-57, AEC, 1964-68, AEC Fellowship Bd., 1964-66, Select Com. Govt. Research, Ho. of Reps., 1964-65, Pres.'s Com. Scientists and Engrs., 1956-58, Dept. of State, 1957, N.Y. Univ. planning internat. activities, 1958-59; Mem. Commn. on Survey of Dentistry; chmn. atomic energy panel Engrs. Joint Council, 1956-58; ex-officio mem. Ind. Gov.'s Energy Com., 1973-76; mem. Congressmen Landgrebe's Energy Crisis Study Commn., 1973-74; mem. panel Nat. Acad. Scis. for Korea-U.S. Joint Com. for Sci. Cooperation, 1973; mem. exec. com. Ind. Gov.'s Energy Com., 1974-78; mem. ad hoc panel on mechanisms for providing sci. advice to State Ind., 1974-76; chmn. Ind. Select Com. on Energy Research and Devel., 1977; dir. U.S. Nat. Com. World Energy Conf., 1977-79; mem. adv. bd. Schnurmacher Inst. Vision Research, SUNY/State Coll. Optometry, 1983-86; cons. Commonwealth Edison Co., 1978-79. Series editor: Energy, Power and the Environment, Marcel-Dekker, Inc., 1976-88. Trustee Optometric Ctr. N.Y.,

1986-88. Recipient Meritorious Civilian Service award USN, 1946; Robert C. Morris award State of Ind., 1978; named Sagamore of the Wabash, 1978. Fellow AAAS; mem. Am. Nuclear Soc. (dir. 1963-66, mem. exec. com. aerospace div. 1963-65), Am. Soc. for Engring. Edn. (chmn. atomic energy edn. com. 1953-57, chmn. com. on space engring. 1962-66, chmn. grad. studies div. 1965-66), U.S. C. of C. (nat. def. com. 1953-59, com. on comml. uses atomic energy 1959-62, com. on new frontiers of tech. 1960-63), Am. Nuclear Soc., Am. Soc. Engring. Edn., Ind. Acad. Scis., Sigma Xi. Home: New York N.Y. Died Apr. 26, 1988.

POWERS, WILLIAM EDMONDS, state justice; b. Valley Falls, R.I., Dec. 8, 1907; s. William F. and Cecilia T. (Edmonds) P.; m. Esther J. Johnson, Sept. 2, 1932 (dec. July 1969); children: Esther Mary, Barbara Ann, Michael Andrew; m. Olive D. Higgins, Dec. 28, 1970. BS, Perkins Inst., 1932; JD, Boston U., 1935, LLD (hon.), 1958; DSc (hon.), Bryant Coll., 1951; DJS (hon.), Suffolk U., 1970. Bar: Mass. 1935, R.I., U.S Dist. Ct. R.I., U.S. Supreme Ct. Pvt. practice Bristol County, 1935-46, R.I., 1946-89; judge Cumberland Probate Ct., 1936-49; atty. gen. State of R.I., 1949-58; assoc. justice R.I. Supreme Ct., 1958-73. Mem. R.I. Ho. of Reps., 1939-40, chmn. com. on rules and order, 1947-49, on judiciary, 1941-49, chmn. legis. exec. joint com. on ins., 1946-49, mem. Commn. on Inter-State Govt., from 1946; pres. R.I. Constl. Conv., 1973. Mem. AMA, R.I. Bar Assn., Elks, KC, Phi Delta Phi. Home: Providence R.I. Died Jan. 7, 1989.

PRAEGER, EMIL HUGH, civil engineer, business executive; b. Guatemala City, Aug. 2, 1892; s. Seaman and Rosalin (Stinson) P.; m. Edna D. Quinn, Feb. 12, 1918; children: Mary Rose Praeger White, Richard Quinn, Elizabeth Stinson Praeger Branigan. BCE, Rensselaer Poly. Inst., 1915, D Engring. (hon.), 1954; D Engring. (hon.), Manhattan Coll., St. John's U. Engr. Fireproof Contractors Corp., 1916-17, Todd-Robertson-Todd, Engrs., 1920; chief engr. Bertram G. Goodhue, Architect, 1921-28; asst. chief engr. Curtis Wright Airport Corp., 1929; pvt. practice, cons. engr. from 1930; chief engr. Madigan-Hyland, 1934-46, ptnr., 1946; later ptnr. Praeger, Kavanaugh, Waterbury; cons. engr. renovation of the White House, Washington, planning office UN Hdqrs.; head dept. civil engring. Rensselaer Poly. Inst., 1939-46. Contbr. articles to profl. jours. With C.E. USN, World War I, capt. USNR, World War II. Decorated Legion of Merit; recipient Gold medal Archtl. League N.Y., Disting. Service award Rensselaer Poly. Inst., Engring. award Cons. Engrs. Council, award N.Y. Soc. Profl. Engrs. Mem. ASCE (hon., Engr. of Yr. award), Am. Inst. Cons. Engrs., Am. Soc. Landscape Architects (hon.), Newcomen Soc., Century Club, Engrs. Club (N.Y.), Tau Beta Pi, Sigma Xi, Chi Epsilon, Theat Xi. Home: Douglaston N.Y. †

PRANGE, CHARLES H., research executive; b. N.Y.C., Feb. 25, 1892; s. Herman and Sophie (Koster) P.; m. Constance Erdle, Nov. 27, 1919; children: Paula (Mrs. Walter Klingensmith), Carol (Mrs. Philip Drake). ME, Stevens Inst. Tech., 1914, DEng (hon.), 1961. Products designer Weber Electric Co., 1914-15, engr. designer, 1920-26; test engr. GE, 1915; engr. U.S. Steel Corp., 1916-19; ptnr. dental rsch. Erdle & Prange, 1926-28; v.p. Austenal Co. div. Howe Sound Co. (formerly Austenal, Inc.), 1928-47, pres., 1947, spl. cons. Recipient Modern Pioneers award Nat. Assn. Mfrs., 1940. Mem. ASME (life), Am. Soc. Metals, Fed. Union (bd. dirs.), Chemists Club, Engineers Club, Stevens Met. Club. †

PRASHKER, HERBERT, lawyer; b. N.Y.C., July 10, 1922; s. Louis and Sarah (Solomon) P.; m. Betty Arnoff, Dec. 10, 1950 (div. 1974); children: Susan, Lucy, Martha Louise. BA, Columbia U., 1942, LLB, 1943. Bar: N.Y. 1943, Mass. 1971, D.C. 1972. Atty. U.S. Dept. Justice, 1943-44; law clk. to chief judge N.Y. Ct. Appeals, 1944-45; law clk. to chief justice U.S. Supreme Ct., 1945-46; assoc., then ptnr. Poletti Freidin Prashker & Gartner (and predecessors), N.Y.C., 1946-85. Pres. N.Y. Young Dems., 1952-53; bd. dirs. Northside Ctr. Child Devel., 1964-85, ACLU, 1964-70. Mem. ABA, Assn. of Bar of City of N.Y., N.Y. State Bar Assn., N.Y. County Lawyers Assn. Home: Great Barrington Mass. Died Nov. 27, 1985; buried Alford, Mass.

PRATHER, JACK LEON, manufacturing company executive; b. Sherman, Tex., Apr. 9, 1918; s. William Henry and Emma Virginia (Graham) P.; m. Louise Vehle, July 4, 1937; 1 child, Virginia Lou. BSMechE, Tex. A&M U., 1941; JD, So. Meth. U., 1948. Bar: D.C. 1949. Sales engr. Crane Co., Dallas, 1941-42; with U.S C.E., Denison, Tex., 1942-43; examiner U.S. Patent Office, Washington, 1948-49, patent atty., gen. counsel, 1949-54; asst. to pres. Fuller Co., Catasauqua, Pa., 1955-62, v.p., 1962-81, also bd. dirs.; bd. dirs. Indsl. Devel. Corp., Indsl. Devel. Authority. Mem. adv. bd. Salvation Army. Lt. (j.g.) USNR, 1943-46. Mem. Internat. Bar Assn., Hon. First Defenders, Lehigh Country Club (Allentown, Pa.). Home: Allentown Pa. Died Apr. 14, 1987; cremated.

PRATT, DOUGLAS MCLAIN, transportation company executive; b. Omaha, 1911. Pres. Balt. Transit Co., 1952-55, Phila. Transit Co., 1955-62; pres., chief exec. officer, gen. mgr. Nat. City Lines, Inc., Denver, San Antonio, from 1962; chmn. exec. com., chief exec. officer, dir. TIME-DC, Inc. Deceased.

PRATT, EDWARD LOWELL, physician, educator; b. Great Barrington, Mass., Dec. 19, 1913; s. Albert Stone and Anna (Lowell) P.; m. Esther Fillmore, Aug. 28, 1940; 1 son, Lowell Albert. Grad., Peddie Sch., 1932; B.S., Mass. Inst. Tech., 1936; M.D., Harvard U., 1940. Diplomate: Am. Bd. Pediatrics. Intern bacteriology and pathology Infants and Childrens Hosp., Boston, 1940-41; asst. resident pediatrics Childrens Hosp., Boston, 1942-43; sr. resident pediatrics Childrens Hosp., 1943-44; sr. fellow pediatrics NRC at Yale, 1946-48, Cambridge (Eng.) U., 1948-49; asso. prof. pediatrics N.Y. U. Coll. Medicine; vis. physician Bellevue Hosp. and attending physician Univ. Hosp., 1949-54; prof. pediatrics, chmn. dept. U. Tex. Southwestern Med. Sch., also chief staff Childrens Med. Center and Parkland Meml. Hosp., Dallas, 1954-63; B. K. Rachford prof. pediatrics, dir. dept. U. Cin. (Coll. Medicine), 1963-79, prof. pediatrics, 1979-88; physician exec. dir. Childrens Hosp., Cin., also dir. Childrens Hosp. Research Found., 1963-79; dir. pediatrics and contagious div. Cin. Gen. Hosp., 1963-79. Mem. med. exchange teams to, Greece and Italy, 1947, Turkey, Lebanon and Israel, 1958. Mem. Am. Pediatric Soc. (pres. 1976), Soc. Pediatric Research (pres. 1958), Am. Soc. Clin. Investigation, Alpha Omega Alpha. Home: Cincinnati Ohio Died Mar. 20, 1988; buried Spring Grove Cemetery, Cin.

PRATT, EUGENE ELLIOT, government official; b. Salt Lake City, May 21, 1892; s. Arthur Eugene and Josephine (Crim) P.; m. Eva Lee Place, Apr. 14, 1918; children: Elliot Lee, Geneva, Betty Jane. Student, U. Utah, 1911-12; LLB, Leland Stanford Jr. U., 1916. Bar: Utah 1916. Pvt. practice 1916-17, 20-29; judge 2d Jud. Dist. Ct., 1929-39; justice Supreme Ct. State of Utah, 1939-49, chief justice, 1949 and 50; mem. Armed Svcs. Bd. Contract Appeals Def. Dept., Washington, from 1951; part-time instr. law Washington Coll. Law, from 1956; lectr. on law U. Utah. Lt., inf., U.S. Army, 1917-20; capt., maj., lt. col. Judge Adv. Gen. Dept., USAR, since 1925; in active svc. 1942-46; cited for meritorious svc. as mem. War Dept. bd. of contract appeals, Office of Under Sec. of War, Washington; promoted to lt. col., USAR, 1942, ret. 1952. Mem. Utah Bar Assn., Phi Delta Phi. Democrat. Home: Washington D.C. †

PRATT, HARADEN, communications consultant; b. San Francisco, July 18, 1891; s. John Haraden and Sophie (Christian) P.; m. Florence Bacon, Oct. 31, 1924. BS, U. Calif., 1914. Oper., installer United Wireless Telegraph Co. and Marconi Wireless Telegraph Co., San Francisco, 1910-14; engr. constrn. and operation trans-Pacific radio sta. Marconi Wireless Telegraphy Co., Bolinas, Calif., 1914-15; radio aide charge constrn. and maintenance all naval radio stas. bur. steam engring. U.S. Dept. Navy, 1915-20; engr. Fed. Telegraph Co., Palo Alto, Calif., 1920-23; constructed radio telegraphy system Western Air Express, 1925-27; developer radio aids for air navigation Bur. Standards, Dept. Commerce, Washington, 1927-28; v.p., chief engr., bd. dirs. Mackay Radio & Telegraph Co., N.Y.C., 1928-51; v.p. Am. Cable & Radio Corp., Dualex Corp., 1953-58; chmn. Radio Tech. Planning Bd., 1945-48; telecommunications adviser to U.S. Pres., 1951-53; U.S. govt. tech. adviser Internat. Radio Telegraph Conf., Washington, 1927, Internat. Radio Consultative Com., Copenhagen, Denmark, 1931; co. rep. Internat. Telecommunications Conf., Bucharest, Romania, 1937, Cairo, 1938, Atlantic City, 1947, Paris, 1949, Geneva, 1951. Recipient medal of honor Inst. Radio Engrs., 1944, Founders award, 1960, Presdl. cert. of merit, 1948. Fellow IEEE (sec., bd. dirs.), Radio Club Am., AIAA (assoc.); mem. Inst. Radio Engrs. Australia (hon. life), Am. Standards Assn. (bd. dirs. 1939-42), Sigma Xi. Home: Pompano Beach Fla. †

PRATT, PHILIP, judge; b. Pontiac, Mich., July 14, 1924; s. Peter and Helen (Stathis) P.; m. Mary C. Hill, July 26, 1952; children—Peter, Laura, Kathleen. Student (Alumni scholar), U. Mich., 1942-43, LLB, 1950; student, U. Chgo., 1943-44. Bar: Mich. 1951. Title examiner Abstract & Title Co., Pontiac, 1951; asst. pros. atty. Oakland County, Mich., 1952; mem. firm Smith & Pratt, Pontiac, 1953-63; circuit judge 6th Jud. Circuit of Mich., Pontiac, 1963-70; U.S. dist. judge Ea. Dist. Mich., 1970-86, chief judge, 1986-89. Served with OSS AUS, 1943-46. Decorated Bronze Star medal. Mem. ABA, Oakland County Bar Assn. (pres. 1961), State Bar Mich., Am. Judicature Soc., Jud. Conf. U.S. Home: Bloomfield Hills Mich. Died Feb. 7, 1989; buried Ottawa Park Cemetery, Clarkston, Mich.

PRATTE, YVES, manufacturing executive, lawyer, former judge; b. Quebec, Que., Can., Mar. 7, 1925; s. Garon and Georgine (Rivard) P.; m. Paule Gauureau, Mar. 1, 1963; children: Josette, Guy, André. B.A., Coll. Garnier, Quebec, 1944; LL.L., Laval U., 1947; post-grad., U. Toronto, 1947-48. Bar: Que. 1947, Ont. 1980, created Queen's Counsel 1958. Mem. firm St. Laurent, Taschereau, Noel and Pratte, Quebec, 1948-53; sr. ptnr. Pratte, Cote, Tremblay, Beauvais, Bouchard, Garneau & Truchon, Quebec, 1954-68; dean Faculty of Law Laval U., 1962-65; spl. legal counsel Prime Ministers Jean Lesage and Daniel Johnson, 1965-68; mem. Royal Commn. Security, 1966-68; bd. dirs. Can. Nat. Railways, 1968-75; sr. ptnr. Desjardins, Ducharme, Bourque & Pratte, Montreal, 1976-77; justice Supreme Ct. of Can., Ottawa, 1977-79; ptnr. Courtois, Clarkson, Parsons & Tetrault, Montreal, Que., 1979-80, Clarkson & Tetrault, Montreal, 1979-88; chmn. bd., chief exec. officer Air Can., 1968-75; chmn. bd. Domtar Inc., Montreal, 1982-88. Roman Catholic. Home: Montreal Que., Canada. Died June 26, 1988.

PREBISCH, RAUL, economist; b. Tucuman, Argentina, Apr. 17, 1901; m. Elena Prebisch; 1 child, Raul. Student, Buenos Aires U.; hon. degrees, Univ. de los Los Andes, Colombia, Columbia U., N.Y.C., Univ. de Montevideo, Uruguay, U. Punjab, India. Prof. polit. economy Buenos Aires U., 1925-48, hon. prof., 1955-86; dep. dir. Dept. Stats. Govt. of Argentina, Argentina, 1925-27; adviser to Minister Fin., Minister of Agr. Govt. of Argentina, 1933-35; dir. econ. research Nat. Bank Argentina, 1927-30, undersec. for fin., 1930-32; organizer, first dir. gen. Cen. Bank of Republic of Argentina, 1935-43; exec. sec. UN Econ. Com. for Latin Am., 1948-62; dir. gen. Latin Am. Inst. for Econ. and Social Planning, 1962-64, 69-86; sec. gen. UN Conf. Trade and Devel., Geneva, Switzerland, 1964-69; invited economist Alliance for Progress Progam, Washington, 1960; hon. mem. faculty econs U. Chile, U. San Andrés, La Paz, Bolivia, U. San Marcos, Lima, Peru. Home: Santiago Chile. Died Apr. 29, 1986.

PREMINGER, OTTO, motion picture and stage producer and director; b. Vienna, Austria, Dec. 5, 1906; LL.D., U. Vienna, m. Marion Mill; m. 2d, Mary Gardner (div.); m. 3d, Patricia Hope Bryce, Mar. 1960; children—Erik, Victoria and Mark (twins). Came to U.S., 1935. Producer, dir. Max Reinhardt Theatre in der Josefstadt, Vienna; dir. Libel, In Time To Come, Howard Koch play about Woodrow Wilson, Outward Bound, The Moon in Blue, Critic's Choice, Full Circle; dir., starred in Margin For Error (all N.Y.C.); producer, dir. motion pictures, including: Laura, Fallen Angel, Centennial Summer, A Royal Scandal, Forever Amber, Daisy Kenyon, Whirlpool, Where The Sidewalk Ends, The Thirteenth Letter, The Moon Is Blue, Angel Face, River of No Return, Carmen Jones, The Man with the Golden Arm, Saint Joan, Bonjour Trustesse, Porgy and Bess, Anatomy of a Murder, Exodus, Advise and Consent, The Cardinal, In Harm's Way, Bunny Lake is Missing, Hurry Sundown, Skidoo, Tell Me That You Love Me, Junie Moon, Such Good Friends, Rosebud, The Human Factor: appeared in Hollywood on Trial, 1977. Author: Preminger: An Autobiography, 1977. Died Apr. 23, 1986; buried Woodlawn Cemetery, N.Y.C. Address: For estate of Mr Preminger Mrs Hope B Preminger 201 E 69th St Sta 11F NYC 10021.

PRENTICE, JOHN GERALD, forest products executive; b. Vienna, Austria, Feb. 27, 1907; s. Otto and Katherine (Pollack-Parnau) Pick; m. Eve Schlesinger-Acs, May 24, 1932; 2 daus. LL.D., U. Vienna; grad., Textile Engring. Sch., Reutlingen, Germany. dir. Canfor Corp., Can. Forest Products Ltd. Vancouver B.C., Canfor Ltd., Prince George Pulp and Paper Ltd., Intercontinental Pulp Co. Ltd. mem. Vancouver Bd. Trade; founder Simon Fraser U., Burnaby, B.C.; hon. life pres. Playhouse Theatre Co. Decorated officer Order of Can. Mem. B.C. Research Council, Can. C. of C., Newcomen Soc. N. Am., Chess Fedn. of Can. (rep.), Fedn. Internationale d'Echecs (exec. council), Can. Council Christians and Jews, U.S. Chess Fedn., B.C. Chess Fedn. Clubs: Men's Canadian, Southlands Riding and Polo, Vancouver Lawn-Tennis and Badminton, Capilano Golf and Country; Manhattan Chess (N.Y.). Died Feb. 19, 1987.

PRENTICE, PIERREPONT ISHAM, publisher; b. Newark, Sept. 10, 1899; s. Sartell and Lydia Beekman (Vanderpoel) P.; m. Mildred Belcher, Sept. 30, 1922; children: Mildred Barbara Prentice Kulesh, Carolyn Sumner Prentice Falies; m. Janet McNair Pffieger, Nov. 1, 1944. BA cum laude, Yale U., 1920. Reporter N.Y. Tribune, 1921-24; editor, pub. Camden Post Telegram (N.J.), 1924-26; mng. editor New Bedford Times (Mass.), 1926-29; news editor Phila. Record, 1929-30; bus. mgr. Fortune mag., 1930-34; circulation dir. Time, Life and Fortune mags., 1934-41; v.p. Time, Inc., 1939-65, v.p. corp. affairs, 1945-49, prin. officer in charge problems of housing and urban affairs, 1949-65; pub. Time mag., 1941-45; editor, pub. Archtl. Forum, 1949-54; founder, editor, pub. House and Home mag., 1952-62; v.p., bd. dirs. Nat. Assn. Homebuilders Research Found., 1965-69; cons. on housing mktg. Belleair, Fla., from 1965; mem. adv. com. FHA, 1954-56; founder, dir. Housing Industry Pres.'s Council, 1954-67; mem. housing fin. com. Com. Econ. Devel., 1966-67; mem. property tax com. Nat. Tax. Assn., from 1976; chmn. Nat. Council for Property Tax Reform, from 1976. Bd. dirs. Lincoln Found., 1963-71; bd. dirs. Robert Schalkenbach Found., from 1963, pres., 1973-81; bd. dirs. Internat. Union for Land Value Taxation and Free Trade, from 1966, v.p., from 1980. Served as 2d lt. U.S. Army, 1918-19. Recipient Disting. Service award Nat. Assn. Homebuilders, 1951, 58; named to Housing Hall of Fame, 1978; recipient Jesse H. Neal 1st award for ediotrial achievement Assoc. Bus. Publs., 1958, 59, 60, 62, F. Stuart Fitzpatrick Meml. award for Outstanding Service and Achievement on behalf constrn. industry AIA, Nat. Assn. Homebuilders, Producers Council, Assoc. Bldg. Contractors and Bldg. Research Inst., 1963, award of honor as one of 25 Ams. who had made most outstanding contbrn. to housing progress form 1950-75 Bldg. Research Adv. Bd., 1977; named Man of Yr. Turntable Builders, 1966; recipient Henry George Found. Incentive award, 1982. Mem. AIA (trustee AIA Found. 1966-68), U.S. C. of C. (task force for econ. growth and opportunity 1965-66, urban and regional affairs com. 1968-74). Presbyterian. Home: Belleair Fla. Died Feb. 2, 1989.

PRESCOTT, JAMES ARTHUR, agricultural chemist; b. Bolton, Eng., Oct. 7, 1890; s. Joseph Arthur and Mary Alice (Garsden) P.; m. Elsie Mason, Oct. 12, 1915; 1 son, John Russell. B.Sc., Manchester U., 1911; D.Sc., Adelaide U., 1932; D.Agr.Sci., Melbourne U., 1956. Ministry Agr. rsch. scholar Rothamsted Exptl. Sta., 1912-16; chief chemist Sultanic Agrl. Soc., Cairo, 1916-24; prof. agrl. chemistry Adelaide U., 1924-25, prof. emeritus, from 1956; chief div. soils Commonwealth Sci. and Indsl. Rsch. Orgn., 1929-47; chmn. oenological rsch. com., 1935-56; dir. Waite Agrl. Rsch. Inst., 1938-55; mem. coun. Australia Wine Rsch. Inst., from 1955; chmn. working group climate and agr., commn. climatology World Meteorol. Orgn., from 1956. Editor Royal Soc. of South Australia. Mem. coun. govs. Scotch Coll., South Australia, 1938-61, chmn. of coun. 1953-61. Decorated Comdr. Order of Brit. Empire; recipient Mueller medal Australian and New Zealand Assn. Advancement Sci. Fellow Royal So. London, Australian Acad. Sci., Royal Australian Chem. Inst., Australian Inst. Agrl. Sci. Home: Myrtle Bank Australia. †

PRESSER, JACKIE, labor union official; b. Cleve., Aug. 6, 1926; s. William and Faye P. Mem. Hotel and Restaurant Employees Union, Cleve., 1946-48, pres., 1948-52; organizer Teamsters Joint Council #41, Cleve., 1952-66, recording sec., 1972-81, chmn. DRIVE, 1983-88, pres., 1983-88, adminstr. trustee severance plan, 1983-88; sec.-treas., bus. mgr. Teamsters Local Union #507, Cleve., 1968-88; v.p. Ohio Conf. Teamsters, Cleve., 1974-81, pres., 1981-88; v.p. IBT Exec. Bd., Cleve., 1976-83; pres. IBT DRIVE, 1983-88; trustee IBT Health and Welfare Fund, Washington, 1983-88; gen. pres. Internat. Brotherhood of Teamsters, Washington, 1983-88; pres. Internat. Bldg. Corp., Washington, 1983-88, Teamsters Internat., Inc., Washington, 1983-88; chmn. Central Conf. Teamsters, Washington, 1983-88; trustee Teamster Affiliates Pension Fund, Washington, 1983-88; vice chmn. Cleve. Fin. Planning and Supervision Commn., Greater Cleve. Roundtable; trustee United Way Services, 1983-86, Greater Cleve. Rountable; chmn. Greater Cleve. Sports Hall of Fame Found. Inc.; co-chmn. Conv. Ctr. Liaison Com., Bus., Labor and Community Fund Raising Com.; labor chmn. New Cleve. Campaign; bd. dirs. Cleve. Conv. and Visitors Bur. Inc., Cleve State U. Devel. Found. Inc., Cleve. Editor: Internat. Teamster mag., Ohio Teamster newspaper. Vice-pres. Muscular Dystrophy Assn.; mem. City of Cleve. Labor Mgmt. Com., Cleve. Conv. Adv. Bd., Adv. Com. to Indsl. Relations Ctr. Cleve. State U., Fedn. for Community Planning, Parent Vol. Assn. for Retarded Ind., Blue Cross of Northeast Ohio Labor Adv. Council, Project Awareness Adv. Com., Hunger Task Force, Jewish Community Fedn., Nat. Conf. Christians and Jews, Citizens League Greater Cleve., YMCA, Divot Diggers, 48.7 Com. Women Space, Coalition of Labor Union Women, Task Force on Urban Problems, Adv. Com. Profl. Golfer's Assn. (No. Ohio sect.), Clevelanders for 100,000 Families Inc.; exec. com. Work in N.E. Ohio Council; rep. Kidney Dialysis Program; campaign worker Israel Bonds. Served with USN, 1943-46. Recipient Man of Yr. award B'nai B'rith Lodge 2201 of N.Y. Jewish. Clubs: Cleveland, University. Home: Cleveland Ohio. Died July 9, 1988.

PRESTON, ROBERT, actor; b. Newton Highlands, Mass., June 8, 1918; s. Frank W. and Ruth (Rea) Meservey; m. Catherine Craig, Nov. 8, 1940. Mem. gov. bd. Actors' Equity. Motion pictures include Union Pacific, 1938, Northwest Mounted Police, 1939, Beau Geste, 1940, Wake Island, 1941, The Macomber Affair, 1946, The Bride Comes to Yellow Sky, 1951, The Dark at the Top of the Stairs, 1960, The Music Man, 1962, How the West Was Won, 1963, All The Way Home, 1963, Junior Bonner, 1972, Child's Play, 1972, Mame, 1973, Semi-Tough, 1977, S.O.B, 1981, Victor/Victoria, 1982, The Last Starfighter, 1984; Broadway plays include Twentieth Century, 1951, The Male Animal, 1952, His and Hers, 1953, The Magic and the Loss, 1954, The Tender Trap, 1954, Janus, 1955, The Hidden River, 1957, The Music Man, 1957, Too True to be Good, 1963, Nobody Loves an Albatross, 1963, Ben Franklin in Paris, 1964-65, A Lion in Winter, 1966, I Do, I Do, 1966-67, Mack and Mabel, 1974, Sly Fox, 1977; TV work includes The Chisholms, 1979, Rehearsal for Murder, 1982, Finnegan Begin Again, 1985, Outrage, 1986; star TV series The Chisholms II, 1980-87, September Gun, 1984. Served from pvt. to capt. USAAF, World War II. Recipient Antoinette Perry award as best musical male star, 1958, 67, Lawrence Langner award for lifetime achievement in theatre, 1987. Died Mar. 21, 1987.

PRESTON, WILL MANIER, lawyer; b. Nashville, May 27, 1904; s. Robert Hatton and Dayse (High) P.; m. Eunice Lannom, Dec. 29, 1926; 1 child, Dolores Clyntelle Preston Fields. LLB, Vanderbilt U., 1925. Bar: Tenn. 1925, Fla. 1926. Pvt. practice Miami, Fla., from 1926; ptnr. Scott, McCarty, Preston & Steel, 1943-66; cons. Scott, McCarthy, Steel, Hector & Davis, 1966-75, Steel, Hector & Davis, 1975-86; gen. counsel Everglades Nat. Park Assn., from 1947; chmn. bd. Dade Nat. Bank, Miami, 1956-69. Charter mem., past pres., dir. Orange Bowl Com. Mem. ABA, Fla. Bar Assn., Dade County Bar Assn. (past pres.), Lions (past pres. Miami), Kiwanis (past pres. Miami). Home: Miami Fla. Died May 22, 1986, interred Woodlawn Cemetery, Miami, Fla.

PRESTOPINO, GREGORIO, artist; b. N.Y.C., June 21, 1907; s. Anthony and Lillian (Rando) P.; m. Elizabeth Dauber, June 21, 1931; children: Paul, Gregory. Student, NAD, N.Y.C., 1922-28. Tchr. art New Sch., N.Y.C.; dir. Edward McDowell Colony; lectr. Mus. Modern Art, N.Y.C., Bklyn. Mus. Exhibited in numerous shows including Whitney Mus., N.Y.C., Mus. Modern Art, N.Y.C., Corcoran Art Gallery, Washington, Pa. Acad. Fine Art, St. Louis Art Mus.; retrospective exbns. Mus. Art., Ft. Lauderdale, Fla., 1978, State Mus., Trenton, N.J., Sharon (N.H.) Art Ctr., 1985, Midtown Galleries, N.Y.C., 1985; represented in permanent collections including Joseph H. Hirshhorn Mus., Mus. U. Minn., Walker Art Gallery, Mpls., Philips Meml. Gallery, Washington, Mus. Modern Art, N.Y.C., Whitney Mus., Rochester (N.Y.) Mus., U. Neb., U. Ill., U. Okla., Hawaii Mus. Art, Butler Art Inst., U. Notre Dame, Montclair (N.J.) Mus. Art, Nat. Inst. Arts and Letters, Keen (N.H.) State Coll., Currier Gallery Mus., Manchester, N.H.; numerous pvt. collections. Recipient 3d prize Second Ann. Portrait of Am. Competition, 1946, Temple Gold medal Pa. Acad. Fine Arts, 1946, Benjamin Altman prize NAD, 1972; Nat. Inst. Arts and Letters grantee, 1961. Home: Roosevelt N.J. Died Dec. 16, 1984, buried Roosevelt, N.J.

PRICE, CHARLES MORGAN, lawyer; b. Chgo., July 17, 1898; s. L. Morgan and Eva (Lapham) P.; m. Elinor Rew, Oct. 8, 1932; children Henry Morgan, Rew Price Carne. AB, Northwestern U., 1920, JD, 1923. Bar: Ill., 1923. Ptnr. Price, Cushman, Keck, Mahin & Cate and predecessor firms, from 1923. Mem. ABA, Ill. Bar Assn., Chgo. Bar Assn., Chgo. Club, Glen View Club, Delta Upsilon, Phi Delta Phi. Home: Chicago Ill. Deceased.

PRICE, MELVIN, congressman; b. East St. Louis, Ill., Jan. 1, 1905; s. Lawrence Wood and Margaret Elizabeth (Connolly) P.; m. Garaldine Freelin, July 7, 1952; 1 child, William Melvin. Ed. parochial schs., East St. Louis; grad., St. Louis U. High Sch.; student, St. Louis U., 1923-25. Sports writer East St. Louis News-Rev., 1925-27; corr. East St. Louis Jour., 1927-33, St. Louis Globe-Democrat, 1943; sec. to Congressman Edwin M. Schaefer, 1933-43; mem. 79th and 80th Congresses (1945-49) from 22d Ill. Dist., 81st to 82d Congresses from 25th Ill. Dist., 1949-53, 83-92d Congresses from 24th Ill. Dist., 1953-73, 93d-100th Congresses from 23d Ill. Dist., 1973—; chmn. house armed service com. mem. commn. adminstrv. rev. Mem. St. Clair County Bd. Suprs., 1929-31. Served with AUS, 1943-44. Mem. Am. Legion, Amvets. Democrat. Roman Catholic. Clubs: KC, Moose, Eagle, Elk, Ancient Order of Hibernians; Nat. Press (Washington). Home: East Saint Louis Mo. Died Apr. 22, 1988.

PRICE, MILTON D., insurance executive; b. Noble, Ill., July 22, 1888; s. Warren and Ada (Curtis) P.; m. Ethel Lewis, June 28, 1917; children: Patricia, Milton D. Ed. pub. schs. of Noble. Assoc. gen. mdse. bus. 1906-11; salesman real estate, insurance, 1911-17; state and spl. agt. 1920-26; with St. Paul-Mercury Indemnity Co., from 1926, pres., from 1948. Mem. Minnesota Club, St. Paul Athletic Club, Somerset Country Club (St. Paul). Presbyterian. Home: Saint Paul Minn. †

PRICE, RAYMOND GLENN, business education educator, author; b. Catlin, Ind., July 7, 1903; s. William and Ada (Gatt) P.; m. Katherine Travers, Dec. 28, 1932; children: Ray G., Roberta Gail Price Mays. BS, Ind. State Tchrs. Coll., 1928; MA, U. Chgo., 1932; EdD, U. Cin., 1944. Tchr. Ind. pub. schs., 1928-35; instr. commerce Ind. State Tchrs. Coll., 1936; dir. bus. tchr. tng. U. Cin., 1936-48; prof. edn. U. Minn., 1948-72, emeritus from 1972; vis. prof. Okla. A&M Coll., 1940, Northwestern U., 1946, U. Chgo., 1947, U. Denver, 1952, Mont. State U., 1957, Utah State U., 1960, Mont. State Coll., 1963, Wayne State U., 1964, Brigham Young U., 1967, Portland State Coll., 1967, N. Tex. State, 1972, Va. Commonwealth U., 1973; disting. lectr. Oklahoma State U., 1972; George A. Ball Disting. Prof. Ball State U., 1978-79; charter mem. Am. Council on Consumer Interests (pres. 1954-56); bd. dirs. Consumers Union Inc., 1956-68, ednl. cons. 1970-87; sec. Minn. Council Econ. Edn., 1962-72; trustee Joint Council Econ. Edn., 1962-71; consumer cons. to Pres. Nixon's Price Commn., 1971; cons. Nat. Bur. Standards, 1969-75; mem. Minn. gov.'s adv. council on consumer affairs, from 1971. Co-author: Functions of Business, 1941, Modern Business: An Introduction to Principles and Problems, 1948, General Business for Everyday Living, 4th edit., 1972, Business and You, 1979; contbr. chpts. in books, articles to profl. jours. Recipient Disting. Alumnus award Ind. State U., 1964, Gregge award for outstanding contbn. to bus. edn., 1965, Disting. Fellowship award Am. Council on Consumer Interest, 1973. Mem. Nat. Bus. Tchrs. Assn. (pres. 1949), United Bus. Edn. Assn. (pres. 1951-52), Am. Acad. Polit. Sci., Am. Ednl. Research Assn., Delta Pi Epsilon (hon., past. nat. dir. research and service projects, faculty adviser Phi chpt.), Phi Delta Kappa (award Alpha Iota chpt. 1945). Home: Minneapolis Minn. Died Dec. 19, 1987; cremated.

PRICE, WILLARD, explorer, naturalist; b. Peterborough, Ont., Can., July 28, 1887; s. Albert and Estella (Martin) P.; m. Jean Reeve, Aug. 4, 1914 (dec. 1929); 1 son, Robert; m. 2d, Mary Virginia Selden, May 28, 1932. BA, Western Res. U., 1909; MA, Columbia U., 1914, LittD, 1930. Mem. editorial staff Survey, 1912-13; editor World Outlook and other publs. on world affairs, 1915-20; fgn. corr. 1933-37; mem. ethnographic expdns. in Micronesia, China, Philippines, Sumatra, India, Nile basin, Sahara Desert, Amazon jungle for Am. Mus. Natural History and Nat. Geog. Soc. Traveled in 133 countries. Author: Ancient Peoples at New Tasks, Pacific Adventure, Children of the Rising Sun, Barbarian (novel), Japan Rides the Tiger, Japan's Islands of Mystery, Japan and the Son of Heaven, Key to Japan, Roving South-Rio Grande to Patagonia, I Cannot Rest from Travel, The Amazing Amazon, Journey by Junk, Adventures in Paradise, Tahiti and Beyond, Roaming Britain, Incredible Africa, The Amazing Mississippi, Rivers I Have Known, America's Paradise Lost, Odd Way Round the World, The Japanese Miracle; (novels for boys) Amazon Adventure, South Sea Adventure, Underwater Adventure, Volcano Adventure, Whale Adventure, African Adventure, Elephant Adventure, Safari Adventure, Lion Adventure, Gorilla Adventure, Diving Adventure, Cannibal Adventure; contbr. articles to nat. mags., Ency. Brit. Home: Laguna Beach Calif. †

PRIDDY, ASHLEY HORNE, oil and gas executive; b. Wichita Falls, Kans., Apr. 1, 1922; s. Walter Mason and Swannonoa (Horne) P.; m. Kathryn Amsler, Dec. 30, 1947; children: Hervey, Betty, Ann. Student, Rice U., 1939-41; BBA, BS in Petroleum Engring., U. Tex., 1949. With Sabine Royalty Corp. (name now Sabine Corp.), Dallas, 1949-84, petroleum engr., 1949-55, v.p., 1958-68, pres., chief exec. officer, 1968-84; bd. dirs. First Nat. Bank Dallas. Mem. town council Highland Park, Tex., 1966-70, mayor, 1970-76; pres. Dallas Wildcat Com., 1978; trustee Hochkaday Sch., Dallas, chmn. bd., 1974-78; trustee Engring Sch. Found., U. Tex., 1973-77; pres. Friends of Gov.'s Mansion, 1980-84. 1st lt. USNR, 1943-46, PTO. Named Disting. Grad. U. Tex. Sch. Engring., 1978. Mem. Tex. Mid-Continent Oil and Gas Assn. (dir. 1980-84), Dallas Petroleum Club, Dallas Couintry Club, Brook Hollow Golf Club (Dallas), Beta Theta Pi, Tau Beta Pi, Tau Sigma. Home: Dallas Tex. Died Mar. 5, 1984, buried Sparkman-Hillcrest Cemetery, Tex.

PRIDE, ALFRED MELVILLE, naval officer; b. Somerville, Mass., Sept. 10, 1897; s. Alfred Morine and Grace (White) P.; m. Helen Nickerson Burrell, June 1, 1921; children: Carol Stanton (wife of Ensign Andrew A. Lemeshewsky, USN, Alfred Morine. Grad., Somerville (Mass.) High Sch., 1916; student, Tufts Coll. Engring. Sch., 1916-18; postgrad. in aeronautical engring., MIT, 1925-26. Commd. ensign, naval aviator USNR, 1918; transferred with rank of lt. USN, 1921, advanced through grades to rear adm., 1944, on duty with Amphibious Force, Pacific Fleet, past chief, Bur. Aero., Navy Dept., comdr. Seventh Fleet, cmdr. Pacific Fleet air arm, 1956-59, ret., 1959. Decorated Victory medal, Commendation Ribbon, various area ribbons. Home: Arlington Va. Died Dec. 24, 1988.

PRINCE, HARRY M., architect; b. N.Y.C., Jan. 22, 1889; s. John J. and Susie (Simmonds) P.; m. Caroline Krooks, June 29, 1924; 1 son, John Jay. Grad. architecture, Cooper Union, 1909; student, Carnegie Inst. Tech., AEF U., France. Registered architect, N.Y., Pa., D.C. Ptnr. Bien & Prince, architects, 1925-38; propr. Harry M. Prince, architect, N.Y.C., 1941-64; sr. ptnr. Harry M. Prince & Assocs., N.Y.C., from 1964. Princ. works include Coney Island Housing Project, 1956, House of Living Judaism, 1957, Jr. High Sch., 1957, Jackson Houses, pub. housing project, 1958, Bloomingdale Libr., 1958, Riverside Health Ctr., 1958, Nurses Residence and Sch., 1958, Madison Houses, pub. housing project, 1959, Concourse Village Housing Project, 1960 (all N.Y.C.). Commr. Tenement House Dept. N.Y.C., 1934-38; dep. commr. housing Dept. Housing and Bldgs., 1938-41; mem. U.S. commn. in Eng. to study effects of bombs on bldgs., 1941; archtl. cons. Housing Authority N.Y.C., 1941-45; commr. water takings N.Y. State, 1942-43; archtl. cons. N.Y. State joint legis. com. housing and multiple dwellings, from 1947; chmn. nat. architect panel synagogue planning Union Am. Hebrew Congregations, 1950-60, Mayor's Com. Better Housing, N.Y.C., from 1955. With A.C., U.S. Army, World War I, AEF in France, Germany. Fellow AIA (past pres. N.Y.C.); mem. N.Y.Soc. Architects, N.Y. Stae Assn. rchitects (past pres.), Am. Arbitration Assn. (U.S. panel), Assn. Presidents Reform Synagogues (chm. 1943-44), Synagogue Council Am. (Union Hebrew Congregation del. 1947-54. Jewish (congregation trustee, pres. 1935-48). Home: New York N.Y. †

PRINCE, JEROME, lawyer, academic administrator, educator; b. N.Y.C., Aug. 26, 1907; s. Henry and Mary (Hoffman) P.; m. Martha Kenith, July 9, 1947 (dec. July 1973); children: Elayne, Karen Prince Gerstl; m. Elaine Lederman, July 29, 1975. BS, CCNY, 1930; LLB, Bklyn. Law Sch., CCNY, 1933, JSD, 1934, LLD (hon.), 1965. Bar: N.Y. 1933. Instr. Bklyn. Law Sch., 1934-36, prof. law and law of evidence, 1936-88, asst. to dean., 1940-45, vice dean, 1945-50, assoc. dean, 1950-53, dean, 1953-71, dean emeritus, from 1971; chief counsel N.Y. State Joint Legis. Com. on Ct. Reorgn., 1965-68; chmn. N.Y.C. Conciliation and Appeal Bd., from 1974. Author: Outline of Evidence, 1949, 2d edit., 1963; co-author: (with Harold Prince) detective and mystery short stories pub. in mags. and anthologies, from 1944; editor, reviser: Richardson on Evidence, 10th edit., 1973; editor: (with George Folwell) Cases on Criminal Law, 1936, (with George N. Matheson) Cases on Evidence, 1949, Cases and Materials on Evidence, 1972. Mem. ABA, N.Y. State Bar Assn., Bklyn. Bar Assn., Assn. of Bar City of N.Y., Phi Delta Phi, Phi Beta Kappa. Home: New York N.Y. Died Dec. 24, 1988.

PRINZ, JOACHIM, clergyman; b. Burkhardsdorf, Germany, May 10, 1902; came to U.S., 1937, naturalized, 1944; s. Joseph and Nani (Berg) P.; m. Lucie Horovitz, Dec. 25, 1925 (dec. Jan. 1931); 1 dau., Lucie Berkowitz; m. Hilde Goldschmidt, May 24, 1932; children—Michael, Jonathan, Deborah. Rabbi, Jewish Theol. Sem., Breslau, Germany, 1925; student, U. Berlin, Germany, 1922-23; Ph.D., U. Giessen, Germany, 1924. Rabbi Jewish community, Berlin, 1926-37; expelled by gestapo 1937; lectr. European and Near Eastern policies, U.S., 1937-39; rabbi Temple B'nai Abraham, Newark, 1939-88. Author: Judische Geschichte, 1931, Illustratierte Judische Geschichte, 1933, Die Geschichten der Bible, 1934, Wir Juden, 1934, Die Reiche Israel and Juda, 1935, Der Freitagabend, 1935, Das Leben Im Ghetto, 1937, Relatos de la Biblia, 1941, Heroes y Principes Hebroes, 1941, Cartes Cartolor, 1946, The Great Jewish Books (edited by S. Caplan and H. U. Ribalow), 1952, The Dilemma of the Modern Jew, 1962, Popes from the Ghetto, 1966, The Secret Jews, 1973; Editorial bds.: Reconstruction, 1958, Judaism, 1958-88. Nat. pres. Am. Jewish Congress, 1958-66, chmn. commn. internat. affairs, 1966-68; chmn. Conf. Pres.'s Maj. Am. Jewish Orgns., 1966-69, World Conf. of Jewish Orgns., 1975-88; exec. bd. World Jewish Congress, 1946, chmn. gov. council, 1967-75, v.p., 1975-88; dir. Conf. Jewish Materials Claims Against Germany, Inc., 1956; Chmn United Jewish Appeal Essex County, N.J., 1945; pres. Jewish Edn. Assn. Essex County, 1944; bd. dirs. Jewish Community Council Essex County, Essex County Heart Assn. Home: Brookside N.J. Died Sept. 30, 1988.

PRITZKER, A(BRAM) N(ICHOLAS), business executive, lawyer, philanthropist; b. Chgo., Jan. 6, 1896; s. Nicholas J. and Annie (Cohen) P.; m. Fanny L. Doppelt, 1921 (dec. 1970); children: Jay A., Robert A., Donald N. (dec.); m. Lorraine Pritzker. Student, Northwestern U., 1913-14; PhB, U. Chgo., 1916; LLB, Harvard U., 1920; LLB (hon.), Gettysburg Coll., 1979. Bar: Ill. 1920. Ptnr. firm Pritzker & Pritzker, Chgo., 1920; chmn. Cory Corp., Chgo., 1946-67; dir. Marmon Group, Chgo., from 1964, Hyatt Corp., Chgo., from 1973, Braniff Internat. Airways, McCall's mag.; dir. Pritzker Found. Active Jewish Fedn. Chgo., Combined Jewish Appeal, Young Mens Jewish Council, Jewish Charities Chgo., Anti-Defamation League, Boys Clubs Chgo. Served as petty officer USN, 1917-19. Recipient numerous honors for his achievements and philanthropies. Mem. Chgo. Bar Assn., Standard Club (Chgo.), Carleton Club (Chgo.). Home: Chicago Ill. Died Feb. 8, 1986, buried Chgo.

PROBST, GEORGE EDGAR, historian, broadcaster, educator; b. Hardtner, Kan., July 6, 1917; s. George Ernest and Helen Jacques (Brock) P; m. Audrey Neff, Dec. 23, 1939 (div. 1954); children: Patricia, Barbara Probst Morrow; m. Catherine Dunning Johnson, 1955 (div. 1962); m. Annice Lee Mills, 1962; children: Joyce, Helen, Claudia. BA in Polit. Sci., U. Chgo., 1939, MA in Social Sci., 1954. Research dir. radio office U. Chgo., 1941-44, instr. Am. history, 1944-47, exec. sec. radio office, producer and dir. Chicago Round Table, 1945-54, sec. to faculty, 1945-47, asst. prof. social scis. in the coll., 1947-54; exec. dir. Thomas Alva Edison Found., 1955-67; adj. assoc. prof. Am. history NYU, 1955-70; organizer, chmn. com. presented case to FCC for assigning TV channels for edn., 1950; chmn. fin. com. Joint Com. Ednl.TV, 1950-52; chmn. com. all ednl. instns. Chgo. Met. Area Ednl. TV, 1951-53;chmn. adult edn. com. administering Fund for Adult Edn. grant for prodn. radio series The Jeffersonian Heritage (co-author), Ways of Mankind, People Under Communicsm, Voice of Europe, Nat. Assn. Ednl. Broadcasters, 1951-53; dir. programs Sta WGBH-TV, Boston, 1954; producer, dir., writer series on Alexis de Tocqueville's Democracy in Action, 1958; dir. Nat. Ednl. TV and Radio Ctr., 1960-66; exec. dir. Nat. Commn. Coop. Edn., from 1962. Editor: The Happy Republic, 1962; co-editor: The The People Shall Judge, 2 vols., 1949-51. Mem. Council on Fgn. Relations, NYU Club, Metropolitan Club (N.Y.C.). Presbyterian. Home: Spencertown N.Y. Died Sept. 9, 1986, buried Spencertown, N.Y.

PROBST, GERALD GRAHAM, computer company executive; b. Ogden, Utah, Sept. 11, 1923; s. Keiner Sawyer and Ruth (Graham) P.; m. Betty Ann Forbes, Oct. 16, 1943; children: Susan Stevens, Kevin Forbes, Kathleen Hess, Marcus Forbes. BS with high honors, U. Utah, 1951; MS, MIT, 1956. With Univac div. Sperry Corp., Blue Bell, Pa., from 1961; v.p., gen. mgr. data processing div. Univac div. Sperry Corp., 1968-70, exec. v.p. world wide devel. and mfg., 1970-71, pres., 1971-78; v.p. Sperry Rand Corp., 1974, exec. v.p., 1975-78, group exec. v.p., 1978-80; pres., chief operating officer Sperry Corp., 1980-82, chmn., chief exec. officer, 1982-89, also dir.; dir. Mellon N.A. Corp., Phila. With USAAF, 1942-47, USAF, 1952-61. Decorated DFC.; Air medal with 5 oak leaf clusters; Commendation medal; recipient Outstanding Alumni award U. Utah, 1970, Disting. Corp. Leadership award MIT, 1980. Mem. IEEE, AIAA, Tau Beta Pi, Phi Kappa Phi. Home: Salt Lake City Utah Died Jan. 15, 1989.

PROCTER, RUSSELL, wholesale hardware executive; b. Auburn, Ky., Dec. 3, 1903; s. Robert Emmett and Mary Holland (Mobley) P.; m. Nancy Waples Dunn, Dec. 9, 1933; 1 dau., Mary Nancy (Mrs. John W. Saltsman). Student, pub. schs. With Belknap Hardware & Mfg. Co. (co. name changed to Belknap, Inc.), Louisville, from 1925; successively order clk., checker, stocktaker, splty. harness salesman, gen. hardware sales in Tex., Okla., buyer sporting goods, mng. buyer Belknap Hardware & Mfg. Co. (co. name changed to Belknap, Inc.), 1925-55, pres., 1955-69, chmn. bd., from 1969, also dir.; former dir. First Nat. Bank, 1st Ky. Trust Co., Louisville, 1st Ky. Co., Louisville. Overseer Ky. So. Coll.; bd. dirs. Asso. Industries Ky.; trustee So. Bapt. Theol. Sem., Shaker Mus., South Union, lKy.; mem. Historic Homes Found., Louisville. Named Hardware Man of Yr. Phila., 1957. Mem. Ducks Unltd., Bklyn. Botanic Garden, Ky. Bot. Garden, Nat. Wildlife Fedn., Nat. Audubon Soc., Friends of Bernheim Forest, Nat. Trust, C. of C. Baptist. Clubs: Pendennis (Louisville), Agricultural (Louisville), Filson (Louisville). Home: Louisville Ky. Deceased.

PROFFITT, DAVID WILSON, retail executive; b. Maryville, Tenn., July 27, 1891; s. Nicholas W. and M. Alice (Lowry) P.; m. Lillian Gay Webb, Apr. 12, 1917; children: Harwell W., John W., R. Neil, M. Lillian Proffitt Lyle. BA, Maryville Coll., 1916, LLD (hon.), 1956; LLD (hon.), Hanover Coll., 1956. Pres. Proffitt's Dept. Store, 1919, later chmn.; v.p., bd. dirs. Proffitt's Dept. Store, Inc., Morristown, Athens, and Cleveland, Tenn.; chmn. bd. Proffitt's, Inc.; owner, operator farm Maryville; chmn. bd. 1st Fed. Savs. & Loan Assn., Maryville. Pres. Nat. Council Presbyn. U.S. Men, 1951-52; moderator Presbyn. Ch. U.S., 1956-57; sr. v.p. Found. United Presbyn. Ch. U.S.; mem. gen. bd. Nat. Council Chs., from 1955; lay rep. inspection refugee needs and conditions Presbyn. Ch.; mem. ch. bd. dirs. Home for Aged.; mem. Draft Appeal Bd. World War II; past chmn., dir. Blount County (Tenn.) United Fund Dr.; chmn. Blount County chpt. ARC, World War II; trustee Maryville Coll., Warren Wilson Coll. Mem. Maryville C. of C. (past pres.), Kiwanis (past pres., dir. Maryville). Home: Alcoa Tenn. †

PROGER, SAMUEL HERSCHEL, physician, educator; b. Jan. 21, 1906; s. Louis Proger; m. Evelyn Levinson, Sept. 8, 1929; children: Susan Jean, Nancy Lane. BS, Emory U., 1925, MD, 1928, DSc (hon.), 1975; DSc (hon.), Tufts U., 1952. Mem. staff New Eng. Med Ctr., Boston, from 1931, physician-in-chief, 1948-71; prof. medicine, chmn. dept., Sch. Medicine Tufts U., 1948-71; pres. Bingham Assocs. Fund; former med. cons. VA, NIH; chmn. bd. trustees, past pres. New Eng. Med. Ctr. Hosp.; past chmn. adminstrv. bd. Tufts-New Eng. Med. Ctr.; chmn. Mass. Health and Welfare Commn., 1967-69. Author articles on cardiovascular disease and med. edn. Trustee Wellesley Coll., Boston Med. Library, Med. Found., Inc.; former mem. adv. com. W.K. Kellogg Found., Commonwealth Fund, Robert Wood Johnson Found. Recipient Am. Design award, 1951, Robert Williams Disting. Chmn. Medicine award, 1980; named one of 350 Jubilee Bostonians, 1980. Fellow Am. Coll. Csrdiology, ACP; mem. Assn. Am. Physicians, Am. Soc. Clin. Investigation, Am. Acad. Arts and Scis., Am. Heart Assn., AMA, Mass. Heart Assn. (past pres.), New Eng. Cardiovascular Soc. (past pres.), Phi Beta Kappa, Alpha Omega Alpha. Home: Chestnut Hill Mass. Died May 29, 1984, buried Wakefield, Mass.

PROTHRO, JAMES WARREN, political scientist, educator; b. Robeline, La., Apr. 15, 1922; s. Edwin Thomas and Frances (Terry) P.; m. Mary Frances Harris, Oct. 17, 1943 (div. Feb. 1971); children: Pamela, Barbara, Susan.; m. Ana Posada Samper, Sept. 10, 1971. BA, N. Tex. State U., 1943; MA, La. State U., 1948, Princeton U., 1949; PhD, Princeton U., 1952. Ast. prof. polit. sci. Fla. State U., 1950-53, assoc. prof., 1953-57; vis. prof. U. N.C., Chapel Hill, 1960-61, prof. polit. sci., also rsch. prof. Inst. for Rsch. to Social Sci., from 1961, dir. of inst., 1967-73, Alumni Disting. prof., from 1975, chmn. dept. polit. sci., from 1980, dir. Louis Harris Data Ctr., 1965-73; vis. prof. Escuela Latinoamericana de Cienca Politica y Adminstracion Publica, Chile, 1966-67; con. U.S. Commn. on Civil Rights, 1964-65. Author: Dollar Decade: Business Ideas in the 1920's, 1954, (with Richard Richardson) The Politics of American Democracy, 7th edit., 1981, (with Donald R. Matthews) Negroes and the New Southern Politics, 1966, (with David Kovenock) Explaining the Vote: Presidential Choices in the Nation and the States, 1973; book rev. editor Am. Polit. Sci. Rev., 1965-68, editorial bd., 1965-69; adv. bd. Jour. of Politics, 1965-76; contbr. articles to profl. jours.; rsch. and publs. on Negro polit. participation in the South combining aggregate data, opinion survey data, depth community studies in a single explanatory model. Rockefeller Found. grantee, 1960-64, Social Sci. Rsch. Council grantee, 1963-64; Ford Found. grantee, 1960-64; Fgn. Area fellow, Chile, 1972. Mem. Am. Polit. Sci. Assn. (exec. council 1970-73), So. Polit. Sci. Assn. (pres. 1970-71), AAUP. Home: Chapel Hill N.C. Died Feb. 7, 1986; cremated.

PROVENSEN, MARTIN ELIAS, author, illustrator; b. Chgo., July 10, 1916; s. Marthin C. and Berendina (Kruger) P.; m. Alice Twitchell, Apr. 17, 1944; 1 dau., Karen Anna. Ed., U. Calif., Berkeley. Exhbns. (with wife) include, Balt. Mus., 1954, Am. Inst. Graphic Arts, N.Y.C., 1959, Botolph Group, Boston, 1964; illustrator: children's books The Fireside Book of Folk Songs, 1949, The New Testament, 1953, The Iliad and Oddysey, 1956, Myths and Legends, 1969, Aesop's Fables, 1965, Fun and Nonsense, 1970, The Provensen Book of Fairy Tales, 1971, A Peaceable Kingdom, 1978, The Golden Serpent, 1980, A Visit to William Blake's Inn, 1981, Birds, Beasts and the Third Thing, 1982; also, Shakespeare, 10 Great Plays, 1961; and text books; author-illustrator: (with wife) The Animal Fair, 1952, Karen's Opposites, 1963, Karen's Curiosity, 1963, What Is a Color, 1967, Who's in The Egg, 1970, Play on Words, 1972, My Little Hen, 1973, Roses Are Red, 1973, Our Animal Friends, 1974, The Book of Seasons, 1976, The Year at Maple Hill Farm, 1978, A Horse and a Hound, A Goat and a Gander, 1979, An Owl and Three Pussycats, 1981, The Glorious Flight, 1983, Leonardo DaVinci, Shaker Lane, 1987; illustrated: The Voyage of the Ludgate Hill, 1987; (with wife) books rep. Fifty Book Year selections, Am. Inst. Graphic Arts, 1947, 48, 72. Served with USNR, 1941-45. Recipient Best Illustrated Book of Year award for Charge of Light Brigade, N.Y. Times, 1964; Best of Year citation, 1952, 53, 59, 63, 64, 76, 78; co-recipient Gold medal Soc. Illustrators, 1960; Art Books for Children citation Bklyn. Mus., 1975; Caldecott and Boston Globe awards for A Visit to William Blake's Inn; Caldecott Medal for The Glorious Flight, 1984. Home: Staatsburg N.Y. Died Mar. 27, 1987.

PUGH, HERBERT LAMONT, physician, naval officer, author; b. Batesville, Va., Feb. 5, 1895; s. Samuel Eli and Mary Elizabeth (Thompson) P.; m. Martha Catherine Schmidt, June 30, 1926; 1 son, Lamont. BS, MD, U. Va., 1923; postgrad. surgery, U. Pa., 1928; postgrad. thoracic surgery, Barnes Hosp., St. Louis, 1940; LLD, Wagner Coll. Diplomate: Am. Bd. Surgery, Am. Bd. Preventative Medicine and Pub. Health, Nat. Bd. Med. Examiners (former mem.). Student intern Martha Jefferson Hosp., Charlottesville, Va., 1923; commd. lt. (j.g.) USN, 1923, advanced through grades to rear adm., 1946; dep. and asst. chief Bur. Medicine and Surgery, Dept. Navy, 1946-51; surgeon gen. USN, chief, 1951-55, insp. gen., med. dept., 1955; comdg. officer Nat. Naval Med. Ctr., Bethesda, Md., 1955-56, ret., 1956; univ. physician George Washington U., 1956-68; med. dir. Navy-Marine Corps-Coast Guard Residence (Vinson Hall), 1969-79; profl. attendance at various med. facilities, including clinics of Vienna. Author: History of the Medical Department of U.S. Navy, 1945-55, 1958, Navy Surgeon, 1959; contbr. articles to sci. jours. and lay publs. Trustee Navy-Marine Corps-Coast Guard Residence Found.; past bd. govs. ARC. With USMC, World War I. Decorated numerous numerous service and area medals; recipient Outstanding Alumnus award U. Va. Club of Washington, Disting. Service award Am. Podiatry Assn. Fellow ACS, Am. Surg. Assn.; hon. fellow Internat. Coll. Surgeons, Am. Assn. for Surgery of Trauma, Am. Coll. Hosp. Adminstrs., Am. Coll. Chest Physicians; mem. Med. Soc. of Va., Alexandria Med. Soc., AMA (past mem. ho. of dels., past chmn. mil. med. sect.), Assn. Mil. Surgeons, Soc. Med. Cons. to Armed Forces, Med. Soc. D.C. (emeritus), Washington Acad. Surgery (hon.), Acad. Medicine Washington (hon.), U. Va. Med. Alumni Assn., Soc. of Con., Mil. Order World Wars (companion), Raven Soc., Masons, Cosmos Club (Washington), Explorers Club, Farmington Country Club (Charlottesville, Va.), Alpha Omega Alpha, Phi Beta KAppa, Omicron DeltaKappa. Presbyterian. Home: McLean Va. Died Dec. 3, 1984.

PULLMAN, GEORGE CONRAD, clergyman; b. Urbana, Ind., Dec. 11, 1887; s. Oscar and Elizabeth (Tramer) P.; m. Edith Christine Brembeck, Dec. 12, 1916; children: George Robert, Marjorie Edith. BA, North Central Coll., Naperville, Ill., 1912; BD, Evang. Theol. Sem., Naperville, Ill., 1914; STM, Evang. Theol. Sem., 1923; DD, Yankton (S.D.) Coll., 1935. Ordained to ministry Evang. Ch., 1914. Pastor Trinity Ch., Rochester, Ind., 1914-18; religious sec. YMCA, Camp Funston, Kans. and Great Lakes lNaval Tng. Sta., Ill., 1918-19; pastor Trinity Ch., Louisville, Ky., 1919-23, 1st Ch., Elkhart, Ind., 1923-26; student sec. YMCA, Chgo., 1926-29; assoc. pastor 1st Congl. Ch., Chgo., 1929-31; pastor 1st Congl. Ch., Sioux City, Iowa, 1931-

46, Bklyn. Hgts. Congl. Ch., Cleve., 1946-54; pastor N. Miami Community Ch., Miami, Fla., 1954-57, ch. fin. counselor, from 1957. Contbr. poems and articles to mags. and to devotional books. Mem. bd. control Yankton Coll. Mem. Kiwanis Club. Republican. Home: Lake Worth Fla. †

PUSEY, MERLO, writer; b. Woodruff, Utah, Feb. 3, 1902; s. John Sidney and Nellie (Quibell) P.; m. Dorothy Richards, Sept. 5, 1928; children: Conway Richards, David Richards, John Richards. Grad., Latter-Day Saints U., 1922; AB, U. Utah, 1928, LLD (hon.), 1975; LittD (hon.), Brigham Young U., 1952. Reporter, asst. city editor Deseret News, Salt Lake City, 1922-28, asst. city editor, 1926-28; copyreader Daily News, Washington, 1928; editorial writer Washington Post, 1928-71, assoc. editor, 1945-71; instr. journalism George Washington U., 1939-42. Author: The Supreme Court Crisis, 1937, Big Government; Can We Control It?, 1945, (authorized biography) Charles Evans Hughes, 2 vols., 1951 (Pulitzer prize, Bancroft prize), Eisenhower The President, 1956, The Way We Go To War, 1969, The U.S.A. Astride the Globe, 1971, Eugene Meyer, 1974, also pamphlets, contbr. articles to nat. mags. Recipient Tamiment Inst. prize, 1952, ABA Gavel award, 1960, Frank Luther Mott Research award Kappa Tau Alpha, 1975. Mem. Am. Polit. Sci. Assn., Cosmos Club, Nat. Press Club. Mormon. Home: Dickerson Md. Died Nov. 22, 1985.

PYATT, CHARLES LYNN, theologian; b. Jacksonville, Ill., Feb. 25, 1886; s. John Cassell and Mary Belle (Cheaney) P.; m. Grace Strawn, Sept. 6, 1910 (dec. Sept. 1936). AB, Transylvania Coll., 1911, AM, 1912, LLD (hon.), 1955; classical diploma, Coll. of the Bible, Lexington, Ky., 1912; BD, Yale Divinity Sch., 1913; ThD, Harvard Divinity Sch., 1916; postdoctoral sties, Johns Hopkins U., 1942-42; DD, Atlantic Christian Coll., 1957. Pastor Cen. Christian Ch., Gary, Ind., 1916, Centenary Christian Ch., Indpls., 1919-20; prof. Old Testament Coll. of the Bible, 1920-53, chmn. faculty, 1928-37, dean, 1938-53, emeritus, from 1953, asst. to pres., from 1953; Dir. Bd. Higher Edn. of Disciples of Christ from 1934, v.p. 1936-38; assoc. in coun., Coun. for Clin. Tng. of Theol. Students, 1936-44; mem. Commn. on Religion and Health of Fed. Coun. of Chs. of Christ, 1940-46, Commn. on Clin. Tng., 1940-42; chmn. S.E. Regional conf., Am. Assn. Theol. Schs., 1940-42; exec. sec. Am. Assn. Theol. Schs. from 1946, mem. exec. com. from 1950. Editor and contbr. the Coll. of the Bible Quarterly. With YMCA in France, 1917-19. Mem. Am. Oriental Soc., Soc. Bibl. Lit. and Exegesis, Nat. Assn. Bibl. Instrs., Masons (K.T., Shriner), Kiwanis, Phi Kappa Tau, Theta Phi (mem. senate). Home: Lexington Ky. †

PYLE, FRANCIS JOHNSON, music educator; b. South Bend, Ind., Sept. 13, 1901; s. Dan and Zoula Angie (Johnson) P.; m. Eleanor Meneghel, Apr. 14, 1927; 1 child, Zoula Pauline Pyle Zein-Eldin. BA, Oberlin Coll., 1923; MA, U. Wash., 1932; PhD, U. Rochester, 1945. Dir. instrumental music Wash. pub. schs., 1927-29; dir. instrumental music, asst. prof. music theory Cen. State Coll., 1929-37; prof. theory and musicology, head dept. Drake U., Des Moines, Iowa, from 1937; vis. prof. theory UCLA, summer, 1955; bicentennial composer-in-residence St. Cloud (Minn.) State U., 1976; vis. prof. orch. dir. Cen. Coll., Pella, Iowa; composer, editor, lectr., guest condr., program annotator Des Moines Symphony Orch.; music advisor Iowa Fine Arts Council; participant Profl. Mentor Project, es Moines pub. schs., 1981. Composer Pictures for Suzanne, 1958, Woodwind Quintet, 1959, Sonata for Clarinet and Piano, 1959, Sonata for Three, 1964, Violin Piano Sonata, 1964, Far Dominion, 1966, TeDeum, 1962, Concerto for trumpet and wind ensemble, 1966, Symphony in One Movement for accordion orch., 1966, Concerto Giubilante for organ, 19 winds and percussion, 1967, Mountain Tarn, Henry Was a Worthy King, Elkan-Vogel, 1967, Four Dialogues for harp and orch., 1969, Sonata for piano, 1968, Full Stature, 1968, Sonatas Nos. 1 and 2 for free bass accordion, 1968-69, Overture for accordion orch., 1969, I Have Chosen Thee, 1968, Canticle of the Sun for brass sextet or piano, 1970, Three Psalms for orch., chorus and brass choir, 1971, Studies in 20th Century Idioms, 8 etudes for free bass accordion, 1971, Sonata for flute and piano, 1970, Sinfonietta No. 1 for chamber orch., 1971, Overture Pasadena for concert band, 1971, Psalm 133 for male chorus and keyboard, 1972, For Those Who Seek for trumpet solo, double brass sextet, percussion, 1972, Symphony No. 1 for concert band, 1973, Dialogues for piano duet, 1974, Quartet for saxaphones, 1974, Sonata No. 3 for piano, 1975, Memorial Chorus, 1975, Sinfonietta No. 3 for orch. (joint commn. Ft. Dodge Symphony-Iowa Arts Council), 1977, Melodic Sketch for violin and piano, 1978, Wedding Music for organ and violin, 1979, Brazos Suiter, 1981, hymn When in Our Music God is Glorified, 1981. Recipient Disting. Service award to music educators, 1970, Robert M. McCowan Meml. award for outstanding contbn. to choral music, 1970. Mem. Nat. Assn. Music Tchrs. (nat. exec. bd.), Music Educators Nat. Conf. (Iowa exec. bd.), Nat. Fedn. Music Clubs (exec. com. Iowa Bicentennial 1976), Am. Musicol. Soc., ASCAP, Masons, Sigma Alpha Iota, Phi Mu Alpha, Pi Kappa Lambda. Presbyterian. Home: Des Moines Iowa.

PYM, MICHAEL (MRS. MARIE LOUISE LUCIA MICHAEL NUNEHAM PYM), writer; b. London, Oct. 20, 1889; d. William Edwin and Marie Louise (de Tongres) Pym; m. Capt. Samuel Newton Branch, 1919 (div. 1925). Student, Pensionnat de Melsele and Sorbonne. Mem. staff La Reina de la Moda, S.Am., Milw. Jour., Pitts. Dispatch, until 1922; spl. corr. N.Y. Annalist, 1925, N.Y. Herald Tribune, India, 1926-30, at Round Table Conf., London, 1930-31; Spl. del. to All India Women's Conf. on Ednl. Reform, 1929. Author: The Power of India, 1930; contbr. articles on Islamic themes to specialized jours. Decorated Officier d'Academie (France). Mem. Royal Cen. Asian Soc., Soc. Woman Geographers, Women's University Club (N.Y.C.); Brit. Automobile Racing Club, Royal Automobile Club, Can. Welsh Corgi Club (Am., Wales); Welsh Corgi Club (Britain). Home: Miami Fla. †

QUALEY, CARLTON CHESTER, historian, educator; b. Spring Grove, Minn., Dec. 17, 1904; s. Ole O. and Clara (Knatterud) Q.; m. Elizabeth Frances Cummings, Apr. 29, 1933 (dec. July 1980); children: John, Mary. B.A., St. Olaf Coll., 1929; M.A., U. Minn., 1930; Ph.D., Columbia U., 1938. From lectr. to assoc. prof. history Bard Coll. of Columbia, 1936-44, assoc. prof. at univ., 1945-46, vis. summer prof., 1938-46; assoc. prof. Swarthmore Coll., 1944-45; prof. Am. history Carleton Coll., 1946-67, Laird Bell prof. history, 1967-70, chmn. dept., 1960-67, vis. prof., fall 1972; part-time dir. Minn. Hist. Soc., 1947-48, research fellow, 1970-88 ; dir. Minn. Ethnic History Project, 1973-78; vis. prof. Northwestern U., summer 1951, Cleve. State U., 1971-72, Augsburg Coll., fall 1976; vis. Coe prof. Am. history Stanford U., summer 1966; vis. lectr. U. Minn., 1976-81. Author: Norwegian Settlement in the United States, 1938, 70, Thorstein Veblen, 1968, On Being an Ethnic Historian, 1972; also articles on immigration, book revs.; contbg. author, dir. research: They Chose Minnesota, 1981. Participant Minn. Russian Seminar, USSR, 1958; Participant Internat. Congress Hist. Scis., Stockholm, 1960, San Francisco, 1975. Shevlin fellow U. Minn., 1931-32; Univ. fellow Columbia U., 1932-33; travel grantee Social Sci. Research Council, 1960; research grantee Hill Found., St. Paul, 1954-55; research grantee Am. Council Learned Socs., 1962-63; research grantee Huntington Library, 1968; research grantee Bush Found., 1973-75; research grantee Nat. Endowment for Humanities, 1975-77. Mem. Orgn. Am. Historians (mem. nominating com. 1966-68), Am. Hist. Assn., Norwegian-Am. Hist. Assn. (bd. editors), Western Hist. Assn., Upper Midwest Hist. Conf. (pres. 1980-81), Minn. Hist. Soc., Immigration Hist. Soc. (treas., editor newsletter since 1973), AAUP. Unitarian. Home: Saint Paul Minn. Died Mar. 25, 1988.

QUASTEL, JUDA HIRSCH, former neurochemistry educator; b. Sheffield, Eng., Oct. 2, 1899; s. Jonas and Flora Quastel; m. Henrietta Jungman, Dec. 27, 1931 (dec. 1973); children—Michael Reuben, David Murray Joseph, Barbara Joan Quastel Glick; m. Susan Ricardo, July 14, 1975. B.S., Imperial Coll. Sci., London, 1921, D.Sc., 1926; Ph.D., Trinity Coll., Cambridge, Eng., 1924; D.Sc. (hon.), McGill U., Montreal, Que., Can., 1969; Ph.D. (hon.), Hebrew U., Jerusalem, 1970. Fellow Trinity Coll., Cambridge, 1924-29; dir. research Cardiff City Mental Hosp., Wales, 1930-41; dir. soil biochemistry research Agrl. Research Council, 1941-47; prof. biochemistry McGill U., Montreal, 1947-66, dir. unit for research in cell metabolism, 1965-66; prof. neurochemistry U. B.C., Vancouver, Can., 1966-83, prof. emeritus, 1983-87; dir. McGill-Montreal Gen. Hosp. Research Inst., 1948-65. Author, editor: (with C. C. Thomas) Neurochemistry, 1955, 2d edit., 1962, Chemistry of Brain Metabolism, 1961, Methods in Medical Research, Vol. 9, 1961; contbr. over 350 articles to profl. jours. Decorated companion Order of Can.; recipient Sr. Gairdner Internat. award for med. research, 1974. Fellow Royal Soc. (London), Royal Soc. Can., Royal Soc. Edinburgh (hon.), Royal Soc. Chemistry (U.K.), Can. Biochem. Soc. (pres. 1963), Biochem. Soc. (U.K. jubilee lectr.) (hon.); mem. Can. Microbiol. Soc. (award 1963). Home: Vancouver B.C., Canada. Died Oct. 15, 1987; buried Vancouver, B.C., Can.

QUINTRELL, CLAYTON A., lawyer; b. Cleve., Mar. 12, 1892; s. Thomas and Sarah Jane (Clayton) Q.; m. Margaret Armstrong, Oct. 30, 1917; 1 son, Thomas A. AB, Western Res. U., 1913; LLB, Harvard U., 1917. Bar: Ohio 1919. Pvt. practice Cleve., from 1919; ptnr. firm Copeland & Quintrell, Cleve., 1919-26, Baker, Hostetler & Patterson, Cleve., from 1926. With U.S. Army, World War I. Mem. Am., Ohio, Cleve. bar assns., Am. Judicature Soc., Beta Theta Pi, Phi Delta Phi. Republican. Episcopalian. Home: Lakewood Ohio. †

RAASCH, JOHN E(MIL), merchant; b. Staten Island, N.Y., Oct. 2, 1891; s. J. Hermann and Louisa (Nunaman) R.; m. Helen Kerr, June 11, 1919. BCS, NYU, 1917. Jr. officer Fed. Res. Bank, N.Y.C., 1914-22; with H.A. Hopf & Co., mgmt. engrs., N.Y.C., 1922-35; exec. v.p. John Wanamaker, N.Y.C., 1935-47, dir., from 1945, pres., 1947-66; dir. John Wanamaker, Phila, from 1945, v.p., 1942-47, pres., 1947-66; also John Wanamaker, Wilmington; chmn. bd., dir. Grand Union Co., East Paterson, N.J.; bd. dirs. Eastern Shopping Ctrs., Inc., John Wanamaker Liberty St., Inc., John Wanamaker, Ltd., London, Agy John Wanamaker, S.A., Paris, Products of Asia, N.Y.C., Products of India, N.Y.C. Trustee emeritus NYU. Recipient Madden Meml. award, Presdl. citation NYU. Mem. Mchts. Coun. NYU Sch. Retailing, NYU Alumni Fedn. (meritorious svc. medal), Arch and Square, Ridgewood Country Club, N.Y. University Club, Alpha Kappa Psi, Eta Mu Pi, Phi Alpha Kappa. Home: Ridgewood N.J.†

RABB, SIDNEY R., retail food and mercantile executive; b. Boston, Oct. 20, 1900; s. Joseph and Lottie Rebeca (Wolf) R.; m. Esther Vera Cohn, Feb. 29, 1920; children: Helene J. Rabb Cahners, Carol P. Rabb Goldberg. Student, Harvard U., 1920, M.A. (hon.), 1962; LL.D., Tufts U., 1961; D.C.S., Suffolk U., 1966; L.H.D., Boston Coll., 1964; D.H., Northeastern U., 1976; D.H.L., Brandeis U., 1977. With Economy Grocery Store Corp., now The Stop & Shop, Cos. (named change 1946), Boston, 1918-85, treas., 1925-65, chmn. bd., 1930-85; v.p., dir. Nathan H. Gordon Corp.; hon. dir. Boston Safe Deposit & Trust Co. Hon. life trustee, exec. com., past pres. Beth Israel Hosp.; hon. life trustee Combined Jewish Philanthropies; hon. trustee Mass. Gen. Hosp., McLean Hosp.; bd. overseers Boys Clubs Boston; hon. trustee Hebrew Rehab. Center for Aged, Boston Mus. Fine Arts, Recuperative Center; past pres. Boston Pub. Library; vice chmn., mem. exec. com. Mass. Com. Catholics, Protestants and Jews; fellow Brandeis U.; com. univ. resources bd. overseers Harvard U.; mem. corp. Mus. of Sci., Boston; mem. nat. bd. govs. Israel Bond Orgn.; hon. bd. dirs. Food Mktg. Inst. Served with USMC, World War I. Fellow Am. Acad. Arts and Scis. Jewish (dir. Kehillath Israel Synagogue, hon. life trustee Temple Israel). Clubs: Masons (Boston), Harvard (Boston), Commercial (Boston); Palm Beach Country. Home: Boston Mass. Died Oct. 13, 1985.

RABI, ISIDOR ISAAC, physics educator; b. Austria, July 29, 1898; came to U.S. in infancy; s. David and Jennie (Teig) R.; m. Helen Newark, 1926; children: Nancy Elizabeth, Margaret Joella. BS in Chemistry, Cornell U., 1919; PhD, Columbia U., 1927; research grad. study in Munich, Copenhagen, Hamburg, Leipzig, Zurich, 1927-29; DSc (hon.), Princeton U., 1947, Dickenson Coll., 1954, Harvard U., 1955, Birmingham (Eng.) U., 1957, Williams Coll., 1958, U. Birmingham, 1960, Clark U., 1962, Adelphi Coll., 1962, Technion, 1963, Franklin Marshall Coll., 1964, Brandeis U., 1965, U. Coimbra, Portugal, 1966, Columbia U., 1968, CCNY, 1968, 1977, Hebrew U., Jerusalem, 1972, Bates Coll., 1977, L.I. U., 1977; LHD (hon.), Hebrew Union Coll., Cin., 1958, Oklahoma City U., 1960; LLD (hon.), Dropsie Coll., 1956; DHL (hon.), Yeshiva U., 1964, Rockefeller U. 1979; LittD (hon.), Jewish Theol. Sem., 1966, Hamburg 1985; PhD (hon.) Bar-Ilan U., Israel, 1987. Tutor in physics, CCNY, 1924-27; lectr. Columbia U., 1929-30, asst. prof., 1930-35, asso. prof., 1935-37, prof., 1937-64, Higgins prof., 1950-64, U. prof., 1964-67, U. prof. emeritus, 1967-88, also exec. officer, dept. physics, 1945-49; Karl Taylor Compton vis. prof. physics, 1968-69; lectr. U. Mich., summer 1936, Stanford U., summer 1938; cons. sci. adv. com. Ballistic Research Lab., Aberdeen, 1939-65; mem. sci. bd. Itek Corp. Staff mem. and asso. dir., Radiation Lab., M.I.T., 1940-45; mem. gen. adv. com. AEC, from 1946, chmn., 1952-56, cons., from 1956; originator idea for European Ctr. for Nuclear Research, Geneva, Switzerland; active in creation of Brookhaven Nat. Lab., L.I.; chmn. sci. adv. Com. ODM, 1953-57; cons. Dept. State, 1955-80; mem. Naval Research Adv. Com., from 1952, cons., sci. adv. com., v.p. Internat. Conf. on Peaceful Uses Atomic Energy, Geneva, 1955, 58, 64; v.p. UN Conf. on Peaceful Uses Atomic Energy, from 1971; U.S. rep. adv. com. to sec. gen. UN, from 1955; mem. President's Sci. Adv. Com., 1957-68, chmn., 1957; cons. Los Alamos Sci. Lab., 1943-45, and from 56; mem. NATO Sci. Com., from 1958; cons. Research and Devel. Bd., 1946-49; U.S. del. UNESCO Conf., Florence, Italy, 1950; mem. U.S. Nat. Commn. UNESCO, 1950-53, 58; mem. UN Sci. Com., from 1954; mem. IAEA Sci. Com., 1958-72; vis. prof. Rockefeller U. (formerly Inst.), 1957-79; Shreve fellow Princeton, 1961-62; Karl Taylor Compton lectr. Mass. Inst. Tech., 1962; gen. adv. com. ACDA, 1962—. Author: My Life and Times as a Physicist, 1960, Science: The Center of Culture, 1970; assoc. editor: Physical Review, 1935-38, 41-44; contbr. to sci. jours. in field. Served in S.A.T.C., 1918. Decorated Officer French Legion of Honor, 1956; comdr., 1968. Barnard fellow, 1927-28; Internat. Ednl. Bd. fellow, 1928-29; Ernest Kempton Adams fellow, 1935; Sigma Xi Semicentennial prize for physical scis., 1936; Henrietta Szold award, 1956; $1,000 prize from AAAS, for study of radio frequency spectra of atoms and molecules, 1939; Elliot Cresson medal of Franklin Inst., 1942; Nobel Prize in Physics, 1944; Barnard medal, 1960; U.S. Medal for Merit, 1948; King's Medal (British, 1948); Comdr., Order So. Cross, Brazil, 1952; Priestley Meml. award Dickenson Coll., 1964; Niels Bohr Internat. Gold Medal, 1967; co-recipient, Atoms for Peace award, 1967; Tribute of Appreciation, State Dept., 1978; Pupin Gold medal Columbia U. Sch. Engring., 1981, Mayor Koch award for Sci. Technology, 1985; Weizmann Medallion award, 1987; Vannevar Bush award, 1986. Trustee Assoc. Univs., Inc., from 1946, pres., 1961-62, chmn. bd., 1962-63; bd. govs. Weizmann Inst. Sci., Rehovoth, Israel, from 1949, v.p. 1986; trustee Mt. Sinai Hosp., from 1960. Fellow Am.

Phys. Soc. (pres. 1950-51); mem. Council on Fgn. Relations, Am. Philos. Soc., Japan Acad. Sci. (fgn. mem.), Nat. Acad. Scis., N.Y. Acad. Scis., Sigma Xi. Clubs: Century, Cosmos (Washington); Faculty (Columbia U.); Athenaeum (London), Century. Died Jan. 11, 1988. Home: New York N.Y.

RADINSKY, LEONARD, anatomy and evolutionary biology educator; b. N.Y.C., July 16, 1937; s. Jacob and Frieda (Groskin) R.; children: Adam, Joshua, Leah. BA, Cornell U., 1958; MS, Yale U., 1960, PhD, 1962. Postdoctoral fellow dept. vertebrate paleontology Am. Mus. Nat. History, N.Y.C., 1962-63; asst. prof. biology Boston U., 1963-64, Bklyn. Coll., CUNY, 1964-67; asst. prof. U. Chgo., 1967-70, assoc. prof., 1970-76, prof. anatomy and evolutionary biology, 1976-85, chmn. dept. anatomy, 1977-85. Contbr. articles to profl. jours. NSF grantee, 1965-85. Mem. AAAS, Soc. Vertebrate Paleontology, Am. Soc. Zoologists, Am. Soc. Mammalogists, Soc. for Study Evolution. Died Aug. 30, 1985.

RADNITZER, ADOLPH, lawyer, corporate executive; b. Chgo., May 31, 1892; m. Charlotte Z. Lisberg, May 28, 1937; children: Edith Pauline, Kenneth. PhB, U. Chgo., 1913, JD cum laude, 1915. Bar: Ill. 1915, N.Y. 1939. Pvt. practice law Chgo., 1916-17; asst. corp. counsel City of Chgo., 1919-20; later sec. reorgn. com. McCrory Stores, Inc.; then sec. Universal Am. Corp., N.Y.C. Mem. Advt. Club. N.Y.C., Masons. Home: New York N.Y. †

RAFTERY, SYLVESTER FRANK, labor union official; b. St. Louis, Nov. 30, 1918; s. Lawrence Michael and Enid Vale (King) R.; m. Marjorie Jane Belt, May 24, 1941; children: Marjorie Jo, Barbara Sue, Mary Ann, Virginia Louise, James Patrick, Jane Marie. Student, St. Louis U., 1950-53. Affiliated with labor movement 1935-84; bus. agt., then fin. sec. Painters Local, St. Louis, mem. local apprenticeship com., del. confs., v.p. Glazier Nat. Conf., gen. organizer, nat. coordinator apprenticeship and tng. for painters, sign painters, glaziers, auto glass workers, stained glass workers, carpet and linoleum layers; acting gen. sec.-treas. Internat. Brotherhood of Painters and Allied Trades, Washington, gen. pres., 1965-84, establisher first nat. pension fund, 1967; v.p. exec. council AFL-CIO; mem. nat. joint trade adv. com. glass and glazing industry; labor mem. Nat. Joinmt Bd. for Settlement Jurisdictional Disputes; mem. screeing com. internal disputes bldg. trades dept. AFL-CIO; mem. joint jurisdictional com. stained glass industry; lectr. ILO; mem. apprenticeship com. metal trades dept. AFL-CIO; chmn. joint jurisidictional com. Gypsum Drywall Contractors Internat.; chmn. painting and decoration nat. joint industry promotion program; mem. steering com. Bldg. Research Inst.; rep. AFL-CIO at Can. Labor Congress, Can. Nat. Expn.; vice chmn. Histadrut, Am. Trade Union Council of Nat. Com. for Labor Israel; sec. navy's goodwill ambassador maritime trades dept. AFL-CIO to Latin Am. trade unions; mem. exec. bd. indsl. trades dept. AFL-CIO, v.p. bldg. constrn. trades and metal trades depts.; mem. nat. appeals bd. bldg. and constrn. industry; bd. dirs. Union Labor Life Ins. Co. Mem. nat. adv. council Peace Corps; citizen's adv. council White House Conf. Children and Youth; Democratic judge elections, Montgomery County, Md.; trustee George Meany Found.; bd. dirs. Am. Inst. Human Engring. With USNR, World War II. Mem. Nat. Planning Assn., Holy Name Soc., K.C. Home: Washington D.C. Died Nov. 20, 1986, buried Gate of Heaven Cemetery, Silver Spring, Md.

RAGSDALE, JESSE G(RANT), principal; b. Half Way, Mo., Oct. 6, 1890; s. James Grant and Eliza Anne (Redd) R.; m. Helen E. Shepherd, July 6, 1918; children: Doris Jean (Mrs. Keith S. Sherburne), Janet Helen (Mrs. Louis T. Renz). AB, Coll. Idaho, 1915; AM, Columbia U., 1922. Tchr. schs. Idaho, 1915-17; tchr. Boise (Idaho) High Sch., 1919-20; prin. Chouteau County High Sch., Ft. Benton, Mont., 1920-21; prin. high sch. Butte, Mont., 1922-30; supt. of schs. City of Butte, 1930-34; supt. Gallatin County High Sch., 1935-45; prin. Billings (Mont.) Sr. High Sch., from 1945; instr. summers Bates Coll., Lewiston, Maine, 1922, Mont. Normal Coll., 1926; compiler schedule card-index system for high sch. enrollment. Author: Making the Most of High School, 1927. Mem. Tri-Partite Panel War Labor Bd., 1942-45. Capt. inf. U.S. Army, World War II. Recipient Sci. Rsch. Assocs. Nat. award, 1951. Mem. Mont. Edn. Assn., Va. Hist. Soc., Am. Acad. Polit. and Social Sci., Mont. Soc. for Study of Edn. (pres. 1947), Kiwanis, Phi Delta Kappa, Pi Gamma Mu. Presbyterian. Home: Alpine Calif. †

RAGSDALE, WARNER BERNICE, journalist, editor; b. Hiram, Ga., Dec. 21, 1898; s. Joseph Robert and Sarah Emma (Bullard) R.; m. Claribel Kemp, Oct 21, 1922; children: Warner Bernice, Ruthmary. Student, Young Harris Coll., 1914-17, Ga. Sch. Tech., 1917-18. Reporter Jacksonville (Fla.) Metropolis, 1920, Hendersonville (N.C.) News, 1921, Charlotte (N.C.) News, 1921, Charlotte Observer, 1921-22, 23-24, AP, Atlanta, 1922, Internat. News Service, Birmingham, Ala., 1922, Phila. Evening Ledger, 1924; with AP, 1924-41; early, night and day editor AP, Atlanta, 1924-26; early editor AP, Louisville, 1925; corr. AP, New Orleans, 1926-27; reporter, editor and spl. writer on govt. and politics AP, Washington, 1927-41; polit. editor U.S. News & World Report, 1941-69. Author: The Origins of the Constitution, 1937, U.S. Politics-Inside and Out, 1970, Guide to 1972 Elections, 1972, Three Weeks in Dayton, 1975, also numerous serialized studies on taxes, govt., trade, nat. def. Exec. com. Periodical Press Galleries, 1949-69, chmn., 1963-65, 67-69. With Students Army Tng. Corps, 1918. Mem. Headliners Club (best feature story award 1937), Nat. Press Club (Washington). Home: Silver Spring Md. Died Dec. 25, 1986; buried Parklawn Cemetery, Rockville, Md.

RAHILLY, THOMAS FRANCIS, foundry executive; b. Diorite, Mich., Oct. 6, 1892; s. Daniel and Josephine (Holley) R.; m. Violet Kennedy, Feb. 15, 1915; children: Thomas Francis, Bernard J., Vernon J., Donald H. Ed. high sch. Pres., chmn. Can. Iron Foundries, Ltd., Montreal; bd. dirs. Dominion Foundries & Steel, Ltd., Hamilton, Ont., Can., John Wood Industries, Ltd., Toronto, Can., Walworth Co., Boston, Electric Tamper & Mfg. Co., Montreal, Bank N.S.., Toronto, Can. Refractories, Ltd., Montreal. Mem. Am. Iron and Steel Inst., Sault Sainte Marie Country Club, Seigniory York Club, Granite Club, Rideau Club, St. James Club, Royal Montreal Golf Club. Home: Mount Royal Can. †

RAHMAN, ANEESUR, physicist; b. Hyderabad, India, Aug. 24, 1927; came to U.S., 1960; s. Habibur and Aisha (Abdullah) R.; m. Yueh-Erh Li, Nov. 3, 1956; 1 child, Aneesa. BS, Osmania (India) U., 1946; MA, Cambridge (Eng.) U., 1948; DSc, Louvain (Belgium) U., 1953. Lectr. Osmania U., Hyderabad, 1949-57; scientist Tata Inst. of Fundamental Research, Bombay, India, 1957-60; sr. scientist, theoretical physicist Argonne (Ill.) Nat. Lab., 1960-85; prof. physics U. Minn., Mpls., 1985-87, also fellow Supercomputer Inst. Home: Minneapolis Minn. Died June 6, 1987; buried Mpls.

RAICHLE, FRANK G., lawyer; b. Mpls., Aug. 28, 1898; s. Frank G. and Grace (Lyons) R.; m. Gladys Ferrin, June 27, 1929. LLB, U. Buffalo, 1919; DHL (hon.), Canisus Coll., 1969. Bar: N.Y. 1920. Pvt. practice Buffalo; ptnr. Raichle, Banning, Weiss and Halpern and predecessors, 1923-86; lectr. U. Buffalo Law Sch., 1925-30; spl. asst. to dist. atty. Erie County, 1938-39; adv. com. to establish uniform rules of evidence for fed. cts. U.S. Jud. Conf., 1965. Bd. regents Canisus Coll., 1965-86. Fellow Am. Coll. Trial Lawyers (prees. 1967-68), Internat. Acad. Tila Lawyers, Am. Bar Found.; mem. ABA, N.Y. State Bar Assn., Erie County Bar Assn., Assn. of Bar of City of N.Y., Am. Law Inst., Am. Judicare Soc., Buffalo Club, Country Club of Buffalo, Saturn Club (Buffalo), Racquet and Tennis Club (N.Y.C.). Home: Buffalo N.Y. Address: For the late Frank G Raichle 88 Middlesex Rd Buffalo NY 14216 Died Jan. 24, 1986.

RAINEY, HOMER PRICE, educator, academic administrator; b. Clarksville, Tex., Jan. 19, 1896; s. Edward and Jenny (Price) R.; m. Mildred Collins, July 28, 1920; children: Helen Collins, Lenore. AB, Austin Coll., Sherman, Tex., 1919, LLD(hon.); AM, U. Chgo., 1923, PhD, 1924; LLD (hon.), Denison U., Washington and Jefferson Coll., U. N.Mex. Instr. Austin Coll., 1919-22; assoc. prof. edn. U. Oreg., 1924-26, prof., 1926-27; pres. Franklin (Ind.) Coll., 1927-31, Bucknell U., Lewisburg, Pa., 1931-35; dir. Am. Youth Commn., 1935-39; pres. U. Tex., 1939-44, Stephens Coll., Columbia, Mo., 1947-56; prof. edn. U. Colo., Boulder, from 1956. Author: Public School Finance, 1929, How Fare American Youth, 1937, also monographs: A Study of School Finance in Oregon, 1925, The Distribution of School Funds in Oregon, 1926, The Achievement of Elementary School Pupils in Oregon, 1927; contbr. to profl. jours. Recipient Thomas Jefferson award 1946. Mem. Phi Beta Kappa, Phi Delta Kappa, Pi Kappa Delta, Masons (Knight Templar). Democrat. Baptist. Home: Boulder Colo. Died Dec. 19, 1985.

RAINWATER, JAMES, physicist, educator; b. Council, Idaho, Dec. 9, 1917; s. Leo J. and Edna E. (Teague) R.; m. Emma Louise Smith, Mar. 7, 1942; children: James Carlton, Robert Stephen, Elizabeth (dec.), William George. BS, Calif. Inst. Tech., 1939, PhD, Columbia U., 1946. Asst. physics Columbia U., 1939-42, scientist OSRD and Manhattan dist., 1942-46, instr., 1946-47, asst. prof. physics, 1947-49, assoc. prof. physics, 1949-52, prof. physics, 1952-82, Michael I. Pupin prof. emeritus of physics, 1982-86; dir. Nevis Cyclotron Lab., 1951-53, 56-61, research scientist AEC, ERDA, NSF and Office Naval Research projects, 1947-86. Recipient Ernest Orlando Laurence award AEC, 1963, Nobel prize in physics, 1975. Fellow AAAS, Am. Phys. Soc., IEEE, Optical Soc. Am., N.Y. Acad. Scis.; mem. Am. Inst. Physics, Am. Assn. Physics Tchrs., Nat. Acad. Scis., Swedish Royal Soc. (hon.). Contbr. articles to profl. jours. Home: Hastings-on-the-Hudson. Died May 31, 1986.

RAKER, JOHN PETER, judge; b. Shamokin, Pa., Feb. 27, 1914; s. Edward and Bertha Edith (Graeber) R.; m. Rita Quitugua, Apr. 15, 1953; 1 son, Frank. AB, Muhlenberg Coll., 1936; JD, George Washington U., 1940. Bar: D.C. 1940, Ter. Guam 1950. Pvt. practice Washington, 1940-41; atty. Dept. Army, 1945-47, Govt. Guam, 1948-51, 62-75, OPA, 1952; U.S. atty. Ter. Guam, 1952-54; atty. Dept. Navy, 1954-62; judge Guam Superior Ct., Agana, from 1975. With U.S. Army, 1942-45. Mem. Am., Fed. bar assns., Windward Hills Golf and Country Club, Elks, Phi Alpha Delta. Lutheran. Deceased.

RALL, OWEN, lawyer; b. Cedar Rapids, Iowa, Dec. 1, 1901; s. Julius Frederick and Flora Ellen (Ashby) R.; m. Bertha L. Biedermann, Mar. 19, 1923 (dec. Apr. 1976); 1 dau., Kathryn Rall Jacky. A.B. magna cum laude, Coe Coll., 1921; J.D., Northwestern U., 1924. Bar: Ill. Bar 1924. Practiced in Chgo.; of counsel firm Peterson, Ross, Schloerb & Seidel, 1933-87; Mem. com. character and fitness Ill. Supreme Ct., 1937-42, chmn., 1942; adv. council U. Ill. Law Forum, 1950-52; chmn. joint com. Ill. civil procedure which revised procedural statutes and Ill. Supreme Ct. and Appellate Ct. rules, 1950-55; mem. Jud. Adv. Council Ill., 1957-61; active constl. revision Ill., legis. reapportionment, jud. reorgn.; chmn. Ill. Supreme Ct. Rules Com., 1963-67. Author articles legal jours. Fellow Am. Coll. Trial Lawyers; mem. ABA, Ill. Bar Assn. (pres. 1961-62, award of Merit 1972), Chgo. Bar Assn. (librarian, bd. mgrs. 1942-43, 46-49), Bar Assn. Seventh Fed. Circuit (pres. 1966-67), Am. Judicature Soc. (Herbert Lincoln Harley award 1973), ADA (hon.), Scabbard and Blade (nat. v.p. 1924-26), Delta Theta Phi (nat. sec., editor 1927-29). Republican. Presbyn. Clubs: Union League (Chgo.) (chmn. modern cts. com. 1958), Plaza (Chgo.). Home: Evanston Ill. Died June 24, 1987; buried Mitchell, Iowa.

RAMBO, VICTOR CLOUGH, ophthalmologist, missionary; b. Landour, Mussoorie, India, July 6, 1894; s. William Eagle and Kate (Clough) R.; m. Louise Steinmetz Birch, Oct. 8, 1923; children: Helen Elizabeth, Victor Birch, William Milton, Barbara Louise, Thomas Clough. Student, Fairmount Coll., Wichita, Kans., 1915-17; BA, Wichita State U.; MD, U. Pa., 1921. Diplomate Am. Bd. Ophthalmology, Nat. Bd. Med. Examiners. Intern Pa. Hosp., Phila., 1921-23; surgeon, opthalmologist Christian Hosp., Mungeli, India, 1923-47; prof. opthalmology Christian Med. Coll., Vellore, India, 1947-57; inaugurator mobile eye hosps. Vellore, 1947; prof. opthalmology Christian Med. Coll., Ludhiana, India, 1957-67, prof. emeritus, 1967-87; pres. Rambo Com., Inc., Sight for Curable Blind, Phila., 1973-87; opthalmologist numerous sight-restoring operations for blind; affiliated with research demonstration project for mobile opthal. units, Ctr. NSEW, from 1930; served with United Christian Missionary Soc., 1923-73. Author: (with Arin Chatterjee) The Curable Blind—A Guide for Establishing and Maintaining Mobile Eye Hospitals, 1974, also numerous articles in field. Life and work subject of book Apostle of Sight, The Story of Victor Rambo, Surgeon to India's Blind (Dorothy Clarke Wilson). Recipient Kaisar I Hind Gold medal for pub. service in India King George VI, 1947, Ehrenzeller award Pa. Hosp., 1972, Cert. Appreciation World Conv. Chs. Christ, 1974, Pranam Patra award Punjab Govt. Fellow ACS, Royal Coll. Surgeons Edinburgh (Scotland); mem. All-India Opthal. Soc. (pres. 1957), AMA, Pa. Med. Soc., Phila. County Med. Soc., Internat. Congress Opthalmology, Oxford Opthalmic Congress, Sigma Xi. Mem. Christian Ch. Home: California Ky. Died May 23,1987; buried Grandview Cemetery, Mentor, Ky.

RAMSEY, ARTHUR MICHAEL (LORD RAMSEY OF CANTERBURY), archbishop; b. Cambridge, Eng., Nov. 14, 1904; s. Arthur Stanley and Agnes (Wilson) R.; m. JOan Alice Hamilton, Apr. 8, 1942. Student, Repton Sch., Magdalene Coll., Cambridge U., Cuddesdon Theol. Coll. Oradined deacon Ch. of Eng., 1928, priest, 1929. Curate Liverpool Parish Ch., 1928-30; subwarden Lincoln Theol. Coll., 1930-36; lectr. Boston Parish Ch., 1936-38; vicar St. Benedict's, Cambridge, 1939-40; canon Durham Cathedral, prof. div. U. Durham, 1940-50; Regious prof. div. U. Cambridge, 1950-52; bishop of Durham 1952-56, archbishop of York, 1956-61, archbishop of Canterbury, 1961-74; spiritual head of Ch. of Eng. and leader worldwide Anglican Ch.; made first offical visit in 400 yrs. by head of the Anglican Ch. to Cath. pope in Rome, 1966. Mem. Athenaeum Club (London); Cambridge Union Club (pres. 1926). Home: London England. also: Canterbury England. Died Apr. 23, 1988.

RAMSEY, HOBART C., corporate professional; b. Chgo., July 24, 1891; s. Charles DeForest and Jennie (Houston) R.; m. Collette Nicks, Sept. 30, 1936; children: Collette Christian, Janet Houston. Ed., U.S. Naval Acad., 1915; LLB (hon.), U. Miami, Fla. Joined Worthington Corp., 1919; joined Worthington Corp., in Europe, 1928-33, reorganizing Worthington European affiliated cos., v.p., 1929-45, exec. v.p., 1945-49, pres., chief exec. officer, 1949-55, chmn., chief exec. officer, 1955-61, chmn., 1961-62; dir. Nat. State Bank Newark, Armstrong Cork Co., Symington-Wayne Corp., N.Y.C., Livestock Fin. Corp., Triangle Conduit & Cable Co., New Brunswick, N.J.; ltd. ptnr. Glore, Forgan & Co., N.Y.C., from 1963; dir., mem. exec. com. Prudential Ins. Co. Am., Tropical Gas Co., N.J. Bell Telephone Co. Trustee Thomas A. Edison Found., St. Barnabas Med. Ctr., Springfield, N.J.; bd. dirs. Nat. Indsl. Conf. Bd.; adv. com. Nat. Security Indsl. Assn. Lt. comdr. USN, World War I. Mem. Am. Enterprise Assn. (trustee), Am. Petroleum Inst., Soc. Naval Architects and Marine Engrs., Naval Order U.S., N.J. C. of C. (bd. dirs.), Union League Club, Cloud Club (N.Y.C.), Short Hills

Club, Quaker Country (N.Y.), Quaker Hill Club (N.Y.), Essex Club (N.Y.C.), Pine Valley Country Club, Lyford Cay Club (Bahamas). Home: Short Hills N.J. †

RAMSEY, JOSEPH ROBERT, lawyer; b. Dothan, Ala., July 26, 1906; s. Richard Hawthorne and Cora (Dowling) R.; m. Hilda Hawkins, May 3, 1936; children: Philip H., Edward L., Joel W., William A. LLB, U. Ala., 1929. Bar: Ala. 1929, U.S. Supreme Ct. Practice law Dothan, 1929-79; ptnr. Ramsey and Baxley; pres. Houston Hotel Corp., 1959-79, City Realty Co., 1956-79; v.p. City Nat. Bank Dothan, 1952-79. Active local boys club, The Haven; pres. Ramsey Found. Mem. ABA, Ala. Bar Assn., Houston County Bar Assn., Def. Research Inst., Ala. Def. Lawyers Assn., Am. Judicare Soc., Phi Alpha Delta, Pi Kappa Phi. Baptist (past chmn. deacons). Home: Dothan Ala. Died Nov. 20, 1979, buried Dothan City Cemetery.

RAMSEY, ROBERT PAUL, theologian, educator; b. Mendenhall, Miss., Dec. 10, 1913; s. John William and Mamie (McCay) R.; m. Effie Register, June 23, 1937; children—Marcia Neal, Janet, Jennifer. B.S., Millsaps Coll., Jackson, Miss., 1935; H.L.D. (hon.), Millsaps Coll., 1974; B.D., Yale U., 1940, Ph.D., 1943; Litt.D. (hon.), Marquette U., 1968, Emory U., 1983; Sc.D. (hon.), Worcester Poly. Inst., 1972; H.L.D. (hon.), Rockford Coll., 1973, Fairfield U., 1976, Monmouth Coll., 1980; D.D. (hon.), St. Anselm's Coll., 1978. Instr. history and social sci. Millsaps Coll., 1937-39; asst. instr. social philosophy Yale U., New Haven, 1941-42; asst. prof. Christian ethics Garrett Bibl. Inst., Evanston, Ill., 1942-44; vis. prof. Garrett Bibl. Inst., summer 1950; asst. prof. religion Princeton U., N.J., 1944-47; assoc. prof. Princeton U., 1947-54, prof., 1954-82, emeritus, 1982-88, Harrington Spear Paine prof. religion, 1957-82, chmn. dept., 1959-63, acting chmn., 1973, 76, sr. fellow Council Humanities, 1958-59, McCosh faculty fellow, 1965-66; vis. prof. Colgate U., 1945, U. Chgo. Div. Sch., 1949, Garret Bible Inst., 1950, Pacific Sch. Religion, 1952, Perkins Sch. Theology, 1953, Yale Div. Sch., 1963; Joseph P. Kennedy, Jr. Found. vis. prof. genetic ethics Georgetown U. Med. Sch., 1968-69; Ashley Meml. lectr. NYU Law Sch., 1958; Thomas White Curry lectr. Austin Presbyn. Sem., 1967; Gray lectr. Duke U., 1967, 1974, Gray M. Blandy lectr. Episc. Theol. Sem. S.W., 1968; Lyman Beecher lectr. Yale U., 1969; Christian A. Herter lectr. Johns Hopkins U.; Bampton lectr. Columbia U., 1975; Whidden lectr. McMaster U., 1978; T.V. Moore lectr. St. Anselm's Abbey, Cath. U. Am., 1979 Tate-Willson lectr. So. Meth. U., 1980; fellow Ctr. for Theol. Inquiry, Princeton, 1982-88; Mueller fellow lectr. Franklin and Marshall Coll., 1983. Author: Basic Christian Ethics, 1950; War and the Christian Conscience, 1961; Christian Ethics and the Sit-In, 1961; Nine Modern Moralists, 1962; Deeds and Rules in Christian Ethics, 1967; Who Speaks for the Church, 1967; The Just War: Force and Political Responsibility, 1968; Fabricated Man: The Ethics of Genetic Control, 1970; The Patient as Person: Explorations of Medical Ethics, 1971; The Ethics of Fetal Research, 1975; Ethics at the Edges of Life: Medical and Legal Intersections, 1978, Speak Up for Just War or Pacifism, 1988; editor: Freedom of the Will (Jonathan Edwards), 1957; Faith and Ethics: The Theology of H. Richard Niebuhr, 1957; Religion, 1965; Ethical Writings of Jonathan Edwards, 1988; co-editor: Norm and Context in Christian Ethics, 1968; The Study of Religion in Colleges and Universities, 1970; Doing Evil to Achieve Good, 1978; editorial bd. Works of Jonathan Edwards, Theology Today, Worldview, Jour. Religious Ethics, Linacre Qur.; contbr. articles to philos. jours. Trustee Council Religion and Internat. Affairs, 1968-75, Drew U., 1968-75; mem. adv. council Kennedy Ctr. for Bioethics, Georgetown U. Recipient Henry K. Beecher award in Med. Ethics, 1981; NEH sr. fellow, 1973-74; Guggenheim fellow, 1978. Mem. Inst. Soc., Ethics and Life Scis. (bd. dirs.), Am. Theol. Soc. (v.p. 1959-60, nat. pres. 1964-65), Am. Soc. Christian Ethics (pres. 1962-63), Inst. Medicine, NAS. Home: Princeton N.J. Died Feb. 29, 1988; buried Princeton.

RANCANS, JOSEPH, bishop; b. Lyuziniki, Latvia, Oct. 25, 1886; came to U.S., 1951; s. Francis and Joann (Swagis) R. Ordained priest Roman Catholic Ch., 1911, consecrated bishop, 1924. Prof. St. Petersburg (Russia) Sem., 1911; envoy Latvian Govt. to Holy See, 1919; dean. dept. Cath. theology U. Latvia, 1938; Cath. dep. Constl. Assembly of Latvia, 1922; v.p. Latvian Parliament Riga, 1923. Chaplain Russian Army, 1914-16. Home: Grand Rapids Mich. †

RAND, NORFLEET HALE, shoe manufacturing executive; b. St. Louis, Dec. 8, 1913; s. Frank Chambless and Nettie Lumpkin (Hale) R.; m. Eloise Alice Stephens, Oct. 13, 1948; children: Miriam McLeod, Helen Norfleet, Norfleet Hale, Edgar Stephens. BA, Vanderbilt U., 1934. With Internat. Shoe Co., St. Louis, 1935-65, mgr. upper leather procurement supply, 1950-57, dir. in charge merchandising and mfg., 1956-65, v.p., 1957-65, also treas.; vice chmn. bd., treas. Interco, Inc., St. Louis, 1965-74, bd. dirs., mem. exec. com., from 1974; bd. dirs. Mercantile Commerce Nat. Bank, Am. Investment Co. Exec. bd. St. Louis council Boy Scouts Am.; bd. dirs. Big Bros. Am., Inc., Big Bros. Orgn. of St. Louis, Ins., Thomas Dunn Meml.; pres. Barnard Free Skin and Cancer Hosp., 1967-72. Recpient Brother of Yr. award, St. Louis, 1959. Mem. St. Louis Country Club, Univeristy Club, Log Cabin Club (St. Louis), Delta Kappa Epsilon. Home: Clayton Mo. Deceased.

RAND, WILLIAM MCNEAR, chemical company executive; b. Watertown, Mass., Apr. 7, 1886; s. William Dwight and Emily (McNear) R.; m. Lucy Kimball Robbins, Sept. 17, 1914; children: Emily L. (Mrs. William F. Herman), William M., Lucy (Mrs. Albert P. Everts Jr.), John R., Peter W. Student, Phillips Exeter Acad., 1903-05; AB, Harvard U., 1909; LLD (hon.), Northeastern U., 1946. Bank messenger 1909-11; teller Mut. Nat. Bank, Boston, 1911-13; treas. City Fuel Co., 1913-19; with Merrimac Chem. Co., Everett, Mass., 1919-21, v.p., 1921-35, pres., 1935-38; pres., mem. exec. com. Monsanto Chem. Co. and successor, St. Louis, 1945-51; dir. Fgn. Operation Adminstrn., 1933-53, dep. dir., 1953-54; trustee Shareholders' Trust, Chase Fund Boston; bd. dirs., mem. fin. com. John Hancock Mut. Life Ins. Co., Liberty Mut. Ins. Co., Liberty Mut. Fire Ins. Co. Pres., bd. dirs. Greater St. Louis Community Chest, 1950; mem. exec. com. United Carr Fastener Corp., Comstock and Wescott; trustee Northeastern U., New Eng. Deaconess Hosp.; past mem. bd. overseers Harvard Coll. Lt. (s.g.) USN, 1917-19. Fellow Soc. Am. Arts and Scis.; mem. Mfg. Chemists Assn. (past chmn. bd.), N.A.M. (past v.p.), Harvard Alumni Assn. (past pres.), Associated Industry Mass. (past pres.), Soc. Chem. Industries (hon. fgn. mem.), Cruising Club Am., Harvard Club, Somerset Club, Union Club, Beta Gamma Sigma. Republican. Home: Lincoln Mass. †

RANDALL, EDWARD, JR., physician; b. Galveston, Tex., Oct. 5, 1891; s. Edward and Laura (Ballinger) R.; m. Katharine Risher, Jan. 23, 1926; children: Edward III, Risher, Laura. BA, Yale U., 1913; postgrad., U. Tex., U. Chgo.; MD, U. Pa., 1919. Diplomate Nat. Bd. Med. Examiners. Intern Pa. Hosp., Phila., 1917-18; prof. medicine U. Tex., from 1928; med. dir. Am. Nat. Ins. Co., from 1955; bd. dirs. Internat. Creosote Co. Bd. dirs. Rosenberg Pub. Library, Sealy & Smith Found. 1st lt. M.C., U.S. Army, 1918-19. Fellow ACP; mem. Tex. Philos. Soc. †

RANDEL, JAMES BUFORD, JR., utilities executive; b. Okla., June 5, 1925; s. James Buford and Clara Marie (Richards) R.; m. Emma Elizabeth French, Apr. 28, 1951; children: James Buford III, Ellen, Carrie, Sally, Nathan. BS, U. Okla., 1950. Engr. FPC, Washington, 1950-53; with Pub. Svc. Electric & Gas Co., Newark, 1953-77, sr. v.p. engring. and prodn., then sr. v.p. cons., 1974-77; sr. v.p. corp., pres. Energy Devel. Corp., 1977-85. With USNR, 1943-45. Mem. Soc. Gas Lighting, Soc. Petroleum Engrs., Am. Gas Assn. Methodist. Died June 16, 1985.

RANDOLPH, ROBERT DECAN, banker; b. Washington, Mar. 20, 1891; s. Thomas Peter and Jane (Decan) R.; m. Frankie Carter, June 14, 1918; children: Aubrey (Mrs. Parker Cushman), Jean (Mrs. Sam Pancoast). Student, U. Va. V.p. J.H. Richardson Contracting Co., Houston, 1914-16, A.L. Carter Lumber Co., Beaumont, Tex., 1916-17; with W.T. Carter & Bros., Camden, Tex., from 1919; v.p., gen. mgr. Moscow, Camden & San Augustine R.R. Co., Camden, from 1921; exec. v.p., trust officer, bd. dirs. Union Nat. Bank, Houston, 1921-53; sr. v.p., vice chmn. bd. Tex. Nat. Bank, Houston, 1953-64; vice chmn. exec. com. Tex. Nat. Bank Commerce, Houston, from 1964, also bd. dirs. Lt. (j.g.) USNR, 1917-19. Mem. Eagle Lake Rod and Gun Club, River Oaks Country Club, Bayou Club, Phi Kappa Sigma. Home: Houston Tex. †

RANDOLPH, VANCE, author; b. Pitts., Kans., Feb. 23, 1892; s. John and Theresa (Gould) R.; m. Marie Wardlaw Wilbur, Mar. 27, 1930 (dec.). AB, Kans. State Tchrs. Coll., 1914; MA, Clark U., 1915; grad. study, U. Kans., 1922-24; LittD, U. Ark., 1951. Staff writer Appeal to Reason, 1917; asst. instr. in psychology U. Kans., 1924; scenario writer Metro-Goldwyn -Mayer Studios, Culver City, Calif., 1933-34; asst. state supr. Fed. Writers Project, 1936-37. Author or co-author numerous books, including: Ozark Superstitions, 1947, We Always Lie to Strangers, 1951, Who Blowed Up the Church House, 1952, (with George P. Wilson) Down in the Holler, 1953; author: The Devil's Pretty Daughter, 1955, The Talking Turtle and Other Ozark Folktales, 1957, Sticks in Knapsack and Other Ozark Folktales, 1958; editor: An Ozark Anthology, 1940, Ozark Folksongs, 4 vols., 1946-50; field worker Archive of Am. Folksong, Libr. of Congress, 1941-43. Pvt. Inf., U.S. Army, World War I. Mem. Am. Legion, Disabled Am. Vets., Authors' League, Am. Folklore Soc., Am. Dialect Soc., Elks Club, Sigma Xi, Psi Chi, Sigma Pi Sigma. Democrat. Home: Eureka Springs Ark. †

RANKIN, ROLFE M(ONTGOMERY), college professor; b. Jefferson City, Tenn., Dec. 17, 1892; s. Jmaes L. and Martha C. (Corbett) R.; m. Lula B. Creswell, May 13, 1918; children: Robert C., Norman O., Carolyn J.; m. 2d, Martha Horton, Jan. 16, 1960. AB, Maryville (Tenn.) Coll., 1916; AM, U. Chgo., 1922; BSCE, Mo. Sch. of Mines, 1927; student, U. Mich., 1933-35. Tchr. math. and sci. Wastch. Acad., Mt. Pleasant, Utah, 1916-17, Westminster Coll., Salt Lake City, 1918-21; tchr. math. and sci. Mo. Sch. of Mines, Rolla, Mo., from 1922, prof. and head dept., from 1942. Radio specialist U.S. Army, 1918. Mem. Math. Assn. of Am., Am. Legion, Lions Club, Masons, Tau Beta Pi, Phi Kappa Phi. Presbyterian. Home: Rolla Mo. †

RANKIN, RUFUS GRADY, utilities executive; b. Belmont, N.C., Feb. 25, 1891; s. Rufus Pink and Zoe (Hand) R.; m. Ruth Boyce, Jan. 22, 1913; children: Anna Boyce (Mrs. Joe W. Lineberger), Rufus Grady, David H., George Mason. Student, U. N.C., 1907-09; LLD, Belmont Abbey Coll., 1948. Various positions in textile industry 1917-36; pres. Superior Yarn Mills, from 1941; bd. dirs. Duke Power Co., Wachovia Bank & Trust. Mem. bd. commrs. Gaston County; mem. N.C. Senate, 1931-53; chmn. bd. advisers Belmont Abbey Coll.; trustee Duke Endowment; chmn. standards Meth. ch. †

RANSON, CHARLES WESLEY, clergyman; b. Ballyclare, Ireland, June 15, 1903; came to U.S., 1948; s. Henry John Frederick and Elizabeth (Clarke) R.; m. Jessie Grace Margaret Gibb, 1932 (dec. 1957); children: Mary Elizabeth, John Hugh, Kathleen Anne; m. Barbara Buttenheim Hicks, Aug. 22 1962 (dec.); m. Mary Claire Allen, 1978. BL (Oxon), Methodist Coll., Belfast, Queen's U., Belfast, Oriel Coll., Oxford; ThD, U. Kiel; STD (hon.), Dickinson Coll. Ordained to ministry Meth. Ch., Cork, Ireland, 1929. Missionary Madras, India, 1929-43; sec. Nat. Christian Council India, Burma and Ceylan, 1943-45; research sec. Internat. Missionary Council, London, 1946-47, gen. sec., 1948-58, dir. theol. edn. fund, 1958-64; prof. ecumenical theology, dean Theol. Sch., Drew U., Madison, N.J., 1965-68; prof. Hartford (Conn.) Sem. Found., 1968-72; minister Salisbury (Conn.) Congl. Ch., 1971-75; vis. lectr. Princeton Theol. Sem., Episc. Theol. Sch., Cambridge, Mass.; Otts lectr. Davidson Coll.; Earl lectr. Pacific Sch. Religion; Fondren lectr. So. Meth. U., 1964; pres. Meth. Ch. in Ireland, 1961-62. Author: A City in Transition, 1937, The Things That Abide, 1940, The Christian Minister in India, 1946, That the World May Know, 1953, (autobiography) A Missionary Pilgrimage, 1988; author, editor: Renewal and Advance, 1948. Fellow Royal Econ. Soc.; mem. Royal Inst. Internat. Affairs, Athenaeum Club (London), University Club (Dublin), Country Club of Sharon (Conn.). Home: Lakeville Conn. also: Delray Beach Fla. Died Jan. 23, 1988, buried Salisbury, Conn.

RANSONE, COLEMAN BERNARD, JR., political scientist, educator; b. Norfolk, Va., Jan. 27, 1920; s. Coleman Bernard and Natalie (Neblett) R.; m. Katherine May, Dec. 19, 1949; children—Natalie Gray, Kathleen Susan, Katherine Neblett. A.B., Coll. William and Mary, 1941; M. Public Adminstrn., Harvard U., 1947; Ph.D., 1950. Instr. to assoc. prof. polit. sci. U. Ala., 1947-57; prof. govt. Coll. William and Mary, 1957-58; prof. polit. sci. U. Ala., University, 1958-85, prof. emeritus, 1985-86, dir. So. regional tng. program in pub. adminstrn., 1958-80. Author: The Office of Governor in the South, 1951, The Office of Governor in the United States, 1956, Ethics in Alabama State Government, 1972, The Alabama Government Manual, 1967, 70, 73, 77, The American Governorship, 1982; mem. editorial bd.: Pub. Adminstr. Rev, 1967-70, Internat. Jour. Public Adminstrn, 1979-86. Mem. Ala. Constl. Commn., 1970-76. Served to 1st lt. USAAF, 1943-46. Fund for Advancement Edn. faculty fellow, 1953-54. Mem. Am. Polit. Sci. Assn., So. Polit. Sci. Assn. (v.p. 1963), Ala. Polit. Sci. Assn. (pres. 1979-80), Am. Soc. Pub. Adminstrn. (sr.), Nat. Assn. Schs. for Pub. Affairs and Adminstrn. (exec. com. 1962-65), Phi Beta Kappa (pres. Alpha of Ala. chpt. 1961-62, 74-75), Pi Sigma Alpha. Episcopalian (lay reader). Home: Tuscaloosa Ala. Died July, 11, 1986; buried Tuscaloosa Meml. Pk., Ala.

RANTA, HUGO ARMAS, government official, lawyer; b. Maple, Wis., Mar. 20, 1914; s. John and Aurora (Aho) R.; m. Mary Naomi Hayden, Apr. 24, 1948 (dec 1979); 1 son, Jeffrey Alan.; m. Julia Miller, May 8, 1982. Ed.B., Superior (Wis.) State Tchrs. Coll., 1934; LL.B., U. Wis., 1940. Bar: Wis. bar 1941. Tchr. schs. Douglas County, Wis., 1934-36, 37- 38; atty. Treasury Dept., 1941-48, asst. to gen. counsel, 1949-62, asst. gen. counsel, 1962-79. Home: Silver Spring Md. Deceased.

RAO, PAUL PETER, federal judge; b. Prizzi, Italy, June 15, 1899; s. Vincent and Anna (Fugarini) R.; m. Grace Malatino, June 22, 1922 (dec.); children: Nina Rao Gewald, Grayce Rao Visconti, Paul Peter; m. Catherine Marolla, 1973. LL.B., Fordham U., 1923; H.H.D., Philathea Coll., London, Ont., Can., 1958; LL.D., Manhattan Coll., 1971, Pace Coll., 1972. Bar: N.Y. 1924, U.S. Supreme Ct., U.S. Ct. Appeals, U.S. Ct. Customs and Patent Appeals, other fed. cts. Asst. dist. atty. New York County, 1925-27; pvt. practice 1927-41, asst. atty. gen. U.S. in charge customs, 1941-48; judge U.S. Customs Ct. (now U.S. Ct. Internat. Trade), 1948—, chief judge, 1965-71, asso. judge, 1971—. Trustee Ch. of Our Lady of Peace; bd. dirs. Nat. Cath. Community Service, Fordham Law Alumni Assn., Sons Union Vets. of Civil War (hon. asso. N.Y. dept.). Served in U.S. Navy, 1917-19; ofcl. French interpreter with French Cruiser Div. Decorated knight Order of St. Hubert, Knight of Lateran, Italian Star of Solidarity, Grand Cross Eloy Alfaro Internat. Found., Republic Panama, 1959; Knight of Malta of Am. chpt., 1962; Mil. Order of Lafayette, 1963; comdr. Order of Merit Italian Republic, 1968; commendatore Republic of San Marino;

recipient Charles A. Rapallo award, 1970; Gold medal Nat. Acad. Sci. in Rome, 1973; Pub. Service award Italian Hist. Soc. Am., 1974; citation Am. Com. for Italian Migration, 1980. Mem. ABA, Fed. Bar Assn. N.Y., N.J. and Conn., Fed. Bus. Assn. N.Y. (exec. com., citation 1962), Am. Legion (past post comdr., life mem.), VFW (hon. comdr. N.Y. County council 1951-56, 57-62), Am. Internat. Acad. U.S.A. (star and cross; hon. life mem. 1958), DAV (citation 1957), Cath. War Vets. (Americanism award 1949), Am. Justinian Soc. Jurists (founder, 1st pres.), Cath. Ct. Attaches Guild N.Y.C. (hon.), Bklyn.-Manhattan Trial Counsel Assn. (hon.), Phi Alpha Delta (hon.). Democrat. Catholic. Home: New York N.Y. Died Nov. 30, 1988.

RAPHEL, ARNOLD LEWIS, ambassador; b. Troy, N.Y., Mar. 16, 1943; s. Harry and Sara (Rosen) R.; m. Nancy Halliday Ely, May 30, 1987; children: Stephanie, John, Robert. B.A., Hamilton Coll., 1964; M.A., Syracuse U., 1966. Spl. asst. to undersec. of state Dept. State, Washington, 1973-75; polit. officer U.S. Embassy, Islamabad, Pakistan, 1975-78; sr. spl. asst. to sec. of state Dept. State, Washington, 1979-81, sr. dep. asst. sec. for polit.-mil. affairs, 1982-84, sr. dep. asst. sec. of state for Near Eastern and South Asian affairs, 1984-87; U.S. ambassador to Pakistan, Islamabad, 1987-88. Home: Washington D.C. Died Aug. 18, 1988.

RAPORTE, ARTHUR JAMES, corporate executive; b. N.Y.C., May 31, 1917; s. Samuel and Florence (Aronson) R.; m. Bernice Mary Olcott, Feb. 21, 1945; children—Stephanie Ina Lindquist, Arthur James. A.B., U. Mich., 1938; LL.B., Harvard, 1941. Bar: N.Y. bar 1941. With firm Van Vorst, Siegel & Smith, 1942, Harris Berlack, 1944-48; counsel, dir. Welch Grape Juice Co., 1948-58; atty. firm Wien, Lane, Klein & Purcell, N.Y.C., 1958-60; dir. real estate Loews Corp., N.Y.C., 1960-82; v.p. Loews Corp., 1962-82; sr. v.p. James Felt Realty Services, 1982-88. Contbr. articles to The N.Y. Times and Gannett Westchester Newspapers. Mem. 3d Assembly Dist. Democratic Orgn.; Bd. dirs., v.p., exec. com. Asthma and Allergy Found. Am., 1972-88. Served to 2d lt. AUS, 1942-44. Mem. N.Y. County Lawyers Assn., Real Estate Bd. N.Y.C., Phi Beta Kappa, Phi Kappa Phi. Club: Harvard (N.Y.C.). Home: Rye N.Y. Died Jan. 24, 1988; interred Ferncliff Cemetery, Hartsdale, N.Y.

RAPOSO, JOSEPH GUILHERME, composer, television show producer, publisher; b. Fall River, Mass., Feb. 8, 1938; s. Jose Soares and Maria Ascencao (Victorine) R.; m. Patricia G. Collins, Jan. 26, 1976; children: Elizabeth C., W. Andrew; children by previous marriage: Joseph R., Nicolas A. AB, Harvard Coll., 1958; diplome, Ecole Normale de Musique, Paris, 1960; PhD (hon.), U. Mass., 1973, Southeastern Mass. U., Hope Coll., Mt. St. Mary's Coll. pres. Jonico Music, Inc.; chmn. bd. dirs. Music Pub. Internat.; guest lectr. Harvard U., Yale U., So. Mass. U.; guest condr. Boston Pops and other maj. symphonies. Music dir.: Loeb Drama Center, Harvard U., 1960-61, Boston Conservatory, 1961-64, Exptl. Theatre, 1961-64, Lincoln Center, N.Y.C., 1965-66, New Theatre, 1965-67, Am. Theatre Lab., N.Y.C., 1967, Metromedia Television, 1967-69, ABC-CBS-NBC Networks, 1967-69, numerous motion pictures, television programs including Sesame St. (recipient TV Acad. awards and nominations for music, lyrics, music direction, 4 Recording Industry Acad. awards as producer, composer and music dir., numerous citations from schs., charities, civic groups), stage plays; mus. dir., composer, lyricist: Childrens Television Workshop, 1969-74; composer: (theme music) Sesame St., Electric Co., Three's Company, CBS Morning News, (animated mus.) Raggedy Ann, 1977; major symphonic work From the Diary of Johann Sutter commd. by, Boston Symphony Orch., 1980; scored 2d Muppet Movie, 1981; popular song writer; producer entertainment projects with major film studios and TV networks; author: Sesame Street Songbook, 1971, It's Not Easy Being Green, 1972; composer: Sing, 1971, Sesame Street, 1969, Being Green, 1970, You Will Be My Music, 1974. Mem. vis. com., bd. overseers Harvard U.; bd. dirs. 3d St. Music Sch. Recipient 5 Grammy awards; producer several gold and platinum records; recipient Oscar nomination for film The Great Muppet Caper. Mem. ASCAP (numerous citations for hit songs), Nat. Acad. Recording Arts and Scis. (bd. govs., numerous Gold Records), Am. Fedn. Musicians, Screen Actors Guild, AFTRA. Roman Catholic. Clubs: Hasty Pudding, Signet Soc. Harvard Coll. Home: New York N.Y. Died Feb. 5, 1989; buried Chatham, Mass.

RAPPAPORT, SYDNEY CHARLES, dentist, educator; b. N.Y.C., Nov. 16, 1919; s. Louis and Helen (Mermelstein) R.; m. Rosalind Appel, July31, 1949; children: Elizabeth Appel, Suzanne Helen. BS, CCNY, 1964; DDS, U. Pa., 1942. Diplomate Am. Bd. Oral Medicine, N.Y. Bd. Oral Surgery. Pvt. practice N.Y.C., 1947-88; rsch. assoc. Columbia Sch. Dentistry, 1950-58; faculty N.Y. Med. Coll., 1969-88, prof., chmn. dept. dentistry, 1972-88; dir. dept. dentistry Met. Hosp., N.Y.C., 1967-88, Bird S. Coler Hosp., Roosevelt Island, N.Y., 1967-88; dir. dentistry Mental Retardation Inst., N.Y. Med. Coll., Valhalla. Capt. AUS, 1943-46. Fellow Am. Coll. Dentists, N.Y. Acad. Dentistry; mem. ADA, AAAS, Am. Assn. Hosp. Dentists (pres. 1978). Home: New York N.Y. Died Dec. 17, 1988.

RASHKIND, WILLIAM JACOBSON, pediatric cardiologist; b. Patterson, N.J., Feb. 12, 1922; s. Jacob Louis and Charlotte Florence (Jacobson) R.; m. Rita Shirley Leisten, Dec. 17, 1949; children: Marilyn, Jean, Charles. AB, U. Louisville, 1943, MD, 1946. Diplomate Am. Bd. Pediatrics. Intern Michael Reese Hosp., Chgo., 1946-47; resident in pediatrics U. Pa. Hosp., Phila., 1953-55; asst. prof. physiology U. Pa. Sch. Medicine, Phila., 1950-53, asst. prof. pediatrics, 1959-63, assoc. prof., 1963-71, prof., 1971-86; dir. cardiovascular labs. Children's Hosp., Phila., 1955-84, dir. div. cardiology, 1984-86; mem. internat. com. coding congenital heart disease, 1969-72, mem. intersoc. commn. heart disease resources, 1971-74; mem. exec. com., congenital heart disease com. Am. Heart Assn., 1970-74. Contbr. articles to med. jours. Served with USN, 1943-49. Nat. Heart and Lung Inst. fellow, 1949-50; NIH grantee, 1952-86. Mem. Am. Pediatric Soc., Soc. Pediatrics Research, Am. Physiol. Soc., Am. Acad. Pediatrics, Am. Soc. Artificial Internal Organs, Assn. European Pediatric Cardiologists, Alpha Omega Alpha. Home: Merion Pa. Died July 6, 1986, buried Iselin, N.J.

RASKIN, ELLEN, writer, illustrator; b. Milw., Mar. 13, 1928; d. Sol and Margaret (Goldfisch) R.; m. Dennis Flanagan, Oct. 17, 1966; 1 dau., Susan Kuhlman Metcalfe. Student, U. Wis., Madison, 1945-48. instr. in illustration Pratt Inst., 1963; instr. in illustration Syracuse U., 1976; guest lectr. U. Berkeley, 1969, 72, 77. Free-lance illustrator, N.Y.C., 1955-68; writer, illustrator: children's books Nothing Ever Happens on My Block, 1966, Silly Songs and Sad, 1967, Ghost in a Four-Room Apartment, 1969, And It Rained, 1969, A & The, 1970, The World's Greatest Freak Show, 1971, The Mysterious Disapperance of Leon (I Mean Noel), 1971, Franklin Stein, 1972, Who, Said Sue, Said Whoo'9 , 1973, Figgs & Phantoms, 1974, Moose, Goose and Little Nobody, 1974, The Tattooed Potato and Other Clues, 1975, Twenty-two, Twenty-three, 1976, The Westing Game, 1978; exhibited: illustrations in group shows AIGA 50 Years of Graphic Arts in America, 1966, Biennale of Illustrations, Bratislava, Czechoslovakia, 1969, Biennale of Applied Graphic Art, Brno, Czechoslovakia, 1972, Contemporary Am. Illustrators of Children's Books, 1974-75. Recipient Distinctive Merit award Art Dirs. Clubs, 1958, Silver medal, 1959; citation of merit Soc. Illustrators, 1966, 70, 71; Best Picture Book award World-Jour.-Tribune, 1966; Honor Book award Boston Globe-Horn Book, 1973; citation Bklyn. Mus. Art, 1973, 74; Edgar Allan Poe Spl. award Mystery Writers Am., 1975; Newbery Honor Book award ALA, 1975; Best Fiction award Boston Globe-Horn Book, 1978; John Newbery medal for The Westing Game, 1979; Notable Wisconsin Author, 1981; book named to Am. Inst. Graphic Arts 50 Books of Yr., 1966, 68; N.Y. Times 10 Best Books, 1966, 68. Mem. Authors Guild, Graphic Artists Guild. Home: New York N.Y. Died Aug. 8, 1984.

RASMUSSEN, AARON FREDERICK, microbiologist and immunologist, educator; b. St. Anthony, Idaho, May 27, 1915; s. Aaron Frederick and Nancy Blanche (Costley) R.; m. Besse Carol Tatum, June 12, 1941; children: Frederick Tatum, Nancy Mabel, Carol Irene. BS, U. Idaho, 1937; MS, U. Wis., 1940, PhD, 1941, MD, 1943. Diplomate Am. Bd. Pathology, Am. Bd. Microbiology. Research assoc. U. Wis. Sch. Medicine, 1941-42, assoc. prof. microbiology and preventive medicine, 1948-51, prof., 1951-52; prof., chmn. med. microbiology and immunology Sch. Medicine, UCLA, 1962-69, also assoc. dean; chief chemotherapy research sect., dept. viral and rickettsial diseases Army Med. Ctr., Wis., 1947-48; vis. scientist U.S. Naval Research Unit 2, Tapei, Taiwan, 1960-61; cons. microbiology br. Office of Naval Research; assoc. Armed Forces Commn. on Influenza; cons. div. gen. med. scis. NIH. With M.C AUS, 1943-47. Mem. Am. Soc. Microbiology (v.p. 1976-77, pres. 1977-78), Am. Acad. Microbiology, Assn. Immunologists, Soc. Clin. Investigation, Western Assn. Physicians. Home: Santa Monica Calif. Died Mar. 17, 1984.

RASMUSSEN, ROBERT VERNON, food store executive, cattle breeder; b. Chgo., Feb. 9, 1907; s. George and Nanna F (Hansen) R.; children: Ritchey Rasmussen Goodwin, Fontaine Rasmussen Christensen. Clk. Nat. Tea Co., Chgo., 1927, v.p., 1936, also bd. dirs., pres., 1943-47, chmn. bd., 1946-47; owner, breeder registered Holsteins Elmwood Farms, Antioch, Ill., from 1924. Mem. Everglades Club (Palm Beach, Fla.), Racquet Club (Chgo.). Home: Lake Forest Ill. also: Palm Beach Fla. Died Jan. 21, 1986.

RASSMAN, EMIL CHARLES, lawyer; b. Indpls., July 27, 1919; s. Fred Wolf and Helen (Leming) R.; m. Annie de Montel, Jan. 31, 1943; children: Laura Helen Rassman Bates, James Neal. BA, Washington and Lee U., 1941; LLB, U. Tex., 1947; LLD (hon.), Baylor U., 1977. Bar: Tex. 1947, U.S. Supreme Ct., 1951. Ptnr. Rassman, Gunter & Boldrick, Midland, Tex.; bd. dirs. Comml. Bank & Trust Co., Midland; mem. Tex. Jud. Council, 1958-61. Campaign chmn., pres. Midland County United Fund, 1956-57; chmn. Midland County chpt. ARC, 1971-73; trustee Midland Ind. Sch. Dist., 1958-61; bd. regents Tex. State U. System, 1961-79, chmn. bd., 1967-69; chmn. bd. Permian Basin Petroleum Mus., Library and Hall of Fame, 1973-78. Capt. AUS, 1941-46. Fellow Am. Coll. Trial Lawyers, Am. Bar Found., Tex. Bar Found., Internat. Aacad. Trial Lawyers, Am. Coll. Probate Counsel; mem. Internat. Assn. Ins. Counsel, Fedn. Ins. Counsel, Midland County Bar Assn. (pres. 1960), State Bar Assn. Tex. (bd. dirs. 1972-75, chmn. bd. 1974-75), West Tex. C. of C. (pres. 1973-74), Tex. State C. of C. (pres. 1973-74), Philos. Soc. Tex., Masons, Phi Delta Phi, Delat Tau Delta. Episcopalian. Home: Rockport Tex. Died Dec. 3, 1983, buried Rockport, Tex.

RATIGAN, WILLIAM, author, historian; b. Detroit; s. Bernard Joseph and Bertie (Laing) R.; m. Eleanor Dee Eldridge, Sept. 12, 1935 (dec.); children—Patricia Lee (Mrs. Arthur A. Ranger), Anesta Colleen (Mrs. Arthur J. Pelton), Bobbie Laing (dec.), Shannon Leitrim. Student, U. Detroit, 1931, 33; A.B., U. Tenn., Chattanooga, 1935; M.A., Mich. State U., 1961, Ph.D., 1963. Continuity dir., producer NBC, Denver, 1937-40; pioneered news dept. NBC, 1939; supr. NBC (Far East listening post), 1940-42; mng. news editor Western div., supr. commentators and war corrs. NBC (Far East listening post), PTO, 1942-45; news editor, scriptwriter NBC (UN Conf.), 1945; staff mem. NDEA Counseling and Guidance Inst. of Mich. State U., 1962; sr. extension lectr. Mich. State U., from 1962; vis. lectr. Fla. State U., 1965, U. Wis., 1966, 68, U. Miami, 1967; founder The Dockside Press, 1953; mem.-at-large Adv. Council Naval Affairs, from 1957; cons. Smithsonian Instn., tech. devel. Great Lakes craft, from 1959. Short story, serial writer, Curtis Pub. Co., other mags., from 1946; author: poems NBC War Poems, 1945, Great Lakes Chanteys, 1948-56; books Soo Canal (foreward by Gen. Douglas MacArthur), 1954, 68, Young Mr. Big, 1955, Hiawatha and America's Mightiest Mile, 1955; editor: books The Adventures of Capt. McCargo, 1956, Straits of Mackinac, 1957, The Blue Snow, 1958, Tiny Tim Pine, 1958, Adventures of Paul Bunyan and Babe, 1958, The Long Crossing, 1959, Highways Over Broad Waters, 1959, Great Lakes Shipwrecks & Survivals, Carl D. Bradley book, 1960, Daniel J. Morrell book, 1969, Conflicts Within Counseling and Guidance, 1964; co-author: books Theories of Counseling, 1965, 72, School Counseling: View from Within, American School Counselors Association's First Yearbook, 1967, Great Lakes History: Steamer Edmund Fitzgerald Edition: Great Lakes Shipwrecks & Survivals, 1977; contbr. to: books Great Lakes Reader, 1966, 78, Ency. Americana, from 1968. Recipient inter-collegiate Odes of Horace award, 1935; Calif. Chaparral poetry prize, 1944; named chief Ottawa tribe, Opwanan iian Kanotong, Interpreter of Dreams, 1957; recipient Distinguished Alumni award U. Tenn. at Chattanooga, 1963, Distinguished Alumni award Dean Jr. Coll., 1966. Mem. Am. Psychol. Assn., Blue Key (pres. 1935, Distinguished mem. 1967). Clubs: Authors (Hollywood, Calif.); Press; Authors (San Francisco); Camp Lucas Officers Open Mess (Sault Ste. Marie). Deceased.

RATNER, IRVING MAURICE, pathologist; b. N.Y.C., Aug. 23, 1915; s. Philip Nachman and Libbie (Forscher) R.; m. Vivienne Drossin, Sept. 11, 1955; children: Michael, Philip, Jeremiah. BS, CCNY, 1934; MD, U. Glasgow, 1947. Intern Lebanon Hosp., Bronx, N.Y., 1947-48; resident Fordham Hosp., Bronx, 1950-51, Mt. Sinai Hosp., N.Y.C., 1952-53; pvt. practice N.Y.C., from 1954; mem. attending staff Bronx Mcpl. Hosp., Center Hosp.; attending staff and faculty Albert Einstein Coll. Medicine, Bronx, from 1956, clin. prof. pathology, from 1977. Capt. U.S. Army, 1942-46. Fellow Coll. Am. Pathologists, N.Y. Acad. Medicine; mem. AAAS, N.Y. State Pathologists (pres.), N.Y. Pathologists Soc., N.Y. State Med. Soc., Pathologists Club N.Y. (pres.). Home: South Salem N.Y. Deceased.

RAUBENHEIMER, ALBERT SYDNEY, educator; b. George, Republic of South Africa, May 18, 1892; came to U.S., 1920; naturalized; s. Hendrik Jacobus and Susannah (Zondagh) R.; m. Mary Elizabeth de Golyer, June 9, 1926; children: Mary Susannah, Judith Elizabeth. AB, U. of Cape of Good Hope, 1919; MA, U. Capetown, 1919, olumbia U., 1921; PhD, Stanford U., 1923; DSc (hon.), U. So. Calif., 1960. Lectr. U. Cape Town, 1918-19; instr. extension dept. Columbia U., 1921; rsch. asst. Stanford U., 1922-23; prof. edn. U. So. Calif., from 1923, v.p. acad. affairs, 1948-60; instr. State Tchrs. Coll., Chico, Calif., summer, 1922, Colo. State Tchrs. Coll., summer 1923, U. of Calif., summers, 1929, 32, Sch. of Edn., Victoria, B.C., summer 1939, U. of Brit. Columbia, Vancouver, summer 1941; chmn. Republic Fed. Savs. and Loan Assn. Contbr. to Genetic Studies of Genius, Vol. I, 1925; also articles to ednl. and psychol. jours. Chmn. gov.'s com. on mental health, 1949-51; chmn. gov.'s com. on penal insts., 1950-51. Mem. Western Psychol. Assn., Am. Psychol. Assn. (assoc.), Phi Beta Kappa, Sigma Xi, Phi Kappa Phi, Phi Delta Kappa, Sigma Alpha Epsilon. Home: Los Angeles Calif. †

RAUCH, BASIL, historian; b. Dubuque, Iowa, Sept. 6, 1908; s. William H. and Elizabeth (Wordehoff) R.; m. Roberta Bruce Brown, 1936 (div. 1963); m. Elizabeth Flower Hird, 1964. A.B., U. Notre Dame, 1929; post-grad. drama and English, Yale, 1929-33; Ph.D. in History, Columbia, 1946. Tchr. various pvt. schs. 1931-40; lectr. history Columbia U. extension, 1940-41; instr. in history Barnard Coll., Columbia U., 1941-43, asst. prof., 1946-49, asso. prof., exec. officer dept. history, 1949-52, prof. history, 1952-74, prof. emeritus history, 1974-86;

chmn. Barnard Coll., Columbia U. (Am. studies program), 1962-66, chmn. dept. history, 1966-70; faculty Seminar in Am. Studies, Salzburg, 1955, 79; Walter Prescott Webb lectr. U. Tex., 1971. Author: The History of the New Deal, 1933-38, 1944, 63, 75, American Interest in Cuba: 1848-1855, 1947, 73, Roosevelt: From Munich to Pearl Harbor, 1950, rev. edit., 1967, 75, Empire for Liberty: The Genesis and Growth of the U.S. of America, 2 vols, (with Dumas Malone), 1960, 6 vols., 1965, also hist. articles.; Editor: Franklin D. Roosevelt: Selected Speeches, Messages, Press Conferences and Letters, 1957. Chmn. acad. adv. council Marlboro Coll., 1956-63. Served as lt. USNR; on faculty U.S. Naval Acad. 1943-46, Annapolis, Md. Recipient Edmund Campion award for service to soc. Campion Sch., 1972. Mem. Am. Hist. Assn., Nat. Archives Assos., Thimble Islands Assn. (gov.), Phi Beta Kappa (hon.). Clubs: Century, Yale, New York, Lawn, New Haven. Home: Killingworth Conn. Died July 19, 1986.

RAUNBORG, JOHN DEE, oil company executive; b. Waco, Tex., Dec. 16, 1926; s. John Oscar and Grace (Duckworeth) R.; m. Betty L. Daffron, July 28, 1973; children by previous marriage: Sharon Lynn. Ronald Ryan, Rhonda Ruth, Randall Ralph. Student, Rutgers U., 1945; BS in Commerce, La. State U., 1949; postgrad., U. Tex., 1949-50. CPA, Tex. Staff auditor Arthur Andersen & Co., Houston, 1950-57; mgr. internal auditing Kerr-McGee Corp., Oklahoma City, 1957-59, asst. to contr., 1960-62, contr. oil and gas div., 1963-67, asst. contr., 1968, contr., from 1969. With AUS, 1944-47. Mem. Am. Petroleum Inst., Am. Inst. CPA's, Oklahoma City C. of C., Fin. Execs. Inst. Methodist. Home: Oklahoma City Okla. Deceased.

RAVICH, ABRAHAM, urologist; b. near Slonim, Poland, June 10, 1899; came to U.S., 1893, citizen through father, 1898; s. Isadore and Ida (Karelitz) R.; m. Martha L. Zuckert, Sept. 3, 1918 (dec. Sept. 22, 1971); 1 child, Robert Alan; m. Charlotte Nathan, Mar. 22, 1973. AB, CCNY, 1908; AM, Columbia U., 1912, MD, 1912. Intern Jewish Hosp., Bklyn., 1912-14, asst., 1914-18, assoc., 1918-25, chief attending urologist, 1925-34; dir. Ravish Urol. Inst., 1934-40; founder Trafalgar Hosp., N.Y.C., 1956; assoc. urologist Beth Moses Hosp., 1920-23, attending physician, 1920-24, chief urologist, 1936-39; chief urologist Bklyn. Hewbrew Home and Hosp. for Aged, 1925-28, dir. urology, 1938-48; cons. Menorah Home for Aged., from 1930; attending urologist Israel Zio Hosp., 1922-34, Adelphi Hosp., 1940-49, cons. from 1950; asst. clin. prof. urology L.I. Coll. Medicine, 1934; exec. dir. Cancer Research and Hosp. Found., 1947-58, sec., treas., from 1958; pres., exec. dir. Inst. Applied Biology, 1947-57; bd. visitors Creedmore State Hosp., 1946-57. Author: Preventing VD and Cancer by Circumcision, 1973; mem. editorial bd. Clinical Abstracts, 1934-37; contbr. articles to profl. jours. Investor Ravich cystoscope, visualized cautery prostatic punch, lithotriptoscope, other devices. Recipient Townsend Harris medal of achievement Associated Alumni CCNY, 1950. Named hon. surgeon Honor Legion N.Y. City Police Dept. Fellow ACS, AMA; mem. Am. Urol. Assn., Masons (32 deg.), Shriners, Physicians Sq. L.I., N.Y. (past pres.). Died Dec., 1984.

RAWLINS, LESTER, actor, production company executive; b. Sharon, Pa., Sept. 24, 1924; s. Ben and Leona (Verier) Rosenberg. B.F.A. in Drama, Carnegie-Mellon U., 1950. Pres. Addison Prodns., Inc., N.Y.C., 1975-88. Charter mem., Arena Stage, Washington, 1950; N.Y.C. debut in Othello, 1956; appeared on Broadway, including: N.Y.C. debut in Nightride, 1971-72 (Drama Desk award 1972), as Mr. Drumm in Da, 1978-79 (Tony award 1978); appeared in: off-Broadway plays, including The Quare fellow, 1958-59 (Obie award 1959), Hedda Gabler, 1960-61 (Obie award 1961), Benito Cereno, 1964-65 (Obie award 1965); movies include Dairy of a Mad Housewife, 1974, They Might Be Giants, 1976; Lovesick, 1983; guest appearances on numerous TV shows, including Starsky and Hutch; TV and radio comml. voice-over announcer guest appearances on numerous TV shows. Served as 1st sgt. USAAF, 1943-46. Mem. Actors Equity Assn., Screen Actors Guild, AFTRA, Assn. Can. TV and Radio Artists. Club: Players. Home: New York N.Y. Died Mar. 22, 1988.

RAWLS, FLORA HAYES, academic administrator; b. Cerulean, Ky., Sept. 17, 1899; d. Foster Addison and Olive (Hayes) R. Student, Ky. State Coll. for Women, 1917-19; BA, Vanderbilt U., 1925, MA, 1930; postgrad., U. Wis., Peabody Coll. Tchr. Latin Monticello (Ky.) High Sch., 1919-20; prin. Cerulean High Sch., 1920-23; tchr. Latin Hopkinsville (Ky.) High Sch., 1925-29; supervising tchr. Memphis State Coll. Tng. Sch., 1930-38, prin., 1938-47; prof. edn., dean women Memphis State U., 1947-70. Bd. dirs. YWCA, 1948-54, pres., 1955-57, exec. dir. Memphis, 1970-73; mem. Gov.'s Commn. Status of Women. Mem. Tenn. Edn. Assn., Nat. Assn. Women Deans and Counselors, AAUW (pres. state div. 1952-53, chmn. nat. conv. com. 1955, chmn. nomimnating com. 1957), Deans of Women in Tenn. (pres. 1950-51), Zonta (Memphis pres. 1948-49), Phi Beta Kappa, Delta Kappa Gamma (state pres. 1944-46, pres. Epsilon chpt. 1970-72), Sigma Kappa. Methodist. Home: Memphis Tenn. Died July 16, 1988.

RAY, GORDON NORTON, educator, foundation executive; b. N.Y.C., Sept. 8, 1915; s. Jess Gordon and Jessie (Norton) R. A.B., Ind. U., 1936, A.M., 1936, L.H.D. (hon.), 1964; A.M., Harvard U., 1938, Ph.D., 1940, Dexter fellow, 1940-41, Guggenheim fellow, 1941-42, 46, 56-57; Rockefeller fellow, 1948-49; Litt.D., Monmouth Coll., 1959, Syracuse U., 1961, Duke U., 1965, U. Ill., 1968, Northwestern U., 1974, U. Md., 1982; LL.D., NYU, 1961, Tulane U., 1963, U. Calif., 1968, Columbia U., 1969, U. So. Calif., 1974; L.H.D., U. Pa., 1978. Instr. English, Harvard U., 1940-42; prof. English, U. Ill., 1946-60, head dept., 1950-57, v.p., provost, 1957-60; vis. prof. U. Oreg., summer 1948; Berg prof. NYU, 1952-53, prof. English,, 1962-80, emeritus, 1980-86; Lowell lectr., Boston, 1950; Walls lectr. Pierpont Morgan Library, 1982; Lyell lectr. Oxford U., 1985; adviser in lit. Houghton, Mifflin Co., 1954-71; mem. adv. bd. Soho Bibliographies, 1968-79; asso. sec. gen. John Simon Guggenheim Meml. Found, 1960-61, sec. gen., trustee, 1963-86, pres., 1963-85, pres. emeritus, 1985-86; mem. adv. council Smithsonian Instn., 1967-84, chmn., 1970-86; treas., dir. Am. Council Learned Socs., 1973-85; trustee Found. Library Center, 1962-68, chmn. bd., 1965-68; trustee Pierpont Morgan Library, N.Y. Pub. Library, Winterthur Mus., 1977-85; dir. Yaddo, 1979-85, Am. Council Edn., 1980-81. Author: Letters and Private Papers of William Makepeace Thackeray, 4 vols, 1945-46, The Buried Life, 1952, Thackeray: The Uses of Adversity, 1811-1846, 1955, Thackeray: The Age of Wisdom, 1847-1863, 1958, (with Leon Edal) Henry James and H.G. Wells, 1958, H.G. Wells and Rebecca West, 1974, The Illustrator and the Book in England from 1790 to 1914, 1976, The Art of the French Illustrated Book 1700-1914, 2 vols., 1982. Served to lt. USNR, 1942-46. Recipient Joseph Henry medal Smithsonian Instn., 1980. Fellow Am. Acad. Arts and Scis., Royal Soc. Lit.; mem. Am. Philos. Soc. (v.p. 1986), MLA (mng. trustee), Phi Beta Kappa. Clubs: Harvard (N.Y.C.), Grolier (N.Y.C.) (past pres.), Century Assn. (N.Y.C.); Athenaeum, Roxburghe (London). Home: New York N.Y. Died Dec. 15, 1986.

RAY, PHILIP LACEY, mining executive, banker; b. Mankato, Minn., July 10, 1890; s. John H. and Genevieve (Eldredge) R.; m. Berenice Steuerwald, Apr. 5, 1924; children: Patricia (Mrs. Harry L. Bratnober), Georgia (Mrs. Donald W. DeCoster Jr.). BA, U. Minn., 1912. With various mining, timber, bus. corps. Duluth, Minn., 1912-17; ptnr. Philip L. Ray & Co., 1917-26; asst. to pres. 1st Nat. Bank Duluth, 1926; exec. v.p., bd. dirs. 1st and Am. Nat. Bank Duluth; with J.&W. Seligman & Co., N.Y.C., 1929-30; pres., bd. dirs. 1st Trust Co. St. Paul, 1930-45, chmn. bd., 1945-61; v.p., bd. dirs. 1st Nat. Bank St. Paul, 1930-45, chmn. exec. com., bd. dirs., 1945-57, chmn. bd., 1957-58; pres., trustee Gt. No. Iron Ore Properties; chmn. bd. Bliss and Laughlin, Inc., 1960-63; bd. dirs. No. Pacific-Ry., St. Paul Fire & Marine Ins. Co.; trustee Minn. Mut. Life Ins. Co. V.p., bd. dirs. Louis W. and Maud Hill Family Found.; bd. dirs. Charles T. Miller Hosp.; vice chmn., trustee Bigelow Found., F.R. Bigelow Found. Mem. AIME, Chicago Club, Minnesota Club, Somerset Country Club, St. Paul Athletic Club, University Club, Links, Kitchi Gammi Club. Home: Saint Paul Minn. †

RAYMOND, ELEANOR, architect; b. Cambridge, Mass., Mar. 23, 1887; d. Thomas C. and Josephine (Watt) Raymond. AB, Wellesly Coll., 1909; MArch, Smith Coll., 1934. Prin. own archtl. practice, Boston, from 1935. Compiler: Early Domestic Architecture of Pennsylvania. Pioneer sun-heated houses; trustee Smith Coll., 1939. Fellow AIA. Home: Cambridge Mass. †

REARDON, JOHN, baritone, actor; b. N.Y.C., Apr. 8, 1930. BA, Rollins Coll., 1952, MusD (hon.), 1976; studied voice with Martial Singher and Margaret Harshaw. Recorded with various record labels including RCA, Deutsche Grammophon, Columbia, Vox, Seraphim and Serenus; head voice dept. Music Acad. of West, Santa Barbara, Calif., 1987—. Baritone with Met. Opera, Washington Opera Soc., Dallas Opera Co., Santa Fe Opera, San Francisco Opera, Teatro La Venice, Italy, N.Y. City Opera Co.; roles include Guglielmo in Cosi Fan Tutte, title role in Gianni Schicchi, Pelleas in Pelleas et Melisande, Doctor in Vanessa, title role in Don Giovanni, Valentine in Faust, Eisenstein in Die Fledermaus, Belaev in Natalie Petrovna, Miles Dunster in Wings of the Dove, Scarpia in Tosca, Nick Shadow in The Rake's Progress, Escamilio in Carmen, Count Almaviva in The Marriage of Figaro, Abdul in The Last Savage, Marcello in La Boheme, Prince Danilo in The Merry Widow, Dandini in La Cenerentola, Sharpless in Nat. Ednl. TV prodns. From the House of the Dead; Broadway debut in The Saint of Bleecker Street, 1954; appeared in Kismet, San Francisco, London, Republic of South Africa; appeared in world premieres Mourning Becomes Electra, The Sea Gull, Am. premiere The Nose; also other TV appearances including children's show Mister Roger's Neighborhood; recs. include Lady in the Dark, Songfest, La Boheme, On The Town; also solo album contemporary art songs. Home: Santa Fe N.Mex. Died Apr. 16, 1988, buried Santa Fe.

REARDON, PAUL CASHMAN, judge; b. Quincy, Mass., Dec. 23, 1909; s. Daniel B. and Mary (Cashman) R.; m. Ann Leich, June 17, 1939; children: Martha, David, Jane Reardon Labys, Thomas. Grad., Phillips Acad., Andover, Mass., 1928; AB, Harvard U., 1932, LLB, 1935. Bar: Mass. 1935. Practice Boston, 1935-55; mng. ptnr. Hausserman, Davidson & Shattuck, 1948-55; gen. counsel Boston C. of C.; spl. counsel to Gov. of Mass., 1953-55; chief justice Mass. Superior Ct., 1955-62; assoc. justice Mass. Supreme Judicial Ct., 1962-76; pres. Nat. Ctr. for State Cts. Mem. exec. com. Mass. Com. Caths., Protestants and Jews; former trustee New Eng. Conservatory Music, World Peace Found., Boston, Thayer Acad.; vis. com. Harvard Law Sch.; overseer Harvard Coll., 1961-67, chmn. exec. com., 1966-67; trustee Boston Symphony Orch., Plimouth Plantation. With USNR, World War II. Mem. ABA (past chmn. sect. jud. adminstrn., chmn. adv. com. fair trial-free press), Mass. Bar Assn., Boston Bar Assn., Harvard Alumni Assn. (past pres.), Nat. Conf. State Trial Judges (past chmn.), Am. Law Inst., Inst. Jud. Adminstrn. (past pres.-elect), Am. Judicare Soc. (past dir.), Am. Bar Found, Am. Acad. Arts and Scis., Tavern Club, Tihonet Club, Union Club (Boston), Phi Beta Kappa, Phi Alpha Delta. Home: Hingham Mass. Died July 29, 1988; buried Mt. Wollaston Cemetery, Quincy, Mass.

REAVIS, JOHN WALLACE, lawyer; b. Falls City, Nebr., Nov. 13, 1899; s. Charles Frank and Myrta A. Reavis; m. Helen Lincoln, May 3, 1924 (dec.); children: John W., Lincoln. LLB, Cornell U., 1921. Assoc. Tolles, Hogsett, Ginn & Morley, Cleve.; sr. ptnr. successor firm Jones, Day, Reavis & Pogue. Served with Flying Corps USN, World War I. Home: Shaker Heights Ohio Deceased.

REBOLLO, ANTHONY ERNEST, corporate executive; b. Huatusco, Veracruz, Mex., Mar. 7, 1892; came to U.S., 1912, naturalized, 1942; s. Francisco and Maclovia (Rincon) R.; m. Eleanor Gibney, Oct. 14, 1929; children: Ernest William, Rosa Leonor, Anthony Ernest. Student, Colegio Cantonal Sanchez Oropeza, Huatusco. Latin Am. rep. Goldsmith & Co., Inc., N.Y.C., 1912-30; with Johnson & Johnson Internat., New Brunswick, N.J., from 1931, successively asst. sec., v.p., bd. dirs., 1931-55; pres., bd. dirs. Pan Am., from 1955; mem. Philippine-Am. Trade Arbitration Commn. Mem. Pan-Am. Soc. U.S. Inc., Am. Mgmt. Assn., Nat. Fgn. Trade Coun., Export Mgrs. Club. Home: Metuchen N.J. †

REDFERN, JOHN JOSEPH, JR., oil and gas producer; b. Jersey City, Oct. 4, 1912; s. John Joseph and Margaret A. (Barry) R.; m. Rosalind Kapps, June 26, 1936; children: John Joseph III, Rosalind, Roberta. C.E., Rensselaer Poly. Inst., 1934, LL.D. hon., 1983; postgrad., U. Okla., 1938-39. Engr. Hoy & Co., Inc., Albany, N.Y., 1934-36; ind. oil operator Oklahoma City, 1937-39, Midland, Tex., 1939-86; pres. Flag-Redfern Oil Co., 1960-83, chmn. bd., 1983-86; pres. Pennant Oils Ltd., Calgary, Can., 1966-73; chmn. bd. Pennant-Puma Oils Ltd., 1973-76; chmn. Midland Map Co., 1950-86; chmn. bd. Leamco Services Inc., 1982-86. Trustee Rensselaer Poly. Inst., 1958-81, hon. trustee, 1981-86, sec. bd., 1965-70, vice chmn., 1970-81; chmn. Midland Meml. Found., 1977-84; bd. dirs. Redfern Found., 1979-86. Mem. Ind. Petroleum Assn. Am. (dir.), Tex. Ind. Petroleum and Royalty Owners (dir.), Ind. Petroleum Assn. N.Mex. (dir.), Tex. Assn. Taxpayers, Inc. (sec. 1985), Mountain States Legal Found. (bd. dirs. 1985-86), Petroleum Mus. (bd. execs. 1984-86). Clubs: Plaza, Midland Country, Midland Petroleum. Home: Midland Tex. Died Sept. 28, 1986; buried Resthaven Meml. Park, Midland, Tex.

REDFIELD, ALFRED CLARENCE, oceanographer, educator; b. Phila., Nov. 15, 1890; s. Robert Stuart and Mary Thibault (Guillou) R.; m. Martha Putnam, June 7, 1921; children: Elizabeth Redfield Marsh, Martha Washburn Koch, Alfred Guillou. Student, Haverford Coll., 1909-10; BS, Harvard U., 1913, PhD, 1917; postgrad., Cambridge U., Eng., 1920, U. Munich, Germany, 1931; PhD (hon.), U. Oslo, 1956; DSc (hon.), Lehigh U., 1965, Meml. U. Nfld., 1967, U. Alaska, 1971. Instr. physiology Harvard U., 1918-19, asst. prof. physiology, 1921-30, assoc. prof., 1930-31, prof., 1931-56, prof. emeritus, from 1956; mng. editor Biol. Bull., 1930-41; assoc. dir. Woods Hole Oceanographic Instn., 1942-56, sr. oceanographer, emeritus, from 1956; asst. prof. physiology U. Toronto, 1919-20. Mem. Nat. Acad. Scis., Marine Biol. Assn. U.K., Am. Acad. Arts and Scis., Am. Physiol. Soc., Am. Soc. Zoologists, Ecol. Soc. Am., Am. Soc. Limnology and Oceanography, Phi Beta Kappa. Home: Woods Hole Mass. Died Mar. 17, 1983.

REDFIELD, EMANUEL, lawyer; b. N.Y.C., Feb. 28, 1904; s. Morris and Rose (Berkowitz) R.; m. Mildred Russell, Feb. 7, 1935; children: Richard, William. AB, NYU, 1922; LLB, Fordham U., 1926; postgrad. in polit. sci., Columbia U., 1932-36. Bar: N.Y. 1927, U.S. Supreme Ct. 1934, other fed. ct. bars. Asst. editor Shepard's Citations, 1922; title examiner N.Y. Title & Mortgage Co., 1923-36; pvt. practice N.Y.C., 1927-31, 38-83; ptnr. Dwyer & Redfield, N.Y.C., 1931-38, Redfield & Georgiopoulos, N.Y.C., 1978-83; guest numerous radio and TV shows. Author: Artists Estates and Taxes; contbr. articles and revs. to profl. jours. Cofounder, gen. council N.Y. Civil Liberties Union, 1955-67, bd. dirs. 1941-68; counsel Artists Equity Assn. N.Y., 1950-74, Internat. Assn. Arts, 1955-65, Internat. Percy Grainger Soc. (formerly Percy Grainger Library Soc.), 1977-83; past. mem. adv. com. Bd. Edn. N.Y.C.; cofounder Riverdale Soc. Ethical Culture, 1950; active Boy Scouts Am., Riverdale Art Com. Recipient citation Artists Equity Assn., 1974. Mem. N.Y. County

Lawyers Assn., Am. Arbitration Assn., Riverdale Camera Club, N.Y.-N.J. Trail Conf. (legal com.), Appalachian Mountain Club, Wall St. Ski Club (past dir.), Woodland Trail Walkers, Westchester Trails Assn., Compo Beach Assn. (Westport, Conn.) (dir.). Democrat. Home: Riverdale N.Y. Died Jan. 20, 1983, buried Ferncliff Cemetery, Hartsdale, N.Y.

REDPATH, ROBERT UPJOHN, JR., insurance executive; b. South Orange, N.J., Aug. 25, 1906; s. Dr. Robert Upjohn and Clara May (Sloneker) R.; m. Nancy Shaw Miller, June 28, 1930; children—Robert Upjohn III, Nancy M., William M., Jean C. (Mrs. Henry P. Becton, Jr.). Grad., Phillips Acad., 1924; student, U. Mich., summer 1925; A.B., Yale, 1928, postgrad. Law Sch., 1928-29; postgrad., New Sch. Social Research, N.Y.U., Columbia, Am. Coll.; C.L.U.s. C.L.U. With Lawyers Mortgage Co., N.Y.C., 1929-33; life underwriter 1933-87; dir. Ohio Casualty Corp., Hamilton, Ohio Life Ins. Co., Hamilton.; lectr. gen. semantics Denver U., 1952; tchr. gen. semantics Adult Schs. of, South Orange-Maplewood and Montclair, N.J., 1954-61. Trustee South Orange-Maplewood (N.J.) Adult Sch., 1965-87; chmn. planning and devel. bd. Village of South Orange, 1947-49; Trustee Inst. Gen. Semantics, 1946-87, pres. bd. trustees, 1946-83; co-founder, trustee Blue Hill Found., 1941-76, New Eyes for the Needy, Short Hills, N.J., 1969-74; bd. mgrs. Vocat. Services br. YMCA, N.Y.C., 1944-87; mem. bd. pensions U.P. Ch. of U.S.A., 1947-62; Trustee Phillips Acad., 1950-52, Susquehanna U., 1960-84, Ethel Walker Sch., 1952-55, Rosemary Hall Found., 1960-63, Phillips Acad. Mem. Million Dollar Round Table (life), Nat. Assn. Life Underwriters, Yale Alumni Assn. (active alumni affairs, Yale medal 1968), Beta Theta Phi, Elihu. Presbyn. Clubs: Graduates (New Haven); Essex County Country; Yale (N.Y.C.). Home: South Orange N.J. Died Dec. 28, 1987.

REDPATH, WILLIAM STANLEY, advertising executive; b. County Antrim, Ireland, Oct. 14, 1903; came to U.S., 1925, nAturalized, 1931; s. William and Isabel (Woodside) R.; m. Ann Mills Baughman, July 29, 1933; children: Nancie J. Redpath Eskey, Virginia E. Redpath Phillips. BSMechE, Queen's U., Belfast, Ireland, 1923. Trainee, salesperson Westinghouse Electric Co., 1925-28; indsl. sales rep., sales mgr., promotion coordinator Duquesne Light Co., Pitts., 1928-39; sales promotion mgr. Equitable Gas Co., Pitts., 1939-44; account exec., account supr. Ketchum, MacLeon & Grove, Inc., Pitts., 1944-50, v.p., 1950-55, exec. v.p., 1955-62, chmn. bd., 1967-69, chmn. exec. com., 1965-67, 70-71, also dir., chief exec. N.Y. office, 1967-69; pres. Ketchum Internat., Inc., Pitts., 1970-71. Mem. University Club, Duquesne Club, St. Clair Club (Pitts.). Republican. Presbyterian. Home: Pittsburgh Pa. Died Feb. 14, 1987.

REED, CLARENCE C., surgeon, rancher; b. Lewisville, Ohio, June 26, 1902; s. John C. and Rosa (McVay) R.; m. Elvira Arman, Dec. 21, 1973; 1 child by previous marriage, Linda. AB, Mt. Union Coll., 1920; MD, U. Chgo., 1925. Diplomate Am. Bd. Plastic Surgery. Resident in surgery U. Chgo., 1926-29; pvt. practice Downey, Calif., from 1933, from 1933; sr. attending surgeon St. Francis Hosp., Lynwood, Calif., from 1945, Downey Community Hosp., from 1970; cattle rancher San Luis Obispo County, Calif., from 1942; asst. prof. surgery U. So. Calif., 1934-44. Founder Reed Meml Found., 1959, Reed Neurol. Research Ctr. UCLA Med. Sch., 1965, Reed Surg. Bldg. U. Chgo., 1966. With AUS, 1919. Recipient Highest award of merit, UCLA Med. Sch., 1972, Gold Key award U. Chgo. Med. Sch. Fellow ACS, Am. Soc. Abdominable Surgeons; mem. AMA, Shriners, Sigma Nu, Mu Sigma Nu. Home: San Marino Calif. Died Sept. 16, 1986, buried Forest Lawn, Cypress, Calif.

REED, DONNA, actress; b. Denison, Iowa, 1922; d. William R. and Hazel Mullenger; m. William Tuttle, Jan. 30, 1943 (div. 1944); m. Anthony Owens, June 15, 1945 (div. 1972); children: Penny Jane, Anthony Jr., Timothy Grant, Mary Ann; m. Grover Asmus. Student, Los Angeles City Coll., 1938-40. Appeared in motion pictures The Courtship of Andy Hardy, 1941, The Get-Away, Shadow of the Thin Man, The Bugle Sounds, Mokey, Apache Trail, Calling Dr. Gillespie, Eyes in the Night, Dr. Gillespie's Criminal Case, 1942, The HUman Comedy, The Man From Down Under, Thousands Cheer, See Here, Private Hargrove, 1943, Gentle Annie, 1944, Picture of Dorian Gray, They Were Expendable, Faithful in My Fashion, 1945, Its a Wonderful Life, Green Dolphin Street, 1946, Beyond Glory, 1947, Chicago Deadline, 1948, The Hero, 1950, Scandal Sheet, 1951, Hangman's Noose, 1952, Barbarossa, 1952, Trouble Along the Way, The Caddy, Gun Fury, From Here to Eternity, 1953 (Oscar award), The Last Time I Saw Paris, The Far Horizons, 3 Hours To Kill, They Rode West, 1954, Ransom, Backlash, 1955, Benny Goodman Story, 1956, Beyond Mombasa, 1957; star TV series The Donna Reed Show, ABCúTV, 1957-66; appeared in TV movie The Best Place To Be, 1979 (Best Supporting Actress award Aca. Motion Picture Arts and Scis. 1954. Named Princess Young Victory Flathead Indian Tribes, 1952. Home: Beverly Hills Calif. Died Dec. 1, 1986.

REED, MARSHALL RUSSELL, bishop; b. Onsted, Mich., Sept. 15, 1891; s. Fred Pitts and Elsie Adelphia (Russell) R.; m. Mary Esther Kirkendall, May 14, 1917; children: Elizabeth Jane, Elsie Mae, Mary Louise. AB, Albion Coll., 1914, DD, 1931; postgrad., Drew Theol. Sem., 1914-15; BD, Garrett Bibl. Inst., 1916, DD, 1940; MA, Northwestern U., 1917, DST, 1953; LLD, Adrian Coll., 1959. Ordained to ministry Meth. Ch., 1917. Pastor Gaines, Mich., 1917-18, Onaway, Mich., 1918-19; pastor Calvary Meth. Ch., Detroit, 1919-23, Jefferson Ave. Meth. Ch., Detroit, 1923-28, Ypsilanti, Mich., 1928-34, Nardin Park Meth. Ch., Detroit, 1934-48; elected bishop of Meth. Ch. 1948, assigned to Detroit area; pres. Coun. of Bishops, 1962-63. Mem. Masons, Phi Beta Kappa, Delta Tau Delta, Delta Sigma Rho. Republican. Home: Detroit Mich. †

REED, VERGIL DANIEL, economics educator; b. Muncie, Ind., Dec. 20, 1896; s. Alonzo Franklin and Florence May (Hayden) R.; m. Ruth Amelia Roberston, Apr. 22, 1924. BS, Ind. U., 1922; MS, Columbia U., 1928, PhD, 1935. With W.R. Grace & Co., 1922-26; with advt. firms 1926-28; v.p., dir. research Wells Advt. Agy., 1929-33; chief reatail and wholesale trade div. U.S. Census Bur., 1935-36, asst. dir., 1936-42; chief gen. stats. staff, chiefindustry and facilities br. stats. div. War Prodn. Bd., 1942-44; assoc. dir. J. Walter Thompson Co., 1944-50, v.p., 1950-58; prof. mktg. and transp. adminstrn. Coll. Bus. and Pub. Service, Mich. State U., 1958-62; prof. mktg. Grad. Sch. Bus., Columbia U., N.Y.C., 1962-65; prof. mktg. Sch. Bus. Adminstrn., Am. U., Washington, 1965-67, prof. emeritus, from 1967. Author: Planned Marketing, 1929, Principles of Economic Geography, 1933, Advertising and Selling Industrial Goods, 1936, Population and Purchasing Power, 1945, (booklet) The Farm Market-Some Basic Trends and Changes, 1949, (with others) U.S.A. Market for Overseas Goods, 1950; editor: Population and Its Distribution, 1951, World Markets, 1954; contbr. reports and articles to tech. and profl. jours. 2d lt. F.A., AUS, World War I. Fellow Am. Statis. Assn.; mem. Am. Mktg. Assn. (pres. 1942), Market Research Council (pres. 1949-50), Population Assn. Am., Cosmos Club (Washington), Alpha Delta Sigma (hon.), Beta Gamma Sigma, Delta Phi Epsilon, Theta Chi. Home: Washington D.C. Died Apr. 9, 1986.

REED, WILLIAM VERNON, architect; b. Monticello, Ill., Nov. 4, 1907; s. Carl Seward and Ida (Vaughan) R.; m. Giuliana Nardi, June 21, 1947; children: Carl Christopher, Giuliana Virginia Maria Reed Keller. B.Arch. cum laude, U. Ill. at Urbana, 1930; certificate, Beaux Arts Inst. Design, 1930; M. Arch. (grad. fellow), Mass. Inst. Tech., 1933. Mem. faculty U. Ill. at Urbana, 1930-31, U. Man. (Can.), 1931-32, Mass. Inst. Tech., 1933-34; cons. fgn. housing, housing div. PWA, 1935-36; prin. project planner S.E. region U.S. Housing Authority, 1937-40; dir. div. housing standards Office Def. Housing Coordinator, Washington, 1940-42; mem.-in-charge tech. investigations President's Housing Mission to Great Britain, 1943; dep. housing expediter, dir. tech. office Nat. Housing Agy., 1946-47; v.p. So. Calif. Homes, 1947-48, IBEC Housing Corp., N.Y.C. and San Juan, P.R., 1948-57; practice architecture San Juan, 1957-75; prin. Reed, Torres, Beauchamp, Marvel, 1963-75; vis. lectr. univs. in U.S. and P.R. Prin. works include P.R. comprehensive plan for outdoor recreation, 1970, (with E.L. Barnes) El Monte Urban Renewal Project, Rio Piedras, P.R., 1960-68; Quintana High Rise Housing Project, Rio Piedras, 1966, Commonwealth Housing Center, Rio Piedras, 1965, Dorado (P.R.) Beach Hotel staff housing, 1965, Housing Investment Corp. Bldg, Rio Piedras, 1962, Psychiat. Treatment Center, Ponce, P.R., 1963; Author: New Homes for Old, 1940, also articles. Dir. Nat. Housing Conf., 1965—; mem. council Casa del Libro, 1960-75; mem. citizen's adv. com. to mayor of San Juan, 1965-68; mem. citizen's com. Nuevo Centro de San Juan, 1967-75, treas., 1970-71; Adv. bd. P.R. Salvation Army. Served to maj. USMCR, 1942-45. Allerton Am. travelling scholar, 1929; fellow Lake Forest Found. Architects and Landscape Architects, 1930; Francis Plym fellow, 1935-36. Fellow A.I.A. (pres. P.R. 1968-70); mem. Am. Inst. Planners, Am. Arbitration Assn. (arbitrator 1976—), Inst. de Arquitectos P.R., Colegio de Ingenieros, Arquitectos Y Agrimensores P.R., Tau Beta Pi, Beta Theta Pi. Club: Cosmos (Washington). Home: Sarasota Fla. Died Apr. 16, 1987; buried Monticello, Ill.

REEDER, LEE, lawyer; b. LaPorte, Ind., Oct. 14, 1909; s. David Huse and Maude Angela (Warner) R.; m. Madaline Flo Brown, June 8, 1935; children: Douglas Lee, Jennifer Ann, Madaline Brown, Jr. Student, Kansas City Jr. Coll., 1926-28; J.D., U. Mo., Kansas City, 1932. Bar: Mo. 1932. Since practiced in Kansas City; dir. numerous firms; spl. counsel, dir. C.L.C. of Am., 1962-78; dir. W.S.C. Group, Inc.; Mem. spl. adv. com. to ICC. Chmn. Citizens Sch. Plant Com., Kansas City, 1950, Citizens Com. on Human Relations, 1950-52, Sch. Bond Com. Kansas City Sch. Dist., 1948; chmn. bd. Youth Symphony of Heart of Am.; founding mem., chmn. Kansas City Commn. Human Relations, 1952-60; bd. dirs., gen. counsel Heart of Am. council Boy Scouts Am., scoutmaster, troop committeeman, Eagle Scout, Silver Beaver award; trustee, chmn. Law Found. U. Mo., Kansas City, 1972-75; trustee, chmn. Leelanau Schs., 1972-75; bd. dirs., gen. counsel Am. Humanics. Recipient Silver Beaver award Boy Scouts Am. Mem. ABA, Mo. Bar Assn. (dir. dept. adminstrv. law 1960), Kansas City Bar Assn., Motor Carrier Lawyers Assn. (pres. 1952-53), Lawyers Assn. Kansas City, ICC Practitioners Assn. (chmn. nat. assn. ethics com. 1960-62), Kansas City Met. Bar Assn., Delta Theta Phi, Alpha Phi Omega (hon.), Bench and Robe Soc. Clubs: Kansas City (Kansas City), Carriage (Kansas City). Lodge: Rotary, Masons, Shriners. Died June 19, 1988.

REESE, HANS H. F., university professor, psychiatrist; b. Bordesholm, Germany, Sept. 17, 1891; came to U.S., 1923; naturalized, 1929; s. H.C. and D.K. Reese; m. Tessa Schmidt, Apr. 12, 1927; children: Sibyl Dorothy, Ernst Schmidt, Alma Hay. Student, U. Munich, Germany, 1913-14; tentamen physicum, U. Kiel, Germany, 1914; MD, U. Kiel, 1917. Asst. surgeon German Navy, 1917-18, U. Hamburg, Germany, 1918-23; prof. of neurology and psychiatry U. Wis., from 1924, chmn. dept., 1924-58. Contbr. articles on history and profl. subjects to med. and neurol. jours. Fulbright professor U. Alexandria, 1961. em. AMA (house of dels. from 1951), Wis. Med. Soc., Coll. Physicians and Surgeons, Am. Neurol. Assn. (pres. 1952-53), Cen. Neuropsychiatric Assn. (pres. 1933), Mex. Soc. Surgery and Neurosurgery (hon.), German Neurol. and Neurosurg. Soc. (corr. hon. mem.), Milw. Neuropsychiatric Soc. (pres. 1940-41), Chgo. Neurol. Soc., University Club (Madison. Home: Madison Wis. †

REEVES, ALBERT LEE, lawyer, executive; b. Steelville, Mo., May 31, 1906; s. Albert L. and Martha (Ferguson) R.; m. Eleanor Louise Glasner, Oct. 3, 1935; children: Elaine L., Martha E., Nancy L. B.A., William Jewell College, 1927; J.D., U. Mo., 1931. Bar: Mo. 1931, D.C. 1949. Instr. Baylor Coll., Belton, Tex., 1927-28; former partner McKenna, Conner & Cuneo (and predecessor firms), Washington, Los Angeles and San Francisco; sr. v.p., sec., mem. exec. com., dir. Utah Internat., Inc. and subsidiaries and affiliates, 1958-75; sr. v.p. cons. Marcona Corp., Marcona Internat., San Francisco, 1975-76; dir. KQED, 1970-76, French Bank Calif.; Mem. 80th U.S. Congress from 5th Dist. Mo. Treas. Jackson County Republican Com., 1934-36; mem. chancellor's assocs. Calif. State Univ.; bd. dirs. St. Luke's Hosp. Served from capt. to lt. col. C.E. AUS, 1942-46, CBI. Decorated Order of Cristobal Colon, Order of Juan Pablo Duarte Dominican Republic; Order of Maritime Merit; San Francisco Port Authority, 1967; Mem. DeMolay Legion of Honor. Mem. ABA, Mo., Fed. bar assns., Bar Assn. D.C., Am. Soc. Polit. Law, Acad. Polit. Sci., Mil. Order World Wars, World Affairs Council No. Calif. (pres. 1966-69), S.A.R., Pi Kappa Delta, Kappa Sigma, Phi Delta Phi, Delta Sigma Rho. Episcopalian. Clubs: Nat. Lawyers, Metropolitan (Washington); Burlingame Country, Pauma Valley Country, Bankers; World Trade (hon. life mem.; pres., dir. 1965-69) (San Francisco). Home: Pauma Valley Calif. Died Apr. 15, 1987; buried St. Francis Episcopal Ch. Meml. Garden, Pauma Valley.

REHG, NORMAN MELCHIOR, mining executive; b. Summerfield, Ill., Jan. 20, 1892; s. Conrad G. and Mary Margaret (Antoine) R.; m. Julie Margaret Nungesser, July 25, 1915 (dec.); children: Julie Norma Stoner, Norman M.; m. 2d, Nellie May Davis, Jan. 19, 1954 (dec.); m. 3d, Mary Lily Rough, Dec. 30, 1963. Student, pub. schs., St. Louis. Pres. Keystone Copper Mining Co., Dragoon, Ariz.; owner, operator Rehg's Copper Mines. Inventor device for moving bed-ridden patients to and rom wheelchair; author: Politics vs. Justice: Pretty Boy Floyd and Me. Active in prosecuting state and fed. criminals. Mem. Masons (K.T.). Home: El Doradao Kans. †

REICH, JOHN, director; b. Vienna, Austria, Sept. 30, 1906; came to U.S., 1938, naturalized, 1944; s. Leopold and Martha (Baxter) R.; m. Friederike Karoline Kurzweil, Oct. 31, 1932 (dec. Feb. 1945); m. Karen Ruth Lasker, July 9, 1957 (dec. Apr. 1983). Baccalaureate with highest honors, Realgymnasium I. Vienna, 1925; Director's Diploma, U. Vienna, 1931; Ph.D., Cornell U., Ithaca, N.Y., 1944. Asst. producer, dir. Burgtheater, Vienna, 1931-32; dir. Max Reinhardt Co., Vienna, 1932-38; from asst. to assoc. prof. Ithaca (N.Y.) Coll., 1938-44; vis. prof. N.Y. U., 1945-46, Smith Coll., 1946-48; dramatic dir. CBS-TV, 1945-46; lectr. Barnard Coll., 1951-53; lectr. Columbia, 1953-56, asst. prof., 1956-57; mem. Fulbright Selection Commn., 1949. Producer, dir., Reinhardt Theatres, Vienna, 1932-38, also Salzburg Festival, summer 1934-37, producing dir., Goodman Theatre and Sch. of Drama, Art Inst. Chgo., 1957-72, Goodman Resident Profl. Co., 1969-72, guest dir., U. Miami, U. Ga., U. Kans., Pa. State U., Cornell U., U. Santa Clara, U. So. Calif., SUNY, Stony Brook, U. Wis., Dallas Theatre Center, Calif. Actors Theatre, Mo. Repertory Theatre, Great Lakes Shakespeare Festival, Julliard, Asolo State Theatre Fla., PAF Playhouse of L.I.; N.Y. stage prodns. include The Sacred Flame (Maugham); (Recipient Ford Found. award for stage and theatre direction, 1959, treas. theatre communications group 1961). Mem. Mayor's Com. Econ. and Cultural Devel., 1964. Decorated chevalier de l'Ordre des Arts et des Lettres France; Grand Badge of Honor Austria). Mem. Nat. Theatre Conf., ANTA (Man of Year award Chgo. 1961). Roman Catholic. Club: Cliff Dwellers. Home: Sarasota Fla. Died Feb. 9, 1988.

REICHBERG, DAVID, marketing executive; b. Newark, Apr. 19, 1926; s. Jacob and Sadie (Goldin) R.; m. Mary Fine, Aug. 7, 1979; children: Debra, Gregory,

Ethan, Brian, Raifiel. B.A., Rutgers U., 1950; M.A., Columbia U., 1951. Sales analyst Tidewater Oil Co., N.Y.C., 1951-54; dir. mktg. Popular Mdse. Co., Passaic, N.J., 1954-61; pres. Reston & Carroll, Inc., N.Y.C., 1961-63; v.p. Harry Schneiderman, Inc., Chgo., 1963-64; exec. v.p. Altman, Vos & Reichberg, N.Y.C., 1964-74; pres. Altman, Vos & Reichberg, 1974-76, dir., 1964-79; pres. Direct Mass Mktg., Inc., 1976—, Syndicated Group Plans, Inc., from 1976, Assn. Informed Travelers, Inc., 1978-80; chmn. Group Direct Mktg. Inc., 1976-78, Overseas Discount Shopping Service, 1974-79; pres. Nat. Group Mgmt. Services, Inc., 1980-82. Mem. Com. on City Waterfront and Waterways, N.Y.C., from 1972, chmn., from 1974; pres. Am. Family Inst., Inc., from 1976. Served with AUS, 1944-46. Mem. Am. Soc. Profl. Consultants (bd. govs. 1980-82). Clubs: Rutgers U. (N.Y.C.), Columbia U. (N.Y.C.); New Rochelle (N.Y.); Tennis, Princeton U. Home: New Rochelle N.Y. Deceased.

REICHERT, PHILIP, medical consultant, cardiologist; b. N.Y.C., Mar. 29, 1897; s. Nathaniel and Charlotte (Fishel) R.; m. Helen F. Keane, Sept. 29, 1939. AB, CCNY, 1918; MD, Cornell U., 1923. Diplomate Nat. Bd. Med. Examiners. Postdocotral fellow, asst. Rockefeller Inst. Med. Research, 1923-25; acting dir. Witkin Found. Cardiol. Research, 1938-40; v.p., dir. profl. div. Doherty, Clifford, Steers & Shenfield, N.Y.C., 1947; dir. research Yorktown Products Corp., N.Y.C., from 1956; dir. course med. advt. and promotion NYU, from 1956. Contbr. numerous articles to profl. jours. Sgt. U.S. Army, World War I; maj. detached duty M.C. Res., World War II. Fellow ACP (life), Am. Coll. Legal Medicine (trustee), Am. Coll. Cardiology (disting. fellow, nat. sec., trustee, gov.), N.Y. Acad. Medicine; mem. Assn. Mil. Surgeons, N.Y. Microscopical Soc., Soc. History, Medicine. Home: New York N.Y. Died Mar. 19, 1985.

REICHLER, OXIE, newspaper editor; b. Utica, N.Y., Dec. 25, 1898; s. Moses and Gertrude (Segal) R.; m. Bertha Emma Schnitzer, Dec. 28, 1924; 1 child, Merton Lawrence. Student, Columbia U., 1916-17, CCNY, 1917-20. Reporter, state editor, night city editor Utica Daily Press, 1920-25; editor, co-pub. N.Y. State Sq. and Compass (Masonic weekly newspaper-mag.), 1924-27; spl. assignment and feature writer Utica Observer-Dispatch, 1927-28; dep. pub. safety commr. City of Utica, 1928-29; assoc. editor Yonkers (N.Y.) Statesman, 1930-32; assoc. editor Yonkers Herald Statesman, 1932-38, editor, 1938-67, editor emeritus, cons., from 1967; daily columnist Prayer for Today Herald Statesman and other newspapers, from 1942; assoc., then v.p. Westchester Rockland Newspapers, from 1957; lectr., radio speaker; mem. Pulitzer Prize jury, 1964. With U.S. Army, 1918. Recipient George K. Polk award for disting. reporting and editorial writing L.I. U., 1952, LaGuardia Meml. award, 1956, Disting. Citizen award Nat. Mcpl. League, 1957. Mem. Am. Soc. Newspaper Editors, N.Y. State Soc. Newspaper Editors (past pres.), Nat. Editorial Writers Conf. N.Y. State Pubs. Assn., N.Y. State Assoc. Dailies, Nat. Civic League (contbr. articles to rev.), Proportional Representation League (trustee), Citizenship Clearing House, Westchester County Hist. Soc., Yonkers Hist. Soc. (hon.), Yonkers C. of C., B'nai B'rith, Masons, Rotary, Sigma Delta Chi. Republican. Jewish. Home: Port Jefferson Station N.Y. Died July 7, 1986; buried Coram, N.Y.

REIGNER, CHARLES GOTTSHALL, publisher; b. Pottstown, Pa., Nov. 14, 1888; s. Henry and Katherine (Gottshall), R.; m. Beatrice Stella Charles; children: Meryle Woodrow, Janice Antoinette Mansfield, Carl William (dec.), Alfred (dec.), Paul Wentworth, Julian Eileen Herr, Roger Sherman, James Harris Norman. AB, U. Pitts., 1915, EdB, 1915; student, Princeton U., U. Pa., N.Y.U.; LittD, Hampden Sydney Coll., 1950; LLD, Waynesburg Coll., 1953, EdD, 1956. Tchr. Strayer Sch., Wanamaker Inst. Industries (Phila.), Bus. and Westinghouse high schs. (Pitts.); mem. teaching staff summer sessions Bowling Green (Ky.) Coll. Commerce, Syracuse U., U. Calif. (Berkeley, Los Angeles), U. Washington; editor The H.M. Rowe Co., Balt., 1919-1927, pres., from 1927; exec. sec. to dir. of purchase, storage and traffic, Q.M.C., U.S. Army, 1918; official reporter Ct. of Claims, 1918-19. Author: Beginnings of the Business School, numerous textbooks in field of bus. edn. Mem. Selective Service Appeal Bd. for Balt. City, World War II. Recipient selective service medal and cert. of merit, citation of merit, N.J. Assn. Schs. of Bus., 1950, Disting. Svc. award, Nat. Assn. and Council of Bus. Schs., 1953, cert. and award of merit City of Balt., 1960, Disting. Citizen award State Md., 1960. Mem. Horace Mann League, NEA (life), Nat. Bus. Tchrs. Assn. (pres. Nat. Shorthand Tchrs. Assn. 1914), Eastern Bus. Edn. Assn., United Bus. Edn. Assn., Nat. Shorthand Reporters Assn. (life), Travelers Protective Assn. Am. (pres. Md. div. 1949), Philalethes Soc. (past pres.), Masons (Shriner 33, K.T.), Kiwanis (pres. Balt. 1940, lt. gov. 1959), Chi Rho Internat., Sigma Mu Sigma, Omicron Delta Kappa, Phi Delta Kappa (pres. Alpha Rho chpt. 1939), Delta Pi Epsilon. Presbyterian (ruling elder; past chmn. com. ednl. instns. Va. Synod, Presbyn. Ch. U.S.). Home: Baltimore Md. †

REINECKE, JEAN OTIS, industrial designer; b. Ft. Scott, Kans., July 9, 1909; s. Henry Hamon and Mary Estella (Knight) R.; 1 child, Barbra. Ptnr. Gen. Displays, Barnes & Reinecke, 1933-47; pres. Reinecke Assocs., Flintridge, Calif., 1947-87; cons. MITI, Japan; instr. New Bauhaus; lectr. Northwestern U., Ill. Inst. Tech., Calif. Inst. Tech., UCLA, MIT, others. designer for firms including 3M, McGraw-Edison, Caterpillar, ITT, Hewlett-Packard Contbr. articles to profl. jours.; design editor Bus. Screen. Bd. dirs. Color Research Inst., Humanics Found.; adv. bd. Art Ctr. Coll. Design. Recipient Design awards Am. Designers Inst., Modern Plastics, Art Dirs. Club, Koppers Steel Packaging. Fellow Indsl. Designers Soc. Am. (chmn. bd., pres.); mem. Soc. Plastics Engrs. (bd. dirs.),. Clubs: Fin 'n' Feather, Riverside. Died Dec. 18, 1987.

REINER, IRVING, mathematician, educator; b. Bklyn., Feb. 8, 1924; s. Max and Mollie (Bolotin) R.; m. Irma Ruth Moses, Aug. 22, 1948; children: David, Peter. B.A., Bklyn. Coll., 1944; M.A., Cornell U., 1945, Ph.D., 1947. Mem. Inst. for Advanced Study, Princeton, N.J., 1947-48, 54-56; mem. faculty U. Ill. at Urbana, 1948-54, 56-86, prof. math., 1958-88; sabbatical leave U. London, fall 1966, spring 1973, U. Paris, U. London, U. Warwick, spring 1977, U. London, 1980. Author: (with C.W. Curtis) Representation Theory of Finite Groups and Associative Algebras, 1962, Methods of Representation Theory, Vol. I, 1981, Vol. II, 1987; Introduction to Matrix Theory and Linear Algebra, 1971, Maximal Orders, 1975, Class Groups and Picard Groups of Integral Group Rings and Orders, 1976, (with K.W. Roggenkamp) Topics in Integral Representation Theory, 1979. Editor procs.: Symposium Representation Theory of Finite Groups, 1970, Ill. Jour. Math, 1978-85; mem. editorial bd. Contemporary Mathematics. Contbr. articles to profl. jours. Guggenheim fellow U. Paris, France, 1962-63; sr. fellow Sci. Research Council, U. London, 1980; Recipient Disting. Alumnus award Bklyn. Coll., 1963; NATO sr. fellow in sci., 1977; sr. vis. fellow Sci. Research Council, fall 1980, Spring 1984. Mem. Am. Math. Soc. (editor procs. 1966-70), Math. Assn. Am., Sigma Xi, Pi Mu Epsilon (nat. councillor 1967-72). Home: Urbana Ill. Died Oct. 28, 1986.

REINHART, BRUCE LLOYD, educator, mathematician; b. Wernersville, Pa., Oct. 20, 1930; s. Russell Lloyd and Ruth (Snyder) R.; m. Virginia May Seems, Jan. 29, 1955; children: Gail, Davis, Hugh. B.A., Lehigh U., 1952; M.A., Princeton U., 1954, Ph.D., 1956. Instr. Princeton U., 1955-56; instr. U. Chgo., 1956-58; research assoc. U. Mich., Ann Arbor, 1958-59; faculty U. Md., College Park, 1959-88; prof. math. U. Md., 1965-88; research scientist Research Inst. Advanced Studies, Balt., 1959-64. Author: Differential Geometry of Foliations, 1983, also articles. NATO fellow U. Strasbourg, France, 1961-62; Fulbright fellow U. Pisa, Italy, 1965-66. Mem. Am. Math. Soc., Math. Assn. Am., Société Mathématique de France. Home: University Park Md. Died July 19, 1988.

REINING, HENRY, JR., academic administrator, government affairs educator; b. Akron, Ohio, Sept. 15, 1907; s. Henry and Elizabeth (Schilling) R.; m. Janet Bolton, June 27, 1934 (dec. 1948); children: William Henry, Judith Ellen; m. Darline Diekmann, June 11, 1950 (dec. Nov. 1988); children: Susan, Barbara (dec.), Richard. BA, U. Akron, 1929, LLD (hon.), 1963; MA, Princeton U., 1930, PhD, 1932; Dr honoris causa, Brazilian Sch. Pub. Adminstrn., Rio de Janeiro, 1964, U. Bahia, Salvador, Brazil, 1964. Instr., asst. prof. govt. U. So. Calif., L.A., 1932-34, prof. pub. adminstrn., from 1947, dean Von Kleinsmid Ctr. Internat. and Pub. Affairs, 1967-73, dean emeritus and spl. asst. to pres. for govtl. relations, from 1973; instr. politics, rsch. assoc. local govt. surveys Princeton (N.J.) U., 1934-36; ednl. dir. Nat. Inst. Pub. Affairs, Washington, 1935-45; adj. prof. Am. U., 1936-42; professorial lectr. George Washington U., 1940-42; mgmt. cons. Rogers and Slade, N.Y.C., 1945-46; asst. to exec. dir. Port of N.Y. Authority, 1946-47; cons. various nat., internat. govtl. agys.; mem. regional loyalty bd. 12th Civil Svc. Region, 1949-51, U.S. Loyalty Rev. Bd., 1951-53; mem. safety adv. panel NASA, from 1968; mem. nat. adv. bd. Fed. Execs. Inst., 1968-73; prin. adviser So. Calif. Assn. Govts., 1969-70; chmn. L.A. County Charter Study Commn., 1957-58, L.A. City Charter Commn., 1966-70. Author: (with George A. Graham) Regulatory Administration, 1944, (with others) Elements of Public Administration, 1960, Cases of Public Personnel Administration, 1949. Mem. bd. regents Calif. Luth. Coll., from 1958. Mem. Fed. Coll. Coun. So. Calif. (hon. life), Am. Soc. Pub. Adminstrn. (past pres.), Nat. Assn. Schs. Pub. Affairs and Adminstrn. (past pres.), Nat. Civil Svc.League (past mem. nat. coun.), Civil Svc. League So. Calif. (past pres.), Soc. Personnel Adminstrn., Am. Polit. Sci. Assn. Lutheran. Home: Los Angeles Calif. Died Dec. 7, 1988; buried Inglewood (Calif.) Park Cemetary.

REISS, ERIC, physician; b. Vienna, Austria, Feb. 29, 1924; came to U.S., 1939, naturalized, 1944; s. Leo Josef and Marianne (Schrecker) R.; m. Louise Marie Zibold, Oct. 7, 1950; 1 son, Eric Leo. B.S., Randolph Macon Coll., 1943; M.D., Med. Coll. Va., 1948. Intern Phila. Gen. Hosp., 1948-50; asst. resident Barnes Hosp., 1954-55; Am. Cancer Soc. scholar metabolism div. dept. medicine Wash. U. Sch., Medicine, 1955-60, instr. medicine, 1956-58, asst. prof. medicine and preventive medicine, 1958-62; dir. Irene Walter Johnson Inst. Rehab., 1958-64, asso. prof. medicine, preventive medicine, 1962-64; chmn. dept. medicine Michael Reese Hosp. & Med. Center, Chgo., 1964-71; prof. medicine Chgo. Med. Sch., 1964-66, U. Chgo., 1969-72; prof., vice chmn. dept. medicine U. Miami (Fla.) Sch. Medicine, 1972-78, acting chmn., 1978-79, prof. medicine, 1979-88. Author: The Treatment of Burns, 1957. Served to maj. AUS, 1943-44, 1950-54. Fellow ACP; mem. Endocrine Soc., Am., So. socs. for clin. investigation, Soc. Exptl. Biology and Medicine, Am. Soc. Nephrology, Am. Fedn. Clin. Research, Central Soc. for Clin. Research, Assn. Am. Physicians, Phi Beta Kappa, Alpha Omega Alpha. Democrat. Home: Miami Fla. Died Jan. 27, 1988.

REITMAN, FRANK H., beverage company executive; b. Austria, 1886. Chmn. Reitman Industries, Newark, Galsworthy Inc., Newark; bd. dirs. Crest Wine & Spirits, Fleming & McClurg. Home: Orange N.J. †

REMEIKA, JOSEPH PETER, materials science researcher; b. Newark, N.J., Jan. 20, 1924; s. Joseph Frank and Eleanor (Machonis) R.; m. Marjorie R.; children—Virginia, Shirley. Mem. disting. tech. staff AT&T Bell Labs., Murray Hill, N.J., 1949-88. Contbr. over 300 articles to profl. jours. Patentee (25) in new materials and processes in physics. Fellow AAAS, Am. Phys. Soc. (Internat. Prize for New Materials 1984); mem. Materials Research Soc., N.Y. Acad. Scis. Died June 17, 1988.

REMINGTON, PAUL ELLSWORTH, utility consultant; b. Boulder, Colo., Nov. 29, 1894; s. Walter Wood and Sarah Lucinda (Porter) R.; m. Nondus Idona Maurer, Sept. 1, 1979. B.A. magna cum laude, U. Colo., 1917. With Mountain States Tel.&Tel. Co., 1912-58, auditor disbursements, 1924-28, chief accountant, 1928-36, comptroller, 1936-51, v.p., 1951-58; pub. utility cons. from 1958; lectr. Bus. U. Colo., 1960-65. Sec., dir., trustee, chmn. bldg. com. Denver Met. YMCA, from 1950. Mem. Nat. Accounting Assn. (past nat. dir., pres. Denver), Phi Beta Kappa, Phi Beta Kappa Assos., Beta Gamma Sigma, Beta Alpha Psi, Delta Sigma Pi, Acacia. Methodist. Clubs: Kiwanis (Boulder), Univ. (Boulder); Masons (32 deg.), Shriners. Home: Boulder Colo. Deceased.

RENDER, SYLVIA LYONS, literary critic, consultant; b. Atlanta, June 8, 1913; d. Lewis Rudolph and Mamie Beatrice (Foster) Lyons; married, July 14, 1935 (div. 1943); 1 son, Frank Wyatt II. B.S., Tenn. State U., 1934; postgrad., U. Chgo., 1934-35; M.A., Ohio State U., 1952; Ph.D., George Peabody Coll. for Tchrs., 1962. Employment interviewer, asst. statistician U.S. Employment Service, Columbus, Ohio, 1943-46; corr. analyst VA, Columbus, 1946-50; instr. Fla. A&M U., Tallahassee, 1952-56; asst. prof. English Fla. A&M U., 1960-62, assoc. prof., 1960-62, prof., 1962-63; prof. N.C. Central U., Durham, 1964-75; specialist in Afro-Am. History and culture, manuscript div. Library of Congress, Washington, 1973-82; free lance lectr., cons. Afro-Am. History and criticism, research and writer in lit. Alexandria, Va., from 1983; mem. adj. faculty George Peabody Coll. for Tchrs., Nashville, 1970, George Washington U., Washington, 1974-77. Author: Charles W. Chesnutt, 1980; editor: The Short Fiction of Charles W. Chesnutt, 1974, The Short Fiction of Charles W. Chestnutt, rev. edit. 1981. Bd. dirs. Hopkins House, Alexandria, 1980-81. Fellow So. Edn. Found., 1960-62; fellow Coop. Program in Humanities, Duke U., 1967-68; grantee Ford. Found., 1971, NEH, 1976. Mem. MLS (del. assembly 1975-77), Nat. Council Tchrs. English (workshop dir. 1982); grantee Daniel A.P. Murray Afro-Am. Culture Assn. (founder); mem. (pres. 1980-81 scholarship in her named), Afro-Am. Hist. and General Soc. (charter). Home: Alexandria Va. Deceased.

RENG, CARL R., academic administrator; b. Sioux Rapids, Iowa, May 13, 1910; s. John G. and Anna Marie (Severson) R.; m. Ruby I. McLaughlin, Aug. 15, 1935; children: Marilyn Ann, Barbara Diane. AB, Buena Vista Coll., 1932, LLD (hon.), 1952; MS, Drake U., 1940; EdD, U. Mo., 1948. High sch. prin. and coach Cooper, Iowa, 1932-35; supt. schs. Huxley, Iowa, 1935-40, Dunlap, Iowa, 1940-43; prof. ednl. adminstrn. U. Ark., 1948-51; pres. Ark. State U., from 1951. Lt. comdr. coll. V-12 program USN, 1943-46. Mem. Am. Assn. Sch. Adminstrs., NEA, Ark. Edn. Assn., Mason, Rotary, Phi Delta Kappa, Kappa Delta Pi. Methodist. Home: Jonesboro Ark. Died Feb. 12, 1988.

RENKEN, HENRY ALGERNON, naval officer, industry executive; b. Waynesboro, Va., Feb. 28, 1908; s. Henry John and Willie Viola (Koiner) R.; m. Isabel Bonvillian, May 30, 1938; children—Marian Souidee (Mrs. W.R. Hjortsberg), Rosalyn (Mrs. M.E. Mina); m. Ruth Virginia Schmidt, July 26, 1952; 1 son, Henry Carl. Student, Washington and Lee U., 1925-26; B.S., U.S. Naval Acad., 1931; student, U.S. Navy Postgrad. Sch., 1938-39, Naval War Coll., 1945. Commd. ensign U.S. Navy, 1931, advanced through grades to rear adm., 1959; served destroyers, battleships, logistic support ships 1931-38, in destroyers, 1940-44; comdr. destroyer (U.S.S. Hambleton), 1942-44; mem. staff (CINC Atlantic Fleet), 1946; planner (Navy Examining Center), 1947; supr. devel. post World War II (Navy Tng. Courses), 1947-49; comdr. (Destroyer Div. 102), 1949-50; supr. revision (Navy Tact. Doctrine), 1951-53; mem.

staff (COM1stFLT), 1953-55; comdr. amphibious flagship (U.S.S. Mt. McKinley), 1956; command ship (U.S.S. Northampton), 1957-59; dir. logistics plans (Navy Dept.), 1959-60; comdr. logistics (7th Fleet), 1961-62; asst. chief naval operations for gen. planning and programming (Navy Dept.), 1963-65; comdr. service force (Atlantic fleet), 1965-67; comdt. (9th Naval Dist.), Great Lakes, Ill., 1967-70; ret.; v.p. Tempel Steel Co., Chgo., 1970-71; v.p. Inter-Probe Inc., North Chicago, Ill., 1973-86. Decorated Silver Star medal, Legion of Merit with 3 gold stars, Bronze Star medal, D.S.M. Home: Lake Bluff Ill. Died July 20, 1986; buried Arlington (Va.) Nat. Cemetery.

REVZIN, MARVIN E., oral surgeaon; b. Detroit, May 28, 1922; s. Samuel and Sarah (Baxter) R.; m. Elaine Levy, Feb. 14, 1948; children: Michael, Susan. BA, Wayne State U., 1942, MA, 1952; DDS, U. Detroit, 1951, MS, 1954. Diplomate Am. Bd. Oral Surgeons (sec.-treas. 1972, v.p. 1977, pres. 1978). Intern Detroit Receiving Hosp., 1951-52, resident, 1952-54; asst. oral surgeon, dir. dental edn. Henry Ford Hosp., Detroit, 1954-62; lectr. oral surgery U. Detroit Sch. Dentistry, 1954-62, prof., chmn. dept. oral surgery and radiology, 1962-65, asst. dean, prof., chmn. dept., 1965-66, assoc. dean., prof., chmn. dept., 1966-67, acting dean, 1967; assoc. dean for hosp. affairs, prof., chmn. oral surgery U. So. Calif. Sch. Dentistry, L.A., 1970-75; dean, prof. oral and maxillofacial surgery U. Mo. Dch. Dentistry, Kansas City, from 1975; mem. hosp. adv. com. USPHS Hosp., Detroit, 1963-67; dir. dental edn. ADA project, Vietnam, 1967-73; external assessor U. Malaya, 1973; grad. lect. speech pathology Wayne State U., 1947-51; first oral surgeon Project HOPE, Indonesia, 1961; cons. U.S. Naval Hosp., San Diego, 1973-75, VA Hosp., Long Beach, Calif., 1974-74, VA Ctr., Leavenworth, Kans., 1975-76, VA Hosp., Kansas City, Kans., 1976, VA Hosp., Topeka, 1976; mem. exec. com. Profl. Staff Assn. L.A. County/U. So. Calif. Med. Ctr., 1970-75; mem. dental hygiene adv. com. Johnson County (Kans.) Community Coll., 1975-76. Editorial bd. Jour. Dental Edn., from 1970; contbr. articles to profl. jours. Mem. profl. adv. com. Mayor's Com. for Health Care, Detroit, 1966-67; bd. dirs. Truman Med. Ctr.; trustee U. Kansas City, Mo. Cancer Found. With USAAF, 1941-45. Recipient Outstanding Tchr. awards U. Detroit, 1962-64, Mayor's Commendation City of Detroit, 1967, Chuong My Bio Tihn award Govt. of S. Vietnam, 1973, Meritorious award medal Vietnam Council on Fgn. Relations, 1973, Cogswell award in oral surgery, 1973, Service award Marsh Robinson Acad. Oral Surgeons, 1975, William Gies Found. award for outstanding achievement in field, 1982; named Man of Year U. Detroit. Fellow Am. Coll. Dentists, Internat. Assn. Oral Surgeons; mem. ADA (chmn. council Nat. Bd. Dental Examiners 1977), Mich. Dental Assn., Mo. Dental Assn., Detroit Dental Assn. (pres. 1963-64), Greater Kansas City Dental Soc., Am. Soc. Oral Surgeons (com. chmn.), Gt. Lakes Soc. Oral Surgeons, So. Calif. Soc. Oral Surgeons, Chalmers J. Lyons Acad. Oral Surgeons (pres. 1961), AAAS, Internat. Assn. Dental Rsch., Am. Speech and Hearing Assn., AAUP, So. Calif. Acad. Oral Pathology, Soc. for Internat. Devel., Fedn. Dentaire Internat., Arista, Omicron Kappa Upsilon. Home: Kansas City Mo. Died Nov. 29, 1985.

REY, ALEJANDRO, actor; b. Buenos Aires, Feb. 8, 1930; came to U.S., 1960, naturalized, 1967; s. Jose and Joaquina (Pereiro) R.; m. Joyce Evelyn Bowman, May 24, 1969 (div.); 1 child, Brandon. Appeared in numerous motion pictures including Guacho (selected for Venice Flim Festival), 1952, Tea and Sympathy, 1955, Desperate Hours, 1957, Five Finger Exersize, 1958, Bajo el Cielo Andaluz, 1959, Fun in Acuapulco, 1963, Synanon, 1964, Blindfold, 1965, Sandpit Generals, 1970, Imulsion, 1970, The Wild Pack, 1972, Moscow on the Hudson, Mr. Majestyk, Blindfold, Swarm, Cuba, Synanon, Terrorvision, The Ninth Configuration; co-starred in TV series Slattery's People, 1964, The Flying Nun, 1964-70; guest star TV series Dallas, Gunsmoke, Naked City, Fantasy Island, Love Boat, others; dir. episodes TV shows Mary Hartman, Mary Hartman, The Facts of Life. Served with Argentine Army, 1950-51. Mem. Actors Studio West (trustee). Home: Los Angeles Calif. Died May 21, 1987.

REYNOLDS, FRED CURTIS, physician; b. Texarkana, Tex., Feb. 19, 1908; s. Joel Burr and Nellie (Sain) R.; m. Phyllis M. Terry, Feb. 1, 1945; children: Mary Ann Reynolds Krey, Barbara Jane Reynolds Wingle, Fred Curtis. A.B., Washington U., 1931, M.D., 1934. Intern surgery Barnes Hosp., St. Louis, 1934-35; asst. resident surgery 1935-36, neurosurgery fellow, 1936-37; preceptorship orthopedic surgery under Dr. E.B. Mumford, Indpls., 1937-43; practice medicine, specializing orthopedic surgery St. Louis, 1946-86; staff Barnes Hosp. Group, 1946-86, St. Luke's West Hosp., 1980-86; asst. Washington U. Sch. Medicine, 1946-55, prof. orthopedic surgery, 1956-72, prof. emeritus, 1972-86; chmn. residency review com. orthopedic surgery Am. Bd. Orthopedic Surgery, 1958-61, v.p. bd., 1961, pres., 1962-64; mem. com. on skeletal system NRC, 1958-63, 66-70; mem. surgery study section NIH, 1962-65, mem. tng. grant com., 1968-72; team physician St. Louis Football Cardinals, 1962-72. Editor: Fractures, Dislocations and Sprains (Key, Conwell), rev. edit, 1960; editorial bd.: Jour. Bone and Joint Surgery, 1954-61; contbr. articles to profl. publs. Trustee Orthopaedic Research and Edn. Found., 1968-74. Served with M.C. U.S. Army, 1943-46. Recipient Alumni citation Washington U., 1978. Mem. A.C.S. (gov. 1956-59, 65-68), Am. Surg. Assn., AMA, Am. Orthopedic Assn., Clin. Orthopedic Soc. (pres. 1960), Am. Acad. Orthopedic Surgeons (chmn. instructional course com., editor instructional course lectures 1959-61, chmn. com. on grad. edn. 1961-64, pres. 1965, mem. com. on chymopapain 1974), Assn. Orthopedic Chmn. (pres. 1972), St. Louis Med. Soc. (hon.). Home: Saint Louis Mo. Died Oct. 10, 1986.

REYNOLDS, GEORGE STANLEY, psychology educator; b. Waterville, Maine, May 18, 1936; s. George Stanley and Mildred Philips (Chapman) R.; m. Dalia Veronika Grebliunas, Sept. 7, 1963; children: Susan Anastazija, Andrew George. AB summa cum laude, Harvard U., 1957, PhD, 1960. Instr. Harvard U., Boston, 1960-62; from asst. to assoc. prof. U. Chgo., 1962-66; prof. psychology U. Calif.-San Diego, 1966-87, chmn. dept., 1970-74; cons. various pub. firms. Author: A Primer of Operant Conditioning; co-author: Introduction to Contemporary Psychology; contbr. articles to profl. jours. Mem. Psychonomic Soc., Phi Beta Kappa, Sigma Xi. Home: Rancho Santa Fe Calif. Died Sept. 7, 1987; cremated.

REYNOLDS, JOSEPH GARDINER, JR., stained glass artist; b. Wickford, R.I., Apr. 9, 1886; s. Joseph Gardiner and Rebecca Granger (Tillinghast) R.; m. Bertha Clogston, Aug. 22, 1911 (dec. May 1962); m. 2d, Katherine MacKillop, June 17, 1963. Ed., R.I. pub. sch.; grad., R.I. Sch. Design, 1907; student, Eng., France, Italy, Spain, 1920, 21, 35, 37. Designer stained glass windows 1907-20; owner studio, dir. partnership(designing and making stained glass windows) Reynolds, Francis & Rohnstock, Belmont, Mass., from from 1921; pres. corp. Reynolds, Francis & Rohnstock Inc. (then Joseph G. Reynolds Asscs. Inc.), Belmont, 1948-66. Prin. workds appear in Princeton U. Chapel, St. Bartholomews Church, N.Y.C., Riverside Ch., N.Y.C., Cathedral St. John the Divine, N.Y.C., East Liberty Presbyn. Ch., Pitts., Presbyn. Ch., Glens Falls, N.Y., Mercersburg (Pa.) Acad. Chapel, Houghton Meml. Chapel, Wellesly Coll., Am. Meml. Cemetery Chapel, Belleau, France, American Ch. in Paris, France, Quai d'Orsay, and numerous other places; co-author apse windows and Declaration-Constitution window of Washington Cathedral, south transept Rose window and the lancets beneath Washington Cathedral, others. Awarded Medal of Merit Boston Soc. Arts and Crafts, 1929, gold medal Boston Tercentenary Art Exhbn., 1930, Medal of Merit Paris Internat. Expn., 1937, AIA Craftsmanship Gold Medal, 1950, R.I. Sch. of Design Alumni award, 1963. Mem. Medieval Acad. of Am., Am. Fedn. of Arts, Nat. Inst. of Soc. Scis., Masons, Providence Art Club, Nat. Early Am. Glass Club. Baptist. Home: Belmont Mass. †

REYNOLDS, PAUL REVERE, literary agent, author; b. N.Y.C., July 21, 1904; s. Paul R. and Amelia (Stead) R.; m. Ruth Wood, Mar. 21, 1940; children: Robin Reynolds, Rebecca Reynolds Wells, Jane Reynolds Swain. BA, Williams Coll., 1926. Lit. agt. 1927-78; pres. Paul R. Reynolds, Inc., N.Y.C., 1956-78. Author: The Writing Trade, 1949, The Writer and His Markets, 1959, The Writing and Selling of Non-Fiction, 1963, The Writing and Selling of Fiction, 1965, A Professional Guide to Marketing Manuscripts, 1968, The Non-Fiction Book, 1969, The Middle Man: Adventures of a Literary Agent, 1972, biography Guy Carleton. Mem. Soc. Author's Reps. (founder, pres. numerous yrs.). Home: Southbury Conn. Died June 10, 1988.

REYNOLDS, PAUL RUSSELL, clergyman; b. Bushnell, Ill., Jan. 15, 1891; s. Othello E. and Mary Katherine (Caldwell) R.; m. Charlotte Louise Belknap, May 30, 1921; children: Robert Belknap, Helen Belknap (dec.), Paul Russell, Barbara Louise. AB, Ellsworth Coll., 1914; BD, Chgo. Theol. Sem., 1918, DD, 1928; AM, Columbia U., 1928. Ordained to ministry Congl. Ch., 1918. Pastor Congl. Ch., Blencoe, Iowa, 1914-15; assoc. Western Office Congl. Edn. Soc., 1919-21; missionary Am. Bd. Commrs. for Fgn. Missions, Fenchow, China, 1921-36; field sec. Div. Christian Edn. Congl. and Christian Chs., from 1936; nat. sec. Young Adult and Family Life Program Div. Christian Edn., Congl. and Christian Chs., 1944-54; dir. Pleasant Hill (Tenn.) Community Ctr., minister Community Ch. Contbr. articles to religious jours. Army sec. YMCA, 1918; bd. dirs. Merom (Ind.) Inst. Chaplain U.S. Army, 1918-19. Mem. Internat. Coun. Religious Edn. (bd. dirs.), Am. Legion. Home: Pleasant Hill Tenn. †

REYNOLDS, SAMUEL WILLIAMS, coal company executive; b. Omaha, Aug. 11, 1890; s. Joel Barlow and Emily (Van Blarcom) R.; m. Louise Northrup, July 15, 1916; children: Louise Reynolds Haugh, Emily Reynolds Baker, Aurel Reynolds Couch. Student pub. schs., Omaha. Pres. Reynolds-Updike Coal Co., Omaha, 1924-88; interim U.S. senator, 1954. With AC, 1917-18; col. Specialist Corps U.S. Army, World War II. Recipient Freedom Found. award for 1952 Mo. River flood fight, 1953. Mem. Am. Legion, Masons, Shriners. Home: Omaha Nebr. Died Mar. 20, 1988, buried Omaha.

REYNOLDS, THOMAS JAMES, lawyer; b. North Vassalboro, Maine, Mar. 17, 1892; s. Thomas Lang and Lucy Upton (Brown) R.; m. Valdemir Munro, Mar. 4, 1919; children: Priseilla Alden, Ruth Munro. AB, Colby Coll., 1914; LLB, Harvard U., 1917; grad., Harvard Ensign Sch., 1918. Bar: Maine 1917, Calif. 1920. Pvt. practice Waterville, Maine, 1917-18; v.p., gen. counsel So. Calif. Gas Co. Ensign USNR, 1918-19. Mem. Am. Legion, California club, Downtown Bus. Men's Assn., Alpha Tau Omega. Republican. Congregationalist. Home: Beverly Hills Calif. †

REYNOLDS, WILLIAM GLASGOW, lawyer; b. Dover, Tenn., July 15, 1911; s. John Lacey and Harriett Edwina (Glasgow) R.; m. Nancy Bradford du Pont, May 18, 1940; children: Katherine Glasgow (Mrs. John M. Sturges, Jr.), William Bradford, Mary Parminter (Mrs. John Schofield Savage), Cynthia du Pont (Mrs. Kermit Nelson Farris). A.B., Vanderbilt U., 1932, J.D. summa cum laude, 1935. Bar: Tenn. 1935, D.C. bar 1964, also U.S. Supreme Ct 1945. Gen. practice Nashville, 1934-35; with E. I. du Pont de Nemours & Co., 1935-71, chief counsel advt., pub. relations and cen. research depts., 1954-71; with firm Morris, Nichols, Arsht & Tunnell, Wilmington, Del., 1972-87; resident counsel Remington Arms Co., Bridgeport, Conn., 1940-41; with Office Gen. Counsel, U.S. Navy, 1942-43, Exec. Office Sec. Navy, 1944, Office Asst. Sec. Navy, 1945; Permanent mem. jud. conf. 3d Jud. Circuit U.S., 1955-87; rep. chem. industry Water Resources Policy Com., 1950; mem. adv. com. Patent Office, Dept. Commerce, 1954; mem. Internat. Conf. Indsl. and Mcpl. Air Pollution, 1949; chmn. Nat. Com. Assay U.S. Mints, 1958; Am. indsl. rep. Com. Experts on Internat. Trademark Treaties, 1969-71, U.S. Govt. rep., 1972-73; del. numerous internat. confs.; dir. Del. Trust Co., Wilmington, 1974-85, mem. exec. com., 1976-85, trust com., 1976-85; mem. vis. com. Law Sch., Vanderbilt U., 1968, mem. chancellor's council, 1968-87, chmn. Law Sch. devel. council, 1968. Author: The Law of Water and Water Rights in the Tenn. River Valley, 1934, Local Restrictions on the Pollution of Inland Waters, 1948, Trademark Management—A Guide for Businessmen, 1955, Trademark Selection, 1960, The Chemical Engineer and Public Liability Law, 1962, A Brief for Corporate Counsel, 1964, Legal Servicing of Industrial Publicity, 1967, Planning a Bonsai Collection, 1968, Reynolds History Annotated, 1978, also numerous articles, treatises. Alt. del. Rep. Nat. Conv., 1956; mem. Rep. Nat. Com. Assos., 1956-65; bd. dirs., sec. Rencourt Found. Del., 1955-87; bd. dirs. United Community Fund No. Del., 1948-53, exec. com., 1949-51; trustee, chmn. bldg. com. Children's Home, Claymont and Wilmington, 1946-47, pres., 1947-51; bd. dir., mem. bldg. com. Del. Art Center, 1948-64. Recipient Founders medal Vanderbilt U. Law Sch., 1935, U.S. Navy commendations, 1943, 45. Mem. Mfg. Chemists Assn. (chmn. lawyers adv. com. 1954), U.S. Trademark Assn. (chmn. bd., pres. 1964-65), Assn. Internationale pour la Protection de la Propertie Industrielle, Am., Fed., D.C., Del. bar assns., Del., Tenn. trial lawyers assns., Nashville Bar Assn., Navy League U.S., Vanderbilt Alumni Assn. (bd. dirs. 1961-64), Vanderbilt Law Alumni (pres. 1970-71), Am., Pa. Bonsai societies, Sons Colonial Wars in Am., SAR, Order of Coif, Phi Kappa Psi. Episcopalian (past warden, vestryman, chmn. bldg. com.). Clubs: Confrerie des Chevaliers du Tastevin (grand officier Wilmington chpt. 1972, mem. nat. council 1973, grant intendant Eastern U.S. 1975, delé ge general 1976, grand pelier gen. U.S. 1977, of N. Am. 1978, bd. dirs., pres. found. 1979-81), Chevy Chase (Md.) Country; Griffith Island (Ont., Can.); Aurora Gun (Greenville, Del.), Greenville Country (Greenville, Del.) (bd. dirs. 1962-65), Vicmead Hunt (Greenville, Del.); Wilmington. Home: Wilmington Del. Died Jan. 29, 1987; buried Greenville, Del.

RHINELANDER, PHILIP HAMILTON, educator; b. Cambridge, Mass., Jan. 1, 1908; s. Philip M. and Helen (Hamilton) R.; m. Virginia Roberts, July 9, 1932; children: Helen H., Virginia K., Philip M., Elizabeth Jane. AB summa cum laude, Harvard U., 1929, LLB, 1932, PhD, 1949. Bar: Mass. 1932. Assoc. Choate, Hall & Stewart, Boston, 1932-40; instr. Harvard U., Boston, 1949-51, lectr. philosophy and gen. edn., 1952, chmn. com. on gen. edn., dir. gen. edn., 1952-55; dean Sch. Humanities and Scis. Stanford (Calif.) U., 1956-61, subsquently prof. philosophy, Olive Palmer prof. humanities emeritus. Mem. Medieval Acad. Am., Phi Beta Kappa. Home: Stanford Calif. Died Mar. 20, 1987.

RHOADES, OTTO L., electric company executive; b. Logan, Kans., July 6, 1889; s. Joseph R. and Laura (Stephenson) R.; m. Hazel T. Wilcop, June 25, 1924. Student pub. schs. Founder, chmn., gen. mgr. Sun Electric Corp., Chgo., later chmn. bd. dirs. Mem. Masons. Home: Crystal Lake Ill. †

RHOADS, PAUL SPOTSWOOD, physician, educator; b. Terre Haute, Ind., Mar. 12, 1898; s. Harry B. and Mary (Spotswood) R.; m. Hester Chapin, Dec. 25, 1924; children: George, Paula Rhoads Menary, Hester, Mary, Emily Rhoads Johnson; m. Mila Pierce. BS, U. Chgo., 1922; MD, Rush Med. Coll., 1924; honorary doctoral degrees, Earlham Coll., Ind. U. With faculty Rush Med. Coll., Chgo., 1926-35; prof. medicine, then prof. emeritus Northwestern U. Med. Sch., 1935-71; formerly chief, then chmn. emeritus dept. medicine Chgo. Wesley Meml. Hosp.; pvt. practice Chgo., Evanston, Ill. and Richmond, Ind.; dir. patient care Cook County Hosp., TB and Contagious Diseases Hosps. Cook County, Ill., Presby. Hosp., Chgo.; researcher McCormick Inst. (now Hoektoen Inst.), Chgo.; chmn. bd. govs. Inst. of Medicine, Chgo., editor quar. publ.; developer programs of med. edn. Reid Meml. Hosp., Richmond. Contbr. research papers to profl. jours. Mem. mem. com. fgn. bd. Am. Presby. Ch. Recipient numerous honors Ind. State Tchrs. Coll., Rush Med. Sch., Greater Chgo. Ch. Fedn., Inst. Medicine, Chgo., AMA, Northwestern U. Med. Ctr., including Ann. Rhoads Lectureship-Infectious Disease Day held at Northwestern U. Med. Ctr., Ann. Rhoads Lectr. in Humanity and Medicine Reid Meml. Hosp. Mem. AMA (editor-in-chief Archives of Internal Medicine 11 yrs., organizer com. on medicine and religion 1960), Am. Soc. Profl. Microbiologists, Cen. Soc. Clin. Research, Soc. Exptl. Biology in Medicine, Chgo. Inst. Medicine . Home: Richmond Ind. Died Jan. 24, 1987.

RHODES, FRED H(OFFMAN), chemical engineer; b. Rochester, Ind., June 30, 1889; s. Eden Ellsworth and Clara Louise (Hoffman) R.; m. Ethel Marion Bundy, Aug. 11, 1915; 1 dau., Clara Helen. AB, Wabash Coll., 1910; PhD, Cornell U., 1914. Asst. in chemistry Cornell U., 1910-14; instr. in chemistry U. Mont., 1914-15, Cornell U., 1915-17; dir. rsch., chem. dept. Barrett Co., mfrs. coal tar products, Frankford, Pa., 1917-20; prof. indsl. chemistry Cornell U., 1920, then dir. Sch. Chem. and Metall. Engring. and Herbert Fisk Johnson prof. indsl. chemistry emeritus., trustee. Author: Patent Law for Chemists, Engineers and Executives, 1931, Technical Report Writing, 1941, Elements of Patent Law, 1950; contbr. to indsl. and engring. chem. publs.; holder several patents covering improvements in refining coal tar products. Mem. Am. Chem. Soc., Phi Beta Kappa, Sigma Xi, Alpha Chi Sigma, Tau Beta Pi, Phi Kappa Phi. Home: DeLand Fla. †

RHODES, IRWIN SEYMOUR, lawyer; b. Cin., Nov. 21, 1901; s. Solomon and Lina (Silberberg) R.; m. Mary Elizabeth Frechtling, Dec. 12, 1941; children: Elana Rhodes Byrd, Irwin Lawrence. BA, U. Cin., 1921; LLB, Harvard U., 1924; MA, Xavier U., 1962. Bar: Ill. 1924, Ohio 1925, D.C. 1978. Pvt. practice Chgo., 1924-29, Cin., from 1929; cons. jud. recs. Gen. Svcs. Adminstrn., 1969; co-dir. Irwin S. and Elizabeth F. Rhodes Legal History Collection, U. Okla.; chmn. com. for Preservation John Marshall Papers, 1953, mem. editorial bd., 1958-59, chmn. spl. com., 1957-59. Author-editor: The Papers of John Marshall, A Descriptive Calendar, 1969; editor Pub. Utilities and Carrier Svc., 1926-29; contbg. editor Ohio Jurisprudence, 1933-35; contbr. articles to legal jours. Bd. fellows U. Okla., from 1970. Named hon. Ky. col. Mem. ABA (chmn. communist tactics, strategy and objectives com. 1962), Fed. Bar Assn. (nat. law observance com.), Cin. Bar Assn. (chmn. com. for preservation legal hist. documents 1961), Cin. Law Library Assn., Md. Hist. Soc., Cin. Hist. Soc., Cosmos Club, Nat. Lawyers Club (Washington), Harvard Bus. Sch. Club, Cincinnati Club, Phi Beta Kappa (hon.). Home: Cincinnati Ohio. Died Mar. 17, 1985; buried Spring Grove Cemetery Mausoleum, Cin.

RHODES, WILLIAM LUTHER, JR., state justice; b. Loris, S.C., May 14, 1918; s. William Luther and Gussie Jane (Worley) R.; m. Margaret Elizabeth Rentz, Apr. 23, 1947; children—Nancy Elizabeth, Jane, Jennifer Ethel. B.A., Duke U., 1939; LL.B., U. S.C., 1942, J.D., 1970. Bar: S.C. bar 1942. Practiced law Hampton, S.C., 1946-60; resident judge 14th Jud. Circuit Ct. of S.C., 1960-75; assoc. justice S.C. Supreme Ct., 1975-86. Mem. S.C. Ho. of Reps., 1950-60, chmn. ways and means com. Served with USAAF, 1942-46. Baptist. Home: Varnville S.C. Died Apr. 8, 1986; buried Varnville Cemetery.

RIBOUD, JEAN, oil service and electronics company executive; b. Lyon, France, Nov. 15, 1919; s. Camille and Helene (Frachon) R.; m. Krishna Roy, Oct. 1, 1949; 1 son, Christophe. Grad., Faculte de Droit, Ecoles des Scis. Politiques, Paris, 1939. Exec. v.p. Schlumberger Ltd., 1963-65, pres., chief exec. officer, 1965-75, chmn. bd., pres., chief exec. officer, 1975-83, chmn. bd., chief exec. officer, 1983-85; mem. internat. council Morgan Guaranty Trust Co. Mem. MIT Corp. Clubs: Links (N.Y.C.), Sky (N.Y.C.), Links Golf (N.Y.C.), Blind Brook (N.Y.C.); Desert Forest Golf (Carefree, Ariz.); Augusta (Ga.) Nat. Golf; La Boulie (Paris). Home: New York N.Y. Died Oct. 20, 1985.

RICCHIUTO, D. EDWARD, advertising executive; b. Jersey City, Mar. 30, 1930; s. Angelo and Concetta (D'Amico) R.; m. Louise Jean Maino, Apr. 25, 1955; children: Edward, Steven. B.B.A., Pace Coll., 1951; M.B.A., CCNY, 1953. Ptnr. Bklyn. Deer Distbn., 1951-53; pres. H. & G. Promotions, Inc., N.Y.C., 1959-87; exec. v.p. Hicks & Griest, Inc., N.Y.C., 1963-87; chief exec. officer Hicks & Greist Advt. Inc., 1974-87, chief exec. officer, pres., 1976-87; v.p., dir. Ricchi Realty Co., Jersey City, 1960-87; exec. v.p., dir. Ramm-Retail Action Micro Market, Inc.; ptnr. A & D Mgmt. Real Estate, Greenwood Village Mgmt., Norwood Gardens Mgmt., Franklyn Gardens Realty; dir. I.S. Kogan Pub. Relations., Transmedia. Mem. Internat. Radio and TV Soc., Sale Execs. Club N.Y.C., Internat. Platform Assn. Club: N.Y. Athletic. Home: Ridgefield N.J. Died Apr. 8, 1987.

RICE, EUGENE FRANKLIN, sugar producer; b. Louisville, Apr. 1, 1892; s. Ellsworth and Louana (Radcliff) R.; m. Lula A. Piper, June 21, 1920; children: Eugene Franklin, Lucy Willard. Student, U. Pa., 1919-20. With L.&N. R.R., Louisville, 1911-14; asst. engr. on r.r. valuation ICC, Chattanooga, 1915-16; resident engr. r.r. constrn. dept. N.C.& St. Louis Ry., Nashville, 1916-17; asst. engr. Cen. Aquirre Sugar Co., P.R., 1920-24, v.p., mgr., 1936-46, exec. v.p., gen. mgr., 1946-53, pres., trustee; mgr. Cen. Machete Co., Guayama, P.R., 1924-30, pres., bd. dirs.; mgr. Cen. Cortada, Santa Isabel, P.R., 1930-36; pres., bd. dirs. Ponce and Guayama R.R. Co.; bd. dirs. P.R.&Am. Ins. Co., Commonwealth Oil Refining Co. Contbr. articles to profl. jours. With Am. Expeditionary Force, 1918, Capt. P.R. State Guard, 1942-45. Mem. Asociaciòn de Productores de Azucar de P.R. (bd. dirs.), ASCE, Colegio de Ingenieros de P.R., P.R. Sugar Technologists Assn., Masons (32 degree), Shriners. Home: Aquirre P.R. †

RICE, JOHN STANLEY, diplomat, business executive; b. Arendtsville, Pa., Jan. 28, 1899; s. Leighton H. and Florence Jane (Hartman) R.; m. Luene Rogers, Nov. 10, 1934; 1 child, Ellen Frances. BS, Gettysburg Coll., 1921. Pres. Rice Trew & Rice Co., Biglerville, Pa., 1929-58; senator State of Pa., 1932-40, senate pres. pro tem, mem. Pa. Liquor Control Bd., 1955-56, mem. Gov.'s cabinet, sec. property and supplies, 1956-57; sec. of Commonwealth of Pa., 1958-61; ambassador to The Netherlands from 1961. Chmn. bd. trustees Gettysburg Coll., 1939-72, acting pres., 1955-56; trustee Luth. Theol. Sem., Gettysburg, mem. bd. pensions United Luth. Ch. in Am.; Dem. nominee for gov. Pa., 1946; chmn. Dem. State Cen. Com., 1959-61. Col. USAAF, 1942-45. Decorated Legion of Merit. Mem. Am. Legion, VFW, Elks, Masons, Phi Gamma Delta, Phi Beta Kappa. Home: Fort Lauderdale Fla. Died Aug. 2, 1985.

RICE, LEONARD WILLIAM, academic administrator; b. Garland, Utah, Dec. 9, 1913; s. Ira Quince and Myra (Winegar) R.; m. Ruth D. Miller, May 4, 1941; children: Michael Cutler, Julia Ellen. BA in English, Brigham YOung U., 1941; MA, U. Wash., 1943, PhD, 1950; postdoctoral student English, Yale U., 1959-60. Prof. English Brigham Young U., 1941-59, chmn. dept., 1955-57, dean Coll. Humanities and Social Scis., 1957-59; prof. English R.I. Coll., 1969-62; pres. Oreg. Coll. Edn. (now Western Oreg. State Coll.), Monmouth, 1962-77; pres. Utah Council Tchrs. English, 1957-59; pres. N.W. Assn. Secondary and Higher Schs., 1971-74. With AUS, 1943-46, PTO. Home: Salem Oreg. Died Aug. 1, 1986; buried Belcrest Meml. Cemetery, Salem, Oreg.

RICE, NEIL W., business executive; b. Boston, Nov. 7, 1892; s. Charles G. and Anne (Proctor) R.; m. Emma Mandell, June 9, 1917 (div.); children: Charles G. II, Emily P. (Mrs. George C. Scott Jr.), Anne (Mrs. Carl E. Berntsen Jr.); m. Helen Shigo Pryor, Feb. 1, 1947. Student pvt. sch. With U.S. Smelting, Refining & Mining Co., from 1914, asst. to the pres., 1916-19, 2d v.p., 1919-22, v.p., 1922-23, 34-38, v.p. in charge Western ops., 1923-34, pres., 1938-45, chmn. bd., from 1945; pres., bd. dirs. N.W. Rice Co., Richmond-Eureka Mining Co.; bd. dirs. U.S. Fuel Co., Agawam Oil Co., Island Creek Coal Co., 1st Nat. Bank Boston, United Shoe Machinery Corp. Home: Hardwick Mass. †

RICE, PHILIP LAVERGNE, judge; b. Lihue, Hawaii, July 22, 1886; s. William Hyde and Mary (Waterhouse) R.; m. Flora Benton, Sept. 12, 1911. Student, U. Chgo., 1914-16. Supr. sugar plantation Koloa, Hawaii, 1907-10; ins. agt. 1913-14, pvt. practice, 1916-43; judge cir. and juvenile cts. 5th (Jud.) Cir., Lihue, Hawaii; assoc. justice Supreme Ct. Hawaii, until 1956, chief justice, from 1956. With U.S. Army, 1917-18. Mem. ABA, Inst. Jud. Adminstrn., Conf. Chief Justices, Social Sci. Assn. Honolulu, Bar Assn. Hawaii, Am. Legion (past dept. comdr.), Pacific Club, Kauai Yacht Club, Phi Delta Phi. Republican. Home: Honolulu Hawaii. †

RICE, STEPHEN OSWALD, communications engineer; b. Shedds, Oreg., Nov. 29, 1907; s. Stephen Rice and Selma Bergren (Rice); m. Inez Biersdorf, Feb. 26, 1931; children: Carole, Joan, Stephen. B.S. in Elec. Engring., Oreg. State U., 1929, Sc.D. (hon.), 1961. Mem. tech. staff Bell Telephone Labs., N.Y.C., 1930-58, Murray Hill, N.J., 1958-72; vis. lectr. applied physics Harvard U., Cambridge, Mass., 1958. Fellow IEEE (Mervin J. Kelley award 1965, Nat. Telecom '74 award, Alexander Graham Bell medal 1983); mem. Nat. Acad. Engring. Died Nov. 18, 1986, buried El Camino Meml. Park, San Diego.

RICH, BUDDY (BERNARD RICH), drummer; b. Bklyn., June 30, 1917; m. Marie Rich, Aug 1952; 1 dau. Appeared with: Joe Marsala at Hickory House, 1938; with other bands including, Bunny Berigan, 1938, Artie Shaw, 1939, Tommy Dorsey, 1939-42, Benny Carter, 1942, 44-46; organized own band, 1946; toured with, Jazz at the Philharmonic, 1947, Ventura and Chubby Jackson in the Big Four, 1951, with, Harry James, 1953-54, European tour, 1957; actor TV, 1957-58; also singer and tap dancer.; Recs. include Take It Away. Served with USMCR, 1942-44. Recipient Metronome mag. award, 1948, award Down Beat mag., 1941, 42, 44, 67, 70-72, gold award Esquire mag., 1947, critics poll award Down Beat, 1953-54, 68; named to Down Beat Hall of Fame, 1974. Died Apr. 2, 1987.

RICH, JOHN FLETCHER, lawyer; b. Lincoln, R.I., Apr. 3, 1908; s. William G. and Bessie G. (Fletcher) R.; A.B., Dartmouth Coll., 1930; LL.B., Harvard U., 1933; m. Dorothy N. Pettingell, Dec. 23, 1933; children—Nancy W., Cynthia C., Susan D., William P. Bar:N.Y., 1934, Mass., 1933; practiced in Buffalo, N.Y. and Boston; counsel Rich, May, Bilodeau, & Flaherty, Boston; chmn., trustee Commonwealth Energy System; dir. Palm Beach Inc., Algonquin Gas Trans. Co. Mem. ABA, Mass. Bar Assn., Boston Bar Assn., Phi Beta Kappa. Congregationalist. Clubs: Athletic (N.Y.C.); Union, Harvard (Boston). Died 1987. Home: Jaffrey N.H.

RICHARDS, FLETCHER D(OUGHITT), advertising company executive; b. New Philadelphia, Ohio, Aug. 2, 1892; s. Thomas Jerman Walker and Anna L. (Luethi) R.; m. Elsa Lillian Schoenberg, May 3, 1924; 1 son, Fletcher Doughitt. AB, Ohio State U., 1916. Advt. solicitor Columbua (Ohio) Citizen, summer 1916; salesman E.T. Miller Co., 1916-17; v.p., treas. Campbell-Ewald Co., Detroit, 1928-35; pres. Campbell-Ewald Co. of N.Y., Inc., advt., 1935-42, pres., gen. mgr., 1942-48; pres., chmn. Fletcher D. Richards, Inc., 1948-55, chmn., 1955-59; pres., chief exec. officer Fletcher Richards, Calkins & Holden, Inc., 1959-60, chmn. exec. com, 1960-64, hon. chmn., 1964-66; hon. chmn. Fletcher Richards, Inc., from 1966. Trustee Greenwich (Conn.) Hosp., from 1959, pres., 1961-63; trustee Conn. Hosp. Assn. Mem. Am. Assn. Advt. Agencies (dir.), Nat. Outdoor Advt. Bur. (pres., dir.), Ohio Alumni Assn., Advt. Coun. Inc. (dir.), Advt. Club, Faculty Club (Ohio), Advt. Club, Metropolitan Club (N.Y.C), Round Hill Club (gov.), Links, Pi Kappa Alpha, Sigma Delta Chi. Republican. Lutheran. Home: Greenwich Conn. †

RICHARDS, JAMES MCDOWELL, theologian, seminary president; b. Statesville, N.C., Nov. 6, 1902; s. Charles Malone and Jane Leighton (McDowell) R.; m. Mary Evelyn Knight, Dec. 31, 1929; children: James McDowell, Mary Makemie, Charles Malone II. Grad., McCallie Sch., Chattanooga, 1918; BA, Davidson (N.C.) Coll., 1922, DD, 1933; MA, Princeton U., 1923; BA, Oxford U., Eng., 1925; MA (Rhodes scholar), Oxford U., 1930; BD, Columbia Theol. Sem., Decatur, Ga., 1928; LLD, King Coll., 1956. Ordained to ministry Presbyn. Ch., 1928. Pastor successively at Clarkesville, Nacoochee and Helen, Ga. 1928-31; pastor 1st Ch., Thomasville, Ga., 1931-32; pres. Columbia Theol. Sem., prof. practical theology, 1932-71, pres. emeritus, form 1971; mem. permanent com. on Christian rels., chmn. com. on Negro work Presbyn. Ch. U.S., 1947-50, chmn. bd. ch. extension, 1950-56; moderator Gen. Assembly, Presbyn. Ch. U.S., 1955-56, S.E. Synod, from 1973, mem. bd. world missions; v.p. Fed. Coun. Chs. Christ Am., 1942-44, mem. exec. com.; mem. gen. bd. Nat. Coun. Chs., 1950-52. Author: Change and the Changeless, 1972; editor: Soli Deo Gloria, 1968; mem. editorial bd. Theology Today. Pres. bd. trustees Davidson Coll., 1940-66, also mem. exec. com.; bd. dirs. Presbyn. Ministers Fund, Phila. Mem. Rotary, Phi Beta Kappa, Kappa Alpha, Omicron Delta Kappa. Democrat. Home: Summerville S.C. Died Aug. 10, 1986; buried Liberty Hill, S.C.

RICHARDS, JOHN STEWART, librarian; b. Chgo., Feb. 16, 1892; s. Milton Nash and Minnie Cunningham (Stewart) R.; m. irene Fry, Apr. 14, 1919; children: Robert Milton, Lynn Stewart. BA, U. Wash., 1916; postgrad., N.Y. State Library Sch., 1919-20; MA, U. Calif., 1932. Librarian Marshfield (Oreg.) Pub. Library, 1916-18, ALA War Svc., Camp Fremont, Calif., 1918-19, Idaho Tech. Inst., Pocatello, 1920-23, Wash. State Normal Sch., Ellensburg, 1923-26; supt. circulation U. Calif. Library, Berkeley, 1926-29, asst. librarian, 1929-34; exec. asst. U. Wash. Library, Seattle, 1934-41, assoc. librarian, 1941-42; lectr. Sch. Librarianship U. Wash., 1938-42; librarian Seattle Pub. Library, from 1942. Mem. ALA (pres. 1955-56), Pacific N.W., Pacific (pres. 1937-38), Wash. library assns., Deattle Coll. Club, Mcpl. League, Rotary. Home: Seattle Wash. †

RICHARDS, PAUL RAPIER, baseball company executive; b. Waxahachie, Tex., Nov. 21, 1908; s. Jesse Thoams and Sarah (McGowen) R; m. Margie McDonald, Feb. 14, 1932; 1 child, Paula Del. Baseball player with Bklyn. Dodgers, N.Y. Giants, Phila. Athletics, Detroit Tigers, 1926-36; mgr. Atlanta Baseball Club, 1938-42, Buffalo Baseball Club, 1947-49, Seattle Baseball Club, 1950, Chgo. White Sox, 1951-54; gen. mgr., field mgr. Balt. Orioles, 1955-59, field mgr., 1960-61; gen. mgr. Houston Colt 45s, 1962-66; v.p. player personnel Atlanta Braves, from 1966; mgr. Am. League All Stars Team, 1961; part-owner Waxahachie Daily Light, 1935-47; former bd. dirs. Assn. Profl. Ball Players Am. Author: Modern Baseball Strategy, 3d edit., 1951. Named to Tex. Hall of Fame, 1960; named Southwesterner of Yr., 1961, Texan of Yr., 1961. Mem. Rotary (hon. life). Baptist. Home: Waxahachie Tex. Died May 4, 1986.

RICHARDSON, L. JANETTE, literature educator; b. Ontario, Oreg., Aug. 18, 1925; d. Joel Henry and Helen King R. BA, U. Oreg., 1946, MA, 1953; PhD, U. Calif., Berkeley, 1962. Tchr. English and drama Gresham (Oreg.) High Sch., 1947-56; asst. prof. rhetoric and comparative lit. U. Calif., Berkeley, 1962-67, assoc. prof., 1967-74, prof., 1974-89, chmn. dept. comparative lit., 1974-79, chmn. dept. rhetoric, 1981-86. Author: Blameth Nat Me, 1970; contbr. articles to profl. jours. Mem. Mediaeval Acad. Am., MLA, Am. Comparative Lit. Assn., Mediaeval Assn. Pacific, Philol. Assn. Pacific Coast, U. Calif.-Berkeley Faculty Club (bd. dirs.), Phi Beta Kappa (treas. Berkeley chpt. 1981-89). Home: Oakland Calif. Died Jan. 28, 1989; buried Grandview Cemetery, LaGrande, Oreg.

RICHARDSON, LOUISE, librarian; b. Gaffney, S.C., Nov. 22, 1889; d. William Henry and Anna Olivia (Wingo) R. AB, Limestone Coll., 1909; BLS, Pratt Inst. Library Sch., 1913; postgrad., U. Chgo., 1925, Columbia U., 1931; AM, U. S.C., 1927. Asst. librarian U. N.C., 1913-14; children's librarian Hibbing (Minn.) Pub. Library, 1914-15, Eveleth Pub. Library, 1915-17; librarian Meredith Coll., 1917-18, Homewood br. Carnegie Library, Pitts., 1918-19; librarian Fla. State U., 1919-53, librarian archives and spl. collections, from 1954. Contbr. articles to profl. jours. Mem. ALA, DAR, Southeastern (TVA Project com. 1951-52), Fla. (treas. 1928-30, pres. 1932-33) library assns., Fla. Hist. Soc., Fla. Edn. Assn., U.D.C., Phi Kappa Phi. Democrat. Baptist. Home: Tallahassee Fla. †

RICHARDSON, RUPERT NORVAL, history educator, author; b. nr. Caddo, Tex., Apr. 28, 1891; s. Willie Baker and Nannie (Coon) R.; A.B., Hardin-Simmons U., Abilene, Tex., 1912; Ph.B., U. Chgo., 1914; A.M., U. Tex., 1922, Ph.D., 1928; LL.D., Baylor U., 1982; m. Pauline Mayes, Dec. 28, 1915; 1 son, Rupert Norval. Prin. high sch., Cisco, Tex., 1915-16, Sweetwater, 1916-17; prof. history Hardin-Simmons U., 1917—, dean students, 1926-28, v.p., 1928-38, exec. v.p., 1938-40, acting pres., 1943-45, pres., 1945-53, pres. emeritus, prof., 1953-67, Piper prof., 1963, Distinguished prof., 1967-88; assoc. prof., prof. history U. Tex. 8 summers, also 1940-41. Mem. So. Bapt. Edn. Commn., 1952-55; mem. Tex. Hist. Survey Com., 1953-67, pres., 1961-63. Served 2d lt. U.S. Army, 1918. Recipient Cultural Achievement in Lit. award West Tex. C. of C., 1967; Ruth Lester award Tex. Hist. Commn., 1972; award of merit Nat. Assn. State and Local History, 1953, 76; Leadership award Tex. State Hist. Assn., 1976; Citizen of Year award Abilene C. of C., 1975; citation of honor Tex. Soc. Architects, 1978. Fellow Tex. State Hist. Assn. (pres. 1969-70); mem. Tex. Philos. Soc. (pres. 1962-63). Baptist. Mason. Lion (past pres., dist. gov.). Author: The Comanche Barrier to the South Plains Settlement, 1933; (with C. C. Rister) The Greater Southwest, 1934; Texas: the Lone Star State, 1943; Adventuring with a Purpose, 1952; The Frontier of Northwest Texas, 1963; Colonel Edward M. House: The Texas Years, 1964; Famous Are The Halls: Hardwin-Simmons University as I Have Seen It, 1975; Caddo, Texas: The Biography of a Community, 1966; Along Texas Old Forts Trail, Abilene, 1972; This I Remember, 1983. Editor: West Tex. Hist. Assn. Yearbook, 1929-88. Contbr. to hist., ednl. publs. Died Apr. 14, 1988. Address: 2220 Simmons Ave, Abilene, Tex. 78601. Home: Abilene Tex. †

RICHARDSON, THOMAS FRANKLIN, banker; b. Hackensack, N.J., Dec. 31, 1922; s. Luther Locke and Ruth (Fisher) R.; m. Patricia Gill, Oct. 12, 1963; children: Yvonne Richardson Farley, Jennifer. A.B., Colgate U., 1945. With Union Trust Co., New Haven, 1947-87; investment analyst, asst. trust office, asst. v.p., v.p., pres., dir. Union Trust Co., 1947-67, chief exec. officer, 1967-87, also chmn., dir.; pres., chief exec. officer, dir. N.E. Bancorp, 1973-78, chmn. bd., chief exec. officer, 1978-87; dir. Stamford Water Co. Pres. Stamford Hosp., 1969-72, Fairfield County Boy Scouts Am., 1973-74. Served with USNR, World War II and Korea. Mem. U.S. C. of C., Am. Bankers Assn., Conn. Bankers Assn. (past pres.). Episcopalian. Clubs: Circumnavigators, Landmark of Stamford (dir.); Graduates Club Assn. (New Haven). Died Mar. 11, 1987.

RICHEY, MARY ANNE REIMANN, district judge; b. Shelbyville, Ind., Oct. 24, 1917; d. H. Wallace and Emma (Nading) Reimann; m. William K. Richey, Oct. 8, 1959; 1 dau., Anne Marie. Student, Purdue U., 1937-40; JD, U. Ariz., 1951. Bar: Ariz. 1951. Dep. county atty. Pima County, Ariz., 1952-54; asst. U.S. atty. Dist. Ariz. Tucson, 1954-59; U.S. atty. 1960; judge Superior Ct. Pima County, Ariz., 1964-76; assoc. presiding judge 1972-76, U.S. dist. judge for Dist. Ariz., 1976-83; mem. exec. com. 99th Cir.), 1978-81. Mem. Jud. Qualification Commn., 1970-76, Criminal Code Rev. Commn., 1973-76, Gov.'s Commn. on Status of Women, 1971-73; co-chmn. Supreme Ct. Com. to Rev. Civil Jury Instrns., 1971-73; mem. adv. bd. Salvation Army, 1968-83; pres. bd. dirs. YWCA, Tucson, 1968-69. Served with WASP, 1944-45. Mem. Am., Pima County bar assns., State Bar Ariz. Home: Tucson Ariz. Died Nov. 25, 1983; buried Tucson.

RICHMAN, MILTON SAUL, newspaperman; b. N.Y.C., Jan. 29, 1922; s. Samuel Abraham and Clara (Ganbarg) R. Student pub. schs., N.Y.C. Minor league baseball player 1939-41; with UPI, 1944-86, sports columnist, 1964-86, sports editor, 1972-85, sr. editor, 1985-86; Mem. com. on baseball vets. Baseball Hall of Fame. Served with M.C. AUS, 1942-44. Recipient Headliners award, 1957; E.P. Dutton Best Sports Stories award, 1957; inducted into Baseball Hall of Fame (writers wing), 1981. Mem. Assn. Profl. Baseball Players Am., Baseball Writers Assn. Am., Profl. Football Writers Assn. Am., Boxing Writers Assn. Club: Headliners. Home: New York City N.Y. Died June 9, 1986; buried Mt. Ararat Cemetery, Farmingdale, N.Y.

RICHTER, CHARLES FRANCIS, seismologist; b. nr. Hamilton, Ohio, Apr. 26, 1900; m. Lillian Brand, July 18, 1928 (dec. Nov. 1972). Student, U. So. Calif., 1916-17; AB, Stanford U., 1920; PhD, Calif. Inst. Tech., 1928; DSc (hon.), Calif. Luth. Coll., 1977. Asst. Seismol. Lab, Carnegie Inst. of Washington, Pasadena, Calif., 1927-36; asst. prof. seismology Calif. Inst. Tech., 1937-47, assoc. prof., 1947-52, prof., 1952-70, emeritus, 1970-85; mem. Lindvall, Richter & Assocs., Los Angeles; cons. Mem. Calif. Bd. Registration Geologists and Geophysicists, 1973-77, Calif. Atty. Gen.'s Environ. Task Force. Author: (with B. Gutenberg) Seismicity of the Earth, rev. edit. 1954, Elementary Seismology, 1958; contbr. to Internat. Constitution of the Earth, rev. edit. 1951. Fulbright rsch. scholar Tokyo U., Japan, 1959-60. Fellow Geol. Soc. Am., Royal Astron. Soc., Am. Geophys. Union, Royal Soc. New Zealand, Town Hall Los Angeles, Seismol. Soc. Am. (hon. medalist 1977), Assn. Engr. Geologists (hon.), Sigma Xi. Home: Pasadena Calif. Died Sept. 31, 1985.

RICHTER, CURT PAUL, psychobiologist, researcher, former educator; b. Denver, Feb. 20, 1894; s. Paul Ernst and Martha (Dressler) R.; m. Phyllis Greenacre; children—Ann Richter Roy, Peter; m. Leslie Prince Bidwell, Apr. 11, 1937; 1 child, Martha Richter Bailey. BS, Harvard U., 1917; PhD, Johns Hopkins U., 1921, LLD (hon.), 1970; DSc (hon.), U. Chgo., 1968, U. Pa., 1976. Assoc. in psychobiology Johns Hopkins Med. Sch., Balt., 1921-22, dir. psychobiology lab. Phipps Psychiat. Clinic, 1922-57, assoc. prof., 1923-57, prof. psychobiology, 1957-60, prof. emeritus, 1960-88; faculty Inst. of Advanced Study at Princeton U., 1957, 58; researcher Smithsonian Tropical Research Inst., Panama, summers 1925, 26, 27; mem. com. NRC, 1941-46. Author: Biological Clocks in Medicine and Psychiatry, 1965; contbg. author: Leaders in the Study of Animal Behavior, 1985. Organizer, dir. Exptl. Rat Control Campaign, Balt., 1942-44; hon. co-chmn. Internat. Com. Study Hunger, Thirst, Jerusalem, 1974. Served with U.S. Army, 1917-19. Recipient Warren medal Soc. Exptl. Psychology, 1950, medal Am. Psychopathol. Soc., 1977, Passano award, 1977, Lashley award, 1980. Mem. Nat. Acad. Scis., Am. Philos. Soc., Nat. Acad. Scis., Am. Acad. Arts and Scis., Halsted Soc., Am. Neurol. Assn. (hon.). Club: Elkridge (Balt.). Home: Baltimore Md. Died Dec. 21, 1988.

RICKETSON, FRANK HENRY, JR., foundation trustee; b. Leavenworth, Kans., Oct. 22, 1895; s. Frank H. and Mary M. (Connor) R.; m. Maizie Donnegan (dec.); 1 son, Frank Henry III (dec.). Student, U. Ky., 1916-17; LL.B., U. Denver, 1919. Staff writer Kansas City Star and Denver Post; then engaged in motion picture prodn.; pres. Fox Inter-Mountain Theatres, 1934-56, Roxy Theatre Co., 1956-62; v.p., gen. mgr. Nat. Theatres, 1956-62; pres. Nat. War Fund of Colo., 1941-46; dir. Pub. Service Co. of Colo., 1946-78, United Banks Colo., Inc., 1944-78, Cheyenne Newspapers, Inc. Author: The Management of Motion Picture Theatres, 1938, Opportunity Needs Selling, 1946, Europe After the Marshall Plan, 1952, Gems From a Thousand Sources, 1964. Trustee John F. Kennedy Center for Performing Arts, 1958-68; chmn. emeritus Central City Opera House Assn.; pres. Roundup Riders of Rockies, 1947-73, chmn. bd., 1973-87; Past campaign mgr., pres., chmn. bd. Mile High United Way (hon. mem. award 1964); v.p. United Community Funds and Councils; Am. Hon. life trustee U. Denver; hon. life trustee Denver Mus., Natural History. Recipient Denver Creativity award, 1957, Civis Princeps Regis Coll., 1961, Internat. Sertoma, outstanding citizen award, 1964, Nat. Exec. award Delta Sigma Phi; citation NCCJ, 1973. Mem. Phi Delta Theta, Phi Alpha Delta, Tau Kappa Alpha, Delta Sigma Pi. Clubs: Denver Country, Denver, Denver Athletic. Home: Denver Colo. Died June 18, 1987; buried Mount Olivet Cemetery, Jefferson County, Colo.

RICKOVER, HYMAN GEORGE, naval officer, government official; b. Jan. 27, 1900; s. Abraham R. and Rachel (Rickover); m. Ruth D. Masters (dec. 1972); 1 son, Robert Masters; m. Eleonore Ann Bednowicz, 1974. B.S., U.S. Naval Acad., 1922; M.S. in Elec. Engring., U.S. Naval Postgrad. Sch., Columbia U., 1929; numerous hon. degress. Commd. ensign U.S. Navy, 1922, advanced through grades to adm., 1973, qualified submariner, 1931, served in U.S.S. La Vellette, 1922-27, served in U.S.S. Nevada, 1922-27, served in U.S.S. S-9, 1929-33, served in U.S.S. S-48, 1929-33; assigned to Office Insp. Naval Material U.S. Navy, Phila., 1933-35; engring. officer U.S.S. New Mexico U.S. Navy, 1935-37, comdg. officer U.S.S. Finch, 1937; assigned to Navy Yard U.S. Navy, Cavite, Philippines, 1937-39; head elec. sect. Bur. Ships Dept. Navy U.S. Navy, Washington, Philippines, 1939-45; indsl. mgr. U.S. Navy, Okinawa, comdg. officer Naval Repair Base, 1945; insp. gen. 19th Fleet U.S. Navy, San Francisco, 1945-46; assigned to atomic submarine project with AEC U.S. Navy, Oak Ridge, 1946; continued in devel. atomic submarine Bur. Ships U.S. Navy, 1947-81, responsible for devel. and constrn. world's 1st submarine U.S.S. Natilus; responsible for 1st nuclear powered electric utility sta. U.S. Navy, Shippingport, Pa.; dir. div. naval reactors U.S. Dept. Energy; comdr. for nuclear propulsion Naval Sea Systems Command, U.S. Navy, to 1981, on active duty 63 yrs. Author: Education and Freedom, 1959, Swiss Schools and Ours: Why Theirs Are Better, 1962, American Education-A National Failure, 1963, Eminent Americans-Namesakes of the Polaris Submarine Fleet, 1972, How the Battleship Maine Was Destroyed, 1976; contbr. numerous articles to profl. jours. Decorated 3 D.S.M. with gold star; decorated Legion of Merit with gold star, hon. comdr. mil. div. Most Excellent Order Brit. Empire; recipient numerous awards including Egleston medal Columbia Engring. Alumni Assn., 1955, Cristoforo Columbo gold medal, 1957, Pupin medal, 1958, spl. gold medal U.S. Congress, 1959, Enrico Fermi award for contbn. to atomic sci. AEC, 1965, Presdl. Medal of Freedom, 1980, Congl. Gold medal, named Father of the Nuclear Navy, 1982. Home: Arlington Va. Died July 8, 1986, buried Arlington Nat. Cemetery.

RICKS, VICTOR E., educator; b. Winfield, Mo., Oct. 15, 1914; s. Willie Eugene and Edna Earl (Myers) R.; m. Harriet J. Sterling, Oct. 15, 1943; children: Marilyn J. Trotter, Cynthia S. Student, Culver-Stockton Coll., 1932-34; BA, U. Mo., 1937, MA, 1941; PhD, U. Chgo., 1950. Elem. sch. tchr. Troy, Mo., 1934-36, Columbia, Mo., 1937-41; instr. speech and radio Stephens Coll., Columbia, 1941-43; counselor to men U. Okla., 1946-48; dean students SUNY, Oswego, 1950-52; prof. edn. div. edn. U. Ill., Chgo., 1952-68, prof. edn., 1968-72; spl. cons. edn. Coll. Dentistry, 1959-65; mem. faculty Fresno (Cal.) State Coll., summer 1959; dir. Nat. Hide Assn. Tng. Sch., 1953-58; dir. Am. Dietetic Assn. Workshop on Teaching, 1961, 63. Contbr. articles to profl. jours. Chmn. Ill. Commn. for Tchr. Edn. and Profl. Standards, 1960-65; pres. Whittier Sch. PTA, Oak Park, Ill., 1961; mem. Commn. on Higher Edn. for Ill. Disciples of Christ, 1967-72. Lt. USNR, 1943-46. Mem. NEA, Ill. Edn. Assn., Assn. for Higher Edn., AAUP, Assn. Sch. Curriculum and Devel., Phi Delta Kappa. Mem. Christian Ch. (elder). Home: Oak Park Ill. Died Aug. 24, 1986.

RIDER, PAUL REECE, mathematician; b. Independence, Mo., Oct. 14, 1888; s. Walter and Alwilda (Reece) R.; m. Madeline Elizabeth Bostian, Oct. 5, 1918 (dec. Oct. 1974); children: Paul Reece, William Bostian, Margaret Rider Moore. AB, William Jewell Coll., Liberty, Mo., 1909, Am, 1910; AM, Yale U., 1914, PhD, 1915. Instr. math. Yale U., 1915-16; instr. Wash. U., 1916-18, asst. prof., 1918-21, assoc. prof., 1921-39, prof., 1939-54, prof. emeritus, from 1954; adj. prof. U. Tex., summer 1920; U.S. Exchange prof. Nat. U. of Mexico, 1942-43, under Buenos Aires Conv. of 1936 for Promotion of Inter. Am. Cultural Relations; vis. prof. U. of Puerto Rico, 1965; mem. faculty U.S. Army U. Shrivenham, Eng., and comd. sch. in Germany, 1945-46; cons. USAF, S.W. Bell Telephone Co., Am. Ordnance Assn., Ohio State U. Rsch. Found. and others; chief statistician Aerospace Rsch. Labs., Wright-Patterson AFB, 1951-64; vis. prof. Rose Poly. Inst., 1965-67; mem. Joint Svcs. Adv. Com. Dept. Def., 1953-55. 2d lt. CAC, World War I, 1918. Author or co-author numerous books relating to field. Fellow Am. Statis. Assn. (chmn. sect. phys. and engring. scis. 1960, coun.), Inst. Math. Statistics (v.p. 1937-38, pres. 1939, sec.-treas. 1940), Am. Soc. Quality Control; mem. Internat. Assn. Statistics in Phys. Scis., Internat. Inter-Am. Statis. Insts., Am. Math Soc., Math. Assn. Am., Econometric Soc., Sociedad Matemática Mexicana, AAUP, SAR, University Club (St. Louis), Cosmos Club (Washington), Acacia, Phi Beta Kappa, Sigma Xi, Kappa Alpha, Gamma Alpha, Pi Mu Epsilon, Omicron Delta Kappa. Home: Laguna Hills Calif. †

RIEBEN, LOUIS, manufacturing executive; b. 1890. Chmn. bd. Triangle Radio Tubes, Inc., Tung-Sol Sales Corp.; chmn. Tung-Sol Electric, Inc. Home: South Orange N.J. †

RIEGEL, JOHN LAWRENCE, paper and textile manufacturer; b. Riegelsville, Pa., Sept. 20, 1897; s. John S. and Marion (Griffin) R.; m. Margaret Murchie, Nov. 28, 1922; children: Mary Ann Lockhart, John L., William M. Student, Collegiate sch., N.Y.C., 1907-12, The Hill Sch., Pottstown, Pa., 1912-15; BS, MIT, 1918. With Riegel Paper Corp., N.Y.C., 1918-87, pres., 1936-59, chmn. bd., 1951-68; chmn. bd. Riegel Textile Corp, 1941-63; trustee Inst. Paper Chemistry, Appleton, Wis.; pres. Am. Paper and Pulp Assn., 1940-42. Mem. University Club, Pinnacle Club (N.Y.C.), Am. Yacht Club (Rye, N.Y.), Fox Meadow Tennis Club (Scarsdale, N.Y.), St. Andrews Golf Club (Hastings-on-Hudson, N.Y.), Phi Gamma Delta. Episcopalian. Home: Hartsdale N.Y. Died May 1, 1987; buried Riegelsville Cemetery.

RIELY, JOHN WILLIAM, lawyer; b. Richmond, Va., Mar. 9, 1917; s. Henry Carrington and Marie Antoinette (Evans) R.; m. Jean Roy Jones, July 2, 1941; children—Caroline A., Henry Carrington. B.A., U. Va.,

1938; LL.B., Harvard U., 1941. Bar: Va. 1941. Assoc. firm Hunton & Williams and predecessors, Richmond, 1941-42, 45-48; partner Hunton & Williams and predecessors, 1949-86. Past pres. Historic Richmond Found. Served to lt. comdr. USNR, 1942-45. Fellow Am. Bar Found.; mem. Jud. Council Va., ABA, Richmond Bar Assn., Bar Assn. City N.Y. Episcopalian. Clubs: Commonwealth, Country of Va, Downtown. Home: Richmond Va. Died Sept. 14, 1986.

RIES, EDWARD J., manufacturing executive; b. Rochester, N.Y., Dec. 28, 1889; s. Peter M. and Hannah (Seiler) R.; m. Pauline Welch, Jan. 17, 1923. Student pub. schs., Rochester. Apprentice elec. dept. Ritter Dental Mfg. Co. (name now Ritter Co., Inc.), 1904-09; serviceman Ritter Dental Mfg. Co. (name now Ritter Co., Inc.), N.Y.C., 1909-12; salesman dental equipment in charge 12 So. states Ritter Dental Mfg. Co. (name now Ritter Co., Inc.), 1912-18, mgr. Phila. office, 1919-26, asst. sales mgr., 1926-28, European rep., 1928-39, v.p., gen. mgr., 1939-41, pres., 1941-53, chmn. bd., from 1953; mem. adv. com. bd. Lincoln-Rochester Trust Co.; bd. dirs. Cap-Roc Inc. Mem. adv. com. bd. Rochester Inst. Tech. 2d lt. A.S., U.S. Army, 1918-19. Mem. Masons, Country Club, Genesce Valley Club, Rochester Club. †

RIESENKONIG, HERMAN FRANK, lithographer; b. N.Y.C., Jan. 29, 1911; s. Hans and Carrie (Seyferth) R.; m. Lois M. Sterling, Sept. 7, 1935; children: Peter, Pamela, John. E.e., Rensselaer Poly. Inst., Troy, N.Y., 1932. With Lithoprint Co. N.Y. Inc., N.Y.C., from 1932, pres., from 1935, dir., from 1935. Inventor specialized equipment for lithoprint process. Active Scarsdale (N.Y.) Vol. Fire Dept. Mem. Scarsdale Golf Club, Town Club (Scarsdale). Presbyterian. Home: Scarsdale N.Y. Deceased.

RIFFLE, JACK BURDETTE, insurance company executive; b. Rochester, N.Y., Sept. 19, 1928; s. Arvis B. and Eleanor (Taft) R.; m. Suzanne Gregg, Apr. 2, 1955; children: Roberta, Gregg, Martha, Scott. B.A., Hamilton Coll., Clinton, N.Y., 1950. Dist. sales mgr. Kemper Ins. Co., 1950-52, spl. risks rep., 1955-56; mgr. Scautub Ins. Agy., Schenectady, 1956-58; dist. sales mgr. Allstate Ins. Co., Rochester, 1958-65; with Utica Mut. Ins. Co., N.Y., 1965-86; exec. v.p. Utica Mut. Ins. Co., 1972-86, pres., 1974-86, chmn., chief exec. officer, 1984-86, also dir.; pres., chief exec. officer Graphic Arts Mut. Ins. Co., 1979-86; pres., chief exec. officer Utica Nat. Life Ins. Co., 1979-86, chmn., 1986; also pres. Utica Nat. Ins. Co. of Tex.; bd. dirs. Ins. Info. Inst., 1979-86, chmn., 1983-85; bd. dirs. Alliance Am. Insurers, 1979-86, Property Loss Research Bur., 1979-86, Property-Casualty Ins. Council, 1981-86, Nat. Council on Compensation Ins., 1984-86; chmn. IRM, 1985-86. Regional pres. Boy Scouts Am., 1980-83, exec. v.p., 1986; pres. Utica United Way, 1977-79; bd. dirs. N.Y. State Traffic Safety Council, 1970-82; charter trustee Hamilton Coll., 1984-86; bd. mgrs. Faxton Hosp., 1985-86; mem. Nat. Commn. Against Drunk Driving, 1985-86. Served with USNR, 1952-55. Recipient Silver Beaver award Boy Scouts Am., 1976, Silver Antelope award, 1979. Mem. Utica C. of C. (dir. 1976-86). Clubs: Ft. Schuyler, Ft. Schuyler Yacht Squadron, Yahnundasis Golf; Union League (N.Y.C.). Home: Clinton N.Y. Died Dec. 13, 1986.

RIFORD, LLOYD STEPHEN, farmer, cattle breeder; b. Randolph, Vt., Apr. 22, 1889; s. Horace Payne and Clarissa (Walker) R.; m. Florence Trimmer, June 16, 1917; children: Lloyd Stephen, Nancy Elena (Mrs. Richard L. Turner). Student, Dartmouth Coll., 1909-10; BS, U. N.H., 1914; MA, U. Mo., 1915. Mem. faculty Rutgers Coll., 1915-17; prodn. mgr. Walker-Gordon Lab. Co., Plainsboro, N.J., 1917-20; an organizer Beacon Milling Co., Cayuga, N.Y., 1920, sec., 1920-28, v.p., 1928-36, pres., 1936-50, chmn. bd., 1950-59; owner, operator Greystone Farm, Auburn, N.Y., from 1925; pres. Auburn Guernsey Farms, Inc., from 1936; bd. dirs. Nat. Bank Auburn, Cayuga County Savs. Bank, Auburn, , Utica (N.Y.) Mut. Ins. Co. Campaign chmn. Cayuga County United Fund, 1941, 50; pres. Cayuga County coun. Boy Scouts Am., 1934-37; del. Rep. Nat. Coinv., 1952; trustee Auburn Meml. Hosp.; Presbyn. ch.; trustee, former chmn. bd. Wells Coll.; bd. dirs. Auburn YMCA. Recipient Citizen of Yr. award B'nai B'rith Cen. N.Y., 1962. Mem. N.A.M. (bd. dirs. 1943, 48), Am. Guernsey Cattle Club (pres. 1963-65), Masons, Sigma Xi, Sigma Nu, Alpha Zeta. Home: Auburn N.Y. †

RIGGS, JAMES LEAR, industrial engineering educator; b. Webster City, Iowa, Sept. 23, 1929; s. Max Elwood and Dixie Ann (Wyckoff) R.; m. Doris Jean Miller, Dec. 23, 1951; children: James Randall, Robin Lee. B.S., Oreg. State U., 1951, M.S., 1958, Ph.D., 1962. Registered profl. engr., Calif. With Mater Machine Works, 1958; asst. prof. indsl. engring. Oreg. State U., 1959-62, asso. prof., 1962-67, prof., 1967-86, head dept., 1968-86; affiliate faculty Japan-Am. Inst. Mgmt. Sci., Hawaii; dir. Oreg. Productivity Center, 1980-86, productivity chair, 1986; cons. editor McGraw-Hill; cons. in field. Author: Economic Decision Models, 1968, Production Systems: Planning, Analysis and Control, 4th edit., 1987, Industrial Organization and Management, 6th edit, 1979, The Art of Management, 1974, Introduction to Operations Research and Management Science, 1975, Engineering Economics, 1977, 3d edit., 1986, Productivity by Objectives, 1983, Productive Supervision, 1985; also articles. Served with USMC, 1951-56. Recipient Carter award for Outstanding Teaching, 1967; Faraday medal, 1986; Fulbright lectr. Yugoslavia, 1975. Mem. Am. Soc. Engring. Edn., World Confedn. Productivity Sci. (pres. 1981-84, chmn. internat. council 1984-86), Inst. Mgmt. Sci., Am. Inst. Indsl. Engrs. (v.p. 1978-79), Sigma Xi, Alpha Pi Mu. Republican. Presbyterian. Home: Corvallis Oreg. Died May 19, 1986; cremated.

RIGHTER, CARROLL BURCH, astrologer, columnist; b. Salem, N.J., Feb. 2, 1900; s. John Charles and Mary Caroline (Burch) R.; student U. Pa., 1918-19; LLB, Dickinson Sch. Law, 1922, LLD (hon.), 1971. Law clk. firm Norman Grey, Esquire, Phila., 1923-25; practicing astrologer, Hollywood, Calif., 1938-88; syndicated columnist, 1950-88; lectr., 1939—; founder, pres. Carroll Righter Astrological Found., Inc., Los Angeles, 1963-88; practicing astrologer England, Sweden, Netherlands, Germany, and France, 1977-86; radio personality Bild Newspaper Chain's Hot Line, 3 hours daily in Germany. Chmn. jr. com. Phila. Summer Concert Orch., 1928; chmn. Profl. Players, Phila., 1929; exec. sec. bd. Pa. Grand Opera Co., 1925-30. Mem. Chirothesian Ch. of Faith (chmn. bd., pres. 1968—). Author: Astrology and You, 1957; Astrological Guide to Health and Diet, 1968; Astrological Guide to Marriage and Family Relations, 1970; Dollar Signs, 1972; prepared Monthly astrological forecasts, 1951-75.Died Apr. 30, 1988.

RILEY, LEONARD JOSEPH, army officer; b. New Bedford, Mass., Dec. 27, 1931; s. Charles Leo and Mary Theresa (Donaghy) R.; m. Annmarie O'Leary, Oct. 22, 1955; children: Mark S., Erin S., Maureen, Michael L., Colleen M., Tara A. B.S., Providence Coll., 1955; M.B.A., U. Ariz., 1965; postgrad., U.S. Army Command and Gen. Staff Coll., 1965-66, U.S. Army War Coll., 1971-72. Commd. 2d lt. U.S. Army, 1955, advanced through grades to brig. gen., 1977; chief equipment br., then chief system devel. U.S. Army Tactical Ops. System Devel. Group Heidelberg, W. Ger., 1966-68; brigade signal officer 4th Inf. Div. Pleiku, Vietnam, 1968; comdr. Phu Lam Signal Bn. Cholon, Vietnam, 1969; exec. officer mgmt. info. systems directorate Office of Chief of Staff, Hdqrs. U.S. Army Washington, 1971; staff officer Worldwide Mil. Command and Control System, Office of Joint Chiefs of Staff 1972-74; comdr. U.S. Army Communications Command-Alaska Fort Richardson, 1974-75; comdr. White House Communications Agy. Washington, 1975-77; dep. comdr., then comdr. U.S. Army Computer Systems Command Ft. Belvoir, Va., 1977-79; comdr. 7th Signal Command and Ft. Ritchie Md., from 1979. Decorated Legion of Merit with oak leaf cluster, Def. Superior Service medal, Bronze Star, Air medals, Army Commendation medal, others. Mem. Assn. U.S. Army, Armed Forces Communications-Electronics Assn., Providence Coll. Alumni Assn., U. Ariz. Alumni Assn., U.S. Army War Coll. Alumni Assn., Beta Gamma Sigma. Home: Mashpec Mass. Died Oct. 13, 1985, buried Nat. Cemetery, Otis AFB, Mass.

RIMLINGER, GASTON VICTOR, educator; b. Strasbourg, France, Aug. 16, 1926; came to U.S., 1947; naturalized, 1953.; s. Victor Joseph and Anna (Glaser) R.; m. Lorraine M. Stewart, Sept. 1, 1951; children: Yvonne, Claire, Francis, Catherine, Christopher. BA summa cum laude, U. Wash., 1951; PhD, U. Calif., Berkeley, 1956. Interpreter U.S. Mil. Govt., Federal Republic of Germany, 1945-47; grad. rsch. economist Inst. Indsl. Relations, Berkeley, 1954-55; instr., then asst. prof. Princeton U., 1955-60; mem. faculty Rice U., Houston, 1960-88, Henry S. Fox prof. econs., chmn. dept., 1964-69, Reginald Henry Hargrove prof. econs., 1972-88; program adviser for econ. planning and rsch. Ford Found., West Africa, 1969-72; cons. for Choice Books for Coll. Libraries, 1965-88, Ford Found., 1972-88. Author: Welfare Policy and Industrialization in Europe, America and Russia, 1971, Indigenisation and Management Development in Nigeria, 1974; contbr. articles to profl. jours. Bd. dirs. Houston Vocat. Guidance Svc., 1966-69. Ford Faculty fellow, 1963-64. Mem. Am., So., Southwestern (pres. 1968-69) econ. assns., Econ. History Assn., Econ. History Soc., Phi Beta Kappa. Roman Catholic. Home: Houston Tex. Died June 12, 1988; buried Brookside Cemetery, Houston.

RINDGE, SAMUEL KNIGHT, investment and property management executive; b. L.A., Apr. 9, 1888; s. Frederick Hastings and Rhoda May (Knight) R.; m. Agnes Marion Hole, July 12, 1911; children: Samuel Hole, Ramona, Frederick Hastings. AB, Harvard U., 1911. In corp. property mgmt. bus. from 1911; sec.-trustee Seaside Water Co.; bd. dirs. Crocker-Citizens Nat. Bank, Rosedale Cemetery Assn.; pres., bd. dirs. Artesian Water Co. Sgt. U.S. Army, 1917-19, capt. Res. Mem. Army Ordnance Assn., Masons, California Club, L.A. Country Club, Newport Harbor Yacht Club, Pi Eta. †

RINGLER, WILLIAM ANDREW, JR., English educator; b. Montclair, N.J., May 17, 1912; s. William Andrew and Anna (Holzborn) R.; m. Evelyn Anne Dressner, June 25, 1946; children: Anne Marie Bower, Robert William, Susan Jane. A.B., Princeton U., 1934, M.A., 1935, Ph.D., 1937. Instr. English Princeton U., 1937-41, asst. prof., 1941-42, 46-50; prof. Washington U., St. Louis, 1950-62; prof. U. Chgo., 1962-79, prof. emeritus, 1980-87; Charles K. Colver lectr. Brown U., 1953; sr. research assoc. H.E. Huntington Library, San Marino, Calif., 1979-87; faculty assoc. in lit. Calif. Inst. Tech., 1982-87. Author: Stephen Gosson, A Biographical and Critical Study, 1942, The Poems of Sir Philip Sidney, 1962, Sir Philip Sidney: The Myth and the Man, 1986, Capystranos, 1986, (with Michael Flachmann) Beware the Cat: The First English Novel, 1988, Bibliography and Index of English Verse Printed 1476-1558, 1989; editor, translator: (with Walter Allen, Jr.) John Rainolds Oratio in Laudem Artis Poeticae, 1940; editor: (with Denton Fox) The Bannatyne Manuscript, 1980; contbr. articles to profl. jours. Mem. nat. com. Shakespeare Anniversary Com., 1964. Served to maj. USAAF, 1942-46. Fellow Guggenheim Found., 1947-48, 57-58; fellow Folger Shakespeare Library, 1952; Fulbright sr. scholar Australia, 1972, Huntington Library-NEH, 1976-77; grantee NEH, 1979-83, British Acad., 1982. Mem. Zamorano Club, Phi Beta Kappa. Democrat. Home: Pasadena Calif. Died Jan. 1, 1987; buried Resurrection Cemetery, San Gabriel Calif.

RIOCH, DAVID MCKENZIE, physician, educator, academic administrator; b. Mussoorie, U.P., India, July 6, 1900; s. David and Minnie (Henly) R.; m. Margaret Jeffrey, Dec. 23, 1938. Student, Philander-Smith Naini Tal, U.P., India, 1913-15; AB, Butler U., 1920; MD, Johns Hopkins Med. Sch., 1924; LHD, Exptl. Coll., Inst. Behavioral Rsch., 1973. House officer Peter Bent Brigham Hosp., Boston, 1924-26; asst. resident in medicine Strong Meml. Hosp., Rochester, N.Y., 1926-28; med. fellow NRC, 1928-30, Dept. Anatomy, U. Mich., Cen. Inst. for Brain Rsch., Ann Arbor and Amsterdam, Holland, 1928-29; med. fellow physiology lab., Oxford U., 1929-30, instr., 1930; assoc. in physiology Johns Hopkins U. Med. Sch., 1930-31; asst. prof. anatomy Harvard U., 1931-38; chmn. dept. neuropsychiatry Washington U. Med. Sch., 1938-42, prof. neurology, 1938-43; dir. rsch. Chestnut Lodge Sanatarium, Rockville, Md., 1943-51; fellow Washington Sch. Psychiatry, 1943-54; dir. div. neuropsychiatry Walter Reed Army Inst. Rsch., Walter Reed Army Med. Ctr., Washington, 1951-70; coordinator Adult Learning Ctr., Inst. for Behavioral Rsch., Silver Spring, Md., 1970-73, prin. scientist, 1973-80; mem. Inst. for Advanced Study, Princeton, N.J., 1958-59; vis. prof. dept. psychiatry U. Chgo., 1968-85, vis. lectr. dept. psychiatry Johns Hopkins U. Sch. Medicine, 1970-72; vis. lectr. emeritus, 1972-85. Writer on neuroanatomy, physiology and neuropsychiat. rsch. With RCAF, 1918. Recipient Exceptional Civilian Service award Dept. Army, 1961, Achievement award, 1961, Walter Reed medal Walter Reed Army Med. Ct., 1970, Van Giesen award N.Y. State Psychiat. Inst., 1973, Thomas W. Salmon award N.Y. Psychiat. Soc., 1976. Fellow N.Y. Acad. Scis., Am. Psychiat. Assn., Am. Neurol. Assn. (hon.), Am. Acad. Arts and Scis., Washington Acad. Medicine, Washington Acad. Sci., Am. Psychopath. Assn., AAAS, Am. Assn. Anatomists, Am. Physiol. Soc., Am. Assn. Rsch. in Nervous and Mental Diseases, Am. Acad. Neurology (assoc.), Psychonomic Soc., Pavlovian Soc., Phi Beta Kappa, Alpha Omega Alpha. Home: Silver Spring Md. Died Sept. 11, 1985.

RIPPY, JAMES FRED, educator; b. Summer County, Tenn., Oct. 27, 1892; m. Mary Dozier Allen, Aug. 19, 1915; children: James Fred, Robert Allen, Frazier Winston. AB, Southwestern U., 1913; AM, Vanderbilt U., 1915; Native Sons fellow, U. Calif., 1917-18, PhD, 1920; Guggenheim fellow, 1927, Carnegie fellow, 1928; DLitt (hon.), Southwestern U., 1961. Asst. in history U. Calif., 1917-20; instr. in history U. Chgo., 1920-23, asst. prof. history, 1923-24, assoc. prof. history, 1924-26; prof. history Duke U., 1926-36; prof. history U. Chgo., 1936-58, prof. emeritus Am. history, from 1958; Albert Shaw lectr. in Am. Diplomacy, Johns Hopkins U., 1928; lectr. Inst. Interamericano of Nat. U. Mex., 1929; Walter Fleming lectr. U. La., 1941; Walker Ames lectr. U. Wash., 1945. mem. editorial staff Hispanic Am. Hist. Rev. from 1926; mem. editorial bd. Am. Hist. Rev., 1933-38; editor Duke U. Press, 1929-36; author or co-author of several books relating to field, among them: The U.S. and Mexico, 1931, Historical Evolution of Hispanic America, 1945, Latin America and the Industrial Age, 1947, Latin America: Land of Conquest and Turmoil, 1958, Modern Latin America, 1958, Globe and Hemisphere, 1959, British Investments in Latin America, 1959; editor various other publs. Mem. U.S. Nat. Com. on History and Geography; del. Pan-Am. Conf. on History and Geography, 1935. Recipient William Volker award, 1960. Mem. Am. Acad. Polit. and Social Sci., Am. Hist. Assn., Miss. Valley Hist. Assn., N.C. Hist. and Lit. Soc. (pres. 1933-34), AAUP, Cosmos Club (Washington), Phi Beta Kappa, Kappa Alpha, Phi Alpha Theta. Home: Durham N.C. †

RITCHEY, JAMES OSCAR, physician; b. Owasco, Ind., Feb. 1, 1891; s. Aaron F. and Christina (Batzell) R.; m. Helen Hare, Aug. 25, 1922. BS, Ind. U., 1916, MD, MS, 1918. Intern Ind. U. Hosp., 1918-19; resident Robert W. Long Hosp., Indpls., 1919-21; pvt. practice from 1921; instr. medicine Ind. U., 1921-23, asst., 1923-27, asst. prof., 1927-28, assoc. prof., 1928-32, prof., from

1932, chmn. med. dept., 1932-56. Fellow ACP; mem. AMA, Ind., Indpls. med. socs., Indpls. Athletic Clukb, Indpls. Literary Club, Phi Chi, Alpha Omega Alpha. Mem. Christian Ch. Home: Indianapolis Ind. †

RITCHIE, ROBERT ESTES, utilities executive; b. Hancock County, Tenn., Sept. 2, 1892; s. Hiram K. and Fannie Marie (Estes) R.; m. Mary Reeves, Sept. 17, 1913; 1 child, Reeves Estes. Student, Poly. Coll., Ft. Worth, 1909-10. With Ft. Worth & Denver R.R., 1910-11, Santa Fe R.R., 1912-17, T.&P. Ry., 1917-18, M.-K.—T. R.R., 1918-20; chief clk., supt. St. Louis-Southwestern R.R., 1920-23; chief clk. to pres. Ark. Power & Light Co., 1923-35, asst. to pres., mgr. Little Rock div., 1935-40, v.p., 1940-52, div. mgr., 1940-45, pres., from 1952, chmn. bd., from 1956; bd. dirs. Mid. S. Utilites, Inc. Deacon local ch. Christian Ch. Mem. Nat. Assn. Electric Cos. (bd. dirs. from 1952), Ark. (bd. dirs., econ. coun.), Little Rock (pres. 1940) C.'s of C., Masons (potentate 1933), Shriners, Little Rock Country Club. Home: Little Rock Ark. †

RITCHIE, ROLAND ALMON, judge; b. Halifax, N.S., Can., June 19, 1910; s. William B. and Lillian C. (Stewart) R.; m. Mary Lippincot Wylde; 1 dau., Elizabeth Stewart. Student, Trinity Coll. Sch., Port Hope, Ont., Univ. King's Coll., Halifax, Pembroke Coll., Oxford U. Bar: N.S. 1934; created king's counsel 1950. With Stewart, Smith, MacKeen & Rogers, Halifax, 1934-40; ptnr. Daley, Ritchie, Black & Moriera (and predecessor), Halifax, 1945-59; puisne judge Supreme Ct. Can., 1959-84; Former mem. bd. govs. Dalhousie U., Halifax; chancellor Univ. King's Coll., 1974-88. Mem. N.S. Barrister Soc. (formerly 1st v.p.), Can. Bar Assn. Home: Ottawa Ont., Canada. Died June 6, 1988.

RITZ, CHARLES, businessman; b. Mitchell, Ont., Can., Feb. 15, 1891; s. George Henry and Elizabeth (Vock) R.; m. Evelyn Millicent Herron, July 22, 1924; children: Gordon Herron, Norma Elizabeth Ritz Phelps. Student, Cen. Bus. Coll., Stratford, Ont., 1906. Stenographer Borland Carriage Co., Stratford, 1907-08, Temiskaming and Northern Ont. Ry., North Bay, Ont., 1908-10; stenographer, sales corr. Robin Hood Flour Mills, Moose Jaw, Sask., 1910-12; sales mgr. in Calgary Robin Hood Flour Mills, Alta., 1912-14; eastern mgr. in Montreal Robin Hood Flour Mills, 1914-31, gen. mgr., 1931-37, pres., 1938-61, chmn. exec. com., from 1961; v.p. Internat. Milling Co., Mpls., 1937-43, pres., 1943-55, chmn. bd., 1955-65, hon. chmn., from 1965; dir. Investors Diversified Svcs., Inc., Mpls., MSL Industries, Inc. Bd. dirs. Mpls. YMCA. Mem. Minneapolis Club, Minikahda Club (Mpls.), Thunderbird Club (Calif.), Masons, Shriners. Home: Wayzata Minn. †

RIVERA, JOSÉ DE, sculptor; b. Baton Rouge, Sept. 18, 1904. Pupil drawing, John W. Norton; LittD (Hon.), Washington U., St. Louis, 1974. Mem. dept . art, grantee Nat. Inst. Arts and Letters, 1959. Exhibited in numerous one man and group shows, including: Whitney Mus., Seattle World's Fair, Battersea Park, London, Eng., Arts Club, Chgo., The White House, Washington, U. N.Mex., Los Angeles County Mus., Phila. Mus. Art;, maj. retrospective shows, La Jolla (Calif.) Mus. Comtemporary Art, 1972, Whitney Mus., numerous commns. including: U. Rochester, City of Lansing (Mich.); represented in permanent collections in maj. museums throughout U.S. including Mus. Modern Art, N.Y.C. Met. Mus. Art, N.Y.C., Art Inst. Chgo., Smithsonian Instn., Tate Gallery, Eng., Art Gallery Toronto, Ont., Can., Hirshhorn Mus., Washington, others. Reipient Watson F. Blair prize Chgo. Art Inst., 1957, Creative Arts medal Brandeis U., 1969, sculpture commn. Am. Iron and Steel Inst., 1965. Work subject of book: José de Rivera Constructions (Dore Ashton and Joan M. Marter) 1980. Home: New York N.Y. Died Mar. 19, 1985.

ROBBINS, WILLIAM JACOB, educator; b. North Platte, Nebr., Feb. 22, 1890; s. Frederick Woods and Clara (Federhoof) R.; m. Christine F. Chapman, July 15, 1915; children: Frederick Chapman, William Clinton, Daniel Harvey. AB, Lehigh U., 1910, DSc, 1937; PhD, Cornell U., 1915; DSc, Fordham U., 1945. Instr. biology Lehigh U., 1910-11; instr. plant physiology Cornell U., 1912-16; asst. in plant physiology Marine Biol. Lab., Woods Hole, Mass., summers 1912, 13; prof. botany Ala. Poly. Inst., 1916-17; plant physiologist Agrl. Expt. Sta., 1916-17; soil biochemist Bur. Plant Industry, U.S. Dept. Agr., 1919; prof. botany U. Mo., 1919-37, dean Grad. Sch., 1930-37, acting pres., Sept. 1933-May 1934; prof. Columbia U., 1937-58, prof. emeritus, from 1958.; bd. dirs. N.Y. Bot. Garden, 1937-58; pres. Fairchild Tropical Garden, 1962-69; assoc. dir. internat. sci. activities NSF, 1962-63; trustee Rockefeller U., from 1956. Author of text on botany and contbr. on physiology of plants. Connected with European office Rockefeller Found., 1928-30; chmn. Nat. Rsch. Fellowship Bd. in Biol. Scis., 1931-37; spl. investigator Citrus Expt. Sta., U. Cal., summer 1924. 2d lt. San. Corp., U.S. Army, 1918. Fellow Am. Acad. Arts and Scis., AAAS; mem. NAS (treas. 1948-60), Am. Philos. Soc. (pres. 1956-59, exec. officer 1959-60), Bot. Soc. Am., Cosmos Club, Century Club, Phi Beta Kappa, Sigma Xi, Phi Kappa Phi, Gamma Alpha. Home: New York N.Y. †

ROBERTS, ROSS T., federal judge; b. 1938. B.A., DePauw U., 1960; J.D., U. Mo., 1963. Ptnr. Roberts & Fleischaker, Joplin, Mo., 1963; ptnr. Shook, Hardy, Ottman, Mitchell & Bacon, Kansas City, Mo., 1968-70, Roberts & Fleischaker, Joplin, 1970-82; pros. atty. Jasper County, Joplin, 1971-77; judge U.S. Dist. Ct. (we. dist.) Mo., Kansas City, from 1982. Died Apr. 24, 1987.

ROBERTS, SAMUEL JACOB, state justice; b. Bklyn., Feb. 18, 1907; s. Jacob and Anna (Wexler) R.; m. Helen G. Blumberg, Dec. 14, 1934 (dec. 1963); 1 child, Barbara; m. Marian S. Zurn, Dec. 12, 1970. BS in Econs., U. Pa., 1928, LLB, 1930; LLD, Gannon U., 1963, Dickinson Sch. Law, 1966, Villa Maria Coll., 1968; postgrad., Phila. Coll. Osteo. Medicine, 1972, Allegheny Coll., 1983. Bar: Pa. 1931. Pvt. practice Erie, Pa., 1931-52; asst. dist. atty. Erie County, 1935-38; referee in unemployment compensations, also spl. dept. atty. gen. Commonwealth Pa., 1939-52; judge Orphans Ct., Erie County, Pa., 1952-63, presiding judge, 1953-63; justice Supreme Ct. Pa., 1963-83, chief justice, 1983-87; bd. commrs. Uniform State Laws, 1981-87; mem. faculty Appellate Judges Seminar, Inst. Jud. Adminstrn., NYU, 1966-87. Contbr. to various legal publs. Trustee Gannon U.; bd. overseers U. Pa. Law Sch.; bd. visitors U. Pitts. Law Sch.; bd. trustees Phila. Coll. Osteo. Medicine; bd. incorporators Hamot Hosp., St. Vincent Hosp.; chmn. Commonwealth Pa. Commn. Bicentennial U.S. Constn. Served to lt. comdr. USNR, 1944-46. Recipient 16th ann. Max C. Currick Brotherhood award, Merit award Erie County Social Agys., Pa. Soc.'s Disting. Citizen of Commonwealth award, 1986; named Man of Yr., 11th ann. award Erie Tchrs. Assn. Mem. ABA (council, chmn. sect. legal edn. and admission to bar 1984-85, com. appellate advocacy), Am. Bar Found. (fellows adv. research com.), Masons (32 degree). Clubs: Kahkwa Country, Erie, Erie County Motor (bd. dirs.), University, Aviation; Concordia (Pitts.); Franklin Inn (Phila.). Home: Erie Pa. Died June 5, 1987; buried Laurel Hill Cemetery, Erie, Pa.

ROBIDOUX, OMER ALFRED, missionary, bishop; b. St. Pierre Jolys, Man., Can., Nov. 19, 1913; s. Joseph and Jeanne (Tanguay) R. B.A., U. Ottawa, 1940; D.D., U. Man., 1970. Oblate of Mary Immaculate, 1934; ordained priest Roman Catholic Ch., 1939, consecrated bishop, 1970; worked with natives in Lestock (Sask.) Missions and Schs., 1941-51, Lebret (Sask.) Missions and High and Elementary Sch., 1951-58, Winnipeg Assiniboia High Sch. and Missions, 1958-65; prin. Assiniboia Sch., Winnipeg, 1958-65; tchr. adult edn. programs 1965-70; bishop of Churchill, 1970-86. Bd. dirs. Churchill Health Centre, 1972-86, mem. exec. com., 1974-86; chmn. Churchill Community Devel. Corp., 1974-86, Churchill No. Studies Centre, from 1976, Cadet instr. Army, 1943-65. Home: Churchill Man., Canada. Died Nov. 12, 1986.

ROBINSON, ALICE GRAM, editor, publisher; b. Omaha; d. Andrew Peter and Carrie (Jensen) Gram; m. Norborne Thomas Nelson Robinson Jr.; 1 son, Norborne Thomas Nelson III. Student, U. Oreg., U. Calif. With press dept. Nat. Woman's Party; mem. Brewer, Taylor, Gram Co.; pvt. practice public relations; spl. Washington writer Good Housekeeping, Fashion Art, Farmer's Wife mags., others; mem. editorial dept. Community Ctr., Washington; founder, pub. Congressional Digest, Washington; pres. C.D. Corp.; dir. women's div. Rep. Nat. Com. Author: Congressional Committee Method of Classroom Study, 1948. Mem. Acad. Polit Sci., Am. Contract Bridge League (life master), Women's Nat. Press Club (a founder), City Tavern Club, Kappa Alpha Theta. Christian Scientist. Home: Washington D.C. Died Jan. 1, 1984.

ROBINSON, HAMPTON CARROLL, JR., surgeon; b. Missouri City, Tex., Oct. 20, 1914; s. Hamptom Carroll and Dannie Joe (DeWalt) R.; m. Patricia Welder, July 12, 1947 (dec. June 1965); children: Hampton Carroll, Patricia W. Robinson, Patrick Welder, Justin Hughes; m. 2d, Mary Louise Fenton, May 29, 1967. Student, U. Houston, 1931-36, U. Tex., Austin, 1934-36; MD, Baylor U., 1940. Intern Rsch. Hosp., Kansas City, Mo., 1940-41; resident St. Joseph's Infirmary, Houston, 1941; pvt. practics specializing in surgery Houston, 1946-88; chmn. Houston Acad. Medicine, 1956-62, Tex. Bd. Health, 1963-75; mem. cons. staff Tex. Children's Meth., Hermann hosps; clin. asst. prof. surgery Baylor Coll. Medicine, 1949-88; adj. prof. community health U. Tex. Health Sci. Ctr., Houston, 1971-88. Bd. dirs. Houston Soc. for Performing Arts; trustee Houston Symphony Soc., Houston Found., U. St. Thomas, Tex. Childrens Hosp. and Catholic Community Svcs. With AUS, USAAF, 1941-45. Decorated Knight of Malta; recipient Commendation award Sec. War, 1945, Brotherhood award NCCJ, 1964. Mem. AMA, Tex. Med. Assn., Harris County Med. Soc., Houston C. of C. (dir.), River Oaks Country Club, Houston Country Club, Ramada Club, El Dorado Club (Indian Wells, Calif.). Home: Houston Tex. Died Feb. 7, 1988; buried Forest Park West, Houston.

ROBINSON, HAROLD FRANK, university chancellor emeritus; b. Bandana, N.C., Oct. 28, 1918; s. Fred Herbert and Geneva (Jarrett) R.; m. Katherine Palmer, Feb. 9, 1944; children: Karen Elizabeth Dail, Mary JoAnne Bewsey. B.S. with high honors, N.C. State Coll., 1939, M.S., 1940; Ph.D., U. Nebr., 1948, D.Sc., 1966. Seed specialist N.C. Crop Improvement Assn., 1940-41; mem. faculty N.C. State Coll., 1945-68, prof., head dept. genetics, 1958-62; dir. Inst. Biol. Scis.; also asst. dir. Agrl. Expt. Sta., 1962-65; adminstrv. dean for research N.C. State U., 1965-68; vice chancellor Univ. System Ga., 1968-71; provost Purdue U., 1971-74; chancellor Western Carolina U., Cullowhee, N.C., 1974-84; dir. Office Univ. Studies Western Carolina U., 1984-88; cons. internat. maize program Rockefeller Found., 1955-65; exec. dir. Pres.'s Sci. Adv. Com. Panel on World Food Supply, 1966-68; mem. cons.'s bur. Nat. Commn. Undergrad. Edn. Biol. Scis., 1963-65; mem. N.C. Bd. Sci. and Tech., 1965-68, Pres.'s Sci. Adv. Panel Internat. Tech. Coop. and Assistance, 1967-68; chmn. panel food crisis in Indonesia Nat. Acad. Scis., 1968, mem. bd. sci. and tech. in internat. devel., 1968-72; mem. panel Korea tech. assistance study, 1969, mem. planning com. on world food, health and population Nat. Acad. Scis.-NSF, 1974-75; mem. world food and nutrition study Nat. Acad. Scis., 1976-77; mem. com. agrl. devel. Bd. Internat. Food and Agrl. Devel., 1977-80; mem. Joint Council Food and Agrl. Scis., U.S. Dept. Agr., 1978-82, mem. exec. com., 1981-82; mem. study group of exec. com., 1978-80; chmn. vis. team to rev. wheat and maize program FAO, Ecuador, 1982, mem. internat. panel to conduct quinquennial rev. of UN FAO Orgn. Research Ctr., El-Baton, Mex., 1982; mem. com. on competency needs in agr. research personnel USDA, 1983-84; mem. presdl. agrl. task force to Zaire, 1985; bd. dirs. N.C. Biotech. Ctr., 1985-88; long-range planning com. Western N.C. Arboretum, Inc., 1985-87, site selection com., 1985-87; bd. dirs. MDC Inc., 1985-87; bd. dirs., exec. com. N.C. Rural Econ. Devel. Ctr., 1986. Asso. editor: Crop Sci, 1962-65. Trustee Coll. Entrance Exam. Bd., 1971-75, mem. fin. com., 1975; bd. dirs. Mountain Area Health Edn. Found., Asheville, N.C., 1975-88, Western N.C. Arboretum, 1986-88, TVA Indsl. Devel. Adv. Council, 1984-88; mem. Nat. Plant Genetics Resources Bd., 1975-81; chmn. joint adv. com. U. N.C.-Community Coll. System-pvt. instns., 1976-79; chmn. instl. heads of So. Conf., 1979-81; co-chmn. Joint PVO/Univ. Rural Devel. Ctr., 1979-88; mem. Bd. Internat. Food and Agrl. Devel., 1980-83; mem. joint adv. com. on higher edn. N.C. Conf., United Meth. Ch., 1979-81; mem. blue ribbon study commn. to explore establishment of rural devel. corp. in N.C., 1980; mem. found. com. to establish Sultan Qaboos U., Sultanate of Oman, 1981-86; mem. N.C. Legis. Study Commn. on Higher Edn., 1983-84, N.C. Awards Com., 1981-84; N.C. Ctr. for Advancement of Teaching, 1984, N.C. Nature Conservancy, 1986-88; community adv. bd. Pub. Radio Sta. WCQS-FM, Asheville, 1986-88; steering com. WNCT Regional Econ. Devel. Project, 1986-88; chmn. Senator Terry Sanford's Western N.C. Adv. Council, 1987-88, I-26 Corridor Assn., 1988; elected del. to Dem. Nat. Conv., 1988. Served with USN, 1941-45. Recipient award Nat. Council Comml. Plant Breeders, 1964. Fellow Am. Soc. Agronomy, AAAS; mem. Am. Inst. Biol. Scis., Assn. Allied Health Professions, Am. Assn. State Colls. and Univs. (com. on allied health professions 1975, chmn. com. on agr., renewable resources and rural devel., 1977-81, mem. team to study higher edn. in Cuba 1978, mem. com. internat. programs 1980-84), Biometric Soc., Genetics Soc. Am., N.C. Assn. Colls. and Univs. (exec. com. 1978-81, Hugh McEniry award com. 1982), Am. Council Edn. (ad hoc com. on problems major intercollegiate athletic programs 1982, div. I reorgn. subcom. of com. on athletics 1983-84), Cherokee Hist. Assn., Western N.C. Devel. Assn., N.C. Retired Govt. Employees Assn. (bd. dirs. 1985-88), Tenn. River Valley Assn. (bd. dirs. TVA com. 1986-88), Nat. Research Council/Nat. Acad. Scis. (com. competency needs in agrl. research 1984-86), Asheville Area C. of C. (bd. dirs. 1983-84), Sigma Xi, Gamma Sigma Delta, Phi Kappa Phi, Phi Sigma, Omicron Delta Kappa, Alpha Kappa Psi (hon.). Died July 3, 1988, buried Greenhill Cemetery, Waynesville, N.C.

ROBINSON, LAWRENCE MARSHALL, electric utility executive, consulting engineer; b. Denver, Jan. 20, 1900; s. Hugh Lawrence and Grace (Worden) R.; m. Mildred Eleanor Blackwood, Nov. 15, 1924 (dec. 1971);1 son, Lawrence Marshall. BSEE with honors, U. Colo., 1922, EE, 1927, MSEE, 1938, D Engring. (hon.), 1955; JD, U. Denver, 1979. Registered profl. engr. Colo., Calif., Wash., Wyo., Ill., N.Y. Engr. to chief elec. engr., mgr. engring. Pub. Svc. Co. Colo., Denver, 1922-53, chief elec. engr., mgr. engring., 1953-59, mng. engr., v.p. engring, 1959-68; cons. engr. elec. utilities Colo. Wash., Ill., Argentina, Dominican Republic., 1968-88, U.S. Bur. Reclamation, Denver, 1969, Pub. Utilities Dist., Wenatchee, Wash., 1975-79, Power Authority Buenos Aires, 1969, Dominican Republic, 1981. Contbr. chpts. to books, articles to publs. Chmn. Solid Waste Disposal Denver Region, 1968-71; mem. Fed Power Commn. Adv. Com., Washington, 1962-67 mem., pres. State Bd. Registered Profl. Engrs., 1957-69. With U.S. Army, 1918. Named Disting. Engring. Alumnus, U. Colo., 1968; recipient Gold Medal award Colo. Engring. Coun., 1954. Life fellow IEEE (v.p. 1945, dir. 1956, Habirshaw award 1963, Centennial award 1984); mem. Profl. Engrs. Colo. (A.J. Ryan award 1969), Masons, Shriners, Sigma Xi, Alpha Tau Omega. Republican. Methodist. Home: Denver Colo. Died July 23, 1988.

ROBINSON, WILLIAM DODD, physician, educator; b. Hoosac, N.Y., Aug. 8, 1911; s. William Goodwin and Catherine Bradford (Dodd) R.; m. Anna Louise Ebert, Sept. 8, 1932; children: William Harvey, David Wells, Peter Dodd. AB, Albion Coll., 1931; MD, U. Mich., 1934. Diplomate Am. Bd. Internal Medicine. Intern, resident, instr. dept. internal medicine U. Mich., 1934-38, rsch. fellow internal medicine, 1938-40, asst. prof., in charge Rackham Arthritis Rsch. unit, 1944-53, assoc. prof. medicine, 1946-52, prof. internal medicine, 1952-79, chmn. dept., 1958-75, prof. emeritus, 1979-88; mem. sci. adv. com. Nat. Vitamin Found., 1957-60; cons. Surg. Gen., USPHS, 1954-61, nat. adv. arthritis and metabolic diseases coun., 1963-67; with field studies internat. health div. Rockefeller Found., Tenn., Spain, Mex., 1940-43; instr. medicine Vanderbilt U., 1943-44. Editor U. Mich. Med. Bull., 1950-54, Rheumatism Revs., 1952-56, Jour. Lab. and Clin. Medicine, 1955-60. Bd. dirs. Mich. chpt. Arthritis and Rheumatism Found.; cons. to surgeon gen. U.S. Army, 1945-46. Master ACP; mem. AMA (mem. coun. food and nutrition 1966-67), Am. Rheumatism Assn., Assn. Am. Physicians, Cen. Soc. Clin. Rsch., Am. Fedn. Clin. Rsch., Mich. Rheumatism Soc., Phi Beta Kappa, Sigma Xi, Sigma Chi, Phi Rho Sigma, Alpha Omega Alpha, Phi Kappa Phi. Home: Ann Arbor Mich. died Sept. 11, 1988.

ROBISON, HOWARD W(INFIELD), former congressman; b. Owego, N.Y., Oct. 30, 1915; s. Addison J. and Pluma L. (Moe) R.; m. Gertrude L. Frederick, Nov. 1, 1946; children, Howard Winfield, Douglas E. AB, Cornell U., 1937, LLB, 1939. Bar: N.Y. 1939. Pvt. practice Owego, N.Y., 1939-87; county atty. Tioga County, N.Y, 1946-57; mem. Town bd., Owego, N.Y., 1947-56; town atty. Owego, N.Y., 1957-58; mem. 85th-87th congresses 33d N.Y. Dist., dist. mem. 88th-92d congresses, mem. com. on appropriations; mem. 93d Congress from 27th N.Y. Dist. Bd. dirs. Tioga County Gen. Hosp. With AUS, 1942-46. Mem. N.Y. State, Tioga County, 6th Jud. Dist. bar assns., Masons, Elks, Kiwanis. Republican. Methodist. Home: Candor N.Y. Died Sept. 26, 1987; buried Evergreen Cemetry, Owego, N.Y.

ROBLIN, DANIEL ARTHUR, JR., corporate executive; b. Buffalo, Oct. 3, 1918; s. Daniel Arthur and Emma (Goldstein) R.; m. Gloria Landsman, May 22, 1949; children: Diane Roblin Finlayson, Daniel Arthur III. B.S. in Metallurgy, Lehigh U., 1939; D.B.A. (hon.), D'Youville Coll., 1980. With Am. Smelting & Refining Co., 1939-41; v.p. Buffalo Housewrecking Co.; also chmn. Seaway Steel Corp., 1946-57; pres. Roblin Inc., 1957-61; pres., chmn. Roblin Industries Inc., 1961-84, chmn., 1985-86; dir. Niagara Frontier Transit Co., 1962-83, Marine Midland Trust Co., Western N.Y., 1968-83, Bisonite Corp., 1969-83, Rand Capitol Corp., 1970-83, Empire of Am. Savs. Assn.; trustee Erie County Savs. Bank. Pres. Erie County chpt. Nat. Found. Infantile Paralysis, 1953-55; mem.-at-large Boy Scouts Am., 1954-86; v.p. Erie County council, 1954-57; chmn. Buffalo and Erie County Econ. Devel. Corp., 1962-69; exec. com., bd. dirs. Greater Buffalo Devel. Found., 1964-86; treas., mem. exec. com. Erie County Republican Com., 1951-66; trustee Edward J. Meyer Meml. Hosp., 1956-64; trustee Buffalo Gen. Hosp., 1966-86, chmn., 1980-83; mem. exec. com., bd. dirs. Buffalo Philharmonic Orch., 1965-68; exec. com., trustee SUNY at Buffalo Found., 1966-86, chmn., 1973-79; co-chmn. Buffalo and Erie County Labor/Mgmt. Council, 1975-83; bd. advisers Villa Maria Coll., 1967-72; mem. adminstrn. bd. advisers Canisius Coll. Sch. Bus., Buffalo, 1969; chmn. exec. com. Erie County Indsl. Devel. Agy.; del. Republican Nat. Conv., 1980. Served with USNR, 1941-46. Recipient Chancellor's medal State U. N.Y. at Buffalo, 1980. Mem. Am. Iron and Steel Inst. (dir. 1980-86), Greater Buffalo Area C. of C. (dir. 1967-69, v.p. 1968-69, 79-86), Empire State C. of C. (dir. 1979-86), NAM (dir. 1977-86). Clubs: Buffalo, Westwood Country (Buffalo), Marco Polo, Harmonie, Metropolitan (N.Y.C.), Capitol Hill (Washington). Home: Buffalo N.Y. Died Dec. 9, 1986.

ROBSON, EDWIN ALBERT, judge; b. Chgo., Apr. 16, 1905; s. Clarence T. and Alice B. (Andres) R.; m. Leah M. Kinne, Sept. 15, 1928; children: Edwin Albert, Clark K., David K. LL.B., DePaul U., 1928. Bar: Ill. 1928. Practiced with Kinne, Scovel & Robson, Chgo., 1928-45; judge Superior Ct. Cook County, 1945-51, dir., organizer central assignment system and pretrial conf. of civil cases, 1948-50, chief justice, 1950-51; judge Ill. Appellate Ct., 1951-58; judge U.S. Dist. Ct. for No. Dist. of Ill. Ct., 1958-86, chief judge, 1970-75, sr. judge, 1975-86. Bd. editors: Manual for Complex and Multidistrict Litigation, 1968. Mem. Am. Judicature Soc., Am., Ill., Chgo. bar assns., Phi Alpha Delta. Methodist. Clubs: Law (Chgo.), Legal (Chgo.), Union League (Chgo.), Standard (Chgo.). Home: Wilmette Ill. Died Oct. 21, 1986; interned Memorial Gardens, Trinity Ch. of the North Shore.

ROCKWELL, KATHARINE LAMBERT RICHARDS, writer, lecturer; b. Orange, N.J., June 10, 1891; d. Dickinson Woodruff and Sally (Lambert) Richards; m. William Walker Rockwell, Nov. 8, 1934. AB, Smith Coll., 1913; student, Nat. Tng. Sch. of YWCA, 1917-18; AM, Columbia U., 1923, PhD, 1934. Sec. YWCA in the Oranges, 1915-17; nat. student sec. YWCA in Pa., Md., Del., 1918-22; dir. religious activities YWCA, City of New York, Harlem Br., 1923-25; instr. dept. of religious edn. Teachers Coll., Columbia U., 1924-25, asst., 1925-27; asst. prof. dept. religion and biblical lit. Smith Coll., 1928-34. Author: The Golden Word, 1919, How Christmas Came to the Sunday Schools (a hist. survey), 1934. Early Portraits of Jesus, 1936. Mem. Nat. Bd. YWCA, 1937-58, hon. me. from 1958 (chmn. res. com. stuent div. 1937-43, chmn. program subject div., 1944-50, 3d v.p. 1946-47, vice chmn. com. on cooperation 1950-53); mem. exec. com. of Fed. Coun. Chs. of Christ in Am., 1947-52; mem. Assoc. Bd. of Christian Colls. in China 1940-46; mem. bd. founders Ginling Coll., Nanking, China, 1935-46. Mem. Am. Soc. Ch. History, Nat. Assn. of Biblical Instrs., Hymn Soc. of Am., Smith Coll. of N.Y.C., Phi Beta Kappa. Home: New York N.Y. †

RODDIS, LOUIS HARRY, naval medical historian; b. Cherokee, Iowa, Feb. 16, 1886; s. Henry and Clara Eva (Schlinger) R.; m. Winifred Emily Stiles, Sept. 27, 1916; children: Louis H., Richard S.L. MD, U. Minn., 1913; student, U.S. Naval Med. Sch., Washington, 1914. Diplomate Am. Bd. Internal Medicine. Apptd. asst. surgeon USN, May 30, 1914, commd. lt. comdr., Feb. 1, 1918; served in various parts of the world; lectr. on med. history U.S. Naval Med. Sch., 1933-37; exec. officer U.S. Naval Hosp., Pearl Harbour, 1937-39; sr. med. officer of U.S. Naval Hosp. Ship Relief, Pacific Theater during Marshall Island and Marianas Islands campaign, 1944. Editor: U.S. Naval Med. Bull., Washington, 1933-37, 1941-48, Naval Med. History of World War II; author: Life of Edward Jenner, 1930, William Withering, 1935, A Short History of Nautical Medicine, 1941, James Lind--Founder of Nautical Medicine, 1950, The Indian Wars of Minnesota, 1956, The First European Medical Men in the New World, 1964; contbr. numerous articles on med. and pharm. history and sci. subjects to profl. publs. Recipient Sir Henry Wellcome prize and medal in mil. medicine, 1943, Commendation letter and medal Sec. of Navy, Outstanding Achievement award U. Minn., 1957; decorated campaign ribbons: Mex. 1914 Victory medal, Am. defense, Am. theater ribbons, Asiatic Pacific with 3 operation stars. Fellow ACP; mem. AMA, Assn. of Mil. Surgeons, Minn. Hist. Soc., Masons, Order of the Carabao, Army and Navy Club (Washington); Liars Club (Burlington, Wis.), Theta Kappa Phi. Democrat. Episcopalian. Home: San Diego Calif. †

RODENBERG, SIDNEY DAN, university dean, microbiology educator; b. St. Louis, Apr. 5, 1926; s. Martin and Etta (Goldfried) R.; m. Dolores Knight, Dec. 21, 1950 (dec.); children: Nancy, Wendy, Amy, Philip. A.B. in Zoology, Washington U., St. Louis, 1948, A.M. in Microbiology, 1950, Ph.D. in Botany (NSF fellow), 1953; M.A. (hon.), U. Pa., 1971. Mem. faculty U. Pa., 1953-75, asso. prof. microbiology, 1961-69, prof., 1969-75; dean U. Pa. (Sch. Allied Med. Professions), 1969-75; prof. microbiology and health sci., dean Coll. Health Professions, Wichita State U., 1976-86; clin. prof. pathology U. Kans. Sch. Medicine, Wichita. Chmn. Upper Merion Student Loan Fund, 1962-64; chmn. Upper Merion Parent-Tchr. Council, 1962-63; mem. Upper Merion San. Bd., 1965-66; mem. health manpower review and study commn. Pa. Regional Comprehensive Health Planning Council, 1971-74; mem. task force on allied health edn. Pa. Dept. Edn., 1972; mem. Pa. Gov.'s Com. on Health Edn., 1974-75; mem. accreditation rev. bd. Nat. Accrediting Agy. for Clin. Lab. Scis., 1974-79; mem. Com. Allied Health Edn. and Accreditation, 1980-85; Bd. dirs. Upper Merion Area Sch. System, 1969-75, pres., 1974-75; bd. dirs. Kans. region NCCJ, 1084-86, Midwest Heart Inst., Wichita, 1985. Served with AUS, 1944-46. NSF Postdoctoral fellow, 1966-67; recipient Lindback award Lindback Found., 1964. Mem. AAAS, Am. Inst. Biol. Scis., Am. Soc. Microbiology, Am. Soc. Allied Health Professionals (dir. 1973-79, mem. adv. com. regional tng. insts. 1972-74, treas. 1974-76, pres. 1976-79), Sigma Xi, Alpha Eta (pres. 1985-86). Home: Wichita Kans. Died Aug. 1986.

ROEDEL, PHILIP MORGAN, international fisheries consultant; b. San Jose, Calif., Aug. 24, 1913; s. Wilhelm vonBrinken and Alice (Morgan) R.; m. Geraldine Harney, June 30, 1939; children: David H., Deborah Ann (Mrs. Christadore). AB in Biology, Stanford U., 1935, AM, 1952. With Calif. Dept. Fish and Game, 1936-69; dir. marine fisheries rsch. program Calif. Fisheries Lab., 1957-69; dir. Bur. Comml. Fisheries, Dept. Interior, 1970; dir. Nat. Marine Fisheries Svc., Nat. Oceanic and Atmospheric Adminstrn., U.S. Dept. Commerce, 1970-73, coord. marine recreation, 1973-75; fisheries advisor AID, 1975-80; cons. fisheries policy, adminstrn. and mgmt. 1980-85; spl. advisor Internat. Ctr. for Living Aquatic Resources Mgmt., Manila, 1980-85; cons. NAS, 1980, Omani-Am. Joint Commn., 1981, Republic of Korea, 1968, Saudi Arabia, 1974; commr. Internat. No. Pacific Fisheries Commn., 1971-74; sec. Calif. Marine Rsch. Com., 1963-69; mem. or chief del. various U.S. fisheries dels., 1965-85; bd. dirs. Resources Devel. Assocs. Inc. Contbr. articles to profl. jours. With AUS, 1943-46. Fellow Am. Inst. Fishery Rsch. Biologists; mem. Gulf and Caribbean Fisheries Inst. (bd. dirs.), Cosmos Club. Home: Novato Calif. Died Mar. 29, 1985.

ROGERS, A. ROBERT, librarian; b. Moncton, N.B., Can., Sept. 9, 1927; came to U.S., 1956, naturalized, 1965; s. Amos R. and Ethel L. (Lutes) R.; m. Rhoda M. Page, Dec. 18, 1960; 1 son, Mark Alan. B.A., U. N.B., 1948; M.A., U. Toronto, 1950; Diploma in Librarianship, U. London, 1953; Ph.D. U. Mich, 1964. Asst. librarian U. N.B., 1951-55, librarian, 1955-56; adult asst. home reading services Detroit Pub. Library, 1957-58, adult asst. reference services, 1958-59; asst. to dir. Bowling Green (Ohio) U. Library, 1959-61, acting dir., 1961-64, dir., 1964-69; prof. library sci. Kent State U., 1969-85; acting dean Kent State U. (Sch. Library Sci.), 1977-78, dean, 1978-85; vis. prof. library sci. Pahlavi U., Shiraz, Iran, 1976-77; Mem. Adv. Council on Fed. Library Programs, 1971-76, 78-82; tech. cons. Touche Ross, 1982-83. Author: poetry The White Monument, 1955, The Humanities; A Selective Guide to Information Sources, 1974, 2d edit., 1980; co-author: The Library in Society, 1984. Trustee Ohio Coll. Library Center, 1967-69; vice chmn. Pub. Library Financing and Support Com., 1983-85. Recipient Gov. Gen.'s Gold medal. Mem. ALA (council 1972-76), Ohio Library Assn. (dir. 1968-76, pres. 1979-80, Librarian of Yr. award 1976), Library Assn. Gt. Britain, Bibliog. Soc. Can., Ohio Coll. Assn. (pres. librarians sect. 1964-65, chmn. library cooperation com. 1966-67, Ohio multitype interlibrary coop. com. 1980-83). Methodist (ch. sch. supt. 1965-68, chmn. Commn. on Edn. 1973-76, 78-80, chmn. adminstrv. bd. 1980-85). Home: Kent Ohio Died June 22, 1985; buried Standing Rock Cemetery, Kent, Ohio.

ROGERS, CARL RANSOM, psychologist, educator; b. Oak Park, Ill., Jan. 8, 1902; s. Walter A. and Julia (Cushing) R.; m. Helen Elliott, Aug. 28, 1924 (dec. 1979); children: David, Natalie. B.A., U. Wis., 1924; M.A., Columbia U., 1928, Ph.D., 1931; L.H.D., Lawrence Coll., 1956, U. Santa Clara, 1971; Litt.D., Gonzaga U., 1968; D.Sc., U. Cin., 1974; Ph.D., U. Hamburg, 1975; Dr. Social Scis., Leiden U., Netherlands, 1975; Sc.D., Northwestern U., 1978; Ph.D. (hon.), Union Exptl. Colls. and Univs., 1984. Psychologist in child study dept. Soc. for Prevention Cruelty to Children, Rochester, N.Y., 1928-30, dir., 1930-39; dir. Rochester Guidance Center, 1939; prof. clin. psychology Ohio State U., 1940-45; dir. counseling services USO, 1944-45; prof. psychology, exec. sec. Counseling Center, U. Chgo., 1945-57; Knapp prof. U. Wis., 1957, prof. psychology and psychiatry, 1957-63; resident fellow Western Behavioral Scis. Inst., La Jolla, Calif., 1964-68, Center Studies of the Person, La Jolla, 1968-87; vis. prof. at various times U. Rochester, Columbia U. Tchrs. Coll., UCLA, Harvard U., Occidental Coll., U. Calif.-Berkeley, Brandeis U. Author: Measuring Personality Adjustment in Children, 1931, Clinical Treatment of the Problem Child, 1939, Counseling and Psychotherapy, 1942, (with J. Wallen) Counseling with Returned Servicemen, 1946, Client-Centered Therapy, 1951, (with others) Psychotherapy and Personality Change, 1954, On Becoming a Person, 1961, (with E.T. Gendlin, D.J. Kiesler, C.B. Truax) The Therapeutic Relationship and its Impact: A Study of Psychotherapy with Schizophrenics, 1967, Freedom to Learn, 1969, Carl Rogers on Encounter Groups, 1970, Becoming Partners: Marriage and Its Alternatives, 1972, Carl Rogers on Personal Power, 1977, A Way of Being, 1980, Freedom to Learn for the 80's, 1983; also numerous articles. Recipient Disting. Sci. Contbn. award Am. Psychol. Assn., 1956, 1st Disting. Profl. Contbn. award, 1972; Nicholas Murray Butler medal Columbia U., 1955; Disting. Contbn. award Am. Pastoral Counselors Assn., 1967; Profl. award Am. Bd. Profl. Psychology, 1968; medal for disting. service Columbia U. Tchrs. Coll., 1986; fellow Center Advanced Study in Behavioral Scis., 1962-63; named Humanist of Year, Am. Humanist Assn., 1964. Fellow Am. Acad. Arts and Scis.; mem. Am. Acad. Psychotherapists (pres. 1956-58), Am. Orthopsychiat. Assn. (v.p. 1941-42), Am. Assn. Applied Psychology (pres. 1944-45), Am. Psychol. Assn. (pres. 1946-47), Phi Beta Kappa. Home: La Jolla Calif. Died Feb. 4, 1987.

ROGERS, CHARLES ELKINS, government official; b. Ozark, Mo., May 5, 1892; s. John Clarke and Ivie E. (Southwick) R.; m. Sadie Berns, May 18, 1918 (dec. Aug. 1952); 1 child, William Cecil; m. Rosemary Fleming, Oct. 15, 1960. AB, U. Okla., 1914; MS, Kans. State Coll., 1926; AM, Stanford U., 1932; PhD, U. Minn., 1948. Reporter Tulsa World, 1914; copy reader, feature writer Kansas City Star, 1915; assoc. prof. Kans. State Coll., 1919; prof., head dept. indsl. journalism 1925-39; head dept. tech. journalism Iowa State Coll., 1940-45; ednl. relations officer FAO, 1946-51; info. specialist Econ. Rsch. Svc., USDA, 1951-63; writer, editor Grad. Sch. USDA, from 1963; vis. instr. journalism Stanford U., 1931-32, U. So. Calif., summer 1939; with div. info. AAA, Washington, 1934-35. 1st lt. U.S. Army. Author: Journalistic Vocations, 1931, rev. edit., 1937, Reporting FFA News, 1941; co-author: Agricultural Journalism, 1926; contbr. aricles to newspapers and mags. Mem. Am. Polit. Sci. Assn., Masons, Cosmos Club, Phi Beta Kappa. Unitarian. Home: Washington D.C. †

ROGERS, DAVID P., utility executive; b. Toronto, Ont., Can., June 29, 1891; s. J.P. and Jessie (Carlyle) R.; m. Elsie M. Bartle, Feb. 25, 1927; children: Marjory Rogers Austin, Jane Rogers Wright. BA, U. Toronto, 1912; BS, MIT, 1915. With Union Gas Co. Can. Ltd., Toronto, from 1930; pres. Union Gas Co. Can. Ltd., 1942-63, chmn. bd., dir., 1963-73; bd. dirs. Union Gas

Co. Ltd., Can. Permanent Trust Co., A.E. Long & Co. Ltd. Home: Toronto Can. †

ROGERS, DONALD LEE, lawyer, trade association executive; b. East Steubenville, W. Va., Mar. 31, 1928; s. Mark Whittaker and Virginia (Campbell) R.; m. Helen E. Long, 1960. A.B., Miami U., Oxford, Ohio, 1951; J.D., Ohio State U., 1953. Bar: Ohio 1953, U.S. Supreme Ct. 1957. Asst. counsel U.S. Senate Com. on Banking and Currency, Washington, 1953-54, counsel, 1955-58; exec. dir. Assn. Bank Holding Cos., Washington, 1958-76, pres., 1976-88. Mem. ABA (banking com.), Fed. Bar Assn., Order of Coif. Methodist. Clubs: Capitol Hill, Nat. Press, Exchequer (pres. 1962), City Tavern, 1925 F St. (Washington). Home: Washington D.C. Died Jan. 18, 1988; buried Metropolitan Meml. Cemetery, Washington.

ROGERS, DOROTHY, psychologist, educator, writer; b. Ashburn, Ga., May 31, 1914; d. Edwin Augustus and Ella Mae (Evans) R.;. AB, U. Ga., 1934, MA, 1936; PhD (fellow 1945-46), Duke U., 1947; postgrad., NYU, 1947-48, Nat. U. Chile, 1942. Tchr. Birmingham, Ala., 1935-44; mem. psychology dept. State U. Coll., Oswego, N.Y., 1946-85, prof. psychology, 1950-85, disting. svc. prof., 1979-85. Author textbooks including Adolescence: A Psychological Perspective, 1972, 78, Child Psychology, 1969, 77, Highways across the Horizon, 1966, Issues in Adolescent Psychology, 1969, 72, 77, Issues in Adult Development, 1980, Issues in Child Psychology, 1969, 77, Issues in Life Span Human Development, 1980, Jeopardy and a Jeep (Am. edit.), 1957, Brit. edit., 1957, Oswego: Fountainhead of Teacher Education, 1961, Mental Hygiene in Elementary Education (Delta Kappa Gamma internat. award), 1957, Psychology of Adolescence, 1962, 72, 77, Adolescence and Youth, 1981, Readings in Child Psychology, 1969, The Adult Years, 1979; contbr. articles to profl. jours. Active Women's Caucus State U. Coll., nat. coun. Nat. Woman's Party; adv. bd. Human Rights for Women. Mem. Am. Psychol. Assn., Eastern Psychol. Assn., Nat. Coun. on Family Relations, Phi Beta Kappa, Kappa Delta Pi, Phi Kappa Phi. Republican. Home: Oswego N.Y. Died Jan. 7, 1985, buried Rose Hill Cemetery, Ashburn. Ga.

ROGERS, EDMUND BURRELL, national park administrator; b. Denver, Dec. 28, 1891; s. Edmund James Armstrong and Maria Georgina Dare (Burrell) R.; m. Sarah Elder Vaille, June 5, 1926. Student, Cornell U., 1910-11; AB, Yale U., 1915. With mountain div. ARC, 1917-19; from asst. to trust officer Colo. Nat. Bank, 1919-29; supt. Rocky Mountain Nat. Park, 1929-36, Yellowstone Nat. Park, 1936-56; spl. asst. to dir. Nat. Park Svc., Denver, from 1956. Editor: Rocky Mountain Letters—1869 (William H. Brewer), 1930. Pvt. U.S. Army, 1918-19. Mem. Am. Planning and Civic Assn., Colo. Mountain Club (charter, pres. 1925, 27), University Club, Mile High Club, Cactus Club, Rotary (hon.). Home: Denver Colo. †

ROGERS, HARRY E(DWARD), manufacturing executive; b. St. Louis, June 17, 1891; s. George O. and Edith J. (Sears) R.; m. Vivian Davis, Jan. 20, 1917; children: George Thomas, Charlotte Patricia. Student, Washington U., 1909; BCS, St. Louis U., 1921. With engring. dept. Am. Car & Foundry Co., St. Louis, 1910-12; with Commonwealth Steel Co., Granite City, Ill., 1912-29; asst. works mgr., works mgr. Gen. Steel Castings Corp., Eddystone, Pa., 1929-40; plant mgr. Nordberg Mfg. Co., Milw., 1940-45; plant mgr. Hughes Tool Co., Houston, from 1945, v.p. mfg., from 1948, also bd. dirs.; bd. dirs. TWA. Mem. Am. Soc. Tool Engrs., NAM, Am. Mgmt. Assn., Army Ordnance Assn., Houston C. of C., Houston Club, Cork Club, River Oaks Country Club. Episcopalian. Home: Houston Tex. †

ROGERS, LINDSAY, law and political science educator; b. Balt., May 13, 1891; s. George Wilson and Emma K. (Gore) R.; m. Oona Staples, June 9, 1917 (dec. 1965). Grad., Balt. City Coll., 1908; AB, Johns Hopkins U., 1912, PhD, 1915, LLD (hon.), 1948; LLB, U. Md., 1915. Newspaper corr. Balt., 1909-15; tchr. Balt. City Coll., 1910-15; adj. prof. polit. sci. U. Va., 1915-18, assoc. prof., 1918-21; lectr. on govt. Harvard U., 1920-21, assoc. prof. govt., 1921-27, prof. pub. law, 1927-29; Burgess prof. pub. law Columbia U., 1929-59, emeritus, from 1959; vis. lectr., spl. lectr. numerous univs. and colls., from 1921; served on spl. govt. coms. and commns., spl. study and rsch. groups; asst. dir. Internat. Labour Office, Montreal, Can., 1942-47; cons. com. fgn. relations U.S. Senate, from 1965. Author several books in field of govt.; editor-in-chief U. Va. Alumni Bull., 1915-21; assoc. editor Polit. Sci. Quar., 1921-59; contbr. articles to profl. publs. Mem. Superior Edn. Coun., P.R., 1942-65. Mem. Century Assn. (N.Y.), Cosmos Club (Washington), Athenaeum Club (London), numerous profl. assns. and orgns. Home: New York N.Y. †

ROGERS, MAX TOFIELD, educator; b. Edmonton, Alta., Can., Jan. 12, 1917; came to U.S., 1938; naturalized, 1944; s. Harry Earlby and Edith (Tofield) R.; m. Ethel Pearce McMaster, 1943; children: Richard Eugene, Kathleen Elaine. BSC, U. Alta., 1937, MSc, 1938; PhD, Calif. Inst. Tech., 1941. Postdoctoral fellow Calif. Inst. Tech., Pasadena, 1941-42; instr. chemistry U. Calif., Los Angeles, 1942-46; mem. faculty Mich. State U., East Lansing, 1946-85, assoc. prof., 1948-55, prof., 1955-85. Robert Tegler fellow,1937-38, Guggenheim Found. fellow, 1954-55, NSF sr. postdoctoral fellow, 1962-63. Fellow AAAS; mem. Am. Chem. Soc. (chmn. phys. chemistry div. 1969-70), Am. Phys. Soc., Chem. Soc. London, AAAU, Sigma Xi. Home: East Lansing Mich. Died Oct. 22, 1985; buried Tofield, Alta., Can.

ROLFE, FRANKLIN P., college dean; b. Concord, N.H., Nov. 15, 1902; s. Harlow Foster and Harriett (Smith) R.; m. Katharine Taylor, June 20, 1931. BS, Dartmouth Coll., 1924, MA, 1925; PhD, Harvard U., 1931. Instr. in English Stanford U., 1925-27; instr., asst. prof. and assoc. prof. U. Calif., Los Angeles, 1932-48, dean Div. Hunanities, 1946-61, dean Coll. Letters and Sci., 1961-85. Mem. bd. editors The Quarterly of Film, Radio and Television; contbr. articles to learned periodicals. Sheldon Traveling Fellow of Harvard, 1931-32. Mem. Western Coll. Assn. (pres. 1966-85), Phi Beta Kappa. Home: Los Angeles Calif. Died July 26, 1985.

ROLL, MARLIN HENRY, health services facility executive; b. Pacific Junction, Iowa, July 6, 1927; s. Dorsey Lee and Edythe Marie (Hanfeld) R.; m. Janice C. Wheeler, Feb. 5, 1949; children: Elizabeth Marie, Clark Stanton, Paul Wheeler, Tiffany Lynne. B.A., State U. Iowa, 1949, M.A., 1951, Ph.D., 1959. Asst. prof. ednl. psychology State U. Iowa, 1956-62; exec. dir. South Suburban Pub. Sch. Coop. Assn. of Cook County, Ill., 1962-64; asso. prof. U. Houston, 1964-66; dir. interagy. commn. on mental retardation Office of Gov., State of Del., Dover, 1966-69; regional adminstr. for mental retardation, supt. dept. mental health State of Mass., 1969-73; dir. Caro (Mich.) Regional Center, 1973-88. Mem. Am. Assn. Mental Deficiency (life), N.E.A. (life), Am. Psychol. Assn., Phi Delta Kappa. Home: Caro Mich. Died July 23, 1988, buried Wahjamega Cemetery, Caro.

ROMA, LISA (LISA ROMA TROMPETER), soprano; b. Phila., Feb. 29, 1892; d. Henry Louis and Lisa (Rome) Stone; m. David Trompeter, Dec. 3, 1936. Student, U. Pa., Sorbonne U.; MusM, U. So. Calif., 1929. Prima donna soprano State Opera, Berlin; concert and opera appearances U.S. and Can.; soloist Chgo. Symphony Orch., Boston Symphony Orch., Cleve. Symphony Orch., San Fransicso Symphony Orch, Met. Opera Orch., N.Y.C. Symphony Orch.; owner, pub., editor Musical Courier mag.; tchr. profl. singing U. So. Calif., 1929-32, adj. prof. voice, 1956; author: The Science and Art of Singing, 1956, Key to Singing and Speech, 1957, Song and Speech, 1958. Recipient Florence Nightingale award, 1929. Mem. Sigma Alpha Iota (hon.). Home: Greenwich Conn. †

ROMAN, STEPHEN BOLESLAV, mining executive; b. Slovakia, Apr. 17, 1921; came to Can. 1937; s. George and Helen R.; m. Betty Gardon, Oct. 20, 1945; children—Helen Elizabeth, Angela Marie, Stephen George, Paul Michael, John Peter, David Andrew, Anne Catherine Ruth. Student, Agrl. Coll. Chmn. bd., chief exec. officer, dir. Denison Mines Ltd., Toronto, Ont., Can.; chmn. bd., dir. Roman Corp., Ltd., Toronto; chmn., dir. Standard Trust Co., Toronto, Lawson Mardon Group Ltd., Seagull Petroleum Ltd.; bd. dirs. Zemex Corp.; pres. Slovak World Congress. Hon. bd. dirs. Royal Agrl. Winter Fair Assn. Can.; bd. dirs. John C. Diefenbaker Meml. Found., Inc., Father John Kelly Found. Served with Can. Army, World War II. Mem. Slovak World Congress (pres.), Bd. Trade Met. Toronto, Royal Can. Mil. Inst. (hon.). Greek Catholic. Clubs: Engineers, Empire, Capitol Hill, Lyford Cay. Home: Toronto Ont., Canada Died Mar. 23, 1988.

ROMANOFF, ALEXIS LAWRENCE, educator; b. St. Petersburg, Russia, May 17, 1892; came to U.S., 1921, naturalized, 1927; s. Lawrence Mercury and Daria (Kondratieff) R.; m. Anastasia J. Sayenko, Sept. 1, 1928. Student, St. Petersburg Tchrs. Coll., 1910-15, Acad. Fine Arts, St. Petersburg, 1912-14, Tomsk U., 1918-19, Vladivostok Poly. Inst., 1919-20; BS, Cornell U., 1925, MS, 1926, PhD, 1928. Rsch. asst. Cornell U., 1924, 26-28, resident dr., 1928-29, rsch. instr., 1928-32, rsch. asst. prof., 1932-43, assoc. prof., 1943-48, prof. chem. embryology, 1948-60, prof. emeritus, from 1960; rsch. fellow biology Harvard U., 1939-40; rsch. fellow Yale U., 1940-41; rsch. assoc. physics U. Fla., 1942. Author: The Avian Egg, 1949, The Avian Embryo, 1960, The University Campus, 1960, Ithaca, 1962, Profiles of American Heritage, 1963, Reflective Poems, 1964; contbr. to Encyclopedia Chemical Technology, 1950; illustrator: Avian Egg, Avian Embryo, (ednl. film) Where Chick Life Begins, 1937; contbr. numerous articles to profl jours.; inventor humidifier, 1931, electronic egg sorting mechanism, 1944. Mil. comdr., tech. adviser Provisional Govt., Saratov, Russia, 1917. Lt. C.E., Russian Army, 1915-17. Recipient Borden award, 1950. Fellow AAAS, N.Y. Acad. Sci., Poultry Sci. Assn.; mem. Am. Physiol. Soc., Am. Chem. Soc., Soc. Exptl. Biology and Medicine, Am. Soc. Zoologists, Am. Genetic Assn., Statler Club, Cornell U. Club, Rotary, Sigma Xi. Greek Orthodox. Home: Ithaca N.Y. †

ROME, EDWIN PHILLIPS, lawyer; b. Phila., Oct. 7, 1915; s. John Jacob and Etta (Phillips) R.; m. Chloe Denham, Oct. 30, 1946 (div. 1969); m. Rita Joseph, Aug. 19, 1969. B.A., Swarthmore Coll., 1937; LL.B., U. Pa., 1940. Bar: Pa. Law clk. Pa. Supreme Ct., Phila., 1940-42; assoc. William A. Gray, Phila., 1942-47; ptnr. Gray, Anderson, Schaffer & Rome, Phila., 1947-54, Blank, Rome, Comisky & McCauley, Phila., 1954-88. Author: Arizona Annotations to the Restatement of the Law of Agency, The Child and the Law in Pennsylvania, Corporate and Commercial Free Speech; contbr. articles to profl. jours. Trustee William Penn Found., 1973-79, Phila. Mus. Art; bd. dirs. Phila. Opera Co.; pres. bd. Walnut Street Theatre, 1983-86; bd. overseers U. Pa. Law Sch. Fellow Am. Bar Found., Internat. Acad. Trial Lawyers; mem. ABA, Phila. Bar Assn., Pa. Bar Assn., Lawyers' Club Phila., Am. Coll. Trial Lawyers, Soc. Archtl. Historians (hon. counsel), Phi Beta Kappa. Democrat. Jewish. Club: Down Town (Phila.). Home: Gladwyne Pa. Died July 2, 1987.

ROMNEY, MARION GEORGE, religious official, lawyer; b. Colonia Juarez, Chihuahua, Mexico, Sept. 19, 1897; s. George Samuel and Artemisia (Redd) R. (parents Am. citizens); m. Ida Olivia Jensen, Sept. 12, 1924; children: Richard J., Janet Ida (dec.), George J. Grad., Ricks Acad., 1918, Ricks Normal Jr. Coll. 1920; student, Brigham Young U., 1924; B.S., U. Utah, 1926, J.D., 1932. Bar: Utah 1929. Asst. atty. Salt Lake County, 1935; asst. dist. atty. 4th Jud. dist. State Utah, 1937-38; asst. atty. Salt Lake City, 1940; treas. Zions Securities Corp., 1947-59, chmn. exec. com. bd. dirs. 1961-82, dir., 1958-82, chmn. bd., 1975-82; chmn. bd. Beneficial Life Ins. Co., Hotel Utah Corp., until 1982; Beneficial Devel. Corp.; dir. Bonneville Internat. Corp. Missionary Ch. of Jesus Christ of Latter-day Saints, Australia, 1920-23; sec. Australian Mission Ch. of Jesus Christ of Latter-day Saints, pres. New South Wales Conf., 1921-23, bishop 33d Ward, 1935-38, pres. Bonneville Stake, 1938-41, asst. to Council of Twelve Apostles, 1941-51, mem. Council of Twelve Apostles 1951-72, 2d counselor in 1st presidency, 1972-82, 1st counselor in 1st presidency, 1982-85; mng. dir. (Gen. Ch. Welfare Com.), 1959, chmn., 1959-63, mem. com. on expenditures, 1963-88; supr. Latin Am. mission 1961-68, Scandinavian, West European, South African missions, 1968-71; dir. Asian missions, 1971-72; Rep. Utah State Legislature, 1935-36; adv. welfare div. Utah State Civil Def. Council, 1950. Trustee Brigham Young U., Provo, Utah. Served as pvt. U.S. Army, 1918. Mem. ABA, Order of Coif, Phi Alpha Delta, Phi Kappa Phi. Home: Salt Lake City Utah. Died May 20, 1988, buried Salt Lake City.

ROMULO, CARLOS P(ENA), editor, author, university president, secretary of education; b. Manila, P.I. Jan. 14, 1901; s. Gregorio and Maria Pena (de Romulo) R.; m. Virginia Llamas, July 1, 1924; children: Carlos Llamas, Gregorio, Ricardo, Roberto. AM, Columbia U., 1921; hon. degrees, many colls. and univs., U.S., P.I. and other countries, 1935-85. Editor several P.I. newspapers, 1919-41; mng. dir. radio stas. KZRM and KZRF, Manila, 1939-41; mem. faculty U. Philippines 1923-28, mem. bd. of regents, 1929-45; mem. Philippine Independence Mission to U.S., 1921, 24, 29, 33; maj. Philippine Army Reserve, U.S. Army, 1941; lt. col. U.S. Army, Bataan, 1942; col. U.S. Army, 1942; aide-de-camp to Gen. MacArthur, brig. gen. 1944; sec. of info. and pub. relations Pres. Quezon's War Cabinet, 1943; sec. pub. instr., 1944; resident commr. of Philippines to U.S. 1944; permanent del. of Republic of Philippines UN, 1952-53; A.E. & P. of P.I. to U.S. 1954-62; pres. U. Philippines, Quezon City, 1962-68; sec. of edn. Philippines, 1966-68; 194; pres. of UN General Assembly 1949; chief del. on Far Eastern Commn.; sec. fgn. affairs, Philippines, 1950-52, 69-85; chmn. P.I.del. 9th session General Assembly UN, 1954; spl. Presdl. adviser on fgn. affairs, 1963-85. Author numerous books including The United, 1951, Crusade in Asia, 1955, The Meaning of Bandung, 1956, The Magsaysay Story (with Marvin Gray), 1956, Friend to Friend, 1958, I Walked with Heroes, 1961, Mission to Asia: The Dialogue Begins, 1964, Contemporary Nationalism and the World Order, 1964, Identity and Change Towards a Definition 1965, Evasions and Response, 1966, Clarifying Asian Mystique, 1969. Recipient Pulitzer prize for disting. correspondence, 1941, numerous other citations and awards. Mem. Philippine Acad. Scis. and Humanities (pres.), Gridiron Club (pres. 1931), Rotary (v.p. 1931, pres. 1935, v.p. Rotary Internat. 1938-50), Metropolitan Club, Cosmos Club, Nat. Press Club, Sigma Delta Chi, Tau Kappa Alpha, Phi Kappa Phi. Home: Makati The Philippines. Died Dec. 15, 1985.

ROOKS, R(AYMOND) NEWTON, lawyer; b. Nevada, Mo., Dec. 23, 1910; s. Ola Raymond and Amy Pearl (Ratliff) R.; m. Ruth Dunlop Darling, June 1, 1940; children: Melissa Darling, Mary Ratliff, John Newton. Student, Trenton (Mo.) Jr. Coll., 1928-30; BS cum laude, U. Ill., 1932, LLB, 1934. Bar: Ill. 1934. With law and claim dept. N.Am. Accident Ins. Co., Chgo., 1934-37; pvt. practice Chgo., 1937-84; mem. Rooks, Pitts, Fullagar & Poust (and predecessors), 1943-84. 1st dist. commr. character and fitness, 1963-73, chmn., 1971-72. Fellow Am., Chgo. bar founds.; mem. ABA (ho. dels. 1955-56, 60-61), Ill. Bar Assn., Chgo. Bar Assn. (bd. mgrs. 1949-51, 59-63, treas. 1954-57, pres. 1961-62), 7th Fed. Cir. Bar Assn., Nat. Conf. Bar Pres., Am. Law Inst., Am. Judicature Soc., Legal Club (pres. 1958-59), Law Club (pres. Chgo. chpt. 1967-68), Mich. Shores Club, Delta Kappa Epsilon. Republican.

Presbyterian. Home: Wilmette Ill. Died July 16, 1984; buried Meml. Pk. Cemetery, Skokie, Ill.

ROON, LEO, chemical engineer; b. N.Y.C., Aug. 6, 1892; s. Julius and Gizella (Goodman) R.; m. Anna Marie Miesem, Oct. 25, 1917; children: Donald, Lois Anne. PhC, Columbia U., 1910; MS, NYU, 1916. Instr. Columbia U., 1912-15, NYU, 1915-16; rsch. chemist, chief chem. div. E.R. Squibb & Sons, 1916-19; cons. 1919-24; pres. Roxalin Flexible Finishes, 1924-47, Nuodex Products Co. and subs., 1932-54; chmn. Hysol Corp., Olean, N.Y.; dir. Canciro Inc., N.Y.C., Hysol, Toronto, Ont. Chmn. bd. trustees Columbia U. Coll. Pharmacy, 1957-60; pres. Ea. L.I. Hosp., Greenport, 1960-61, also bd. dirs.; bd. dirs. Roon Found. Fellow Am. Inst. Chemists; mem. Am. Chem. Soc., N.Y. Paint, Varnish and Lacquer Assn. (hon., pres. 1941), Paint Rsch. Inst. (trustee), Columbia Univ. Club. Home: La Jolla Calif. †

ROONEY, ARTHUR JOSEPH, professional football club executive; b. Coulter, Pa., Jan. 27, 1901; s. Daniel and Margaret (Murray) R.; m. Kathleen McNulty, June 10, 1931; children: Daniel, Arthur, Timothy, Patrick, John. B.C.S., Georgetown U., 1920; student, Duquesne U., 1923. Chmn. bd. Pitts. Steelers Profl. Football Club, 1933-88; dir. William Penn Raceway, 1962, Pompano Raceway, 1965-88; promoter prize fights, 1928-88, horse race breeder, 1930-88. Mem. Holy Name Soc., St. Vincent De Paul Soc. Club: K.C. Home: Pittsburgh Pa. Died Aug. 25, 1988.

ROOS, JEAN CAROLYN, librarian; b. Buffalo, Mar. 9, 1891; d. Henry E. and Lydia (Siegel) Roos. Student, U. Buffalo, Cleve. Coll.; cert., Sch. Libr. Sci., Western Res. U., 1928. Asst. supr. sch. dept. Cleve. Pub. Libr., 1922-40, head Stevenson Room for young people, 1925-40, supr. youth dept., 1940-59; lectr. young people's lit., Sch. Libr. Sci., Western Res. U., 1929-59, Sch. Library Sci., Columbia U., summers 1931, 38. Compiler: Recreational Reading for Young People, 1931, By Way of Introduction, 1938, Patterns in Reading, 1954, Young Adults and the Public library, 1960. Mem. exec. bd., coun. ALA, Cleve. exec. bd. YWCA, Cleve. Consumer League, Women's Nat. Book Assn., Delta Kappa Gamma. Home: Jensen Beach Fla. †

ROOSEVELT, FRANKLIN DELANO, JR., lawyer; b. Campobello Island, N.B., Aug. 17, 1914; s. Franklin Delano Roosevelt (31st Pres. of U.S.) and Eleanor (Roosevelt) R.; m. Felicia Warburg Sarnoff, July 1, 1970; children by previous marriage: Franklin Delano III, Christopher duPont, Nancy S., Laura D. AB, Harvard U., 1937; LLB, U. Va., 1940. Elected mem. 81st Congress, 20th N.Y. Dist., May, 1949; re-elected 82d, 83d Congresses from 20th N.Y. Dist.; chmn. bd. Fiat Distbrs. Inc., Mickelberry Corp.; former undersec. of commerce; chmn. Equal Employment Opportunity Commn. after 1965; Liberal Party candidate for gov. of N.Y., 1966. With USNR, 1941-45. Decorated Legion of Merit with Combat V. Silver Star, Purple Heart, Sec. Navy Commendation ribbon. Mem. N.Y. Yacht Club, Racquet and Tennis Club (N.Y.C.), Masons. Episcopalian. Home: Poughquag N.Y. Died August 17, 1988.

ROOSEVELT, JULIAN KEAN, investment banker; b. N.Y.C., Nov. 14, 1924; s. George Emlen and Julia (Addison) R.; m. F. Madeleine Graham, July 26, 1946; children: Nicholas Paul, George Emlen III, Robin Addison, Fay Satterfield; m. 2d, Margaret Fay Schantz, Dec. 30, 1957. Grad., Phillips Exeter Acad., 1943; AB, Harvard U., 1950. V.p. Sterling Grace & Co. Inc. (investment bankers), N.Y.C. Mem. exec. bd. U.S. Olympic Com,, exec. com. Internat. Olympic Com. for U.S., coun. N.Y. State Maritime Coll., U.S. Coast Guard Acad., N.Y. State Maritime Coun. With USNR, 1947; 1st lt. F.A., AUS, 1948-55. Mem. U.S. olympic Teams, 1948, 52, 56; ofcl. 1969, 64, 68, 72, 76; recipient Gold medal. Mem. Am. Seamen's Friend Soc. (trustee), Am. Hist. Assn. (pres.), Desc. Colonial Wars, Soc. War 1812, SAR, N.Y. Yacht Club (life), Bond of N.Y. Club (N.Y.C.); Seawanhake Corinthian Yacht Club (Oyster Bay); Cruising of Am. Club (life), Storm Trysail Club, Hanko Yacht Club, Royal Norwegian Yacht Club (Oslo), Royal Swedish Yacht Club, Royal Bermuda Yacht Club, Transpacific Yacht Club (Calif.), Imperial Poona Yacht Club, Royal Danish Yacht Club; Royal Cork Yacht Club (Ireland); Fishers Island Yacht Club; Kanto Yacht Club (Japan); North American Yacht Racing Union, Sagamore Yacht Club, Far East Yacht Racing Fedn. Died Mar. 27, 1986.

ROPER, WILFRED ALLEN, banker; b. Richmond, Va., Feb. 13, 1892; s. George K. and Kate Cowles (Childrey) R.; m. Grace S. Gathright, Sept. 29, 1914; children: Robert P., Doris L. (Mrs. George D. Vaughan), George Kinsey. Student, Am. Inst. Banking. With Bank of Commerce and Trusts, Richmon, Va., from 1907, asst. cashier, 1916, v.p., chashier, 1919, pres., from 1935; chmn. bd. and chmn. exec. com. Bank of Commerce and Trusts, Richmond, Va., from 1959; bd. chmn. State-Planters Bank of Commerce and Trusts, Richmond, Va., from 1956, chmn. exec. com., from 1958. Mem. Va. Bankers Assn. (past pres.), Va. C. of C. (past pres.), Clearing House Assn. Richmond (past pres.). Home: Richmond Va. †

ROREM, CLARENCE RUFUS, accountant; b. Radcliffe, Iowa, Nov. 17, 1894; s. Ole John and Sine (Thompson) R.; m. Gladys Winifred Miller, Aug. 10, 1920; children: Rosemary (Mrs. John M. Marshall Jr.), Ned. AB cum laude, Oberlin Coll., 1916; AM, U. Chgo., 1925, PhD, 1929; LLD, Yankton Coll., 1935. CPA, Ind. Field rep. Goodyear Tire & Rubber Co., 1916-17, 19-22; asst. prof. econs., dean of men Earlham Coll., Richmond, Ind., 1922-24; instr. acctg. U. Chgo., 1924-27, asst. to dean Sch. Commerce and Adminstrn., 1925-28, asst. prof., 1927-29, asst. dean, 1928-29, assoc. prof., 1929; economist, acct. Com. on Cost of Med. Care, Washington, 1929-31; assoc. dir. med. svc. Julius Rosenwald Fund, Chgo., 1931-36; dir. com. on hosp. svc. Am. Hosp. Assn., Chgo., 1937-46; cons. Blue Cross Commn., 1947; exec. dir. Hosp. Coun. Phila., 1947-60, Hosp. Planning Assn. Allegheny County, Pitts., 1960-64; spl. cons. Hosp. Rev. and Planning Coun. So. N.Y., 1964-88; cons. several govtl., pvt. orgns. and assns. Author numerous books including Physicians' Private Offices at Hospitals, 1958, Health Service and Urban Sprawl, 1965. 2d lt. U.S. Army, 1917-19. Recipient Justin Ford Kimball award Am. Hosp. Assn., 1960. Fellow Am. Inst. Accts., Am. Pub. Health Assn., ; mem. Am. Acctg. Assn., Am. Hosp. Assn., Am. Econ. Assn., Am. Acad. Polit. and Social Sci., Cosmos Club, Phi Beta Kappa. Home: New York N.Y. Died Sept. 19, 1988.

ROSATI, JAMES, sculptor; b. Washington, Pa., June 9, 1912; s. Joseph and Lucia (Spagnola) R.; m. Carmel Greco, Sept. 1, 1931; children: Margaret Elizabeth Norton, Anthony John, Mary Joset, Phillippe Cecilia Tuscano. Grad., high sch. prof. sculpture Yale U., 1964-88; violinist Pitts. Symphony, 1928-30. Exhibited one man shows at Peridot Gallery, N.Y.C., 1954, Otto Gerson Gallery, N.Y.C., 1959, 62, Hopkins Art Ctr., Dartmouth Coll., 1963, Charles A. Dana Creative Arts Ctr., Colgate U., 1968, Rose Art Mus., Brandeis U., 1969-70, Albright-Knox Art Gallery, Buffalo, N.Y., Yale U. Art Gallery, Marlborough-Gerson Gallery, N.Y., Marlborough Gallery, N.Y., 1977, 1981-82, 1984, 1988, Gibbes Art Gallery, Charleston, S.C.; exhibited in group shows at 9th St. Show, 1951, Whitney Mus., 1952-54, 60, 62, 64, 67, Carnegie Internat., 1958, 61, 64, 1970-71, London County Coun., Battersea Pk., 1963, Mus. Modern Art Circulating Show, 1964-65, Internat. Coun. Mus. Modern Art, Paris, Berlin, 1965-66, Colby Coll., 1967, Mus. Contemporary Arts traveling exhbn., 1967-68, Grand Rapids Art Mus., Mich., 1969, New Sch. Art Ctr. N.Y., 1969, Fondation Maeght, Paris, 1970, Balt. Mus. of Art, 1970, Hudson River Mus., Yonkers, N.Y., 1971, 11th Biennale Middelheim, Antwerp, Belgium, 1971, Summit Art Ctr., N.J., 1974, Kennedy Galleries, N.Y., Greenwich Arts Coun., Conn., 1976, Museo Rufino Tamayo, Mexico City, 1981, Museo Angel Orensanz y Artes del Serrablo, Sabiñanigo, Spain, 1982, Sonoma State U. Gallery, 1984, Redding Mus. and Art Ctr., Ca., 1984, Palm Springs Desert Mus., Ca., 1984, Boise Gallery Art, Idaho, 1984, Cheney Cowles Meml. Mus., Spokane, Wash., 1984, Nohra Haime Gallery, N.Y., 1986; represented in permanent collections at Whitney Mus., Yale U., U. Mus., Geigy Chem. Corp., Arsley, N.Y., NYU Mus., Hopkins Art Ctr. of Dartmouth Coll.; also pvt. collects. Bd. govs. Skowhegan Sch. Painting nd Sculpture. Recipient Brandeis Creative Arts award, 1960, Frank Logan Gold medal and prize for sculpture Chgo. Inst., 1962, Arts Club prize Providence, 1962, Carborundum Major Abrasive Mktg. award, 1963, Design in Steel award Am. Iron Steel Inst., 1973; Guggenheim fellow, 1964; grantee Nat. Found. Arts and Humanties, 1966, Nat. Arts Coun. grantee, 1968. Died Feb. 24, 1988; buried Immaculate Conception Cemetery, Washington, Pa.

ROSE, ALFRED LEOPOLD, lawyer; b. N.Y.C., June 21, 1886; s. William Raphael and Clara (Siegel) R.; m. Dorothy M. Becker, Nov. 8, 1920; 1 son, William Ralph. AB, Princeton U., 1908; LLB, N.Y. Law Sch., 1910; MD, Harvard U., 1932. Bar: N.Y. 1911. With firm Rose & Paskus, 1911-30, Proskauer, Rose & Paskus (now Proskauer, Rose, Goetz & Mendelsohn), from 1930; hon. dir. May Dept. Stores Co. Past pres., trustee Mt. Sinai Hosp., N.Y.C. Mem. Am., N.Y. State, City N.Y. bar assns, N.Y. County Lawyers' Assn. Home: New York N.Y. †

ROSE, HARRY MELVIN, physician, educator; b. Niles, Ohio, May 30, 1906; s. Charles Homer and Anna Beatrice (Stevens) R.; m. Elizabeth Dryden Ramage, June 26, 1930 (dec. Apr. 1978); children: Ann Elizabeth (Mrs. Rene Alexandre Isaac), Frank Stevens, Stuart Ramage; m. Helen R. Buxton, July 30, 1979. A.B., Yale U., 1928; M.D., Cornell U., 1932; Sc.D. (hon.), Columbia U., 1980. Diplomate: in pub. health and med. lab. microbiology Am. Bd. Microbiology, Am. Bd. Internal Medicine. Intern Springfield (Mass.) Hosp., 1932; asst. physician N.Y. State Tb Hosp., Raybrook, 1933-35; sr. physician N.Y. State Tb Hosp., 1935-38; intern Presbyn. Hosp., N.Y.C., 1938; resident bacteriology Presbyn. Hosp., 1938-42, mem. hosp. staff, 1943-86, attending microbiologist, 1950-72; faculty Columbia U., 1940-73, prof. microbiology, 1950-73, John E. Borne prof. med. and surg. research, chmn. dept. microbiology, 1952-73; active staff Lakes Region Gen. Hosp., Laconia, N.H., 1973-86, Huggins Hosp., Wolfeboro, N.H., 1973-86; mem. Nat. Bd. Med. Examiners, 1958-62; Mem. Commn. on Influenza, Armed Forces Epidemiological Bd., 1949-71; cons. Sec. of War on epidemic diseases, 1941-46; cons. to surg. gen., 1956-72; cons. med. com. U.S. Army Chem. Corps Adv. Council, 1962-66. Editor-in-chief: Jour. Immunology, 1968-72. Recipient award Gairdner Charitable Found., Can., 1959. Fellow ACP, Am. Pub. Health Assn., Am. Acad. Microbiology; mem. AMA, Assn. Am. Physicians, AAAS, Am. Assn. Immunologists, Am. Soc. Clin. Investigation, Harvey Soc., Soc. Exptl. Biology and Medicine, Am. Soc. Microbiologists, Am. Rheumatism Assn. (hon.), N.Y. Soc. Electron Microscopists, N.Y. Acad. Medicine, N.Y. Acad. Scis., N.H. Med. Soc., Alpha Omega Alpha, Sigma Xi, Nu Sigma Nu. Club: Bald Peak Colony (Melvin Village, N.H.). Home: Sandwich N.H. Died Nov. 4, 1986.

ROSE, WILLIAM ALFRED, lawyer; b. Pulaski, Tenn., Oct. 7, 1900; s. William Alfred and Sarah Lilian (Tardy) Rl; m. Anne Elizabeth Travis, May 2, 1942; children: William Alfred, Elizabeth Travis Rose Sledge. AB, U. Ala., 1921, LLB, 1923; JD, Yale U., 1924. Pvt. practice Birmingham, Ala., 1923-81; ct. apptd. atty. for receiver in extensive litigation in Fed. Dist. and Appellate cts., 1933-37; mem. firm Bradley, Arant, Rose & White and predecessors, 1935-81. Mem. ABA (coun. sects. local govt. law and legal edn.), Ala., Birmingham bar assns., Am. Judicature Soc. Nat. Conf. Commrs. Uniform State Laws (life), Assn. Bar City N.Y., Sons Colonial Wars, S.O.R., St. Andrew's Soc. Middle South, Birmingham Little Theater (pres. 1942-43), Mountain Brook Country Club, Relay House, Execs. Club (pres. 1947-48), Phi Beta Kappa, Phi Delta Phi (nat. pres. 1939-41), Phi Gamma Delta. Episcopalian (treas., mem. exec. coun. Diocese of Ala. 1946-71, chmn. diocesan endowment fund 1965-71. warden emeritus ch. 1961-81). Home: Birmingham Ala. Died Nov. 25, 1981.

ROSE, WILLIAM CUMMING, biochemist, educator; b. Greenville, S.C., Apr. 4, 1887; s. John McAden and Mary Evans (Santos) R.; m. Zula Franklin Hedrick, Sept 3, 1913. BS, Davidson (N.C.)(Coll., 1907, ScD, 1947; PhD, Yale U., 1911, ScD, 1947; postgrad., U. Freiburg, Germany, 1913; ScD, U. Chgo., 1956; DSc, U. Ill., 1962. Asst. in physiology and chemistry Yale U., New Haven, Conn., 1908-11; instr. in physiology and chemistry U. Pa., 1911-13; assoc. prof. biol. chemistry Coll. of Medicine, U. Tex., 1913-14, prof. and head of dept., 1914-22; prof. physiol. chemistry U. Ill., 1922-36, prof. biochemistry, 1936-53, rsch. prof. biochemistry, 1953-55, emeritus, 1955-85, acting head chemistry dept., 1942-45; vis. lectr. U. Mich., summer 1938, Fourteenth Hektoen lectr., Inst. Medicine of Chgo., 1938; assoc. fellow AMA (mem. Coun. on Pharmacy and Chemistry 1936-43); mem. adv. bd. Wistar Inst., 1936-40; mem. food and nutrition bd., chmn. com. Protein Foods, Nat. Rsch. Coun., 1940-47, Nat. Adv. Health Coun., 1944-49; mem. adv. com. Nutrition Found., 1943-57. Mem. editorial bd. Jour. Nutrition (1935-39), Jour. Biol. Chemistry (1936-49). Discovered and identified the amino acid threonine. Contbr. papers on nutrition and intermediary metabolism and biochemistry of the amino acids to Jour. Biol. Chemistry, Jour. Nutrition, Jour. Pharmacology and Exptl. Therapeutics, Am. Jour. Physiology and Physiology Revs. Recipient Sci. award Grocery Mfrs. Am., 1947, Osborne-Mendel award Am. Inst. of Nutrition, 1949, Willard Gibbs Medal of Am. Chem. Soc., 1952, Charles F. Spencer award Am. Chem. Soc., 1957, 20th Anniversary award Nutrition Found., 1961, Nat. medal of Sci., 1966. Fellow AAAS; mem. Biochemistry Soc. of Great Britain, Am. Soc. of Biol. Chemists (councillor 1931-34, 1936-37, v.p. 1937-39; pres. 1939-41), Am. Chem. Soc., Soc. Exptl. Biology and Medicine, Am. Inst. Nutrition (pres. 1945-46, hon. fellow), Ill. Acad. Sci., Harvey Soc. (hon.), University Club (Urbana), Chaos Club (Chgo.), Phi Beta Kappa, Sigma Xi, Phi Kappa Phi, Phi Lambda Upsilon, Sigma Alpha Epsilon, Phi Beta Pi, Alpha Chi Sigma. Presbyterian. Home: Champaign Ill. Died Sept. 25, 1985.

ROSELIEP, RAYMOND, clergyman, author; b. Farley, Iowa, Aug. 11, 1917; s. John Albert and Anna Elizabeth (Andeson) R. BA, Lora Coll., 1939; postgrad., Cath. U. Am., 1939-43; PhD, U. Notre Dame, 1954. Ordained secular priest Roman Catholic Ch., 1943. Asst. pastor Immaculate Conception Ch., Gilbertville, Iowa, 1943-45; mng. editor Witness, 1945-46; mem. faculty dept. English Loras Coll., Dubuque, Iowa, 1946-66; prof. emeritus Loras Coll., 1982-83; resident chaplain Holy Family Hall Mt. St. Francis, Dubuque, 1966-83; poet-in-residence Georgetown U., summer 1964. Author: Some Letters of Lionel Johnson, 1955; poetry: The Linen Bands, 1961, The Small Rain, 1963, Love Makes the Air Light, 1965; poetry and prose: Voyages to the Inland Sea, IV, 1974; poetry: Flute over Walden, 1976, Light Footsteps, 1976, Walk in Love, 1976, A Beautiful Woman Moves with Grace, 1976, Sun in His Belly, 1977, Step on the Rain, 1977, Wake to the Bell, 1977, A Day in the Life of Sobi-Shi, 1978, Sailing Bones, 1978, Sky in My Legs, 1979, Firefly in My Eyecup, 1979, The Still Point, 1979, Listen to Light, 1980; poetry and prose: A Roseliep Retrospective, 1980, Swish of Cow Tail, 1982, Rabbit in the Moon, 1983, The Earth We Swing On, 1984; contbr. poetry and revs. to numerous mags. Recipient Montgomery Poetry award Soc. Midland Authors, 1968, Henderson award Haiku Soc. Am., 1977, Biennial Merit Book award Haiku Soc. Am., 1981, Shugyo Takaha award Yuki Teikei Haiku Soc. of U.S. and Can., 1980, Poetry award Yankee Mag., 1970, 81, 82. Mem. Acad. Am. Poets, Hist. Soc. Iowa, Delta Epsilon. Home: Dubuque Iowa. Died Dec. 6, 1983; buried Mt. Calvary Cemetery, Dubuque, Iowa.

ROSEN, CARL GEORGE ARTHUR, engineer; b. San Francisco, July 14, 1891; s. Carl A. and Hanna M. (Peterson) R.; m. Alice Stelling, Oct. 6, 1923. Grad., Cogswell Poly. Coll., 1910; BS, U. Calif., 1914, ME (hon.), 1925; ScD, Bradley U., 1955; LLD, Capital U., 1956. Registered prof. engr., Ill. Chief engr. Dow Pump & Diesel Engine Co., 1915-22, cons. engr., 1922-28; chief engr. Pacific Diesel Engine Co., 1923-24; engr. in charge diesel devel. Caterpillar Tractor Co., 1928-38, asst. chief engr. in charge diesel rsch., 1938-42, dir. rsch., 1942-49, cons. engr. adminstrv. dept., 1949-57; v.p., ptnr. List Rosen Wittek Assocs., Inc., Chicago Heights, Ill., from 1963; cons. R&D Dept. of Def.; cons. to industry in Europe and U.S.; mem. adv. com. to ordnance; Clayton lectr. Inst. Mech. Engrs., U.K., 1950; lect. Stanford U.; regents lectr. Buckendale Medalist, U. Calif., 1955. Author: Marine Diesel Engines; articles. Chmn. planning and constrn. com. Peoria Expn. Garden; mem. Naval Tech. Mission to Europe, 1945. Fellow ASME; mem. AAAS, Soc. Automotive Engrs. (pres. 19550, Am. Soc. Testing Materials, Am. Ordnance Assn., Peoria Acad. Sci., Creve Coeur Club, Engineers Club, Bohemian Club, Rancheros Visitadores, Sigma Xi, Pi Tau Sigma. Lutheran. Home: Woodside Calif. †

ROSENBERG, ALEXANDRE PAUL, art dealer; b. Paris, Mar. 8, 1921; came to U.S., 1946; s. Paul and Marguerite Ida (Loevi) R.; m. Elaine Lois Sobel, Feb. 29, 1948; childreN; Elizabeth Marthe, Marianne Barbara. PhD in Philosophy, Sorbonne, Paris, 1940. With Paul Rosenberg & Co., N.Y.C., 1946-87; pres. Paul Rosenberg & Co., 1959-87; spl. rsch. European art from Renaissance to 20th Century; organizer public exhbns., collector early printed manuscripts and books. Served with Free French Forces, 1940-45. Mem. Art Dealers Assn. Am. (pres. 1962-64, 76-78, dir.), Morgan Library, N.Y. Jock Club, Grolier Club (resident mem. N.Y.). Home: New York N.Y. Died July 10, 1987; buried Paris.

ROSENFELD, HENRY, dress manufacturer and designer; b. N.Y.C., May 17, 1911; s. Max S. and Rose (Brandes) R.; m. Mildred; children, Carole Rosenfeld Katz and Nancy Rosenfeld Upham. Student, N.Y. pub. schs. Shipping clk. Birke & Birke, N.Y.C., 1929; commn. salesman Bedford Dress Co., N.Y.C., 1934, gen. mgr., 1934-42; organizer Henry Rosenfeld Inc., N.Y.C., 1942, pres., chmn., 1974-86; pres. Henry Rosenfeld Luggage, 1975, Martec Co., N.Y. Home: New York N.Y. Died Feb. 5, 1986.

ROSENSAFT, MELVIN, business executive, management consultant, educator; b. N.Y.C., Jan. 28, 1919; s. Nathan and Yetta (Applebaum) R.; m. Beatrice Golombek, June 27, 1954; children: David Norman, Lester Jay, Emily Susan. Cert., State Tchrs. Coll., Paterson, N.J., 1940; B.S. summa cum laude, Rider Coll., 1942; M.B.A. summa cum laude, Suffolk U., 1978; cert. mgmt. cons., Inst. Mgmt. Cons., 1979. Lic. real estate broker, Mass. Field dep. IRS, Newark, 1942-43; with Gt. Am. Plastics Co., Leominster, Mass., 1944-48, 50-52, 56-71; asst. to pres. Gt. Am. Plastics Co., 1950-52, v.p. in charge mfg., 1956-62, exec. v.p., gen. mgr., 1962-71; pres., chief operating officer Artefactos Plasticos, Mexico City, 1948-49; pres., mng. dir. Irwin Products, Toronto, Ont., Can., 1949-50; mgr. plastics div. Ideal Plastics Co., Hollis, N.Y., 1953-55; exec. v.p., gen. mgr. Gt. Am. Chem. Corp., Fitchburg, Mass., 1962-71; pres., chief exec. officer Gt. Am. Chem. Corp., 1971-76, dir., 1969-77; ptnr. Devon Co., N.Y.C., from 1975; pres., chief exec. officer Melvin Rosensaft and Assos. (mgmt. cons.), Leominster, from 1976; chmn. bd., pres., chief exec. officer Cons. to Mgmt., Inc., Boston, N.Y.C., Cleve., from 1980; asso. prof. mgmt. Keene State Coll., from 1979, spl. asst. to pres., from 1981, indsl. liaison and coordinator industry/coll. linkages, from 1981; master lectr. in mgmt. and mktg. Suffolk U. Grad. Sch. Mgmt., from 1977; mem. adj. faculty Fitchburg State Coll., Mt. Wachusett Community Coll.; v.p., gen. mgr. Irwin Corp., N.Y.C., Leominster Plastics Co., Nashua Plastics Co., N.H., Fitchburg Realty Corp., Factory St. Realty Corp., Nashua; v.p., dir. F.I.A. Credit Union; bd. dirs. Lastomerex Inc., Jefferson, Mass., Paramount Systems Design Group, Inc., N.Y.C., Ameritec Corp., N.Y.C., Chipurnoi Inc., Long Island City, N.Y., Kinnerton Industries, N.Y.C. and London; bd. dirs. Small Bus. Inst. div. SBA, from 1982; indsl. lobbyist Mass. Legislature, U.S. Congress. Author: (with Lester J. Rosencraft) Industrial Needs Assessment for the City of Leominster, Massachusetts, 1978; monographs on pragmatic mgmt. edn., strategic planning, and collective bargaining; articles on OSHA compliance, indsl. mktg., and creative product applications in the petrochemical field. Mem. mayoral adv. on econ. and indsl. devel. City of Leominster; mem. adv. com. Leominster Urban Renewal, Mass. Regional Vocat. Tech. Sch.; mem. Fitchburg Indsl. Devel. Commn., SPI polyvinyl chloride task force.; pres., trustee, bd. dirs. Fitchburg—Leominster Community Center; bd. dirs. Fitchburg Gen. Hosp., Wachusett Personnel Services, Wachusett Ednl. and Career Adv. Services; life saving/water safety services examiner ARC; scoutmaster troop 17, Boy Scouts Am., chmn. Nashoba Valley Council; trustee Keene Ministry, from 1982; Chmn. Anti-Defamation League of B'nai B'rith. Served with intelligence division AUS, 1943-44. fellow Scheie Eye Inst. Presbyn. Hosp./U. Pa. Med. Center, Phila. Fellow Benjamin Franklin Assocs. of U. Pa.; mem. Commerce Club (past pres.), Rider Century Club, Fin. Mgmt. Honor Soc., Inst. Mgmt. Sci., Inst. Mgmt. Consultants, Am. Mgmt. Assn., Assn. for Bus. Simulation and Exptl. Learning, Soc. Profl. Mgmt. Consultants, AAUP, Soc. Plastics Engrs. (profl.), Chem. Soc. Gt. Brit., Soc. Plastics Industry, Internat. Platform Assn., Mass. Personnel and Guidance Assn., Leominster C. of C., Leominster Hist. Soc., Delta Mu Delta. Died May 27, 1983; buried Agudas Achim Cemetery, Fitchburg, Mass.

ROSENSTOCK, JOSEPH, orchestra conductor; b. Cracow, Poland, Jan. 27, 1895; came to U.S., 1946; naturalized, 1949; s. Bernard and Sabine (Gelberger) R.; m. Marilou Harrington, 1958. Student, Acad. of Music, Vienna, 1912-19, U. Vienna, 1913-20. Prof. H.C. Federal Republic of Germany, 1967; condr., pianist, composer, asst. condr. Philharmonic Choir, Viena, 1917-20; prof. composition Acad. Music, Berlin, 1920-21; condr. (symphony and opera) Stuttgart, Darmstadt, Wiesbaden, Mannheim, Met. Opera, N.Y.C., Berlin,, Tokyo, 1922-46; condr. N.Y. City Opera, 1948-61, gen. dir., 1952-58; dir. Opera House, Cologne, Federal Republic of Germany, 1958-61, Met. Opera, N.Y., San Francisco Opera, 1961-85; musical dir. Aspen (Colo.) Festivals, 1949-53; hon. mus. dir. and condr. Japanese Broadcasting Orchestra. Composer: A Piano Sonata, 1916, Symphonic Concerto for Piano and Orchestra, 1918, Ouverture for Orchestra, 1920. Awarded Order of the Sacred Treasure, Japan, 1957. Home: New York N.Y. Died Oct. 17, 1985.

ROSOFSKY, SEYMOUR, artist, educator. M.F.A., Art Inst. Chgo. Prof. art Loop City Coll., Chgo. Numerous; one-man shows include, Galerie du Dragon, Paris, France, Art. Inst. Chgo., U. Wis., U. Chgo., B.C. Holland Gallery, Chgo., Richard Feigen Gallery, Chgo., Gallery Odyssia, Rome and N.Y.C., Transart Gallery, Milan, Italy, I Portici Gallery, Turin, Italy, Hank Baum Gallery, San Francisco, Richard Gray Gallery, Chgo., Monique Knowlton Gallery, N.Y.C.; appeared in group shows in, N.Y.C., Chgo., Paris, Rome, Turin, Houston, Detroit, Milw., Brussels, Montreal, Washington; represented in permanent collection, Mus. Modern Art, N.Y.C., Art Inst. Chgo., Mus. Contemporary Art, Chgo., also pvt. collection; rep. by, Richard Gray Gallery, Chgo., Galerie du Dragon, Paris, Odyssia Gallery, Rome, Monique Knowlton Gallery, N.Y.C., Hank Baum Gallery, Galeria Minotauro, Caracas, Venezuela. Fulbright fellow, 1958-59; Guggenheim fellow, 1962-63, 63-64; Tamarind fellow, 1967; Cassandra Found. fellow, 1972. Died 1982.

ROSS, DONALD MURRAY, zoology educator; b. Sydney, N.S., Can., May 11, 1914; s. Murdock Willard and Jennie (Fail) R.; m. Ruth Emily Green, May 31, 1941; children—Mary Isabel, Andrew John. B.A., Dalhousie U., Halifax, N.S., 1934, M.A., 1936; Ph.D., Cambridge U., Eng., 1941, Sc.D., 1966. Research officer Cambridge U., 1941-45; lectr. Univ. Coll., London, 1945-60; prof. zoology U. Alta., Edmonton, Can., 1961-79, head dept., 1961-64, dean Faculty of Sci., 1964-76, prof. emeritus, from 1979. Assoc. editor Marine Behavior and Physiology, 1970; producer 6 sci. films, 1961-84 (Padua Bronze medal 1971); contbr. articles to profl. jours., chpts. to books. Bd. govs. U. Alta., 1967-76. Recipient Gov. Gen.'s Gold medal Dalhousie U., 1934; 1851 Sci. Scholar award 1851 Exhbn. Commn., London, 1937-41, Queen's Jubilee Medal, 1977. Fellow Royal Soc. Can., AAAS; mem. Can. Soc. Zoologists (council 1971-75, Fry medal 1980), Marine Biology Assn. U.K., Am. Soc. Zoologists. Home: Edmonton Alta., Canada. Died Feb. 13, 1986; cremated.

ROSS, EDMUND W., insurance company executive; b. Detroit, 1892. Grad., Detroit Coll. Pres., dir. C.P.A. Ins. Co.; bd. dirs. Pine Ridge Coal Co., Leonard Refineries, Gen. Tire & Rubber Co. Home: Grosse Pointe Mich. †

ROSS, GLENN ROBERT, psychologist, educator, university president; b. Kerens, Tex., Aug. 6, 1928; s. Henry and Cassie (Busher) R.; m. Billye Stricklin, Aug. 28, 1950 (dec. Mar. 1966); children—Mark, Robin; m. Betty Dick Chapin, Aug. 21, 1968. B.S., Tex. A. and M. U., 1949, M.S., 1950; Ph.D., U. Denver, 1955. Men's clothing salesman Conway & Co., Bryan, Tex., 1949-50; dormitory counsellor Tex. A. and M. U., 1950-51; grad. asst. Counselling Center U. Denver, 1953-55; counseling psychologist U. Tex., 1955-56; asst. dean students, asst. prof. psychology, dir. counseling U. Denver, 1956-59; dean student affairs Ball State U., 1959-62; dean student affairs, prof. ednl. psychology, vice chancellor student affairs U. Nebr., Lincoln, 1962-70; v.p., corp. sec., prof. U. Nebr., 1970-73; chancellor U. Ark., Little Rock, 1973-82; pres. Western Wash. U., Bellingham, 1983-87; Vice chmn. Assn. for Internat. Practical Tng., Inc., bd. dirs., 1978-87; former cons. Social Security Administrn., VA; dir. No. Systems Co., Academic Press. Contbr. articles to profl. jours. Apptd. by sec. state to U.S. Nat. Commn. on UNESCO, 1970, vice chmn., 1975; chmn. U.S. del. Western Hemisphere meeting UNESCO, Ottawa, 1971; mem. U.S. del. meeting UNESCO, Bucharest, Rumania, 1973; co-chmn. Ark. Brotherhood Program, 1974-75; mem. Ark. Humanities Council, 1976-80; chmn., 1977-79; regional bd. dirs. NCCJ, 1977; mem. Ark. Com. for Future Directions of Higher Edn.; trustee Mus. of Sci. and History, 1981-83; bd. dirs. United Way; mem. 4th Corner Econ. Devel. Bd. Served with USAF, 1951-53; lt. col. res. Mem. Am. Assn. State Colls. and Univs. (state rep. 1976-79, chmn. urban affairs com. 1978-80, dir. 1980-82, mem. del. to study Israeli higher edn. 1980), Am. Personnel and Guidance Assn. (past dir.), Internat. Assn. Univ. Presidents (steering com. N.Am. Council), Am. Coll. Personnel Assn. (pres. 1972-73), Ark. State Council for Econ. Edn. (dir. 1981-84), Council Presidents Wash. Pub. Colls. and Univs. (chmn.), Commn. on Instns. of Higher Edn. of North Central Assn. (cons.-evaluator 1980-82), Costa Rica Conf. Higher Edn., Greater Little Rock C. of C. (bd. dirs.), Bellingham C. of C. (bd. dirs.), Phi Kappa Phi, Beta Gamma Sigma, Phi Delta Kappa, Omicron Delta Kappa. Presbyn. (elder). Died Nov. 4, 1987.

ROSS, NANCY WILSON (MRS. STANLEY P. YOUNG), author; b. Olympia, Wash.; d. Robert James and Lydia (Giles) Wilson; m. Charles Walton Ross, Jr. (div.); m. Stanley P. Young, 1942. B.A., U. Oreg.; student, Bauhaus, Dessau, 1932, Bauhaus, Berlin, 1933; spl. student, U. Chgo., 1937-38. lectr. on Zen, C.G. Jung Inst., Zû rich, 1964; lectr. Dartington Hall, Devon, Eng., 1977. Writer articles and novels, from 1932; war corr., 1945; Author: Friday to Monday, 1932, Take the Lightning, 1940, Farthest Reach, Oregon and Washington, 1941, The Waves, 1943, Westward the Women, 1944, The Left Hand Is the Dreamer, 1947, I, My Ancestor, 1950, Times Corner, 1952, Joan of Arc, 1953, The Return of Lady Brace, 1957, The World of Zen: An East-West Anthology, 1960, Heroines of the Early West, 1960, Three Ways of Asian Wisdom, Hinduism, Buddhism, Zen and Their Significance for the West, 1966, Buddhism: A Way of Life and Thought, 1980; introdn. to The Notebooks of Martha Graham, 1973. Recipient U. Thant award for cultural bridge-building, 1981. Mem. Asia Soc. (trustee), Kappa Kappa Gamma, Theta Sigma Phi. Home: Old Westbury N.Y. Died Jan. 18, 1986.

ROSSANT, MURRAY J., foundation executive; b. N.Y.C., June 9, 1923; s. Marcus and Anne (Orbach) R.; m. Naima Landman, Nov. 19, 1949 (div.); children: Maxwell (dec.), John, Anne; m. Diane Kemelman, Sept. 23, 1976. Student, Lafayette Coll., 1940-41; AB, Swarthmore Coll., 1943. Contbg. editor Time mag., 1944-45; European rep. Joint Distbn. Com., 1948-49; sr. editor Bus. Week mag., 1952-62; mem. editorial bd., fin. columnist N.Y. Times, N.Y.C., 1962-67; dir. 20th Century Fund, 1967-88. Recipient Loeb Mag. award U. Conn., 1959. Mem. Nat. Press Club. Home: New York N.Y. Died June 28, 1988.

ROSSER, CURTICE, surgeon; b. Dallas, Jan. 3, 1891; s. Charles McDaniel and Elma (Curtice) R.; m. Lillian McCune Parks. BA, U. Tex., 1911; MD cum laude, Northwestern U., 1917; DSc, Southern Meth. U., 1955. Diplomate Am. Bd. Proctology (pres.). House pupil Mass. Gen. Hosp., 1917; practice medicine Dallas, from 1919; specializing proctology from 1928; faculty Southwestern Med. Coll., from 1919, prof., dept. proctology, from 1932. Lt. USNRF, World War I. Recipient Marchman award for oustanding sci. contbn., disting. svc. to medicine, 1951. Fellow Sociedade Brasileira de Proctologia (hon.), ACS (gov.), Internat. Coll. Surgeons (hon., pres. U.S. chpt. 1957-58), Am. (hon., pres.), Phila. (hon.), New York (hon.) proctologic socs., South Surg. Assn.; mem. AMA (hon.), So. Med. Assn., Dallas So. Med. Soc., Dallas So. Clin. Soc. (pres.), Acad. Med. of Sao Paulo (Brazil, corr.), Brook Hollow Golf Club, Dallas Athletic Club, Masons (33 deg.), Alpha Omega Alpha (hon. med.). Episcopalian. Home: Dallas Tex. †

ROTH, FREDERIC HULL, accountant; b. Cleve., Feb. 20, 1914; s. Stanley Edward and Myrtle (Hull) R.; m. Emmy Alice Braun, Aug. 17, 1936; children: Frederic Hull, Robert Allan (dec.). AB, Wooster Coll., 1935; MBA, Harvard U., 1937. CPA, Ohio, La., Va., N.C. With Scovell Wellington & Co., Cleve., 1938-62, sr. supr., 1952-62; ptnr. Coopers & Lybrand Internat. (formerly Lybrand, Roos Bros. & Montgomery), Cleve., 1962-86; bd. dirs. Magnetics Internat., Inc. Bd. dirs., treas. Cleve. Playhouse, 1964-66, bd. dirs., 1967-76; mem. nat. adv. bd. Am. Security Coun. Mem. AICPA (coun. 1966-70, gov. Cleve. chpt.), Ohio Soc. CPA's (pres. Cleve. chpt. 1960-61, state pres. 1967-68), Nat. Assn. Accts., Inst. Internatl Auditors, AIM, Tax Club Cleve., Internat. Platform Assn., Cleve. C. of C., Newcomen Soc. N.Am., Western Res. Hist. Soc., Ohio Hist. Soc., Gt. Lakes Hist. Soc., Early Settlers Assn., Nat. Trust Hist. Preservation, Internat. Soc. Brit. Genealogy and Family History, Order Founders and Patriots Am., SAR, Mil. Order Stars and Bars, SCV, Sons Am. Colonists, Sons and Daus. of Pilgrims, Descendants Colonial Clergy, Sons Union Vets. Civil War, Descendants Colonial Physicians and Surgeons, Soc. Colonial Wars, Soc. War of 1812, Mil. Order Fgn. Wars, Order of Lafayette, Order Blue Gavel (dist. treas. 1973-74, chpt. pres. 1973, dist. pres. 1975, ea. v.p. 1976, internat. pres. 1980), City Club, Harvard Club, Midday Club, Cleve. Yacht Club (treas. 1952-65, fleet capt. 1966, rear commodore 1967, vice commodore 1968, commodore 1969), Westwood Country Club, Catawba Island Club, Union Club Cleve., Clifton Club, Masons, Shriners, Rotary (bd. dirs., treas. Cleve. chpt. 1966-67). Republican. Methodist. Home: Rocky River Ohio. Died Jan. 28, 1986; buried Lakewood Park Cemetery, Rocky River, Ohio.

ROTH, LLOYD JOSEPH, pharmacologist, educator; b. Whittemore, Iowa, Sept. 18, 1911; s. Simon and Sarah (McCabe) R.; m. Mary Jane Morrow, Dec. 23, 1938; children: Dennis M., Marc T., Keven S. BS in Pharmacy, U. Iowa, 1935; MA in Chemistry, Columbia U., 1940, PhD, 1942; MD, U. Chgo., 1952. Rsch. chemist petrogalar labs. Wyeth Co., Chgo., 1936-38; asst. prof. pharm. chemistry U. Iowa, 1946-47; mem. biol. rsch. staff, sci. cons. Los Alamos Sci. Labs., 1944-48, 71-86; rsch. officer Manhattan Project, 1944-46; asst. prof. pharmacology U. Chgo., 1952-56, assoc. prof., 1956-60, prof., 1960-86, chmn. dept., 1957-73; chmn. med. exhibits 2d Internat. Conf. Peaceful Uses Atomic Energy, Geneva, 1958. Capt. AUS, 1942-46; col. Res. ret. Mem. Soc. Pharmacology and Exptl. Therapeutics, German Pharm. Soc. (corr.). Home: Englewood Colo. Died July 25, 1986.

ROTH, STEPHEN ALAN, corporate executive. s. Herman and Rose (Fingerman) R.; m. Paula Susan Goldstein, Oct. 5, 1961; children: Stephanie, Gary, Jill, Gregory. B.B.A., CCNY, 1958; postgrad., Fairleigh Dickenson U., 1964-66. Project supr. NCO div. Dun & Bradstreet, N.Y.C., 1963-65; product planner Sperry Rand, Norwalk, Conn., 1965-66; sr. research analyst SCM Corp., N.Y.C., 1966-68; v.p., dir. market services Doremus & Co. (advt. agy.), N.Y.C., 1968-85; mng. dir. litigation services div. Doremus & Co. (advt. agy.), 1980-85; pres. Litigation Resources, N.Y.C., 1985-86. Mem. Inst. for Mgmt. Sci., Am. Marketing Assn., Am. Statis. Assn., Am. Sociology Soc. Home: Wyckoff N.J. Died Aug. 11, 1986.

ROTHBART, HYMAN, retail apparel company executive; b. Bolechow, Austria, Nov. 11, 1891; came to U.S., 1900; naturalized, 1915; s. David and Lena (Schwartzman) R.; m. Minnie Branower, June 3, 1917; children: Clair Rothbard Wolfand, David. Stidemt, CCNY, 1910-12; LLB, N.Y. U., 1916. Bar: N.Y. 1918, U.S. Supreme Ct. 1925. Counsel Union Underwear Co. Inc., N.Y.C., 1938-75, sec., 1940-75; sec., counsel Goldfarb Investing Corp., N.Y.C., 1955-75. Trustee, treas. Jewish U., University Heights, N.Y., from 1962; mem. pres.'s coun. Brandeis U., Waltham, Mass., from 1965; trustee, bd. dirs. Bonds for Israel. Mem. Am., Bronx County bar assns., Maccabees (state comdr. N.Y. 1962), N.Y. U. Club, Grand Street Boys Club, Masons (Shriner), B'Nai Brith. Home: New York N.Y. †

ROTHSCHILD, LOUIS SAMUEL, business executive; b. Leavenworth, Kans., Mar. 29, 1900; s. Louis Philip and Nora (Westheimer) R.; m. Emily Bettman, Oct. 7, 1929 (dec. June 1988). PhB, Yale U., 1920. With Rothschild & Sons, Inc., Kansas City (Mo.) and Oklahoma City, 1920-56, sec., 1931-34; v.p. Rothschild & Sons, Inc., 1934-42, pres., 1942-55; chmn. bd. Inland Waterways Corp., 1953-59; chmn. Fed. Maritime Bd., 1953-55; maritime adminstr. U.S. Dept. Commerce, 1953-55; undersec. of Commerce for transp. 1955-58; pres., bd. dirs. Transp. Equities Corp., 1958-61, 65-84, Intermediate Credit Corp., 1962-65, Standard R.E. Improvement Co., 1965-75; U.S. del. NATO Planning Bd. for Ocean Shipping, 1953, ILO conf., 1958; chmn. Air Coordinating Com., 1955-58; mem. commn. govt. security, 1955-56. Mem. city planning commn., Kansas City, 1937-53, chmn., 1946-53; chmn. Menorah Found. Med. Rsch.; bd. dirs. Community Studies, Inc., Midwest Rsch. Inst., Kansas City; trustee William Allen White Found. With USN, 1918-19. Recipient Presdl. citation, 1958. Home: Washington D.C. Died Sept. 1, 1984; buried Kansas City, Mo.

ROTHSTEIN, ARTHUR, photographer; b. N.Y.C., July 17, 1915; m. Grace Goodman, July 4, 1947; children: Robert, Ann, Eve, Daniel. B.A., Columbia U., 1935. Photographer Farm Security Asminstrn., 1935-40; photographer Look mag., 1940-43, dir. photography, 1946-71; dir. photography, assoc. editor Parade mag., 1972-85; mem. adj. faculty Columbia U. Grad. Sch. Journalism, 1961-71; prof. emeritus Daytona Beach Community Coll., Fla., 1982; prof. Mercy Coll., 1982, Newhouse Sch. Communications, Syracuse, N.Y., 1983. author: Photojournalism, 1956; Creative Color Photography, 1963; Look at Us, 1970; The Depression Years, 1978; Words and Pictures, 1979; American West, 1981. Served with AUS, 1943-46. Decorated Army Commendation medal; recipient award 1st Internat. Photo Exposition, Syracuse U., N.Y., N.Y. Art Dirs. Club, Photog. Soc. Am., Nat. Press Photographic Scientists and Engrs., Boys Clubs of Am., 1982. Fellow Royal Photog. Soc. Gt. Britain, Photog. Hist. Soc.; mem. Am. Soc. Mag. Photographers (a founder). Home: New Rochelle, N.Y. Died Nov. 11, 1985.

ROTHWELL, CHARLES EASTON, college president; b. Denver, Oct. 9, 1902; s. Charles G. and Winifred (Burns) R.; m. Virginia Sterling, July 30, 1932; 1 child, Marth Anne. AB, Reed Coll., 1924, LLD, 1961; AM, U. Oreg., 1929; PhD, Stanford U., 1938; LLD, U. Calif., 1961, Golden Gate Coll., 1961; DHL, Santa Clara U., 1967. Dir. tchr. tng. in social scis. U. Oreg., 1927-32; instr. citizenship and history Stanford U., 1932-39; asst. prof., adviser to men Reed Coll., 1939-41; with U.S. Dept. State, 1941-46; adv. to U.S. sect. 1st West Indies Conf., Anglo-Am. Caribbean Commn., 1944; exec. sec. UN Conf. Internat. Orgn., San Francisco, 1945; sec. gen. U.S. del. to U.N. 1946; sr. staff mem. Brookings Inst., 1946-47; vice chmn., rsch. prof. Hoover Inst. and Lilbrary, 1947-52, dir., 1952-59; pres. Mills Coll., Oakland, Calif., 1959-67, emeritus, 1967-87; del. Fulbright Conf. Am. Studies, Cambridge (Eng.) U., 1952; mem. staff Nat. War Coll., 1939; trustee Mills Coll.; with Asia Found., 1967-71, AID, 1971-74. Author: (with Alfred N. Lomax) An Economic Geography of the Oregon Region, 1930; (with H.D. Lasswell and D. Lerner) The Comparative Study of Elites, 1952, Power and Peace in the Pacific; contbr. articles to profl. jours. Mem. Am. Polit. Sci. Assn., Am. Hist. Assn., World Affairs Coun. No. Calif., Am. Coun. Edn., Assn. Am. Colls. (coordinating coun. for higher edn.), Bohemian Club. Home: Inverness Calif. Died May 1, 1987; buried Inverness, Calif.

ROTHWELL, PAUL TAYLOR, food manufacturer; b. Dorchester, Mass., Oct. 16, 1892; s. Bernard J. and Emily (Taylor) R.; m. Adeline Gertrude Magrane, Apr. 14, 1920; children: Joan Rothwell Moor, Bernard J. Grad., Worcester Acad., 1911; student, U. Wis., 1913-17. With Bay State Milling Co., Boston, from 1913, successively sweeper, salesman Boston office, asst. to Eastern sales mgr., Eastern sales mgr., asst. to pres., 1915-40, pres., 1940-59, chmn. bd., from 1959; bd. dirs., mem. exec. com. First Fed. Savs. & Loan Assn. Bd. dirs. Mass. Soc. Prevention Cruelty to Children; mem. Boston Coun. Mass. Commn. against Discrimination. With U.S. Army, World War I. Mem. C. of C. (pres. 1952-53), Algonquin Club. Roman Catholic. Home: Wellesley Hills Mass. †

ROUSH, GALEN JAMES, motor freight company executive; b. Akron, Ohio, June 9, 1892; s. George Pendelton and Lucy (James) R.; m. Sarah E. Woodbury, Feb. 8 (dec. 1935); children: Galen James, Sarah E. Roush Werner; m. 2d, Ruth Coates, May 15, 1936; children: Thomas Weld, George Colton. AB, Hiram Coll., 1915; LLB, Western Res. U., 1922. Bar: Ohio 1921, Fla. 1925. Tchr. math. and scis., athletic coach high sch., 1915-17; pvt. practice law Cleve., 1921-25, Fla., 1925-29; organizer Roadway Express Inc., Akron, Ohio, 1930, chmn. bd., chief exec. officer, from 1956. Trustee Akron YMCA, 1942-54, pres., 1955; trustee Hiram (Ohio) Coll., 1950. 1st lt. inf. U.S. Army, 1917-19. Mem. Am. Trucking Assn. (v.p.1960), City Club, University Club, Portage Country Club (Akron). Republican. Mem. Christian Ch. Home: Peninsula Ohio. †

ROUSSELOT, HAROLD ANTHONY, securities and commodities broker; b. N.Y.C., June 13, 1907; s. Louis J. and Louise (Jaeck) R.; m. Elsie Muller, Sept. 2, 1931; 1 child, Anthony Denis. AB, Columbia U., 1929. Joined Orvis Bros. & Co., 1929, ptnr., 1938-50, mng. ptnr., 1950-55; gov. Am. Stock Exchange, 1954-60; gov. Commodity Exchange, Inc., 1954-64, pres., 1958-60; ptnr. Francis I. Du Pont & Co., 1955-66, sr. ptnr., 1966-71, mng. ptnr., 1971; chmn. bd. duPont Glore Forgan Inc., 1971-73; exec. v.p. duPont Walston Inc., 1973-74; sr. adviser, v.p. Drexel Burnham Lambert, Inc., 1974—; mem. N.Y. Produce Exchange, gov., 1953-58; former mem. Chgo. Bd. Trade, N.Y. Cotton Exchange, Boston Stock Exchange; bd. govs. Assn. Stock Exchange Firms, 1963-71, chmn., 1969-70; bd. govs. Assn. Commodity Exchange Firms, 1972-74. Chmn. com. on athletics Columbia U., 1951-60, trustee, 1962-80, emeritus, 1980—; chmn. Columbia Coll. Coun., 1958-59; pres. Columbia Alumni Fedn., 1960-62. 1st lt. USAAC, 1942; lt. col. USAAF, 1945. Decorated knight of Malta. Mem. University Club, N.Y. Stock Exchange Club, Luncheon Club. Republican. Roman Catholic. Home: New York N.Y. Deceased; buried Woodlawn Cemetery.

ROUTH, PORTER WROE, church executive; b. Lockhart, Tex., July 14, 1911; s. Eugene Coke and Mary M. (Wroe) R.; m. Ruth Elizabeth Purtle, June 7, 1936; children—Eugene Charles, Elizabeth Ann, Dorothy Kate, Mary Susan, Leila Ruth. A.B., Okla. Baptist U., 1934, LL.D., 1951; student, So. Bapt. Theol. Sem., 1937, U. Mo., 1938, George Peabody Coll., 1946-47; D.D., Wake Forest U., 1978. Dir. publicity and instr. polit. sci. Okla. Bapt. U., 1935, dir. univ. press, 1936-37; instr. journalism, editorial staff Shawnee News, 1938- 40; asso. sec. Okla. Bapt. Sunday Sch. and Tng. Union Dept., Oklahoma City, 1940-41; sec. Okla. Bapt. Brotherhood and Promotion Dept., 1942-43; sec. dept. survey, statis. and info. Bapt. Sunday Sch. Bd., Nashville, 1945-51; sr. sec. So. Bapt. Conv., 1946-52, exec. sec. of exec. com., 1951-79; vis. prof. So. Bapt. Theol. Sem., Louisville, 1979; exec. com. Bapt. World Alliance, 1955-85, adminstrv. com., 1956-85. Author: My World Too, 1948, Meet the Presidents, 1952, 77,000 Churches, 1964, Chosen for Leadership, 1976, Waiting in the Wings, 1978, Mission to the World, 1979; editor: Okla. Bapt. Messenger, 1943-45, The Quar. Rev, 1945-52. Chmn. Gov.'s Advisory Com. on Developmental Disabilities, Tenn. Mem. Am. Bible Soc. (dir.). Home: Nashville Tenn. Died Nov. 7, 1987.

ROUTTENBERG, MAX JONAH, rabbi; b. Montreal, Que., Can., Mar. 22, 1909; came to U.S., 1927, naturalized, 1940; s. Harry David and Dora (Garmaise) R.; m. Lilly Soloway, Sept. 24, 1931; children: Ruth, Naomi (dec.), Aryeh. Student, McGill U., 1925-27; BSS, NYU, 1931; MHL, Jewish Theol. Sem., 1932, DHL, 1949, DD (hon.), 1966. Ordained rabbi, 1932. Rabbi Kesher Zion Synagogue, Reading, Pa., 1932-48; exec. v.p. Rabbinical Assembly Am., 1948-51, pres., 1964-66, chmn. Jewish law and standards com., 1960-63, chmn. publs. com., 1976-87; exec. v.p. Jewish Theol. Sem., 1951-54, co.-chmn. rabbinic cabinet, 1957-87, bd. dirs., 1962-87, vis. prof. homiletics, 1972-87; dir. Sem. Coll. Jewish Music and Cantors Inst., N.Y.C., 1951-54; rabbi Temple B'nai Sholom, Rockville Centre, N.Y., 1954-72, rabbi emeritus, 1972-87; chmn. Nat. Acad. Jewish Studies, 1956-59; mem. fgn. affairs com. N.Y. Bd. Rabbis, 1958-87; exec. com. Jewish chaplaincy commn. Jewish Welfare Bd., 1962-87; mem. com. Synagogue Coun. Am., 1952-87; mem. Zionist Dist., Rockville Centre, 1954-87; chmn. Met. Rabbinical Assembly, 1958-60. Author: Seedtime and Harvest, 1969, Decades of Decision, 1973, One in a Minyan, 1977; chmn. editorial bd. Conservative Judaism, 1964-87; editor: Rabbinical Assembly Proc, 1940; mem. editorial bd. Jewish Digest, 1963-87; program editor (TV program) The Eternal Light, 1970-87. Mem. Rockville Centre Commn. Human Rights, 1960-87, Nat. Citizens Com. Community Relations Svc., 1964-87; bd. dirs. United Synagogue Am., Radius Inst., 1982-87. Chaplain AUS, 1942-47, ETO. Sabato Morars fellow Jewish Theol. Sem. Mem. Zionist Orgn. Am. (exec. com.), Am. Jewish Hist. Soc., Histadrut Ivrit Am. Home: Yorktown Heights N.Y. Died Jan. 18, 1987; buried L.I., N.Y.

ROUZER, E(NGLAR) MCCLURE, lawyer, business executive; b. Cumberland, Md., May 10, 1887; s. Alexander McClure and Emma Jane (Englar) R. AB, Western Md. Coll., 1907; LLB, U. of Md., 1910; LLD (hon.), Western Md. Coll., 1957. Bar: Md. 1910. Pvt. practice Balt., from 1910; mem. firm France, Rouzer, Mundy & Harris, Balt., from 1917; v.p., sec., dir. Mid-Continent Petroleum Corp., Tulsa, Okla., 1917-55; dir. Sunray-Mid-Continent Oil Co., Tulsa, 1955-59. Trustee Union Meml. Hosp., Western Md. Coll., The Emanuel Chambers Found. Lt., 320th Inf., 80th Div., U.S. Army, 1917-19; participated in Artois, St. Mihiel and Meuse-Argonne offensives. Mem. Am., Md. and Balt. City bar assns., Maryland Club, Elkridge Club, Phi Kappa Sigma. Home: Baltimore Md. †

ROW, WILLIAM STANLEY, mining company executive; b. Curries, Ont., Can., Feb. 1, 1904; s. Frederick and Clara Ann (Putnam) R.; m. Helen Shirley Rogers, Feb. 16, 1933; children: James (dec.), Caroline Margaret. BS in Mining, McGill U., 1927. Registered profl. engr., Ont. With Cerro de Pascoe Copper Corp., 1927-30, Lake Shore Gold Mines Ltd., 1930-37; mgr. Kerr-Addison Mines Ltd., Toronto, Ont., Can., 1937-55, exec. v.p., 1955-58, pres., 1958-66, chmn., 1967-84. Mem. AIME, Ont. Mining Assn. (past pres.), Can. Inst. Mining and Metallurgy (chmn. Toronto chpt. 1960-61), Profl. Engrs. Assn. Ont., National Club, York Downs Golf and Country Club, Goodwood Club. Home: Toronto Ont., Canada. Died Nov. 12, 1984; buried Mt. Pleasant Cemetery, Toronto, Ont., Can.

ROWAN, DAN HALE, actor; b. Beggs, Okla., July 2, 1922; s. Sean (John) and Clella (Hale) R.; m. Phyllis Mathis, 1946; children: Thomas Patrick, Mary Ann, Christie; m. Adriana Van Ballegooygn, June 1963. Student, U. So. Calif., UCLA. Formed team Rowan and Martin, 1952; performed in U.S., Eng. and Australia; TV appearances; summer TV replacement Dean Martin show, 1966; co-star Rowan and Martin's Laugh-In TV show, 1968-72, also co-producer series; charity performances for Eisenhower Heart Fund, ARC, others. Fighter pilot USAAF, 1941-46. Decorated Air medal, Purple Heart, D.F.C. with oak leaf cluster. Mem. Bohemian Club. Home: Englewood Fla. Died Sept. 22, 1987.

ROWAN, JAN CHRISTOPHER, architect; b. Warsaw, Poland, Dec. 24, 1924; came to U.S, 1949; naturalized, 1955; s. George B. and Zofia (Fajans) R.; m. Ursula Miskolczy, June 12, 1955; children: Christopher George, Timothy Roderick, Peter Oliver. B.Commerce, London Sch. Econs., 1944; student, Archtl. Assn. Sch. Architecture, London, 1947-49; B.Arch., McGill U., 1951. Propr. Jan C. Rowan, architect, Stamford, Conn., 1955-85; features editor Progressive Architecture, 1959-61, mng. editor, 1961-63, editor, 1963-69; exec. v.p.pres. R & S Internat. Inc., 1970-71; pres. Rowan Constrn. Co., 1972-85; lectr., instr. Pratt Inst., Cooper Union, R.I. Sch. Design, 1952-56,. With Brit. Liberation Forces, 1942-47. Recipient Jesse H. Neal Editorial Achievement award Am. Bus. Press, 1967. Home: Stamford Conn. Died May 5, 1985; buried Montreal, Can.

ROWAN, M. EDWARD, manufacturing executive; b. St. Louis, Jan. 28, 1891; s. James W. and Cecelia (Jannerette) R.; m. Colleen Wrape, Oct. 12, 1920; children: William H., Edward A., John G., Colleen Audrey (Mrs.J. Farral Browne), Patricia Ann (Mrs. Robert T.

Clark). Student pub. schs. Salesman Ely & Walker, 1916-26; salesman Elder Mfg. Co., 1916-20, dept. mgr., 1921-25, v.p., 1925-49, pres., 1950-59, chmn. bd., from 1959. Bd. dirs. Cath. Charities, USO, Social Planning Coun.. With USN, 1917-18. Mem. Internat. Assn. Garment Mfrs. (pres. 1935-38), C. of C. (bd. dirs.). Home: Clayton Mo. †

ROWE, HARRY WILLISON, college dean; b. Mercer, Maine, Nov. 13, 1887; s. Willison and Fanny Louisa (Groves) R.; m. Eleanor Hope Chandler, Sept. 2, 1913; children: Ruth Rowe Wilson, Robert Chandler, Esther Rowe Tallamy. AB, Bates Coll., 1912, AM (hon.), 1942; LHD, Western New Eng. Coll., 1953; LHD (hon.), U. Maine, 1957. Prin. Troy (Maine) High Sch., 1906-08; field sec. Maine Christian Endeavor Union, 1912-14; sec. No. New Engl. Christian Endeavor Unions, 1914; with Bates Coll., from 1914, successively grad. YMCA sec., alumni sec., bursar, asst. to pres., dean of faculty, 1946-58, dean emeritus, coll. historian, from 1958; trustee Maine Cen. Inst., from 1923, pres. bd., 1924-69; bd. dirs. Portland Jr. Coll., 1933-57, Nyack Boys Sch., 1955-61. Mem. Eastern Assn. Coll. Deans and Advisers of Men (pres. 1952-53), Am. Assn. Acad. Deans, Coll. Entrance Examination Bd., Huguenot Soc. Maine (pres. 1971-73), New Eng. Conf. Grad. Edn., New Eng. Assn. Colls. and Secondary Schs., SAR (pres. 1969-71), Soc. Colonial Wars (gov. 1974-76), Maine League Hist. Socs. and Museums (sec.), Maine (sec. from 1968), Androscoggin County (pres. 1958-61, 64-67, dir.) hist. socs., Christian Endeavor Internat. (trustee), Soc. Descs. Colonial Clergy, Maine Soc. Order of Founders and Patriots Am., Rotary Club (dist. gov. 1956-57, sec. 1959-74), Phi Beta Kappa, Delta Sigma Rho, Tau Kappa Alpha. Republican. Congregationalist. Home: Lewiston Maine. †

ROWE, PAUL NICHOLAS, lawyer; b. Indpls., Aug. 27, 1904; s. Pierce Edward and Cecelia Elizabeth (O'Toole) R.; m. Dorothy Margaret Meier, Apr. 18, 1931; children: Edward Francis, Norman Pierce. Student, U. Notre Dame, 1923-25; SB, Harvard U., 1927, JD, 1930. Bar: Ind. 1930. With Baker & Daniels, 1930-85, ptnr., 1939-76, counsel, 1977-85; sec., bd. dirs. Gov. Ind. Economy Program, 1968-73. Author, editor Indiana Taxes, 1953; author: History of Baker & Daniels, 1979. Bd. dirs. Ind. Continuing Legal Edn. Forum, 1964-67, pres., 1966. Fellow Am. Bar Found., Ind. Bar Found. (bd. dirs., v.p. 1965-66); mem. ABA, Ind. Bar Assn. (treas. 1947, pres. 1953), 7th Cir. Bar Assn., Assn. ICC Practitioners, Am. Law Inst., Ind., Indpls. c. of c.'s, Lawyers Club, Columbia Club, Athenauem Club, Nat. Lawyers Club. Home: Indianapolis Ind. Died Nov. 30, 1985, buried Indpls.

ROY, MAURICE CARDINAL, former archbishop of Quebec; b. Que., Can., Jan. 25, 1905; s. Ferdinand and Mariette (Legendre) R.; B.A., Petit Seminaire, Que., 1923; D.Th. (D.D.), Laval U., 1927; D.Ph., Institutum Angelicum, 1929; student Institut Catholique and Sorbonne, Paris, 1929-30. Ordained priest, 1927; prof. theology Laval U., 1930-46; rector Grand Sem. (Sch. Theology), Laval U., 1946; bishop, Trois-Rivieres, Que., 1946-47; primate of Can., 1946-81; bishop ordinary to Can. Armed Forces, 1946-82; archbishop of Quebec, 1947-81, elevated to Sacred Coll. Cardinals, 1965; named chmn. Council of Lay Apostolate and Pontifical Commn. of Justice and Peace, 1967-77; sec. faculty of philosophy Laval U., 1930-34; organizer Laval Summer Course of Pedagogy, 1935-37. Served as army chaplain (hon. col.) Can. Army Overseas, 1939-45. Decorated Order Brit. Empire; chevalier Legion d'Honneur; comdr. de l'Ordre de Leopold de Belgique; comdr. de l'Ordre d'Orange-Nassau de Holande. Mem. Que. Garrison Club. Address: Quebec. Died Oct. 24, 1985.

RUBIN, AARON, communication executive; b. Bklyn., Aug. 29, 1915; married. Student, CCNY. With acctg. dept. NBC, 1937-42, chief acct., 1954-61, fin. exec. v.p., 1961-77, chmn. pres.'s coun.; also bd. dirs; from asst. compt. to asst. treas. Blue Network (name changed to ABC), 1942-54. With USAAF, World War II. Died Dec. 23, 1987.

RUBINOFF, DAVID, violinist, conductor; b. Grodno, Russia, Sept. 3, 1897; came to U.S., 1912; s. Ruben and Libby (Zaparowitz) R.; m. Mertice Rubinoff (div. 1957); children: Ruby, Rubin. Ed., Forbes Sch., Pitts.; MusD, Warsaw (Poland) Royal Conservatory. Condr. Forbes Sch. Orch.; organizer profl. orch. for U.S. tour; engaged by Loew's Theatres for trans-continental tour; dir. Paramount Orch., N.Y.C.; organizer Dave Rubinoff orchs.; featured with Eddie Cantor in popular radio programs, 1930-35; violin soloist, conductor radio program NBC network, 1935-86; performed at army camps, hosps., schools, other orgns., averaging 300 concerts annually. Composer: Russian Rhapsody, Dance of the Russian Peasants, Slavonic Fantasy, Danse Russe, Fiddlin' the Fiddle, Stringin' Along, Russian Hearts, In a Spanish Garden, Souvenir, Romance, Tango Tzigane, Mon Reve d'Amour, Gypsy Fantasy, Banjo Eyes. Recipient Disting. award Am. Coun. Music; Warsaw Royal Conservatory scholar. Mem. Chgo. Fedn. Musicians (hon.), New Haven Fedn. Musicians (hon.), Kiwanis, Rotary, Optimists, Lions, Exchange Club, B'nai B'rith. Home: Detroit Mich. Died Oct. 6, 1986.

RUBLOFF, ARTHUR, real estate developer; b. Duluth, Minn.; s. Solomon W. and Mary Rubloff; m. Josephine Sheehan (dec.); m. Mary Hilem, June 19, 1980. Chmn. bd. Rubloff Devel. Corp., Chgo., North Kansas City (Mo.) Devel. Co.; pioneer, creator North Mich. Ave-Magnificent Mil, Ft. Dearborn, Old North Town; developer Ebvergreen Park Shopping Plaza, Chgo., 1942, Carl Sandburg Village, Bay Shore Properties, San Francisco; creator, developer Southland, Sun Valley, East Ridge, San Francisco; former cons. World Trade Ctr. Nat. chmn., bd. dirs. Horatio Alger Awards Com., N.Y.C..; mem. citizens bd. U. Chgo.; bd. dirs., life mem. Chgo. Heart Assn.; trust assocs. Chgo. Community Trust; bd. dirs., v.p. 100 Club of Cook County; chmn. library coun. Northwestern U.; life trustee Art Inst. Chgo.; past bd. dirs. Jewsih Fedn. Met. Chgo.; bd. dirs., nat. co-chmn. United Cerebral Palsy Assn., N.Y.C.; chmn., bd. dirs. United Cerebral Palsy Greater Chgo.; bd. dirs. State St. Coun.; mem. Chgo. Com. Urban Opportunity; co-chmn. nat. bd. dirs. NCCJ, also co-chmn., Chgo. Decorated Stella Della Solidarieta Italiana award; recipient award Am. Planning and Civic Assn., 1954, ann. Horatio Alger award Am. Schs. and Colls Assn., 1955, award North Side Civic Com. Chgo., 1955, award of merit VFW,1961, Good Am. award Chgo. Com. 1000, 1962, Man of Yr. award Cath. War Vets., 1963, Outstanding Civic Leader Chgo. Little Flower Sem. Soc., 1969, Chicagoan of Yr. award Chgo. Boys Clubs, 1971, Internat. Humanitarian award B'nai B'rith, 1975; named to Hall of Fame B'nai B'rith Women's Coun., 1966; named hon. fellow Brandeis U. Mem. Internat. Real Estate Fedn. Chgo. Bd., Chgo. Assn. Commerce and Industry (sr. coun. policy com.), Nat. Assn. Housing and Redevel. Ofcls., Chgo. Real Estate Bd., NAREB, Nat. Realty Com. (membership com.), Greater North Mich. Ave. Assn. (founder, past pres., bd. dirs.), Am. Soc. Real Estate Counselors, U.S. C. of C., Harmonie Club, Hemisphere Club, Doubles Club, Standard Club, Executives Club, Oil Men's Club (hon.), Monroe Club, The Arts Club, Mid-Day Club, Economics Club, Mid-Am. Club, Plaza Club, International Club, Poinciana Club, Variety Club (gov. tent 26, King of Hearts award 1973), Lambda Alpha. Home: Palm Beach Fla. Died May 24, 1986; interred Rose Hill Mausoleum, Chgo.

RUDY, CHARLES, sculptor; b. York, Pa., Nov. 14, 1904; s. John Horace and Marian Elizabeth (Emig) R.; m. Lorraine Schwartz, June 13, 1931. Student, Pa. Acad. Fine Arts, 1924-28; LHD (hon.), York Coll. Pa., 1981. Tchr. sculpture Cooper Union, 1931-41, Pa. Acad. Fine Arts, Phila.; artist-in-residence Mich. State Coll. Author: Painters and Sculptors of Modern America; executed sculpture in fed. bldgs., N.Y. World's Fair, Va. Poly. Inst. War Meml.; rep. collections Pa. Acad. Fine Arts, Brookgreen Gardens, Georgetown, S.C., Met. Mus., N.Y.C., others; executed World War II Meml. for Va. Poly. Inst., portrait bust of John Lloyd Newcomb, 1935-47; Sun Seaman's Meml., erected at Marcus Hook, Pa., 1949, war meml. U. Pa. campus, 1952; carving for Audubon Shrine, Montggomery County, Pa., 1955; 7-foot bronze figure Edgar Allen Poe, capitol grounds, Richmond, Va., 1957; meml. tablet of Ormond Rambo for Swedish-Am. Mus., Phila., 1959; sculpture Lehgih County (Pa.) Ct. House, 1964, Pa. Hist. Mus., Harrisburg, 1964; designer Nat. Commemorative Soc. medal, 1967; exhibited one-man show York Art Assn., 1976; group shows included Phila. Mus. Art, 1976, Gov.'s Mansion, Harrisburg, 1982-83; retrospectives included show, Phillips Mill, Pa., 1979, Bucks County Coun. on Arts, 1980. Winner Bronx Post Office Competition, 1936; recipient hon. mention Archtl. League, 1938, Am. Acad. Arts and Letters award, 1944, Dr. Herbert Howe prize, 1947, Percy M. Owens Meml. prize, 1971, 1st prize award and fellowship Pa. Acad. Fine Arts, 1976, Outstanding Artist award Rutgers Fine Arts Mus., 1976, Bucks County C. of C. Fine Arts award, 1980, Excellence in Arts citation Pa. Ho. of Reps., 1980, prize Doylestown Art League, 1984; Guggenheim fellow, 1942; honored with proclamation of Charles Rudy Day, York, Pa., 1976; named to York County Hall of Fame, 1977. Mem. NAD, Nat. Sculpture Soc. (Gold medal 1973). Home: Ottsville Pa. Died Apr. 24, 1986; buried St. Luke's Cemetery, Ottsville, Pa.

RUE, WILLIAM M., banker; b. Cin., Feb. 26, 1930; s. George W. and Anne (Overstreet) R.; m. Elizebeth Lee Altsheler, Dec. 30, 1960; children—Mitch, George, David. B.S. in Commerce, U. N.C., 1952; LL.B., U. Louisville, 1960. Mgmt. trainee to vice chmn., chief fin. officer 1st Ky. Nat. Corp., Louisville, 1954-85; dir Starks Bldg. Corp., Louisville, 1982. Trustee Ducks Ltd., Chgo., 1976; bd. dirs. Ducks Ltd. Can., Winnepeg, 1982; trustee Gheens Found., Louisville, 1983 Served to lt. (j.g.) USNR, 1952-54; Korea. Republican. Presbyterian. Clubs: Pendennis, Harmony Landing, River Valley. Home: Louisville Ky. Died Dec. 16, 1986; buried Cave Hill Cemetery, Louisville, Ky.

RUFI, JOHN, educator; b. Neosho County, Kans., Jan. 22, 1892; s. Jacob and Anna (Schmoker) R.; m. Greta W. Forte, July 1, 1922; 1 dau., Joan Elizabeth. BS, Kans. State Tchrs. Coll., Emporia, 1918; AM, Tchrs. Coll., Columbia, 1921, PhD, 1927. Tchr. rural and village schs., Kans., 1910-13, Jr. High Sch., Emporia, Kans., 1919, N.Y. Vocational Sch., 1919-21; prin. high sch. and asst. supt. Ironwood, Mich., 1921-24; assoc. Columbia, 1924-25; prof. of edn. Mich. State Coll., East Lansing, 1925-28; lectr. summers, Columbia, 1923, 24, 25, 35, Colo. State Tchrs. Coll., 1936, Northwestern U., 1937, U. Minn., 1944, 45, U. Calif., 1948-49, U. Colo., 1955; Fulbright lectr. in Turkey, 1951-52. Author: The Small High School, 1926, (with W.W. Carpenter) The Teacher and the School, 1930, (with W.W. Carpenter) The Teacher and Secondary School Administration, 1931, (with W.W. Carpenter) Study Guide to High School Administration for Teachers, 1933. A Manual of Supplementary Materials in High School Administration, 1940, The Supervision of High School Instruction, 1940, (with C.W. Martin) The Junior High School, Secondary Education in Turkey; contbr. to ednl. jours. Wuth U.S. Army, Mex. Border, 1916; U.S. N.R.F., 1918-19; to Germany for U.S. War Dept, 1947. Mem. NEA (dep. Secondary Sch. Prins.), North Cen. Assn. of Colls. and Secondary Schs. (v.p. mem. commn.), Mo. State Tchrs. Assn. (pres.), Am. Legion, Masons, Rotary, University Club (Columbia, Phi Delta Kappa, Phi Kappa Phi, Kappa Delta Pi. Home: Columbia Mo. †

RUGGIERI, GEORGE DANIEL, marine scientist; b. Phila., Jan. 29, 1925; s. Gervasio and Theresa (DeStefano) R. B.S., St. Joseph's Coll., Phila., 1948, D.Sc. (hon.), 1981; Ph.D., St. Louis U., 1960; D.Sc. (hon.), L.I. U., 1986. Joined S.J., 1950; ordained priest Roman Catholic Ch., 1962; asst. prof. biology St. Joseph's Coll., 1965-67; coordinator research, research biologist, prin. investigator exptl. embryology Osborn Labs. Marine Scis., N.Y. Aquarium, Bklyn., 1967-70; asst. dir. Osborn Labs. Marine Scis. Osborn Labs. Marine Scis., N.Y. Aquarium, 1970-72, dir., 1973-87; assoc. dir. N.Y. Aquarium, 1973-76, dir., 1976-87; mem. subcom. on marine resources Mayor's Oceanographic Adv. Com., N.Y.C., 1969-73; adj. assoc. prof. biology Fordham U. Grad. Sch., NYU 1978-87; mem. staff Louis Calder Conservation and Ecology Ctr., Fordham U., Armonk, N.Y.; research asso. N.Y. Ocean Sci. Lab., N.Y., 1971-82; co-chmn. Food-Drugs from the Sea Symposiums, 1972, 74; mem. Episcopal Diocesan Commn. on Environment and Ecology, L.I., N.Y., 1970-72; mem. marine scis. adv. bd. Coral Reef Soc., 1978-87; bd. adv. Robert Chambers Lab. for Cellular Microsurgery, 1983-87. Co-author: The Healing Sea, 1978; co-editor: Marine Tech. Soc. Food and Drugs from the Sea Proc, 1974; contbr. sci. articles to profl. jours. Mem. exec. com. Gateway Citizens Com., 1979; bd. dirs. N.Y. Inst. Ocean Resources, 1973-74, St. Joseph's Coll., 1973-79, Nat. Theatre Workshop of Handicapped, 1979-87; trustee U. Scranton, Pa., 1970-74, Fordham U., 1978-84, 87, St. Peter's Coll., Jersey City, 1987; mem. adv. com. Gateway Nat. Recreation Area, 1979-87; mem. com. on Peabody Mus., Yale U. Council, 1983-87; mem. U.S. Nat. Com. for Internat. Union of Biol. Scis., 1986-87. Served with AUS, 1943-46. Recipient Alumni Merit award St. Louis U., 1977, NOGI award for Scis. Underwater Soc. Am., 1986. Fellow AAAS, N.Y. Acad. Scis., N.Y. Zool. Soc. (editorial adv. bd. Animal Kingdom, Carter chair marine scis. 1983), Am. Assn. Zool. Parks and Aquariums (bd. dirs. 1986-87); mem. Am. Inst. Biol. Scis., Am. Micros. Soc., Am. Soc. Zoologists, Bermuda Biol. Sta. for Research, Hudson River Environ. Soc., Internat. Union Dirs. Zool. Gardens, Soc. Invertebrate Pathology, Harvey Soc., Wildlife Disease Assn., Coral Reef Soc. (trustee), Am. Littoral Soc. (adv. council 1984-87), Sigma Xi. Died Dec. 1, 1987.

RUGGLES, WILLIAM BRUSH, newspaper editor; b. Austin, Tex., Mar. 7, 1891; s. Gardner and Mary Lee (Grant) R.; m. Dorothy Sheridan, Jan. 30, 1922; children: Margery Alice (Mrs. Margery Gunter), Marilou (Mrs. Jesse R. Core III), Dorothy Clare (Mrs. William Spence Smith), Anne (Mrs. Alan Bromberg). Student, U. Tex., 1907-10. Sports editor Houston Post, 1910-16; spl. writer Houston Chronicle, 1916; sports editor Galveston (Tex.) News, 1916-17; sports editor Dallas News, 1919-25, editorial writer, 1926-37, assoc. editor in chief, 1937-43, editor, from 1943; sec. Dallas Automobile Club, 1920; exec. sec. Ex-Student's Assn., U. Tex., 1925-26; statistician Tex. Baseball League, from 1920, sec., 1921-25, acting pres., 1929. Author: History of the Texas League, 1888-1950; Texas league Record Book, 1888-1950; verse appeared in anthologies of Southwestern verse; editor Alcalde, 1927-41. 2d lt. U.S. Army, 1917-19, col. inf. AUS, 1942-46, col. USAR ret. Decorated Bronze Star, Victory medal with 2 star, German Occupation medal, Am. Theatre medal, S.W. Pacific medal with 3 stars, Philippine Liberation medal with 1 star, World War II medal. Mem. Tex. Geog. Soc., Dallas Hist. Soc., Res. Officers Assn., Soc. 1st Div., Am. Soc. newspaper Editors, Newcomen Soc., Mil. Order World Wars, Poetry Soc. Tex., English-Speaking Union, Phi Kappa Psi. Presbyterian. Home: Dallas Tex. †

RUKEYSER, MERRYLE STANLEY, journalist, lecturer; b. Chgo., Jan. 3, 1897; s. Isaac and Pauline (Solomon) R.; m. Berenice Helene Simon, June 25, 1930 (dec. 1964); children: Merryle Stanley, Louis Richard, William Simon, Robert James; m. Marjorie Ballin Lefler, Aug. 1, 1965 (dec. Apr. 1974). LittB, Columbia U., 1917, MA in Econs., 1925; LLD (hon.), St. Thomas Inst. Advanced Studies, 1984. Reporter Rockaway News, Far Rockaway, N.Y., summers 1914, 15; asst. sports editor and corr. N.Y. Morning Telegraph, N.Y.C., 1915-17; with N.Y. Tribune, N.Y.C., 1917-23, fin. and bus. editor, 1920-23; fin. editor N.Y. Evening

Jour., N.Y.C., 1923-26; fin. columnist Hearst Newspapers and Internat. News Service, 1927-58, editorial writer, 1931-52; mem. teaching staff Sch. Journalism, Columbia U., N.Y.C., 1918-35; former commentator MB; syndicated newspaper columnist Everybody's Money, from 1958. Author: The Common Sense of Money and Investments, 1924, Financial Advice to a Young Man, 1927, Investment and Speculation, 1930, The Doctor and His Investments, 1931, The Diary of a Prudent Investor, 1937, Financial Security in a Changing World, 1940, Life Insurance Property: the Hallmark of Personal Progress, 1958, The Attack on Our Free Choice, 1963, Collective Bargaining: The Power to Destroy, 1968; contbr. articles to fin., trade, nat. affairs jours. Pres. New Rochelle Bd. Edn., N.Y., 1960-62. Mem. Acad. Polit. Sci. (past pres.), Alumni Assn. Columbia U. Sch. Journalism (pres. 1924-27), Sigma Delta Chi. Home: White Plains N.Y. Died Dec. 21, 1988; buried Sharon Gardens, Valhalla, N.Y.

RUNNELLS, RUSSELL A(LGER), veterinary pathologist; b. Oceana, Va., June 21, 1891; s. Fred Augustus and Elizabeth (Scott) R.; m. Laura Theresa Marvin, July ;6, 1918; children: Frances E. (Mrs. Lawrence H. Van Vlack), Mildred V. (Mrs. J. D. Martin). DVM, Mich. State Coll., 1916; MS, U. Mich., 1930. Asst. prof. animal pathology Mich. State Coll., 1919-24, prof., head dept. anatomy, 1943-48, prof., head animal pathology, 1948-55; assoc. Va. Agrl. Expt. Sta., 1924-30; assoc. prof. Iowa State Coll., 1930-43; resident cons. pathology The Upjohn Co., from 1955. Author: Textbook of Animal Pathology, 1938. Lt. U.S. Army, 1914-19. Mem. AVMA, Am. Coll. Vet. Pathologists, Am. Assn. Pathologists and Bacteriologists, Internat. Acad. Pathologists, Sigma Xi, Phi Kappa Phi. †

RUSCH, HAROLD PAUL, oncologist, emeritus educator; b. Merrill, Wis., July 15, 1908; s. Henry Albert and Olga (Brandenburg) R.; m. Lenore Robinson, Aug. 6, 1940 (dec. 1978); children: Carolyn Elizabeth, Judith Ann (dec. 1976); m. Louise Van Wart, Oct. 20, 1979. B.A., U. Wis., 1931, M.D., 1933. Intern Wis. Gen Hosp., Madison, 1933-34; instr. dept. physiology U. Wis., 1934-35, asst. prof. oncology, 1941-43, asso. prof., 1943-45, prof., 1945-79, prof. emeritus, 1979-88, head dept. cancer research, 1940-46; dir. McArdle Lab. for Cancer Research, U. Wis., 1946-72, Wis. Clin. Cancer Center, 1972-78; Mem. nat. cancer com. NRC, 1954-58, com. on growth, 1949-53; research adv. council Am. Cancer Soc., 1962-65, bd. dirs., 1965-88, exec. com., 1970-74, nat. award, 1972, hon. life mem., 1974; mem. Nat. Adv. Cancer Council, 1954-58, Nat. Cancer Adv. Bd., 1972-74; mem. commn. on cancer research Internat. Union Against Cancer, 1954-58; mem. Pres.'s Com. on Heart Disease and Cancer, 1961, U.S. Senate Com. Consultants on Cancer, 1970. Author, contbr. sci. articles.; Editor-in-chief: Cancer Research jour, 1950-65; Editorial bd.: Perspectives in Biology and Medicine, 1959-73. Bowman Cancer fellow, research asso. in medicine, visiting Am. and European Cancer Labs., 1935-39. Fellow AAAS; mem. Am. Assn. Cancer Research (pres. 1953-54), Assn. Am. Cancer Insts. (pres. 1972-74), Am. Soc. Exptl. Pathology, Soc. Exptl. Biology and Medicine, Madison Geol. Soc. (pres. 1946-47), Sigma Xi, Alpha Omega Alpha (hon.), Phi Kappa Phi (Papanicolaou award 1981). Home: Madison Wis. Died May 26, 1988.

RUSCH, WILLIAM GEORGE, clergyman; b. Dunkirk, N.Y., July 22, 1924; s. Raymond and Isabel (Dufton) R.; m. Ruth Jeannette Johnson, Aug. 23, 1947; children: Carolyn Rose Von Endt, Elizabeth Diane Rusch Terry, Kathryn Ann Rusch Rible, Paul Christopher. A.B. magna cum laude, Washington and Jefferson Coll., 1948; M.Div., Western Theol. Sem., 1950; M.Ed., U. Pitts., 1950, Ph.D., 1958; D.Min., Pitts. Theol. Sem., 1975; D.D. (hon.), Grove City (Pa.) Coll., 1968; LL.D. (hon.), Waynesburg Coll., 1972; L.H.D. (hon.), Wilson Coll., 1973, Westminster Coll., 1978; Litt.D. (hon.), Davis and Elkins Coll., 1974, Lafayette Coll., 1975; H.H.D. (hon.), Washington and Jefferson Coll., 1977; D.Litt. (hon.), Beaver Coll., 1981. Ordained to ministry Presbyn. Ch., 1950; pastor in Tarentum, Pa., 1948-51, Pitts., 1951-54; pastor in 2d Presbyn. Ch., Washington, Pa., 1954-60, Ch. of Covenant, Washington, Pa., 1960-67; exec. Synod of Pa., Camp Hill, 1968-72, Synod of Pa.-W.Va., 1972-75, Synod of The Trinity, 1975-87; moderator Washington Presbytery, 1958; chmn. Christian edn. com. Synod Pa., 1960-66, chmn. higher edn. com., 1960-66, moderator, 1966-67; pres. Washington Council Chs., 1967; mem. bd. Christian edn. U.P. Ch., 1967-68, mem. nat. staff, bd. nat. missions, 1968-72; mem. Gen. Assembly Com. on Regional Synod Orgn., 1971-73; mem. council Gen. Assembly of U.P. Ch., 1972-76, mem. churchwide coordinating cabinet, 1972-87; co-chmn. Pa. Conf. on Interch. Coop., 1972-76; mem. Pa. Commn. United Ministries in Higher Edn., 1968-87; pres. Pa. Council Chs., 1977-78; mem. spl. com. on evangelism Gen. Assembly, 1982-85. Co-author: The Incomparable Snowden, 1961. Chmn. Washington Juvenile Commn., 1966-68; Pres. bd. United Fund Washington, 1962; life trustee Washington and Jefferson Coll., 1957-87; chmn. bd. Big Bros. Washington, 1967, Washington Sch. Bd., 1967-68; bd. dirs. Pitts. Theol. Sem., 1971-87. Served to 2d lt. USAAF, 1943-46, PTO. Recipient Ch. History prize, also Hebrew prize Western Theol. Sem., 1950; Disting. Service citation NAACP, 1968; Disting. Alumnus award Pitts. Theol. Sem., 1984. Mem. Phi Beta Kappa, Beta Theta Pi, Delta Sigma Rho, Eta Sigma Phi, Pi Sigma Alpha. Lodge: Masons (33 degree, master 1963, grand chaplain 1971-87, grand prelate commandery K.T. Pa. 1973-74). Home: Camp Hill Pa. Died Apr. 22, 1987.

RUSK, ROGERS D., physicist, educator; b. Washington, Nov. 17, 1892; s. James Madison and Annie Sue (Rogers) R.; m. Sarah Florence Eldredge, Aug. 19, 1931; children: Susannah Margaret, James Rogers. BS, Ohio Wesleyan U., 1916; MA, Ohio State U., 1917; PhD, U. Chgo., 1925. Prof. physics, head dept. North Cen. Coll., Naperville, Ill., 1919-28; assoc. prof. physics Mt. Holyoke Coll., 1928-40, prof., 1941-58, chmn. dept., 1940-46; head dept. physics Holyoke Jr. Coll., 1946-58, 60-61; John Hay Whitney prof. Furman U., 1958-59; vis. prof. Wesleyan U., Middletown, Conn., 1959-60; chmn. dept. physics SUNY, Oswego, 1962-63. Author: How to Teach Physics, 1922, Atoms, Men and Stars, 1937, Forward with Science, 1943, Atomic and Nuclear Physics, rev. edit., 1964, College Physics, rev. edit., 1960; contbr. numerous articles to sci., ednl. jours. With Signal Corps, U.S. Army, 1918-19. Recipient 1st prize for water color Springfield Art League ann. exhbns., 1935, 39, hon. mention, 1936, 37. Fellow Am. Phys. Soc., AAAS; mem. Sigma Xi. Home: South Hadley Mass. †

RUSKA, ERNST AUGUST FRIEDRICH, electrical engineer; b. Heidelberg, Germany, Dec. 25, 1906; s. Julius Ferdinand and Elisabeth (Merx) R.; m. Irmela Ruth Geigis, May 15, 1937; children: Ulrich, Irmtraud, Jürgen. Student, Tech U. Munich, 1925-27; cert. engr., Tech. U. Berlin, 1931, DEng, 1934; D in Medicine honoris causa, Kiel U., 1958; D in Physics honoris causa, Moderna U., 1963. Devel. engr. TV, Berlin, 1934-36; dept. head, head clk. Siemens & Halske AG, Berlin, 1937-55; recognized as lectr. Tech. U. Berlin, 1944, asst. prof., 1959-88; prof. Free U., Berlin, 1949-88; sci. mem. Fritz-Haber Inst. Max Planck Soc. Promotion Scis., 1954-88, dir. Inst. Elctron Miscopy, 1957-88; prin. rsch. in invention, exptl. testing, tech. devel. electron microscope, 1931-88. Contbr. numerous articlews on electron optics and elctron microscopy to profl. ljours. Recipient Senckenberg prize U. Frankfurt am Main, 1939, Silver Leibniz medal Prussian Acad. Scis., 1941, Albert Lasker award Am. Pub. Health Assn., 1960. Fellow Royal Microscopical Soc. (hon.); mem. Deutscher Akademie der Naturforscher Leopoldina. Home: Berlin Federal Republic of Germany. Died May 30, 1988.

RUSSELL, DONALD JOSEPH, transportation executive; b. Denver, Jan. 3, 1900; s. Donald McKay and Josephine (Nunan) R.; m. Mary Louise Herring, Feb. 8, 1921; children: Donna Louise (dec.), Mary Ann (Mrs. Richard Kendall Miller). Student, Stanford U., 1917-20; LLD, Loyola U., L.A., 1955. With engring., constrn., maintenance and oper. depts. So. Pacific Co., 1920-41, asst. to pres., 1941, v.p., 1941-51, exec. v.p., 1951, pres., 1952-64, chmn., 1964-85; mem. exec. com., chmn. bd. St. Louis-Southwestern Railway Co.; bd. dirs. Tenneco, Inc., Fed. Ins. Co., Chubb Corp. Mem. exec. com., bd. dirs. Stanford Rsch. Inst.; bd. regents U. San Francisco; mem. bd. visitors Tulane U. With RAF, 1918-19. Mem. Bus. Coun., Press Club, Pacific Union Club, Burlingame Country Club, Pinnacle Club, The Links, Recess Club, California Club, Boston Club, metropolitan Club, Bohemian Club, Delta Tau Delta, Sigma Phi Upsilon. Republican. Roman Catholic. Home: San Francisco Calif. Died Dec. 13, 1985.

RUSSELL, FREDERIC ARTHUR, business management educator; b. Sioux Falls, S.D., June 22, 1886; s. Marcus and Florence Ida (Knappen) R.; m. Myra Parker, Aug. 5, 1911; children: Carlton (dec.), Helen. AB, Albion (Mich.) Coll., 1908, AM, 1909, LLD (hon.), 1957; PhD, U. Ill., 1916. With various newspapers, 1909-13; instr. U. Ill., 1916-17, asst. prof., 1919-21, assoc. prof. bus. orgn. and operation, 1921-24, prof., head div., 1924-51, prof. emeritus, from 1951; asst. prof. journalism U. Washington, 1917-19, acting dir. Sch. Journalism, 1918-19; tchr. summers U. Washington, Northwestern U., U. Chgo., UCLA. Author: Management of Sales Organization, 1922, Textbook of Salesmanship, 1924, 8th edit., 1969, Speaking Effectively, 1928, (with F.M. Jones) Cases and Problems in Salesmanship, (with Victor Vogt) Verkaufs-Psychologie fur resende Kaufleute, 1930. Mem. Am. Econ. Assn., Am. Mgmt. Assn., Am. Mtg. Assn. (pres. predecessor orgn. 1927), SAR, Soc. Mayflower Descendants, Founders and Patriots Am., Huguenot Soc. Am., Kiwanis, Beta Gamma Sigma, Alpha Kappa Psi, Alpha Delta Sigma, Phi Beta Kappa, Sigma Nu, Sigma Delta Chi. Presbyterian. Home: Northampton Mass. †

RUSSELL, JOHN EDWARD, business executive; b. Manzanita, Calif., Aug. 26, 1889; s. Frederick William and Flora (Philpots) R.; m. Olive Ashton Edgell, June 1, 1918; children: Peter E., Phyllis Ashton Russell Chandler. Ed. high sch., San Francisco. With William Dinswood & Co., San Francisco and N.Y.C., 1908-22; with Theo. H. Davies & Co., Ltd., Honolulu, 1922-61, pres., 1930-55, chmn. bd., 1955-61; bd. dirs. Hawaiian Trust Co., Ltd., First Nat. Bank Hawaii. Trustee S.M. Damon Estate Trust, Honolulu. Mem. Hawaiian Sugar Planters Assn., Hawaiian Sugar Techs. (life), Pacific-Union Club (San Francisco), Pacific Club (Honolulu). Home: Honolulu Hawaii. †

RUSSELL, JOHN MCFARLANE, foundation executive; b. N.Y.C., Apr. 28, 1903; s. James Earl and Agnes (Fletcher) R.; m. Hortense Hoad, Feb. 9, 1929 (dec. Apr. 1958). AB, U. Mich., 1924; DSc (hon.), Woman's Med. Coll. Pa., 1951; LLD, Queen's U., Can., 1954, Duke U., 1966. Rep. Ginn & Co., 1924-29; asst. in survey Carnegie Corp. New Zealand, Australia and Republic of South Africa, 1928; adminstrv. asst., asst. to pres. Carnegie Corp., N.Y., 1930-39; rsch. assoc. radio in edn. project Am. Assn. Adult Edn., 1929-30; asst. to pres. Harvard U., 1940-42; rsch. officer, Allied Geog. Sect., G.H.Q., S.W. Pacific area; exec. dir., sec. Army and Navy Com. on Welfare and Recreation, Washington, 1944-46; v.p., exec. dir. Markle Found., 1946-60, pres., 1960-69; mem. adv. coun. dept. biology Princeton U. Mem. com. on growth NRC, 1947-56; mem. sci. adv. coun. Am. Cancer Soc., 1956-58; dir. Nat. Health Coun., 1962-65, v.p., 1965-69. With U.S. Army, 1942-44. Recipient Russell award, 1962, Rosenberger medal U. Chgo., 1968, Abraham Flaxner award Assn. Am. Med. Colls., 1969. Mem. Trigon, Coffee House Club, Century Club, Union Club, N.Y. Club. Presbyterian. Died Mar. 15, 1986.

RUSSELL, PAUL FARR, physician; b. Boston, Aug. 12, 1894; s. Samuel and Sarah (Woodman) R.; m. Phyllis Additon, 1922; children: Christopher Harvey, Theodore Emery. AB, Boston U., 1916; MD, Cornell U., 1921; MPH, Harvard U., 1929; ScD (hon.), Colby Coll., 1960. Diplomate Am. Bd. Preventive Medicine and Pub. Health. Mem. staff Rockefeller Found., 1923-59; cons. AID, 1957-65; cons., also mem. malaria panel WHO, 1947-83; cons. to surg. gen. U.S. Army, 1947-70; vis. lectr. Harvard U., 1958-60, 63-67, vis. prof., 1960-63. Author: Man's Mastery of Malaria, 1955, others; contbr. articles to profl. jours. Col. M.C., U.S. Army, 1942-45. Decorated Legion of Merit with oak leaf cluster; Mary Kingsley medalist liverpool Sch. Tropical Medicine, 1949, Walter Reed medalist Am. Soc. Tropical Medicine, Cornell Med. Alumni award of distinction, 1958; named to Collegium Disting. Alumni Boston U., 1974. Fellow AAAS (life), Royal Soc. Tropical Medicine (hon.); mem. Am. Pub. Health Assn., am. Soc. Tropical Medicine and Hygiene (LePrince medal 1979), Acad. nacionale Medicine (hon.), Nat. Malaria Soc. (hon.), Cosmos Club, Army and Navy Club, Explorer's Club. Republican. Congregationalist. Home: Richmond Va. Died Nov. 2, 1983.

RUST, RICHARD SUTTON, insurance executive; b. Cin., Oct. 1, 1889; s. Charles and Annie D. (Brown) R.; m. Margery T. Rutter, Sept. 30, 1916; children: Richard Sutton, James Gillespie. AB, Wesleyan U., Middletown, Conn., 1912; LLB, Cin. Law Sch., 1929. With Union Cen. Life Ins. Co., Cin., from 1912, v.p., sec., from 1942. Pres. Cin. Bur. Govtl. Rsch. Mem. SAR (pres. Cin. chpt., pres. Ohio soc.), Soc. Colonial Wars (dep. gov. gen., gov. Ohio soc.), Masons, Cuvier Press Club, University Club, Queen City Club, Country Club (Cin.); Lotus Club (N.Y.C.); Literary Club. Home: Cincinnati Ohio. †

RUSTIN, BAYARD, human rights activist; b. West Chester, Pa., Mar. 17, 1912; s. Florence Rustin. Student, Wilberforce (Ohio) U., 1932-33, Cheyney (Pa.) State Tchrs. Coll., 1933-34, CCNY, 1934-35; 18 hon. degrees including, Harvard U., Brown U., NYU, Yale U. Race relations dir. Fellowship of Reconciliation, 1941-53; field sec. Congress Racial Equality, 1941; exec. sec. War Resisters' League, 1953-55; spl. asst. to Dr. Martin Luther King, Jr., 1955-60; organizer March on Washington for Jobs and Freedom, 1963; pres. A. Philip Randolph Inst., N.Y.C., 1966-79, chmn., 1979-87; pres. A. Philip Randolph Ednl. Fund, N.Y.C., 1967-87; Chmn. Social Democrats U.S.A.; chmn. exec. com. Leadership Conf. on Civil Rights. Author: Down The Line, 1971, Strategies for Freedom, 1976, also articles. Bd. dirs. NAACP Legal Def. Fund, Black Ams. to Support Israel Com., League Indsl. Democracy, AFL-CIO Labor Studies Center, Coalition for Dem. Majority, Com. on Present Danger, Ams. for Energy Independence; Bd. dirs., chmn. exec. com. Freedom House.; Bd. dirs., vice chmn. Internat. Rescue Com.; mem. U.S. Holocaust Meml. Council. Recipient Eleanor Roosevelt award Trade Union Leadership Council, 1966; Man of Year award Pitts. br. NAACP, 1965; Liberty Bell award Howard U. Law Sch., 1967; John Dewey award United Fedn. Tchrs., 1968; Family of Man award Nat. Council Chs., 1969; John F. Kennedy award Nat. Council Jewish Women, 1971; Lyndon Baines Johnson award Urban Coalition, 1974; Murray Green award AFL-CIO, 1980; Stephen Wise award Am. Jewish Com., 1981; John LaFarge Meml. award Cath. Interracial Council of N.Y., 1981. Mem. UN Assn. (dir.), Soc. of Friends. Home: New York N.Y. Died Aug. 24, 1987; interred at pvt. residence, N.Y. State.

RUTSTEIN, DAVID DAVIS, physician, educator; b. Wilkes-Barre, Pa., Feb. 5, 1909; s. Harry and Nellie (Davis) R.; m. Mazie E. Weissman, Feb. 22, 1935; children: Catherine Ann, David Davis; m. Ruth E. Rickel, Aug. 11, 1951 (dec. 1978); m. Beverly Bennett, Nov. 3, 1979. B.S., Harvard U., 1930, M.D., 1934. Asst. in bacteriology, research fellow pediatrics Harvard U. Med. Sch., 1936-37, prof. preventive medicine and head dept., 1947-69, Ridley Watts prof., 1966-75, emeritus, 1975-86; disting. Physician VA, 1976-82; vis. inst. lectr. Mass. Inst. Tech., 1970-71; asst. prof. medicine Albany Med. Coll., 1940-43; asso. vis. physician Bellevue Hosp., 1943-47; cons. preventive medicine Boston Hosp. for Women, Mass. Gen. Hosp.; physician Children's Hosp.; med. cons. pneumonia N.Y. State Dept. Health, Albany, 1937-40, chief cardiac bur., 1940-42; nat. dir. gas protection sect. Office Civilian Def., Washington, 1942-43; dep. commr. health N.Y.C. Dept. Health, 1943-46, dir. bur. labs., 1943-45; med. dir. Am. Heart Assn., Am. Council Rheumatic Fever, N.Y.C., 1946-47; chmn. U.S.-U.K. Coop. Rheumatic Fever Study, 1950-65, Internat. Conf. Hemolytic Streptococcus in Rheumatic Fever, Internat. Children's Centre, Paris, 1956; chmn. expert com. on rheumatic diseases WHO, Geneva, 1956, mem. expert com. cardiovascular diseases and hypertension, 1958, chmn. expert com. on prevention of rheumatic fever, 1966; corp. vis. com., med. dept. Mass. Inst. Tech., 1964-70; mem. nat. adv. council Peace Corps, 1965-69; com. on interplay of engring. with biology and medicine Nat. Acad. Engring., 1967-73; mem. spl. med. adv. group VA, 1968-73; governing bd. Sante, 1975-79, Centre National de la Recherche Scientifique (CNRS), France, 1975-79. Author: Lifetime Health Record, 1958, The Coming Revolution in Medicine, 1967, (with Murray Eden) Engineering and Living Systems, 1970, Blueprint for Medical Care, 1974; also sci. papers. Decorated chevalier Legion of Honor, France; recipient Benjamin Franklin Mag. award, 1957; Jubilee medal Swedish Med. Soc., 1966. Fellow Am. Acad. Arts and Scis. (council); mem. Academie Nationale de Mé decine (Paris) (corr.), Royal Soc. Medicine (London) (hon.), Am. Heart Assn. (v.p. 1954-57, Gold Heart award 1959), Am. Soc. Clin. Investigation, Am. Pub. Health Assn. (governing council), Am. Epidemiol. Soc. (pres. 1966-67), Inst. Medicine, Nat. Acad. Scis., Sigma Xi, Alpha Omega Alpha. Clubs: Aesculapian (Boston), St. Botolph (Boston); Confrerie des Chevaliers du Tastevin, Nuits-St Georges. Home: Cambridge Mass. Died Feb. 14, 1986; cremated.

RYAN, JAMES, Irish government official, physician; b. Tomcoole, Wexford, Ireland, Dec. 6, 1892; s. John and Elizabeth (Sutton) R.; m. Mairin Cregan, Aug., 1919; children: Eoin, Nuala, Seamus. MB, BChir, BA in Obstetrics, U. Coll., Dublin, Ireland, 1917; D in Pub. Health, U. Coll., 1922. Physician Dublin Skin and Cancer Hosp., 1921-25; med. adminstr. New Ireland Assurance Co., 1918-57; mem. Brit. Parliament, 1918-22; mem. Irish Parliament, from 1923, minister for agr., 1932-47, for health and social welfare, 1947-48, 51-54, for fin., from 1957; del. Ottawa Econ. Conf., 1932, Irish-British Peace Conf., 1938, FAO Conf., Copenhagen, 1946; bd. dirs. New Ireland Assurance Co., Irish Nat. Ins. Co., Burnhouse Ireland, Ltd., Nat. Tanners, Ltd. Chmn. Wexford County Council, 1919-22. Served med. dir. Irish Rep. Army, 1916, comdt. bn., 1917-20, brigade, 1920-22, in prison, 1916, 20-21, 22-23. Home: Delgany, County Wicklow Ireland. †

RYDER, PAUL BERNHARD, consul general for Denmark; b. Copenhagen, Nov. 1, 1892; s. Carl S. and Karen H.H. (Shroder) R.; married Tove Ryder (neé Baroness Schaffalitsky de Muckadell); 1 dau., Tove Falch. Candidatus juris, U. Copenhagen, 1916. Atty.'s articled clk. 1916-17; comml. activity U.S.A., Chile, Argentina, 1917-21; entered Danish fgn. svc., 1921; ofcl. assignments Danish fgn. svc., Copenhagen, Reval, Helsingfors, Haag, Bern, Geneva, Madrid, Lisbon, O, slo and Flensburg, from 1957; consul gen. N.Y.C., from 1957. Home: New York N.Y. †

RYERSON, KNOWLES AUGUSTUS, horticulturist; b. Seattle, Oct. 17, 1892; s. Will Augustus and Jessie (Knowles) R.; m. Emma Mary Freeman, Aug. 3, 1916 (dec.); 1 child (dec.); m. 2d, Edith Palmer Popenoe, June 25, 1969. BS, U. Calif., 1916, MS, 1923, LLD, 1961. With Agrl. extension svc. U. Calif., 1919-25; asst. state club leader 1919-21; asst. farm adviser Los Angeles County, Calif., 1922-23, farm adviser, 1924-25; horticulturist Agrl. Svc. Technique, Haiti, 1925-27, Joint Palestine Survey Commn., Palestine and Transjordan, May-Nov. 1927; in charge Div. Fgn. Plant Introduction Bur. Plant Industry, U.S. Dept. Agr., 1928-34; chief Bur. Plant Industry, 1934, in charge subtropical fruit investigations, 1934-37; dir., prof. horticulture U. Calif., Davis, 1937-52; dean Berkeley campus U. Calif., 1952-60, dean, prof. emeritus, from 1960; spl. asst. to chancellor Pacific island studies Santa Cruz campus, also spl. asst. to chancellor Davis campus arboretum from 1960; asst. dir. Agr. Expt. Sta., 1952-60; spl. rep. Bd. Econ. Warfare and Fgn. Econ. Adminstrn,., Pacific Ocean Area, 1943-44; chmn. Dept. State Com. on Inter-Am. Coop. in Agrl. Edn., 1938-43; sr. agrl. officer, spl. tech. econ. mission E.C.A., Thailand, 1950, 51; cons. univ. devel. Thai Govt., 1966; U.S. rep. Pacific Sci. Coun., 1947-61; hon. v.p. Tenth Pacific Sci. Congress, 1961; mem. Rsch. Coun. South Pacific Commn., 1949-53, from 1971; U.S. commr. South Pacific Commn., 1952-62, sr. mem., 1957-62; U.S. rep. Rhinoceros Beetle ops. bd. Joint South Pacific Commn.-UN Spl. Fund Project, from 1964; adminstr. Com. Inter-Am. Inst. Agrl. Sci., Turrialbna, Costa Rica, 1945-54; searcher econ. plants for introduction into U.S. in Can., 1929, Spain, Morocco, Algeria, Tunis, Sicily, France, 1930, Mexico, 1940; mem. Hopkins Commn. on Civilian Govt. for Guam and Am. Samoa, U.S. Navy, 1947, Gov.'s Commn. Social and Econ. Causes of Crime and Delinquency, 1947-49, adv. coun. Nat. Arboretum, 1938-74; trustee Saratoga Hort. Found. Author articles on subtropical, tropical horticulture and agrl. exploration. Mem. Pacific sci. bd. NRC, 1946, chmn., 1946-52; trustee World Affairs Coun. No. Calif., 1954-60. With U.S. Army in France, 1917-19; agrl. damage investigations Am. Peace Commn., Jan.-Mar. 1919; agrl. officer Am. embarkation ctr., France, 1919. Decorated Chevalier du Merite Agricole (France), Ouissam Alaouite (Morocco), bronze medal Soc. d'Acclimitation de la France; recipient Pres.'s Cert. of Merit, 1946, Disting. Svc. award Alpha Kappa Lambda, 1964, Meyer medal Am. Genetics Assn. and U.S. Dept. Agr., 1968, Disting. Svc. Centennial Yr. award U. Calif., 1968; Berkeley fellow, 1968. Fellow AAAS; mem. Astron. Soc. Pacific, Calif. Bot. Soc., Am. Hort. Soc. (v.p. 1930-34), Soc. Am. Naturalists, Soc. Am. Foresters, Am. Polar Soc., Save the Redwoods League, Wilderness Soc., Nat. Parks Assn., Cal. Acad. Scis., Am. Assn. Botanic Gardens and Arboretums, Antarctic Soc. New Zealand, Cosmos Club (Washington; Explorers Club (N.Y.C.), Bohemian Club, Commonwealth Club (bd. govs.) (San Francisco); Rotary (Internat. Peace Grove award 1975) (Berkeley), Scabbard and Blade, Delta Phi Epsilon, Alpha Phi Omega, Hon. mem. Calif. Avocado Assn., Sigma Xi, Alpha Zeta, Alpha Kappa Lambda, Phi Delta Kappa. Congregationalist. Home: Berkeley Calif. †

RYON, THOMAS S(HIPLEY), tobacco company executive; b. Washington, May 29, 1917; s. Norman Eugene and Mary (Shipley) R.; m. Ruth Elizabeth Green, Apr. 12, 1940; children—Thomas Shipley, David Osmond. A.B., Duke U., 1938; postgrad., Law Sch., George Washington U., 1938-40. Real estate and income tax specialist Washington, 1938-39; mgr. A.C. Monk Enterprises, Farmville, N.C., 1940-43; accountant A.C. Monk & Co., Inc., 1940-43, asst. sec., 1943-54, sec., 1954, v.p., 1971-86; v.p. Dixon Hamilton Tobacco Suppliers Co., 1968-86; sec., dir. Mohenco Corp., Wendell, N.C., 1976-86, Eastern Tobacco Co.; sr. v.p. First Fed. Savs. & Loan Pitt County, 1972-85, dir., 1972-86; pres. T.S. Ryon & Co., 1967-86, Ryon & Assos., 1985-86; dir. Security Savs. & Loan, 1959-71, pres., 1962-71; pres. Farmville Tobacco Bd. Trade, 1966-68. Chmn. Farmville Fed. Housing Authority, 1974-79; chmn. Farmville council Boy Scouts Am., 1957-63; bd. dirs. Farmville Little League, Farmville Community Chest, Farmville United Fund; vice chmn. Farmville Sch. Bd., 1957, chmn., 1958-63; treas. Jones for Congress Com., 1967-86. Mem. N.C. World Trade Assn. (dir.), Farmville C. of C. (dir.). Democrat. Episcopalian. Clubs: Wilson Coin, Farmville Coin, Farmville Country (past sec.-treas.). Home: Farmville N.C. Died May 25, 1986.

SACKETT, WALTER WALLACE, JR., physician, surgeon, former state legislator; b. Bridgeport, Conn., Nov. 20, 1905; s. Walter Wallace and Hermine M. (Archambault) S.; m. Sophie Georgeff, Nov. 22, 1972; children by previous marriage: Monica Ann, Walter Wallace III; 1 stepson, Charles A. Dunn; 1 adopted child, John A. (dec.). Student, Harvard U., 1922-23; AB, U. Miami, 1932; postgrad., U. Ala., 1932-34; MD, Rush Med. Coll., 1938. Instr. anatomy U. Ala., 1934-36, instr. obstetrics, student health physician, 1939-40; prof. anatomy Coll. Mortuary Sci., St. Louis, 1936-37; intern Berwyn (Ill.) Hosp., 1937-38, St. Luke's Hosp., St. Louis, 1938-39; resident Charity Hosp., Natchez, Miss., 1940-41; pvt. practice Miami, Fla., 1941-85; mem. Fla. Ho. of Reps., 1966-76; mem. Med. Rsch. Found., U. Miami, 1950-53; mem. staff Drs., Jackson Meml. Coral Gables hosps.; mem. adv. com. poliomyelitis to surgeon gen. U.S., 1960-61; cons. diabetes and arthritis USPHS, 1961-62; pioneer oral polio vaccine in newborns, 1960-61; lectr. in field. Author: Bringing Up Babies, 1962, A Manual on Baby Feeding; contbr. articles to popular mags., profl. jours. Trustee U. Miami, 1961-63. Recipient Outstanding Alumni award U. Miami, 1957. Mem. Am. (bd. dirs. 1960-63, v.p. 1963-64), Fla. (founder-mem., pres. 1965), Dade County (pres. 1951-53) acads. gen. practice, Assn. Am. Physicians and Surgeons (Fla. membership chmn.), U. Miami Alumni Assn. (bd. dirs. 1957-61, pres. 1959), Coral Gables C. of C., Iron Arrow, Sigma Xi, Phi Chi. Roman Catholic. Home: Coral Gables Fla. Died Oct. 5, 1985; buried Flagler Meml. Park, Miami.

SACKHEIM, MAXWELL BYRON, advertising executive; b. Kovna, Russia, Sept. 25, 1890; came to U.S., 1891, naturalized, 1898; s. Simon and Lena (Altschul) S.; m. Sarah Prockter, June 14, 1913; children: Robert Benton, Sherman Prockter; m. Sallie Weir, Oct. 8, 1949. Student pub. schs. Office boy Long-Critchfield Advt. Agy., 1905-12; asst. to advt. mgrs. Sears, Roebuck & Co., Chgo., 1913; copywriter J. Walter Thompson, N.Y.C., 1914; sec. Ruthrauff & Ryan, Inc., 1915-19; pres. Sackheim & Sherman Advt. Agy., 1919-28, The Brown Fence & Wire Co., 1928-44; pres. Maxwell Sackheim & Co., Inc., N.Y.C., 1945-56, chmn., treas., 1956-60; co-founder Book-of-the-Month Club, 1926, Around the World Shoppers Club, 1952. Dir. Abilities, Inc. of Fla., Clearwater, Morton Plant Hosp., Clearwater; head small contbns. div. Rep. Nat. Com., 1945. Mem. Clearwater C. of C. (bd. dirs.), Rotary, Masons. Home: Largo Fla. †

SADAT, ANWAR ES-, president; b. Arab Republic of Egypt, 1918. Ed., Mil. Coll. Cairo. Commd. officer Egyptian Army, 1933; advanced through grades to col; past gen. sec. Islamic Congress; editor newspapers Al Jumhuriya and Al Tahrir, 1955-56; minister of state United Arab Republic, 1955-56, vice chmn. Nat. Assembly, 1957-64, chmn. Nat. Assembly, 1964-69; gen. sec. Egyptian Nat. Union, 1957-61; mem. Presidency Coun., 1962-64; v.p. United Arab Republic, 1969-70, interim pres., 1970, pres., 1970-81; pres. Afro-Asian Conf., Cairo, 1958. Author: Revolt on the Nile, 1957. Died Oct. 6, 1981; buried Cairo.

SADDLER, OWEN LESLIE, television executive; b. Wilmington, Del., Nov. 6, 1911; s. Edward and Georgiana (Longacre) S.; m. Elizabeth Rankin, Apr. 6, 1940; children: Barbara (Mrs. Bruce Georgi), Owen Leslie, David Rankin; m. Jocile Butterfield, Apr. 15, 1972. B.A., Bucknell U., 1934, M.A., 1935; postgrad., Northwestern U., 1937-38. With legal dept. E.I. du Pont de Nemours & Co., Wilmington, 1930-33; reporter Wilmington Jour. Every Evening, 1934; tchr. Warner High Sch., 1936; chmn. bd., dir. May Broadcasting Co., Omaha, Tucson, from 1949; sec. treas., dir. KFAB Broadcasting Co., Omaha, also Bus. Service Co., Omaha and Lincoln, Nebr., from 1957; Mem. affilliates adv. bd. ABC-TV, 1950-53, CBS-TV, 1953-57, NBC-TV, 1963-69. Mem. met. bd. YMCA, 1961-64; presdl. councilor Creighton U., Omaha, from 1969; bd. dirs., v.p. Jr. Achievement; v.p., bd. dirs. Lutheran Med. Center, Omaha; bd. regents UCS Citizens Assembly. Recipient Silver medallion Advt. Fedn. Am.-Advt. Assn. West, 1965; named Boss of Year Nat. Secs. Assn., 1965. Mem. Broadcast Pioneers Am., TV Pioneers Am., Nat. Assn. Broadcasters, Nebr. Broadcasters Assn. (elected to Hall of Fame 1977, Pioneer award in conjunction with NBC 1983), Sigma Delta Chi, Alpha Epsilon Rho. Republican. Mem. United Ch. of Christ. Clubs: Happy Hollow Country (Omaha), Omaha Press (Omaha), Omaha Skeet (Omaha), Quad (Omaha). Home: Omaha Nebr. Deceased.

SAGE, ROBERT FLOYD, foundation executive; b. Battle Creek, Mich.; s. Charles Floyd and Effa Laurinda (Mooney) S.; m. Genevieve Ray Phillips, Nov. 30, 1946; children: Melissa Jane Sage Booth, Anne Elizabeth. Student pub. schs., Hillsdale, Mich.; L.H.D. (hon.), Siena Heights Coll., 1973. Various positions in labor 1933-42, 46-58; profl. pilot, owner-operator fixed base operation Marion, Ohio, 1958-68; v.p., dir. Guest House Inc., Lake Orion, Mich., 1968-76; dir. Guest House Inc., 1963-88; pres. Sage Found., Detroit, 1962-88. Trustee, chmn. student affairs com. Siena Heights Coll., Adrian, Mich., 1969-88; bd. dirs. Cath. Social Service, Adrian, 1976-80, La Lumiere Sch., Laport, Ind.; mem. Franklyn Two. (Mich.) Planning Commn., 1976-78, Congressman Dave Stockman's Indsl. Adv. Com., 1977-81; chmn. com. alcohol studies Mercy Coll., Detroit, 1977-82, trustee, 1974-82; bd. assos. Adrian (Mich.) Coll., 1979-80; bd. visitors Mich. Cancer Found., 1979-82; bd. trustees Bixby Hosp., Adrian Mich., 1986-88, Saline (Mich.) Hosp., 1986-88. Served with USAAF, 1942-46. Recipient Lenawee County Citizen of Yr. award, 1979, Disting. Achievement award Hope Coll., 1979, cert. of recognition Nat. Aborist Assn., 1979; (with Genevieve Sage); Mercy medallion Mercy Coll., 1980; Pres.'s Cabinet award Siena Heights Coll., 1981; named to Order of Owl Regis High Sch. N.Y.C., 1978. Republican. Roman Catholic. Home Tecumseh Mich. Died Apr. 29, 1988; buried Brookside Cemetery, Tecumseh, Mich.

SAHS, ADOLPH LOUIS, neurologist; b. Charles City Iowa, May 27, 1906; s. Herman John and Bertha Emma (Dahse) S.; m. Margaret Alice Weeber, Feb. 8, 1936 children: Margaret, Carolyn, Mary. Student, U. Iowa 1925-27, MD, 1931. Intern Cin. Gen. hosp., 1931-32 resident U. Hosp., 1932-33; prof. neurology, head dept U. Iowa Coll. Medicine, Iowa City, 1948-74, prof emeritus, 1974-86; cons. USPHS, VA. Co-author Textbook of Neurology, 6 ed., 1966. chmn. Cooperative Study of Intracranial Aneurysms and Subarachnoid Hemorrhage, 1969, Joint Com. for Stroke Facilities 1969-78; mem. USPHS (adv. counc. 1966-70, chmn neurology study sect. 1962-66, chmn. neurology tng grants com. 1957-60). Recipient Disting. Alumni award U. Iowa, 1981. Mem. AMA, Am. Acad. Neurology (pres. 1961-63), Am. Neurol. Assn. (pres. 1967-68), Am Bd. Psychiatry and Neurology (dir. 1959-67, pres. 1967) Epilepsy Found. Am. (bd. dirs.), Nat. Multiple Sclerosis Soc. (med. adv. bd.). Republican. Home: Iowa City Iowa. Died Dec. 6, 1986; buried Iowa City.

ST. JOHN, HAROLD, botany educator, explorer; b Pitts., July 25, 1892; s. Charles Elliott and Martha Elizabeth (Everett) St. J.; m. Elizabeth Chandler, June 24, 1922; children: Charles Elliott, Robert Pierce, Mary Merrill, Martha Everett. AB, Harvard U., 1914, AM 1915, PhD, 1917; postgrad., U. Sorbonne, Paris, 1919. Asst. in botany Harvard U. and Radcliffe Coll., 1913-15; asst. botanist Can. Geol. Survey, 1915, 17; asst. i botany Univ. Extension, 1917; asst. prof. State Col Wash., 1920-23, assoc. prof., curator Herbarium,, 192 29; prof. U. Hawaii, 1929-50, chmn. dept., 1929-40, 4 54, sr. prof., 1950-57, Wilder prof., 1957-58; assoc. di Manoa Arboretum, 1953-57, bd. dirs., 1957-58; ass Gray Herbarium, 1913-17, 19-20; botanist B.P. Bisho Mus., Honolulu, from 1929; vis. prof. Yale U., 1939-4 botanist, explored for quinine Andes Mountains, Colombia, 1944-45; J.H. Whitney vis. prof. Chatham Coll., Pitts., 1958-59; Smith-Mundt vis. prof. U. Saigon, U. Hue Vietnam, 1959-61; Fulbright prof. Cairo U., 1963; curator Herbarium, from 1965; made bot. explorations or expdns. to Nfld. and maritime provinces of Can., Hawaiian Islands, Ea. Polynesia, Melanesia, Micronesia, S.E. Asia, Indian Ocean, Africa, northeastern and northwestern U.S. Author: (with E.Y. Hosaka) Weeds of the Pineapple Fields of the Hawaiian Islands, 1932, Flora of Southeastern Washington and of Adjacent Idaho, 1937, Nomenclature of Plants, 1958; founder, 1st editor Rsch. Studies; mem. bd. editors Pacific Sci., 1946-53, 55-58; contbr. articles to profl. jours. 2d lt. inf. U.S. Army, 1918-19. Fellow AAAS, Linnean Soc. London; mem. Bot. Soc. Am., New Eng. Bot. Club, N.W. Sci. Soc., Torrey Bot. Club, Acad. Nat. Scis. Phila., Hawaiian Bot. Soc. (pres. 1932-33), Hawaiian Acad. Sci. (pres. 1947-48), Am. Soc. Plant Taxonomists, Bot. Soc. Japan (hon.), Soc. Internat. Phytosociologie et de Geobontique, Am. Legion, Phi Beta Kappa (hon.), Sigma Xi, Phi Kappa Phi (pres. U. Hawaii chpt. 1945-46). Republican. Unitarian. Home: Honolulu Hawaii. †

SALEMME, ANTONIO, artist; b. Gaeta, Italy, Nov. 2, 1892; s. Nicholas Vincent and Felice (Fedele) S.; m. Elizabeth Hardy, July 1920 (div. June 1932); m. Martha Anna Blomgran, Aug. 5, 1941. Student, Eric Pape Art Sch., Boston Mus. Fine Arts Sch.; student sculpture, Rome, 1912-19. One man shows include Ferargil Gallery, Erich-Newhouse Gallery, Findlay Galleries, Wakefield Bookshop Gallery, Wellons Gallery, Sagittarius Gallery, Robert Schoelkopf Gallery; exhibited group shows NAD, Pa. Acad. Fine Arts, Art Inst. Chgo., Archtl. League N.Y.C., Nat. Sculpture Soc., Allied Artists, Met. Mus. Art, Peitrantonio Gallery, J. and B. Weintraub Gallery, Kent State U., others; represented in permanent collections Newark Mus., Syracuse Mus. Fine Arts, Beinecke Library Yale U., Met. Mus. Art, N.J. Coll. Women, Columbia U., also pvt. collections; tchr. sculpture Nat. Inst. Archtl. Edn., N.Y.C., 1921-22, Roerick Mus. Sch., N.Y.C., 1928-29, Spence Sch., N.Y.C., 1939. With Italian Army, World War I. Decorated War Cross; Guggenheim fellow, 1932, 36; recipient 1st prize sculpture Guild Hall, East Hampton, N.Y., 1958, other awards. Mem. Nat. Inst. Archtl. Edn., (hon. life), Internat. Platform Assn. Home: Easton Pa. †

SALISBURY, EUGENE FRANKLIN, civil engineer; b. Omaha, June 5, 1886; s. Henry Houston and Mary Matilda (Lewis) S.; m. Amanda Herndon Painter, Apr. 7, 1915; children: William Painter, Henry Houston. Student civil engring., U. Mo., 1904-08. Profl. engr. Ark., Kans., Mo. and Tex. With engring. dept. M.P. R.R., 1909-20; instrumentman, asst. engr. Fall City, Nebr., 1909-18; prin. asst. engr. and asst. to engr. maintenance of way Cotton Belt Ry., Tyler, Tex., 1918-19; chief engr. La. & Ark. R.R., Minden and Shreveport, La., from 1920; chief engr. Kans. City So. Ry., Kans. City, Mo., 1941-57, asst. to pres., from 1958. Author treatise: Influence of Diversion on the Mississippi and Atchafalaya Rivrs (ASCE). Mem. U.S. Com. on Large Dams, Miss. River Commn., from 1950, Greater Kansas City Flood Protection Planning Com. Mem. ASCE, Am. Ry. Engring. Assn., S.R., Mystical Seven, Masons, Sigma Chi. Home: Grandview Mo. †

SALOMON, MARDOQUEO ISAAC, physician; b. Minsk, Poland, Jan. 26, 1906; came to U.S., 1942, naturalized, 1947.; s. Joseph S. and Ida (Perkal) S.; m. Sofia Lewin, Oct. 21, 1930; children: Ruth Dalila (Mrs. Edward J. King), Hilel-Benami. D Nat. Sci., U. Brussels, 1929; MD, U. Geneva, 1933. Prof. biology and physiology U. Cochabamba, Bolivia, 1938-42; pvt. practice Bolivia, 1938-42, La Paz, Bolivia, 1940-42; clin. prof. dept. medicine N.Y. Med. Coll.; mem. staff Flower-Fifth Ave. hosp., 1942-84, Met. Hosp., N.Y.C., 1942-84, Logan Meml. Hosp., 1942-84. Contbr. numerous articles to profl. jours. Bd. dirs. United Israel World Union. With Bolivian Army, 1933-35. Recipient Physician's Recognition award, 1969. Fellow Am. Coll. Chest Physicians, Am. Coll. Cardiology, Am. Coll. Angiology. Home: New York N.Y. Died Nov. 18, 1984.

SALOMONE, A. WILLIAM, historian, educator, writer; b. Guardiagrele, Italy, Aug. 18, 1915; came to U.S., 1927, naturalized, 1942; s. Michael and Italia (Scioli) S.; m. Lina Palmerio, Sept. 13, 1941; 1 child, Ilia S. Salomone Smith. B.A., LaSalle Coll., 1938; M.A., U. Pa., 1940, Ph.D. (Social Sci. Research Council fellow), 1943. Instr. history, Italian civilization Haverford Coll., 1942-43; instr. modern European history U. Pa., 1944-45; successively instr., asst. prof., asso. prof., prof. N.Y. U., 1945-62; Wilson prof. modern European and Italian history U. Rochester, 1962-82, emeritus, 1982-89; vis. prof. Columbia U., 1961-62, 64; Pres. Am. div. Instituto per la Storia del Risorgimento, 1959-60; cons. in Italian history Collier's Ency.; Mem. selection com. Italian govt. scholarships, Fulbright Italian history fellowships. Author: Italian Democracy in the Making, 1945, L'Età Giolittiana, 1949, (with A. Baltzly) Readings in Twentieth-Century European History, 1950, Italy in the Giolittian Era, 1960, Italy from the Risorgimento to Fascism, 1970; mem. editorial bd. Jour. Modern History, 1965-68, Italian Quar., 1974—, Jour. Ital. History, 1977-82; editorial coordinator Italian sect. International Dictionary of Great Historians, forthcoming auspice Comité Internationale des Science, Historiques, Commission de l'Historiographie, 1984—, preface to S. Di Scala's Renewing Italian Socialism, 1988; contbr. articles to profl. jours. Recipient Herbert Baxter Adams prize Am. Hist. Assn., 1946; Social Sci. Research Council fellow, 1942-43, 55-56; Guggenheim fellow, 1951- 52; Nat. Found. for Humanities Sr. fellow, 1967-68; decorated knight-officer Order Merit Italian Republic, 1960; recipient citation Soc. Italian Hist. Studies, 1967; synposium held in his honor U. Rochester, 1981; Modern European History prize established in his honor U. Rochester, 1981; conf. in his honor Columbia U., 1982; recipient hon. citizenship Guardiagrele, Italy, 1983, Brother Anselm award West Catholic Alumni Assn., 1988; honored by Comune di Guardiagrele, 1988, Citta di Molfetta, Italy, 1988; recipient Giornate Salveminiane di Molfetta medal, 1988. Mem. Am. Hist. Assn. (session held in his honor 1983), Assn. European Historians N.Y. (pres. 1970-72), Renaissance Soc. Am., Am. Assn. Tchrs. Italian, Am. Acad. Polit. Sci., Soc. for Italian Hist. Studies (pres.), Am.-Italy Soc., Matteotti Internat. Symposium (pres. 1975). Home: Ardmore Pa. Died Jan. 24, 1989; buried Sts. Peter and Paul Cemetery.

SALOUTOS, THEODORE, educator, historian; b. Milw., Aug. 3, 1910; s. Peter and Demetra (Perdikis) S.; m. Florence Louise Schwefel, Sept. 21, 1940; children: Bonita Louise (Mrs. Martin Gilbert), Theodore A. Peter. BE, Milw. State Tchrs. Coll., 1933; postgrad., U. Wis. Law Sch., summers 1934-36; M Philosophy, U. Wis., 1938, PhD, 1940. Tchr. Waukesha (Wis.) Pub. Schs., 1933-36; rsch. asst. history U. Wis., 1937-40, postdoctoral fellow history and agrl. econs., 1940-41, instr., 1941-43; vis. lectr. Oberlin Coll., 1943-45; lectr. UCLA, 1945-46, faculty, 1946-80, prof., 1956-80, chmn. dept., 1956-59; vis. summer prof. U. Minn., 1947, U. Wis., Milw., 1962, U. Hawaii, 1968; Fulbright lectr. U. Freiburg, Fed. Republic Germany, 1959-60; cons., panelist Nat. Endowment Arts and Humanities, 1968-75; mem. nat. adv. bd. Immigration History Rsch. Ctr., U. Minn., 1973-80; cons. Holloman (N.Mex.) AFB, 1958-59. Author: They Remember America, 1956, Farmer Movements in the South, 1865-1933, 1960, The Greeks in the United States, 1964, Twentieth Century Populism, 1964, Farmer Movements in the South, 1964, The Greeks in America, 1967, Populism: Reaction or Reform, 1968; (with John D. Hicks) Agricultural Discontent in the Middle West, 1900-1939, 1951, The American Farmer and the New Deal, 1982 (Henry Wallace book award); mem. editorial bd. Agrl. History, 1957-80, Jour. Am. History. Pres. Mar Vista (Calif.) Dem. Club, 1961-62, Save Cyprus Coun. So. Calif., 1974-77; mem. Friends of Huntington Library, 1964-80. Recipient Disting. Alumnus award U. Wis.-Milw., 1977; Fulbright rsch. scholarship, Greece, 1962. Mem. Am. History Soc., (pres. Pacific Coast Br., 1978-80), Am. (exec. com. Pacific Coast br. 1962-65), Miss. Valley hist. assns., Agrl. History Soc. (pres. 1965-66), Immigration History Soc. (pres. 1973-76), Bus. history Soc., Econ. History Assn., English Econ. History Soc., Pan Arcadian Fedn., Order Ahepa (chmn. edn. com. 1964-65), Hellenic Univ. So. Calif. Club (pres. 1961-63, 69-71). Home: Los Angeles Calif. Died Nov. 5, 1980; buried Woodlawn Cemetery, Santa Monica, Calif.

SALT, WALDO, screenwriter, lyricist; b. Chgo., Oct. 18, 1914; s. William Haslem and Winifred (Porter) S.; m. Ambur Dana, 1939 (div.); m. Mary Davenport, 1942 (div.); children: Jennifer, Deborah; m. Gladys Schwartz, 1968; m. Eve Merriam, Oct. 22, 1983. A.B., Stanford U., 1934. Civilian cons., writer Office of War Info., 1944-45; dir. dramatics and music Menlo Sch. and Jr. Coll., Menlo Park, Calif., 1934-35; lectr. NYU, N.Y.C., 1984-87. Author: (folk opera) Sandhog, 1955, (screenplays) Midnight Cowboy (Acad. award 1969), Serpico (Acad. award nomination, Writers Guild award 1973), Coming Home (Acad. award 1978). Recipient Laurel award Writer's Guild, 1986. Home: New York N.Y. Died 1987.

SALZER, FELIX, author, music educator; b. Vienna, Austria, June 13, 1904; came to U.S., 1939, naturalized, 1945; s. Max and Helene (Wittgenstein) S.; m. Hedi Lemberger-Lindtberg, Sept. 16, 1939. Ph.D., U. Vienna, 1926. Prof., dean, chmn. theory dept. Mannes Coll. Music, N.Y.C., 1940-56, 62-86; prof. music Queens Coll., 1963-86; vis. lectr. U. Calif. at Los Angeles, 1960, Peabody Conservatory Music, 1962, New Sch. Social Research, 1962-63, U. Oreg., summer 1965. Author: Structural Hearing (Tonal Coherence in Music), Vol. I text, Vol. II musical examples and analyses, 2d edit, 1962, German translation, 1960; co-author: Counterpoint in Composition, 1969; Editor: The Music Forum, 5 vols, 1967, 70, 73, 76, 80. Mem. Am. Musicol. Soc. (chmn. N.Y. chpt. 1963-65). Home: New York N.Y. Died Aug. 10, 1986; buried Ferncliff Cemetery, Hartsdale, N.Y.

SAMFORD, FRANK PARK, JR., holding company executive; b. Montgomery, Ala., Jan. 29, 1921; s. Frank Park and Hattie Mae (Noland) S.; m. Virginia Carolyn Suydam, May 27, 1942; children: Frank Park III, Laura Alice, John Singleton Pitts, Mae Virginia. Student, Auburn U., 1937-38; B.A., Yale U., 1942; LL.B., U. Ala., 1947, LL.D., 1980. C.L.U. With Liberty Nat. Life Ins. Co., Birmingham, Ala., 1947-86; v.p. Liberty Nat. Life Ins. Co., 1955-60, pres., 1960-86, chmn. bd., 1973-86, chmn. exec. com., dir., 1973-86; chmn., dir. Torchmark Corp., 1980-86, chmn. exec. com., dir., 1986; chmn. Life Insurers Conf., 1970; former trustee Am. Coll. Life Underwriters; trustee Am. Council Life Ins. Chmn. Jefferson County United Appeal, 1964; trustee Jefferson County Community Chest, pres., 1965; bd. govs. Indian Springs Sch., Helena, Ala.; trustee Auburn U. Served to lt. (s.g.) USNR, 1942-45. Named to Ala. Acad. Honor, 1980. Mem. Alpha Tau Omega, Phi Kappa Phi, Phi Delta Phi, Berzelius. Presbyterian. Clubs: Rotarian. (Birmingham), Birmingham Country (Birmingham), Mountain Brook Country (Birmingham). Home: Birmingham Ala. Died Dec. 6, 1986.

SAMMIS, DONALD STUART, industrialist; b. Stratford, Conn., Nov. 15, 1889; s. Frank Russell and Elizabeth (French) S.; m. Eloise Saeger Howell, Aug. 31, 1929; children: Donald Stuart, Robert Howell, Martha Bouton, Wilson French. PhB, Yale U., 1909, ME, 1911. Engaged in industrial work 1911-17, in managerial capacity, 1919-31; city mgr., Stratford, 1931-34; supt. Underwood Corp., 1935, v.p. and works mgr. Bridgeport works, 1936-47, Hartford, 1947-50; v.p., N.Y.C., 1950-54, then ret.; v.p., sec. Pootatuck Corp., Stratford; chmn. bd. Minshall Organ, Inc., from 1956; bd. dirs. Acme Shear Co., Conn., Nat. Bank, City Savings Bank, Bridgeport, Hansen-Whitney Co. Mem. exec. com. Pomperang coun. Boy Scouts Am.; trustee Am. Shakespeare Festival Theatre and Acad.; trustee, vice chmn., treas. Lebanon Found., New London, Conn.; trustee U. Bridgeport; bd. dirs. Bridgeport Hosp. With U.S. Army, 1917-19. Home: Warner N.H. †

SAMMONS, EDWARD CURF, business executive; b. Portland, Oreg., Aug. 22, 1891; s. George Edward and Mary Jane (DeBoest) S.; m. Florence Knapp, Mar. 10, 1923; children: Edward Curf, Thomas Knapp. Ed. pub. schs., Portland; LLD (hon.), Oreg. State Coll., 1946, U. Portland, 1950. Reporter Morning Oregonian, Portland; associated with Lumberman's Bank, Portland, 1911; v.p. U.S. Nat. Bank (merger with Lumberman's Bank), Portland, 1917-28, chmn. bd., 1960-63; v.p. Iron Fireman Mfg. Co., Portland, 1928-45; bd. dirs. Am. Mail Line; pres. Oreg. War Industries, Inc., 1941-45. Past mem. Oreg. State Bd. Higher Edn. Lt. col. Am. Expeditionary Force. Mem. Masons, Shriners, Waverley Country Club, Multnomah Club, Athletic Club, Arlington Club, University Club. Republican. Home: Newberg Oreg. †

SAMPSELL, DAVID SYLVESTER, lawyer; b. Chgo., Aug. 24, 1908; s. Marshall E. and Edna (Smith) S.; m. Harriet C. Fenner, Sept. 15, 1934; children: David F., Bruce. Grad., Hill Sch., Pottstown, Pa., 1926; AB, Yale U., 1930; JD, Northwestern U., 1933. Bar: Ill. 1933. Assoc. Taylor, Miller, Busch & Boyden, Chgo., 1933-39; with Mid. West Svc. Co., Chgo., 1939-44; with No. Trust Co., Chgo., 1946-73, sr. v.p., gen. counsel, 1962-73. Mem. Evanston Twp. High Sch. Bd. Edn., 1957-63, pres., 1960-63; mem. Chgo. Crime Commn., 1953-86, bd. dirs., 1966-72; bd. dirs. United Charities, 1953-60, Evanston Hosp., 1951-60, 63-73, sec., 1953-60, v.p., 1965-70, vice chmn., 1970. 1st lt. AUS, 1944-46. Mem. Order of Coif, Law Club, Legal Club, University Club, Glen View Club, Old Elm Club, Naples Yacht Club, Hole-in-the-Wall Club, Phi Beta Kappa, Psi Upsilon, Phi Delta Phi. Home: Evanston Ill. Died Mar. 4, 1986.

SAMPSON, ARTHUR FRANCIS, business executive; b. Fall River, Mass., Oct. 8, 1926; s. Arthur F. and Dora (Couturier) S.; m. Blanche Bouffard, Sept. 20, 1947; children: Arthur Francis III, Philip R., Jason E., Matthew S. Student, U. Mass., 1944-45, Sampson Coll., 1947-48; BS, U. R.I., 1951. With GE, Lynn, Mass., 1951-53; with GE, Erie, Pa., 1953-63, mgr. purchasing, 1961-63; dep. sec. procurement Commonwealth of Pa., Harrisburg, 1963-66; sec. adminstrn., budget sec. Gov. Pa. Cabinet, Harrisburg, 1967-69; commr. Fed. Supply Service, commr. Pub. Bldgs. Service, dep. adminstr. for spl. projects GSA, Washington, 1969-72, acting adminstr., 1972-73, adminstr., 1973-76; pres., chief exec. officer, dir. San-Vel Concrete Corp., Littleton, Mass., 1976-77; pres. SEREC Inc., Fairfield, Ala., from 1978; bus. and govtl. cons. 1979-88; v.p. Lone Star Industries, Greenwich, Conn., from 1981; mem. White House Regulations and Purchasing Rev. Bd., from 1970, Pres.'s Commn. on Procurement, from 1970, Nat. Capitol Planning Commn., from 1970, Pres.'s Adv. Coun. on Hist. Preservation, from 1972; lectr. bus. and govt. adminstrn. MIT, Princeton, U. Mich. Bd. dirs. Jr. Achievement Met. Washington, 1972-88, Prestressed Concrete Inst., Nat. Fire Protection Assn.; mem. D.C. Mayor's Devel. Com., from 1972. With USAAF, 1944-47. Recipient Presdl. citation Soc. Am. Value Engrs., 1969, Synergy III award Soc. Am. Registered Architects, 1972, citation Engring. News Record, 1972, top ten pub. works men of the year award Am. Pub. Works Assn., 1973. Mem. Nat. Assn. Purchasing Agts., Nat. Assn. Accountants, AIA (hon.), Fed. Govt. Accountants Assn. (hon.), K.C. Republican. Home: Falls Church Va. Died Mar. 13, 1988, buried Warren, R.I.

SAMS, JAMES C., clergyman; b. Cochran, Ga., Feb. 19, 1909; s. Lonnie and Charlotte S.; m. Cornelia Fleming, Sept. 29, 1930. BS, Fla. A&M Coll., 1946. Ordained to ministry Bapt. Ch. Pastor Jacksonville,

Fla., 32 yrs.; pres. Progressive Bapt. Conv. Fla., 17 yrs.; 1st v.p. Nat. Bapt. Conv. Am., 1961-67, pres., 1967-85. Vice chmn. bd. trustees Fla. Meml. Coll.; trustee Edward Waters Coll. Died Sept. 1985.

SANBORN, RICHARD DYER, railroad executive; b. Sanbornville, N.H., June 3, 1936; s. Richard Dyer and Bernice (McCrillis) S.; m. Marie B. Burgwin, June 3, 1963 (div. 1977); 1 child, Cynthia Marie; m. Hilda Joan Penner, July 1, 1977. BA, U. N.H., 1957; LLB, Harvard U., 1960. Bar: Mass. 1960, Fla. 1966. Atty. Atlantic Coast Line R.R., Jacksonville, Fla., 1961-72; with Family Lines Rail System, Jacksonville, 1972-73, v.p. exec. dept. and asst. to chmn., 1973-80, sr. v.p. adminstrn., 1980-82; pres., chief exec. officer Seaboard System R.R., Jacksonville, 1982-86; pres., chief exec. officer CSX Distbn. Services of CSX Corp., Jacksonville, 1986-88, also dir.; pres., chief operating officer Consol. Rail Corp., Phila., 1988-89; chmn., pres., chief exec. officer Conrail, Phila., Jan.-Feb. 1989; bd. dirs. Alico, Inc., 1st Ky. Nat. Corp., Louisville. Bd. dirs. Md. C. of C., Balt. Symphony, United Way Cen. Md.; trustee Jacksonville U., Goucher Coll., Edward Waters Coll. Mem. ABA, Mass. Bar Assn., Fla. Bar Assn., Assn. Am. R.R.s (dir.), Nat. Devel. Com. U. N.H., Newcomen Soc., Nat. R.R. Labor Conf. Clubs: Commonwealth (Richmond); River (Jacksonville); Maryland (Balt.), Timuquana (Jacksonville), Ponte Vedra (Fla.). League: The Union of Phila. (mem. exec. bd.). Home: Baltimore Md. Died Feb. 12, 1989; buried Sanbornville, N.H.

SAND, HAROLD EUGENE, forest products executive; b. Portland, Oreg., Sept. 2, 1917; s. Charles Edwin Sand and Rae (Anderson) S.; m. Marian Annette Thomas, Nov. 4, 1939; children: Barbara Sand Strader, Kathleen Sand Williams, Thomas C. B.S., U. Oreg., 1941; M.B.A., Calif. Western U., 1980. Pres. Sand Plywood Co., Portland, Oreg., 1941-56; exec. Ga. Pacific Corp., Portland, 1956-82; dir. Ga. Pacific Corp., Atlanta, 1973-86; dir. Oreg. Mut. Savs. Bank, Portland. Trustee Oreg. Grad. Ctr., Portland, 1982-86 ; trustee St. Vincents Hosp., 1982-86 . Republican. Presbyterian. Clubs: Waverley Country (Portland) (pres. 1979), Arlington (Portland) (dir. 1982-86). Home: Portland Oreg. Died Dec. 11, 1986; interred Riverview Cemetery and Mausoleum, Portland, Oreg.

SANDERS, ALLISON, newspaper columnist; b. Washington, Sept. 3, 1902; s. John Wylie and Lela (Allison) S.; m. Thelma Ann McCarty, June 18, 1924 (dec.); children: Gay Sanders Bugbee, Allison (dec.). Student, Tex. A&M U., 1920-24. Reporter Houston Press, 1931-33; reporter Houston Chronicle, from 1933, news reporter, 1933-47, city editor, 1947-56, feature editor, 1956-58, columnist, from 1958. Mem. Press Club of Houston (pres. 1958-59). Republican. Died Aug. 30, 1985.

SANDERS, MURRAY JONATHAN, physician, med. research inst. exec.; b. Chelsea, Mass., Apr. 11, 1910; s. Louis and Rose (Gould) S.; m. Margaret Weatherly, Dec. 19, 1959; children—Frank Weatherly, Andrea Joan, Murray Jonathan. B.S., Tufts Coll., 1931; student (scholar), Heidelberg (Germany) U., 1929; M.D., U. Chgo., 1936. Asst. Office Coroner Cook County, Chgo., 1936; asst. pathology U. Chgo. Rush Med. Coll., 1936; rotating intern Evanston (Ill.) Gen. Hosp., 1936-38; Oliver Rea scholar Columbia Coll. Phys. and Surg., N.Y.C., 1938-40; instr. bacteriology Columbia Coll. Phys. and Surg., 1940-41, asst. prof., 1941-45, asso. prof., 1945-47; prof. bacteriology U. Miami, Coral Gables, Fla., 1948-52; research prof., dir. dept. microbiology U. Miami, South Miami, Fla., 1952-60; med. dir., v.p. Pan Am. Pharms., Inc., Ft. Lauderdale, Fla., 1960-62; founder, med. dir. Sanders Med. Research Found., Delray Beach, Fla., 1971-87; cons. pathology N.Y.C. Dept. Hosp., Harlem Hosp., N.Y.C., 1947-87 ; cons. Biogenix, Inc., 1980-87 ; dir. research Variety Children's Hosp., Miami, 1952-53; cons. Nat. Children's Cardiac Hosp., Miami, 1950-55, Blood Plasma Corp. Japan, Osaka, 1950-87 ; hon. med. staff, cons. Guam Meml. Hosp., Agana, 1950-57; chmn. dept. biol. scis. Fla. Atlantic U., 1962-65; med. dir., v.p. Gray Industries, Inc., Gray Research Found. Editor: Jour. Indsl. Medicine; editor proc.: Internat. Symposium Med. and Applied Virology, 1966; editor: Modern Concepts, Med. Virology, Oncology and Cytology, 1966; Contbr. articles and chpts. to profl. publs. Trustee Palm Beach Atlantic Coll. Served from maj. to lt. col., M.C. AUS, 1940-46; staff officer Gen. MacArthur 1944-45; cons. Sec. of War, also mem. commn. neurotropic virus disease Bd. Investigation and Control Influenza and Other Epidemic Diseases in Army 1942-46. Decorated Legion of Merit, D.S.M.; commendation Med. Intelligence Service, Gen. Eisenhower, 1946; nominee medicine Nobel Prize, 1966; mem. Outstanding Citizen Assn., Miami. Fellow Royal Soc. Health (Eng.), AAAS, N.Y. Acad. Scis. (life), N.Y. Acad. Medicine; mem. Am. Assn. Pathologists and Bacteriologists, Soc. Exptl. Biology and Medicine, Am., Fla. pub. health assns., Am. Fedn. Clin. Research, Soc. Am. Bacteriologists, Internat. Soc. Transfusion, Am. Assn. Blood Banks, Tissue Culture Assn., So. Med. Assn., Fla. Acad. Scis., Sociedad Cubana de Salubridad Publica (corr.), Ret. Officers Assn., Sigma Xi. Club: Cosmos (Washington). Home: Delray Beach Fla. Died June 29, 1987; interred Arlington National Cemetery.

SANDMAIER, PHILIP JAMES, JR., accountant; b. Buffalo, Mar. 21, 1919; s. Philip James and Theresa (Stinely) S.; m. Antoinette C. Pfeiffer, Oct. 6, 1945; children—Donna M., Marian L., Robert J., Philip R. B.S. maxima cum laude, U. Notre Dame, 1940. With Haskins & Sells (C.P.A.'s), 1940—; partner exec. office Haskins & Sells (C.P.A.'s), N.Y.C., 1958-62; mng. partner Haskins & Sells (C.P.A.'s), San Diego, 1962-64, Phila., 1964-69; exec. office Haskins & Sells (C.P.A.'s), N.Y.C., from 1969; dir., treas. Practicing Law Inst., N.Y.C., from 1973, Nat. Bur. Econ. Research, N.Y.C., from 1977. Com. chmn. United Fund, Cleve., 1950-52, Newark, 1956-58, vice chmn., Phila., 1964-65; lay trustee Villanova U., 1965-69; trustee Asia Soc., N.Y.C., 1971. Served to 2d lt. AUS, 1941-45, ETO. Decorated Bronze Star medal. Mem. Am. Inst. C.P.A.'s, Ohio, N.J., N.Y., Calif., Pa. socs. C.P.A.'s. Home: Bryn Mawr Pa. Deceased.

SANDMAN, CHARLES W., JR., judge, former congressman; b. Phila.; s. Charles W. and Rose (Frasch) S.; m. Marion Louise Cooney, Apr. 3, 19948; children: Carol, William, Marion, Robert, Charles, Richard. Student, Temple U., 1940-42; LLB, Rutgers U., 1949. Bar: N.J. 1949. Pvt. practice Cape May, N.J., from 1949; city solicitor Cape May, 1956-61, from 1964; mem. N.J. Senate from Cape May County, 1956-66; acting gov. State of N.J., 1965-66; mem. 90th-93d Congresses from 2d N.J. dist., 1966-74; solicitor First Nat. Bank Stone Harbor (N.J.); chief judge Cape May County Family Ct., 1984-85. Chmn. Cape May County chpt. ARC, from 1957; chmn. Cape May County Rep. Com., from 1958; del. Rep.Nat. Conv., 1956, 60, 64, 68. With USAAF, 1942-45. Decorated Air medal with 3 oak leaf clusters; recipient B'nai B'rith award 1958; named Outstanding Legislator in N.J., N.J. Assn. Chosen Freeholders, 1960, 64. Mem. ABA, N.J. Bar Assn., Theta Kappa Phi. Roman Catholic. Home: Cape May N.J. Died Aug. 26, 1985, buried Cold Spring Cemetery.

SANN, PAUL, newspaperman, author, editor; b. Bklyn., Mar. 7, 1914; s. Harry and Freda (Spilton) S.; m. Birdye Pullman, July 28, 1934 (dec.); children: Eleanor (dec.), Howard. Student, N.Y. Prep. Sch., 1931, Morris High Sch. With N.Y. Post, 1931-44, 44-77, copy boy, reporter, numerous assignments, N.Y.C. and Washington, night city editor, asst. city editor, 1931-44, Washington corr., 1945, news editor, UN Conf. edit., San Francsico, 1945, asst. to exec. editor, then mng. editor N.Y. Post-Bronx Home News, 1945-47, city editor, 1948-49, exec. editor, 1949-77, columnist "It Happened All Over", 1954-61, war corr. Yom Kippur War, Israel, 1973; rewrite man N.Y. Jour.-Am., 1944; enforcement officer Free Trial/Free Press Conf. Author: (nonfiction) (with J.D. Horan) Pictorial History of the Wild West, 1954, The Lawless Decade, 1957, (with Arnold Red Auerbach) Red Auerbach: Winning the Hard Way, 1966, Fads, Follies and Delusions of the American People, 1967, Kill the Dutchman! The Story of Dutch Schultz, 1971, The Angry Decade: The Sixties, 1979, American Panorama, 1980, (fiction) Dead Heat: Love and Money, 1974, Trial in the Upper Room, 1981; contbr. to: A Century of Journalism, 1943, More Post Biographies, 1947, These Were Our Years, 1959, Ain't We Got Fun?, 1980; contbr. to nat. mags. Cons. Mcpl. Housing Authority, Yonkers, N.Y., 1939's. Nominated for Pulitzer prize in internat. reporting; recipient honor for contbn. to journalism City Coun. N.Y.C., 1977. Mem. Am. Newspaper Guild (founding mem.), N.Y. State Soc. Newspaper Editors, N.Y. Press Club. Home: Wilton Conn. Died Sept. 5, 1986, buried Hastings-on-Hudson, N.Y.

SAPP, HENRY GRADY, religious association executive; b. Rogers, Tex., Feb. 27, 1892; s. John W. and Mary L. (Hairrell) S.; m. Lola Mae McBride, July 6, 1935. Grad., S.W. Tex. State Tchrs. Coll., 1910; post-grad., U. Chgo., U. Ga. Tchr., high sch. prin. pub. schs. Tex., 1911-18; pvt. sec., asst. to chmn. bd. Coca-Cola Co., 1925-47; pres. Brotherhood of St. Andrew in U.S., York, Pa., 1957-63, pres. emeritus, from 1963; chmn. laymen's work P.E. Ch., Diocese Atlanta, 1954; lay dep. Gen. Conv., Episcopal Ch., Honolulu, 1955, Miami Beach, Fla., 1958; mem. gen. div., laymen's work com. Nat. Coun. P.E. Ch. in U.S.; v.p. Keep, Inc., Kiyosato Ednl. Expt. Project, Tokyo. Trustee Brotherhood St. Andrew Found.; bd. dirs. Near East Found., N.Y.C.; vestryman local Episc. ch. Cpl. USMC, 1918-19. Mem. Nat. Geog. Soc., Brotherhood St. Andrew Legion. Republican. Home: Columbus Ga. †

SAPPINGTON, THOMAS ASBURY, physician; b. Sycamore, Ga., May 9, 1913; s. Ernest P. and Nell (Whittle) S.; m. A. Phyllis Duncan, Aug. 31, 1940; children: Phyllis (Mrs. S. Monte Kellam Jr.), Kathryn (Mrs. Michael Kellum), Thomas A. BA, Vanderbilt U., 1934, MD, 1937. Diplomate Am. Bd. Family Practice. Med. examiner Ga., from 1953; physician Upson County, Ga., from 1956; clinician Upson County Health Dept., from 1956; preceptor in gen. medicine Med. Coll. Ga., from 1971, asst. prof. dept. family practice; dir. Ga. Blue Shield. Mem. Upson County Blood Program; mem. panel cancer control USPHS, 1960. Lt. col. AUS, 1940-46. Mem. AMA, Upson County Med. Soc. (past pres.), 6th Dist. Med. Soc., Med. Assn. Ga. (named Gen. Practitioner of Yr. 1971), Am. Acad. Gen. Practice (pres. Ga. chpt. 1970, bd. dirs. 1971-84, mem. commn. edn. 1956-59), Ga. Acad. Gen. Practice (chmn. edn. com., plaque for outstanding service as del., Disting. Service award 1977), VFW, Am. Legion, Kiwanis, Masons, Shriners. Home: Thomaston Ga. Died May 31, 1984.

SARGEANT, HOWLAND H., international radio consultant, foundation executive; b. New Bedford, Mass., July 13, 1911; s. M. Motley and Grace E. (Howland) S.; m. Dorothy Psathas; children: Kimon, Paul. AB summa cum laude, Dartmouth, 1932; AB honors sch., Oxford (Eng.) U., 1934, AM, 1938, B.Litt., 1940. With Fed. Home Loan Bank Bd., 1935-40; editor Fed. Home Loan Bank Rev., 1937-40; exec. sec. NSF of NAS, 1940-47; chmn. tech. indsl. intelligence com. U.S. Joint Chiefs of Staff, 1944-46; dep. asst. sec. of state for pub. affairs 1947-51, asst. sec. pub. affairs, 1952-53; cons. State Dept. and Ford Found., 1953-54; pres., trustee Radio Liberty Com. Inc., 1954-75; dir. RFE/RL Inc., 1976-77, Commonwealth Fund's Harkness Fellowships, 1980-84; pres. Magnesium Devel. Corp., 1945-50; pres. UNESCO Gen. Conf., Paris, 1951, chmn. U.S. dels. 5th-7th confs. Author: The Representation of the United States Abroad, 1965, Soviet Propaganda, 1972; contbr. articles to profl. jours. Mem. adv. com. Dartmouth Inst., 1972-80; mem. adv. com. Grad. Sch. Corp. and Polit. Communication, Fairfield U., 1968-84; mem. Panel Ideas and Polit. Communication in Soviet Union, 1976-84; trustee Freedom House; mem. bd. Internat. Broadcasting, 1974-75. Recipient certificate of appreciation U.S. Army, Superior Service award State Dept., Dartmouth Alumni award; Rhodes Scholar 1940. Mem. Assn. Am. Rhodes Scholars, Dartmouth Alumni Coun. (pres. 1968-69), Internat. Radio and TV Execs., Coun. Fgn. Rels., Am. Fgn. Service Assn., West Side Tennis Club, Dartmouth Coll. Club, Century Assn., Sphinx, Phi Beta Kappa, Kappa Kappa Kappa. Home: New York N.Y. Died Feb. 29, 1984; buried New Bedford, Mass.

SARGEANT, WINTHROP, author, critic, translator; b. San Francisco, Dec. 10, 1903; s. Winthrop and Geneve (Rixford) S.; m. Jane Smith, Dec. 23, 1955. Trained in Europe as musician. Violinist, San Francisco Symphony, 1922-24; Violinist N.Y. Symphony, 1926-28, N.Y. Philharm., 1926-28; music critic Bklyn. Daily Eagle, 1934-36, N.Y. Am., 1936-37; music editor Time mag., 1937-39, gen. writer, 1939-45; sr. writer, roving corr. Life mag., 1945-49; music critic New Yorker mag., 1949-72, record critic, 1972-86. Author: Jazz: Hot and Hybrid, 1938, Geniuses, Goddesses and People, 1946, Listening to Music, 1958, In Spite of Myself: A Personal Memoir, 1970, Divas: Impressions of Todays Sopranos, 1973, The Bhagavad Gita, An Interlinear Translation from the Sanskrit, 1979; also numerous articles.; contbr. to: Ency. Americana; mem. adv. bd.: Am. Heritage Dictionary of Am. Lang. Recipient citation for disting. contbn. to Am. music Nat. Assn. Am. Composers and Condrs. Mem. Am. Oriental Soc. Home: Salisbury Conn. Died Aug. 15, 1986.

SARVIS, ARTHUR H., banker; b. Stratford, Ont., Can., 1889. Vice chmn. bd., chmn. exec. com., dir. Citizens Comml. & Savs. Bank, Flint, Mich. Mem. Elks. Home: Flint Mich. †

SATENSTEIN, FRANK, publishing company executive; b. N.Y.C., 1924. Student, Cornell U. Pres., chmn. exec. com., bd. dirs. Am. Book-Stratford Press Inc., N.Y.C., then chmn. bd. dirs.; pres. Cornwall Press. Home: New York N.Y. Died Sept. 30, 1984.

SATHERLY, ARTHUR EDWARD, record producer, inventor; b. Bristol, Eng., Oct. 19, 1889; came to U.S., 1913; Student, Queen Elizabeth Coll. With Wis. Chair Co., Milw.; then with Grafton, New London, Wis., 1913-16, 19; asst. sec. to Thomas A. Edison 1916; pioneer record producer with Paramount Records, QRS Records, N.Y.C., Plaza Records, Am. Record Co., N.Y.C.; then with Columbia Records, 1938-52. Mem. Country Music Assn. (Country Music Hall of Fame 1971), Acad. Country and Western Music (Pioneer award 1969). Home: Fountain Valley Calif. Died Feb. 10, 1986.

SATTERFIELD, DAVID EDWARD, III, congressman; b. Richmond, Va., Dec. 2, 1920; s. David Edward Jr. and Blanche (Kidd) S.; m. Anne Elizabeth Powell, Dec. 27, 1943; children: David Edward IV, John Bacon. Student, U. Richmond, 1939-42; LLB, U. Va., 1948. Bar: Va. 1948. Former ptnr. Satterfield, Haw, Anderson, Parkerson & Beazley; asst. U.S. atty. Ea. Dist., Va., 1950-53; councilman City of Richmond, 1954-56; mem. Va. Gen. Assembly, 1960-64, 89th-96th Congresses from 3d dist. Va. Past sec.-treas., dir. Richmond Baseball, Inc., The Virginians baseball club; trustee U. Richmond, Naval Aviation Mus. Lt. USNR, World War II, PTO; capt. Res. Decorated Purple Heart. Mem. Masons (32 degree), Shriners, Phi Gamma Delta, Phi Alpha Delta. Democrat. Died Sept. 29, 1988.

SAUCIER, LAFAYETTE LUDOVIC, educator; b. Montreal, Que., Can., Dec. 6, 1916; s. Henri Louis and Nelida (LaFayette) S.; m. Florence M. McKeough, June 9, 1945; 1 son, John Robert. AB, St. Michaels Coll., 1940; MEd, U. Vt., 1949, MA, 1950, EdD; C.A.G.S., 1978. Tchr. Winooski (Vt.) Sch. Dist., 1940-56;

supervising prin. Winooski Sch., 1956-63; supt. schs. Winooski (Vt.) Sch. Dist., 1963-74; prof. edn. Coll. Edn., U. Vt., Burlington, from 1974, cons. bilingual edn.; coordinator Vt. Tchrs. Corps, from 1974; prof. edn. John F. Kennedy Sch., Winnoski; travel and study tours Can., Switzerland, Hungary, Bulgaria, USSR, China, Germany; chief adminstr. Handicapped Children Chittenden County, Vt. Mem. adv. coun. Vt. Commr. Edn., 1966-67, Vt. Gov. on Youth Commn., 1965-87; mem. Gov. adv. coun. for Vocational and Tech. Edn.; mem. approval com. Office of Econ. Opportunity for Vt., 1966-67; mem. coun. U. Vt., from 1977; assoc. mem. Smithsonian Instn. With AUS, 1942-45. Deocrated Silver Star, Bronze Star; Winooski High Sch. and Vocat. Community Ctr. dedicated in his honor; recipient Disting. Service award U. Vt. Fellow Nat. Acad. Sch. Execs.; mem. Vt. Hist. Soc., NAt. Hist. Soc., Comparative Edn. Soc., NEA, Am. Assn. Sch. Adminstrs., Dept. Elementary Sch. Prins., Am. Acad. Polit. and Social Sci., Vt. Supt. Assn., New Eng. Supt. Assn., Phi Delta Kappa, K.C. (4 deg.). Roman Catholic. Home: Winooski Vt. Died Nov. 1, 1987; buried St. Stephen's Cemetery, Winooski.

SAUNDERS, BYRON WINTHROP, industrial engineering educator; b. Providence, June 27, 1914; s. Winthrop Henry and Vera (Sweet) S.; m. Miriam Ellis Wise, Dec. 28, 1942; children: William Clinton, Martha Elizabeth, Carolyn Ellis. B.S. in Elec. Engring, R.I. State Coll., 1937; M.S., Stevens Inst. Tech., 1945. With Narragansett Electric Co., 1937-38, Douglas Paton Co., Providence, 1938- 40, RCA, 1940-47; mem. faculty Cornell U., 1947-78, prof. indsl. engring., 1956-78, chmn. dept., 1963-67; dir. Cornell U. (Sch. Indsl. Engring.), 1967-75, also dir. continuing edn. in engring., 1971-74, dean faculty, 1974-78; ret. 1979; Joseph Lucas vis. prof. U. Birmingham, Eng., 1960-61; treas., dir. Wilderness Corp.; cons. in field. Contbg. editor: Industrial Engineering Handbook. Past mem. Ithaca Planning Bd.; Former trustee St. Lawrence Dist. Unitarian Universalist Assn.; Trustee SEA Edn. Assn. (trustee). Fellow Am. Inst. Indsl. Engrs.; mem. ASME, Am. Soc. Engring. Edn., AAAS, Inst. Mgmt. Scis., Tau Kappa Epsilon, Alpha Pi Mu. Unitarian (past pres.). Home: Ithaca N.Y. Died Jan. 4, 1987.

SAUNDERS, JOHN ALLEN, cartoonist, writer; b. Lebanon, Ind., Mar. 24, 1899; s. Fred Clark and Nancy Ellen (Jackson) S.; m. Lois Long, Mar. 27, 1923; children: John Philip, David Allen, Penelope Ellen, Lois Ann. AB, Wabash Coll., MA, LHD (hon.), 1963. Asst. prof. Romance langs. Wabash Coll., 1927-38; comics editor Pubs. Syndicate, Chgo., 1937-45; continuity writer Field Newpaper Syndicate, Chgo. Cocreator: comic strips including Mary Worth and Steve Roper; author: play The Big Cough; contbr. articles and short stories to mags. Mem. Toledo Bd. Edn., Toledo Libr. Bd. Mem. Nat. Cartoonists Soc., Newspaper Comics Coun., Rotary (pres. local chpt.), Players Club (N.Y.C.), Masons. Democrat. Presbyterian. Home: Perrysburg Ohio. Died Jan. 28, 1986.

SAUNDERS, STUART THOMAS, consultant, former railroad executive; b. McDowell, W.Va., July 16, 1909; s. William H. and Lucy (Smith) S.; m. Dorothy Davidson, June 24, 1939; children: Stuart Thomas, Laura Jeter (Mrs. C.V. Spratley III), Jesse Davidson, William Tazewell. AB, Roanoke Coll., 1930, LLD, 1959; LLB, Harvard, 1934; LLD, Hampden-Sydney Coll., 1959, Lynchburg Coll., 1960, Emory and Henry Coll., 1961, Trinity Coll., 1960, Washington and Lee U., 1961, Morris Harvey Coll., 1963, Bradley U., 1964, U. Md., 1964, St. Joseph's Coll., 1965, Dickinson Sch. Law, 1968, Williams Coll., 1968, U. Md., 1968, U. Pa., 1969; LHD, Susquehanna U., 1968. Bar: D.C. 1934, Va. 1938. Practice Washington, 1934-39; mem. Douglas, Obear & Campbell, 1936-39; asst. gen. solicitor Norfolk & Western Ry., 1939-47, asst. gen. counsel, 1947-51, v.p., gen. counsel, 1954-56, exec. v.p., 1956-58, pres., 1958-63; head Pa. R.R., 1964-68; chmn., chief exec. officer Penn Central Transp. Co., 1968-70, ret., 1970; cons. from 1971; bd. dirs. Va. Hot Springs Inc., Hotel Waldorf-Astoria Corp.; mem. Bus. Coun. Chmn. bd. trustees Roanoke Coll.; trustee Va. Found. Ind. Colls., Found. for Pa. Ind. Colls., Hollins Coll., John Fitzgerald Kennedy Libr. Corp., Com. Econ. Devel., Ind. Coll. Funds Am. Tax Found. Inc., U. Va. Grad. Sch. Bus. Sponsors, Va. Theol. Sem. Mem. ABA, Va. Bar Assn., Newcomen Soc. N.Am., Met. Club, Commonwealth Club, Links Club, Omicron Delta Kappa. Episcopalian. Home: Richmond Va. Died Feb. 7, 1987.

SAVAGE, LEON, lawyer; b. Kovna, Lithuania, Mar. 23, 1888; came to U.S., 1914; naturalized, 1921; s. Meyer and Rebecca (Dimenstein) S.; m. Anna Lifschitz, Nov. 28, 1918 (dec. 1960); m. 2d, Rose Gootblat, Mar. 1964. BL, Paris U.; LLB, Columbia U., 1923; JSD, Bklyn. Law Sch., 1952. Bar: N.Y. 1925, Fed. 1925. Journalist on Russian paper Telegraph, Kovna, 1905, later on Russian, Yiddish, English newspapers and mags.; feature writer Phila., North American, 1917-20; spl. writer Am. Alliance for Labor and Democracy in World War I; assoc. rep. Russian press in U.S., 1917-18; publicist, city editor Jewish Daily Day, 1917-48; practiced law in N.Y.C., from 1925. Author: Population and Immigration in United States, Treason and Punishment, (with B. Charney Vladeck) From the Depths of My Heart, Nightmare in the Kremlin (transl.); editor: Washington Heights Dem.; contbg. editor Zionist Announcer, Jewish Forum, Jewish Social Studies, Jewish Tribune and Jewish Rev. Mem. numerous polit. and civic coms. and orgns., N.Y.C., chmn. or pres. of several; also active in Jewish orgns. and zionist movement; hon. pres. Bronx Zionist Region; sec., dir. YMHA and YWHA, Washington Heights, from 1926; bd. dirs. Met. sect. Jewish Welfare Bd. Am.; chmn. spl. groups, mem. ind. citizens coms. in the senatorial campaigns for Herbert H. Lehman; active in campaign for Mayor Wagner, 1952. Mem. N.Y. County Lawyers Assn., Acad. Polit. Sci., and other bus. and profl. orgns., Masons, B'nai B'rith (dep. dist. pres. dist. 1). Home: Brooklyn N.Y. †

SAVAGE, ROBERT H., investment company executive; b. 1916; m. Jean Savage; children: Lawrence, Robert Jr., William, John, Peter, Michael, David, Richard, Holly, Carol. BA, CCNY, 1937. Reporter Wall St. Jour., 1945-50; security analyst Merrill, Lynch, Pierce, Fenner & Smith, 1950-52; sr. security analyst Wood, Struthers & Co., 1952-55; dir. investor rels. Chrysler Corp., 1955-64; with ITT, 1964-79, successively spl. asst. to treas., dir. investment rels. treas. dept., dir. investment rels. fin. and treas. depts., v.p. investor rels.; co-founder, mem. investment firm Kehoe, Towey & Savage, N.Y.C., 1979-86. Home: Stamford Conn. Died Apr. 30, 1986.

SAWHILL, JOHN ELDEN, physician; b. Concordia, Kans., Aug. 26, 1890; s. William F. and Lucy (Campbell) S.; m. Helen Knapp, Aug. 21, 1920; children: John Elden, Robert Arthur, Malcolm Campbell. Student, Coll. Emporia, 1908-11; AB, U. Kans., 1912; MD, NYU, 1918. Univ. physician Washington Sq., NYU, 1924; prof. hygiene Washington Sq. Coll., 1942-62. Fellow N.Y. Acad. Medicine (life); mem. AMA (life), N.Y. County Med. Assn. (life), Am. Coll. Health Assn. (pres. 1952), Nu Sigma Nu, Alpha Omega Alpha. Home: Sarasota Fla. †

SAXE, EMANUEL, accountant, educator; b. N.Y.C., Aug. 23, 1903; s. Bernhard David and Helen (Armsburg) S.; m. Ruth M. Lubell, July 7, 1929; children: Judith Kate Saxe Kuvin (dec.), David Bernhard. B.S. in Social Sci, CCNY, 1925; J.D., NYU, 1929, Ph.D., 1937; D.C.S. (hon.), Pace Coll., 1956; LL.D. (hon.), Baruch Coll., 1974. Bar: N.Y. 1930; C.P.A., N.Y. Staff acct. Klein, Hinds & Finke, C.P.A.s, 1923-26; pvt. practice as C.P.A. 1926-85; faculty Bernard M. Baruch Sch. Bus. and Public Adminstrn., CCNY, 1934-68, sec. faculty, 1941-56, chmn. dept. accountancy, 1950-56, dean, 1956-68; dean emeritus Bernard M. Baruch Sch. Bus. and Public Adminstrn., CCNY (sch. became Bernard M. Baruch Coll.), 1968-87, Morton Wollman disting. prof. accountancy, 1969-70, disting. univ. prof. accountancy, 1970-73; mng. editor N.Y. C.P.A.; dir. tech. services and research N.Y. Soc. C.P.A.s, 1946-56. Author: Estate Accounting, 1939, (with S. B. Tunick) Fundamental Accounting-Theory and Practice, 3d edit, 1963; Contbr. articles to acctg. jours. Spl. examiner N.Y.C. Mcpl. Civil Service Commn., 1941-42; expert examiner acctg. and taxation N.Y. Civil Service Commn., 1949-50; chmn. adv. com. N.Y. Dept. Edn., 1951-52; mem. Nat. Com. Standards Edn. and Experience CPA's, 1952-57; trustee Bronx YM and YWHA, 1934-87, pres., 1947-49; trustee Fedn. Jewish Philanthropies N.Y.C., 1950-53, 61-62, Student Aid Assn. CCNY, 1952-80, City Coll. Fund, 1957-87 , Baruch Coll. Fund, 1969-80; mem. N.Y. State Council on Accountancy, 1967-71, vice chmn., 1971; mem. N.Y. State Bd. Public Accountancy, 1971-73; v.p. Middle Atlantic Assn. Colls. Bus. Adminstrn., 1966-67, pres., 1967-68; mem. N.Y.C. Temporary Commn. on City Finances, 1975-77; chmn. quality control rev. com. Office of Comptroller, City of N.Y., 1978-83; mem. Commr.'s Adv. Panel, Dept. Fin., 1982-85. Recipient Alumni Service award CCNY, 1950, Townsend Harris medal for notable achievement, 1953; Outstanding Service award N.Y. Soc. C.P.A.s, 1957; D.S.M. Baruch Coll., 1972; Emanuel Saxe disting. professorship established at Baruch Coll., 1972, Emanuel Saxe disting. lectures in acctg. established 1973. Member Am. Inst. C.P.A.s (council 1970-73), N.Y. Soc. C.P.A.s (v.p. 1964-65, Cert. of Honor 1981), Am. Acctg. Assn., Alumni Assn. CCNY, Phi Beta Kappa (pres. Gamma chpt. N.Y. 1962), Beta Gamma Sigma, Beta Alpha Psi, Sigma Alpha. Home: Riverdale N.Y. Died Dec. 12, 1987.

SAXON, CHARLES DAVID, cartoonist, artist; b. Bklyn, Nov. 13, 1920; m. Nancy Lee Rogers, July 11, 1940; children: Amanda Irby, Charles Rogers, Peter Cullum. AB, Columbia U., 1940; DHL (hon.), Hamilton Coll., 1972. Editor various mags. Dell Pub. Co., 1940-42, editorial dir. spl. issues dept., 1945-49, editor-in-chief Modern Screen, Screen Stories mags., 1950-56; cartoon editor This Week mag., 1948-49; cartoonist New Yorker mag., 1956-88. Author, illustrator books including: One Man's Fancy (collection Saxon cartoons), 1977; artist 725 drawings, 92 covers for The New Yorker; contbr. cartoonist various mags.;. 1st lt. USAAF, 1943-45. Recipient award for animated films Venice Film Festival, Gold Medal award Art Dirs. Club. Home: New Canaan Conn. Died Dec. 6, 1988.

SAXTON, MARK, writer, editor; b. Mineola, N.Y., Nov. 28, 1914; s. Eugene Francis and Martha (Plaisted) S.; m. Josephine Porter Stocking, June 27, 1940 (dec. 1967); children: Russell Steele, Martha Porter. A.B., Harvard U., 1936. Newspaper, mag. and radio work 1936-38; asst. editor Farrar & Rinehart, N.Y.C., 1938-43; asso. editor Rinehart & Co., 1946; exec. editor William Sloane Assos., 1946-50; editor McGraw-Hill Book Co., 1950-52; promotion mgr., editorial adviser Harvard U. Press, Cambridge, Mass., 1952-68; editor-in-chief, dir. Gambit, Inc., Ipswich, Mass., 1968-80; Mem. staff Breadloaf (Vt.) Writers Conf., summers 1947-51, 60. Author: Danger Road, 1939, The Broken Circle, 1941, The Year of August, 1943, Prepared for Rage, 1947, Paper Chase, 1964, The Islar, 1969, The Two Kingdoms, 1979, Havoc in Islandia, 1982; author short stories. Trustee, v.p. Joseph Collins Found., N.Y.C., 1950-88. Served to lt. (j.g.) USNR, 1943-46. Clubs: Century Assn. (N.Y.C.), Harvard (N.Y.C.); St. Botolph (Boston). Home: New York N.Y. Died Jan. 7, 1988.

SAYRE, JUDSON SHIRLEY, manufacturer; b. Meadville, Pa., Jan. 9, 1899; s. Nichoals W. and Mae (Lamphier) S.; m. Margaret Stewart, Aug. 24, 1924; children: Shirley Jean, Dorothy Nan; m. Louise Weller, July 31, 1942. AB, Ohio Wesleyan U., 1920; postgrad., Columbia, 1923; LHD (hon.), Hartwick Coll., 1962. Dir. slaes tng. Alexander Hamilton Inst., 1920-25; br. mgr., later asst. sales mgr., gen. sales mgr. Kelvinator Corp., 1925-33; appliance sales mgr. Montgomery Ward & Co., 1933-35; asst. to pres. RCA Mfg. Co., 1935-37; v.p. charge sales Bendix Home Appliances, South Bend, Ind., 1937-41, pres., chmn. bd., 1941-51; v.p. AVCO Mfg. Co., gen. mgr. Bendix Home Appliances, 1951-53; merchandising cons. 1953-54; pres., gen. mgr. Norge div. Borg-Warner, 1954-60, chmn. bd., chief exec. officer, 1960-63; v.p. marketing Borg-Warner, 1963-64; cons. from 1964; bd. dirs. St.L.-S.F. R.R., Zions First Nat. Bank, Salt Lake City, Weigh-Tronix, Inc., Fairfield, Iowa. Trustee Ohio Wesleyan U.; bd. dirs. Ill. Masonic Hosp. Assn. Mem. Western Golf Assn. (dir.), Surf Club (Miami Beach), Indian Creek Country Club (Bal Harbour, Fla.), Chicago Club, Mchts. and Mfrs. Club, Mid-Am. Club (Chgo.), Bob O'Link Golf Club, Seignery of Can., Masons (32 degree), Beta Theta Pi. Home: Bal Harbour Fla. Died May 6, 1986; buried North Baltimore, Ohio.

SCARBOROUGH, JULIAN HASKELL, academic administrator; b. Bishopville, S.C., June 16, 1891; s.Orlando C. and Mary (Ambrose) S.; m. Mary Claire Peterson, Jane. 3, 1923; 1 child, Julian Haskell. Student, Furman U., LLD (hon.), 1949; student, Yale U., George Washington U. Pres. Fed. Land Bank of Columbia (S.C.) Dist. No. 3, ret., 1954; adminstrv. dir. Furman U., from 1954; past pres. Prodn. Credit Corp. of Columbia; v.p., bd. dirs. State Life Ins. Co.; bd. dirs. State Capital Life Ins. Co., State Capital Ins. Co. Formerly mem. S.C. Ho. of Reps., S.C. State seantor, treas. State of S.C.; gen. agt. Farm Credit Adminstrn.; treas. S.C. div. Am. Cancer Soc.; chmn. bd. trustee Furmnan U. Mem. Rotary. Democrat. Baptist. Home: Myrtle Beach S.C. †

SCARF, FREDERICK LEONARD, physicist; b. Phila., July 25, 1930; s. Louis Harris and Lena (Elkman) S.; m. Mimi Florence Levin, Aug. 30, 1953; children: Elizabeth Anna, Robert Henry, Daniel Albert. AB, Temple U., Phila., 1951; PhD, MIT, 1955. Rsch. assoc. MIT, 1955-56; asst. prof., then assoc. prof. physics U. Wash., Seattle, 1956-62; mgr. space sci. dept. TRW Def. and Space Systems Group, Redondo Beach, Calif., 1962-88; cons. mission planning NASA; chmn. panel internat. magnetosphere study NAS. Contbr. articles to profl. publs. Recipient Exceptional Scientific Achievement medal NASA, 1981, 86; MIT overseas fellow, summer 1955; NSF postdoctoral fellow, 1958-59. Fellow Am. Geophys. Union; mem. Internat. Radio Sci. Union (chmn. commn. IV 1972-75). Home: Sherman Oaks Calif. Died July 17, 1988.

SCARFF, MAX M., agriculturist; b. New Carlisle, Ohio, Jan. 16, 1892; s. William Neff and Mary E. (Miller) S.; m. Ina Pearl Studebaker, June 5, 1919; children: Mary Ellen (Mrs. Charles F. Martin), Phyllis (Mrs. John E. Milliken), Jane (Mrs. Boyd E. McKinney), Nancy (Mrs. Norman H. Baker), Maxine (Mrs. Richard W. Goodall). BS, Ohio State U., 1914. Ptnr. W.N. Scarff & Sons, New Carlisle, 1914-53; propr. Scarff Seed Co., from 1953; v.p. N.C. Bank; bd. dirs. No. Life Ins., Seattle, new Carlisle Nat. Bank, Nationwide Mut. Ins. Co., Nationwide Mut. Fire Ins. Co., Nationwide Life Ins. Co., Peoples Broadcasting Corp., Brunson Bank & Trust Co., Nationwide Corp. Approved Fin., Mich. Life Ins. Co. With armed forces, World War I. Named Master Farmer, Ohio, 1937. Mem. Newcomen Soc., Am. Seed Trade Assn. (past pres.), Ohio Seed Dealer's Assn. (past pres.), So., Western seedmen's assns., Ohio Seed Improvement Assn. (past pres.), Ohio Hybrid Seed Corn Producers (past pres.), Masons, Sertoma, Sigma Alpha Epsilon. Methodist. Home: New Carlisle Ohio. †

SCHAEFER, HAROLD WILLIAM, business executive; b. Chgo., Feb. 16, 1909; s. Curtis Lewis and Mary Dora (Grouble) S.; m. Mary M. Campbell, June 29, 1940; 1 son, Harold William II. BS in Elec. Engring., Lewis Inst.; student physics, U. Chgo. Asst. to pres. Majestic Radio Corp., Chgo., 1925-31, Gen. Household Utilities, Chgo., 1931-39; chief engr. Harry Alter Co., Chgo., 1939-41; dir. engring. and mfg. proximity fuse program Applied Physics Lab, Johns Hopkins U., 1941-43; mgr. facilities planning, radio and TV mfg. Radio Corp. Am., Camden, N.J., 1943-44; asst. div. mgr. in charge engring. and mfg. Westinghouse Electric Corp., Sunbury, Pa., 1944-50; v.p. appliance engring. Philco Corp., Phila., 1950-56, v.p., gen. mgr. appliances div., 1956-58, v.p. devel. and planning appliances, 1958-61, v.p., dir. engring. consumer and comml. products, 1961-63; v.p., gen. mgr. Eureka Williams Co., Bloomington, Ill., from 1963, then pres., until 1980; v.p., dir. NAt. Union Electric Corp. Dir. Adlai E. Stevenson Lectures, Bloomington-Normal. Mem. AAAS, IRE, Internat. Soc. Bioclimatology and Biometerology, Am. Inst. Med. Climatology, Am. Ordnance Assn., Smithsonian Instn., Franklin Inst. Home: Bloomington Ill. Died Aug. 15, 1988.

SCHAEFER, OTTO GUSTAVE, publishing company executive; b. Washington, Mo., Nov. 14, 1892; s. Louis and Ida (Schnadt) S.; m. Jeanette Bernice Wallen, Dec. 24, 1930; children: Louise Schaefer Dailey, Mary Schaefer Mundy. BS, U. Mo., 1918; MS, U. Minn., 1921. County agrl. agt. Steele County, Minn., 1920-22; diary extension specialist Pa. State Coll., 1922-23; assoc. prof. dairy husbandry U. Minn., 1923-28; with Meredith Pub. Co., from 1928, Ea. mgr., 1949-57, v.p., from 1957, also bd. dirs.; bd. dirs. Mag. Advt. Bur., Pubs. Info. Bur. 2d lt. U.S. Army, World War I. Mem. University Club, Knollwood Country Club (White Plains, N.Y.). Home: Scarsdale N.Y. †

SCHAEFER, PAUL A., lawyer; b. St. Louis, Sept. 23, 1888; s. Henry and Martha (Erck) S.; m. Eleanor Tuegel, Sept. 7, 1911; children: P. James, Eleanor Ruth Schaefer Fleming, Ralph H., Irma Mae Schaefer Milster. Ed. pub. schs., also, Alexander Hamilton Inst. With Cen. Mo. Trust Co., Jefferson City, from 1903, treas., 1918-55, vice chmn., from 1955, also bd. dirs.; v.p., dir. Mut. Savs. and Loan Assn., Jefferson City, from 1932. Treas. Jefferson City Pub. Library, Lincoln U.; chmn. quota and admissions com. Jefferson City United Community Fund. Mem. Mo., Cole County (sec.) bankers assns., Jefferson City C. of C., Kiwanis (pres. Jefferson City 1921, treas. from 1922, chmn. child welfare com., civic award 1953). Lutheran (pres.). Home: Jefferson City Mo. †

SCHAEFER, WALTER V., lawyer, judge; b. Grand Rapids, Mich., Dec. 10, 1904; s. Elmer Philip and Margaret (O'Malley) S.; m. Marguerite Moreland Goff, June 3, 1940; children: James M. Goff, Barlow Goff (stepsons), Nancy, Walter V. Jr. PHB, U. Chgo., 1926, JD, 1928, LLD, 1959; LLD, John Marshall Law Sch., 1950, Northwestern U., 1954, Lake Forest Coll., 1955, Notre Dame U., 1972, DePaul U., 1975. Bar: Ill. 1928. Pvt. and govt. law practice 1929-40; prof. law Northwestern U., 1940-51; referee in bankruptcy U.S. Dist. Ct., 1942-43; justice Ill. Supreme Ct., 1951-76; mem. firm Rothschild, Barry & Myers, from 1976; lectr. Northwestern U., from 1976; E. Freund lectr. U. Chgo., 1956; Holmes lectr. Harvard, 1960; Rosenthal lectr. Northwestern U., 1966; Cardozo lectr. N.Y., 1967. Co-editor: Illinois Civil Practice Act, Annotated, 1934. Mem. ABA (Gold medal 1969), Ill. Bar Assn., Chgo. Bar Assn., Am. Law Inst. (coun.), Am. Acad. Arts and Scis., Legal Club (pres. 1948-49), Univ. Club. Democrat. Home: Lake Bluff Ill. Died June 15, 1986.

SCHAFFNER, ROBERT MICHAEL, food technology consultant; b. Bklyn., Jan. 30, 1915; s. Arthur G. and Helen (Von Holleuffer) S.; m. Blanche Wharton, June 1, 1940; children—Val, Pam, Todd. B.S., Poly Inst. Bklyn., 1936; M.S., W.Va. U., 1939; Ph.D., U. Pitts., 1941. Chem. engr. A. Hess & Co., N.Y.C., 1936-37; teaching asst. W.Va. U., 1937-39; instr. chem. engring. U. Pitts., 1939-41; chem. engr. Standard Oil Co., Ind., 1941-43; dir. research Guardite Corp., Miner Labs., Chgo., 1943-44; chem. engr. Libby McNeill & Libby, 1945-48, asst. to v.p. prodn., 1949-53, plant mgr., 1953; asst. gen. supt. Eastern div., 1954-57, v.p. research and quality control, 1957-70; asso. dir. for tech. Bur. Foods, FDA, Washington, 1971-84; food tech. cons. 1985-88. Author tech. articles; patentee on food dehydration. Mem. Inst. Food Tech., Assn. Food and Drug Assn., Am. Chem. Soc., Am. Inst. Chem. Engrs., Lambda Chi Alpha, Phi Lambda Upsilon. Home: Falls Church Va. Died June 17, 1988.

SCHAFLER, NORMAN I., corporation executive; b. N.Y.C., 1917; m. Rubelle Sanders; children: Julie, Richard. Grad., Pratt Inst., Bklyn. Sales engr. Atlantic Heat and Power Co., N.Y.C., 1938-40; pres. Continental Heat and Power Co., N.Y.C., 1940-42; v.p. Consol. Diesel Electric Corp., Mt. Vernon, N.Y., 1942-49; pres. Consol. Diesel Electric Corp., Stamford, Conn., 1949-64; chmn. bd., chief exec. officer, dir. Condec Corp., Old Greenwich, Conn., from 1964; bd. dirs. United Aircraft Products Corp., Fidelity Trust Co., Bangor Punta Corp., Sun Chem. Corp. Trustee, former pres. Congregation Rodeph Shalom; bd. incorporators Stamford Hosp.; bd. visitors Pratt Inst. Mem. Chief Execs. Forum, World Bus. Council, Econ. Club, Tower Fellows, Birchwood Country Club, Harmonie Club, Lotos Club, Saugatuck Harbor Yacht Club, Metropolis Country Club. Home: New York N.Y. also: Westport Conn. Died July 31, 1986.

SCHALL, LEROY ALLEN, otolaryngologist; b. Latrobe, Pa., Oct. 15, 1892; s. Ephraim A. and Elsie (Scott) S.; m. Mabel Ferguson, Nov. 16, 1921; children: Ethel Schall Gooch, Nancy Schall McCord. MD, Jefferson Coll., Phila., 1917; AM (hon.), Harvard U., 1942; ScD (hon.), Jefferson Med. Coll., 1948. Diplomate Am. Bd. Otolaryngology (asst. to bd. dirs. 1926-39, dir. 1940, pres. 1951-52). Intern Phila. Gen. Hosp. and Meml. Hosp., Johnstown, Pa.; with USPHS, 1920-23; otolaryngologist VA Hosp., Boston; clin. asst. Mass. Eye and Ear Infirmary and Mass. Gen. Hosp., Boston, 1923-25, asst. surgeon, 1925-29, assoc. surgeon, 1935-39, chief otology and laryngology, from 1939; prof. laryngology Harvard U., 1939-59, prof. emeritus, from 1959, also W.A. LeCompte prof. otology emeritus; mgr. Mass. Eye and Ear Infirmary, from 1959; cons. U.S. Marine Hosp. #2, 1923-41, Anna Jaques Hosp., Newburyport, Mass., 1924-27, Jordan Hosp., Plymouth, Mass., 1935-40, N.E. Peabody Home for Crippled Children, from 1940, Palmer Meml. Hosp. from 1940; asst. laryngologist Huntington Meml. Hosp., 1920-40, laryngologist, 1940-41; asst. laryngologist Newton Hosp., 1927-34, Robert Breck Bingham Hosp., 1923-40, Palmer Meml. Hosp., 1930-40; cons. tumor clinic Boston Dispensary, 1923-40, nose and throat clinic, 1936-40. Author: Neoplasms of the Ear in textbook Diseases of the Ear, Nose, Throat; contr. articles to profl. jours. Fellow AMA (sec. otology and laryngology sect. 1938-40, vice chmn. 1937, chmn. 1941), ACS; mem. Mass. Med. Soc., N.E. Otol. and Laryngol. Soc. (pres. 1943), Am. Laryngol., Rhinological and Otol. Soc. (pres. 1954), Am. Acad. Ophthalmology and Otolaryngology (pres. 1958), Am. Otol. Soc., Am. Laryngol. Assn. (pres. 1957),Am. Broncho-Esophagol. Assn. (pres. 1950), Boston Surg. Soc., Newton Med. Club, Aesculpian Club (hon.), P.R. Med. Assn. (hon.), Guatemala Med. Assn. (hon.), Soc. Chilena de Otorhino laryn.Facultad de Biol y Ciencas Medica, U. Chile, Soc. Med. Hungarorum Soc. Rhino., Laryngol. et Otoligie Tenentium, Masons, Harvard Club (Boston), Faculty Club (Cambridge), Brae Burn Country (West Newton), Phi Chi, Alpha Omega Alpha. Home: Boston Mass. †

SCHALLERT, EDWIN F(RANCIS), journalist, lecturer; b. L.A., Apr. 15, 1890; s. John Joseph and Mary Joseph (Lindsay) S.; m. Elza Emily Baumgarten, June 30, 1921; children: William Joseph, John Walter, Roy Edwin. AB, St. Vincent's Coll., 1908, AM, 1911; student, L.A. Bus. Coll., 1909-10. Writer, assoc. editor West Coast Mag., L.A., 1910-11; fin. editor L.A. Times, 1912-15, drama editor, music critic, 1915-17, drama, mtion picture editor, critic, 1919-58, music critic, 1919-34; editor Weekly Motin Picture Preview, 1924-33, Ann. Motion Picture Preview, 1927-58; West Coast co-corr. Picture-Play Mag., 1923-36; weekly radio broadcaster Conversations with Film Personalities, radio stas., L.A., 1934-38; West Coast corr. N.Y. Herald-Tribune, 1948-52; lectr. theatre arts dept. UCLA, 1958; radio gust Elza Schallert Revs., Hollywood on the Air; Westminster Abbey corr. for Elizabeth II coronation, 1953. So. Calif. contbr. The Burns Mantle and Successors Best Plays, 1932-53; mags. With Am. Expeditionary Force, 1917-19. Recipient Screen Publicists Guild Hollywood tribute, 1953; co-recipient honors Loyola U., 1963. Mem. Hollywood Publicists Assn. (hon.), Variety Club Internat., Motion Picture Sound Editors, Hollywood Press Club. Republican. Roman Catholic. Home: Los Angeles Calif. †

SCHEID, VERNON EDWARD, geologist, educator; b. Balt., Sept. 5, 1906; s. Charles Christian and Blanche McLenny (Donaldson) S.; m. Martha Frances Helm, Aug. 17, 1934; children: Donald Edward, Margaret Kathryn. AB, Johns Hopkins U., 1928, PhD, 1946; MS, U. Idaho, 1940. Registered profl. engr., Nev.; registered geologist, Calif. Instr. geology Johns Hopkins, 1931-34, summers 1932, 34; asst. geologist Ark. Geol. Survey, summer 1931; geol. field asst. U.S. Geol. Survey, Idaho and Colo., summers 1929, 30, 35, 36; geologist ore deposits Idaho, summers 1940, 41; asst. geologist Idaho Bur. Mines and Geology, summer 1938; part-time mineralogist 1938-39; instr. U. Idaho, 1934-38, asst. prof., 1938-42, prof. geology, head dept. geology-geography, 1947-51; geologist Strategic Minerals Investigations, Mont., Idaho, Wash., 1942-47; dean Mackay Sch. Mines U. Nev., prof. mineral sci., 1951-72, prof. mineral econs., from 1973; dir. Nev. Bur. Mines and Nev. Mining Analytical Lab., 1951-72; organizer, chmn., dir. Nev. Oil and Gas Conservation Commn., 1953-72; asst. leader Econ. Geol. Excursion, 16th Internat. Geol. Congress, Wash., 1933; collaborator in seismology for Idaho U.S. Coast and Geodetic Survey, 1939-42, 1947; mem. numerous Nev. gov.'s adv. councils on mining, natural resources, maps, water, energy, from 1951; leader People to People Econ. Geology and Mining del., Peoples Republic of China, Brazil, Peru, Republic of South Africa; mem. Nat. Adv. Com. on Oceans and Atmosphere; mining engring., geology cons. fgn. countries UN, from 1973, also pvt. industry. Co-author: Nev. Oil and Gas Conservation Law, 1953; author numerous geological reports. Mem. mineral industry research and edn. adv. com. U. Alaska. Fellow Geol. Soc. Am., AAAS; mem. AIME (Pacific S.W. chmn. indsl. minerals div. 1956-58, gen. chmn. div. conf. 1957, chmn. Nev. sect. 1965, Robert Earll McConnell award 1980), Soc. Mining Engrs. (Disting. mem.), Mineral Soc. Am., Assn. Geoscientists for Internat. Devel., Assn. Am. State Geologists, Soc. Econ. Geologists, Rotary, Sigma Xi, Phi Kappa Phi, Sigma Gamma Epsilon, Tau Beta Pi. Home: Reno Nev. Died June 6, 1987.

SCHELL, ORVILLE HICKOK, JR., lawyer; b. New Rochelle, N.Y., July 11, 1908; s. Dr. Orville Hickok and Marea (Martin) S.; m. Marjorie Elizabeth Bertha, June 29, 1935 (div. 1970); children—Suzanne Elizabeth (Mrs John Pearce), Orville Hickok III, Jonathan Edward; m Elinor Sterling Johnson, June 20, 1970; children—Christopher Sterling, Andrew John, Peter O.H. Grad., Lawrenceville Sch., 1926; A.B., Yale U. 1930; LL.B., Harvard U., 1933. Bar: N.Y. 1934. Assoc. Hughes, Schurman & Dwight, 1933-37, Hughes, Richards, Hubbard & Ewing, 1937-40; Assoc. Hughes, Hubbard & Ewing, 1941-42, partner, 1942-87; with Hughes, Hubbard & Reed.; Sec., asst.-treas., dir. J. Stirling Getchell, Inc. (advt. agy.), 1940-41; exec. compensation com., dir. Merck & Co., Inc.; dir. W. O. Hickok Mfg. Co.; chief counsel bur. ordnance Navy Dept., 1945-46; chmn. N.Y. Lawyers for the Pub. Interest, 1977-87 ; U.S. del. Conf. on Security and Cooperation in Europe, Madrid, 1980. Bd. dirs. Regional Plan Assn., N.Y., 1955-64, New York Urban Coalition, 1974-87 , Council on Pub. Interest Law, 1974-87 , NAACP Legal Def. and Ednl. Fund, 1975-87 ; chmn. N.Y.C. Ballet, 1975-87 ; bd. dirs. N.Y.C. Center Music and Drama, 1980-87 , Lincoln Ctr. for Performing Arts; pres., bd. dirs. Union Settlement Assn., 1971-73; chmn. N.Y. State Moreland Commn., 1975-87 ; co-chmn. joint com. for study N.Y. State narcotics laws of Assn. Bar City N.Y. and Drug Abuse Council; co-chmn. Com. for Pub. Justice, 1977-87 ; mem. com. character and fitness appellate div. 1st Dept. N.Y. State Supreme Ct.; mem. Zoning Bd., Town of Redding (Conn.), 1979; Trustee, vice chmn. Vassar Coll., 1963-73; trustee Town Sch., N.Y.C., 1977-87 , South St. Seaport Mus., 1977-87 ; bd. dirs., vice chmn. U.S. Citizens Helsinki Watch, 1978-87 ; chmn. America's Watch. Served as lt. USNR, 1943-45. Mem. Am. Bar Assn., Assn. Bar City N.Y. (pres. 1972-74), N.Y. State Bar Assn. Clubs: Downtown Assn., Yale, Century Assn. (N.Y.C.); Wilton (Conn.) Riding. Home: Redding Ridge Conn. Died June 17, 1987.

SCHENCK, ROBERT H., lawyer; b. Morristown, N.J., Apr. 19, 1889. Grad., N.Y. Law Sch. Bar: N.J. 1910. Ptnr. Schenck, Price, Smith & King, Morristown; counsel N.J. Firemen's Assn., Newark, from 1932; bd. dirs. 1st Nat. Bank N.J., Morristown. Mem. ABA, N.J. Bar Assn., Morris County Bar Assn., Holland Soc. N.Y., SAR. Home: Morristown N.J. †

SCHERING, HERBERT, educator; b. Berlin, Germany, Nov. 28, 1900; came to U.S., 1923, naturalized, 1929; s. Emil and Mary Anna (Boehm) S.; m. Frances Young, July 12, 1959. AB in Edn., U. Toledo, 1936, MA in History, 1942; MA in German, U. Mich., 1948, PhD in German, 1953. Asst. libr. U. Toledo, 1936-45, mem. faculty, from 1945, prof. German, from 1963, chmn. dept. fgn. langs., 1960-66, asst. to the dean Coll. Arts and Scis., 1966-68, asst. dean, from 1968. Mem. Am. Assn. Tchrs. German, AAUP, MLA, Am. Coun. on Teaching Fgn. Langs., Midwest Modern Lang. Assn. Died Sept. 15, 1985.

SCHIEFFELIN, WILLIAM JAY, JR., business executive; b. N.Y.C., Nov. 30, 1891; s. William Jay and Marla Louise (Shepard) S.; m. Annette Markoe, May 4, 1918; children: Anne Louise, William Jay III. Treas. Schieffelin & Co., 1919-22, pres., 1922-52, chmn. bd., 1952-62, hon. chmn., cons., from 1962; v.p., dir. Am. Kitchen Products Co., 1931-38; trustee Greenwich Savs. Bank, from 1956. Hon. trustee St. Luke's Hosp.; dir. N.Y.C. YMCA, 1925-47. Past pres. Nat. Wholesale Druggists Assn.; v.p., dir. Nat. Assn. Alcoholic Beverage Importers, 1934-44, hon. v.p., from 1944. First lt. 12th N.Y. Inf., 1916-17, Mexican border; 1st lt. to capt. 12th F.A., 2d div. AEF, 1918. Trustee Carnegie Endowment Internat. Peace, 1941-62. Mem. N.Y.C. C. of C. (v.p. 1956-60), Phi Beta Kappa, Sigam Xi, Scroll and Key, Union, Yale, N.Y. Yacht and Century Clubs. Home: New York N.Y. †

SCHILLER, MILTON S., lawyer; b. Boston, Mar. 18, 1914; s. Louis B. and Augusta (Goldberg) S.; m. Muriel Wilson, Mar. 7, 1943; children: Dorothy Ellen (Mrs. Frederic Barton Askin), Leslie Ann (Mrs. Harry J. Philip). AB cum laude, Harvard, 1935, LLB, 1938. Bar: MAss. 1938, Md. 1945. Assoc. firm Slater & Goldman, Boston, 1938-41; with Dept. Justice, Boston and N.Y.C., 1942-43, Tax Ct. U.S., Washington, 1943-45; ptnr. Weinberg & Green, Balt., 1945-80, ptnr. emeritus, 1981-85. Mem. Am., Md., Balt., bar assns., Center Club Inc., Suburban Balt. County Club, Banyan Country Club (Palm Beach, Fla.). Home: Baltimore Md. Died Oct. 5, 1985; buried Balt.

SCHIMPF, ALFRED IRVING, banker, industrial executive; b. Albany, N.Y., Jan. 2, 1891; s. Franklin Frederick and Alica Sophia (DeRouville) S.; m. Evea Brown, Dec. 24, 1941; m. Alba Eminente, 1963. LLB, Union U., Albany, 1914. With Nat. Comml. Bank & Trust Co., Albany, 1920-43, asst. to pres., 1956-62; with Fed. Res. Bank N.Y., 1943-44, Mfrs. Trust Co., N.Y.C., 1944-45; treas. Celotex Corp., Chgo., 1945-56; chmn. bd., chief exec. officer B.T. Babbitt, N.Y.C., from 1960; chmn. bd. Heartland Devel. Corp., Albany, 1956-62. Capt. inf. U.S. Army, 1916-19. Mem. Ft. Orange Club,

University Club, Metropolitan Club, Old Chatham Hunt Club, Delta Chi. †

SCHIOTZ, FREDRIK AXEL, clergyman; b. Chgo., June 15, 1901; s. Jacob and Stina (Akerholt) S.; m. Dagny Aasen, Aug. 23, 1928; children: Lois, nathan, Paul. BA, St. Olaf Coll., 1924; BTh, Luther Theol. Sem., St. Paul, 1930; DD (hon.), Concordia Coll., Moorhead, Minn., 1945, Augustana Theol. Sem., Rock Island, Ill., 1945; ThD (hon.), U. Erlangen, Germany, 1952; LLD (hon.), St. Olaf Coll., 1955, Valparaiso U., 1963; LittD, Pacific Luth. U., 1960; DD, Tex. Luth. Coll., 1961; LHD, Gettysburg Coll., 1964, Thiel Coll., 1965; JCD, Susquehanna U., 1966; DD, Northwestern Luth. Theol. Sem., 1968, Wartburg Theol. Sem., 1970. Ordained to ministry Luth. Ch., 1930. Tchr. high sch. Ladysmith, Wis., 1924-26; pastor Zion Luth. ch., Duluth, Minn., 1930-32, Trinity Luth. Ch., Moorhead, 1932-38, Bklyn., 1945-48; exec. sec. Student Svc. commn. Am. Luth. Conf., 1938-45, Commn. on Younger Chs. and Orphaned Missions, Nat. Luth. Coun., 1948-54; pres. Evang. Luth. Ch., 1954-60; pres. Am. Luth. Ch., 1961-71, pres. emeritus, 1971—; mem. cen. com. World Coun. Chs., 1962-71; del. Luth. world Fedn. convs., Lund, Sweden, 1947, Hanover, Fed. Republic Germany, 1952, Mpls., 1957, Helsinki, Finland, 1963, Evian, France, 1970. Author: Release, 1935. Bd. dirs. Concordia Coll., 1933-40, Student Vol. Movement Fgn. Missions, 1948-54. Decorated comdr. Order St. Olaf with star (Norway); recipient Centennial award Augustana Coll., 1961, award St. Olaf Coll., 1967; named one of 22 Disting. Norwegian-Ams., Norwegian-Am. 1975 Sesquicentennial Assn., 1975. Mem. Luth. World Fedn. (mem. exec. com. 1955—, pres. 1963-70, dir. dept. World Missions 1952-54), Norwegian-Am. Hist. Assn., Am.-Scandinavian Found. Home: Minneapolis Minn. Died Feb. 25, 1989.

SCHLAGLE, FRANK LESLIE, school system administrator; b. Linwood, Kans., Nov. 18, 1892; s. Charles Edgar and Mary Ellen (Kirby) S.; m. Doris Emily Willson, June 20, 1924. BS, Kans. State Tchrs. Coll., 1916; AM, Tchrs. Coll., Columbia U., 1923. Tchr. rural sch. Syracuse, Kans., 1909-11; prin. elem. sch. nr. Kansas City, Kans., 1911-15; asst. prin. Cen. Jr. High Sch., 1916-18; prin. Argentine High Sch., 1919-24, asst. supt. of schs., 1924-32; supt. of schs. City of Kansas City, from 1932; cons. on edn. to U.S. del. UN Conf., San Francisco, 1945; chmn. World Conf. Teaching Profession, Endicott, N.Y., 1946, also preparatory commn. Contbr. numerous articles to ednl. mags. Sec. adv. coun. Kansas City and Wyandotte County Health Dept.; bd. dirs. Kansas City Community Chest, Kansas City Camp Fire Coun.; advisor Kaw coun. Boy Scouts Am.; nat. bd. dirs. Camp Fire Girls, 1947-50; chmn. Gov.'s Def. Commn. on Edn., 1940-47; mem. Kans. State Bd. Edn., 1939-45, Kans. State Bd. for Vocat. Edn., 1939-45; chmn. Kans. State March of Dimes, 1950-53; mem. U.S. del. to Conf. on Ednl., Sci. and Cultural Orgn. UN, London, 1945; treas. Kans. Commn. for UNESCO, 1949-56. Ensign USN, 1918-19. Mem. Kansas City C. of C., NEA (life, pres., chmn. exec. com. 1944-46, trustee from 1944, ednl. policies commn., def. com. 1944-46, war and peace fund campaign com. 1943, bd. dirs. Kans. chpt. from 1932, budget com. 1942-44), Kans. State Tchrs. Assn. (v.p. 1930-31, chmn. bd. 1936-41, chmn. legis. com. 1941-43, chmn. minimum salary schedule com. 1947), Am. Assn. Sch. Adminstrs., Kans. Schoolmasters Club, Am. Legion, Horace Mann League, Masons (32 degree), Shriners, Kiwanis, Phi Delta Kappa. Presbyterian. †

SCHLAMME, MARTHA, folk singer; b. Vienna; arrived in Eng., 1938; came to U.S., 1948; Interned on Isle of Ma; folk singer BBC; recording artist Vanguard Records. Appearances include Habibi Club, Eng., Town Hall, N.Y.C., Gate of Horn, McCormick Place, Chgo., Newport (R.I.) Folk Festival, Edinburgh Festival, Weill cabaret, N.Y.C., Chautauqua Institution. Died Oct. 7, 1985.

SCHMIDT, CARL FREDERIC, educator, pharmacologist, physiologist; b. Lebanon, Pa., July 29, 1893; s. Jacob Charles and Mary Ellen (Greth) S.; A.B., Lebanon Valley Coll., 1914, D.Sc. (hon.), 1955; M.D., U. Pa., 1918, Sc.D. (hon.), 1965; D.S.M., Charles U., Prague, 1963; m. Elizabeth Viola Gruber, June 24, 1920; children—Carl F., Barbara Elizabeth. Intern, Hosp. U. Pa., 1918-19; instr. pharmacology U. Pa., 1919-22, asst. prof., 1924-29, assoc. prof., 1929-31, prof. pharmacology Med. Sch., 1931-59, emeritus prof. pharmacology, 1959-88, Dental Sch., 1949-52; assoc. in pharmacology Peking (China) Union Med. Coll., 1922-24; guest lectr. Portland (Oreg.) Med. Soc., U. Oreg. Med. Sch., 1943; Mary Scott Newbold lectr. Coll. Physicians Phila., 1943; Commonwealth vis. prof. U. Louisville, 1946; Harvey lectr., N.Y., 1949, ann. lectr. in pharmacology U. London, 1949; Henry Lower lectr., Cleve., 1949; Hachmeister Meml. lectr. Georgetown U., 1951; Graves lectr. Ind. U., 1954; chmn. adv. com. Life Ins. Research Fund, 1954-55; cons. surgeon gen. U.S. Army and VA; vis. prof. U. Philippines, 1955; research dir. U.S. Naval Aerospace, med. research dept. Naval Air Devel. Center, Johnsville, 1962-69; clin. prof. pharmacology U. South Fla. Coll. Medicine, from 1970; mem. Unitarian Med. Mission to Germany, 1948; chmn. pharmacology study sect. USPHS, 1947-51, mem. phsyiology study sec., 1947-48; chmn. Internat. Fellowships Com., 1963-64; mem. drug research bd. Nat. Acad. Sci., 1963-69; mem. NRC, 1947-50, sec. subcom. oxygen and anoxia, 1941-45; chmn. panel on physiology Research and Devel. Bd., 1948-50; chmn. subpanel on med. aspects of chem. warfare, 1948-50; mem. adv. panel on physiology Office Naval Research, 1947-52. Served as 1st lt., Med. Res. Corps, U.S. Army, 1918-25. Mem. Internat. Union Physiol. Scis. (v.p., pres. sect. pharmacology 1959-65, pres. 1965-66, hon. pres. 1966-88), Am. Heart Assn., Am. Soc. Pharmacology (v.p. 1940-42, pres. 1948-50), Am. Physiology Soc., Soc. Exptl. Biology and Medicine, Assn. Am. Physicians, AAAS, Physiology Soc. Phila., Penn Valley Assn. (pres. 1944-46), Nat. Acad. Scis., Am. Acad. Arts and Sci., Aerospace Med. Assn., Alpha Omega Alpha, Sigma Xi; hon. mem. Pharmacol. Soc., Argentine Med. Assn., others. Club: Merion Cricket (Haverford, Pa.). Mng. editor Jour. Pharmacology and Exptl. Therapeutics, 1940-42, Circulation Research, 1958-62; asso. editor Chem. Abstracts, 1942-48; author articles on respiration, cerebral and coronary circulation, action of Chinese drugs; kidney function, aerospace pharmacology to profl. jours. Home: Radnor, Pa. Died Apr. 14, 1988, buried Hershey (Pa.) Cemetery.

SCHMIDT, HENRY DUNCAN, paperboard manufacturing company executive; b. York, Pa., Aug. 25, 1892; s. John Charles and Anna M. (Small) S.; m. Margaret M. Hawkins, Feb. 10, 1927; children: Helen Margaret, John Charles. Grad., St. Paul's Sch., 1910; PhB, Yale U., 1913. Sec. Standard Chain Co., York, Pa., 1914-16; v.p., sec., dir. Schmidt & Ault Paper Co., York, 1914-23, pres., treas., dir., 1923-60; pres., treas. Schmidt & Ault Paper Co. (div. St. Regis Paper Co.), York, 1960-62, chmn., 1962-75; bd. dirs. St. Regis Paper Co., pres., treas., dir. John C. Schmidt Terminal Co., 1923-60; receiver Pullman Motor Car Co, 1917; bd. dirs. York Bank & Trust Co.; mem. adv. com. various activities WPB, OPA, 1942-45; mem. York City and County Def. Coun., 1942-45. Mem. Octant Soc. New Haven, Newcomen Soc. N.A., Mfrs. Assn. York (pres. 1933), Paperboard Industries Assn. (pres. 1932-33), Nat. Paperboard Assn. (pres. 1936-39, dir. 1934-60), York Junta, York County Agrl. Soc., Lafayette Club, Rotary, Country Club (York), St. Elmo Club (New Haven), Yale Club (N.Y.C.). Repblican. Episcopalian. Home: York Pa. †

SCHMIDT, J(OHN) RAYMOND, editor, lecturer; b. Mt. Vernon, Ind., Oct. 6, 1886; s. Edward and Henrietta (Fellemende) S.; m. Ruth Andrew, Sept.12, 1923. AB, DePauw U., 1910; LLD, Pasadena Coll., 1942. Asst. chmn. Ind. State Prohibition Com., 1911, chmn., 1914-18; chmn. Ohio State Prohibition Com., 1912; bus. mgr. Am. Advance (nat. prohibition weekly), 1913; field sec. Intercollegiate Prohibition Assn., 1919-20; lectr. for Internat. Reform Fedn., editor 20th Century Progress, 1923-25; sec., gen. supt. Nat. Civic League, editor Civic Forum, from 1935; assoc. editor Nat. Voice (nat. tabloid temperance weekly), from 1936; rep. from D.C., mem. Prohibition Nat. Com., from 1924. Nat. supt legis. work Internat. Order of Good Templars, from 1936mem. Yale Sch. Alcoholic Studies, 1946; v.p. Internat. Fedn. for Narcotic Edn., Anti-Cigarette Alliance of D.C.; pres. United Dry Forces of D.C. Home: Washington D.C. †

SCHMIDT, MOTT B., architect, engineer; b. Middletown, N.Y., Sept. 2, 1889; s. Edward Mott and Frances (Jennett) S.; m. Elena Bachman, June 10, 1922 (dec. 1955); 1 child, Elena Anne (Mrs. William R. Chandler, dec.); m. 2d, Katharine Stone, 1958. Study and travel abroad, 1906-08. Asst. in archtl. offices of N.Y. 1908-12; pvt. practice in architecture and engring., since 1912, including comml., indsl., and residential design. Served as 1st lt., Chem. Warfare Service, 1917-19. Fellow AIA. Clubs: Racquet and Tennis (N.Y.); Knickerbocker (N.Y.); Bedford Golf and Tennis. Home: Katonah N.Y. †

SCHMIDT, WILLIAM GUSTAV, biochemistry educator, university dean, lawyer; b. Phila., May 10, 1891; s. Gustav F. and Catherine (Ackermann) S.; m. Ruth Ischler, June 28, 1919. BS, U. Pa., 1913, AM, 1922, PhD, 1931, MS in Chemistry, 1957; grad. pharmacy, Temple U., 1920, LLB, 1927; MPL, Washington Coll., 1931; LLM, Georgetown U., 1931. Chem. engr. U.S.Bur. Mines, 1913-14; indsl. worker 1914-16; tchr. Phila. high schs., 1916-40; practiced gen. law Phila., from 1927; practiced patent law from 1930; dean Hahnemann Med. Coll., Phila., from 1941, prof. biochemistry, from 1946; rsch. assoc. Pa. Legis. Reference Bur.; asst. counsel Pa. Turnpike Commn., 1952; counsel VA, from 1954. Trustee Eberhard Med. Found.; chmn. com. sci. and arts Franklin Inst., from 1959; Rep. candidate for county commr. of Phila., 1951. Mem. Am. Chem. Soc., Patent Bar Assn., U. Pa. Grad. Sch. Alumni Assn. (pres.), Union League Phila., Masons Blue Key, Sigma Xi, Pi Upsilon Rho, Phi Lambda Upsilon, Phi Beta Phi. Home: Philadelphia Pa. †

SCHMIEDELER, EDGAR, educator, clergyman; b. Kansas City, Kans., Dec. 15, 1892; s. John Baptist and Margaret (Müller) S. AB, St. Vincent's Coll., Latrobe, Pa., 1915; S.T.L., St. Vincent's Sem., Latrobe, Pa., 1916; PhD, Catholic U., 1927; student, U. Notre Dame, 1921, Harvard U., 1927. Ordained priest Roman Catholic Ch., 1918, O.S.B. Prof. dogmatic theology St. Benedict's Sem., Atchison, Kans., 1919-21; prof. sociology St. Benedict's Coll., Atchison, 1922-25, head sociology dept., 1926-29; instr. sociology Cath. U. Am., 1932-33, 1937-45. Author: Introductory Study of the Family, 1930; Readings on the Family, 1932, A Better Rural Life, 1938, The Sacred Bond, 1940, Cooperation, 1941, 25 Years of Uncontrol, 1943, Marriage and the Family, 1946, The Child's World, 1951; also brochures on parent edn. and rural life; co-author: Parent and Child; assoc. editor: the Family Digest. Dir. Family Life Bur., Nat. Cath. Welfare Conf., 1931-56; founder and liaison officer to Cath. Conf. on Family Life; chaplain Ursuline Convent and Acad., Paola, Kans., from 1956. Mem. Internat. Union Family Orgns. Home: Paola Kans. †

SCHMITT, HENRY JOSEPH, publisher; b. Wahpeton, N.D., Aug. 11, 1909; s. Peter and Mary (Ridder) S.; m. Viola Oyhus, Jan. 1, 1937; 1 child, Peter Oyhus. Student, St. John's Parochial Sch., Wahpeton, N.D., 1915-24, Coll. of Science, Wahpeton, 1924-27. Advt. solicitor Aberdeen American News, S.D., 1928-30, Grand Forks (N.D.) Herald, 1930-32; Aberdeen American News, 1932-35, St. Paul (Minn.) Daily News, 1935-36, Duluth (Minn.) Herald, 1936, 37, Ridder-Johns, Inc., N.Y.C., 1937-38; chmn. emeritus Aberdeen News Co., from 1979. Served with AUS, World War II. Mem. Am. Soc. Newspaper Editors, U.S. C. of C. (dir. from 1970, v.p. 1971), Am. Legion, Sigma Delta Chi, Beta Gamma Sigma. Roman Catholic. Clubs: Elk, Moccasin Creek Country. Home: Aberdeen S.D. Died May 25, 1986, buried Riverside Cemetery, Aberdeen, S.D.

SCHNEBLY, MERRILL ISAAC, lawyer, educator; b. Peoria, Ill., Aug. 26, 1888; s. John Rench and Mary Ellen (Brown) S.; m. Bessie Viola Anthony, Nov. 19, 1913 (dec. 1949); children: Merrill Anthony (dec.), Ellen Margaret Schnebly Swartz, Eudora Ann Schnebly McBride, John Rowland; m. 2d, Melitta A. Margaret, Nov. 6, 1950 (dec. 1954); m. 3d, Evangeline G. Hunter, May 4, 1956. Student, Bradley Poly. Inst., Peoria, 1907-10; AB, U. Chgo., 1911, JD cum laude, 1913; JSD cum laude, Yale U., 1926. Bar: Ill. 1913. Pvt. practice Peoria, 1913-17; asst. prof. law George Washington U., 1917-20; prof. law Ind. U., 1920-25; teaching fellow Yale U., 1925-26; prof. law U. Mo., Columbia, 1926-28; prof. law U. Ill., 1928-56, prof. emeritus, from 1956. Contbr. to Harvard Law Rev., Yale Law Jour., Mich. Law Rev., Ill. Law Rev., Law Times, other publs. Mem. Am., Ill. bar assns., AAUP, Order of Coif, Masons, University Club, Urbana Golf and Country Club, Phi Delta Phi, Delta Chi, Delta Sigma Rho. Republican. Methodist. Home: Champaign Ill. †

SCHNEIDER, ERWIN HENRY, music educator; b. St. Louis, Feb. 17, 1920; s. Erwin Louis and Anna Marie (Busse) S.; m. Jenila Marie Adkins, Nov. 29, 1941; 1 dau., Nila Marie. BS, N.W. Mo. State Coll., 1942; MS, U. Kans., 1946, PhD, 1956. Instr. music U. Kans., 1946-47; assoc. prof. music Western State Coll., Gunnison, Colo., 1948-49; prof., head dept. art and music edn. U. Tenn., Knoxville, 1949-60; prof. music Ohio State U., Columbus, 1961-69, acting dir., 1964-65, head div. music edn., 1965-69; prof., head dept. music edn. U. Iowa, Iowa City, from 1969. Mem. Nat. Assn. Music Therapy (pres. 1964-65, editor Bull., Yearbooks), Am. Psychol. Assn., Am. Ednl. Rsch. Assn., AAAS, Music Tchrs. Nat. Assn., Music Educators Nat. Conf., Phi Delta Kappa, Phi Mu Alpha, Phi Kappa Lambda. Home: Coralville Iowa Died Oct. 7, 1985.

SCHNEIDER, FRANZ, business executive; b. Lawrence, Mass., July 11, 1887; s. Franz and Elizabeth (Sweeney) S.; m. Elizabeth Burns, Nov. 6, 1936; children: Elizabeth, Timothea, Katherine, Ann, Franz, Jane. Student, Phillips Acad., Andover, Pa., 1904; BS, MIT, 1909, MA, 1910. Instr. biology, pub. health MIT, 1910-13; sanitarian Russel Sage Found., 1913-17; assoc. mgr. rsch. dept. Am. Internat. Corp., 1919-20; asst. to pres. First Secutrities Corp., 1920; fin. editor N.Y. Eveing Post, 1921-25, N.Y. Sun, 1925-29; v.p. Newmont Mining Corp., 1930-47, exec. v.p., 1947-53, chmn. exec. com., 1931-53, cons., from 1954; bd. dirs. Colonial Growth Shares, Inc., Can. Export Gas & Oil Ltd., Chem. Fund, Inc., Continental Oil Co., Equitable Gas Co., Phelps Dodge Corp., Transcontinental Gas Pipe Line Corp., El Paso Natural Gas Co., Eberstadt Fund, Inc.; trustee Mut. Life Ins. Co. N.Y., 1944-68; mem. staff 2d com. experts apptd. by Reparations Commn., 1929; asst., assoc. dep. adminstr. War Shipping Adminstrn., 1942-44; spl. asst. to dir. Office War Moblzn. and Reconversion, 1944-45; cons. to asst. sec. adminstrn. Dept. State, 1945-47; preparer reports mil. budget for Com. Nat. Security Orgns., Hoover Commn., 1948, Sen. Appropriations Com., 1949; mem. ad hoc com. for rev. budget, rsch. and devel. bd. Dept. Def., 1951; asst. report Nat. Security Act for Preparedness Subcom. Senate Armed Services Com., 1953; mem. task force on bus. orgn. Dept. Def., task force on procurement, Hoover Commn., 1954. Author articles on pub. health, econs., fin. Bd. dirs. Acad. Polit. Sci., Ray C. Fish Found.; trustee L.I. U. Maj. Gen. Staff Corps, U.S. Army, World War I. Recipient Presdl. Certificate of Merit. Mem. Cotton Bay Club (Eleuthra), N.Y. Yacht Club, University Club, Rockefeller Lunch Club (N.Y.C.) Seawanhka Corinthian Yacht Club (Oyster Bay, N.Y.). Home: Oyster Bay N.Y. †

SCHNEIDER, HAROLD K., anthropology educator; b. Aberdeen, S.D., Aug. 24, 1925; s. Frank X. and Bernice (Anderson) S.; m. Carol Snyder, Sept. 11, 1948; children: Ann Elizabeth, Amy, Jane, Caroline, David Paul. B.A., Macalester Coll., 1946; postgrad., Seabury-Western Theol. Sem., 1946-48; Ph.D., Northwestern U., 1953. Mem. faculty Lawrence U., Appleton, Wis., 1953-70; prof. Lawrence U., 1966-70; prof. anthropology Ind. U., Bloomington, 1970-87; Anthrop. field worker, Pokot, Kenya, 1951-52, Nyaturu, Tanzania, 1959-60; Mem. nomad commn. Internat. Union Anthrop. and Ethnol. Scis.; mem. exec. com. Human Relations Area File, Inc. Author: (with E.E. LeClair) Economic Anthropology, 1968, The Wahi Wanyaturu, 1970, Economic Man, 1974, Livestock and Equality in East Africa, The Africans, 1981, Anthropologia Economica, 1985. assoc. editor: An Ethnologist; bd. referees Archivo per L'Antropologie e Ethologia Firenze. Fulbright fellow, 1951-52; NSF Grantee, 1959-60, 66-67. Fellow Current Anthropology; mem. Soc. for Econ. Anthropology (pres.). Home: Bloomington Ind. Died May 2, 1987.

SCHNEIDER, MISCHA, cellist; b. Wilna, Poland, Feb. 5, 1904; came to U.S., 1930, naturalized, 1947; s. Isaac and Chasia (Fajnowska) S.; m. June Holden, Jan. 7, 1947; 4 children. Student, Conservatorium, Leipzig, Germany, Ecole Normale de Musique, Paris. Cellist Budapest String Quartet, 1930-68, in residence Libr. of Congress, 1939-62; prof. cello and chamber music U. Buffalo, 1962-74; concert tours Europe, S.Am., Australia, Asia, Africa. Home: Buffalo N.Y. Died Oct. 3, 1985.

SCHNEIDER, RICHARD COY, physician, educator; b. Newark, May 29, 1913; s. Louis and Elizabeth (Coy) S.; m. Madeleine T. Thomas, Feb. 12, 1943. B.A., Dartmouth, 1935; M.D., U. Pa., 1939; M.S., U. Mich., 1948. Diplomate: Am. Bd. Neurol. Surgery (vice chmn. 1970-72). Intern Newark City Hosp., 1939-41; resident pathology Cleve. City Hosp., 1941-42; resident gen. surgery City of Detroit Receiving Hosp., 1942-43; resident neurosurgery U. Mich., 1946-48; practice medicine specializing in neurosurgery Cleve., 1948-50; asst. prof. neurosurgery U. Mich., Ann Arbor, 1950-52; assoc. prof. U. Mich., 1952-62, prof. neurosurgery, 1962-69, head sect. neurosurgery Med. Center, 1969-79, prof., 1979-83, prof. emeritus, 1983-86; 1st E. Latunde Odeku Meml. lectr. U. Ibadan, Nigeria, 1976; honored guest Congress Neurol. Surgeons, 1977; W. Yandell lectr. Louisville Surg. Soc., U. Louisville, 1979; honored guest Japanese Soc. Neurotraumatology, 1980, Mex. Neurosurg. Soc., 1981; Percival Bailey lectr. 1985, W.J. Gardner lectr., 1985; Mem. Council Med. Splty. Socs., 1974-76. Author: (with others) Correlative Neurosurgery, 1969; sr. editor 3d edit. (with others), 1981, Surgery of the Cranial Nerves, 1973, Head and Neck Injuries in Football, 1973, Sports Injuries: Mechanisms, Prevention and Treatment, 1985. Served to capt. M.C. AUS, 1943-46, ETO. Named Man of Year Culver Mil. Acad., 1970. Mem. ACS, Neurosurg. Soc. Am. (v.p.), Am. Acad. Neurol. Surg., Am. Assn. Neurol. Surgeons (pres. 1974-75, dir. 1970-75), World Fedn. Neurosurg. Socs. (rep., sec., v.p. 1977-86), Aerospace Med. Assn., Am. Epilepsy Soc., Assn. Rsch. on Mental Disease, Am. Soc. for Surgery of Trauma, Pan-Pacific Surg. Assn. (v.p. neurosurgery 1981-83), Phi Kappa Psi, Nu Sigma Nu, Alpha Omega Alpha (hon.). Home: Ann Arbor Mich. Died June 9, 1986; buried Findlay, Ohio.

SCHNEIDER, WILLIAM ALBERT, savings and loan executive; b. Kankakee, Ill., May 4, 1891; s. Albert and Bertha (Birr) S.; m. Dorothy G. Marlow, June 15, 1916; children: William Albert, Robert M. (dec.), James G., Stephen E. BS, U. Chgo., 1913; MA, Columbia U., 1914. With Kankakee Fed. Savs. & Loan Assn., from 1915, sec., 1937-43, pres., mgr., 1943-61, chmn. bd., from 1961. Mem. Ann. Assay Commn., 1958. Recipient Pub. Svc. citation U. Chgo. Alumni, 1956. Mem. Am. Numismatic Assn., Masons (Shriner), Elks, Kiwanis, University Club (Chgo.); Chikaming Country Club, Alpha Tau Omega. Home: Lakeside Mich. †

SCHNIEBS, OTTO EUGEN, physical education educator, ski consultant; b. Esslingen, Germany, Dec. 18, 1892; came to U.S., 1927; naturalized, 1934; s. Gustave and Karoline (Huttenlocher) S.; m. Frida Knepel, Dec. 18, 1922; children: Elvira Schniebs Patnode, Ursula. Master diploma, Handwerkskammer, Stuttgart, Germany, 1911. Coach winter sports Appalachian Mountain Club, 1927-30, Harvard Mountaineering Club, 1927-30; prof. phys. edn., coach winter sports Dartmouth U., 1930-36; founder Am. Ski Sch., Wilmington, N.Y., 1930, pres., 1930-39; mfr., sales rep. Otto E. Schniebs Co., 1933-65; ski cons., Wilmington, from 1939. Author: Modern Ski Technique, 1933, Skiing for All, 1935, American Skiing, 1939. Recipient Silver Bowl award New Eng. Ski Coun., 1963. Mem. U.S. Ski Assn., U.S. Ea. Amateur Ski Assn. (Safety Trophy award 1938-39), U.S. Profl. Ski Instrs. Assn., Whiteface Mountain Ski Coun., Dartmouth Outing Club, Lake Placid C. of C., Wilmington C. of C. Home: Wilmington N.Y. †

SCHNUCK, EDWARD J., retail grocery store company executive; b. 1915. Pres. Schnuck Markets, Inc., Hazelwood, Mo., 1961-70, chmn., 1970-83, treas., from 1976, chmn. exec. com., also dir., 1983-87. Died Feb. 4, 1987.

SCHOENBERG, BRUCE STUART, neuroepidemiologist, neurologist; b. New Brunswick, N.J., Nov. 2, 1942; s. Mitchell and Beatrice (Brodsky) S.; m. Devera Elizabeth Glazer, Aug. 12, 1973; children: Ian Charles, Claire Jennifer. BA summa cum laude, U. Pa., 1964; MD cum laude, Yale U., 1968; MPH, Johns Hopkins U., 1973, DrPH, 1980; MS in Neurology, U. Monn., 1976. Diplomate Am. Bd. Psychiatry and Neurology. Abstractor in enzymology Chem. Abstracts, Columbus, Ohio, 1965-76; staff assoc. Nat. Cancer Inst., Bethesda, Md., 1968-70, cons., 1971-87, mem. rev. com., 1975-78; spl. fellow Nat.Inst. Neurol. Diseases and Stroke, NIH Bethesda, 1971-74; intern Mayo Grad. Sch. Medicine, Rochester, Minn., 1970-71, sr. resident in neurology, 1971-75, instr., 1974-75; chief sect. neuroepidemiology Nat. Inst. Neurol. and Communicative Disorders and Stroke, NIH, Bethesda, 1975-87; lectr. Yale U. Sch. Medicine, 1968-87; vis. scientist dept. neurology Mayo Clinic, Rochester, 1975-87; clin. instr. dept. neurology Georgetown U. Sch. Medicine, 1972-75, clin. asst. prof., 1975-78, clin. assoc. prof., 1978-87; clin. prof. neurology Uniformed Svcs. U. Health Scis., Bethesda, 1980-87; sr. asst. surgeon USPHS, 1968-70, sr. surgeon, 1975-87. Author: Multiple Primary Malignant Neoplasms, 1977; contbr. chpts. to books and articles to profl. jours.; editor: Neurological Epidemiology: Principles and Clinical Applications, 1978; editor-in-chief Neuroepidemiology; adv. editor Jour. Neurol. Scis., 1977-87; bd. editors Minn. Medicine, 1974-87, So. Med. Jour, 1977-87, European Neurology, 1981-87, Epidemiology Monitor, 1981-87. Recipient Richmond award Am. Acad. Cerebral Palsy and Devel. Medicine, 1977, Original Rsch. award So. Med. Assn., 1978, Surgeon General's Medallion, 1987, others; NEH fellow, 1978, Hereditary Disease Found. Selznick fellow, 1978. Fellow ACP, Am. Acad. Cerebral Palsy and Devel. Medicine, Am. Coll. Preventative Medicine, Am. Heart Assn. (Stroke and Epidemiology couns.), Royal Soc. Health, Royal Soc. Medicine, AAAS, Gerontol. Soc., N.Y. Acad. Scis., Soc. Advanced Med. Systems, Med. Soc. London; hon. mem. Brit. Brain Rsch. Assn., European Brain and Behavior Soc. Home: Bethesda Md. Died July 14, 1987; buried Arlington Nat. Cemetery, Washington.

SCHOENBRUN, DAVID FRANZ, broadcaster, author; b. N.Y.C., Mar. 15, 1915; s. Max and Lucy (Cassirer) S.; m. Dorothy Scher, Sept. 23, 1938; 1 dau., Lucy. BA, CCNY, 1934. Tchr. French Townshend Harris High Sch., 1934-35, Far Rockaway High Sch., 1935-37; mem. faculty CCNY, 1938-39; free lance writer 1939-40; editor, French broadcaster Voice of Am., 1941-43; reporter CBS News, Paris, 1945-60, Washington, 1960-63; reporter ABC News Metromedia, 1963-79; news analyst Ind. Network News, N.Y.C., from 1983; sr. lectr. internat. affairs Columbia U., 1967-68, New Sch. Social Rsch., 1968-88. Author: As France Goes, 1957, Three Lives of Charles de Gaulle, 1966, Vietnam, 1968, The New Israelis, 1973, Triumph in Paris, 1976, Soldiers of the Night, 1980. With AUS, 1943-45. Decorated Croix de Guerre, Legion d'Honneur (France). Mem. Anglo-Am. Press Club of Paris (past pres.), Univ. Club, Am. Club (Paris), Nat. Press Club, Overseas Press Club. Jewish. Died May 23, 1988.

SCHOTTERS, BERNARD WILLIAM, business executive; b. Indpls., Dec. 26, 1908; s. Frank J. and Elizabeth (Neuhardt) S.; m. Virginia J. Hubbard, May 25, 1935; children: Sally J., Bernard William II. JD, Ind. U., 1935. With Indpls. Power & Light Co., 1926-74, pres., 1067-71, chmn. bd., chief exec. officer, 1971-74, mem. exec. com., then ret.; pres. Indpls. Better Bus. Bur.; bd. dirs. Am. Fletcher Nat. Bank, St. Francis Hosp., Indpls. Hosp. Devel. Assn. Inc., Ind. Electric Assn., Ind. State Symphony Soc. Inc. Lt. col. USMCR, World War II. Mem. Ind. Bar Assn., Indpls. Bar Assn., Indpls. C. of C., Am. Legion, Masons, Rotary, Shriners, Indpls. Athletic, Columbia, Indpls. Country, Meridian Hills Country clubs, Sigma Delta Kappa. Mem. Christian Ch. (33 deg.). Home: Indianapolis Ind. Died July 10, 1987; buried Crown Hill Cemetery, Indpls.

SCHRAM, EMIL, business executive; b. Peru, Ind., Nov. 23, 1893; s. Emil Alexander and Katharine (Graf) S.; m. Mabel Miller, Dec. 28, 1914 (dec.); children: Robert Miller, James Edward, Daniel Conaway; m. 2d, Margaret Beauchamp Percy, May 7, 1971. Grad., Peru High Sch., 1911; LLD, NYU, 1948, U. Vt., 1948, Franklin Coll., 1961, Ind. U., 1968. Bookkeeper J.O. Cole, Peru, 1910-15; mgr. Hartwell Land Trust, Hillview, Ill., 1915-33; mgr. Community Elevator and Grand Pass Elevator, Hillview, 1915-33; bd. dirs., sec. Hartwell Drainage and Levee Dist., 1915-33; chmn. bd. dirs. Nat. Drainage Assn., 1931-33; chief drainage, levee and irrigation div., Reconstruction Fin. Corp., 1933-36; bd. dirs., 1936-41, chmn., 1939-41; v.p., dir. Fed. Prisons Industries, Inc., 1938-66; chmn. Peru Trust Co.; dir. Assocs. Investment Co.; pres. Valley Farm, Inc.; hon. mem. Bus. Adv. Coun.; dir. Peru Trust Co., Ind. Nat. Bank, CTS Corp., Home Ins. Co. N.Y.; pres. N.Y. Stock Exchange, 1941-51; pres. U.S.O., Inc., 1953-57, vice chmn., 1957-60. Mem. Ind. Acad., Columbia Club, Masons. Democrat. Presbyterian. Home: Peru Ind. Died Sept. 18, 1987.

SCHRAM, LAUREN, insurance executive; b. Albany, N.Y., 1891; s. Clarence and Georgia (Stowitts) S.; m. Katherine Kreidler, Sept. 24, 1919; children: William C., Sarah Jane. Student, Utica Free Acad. With Met. Life Ins. Co., 1911-31; with Western and Southern Life Ins. Co., from 1931, sucessively asst. sec., field sec., supt. agys. to v.p., from 1942. Republican. Presbyterian. Home: Cincinnati Ohio. †

SCHRAMM, WILBUR LANG, communications educator; b. Marietta, Ohio, Aug. 5, 1907; s. Archibald and Louise (Lang) S.; m. Elizabeth Donaldson, Aug. 5, 1934; children: Mary Barbara, Richard Michael. AB, Marietta Coll., 1928, LittD, 1945; AM, Harvard U., 1930; PhD, U. Iowa, 1932; D.Univ. (hon.), Brit. Open U., 1975. Began as newspaper reporter and desk edito; became corr. AP, 1928; post-doctoral and Nat. Rsch. fellow, 1932-35; asst. prof. English, U. Iowa, 1935-38, assoc. prof., 1938-40, prof., 1940-43, dir. Sch. Journalism, 1943-47; asst. to pres., Inst. Communications Rsch., dir. Univ. Press and rsch. prof. U. Ill., 1947-55, dean div. communications, 1950-55; prof. communications and journalism Stanford U., 1955-73, dir. Inst. Communication Rsch., 1957-73, Janet M. Peck prof. internat. communication, 1962-73, emeritus, from 1973; dir. East-West Communication Inst., East-West Ctr., Honolulu, 1973-75, Boon Haw prof. communication Chinese U. Hong Kong, from 1977; vis. prof. Indian Space Rsch. Orgn., 1976; on leave as dir. ednl. service, Office War Info., Washington, 1942-43; cons. U.S. Dept. State, UNESCO, USIA, AID, U.S. Office Edn., U.S. Def. Dept., Ford Found., Nat. Ednl. TV, others; mem. U.S. Def. Bd., 1956-61. Author or coauthor 30 books; latest publs.: Mass Communications, 1949, Process and Effects of Mass Communication, 1954, Four Theories of the Press, 1956, Responsibility in Mass Communication, 1957, One Day in the World's Press, 1959, Television in the Lives of Our Children, 1961, The People Look at Educational Television, 1963, Mass Media and National Development, 1964, The New Media, 1967, Communication and Change, 1967, Learning from Television, 1968, Quality in Instructional Television, 1972, Handbook of Communication, 1973, Men, Messages, Media—a Look at Human Communication, 1973, Communication and Change—The Last Ten Years, 1976, Big Media, Little Media, 1977, Circulation of News in the Third World, 1981. Founder, dir. The Writers Workshop, U. Iowa, 1937-41; founder Ill. Inst. Communications Rsch., 1948; chmn. U.S. del. to Asian Powers Conf. on Communication, Bangkok, 1960. Recipient O. Henry prize for fiction in 1942, George Polk Meml. award for rsch., 1960, gold medal disting. svc. to journalism U. Mo., 1972, Deutschmann prize for communicatin rsch., 1973, awards Nat. Ednl. Broadcasters, 1973, Assn. Ednl. Communications and Tech., 1974; fellow Inst. for Advanced Study in Behavorial Scis., 1959-60; sr. fellow E.-W. Ctr., 1969-70. Mem. Am. Sociol. Assn., Am. Psychol. Assn., Am. Statis. Assn., Am. Assn. Pub. Opinion Rsch., AAAS, Nat. Acad. Edn., Phi Beta Kappa, Delta Upsilon, Sigma Delta Chi, Kappa Tau Alpha. Home: Honolulu Hawaii. Died Dec. 27, 1987, cremated.

SCHREIBER, FLORA RHETA, theatre arts and speech specialist, author, educator; b. N.Y.C., Apr. 24, 1918; d. William and Esther (Aaronson) S. BS, Columbia U., 1938, MA, 1939; cert., U. London, 1937, NYU Radio Workship, 1942. Instr. speech and dramatic art Bklyn. Coll., 1944-46; drama critic Players mag., 1941-46; instr. Exeter Coll., U. S.W., Eng., 1937; asst. prof. Adelphi Coll., Garden City, N.Y., 1947-53; dir. radio-TV div. Center Creative Arts, 1948-51; lectr. New Sch. Social Research, 1952-76; prof. English and speech John Jay Coll. Criminal Justice, City U. N.Y., 1974-88, dir. pub. relations, 1965-80, asst. to pres., 1970-83. Creator, producer Bklyn. Coll. Radio Forum, Sta. WYNC, N.Y.C., 1944-46; Author: William Schuman, 1954, Your Child's Speech, 1956, Jobs with a Future in Law Enforcement, 1970, Sybil, 1973, paperback edit., 1974, fgn. edits., 1974-76, The Shoemaker, 1983, paperback edits., 1984, fgn. edit., 1983-88; also short stories plays, opera libretti and art songs.; contbr. to nat. mags.; columnist nat. mags. including Sci. Digest, 1966-72, Bell McClure, United Features; feature writer: nat. mags. including N.Y. Times Spl. Features; producer radio forum on Community Theater for NBC, 1949; numerous radio and TV appearances in U.S. and Eng. including Oprah Winfrey Show, ABC News, Morton Downey Jr. Show. Cornelia Otis Skinner scholar, 1937; awards Am. Med. Writers Assn., Family Service Assn. Mem. AAUW, AAUP, Speech, Assn. Am., ANTA, Speech Assn. Eastern States, Am. Soc. Journalists and Authors (past v.p., Author of Yr. 1985), Authors League Am., PEN. Club: Overseas Press. Home: New York N.Y. Died Nov. 3, 1988.

SCHRIER, ALLAN MARTIN, educator; b. N.Y.C., Jan. 15, 1930; s. Jack and Jean (Scheinberg) S.; m. Judith E. Sanow, July 4, 1958; children—Marya E., Evan J. B.A., N.Y. U., 1952; M.S., U. Wis., 1954, Ph.D., 1956. Postdoctoral research fellow Calif. Inst. Tech., 1956-58; prof. psychology Brown U., Providence, 1958-87; chmn. com. on nonhuman primates Nat. Acad. Scis., 1976-79; mem. council Inst. Lab. Animal Resources, Nat. Acad. Scis., 1977-80; mem. adv. bd. USPHS. Sr. Editor: Behavior of Nonhuman Primates, Vols. 1 and 2, 1965, Vols. 3 and 4, 1971, Vol. 5, 1974;

editor: Behavioral Primatology: Advances in Research and Theory, Vol. 1, 1977; asso. editor: Animal Learning and Behavior, 1976-79; editor Lab. Primate Newsletter, 1962-87; mem. editorial bds. several jours.; contbr. articles to profl. jours. Fellow Am. Psychol. Assn., AAAS, Internat. Primatological Soc. (sec. gen. 1976-84); mem. Animal Behavior Soc., Psychonomic Soc. Home: Providence R.I. Died Mar. 27, 1987, buried Swan Point Cemetery, Providence.

SCHRIVER, LESTER OSBORNE, clergyman; b. Bristol, Conn., Mar. 7, 1891; s. Milo Seeley and Fannie Caroline (Osborne) S.; m. Blanche Larkin, Sept. 15, 1915; children: Alice Caroline Schriver Suffield, Merritt Larkin. AB, Syracuse U., 1917; postgrad., Wesleyan and Berkeley Sem.; LLD (hon.), Lincoln Meml. U., 1940; LHD (hon.), MacMurray Coll., 1951. Ordained to ministry Conglist. Ch., 1920. Dir. edn. Aetna Life Ins. Co., Hartford, Conn., 1924-29; gen. agt. Peoria, Ill., 1929-53; exec. v.p. Nat. Assn. Life Underwriters, Washington, 1953-66; minister Community Congl. Ch., Mt. Dora, Fla., from 1966. Author: A Sublime Parallel, 1945, Lincoln and Vandalia, 1946, Seven Lincoln Shrines, 1947, Thirty Years on the Firing Line, 1954, As One Man Thinks, 1960, The Price of Liberty, 1964; co-author: The Education of Abraham Lincoln, 1940, Some Religious Influences that Surrounded Lincoln, 1941, others; cons. editor: Life and Health Insurance Handbook, 1959; contbr. articles to profl. jours. Exec. v.p. Religious Heritage Am., Inc., 1962; chmn. Greater Peoria Planning Commn.; mem. Peoria City Council; bd. dirs. Ill. Tchrs. Coll., YMCA; mem. Pub. Health Nursing Bd.; trustee Lincoln Meml. U., MacMurray Coll. Recipient award for best pub. address Freedom Found., 1951, best editorial award, 1952, 63, George Arents Pioneer medal and scroll for outstanding achievement Syracuse U., 1958, John Newton Russell award, 1958, 6th Freedom Found. award for addresses and editorials, 1962. Mem. Nat. Assn. Life Underwriters (past pres.), Civil War Round Table, Nat. Press Club (Washington), Creve Coeur Country Club (Peoria), Union League Club (Chgo.), Advt. Club (N.Y.C.), University Club (pres. Winter Park 1970-71), Rotary, Masons, Theta Alpha, Theta Nu. Republican. Home: Winter Park Fla. †

SCHROEDER, LUTHER H., paint manufacturing company executive; b. Cleve., Mar. 9, 1891; s. Henry C. and Mary A. (Kuhlmeier) S.; m. Catherine E. Shea, May 6, 1942. LLB magna cum laude, Cleve. Law Sch. With Sherwin-Williams Co., from 1908, acct., exec. cashier, then asst. treas, 1908-22, treas., from 1922, v.p., from 1943, also bd. dirs. Home: Lakewood Ohio †

SCHULER, HENRY J., banker; b. Bklyn., July 9, 1890; s. Henry and Mary (Lutz) S.; m. Ethel Forsythe, Nov. 30, 1912; 1 son, Edwin Forsythe. Student pub. schs.; student, L.I. Bus. Coll. With Franklin Trust Co., 1906, asst. treas., 1918; asst. cashier, asst. v.p., v.p. and cashier Franklin Trust Co. (merged with Bank of Am. 1920), 1918-1931; v.p. The Bank of N.Y., 1931, hon. trustee, 1948, trustee, from 1951. Mem. Country Club (Hempstead, N.Y.), North Fork Country Club (Cutchogue, N.Y.); Midday Club (N.Y.C.), Masons. Presbyterian. Home: Lynbrook N.Y. †

SCHULTZ, ADOLPH H(ANS), anthropology educator, researcher; b. Stuttgart, Germany (citizen of Zürich, Switzerland), Nov. 14, 1891; came to U.S., 1916; naturalized, 1934; s. Julius and Sophie (Frick) S.; m. Travis Bader, Dec. 10, 1924. PhD, U. Zürich, 1916; MD honoris causa, U. Bale, 1962. Rsch. assoc. Carnegie Instn. Wash., 1916-25, 37-38; assoc. prof. phys. anthropology Johns Hopkins Med. Sch., 1925-51; prof. anthropology, dir. Anthrop. Inst. U. Zürich, 1951-62, prof. emeritus, from 1962; mem. sci. expdn. to Asia 1937. Editor: Handbook of Primatology; contbr. sci. articles to tech. jours., books. Recipient Viking Fund medal in anthropology, 1948. Fellow Zool. Soc. London (fgn.); mem. Austrian Acad. Scis. (corr.), Am. Philos. Soc., Internat. Congress Anthrop. and Ethnol. Scis. (permanent coun., v.p. 1956), Soc. d'Anthrop. de Paris (hon.), N.Y. Acad. Sci. (hon.), Am. Assn. Phys. Anthropologists, Am. Anthrop. Assn., Am. Soc. Mammalogists, German Anthrop. Soc. (corr.), Swiss Anthrop. Soc., Anthrop. Soc. Italy, Brit. Assn. Anatomists (hon.), Soc. Human Biology (hon.). Home: Zürich Switzerland. †

SCHULTZ, MARTIN C., business executive; b. Bartlett, Ill., 1891. Ed., Beloit Coll. Chmn. bd., dir. Urbana Mills Co., Ohio. Home: Urbana Ohio. †

SCHURMAN, GEORGE MUNRO, business executive; b. Ithaca, N.Y., June 6, 1892; s. Jacob Gould and Barbara Forrest (Munro) S.; m. Kerstin Helena Traube, July 16, 1929; 1 child, Peter. AB, Cornell U., 1913. Founder, pres., treas., dir. Nat. Bag Corp., from 1927; bd. dirs. Am. Brake Co., W.Pa. Power Co., Monongahela Power Co., Centennial Ins. Co.; trustee Atlantic Mut. Ins. Co.; mem. textile bag industry adv. com., War Prodn. Bd., 1942-45; chmn. textile bag industry adv. com., Office Price Adminstrn., 1943-45. Councilman Bedford Twp., Westchester County, N.Y. Capt. 4th F.A. World War I. Mem. University Club, Down Town Assn. (N.Y.C.), Alpha Delta Phi. Home: Katonah N.Y. †

SCHURZ, FRANKLIN D., newspaper executive; b. South Bend, Ind., Mar. 8, 1898; s. John Giles and Grace (Dunn) S.; m. Martha Montgomery, Sept. 11, 1929 (dec. Nov. 1987); children: Franklin D. Jr., James M., Scott Clark, Mary. AB, Harvard U., 1920, MBA, 1921; LLD, Ind. U., U. Notre Dame, St. Mary's Coll. C.P.A. Acct. Calif. Assoc. Food Rsch. Inst., Stanford, 1922-25; with South Bend Tribune, 1925-76, v.p., 1929-46; mgr. sta. WSBT, South Bend, 1936-46; sec., treas., bus. mgr. South Bend Tribune, 1946-54, gen. mgr., 1954-64, editor, pub., 1954-72, pres., 1957-75, chmn. bd., 1975-76; chmn. bd. Schurz Communications, Inc., from 1976, also bd. dirs.; pres. Inland Daily Press Assn.; 1st v.p. AP; bd. dirs. Am. Nespaper Pubs. Assn. 1952-60. Mem. adv. coun. arts and letters, hon. trustee U. Notre Dame, Ind. Recipient U. Minn. disting service award in journalism, 1959, Ind. Newspaper Pubs. 1st Freedom award; named to Ind. Journalism Hall of Fame. Mem. AICPA, Am. Soc. Newspaper Editors, Ind. Acad., Ind. Broadcaster Assn. (named to Hall of Fame), Broadcast Pioneers (Ind. chpt.), Masons, Rotary, Kiwanis, South Bend Press Club, Sigma Delta Chi. Home: South Bend Ind. Died Apr. 12, 1987; buried Riverview Cemetery, South Bend.

SCHWAB, JOSEPH JACKSON, emeritus humanities educator; b. Columbus, Miss., Feb. 2, 1909; s. Samuel Buchsbaum and Hortense (Jackson) S.; m. Rosamond Martin McGill, Sept. 13, 1932; 1 child, Jill McGill Pigorish. Ph.B., U. Chgo., 1930, S.M., 1936, Ph.D., 1938. Research assoc. Columbia U., 1936-37; asst. biology U. Chgo., 1934-36, instr., 1937-39, asst. prof., 1940-44, assoc. prof., 1945-48, prof. biol. scis., prof. edn., 1949-73, William Rainey Harper prof. natural scis., 1950; chmn. natural scis. U. Chgo. (The College), 1945-51; Inglis lectr. Harvard U., 1960. Author: Science, Curriculum and Liberal Education, College Curriculum and Student Protest; author: Teaching of Science as Enquiry, Eros and Education; editor, author: Biology Tchrs.'s Handbook; contbr. articles to profl., popular publs. Recipient teaching award U. Chgo., 1945, 65; fellow Ctr. Advanced Study in Behavioral Scis., 1958-59; Guggenheim fellow, 1971-72; vis. fellow, assoc. Ctr. Study Dem. Instns., 1973-88. Mem. Genetics Soc. Am., Sigma Xi. Home: Lancaster Pa. Died Apr. 13, 1988, cremated.

SCHWACHA, GEORGE, artist; b. Newark, Oct. 2, 1908; s. George and Bertha (Poppele) S.; m. Ruth J. Hunt, 1954; children: Barbara Schwacha Fraccio, Keith, Martin. Student, Art Students League. Pres. Art Centre N.J., 1977-80, treas.; pres. Art Centre Oranges, 1975-76. Exhibited in group shows at Pa. Acad., Corcoran Gallery, Birmingham Art Mus., Butler Art Inst. in Youngstown, Ohio, Conn. Acad. Fine Arts as well as leading N.J. and N.Y. exhibitions. Represented in numerous museums and public collections including Newark Mus., Montclair Mus., Isaac Delgado Mus. in New Orleans as well as those in the following countries: Austria, Belgium, Canada, Egypt, England, France, Germany, Greece, Holland, Hong Kong, Israel, Scotland and Switzerland. Recipient medal for State Exhbn. Montclair Art Mus., 1937, medal of honor Ala. Watercolor Soc., 1954, medal Nat. Soc. Painters in Casein, 1956, 1st prize Washington Watercolor Soc., 1955, 1st oil prize Montclair Art Mus., 1963, best in show award Art Centre N.J., 1985, numerous others. Mem. Audubon Artists (pres.), Am. Water Color Soc., Am. Artists Profl. League (hon. life pres.), Phila. Water Color Club. Home: East Hanover N.J. Died Mar. 5, 1986; buried Restland Memorial Pk., East Hanover.

SCHWARTZ, CHARLES K., lawyer; b. Norway, Mich., Mar. 30, 1891; s. Simon J. and Bertha (Ruwitch) S.; m. Olive Joselit, Feb. 26, 1920; children: Roxie, Denise, Barbara. Student, Gregg Bus. Coll.; LLB, John Marshal Law Sch., 1913. Bar: Ill. 1913. Practiced in Chgo. from 1913; ptnr. Schwartz, Welfeld & Perlman, 1933-36; ptnr. Gottlieb & Schwartz, from 1936, specializing in corp., real estate and tax matters; v.p. Occidental Petroleum Corp.; co-founder Pacific Northwest Pipeline Corp.; asst. state atty. Cook county, 1914-17. Mem. and chmn. Ill. State Tax Commn., 1936-40; counsel Petroleum Co-ordinator for War under Sec. Interior, 1941-44. With Inf., U.S. Army, World War I. Mem. Standard Club (Chgo.), Brentwood Club. Democrat. Home: Los Angeles Calif. †

SCHWARTZ, GEORGE MELVIN, geologist, educator; b. Oakfield, Wis., Sept. 23, 1892; s. George and Hannah (Bastian) S.; m. Ruth Tucker, Sept. 28, 1920; children: George Melvin, John Bernard, Ruth. AB, U. Wis., 1915, AM, 1916; PhD, U. Minn., 1923. Field geologist Wis. Geol. Survey, seasons 1914, 15, 19; asst. U. Wis., 1915-16; geologist Copper Range Co., 1916-18; mem. faculty U. Minn., from 1919, prof. geology, from 1944; field geologist Minn. Geol. Survey, 1921-44, dir., from 1947; geologist U.S. Geol. Survey, 1944-52; lectr. econ. geology Laval U., Can., 1940-41; cons. mining, engring, geology from 1920. Author various Minn. Geol. Survey Bulls. Chmn. Minn. State Mapping Adv. Bd., from 1949. 2d lt. F.A., U.S. Army, 1918-19. Mem. AAAS, Geol. Soc. Am., Soc. Econ. Geologists (pres. 1958-59), Soc. Geologique de Belgique (corr.), AIME, Assn. State Geologists, Mineral Soc. Am., Sigma Xi. Home: Minneapolis Minn. †

SCHWARZKOPF, PAUL, powder metallurgist; b. Prague, Apr. 13, 1886; came to U.S., 1936.; s. Henrich and Adele (Turnovsky) S.; m. Emma Gebauer, 1911; children: Willy (stepson), Henry; m. 2d, Mary Mondini, 1930; 1 child, Max Walter. Organized Wolfram Lab., Berlin, 1911; with Richard Kurtz organized Deutsche Gluehfadenfabrik, Berlin, 1919; with Richard Kurtz and Messrs. von Benthem: Vereenigde Draadfabriken, Nijmegen, Holland, 1920; with Richard Kurtz, Metallwerk Plansee, Reutte, Tyrol, Austria, 1921; with Prince Ernst Heinrich, Duke of Saxony, Molybdenum Co., Amsterdam, Holland, and Am. Electro Metal Corp., Lewistown, Maine, 1929; with Deutsche Edelstahlwerke: Ver. Edelstahlwerke; Glarus, Switzerland, Cutanit Ltd., London, and Am. Cutting Alloys Inc., N.Y.C., 1931; with Fred R. Simms, Compound Electro Metals, Ltd., London, 1936 (merged with Cutanit Ltd. into Metro-Cutanit Ltd., London, 1950, jointly owned with Met. Vickers Elec. Co. Ltd.); with George Cohen Sons & Co. Ltd., formed George Cohen Sinteel Ltd., London, Eng., 1953, becoming dir.; with P.R. Mallory 7 Co., Mallory-Schwarzkopf Metals, Inc., 1955, becoming dir., chmn. bd.; with Firth Sterling Inc., Borolite Corp., 1955, becoming dir., pres.; with S.B. Becker et al, Am. Sinteel Corp., 1955, becoming dir., chmn. bd.; with Hans Petschek established research lab. and mfg. plant Am. Electro Metal Corp. (now Schwarzkopf Devel. Co.), Yonkers, N.Y., 1939, becoming dir. research, pres., from 1946. Author: Powder Metallurgy, 1947; Refractory Hard Metals (with R. Kieffer), 1953; also tech. articles in metall. jours. Publisher Powder Metallurgy Bulletin; Planseeberichte. Patentee in powder metallurgy. Served with Austrian Army, WWI. Recipient Exner Medal, 1955; elected Hon. Senator, U. Innsbruck, Austria, 1956. Mem. AIME, Am. Soc. Metals. Home: Reutte-Tyrol Austria. †

SCHWEICKHARD, DEAN M., state commissioner of education; b. Mankato, Minn., Aug. 5, 1892; s. Daniel Louis and Mary Isabelle (Ashworth) S.; m. Mildred Parmelee, June 14, 1917; 1 dau., Harriet Jean (Mrs. Ray C. Hansen). AB, U. Wis., 1916; MA, U. Minn., 1927; EdD, Hamline U., 1944. Tchr. Lyle, Minn., 1912-13; elem. sch. prin. Kinney, Minn., 1913-14; high sch. tchr. Sioux City, Iowa, 1916-17; prof. edn. Purdue U., 1919-20; dir. vocational edn. Clinton, Iowa, 1920-22; supr. State Dept. Edn., St. Paul, 1922-30; asst. supt. schs. Mpls., 1930-43; summer session lectr. various state tchrs. colls., 1930-42; state commr. edn. Minn., from 1943. Author: Industrial Arts in Education, 1928. Pres. Minn. State Tchrs. Retirement Fund; mem. adv. com. U.S. Armed Forces Inst., edn. mem. War-Navy Com., 1947-50; mem. Fed. Commn. on Life Adjustment Edn. of Youth, 1947-50; exec. sec. Minn. State Commn. on Sch. Dist. Reorgn.; chmn. Minn. State Commn. for Study of Higher Edn.; mem. bd. dirs., Big Brothrs Inc. and Hennepin County Tuberculosis Assn.; mem. bd. and sec. State Tchrs. Coll. Bd.; mem. Pres.' Com. on Edn. beyond High Sch.; pres. coun. of Chief State Sch. Officers, 1957. Mem. Am. Assn. Sch. Adminstrs. (mem. Yearbook commn. 1957), NEA, Minn. Edn. Assn., Am. Vocational Assn., Phi Delta Kappa. Home: Saint Paul Minn. †

SCHWENK, ERWIN, chemist; b. Prague, Czechoslovakia, Oct. 19, 1887; came to U.S., 1933; naturalized, 1939; s. Adolph and Johanna (Reis) S.; m. Rascha Schapiro, Aug. 4, 1914; 1 dau., Lilli (Mrs. Donald F. Hornig). Chem. engr., tech., Hochschule, Vienna, 1909; Dr. Natural Sci., Hochschule, 1910. Asst. Royal Acad. for Wine, Fruit and Garden Sci., Geisenheim a Rhein, Germany, 1910-12, U. Erlangen, Bavaria, 1912-13; asst. and tchr. Tech. Coll., Vienna, 1913-14; asst. Kaiser Wilhelm Inst., Berlin, 1914-16; dir. rsch. Soc. of Chem. and Metall. Products, Aussig a.d. Elbe, Czechoslovakia, 1916-28; asst. dir. rsch. Schering A.G., Berlin, 1928-33; dir. rsch. Schering Corp., Bloomfield, N.J., 1933-48, v.p., 1942-48, cons., 1948-53; rsch. assoc. Worcester Found. Exptl. Biology, Shrewsbury, Mass., from 1949. Author: Grundlagen and Derzeitiger Stand d. Chemotherapie, 1913; contbr. tech. papers to profl. jours. Civilian OSRD, 1944. Fellow AAAS, N.Y. Acad. Scis.; mem. Am. Chem. Soc., London Chem. Soc., Am. Soc. European Chemists and Pharmacists, Am. Inst. Chem. Engrs. Home: Shrewsbury Mass. †

SCHWEPPE, ALFRED JOHN, lawyer; b. Brown County, Minn., Mar. 29, 1895; s. Fred Herman and Alwina (Poehler) S.; m. Dorothy Lawrence Greene, June 30, 1922; children: Elizabeth Scweppe Whistler, Warren Greene. A.B., Northwestern Coll., Watertown, Wis., 1915, U. Wis., 1916; M.A., U. Wis., 1917; LL.B., U. Minn., 1922. Bar: Wash. State 1922. Part-time instr. English U. Wis., 1916-17; tchr. English New Trier High Sch., Kenilworth, Ill., 1917-18, 1919; part-time instr. in English U. Minn., 1919-22; with firm Tanner & Garvin, Seattle, 1922-24; partner firm Long & Schweppe, Seattle, 1924-26; lectr. law U. Wash., 1923-26; dean law sch., also prof. constl. law 1926-30; partner firm McMicken, Rupp & Schweppe, 1930-62, Schweppe, Reiter, Doolittle & Krug, 1962-66, Schweppe, Doolittle, Krug, Tausend, Beezer & Bieierle, Seattle, 1967-83, Schweppe, Krug & Tausend, P.S., Seattle, 1983-87; mem. State Bar Commn., 1933, State Liquor Adv. Commn., 1933, Code Compilation and Revision Com., 1941; exec. sec. Wash. Jud. Council, 1930-57; chmn. Seattle Crime Prevention Commn., 1968-71; mem. Forward Thrust. Author: Simkins' Federal Practice, 1934, rev. edit., 1938, West's

U.S. Court of Appeals Forms, 1952, 64; contbr. numerous articles to legal and other jours. Served in USN, World War I. Mem. Seattle Bar Assn. (exec. sec. 1930-33), Wash. Bar Assn. (exec. sec. 1930-33, pres. 1954-55), Alaska Bar Assn., ABA (chmn. com. jud. councils 1938-39, mem. ho. dels. 1948-60, 66-68, mem. com. peace and law 1948-59, 66-87, chmn. 1949-58, chmn. com. on bill of rights 1959, 61-64, vice chmn. sect. individual rights 1966-87, bd. editors jour. 1949-71, council legal edn. 1949), Am. Judicature Soc. (dir. 1949), Iron Wedge, Order of Coif, Phi Delta Phi. Republican. Clubs: Rainier. Home: Seattle Wash. Died Apr. 12, 1988.

SCHWIEGER, JOHN HENRY, stock exchange official; b. N.Y.C., Jan. 14, 1913; s. John and Charlotte (Floerke) S.; m. Camilla M. Meyer, June 12, 1937; children: Camilla Schwieger Humphreys, Jonathan, Gerret. BS, CCNY, 1936; MA, Columbia U., 1939. V.p. N.Y. Stock Exchange, formerly in charge mem. firm liaison; cons. Paine Webber Jackson & Curtis, Ins., then ptnr.; sr. v.p., sec. Paine Webber Inc., 1972-75; pres. Commodity Exchange, Inc.; gov. Am. Stock Exchange; mem. Cotton Exchange, Merc. Exchange, N.Y. Coffee and Sugar Exchange; dir. N.Y. Bd. Trade. Mem. dist. com. Boy Scouts Am.; bd. dirs. YMCA Greater N.Y.; bd. mgrs. Westchester-Bronx YMCA. Mem. Union League, Stock Exchange Luncheon, City Midday clubs, Phi Beta Kappa. Lutheran (coun.). Home: New Paltz N.Y. Died June 29, 1988, buried New Paltz Rural Cemetery.

SCHWIERING, CONRAD, artist; b. Boulder, Colo., Aug. 8, 1916; s. Oscar C. and Willetta (Jamison) S.; m. Mary Ethel Smith, Sept. 1, 1939. B.A. in Commerce and Law, U. Wyo., 1938; postgrad. Art Students League, N.Y.C., 1939-41, Grand Central Sch. Art, N.Y.C., 1940-41. One-man show: Nat. Cowboy Hall of Fame, 1981; group shows: Nat. Acad. Western Artists, Oklahoma City, Artists of Am., Denver, Settlers West, Tucson, Corpus Christi (Tex.) Miniature Show; represented in permanent collections: Whitney Gallery Western Art, Cody, Wyo., Nat. Cowboy Hall of Fame, Oklahoma City, Wyo. State Mus., Cheyenne, U. Wyo., Laramie, Genesee Country Mus., Rochester, N.Y.; instr. art U. Wyo., 1949, Teton Artists Associated, 1959-64. Active Grad Teton Natural History Assn., Jackson Hole Mus., Mont. Hist. Ctr., Helena. Served to lt. col. C.E., AUS, 1941-46. Conrad Schwiering Day declared by Gov. Wyo., 1981; recipient Trustees Gold medal Nat. Cowboy Hall of Fame and Western Heritage Ctr., 1981; Disting. Alumni award U. Wyo., 1970. Mem. Nat. Acad. Western Art. Republican. Roman Catholic. Clubs: Salmagundi, Rotary. Subject of TV documentaries Conrad Schwiering Mountain Painter, Harriscope Broadcasting Co., 1973, Profiles in American Art, Pub. Broadcasting System, 1982; subject of books; Conrad Schwiering—Painting on the Square (Dean Krakel), 1981; Schwiering and the West (Robert Wakefield). Died Jan. 27, 1986; buried Shadow Mountain, Grand Teton Nat. Park, Wyo.

SCHWOEBEL, WILLIAM SYLVESTER, business executive; b. Pitts., May 29, 1912; s. William L. and Anna (Cotter) S.; m. Georginia E. Connell, Dec. 25, 1946 (dec.); m. 2d, Martha L. Bremer, Dec. 10, 1955; children: Ann, Mary. Student, U. Pitts.; grad. Advanced Mgmt. Program, Harvard U. Auditor Nat. Steel Products Co., Houston, 1939-42; asst. comptroller Nat. Steel Corp., Pitts., 1954-56, controller, 1956-64, v.p., controller, 1964-69, v.p. fin., 1969-72, sr. v.p. fin., 1972-78; chmn., chief exec. officer corp. ins. Reins. Co. Ltd., Bermuda, from 1978; vice chmn. Nat. Underground Storage, Inc., Butler, Pa., from 1978. 1st lt. USAAF, 1942-46. Mem. Fin. Execs. Inst., Am. Iron and Steel Inst., Soc. Fin. Analysts, AIM, Duquesne, St. Clair Country, Williams Country, Rolling Rock clubs. Home: Pittsburgh Pa. Died Aug. 21, 1981; buried Pitts.

SCOTT, FLORA MURRAY, botany educator; b. Craig Manse, Montrose, Scotland, Sept. 6, 1891; came to U.S., 1922, naturalized, 1935; s. Robert and Mary (Jobson) S. MA, St. Andrews U., 1911, BS, 1914; PhD, Stanford U., 1925. Asst. prof. biology Constaninople Coll., 1920-21; staff League of Red Cross Socs., Geneva, Switzerland, 1921-22; faculty UCLA, from 1925, succesively instr., asst. prof., assoc. prof., prof. botany, from 1948. Served with Royal Arsenal, Woolwich, 1916-17, with Q.M. British Expeditionary Force, 1917-19. Decorated Order of Brit. Empire, 1919; Carnegie rsch. scholar, 1914-15. Mem. Bot. Soc. Am., AAAS, Western Naturalists. Home: Los Angeles Calif. †

SCOTT, GEORGE TAYLOR, scientist, zoology educator; b. Stillwater, N.Y., Sept. 10, 1914; s. Robert Winfield and Helen Denison (Taylor) S.; m. Elsie Mae Welling, Oct. 16, 1943; children: Helen Ann, Georganne Elsie. BS, Union Coll., 1938; AM, Harvard U., 1941, PhD, 1943. Austin teaching fellow Harvard U., 1940-43; instr. zoology Oberlin Coll., 1943-45, asst. prof., 1945-49, assoc. prof., 1949-52, prof., 1952-80, emeritus, 1980-87, chmn. dept. biology, 1956-67; assoc. scientist Woods Hole Oceanographic Inst., 1954-59; trustee Bermuda Biol. Sta. for Rsch., from 1955, pres., 1967-77; trustee Marine Biol. Lab., 1956-73. Contbr. articles to profl. jours. Fellow AAAS, Ohio Acad. Sci., N.Y. Acad. Sci.; mem. Am. Soc. Zoologists, Soc. Gen. Physiologists, AAUP, Corp. Marine Biol. Lab., Sigma Xi, Theta Nu Epsilon, Gamma Alpha. Home: Woods Hole Mass. Died Sept. 17, 1987; buried Stillwater Union Cemetery.

SCOTT, HAROLD W(ILLIAM), investment executive; b. N.Y.C., Mar. 29, 1905; s. Robert A. and Leonie M. (Huerstel) S.; m. Kate Ross Billings, Apr. 30, 1926; children: Phyllis Scott Lobdell, Harold W. Grad., Taft Sch., Watertown, Conn., 1924; student, Princeton U., 1925. Entered commodity bus. N.Y.C., 1925; mem. Produce Exchange, N.Y.C., 1927, security bus., N.Y.C., 1927; odd lot broker and mem. N.Y. Stock Exchange, N.Y.C., 1929, gov., 1949, chmn. bd. govs., 1954-56; with Dean Witter & Co., N.Y.C., 1937-71, gen. ptnr., 1937-71. Mem. bd. govs. Monmouth Med. Ctr. Served from capt. to lt. col. USAAF, 1942-45. Mem. N.Y. Stock Exchange Luncheon Club, Racquet and Tennis Club, Veterans 7th Regiment (N.Y.C.); Seabright Club (N.J.), Beach Club, Rumson (N.J.) Country Club. Home: Rumson N.J. Died Mar. 3, 1986.

SCOTT, JOHN ALDEN, newspaper foundation executive; b. Litchfield, Conn., Mar. 11, 1916; s. Alden John and Jennie Eugenia (Wheeler) S.; m. Patricia Jean Myers, Dec. 1, 1945; children: Sally Jean (Mrs. Larry Ogden), Susan Jane (Mrs. Jerry Burns), Steven Carl, John A. A.B., U. Notre Dame, 1938; postgrad., Ind. U., Purdue U. With South Bend (Ind.) Tribune, 1950, Elkhart (Ind.) Truth, 1957-62; pub. Lafayette (Ind.) Jour. and Courier, 1962-70, Olympia (Wash.) Olympian and Bellingham (Wash.) Herald, 1969-70; chief exec., pub. Honolulu Star Bull., 1972-76; pres. Gannett Newspaper Found., Rochester, N.Y., 1976-81; chmn. Gannett Newspaper Found., 1981-86. Mayor of, South Bend, 1952-56. Served as officer USMCR, 1941-45; brig. gen. Res. (ret.). Decorated Silver Star, Bronze Star, Purple Heart; Named Young Man of Year in South Bend Jr. Assn. Commerce, 1949. Mem. Sigma Delta Chi. Club: Rotary. Lodges: Masons; Shriners. Home: Cocoa Beach Fla. Died Oct. 1, 1986.

SCOTT, LESLIE WRIGHT, university official; b. Chgo., July 25, 1913; s. Charles O. and Charlotte (Wright) S.; m. Ellen Meyer, June 6, 1942; children: William, Leslie Ann, Mary Ellen, Timothy. AB, Mich. State U., 1935. Dir. Kellogg Ctr. for Continuing Edn. Mich. State U., 1950-56, dir. Sch. Hotel and Restaurant Mgmt., 1947-55, dean continuing edn., 1955-56; v.p. Fred Harvey, Inc., 1970-72; v.p. for devel., prof. hotel, restaurant and instl. mgmt. Mich. State U., East Lansing, from 1972; dir. Canteen Corp., Win Schulers, Inc., Yellowstone Park Co. Contbr. articles to trade jours. Bd. dirs. St. Lawrence Hosp., Lansing, Lansing Symphony; pres. Mich. State U. Found., from 1976. Lt. USNR, 1942-46. Mem. Nat. Restaurant Assn. (past pres.), Hinsdale Golf, Chicago, University Mich., Country of Lansing, City of Lansing clubs, Rotary. Home: Willowbrook Ill. Died July 18, 1984; buried Chgo.

SCOTT, WILLIAM JOHN, lawyer, attorney general; b. Chgo., Nov. 11, 1926; s. William Earl and Edith (Swanson) S.; m. Dorothy Lorraine Johnson, May 27, 1950 (dic. Sept. 1970); children: Elizabeth Anne, William G. Student, Bucknell U., 1945, U. Pa., 1946; JD, Kent Coll. Law, Chgo., 1950. Bar: Ill. 1950. Practiced in Chgo., 1950-51, 67-69; with LaSalle Nat. Bank, Chgo., 1951-53, Am. Nat. Bank & Trust Co., Chgo., 1953-58; v.p. Nat. Blvd. Bank Chgo., 1959-62; spl. asst U.S. atty., 1959; pres. Holiday Travel House, from 1959; treas. State of Ill., 1963-67, atty. gen., from 1969. Trustee MacMurray Coll., Jacksonville, Ill., 1963-67. With USNR, 1945-46. Mem. ABA, Fed. Bar Assn., Ill. Bar Assn., Chgo. Bar Assn. Republican. Presbyterian. Home: Palos Heights Ill. Died June 22, 1986.

SCRIBNER, GILBERT HILTON, JR., real estate broker; b. Milw., June 1, 1918; s. Gilbert Hilton and Nancy (Van Dyke) S.; m. Helen Shoemaker, Mar. 22, 1941; children: Helen Eaton (Mrs. Gregory E. Euston), Nancy Van Dyke (Mrs. David W. Clarke, Jr.), William Van Dyke, II. B.S., Yale U., 1939. Pres. Scribner & Co., 1962-77, chmn., from 1977; dir. No. Trust Co., No. Trust Corp. Pres. Civic Fedn., 1955-57; mem. Chgo. Pub. Bldgs. Com., 1967-71; trustee Northwestern U.; bd. dirs. Mid-Am. chpt. A.R.C., 1952-57, 67-72; chmn. adv. com. to bd. commrs. Forest Preserve Dist. Cook County, Ill.; chmn. Ill. Commn. for Constnl. Revision, 1958-61; bd. dirs. Northwestern Meml. Hosp. Served as lt. comdr. USNR, 1941-45. Mem. Chgo. Hist. Soc. (trustee 1946-78). Republican. Episcopalian. Clubs: Chicago (Chgo.), Mid-Day (Chgo.), Commercial (Chgo.); Indian Hill (Winnetka); Links (N.Y.C.); Old Elm (Highland Park, Ill.). Home: Northfield Ill. Deceased.

SCRIPPS, JAMES G(EORGE), publisher; b. San Diego, Nov. 24, 1911; s. James G. and Josephine (Stedem) S.; m. Marion Bates, Sept. 11, 1931; children: Sally Estelle, Marion Susan. Ed. pub. schs., San Diego; HHD (hon.), Utah State U. Bd. chmn., pres., bd. dirs. Pioneer Newspapers, James G. Scripps Newspapers. Treas. Scripps League. Served on active duty with USNRF, 1940-45; in Pacific area, including Iwo Jima and Okinawa; rank of rear admiral, ret. Decorated Silver Star, Purple Heart; recipient commendation ribbon. Mem. Rainier Club. Died Jan. 24, 1987.

SCUDDER, TOWNSEND, III, writer, educator; b. Glenwood, L.I., N.Y., Aug. 27, 1900; s. Townsend and Mary Dannat (Thayer) S.; m. Virginia Louise Boody, June 23, 1923; children—Townsend, Thayer. B.A., Yale, 1923, Ph.D., 1933. With book editorial dept. Doubleday, Page & Co., 1923; editorial work Rockefeller Found., 1924; with English dept. Yale, 1924-31; asst. prof. English Swarthmore Coll., 1931-40; asso. prof. 1940-43, on leave, 1943-48, prof., 1943-53; exec. dir. Center for Information on Am., Washington, Conn., 1951-56; pres. Center for Information on Am., 1956-87. Author: Emerson and Some Englishmen, 1935, Jane Welsh Carlyle, 1939, Concord; American Town, 1947; Contbr.: chpt. on Henry David Thoreau to The Literary History of the United States, 1948; various essays, revs. to profl. lit.; Editor: Letters of Jane Welsh Carlyle to Joseph Neuberg, 1931. Trustee Middlesex Coll. Guggenheim fellow, 1943-44; asso. fellow Timothy Dwight Coll., Yale. Mem. Phi Beta Kappa. Club: Coffee House (N.Y.). Home: Woodbury Conn. Died Sept. 30, 1988.

SEABURY, JOHN WARD, business executive; b. Oak Park, Ill., Dec. 1, 1921; s. Charles Ward and Louise (Lovett) S.); m. Charlene Adrienne Brown, Feb. 23, 1946; children: Deborah S. Holloway, Charles Ward II, David Grant. Grad., Choate Sch., 1940; B.S. in Indsl. Adminstrn. and Engring, Yale U., 1943. With Marsh & McLennan, Inc., Chgo., 1946-76; asst. v.p. Marsh & McLennan, Inc., 1952-56, v.p., 1956-76; pres. Hanover Securities Co., from 1966; exec. dir. Seabury Found. Trustee Berea (Ky.) Coll., Seabury-Western Theol. Sem., Evanston, Ill., Lyric Opera Chgo. Served to lt. (j.g.) USNR, 1943-46. Mem. Chgo. Art Inst., Chgo. Hist. Soc., Chgo. Zool. Soc., Field Mus. Natural History, Shedd Aquarium Soc. Chgo., Mus. Sci. and Industry, Orchestral Soc. Chgo., Chi Phi. Republican. Episcopalian. Clubs: Crystal Lake Yacht (Frankfort, Mich.), Crystal Downs Country (Frankfort, Mich.); Tower (Chgo.), University (Chgo.), Yale (Chgo.), Economic (Chgo.); Indian Hill (Winnetka); The Moorings (Vero Beach, Fla.). Home: Winnetka Ill. Died Oct. 18, 1988.

SEAL, CHARLES R(YLAND), state official; b. Hanover County, Va., June 29, 1890; s. William Ryland and Emma Jane (Luck) S.; m. Jessie Larned Dickson, Mar. 27, 1913; 1 dau., Nancy Lee (Mrs. Clarence Eugene Hauss). LLB, Nat. U., 1917. Atty. and examiner ICC, 1918-27; transp. dir. Balt. Assn. of Commerce, 1927-46; dir. bur. of water carriers and freight forwarders ICC, 1946-53; gen. counsel, dir. bur. transp. Va. State Ports Authority, 1953-57; dir. transp. Md. Port Authority, 1957-58; dep. exec. dir., gen. counsel Va. State Port Authority, 1958-60, gen. and commerce counsel, from 1960. Chmn. exec. com. Nat. Indsl. Traffic League, 1943-44; pres. Assn. of ICC Practitioners, 1942-43. Home: Norfolk Va. †

SEAL, JOHN RIDLEY, physician, military officer; b. W.Va., Mar. 10, 1912; s. Gordon S. and Inez A. (Crump) S.; m. Frances C. Shackelford, Jan. 7, 1937. MD, U. Va., 1937. Diplomate Am. Bd. Internal Medicine. Intern Strong Meml. Hosp., Rochester, N.Y., 1937-38; fellow in pathology U. Va. Sch. Medicine, 1938-40; resident in medicine N.Y. Hosp., N.Y.C., 1940-42; commd. lt. (j.g.) USN, 1942, advanced through grades to capt., 1957; officer in charge Naval Med. Rsch. Unit 4, Great Lakes, Ill., 1946-54; dir. communicable disease div. Bur. Medicine and Surgery Navy Dept., Washington, 1954-58; comdg. officer Naval Med. Rsch. Unit 3, Cairo, Ill., 1958-61, Naval Med. Rsch. Inst., Bethesda, Md., 1961-65, ret., 1965; assoc. dir. intramural rsch. Nat. Inst. Allergy and Infectious Diseases NIH, Bethesda, 1965-70, sci. dir., 1970-75, dep. dir. Nat. Inst. Allergy and Infectious Disease, 1975-81, spl. asst. to dir. NIH, from 1981. Rsch., publs. in field. Recipient Superior Service award HEW, 1968, Disting. Service award, 1972, rank of Meritorious Exec., 1980, Stitt award Assn. Mil. Surgeons U.S., 1954, Founders medal, 1963, 68. Fellow ACP; mem. Infectious Disease Soc., Am. Epidemiol. Soc., AAAS, N.Y. Acad. Scis., Am. Soc. Tropical Medicine and Hygiene. Home: Bethesda Md. Died Aug. 11, 1984.

SEAMANS, FRANK L., lawyer; b. Canton, Ill.. AB, U. Ill., 1935; LLB, Harvard U., 1938. Bar: Pa. 1939. Ptnr. firm Eckert, Seamans, Cherin & Mellott, Pitts. Mem. ABA, Pa. Bar Assn., Allegheny County Bar Assn. Home: Pittsburgh Pa. Died Dec. 28, 1984; buried Southminster Presbyn. Ch., Pitts.

SEARS, PAUL BIGELOW, botany educator; b. Bucyrus, Ohio, Dec. 17, 1891; s. Rufus Victor and Sallie Jane (Harris) S.; m. Marjorie Lea McCutcheon, June 22, 1917; children: Paul McCutcheon, Catherine Louise, Sallie Harris. BS, Ohio Weslyan U., 1913; DSc (hon.), Ohio Wesleyan U., 1937; AM, U. Nebr., 1915; PhD, U. Chgo., 1922; DSc (hon.), Oberlin Coll., 1958; LLD (hon.), U. Ark., 1957, U. Nebr., Wayne, 1957; LittD (hon.), Marietta Coll., 1951. Instr. botany Ohio State U., 1915; asst. prof. botany U. Nebr., 1919-25, assoc. prof., 1925-27; prof. botany, head of dept. U. Okla., 1927-38; prof. botany Oberlin Coll., 1938-50; chmn. conservation program Yale U., from 1950, chmn. plant sci. dept., 1953-55; rsch. assoc. Tchrs. Coll., Columbia U., 1936-38; cons., lectr. in field; mem. Nat. Sci. Bd., 1958-64. Author: Deserts on the March, 1935, This is Our World, 1937, Who Are These Americans?, 1939, Life and Environment, 1939, This Useful World, 1941,

Charles Darwin, 1950; contbr. articles to profl jours., mags. With U.S. Army, 1917-18. Fellow AAAS (pres. 1956, chmn. bd. 1957); mem. Bot. Soc. Am. (sec. gen. sect. 1924-28), Am. Soc. Natrualists, Ohio Acad. Sci. (past pres.), Okla. Acad. Sci., Ecol. Soc. Am. (past pres.), Ohio Wildlife Council, Nat. Audubon Soc. (chmn. bd. from 1956), Am. Acad. Arts and Scis., Conn. Acad. Arts and Scis., Phi Beta Kappa, Sigma Xi, Phi Sigma (nat. pres. 1928-29, nat. chancellor 1929-33), Sigma Gamma Epsilon, Delta Tau Delta. Home: New Haven Conn. †

SEED, THOMAS FINIS, lawyer; b. Springfield, Mo., Aug. 30, 1916; s. William Thomas Haydn and Essye Pearl (Peters) S.; m. Magda Monica Vettos, Dec. 31, 1955. A.B., Kans. State Tchrs. Coll., 1941; J.D., U. Kans., 1948. Bar: Kans. 1948, U.S. Supreme Ct. 1966. Sole practice, Wichita, Kans., 1948-50, 53-59, 81-88; county atty. Sedgwick County, Wichita, 1951-53; field atty. VA, Wichita, 1960-77; sec., recorder York Rite, Masons, Wichita, 1978-80. Pres. Wichita Inter-Club Council, 1951. Served to maj. U.S. Army, 1942-46. Mem. Fed. Bar Assn. (pres. Kans. chpt. 1974), Kans. Bar Assn., Wichita Bar Assn., Phi Delta Phi. Republican. Methodist. Club: Nat. Lawyers (Washington). Lodge: Masons. Home: Wichita, Kans. Died May 27, 1988; buried Nat. Cemetery, Springfield, Mo.

SEEGRABER, FRANK JOSEPH, librarian; b. Boston, Oct. 8, 1916; s. Andrew and Emma (Herr) S.; m. Edith Walker, June 24, 1944; children: Barbara, Frank Joseph, Jean, Rita, Claire, Richard, Loretta, Carol, John, Paul. A.B., Holy Cross Coll., 1938; B.S. in L.S, Columbia, 1943; spl. grad. student, Harvard, 1953. Spl. library asst. Littauer Center, Harvard, 1939; asst. gen. reference dept. Boston Pub. Library, 1939-41; grad. asst. Columbia Coll. Library, 1941-42; asst. periodicals dept. N.Y. Pub. Library, 1942-43; inventory supr. Holtzer-Cabot Electric Co., Boston, 1944-47; ednl. counselor Grolier Soc., 1947; asst. Kirstein Bus. Library, Boston, 1948; reference librarian Boston Coll. Library, 1948-58; librarian Merrimack Coll., N. Andover, Mass., 1958-65; asst. librarian U. Mass. (Boston br.), 1965-68; librarian Coll. Bus. Adminstrn. Boston Coll., 1968-69; librarian Boston Coll. (Sch. Mgmt.), 1969-75, spl. collections librarian, 1975-88; lectr. bibliography Boston Coll., 1955-58; lectr. library sci. Northeastern U., 1966-75; sr. lectr., cons., 1975-88. Mem. Area Planning Council, 1968-69. Mem. ALA, New Eng. Library Assn. (bibl. com.), Mass. Library Assn. (chmn. edn. com.), New Eng. Tech. Services Librarians (vice chmn. 1961-62, chmn. 1962-63, exec. com. 1963-65, archivist 1968-88), Spl. Libraries Assn. (chmn. ednl. com. Boston 1955-56), bibliog. socs. Am., U. Va. Roman Catholic. Club: KC. Home: Wollaston Mass. Died May 19, 1988; buried New Calvary Cemetery, Boston.

SEGOVIA, ANDRES, guitarist; b. Linares, Spain, Feb. 18, 1894; m. Emilia, 1962; 1 son; 2 children (by former marriage). Specialized in study guitar, Granada Mus. Inst.; D.Mus. (hon.), Oxford U., 1972. Has taught at Santiago de Compostela, Acad. Chigi, Sienna, U. Calif., Berkeley, other schs. Started playing guitar at age 10, debut in, Granada, Spain, 1909; toured in Europe and S. Am.; made N.Y. debut, Town Hall, 1928; recitals throughout U.S.; adapted works of Bach, Haydn and Mozart; Author: Segovia: An Autobiography of the Years 1893-1920, 1977, Segovia: My book of the Guitar, 1979. Decorated Gran Cruz de Alfonso X el Sabio, Gran Cruz de Isabel la Católica, Gran Cruz de Beneficencia con distintivo blanco (Spain); Caballero de la Gran Cruz de la Orden al Mérito de la República Italiana (Italy); Comemdador de la Orden de las Artes y Letras de la República Francesa (France); Orden del Sol Naciente (Japan); recipient Gold medal for meritorious work, Spain, 1967, Grammy award, 1958, Lifetime Achievement award Nat. Acad. Rec. Arts and Scis., 1986. Mem. Royal Acad. Fine Arts (Spain). Died June 2, 1987; buried Sacramental de San Isidro, Madrid.

SEID, HERMAN, lawyer; b. Bklyn., Aug. 14, 1902; s. Joseph and Ida (Niedelmann) S.; children: John, Richard. Student, Stevens Inst. Tech., 1918-21; LL.B., Bklyn. Law Sch., 1924. Bar: N.Y., Pa., U.S. Supreme Ct. Counsel, then cons. Carrier Corp., Syracuse, N.Y., from 1929; practice corporate, patent and internat. law. Aerofin Corp., Lynchburg, Va., 1935-81; also cos. in, Europe, Japan, S.Am.; pres. River Co. Del.; chmn. SEID Internat. S.A., Brussels; pres. Heart Edn. and Research Found. Inc., N.Y.C. Contbr. articles to profl. jours. Bd. dirs. Northeastern (Dental) Dispensary, N.Y.; Vice pres. Assn. Bds. Edn. of Conn., 1942-47; pres. Met. Com. for Religious Liberty, N.Y., 1951-53; deacon Unitarian Ch. All Souls, N.Y.C.; chmn. East Side Forum, N.Y., 1953-56. Mem. N.A.M. (patents com., spl. rep. India and Caracas), Am. Soc. Corporate Secs. (chmn. stock exchange com. 1960), Internat. Assn. for Protection Indsl. Property, N.Y. Patent Law Assn. (chmn. fgn. patents com. 1967), Am. Patent Law Assn. Clubs: Masons, Squadron A, Talk (N.Y.C.); Pettipaug Yacht (Essex); Black Hall (Old Lyme, Conn.). Home: Essex Conn. Died 1984.

SEIDMAN, JACOB STEWART, accountant; b. N.Y.C., Sept. 8, 1901; s. Louis and Fanny (Goldfarb) S.; m. Jan Sherman, Dec. 29, 1950. B.C.S. magna cum laude, N.Y. U., 1921, B.S. cum laude, 1928; J.D. cum laude, Fordham U., 1924; LL.M. cum laude, St. Lawrence U., 1925. C.P.A., N.Y. State. Founding partner Seidman & Seidman (C.P.A.'s), 1921-41, from 1945; Del. N.Y. State to Nat. Tax Assn. convs., 1926-29; accounting cons. appropriations com. U.S. Ho. Reps., 1948, 50; mem. exec. com. N.Y. Bd. Trade, from 1957; adv. com. comptroller N.Y. State, 1956-59; acad. council Advanced Tng. Center of Internal Revenue Service, 1952-54; mem. accounting task force Hoover Commn., 1953; former chmn. Council Accountancy State U. N.Y.; head U.S. exchange mission on accountancy to, Soviet Union; counsultor taxation adv. bd. Pace Coll.; mem. adv. council Joint Legislative Com. on N.Y. State's Commerce, Econ. Devel. and Tourism; mem. N.Y. State Atty. Gen.'s Adv. Com. on Theatrical Financing and Practices; chmn. com. on econs. Bd. Standards and Planning for Living Theatre. Author: Federal Income and Excess Profits Tax Laws, 4 vols; contbr. newspapers, profl. jours., theatrical mags.; tax columnist: N.Y. Herald Tribune, 1936-57; tax contbr.: N.Y. Times, from 1959. Treas., trustee Am. Acad. Dramatic Arts; bd. dirs. Nat. Parkinson Found., New Dramatists Com., Albert Gallatin Asso. of N.Y. U.; life trustee N.Y. U.; trustee Hosp. Joint Diseases; vice chmn. disaster relief com. N.Y.C. chpt. A.R.C., 1948; adv. com., law com. Fedn. Jewish Philanthropies. Served from lt. comdr. to capt. USNR, World War II. Recipient John T. Madden meml. award N.Y.U., 1955; named hon. fellow in accounting L.I. U., 1956; recipient award for outstanding service to advancement of human rights Joint Def. Appeal, 1956; N.Y. U. Alumni Meritorious Service award, 1962. Mem. Am. Inst. C.P.A.'s (pres. 1959-60, chmn. tax com., mem. council, exec. com., named Accountant of Year 1956, past mem. accounting prins. bd.), N.Y. State Soc. C.P.A.'s (past pres., award of the year 1956), Soc. Bus. Adv. Professions, Am. Accounting Assn., Nat. Assn. Cost Accountants, Nat. Security Indsl. Assn., N.Y. U. Commerce Alumni Fedn. (pres.), N.Y. Alumni Fedn. (exec. com.), N.Y. U. Finance Club (pres. 1961), Navy League U.S., ANTA (dir. Greater New York chpt.), Alpha Epsilon Pi, Beta Gamma Sigma (dir., hon.), Alpha Beta Psi (hon.), Delta Mu Delta (hon.), Sphinx Club, Arch and Square. Clubs: Economic (N.Y.C.), Accountants (N.Y.C.). Home: New York N.Y. Deceased.

SEIFERT, RALPH LOUIS (EDWIN), chemist, educator; b. Posey County, Ind., Feb. 4, 1914; s. Daniel Frederick and Elfrieda Caroline (Ehrhardt) S.; m. Catherine Ford Dyer, June 18, 1938; 1 son, Ralph Louis. AB, U. Evansville, 1934; MA, U. Ill., 1935, PhD, 1937. Instr. U. Ill., 1937-38; instr. to prof. Alma Coll., 1938-44; rsch. chemist Respiration Lab. U. Chgo., summer 1942, rsch. chemist Metall Lab., 1944-46; assoc. prof. Carleton Coll., 1946-49; assoc. prof. Ind. U., 1949-66, prof. chemistry, 1966-77, prof. emeritus, from 1977; cons. Argonne (Ill.) Nat. Lab., 1946-68, rsch. chemist, summers, 1948, 49, 55. Author: (with F.T. Gucker) Physical Chemistry, 1966; editorial bd. Jour. Phys. Chemistry, 1968-72. Fellow AAAS; mem. Am. Chem. Soc., Electrochem. So., Chem. Soc., Ind. Acad. Sci., Sigma Xi, Phi Lambda Upsilon, Alpha Chi Sigma. Home: Bloomington Ind. Died Apr. 23, 1987.

SELDEN, ALBERT W., theatrical producer, composer; b. N.Y.C., Oct. 20, 1922; s. Lynde and Muriel (Wiggin) S.; m. Jean Beaven, Dec. 22, 1943 (div. Feb. 1960); 3 sons, 2 daus.; m. Carlye Rogerson; 2 sons, 2 daus. BA, Yale U., 1943. Founder, producer, mgn. dir. Conn. Landmark Goodspeed Opera House, East Haddam, from 1962. Begam theatrical career at Yale; musician and composer; wdrote: score for Broadway revue Small Wonder; also many TV spls.; produced: Broadway plays , Body Beautiful, His and Hers, The Grey-Eyed People, Man of La Mancha (Critics award 1965, Tony award); producer: Hallelujah, Baby (Tony award 1968), Portrait of a Queen, Come Summer, Irene, all N.Y. Decorated Bronze Star. Mem. Dramatists Guild, ASCAP, League N.Y. Theatres. 1st lt. AUS, 1942-45. Home: Santa Fe N.Mex. Died June 6, 1987; buried Santa Fe.

SELDEN, ARMISTEAD INGE, JR., ambassador, lawyer; b. Greensboro, Ala., Feb. 20, 1921; s. Armistead Inge and Eith Manson (Cobbs) S.; m. Mary Jane Wright, Aug. 21, 1948; children: Armistead Inge III, Martee Graham, Jack Wright, Edith Cobbs, Thomas Lawson. BA, U. of South, 1942, LLB, 1948. Bar: Ala. 1948. Practiced in Greensboro, 1948-52, Washington, 1969-70, 73-74; mem. Ala. Ho. of Reps., 1950-52; mem. 83d to 91st congresses from Ala. dist.; mem. Fgn. Affairs Com., 1955-69, chmn. subcom. on inter-Am. affairs, 1959-69; prin. dep. asst. sec. for internat. security affairs Office Sec. Def., 1970-72, cons. U.S. Dept. Def., 1972-73; A.E. and P. to New Zealand, Western Samoa, Fiji and Tonga, 1974-79. Trustee U. of South. Lt. USNR, 1942-46. Recipient Spl. Order Law and Culture for Inter-Am. Service, Mexican Acad. Internat. Law, 1963, commendation Pres. Philippines, 1968, Disting. Civilian medal U.S. Dept. Def., 1972. Mem. ABA, Ala. Bar Assn., D.C. Bar Assn., Am. Legion, VFW, Blue Key, Sigma Alpha Epsilon, Phi Delta Phi. Episcopalian. Died Nov. 14, 1985.

SELLERS, SANDFORD, JR., educational adviser; b. Lexington, Mo., Feb. 5, 1892; s. Sandford and Lucia Valentine (Rogers) S.; m. Marion Logan Kean, June 8, 1915; children: Lillian Logan (Mrs. Igor DeLissovoy), Marion Stuart (Mrs. John R. Allison), Sandford III, Logan McBrayer. Grad., Wentworth Mil. Acad., Lexington, Mo., 1908; BS, U. Chgo., 1913, MA, 1934. Tchr. and comdt. Wentworth Mil. Acad., 1913-17; served at 1st Officers Tng. Camp, 1917; successively comdt., asst. supt., supt. Wentworth Mil. Acad., 1919-33; ednl. adviser CCC, 6th Army Corps Area, 1934-42; with Nat. Safety Coun., 1942-43; headmaster Elgin (Ill.) Acad., 1943-45; supt. Morgan Park Mil. Acad. and Jr. Coll., 1945-49; ednl. adviser Fourth Army, 1950-57, chief edn. br. hdqrs., from 1957. Capt. Inf., 342d Machine Gun Bn., 89th Div., U.S. Army; commd. maj., staff specialist, O.R.C., 1924; promoted lt. col., 1930; inactive, 1940; col. Ill. Nat. Guard, 1945-49. Awarded 2 battle stars Army of Occupation. Mem. NEA, Nat. Assn. Secondary Sch. Prins., Am. Assn. Sch. Adminstrs., Toastmasters Club, Beta Theta Pi, Phi Delta Kappa. Home: San Antonio Tex. †

SELLS, SAUL B., research psychologist, educator, consultant; b. N.Y.C., Jan. 13, 1913; s. Maxwell I. and Dora B. S.; m. Helen Francis Roberts, July 2, 1939 (dec.). A.B., Bklyn. Coll., 1933; Ph.D., Columbia U., 1936; D.Sc. (hon.), Tex. Christian U., 1983. Research asst., instr. edn. research Tchrs. Coll., Columbia U., N.Y.C., 1934-36; instr. psychology Columbia U., N.Y.C., 1935-37; research assoc. Bd. Edn., N.Y.C., 1935-40; lectr. in psychology Grad. Sch., Bklyn. Coll., 1936-37; research analyst Pub. Work Reserve, Washington, 1940-41; chief statistician Office Price Adminstrn., Washington, 1941-46; asst. to pres. A.B. Frank Co., San Antonio, 1946-68; prof., head dept. med. psychology U.S. Air Force Sch. Aerospace Medicine, Randolph AFB, Tex., 1948-58, cons., 1959-62; adj. prof. Trinity U., San Antonio, 1949-55; vis. prof. U. Tex., Austin, 1950-51, Tex. A&M U., College Station, from 1984; prof. psychology Tex. Christian U., Fort Worth, 1958-62, research prof., dir. inst. behavioral research, 1962-83, research prof. emeritus, 1983-88; pres. IBR Assocs., from 1984; cons. Nat. Ctr. Health Stats., Washington, 1965-70; mem. research career award com. Nat. Inst. Gen. Med. Sci., NIH, Washington; chmn. personality soc. U.S. Office Edn., Washington; research cons. Am., Eastern Pan Am., Trans World, Pan Am, U.S. Air, Fed. Express, COMAIR, other airlines, from 1960; cons.-reviewer VA, Washington, 1981-88, NSF, Washington, 1975-88, Can. Sci. Council, Ottawa, 1980-81; pres. Psychology Press, Inc., Brandon, Vt., 1963-68; cons. WHO, Geneva, Switzerland, 1976; mem. Gov.'s Council on Drug Abuse, Austin, Tex., 1980-88; mem. adv. com. on research Div. Mental Health and Devel. Disorders, State of Ill., Chgo., from 1981; bd. dirs. Commodore Savs. Assn., Dallas. Cons. editor Psychol. Bull., 1955-58, Jour. Clin. Psychology, from 1960, Psychology in Schs., from 1963; editor Behavioral Research Monographs, 1962-88; mng. editor, assoc. editor Multivariate Behavioral Research, from 1966 . Chmn. Tarrant County Heart Assn., Fort Worth; mem. Bexar County Mental Health Assn., San Antonio. Recipient Commendation for Meritorious Civilian Service U.S. Air Force, 1955, Pace Setter award Nat. Inst. Drug Abuse, 1978, Appreciation award, Meritorious Service award Tex. Commn. Alcohol and Drug Abuse, 1986. Fellow Am. Psychol. Assn. (pres. mil. div. 1970), Aerospace Med. Assn. (Longacre award 1956), AAAS; mem. Am. Astronautical Soc. (sr.), Soc. Multivariate Exptl. Psychology (pres. 1964), Am. Ednl. Research Assn., Psychometric Soc., Am. Statis. Assn., Soc. Psychol. Study Social Issues, Southwestern Psychol. Assn. (pres.), Tex. Psychol. Assn. (pres.), Southwest Research Inst. Sigma Xi. Worked on: Application of psychology to behavioral problems involving individual and organizational measurement, personnel selection, personality measurement, organizational climate, management strategies, drug and alcohol abuse, air traffic control, aviation space travel and related areas. Subspecialties: Behavioral psychology; Ecology (environmental science). Died Feb. 4, 1988. Home: Fort Worth Tex.

SELTZER, LEON EUGENE, publisher, copyright lawyer; b. Auburn, Maine, Aug. 14, 1918; s. Samuel and Sadye (Shapiro) S.; m. Lenore Chafetz, Mar. 14, 1948; children—Deborah, Janet, Marcia. A.B., Columbia U., 1940; J.D., Stanford U., 1974. Bar: Calif. 1974, U.S. Dist. Ct. (no. dist.) Calif. 1974. Asst. editor Columbia U. Press, 1939-41, editor, 1946-52, sales promotion mgr., 1952-56; dir. Stanford U. Press, 1956-83, dir. emeritus, 1983-88; of counsel Majestic, Gallagher, Parsons, and Siebert, San Francisco, 1983-88; asst. editor Columbia Ency., 1946-50; editor Columbia Lippincott Gazetteer of the World, 1946-52; scholar-in-residence Center for Advanced Study in Behavioral Scis., 1975-76. Contbr. short stories, articles and verse to nat. mags.; author: Exemptions and Fair Use in Copyright, 1977. Vice pres. Santa Clara County Bd. Edn., 1966-71. Served from pvt. to maj. C.E. AUS, 1941-46, PTO. Guggenheim fellow, 1975-76. Mem. Assn. Am. Univ. Presses (pres. 1968-69), Copyright Soc. U.S.A. Home: Stanford Calif. Died Jan. 11, 1988; buried Waldron, Wash.

SEMPLE, ROBERT BAYLOR, business executive; b. St. Louis, Aug. 18, 1910; s. Nathaniel Meacon and Margery (Ferriss) S.; m. Isabelle Ashby Neer, June 15, 1933 (dec. 1983); children: Robert B. Jr., Lloyd A., Elizabeth H., William T. and Nathaniel M. (twins); m. Holly Reid Fowler, Aug. 31, 1985. BS, MIT, 1932,

MS, 1933. Research chemist Monsanto Chem. Co., 1933-35, pilot plant group leader, mgr. interim mfg. dept., 1935-39, asst. dir., gen. devel. dept., 1939-42, mgr. petroleum chem. sales, 1942-44, dir. gen. devel. dept., 1944-49; pres. Wyandotte Chem. Corp., Mich., 1949-70; pres. BASF Wyandotte Corp., 1970-71, chmn. bd., 1971-79; emeritus dir. Am. Natural Resources Co.; former trustee Atlantic Mut. Ins. Co., Centennial Ins. Co. Pres. Detroit Symphony Orch., 1962-79, chmn. bd. dirs. 1979-81, hon. chmn. 1982-88; emeritus trustee Harper-Grace Hosps.; life mem. corp. MIT. Mem. Com. Econ. Devel. (trustee emeritus), Chem. Mfg. Assn. (past dir., chmn.), Inst. Chem. Engrs., Am. Chem. Soc. Episcopalian. Clubs: Links (N.Y.C.); Detroit, Yondotega; Grosse Pointe (Grosse Pointe, Mich.), Country (Grosse Pointe, Mich.); Bohemian (San Francisco). Home: Grosse Pointe Farms Mich. Died Nov. 4, 1988; interred Emmanuel Church, Delaplane, Va.

SENN, PETTUS HOLMES, university professor; b. Silverstreet, S.C., Oct. 13, 1890; s. Charles Walker and Caroline (Caldwell) S. BS, Clemson Coll., 1915; MS, U. Wis., 1921, PhD, 1931. Agrl. agt. S.C., 1915-18; asst. in genetics U. Wis., 1920-21, asst. in agronomy, 1926-28; plant breeder Clemson Coll., 1922-23; plant microscopist Exptl. Sta., Ky., 1924-25; asst. prof. agronomy U. Fla., 1929-34, assoc. prof., 1935-39, prof. agronomy and head dept. agronomy, from 1940. Contbr. articles to Jour. Heredity, Jour. Phytopathol., Agronomy Jour. Active in Boy Scout Orgn. Med. tech. World War I. Fellow AAAS; mem. Am. Genetic Assn., Genetic Soc. of Am., Am. Soc. Agronomy, Am. Inst. Biol. Scis., Am. Phytopathol. Soc., Fla. Soil and Crop Sci. Soc., Fla. Acad. Sci., Assn. So. Agrl. Workers, Sigma Xi, Gamma Sigma Delta, Phi Kappa Phi, Phi Sigma, Alpha Zeta. Home: Gainesville Fla. †

SERA Y SERRANO, JOSE AGUSTIN, diplomat; b. Holguin, Oriente, Cuba, Apr. 23, 1892; s. Jose Sera Marraro and Dolores Serrano Manduley; m. Dulce Maria Aleman y Velez, Oct. 26, 1935; children: Carlos Manuel Sera y Aleman, Elisa Dulce Laura. Student, Guilford Coll., N.C.; Georgetown U. Sch. Fgn. Service. Consul gen. Govt. of Cuba, Washington, from 1941. Decorated Knight Cuban Red Cross, Nat. Order Merit Carlos Manuel de Cespedes, Medal Gen. Antonio Macco, Order St. Christopher Havana, Cuba, Medal Internat. Found. Elroy Alfaro; recipient Diploma of Honor State Dept. Cuba. Home: Washington D.C. †

SEROTA, HERMAN MICHAEL, psychiatrist, psychoanalyst, educator; b. Chgo., May 1, 1914; s. Hermon and Hannah (Pouhl) S.; m. Hermia Sunshine, 1957. BS, U. Chgo., 1934, MD, 1938, PhD, 1939. Diplomate Am. Bd. Psychiatry and Neurology; cert. (Rockefeller fellow), Inst. for Psychoanalysis, Chgo., 1948. Intern Michael Reese Hosp., Chgo., 1938-39; resident U. Chgo. Hosps., 1939-42; practice medicine, specializing in psychiatry and psychoanalysis Chgo., from 1942; asst. to assoc. prof. psychiatry Northwestern U. Med. Sch., 1950-56, disting. lectr., 1973-74; professorial lectr. U. Chgo., 1956-74, sr. attending psychiatrist Psychiat. and Psychosomatic Inst., 1966-74; dir. liaison psychiatry, 1950-56; mem. staff, tng., supervising analyst Inst. for Psychoanalysis, Chgo., 1956-74; tng. and supervising psychoanalyst San Diego Psychoanalytic Inst., La Jolla, Calif., from 1974; clin. prof. psychiatry U. Calif. at San Diego, from 1974; attending psychiatrist Univ. Hosp., San Diego. Life mem. Art Inst. Chgo.; assoc. life mem. Field Mus. Natural History. Capt. M.C., AUS, 1942-46. Fellow Am. Psychiat. Assn. (life), AAAS (life, chmn. com. on liaison); mem. Am. Psychoanalytic Assn. (councillor-at-large 1971-75, 76-80), Chgo. Psychoanalytic Soc. (pres. 1965-66), Am. EEG Assn. (charter), Phi Beta Kappa, Sigma Xi, Alpha Omega Alpha. Home: La Jolla Calif. Deceased.

SESSA, FRANK BOWMAN, educator, librarian; b. Pitts., June 11, 1911; s. Thomas G. and Margaret Isabelle (Bowman) S.; m. Anne Marshall Johnston, Dec. 19, 1942; children—Anne Marshall, Jane Thomas, Gale Francesca. A.B., U. Pitts., 1933, A.M., 1934, Ph.D., 1950; B.L.S., Carnegie Inst. Tech., 1942. Research fellow Western Pa. Hist. Survey, 1935-36; librarian Hist. Soc. Western Pa., 1936-40; circulation librarian U. Pitts., 1941-42; prof. U. Pitts. (Sch. Library and Info. Sci.), 1966-80, prof. emeritus, 1980-87, acting dean, 1971-74, chmn. dept. library sci., 1973-76; instr. history U. Miami, 1947-50, asst. prof., 1951; dir. libraries City Miami, 1951-66. Contbr. articles to profl. jours. Served as lt. comdr. USNR, 1943-46; capt. Res. ret. Mem. AAUP, ALA (treas. 1972-76), Fla. Library Assn. (pres. 1959-60), Oral History Assn., Fla. Hist. Soc. (pres. 1962-64), Hist. Soc. Western Pa., Beta Phi Mu (exec. sec. 1976-80). Club: Rotarian. Home: Orlando Fla. Died June 24, 1987.

SESSIONS, EDSON OLIVER, U.S. ambassador, corporation executive; b. Toledo, Nov. 5, 1902; s. Edson Oliver and Helen (Potter) S.; m. Frances Cox, Apr. 10, 1937; children: William, Michael. Student, Chgo. Latin Sch.; BS, Harvard U., 1925. V.p. charge constrn. E.O. Sessions Co., Ltd., Chgo., Detroit, N.Y.C., Portland, 1925-30; chief indsl. engr. Bendix Aviation Corp., South Bend, Ind., 1930-32; mgmt. cons. J.O. McKinsey & Co., Chgo., N.Y.C., 1932-34; pres. Sessions Engring. Co., Chgo., mgmt. cons. architects and engrs., 1934-54, cons., 1955-57; cons. Army Ordnance Dept., N.Y. and Chgo. dists., 1943-45; spl. studies China industralization program Chinese Nationalist Govt., 1943; dir. U.S. Ops. Mission FOA, Bangkok, Thailand, 1954-55; leader spl. study group econ. and polit. problems in Cambodia and Laos, State Dept.-ICA, 1956; pres. E.O. Sessions Co. of Fla., 1955-57; pres., dir. Root-Lowell Mfg. Co., Chgo.; mng. dir. various indsl. firms; U.S. dep. postmaster gen., 1957-59; ambassador to Finland, 1959-60; pres. E.O. Sessions Co., Calif., 1960-67; asst. adminstr. Vietnam, AID, 1967-68; ambassador to Ecuador, Quito, 1967-70. Home: Laguna Hills Calif. Died Nov. 15, 1987.

SESSIONS, ROBERT EVANS, lawyer; b. Huntsville, Ala., June 1, 1909; s. Robert Ernest and Yula (Stricklen) S.; m. Janice de la Croix, Dec. 26, 1931; 1 son, Robert Evans. AB, U. Ala., 1930; LLB, Yale U., 1933. Bar: Tenn. Atty. A.A.A., 1933-34; atty., dir. Office Price Adminstrn., 1940-43; ptnr. Alderson & Sessions, mgmt. cons., Phila., 1945-58; pres. Edward Dalton Co. div., exec. v.p., dir., mem. exec. com. Mead Johnson & Co., 1958-62, sr. exec. v.p., vice chmn. bd. exec. com., 1962-64; pres. Robert E. Sessions, mgmt. counsel, 1964-76; pres. Krain & Canton Inc., 1965-68; chmn. bd. Esterbook Pen Co., 1967-68. Mem. Mayor's Pub. Bldg. Commn.; dir. Old Phila. Corp., inter-agy. com. for met. study. Decorated knight officer Order Merit (Italy). Mem. C. of C. Greater Phila. (pres.), Am. Mktg. Assn. (nat. award for contbn. field of theory in mktg., chmn. nat. awards program), Del. Valley Coun. (exec. com.), Am. Mgmt. Assn., Soc. for Advancement Mgmt., Assn. Cons. Mgmt. Engrs., Franklin Inst., Newcomen Soc., Merion Cricket, Phila. Country, Midday, Yale clubs. Democrat. Home: Haverford Pa. Died Jan. 30, 1981; buried Ch. of Redeemer yard, Bryn Mawr, Pa.

SETE, BOLA (DJALMA DE ANDRADE), guitarist; b. Rio de Janeiro, Brazil, July 16, 1923; s. Acacio and Hilda (Santos) de Andrade; m. Glada Anne Hurd, Feb. 17, 1971. M.Mus., Rio de Janeiro Conservatory of Music, 1945. Formed own mus. group, 1950, toured, S.Am., 1950-53, Europe, 1953-58, played in, P.R., 1959, with, Dizzy Gillespie band, 1962, formed new group, 1966, solo acoustical guitar concerts, 1971-87 , recs.: Lost Lake Records;, albums: Ocean, Jungle Suite, Dancing Cat Records, 1985. Named New Guitarist of Year, Down Beat mag. 1965, recipient European Film Festival award for best original music in a documentary film 1967, Cindy award 1968. Home: Marin City Calif. Died Feb. 14, 1987; cremated.

SETTLE, RAYMOND W., clergyman, writer; b. Pleasant Gap, Mo., Mar. 11, 1888; s. Charles Angelo and Emily Luvina (Rogers) S.; m. Mary Anna Lund, Aug. 25, 1914; children: Pauline Marie Settle Sharp, Marilyn Ray Settle Bricker. AB, William Jewell Coll., 1922. Ordained to ministry Baptist Ch., 1910. Pastor First Ch., Erie, Kans., 1912-13, Neodesha, Kans., 1913-15, Beaumont Ch., Kansas City, Mo., 1915-21, Prairie View and Drexel, Mo., chs., 1921-22, First Ch., Mt. Ayr, Iowa, 1922-23; pastor Slater, Mo., 1923-34, Lamar, Colo., 1935-42; pastor First Ch., Lexington, Mo.; then pastor South Fork (Colo.) Community Ch., Emanuel Chapel; chaplain Vets. Ctr. Author: March of the Mounted Riflemen, 1940, (with Mary L. Settle) Empire on Wheels, 1949, Story of Wentworth, 1949, (with Mary L. Settle) Saddles and Spurs: The Saga of the Pony Express, 1955, War Drums and Wagon Wheels, 1966; editorial writer Evangel. Sunday Sch. Lesson Commentary, 1955-62; also numerous articles. Moderator Lafayette County Baptist Assn., 1942-44; dir. Lexington C. of C., 1944-46; mem. Lexington Post-war Planning Commn., 1943; full time sec. Cameron C. of C.; mem. John Phelps Fruit Meml. Commn., 1944; mem. Tri-County Baptist Dist. Bd., 1943-44; pres. Lexington Ministerial Alliance, 1943-45; bd. mgrs. Colo. Bapt. Conv. YMCA, sec. World War, Great Lakes Naval Tng. Sta., Detroit Naval Tng. Sta. and Camp Grant, Rockford, Ill., 1918-19. Mem. Am. Pioneer Trails Assn., Mo. Writer's Guild (pres. 1929-30, award 1949), Mo. Hist. Soc., Mo. Baptist Hist. Soc., Kans. Hist. Soc., Colo. Hist. Soc., Colo. Authors League, SAR, Western History Assn., Masons, Kappa Sigma, Pi Kappa Delta. Democrat. Home: Monte Vista Colo. †

SEVERINGHAUS, JOHN WALTER, architect; b. Seymour, Ind., Dec. 20, 1905; s. Charles Edwin and Ida (Mock) S.; m. Helen Merrill Clark, July 24, 1943; children: John Merrill, Nancy Clark. A.B., Ohio Wesleyan U., 1928; B.Arch., Ohio State U., 1931, L.H.D., 1970. Archtl. designer Adams & Prentice, 1934-37; project mgr. Skidmore, Owings & Merrill, N.Y.C., 1937-42; asso. partner Skidmore, Owings & Merrill, 1946, gen. partner, 1949-75; former partner in charge Chase Manhattan Bank, Hdqrs., N.Y.C.; bd. dirs. N.Y. Bldg. Congress, 1962-64; mem. adv. bd. China Inst. Am., N.Y.C., 1975-78. Projects included Ford Central Staff Office Bldg., Deaborn, Mich., First City Nat. Bank Bldg., U.S. Air Bases, Morocco, Texaco Offices, Harrison, N.Y. Mem. Scarsdale (N.Y.) Bd. Edn., 1964-70; trustee YWCA, White Plains, N.Y. Served to maj. USAAF, 1942-46. Fellow AIA; mem. Am. Bible Soc. (bd. mgrs.), Phi Beta Kappa Assos., Phi Beta Kappa, Tau Beta Pi, Tau Sigma Delta, Alpha Sigma Phi. Methodist. Clubs: Univ. (N.Y.C.) (pres. 1975-78); Scarsdale (N.Y.) Golf. Home: Scarsdale N.Y. Died Oct. 16, 1987.

SEYFERTH, OTTO ADOLPH, gas company executive; b. Grand Rapids, Mich., Sept. 1, 1891; s. Fredric and Caroline Johanna S.; m. Alma Amanda Sundell, Aug. 15, 1912; children: Donald Fredric, James Roger, Thomas Herbert. Chmn. bd., dir. Westran Corp., Muskegon, Mich. Mgmt. mem. Mblzn. Adv. Bd., 1950. Mem. Muskegon C. of C. U.S. (pres. 1950-51, chmn. exec. com. 1952-53). Home: Muskegon Mich. †

SEYMOUR, ANNE, actress; b. N.Y.C., Sept. 11, 1909; d. William Stanley and May Davenport (Seymour) Eckert. Student, Am. Lab. Theatre Sch., N.Y.C., 1927-28. Profl. debut with the, Jitney Players, 1928; appeared in numerous plays, Broadway theatres, East Coast theatres, 1928-88 , including; A School for Scandal, 1931, The Wind and the Rain, 1936, The Romantic Young Lady, 1942, Sunrise at Campobello, 1958; appeared in west coast prodns. Medea, 1965, Ring Round the Moon, 1975, Close Ties, 1982; film debut as Lucy Stark in All the King's Men, 1949; film appearances include Whistle at Eaton Falls, 1951, Man on Fire, 1957, Desire Under the Elms, 1958, Handle with Care, 1958, Pollyanna, 1959, Home from the Hill, 1960, All the Fine Young Cannibals, 1960, Where Love Has Gone, 1964, Stage to Thunder Rock, 1964, How to Succeed in Business Without Really Trying, 1966, Blindfold, 1966, Mirage, 1967, Stay Away, Joe, 1968, Gemini Affair, 1974, Hearts of the West, 1975, Never-Never Land, 1981; radio performances include Grand Hotel, 1933; title role The Story of Mary Marlin, 1936-40, 41-44, A Woman of America, 1943, The Magnificent Montague, 1950; narrator My Secret Story, 1951; radio performances include Ford Mystery Theater, Cavalcade, Theatre Guild of the Air, Philip Morris Playhouse, Inner Sanctum, Somerset Maugham Playhouse, Studio One, Armstrong Theatre of Today, CBS Mystery Theatre, Heartbeat House, Fireside Playhouse; TV appearances include Tim Conway Show, Empire, Perry Mason, Emergency, Mr. Merlin, Cagney and Lacey; appeared in: numerous other TV films and series including The Honeymooners, Robert Montgomery Presents, Studio One, Police Woman, Police Story, Family Ties, T.J. Hooker, Remington Steel, Alfred Hitchcock Presents. Mem. AFTRA (nat. bd. dirs., v.p., sec. 1927-52, v.p. Chgo. chpt. 1927, dir. 1937-40, dir. N.Y.C. chpt. 1940-52), Am. Theatre Wing (bd. 1959-62), Plays for Living (bd. dirs. 1959-73), Plays for Living of So. Calif., Vets. Hosp. Radio and TV Guild (1st v.p. 1961), Actors Fund Am. (bd. dirs. West Coast, chmn. West Coast com. 1982), Episcopal Actors' Guild (dir. 1958-83), Theatre Authority (bd. dirs. West Coast 1977-81), Screen Actors Guild (nat. bd. dirs. 1973-81), ANTA (dir. 1974-77). Home: Studio City Calif. Died Dec. 8, 1988.

SHAARA, MICHAEL JOSEPH, JR., author; b. Jersey City, June 23, 1928; s. Michael Joseph and Florence Alleene (Maxwell) S.; m. Helen Elizabeth Krumwiede, Sept. 16, 1950 (div. June 1980); children: Jeffrey, Lila. B.S., Rutgers U., 1951; postgrad., Columbia U., 1952, U. Vt., 1953-54. Assoc. prof. English Fla. State U., Tallahassee, 1961-73; writer, producer, performer courses ednl. TV 1961-65. Recipient (Pulitzer Prize for fiction 1975); Author: The Broken Place, 1968, The Killer Angels, 1974, The Herald, 1981, Soldier Boy, 1982; Contbr. short stories, articles to Am., fgn. mags. Served with AUS, 1946-47. Recipient award for excellence in med. journalism A.M.A., 1966; Coyle Moore award for classroom excellence, 1967. Mem. AAUP, Internat. Platform Assn., Gold Key Honor Soc., Theta Chi, Omicron Delta Kappa. Home: Tallahassee Fla. Died May 5, 1988; buried Meadow Wood Cemetery, Tallahassee.

SHAHEEN, JOHN MICHAEL, oil company executive; b. Lee County, Ill., Oct. 24, 1915; s. Michael and Sadie (Saied) S.; m. Barbara Tracy, Apr. 21, 1951; children—Tracy, Michael, Bradford. Student, U. Ill., 1934-36, U. Chgo., 1937-38. Pres. Shaheen Natural Resources Co., Inc., N.Y.C., Macmillan Ring-Free Oil Co., Inc., N.Y.C., 1968-85, Golden Eagle Refining Co., Inc., N.Y.C., 1956-60; mem. U.S. Adv. Commn. on Info., 1971-77, Nat. Petroleum Council, 1970-77; spl. U.S. ambassador to Colombia, 1974. Vestryman St. Bartholomew's Episcopal Ch., N.Y.C. Served as capt., OSS USNR, 1941-45. Decorated Silver Star, Legion of Merit; recipient Outstanding Leadership in Energy Resources Devel. award ASME, 1974. Republican. Clubs: Union League, Met. Home: New York N.Y. Died Nov. 1, 1985.

SHAKLEE, FORREST CLELL, SR., nutritional researcher; b. Carlisle, Iowa, Nov. 27, 1894; s. Robert Lenz and Martha Jane (Overton) S.; student D.C. Palmer Coll., 1915; Ph.C., West Coast Chiropractic Coll., Oakland, Calif., 1931; D.D., Calif. Coll., 1933; D.D., Coll. Divine Metaphysics, Indpls., 1933; A.B., Am. Humanist SCh., 1949; Ph.D. in Psychology, Commonwealth U., Los Angeles, 1957; m. Ruth Alice Chapin, Dec. 15, 1915 (dec. 1941); children—Forrest Clell, Raleigh L.; m. 2d, Dorothy Eleanor Potter, Aug. 8, 1957. Pvt. practice as chiropractor, Rockwell City, Iowa, 1915-23, Mason City, Iowa, 1924-30, Oakland, 1931-43; ordained to ministry Ch. of Christ, 1929; pastor, Portland, Iowa, 1928-29; founder Shaklee Corp., Emeryville, Calif., 1956, pres., chmn. bd., 1956-72, chmn. bd., 1972-75, chmn. emeritus, 1975-85; cons. human relations, Oakland, 1941-57. Recipient Outstanding Achievement award Standard Chiropractic

Coll., San Jose, 1937, Spl. Recognition award Calif. Sec. State, 1968, Humanitarian award Nat. Health Fedn. Am., 1973, Ambassador of Good Will award Mayor of Chattanooga, 1977, numerous others. Mem. Hayward C. of C. (dir. 1965-66), Order Ky. Cols., Oakland Mus. Assn., Calif. Hist. Soc., Thoughtsmanship (founder, pres. 1947). Clubs: Masons; Shriners. Author: Thoughtsmanship Life's Questions and Answers, 1951; Thoughtsmanship for Well Being, 1951; Thoughtsmanship for the Salesman, 1951; Thoughtsmanship in Love and Marriage, 1951; Thoughtsmanship for the Bride, 1951; Shaklee Reference Treasure to Better Health Through Better Nutrition, 1960; Reflections on a Philosophy, 1973; When Nature Speaks: The Life of Forrest C. Shaklee, Sr. Died Dec. 15, 1985; buried Chapel of the Chimes, Oakland. Home: Castro Valley Calif.

SHAKMAN, JAMES GLIKAUF, brewing company executive; b. Chgo., Mar. 20, 1894; s. Adolph and Theresa (Glikauf) S.; m. Anne Gerbin, Mar. 26, 1927 (dec.). BS, Ill. Inst. Tech., 1914. Chemist st. dept. City Chgo., then Walter H. Flood Labs., 1915-16; test engr. Wis. Steel Co., South Chgo., 1916-17, Internat. Filter Co., Chgo., 1919-24; field engr. Foote Bros. Gear & Machine Co., Milw., 1925-27; joined Pabst Brewing Co., Chgo., 1928, asst. to v.p., 1928-30, v.p. in charge plant ops. and processing, dir., 1930-59. Mem. Am. Inst. Chem. Engrs., Am. Chem. Soc., ASME, Am. Soc. Brewing Chemists, Master Brewers Assn. Am., AAAS, Masons (32 deg.), Shriners, Jesters. Lt. U.S. Army, 1917-18; expert cons. Q.M.C., U.S. Army, 1944-45. Home: Seattle Wash. Died July 18, 1986.

SHANAHAN, ELWILL MATTSON, state official; b. Salina, Kans., Sept. 22, 1912; d. August G. and Adine (Peterson) Mattson; m. Paul R. Shanahan, Oct. 13, 1951 (dec. Apr. 1966); m. 2d, W. Keith Weltmer, July 11, 1976. Sec. of state State of Kans., Topeka, 1966-78, ret., 1978. Republican. Home: Salina Kans. Died Oct. 5, 1983; interred Topeka.

SHANDS, JOSEPH WALTER, banker; b. Bronson, Fla., Apr. 25, 1891; s. Thomas Walter and Coris Anne (Parker) S.; m. Mary Courtney Harris, Nov. 15, 1924; children: Susan Courtney Shands Murchison, Mary Ann Shands Bryan, Joseph Walter Jr. AB, U. Fla., 1911; LLB, Columbia U., 1914. Pvt. practice Gainesville, Fla., 1914-16; assoc. E.J. L'Engle, Jacksonville, Fla., 1919-25; ptnr. L'Engle and Shands, Jacksonville, 1926-36, L'Engle, Shands, McCarthy & Lane, Jacksonville, 1936-42; pres., dir. Atlantic Nat. Bank, Jacksonville, from 1942; bd. dirs. Pullman Co. Bd. dirs. Daniel Meml. Home for Children; bd. dirs., mem. exec. com. Fla. War Fund, Inc., 1943-44; state chmn, Victory Fund Com., 1942; regional mgr. Fla. War Fin. Com., 1943-45; past chmn. bd. dirs. Community War Chest Jacksonville and Duval County, Fla., pres., 1943; bd. dirs., pres. United Fund, Jackson and Duval County. 2d lt. inf. Fla. NG. Mex. Border Service, 1916-17; capt. inf. AEF, World War I. Mem. Fla. C. of C. (bd. dirs.), Jacksonville Area C. of C. (past dir.), Timuquasna Country Club (Jacksonville), River Club (Jacksonville), Ponte Vedra (Fla.) Beach Club, Kappa Alpha. Home: Jacksonville Fla. †

SHANKLIN, J. GORDON, lawyer, former government official; b. Elkton, Ky., Dec. 10, 1909; s. William S. and Eva J. (Jones) S.; m. Emily Shacklett, July 15, 1933; children—Elizabeth Eve, William Samuel. B.A., Vanderbilt U., 1932, LL.B., 1934. Bar: Tenn. bar 1934, Tex. bar 1975. With FBI, Washington, 1943-75; spl. agt. in charge FBI, Mobile, Ala., 1952-55, FBI (Pitts. office), 1955-56; insp. hdqrs. FBI (Pitts. office), Washington, 1956-58; spl. agt. in charge FBI (El Paso. (Tex.) office), 1958-59; spl. agt. in charge FBI (Honolulu office), 1959-63, Dallas, 1963-75; partner firm Johnson, Guthrie, Nash & Shanklin, Dallas, 1975-78, Johnson, Shanklin, Billings & Porter, Dallas, 1978-84; pvt. practice 1984-88; instr. various police acads. Recipient numerous profl. awards and citations from civil and police orgns. Baptist. Home: Dallas Tex. Died July 11, 1988; buried Sparkman-Hillcrest Cemetery, Dallas.

SHANKMAN, JACOB KESTIN, clergyman; b. Chelsea, Mass., Oct. 22, 1904; s. Isaac and Dina (Kestin) S.; m. Miriam C. Frankenstein, June 12, 1930; children: Judith Bess Shankman Kosak, Diane L. Shankman Panish, Michael David. BA, Harvard U., 1923, MA, 1925; BHL, Hebrew Union Coll., 1926, DD, 1955. Rabbi 1930; student rabbi Danville, Pa., 1926, Binghamton, N.Y., 1927, Portsmouth, Ohio, 1928-29; summer rabbi Kansas City, Mo., 1930; rabbi Congregation Berith Sholom, Troy, N.Y., 1930-37; rabbi Temple Israel, New Rochelle, N.Y., 1937-74, rabbi emeritus, 1974-86, elected to life tenure, 1967; mem. exec. com., chmn. com. on ch. and state; chmn. com. on mediation and ethics Cen. Conf. Am. Rabbis; co-chmn. rabbinic-congl. relationships commn; mem. exec. be. N.Y. Bd. Rabbis; Am. dir. World Union for Progressive Judaism, 1957-64, world pres., 1964-70. Chmn., Coun. Social Agys., Troy, 1937m New Rochelle, 1941-43; chmn. United Hebrew Charities, Troy, 1935-37, New Rochelle, 1942; mem. Human Rights Commn., New Rochelle, 1962-86, pres.'s adv. coun. Coll. New Rochelle; bd. dirs. New Rochelle Community Chest, Salvation Army Adv. Coun., Zionist Orgn. Am., NAACP; bd. govs. Hebrew Union Coll.-Jewish Inst. Religion. Lt. comdr. USNR, 1943-46. Recipient Civic Achievement award New Rochelle, 1962; named Community Chest Man of Yr., 1964. Mem. Westchester Coun. Rabbis (past pres.), Hebrew Union Coll. Jewish Inst. Religion Alumni Assn. (past pres.), Assn. Reform Rabbis N.Y. (past pres.). Home: New Rochelle N.Y. Died Feb. 4, 1986; buried Sharon Gardens, Westchester, N.Y.

SHANNON, HALL, physician, surgeon; b. Burleson, Tex., Dec. 26, 1889; s. J.C. and Rhoda (Jackson) S.; m. Mary Lucile Jordan, Dec. 25, 1917. MD, Baylor U., 1917. Diplomate Am. Bd. Med. Dirs. V.p., med. dir. Southland Life Ins. Co., Dallas, 1939-60, cons. med. dir., 1961-64, hon. med. dir., from 1965, also bd. dirs. Mem. exec. com. Dallas Civic Opera Co. With M.C., U.S. Army, World War I. Fellow ACS (life); mem. AMA, Am. Life Ins. Cos. Assn., Soc. Life Ins. Med. Dirs., Ins. Execs. Tex., Dallas C. of C., Masons. Presbyterian. Home: Dallas Tex. †

SHANNON, LARRY JOSEPH, chemical engineer; b. Williston, N.D., Apr. 10, 1937; s. Harold Joseph and Margaret Mary (Hannegrefs) S.; m. Angela Evans, June 22, 1957; children: Laura, Christina. B.S. in Chem. Engring., Seattle U., 1959; Ph.D., U. Calif., Berkeley, 1963. Sr. engr. United Tech. Corp., Sunnyvale, Calif., 1963-69; sr. engr. Midwest Research Inst., Kansas City, Mo., 1969-72; sect. head Midwest Research Inst., 1972-75, asst. div. dir., 1975, div. dir., 1977-79, exec. dir. engring. and applied scis. group, 1979-84; div. dir. solar heat research div. Solar Energy Research Inst., Golden, Colo., 1984-87; dir. S-G Metal Corp., Kansas City. Western Gear fellow, 1955-59; Dow Chem. fellow, 1960-61. Mem. AIAA, Air Pollution Control Assn., Sigma Xi. Home: Golden Colo. Died Aug. 26, 1987; buried Mt. Olivet Cemetery, Golden, Colo.

SHANNON, WILLIAM VINCENT, educator, former ambassador, former newspaperman; b. Worcester, Mass., Aug. 24, 1927; s. Patrick Joseph and Nora Agnes (McNamara) S.; m. Elizabeth McNelly, Aug. 5, 1961; children: Liam Anthony, Christopher Andrew, David Patrick. AB magna cum laude, Clark U., 1947, DLitt, 1964; MA, Harvard U., 1948; DLitt, New Rochelle Coll., 1971; LHD, Boston U., 1976, Stonehill Coll., 1982, U. Mass., 1987; LL.D., Sacred Heart U., Bridgeport, 1978. Free-lance writer Washington, 1949-51; Washington corr., columnist N.Y. Post, 1951-64; editorial bd. N.Y. Times, 1964-77; ambassador to Ireland 1977-81; Univ. prof. Boston U., 1981-88. Author: (with R.S. Allen) The Truman Merry-Go-Round, 1950, The American Irish, 1964, The Heir Apparent, 1967, They Could Not Trust The King, 1974; contbr. articles to mags. Bd. dirs. Am. Ireland Found. Recipient Page One award for nat. coverage N.Y. Newspaper Guild, 1951, Edward J. Meeman award for conservation writings Scripps-Howard Found., 1968, 76; Gold medal Am. Irish Hist. Soc., 1979; fellow in residence Center Study Democratic Instns., Santa Barbara, Calif., 1961-62; Alicia Patterson Fund fellow London, 1969-70. Mem. Phi Beta Kappa. Roman Catholic. Clubs: Century (N.Y.C.), The Tavern (Boston). Home: Brookline Mass. Died Sept. 27, 1988.

SHAPELY, FERN RUSK, curator; b. Mahomet, Ill., Sept. 20, 1890; d. William Humphrey and Anna Lucinda (Renner) Rusk; m. John Shapley, Sept. 19, 1918; children Dora Shapley Van Wijk, Ellen Shapely Fish. AB, U. Mo., 1913, AM, 1914, PhD (resident fellow), 1916, AFD, 1959. Fellow archeology Bryn Mawr Coll., 1914-15; European fellowship grantee 1915; asst. in art and archaeology U. Mo., 1916-17, asst. prof. art, summer 1925; rsch. asst. Nat. Gallery Art, Washington, 1943-47, curator paintings, 1947-56, asst. chief curator, 1956-60, curator paintings Samuel H. Kress Found., 1960-72. Author: George Caleb Bingham, The Missouri Artist, 1917, European Paintings from the Gulbenkian Collection, 1950, Paintings from the Samuel H. Kress Collection: Italian Schools, vol. 1, 1966, vol. 2, 1968, vol. 3, 1972; co-author: Comparisons in Art, 1957; contbr. articles to profl. jours. Mem. Phi Beta Kappa. Home: Washington D.C. †

SHAPIRO, SAMUEL HARVEY, lawyer, former gov. Ill.; b. Apr. 25, 1907; s. Joseph and Tillie (Bloom) S.; m. Gertrude Adelman, May 21, 1939. Student, St. Viator Coll.; J.D., U. Ill., 1929. Bar: Ill. bar 1929. With Shapiro & Lauridsen, Kankakee, 1969-87; city atty. Kankakee, 1933-35; state's atty. Kankakee County, 1936-40; mem. 65th-71st Ill. gen assemblies, chmn. public aid, health, welfare and safety com., 1959; lt. gov. Ill. 1960-68, gov., 1968-69; dir. Aetna State Bank, Chgo. Pres., Nat. Conf. Lt. Govs., 1960-62; chmn. Ill. Mental Health Commn. Past mem. Council on Improvement Econ. and Social Status Older People; past mem. Intergovtl. and Narcotics commns.; mem. Ill. Legis. Redistricting Commn., 1981; mem. nat. civil rights com. Anti-Defamation League.; Past sec., treas. Young Democratic Club Ill. Served with USNR, World War II. Named Man of Year Jewish Police Soc. Chgo., Man of Year Jewish Nat. Fund, 1968. Mem. Am., Ill., Chgo., Kankakee County bar assns., Kankakee C. of C., Musician's Union (past pres.), Kankakee Fedn. Labor (past pres.), Am. Legion, Amvets, Alpha Epsilon Pi (past nat. pres.), Moose, Kiwanian, Elk; mem. B'nai B'rith. Clubs: Country (Kan Ka Kee);. Home: Kankakee Ill. Died Mar. 16, 1987.

SHAPLEN, ROBERT MODELL, journalist, author; b. Phila., Mar. 22, 1917; s. Joseph and Sonia (Modell) S.; m. Martha Lucas, Apr. 10, 1953 (div. 1962); 1 son, Peter Lucas; m. June Herman, Mar. 31, 1962 (dec. Oct. 1982); children: Peter, Kate, Jason; m. Jayjia Hsia, June 1984. B.A., U. Wis., 1937; M.S. in Journalism, Columbia U., 1938; postgrad. (Nieman fellow), Harvard U., 1947-48. Reporter N.Y. Herald Tribune, 1937-43; S.W. Pacific War corr. Newsweek mag., 1943-45; Far East bur. chief Newsweek mag., Shanghai, 1945-47; writer Fortune mag., 1948-50; mem. fgn. staff Collier's mag., also fgn. corr. 15 newspapers, 1950-52; staff writer New Yorker mag., 1952-88; Far East corr. New Yorker mag., Hong Kong, 1962-78; Disting. vis. Marsh prof. communications U. Mich., 1980. Author: A Corner of the World, 1949, Free Love and Heavenly Sinners, 1954, A Forest of Tigers, 1956, Kreuger: Genius and Swindler, 1960, Toward the Wellbeing of Mankind: 50 Years of the Rockefeller Foundation, 1962, The Lost Revolution, 1965, Time out of Hand: Revolution and Reaction in the Southeast Asia, rev, 1970, The Road from War, rev., 1971; introduction to The Face of Asia, 1972, A Turning Wheel, 1979, Bitter Victory, 1986; also numerous articles, TV documentaries. Club: Harvard (N.Y.C). Home: Princeton N.J. Died May 15, 1988.

SHARP, DUDLEY CRAWFORD, manufacturing executive, former secretary of air force; b. Houston, Mar. 16, 1905; s. Walter Benona and Estelle (Boughton) S.; m. Tina Cleveland, Jan. 8, 1929; children: Dudley Crawford, Julia May. BS, Princeton U., 1927. With Mission Mfg. Co. (formerly Mission Sales Co.), 1927-87, v.p., 1927-35, exec. v.p., 1935-46, pres., 1946-55, chmn. bd., 1955-87; asst. sec. Air Force, 1955-59, under sec., 1959, sec., 1959-61. Former chmn. Harris County Republican party; trustee Colonial Williamsburg Fund; bd. dirs. Houston Lighthouse for Blind, Houston Planned Parenthood Ctr.; bd. visitors M.D. Anderson Hosp. and Tumor Inst.; chmn. Prairie View A. and M. Coll. Found. With USNR, 1942-45. Mem. Houston C. of C. Home: Houston Tex. Died May 17, 1987.

SHARP, GEORGE STEVENSON, surgeon; b. Cadiz, Ohio, Apr. 15, 1901; s. George Cunningham and Agnes (Stevenson) S.; m. Pauline Casebeer, Nov. 15, 1927 (div. 1952); children: George S., Paula Sharp; m. 2d. Cecilia Retinger. MD, Harvard U., 1927. Diplomate Am. Bd. Radiology. Intern Montreal Gen. Hosp., 1927-28; resident in surgery N.Y. Hosp., 1928-29; Rockefeller fellow Meml. Hosp., N.Y.C., 1929-32; assoc. prof. surgery U. So. Calif. Med. Sch., Los Angeles, 1945-50; prof. oral pathology Sch. Dentistry, 1950-70; founder, dir. Pasadena (Calif.) Found. for Cancer Rsch., 1952-88; vis. prof. U. Mex., 1940-88, U. Guadalahara, 1940-88; dir. Pasadena Tumor Inst.; hon. prof. surgery Sch. Medicine, Athens, Greece, 1962. Author: Oral Cancer and Tumors of Jaws; contbr. articles to med. jours. Mem. ACS, Ewing Soc. (pres. 1942-45), Head and Neck Sugeons (co-founder), Valley Hunt Club, Overland Club, Flintridge Riding Club (pres. 1965-67). Home: Laguna Beach Calif. Died Apr. 27, 1988.

SHARPLES, LAURENCE PRICE, association executive, manufacturing company executive; b. West Chester, Pa., Oct. 6, 1891; s. Philip M. and Helen E. (Brinton) S.; m. Rose-Vincent Lyon, June 24, 1934; children Laurence Price, Susan Brinton Abbot; m. 2d, Adrienne Kirby, 1964. AB, Swarthmore Coll., 1912. Pres. Sharples Milker Co., Phila., 1920-27; v.p. Sharples Corp., Phila., 1932-62; airplane pilot from 1930; winner Doherty Cup Fla. air race, 1934; chmn. bd. Aircraft Owners and Pilots Assn., from 1940; mem. Collier Award Com., 1942-44. Mem. bd. Franklin Inst., from 1962, Dunwoody Village, from 1973; hon. chmn. bd. Widener Colls., from 1972. 1st lt. Tank Corps, U.S. Army, World War I.; AEF, France. Mem. Philadelphia Club, Philadelphia Racquet Club, Merion Cricket Club (Haverford, Pa.), Courts Club (pres.1960, Wynnewood, Pa.), Merion Golf Club (Ardmore, Pa.). Home: Bryn Mawr Pa. †

SHARTEL, BURKE WOODS, law educator; b. Sedan, Kans., Jan. 9, 1889; s. John Wilford and Elfrieda (Woods) S.; m. Elisabeth Rott, June 15, 1920; 1 child, Marlou (Mrs. Brooks Crabtree). Student langs., France and Germany, 1909-10; AB, U. Mich., 1911, JD, 1913; SJD, Harvard U., 1919; JD honoris causa, U. Heidelberg, Fed. Republic Germany, 1953. Bar: Okla. 1913. With Shartel, Dudley & Shartel, Oklahoma City, 1913-17; asst. prof. U. Ill. Law Sch., 1919-20; mem. faculty U. Mich. Law Sch., 1920-59, prof., 1921-59, prof. emeritus; apptd. by Dept. State to deliver lectures on Am. law to German lawyers, 1951; guest prof. U. Heidelberg, summers 1951, 53, 55, U. Munich, 1958-59. Author: Our Legal System and How it Operates, 1951, Der Geist des Amerikanischen Rechts, 1951; co-author: The Law of Medical Practice, 1959, Readings in Legal Method, 1959; contbr. articles to profl. jours. With USN, 1918. Mem. ABA, Mich. State Bar Assn. Home: Ann Arbor Mich. †

SHAVER, ERWIN LEANDER, church official; b. Eau Claire, Wis., Dec. 1, 1890; s. Leander and Emma Isabel (Church) S.; m. Ellen Montgomery Griffiths, Aug. 3, 1915 (dec.); children: Doris (Mrs. G. B. Ouderkirk), Robert G.; m. Marjorie F. Kendall, June 21, 1943. AB, Lawrence Coll., 1913, AM, 1914; STB, Garrett Bibl. Inst., 1916; postgrad., Union Theol. Sem., 1917-20; AM,

Columbia U., 1918, postgrad., 1918-20; DD, Northland Coll., 1933. Ordained to ministry Congl. Ch., 1917. Pastor Rosendale and Genoa City, Wis., 1912-16; dir. religious edn. Decatur, Ill., 1916-17; pastor East Rockaway, N.Y., 1917-20; asst. in religious edn. Union Theol. Sem., N.Y.C., 1919-20; prof. religious edn. Hendrix Coll., Conway, Ark., 1920-22; dist. sec. Congl. Edn. Soc., Boston, 1922-26; sec. leadership edn. Bd. Home Missions, 1926-46, sec. weekday religious edn., from 1946; dir. weekday religious edn. Internat. Coun. Religious Edn., 1942-50; exec. dir. weekday religious edn. Nat. Coun. Chs., 1950-58; cons. Christian Edn. Dept. Mass. Coun. Chs., from 1958; instr. U. Chgo., summers, Boston U., Auburn Sch. Religious Edn., Reformed Theol. Sem. Author books on religious edn.; contbr. articles to religious jours. Mem. NEA (dept. suprs.), Religious Edn. Assn. Home: Waltham Mass. †

SHAW, HENRY OVERSTREET, transportation executive; b. Adel, Ga., Oct. 21, 1893; s. Archibald Hiram and Elizabeth (Overstreet) S.; m. Vivian Izona Riggs, June 19, 1920 (dec. May 1967); a dau., Sylvia Byron Blount; m. 2d, Mary H. Garnder, Apr. 28, 1971. Intensive course, U.S. Naval Acad., 1918. With Ga. Lumber & Supply Co. and Shaws Inc., Miami, Fla., 1914-29; v.p., treas. Ga. Lumber & Supply Co. and Shaws Inc., 1923-29; with Shaw Bros. Oil Co. and predecessor cos., Miami, 1916-61, chmn. bd. dirs. and exec. officer, 1950-61; land developer 1916-85; ptnr. Shaw Bros. Docks, Shaw Bros. Shipping Co., 1943-85; pres. Shaw Gold Coast Co., 1955-85; pres. Shaw Marine Co; owner Shaw Fgn. Trade Warehouse; pres. Fla. Fgn. Trade Zone Inc., 1969-85; bd. dirs. Fla. Nat. Bank & Trust Co. of Miami, Nat. Bank at Opa Locka. Bd. dirs. Hist. Assn. So. Fla.; mem. civilian aide com. of comdg. gen. Army Air forces, 1942; chmn. Dade Country Chpt. ARC war fund drive, 1942, dir. county chpt., 1942-43, vice chmn., 1943; pres. So. Atlantic and Fla. Ports Conf., 1945-47; chmn. Miami Rate and Traffic Bd., 1927-33, Port and Harbor Bd., 1937-38, 39; mem. Am. and Fla. petroleum industries coms., 1931-85, Fla. Gov.'s Spl. Com. on Freight Rates, 1940-45, citizens bd. U. Miami, 1946-85, pres. 1950. Ensign Supply corps USNRF, 1918-19. Mem. Miami C. of C. (pres. 1944-46), Greater Miami Traffic Assn., Internat. Platform Assn., Newcomen Soc., Masons (K.T., Shriner), Elks, Rotary. Home: Coral Gables Fla. Died Jan. 13, 1985; buried Miami Woodlawn Pk. Cemetery.

SHAW, IRWIN, author; b. N.Y.C., Feb. 27, 1913; s. William and Rose (Tompkins) S.; 1 son, Adam. A.B., Bklyn Coll., 1934. Drama critic New Republic, 1947-48. Author: plays Bury the Dead, 1936, Siege, 1937, The Gentle People, 1939, Quiet City, 1939, Retreat to Pleasure, 1941, Sons and Soldiers, 1943, The Assassin, 1945, (with Peter Viertel) The Survivors, 1948; books, collections of short stories Sailor Off the Bremen, 1940, Welcome to the City, 1942, Act of Faith, 1946; novel The Young Lions, 1948, The Troubled Air, 1950; (with Robert Capa) non-fiction The Face of Israel, 1950; novel Mixed Company, 1950, Lucy Crown, 1956; short stories Tip on a Dead Jockey, 1957, Selected Short Stories, 1959; novel Two Weeks in Another Town, 1959; play Children From Their Games, 1963; (with Robert Capa) travel In The Company of Dolphins, 1964; novel Voices of a Summer Day, 1965, Love on a Dark Street, 1965, Rich Man, Poor Man, 1970; short stories God Was Here But He Left Early, 1973; novel Evening in Byzantium, 1973, Nightwork, 1975; essays Paris! Paris!, 1977; novel Beggarman, Thief, 1977, Bread Upon the Waters, 1981; (with Robert Capa) Five Decades, 1978; novel The Top of The Hill, 1979, Acceptable Homes, 1982; Contbr. to mags. (Recipient O. Henry Meml. award 1944, 2d prize 1945). Served with AUS, 1942-45. Home: Klosters Switzerland. Died May 16, 1984.

SHAW, JAMES HOWARD, religious administrator, clergyman; b. Nova Scotia, Can., Dec. 1, 1910; s. Daniel and Emma (Huntley) S.; m. Ella von Helmolt, July 12, 1933; children: Beverly Louis Johnson, David Howard, Kenneth Reid. Student, U. N.B., Can., 1930-31; divinity diploma, N.E. Sch. Theology, 1933; ThB, Gordon Coll. theology and Missions, 1933-34, Div. Sch., 1942, Evang. Sem., 1948-49; DD, Aurora Coll., 1968. Ordained to ministry Advent Christian Ch., 1934. Pastor Newport Ctr., Vt., 1934-36, Schenectady, 1936-40, Providence, 1940-47; pastor Coll. Ch., Aurora, Ill., 1947-56; pastor Worcester, Mass., 1956-58, LaGrange, Ill., 1975-81; exec. sec. Advent Christian Gen. Conf. Am., 1958-75, S. Ga. and Fla. Conf. of Advent Christian Chs., 1981-85. Elective officer Advent Christian denomination 1943-60; adv. coun. Am. Bible Soc., 1959-75; bd. dirs. Aurora Coll., 1975-81. Mem. Am. Advent Mission Soc. (rec. sec., dir. 1957-58), R.I. Ministerial Assn. (chmn. dept. evangelism), Greater Worcester Counsc chs. Ministerial Assn., Aurora Ministerial Assn. (pres.), Greater Worcester Ministerial Assn. (pres.), LaGrange Ministerial Assn. (pres.), Rotary. Home: Live Oak Fla. Died May 12, 1986; buried Advent Christian Village, Dowling Pk., Fla.

SHAW, ROBERT NELSON, retail executive; b. Sault Ste. Marie, Mich., Jan. 23, 1912; s. Fred F. and Orpha L. (Lymburner) S.; m. Georgina L. Karlson, June 23, 1937; 1 son, Frederick A. AB, U. Mich., 1934, MBA, 1935. With Merc. Stores Co., Wilmington, Del., 1935-78; v.p. Glass Block Store, Duluth, Minn., 1947-48; pres., gen. mgr. McAlpin Co., Cin., 1948-64, exec. v.p., bd. dirs. parent co., 1962-64, pres. parent co., 1964-72, chmn. bd., chief exec. officer, 1972-75, also bd. dirs., cons.; bd. dirs. Kroger Co., Cin., Cin. Retail Merchants, pres., 1956; pres. Cin. Credit Bur., 1958; chmn. bd., 1959-64; bd. dirs. Cin. Unltd., Cin. Property Owners. Lt. USNR, 1944-46. Mem. Cin. C. of C., Navy League, Internat. Platform Assn., Newcomen Soc., Masons, Shriners, N.Y. Athletic Club, Union League, Kenwood Country Club, Old Pueblo Club, Skyline Country Club, Le Mirador Country Club, Theta Xi. Home: Tucson Ariz. Deceased.

SHAW, WILLIAM HENRY, educator; b. Durham, N.C., Aug. 6, 1902; s. Calvin High and Ora Mozelle (Bevers) S.; m. Mary Louise Carlton, June 1, 1929; children: William Henry, Carlton Reed. BA, Duke U., 1928, MEd, 1929; EdD, Auburn U., 1963. Tchr. Durham County (N.C.) schs., 1924-26, prin., 1926-30; prin. Neehham Broughton High Sch., Raleigh, N.C., 1930-38; supt Sumter (S.C.) City Schs., 1938-45; supt. edn. Muscogee County Sch. Dist., Columbus, Ga., 1945-73; prof. ednl. adminstrn. Columbus (Ga.) Coll., from 1973. Trustee Nat. Inf. Mus. of Ft. Benning, 1970-75; bd. dirs. Mus. Arts and Crafts, Columbus, 1950-75, Columbus YMCA, from 1974. Mem. Ga. Edn. Assn. (pres. 1955-56), Columbus Execs. (pres. 1947), Columbus C. of C. (life mem., dir. 1970-73), Am. Assn. Sch. Adminstrs. (life), NEA (life), Rotary (dist. gov. 1944-45), Phi Beta Kappa, Kappa Delta Pi, Phi Delta Kappa. Methodist. Home: Columbus Ga. Deceased.

SHEAFFER, JOSEPH GUY, business executive; b. Pitts., July 13, 1892; s. Charles Miller and Margaret V. (Culp) S. ME, Cornell U., 1916. Various positions from apprentice to div. supt. Pa. R.R., 1916-36; v.p. St. Louis Stockyards, Ill., 1936-42, pres., 1942-58, dir., from 1936, chmn. bd., from 1958; v.p., dir. East St. Louis Junction R.R. Co., 1936-42, pres., 1942-58, dir., from 1942, chmn. bd., from 1958; bd. dirs. Nat. Stockyards, Nat. Bank. Dir. Boys Club of St. Louis. Lt. 19th Engrs., 1917-19. Mem. Pa. Scotch-Irish Soc., Newcomen Soc. Am., Masons, Athletic Club, Glen Echo Country (St. Louis), Merion (Pa.) Cricket, Delta Kappa Epsilon. Republican. Presbyterian. Home: Saint Louis Mo. †

SHEARMAN, THOMAS BROADUS, newspaper publisher; b. Olympia, Wash., June 27, 1893; s. William Hugh and Caledonia Martha (Pyott) S.; m. Flora Kate Inglis, June 27, 1920; children—William Hugh, Margery, Thomas Broadus, Virginia. Student, U. Wis., 1910, 14. Advt. solicitor Chgo. Tribune, 1914-17, 19-44; pub. Roswell (N.Mex.) Record, Hobbs (N.Mex.) News Sun, Trinidad (Colo.) Chronicle News, from 1944, Lake Charles (La.) Am. Press; oil and gas operator. Served to lt. U.S. Army, 1917-19. Recipient citations U. Wis., citations Lake Charles Meml. Hosp., citations St. Patrick's Hosp. of Lake Charles. Baptist. Home: Lake Charles La. Died Apr. 4, 1988.

SHEATS, PAUL HENRY, educator; b. Tiffin, Ohio, Dec. 5, 1907; s. Edward Hamlin and Katherine Ann (Koch) S.; m. Dorothea Burns, 1929; 1 son, Paul Douglas; m. Helen Johnson Taylor, Nov. 21, 1942 (div. June 1967); children: Peter Warren, Michael Clarron; stepchildren: Vern Taylor, Marion; m. June Maseeger Dow, June 16, 1967. A.B., Heidelberg Coll., Tiffin, 1929; A.M., Columbia U., 1930; Ph.D., Yale U., 1936; LL.D., U. Akron, 1966. Instr. govt. N.Y. State Coll. for Tchrs., Albany, 1930-34; instr. dept. edn. Yale U., 1934-36; dir. Fed. Forum Project, Chattanooga, 1936-37; adminstrn. asst. Fed. Forum Demonstration, U.S. Office Edn., 1937-39; asst. prof. edn. U. Wis., 1939-42; head adult edn. sect. OWI, 1942-43; dir. New Tools for Learning, N.Y.C., 1943-44; ednl. dir. Town Hall, Inc., N.Y.C., 1944-46; assoc. dir. Univ. Extension, U. Calif., 1946-57, dir., 1957-58, univ. dean, 1958-67; assoc. prof. edn. UCLA, 1946-49; prof. edn. U. Calif., 1949-75, prof. emeritus, 1975-84; vis. prof. edn. U. Judaism, 1976, 77; adj. prof. adult edn. Tchrs. Coll. Columbia U., 1982; Kellogg resident fellow Oxford U. Extra-Mural Delegacy, spring 1967; cons. Ford Found. Fund Adult Edn., 1951, Coahoma Jr. Coll., Clarksdale, Miss., 1980; sr. cons. So. Regional Edn. Bd., 1970-73; adv. com. on adult edn. Calif. Dept. Edn., 1968-70; mem. UNESCO Nat. Commn., 1950-56, vice chmn. exec. com., 1954-56; U.S. del. UNESCO conf adult edn., Elsinore, Denmark, 1949, Montreal, 1960; U.S. del. UNESCO conf adult edn. (7th Gen. Conf.), Paris, 1952; mem. Pres.'s Panel on Vocat. Edn., 1961-62; chmn. AID Evaluation Panel for World Edn., 1973. Author: (with R.W. Frederick) Citizenship Education Through the Social Studies, 1936, (with J.W. Studebaker, C.S. Williams) Forums for Young People, 1937, Education and the Quest For a Middle Way, 1938, Forums on the Air, 1939, (with R. Spence, C. Jayne) Adult Education, 1953, (with James Farmer, J. David Deshler) Developing Community Service and Continuing Education Programs in California Higher Education Institutions, 1972, Developing Community Services in the Seventies: New Roles for Higher Education, 1975; editor: Adult Edn. Bull., 1940-42; editorial bd.: Lifelong Learning, The Adult Years, 1977-79; contbr.: Foundations of Education (Kneller), 1963, 67, 70, Handbook of Adult Education in the U.S., 1960, Materials and Methods in Adult Education, 1972, 76, 83. Bd. dirs. Nat. Tng. Labs., 1961-64; chmn. bd. dirs. Internat. Coll., 1970-72; adv. bd. trustees City U. Los Angeles, 1979-84 . Recipient Delbert Clark award, 1970; Los Angeles Human Relations Commn. cert. of merit, 1979. Fellow Nat. Univ. Extension Assn. (dir. 1958-64, pres. 1962-63, Julius M. Nolte award 1975); mem. NEA (pres. dept. adult edn. 1942-44), Am. Ednl. Research Assn., Adult Edn. Assn. U.S. (pres. 1953-54), Assn. State Univs. and Land Grant Colls. (exec. com. 1963-66), UCLA Emerti Assn. (pres. 1977-78). Club: Faculty. Home: Los Angeles Calif. Died Aug. 12, 1984.

SHEETZ, WALTER FRANKLIN, corporation executive; b. Columbus, Ohio, Aug. 5, 1891; s. Frank and Wealthy A. (Neff) S.; m. Estelle Rohe, June 9, 1939. Student pub. schs.; LHD, Laurence Inst. Tech., 1959. Salesman R.C. Mahon Co., Detroit, 1912-16, sec., 1916-28, v.p., 1928-55, chmn. Mem. Engring. Soc. Detroit, Detroit Athletic Club, Recess Club, Union League, Engineers Club, Key Largo Anglers Club. Home: Detroit Mich. †

SHELDON, ROBERT BURNETT, psychiatrist; b. Silsbee, Tex., Sept. 6, 1924; s. Robert Burnett and Mamie Parker (Craiglow) S.; m. Marion LaVelle McSpedden, Aug. 22, 1953; children: Susan, Martha, George, Patti. BA, U. Tex., 1950; MD, Southwestern Med. Sch., Dallas, 1954. Cert. Am. Bd. Psychiatry and Neurology. Intern VA Hosp., Houston, 1954-55; pvt. practice medicine and surgery Beaumont, Tex., 1955-61; resident in psychiatry Baylor U. Coll. Medicine Hosp., Houston, 1961-64; pvt. practice specializing in psychiatry Houston, 1964-68; exec. dir. Waco-McLennan County Mental Health-Mental Retardation Ctr., Waco, Tex., 1969-71; chief psychiatry and neurology svc. Tex. Dept. Corrections, Huntsville, Tex., 1971-72; dir. outpatient svcs. then chief psychiat. svcs. Big Spring (Tex.) State Hosp., 1975-85; spl. cons. Dallas regional office NIMH. Author articles, chpt. in book. With USAAF, 1943-46, comdr. USNR, 1961-77. Mem. Am., So. Tex. med. assns., Cherokee County (pres. 1977) med. socs., Am. Psychiat. Assn., Am. Coll. Legal Medicine, Am. Assn. Psychiatry and Law, Am. Acad. Forensic Scis., Am. Correctional Assn., Am. Geriatric Soc., Lions, Rotary, Shriners. Democrat. Baptist. Home: Rusk Tex. Died Aug. 14, 1985.

SHELDON, WALTER MOORE, insurance executive; b. Evanston, Ill., Oct. 14, 1892; s. Frank Parmalee and Lulu (Moore) S.; m. Laura Hill, Jan. 15, 1937; children: Helenanne (Mrs. Jordan), John Cochran Bryan (dec.), Hedley, Nancy (Mrs. Cassiday), Walter Moore. Student pub. schs., Hinsdale, Ill. With Fireman's Fund Ins. Co., 1909-18, 19; with W.A. Alexander & Co., from 1919, v.p., 1935-48, exec. v.p., 1948-59, pres., 1960-61, ins. broker, from 1961. With AUS, 1918. Mem. Nat. Assn. Casualty and Surety Agts. (pres. 1959-60), Nat. Assn. Ins. Agts. (exec. com. 1947-49, v.p. 1951-52, pres. 1952-53), Chgo. Bd. Underwriters (past pres.), Am. Legion (past comdr.), Masons, Union League, Golf Club, Everglades Club. Home: Hinsdale Ill. †

SHELLENBERGER, JOHN ALFRED, biochemist; b. Moline, Ill., Jan. 8, 1900; s. Wilbur F. and Jennie A. (Johnston) S.; m. Annabel F. Gangnath, June 3, 1939; children: Karen, Joan, Margo. B.S., U. Wash., 1928; M.S., Kans. State U., 1929; Ph.D., U. Minn., 1939. Asst. prof. U. Idaho, Moscow, 1929-32; instr. U. Minn., Mpls., 1932-39; head biochemistry div. Rohm & Haas Co., Phila., 1939-42; head dept. grain sci. Kans. State U., Manhattan, 1944-70, disting. prof. biochemistry, 1970-87; cons. Govt. Argentina, 1942-44, U.S. Dept. State, 1948-51, U.S. Dept. Agr., 1952-56. Author: Bread Science and Technology, 1971. Named Disting. Alumnus U. Minn., 1966; recipient Neumann medal German Cereal Industry, 1969, Gold medal Assn. Operative Millers, 1960. Fellow AAAS; mem. Internat. Assn. Cereal Chemists (pres. 1962-64 C.H. Bailey award), Am. Chem. Soc., Am. Assn. Cereal Chemists (pres. 1950-55), Inst. Food Tech. Club: Country (Manhattan). Lodge: Rotary. Home: Manhattan Kans. Died Aug. 14, 1987; buried Sunset Cemetery, Manhattan, Kans.

SHEPARD, NORMAN ARTHUR, chemical research executive; b. New Haven, Apr. 8, 1890; s. Arthur Lewis and Gizela (Berger) S.; m. Jessie Olive Male, June 19, 1913; children: Berger Male, Louise Male (Mrs. Robert A. Hull Jr.), Molly Elizabeth (Mrs. Molly Wrightington). PhB, Yale U., 1910, PhD, 1913. Instr. chemistry Yale U., 1913-17, asst. prof., 1917-19; dir. organic chem. rsch. Firestone Tire & Rubber Co., 1919-25, dir. chem. rsch., 1925-35; dir. tech. svc. Am. Cyanamid Co., 1936-41, chem. dir., 1941-55; tech. cons. Baruch Survey Com., 1942, Navy Rubber Survey Com., 1942-43, Office of Rubber Dir., 1943-44; cons. self-sealing fuel cells USN, 1942-45; ttech. cons. WPB, 1942; mem. com. on Quartermaster problems, 1943-51; mem. adv. com. on plastics Sch. Engring., Princeton U., 1949-58; mem. com. on equipment and materials R&D Bd., Nat. Mil. Establishment, 1949-52, chmn., 1953; mem. tech. adv. panel on materials Office of Asst. Sec. Def., 1954-56; mem. div. engring. and indsl. rsch. NRC, 1950-58, mem. materials adv. bd., 1957-59, engring. manpower com. Engrs. Joint Coun., 1951-61; chmn. bd. Conn. Coun. Sci. Edn., Inc., 1962-65; treas. TEAM, Inc., from 1960. Contbr. articles in field to profl. jours. Cons., trustee Dorr Found. Fellow Am. Inst. Chemists, N.Y. Acad. Scis.; mem. AAAS, Am. Chem. Soc. (chmn. rubber div. 1935-36), Am. Inst. Chem. Engrs., Indsl.

Rsch. Inst. (pres. 1947-48), Soc. Chem. Industry, N.E. Assn. Chemistry Tchrs., Sigma Xi, Alpha Chi Sigma, Chemists Club, Graduate Club. Home: Stamford Conn.†

SHEPARD, TRENT ALLEN, insurance company executive; b. Normal, Ill., May 20, 1920; s. Lawrence Freeman and Mildred (Oster) S.; m. Myra Jane Rodgers, Dec. 5, 1948; children: Trent Allen, Karen Jane, Gregory Mark, Tracy Morgan. BS in Econs., U. Ill., 1942, LLB, 1945. Bar: Ill. 1946. CLU. Pres., trustee Union Automobile Indemnity Assn., Bloomington, Ill., 1952-85, Prairie State Farmers Ins. Assn., Bloomington, 1952-85; pres., treas., dir. Union Ins. Exchange, Bloomington, 1952-85; founder, pres., chmn. bd. Am. Union Life Ins. Co., Bloomington, 1961-85, Am. Diversified Investors Fund Inc., Bloomington, 1964-85; pres., treas., dir. Farmers Deposit Co., Bloomington; founder, pres., treas. Mid-Am. Fin. Corp., also bd. dirs. Bd. dirs. Bloomington YMCA, Bloomington United Way Fund, Bloomington chpt. Am. Cancer Soc., Brokaw Hosp., Normal. With inf. AUS, 1942-44. Mem. Ill. Bar Assn., Chartered Property and Casualty Underwriters, Chartered Life Underwriters. Mem. Christian Ch. (bd. dirs.). Home: Bloomington Ill. Died Nov. 1, 1985; buried Park Hill Cemetery, Bloomington, Ill.

SHEPLEY, JAMES ROBINSON, communications executive; b. Harrisburg, Pa., Aug. 16, 1917; s. Charles Laurence and Jean (Robinson) S.; m. Jean Stevens, Mar. 27, 1937; children: Steven, Jean Lucile, James, Lynn Hammond; m. Yvonne Hudson, 1 child, Genoa Laurence. Student, Dickinson Coll., 1935-37, LittD, 1959; DSc, Clarkson Coll. Tech., 1966. Corr. Pitts. Press, 1937; Pa. legis. corr. UPI, 1937-40, Washington corr., 1940-42; Washington corr. Time mag., 1942, fgn. policy corr., 1946-48; war corr. Time and Life mags, CBI, S.W. Pacific Theatre, ETO, 1942-44; chief Washington corr. Time and Life mags, 1948-57, chief corr. for U.S. and Can. news svc., 1957-60; asst. pub. Life mag., 1960-63; pub. Fortune mag., 1964-67, Time mag., 1967-69; pres. Time, Inc., 1969-80, chmn. exec. com., 1980-82; chmn. bd. Washington Star; U.S. staff officer at Potsdam Conf., 1945; collaborator Gen. Marshall's ofcl. report World War II, 1945; attache to Chief of Staff Gen. G.C. Marshall, 1945-46; attache to spl. presdl. envoy to China, 1946. Co-author: The Hydrogen Bomb. Capt. USAR, 1946-50; maj. USAFR. Awarded War Dept. Letter of Commendation. Mem. Manhasset Bay Yacht Club, F St. Club, Metropolitan Club, N.Y. Yacht Club, Nat. Press Club, Conquistadores del Cielo, Storm Trysail Club, Cruising Club of Am. Died Nov. 2, 1988.

SHER, DAVID, lawyer; b. Omaha, Jan. 27, 1908; s. Philip and Rebecca (Saxe) S.; m. Phyllis Tulin, Nov. 30, 1934; 1 son, Michael. BS, Harvard U., 1928, LLB, 1931. Bar: N.Y. 1932. Asst. to gen. counsel Gen. Motors Corp., 1931-46; ptnr. Stroock & Stroock & Lavan, N.Y.C., from 1946; bd. dirs. Tosco Corp. Pres. Jewish Family Service N.Y.; chmn. Nat. Community Relations Adv Coun.; chmn. publ. com. Commentary mag.; chmn. bd. Community Coun. Greater N.Y.; assoc. chmn. bd. N.Y. Fedn. Jewish Philanthropies; chmn. exec. com. Internat. Rescue Com. Mem. Am. Coun. on Germany, Am. Soc. for Technion (v.p), Harmonie Club, Lotos Club, Century County Club (N.Y.C.). Home: New York N.Y. Deceased.

SHERER, ALBERT WILLIAM, JR,, foreign service officer; b. Wheaton, Ill., Jan. 16, 1916; s. Albert William and Linda (Van Nostran) S.; m. Carroll Russell, Oct. 24, 1944; children: Peter, Susan, Anthony. AB, Yale U., 1938; LLB, Harvard U., 1941. Fgn. svc. officer 1946-75; assigned Tangier, Morocco, 1946-49, Budapest, Hungary, 1949-51, Office Ea. European Affairs, Dept. State, 1951-54, 57-61; 1st sec. Prague, Czechoslovakia, 1955-57; dep. chief of mission Warsaw, Poland, 1961-66; fgn. svc. insp. Dept. State, Washington, 1966-87; ambassador to Togo,1967-68, to Togo and Equatorial Guinea, 1968-70, to Republic of Guinea, 1970-72, to Czechoslovak Socialist Republic,1972-75; chief U.S. del. to Conf. Security and Cooperation Europe, 1974-75; dep. rep. of U.S. to UN Security Coun., 1975-87. With USAAF, 1941-45. Home: Greenwich Conn. Died Jan. 24, 1987; buried Greenwich, Conn.

SHERIF, MUZAFER, social psychologist, author; b. Ödemis, Izmir, Turkey, July 29, 1906; s. Serif and Emine Basoglu; m. Carolyn Wood, Dec. 29, 1945; children: Sue, Joan, Ann. BA, Am. Internat. Coll., Izmir, Turkey, 1927; MA, Istanbul U., 1929, Harvard U., 1932; PhD, Columbia U., 1936. Rsch. fellow Princeton U., 1945-47, Yale U., 1947-49; prof., dir. Inst. Group Relations U. Okla., 1949-66, rsch. prof. psychology, on leave, 1965-66; vis. prof. program for excellence U. Tex., 1958-59; Ford vis. prof. U. Wash., Settle, 1960; Disting. vis. prof. Pa. State U., 1965-66, prof. sociology, 1966-72, emertius, 1972-88. Author: An Outline of Social Psychology, rev. edit., 1956, Reference Groups, 1964, Social Judgment, 1965, Groups in Harmony in Tension, 1965, The Psychology of Ego-Involvments, 1965, Psychology of Social Norms, 1965, Attitude and Attitude Change, 1965, In Common Predicament, 1966, Social Interaction: Process and Products, 1967, Social Psychology, 1969; contbr. numerous articles to profl. jours. Recipient Kurt Lewin Meml. award, 1967. Fellow Am. Psychol. Assn. (coun. civ. 9, 1963-65, Disting Contbn. award 1968), Am. Sociol. Assn.; mem. Sigma Xi. Home: Fairbanks Alaska. Died Oct. 16, 1988.

SHERIFF, HILLA, physician; b. Easley, S.C., May 29, 1903; d. John Washington and Mary Lenora (Smith) S.; m. George Henry Zerbst, July 10, 1940 (dec.). Student, Coll. Charleston (S.C.), 1920-22; MD, Med. U. S.C., Charleston, 1926; MPH, Harvard U., 1937; LHD (hon.), Coll. Charleston, 1985. Diplomate: Am. Bd. Preventive Medicine. Intern Hosp. of Woman's Med. Coll., Phila., 1926-27, Children's Hosp., Washington, 1928-29, Willard Parker Contagious Disease Hosp., N.Y.C, 1929; practice pediatrics Spartanburg, S.C., 1929-33; dir. Spartanburg County Health Dept., 1933-40; med. staff Spartanburg Gen. Hosp.; med. dir. Am. Women's Hosp. Units, Spartanburg and Greenville Counties, S.C., 1931-36; med. dir. research study in, Spartanburg County, S.C.; for Milbank Meml. Fund, N.Y.C., 1935-39; asst. dir. div. maternal and child health S.C. Dept. Health and Environ. Control, Columbia, 1940-41, dir., 1941-74, chief bur. community health services, asst. state health officer, 1968-73; dep. commr. personal health services, past dir. crippled children's services; clin. prof. pediatrics Med. U. S.C., from 1972; clin. prof. pediatrics, preventive medicine and community health U. S.C. Sch. Medicine, from 1985. Mem. S.C. State Youth Conservation Com., chmn. health and med. care sub com.; rep. from S.C. to White House Conf., 1940, 50, 60; mem. State Adv. Com. on Adult Edn., 1947; Mem. S.C. Council for Handicapped Children, Gov.'s Interagy. Council on Mental Retardation Planning; chmn. S.C. State Nutrition Com.; bd. dirs. Winthrop Coll. Found., Rock Hill, S.C. Recipient Meritorious award S.C. Mental Health Assn., 1972, Disting. Alumnus award Med. Alumni Assn., 1981, Outstanding State Employee award S.C. State Employees Assn., 1974, Sims award S.C. Dept. Health and Environ. Control, 1974, award S.C. Hosp. Assn., 1975, 86; Wm. Weston Disting. Service award U. S.C. Sch. Medicine, 1983; named to Order of Palmetto Gov. S.C.; honored in career documentary Carrying Helath to the County, by U. S.C. Sch. Medicine, Dept. Preventive Medicine and Community Health and Dept. Pediatrics. Fellow Am. Pub. Health Assn. (council mem. maternal and child health sect., Ross award 1969), Am. Acad. Pediatrics (chpt. pres. 1972, Career Achievement award 1986), Assn. State Maternal and Child Health and Crippled Children's Dirs. (pres. 1960-62), Am. Assn. Pub. Health Physicians, Columbia Med. Soc. (v.p. 1962), Am. Med. Women's Assn. (2d v.p. 1946); mem. Am., So., S.C. med. assns., S.C. Pub. Health Assn. (pres. 1947), Pan Am. Med. Women's Alliance; Fellow S.C. Obstetrical and Gynecol. Soc. (hon. mem.); mem. S.C. Pediatric Soc. (sec.-treas. 1941-46, pres. 1972-73, Career Achievement award 1986), S.C. Mental and Social Hygiene Soc. (pres. 1948-49), S.C. Thoracic Soc., S.C. Conf. Social Work, Delta Kappa Gamma, Alpha Epsilon Iota. Episcopalian. Clubs: S.C. (Columbia), Federation of Women's (Columbia), Business and Professional Women's (Columbia) (charter mem. Spartanburg club), Survey (Columbia); Harvard of S.C. (sec.-treas. 1977-79). Home: Columbia S.C. Died Sept. 10, 1988, buried Greenlawn Meml. Park, Columbia, S.C.

SHERMAN, RONALD KING, advertising agency executive; b. N.Y.C., Aug. 28, 1933; s. Harry and Sylvia (Glasser) S.; m. Wendy Joan Kupsick, May 13, 1962; children—Derek, Samantha. B.A., Princeton U., 1955; M.B.A., Columbia U., 1957. Account rep. J. Walter Thompson Co., N.Y.C., 1957-60; asst. to pres., dir. pub. relations Kayser Roth Corp., N.Y.C., 1960-63; with J. Walter Thompson Co., 1964-82; sr. v.p., group mgmt. supr. J. Walter Thompson Co., Detroit, 1973-75; exec. v.p., gen. mgr. J. Walter Thompson Co., N.Y.C., 1975, pres. Eastern div., 1977-80, dir., 1977-82, pres. entertainment div., 1980-82; pres. dir. Wells, Rich, Greene Worldwide, N.Y.C., 1982-86; vice chmn. Wells, Rich, Greene, Inc., N.Y.C., 1986; pres. Calet, Hirsch and Spector, N.Y.C., 1987-88; bd. dirs. Ross Roy Group, Inc. Chmn. Internat. Film and TV Festival N.Y., N.Y.C., 1984-87. Mem. Am. Assn. Advt. Agys. (client services com.). Home: New York N.Y. Died Sept. 10, 1988.

SHERMAN, VERNON WESLEY, electrical engineer; b. Oscoda, Mich., Apr. 7, 1907; s. Henry C. and Mabel (Nolan) S.; m. June Roach, Sept 2, 1930; children: Nola Marie, Vernon Clayton; m. Helen L. McNair, July 28, 1948; 1 son, Vernon Wesley. AB, Coll. City of Detroit, 1931; BS in Mech. Engring., Wayne U., 1937, MS in Elec. Engring., 1941; BS in Edn., Cen. Mich. U., 1964. Registered profl. engr., Mich., N.J. Asst. to supt. Gen. Elec. Co., Detroit, 1925-33; project engr. Chrysler Corp., Detroit, 1933-42; mgr. indsl. electronics div. Fed. Telephone & Radio Corp., Newark, 1942-45; pres., chief engr. Sherman Indsl. Electronics Co., Belleville, N.J., 1945-58; gen. mgr. Sherman Indsl. Electronics div. Engring. Design Inc., State College, Pa., 1958-59; prop. Lake City Marine, Mich., 1959-64; tchr. math. and sci. dept. Manton (Mich.) High Sch., 1964-72. Author several tech. papers including Thin Case Hardening with Radio Frequency Energy, 1943, Electronic Heating of Food, 1944, Dehydration of Food, 1944, Electronic Heating of Preforms, 1944, Case Hardening by Megacycle Induction Heat, 1944, New Induction Heater,1950, Passive Solar Heating, 1980; contbr. to New Voices in American Poetry, 1977, 78, 79, 80; holder of 23 patents granted or applied for in field of high frequency induction and dielec. heating. Chmn. bd. Civilian Def. Communications, Belleville, 1953-57. Recipient War Dept. Atomic Bomb cert., 1945, Disting. Alumnus award Coll. Engring. Wayne State U., 1958; Order of Engr., 1974. Mem. Am. Soc. for Metals, Quarter Century Wireless Assn. (life mem.), Mich. Soc. Profl. Engrs. (edn. com. 1969-71, pres. No. chpt. 1974-75), IEEE (sr. mem., bd. editors 1943-54, mem. indsl. electronics com. 1946-48), Am. Assn. Physics Tchrs., Nat. Coun. Tchrs. Math. (life mem.), Kiwanis, Epsilon Sigma. Presbyterian. Home: Manton Mich. Died Sept. 16, 1983; buried Caldwell Twp. Cemetery, Mich.

SHERRILL, MARY LURA, college professor; b. Salisbury, N.C., July 14, 1888; d. Miles Osborne and Sarah Rosanna (Bost) Sherrill. AB, Randolph-Macon Woman's Coll., 1909, AM, 1911; PhD, U. Chgo., 1923; DSc (hon.), Womens Coll. of U. of N.C., 1948. Instr. chemistry Randolph-Macon Woman's Coll., 1911-16, adj. prof., 1916-18; assoc. prof. chemistry N.C. Coll. for Women, 1918-20; asst. prof. chemistry Mt. Holyoke Coll., 1921-24, assoc. prof., 1924-30, prof. chemistry, 1930-54, emeritus, chmn. dept., from 1954; rsch. worker U. Brussels, 1928-29 as holder of Com. for Relief in Belgium Ednl. Found. fellowship, also in Brussels, Oxford, Eng. and Vienna, 1936. Contbr. scientific articles to chem. publs. Trustee Randolph-Macon Woman's Coll. from 1954. Served as assoc. chemist CWS, Edgewood Arsenal, 1920-21. Fellow AAAS; mem. Am. Chem. Soc. (councillor 1940-43, sec. Conn. Valley sect. 1925-28, chmn. 1931-33; recipient James Flack Norris award Northeastern Sect. 1957, Garvan medal, 1947), AAUW (recipient Sarah Berliner fellowship), AAUP, Sigma Xi, Phi Beta Kappa, Phi Mu, Sigma Delta Epsilon (hon.). Methodist. Home: South Hadley Mass. †

SHERROUSE, CHARLES BEN, farmer, banker; b. Gilbert, La., Aug. 15, 1891; s. William Jasper and Lottie (Campbell) S.; m. Clarissa Butler, Aug. 7, 1913; children: Dorothy Mae (Mrs. George Gear), June Clarissa (Mrs. Edward Holmes). BA, La. State U., 1911. Operator cattle and farming bus. Monroe, La., from 1911; v.p. Winnsboro State Bank & Trust Co., La., from 1935; bd. dirs. Ouchita Nat. Bank, Monroe, Hibernia Nat. Bank, New Orleans, La. Power & Light Co., New Orleans, Gen. Am. Oil Co. Tex., Dallas. Chmn. Monroe War Bond dr., 1943-45; del. Dem. Nat. Conv., 1924, 44; presdl. elector, 1944; mem. bd. suprs. La. State U., 1944-58. Mem. Masons (32 degree), Shriners. Methodist. Home: Monroe La. †

SHERWOOD, GRACE MABEL, state librarian; b. Buxton, Maine, Oct. 24, 1886; d. Benjamin Atherton and Elizabeth May (Murray) S. AB, Pembroke Coll., 1906; LittD, R.I. Coll. Edn., 1938; LHD, Brown U., 1951. Dir. legis reference bur. R.I. State Library, 1907-37; state librarian, state record commr. State of R.I., from 1937, dir. state library book pool for fighting svcs., 1941; writer digests of legis., history, verse, law drafting for R.I. Gen. Assembly. Author: Gifts, Navigators; musical plays. Served in leave areas as writer, dir. soldier shows, Eng., France, World War I. recipient hon. citation, 1944, 48. Mem. ALA, Nat. Assn. State Libraries (pres. 1952-53), R.I. Library Assn., Art Club. Baptist. Home: Providence R.I. †

SHETLER, CURTIS MONROE, communications executive; b. Navarre, Ohio, Nov. 28, 1891; s. John Henry and Margaret (Bach) S.; m. Clara E. Baldwin, June 5, 1916; children: June Shetler Stow, Jean Shetler Jones. Student, Mt. Union Coll., 1912-14; LLB, Ohio Northern U., 1916, LLD, 1945. Bar: Ohio 1916. City atty. Alliance, Ohio, 1918-24; claim agt., claims atty., later gen. counsel Stark Electric R.R. Co., 1924-29, pres., until 1929; pres. Ohio Svc. Holding Corp. (renamed Tel. Svc. Co. of Ohio), Eastern Telephone Svc. Co., Ohio Cen. Telephone Corp., The Lima Telephone Co., until 1967; chmn. bd. United Telephone Co. of Ohio; v.p. Tri-City Transit Inc.; pres. Citizens Ice Co. Mem. Ohio Bas Assn., Stark County Bar Assn. (past pres.), Ohio State Skeet Assn. (past pres.), Gulf Stream Bath and Tennis Club, Canton City Club, The Little Club (Gulf Stream, Fla.); Delray Beach Yacht Club, Sigma Nu, Kappa Phi Gamma. Republican. Presbyterian. Home: Delray Beach Fla. †

SHEWMAKER, RUSSELL NEWTON, lawyer, government official; b. Washington, Mar. 15, 1915; s. Ulysses S. and Adelle (Weddington) S.; m. Ruth Lenore Horn, Aug. 3, 1940; children: John Russell, Wayne Allan, Dale Pryor, Diane Ruth, Roger Brett. J.D., George Washington U., 1941, A.B., 1942. Bar: D.C. 1941. With Bur. Customs, Treasury Dept., 1935- 51; practice law in Washington, from 1941; atty. U.S. Internat. Trade Commn. (formerly U.S. Tariff Commn.), 1951-56, asst. gen. counsel, 1956-63, gen. counsel, 1964-77, 79-80, sr. adviser, 1978-79, 80-81; pvt. practice from 1981; Drafted Tariff Classsification Act, 1962, organized, drafted Tariff Schedules of U.S., 1963; liaison officer, cons. House Ways and Means Com. and Senate Finance Com. on tariff and trade matters, 1964-76; U.S. rep. to EEC on tariff nomenclature, Brussels, 1963, Geneva, 1964; del. Customs Cooperation Council, Brussels, 1964-65; mem. U.S. delegation GATT, Geneva, 1967. Cubmaster, committeeman Nat. Capital area council Boy Scouts Am., 1950-57; legislative chmn.

D.C. Congress Parents and Tchrs., 1955-58. Recipient letters of commendation Pres. Kennedy, 1962. Mem. ABA; Mem. Fed., D.C. bar assns., Phi Eta Sigma, Phi Delta Phi. Home: Washington D.C. Died Jan. 4, 1988; buried Ft. Lincoln Cemetery, Brentwood, Md.

SHIDELER, ERNEST HUGH, college professor; b. Logansport, Ind., Mar. 20, 1891; s. William Jonathan and Josephine (Freeman) S.; m. Bertha Lee Odor, Sept. 10, 1919; children: Ross Odor, Kenneth Dale, Royal William. AB, Ottawa (Kans.) U., 1915; AM, U. Chgo., 1917, PhD, 1927; grad. study, U. Wis., 1921. Instr. social sci. Leavenworth (Kans.) High Sch., 1915-16, Univ. High Sch., Chgo., 1919-20; assoc. prof. econ. and sociology Franklin (Ind.) Coll., 1920-22, prof., head of dept., 1924-36; on leave as Ind. State dir. rural rehabilitation, Gov.'s Commn. on Unemployment Relief 1934-35, on leave as Ind. State dir. Resettlement adminstrn., 1935-36; Ind. State dir. Farm Security Adminstrn., 1937-47; chmn. div. commerce and bus. adminstrn. U. Ill. (Galesburg div.), 1947-48; assoc. prof. sociology U. Ill., Urbana, 1949-59; fellow and instr. in sociology U. Chgo., 1922-23, also rsch. asst.; vis. prof. (summers) U. of So. Calif., 1924, Butler U., 1928, Ind. State Tchrs. Coll., 1929; lectr. in field. Author: Group Life and Social Problems, 1929; contbr. to profl. jours. Vice-chmn. Ind. War Bd., U.S. Dept. Agr., 1941-45. Sgt. 110th Telegraph Battalion, 2d lt., 1st lt. 305th Field Signal Battalion, acting adj., later battalion supply officer, Div. Hdqrs. staff, acting signal officer 80th Div., AEF, 1917-19, France. Mem. Ind. Mktg. Rsch. Club (bd. dirs.), Am. Sociol. Soc., AAUP, Nat. Conf. Social Work, AAAU, Soc. Social Rsch. (past sec.), Ind. Acad. Social Scis. (ex-pres.), Am. Economic Assn., Rural Sociol. Soc. Am., Ind. Schoolmen's Club, Am. Legion, Exchange Club, University Club, Pi Kappa Delta, Pi Gamma Mu. Baptist. Home: Urbana Ill. Died Nov. 6, 1972; buried Eastlawn Cemetery, Urbana, Ill.

SHIDEMAN, FREDERICK EARL, pharmacologist, educator; b. Albion, Mich., Oct. 16, 1915; s. George Washington and Mary Anne (Klein) S.; m. Margaret Elizabeth Reiner, Aug. 12, 1939; children—Frederick C., Jeffrey R., Ethel M., Elizabeth M. B.A., Albion Coll., 1936; Ph.D. (Wis. Alumni Research Found. research asst.), U. Wis., 1941, postdoctoral fellow, 1941-42; M.D., U. Mich., 1946; LL.D. (hon.), Yonsei U., 1978. Instr. U. Mich., 1943-47, asst. prof. pharmacology, 1947-49, assoc. prof., 1949-52; prof. pharmacology and toxicology U. Wis., 1952-62, chmn. dept., 1954-62; prof. and head dept. pharmacology U. Minn., 1962-87, prof. emeritus pharmacology, 1987-88; Chmn. adv. com. abuse of depressant and stimulant drugs FDA, HEW, 1966-68; chmn. sci. adv. com. on drugs Bur. Narcotics and Dangerous Drugs, U.S. Dept. Justice, 1968-72; chmn. pharmacology and exptl. therapeutics study sect. NIH, 1960-65; mem. pharmacology and toxicolgy tng. com.; mem. com. Narcotic Addiction and Drug Abuse, NIMH, 1971-75; chmn. Pharmacology com. Nat. Bd. Med. Examiners, 1967-72; chmn. drug research bd. Nat. Acad. Scis.-NRC, 1972-76; mem. adv. com. on personnel for research Am. Cancer Soc., 1974-88 , chmn., 1976-78; trustee U.S. Pharmacopeial Conv., 1975-88, v.p., 1975-80, pres., 1980-85; vice chmn. Nat. Council on Drugs, 1976-78, chmn., 1978-80. Editor: Take As Directed; cons. editor: Am. Scientist; Contbr. articles to profl. jours. Recipient travel award Am. Physiol. Soc. to XVIII Internat. Physiol. Congress, Copenhagen, Denmark, 1950. Fellow Royal Soc. Medicine; mem. Am. Soc. Pharmacology and Exptl. Therapeutics (pres. 1963-64), Soc. Exptl. Biology and Medicine, AAAS, Wis. Med. Soc. (hon.), Japanese Pharmacology Soc., Peruvian Pharmacology Soc. (hon.), Korean Med. Assn. (hon.). Home: Minneapolis Minn. Died Apr. 21, 1988.

SHILENSKY, MORRIS, lawyer; b. Oserany, Poland, Nov. 20, 1910; came to U.S., 1912, naturalized, 1925; s. Louis and Esther (Kachonofsky) S.; m. Celia Binder, Nov. 6, 1932; children: Sylvia E. (Mrs. Gerald Freed), Michael. Student, Columbia U., 1929; LLB, St. Lawrence U., 1932. Bar: N.Y. 1933. Assoc. Hays, St. John, Abramson & Heilbron, 1928-38, ptnr., from 1938; counsel Vedder, Price, Kaufman, Kammholz & Day; sec., bd. dirs. Henry I Siegel Co. Inc.; bd. dirs. Alfred Dunhill of London Inc. Pres., bd. dirs. Billy Rose found.; bd. dirs. Am. Friends Israel Mus.; bd. dirs., v.p. Samuel Schulman Inst. Mem. N.Y. County Lawyers Assn. Home: Rego Park N.Y. Died Aug. 19, 1987.

SHIMKIN, LEON, book publisher; b. Bklyn., Apr. 7, 1907; s. Max and Fannie (Nickelsberg) S.; m. Rebecca Rabinowitz, Aug. 17, 1930; children: Emily, Michael. BCS, NYU, 1926. Acct. N.Y.C.; bus. mgr., treas., dir. various book pub. enterprises; pres. and dir. Simon & Schuster Inc., N.Y.C., 1924; co-chmn. emeritus Simon & Schuster Inc., 1984-88; co-founder Pocket Books Inc., 1939. Trustee Com. Econ. Devel. NYU, N.Y.C., Westchester Jewish Community Svcs. Mem. Rockefeller Ctr. City Athletic Club, Rock Rimmon Country (Pound Ridge, N.Y.); Beach Point (Mamaroneck, N.Y.). Home: Larchmont N.Y. Died May 25, 1988.

SHIMKIN, MICHAEL BORIS, physician, educator; b. Tomsk, Siberia, USSR, Oct. 7, 1912; came to U.S., 1923, naturalized, 1928; s. Boris Michael and Lydia (Serebrova) S.; m. Mary Louisa North, July 2, 1938; children—Peter Michael, Ann Mary Shimkin Segal, Philip North. AB, U. Calif., Berkeley, 1933; MD, U. Calif., San Francisco, 1937. Diplomate: Am. Bd. Internal Med., Am. Bd. Preventive Med. Resident medicine U. Tex., 1937-38; research fellow Harvard, 1938-39; officer USPHS, 1939-63, med. dir., 1950; with Nat. Cancer Inst., NIH, 1939-44, 46-63, chief biometry and epidemiology br., 1954-60, asso. dir. field studies, 1960-63; asst. chief Office Internat. Health, USPHS, 1945-46; clin. prof. oncology, chief lab. exptl. oncology U. Calif. Sch. Medicine, San Francisco, 1947-54; prof. medicine Temple U. Sch. Medicine, 1963-69; asst. v.p. research Temple U. Sch. Medicine (Health Scis. Center), 1966-69; chief cancer biology (Fels Research), 1963-69; prof. community medicine and oncology U. Calif., San Diego, 1969-80; prof. emeritus U. Calif., 1980-89; asso. dean for health manpower, 1970-72; Coordinator regional med. program San Diego & Imperial Co., 1969-73; Advisor U.S. delegation WHO constn. conv., 1945-46, OSRD, 1943-44; med. officer UNRRA, 1944-45; pub. health ofcr. G-5, 3rd Army, 1944-45; adviser Am. Cancer Soc. Author: Science and Cancer, 1964, 4th edit., 1980, Contrary to Nature, 1977, Sci. editor Jour. Nat. Cancer Inst, 1955-60; Editor: Cancer Research, 1964-69; author over 300 articles in field. Fellow A.C.P., Am. Coll. Preventive Medicine; mem. Am. Assn. Cancer Research (pres. 1973), Soc. Exptl. Biology and Medicine, Phi Beta Kappa, Sigma Xi. Home: La Jolla Calif. Died Jan. 16, 1989; cremated.

SHIP, IRWIN, dental educator; b. N.Y.C., July 11, 1932; s. Max and Lillian (Gootnick) S.; m. Gabriella Wolfsohn, June 24, 1956; children: Jonathan Avram, Sara Ann, Jordan Robert. Student, Columbia U., 1949-52; DMD, Harvard U., 1956; MS in Epidemiology and Preventive Medicine, U. Pa., 1965. Intern in oral surgery and oral medicine Mass. Gen. Hosp., Boston, 1956-57; prin. investigator clin. br. NIH, Bethesda, Md., 1957-60, clin. assoc., cons. oral medicine, 1962-73; asst. chief dental rsch. Phila. Gen. Hosp., 1960-62, rsch. com., 1962-73, chief dental rsch, 1962-73, sr. attending dentist, 1973-74; attending dentist Children's Hosp., Phila., 1962-84; asst. prof. oral medicine U. Pa. Sch. Dental Medicine, Phila., 1960-63; assoc. prof. U. Pa. Sch. Dental Medicine, 1963-66, prof., 1966-84, dir. hosp. edn., 1963073, chmn. dept. oral medicine, 1973-78, prof. dept. otorhinolaryngology, 1974-84, dir. Clin. Rsch. Ctr., 1978-84; mem. staff Hosp. U. Pa., Presbyn. U. Hosp.; vis. prof. oral medicine Hebrew U., Jerusalem, 1968, 69-70, 72; dir. affiliated program, 1975-84; vis. prof. Japan, 1976; dir. Robert Wood Johnson Found. Rural Dental Health Program, U. Pa., 1975-81; cons. WHO.; cons. to editorial bds.; reviewer for med. and dental jours.; contbr. chpts. to books, articles to profl. publs. Chmn. adult edn. program Temple Beth Hillel, 1964-69, bd. dirs., 1965-70, mem. exec. com.. 1966-80, vice chmn., 1978, 80; vice chmn. dental div. Am. Friends of Hebrew U., 1978-84. With USPHS, 1957-60. Recipient Grace Millliken award Harvard U., 1956, Myrtle Wreath award Phila. chpt. Hadassh, 1973, spl. citation Am. Friends Hebrew U., 1978; Fogerty sr. internat. fellow, 1982-83. Mem. ADA, Am. Pub. Health Assn., Soc. Hosp. Dentists, Am. Bd. Oral Medicine (bd. examiners 1979-84, chmn. 1981-84), Am. Soc. Dentistry for Handica,pped, Internat. Assn. Dental Rsch. (sec.-treas. 1963-66, pres. Phila. sect. 1965-67, counsellor 1967-68), Coll. Physicians Phila. Home: Wynnewood Pa. Died Apr. 16, 1984; interred Frazer, Pa.

SHIPLEY, JOSEPH T., editor, writer, radio commentator; b. Bklyn., Aug. 19, 1893; s. Jay R. and Jennie (Fragner) S.; m. Helen Bleet; children: Margaret (Mrs. Fiedler), Paul D.; m. Ann Ziporkes; children: J. Burke, H. Thorne; m. Shirley Hector. A.B., Coll. City N.Y., 1912; A.M., Columbia U., 1914, Ph.D., 1931. Instr. in English Stuyvesant High Sch., 1914-57; lecturer on poetry Bd. of Edn., 1916-20; instr. in lit. criticism Coll. City of N.Y., 1928-38, Bklyn. Coll., 1932-38; sec. of faculty, successively asst. prof., assoc. prof. English; Yeshiva Coll., 1928-44; drama critic New Leader, 1922-62, radio station WEVD, 1940-84; Am. corr. Assn. pour le Rencontre des Cultures, 1965-88; Vocabulary cons. Sci. Research Assocs.; instr. Playwrights Seminar Dramatic Workshop, dean, 1952-54; mng. dir. Theatre of UN; apptd. to make survey and scenarios for motion picture survey of N.Y. C. Sch. System, 1939; founder and exec. sec. Inst. Pub. Arts in Edn., 1939-41. Fgn. editor: Contemporary Verse, 1919-26; asst. editor: Jour. History of Ideas, 1940-44; assoc. editor: Jour. Aesthetics; editor: American Bookman; Dictionary of World Lit, 1943, Ency. of Lit, 1946; editorial assoc.: Philos. Library; Author translations from the French; Trends in Literature, 1948, Guide to Great Plays, 1952, Dictionary of Forgotten Words, 1953, Dictionary of World Literary Terms, 1955, rev. 1968, 72, Playing with Words, 1960, Word Play, 1972, Mentally Disturbed Teacher, 1961, Word Games for Play and Power, 1962, Five plays by Ibsen, 1965, Vocabulab, 1968, Anthology: Modern French Poetry, 1975, In Praise of English, 1977, Discursive Dictionary of Indo-European Roots in English Words, 1984, New Guide to Great Plays, 1984; Contbr. to: also articles, poems and critical essays to mags. Ency. Brit, in U.S., Eng., France, India, Pakistan.; Editor: Study-Master Guides to Drama. Chmn. Nat. Com. on Edn. in Public Arts; Am. rep. Theatre des Nations Festival, Paris.; Am. director Far East Research Inst.; mem. cultural adv. bd. American Coll. in Paris; hon. trustee Hwa Kiu U. (Macao), Canton U., Hong Kong. Recipient Townsend Harris medal for distinguished contbns. in field, 1975. Mem. Assn. Internationale de la Critique Dramatique (U.S. v.p.), Drama Critics Circle London (hon.), English Assn., N.Y. Drama Critics' Circle (pres. 1952-54, sec.), Phi Beta Kappa. Home: New York N.Y. Died May 11, 1988, cremated.

SHIRLEY, JAMES CLIFFORD, academic administrator; b. Superior, Nebr., Sept. 24, 1892; s. William Martin and Effie Caroline (Barringer) S.; m. Tonnie Adeline Wilson, Aug. 16, 1917; children: James Clifford (dec.), Todd Wilson, Patricia Ann (dec.), Dorothy Caroline, Donald Allen. AB, Phillips U., 1917; MA, U. Mo., 1920; student summers, U. Chgo., 1917, 25, Stanford U., 1929; PhD, U. Calif., 1937. Instr. Biol. sci. Phillips U., Enid, Okla., 1917-19, prof. biology, from 1922, acting dean, 1935-37, dean coll. arts, from 1937; instr. biology Christian Coll., 1920; ranger naturalist, lectr. botany Govt. Field Sch. Natural History, Yosemite Park, summers, 1931-38. Author: Redwoods of Coast and Sierra, 1936. Mem. AAAS, Okla. Acad. Sci., Kiwanis, Masons, Civic Garden Club (Enid), Sigma Xi, Phi Sigma. Home: Enid Okla. †

SHOEMAKER, FLOYD CALVIN, historian; b. Kissimmee, Fla., May 7, 1886; s. Frank Calvin and Emma Viola (Dreyer) S.; m. Caroline Tull, June 2, 1911 (div.); 1 child, Evelyn; m. L. Pearle McCown, July 2, 1944. PhB, Kirksville (Mo.) State Normal Sch., 1906; AB, U. Mo., 1909, AM, 1911, LLD, 1954; LLD, Cen. Coll., 1942. Tchr. history and Latin Gallatin (Mo.) High Sch., 1909; asst. prof. polit. sci. and pub. law U. Mo., 1909-11; asst. sec., librarian State hist. Soc. Mo., 1910-15, sec., librarian, 1915-60, cons., from 1960. Author books relating to field; editor Mo. Hist. Rev., 1915-60; co-editor hist. publs. Recipient merit award Rockhurst Coll., 1960, merit award Mo. Press Assn., 1960; named Mr. Mo. Mo. State Senate, 1955. Mem. Am., Miss. Valley hist. assns., Am. Assn. State and Local History (merit award 1955, 59), Assn. Am. Archivists, Soc. Am. Historians, Masons, Phi Beta Kappa, Sigma Delta Chi (life, Wells Key 1941). Democrat. †

SHORE, NATHAN ALLEN, dentist; b. N.Y.C., Feb. 2, 1914; s. Moritz and Jeanette (Bricianer) Shapiro; m. Miriam Felder, Feb. 4, 1943; 1 child, Elizabeth Ann. DDS, Marquette U., 1938. Pvt. practice N.Y.C.; lectr. NYU, Loma Linda U.; lectr. in field to profl. socs., seminars. Author: Temporomandibular Joint Dysfunction and Occlusion Equilibration, 2d edit., 1976; (with Miriam Felder Shore) How to Test and Hire for the Professional Office, 1967; producer two tech. films; contbr. numerous articles to profl. jours. With Dental Corps, U.S. Army, 1943-46. Recipient Presdl. Citation award Govt. of Belgium, Most Valuable Tchr. award Conn. Dental Assn., 1981. Fellow Am. Coll. Dentists, Internat. Coll. Dentists; mem. Soc. Oral Physiology, Occlusion (founder 1954, pres. 1955-59, Steven W. Brown Gold medal 1968), Am. Equilibration Soc., Royal Soc. Medicine, Periodontal Soc. Rome (hon.). Home: New York N.Y. Died Mar. 21, 1984.

SHOUP, ROBERT JOHN, lawyer; b. Xenia, Ohio, Jan. 30, 1911; s. Marcus and Mary (Mahanna) S.; m. Madeleine Marchand Cole, Sept. 4, 1937; children—Suzanne (Mrs. William M. Wehner), Carol (Sister Carol Shoup), Robert G., Bruce D., Charles C. B.S. in Econs, U. Pa., 1933; LL.B., U. Cin., 1936. Former partner firm Baker & Hostetler, Cleve.; of counsel. Baker & Hostetler. Fellow Am., Ohio bar assn. founds. Home: Chagrin Falls Ohio. Died May 21, 1984; buried Xenia, Ohio.

SHOVE, BENJAMIN E., lawyer; b. Syracuse, N.Y., 1892. AB, Yale U., 1914; LLB, Columbia U., 1917. Bar: N.Y. 1919. Ptnr. Hancock, Ryan, Shove & Hust and predecessor firms, Syracuse. Mem. ABA, N.Y. State Bar Assn., Onondaga County Bar Assn. (pres. 1939). †

SHRIVER, HARRY CLAIR, administrative law judge; b. Gettysburg, Pa., Oct. 2, 1904; s. Edward Simpson and Minnie B. (Snyder) S.; m. Florence Basehoar, Oct. 10, 1944; children: Anne Basehoar Bielot, Harry Clair, Florence Louise Armstrong. Student, Shippensburg State U., 1924, Dickinson Coll., 1925-26, Gettysburg Coll., 1926-27; J.D., George Washington U., 1930, LL.M., 1931, A.B., 1932. Bar: D.C. 1931, U.S. Supreme Ct 1935, U.S. Ct. Claims 1945. Tchr. Adams County, Pa., 1924-25; staff Library of Congress, 1928; practice law Washington, 1932-37, 47; staff Law Library of Congress, 1935, spl. agt., 1936; del. D.C. Bar Assn., 2d Congress Internat. and Comparative Law, 1937; atty. FTC, 1942, War Shipping Adminstrn., 1944, Maritime Commn., 1946, Maritime Adminstrn., 1950; asst. gen counsel, gen. counsel St. Lawrence Seaway Devel. Corp., 1958-62; hearing examiner FPC, 1963-72, adminstrv. law judge, 1972-86; dir., pub. The Fox Hills Press, Annapolis, Md., 1970-86. Author: Justice Oliver Wendell Holmes: His Book Notices and Uncollected Letters and Papers, 1936, How to Find the Law of Administrative Agencies, 1940, Judicial Opinions of Oliver Wendell Holmes, 1940, History of the Shriver Family, 1962, What Gusto, 1970, The Government Lawyer, 1975, What Justice Holmes Wrote; And What Has Been Written About Him, 1978, How to Tell a Story and

How to Have One for Any Occasion, 1981, Gettysburg to Washington, 1984; contbr. articles to law jours., periodicals. Mem. Am., Fed. bar assns., Pa. Hist. Junto (pres. 1968-72), Phi Beta Gamma, Theta Chi. Republican. Lutheran. Clubs: Rotary; Old Georgetown (Washington) (co-founder, dir.). Home: Annapolis Md. also: New Smyrna Beach Fla. Died Apr. 29, 1986; buried Mount Olivet Cemetery, Hanover, Pa.

SHULL, HENRY CARLTON, lawyer; b. Sioux City, Iowa, Jan. 16, 1892; s. Deloss Carlton and Fannie E. (Mitchell) S.; m. Alice Lincoln, Aug. 15, 1921. Student, Harvard U., 1914-15; PhB, U. Chgo., 1914, JD, 1916; LLD (hon.), Parsons Coll., Fairfield, Iowa, 1947. Bar: Iowa 1916. Practiced in Sioux City; ptnr. Shull, Marshall, Nayne, Marks & Vizinros and predecessor firms, from 1940. Mem. Iowa State Bd. Regents, 1925-51, pres., 1940-51; mem. State Bd. Vocat. Edn., 1941-51; chmn. Midwest dist. com. selection Rhodes Scholars, 1948-56; trustee Sioux Falls (S.D.) Coll. With USN, World War I. Recipient citation for pub. service U. Chgo., 1944. Republican. Baptist. Home: Sioux City Iowa. †

SHULMAN, MAX, author; b. St. Paul, Mar. 14, 1919; s. Abraham and Bessie (Karchmer) S.; m. Carol Rees, Dec. 21, 1941 (dec. 1963); children—Daniel, Max, Peter, Martha; m. Mary G. Bryant, 1964. A.B., U. Minn., 1942. Freelance writer, 1942-88 ; author: Barefoot Boy with Cheek, 1943 (musical comedy version produced by George Abbott, 1947), The Feather Merchants, 1944, The Zebra Derby, 1946, Sleep Till Noon, 1949, Rally Round the Flag, Boys, 1957; also movies House Calls, (with Julius J. Epstein) Confidentially Connie, (with Herman Wouk) Affairs of Dobie Gillis, Half A Hero, The Tender Trap; play, 1954, I Was a Teen Age Dwarf, 1959, Anyone Got a Match?, 1964; musical comedy How Now Dow Jones, 1967, Potatoes Are Cheaper, 1971; also short stories in Mademoiselle; others; author: TV series Dobie Gillis. Served with USAAF, 1942-44. Mem. Authors Guild, Dramatists Guild, Writers Guild Am. Home: Los Angeles Calif. Died Aug. 28, 1988.

SHUSTER, CARL NATHANIEL, mathematician, educator; b. Frenchtown, N.J., Feb. 16, 1890; s. Nathaniel Rittenhouse and Catharine Pickell (Draucker) S.; m. Edith Gilman, June 5, 1918; children: Carl Nathaniel, John Gilman, Jean S. PhD, Columbia U. Tchr. jr. high sch.; mem. faculty Columbia U.; mem. faculty Trenton State Coll., prof. emeritus; v.p. Yeshiva U.; lectr. numerous univs. Author 63 books; contbr. numerous articles to profl. jours.; inventor; originator project method field work in math. With USN, World War I. Recipient Gold Key Columbia U. Press Assn., Alumni citation Trenton State Coll. Mem. Assn. Math. Tchrs. N.J. (past pres.), Nat. Coun. Tchrs. Math., Lions Club, Torch Club, Phi Delta Kappa. Home: Saint Petersburg Fla. †

SIBLEY, JOHN ADAMS, lawyer; b. Milledgeville, Ga., Jan. 4, 1888; s. James Longstreet and Mattie (Erwin) S.; m. Nettie Whitaker Cone, Nov. 25, 1914 (dec. Mar. 1934); children: John A. (dec.), James Malcolm, Jeannette Sibley Yow (dec.), Martha Sibley George; m. Barbara Sanford Thayer, Mar. 29, 1937; children: Barbara Thayer, Horace Holden, John Adams, III, Stephen Thayer. Prep. course, Ga. Mil. Coll., Milledgeville, Ga.; LL.B., U. Ga., 1911; LL.D., Oglethorpe U., 1950, Mercer U., 1952, Emory U., 1962, Berry Coll., 1981; D.Nu.L., Morris Brown Coll., 1980. Bar: Ga. 1911. Began practice under title of Sibley & Sibley, Milledgeville; mem. firm King & Spalding, Atlanta, Spalding, Sibley & Troutman, 1918-46; judge County Ct., Baldwin County, Ga., 1914-18; chmn. bd. Trust Co. Ga., 1946-63, adv. dir., chmn. adv. council, dir.; dir. Trust Co. of Ga. Assocs., Coca-Cola Co., Coca-Cola Export Corp. Hon. chmn. bd. trustees Henrietta Egleston Hosp. for Children; chmn. Gen. Assembly Com. on Schs. (Sibley Commn.), 1960-61, Higher Ednl. Facilities Commn. for Ga., 1963-66; past chmn. bd. trustees Berry Schs., Mount Berry, Ga.; past trustee Agnes Scott Coll., Atlanta. Mem. Am. (v.p. 1922), Ga., Atlanta bar assns. Democrat. Presbyn. Clubs: Rotarian. (Atlanta), Capital City (Atlanta), Piedmont Driving (Atlanta), The Ten (Atlanta). Home: Atlanta Ga. Died Oct. 25, 1986.

SICKMAN, LAURENCE CHALFONT STEVENS, art museum official; b. Denver, Aug. 27, 1906; s. D. Vance and May Ridding (Fuller) S. AB cum laude, Harvard U., 1930; Harvard-Yenching fellow, Peking, China, 1930-35; hon. doctorate, Rockhurst Coll., 1972; LHD, Baker U., 1973, Columbia U., 1977; DLitt, U. Mo., 1974; LLD, U. Mo., Kans. City Art Inst. Curator oriental art Nelson Gallery Art-Atkins Mus., Kansas City, Mo., 1935-45, vice dir., 1946-53, dir., 1953-77, dir. emeritus, cons. to trustees, 1977-88; lectr., resident fellow Fogg Mus., Harvard U., 1937-39. Author: (with Alexander Soper) The Art and Architecture of China, 1956; editor, contbr. Chinese Calligraphy and Painting, 1962; editor Archives of Asian Art, 1966-73; contbr. articles to profl. publs. Mem. exec. com. Art in Embassies program State Dept., 1965-88. Maj. combat intelligence USAAF, 1942-45. Decorated Legion of Merit; knight comdr. Royal Order of North Star (Sweden); recipient Charles Lang Freer medal, 1973. Mem. Chinese Art Soc. Am. (gov. editor Archives 1948-66), Am. Coun. Learned Socs. (com. on Far Eastern studies 1948-53, joint com. Asian studies1967-69), Far Eastern Assn. (gov. 1951-53), Am. Mus. Dirs., Am. Oriental Soc., Japan Soc., Far Eastern Ceramic Group, Assn. Art Mus. Dirs. U.S.A. and Can. (pres.), Coll. Art Assn. (dir.), Kansas City Country Club, River Club, Rotary (Kansas City, Mo.). Home: Kansas City Mo. Died May 7, 1988; buried Columbia Cemetery, Boulder, Colo.

SIEBENTHALER, HAROLD JACOB, lawyer; b. Cin., Oct. 23, 1892; s. Louis F. and Mollie (Mohlenhoff) S.; m. Florence Burkhardt, Mar. 20, 1920; 1 dau., Phyllis A. (Mrs. William H. Hopple Jr.). J.D., Salmon P. Chase Coll. Law, Cin., 1914, LLD, 1964. Bar: Ohio 1914. Pvt. practice Cin., 1915-88; of counsel Frost & Jacobs, Cin., 1915-88; dir. emeritus Witt Co.; dir. Charles V. Maescher & Co. Inc., W.A. Natorp Co. Inc., F.F. Co.; former pres. Salmon P. Chase Coll. Law. Mem. Am., Ohio, Cin. bar assns., Cincinnati County Club, Queen City Club, Cincinnati Club, Rotary, Shriners, Jesters, Masons (33d deg.). Home: Cincinnati Ohio. Died July 17, 1988.

SIEDLE, E. GEORGE, federal agency administrator; b. Chgo., July 5, 1889; s. Emil and Anna (Mussman) S.; m. Claire Katherine McQuaide, Oct. 1, 1910; 1 child, Anna Claire Siedle LaBarbara. Student, Duquesne U. With freight traffic depts. of railroads in Pitts; then gen. traffic mgr. Armstrong Cork Co., Lancaster, Pa.; asst. postmaster gen. Bur. Transp., Post Office Dept., Washington, from 1954; v.p., exec. and liaison com. Universal Postal Union; chmn. Lancaster Traffic Study and Safety Com.; mem. Gov.'s Hwy. Safety Com. Pa.; sponsor Lancaster Mcpl. Airport; pub. rep. Airport Commn.; mem. adv. bd. Atlantic State Shippers. Author articles in field. Mem. Assn. Traffic Clubs Am. (past pres.), Glass Container Mfrs. Inst. (chmn. traffic com.), Eastern Hard Surface Floor Covering Mfrs. Council (chmn.), Nat. Indsl. Traffic League, Eastern Indsl. Traffic League (v.p.), ICC Practitioners, Asphalt Tile Inst., Wallboard Traffic League, Am. Soc. Traffic and Transp. Home: Washington D.C. †

SIEGBAHN, KARL MANNE GEORG, physicist; b. Örebo, Sweden, Dec. 3, 1886; s. Nils Reihold Georg and Emma Sofia Mathilda (Zetterberg) S.; m. Karin Högbom, May 23, 1914; children: Bo Lennart Georg, Kai Manne Börje. DSc, U. Lund, 1911; Dr honoris causa, Freiberg U., 1931, U. Bucharest, 1940, U. Oslo, 1946. Prof. physics U. Lund, Sweden, 1914-23, U. Upsala, Sweden, 1923-37; dir. Nobel Inst. Physics Acad. Sci., Stockholm, 1937-64, emeritus, from 1964; mem. Internat. Com. for Weights and Measures, from 1937. Recipient Nobel prize in physics, 1925, Hughes medal, 1934 and Rumford medal, 1940 Royal Soc. London, Duddell medal Phys. Soc. London, 1948. Mem. Internat. Union Physics (pres. 1938-47), Royal Swedish Acad. Sci., Nat. Acad. Sci. Denmark, Nat. Acad. Sci. Norway, Nat. Acad. Sci. Finland, Acad. de Scis. Paris, Royal Soc. London, Royal Soc. Edinburgh. Home: Stockholm Sweden. †

SIEGEL, SEYMOUR, clergyman, educator; b. Chgo., Sept. 12, 1927; s. David and Jeanette (Morris) S. B.A., U. Chgo., 1947; M.H.L., Jewish Theol. Sem., 1951, D.H.L., 1958. Rabbi 1951; registrar, postgrad. dept. Jewish Theol. Sem. Am., 1951-59, assoc. prof. theology, 1959-67, sem. prof. theology, Young Men's Philanthropic League prof. ethics and rabbinic though' 1967-88, Ralph Simon prof. ethics and theology, 1976-88; asst. dean Herbert H. Lehman Inst. Ethics, 1962-88; vis. prof. Seminario Rabinico, Buenos Aires, Argentina, 1962-64; adj. prof. Jewish studies; Coll. City N.Y., 1971-73; lectr. ethics Union Theol. Sem.; sr. research fellow Kennedy Inst. for Bioethics, 1976-77; Humanities fellow and lectr. Med. Coll. Pa.; fellow Woodrow Wilson Center for Scholars, 1981; vis. prof. George Washington U.; mem. Pres.'s Commn. for Study of Ethical Problems in Medicine and Behavioral Research, 1982-83; exec. dir. U.S. Holocaust Meml. Council, 1982-88 ; adj. scholar Heritage Found., 1981-88. Author: Conservative Judasim and Jewish Law, 1976, The Jewish Dietary Laws, Contemporary Issues in Jewish Ethics, 1980, God in Conservative Judaism; mem. editorial bd.: Jewish Publ. Soc; mem. editorial adv. bd.: Kennedy Inst. for Study Human Reprodn. and Bioethics; div. editor: Ency. Judaica; editor: This World mag.; bd. editors: Ency. Bio-Med. Ethics. Fellow Inst. Religious and Social Studies, Soc. for Religion in Higher Edn., Conf. on Sci., Philosophy and Religion, Am. Jewish Forum (pres.), World Union of Jewish Studies (council 1981); Mem. B'nai B'rith. Home: New York N.Y. Died Feb. 24, 1988, buried Riverside Cemetery, Rochelle Park, N.J.

SIENA, JAMES VINCENT, lawyer; b. Cleve., Sept. 25, 1932; s. Vincent James and Virginia Catherine (Johnson) S.; m. June Elizabeth Harvey, 1954 (dec. 1974); children: Katherine June, James Harvey, Margaret Johnson; m. Lynn Bonde, Dec. 31, 1978. Student, Miami U., 1951-52; B.A., Western Res. U., 1955; LL.B., Stanford U., 1961. Bar: D.C. 1962, Calif. 1976. Assoc. Covington & Burling, Washington, 1961-67; dep. undersec. Army for internat. affairs, Washington, 1967-69; legal adv. to pres. Stanford U., 1970-77; dep. asst. sec. Def. for European and NATO affairs Dept. Def., Washington, 1977-81; ptnr. Davis Simpich & Siena, 1981-88; cons. OEO, 1964-65. Editor: Antitrust and Local Government, 1981. Bd. dirs. ACLU, Washington, 1963-67, Sierra Club Legal Def. Fund, 1972-77, Internat. Inst. Strategic Studies, 1981-88 . Served with USMCR, 1955-58. Mem. Calif. Bar Assn., D.C. Bar Assn. Democrat. Home: Washington D.C. Died Jan. 3, 1988.

SIENKIEWICZ, CASIMIR A., banker; b. 1892; m. Jane Patton; children: John Wilbur, Michael. Ed. abroad; LLD)hon.), Internat. Coll.; student, Princeton U. Chmn., chief exec. officer, bd. dirs. Central-Penn Nat. Bank, Phila.; former v.p. Fed. Res. Bank Phila.; bd. dirs. Tasty Baking Co., Phila., Port Reading R.R. Co., Ben Franklin Hotel; mem., dir. fed. adv. council 3d Fed. Res. Dist.; cons. Depts. Commerce, Labor and Treasury; cons. spl. bipartisan com. on postward policy and planning, Ho. of Reps., 1945-46. Trustee Assoc. Hosp. Service, Phila., Drexel Inst. Tech., Solebury Sch., New Hope; chmn. adv. com. Econs. and Social Service Depts., Princeton U. Mem. Am. Bankers Assn. (mem. exec. council), Pa. Bankers Assn. (past pres.), Pa. Acad. Fine Arts, Union League Club, Racquet Club, Midday Club, Down Town Club, Princeton Club, Sunnybrook Golf Club, Pine Valley Golf Club, Seaview & Doyleston Country Club, Rotary. †

SIGNORET, SIMONE (SIMONE-HENRIETTE-CHARLOTTE KAMINKER), actress; b. Wiesbaden, Germany, Mar. 25, 1921; d. Andre and Georgette (Signoret) Kaminker; ed. Solange Sicard Sch., Paris; m. Marc Allegret, 1947 (div.); 1 dau., Catherine; m. 2d Yves Montand, June 15, 1950. Tutor, English and Latin, Paris; typist for newspaper Le Nouveau Temps; appeared in motion picture Des Demons d l'Aube, 1946, other roles in Dédée d'Anvers, La Ronde, 1950, Thérèse Raquin, 1953, La mort en ce jardin, Diabolique, 1955, Les Sorcières de Salem (with husband in play version Paris stage, 1954)), 1958, Room at the Top, 1958, also appeared as Roberte in Naked Autumn, 1963, Adua e le Compagne, Term of Trial, 1963, Ship of Fools, 1965, The Sleeping Car Murders, 1966, The Deadly Affair, 1967, Games, 1967, The Seagull, 1968, The Confession, 1971, Madame Rosa, 1978, I Sent a Letter to My Love, 1981; L'Etoile du Nord, 1983; TV acting debut in Don't You Remember, Gen. Electric Theater, 1960; TV appearance A Small Rebellion (Emmy award), 1966. Recipient Prix Suzanne Bianchetti for performance in Macadam, 1946, Prix Féminin du Cinéma, 1952, Grand Prix d'Intérpretation féminine de l'Académie du Cinema, 1953; Brit. Film Acad. award for performance as queen of Apaches in Casque d'Or, 1951; Best Actress award Brit. Film Acad. and Cannes Film Festival, 1959; prize as best fgn. actress German Film Critics, 1959; Acad. Award for best actress of 1959. Author: Nostalgia Isn't What It Used to Be, 1978. Died Sept. 31, 1985. Home: Paris France.

SIK, ENDRE, government official; b. Budapest, Hungary, Apr. 2, 1891; s. Sandor and Flora (Winternitz) S.; m. Katharine Toezky, Aug. 11, 1918; children: Irina (Mrs. Sergei Sokolow), Igor. Student, Univ. Law, Budapest, 1912. With sci. insts. USSR, 1923-45; prof. history U. Moscow, 1939-45; with Hungarian Ministry Fgn. Affairs, from 1945, minister in Washington, 1948-49, head polit. dept., 1949-53, dep. minister, 1953-54, 1st dep. minister, 1954-58, minister, from 1958. Prisoner of war, Russia, World War I. †

SILL, WEBSTER HARRISON, JR., plant pathologist, educator; b. Wheeling, W.Va., Dec. 4, 1916; s. Webster Harrison and Grace Elaine (Clark) S.; m. Charlyn Alice Adams, July 25, 1943; children—Webster Harrison III, Susan C. (Mrs. Pat Moore), Warren T. B.S., W.Va. Wesleyan Coll., 1939; postgrad., Pa. State U., 1942; M.A., Boston U., 1947; Ph.D., U. Wis., 1951. Research asso. U. Wis., Madison, 1951-52; asst. prof. botany and plant pathology Kans. State U., 1952-56, asso. prof., 1956-63, prof., 1963-69; chmn. dept. biology, prof. U. S.D., Vermillion, from 1969; dir. Black Hills Natural Scis. Field Sta., 1970-73, Center for Environ. Studies, from 1972; food and agrl. officer FAO, UN, 1962-63; dir. research Andhra Pradesh Agrl. U., Hyderabad, India, AID, 1966-68; pres. Environ. Cons., Inc., 1971-87; cons. H.J. Heinz Co., Gen. Foods Corp., Frontier Chem. Co., Eli Lilly Co. Author: The Plant Protection Discipline, Integrated Plant Protection. Co-author: Sourcebook of Laboratory Exercises in Plant Pathology; also numerous articles on research. Co-chmn. Kans. Centennial Com., 1961; active Boy Scouts Am., from 1952; bd. dirs. Sioux council, from 1968; chmn. United Campus Christian Fellowship; hon. life PTA, P.T.A.; pres. Westminster Found., 1964. Served to 1st lt. USMCR, 1941-46. Wis. Alumni Research fellow, 1948-51; Lisle fellow, 1937; Danforth fellow, 1957; NSF sr. postdoctoral fellow Marine Lab., Duke, 1972; Food Inst., East-West Center sr. fellow Honolulu, 1974-75; Ace govtl. fellow, 1976-77; holder spl. chair Nat. Chung Hsing U.-Nat. Sci. Council, Taiwan, 1980-81. Mem. Am. Phytopath. Soc., Bot. Soc. Am., AAAS, Am. Inst. Biol. Scis., N.Y. Acad. Scis., Internat. Platform Assn., Sigma Xi, Phi Sigma, Gamma Sigma Delta, Gamma Alpha, Pi Sigma Alpha. Republican. Methodist (lay minister 1939-68; named Kans. Layman of Year 1957). Lodges: Kiwanis, Rotary. Home: Vermillion S.D. Died Feb. 11, 1987; buried Bluff View Cemetery, Vermillion, S.D.

SILVER, JAMES WESLEY, educator; b. Rochester, N.Y., June 28, 1907; s. Henry Dayton and Elizabeth (Squier) S.; m. Margaret McLean Thompson, Dec. 31, 1935; children: James William, Virginia Margaret. AB, U. N.C., 1927; AM, Peabody Coll., 1929; PhD, Vanderbilt U., 1935; hon. doctoral degree, Morehouse Coll., 1967, U. So. Fla., 1976. Assoc. prof. history Southwestern Coll., Winfield, Kans., 1935-36; asst. prof. history U. Miss., 1936-42, assoc. prof., 1942-46, chmn. dept., 1946-57; prof. history U. Notre Dame, South Bend, Ind., 1965; prof. history U. South Fla., Tampa, 1965-79, prof. emeritus, 1979-88; summer lectr. Emory U., Harvard U., others. Author: Edmund Pendleton Gaines: Frontier General, 1949, Confederate Morale and Church Propaganda, 1957, A Life for the Confederacy, 1959, Missssissippi in the Confedercy. 1961, Mississippi: The Closed Society (Sidney Hillman Found. award for 1964), The 1947-48 Jour. So. History, 1952-56, Mississippi Valley Hist. Rev., 1963-88; contbr. articles to various hist. jours, Dictionary Am. History. Mem. State Hist. Commn., Miss., 1948-57, South Bend Human Relations Commn.; bd. dirs. Forest History Found. With ARC in Pacific area, 1945. Fulbright scholar U. Aberdeen, Scotland, 1949-50, Ford Found. scholar Harvard U., 1951-52; recipient Anisfield-Wolfe Race Relations award, 1965. Mem. Am. Acad. Arts and Scis., Am. SoSo. (mem. exec. coun., pres.) hist. assns., Orgn. Am. Historians, Miss. Hist. Soc., Rotary, Phi Beta Kappa, Omicron Delta Kappa, Tau Kappa Alpha, Pi Gamma Mu, Phi Kappa Phi. Home: Cape Coral Fla. Died July 25, 1988.

SILVER, JOE, actor; b. Chgo., Sept. 28, 1922; s. Morris and Sonia (Genis) S.; m. Evelyn Colton, Jan. 8, 1950; children: Christopher, Jennifer. Student, U. Wis., 1940-42. Broadway debut in Tobacco Road, 1942, other Broadway shows inculde Gypsy, 1959, Lenny (Tony award nominee), 1972, Promises, Promises (N.J. Drama Critics award nominee), 1973; other N.Y. stage appearances include The Zulu and The Zayda, 1965, You Know I Can't Hear You When the Water's Running, 1967, Old Business at N.Y. Shapkespeare Festival Pub. Theatre; appeared in numerous motion pictures, 1950-88, including Switching Channels, The Gig, Almost You, Rhinoceros, 1973, The Apprenticeship of Duddy Kravitz, 1974; over 1000 TV shows from 1947; panelist What's It Worth, Red Button's series, 1950s. With Signal Corps, AUS, 1944-47. Mem. Screen Actors Guild (bd. dirs. from 1967), AFTRA, Actors Equity Assn. Died Feb. 27, 1989.

SILVERMAN, FRED, hospital executive; b. N.Y.C., May 31, 1935; s. Joseph and Bella (Brenman) S.; m. Lois Leichtman, Dec. 3, 1972; children: Mark, Gail, Karyn, Jeffrey. B.B.A. in Indsl. Engring, CCNY, 1958; postgrad., N.Y. U. Sch. Bus. Adminstrn., 1962-68. Mgr. central supply dept. Montefiore Hosp., Bronx, N.Y., 1958-62; asst. adminstr. for method and procedures Montefiore Hosp., 1962-63, asst. adminstr., 1963-68, dep. dir., 1972-77; adminstr. Hosp. of Albert Einstein Coll. Medicine, 1969-72; pres. Bronx-Lebanon Hosp. Ctr., 1977-87, Bronx-Lebanon Hosp. Ctr. Housing Corp., 1985-87, Bronx-Lebanon New Directions Fund, Inc., 1984-87, Nutri-Health, Inc.; asst. prof. hosp. adminstrn. CCNY, 1970-87 ; assoc. clin. prof. NYU Sch. Public Adminstrn.; dir. FOJP Service Corp. (malpractice ins. co.), 1977-83; mem. Ins. Profl. Adv. Com.; mem. health com. Task Force on N.Y. Crisis, 1978-83; chmn. Coalition of Distressed Hosps., N.Y.C., 1985-87. Mem. Bronx Borough Pres.'s Econ. Devel. Com., 1980; mem. N.Y.C. Community Bd. 3, 1981-83; chmn. bd. Stratton Mountain (Vt.) Village, 1986-87. Served with M.C. U.S. Army, 1958. Recipient citation med. bd. Bronx-Lebanon Hosp., 1978, citation med. bd. Patrolmen's Benevolent Assn. N.Y.C., 1978, citation med. bd. 11th Dist. N.Y.C. Transit Police Dept., 1979; Community Leadership award Bronx aux. bd. N.Y. Urban League, Inc., 1981; Community service award Bronx Council on Arts, 1986; cited in Congl. Record, 1981; Award of Merit Bronx div. Council Chs., 1983. Mem. Am. Coll. Hosp. Adminstrs., Am. Hosp. Assn., Am. Public Health Assn., Greater N.Y. Hosp. Assn. (bd. govs.), Hosp. Assn. N.Y. State (com. govt. relations , co-chmn. regional polit. action com.), Public Health Assn. N.Y.C., Bronx C. of C. (health and hosp. com. 1977-87). Died Apr. 16, 1987; buried Sharon Gardens, Valhalla, N.Y.

SILVERMAN, HARRY T., metal processing executive; b. N.Y.C., Mar. 9, 1910; s. Isadore and Stella (Rubell); m. Miriam Neuhoff; children: Richard, Barry, Jeffrey, Kenneth. Student, U. Ala., St. John's Law Sch. Pres., chmn. bd. Landers, Frary & Clark, N.Y.C., 1959-61; pres. Dorset Rex Inc., N.Y.C. and Thomaston, Conn., 1959-61; pres. Plume & Atwood Brass & Copper Corp., Thomaston, 1958-69, chmn., 1969; pres., dir. Thomaston Plume & Atwood Brass & Copper Corp., 1958-87, Dorset Products Inc., N.Y.C.; bd. dirs. Pref. Life Ins. Co. N.Y., Capitol Pine & Steel Products. Pres., treas. Silverman Found.; founder Albert Einstein Coll. Medicine; mem. Mayor's Olympic Com., 1960; trustee League for Cardiac Children. Mem. Young Men's Philanthropic League (v.p., dir.), Mason (Shriner). Home: New York N.Y. Died June 2, 1987.

SILVERS, PHIL, actor; b. Bklyn., May 11, 1912; m. Jo Carroll Dennison, Mar. 2, 1945 (div.); m. 2d, Evelyn Patrick, Oct. 21, 1956 (div.); five daus. First appeared: on stage in vaudeville act in Gus Edwards' School Days Revue, 1925-28; later toured in: vaudeville with Morris and Campbell; toured with: Minsky Burlesque troupse, 1934-39; on: legitimate stage in Yokel Boy; musical, 1939; made film debut in Hit Parade, 1940; appeared in numerous pictures, the latest being You'll Never Get Rich, 1955, 40 Pounds of Trouble, 1963, It's a Mad, Mad, Mad World, 1963, A Guide for the Married Man, 1967, Buona Sera, Mrs. Campbell, 1969, The Boatniks, 1970, The Strongest Man in the World, 1975, WonTonTon, the Dog Who Saved Hollywood, 1976, The Chicken Chronicles, 1977, The Cheap Detective, 1978; in USO performnces in Mediterranean area, World War II; leading role in: Broadway prodn. High Button Shoes, 1947-50; leading role: Top Banana, 1951-52; on tour, 1953, and in film of same name, 1954; with CBS-TV, after 1955; in role of Sgt. Bilko in the Phil Silvers TV Show (first named You'll Never Get Rich, 1955-59; leading role in: Broadway prodn. Do-Re-Mi, 1960, A Funny Thing Happened on the Way to the Forum, 1972; has appeared as entertainer in night clubs and: as guest on radio shows; appeared in: TV movie The Night They Took Miss Beautiful, 1977 (recipient triple citation for best comedian, best comedy series, best actor in continuing performance Acad. TV Arts and Scis. 1955, Emmy award for best comedy series show 1957, Tony awards 1951, 72); author: (with Robert Saffron) The Laugh Is On Me: The Phil Silvers Story, 1973. Mem. Screen Actors Guild, AFTRA, Am. Guild Variety Artists, Friars Club, Calif. Country Club. Home: Beverly Hills Calif. Died Nov. 1, 1985.

SIMAK, CLIFFORD D(ONALD), author; b. Millville, Wis., Aug. 3, 1904; s. John Lewis and Margaret (Wiseman) S.; m. Agnes Kuchenberg, Apr. 13, 1929; children: Richard Scott, Shelley Ellen. Student, U. Wis. Reporter Iron River Reporter (Mich.), Spencer Reporter (Iowa), Dickinson Press (N.D,), Brainerd Dispatch (Minn.); with Mpls. Star, 1939-76, news editor, 1949-76. Author: (novels) The Creator, 1935, Cosmic Engineers, 1939, Time and Again, 1950, City, 1952, Time Is the Simplest Thing, 1961, Way Station, 1963, All Flesh Is Grass, 1965, The Werewolf Principle, 1967, The Goblin Reservation, 1968, Out of Their Minds, 1970, A Choice of Gods, 1972, Shakespeare's Planet, 1976, A Heritage of Stars, 1977, Mastgodonia, 1978, Project Pope, 1981, Special Deliverance, 1982, Highway of Eternity, 1986; (nonfiction) The Solar System: Our New Front Yard, 1962, Geology, 1965, Trilobite, Dinosaur and Man: The Earth's Story, 1966, Wonder and Glory: The Story of the Universe, 1969, Prehistoric Man, 1971, others; (short stories) Strangers in the Universe, 1956, The Worlds of Clifford Simak, 1960, All the Traps of Earth and Other Stories, 1962, Skirmish: The Great Short Science Fiction of Clifford D. Simak, 1977, others; contbr. lit. to Astounding Sci. Fiction mag., Galaxy Sci. Fiction. Recipient Internat. Fantasy award, 1953, Hugo award, 1959, 64, 80, Grand Masters award Sci. Fiction Writers Am., 1977, Jupiter award, 1978, Nebula award Sci. Fiction Writers Am., 1980. Died Apr. 25, 1988; interred Lakewood Cemetary, Mpls.

SIMMONS, JOHN EDWARDS, publisher; b. Osceola, Iowa, May 30, 1918; s. Paul Murray and Gladys (Edwards) S.; m. Eleanor Pownall, Apr. 1, 1947; children: Frederick Pownall, Mary Murray. BA, U. Iowa, 1947. Bus. mgr. U. Pa. Press, 1950-54; asst. mgr. Cornell U. Press, 1954-60; sr. editor U. Chgo. Press, 1960-61; dir. publs. U. Iowa, Iowa City, 1961-77; dir. U. Iowa Press, 1970-86. With U.S. Army, 1941-45. Home: Iowa City Iowa. Died July, 1986.

SIMMONS, OZZIE GORDON, sociologist, educator; b. Winnipeg, Man., Can., Oct. 9, 1919; s. Max and Rose (Goldstone) S.; m. Charlotte Sonenklar, Dec. 9, 1942; children: Gregor, Lauren, Paula. B.S., Northwestern U., 1941; M.A., Harvard U., 1948, Ph.D., 1952. Dir. in Peru for Inst. Social Anthropology, Smithsonian Instn., also vis. prof. U. San Marcos, Lima, Peru, 1949-52; cons. anthropologist Inst. Inter-Am. Affairs, Santiago, Chile, 1953; asso. prof. anthropology Harvard U. Sch. Public Health, 1953-61; prof. sociology, also dir. Inst. Behavioral Sci., U. Colo., Boulder, 1961-68; sr. faculty research asso. Brandeis U., 1961-65; program officer internat. div. Ford Found., 1968-81; lectr. behavioral sci. Johns Hopkins U., Balt., 1968-71; disting. vis. prof. sociology Fordham U., 1981-84, prof., chmn. dept. sociology and anthropology, 1984-86, disting. lectr. dept. sociology and anthropology, sr. research assoc. Hispanic Research Ctr., 1986-88; cons. NIH, also mem. health services research study sect., 1961-65; cons. VA, Ford Found.; chmn. research study sect. alcoholism and alcohol-related problems Nat. Center Prevention and Control of Alcoholism, NIMH, 1967-68. Author: Social Status and Public Health, 1958, After Hospitalization: The Mental Patient and his Family, 1960, (with Howard E. Freeman) The Mental Patient Comes Home, 1963, Work and Mental Illness: Eight Case Studies, 1965, Mexican Americans and Anglo Americans in South Texas, 1974, Development Perspectives and Population Change, 1983, Perspectives on Development and Population Change in the Third World, 1988, also numerous research articles on behavioral and health scis.; assoc. editor Am. Sociol. Review, 1959-62, Jour. Health and Human Behavior, 1959-66; Asso. editor: Social Sci. and Medicine, 1966-76; Assoc. editor: Jour. Health and Social Behavior, 1967-71, Evaluation Rev, 1980-84. Served with USAAF, 1942-46. Co-recipient Hofheimer prize Am. Psychiat. Assn., 1963; Sigmund Livingston fellow, Arnold traveling fellow Harvard. Fellow Am. Sociol. Assn. (past mem. exec. council sect. med. sociology), Population Assn. Am., Internat. Union Sci. Study Population; mem. Phi Beta Kappa. Home: River Vale N.J. Died Nov. 26, 1988; buried Garden of Memories, Washington Township, N.J.

SIMMONS, ROBERT GLENMORE, judge; b. Scotts Bluff County, Nebr., Dec. 25, 1891; s. Charles H. and lice May (Sheldon) S.; m. Gladyce Weil, June 23, 1917; children: Robert G., Marian Jean, Ray Clifford. Student, Hastings Coll., 1909-11, LLD, 1942; LLB, U. Nebr., 1915. Pvt. practice Gering, 1915; county atty. Scotts Bluff County, 1916-17; mem. 68th to 72d U.S. Congresses 6th Nebr. dist., 1923-33; chief justice Nebr. Supreme Ct., from 1938; mem. Pres. Emergency bds.; arbitrator Nat. Mediation Bd.; neutral mem., referee Nat. R.R. adjustment Bd.; designated dep. judge adminstrv. tribunal ILO, Geneva, 1955, 58; sent to Orient by Dept. State, 1952, 53, Mid. East, Gold Coast, 1956; apptd. chmn. legal group Pres. eisenhower's People-to-People Program, 1956. Contbr. articles to profl. jours. Rep. nominee for U.S. Senate, 1934, 36. 2d lt. U.S. Army, 1917-19. Recipient Order Kalantiao Cen. Philippine U., 1955, cert. of merit USIA, 1956, award Freedom's Found., 1960. Mem. ABA (mem. Ho. Dels. 1946-48, chmn. spl. com. on improving adminstrn. of njustice, adv. bd. jour. 1958-61), Nebr. Bar Assn., Conf. Chief Justices (exec. coun. 1959-60), Am. Legion (comdr. Dept. Nebr. 1920-21), U. Nebr. Alumni Assn. (pres. 1921), Masons (33 degree), Shriners, Order of Coif. Congregationalist. †

SIMMS, BENNETT THOMAS, federal agency executive, veterinarian; b. Emelle, Ala., Jan. 26, 1888; s. John Thomas and N. Enes (Thomas) S.; m. Lillian Elizabeth LaLonde, June 21, 1922; children: Bennett Thomas, Elizabeth LaLonde, John Donald, Marjorie Epes. DVM, Ala. Poly. Inst., 1911; student, U. Chgo., 1912-13. Instr. vet. dept. N.C. State Coll., 1911; asst. prof. vet. medicine Oreg. State Coll., 1913-14, prof., dept. head and exptl. sta. veterinarian, 1914-38; dir. regional animal disease rsch. lab Bur. Animal Husbandry, USDA, Auburn, Ala., 1938-45, chief, 1945-54, chief animal disease and parasite rsch. br., 1954-55, dir. livestock rsch., 1955-57, asst. adminstr., prodn. rsch., 1957; vet. specialist Nebr. unit Internat. Commodity Agreement, USDA, Turkey, from 1957. Fellow AAAS; mem. N.Y. Acad. Scis., Washington Acad. Scis., AVMA (pres.), Am. Soc. Parasitologists, Sigma Xi, Gamma Sigma Delta, Alpha Zeta, Alpha Psi, Beta Theta Pi. Home: South Arlington Va. †

SIMONDS, RALPH WARNER, investment banker; b. Burlington, Vt., Apr. 16, 1891; s. Abram B. and Helen (Warner) S.; m. Bernardine Kimball, 1915; children: Elizabeth Simonds Seelbach, Barbara Simonds Hibbard, Ralph Warner, Richard, Bernardine Simonds Templeton. BS, U. Vt., 1913; LLB, Detroit Coll. Law, 1918. Pres. Baker, Simonds & Co., Inc., from 1923; bd. dirs. Ex-Cello-O Corp.; cons. E.F. Hutton & Co., Inc. Co-chmn. war fin. com., bond drives, 1942-45; vice chmn. sponsors Grad. Sch. Bus. Adminstrn. U. Va. Mem. Blue Ridge Swimming Club (pres.), Farmington Hunt Club, Farmington Country Club (Charlottesville, Va.), Lost Tree Club (Lost Tree Village, Fla.). Home: Ivy Va. †

SIMONETTO, JOHN AMBROSE, industrial contracting executive; b. Albia, Iowa, Dec. 12, 1915; s. John and Catherine Theresa (Cappellin) S.; m. Theres Rita Cassidy, Jan. 3, 1938; children: Patrician Simonetto Scubelek, Joseph, Pamela Simonetto Pampe, Michael, John. Student pub. schs., Albia, Iowa. V.p. J.M.Foster Inc., Gary, Ind., 1963-70, exec. v.p., 1970-86; bd. dirs. Lake County Sheriff's Merit Bd., 1982-84. Mem. Nat. Erectors Assn. (dir. nat. maintenance agreements policy com.). Home: Crown Point Ind. Died Apr. 12, 1986; buried Valparaiso, Ind.

SIMONPIETRI, ANDRE C., foreign service officer; b. Richmond, Va., July 23, 1911; s. Auguste and Alma Cecilia (Dominici) S.; m. Grace Marie Boland, May 24, 1941; children: Andre C., Grace Alma Brix, D. Augustine III, Pierre Antoine, Raymond, Paul Philippe. AB, Università Urbana, Rome, 1931, MA, 1932, PhD, 1935; S.T.B., Università, Rome, 1934. Instr. U. Md., 1936-37, pub. agt., 1937-38; exec. asst. div. internat. confs. Dept. State, 1938-42; lectr. Washington Coll. of Fgn. Svc., 1939-41; sec. Commn. on Cartography Pan-Am. Inst. of Geography and History, 1942-51; sec. gen. Mexico city, 1951-56; spl. adviser on cartography Dept. State, 1945-51; liaison officer Joint Chiefs of Staff, 1947-51; assoc. dir. Office Internat. Relations Nat. Acad. Scis., Nat. Rsch. Coun., Washington, 1956-62; appt. sci. offier Fgn. Svc. Res., 1962; sci. attache Am. Embassy, Rio de Janeiro, 1962-67; assigned Am. Embassy, Buenos Aires, 1967-71, counselor for sci. affairs, 1970-71; counselor for sci. and technol. affairs Am. Embassy, Mexico City, 1971-75; cons. Dept. State, 1975-80; liaison officer Internat. Union Geodesy and Geophysics-Pan-Am. Inst. Geography and History, 1957-63; chmn. U.S. Regional Sci. Office for Latin Am., 1962-67; chmn. del. to numerous internat. confs.; mem. bd. U.S.-Brazil Ednl. (Fulbright) Commn., 1964-67, U.S.-Argentina, 1970-71; mem. Inter-Am. Com. on Sci. and Tech. OAS, 1974-78.

Editor, author, linguist, internat. sci. affairs authority. Mem. numerous U.S. and fgn. profl. assns.; Cosmos Club (Washington), Clube de Golfe de Brasilia, San Andres Club (Buenos Aires), Gavea Golf Club (Rio de Janeiro), Club de Golf Mexico, Culpeper (Va.) Country Club. Home: Rixeyville Va. Died Feb. 12, 1986; buried Culpeper, Va.

SIMONS, ALBERT, architect; b. Charleston, S.C., July 6, 1890; s. Thomas Grangee III and Serena Daniel (Aiken) S.; m. Harriet Porcher Stoney, Dec. 1, 1917; children: Albert, Samuel Stoney, Serena Aiken, Harriet Porcher. Student, Coll. Charleston, 1906-07, LittD, 1970; BS, U. Pa., 1911, MS, 1912; student, Atelier of Ernest Hebrard, Paris, 1912; traveled and studied in Europe, 1912-13. Draftsman with Lawrence Hall Fowler, Balt., 1914; instr. dept. architecture Clemson (S.C.) Coll., 1915-16; ptnr. Todd, Simons & Todd, Charleston, 1916-17, Simons and Lapham, 1920-55, Simons, Lapham & Mitchell, 1955-64, Simons, Lapham, Mitchell & Small, 1964-72, Simons, Mitchell, Small & Donahue, from 1973. Mem. Planning and Zoning Commn. of Charleston; mem. Charleston County Planning Bd. With U.S. Army A.E.F., 1917-19; served to maj. AUS, 1943-45. Recipient award So. Acad. Letters, Arts and Scis., 1973. Fellow AIA, Royal Soc. Arts; mem. NAD (assoc.), Nat. Soc. Lit. and the Arts, Soc. of Cin., St. Cecilia Soc., Masons, Alpha Tau Omega. Home: Charleston S.C. †

SIMONS, DOLPH COLLINS, newspaper publisher, editor; b. Lawrence, Kans., Nov. 24, 1904; s. W.C. and Gertrude (Reineke) S.; m. Marie Nelson, Feb. 16, 1929; children: Dolph Collins, John Nelson. AB, U. Kans., 1925. Reporter AP, Chgo., 1924; office mgr. Lawrence Daily Jour.-World, 1925, editor, 1950-79, pub., 1944-63; pres. World Co., 1951-69, chmn. bd., 1969-89; dir. Fed. Res. Bd., Kansas City, 1962-70, dep. chmn., 1963-66, chmn., 1967-70. Author: Germany and Austria, May-June 1947, A Globe-Circler's Diary, 1949. Mem. Pulitzer Awards Jury, 1962-63; del. Rep. Nat. Conv., 1944, 60; v.p. Eisenhower Found., 1951-89; trustee, past pres. U. Kans. Endowment Assn.; v.p., past chmn. bd. trustees Kans. 4-H Found.; trustee Midwest Research Inst., Kansas City; past pres. William Allen White Found.; civilian observer round-the-world Navy Flight, 1949. Recipient Disting. Service citation U. Kans., 1956, Ellsworth award, 1975, Dolph Simons Sr. Research award in biomed. scis., 1981; Pub. Service award Baker U., 1976; Disting. Service in Journalism award U. Minn., 1966. Mem. Lawrence C. of C. (past pres., dir.), U. Kans. Alumni Assn. (dir., past pres.), Kans. Press Assn. (past dir. and pres.), Am. Soc. Newspaper Editors (dir. AP 1951-60, v.p. 1950-51, 59-60), Kans. Hist. Soc. (dir.), Lawrence Hist. Soc. (past pres.), Phi Kappa Psi, Sigma Delta Chi. Baptist. Clubs: Lawrence Country; River, Kansas City Country, Mercury (Kansas City, Mo.); Kansas Day Rep. (past pres.); Garden of Gods (Colorado Springs, Colo.); Valley Country (Scottsdale, Ariz.). Lodges: Masons, Rotary. Home: Lawrence Kans. also: Scottsdale Ariz. Died Feb. 14, 1989.

SIMPSON, BRYAN, federal judge; b. Kissimmee, Fla., May 30, 1903; s. Arthur Allen and Mary Elizabeth (Bryan); LLB, U. Fla., 1926; LLD (hon.), Stetson U., 1958; m. Sarah George Hall (Hixon), Feb. 15, 1941; children: John H. Hixon, George C. Hixon, Joseph M. Hixon (stepsons); 1 son, Bryan; m. 2d, Sally Thompson Jones, Mar. 1, 1968; stepchildren: Eve Dunbar Jones, Isaac F. Jones, III. Bar: Fla. 1926; pvt. practice Jacksonville, 1926-39; asst. states atty. 4th Fla. Cir., 1933-37; judge Criminal Ct. of Record, Duval County, Fla., 1939-46; cir. judge Fourth Fla. Cir., 1946-50; U.S. dist. judge So. Dist. Fla., 1950-60; chief judge U.S. Ct. Appeals, 5th Cir., 1966-75. Trustee Cummer Gallery Art; trustee emeritus Bolles Sch., Jacksonville; bd. dirs. Children's Home Soc. Fla. 1st lt. AUS, 1943-45, ETO. Mem. Am., Jacksonville, Fed. bar assns., Maritime Law Assn., U.S., Fla. Bar, Rotary , Timuquana Country Club, River Club, Fla. Yacht, Saw Grass Club, Ponte Vedra (Jacksonville), Ft. Worth Club, Nat. Lawyers Club (hon.) (Washington), Phi Delta Phi, Kappa Alpha. Democrat. Episcopalian. Died Aug. 22, 1987.

SIMPSON, EDNA (MRS. SIDNEY SIMPSON), congresswoman; b. Carrollton, Ill., Oct. 26, 1891; m. Sidney Simpson, Feb. 1, 1920 (dec.); children: Martha Simpson Stoffel, Janet. Mem 86th Congress, 20th Ill. Dist., 1958. Republican. Home: Carrollton Ill. †

SIMPSON, GEORGE GAYLORD, educator, vertebrate paleontologist; b. Chgo., June 16, 1902; s. Joseph Alexander and Helen Julia (Kinney) S.; m. Lydia Pedroja, Feb. 2, 1923 (div. Apr. 1938); children: Helen Frances, Patricia (dec.), Joan, Elizabeth; m. 2d. Anne Roe, May 27, 1938. Student, U. Colo., 1918-19, 20-22; PhB, Yale U., 1923, PhD, 1926, ScD, 1946; ScD, Princeton, 1947, U. Durham, 1951, Oxford U., 1951, U. N.Mex., 1954, U. Chgo., 1959, Cambridge (Eng.) U., 1965, York U., 1966, Kenyon Coll., 1968, U. Colo., 1968; LLD, U. Glasgow, 1951; Dr. h.c., U. Paris, France, 1965, Universidad de la Plata, Argentina, 1977. Marsh fellow, rsch. on Mesozoic mammals Peabody Mus., Yale, 1924-26; field asst. Am. Mus. Nat. History, N.Y.C., 1924, asst. curator of vertebrate paleontology, 1927, assoc. curator, 1928-42, curator of fossil mammals, 1942-59, chmn. dept. geology and paleontology, 1944-58; prof. vertebrate paleontology Columbia, 1945-59; Agassiz prof. vertebrate paleontology Mus. Comparative Zoology, Harvard, 1959-70; prof. geoscis. U. Ariz., Tucson, 1967-84; pres., trustee Simroe Found., 1968-84; NRC and Internat. Edn. Bd. fellow in work on early fossil mammals, chiefly in Brit. Mus., London, also other instns., Eng., France and Germany, 1926-27; expdns. to collect fossil animals include No. Tex., Mont., N.Mex., Fla. and S.E. States, Argentina, Venezuala, Brazil. Author: The Meaning of Evolution, rev. edit., 1967, Horses, 1951, Life of the Past, 1953, The Major Features of Evolution, 1953, Evolution and Geography, 1953, Life, 1957, Quantitative Zoology, 1960, Principles of Animal Taxonomy, 1961, This View of Life: The World of an Evolutionist, 1964, The Geography of Evolution, 1965, Biology and Man, 1969, Penguins, 1976, Concession to the Improbable, an Unconventional Autobiography, 1978, Splendid Isolation, The Curious History of South American Mammals, 1980, Why and How, Some Problems and Methods in Historical Biology, 1980. Served to maj. U.S. Army, 1942-44. Recipient Cross medal Yale Grad. Assn., 1969, Lewis prize Am. Philos. Soc., 1942, Thompson medal NAS, 1943, Elliot medal, 1944, 65, Gaudry medal Geol. Soc. France, 1947, Hayden medal, 1951, Penrose medal Geol. Soc. Am., 1952, André H. Dumont medal Geol. Soc. Belgium, 1953, Darwin-Wallace medal Linnean Soc., 1958, Darwin Plakette, Deutsche Akad. Naturforscher Leopoldina, 1959, Gold Medal Linnean Soc., 1962, Darwin medal Royal Soc., 1962, Nat. Medal Sci., 1966, disting. achievement medal Am. Mus., 1969, Paleontol. Soc. medal, 1973, Internat. award Nat. Mus. Natural History, 1976. Fellow Am. Acad. Arts and Scis., NAS, Am. Philos. Soc., Geol. Soc. Am., Paleontol. Soc., AAAS; mem. Soc. Vertebrate Paleontology (sec.-treas. 1940-41, pres. 1942), Soc. Study Evolution (pres. 1946), Am. Soc. Mammologists, Soc. Systematic Zoology (pres. 1962), Am. Soc. Zoologists (pres. 1964), Academia Nazionale dei Lincei (Italy), Academia Nazionale dei XL (Italy), Sociedad Argentina de Estudios Geog. Gaea (hon. corr.), Zool. Soc. London (fgn. mem.), Royal Soc. (fgn. mem.), Linnean Soc. London (fgn. mem.), Academia de Ciencias (Venezuela, Brazil, Argentina), Asociacion Paleontologica Argentina (hon. mem.), Deutsch Gesellschaft für Saugetierkunde (hon.), Senkenbergische Naturforschende Gesellschaft, Phi Beta Kappa, Sigma Xi. Home: Tucson Ariz. Died Oct. 6, 1984.

SIMPSON, GORDON, lawyer; b. Gilmer, Tex., Oct. 30, 1894; s. Robert Walton and Adeline (Fuller) S.; m. Grace Jones, Sept. 20, 1921; children—Mary Margaret (Mrs. Harry Edward Carloss, Jr.), Barbara (Mrs. John Charles Cooper). Student, Baylor U., 1911-13; A.B., U. Tex., 1915, J.D., 1919. Bar: Tex. bar 1919, U.S. Supreme Ct 1942. Practiced law Tyler, Tex., 1920-42; mem. Tex. Ho. Reps., 1923-27; judge 7th dist. Tex., 1930; asso. justice Tex. Supreme Ct., 1945-49; pvt. practice Dallas, 1949-87; pres. Gen. Am. Oil Co., Texas, 1955-60; assoc. firm Thompson & Knight (and predecessor), 1960-87; Mem. Tex. Civil Jud. Council, 1946-56, pres., 1955-56. Chmn. commn. for investigation war crime cases Dept. Army, Dachau, Germany, 1948. Served to lt. U.S. Army, 1917-19; lt. col. JAG. dept. AUS, 1942-44; col. Res. ret. Decorated Bronze Star. Fellow Am. Bar Found.; mem. Internat., Am., Smith County, Dallas bar assns., Judge Adv. Assn. (pres. 1955-56), Am. Law Inst. (life), Tex. Presbyn. Found. (chmn. 1953-57, 60-62, 63-66), State Bar Tex. (pres. 1941-42), Ind. Petroleum Assn. Am. (pres. 1958-59, life mem.), Am. Petroleum Inst., Delta Chi. Democrat. Presbyterian. Clubs: Mason, Elk, Town and Gown, Petroleum, Dallas Country. Home: Dallas Tex. Died Feb. 13, 1987.

SIMPSON, HARRELL ABNER, lawyer, judge; b. Evening Shade, Ark., Feb. 19, 1913; s. James Monroe and Laura Frances (Harrell) S.; m. Norma Jeanne Belford, Oct. 24, 1941; children: Harrell Abner, Anne Belford. Grad., Ark. Tech., Russellville, 1933; LLB, U. Ark., 1938; student, Nat. Coll. State Trial Judges, 1968. Bar: Ark. 1938, U.S. Supreme Ct. 1952. Tchr. rural schs. Lawrence County, Ark., 1933-35; dep. pros. atty. Randolph County, Ark., 1939-44; dep. 16th Jud. Cir., Pocahontas, Ark., 1944, pros. atty., 1945-48, judge, 1954-79; chmn. com. for revision Ark. Criminal Code; mem. Ark. Jud. Coun., pres., 1972-73; mem. State-Fed. Jud. Coun.; mem. com. on model jury instrn. under criminal code Ark. Supreme Ct. Chmn. March of Dimes; commr. Little League Baseball; cub master Cub Scouts Am. Nat. Coll. State Trial Judges fellow. Mem. Am. Judicature Soc., Am., Ark., Randolph-Lawrence, Eight Chancery bar assns., Pocahontas C. of C. (past sec.), Masons, Order Eastern Star, Pi Kappa Alpha. Methodist (bd. stewards). Home: Pocahontas Ark. Died July 9, 1984.

SIMS, VAN BUREN, retail executive; b. Cedartown, Ga., Mar. 4, 1890; s. John Warren and Alilce Rosalie (Locke) S.; m. Anne Lindsay, Nov. 12, 1913. Student, Ouachita Coll., 1907-08. Various clerical positions 1910-13, legis. sec. to gov. of Ark., 1913, 17; fin. clk. U.S. Indian Svc., Wahpeton (N.D.) and Pawnee (Okla.), 1914-15; warrant clk. Ark. State Treasury, 1915-16; asst. state compt. Office State Comptr. State of Ark., 1917-20, state compt., 1920-25; asst. treas. James McCreery & Co., N.Y.C., 1925-27; with Lord & Taylor, N.Y.C., from 1927, treas., 1927-46, exec. v.p., 1931-46, 1st v.p., 1946-59, chmn. bd., from 1959, also bd. dirs. Chmn. fund raising campaigns for civic, religious, charitable and polit. causes. Mem. N.Y. State Coun. Retail Mchts., 60 East Club. Baptist. Home: New York N.Y.†

SINCLAIR, GREGG MANNERS, university president; b. St. Marys, Ont., Can., May 20, 1890; came to U.S., 1893; s. John and Frances Ann (Henderson) S.; m. Marjorie Putnam, May 20, 1939. BA, U. Minn., 1912, LLD, 1949; MA, Columbia U., 1919, LLD, 1954; LLD, Ohio State U., 1951, U. Calif., 1955; HHD, U. Hawaii, 1956; DLitt, Kelo U., Japan, 1960. Tchr. English various schs., Kyoto, Japan, 1912-15; with bond and mortgage bus. Mpls., 1915-17, 21-23; tchr. Hikone (Japan) Coll. Commerce, 1923-26; asst. prof. English U. Hawaii, 1928-31, assoc. prof., 1931-36, prof., from 1936, dir. Oriental Inst., 1936-40, pres., 1942-55. Translator: (with B. Mitsui) an Adopted Husband, 1919; (with J. K. Suita) Tokyo People, 1926; editor: Ten Short Stories by Henry James (2 vols.), 1925; contbr. articles to jours. Active in war svc. YMCA, Camp Grant, Ill., 1918; pres. Footlights, Honolulu, 1930-31; bd. dirs. Honolulu Community Theatre, 1935-47; mem. U.S. Loyalty Rev. Bd., 1949-51; chmn. citizens adv. com. Hawaii Statehood Commn.; vice chmn. com. civil rights, State of Hawaii. Mem. Bengal, Japan Asiatic Socs., Newcomen Soc., Hawaiian Acad. Sci., Dickens Fellowship, Bronte Soc., Outrigger Canoe, Pacific Club, Phi Beta Kappa, Phi Kappa Phi, Pi Gamma Mu. Democrat. Home: Honolulu Hawaii. †

SINGLETON, CHARLES SOUTHWARD, Romance language educator; b. McLoud, Okla., Apr. 21, 1909; s. Ellison Oliver and Lucy (Pennington) S.; m. Eula Duke, June 27, 1935. AB, U. Mo., 1931; PhD, U. Calif., 1936; MA (hon.), Harvard, 1948; DLitt (hon.), U. Mo., U. Bologna, Italy, Western Md. Coll.; LHD (hon.), Middlebury (Vt.) Coll. Exchange fellow from Berkeley (Calif.) Internat. House Italy, 1934-36; instr. Italian U. Calif., 1936; instr. French and Italian U. Mo., 1936-37; succeseively assoc. in Italian, assoc. prof., prof. Italian lit., chmn. dept. Romance langs. Johns Hopkins U., 1937-48; vis. lectr. Italian lit. Harvard, 1947, prof. Romance langs., 1948-57, chmn. dept., 1950-52; prof. humanistic studies Johns Hopkins U., 1957-85, dir. Humanities Ctr., 1966-85; prof.-at-large Cornell U. Author: Canti carnascialeschi del Rinascimento (Scrittori d'Italia), 1936, Nuovi canti carnascialeschi del Rinascimento, 1940, An Essay on the Vita Nuova, 1949, Dante Studies, 1954, Il Decameron, 1955, Journey to Beatrice, 1958; editor: Art, Science and History in the Renaissance, 1967, Modern Language Notes: Toynbee Dante Dictionary, 1968, Interpretation, Theory and Practice, 1969; contbr. articles to profl. jours. Decorated Commendatore dell 'ordine al merito della Republica, Italy; recipient Internat. prize Italian lit. Forte dei Marmi, Italy; Guggenheim fellow, 1962. Mem. Am. Philos. Soc., AAUP, MLA, Arcadia, Phi Beta Kappa. Home: New Windsor Md. Died Oct. 10, 1985.

SIPP, JOHN LOUIS FRANCIS, banker; b. Staten Island, N.Y., Feb. 7, 1919; s. John L. and Margaret (Kiernan) S.; m. Virginia Fach, Dec. 11, 1944; children: John Jeffrey, Gregory David. B.A., Lehigh U., 1941; J.D., Bklyn. Law Sch., 1949. Bar: N.Y. 1949. Trainee Gen. Cable Corp., Rome, N.Y., 1941-42; prodn. engr. Perth Amboy, N.J., 1946-47; prnt. Fach & Sipps, S.I., N.Y., 1949-67, Fach & Sipps & Hall, S.I., N.Y., 1967-74; chmn. bd., chief exec. officer S.I. Savs. Bank, 1974-87, also dir., 1974-87; dir. Instl. Investors Mut. Found., N.Y.C., 1977; trustee Savs. Banks Retirement System. Bd. dirs. N.Y.C. Partnership, 1980-87 ; bd. dirs. Partnership for Neighborhood Safety, N.Y.C., 1982-87 ; mem. Com. on Character and Fitness 2d Jud. Dept., Bklyn., 1971-87 , Temporary Commn. of City Finances, N.Y.C., 1975-77, N.Y.C. Port Council on Devel. and Promotion, 1982-87 ; bd. dirs. Snug Harbor Cultural Ctr., 1979-87 ; mem. St. John's U. Council, 1976-87 . Served to capt. USAAF, 1943-46. Recipient Anchor award Soc. for Seaman's Children, 1979; recipient Disting Service award ARC, 1982, Community Service award Salvation Army, 1982. Mem. ABA, N.Y. State Bar Assn., Richmond County Bar Assn., Nat. Assn. Mut. Savs. Banks (bd. dirs. 1979-82). Roman Catholic. Clubs: Richmond County Country (gov.), Seaview Country, Club at World Trade Ctr. Lodge: Rotary. Home: Staten Island N.Y. Died May 4, 1987.

SIQVELAND, THORGEIR, foreign service officer; b. Kristanssand, Norway, July 15, 1892; s. Caspar Fredrik and Charlotte Aall (Buch) S.; m. Marie Didrikke Cappelen Flood, Jan. 7, 1944. BA, Oslo Katedralskole, 1911; res. officer, Royal Norwegian Officers Acad., 1913; LLB, Oslo U., 1920; LLD (hon.), Luther Coll., 1959. Asst. judge Mandal, Norway, 1921; attaché Norwegian Consulate Gen., Antwerp, Belgium, 1921; sec. Ministry Fgn. Affairs, Oslo, 1922-23; vice consul Shanghai, China, 1923-28; acting consul gen., Norwegian Consular judge for China 1925, 27; judge Internat. Mixed Ct. Shanghai, 1923-26; Norwegian consular rep. Provisional Ct. Shanghai, 1927-28; sec. legation Washington, 1928-31; 1st sec. Ministry Fgn. Affairs, Oslo, 1931-35, dir. legal div., 1935-46; consul gen. for Minn., N.D., S.D., Mont. Govt. of Norway, Mpls., from 1946, for Iowa, Nebr., from 1953. Capt. Norwegian Army, from 1939. Decorated comdr. Polonia Restitua; officer Portugese Order of Christ; officer Lithuanian Order Gdediminas, officer Red Cross Decoration; knight (1st class) Order St. Olav (Norway), comdr.; Cravat Order Brilliant Star (China); recipient Medal of Merit, 1957. Mem. Nordmanns-Forbundet (bd. dirs., coun., diploma), Assn. Res. Officers Norway, Adminstrv. League No. Countries, Sons of Norway (Mpls. chpt.), Minn. Leif Erikson Monument Assn., Norwegian-Am. Hist. Assn., Am. Automobile Assn., Six O'clock Club, Norwegian Luncheon Club, Minneapolis Club (hon.), Skylight Club, Minnesota Club. Lutheran. †

SITTLER, JOSEPH, educator, clergyman; b. Upper Sandusky, Ohio, Sept. 26, 1904; s. Joseph and Minnie (Vieth) S.; m. Jeanne Seitz, Aug. 10, 1939; children: Stephen, Joseph IV, Edward, Barbara, Philip, Bay. AB, Wittenberg Coll., 1927, LLD, 1956; BD, Hamma Div. Sch., 1930; DD, Wagner Coll., 1948, Eureka Coll., 1960, Gettysburg Coll., 1962, Thiel Coll., 1975, Carleton Coll., 1976; LHD, Alfred U., 1959; LLD, Notre Dame, 1966, Loyola U., 1969; LittD, Meadville Theol. Sem., 1970. Ordained to ministry Luth. United Luth. Ch., 1930. Pastor, Cleve., 1930-43; prof. theology Chgo. Luth. Theol. Sem., Maywood, Ill., 1943-57; prof. theology U. Chgo., 1957-73, prof. emeritus, 1973-87; disting. prof. in residence Lutheran Sch. Theology, Chgo.; Lyman-Beecher lectr. Yale U., 1959; William Belden Noble lectr. Harvard U., 1959. Author: Doctrine of the Word, 1948, Structure of Christian Ethics, 1958, Ecology of Faith, 1961, Care of the Earth, 1964, The Anguish of Preaching, 1966, Essays on Nature and Grace, 1972, Gravity and Grace: Reflections & Provocations, 1986. Mem. Am. Theol. Soc. Home: Chicago Ill. Died Dec. 28, 1987.

SIX, ROBERT FORMAN, airline executive; b. Stockton, Calif., June 25, 1907; s. Clarence Logan and Genevieve (Peters) S.; m. Audrey Meadows, Aug. 1961. Ed. pub. schs., Stockton; DSc (hon.), U. Colo. Instr. Stockton and Frisco, Stockton, 1929-33; dist. circulation mgr. San Francisco Chronicle, 1933-35; owner Mouton & Six, 1935-37; pres., dir. Continental Airlines, 1938-82; chmn. bd. Continental Air Services, 1938-82. Mem. nat. citizens bd. Eisenhower Med. Ctr.; mem. Airlift Com. Nat. Def. Transp., Wright Bros. Hall of Fame Com., Air Force Acad. Found., Nat. Football Found. and Hall of Fame; mem. bd. nominators Internat. Aerospace Hall of Fame; mem. Gen. McArthur Adv. Bd.; vice chmn. UN Day Com., 1973; trustee City of Hope Med. Ctr. Lt. Col. USAAF, 1942-44, PTO. Decorated Army Commendation medal. Mem. Wings Club of Am., Conquistadores del Cielo, Nat. Aviation Club, Sky Club, Rocky Mountain Food and Wine Soc., Chevaliers du Tastevin, Confrerie de la Chaine des Rotiesseurs, First Flight Soc., Nat. Aeros. Assn., Colo. Aviation History Soc., Brown Palace Club, Denver Club, Aero Club (Washington), Brook Club (N.Y.C.), Travellers Club (Paris), Vallejo Gun Club, Am. Sportsman, Raffles Club. Home: Beverly Hills Calif. Died Oct. 6, 1986; buried Holy Cross Cemetery, L.A.

SKALLERUP, WALTER THORWALD, JR., lawyer; b. Chgo., Feb. 17, 1921; s. Walter Thorwald and Ruth (White) S.; m. Nancy McGhee Baxter, Dec. 16, 1950 (dec.); children: Paula Skallerup Osborn, Walter Thorwald III, Andrew (dec.), Nancy.; m. Margaret Perkins Bouhafa, Dec. 24, 1983. B.A., Swarthmore Coll., 1942; LL.B., Yale U., 1947. Bar: D.C. 1948. Atty. AEC, 1947-52; partner Volpe, Boskey & Skallerup, Washington, 1953-61; dep. asst. sec. for security policy U.S. Dept. Def. 1962-67; partner Cox, Langford & Brown, Washington, 1968-71; pvt. practice 1973-81; gen. counsel Dept. Navy, Washington., 1981-87 ; spl. cons. to undersec. state, 1968-69; legal cons. Joint Congressional Com. on Atomic Energy, 1973-74; mem. panel U.S. AEC Atomic Safety and Licensing Bd., 1970-71. Treas. Citizens for Senator Henry M. Jackson campaign, 1971-72; treas., counsel Senator Henry M. Jackson for Pres. Com., 1974-76; bd. mgrs. Swarthmore (Pa.) Coll., 1977-87 . Served with USNR, 1943-45. Home: McLean Va. Died July 29, 1987.

SKLAR, GEORGE, writer; b. Meriden, Conn., June 1, 1908; s. Ezak and Bertha (Marshak) S.; m. Miriam Blecher, Aug. 22, 1935; children—Judith, Daniel, Zachary. B.A., Yale, 1929; postgrad. dept. drama, 1929-31. Author: (with Albert Maltz) plays Merry Go Round; produced plays, Avon Theatre, New York, 1932, Peace On Earth, (with Albert Maltz), Theatre Union, 1933, Stevedore, (with Paul Peters), Theatre Union, 1934, Parade, (with Paul Peters), Theatre Guild, N.Y.C., 1935, Life and Death of An American; produced by plays, Fed. Theatre Project, 1939; novel The Two Worlds of Johnny Truro, 1947; (with Vera Caspary) play Laura; produced as play, Cort Theatre, N.Y.C., 1947; novel The Promising Young Men, 1951, The Housewarming, 1953, The Identity of Dr. Frazier, 1961; play And People All Around, 1966 (1966-67 selection Am. Playwrights Theatre), Brown Pelican, 1972. John Golden fellow, 1939. Mem. Dramatists' Guild, Authors' Guild, Phi Beta Kappa. Home: Los Angeles Calif. Died May 15, 1988.

SLACK, FRANCIS GODDARD, physics educator; b. Superior, Wis., Nov. 1, 1897; s. William H. and Enid (Warner) S.; m. Belle Hunt, June 30, 1923. BS, U. Ga., 1918; PhD, Columbia, 1926; student, U. Munich, Germany, 1926-27. Test engr. Gen. Electric Co., Schenectady, N.Y., 1920-21; assoc. prof. physics Vanderbilt U., Nashville, 1928-38, prof. physics, chmn. dept., from 1938; divisional dir. Div. War Rsch., Columbia, 1941-45. Contbr. articles on radiation, optics, and nuclear physics to sci. pubs. With. U.S. Army Air Service, 1918-19; 2d lt. Army Air Service Res. Fellow Am. Phys. Soc. (past. chmn. Southeastern sect.), AAAS; mem. Optical Soc. Am., Am. Soc. Engring Edn., Am. Assn. Physics Tchrs. (mem. coun. and bd. editors 1941-43), Tenn. Acad. Sci. (past pres.), Bellemeade Country Club of Nashville, Sigma Xi. Democrat. Presbyterian. Died Feb. 26, 1985.

SLATER, JOHN ELLIOT, consulting engineer; b. Somerville, Mass., Aug. 11, 1891; s. Fred Raymond and Millie Eva (Gilcreast) S.; m. Pauline Mabie Holman, June 7, 1916; children: Marilyn, Dorothy Holman, Philip Elliot. AB, Harvard U., 1913, grad. Sch. Bus. Adminstrn., 1913. With U.P. R.R., 1913-14; with N.Y., N.H.&H R.R., 1914-25, statistician, analyst, asst. to gen. mgr., chmn. bd., dir.; prof. transportation U. Ill., 1925-26; sec. and treas. Am. Brown Boveri Electric Corp., Camden, N.J., 1926-29; with Coverdale & Colpitts, cons. engrs., N.Y.C., 1929-66; mem. firm, 1931-66, then cons.; exec. v.p., pres., dir. Am. Export Lines, Inc., 1936-56; chmn. bd. N.Y. Shipbuilding Corp., 1951-53; trustee Atlantic Mut. Ins. Co. Regional dir. for North and N.Y. Africa for U.S. War Shipping Adminstrn., 1942-43. 1st lt. engrs. U.S. Army, Feb.-Oct. 1918; commd. capt. Transportation Corps, Oct. 1918; overseas, 1918-19. Mem. Soc. Naval Architecs and Marine Engrs. (assoc.), Essex Fells Country Club, Phi Beta Kappa. Episcopalian. Home: Essex Fells N.J. †

SLAVEN, LANT RADER, lawyer; b. Lewisburg, W.Va., Aug. 16, 1891; s. Wilbur Decatur and Nannie Waddel (Montgomery) S.; m. Rowena Rardon, Oct. 5, 1920; children: Margaret Slaven Canada, Nancy Slaven Davis, Katharine Slaven, Levis. AB, U. Va., 1911, LLB, 1914. Bar: W.Va. 1914. Assoc. Edward C. Lyon, N.Y.C., 1914-15; pvt. practice Williamson, W.Va., 1915-72; ptnr. firm Slaven, Staker & Smith (and predecessor law firm partnerships), Williamson, 1922-72; pres. Mingo Oil & Gas Co., Burning Creek Marrowbone Land Co.; chmn. bd., dir. Nat. Bank of Commerce (all Williamson). 2d lt. USAC, World War I. Mem. W.Va. Bar Assn. (pres, 1953-54), Raven Soc., Phi Beta Kappa, Order of Coif, Phi Delta Phi, Sigma Alpha Epsilon. Presbyterian. Home: Williamson W.Va. †

SLICHTER, HARRY CORMANY, editor; b. Kansas City, Mo., June 22, 1891; s. Samuel Cormany and Fanny (Smith) S.;.m. Gail Binkley, May 6, 1924; 1 child, Jane. Student, U. Mo., 1914-15; AB, Cornell U., 1920. Trombonist Kansas City, Chgo. and N.Y. orchs., 1909-20; actor road shows and vaudeville 1911-12; chemist packing house labs. Kansas City and Chgo., 1910-14; copy reader Waterbury (Conn.) Republican and Lynn (Mass.) Telegram-News, 1920-22; mng. editor Tampa (Fla.) Times, 1922-33; editorial writer St. Peterburg (Fla.) Independent, 1933-36; editor, mng. editor, radio commentator Telegraph-Herald, Dubuque, Iowa, from 1936. With Chem. Warfare Service, U.S. Army, World War I, also band leader. Mem. Dubuque C. of C., Dubuque Golf Club, Rotary. Methodist. Home: Dubuque Iowa. †

SLINGLUFF, THOMAS ROWLAND, JR., publishing company executive; b. Balt., Aug. 10, 1919; s. Thomas Rowland and Gertrude Seckel (Jenkins) S.; m. Pamela Lloyd, Mar. 30, 1953; children: Michael St. Clair, Pamela Devereux, Deirdre Ann. B.A., Stanford, 1948; diplôme d'Études, Sorbonne U. Paris, France, 1949. Staff officer London (Eng.) Embassy U.S. Foreign Service, 1949-52, Paris (France) Embassy, 1952-53; dir. Pa. State U. Press, University Park, Pa., 1958-72; treas., gen. mgr. Am. U. Pubs. Group Ltd., London, 1965-72; chmn., chief exec. officer Univ. Park Press Inc., Balt., 1967-81; chmn. Am. Pub. Co., Balt., 1981-84; pres. Olympia Holdings, Ltd., N.Y.C., 1981-84; owner Augean Stables, Balt. Trustee Walters Art Gallery, Balt., Md. Hist. Soc. Served with USAAC, 1942-45. Decorated D.F.C. with oak leaf cluster, Air medal. Mem. Soc. Colonial Wars, Pi Gamma Mu. Clubs: Md. (Balt.), Elkridge (Balt.), Greenspring Hunt (Balt.); Hurlingham (London); Brook (N.Y.C.). Home: Baltimore Md. Died Feb. 1984.

SLIVINSKY, CORNELL, engineering consultant; b. Sewickley, Pa., Sept. 18, 1925; s. Joseph J. and Florence M. (Cornell) S.; m. Ann M. Campolongo, July 24, 1948; children: Kyra, Valerie. BS, Tulsa U., 1944. Structural engr. Kellett Aircraft Corp., Phila., 1947-49; project engr. Vertol div. Boeing Co., Phila., 1949-60; v.p., gen. mgr. Parsons Corp., Traverse City, Mich., 1960-68; dir. plans and programs Gates Learjet Corp., Wichita, Kans., 1968-71; v.p., gen. mgr. Vero Beach Facility, Piper Aircraft Corp., Lock Haven, Pa., 1971-74; pres. Gen. Aviation div. Rockwell Internat., Bethany, Okla., 1974-81, v.p. adminstrn., El Segundo, Calif. br., 1981-83. cons. from 1983. Patentee in field. Mem. adv. bd. Okla. U. Aerospace Sch. With USAAF, 1944-47. Home: Palm Desert Calif. Died Feb. 1, 1986; interred West Newton, Pa.

SLOAN, HAROLD STEPHENSON, economist; b. Bklyn., Nov. 23, 1887; s. Alfred Pritchard and Katharine (Mead) S.; m. Bertha Louis Florey, Sept. 14, 1910; 1 child, Alvin Florey. BS, Columbia U., 1909, MA, 1926; LLD, U. Denver, 1946; DSc, Fairleigh Dickinson U., 1960. Treas., gen. mgr. De Camp & Sloan, Inc., Newark, 1908-25; clk. Bennett-Sloan & Co., 1909; tchr. econs. Marquand Sch., Bklyn., 1925-27, N.J. State Normal Sch., Newark, 1927-29; asst., later assoc. prof. N.J. State Tchrs. Coll., Upper Montclair, 1929-36; v.p., exec. dir. Alfred P. Sloan Found., 1936-45; vis. prof. NYU, 1941-58; dir. rsch. Fairleigh Dickinson U., Rutherford, N.J., 1957-71; vis. prof. NYU Grad. Sch., Columbia Tchrs. Coll., 1945-58; prof. interamerican course on edn. and econ. devel. Bogota, Colombia, 1959. Author: Today's Economics, 1936, Farming in America, 1947; co-author: Dictionary of Economics, 1948, Classrooms in the Factories, 1958, Classrooms in the Stores, 1962, Classrooms in the Military, 1964, Classrooms in Main Street, 1966; contbr. articles on econs. to publs. Pres. Inst. for Instructional Improvement. Mem. University Club, Alpha Delta Phi, Phi Delta Kappa. Unitarian. Home: New York N.Y. Died Nov. 5, 1988.

SLOAN, LAWRENCE WELLS, surgeon; b. Salt Lake City, June 13, 1896; s. Thomas Watts and Edna Margaret (Wells) S; m. Fulvia Ivins, Sept. 19, 1924; children: Carolyn Ivins, Ann-Lawrie, Margaret Elizabeth; m. 2d Natalie Norton, Dec. 22, 1963; stepchildren: William Blachly, Barbara Carpenter. Student, U. Utah, 1916-17; MD, Harvard, 1925. Missionary Ch. of Jesus Christ of Latter Day Saints, Germany and Eastern U.S., 1914; asst. in anatomy Harvard MEd. Sch.; asst. resident in pathology Boston City Hosp., 1925-26; surgical tng. Presbyn. Hosp., N.Y.C., 1926-31; practiced surgery N.Y.C., 1931-86; surgeon, cons. in surgery Presbyn. Hosp., 1961-86; assoc. prof. clin. surgery Columbia U., 1947-61, prof. clin. surgery emeritus, 1961-86; prof. clin. surgery Columbia-Presbyn. Hosp. Med. Ctr. Contbr. articles to profl. jours. 1st lt. F.A., U.S. Army, 1917-19; to lt. col. Med. Corps, 1942-45. Recipient Bronze Star. Mem. Am. Surg. Assn., Acad. of Medicine N.Y.C., N.Y. Surg. Soc., Am. Bd. Surgery, Century Assn. Internat. Soc. Surgery, Am. Goiter Assn., Am. Thyroid Assn. (dir. 1960-63, pres. 1966). Mormon. Home: Bronx N.Y. Died Apr. 29, 1986.

SLOTNICK, DANIEL LEONID, computer scientist, educator; b. N.Y.C., Nov. 12, 1931; s. Leonid and Sara (Janowski) S.; m. Joan Katherine Heil, Spet. 19, 1952; children: Ellen, Clare. BA, Columbia U., 1951; MA, NYU, 1952, PhD in Applied Math, 1956. Mem. staff Inst. Advanced Study Electronic Computer Project, Princeton, N.J., 1952-54, Princeton U., 1956-57; with IBM, Poughkeepsie and Yorktown Heights, N.Y., 1957-61, Westinghouse Corp., Balt., 1961-65; mem. faculty U. Ill., Urbana, 1965-85, prof. computer sci., 1965-85; cons. industry and govt.; chmn. bd. 6 pvt. corps. Author: Computers: Their Structure, Use, and Influence, 1979; contbr. articles to profl. jours. Recipient prize Am. Fedn. Info Processing Socs., 1962, W. Wallace McDowell award IEEE Computer Soc., 1983. Fellow IEEE. Home: Urbana Ill. Died Oct. 25, 1985.

SLOWINSKI, WALTER ALOYSIUS, educator, lawyer; b. Newark, Oct. 28, 1920; s. Walter A. and Eugenia (Stawski) S.; m. Annette Carter Roberts, Jan. 31, 1953; children—Francis Hill, John Bowie, Mary Carroll, Walter Kent, Annette Carter, Elizabeth Snowden, Eugenia Calvert, Richard Lee. B.S., St. Vincent Coll., 1941, LL.D. (hon.), 1975; J.D., Cath. U., 1948. Bar: D.C. bar 1947, Ill. bar 1957. Resident partner Baker & McKenzie, Washington, 1957-87; adj. prof. Georgetown U. Grad. Law Sch., 1956-70; gen. counsel Council of Americas, Assn. Am. Chambers Commerce Latin Am., Fund for Multinat. Mgmt. Edn., Internat. Mgmt. and Devel. Inst.; mem. adv. com. transnat. enterprises U.S. Dept. State, 1975-87 ; lectr. U. Va. Law Sch., Dept. Commerce Seminars for Comml. Attaches, Dept. State Fgn. Service Inst., Am. Mgmt. Assn., Columbia U., George Washington U. Mem. editorial bd.: The Tax Adviser, 1970-75. Trustee Nat. Catholic Ednl. Assn., 1976-87 . Served with USNR, 1942-45, 50-53. Recipient Distinguished Service award Sch. Govt. and Bus. Adminstrn., George Washington U., 1974. Fellow Am. Bar Found.; mem. Washington Fgn. Law Soc. (pres. 1969-70), Am. Bar Assn. (sec. sect. taxation 1952-53, mem. com. fgn. tax problems 1957-87 , mem. council sect. internat. and comparative law 1968-70, vice chmn. com. treasury dept. sect. adminstrv. law 1970-74), Am. Law Inst., Am. Judicature Soc., Tax Inst. Am. (past gov.), Soc. Cincinnati, Internat. Fiscal Assn., Bar Assn. D.C. (dir. 1970-72, pres. research found. 1970-72). Clubs: Knights of Malta; Cosmos (Washington) (pres. 1978-79). Home: Washington D.C. Died May 18, 1987, buried Arlington Nat. Cemetery, Washington.

SMALL, STANTON HARRISON, manufacturing company executive; b. San Francisco, Aug. 8, 1922; s. Cecil Stanton and Helena Clara (Newton) S.; m. Evaline Agnes Morton, Aug. 16, 1945; children: Katherine Claire, David Stanton. BA in Econs. and Bus., U. Wash., 1949. With Gen. Electric Co., 1949-70, mgr. fin. med. systems dept., 1964-70; v.p. fin., treas. Allen-Bradley Co., Milw., 1970-82, ret. Chmn. Benton (Wash.) unit Am. Cancer Soc., 1962-64; trustee, chmn.

planning com. St. Francis Hosp., Milw.; bd. dirs. Better Bus. Bur., Milw. With USAAF, 1941-45. Decorated D.F.C., Air medal. Mem. Fin. Execs. Inst. Home: Brookfield Wis. Died Aug. 24, 1986; cremated.

SMALLS, CHARLIE, composer, lyricist; b. N.Y.C., Oct. 25, 1943; s. Charles Henry and Rebecca Derotha (McNeil) S.; m. Marilyn Rose Simson, May 3, 1964; 1 son, Charles Michael. Grad., Juilliard Sch. Music, N.Y.C., 1961. Mus. dir., Club Improvisation, N.Y.C., 1960, The Scene, N.Y.C., 1960, Harry Belafonte on tour in, Paris and Stockholm, 1964, Hugh Masekela Group, 1966; composer: theme film Faces, 1967-68; scores for film Drum, 1976; composer, lyricist: stage prodn. The Wiz, 1974; film version, 1977; songs included Lena Horne Broadway show; (Recipient Drama Desk award 1974, 75, Show of Month award Tour-A-Trail Cultural Club 1976, Grammy award Best Cast Show Album for The Wiz 1976, Tony awards best mus. score (music and lyrics) for The Wiz 1975). Served with USAF, 1961-63. Mem. Broadcast Music Inc. Home: New York N.Y. Died Aug. 27, 1987.

SMITH, ALBERT (ALBERT SCHMIDT), comic artist, editor; b. Bklyn., Mar. 21, 1902; s. Henry Schmidt and Josephine (Dice) S.; m. Erna Anna Strasser, May 25, 1921; children: Rose Erna, Marie Emma Smith Schiller, Dorothea Josephine Coates. Student public schs. of, Bklyn. Artist, editor syndicate dept. New York World, 1920-30; comic artist United Features Syndicate, 1930-32; ghost artist, writer several well-known comic strips 1932-86; became head Smith Service, 1950; feature editor Smith Service div. Am. Press Assn. Writer, comic artist: Remember When, 1950-86 ; artist: Bell Syndicate, from 1932, Mutt and Jeff comic strip, from 1932, Life in the Suburbs, Cicero's Cat, Rural Delivery, Bumbles. Mem. Nat. Cartoonists Soc. (pres.), Am. Newspaper Comic Council, Inc. Club: Lambs. Home: Bomoseen Vt. Died Nov. 24, 1986; buried Castleton, Vt.

SMITH, ALFRED GLAZE, JR., economist, educator; b. Urbana, Ill., Dec. 28, 1913; s. Alfred Glaze and Lucy Catherine (Prutsman) S.; m. Katherine Cushing Brown, May 9, 1936; children: Alfred Glaze III, LeRoy Fairchild. AB, Columbia U., 1934, AM, 1939, PhD, 1954. With personnel div. S.H. Kress & Co., 1936-38; instr. econs. U. S.C., Columbia, 1938-42, asst. prof., 1942-47, assoc. prof., 1947-54, prof., from 1954, head dept. econs., 1958-70, acting assoc. v.p. for instrn., 1974-76; discussant 1st Ann. Conf. Econ. Devel. South, 1960; Fulbright prof., Bologna, Italy, 1963-64; owner, operator farm, Lexington County, S.C. Author: Economic Readjustment of an Old Cotton State: South Carolina, 1820-1860, 1958. Served as officer USNR, 1943-46; comdr. res. Mem. Am. Econ. Assn., Econ. History Assn., Torch Club. Home: Columbia S.C. Deceased.

SMITH, ARTHUR EDWARD, aircraft company executive; b. Malden, Mass., July 7, 1911; s. George August and Mary (Wardwell) S.; m. Frances Kenworthy, Oct. 17, 1936; children: David K., Kenneth W., Francie. BS, Worcester Poly. Inst., 1933, D in Engring. (hon.), 1969. Test engr. Internat. Motors, Allentown, Pa., 1933-34; salesman Manning, Maxwell & Moore, N.Y.C., 1934-35; test engr., asst. project engr., project engr. Pratt & Whitney Aircraft Co., East Hartford, Conn., 1935-42, asst. chief engr., 1944-49, chief engr., 1949-52, asst. engring mgr., 1952-56, engring. mgr., 1956-57, div. exec. v.p., 1957-67, div. pres., 1967; chief engr. Pratt & Whitney Aircraft Corp. of Mo., Kansas City, 1942-44; exec v.p. United Aircraft Corp. (now United Technologies), East Hartford, 1968, pres., 1968-71, also bd. dirs., chmn. bd., 1972-74; bd. dirs. United Aircraft of Can. Ltd., Orenda Ltd., United Aircraft Internat., Conn. Bank & Trust Co., Hartford Fire Ins. Co., Hartford Accident & Indemnity Co., Savs. Bank of Manchester, Travelers Ins. Co. Mem. engring adv. com. U. Hartford; bd. dirs. Manchester Meml. Hosp., Greater Hartford Community Chest, Manchester Redevel. Agy. Recipient Robert H. Goddard award Worcester Poly. Inst., 1967. Mem. Soc. Automotive Engrs., Nat. Aero. Assn., Conn. C. of C. Home: Manchester Conn. Died Aug. 6, 1985.

SMITH, BRADFORD, JR., insurance company executive; b. Cynwyd, Pa., Dec. 15, 1901; s. Bradford and Helen H. (Rhein) S.; m. Henrietta H. Dunne, Nov. 12, 1926 (dec.); children: Louisa Smith Heilman, Bradford III. Grad., Haverford (Pa.) Sch., 1920; student, Dartmouth Coll., 1921-23. With L.M. Addis & Co., ins. brokers and agts., Phila., 1923-26, Robert Hampson & Sons Ltd., gen. agts., Montreal, Can., 1926-29; with Ins. Co. N.Am., Phila., 1929-69, spl. agt., asst. sec., fire sec., v.p., 1929-56, exec. v.p., dir., 1956-61; v.p. Life Ins. Co. N.Am., Phila., 1957-61, pres., 1961-66; dir., pres. Ins. Co. N.Am., Phila., 1961-66, chmn., chief exec. officer, 1964-69; dir., chmn., pres INA Corp., Phila., 1968-69; bd. dirs. Fidelity Bank, Fidelity Corp., I.T.E. Circuit Breaker Co., Phila. Pres., chmn. bd. Haverford Sch., 1945-62. Mem. Union League Club, Corinthian Yacht Club, (Phila.); Merion Cricket Club (Haverford). Republican. Home: Centreville Md. Died Sept. 13, 1988.

SMITH, BROMLEY KEABLES, government official; b. Muscatine, Iowa, Apr. 21, 1911; s. John Bunyan and May (Keables) S.; m. Chloethiel Woodard, Apr. 5, 1940; children: Bromley Keables, Susanne Woodard. AB, Stanford, 1933; grad., Nat. War Coll., 1952. Researcher Code Authority, 1934-35; news editor 1938-40; vice consul Am. Embassy, Montreal, Can., 1940; 3d sec., vice consul Am. Embassy, La Paz, Bolivia, 1941-45; liaison officer U.S. delegation UN Conf. Internat. Orgn., San Francisco, 1945; mem. staff Office Sec. State, 1945-48; asst. to U.S. mem. Coun. Fgn. Ministers, Moscow, 1947, London, 1947; spl. asst. to asst. sec. state 1949, spl. asst. to sec. state, 1950; adviser U.S. delegation to NATO, Brussels, 1950, 4-Power Exploratory Talks, Paris, 1951; alternate State Dept. mem. NSC Planning Bd.; mem. State Dept. policy planning staff, 1953; sr. mem. spl. staff NSC, 1953-58; exec. officer Ops. Coordinating Bd., 1959-61; exec. sec. NSC, 1961-69, cons., 1970-87; to asst. dir. internat. communications policy Office of Telecommunications Policy, Exec. Office of the Pres., 1972-75. Author: commentary in U.S.-Soviet Summitry—Roosevelt through Carter (Ctr. Study of Fgn. Affairs), 1987, Organizational History of the National Security Council during the Kennedy and Johnson Administrations, 1987. Recipient Pres. award for disting. fed. civilian service, 1964. Mem. Phi Beta Kappa. Home: Washington D.C. Died Mar. 1, 1987; buried Oak Hill Cemetery, Washington.

SMITH, C. RAY, interior designer, author, editor; b. Birmingham, Ala., Mar. 3, 1929; s. Calvin Ray and Sara Amanda (Kelly) S.; m. Leslie Armstrong, Dec. 17, 1971 (div.); 1 son, Sinclair Scott. B.A. in English, Kenyon Coll., 1951; M.A. in English, Yale U., 1958; student, Royal Acad. Dramatic Art, London, 1956-57. Asst. editor Interior Design mag., 1959-60; from assoc. editor to sr. and features editor Progressive Architecture mag., 1961-70; editor Theatre Crafts Mag., 1969-74; editor-in-chief Interiors and Residential Interiors mags., 1974-77; freelance author, editor, lectr.; cons. pub. relations, design; tchr. Parsons Sch. Design, N.Y.C., 1978-86; tchr. Fashion Inst. Tech., 1985-86. Author: books including: The American Endless Weekend, 1972, Supermanerism: New Attitudes in Post-Modern Architecture, 1977, AIGA Graphic Design USA: 1, 1980, Interior Design in 20th Century America: A History, 1987; co-author: Interior Design in the 20th Century, 1986; editor: books including: The Theatre Crafts Book of Costume, 1973, The Theatre Crafts Book of Makeup, Masks and Wigs, 1974; contbr. articles to newspaper, profl. jours., periodicals, encys. Exec. dir. Aston Magna Found. for Music, 1972-75. Served with AUS, 1952-54, ETO. Nat. Endowment for Arts grantee, 1972, 77; Graham Found. grantee, 1971, 85; Ednl. Facilities Lab. grantee, 1980. Fellow AIA, U.S. Inst. for Theatre Tech. (pres. 1968-71); mem. Soc. Archtl. Historians, Archtl. League N.Y. Episcopalian. Home: Krumsville Pa. Died Aug. 18, 1988.

SMITH, CECIL WELDON, public utility executive; b. Clifton, Ill., Sept. 29, 1890; s. Weldon Charles and Alice Mary (Colby) S.; m. Lucile Heskett, July 28, 1917; children: Margaret (Mrs. Robert R. Hackford), Joan (Mrs. Patrick A. Requa). BS, U. Ill., 1913. With Ill. Geol. Survey, 1912-13; mining engr. Nokomis (Ill.) Coal Co., 1913-17, U.S. Bur. Mines, Pitts., 1917; constrn. engr. Ill. Coal Corp., Chgo., 1918-26; asst. gen. mgr. O'Gara Coal Co., Chgo., 1926-27; with Mont.-Dakota Utilities Co. and predecessors, from 1927, v.p., 1944-53, pres., 1953-65, chmn. bd., 1965-74; chmn. Midwest com. preparation nat. electric poer survey FPC, 1962-63. Mem. AIME (Legion of Honor mem.). Home: Minneapolis Minn. †

SMITH, CHARLES BUNYAN, college president; b. Geneva County, Ala., June 5, 1891; s. Isaac Bryan and Ida Elaine (Brunson) S.; m. Annie Pearl Newell, Dec. 20, 1925; 1 child, Martha Ann. Diploma, State Normal Sch., Troy, Ala., 1917; BS, Peabody Coll., 1922, MA, 1927; postgrad., Duke U., summers 1933, 34; EdD, Columbia U., 1940. Tchr. rural schs. Crenshaw County, 1910; tchr. Montgomery and Madison counties, 1917-28; supt. Tallassee, 1923-35; dir. div. instrn. Ala. Dept. Edn., 1935-37; pres. State Tchrs. Coll., Troy, from 1937. With armed forces World War I. Mem. Masons, Rotary, Kappa Delta Pi. Democrat. Methodist. Home: Troy Ala. †

SMITH, CLAUDE EARLE, botany educator; b. Boston, Mar. 8, 1922; s. Claude E. and Pearl (Morgan) S.; m. Roberta Jean Klages, June 9, 1948; children: Deborah Joann, Sandra Lee, Richard Randall, Darrell Lance. A.B., Harvard U., 1949, A.M., 1951, Ph.D., 1953. Asst. curator botany Acad. Nat. Scis., Phila., 1953-58; assoc. curator botany Field Mus. Nat. History, Chgo., 1959-61; sr. research botanist U.S. Dept. Agr., Beltsville, Md., 1962-69; prof. anthropology and biology U. Ala., University, 1970-87; cons. Smith, Kline and French, Phila., 1953-58, Scott, Forsman Co., 1959-61; acting dir. Taylor Meml. Arboretum, Chester, Pa., 1954-58; botanist Tehuacan Archaelogical-Bot. Project, 1961-64, Prehistory and Human Ecology Valley of Oaxaca Project, Mexico, 1966-70; bot. analysis of plant remains Guitarrero Cave, Peru, 1970-72, Parmana, Venezuela, 1976-78, La Galgada, Peru, 1982-83. Editor: Man and His Food, 1973. Asst. scoutmaster Phila. chpt. Boy Scouts Am., 1953-58; asst. scoutmaster Laurel, Md. chpt. Boy Scouts Am., 1962-69; nature councilor Girl Scouts U.S.A., Phila., 1953-58. Served with USN, 1942-45. Am. Philos. Soc. grantee, 1957. Fellow Explorers Club; mem. Soc. Econ. Botany (pres. 1979-80), Internat. Assn. Plant Taxonomy, Soc. Am. Archaeology, Am. Soc. Plant Taxonomy. Home: Tuscaloosa Ala. Died Oct. 19, 1987, cremated.

SMITH, CLEMENT ANDREW, pediatrician, educator; b. Ann Arbor, Mich., Nov. 19, 1901; s. Shirley Wheeler and Sara Spencer (Browne) S.; m. Margaret Beal Earhart, Feb. 6, 1926 (dec. 1960); children: Pamela, Maragaret Smith Biggar, Reynolds Rich, Hilary Janet; m. Mary Bunting, May, 1979. AB, U. Mich., 1923, AM, 1925, MD, 1928; AM, Harvard U., 1949; DSc (hon.), Colby Coll., 1958; MD (hon.), Groningen U., 1964. Diplomate Am. Bd. Pediatrics. Intern, resident pediatrics Univ. Hosp., Ann Arbor, 1928-30; resident Children's Hosp., Boston, 1930-31, chief infants svc., 1949-56; instr. pediatrics U. Mich., 1932; teaching staff pediatrics Harvard Med. Sch., 1933-43, assoc. prof., 1945-49; prof. pediatrics Wayne State U., 1943-45; med. dir. Children's Hosp. of Mich., Detroit, 1943-45; assoc. prof. pediatrics, dir. rsch. on newborns Boston Lying-In Hosp., 1949-63; prof. pediatrics Boston Lying-In Hosp. and Harvard Med. Sch., 1963-68, prof. emeritus, from 1968; cons. children's med. svc. Mass. Gen. Hosp.; praelator in pediatrics Queen's Coll., U. St. Andrews. Author: The Physiology of the Newborn Infant, 1945, 4th edit., 1976; editor: Pediatrics jour., 1961-74; editorial bd. Biologica Neonatorum, Paris; contbr. articles to profl. jours. Recipient Arvo Yippö medal Helsinki, Finland, 1957. Mem. AM. Acad. Arts and Scis., Am. Acad. Pediatrics, Soc. Pediatric Rsch., Am. Pediatric Soc. (pres. 1965-66), Swedish Pediatric Soc. (hon.), Brit. Paediatric Assn. (hon.), Soc. Pediatrie (Paris), Neonatal Soc. London (hon.), Harvard Club (Boston), Sigma Xi, Phi Gamma Delta, Alpha Omega Alpha. Home: Cambridge Mass. Died Dec. 31, 1988.

SMITH, DENTON HENRY, manufacturing company executive; b. Greene County, Mo., Jan. 19, 1910; s. Oren H. and Bessie E. (Goodin) S.; m. Kathryn E. Gilmore, Aug. 13, 1938; children: Judy Kay Smith Sipe, Allen J., Rebecca E. Smith Bowman (dec.), Eleanor Anne O'Connell. Student, Drury Coll., 1929-30. Pres. Springfield (Mo.) Motor Sales; distbr. Willys-Overland, 1944-51; pres., chmn. bd. Mono Mfg. Co., mfr., distbr. garden tillers, poer mowers, brush cutters, Springield, 1951-84; dir. Ozark Air Lines Inc., St. Louis, 1969-73, vice-chmn. bd., from 1973; chmn. bd. Northpark Properties Inc., Springfield; pres. Smith Investment Co., Springfield, Denton H. Smith Warehouse Corp., Springfield; dir. Blue Springs Bank, Mo., Commerce Bank of Willard, Mo., First State Bank, Raytown, Mo., Jackson County State Bank, Kansas City, Mo. Trustee Drury Coll., 1971-84; mem. Mo. Dem. Com.; del. Dem. Nat. Conv. Mem. Elks. Presbyterian. Home: Springfield Mo. Died July 6, 1984; buried Greenlawn North Cemetery.

SMITH, DEWITT C(LINTON), social services administrator; b. Hagerstown, Md., Oct. 30, 1892; s. Curtis S. and Carrie T. (Stottlemyer) S.; m. Mary Gladys Benson, Oct. 30, 1919; children: DeWitt Clinton, Phyllis (Mrs. Edward S. Crawford). Ed., Georgetown U. Law Sch. Asst. sec. bd. commrs Govt. D.C., 1916-17; with ARC, 1919-58, asst. to gen. mgr., 1919-21, dir. fiscal svc., 1921, asst. to vice chmn., 1921-32, mgr. ea. area, 1932-33, asst. dir. domestic ops., 1933-39, dir. domestic ops., nat. dir. disaster felief, 1939-43, vice chmn., 1943-47, trustee, vice chmn. retirement system, 1949-58, in charge svcs. in continental U.S., v.p. in charge social welfare svcs., 1950-51, asst. gen. mgr., 1951-54, v.p. ops., 1954-58; spl. planning cons. Exec. Dept. State of Tex., 1958-59; mem. adv. bd. region 2 Office Civil and Def. Moblzn., from 1959; dir. field ops. Miss. Valley flood relief, 1927, gen. dir. drought relief, 1930-31; gen. dir. Ohio and Miss. Valley flood relief; active relief work, Fla., 1926, 28, 35; chmn. spl. com. plan with Army and Navy, 1935-41; chmn. Nat. Conf. on Home Safety, 1946-47; mem. exec. com. Nat. Social Welfare Assembly, 1946-53; mem. exec. bd., bd. dirs. Nat. Safety Coun., 1946-48. Editor Annals Am. Acad. Polit. and Social Sci. on Disasters and Disaster Relief, 1957. Mem. adv. com. on civil def. planning Office Sec. of Def., 1948-49; mem. adv. com. on emergency welfare svcs. Fed. Civil Def. Adminstrn., 1951-53. Lt. inf. U.S. Army, 1917-19. Mem. Nat. Assn. for Employment of Handicapped (policy com. 1947), Masons. Presbyterian. Home: Bethesda Md. †

SMITH, DONALD S(HOECRAFT), manufacturing executive; b. Cleve., Mar. 12, 1892; s. Edward Ward and Ida (Amsden) S.; m. Edith Stringer, Feb. 14, 1936; 1 child, Marilyn (Mrs. David Cooper). Student pub. schs., Cleve. From acct. to pres., chmn. bd. Perfection Stove Co., 1910-56; pres. Hupp Internat.; v.p., bd. dirs. Hupp Corp.; mem. adv. bd. Mut. Machinery & Boiler Ins. Co., Boston; bd. dirs. Arkwright Mut. Fire Ins. Co., Boston, Gibson Refrigerator Co. Can., Ltd. Mem. Nat. Assn. Cost Accts. (past pres.), Am. Mgmt. Assn., AIM, C. of C., Masons, Cleveland Club, Athletic Club, Madison Golf and Country Club, Mentor Yacht Club, Gyro Internat. Club. Home: Shaker Heights Ohio. †

SMITH, ELLIOTT DUNLAP, lawyer, economics educator; b. Chgo., Jan. 23, 1891; s. Dunlap and Harriet (Flower) S.; m. Marie Francke, May 19, 1917; children: Lucy Dunlap Smith Adams, Katherine Dunlap Smith Welch, Hugo Francke Dunlap. AB, Harvard U., 1913, LLB, 1916; AM (hon.), Yale U., 1928; LHD (hon.), Washington and Jefferson Coll., 1949. Bar: Ill. 1916.

Practice law Chgo., 1916; with Coun. Nat. Def., becoming chief orgn. field div., 1917-18; dir. investigations, U.S. Tariff Commn., 1919; personnel mgr. and div. mgr. Dennison Mfg. Co., Framingham, Mass., 1919-28; lectr. social ethics, Harvard, 1926, 27; prof. econs., Yale U., 1928-46, chmn. dept. econs., 1939-45, dir. com. preparation for War Svc., 1942-43, master Saybrook Coll., 1932-46; provost and Falk prof. social rels. Carnegie Inst. Tech., 1946-58, then emeritus; overseer Harvard U., 1951-57; Navy Coll. Curriculum cons. (USN), 1942-46; cons. Wider City Parish, New Haven, from 1963. Author: Psychology for Executives, 1928, rev. edit., 1934, Technology and Labor, 1939; co-author: Union Management Cooperation in the Stretch-Out, 1934; contbr. numerous articles on indsl. and ednl. subjects. Mem. adv. com. indsl. rels. Nat. Indsl. Conf. Bd., 1936-46; trustee Sarah Lawrence Coll., 1935-43, then from 1960, chmn. 1935-39; bd. visitors U.S. Air Univ., 1946-49. Mem. Soc. Engring. Edn. Home: New Haven Conn. †

SMITH, EUGENE M., lawyer, railroad executive; b. Chgo., June 7, 1891; s. Felix F. and Claribel (Hooker) S. LLB, U. Chgo., 1914. With N.Y. R.R., 1909-17; with N.Y.C. & St.Louis R.R., from 1917, atty., gen. land and tax atty., gen. atty., asst. to gen. counsel, then gen. counsel, from 1947, v.p., from 1949. Home: Shaker Heights Ohio. †

SMITH, FRED WILDON, business and ranching executive; b. Alamosa, Colo., May 22, 1892; s. Otis Grand and Edith Rockwell (Mingay) S.; m. Grace Hobson, July 22, 1917 (dec. 1968); children: Rodney (dec.), Barbara Barnard, Helen M. Student, The Principia, St. Louis, 1906-07, U. Calif., 1916. With Hobson Bros. Packing Co., from 1916, acct., sec., 1916-30, pres., from 1930; assisted in orgn. Ventura Investment Co., 1920; pres. Ventura Securities Co., 1931-71; pres. Salinas Land Co., from 1930; pres. Saticoy Rock Co., 1920-35, v.p. , 1936-59; v.p. Calif Orchard Co.; chmn. adv. bd. Ventura Bank of Am., exec. mgr. Smith-Hobson; v.p. Ivy Lawn Cemetery Assn. Mem. Ventura War Price and Rationing Bd.; hon. trustee Pomona Coll., Claremenot; mem. Calif. Bd. Edn., 1943-49, pres., 1943-47. Mem. Ventura C. of C. (pres. 1957), Ventura Lions Club, Internat. Assn. of Lions Clubs (pres.), 1947-48, Elks (charter mem. lodge 1430). Home: Ventura Calif. †

SMITH, FREDERICK DANESBURY, college dean; b. Keighley, Yorkshire, Eng., Aug. 21, 1887; s. Addyman and Margaret (Ackroyd) S.; m. Fannie Elizabeth Putcamp, Aug. 30, 1922. AB, Stetson U., 1909, PhD, 1916; postgrad., U. Montpellier, France, 1919. Asst. prof. Latin Miami U., Oxford, Ohio, 1910; instr. Greek Lawrence Coll., Appleton, Wis., 1911; instr. Greek and Latin Bradley Poly. Inst., Peoria, Ill., 1912-13; fellow in Greek U. Chgo., 1914-15, instr. in Greek, summer 1920; instr. classical lang. and lit. U. N.D., 1916-18, asst. prof., 1919; asst. prof. gen. lit. So. Meth. U., Dallas, 1920-21, assoc. prof., 1922, prof., head dept., from 1923, acting dean Coll. Arts and Scis., 1937-40, dean instrn., 1940-58, emeritus coll. dean, from 1958. Author: Athenian Political Commissions, 1920. With Am. Expeditionary Force, 1918-19. Mem. AAUP, MLA, Tex. Coun. Ch.-Related Colls. (past pres.), Assn. Tex. Colls. (past pres.), Conf. Acad. Deans So. States (chmn. 1955), Masons, Town and Gown Club, Eta Sigma Phi, Pi Gamma Mu, Phi Alpha Theta. Republican. Methodist. Home: Dallas Tex. †

SMITH, GEORGE (WILLIAM), business executive; b. Newport, R.I., Mar. 28, 1891; s. George William and Bessier (Carr) S.; m. Alice Bertha Wood, Sept. 24, 1913; 1 child, Stedman West. BS, Worcester Poly. Inst., 1915, ME, 1917. Rsch. engr. White Motor Co., Cleve., 1915-17; chief engr. U.S. Naval Aircraft Factory, Phila., 1917-19; works mgr. Victor Talking Machine Co., Camden, N.J., 1919-25; v.p. White Motor Co., Cleve., 1925-35; cons. engr., pres. Smith & Wood Inc., N.Y.C., 1935-47; chmn. bd. dirs. DeLAval Steam Turbine Co., Trenton, N.J. Trustee Worcester Poly. Inst. Mem. Inst. Aeronautical Scis., Naval Architects and Marine Engrs. Soc. Automotive Engrs., N.Y. State Soc. Profl. Engrs., Am. Assn. Naval Engrs., Nat. Security Indsl. Assn., Swedish C. of C., Wings Club, Pinnacle Club, Gibson Island (Md.) Club, Nat. Aviation Club (Washington), Sigma Xi, Tau Beta Pi, Alpha Tau Omega. Republican. Episcopalian. Home: Greenwich Conn. †

SMITH, GUY LINCOLN, III, zoological park administrator; b. Johnson City, Tenn., Mar. 4, 1922; s. Guy Lincoln and Thelma (McNab) S.; m. Laura Orr, Oct. 9, 1946; children: Guy Lincoln IV, Marie Louise Camors, Christopher Zachary. Student, U. Tenn., 1940-41. Sales mgr. Radio Sta. WKGN, Knoxville, Tenn., 1951-53; gen. sales mgr. Sta. WTVK-TV, Knoxville, 1953-61, 65-74; pres. Nelson-Chessman Advt. and Mktg. Agy., Knoxville, 1962-64; acting zoo dir. Knoxville Zool. Park., 1971-74, exec. dir., from 1974; cons., bd. dirs. Kaosiung City Zoo, from 1976, City of Taipei New Zoo, from 1979; internat. studbook keeper Indian lion. Author: A House for Joshua, the Building of the Knoxville Zoo, 1985. Bd. dirs. Knoxville Internat. Trade Mart, 1974-80; founder, bd. dirs. Knoxville Sister City Program, 1974-80. Served to lt. USAF, 1943-45. Recipient Community Service award Knoxville C. of C., 1973; commendation for exemplary achievement Sister Cities Internat., 1981; named Hon. Citizen City of Kaohsiung, 1976, other awards. Fellow Am. Assn. Zool. Parks and Aquariums (species coordinator Indian lion), Kappa Sigma. Republican. Roman Catholic. Home: Knoxville Tenn. Died Feb. 18, 1987.

SMITH, H. DEWITT, mining engineer; b. Plantsville, Conn., Sept. 30, 1888; s. Charles Dwight and Lillian M. (Hough) s.; m. Ellen Dawson Burke, Apr. 3, 1916; children: Charles DeWitt, Elizabeth Cass (Mrs. Alfred F. Sanford II), Jeannette (Mrs. J. Clifton Rodes). PhB, Yale U., 1908, EM, 1910. Engr. J.E. Spurr, Inc., western U.S. and Mex., 1910-13; foreman, mine supt., asst. mgr. Kennecott (Alaska) Copper Corp., 1914-17; mine supt., gen. supt. United Verde Copper Co., Jerome, Ariz., 1917-24; mgr. sales United Verde Copper Co., N.Y.C., 1927-30; engr. indsl. dept. N.Y. Trust Co., 1924-27; mem. exec. com., bd. dirs. Phelps Dodge Corp., St. Joseph Lead Co.; chmn. bd. O'Okiep Copper Co., Ltd.; adviser, exec. v.p. Metals Res. Co. subs. R.F.C., Washington, 1941-44; bd. dirs. Tsumeb Corp., Ltd. Mem. AIME (past pres.), Mining and Metall. Soc. Am. (past pres.), Downtown Assn., Mining Club (past pres.), University Club, Metropolitan Club, Chevy Chase Club. Republican. Presbyterian. †

SMITH, HAROLD ARMSTRONG, lawyer; b. Albany, Ill., Aug. 27, 1898; s. Afred B. and Louise (Rosenkrans) S.; m. Ruth Gilbert, June 16, 1926; 1 dau., Elizabeth Ann. LLB, Northwestern U. Law Sch., 1921; LLD, John Marshall Law Sch., 1949, Tri-State Coll., 1953. Bar: Ill. 1921. Ptnr. Winston, Strawn, Smith & Patterson, Chgo., from 1921; bd. dirs. First Nat. Bank, Chgo., Comml. Credit Co., Balt. Mem. Permanent Ct. of Arbitration, The Hague, The Netherlands; trustee Wesley Meml. Hosp., Chgo. YMCA, Northwestern U. With ROTC, Camp Grant, World War I. Recipient award of merit Northwestern U. Alumni Assn., 1949. Mem. Am., Ill. State and Chgo. (past pres.) bar assns., Am. Soc. of Internat. Law, Gen. Alumni Assn. Northwestern U. (pres.), Union League Club, Mid-Day Club, Westmoreland Country Club, Law Club, Commercial Club, Chicago Club, Trial Lawyers Soc. Chgo., Crime Commn. (pres.), Lambda Chi Aalpha, Delta Theta Phi. Republican. Methodist. Home: Evanston Ill. †

SMITH, HAROLD MORRISON, headmaster; b. Falls City, Nebr., Jan. 22, 1888; s. Alvin Leroy and Annie Laurie (Campbell) S.; m. Bessie S. Braley, Dec. 24, 1910; 1 son, Morris Wadleigh. Grad., Proctor Acad., Andover, N.H., 1909; AB, Bates Coll., 1914; MA, Columbia U., 1929; LHD, Pa. Mil. Coll., 1951; LLD, Bucknell U., 1952; LittD, Norwich U., 1954. Asst. and instr. dept. geology and astronomy Bates Coll., 1914-15; prin. Norridgewock (Maine) High Sch., 1915-16, Hopkinton High Sch., Contoocook, N.H., 1916-18, New Hampton Lit. Inst., 1918-21; headmaster Pembroke Acad., N.H., 1921-32; dean Bordentown (N.J.) Mil. Inst., 1932, co-prin., 1936-56, headmaster, from 1956, pres. bd., from 1956; Del. to Coll. Entrance Examination Bd. Mem. Boarding Sch. Assn. Phila. Region (pres.), Assn. Mil. Colls. and Schs. (pres. 1950-52), Trenton Assn. Bapt. Chs. (moderator), Nat. Assn. Secondary Sch. Prins., Am. Numismatic Assn., N.J. Archeol. Soc., AAAS, Mason (33 degree Shriner), Rotary (past pres.), Trenton Symposium (pres.), Phi Beta Kappa. Republican. Baptist. Home: Bordentown N.J. †

SMITH, HENRY J., lawyer; b. N.Y.C., Jan. 2, 1919; m. Greta Olson; children: Henry, Kenneth, Theresa. AB, Fordham U., 1940; JD, Harvard U., 1947. Bar: N.Y. 1948. With firm McCarthy, Fingar, Donovan, Glatthaar, Drazen & Smith, White Plains, N.Y.; treas. Legal Aid of Westchester (N.Y.), 1962-72, dir., 1964-72, mem. exec. com., 1968-72; spl. counsel Town of Greenburgh, 1963-69, City of White Plains, 1967-68, City of New Rochelle (N.Y.), 1969, County of Westchester, 1971-74, other municipalities, 1974-86. Bd. dirs. Welserv OEO, 1968-72. Fellow Am. Bar Found., N.Y. Bar Found., Am. Coll. Trial Lawyers; mem. ABA, (ho. of dels. 1978-86), White Plains Bar Assn. (dir. 1957-66), Westchester County (pres. 1963-65, dirs. coun. 1965-86), N.Y. State Bar Assn. (del. 1972-86, exec. com. 1972-79, pres. 1977-78), Am. Judicature Soc. Home: Greenburgh N.Y. Died Aug. 5, 1986; buried Immaculate Conception Cemetery, New Hartford, Conn.

SMITH, HENRY NASH, educator; b. Dallas, Sept. 29, 1906; s. Loyd Bond and Elizabeth (Nash) S.; m. Elinor Lucas, Apr. 10, 1936; children: Loyd Mayne, Janet Carol, Harriet Elinor. AB, So. Meth. U., 1925, LLD, 1966; AM, Harvard, 1929, PhD, 1940; LittD, Colo. State U., 1970. Mem. faculty So. Meth. U., 1927-41, assoc. prof. English, 1940-41; prof. English and Am. history U. Tex., 1941-47; prof. English U. Minn., 1947-53; prof. English U. Calif., Berkeley, 1953-74, prof. emeritus, 1974-86, chmn. dept., 1957-60; vis. lectr. Am. lit. Harvard, 1945-46, Washington U., St. Louis, 1974; fellow Huntington Libr., 1946-47, Ctr. Advanced Studies Behavioral Scis., Stanford, 1960-61; Fulbright lectr., Italy, 1965. Author: Virgin Land: The American West as Symbol and Myth, 1950 (John H. Dunning prize in Am. history Am. Hist. Assn. 1950, Bancroft award in Am. History, Columbia 1951), Mark Twain: The Development of a Writer, 1962, Mark Twain's Fable of Progress, 1964; editor: James Fenimore Cooper's The Prairie, 1950, Mark Twain of the Enterprise, 1957, Mark Twain, San Francisco Correspondent, 1957, Mark Twain's Huckleberry Finn, 1958, Popular Culture and Industrialism, 1865-1890, 1967; co-editor: Mark Twain-Howells Letters (2 vols.), 1960; mem. editorial staff Southwest Review, 1927-41; contbr. Literary History of U.S. (edited by Robert E. Spiler and others), 1948. Mem. editorial bd. John Harvard Libr., 1959-69. Woodrow Wilson Internat. Ctr. fellow, 1975; Guggenheim fellow, 1975. Fellow Am. Acad. Arts and Scis.; mem. MLA (pres. 1969). Home: Berkeley Calif. Died May 30, 1986.

SMITH, HOWARD, research laboratory executive; b. Conneaut, Ohio, Sept. 29, 1891; s. Charles W. and Evelyn J. (Howard) S.; m. Irma Rahwyter, June 19, 1931. Student, Stanford U., 1909-10. Founder, v.p. Indsl. Rsch. Labs., L.A., from 1931; with Honolulu Oil Corp., from 1936, v.p., from 1955. Mem. Petroleum Club, University Club. Home: Laguna Beach Calif. †

SMITH, JESSE SHERWOOD, advertising executive; b. Elmira, N.Y., June 2, 1892; s. Milton Y. and Mary (Sherwood) S.; m. Agnes Sickels, Dec. 14, 1917; children: Walter Sherwood (dec.), Milton, Galen Burritt. AB, Cornell U., 1914. Sales corr. Home Pattern Co., N.Y.C., 1914-15; advt. salesman Internat. Mag. Co., N.Y.C. and Chgo., 1915-17, ea. advt. mgr., 1919-27, advt. mgr., 1925-27; with Calkins & Holden (name changed to Fletcher, Richlands, Calkins & Holden, Inc.), N.Y.C., from 1927, v.p., 1928-38, pres., from 1938, chmn. bd., from 1950, chmn. exec. com., from 1959. 2d lt. F.A., Am. Expeditionary Force, 1917-19. Mem. Cornell Club, Phi Beta Kappa. Republican. Home: West Nyack N.Y. †

SMITH, KATE (KATHRYN ELIZABETH SMITH), singer; b. Washington, May 1, 1907. Singer in public since early yrs.; stage debut in Honeymoon Lane, 1926; appeared in: road show Hit the Deck; co-starred in: Broadway mus. Flying High; made debut on radio in 1931; with own show Kate Smith Sings; helped write: lyrics for theme song When The Moon Comes Over The Mountain; star: radio program Kate Smith Speaks, 1938-51; introduced: song God Bless America, 1938; TV debut in 1950; starred in own show, 1950-54; guest appearances on Ed Sullivan show, 1955;, Jack Paar Show, 1964, Donny and Marie Osmond Show, 1975; TV spls. include The Stars and Stripes Show, 1976, Women of the Year, 1976; appeared in concert at Carnegie Hall, 1963; numerous motion pictures; made numerous records; introduced over 700 songs which made The Hit Parade, 19 of them selling over a million copies. Home: Raleigh N.C. Died June 17, 1986; interred St. Agnes Roman Cath. Cemetery, Lake Placid, N.Y.

SMITH, KENDRICK, fund-raising consultant; b. N.Y.C., Jan. 6, 1922; s. Walter Murray and Doramont (Kendrick) S.; m. Martha B. Seymour, May 29, 1943 (div. Nov. 1964); children: Beverly T. (Mrs. Amell), Laura K. (Mrs. Laura Carstoiu), James D.; m. Margaret Ross Gray Sturtevant, Nov. 26, 1966; 1 child, K. Tasker; stepchildren: Deborah R. Sturtevant, Thomas C. Sturtevant, Jr., Kristin F. Sturtevant, Susan G. Sturtevant. B.A., Amherst Coll., 1943. With Kersting Brown & Co., N.Y.C., 1946-63; v.p. Kersting Brown & Co., 1955-63, sec., 1960-63, also dir.; cons. fundraising, Wayland, Mass., 1963-87; owner Info. Research Service, Execs. in Edn., search orgn.; guest lectr. Harvard U. Sch. Edn., 1975. Author: Boston-How You Can Plan a Perfect Visit, 1979. Trustee Beaver Country Day Sch., 1973-75; v.p., bd. dirs. Mass. Children's Lobby, 1975-76; judge Lilly Endowment Competition, 1976, 78. Served as cryptographer USAAF, 1943-46, ETO. Died Apr. 8, 1987.

SMITH, KIRK, lawyer; b. Fairview, Ohio, Aug. 22, 1891; m. Corinne L. Harris; children: Corinne Smith Richardson, Cynthia Smith Varton. AB, Brown U.; LLB, Harvard U. Bar: R.I. 1918. Ptnr. firm Edwards & Angell, Providence; of counsel Edwards & Angell. Dir., mem. exec. com. Citizens Trust Co; bd. dirs. Legal Aid Soc. R.I., Children's Friend and Svc.; trustee Bryant Coll. Bus. Adminstrn.; hon. trustee Andover-Newton Theol. Sch. Home: Providence R.I. †

SMITH, LEE IRVIN, chemistry educator; b. Indpls., July 22, 1891; s. Edgar Poe and Susie Louise (Amberg) S. AB, Ohio State U., 1913, AM, 1915; AM, Harvard U., 1917, PhD, 1920. Asst. in chemistry Ohio State U., 1913-15; Austin teaching fellow Harvard U., 1915-17, instr., 1919-20; instr. in organic chemistry U. Minn., 1920-21, asst. prof., 1921-28, assoc. prof., 1928-33, acting chief div. organic chemistry, 1931-33, prof., chief div., 1933-60, adminstrv. asst., 1937-38, prof. emeritus. Contbr. articles to profl. jours. 1st lt. CWS, U.S. Army, 1918. Fellow AAAS; mem. Am. Chem. Soc., Brit. Chem. Soc., NAS, Swiss Chem. Soc., Masons, Campus Club, Phi Beta Kappa, Sigma Xi, Phi Lambda Upsilon, Gamma Alpha, Alpha Chi Sigma. Home: Minneapolis Minn. †

SMITH, LLOYD PRESTON, management consultant; b. Reno, Nov. 6, 1903; s. Preston Brooks and Ida (Sauer) S.; m. Florence S. Hunkin, Sept. 16, 1928 (dec.); children: Sandra Lee Reynolds, Jacqueline Sue Sullivan; m. F. Irene Anderson, 1971 (dec. 1984). B.E.E., U. Nev., 1925; Ph.D., Cornell U., 1930; D.Sc., U. Nev., 1961. Research engr. Gen. Electric Co., Schenectady,

1925-26; Coffin fellow physics Cornell U., 1926-27, instr. physics, 1927-30, asst. prof., 1932-36, prof., 1936-56, chmn. dept. physics, dir. dept. engring. physics, 1946-56, dir. Research Found., 1948-56, chmn. corp. com. Cornell U. Council, mem. council for Coll. Engring., 1956-64, faculty mem. bd. trustees, 1952-56; NRC fellow Calif. Inst. Tech., 1930-31; Internat. Research fellow U. Munich, U. Utrecht, 1931-32; lectr. Stanford U., 1935; research physicist RCA Labs., Princeton, N.J., 1939; cons. war research RCA Labs., 1941-45, assoc. research dir., 1945-46, cons., 1946-55, mem. research planning commn., 1952-55; mem. council Fund for Peaceful Atomic Devel., 1956-58; cons. atomic bomb research U. Calif., 1942; cons. Union Carbide Nuclear Co. (formerly Carbide & Carbon Chems. Corp.), Oak Ridge, 1947-88, Brookhaven Nat. Labs., Upton, L.I., 1947-49, Haloid Co., 1952-53, Detroit-Edison Co., 1953-56; cons. AVCO Mfg. Corp., 1956, 1959, v.p., dir., 1956-59, pres. research and advanced devel. div., 1956-58; research dir. research lab. Aeronutronic div. Ford Motor Co., 1959-63; v.p., dir. applied research labs. Aeronutronic div. Philco Research Labs., 1964-65; v.p. phys. scis. Stanford Research Inst., Menlo Park, Calif., 1965-69; sr. sci. adviser Stanford Research Inst. (Office Research Ops.), 1969-71; cons. on tech. research and devel. of bus. mgmt. 1965-88; pres. Lloyd P. Smith and Assocs., 1972-88, Desert Research Inst., U. Nev., 1975-80, Wright Energy Nev. Corp., 1980-81; dir. Research Corp. N.Y.; cons. Union Carbide Corp., Douglas Aircraft, Inc., 1959, Crown Zellerbach Corp., 1983-85; mem. exec. com. Def. Sci. Bd., 1961-65; adv. panel for physics NSF, 1956-59; mem. adv. com. anti-submarine warfare Nat. Security Indsl. Assn. Author: Mathematical Methods for Scientists and Engineers, 1953; contbr. articles sci. jours. Bd. dirs. Orange County Philharmonic Soc. Recipient certificate of merit USN, 1947. Mem. Am. Phys. Soc., Am. Assn. Physics Tchrs. (chmn. com. physics engring. edn. 1955-56), Am. Ordnance Assn. (chmn. physics sect. 1959-88), Am. Inst. Physics, Am. Soc. Engring. Edn., N.Y. Acad. Scis., Sigma Xi, Theta Chi, Phi Kappa Phi. Club: University (N.Y.C.). Lodge: Masons. Home: Menlo Park Calif. Died June 17, 1988.

SMITH, MATTHEW DINSDALE, university administrator; b. Montfort, Wis., Feb. 1, 1891; s. Albert Francis and Alice Jane (Dinsdale) S.; m. Loretta Fern Sage, Dec. 29, 1920; children: Matthew Dinsdale, Albert Francis, Miriam Jane (Mrs. Baltus Fritzmeier), Loretta Fern (Mrs. Leonard S. Buxton). AB, Dakota Wesleyan U., 1912, LHD, 1959; AM, Columbia U., 1914; postgrad., U. Chgo., 1921; EdD, U. Calif., Berkeley, 1930. Tchr. high sch. Huron, S.D., 1914-15; prin. high sch. Belle Fourche, 1915-17, Callao, Peru, 1917-20; pres. Mexican Meth. Inst., Puebla, Mex., 1922-32; dean Kans. Wesleyan U., 1933-36; dean Dakota Wesleyan U., 1936-44, pres., 1952-58; dir. Pan Am. Inst., Republic of Panama, 1944-52; exec. sec. S.D. Found. Pvt. Colls., 1958-60. Mem. gen. edn. bd. Meth. Ch., 1940-44, 52-60. Recipient diploma distinction S.D. State Coll., 1959. Mem. NEA, S.D. Edn. Assn., S.D. Assn. Coll. Deans and Registrars (past pres.), Masons, Kiwanis, Phi Delta Kappa, Phi Kappa Phi, Pi Gamma Mu. Home: Mitchell S.D. †

SMITH, (IRVING) NORMAN, editor; b. Ottawa, Ont., Can., Oct. 28, 1909; s. Ernest Norman and Bessie (Irving) S.; m. Mary Frances O'Neil, May 26, 1936. Grad., Lakefield Coll. Sch., 1928; LLD. Reporter Ottawa Jour., 1929-32; reporter, editor Can. Press, various Can. cities, London, N.Y.C., 1932-39; assoc. editor Ottawa Jour., 1939-67, editor, pres., 1967-73. Author: J.F.B. Livesay, A Memoir, 1944, A Reporter Reports, 1960, The Journal Men, 1974; also booklets, articles; editor: The Diary of E.W. Harrold, 1947; The Unbelievable Land (Arctic Canada). Mem. N.W.T. Coun., 1961-64; chmn. Ottawa Community Chest, 1962l bd. dirs. Lakefield (Ont.) Coll. Sch., from 1945; bd. govs. Carleton U., from 1974. Recipient Nat. Newspaper award for fgn. corr. Can. Nat. Press Club, 1955; decorated officer Order Can. Mem. Can. Press (pres. 1970-72), Commonwealth Press Union (chmn. Can. sect. 1960-65), Can. Geog. Soc. (dir.), Rideau Club, Royal Ottawa Golf Club, Ottawa Ski Club, Can. Club (pres. 1958-59) (Ottawa). Home: Ottawa Can. Died Jan. 28, 1989.

SMITH, ORMA RINEHART, judge; b. Booneville, Miss., Sept. 25, 1904; s. Jefferson Davis and Lena (Rinehart) S.; m. Margaret Elizabeth Fernandez, June 17, 1930; 1 son, Orma Rinehart Jr. JD, U. Miss., 1927. Bar: Miss. 1927. Practice Corinth, Miss., 1928-68; mem. firm Smith & Smith, 1959-68; judge U.S. Dist. Ct. (no. dist.) Miss., 1968-82; bd. dirs. Nat. Bank of Commerce of Corinth, 1946-68, Fidelity Fed. Savs. & Loan Assn. of Corinth, 1957-68. Trustee Corinth Separate Sch. Dist., 1940-55. Fellow Miss. Bar Found.; mem. ABA, Alcorn County Bar Assn., Miss. State Bar (past pres.), U. Miss. Alumni Assn. (pres. 1961-62), Masons (33 deg.), Shriners, K.T., Alpha Tau Omega. Baptist (past chmn. bd. deacons). Home: Corinth Miss. Died July 5, 1982; buried Corinth.

SMITH, PARKE GILLESPIE, surgeon; b. Reiley, Ohio, Aug. 13, 1890; s. Henry Harrison and Sarah Louise (Gillespie) S.; m. Dorothy K. Daugherty. AB, Miami U., Oxford, Ohio, 1907-10; MD, U. Cin., 1917. Diplomate Am. Bd. Urology. Intern Christ Hosp. Cin., 1916-17, housemanship, 1917-18, mem. attending urologic staff; urol. surgeon Cin., from 1918, asst. to Dr. Gordon S. McKim, 1919-22, assoc., then ptnr., 1922-44; mem. attending urologic staff Holmes, Children's hosps., Cin.; clinician in charge urologic div. Outpatient Dispensary, Holmes, Children's hosps., 1935-53; asst. dir. dept. urology, div. surgery Cin. Gen. Hosp., 1937-46, dir. dept., 1947; assoc. prof. urologic div. Med. Dept., U. Cin., 1937-46, clinicain in charge urologic div., 1947; Dir. Frontier Nursing Svc.; mem. urol. svc. and adv. bd. Mercy Hosp., Miami, Fla.; cons. St. Francis Hosp., Miami Beach, Fla. Contbr. numerous articles to profl. jours. Mem. Cin. Bd. Health, 1939-53. Capt. U.S. Army, World War I. Fellow ACS; mem. AMA (v.p. 1940-41), Cin. Acad. Medicine (pres. 1932), Ohio State Med. Assn. (pres. 1939-50), Am. Urologic Assn. (pres. North Cen. br. 1935-36), Am. Assn. Genito-Urinary Surgeons, Uro-Surg. Soc., So. Surg. Soc., Internat. Soc. Urologists, Fla. Med. Assn., Masons (32 degree), Shriners, University Club, Ft. Mitchell Country Club, Phi Delta Theta, Alpha Kappa Kappa. Republican. Presbyterian. Home: Coral Gables Fla. †

SMITH, RAY VICTOR, dentist, educator; b. Fairbault County, Minn., July 28, 1891; s. Martin Henry and Clara Pauline (Krosch) S.; m. Hazel Ferne Pilcher, Sept. 10, 1912; 1 child, Ronald Ray. DDS, U. Iowa, 1914. Pvt. practice Spirit Lake, Iowa, 1914-16; mem. faculty Coll. Dentistry, U. Iowa, from instr. prosthetic technic to prof., head prosthetic and crown and bridge technic, 1916-55, prof., head crown and bridge dept., from 1955; cons. prosthetics VA. Contbr. articles to profl. jours. Fellow Am. Coll. Dentists; mem. ADA (cons. dental edn), Iowa Dental Soc., Am. Assn. Dental Schs. (chmn. com. aptitude testing 1937-52), Masons, Sigma Xi, Xi Psi Phi, Omicron Kappa Upsilon. Methodist. Home: Iowa City Iowa. †

SMITH, RAY WINFIELD, educator; b. Marlboro, N.H., June 4, 1897; s. John Henry and Ellen Maria (Stone) S.; m. Bonnie D. Jones, Oct. 20, 1923; children: Michel Frans, Champney Fowlis. BS, Dartmouth, 1918, LHD (hon.), 1958. With Am. oil interest, Belgium, The Netherlands, Germany, 1922-36; propr. import-export firm Houston, 1936-42; govt. ofcl. 1946-55; econ. adviser U.S. comdt., Berlin, Germany, 1951-52; U.S. commr. Mil. Security Bd., Germany, 1952-55; pres. Ray Winfield Smith Found., 1955-73; mem. faculty, mem. supervising com. for Ray Winfield Smith lectures on origins, devel. and future of mankind Dartmouth, from 1974; dir. Alhenaten Temple Project in U.A.R., 1965-72; dir. rsch. project on City of Isfahan, Iran; cons. Brookhaven Nat. Lab. Author: Glass from the Ancient World, 1957; numerous articles on ancient glass; bd. editorial rev. Jour. Glass Studies; sr. editor The Akhenaten Temple Project; patentee in fields directional drilling, elevator safety. Bd. visitors Boston Mus. Fine Arts, 1956-62; v.p., exec. dir. Eisenhower-Nixon Club, Washington, 1956; gen. chmn. N.H. Vols. for Nixon-Lodge, 1960; officer of inaugural com., Washington, 1957. 2d lt. Ordnance Dept., AEF, 1918-19; lt. col. USAAF, 1944-45. Decorated Purple Heart, Legion of Merit; recipient 1st award AIA. Fellow German Archeol. Inst., AAAS (coun. mem.); mem. Internat. Com. Ancient Glass (chmn. 1948-68), Archeol. Inst. Am. (bd. trustees 1957-66, chmn. com. ancient glass, 1955-68), Am. Rsch. Ctr. Egypt, Cairo (dir. 1963-65), Army and Navy Club, Sigma Alpha Epsilon. Home: Houston Tex. Died Apr. 17, 1982.

SMITH, RAYMOND D(ANIEL), publishing company executive; b. St. Johnsville, N.Y., Aug. 4, 1912; s. Emery Augustus and Ada (Groff) S.; m. Blanche Virginia Wolfram, Feb. 11, 1960; 1 stepson, Charles H. Copeland. Student, NYU, 1949. With newspaper advt. dept. Union Star, Schenectady, N.Y., 1929-31; pub. Schenectady Neighborhood News, 1932; laborer PWA and WPA, 1933-34; chemist, dispatcher, gen. office Standard Oil N.J., 1934-51; free-lance photographer 1944-50; pub. Cats mag., Pitts. and Washington, 1951-79, Port Orange, Fla., from 1979; assoc. pub. Cats mag., Japan, 1977-82; editor Mag. Index, 1958; instr. Henry George Sch. Social Sci., 1948-50. Editor: (with Blanche V. Smith) Complete Cat Ency., 1972, Rand McNally Pictorial Ency. of Cats, 1980; author: poetry in Praise of Cats; contbr. articles and poems to profl. jours., encys., and anthologies. Mem. AAAS, Henry George Found. Am., Am. Cat Fanciers Assn., Crown Cat Fanciers Fedn. Democrat. Presbyterian (elder). Home: South Daytona Fla. Died Aug. 22, 1985; buried Greenwood Cemetery, Daytona Beach, Fla.

SMITH, RAYMOND G., insurance company executive; b. Columbus, Ohio, Nov. 20, 1916; s. Raymond G. and Nellie (Dorbert) S.; m. Louise Lenora Patton, Nov. 3, 1939; children: David R., Donald R., Barbara Louise. Student, Ohio State U.; also student mgmt. devel. program, Case Inst. Tech., 1958. With Nationwide Ins. Cos., from 1937; sr. v.p. fin. Office Pres., Nationwide Mut. Ins. Co., Nationwide Mut. Fire Ins. Co., Nationwide Life Ins. Co., Nationwide Gen. Ins. Co., Nationwide Variable Life Ins. Co., Nationwide Found., Nationwide Premium Accounts Inc., Nationwide Transport Inc., Nationwide Property and Casualty Ins. Co., Automotive Recycling Ctr. In., Nationwide Profl. Svcs. Inc. Served with AUS, 1943-46. Mem. Am. Mgmt. Assn., Treas.'s Club, Columbus Area C. of C., Fin. Execs. Inst. Home: Columbus Ohio. Died July 1, 1987; buried Union Cemetery, Columbus.

SMITH, ROBERT M., retail executive; b. Talbot County, Ga., June 9, 1892; s. William M. and Alice E. (Kennedy) S.; m. Elsie Cochran, Oct. 5, 1932; 1 child, Robert M. Ed. pub. schs., Ga. With Gt. Atlantic and Pacific Tea Co., from 1911; pres. so. div. Gt. Atlantic and Pacific Tea Co., Jacksonville, Fla., from 1938; bd. dirs. Gt. Atlantic and Pacific Tea Co. of N.J., Gt. Atlantic and Pacific Tea Co of Md.; bd. dirs. Atlantic Nat. Bank, Jacksonville, 1st Fed. Loan & Savs. Co., T.&G. R.R. Co. subs. Seaboard Ry. Mem. Kiwanis, Seminole Club, Timuquana Country Club. Democrat. Presbyterian. Home: Jacksonville Fla. †

SMITH, SOLOMON BYRON, banker; b. Chgo., Apr. 20, 1905; s. Solomon Albert and Fredrika (Shumway) S.; m. Barbara Neff, May 14, 1932 (dec. 1977); children: Wendy Byron and Solomon Albert II. Grad., Hill Sch., Pottstown, Pa., 1924; AB, Yale, 1928. With No. Trust Co., Chgo., 1928-70, successively clk., asst. cashier, asst. sec., 2d v.p., v.p., 1928-49, exec. v.p., 1949-57, vice chmn., 1957-63, chmn. exec. com., 1963-70, bd. dirs., 1970-86; bd. dirs. Ill. Tool Works Inc. Trustee John Crerar Libr., Rush-Presbyn.-St. Luke's Hosp.; hon. trustee Chgo. Mus. Sci. and Industry; treas. Glenwood Sch. for Boys; trustee James C. King Home, Yale U. Art Gallery Assocs.; treas. Chgo. Sunday Evening Club, Protestant Found. Greater Chgo.; gov. mem. Art Inst. Chgo.; life mem. Mus. Contemporary Art, Chgo. Hist. Soc. Mem. River Club, Brook Club (N.Y.C.), Yale Club, Racquet Club, Univ. Club, Chgo. Club, Casino Club, Onwentsia Club, Old Elm Club, Shoreacres Club (Lake Bluff, Ill.). Home: Lake Forest Ill. Died Oct. 9, 1986; buried Rose Hill Cemetery, Chgo.

SMITH, THOMAS WILLIAM MACAULAY, ambassador; b. Boston, Apr. 18, 1930; s. A. William and Isadore (Luce) S.; m. Jane Stuart McDill, May 23, 1959; children: Julia H.M., Ann L.M., Sarah S.M. A.B., Harvard U., 1951; B.A., Cambridge U., 1953, M.A., 1956; M.A., U. Wis., 1970. Commd. fgn. service officer Dept. State, 1956; 3d sec. Am. Embassy, Tunis, Tunisia, 1958-60; 2d sec. Am. Embassy, Paris, 1961-65, Lagos, Nigeria, 1966-68; 2d. sec. Nat. War Coll., 1971-72; 1st sec. Am. Embassy, London, 1972-75; dir. Office of West African Affairs Dept. State, 1975-79; U.S. ambassador to Ghana Accra, 1979-83; U.S. ambassador to Nigeria Lagos, 1983-86; dep. asst. sec. program and policy rev. Dept. State, 1986-87. Served to 1st lt. USMC, 1953-56. Clubs: Metropolitan (Washington); Reform, Flyfishers (London). Home: Washington D.C. Died July 22, 1987, buried River St. Cemetery, Woodstock, Vt.

SMITH, WILLI DONNELL, fashion designer; b. Phila., Feb. 29, 1948; s. Willie Lee and June Eileen (Bush) S. Student, Phila. Coll. Art, 1962-65, Parsons Sch. Design, N.Y.C., N.Y. U., 1965-69. Lectr. fashion history Fashion Inst. Tech. Sketcher, Bobbie Brooks, N.Y.C., 1969, designer, Digits, N.Y.C., 1969-75, designer, v.p., Willi Wear, Ltd., N.Y.C., 1976-87 , also London; designer patterns for, McCall's Co., furniture for, Kroll Assocs., textiles for Bedford Stuyvesant Workshop. Recipient Coty award, 1983, Cutty Sark award, 1986; named Designer of Year, Internat. Mannequins, 1978. Mem. League in Aid for Crippled Children, Bedford Stuyvesant Children's Assn. Democrat. Home: New York N.Y. Died Apr. 17, 1987.

SMITH, WILLIAM ERNEST, history educator; b. Licking, Mo., Apr. 30, 1892; s. William and Laura (Ray) S.; m. Ophia D. Smith, July 22, 1916; children: Laura J. (dec.), Joseph W. Student, State Tchrs. Coll., Warrensburg, 1923; grad., S.W. Mo. State Tchrs. Coll., Springfield; MPh, U. Wis., 1924, PhD, 1927; LittD (hon.), Miami U., 1962. Tchr. Mo. pub. schs. 1910-13; prin. high sch. Walnut Grove, Mo., 1913-18; supt. schs. Belton, Mo., 1918-23; instr. history S.W. Mo. State Tchrs. Coll., summers 1924, 25; lectr. Am. history U. Wis., summer 1926, 30; asst. prof. history Miami U., Oxford, Ohio, 1928-29, assoc. prof., 1929-31, prof., 1931-59, chmn. dept. history, 1935-57, rsch. prof. history, 1959-66, prof. history emeritus, from 1966; lectr. contemporary world affairs, U. Cin., 1932-53, U. Nebr., summer 1941, U. Calif., summer 1949. Author, coauthor or editor books relating to fields including: The Francis Boston Blair Family in Politics, The American Civil War: An Interpretation, A.W. Gilbert: Citizen-Soldier of Cincinnati, A. Buekeye Titan, 1953; editor: Fair Oxford, 1949, Lafayette, Guest of the Nation, 3 vols., 1950, 54, 59, History of Southwestern Ohio: The Miami Valleys, 3 vols., 1964; contbr. Dictionary Am. Biography, Peoples Ency., Ency. Brit. Chmn. bd. First Citizens Bank, Oxford, Ohio; chmn. com. to write war history Miami U.; sec.-treas. Federated McGuffey Socs. Am., pres. 2 yrs.; curator McFuffey Library and Mus., from 1947, also dir.; historian-mem. Mad Anthony Wayne Pkwy. Bd., 1953-63. Recipient rsch. award Ohio Library Assn., 1949, 50. Mem. Am., Miss Valley, Mo., Butler County, Clermont County hist. assns., Oxford Mus. Assn., Ohio Archeol. and Hist. Soc., Acacia, Torch Club, Masons, Kiwanis. Presbyterian. Home: Oxford Ohio. †

SMITH, WILMOT MOTT, insurance executive; b. Patchogue, N.Y., Mar. 18, 1887; s. Wilmot M. and

Elizabeth (Mott) S.; m. Kathryn Henss, Aug.,12, 1911; children: Carol Smith Patton, Peggy Smith Marsh. Student, N.Y. Mil. Acad., 1903-05, N.Y. Law Sch., 1906-07. Asst. sec. Aetna Indemnity Co., N.Y.C., 1907-11; supt. Eastern dept., bonding dept. Royal Indemnity Co., 1911-12; mgr. N.Y. bonding dept. Aetna Casualty & Surety Co., Hartford, Conn., 1912-23, sec., 1923-26, v.p., from 1926; bd. dirs. Standard Fire Ins. Co. Fellow Ins. Inst. Am.; mem. U.S. Srs. Golf Assn., S.R. (nat. and N.Y. state), Hartford Golf Club, Hartford Club, Tin Whistles Club (Pinehurst, N.C.), Chi Sigma Chi. Home: West Hartford Conn. †

SMOLAR, BORIS (BER), editor, author; b. Rovno, Ukraine, May 27, 1897; came to U.S., 1919, naturalized, 1927; s. Leizer-Levy and Miriam (Shearer) S.; m. Genia Lewin, Feb. 26, 1934 (dec. Jan. 1986). Student, Lewis Inst., Chgo., 1921, Medill Sch. Journalism, Northwestern U., 1923-24; D.Hebrew Letters, Balt. Hebrew Coll., 1973. Mem. editorial staff Jewish Daily Forward, 1920-24; roving corr. N.Y. World, 1928-30; editor-in-chief Jewish Telegraphic Agy., N.Y.C., 1924-67, editor in chief emeritus, 1967-86, European dir., London, Eng., 1925-40, chief corr., Europe, 1925-40. Author: Soviet Jewry Today and Tomorrow, 1971; also books for children; column Between You and Me, English-Jewish Press. Bd. dirs. Am. Jewish Joint Distbn. Com., YIVO-Jewish Rsch. Inst. Decorated Medal Amoris Alumna Pax, Pope Paul VI, 1965; Silver medal, Bronze Peace medal (Israel); Smolar award for excellence in Am. Jewish Journalism established by Coun. Jewish Fedns. and Welfare Funds, 1975. Mem. UN Corrs. Assn., Jewish Writers Union, Christian-Jewish Amity U.S., PEN Club. Home: New York N.Y. Died Jan. 31, 1986.

SMUCKLER, EDWARD AARON, physician, educator; b. N.Y.C., Feb. 10, 1931; s. Abraham Franklin and Agnes Lydia (Jacobson) S.; m. Judith Carole Becker, Mar. 28, 1954; children: Cynthia L., Douglas E., Alison, L., Elizabeth L., Daniel J. AB, Dartmouth Coll., 1952; MD, Tufts U., 1956; PhD, U. Wash., 1963. Intern U.S. Naval Hosp., Bethesda, Md., 1956-57; postdoctoral fellow U. Wash. Med. Sch., Seattle, 1959-61, mem. faculty, 1961-76, prof. pathology, 1969-76; prof., chmn. dept. pathology U. Calif., San Francisco, 1976-86; cons. No. State Hosp., Sedro Woolley, Wash., 1961-63, VA Hosp., 1963-76; mem. pathology B Study sect. NIH, 1971; nat. adv. toxicology com. FDA, 1975-78; sci. adv. panel EPA, 1975-82; regional med. adviser Nat. Ski Patrol System, 1971-86. Lt. M.C. USNR, 1956-59. NSF sr. postdoctoral fellow Wennergren Inst., Stockholm, 1965-66; Guggenheim fellow Nat. Inst. Med. Rsch., London, 1970-71. Mem. ACS, AAAS, Biochem. Soc., Am. Soc. Exptl. Pathology, Am. Assn. Pathologists and Bacterioloists, Am. Assn. Cancer Rsch., Am. Soc. Biol. Chemistry. Home: Sausalito Calif. Died Mar. 6, 1986.

SMYTH, HENRY DEWOLF, physicist; b. Clinton, N.Y., May 1, 1898; s. Charles Henry Jr. and Ruth Anna (Phelps) S.; m. Mary de Coningh, June 30, 1936. BA, Princeton, 1918, MA, 1920, PhD, 1921; PhD, Cambridge (Eng.) U., 1923; DSc, Drexel Inst., 1950, Case Inst. Tech., 1953, Hamilton Coll., 1965; LLD, Rutgers U., 1968. NRC fellow Cambridge, Eng., 1921-23; NRC fellow Princeton U., 1923-24, instr. in physics, 1924-25, asst. prof., 1925-29, assoc. prof., 1929-36, prof., 1936-66, Joseph Henry prof. physics, 1946-66, emeritus prof., 1966-86, chmn. dept. physics, 1935-50, chmn. bd. Sci. and Engring Rsch., 1955-59, chmn. Univ. Rsch. Bd., 1959-66; cons. on war rsch. projects to NRC and to Office of Sci. R. & D., 1940-45; cons. Manhattan Dist. project (atomic bombs), U.S. Engrs. 1943-45; mem. AEC, 1949-54; U.S. rep. Internat. Atomic Energy Agy., 1961-70. Author: Matter, Motion and Electricity, 1939, Atomic Energy for Military Purposes (Official War Report on Atomic Bombs), 1945; contbr. articles to Phys. Rev. and other sci. jours.; mem. editorial bd. Princeton Univ. Press, 1946-49, 59-61; assoc. editor Phys. Rev., 1927-30. Trustee Assoc. Univs. Inc. (Brookhaven Nat. Lab.), 1946-49; chmn. bd. trustees Univ. Rsch. Assocs., 1965-70, mem.-at-large, from 1970. Recipient Woodrow Wilson award Princeton, 1964, citation AEC, 1967, Atoms for Peace award, 1968, Disting. Honor award Dept. State, 1970, 1st Henry DeWolf Smyth award for nuclear statesmanship Am. Nuclear Soc.-Atomic Indsl. Forum, 1972. Fellow Am. Phys. Soc. (coun. 1940-44, v.p. 1956, pres. 1957); mem. Am. Acad. Arts and Scis., Am. Philos. Soc., Phi Beta Kappa, Sigma Xi. Home: Princeton N.J. Died Sept. 11, 1986; buried Princeton, N.J.

SMYTHE, CHAUNCEY B., business executive; b. Charleston, Ill., 1888. Grad., MIT, 1911. Pres., bd. dirs. Thew Lorain Co. div. Koehring Co., Milw.; bd. dirs. Koehring Co.; bd. dirs. Lorain County Savs. & Trust Co., Elyria, Ohio. Pres. Elyria Meml. Hosp. Co. Home: Elyria Ohio. †

SNEIDER, RICHARD LEE, ambassador; b. N.Y.C., June 29, 1922; s. Leopold J. and Frances (Magid) S.; m. Lea Ruth Tartalsky, Oct. 1, 1944; children: Dena Ann, Daniel Charles, David Abbott. A.B., Brown U., 1943; M.I.A., Columbia, 1948. Joined U.S. Fgn. Service, 1955; fgn. affairs officer State Dept., 1948-54; 2d sec., later 1st sec. Am. Embassy, Tokyo, Japan, 1954-58; officer charge Japanese affairs State Dept., 1958-61; assigned Nat. War Coll., 1961-62; polit. counselor Am. Embassy, Karachi, Pakistan, 1962-65; country dir. Japan, 1966-68; sr. staff mem. Nat. Security Coun., 1969; dep. chief mission, minister for Okinawa Reversion Negotiations Nat. Security Coun., Tokyo, 1969-72; dep. asst. sec. bur. East Asian-Pacific affairs State Dept., 1972-74; ambassador to Korea 1974-78; fellow Inst. Politics, Harvard U., 1978; adj. prof. Columbia U., 1979. 1st lt. AUS, 1943-46. Mem. Asia Soc. (trustee 1979-86). Home: New York N.Y. Died Aug. 15, 1986; buried Arlington Nat. Cemetery.

SNELL, WILLIS BYRON, glass company executive; b. Cin., June 10, 1892; s. Willis B. and Laura A. (Harris) S.; m. Hazel Arnett, July 26, 1950; children: Willis Byron 3d, Betty (Mrs. Roger H. Smith). Asst. gen. mgr. Charles Boldt Glass Co., Cin., 1918-25; gen. mgr. Olean Glass Co., N.Y., 1926-30; plant mgr. Hazel Atlas Glass Co., Washington, Pa., 1930-32, Owens-Ill. Glass Co., Columbus, Ohio, 1932-37; v.p. mfg. Anchor Hocking Glass Co., Lancaster, Ohio, 1937-61. Mem. Masons, Elks. Methodist. Home: Cincinnati Ohio. †

SNELLGROVE, HAROLD SINCLAIR, educator; b. Meridian, Miss., May 18, 1913; s. Edwin Doty and Laura (Sinclair) S. B.A., Duke, 1936, M.A., 1940; Ph.D., U. N.Mex., 1948. Instr. Gulf Coast Mil. Acad., 1936-41; teaching fellow U. N.C., 1941-42; instr. history U. N.Mex., 1946-47, vis. prof., summer 1951; mem. faculty Miss. State U., from 1947, prof. history, 1957-78, head dept., 1961-78, prof. and head emeritus, from 1978. Author: The Lusignanas in England, 1247-1258, 1950, also articles. Served with AUS, 1942-46. Mem. Mediaeval Acad. Am., Am., So. hist. assns., Phi Kappa Phi, Omicron Delta Kappa, Phi Alpha Theta, Alpha Psi Omega, Pi Delta Phi, Sigma Delta Pi. Republican. Episcopalian. Home: Starkville Miss. Died Nov. 5, 1985.

SNOOK, JOHN ORLA, lawyer, foundation executive; b. Sterling, Kans., Aug. 31, 1902; s. Arthur Jordan and Rachel P. (Dawson) S.; m. Kathryn Koons, Oct. 14, 1934. AB, Sterling Coll., 1924, LLD, 1963; JD, Northwestern U., 1928. Bar: Ill. 1929. Since practiced in Chgo.; mem. firm Concannon, Dillon, Snook & Morton, 1937-85; bd. dirs. Kellogg Co., 1965-80. Trustee La Rabida Children's Hosp. and Rsch. Ctr., 1945-79, W.K. Kellogg Found., 1953-85. Mem. ABA, Ill. Bar Assn., Chgo. Bar Assn., Am. Arbitration Assn. (arbitrator), Pi Kappa Delta. Home: Glencoe Ill. Died Apr. 11, 1985.

SNOW, HERMAN BERNARD, physician, consulting psychiatrist; b. N.Y.C., Mar. 6, 1909; s. Harry and Sarah (Mistofsky) Snofsky; m. Reta Mae Gullackson, Dec. 12, 1982; 1 son, Robert. B.A., Syracuse U., 1929, M.D., 1933. Diplomate: Am. Bd. Psychiatry and Neurology. Intern Univ. Hosp., Syracuse, 1933-34; resident psychiatrist Binghamton (N.Y.) State Hosp., 1934-36, sr. psychiatrist, 1936-39, supervising psychiatrist, 1939; practice medicine specializing in cons. psychiatry Binghamton, 1946-48, Utica, N.Y., 1948-54, Ogdensburg, N.Y., 1954-62, Poughkeepsie, N.Y., 1962-79; asst. dir. Utica State Hosp., 1948; med. insp. Dept. Mental Hygiene, Albany, N.Y., 1949-51; dir. St. Lawrence State Hosp., Ogdensburg, 1954-62; psychiat. cons. VA Hosp., Sunmount, N.Y., 1957-62, Postdam (N.Y.) Hosp., 1959-62; dir. Hudson River State Hosp., Poughkeepsie, 1962-79; psychiat. cons. Vassar Bros., St. Francis hosps.; mem. Gov.'s Prison Commn., 1963-87; cons. Hudson River Psychiat. Center; Mem. N.Y. State Bd. Medicine, 1963-75. Contbr. articles to profl. jours. Served to capt. N.Y. N.G. 1935-39; to lt. col. M.C. AUS, 1940-46. Recipient citations St. Lawrence U., 1958, citations Congregation Anshe Zophen, 1958, Adolf Meyer award for distinguished service in behalf of improved care and treatment of mentally ill, 1959; named Ky. col., 1963. Fellow Am. Psychiat. Assn. (life fellow; pres. Mid. Hudson br. 1965-66), Am. Coll. Psychiatry (emeritus); mem. Med. Soc. State N.Y. (life), AMA, Assn. Med. Supts. Mental Hosps. (pres. 1965), Dutchess County Med. Soc. (pres. 1967), 50 yr. Club Am. Medicine. Home: Hyde Park N.Y. Died Apr. 12, 1987; entombed Community Chapel Mausoleum, Poughkeepsie Rural Cemetery, N.Y.

SNYDER, JOHN WESLEY, business executive; b. Jonesboro, Ark., June 21, 1895; s. Jere Hartwell and Ellen (Hatcher) S.; m. Evlyn Cook, Jan. 5, 1920 (dec. May 1956); 1 dau., Edith Cook Snyder Horton. Student, Vanderbilt U., 1914-15; hon. degrees., 8 U.S. univs. Banker Ark. and Mo., 1919-30; nat. bank receiver Office of Comptroller of Currency, Washington, 1931-37; mgr. St. Louis Loan Agy., RFC, 1937-43, asst. to dirs., 1940-44; exec. v.p. and dir. Def. Plant Corp., Washington, 1940-43; apptd. fed. loan adminstr. Apr. 1945, resigned; apptd. dir. Office War Mblzn. and Reconversion, July 1945; v.p. First Nat. Bank, St. Louis, 1943-45; sec. treasury 1946-53; chmn. fin. com., pres. Overland Corp., Toledo, 1953-66, also bd. dirs.; del. Internat. Fin. Confs., Mexico City, 1945-52, Rio de Janeiro, 1947, London, 1947, Paris, 1950-52, Ottawa, 1951, Rome, 1951, Lisbon, 1952; adviser U.S. Treasury, 1955-76. Mem. coun. adv. bd. Boy Scouts Am.; chmn. Georgetown U. Libr. Assocs.; mem. bd., fin. com. Consortium Univs. of Washngton Met. Area; chmn. bd. trustees Harry S. Truman Scholarship Found.; chmn. spl. fin. com. Washington Nat. Cathedral; trustee Harry S. Truman Libr.; past chmn. bd. regents Georgetown U. Capt. 57th F.A. Brigade, 32 Div., World War I; ret. col. U.S. Army, 1955. Mem. Am. Legion, Res. Officer Assn. (life; past pres. Mo. dept.), Bus. Council, Mo. Athletic Club (St. Louis), Chevy Chase Club, Alfalfa Club, Met. Club (Washington), Masons (33 deg.), Rotary (past pres. Toledo, hon. mem. Washington), Omicron Delta Kappa, Alpha Tau Omega. Episcopalian. Home: Seabrook Island S.C. Died Oct. 8, 1985.

SNYDER, LEON CARLETON, horticulture educator; b. Shepherd, Mich., Mar. 11, 1908; s. Charles N. and Emiline (Robinson) S.; m. Vera A. Ferch, Mar. 29, 1934; children: Ann Marie, Leon Carleton, Mary Carol, Erva May. Student, Central State Tchrs. Coll., Mt. Pleasant, Mich., 1925-28; B.S., U. Wash., 1931, M.S., 1931, Ph.D., 1935. Instr. botany U. Wyo., 1935-36; instr. botany S.D. State Coll., 1936-42, asst. prof. horticulture, 1942-45; with U. Minn., from 1945, successively assoc. prof., extension horticulturist, prof., head horticulture dept., supt. Fruit Breeding Farm, from 1953, dir. Landscape Arboretum, from 1969, prof. emeritus, from 1977; mem. bd. experts Home and Hobby Sect., Mpls. Star & Tribune, from 1954, garden editor, from 1966. Author: Gardening in the Upper Midwest, 1978, Trees and Shrubs for Northern Gardens, 1980, How Does Your Garden Grow? 1982, Flowers for Northern Gardens, 1983; co-author: Minnesota Gardener's Companion, 1981; editor: garden column Mpls. Star & Tribune. Bd. dirs. Minn. Zool. Soc. Recipient Good Neighbor award WCCO Radio, 1968, 69, 76; Greater Mpls. Outstanding Achievement awards; George Robert White medal of honor Mass. Hort. Soc., 1974; medal of honor Garden Club Am., 1974; Norman Jay Colman award Am. Assn. Nurserymen, 1974; Disting. Service to Agr. award Gamma Sigma Delta, 1976; Liberty Hyde Bailey medal Am. Hort. Soc., 1976; John Robertson Meml. award S.D. Hort. Soc., 1976; Meritorious Service cert. Epsilon Sigma Phi, 1976; Outstanding Alumnus award Central Mich. U., 1983; honored by proclamation of Leon C. Snyder Day in State of Minn.; dedication of Leon C. Snyder edn. bldg. at Arboretum and establishment Leon C. Snyder Scholarship program, 1976; Silver Seal award Nat. Council State Garden Clubs, Inc., 1986; Hon. Life Cons. Rosarian Cert., 1984. Fellow Am. Soc. Hort. Sci. (sec. Gt. Plains sect. 1958, pres. 1959, chmn. 1959, chmn. floriculture, ornamental and landscape hort. sect. 1966-67), Am. Hort. Soc. (dir.), Royal Hort. Soc. Eng.; hon. life mem. Minn. Hort. Soc. (exec. bd. 1953, fruit list com. from 1945); mem. Am. Assn. Bot. Gardens and Arboreta (dir. 1960-63, award for arboretum devel. 1974), AAUP, Federated Garden Clubs Minn. (life), Men's Garden Club Am. (Gold medal 1963), Phi Beta Kappa, Sigma Xi, Gamma Sigma Delta, Phi Sigma, Pi Alpha Xi, Epsilon Sigma Phi. Home: Minnetonka Minn. Deceased.

SNYDER, MELVIN HAROLD, clergyman, evangelist; b. Evansville, Ind., Jan. 1, 1912; s. Harold M. and Lucille (Myers) S.; m. Eloise May Brown, July 30, 1933; children: Ina Ruth Synder Buckles, Mary Katherine Snyder McGinnis, Evangeline May Snyder Greves, Harold DeWayne, David Leroy, Margaret Frances Snyder McFrederick, Mark Wesley. Student, Frankfort Pilgrim Coll., 1927-31; D.D., Eastern Pilgrim Coll., 1960. Ordained to ministry Pilgrim Holiness Ch., 1938. Evangelist 1930-35; pastor Marion, Ind., 1935-42; asst. dist. supt. Ind. Pilgrim Holiness Ch., Frankfort, 1942-44, dist. supt., 1944-48; dist. supt. Ind. Pilgrim Holiness Ch., Terre Haute and Bedford, 1948-56; asst. gen. supt. Ind. Pilgrim Holiness Ch., Indpls., 1954-58, gen. supt., 1958-68; gen. supt. Wesleyan Ch., Marion, 1968-80, gen. evangelist, 1980-84, mem. bd. pensions, 1980-84; chmn. polity com. Wesleyan Meth. and Pilgrim Holiness Chs., 1962-68; co-chmn. Wesleyan Ch. and Free Meth. Ch. Commn. on Merger, 1970-76; pres. bd. trustees Frankfort Pilgrim Coll., 1947-58, Wesleyan Ch. Corp., 1969-72, Houghton (N.Y.) Coll., 1970-72; chmn. Wesleyan World Fellowship, 1972-76; pres. Pilgeim Holiness Ch. Corp., 1966-68. Contbr., editor: Pilgrim Holiness Advocate, 1958-68, Wesleyan Advocate, 1968-80, The Preachers Mag., 1973-80, other periodicals; composer: The Prince of Bethlehem, 1946, Suffer the Children to Come Unto Me, 1944, There's Music in My Soul, 1942. Recipient Alumni award Frankfort Pilgrim Coll., 1951, Holiness Exponent of Yr. award Christian Holiness Assn., 1981. Mem. Nat. Holiness Assn. (bd. adminstrn., treas. 1964-69), Nat. Assn. Evangelicals (commn. chaplains 1964-68, bd. adminstrn. 1966-84, exec. com. 1974-78). Home: Marion Ind. Died Apr. 4, 1984; buried Frankfort, Ind.

SNYDER, WILLIAM CORDES, JR., business executive; b. Snow Shoe, Pa., June 12, 1903; s. William Cordes and Mary Allen (Perry) S.; m. Virginia Harper, June 4, 1932; children: Virginia, William Cordes. G-rad., Lehigh U., 1926, DEng (hon.), 1963. With Wheeling (W.Va.) Mold and Foundry Co., 1925-27, chemist, 1926, metallurgist, 1927; metallurgist and roll maker Lewis Foundry & Machine Co., Pitts., 1927-35; v.p. in charge of sales Lewis Foundry & Machine Co., 1935, pres., gen. mgr., until 1937, dir., mem. exec. com., 1937-45; pres., gen. mgr., dir., mem. exec. com. Continental Foundry & Machine Co., 1945-47; v.p. in charge of metall. dept. Koppers Co. Inc.; also in charge Chile mgmt. and constrn. and operation of completely integrated steel plant Koppers Co. Inc., Concepcil,

Chile, 1947-51; pres., chmn. chief exec. officer Blaw-Knox Co., 1951-68, chmn. bd. dirs., 1968-85. Mem. fund-raising coms. Community Fund, Red Cross, Salvation Army; bd. dirs. Nat. Indsl. Conf Bd., Boy Scouts Am., Pitts. YMCA; trustee Sewickley Valley Hosp. Recipient Horatio Alger award, 1956. Mem. Tri-State Indsl. Assn., Am. Iron and Steel Inst., Iron and Steel Engrs., Am. Inst. Mining and Metall. Engrs., Engrs. Soc. Western Pa., Duquesne Club, Univ. Club (Pitts.), Allegheny Country Club, Rolling Rock Club, Laurel Valley Golf Club (Ligonier, Pa.), Met. Club, Internat. Club, Capitol Hill Club (Washington), Saucon Valley Country Club (Bethlehem, Pa.), Castalia (Ohio) Trout Club, Pine Valley Golf Club, Gulf Stream Golf Club, Gulf Stream Bath and Tennis Club (Delray Beach, Fla.). Home: Sewickley Pa. Died July 16, 1985; buried Greenwood Cemetery, Wheeling, W.Va.

SOBEL, ELI, educator; b. N.Y.C., Jan. 17, 1915; s. Martin David and Lean (Filenbaum) S.; m. J. Margaret Forster, Dec. 2, 1944; 1 son, Jeffrey Abbott. A.B., U. Ala., 1937, M.A., 1938; Ph.D., U. Calif. at Berkeley, 1947. Instr. U. Ala., 1938-39; teaching fellow U. Calif. at Berkeley, 1939-42; mem. faculty U. Calif. at Los Angeles, 1946-87, prof. German, 1957-87; assoc. dean U. Calif. at Los Angeles (Coll. Letters and Sci.), 1957-64, chmn. faculty, 1975-76, chmn. dept. Germanic langs., 1964-69; Cons. Council Grad. Schs. U.S., 1966-76 , Can. Council, 1970-76 ; mem. sr. accrediting commn. Western Assn. Schs. and Colls., 1965; panelist cons. Nat. Endowment for the Humanities, 1971-79. Author: Sebastian Brant and Ovid, 1952, Alte Newe Zeitung: A Sixteenth-Century Collection of Fables, 1958, The Tristan Romance in the Meisterlieder of Hans Sachs, 1963; Editor: Pacific Coast Philology, 1974-75; Contbr. numerous articles, revs. to jours. Served to lt. comdr. USNR, 1942-45. Decorated Silver Star, Presdl. citation with bronze star; citation President Philippines; Guggenheim fellow, 1959-60. Mem. Modern Lang. Assn. Am., Renaissance Soc. Am. (a founder), Philol. Assn. Pacific Coast (pres. 1974-75), Medieval Acad., Phi Sigma Delta. Jewish. Home: Los Angeles Calif. Died Apr. 1, 1987; buried Los Angeles.

SOBOL, LOUIS, columnist; b. New Haven, Aug. 10, 1896; s. Jacob and Sonya (Secoll) S.; m. Lee Helen Cantor, Apr. 26, 1919 (dec. 1948); 1 dau., Natalie (dec.); m. 2d, Peggy Antman, July 28, 1950. Student, Crosby Sch., 1910-14. Reporter Waterbury (Conn.) Repulican, 1913, various newspapers, Conn. and N.Y.; Manhattan columnist Hearst newspapers, King Features Syndicate, 1927-67; former commentator ABC radio network. Author: High Hatters (play), 1928, Six Lost Women, 1936, Some Days Were Happy, 1947, Along the Broadway Beat, 1950; contbr. articles and fiction to leading nat. mags. Served in AUS, 1917-19. Decorated Knight Comdr. Order St. Andrew of Caffa. Mem. Artists and Writers, Authors Guild of Am., Silurians. Home: New York N.Y. Died Feb. 9, 1986.

SOLIS, SEIFERTH, architect; b. New Orleans, Feb. 13, 1895; s. Herman Joshua and Cecelia (Cohen) S.; m. Helen B. Stern, Feb. 7, 1923; 1 dau., Celia Seiferth Kornfeld. BArch, Tulane U., 1915. Practice architecture New Orleans, from 1920; chief archtl. supr. for La. FHA, 1934-36; pres. La. Bd. Archtl. Examiners, 1940-48, Nat. Coun. Archtl. Registration Bds., 1945-48; chmn. zoning and major st. plan-coms. New Orleans City Planning and Zoning Commn., 1923-30; mem. New Orleans Vieux Carre Commn., 1966-72. Prin. works include La. State Capitol, Baton Rouge, 1930, bldgs. La. State U., 1932-59, Southeastern La. Coll., 1934-38, Southwestern La. U., 1935-38, Charity Hosp., New Orleans, 1938, Touro Infirmary, New Orleans, 1938-61, IBM bldg., New Orleans, 1956, also schs., hotels, stores, residences. Pres. New Orleans Cultural Centre Commn., 1961-71; pres. Jewish Children's Home, New Orleans, 1950-58, trustee trust funds, from 1960; sec., trustee Newman Sch., New Orleans, 1940-60; trustee F.P. Keyes Found., from 1970; bd. dirs. Friends Tulane U. Library. Capt. U.S. Army, 1917-19; maj. AUS, 1942-45. Recipient cert. of appreciation State of La., 1983. Fellow AIA (pres. New Orleans 1928-30, 58-60, Faget award 1973); mem. Am. Geog. Soc., Soc. Archtl. Historians, La. Architects Assn., La. Landmarks Soc. (dir.), Nat. Trust Hist. Preservation, La. Engring. Soc., La. Hist. Soc. Home: New Orleans La. Died Oct. 11, 1987; buried Metairie Cemetery, New Orleans.

SOLLENBERGER, ISAAC JACOB, finance educator; b. Fidelty, Ohio, Apr. 3, 1891; s. David P. and Rebecca Ann (Yount) S.; m. Mary Hoke, May 23, 1914; children: Talmadge Eugene, Guinevere, Lowel Dwight, Mary Margaret, Martha Eleen, John David. AB, Manchester Coll., 1914; MS, Ohio State U., 1920; postgrad., Columbia U., 1927. Asst. Manchester Coll., 1912-14, instr., 1914-16; asst. Ohio State U., 1920-21; instr. Ohio Wesleyan U., 1921-23; instr. U. Okla., Norman, from 1923, prof. finance, from 1942, chmn. dept. finance, Coll. Bus. Adminstrn., 1943-56; cons. economist govtl. and pvt. agys., from 1930. Author booklets; contbr. articles to econ. publs. Mem. Am. Econ. Assn., Am. Finance Assn., Am. Assn. Univ. Tchrs. Ins., Beta Gamma Sigma. Home: Norman Okla. †

SOLOMON, GUS J., judge; b. Portland, Oreg., Aug. 29, 1906; s. Jacob and Rose (Rosencrantz) S.; m. Elisabeth Willer, Mar. 18, 1939; children—Gerald, Philip, Richard. Student, Reed Coll., 1923-25, LL.D. (hon.), 1975; Ph.B., U. Chgo., 1926, Columbia U., 1926-27; LL.B., Stanford U., 1929; LL.D (hon.), Lewis & Clark Coll., 1986. Pvt. practice 1929-49, U.S. Dist. judge, 1949-87, chief judge, 1959-71, sr. judge, 1971-87; dist. judges rep. for 9th Circuit, Jud. Conf. U.S., 1963-66. Recipient Portland First Citizen for 1970 award, Disting. Service award Portland State U., 1980; Aubrey Watzek award Lewis and Clark Coll., 1984. Mem. Dist. Judges Assn. 9th Circuit (pres. 1968-69). Democrat. Jewish. Home: Portland Oreg. Died Feb. 15, 1987.

SONDERGAARD, GALE, actress; b. Litchfield, Minn.; m. Herbert J. Biberman, 1930 (dec.). AB, U. Minn. Appeared in Theater Guild productions including Major Barbara, 1928 and Broadway plays including Strange Interlude, Red Rus, others; appeared in films Anthony Adverse, Maid of Salem, Seventh Heaven, Cat and the Canary, The Life of Emile Zola, The Blue Bird, The Strange Death of Adolph Hitler, Mark of Zoro, Never Say Die, The Letter, The Spider Woman, The Spider Woman Strikes Back, The Climax, The Invisible Man's Revenge, Gypsy Wildcat, Chhristmas Holiday, Anna and the King of Siam, Road to Rio, Pirates of Monterey, East Side, West Side, Hollywood on Trial, 1977, others. Recipient Acad. award as best actress in supporting role Anthony Adverse, 1936, Outstanding Achievement award U. Minn., 1968; nominated Acad. award for best actress supporting role for Anna and the King of Siam, 1946. Home: Los Angeles Calif. Died Aug. 14, 1985.

SONES, FRANK MASON, JR., physician; b. Noxapater, Miss., Oct. 28, 1918; s. Frank Mason and Myrtle Carrie (Bryan) S.; m. Geraldine Newton, Apr. 2, 1942; children—Frank Mason, Geraldine Patricia, Steven Newton, David Bryan. A.B., Western Md. Coll., Westminster, 1940; M.D., U. Md., Balt., 1943; D.Sc. (hon.), Western Md. Coll., Westminster, 1969; D.H.C., Fed. U. Rio De Janeiro, Argentina, 1969, Fed. U. La Plata, Argentina, 1979. Lic. physician Ohio. Intern U. Md. Hosp., Balt., 1944; resident in internal medicine and cardiovascular disease Henry Ford Hosp., Detroit, 1946-50; dir. Cardiac Lab. and Pediatric Cardiology Cleve. Clinic Found., 1950-66, dir. dept. cardiovascular disease and cardiac lab., 1966-75, sr. physician dept. cardiology, from 1975; cons. and lectr. in field. Contbr. chpts. to books, articles to profl. jours. Nat. cons. in cardiovascular disease to Surgeon Gen., USAF, 1968-77. Served to capt. MC, USAF, 1944-46, World War II. Recipient numerous awards for excellence in medicine most recent: Galen medal Royal Soc. Apothecaries, London, 1985; grantee in field. Fellow Am. Coll. Chest Physicians, Am. Coll. Cardiology, Am. Heart Assn. (Council on Clin. Cardiology, Council on Epidemiology, Council on Radiology), Soc. Cardiac Angiography, Am. Coll. Radiology (hon.), Peruvian Heart Assn. (hon.), Columbian Heart Assn. (hon.), Chilean Soc. Cardiology (hon.), Argentine Fedn. Cardiology (hon.), Nat. Acad. Medicine Brazil (hon.). Home: Solon Ohio. Died Aug. 29, 1985; buried Chagrin Falls, Ohio.

SONNE, HANS CHRISTIAN, business executive; b. Maribo, Denmark, June 19, 1891; s. Christian and Sophia (Gottig) S.; m. Carol H. Mulford, Nov. 10, 1928; children: Sophia Anne, Carol Louise, Christian Richard, Sheila B. A. Grad., U. Copenhagen, 1912. With Frederick Huth & Co., London, 1912-17; sr. ptnr. Huth & Co., N.Y.C., 1917-23; chmn. Amsinck, Sonne & Co., merchant bankers, N.Y.C., 1923-55; chmn. Christian Hansen's Lab. Inc., Little Falls, N.Y. Constitution Ins. Corp.; trustee, treas. Twentieth Century Fund; trustee Com. for Econ. Devel. Author: The City Its Finance July 1914 to July 1915 and Future (London) 1915, Whither America--Common Sense and Better Times (N.Y.). 1938, Enterprise Island, 1948, Our Achilles Heel: World Liquidity, 1967, Gold: A World Asset or a Strait Jacket, 1968. Mem. Nat. Planning Assn. (chmn. bd. trustees), Am. Scandinavian Found. (chmn. bd. trustes), Metropolitan Club, Tuxedo Club. Episcopalian. Home: New York N.Y. †

SONNEBORN, RUDOLF GOLDSCHMID, petroleum executive; b. Balt., June 22, 1898; s. Siegmund B. and Camille K. (Goldschmid) S.; m. 2d. Dorothy Schiff, 1953. Student, Park Sch., Johns Hopkins U., 1918; postgrad., Harvard Bus. Sch., 1919-20. Dir., sec., treas. Sonneborn Chem. and Refining Co. (became part of Witco Chem. Co. Inc., 1960), pres., until 1960; pres., dir. Petroleum Transport & Trading Corp., Sonneborn Assocs. Petroleum Corp., N.Y. Post Corp., Sonapco Bank St. Corp. Alliance Indsl. Devel. Corp., Alliance Industries Inc., Pan Alliance Corp., Del Amkor Corp., Ampak-Am. Israel Corp., Israel Devel. Corp., Israel Am. Indsl Devel. Bank Ltd., Palestine Econ. Corp., Am. Israeli Fin. Corp.; chmn. bd. Am. Palestine Trading Corp.; pres. Israel Am. Petroleum Corp.; founder Material for Israel; dir. Am. Com. for Weizmann Inst. Sci., Am. Friends of Hebrew U., Coun. Jewish Fedns. & Welfare Funds; treas., dir. Breth Found., Bezalel Found.; dir. Hirschman Found., Post Found; nat. chmn. United Jewish Appeal, 1950-44; hon. co-chmn. United Jewish Appeal Greater N.Y.; past pres. Oil Trades Assn. Inc., N.Y. Mem. Nat. Petroleum Assn. (trustee), Pa. Grade Crude Oil Assn. (dir.), Am. Petroleum Inst. (past dir.), Advertising Club, Johns Hopkins Club, Pinnacle Club, Oil City Club, Twenty-Five Yrs. of Petroleum industry, Harvard Bus. Sch. Club, Young Men's Philanthropic League. Home: New York N.Y. Died June 1, 1986.

SOOY, FRANCIS ADRIAN, physician, educator; b. Coalinga, Calif., July 1, 1915; s. Francis Adrian and Mabel Maleta (Boone) S.; m. Elizabeth Dean Thompson, Apr. 17, 1944; children: Charles Daniel, Jane Anne, Elizabeth Dean, Frances McAllister, Adrian Thompson. B.A., U. Calif. at Berkeley, 1937; M.D., U. Calif. at Francisco, 1941, postdoctoral tng. surgery and otolaryngology, 1941-42; postdoctoral tng. otolaryngology, Washington U. Med. Sch., St. Louis, 1942-44. Diplomate: Am. Bd. Otolaryngology (dir. 1968-86). Mem. faculty U. Calif. Sch. Medicine, San Francisco, 1946-86; prof. otolarynology U. Calif. Sch. Medicine, 1961-86, dir. audiology and speech clinic, 1953-72, chmn. div. otolaryngology, 1958-67, chmn. dept. otol., 1967-72, chmn. acad. council, chmn. acad. assembly, 1969-70, Univ. chancellor, 1972-82; Mem. otolaryngology tng. grant com. NIH, 1959-63, nat. adv. council neurol. diseases and blindness, 1964-68; bd. dirs. Am. Council Otolaryngology. Editorial bd.: Annals Otology, Rhinology and Laryngology. Served with USNR, 1944-46. Elected to Shoong Hall of Fame, 1983. Mem. Am. Acad. Ophthalmology and Otalaryngology, Am. Laryngol. Assn., Am. Laryngol., Rhinol. and Otol. Soc. (pres. elect 1977), Am. Otol. Soc. (pres. 1984), Pacific Coast Oto-Ophthal. Soc. (exec. sec.-treas. 1968-86), Collegium ORL Amicitiae Sacrum (pres. 1980), Otosclerosis Study Group (pres. 1985). Home: San Francisco Calif. Died Sept. 12, 1986.

SORKIN, LEONARD, violinist, educator; b. Chgo., Jan. 12, 1916; s. David and Rebecca (Azef) S.; m. Aviva B. Dolnick, July 6, 1939; children: Rafael, Naomi Sorkin Shapiro. Student, Chgo. Musical Coll., Am. Conservatory; MusD (hon.), Northland Coll., 1977. Founder, dir. Summer Evenings of Music Festival, U. Wis., Milw., 1954-85, artist-in-residence Sch. Fine Arts, 1962-85, prof. music, 1967-85, Disting. prof., 1977-85, founder, dir. Inst. Chamber Music, 1982-85; artist-in-residence Festival do Music de Camera, San Miguel, Mex., 1979-80. Mem. 1st violin sect. Chgo. Symphony, 1936-43; soloist in recital with orchs., including Chgo. Symphony, Ill. Symphony, Mid. West concerts; concertmaster Seidenberg Symphonette, Chgo. and Midwest; organizer Fine Arts Quartet, 1940-43; with Staff ABC, 1946-54, quartet in residence Northwestern U., 1953-55, Community Music Sch. north Shore, Winnetka, Ill., 1960-64, 1st violinist, 1982; participant June Music Festival, Albuquerque, 1968-78; pioneer stereophonic recs., Concert Disc Records, ednl. films for Ency. Britannica Films, also ednl. series for Nat. Ednl. and TV Ctr.; toured Europe, 1958-59, 59-60, 60-61, 62, 63, 70-77, 78, 80-81, Australia-New Zealand tour, 1961, the Orient, 1967; performer Edinburgh Festival, 1971. With AUS, 1943-46. Recipient Wis. Gov.'s award, 1968; named laureat and mem. Lincoln Acad., 1967; named Artist of Yr. Am. String Tchrs. Assn., 1970. Home: Milwaukee Wis. Died June 7, 1985.

SOSTRIN, MOREY, merchant; b. Russia, Jan. 10, 1904; came to U.S., 1909, naturalized, 1920; s. Jacob and Anna (Bush) S.; m. Anne Ferer, Aug. 22, 1964. Student, U. Chgo., 1920, Northwestern U., 1921. With Fair Dept. Store, Chgo., 1921; mdse. mgr. J. N. Adam Co., Buffalo, 1924; v.p. J. N. Adam Co., 1928; mdse. mgr. Loesers, Bklyn., 1933; pres. McAlpin Co., Cin., 1936; with Younker Bros., Inc., Des Moines, 1938-87; v.p. Younker Bros., Inc., 1942, pres., dir., 1944-69, chmn., 1965-87, cons., 1969-87. Club: Des Moines, Embassy, Wakonda; Poinciana (Fla.). Home: Palm Beach Fla. Died Jan. 17, 1987; cremated.

SOTTILE, JAMES, III, mining company executive; b. Miami, Fla., Aug. 3, 1940; s. James and Ethel (Hooks) S.; children—James IV, Michael, Scott, Thomas, Jennifer. B.S. cum laude, U. Fla., 1962. Vice pres. Goldfield Corp., Melbourne, Fla., 1970-71; pres., dir. Goldfield Corp., 1971-83; v.p., dir. Canaveral Indian River Groves, Inc., Micco, Fla., 1964-70, Brevard-Indian River Groves, Inc., Micco, 1964-69, Indian River Shores Groves, Inc., 1962-64; pres., dir. Indian Mound Corp., Micco, 1963-69, Original 51 Corp., Micco, 1966-69, Harlan Fuel Co., Ky., 1975-83; v.p. Lake Byrd Citrus Packing Co., Melbourne, 1963-71; pres. Lake Byrd Citrus Packing Co., 1971-83; also dir.; v.p. Indian River Orange Groves, Inc., Melbourne, 1963-69; pres. Indian River Orange Groves, Inc., 1969-74; also dir.; pres., dir. Citrus Growers of Fla., Inc., Melbourne, 1970-83; v.p., dir. No. Goldfield Investments Ltd., Inc., Melbourne, Fla., 1971-79; pres. No. Goldfield Investments Ltd., Inc., 1979-83; v.p., dir. Mamba Engring. Co., Inc., Titusville, Fla., 1972-83; pres., dir. Black Range Mining Corp., Albuquerque, 1972-83, Goldfield Consol. Mines Co., Albuquerque, 1972-83, San Pedro Mining Corp., Albuquerque, 1972-83; v.p., dir. Valencia Center, Inc., Coral Gables, Fla., 1964-83. Supr., sec. San Sebastian Drainage Dist., Melbourne, 1965-78. Mem. Fla. C. of C. (dir. 1972), Young Pres.'s Orgn. Democrat. Roman Catholic. Clubs: Eau Gallie Yacht; Cat Cay (Bahamas). Home: Melbourne Fla. Died June 10, 1983.

SOULE, ARTHUR BRADLEY, radiologist, educator; b. St. Albans, Vt., Oct. 22, 1903; s. Arthur Bradley and Minnie (Miller) S.; m. June Yale Crouter, June 29, 1931; children: Caroline Yale, Arthur Bradley III. AB, U. Vt., 1925, MD, 1928. Pvt. practice specializing in radiology Burlington, Vt., 1929-76; chief radiology svc. Mary Fletcher Hosp., Burlington, 1933-70; prof. radiology Coll. Medicine, U. Vt., Burlington, 1936-70, chmn. dept., 37-70, prof. emeritus, 1970-83; bd. dirs. med. alumni affairs, 1976-83; mem. com. acad. radiology NAS-NRC; mem. tng. grants com. USPHS. Contbr. articles to profl. jours. Recipient Excellence in Teaching award Nu Sigma Nu, 1964, Disting. Svc. medal U. Vt. Med. Alumni Assn., 1970, Cert. of Honor, A.S.R.T., 1969, Citation of Honor Coun. Med. Edn., AMA, 1969, citation for contbns. to allied health edn, 1980. Fellow Am. Coll. Radiology (commn. chmn., gold medal 1974); mem. Am. Roentgen Ray Soc. (2d v.p. 1957, 68), Radiol. Soc. N.Am., New Eng. Cancer Soc. (pres.). Home: South Burlington Vt. Died July 1, 1983; buried Meml. Garden, St. Paul's Cathedral, Burlington, Vt.

SOULE, FRANK F(LINT), publisher; b. Benton Harbor, Mich., Apr. 10, 1889; s. John F. and Carrie H. (Doyle) S.; m. Ruth H. Harrower, Oct. 18, 1913; children: Lois Virginia (Mrs. John Gully Cole), Frank Flint. AB, U. Chgo., 1912. With Lord & Thomas Advt. Agy., Chgo., 1911; advt. solicitor Leslie-Judge Co., 1912-18; western mgr. Christian herald, 1918-21, McCall's mag., 1921, Conde Nast Publs., Inc., Chgo., 1921-31; bus. and advt. dir. Conde Nast Publs., Inc., N.Y.C., from 1931, v.p., 1947-57, gen. sales counsel, from 1957, also bd. dirs. Dir. Nat. Better Bus. Bur. Mem. University Club, Union League, Apawamis Club, Beverly Hills Club. Home: Los Angeles Calif. †

SOULE, GEORGE, college president; b. New Orleans, Nov. 24, 1896; s. Albert Lee and Anna Sophronia (Cooper) S.; m. Mary Brooks Ragland, Feb. 21, 1922; children, George, Evan R., Mary Brooks. Student, Isadore Newman Sch., Ga. Mil. Acad., Acad. Soulé Coll., La. State U. Clk., asst. instr. Soulé Coll., 1919-26, tchr., asst. treas,, 1926-1929, sec., mgr. in charge of adminstrn., 1929-83; ptnr. in firm of A.L.E.E. and George Soulé, owners of Soulé Coll. Inc., 1936-48; past v.p. Am. Empire Ins. Co.; bd. dirs. Union Savs. & Loan Assn.; bd. dis., past v.p. Bur. Govtl. Rsch. of New Orleans. Past pres. New Orleans chpt. Nat. Officers Mgmt. Assn.; former dir. Magnolia Sch. for Exceptional Children (pres. 1945, 46); chmn. campaign executives com. United Community and War Chest, 1945; past pres. New Orleans Community Chest; chmn. New Orleans Ednl. Fund; past vice chmn. City Planning and Zoning Commn. of New Orleans; campaign vice chmn., United Fund, 1952; gen. chmn. Congress Freedom nat. conv., 1963. 2d lt., U.S. Field Arty., 1917-18. Recipient Americanism award Am. Legion, 1960. Mem. New Orleans C. of C., Young Men's Bus. Club, Discussions Unlimited (hon. life), Boston Club (hon. life mem.), Pendennis Club (pres. 1970-71), Gyro Club (past pres., past dist. gov.) (New Orleans), New Orleans Executive of Louisiana (pres. 2 terms), Juanita Club (hon. life mem.). Anglican Catholic. Home: New Orleans La. Died 1983; buried New Orleans.

SOYER, RAPHAEL, artist; b. Russia, Dec. 25, 1899; came to U.S., 1912; s. Abraham and Bella (Schneyer) S.; m. Rebecca Letz, Feb. 8, 1931; 1 dau., Mary. Student, Cooper Union, N.A.D., Art Students League. Exhibitor in nat. and internat. shows, Corcoran Mus., Washington, Carnegie Internat., Chgo., Phila., one-man shows since 1929 at following galleries, Daniel, Rehn, Valentine, Macbeth, A.C.A., Weyhe, Assoc. Am. Artists, Forum Gallery, retrospective exhbn., Whitney Mus. Am. Art, 1967; Author: Self Revealment; Diary of an Artist; illustrator: Adventures of Yemima and Other Stories (Abraham Soyer). Subject of book by Lloyd Goodrich, 1972; Recipient 1000 prize for art USA, 1959; Gold medal Am. Acad. and Inst. Arts and Letters, 1981. Mem. Artists Equity Assn., Am. Art Group, Soc. Painters, Sculptors and Gravers, Nat. Inst. Arts and Letters (council), N.A.D. (asso.), Am. Acad. Arts and Letters. Home: New York N.Y. Died Nov. 2, 1987.

SPAIN, FRANK EDWARD, lawyer; b. Memphis, Oct. 11, 1891; s. John Batt Kennedy and Ida (Lockard) S.; m. Margaret Cameron, July 21, 1917 (dec. 1971); children: Margaret C. (Mrs. W. C. McDonald, Jr.), Frances (Mrs. J. C. Hodges, Jr.) (dec.); m. Nettie Elizabeth Edwards, 1974. A.B., So. U. (now Birmingham- So. U.), 1910, LL.D. (hon.), 1955; LL.B., U. Ala., 1913, LL.D. (hon.), 1962. Bar: Ala. 1913. Practiced in Birmingham 1980, asst. city atty., 1917; mem. Spain, Gillon, Riley, Tate & Etheredge; dir. emeritus Liberty Nat. Life Ins. Co.; formerly gen. counsel U.S. Fidelity & Guaranty Co., Ala.; formerly sec. and dir. Odum Bowers & White Corp.; Food adminstr. for Jefferson County, 1917; fair price commr. for, Ala., 1919. Chmn. Housing Authority of Birmingham Dist., 1938-43, Ala. Assn. of Housing Authorities, 1938-43; appeal chmn. Jefferson County Community and War Chest Drive, 1943, Ala. War Chest, 1945; pres. Community Chest of Birmingham, 1946-47; mem. State Adv. Council Constrn. Mental Retardation Facilities.; mem. Coll. Electors N.Y.U. Hall Fame Gt. Ams.; past dir. U. Ala. Med. Center Found., Ala. Soc. Crippled Children and Adults, Eye Found.; adv. bd. Cumberland Law Sch.; trustee Birmingham-So. Coll.; hon. mem. pres.'s council U. Ala., Birmingham. 2d lt. heavy arty., 1918. Decorated chevalier Legion of Honor France; Gorgas award Ala. Medical Assn., 1964; named Outstanding Philanthropist Ala. Soc. Fundraising Execs., 1984; named to Ala. Acad. Honor, 1973; Ala. Bus. Hall of Fame, 1980; Gallery of Leaders Torchmack Corp., 1984; Gallery of Disting. Citizens Birmingham City Council, 1984. Mem. Rotary Internat. (pres. 1951-52), Birmingham C. of C. (pres. 1953), Ala. Motorists Assn. (pres. 1930-41), ABA (chmn. ins. sect. 1944-46), Ala. Bar Assn., Birmingham Bar Assn. (Man of Year nominee 1973), past mem. Judicial Council Ala., mem. Assn. Life Ins. Counsel, Am. Life Conv. (past chmn. legal section), Sigma Alpha Epsilon, Phi Beta Kappa, Omicron Delta Kappa. Republican. Episcopalian. Clubs: Rotary (pres. 1942-43, Paul Harris fellow, citation for service above self 1977), Mountain Brook, The Club, The Relay House; Lakeview Country (Greensboro, Ala.); N. River Yacht (Tuscaloosa, Ala.). Deceased.

SPANTON, WILLIAM T., vocational educator; b. Independence, Ky., Oct. 25, 1891; s. Thomas M. and Frances E. (Nugent) S.; m. Ethel O. Schramm, Oct. 28, 1916; 1 child, William F. AB, Ohio State U., 1915, BS in Edn., Agr., 1916; AM, Brown U., 1924; PhD, Am. U., 1932. Tchr. high sch. Plain City, Ohio, 1916-17; supt. schs. Litchfield, Ohio, 1917-18; head agrl. dept. East Tech. High Sch., Cleve., 1918-19; prof. agrl. edn. R.I. State Coll., 1919-20; state high sch. insp., state supr. agrl. edn. Jefferson City, Mo., 1920-25; fed. agt. for agrl. edn. U.S. Office Edn., 1925-41, dir. agrl. edn. svc., from 1944. Pres. Future Farmers Am. Found., from 1950; mem. bd. govs. Agrl. Hall of Fame; mem. Nat. Coun., Boy Scouts Am.; bd. dirs. Farm Film Found. Recipient Silver Buffalo award Boy Scouts Am., 1961. mem. Nat. Safety Coun. (farm div.), Am. Vocat. Assn. (life), Masons, KT, Phi Delta Kappa, Alpha Tau Alpha, Alpha Zeta (hon. at large). Home: Hyattsville Md. †

SPARKMAN, JOHN JACKSON, U.S. senator; b. Morgan County, Ala., Dec. 20, 1899; s. Whitten J. and Julia Mitchell (Kent) S.; m. Ivo Hall, June 2, 1923; 1 dau., Julia Ann Shepard. AB, U. Ala., 1921, LLB, 1923, LLD, 1968; LLD, Spring Hill Coll., Mobile, Ala., 1956, Auburn U., 1960, Nat. U. Seoul (Korea), 1969. Bar: Ala. 1925. YMCA sec. U. Ala., 1923-25; instr. Huntsville (Ala.) Coll., 1925-28; pvt. practice Huntsville, 1925-36; U.S. Commr. 930-31, mem. 75th-80th congresses from 8th Ala. Dist., apptd. to U.S. Senate to fill uenexpired term of late Senator Bankhead, 1946, U.S. Senator, 1936-79; Democratic nominee for v.p., 1952; trustee Am. U., Athens (Ala.) Coll.; U.S. del. 5th Session UN Gen. Assembly; chmn. Senate Com. on Banking, Housing and Urban Affairs, 1967-74, Fgn. Relations Com., 1974-79. Served in Students' Army Tng. Corps, 1918. Col. U.S. Res. Corps (ret.). Mem. Am. Legion (past comdr.), Huntsville C. of C. (pres. 1935-36), Masons, Order Eastern Star, Woodman, Kiwanis, Phi Beta Kappa, Pi Kappa Alpha, Phi Alpha Delta. Democrat. Methodist (list lay leader). Home: Huntsville Ala. Died Nov. 16, 1985.

SPATAFORA, ANTHONY FRANK, hotel executive; b. New Orleans, Apr. 29, 1891; s. Mariano and Croce (Crapa) S.; m. Mary Lucy Noto, Dec. 18, 1912. Student, pub. schs., New Orleans. Bellboy Monteleone Hotel, New Orleans, 1904-08, asst. clk., 1908-18, night mgr., 1918-22, exec. asst. mgr., 1922-30, gen. mgr., 1930-70, sec., treas., 1949-70, v.p., gen. mgr. Named Hotelman of Yr., So. Hotel Jour., 1944, hon. col. La. Mem. Hotel Greeters Am. (internat. pres. 1930-33), New Orleans C. of C. (bd. dirs.), Nat. Hotel Sales Mgmt. Assn., Internat., Am., La., New Orleans (past pres.) hotel assns., United Comml. Travelers Protective Assn. Am., KC, Kiwanis. Home: New Orleans La. †

SPAULDING, CHARLES CLINTON, JR., lawyer; b. Durham, N.C., Nov. 10, 1907; s. Charles Clinton and Fannie (Jones) S.; m. Mae Frances Bass, Sept.1, 1936 (dec.); 1 son, Charles Clinton; m. 2d, Minnie Pearson Turner, June 5, 1960. AB, Clark U., 1930; LLB, St. Johns U., 1935, JD, 1968. Bar: N.C. 1946. With N.C. Mut. Life Ins. Co., Durham, 1936-87, spl. rep. investment, 1936-41, asst. to treas., then asst. treas., 1941-1946, asst. treas. atty., 1946-51, counsel, 1951-58, gen. counsel, dir., 1958-80, v.p., gen. counsel, 1962-73; ptnr. Malone, Johnson, De Jarmon & Spaulding, Durham, 1973-87; chmn. bd., dir. Mechanics & Farmers Bank, 1952-87; past cons. legal svcs. div. OEO, Washington. Past treas., v.p., pres. Durham County unit Am. Cancer Soc.; now bd. dirs.; past chmn. Citizens Adv. Com. Workable Program under HUD; trustee St. Augustine's Coll., Raleigh, N.C., 1971-79, 81-87, N.C. Cancer Inst.; charter mem. N.C. for Better Libraries; Mem. N.C. Commn. for Study Cancer, 1972-74, Criminal Code Commn. N.C., 1975-78. Recipient award pub. svc. Durham County unit Am. Cancer Soc., 1968-70, award leadership sales program Balt. N.C. Mut. Life Ins. Co., 1966. Mem. Assn. Life Ins. Counsel (emeritus), Nat. Bar Found., Nat. Bar Assn. (life, past treas., exec. com., C. Francis Stradford award 1973), Am. (past chmn., subcom. in taxation sect.) Bar Assn. Democrat. Baptist (deacon, trustee, bus. mgr., treas. ch.; award for svcs. 1968). Home: Durham N.C. Died Sept. 10, 1987; buried Durham, N.C.

SPEAKE, S. A., advertising executive; b. Closter, N.J., 1891. Sr. v.p., treas., dir. Albert Frank - Guenther Law Inc., Closter, N.J. Home: Closter N.J. †

SPEAR, JOSEPH, mathematics educator; b. Boston, Aug. 25, 1891; s. Jacob and Mary (Rosenberg) s.; m. Gertrude Mandelstam, July 17, 1921; children: Charles George, Harold Samuel. AB, Harvard U., 1913; AM, Boston U., 1933. With astron. computer project with Dr. Percival Lowell Boston, 1913; instr. math. and German U. Maine, 1913-15; assoc. editor U.S. Investor, Boston, 1915-18; instr. math. Northeastern U., 1919, prof., chmn. dept., 1920-58, prof., from 1958; TV lectr. on math., from 1957. Author: Mathematics, To Reason, 1938, Introduction to Calculus, 1938, Differential Calculus of Algebraic Functions, 1946. Lt. F.A., U.S. Army, World War I. Fellow AAAS; mem. Math. Assn. Am., Am. Math. Soc., Am. Soc. Engring. Edn., Assn. Tchrs. Math. New Eng., N.E. Track and Field Ofcls. Assn., N.E. Amateur Athletic Union, 301st F.A. Vets. Assn., Masons. Home: Brighton Mass. †

SPEAR, WILLIAM WILSON, lawyer; b. Genoa, Nebr., May 8, 1911; s. Edward McGraw and Lucia (Wilson) S.; m. Louise Boles, Apr. 7, 1942 (div. Mar. 1961); children: William E., Andrew M., Loraine; m. Sylvia C. Gunnlaugson, Aug. 1963. AB, U. Nebr., 1933; JD, George Washington U., 1936. Bar: D.C. 1936, N.Y. 1938, Nebr. 1945, W.Va. 1968. Atty. Chesapeake & Potomac Telephone Co., Washington, 1936-37, Bklyn. Manhattan Transit Corp., N.Y.C., 1937-40; asst. div. atty AT&T, Washington, 1946-50; mem. firm Spear Lamme & Simmons (and predecessors), Fremont, Nebr., 1951-58; sr. atty. Standard Oil Co., Ind., 1958-70, v.p., 1970-76, v.p. govt. relations ret., 1976; pvt. practice Martinsburg, W.Va., 1976-84. Mem. Rep. Nat. Com., 1954-56; chmn. State Cen. Com., 1954-56; chmn. call com., 1956; nat. conv.; bd. regents Georgetown U., Washington, 1971-84. Maj. USAAF, 1942-46. Mem. Fed. City, Univ., Capitol Hill Clubs (Washington), Phi Alpha Delta, Chi Phi. Home: Martinsburg W.Va. Died Aug. 15, 1984; buried Harper Cemetery, Harpers Ferry, W.Va.

SPEED, JAMES SPENCER, orthopaedic surgeon; b. Rapid City, S.D., July 30, 1890; s. Edward Watkins and Mary (Spencer) S.; m. Elizabeth Broaddus, June 6, 1927. AB, U. Va., 1913; MD, Johns Hopkins U., 1916. Diplomate Am. Bd. Orthopaedic Surgery. Pvt. practice from 1920; chief of staff Willis C. Campbell Clinic, Crippled Children's Hosp. Sch., Hosp. for Crippled Adults, from 1941. Contbr. numerous articles to profl. jours. 1st lt. M.C., U.S. Army, 1917-19. Fellow ACS; mem. AMA, Am. Orthopaedic Assn., Am. Acad. Orthopaedic Surgeons, So. Med. Assn., So. Surg. Assn., Robert Jones Club, Memphis Country Club, Rotary,, Sigma Chi, Alpha Omega Alpha. †

SPEER, EUGENE EAVEN, JR., medical center administrator; b. Decatur, Ala., Nov. 10, 1911; s. Eugene Eaven and Emma (Shoemaker) S.; m. Jessie M. Pridmore, Mar. 1, 1946 (dec. 1977); m. Johanna Sachs, Dec. 14, 1984. B.S., Athens Coll., 1937; student, U. Ala., 1935-38. Tchr. Decatur pub. schs., 1933-38, prin., 1938-41, vocat. adviser, 1937-38; first aid and water safety field rep. East-Coast Am. Nat. Red Cross, 1941-42; with VA 1946-85, nat. dir. med. adminstrn., 1963-66; hosp. dir. Louisville, 1966-69, Buffalo, 1969-71, Augusta, Ga., 1971-85; ret. 1985; vis. lectr., preceptor George Washington U. Grad. Sch. Health Care Adminstrn.; preceptor health care adminstrv. residents U. Ottawa; faculty Med. Coll. Ga. Bd. dirs. numerous community agy. bds. including chmn., pres., bd. dirs. East Central Ga. Health Services Agy. Served to capt. AUS, 1942-46. Recipient service citations VFW, Am. Legion, DAV, Paralyzed Vets. Am., Amvets, Order of Purple Heart; named Fed. Civil Servant of Yr. Greater Kansas City Area, 1962. Fellow Am. Coll. Hosp. Adminstrs.; life mem. DAV AMVETS, Am. Legion, VFW, Paralyzed Vets. Am.; mem. Nat. Council Tchrs. Math. (Ala. pres. 1937), Tenn. Valley Council Tchrs. Math., Am. Hosp. Assn., Western Hosp. Assn., N.Y. Hosp. Assn., Assn. Mil. Surgeons U.S., Fed. Exec. Assn. (pres. 1969, bd. dirs. Frontier Niagara chpt. 1970-71), Greater Augusta Hosp. Adminstrs. (chmn.). Club: Civitan. Lodge: Kiwanis. Home: Evans Ga. Died Apr. 19, 1987; buried Nat. Cemetery, Beaufort, S.C.

SPEER, PAUL, lawyer; b. Oil City, Pa., July 29, 1892; s. Peter M. and Isabella A. (Paul) S.; m. Laura L. Detwiller, Nov. 29, 1924 (div.); 1 child, Laurette; m. Margaret S. Buckley, Nov. 7, 1957. AB, Harvard U., 1913, LLB, 1917. Bar: N.Y. 1920. Spl. asst. to Atty. Gen. of U.S. 1920-21; v.p., gen. counsel, bd. dirs. U.S. Potash Co., 1930-56; (merger of U.S. Potash Co. and U.S. Borax and Chem. Corp.); counsel Macklin, Speer, Hanan & McKernan, N.Y.C., from 1946; v.p., bd. dirs. U.S. Borax and Chem. Corp., 1956-59, cons., bd. dirs. from 1959; counsel M&J Tracy, Inc., N.Y.C., from 1962; Mayor Roslyn Estates, N.Y., 1931-33, trustee 1939-41. Capt. inf. AUS, 1917-19. Mem. Potash Export Assn. (pres. 1940-55, past bd. dirs.), Am. Potash Inst. (bd. dirs. 1935-59), Assn. of Bar of City of N.Y. Maritime Law Assn. U.S., Pa. Soc. (v.p.), Downtown Assn., Harvard Club, Metropolitan Club. Republican. Presbyterian. Home: New York N.Y. †

SPEER, TALBOT TAYLOR, publisher; b. Pitts., Jan 7, 1895; s. John L. Dawson and Margaret (Taylor) S. m. Mary Washington Stewart, Dec. 8, 1920 (dec. 1926) 1 child, Mary Washington; m. Louise Pierce Leetch Nov. 1928 (div.); children: Louise Pierce, Margaret

Taylor, Eleanor Talbot; m. Jane Turner, Oct. 5, 1943; children: Talbot Taylor, J.L. Dawson, Jane Alexander, Ramsey Clarke. Student, Brennens and Bradshaw Schs., Pitts., 1900-07, Episcopal High Sch., Alexandria, Va., 1907-13, U. Va., 1913-15, U. Md., 1915-16; LL.D., U. Balt., 1974. Salesman The Daniel Miller Co., Balt., 1919-21; asst. to pres. Balt. Salesbrook Co., 1922, pres. and chmn. of bd., 1922—; pres., chmn. bd. The Capital-Gazette Press, Annapolis, Md., 1926; pub. since 1926 of Daily Evening Capital; pub. from 1926 of Md. Gazette, So. Md. Times, U.S. Coast Guard Mag., Chesapeake Skipper, Prince George County News, Md., Capital-Gazette News, Ann Arundel County, Md.; pres. Speer Pubs., from 1951; pub. St. Mary's Beacon, Waldorf Leaf; dir. Union Trust Co. Med., from 1947. Founder, pres. Nat. Ednl. Found, Inc., Balt.; pres. Talbot T. Speer Found., Inc., 1951-75; Dir. Balt. Assn. of Commerce, 1935-40, Balt. Conv. Bur., 1946-48, County Taxpayers League, 1945—; Dir. U.S. Naval Acad. Found., 1950-54, mem. higher edn. com., Md., from 1945 ; mem. higher edn. com. prison bd., 1948-50; mem. W.P.B., 1940-45, Indsl. Moblzn. Com., from 1950, U.S. Army Adv. Com., since 1947. Served as 2d lt. Am. 1st div. in France U.S. Army, 1917-18; resigned with rank of capt. 1918. Decorated Purple Heart, Silver Star U.S.; Fourrogere Croix de Guerre France; cited by U.S. Govt., certificate of merit for services to Nat. War Effort; recipient Certificate Distinguished Citizenship for 40 yrs. outstanding Service as leading newspaper pub., industrialist and philanthropist Gov. Md., 1965, 73, Certificate Distinguished Citizenship for 40 yrs. outstanding Service as leading newspaper pub., industrialist and philanthropist Mayor Balt., 1973. Mem. N.A.M. (sr. dir., rep. Md. 1947-50), Splty. Accounting Supply Mfrs. Assn. dir., Asso. Industries Md. (pres., dir. 1949-51), Newcomen Soc. (award 1961), Mil. Order Fgn. Wars, Salesbook Mfrs. Assn, Alumni Assn. U. Md. (pres. 1950-52), Soc. 1st div. A.E.F., Am. Legion, Mems. of the Purple Heart, Delta Psi. Episcopalian (mem. lay council procathedral of Md. 1925-54). Clubs: Rotary, Maryland, Bachelors Cotillion, Elkridge Kennels, Greenspring Valley Hunt, Carrollton Hounds, Wythmore Hounds, Baltimore Country, Annapolis Yacht, Annapolitan, St. Anthony, Lake Placid, Everglades, Nat. Press, Gulf Stream Golf; Rolling Rock (Ligonier, Pa.); Delray Beach (Fla.) Bath and Tennis. Home: Delray Beach Fla. Deceased.

SPELLMAN, GLADYS NOON, congresswoman; b. N.Y.C., Mar. 2, 1918; d. Henry and Bessie G. Noon; m. Reuben Spellman: children: Stephen Louis, Richard Eric, Dana Spellman O'Neill. Ed., George Washington U. and Grad. Sch. of Dept. Agr. Tchr. Prince George's County (Md.) Pub. Schs.; mem. Prince George's County Bd. Commrs., 1962-70, Prince George's County Coun., 1971-74, 94th-97th Congresses from 5th Md. Dist., Adv. Com. Intergovtl. Relations, 1967-69, Gov.'s Commn. on Law Enforcement and Adminstrn. Justice, Gov.'s Commn. on Functions of Govt.; vice chmn. Gov.'s Commn. to Determine State's Role in Financing Pub. Edn.; chmn. Md. State Comprehensive Health Planning Adv. Coun., Washington Suburban transit Comm., Regional Planning Bd. IV, Fed. Omnibus Crime Control and Safe Sts. Act. Bd. dirs. Washington Met. Area Transit Authority; mem. Dem. Adv. Com. Elected Ofcls; v.p. Met. Washington Coun. Govts.; chmn. bd. trustees Prince George's Gen. Hosp., 1962-70. Mem. Md. Assn. Counties (past dir., chmn. edn. com.), Nat. Assn. Counties (past pres.), Nat. Labor-Mgmt. Relations Svc., Nat. Coun. State Govts. (steering com. of urban affairs com.), Nat. Assn. Regional Couns. (dir.). Home: Laurel Md. Died June 19, 1988; buried Arlington Nat. Cemetery, Washington.

SPENCE, ARTHUR MEARNS, publishing company executive; b. N.Y.C., May 11, 1917; s. James Williams and Margaret Mary (Mearns) S.; m. Jean Gunnip, Mar. 22, 1941; children: Marilyn, Helen Spence Tschantre. BS, NYU, 1943. Various positions Guaranty Trust Co., N.Y.C., 1933-42; regional auditor Reuben H. Donnelley Pub. Co., N.Y.C., 1946-49; controller Geyer-McAllister Publs., N.Y.C., 1949-65, treas., 1965-69, v.p., treas., 1969-72, exec. v.p., 1972-74, pres., 1974-86, dir., 1974-86; bd. dirs. Am. Bus. Press. Lt. AUS, 1943-46, ETO. Decorated Purple Heart. Mem. Assn. Paid Circulation Pubs. (past chmn. bd.), University Club, Orienta Yacht Club, St. Andrew's Soc., Westchester Hills Golf Glub. Republican. Methodist. Home: Mamaroneck N.Y. Died June 10, 1986; buried Cypress Hills Cemetery.

SPENCER, DALE RAY, journalism educator; b. Pocatello, Idaho, Oct. 21, 1925; s. Howard Harris and Eleda (Eastman) S.; m. Lillian Joy Hodkins, Dec. 21, 1947; children: Melinda Sue, Jennifer Joy. Student, Idaho State U., 1944-45, U. N.Mex., 1945-46; BJ, U. Mo., 1948, MA, 1955, JD, 1968. Bar: Mo. 1969. Mem. faculty U. Mo., Columbia, 1950-89; prof. journalism U. Mo., 1971-89, chmn. news editorial dept., 1979-80, lectr. communications law, 1958-89; founder, 1st pres. Mo. Assembly of Faculty in Higher Edn., 1975-76; mem. bar relations com. Am. Newspaper Pubs. Assn., 1976-82, mem. legal affairs com., 1982-86; mem. bar task force ABA-Am. Newspaper Pubs. Assn., 1981-86, mem. governing com. of forum com. on communications law, 1981-89; mem. adv. bd. 13th Jud. Circuit Juvenile Ct., 1984-89; mem. bicentennial com. on community forums Mo. Press Bar Commn., 1987-89; mem. Mo. Freedom of Council, 1987-89; mem. adv. bd. FirstNet USA, 1987-89. Editor: Columbia Missourian, 1950-73. Bd. dirs. Wonderland Camp for Handicapped Children, from 1973; v.p. Freedom of Info. Found., from 1979. Served with USNR, 1943-46. Recipient Joyce Swan Disting. Faculty award U. Mo. Journalism Sch., 1967. Mem. ABA, Mo. Bar (chmn. pub. info. com. 1981-83), Investigative Reporters and Editors, Mo. Press Law Group (organizer, acting chmn. 1982-89), Assn. for Edn. in Journalism and Mass Communication, Am. Judicature Soc., Sigma Delta Chi (nat. v.p. 1951-53), Kappa Tau Alpha, Kappa Alpha Mu. Club: Kiwanis. Home: Columbia Mo. Died Dec. 23, 1988.

SPENGLER, EDWIN HAROLD, educator; b. Bklyn., Apr. 4, 1906; s. John P. and Louise A. (Wurst) S.; m. Helen L. Herold, 1934. BS, CCNY, 1925; AM, Columbia U., 1928, PhD, 1930. Instr. CCNY, 1925-30; instr. Bklyn. Coll., 1930-35, asst. prof., 1936-41, assoc. prof., 1941-49, prof., 1949-70, prof., dean emeritus, 1971-81; rsch. staff N.Y. State Commn. Revision Tax Laws, 1931-32, commn. on State Aid, 1935; lectr. Columbia U., 1941-43; cons. Nat. Resources Planning Bd., 1942-43; MIT Urban Redevel. Sta., 1942; hist. editor Air Tech. Service Command AAF, 1944-46; cons. Mcpl. Fin. Study, Mayor's Com. Mgmt. Survey, N.Y.C., 1950-51; exec. sec treas. Assn. U. Evening Colls., 1954-63; Fulbright lectr., 1957-58. Author: Land Values in N.y., 1930, Introduction to Economics, 1931, Introduction to Business, 4th Edit, 1955, Urban Taxation, 1943; numerous monographs and articles. Bd. dirs. Citizens' Housing and Planning Coun. N.Y., 1943-81; cons. N.Y.State-City Fiscal Affairs Com., 1955-56; trustee Silver Bay Assn., 1964-81. Mem. Freedom House, Am. Econ. Assn., Adir Mountain Club, Phi Beta Kappa, Lambda Alpha. Home: Rockville Centre N.Y. Died 1981.

SPERONI, CHARLES, college dean; b. Santa Fiora, Italy, Nov. 2, 1911; came to U.S., 1929; naturalized, 1941; s. Edoardo and Aida (Falchi) S.; m. Carmela Helen Corica, June 15, 1938. AB, U. Calif., Berkeley, 1933, PhD, 1838. Assoc. in Italian UCLA, 1935-38, instr., 1938-41, asst. prof., 1941-47, assoc. prof., 1947-53, prof., 1953-84, chmn. dept., 1949-56, dir. summer sessions, 1956-68, acting dean Coll. Fine Arts, 1967-68, dean, 1968-84. Author: Proverbs and Proverbial Phrases in Basile's Pentameron, 1941, Merbury's Proverbi Vulgari, 1946; (with others) Spoken Italian for Travellers and Students, 1946, Decca's Italian Course, 1947; The Italian Wellerism to the End of the Seventeenth Centrury, 1953; (with others) Basic Italian, 1958; Panorama Italiano, 1960, Michelangelo Letters, 1960, Wit and Wisdom of the Italian Renaissance, 1964; (with others) Leggendo e ripassando, 1968, The Aphorisms of Orazio Rinaldi, Robert Greene, Lucas Gracian Dantisco, 1968; (with others) L'Italia Oggi, 1976; asst. editor Modern Language Forum, 1943-47, editor 1947-49; chmn. bd. editors U. Calif. Press Modern Philology Series, 1949-54; editorial cons. Ency. Britannica's World Lang. Dictionary, 1954. Decorated Star of Italian Solidarity, Cavaliere Ufficiale della Repubblica Italiana, Commendatore dell'Ordine al Merito della Repubblica Italiana; chevalier dans l'Ordre des Palmes Académiques. Mem. Modern Lang. Assn., Philol. Assn. Pacific Coast, Assn. Am. Tchrs. Italian (pres. 1949), Folklore Soc. Calif., U. Calif. Club, Phi Beta Kappa. Home: Los Angeles Calif. Died Aug. 28, 1984.

SPEYER, A. JAMES, curator; b. Pitts. B.S., Carnegie-Mellon U.; postgrad., Chelsea Polytechnique, London, Sorbonne, U. Paris; M.A., Ill. Inst. Tech.; studied under, Mies van der Rohe. Architect Chgo., 1946-47; prof. advanced architecture Ill. Inst. Tech., Chgo., 1946-61; curator contemporary art Art Inst. Chgo., from 1961; vis. prof. architecture Nat. U. Athens, Greece, 1957-60; instr. modern art Ford Found. seminar Art Inst. Chgo.; Chgo. corr. Art News Mag., 1955-57. Home: Chicago Ill. Died Nov. 9, 1986.

SPIEGEL, ERNEST ADOLF, neurologist; b. Vienna, Austria, July 24, 1895; came to U.S., 1930; naturalized, 1936; s. Dr. Ignaz and Elise (Fuchs) S.; m. Anna Simona (Mona) Adolf, Aug. 1, 1925. Student, Gymnasium, Vienna, 1905-13; MD, U. Vienna Med. Sch., 1918; Dr. honoris causa, U. Zurich, Switzerland, 1965. Asst. Neurol. Inst. and Policlinic, U. Vienna, 1919-30, docent, 1924-30; prof. exptl. neurology and head dept. Temple U. Sch. Medicine, Phila., 1930-66, prof. emeritus, 1966-85. Former editor Confinia Neurologica, Progress in Neurology and Psychiatry; author numerous sci. articles and books on nervous system and nervous diseases. Recipient Otto Foerster medal, 1965. Fellow Coll. Physicians Phila., AMA; mem. Am. Electroencephalograghy Soc. (Hon.), Am. Neurol. Assn., Am. Therapeutic Soc., Phila. Neurol Soc., Assn. Rsch. Nervous and Mental Diseases, Internat. Soc. Functional and Stereotactic Neurosurgery (hon. pres), German Neurosurgical Soc. (hon.); corr. mem. Vienna Med. Soc., Vienna Psychiat.-Neurol. Soc. Home: Philadelphia Pa. Died Jan. 26, 1985.

SPIEGEL, SAM, film producer; b. Jaroslaw, Poland, Nov. 11, 1903; m. 3d, Betty Benson; children: Alisa Freeman, Adam. Ed., U. Vienna. Producer Universal Pictures, Berlin, 1933-37; ind. producer Europe, 1933-37; story translator Hollywood, Calif., 1927; producer Hollywood, 1939-85; founder (with John Huston) Horizon Pictures Inc., Calif., 1948, pres, 1948. Producer: (with Boris Morris) Tales of Manhattan, 1942, The Stranger, 1945, The African Queen, 1953, On the Waterfront, 1954 (Acad. award), The Bridge on the River Kwai, 1957 (Acad. award), The Strange One, 1957, Suddenly Last Summer, 1960, Lawrence of Arabia, 1962 (Acad. award), The Chase, 1966, Mr. Innocence, The Night of the Generals, 1966, The Swimmer, 1968, Nicholas and Alexandra, 1971, The Last Tycoon, 1976; co-producer: We Were Strangers, 1949. Home: Hollywood Calif. Died Dec. 31, 1985.

SPIETH, HERMAN THEODORE, educator; b. Charlestown, Ind., Aug. 21, 1905; s. Henry Herman and Lydia (Schulte-Wieking) S.; m. Evelyn E. Wilkinson, Aug. 30, 1931; 1 son, Philip. AB, Ind. Cen. Coll., 1926, LLD, 1958; PhD, Ind. U., 1931. Instr. zoology Ind. U., 1931-32; successively instr., asst. prof., assoc. prof. biology CCNY, 1932-53; prof. zoology U. Calif., Riverside, 1953-64, chmn. div. life scis., 1953-56, 2d provost, 1956-58, 1st chancellor, 1958-64; prof. zoology, chmn. dept. U. Calif., Davis, 1964-74, prof. emeritus, 1974-88; guest investigator U. Tex., 1949-50, 64-65; vis. colleague U. Hawaii, summers 1963, 64, 65, 66, 68, 69, 74; lectr. zoology Columbia U., 1938-52; head marine and fresh water zoology Cold Spring Harbor Biol. Lab. , L.I., summers 1931-38; rsch. assoc. Am. Mus. Natural History, 1943-62. Author articles on ephemeropteran taxonomy, evolution and behavior in Drosophila. Served from lt. to capt. USAAF, 1943-45. Fellow AAAS, Animal Behavior Soc., Entomol. Soc. Am., Calif. Acad. Sci.; mem. Am. Inst. Biol. Scis., Soc. Systematic Zoology, Am. Soc. Naturalists, Soc. for Study Evolution, N.Y. Entomol. Soc., Am. Soc. Zoologists, Am. Soc. Limnology and Ocenography, Sierra Club, Sigma Xi, Delta Chi. Home: Davis Calif. Died Oct. 20, 1988.

SPINK, WESLEY W., physician, educator; b. Duluth, Dec. 17, 1904; s. George Charles W. and Caroline (Kuntz) S.; m. Elizabeth Hamilton Hurd, Aug. 29, 1935; children: Helen Gayden (Mrs. Robert DuPont, Jr.), George Wesley (dec.), William Wesley. A.B., Carleton Coll., 1926, D. Sc. (hon.), 1950; M.D., Harvard U., 1932; research scholar, Harvard Med. Sch., 1932-33. Diplomate: Am. Bd. Internal Medicine. Intern IV Med. Service (Harvard), 1933-34; resident physician Thorndike Memorial Lab. (both Boston City Hosp.), 1934-37; asst. in medicine Harvard Med. Sch., 1934-37; asst. prof. medicine U. Minn. Med. Sch., 1937-41, asso. prof., 1941-47, prof., 1947-67, Regents' prof. medicine, 1967-73, prof. comparative medicine, 1970-73; emeritus Regents' prof. medicine and comparative medicine 1973-88; Cons. brucellosis to WHO; dir. Brucellosis Research Center of the U.S., 1951-73, WHO, FAO, UN. Author: Sulfanilamide and Related Compounds in General Practice, 1941, rev. edit., 1942, Nature of Brucellosis, 1956, Infectious Diseases: Prevention and Treatment in the 19th and 20th Centuries, 1978; contbr. med. publs. Recipient Chapin medal City of Providence, 1964; Distinguished Scholar award Nat. Library of Medicine, 1973. Charter mem. Am. Bd. Microbiology.; Master A.C.P. (bd. regents 1960-66, pres. 1963-64); fellow AAAS; hon. fellow Royal Australasian Coll. Physicians; mem. AVMA (hon.), N.Y. Acad. Scis. (hon.), Am. Soc. Clin. Investigation (pres. 1949), Am. Clin. and Climatological Assn., Assn. Am. Physicians (emeritus), Am. Assn. Immunologists, Soc. U.S. Air Force Internists and Allied Specialists (hon.), Central Soc. Clin. Research (pres. 1950), Soc. Exptl. Biology and Medicine, Minn. Acad. Medicine, Harvard Med. Alumni Assn. (pres. 1967-68), Minn. Med. Assn., Mpls. Soc. Internal Medicine (hon.), Infectious Disease Soc. Am. (emeritus, Bristol award 1983), Minn. Pathol. Soc. (pres. 1944), Mpls. Acad. Medicine, Phi Beta Kappa, Alpha Omega Alpha. Home: Minneapolis Minn. Died May 14, 1988.

SPIVAK, JOHN LOUIS, journalist, author; b. New Haven, June 3, 1897; s. Louis and Ida Sara Fanny (Sukloff) S.; m. Mable Mae Fry, July 2, 1917; a dau., Jacqueline Spivak Klein. Ed., pub. schs. Reporter New Haven Union, 1914-17, N.Y. Sun, 1917-19, N.Y. Call, 1919-21; corr. INS, Berlin, Moscow, 1922-23. Author: The Devil's Brigade, 1930, Georgia Nigger, 1932, Plotting America's Pogroms, 1934, America Faces the Barricades, 1935, Europe under the Terror, 1936, Secret Armies, 1939, Honorable Spy, 1939, Shrine of the Silver Dollar, 1940, A Pattern for American Fascism, 1947, A Man in His Time, 1967. Mem. Authors League Am. Home: Riegelsville PA 18077 Died Oct. 2, 1981.

SPRAGUE, ATHERTON H(ALL), educator; b. Amherst, Mass., Dec. 19, 1897; s. David and Anna Hubbell (Gardiner) S.; m. Mary Ann Whittemore, June 20, 1925; 1 dau., Rosemary. BA, Amherst Coll., 1920; MA, Princeton U., 1923, PhD, 1941. Instr. math. Amherst Coll., 1920-22, 23-26, assoc. prof., 1926-40, prof., 1940-86, dean of freshmen, 1928-33; vis. prof. or lectr. Mt. Holyoke Coll., Smith Coll., others. Author: Plane and Spherical Trigonometry, 1942, Trigonometry and Analytic Geometry, 1932, Calculus, 1952. Mem. Am. Math. Soc., Sigma Xi, Delta Upsilon. Home: Amherst Mass. Died Jan. 17, 1986.

SPRUILL, CORYDON PERRY, economist, professor, university dean; b. Raleigh, N.C., Feb. 5, 1899; s. Corydon Perry and Sadie Richard (Short) S.; m. Julia Grimes Cherry, Sept. 14, 1922. AB, U. N.C., 1920; BLitt, Oxford U., Eng., 1922; postgrad., Harvard U.,

1928-30. Asst. prof. econs. U. N.C., Chapel Hill, 1922-26, assoc. prof., 1926-32, prof., 1932-61, alumnus dist. prof. econs., 1961-68, prof. emeritus, 1968-88, dean of faculty, 1955-57, chmn. faculty, 1964-66; instr., tutor Harvard U., 1929-30; economist OPA, Washington, 1944-45; dir. study, editor report N.C. Com. for Study Pub. Sch. Fin., 1958. Sec. Chapel Hill Hist. Soc., 1969-72; trustee Preservation Soc. Chapel Hill, 1972-75. With USAAF, 1918; from maj. to lt. col. QMC, AUS, 1942-44. Mem. Royal Econ. Soc., Phi Beta Kappa, Pi Kappa Phi. Democrat. Baptist. Home: Chapel Hill N.C. Died Apr. 19, 1988.

STAERKEL, WILLIAM MAX, college president; b. Newton, Kans., Apr. 14, 1921; s. Otto and Grace Hazel (Williams) S.; m. Mary Lou Plumb, Apr. 15, 1943; children—Scott William, Richard Plumb. B.A., Bethel Coll., 1942; M.Ed., U. Kans., 1948; Ed.D., Stanford U., 1953. Prin. El Dorado (Kans.) High Sch., 1950-54; supt. schs. Beatrice (Nebr.) public schs., 1954-57; Arcadia (Calif.) Unified Sch. Dist., 1957-60; dir. ednl. services Booz, Allen & Hamilton, Chgo., 1960-67; founding pres. Parkland Coll., 1967-87. Served to lt. USN, 1942-46. Decorated Bronze Star. Mem. Am. Assn. Community and Jr. Colls. (chmn. council public community coll. presidents 1969-70), Phi Delta Kappa. Presbyterian. Club: Rotary. Home: Champaign Ill. Died Dec. 10, 1987; buried Champaign, Ill.

STAHL, BEN, artist, author; b. Chgo., Sept. 7, 1910; s. Ben F. and Grace (Meyer) S.; m. Ella M. Lehocky, Dec. 19, 1940; children—Ben F., Gail, Regina, David. Student pub. schs. Mem. founding faculty Famous Artists Schs., Westport, Conn., 1949—; founder, v.p. Sarasota Mus. of Cross (created all paintings and drawings exhibited) (all paintings stolen 1968)). Illustrator, Sat. Evening Post, other nat. mags., 1933—, exhibitor, NAD, Chgo. Art Inst., Carnegie Internat., Pitts., others, one-man shows, Soc. Ill., N.Y.C., 1945, Stevens Gross Galleries, Chgo., 1950, Scarab Club, Detroit, 1951, Sarasota Art Assn., 1950, Chgo., 1969, Bridgeport U., 1969, Ft. Lauderdale, Fla., 1970, Top-flight Gallery, 1971, Parker Playhouse Gallery, 1971, Red Piano Gallery, Hilton Head, S.C., 1975, Columbia (S.C.) Mus. Art, 1976, Fenn Galleries Ltd., 1978, Gallerie Macler, 1981; painter, exhibitor 14 stas. of cross for, Cath. Bible and Cath. Press, Chgo., 1955; illustrator 2 vols.: Gone With the Wind, 1960, Madame Bovary, Little Women; condr.: TV series Journey into Art with Ben Stahl for, S.C. Ednl. TV network, 1976; (Recipient 62 nat. awards for painting and illustration including, Saltus gold medal NAD 1949); author, illustrator: Blackbeard's Ghost, 1965 (Sequoia Book award for best children's book 1966, Walt Disney film 1968); author: The Secret of Red Skull, 1971; inventor spray glazing medium for painters. Mem. Fla. Art Commn., 1965-87 . named to Soc. Illustrators Hall of Fame, 1979. Home: Guanajuato Mexico.

STAHL, CHARLES ROBERT, publisher; b. Lwow, Poland, Oct. 23, 1921; s. Artur Roman and Regina S.; m. Janina A. Zipper-Zakrzewska. Mar. 8, 1940; children: Sandra, Jeanie. Student, U. Lwow, 1939-41, U. Budapest, Hungary, 1941-44. Pres. Econ. News Agy. Inc., Princeton, N.J., 1948-85; cons. in precious metals and monetary matters. Editor: Green's Commodity Market Comments, 1964-85. Mem. Nat. Assn. Bus. Economists, Am. Statis. Assn., Nat. Assn. Futures Trading Advisers, Nassau Tennis Club (Princeton), Golf d'Onex Club (Geneva). Republican. Roman Catholic. Home: Princeton N.J. Died Nov. 11, 1985; buried Princeton, N.J.

STALEY, OREN LEE, farmer's organization executive; b. Rea, Mo., May 6, 1923; s. Elmer Lee and Avis (Thompson) S.; m. Ruth Margaret Turner, Aug. 11, 1946; children: Janice Lee Staley Utley, Gregg Thompson, Cathy Lynn. Student, N.W. Mo. State Coll., 1940-41, 46-47. Farmer Rea, Mo., 1934-88; regional v.p. Nat. Farmers Orgn., Corning, Iowa, 1955, 1st nat. pres., 1955-79. Bd. govs. Agrl. Hall of Fame. Served with USN, 1944-45. Mem. Masons. Baptist. Home: Rea Mo. Died Sept. 19, 1988.

STALLONES, REUEL ARTHUR, university dean; b. North Little Rock, Ark., Oct. 10, 1923; s. Wilner Leroy and Jet (Wilson) S.; m. E. Joyce Graves, Aug. 14, 1945 (div. 1977); children—Jorel, Loran, Jared. Student, Visalia Jr. Coll., 1941-42, Ripon Coll., 1943-44, U. Mich., 1944-45; M.D., Case-Western U., 1949; M.P.H., U. Calif. at Berkeley, 1952. Intern Letterman Hosp., San Francisco, 1949-50; asst. chief dept. epidemiology Walter Reed Army Inst. Research, Washington, 1954-56; lectr., prof. U. Calif. at Berkeley, 1956-68; prof., dean Sch. Pub. Health, U. Tex. at Houston, from 1968. Served with AUS, 1943-46, 49-56. Fellow Am. Pub. Health Assn., Am. Coll. Preventive Medicine; mem. Am. Epidemiology, Assn. Tchrs. Preventive Medicine, Hamann Soc., Delta Omega, Sigma Xi. Home: Houston Tex. Died June 22, 1986.

STANFORD, ANN, educator, author; b. LaHabra, Calif.; d. Bruce and Rose (Corrigan) S.; m. Ronald Arthur White, Sept. 18, 1942; children: Rosanna, Patricia, Susan, Arthur Bruce. B.A., Stanford, 1938; M.A. in Journalism, U. Calif., Los Angeles, 1958, M.A. in English, 1961, Ph.D., 1962. Asst. prof. English Calif. State U., Northridge, 1962-66; assoc. prof. Calif. State U., 1966-68, prof., 1968—; co-founder Calif. State U. Northridge Renaissance Edits., 1969-72. Author: poetry In Narrow Bound, 1943, The White Bird, 1949, Magellan: A Poem to Be Read by Several Voices, 1958, The Weathercock, 1966, The Descent, 1970, The Bhagavad Gita: A New Verse Translation, 1970, Anne Bradstreet: The Worldly Puritan, An Introduction to Her Poetry, 1975, In Mediterranean Air, 1977; The Countess of Forli: A Poem for Voices, 1985; editor: poetry The Women Poets in English—An Anthology, 1973; editor: (with Pattie Cowell) Critical Essays on Anne Bradstreet, 1983; editorial bd.: Early Am. Lit, 1971-73. Recipient Lit. award Nat. Inst.-Am. Acad. Arts and Letters, 1972; Silver medal Commonwealth Club Calif., 1959, 78, 86; Outstanding Prof. award Calif. State U. and Coll. System, 1974; James D. Phelan fellow, 1938-39; Nat. Endowment for Arts grantee in writing, 1974-75. Mem. Poetry Soc. Am. (Shelley Meml. award 1969, DiCastagnola award 1976, v.p. West Coast 1970-78, v.p. Southwest 1978-87), P.E.N. Internat., Asso. Writing Programs (dir. 1981-84, pres. 1983-84), Phi Beta Kappa. Home: Beverly Hills Calif. Died July 12, 1987.

STANFORD, ERNEST ELWOOD, botanist, author; b. Rowe, Mass., Apr. 17, 1888; s. George Elwin and Minnie Emily (Peck) S.; m. Alice Lyndon Carroll, Dec. 20, 1911; children: Donald Elwin, Mary Lyndon, David Elwood. BS, U. Mass., 1915, ScD, 1950; MS, N.C. State Coll., 1917; PhD, Harvard U., 1924. Asst. in plant pathology N.C. Expt. Sta., 1915-17; asst. plant pathologist USDA, 1917-19; bot. expert U.S. Tariff Commn., Washington, 1918-19, 20, 28; prof. pharmacognosy Western Res. U., 1919-26; prof. botany Coll. of the Pacific, 1926-58; chmn. div. sci. and math. Pikeville Coll., Ky., from 1959; part-time faculty Stockton Coll., 1935-53. Author: Economic Plants, 1934, General and Economic Botany, 1937, man and the Living World, 1940; adv. editor: Economic Botany, 1946; short stories; contbr. articles on botany to profl. jours. Fellow AAAS; mem. Bot. Soc. Am., Calif. Bot. Soc., Phi Kappa Phi, Pi Gamma Mu. Republican. Congregationalist. Home: Pikeville Ky. †

STANFORD, WILLIAM RANEY, physician; b. Teer, N.C., Nov. 28, 1892; s. Charles Whitson and Emma Graves (Baynes) s.; m. Lois Brooke Foote, July 11, 1923; children: Raney Baynes, Stephen Dunlap. AB, U. N.C., 1915; MD, U. Pa., 1919. Diplomate Am. Bd. Internal Medicine. Intern St. Vincent's Maternity and Children's Hosp., 1919; regular intern U. Pa. Hosp., 1919-21, resident, 1922; pvt. practice Durham, N.C., from 1922; mem. vis. staff, former med. cons. Lincoln Hosp., from 1922; chief med. staff Watts Hosp., 1937-49, cons. staff; mem. vis. staff Duke Hosp., from 1930; mem. N.C. Med. Care Commn., from 1949; former med. cons. athletic dept. U. N.C., assoc. clin. prof. medicine emeritus; bd. dirs. N.C. State Hosp. for Insane, 1931-43. Contbr. articles to profl. jours. Med. examiner local draft bd., 1941-45; former examiner medicine part III Nat. Bd.; pres. Ednl. Found. Inc. U. N.C., 1943-47, Durham chpt. N.C. Wildlife Fedn., 1945-46. Surgeon USPHS, 1943. Fellow ACP, AMA; mem. Durham-Orange County Med. Soc. (pres. 1930), 6th Dist. Med. Soc. (past pres.), N.C. State Med. Soc., So. Med. Assn., Am. Heart Assn., N.C. Mental Hygiene Soc. (past pres.). Democrat. Presbyterian. †

STANLEY, LOWELL, business executive; b. Long Beach, Calif., Aug. 10, 1934; s. George Tatum and Clara (Graves) S.; m. Helene Archer, Nov. 21, 1934. AB, UCLA, 1928. With Jergins Oil Co., 1933-52, pres., 1950-51, chmn. bd., 1951-52; chmn. exec. com. Monterey Oil Co., 1952-55; dir. Petrolane Inc., from 1943, chmn. bd., 1961-71, chmn. exec. com., 1971-83; bd. dirs. Beckman Instruments Inc., Beckman Instruments Ltd., Eng., Beneficial Standard Corp., Gt. Western Standard Corp., Gt. Western Savs. and Loan Assn.; panelist fed. tax policy for econ. growth and stability, joint econ. com. U.S. Congress, 1955. Mem. Ind. Petroleum Assn. Am. (bd. dirs.), Am. Inst. CPAs, Calif. Club (Los Angeles), Los Angeles Country Club. Home: Beverly Hills Calif. Died May 25, 1984, buried Forest Lawn, Glendale, Calif.

STANLEY, MARVIN MILES, business educator, management consultant, air force officer; b. Lexington, Miss., Mar. 1, 1922; s. Marvin and Leila Virginia (Miles) S.; m. Rebecca Anne Matchett, May 21, 1943 (dec. Jan., 1983); children: Richard Matchett, Virginia Miles, Lynne Anne.; m. Shirley Grace Davis, Dec. 18, 1983; stepchildren: Charles Coble, Jennifer Susan Farmer. Student, Miss. State U., 1939-42; A.B., George Washington U., 1956; M.B.A. with distinction (Baker scholar), Harvard U., 1959; Ph.D., Am. U., 1972; grad., Air Tactical Sch., 1948, Air Command Staff Coll., 1950, Indsl. Coll. Armed Forces, 1963. Commd. 2d lt. USAF, 1943, advanced through grades to col., 1964; command pilo; chief plans and programs div., chief public info. div. Office Sec. of Air Force, 1964-67; dir. info. Tactical Air Command, 1967-68; ret. 1968; asst. prof. Coll. William and Mary, Williamsburg, Va., 1968-71, assoc. prof., 1971-74; prof. Coll. William and Mary, 1974-77, Chessie prof. bus. adminstrn., 1977-88; assoc. dean Sch. Bus. Adminstrn., 1971-74; cons. Coca-Cola Co., Chessie System, 1974-80, CSX, Inc.; v.p. Mid-Atlantic Research, Inc.; dir. 1st Va. Bank Commonwealth; chmn. bd. Queens Lake, Inc., 1971-73; mem. Va. Indsl. Devel. Commn., 1985-88, Gov.'s Bd. Adv. Economists, 1978-82; mem. commn. to study acquisition of Washington Nat. and Dulles Airports by State of Va., 1971-73. Author: Total Modal, The Story of CSX Corporation, 1986. Decorated Legion of Merit with oak leaf cluster, Air medal with oak leaf cluster, Air Force Commendation medal (3); recipient Silver Anvil award Am. Public Relations Assn., 1960; established Shirley Grace Davis-Marvin M. Stanley MBA Scholarship Coll. William and Mary, 1988. Mem. Acad. Mgmt., Eastern Acad. Mgmt. (dir. 1971-74), Air Force Assn., Ret. Officers Assn., Newcomen Soc. N.Am., Rotary, Beta Gamma Sigma. Republican. Episcopalian. Clubs: Army-Navy Country, So. Srs. Golf Assn, Golden Horseshoe Golf Assn. Home: Williamsburg Va. Died Oct. 6, 1988; buried Arlington (Va.) Nat. Cemetery.

STANTON, FRED L., banker; b. Anaconda, Mont., July 17, 1886; s. Edgar Henry and Cora Edith (Conley) S.; m. Violet Elmira Baker, June 5, 1918 (dec.). Student, Stanford U., 1910. Chmn. bd., dir. Washington Trust Bank, Spokane, Wash. 2d lt. F.A., U.S. Army, World War I. Home: Spokane Wash. †

STANTON, SEABURY, textile manufacturing executive; b. New Bedford, Mass., Oct. 9, 1892; s. James Easton Jr. and Mary Thomas (Cook) S.; m. Jean Kellogg Austin, Dec. 21, 1916, children: Jean (dec. 1960), James Easton 3rd, John Kellogg. AB, Harvard U., 1915; postgrad., New Bedford Textile Sch., evenings 1915-17. With Hathaway Mfg. Co., New Bedford, 1915-17 and from 1919, asst. treas., 1922-32, treas., from 1932, also bd. dirs., pres., 1939-55, chmn. exec. com., from 1955; vice chmn. bd. Berkshire Hathaway, Inc., New Bedford, from 155, pres., from 1957; trustee, mem. bd. investment New Bedford Inst. for Savs., Mchts. Nat. Bank New Bedford; mem. exec. com. Associated Industries of Mass.; bd. dirs. New Bedford Hotel Corp. Bd. dirs. New Bedford Bd. Commerce, Taxpayers Assn., Old Dartmouth Hist. Soc. and Whaling Mus.; hon. trustee St. Luke's Hosp., New Bedford. 2d lt. inf. U.S. Army, 1917-19, ETO. Mem. No. Textile Assn. (bd. dirs.) Harvard Club, Algonquin Club (Boston), Wamsutta Yacht Club (New Bedford), Key Largo (Fla.) Anglers Club. Republican. Unitarian. Home: New Bedford Mass. †

STAPLES, HAROLD ELMER, lawyer; b. Brattleboro, Vt., June 9, 1892; s. Charles and Florence (Elmer) S.; m. Margaret Dorothy Smith, May 6, 1918; children: Richard F., Margaret E. Staples Morrow, Charles G., Jeanne Elizabeth Staples Busch. AB, Harvard U., 1914, LLB, 1917. Bar: Mass. 1917, R.I. 1918. Practice in Providence from 1918; ptnr. Tillinghast, Collins & Tanner, from 1926; 1st asst. atty gen., R.I., 1925-27. Trustee Marlboro (Vt.) Coll., from 1948; pres. Family Welfare Soc. Providence, 1933-36, Providence Animal Rescue League, from 1951, Internat. Inst. Providence, 1950-61; bd. dirs. Am. Coun. for Nationalities Svc.; nat. coun. U.S. Com. Refugees. With USNRF, 1918-19. Fellow Am. Coll. Trial Lawyers; mem. Am. Inter-Am. Bar Assn., R.I. Bar Assn., Am. Law Inst., Am. Judicature Soc., Soc. Colonial Wars, Appalachian Mountain Club, Green Mountain Club (Vt.), Hope Club, Art Club, Agawam Hunt Club, Rotary, Masons, Phi Beta Kappa. Home: Providence R.I. †

STARK, LELAND WILLIAM FREDERICK, bishop; b. Evanston, Ill., Sept. 5, 1907; s. Rev. Gustaf Knute and Jennie (Peterson) S.; m. Phyllis Wilma Anderson, Sept. 10, 1935; children: Craig Latimer, Leighton Bradley. Student, U. Minn., 1927; BA, Gustavus Adolphus Coll., St. Peter, Minn., 1932; postgrad., Chgo. theol. Sem., 1932-34; ThB, Seabury-Western Theol. Sem., Evanston, Ill., 1935, DD, 1953; LHD, Seton Hall U., South Orange, N.J., 1966. Ordained priest, deacon P.E. Ch., 1935. Vicar Episcopalian chs., New Ulm, Sleepy Eye, St. James, Windom, Minn., 1935-38; rector Ascension Ch., Stillwater, Minn., 1938-40; dean Calvary Cathedral, Sioux Falls, S.D., 1940-48; rector Ch. of Epiphany, Washington, 1948-53; bishop coadjutor Episcopal Diocese, Newark, 1953-58, bishop, 1958-73; pres. N.J. Coun. Chs., 1964-66. Pres. coun. Christ Hosp., N.J., 1953-59; trustee Newark Mus. Decorated Liberian Humane Order African Redemption. Mem. House of Bishops, Glen Ridge Country Club, Rock Spring Golf Club, Rotary. Home: Montclair N.J. Died May 8, 1986; buried Holy Innocents Churchyard, West Orange, N.J.

STARK, THOMAS FRANCIS, university president; b. Duluth, Minn., Mar. 18, 1935; s. Bernard Francis and Emma (Harris) S.; m. Judith Olsen, July 26, 1958; children: Bradley, Kathryn, Cynthia. BS, U. Minn., 1957; MS, So. Ill. U., 1959; PhD, Mich. State U., 1966; postdoctoral in ednl. mgmt., Harvard U., 1985. Supt. schs. City of Grand Rapids, Minn., 1966-69; assoc. prof. U. Minn., Mpls., 1969-74; supt. schs. Mankato (Minn.) Pub. Schs., 1974-80; v.p. fiscal affairs Mankato State U., 1980-83; pres. Winona (Minn.) State U., 1983-88; adv. bd. inst. ednl. mgmt. Harvard U., 1985—. Bd. dirs. Found. for Minn. Progress, 1969-74, United Way, Mankato and Winona. NDEA fellow, 1960; Bush fellow, 1985. Mem. Am. State Colls. and Univs. Assn., Winona C. of C. (bd. dirs.), Phi Delta Kappa. Lutheran. Lodge: Kiwanis (bd. dirs. Grand Rapids, Mankato and Winona chpts. 1962—). Died Aug. 21, 1988.

STARKEY, OTIS P(AUL), economic geographer; b. Buffalo, Apr. 14, 1906; s. Frederick Robinson and Laura Magdalene (Hirsch) S.; m. Eleanor De Vere Stoddard, Nov. 24, 1932 (dec. July 1958); m. 2d, Evelyn Saxton Locke, June 25, 1960. BS, Columbia U., 1927, AM, 1930, PhD, 1939. Instr. econs. Washington and Jefferson Coll., Washington, Pa., 1927-28, editorial work on texts, 1928-31; instr., later asst. prof. geography U. Pa., 1931-42; lectr. Columbia U., 1945-46, summer 1948; prof. geography Ind. U., 1946-86, chmn. dept., 1946-56. Author: The Economic Geography of Barbados, 1939, Introductory Economic Geography (with L.E. Klimm and N.F. Hall), 1937, 40, 56, Exploring Our Industrial World (with W.F. Christians), 1938; contbr. articles to profl. jours. Geographer Mil. Intelligence, G/2 War Dept., 1942-45; with Office of Fgn. Liquidation Commr., State Dept., 1945-46. Reipient Meritorious Civilian Service award War Dept., 1946. Mem. Assn. Am. Geographers, Am. Geog. Soc., AAAS, Nat. Coun. Geography Tchrs., Ind. Acad. Sci., Ind. State Tchrs. Assn., Beta Gamma Sigma, Pi Gamma Mu. Home: Bloomington Ind. Died Jan. 27, 1986.

STARLING, JAMES HOLT, biologist, educator; b. Troy, Ala., June 28, 1912; s. James Jefferson and Minnie (Radford) S.; m. Mary Nell Lewis, Nov. 14, 1936; 1 son, John Lewis. B.A., U. Ala., 1933, M.A., 1937; Ph.D., Duke, 1942; student summers, Brit. Mus. Natural History, 1953, Oak Ridge Inst. Nuclear Studies, 1961. Sci. tchr. Troy High Sch., 1934-39; grad. asst. zoology Duke U., 1939-42; mem. faculty Washington and Lee U., Lexington, Va., 1942-83; prof. biology Washington and Lee U., 1951-83, prof. emeritus, from 1983, faculty marshall, 1960-74, coordinator premed. studies, 1964-83, chmn. dept. biology, 1976-78; vis. prof., cons. NSF Insts., summers 1955-65. Contbr. research to profl. publs. Pres. Rockbridge Tb Assn., 1948-50; Bd. dirs. Va. Tb Assn., 1948-50. Served to capt. AUS, 1943-46. Mem. Va. Acad. Sci., AAAS, Southeastern Biologists Assn., Sigma Xi, Alpha Epsilon Delta, Sigma Alpha Epsilon. Presbyterian. (deacon, elder). Home: Lexington Va. Died Apr. 20, 1987, buried Stonewall Jackson Cemetery, Lexington, Va.

STARR, EUGENE GRANT, oil executive; b. Tucson, 1888. Pres. Universal Consol. Oil Co., also bd. dirs. Home: Los Angeles Calif. †

STARR, GEORGE W(ASHINGTON), economist; b. Greenville, Ohio, Dec. 11, 1892; s. George Washington and Ada (Cozier) S.; m. Cecile C. Stocker, May 26, 1920; children: Richard, Margery. BS, Ohio State U., 1921, MS, 1924. Asst. dir. Bur. Bus. Rsch., Ohio State U., 1925-26; dir. Bur. Bus. Rsch., Ind. U., 1927-54; prof. pub. utilities and transp. Ind. U., from 1954; economist Conf. Am. Small Bus. Orgns., Chgo., 1945-46. Author, co-author books in field; editor Ind. Bus. Rev., 1927-54; fin. writer Indpls. Star, 1930-42. Mem. Ind. Econ. Coun.; chmn. Aero. Commn. Ind., 1944-53; asst. commr. revenue, dir. Gross Income Tax Div., State of Ind., 1953-54; state price exec. Ind. OPA, 1942. Mem. Am. Mktg. Assn., Am. Transp. Soc., Am. Statis. Assn., Beta Gamma Sigma, Alpha Kappa Psi, Lambda Chi Alpha. Republican. Methodist. Home: Bloomington Ind. †

STARRING, MASON BRAYMAN, JR., investment banker; b. Chgo., Aug. 16, 1889; s. Mason Brayman and Helen Bath (Swing) S.; m. Gertrude Farquhar Lathrop, Oct. 28, 1916; children: Eleanor Lathrop Starring von Kenschitski, Mason B. III. AB, Yale U., 1911. Ptnr. A.C. Allyn & Co.; pres. Permain Oil & Gas Co. 1st lt. U.S. Army, World War I. Mem. Blind Brook Golf Club (Harrison, N.Y.), Recess Club, Yale Club, Downtown Athletic Club, Yale Golf Club (N.Y.C.), Mill Reef Club (Antigua, B.W.I.), Golf and Tennis Club (Bedford, N.Y.), Zeta Psi. Home: Stamford Conn. †

STARRS, JOHN RICHARD, lawyer; b. Detroit, Aug. 15, 1913; s. Thomas Charles and Nora Ellen (Command) S.; m. Geraldine Leigh Poe, Sept. 26, 1948 (dec. Jan. 1950); 1 child, Thomas; m. Mabel Angeline Gilchrist, May 26, 1951; children: Mary, Elizabeth, William, Kathleen, Michael, margaretta, John. AB, U. Detroit, 1934, JD, 1938. Bar: Mich. 1938, U.S. Surpeme Ct. 1943. Pvt. practice Detroit, 1938-84; sr. ptnr. Higgins, Starrs & Macdonell; faculty U. Detroit Law Sch., 1949-65; bd. dirs. Am. Elec. Heater Co. Contbr. articles to profl. jours. Mich. corr. Selden Soc.; active as trained adult in scouting movement, 1959-66; founder, past pres. Friends of U. Detroit Library; trustee Cath. Social Svcs. Wayne County. Lt. USNR, 1942-46. Mem. State Bar Mich. (chmn. hearing panel atty. discipline bd.), Detroit Bar Assn., Am. Arbitration Assn. (panel arbitrators), Alpha Sigma Nu. Roman Catholic. Home: Grosse Pointe Park Mich. Died Oct. 29, 1984.

STARS, WILLIAM KENNETH, museum director, educator; b. DePauw, Ind., Mar. 12, 1921; s. Robert Emmett and Edna Mary (Crider) S.; m. Martha Vickers, Oct. 2, 1945. BA, Duke U., 1948; MA, U. N.C., 1951; postgrad. in art edn., NYU, 1954-67. Tchr. art Durham (N.C.) High Sch., 1950-66; instr. studio art Duke U., Durham, 1953-67, asst. prof. art, 1967-75, assoc. prof., 1975-85; conservator Mus. Art, Durham, 1967-85, dir., 1973-85; cons. singer Co., Craftool Inc.; mem. Burroughs Wellcome art Adv. Bd., 1978-85; juror R.J. Reynolds N.C. Artist Competition, 1977. Author: catalogues Raimondo Puccinelli, 1974, The Italian Paintings from the Mary and Harry L. Dalton Collection, 1974, Selected Works from the Benenson Collection, 1976, America the Beautiful: A Bicentennial Exhibition of American Art from the Dalton Collection, 1976; producer films Crayon Techniques, 1954, Three Billy Goats Gruff, 1956, How To Use the Library, 1958; patentee in U.S. and fgn. countries. Mem. Durham Bicentennial Steering Com., 1974; bd. dirs. Allied Arts Inc., Durham, 1960-62, With USNR, 1942-45. Named Outstanding Prof. Duke U., 1966; Nat. Endowment for Arts grantee, 1975, 76; Fulbright-Hayes grantee, 1977. Mem. Coll. Art Assn., Internat. Inst. for Conservation, Southeastern Coll. Art conf., Nat. Art Edn. Assn., N.C. Art Edn. Assn., Am. Inst. for Conservation, Internat. Com. on Museums, Durham Art Guild (pres. 1954-55), Kappa Delta Pi. Methodist. Home: Durham N.C. Died Oct. 28, 1985; buried Durham, N.C.

STAUB, JOHN F., architect; b. Knoxville, Tenn., Sept. 12, 1892; s. Frederick and Anna Cornelia (Fanz) S.; m. Madeleine Louise Delabarre, Oct. 4, 1919; children: John Delabarre, Nancy Delabarre (Mrs. William A. Wareing Jr.), Caroline (Mrs. Charles Callery). BS, U. Tenn., 1913; BS in Architecture, MIT, 1915, MS, 1916. Archtl. designer assoc. with H.T. Lindeberg, architect, N.Y.C., 1916-23; pvt. practice 1923-71. Archtl. works include Tex. Meml. Mus., Austin, Rice U. Libr., Houston, Bayou Bend Mus., office bldgs., schs. and large country houses in many So. states. Mem. City Planning Commn. Houston, 1926-38; cons. architect Houston Housing Authority, 1939. Naval aviator World War I; comdg. officer USNR, 1942-44. Decorated Navy Cross. Fellow AIA (past pres. So. Tex. chpt., nat. dir. 1942); mem. Bayou Club, Sigma Alpha Epsilon, Phi Kappa Phi. Home: Houston Tex. †

STAVELY, EARL BAKER, electrical engineering educator; b. Littlestown, Pa., Mar. 5, 1892; s. Charles Henry and Alverta May (Baker) S.; m. Helen Amanda Markle, Oct. 17, 1918; children: Earl Baker, James Markle, Donald Charles. BSEE, Pa. State U., 1912, degree in EE, 1915. Asst. instr. elec. engring. Columbia U., 1912-13; design engr. Crocker-Wheeler Electric Co., Ampere, N.J., 1913-16; mem. faculty Pa. State U., 1916-59, prof., 1926-59, asst. dean Coll. Engring. and Architecture, 1948-57, assoc. dean, 1957-59, prof. emeritus, from 1959. Pres. State College (Pa.) Coun. Chs., 1946-48; bd. dirs. State College Welfare Fund, from 1936; sec. State College Concerts Assn., 1953-57; elder, treas. Evang. and Reformed Ch. Mem. AIEE, IRE, Triangle, Am. Soc. Engring. Edn (chmn. Allegheny sect. 1952-54, ednl. methods div. 1954-56, gen. coun. 1955-56), Masons, Phi Kappa Phi, Tau Beta Pi, Sigma Tau, Eta Kappa Nu, Sigma Phi Sigma. Home: State College Pa. †

STEBBINS, ERNEST LYMAN, university dean; b. Oelwein, Iowa, Dec. 25, 1901; s. Francis Willard and Harriet May (Slayton) S.; m. Helen Bardwell Ross, Sept.2, 1928; children: Bardwell Ross, Jonathan Lyman. BS, Dartmouth Coll., 1925; student, Dartmouth Med. Coll., 1925-27; MD, Rush Med. Coll., 1929; MPH, Johns Hopkins U., 1932. Epidemiologist Va. State Dept. of Health, 1931; health officer Henrico County, Va., 1932-34; epidemiologist N.Y. State Dept. Health, 1934-36, dist. state health officer, 1936-37, dir. Div. of Communicable Diseases, 1937-38, asst. commr. of health, 1938-40; prof. epidemiology Coll. Physicians and Surgeons, Columbia U., 1940-42; commr. of health N.Y.C., 1942-46; prof. of Pub. Health Adminstrn. and dean Sch. of Hygiene and Pub. Health Johns Hopkins U., 1946-65, dean Sch. Hygiene and Pub. Health, 1965-84; pres. Nat. Health Coun.; cons. to surgeons gen. U.S. Army, U.S. Navy, USPHS, Nat. Found.; pres. Adv. Bd. for Med. Spltys.; dir. Am. Cancer Soc.; chmn. Am. Bd. Preventive Medicine and Pub. Health; mem. Armed Forces Epidemiological Bd.; cons. N.Y., Md., Del. state depts. health; vice chmn. Md. Hosp. Planning Bd.; chmn. Balt. City Med. Adv. Com., mem. adv. com. W.K. Kellogg Found. Author pub. health texts; contbr. papers to profl. jours. Fellow AMA, Am. Pub. Health Assn. (pres. 1965-66), N.Y. Acad. Medicine; mem. Am. Epidemiological Soc., Alpha Omega Alpha, Delta Omega, Sigma Alpha Epsilon, Alpha Kappa Kappa. Mem. Ch. of Christ. Home: Baltimore Md. Died April 30, 1987.

STEDMAN, ALFRED DELOS, newspaper editor; b. Boone, Iowa, Sept. 21, 1891; s. Arthur Beach and Ada Prudence (Millard) S.; m. Hazel E. Dingle, Mar. 8, 1918; children: Richard, Carol Stedman Johansen, John. BA, Hamline U., 1919, LLD (hon.), 1940. Reporter St. Paul Dispatch and Pioneer Press, 1915-17, copy reader, 1919-21; assoc. editor Farmers Dispatch, St. Paul, 1922; news editor and city editor St. Paul Pioneer Press, 1922-24, editorial writer, 1924-29, Washington corr., 1929-33; apptd. dir. info. Agrl. Adjustment Adminstrn., 1933, apptd. asst. adminstrn., 1934; resumed position as Washington corr., St. Paul Pioneer and Dispatch, 1939; bd. editors U.S. News, Washington, 1941, asst. exec. editor 1944; assoc. editor St. Paul Pioneer Press and Dispatch, 1945-60, ret., 1960. Author articles and papers. 1st sgt. U.S. Army, World War I. Home: Saint Paul Minn. †

STEEN, WILLIAM BROOKS, foundation executive, physician; b. Joliet, Ill., July 14, 1904; s. Earl R. and Sarah Lavinia (Brooks) S.; m. Rose Thacker, Oct. 19, 1942; 1 son, William Brooks. Student, Joliet Jr. Coll., 1922-24; BS, U. Chgo., 1925, PhD, 1931, MD, 1931. Intern Cook County Hosp., Chgo., 1931-33, resident pathology, 1934; instr. anatomy U. Chgo., 1926-31, asst. medicine, 1934-37; assoc. physician Desert Sanitarium, Tucson, 1937-38; resident physician Pima County Gen. Hosp., 1938-39; physician Tucson Clinic, 1939-84; med. dir. Oshrin Hosp., 1952-66, Elks State Assn. Hosp., 1951-67; pres. Nat. Asthmatic Found., 1966-84; chief staff St. Mary's Hosp., 1955. Mem. Bd. Nat. Found. Asthmatic Children, 1954-84, med. dir., 1955-84, exec. com., 1954-84, pres., 1966-84; mem. Hosp. Adv. Survey and Constrn. Council, Ariz., 1957-65, Ariz. Bd. Health, 1965-70, sec. 1966-67, vice chmn. bd., 1968, pres., 1970-84; pres. Bd. Health City Tucson-Pima County, 1952-56; med. dir., mem. exec. com. Nat. Found. Asthmatic Children, 1954-84, v.p., 1965, pres. 1966-84; pres. Navajo Health Assn., 1955-56. Maj. AUS, 1942-46. Fellow ACP, Am. Coll. Chest Physicians (past pres. Ariz.), Am. Acad. Allergy (v.p. 1965-66), Am. Coll. Allergists (sec. bd. regents), AAAS; mem. AMA (del. from Ariz. 1966-84), Ariz. (pres. 1963-64), Pima County (past pres.) med. socs., Assn. Physicians and Surgeons, Ariz., Am. Trudeau socs., Ariz. Soc. Internists, Ariz. Soc. Allergy, Ariz. Acad. Sci., SAR (pres. Tucson chpt. 1965-67, pres. state soc. 1967-84), Am. Thoracic Soc., Am. Soc. Internal Medicine, Tucson Literary Club (sec. 1967-84), Old Pueblo Club, Rotary, Mountain Oyster Club, Sigma Xi, Beta Theta Pi, Nu Sigma Nu. Presbyterian. Home: Tucson Ariz. Deceased.

STEERE, DAVID D., insurance executive. m. Cherrie Perkins; children: Catherine, Shirley, Kenneth, Anne. Grad., Yale U., 1937; M.B.A.,, Harvard Grad. Sch. Bus., 1939. Chmn. bd., pres. Allied Fin. Co.; chmn. bd. Steere Tank Lines; former sec., chmn. Republic Ins. Co.; chmn. exec., finance coms. Mem. Nat. Consumer Finance Assn. (past dir., past pres. Am. Finance Conf.). Clubs: Terpsichorian (Dallas), Brook Hollow (Dallas), Idlewild (Dallas); Bath and Tennis (Palm Beach, Fla.), Everglades (Palm Beach, Fla.); Koon Kreek (Athens, Tex.); N.Y. Yacht (N.Y.C.); Stone Horse Yacht (Harwichport, Mass.); Eastward Ho Country (Chatham, Mass.); St. Petersburg (Fla.) Yacht; Yale Sailing Assos. (New Haven) (trustee). Home: Dallas Tex. Died Mar. 21, 1987; buried Sparkman Hillcrest Cemetery, Dallas.

STEERE, WILLIAM CAMPBELL, botanist, educator; b. Muskegon, Mich., Nov. 4, 1907; s. James A. and Lois (Campbell) S.; m. Dorothy Clara Osborne, June 14, 1927; children: Lois Steere Beattie, Alice Steere Coulombe, William Campbell. BS, U. Mich., 1929, AM, 1931, PhD, 1932, DSc (hon.), 1962; postgrad., U. Pa., 1929-31; DSc (hon.), Montreal, 1959, U. Alaska, 1982. Instr. botany Temple U., Phila., 1929-31; instr. U. Mich., 1931-36, prof., 1946-50, chmn. dept., 1947-50, curator bryophytes, 1945-50; prof. biology (botany) Stanford (Calif.) U., 1950-58, dean grad. div., 1950-58; dir. N.Y. Bot. Garden, 1958-70, pres., 1970-72, pres. emeritus, sr. scientist, 1973-89; prof. botany Columbia U., 1958-76, prof. emeritus, 1976-89; Botanist U. Mich.-Carnegie Instn. expdn. to Yucatan, 1932; U.S. Cinchona Mission to Colombia and Ecuador, 1942-44; leader U. Mich. expdn. to Great Bear Lake, N.W. Ty., 1948; exchange prof. U. P.R., 1939-40; botanist U.S. Geol. Survey, Alaska, 1949, Arctic Rsch. Lab., Point Barrow, Alaska, summers 1951-53, 60, 61, 63, 72, 74, Greenland, 1962; program dir. systematic biology NSF, 1954-55; pres. bryol. sect. 8th, 9th Internat. Bot. Congresses, Paris, 1954, Montreal, 1959. Editor: Fifty Years of Botany, 1958, Am. Jour. Botany, 1953-57; asso. editor: Annales Bryologici, 1936-39; editor-in-chief: The Bryologist, 1938-54; co-editor: This is Life, 1962, Evolutionary Biology, 1966; Author: Liverworts of Southern Michigan, 1940, Lab. Outline for Elementary Botany, (with others), 1937, Biological Abstracts-Biosis. The First 50 Years, 1976, The Mosses of Arctic Alaska, 1978, numerous tech. articles on cytology and systematics of petunia, musci and hepaticae of Mich., musci of tropical Am., Arctic Am., spl. problems of bryogeog., fossil bryophytes from Pleistocene and earlier times. Decorated Order of Sacred Treasure Japan; recipient Liberty Hyde Bailey medal Am. Hort. Soc., 1965, Mary Soper Pope medal Cranbrook Inst. Scis., 1970, Meritorious award Coun. Biology Editors, 1981, Hedevig medal, 1987, ASC award for sci.; Benjamin Franklin fellow Royal Soc. Arts London. Fellow AAAS (v.p. 1949, 66, 67), Calif. Acad. Scis., Am. Geog. Soc.; mem. Am. Fern Soc., Am. Soc. Plant Taxonomists (pres. 1959), Assn. Tropical Biology, Internat. Assn. Bryologists (pres. 1969-75), New Eng. Bot. Club, So. Appalachian Bot. Club, Torrey Bot. Club (pres. 1961), Bot. Soc. Am. (pres. 1959), Inst. Ecuatoriano de Ciencias Naturales (hon.), Finnish Bot. Soc. (corr.), Calif. Bot. Soc., Zool. Soc. Vanamo (corr.), Mich. Acad. Sci., Arts and Letters (editor 1936-40), Rsch. Club U. Mich., Sci. Rsch. Club U. Mich. (pres. 1941-42), Soc. Venezolana de Ciencias Naturales (corr.), Brit. Bryological Soc., Japanese Bryological Soc., Am. Bryological Soc. (pres. 1936-37), Assn. Sudamericana de Fitotaxonomists, Am. Soc. Naturalists (pres. 1957-58), Soc. for Study Evolution, Arctic Inst. N.Am., Am. Assn. Mus. (pres. 1968-70), N.Y. State Assn. Mus. (pres. 1961-62), Sigma Xi. Clubs: Cosmos (Washington); Century Assn. (N.Y.C.), University (N.Y.C.). Home: Bronx N.Y. Died Feb. 7, 1989.

STEIMLE, EDMUND AUGUSTUS, clergyman, educator; b. Allentown, Pa., Sept. 19, 1907; s. Augustus and Emily (Bruning) S.; m. Rosalind Weinert Ball, Apr. 24, 1936 (dec.); children: Sondra (Mrs. David R. Offord), Rosalind Ball (Mrs. David J. Horn), Edmund Augustus; m. Eleanor Floyd Wadleigh, Jan. 23, 1971. Grad., Philips Acad., Andover, Mass., 1926; AB, Princeton U., 1930; BD, Lutheran Theol. Sem., Phila., 1935; AM, U. Pa., 1934; DD, Wagner Coll., 1950, Pacific Luth. U., 1977; LittD, Muhlenberg Coll., 1957; LLD, Roanoke Coll., 1960, Gettysburg Coll., 1962; LHD, Hamilton Coll., 1974. Ordained to ministry Luth. Ch., 1933. Teaching fellow Luth. Theol. Sem., Phila., 1933-35, Hagan prof. practical theology, 1952-61; pastor Jersey City, 1935-40, Cambridge, Mass., 1940-52; Brown prof. homiletics Union Theol. Sem., N.Y.C., 1961-75, emeritus, 1975-88; vis. prof. preaching Louisville Prebyn. Theol. Sem., 1976; adj. prof. preaching Wesley Theol. Sem., Washington, 1976-82; Zimmerman lectr. Gettysburg Theol. Sem., 1960; Gray lectr. Duke Div. Sch., 1966; preacher on radio, 1955-74. Author: Are You Looking for God?, 1957, Disturbed by Joy, 1967, From Death to Birth, 1973, God the Stranger, 1978, (with others) Preaching the Story, 1980; editor: Renewal in the Pulpit, 1966; cons. editor: Preacher's Paperback Library. Home: Annapolis Md. Died Feb. 16, 1988; buried Laurel Hill Cemetery, Phila.

STEIN, AARON MARC, novelist; b. N.Y.C., Nov. 15, 1906; s. Max and Fannie (Blumberg) S. AB summa cum laude, Princeton U., 1927. Reporter, editor, critic, columnist N.Y. Evening Post, 1927-38; contbg. editor Time, 1938; reports editor, media div. Bur. Intelligenece, Office War Info., 1942-43. Author: Spirals, 1930, The Sun is a Witness, 1940, The Case of the Absent-Minded Professor, 1943, ...and High Water, 1946, The Cradle and the Grave, 1948, Pistols for Two, 1951, Mask for Murder, 1970, Lock and Key, 1973, Lend Me Your Ears, 1976, Chill Factor, 1978, One Dip Dead, 1979, The Cheating Butcher, 1980, others; novels pub. under pseudonym George Bagby include Murder at the Piano, 1935, Murder on the Nose, 1938, The Twin Killing, 1947, Scared to Death, 1952, Dead Drunk, 1953, Cop Killer, 1956, Dirty Pool, 1966, Two in the Bush, 1976, Innocent Bystander, 1977, Country and Fatal, 1980; novels pub. under pseudonym Hampton Stone include The Corpse That Refused to Stay Dead, 1952, The Man Who Was Three Jumps Ahead, 1959, The Babe with the Twistable Arm, 1962, The Funniest Killer in Town, 1967, The Swinger Who Swung by the Neck, 1970, The Kid Who Came Home with a Corpse, 1972; short stories, articles, critical essays. With U.S. Army, 1943-45. Mem. Mystery Writers Am. (pres. 1974, Grand Master Edgar award, 1979), Princeton Club (N.Y.), Nassau Club, Phi Beta Kappa. Died Aug. 29, 1985.

STEIN, JESS, publisher, editor; b. N.Y.C., June 23, 1914; s. Elias and Regina (Goldenberg) S.; m. Dorothy Gerner, Mar. 7, 1943; children: Regina (Mrs. Bruce H. Wilson), Eric. A.B., Wayne State U., 1933; M.A., U. Chgo., 1934, postgrad., 1934-36. Editor Scott Foresman & Co., Chgo., 1934-42; with Office of Censorship, Washington, 1942-45, Random House, Inc., N.Y.C., 1945-80; head coll. and reference depts. Random House, Inc., 1950-59, v.p., 1959-80, editor-in-chief emeritus, 1980-84, dir., 1967-74; v.p. Alfred A. Knopf, Inc., N.Y.C., 1967-74; pres. Jess Stein Assocs., 1974-84; pres. Bookmark Pub. Assocs., Ltd., 1980-84; cons. Internat. Reading Assn., 1976-81, U. Mass. Press, 1975-79; mem. adv. com. Scarsdale Adult Sch., 1980-83, trustee, 1983-84; dir. L.W. Singer Co., N.Y.C., Random House Can. Ltd., Toronto, RH Sch. and Library Services, Inc. Author: (with R.N. Linscott) Why You Do What You Do, 1956; mng. editor: Am. Coll. Dictionary, 1947-80; editor, translator (pseudonym Isai Kamen): Tolstoy's The Kreutzer Sonata, 1957, Great Russian Stories, 1959; editor: Am. Everyday Dictionary, 1949-80, Am. Vest Pocket Dictionary, 1951-80, Basic Everyday Ency, 1954-80, Vest Pocket Rhyming Dictionary, 1951-80, Modern Am. Dictionary, 1957-80, Irving's Life of George Washington, 1975, Random House Coll. Dictionary, rev, 1975-80; editor-in-chief: Random House Dictionary of the English Language, 1966-80; editorial dir.: Random House Ency, 1977-80, RH dictionaries, 1966-80; editor: Random House Speller/Divider, 1981-84, (with Stuart B. Flexner) Random House Thesaurus, 1984; cons.: (edited by Jones, Hoerr and Osol) New Gould Med. Dictionary, 1949, (edited by Avis) Dictionary of Canadianisms, 1967. Mem. White Plains (N.Y.) City Democratic Com., 1954-58, Westchester County (N.Y.) Dem. Com., 1956-58; mem. govt. adv. com. on internat. book programs U.S. Dept. State, 1964-67; adviser proposed Hall of Fame, Jerusalem, 1976-84. Recipient Wayne State U. Alumni award, 1969; recipient Corp. Leadership award, 1982. Mem. Am. Textbook Publs. Inst. (dir. 1961-64, treas. 1964), Linguistic Soc. Am., Nat. Council Tchrs. English, Coll. Pub. Group (chmn. 1960-61), MLA, Dictionary Soc. Am., Coll. English Assn., Dialect Soc., NAACP, ACLU, Urban League. Club: Dutch Treat (N.Y.C.). Home: White Plains N.Y. Died June 23, 1984.

STEINBREDER, HARRY JOHN, JR., publishing executive; b. St. Louis, Aug. 21, 1930; s. Harry John and Susan (Fritch) S.; m. Cynthia Means, Feb. 26, 1955; children: Harry John III, Susan Gay, Gillett, Sarah Cole. BA in History, Washington U., St. Louis, 1952. With Life SMR, Time, Inc., St. Louis, 1954; advt. salesman Fortune mag., 1955-59; advt. salesman Sports Illustrated, N.Y.C., 1959-66, mgr., 1966-67, advt. dir., 1967-72, assoc. pub., 1972-73; pub. Money mag., 1973-76; dir. spl. projects Time mag., 1976-85. Bd. dirs. Audubon Soc., Conn., 1965-68, Franklin Coll., Lugano, Switzerland; mem. adv. com. U.S. Ski Team. 1st lt. arty. AUS, 1952-54. Mem. Fairfield County Hunt Club, Fairfield Country Club, Mashomack Fish and Game Preserve Club, Seminole-Fla. Club, Ekwanok Club, Ducks Unltd. Home: Fairfield Conn. Died Nov. 15, 1985.

STEINCROHN, PETER JOSEPH, physician, author; b. Hartford, Conn., Nov. 28, 1899; s. Myer and Pearl (Brownstein) S.; m. Patti Chapin, Feb. 8, 1936; 1 dau., Barbara Jane. Student, N.Y. U., 1917-19; M.D., U. Md., 1923. Intern Muhlenberg Hosp., Plainfield, N.J., 1923-25; postgrad. Mass. Gen., Beth Israel hosps., Boston, Mt. Sinai Hosp., N.Y.C.; practice medicine specializing in internal medicine and cardiology Hartford, 1925-86; attending physician Mt. Sinai Hosp., Hartford, 1930-54; chief staff Mt. Sinai Hosp., 1940-41; now cons.; attending physician McCook Meml. Hosp., 1930-54; now cons.; ex-cons. internal medicine, cardiologist Hartford Inst. Living; columinst Bell Newspaper Syndicate, N.Y.C., 1954-68; columnist McNaught Newspaper Syndicate, 1968-86; former radio broadcaster health programs WKAT and WINZ, Miami; moderator weekly program WTHS-TV; med. editor WTVJ-TV, Miami, Fla., 1965-67; Med. co-chmn. Hartford Rehab. Soc., 1950-55; adviser Hartford Vis. Nurse Assn., Cerebral Palsy Assn. Author: More Years for the Asking, 1940, How to Keep Fit Without Exercise, 1942, Heart Disease is Curable, 1943, How to Stop Killing Yourself, 1950, How to Master Your Fears, 1952, Doctor Looks at Life, 1953, Live Longer and Enjoy It, 1956, You Can Increase Your Heart Power, 1958, Mr. Executive-Keep Well-Live Longer, 1960, Your Life to Enjoy, 1963, Common Sense Coronary Care and Prevention, 1963, You Live as You Breathe, 1967, How to Get a Good Night's Sleep, 1968, How to be Lazy, Healthy and Fit, 1969, Your Heart is Stronger than You Think, 1970, How to Master Your Nerves, 1970, Don't Die Before Your Time, 1971, Antidotes For Anxiety, 1971, Low Blood Sugar, 1972, Questions and Answers About Nerves, Tension and Fatigue, 1973, Ask Dr. Steincrohn, 1979, How To Cure Your Joggermania!, 1979; Contbr. articles to nat. mags. and prof. jours. Mem. exec. council Friends of U. Miami Library. Served as pvt. U.S. Army, World War I. Fellow A.C.P.; mem. AMA, Conn. Med. Soc. (1st v.p. 1940), Hartford County Med. Soc. (dir.), Hartford Med. Soc., Hartford Heart Assn. (v.p. 1950), Greater Miami Heart Assn. (co-chmn edn. com., dir.), Hartford Cancer Soc. (dir.), Hartford Tb Soc. (dir.), Tau Epsilon Phi. Club: Mason. Home: Coral Gables Fla. Died Feb. 17, 1986.

STEINER, STAN, author, conservationist. Lectr. U. N.Mex., U. Calif., Colo. Coll., Sorbonne, U. Budapest, U. Wyo., U. Nebr., Inst. Am. West, U. Tex.-El Paso; guest prof. U. Paris, France, 1974-75; faculty Nat. Collegiate Honors Council Seminars, U. N.Mex., 1982. Author: George Washington: the Indian Influence, 1970, New Indians, 1968, Raza: the Mexican Americans, 1970, The Tiguas: the Lost Tribe of City Indians, 1972, (with Luis Valdez) Aztlan: an Anthology of Mexican American Literature, 1972, (with Shirley Witt) The Way: an Anthology of American Indian Literature, 1972, The Islands: The Worlds of the Puerto Ricans, 1974, (with Maria Teresa Babin) Borinquen: An Anthology of Puerto Rican Literature, 1974, The Vanishing Whiteman, 1976; The Spirit Woman, 1979, Fusang: The Chinese Who Built America, 1979, In Search of the Jaguar, 1979, The Ranchers: A Book of Generations, 1980, The Westerners, 1987, Lost Dreams: The New Indian Movements, 1987; editor: Dark and Dashing Horsemen, 1981; gen. editor series: Western History From a Western Viewpoint, 1981-87 ; mem. editorial bd.: The American West, 1981-87 ; TV documentary Meanwhile Back at the Ranch; also articles in N.Y. Times, Los Angeles Times, Forbes, N.Mex. Mag.; panelist Western Film Festival, 1986. Recipient Golden Spur award Western Writers Am., 1973, 77, Anisfield award Saturday Rev., 1971. Home: Santa Fe N.Mex. Died Jan. 12, 1987.

STEINHAUER, RALPH, former lieutenant governor; b. Morley, Alta., Can., 1905; m. 1928; 4 daus., 1 son. Councilor, chief Saddle LAke Indian Band, Alta., Can.; lt. gov. Province of Alta., 1974-79, ret., 1979. Mem. Indian Assn. Alta. (co-founder). Died 1987.

STEINHOFF, DAN, management educator; b. Spokane, Wash., Dec. 16, 1911; s. Dan and Bertha (Van Os) S.; m. Jill Hegner, June 1, 1962. BBA, U. Wash., 1934, teaching diploma, 1939; postgrad., Northwestern U. Coll. Law, 1935-36; MS, U. Mich., 1941; D.SocialSci. in Econs., U. Havana, Cuba, 1952. Credit exec. Bank of Calif., Portland, Oreg., 1934-37; teaching fellow econs. U. Wash., 1937-39; instr. econs. U. Mich., 1939-41; asst. prof. bus. adminstrn. Antioch Coll., 1941-42; pub. utilities cons. 1946-52; from asst. prof. to prof. mgmt. U. Miami, 1946-50, dean evening div., prof. mgmt., 1950-62, dean div. continuing edn., 1962-63, prof. mgmt., 1963-81, chmn. mgmt. dept., 1969-73; prof. mgmt., bd. govs. Concordia Coll., Portland, Oreg., 1981-85; dir. Indsl. Rsch. Inc. Author: Small Business Management Fundamentals, 1974, 78, 82, Small Business: Cases and Essays, 1975, Developing Managers in Organizations, 1976, 80, World of Business, 1979. With AUS, 1942-45. Mem. Assn. Univ. Evening Colls., Assn. Urban Univs., Southeastern Adult Edn. Assn., Small Bus. Inst. Dirs. Assn., Internat. Coun. Small Bus., Newcomen Soc., Srtus, Chi Phi, Delta Sigma Pi, Beta Gamma Sigma, Phi Delta Kappa. Methodist. Home: Vancouver Wash. Died Nov. 1985.

STENBECK, HUGO EDVARD, business executive, lawyer; b. Uppsala, Sweden, Oct. 15, 1890; s. Nils and Maria (Rydberg) S.; m. Martha Odelfelt, Oct. 1, 1932; children: Nils Hugo Andreas, Elisabeth Silfverstolpe, Margaretha af Ugglas, Jan Hugo. LLB, U. Uppsala, 1914. Sr. ptnr. Advokatfirman Lagerlöf, Stockholm, from 1923; chmn. bd. dirs. Korsnäs-Marma AB, Sandvik AB, Investment AB Kinnevik, Halmstads Järnverks AB, AB Partner, Rydboholms AB. Decorated knight Royal Order of No. Star, knight comdr. Royal Order of Casa. Mem. Swedish Bar Assn. Home: Stockholm Sweden †

STENSIÖ, ERIK ANDERSON, paleontologist, educator; b. Döderhult, Sweden, Oct. 2, 1891; s. Johan Anderson and Tili (Erlandsson) S. Doctorate, U. Uppsala, 1921. Prof. paleontology Swedish Mus. Natural History, Stockholm, from 1923. Mem. Acad. Sci. Stockholm; fgn. mem. Royal Soc. London, Acad. Sci. Phila., Geol. Soc. Am., Paleontol. Soc. Am.; hon. mem. Vertebrate Paleontol. Soc. Am., Am. Acad. Scis., N.Y. Acad. Scis., Oslo Acad. Scis., Copenhagen Acad. Scis., Netherlands Acad. Scis., Munich Acad. Scis., Vienna Acad. Scis., Halle Acad. Sics., Geol. Soc. London, Geol. Soc. France, Geol. Soc. Poland, Royal Soc. Edinburgh, Zool. Soc. London, Linnean Soc. London. Home: Stockholm Sweden †

STEPAN, ALFRED CHARLES, JR., chemical manufacturing executive; b. N.Y.C., Apr. 17, 1909; s. Alfred Charles and Charlotte (Corbett) S.; m. Mary Louise Quinn, Feb, 10, 1934; children: Marilee (Mrs. Richard Wehman), Alfred Charles, F. Quinn, Stratford, Charlotte (Mrs. Joseph Flanagan), Paul, John. BA, U. Notre Dame, 1931, LLD (hon.), 1963; student, Northwestern U., 1931-33, Ill. Inst. Tech., 1933-34. Founder Stepan Chem. Co., Northfield, Ill., 1932, chmn., chief exec. officer, 1973-84; bd. dirs. 1st Nat. Bank Winnetka, Chgo. Helicopter Airways Inc., Thor Power Tool Co. Bd. dirs. Ravinia Festival Assn., Lyric Opera of Chgo., pres. 1959-61; pres. Lyric Opera Ctr. for Am. Artists, Chgo., 1974-83, chmn. bd. dirs. 1983-84; mem. vis. com. humanities U. Chgo.; trustee U. Notre Dame, 1957-79, Orchestral Assn. Recipient Carol Fox award for Disting. Service to Opera, Lyric Opera, 1984; Stepan Ctr. and Stepan Chemistry Hallnamed in his honor, Notre Dame U. Mem. Arts Club, Comml. Club, Chgo. Club, Bob O'Link Golf Club (Highland Park, Ill.), Glen View Club, Everglades Club, Seminole Golf, Bath and Tennis Club (Palm Beach Fla.). Republican. Home: Winnetka Ill. Died Dec. 1, 1984.

STEPHENS, JOHN CALHOUN, JR., educator, dean; b. Augusta, Ga., July 23, 1916; s. John Calhoun and Lillian (Cason) S.; m. Enid Leslie Bryan, June 7, 1947; 1 child, Anne Howard. AB, Emory U., 1937, MA, 1938; PhD, Harvard, 1950. Ordained to ministry Protestant Episcopal Ch. as perpetual deacon, 1957. Tchr. Dalton (Ga.) High Sch., 1938-39; instr. English Clemson Coll., 1939-41; mem. faculty Emory U., Atlanta, 1946-73, prof. English, 1960-73, chmn. dept., 1959-61, dean. Coll., 1961-73; prof. English U. Ga., Athens, 1973-83, prof. emeritus, 1983-85; dean Franklin Coll. Arts and Scis., Athens, 1973-77, dean emeritus, 1983-85; mem. policy Coun. Undergrad. Assessment Program Ednl. Testing Service, 1976-80. Author articels, essays, poems, revs.; editor: Longsword, 1957, Georgia, A Poem, 1736, 1950, Poems of Zechariah Worrell, 1764-1834, 1958, The Guardian, 1982. Maj. USAAF, 1941-46; lt. col. USAF Res. ret. Guggenheim fellow, 1957-58. Mem. So. Atlantic MLA, Ga., Richmond County hist. socs., English-Speaking Union, MLA, Am. Soc. Eighteenth Century Studies, Southeast Soc. 18th Century Studies, Internat. Berkeley Soc., DeKalb County Hist. Soc., Harvard Club (Atlanta), Phi Beta Kappa, Sigma Alpha Epsilon, Omicron Delta Kappa. Home: Atlanta Ga. Died May 23, 1985; buried Cathedral of St. Philip, Atlanta.

STEPHENS, THOMAS EDWIN, lawyer, presidential aide; b. Ireland, Oct. 18, 1903; s. William Henry and Eleanor Annie (Saunders) S.; m. Mary Culver, Dec. 9, 1942. LLD, St. Lawrence U., 1932; grad., Bklyn. Law Sch. Real estate title examiner Title Guarantee & Trust Co., N.Y.C., Chgo. Title and Trust Co., 1925-26; fraud investigator Royal Indemnity Co., N.Y.C., 1927-32; asst. corp. counselor City of N.Y., 1934-36; assoc. firm Lord, Day & Lord, 1936-37; adminstrv. asst. to pres. Coun. of City of N.Y., 1938-42; dir. campaign div. Rep. Nat. Com., Washington, 1945-46; asst. to Rep. nat. campaign mgr. 1948; adminstrv. asst. to Sen. John Foster Dulles, 1949; sec. N.Y. State Rep. Com., 1950-52; appointment sec. Gen. Dwight D. Eisenhower, 1952-53; sec. Pres. Dwight D. Eisenhower, from 1953. Maj. Army Air Corps, World War II, ETO. Mem. Phi Delta Phi. Home: Clearwater Fla. Died May 15, 1988.

STEPHENS, WILL BETH DODSON, psychologist, educator; b. Van Horn, Tex., July 14, 1918; d. John

Lester and Almeda (Garner) Dodson; m. Jack Howard Stephens, Feb. 18, 1944; children: Jack Howard, Jill Johnstone. B.F.A., U. Tex., 1942, M.Ed., 1958, Ph.D., 1964. Asst. dir. USO, Del Rio, Tex., 1942-45, YWCA, Austin, Tex., 1946-47; spl. edn. tchr. Tyler, Tex., 1956-60; research assoc. U. Tex., 1962-64; research asst. prof. Inst. for Research on Exceptional Children, U. Ill., Urbana, 1965-66; assoc. prof. ednl. psychology Temple U., Phila., 1966-70, prof. spl. edn., 1970-75; head spl. edn. program U. Tex.-Dallas, 1975-80; dir. Dept. Def. Dependents Schs., Alexandria, Va., 1982-87; mem. Pres.'s Com. on Mental Retardation, 1971-78. Editorial bd.: Topics in Early Childhood Edn., Jour. Assn. of Severely Handicapped; contbr. articles to profl. jours. Dir., past pres. Found. Exceptional Children; mem. adv. bd. Tex. Easter Seal Soc.; mem. ednl. adv. bd. Am. Found. for Blind. Vocat. Rehab. Adminstrn. fellow U. Geneva, 1964-65. Fellow Am. Psychol. Assn., Pa. Psychol. Assn., Am. Assn. on Mental Deficiency (v.p. ednl. div. 1977-79); mem. Council for Exceptional Children (past pres. div. mental retardation, chmn. nat. research coms.), Nat. Assn. Retarded Children (nat. edn. com.), Jean Piaget Soc., Soc. for Research in Child Devel., Am. News Women's Club, Internat. Assn. Sci. Study Mental Deficiency, Am. Ednl. Research Assn., DAR. Episcopalian. Home: Alexandria Va. Died Mar. 7, 1987.

STEPHENS, WILLIAM RICHMOND, chemistry educator; b. Stroud, Ala., Mar. 27, 1892; s. Marion R. and Martha Jane (Muldrew) S.; m. Abbie Williams, Dec. 26, 1912. BS, Ala. Polytech. Inst., 1919, MS, 1922; student, U. Chgo., 1922, 23; PhD, U. Iowa, 1929. Pub. sch. tchr. Stroud, 1912-14, Loachapoka, Ala., 1914-16; prof. sci. Meridian Coll., Tex., 1919-22, dean, 1920-22; asst. prof. chemistry Baylor U., 1922-25, assoc. prof., 1925-29, prof. chemistry, from 1929, chmn. dept., 1949-65. Mem. Am. Chem. Soc., AAAS, Am. Assn. U. Profs., Tex. Acad. Sci., Sigma Xi, Phi Lambda Upsilon. Baptist. Home: Waco Tex. †

STEPHENSON, HERBERT ROY, insurance executive; b. Buffalo, Oct. 25, 1888; s. George Herbert and Rosanna (Baille) S.; m. Hazel Myrtle Evans, 1926. Ed. pub. schs., Markham, Ont., Can.; student, Jarvis Collegiate Inst., Toronto, Ont. With Mfrs. Life Ins. Co., Toronto, 1905-12; actuary, then sucessively asst. gen. mgr., gen. mgr., v.p., mng. dir. then pres. Crown Life Ins. Co., Toronto, 1912-59, chmn., from 1959. Fellow Soc. Actuaries; assoc. fellow Inst. Actuaries Gt. Britain. Home: Toronto Ont., Canada. †

STERLING, CHANDLER WINFIELD, bishop; b. Dixon, Ill., Jan. 28, 1911; s. Robert and Mary Eleanor (Chandler) S.; m. Catherine Ricker, June 17, 1935; children: Mary, Margaret, Kathy, Ann, Beth, Sarah, Jonathan, Julia. BA, Seabury-Western Sem., 1938, DD, 1957. Ordained to ministry Protestant Episcopal Ch. as deacon, 1938, as priest, 1938. Minister Wilmette, Ill., 1938-40, Oak Park, Ill., 1941-42, Milw., 1942-43, Freeport, Ill., 1943-44, Elmhurst, Ill., 1944-50, Chadron, Nebr., 1950-56; bishop Mont., 1956-68; asst. bishop Pa., 1968-76. Author: Little Malice in Blunderland, 1965, The Holroyd Papers, 1969, The Eighth Square, 1969, Arrogance of Piety, 1969, The Icehouse Gang, 1972, Beyond This Land of Whoa, 1973, The Doors to Perception, 1974, The Witnesses, 1975; contbr. articles to nat. mags. Mem. staff exptl. programs Western Nebr. Mission Fields; chmn. Youth Commn., Chgo., 1944-50; mem. bd. Nat. Parks Ministry. Recipient Silver Beaver award Boy Scouts Am., 1947. Home: Oconomowoc Wis. Died Mar. 3, 1984.

STERLING, GORDON DONALD, chemical company executive; b. White Plains, N.Y., Feb. 6, 1935; s. Daniel Henry and Margery Washburn (Cornell) S.; m. Nancy Louise Johnson, Apr. 4, 1959; children: Pamela Anne, Sandra Lynn, Jeffrey Glen. AB, Hamilton Coll., 1957. Loss prevention engr. Factory Mut. Co., Montclair, N.J., 1957-60, Fairfield & Ellis, Boston, 1960-63; with Am. Cynamid Co., 1963-85, pres. organic chems. div., 1979-81; pres. Formica Corp. subs. Am. Cynamid Co., 1981-85; chmn., chief exec. Formica Corp., 1985-88. Chmn. Placer County (Calif.) Econ. Devel. Coun., 1971-73. Mem. Synthetic Organic Chems. Assn. (bd. govs.). Died May 11, 1988.

STERLING, HENRY SOMERS, educator, geographer; b. N.Y.C., Mar. 4, 1905; s. Warner Strong and Alice May (Habberton) S.; m. Noël deWetter, Nov. 10, 1930; children: Keir Brooks, Christopher Hastings. Grad., St. Mark's Sch., Southboro, Mass., 1922; BA, Columbia, 1927, MA, 1934; PhD, U. Wis., 1939. Mem. fgn. dept. Nat. Automobile C. of C., 1928-32, Latin Am. rep., 1930-31; mem. faculty U. Wis., Madison, 1937-73, prof. geography, 1957-73, prof. emeritus, 1973-87, chmn. dept., 1962-63, 65-66; with rsch. and analysis br. OSS, 1941-45; dir. inter-disciplinary rsch. program in Venezuelan Andes, Consejo de Bienestar Rural, 1952-53. Co-author: Economic and Social Problems of the Venezuelan Andes, 2 vols. (in Spanish), 1955-56. Social Sci. Rsch. Coun. fellow 1946-47; recipient Medal of Freedom, 1946, Atwood medal Pan. Am. Inst. Geography and History, 1959. Mem. Assn. Am. Geographers, Am. Geog. Soc., Conf. Latin Americanist Geographers, Delta Psi. Home: Madison Wis. Died Sept. 3, 1987.

STERLING, ROSS N., federal judge; b. 1931. B.A., U. Tex., 1956, LL.B., 1957. With Vinson & Elkins, 1958-76; judge U.S. Dist. Ct. (so. dist.) Tex., 1976-88. Home: Houston Tex. Died Jan. 14, 1988.

STERN, OTTO, physicist; b. Sohau, Germany, Feb. 17, 1888. Ph.D., Breslau, 1912; LLD, U. Calif., 1930. Private-docent. Tech. Hochschule, Zürich, 1913-14, Frankfurt, 1914-21; prof. Rostock, 1921-22, Hamburg, 1923-33; rsch. prof. physics dept. Carnegie Inst. Tech., 1933, prof. emeritus. Recipient Nobel prize in physics, 1943. Mem. Danish Royal Akad. Home: Pittsburgh Pa. †

STERNBERG, ELI, mechanics and applied mathematics educator; b. Vienna, Nov. 13, 1917; s. Philip and Eva (Makowska) S.; m. Rae A. Shifrin, 1955; children: Eve Louise, Peter Joshua. BCE, N.C. State U., 1941, DSc (hon.), 1963; MS, Ill. Inst. Tech., 1942, PhD, 1945; DSc (hon.), Technion, Israel, 1984, U. N.C., 1984. Asst. prof. Ill. Inst. Tech., Chgo., 1945-47, assoc. prof., 1947-51, prof., 1951-56; vis. prof. Tech Hogesch., Delft, Netherlands, 1956-57; prof. Brown U., Providence, 1957-64; prof. applied mechanics Calif. Inst. Tech., Pasadena, 1964-70, prof. mechanics, 1970-88, emeritus, 1988; vis. prof. Keio U., Tokyo, 1963-64, U. Chile, Santiago, 1970-71, U. Calif., Berkeley, 1979. Proceedings editor 1st U.S. Nat. Congress Applied Mechanics, 1951; mem. editorial bd. Jour. Elasticity, 1971-88, Archive for Rational Mechanics and Analysis, from 1957; contbr. articles on continuum mechanics, elasticity theory to profl. jours. Guggenheim fellow, 1963, Fulbright fellow, 1970; recipient Timoshenko medal ASME, 1985. Fellow Am. Acad. Arts and Scis.; mem. Nat. Acad. Engring., Nat. Acad. Scis. Home: Altadena Calif.

STERNE, AUGUSTUS HERRINGTON, university dean, former banker; b. Montgomery, Ala., Feb. 28, 1913; s. Adolph Herrington and Sue Evans (Brown) S.; m. Helen Hill Hopkins, Apr. 29, 1938; children: Helen (Mrs. James S. Anderson), William A., Carroll P., Augusta H., Nancy Evans. A.B., U. Ga., 1934; student, Emory U. Law Sch., 1934-35. With Retail Credit Co., Atlanta, 1935-36; with Trust Co. of Ga., Atlanta, 1936-78; sr. v.p. Trust Co. of Ga., 1957-64, pres., dir., 1964-73, chmn., 1973-78, ret., 1978; chmn. adv. council; dean Grad. Sch. Bus. Adminstrn., Atlanta U., 1978-82; dir. Atlantic Steel Co. Served with USMCR, 1942-45. Mem. Sigma Alpha Epsilon, Phi Delta Phi. Episcopalian. Clubs: Peachtree Golf, Piedmont Driving, Commerce (dir.), Nine O'Clocks, Capital City, Augusta Nat. Golf. Home: Atlanta Ga. Died Oct. 13, 1986; interred Arlington Cemetery, Atlanta, Ga.

STERNE, MERVYN HAYDEN, investment banker; b. Anniston, Ala., Aug. 2, 1892; s. Anselm and Henrietta (Smith) S.; m. Dorah Heyman, Nov. 28, 1922; 1 child, Dorah Rosen. Student pub. schs.; LHD, Howard Coll., 1948; DLitt, Birmingham-So. Coll., 1967; LLD, U. Ala., 1969. Stenographer L.&N. R.R., Annisotn, 1907-09; asst. cashier Traders Nat. Bank of Birmingham, 1909-16; treas. Realty Trust Co., 1911-16; investment banker Sterne, Aggee & Leach, Birmingham and Montgomery, Ala., 1916-73; bd. dirs. Ala. By-Products Corp., Ensley Co., Avondale Mills, Classe Ribbon Co., Ramsay-McCormack Land Co., Hayes Internat. Corp. Author reports, surveys on state and city financial problems. Bd. dirs. Community Chest, Birmingham Libr., United Jewish Fund, Birmingham Mus. Art; trustee Birmingham-So. Coll. Capt. inf. U.S. Army, 1917-19; served to col. ASF, 1942-46. Decorated Legion of Merit. Mem. Investment Bankers Assn. Am., Nat. Assn. Security Dealers, Ala. Bankers Assn., Omicron Delta Kappa (hon.). Jewish. Home: Birmingham Ala. †

STERNFELD, HARRY, architect; b. Phila., Nov. 21, 1888; s. Isidor and Bertha (Daiber) S.; m. Flora Maxwell, July 17, 1912. AB, Central High Sch., Phila., 1907; BS in Architecture, U. Pa., 1911, MS in Architecture, 1914; diploma, Ecole des Beaux Arts, Paris, 1920. Practice architecture from 1911; asst. prof. architecture Carnegie Inst. Tech., Phila., 1914-18, head. dept., 1918-23; prof. design U. Pa., Phila., 1923-59, prof. emeritus, from 1959; lectr. Temple U., Phila., 1965-66; vis. fellow Am. Acad., Rome, 1920-21. Prin. works (sole projects or with others) include: Slovak Girls' Acad., Danville, Pa., Harrisburg (Pa.) Cath. High Sch., City Planning of Rome, N.Y., Pitts. Bldg. at Sesquicentennial Expn., Phila., War MEml., Audenarde, Belgium, Appomattox MEml. marking spot of Gen. Lee's surrender, U.S. Ct. House, Phila., Hdqrs. Bldg., Ft. Monmouth, N.J., U.S. P.O., Milton, Pa., A&P Bakery Bldg., Phila., Pa. State Driver Exam Stas., Morristown, Bortondale, Selinsgrove, State Coll.; architect in assn. for Eastern Pa. Psychiat. Assn., Germantown Jewish Ctr., John Wister Sch., White Rock Bapt. Ch., Woman's Christian Alliance Bldg., U.S. Courthouse Expansion, Phila. Served with inf., F.A., U.S. Army, 1918; with S.C., AUS, World War II. Fellow AIA; mem. Phila. Art Alliance, T-Square Club, Phila. Sketch Club, Scarab, Sigma Xi, Tau Sigma Delta. Recipient Paris prize scholarship, 1914; awarded dipl. and medal Montevideo, S.A. Home: Atlantic City N.J. †

STEUDEL, ARTHUR WILLIAM, manufacturing executive; b. Cleve., Aug. 28, 1892; s. Richard and Julia (Conrad) S.; m. Frieda M. Bohnert, June 30, 1915; children: Richard A., Gloria. Student pub. schs. With Sherwin-Williams Co., from 1908, with dye, chem. and color dept., 1915-17; mgr. sales ea. region Sherwin-Williams Co., Chgo., 1917-19, N.Y.C., 1919-23; asst. to pres., mgr. dye, chem. and color sales dept. Sherwin-Williams Co., Cleve., 1928-29, v.p., 1929-36, successively v.p., gen. mgr., pres., 1940-60, chmn., chief exec. officer, from 1960, also bd. dirs.; bd. dirs. Wilson & Co., Inc., Chgo., B.&O. R.R., Cleve. Trust Co., Republic Steel Corp. Mem. Masons, Westwood Country Club, Union Club, Pepper Pike Country Club, Tavern Club, Metropolitan Club, Brook Club, Clifton Club. Home: Lakewood Ohio. †

STEVENS, HALSEY, composer, educator, author; b. Scott, N.Y., Dec. 3, 1908; s. Horace B. and Mary Colenia (Churchill) S.; m. Harriett Elizabeth Merritt, Sept. 2, 1939; children: Christopher, Ann Stevens Naftel, Joanna StevensShields. Ed., Syracuse U., U. Calif.; pvt. study; LittD (hon.), Syracuse U., 1966. Asst. instr. Syracuse U., 1935-37; assoc. prof. Dakota Wesleyan U., 1937-41; prof., dir. coll. music Bradley U., 1941-46; prof. U. Redlands, 1946; asst. prof. U. So. Calif., Los Angeles, 1946-48, assoc. prof., 1948-51, chmn. composition dept., 1949-74, prof., 1951-76, mem. grad. sch. adminstrv. council, 1961-63, grad. sch. research lectr., 1956, composer in residence, 1972-76, Mellon prof., 1974-76, prof. emeritus, 1976; program annotator Los Angeles Philharmonic Orch., 1946-51; Phoenix Symphony, 1947-48, Coleman chamber concerts, 1967-82; vis. prof. Pomona Coll., 1954, U. Wash., summer 1958, Yale U., 1960-61, U. Cin., 1968, Williams Coll., 1969; resident scholar Rockefeller Found., Villa Serbelloni, Italy, 1971. Composer: Symphony No. 1, Sinfonia breve, Symphonic Dances, Triskelion, Cello Concerto, Clarinet Concerto, Double Concerto (violin and cello), Viola Concerto, Threnos, Ballad of William Sycamore, A Testament of Life; also other orchestral, chamber, piano, choral music; guest condr., San Francisco Symphony, Los Angeles Philharmonic orchs., (Recipient Sinfonia Nat. award 1943, 46, Chamber Music award Nat. Fedn. Music Clubs 1945, Publ. awards Middlebury Coll. Composers Conf. 1946, Soc. Pub. Am. Music 1948, Nat. Assn. Coll. Wind and Percussion Instrs. 1954, Friends of Harvey Gaul award 1960, award Nat. Inst. Arts and Letters 1961, Ramo Disting. Faculty award U. So. Calif. 1974, Abraham Lincoln award Am. Hungarian Found. 1978); Author: The Life and Music of Bela Bartok, 1953, rev., 1964; Co-editor: Festival Essays for Pauline Alderman, 1976; Contbr. articles to periodicals, also East Central Europe: A Guide to Basic Publications. Served with USNR, 1943-45. Recipient commns. from Louisville Philharmonic Soc., 1953, 57; recipient commns. from U. Redlands, 1953, commns. from U. So. Calif., 1955, commns. from Fromm Found., 1956, commns. from San Francisco Symphony, 1958, commns. from Almand Meml. Fund, 1958, commns. from Sigma Alpha Iota, 1962, commns. from Pi Kappa Lambda (No. Tex. State U.), 1962, commns. from Ga. So. Coll., 1967, commns. from New Haven Symphony, 1968, commns. from Friends and Students of Lee Gibson, 1969, commns. from Alchin Fund, 1972, commns. from Nat. Endowment for Arts, 1975, Music Tchrs. Nat. Assn., 1975, Draco Found., 1976, Disting. Emeriti award U. So. Calif., 1980, Centennial award U. So. Calif., 1984; Guggenheim fellow, 1964-65, 71-72. Mem. Nat. Assn. Am. Composers and Condrs. (v.p. So. Calif. chpt.), Nat. Assn. Composers U.S.A. (adv. bd.), Am. Musicological Soc. (v.p. So. Calif. chpt. 1968-70), Am. Liszt Soc. (dir. 1968-78, nat. adv. com. from 1978), Am. Composers Alliance (bd. govs. 1960-61, nat. adv. bd. 1976-79), Music Library Assn., Conf. Bd. Asso. Research Councils (adv. com.), Com. Internat. Exchange Persons (chmn. 1961-63), Phi Beta Kappa, Phi Mu Alpha, Phi Kappa Phi, Pi Kappa Lambda. Home: Englewood Calif. Died Jan. 20, 1989.

STEVENS, HARVEY ALONZO, educator; b. West Allis, Wis., Oct. 20, 1913; s. Daniel A. and Genevieve (Kingston) S.; m. Irene Borkowski, June 22, 1940; 1 dau., Patricia Ann. B.S., U. Wis.-Milw., 1939; post-grad., U. Wis.-Milw., Madison, 1946-48. Tchr. South Milwaukee (Wis.) High Sch., 1939-43; prin. No. Wis. Center for Developmentally Disabled, Chippewa Falls, Wis., 1944-46; supr. classes mentally retarded Wis. Dept. Pub. Instrn., Madison, 1946-48; supt. So. Wis. Center for Developmentally Disabled, Union Grove, Wis., 1948-55, Johnstone Tng. and Research Center, Bordentown, N.J., 1955-58, Central Wis. Center Developmentally Disabled, Madison, 1958-69; dir. Bur. for Developmentally Disabled, Wis. Dept. Health and Social Services, 1969-72; program adminstr. Waisman Center on Mental Retardation and Human Devel., U. Wis., Madison, 1972-79; program adminstr. emeritus Waisman Center on Mental Retardation and Human Devel., U. Wis., 1979-86; outreach coordinator rehab. research and tng. ctr. U. Wis., Madison, 1985-86; dir. mental retardation services Wis. Dept. Health and Social Services, 1963-66; Cons. Office Spl. Asst. of Pres. for Mental Retardation Internat. Activities, 1963-65; cons. USPHS, hosp. and med. facilities sect., mental retardation br., 1965-67; regional dir. Council Exceptional Children, Madison, 1950-52; rep. Wis. to bd. govs. Council on Exception Children, 1962; spl. adv. Pres.'s Panel on Mental Retardation, 1961-62; chmn. Joint Commn. Internat. Aspects Mental Retardation; past mem. profl. adv. com. mentally retarded and law. Nat. Law Center George Washington U.; mem. Fed. Hosp. Council, 1972-76, Wis. Council Developmental Disabilities, 1977-79; adv. com. U. Ala. Mgmt. Tng. Inst., 1973-79, U. Mo. Career Mgmt. Project, 1978-79. Author: (with Heber) Mental Retardation, a Review of Research, 1964, (with Bathazar) Emotionally Disturbed, Mentally Retarded, 1975, (with Sloan) A Century of Concern: A History of American Association on Mental Deficiency: 1876-1976; Contbr. (with Sloan) articles to profl. jours. Served with AUS, 1943-44. Recipient Joseph P. Kennedy Found. Internat. Leadership award, 1968; Distinguished Alumni award U. Wis.-Milw., 1968; Distinguished Service award Wis. Acad. Arts, Letters and Dance, 1969. Fellow Am. Assn. Mental Deficiency (Leadership award 1973, pres. 1964-65, mem. profl. adv. com. standards for state residential facilities for mentally retarded); mem. Internat. London Congress for Sci. Study Mental Deficiency (co-chmn. 1960), Am. Assn. Univ. Affiliated Programs for Developmentally Disabled (pres. 1974-75), Internat. Assn. for Sci. Study Mental Deficiency (pres. 1964-67), Mexican Assn. for Study Mental Deficiency (hon. pres.), Venezuelan Assn. for Study Mental Deficiency (hon.), Brazilian Assn. for Scientific Study Mental Deficiency (hon. pres.). Home: Evansville Wis. Died Oct. 26, 1927.

STEVENS, LEE, talent agency executive; b. Bklyn., Mar. 10, 1930; s. Joseph and Helen (Zlotnik) Silverman; m. Lizabeth Silverman, Apr. 11, 1954; children—Todd Lowell, Claudia Michelle, Jennifer Susan. BS, NYU, 1951, JD, 1957. Bar: N.Y. 1957. Sec. William Morris Agy., N.Y.C., 1953-57, with bus. affairs dept., 1957-62, exec. asst. to pres., 1962-80, exec. v.p., chief operating officer N.Y. office, 1980-84, pres., dir., chief exec. officer, 1984-88; vice chmn. adv. bd. Tisch Sch. of Arts, NYU, N.Y.C., 1983-88; mem. NYU Med. Ctr. Bd., 1987-88. Pres. Grace Harbor Assn., Kings Point, N.Y., 1967-69; chmn. Show Biz Bash East, Big Bros.-Big Sisters, N.Y.C., 1979; mem. exec. com. United Jewish Appeal/Fedn.-Entertainment Div., N.Y.C., 1982-88; mem. arts and entertainment adv. com. N.Y.C. Partnership, 1984; bd. dirs. USO of Met. N.Y., N.Y.C., 1985-88; v.p. Western States Friends of Hebrew Univ., 1987-88. Served to cpl. U.S. Army, 1951-53. Mem. Internat. Radio and TV Soc., Nat. Acad. TV Arts and Scis., Country Music Assn., Acad. Motion Picture Arts and Scis., Psi Chi Omega, Phi Lambda Delta. Clubs: City Athletic (N.Y.C.); Hillcrest Country (Los Angeles). Home: New York N.Y. Died Feb. 2, 1989.

STEVENS, MARK CHANCELLOR, banker; b. Detroit, Dec. 17, 1906; s. Mark Burnham and Emily M.C.E. (Gilmore) S.; m. Betsy Dawson, Apr. 29, 1933 (dec. Dec. 1964); children: Betsy Ann Stevens Sutton, Mark C., Thomas B.; m. Serena Ailes, Apr. 3, 1969. A.B. magna cum laude, Harvard U., 1927; B.A. magna cum laude, Trinity Coll., Cambridge U., Eng., 1928. With Comerica (formerly Detroit Bank & Trust Co.), 1928-72, successively trust officer, asst. v.p., v.p., 1928-67, officer in charge personal trust dept., 1957-72; sr. v.p. Comerica (Formerly Detroit Bank & Trust Co.), 1967-72; consul gen. Thailand, 1957-87; councilman, Grosse Pointe Farms, Mich., 1965-75. Treas. Alvin M. Bentley Found., 1964-76, v.p., 1978-79, pres., 1979-87 , trustee, 1964-87 ; mem. exec. com. Alvin M. Bentley Hist. Libr.; trustee Merrill Palmer Inst., 1967-75, Children's Home of Detroit, 1974-87 ; trustee Elmwood Cemetery, 1946-87 , sec.-treas., 1946-87 ; trustee Detroit Hist. Soc., 1961-87 , pres., 1969-71. Decorated Order Crown of Thailand (2). Mem. English Speaking Union (pres. Detroit chpt. 1956-63, now trustee, nat. dir., chmn. exec. com. 1976-87), Circumnavigators Club (pres. Detroit chpt. 1969-71, internat. pres. 1972), Detroit Com. on Fgn. Relations (chmn. 1966-68), C. of C. Clubs: Detroit, Grosse Pointe Country, Detroit Yacht, Economic, Recess, Consular Corps, Bayview Yacht, The Players; Farmington Country (Charlottesville, Va.); Trinity Boat (Cambridge, Eng.). Home: Grosse Pointe Farms Mich. Died Nov. 19, 1987; buried Elmwood Cemetery, Detroit.

STEVENS, OLIVER M., transportation executive; b. Culver, Ind., June 30, 1891; s. Aden B. and Amanda (Louden) S.; m. Eleanor Sawyer, Aug. 18, 1917; children: Canstance, Douglas. LLB, Lincoln Jefferson Law Sch., 1912. Various positions on R.R.'s 1905-15; supt. refrigerator service C.B.&Q. R.R., 1915-17; asst. to operating v.p. C., M., St. P.&P. R.R., 1919-23, div. supt., 1923-25, asst. to pres., 1925-26; trainmaster Mo. Pacific R.R., Atchison, Kans., June-Nov., 1926, Wichita, Kans., 1926-37; exec. rep. Mo. Pacific R.R., Denver; v.p., dir. Denver & Salt Lake Ry., 1937-42; pres., gen. mgr. Am. Refrigerator Transit Co., St. Louis, from 1942; former dir. D. & R.G. W., D.S.L. & W., D.S.L. & P. Stage Lines; chief U.S. Ry. Mission, Mexico City, 1942-44. Maj. arty. U.S. Army, 1917-19. Mem. Denver Club, Noonday Club (St. Louis), Mo. Athletic Club (St. Louis), Racquet Club (St. Louis), Union League (Chgo. Republican. Episcopalian. Home: Saint Louis Mo. †

STEVENS, STODDARD MORE, lawyer; b. Rome, N.Y., Oct. 19, 1891; s. Stoddard More and Katharine (May) S.; m. Marion Olney, Aug. 24, 1918; children: Adele Olney (Mrs. William Davis Vail), Katharine More (Mrs. Roger Coursen Ward), Marion Hoyt (Mrs. Edward M. Harris Jr.). AB, Cornell, 1914; LLB, Columbia, 1917; LLD, St. Lawrence U., 1967. Bar: N.Y. 1917. With Sullivan & Cromwell, N.Y.C., from 1917, mem. firm, from 1929. Mem. adminstrv. com. Ctr. Hellenic Studies (Wash.); trustee emeritus Abbot Acad., Andover, Mass.; trustee Andrew W. Mellon Found., N.J. Hist. Soc.; hon. trustee St. Barnabas Med. Ctr., N.J.; gen. trustee Nat. Gallery Art, Washington; pres., bd. dirs. Stevens Kingsley Found., N.Y.C. Mem. ABA, N.Y. Bar Assn., Bar Assn. City N.Y., Am. Law Inst., N.Y. Law Inst., Baltusrol Golf Club (Springfield, N.J.), Short Hills (N.J.) Club, India House Club, Univ. Club, Down Town Assn., Knickerbocker Club, Anglers Club, Metropolitan Club (Washington), Sankaty Head Golf Club (Nantucket, Mass.), Psi Upsilon. Home: Short Hills N.J. †

STEVENSON, JOHN ELLSWORTH, banker; b. Columbus, Ohio, Apr. 18, 1892; s. William Cage and Jane Mary (Dickson) S.; m. Rhea Vanston Dickson, Jan. 14, 1924; children: John Ellsworth, Mary Jane. Ed. pub. schs., Columbus. With Deshler Nat. Bank, Columbus, 1907; pres. Huntington Nat. Bank, Columbus, 1949-58, chief exec. officer, chmn. bd., 1958-63, hon. chmn., from 1964, also bd. dirs. Mem. Columbus C. of C., Masons, Shriners, Scioto Country Club. Episcopalian. Home: Columbus Ohio. †

STEVENSON, JOHN SINCLAIR, geologist, educator; b. New Westminster, C., Can., Sept. 21, 1908; s. Ben and Emelia (Johnston) S.; m. Louise Francis Stevens, Jan. 22, 1935; children: John Stevens, Robert Francis. B.A., U. B.C., 1929, B.Applied Sci., 1930; Ph.D., MIT, 1934. Instr., asst. in geology MIT, 1931-34; engr.-in-charge Longacre Longlac Gold Mines, Ont., 1934-35; asst. mining engr. B.C. Dept. Mines, Victoria, 1935-36; asso. mining engr. B.C. Dept. Mines, 1936-41, mining engr., 1941-50; asso. prof. mineralogy McGill U., Montreal, Que., 1950-61; prof. McGill U., 1961-87, chmn. dept. geol. scis., 1966-68, Sir William Dawson prof. geology, 1971-78; Canadian fellow Guggenheim Meml. Found., 1947-48; cons. geologist, 1950-87, cons. grad. edn., Ont., 1969. Fellow Royal Soc. Can., Geol. Soc. Am., Geol. Assn. Can., Mineral. Soc. Am.; mem. Mineral. Soc. London, Canadian Inst. Mining and Metallurgy, Soc. Econ. Geologists, Mineral. Assn. Can. (past pres.), Sigma Xi. Mem. United Ch. (elder). Clubs: McGill Faculty (Montreal); Hudson (Que.); Yacht Whitlock Golf (Hudson Heights). Home: Hudson Heights Que., Canada. Died Sept. 7, 1987; buried Cote St. Charles Churchyard, Hudson Heights, Que., Can.

STEVENSON, LANGDON RIDDLE, investment banker; b. Tarrytown, N.Y., May 11, 1935; s. Stuart Riddle and Irene (Davis) S.; m. Mary Harman Biggs, Apr. 22, 1972; children: Charlotte, John, Alexander; stepchildren—Elizabeth, Susannah, Jennifer Smith. B.A., Princeton U., 1957. V.p. Bankers Trust Co., N.Y.C., 1958-69; 1st v.p. Bache & Co., Inc., N.Y.C., 1969-75; 1st v.p., treas. Bache Halsey Stuart Shields Inc., N.Y.C., 1975-78; sr. v.p., treas. Bache Halsey Stuart Shields Inc., 1978-82; sr. v.p., treas. Prudential-Bache Securities, from 1982, also dir.; treas. Bache Group Inc., 1978-82; treas., dir. Prudential Bache Trade Corp., 1984-85, pres., chief exec. officer, 1985-87; trustee Command Money Fund, from 1982, Command Tax Free Fund, from 1982, Command Govt. Fund, from 1982; mem. adv. bd. Nat. Enterprise Bank, Washington, from 1983; chmn. PB Internat. Bank, Luxembourg, 1986-88. Trustee Village of Irvington-on-Hudson, N.Y., 1967-70, mayor, 1970-71; v.p., bd. dirs. Hudson Valley chpt. Nat. Audubon Soc., 1974-80, editor newsletter, 1974-78. Served with USAF, 1961-62. Republican. Presbyterian. Clubs: Down Town Assn. (N.Y.C.), Racquet and Tennis (N.Y.C.); Ardsley Country. Deceased.

STEVENSON, ROBERT, film director; b. London, 1905; came to U.S., naturalized, 1940; m. Ursula Stevenson; 2 children. Ed., Cambridge U. Dir. motion pictures including: Dishonored Lady, 1947, To the Victor, 1948, To the Ends of the Earth, 1948, Walk Softly, Stranger, 1950, My Forbidden Past, 1951, Las Vegas Story, 1952, Johnny Tremaine, 1957, Old Yeller, 1958, Darby O'Gill and the Little People, 1959, Kidnapped, 1960, The Absent-Minded Professor, 1961, In Search of the Castaways, 1962, Son of Flubber, 1963, The Misadventures of Merlin Jones, 1964, Mary Poppins, 1964, Monkey's Uncle, 1965, That Darn Cat, 1965, The Gnome-Mobile, 1967, The Love Bug, 1969, Bedknobs and Broomsticks, 1971, Herbie Rides Again, 1974, Island at the Top of the World, 1974, One of Our Dinosaurs is Missing, 1975, The Shaggy D.A., 1976; dir. over 100 TV shows including Cavalcade of America, Ford Theatre, Playhouse of Stars, G.E. Theatre, Hitchcock Presents, 20th Century-Fox Hour, Gunsmoke, Walt Disney. Home: Santa Barbara Calif. Died Apr. 30, 1986.

STEVERS, MARTIN DELAWAY, editor, writer; b. Chgo., June 28, 1892; s. Frederick Delaway and Ida Louise (Morse) S.; m. Margaret Marie Reidy, June 10, 1922. PhB, U. Chgo., 1914. Writer on staff Am. School and Illustrated World, 1914-16, 20-21, staff editor, assoc. mng. editor, 1933-46, mng. editor, 1946-59; staff editor Compton's Pictured Ency., 1921-23; mem. editorial staff Liberty, 1924-25; copywriter, copy chief Bus. Survey, Chgo. Tribune, 1926-29; treas. Crowell, Crane, Williams & Co., Chgo. and N.Y.C., 1929-31. Author: Steel Trails, 1933, Mind Through the Ages, 1940; (with Jonas Pendlebury) Sea Lanes, 1935; contbr. articles to mags. Lt. U.S. Army, 1916-19. Mem. Midland Authors Club, Tavern Club, Sigma nu. Episcopalian. Home: Chicago Ill. †

STEWART, BENNETT MCVEY, former congressman; b. Huntsville, Ala., Aug. 6, 1914; s. Bennett and Cathleen (Jones) S.; m. Pattye Crittenden, Sept. 1938; children: Bennett Michael, Ronald Patrick, Miriam Kay Stewart Early. BA, Miles Coll., 1938-40. Asst. prin. Irondale High Sch., Birmingham, Ala., 1936; assoc. prof. sociology Miles Coll., 1938-40; ins. exec. Atlanta Life Ins. Co., 1940-50; dir. Ill. Atlanta Life Ins. Co., Chgo., 1950-68; insp. Chgo. Bldg. Dept., 1968; rehab. specialist Chgo. Dept. Urban Renewal, 1968-71; alderman from 21st ward Chgo. City Coun., from 1971; mem. 96th Congress from 1st Ill. dist. Bd. dirs. Wabash YMCA; mem. Chesterfield Community Coun.; mem. Dem. Ward Com., Chgo., 1972-88. Mem. Chgo. Ins. Assn. (past pres.), Alpha Psi Alpha (past Chgo. grad. chpt. pres., bd. dirs.). Christian Methodist Episcopalian. Home: Chicago Ill. Died Apr. 26, 1988.

STEWART, J. GEORGE, architect; b. Wilmington, Del., June 2, 1890. Student, U. Del. Mem., del. at large Congress, Washington, 1935-37; architect Capitol, Washington, from 1954; acting dir. Botanic Garden, Washington. Mem. Capitol Police Bd., Commn. for Extension U.S. Capitol, AIA (hon.). Home: Washington D.C. †

STEWART, JOHN WALKER, surgeon, educator; b. Ewing, Ill., June 30, 1892; s. Towner Kent and Nancy Jane (Webb) S. Student, Ewing Coll., 1900-11; MD, St. Louis U., 1915. Diplomate Am. Bd. Surgery (founder). Intern St. Louis City Hosp., 1915-17, resident surgeon, 1917-20, asst. surgeon, 1921-26, assoc. surgeon, 1926-33, surgeon, 1939-45; asst. surg. St. Mary's Group of Hosps., 1924-25, assoc. surgeon, 1925-46, acting surgeon-in-chief, from 1946; dir. surgery St. Louis City Hosp. for the Colored, 1935-37; chief staff Bethesda Gen. Hosp., St. Louis, from 1943; asst. in surgery St. Louis U., 1920-21, instr. 1921-28, sr. instr., 1928-33, asst. prof., 1933-41, assoc. prof. surgery, 1941-50, chmn. dept., 1946-50, prof. surgery, from 1950. Mem. bd. govs. Am. Nat. Red Cross. Lt. Med. Res. Corps., World War I; col. M.C., World War II. Decorated Legion of Merit. Fellow ACS; mem. AMA, St. Louis, Mo. State med. socs., Western, St. Louis surg. socs., Phthagorean Literary Soc., Phi Chi, Alpha Omega Alpha. Home: Saint Louis Mo. †

STEWART, JOSEPH KYLE, educator; b. Oceana, W.Va., Mar. 24, 1906; s. Charles B. and Nina (Swope) S.; m. Marjorie Thorn, July 3, 1934 (dec. 1954); 1 son, John E.; m. Irene Kersey Baker, Mar. 24, 1957; stepchildren: William P. Baker, Jennifer L. Baker. AB, Marshall Coll., 1927; MS, W.Va. U., 1931, PhD, 1934; postgrad., Harvard, MIT, 1943. Math tchr. Charleston, W.Va., 1927, Gauley Bridge, W.Va., 1928-30; instr. W.Va. U., Morgantown, 1932-37, asst. prof., 1937-46, assoc. prof., 1946-50, prof., 1950-72, prof. emeritus, 1972-87, head dept. math, 1960-65, asst. grad. dean, 1963-65; dir. Kanawha Valley Grad. Ctr. Sci. and Engring., Inst. W.Va., 1958-60, Ctr. Rsch. Devel., 1961-62. Author: Intermediate Algebra, 1942; contbr. articles to profl. jours. With USN, World War II. Mem. Am. Math. Soc., Naval Res. Assn., Math. Assn. Am., AAUP, U.S. Naval Inst., W.Va. Acad. Sci. (pres. 1965), Rotary, Sigma Xi. Home: Morgantown W.Va. Died Nov. 21, 1987; buried Beverly Hills Meml. Garden, Morgantown, W.Va.

STEWART, LEROY ELLIOTT (SLAM STEWART), string bassist; b. Englewood, N.J., Sept. 21, 1914; s. Elliott Edward and Mary (Harris) S.; m. Claire Louise Wood, Jan. 11, 1969. Student, Boston Conservatory Music, 1934-35; Dr. Music, 1985. faculty State U. N.Y.; dir. jazz workshops Newing Coll., Binghamton, 1971-87 ; lectr., performer Roberson Center Ednl. Services.; Cons. Roberson Center. Appeared in Boston night clubs with, Jabbo Jenkins, Dean Earl and, Sabby Lewis, 1935-36, joined Peanuts Holland in, Buffalo, 1936; formed guitar and bass duo with Slim Gaillard at Jock's Place, N.Y.C., 1935-37; appeared on radio WNEW, N.Y.C., 1937-41, mem. Art Tatum Trio, 1941-56, Benny Goodman Sextet, 1945-47, 73-85, appeared at Monterey Jazz Festival with Slim Gaillard, 1970, with, Benny Goodman Sextet at Kennedy Center, Washington, Red Rock Amphitheater, Denver, Wolf Trap Farm Park, Va., Saratoga Performing Arts Theater, Royal Albert Hall, London, Carnegie Hall, Town Hall and, Lincoln Center, N.Y.C., also in, Dublin, Hamburg, Helsinki, Vienna and, Alaska, Kool Jazz Festival, Montreux Jazz Festival, 1984; appeared in movies, on Broadway and television; guest soloist with symphony orchs. and chamber music quartets; (Recipient Esquire Silver award 1945-46, Downbeat award for best bassist of year 1945, Metronome award for best all-Am. jazz bassist 1946, Prez award for contribution to jazz N.Y.C. Dept. Cultural Affairs 1979, Highest Honor award Berklee Coll. Music 1979, Grammy award nominee 1981); Author: Styles in Jazz Bass, 1944; Composer: Flat Foot Floogie, 1937. Fellow Yale U.; Fellow Newing Coll.; Fellow State U. N.Y., Binghamton. Mem. ASCAP, Am. Fedn. Musicians (High Honor Achievement award 1985), Am. Soc. Bassists. Russian Orthodox. Club: Sertoma.

Home: Binghamton N.Y. Died Dec. 9, 1987; buried Vestal Hills Meml. Pk., Binghamton, N.Y.

STEWART, MICHAEL, playwright, lyricist; b. N.Y.C., Aug. 1, 1929. M.F.A., Yale U. Sch. Drama. Author: librettos Bye Bye Birdie, 1961, Carnival, Hello Dolly; author: books for Broadway shows The Grand Tour; book and lyrics I Love My Wife; lyrics Barnum (Recipient Tony award 1961, 64, Drama Critics Circle award (2).). Home: New York N.Y. Died Sept. 20, 1987.

STEWART, PATRICK BRIAN, pharmaceutical company research and development executive, physician; b. Champion Reef, Mysore State, India, Aug. 7, 1922; came to U.S., 1977; s. James and Lily (Wallace) S.; M.B.B.S., Middlesex Hosp. Med. Sch., U. London, 1950; m. Eunice Lily Sixsmith, Jan. 11, 1949; children—Jennifer, Duncan, Katharine. Intern, resident Brompton Hosp., London; resident Middlesex Hosp., London, 1950-51, Brompton Hosp. for Diseases of Chest, London, 1951-52; gen. practice medicine, Barnstaple, Eng., 1952-54; med. dir. Geigy Pharms., Can., 1957-62; dir. research Pharma-Research Can. Ltd., Montreal, Que., 1962-77; sr. v.p. research and devel. Boehringer Ingelheim, Ridgefield, Conn., from 1977; research fellow dept. physiology McGill U., Montreal, 1954-56, lectr. in physiology, 1956-57, asst. prof. clin. medicine, 1958-74, assoc. prof. medicine and clin. medicine, 1974-77; asst. physician Royal Victoria Hosp., Montreal, 1957-69, assoc. physician, 1969-77; research assoc. NRC Can., 1956-57; research fellow dept. allergy, immunology and rheumatic diseases Scripps Clinic and Research Found., La Jolla, Calif., 1963-64. Served with Brit. Royal Air Force, 1940-45. Decorated D.F.C. Mem. AAAS, Am. Physiol. Soc., Am. Assn. Immunologists, Am. Physiol. Soc., Can. Med. Assn., N.Y. Acad. Scis., Ont. Coll. Physicians and Surgeons, Transplantation Soc., Royal Coll. Physicians (London). Contbr. chpts., articles to profl. publs. Home: Washington Depot, Conn. Deceased.

STEWART, PERCY MERRITT, investment banker; b. N.Y.C., Dec. 29, 1890; s. Charles Alexander and Mary (McAllister) S.; m. Ruth Davison, Sept. 23, 1916 (dec. 1938); children: Ruth Doris (Mrs. William J. Fleming), Shirley Jean (Mrs. Henry O. Clutsam), Robert Davison; m. 2d, Betty Holloway, June 25, 1938. With Kuhn, Loeb & Co., from 1906, ptnr., from 1941, later ltd. ptnr; gov. N.Y. Stock Exchange, 1943-48; hon. dir. Metromedia Inc.; former gov. Fed. Hall Meml. Assocs. Inc. Mem. Investment Bankers Assn. Am. (R.R. securities com. 1947-48), Union League, Bankers Club, Bond Club, Regency Club Inc., Am. Yacht Club, Apawamis Club, Shenorock Shore Club (Rye, N.Y.), Ocean Club of Fla. Inc., The Little Club Inc. (Fla.). Republican. Presbyterian. Home: Rye N.Y. †

STEWART, REGINALD, pianist, conductor, conservatory director; b. Edinburgh, Scotland, Apr. 20, 1900; s. George Watson and Elizabeth (Drysdale) S.; m. Ruby McLean Glasgow, July 4, 1921 (dec. Mar. 1987); children: Delphine Glasgow, Ursula Drysdale. Ed. pvt. tutors; student, St. Mary's Coll., Edinburgh, D.Music (hon.); studied with, Arthur Friedheim, Isidor Phillipp, Nadia Boulanger, Mark Hambourg. Tchr. piano Can. Acad. Music, 1920; dir. Hart House, U. Toronto, 1922; formed Bach Soc., Toronto, 1933, Toronto Philharm. Orch., 1934; condr. Balt. Symphony Orch., 1942-52; dir. Peabody Conservatory of Music, Balt., 1941-58; artist-in-residence Music Acad. of West, Santa Barbara, Calif., 1960-82. Pianist, 1919; mus. dir. Can. Operatic Soc.; pianist, Hambourg Trio, 1921; toured as concert pianist, Eng., 1924, Can., 1925; condr. London Symphony Orch., Albert Hall; also soloist, 1930, series of concerts over Can. radio network, 1931; condr. BBC Symphony Orch.; piano recitals in Eng., 1932, many cantatas, to 1941; radio broadcasts Gen. Motors Hour, N.Y.C., 1935, Ford Hour; N.Y.C. debut as pianist Town Hall, 1937; condr. Nat. Symphony Orch., Washington, 1938; toured U.S., Can. as pianist, 1938-39; condr. N.Y.C. Orch. and N.Y. Philharm. Orch., 1940, Detroit Symphony Orch., 1940-41; 2 piano recitals Town Hall, N.Y.C., 1940-41, NBC Symphony Orch.; soloist with N.Y. Philharm., Chgo. Symphony Orchs., 1941, Santa Barbara Symphony Orch.; guest condr. London Philharmonia, 1956, Stratford Festival, Can., with leading symphony orchs., Cen. Am., S.Am., The Netherlands, Switzerland, Mexico, Eng., Italy, Greece; transcribed many works for orchs.; recs. for Victor, Vanguard and Educo. Mem. Canadian Club, Bohemian Club (N.Y.C.), Hamilton Club (Balt.), Arts and Letters Club (Toronto). Home: Montecito Calif. Died July 8, 1984; interred Toronto, Can.

STEWART, ROBERT BRUCE, educator; b. Duluth, Minn., Mar. 31, 1896; s. Frederick C. and Alice (Warnock) S.; m. Lillian V. Olssen, June 15, 1918; 1 son, Robert Bruce (dec.). AB, U. Wis., 1923, AM, 1926; LLD, Butler U., 1943; DCL, Ind. Tech. Coll., 1947; LLD, Tri-State Coll., 1961; DEdnl Adminstrn., Purdue U., 1968; DBA, St. Thomas Inst., 1968. Tchr. Wis. Bus. Coll., Kenosha, 1913, Cental Bus. Coll., Duluth, 1914, pub. high schs., Houghton, Mich., Duluth, Madison, Wis., 1915-23; bus. mgr. Albion (Mich.) Coll., 1923-25; controller Purdue U., 1925-49, v.p., treas., 1945-61, lectr. acctg., instr. sch. budgets and acctg., 1928-46, prof. sch. fon, from 1946; sec.-treas., dir. Varsity Realty Corp., 1928-32, 40-57; dir. Standard Life Ins. Co. Ind., from 1939, v.p. from 1944; pres. Lake Cen. Air Lines, 1953-54, chmn. bd. 1954-60, dir. 1965-68; treas. Ross-Ade Found., 1925-40, sec.-treas., 1940-61; sec.-treas. Purdue Rsch. Found., 1929-60, dir., v.p., gen. mgr., 1960-62, v.p. for spl. projects, 1962-67; v.p., dir. E. Chgo. Housing Corp., 1956-67, Housing Progress Inc., 1964-67; treas. Better Homes in Am. Inc., Lafayette, 1935-38; dir., sec.-treas. Purdue Aeros. Corp., 1942-61; dir. Nat. Homes Inc., Allegheny Airlines, 1968-75; chmn. Bd. Tax Commrs., 1965-67; cons. various ednl. movements and surveys, U.S. govt. on ednl. facilities. Co-author: Debt Financing of Plant Additions for State Colleges and Universities, 1948; contbr. articles to profl. jours. Trustee Tri-State Coll.; pres. bd. dirs. Delta Phi Delta Scholarship Found., from 1973. Mem. Univ. Club, La Fayette Country Club, Parlor Club, Indpls. Athletic Club, Masons, numerous profl. assns. Presbyterian. Home: Boca Raton Fla. Died June 10, 1988.

STEWART, ROBERT FLETCHER, corporate executive; b. Gardner, Mass., Aug. 6, 1927; s. Arlington K. and Edith (Fletcher) S.; m. Joan Marshall, June 23, 1951; children—Carolyn, Eleanor. B.S., Worcester Poly. Inst., 1950, D.Engring. (hon.), 1978; postgrad., Babson Inst. Bus. Adminstrn., 1950-51, Boston U. Grad. Sch. Bus., 1957-58. Pres. Royal Typewriter Co. div. Litton Industries, Inc., Hartford, Conn., 1969-70; group exec. machine tool systems group, corp. v.p. Litton Industries, Inc., Hartford, 1970-71; pres. indsl. products group, corp. v.p. Rockwell Internat. Corp., Pitts., 1971-75; sr. v.p. strategic planning, grouphead Flight Systems Group, United Techs. Corp., Hartford, 1975-78; pres. Arlen Realty & Devel. Corp., 1978-79; sr. v.p. corp. planning and devel. IC Industries Inc., Chgo., 1979-82, exec. v.p., dir., 1982-84, sr. exec. v.p., dir., 1984-87. Trustee Worcester (Mass.) Poly. Inst. Served with USNR, 1945-46. Home: Prospect Heights Ill.

STEWART, SLAM See STEWART, LEROY ELLIOTT

STEWART, WELLINGTON BUEL, pathologist, educator; b. Chgo., June 18, 1920; s. George Ross and Helen Isabel (Skinner) S.; m. Helen M. Zimmerman, June 16, 1945; children—Douglas Peter, Thomas Hale, John Gilman. B.S., U. Notre Dame, 1942; M.D., U. Rochester, 1945. Diplomate Nat. Bd. Med. Examiners, Am. Bd. Pathology (anat. and clin. pathology). Intern in pathology Strong Meml. Hosp., Rochester, N.Y., 1945-46; Rockefeller fellow pathology U. Rochester, 1948-49, Vet. Postgrad. fellow pathology, 1948-50; from assoc. pathology to assoc. prof. pathology Columbia, 1950-60; prof. pathology, chmn. dept. U. Ky. Coll. Medicine, 1960-70; prof. pathology, dir. med. computer center U. Mo., Columbia, 1970-75; dir. labs. U. Mo., 1975-85, cons. in clin. pathology, 1985-88, prof. emeritus pathology, 1985-88. Contbr. articles to sci. publs. Served to capt. M.C. AUS, 1946-48. Fellow Coll. Am. Pathologists; mem. Am. Assn. Pathologists, Mo. Soc. Pathologists (sec.-treas. 1978-84), Harvey Soc., Am. Assn. Blood Banks, Soc. Computer Medicine (pres. 1978), Am. Soc. Exptl. Biology and Medicine, AMA, Mo. Med. Assn., Ky. Soc. Pathologists (pres. 1965-66), Am. Soc. Clin. Pathlogists (chmn. bd. registry med. technologists 1964-67, commr. for med. tech. 1967-71), Sigma Xi, Alpha Omega Alpha. Club: Cosmos. Home: Columbia Mo. Died Mar. 16, 1988; buried Columbia, Mo.

STEYERMARK, JULIAN ALFRED, botanist; b. St. Louis, Jan. 27, 1909; s. Leo and Mamie (Isaacs) S.; m. Cora Shoop, Sept. 1, 1937. A.B., Washington U., 1929, M.S., 1930, Ph.D., 1933; M.A. (grad. scholar), Harvard U., 1931. Rufus J. Lackland research fellow Mo. Bot. Garden, 1932-33; research asst. to Dr. Robert E. Woodson, Jr.; mem. expdn. to Panama, 1934-35; hon. research assoc. Dr. Robert E. Woodson, Jr., 1948-88; instr. biology University City (Mo.) Sr. High Sch., 1935-37; taxonomist, ecologist U.S. Forest Service, summers 1936-37; asst. curator herbarium Chgo. Natural History Mus., 1937-47, assoc. curator, 1948-49, curator, 1950-58; botanist Instituto Botanico, Ministerio de Agricultura and Cria, Caracas, Venezuela, 1959-88; curator herbarium Instituto Botanico, Ministerio de Agricultura and Cria, 1975-81, assessor to dir., 1982-84; curator Mo. Bot. Garden, 1984-88; research assoc. emeritus Instituto Botanico and Instituto Nacional de Parques,, 1985-88; leader bot. expdn. Guatemala, 1939-40, 41-42; to Venezuela, 1944-45, 53; del. to Conservation Council Chgo., 1939-58; botanist Cinchona Mission to Ecuador for U.S. Govt., 1943, Venezuela, 1943-44; hon. 1st v.p. First Latin Am. Bot. Congress; co-leader bot. expdn. to Venezuela, 1954-55, expdns. in, 1959-88; vis. curator N.Y. Bot. Garden, 1961-65, 68-69; Mem. Gov.'s Natural History Adv. Com. for Ill. Beach State Park, 1950; gov. Nature Conservancy, 1953-56; trustee Nature Conservancy (Mo. chpt.); mem. Commn. Preservation Natural Area Venezuela; mem. adv. bd. Audubon Soc. Venezuela, 1976-88; cons. Humid Forests of Venezuela, Sierra Club. Author: Spring Flora of Missouri, 1940, (with Paul C. Standley) Flora of Guatemala, 1946-58, Vegetational History of the Ozark Forest, Flora of Missouri, Rubiaceae of the Guayana Highlands, Flora of Auyan-tepui, Venezuela, Flora of the Meseta del Cerro Jaua, Venezuela, Flora of Ptari-tepui, Venezuela, Rubiaceae of Venezuela, 3 vols, 1974, (with Charles Brewer-Carias) Venezuela, 1975, (with Otto Huber) Flora del Avila, (with Gondelles and Garcia) National Parks of Venezuela; Contbr. to: Flora of Venezuela. Decorated Order of Quetzal Govt. Guatemala; Gold medal Order Merit Work Order Andres Bello, Venezuela; Order Henri Pittier 1st class; recipient disting. service awards; award Amigos Venezuela, 1972; William H. Phelps Conservation award, 1983; Gold medal Mo. Bot. Garden, 1979; recipient Spl. Plaque, Herbarium of Instituto Botanico, Caracas, Venezuela, Instituto Nacional de Parques, Venezuela, with Terramar Found., 1983-86; Spl. Homage, Orchid Soc. of Venezuelan Soc. Natural Scis., 1985, also Plaque; NSF grantee, 1958-59, 86-88, Nat. Geog. Soc. grantee, 1986-88; Steyermark Woods Preserve named in his honor Mo. Dept. Conservation. Fellow AAAS; mem. Bot. Soc. Am., Am. Soc. Plant Taxonomists, Ecol. Soc. Am., Friends of Our Native Landscape (hon.), Venezuela Soc. Natural Sci. (hon.), Ecuador Inst. Natural Scis. (hon.), Barrington Natural History Soc. (pres.), Sigma Xi. Clubs: St. Louis Wild Flower (hon. mem.), Kennicott. Home: Saint Louis Mo. Died Oct. 15, 1988.

STICKELL, VANCE L., newspaper marketing and advertising executive; b. Ong, Nebr., Feb. 15, 1925; s. Ora F. and Helen (Swanson) S.; m. Betty Lee Allen, July 11, 1953. B.A., DePauw U., 1948; postgrad., UCLA, 1960. Merchandising field trainee Los Angeles Times, 1948-49, asst. display advt. mgr., 1959-62, display advt. mgr., 1962-68, advt. dir., 1968, v.p. sales, 1968-81, exec. v.p. mktg., 1981—; bd. dirs. Bromar, Inc., Newport Beach, Calif. Mem. adv. bd. Skid Row Devel. Corp., Los Angeles; chmn. ARC, Los Angeles, 1980-81; mem. bd. dirs. Better Bus. Bur., Los Angeles, Central City Assn., Los Angeles; pres Greater Los Angeles Visitors and Conv. Bur., 1981-82. Served with USN. Recipient Humanitarian of Yr. award Nat. Jewish Ctr. Immunology and Respiratory Medicine, 1985; Vance Stickell Retail Mktg. scholarship established in his honor at Calif. State U., Los Angeles, 1985; elected to Advt. Hall of Fame posthumously, 1987; Vance Stickell Meml. Fund for Blood Services established by L.A. chpt. ARC; Vance Stickell Meml. Student Internship Program sponsored by Am. Advt. Fedn. and L.A. Times. Mem. Am. Advt. Fedn. (chmn. 1983-84, chmn. Council Judges Advt. Hall of Fame, 1986), The Advt. Council (1st. vice chmn. 1985-87), Newspaper Advertising Bur. (mem. plans commn. 1974-87, chmn. sales structure task force for Future Advt. Com.), Internat. Newspaper Advt. and Mktg. Execs. (hon. life mem.), Los Angeles Advt. Club (Silver Medal award 1986). Clubs: Wilshire Country (Los Angeles) (pres. 1972-73), Pauma Valley Country (San Diego); PGA West Country (LaQuinta, Calif.). Home: Pasadena Calif. Died Oct. 19, 1987; buried Laguna Beach, Calif.

STILLMAN, CHARLES LATIMER, management consultant; b. N.Y.C., 1904; s. Leland Stanford and Ada Lombard (Latimer) S.; m. Frances Disoway Johnson, Nov. 19, 1932 (div.); children: Charles Latimer, Stanley Wells, Louise Lombard; m. Marjorie Hodgsdon Peters, 1950. Grad., Phillips Acad., 1922; AB, Yale, 1926. With So. States Devel. Co., Hazelhurst, Ga., 1926-28; with Time Inc., N.Y.C., 1928-71, treas., 1930-60, v.p., 1939-49, exec. v.p., 1949-59, chmn. fin. com., 1960-69, adv. dir., 1969-71; mgmt. cons. N.Y.C., from 1971; chmn. bd. dirs. Eastex Inc., Rock-Time Inc.; pres., dir. Jasper Timber Co.; chmn. bd., pres., dir. Rayburn Land Co.; bd. dirs. Printing Devels. Inc.; head Fed. Econ. Coop. Adminstrn. Tech. (Indsl.) Mission, China, 1948. Trustee Escuela Agricola Panamericana; bd. dirs., v.p., sec.-treas. Henry Luce Found. Mem. Univ. Club, Fairfield Hunt Club, River Club. Republican. Home: Fairfield Conn. Died June 8, 1986.

STITES, HENRY J., lawyer; b. Hopkinsville, Ky., Aug. 2, 1889; s. Henry J. and Susan (Edmunds) S.; m. Alice Beattie, Nov. 16, 1932; children: Henry J. IV, Anne Campbell. AB, Georgetown Coll., 1909, Yale U., 1910; LLB, Yale U., 1912, Louisville U., 1911. Bar: Ky. 1911, Conn. 1912. Mem. Stites & Stites, Louisville; spl. asst. to U.S. Atty. Gen., from 1954; bd. dirs. various corps. Pres. bd. Hindman Settlement Sch.; trustee Georgetown Coll., 1916, 32; regent Western State Coll., 1924-27; chmn. Rep. city, state, nat. elections, 1927-28, 30, state treas., 1927-31. With U.S. Army, 1917-19, col. Ky. N.G. Mem. ABA (chmn. bar bldg. com. 1954-55, Louisville chmn. membership com. 1956), Louisville (exec. com. 1945-46), Ky. (chmn. war work com. 1941-46, state bd. bar commrs., chmn. state dist. bar conf. 1943-49) bar assns., Assn. of Bar of City of N.Y., Am. Legion (charter), Pendennis Club, Filson Club, Louisville Country Club, Phi Delta Phi, Kappa Alpha. Baptist. †

STOCK, VALENTINE NORBERT, food processing executive; b. Toronto, Ont., Can., May 14, 1923; s. Valentine F. and Olga A. (Wallace) S.; B.A.Sc. U. Toronto, 1946; m. Georgia I. Knowles, 1955; children—Michael, Andrew, Barbara. With Duplate Can. Ltd., 1947-54, Henry A. Martin Ltd., Mgmt. Cons., 1954-57; with Can. Packers Ltd., Toronto, 1958-87, dir., 1974-87, pres., 1978-87, chmn., chief exec. officer, 1980-85; pres. Can. Chromalox Co. Ltd., 1967; dir., chmn. Norwich Union Life Soc.; exec. v.p. Can. Corp. Mgmt. Co. Ltd., 1971; pres. Can. Corp. Mgmt. Co., 1972-78; vice-chmn., dir. Consumers Glass Co. Ltd.; dir. Eaton's of Can. Ltd., PPG Can. Inc., Dome Mines Ltd., CAE

Industries Ltd., Falconridge Ltd., Can. Liquid Air Ltd. Pres. Art Gallery of Ont., 1986-87; chmn. Olympic Trust Can. Served to sub-lt. RCNVR, 1944-45. Mem. Assn. Profl. Engrs. Clubs: Toronto, Toronto Golf, York, Badminton & Racquet, Mount Royal, Osler Bluff Ski. Died Jan. 2, 1987, buried Mt. Pleasant Cemetery, Toronto.

STOCKTON, GILCHRIST BAKER, military officer, business executive; b. Jacksonville, Fla., Aug. 20, 1890; s. John Noble Cumming and Fannie (Baker) S.; m. Mildred Churchwell, Oct. 14, 1925; children: Mildred Stockton Adams, Gilchrist B. Student, U. N.C., 1909-10; LittB, Princeton U., 1914; postgrad. (Rhodes scholar), Christ Church, Oxford, 1914-17, B.A., 1917, M.A., 1927. Commd. lt. (j.g.) USNRF, 1917; advanced through to rear adm. USN, 1945; naval aide and liaison offcer to U.S. high commr. Philippines, 1945-46; mem. U.S. Commn. Relief in Belgium, 1915-16; spl. asst. to Am. ambassador, London, 1916-17; aide Adm. W.S. Sims, comdr. USNRF, 1917-19; chief of mission to Austria Am. Relief Adminstrn. under Herbert Hoover, 1919-20; pres. Ortega Co., real estate, Jacksonville, Fla., 1922-30; E.E. and M.P. Austria, 1930-33; exec. v.p. Mail Order Assn. Am., 1934-36; pres. Ortega Co., 1936-67. Dir. fin. for Fla., Dem. Nat. Com., 1924; del. Dem. Nat. Conv., 1928, alternate del., 1940. Awarded Mil. Merit medal Philippines. Decorated chevalier Order of Crown (Belgium), Gold Cross of Honor, Order of Merit of Austrian Republic, medal City of St. Quentin, medal Salvator, City of Vienna, Great Golden Cross of Honor with ribbon and star for svc. to Austrian Republic. Mem. Am. Legion (past post comdr.), Florida Yacht Club, Timuquana Country Club (Jacksonville), Phi Beta Kappa, Sigma Nu. Episcopalian. Home: Jacksonville Fla. †

STOCKTON, RICHARD GORDON, banker; b. Winston-Salem, N.C., Feb. 12, 1892; s. Madison Doughty and Martha (Vaughn) S.; m. Hortense Jones, Oct. 13, 1917; children: Sara Stockton Hill, Jean Rhodes. BA, U. N.C., 1911; postgrad., Columbia U. Law Sch., 1912. Pvt. practice 1913-22; trust officer Wachovia Bank & Trust co., Winston-Salem, 1922-30, v.p., trust officer, from 1930, acting pres., sr. trust officer, 1949-51, chmn. bd., 1951-55, chmn. exec. com., from 1955. Trustee Greensboro Coll. for Women; pres. Children's Home, Inc., N.C. Found. Ch.-Related Coll., from 1956; state chmn. Boys' Clubs Am.; state treas. Crusade for Freedom, 1953; past pres. Carolinas United Red Feather Svcs., 1953. Mem. ABA, Winston-Salem C. of C., Am. Bankers Assn. (past pres. trust div.), Rotary, Beta Theta Pi. Democrat. Methodist. †

STOESSEL, WALTER JOHN, JR., diplomat; b. Manhattan, Kans., Jan. 24, 1920; s. Walter John and Katherine (Haston) S.; m. Mary Ann Ferrandou, June 20, 1946; children: Katherine, Suzanne, Christine. A.B., Stanford, 1941; student, Russian Inst., Columbia U., 1949-50, Center Internat. Affairs, Harvard U., 1959-60. Fgn. service officer 1942-86; vice consul, 3d sec. embassy Caracas, Venezuela, 1942-44; 2d sec., vice consul Moscow, USSR, 1947-49; polit. officer Bad Nauheim, also Bad Homburg, Germany, 1950-52; officer charge USSR affairs Dept. State, 1952-56; assigned White House, 1956; 1st sec., consul Paris, 1956-59; dir. exec. secretariat Dept. State, 1960-61; counselor embassy Paris, 1961-63; minister-counselor Moscow, USSR, 1963-65; dep. asst. sec. state Europe, 1965-68; ambassador to Poland, 1968-72; asst. sec. state for European affairs 1972-74; ambassador to USSR Moscow, 1974-76; to Fed. Republic of Germany Bonn, 1976-81; undersec. for polit. affairs Dept. State, 1981-82, dep. sec. state, 1982; dir. Lockheed Corp., Hartford Group, Allen Group; chmn. Pres.' Commn. on Chem. Warfare, 1985, U.S. Del. to Budapest Cultural Forum, 1985. Served with USNR, 1944-46. Mem. Council Fgn. Relations, German Marshall Fund U.S., Atlantic Council, UN Assn. U.S. (chmn. parallel studies program with USSR), Phi Delta Theta. Clubs: Chevy Chase, Metropolitan, Alibi. Home: Washington D.C. Died Dec. 9, 1986.

STOKES, ANSON PHELPS, JR., clergyman; b. New Haven, Jan. 11, 1905; s. Anson Phelps and Carol G. (Mitchell) S.; m. Hope Procter, July 10, 1943; children: Hope Carol (Mrs. Paul Fremont-Smith), Mary Elizabeth. Student, St. Paul's Sch., Concord, N.H., Corpus Christi Coll., Cambridge, Eng.; BA, Yale, 1927; BD, Episcopal Theol. Sem., Cambridge, Mass.; DD, Kenyon Coll., 1953; STD, Columbia, 1954, Berkley Div. Sch., New Haven, 1962, Suffolk U., 1968. Ordained to ministry Protestant Episcopal Ch. as deacon, 1932, as priest, 1933. Asst. minister St. Mark's Ch., Shreveport, La., 1932, assoc. rector, 1933-36; rector Trinity Ch., Columbus, Ohio, 1937-45; rector, canon St. Andrew's Cathedral Parish, Honolulu, 1945-50; rector St. Bartholomew's Ch., N.Y.C., 1950-54; bishop coadjutor Diocese Mass., 1954-56, bishop, 1956-70; dep. to gen. cov. Protestant Episcopal Ch., 1940, 43. Trustee Lenox (Mass.) Sch., Phelps Stokes Fund, N.Y.C. Mem. Century Assn., Yale Club (N.Y.C.), Country Club (Brookline), Union Club (Boston), Alpha Delta Phi. Home: Brookline Mass. Died Nov. 7, 1986.

STOLZ, LOIS MEEK, psychologist, educator; b. Washington, Oct. 19, 1891; d. Alexander Kennedy and Fanny Virginia (Price) Meek; m. Herbert Rowell Stolz, Mar. 7, 1938. AB cum laude, George Washington U.,

1921; MA, Columbia U., 1922, PhD, 1925. Ednl. sec. AAUW, 1924-29; prof. edn., dir. Child Devel. Inst. Columbia U., 1929-39; rsch. assoc. Com. for Study Adolescents, Progressive Edn. Assn., 1938-39, Com. on Child Devel., U. Chgo., 1939, Inst. Child Welfare U. Calif., 1940-50; prof. psychology Stanford U., 1947-57, prof. emerita, from 1957; rsch. assoc. Study Parental Practices and Communication, from 1957; organizer, dir. Child Svc. Ctrs., Kaiser Shipyards, Portland, Oreg., 1943-45. Author: A Study of Learning and Retention of Young Children, 1925, Personal-Social Development of Boys and Girls, 1940, (with H. R. Stolz) Somatic Development of Adolescent Boys, 1951; (with others) Father Relations of War-born Children, 1954; contbr. articles to mags. Mem. Pres. Hoover's Com. Advancement Edn., 1926-28, Nat. Com. Nursery Schs., 1929-31; mem. nat. adv. com. Fed. Emergency Relief Adminstrn. and Works Projects Adminstrn. nursery schs., 1932-38; pres. gov.'s asst. as coord. child care State of Calif., World War II. Mem. Progressive Edn. Assn. (v.p. 1937), Mental Health Soc. Calif. (pres. 1945-46), Am. Psychol. Assn., AAUW, Internat. Fedn. Univ. Women (panel fellowship com.), Nat. Assn. Nursery Edn., Soc. Rsch. in Child Devel. (bd. dirs.). Home: Portola Valley Calif. †

STONE, CLEMENT, financial investment executive; b. Evanston, Ill., June 12, 1928; s. William Clement and Jessie Verna (Tarson) S.; m. Pamela Hahn, June 14, 1986; children by previous marriages: Steven, Sandra, Michael, Deborah, David Charles and Sara Michelle (twins). B.S., U. Ill., 1950; Life Ins. Mktg. degree, So. Meth. U., 1951; postgrad., Northwestern U., 1963; M.B.A., Harvard U., 1965. With Combined Internat. Corp., Northbrook, Ill., 1942-82; salesman Combined Internat. Corp., 1942-52, dir., 1952-82, asst. to pres., 1952-56, exec. v.p. sales, 1956-61, exec. v.p. sales and mktg., resident v.p., mng. dir. U.K., 1966-69, mng. dir. U.K., exec. v.p. European ops., 1969-70, pres. European ops., mng. dir. U.K., 1970-72, pres., chief operating officer, 1972-73, pres., chief exec. officer, chief operating officer, 1973-82; v.p., dir. Combined Am. Ins. Co., from 1953, asst. to pres., 1954-62; pres., chief operating officer, dir. Combined Ins. Co. Wis.; 1st v.p., dir. Combined Life Ins. N.Y.; v.p., dir. Combined Registry Co.; vice chmn. bd. Combined Opportunities, Inc.; chmn., chief exec. officer Universal Fin. Corp. and subs., Northbrook, 1983-86. Trustee Coll. Ins., N.Y.C.; bd. dirs., v.p. W. Clement and Jessie V. Stone Found. Mem. Delta Sigma Pi. Clubs: Harvard Alumni Chgo. (Chgo.), Met. (Chgo.), Mid-Am. (Chgo.), Univ. (Chgo.), Michigan Shores (Wilmette, Ill.). Home: Lake Forest Ill. Died Dec. 12, 1986; buried Lake Forest Cemetery.

STONE, ERNEST, education educator; b. Crossville, Ala., Dec. 24, 1912; s. Samule W. and Belinda K. (McDaniel) S.; m. Katherine Gann, Aug. 18, 1934; 1 child, William Ernest. BA, U. Ala., 1938, MA, 1939, LLD (hon.), 1970; LLD (hon.), Samford U., 1962. Prin. Kilpatrick Jr. High Sch., Crossville, 1933-36, Crossville High Sch., 1936-42; supt. schs. DeKalb County, Ft. Payne, Ala., 1942-43; supt. city schs. Jacksonville, Ala., 1946-66; supt. edn. State of Ala., 1966-71; pres. Jacksonville State U., from 1971; bd. dirs. Ft. Payne Bank; past pres. Edn. Investment Corp., Birmingham, Ala.; mem. Lackey-Edwards Com. on Sch. Fin., 1958; mem. Ala. Edn. Study Commns., 1967-69, rep. exploration ednl. needs for sci. future, 1960. Author: Preventive Medicine in Public Schools; Individual Difficulties of High School Students in DeKalb County, Ala. Del. Nat. Dem. Conv., 1956, presdl. elector, 1968; trustee U. Ala., Auburn U., Ala. Coll. U. Ala., Tuskegee Inst. With USNR, 1943-46. Recipient Ala. Most Promising Young Educator award, 1948, Most Promising Educator award Phi Kappa Phi, 1969, 1st citation for outstanding svcs. to youth Ala. Congress Parents and Tchrs., 1970; named to Ala. Acad. Honor, 1973. Mem. Ala. Edn. Assn. (past pres.), Ala. Assn. Secondary Sch. Prins., Am. Legion (past comdr. Ala. dept. 1971-72), Rotary, Masons, Shriners. Baptist (deacon). Home: Jacksonville Ala. Mailing: Estate of Ernest Stone Mrs Katherine Stone 403 6th St Jacksonville AL 36265 Died Feb. 7, 1989.

STONE, MARSHALL HARVEY, mathematician, educator; b. N.Y.C., Apr. 8, 1903; s. Harlan Fiske and Agnes (Harvey) S.; m. Emmy Portman, June 15, 1927 (div. July 1962); children: Doris Portman, Cynthia Harvey, Phoebe Goodrich; m. Raviojla Perendija Kostic, Aug. 8, 1962; 1 child, Svetlana Kostic-Stone. AB, Harvard U., 1922, AM, 1924, PhD, 1926; postgrad., U. Paris, France, 1924-25; ScD, Kenyon Coll., 1939; hon. doctorate, Universidad de San Marcos, Lima, Peru, 1943, Universidad de Buenos Aires, 1947, U. Athens, 1954; ScD (hon.), Amherst Coll., 1954, Colby Coll., 1959, U. Mass., 1966. Part-time instr. Harvard U., 1922-23, instr., 1927-28, asst. prof. math., 1928-31, assoc. prof., 1933-37; instr. Columbia U., 1925-27; assoc. prof. math. Yale U., 1931-33; acting assoc. prof. Stanford U., summer 1933; prof. math. Harvard U., 1937-46, chmn. dept., 1942; Andrew MacLeish Disting. Service prof. math. U. Chgo., 1946-68, chmn. dept. math., 1946-52, mem. com. on social thought, from 1962, prof. emeritus, 1968; George David Birkhoff prof. math. U. Mass., 1968-73 prof., 1973-80, emeritus, 1980-89; Walker Ames lectr. U. Wash., summer 1942; vis. lectr. Facultad de Ingenieria, U. Buenos Aires, 1943, U. do Brasil, Rio de Janeiro, 1947, Tata Inst. Funda-

mental Research, Bombay, 1949-50, Am. Math. Soc., 1951-52, College de France, 1953, Australian Math. Soc., 1959, Middle East Tech. U., Ankara, 1963, Pakistan Acad. Sci., 1964, U. Geneva, 1964; 1st Ramanujan vis. prof. Inst. Math Scis. Madras, 1963; vis. prof. Research Inst. Math. Scis., Kyoto, Japan, 1965; vis. scientist C.E.R.N., Geneva, 1966; Fulbright lectr. Australian Nat. U., 1967; hon. prof. Madurai Kamaraj U., South India, from 1967; hon. Disting. prof. Tchrs. Coll., Columbia U., from 1978; vis. lectr. U. Campinas (Brazil), 1979, U. Técnica, Santiago, Chile, 1979, Academia Sinica, China, 1979; Fulbright travel grantee, vis. prof. Tata Inst., Bombay, 1980-81; cons. to USN Dept. Bur. Ordnance and Office Vice Chief Naval Operations, 1942-43; Civil Service employee U.S. War Dept. office chief of staff MIS, spl. br., 1944-45; with overseas service U.S. War Dept. office chief of staff, CBI, ETO; Cons. State Dept., India, 1961, NSF-AID, India, 1968-69, 73; vis. prof. U. Islamabad, Pakistan, 1968-69; pres. Inter-Am. Com. Math. Edn., 1961-72, hon. pres., 1972; vice chmn. div. math. NRC, 1951-52. Author: Linear Transformations in Hilbert Space and Their Applications to Analysis, 1932; Contbr. articles on math. and math. edn. to profl. jours. Pres. Internat. Math. Union, 1952-54, Internat. Commn. on Math. Instrn., 1959-62, Inter Union Com. Teaching Sci., Internat. Council Sci. Unions, 1962-65. Recipient Nat. Medal of Sci., 1983. Mem. Am. Math. Soc. (pres. 1943-44), Nat. Acad. Scis., Am. Philos. Soc., Union Mathematica Argentine (hon.), Indian Math. Soc. (hon.), Centre International de Mathematiques Pures et Appliquees (adminstrv. and sci. councils), Acad. Brasileira de Ciencias, Lund (Sweden) Physiographical Soc., Bologna (Italy) Acad., Explorers Club (N.Y.C.). Home: Amherst Mass. Died Jan. 9, 1989; buried Wildwood Cemetery, Amherst, Mass.

STORK, WILLIS WILLIAM, educational consultant, headmaster; b. Enola, Nebr., Dec. 14, 1911; s. William Willis and Fannie Jane (Bryant) S.; m. Helen Baldwin, Aug. 14, 1936; children: William Willis, Cynthia (Mrs. Jay Thomas Gerber). A.B., U. Nebr., 1933, M.S., 1935; postgrad., Harvard U., summers 1936, 37, U. Mich., summers 1938, 39. Prin. Mt. Hope High Sch., Meadow Grove, Nebr., 1930-32; tchr. Norfolk (Nebr.) High Sch., 1935-36; prin. West Point (Nebr.) High Sch., 1936-37; headmaster Maumee Valley Country Day Sch., Ohio, 1937-55, Polytechnic Sch., Pasadena, Calif., 1955-76; Chmn. Nat. Assn. Ind. Schs., 1972-76. Chmn., moderator Toledo Town Meeting of Air, 1946-49; committeeman Pasadena Tournament of Roses Assn., 1960-80; mem. Pasadena Cultural Heritage Commn., 1976-86; bd. dirs. Toledo Little Repertoire Theatre, 1938-42, Toledo Mental Hygiene Center, 1942-50, Pasadena Child Health Found., 1962-61, Pasadena Art Council; trustee Pasadena Library Bd., 1959-64, Pasadena Art Mus., 1960-66, Cate Sch. Served with USNR, 1943-46. Mem. Country Day Sch. Headmasters Assn. (pres. 1971-72), Headmasters Assn., Calif. Assn. Ind. Schs. (pres. 1968-70), Pasadena Hist. Soc. (pres. 1981-86), Pasadena C. of C. (bd. dirs.). Clubs: Rotarian (pres. Toledo 1948-49, Pasadena 1963-64), Twilight (pres. 1980-81), Valley Hunt, Breakfast Forum, University. Home: Pasadena Calif. Died May 5, 1986, cremated.

STORKE, HARRY PURNELL, college president, former army officer; b. Balt., Mar. 8, 1905; s. Richard William and Laura Belle (Taylor) S.; m. Lois Mason Sawyer, Sept. 4, 1928; children: Lois (Mrs. Thomas E. Davenport), Carolyn Mason (Mrs. Richard E. Mueser); m. 2d Elizabeth Davidson Benson, May 3, 1975. BS, U.S. Mil. Acad., 1926; student, Nat. War Coll., Washington, 1948-49; LLD, Am. Internat. Coll., 1964; LittD, Holy Cross Coll., 1965; DEng, Worcester Poly. Inst., 1965. Commd. 2d lt. U.S. Army, 1926, advanced through grades to lt. gen., 1960; instr. English U.S. Mil. Acad., 1939-43; arty. officer 2d Corps, Sicily, 1943-45; mem. U.S. staff Standing Group NATO, 1949-51; comdg. gen. Camp Desert Rock, AEC Proving Grounds, Nev., 1952; dep. J3 Hdqrs. European Command, 1952-53; chief logistics G-4 Hdqrs. USAREUR, Heidelberg, Germany, 1954-56; comdg. 9th Inf. Div., Goeppingen, Germany and Fort Carson, Colo., 1956-57; comdg. gen. I Corps (Group), 1959-60; comdr. Allied Land Forces S.E. Europe, Ismir, Turkey, 1960-61, ret.; pres. Worcester Poly. Inst., 1962-69. Decorated D.S.M., Legion of Merit (U.S.); Order of Brit. Empire; Croix de Guerre, Medaille de la Reconnaissance (France); Legion of Valour (Italy); Order Taeguk (Korea); Royal Order Phoenix (Greece). Died Dec. 11, 1984.

STOUCH, CLARENCE EDGAR, publisher; b. Westminster, Md., Aug. 9, 1891; s. Joseph and Alverta (Geiselman) S.; m. Margaret Standing, 1929; 1 child, Patricia Nancy. Student pub. schs. With Pa. R.R. Co., Balt., Phila., 1910-17; pvt. sec. ARC, Washington, 1917-19; pvt. sec. to H.P. Davison, J.P. Morgan & Co. N.Y.C., 1919-23; pres. Publ. Corp., N.Y.C., 1941-53, chmn. bd., 1954-69, chmn. emeritus, from 1969; pres. Crowell-Collier, 1951-53, chmn. bd., 1954-55. Pres. trustee Knapp Found. N.Y. N.C. Republican. Home: Greenwich Conn. †

STOUT, MYRON STEDMAN, artist; b. Denton, Tex., Dec. 5, 1908; s. Myron Stedman and Alberta (Inge) Stout. B.S., North Tex. State U., 1930; student, Acad. San Carlos, Mexico City, 1933; M.A., Columbia U., 1938, Hans Hofmann Sch. Art, intermittently 1946-52.

One-man shows include, Stable Gallery, N.Y.C., 1954, Hansa Gallery, N.Y.C., 1957, Contemporary Arts Mus., Houston, 1977, Whitney Mus., 1980, 85, Cherrystone Gallery, Wellfleet, Mass., 1980, exhbns. include, Carnegie Inst. Internat., 1958, Whitney Mus., 1958, 62, 64, 73, 78, 81, 86, Mus. Modern Art, 1959, 81, 86, travelling show, 1975-77, Inst. Contemporary Art, Boston, 1959, Am. Fedn. Arts travelling show, 1960-61, Jewish Mus., N.Y.C., 1963, Guggenheim Mus., 1964, also travelling, 1964-65, 69, 81, Sidney Janis Gallery, N.Y.C., 1964, Albright-Knox Gallery, Buffalo, 1968, Corcoran Gallery Art Biennial, 1969, Everson Mus. and Travelling, Syracuse, 1977, McCrory Found. Collection Travelling Show, 1979-81, Washington State Art Consortium Collection, 1977; represented in permanent collections, Bklyn. Mus., Carnegie Inst., Guggenheim Mus., Art Inst. Chgo., Hirshhorn Mus., Nat. Gallery, Mus. Modern Art, McCrory Found. Collection, Wash. Art Consortium, Seattle, Albright-Knox Gallery, Portland Mus., Maine, also pvt. collections. Trustee Fine Arts Work Center, Provincetown, Mass. Served with USAAC, 1943-45. Recipient award Nat. Found. Arts and Humanities, 1967, Award of Merit, Distinction in Painting Am. Acad. and Inst. Arts and Letters, 1982; Guggenheim fellow, 1969. Home: Provincetown Mass. Died Aug. 2, 1987, buried I.O.O.F. Cemetery, Denton, Tex.

STOWE, ROBERT LEE, JR., textile company executive; b. Belmont, N.C., Aug. 17, 1902; m. Ruth Link Harding; children: Robert Lee III, Daniel Harding, Richmond Harding. BS, Davidson Coll., 1924. Pres., treas., dir. Chronicle Mills, Nat. Yarn Mills Inc., Stowe Spinning Co.; pres., dir. Bank of Belmont, Atlas REal Estate Co., Belmont Syndicate; v.p., treas., dir. Belmont Converting Co.; dir. Stowe Merc. Co., Lakeview Farms. Mem. Belmont City Coun., 1953-67; former trustee N.C. Vocat. Textile Sch.; mem. nat. adv. bd. MacArthur Meml. Found.; founder Stowe Park. Named Belmont Man of Yr., 1963; Stowe Galleries and Robert LEe Stowe Jr. Tennis House, Davidson Coll. named in his honor. Mem. Newcomen Soc. N.Am., Charlotte (N.C.) Country Club, Dunes Golf and Beach Club (Myrtle Beach, S.C.), Phi Gamma Delta. Presbyterian (past. tchr. Sunday sch.; deacon, later elder). Home: Belmont N.C. Died Apr. 8, 1984; buried Belmont.

STRAKA, JEROME A., toiletries company executive; b. Milw., Jan. 26, 1903; s. Edward A. and Anna (Kolman) S.; m. Mary Jane Lucas, Oct. 24, 1925; children: Jane Anne (Mrs. Edward A. Bosshart), James J. BA, U. Wis., 1924. With Colgate-Palmolive, 1924-53, gen. mgr. Polish subs., 1931-39, gen. mgr. Kirkman & Son div., 1939-43, v.p., 1944-45, v.p., gen. mgr. toilet goods div., 1947-52, exec. v.p. div., 1952-53, dir., 1949-53, pres. Kay Daumit div., 1947-53; exec. v.p. Yardley of London Inc., 1945-47; exec. v.p. Chesebrough Mfg. Co. Consol., 1954, pres., 1955; pres., chief exec. officer, dir. Chesebrough-Pond's Inc., 1955-68, chmn bd., 1968-69, dir., 1954-69; bd. dirs. Rexham Corp., Twentieth Century-Fox Film Corp., Keuffel & Esser Co. Bd. dirs. Am. Assn. for Gifted Children, Koscisko Found., Calvin Coolidge Meml. Found. Mem. Wine and Food Soc. London and N.Y., Council Fgn. Rels., Univ. Club, Nat. Arts Club, Hajji Baba Rug Club, Grolier Club, Lucullus Circle, Commanderie de Bordeaux, Men's Garden, Phi Beta Kappa, Lambda Chi Alpha. Presbyterian. Home: Highstown N.J. Died Apr. 22, 1986; interred Presbyterian Churchyard, Basking Ridge, N.J.

STRATER, HENRY (MIKE), artist; b. Louisville, Jan. 21, 1896; s. Charles Godfrey and Adeline (Helme) S.; m. Margaret Y. Conner, June 26, 1920 (div. 1942); children: David, Martha, Michael Henry, Nicholas Appleby; m. Janet M. Orr, June 5, 1942 (div. 1946); 1 child, Jeremy Meacham; m. Lois A. Thompson, Aug. 5, 1951 (div. 1967); children: Pompe Ann, William T., Matthew Helme. One-man shows include Montross Gallery, N.Y.C., 1931, 32, 34, 36, 38, 40, Speed Mus., Louisville, 1936, 64, Portland (Maine) Mus., 1938, Bowdoin Coll., 1940, 50, Horne Gallery, Boston, 1939, Abbot Acad., 1940, Gov. Dummer Acad., 1940, Ind. U., 1951, Louisville Arts Club, 1952, 62, Art Mus., Princeton, 1951, 69, Frank Rehn Gallery, N.Y.C., 1961, 63, 65, 68, 70, Thieme Gallery, Palm Beach, Fla., 1961, 62, 64, U. Louisville, 1951, Norton Gallery, Palm Beach, Fla., 1962, 67, Mus. Art of Ogunquit (Maine), 1963, 74, 77, 81, Lawrenceville (N.J.) Sch., 1965, Swope Gallery, Indpls., 1964, Butler Inst. Am. Art, 1966, First Nat. Bank, Palm Beach, 1967, 69, 71, 73, 75, Heath Gallery, Atlanta, 1967, Ogunquit Gallery, 1970, Lighthouse Gallery, Fla., 1971, Allentown (Pa.) Art Mus., 1971, Art Mus. Palm Beaches, 1977, Gallery Gemini, Palm Beach, 1977, Ariz. State U., 1979; exhibited in group shows including Salon d'Automne, Paris, 1922, also 150 others; represented in pub. and pvt. collections museums, univs. and schs. in U.S., also Am. embassy, London; exhibiting mem. Whitney Studio Club, 1926; supervising architect Ogunquit Mus. Art, 1950-51, trustee, 1952-73, dir., 1960-87; numerous appearances radio and TV. Trustee Ogunquit Pub. Libr., York (Maine) Hosp., 1938-73, pres., 1958-72. Recipient 2d prize Golden Gate Exhbn., 1939, citation for achievements in the arts and humanities Gov. of Maine, 1975. Mem. Princeton Club, Sailfish Club of Fla., York Harbor Reading Room, Everglades Club, Players Club. Episcopalian. Home: Ogunquit Maine. Died Dec. 22, 1987.

STRATFORD, HERBERT RIDLEY, business executive; b. Jersey City, Oct. 4, 1905; s. Herbert Ridley and Kathleen Augusta (Luckenbach) S.; m. Margo Wyeth, June 8, 1935; children: Herbert Ridley III, Margo. Grad., Hill Sch., 1924; BS, Princeton U., 1928. Stockbroker Smith, Graham & Rockwell, N.Y.C., 1928-32; salesman Morton Salt Co., 1932, asst. ea. sales mgr., Washington, 1933-38, staff gen. office sales, Chgo., 1938-42, gen. sales mgr., v.p., 1942-52, exec. v.p., 1952-65, pres., 1966-69; exec. v.p. Morotn Internat., Inc., 1965-69, chmn. exec. com., 1969-71; pres. Imperial Thermal Products, Inc. div., to 1969; past pres., bd. dirs. Cedar St. Corp. Hon. trustee, past pres. Ill. Children's Home and ASid Soc.; past v.p., past trustee Chgo. Sunday Evening Club; hon. trustee, past chmn. devel. com. Orchestral Assn.; former trustee English Speaking Union; pres. Saddle & Cycle Club, Chgo., 1947, 48. Mem. Brookfield Chgo. Zool. Soc., Chgo. Hist. Soc., Ill. Mfrs. Assn., Chicago Club, Tower Club, Princeton Club, Commercial Club, Casino Club (all Chgo.), Cap and Gown Club (Princeton, N.J.), Princeton Club (N.Y.C.). Republican. Episcopalian. Home: Cody Wyo. also: Tucson Ariz. Died Jan. 6, 1989.

STRAUS, JACK ISIDOR, department store executive; b. N.Y.C., Jan. 13, 1900; s. Jesse I. and Irma (Nathan) S.; m. Margaret Hollister, Apr. 29, 1924 (dec. Apr. 1974); children: Kenneth Hollister, Patricia Straus Harrah, Pamela Straus Haber; m. Virginia Megear, Jan. 11, 1975. AB, Harvard U., 1921; LLD (hon.), Adelphi Coll., 1955; DCS, NYU, 1958. With R.H. Macy & Co., N.Y.C., 1921-85, v.p., 1933-39, acting pres., 1939-40, pres., chief exec. officer, 1940-56, chmn., chief exec. officer, 1956-68, chmn. exec. com., 1968-76, hon. chmn. and dir. emeritus, 1977-85; pub. gov. N.Y. Stock Exchange, 1964-68; dir., mem. N.Y.C. Econ. Devel. Council, 1965-76. Trustee Roosevelt Hosp., N.Y.C., 1944-74, chmn. bd. trustees, 1965-74; bd. overseers Harvard U., 1950-54; mem. vis. com. Sch. Bus. Adminstrn., 1938-65, Univ. Resources, 1964-67; mem.-at-large bd. dirs. Empire State Found., 1952-72; bd. dirs. Police Athletic League, N.Y.C., 1961-75, v.p. 1964-75; bd. dirs. United Way, N.Y.C., 1969-85; bd. govs. Hundred Year Assn., N.Y., 1961-74; hon. trustee St. Luke's-Roosevelt Hosp., 1979-85. 2d lt. U.S. Army, 1919. Decorated cross of officer Order Leopold II, Belgium; chevalier Order Legion of Honor, France; Stella della Solidariety Italiana de 2d classe; commendatore Order of Merit, Italian Republic. Mem. Harvard Club, Union Club, Piping Rock Club, Creek Club (Locust Valley, N.Y.). Home: New York N.Y. Died Sept. 19, 1985; buried Woodlawn Cemetery, N.Y.C.

STRAYER, JOSEPH REESE, educator; b. Balt., Aug. 20, 1904; s. George Drayton and Cora (Bell) S.; m. Lois Curry, Sept. 12, 1929 (dec. Feb. 1984); children—Charles Drayton, Elizabeth Anne Strayer Corson; m. Sylvia Thrupp, Aug. 14, 1986. A.B., Princeton, 1925, L.H.D., 1980; M.A., Harvard, 1926, Ph.D., 1930; postgrad., U. Paris, 1928-29; LL.D., Caen U., 1957; L.H.D., Lehigh U., 1976. Instr. history Stevens Inst. Tech., 1929-30; instr. history Princeton, 1930-35, Shreve fellow, 1935-36, asst. prof., 1936-40, assoc. prof., 1940-42, Henry Charles Lea prof. history, 1942-49, Dayton-Stockton prof. history, 1949-73, prof. emeritus, 1973-87; chmn. dept., 1941-61. Author: Western Europe in the Middle Ages, 1954, Feudalism, 1965, The Medieval Origins of the Modern State, 1970, Les Gens de Justice du Languedoc, 1970, The Albigensian Crusades, 1971, Medieval Statecraft and the Perspectives of History, 1971, The Reign of Philip the Fair, 1980; Author, co-author or editor books relating to field; contbr. to mags. Councilman of Borough of Princeton, 1964-67. Fellow Am. Acad. Arts and Scis., Brit. Acad., Mediaeval Acad. Am. (pres. 1966-69); mem. Am. Philos. Soc., Am. Hist. Assn. (pres. 1971), Am. Council Learned Socs. (bd. dirs. 1948-51), Phi Beta Kappa. Home: Princeton N.J. Died July 2, 1987.

STREET, CHARLES LARRABEE, clergyman; b. Chgo., Apr. 25, 1891; s. Charles Arthur and Rosalind Carden (Larrabee) S.; m. Mary Rouse, Jan. 31, 1922; children: Mary Louise, Dorothy Rouse, John Charles. AB, Yale U., 1914; BD, Gen. Theol. Sem., 1919, STD, 1950; PhD, Columbia U., 1926. Ordained to ministry Protestant Episcopal Ch., 1917. With St. Paul's Ch., Chgo., 1917-18, Cathedral S.S. Peter and Paul, Chgo., 1918-21; supt. City Mission, Chgo., 1919-24; student chaplain U. Chgo., 1924-28; headmaster St. Alban's Sch., Sycamore, Ill., 1928-38, Sherwood Hall, Laramie, Wyo., 1939-41; priest-in-charge Christ Ch., Dallas, 1941-45; rector St. Christopher's Ch., Oak Park, Ill., 1945-49; Suffragan bishop Episcopal Diocese Chgo., from 1949. Assoc. editor Anglican Theol. Rev. Mem. University Club, Yale Club, Beta Theta Pi. Home: Oak Park Ill. †

STREET, CLARENCE PARK, construction contractor; b. Cadiz, Ky., Nov. 11, 1900; s. Edward Roberts and Mary (Grinter) S.; m. Ruth Howerton Wallace, Dec. 3, 1935; children: Ruth Wallace (Mrs. Charles E. Ide Jr.) (dec.), Mary Grinter (Mrs. George E.N. Montague), Jane Harrison Liles, Edward Robert. With McDevitt-Fleming Co., Chattanooga, 1922-25, J.J. McDevitt Co., Charlotte, N.C., 1925-41; with McDevitt & Street Co., 1941-84, sec., gen. mgr., 1941-60, pres., 1961-66, chmn. bd. dirs., 1966-84. Mem. Airport Adv. Bd., Charlotte, 1946-75; trustee, mem. exec. com. Queens Coll., 1948-84, chmn. bd. trustees, 1967-74; trustee Presbyn. Hosp. Mem. Assn. Gen. Contractors Am. (treas. Carolinas br. 1939-41, 45-51, v.p. 1942-43, pres. 1944, chmn. nat. pub. relations com., pres. 1944-49, vice chmn. bldg. div. 1947, chmn. 1948, nat. v.p. 1952, nat. pres. 1953), Cons. Constructors Coun. Am., Vanderbilt Alumni Assn., Nat. Planning Assn., Newcomen Soc. N.Am., Phi Beta Kappa, Phi Delta Theta. Presbyterian (elder). Home: Charlotte N.C. Died Aug. 16, 1984.

STREET, JAMES HARRY, economics educator; b. New Braunfels, Tex., Nov. 17, 1915; s. James William and Kate (Goldenbagen) S.; m. Mabel Carroll, Jan. 16, 1944; children: John William, Janet Pauline. B.A. magna cum laude, U. Tex., 1940, M.A., 1947; Ph.D., U. Pa., 1953; D.Econ. Scis. (hon.), Nat. U. Asuncion, Paraguay, 1955; M.A. (hon.), U. Cambridge, Eng., 1972. Reporter, editor New Braunfels Herald, 1933-36; social sci. analyst U.S. Bur. Agr. Econs., Washington, 1941-43; civilian pub. service employee U.S. Forest Service, Cooperstown, N.Y. and Phila., 1943-46; instr. econs. U. Pa., Phila., 1946-48; asst. prof. econs. Haverford (Pa.) Coll., 1948-52; asst. prof. Rutgers U., New Brunswick, N.J., 1952-55; assoc. prof. Rutgers U., 1955-59, prof. econs., 1959-76, disting. prof. econs., 1976-86, prof. emeritus, 1986-88, chmn. econs. dept., 1977-81, dean Univ. Coll., 1983-84; vis. prof. Nat. U. Asuncion, Paraguay, 1955; vis. lectr. various univs. in, Argentina, 1957-58; Fulbright lectr. U. San Marcos, Peru, 1963; econ. specialist Central Am. social studies seminars, summers 1965-72; Fulbright lectr. Nat. U. Mex., 1970; vis. scholar U. Cambridge, 1972-73. Editor: Ideas and Issues in the Social Sciences, 1950; author: The New Revolution in the Cotton Economy, 1957, (with others) Technological Progress in Latin America, 1979, Latin America's Economic Problems, 1987; contbr. articles to profl. jours. Bd. dirs. Metuchen Free Pub. Library, 1963-68. Fellow AAAS; mem. Am. Econ. Assn., Assn. Evolutionary Econs. (v.p. 1981, pres. 1982, Veblen-Commons award 1987), N.Am. Econs. and Fin. Assn. (v.p. 1985), Conf. Latin Am. History; Mem. Latin Am. Studies Assn., Royal Econ. Soc., Council Internat. Exchange Scholars, Phi Beta Kappa (chpt. pres. 1967-68). Home: Metuchen N.J. Died June 20, 1988, buried Beth Israel Cemetery, Woodbridge, N.J.

STREIBERT, THEODORE CUYLER, communications executive; b. Albany, N.Y., Aug. 29, 1899; s. Henry and Catherine (Kaiser) S.; m. Margaret Grout, Mar. 6, 1935 (dec. July 1986); children: Catherine, Marshall, Theodore Paul. BS, Wesleyan U., 1921; MBA, Harvard, 1923. Rsch. staff, bur. bus. rsch. Harvard Bus. Sch., 1923-25, asst. dean, 1929-33; treas. Cinema Credits Corp.; asst. sec. FBO Pictures Corp., 1926-28; asst. to exec. v.p. Pathe Exchange Inc., 1928-29, dir., 1933-35; dir., v.p. radio sta. WOR, Bamberber Broadcasting Service Inc., 1935-44, pres., 1945-53; treas. MBS, 1935-37, v.p., 1938-44, chmn. bd., 1949-51; dir. USIA, 1953-56; mem. bus. staff Nelson and Lawrence Rockefeller, 1957-60; v.p. Time-Life Broadcast Inc.; mgr. WTCN-TV and Radio, Mpls., 1960-62; dir. Free Europe Com., pres., dir. Radio Free Europe Fund, 1962-65; exec. sec. Dr. Goheen's Com. Higher Edn., 1965-68; v.p. N.J. Hist. Soc., 1968-69; spl. asst. to dean Sch. Internat. Affairs, Columbia, 1970-72; spl. asst. to chancellor L.I. U., 1972-76. Former trustee Village of Laurel Hollow; pres., bd. dirs. Vis. Nurse Service N.Y., Legal Aid Soc. N.Y.; hon. trustee Carnegie Endowment for Peace. Mem. Harvard Club (N.Y.C.), Piping Rock Club, Phi Beta Kappa, Alpha Delta Phi. Episcopalian (mem. vestry). Home: Syosset N.Y. Died Jan. 18, 1987; buried Locust Valley Cemetery, Locust Valley, N.Y.

STREISINGER, GEORGE, biologist; b. Budapest, Hungary, Dec. 27, 1927; s. Andor and Margit (Freund) S.; m. Lotte Sielman, June 12, 1949; children: Lisa, Cory. BS, Cornell U., 1950; PhD, U. Ill., 1953. Assoc. geneticist Carnegie Instn. of Washington, Cold Spring Harbor, N.Y., 1956-60; assoc. prof. dept. biology U. Oreg., Eugene, 1960-65, prof., 1965-84, co-chmn. dept., 1968-71, rsch. assoc. Inst. Molecular Biology, 1960-84, acting dir., 1967-68; mem. genetics study sect., div. rsch. grants NIH, 1976-80; mem. Med. Rsch. Coun. Unit for Molecular Biology, Cambridge, Eng., 1957-58. Contbr. articles to profl. jours.; developed zebra fish for genetic rsch. Nat. Found. for Infantile Paralysis rsch. fellow Calif. Inst. Tech., 1953-56; Guggenheim fellow, 1971-72. Mem. NAS. Died Aug. 11, 1984; cremated.

STREIT, CLARENCE KIRSHMAN, author; b. California, Mo., Jan. 21, 1896; s. Louis Leland and Emma (Kirshman) S.; m. Jeanne Defrance, Sept. 26, 1921; children: Travan Pierre Defrance (dec.) Jeanne (Mrs. Felix Rohatyn), Colette (Mrs René Perret). AB, U. Mont., 1919, LLD, 1939; postgrad., Sorbonne, 1919; Rhodes scholar, Oxford U., 1920-21; LLD, Colby Coll., 1941; D.Litt., Oberlin, 1940, Hobart Coll., 1941; LHD, Ill. Coll., Jacksonville, 1966. With Phila. Pub. Ledger, 1920-24, with Paris bur., 1920, 24, Turko-Greek War corr., 1921, Rome corr., 1922-23, Constantinople corr., 1923-24; with N.Y. Times, 1925-39, at Carthage excavation, Riff war corr., 1925, Vienna corr., 1925-27, N.Y. staff, 1927-28, League of Nations corr., 1929-39, with Washington bur., 1939; pres. Fed. Union Inc.,

1939-86; editor Freedom and Union, 1946-75; mem. bd. Atlantic Union Com., 1949-62; pres. Internat. Movement for Atlantic Union, 1958-86. Author: Where Iron Is, There Is the Fatherland, 1920, Hafiz—The Tongue of the Hidden (Rubaiyat), 1928, rev. as Hafiz in Quatrains, 1946, Union Now, 1939, rev. 199948, Union Now With Britain, 1941, Freedom Against Itself, 1954, Freedom's Fromtier, Atlantic Union Now, 1960; co-author: The New Federalist, 1950. With U.S. Army, 1917-19, AEF. Recipient Kefauver Union of Free award, 1968. Mem. Phi Beta Kappa, Sigma Delta Chi, Sigma Chi. Home: Washington D.C. Died July 6, 1986.

STREITZ, RUTH, educator; b. North Platte, Nebr., Sept. 19, 1892; d. Alexander Frederick and Grace Agnes (Stewart) Steitz. PhB, U. Chgo., 1921, MA, 1922; PhD, Columbia U., 1926. Tchr. pub. schs., Lincoln, Nebr., 1914-17; chief clk. State Banking Bd., Lincoln, 1917-19; dir. child welfare Madison, Wis., 1919-21; assoc. Bur. Ednl. Rsch. and in Coll. Edn., U. Ill., 1922-24; prof. edn., chmn. dept. U. Cin., 1926-38; prof. edn. Ohio State U., Columbus, 1938-70; prof. emerita Ohio State U., from 1970; lectr. U. Maine. Author: Safety Education in the Elementary School, 1926, Directing Learning in the Elementary School, 1932; contbr. John Dewey Soc. 13th Yearbook, Educational Leadership, Saturday Rev. Lit. Mem. Am. Rsch. Assn., AAUP, Nat. Soc. for Study Edn., Nat. Assn. Coll. Tchrs. Edn., AAUW, Zonta, Women's Club, Golf Club, College Club, Kappa Delta Pi, Pi Lambda Theta, Pi Theta, Alpha Lambda Delta (hon.). Home: Columbus Ohio. †

STRETCH, LORENA B., educator; b. Meridian, Tex., Aug. 2, 1891; d. William Mason and Florence Mildred (Womack) S. Student, Meridian Coll., 1910-12; AB, Baylor U., 1924, AM, 1927; postgrad, U. Chgo., 1928; PhD, George Peabody Coll. for Tchrs., 1931. Supt. pub. sch., Hill County, Tex., 1915-26; instr. edn. Baylor U., 1926-28, prof. edn., 1928-34, chmn. Sch. Edn., from 1934; dir. Baylor U. summer sch., 1941-42; vis. summer prof. ednl. psychol. George Peabody Coll., 1931-32, Duke U., 1933-36. Author: Guiding Child Development in the Elementary School, other books relating to field. Trustee McLennan County Bd. Edn., Tex. Mem. Tex. State Tchrs. Assn., Nat. Soc. Curriculum Study, Nat. Coun. Com. on Arithmetic, NEA, Kappa Delta Pi, Alpha Chi. Home: Waco Tex. †

STRINGFELLOW, GEORGE EDWARD, manufacturing executive; b. Reva, Va., Dec. 2, 1892; s. James W. and Elizabeth F. (Bowers) S.; m. Carrie M. Fearnow, Dec. 31, 1912 (dec. Dec. 1961). Ed. pub. schs., Va. Mem. cons. com. Inter-County Title Guaranty & Mortgage Co., N.Y.; bd. dirs. Mine Safety Appliances Co., Pitts. Trustee Ind. Inst. Tech., James Monroe Found.; gov. Am. Found. Religion and Psychiatry; bd. dirs. Freedoms Found. Valley Forge; mem., past pres. N.J. div. Am. Cancer Soc.; mem. civic orgns., Orange and Maplewood, N.J. Mem. N.J. Taxpayers Assn. (past pres.), Orange C. of C., Maplewood C. of C. (past pres.), Masons (imperial potentate 1958-59), Shriners, Kiwanis, Duquesne Club, Montclair Golf Club. Presbyterian. Home: East Orange N.J. †

STROBOS, ROBERT JULIUS, educator, neurologist; b. The Hague, Holland, July 2, 1921; came to U.S., 1949, naturalized, 1959; s. Harm and Anna (Ritzenhofer) S.; m. Virginia L. Gaskin, Feb. 10, 1967; children—Semon, Jur, Carolyn, Katharine, Eben. B.A., U. Amsterdam, Holland, 1941, M.D., 1945. Rotating intern Univ. Hosp., Amsterdam, 1945-47; physician Lago Oil Co., Aruba, N.W. I., 1947-49; resident neurology and psychiatry Montefiore Hosp., N.Y.C., Neurol. Inst., N.Y.C., Nat. Hosp., London, Eng. and N.Y. Hosp., 1950-54; asst. prof., asso. prof. neurology Bowman Gray Sch. Medicine, Winston-Salem, N.C., 1954-60; prof. neurology, chmn. dept. N.Y. Med. Coll., 1960-87; attending neurologist Lincoln, Met., Bird S. Coler hosps., N.Y.C.; Westchester County Med. Center, Valhalla, N.Y. Author: novel Treading Water, 1980; contbr. profl. jours. Fellow Am. Acad. Neurology, Am. EEG Soc.; mem. Assn. Research Nervous and Mental Diseases, Am. Epilepsy Soc., Assn. U. Profs. Neurology. Home: New York N.Y. Died Mar. 16, 1987.

STROHM, JOHN LOUIS, author, editor, radio commentator, business executive; b. nr. West Union, Ill., June 22, 1912; s. Charles Gottlieb and Nellie Ethel (Davidson) S.; m. Lillian Ann Murphy, Sept. 8, 1941; children: Terry John, Karen Nell, Robert Dean, Cheryl Ann, David Charles, Colleen Ruth. With publicity dept. Owens-Ill. Glass Co., 1935-36; journalist, freelance writer world-wide, 1937-38; field editor Prairie Farmer, 1938-41; traveled in Latin Am., gathered material for writing and radio 1941; asst. editor Prairie Farmer, 1941-43, mng. editor, 1943-46; traveled in Europe extensively, writing for farm mags. 1946, NANA broadcasting for CBS, traveled in Soviet Union extensively, broadcasting, writing articles for NEA syndicate; pres. No. Ill. Publs. Inc., 1945-50; pres. Publs. Inc., editor Nat. Wildlife, Internat. Wildlife Mag.; mgr. Nat. Corn Husking Contest, 1941; chmn. 1952 Nat. Rural Electrification Conf.; conducted radio program, World Neighbor, WLS, 1944-46; fgn. corr., Europe, Middle East, 1948, S.E. Asia, 1950, Europe, 1954; ofcl. escort to Russian farm ofcls. on U.S. trip, 1955; worked for Pres. Eisenhower, Washington, 1956; first Am. corr. with State Dept. permission to travel in Red China for NEA syndicate, Readers' Digest, NBC, Look mag., 1958; pres. John Strohm Assocs. Inc.; sec., dir., organizer Terra Chems. Internat. Inc., Sioux City, Iowa; organizer World Seeds Inc.; cons. to Sec. Agr. Author: I Lived With Latin Americans, 1943, Just Tell the Truth, 1947; editor: Ford Almanac; assoc. editor Country Gentleman, 1947-55; contbr. to Readers' Digest. Pres. U. Ill. Found. Recipient Sigma Delta Chi Disting. Service award, 1947, 59, Overseas Press Club award, 1959, Pres.'s award, 1978. Mem. Pan.-Am. Council (past pres.), Nat. Corn Husking Contest Assn. (pres.), U. Ill. Alumni Assn. (bd. dirs.), U. Ill. Journalism Alumni Assn. (bd. dirs.), Am. Agrl. Editors Assn. (sec.; pres. 1946), Overseas Press Club, Chgo. Press Club. Clubs: Players (N.Y.C.); Cliff Dwellers, Adventurers (Chgo.). Home: Washington D.C. Died Dec. 5, 1987; buried St. Mary's Cemetery, Woodstock, Ill.

STRÖMGREN, BENGT GEORG DANIEL, astronomer, educator; b. Göteborg, Sweden, Jan. 21, 1908; s. Svante Elis and Hedvig (Lidforss) S.; m. Sigrid Caja Hartz, Mar. 31, 1931. MS, Copenhagen U., 1927, PhD, 1929. Lectr. Copenhagen (Denmark) U., 1933, prof., 1938-40; dir. Observatory, 1940; asst. prof. U. Chgo., 1936-37, assoc. prof., 1937-38, vis. prof., 1946-47, Sewell Avery disting. svc. prof., 1952; prof., dir. Yerkes and McDonald Obs., Williams Bay, Wis., 1951-57; spl. lectr. astronomy U. London, 1949; vis. prof. Calif. Inst. Tech., Princeton (N.J.) U., 1950; mem. Inst. for Advanced Study, Princeton, 1957-87. Author: (with Elis Strömgren) Laerebog i Astronomi, 1931, Lehrbuch der Astronomie, 1933; editor: Handbuch der Experimentalphysik, Vol. 26 (Astrophysik), 1937. Recipient Augustinus prize, 1950. Mem. Royal Danish Acad. Scis. and Letters, Danish Acad. Tech. Scis., Am. Acad. Arts and Scis., Royal Astron. Soc. (assoc.), Societe Royale des Scis. de Liege, Am. Astron. Soc. (hon.), Acad. Coimbra, Royal Swedish Acad. Scis., Physiographic Soc., Koninklijke Nederlandse Akademie van Wetenschappen, Internat. Astron. Unions (gen. sec. 1948), Internat. Coun. Sci. Unions (exec. com. 1948), Quadrangle Club. Died July 4, 1987.

STRONG, BENJAMIN, banker; b. Plainfield, N.J., Aug. 3, 1896; s. Benjamin and Margaret Guitton (LeBoutillier) S.; m. Laura Beaumont Pratt, May 27, 1924; children: Benjamin, John Erwin, Laura Guitton. Grad., Phillips Exeter Acad., 1919; LLD, NYU, 1948. Clk. Nat. Bank Commerce, N.Y.C., 1921-22, J. Henry Schroder & Co., London, 1922-23; with Internat. Acceptance Bank, Inc., N.Y.C., 1923-30; asst. v.p. Bank of the Manhattan Co., 1930-32, v.p., 1932; v.p. U.S. Trust Co. N.Y., 1933-38, trustee, 1937-62, 1st v.p., 1938-47, pres., 1947-58, chmn. bd., 1958-62; bd. dirs. Atlantic Mut. Cos., Home Life Ins. Co.; chmn. investment com. Royal Globe Group; trustee Seamen's Bank for Savs. Bd. dirs. Union Theol. Seminary, Met. Opera Assn.; trustee Presbyn. Hosp.; v.p. J.P. Morgan Library. 1st lt. Am. Expeditionary Force, 1917-19. Mem. Acad. Polit. Sci., N.Y. State C. of C. (v.p.), English-Speaking Union, Pilgrims of U.S., Soc. Cin., Hugenot Soc., Coun. on Fgn. Relations, Pinnacle Club, Met. Opera Club, Bankers, Links, Century Assn., Downtown Assn., University Club, Am. Yacht Club. Republican. Presbyterian. Home: New York N.Y. Died May 2, 1986.

STRONG, FREDERICK SMITH, JR., army officer; b. Orchard Lake, Mich., May 16, 1887; s. Frederick Smith and Alice Marion (Johnston) S.; m. Marjorie Lee Ward, Oct. 9, 1912 (dec. Feb. 1970); children: Frederick Smith III, John Ward (dec.), Marjorie (Mrs. William A. Richardson), Rosamond (Mrs. Wm. L. Fisher). B.S., U.S. Mil. Acad., 1910; grad., Engrs. Sch., Washington, D.C., 1912. Commd. 2d lt. C.E. U.S. Army, 1910, advanced through grades to brig. gen., 1944; served with 7th and 2d divs., France, 1918; with Service of Supply, 1918-19, resigned, 1919; commd. col. Q.M. Res., U.S. Army, 1941; zone constructing quartermaster IV Zone, Atlanta, 1941; War Dept. Gen. Staff, 1942, Office of Chief of Engrs., 1942-43; chief engr. Service of Supply, China-Burma-India, 1943; in hosp. on sick leave 1943-44; comdg. officer Northwest Service Command, 1944-45; hdqrs. A.S.F., to 1945; comdg. U.K. base 1945, Reverted to inactive status, 1946; Exec. dir. com. on artificial limbs NRC, 1946-55, chmn. prosthetics research board, 1955-59; engaged in real estate and land devel. bus., Orchard Lake, Mich., from 1919; v.p., dir. Ind. Limestone Co., Chgo., 1926-27; with Booth Investment Co., Detroit, 1927-41, successively v.p., pres., gen. mgr. and dir. Commr. Village of Orchard Lake, Mich., 1928-40, pres., 1941, resigning to re-enter active mil. service, council member at, City of Orchard Lake Village, Mich., 1964. Decorated D.S.M., Legion of Merit. Mem. Am. Soc. Mil. Engrs., West Point Soc. Mich. (pres. from 1975). Clubs: Army and Navy (Washington); Orchard Lake (Mich.) Country. Home: Sylvania Ohio. Deceased.

STRONG, L(ESTER) CORRIN, foundation executive, ambassador; b. Tacoma, Nov. 25, 1892; s. Lester B. and Hattie Maria (Corrin) Lockwood; m. Alice Trowbridge, Sept.23, 1922; children: Henry, Trowbridge, Corrin Peter. PhB, Yale U., 1916; postgrad., Columbia U. Law Sch., 1924-25; LLD (hon.), Keuka Coll. With trust dept. Guaranty Trust Co., N.Y.C., 1925-27; with trust dept. Nat. Savs. & Trust Co., Washington, 1927-29, also bd. dirs.; organizer, pres. Hattie M. Strong Found., from 1928; U.S. Ambassador to Norway 1953-57. Trustee Rollins Coll., Children's Hosp., 1932-36, George Washington U.; bd. dirs. Washington chpt. Boy Scouts Am., 1938-41; adv. trustee YWCA, 1939-41; chmn. exec. com. Washington Cathedral Bldg. Fund, 1946; dir. loan div. Econ. Coop. Adminstrn., 1948; dep. dir. Internat. Trade Promotion Div., 1949-50. 2d lt. arty French Army, 1917-18; col. gen. staff corps, chief liaison br. internat. div. Army, 1943-46. Decorated Legion of Merit, Officer Legion of Honor (France), Order of the White Cloud Banner (China), Cross of Liberation (Norway), Grand Officer Order of Orange of Nassau (Netherlands), Officer Order of Leopold (Belgium), Grand Cross Norwegian Order of St. Olav. Mem. Nat. Symphony Orch. Assn. (pres. 1939-41), Yale Club, Coffee House Club (N.Y.C), Metropolitan Club, Chevy Chase Club (Washington). Home: Washington D.C. †

STRUTHERS, P(ARKE) H(ARDY), zoology educator; b. Mpls., May 29, 1891; s. Alfred Luther and Carrie Elizabeth (Hardy) S.; m. Mildred Lucebia Morgan, Oct. 1, 1918 (dec. July 1942); children: Jane Mildred (Mrs. Ward), Alfred Morgan, Parke Hardy Jr., John Hodgkiss, Robert Claflin, Carolyn. PhB, Brown U., 1915; MA, Syracuse U., 1924, PhD, 1927. Instr. zoology Pa. State Coll., 1915-17; prof. botany U. P.R., 1920-22; rsch. collector vertebrates Am. Mus. Nat. History, Carribean Sea, 1920-22; instr. zoology Syracuse (N.Y.) U., 1922-27, asst. prof., 1927-29, assoc. prof., 1929-39, prof., 1939-56, prof. emeritus, from 1956; dir. Mus. Natural Sci., Syracuse, 1926-33; dir. carp control studies Conservation Dept. N.Y., 1927-31; founder Merriconn Biol. Lab., Nelson, N.H., 1933, dir. tropical br. lab., Santiago, Republic of Panama, from 1948; dir. expdns., P.R., 1926, Andean Mountains, 1931, Republic of Panama, 1948. Author: Birds of Puerto Rico, 1922, Birds of Mona Island, 1926, the Prenatal Skull of the Canadian Porcupine, 1927, Carp Control Studies, 1927-31, Breeding Habits of the Porcupine, The Cervical Vertebrae of the Porcupine, 1928, Development of the Aortic Arches in the Porcupine, 1936, Development of the Extrahepatic Ducts in the Porcupine, 1941, Prenatal Heart of the Porcupine, Mammalian Annomalies, 1948, others. With U.S. Army, 1917-19. Mem. Am. Soc. Zoologists, Am. Soc. Mammalogists, Am. Fisheries Soc., Audubon Soc., Explorers Club, Sigma Xi, Kappa Phi. Republican. Congregationalist. Home: Syracuse N.Y. †

STUDENROTH, CARL WILSON, labor union official; b. Columbia, Pa., Apr. 14, 1915; s. Frederick Melvin and Priscilla Mary (Crist) S.; married, Apr. 1937; children: Wanda Faye, Donna Marie. Student, Pa. State Coll., 1933-35. Laborer Pa. R.R., 1935-36; molder and foundry worker Grinnell Corp., 1936-44; organizer, dist. rep., v.p. Internat. Molders and Allied Workers Union, AFL-CIO-CLC, Cin., 1944-55, pres., 1976-83; mem. exec. bd. Indsl. Union Dept., AFL-CIO, Metal Trades AFL-CIO; adv. various govt. commns.; pres. Labor Adv.; mem. labor sector adv. Strauss Trade Commn. Democrat. Lutheran. Died Nov. 13, 1983; cremated.

STUTLER, BOYD BLYNN, editor; b. Cox Mills, W.Va., July 10, 1889; s. Daniel Elias and Emily Bird (Heckert) S.; m. Catheolene May Huffman, Nov. 26, 1911; children: William Morris, Warren Harding. Ed. pub. schs., Gilmer and Calhoun Counties, W.Va.; LittD, Alderson-Broadus Coll., 1961. Printer W.Va. newspapers, 1900-07; joint editor, pub. The Sunbeam, Grantsville, W.Va., 1904; editor Grantsville News, 1907-17, Logan (W.Va.) Banner and State Gazette, 1919; chief W.Va. Div. Pub. Printing, 1920-28; asst. editor, contbr. W.Va. Handbook and Manual, 1920-28; editor Svc. Mag., Charleston, W.Va., 1925-26; contbr. editor Svc. Mag., Pitts., 1926-39; editor W.Va. Legionnaire, 1928-29; mng. editor W.Va. Rev., 1929-32, Am. Legion Mag., 1936-54, Edn. Found., W.Va., from 1954; war corr. s.w. Pacific Theatre, 1944-45. Author: Captain John Brown and Harper's Ferry, 1926, Glory, Glory, Hallelujah, 1960, West Virginia in the Civil War, 1963; (with Phil Conley) West Virginia Yesterday and Today, 1952; editor Nat. Legionnaire, Indpls., 1942-44; contbr. articles to mags., newspapers and radio. Mayor City of Grantsville, 1911-12; pres. Bd. Edn., Grantsville, 1915-16; mem. W.Va. War History Commn., 1944, W.Va. Civil War Centennial Commn., from 1958; adv. mem. U.S. Civil War Centennial Commn., from 1959; chmn. John Brown Centennial Com, W.Va., 1958-59. Sgt. U.S. Army, 1917-19. Mem. Am. Legion (post comdr. 1927-28, adj. Dept. W.Va. 1928-29, asst. nat. publicity dir., field sec. to nat. comdr. 1932-36), 80th Div. Vets. Assn. (assisted orgn. in France 1919, nat. exec. coun. 1921-23, resident sec. 1925-26, nat. vice comdr. 1926-31, nat. comdr. 1932-33), Bibliog. Soc. Am., Ohio, Kans., W.Va. (pres. 1958-59) hist. socs. Republican. Home: Charleston W.Va. †

STUTSMAN, OSCAR T., chemical company financial executive; b. New Orleans, Mar. 4, 1923; s. Thaddeus Oscar and Kate (Mandeville) Adams; m. Barbara Porter, Apr. 6, 1943; children: Richard Allen, Louise Ann, Donald William. Student, U. Tex., El Paso, 1941, George Washington U., 1941-43. Fingerprint technician FBI, Washington, 1941-43; acct. IMC, Carlsbad, N.Mex., 1946-63; adminstrv. mgr. IMC, Lakeland, Fla., 1963-71; div. v.p. IMC, Libertyville, Ill., 1971-79; v.p. fin. IMC, Northbrook, Ill., 1979-85. Bd. dirs. 100 Club,

Lake County, Ill., 1979-83, Hull House Assn., Chgo., 1982-83. Sgt. U.S. Army, 1943-46. Mem. Fin. Execs. Inst. Republican. Home: Lincolnshire Ill. Died Oct. 22, 1985; buried Kelley & Spaulding Funeral Home, Highland Park, Ill.

SUGARMAN, NORMAN ALFRED, lawyer; b. Cleve., Sept. 12, 1916; s. Simon and Esther (Goldstein) S.; m. Joan Katherine Green, Oct. 20, 1940; children: Joel, Janet, Elaine, Nancy, Laurence. A.B., Case Western Res. U., 1938, J.D., 1940; D.H.L. (hon.), Duke U., 1981. Bar: Ohio 1940, D.C. 1955, U.S. Supreme Ct. 1947, U.S. Tax Ct. 1949. Atty. Office of Chief Counsel, Bur. Internal Revenue, 1940-43, 45-49, spl. asst. to chief counsel, 1949-51, asst. head mgmt. staff, 1951-52, asst. commrs., supervising tech. tax work, 1952-54; partner law firm Baker & Hostetler, Washington; with offices in Baker & Hostetler, Cleve. and Columbus, Ohio, Orlando, Fla. and Denver, 1954-86; lectr. law, law sch. George Washington U., 1950-52, U. Miami, 1976-79; lectr. law insts. and tax forums. Editor: Fed. Bar Jour, 1950-52; co-author: Tax Exempt Charitable Organizations 2d edit., 1983; Contbr. to various legal and tax publs. Spl. counsel on community found. matters Council on Founds., Inc.; gen. counsel Jewish Community Fedn. Cleve., 1971-75, mem. endowment fund com.; chmn. tax policy affecting philanthropy com., mem. bd. dirs. Council Jewish Fedns., N.Y.C.; Trustee Dyke Coll., 1966-72, 75-76, Case Western Res. U., 1977-86 , Endowment Fund United Jewish Appeal of Greater Washington. Served with F.A. AUS, 1943-45, France and Germany. Mem. ABA (mem. tax sect. com. on exempt orgns., spl. com. on simplification, planning com.), Cleve. Bar Assn., Bar Assn. D.C., Washington Estate Planning Council, Tax Club Cleve. (pres. 1967). Home: Washington D.C. Died Feb. 18, 1986, buried Washington.

SULLIVAN, JOSEPH TIMOTHY PATRICK, lawyer; b. N.Y.C., Nov. 17, 1895; s. Timothy Patrick and Hannah (McCarthy) S.; m. Grace Darby, Jan. 25, 1933 (dec. 1940); children: Sally Sullivan Fox, Maureen Sullivan Rollins, Timothy Patrick. PhB, Yale U., 1916; LLB, Fordham U., 1924. Bar: N.Y. 1925. Pvt. practice N.Y.C., from 1925; pres. Sullivan Enterprises, Inc., N.Y.C., from 1950; foreman emeritus 2d Panel Sheriff's Jury, N.Y. County; mem. com. on character and fitness N.Y. State Supreme Ct., 1st dept. ; co-founder Just One Break, Inc. Del. Dem. Nat. Conv., 1952, 56, 60. Mem. ABA, N.Y. State Bar Assn., Assn. of Bar of City of N.Y., Am. Irish Hist. Soc. (pres. gen. emeritus), Yale Club, Brook Club (N.Y.C.), California Club (L.A.), Knight of Malta. Home: Manhattan N.Y. Died Feb. 5, 1989.

SULLIVAN, LEONOR KRETZER, congressman; b. St. Louis; d. Frederick William and Nora (Jostrand) Kretzer; m. John Berchmans Sullivan, Dec. 27, 1941 (dec. Jan. 1951). Student, Washington U., St. Louis; LLD, Lindenwood Coll., U. Mo., St. Louis, St. Louis U., Rockhurst Coll., Georgetown U. Former tchr. and dir. St. Louis Comptometer Sch.; adminstrv. aide Office of Rep. Sullivan, Washington, 1942-51, Rep. Irving, 1951-52; mem. 83d-94th Congresses from 3d dist. Mo., chmn. mcht. marine and fisheries com., mem. baking and currency com. Mem. LWV, Am. Legion Aux. Democrat. Died Sept. 1, 1988.

SULLIVAN, MATTHEW GERARD, clergyman, educator; b. N.Y.C., May 28, 1911; s. Matthew and Nellie (Harrington) S. AB, Boston Coll., 1933, AM, 1934; postgrad., Fordham U., 1935-37; STL, Woodstock Coll., 1941. Joined S.J., 1927; ordained priest Roman Cath. Ch., 1940. Tchr. classics Fordham Prep. Sch., 1934-37; asst. prof. Loyola Coll., Balt., 1942-44, prof. psychology, 1944-48; dir. VA Guidance Ctr., 1945-49, dean, 1947-50; dean, acad. v.p. St. Joseph's Coll., 1950-87. Chmn. Sect. Higher Edn., State of Md., 1949-50. Mem. Assn. Am. Colls., Jesuit Ednl. Assn., Nat. Cath. Edn. Assn., Ea. Assn. Coll. Deans and ADvisers of Men (v.p.), Mid. States Assn. Colls. and Secondary Schs., Pa. Assn. Colls. and Univs. Died Nov. 2, 1987.

SULZBERGER, IPHIGENE OCHS, publishing company executive; b. Cin., Sept. 19, 1892; d. Adolph S. and Effie (Wise) Ochs; m. Arthur Hays Sulzberger, Nov. 17, 1917; children: Marian Effie (Mrs. Orvil E. Dryfoos), Ruth Rachel (Mrs. Ben Hale Golden), Judith Peixotto (Mrs. Richard Cohen), Arthur Ochs. AB, Barnard Coll., 1914; LLD, U. Chattanooga, 1944, Columbia U., 1951. Dir. spl. activities Times Printing Co., Chattanooga, from 1914, N.Y. Times, N.Y. Times Co., from 1917. Trustee Barnard Coll., U. Chattanooga, Assn. on Am. Indian Affairs; mem. bd. govs. Hebrew Union Coll.; v.p., bd. dirs. Girl Scout Coun. Greater N.Y., Inc.; chmn. bd. Park Assn. N.Y.C., Inc., from 1951. Mem. Barnard Coll. Club, Women's Univ. Club, Cosmopolitan Club. Home: New York N.Y. †

SUMAN, JOHN ROBERT, oil executive; b. Daleville, Ind., Apr. 9, 1890; s. George O. and Nora (Way) S.; m. Beatrice Mary Mowers, Dec. 16, 1912; children: John Robert Jr., Richard Harlan. Student, U. So. Calif., 1908-10; BS, U. Calif., 1912; DEng (hon.), S.D. Sch. Mines, 1941. Asst. assayer, surveyor Yellow Aster Mining & Milling Co., 1911; asst. geologist Rio Bravo Oil Co., 1912-13, chief engr., 1913-17, asst. to v.p., gen. mgr., 1919-25, v.p., gen. mgr., 1925-27; tech. supt. Roxana Petroleum Corp., Tex. and La., 1917-19; asst. mgr. East Coast Oil Co. subs. So. Pacific, 1922, mgr., 1923; gen. mgr. Tex. ops. Associated Oil Co. Calif., 1923-26; bd. dirs. Humble Oil & Refining Co., 1927-33, v.p. in charge prodn., bd. dirs., 1933-45; v.p., mem. exec. com., bd. dirs. Standard Oil Co., N.J., 1945-55; cons. Schlumberger, Inc. Author: Petroleum Production Methods. Mem. bd. govs. advisors Rice U.; bd. dirs., mem. exec. com. Jr. Achievement, Inc.; bd. dirs. Houston Symphony Soc., Tex. Delta Upsilon Found. Recipient John Fritz medal, 1958, Howard Coonley medal Am. Standard Assn., 1958; decorated Legion of Honor medal (France). Mem. Am. Assn. Petroleum Geologists, AIME (past pres., Anthony F. Lucas medalist 1943), Tex. Mid-Continent Oil and Gass Assn. (bd. dirs., hon. bd. dirs.), Am. Petroleum Inst. (hon. bd. dirs.), Ind. Petroleum Assn. Am., Ducks Unltd. (hon. trustee), Houston Geol. Soc., Houston Country Club, Houston Club, Ramada Club, 29 Club, University Club. Home: Houston Tex. †

SUMMERS, HOLLIS, writer, educator; b. Eminence, Ky., June 21, 1916; s. Hollis S. and Hazel (Holmes) S.; m. Laura Clarke, June 30, 1943; children—Hollis III, David Clarke. A.B., Georgetown Coll., 1937, Litt.D., 1965; M.A., Middlebury Coll., 1943; Ph.D., State U. Iowa, 1949. Instr. writing Georgetown (Ky.) Coll., 1944-49, U. Ky., Lexington, 1940-59, Ohio U., Athens, 1959-87; mem. staff Writers Confs., Bread Loaf, Vt., Antioch, Ohio, Morehead, Ky., Grinnel, Iowa, others; adviser Conf. on Writers in Am., Ford Found., 1958; lectr. arts program Assn. Am. Colls., 1958-63; Danforth lectr., 1963-66, 71; Fulbright lectr. U. Canterbury, Christchurch, N.Z., 1978; mem. Ohio Council for Humanities. Author: novels City Limit, 1948, Brighten the Corner, 1952, The Weather of February, 1957, The Day After Sunday, 1968, The Garden, 1972, (with James Rourke) Teach You A Lesson, 1955; poetry The Walks Near Athens, 1959, Someone Else, 1962, Seven Occasions, 1965, The Peddler and Other Domestic Matters, 1967 (Ohloana Poetry award 1968), Sit Opposite Each Other, 1970, Start from Home, 1972; short stories How They Chose the Dead, 1973, Standing Room, 1984; poetry, Occupant Please Forward, 1976; Editor: Kentucky Story, 1954, (with Edgar Whan) Literature: An Introduction, 1960, Discussions of the Short Story, 1963; poetry Dinosaurs, 1977, After the Twelve Days, 1987, After the Twelve Days, 1988, Other Concerns and Brother Clark, 1989. Named Distinguished Prof. of Year U. Ky. Coll. Arts and Scis., 1959, Distinguished Prof. Ohio U., 1964; recipient Poetry award Sat. Rev., 1959; Ohio Arts Council award 1976; Nat. Endowment for Arts fellow, 1974; grantee, 1975. Home: Athens Ohio. Died Nov. 14, 1987; buried Millersburg Cemetery, Ky.

SUMMERSELL, CHARLES GRAYSON, history educator; b. Mobile, Ala., Feb. 25, 1908; s. Charles Fishweek and Sallie Rebecca (Grayson) S.; m. Frances Sharpley, Nov. 10, 1934. A.B., U. Ala., 1929, A.M., 1930; Ph.D., Vanderbilt U., 1940. Instr. history U. Ala., 1935-40, asst. prof., 1940-46, assoc. prof., 1946-47, prof. history, 1947-78, head dept., 1954-71, retired, 1978; disting. fellow Ctr. for Study of So. History and Culture, U. Ala., from 1978; radio commentator, Tuscaloosa and Selma, Ala., 1941-43. Author: Historical Foundations of Mobile, 1949, Mobile History of a Seaport Town, 1949, Alabama History for Schools, 1957, rev. edit., 1961, 70, 75, 82, 85, Alabama Past and Future, (with Howard W. Odum and G. H. Yeuell), 1941, rev. edit. (with G. H. Yeuell & W. R. Higgs), 1950, (with Frances C. Roberts) Exploring Alabama, 1957, rev. edit., 1961, The Cruise of CSS Sumter, 1965, Alabama History Filmstrips, 1961, (with Rembert Patrick and Frances S. Summersell) Florida History Filmstrips, (with W.T. Chambers and Frances S. Summersell) Texas History Flimstrips, 1965, Ohio History Filmstrips, 1966, (with Andrew Rolle and Frances S. Summersell) California History Filmstrips, 1967, (with Robert Sutton and Frances S. Summersell) Illinois History Filmstrips, 1971; CSS Alabama Builder, Captain and Plans, 1985; editor; The Journal of George Townley Fullam, Boarding Officer of the Confederate Sea Raider Alabama, 1973, CSS Alabama; Builder, Captain and Plans, 1985 (History Book Club Selection 1986); editor; author introduction: Colonial Mobile (by Peter J. Hamilton), 1976; mem. editorial adv. bd. American Neptune, 1946-83, The Ala. Rev, 1964-71; contbr. articles and revs. to encys. and profl. jours. Mem. Ala. Hist. Commn., 1966-87, Ala. State Records Commn., Ala. Bicentennial Commn., 1971-72, Tannehill Furnace and Foundry Commn., 1969-87 (chmn. 1980-82); mem. Tuscaloosa Heritage Commn. (formerly County Preservation Authority), 1973-83, chmn., 1979-80. Served from lt. (j.g.) to lt. comdr. USNR, 1942-46, PTO; comdr. 1954; officer charge Naval Intelligence Sch. 1951-53, Norfolk, Va.; mem. steering com. organized Tuscaloosa Unit of Organized Res. Navy 1947; officer in charge 1955. Recipient Letter of Commendation USNR, 1945, Outstanding Tchr. award U. Ala. Nat. Alumni, 1978, Ramsey award Ala. Assn. Historians, 1981, Pritchett award Tuscaloosa County Heritage Commn., 1982. Mem. Orgn. Am. Historians, English Speaking Union, So. Hist. Assn., Am. Hist. Assn., Ala. Hist. Assn. (pres. 1965-56, emeritus 1982), U.S. Naval Inst., Naval Hist. Found., S.A.R. (pres. Ala. Soc. 1957-58), Am. Assn. State and Local History (Southeastern area chmn. regional awards com.), Newcomen Soc. N.Am., Soc. Nautical Research (London, Eng.), Hakluyt Soc. (London), Phi Beta Kappa (pres. Ala. chpt. 1953-54), Phi Alpha Theta. Democrat. Clubs: University, Tuscaloosa Country; Army-Navy (Washington). Home: Tsucaloosa Ala. Died Oct. 9, 1987; buried Oak Hill Cemetery, Birmingham, Ala.

SUSSKIND, DAVID HOWARD, television, motion picture and theatre producer; b. N.Y.C., Dec. 19, 1920; s. Benjamin and Frances (Lear) S.; m. Phyllis Briskin, Aug. 23, 1939; children: Pamela, Diana, Andrew; m. Joyce Davidson, Apr. 22, 1966; 1 dau., Samantha. B.S., Harvard U., 1942. With publicity dept. Warner Bros., also Universal Picture Corp., 1946-48; talent agt. Century Artists also, Music Corp. Am., 1949-52; co-owner, pres. TV, theatre and motion picture prodns. Talent Assos., Ltd., N.Y.C.; (merged with Time-Life Films, Inc. 1977), 1952-87. Producer: Broadway shows A Very Special Baby, 1956, A Handful of Fire, 1958, Rashomon, 1959, Kelly, 1965, All in Good Time, 1965, Brief Lives, 1968; motion pictures Edge of the City, 1957, Raisin in the Sun, 1961, Requiem for a Heavyweight, 1962, All the Way Home, 1963, Lovers and Other Strangers, 1969, Straw Dogs, 1971, The Pursuit of Happiness, 1971, Alice Doesn't Live Here Anymore, 1975, All Creatures Great and Small, 1974, All Things Bright and Beautiful, 1979, Buffalo Bill and the Indians, 1976, Loving Couples, 1980, Fort Apache, The Bronx, 1981; moderator: TV discussion program Open End, 1958-67, The David Susskind Show, 1967-87 (numerous Emmy awards); TV producer: Kaiser Aluminum Hour, 1956-57, Rexall TV Specials, 1957-60, Oldsmobile Music Theatre, 1959, Play of the Week, 1959-60, Art Carney shows, 1959-61, Westclox-General Mills, 1959-60, Breck Golden Theater, 1961-62, Festival of the Performing Arts, 1962-63, Esso Repertory Theatre, 1964-65, Dupont Shows, 1957-64, Kraft Theatre, 1957-58, Armstrong Circle Theatre, 1954-58, 58-63, Philco-Goodyear Playhouse, 1948-52, Justice, 1954-56, Family Classics, 1960-61, The Witness, 1960-61, East Side, West Side, 1963-64, Get Smart, 1965-70, He & She, 1967-68, N.Y.P.D., 1967-69 others; TV discussion program The Price, 1971 (Hallmark Hall of Fame); The Moon and Sixpence, 1959, The Power and the Glory, 1961, Way Out, 1961, Hedda Gabler, 1963, Mr. Broadway, 1964, Death of a Salesman, 1966, Dial M for Murder, 1967, Diary of Anne Frank, 1967, Mark Twain Tonight, 1967, The Crucible, 1967, Johnny Belinda, 1967, The Human Voice, 1967, A Case of Libel, 1968, Of Mice and Men, 1968, From Chekhov with Love, 1968, The Choice, 1969, Look Homeward Angel, 1972, Straw Dogs, 1972, All the Way Home, 1972, If You Give a Dance, You Gotta Pay the Band, 1972, Harvey, 1972, The Shenyang Acrobatic Troupe Special, 1973, The Glass Menagerie, 1973, The Magic Show, 1975, A Moon for the Misbegotten, 1975, Caesar and Cleopatra, 1976, Eleanor and Franklin, 1976 (12 Emmy awards), Truman at Potsdam, 1976, Harry S. Truman: Plain Speaking, 1976, Richard Rodgers: The Sound of His Music, 1976, Eleanor and Franklin: The White House Years (TV Critics Circle award for best drama of year), 1977 (Emmy awards), Johnny We Hardly Knew Ye, 1977, The TV Critics Circle Awards Show, 1977, The War Between the Tates, 1977, Goldenrod, 1977, World of Darkness, 1977, Breaking Up, 1977, Tell Me My Name, 1977, Norman Conquests, 1978, Blind Ambition, 1979, Mr. Lincoln, 1981, The Bunker, 1981, The Wall, 1982, Casey Stengle, 1980, Dear Liar, 1980-81, Ian McKellum: Acting Shakespeare, 1981, JFK: A One-Man Show, 1984, Winston Churchill, 1986, Ike, 1986, Lyndon Johnson, 1987, I Would Be Called John: Pope John XXII, 1987; also TV series pilot for Alice, 1976, On Our Own, 1977; (Recipient Peabody TV award, Sylvania TV awards, Robert Sherwood award 1957, Newspaper Guild awards, Christopher awards). Served to lt. (s.g.) USNR, 1942-46. Home: New York N.Y. Died Feb. 22, 1987.

SUSSMAN, JERRY, resort hotel operator; b. N.Y.C., Mar. 20, 1922; s. Louis J. and Bessie (Levinson) S.; m. Esther Waldman, Mar. 20, 1946; children—Kenneth, Marc, Lester, David. B.B.A., Coll. City N.Y., 1942. Asst. mgr. Tamarack Lodge, Greenfield Park, N.Y., 1936-42; gen. mgr. Ritz Plaza Hotel, Miami Beach, Fla., 1946-49, Sorrento Hotel, 1949-52; mng. partner Johnina Hotel, Miami Beach, 1952-57, Crown Hotel, Miami Beach, 1957-59; exec. dir. Carillon Hotel, Miami Beach, 1959-74, Holiday Inn at Calder, 1974-75; partner, exec. dir. R.S.M. Mgmt. Corp., 1974-86; adv. bd. Jefferson

Nat. Bank, Miami Beach, 1975-80; partner Howard Johnson Motor Lodges, Pompano Beach, St. Petersburg Beach, Treasure Island and Hollywood Beach, Fla., Gateway Inn, Archway Inn, Orlando, Fla., Holiday Inns, Coral Gables, Coral Springs, Fla.; mem. Miami Beach Planning Commn., 1968-72; chmn. Gov. Fla.'s Tourism adv. com., 1972-76. Bd. dirs. United Fund Dade County. Served to 1st lt. AUS, 1942-46. Elected to Hotel Hall of Fame, 1968. Mem. Miami Beach C. of C. (pres. 1968-70), South Fla. Hotel and Motel Assn. (pres. 1971-75), Beta Gamma Sigma., B'nai B'rith. Jewish religion (v.p. temple 1949-59; v.p. United Synagogue Am. 1969-73). Home: Miami Beach Fla. Died Mar. 9, 1986.

SUTHERLAND, DONALD WAYNE, historian, educator; b. Sioux Falls, S.D., Jan. 24, 1931; s. Donald Wayne and Kathleen Gertrude (Bickert) S.; m. Janet Meager, July 27, 1957; m. Judith Lynne Cleveland, Dec. 17, 1961; children—Anne, Jean, Kathleen, Ian James. B.A., Swarthmore Coll., 1953; D.Phil., Oxford U., Eng., 1957. Instr. dept. history U. Iowa, Iowa City, 1958-60; asst. prof. U. Iowa, 1960-64, assoc. prof., 1964-67, prof., 1967-86, adj. prof. law, 1981-86, Carver prof. history and law, 1985-86; vis. prof. N.E. Normal U., Changchun, China, 1985. Author: Quo Warranto Proceedings in the Reign of Edward I, 1278-1294, 1963, The Assize of Novel Disseisin, 1973; editor: The Eyre of Northamptonshire 3-4 Edward III, a.d. 1329-1330, 1983. Served with AUS, 1956-58. Research fellow Am. Council Learned Socs., 1964-65, Social Sci. Research Council, 1964-65, Nat. Endowment for Humanities, 1971-72, Guggenheim Found., 1973-74, Nat. Humanities Ctr., 1985-86. Fellow Medieval Acad. Am.; mem. Royal Hist. Soc., Conf. on Brit. Studies, Am. Soc. for Legal History, Midwest Medieval History Conf., Selden Soc. Lutheran. Home: Iowa City Iowa. Died Sept. 9, 1986.

SUTLEY, MELVIN LOCKETT, hospital administrator; b. Center, Colo., Mar. 13, 1892; s. Myron M. and Annie Lee (Chrisman) S.; m. Margaret Hutchinson, July 1, 1917 (dec. July 1947). BA, U. Colo., 1913, LLB, 1917. Bar: Colo. 1917. Practice law 1917-19; instr. U. Hokkaido, Japan, 1919-22; supt. St. Luke's Internat. Hosp., Tokyo, 1922-25; asst. supt. Pa. Hosp., Phila., 1926-27, Delaware County Hosp., Drexel Hill, Pa., 1927-41; adminstr. Wills Eye Hosp., Phila., 1941-62; pres. Hosp. Purchasing Svc. Pa., 1952-62. Organized project to study eye conditions in India, 1965. Fellow Am. Coll. Hosp. Adminstrs. (pres. 1960-61); mem. Am. Hosp. Assn., Pa. Hosp. Assn. (pres. 1935-36), Phila. Regional Writers Conf. (dir. from 1960), Masons (33 deg.). Methodist. Home: Philadelphia Pa.†

SUTPHIN, SAMUEL REID, paper company executive; b. Indpls., Dec. 28, 1911; s. Samuel Brady and Agatha (Reid) S.; m. Lisa Polk Spilman, Oct. 30, 1948; children: Agatha Reid, Lisa (dec.), Samuel Brady II. A.B., Yale U., 1934; student, Inst. Paper Chemistry, Appleton, Wis., 1934-36; LL.D. (hon.), Franklin Coll., Ind. State U. With Kimberly-Clark, 1936-38; with Beveridge Paper Co., Indpls., 1938-69; exec. v.p. Beveridge Paper Co., 1952-58, chmn., 1958-69; chmn., dir. Tecnifax Corp., 1964-68, Plastic Coating Corp., Holyoke, Mass., 1958-68; chmn. adv. bd. Plastic Coating Corp., 1968-69; v.p. Scott Paper Co., 1965-69, dir., 1965-82; pres. Madeira Enterprises, 1971-88; former dir. Norfolk and Western Ry. Co., P.R. Mallory & Co., Inland Container Corp., Crane Co., Ind. Bell, Ind. Nat. Bank of Indpls., Ind. Nat. Corp., Medusa Corp., Norfolk So. Corp. Trustee Indpls. Mus. Art; trustee emeritus Nat. Trust Hist. Preservation; chmn. Ind. State Scholarship Commn., 1965-66, Kent Sch., 1969-72; bd. dirs. Nat. Audubon Soc., 1976-82, Royal Oak Found., 1979-88. Served to comdr. USNR, 1941-46. Decorated Legion of Merit with Combat V. Republican. Episcopalian. Clubs: Links (N.Y.C.); Nantucket (Mass.) Yacht; Univ., Woodstock (Indpls.), Columbia (Indpls.); Rolling Rock (Ligonier, Pa.). Home: Zionsville Ill. Died May 24, 1988.

SUTTON, OTTIS ALTON, oil executive; b. Dubberly, La., Oct. 27, 1906; s. Henry Otis and Nettie (Warren) S.; m. Neva Anderson, Oct. 1, 1954; children: Dianne, Mike. Student, Centenary Coll., 1926-29. Various exec. positions Air Reduction Co., 1930-39; founder The O.A. Sutton Corp., Inc., Wichita, Kans., 1940, Alloys Foundry, Inc., 1943-47; ptnr. Sumac Oil & Gas Co.; oil operator under name O.A. Sutto; chmn. bd. Kans. State Bank, Wichita, 1957-61; owner Bar S Ranch, Eureka, Kans., Carter-Raymond Mines, Gunnison, Colo., Sutton Pl., Wichita; pres., chmn. bd. Oasis Petroleum, Inc., Wichita, 1969-73, Atlantic Bldg. Corp., Boynton Beach, Fla., 1973-87; chmn. bd. 1st Bank & Trust, Boynton Beach, 1968-81, 1st Bank, Delray Beach, Fla., 1973-87, 1st Bank West, Lake Worth, Fla., 1973-87, 1st Bank & Trust Palm Beach County, Delray Beach; owner O.A. Sutton Investments, Delray Beach, 1981-87. Mem. bd. govs. Am. Royal; pres., bd. dirs. Wichita Community Chest and United Fund. Mem. NAM (bd. dirs.), Wichita C. of C. (past bd. dirs.), Masons, Shriners, Wichita Country Club, Wichita Club, Petroleum Club, Pine Tree Golf Club, La Coquille Club, N.Y. Yacht Club, Bob'O'Link Golf Club, Boynton Beach Club, Alpha Kappa Psi. Methodist. Home: Delray Beach Fla. Died Nov. 7, 1987; interred Old Mission Mausoleum, Wichita.

SVARTZ, NANNA CHARLOTTA, physician; b. Vasteras, Sweden, July 25, 1890; d. Johan Anshelm Ferdinand and Anna Charlotta (Moxen) Svartz; m. Nils Magnus Malmberg, Oct. 12, 1918; 1 dau., Gunvor. M.D., Karolinska Inst., Stockholm, 1927; D.Sc. (hon.), Rockford (Ill.) Coll., 1948; M.D. (hon.), Turku U., Finlans, 1970. Asst. physician 1st med. dept. U. Hosp. Serafimerlasarettet, Stockholm, 1918-28, dir. outpatient dept., 1929-30, dir. cen. labs., 1931-34; head physician St. Erik Hosp., Stockholm, 1934-37; prof. internal medicine Karolinska Inst., 1937-57; mem. bd. Univ. Hosp. Karolinska Sjukhuset, 1938-43; mem. sci. sect Royal Swedish Med. Bd., 1937-53; dir. King Gustav V Rsch. Inst., 1948-60; chmn. Health Orgn. Stockholm Students, 1960-66. Contbr. numerous papers on ulcerative colitis, rheumatic diseases, especially isolation rheumatoid factor, chemotherapy, asulfidine. Pres. 3d Internat. Congress Internat. Medicine, Stockholm, 1954; mem. directing bd. King Gustav V 80th Birthday Found., from 1938, v.p. from 1953; mem. Swedish delegation Centennial Jubilee Settlement Swedes in Middle West, 1948. Named knight comdr. 1st class Order Pole Star, also Finnish Order White Rose, Illis quorum meruere labores medal, 12 size; recipient City of Hope award, 1962, San Remo prize, 1963, medal U. Liege (Belgium), 1963, several others. Fellow Royal Coll. Physicians (London); mem. Internat. Soc. Internat. Medicine (pres. 1952-62, hon. pres. 1956; hon. mem. Swiss, Italian, Argentinian, Belgian acads. medicine; corr. mem. French Acad. Medicine; hon. mem. other Swedish and fgn. med. socs. Home: Stockholm Sweden. †

SWAIN, JAMES OBED, educator; b. Greenfield, Ind., Dec. 31, 1896; s. Ashbell Willard and Laetitia (Lambert) S.; m. Nancy Jane Cox, June 19, 1923; children: James Maurice, Juan Robert. AB, Ind. U., 1921, AM, 1923; PhD, U. Ill., 1932; postgrad., U. Madrid, summer 1933, U. Chile, 1951-52. Mem. faculty Mich. State Coll., 1931-37; asst. prof. modern fgn. langs., then prof. U. Tenn., Knoxville, 1937-64; chmn. dept. U. Tenn., 1937-58; vis. prof. modern Fgn. langs. U. Ky., 1964-66, Spanish Appalachian State Tchrs. Coll., summer 1966, French Maryville (Tenn.) Coll., 1966, Romance langs. Roanoke (Va.) Coll., 1967, Lee Coll., Cleve., Tenn.; guest dir. summer langs. sch. Western Colo. Coll., 1937; guest lectr. Am. lit. U.Chile, summer 1952, U. Madrid, summer, 1958. Author: Rumbo a Mexico, 1942, Ruedo Antillano, 1946; joint author: Funcciòn y Alcance de las Escuelas de Temporada, 1955, Juan Marin--Chilean, the Man and His Writings, 19711 assoc. editor: Hispania, 1936-42; asst. bus. mgr.: Modern Lang. Jour., 1938-51. With C.E. U.S. Army, 1918-19. Mem. MLA Am. (sect. officer various times), Cen. So. States Modern Lang. Tchrs. Spanish (mem. exec. com. 1949-52), Am. Assn. Tchrs. French, Sigma Delta Pi (exec. sec. 1947-62, nat. hon. pres. 1979-80, sr. hon. pres. from 1980). Methodist (deacon). Home: Knoxville Tenn. Died Feb. 10, 1986; buried Knoxville, Tenn.

SWAIN, ROBERT CUTHBERTSON, chemical company executive; b. Palo Alto, Calif., Sept. 14, 1907; s. Robert Eckles and Harriet King (Cuthbertson) S.; m. Frances Grace Johnson, Aug. 27, 1929 (dec.); children: Mary Frances Swain Cole, Robert, Nancy (dec.). AB, Stanford U., 1928; student, U. Heidelberg, Germany, 1928, U. Berlin, 1928-32. Rsch. chemist Am. Cyanamid Co., 1934-42, dir. rsch. div. Stamford (Conn.) Labs., 1942-45, rsch. dir., 1945-46, v.p. charge rsch. and devel., 1946-59, v.p. internat. relations, 1959-65, exec. v.p., 1965-73, ret., also bd. dirs.; pres. Cyanamid Internat. Corp., 1959-65; bd. dirs. Perkin-Elmer Corp., Norwalk, Conn.; cons. OSRD, 1943-45; mem. U.S. del., mem. Coun. Internat. Congress Pure and Applied Chemistry, London, 1947; mem. panel on nations' potential for basic rsch. in chemistry, NRC, 1947-50; chmn. chem. warfare com. Nat. Mil. Bd. R & D, 1950-51. Past bd. dirs. Herbert Hoover Found., N.Y.C.; past bd. overseers Hoover Instn. on War, Revolution and Peace, Stanford, Calif. Recipient Castner Meml. medal Eng., 1953, James Moorhead Turner medal, 1958for contbns. to chemistry; NRC fellow, 1932-34, Alexander von Humboldt fellow, 1928-32. Mem. Am. Chem. Soc. (chmn. Western Conn. sect. 1945-46, chmn. new activities com. 1946-47), Internat. Union Chemistry (adv. com. 1947-49), Soc. Chem. Industry (chmn. 1951-52), Am. Inst. Chemists, Mfg. Chemists Assn., Chemists Club (N.Y.C.), Greenwich (Conn.) Country Club, Riverside (Conn.) Yacht Club, Bohemian Club (San Francisco), Phi Lamba Upsilon, Alpha Chi Sigma, Sigma Nu., Sigma Xi. Home: Riverside Conn. Died Feb. 12, 1989.

SWANSON, W(ILLIAM) F(REDIN), university dean; b. Arroyo, Pa., Dec. 19, 1892; s. Joseph and Anna Elizabeth (Lundberg) S.; m. Anna Ida Moore, Aug. 24, 1917; children: Ruth Bernice (Mrs. Reginald George Farrar), William Fredin. BS, Pa. State U., 1915; DDS, U. Pitts., 1920, MS, 1930. Pvt. practice Phila., 1920-23; asst. prof. bacteriology and histology U. Pitts., 1923-37, assoc. prof., 1937-45, prof., from 1945, assoc. dean, 1947-53, acting dean, 1953, dean, from 1954; chief dental svcs., staff Psychiat. Hosp., Falk Clinic; cons. Oakland VA Hosp., Leech Farm VA Hosp. Author: Regeneration of Tissue in Frogs, 1942, Dens in Dente, 1947; editor Odontological Bull., 1925-42; contbr. articles to profl. jours. Mem. Mayor's Health Coun., 13 Citizens' Com.; bd. mgrs. Oakland YMCA, pres., 1952; mem. Pitts. com. Am. Heart Assn. Mem. ADA, AAAS, Am. Coll. Dentists (councilor from 1944), Internat. Assn. Dental Rsch., Odontological Soc. Western Pa. (pres. 1938, bd. dirs.), Pa. Dental Soc., Pitts. Acad. Dentists, Nat. Sci. Orgn., Am. Assn. Dental Schs.l, Soc. Am. Bacteriologists, Federacion Dentaire Internacionale, Druids, Masons (32 degree), University Club, Rotary, Sigma Xi, Phi Sigma, Omicron Kappa Upsilon, Omicron Delta Kappa, Psi Omega (nat. pres. 1931), Delta Tau Delta. Home: Pittsburgh Pa. †

SWARTWOUT, DENTON KENYON, manufacturing executive; b. Saginaw, Mich., July 5, 1892; s. Denton K. and Gertrude (Final) S.; m. Frances Willard Preyer, Aug. 23, 1916; children: Denton Kenyon III, Charles Julius. BSME, Cast Inst. Tech., 1915. With The Swartwout Co., Cleve., 1915-60, pres., 1935-56, chmn. bd., 1957-60; bd. dirs. Swartwout Fabricators, Inc., Kokomo, Ind. Mayor Moreland Hills Village, Ohio, 1948-53; trustee, treas. Am. Youth Found., St. Louis; trustee Coun. Profit Sharing Industries, from 1949. Mem. Citizens League Cleve., Sigma Xi, Tau Beta Pi, Sigma Alpha Epsilon. Congregationalist. Home: Chagrin Falls Ohio. †

SWEATT, HAROLD W., corporate executive; b. Mpls., Nov. 9, 1891; s. William R. and Jessie (Wilson) S.; m. Mary Buchanan, Apr. 17, 1915. BA, U. Minn., 1913. With Minneapolis-Honeywell Regulator Co., as v.p. and gen. mgr., pres., 1934-53, chmn. bd., 1953, chmn. fin. com., 1961; then hon. chmn. bd. Honeywell, Inc.; bd. dirs. Northwestern Nat. Bank and Trust Co., N.W. Banccorp., Gen. Mills, Inc., Minn. & Ont. Paper Co. Co-chmn. Can. Am. Com. Mem. Minneapolis, Woodhill, Links (N.Y.C.), Chicago, Minnikahda, Everglades, Seminole, Bath and Tennis (Palm Beach), Gulf Stream Golf (Delray Beach) clubs. Home: Palm Beach Fla. †

SWEENEY, JAMES JOHNSON, writer, museum director; b. Bklyn., May 30, 1900; s. Patrick M. and Mary (Johnson) S.; m. Laura Harden, May 17, 1927; children: Ann Sweeney Baxter, Sean, Siadhal, Tadhg, Ciannait Sweeney Tait. AB, Georgetown U., 1922, LHD, 1963; postgrad., Jesus Coll., Cambridge, Eng., 1922-24, U. Sorbonne, Paris, 1925, U. Siena, Italy, 1926; DFA (hon.), Grinnell Coll., 1957, U. Mich., 1960, U. Notre Dame, 1961, U. Buffalo, 1962; ArtsD, Ripons Coll., 1960; LHD, Rollins Coll., 1960, Coll. of the Holy Cross, U. Miami, Georgetown U., 1963; LLD, Nat. U., Dublin, Ireland, 1978. N.Y. corr. Chgo. Evening Post Art World, 1931-32; dir. exbhn. 20th Century Painting and Sculpture U. Chgo., 1933-34; lectr. fine arts Inst. Fine Arts, NYU, 1935-40; vis. scholar U. Ga., 1950, 51; lectr. fine arts Harvard U., 1961; dir. exhbn. African Negro art, Mus. Modern Art, N.Y.C., 1935, dir. exhbn. of work by Joan Miro, 1941, exhbn. of sculpture and constrns. by Alexander Calder, 1943, Alfred Stieglitz exhbn., 19047, dir. dept. painting and sculpture, 1945-46; dir. Picasso exhbn. Art Gallery Toronto, 1949; dir. commentary film on Henry Moore, 1948; dir. exhbns. 12 Am. Painters, Dublin, 1963; dir. Va. Biennial Exhbn., 1950; resident scholar U. Ga., 1950-51; dir. exbhn. Sculpture by Alexander Calder, MIT, 1950-51, Masterpieces of XXth Century, Musé d'Art Moderne, Paris, Tate Gallery, London, 1952; installation U.S. Pavillon Biennale, Venice, Itraly, 1952; mem. jury Carnegie Internat., July, 1958, 76, Message on the Plastic Arts, Brussels Expn., 1958, Internat. Biennal Exhbn. of Prints, Tokyo, 1966, Rosc Exhbn., Dublin, 1967, UNESCO Prize, Venice, 1968; dir. Burlington Mag., London, 19652-61, mem. cons. com., 1961-86; dir. Alexander Calder Exhbn. Tate Gallery, London, 1962, Signals in the Sixties, Honolulu Acad. Arts, 1968; contbg. critic New Republic mag., 1952-53; art adv. com. Chase Manhattan Bank, N.Y.C., 1958-86; mem. adv. com. The Arts Ctr. Program, Columbia U., mem. adv. coun. art and archaeology; mem. curriculum adv. bd. art edn. dept. NYU. Author, co-author and/or editor: Alexander Calder, 1951; Burri, 1955, Atmosphere Miro, 1959, AFRO, 1961, Irish Illuminated Manuscripts, 1965, Vision and Image, 1968, Joan Miro, 1970, Eduardo Chillida, 1970, Pierre Soulages, 1972, Contemporaries and Predecessors, 1973; (with Paul Radin) African Folk Tales and Sculpture, 1952, rev. edit., 1965; (with José Luis Sert) Antoni Gaudi, 1960; asst. editor. Partisan Rev., 1948-63. Mem. adv. com. Bennington (Vt.) Coll.; trustee Bauhaus-Archive, Am. Acad. in Rome, 1962; mem. art com. Addison Gallery; mem. W.B. Yeats Meml. Com., Dublin; mem. Am. Revolution Bicentennial Commn., 1967-69; bd. dirs. Am. Irish Found.; mem. vis. com. on fine arts Fogg Mus., Harvard U.; hon. pres. Fedn. Internationale du Film d'Art, Paris; dir. Mus. Fine Arts, Houston, 1961-68, cons. dir., 1968-86; gallery cons. Nat. Gallery, Canberra, Australia, 1968-86; mem. art adv. com. U. Notre Dame, 1968-86; art adviser Israel Mus., Jerusalem, 1972-86; adviser on purchase Arts Coun. No. Ireland, Belfast, 1970. Decorated chevalier Legion d'Honneur, 1955; officer de l'ordre des Arts et des lettres, 1959; knight comdr. Order of Isabel lat Catolica, 1977; recipient Art in Am. award, 1963. Fellow Am. Acad. Arts and Scis., Royal Soc. Antiquaries Ireland; mem. Assn. Art Mus. Dirs., Edward MacDowell Assn. (pres. 1955-62, counselor 1964-86), Internat. Assn. Art Critics (pres. 1957-63, bd. dirs. 1963-86), Buffalo Fine Arts Inst. (hon.), Iran Am. Soc. (bd. dirs. 1964-86), Société Europeé de la Culture, Mediaeval Acad. Am. (councillor), Art Coun.

Dublin, Nat. Coun. Arts, Internat. Coun. Mus. Modern Art (hon.), Yeats Assn. Dublin (hon.), Nat. Coun. Arts, Soc. Internat. des Arts Chretiens (v.p.), Liturg. Arts Soc. (bd. dirs.), Century Club, Grolier Club, Players Club, Brook Club, River Club, Cosmos Club, Athenaeum Club, Kildare St. Club, University Club, Hibernian United Svc., Stephen's Green Club, Phi Beta Kappa. Home: New York N.Y. Died Apr. 14, 1986.

SWEENY, DONALD N., lawyer; b. Detroit, Aug. 7, 1891; s. Frank N. and Anne (Brown) S.; m. Avis M. Allen, Sept. 7, 1914; children: Donald N., Allen N. Student, U. Mich., 1909-11; LLB, Detroit Coll. Law, 1914. Bar: Mich. 1914. Clk. Peoples State Bank, Detroit, 1911; pres. First Nat. Bank Detroit, 1932; mem. law firm Kerr, Wattles & Russell, Detroit. Mem. Am., Mich., Detroit bar assns., Assn. Interstate Commerce Commn., Practitioners, Detroit Club, Grosse Pointe Club, Delta Theta Phi. Episcopalian (vestryman). Home: Grosse Pointe Park Mich. †

SWEET, DAVID EMERY, college president; b. Holyoke, Mass., July 9, 1933; s. Adrian John and Elsie King (Jocelyn) S.; m. Arleene Pachl, June 4, 1954; children: Karen Joy, Jocelyn Sue. AB, Drury coll., 1955; MA, Duke U., 1958, PhD, 1967. Instr. Ohio U., 1959-60; assoc. prof. polit. sci. Ill. State U., 1960-69; vice chancellor acad. affairs Minn. State U., St. Paul, 1969-71; founding pres. Met. State U., St. Paul, 1971-77; pres. R.I. Coll., 1977-84. Woodrow Wilson fellow, 1955-56, Commonwealth Studies fellow, 1958-59. Died Sept. 16, 1984.

SWEET, JOHN HOWARD, publisher; b. Emerson, Man., Can., Mar. 21, 1907; s. Henry Charles and Hannah (Mooney) S.; m. Lillian Flora Martin, Sept. 11, 1926; 1 son, John Allan; m. Anne Ethel Wallace, Oct. 4, 1940; children—Anthony Howard, Elizabeth Anne. Student, U. Man., 1923-26. Asst. circulation mgr. AMA, 1926-29; circulation mgr. Traffic World, 1929-37; v.p. Poor's Pub. Co., 1937-40, Dickie Raymond, Inc., 1940-42; circulation mgr. World Report, 1946-48; with U.S. News and World Report, 1948-88, circulation dir., 1948-51, exec. v.p., 1951-59, pres., 1959-81, pub., 1951-78, chmn. bd., 1973-83, chmn. emeritus, 1983-88, chief exec. officer, 1973-81. Served as lt. comdr. USNR, 1943-45. Mem. Conf. Bd. Presbyn. (trustee). Clubs: Princess Anne Country (Virginia Beach); Nat. Press (Washington), Army and Navy (Washington), Congressional Country (Washington), Metropolitan (Washington). Home: Washington D.C. Died Aug. 14, 1988.

SWIGERT, ERNEST GOODNOUGH, manufacturing executive; b. Portland, Oreg., Aug. 4, 1892; s. Charles F. and Rena (Goodnough) S.; m. Frances Turrish, Nov. 8, 1921; children: Nannie M. (Mrs. Robert C. Warren), Ernest C., Henry T., Elizabeth G. (Mrs. Richard Panzer). BS, Harvard U., 1915. With Electric Steel Foundry, Portland, from 1916, v.p., from 1927, also bd. dirs.; v.p., bd. dirs. ESCO Corp.; chmn. bd. Hyster Co., Portland. Mem. Nat. Assn. Mfrs. (pres. 1957), Arlington Club, Racquet Club, Multnomah Athletic Club, Portland Yacht Club, Tavern Club, Harvard Club. Home: Portland Oreg. †

SWINGLE, WILBUR WILLIS, zoology educator; b. Warrensburg, Mo., Jan. 11, 1891; s. Jacob and Emma Lucy Swingle; m. Emily Gerken, Nov. 2, 1916 (div.); m. Alice Sullivan, Apr. 1929; children: Stephen Grey, Philip Colin. AB, AM, U. Kans., 1916; PhD, Princeton U., 1920. Fellow in zoology U. Kans., 1916, instr., 1917-18; instr. zoology Yale U., 1920, asst. prof., 1921-26; prof., head dept. zoology State U. Iowa, 1926-29; prof. biology Princeton U., from 1929, Edwin Grant Conklin prof., 1933-56, Henry Fairfield Osborn rsch. prof., 1956-59, sr. rsch. assoc. biology, 1959-63; head sect. adrenal physiology Bur. Rsch. in Neurology and Psychiatry, N.J. Neuro-psychiat. Inst., Princeton, N.J., from 1963. Contbr. numerous articles in exptl. zoology and physiology to profl. jours. Recipient medal Endocrine Soc., 1959. Fellow N.Y. Acad. Sci.; mem. Am. Soc. Zoologists, Am. Assn. Anatomists, Am. Soc. Physiologists, Soc. Exptl. Biology and Medicine, Assn. for Study of Internal Secretion (coun. 1931-32), Am. Soc. Naturalists, Princeton Club, Sigma Xi, Sigma Alpha Epsilon, Phi Chi. Republican. Home: Princeton N.J. †

SWISHER, CHARLES F., lawyer. m. Helen Johnson, 1949; children: Nancy Swisher Thomas, Mary Swisher Ewing, Benjamin F. B.A., U. Ariz.; J.D., U. Iowa. Mem. firm Swisher & Court; gen. counsel The Rath Packing Co., Waterloo, Iowa, 1960-84; dir. The Rath Packing Co., 1969-84, chmn. bd., 1975-84; chmn. bd., dir. Waterloo Savs. Bank; gen. counsel, dir. Waterloo Industries Inc.; dir. Central United Corp., Sioux City, Iowa, Central United Life Ins. Co., Sioux City, Allbee & Sons Printing Co., Waterloo, Inland Litho Plate & Engraving Co., Waterloo; bd. dirs. Waterloo Indsl. Devel. Assn., from 1984. Home: Waterloo Iowa. Deceased.

SWYGERT, LUTHER MERRITT, judge; b. Miami County, Ind., Feb. 7, 1905; s. Irven W. and Catherine (Hoover) S.; m. Mildred Kercher, Oct. 10, 1931 (dec. Jan. 1969); m. Mrs. Gari Pancoe, July 1, 1969; children—Robert L. (dec.), Michael I. LL.B. magna cum laude, Notre Dame U., 1927; LL.D., Valparaiso Sch. Law, 1964, U. Notre Dame, 1969, Stetson U., 1982. Bar: Ind. bar. Pvt. practice 1927-31; dep. pros. atty. Lake Co., Ind., 1931-33; asst. U.S. atty.; asst. No. Dist. Ind., 1934-43, U.S. dist. judge, 1943-61, chief judge, 1954-61; judge U.S. Circuit Ct. Appeals, 1961-88, chief judge, 1970-75, sr. cir. judge, 1981. Mem. ABA, Ind. Bar Assn. Home: Chicago Ill. Died Mar. 16, 1988.

SYLLA, JAMES R., petroleum company executive; m. Virginia E. Sylla; children: John, Thomas, Mary. B.S. in Chem. Engring., Cornell U.; MBA, U. Chgo. With Chevron, 1957-87; v.p. Chevron Corp., San Francisco, 1979-87; pres. Chevron Shipping Co., 1984; pres., dir. Chevron U.S.A., Inc., San Francisco, 1984-87, mem. exec. com., 1986-87. Pres. bd. trustees Golden Gate U.; bd. govs. San Francisco Symphony; bd. trustees Marin Ednl. Found. Mem. San Francisco C. of C. Died Dec. 7, 1987. Address: for estate of J R Sylla Mrs Virginia E Sylla PO Box 864 Kentfield CA 94914.

SYMINGTON, LLOYD, lawyer; b. N.Y.C., Sept. 28, 1913; s. Charles J. and Elizabeth (Lloyd) S.; m. Nancy E. Glover, Sept. 6, 1941; children: Lloyd, Donald, Marion, Nicholas. AB cum laude, Princeton U., 1936; LLB, U. Va., 1939. Bar: D.C. 1941. With Office Gen. Counsel, WPB, 1942-46; ptnr. Fowler & symington (name now Leva, Hawes, Symington & Martin), 1946-84; sec. Fiat-Roosevelt Motors, 1966-70. Mem. chpt. Washington Cathedral, 1953-73; D.C. del. Dem. Nat. Conv., 1968; bd. dirs. Nat. Symphony Orch. Assn., pres., 1968-70; bd. govs. St. Albans Sch., 1952-72, chmn., 1955-57; trustee Potomac Sch., 1951-61. Mem. ABA, Fed., D.C. bar assns., Defenders of Wildlife (bd. dirs., gen. counsel), Order of Coif, Fed. City Club, Metropolitan Club, Phi Beta Kappa. Home: Bethesda Md. Died Nov. 18, 1984.

SYMINGTON, STUART, U.S. senator, banker; b. Amherst, Mass., June 26, 1901; s. William Stuart and Emily Haxall (Harrison) S.; m. Evelyn Wadsworth, Mar. 1, 1924 (dec.); children: Stuart, James Wadsworth; m. Ann Hemingway Watson, June 14, 1978. B.A., Yale U., 1923; student, Internat. Corr. Schs. Pres. Eastern Clay Products, 1925-27, Valley Appliances, 1927-30, Colonial Radio Co., Rochester and Buffalo, N.Y., 1930-35, Rustless Iron & Steel Co., Balt., 1935-37; pres., chmn. bd. Emerson Electric Mfg. Co., St. Louis, 1938-45; surplus property adminstr. Washington, 1945-46; asst. sec. of war for air 1946-47; sec. Air Force, 1947-50; chmn. Nat. Security Resources Bd., 1950-51; adminstr. RFC, 1951; U.S. senator from Mo. 1952-77; vice chmn., dir. 1st Am. Bankshares, Washington, 1980-88. Pres. Nat. Cathedral Assn., Washington, 1974-77. Served with U.S. Army, 1918-19. Home: New Canaan Conn. Died Dec. 14, 1988.

SYRKIN, MARIE, editor; b. Bern, Switzerland, Mar. 22, 1899; came to U.S., 1907, naturalized, 1915; s. Nachman and Batya (Osnos) S.; m. Charles Reznikoff, May 27, 1930; 1 son, David. BA, Cornell U., 1920, MA, 1922; hon. doctorate, Jewish Tchrs. Sem., 1976, Brandeis U., 1979, Hebrew Union Coll., 1981, Reconstructionist Rabbinical Coll., 1988. Tchr. English, N.Y. high schs., 1925-50; faculty dept. humanities Brandeis U., Waltham, Mass., 1950-66; prof. emeritus Brandeis U., from 1966; editor Herzl Press, N.Y.C., from 1971. Author: Your School, Your Children, 1944, Blessed Is the Match, The Story of Jewish Resistance, 1957, Nachman Syrkin: A Memoir, 1960, Golda Meir: A Biography, 1969, Gleanings: A Diary in Verse, 1979, The State of the Jews, 1980; editor: Jewish Frontier, 1950-71; editorial bd.: Midstream, from 1968; contbr. articles and essays to various publs. Mem. exec. World Zionist Movement, 1965-69; hon. pres. Labor Zionist Movement U.S., 1965-70. Recipient Woman of Year award Jewish War Vets. Women's Aux., 1964; Woman of Year award Univ. Women-U. Judaism, 1973; Lit. award; Pioneer Women-25th Anniversary Israel award, 1973; Myrtle Wreath award Hadassah, 1976; Bublick prize Hebrew U. Jerusalem, 1981; Golda Meir award, Na'amath, 1987; Histadrut Menorah award, 1987. Mem. Am. Profs. for Peace in Middle East (exec. from 1968). Home: Santa Monica Calif. Died Feb. 1, 1989; buried L.A.

SZENT-GYORGYI, ALBERT, biochemist; b. Budapest, Hungary, Sept. 16, 1893; came to U.S., 1947, naturalized, 1955; s. Nicholas and Josephine (Lenhossek) Szent-G.; 1 dau., Cornelia Szent-Gyorgyi Pollit. M.D., U. Budapest, 1917; Ph.D., Cambridge U., Eng., 1927. Prof. med. chemistry Szeged, 1931-45; prof. biochemistry U. Budapest, 1945-47; sci. dir. Nat. Found. Cancer Research Marine Biol. Labs., Woods Hole, Mass., 1947-86. Author: Oxidation, Fermentation, Vitamins, Health and Disease, 1939, Muscular Contraction, 1947, The Nature of Life, 1947, Contraction in Body and Heart Muscle, 1953, Bioenergetics, 1957, Submolecular Biology, 1960, Bioelectronics, 1968, The Crazy Ape, 1970, What Next?, 1971, The Living State, 1972, Electronic Biology and Cancer, 1976, The Living State and Cancer, 1978. Recipient Nobel prize in medicine, 1937, 55; recipient Lasker award Heart Association, 1954. Mem. Acad. Scis. Budapest (pres.), Nat. Acad. Budapest (v.p.), Nat. Acad. Scis., Council of Edn. (chmn.). Died Oct. 22, 1986.

SZERYNG, HENRYK, violinist; b. Zelazowa Wola, Poland, Sept. 22, 1918; naturalized, 1946; s. Szymon and Aline Woznicka Z.; m. Waltraud Büscher, 1984. Studied with Carl Flesch, Gabriel Bouillon, Nadia Boulanger; attended Sorbonne U., Paris; Dr. h.c., Georgetown U., Washington. Became dir. string dept. Nat. U., Mexico City. Made first concert tour in 1933, performing in Warsaw, Bucharest, Vienna, Paris; Carnegie Hall debut, 1943; recorded for RCA, Philips, CBS, Mercury, EMi, Edison, Wiener Flötenuhr, Golden Records; Grammy award; numerous concert tours. Decorated knight comdr. Order Polonia Restituta; comdr. Order Arts and Letters; Legion of Honor both France; comdr. Order Lion Finland; comdr. Order of Merit Italy; comdr. Order of Merit Rumania; comdr. Order of Merit Poland; officer Order Crown Belgium; comdr. Ordre Mérte Culturel et Artistique, France, 1966; comdr. Alfonso X el Sabio, Spain 1971; comdr. Order St. Charles, Monaco, 1985; recipient Grand prix du Disque (6); apptd. goodwill ambassador by Mexican govt., 1956; named cultural advisor to Mexican del. UNESCO and Mexican Fgn. Ministry; Silver medal City of Paris, 1963; Gold medal, 1980; Mozart medal, 1971; Gran Premio Nacional Mexico, 1979; Golden medal City of Paris, 1981, City of Jerusalem, 1983; officer Legion d'Honneur, 1984; Golden medal of Merit, Poland, 1987; Cross of Merit, 1987; recipient Arturo Toscanini Music Critics award, 1987. Home: New York N.Y. Died Mar. 3, 1988; buried Monaco.

TAFT, ROBERT STEPHEN, lawyer, educator; b. N.Y.C., Nov. 1, 1934; s. Harold A. and Mae Vivian (Gray) T.; m. Marlene Rosalie Medwin, June 22, 1958; children: Leslie Ann Taft Aiuto, Peter Stephen. B.A., Dartmouth U., 1956; LL.B., Columbia U., 1959; LL.M., N.Y. Law Sch., 1960. Bar: N.Y. 1959, Fla. 1978, D.C. 1981. Practiced in N.Y.C., 1960-87; assoc. Reid and Priest, 1960-67; ptnr. Hatfield, Brady and Taft, 1967-77, Miller, Montgomery, Sogi, Brady & Taft, 1977-81, Botein, Hays, Sklar & Herzberg, 1981-85; sr. tax ptnr. Certilman, Haft, Lebow, Balin, Buckley & Kremer, 1985-87; lectr. N.Y. U. Tax Inst., N.Y.C., 1973-87; prof. law N.Y. Law Sch., 1972-87. Author: (with Arnold S. Anderson) New York Practice-Personal Taxes, 1975, Tax Aspects of Separation and Divorce, 1984; contbr. articles to legal jours.; tax columnist: N.Y. Law Jour, 1972-87. Pres. Gt. Neck (N.Y.) Grace Ave. Sch. PTA, 1971-72; mem. adv. bd. Odyssey House, 1970-84, bd. dirs., 1976-82; trustee Practicing Law Inst. Found., 1970-87. Mem. ABA, N.Y. State Bar Assn., Nassau County Bar Assn., Soc. Am. Magicians. Home: Great Neck N.Y. Died Dec. 10, 1987, buried N.Y.

TALBERT, ANSEL EDWARD MCLAURINE, magazine editor; b. Washington, Jan. 6, 1912; s. Ansel D. and Lily (McLaurine) T.; m. Marlene Zimmer, 1951 (div. 1969). Grad., Landon Sch., Bethesda, Md., 1930; A.B., Columbia, 1934, Litt.B., 1935, M.S. (Henry Woodward Sackett fellow), 1935; spl. student, McGill U. N.Y. corr. Sci. Service, 1935-36; with N.Y. Herald Tribune, 1936-58; spl. assignment N.Y. Herald Tribune, Europe, 1939, Far East, 1940; Korean war corr., chief Tokyo bur. N.Y. Herald Tribune, 1950-51; assigned N.Y. Herald Tribune (Middle East, Japan, Korea, Alaska, Eng., France), 1951-53, N.Y. Herald Tribune (Thule, Greenland, Ice Island T-3, North Pole), 1954; assigned N.Y. Herald Tribune (operation Deep Freeze, McMurdo Sound, Antarctica, also four flights over South Pole), 1956, Soviet Union, 1956, Scandinavia, Pakistan, Iran, 1957; mil. and aviation editor N.Y. Herald Tribune (operation Deep Freeze, McMurdo Sound, Antarctica, also four flights over South Pole), 1954-58; writer nationally syndicated column Def. and Aviation; exec. editor publs., v.p. Flight Safety Found., 1959-67; mng. editor Air Transport World mag., 1967-70, exec. editor, from 1970; sr. editor Travel Agt. mag., Travel Agt. Internat., Interline Reporter.; Panelist CBS-TV show Longines Chronoscope, 1952-54; spl. broadcasts aerospace, mil. devels. WQXR, 1960-61, WRUL-Worldwide Broadcasting System, 1962-63; mem. exec. com. Editorial Opinion Research, 1970-87. Author: Famous Airports of the World, 1953, Newsbreak, 1977; Co-author: How I Got That Story, 1967, The Grand Original - A Biography of Randolph Churchill, 1971; Mem. editorial bd.: Mil. Pub. Inst, 1958-65. Trustee, past mem. adv. com. Harmon Internat. Aviation Trophies; past mem. Collier Trophy Com. Served from pvt. to lt. col. AUS, 1941-46; chief ultra intelligence for 8th Air Force Eng. Decorated chevalier Legion of Honor, France; Royal Yugoslav War Cross of St. Andrew; Medal of Merit of Santos Dumont Brazil; recipient James J.; Strebig trophy for outstanding writing on aviation, 1957; Gold medal Adventures Club, 1959; TWA Nat. award for outstanding mag. writing on bus. subjects, 1970. Mem. Aviation Space Writers Assn. (past pres.), Am. Polar Soc., Arctic Inst. N. Am., Elbeetian Legion, S.A.R., Am. Legion (past post comdr.), Woodmen of World, Air Force Assn., Civil

War Round Table, Columbia U. Alumni Assn., Vet. Corps Artillery N.Y., V.F.W., Zeta Psi. Clubs: Wings (past v.p.), Adventurers (past pres.), Dutch Treat, St. Hubert's Soc, N.Y. Athletic, Overseas Press (N.Y.C.), National Press (Washington). Home: Bridgeport Conn. Died Oct. 7, 1987.

TALBERT, ERNEST WILLIAM, educator; b. San Jose, Calif., Apr. 3, 1909; s. Franklin Lilburn and Edith Blake (Leach) T.; m. Marion Katherine Tuttle, Dec. 22, 1934 (dec. Apr. 1977); children: Peter Scott, Katherine Talbert Gerritsen; m. Floy E. Coleman, Aug. 28, 1979. AB, San Jose State Coll., 1929; MA, Stanford U., 1931, PhD, 1936. Instr. Compton (Calif.) Dist. Jr. Coll., 1934-36, U. Idaho, 1936-38, U. Tex., 1938-42; asst. prof., then assoc. prof. English Duke U., 1942-49; prof., then Alumni Disting. prof. U. N.C., Chapel Hill, 1949-74, prof. emeritus, 1974-85, mem. adminstrv. bd. Grad. Sch., 1965-70, dir. grad. studies English, 1966-69, bd. govs. U. N.C. Press, 1961-74. Author: Problem of Order: Elizabethan Political Thought and an Example of Shakespeare's Art, 1962, Elizabethan Drama and Shakespeare's Early Plays, 2d edit., 1973; co-author: Classical Myth and Legend in Renaissance Dictionaries, 2d edit., 1973, Critical Approaches to Six Major English Works: Beowulf through Paradise Lost, 2d edit., 1973, Manual of Writings in Middle English, 1050-1500, II, 1970; editor Recent Lit. of English Renaissance in Studies in Philology, 1948-53, Recent Lit. of English Renaissance Studies in Philology, 1969-74; contbr. numerous articles to profl. jours. Carnegie grantee, 1947, 48, Kenan rsch. grantee, 1968; Victor fellow Stanford U., Univ. fellow Stanford U., Folger fellow, 1950; sr. fellow S.E. Inst. Medieval and Renaissance Studies, 1965; Grad. scholar Stanford U. Mem. MLA, Acad. Lit. Studies, Renaissance Soc. Am., S.E. Renaissance Conf. (past pres.). Episcopalian. Home: Walnut Creek Calif. Died Aug. 10, 1985; cremated.

TALBOTT, FRANCIS LEO, physicist, educator; b. Lancaster, Ohio, July 17, 1903; s. Ernest Edgar and Mary A. (Light) T.; m. Gertrude Louise Ferguson, June 4, 1963. AB, St. John's U., Toledo, 1924; MA, Cath. U., 1926, PhD, 1928. Mem. faculty Cath. U., 1926-85, prof., 1953-69, reactor supr., summers 1947-69, chmn. dept. physics, 1947-69, prof. emeritus, 1969-85; prof., rsch. coord., chmn. dept. physics Allentown Coll. St. Francis de Sales, Center Valley, Pa., 1970-85; physicist proximity fuze project Johns Hopkins U., 1943-46; participant Oak Ridge Nat. Lab., 1947-85; mem. coun. Oak Ridge Inst. Nuclear Studies, 1964-86; cons. Naval Rsch. Lab., 1954-56. Recipient De Sales medal Allentown Coll., 1973, award Alumni Cath. U., 1973. Mem. AAUP, Am. Phys. Soc., Optical Soc. (Bene Merenti medal 1960), Sigma Xi. Home: Bethlehem Pa. Died Dec. 25, 1985.

TAMM, EDWARD ALLEN, circuit judge; b. St. Paul, Apr. 21, 1906; s. Edward Allen and Lucille Catherine (Buckley) T.; m. Grace Monica Sullivan, Jan. 30, 1934; children—Edward Allen, Grace Escudero. Student, Mt. St. Charles Coll., Helena, Mont., 1923-25, U. Mont., 1926-28; LL.B., Georgetown U., 1928-30, LL.D., 1965; J.S.D., Suffolk U., 1971; LL.D. hon.), Carroll Coll., 1974, N.Y. Law Sch., 1980. Bar: bar Minn. and U.S. Supreme Ct. Ofcl. FBI, 1930-48; judge U.S. Dist. Court for D.C., 1948-65, U.S. Ct. Appeals for D.C., Circuit, 1965-85; chief judge U.S. Temporary Emergency Court of Appeals, 1972-85; Spl. adviser to U.S. delegation UN Conf. on Internat. Orgn., 1945; mem. com. on jud. adminstrn. Jud. Conf. U.S., 1969-85, chmn. rev. com., 1969-78, chmn. jud. ethics com., 1978-85. Trustee Saint Joseph Coll.; bd. dirs. Police Boys Club, Washington. Formerly lt. comdr. USNR. Decorated comdr.; Legion of Merit Ecuador, 1942; Order of Balboa Panama, 1945; recipient Judiciary award, 1970, Distinguished Alumnus award Georgetown U., 1964. Mem. Met. Bd. Trade, USCG Aux., ABA (mem. adv. com. on judges function 1969-85, spl. com. on prevention and control crime 1969-85), Fed. Bar Assn., D.C. Bar Assn. (hon.), Am. Law Inst., Gourmet Soc., Am. Judicature Soc., Friendly Sons St. Patrick, U.S. Power Squadron, Sons Union Vets, John Carroll Soc., Pres.'s Cup Regatta Assn., La Confrerie des Chevaliers du Tasterin, Confrerie de la Chaine des Rotisseurs, Newcomen Soc., Sigma Nu. Roman Catholic. Clubs: Columbia Country, Ocean City Light, Tackle, Nat. Lawyers, Seaview Country. Home: Washington D.C. Died Sept. 22, 1985; buried Gate of Heaven, Washington.

TAMS, JAMES ELMORE MOFFETT, lawyer; b. Trenton, N.J., Mar. 9, 1891; s. William Henry and Ella Theresa (Moffett) T.; m. Gladys Honore Cole, Nov. 20, 1915; children: Helen Cole Tams Twitchell, Barbara Moffett Tams Ferguson, Anne Yard. BA, Princeton U., 1911; LLB, Harvard U., 1914. Bar: N.J. 1915. With Stryker, Tams & Dill, and predecessors, Newark, from 1914, ptnr., from 1926. Mem. ABA, N.J. Bar Assn. Episcopalian. Home: Madison N.J. †

TANNEHILL, URBAN ROY, corporate official; b. McConnelsville, Ohio, May 1, 1891; s. James Boggs and Sarah Isabel (Crouch) T.; m. Verna Vigar, June 2, 1917; 1 child, James Robert. Student, Denison U., Granville, Ohio, 1909-12. V.p. Kalamazoo (Mich.) Stationery Co., 1932-42, pres., 1942-48; v.p. Western Tablet & Stationery Corp., Dayton, Ohio, 1948-51, exec. v.p., 1951-53, pres., dir., from 1953. Mem. Paper Stationery and Tablet Mfrs. Assn. (v.p., dir.), Phi Delta Theta. Home: Dayton Ohio. †

TANNIAN, JOY, lawyer, utility executive; b. N.Y.C., Sept. 30, 1932; d. Constantine and Aphrodite (Menex) Xenis; 1 child, Sean P. B.A., U. Mich., 1953, J.D., 1956. Bar: N.Y. 1957. Atty. Consol. Edison Co. N.Y. Inc., N.Y.C., 1957-73, asst. v.p., asst. gen. counsel, 1973-76, v.p., 1976-80, v.p., assoc. gen. counsel, 1980-84, sr. v.p., gen. counsel, 1984-88. Mem. N.Y. State Bar Assn. (exec. com. corp. counsel sect. 1982-88), Edison Electric Inst. (econ. exec. adv. com. 1981-88, legal com. 1984-88), Order of Coif, Phi Beta Kappa. Home: Sands Point N.Y. Died Aug. 3, 1988.

TATE, ALBERT, JR., federal judge; b. Opelousas, La., Sept. 23, 1920; s. Albert and Adelaide (Therry) T.; m. Claire Jeanmard, Apr. 23, 1949; children: Albert III, Emma Adelaide, George J., Michael F., Charles E. Student, Yale, 1937-38, La. State U., 1938-39; B.A., George Washington U., 1941; LL.B., Yale U., 1947; certificate, La. State U., 1948. Bar: La. 1948. Practice law Ville Platte, La., 1948-54; judge Ct. Appeals, 1st Circuit La., Baton Rouge, 1954-60; presiding judge 3d Circuit, Lakes Charles, La., 1960-70; assoc. justice La. Supreme Ct., 1958, 70-79; judge U.S. Ct. Appeals (5th cir.), 1979-86; prof. law La. State U., 1967-68; mem. faculty Inst. Jud. Adminstrn., N.Y. U., 1965-76; appellate judges seminar U. Ala., 1966, 68, 69, U. Nev., 1967; Vice chmn. study adminstrn. appelate cts. Am. Bar Found., 1970-76; Am. Bar Assn. rep. adv. council Nat. Center for State Cts., Washington, 1971-72; mem. adv. Council for Appellate Justice, 1971-75; mem. com. and council La. State Law Inst., 1954-59; chmn. Jud. Com. La., 1968-70; mem. jud. council Supreme Ct. La., 1960-70; chmn. La. Jud. Planning Council, 1976-79; del. Constl. Conv. La., 1973-74. Author: Louisiana Civil Procedure, 1968, 3d edit., 1977, Treatises for Judges: A Selected Bibliography, 1971, 2d edit., 1972, 3d edit., 1976; Contbr. articles to profl. jours. Chmn. La. Commn. on Aging, 1956-59; pres. La. Cotton Festival, 1955-57; mem. Evangeline Area council Boy Scouts Am., 1948-86, dist. chmn., 1949-50; mem. La. Gov.'s Commn. on Rehab. and Corrections, 1970-75; Bd. dirs. La. State U. Found. Served with CIC AUS, 1942-45, PTO. Recipient Nat. Jud. award of merit Am. Trial Lawyers Assn., 1972; inducted La. State U. Hall of Distinction. Mem. ABA (chmn. exec. com. appellate judges conf. 1966-76, chmn. com. appellate advocacy 1974-78, mem. com. tech. in courts 1973-78, chmn. 1974-76), La. Bar Assn., Am. Judicature Soc. (dir. 1969-73), La. Conf. Ct. Appeal Judges (pres. 1967-70), Am. Legion, V.F.W., Woodmen of World, Delta Kappa Epsilon, K.C., Rotarian. Home: Ville Platte La. Died Mar. 27, 1986; buried Ville Platte, La.

TATHAM, ARTHUR EDWARD, advertising executive; b. nr. Webster City, Iowa, Sept. 17, 1907; s. John William and Libby (Hoag) T.; m. Angela Bolas, Feb. 29, 1932; children: Judith Ann, Jane Bonner, Jonathan Chase. BS, Northwestern U., 1929. Advt. dir. Bauer & Black div. Kendall Co., Chgo., 1933-38; v.p. Young & Rubicam, Inc., Chgo. and N.Y.C., 1938-44; pres. Tatham-Laird, Inc., Chgo., 1946-55, chmn., 1955-65; chmn. exec. com. Tatham-Laird & Kudner, Inc., Chgo., 1965-73; bd. dirs. Gen. Fin. Corp.; spl. asst. to Undersec. of Navy, 1945-46. Trustee, former chmn. bd. regents Northwestern U.; bd. dirs. Evanston Hosp. Comdr. USNR, 1944-46. Mem. Am. Assn. Advt. Agys. (chmn. bd. 1963-64), Assn. Nat. Advertisers (past bd. dirs.), Naval Air Res. (adv. coun.), Chgo. Federated Advt. Club (past pres.), Chgo. Athletic Assn., Chicago Club, Skokie Country Club. Home: Winnetka Ill. Died Sept. 9, 1985; interred Christ Ch., Winnetka.

TAUCH, WALDINE, sculptor; b. Schulenburg, Tex., Jan. 28, 1892; d. William and Elizabeth (Helman) T. Ed. high sch.; studied with, Pompeo Coppini (sculptor); DFA (hon.), Howard Payne U., Brownwood, Tex., 1941. Assoc. prof. fine art dept. Trinity U., San Antonio, 1943-45; dir. arts Panhandle Plains Hist. Soc. and Mus., 1972-73. Works include: Henderson Meml., Richmond, Ky.; Soldiers, Sailors and Pioneer Monument, Bedford, Ind.; Le Seuer Smith Children, portrait fountain group, Pelham Manor, N.Y.; portrait bust Mrs. Eli Hertzberg, Mcpl. Auditorium, San Antonio; basrelief Children's Reading Room, Jersey City Libr.; portrait relief George Washington, Washington Jr. High Sch., Mt. Vernon, N.Y.; Tex. Independence Monument, Gonzales, Tex.; portrait monument Mr. and Mrs. Isaac Van Zandt, Canton, Tex.; Moses Austin Monument, San Antonio; Gulf Breeze, Witte Meml. Mus., San Antonio; Innocence, ideal head, Woman's Club, San Antonio; meml. relief John Allen Walker, Howard Payne U., Brownwood; Genius of Music, Ann Hertzberg Meml.; bust of Mirabeau Lamar, Alamo Libr., San Antonio; heroic portrait statue group Buckner Ranch for Boys, Burnet, Tex.; Louis Kocurek, Sr. children, garden group, San Antonio; life size figure of Pippa Passes, Baylor U.; heroic figure The Texas Ranger of Today, Dallas; portrait fountain group Louis Kocurek, Jr. children, San Antonio; heroic portrait figure former mayor Dallas; heroic figure Gen. Douglas MacArthur, MacArthur Acad. Freedom, Brownwood, large heroic sized ideal figure representing higher edn. Trinity U., San Antonio; Am. doughboy in front of Am. Legion, Austin, others. Charter mem., sponsor Coppini Acad. Fine Arts. Fellow Nat. Sculptor Soc.; mem. Nat. Soc. Arts and Letters, Artists and Craftsmen, San Antonio Art League, Tues. Musical Club, Women's Club (San Antonio), Brady (Tex.) Tues. Club. Home: San Antonio Tex. †

TAULBEE, ORRIN EDISON, computer science and mathematics educator; b. Taulbee, Ky., Oct. 18, 1927; s. William Perry and Virgie (Carpenter); m. Margaret Janet MacDougall, Sept. 3, 1955; children: Gregor, Edison, George, Scott. B.A., Berea Coll., 1950; M.A., Mich. State U., 1951, Ph.D., 1957. Research mathematician Remington Rand Univac, St. Paul, 1955-58, Lockheed Aircraft Corp., Marietta, Ga., 1958-59; asso. prof. math. Mich. State U., 1959-61; mgr. information sci. Goodyear Aerospace Corp., Akron, Ohio, 1961-66; dir. mgmt. information systems, dir. Computer Center, U. Pitts., 1966-70; prof. computer sci., math., info. sci., chmn. dept. computer sci., 1966-84, founder computer sci. dept. four yr. undergraduate scholarship, 1966; vis. scientist Nat. Bur. Standards, 1971; rep. U. Pitts. as lectr. and adv. in computer sci. several western Eur. countries, 1970, Taiwan, 1974, People's Republic China, 1978; cons. in field. Editorial bd.: Ency. Library and Info. Sci, 1965-87, Jour. Info. Systems, 1973-87; Contbr. articles to profl. jours. Bd. visitors Ohio U., 1981-87. Served with AUS, 1946-48. Mem. Am. Soc. Info. Sci., Am. Math. Soc., Math. Assn. Am., Data Processing Mgmt. Assn., N.Y. Acad. Scis., Assn. Computing Machinery (nat. lectr. 1967-68, chmn. Pitts. chpt. 1971-74, chmn. computer sci. conf. com. 1973-87, dir. computer sci. employment register 1973-87, mem. conf. bd. com. 1977-87, Outstanding Contribution award 1984). Home: Pittsburgh PA. Died May 4, 1987. †

TAUSSIG, EDWARD HOLMES, automobile retail executive; b. Wheeling, W.Va., Oct. 23, 1892; s. James Edward and Harriet (Holmes) T.; m. Renza Brown, Apr. 11, 1923 (div. 1934); 1 child, Renza (Mrs. Junk); m. Florence Streater, July 21, 1935; 1 child, James Edward. Student pub. schs., St. Louis. Clk. Tex. Oil Co., Houston, 1911-12; stockbroker's asst. Houston, 1912-14, traveling rep. cotton factorage bus., 1915-17; founder Towles & Taussig, 1919, ptnr., 1919-26; mem. Dufton, Taussig & Co., 1926-41; pres. Ed Taussig Ford, Inc., Lake Charles, La., from 1941, Sulphur (La.) Motor Co., 1941-63; pres.. Ed. Taussig Lincoln-Mercury, Inc., Auto Leasing & Sales Co., Inc., Lake Charles, from 1950, Calcam Tractor & Equipment Co., Lake Charles, from 1946; v.p. Donaldson Ford Co., Inc., Sulphur; adv. dir. Gulf States Utilities Co., Beaumont, Tex.; bd. dirs. La. & So. Life Ins. Co., Inc., New Orleans. Pub. mem. War Manpower Commn. for S.W. La., 1942-46, La. State Labor Bd., 1948-52; chmn. La. Motor Vehicle Commn.; dir. Lake Charles chpt. ARC. Capt. U.S. Army, 1917-18. Mem. Lake Charles Assn. Commerce (past pres.), La. Automobile Dealer Assn., S.W. La. Hosp. Assn. (v.p., exec. com.), Pub. Affairs Rsch. Coun. La. (exec. com., past pres.), Am. Legion, VFW, Travelers Protection Assn., Pioneer Club, Rotary (past pres. local chpt.), Golf and Country Club (past pres.). Home: Lake Charles La. †

TAUSSIG, HELEN BROOKE, physician; b. Cambridge, Mass., May 24, 1898; d. Frank William and Edith (Guild) T. Student, Radcliffe Coll., 1917-19; AB, U. Calif., 1921; rsch., postgrad., Boston U., 1922-24; MD, Johns Hopkins U., 1927. Fellow heart sta. Johns Hopkins Hosp., 1927-28, intern pediatrics, 1928-30; charge children's heart clinic Harriet Lane Home, Balt., 1930-63; faculty Johns Hopkins Sch. Medicine, 1930-63, prof., 1959-63, prof. emeritus, 1963-86. Co-inventor Blalock/Taussig blue baby oper. Named chevalier Legion of Honor (France); co-recipient Passano award, 1948, Gardiner award, 1959; recipient hon. medal Am. Coll. Chest Physicians, 1953, Antonio Feltrinelli prize, 1954, Lasker award Am. Pub. Health Assn., 1954, 1st Thomas River Meml. Rsch. Fellowship award Nat. Found, 1963, Medal of Freedom, 1964, Founders award Radcliffe Coll., 1966, Carl Ludwig Medal of Honor, 1967, william F. Faulkner Nat. Rehab. award, 1971; named to Women's Hall of Fame, 1973. Mem. ACP, NAS, Am. Heart Assn (pres. 1965-66, Gold Heart award 1963, James B. Herrick award 1974), Assn. Am. Physicians, Am. Acad. Arts and Scis., Md. Soc. Med. Rsch. (pres. 1969-86), Soc. Pediatric Rsch., Am. Pediatric Soc. (Howland award 1971), Am. Acad. Pediatrics, Am. Philos. Soc., Phi Beta Kappa, Alpha Omega Alpha. Home: Kennett Square Pa. Died May 20, 1986; interred Mt. Auburn Cemetery, Cambridge.

TAYLOR, A(USTIN) STARKE, cotton industry executive; b. Mason, Tenn., Feb. 19, 1890; s. William Lee and Betty (Claiborne) T.; m. Veryl Lamb, Aug. 4, 1918; children: A. Starke, Veryl Evelyn, Miles Cary. Student, Mmephis U., 1906-10. With cotton shiping firm Cohn & Ellett, Memphis, 1912-16; participating ptnr. Dallas and Calexico, Calif., Silvan Newburger & Son, New Orleans, 1916-18, M. Hohenberg & Co., Memphis, 1928-42; founder, sr. ptnr., then pres. Starke Taylor & Son, Dallas, from 1942, also bd. dirs. Mayor Highland Park, Tex., 1946-48. Mem. Am. Cotton Shippers Assn. (past pres.), Dallas Cotton Shippers Assn. (past pres.), Dallas Cotton Exchange (past pres.), N.Y. Cotton Exchange (past dir., mem.adv. com.), Tex. Cotton Assn., Liverpool Cotton Assn. (assoc. mem.), Dallas Country Club (past pres.). Democrat. Presbyterian. Home: Dallas Tex. Deceased.

TAYLOR, EARL HOWARD, writer, editor; b. Yates Center, Kans., Feb. 15, 1891; s. Jacob Andrew and Lillian Virginia (Powell) T.; m. Helen Moore Martin, June 7, 1924; 1 child, Richard Powell. Student, U. Nebr., 1911-13. With Omaha Daily News, 1913-14; feature writer Kansas City Star, 1915-16, 19; assoc. editor The Country Gentleman, Phila., 1920-55. Author: Our Changing Land Policy; editorial writer on econ. and conservation issues. Polit. aide Gov. Alfred M. Landon, 1936. With U.S. Naval Armed Guard, World War I. Mem. Nat. Press Club, Chi Phi. Republican. Home: Swarthmore Pa. †

TAYLOR, JOHN INGALLS, newspaper executive; b. Dedham, Mass., July 26, 1911; s. John I. and Cornelia (Van Ness) T.; m. Margaret Blake, Apr. 16, 1939; children: John, Timothy, David, Benjamin. AB, Harvard U., 1933. With Boston Globe, 1933-80, treas., 1952-60, pres., 1961-65, also bd. dirs.; bd. dirs. Million Markets Newspapers, Inc., Bur. Advt., Am. Newspapers Pubs. Assn.; pres. Globe Newspaper Co.; pres., bd. dirs. Affiliated Publs., Inc.; chmn. bd. Affiliated Broadcasting. Trustee Milton Acad.; bd. dirs. Advt. Rsch. Found., Gesell Inst. Child Behavior. With USN, 1943-45. Home: South Natick Mass. Died June 8, 1987; buried Forest Hills, Mass.

TAYLOR, MAXWELL DAVENPORT, army officer, government official, ambassador; b. Keystesville, Mo., Aug. 26, 1901; s. John Earle Maxwell and Pearle (Davenport) T.; m. Lydia Gardner Happer, Jan. 26, 1925; children: John Maxwell, Thomas Happer. BS, U.S. Mil. Acad., 1922; postgrad., Engr. Sch., 1922-23, F.A. Sch., 1932-33, Command and Gen. Staff Sch., 1933-35, Army War Coll., 1939-40; DEng (hon.), NYU, 1946; LLD, Bowdoin Coll., 1948, U. Mo., 1951, Williams Coll., 1952, Pa. Mil. Coll., 1956, Trinity Coll., Yale U., 1956, Phillips Coll., Lafayette Coll., 1956, Seoul U., 1958, U. Pitts., 1962, U. Akron, 1966, Tarkio Coll., 1966, Norwich U., 1967, Worcester Poly. Inst., 1968, Parsons Coll., 1970, William Jewell Coll., 1970. Commd. 2d lt. U.S. Army, 1922, advanced through grades to gen., 1953, transferred from C.E. to F.A., 1926; instr. French and Spanish U.S. Mil. Acad., 1927-32; studied Japanese lang. Tokyo, 1935-39; asst. mil. attache Beijing, 1937; spl. mission to Latin Am. countries 1940, chief of staff, arty. comdr., 1942, served overseas, 1943-44, div. comdr., 1944-45; supt. U.S. Mil. Acad., 1945-49; chief of staff Am. Army Forces in Europe, 1949; comdr. Am. Mil. Govt. and Army Forces, Berlin, 1949-51; dep. chief of staff for ops. and adminstrn. U.S. Army, 1951-53; comdr. Korea, U.S. Army Forces, Far East, 1954; U.S. and UN comdr. in Far East 1955; chief of staff U.S. Army, 1955-59; chmn. bd., chief exec. officer, bd. dirs. Mexican Light & Power Co., 1959-60; pres. Lincoln Ctr. for the Performing Arts, 1961; mil. rep. of Pres. of U.S. 1961-62; chmn. Joint Chiefs of Staff, 1962-64; amb. to Vietnam 1964-65, spl. cons. to Pres. of U.S., 1965-69; pres. Inst. Def. Analyses, 1966-69; mem., chmn. Pres.'s Fgn. Intelligence Adv. Bd., 1965-69. Author: the Uncertain Trumpet, 1960, Responsibility and Response, 1967, Swords and Plowshares, 1972, Precarious Security, 1976. Decoarted Silver Star with oak leaf cluster, D.S.C., D.S.M. with 3 oak leaf clusters, Legion of Merit, Bronze Star, Purple Heart; hon. knight comdr. Order Brit. Empire, hon. companion Order of Bath (mil. div.), D.S.O. (Gt. Britain); comdr. Legion of Honor, Croix de Guerre with palm (France); cross of grand officer Order of Leopold, Order of Crown with palm, grand officer Croix de Guerre with palm (Belgium); Order Mil. Merit, 1st class (Mex.); chief comdr. Legion of Honor, P.I., grand officer Order of Boyaca (Colombia); Taeguk Disting. Mil. Svc. medal, 1st and 2d awards (Republic of Korea); grand officer Order of Mil. Merit (Brazil); comdr. Mil. Order of Ayacucho (Peru); Cloud and Banner medal with grand cordon (Peoples Republic of China); comdr. Mil. Order of Italy, grand ofcl. Order of Mil. Merit (Italy); Militaire Willems-Orde, 4th class (The Netherlands); Thai Most Noble Order of the Crown of Thailand, 1st class (Thailand); Cordon of Trinity medal with placque (Ethiopia); higher comdr.'s cross Order of George the 1st (Greece); Gt. Cross of Nat. Order (South Vietnam); Order Rising Sun (Japan); grand cross Order Mil. Merit (Spain). Mem. University Club, Lotus Club, Chevy Chase Club, Army and Navy Club, Alibi Club, International Club. Home: Washington D.C. Died Apr. 19, 1987; buried Arlington (Va.) Nat. Cemetery.

TAYLOR, ROBERT L., judge; b. Embreeville, Tenn., Dec. 20, 1899; s. Alfred Alexander and Florence Jane (Anderson) T.; m. Florence Fairfax McCain, May 27, 1933; children—Ann, Robert. Ph.B., Milligan Coll., 1921; student, Vanderbilt Law Sch., 1922-23; LL.B., Yale, 1924. Bar: Tenn. bar 1923. Practice law Johnson City, 1924-49; U.S. judge Eastern Dist. Tenn., from 1949. Trustee Milligan Coll. Mem. Am., Fed., Tenn. bar assns., Jud. Conf. U.S., Am. Judicature Soc., Sigma Alpha Epsilon, Phi Delta Phi, Corby Court. Mem. Christian Ch. Home: Knoxville Tenn. Died July 11, 1987; buried Monte Vista Cemetery, Johnson City, Tenn.

TEICHMANN, HOWARD MILES, author, educator; b. Chgo., Jan. 22, 1916; s. Jack and Rose (Berliner) T.; m. Evelyn Jane Goldstein, Apr. 2, 1939; 1 dau., Judith Robin Teichmann Steckler. B.A., U. Wis., 1938. Prof. English Barnard Coll., Columbia U., 1946-87; Stage mgr., script writer Mercury Theatre, N.Y.C., 1938; writer, dir., producer radio and television plays 1939-53; sr. editor overseas br. OWI, 1942-43; expert cons. in radio Staff of Gen. of Army Brehon Sommerville, 1943-45; exec. v.p. Shubert Theaters, 1962-72; Mem. mayor's adv. bd. WNYC-AM-FM-TV, 1979; adminstr. Sam S. Shubert Found., 1962-72. Author: (with George S. Kaufman) plays The Solid Gold Cadillac, 1953, Miss Lonelyhearts, 1955, The Girls in 509, 1958, Julia, Jake and Uncle Joe, 1960, A Rainy Day in Newark, 1962, Smart Aleck-Alexander Woollcott at 8:40, 1979; biographies George S. Kaufman: An Intimate Portrait, 1972; Smart Aleck, The Wit, World and Life of Alexander Woollcott, 1976, Alice: The Life and Times of Alice Roosevelt Longworth, 56721979, Fonda, My Life, 1981. Recipient Peabody award, 1953; Emmy award, 1954; Disting. Service award Sch. Journalism, U. Wis., 1959; Howard M. Teichmann scholarship fund established Columbia U., 1987; Howard M. Teichmann Writing Prize in his honor Barnard Coll., 1987. Mem. Dramatists Guild (council 1953-73), Dramatists Play Service (dir.), Dramatists Guild Fund (treas.), Writers Guild East, PEN. Home: New York N.Y. Died July 7, 1987.

TEICHNER, VICTOR JEROME, psychiatrist, psychoanalyst, hospital administrator, educator; b. N.Y.C., Oct. 22, 1926; s. William Isaiah and Sonya Clare (Breitman) T.; m. Gail W. Berry, Jan. 8, 1978; 1 child from previous marriage, William A. Student, Bklyn. Coll., 1943, U. Wis., 1944-45; MD, Temple U., 1949; cert. in psychoanalytic medicine, Columbia U., 1963. Diplomate Am. Bd. Psychiatry and Neurology. Intern Harlem Hosp., N.Y.C., 1949-50; dresident Bellevue Hosp., N.Y.C., 1950-53, sr. psychiatrist, 1954-59; rsch. psychiatrist Ittleson Ctr. for Child Rsch., N.Y.C., 1959-60; clin. instr. psychiatry Columbia U., 1961-71; mem. faculty, tng. and supervising psychoanalyst N.Y. Med. Coll., N.Y.C., 1971-83, clin. prof., 1973-83; dir. dept. psychiatry Met. Hosp., N.Y.C., 1972-83; dir. Nat. Commn. on Confidentiality of Health Records, 1975-78. Mem. editorial bd. Jour. Psychiat. Treatment and Evaluation, 1980-83; contbr. articles on ethics, confidentiality, transcultural psychiatry to profl. jours. With USNR, 1945-52. Fellow Am. Psychiat. Assn. (pres. N.Y. County dist. br. 1980-81), N.Y. Acad. Medicine, Am. Acad. Psychoanalysis (asst. editor jour. 1972-83, pres. 1983); mem. Assn. Psychoanalytic Medicine (editor bull. 1970-75), Soc. Med. Psychoanalysts (pres. 1980-81). Home: New York N.Y. Died May 3, 1983; buried Union Fields, Queens, N.Y.

TEITEL, CAROL, actress; b. Bklyn., Aug. 1, 1929; d. Henry and Blanche Kahn Reisman; m. Nathan Teitel. Appeared in Broadway plays: All Over Town, A Flea in Her Ear, Crown Matrimonial, Marat/Sade, Hamlet, The Entertainer, The Country Wife, The Little Foxes; Off-Broadway plays include: Under Milk Wood (Obie award), The Country Scandal (Obie award), Fallen Angels, The Way of the World, The Misanthrope, Long Days Journey into Night, The Keymaker, The Old Ones, Colombe, Juana La Loca (title role), Am. Place Theater, The Flight of the Earls, The Marriage of Figaro, Circle in the Square, 1985; appeared at Met. Opera House as female lead in Every Good Boy Deserves Favor; founding mem. Am. Conservatory Theater, San Francisco; leading regional theatre roles: Glass Menagerie and The Importance of Being Earnest, Pitts. Pub. Theatre, Night of the Iguana, Man. Theatre Ctr., Winnipeg, Can., Macbeth and Weekends Like Other People, Actors' Theatre of Louisville, The Hollow, Arena Stage, Washington, The Price, Olney Theatre; TV appearances include: Woman of Valor (Am. Women in Radio and TV Best Performance award, Emmy nominee), Lovers and Other Strangers (NBC); has appeared on numerous dramatic spls. and soap operas including The Edge of Night; also commercials and radio assignments; one-woman show The Faces of Love, The Roundabout, N.Y.C., also tours in U.S. and Eng.; guest artist in Long Day's Journey Into Night Nottingham Repertory Theatre, Eng.; appeared in Mary Stuart, Ah, Wilderness, Juno and the Paycock, Misalliance, Trelawney of the Hills, Undiscovered Country, Williamstown Festival, 5 seasons; played Judith Bliss in Hay Fever, Am. Shaw Festival, 1983, also in Faces of Love, 1985; appeared as Dolly Levy in: The Matchmaker, Nottingham Playhouse, 1983, as Jacqueline in La Cage aux Folles, San Francisco/Los Angeles, 1985. Mem. Actors Equity (exchange actor in Eng.). Home: New York N.Y. Died July 27, 1986; buried Valhalla (N.Y.) Gardens Cemetery.

TEITLER, SAMUEL L., lawyer, electronics executive; b. N.Y.C., Apr. 26, 1906; s. Julius and Sarah Teitler; m. Beatrice Ostroleng, Mar. 29, 1931; children: Michael, Robert, Ann T. (Mrs. Ozer). LLB, St. Lawrence U., 1927. Bar: N.Y. 1929. Pres. Lepel Corp., Maspeth, N.Y., 1942-46, chmn. bd.; mem. Teitler & Teitler, N.Y.C., 1964-86; counsel World Airways, Inc., Oakland, Calif., vice chmn., 1971-86, also bd. dirs. Pres. Kew Gardens Community Coun., 1954-57; pres. Jewish temple, 1955-56. Mem. ABA, Am. Soc. Tool and Mfg. Engrs., Am. Soc. Metals, Soc. Plastics Industry, N.Y. County Lawyers Assn., World Trade Ctr. Club. Home: New York N.Y. Died 1986.

TEMPLETON, H. R., banker; b. 1889; m. Alma M. Templeton. Mem. exec. com., v.p. Cleveland Trust Co.; dir. Cleve. Inst. Radio Electronics Inc., The 1737 Euclid Ave.; guest speaker rutgers Sch. Banking, Pacific Coast Banking Sch., U. Wash. Past trustee Hiram Coll. Mem. Mortgage Bankers Assn. (former mem. bd. govs.), Am. Bankers Assn. (pres. savs.and mortgage div. 1944-45). Home: Cleveland Ohio. †

TEMPLETON, JOHN BENJAMIN, construction executive; b. Waxahachie, Tex., Feb. 23, 1892; s. Patrick Henry and Nancy (Watson) T.; m. Ethel Templeton, Oct. 10, 1921. Ed. pub. schs., Tex. Pres. Austin (Tex.) Bridge Co.; v.p. So. Bridge Co., Servis Equipment Co., Coastal Constrn. Co., Austin Bldg. Co., Austin Contracting Co., Austin Asphalt Co., South Builders, Inc., Austin Road Co., Worth Constrn. Co., Austin-Worth Constrn. Co., Austin Paving Co. Home: Dallas Tex. †

TENNYSON, ALFRED (LIONEL), lawyer, government official; b. Washington, Mar. 25, 1892; s. Francis I. and Ellen F. (Talbot) T.; m. Margaret D. Davis, June 9, 1945. Student, George Washington U., 1915-16; LLM, Georgetown U., 1923. Bar: D.C. 1922, U.S. Supreme Ct. Pvt. practice Washington, 1922-25; interested in legal aspects of Fed. Narcotic Law enforcement work from 1920; chief counsel Bur. of Narcotics, from 1934; tech. adviser to U.S. del. to UN Commn. on narcotic drugs, 1949-58; alternate U.S. del. to UN Opium Conf., 1953. Home: Washington D.C. †

TENZING, NORGAY, mountaineer; b. Thamy, Solokhumbu, Nepal, May 15, 1916; s. Mingma and Kinsum Norgay; m. Dawa Phuty, 1936; children: Pem Pem (Mrs. Thundup Tshering), Neema (Mrs. Nole Gyalong). Grad. high sch. Profl. mountaineer 1935-86; dir. field tng. Himalayan Mountaineering Inst., Darjeeling, India; climbed Mt. Everest 1953. Author: Man of Everest (as told to James Ramsey Ullman), Tiger of the Snow. Recipient tiger medal Himalayan Club Calcutta, 1938, Nepal Tara I, 1953, George medal Queen Elizabeth, Iran's hightest sports medal Shah of Iran, gold medal Dr. Rajendra Prasad Pres. of India, U.S. Hubbard medal, 1954, highest medal for outstanding achievement Union Sports Socs. Soviet Union, 1962, Sports medal Ministry Sports Italy, Sports medal Govt. France. Mem. Mountaineering Assn. Club, Sherpa Climbers Assn. (pres.), Sherpa Buddhist Assn. Darjeeling (pres.). Home: Darjeeling India. Died May 9, 1986.

TEPER, LAZARE, economist; b. Odessa, Russia, Jan. 16, 1908; came to U.S., 1927, naturalized, 1938; s. Gedeon and Esther (Bogatirsky) T. Student, U. Populaire Russe, 1924-26, U. Paris, 1926-27; AM, Johns Hopkins U., 1930, PhD, 1931. Student asst. Johns Hopkins U., 1929-31; rsch. asst. Walter Hines Page Sch. Internat. Relations, 1931-34; instr. econs. Brookwood, Inc., 1934-36; dir. rsch. Joint Bd. Dressmakers Union, 1935-37; dir. rsch. Internat. Ladies Garment Workers Union, 1937-80, dir. spl. projects, 1980-85; cons. to rsch. div. Social Security Bd., 1938-43; mem. com. seasonalty in industry N.Y. Dept. Labor, 1939-40; del. White House Conf. Nutrition for Def., 1941; U.S. del. to World Statis. Congress, 1947; AFL and Internat. Conf. Trade Unions rep. to UN Statis. Commn., 1947-85; del. Nat. Health Assembly, 1948; cons. N.Y. State Legis. Com. Nutrition, 1942-43; active miscellaneous rationing div. OPA, 1942-43; with div. stats. and standards U.S Budget Bar., 1950-51; mem. intensive rev. com. Bur. of Census, 1953; mem. Spl. Com. Employment Stats., 1954; mem. com. stats. Program for City N.Y., 1954; seminar assoc. Columbia U., 1961; mem. com. on work in industry NAS NCR; mem. joint labor adv. coun. Bur. Labor Stats.; mem. com. nat. policy Nat. Planning Assn.; mem. com. employment 20th Century Fund; mem. exec. com. Productivity Conf.; dir., mem. exec. com. Fedn. Employment and Guidance Svc.; trustee Fed. Stats. Users Conf., chmn., 1979-80. Author: Hours of Labor, 1932, Women's Garment Industry, 1937; contbr. articles to profl. jours. mem. Nat. Pub. Adv. Com. on Area Redevel., 1963-85, Mgmt.-Labor Textile Adv. Com., 1962-85; dir.-at-large Nat. Bur. Econ. Rsch., 1970-85. With AUS, World War II. Fellow AAAS, Am. Statis. Assn.; mem. Am. Econ. Assn., Nat. Assn. Bus. Economists, Am. Mktg. Assn., Acad. Polit. Sci., Indsl. Relations Rsch. Assn., Econometric Soc., Met. Econ. Assn. (pres. 1975). Home: New York N.Y. Died Apr. 25, 1985; cremated.

TERREL, CHARLES LYNN, consultant; b. DeGraff, Ohio, Apr. 19, 1904; s. Charles and Rose B. (Pence) T.; m. Lela Fern Heaston, June 15, 1935; children: Sondra Lee, Mark Heaston; m. Mary Emily Masterson, Sept. 3, 1956. B.A., Ohio State U., 1928; M.B.A. cum laude, Harvard U., 1932. Engr., Western Electric Co., 1926-32; credit dept. Continental Ill. Nat. Bank & Trust Co., Chgo., 1932-36; pres. Jones Abstract Co., 1936-43; treas. Albra Casting Co., 1938-43; asst. adminstr. Lend Lease Adminstrn., 1941-42; program dir. Allied Combined Chiefs of Staff, 1942; chmn. North African Econ. Bd., Algiers, 1943; pres. mgmt. Service Co., 1943-48; v.p. Terrel Estate, Inc., 1943-48; fgn. trade cons. Dept. State, 1948; fgn. trade adminstr. Greek Govt., Athens, 1948-51; dep. chief U.S. spl. mission to Taiwan Formosa, 1951-53; pres. Internat. Cons., Inc., 1953-60; chief indsl. devel. div. Dept. State, Nigeria, 1960-63; dir. Devel. Service Inst., Nat. Investment Bank, Accra, Ghana, 1963-66; fin. advisor Devel. Service Inst., Nat. Investment Bank, 1966-68, Korea Devel. Finance Corp.,

1968-73, Korea Investment and Finance Corp., 1971-73, Korea Capital Corp., Seoul, 1973-74, Indsl. Devel. Bank, Saigon, 1973-75, Kuwait Indsl. Devel. Bank, 1974, Banco Unido de Fomento, Santiago, Chile, 1974; mission chief Internat. Finance Corp. (World Bank), Washington, 1974; fin. adviser Compagnie Financiere et Touristique, Tunis, 1975-78; program evaluator AID, Abidjan, Ivory Coast, 1978; fin. advisor Saudi Indsl. Devel. Fund, Riyadh, Saudi Arabia, 1979, Devel. Indsl. Bank, Cairo, 1981-82, Caribbean Fin. Services Co., Barbados, 1983; investment advisor Caribbean area, 1980; pres. Internat. Devel. Cons., Inc., 1965-87; asst. prof. bus. adminstrn. San Diego State Coll., 1957-60. Decorated Order of Bn. of George I (Greece). Mem. Ops. Research Soc. Home: Alexandria Va. Died May 13, 1987; buried DeGraff, Ohio.

TERRY, LYON FRANK, petroleum engineer; b. Rochester, Ind., Sept. 4, 1892; s. Frank H. and Gertrude A. (Lyon) T.; m. Edna Brubaker, Sept. 29, 1920; children: Julia Lee, Nancy (Mrs. William I. Thompson). BSCE, U. Mich., 1915. Field engr. Wolverine Oil Co., Okla. and Kans., 1915-16; asst. gen. supt. Mid-Co Gasoline Co., Tulsa, 1917-19; ind. cons. engr. N.Y.C., 1921-24; gas engr. Standard Oil Co., N.J., 1924-27; v.p. firm Ralph E. Davis, Pitts. and N.Y.C., 1927-36; oil and gas engr. Chase Manhattan Bank, 1936-49, v.p., 1949-57; assoc. Lehman Bros., N.Y.C., from 1957; Gas and oil valuation engr. WPB, Washington, during World War II. 2d lt., F.A., U.S. Army, 1918. Mem. AIME (Anthony F. Lucas gold medal 1963), Am. Gas Assn. (vice chmn. com. on natural gas res. 1944-47), Am. Assn. Petroleum Geologists, Am. Petroleum Inst., Ind. Natural Gas Assn. Am. Home: Ridgewood N.J. †

TERRY, SONNY (SAUNDERS TERRELL), musician; b. Durham, N.C., Oct. 24, 1911; s. Reuben and Massiline (Smith) Terrell; m. Roxie, 1948 (div. 1967); m. 2d Emma Taylor, 1968. Blind from age 1, formerly worked with Blind Boy Fuller, worked with Brownie McGhee, 1939-86; rec. artist Folkways Records, Prestige Records, Fantasy Records, Vanguard Records. Appeared in Spirituals to Swing Concert, N.Y.C., 1938; (plays) Finian's Rainbow, 1947-48, Cat on a Hot Tin Roof, 1955-57; (films) The Jerk, 1979, The Color Purple, 1985; albums include (with Brownie MCGhee) Brownie and Sonny, Blues and Shouts, Brownie McGhee and Sonny Terry, Blues from Everywhere, Blues and Folk, Blues All Round, Blues in My Soul, Down Home Blues, Going Down Slow, Guitar Highway, Get on Board, Get Together, Hometown Blues, Hootin' and Hollerin', Key to the Highway, Long Way from Home, Midnight Special, On the Road, Preachin' the Blues, Penitentiary Blues, Sonny is King, Terry and McGhee, Traditional Blues, Walk On, Where the Blues Began, You Hear Me Talking; author: The Harp Styles of Sonny Terry, 1975. Home: Holliswood L.I. N.Y. Died Mar. 11, 1986.

TERSTEGGE, WILTON HENRY, retail executive; b. New Albany, Ind., Aug. 22, 1892; s. Henry and Floy E. (Gates) T.; m. Anne Murnan, Nov. 20, 1919 (dec. 1956); children: Martha Anne, Floy Gates, Mary; m. Dorothy C. Besten, Apr. 15, 1961. Student pub. schs. With Stratton & Terstegge Co., Louisville, from 1913, chmn., from 1960; bd. dirs. Liberty Nat. Bank & Trust Co. Mem. C. of C., Louisville Amphitheatre Assn. (bd. dirs.), Louisville Theatrical Assn. (bd. dirs.), Rotary, Audubon Country Club, Pendennis Club. Home: Louisville Ky. †

THALHIMER, MORTON GUSTAVUS, real estate, theatre executive; b. Richmond, Va., Oct. 17, 1889; s. Gustavus and Pauline (Lohnstader) T.; m. Ruth Wallerstein, Oct. 11, 1920. Ed., U. Pa. Pres. Morton G. Thalhimer Inc., Richmond, Va.; chmn. bd. Neighborhood Theatre Inc.; bd. dirs. Fireman's Mut. Aid Assn. of Richmond, State Planters Bank of Commerce and Trusts, M.P.T.O. Va. Trustee Grad. Sch. U. Va.; past pres. Real Estate Bd., Richmond; bd. dirs. Variety Club's Will Rogers Hosp., Saranac Lake, N.Y., Va. Home for Incurables, Richmond Meml. Hosp., Va. Mus. Fine Arts, Sheltering Arms Hosp. Mem. Va. Real Estate Assn. (past pres.), Richmond Real Estate Exch., Am. Soc. Real Estate Counselors, YWCA, Am. Inst. Real Estate Appraisers, Columbia Assns., Internat. Real Estate Fedn., Masons, Jefferson-Lakeside Club, Variety Club. Home: Richmond Va. †

THARP, CARTER B., banker; b. Indpls., Aug. 10, 1918; s. Harod Bland and Emily (List) T.; m. Esthermae Myers, Apr. 23, 1949; children: Carter Allen, Riley Bland. AB, Wabash Coll., 1939; JD, Harvard U., 1942. Bar: Ind. 1942. With Am. Fletcher Nat. Bank and Trust Co. and predeccessor, 1949-85, sr. v.p., economist, 1967-85; pres. Tecumsah Ins. Co., 1969-71; v.p. Am. Fletcher Corp., Indpls.; bd. dirs. Rex Underwriters, Inc. Past treas. Community Svc. Coun.; pres. Home Care Agy., 1965-69; pres. Cen. Ind. Health Systems Agy.; past v.p. Indpls. Tb Assn.; past mem. met. sch. bd. Washington Twp., Marion County, 1962-66; past trustee United Meth. Home, Franklin, Ind. Capt. AUS, 1942-46. Mem. Indpls. Bar Assn., Indpls. Literary Club, Phi Beta Kappa, Delta Tau Delta. Methodist. Home: Indianapolis Ind. Died Mar. 13, 1985.

THATCHER, HAROLD W., lawyer; b. New Haven, Oct. 16, 1886. LLB, Yale University. Bar: Conn. 1908, R.I. 1909. Mem. firm Swan, Keeney & Jenckes, Providence. Mem. R.I. Bar Assn., Phi Alpha Delta. Home: Providence R.I. †

THATCHER, HERBERT BISHOP, air force officer; b. East Orange, N.J., May 1, 1909; s. Harry Morse and Maude (Eastor) T.; m. Frances Brooks, June 9, 1934; children: Elizabeth Brooks (Mrs. Rafloski), Peter Brooks. Student, U. Hawaii, 1926-27; BS, AB, U.S. Mil. Acad., 1932. Commd. 2d lt. U.S. Army, 1932, advanced through grades to brig. gen., 1944; lt. gen. USAF; comdg. officer various units U.S., 1932-45; comdg. gen. 1944; asst. chief staff A-3 Div., SHAEF, Air Staff, 1944; comdg. gen. 314th Composite Wing USAF, Japan; dir. plans USAF, 1942-56; vice comdr. USAF Europe, Wesbaden, Fed. Republic Germany, 1956-58; chief MAAG Fed. Republic Germany, 1958-60; spl. asst. Joint Chiefs of Staff, 1960; past chief of staff U.S. Forces, Korea, UN Command, Korea; head Air Def. Command, Ent. AFB, Colorado Springs, Colo., 1963-67. Decorated Legion of Merit, Silver Star, D.F.C. with cluster, Air medal with 7 clusters; Disting. Flying Cross (Gt. Britain); Legion of Merit, Croix de Guerre with palm (France). Mem. Army-Navy Country Club (pres. 1961). Home: Colorado Springs Colo. Died June 6, 1986; buried Air Force Acad., Colorado Springs.

THAYER, LUCIUS HARRISON, II, lawyer; b. Boston, Oct. 13, 1927; s. Lucius Ellsworth and Virginia (Speare) T.; m. E. Sherrill Smith, June 24, 1949; children—L. Harrison, Richard E., Alexa S. Thayer Fuller, Lynda R.; m. 2d, Constance E. Yerxa, Apr. 2, 1982. A.B. cum laude, Amherst Coll., 1949; J.D. magna cum laude, Harvard U., 1952. Bar: N.Y. 1953, Mass. 1961; U.S. Supreme Ct. 1956. Law clk. U.S. Ct. Appeals (2d cir.) 1952-53; assoc. Davis Polk Wardwell Sunderland & Kiendl, N.Y.C., 1953-55; atty. adviser Dept. Justice, Washington, 1955-56; assoc. Patterson, Belknap & Webb, N.Y.C., 1956-60; assoc. Hale and Dorr, Boston, 1961-62, ptnr., from 1962; asst. treas., clk., dir. Exolon-Esk Co., Tonawanda, N.Y., from 1958; asst. clk. Augat Inc., Attleboro, Mass., from 1969; clk. Inconix Corp., Natick, Mass., from 1958; v.p., clk., dir. Sherwood Investors, Inc., Boston, from 1963. Chmn. N.Y.C. Young Republicans, 1958; bd. dirs. Am. Congl. Assn., from 1967, 1st v.p., from 1974. Mem. ABA, Mass. Bar Assn., Boston Bar Assn., Phi Beta Kappa. Editor Harvard Law Rev., 1950-52. Clubs: Dublin Lake (N.H.); Hollywood (Childwood, N.Y.). Home: Boston, Mass. Deceased. Home: Boston Mass.

THEOBALD, JOHN J., academic administrator; b. N.Y.C., Sept. 8, 1904. AB, Columbia U., 1925, BS, 1926, degree in CE, 1928, PhD in Polit. Sci., 1935, LLD, 1954; LLD, Syracuse U., 1956, L.I. U., 1958; ScD (hon.), Wagner Coll., 1956; LHD, St. John's U., 1956; EdD, Poly. Inst., 1957; lic. naval architect for boats 40' and under, Westlawn Sch. Naval Architects. Instr. math. CCNY, 1926-28, from instr. to prof. civil engring., 1931-85, dean adminstrn., 1946-49; supt. Pub. Works Village of Lawrence, 1929-31; cons. engr. Villages of Lawrence, Hewlett, Bay Park, Village of Cedarhurst, 1929-35; adminstrv. cons. Westchester Charter Revision Commn., 1933, N.Y. Stte Senate Com. for Revision of Tax Laws, 1934-35; cons. engr. statis. div. Works Progress Adminstrn., Washington, 1935-39; adminstrv. cons. U.S. Bur. of Budget, Washington, 1939-41; spl. lectr. Sch. Engring., Columbia U., 1943-49, spl. lectr. Sch. Architecture, 1944-49; pres. Queens Coll., 1949-58, pres. emeritus; dep. mayor City of N.Y., 1956-58; supt. schs. N.Y.C., 1958-62; v.p. U.S. Industries, Inc., 1962-66; exec. v.p. N.Y. Inst. Tech., Old Westbury, 1966-85, dean grad. studies, bd. dirs. sch. devel., until 1985; cons. div. orgn. adminstrn., control NEA, 1949; trustee Jamaica Savs. Bank. Author: An Economic Analysis of Highway Administration in the State of New York, Hydraulics for Firemen, Civil Engineering: Engineering for Society. Bd. dirs. NCCJ, Found. on Automation and Employment, Inc., YMCA, Boy Scouts Am. Mem. Brooklyn Club, Lotos Club. Home: Port Washington N.Y. Died Sept. 6, 1985; body donated to sci.

THEODORE, LEE BECKER, dancer, choreographer, dance archivist; b. Newark, Aug. 13, 1933; d. Zena and Gayna (Klasner) Becker; m. Paris Theodore, Aug. 27, 1962; children: Said, Ali. Grad., High Sch. of Performing Arts, N.Y.C., 1949. Founder, dir. Jazz Ballet Theatre, 1961-63, The Am. Dance Machine, N.Y.C., 1975-87; guest instr. Am. Theatre Assn., Soc. Stage Dirs. and Choreographers, Lincoln Ctr. Library Performing Arts. Guest artist, N.Y.C. Ballet, Donald McKayle Co.; appeared in Broadway musical productions of The King and I, Damn Yankees, West Side Story (originator role of tomboy "Anybodys" 1957); choreographer film The Song of Norway; TV show Kraft Music Hall; Broadway prdns. Baker St., Flora, The Red Menace, The Apple Tree (Tony award nomination 1967); creator (dance), Internat. Jazz Festival, Washington, 1962. Mem. Pres.'s Music Com., 1962. Recipient award Dance Mag., 1982; recipient trophy Dance Educators Am., 1982. Mem. NEA, N.Y. State Choreographers Assn., Soc. Stage Dirs. and Choreographers, Actors Equity Assn., Am. Guild Mus. Artists, AFTRA. Home: New York N.Y. Died Sept. 3, 1987.

THIBAUT, JOHN WALTER, psychology educator; b. Marion, Ohio, Apr. 30, 1917; s. Ralph Gooding and Marie (Walter) T.; m. Ann Elliot Hommann, Jan. 5, 1944; children: Constantia, Charles. AB, U. N.C., 1939; PhD, MIT, 1949. Instr. philosophy U. N.C., Chapel Hill, 1941-42, assoc. prof. psychology, 1953-55, prof., 1955-62, Alumni Disting. prof., from 1962, chmn. psychology dept., 1960-66; rsch. assoc. U. Mich., 1948-49; asst. prof. psychology Boston U., 1949-51; lectr., rsch. assoc. Harvard U., 1951-53; bd. dirs. Social Sci. Rsch. Coun., 1966-69. Author: (with Harold Kelley) The Social Psychology of Groups, 1959; editor Jour. Exptl. Social Psychology, 1965-70; contbr. profl. jours. 1st lt. AUS, 1942-46. Fellow Ctr. Advance Study Behavioral Scis., Stanford, 1956-57, USPHS Spl. fellow Sorbonne, Paris, 1963-64. Fellow Am. Psychol. Assn., Soc. Psychol. Study Social Issues. Home: Chapel Hill N.C. Died Feb. 26, 1986.

THIEL, GEORGE A., geology educator; b. Staples, Minn., Nov. 19, 1892; s. Frederick and Amelia (Lenz) T.; m. Inez Lillian Erickson, July 12, 1923; 1 child, Marianne Southerland (Mrs. Marshall Battig). BA, U. Minn., 1917, MA, 1920, PhD, 1923. Mem. faculty U. Minn., 1921-61, prof. geology, chmn. dept., 1945-61. Co-author: Geology—Principles and Processes, 1960; contbr. articles to profl. jours. 1st lt. San. Corps, U.S. Army, 1917-19. Named Outstanding Geology Tchr. Assn. Geology Tchrs., 1954. Mem. Geol. Soc. Am., Soc. Econ. Geologists, Am. Assn. Petroleum Geologists, Minn. Acad. Sci., Phi Beta kappa, Sigma Xi. Home: Minneapolis Minn. †

THIEM, EZRA GEORGE, journalist, writer; b. Chgo., July 8, 1897; s. Theodore John and Sophia Caroline (Offner) T.; m. Jane P. Weaver, July 8, 1926; children: Mrs. Jane T. Hill, Theodore George. BS cum laude, U. Ill., 1921; postgrad. Medill Sch. Journalism,, Northwestern U., 1924; postgrad., John Marshall Law Sch., 1927-28. Asst. editor Prairie Farmer, Chgo., 1923-26; editor, dir. info. Ill. Agrl. Assn., 1926-39; reporter, agrl. editor, staff writer Chgo. Daily News, 1940-62, writer, editor garden page, 1962-66, free-lance writer, 1962-87; mem. Ill. Ho. of Reps., 1965-66. Author: (series) The Keys to Better Relations Between Management and Labor, 1945, The Hodge Scandal, 1963; editor sesqui-centennial edit. of history of Carroll County, Ill., 1968; contbr. numerous articles to agrl. mags. Trustee Met. Sanitary Dist. Greater Chgo., 1967-72; mem. Res. Officers' tng. Corps, 1916-18. Joint winner Pulitzer prize, 1949; recipient Pulitzer Pub. Svc. award, 1956, Rotary Club Chgo. award and citation, 1956, citation and award Ill. Press. Assn., 1956, citation Freedom Found., 1951. Fellow Sigma Delta Chi; mem. Farm House, Chgo. Newspaper Vets., Healiners, Ill. Hist. Soc., Chgo. Press, Chgo. Farmers, Masons, Alpha Zeta. Republican. Christian Scientist. Home: Evanston Ill. Died July 8, 1987.

THIMMESCH, NICHOLAS PALEN, columnist; b. Dubuque, Iowa, Nov. 13, 1927; s. Leo Nicholas and Victoria Maria (Glatzmaier) T.; m. Wynora Susan Plum, Apr. 17, 1953 (div. 1975); children: Nicholas Palen, Elizabeth, Martha, Peter, Michael. B.A., State U. Iowa, 1950; postgrad., Iowa State U., 1955. Reporter Davenport (Iowa) Times, 1950-52, Des Moines Register, 1953-55; corr. Time Mag., 1955-67; Washington Bur. chief Newsday, 1967-69; syndicated columnist Washington, 1969-85; resident journalist Am. Enterprise Inst., 1981-85. Contbg. editor: New York mag, 1976-78; commentator, Cable News Network, 1981; author: (with William Johnson) Robert Kennedy at 40, 1965, The Bobby Kennedy Nobody Knows, 1966, Condition of Republicanism, 1968. Mem. Nat. Commn. for Observance of World Population Year, 1974-75; nat. adv. council St. John's U., Minn. Served with U.S. Mcht. Marines, 1945-47. Fellow Inst. of Politics; Fellow John F. Kennedy Sch. Govt.; Fellow Harvard U., 1980-81. Mem. H.L. Mencken Soc. Roman Catholic. Home: Chevy Chase Md. Died July 11, 1985.

THOMAS, CHARLES DANSER, educator, physicist; b. Weston, W.Va., Nov. 8, 1908; s. Albert R. and Amy L. (Danser) T.; m. Ada G. Zickefoose, May 28, 1935; children: Charles Danser, Richard Karl. AB, W.Va. U., 1930, MS, 1931; PhD, U. Chgo., 1937. Mem. faculty W.Va. U., Morgantown, from 1931, prof. physics, 1946-74, prof. emeritus, 1974-81, chmn. dept., 1954-69; physicist Armour Rsch. Found., 1946. Mem. Am. Physics Soc., Am. Assn. Physics Tchrs., Am. Nuclear Soc., Rotary, Phi Beta Kappa, Sigma Xi, Beta Theta Pi, Sigma Pi Sigma, Gamma Alpha. Home: Morgantown W.Va. Died June 21, 1981.

THOMAS, DAVID DIPLOCK, resource company executive; b. Winnipeg, Man., Can., July 23, 1924; s. Edgar James and Blanche Elizabeth (Stevens) T.; m. Eva Josephine Johnston, Nov. 16, 1968; children: Nancy Elizabeth, John Edgar, Gordon James, Patricia Ann. Chartered acct., Man. Inst. Chartered Accts., Winnipeg, 1947. Chartered acct. trainee Millar Macdonald & Co., Winnipeg, 1941-47; with Sherritt Gordon Mines Ltd., Toronto, from 1947, treas., 1964-67, pres., chief exec. officer, from 1967, also bd. dirs.; mem. Nat. Adv. Com. on Mining Industry; dir. Ingersoll-Rand Can. Bd. dirs. Queen's U. Mem. Can. Inst. Mining and Metallurgy, Mining Assn. Can. (pres., dir.), Can. Bus. Coun. on Nat. Issues, Can. Inst. Chartered Accts., Inst. Chartered Accts. Man., Inst. Chartered

Accts. Ont., Toronto Club, Donalda Club, Bd. Trade Club. Home: Toronto Canada. Deceased.

THOMAS, FRED BENJAMIN, organization executive, educator; b. Ulysses, Nebr., June 16, 1891; s. Dudley Nicholas and Orie Emma (Streeter) T.; m. Nina Searles, Oct. 20, 1932. Engaged in radio and theatre, 1912-32; ednl. dir. Hermetic Brotherhood inc., religio-philosophic order, Oakland, Calif., from 1929; dir. Sr. Peacebuilders Inc., Oakland, 1959-70. Author study material, specialized articles in field. Mem. Am. Philatelic Soc. (recorder bd. v.p.s 1957-61, pres. 1961-65), Philatelic Rsch. Soc. (co-organizer, trustee, curator from 1953), Assn. Western Pilatelic Exhbns. Inc. (organizer, dir. from 1957). Home: Oakland Calif. †

THOMAS, J(ULIAN) B(ALDWIN), public utilities executive, consultant; b. San Marcos, Tex., July 19, 1891; s. John Adolphus and Nellie Rebecca (Julian) T.; m. Beatrix Hemkens, Nov. 15, 1920; 1 dau., Nellie Frances. BS, Tex. A.&M. Coll., 1911, ME, 1931. With Greenville Foundry and Machine Co., 1907-08; student engr. Houston Cotton Oil Co., 1911-12; supt. Mcpl. Electric Plant, Greenville, Tex., 1912; draftsman and engr. Russsell Machine Co., Dallas, 1912, Tex. Power & Light Co., 1912-17, engr. and chief engr., 1919-30; v.p. charge ops. Tex. Electric Svc. Co., Ft. Worth, 1930-38, dir. from 1933, exec. v.p., 1938-40, v.p. and gen. mgr., 1940-41, pres., gen. mgr., 1941-61, chmn. bd., 1961-63, engring. cons. from 1963; v.p., dir. Tex. Utilities Co., Ft. Worth, 1945-61; dir. Fed. Res. Bank Dallas, 1955-58; dir. Old Ocean Fuel Co., pres., 1959-61; chmn. elec. power surveys, Taiwan, 1963-64, Korea, 1964-65, Philippines, 1964-65. Mem. Tex. Bd. Registration Profl. Engrs., 1941-51, chmn., 1949; bd. dirs. YMCA; bd. dirs. Tex. Atomic Energy Rsch. Found., 1957-62, pres. 1958-59; chmn. Gov.'s Com. on Water Conservation in Tex., 1952-57, Tex. Rsch. League, 1958. Capt. Coast Artillery Air Army Corps, 1917-19. Fellow AIEE, Am. Soc. Mech. Engrs.; mem. Tex. Agrl. and Mech. Ex-students Assn. (pres.), West Tex. C. of C. (bd. dirs. 1943-61), Edison Electric Inst. (dir. 1948-51, 52-55, 61-62), Ft. Worth Club, Steeplechase Club, River Crest Country Club, Colonial Club, Exchange Club, Ft. Worth Boat Club, Shady Oaks Country Club, Tau Beta Pi. Episcopalian. Home: Fort Worth Tex. †

THOMAS, LEE BALDWIN, SR., manufacturing company executive; b. Alma, Nebr., Sept. 17, 1900; s. Rees and Fannie (Baldwin) T.; m. Margaret Thomas, 1924 (dec.); children: Lee Baldwin, Margaret Ellen (Mrs. Wallace H. Dunbar), Susan Jane (Mrs. A. Scott Hamilton, Jr.); m. Elizabeth C. Bromley. B.B.A., U. Wash., 1923. Advt. mgr. Ernst Hardware Co., Seattle, 1923-24, sales mgr., 1926-29; buyer R.H. Macy Co., N.Y.C., 1924-25; dir. home goods merchandising Butler Bros., Chgo., 1929-41; pres. Ekco Products Co., Chgo., 1941-47; with Am. Elevator & Machine Co., Louisville, 1947-48; dir. Thomas Industries, Louisville; chmn. exec. com. Vt. Am. Corp., Louisville; owner Honey Locust Valley Farms, Cloverport, Ky. Bd. dirs. Honey Locust Found., Louisville. Episcopalian. Clubs: Owl Creek Country (Anchorage, Ky.); Harmony Landing Country (Goshen, Ky.); Hunting Creek Country (Prospect, Ky.); Jefferson, Pendennis (Louisville); Union League, Mid-Day (Chgo.); Lake Region Yacht and Country (Winter Haven, Fla.); Mountain Lake (Lake Wales, Fla.); Delray (Fla.); Dunes Country. Died Mar. 21, 1988.

THOMAS, O. PENDLETON, financial services company executive; b. Forney, Tex., June 14, 1914; s. William Pendleton and Lottye (Trail) T.; m. Anne Swindell; children: William Pendleton II, Alexander Cole, James Trail. BS, East Tex. State U., 1935, LLD (hon.), 1972; MBA, U. Tex., 1941; grad. Advanced Mgmt. Program, Harvard U., 1955. With Sinclair Oil Corp., N.Y.C., 1945-69, pres., 1964-69, chief exec. officer, 1968-69; chmn. exec. com., dir. Atlantic Richfield Co., N.Y.C., 1969-71; chmn. bd. B.F. Goodrich Co., Akron, Ohio, 1971-79, then dir.; chmn. bd., pres. PenVest, Inc., Houston, from 1980; trustee Mut. Life Ins. Co. N.Y.; dir. Armco Inc., Westinghouse Corp., Jim Walter Corp. Bd. visitors U. Tex. System Cancer Ctr. at M.D. Anderson Hosp. and Tumor Inst., Houston; bd. dirs., exec. com. W.M. Keck Found. Lt. USNR, 1942-45. Named Disting. Grad. U. Tex. Coll. Bus. Adminstrn., 1964, Disting. Alumnus U. Tex., 1969. Mem. Am. Petroleum Inst. (hon. dir.), Conf. Bd. (sr.), UN Assn. U.S. (gov., dir.), River, Links, Blind Brook, Round Hill, Augusta, National, Bohemian, Petroleum, Ramada, Houston Country clubs. Home: Houston Tex. Died Feb. 8, 1985; buried Meml. Oaks Cemetery, Houston.

THOMAS, WALTER F., banker; b. 1910; married; children: Roger, Walter F. Jr. AB, Princeton U., 1931. With Mfrs. Hanover Trust Co. and predecessor, from 1931, v.p., 1948-57, sr. v.p., 1957-61, v.p. ops., 1961-63, exec. v.p., 1963-70, vice chmn., 1970-74, ret., 1977, dir., from 1976. With USN, World War II. Home: Boca Raton Fla. Died Nov. 7, 1987.

THOMPSON, BARD, university dean; b. Waynesboro, Pa., June 18, 1925; s. Charles Herbert and Frances (Beard) T.; m. Bertha Denning, Sept. 1, 1951; children: Andrew Bard, Frances Rutledge. Grad., Mercersburg Acad., 1944; A.B., Haverford Coll., 1947; B.D., Union Theol. Sem., N.Y.C., 1949; Ph.D., Columbia, 1953. Instr., then asst. prof. ch. history Emory U., Atlanta, 1951-55; asso. prof. ch. history Vanderbilt U., Nashville, 1955-59; Buffington prof. ch. history Vanderbilt U., 1959-62; Heilman prof. ch. history Lancaster Theol. Sem., 1962-65; prof. ch. history Drew U., Madison, N.J., 1965-87; dean Grad. Sch., Drew U., 1969-87, adj. prof. history Coll. Liberal Arts, 1985-87; mem. Ctr. Theol. Inquiry, Princeton, N.J., 1986-87. Author: Liturgies of the Western Church, 1961, Renaissance and Reformation, A Bibliography of Christian Worship; (with others) Essays on the Heidelberg Catechism, 1963; co-editor: (with others) Principle of Protestantism, 1964, Mystical Presence and Other Writings on the Eucharist, 1966; research on Renaissance and Reformation history. Trustee N.J. Shakespeare Festival, 1973-78, Gill/St. Bernard's Sch., 1975-80, Summit Art Ctr., 1982-87; Ofcl. observer Vatican II, 1964. Mem. Am. Soc. Ch. History, Phi Beta Kappa (pres. Gamma chpt. 1986-87). Club: Morristown (N.J.). Home: Morristown N.J. Died Aug. 12, 1987; interred Green Hill Cemetery, Waynesboro, Pa.

THOMPSON, ERA BELL, magazine editor; b. Des Moines; d. Stewart C. and Mary (Logan) T. Student (Wesleyan Service Guild scholar 1931), U. N.D., 1929-31, L.H.D., 1969; B.A., Morningside Coll., 1933, LL.D., 1965; postgrad., Northwesten U. Sch. Journalism, 1938, 40. Sr. interviewer U.S. and Ill. Employment Service, 1942-47; asso. editor Johnson Pub. Co., Chgo., 1947-51; co-mng. editor Ebony mag., 1951-64; internat. editor 1964-70; mem. N. Central Region Manpower Adv. Com., 1965-67; pub. mem. USIA Fgn. Service Selection Bds., Washington, 1976. Author: (autobiography for which she had received Newberry Library-Rockefeller Found. fellowship to write) American Daughter, 1946, Africa, Land of My Fathers, 1954; co-editor: White on Black, 1963. Mem. Community Art Center, Chgo., 1942-44; mem. Chgo. met. bd. YWCA, 1944-47; trustee Hull House, Chgo., 1960-64. Recipient Soc. Midland Authors Patron Saints award, 1968; Theodore Roosevelt Roughrider award, 1976; named to Athletic Hall of Fame U. N.D., 1981; fellow Bread Loaf Writers Conf., 1949. Mem. Soc. Midland Authors (dir. 1961-75), Urban League (Chgo. edn. com. 1953-56), Friends Chgo. Pub. Library (bd. 1959-60), NAACP, Assn. Study of Afro-Am. Life and History, Iota Phi Lambda (Woman of Year 1965), Sigma Gamma Rho (hon.). Home: Chicago Ill. Died Dec. 30, 1986.

THOMPSON, FREDERICK DELOS, publisher, advertising executive; b. San Antonio, Dec. 27, 1915; s. Frederick Delos and Ruth Margaret (Platt) T.; m. Julia L. Acheson, May 17, 1939; children: Geoffrey, Jonathan, Kathleen Thompson McCurdy, Cameron, Kimberley. Student, U. Beirut, Lebanon, 1933; BA, Columbia U., 1937. V.p. Reader's Digest, Pleasantville, N.Y., 1939-69; pres. Family Circle Co., N.Y.C., 1969-75; v.p. N.Y. Times Co., N.Y.C., 1975-79, asst. to pres., 1979-81. Chmn. ARC Greater N.Y., Am. Fedn. for Aging Rsch.; bd. dirs. N.Y. Blood Ctr. Died Sept. 17, 1988.

THOMPSON, G(EORGE) K(ING), judge; b. Jamaica, Iowa, Nov. 24, 1887; s. William J. and Ida A. (King) T.; m. Grace I. Byfield, Dec. 17, 1921; children: George K., William B. AB, U. Iowa, 1911, LLB, 1914. Bar: Iowa 1914. Pvt. practice Cedar Rapids, Iowa, 1915-33; atty. Linn Co., Cedar Rapids, 1933-40; judge dist. ct., Iowa, 1941-50; dist. ct., supreme ct., Iowa, 1951—; chief justice of ct. 1952, 56, 59. Mem. Masons (32 degree, Shriner). Republican. Presbyterian. Home: Cedar Rapids Iowa. †

THOMPSON, GEORGE ROBERT, travel consultant; b. Brunswick, Maine, Mar. 29, 1917; s. Albert E. and Mabel (Burditt) T.; m. Ruth Eleanor Blake, May 3, 1941; children: William, Mary Louise, Robert, James. B.A., Brown U., 1940. With Am. Mut. Liability Ins. Co., Boston, 1940-41; Devonshire Financial Service Am. Mut. Liability Ins. Co., Portland, Maine, 1941-56; with Nat. Life Ins. Co., Montpelier, Vt., 1956-80; treas. Nat. Life Ins. Co., 1967-74, v.p. policyholder services, 1974-80; New Eng. rep. Dominican Republic Tourist Bd., 1980-85. Trustee Montpelier Home for Aged, 1971-81. Served with USAAF, 1943-46. Lodges: Masons; Rotary. Home: Montpelier Vt. Died Feb. 4, 1987, cremated.

THOMPSON, HAROLD WILLIAM, educator; b. Buffalo, June 5, 1891; s. Samuel Joseph and Katherine (Kernahan) T.; m. Jean Alma Saunders, Sept. 5, 1916; children: Arthur Stuart, Katherine; m. Marion H. Chesebrough, June 27, 1942. PhB, Hamilton Coll., 1912, MusD, 1947; AM, Harvard U., 1913, PhD, 1915; DLitt, Edinburgh U., 1929; LHD, Union Coll., 1940. With N.Y. State Coll. for Tchrs., 1915-40, dir. music dept., 1920-24, prof. English, 1921-40; vis. instr. Cornell U., summers 1932-39, prof., 1940-59, Goldwin Smith prof., 1951-59, prof. emeritus, 1959; organist, choirmaster Hamilton Coll., 1908-12, 1st Presbyn. Ch., Albany, 1915-24; folklore rsch. aided by Rockefeller Found., 1938-39; lectr. Ind. U., summer 1942. Author, co-author, editor books relating to lit., folklore and music; contbg. editor The Diapason, 1918-50; editor N.Y. Folklore Quar., 1950-55; 1st editor Cornell Studies in Am. History, Lit. and Folklore. Trustee Hamilton Coll., 1937-41; mem. Nat. Com. on Folk Arts U.S., from 1954. Guggenheim Found. fellow, 1925-27. Fellow Royal Soc. Edinburgh, Soc. Antiquaries Scotland, Rochester Mus. Arts and Scis.; mem. MLA, Am., N.Y. State (trustee 1945-55) hist. assns., Am. (pres. 1942), N.Y. (pres. 1943-49), Pa. (coun.) folklore socs., Am. Guild Organists, Emerson Lit. Soc., Medieval Acad. Am., Savage, Book and Bowl Club, Phi Beta Kappa. Presbyterian. Home: Cortland N.Y. †

THOMPSON, JAMES STACY, publisher; b. Ligonier, Ind., Sept. 2, 1887; s. Edwin G. and Ella (Kennedy) T.; m. Dorothy Marie Burnham, Dec. 23, 1911 (dec. 1951); children, James S., Nancy Thompson Kelsey; m. 2d, Doris Renton Taylor, Dec. 1952. AB, U. Wis., 1910. Coll. rep. McGraw-Hill Book Co., 1910-18, sec., 1918-26, v.p., 1926-44, pres., 1944-47, vice chmn. bd., 1947-49, ret., 1949; cons. Dept.of State, 1952. Trustee Columbus Boys Choir Sch., 1956—. Recipient Journalism citation U. Wis., 1956. Mem. Am. Soc. Engring. Edn. (hon. mem., treas. 1942-50), Nassau Club (Princeton); Cosmos Club (Washington). Republican. Presbyterian. Home: Princeton N.J. †

THOMPSON, JOSEPH TRUEMAN, engineer, educator; b. Balt., Mar. 28, 1891; s. Joseph Camillus and Frances Elizabeth (Slingluff) T.; m. Sarah Madison Brockenbrough, July 7, 1917; 1 child, Elizabeth Madison. BS, Johns Hopkins U., 1917. Mem. faculty dept. civil engring. Johns Hopkins U., from 1919, prof., 1930-58, chmn. dept. civil engring., 1930-56, prof. emeritus, prin. rsch. scientist, from 1958; hwy. rsch. specialist to chief hwy. engr. U.S. Bur. Pub. Rds., 1926-41; mgr. 6th Internat. Rds. Congress, 1930. Contbr. articles to profl. jours. Mem. Gov.'s Com. to Revise Md. Motor Vehicle Laws, 1941-42, Bd. Sch. Commrs., Balt., 1944-54, Md. State Hwy. Adv. Com., 1947-50, Gov.s Com. on Effect of heavy Motor Vehicles on Hwys. and Bridges, 1949-51; mem. dir. hwy. traffic adv. com. to War Dept., 1942-43; chmn. adv. com. Balt. Met. area traffic study, 1945-46. Capt. C.E., U.S. Army, 1917-19. Mem. ASCE (pres. Md. sect. 1933), Hwy. Rsch. Bd., Johns Hopkins Club, Sigma Xi, Tau Beta Pi, Omicron Delta Kappa. Home: Baltimore Md. †

THOMPSON, LAROY BERNARD, university administrator; b. Laconia, N.H., Oct. 16, 1920; s. John Fawdrey and Anna (Hildebr) T.; m. Edwina Brown Graf, June 12, 1948; children: Virginia K. Turner, Steven M. B in Chem. Engring., Cornell U., 1943. Engring. lab. adminstr. U. Chgo., 1943-44; engring. rsch. asst. U. Calif., Los Alamos, N.Mex., 1944-46; adminstrv. aide U. Rochester (N.Y.), Cyclotron Lab.; engring., rsch. asst. Cornell U., 1947-49; dir. rsch. U. Rochester, 1949-57, assoc. treas., 1957-59, v.p., treas., 1959-70, sr. v.p., treas., from 1970; dir. Voplex Corp., Lincoln 1st Bank Rochester, Info. Assocs., Inc., Star Supermarkets, Inc. Bd. dirs. Rochester Area Hosps. Corp., Rochester Hosp. Svc., United Way, Rochester; bd. overseers Ctr. Naval Analyses; trustee Tilton (N.H.) Sch., Assoc. Univs., Inc.; bd. mgrs. Meml. Art Gallery. Mem. Country Club of Rochester. Home: Rochester N.Y. Died Oct. 23, 1985; buried White Haven, Rochester.

THOMPSON, LAWRENCE SIDNEY, classics educator; b. Raleigh, N.C., Dec. 21, 1916; s. Lawrence Sidney and Elizabeth Luraa (Jones) T.; m. Algernon Smith Dickson, Sept. 23, 1950 (dec. July 1962); children: Sarah E., Mary L., Richard; m. Ellen Marshall Dunlap, May 18, 1968 (dec. Feb. 1975); m. Anna Murashko O'Brien, Aug. 16, 1975 (div. Mar. 1979). AB, U. N.C., 1934, PhD, 1938; AM, U. Chgo., 1935; ABLS, U. Mich., 1940. Fellow Am.-Scandinavian Found., Uppsala and Lund, Sweden, 1938-39; asst. to librarian Iowa State Coll., 1940-42; spl. agt. FBI, Washington, 1942-45; bibliographer USDA Library, 1945-46; head librarian Western Mich. Coll., 1946-48; dir. libraries U. Ky., Lexington, 1948-65, prof. classics, 1948-86; cons. Erasmus Press, Lexington; advisor on library problems Ministry of Edn. Govt. of Turkey, Ankara, 1951-52; conducted survey of library of Caribbean Commn., Port-of-spain, Trinidad and Tobago, 1953. Author: Folkore of the Chapel, 1950, The Kentucky Novel, 1953, Wilhelm Waiblinger in Italy, 1953, Foreign Travellers in the South, 1900-1950, The Club Bindery, 1955, Kentucky Tradition, 1956, Kurze Geschichte des Handeinbandes in den Vereinigten Staaten von Amerika, 1955, Boktryckarkonstens uppkomst Förenta staterna, 1956, History of Printing in Colonial Spanish America, 1962, A Bibliogrpahy of American Doctoral Dissertations in Classical Studies and Related Fields, 1968, Bibliologia Comica, 1968, A Bibliography of Spanish Plays on Microcard, 1967, Essays in Hispanic Bibliography, 1970, The Southern Black: A Bibliography of Books in Microform, 1970, Books In Our Time, 1972, The New Sabin, Vol. I-VII, 1974-86, A Bibliography of Dissertations in Classical Studies, American, 1964-72; British, 1950-72; with a Cumulative Index, 1861-1972, 1976; pub.: American Notes and Queries, 1962-86, Germanic Notes, 1969-86, Appalachian Notes, 1972-86; contbr. on lit., bibliog. and hist. subjects to learned jours., Am. Scandinavia, Fed. Republic Germany. Mem. ALA, Southeastern Library Assn. (hon.), Bibliog. Soc. Am., Saellskapet Bokvaennerna, Ky. Library Assn., Ky. Folklore Soc. (pres. 1963-64), Ky. Hist. Soc., Sociedad de Bibliófilos de Argentina, Soc. Colonial Wars in Commonwealth of Ky., Soc. Cin., Caxton Club, Rowfant Club, Grolier Club, Rounce and Coffin Club, Filson Club, Gutenberg-Gesellschaft Club, Rotary, Phi Beta Kappa, Beta Theta Pi, Beta Phi Mu (founder).

Democrat. Presbyterian. Home: Lexington Ky. Died Apr. 19, 1986.

THOMPSON, PORTER, lawyer; b. Berlin, N.H., Aug. 1, 1904; s. Frederick William and Grace (Porter) T.; m. Fanny Lois Mapel, July 31, 1928. Grad., Phillips Exeter Acad., 1922; B.S., Bowdoin Coll., 1926; LL.B., Harvard, 1929. Bar: Mass. and Maine bars 1929. Asso. firm Warner, Stackpole, Bradlee & Cabot, Boston, 1929-31; partner firm Linnell, Perkins, Thompson, Hinckley & Keddy, Portland, Maine, 1931-73; of counsel Linnell, Perkins, Thompson, Hinckley & Keddy, 1973-86; dir. Canal Nat. Bank, Portland, 1953-80, Am. Hoist & Derick Co., 1959-66, United Bancorp Maine, 1969-71. Trustee Maine Eye and Ear Infirmary, 1950-86, pres., 1972-80; trustee Maine Med. Center, 1971-78, bd. incorporators, 1951-86. Served to maj. USAAF, 1942-45, PTO. Decorated Legion of Merit. Mem. Am., Maine, Cumberland County bar assns. Home: Falmouth Maine. Died Oct. 19, 1986.

THOMPSON, VAN DENMAN, musician; b. Andover, N.H., Dec. 10, 1890; s. Burt Fenton and Callie Berry (Morey) T.; m. Eula Mai Bogle, Apr. 14, 1911; children: Gwendolen Thompson Crawley, Constance (dec.), Patience Thompson Berg, Van Denman, Cynthia Thompson Bartley, Winston, Lynnwood. Grad., Colby Acad., New London, N.H., 1908, New Eng. Conservatory Music, Boston, 1909; postgrad. student, New Eng. Conservatory Music, Boston, 1909-10; student, Harvard U., 1908-09; MusB, Lincoln-Jefferson U., Chgo., 1919; MusD, DePauw U., 1935. Head dept. music Woodland Coll., Jonesboro, Ark., 1910-11; prof. organ and composition, univ. organist DePauw U., from 1911, head Sch. Music, from 1937; has given many organ recitals in Cen. and Ea. States. Author: (with others) Better Music in Our Churches, 1923; composer ch. anthems, organ and piano pieces; commd. to write mus. work for 150th anniversary M.E. Ch. (oratorio, The Evangel of the New World), 1934; contbr. to mus. jours. Recipient 1st prize in organ composition conducted by Nat. Fedn. Music Clubs, 1919. Fellow Am. Guild Organists; mem. Phi Mu Alpha, Pi Kappa Lambda. Democrat. Methodist. Home: Greencastle Ind. †

THOMSON, HARRY PLEASANT, JR., lawyer; b. Kansas City, Mo., May 9, 1917; s. Harry Pleasant and Alice F. (DeWolff) T.; m. Martha Jean Martin, May 3, 1941 (dec. 1981); children: Jane Anne Thomson McCarthy, Carol Lee, Lisa Clair Thomson Porter. AB, U. Mo., 1937, JD, 1939. Bar: Mo. 1939, U.S. Supreme Ct. 1959. Practiced in Kansas City; co-founder Shughart, Thomson & Kilroy (P.C.), Kansas City, 1939, ptnr., 1939-81, of counsel, 1981-88; lectr. Mo. Continuing Legal Edn. Programs, 1961-78; Mem. Mo. Supreme Ct. Com. on Jury Instrns., 1962-81, chmn., 1977-81; mem. Commn. on Retirement, Removal & Discipline of Judges, 1972-81, chmn., 1980-81. Author: (with others) Missouri Approved Jury Instructions, 1964, 69, 73, 76, 78, 80; Mem. bd. editors: Mo. Law Rev, 1938-39; editorial adv. bd. Antitrust Law & Econs. Rev.; contbr. articles to profl. jours. Trustee U. Mo. Law Sch. Found., 1975-87, pres., 1979-81. Lt. comdr. USN, World War II. Recipient certificate of appreciation for disting. service Mo. Bar, 1964, Spurgeon Smithson award Mo. Bar Found., 1979; Charles E. Whittaker award Kansas City Lawyers Assn., 1984; Litigator Emeritus award Kansas City Met. Bar Assn., 1985. Fellow Am. Coll. Trial Lawyers (regent 1967-68), Am. Bar Found.; mem. Lawyers Assn. Kansas City (past pres.), Kansas City Claims Assn. (past pres.), Internat. Assn. Ins. Counsel, Mo. Bar Assn. (bd. govs. 1967-71, exec. com. 1970-71), ABA, Am. Judicature Soc., Internat. Soc. Barristers, Order DeMolay Legion of Honor, Phi Beta Kappa, Order of Coif, Psi Chi, Sigma Chi, Delta Theta Phi. Clubs: University (pres. 1977), Carriage, Kansas City. Lodge: Rotary. Died Sept. 16, 1988.

THOMSON, VERNON WALLACE, congressman, government official; b. Richland Center, Wis., Nov. 5, 1905; s. Alva A. and Ella M. (Wallace) T.; m. Helen Davis, June 6, 1936 (dec. 1973); children: Patricia, Susan Thomson Turner, Vernon Wallace Jr. Student, Carroll Coll., 1923-25, LLD, 1956; BA, U. Wis., 1927, LLB, 1932. Bar: Wis. 1932. Tchr. Viroqua (Wis.) High Sch., 1927-29, Madison (Wis.) Vocational Sch.; practiced law, Richland Ctr., until 1951; enrolling officer Civilian Conservation Corps, 1933-35; asst. dist. atty. Richland County, 1933-35; city atty. Richland Ctr., 1933-37, 42-44; mem. Wis. Assembly, 1935-51, speaker, 1939, 41, 43, Rep. floor leader, 1945, 47, 49; mayor Richland Ctr., 1944-51; atty. gen. Wis., 1951-57; gov. Wis., 1956-58; practiced law, Madison, 1959-60; mem. 87th-93d congresses 3d Dist. Wis.; mem. house com. on fgn. affairs, house select com. on small bus.; mem. Fed. Election Commn., from 1975, chmn., 1976-77; mem. adv. com. on rules, pleadings, practice, procedure Wis. Supreme Ct., 1945-51; mem., sec. Wis. Legis. Coun., 1949-51; mem. Wis. Jud. Coun. from 1951. Pres. Richland Ctr. Library Bd., 1939-51; del. to Rep. nat. convs., 1936, 40, 52, 56; presdl. elector, 1952, 56. Mem. Order of Coif, Masons (33 deg.), Chi Phi, Phi Delta Phi. Home: McLean Va. Died Apr. 2, 1988; buried Richland Ctr. (Wis.) Cemetery.

THORMODSGARD, OLAF H., law educator; b. Carrington, N.D., Sept. 15, 1891; s. Halvor O. and Andrea (Gunnarson) T.; m. Marie Bentégast, June 9, 1928. BA, Spokane U., 1913; MA, St. Olaf Coll., Minn., 1916; JD, U. Chgo., 1923; postgrad., Harvard U., 1925-26. Instr. high sch. Fergus Falls, Minn., 1916-18; prof. econs. St. Olaf Coll., 1919-25; assoc. prof. law U. N.D., 1926-29, prof. law, from 1929, dean, 1933-62, dean emeritus, from 1962; mem. Commn. on Uniform State Laws for N.D.; mem. Jud. Council N.D. With Wash. State NG, 1910-13, Am. Expeditionary Force, 1918-19. Decorated Medalle d'Honneur des Epidemie (France), 1918; Carnegie Endowment for Internat. Peace fellow, 1925-26. Mem. ABA, Minn. Bar Assn., N.D. Bar Assn., Newcomen Soc., Am. Legion, Fornightly Club (Grand Forks, N.D.), Masons (32d degree), Shriners, Order of Coif., Delta Phi, Tau Kappa Epsilon. Home: Bordeaux France. †

THORNBURG, MARTIN LYNN, educator; b. Monon, Ind., July 25, 1892; s. Thomas Sherman and Rhosa (Bringham) T.; m. Lucille Bitting, Nov. 28, 1918; children: Dale Lynn, Marilyn Ada. BS, Purdue U., 1915, ME, 1922. Registered profl. engr., Ariz. With Am. Rolling Mills, 1915; instr. mech. engring. N.C. State U., 1916; asst. prof. mech. engring. Purdue U., Lafayette, Ind., 1919-24; assoc. prof. U. Ariz., Tucson, 1924-27, prof., head dept., 1927-58. Cons. power plants, heat transfer. With USAAF, 1917-18. Recipient Engr. of Yr. award So. br. Ariz. Soc. Profl. Engrs. Mem. ASME, Am. Soc. for Engring. Edn., Am. Assn. Engrs, Masons, Tau Beta Pi, Theta Tau. Home: Tucson Ariz. †

THORNBURG, MAX WESTON, educator; b. Long Beach, Calif., Oct. 3, 1892; s. Charles H. and Eva L. (Holbrook) T.; m. Leila B. Berry, Mar. 30, 1918; children: Roann E. (Mrs. Laurence Davis), Priscilla L. (Mrs. L. Lee), Russell B. AB, U. Calif., 1917, BS, 1921, degree in CE, 1933; postgrad., U. Grenoble, France, 1919. With Standard Oil Co., Calif., 1920-36, chief engr. mfg. dept., 1924-29, mgr. Richmond refinery, 1929-31, chmn. bd. engrs., 1931-36; v.p. Bahrein Petroleum Co. and Calif. Tex. Oil Co., 1936-41; spl. asst. to undersec., petroleum adviser, chmn. fgn. petroleum policy com. Dept. State, 1941-43; rsch. dir. econ. survey of Turkey 20th Fund, 1947; adviser 7 yr. plan Govt. of Iran, 1948-51; with industrialization plan Govt. of Turkey, 1954-55; Regents prof. polit. sci. U. Calif., 1955-56; rsch. assoc. Ctr. for Internat. Affairs Harvard U., from 1958. Author: The Design of a Petroleum Law, Turkey—An Economic Appraisal, 1949. contbr. articles to profl. jours. Capt. U.S. Army, 1917-20. Mem. Coun. Fgn. Relations, Royal Asiatic Soc., East India Assn., Am. Acad. Polit. Sci., Am. Geog. Soc., Pacific Union Club, Athenaeum, Royal Thames Yacht Club, Sigma xi, Phi Kappa Sigma, Tau Beta Pi. †

THORNDIKE, CHARLES JESSE (CHUCK THORNDIKE), cartoonist; b. Seattle, Jan. 20, 1897; s. Charles Adelbert and Hortense Victoria T.; m. Anne Lee; 1 dau., Barbara Ann. Student, U. Wash., 1919-20, U. Calif., 1920-22. Co-founder AA group, So. Calif., 1939; lectr. schs. and clubs. Began as cartoonist, 1916; successively with: San Francisco Bull, Animated Cartoon Film Corp., N.Y. Herald-Tribune Syndicate, Van Tine Syndicate; art dir. for Gen. Motors Corp., Forbes Mag., A.M. Walzer Co., Dover, N.J.; artist for Fox Films, United Artists, Universal and Ednl. Films; has conducted cartoon classes in N.Y.C., for 3 yrs.; on radio programs Behind the Cartoon; mem. adv. bd. Washington Sch. Art; sr. visual info. specialist, USN, from 1941; art. dir., OAS; did articles and cartoons for Carter. Author: several books, latest being Susie and Sam in Silver Springs, 1949, Susie and Sam at Rock City, 1950, New Secrets of Carooning, 1957, How to Enjoy Good Health, 1966; originator of: nespapers sydicate feature Oddities of Nature; writer: Syndicated newspaper feature World of Tomorrow; contbr. cartoons to New Yorker; others; contbr. Community Reporter, 1969-71; cartoonist for Winner's Circle; creator instrn. course for Cartoonists Profiles. With USMC, 1918-19. Mem. Jockey Club, Pi Kappa Alpha. Democrat. Episcopalian. Home: Miami Fla. Died Mar. 22, 1986.

THORNTON, FRANK EBERLE, orthopaedic surgeon; b. Valley Junction, Iowa, Nov. 21, 1912; s. Frank E. and Eva (Tussing) T.; m. Carol Edgington, Sept. 2, 1936; children: Richard, Thomas, Jerry. MD, State U. Iowa, 1937. Rotating intern Meth. Hosp., Indpls., 1937-38; staff Meth. Hosp., Des Moines, from 1945, chief orthopedics, 1950-72, pres.-elect staff, 1966, chief of staff, 1968-70; resident orthopedics State U. Iowa Hosp., 1938-41, asst. prof. orthopedic surgery, 1041-46; pvt. practice Des Moines, 1945-52, 54-72, Spencer, Iowa, 1972-76; chief orthopedic sect. surgery VA Hosp., Des Moines, from 1976; chief surgery Broadlawn Polk County Hosp., 1970-72; clin. asst. prof. U. Iowa, from 1980. Lt. comdr. M.C., USNR, 1952-54. Mem. Am. Acad. Orthopaedic Surgery, ACS, Clin. Orthopaedic Soc., Cen. Iowa, Mid. Cen. States (pres. 1969-69), Iowa orthopaedic socs. Home: Des Moines Iowa. Died Dec. 27, 1982; buried Masonic Cemetery, Des Moines.

THORSON, RALPH EDWARD, educator, biologist; b. Chatfield, Minn., June 25, 1923; s. Edne Odin and Grace Margaret (Tuohy) T.; m. Margaret Elizabeth Voith, Oct. 4, 1952; children—Margaret Jane, Kristin Inger, Julianne. B.S., U. Notre Dame, 1948, M.S. in Zoology, 1949; Sc.D. in Hygiene, Johns Hopkins, 1952. Instr. parasitology Johns Hopkins, 1952-53; asso. prof. parasitology Auburn U., 1953-57, prof., 1958-59; group leader parasitic chemotherapy Am. Cyanamid Co., 1957-58; prof. biology, head dept. U. Notre Dame, Ind., 1959-64; prof. U. Notre Dame, from 1966, acting chmn. dept., 1967-68; mem. U. Notre Dame (Grad. Council), 1959-64, 67-71, U. Notre Dame (Research Council), 1961-63, 71-73; prof., chmn. dept. tropical health Am. U. Beirut, 1964-66. Served as 1st lt., navigator USAAF, 1942-45. Decorated D.F.C., Air medal with four oak leaf clusters. Fellow AAAS, Am. Acad. Microbiology; mem. Am. Soc. Parasitologists (editorial bd., v.p. 1981), Am. Soc. Tropical Medicine and Hygiene, Sigma Xi (grants-in-aid research com.). Home: South Bend Ind. Deceased.

THREET, MARTIN ALBRO, lawyer; b. Sheridan, Ark., Dec. 10, 1892; s. James Monroe and Flora (Braden) T.; m. Fanchon E. Mitchell, Apr. 1, 1922; 1 child, Martin Edwin. Ed., Ouachita Coll.; LLB, Cumberland U., 1920. Bar: Ark. 1920. Pvt. practice Dermott, Ark., 1922-26, Las Cruces, N.Mex., 1926; dist. atty. 3d Jud. Dist. N.Mex., 1932-43; mem. Supreme Ct. N.Mex., 1943; atty. Interstate Streams Commn. State of N.Mex., 1945-51; counsel Mid. Rio Grande Conservancy Dist. Past pres. bd. regents N.Mex. Coll. Agr. and Mechanic Arts, Las Cruces. With U.S. Army, World War I. Mem. ABA, N.Mex. Bar Assn., Am. Legion, 40 and 8, Country Club, Knife and Fork Club, Lions, Albuquerque Country Club. Home: Albuquerque N.Mex. †

THROCKMORTON, JOHN LATHROP, army officer; b. Kansas City, Mo., Feb. 28, 1913; s. Russell Conwell and Ruth Amarette (Bullene) T.; m. Regina Theresa Higgins, Oct. 16, 1937; children: Thomas Bullene, Edward Russell, John Lathrop, David Kerwin. Grad., Culver Mil. Acad., 1931; BS, U.S. Mil. Acad., 1935; grad., Nat. War Coll., 1954. Commd. 2d lt. U.S. Army, 1935, advanced through grades to gen., 1969; comdr. 5th Rgt. Combat Team, Korean War, 1950-51; comdt. cadets U.S. Mil. Acad., 1956-59; div. comdr. 82d Airborne Div., Ft. Bragg, N.C., 1962-64; comdg. gen. Third U.S. Army, 1967-69; comdr. in chief U.S. Strike Command, MacDill AFB, Fla., from 1969. Mem. Soc. Colonial Wars, Army-Navy Club, Tampa Yacht Club. Episcopalian. Died Feb. 13, 1986.

THROOP, ALLEN EATON, lawyer; b. Niagara Falls, N.Y., Jan. 2, 1900; s. Augustus Thompson and Helen Maria (Eaton) T.; m. E. Wilhelmina Westbrook, Jan. 19, 1929; children: Thomas Augustus, Adrian Westbrook. AB, Hamilton Coll., 1921; AM, Harvard U., 1922, LLB, 1925, SJD, 1926. Bar: N.Y. 1928, D.C. 1966. Practiced with Cotton & Franklin (later Cotton, Franklin, Wright & Gordon), N.Y.C., 1926-34; counsel RFC, Washington, 1932; sec. Fgn. Bondholders Protective Council, N.Y.C., 1934; asst. gen. counsel SEC, Washington, 1934-37; gen. counsel SEC, 1937-38; assoc. prof. Yale U., 1938-40; gen. counsel Trustees of Associated Gas & Electric Corp., N.Y.C., 1940-46; trustee corp. Trustees of Associated Gas & Electric Corp., 1946-55; mem. firm Shearman & Sterling, N.Y.C., 1945-63; v.p., gen. counsel Communications Satellite Corp., Washington, 1963-66; assoc. firm Corcoran, Youngman & Rowe, Washington, 1967-82; Edwin A. Mooers lectr. Washington Coll. Law, Am. U., Washington, 1967; adviser fed. securities code project Am. Law Inst., 1969-80; mem. adv. bd. Securities Regulation and Law Report, 1969-83. Contbg. author: A Lawyer's Guide to International Business Transactions; contbr. articles to law jours. Mem. ABA (chmn. com. fed. regulation securities 1960-62), D.C. Bar, D.C. Bar Assn., Am. Law Inst., Am. Bar Found., University Club (Washington), Phi Beta Kappa. Presbyterian. Home: Falls Church Va. Died Feb. 19, 1989.

THUN, RUDOLF EDUARD, electronics engineer; b. Berlin, Jan. 30, 1921; came to U.S., 1955, naturalized, 1961; s. Rudolph and Katharina (Schmidt) T.; m. Brigitte Martha Roeder, Jan. 24, 1944; children: Rudolf Paul, Hans Ulrich. Physics Diploma, U. Frankfurt, 1954, Ph.D., 1955. Research physicist Degussa, Hanau, W. Ger., 1951-55; electronics engr. U.S. Army Engr. Research and Devel. Lab., Ft. Belvoir, Va., 1955-59; with IBM, 1959-67, Raytheon Corp., 1967-87; dir. Device Tech. corp. staff Raytheon Corp., Lexington, Mass., 1983-87. Co-editor: Physics of Thin Films, II-VI, 1964-69; authored articles in field. Recipient Tech. Achievement award U.S. Army C.E., 1959. Fellow IEEE (contbn. award 1975), Am. Phys. Soc.; mem. Am. Vacuum Soc. (dir.), Optical Soc. Am., Electron Microscope Soc., Internat. Soc. for Hybrid Microelectronics, Sigma Xi. Home: Carlisle Mass. Died July 5, 1987; buried Green Cemetery, Carlisle, Mass.

THURSTON, CARL GIVENS, hotel executive; b. Glen Wilton, Va., Dec. 28, 1917; s. Arthur Lynwood and Merle (Hill) T.; m. Dorothy Louise Deppensmith, Feb. 16, 1945; children: John Kent, Carole Anne Thurston Ryczek, Robert Gordon. Grad., Roanoke (Va.) Bus. Coll., 1938; student bus. courses, U. Buffalo, 1947, Cornell U., 1949, U. Minn., 1950. Cert. hotel adminstr. Ednl. Inst., Am. Hotel and Motel Assn. With Appalachian Elec. Co., 1938-41; dir. pers. Hotel Statler, Buffalo, 1947-48, N.Y.C., 1948-51; pers. asst. Hotel

Statler Co., 1951-54; resident mgr. Hotel Statler, Buffalo, 1955-58, gen. mgr. Statler-Hilton Hotel, Buffalo, 1958-61; mgr. Waldorf-Astoria Hotel, N.Y.C., 1961-62, Hilton Hawaiian Village, Honolulu, 1962-64; gen. mgr. Hotel Roanoke, 1964-69; hotel cons., 1969-70; v.p., mng. dir. Hunt Valley (Md.) Inn, Inc., 1970-71; hotel cons., 1971-73; exec. v.p. Leisure Mgmt. Corp. (hotel mgmt., devel.), Lansing, Mich., 1973-74, Carl G. Thurston Assocs. Hotel Mgmt. and Devel., Plymouth, Mich., 1974-76, Carl G. Thurston & Assocs., Roanoke, 1976-80; mng. dir. Bay Harbor Club, Stuart, Fla., from 1980; dir. Bank Va., Internat. Exec. Svc. Corp., N.Y.C. Chmn. design and constrn. com. Roanoke Civic Ctr.; mem. Statler Found. Scholarship Com., adv. coun. U.S. Job Corps.; bd. dirs. Roanoke Conv. Bur. Capt. AUS, 1941-46. Mem. Va., Roanoke chambers commerce, Internat. Exec. Svc. Corp., Newcomen Soc. N.Am., Internat., Am. (dir.), So. (dir.), Va. (dir.), Md. (dir.), Mich. hotel assns., Hotels Greeters Am. (pres.), Va. Travel Coun., Nat., Va. restaurant assns., Assn. U.S. Army (cons. directory 1977), Pickwick Roanoke Country Club, Rotary. Republican. Methodist. Home: Roanoke Va. Died Aug. 6, 1985; buried Blue Ridge Meml. Gardens.

TIEDEMAN, WALTER VON DOHLEN, scientist; b. Bklyn., Apr. 23, 1891; s. John Albert and Antionette Marie (von Dohlen) T.; m. Edna Marie Komfort, Aug. 3, 1915; children: Robert Komfort, David Valentine, Walter von Dohlen Jr., Emma Jean Fallon, Doris Anne Johnson. BS, Union Coll., 1913, MCE, 1914. Sanitary bacteriologist investigating pollution of Ohio River. USPHS, Cin., 1915-17; asst. sanitary engr. in charge extra-cantonment sanitation USPHS, Souther Field and Americus, Ga., 1918-29; cons. USPHS, 1947-59; asst. sanitary engr. Cleve., 1917-18; city engr., supt. water Americus, Ga., 1920-22; spl. staff mem. in charge malaria survey and control demonstration in P.I. Internat. Health Bd. of Rockefeller Found., 1922-25; asst. sanitary engr. to chief of milk and restaurant sanitation N.Y. State dept. Health, 1925-40; resident lectr. on pub. health engring. Sch. Pub Health, U. Mich., 1958-59; dir. testing lab. Nat. Sanitation Found., 1956-59, spl. cons., 1960—; chmn. subcom. food san. Div. Med. Scis., NRC, Washington. 1945-62; mem. commn. on environ. hygiene Armed Forces Epidemiol. Bd., 1952. Author: (with Dr. Haven Emerson) Administrative Medicine, 1951, (with Earle B. Phelps) Public Health Engineering, Vol. II, 1950; contr. articles to tech. jours.; author and tech. adviser in producing motion picture 'Twixt the Cup and the Lip. Mem. WHO adv. panel, environ. sanitation, 1951-60. Mem. Royal Soc. Health, Am. Pub. Health Assn., AAAS, Internat. Assn. Milk and Food Sanitarians, Inst. Food Tech., Sigma Xi, Delta Omega. Home: Wayne N.J. †

TIEGS, ERNEST WALTER, education educator; b. Oconto, Wis., July 25, 1891; s. August and Adeline (Marck) T.; m. Bernice Vida Ross, Aug. 24, 1916; children: Carol Lois, Leah Marie, Virginia Anne; m. 2d, Fay Adams, Sept. 1, 1949. BA, Lawrence Coll., Appleton, Wis., 1913; student, U. Wis., summer 1915, U. Chgo., summer 1916; MA, U. Minn., 1922, PhD, 1927. Prin. graded sch. Royalton, Wis., 1911-13; supt. schs. Peshtigo, Wis., 1914-16; supervising prin. elem. schs., Crystal Falls, Mich., 1916-19; prin. elem. and grammar sch., Mpls., 1919-21, 23-24; asst. to supt. schs., Mpls., 1924-27; acting dean and assoc. prof. edn. U. So. Calif., 1927-28, dean Univ. Coll., prof. edn., 1928-46; editor-in-chief Calif. Test Bur., 1947-53; prof. edn. L.A. State Coll., 1953-61. Author, co-author or co-editor books relating to field; author monograph; editor: (with Fay Adams) Tiegs-Adams Social Studies Series: Teaching the Social Studies, 1959. Mem. NEA (life), Calif. Rsch. and Guidance Assn. (pres. so. sect.), Masons, Phi Beta Kappa, Phi Kappa Phi, Phi Delta Kappa, Tau Kappa Alpha, Sigma Phi Epsilon. Republican. Methodist. Home: Los Angeles Calif. †

TIFFEAU, JACQUES EMILE, fashion designer; b. Poitou, France, Oct. 11, 1927; came to U.S., 1931.; s. Auguste and Celine (Meunier) T. Fashion designer Monte-Sano & Pruzan, Ltd., N.Y.C., from 1951; v.p., treas. Tiffeau & Busch, Ltd., N.Y.C., 1958-70; designer Originala, N.Y.C.; fashion critic Parsons Sch. Design; with Rive Gauche div. Yves Saint Laurent, Paris, from 1975; instr. fashion design, Inst. de la Mode, Paris. With French Army Air Force, World War II. Recipient Coty Design award, 1960, 64, Nat. Cotton award, 1961, Internat. Fashion award London (Eng.) Sunday Times, 1964, Tobe-CoBurn Fashion award, numerous others. Home: Paris France. Died Feb. 29, 1988.

TIGRAK, MEHMET FAUT, structural engineer; b. Istanbul, Turkey, Aug. 26, 1911; came to U.S., 1958; naturalized; s. M. Suleyman and Hediye (Harputlu) T.; m. Mary Louise Evans; children: William M.U., James A.F., Hediye L. Diploma, Mil. Coll., Habiye-Istanbul, 1932; Diploma Mil. Engring., 1934; Certificate, U. Berlin, Germany, 1938; student, Technische Hochschule, Berlin, 1938-39; BS, U. Ill., 1942, MS, 1943, PhD, 1945. Registered profl. engr., Ill., Ind., Mo., Ky., Tenn., Wis., Turkey; registered structural engr., Ill., Ky., Turkey. With Turkish Army Corps Engrs., 1934-51, resigned sr. maj., 1951; tech. dir. Turk Yapi Ltd. Co., Ankara, 1951; dept. head Metcalf, Hamilton, Grove, Kansas City, Mo., 1951-53; prin. engr. project coordinator Hamilton Co., Kansas City, 1953-54; owner, operator Tigrak Cons. Engring. Co., Tigrak Constrn. Co., Ankara, 1954-58; prin. ptnr., mgr. Tigrak & Kolbasi, Engrs.-Contractors, Ankara, 1956-58; assoc. in charge structure Clark, Daily, Dietz & Assocs., Urbana, Ill., 1958-62; v.p. in charge structure and hwy. div. Clark, Dietz & Assocs., Engrs. Inc., Urbana, 1962-66, v.p. in charge fed. and R.R. projects, from 1966. Recipient Honorable Mention award for Findlay Bridge (Shelbyville, Ill.), U.S. Army C.E., 1969. Mem. ASCE (life), AAAS, Ill. Assn. Professions, Nat., Ill. socs. profl. engrs., Am. Concrete Inst., Am. Ry. Engring. Assn., Soc. Am. Mil. Engrs., Chamber Architects and Engrs. Turkey, Masons (32 deg.), Shriners, Sigma Xi, Chi Epsilon, Phi Kappa Epsilon. Home: Mahomet Ill. Deceased.

TILLEY, ROBERT JAMES, editor; b. Terre Haute, Ind., July 16, 1925; s. Robert Light and Ethel Emeline (Hadden) T.; m. Mary Frances Torbert, Dec. 21, 1957. BA, DePauw U., 1948; postgrad. Russian Inst., Columbia U., 1948-49. Project officer U.S. Civil Svc., 1949-53; with John Wiley & Sons, Inc., N.Y.C., 1953-59, assoc. editor, 1957-59; with Columbia U. Press, N.Y.C., 1959-80, exec. editor, 1960-62, asst. dir., 1962-71, editor-in-chief, 1971-80; editor Oxford U. Press, 1974-80; mem. staff world hdqrs. ITT Corp., N.Y.C., from 1981. Mem. Govt. Adv. Com. on Internat. Book and Library Programs, 1972-76; v.p. Madison Sq. Ch. House, 1966-68, pres., 1968-70. With USNR, 1943-45. Mem. Am. Inst. Biol. Scis., Princeton, Washington clubs. Presbyterian (elder from 1960). Home: New Preston Conn. Deceased.

TILLSTROM, BURR, television performer; b. Chgo., Oct. 13, 1917; s. Bert F. and Alice (Burr) T. Student, U. Chgo.; DLitt, Hope Coll., Holland, Mich., 1972. With WPA-Chgo. Park Dist. Theatre, 1936; traveled with puppet, marionette and stock shows; mgr. puppet exhibits and Marionette Theatre, Marshall Field & Co., Chgo. (performed on exptl. TV for RCA), 1939; sent to Bermuda by RCA to do ship to shore TV broadcasts, 1940; creator and impressario: puppet show Kukla, Fran and Ollie with Fran Allison, from 1947. Pioneer in TV when he presented puppets on Balaban and Katz first telecast, sta. WBKB, Chgo., 1941; show developed by and for TV. Recipient George Peabody award, 1949, 64, NATAS, Emmy award, 1953, 65, 71, more than 50 other awards. Home: Palm Springs Calif. Died Dec. 6, 1985; buried Chgo.

TILSON, HOWARD, industrial engineer; b. N.Y.C., May 30, 1891; s. William Richard and Martha Elizabeth (McNair) T.; m. MArgaret Barnard, June 19, 1917; 1 child, Barnard. M.E., Cornell U., 1913. Profl. engr. Mass., Conn. Minn. and Ill. mgr. Casualty Ins. Rating Bur., 1913-17; supt. Celluloid Co., Newark, 1919-20; prodn. mgr. Monroe Calculating Machine Co., Orange, N.J., 1920-21; cons. indsl. engr. 1921-24; field engr. C.L. Stevens & Co., Boston, 1924-28; indsl. engr., asst. to v.p. A. G. Spaulding & Bros., Chicopee, Mass., 1928-37; field engr. Rath & Strong, Boston, 1937-40; v.p. Proctor Electric Co., Phila., 1940-42; works mgr. Franklin Machine & Foundry, Providence, 1942-43; cons. indsl. engr. 1943-46; pres. Donnelly Elec. & Mfg. Co., 1946-47; propr. Chain Mfg. Co., 1947-51; cons. ECA, Paris, 1951-52; chief industry office Mission to France ECA, 1952-55; chief prodn. engring. div., ammo dept. Frankford Arsenal, Phila., 1955-57; chief industry, mining and transp. div. ICA, U.S. Ops. Mission, Israel, from 1957. Capt. Ordnance Corps, U.S. Army, World War I. Mem. ASME, Am. Soc. Tool Engrs., Am. Legion, Sigma Alpha Epsilon. Episcopalian. Home: Avon Conn. †

TILTON, JOHN NEAL, architect, educator; b. Chgo., June 16, 1891; s. John Neal and Emily Wood (Larrabee) T.; m. Hazel Davidson, Sept. 14, 1940. BArch, Cornell U., 1913, MArch, 1914. Registered architect, Ill., 1919. Designer Marshall and Fox, architects, Chgo., 1914-17, 19-26; ptnr. John A. Armstrong, John N. Tilton and William H. Furst, Chgo., 1926-32; ptnr. (part-time) John A. Armstrong, John N. Tilton and William H. Furst, from 1932, firm name Furst and Tilton, from 1952; asst. prof. architecture, Cornell U., 1932-36, prof. architecture, 1936-59, emeritus prof., from 1959, acting dean Coll. Architecture, 1937-38, asst. dean, 1938-40; cons. at bldgs. and properties Cornell U., from 1959. Specialist in church architecture and design; prin. works include Emmanuel Ch., LaGrange, Ill., Seabury Western Sem. Group, Evanston, Ill., Trinity Ch., Reno, Nev., Capital Drive Luth. Ch., Milwaukee, etc. Commd. 2d lt. U.S. Army Signal Corps, 1917, served, 1918-19. Recipient citation Assn. Collegiate Schs. Architecture, 1958. Mem. AIA, N.Y. State Assn. Architects, Statler Club, Rotary, Tau Beta Pi. Republican. Episcopalian (vestryman). Home: Ithaca N.Y. †

TIMMONS, BASCOM N., newspaper writer; b. Collin County, Tex., Mar. 31, 1890; s. Commodore Amplias and Martha Ann (Crenshaw) T.; m. Ethel Boardman, Aug. 8, 1925 (dec. Oct. 1970). Ed. pub. schs. and mil. acad. Began as reporter Ft. Worth Record, 1906; with Dallas Times Herald, 1907; mng. editor Amarillo News, 1910; with Milw. Sentinel, 1911, Washington Post, 1912-13; editor and owner Daily Panhandle, Amarillo, Tex., 1914-16; Washington corr. for Houston Chronicle, 1917-73 (except for leave military service World War I). Author: Jesse H. Jones, The Man and The Statesman. Recipient award Biography Tex. Heritage Found., 1958. Mem. Philos. Soc. of Tex. Methodist. Clubs: Elk, Nat. Press (pres. 1932), Gridiron. Home: Washington D.C. Died May 31, 1987.

TINBERGEN, NIKOLAAS, zoologist; b. The Hague, The Netherlands, Apr. 15, 1907; s. Dirk Cornelis and Jeannette (Van Eek) T.; m. Elisabeth Amelie Rutten, Apr. 14, 1932; children: Jacob, Catharina Tinbergen Loman, Dirk, Jannetje, Gerardina Tinbergen Carleston. PhD, Leiden (Netherlands) U., 1932. Faculty Leiden U., 1933-49, prof. exptl. zoology, 1947-49; ethology lectr. Oxford (Eng.) U., from 1949, reader animal behavior, 1962-66, prof. in animal behavior, 1966-74, emeritus, 1974-88. Author: The Study of Instinct, 1951, Social Behaviour in Animals, 1953, The Herring Gull's World, 1953, Curious Naturalists, 1956, Animal Behavior, 1965, Signal for Survival, 1970, The Animal in its World, 2 vols., 1974; (with E.A. Tinbergen) Autistic Children, New Hope for a Cure, 1983; also articles and films including Signals for Survival (Italia prize 1969, Blue Ribbon N.Y. Film Festival 1971). Recipient Joint Nobel prize for physiology or medicine, 1973, Swammerdan medal, 1973, other awards. Fellow Royal Soc., 1962; mem. Nat. Acad. Scis., Am. Philos. Soc., Am. Acad. Arts and Scis. (fgn.), Akademie van Wetenschappen, Am. Mus. Natural History, Max Planck Gesellschaft, others. Home: Oxford England. Died Dec. 21, 1988.

TINDALL, CHARLES WILLIAM, JR., consumer electronics company executive; b. Kirksville, Mo., Feb. 7, 1926; s. Charles William and Lottie Belle (Rowe) T.; children: Jerry Ann Taylor, John Scott.; m. Raeia Jean Chandler, 1982; step-children: Angela Jean Goodman, David Bruce Goodman, Jr. B.S., U. Mo., 1950. C.P.A., Tex. Mng. acct. Price Waterhouse & Co., 1951-66; v.p., treas. Tandy Corp., Ft. Worth, 1966-79; sr. v.p., treas. Tandy Corp., 1979-86; past dir. Pier I Imports, Tex. Commerce Bank, Tex. Greenhouse Co., all Ft. Worth. Sect. chmn. United Way, Ft. Worth, 1981, div. chmn., 1982; past dir. Fort Worth Ballet, Osteopathic Med. Ctr., Ft. Worth. Served with USMC, 1944-46. Decorated Purple Heart. Mem. Am. Inst. CPAs, Fin. Execs. Inst., Tex. Soc. CPAs. Mem. Ch. of Christ. Clubs: Colonial Country, Shady Oaks Country, Century II, Petroleum. Home: Fort Worth Tex. Died Apr. 1, 1987; interred Greenwood Mausoleum, Ft. Worth, Tex.

TINDALL, WILLIAM YORK, language educator; b. Williamstown, Vt., Mar. 7, 1903; s. William John and Barbara (Chudoba) T.; m. Cecilia Herkenhoff Kramer, Dec. 22, 1937; 1 dau., Elizabeth Tindall Layton. AB, Columbia U., 1925, AM, 1926, PhD, 1934; LLD (hon.), Iona Coll., 1968. Instr. in English NYU, 1926-31; instr. in English Columbia U., 1931-37, asst. prof., 1937-45, assoc. prof., 1945-50, prof. English, 1950-71, prof. emeritus, 1971-81; vis. lectr. Northwestern U., 1950, U. Tex., 1956, U. Pa., 1953-60, Occidental Coll., 1957, Brown U., 1959, Howard U., 1960. Author: John Bunyan, Mechanick Preacher, 1934, D.H. Lawrence and Susan, his Cow, 1939, Forces in Modern British Literature, 1947, rev. edit., 1956, James Joyce, 1950, The Literary Symbol, 1955, A Reader's Guide to James Joyce, 1959, Beckett's Bums, 1960, The Joyce Country, 1960, Wallace Stevens, 1961, A Reader's Guide to Dylan Thomas, 1962, Samuel Beckett, 1964, W.B. Yeats, 1966, A Reader's Guide to Finnegans Wake, 1968; editor: The Later D.H. Lawrence, 1952, James Joyce's Chamber Music, 1954, The Poems of W.B. Yeats, 1969, Columbia Essays on Modern Writers, 1964-71. Recipient Horace Gregory award, 1974; John Simon Guggenheim Found. fellow, 1954. Mem. Modern Lang. Assn., James Joyce Soc., AAUP, Phi Beta Kappa. Democrat. Home: New York N.Y. Died Sept. 8, 1981.

TITO, MARSHALL (JOSSIP BROZ), president of Yugoslavia; b. 1892. Pvt. Austro-Hungarian Army, 1914; imprisoned Russian comps 1915-17, fought with Red Army, 1917-21, returned to Yugosalvia, became Croatian labor leader (with Metal Worker's Union), accused of Communist conspiracy, 1928, sentenced to 5 yrs. hard labor; an organizer of The Internat. Brigade Spain; comdr. Yugoslav Nat. Army Liberation; chmn. Com. and Commr. for Nat. Def. Nat. Com. Liberation; mem. Presidium Anti-Facsist; premier Govt. of Yugoslavia, 1944-53, minister of nat. def., pres., 1953-80. Address: Belgrade Yugoslavia. Died May 4, 1980; buried House of Flowers, Belgrade, Yugoslavia.

TOBIAS, CHARLES HARRISON, broker; b. Cin., Nov. 12, 1888; s. Morris H. and Mary (Leszinsky) T.; m. Charlotte Westheimer, Feb. 17, 1920; children: Charles H., John E., Paul H. Student, U. Cin., 1908. Ptnr. Chas. Tobias Bros. & Co., cap mfr., Cin., 1910-26, Julian Behr Co., advt., Cin., 1926-28, Westheimer & Co., brokers, Cin., 1928-63; divisional dir. Hayden, Stone, Inc., brokers, Cin., from 1963; pres. Cin. Stock Exchange, 1949-51. Trustee Jewish Hosp., Cin., 1930-50, Cin. Boxing Commn., 1930-50, Ohio Valley Tennis Assn., 1937-50. Capt. U.S. Army, 1917-19; maj. AUS, 1942-45. Mem. Bankers Club, Losantiville Country Club, Masons. Home: Cincinnati Ohio. †

TOBRINER, MATHEW OSCAR, state justice; b. San Francisco, Apr. 2, 1904; s. Oscar and Maude (Lezinsky) T.; m. Rosabelle Rose, May 19, 1939; children: Michael Charles, Stephen Oscar. AB, Stanford U., 1924, MA,

1925; LLB, Harvard U., 1927; SJD, U. Calif., 1932; LLD, U. Santa Clara, U. San Diego. Bar: Calif. 1928. Sr. ptnr. Tobriner, Lazarus, Brundage & Neyhart, San Francisco and L.A., 1928-59; justice Dist. Ct. Appeal, 1st Dist. Calif., 1956-62; assoc. justice Supreme Ct. Calif., from 1962; chief atty. solicitor's office Dept. Agr., 1932-36; atty. various unions AFL, counsel before Calif. Supreme Ct. on major labor issues; assoc. prof. Hastings Law Sch., 1958-59; mem. Jud. Coun. Calif., 1965-67, 78-79, 81-82. Author: (with E.G. Mears) Principles and Practices of Cooperative Marketing; adv. com. Hastings Law Jour., from 1959; contbr. articles to legal jours. Del. Dem. Nat. Conv., 1956; exec. com. gubernatorial campaign, 1958. Mem. San Francisco Legal Aid Soc. (pres. 1961), Jewish Community Rels. Coun. (chmn. 1962-64), Order of Coif (hon.), Phi Beta Kappa, Delta Sigma Rho. Home: San Francisco Calif. Died Apr. 1982.

TOLSON, JULIUS HENRY, lawyer; b. Phila., Apr. 11, 1904; s. Henry F. and Lena (Segal) T.; m. Lois C. Leidich, June 29, 1934; children: Jay H., Jayne E., Ann R. (Mrs. Richard D. Lippe). B.S. in Edn. U. Pa., 1925, M.A., 1932, Ph.D., 1951; postgrad., Exeter Coll., Oxford U., Eng., 1925-26, Temple U. Law Sch., 1926-30. Bar: Pa. 1931. Atty. firm Jenkins & Bennett, Phila., 1926-30; head English dept. La Salle Coll., Phila., 1931-32; chief claims settlement, spl. dep. atty. gen. Dept. Pub. Assistance, Commonwealth of Pa., 1932-45; mem. firm Solomon, Tolson & Resnick, 1953-69; ptnr. firm Malis, Tolson & Malis, 1969-83; ptnr. Mesirov; Gelman, Jaffe, Cramer & Jamieson, 1984-87; past dir., gen. counsel Fischer & Porter Co. Asso. editor: Temple U. Law Quarterly, 1928-30. Served to lt. comdr. USNR, 1942-45. Mem. Pa., Phila. bar assns., Am. Vets. World War II (past county comdr. Phila.), China Stamp Soc. (v.p.). Clubs: Masons, Explorers. Home: Philadelphia Pa. Died July 21, 1987; buried Mt. Sinai Cemetery, Phila.

TOMPKINS, LESLIE JAMES, association executive; b. Yonkers, N.Y., July 21, 1892; s. William J. and Adah R. (Webb) T.; m. Beulah M. Tayntor, Mar. 25, 1918; children: James B., Barbara R. Spack. B in Humanics, Springfield (Mass.) Coll., 1918; MA, NYU, 1938. Gen. sec. Gloversville (N.Y.) YMCA, 1919-23, Amsterdam (N.Y.) YMCA, 1923-29; assoc. exec. N.Y. State YMCA, 1929-36; exec. for personnel Nat. YMCA, 1937-46, exec. for field svcs., 1946-58; exec. sec. N.Am. Assn. YMCA Secs., 1958—. Author: Boards and Committees in YMCA, 1958, Association Accounting, 1954, Operating Ratios in the YMCA, 1954, Survey Techniques in Studying Local YMCAs. Trustee Springfield Coll.; pres., trustee Bethel Home for Aged, Ossining, N.Y. With U.S. Army, 1918. Mem. Nat. Assn. Social Workers, Nat. Vocational Guidance Assn., Adult Edn. Assn., Springfield Coll. Alumni Assn. (Tarbell Medallion 1946). Methodist (trustee). Home: Yonkers N.Y. †

TORGERSON, SVERRE, editor, clergyman; b. Stavanger, Norway, Sept. 21, 1890; came to U.S., 1909; naturalized, 1921; s. Emanuel and Lina (Johansen) T.; m. Ruth Marie Anderson, Nov. 25, 1923. Student, Bethany High Sch., Everett, Wash., 1915-16; candidate of Theology, Augsburg Coll. and Sem., 1921; student, Biblical Sem. in N.Y., 1929-30. Ordained to ministry Lutheran Ch., 1921. Pastor Lutheran Ch., Duluth, Minn., 1921-22, Superior, Wis., 1922-25, Racine, Wis., 1925-31, Bronx, N.Y., 1931-33, Morris, Minn., 1933-45; editor The Lutheran Messenger, Mpls., 1945-53, Folkebladet (Norwegian ch. paper), 1947-52; sec. Luth. Free Ch., 1940-50. Home: Minneapolis Minn. †

TORMEY, THOMAS JAMES, industrial relations director; b. Missouri Valley, Iowa, Aug. 13, 1892; s. William Edward and Ida Helen (Evans) T.; m. Claire Vaughn Lynch, June 15, 1920; children: Truman Lynch, Thomas James. BS, Coe Coll., 1914; PhD, U. Iowa, 1932. Tchr. Independence, Iowa, 1914-16, supr. schs., 1916-17, supt., 1917-18; supt. Grundy Ctr., 1921-31; instr. Iowa State Tchrs. Coll., summers 1926-30; rsch. fellow U. Iowa, 1932-33; pres. Ariz. State Tchrs. Coll., 1933-44; dir. indsl. relations Menasco Mfg. Co. Co-author: First Days in School, 1924, Work Book Readers, 1927, Study Guides to American History, 1930. Mem. Personnel and Indsl. Relations Assn., Masons, Phi Delta Kappa. Home: Altadena Calif. †

TORREY, THEODORE WILLETT, zoologist, educator; b. Woodbine, Iowa, Jan. 15, 1907; s. Henry Lee and Pansy Margaret (Willett) T.; m. Marcella Loge, Aug. 14, 1938. AB, U. Denver, 1927; AM, Harvard U., 1929, PhD, 1932. Teaching fellow Harvard U., 1929-32; mem. faculty Ind. U., from 1932, prof. zoology, 1947-72, prof. emeritus, 1972-86, also chmn. dept. zoology, 1948-66. Author: Laboratory Manual for Embryology, 1948, Laboratory Studies in Comparative Vertebrate Anatomy, 1948, Morphogenis of the Vertebrates, 1962, 67, 71, Laboratory Studies in Developmental Anatomy, 1962, 67; contbr. rsch. papers in embryology. Mem. AAAS, Am. Soc. Zoology, Ind. Acad. Sci., Sigma Xi, Phi Sigma, Lambda Chi Alpha. Home: Bloomington Ind. Died Aug. 31, 1986.

TOSTLEBE, ALVIN SAMUEL, economist, educator; b. Cedar Falls, Iowa, Dec. 27, 1894; s. Herman Julius and Emma Walpurga (Eck) T.; m. Pearle Childress, Aug. 30, 1922; children: John Herman (dec.), Patricia

Jane Tostlebe, Marcia Luanne Tostlebe Davis, Miriam Childress Tostlebe Thompson. AB, Iowa State Tchrs. Coll., 1916; AM, Columbia U., 1920, PhD, 1924. Instr. Sioux Ctr. (Iowa) High Sch., 1916-17; asst. prof. econs. U. Vt., 1920; instr. fin., Wharton Sch., U. Pa., 1920-21; instr. econs., Columbia U., 1921-24, assoc. in econs., 1924-27; prof. econs., Coll. Wooster, from 1927, head dept., 1931-60; sr. agrl. economist U.S. Dept. Agr., Washington, 1940-41, prin. agrl. economist, 1944-45, 50-53, cons. 1946-49. Author: The Bank of North Dakota, 1924, (with W.E. Weld) A Casebook for Economics, 1927, (with others) Impact of the War on the Financial Structure of Agriculture, 1944, The Growth of Physical Capital in Agriculture 1870-1950, 1954, Capital in Agriculture: Its Formation and Financing Since 1870, 1957; also articles and revs. Enlisted USN, 1917; commd. ensign USNRF, 1918, assigned to U.S.S. Glacier. Mem. Am. Econ. Assn., Ohio Assn. Economists and Polit. Scientists (pres. 1961-62). Methodist. Home: Wooster Ohio. Died Dec. 12, 1986, buried Wooster Cemetery.

TOUBIN, ISAAC, clergyman; b. N.Y.C., May 22, 1915; s. Samuel and Anna (Finer) T.; m. Henriette Rabinowitz, Oct. 11, 1936; 1 dau., Serena Toubin Seligman. BA, Yeshiva Coll., 1934; rabbi, Jewish Theol. Sem., 1939, M Hebrew Lit., 1940; postgrad., NYU, Columbia U. Ordained rabbi, 1939. dir. Jewish Welfare bd. army and navy activities, greater N.Y. area, 1941-43, assoc. dir. army and navy religious activities, 1943-44; dir. European Office, 1944-46; asst. exec. dir. Am. Jewish Congress, 1946-56, exec. dir., 1956-60; exec. dir. Am. Assn. for Jewish Edn., then exec. v.p., mem. exec. com. World Jewish Congress. Mem. Nat. Community Rels. Adv. Coun., from 1946; Rabbinical Assembly Am. Collector Judaica; sculptor in wood bibl. subjects. Home: Manhattan N.Y. Died Mar. 23, 1986.

TOUSLEY, BENNETT EDWIN, hotel executive; b. New Haven, May 24, 1892; s. Bennett Edwin and Anna J. (Fitch) T.; m. Katherine M. Tunney, June 10, 1916 (dec.); 1 son, Bennett Edwin III; m. 2d, Pauling Maujean Downey, Oct. 12, 1968. Student, Boardman Sci. Sch., Phillips Exeter Acad., NYU, Georgetown U. Reporter N.Y. Sun, 1913-16; publicity , promotion dir. Episcopal Ch. Pension Fund, 1916; asst. to pres. Mfrs. Trust Co. of N.Y., 1919-20; acct. exec. W.S. Hill Co., N.Y.C. and Pitts., 1921-22; assoc. mgr. Warwick Hotel, N.Y.C., Phila., 1926-27; v.p. mng. dir. Warwick Hotel, Phila., 1928-35; v.p. gen. mgr. Jermyn Hotel, Scranton, Pa., 1927-28; gen. mgr. Traymore Hotel, Atlantic City, 1935-41, Chelsea Hotel, Atlantic City, 1942-45; mng. dir. Ambassador Hotel, Atlantic City, 1941-46; v.p., gen. mgr. Bellevue-Stratford Hotel, Phila., 1946-55; gen. mgr. Penn Sherwood Hotel, Phila., 1956-58, Adelphia Hotel, Phila., from 1958. Assoc. editor: Flying, Aerial Age, 1918. Exec. sec., dir. French Aviation Mission to U.S., 1918; dir. Miss America Pageant, Atlantic City, 1935-46, dir.-gen., 1940-41; dir. bur. coordination ARC, Washington, 1918, chmn. fund dr. Atlantic County, 1943-44, chmn. Phila. chpt., 1953-54; 1st pres. Atlantic County chpt. Am. Cancer Soc., 1945-46; del. Rep. Nat. Conv., 1940. Decorated Officier d'Academie, Palmes Academique (France), 1932. Mem. N.W. Hist. and Geneal. Soc., Soc. Descs. Colonial Clergy, Aerial League Am. (organizer), Silurian Soc., N.Y., Pa., W. Phila. (dir. 1957-58), Greater Phila. (dir. 1950-54) C. of Cs, Soc. Colonial Wars, S.R., SAR, Acad. Polit. Sci., Pa. Hotels Assn. (pres. 1956, internat. coun. 1935, dir. 1958), U.S. Army Assn., N.J. (past pres.), Phila. (five times pres.) hotel assns., Phila. Safety Coun., English Speaking Union, Soc. Friendly Sons St. Patrick (pres. nat. coun. from 1955, pres. Phila. chpt. 1954-55), Am. Soc. Travel Agts., N.E. Soc. Phila., Welsh Soc. Phila. (pres. 1959), Pub. Relations Assn. Phila., Phillips Exeter Alumni Assn. Phila. (pres. 1958), Moose, Poor Richard Club, Skal Club, Variety Club, Rotary (Phila.), Lions (dist. gov. 1943-44, pres. Atlantic City 1941-42). Home: Northfield N.J. †

TOWLE, KATHERINE AMELIA, college dean; b. Towle, Calif., Apr. 30, 1898; d. George Gould and Katherine (Meister) Towle. AB, U. Calif., Berkeley, 1920, MA, 1925; LLD (hon.), Mills Coll., 1952. Resident dean Miss Ransom and Miss Bridges Sch., 1927-29, headmistress, 1929-32; sr. editor U. Calif. Press, 1935-43; adminstrv. asst. to v.p. and provost, U. Calif., 1946-47, asst. dean women, 1947-48, on mil. leave, 1943-46; dean women, assoc. dean students, U. Calif., Berkeley, 1953-62, dean students, from 1962. Commd. capt. USMCR, 1943, advanced through ranks to col., 1945; asst. dir. USMC Women's Res., 1944-45, dir., 1945-46; appointed 1st dir. Woman Marines in regular Marine Corps, 1948, col. USMC, ret. 1953. Decorated Legion of Merit. Mem. Am. Pers. and Guidance Assn., Nat. Assn. Pers. Adminstrs., Nat. Assn. Women Deans and Counselors (pres. 1957-59), AAUW, Women's Faculty Club, Town and Gown Club, Sulgrave Club, Town and Country Club, Kappa Alpha Theta. Episcopalian. Died Mar. 1, 1986.

TOWNSEND, EDWARD, banker; b. Pelham, N.Y., Aug. 26, 1912; s. Myron Turner and Gertrude (Barnard) T.; m. Felicia Thomas; children: Valoise Townsend Hodgkins, Victoria Townsend Roschen. Grad., Hotchkiss Sch., 1931; BA, Yale U., 1934. With Hanover Bank, 1935-42; with The First Boston Corp., 1946-77, v.p., 1955-64, sr. v.p., 1964-77, ret., 1977, also

bd. dirs.; dir. Dundee Cement Co., Mich. Pres. Met. Opera Club, 1978-80; chmn. Peoples' Symphony Concert. Ordnance maj. U.S. Army, World War II. Home: New York N.Y. Died July 19, 1986.

TOWNSEND, IRVING JOSEPH, producer phonograph records, writer; b. Springfield, Mass., Nov. 27, 1920; s. Irving Joseph and Marguerite (Noble) T.; married; children: Nicole L., Jeremy N. AB, Princeton U., 1943. Profl. musician to 1950; v.p.; producer Columbia Records, Hollywood, Calif., from 1950; columnist Santa Barbara (Calif.) News-Press, 1972-74. Author: The Less Expensive Spread, 1971, John Hammond on Records, 1977, The Tavern, 1978, Separate Lifetimes, 1986; contbr. articles to mags. Lt. USNR, 1943-46. Mem. NARAS (pres.). Home: Santa Inez Calif. Died Dec. 17, 1981; buried Ballard, Calif.

TOWNSHEND, WILSON LEWIS, lawyer; b. Washington, Oct. 19, 1890; s. John Wilson and Elizabeth Morrow (Gayley) T.; m. Virginia Ray Wilson, Jan. 21, 1920; children: Elizabeth Gayley (Mrs. Horace Lincoln Jacobs III), Wilson Lewis. LLB, George Washington U., 1913. Bar: D.C. 1912, Md. 1916. Gen. practice Washington and Md., 1916-40; dep. register of wills Washington, 1919; spl. asst. to atty. gen., establishing title of U.S. in waterfront land in Washington 1932-33; became gen. counsel Export-Import Bank of Washington, 1949, dir., 1952-53; bd. dirs. Equitable Coop. Bldg. Assn., Montgomery Mut. Bldg. Assn. Corp. counsel Town of Kensington, 1920-40. Capt. inf. U.S. Army, 1917-19; asst. intelligence officer Mil. Intelligence div. War Dept. Gen. Staff, 1940-46; chief Latin Am. br. and Western Hemisphere specialist; col. Mil. Intelligence Res. from 1943. Decorated Legion of Merit, 1945. Mem. Am., Fed., D.C. and Md. bar assns., Am. Legion, Res. Officers Assn., Cosmos Club, Masons, Kappa Alpha. Presbyterian. Home: Kensington Md. †

TOWNSON, DOUGLAS C., newspaper executive; b. Rochester, N.Y., 1891; m. Marie Werner, Apr. 3, 1916; children: Marie, William, Barbara, Andrea. BA, Yale U., 1914. V.p., dir. Gannett Co., Inc., Rochester, Frank E. Gannett Newspaper Found.; mem. adv. com. Lincoln-Rochester Trust Co.; bd. dirs. Rochester Telephone Corp. Home: Rochester N.Y. †

TRAFFORD, WILLIAM BRADFORD, lawyer; b. N.Y.C., Mar. 22, 1910; s. Perry D. and Elizabeth (Meeker) T.; m. Abigail Sard, Jan. 26, 1937 (div. 1965); children: Abigail (Mrs. P. Robin Brett), Elizabeth, William Bradford; m. Stella M. Champollion, Sept. 3, 1965. Grad., St. Paul's Sch., 1927; student, U. Freiburg, Germany, 1927-28; AB, Harvard U., 1932, LLB, 1936. Bar: Mass. 1936, N.Y. 1937. Law clk. to judge U.S. Ct. Appeals, 1937-39; asst. corp. counsel N.Y.C., 1939-42; mem. Peabody, Brown, Rowley & Storey, Boston, 1946-85; town counsel Wenham, Mass., 1948-65. Bd. dirs. Mass. Soc. Prevention of Cruelty to Children. 1st lt. inf., AUS, 1942-45, ETO. Decorated Bronze Star, Purple Heart. Mem. Am. Law Inst., Boston Bar Assn., Mass. Hist. Soc., City Club, Tavern Club. Home: Boston Mass. Died Feb. 20, 1983; cremated.

TRAMMELL, CHARLES MONROE, lawyer; b. Lakeland, Fla., June 6, 1886; s. Erasmus Ripley and Sarah Roberta (Germany) T.; m. Iris May Robertson, June 29, 1910; children: Charles Monroe, Mary Virginia. PhB, Emory Coll., Oxford, Ga., 1907; LLB, Vanderbilt U., 1909; postgrad., George Washington U., 1920, Am. U., 1921. Bar: Fla. 1909, U.S. Tax Ct. 1924. Practiced in Lakeland, 1909; county judge Polk County, Fla., 1913-17; spl. atty. in office solicitor internal revenue, 1920-24; mem. U.S. Bd. Tax Appeals (now U.S. Tax Ct.), 1924-36; ptnr. Trammell, Rand & Nathan, Washington, from 1936; pres. Lexington Mining Co., tech. advisor IRS. Econ. advisor Bd. Econ. Warfare; chief Civil Affairs Br. Mil. Dist. Washington; counsel for Chinese Air Forces. Commd. 2d lt. Air Svc., 1918, capt., Mar. 1919, maj., July 1919; discharged, 1920; col., dir. Army Indsl. Coll. Mem. ABA, Fed. Bar Assn., Bar Assn. D.C., Fla. Bar Assn., Am. Law Inst., Am. Judicature Soc., Mil. Order World War, SAR, Sojourners, Masons (32 deg.). Democrat. Methodist. Home: Washington D.C. †

TRAPP, WILLIAM O(SCAR), educator, newspaperman; b. N.Y.C., Mar. 9, 1889; s. Carl and Elizabeth (Neilson) T.; m. Hilda Lankering, Aug. 30, 1935. Grad., Montclair (N.J.) State Normal Sch., 1910; AB, Ind. U., 1912; AM, Cornell U., 1941, PhD, 1943. Teaching fellow philosophy Ind. U., 1912-13, instr. English, 1913-14; reporter, polit. writer, subeditor Phila. newspapers, 1914-25; asst. Am. History Cornell U., 1942-43; reporter, polit. editor, legis. corr. N.Y. Eve. World (conducted campaign against ambulance chasing which won Pulitzer prize for paper, 1929) and N.Y. World Telegram, 1925-38; publicity dir. Gov. Herbert H. Lehman, N.Y., 1938; dir. pub. relations N.Y. State Ins. fund, 1938-40; assoc. prof. journalism Columbia U., 1943-45; mem. univ. coun., 1945-50, coun. edn. journalism, 1946-50; lectr. communication arts Fordham U. 1954—, adj. prof., 1958—. Author: Constitutional Doctrines of Owen J. Roberts, 1943; contbr. articles to periodicals. Mem. N.Y. State and Am. polit. sci. assns., Am. Acad. Polit. and Social Sci., Am. Soc. Pub. Adminstrn., Acad. Polit. sci., Nat. Mcpl. League, Am.

Hist. Assn., N.Y. Hist. Soc., Assn. Edn. Journalism, AAUP, N.Y. Legis. Corrs. Assn., Masons (K.T., Shriner), Inner Circle Club (N.Y.), Phi Beta Kappa, Sigma Delta Chi, Phi Kappa Phi. Democrat. Episcopalian (warden). Home: New York N.Y. †

TRESEDER, ROSS CLEMO, business executive; b. Ridgeway, Wis., Mar. 31, 1891; s. Martin and Elizabeth (Rundall) T.; m. Elizabeth Pace, Dec. 30, 1914; children: Elizabeth Treseder Land, Jane Treseder Low. Student, pub. schs., Ridgeway, Wis. With Coca Cola Co., Atlanta, 1912-34, v.p., advt. mgr., 1922-30, v.p., sales mgr., 1930-34; v.p. Nat. Distillers Products Corp., N.Y.C., 1934-37; v.p., dir. Lorr Labs., Paterson, N.J., 1938-50, exec. v.p., dir., chmn. exec. com., 1952-53, pres., dir., chmn. exec. com., 1953-54; exec. v.p., dir. Milkmaid Inc., Paterson, 1952-53; with A.R. Winarick Inc., N.Y.C., from 1954. Mem. Union League (N.Y.C.). Episcopalian. Home: New York N.Y. †

TREUHAFT, WILLIAM COLUMBUS, paint manufacturing company executive; b. Cleve., Oct. 21, 1892; s. Morris and Bertha (Goodman) T.; m. Elizabeth Marting, May 1934. Student, Adelbert Coll., Western Res. U., 1910-13, LHD; student, Case Inst. Tech., 1910-14, LLD. Pres. Sterling Products Co., Cleve., 1916-28; founder, chmn. Tremco Inc., Cleve., from 1928, Tremco (Can.) Ltd., Toronto, 1928-66; dir. Tremco Ltd., Eng.; chmn. Univ. Circle Inc. Pres. Cleve. Community Fund, 1956-57; chmn. endowment fund com., hon. life trustee Jewish Community Fedn.; mem. health planning and devel. commn. Cleve. Welfare Fedn.; pres. United Appeal Greater Cleve., 1966-67; chmn. Cancer Ctr. Inc.; mem. Cleve. Little Hoover Commn.; trustee Ursuline Coll. for Women, Case Western Res. U. Lt. (j.g.) USNRF, World War I. Recipient Charles Eisenman award for community service, 1951, Disting. Service award Community Chest, 1954, Cleve. medal for pub. service Cleve. C. of C., 1958, Bus. Statesmanship award Harvard Bus. Sch. Club, Cleve., 1969, Ursula Laurus award Ursuline Coll., 1970, Disting. Service award Coun. on Social Work Edn., 1971, Human Relations award NCCJ, 1972. Mem. Am. Mgmt. Assn. (bd. dirs., chmn. emeritus fin. com.), Coun. Social Work Edn. (chmn. nat. com.), The 50 Club, Union Club, Kirtland Country Club (Cleve.), Mentor (Ohio) Harbor Yachting Club. Home: Cleveland Ohio. †

TREUTING, WALDO LOUIS, physician, educator; b. New Orleans, Apr. 28, 1911; s. Henry Louis and Lydia Amanda (Waldo) T.; m. Alida Mary Jauchler, May 6, 1936; children: Waldo Louis, Robert E., Walida L. Treuting Enochs. BS, Tulane U., 1930, MD, 1934; MPH, John Hopkins, 1939. Diplomate Am. Bd. Preventive Medicine. Intern Charity Hosp., New Orleans, 1934-35; dir. Parish Health Unit, La., 1935-38; dir. crippled children's program, state epidemiologist, dir. preventive medicine div. La. State Dept. Health, 1939-46; state health officer, pres. La. State Bd. Health, 1946-48; prof. pub. health adminstrn., sch. medicine, Tulane U., 1948-58, acting chmn. dept. tropical medicine and pub. health, 1953-58; prof. and head dept. pub. health practice, grad. sch. pub. health. U. Pitts., from 1958; dir. Allegheny County Health Dept., Health Programs to Govt. of Egypt, 1953; mem. nat. adv. com. on Pub. Health Traineeship, USPHS, 1956-59; dir. La. div. Am. Cancer Soc., New Orleans Coun. Social Agys., La. Health Coun. Fellow Am. Pub. Health Assn., Am. Coll. Preventive Medicine (treas., regent 1955); mem. Am. Social Hygiene Assn. (dir. 1949), Community Health Assn. (dir.), So. Med. Assn. (sec. sect. pub. health 1949-51, chmn. 1952), Pa. Acad. Preventive Medicine (sec., treas. 1959-60), Allegheny County Med. Soc., Pa. Pub. Health Assn. (pres. 1964-65), Sigma Xi, Alpha Omega Alpha, Delta Omega (nat. pres. 1961). Home: Pittsburgh Pa. Died Aug. 4, 1985.

TRIBBLE, HAROLD WAYLAND, theologian, educator; b. Charlottesville, Va., Nov. 18, 1899; s. Henry Wise and Estelle Carlton (Rawlings) T.; m. Nelle Futch, June 10, 1925; children: Harold Wayland, Betty May Tribble Barnett, Barbara Ann Tribble Holding. Student, Columbia Coll., Lake City, Fla., 1915-17; AB, Richmond (Va.) Coll., 1919; ThM, Southern Bapt. Theol. Sem., Louisville, Ky., 1922, ThD, 1925; AM, U. Louisville, 1927; PhD, U. Edinburgh, Scotland, 1937; student, U. Bonn, Germany, 1931, U. Basel, Switzerland, 1936; DD, Stetson U., Fla., 1930; LLD, Union U., Jackson, Tenn., 1939, Wake Forest Coll., 1948, U. Richmond, 1949, Duke U., 1952, U. N.C., 1952. Ordained ministry Bapt. Ch., 1919. pastor successively Cropper, Christiansburg, New Castle, Simpsonville, Ky., 1920-30; asst. prof. theology, Southern Bapt. Theol. Sem., 1925-29, prof., 1929-47, pres. Andover Newton Theol. Sch., Newton Centre, Mass., 1947-50; pres. Wake Forest Coll., 1950-67; pres. Southern U. Conf., 1965-66. Author: Our Doctrines, 1929, From Adam to Moses, 1934, Salvation, 1940; rev. E.Y. Mullins', The Baptist Faith, 1935; contbr. theol. articles to jours. Mem. Old Town Club, Masons, Phi Beta Kappa, Omicron Delta Kappa, Kappa Sigma, Tau Kappa Alpha. Home: Winston-Salem N.C. Died June 17, 1986; cremated.

TRIBLE, WILLIAM MACLOHON, otolaryngologist; b. Washington, July 3, 1924; s. George Barnett and Letha (MacLohon) T.; m. Elizabeth Stuart Henley, Feb. 3, 1956; children: Letha, George, Elizabeth, Annadelia; m. Gwendolyn Quodling Shields, Feb. 11, 1982. AB, Princeton U., 1943; MD, George Washington U., 1950; MS, U. Pa., 1956. Diplomate Am. Bd. Otolaryngology. Intern George Washington U. Hosp., 1950-51; resident in otolaryngology Manhattan Eye, Ear and Throat Hosp., 1952-55; pvt. practice Washington, from 1955; clin. asst. prof. Howard U. and Freedman's Hosp., Washington, 1959-66; clin. asst. George Washington Sch. Medicine, 1956-58, assoc., 1958-60, clin. asst. prof. 1961-68, clin. prof. otolaryngology, 1969-84, chief otolaryngology, Washington Hosp. Ctr., 1972-78. Contbr. articles to profl. jours. With AUS, 1943-46. Fellow ACS (gov. 1972-78); mem. Am. Soc. Head and Neck Surgery (pres. 1978-79), Am. Laryngol. Assn. (sec. from 1977), Am. Coun. Otolaryngology (treas. from 1974), Soc. Surg., Oncology, Am. Laryngol., Rhinol. and Otol. Soc. (sec. from 1980), Metropolitan Club, Chevy Chase Club, City Tavern Club. Republican. Episcopalian. Home: Bethesda Md. Died July 27, 1984; buried Rock Creek Cemetery, Washington.

TRIMBLE, LESTER ALBERT, composer; b. Bangor, Wis., Aug. 29, 1923; s. John Lester and Clara Frieda Amanda (Piske) T.; m. Mary Constance Wilhelm, July 5, 1947. Studied with, Darius Milhaud, Nikolai Lopatnikoff, Arthur Honegger, Nadia Boulanger; M.F.A., Carnegie Inst. Tech., 1948; student, Conservatoire Nat. de Musique, Paris, 1951, Ecole Normale De Musique, Paris, 1951, Berkshire (Mass.) Music Center, summer 1947; student electronic music, Columbia, 1969; D.Mus. (hon.), St. John's U., 1986. Mem. faculty Chatham Coll., Pitts., 1949-50; music criticis for N.Y. Herald Tribune, 1952-60, The Nation, 1956-61, Washington Star, 1963-64, Notes mag., the Music Quar., occasionally 1952-62; gen. mgr. Am. Music Center, N.Y.C., 1960-62; bd. dirs. Am. Music Center, 1959-86; prof. music U. Md., 1963-68; music critic Stereo Rev. mag., 1970-73; mem. faculty Juilliard Sch., 1971-85, New Sch. Social Research, 1969-70; judge numerous composition competitions; mem. rec. com. Walter W. Naumburg Found.; Bd. dirs. MacDowell Colony, Am. Composers Alliance, Bennington Composers Conf., Music in Our Time, Concert Artists Guild. Composer-in-residence, N.Y. Philharmonic Orch., 1967-68, (Dial Press Creative Writing award 1947), Wolf Trap Farm Park, Va., 1973-74; performance of music with maj. symphony orchs. and chamber ensembles throughout world, recs. on, Columbia, Desto, C.R.I. records. Served with USAAF, 1942-44. Guggenheim fellow, 1964; recipient award and citation Nat. Inst. Arts and Letters, 1961; award Soc. Publn. Am. Music, 1964; Thorne Fund award, 1968-69; award Columbia Records Modern Music Series, 1958; Ford Found. Publn.-Rec. award, 1972; Alice Ditson award, 1957; Sigma Alpha Iota Publn. award, 1964; Rockefeller grant, 1967; fellow MacDowell Colony, 1958-59; fellow Yaddo Found., 1959; fellow Huntington Hartford Found., 1957. Home: New York City N.Y. Died Dec. 31, 1986.

TRIVERS, HOWARD, educator, foreign service officer; b. N.Y.C., Sept. 30, 1909; m. Mildred Raynolds, Dec. 22, 1934; children: Aylmer, Robert, Jonathan, Kate, Ruth, Mildred, Howard E. Grad., Worcester Acad., 1926; AB, Princeton U., 1930; MA, Harvard U., 1932, PhD, 1941; student, Heidelberg U., Germany, 1932-33, U. Freiburg, Germany, 1935-38; grad., Nat. War Coll., 1950. Teaching asst. Harvard U., 1934-35; with Dept. State, 1941-69, staff European div., 1941-43, div. territorial studies, 1943-45, staff Cen European div., participant Postdam Conf., Moscow Conf., Berlin blockade meeting, 1945-49, staff No. European div., 1952-54, officer-in-charge Czechoslovak, Polish, Baltic affairs, 1955-57, assigned Am. embassasy, Copenhagen, 1950-52, chief Eastern affairs sect. U.S. mission, Berlin, 1957-60, dep. to asst. chief mission, 1960-62, dir. Office Research and Analysis for Sino-Soviet Bloc, 1962-65; sr. examiner Bd. Examiners Fgn. Service, 1965-66; Am. consul gen. Zurich, Switzerland, 1966-69; mem. faculty Nat. War Coll., 1954-55; vis. prof. dept. govt. So. Ill. U., Carbondale, 1969-72; vis. prof. polit. sci. Ball State U., Muncie, Ind., 1972-74, adj. prof., 1974-87. Author: Three Crisis in American Foreign Affairs and a Continuing Revolution, 1972. Mem. Am. Philos. Assn., Fssn. Fgn. Service Assn., Am. Polit. Sci. Assn. Home: Muncie Ind. Died Mar. 27, 1987.

TROMPETER, LISA ROMA See ROMA, LISA

TROTT, RAYMOND HARRIS, banker; b. Bath, Maine, Aug. 3, 1892; s. Joseph McCobb and Annie (Harris) T.; m. Elisabeth McIlwain Houghton, Apr. 7, 1920; children: Houghton McCobb, Virginia Trott Rothschild, Elisabeth Trott Hazard. AB, Dartmouth Coll., 1914; student, Harvard Law Sch. extension, 1918. Bar: Maine 1918, Mass. 1918. Successively asst. trust officer, trust officer, v.p. R.I. Hosp. Trust Co., 1920-47, pres., 1947, then chmn. bd., dir.; dir. Gorham Mfg. Co., Congdon & Carpenter Co.; chmn. bd. Gorham Corp., R.I. Hosp. Trust Co., R.I. Hosp., Nat. Bank. Chmn. R.I. Community Chest Campaign, 1943-44, v.p., 1945-47; trustee, treas. Providence Lying-In Hosp.; mem. ARC Fgn. Svc., 1918. Mem. ABA, Am. Bankers Assn., Agawam Hunt Club, Providence Art Club, Hope Club, Turks Head Club, University Club (N.Y.). Home: Providence R.I. †

TROTTER, JOHN ELLIS, geography educator; b. Chgo., May 18, 1921; s. John William and Helen (Ellis) T.; m. Twanette M. Watterson. MS, U. Chgo., 1953, PhD, 1962. Faculty Ill. State U., Normal, 1956-85, prof. geography, 1965-85, head dept. geography and geology, 1967-78. Contbr. articles to profl. jours. With USAAF, 1943-45. Decorated D.F.C., Air medal. Mem. Assn. Am. Geographers, Am. Geog. Soc. Home: Normal Ill. Died Apr. 7, 1985; buried Park Hill Cemetery, Bloomington, Ill.

TRYON, LAWRENCE EDWIN, lawyer; b. Channahon, Ill., Nov. 25, 1899; s. Allison and Mary (Alexander) T.; m. Mary A. Bradshaw, Apr. 12, 1925; children: Myrna Jewell Tryon Thomas, Allison Charles, Mary Kathryn Tryon Carter; m. Eugenia Shaw, June 11, 1953. Student, Northwestern U., Salt City Bus. Coll., Hutchinson, Kans., LaSalle Extension U. Bar: Okla. 1929. County judge Texas County, Okla., 1931-36, county atty., 1937-38; pvt. practice in Guymon, Okla., from 1938; ptnr. Tryon & Field, Guymon; bd. dirs. City Nat. Bank & Trust Co., Guymon. Author: I Say, Say I, 1981, Travelling on the Road to Damascus, 1983. Del. Gen. Conf. Meth. Ch., 1936; Rep. nominee Supreme Ct. Okla., 1950; del. Rep. Nat. Conv., 1960; pres. bd. control Meml. Hosp., Guymon, 1948-79. With U.S. Army, World War I. Fellow Am. Coll. Probate Counsel; mem. ABA, Okla Bar Assn., Lions Club (dist. gov.), Masons (32 deg.), K.T. (dep. grand comdr.), Shriners. Home: Guymon Okla. Died Apr. 16, 1985.

TUCHMAN, BARBARA WERTHEIM, historian, writer; b. N.Y.C., Jan. 30, 1912; d. Maurice and Alma (Morgenthau) Wertheim; m. Lester R. Tuchman, 1940; children: Lucy, Jessica, Alma. B.A., Radcliffe Coll., 1933; D.Litt., Yale U., Columbia U., Harvard U., Brown U., N.Y. U., Norte Dame U., Smith Coll., William and Mary Coll., Darmouth Coll. Research asst. Inst. Pacific Relations, N.Y.C., 1934, Tokyo, 1935; editorial asst. The Nation, N.Y.C., 1936, Spain, 1937; staff writer War in Spain, London, 1937-38; Am. corr. New Statesman and Nation, London, 1939; with Far East news desk, OWI, N.Y.C., 1944-45; Jefferson lectr., 1980. Author: The Lost British Policy, 1938, Bible and Sword, 1956, The Zimmerman Telegram, 1958, The Guns of August, 1962 (Pulitzer prize), The Proud Tower, 1966, Stilwell and the American Experience in China, 1971 (Pulitzer prize), Notes from China, 1972, A Distant Mirror, 1978, Practising History, 1981, The March of Folly, 1984, The First Salute, 1988; contbr. to Fgn. Affairs, N.Y. Times, others. Trustee Radcliffe Coll., 1960-72, N.Y. Public Library, 1980—. Decorated Order Leopold 1st class Belgium. Fellow Am. Acad. Arts and Letters (pres. 1978-80), Smithsonian Council, AAAL (Gold medal for history 1978); mem. Authors Guild (treas.), Authors League (council), Soc. Am. Historians (pres. 1971-73). Club: Cosmopolitan. Home: Cos Cob Conn. Died Feb. 6, 1989; buried Temple of Israel, Mount Hope Cemetery, Hastings on Hudson, N.Y.

TUCKER, FORREST MEREDITH, actor; b. Plainfield, Ind., Feb. 12, 1919; s. Forrest A. and Doris P. (Heringlake) T.; 1 dau., Pamela Brooke; m. Marilyn Johnson, Mar. 28, 1950 (dec. July 1960); m. Marilyn Fisk, Oct. 23, 1961; children: Cynthia Brooke, Forrest Sean. Student, Mt. Hermon (Mass.) Prep., 1933. Motion picture debut in: The Westerner, 1939; actor, Columbia Pictures, 1940-42, Warner Bros., 1946-48, Republic Pictures, 1948-55; appeared in TV series Crunch and Des, NBC-TV, 1956; star mus. prodn. on tour Music Man, 1958; TV series F Troop, 1966-69, Dusty's Trail, 1974, Ghost Busters, 1975; assoc. producer TV series, Drury Lane Theatre, Chgo., 1969; mem. nat. co. TV series That Championship Season, 1972-73, Plaza Suite, 1971-72; appeared in TV series The Confidence Game; appeared in numerous movies including: Sands of Iwo Jima, 1950, Auntie Mame, 1958, The Night They Raided Minsky's, 1968, Wild McCullochs, 1975; appeared in TV movie The Incredible Rocky Mountain Race, 1977, Blood Feud, 1983. Served to 2d lt. Signal Corps U.S. Army, 1942-45. Clubs: Am. (London), Stage Golfing (London); Masquers (Hollywood, Calif.) (dir.); Players (N.Y.C.), Lambs (N.Y.C.), Friar's (N.Y.C.); Variety Internat. (dir.). Home: Los Angeles Calif. Died Oct. 25, 1986.

TUCKER, GABRIEL FREDERICK, JR., physician-surgeon; b. Bryn Mawr, Pa., June 18, 1924; s. Gabriel Frederick and Beatrice (Jarvis) T.; m. Mary Elizabeth O'Brien, June 30, 1947; children: Beatrice, Gabriel, Mark, Michael, William, Patrick. A.B., Princeton U., 1947; M.D. (Henry Strong Denison scholar), Johns Hopkins U., 1951. Diplomate Am. Bd. Otolaryngology. Intern Grad. Hosp. of U. Pa., Phila., 1951-52; fellow in bronchoesophagology and laryngeal surgery U. Pa. Sch. Medicine, 1953-54; resident in otolaryngology Johns Hopkins U., 1954-56, instr., 1956, asst. prof. laryngology and otology, 1958-62, in charge bronchoscopic clinic, 1961-62; instr. surgery and pharmacology U. N.C., Chapel Hill, 1956-58; former clin. prof. laryngology and bronchoesophagology Temple U., Phila.; prof. assoc. Chevalier Jackson Clinic, Phila., 1962-75; previously prof. otolaryngology and maxillofacial surgery Northwestern U. Sch. Medicine; head div. bronchoesophagology-otolaryngology, dept. communicative disorders Children's Meml. Hosp., Chgo., 1975-86; vis. faculty U. Pa., from 1967, Temple U., 1975-81, Hahnemann Med. Coll., 1972-81; cons. otolaryngology Armed Forces Inst. Pathology, Washington, 1976-86, Cook County Hosp., Chgo., 1976-86, Lakeside VA Hosp., Chgo., 1976-86, Rehab. Inst. Chgo., 1981-86. Author: Human Larynx, 1971, trans. Am. Broncho-Esophagological Assn., 1968-72; co-author: Ear, Nose and Throat Disorders in Children, 1985, others; contbd. chpts. to books, articles to profl. jours.; editor: Am. Laryngol. Assn., 1977-83. Bd. dirs. Family Services Phila., 1966-69. Served as ensign USNR, 1943-46. grantee Edward Shedd Wells Fund, 1975-86; grantee Helen Mayer Medgyesy Fund, 1979-81. Hon. mem. Irish Otolaryn. Soc. (Sir William Wilde medal 1977), Pacific Coast Ophthal. and Otolaryng. Soc., Soc. Mil. Otolaryngologists, Australian Otolaryng. Soc., Ill. Soc. Otolaryngology; mem. Am. Bronchoesophagological Assn. (council 1968-86, pres. 1974, Chevalier lectr. 1979, Chevalier Jackson award 1982), Am. Laryngol. Assn. (librarian, historian, editor 1977-83, pres. 1984-85), Am. Council Otolaryngology (pres. 1975), ACS (bd. govs. 1978-86), Am. Acad. Pediatrics (chmn. sect. otolaryngology and bronchoesophagology 1981-83, program chmn. 1983), Internat. Bronchoesophagological Soc. (exec. sec.-treas. 1983-86), Pan Am. Assn. Oto-Rhino-Laryngology and Bronchoesophagology, Royal Soc. Medicine, Brazilian Soc. Bronchoesophagology, Am. Acad. Ophthalmology and Otolaryngology (Honor award 1969), Johns Hopkins Med. and Surg. Assn., Soc. U. Otolaryngologists, Am. Laryngol. Rhinol. and Otol. Soc., Assn. for Research in Otolaryngology, Soc. for Ear Nose and Throat Advances in Children, Pa. Acad. Ophthalmology and Otolaryngology, Philadelphia County Med. Soc., Phila. Laryngol. Soc. (pres. 1974), Coll. Physicians Phila., Chgo. Laryngol. Soc., Inst. Medicine Chgo. Clubs: Phila. Bronchoscopic Soc. (pres. 1975-78), N.Y. Bronchoscopic Soc. (pres. 1976-77). Home: Chicago Ill. Died Dec. 8, 1986.

TUCKER, JOHN HELLUMS, JR., lawyer; b. Pine Bluff, Ark., Feb. 25, 1891; s. John Hellums and Lucille (LePhiew) T.; m. Hortense Rigby, Apr. 23, 1924. AB, Washington and Lee U., 1910, LLD (hon.), 1958; LLB, La. State U., 1920, LLD (hon.), 1956; LLD (hon.), Tulane U., 1959, Loyola U., 1966; DHL (hon.), Centenary Coll., 1972. Bar: La. 1920. Practiced in Shreveport, La., from 1920; ptnr. Tucker, Jeter & Jackson; agt. Consulaire de France in Shreveport. Author: Ssource Bbooks on Louisiana Law (vols. VI-1X, Tulane Law Rev.), 1931-35, Bartolus Soc. Juridical Studies 1, Effects on the Civil Law of La. Brought About by the Changes in its Sovereignty, Tradition and Techniques of Codification: The Louisiana Experieince, Au-Delá du Code Civil, Mais Par le Code Civil. Chmn. La. State Law Inst.; mem. Gen. Staff Com. on Res. and N.GH. Policy, 1946-49. Served to sgt. U. S. Army, 1916, Mexican border, 1st lt. World War I, col. inf., col. inf. World War II; col. inf. res., 1943-51. Decorated French Legion of Honor, 1956. Mem. La. Bar Assn. (former gov.), Shreveport Bar Assn., Internat. House (Boston), Pickwick Club, New Orleans Country Club, Limsoll Club (New Orleans), Union Club (Cleve.), Westbrook Club (Mansfield, Ohio), Shreveport Club, Shreveport Country Club, Army and Navy Club (Washington), Confrérie de Chevaliers du Tastevin (grand officer), Phi Beta Kappa, Sigma Nu, Phi Delta Phi, Omicron Delta Kappa, Order of Coif. Home: Shreveport La. Died 1984.

TUCKER, WILLIAM EARLE, lawyer; b. Plant City, Fla., Sept. 12, 1921; s. Jasper William and Lillian (Turner) T.; m. Gloria B. Wright, Dec. 3, 1944; children: Pamela Suzanne, Karen Lee Kuykendall. Student, Fla. So. Coll., 1939-42; J.D., Washington and Lee U., 1948. Bar: Fla. 1948. With firm Cooper, Cooper & Tucker (and predecessor), Tampa, Fla., 1948-54; asst. county solicitor Hillsborough County, Fla., 1954-57; partner Gibbons, Tucker, Miller, Whatley & Stein, P.A., Tampa, 1957-87; dir., atty. First Ruskin Bank, Fla., 1962-84; v.p., atty., dir. Sun City Center Bank, Fla., 1971-83. Served with USAAF, 1942-45. Mem. Am., Fla., Tampa, Hillsborough County bar assns., C. of C. Temple Terrace (sec. 1969), Phi Alpha Delta. Democrat. Baptist. Clubs: Exchange (Tampa), University (Tampa), Tower (Tampa); Temple Terrace Golf and Country. Home: Temple Terrace Fla. Died Mar. 6, 1987, buried Hillsboro Meml. Cemetery.

TUCKEY, JOHN SUTTON, educator; b. Washington, July 27, 1921; s. William Dyson and Nellie (Sutton) T.; m. Irene Louise Swinehart, Nov. 18, 1945; children: Alan, Janis. A.B., U. Notre Dame, 1943, M.A., 1949, Ph.D., 1953. Instr. English Purdue U., Hammond, Ind., 1953-55; asst. prof. English Purdue U., 1956-59, asso. prof. English, 1960-64, prof. English, 1965-87, F.L. Hovde Disting. Service prof., 1981-87; chmn. dept. English Purdue U., 1963-83, asst. dean grad. sch., 1974—. Author: Mark Twain and Little Satan-The Writing of the Mysterious Stranger, 1963; Editor: Mark Twain's Which Was the Dream and other Symbolical Writings of the Later Years, 1967, Mark Twain's Mysterious Stranger—and the Critics, 1968, Mark Twain's Fables of Man, 1972, The Devil's Race Track: Mark Twain's Great Dark Writings, 1980. Served to lt. (j.g.) USNR, 1944-46. Purdue Research Found. grantee, 1961, 62, 64; Am. Philos. Soc. grantee, 1965; NEH sr. fellow, 1973. Mem. MLA, Coll. English Assn., Ind. Coll. English Assn. (pres. 1965), Midwest MLA, Am. Studies Assn. Home: Crown Point Ind. Died Sept. 4, 1987; buried Elkhart, Ind.

TUDOR, ANTONY (WILLIAM COOK), choreographer, former dancer; b. London, Apr. 4, 1908; came to U.S., 1938.; Studied dancing with, Marie Rambert, Pearl Argyle, Harold Turner, Margaret Craske; D.Litt. (hon.), St. Andrew's U., 1970. Prin. ballet dancer various cos., 1930-50; dir., choreographer Ballet Rambert, London, 1930-38; with Sadler's-Wells Royal Ballet, 1931-36; choreographer Royal Opera House Covent Garden, 1935-38; founder London Ballet, 1930's; choreographer Am. Ballet Theatre (formerly Ballet Theatre), 1939-80, assoc. dir., 1974-80, choreographer emeritus, 1980-87; head faculty Met. Opera Ballet Sch., 1950-63, ballet dir., 1957-63; artistic dir. Royal Swedish Ballet, 1963-64; tchr. dance Juilliard Sch.; choreographer N.Y.C. Ballet, 1951-52. Producer ballets in Japan, Sweden, Greece, Can., Australia; choreographed numerous dances for BBC Prodns. including Paleface, 1937, Fugue for Four Cameras, 1937, Portsmouth Point, 1937, Tristan and Isolda, 1938, The Emperor Jones, 1938, The Tempest, 1939, The Pilgrim's Progress, 1939; choreography for film In a Monastery Garden, 1932; London theater choreography includes The Happy Hypocrite, 1936, To and Fro, 1936, Johnson over Jordan, 1939, Hollywood Pinafore, 1945, The Day Before Spring, 1945; other works choreographed include Cross-Garter'd, 1931, Mr. Roll's Quadrilles, 1932, Constanza's Lament, 1932, Lysistrata, 1932, Adam and Eve, 1932, Pavanne Pour une Infante Defunte, 1933, Atlanta of the East, 1933, Paramour, 1934, The Legend of Dick Whittington, 1934 (as an interlude in T.S. Eliot's The Rock), The Planets, 1934, The Descent of Hebe, 1935, Jardin aux Lilas, 1936, Dark Elegies, 1937, Suite of Airs, 1937, Gallant Assembly, 1937, Judgement of Paris, 1983, Soiree Musicale, 1938, Gala Performance, 1938, Goya Pastoral, 1940, Time Table, 1941, Pillar of Fire, 1942, The Tragedy of Romeo and Juliet, 1943, Dim Lustre, 1943, Undertow, 1945, Shadow of the Wind, 1948, The Dear Departed, 1949, Nimbus, 1950, Lady of the Camilias, 1951, Les Mains Gauches, 1951, Ronde Du Printemps, 1951, La Gloire, 1952, Trio Con Brio, 1952, Exercise Piece, 1953, Little Improvisations, 1953, Elizabethan Dances, 1953, Britannia Triumphs, 1953, Offenbach in the Underworld, 1954, La Leyenda de Jose, 1958, Hail and Farewell, 1959, A Choreographer Comments, 1960, Gradus Ad Parnassus, 1962, Fandango, 1963, Ekon Av Trunpeter (Echoes of Trumpets) 1963, Concerning Oracles, 1966, Shadowplay, 1967, Knight Errant, 1968, Divine Horseman, 1969, Continuo, 1971, Sunflowers, 1971, Cereus, 1972, The Leaves Are Fading, 1975, Tiller in the Fields, 1978. Recipient Carina Ari Gold medal, 1973; Dance Mag. award, 1974; Creative Arts medal Brandeis U., 1976; Capezio Dance award, 1986; Handel Medallion, 1986. Home: New York N.Y. Died Apr. 19, 1987.

TUFTY, ESTHER VAN WAGONER, news correspondent; b. Kingston, Mich., 1897; d. James and Florence (Loomis) Van Wagoner; m. Harold Tufty, Sept. 17, 1921 (div.); children: Harold Guilford, James Van Wagoner. BA, U. Wis., 1921. Reporter Madison (Wis.) Democrat, 1915-19, Capitol Times, Madison, 1919-21; with editorial staff Evanston (Ill.) News Index, 1923-33, mng. editor, 1932-33; fgn. corr. 1933-34; founder, chief, Washington corr., polit. columnist Tufty News Bur. (Mich. League of Home Dailies), servicing Owosso (Mich.) Argus Press, Ogdensburg (N.Y.) Jour., Macomb Daily, Mt. Clemens, Mich., numerous others; also TV news commentator NBC-TV network; radio news commentator, Washington corr. Central Press; invited as war corr. Brit. Ministry of Information; lectr. Regent Woodrow Wilson Birthplace Found.; exec. com. Pres.'s Com. to Help Emnploy the Physically Handicapped; mem. Def. Adv. Com. Women in Service. Hon. mayor Traverse City, Mich.; recipient U.S. Pres.' Disting. Service award, 1966. Mem. Am. Women in Radio and TV (nat. pres.), Am. Newspaper Women's Club (pres. 1969-70), Women's Nat. Press Club Washington (past pres.), Zonta, Theta Sigma Phi (Headliner award 1966). Died May 4, 1986.

TULLY, JASPER WILLIAM, oil and gas company executive; b. San Francisco, Nov. 3, 1891; s. John J. and Emily (Learned) T.; m. Leslie Brown, Sept. 25, 1919 (dec. 1929); children: Robert, Thomas; m. 2d, Ruth Hitch, May 12, 1933. BS, U. Calif., 1915. Salesman Blyth, Witter & Co., San Francisco, 1915-20; ptnr. Mitchum, Tully & Co., 1920-54; pres. Reserve Oil & Gas Co., 1934-63, dir., from 1932, chmn., 1963-66, chmn. emeritus, from 1966. 1st lt. Inf., U.S. Army, 1917-19. Mem. Ind. Petroleum Assn. Am., Newcomen Soc. Am., Commercial Club, Sierra Club, Pacific Union Club, California Club, Sigma Nu. Home: San Francisco Calif. †

TULLY, JOHN PATRICK, oceanographer; b. Brandon, Man., Can., Nov. 29, 1906; s. John and Agnes (Mott) T.; m. E. Lorraine Hamilton; children—Jean Agnes, Anne Lorraine, James Hamilton. B.S., U. Man., 1932; Ph.D., U. Wash., 1947. Asst. chemist Fisheries Research Bd., Nanaimo, B.C., Can., 1931-69, oceanographer in charge, 1940-69; cons. B.C. Electric Co. until 1987. Contbd. articles to profl. jours. Trustee Nanaimo Sch. Bd., 1953-54; active Emergency Measures Nanaimo, 1947-54. Decorated Order of Brit. Empire; recipient Manley Bendal prize French Govt., 1967, medal of Merit Port and Harbor Assn., 1985, other medals and awards; CSS John P. Tully named in his honor, 1984. Fellow Royal Soc. Can.; mem. Estuarine Research Assn. (life), Am. Geophys. Union (life). Home: Nanaimo B.C., Canada Died May 19, 1987; cremated.

TUNICK, STANLEY BLOCH, lawyer, accountant, consultant; b. N.Y.C., Mar. 6, 1900; s. Abraham and Mary (Bloch) T.; m. Mildred P. Superior, June 26, 1942; children: Andrew Jeffrey, Richard David. AB, CCNY, 1919, MBA, 1923; JD, St. Lawrence U., 1928; PhD, NYU, 1938. Bar: N.Y. 1929, U.S. Tax Ct. 1934, U.S. Dist. Ct. 1945; C.P.A., N.Y., Pa., N.J., Fla. Fgn. corr. export Loeb & Schoenfeld Co., 1919-20; chief acct. motion pictures Assoc. Exhibitors, Inc., 1920-24; traveling auditor motion pictures Pathe Exchange, Inc., 1924-25; auditor Pathex, Inc., 1925-26; sr. acct., mem. staff various acctg. firms, 1926-28; pvt. practice acctg. from 1928; ptnr., acct. Tunick & Platkin, 1941-71, cons., 1971-78; cons. Buchbinder, Stein, Tunick & Platkin, 1978-88; tchr. bookkeeping Haaren High Sch., N.Y.C., 1928-31; practice law, 1929-87; instr. Baruch Sch. Bus. and Public Adminstrn. of CCNY, 1931-42, asst. prof., 1942-48, asso. prof., 1948-51, prof., 1951-62, chmn. accountancy dept., 1956-62; mem. N.Y. State Bd. C.P.A. Examiners, 1962-70, sec., 1964-65, vice chmn., 1965-67, chmn., 1967-69; formerly trustee Abraham Kamber Co., Broad Street Properties. Author: (with E. Saxe) Fundamental Accounting-Theory and Practice, 1950, rev., 1956, 63; author of: Accounting I, II, III; Collaborating editor: N.Y. Tax Course Annual, 1939-62; cons. editor: Fed. Tax Course Annual, 1952-63; contbd. articles to profl. jours., mags. Past dir. Camp Loyaltown, Inc.; past bd. dirs. City Coll. Fund, United Jewish Appeal Greater N.Y.; bd. of overseers Combined United Jewish Appeal/Fedn. of Jewish Charities, 1986-88; council of govs. Albert Einstein Coll. Medicine, Yeshiva U., 1979-83; bd. dirs. Palm Beach chpt. Am. Jewish Com., 1981-88; trustee Student Aid Assn. City Coll., 1958-88; mem. nat. council Joint Distbn. Com., 1967-88; v.p., sec., bd. dirs. James Charles O'Connor Found., Inc., 1982-88. Served as pvt., inf. U.S. Army, World War I; lt. col. C.E. AUS, World War II; lt. col. O.R.C. until 1987. Decorated Army Commendation medal; recipient Townsend Harris medal Alumni City Coll., N.Y., 1966; medallion Baruch Sch. Alumni Soc., 1968; 125th Anniversary medal City Coll. N.Y., 1973; honored by Israel Bond Orgn., 1958; honored by United Jewish Appeal, 1964, 80; honored by Fedn. Jewish Philanthropies, 1969; honored by Albert Einstein Coll. Medicine, 1973; honored by Am. Jewish Com., 1974; honored by Town Club N.Y.-Fedn. Jewish Philanthropies, 1972. Mem. N.Y. State Soc. C.P.A.s (award for contbn. to profession 1965, dir. 1948-51, treas. 1951-53, v.p. 1955-56, trustee disability ins. trust 1956-85, 50 yr. membership cert. 1978), Am. Inst. C.P.A.s (hon. mem. 1985; nat. council 1967-70), Am. Legion, Res. Officers Assn., AAUP, Am. Arbitration Assn. (nat. panel arbitrators), Assn. Alumni City Coll. N.Y. (dir. 1952-58, hon. dir. 1959-87, dir. Palm Beach chpt. 1976-87, Alumni Service medal 1940), UN Assn., Internat. Brotherhood Magicians, Phi Beta Kappa, Phi Delta Kappa, Beta Gamma Sigma, Beta Alpha Psi, Delta Pi Epsilon, Iota Theta. Clubs: Accountants of America, Town of City of N.Y, The 100 (pres. 1972-73), N.Y. University, Soc. of Four Arts. Home: Palm Beach Fla. Died July 12, 1988; buried Mt. Hebron Cemetery, N.Y.

TUNKS, LEHAN KENT, law educator; b. Gibbon, Nebr., Aug. 14, 1915; s. Earl G. and Belle (Reddy) T.; m. Margaret Cary, June 1, 1940; children: Lehan Kent II, Timothy Earl. AB, U. Nebr., 1935; JD, Northwestern U., 1938; Sterling fellow, Yale U., 1938-39, JSD, 1947. Bar: Ill. 1938, N.J. 1962. Instr. law U. Iowa, 1939-40, asst. prof., 1940-46, assoc. prof. to prof., 1946-49; dean law sch., prof. law Rutgers U., 1953-62; dean law sch. U. Wash., Seattle, 1962-84; summer lectr. law Northwestern U., 1941, U. Ill, 1947, Stanford U., 1948, U. Calif., Berkeley, 1949, U. Pitts, 1953; law sch. adviser Assn. Am. Law Schs., 1951-54; atty. Office Price Adminstn., 1941-44, dir. bds. rev., 1944-46. Author: (with Michael Adams) Iowa Legal Aptitude Test, 1st edition, (with M. Adams and Dewey Stuit) 2d edition, 1941; contbg. editor: Anatomy of Legal Education, 1961; editor: Cases and Materials on Corporate Finance, Iowa Model Municipal Ordinances, 1941; contbr. articles to profl. jours. Recipient Notable Nebraskan award, 1967. Mem. Am. Judicare Soc., ABA, AAUP, Am. Acad. Polit. Sci., Order of Coif (nat. pres. 1970-73) Order of Artus, Phi Delta Phi. Home: Seattle Wash. Died Nov. 9, 1987.

TURCK, CHARLES JOSEPH, college president, law educator; b. New Orleans, Sept. 13, 1890; s. Charles Edwin and Louisa Bertha (Frank) T.; m. Emma Fuller, Sept. 28, 1914; children: Viola Turck Giben, Emma Louise Turck Wine. AB, Tulane U., 1911; AM, Columbia U., 1912, LLB, 1913; LLD, Ky. Wesleyan, 1928, Cumberland U., 1930, Tulane U., 1935, U. Ill., 1956; grad., Sch. Mil. Govt., Charlottesville, Va. Bar: N.Y. 1913, later La., Tenn., Ky. Practiced with Lord, Day & Lord, N.Y.C., until 1916; prof. law Tulane U., 1916-20; prof. law Vanderbilt U., 1920-24, also sec. Law Sch.; prof. law, dean Law Sch. U. Ky., 1924-27; pres. Centre Coll., 1927-36; dir. dept. spl. edn. and action Bd. of Christian Edn. Presbyn Ch. U.S.A., 1936-39; faculty Provost Marshal Gen.'s Sch., Ft. Custer, Mich.; pres. Macalester Coll., St. Paul, 1939-58; exec. dir. Japan Internat. Christian U. Found., 1958-60; pres. M.J. Lewi Coll. Podiatry, N.Y.C., from 1967. Editor: Anson on

Contracts, 1929. Pres. Assn. Am. Colls., 1946, Nat. Coun. Presbyn. Men, 1948-49; mem. Fact-Finding Commn. on Jerusalem, 1950; chmn. Gov.'s Com. on Ethics and Govt. Minn., 1958; mem. com. on aging Community Svc. Soc. N.Y., Ky. State Reorgn. Commn., Ky. State Tax Commn.; del. World Conf. Oxford and Edinburgh, 1937.; ednl. dir. War Work YMCA, Pensacola, Fla., Parris Island, S.C., 1918-19; ednl. cons. various religious and ednl. groups, from 1960. Maj. U.S. Army, 1948-44. Mem. Nat. Coun. Accreditation Tchr. Edn. (chmn. 1955-56), Masons, Rotary (gov. 18th dist. 1932-33), Phi Beta Kappa, Sigma Nu, Phi Delta Phi. Presbyterian (chmn. laymen's com. and vice-moderator, 1945-46). Home: New York N.Y. Died Jan. 12, 1989.

TURNBULL, WILLIAM WATSON, educational testing firm executive; b. St. Thomas, Ont., Can., Dec. 26, 1919; came to U.S., 1942, naturalized, 1953; s. William Watson and Elsie (Rodd) T.; m. Mary Elizabeth Sinclair, June 30, 1944; 1 child, Brenda Jean. B.A., U. Western Ont., 1942; A.M., Princeton U., 1943, Ph.D., 1944; LL.D. and Ed.D hon. degrees. Head dept. test constrn. Coll. Entrance Exam. Bd., Princeton, 1944-48; sec. Coll. Entrance Exam. Bd., 1946-48; dir. test constrn., analysis and research Ednl. Testing Service, Princeton, 1948-49; v.p. test devel., analysis and research Ednl. Testing Service, 1949-53, v.p. for testing ops., 1953-56, exec. v.p., 1956-70, pres., 1970-81, disting. scholar in residence, 1981-87; past chmn. bd. Mason Early Edn. Found.; past chmn., trustee Ctr. for Applied Linguistics; past trustee, mem. exec. com. Ednl. Products Info. Exchange, Nat. Found. Advancement in the Arts; past sec. Am. Lang. Acad. Vis. scholar Ctr. Advanced Study in Behavioral Scis., 1981-82. Mem. Internat. Assn. Ednl. Assessment (pres., chmn., trustee), AAAS, Am. Ednl. Research Assn., Am. Assn. Higher Edn., Internat. Assn. Applied Psychology, Am. Psychol. Assn., Internat. Council Psychologists (trustee), Nat. Council Measurement in Edn., Psychometric Soc., Sigma Xi. Clubs: Nassau (Princeton); Century Assn, Princeton of N.Y.C. Home: Princeton N.J. Died May 21, 1987, St. Thomas (Ont., Can.) Mausoleum.

TURNER, ALBERT, clothing manufacturer; b. N.Y.C., Nov. 1, 1891; s. Joseph and Anne Ruth T.; m. Rose Zoller. Pres. Albert Turner & Co. Inc., N.Y.C. Home: Katonah N.Y. †

TURNER, DON ABBOTT, business executive; b. Macon, Ga., 1892; married; children: Mrs. C.C. Butler, Mrs. L.P. Corn, William B. Chmn. bd. dirs. W.C. Bradley Co., Columbus Bank & Trust Co.; bd. dirs. Coca-Cola Co., Coca-Cola Internat. Corp., Central of Ga. Ry. Co., Atlanta. Home: Columbus Ga. †

TURNER, HERMAN LEE, clergyman; b. nr. Lacey Springs, Ala., Aug. 5, 1891; s. Elijah Howard and Sabrina Allen (Hornbuckle) T.; m. Ann Grace Hartung, Mar. 18, 1911; children: Margaret Elizabeth (Mrs. Thomas E. Bryant), Herman Lee, Donald Bernarr, Paul Gray. DD (hon.), Cumberland U., 1934, Mercer U., 1943; LLD, Tusculum Coll., 1940; LHD, John S. Smith U., 1958. Ordained to ministry Presbyn. Ch., 1919. Various positions with local firms Decatur, Ala., 1906-14; membership sec. YMCA, Decatur, 1915-16; Sabbath Sch. missionary Presbyn. Ch. in U.S.A., 1916-19; pastor Columbia Ave. Ch., Sheffield, Ala., 1919-24; synodical exec. Ala. and Miss. Presbyn. Ch. U.S.A., 1924-27; assoc. pastor Ind. Presbyn. Ch., Birmingham, Ala., 1927-30; pastor Covenant Presbyn. Ch., Atlanta, from 1930; condr. weekly religious news broadcast, St. WSB, Atlanta, from 1945; mem. bd. nat. missions, moderator gen. assembly United Presbyn. Ch. U.S.A., from 1960. Pres. Atlanta Area Social Planning Coun., 1934-35, Atlanta area Boy Scouts Am., 1935-37, USO Coun., 1942-46, Ga. Soc. Crippled Children and Adults, 1950-52; pres. Ga. Citizens Coun., 1945, Am. Christian Palestine Com., 1947-48; bd. dirs. Atlanta YMCA, 1952, Protestant Radio and TV Ctr., Atlanta, 1952; trustee Maryville Coll., 1949, NCCJ, from 1959. Recipient Silver Beaver award Boy Scouts Am., Silver Antelope award Boy Scouts Am., Silver Buffalo award Boy Scouts Am. Mem. Nat. (chmn. Soc. office 1955-57), Ga. (pres. 1956-58) coun. chs., Atlanta christian Coun. (pres. 1933), Atlanta C. of C., Rotary (pres. Atlanta chpt. 1941-42, past dist. gov., Armin Maier award 1945). Home: Atlanta Ga. †

TURNER, JANET E., artist; b. Kansas City, Mo., 1914; d. James Ernest and Hortense (Taylor) T. A.B., Stanford U., 1936; diploma, postgrad., Kansas City Art Inst. (under Thomas H. Benton, John de Martelly), 5 years; postgrad., Claremont Grad. Sch. (Millard Sheets, Henry McFee), 2 years, M.F.A., 1947; student serigraphy, Edward Landon; Ed.D., Columbia, 1960. Faculty Girls Collegiate Sch., Claremont, Calif., 1942-47; asst. prof. art Stephen F. Austin State Coll., Nacogdoches, Tex., 1947-56; asst. prof. Chico State U., 1959-63, assoc. prof., 1963-68, prof., 1968-80. Works have been shown in painting, water colors and prints exhbns. throughout U.S.; exhibited over 200 one-man shows in U.S., Israel, Japan; exhibited in Internat. Biannual of Graphics, Krakow, Poland, Internat. Exchange Exhbn., Seoul, Korea, Artistes Contemporains Americains, Le Salon des Nations, Paris; represented in collections in U.S., fgn. countries. Illustrator: F. Smith. Recipient prizes including: (painting) 1st prize Tex. Fine Arts Assn., 1948; Dealey purchase prize and Comini popular prize 11th Tex. Gen. Exhbn.; R.D. Straus prize 13th Tex. Gen. Exhbn.; 3 prize oils 50th Anniversary Exhbn. Art Assn. New Orleans; S. Karasick prize 59th Ann. Nat. Assn. Women Artists; water colors purchase prize 2d Tex. Water Color Soc.; Sun Carnival prize 3d Ann. Southwestern Sun Carnival Fine Arts Exhbn., El Paso; purchase prize Smith Coll. Mus. Art, 37th Ann. Exhbn. Western Art, Denver; Marcia Tucker prize Nat. Assn. Women Artists; prints Nat. Assn. Women Artists, 1950; graphics 1st prize Painters and Sculptors Soc. N.J., 32d Ann. Springfield (Mass.) Art League, Pen and Brush Black and White Exhbn., N.Y.C.; purchase prize Soc. Am. Graphic Artists 36th Ann. A.N.A.; 2d prize, Springfield Art League, Mass., 1955; 1st prize, Pen and Brush, 1956; 8th ann. Boston Printmakers purchase prize; 6th Southwestern Dallas Mus. Fine Arts, 1st prize graphics, Painters Sculptors Soc. of N.J.; Tupperware Art Fund Fellowship award for painting; Los Angeles County Nat. purchase prize; purchase prize Calif. State Fair, 1960; Cannon prize N.A.D., 1961; Medal of Honor and Alice S. Buell Meml. prize Nat. Assn. Women Artists, 1963; Katheryn Colton prize, Medal of Honor and Mabel M. Garner award, 1967; A.P. Hankins Meml. prize Print Club Pa., 1972; Lessig Rosenwald prize Print Club, 1975; Medal of Honor, Nat. Assn. Women Artists, 1977; Guggenheim fellow, 1952; Tupperware fellow, 1956-87; co-recipient Outstanding Prof. award Calif. State U. and Colls., 1975. Mem. League Am. Pen Women, Los Angeles Printmaking Soc. (Purchase prize 1971), Nat. Assn. Women Artists (Schafer prize 1983), Audubon Artists (award 1981), Am. Color Print Soc. (award 1981), Soc. Am. Graphic Artists (award 1982), N.A.D. (academician, Cook award 1985), AAUW, Calif. Soc. Printmakers, Los Angeles Printmaking Soc., Centro Studie Scambi Internazionale, DAR, Delta Kappa Gamma, Alpha Omicron Pi, Kappa Delta Pi, Pi Lambda Theta. Home: Chico Calif. Died June 27, 1988; cremated.

TURNER, RICHARD LAZEAR, diversified manufacturing company executive, lawyer; b. Huntington, Va., Feb. 22, 1925; s. Clyde Baker and Jess L. (Lazear) T.; m. Nancy Elena Riford, June 9, 1951; children: Richard R., Sarah L., James R., Molly L. BA, Yale U., 1948, LLB, 1951. Bar: N.Y. 1952. Assoc., then ptnr. Nixon, Hargrave, Devans and Dey, Rochester, N.Y., 1951-62; chmn. bd. Schlegel Corp. (and predecessor), Rochester, 1962-86, chief exec. officer, 1964-86, pres., 1972-86; bd. dirs. Forbes Products Corp., Genesee Brewing Co., Rochester Marine Midland Bank, Rochester Telephone Corp. Trustee Genesee Country Mus., Mumford, N.Y., Univ. Rochester, Rochester Mus. and Sci. Ctr.; former trustee Preservation League N.Y. State; bd. dirs., past chmn. bd. Hochstein Sch. Music, Rochester; mem. City of Rochester Fin. Rev. Com.; vice chmn. Bus. Commn. for Our Community's Future; chmn. Indsl. Mgmt. Task Force on Community Problems. With USMC, 1943-46. Recipient (with wife) Oakleigh Thorne medal Garden Clubs Am. Rochester Indsl. Mgmt. Council (dir., former chmn.), Rochester Area C. of C. (trustee). Home: Pittsford N.Y. Died Feb. 2, 1986.

TURNER, WILLIAM WIRT, university professor, author; b. Matville, W.Va., Nov. 27, 1889; s. Capt. William and Martha Dolliver (Hinchman) T.; m. Grace Luella Robertson, June 23, 1921 (dec. Apr. 1960); children, William, Virginia Ann Hull; m. 2d, Julia Dickinson Secrest, Mar. 22, 1962. AB, Morris Harvey Coll., Charleston, W.Va., 1911; BS in Architecture, U. of Notre Dame, 1916, MArch, 1918. Mem. staff Cen. Sr. High Sch., South Bend, Ind., 1929-35; asst. prof. architecture U. of Notre Dame, South Bend, 1936-39, assoc. prof., 1940-44, head dept. engring. drawing, 1942-57, prof. engring. drawing, 1945-57, emeritus, 1957—. Author books relating to field; latest publs.: Projection Drawing for Architects, 1950, Shades and Shadows, 1951, Integrated Problems in Engineering Drawing and Descriptive Geometry, 1953, Graphic Statics and Structural Steel Technology. Mem. Am. Soc. Engring. Edn., Masons (Scottish Rite, Shriner). Republican. Methodist. Home: Wilmington N.C. †

TUTTLE, ALBERT THEODORE, clergyman; b. Manti, Utah, Mar. 2, 1919; s. Albert Mervin and Clarice (Beal) T.; m. Marne Whitaker, July 26, 1943; children—David M., Diane, Robert T., Clarissa Marne, Jonathan W., Melissa, Boyd Jeremy. A.B., Brigham Young U., 1943; M.A., Stanford U., 1949; postgrad., U. Utah. Missionary No. States Mission, 1939-41; sem. tchr. Menan, Idaho, Brigham City, Kaysville, Utah, Salt Lake City, 1946-52; dir. Inst. of Religion, U. Nev., 1952; supr. sems. and insts. Latter-day Saints Dept. Edn., from 1953; pres. Provo Temple, 1980-82; supr. S.Am. missions, 1961, 75, pres. S. area, 1984-85, NW area, from 1985; gen. authority Latter-day Saints Ch., First Council of Seventy, from 1958; area adminstr., Spain, Italy, Portugal, 1982-84. Served as 1st lt. 5th Div. USMCR, 1943-46. Named Outstanding Student in Religion, Brigham Young U., 1943. Mem. Phi Delta Kappa, Delta Phi (past pres.), Blue Key. Deceased.

TUTTLE, DONALD SEYMOUR, business executive; b. Naugatuck, Conn., Feb. 4, 1890; s. Howard Beecher and Jeannette Phelps (Seymour) T.; m. Rachel Dinsmore, Mar. 1, 1917; children: Donald Seymour, Charles Dinsmore, Mary Ann Tuttle Carley. Grad., Hotchkiss Sch., Lakeville, Conn., 1909; PhB, Sheffield Sci. Sch., Yale U., 1912. Chmn. Naugatuck Water Co. (until merger with other cos. to become Conn. Water Co.); dir., chmn. bd. Naugatuck Nat. Bank (merged with Colonial Trust Co.), 1957; dir., trust com. Colonial Trust Co., 1957-59, Citizens and Mfrs. Bank and Trust Co., 1959—; assoc. dir. Colonial Bank and Trust Co., 1959—; bd. dirs., mem. exec. com. Risdon Mfg. Co., Naugatuck, Ea. Malleable Iron Co.; trustee and exec. com. Naugatuck Savs. Bank. Mem. YMCA. Ordnance Dept, AUS, 1917-19; 2d lt. Ordnance Reserves, 1919-24. Mem. C. of C. (former dir. and treas.), Yale Club, Grolier Club (N.Y.C.); Elizabethan Club, Graduates Club (New Haven). Home: Naugatuck Conn. †

TWAITS, WILLIAM OSBORN, oil company executive; b. Galt, Ont., Can.; s. William and Laura (Osborn) T.; m. Frances Begg, May 29, 1937; children: Judith Twaits Allan, Sheryl Twaits Young. B.Commerce, U. Toronto, 1933; DCL, Acadia U.; D.Bus.Adminstrn., U. Ottawa; LLD, U. Windsor. With Imperial Oil Ltd., Toronto, Ont., Can., 1933-74, served in refining, rsch., crude oil prodn., supply and transp., petroleum econs. and other phases of petroleum and petrochem. industries, exec. v.p., 1956-60, pres., 1960-73, chmn., 1973-74, bd. dirs., 1950-74; v.p., dir. Royal Bank Can.; pres. Sarcalto Ltd.; bd. dirs. Alcan Aluminium Ltd., N.Y. Life Ins. Co. Sr. mem. Bus. Coun. on Nat. Issues; mem. exec. com. Brit.-N.Am. com.; mem. C.D. Howe Inst.; bd. govs., hon. treas. Olympic Trust Can.; mem. coun. of honor Stanford Rsch. Inst.; hon. pres. The Arthritis Soc.; councillor Conf. Bd.; hon. assoc. Conf. Bd. Can.; hon. bd. dirs. Can.'s Aviation Hall of Fame. Decorated companion Order of Can. Fellow Royal Soc. Arts; mem. York Club, Rosedale Golf Club (Toronto), Augusta Nat. Club, Rideau Club (Ottawa), Delta Kappa Epsilon. Home: Toronto Ont., Canada. Died Apr. 3, 1986.

TWEEDY, GORDON BRADFORD, insurance company executive; b. Bridgeport, Conn., Feb. 8, 1907; s. Henry Hallam and Grace Hannah (Landfield) T.; m. Mary Johnson, June 7, 1944; children: Clare Bradford, Ann Sellett, Margot Martin. Grad., Taft Sch., 1924, Phillips Andover Acad., 1925; AB, Yale U., 1929, LLB cum laude, 1932. Bar: Conn. 1933, N.Y. 1934, U.S. Supreme Ct. 1935, Vt. 1973. Instr. Yale Law Sch., 1933-34; assoc. Sullivan and Cromwell, N.Y.C. and Paris, 1934-38; spl. counsel SEC, Washington, 1938-39, tax div. Dept. Justice, Washington, 1939-41; v.p., dir. China Nat. Aviation Corp., 1944-48; v.p., gen. counsel C.V. Starr & Co., Inc., N.Y.C., 1948-61, sr. exec. v.p., 1961-68, chmn. bd., 1968-72; bd. dirs. Am. Internat. Group, Consol. Securities Corp. Trustee China Inst. Mem. Council on Fgn. Relations, Assocs. Fgn. Policy Assn., Far East Am. Council, Council for Latin Am., Down Town Assn., River Club, Yale Club, Century Club (N.Y.C.), Mill Reef Club (Antigua), Metropolitan (Washington), Royal Bermuda Yacht, Order of Coif. Home: Brewster N.Y. Died June 25, 1985.

TWEEDY, WILLIAM ELWYN, lawyer; b. Bklyn.; s. Joseph H. and Amy (Bogardus) T.; m. Elizabeth Coote Clark, June 20, 1936; children—Jeffrey Clark, Elizabeth Tweedy Morash. B.B.S., Syracuse U., 1924; J.D., Harvard U., 1927. Bar: N.Y. 1929. Sole practice, Bklyn., 1927-51, N.Y.C., 1951-58, Ft. Salonga, Northport, N.Y., 1950-76, East Chatham, N.Y., 1976-87. Mem. ABA, N.Y. State Bar Assn., Suffolk County Bar Assn., Columbia Bar Assn., Phi Gamma Delta, Phi Delta Phi. Republican. Methodist. Clubs: Rotary (bd. dirs), Masons. Home: East Chatham, N.Y. Died Sept. 9, 1987; cremated. Address: for estate of W E Tweedy Mrs Elizabeth Tweedy PO Box 64 East Chatham NY 12060. Home: East Chatham N.Y.

TWOHY, JAMES FRANCIS, finance executive; b. St. Paul, Jan. 30, 1889; s. John and Mary Agnes (Rogers) T.; m.Freda Rau, Feb. 15, 1911 (dec.): children: James, Richard, Kevin Rogers, Mary Ann; m. 2d, Cecile Boyd, Oct. 1, 1926. AB, U. of Santa Clara, Calif., 1907; student, Harvard U., 1907-09. Sec., sec.-treas., v.p., pres. Twohy Bros. Co., 1910-35; founder, with William Pigott, Seattle Pacific Car and Foundry Co., 1916, v.p., treas., dir., 1916-35; organized with brothers Seattle, North Pacific Shipbuilding Co., 1917, dir., sec.-treas., chmn. exec. com., 1917—; regional mgr. Home Owners Loan Corp. for nine western states, 1935-39; gov. Fed. Home Loan Bank System, 1939-46; chmn. bd. dirs. Allied Bldg. Credits Inc., 1946-47, Investors Diversified Svcs. Inc., 1948-50; former pres. Twohy Fin. Co., Los Angeles; lectr. U. of Santa Clara. Mem. loyalty rev. bd., U.S. Civil Svc. Commn., NCCJ, Cath. Commn. for Intellectual and Cultural Affairs. Mem. Knights of Malta. Democrat. Roman Catholic. Home: San Jose Calif. †

TYLER, MAX EZRA, bacteriologist, microbiology educator; b. Groveland, N.Y., June 1, 1916; s. Leon Charles and Bessie L (Dorn) T.; m. Charlotte Dean Moelchert, May 3, 1945; children: Gail Ann, Scott Dean. BS, Cornell U., 1938; MS, Ohio State U., 1940, PhD, 1948. Asst. bacteriologist, grad. asst. Ohio State U., 1938-41; instr., research assoc. bacteriology Colo. Coll. A&M, 1941-42; research bacteriologist, br. chief Camp Detrick, Md., 1946-53; chmn., prof. dept. bacteriology U. Fla., Gainesville, 1953-71, prof. microbiology, 1971-86; cons. U.S. Chem. Corps, Biol. Warfare Ctr., 1953-56. Contbr. articles to nat. and fgn. sci. jours. Lt. San. Corps AUS, 1943-46. Fellow AAAS, Am. Pub.

Health Assn.; mem. Am. Soc. Microbiology (pres. S.E. br. 1959, nat. councilor 1963-86), Soc. for Gen. Microbiology (Eng.), Sigma Xi (pres. Fla. 1960), Gamma Sigma Delta (pres. Fla. 1960). Home: Gainesville Fla. Died 1986; buried Gainesville.

TYLER, PAUL MCINTOSH, mineral technologist, economics consultant; b. Oberlin, Ohio, Apr. 18, 1889; s. George Wells and Merion (McIntosh) T.; m. Dorothy Neff, Oct. 7, 1920 (dec. Mar. 1961). SB in Mining Engring. and Metallurgy, MIT, 1912. Asst. instr. MIT, 1912-13; researcher in metallurgy 1914-15, 18; mine supt. Colo., 1915-17; chief metals and ceramics divs. U.S. Tariff Commn., 1918-23, spl. expert, 1925-28; cons. in market rsch. 1924; from asst. chief econs. br. to regional engr. Ea. region U.S. Bur. Mines, 1928-45; with Bd. Econ. Warfare, 1942-43; European rep. metals and minerals Tech. Indsl. Intelligence Com., 1945-46; exec. officer MIT Metall. Lab., Watertown Arsenal, 1946-47; econ. cons. Am. Mining Congress, 1945-46, N.J. State Minerals Rsch. Bur., from 1945; cons. expert Fin. Com., U.S. Senate, 1922; mem. joint congl. com. Econ. Coop., 1949; investigated metal industries and gen. conditions in Europe for U.S. Govt., 1919-20, 21, 49, also in Turkey, North Africa and Spain. Author: From the Ground Up, 1948; contbr. numerous articles to profl. jours. Mem. AIME (past chmn. rare metals com., milling methods com., mineral econs. com., chmn. industrial minerals div. 1941-42, sec.-treas. Washington sect. 1928-30, chmn. 1951-52), NAS, Nat. Rsch. Coun. Adv. Com. on Metals and Minerals (sec. non-metallic minerals group 1941-45, metall. cons. 1951-53, from 1957), Mining Club, Cosmos Club. Home: Bethesda Md. †

TYLER, ROGER BROWNE, lawyer; b. Bernardston, Mass., July 19, 1896; s. William J. and Susie Noyes (Browne) T.; m. Margaret L. Blakely, Oct. 4, 1924 (dec. 1955) children: William B., Martha Ann Tyler Saunders, Margaret C. Tyler Stetson; m. Beatrice M. Lowell Colby, Aug. 29, 1956. Grad., Boston Latin Sch., 1913; AB, Harvard U., 1917, LLB, 1920; LLD (hon.), Emerson Coll., 1065. Bar: Mass 1920. Assoc. Goodwin, Proctor, Field & Hoar, Boston, 1920-26; assoc. Rackemann, Sawyer, & Brewster, Boston, 1926-30, ptnr., 1930-85, sr. ptnr., 1971-78, of counsel, 1978-85; bd. dirs., also chmn. bd. Workingmens Coop. Bank, Boston, 1923-71, pres., 1947-52; past trustee Warren Instn. Savs.; past incorporator Union-Warren Savs. Bank; former corporator Newton Savs. Bank; trustee Thomas Thompson Trust, Ogden Codman Trust. Chmn. Brookline Community Council, 1955-58; mem. Brookline Bicentennial Commn., , Brookline Town Meeting, 1955-74; vp. , dir. Bunker Hill Monument Assn.; corporator Brattleboro Meml. Hosp.; trustee, past chmn. Walnut Hills Cemetery, Emerson Coll.; past pres., trustee Rivers Country Day Sch.; past trustee Marlboro Coll., Beaver County Day Sch.; sec. Harvard Class of 1917. Ensign USNR, 1918-1919. Mem. ABA, Mass. Bar Assn. (past pres., dir.), Boston Bar Assn. (past council mem.), Norfolk County Bar Assn., Mass. Conveyancers Assn. (exec. com., past pres.),Bostonian Soc. (past pres., dir.), New Eng. Historic Geneal. Soc. (past council mem.), Boston Latin Sch. Assn. (trustee, past pres.), Soc. Cin. N.H. (standing com.), Soc. Colonial Wars Mass. (past lt. gov.), Am. Philaletic Soc. (life), Mass. Audubon Soc., Nantucket Hist. Soc., Brookline Hist. Soc., Bernardson Hist. Soc., Dorchester Hist. Soc., Soc. Preservation New Eng. Antiquities, Navy League, The Country Club (Brookline), Curtis Club, Abstract Club., Masons. Republican. Unitarian. Home: Chestnut Hill Mass. Died 1985.

TYREE, SHEPPARD YOUNG, JR., chemistry educator; b. Richmond, Va., July 4, 1920; s. Sheppard Young and Rosa Dove (Burton) T.; m. Barbara Doris Jones, June 5, 1943; children: Susan Scott, Pamela Fore, Peter Burton, Sally Blair, Rebecca Young. B.Sc. in Chemistry, MIT, 1942, Ph.D., 1946. Instr. MIT, 1943-46; asst. prof., then asso. prof. U. N.C., 1946-58; sci. officer Office Naval Research, 1954-55; prof. U. N.C., 1958-66; liaison scientist Office Naval Research, London, 1965-66; prof. chemistry Coll. William and Mary, 1966-84, head dept., 1968-73; research chemist Oak Ridge Nat. Lab., summer 1949; lectr., operator Morehead Planetarium, 1951-52; gen. coll. adviser U. N.C., 1956-58; dir. 4th Summer Inst. Coll. Chemistry Tchrs., 1957; vis. prof. U. P.R., summer 1963; chem. cons. to pvt. industry, govt. agys. Chmn. Gordon Research Cong. Inorganic Chemistry, 1957, mem. com., 1955-56, 61, 67; lectr. NSF Summer Inst., 1956-68; mem. bd. Inorganic syntheses, Inc., 1957-73, sec.-treas., 1968-72; chmn. Council Oak Ridge Asso. Univs., 1973-76, bd. dirs., 1973-79; cons. Titanium Alloy Mfg. Co., 1953-61, Climax Molybdenum Co., 1957-62, Chemistry Div. U.S. Naval Rsch. Lab., 1967-72, Vulcan Materials Co., 1969-73, The Gillette Co., 1973-83, The Nat. Pk. Svc., 1974, Edison Elec. Inst., 1981-82, Chem. & Metal Industries Inc., 1981-87. Author: (with K. Knox) Inorganic Chemistry, 1961; Editor: Inorganic Syntheses, Vol. IX, 1967; contbr. over 74 publs. to sci. jours. Panel mem. NATO postdoctoral fellowships, 1967-70; tech. adv. com. Va. State Air Polution Control Bd., 1981-87; active local Boy Scouts Am. Served with USNR, 1942. Recipient Herty medal Am. Chem. Soc., 1964; recipient grants NASA, 1975-77, EPA, 1976-79, 78-80. Fellow AAAS; mem. Va. Acad. Sci., Am. Chem. Soc. (tour speaker 1959, 61, 64, 77, vis. scientist 1958-63, chmn. N.C. sect. 1960, councillor 1963-66, exams. com., chmn. subcom. Inorganic Chemistry 1957-62, coll. chemistry cons. svc., 1968-75d), NSF (vis. lectr.), Phi Beta Kappa, Sigma Xi (pres. U. N.C. chpt. 1964-65), Alpha Chi Sigma, Phi Gamma Delta (purple legionnaire 1943-45, 63-65). Mem. Protestant-Episcopal Ch. Home: Floyd Va. Died July 17, 1987; buried Floyd County, Va.

UHLENBECK, GEORGE EUGENE, physicist; b. Batavia, Java, Dutch East Indies, Dec. 6, 1901; came to U.S., 1927; s. Eugenius Marius and Annie Marie Constance Julie (Beeger) U.; m. Else Renee Ophorst, Aug. 23, 1927. Ph.D., U. Leyden, 1927; Sc.D. (hon.), Notre Dame U., 1953, Case Inst. Tech., 1960, U. Colo., 1965, Yeshiva U., 1967. Asst. in theoretical physics U. Leyden, 1925-27; instr. physics U. Mich., 1927-28, asst. prof., 1928-30, assoc. prof., 1930-35, prof. theoretical physics, 1939-59; Henry S. Carhart Prof., prof. theoretical physics Utrecht, Holland, 1935-39; war researcher(radar) 1943-45; with radiation lab., MIT, Cambridge, 1961-71; prof. physics Rockefeller U., 1961-71, prof. emeritus, 1971-74. Recipient Max Planck medal, 1964, Lorentz medal, 1970, Nat. Med. of Science, 1977, Wolf prize (co-recipient), 1979; cmdr. of Order of Orange-Nassau, Netherlands. Fellow Am. Phys. (pres. 1959), Dutch phys. socs.; mem. Am. Philos. Soc., NAS, Dutch Royal Acad., Acad. dei Lincei (Rome). Died Oct. 31, 1988.

ULLMAN, ALBERT CONRAD, former congressman; b. Great Falls, Mont., Mar. 9, 1914; s. Albert C. and Julia (Miller) U.; m. Audrey K. Manuel, Aug. 1972; 4 children. A.B., Whitman Coll., 1935; M.A., Columbia U., 1939. Pub. sch. tchr. Port Angeles (Wash.) High Sch., 1935-37; real estate broker, builder Baker, Oreg., 1945-57; mem. 85th-96th congresses from 2d Dist. Oreg.; chmn. House Budget Com., 1974, Ways and Means Com., 1975-81, Joint Com. on Taxation, 1975, 77, 79. Served with USNR, 1942-45; capt. Res. until 1986. Mem. Beta Theta Pi. Democrat. Presbyterian. Home: Arlington Va. Died Oct. 11, 1986.

ULMAN, LEWIS HOLMES, lawyer, former telephone company executive; b. Washington, Apr. 28, 1916; s. Leon Simon and Lilly Caudry (Hawkins) U.; m. Suzanne Preston, Apr. 5, 1941; children: Michael H., Craig H. A.B., Princeton U., 1938; J.D., Georgetown U., 1942. Bar: D.C. 1941, N.Y. 1968, Conn. 1972. Asso. Cravath, Swaine & Moore, N.Y.C., 1941-43; atty. NLRB, Washington, 1946-54; gen. atty. Chespeake & Potomac Telephone Cos., Washington, 1954-66; atty. AT&T, N.Y.C., 1966-70; v.p., gen. counsel So. New Eng. Telephone Co., New Haven, 1971-81. Mem. D.C. Democratic Central Com., 1964-68; mem. Woodbridge (Conn.) Dem. Town Com., 1973-81; former exec. v.p., bd. dirs. House of Mercy; past bd. govs. St. Albans Sch.; past bd. dirs. Conn. Bar Found. Served with AUS, 1943-46, ETO. Episcopalian. Clubs: Metropolitan, Chevy Chase (Washington). Home: Chevy Chase Md. Died Feb. 23, 1988.

UNDERWOOD, DON, public relations and advertising executive; b. Thomas, W.Va., Feb. 20, 1918; s. Roy L. and Helen (Brown) U.; m. Miriam L. Ellison, Apr. 21, 1941 (div. 1960); 1 child, Donald M.; m. Nancy M. Costlow, May 28, '1966. Student, pub. schs., Indpls. News editor Indpls. News, 1936-42, chief polit. writer, 1945-47, chief Washington bur., 1947-49; v.p., Washington mgr. Bozell and Jacobs, Inc., 1949-56, exec. v.p. N.Y.C., 1956-64, pres., from 1964, chief exec. officer, 1967; co-founder, chmn. bd. Underwood Jordan Assocs. (subs. Ogilvy & Mather, Internat. Pub. Relations 1981), 1968, sr. cons., 1982-86; chmn. bd. Underwood Jordan McLeish, London, 1970-82; bd. dirs. Inside Can. Pub. Relations Ltd.; founder, chmn. Pinnacle Group, internat. pub. relaitons, U.S., Can., Gt. Britain, Tokyo, 1976-85. Cons. Pres.'s Task Force Pvt. Sector Initiatives, 1982. Capt. AUS, 1942-45, ETO. Decorated Bronze Star, Fourragére (Belgium). Mem. Internat. Pub. Relations Assn., Pub. Relations Soc. Am., Pub. Utilities Advt. Assn., Am. Legion, Nat. Press Club (Washington), N.Y. Athletic, Marco Polo Club (N.Y.C.), Indpls. Press Club, Poor Richard Club (Phila.), LeMirador Country Club (Vevey, Switzerland), Sigma Delta Chi. Home: New York N.Y. Died Mar. 29, 1985; buried Holy Rood Cemetery, Westbury, N.Y.

UNDERWOOD, ROBERT CHARLES, former state supreme court justice, lawyer; b. Gardner, Ill., Oct. 27, 1915; s. Marion L. and Edith L. (Frazee) U.; m. Dorothy Louise Roy, Feb. 2, 1939; 1 child, Susan Louise Underwood Barcalow. BA, Ill. Wesleyan U., 1937, LLD, 1970; JD, U. Ill., 1939; LLD, Eureka Coll., 1970, Loyola U., Chgo., 1969, Ill. State U., Normal, 1984. Bar: Ill. 1939. Sole practice Bloomington, Ill., 1939-46; city atty. Normal, Ill., 1942-43; asst. state's atty. McLean County, Ill., 1942-46; county judge 1946-62; justice Ill. Supreme Ct., 1962-84, chief justice, 1969-75; previously of counsel Dunn, Goebel, Ulbrich, Morel and Hundman, Bloomington; mem. Conf. Chief Justices, 1969-75, mem. exec. council, 1971-75, vice chmn., 1974-75; Ill. rep. Nat. Center for State Cts., 1978-79; past bd. dirs. Champion Fed. Savs. & Loan Assn. Contbd. articles to profl. jours. Vice chmn. Ill. Commn. Children, 1953-55; trustee Ill. Wesleyan U., 1957-59, 85-87; past mem. bd. dirs. McLean County Mental Health Center, Bloomington, Westminster Found.; chmn. com. to survey legal edn. needs in Ill., Bd. Higher Edn., 1968; numerous other civic activities. Recipient Disting. Service award U.S. Jaycees, 1948, Good Govt. award, 1953, Outstanding Citizen award Normal C. of C., 1962, Ann. Pub. Service citation Ill. Welfare Assn., 1960, Outstanding Achievement cert. U. Ill. Coll. Law, 1969, Lincoln the Lawyer award Abraham Lincoln Assn., 1986, Alumni Achievement award U. Ill., 1987. Fellow Ill. State Bar Found. (hon.), Pa. Mason Juvenile Ct. Inst., Ill. Bar Assn. (award of Merit 1976), Ill. State Bar Assn.; mem. ABA, McLean County Bar Assn. (past pres.), Ill. County and Probate Judges Assn. (past pres.), Am. Judicature Soc. (bd. dirs. 1974-79, Herbert Harley award 1986), Sigma Chi, Pi Kappa Delta. Republican. Methodist. Clubs: Bloomington, Bloomington Country. Lodges: Rotary (hon.), Masons (33 deg.), Kiwanis (hon.). Home: Normal Ill. Died Mar. 30, 1988; buried Funks Grove (Ill.) Cemetery.

UNGAR, FREDERICK, publishing executive; b. Vienna, Austria, Sept. 5, 1898; came to U.S., 1939, naturalized, 1945; s. Moriz and Bertha (Kobler) U.; m. Hansi Beck, Apr. 17, 1948; 1 son, Bertrand Theodore. Dr. Law, U. Vienna, 1923; Litt.D. (hon.), Suffolk U., 1982. Founder Phaidon Verlag, Vienna, 1924; founder Saturn Verlag, 1926-38; pub. Frederick Ungar Pub. Co., N.Y.C., 1940-88, pub. emeritus; pub. Stephen Daye Press, N.Y.C., 1945-88. Editor: (introduction) To Mother with Love, 1951; (introduction) What's Right with America, 1952; Friedrich Schiller, An Anthology for Our Time, With an Account of His Life and Work, 1959; (introduction) Goethe's World View, 1963; (with Alexander Gode) Anthology of German Poetry through the 19th Century, 1964; (introduction) Handbook of Austrian Literature, 1973; (introduction) The Last Days of Mankind (Karl Kraus), 1974; (with Lina Mainiero) Encyclopedia of World Literature in the 20th Century, Vol. 4, 1975; (introduction) No Compromise: Selected Writings of Karl Kraus, 1977; (introduction) Practical Wisdom; A Treasury of Alphorisms and Reflections from the German, 1977; (introduction) Austria in Poetry and History, 1984; (introduction) Arthur Schnitzler, The Little Comedy and Other Stories, 1978; editor: (introduction) The Eternal Feminine: Selected Poems of Goethe, billingual edit., 1980; (preface) E. Fritz Schmerl, The Challenge of Age, 1986. Recipient Alexander Gode medal Am. Translators Assn., 1975; named hon. prof. Austrian Govt., 1976; recipient Service award German Book Trade Assn., 1980; SilverCross for meritorius service to Vienna. Mem. Ethical Soc. No. Westchester, N.Am. Com. for Humanism (hon.). Home: Scarborough N.Y. Died Nov. 16, 1988; cremated.

UNNA, KLAUS ROBERT WALTER, pharmacologist, educator; b. Hamburg, Germany, July 30, 1908; came to U.S., 1937, naturalized, 1944.; s. Karl and Marie (Boehm) U.; m. Maya Stromberg-Grossmann, May 25, 1939; 1 child, Jan Erik. MD, U. Freiburg, Germany, 1930. Intern univs. hosps., Berlin, Hamburg, Cologne, 1931; faculty U. Vienna, 1933; asst. phramacologist Merck Inst. Therapeutic Research, 1937-44; instr. pharmacology U. Pa., 1944-45; asst .prof. U. Ill.-Chgo., 1945-48, assoc. prof., 1948-51, prof., then prof. emeritus, from 1951, head dept. pharmacology, 1955-74; exec. sec. Internat. Brain Research Orgn. of UNESCO; mem.Com. on Drug Abuse Dept. Justice, Research Council on Brain Scis. Nat. Acad. Scis.; cons. USPHS, NIH, NIMH. Editorial bd. Jour. Pharmacology and Exptl. Therapeutics, 1953-57; co-editor Exptl. Brain Research, 1967; contbr. various sci. jours. and publs. Mem. Am. Physiol. Soc., Am. Soc. Pharmacology and Exptl. Therapeutics, AAAS, Am. Inst. Nutrition, Soc. Exptl. Biology and Medicine (assoc. editor proc. 1959), Soc. for Neurosci., German Pharmacological Soc. (hon.), Viennese Acad. Sci., Sigma Xi. Home: Santa Fe N. Mex. Died June 30, 1987.

UNRUH, JESSE MARVIN, state official; b. Newton, Kans., Sept. 30, 1922; s. Isaac P. and Nettie Laura (Kessler) U.; m. Virginia June Lemon, Nov. 2, 1943 (div.); children—Bruce, Bradley, Robert, Randall, Linda Lu; m. Chris Edwards, 1986. B.A., U. So. Calif., 1948, postgrad., 1949, LL.D., 1967. Dist. staff dir. Fed. Census, 1950; with Pacific Car Demurrage Bur., 1950-54; mem. Calif. Assembly, 1954-70, chmn. com. fin. and ins., 1957-59, chmn. ways and means com., 1959-61, speaker of assembly, 1961-68, Democratic leader, 1968-70, mem. adv. commn. on intergovtl. relations, 1967-70; vis. prof. polit. sci. San Fernando Valley State Coll., 1970; vis. prof. U. So. Calif. Sch. Law, 1971-72; treas. State of Calif., from 1972; cons., prof. polit. sci. Eagleton Inst. Politics, Rutgers U., from 1965; past co-chmn. Seminar Young Legislators, Carnegie Corp.; Chubb fellow Yale, 1962. Mem. Calif. Central Democratic Com., 1954-87; So. Calif. mgr. John F. Kennedy presdl. campaign, 1960, So. Calif. co-chmn. gubernatorial campaign, 1962, statewide coordinator assembly, congl. campaigns, 1962; chmn. Robert F. Kennedy's Calif. presdl. campaign, 1968; chmn. Calif. del. Dem. Nat. Conv., 1968; pres. Nat. Conf. State Legis. Leaders, 1966; Dem. candidate for gov. Calif., 1970; bd. regents U. Calif., 1961-68; trustee Calif. State Colls., 1961-68, Inst. for Am. Univs., Citizens Conf. on State Legislatures, from 1968. Served with USNR, 1942-45. Home: Sacramento Calif. Died Aug. 4, 1987.

UNTERECKER, JOHN EUGENE, English language educator, author; b. Buffalo, Dec. 14, 1922; s. John G.

and Bertha (Ellinger) U.; m. Ann Apalian, Feb. 28, 1953 (div. 1973). BA, Middlebury Coll., 1944; MA, Columbia, 1948; PhD, Columbia U., 1958. Radio announcer Sta. WBNY, Buffalo, 1944; Off-Broadway, stock and TV actor 1945-46; instr. CCNY, 1946-58; mem. faculty Columbia, 1958-74, prof. English lit., 1966-74; prof. English U. Hawaii, Honolulu, 1974-89; Vis. prof. U. Hawaii, 1969, U. Tex., 1974, Flinders U., Australia, 1979; lectr. Yeats Internat. Summer Sch., Ireland, 1972, 73-75, 77, 78, 79, 80, 82, 84 mem. book reviewer N.Y. Times, New Leader, Sat. Rev. Pres. Hawaii Lit. Council, 1975, mem. bd., 1975-78. Author: A Reader's Guide to W.B. Yeats, 1959, Lawrence Durrell, 1964, The Dreaming Zoo, 1965, Voyager: A Life of Hart Crane, 1969, Dance Sequence, 1975, Stone, 1977; editor: (with Frank Stewart) Poetry Hawaii: A Contemporary Anthology, 1979; gen. editor Columbia U. Press 20th Century Am. Poets series, from 1966; contbr. poetry to major mags. Guggenheim fellow, 1964-65, Yaddo fellow, 1967, 68, 69, 70, 72, 74, 79, NEA fellow, 1980; grantee Am. Philos. Soc., 1962, grantee Am. Council Learned Socs., 1962, 72; recipient Hawaii award for literature, 1985. Mem. Author's Guild, P.E.N., MLA, James Joyce Soc., Lawrence Durrell Soc., Am. Com. Irish Studies, Am. Gloxinia Soc. Home: Honolulu Hawaii. Died Jan. 2, 1989.

UPGREN, ARTHUR REINHOLD, economist, educator; b. River Falls, Wis., Jan. 18, 1897; s. Charles August and Emily Matilda (Carlson) U.; m. Marion Elizabeth Andrews, Feb. 26, 1926; children: Emily Andrews, Arthur Reinhold Jr.; m. Anna B. Kerr, June 5, 1954; m. Irene M. Matlock, Oct. 19, 1974; m. Elizabeth Moretz Aldrich, July 28, 1976. AB, U. Wis., 1920; PhD, U. Minn., 1937. Teller First Nat. Bank, River Falls, 1914-16; credit analyst, credit dept. Chase Nat. Bank, N.Y.C., 1925-27; econ. statistician Eastman, Dillon & Co., 1927-29; sec. All Am. Gen. Corp., 1929-30; v.p., economist Mpls. Fed. Res. Bank, 1942-45; instr. Sch. Bus. Adminstrn., U. Minn., 1930-37, assoc. prof., 1937-42, prof. econs. and fin., 1942-51; dean Amos Tuck Sch. Bus. Adminstrn., Dartmouth Coll., 1952-57; Frederic R. Bigelow prof. econs. Macalester Coll., St. Paul, 1957-66; bd. dirs., econ. adviser Bank Mpls.; hon. dir. Green Giant Co., Cherne Indsl., Inc.; econ. cons. Mpls. Star and Tribune; research assoc. Hutchings Commn. on Internat. Relations, N.Y.C., 1933-34; econ. analyst trade agreements div. Dept. State, 1934-35; econ. cons. Govt. of Man., Can., 1937-38; research sec. Council on Fgn. Relations, 1940-41; 1st chief nat. econs. div. Dept. Commerce, World War II; observer for FRS, Bretton Woods Internat. Money Conf., 1944; vis. prof. U. Fla., 1966-70; mem. Mayor's Fin. and Taxation Commn., Mpls., 1946-48, sch. emergency tax com., 1947. Author: (with Stahrl Edmunds) Economics For You and Me, 1953, also econ. bulls.; contbr. to mags. Developer Upgren Swimpond, 1948. Decorated Knight Royal Order North Star (Sweden), 1952; named Minnesotan of Yr., 1975. Mem. Mpls. Club, Gammon Club (Pompano Beach, Fla.), Cosmos (Washington), Coral Ridge Yacht (Ft. Lauderdale, Fla), Kiwanis (hon.). Home: Boca Raton Fla. Died Sept. 1, 1986, buried River Falls, Wis.

UPTON, FREDERICK STANLEY, corporation executive; b. Battle Creek, Mich., June 20, 1890; s. Cassius M. and Carrie A. (Blodgett) U.; m. Margaret Beckley, Dec. 26, 1917; children: David F., Stephen E., Priscilla J. Byrns, Sylvia C. Fowler. Grad., high sch. Sec.-treas., dir. Upton Machine Co., 1912-29, Nineteen Hundred Washer Co. (merged with Upton Machine Co.), 1929-50; v.p., dir., treas. Whirlpool Corp. (name changed from Nineteen Hundred Washer Co., 1950), 1937-54; dir., Sr. v.p. Whirlpool Corp., 1954-55, dir., 1955—; former v.p., now dir. Peoples State Bank. Vice chmn. Mich. Rep. Fin. Com.; del.-at-large Rep. Nat. Conv., 1956; pres. Whirlpool Found.; trustee Kalamazoo Coll.; pres. St. Joseph-Benton Harbor Meml. Hosp. Assn.; past v.p. Berrien-Cass coun. Boy Scouts Am. (Silver Beaver award). Lt. U.S. Army, World War I. Mem. Am. Legion, Union League Club (Chgo.); Point O'Woods Golf and Country Club (1st pres.), Twin City Rotary (past pres.). Congregationalist. Home: Saint Joseph Mich. †

URQUHART, JOHN E., manufacturing executive; b. Ashfield, Mass., Apr. 9, 1889; s. John Edwin and Helen (Slicer) U.; m. Loretta Syburg; 1 dau., Martha Urquhart Lord. AB, Yale U., 1910. With Semet-Solvay Co., div. Allied Chem. & Dye Corp., 1910-33; gen. supt. Woodward Iron Co., 1933-34, pres., 1953-58, chmn., 1958—; bd. dirs. Birmingham br. Fed. Res. Bank of Atlanta. Mem. exec. com. Birmingham Com. of 100. Mem. Assoc. Industries Ala. (dir.), Ala. Mining Inst. (bd. govs.), Am. Iron and Steel Inst., Newcomen Soc. Home: Birmingham Ala. †

UTRECHT, JAMES C., lawyer; b. Cin., May 26, 1922; s. Arthur C. and Alma (Schnieders) U.; m. Zena B. Utrecht; children-James D., Steven T., Daniel S., Gregory F., Jonathan A., Teresa S. B.A., U. Cin., 1947, J.D., 1948. Bar: Ohio bar 1948, U.S. Ct. Mil. Appeals bar 1953, U.S. Supreme Ct. bar 1953. Practiced in Cin., 1948-56, Troy, Ohio, 1956-85; pres. Shipman, Utrecht & Dixon Co. (L.P.A.), 1956-85; past asst. pros. atty., Hamilton County, Ohio, past spl. counsel atty. gen., Ohio. Past trustee Stouder Meml. Hosp., Troy. Served to lt. col. USAR, 1943-45, 51-53. Decorated Bronze Star. Fellow Am. Coll. Trial Lawyers, Ohio Bar Assn. Found.; mem. ABA, Ohio Bar Assn. (past council dels.), Miami County Bar Assn. (past pres.), Cin. Bar Assn., Am. Judicature Soc., Am. Soc. Hosp. Attys., Internat. Assn. Ins. Counsel, Charles McMicken Soc. Roman Catholic. Club: Rotarian (Troy) (past pres.). Home: Troy Ohio. Died Aug. 20, 1985; buried Riverside Cemetery, Troy.

VACANO, WOLFGANG, orchestra conductor, educator; b. Cologne, Germany, Dec. 23, 1906; came to U.S., 1951, naturalized, 1957; s. Stephen and Charlotte (Schirmann) V. Diploma, Berlin State Acad. Music, 1928; PhD (hon.), Marion Coll., Indpsl., 1977. Prof. music, opera condr. Ind U. Sch. Music, Bloomington, 1951-85, Aspen (Colo.) Festivals and Music Sch., 1952-54, 61-64. condr. Indpls. Philharm. Orch. from 1963; vis. prof. music U. Wis. Milw., 1967-68, mus. dir. Music for Youth, Milw., 1967-70; artistic dir. Brigham Young U., Provo, Utah, 1972-47; condr. mcpl. opera houses in Germany, Switzerland, 1928-39; condr. Teatro Argentino, La Plata, 1947-51, Teatro Municipal, Santiago, Chile, 1942-43, Teatro El Sodre, Montevideo, Uruguay, 1945, Teatro Colon, Buenos Aires, 1949-51, Nat. Symphony Orch., Nicaragua, 1977, Opera Co., Peoria, Ill., 1977-78. Named Hon. Citizen Indpls., 1966. Home: Bloomington Ind. Died Jan. 3, 1985; buried Park Hill Cemetery, Bloomington.

VALENTINE, ITIMOUS T., lawyer; b. Spring Hope, N.C., Nov. 14, 1887; s. James May and Susan Ella (May) V.; m. Hazel Graham Armstrong, Sept. 8, 1922; children: Hazel Valentine Jessup, Itimous T. Jr., Elizabeth Valentine Fuller, James F., Mary Hobbs Armstrong. Student, Mars Hill Coll., N.C., 1912-14; BA, Guilford Coll., N.C., 1917. Bar: N.C. 1915. Pvt. practice Middlesex, 1917, Springhope, 1919-34, Nashville, 1934-43, 47-51, 52—; sr. mem. Valentine & Valentine, Nashville, 1952—; pros. atty. Nash County, N.C., 1922-34; assoc. justice N.C. Supreme Ct., 1951-52. Mem. N.C. bd. Charities and Pub. Welfare, 1940-44. Col. judge adv. gen. dept. U.S. Army, 1943-47, office undersec. war, 1945-47. Mem. N.C., Rocky Mount-Nash County bar assns., Phi Alpha Delta. Baptist (past deacon). Home: Nashville N.C. †

VALLEE, HUBERT PRIOR RUDY, orchestra leader; b. Island Pond, Vt., July 28, 1901; s. Charles Alphonse and Katherine (Lynch) V.; m. Fay Webb, July 6, 1931 (dec. Nov. 1936); m. Bette Jane Greer, Dec. 1943 (div. 1944); m. Eleanor Kathleen Norris, Sept. 3, 1949. Student, U. Maine, 1921; Ph.B., Yale, 1927. Pres. Am. Fedn. Actors, 1937. Played with Savoy Havana Band at Hotel Savoy, London, Eng., 1924-25, broadcast and recorded while there, played with band at Yale and led Yale football band during sr. year; toured U.S. with coll. band, formed Connecticut Yankees, 1928; first U.S. broadcasts, 1928; performed with orch., for 10 yrs; on NBC's Fleischmann Variety Hour, appeared at Paramount (N.Y.) and Paramount (Bklyn.), 10 weeks spring of 1929, returning in Oct. for run of nearly two years; starred in motion pictures Vagabond Lover, 1929, George White's Scandals, 1934, Sweet Music, 1935, Gold Diggers in Paris, 1938, Second Fiddle, 1939, Time Out for Rhythm and Too Many Blondes, 1941, also Man Alive, People Are Funny, It's in the Bag, The Fabulous Suzanne, I Remember Mamma, The Bachelor and the Bobby Soxer, Beautiful Blonde from Bashful Bend, Father Was a Fullback, Mother Is a Freshman, The Admiral Was a Lady, Mad Wednesday, Ricochet Romance, Gentlemen Marry Brunettes, How to Succeed in Business Without Really Trying, Live a Little, Love a Little; appeared in stage show of George White's Scandals, 1931, 36; played stage show of Coronation Week engagement in London, 1937, Cocoanut Grove, Los Angeles, 1937, 38, broadcasted weekly for Standard Brands, 1929-39, for Nat. Dairies, Sealtest program, 1940-41, Drene Show, 1944-46, Philip Morris, 1946-47, Rudy Vallee Show, 1950; frequent night club appearances; appeared in musical comedy How To Succeed in Business Without Really Trying, N.Y.C., 1961-64; has appeared on TV variety shows; tours with one-man multi-media show.; composer of songs and musical numbers. Author: Vagabond Dreams Come True, 1930, Let the Chips Fall, 1975. Served in USN, World War I; Served in USCG., World War II. Recipient N.Y. Critics award 1962. Mem. Am. Fedn. Musicians, Am. Soc. of Authors and Composers, Acad. Motion Picture Arts and Scis., Amateur Cinema League, Nat. Assn. Performing Artists, Screen Actors' Guild, Am. Arbitration Assn., Am. Legion, La Société des 40 Hommes et 8 Chevaux, Sigma Alpha Epsilon. Clubs: N.Y. Athletic, Lambs, Friars, Yale (N.Y.C.). Lodge: Elks. Home: North Hollywood Calif. Died July 3, 1986.

VALLÉE, PAUL, judge; b. Island Pond, Vt., July 6, 1891; s. George H. and Catherine (Monahan) V.; m. Catherine McWeeny, Aug. 30, 1932; children: Ruth Ann, Mary. LLB, U. So. Calif., 1914. Bar: Calif. 1913, U.S. Supreme Ct. 1923. Dep. pub. defender L.A. County, 1914-18, dep. county counsel, 1918-19, chief dep. county counsel, 1919-22; asst. counsel Union Oil Co. Calif., 1922-23; ptnr. Mott & Vallée, L.A., 1923-26, Mott, Vallée & Grant, 1926-39, Vallée, Beilenson & Kenny, 1939; pvt. practice L.A., 1939-47; judge Calif. Superior Ct., 1947-48; justice Calif. Dist. Ct. Appeal, from 1948; instr. Sch. Law, U. So. Calif., 1919-49; lectr. on wills, will contests, probate adminstrn. Stanford Law Soc., Bar Assn. City and County of Sacramento, Bar Assn. for City and County of Salt Lake, other legal insts. Mem. Calif. State Bar (bd. govs. 1936-39, pres. 1938-39), L.A. Bar Assn. (lectr.), Law Soc., Law Alumni Assn. (bd. dirs. U. So. Calif. chpt. 1941, pres. 1942-45), Gen. Alumni Assn. (bd. dirs. U. So. Calif. 1942-45), Order of Coif (hon.), Phi Alpha Delta. Democrat. †

VALLOTTON, WILLIAM WISE, surgeon, educator; b. Valdosta, Ga., Nov. 26, 1927; s. Joseph Edward and Mattie (Rouse) V.; m. Hilda Roberta Jones, Sept. 3, 1950; children: Stephen Ralph, Amie, Mark Hugh, William Wise. A.B., Duke U., 1947; M.D., Med. Coll. Ga., 1952; postgrad., Harvard U., 1956. Diplomate: Am. Bd. Ophthalmology. Intern U. Wis., 1952-53; resident in ophthalmology Duke U., 1953-55, instr., 1953-55, assoc., 1955-56; assoc. prof. ophthalmology Med. U. S.C., Charleston, 1958-65, prof., 1965-88, dir. residency program ophthalmology, 1960-70, chmn. dept. ophthalmology, 1967-86; dir. Storm Eye Inst., 1976-86; v.p. Vallorbe Inc., Valdosta, 1955-88; cons. USN Hosp., Charleston, 1962-88, State Hosp. S.C., Columbia, 1963-88, VA Hosp., Charleston, 1966-88; faculty home study Am. Acad. Ophthalmology and Otolaryngology. Contbr. articles to profl. jours. Bd. dirs. S.C. Commn. for Blind, 1975-76. Served to lt. M.C. USNR, 1956-58. Fellow A.C.S.; mem. S.C. Ophthal. and Otolaryn. Soc. (pres. 1965), Assn. Research in Ophthalmology (chmn. S.E. sect. 1966-67), Am. Acad. Ophthalmology and Otolaryngology (Honors award 1968), So. Med. Assn. (asso. councilor 1972-75, councilor 1975-80), N.Y. Acad. Scis., Charleston Duke Alumni Assn. (past pres.), J.C.A.H.P.O. (commr. 1981-86), Pi Kappa Phi, Alpha Kappa Kappa, Alpha Omega Alpha. Republican. Methodist. Clubs: Charleston Country, Elks. Home: Charleston S.C. Died Sept. 4, 1988; buried Valdosta, Ga.

VAN ALLEN, MAURICE WRIGHT, physician; b. Mt. Pleasant, Iowa, Apr. 3, 1918; s. Alfred Maurice and Alma E. (Olney) Van A.; m. Janet Hunt, Aug. 20, 1949; children: David, Martha, Evalyn, Jonathan. B.A., Iowa Wesleyan Coll., 1939; M.D., U. Iowa, 1942. Diplomate Am. Psychiatry and Neurology, Am. Bd. Neurol. Surgery. Intern Pa. Hosp., Phila., 1942-43; tng. in neurology and neurosurger; practice medicine specializing in neurology Iowa City, Iowa, from 1954; chief neurol. sect. VA Hosp., Iowa City, 1954-59; asso. prof. dept. neurology Coll. Medicine, U. Iowa, 1959-65, prof., 1965-86, head dept., 1974-86; mem. coun. Nat. Inst. Dental Rsch. Author book in field; contbr. articles to profl. jours.; editor Archives of Neurology, 1976-82. With M.C., U.S. Army, 1943-46. Mem. AMA, Am. Acad. Neurology, Am. Neurol. Assn., Assn. Rsch. and Nervous and Mental Disease, Sigma Xi, Alpha Omega Alpha. Republican. Episcopalian. Home: Iowa City Iowa. Died May 2, 1986; buried Memory Gardens Cemetery & Chapel Mausoleum Inc., Iowa City.

VANAMAN, ARTHUR WILLIAM, corporate consultant, military officer; b. Millville, N.J., May 9, 1892; s. William Augustus and Mary (Young) V.; m. Blanche V. Garroway, Apr. 6, 1918; children: Mary McKee (Mrs. J. M. O'Gorman), Arthur William. BSEE, Drexel Inst. Tech., 1915, hon. DSc, 1942; student, Postgrad. Sch. of Westinghouse Electric Co., 1915-16; grad., Flying Sch., 1918, MIT (advanced aeronautical engring.), 1918, Air Corps Engring Sch., 1930, Air Corps Tactical Sch., 1935, Army Indsl. Coll., 1936, Army War Coll., 1937. Promoted through grades to maj. gen. USAAF, 1944; chief procurement engring., asst. chief procurement Air Force, Hdqrs. Air Service Command, Dayton, Ohio, 1930-34; air attache Berlin, 1937-41; sec. air staff Hdqrs. A.A.F., Washington, 1941-42; comdg. gen. USAAF Materiel Ctr., Wright Field, Ohio, 1942-43, Oklahoma City Air Service Command, Kelly Field, 1944; A-2 Hdqrs. 8th Air Force, ETO, May-June 1944; prisoner of war Germany, 1944-45; dep. chief staff Prisoner of War Affairs, U.S. S.T.A.F., France, May-June 1945; comdg. gen. Mobile Air TEch. Service Command, Brookley Field, Ala. (area command), 1946-48; comdt. Indsl. Coll. of Armed Forces, Washington, 1948-52; CG Sacramento Air Material Area, McClellan AFB, Calif., 1952-54; cons. and mem. tech. adv. com. Aerojet Gen. Corp., 1954-58, asst. to pres., from 1958. Decorated D.S.M., Legion of Merit with 2 oak leaf clusters, Bronze Star, Air medal, Commendation Ribbon with oak leaf cluster, Purple Heart, Victory Medal (World War I and World War II), European, African and Middle Eastern Campaign medal, Am. Def. Service medal, Am. Campaign medal; Croix de Guerre with Palme (Belgium). Mem. Army and Navy Club, Columbia Country Club, Del Paso Country Club, Rotary, Masons, Shriners. Home: Fair Oaks Calif. †

VAN BAALEN, CHASE, microbiologist; b. Detroit, Sept. 12, 1925; s. Harold and Lillian (Netzorg) Van B.; m. Donna Gale Ems, June 20, 1954; children: Patricia, Aaron, Julie. BS, U. Ala., 1948; MS, U. Detroit, 1950; PhD, U. Tex., 1957. Rsch. scientist Kitchawan Rsch. Lab., Bklyn. Bot. Garden, Ossining, N.Y., 1958-61; lectr. U. Tex. Marine Sci. Inst., Port Aransas, 1961-64, asst. prof. botany, 1965-67, assoc. prof., 1968-72; prof. botany and marine studies Port Aransas Marine Lab., from 1972. Contbr. numerous articles, revs. to profl. publs.; mem. editorial bd. Handbook Microbiology, 1978-79; assoc. editor Jour. Phycology, from 1979. NSF grantee, from 1961. Mem. Am. Soc. Microbiology, Am. Soc. Photobiology, Am. Soc. Plant Physiology, Phycological Soc. Am., Soc. Gen. Microbiology, Japanese Soc. Plant Physiology, Scandinavian Soc. Plant Physiology, Sigma Xi. Home: Port Aransas Tex. Died Jan. 20, 1986; interred Seaside, Corpus Christi, Tex.

VAN BORTEL, FRANCIS JOHN, advertising executive; b. Macedon, N.Y., June 2, 1921; s. Peter Marvin and Margaret (Blankenberg) Van B.; m. Dorothy Matilda Greey, Aug. 18, 1953. MA, U. Chgo., 1952. Instr. U. Chgo., 1952-54; dir. research McCann-Erickson, Chgo., 1954-65; dir. Western Region Marplan, Chgo., 1965-69; pres. Western Region Marplan, 1969-70; exec. v.p. McCann Erickson, Inc., N.Y.C., 1970-86, Van Bortel Assocs., Rye, N.Y., 1986-89. Served with USAAF, 1942-46. Mem. Sigma Xi. Clubs: Coveleigh (Rye, N.Y.), Apawamis (Palmyra, N.Y.). Home: Rye N.Y. Died Jan. 2, 1989; buried Palmyra.

VAN CAMPEN, MARION (KELLY), educator; b. Laramie City, Wyo., Mar. 30, 1891; d. Anson Cyrus and Marion Josephine (Kelly) Van C. AB, U. Tenn., 1911; PhB, U. Chgo., 1912; AM, Columbia U., 1935, EdD, 1938. Kindergarten dir. Park Sch., Cooley Settlement House, Knoxville, 1912-17; instr. Sch. Childhood U. Pitts., 1917-19; tchr. Oak Lane (Pa.) Country Day Sch., 1919-21; supr. elem. dept. Longwood Day Sch., Boston, 1921-25; supr. Norristown (Pa.) Pub. Schs., 1925-28; asst. prof. edn. Pa. State U., 1928-35; instr. summer sch. Kent State U., 1936-38, asst. prof., 1938-45, prof., head elem. edn. dept., from 1945; instr. summer sch. U. Tenn., 1912-15, 20-23, U. Pitts., 1918, Asheville, N.C., 1924-25, Pa., 1928-34, 45; cons. in field. mem. Portage County Youth Commn. Mem. NEA, AAUP, AAUW, Am. Edn. Found., Childhood Edn. Assn., North Ea. Ohio Tchrs. Assn., Ohio Edn. Assn., Progressive Edn. Assn. (pres. region Pitts. 1934-35), Delta Kappa Gamma, Kappa Delta Pi. Democrat. Home: Kent Ohio. †

VANCE, VIVIAN, actress; b. Cherryvale, Kans.; d. Robert A. and Mae (Ragan) Jones; m. John Dodds, Jan. 16, 1961. Ed. pub. schs., Independence, Kans. Understudy to Ethel Merman in Anything Goes, 1934; featured opposite Ed Wynn in Hooray for What, 1937, Danny Kaye in Let's Face It, 1941; appeared in plays Kiss The Boys Good-bye, 1939, Skylark with Gertrude Lawrence, 1940, Voice of the Turtle (Chgo. and San Francisco), 1946-47, The Cradle Will Rock, 1947; co-starred in (TV shows) I Love Lucy, 1951-59, The Lucy Show, 1962-65; TV guest appeances include The Jack Paar Show. Chmn. Conn. Mental Health Assn.; est. Vivian Vance Fund in gratitude to Dr. Eleanor Steele, Phila. Psychoanalytic Inst., 1946. Recipient Emmy award Acad. TV Arts and Scis., 1953, Genii award L.A. Profl. Women, 1964; named Best Supporting Actress TV Writers and Critics, 1964, 65. Died Aug. 17, 1979.

VANDER SLUIS, GEORGE JACOB, artist; b. Cleve., Dec. 18, 1915; s. Gerrit and Hilda (Koopman) Vander Sluis; m. Hildegarde Bristol, Oct. 24, 1948; children: Sylvia, Peter, Jeffrey. Diploma, Cleve. Inst. Art, 1939; student, Colo. Springs Fine Arts Ctr., 1940. Prof. painting Syracuse (N.Y.) U., 1947-84, chmn. grad. div. Coll. Visual and Performing Arts, 1970-77. One-man shows include Seligmann Gallery, N.Y.C., 1959, Royal Marks Galler, N.Y.C., 1962, 63, 64, Krasner Gallery, N.Y.C., 1968, 69, 71; exhibited group shows at Whitney Art Mus., N.Y.C., 1954, Mpls. Inst. Art, 1957, U. Ill., 1961, White House, 1966, Mus. Contemporary Crafts, N.Y.C., 1968, Enviro-Vision N.Y. State Expo, Syracuse, 1972; represented in permanent collections Everson Mus., Syracuse, Rochester (N.Y.) Meml. Art Gallery, Colorado Springs Fine Arts Ctr.; painted mural Rena Pierson Meml. Chapel, Syracuse U., 1981. With U.S. Army, 1942-45. Fulbright grantee, 1951-52, N.Y. State Council Arts grantee, 1966, Ford Found. grantee, 1978, 79. Home: Camillus N.Y. Died Mar. 2, 1984; buried Syracuse, N.Y.

VAN DER VRIES, BERNICE TABER, transit official; b. Holton, Kans., Feb. 14, 1890; d. Otis G. and May (Thomas) Taber; m. John Nicholas Van der Vries, June 9, 1910 (dec.); 1 son, John Nicholas. Student, U. Kans., 1907-1909, Barnard Coll., 1909-10. Mem. Village Coun., Winnetka, Ill., 1931-35; rep. 7th Dist. Ill. Ho. of Reps., Springfield, 1934-56; dir. Chgo. Transit Authority, from 1957. Bd. mgrs. Coun. State Govts., 1937-60, chmn. bd., 1950; chmn. adv. com. Community Mental Health Svcs., Dept. Mental Health, State Ill.; mem. bd. Nat. Safety Coun., 1959-65; vice chmn. adv. com. Ill. Children's Hosp. Sch.; trustee Nat. Soc. Crippled Children and Adults, 1957-66; gov. Am. Nat. Red Cross, 1952-58; bd. trustees Hull House, 1945-59, Shimer Coll.; dir. Chgo. Met. Welfare Coun. Recipient Jane Addams medal, 1956, citations Ill. State Nurses Assn., Ill. Soc. for Mental Health, Ill. Inter-profl. Coun., U. Kans., 1st Dirs. award Ill. Dept. Mental Health, 1966. Mem. Winnitka League Women Voters, Woman's Club (Winnetka), Zonta (Evanston), Pi Beta Phi. Episcopalian. Home: Evanston Ill. †

VANDERWERF, CALVIN ANTHONY, academic administrator, chemistry educator; b. Friesland, Wis., Jan. 2, 1917; s. Anthony and Anna (Schaafsma) V.; m. Rachel Anna Good, Aug. 22, 1942; children: Gretchen VanderWerf Jones, Klasina, Julie, Lisa VanderWerf Hawkins, Pieter, Marte VanderWerf Singerman. AB, Hope Coll., 1937, ScD (hon.), 1963; PhD, Ohio State U., 1941; LLD (hon.), St. Benedict's Coll., Atchison, Kans., 1966; ScD (hon.), Rose Poly. Inst., 1966. Instr. U. Kans., 1941-42, faculty mem., 1943-63, prof. chemistry, 1949-63, chmn. dept., 1961-63; pres. Hope Coll., Holland, Mich., 1963-70; vis. prof. Colo. State U., 1970-71; prof. chemistry U. Fla., Gainesville, dean Coll. Arts and Scis., 1971-88; vis. scientist NSF, 1955-88; guest lectr. Continental Classroom, 1959; cons. NU.S. Naval Ordnance Test Sta., China Lake, Calif., 1951-60; mem. Petroleum Fund Adv. Bd., 1957-63; cons. Smith, Kline & French Co., 1947-63, Spencer Chem. Co., 1952-63, Pan Am. Petroleum Co., 1958-63; bd. dirs. Kativo Chem. Co., Ltd., Costa Rica; chmn. discipline com. in chemistry Ednl. Testing Service; mem. Danforth Grad. Fellowship Reading Com.; rep. U.S. Dept. State 9th Internat. Conf. on Higher Edn., Yugoslav univs., Dubrovnik; lectr., cons. on sci. edn. OAS, Buenos Aires, 1965; trustee, mem. exec. com. Research Corp. Author: (with Sisler and Davidson) General Chemistry, 2d edit., 1959, Korean transl., 1959, Acids, Bases and the Chemistry of the Covalent Bond, 1961, College Chemistry, A Systematic Approach, 2d edit., 1959, 3d edit., 1967, Korean transl., 1964, Asian edit., 1964, also Japanese, French, Spanish and Italian transls., (with Brewster and McEwen) Unitized Experiments in Organic Chemistry, 3d edit., 1969, A Brief Course in Experimental Organic Chemistry, 1972; editor Organic Chemistry Series; mem. editorial bd. Jour. Chem. Edn.; contbr. numerous articles to profl. jours. Pres. Christian Reformed Ch. Sch., Holland, 1963-70. Petroleum Research Fund grantee, 1962. Fellow N.Y. Acad. Scis.; mem. Am. Chem. Soc. (com. on chemistry and pub. affairs), Chem. Soc. London, Sigma Xi, Phi Lambda Upsilon, Gamma Alpha. Home: Gainesville Fla. Died July 19, 1988.

VAN DEVENTER, JOHN FRANCIS, investment executive; b. Passaic, N.J., Aug. 30, 1909; s. William and Irma (Fowler) V.; m. Ellenor Sowerbutt Vandermade, Jan. 19, 1946; children: Tina Maillefert, John Francis. BA, Hamilton Coll., 1932; MS, Columbia U., 1935. With trust dept. Bankers Trust Co., N.Y.C., 1935-41; with Van Alstyne, Noel & Co., 1946-47, treas. dept. Gen. Aniline & Film Corp., 1947-49, Southport Distbrs., Inc., 1950, investments Chem. Fund., Inc., later sr. investment officer, dir.; v.p., dir. F. Eberstadt & Co., Inc., N.Y.C., 1951-77, Mgrs. & Distbrs., Inc.; dir., vice chmn. trust investment com. First Nat. Bank of Litchfield. Lt. comdr. USNR, 1942-46, comdr. Res. Mem. Holland Soc. N.Y., Down Town Assn., Hamilton Club, Washington Club (Conn.), University Club, Univ. Glee Club (N.Y.C.), Down Town Athletic Club, Shinnecock Hills Golf Club, Meadow Club, Bathing Corp. Southampton (N.Y.). Home: Washington Conn. Died Feb. 6, 1986; buried Washington, Conn.

VAN DYCK, LEO, manufacturing executive; b. Antwerp, Belgium, Mar. 12, 1888; s. Joannes and Antoinette (Wauters) Van D.; m. Hedwige Pflügl, Dec. 20, 1913; children: Louise Mertens, Alfrieda Mariën, Eugene. Works mgr. Bell Telephone Mfg. Co. S.A., Antwerp, 1930-35, mng. dir., from 1935, pres. bd., 1952-61, hon. pres., 1961; v.p. Internat. Standard Electric Corp., Fabrimetal, Brussels; v.p., bd. dirs. Standard Electric A/S, Copenhagen, Denmark; bd. Radio Rediffusion S.A. Verviers, Belgium, Lab. Cen. Telecommunications, Paris, Standard Telephone et Radio S.A., Zurich, Switzerland, Kredietbank, Belgium, Nederlandsche Standard Electric Mij., The Hague, The Netherlands. Knighted as baron; decorated comdr. Order of Leopold, Order of Crown, Grand Officer Order Leopold II; officer Legion of Honor (France); officer Order Orange-Nassau (The Netherlands); comdr. Order St. Sylvester. Home: Antwerp Belgium. †

VAN DYKE, WILLARD AMES, motion picture, photographer, educator; b. Denver, Dec. 5, 1906; s. Louis and Pearl (Ames) Van D.; m. Mary Gray Barnett, Jan. 2, 1938 (div. Mar. 1950); children: Alison Van Dyke Shank, Peter; m. Margaret Barbara Murray Milikin, June 17, 1950; children: Murray, Cornelius. Co-founder (including Edward Weston, Ansel Adams, Imogen Cunningham) Group f.64, 1932; photographer art project Pub. Works Adminstrn., San Francisco, 1934, Harper's Bazaar, 1935; dir. dept. film Mus. Modern Art, N.Y.C., 1965-74; prof. SUNY at Purchase, 1973-81; vis. prof. U. N.H., 1968, 69; bd. dirs. Anthology Film Archives, 1977. Dir. documentary films including The City, 1939, Valleytown, 1940, The Children Must Learn, 1940, The Bridge, 1942, San Francisco, 1945, The Photographer, 1947, Skyscraper, 1958, Rice, 1964; dir. TV programs including High Adventure, 1958, 20th Century, 1963-65, 21st Century, 1968; photographs exhibited in one-man shows De Young Meml. Mus., San Francisco, 1933, San Diego Mus., 1934, Pa. State U., 1970, Budapest, 1974, Witkin Gallery, N.Y.C., 1977, Wirtz Gallery, San Francisco, 1977, Kenyon Gallery, Chgo., 1981, others. Mem. Yale Art Council, 1976-86; mem. vis. com. in environ. studies Harvard U., 1981-86; trustee Internat. Film Sems., pres. 1965-72; mem. Brandeis U. Commn. for Awards in Creative Arts, 1977. Recipient Spl. award Internat. Mus. Photography, 1978; named Laureate Artist in Residence Harvard U. Mem. Century Club (N.Y.C.). Home: Santa Fe N.Mex. Died Jan. 23, 1986.

VAN HOOSE, WILLIAM HENRY, educational psychology educator; b. Louisa, Ky., Sept. 20, 1929; s. Millard and Elizabeth (Moore) Van H.; children—Frederick, Pamela. A.B., Morehead State U., 1951; M.S., Ind. U., 1957; Ph.D., Ohio State U., 1965. Psychologist, Akron pub. schs., Ohio, 1960-62; asst. prof. ednl. psychology U. Mich., Ann Arbor, 1962-65; prof. Wayne State U., Detroit, 1965-72; prof. counselor edn. U. Va., Charlottesville, from 1972, dir. Ctr. for Research and Career Devel., from 1979. Author: Midlife: Myths and Realities, 1985; Tecumseh: An Indian Moses, 1984. Contbr. articles to profl. jours. Mem. citizens adv. com. on developmental counseling Va. Gen. Assembly, 1980-84. Served with U.S. Army, 1951-53. Named Outstanding Ph.D. Grad., Ohio State U., 1983. Mem. Am. Psychol. Assn. Democrat. Presbyterian. Avocations: fishing; golf. Home: Charlottesville, Va. Deceased.

VAN HOUTEN, ROBERT WALLACE, academic administrator, civil engineering educator; b. Newark, Jan. 31, 1905; s. Wilford Bush and Ellen (Sandford) Van H.; m. Martha Fairchild Tuckley, Sept. 3, 1930; children: James Wallace, Donald Roger, Valerie. BS, Newark Coll. Engring. (now N.J. Inst. Tech.), MCE, 1932, D Engring., 1970; DSc (hon.), Rider Coll., 1955, Clarkson Coll. Tech., 1956; D Engring. (hon.), Stevens Inst. Tech., 1955; LHD (hon.), Newark State Coll. (now Kean State Coll.), 1961; LLD (hon.), Seton Hall U., 1966. Sch. tchr. Essex Fells and Roselle, N.J., 1924-26; constrn. insp. A.C. Windsor Constrn. Co., Newark, 1928-29; researcher Wallace & Tiernan Co., Belleville, N.J., 1929-30; instr. civil engring. Newark Coll. Engring. (now N.J. Inst. Tech.), 1930-36, asst. prof., 1936-41, assoc. prof., 1941, asst. to pres., 1938-40, asst. dean, 1941-43, dean, 1943-47, pres., 1947-70, pres. emeritus, 1970-86; trustee Howard Savs. Bank, 1957-86; mem. adv. bd. Liberty Nut. Inst. Co., 1968-86; bd. dirs. Prudential Ins. Co., Gibraltor Fund, 1968-86; pres. Newark Coll. Engring. Research Found., 1959-65; bd. overseers Found. Newark Coll. Engring., 1965-76, pres., 1965-70, sec., 1970-75; adv. panel ROTC affairs U.S. Dept. Def., 1954-61, AFROTC panel, 1963-65; mem. nat. Commn. on Accrediting, 1964-70, N.J. State Com. Adminstrn. Higher Edn. Facilities Act, 1964-68. Bd. dirs. N.J. Safety Council, 1950-70, Newark ARC, 1955-60; chmn. N.J. Brotherhood Week, NCCJ, 1968; trustee United Hosps. Newark, 1960-74, Symphony Hall, 1964-70; trustee Milburn Pub. Library. 1960-73, pres., 1968-73; dir. Jr. Achievement Essex, West Hudson, 1949-70. Fellow ASCE (life); mem. Am. Soc. Engring. Edn. (life, chmn. evening engring. edn. div. 1952-53, gen. council, 1953-57, v.p. 1957-59, pres. 1961-62, dir. 1962-64), Am. Council on Edn. (vice chmn. 1956-57), Assn. Urban Univs. (pres. 1953-54), N.J. Assn. Colls. and Univs. (pres. 1955-56), NSPE, N.J. Soc. Profl. Engrs. (Citizen of Yr. award 1958), Rotary, Tau Beta Pi, Omicron Delta Kappa, Sigma Pi (Nat. Founders award 1962) Chi Epsilon, Pi Delta Epsilon, Alpha Phi Omega. Methodist. Home: Short Hills N.J. Died Jan. 6, 1986.

VAN NOTE, WILLIAM GARDNER, college president; b. Atlantic Highlands, N.J., Mar. 9, 1906; s. Henry Clay and Anna Elizabeth (Gardner) Van N; m. Rachel Poling, Nov. 9, 1929 (div. 1961); children: William Gardner, Gretchen; m. Bettina Van Camp, Dec. 16, 1961. BChemE, Rensselaer Poly. Inst., 1929; MS, U. Vt., 1933; PhD, Pa. State Coll., 1941; LLD (hon.), St. Lawrence U., 1957; ScD (hon.), N.C. State Coll., 1958. Registered profl. engr., N.J. Metallurgist Babcock & Wilcox Co., Bayonne, N.J., 1930; teaching and research fellow dept. metall. engring. McGill U., Toronto, Ont., Can., 1931; instr. U. Vt., 1931-33; instr. chem. engring. N.C. State Coll., 1933-35, asst. prof., 1936-39, assoc. prof., 1941-42, assoc. prof. metallurgy, 1942-44, prof., 1944-51, dir. dept. engring. research, 1946-51; pres. Clarkson Coll. Tech., 1951-61; pres. Monmouth Coll., West Long Br., N.J., 1962-71, pres. emeritus, 1971-85; adj. prof. Brookdale Community Coll., 1971-72; teaching fellow metall. engring. Carnegie Inst. Tech., 1935-36; liason N.C. State Coll. faculty mem. for local Bur. Mines Sta., 1944-46; acting asst. dir. engring. exptl. sta. N.C. State Coll., 1944-45, asst. dir., 1945-46; liason rep. with Oak Ridge Inst. Nuclear Studies, 1949; research metallurgist GE, Schenectady, summers 1944, 45; mem. adv. bd. N.J. Nat. Bank & Trust Co.; chmn. Commn. Non-tax Supported Colls. and Univs. N.Y., 1956-58. Contbr. articles to profl. jours. Mem. Gov.'s Commn. to Study Capital Punishment; v.p. N.J. Coll. Fund, 1965-67. Mem. N.J. Assn. Colls. and Univs. (pres. 1967), N.J. Coll. Fund Assn. (v.p. 1965-69), Assn. N.Y. State Colls. and Univs. (v.p. 1960-61), Middle States Assn. Coll. and Secondary Schs. (com. instns. higher edn. 1960-65), Am. Soc. Metallurgy, Am. Soc. Engring. Edn. (chmn. research br S.E. sect), Rotary, Sigma Xi, Phi Lambada Upsilon, Sigma Pi Alpha, Delta Phi, Tau Beta Pi. Presbyterian. Home: Sun City Center Fla. Died Aug. 31, 1985.

VAN PETTEN, OLIVER W(ILLIAM), engineer; b. Cramer, Ill., Aug. 25, 1891; s. William Johnston and Margaret Elizabeth (Buchanan) Van P.; m. Mary Faith Archer, May 18, 1921; children: Oliver William, Albert Archer, Emilie Margaret. Student, Ill. Coll. Engring., 1909-13. Constrn. work L.A. Aqueduct; ry. and bridge constrn. work Oreg. Short Line R.R.; constrn. work East Side Levee and Sanitary Dist., East St. Louis, Ill.; street paving W.Va. and Ky.; v.p. Union Constrn. Co.;

engaged in devel. of coal, oil and natural gas properties in Appalachian area and supervisor gas exploratory work P.Q., 1914-28; with Columbian Carbon Co. in oil and natural gas devel., 1932-59, v.p., dir.; cons. natural gas transp. and devel. W.Va. state chmn. Crusade for Freedom, 1956, 57; bd. dirs. Charleston Meml. Hosp. With F.A., U.S. Army, World War I. Mem. Am. Petroleum Inst., Ky. Oil and Gas Assn., Edgewood Country Club (pres. 1943, 44), Berry Hills Country Club (charter mem.), Army and Navy Club (Charleston), Rotary (pres. 1946), Masons, Alpha Delta Phi. Presbyterian. Home: La Jolla Calif. †

VAN SICKLE, CLARENCE L(OTT), business management educator; b. Frankfort, Ind., Mar. 16, 1892; s. Samuel and Catherine (McDowell) Van S.; m. Della B. Tschappat, Apr. 9, 1921. BS, U. Pitts., 1923, AM, 1925. Acct. various R.R. cos. Chgo., 1910-17; instr. acctg. and econs. Carnegie Inst. Tech., 1923-24; prof. acctg. U. Pitts., from 1924, coordinator exec. devel. course, from 1962. Author: Accounting System Installation, 1934, Cost Accounting Fundamentals and Procedures, 1928, Cases in Cost Accounting, 1955; contbr. articles to profl. jours. Served with Q.M.C. U.S. Army, 1917-18. Mem. Am. Acctg. Assn., Controllers Inst. Am., Sales Exec. Club, Nat. Assn. Accts. (pres. Pitts. chpt. 1931-32), Theta Chi, Beta Gamma Sigma, Alpha Kappa Psi. Methodist. Episcopalian. Home: Pittsburgh Pa. †

VAN SICKLE, JOHN V(ALENTINE), economist; b. Denver, Apr. 30, 1892; s. James Hixon and Mary (Valentine) Van S.; m. B. Louise Patterson, June 12, 1926; children: Patricia, James Hixon, Shaila V. AB, Haverford Coll., 1913; MA, Harvard U., 1921, PhD, 1924. Tutor div. history, govt. end econs., asst. econs. Haverford Coll., 1915-17; asst. U.S. Embassy, France, 1919-20; asst. sec. Am. unofficial del. Reparations Commn., Vienna, 1920-21; asst. to tech. adv. to Austrian Govt., 1921-23; asst. prof. U. Mich., 1924-26, assoc. prof., 1926-28; fellow, grant-in-aid sec. Social Sci. Rsch. Coun., 1928-29; asst. dir. social scis. Rockefeller Found., Paris, 1929-34, New York, 1934-38; prof. econs., Vanderbilt U., 1938-46; chmn. dept. econs. Wabash Coll., from 1946; mem. adv. bd. Am. Enterprise Assn., 1944-56; tax cons. Chinese Nationalist Govt., Formosa, 1954. Author: Direct Taxation in Austria, 1931, Planning for the South: An Inquiry into the Economics of Regionalism, 1943; co-author: Introduction to Economics, 1954; contbr. to econ. jours. Mem. Conseil Supericur de la Faculté Internat. d'Economie Comparée dé l' Universite Internat. de Sciences Comparés, Luxembourg. 1st lt. and supply officer U.S. Air Svc., 1917-19. Mem. The Mont Pèlerin Soc., Phi Beta Kappa. Home: Crawfordsville Ind. †

VAN SINDEREN, HENRY BRINSMADE, businessman; b. Bklyn., June 19, 1889; s. William Leslie and Mary (Brinsmade) Van S.; m. Katharine Lyman White, Apr. 8, 1915 (dec. Dec. 1918). Prep. edn., Ridge Sch., Washington, Conn., 1905-07; AB, Yale U., 1911. With Am. Trading Co., 1911-17, U.S. War Trade Bd., 1917-18; assoc. C. Tennant, Sons & Co., from 1919, v.p., 1919-45, pres., 1945-51, chmn. bd., from 1952. Chmn. Wash. Planning Commn.; sec. Wash. Redevelopment Agy. Mem. River, Pinnacle, University, Yale clubs (all of N.Y.C.). Congregationalist. Home: Washington Conn. †

VAN SMITH, HOWARD, writer; b. Forest Hill, N.J., Apr. 6, 1909; s. Arthur Lockwood and Florence (Garrettson) S.; m. Anne McCarron, June 21, 1938 (div. 1965); children: Garrett, Parris, Antony, William; m. Micheline Mathews, Nov. 26, 1965. Student, Pennington Prep., 1927-29, Franklyn Union, 1936-37. Staff reporter N.Y. Times, 1930-32; free-lance writer 1933-35, heating and hydraulics engr., 1935-42; civilian engr. Air Force, Warner-Robins Airfield, Ga., 1942-44; reporter Orlando (Fla.) Sentinel, 1944; Sunday editor Miami (Fla.) News, 1945-57, spl. writer, 1957-65; spl. writer Ft. Lauderdale (Fla.) News, 1965-77; adminstrv. asst. Fla. Dept. Agr., Davie, 1978-80; editor Fla. Nurseryman, 1981-86; lectr. U. Miami, 1948-54. Author: (with C. Raymond Van Dusen) The New Speech-O-Gram Technique for Persuasive Public Speaking, 1962, The Education of Juan, 1973; contbr. articles, short stories to nat. mags. Recipient Pulitzer prize for nat. reporting, 1959; meritorious award Fla. Pub. Health Assn., 1959; Service to Mankind award, 1961; named to Hort. Hall of Fame, 1976; named foremost gardening writer in Am. and Can. Am. Assn. Nurserymen, 1978; N.Y. State Center for Migrant Studies fellow N.Y. State U. at Geneseo. Home: Fort Lauderdale Fla. Died Aug. 14, 1986; buried Miami, Fla.

VAN VALKENBURG, SAMUEL, geographer; b. Leeuwarden, The Netherlands, Sept. 14, 1891; s. Frederick Alexander and Maria Leonarda Adriana (Jolles) Van V.; m. Erica Ashauer, May 16, 1918; children: Frederik Alexander, Mariane, Denise. Ed., U. Utrecht, The Netherlands, U. Berlin; PhD, U. Zurich, Switzerland. Head geog. sect. Royal Topog. Svc., Netherlands East Indies, 1921-26; asst. prof. geography Clark U., Worcester, Mass., 1927-29; assoc. prof. Grad. Sch. Geography Clark U., 1932-37, prof., from 1937, dir. Grad. Sch. Geography, from 1946; asst. prof. geography Wayne U., Detroit, 1929-32. Author: (with E. Huntington and F.E. Williams) Economic and Social Geography, 1934; (with E. Huntington) Europe, 1935, Elements of Political Geography, 1939, European Jigsaw, 1945, Whose Promised Lands?, 1946; (with C.C. Held) Europe, 1952; (with C.L. Stotz) Elements of Political Geography, 1954; mng. editor Econ. Geography. Mem. Assn. Am. Geographers. Unitarian. Home: Worcester Mass. †

VAN VEEN, STUYVESANT, artist, educator, semiotographer; b. N.Y.C., Sept. 12, 1910; s. Arthur Lewis and Marcella Reutlinger (Marks) Van V.; m. Felicia Geffen, Aug. 10, 1962. Student, Pa. Acad. Fine Arts, summers 1927-28, N.Y. Sch. Indsl. Art, 1928, NAD, 1929, CCNY, 1931, Art Students League, 1933-34. Tchr. painting and drawing classes for writers N.Y.C., 1932-34; lectr. Coll. Art Assn., 1940-41; supr., instr. Cin. Art Acad., 1946-49; assoc. prof. CCNY, CUNY, 1949-74. Illustrator: 8 books including Gesture, Race and Culture, 1972; murals executed bldgs. throughout U.S.; numerous one-man exhbns. including, ACA Gallery, N.Y.C., 1964, 68, 73, Maurice M. Pine Free Pub. Library, Fairlawn, N.J., 1978, Mid-Hudson Art and Sci. Ctr., Poughkeepsie, N.Y., 1981; exhibited in numerous group shows including, Am. Water Color Soc., 1932, 34, 36, 40, 42, 56, 67, N.A.D., 1956, 65, ASCA anns., 1966-85, Audubon Artists, 1977-87, 88, N.S.P.C. anns., 1956-87, 88, Riverside Mus., 1955, 57, 59, 61, 64, 66, Plastics U.S.A. Year Tour of USSR, 1961-62, Eastern States Exhbn., Springfield (Mass.) Mus. Art, 1963, 64, Archtl. League of N.Y., 1965, Art Students League Centennial, Mus. of N.Y.C., 1975-76, New Deal for Art, 1977-78, N.Y. WPA Artists Then and Now, 1977, Emily Lowe Gallery, Parsons Sch. Art Gallery, Hofstra U., Hempstead, L.I., 1978, Dawn of a New Day, Queens Mus., 1980, WPA Artists Inc., N.Y.C. and Passaic, N.J., 1984, ACA, 1986, Mary Ryan Gallery, 1981, 82, 83, ACA 50th Anniversary of Am. Artists Congress, 1986, Am. Acad. Arts and Letters, 1987; represented in permanent collections including, U. Wichita, U. Minn., Coll. Fine Arts at Ohio U., Lincoln Ctr. Mus. Performing Arts, Columbia Anthropology Archives, N.Y. State U. Mus., New Paltz, Norfolk Mus. Art, Newark Mus., Syracuse Mus., Smithsonian Instn., Fairleigh Dickinson U., N.Y. U., Burke Mus., Seattle, Yale U. Art Gallery; art dir., prodn. mgr., Fox Features Syndicate, 1940-41, art dir., Cin. Ordnance Dist., U.S. War Dept., 1942-43, publs. illustrator, USAAF, 1944-45, reviewer, Cin. Enquirer, 1946-49, stage designer, Stage, Inc., Cin. Civic Theater, 1948-49, mural cons., Internat. Fair Consultants, 1961-62, Pres., mem. adv. bd., Artists Tech. Research Inst., 1963-75, co-founder, Nat. Com. Arts and Govt., 1952. Served with USAAF, 1943-45. Recipient numerous awards including Childe Hassam Purchase award Am. Acad. Arts and Letters, 1961; prize Am. Soc. Contemporary Artists, 1966, 79; award Silvermine Artists Guild, New Eng. Ann., 1969; Audubon Artists Silver medal, 1982; MacDowell fellow, 1931, 35, 38; Yaddo fellow, 1932. Mem. Am. Acad. and Inst. Arts and Letters, Artists Equity Assn. (pres. N.Y. chpt. 1958-59, hon. adv. bd. mem.), Nat. Orgn. Arts Equity (v.p. 1956-58), Am. Watercolor Soc., Nat. Soc. Painters in Casein (award winners spl. exhibition at Lotus Club 1986), Nat. Soc. Mural Painters, Art Students League (life), Am. Soc. Contemporary Artists, Art League Hudson Valley (hon.), Townsend Harris Alumni Assn. (hon. dir.), Audubon Artists Soc. Home: New York N.Y. Died May 28, 1988; cremated.

VAN VLISSINGEN, ARTHUR, writer; b. Chgo., Nov. 2, 1894; s. Arthur and Sophia Evans (Levering) Van V.; m. Ruth Lindsey, Sept. 22, 1917; children: Lindsey, Carol Van Vlissingen Carpenter, Marcia Van Vlissingen Wire. AB, Northwestern U., 1915. Mem. editorial staff The Mag. Bus., 1916-20, mng. editor, 1920-22; editor Factory mag., 1927, Factory and Indsl. Mgmt. mag., 1928; cons. editor Factory Mgmt. and Maintenance mag., 1936-42; chief Chgo. bur. Business Week mag., 1938-47. Author: The Yankee of the Yards; contbr. numerous articles and short stories to mags. With USNR, World War I. Mem. Am. Philaletic Soc., Trans-Miss. Philaletic Soc., Chgo. Philaletic Soc., Wis. Postal History Soc. (pres. 1963-75), Ill. Postal History Soc., Iowa Postal History Soc., U.S. Cancellation Club (pres. 1964-67), Sigma Alpha Epsilon. Republican. Episcopalian. Home: Lake Forest Ill. Died Oct. 20, 1986.

VAN WAGONER, MURRAY DELES, governor, civil engineer; b. Kingston, Mich., Mar. 18, 1898; s. James and Florence (Loomis) Van W.; m. Helen Jossman, June, 1924 (dec. Apr. 1986); children: Ellen Louise Van Wagoner Wikel, Jo Ann Van Wagoner Karohs. BSCE, U. Mich., 1921. Civil engr. then div. bridge engr. Mich. State Hwy. Dept., 1921-24; engr. McGaughan & Ransom, Pontiac, Mich., 1924-26; owner pvt. engring. co. Pontiac, 1926-30; drain commr. Oakland County (Mich.), 1930-33; state hwy. commr. Mich., 1933-40; gov. State of Mich., 1941-42; cons. engr. 1943-47; apptd. dir. Office of Mil. Govt., Bavaria, Germany, 1948; civil gov. State of Bavaria, Fed. Republic Germany, 1949; mem. Mackinac Bridge Authority, Mich., 1950-86; del. Internat. Rd. Congress, 1938; v.p. Byrne Door Co., Inc., 1945. Mem. Am. Rd. Builders Assn. (pres. 1938-40, bd. dirs.), ASCE, Mich. Engring. Soc., Masons, Elks, Eagles, Detroit Club, Economic Club. Democrat. Episcopalian. Died June 12, 1986.

VAN ZANDT, JAMES EDWARD, congressman; b. Altoona, Pa., Dec. 18, 1898; s. James Theodore and Katherine (Smith) Van Z.; m. Esther Meisenhoelder, Sept. 21, 1947; 1 child, James Edward II. Ed., Altoona pub. schs., Ry. Apprentice Sch.; LLD (hon.), Rider Coll., 1956. Molder apprentice Pa. Ry. shops, Altoona, 1916; with various depts. Pa. R.R., to dist. passenger agt., 1938; mem. 76th to 82d Congresses 22d Pa. dist., 1938-43, 83d to 87th Congresses 20th Pa. dist., 1946-62; ranking House Rep., mem. Joint Atomic Energy Com. and House Armed Services Com. With USN, 1917-19, lt. to capt. active duty, USN, 1941-46; rear adm. ret., USNR; also served in Korea. Mem. VFW (comdr. Pa. dept. 1928-29, nar. comdr. in chief 1933-35), Am. Legion, Amvets, Grange, Masons, Shriners, KP, Eagles. Republican. Lutheran. Home: Altoona Pa. Died Jan. 6, 1986.

VARGAS, GEORGE LELAND, lawyer; b. Winnemucca, Nev., Aug. 31, 1909; s. John Dorsey and Margaret Harriet (Wilkinson) V.; m. Phyllis Balzar, Aug. 1928 (div. 1943); children: Del, George Leland II (dec.), Susan, Linda; m. Andrea Drumm, 1948 (div. 1950); m. Josephine Berliner, Oct 17, 1950; 1 dau., Nola. AB, U. Nev., 1931; JD, Stanford U., 1934. Bar: Nev. 1934, Calif. 1934. R.R. public rels. counsel 1937-41; nat. counsel Nat. Bd. Fire Underwriters, 1944-46, Western gen. counsel, 1946-65; practiced in Reno from 1934; chmn. bd. Vargas & Bartlett Ltd. (Organizer), 1946-68; dir., counsel Bonanza Lines, 1946-68; dir., sr. counsel Valley Bank Nev.; dir., mem. exec. com. Air West, 1968-70; gen. counsel Nev. Bankers Assn., 1978-85; dir. Johnson Controls, Inc., Milw.; gen. counsel Nat. Jud. Coll. Fellow Am. Acad. Matrimonial Lawyers; mem. Stanford Assocs., ABA, Internat. Assn. Ins. Counsel, Am. Coll. Trial Lawyers, Am. Coll. Probate Counsel, Elks (exalted ruler Reno, Mexico), Balboa de Mazatlan Club (dir.), Alpha Tau Omega. Episcopalian. Home: Reno Nev. Died Sept. 7, 1985; buried Mountain View Cemetery, Reno, Nev.

VARIAN, ELAYNE H., art museum administrator; b. San Francisco; m. John Varian. Student, Art Inst. Chgo; AM, U. Chgo.; postgrad., NYU. Asst. to pres. Duveen Bros., Inc. gallery, 1953-62; exec. dir. Village Art Ctr., 1962-64; dir. contemporary wing, curator Finch Coll. Mus. of Art, N.Y.C., 1964-75; adviser N.Y. State Council on Arts, from 1967; lectr. contemporary art history; contemporary curator Ringling Mus., Sarasota, Fla., 3 yrs.; tchr. Ill. Inst. Tech., Chgo., Chgo. Art Inst. Contbr. articles in field to scholarly publs. Pres. Am. Friends Attingham Cons. Everson Mus. Art, Syracuse, N.Y., 1969; mem. Mayor's Citizen' Adv. Com., N.Y.C., 1967-69; bd. dirs. Heathcote Art Found., N.Y.C. MacDowell Colony fellow, 1970; Sussman Traveling grantee, 1970-71. Mem. Gallery Assn. N.Y. State (dir. 1972, co-dir. exhbn. com.), Am. Assn. Museums, Internat. Council Museums, Coll. Arts Assn. Died Nov. 4, 1987.

VARTAN, VARTANIG GARABED, journalist; b. Pasadena, Calif., June 28, 1923; s. Garabed S. and Yeranig (Saxenian) V.; m. Cynthia Kirk Smith, Nov. 18, 1961; 1 child, Kirk Spencer. B.A., Yale U., 1948. Reporter Laurel (Miss.) Leader-Call, 1948-49, Tupelo (Miss.) Jour., 1949-52, United Press, 1952-55; financial writer N.Y. Herald Tribune, 1955-62; Wall St. columnist Christian Sci. Monitor, 1957-62; financial writer N.Y. Times, 1963-88; pres. Microsurg. Research Found., Inc., 1982-88; freelance writer. Author: 50 Wall Street, 1968, The Dinosaur Fund, 1972. Served with AUS, 1943-45. Episcopalian. Club: Century Assn. (N.Y.C.). Home: New York N.Y. Died May 24, 1988; buried Providence.

VATH, JOSEPH G., bishop; b. New Orleans, Mar. 12, 1918. Ed., Notre Dame Sem., New Orleans, 1935-41; J.C.L., Catholic U. Am., 1948. Ordained priest Roman Catholic Ch., 1941; asst. pastor Ascension Ch., Donaldsonville, La., 1941-46, Incarnate Word Ch., New Orleans, 1948, St. Michael's Ch., 1948-49; vice-chancellor Archdiocese of New Orleans 1948-66, sec. to bishop, 1949-62, sec. diocesan tribunal, 1955; adminstr. Our Lady of Perpetual Help Ch., Kenner, La., 1952; pastor Little Flower Ch., 1966-69; consecrated bishop 1966; vicar gen., aux. bishop Mobile-Birmingham (Ala.) and titular bishop of Novaliciana, 1966-69; bishop of Birmingham 1969-87. Home: Birmingham Ala. Died July 14, 1987; buried Bishop's Garden, St. Paul's Cathedral, Birmingham, Ala.

VAUGHAN, HENRY FRIEZE, public health administrator; b. Ann Arbor, Mich., Oct. 12, 1889; s. Victor and Dora (Taylor) V.; m. Grace Seeley, Sept. 19, 1914; 1 son, Henry F. BS, U. Mich., 1912, MS, 1913, DrPH, 1916. Diplomate Am. Acad. San. Engrs. Pvt. practice san. engring. and pub. health 1913-17; assoc. prof. pub. health Wayne State U., Detroit, 1915-37, prof., 1937-41; commr. of health City of Detroit, 1918-41; spl. lectr. in pub. health adminstrn. U. Mich., 1922—, prof. pub. health, dean sh. pub. health, 1941-60, dean emeritus, 1960—; spl. lectr. Vanderbilt U., 1935-43. Author: (with Victor C. Vaughan and George T. Palmer) Epidemioogy and Public Health; editor: Am. Jour. of Pub. Health, 1922-24; editorial bd. Mcpl. Sanitation, 1930-36,. Trustee W.K. Kellogg Found.; president Nat. Sanitation Found.; chmn. com. on Mcpl. Health Orgn. of Pres. Hoover's Conf. on Child Health and Protection; chm. Com. Nat. Health Conservation Contest, 1935-44; promoter since 1928 plan med. and and indsl. participation in pub. health svc. now being extensively adopted;; mem. adv. bd. Nat. Orgn. for Pub. Health Nursing, 1925-50; cons. USAF, USPHS; sec. Assn. of Schs. of Pub. Health, 1942-46; mem. Mich. Bd. Examiners of Basic Scis., 1941-52; mem. nat. adv. health coun. USPHS, 1942-46; cons. USAF; mem. nat. adv. coun. Cleve. Health Mus., nat. adv. dental rsch. coun. USPHS, 1947-51, adv. com. to review activies FDA. Commd. capt. San. Corps., U.S. Army, Dec. 12, 1917; in charge san. dept. at Camp Upton, L.I. and Camp Wheeler, Ga.; ; mem. Pneumonia Commn., apptd. by surgeon gen.; hon. discharged Jan. 28, 1919. Recipient Sedgwick Meml. medal Am. Pub. Health Assn., 1949, Mich. Trudeau award, 1958. Fellow Am. Pub. Health Assn. (pres. 1925), Royal San. Inst. (hon.); mem. AMA (hon.), Am. Trudeau Soc. (hon.), Am. Acad. Pediatrics, Mich. Pub. Health Assn. (pres. 1940), Nat. Tuberculosis Assn. (mem. bd. dirs.), Am. Soc. CE State and Provincial Health Officers Assn., Acanthus Club, Detroit Athletic Club, Philatelic Club, Country Club, Beta Thea Pi, Delta Omega, Phi Kappa Phi. Episcopalian. Home: Ann Arbor Mich. †

VEECK, BILL (WILLIAM LOUIS), JR., professional sports executive; b. Chgo., Feb. 9, 1914; s. William L. and Grace Greenwood (De Forrest) V.; m. Eleanor Raymond, Dec. 8, 1935 (div. 1949); m. Mary Frances Ackerman, Apr. 29, 1950; 9 children. Student, Kenyon Coll. With Chgo. Cubs profl. baseball team, 1933-41, treas., asst. sec., 1940-41; pres., owner profl. baseball teams Milw. Brewers (Am. Assn.), 1941-45, Cleve. Indians, 1946-49, St. Louis Browns, 1951-53, Chgo. White Sox, 1959-61, 76-81; sports announcer NBC-TV, 1957-58; pres., owner Suffolk Downs, Boston, 1969-71; co-host (with Mary-Frances Veeck) radio and TV shows, Cleve., St. Louis, Chgo. Author: (with Ed Linn) Veeck-As in Wreck, 1962, The Hustler's Handbook, 1965, Thirty Tons a Day, 1972. With USMCR, 1943-45. Named Minor League Exec. of Yr., Sporting News, 1942, Maj. League Exec. of Yr., 1948, 77. Roman Catholic. Died Jan. 2, 1986; cremated.

VERNON, GLENN MORLEY, sociologist, educator; b. Vernal, Utah, Apr. 6, 1920; s. William Morley and Roseltha (Bingham) V.; m. June Andersen, Dec. 24, 1941; children: Gregory Glenn, Rebecca, Paul Binghgam. BS, Brigham Young U., 1947, MS in Sociology, 1950; PhD, Wash. State U., 1953. Asst. prof. Auburn U., 1953-54; asst. prof. then assoc. prof. Cen. Mich. U., 1954-59; assoc. prof. Brigham Young U., Provo, Utah, 1959-63, prof. sociology, head. dept. sociology and anthropology, 1963-68; prof. anthropology U. Maine, 1963-68; prof. sociology U. Utah, 1968-85, chmn. dept., 1970-73; vis. prof. McMaster U., Hamilton, Ont., Can., summer 1959, U. Utah, summer 1966, U. Maine, U. Del., summer 1976. Author: Sociology of Religion, 1962, Human Interaction, An Introduction to Sociology, 1965, 2d edit., 1972, Sociology of Death, 1970, (with Jerry D. Cardwell) Social Psychology: Shared Symboled and Situated Behavior, 1981; contbr. articles to profl. jours. Pilot USAAF, 1942-45. Fellow Am. Sociol. Assn.; mem. Insts. Religion and Health, Found. of Thanatology, Internat. Conf. for Sociology of Religion, Soc. Sci.Study Religion, Internat. Conf. for Sociology of Religion, Soc. for Study Symbolic Interaction, Religious Research Assn., Pacific Sociol. Assn., Utah Sociol. Soc. (pres. 1976-77), Internat. Sociol. Assn., Internat. Assn. for Near-Death Studies, Soc. for Sociol. Study of Mormon Life (pres. 1978-80), Sigma X, Phi Kappa Phi. Mormon. Home: Salt Lake City Utah. Died Oct. 11, 1985; buried Salt Lake City.

VERSENYI, LASZLO GASPAR, philosophy educator; b. Baja, Hungary, Apr. 3, 1928; came to U.S., 1949; s. Jeno and Andrea (Csoor) V.; m. Diana Abelson, Sept. 1, 1953; children—Adam Nathaniel, Andrea Sarah. Student, U. Heidelberg, Fed. Republic Germany, 1948-50, postgrad., 1952-53; B.A., Yale U., 1952, Ph.D., 1955. Instr. Yale U., New Haven, Conn., 1955-58; from instr. to Mark Hopkins prof. philosophy, chmn. dept. Williams Coll., Williamstown, Mass., 1958-87. Author: Socratic Humanism, 1963; Heidegger, Being and Truth, 1965; Man's Measure, 1974; Holiness and Justice, 1982; contbd. articles to scholarly publs. Grantee Am. Council Learned Socs., 1963, Am. Philos. Soc., 1963; NEH fellow, 1970. Home: Williamstown Mass. Died Feb. 23, 1988, buried Williams Coll. Cemetery, Williamston.

VICTORY, JOHN FRANCIS, government official; b. N.Y.C., Jan. 23, 1892; s. John Francis and Ellen (Hines) V.; m. Marie Frances Brennan, Oct. 17, 1917; children: Elizabeth Marie (dec.), John Robert, Elizabeth Jeanne, William Charles Walcott. LLB, Georgetown U., 1923, LLM, 1924; LLD (hon.), Norwich U., 1950. Bar: D.C. 1923. Congl. reporter 1911-15, shorthand instr., later propr. of shorthand sch., 1913-18; 1st employee Nat. Adv. Com. for Aeros., 1915, asst. sec., 1917-27, sec., 1927-45, exec. sec., 1945-58; asst. to adminstr. NASA, 1958-60; chmn. Internat. Civil Aeros. Conf. Pilgrimage to Kitty Hawk, N.C., 1928; mem. Collier Trophy Com., from 1946, chmn., 1948; chmn. award com. Wright Bros. Meml. Trophy, 1948-51; organizer 1st Internat. Air Pioneers Reunion, Washington, 1953; pres. Victory Lecture Svc., Colorado Springs, Colo., from 1960. V.p. Washington Community Chest, 1939, sec., 1940-50. Recipient Presdl. Medal for Merit, 1947, Wright Bros. Meml. Trophy, 1958; named Elder Statesman of Aviation, 1957. Mem. Washington Bd. Trade (chmn. com. charities and corrections 1936-40, chmn. aviation com. 1945-47, 50-51), Inst. Aero. Sci., Nat. Aero. Assn. (chmn. ann. convs. 1926-30, treas. 1929-35, bd. dirs. 1950-54, chmn. exec. com. 1952-54, v.p. from 1955), Shakespeare Soc., KC, Aero Club (pres. 1937-39), Manor Club, Nat. Aviation Club, Torch Club (pres. 1944), Cosmos Club. Roman Catholic. †

VIDAL DE LA FUENTE, JORGE, nitrate company executive; b. Valparaiso, Chile, Apr. 11, 1892; s. Ramon Vidal and Teresa de la Fuente (Duenas) Aguayo; m. Adelina Casanova, Jan. 25, 1941; children: Jorge, Teresa (dec.), Marta. B Humanities, U. Chile, 1910. Exec. v.p. Corporacion de Ventas de Salitre y Yodo de Chile, 1941-61, then dir.; pres. Compania Salitrera Anglo Lautaro, Santiago, from 1961; pres., dir. Anglo Lautro Nitrate Corp., from 1967; bd. dirs. Banco Central de Chile, Banco Sud-Americano, La Estrella Ins. Co., La Chilena Consolidada Ins. Co., Cia Minera de Oruro; chmn. bd. dirs. El Mercurio de Antofagasta, La Prensa de Tocopilla. Author: The Chilean Nitrate Tragedy, rev. edit., 1953. Decorated Order Brit. Empire; Legion Honour (France); Mil. Order Christ (Portugal). Home: Santiago Chile. †

VIESULAS, ROMAS, artist, educator; b. USSR, Sept. 11, 1918; s. Kazimieras and Juzefa (Kozukauskas) V.; m. Jura Gailiusis, June 22, 1968; children: Romas-Tauras, Vytautas-Kostas, Auste-Neringa. Diploma, Ecole des Arts et Metiers, Freiburg, Fed. Republic Germany, 1949, Ecole Nat. Superieure des Beaux Arts, Paris, 1950. Faculty, chmn. dept. printmaking Tyler Sch. Art-Temple U., Phila., 1960-85, prof., 1969-85; vis. artist Am. Acad. in Rome, 1964-65, 79; artist-in-residence Biennial of Venice, 1970. One-man shows include: Le Soleil dans la Tete, Paris, 1959, Yoseido Gallery, Tokyo, 1964, Il Torcoliere, Rome, 1965, Cin. Art Mus., 1967, Oxford (Eng.) Gallery, 1968; represented in permanent collections: Met. Mus. Art, N.Y.C., Mus. Modern Art, N.Y.C., Nat. Gallery, Washington, Art Inst. Chgo., Biblioteque Nationale, Paris, Nat. Mus., Krakow, Poland, Mus. Modern Art, Kamakura, Japan, Mus. Contemporary Art, Skopje, Yugoslavia, Bklyn. Mus., Library of Congress, Washington, Vatican Mus., Rome, Frederikshavn (Denmark) Art Mus., numerous others. Mem. AAUP, Soc. Am. Graphic Artists, Inst. Lithuanian Studies, Lithuanian Cath. Acad. Scis., Assn. for the Advancement of Baltic Study, Phila. Print Club. Died 1986.

VILAS, HOMER ALBON, broker; b. Ogdensburg, N.Y., Mar. 27, 1891; s. Albon W. and Jennie M. (Welch) V.; m. Elizabeth Margaret Waters, Oct. 12, 1916; children: Richard Winchester, Homer Albon. BS, St. Lawrence U., 1913, LLD (hon.), 1958. With Equitable Trust Co. of N.Y., 1913-15, L. M. Prince and Co., 1915-18, Vilas and Hickey, 1918-29; v.p. F. L. Carlisle, 1929-31; ptnr. Cyrus J. Lawrence and Sons, 1931-67, ltd. ptnr., 1967-73; hon. chmn. bd. Cyrus J. Lawrence Inc., from 1973; dir. Union Camp Corp., Milmine Bodman & Co. Inc.; mem. bd. mgrs. Montclair Savs. Bank, 1947, 1949-55; gov. Assn. Stock Exchange Firms, 1941-47, pres. 1948. Trustee Mountainside Hosp., Montclair, N.J., 1945-60, 64-66, hon. chmn. bd., 1960-64, hon. trustee, 1960-64, from 1966, treas. 1947-48, v.p., 1949-52, pres., 1952-60, 64-66; trustee Edward J. Noble Found., Greenwich, Conn., 1952-59; pres. Bodman Found., from 1963; trustee St. Lawrence U., 1929-68, trustee emeritus, from 1968, chmn. exec. com., chmn. bd., 1954-68, hon. chmn., from 1968; past dir. Deafness Rsch. Found. Mem. Down Town Club, Union League, Links Club, Pinnacle Club, Upper Montclair Country Club, Alpha Tau Omega. Republican. Congregationalist. Home: Upper Montclair N.J. †

VINAL, ALBERT, shoe manufacturer; b. Cambridge, Mass., Sept. 28, 1891; s. Charles Albert and Nellie (Furber) V.; m. Margaret Heald, June 2, 1915; children: Albert, Arthur Heald, Helen Furber. AB, Williams Coll., 1914. With Stetson Shoe Co. Inc., South Weymouth, Mass., 1914—, chmn., dir.; pres. John Furber Lumber Co., Weymouth Lumber Co.; dir. South Shore Nat. Bank of Quincy, Am. Mut. Liability Ins. Co., Am. Policyholders Ins. Co., Tubular Rivet & Stud Co., Weymouth Light and Power Co.. Trustee Williams Coll., South Shore Hosp., Fogg Libr. Home: South Weymouth Mass. †

VINCENT, HOWARD P(ATON), English educator; b. Galesburg, Ill., Oct. 9, 1904; s. Clarence and Lucy Seymour (Hall) V.; m. Mary Wilson Smith, Sept. 4, 1931; children: Judith Hall, John Way. AB, Oberlin Coll., 1926; MA, Harvard U., 1927, PhD, 1933; Litt.D. (hon.), Hillsdale Coll., 1958. Instr. composition and lit. W.Va. U., 1927-28; tchr. Park Sch., Cleve., 1931-32; supr. Blair County Office of Relief, Altoona, Pa., 1935; Ezra L. Koon prof. English, head dept. Hillsdale (Mich.) Coll., 1935-42; asst. prof. Ill. Inst. Tech., Chgo., 1942-44, assoc. prof., 1944-47, prof. English, chmn. lang., lit. and philosophy, 1947-62; prof. English and Am. Lit. Kent (Ohio) State U., from 1962; Fulbright lectr. Am. civilization and lit. France, 1954-55, Belgium, 1961-62, Italy, 1967; dir. French library service U.S. Info. Service, 1955-58. Author: The Trying Out of Moby Dick, 1949; editor: Letters of Dora Wordsworth, 1944, Collected Poems of Herman Melville, 1947, Critique of Moby Dick, 1952, (with H. Hayford) Reader and Writer, 1954, Bartleby the Scrivener: A Symposium, 1966, Melville and Hawthorne in the Berkshires, 1968, Dammier and His World, 1969. Fellow Fund for Advancement of Edn., 1951-52. Mem. MLA, Nat. Council Tchrs. English, Coll. English Assn., AAUP, Melville Soc. Am. (pres. 1951, 69-70, sec. 1963-69), Keats-Shelley Assn. Am. Home: Kent Ohio. Died Sept. 24, 1985.

VINCIGUERRA, FRANCESCA See **WINWAR, FRANCES**

VINEBERG, ARTHUR MARTIN, heart surgeon; b. Montreal, May 24, 1903; s. Abraham Moses and Anna (Berman) V.; m. Ann Porter, Dec. 28, 1942; stepchild: Brian Buckley. BS, McGill U., 1924, MD, CM, MSc in Biochemistry, 1928, Rockefeller fellow in exptl. physiology, 1929-30, PhD in Physiology, 1933. Diplomate Am. Bd. Thoracic Surgery (founder). Surg. houseman Presbyn.-Bellevue Hosp., N.Y.C., 1928-29, Royal Victoria Hosp.-McGill U., Montreal, 1931-33; instr. anatomy McGill U., Montreal, 1933-42; lectr. surgery McGill U., 1945-58; studies in exptl. surgery Montreal, 1945-87, surg. cardiac cons. Queen Mary Vets. Hosp., 1951-87; surg. cardiac cons. Queen Mary Vets. Hosp. Jewish Gen. Hosp., Montreal, 1957-87; head cardiac surgery Royal Victoria Hosp., 1957-87. With M.C. Royal Can. Army, 1942-45. Recipient Med. Undergraduate Prize McGill U., 1928, Casgrain-Charbonneau Prize, 1942. Fellow Am. Coll. Chest Physicians, ACS, Am. Heart Assn., Royal Coll. Surgeons; mem. Am. Coll Cardiology, Que. Cardiovascular and Thoracic Surgery Soc. (co-founder), Can. Heart Assn., Que. Heart Assn. (past med. adv. com.), Montreal Heart Assn., Can. Med. Assn., Montreal Clin. Soc., Montreal Chirurg. Soc., Can. Physiol. Soc., Montreal Physiol. Soc. Home: Montreal, P.Q. Canada. Died Mar. 20, 1988.

VINEBERG, PHILIP FISCHEL, lawyer; b. Mattawa, Ont., Can., July 21, 1914; s. Malcolm and Rebecca (Phillips) V.; m. Miriam S. Schachter, Dec. 19, 1939; children: Robert S., Michael D. B.A., McGill U., 1935, M.A., 1936, B.C.L., 1939; postgrad., Ecole Libre des Scis. Politiques, Paris, France, 1935-36; LL.D. (hon.), 1980. Bar: Called to bar, Que. 1939, appointed Queen's Counsel 1959. Practiced in Montreal; mem. firm Phillips & Vineberg, 1939-87; various lectureships and profesorships in econs., polit. sci., comml/ law and corp. law McGill U., 1939-68; past chmn. consultative com. Que. Dept. Revenue. Author: The French Franc and the Gold Standard, 1936; Contbr.: chpts. to Money Credit and Banking, 1940, Studies in Canadian Company Law, 1968; contbg. editor: chpts. to Prentice Hall Income Taxation in Canada; contbd. articles to profl. jours. Mem. Ry. Conciliation Bd., 1958, 60; past v.p. Canadian Friends of Alliance Israelite Universelle; past trustee Jewish Gen. Hosp., Canadian Inst. Research Pub. Policy, Inst. for Research on Pub. Policy; chmn. bd. govs. Canadian Tax Found., 1966-67; former bd. govs. YMHA, McGill U., Cardoza Law Sch., Bar-Ilan U.; pres. fellows Found. for Legal Research in Can., 1973-76. Fellow Brandeis U., Bar-Ilan U., U.S. Coll. Trial Lawyers; apptd. officer Order of Canada, 1974. Mem. Canadian Bar Assn. (pres. Que. br. 1973-74, nat. exec. com. 1974-75), Bar Province Que. (vice chmn. 1969-70), Bar of Montreal (batonnier 1969-70), Internat. Fiscal Assn. (pres. Canadian br. 1974-76, past internat. exec.). Home: Westmount Que., Canada. Died Nov. 24, 1987.

VINEYARD, GEORGE HOAGLAND, physicist, former laboratory administrator; b. St. Joseph, Mo., Apr. 28, 1920; s. George Hoagland and Mildred M. (Barkley) V.; m. Phyllis Ainsworth Smith, Feb. 3, 1945; children: John H., Barbara Gale. B.S., Mass. Inst. Tech., 1941, Ph.D., 1943; Sc.D. (hon.), L.I.U., 1977, U. Mo., 1986. Mem. staff Radiation Lab., Mass. Inst. Tech., 1943-45; mem. faculty U. Mo., Columbia, 1946-54; prof. U. Mo., 1952-54; mem. staff Brookhaven Nat. Lab., Upton, N.Y., 1954-86; sr. physicist Brookhaven Nat. Lab., 1960-86, chmn. dept. physics, 1961-66, dep. dir. lab., 1966-72, dir. lab., 1973-81; cons. to govt. and industry; fellow Poly. Inst. N.Y., 1978-86; mem. vis. com. Materials Sci. Center, Cornell U., 1964-67; dept. physics Mass. Inst. Tech., 1969-73; mem. president's sci. and ednl. adv. com. for Lawrence Berkeley Lab., U. Calif., 1977-81; adv. com. Nat. Magnet Lab., 1963-67; adv. com. math. and phys. scis. NSF, 1966-71, chmn., 1971; mem. sci. policy bd. Stanford Synchotron Radiation Project, 1977-81; mem. solid state scis. panel NRC, 1954-86, chmn., 1965-71, chmn. solid state scis. com., 1970-72; chmn. panel condensed matter, physics survey com. Nat. Acad. Scis., 1969-72; mem. materials research council ARPA, 1967-86; mem. Sec. State ad hoc com. U.S. participation IAEA, 1970-72; chmn. nat. allocation com. JVNC Computer Ctr., 1985-86. Co-editor: series Documents in Modern Physics, 1964-78; editor Phys. Rev. Letters, 1983-85; bd. asso. editors series Am. Jour. Physics, 1948-50, Phys. Rev., 1959-61; bd. editors series Physics, 1964-68, Jour. Computational Physics, 1966-70, Physics and Chemistry of Liquids, 1968-86. Bd. dirs. L.I. Action Com., 1979-82; mem. adv. com. on sci. and tech. N.Y. State Legis. Commn., 1980-86. Recipient award distinguished contbns. to higher edn. Stony Brook Found., 1975. Fellow Am. Acad. Arts and Scis., Am. Phys. Soc. (chmn. div. solid state physics 1972-73, councillor at large 1974-78, chmn. div. condensed matter physics 1984-85, v.p. 1986), AAAS; mem. L.I. Assn. Commerce and Industry (dir. 1975-82), Sigma Xi.

Home: Bellport N.Y. Died Feb. 21, 1987; buried St. Joseph, Mo.

VOELKEL, ROBERT T(OWNSEND), religion educator; b. Cleve., Feb. 26, 1933; s. Elmer E. and Mercy (Townsend) V.; m. Martha Ann Bousman, Dec. 21, 1955; children—Andrew, Thomas, James. B.A., Coll. of Wooster, 1954; postgrad. (Fulbright scholar), New Coll. U. Edinburgh, Scotland, 1954-55; B.D. in N.T. and Ch. History, 1957, Th.D. in Systematic Theology, 1962. Instr. religion Coll. of Wooster, 1957-59; instr. Pomona Coll., 1962-64, asst. prof. religion, 1964-67, assoc. prof., 1967-73, prof., 1973-87, William M. Keck disting. service prof., 1986-87, chmn. dept. religion, 1969-75, v.p., dean of coll., 1975-86; vis. prof. Philipps-Universitat, Marburg/Lahn, W. Ger., 1975-76; mem. com. on ecumenics and liturgics So. Calif. Conf. United Ch. of Christ, 1966-68; sec. exec. com. United Ministries in Higher Edn. Regional Commn., So. Calif., 1966-68. Author: The Shape of the Theological Task, 1968; editor, author: intro., critical notes and bibliography The Communion of the Christian with God (Wilhelm Herrmann), 1971. Mem. bd. deacons Claremont (Calif.) United Ch. of Christ, 1971-74, mem. bd. Christian edn., 1964-66; mem. corp. Pilgrim Pl. Retirement Ctr., Claremont, 1973-76. Recipient Wig Disting. Prof. award Pomona Coll., 1966; Fulbright travel grantee, 1975-76. Mem. Am. Soc. Ch. History, Am. Acad. Religion, Pacific Coast Theol. Soc., So. Calif. Conf. Acad. Deans (chmn. 1980), Phi Beta Kappa. Home: Claremont Calif. Died Oct. 8, 1987.

VOIGT, EDWIN EDGAR, college president; b. Kankakee County, Ill., Feb. 13, 1892; s. Theodore G. and Dorothea (Kukuck) V.; m. Eleanor Hemsted Dodge, Aug. 27, 1921; children: Paul Stuart, Nancy. BS, Northwestern U., 1917, MA, 1922; BD, Garrett Bibl. Inst., 1921, DD, 1942; PhD, Yale U., 1924; LLD, Simpson Coll., 1954; LittD (hon.), Dakota Wesleyan U., 1960; LHD, Ill. Wesleyan U., 1961, McKendree Coll., 1961. Instr. bibl. lit. Northwestern U., 1920-21; asst. prof. Old Testament Interpretation, Garrett Bibl. Inst., 1924-28, assoc. prof., 1928-32; assoc. pastor First Meth. Ch., Evanston, Ill., 1932-36; pastor First Meth. Ch. and dir. Wesley Found., Iowa City, Iowa, 1936-42; pres. Simpson Coll., 1942-52; bishop Dakota area, 1952-60, Ill. area, 1960-64; pres. McKendree Coll., Lebanon, Ill., from 1964. Author: Latin Versions of Judith, 1925, (with O.R. Sellers) Biblical Hebrew for Begineers, 1941, Methodist Worship in Church Universal, 1965; contbr. articles to ch. sch. publs. of Meth. Ch. 2d lt. U.S. Army, World War I. Fellow Nat. Coun. Religion in Higher Edn.; mem. Soc. Bibl. Lit., Masons, Rotary, Beta Theta Pi, Delta Sigma Rho, Phi Mu Alpha (hon.). Home: Lebanon Ill. †

VOLK, GARTH WILLIAM, agronomist; b. Maple Valley, Wis., June 13, 1905; s. James R. and Marietta (McKenney) V.; m. Alice Marie Peters, June 15, 1935; children: Veril Van, Bob Garth. BS, U. Wis., 1934, MS, 1935, PhD, 1936. Soil chemist United Fruit Co., 1928-33; asst. prof. soils Okla. State U., 1936-38; assoc. prof. soils Auburn (Ala.) U., 1938-42, prof., 1942-44; soil chemist Ohio Agrl. Experiment Sta., 1944-47; chmn. dept. agronomy Ohio State U., Columbus, 1947-75; former cons. I.D.I. Co., Ltd., Nassau, Bahamas, D.C.I. Co., Washington, Standard Fruit Co., New Orleans, U.S. AID. Fellow Am. Soc. Agronomy; mem. Soil Sci. Soc. Am. (chmn. soil chemistry sect. 1946, sec. nat soil research com. 1954), Internat. Soil Sci. Soc. Home: Worthington Ohio. Died June 8, 1986; buried Oaklawn Meml. Cemetery, Corvallis, Oreg.

VOLLMER, WILLIAM G., railroad executive; b. Cin., July 30, 1886; s. Louis and Elizabeth Vollmer; m. Alice Margaret Brangle, June 11, 1910; children: William G. Jr., Mary Elizabeth (Mrs. Isaac H. Clucas Jr.), Edward Louis, John James. Student, Bartlett's Business Coll., Cin. Began as stenographer Pa. R.R., 1902; served in passenger traffic, maintenance, engring. and operating depts. Pa. R.R., Balt. & Ohio R.R., Rock Island Lines and Mo. Pacific R.R., 1902-17; asst. to pres. Mo. Pacific R.R., 1917-18; asst. regional dir., southwestern region U.S. R.R. Adminstrn., 1918-20; asst. to pres. Mo. Pacific Lines, 1920-33; exec. asst. 1933-45; pres. Tex. & Pacific Ry. Co., 1945, ret. Mem. Am. Ry. Engring Assn., Mo. Athletic Club, Noonday Club (st. Louis), Traffic Club, Railroad Club (Chgo.), Dallas Athletic Club, City Club, Downtown Club, Fort Worth Club, Internat. House (New Orleans), Boston Club (New Orleans). Home: Dallas Tex. †

VOLLUM, HOWARD, corporate executive; b. 1913; married. B.A., Reed Coll., 1936. With Murdock Radio & Appliance Co., 1936-41; founder Tektronix, Inc., 1946, pres., 1946-71, chmn., 1971-85; past dir. U.S. Nat. Bank Oreg., Pacific Power & Light Co. Served with Signal Corps, U.S. Army, 1941-45. Died Feb. 3, 1986.

VON DER AHE, CHARLES T., grocery company executive; b. Denmark, Aug. 29, 1892; s. Rudolph and Carolyn (Larsen) Von Der A.; m. Linda A. Luer, Jan. 22, 1907. Founder Von's Grocery Co., L.A., then chmn. bd. Home: Los Angeles Calif. †

VON NEUMANN, ROBERT FRANZ ALBERT, artist; b. Rostock, Germany, Sept. 10, 1888; came to U.S., 1926, naturalized, 1930; s. Franz and Marie (Rohn) Von N.; m. Katherine Fisher; children: Robert, Angela (Mrs. John Ulbricht); m. 2d, Hildegard Oesten. Grad., Real Sch., Rostock, Kuntsgewerbe Sch., Rostock; student, Rotal Acad., Berlin, 1910-14, 18-19; studoed with, Hans Hofmann Glaucester, 1935; DFA honoris causa, U. Milw., 1972. Prof. Wis. State Coll., 1945-47; instr. painting Chgo. Art Inst., 1942-47, Summer Sch. of Srta, Saugatuck, Mich. Works in collections U. Jerusalem, Israel, Warsaw, Poland, Berlin, Germany, Nat. Libr., Paris, Libr. of San Francisco, Libr. of Congress. Recipient Jules Brower prize Chgo. Art Inst., 1936, Frederick Talbott prize Am. Etchers, N.Y.V., 1942, Wis. Painters and Sculptors prize, 1943, prize for print Assoc. Am. Artists, 1948, prize for lithograph Nat. Acad., 1949, 1st prize Chgo. Etchers, 1954, Steuben award, 1972, others. Mem. NAD (assoc.), Chgo. Etchers, Wis. Painters and Sculptors (past pres.), Milw. Printmakers, Artists Equity (past pres. Milw. chpt.), Am. Graphic Artists. Home: Milwaukee Wis. †

VON THADDEN-TRIEGLAFF, REINOLD, church organization executive; b. Mohrungen, East Prussia, Germany, Aug. 13, 1891; s. Adolf von Thadden and Ehrengard von Gerlach; m. Elizabeth Freiin von Thüngen, Jan. 19, 1921; children: Ernst-Dietrich, Leopold, Franz-Lorenz, Bogislav, Rudolf. Student, Sorbonne, Paris, also univs. Leipzig, Munich, Greifswald; LLD, 1920; ThD (hon.), U. Kiel, 1948, U. Paris, 1959; DD, U. Aberdeen, 1953, U. Chgo., 1954; LLD, Wittenberg Coll., 1955. Pres. Student Christian Movement, Germany, 1928; v.p. Pomeranian Provincial Synod, mem. Prussian Gen. Synod in Berlin, 1929; vice chmn. World's Student Christian Fedn., 1937-49; pres. Pomeranian Coun. of Brethren, mem. Nat. Coun. Brethren; spokesman German laity to World Conf. on Life and Work, Oxford, 1937; assisted establishment World Coun. Chs. in Geneva, also Ecumenical Inst. at Bossey, mem. cen. com. World Coun. Chs., chmn. Ecumenical Inst., 1948-54; founder Deutscher Evangelischer Kirchentag, rally of Protestant laity, 1949, pres., 1949-64, hon. pres., from 1964. Author: Das Laienamt der Kirche, 1936, Jüngerschaft, 1937, Kirche im Kampf, 1947, Aufverlorenem Posten?, 1948, Der junge Bismarck, 1950. Served as maj. during war-time occupation of Belgium; arrested, imprisoned as civilian, by Russian Army. Decorated Grand Cross of Merit, Fed. Rep. Germany, 1955. Home: Fulda Federal Republic of Germany. †

VON WENING, EUGENE, JR., construction company executive; b. Bklyn., Sept. 3, 1926; s. Eugene Maxmillian von Wening and Helen Levenia (Walther) von Wening Caller; m. Virginia Ann Turner, June 29, 1951 (div. Oct. 1969); children—Virginia M. von Wening-Stricklin, Helen Kari von Wening-Sperry, Eugene T.; m. Marilyn Adam, Dec. 23, 1983. Diploma, N.Y. State Maritime Acad., 1946; B.A., Cornell U., 1950. Lic. maritime officer. Third officer U.S. Lines, N.Y., 1946-47; third officer Mobile Oil (shipping), N.Y., 1947; exec. v.p. Turner Constrn. Co. N.Y., San Francisco, 1950-87; chmn. Turner Internat. Industries N.Y.C., 1982-87; dir. Turner Corp. N.Y.; pres. Constrn. Industry Council of Calif., 1976-77. Rep. to town meeting, Greenwich, Conn., 1962-63; trustee Pacific Legal Found., Sacramento, 1983-87, vice chmn., Calif. Devel. Found., Los Angeles, 1980-87. Served with U.S. Maritime Service, 1944-46; served to lt. USNR, 1952-54. Mem. Cons. Constructors' Council of Am., Assoc. Gen. Contractors of Calif. (pres. 1981), Assoc. Gen. Contractors of Am. (bd. dirs. 1982-88), Western Fedn. of Regional Constrn. Employers (bd. dirs. 1977-81). Republican. Clubs: Innis Arden Golf Country (v.p.) (Greenwich, Conn.), Bankers, Olympic (San Francisco), Ironwood Country (Palm Desert, Calif.), Tiburon Peninsula. Died Apr. 10, 1987.

VOORHEES, DONALD, orchestra conductor; b. Allentown, Pa., July 26, 1903; m. Marni Voorhees; children: Dorothy Voorhees Taylor, David Voorhees; stepchildren: Owne Murphy, Dennis Murphy, Susan Ballard. Hon. degrees, Bates Coll., Muhlenberg Coll. Began career at age 11, choir master and organist, pianist Lyric Theatre Orch., Allentown, condr. orch. at age 15; Broadway debut as condr. Winter Garden Theater orch., 1920; condr. musical comedies, Earl Carroll's Vanities, 1920-25; presented radio musical program from stage Earl Carroll Theatre for Sta. WEAF-Radio, 1925; condr. Atwater Kent Hour, pioneer network music program, also GM Hour presenting stars of Met. Opera; musical dir. DuPont's Cavalcade of Am., Ezio Pinza TV shows; condr., musical dir. Bell Telephone Hour radio program, 1940-58, for NBC-TV, from 1958, composer Bell Waltz, show theme; regular condr. Allentown Symphony. Recipient numerous awards including Lowell Mason award for contbns. to music edn. Home: Stone Harbor N.J. Died Jan. 10, 1989.

VOORHEES, WILLIAM DELANO, JR., psychiatrist, hospital administrator; b. Bklyn., Dec. 29, 1920; s. William Delano and Thekla (Grimmell) V.; m. Selma Jean Schurmann, Dec. 8, 1945; children: Carol Ann, Susan Jean, William Delano III. BA, Johns Hopkins U., 1942, MD, 1945. Diplomate Am. Bd. Neurology and Psychiatry. Intern Hartford (Conn.) Hosp., 1945-46; resident in psychiatry Payne-Whitney Psychiatric Clinic, N.Y.C., 1948-53; asst. in psychiatry Cornell U., N.Y.C., 1949-51, instr., 1951-53; instr. psychiatry U. Wash., Seattle, 1953-56; dir. extramural services Western State Hosp., Ft. Steilacoom, Wash., 1956-60, dir. forensic unit, 1977-87; supt. No. State Hosp., Sedro-Woolley, Wash., 1960-68; assoc. commr. div. local services N.Y. State Dept. Mental Hygiene, 1968, 1st dep. commr., then regional dir., 1968-77; cons. NIMH, 1963-71. Served to capt. M.C., AUS, 1946-48. Mem. Am. Psychiat. Assn. Home: Tacoma Wash. Died Nov. 22, 1987.

VOORHIS, HAROLD OLIVER, university administrator; b. Kokomo, Ind., July 29, 1896; s. Warren R. and Edna (Curlee) V.; m. Rosalie Voorhis (dec. 1980); children: Patricia Voorhis Grinnell, Joanna Voorhis Beattie, Katrina Voorhis Mabon. BS, Colgate U., 1919, JD, 1945; postgrad. in law, Columbia U., 1920-21; MA, NYU, 1922, Litt.D. (hon.), 1961. Surveyor's asst. Sask., Can., 1914-15; sec. to pres. Colgate U., Hamilton, N.Y., 1916-19, Chautauqua (N.Y.) Instn., 1919; sec. to v.p. Nat. Bank Commerce, N.Y.C., 1920; instr. in econs. NYU, 1920-25, sec. Bd. Trustees, 1924-61; vice chancellor univ. 1945-56, v.p., 1956-61, v.p., sec. emeritus, from 1961. Past trustee Colgate U., v.p., bd. dirs. Alumni Corp., 1940-46; past bd. dirs. N.Y.C. YMCAs, past chmn. Greater N.Y. Gen. Assembly; pres. Greater N.Y. Council for Fgn. Students, 1950-52, Netherlands-Am. Found., 1952-58; past trustee Parsons Sch. Design, N.Y.C. With U.S. Army, 1918-19. Decorated Comdr. Netherlands Order. Mem. Holland Soc. N.Y. (past trustee, pres. 1947-50), Am. Legion, Phi Beta Kappa, Pi Delta Epsilon, Beta Theta Pi, Alpha Kappa Psi, Sigma Sigma Omega. Republican. Presbyterian. Clubs: University, Faculty; Tokeneke (Darien, Conn.). Home: Darien Conn. Died Aug. 31, 1985.

VORBECK, MARIE LUDMILLA, biochemistry and pathology educator, researcher; b. Rochester, N.Y., June 24, 1933; d. Joseph and Maria (Klein) V. B.S., Cornell U., 1955; M.S., Pa. State U., 1958; Ph.D., Cornell U., 1962. Fellow U. Rochester Med. Sch., N.Y., 1962-64; asst. prof. Temple U. Med. Sch., Phila., 1964-66, Jefferson Med. Sch., Phila., 1966-68; assoc. prof. U. Mo., Columbia, 1968-74, prof. dept. biochemistry and pathology Sch. Medicine, 1974-86; cons. NIH, Bethesda, Md., 1982; mem. ad hoc animal adv. com. Nat. Inst. Aging, 1982-86. Contbr. articles to profl. jours. Recipient Phi Tau Sigma Cornell U., 1960; recipient Faculty-Alumni award Alumni Assn. U. Mo.-Columbia, 1983. Mem. Am. Soc. Cell Biology, Tissue Culture Soc. Roman Catholic. Home: Columbia Mo. Died Nov. 24, 1986; buried Columbia, Mo.

VORENBERG, F. FRANK, retail executive; b. Boston, Feb. 8, 1900; s. Felix and Rose (Frankenstein) V.; m. Ida Muhlfelder, Mar. 3, 1924 (dec.); children: John, James. With Gilchrist's Dept. Stores, Boston, 1921-75, pres., 1942-75. Mem. panel U.S. War Labor Bd., 1943-45, adv. com. Office of Price Stabilization, 1950-52; past trustee Mt. Auburn Hosp., Cambridge, Mass., Beth Israel Hosp., Boston, Boston Family Service Assn. Served with AUS, 1918-19. Home: Cambridge Mass. Died Mar. 13, 1988; buried Mt. Auburn Cemetery, Cambridge, Mass.

WACHTEL, HOWARD RICHARD, lawyer; b. Bklyn., Mar. 28, 1927; s. Stanley and Miriam (Ducoffe) W.; m. Audrey Berk, Sept. 17, 1954; children—Julia, Emily Louise Gill. Student, U. Ill., 1946-48; LL.B., Columbia U., 1951. Bar: N.Y. U.S. Dist. Ct., U.S. Ct. Appeals, U.S. Supreme Ct. Assoc. to ptnr. LeBoeuf, Lamb, Leiby & MacRae, N.Y.C., 1953-88. Contbr. articles to profl. jours. Chmn. N.Y.C. com. N.Y. Young Republican Club, 1954. Served with USCG, 1951-53, lt. comdr. U.S. Mcht. Marine, 1944-46. Mem. ABA (chmn. trade assn. com. antitrust sect. 1972-75, lectr. antitrust insts. 1974, 78), Assn. Bar City of N.Y. Home: Stamford Conn. Died Dec. 26, 1986.

WACHTEL, WILLIAM W., association executive; b. Milw., Feb. 2, 1892; s. Jack and Susan (Gegusan) W.; m. Helen Chan, June 6, 1923; 1 child, Jack S. Student, grammar sch., Wis. Sec. Bd. of Pub. Safety, Terre Haute, Ind., 1907; asst. sales mgr. Elec. div. Johns-MAnville Co., New Orleans, 1908; successively clk., sales statistician in purchasing dept., accountant, advt. mgr., sales mgr., v.p. in charge sales and advt. Loose-Wiles Biscuit Co., 1910-36; v.p., dir. Calvert Distillers Corp., N.Y.C., 1936-38, pres., from 1938; bd. dirs. Distillers Corp., Seagram Ltd., Montreal, Can., from 1943, Joseph E. Seagram & Sons, N.Y.C., from 1945; pres. Inst. Pub. Information, N.Y.C., from 1959. Home: New York N.Y. †

WADE, W(ILLIAM) WALLACE, athletic association administrator; b. Trenton, Tenn., June 15, 1892; s. Robert Bruce and Sarah Ann (Mitchell) W.; m. Frances Bell, July 1, 1917 (dec.); children: William W., Frances Margaret; m. 2d Virginia M. Jones, Nov. 29, 1950. AB, Brown U., 1917. Athletic dir. Fitzgerald Clarke Sch., Tullahoma, Tenn., 1919-21; asst. athletic dir. Vanderbilt U., 1921-23; athletic dir. and football coach U. Ala., 1923-31; athletic dir. and football coach Duke U., 1931-42, dir. physical edn. and athletics, 1945-50; commr. Southern Conf., from 1951. Tenn. N.G., 1917; served to capt. U.S. Army, World War I; lt. col., World War II, ETO. Decorated 4 Battle Stars, Bronze Star, Croix de Guerre; named to Nat. Football Hall of Fame. Mem.

Durham Rotary Club, Delta Phi. Presbyterian. Home: Bahama N.C. †

WADEWITZ, WILLIAM ROBERT, publishing company executive; b. Iron Mountain, Mich., Sept. 25, 1890; s. Henry and Augusta (Mehlberg) W.; m. Eleanor Sheakley (dec.); m. 2d, Evelyn Graves, 1960. Ed., Lawrence Coll. With Western Pub. Co., Racine, Wis., 1907—, pres., 1953-57, chmn. bd., pres., 1957-58, chmn. bd., 1958—; bd. dirs. First Nat. Bank & Trust Co., Racine. Chmn. Racine Cemetery Commn.; presented W.R. Wadewitz Meml. Ct. of Honor to Graceland Cemetery, Racine, 1948; air-conditioned all rooms and facilities St. Luke's Hosp., Racine, 1957; adv. bd. Dominican Coll., Racine; past dir. Goodwill of Racine. 2d lt. F.A., U.S. Army, World War I. Named Man of Yr. VFW, Racine, 1948. Mem. Racine Mfrs. Assn. (gov.), Racine C. of C. (past v.p., dir.), Am. Legion 32d Div. Vets, Elks (trustee), Racine Country Club, Last Man's Club (Racine); Meadowbrook Country Club, Somerset Club. Home: Racine Wis. †

WADLEIGH, WINTHROP, lawyer; b. Milford, N.H., Jan. 23, 1902; s. Fred Tilton and Alice Bancroft (Conant) W.; m. Sylvia Moore Leach, June 11, 1932 (dec. Sept. 1967); children: Theodore, James L.; m. Faith Preston, Dec. 19, 1970. A.B. magna cum laude, Dartmouth Coll., 1923; J.D., Harvard U., 1927. Bar: N.H. bar 1927. Practiced in Concord, 1927-29, Manchester, 1931-86; asso. Robert W. Upton (Esq.), 1927- 29; asst. atty. gen. N.H., 1929-31; partner Wadleigh, Starr, Peters, Dunn & Chiesa, 1931-86, now sr. partner.; Dir. Mchts. Nat. Bank of Manchester, 1938-74, Osceola Shoe Co., Inc. Contbr.: chpt. to Religion Ponders Science, 1964; articles to profl. publs. Del. N.H. Constl. Conv., 1930; mem. Commn. to Revise Corp. Laws of N.H., 1932; moderator Ward I, Manchester, 1942-46; sec. Amoskeag Co., 1957-65, now hon. sec.; chmn. Christian Friends Drive, United Jewish Appeal, 1964; pres. Manchester br. NAACP, 1965-67; treas. Fund for Animals, Inc., N.Y.C., 1967-75; chmn. investment com. N.H. Conf. United Ch. of Christ, 1967-86; vice-chmn., bd. dirs. N.H. Civil Liberties Union, 1967-86; mem. N.H. Commn. for Human Rights, 1967-70; chmn. Brotherhood Week in N.H., 1968, SPACE, 1968-75; treas. ACLU, N.Y.C., 1969-75, bd. dirs., 1967-73; bd. dirs. N.H. chpt. NCCJ, 1965-75; trustee White Pines Coll., Chester, N.H., 1969-86, Gale Home, Cogswell Benevolent Trust, Blanche A. Bruce Charitable Trust; pres. Havenwood Retirement Community, 1977-81. Recipient Brotherhood award N.H. chpt. Nat. Conf. Christians and Jews, 1970. Mem. ABA, N.H. Bar Assn., Manchester Bar Assn., Dartmouth Assn. of Manchester (pres.), Audubon Soc. N.H. (life), Soc. for Protection N.H. Forests (life), Phi Beta Kappa Assos. (life), Phi Beta Kappa. Conglist. (trustee, deacon). Lodges: Mason, Kiwanis. Home: Chester N.H. Died Mar. 3, 1986; buried Manchester, N.H.

WADMOND, LOWELL CURTIS, lawyer; b. Racine, Wis., Mar. 16, 1896; s. Christian George and Celia (Jensen) W.; m. Mary Elita Cason, July 27, 1938. Mus.B. cum laude, Chgo. Mus. Coll., 1921; Ph.B. cum laude, U. Chgo., 1922, J.D. cum laude, 1924. Bar: Ill. 1924, Wis. 1925, N.Y. 1926, U.S. Supreme Ct. 1940. With Tolman, Sexton & Chandler, Chgo., 1924-26; asst. U.S. atty. for So. dist. N.Y., 1926-30; spl. asst. atty. gen. N.Y. State, 1929-31; spl. asst. to atty. gen. of U.S., 1930; mem. com. character and fitness, appellate div. Supreme Ct. of N.Y. (1st dept.), 1934-86, chmn., 1959-86; mem. firm White & Case, N.Y.C., 1935-86; dir. Texasgulf, Inc., 1949-73, hon. dir., 1973-86; dir. Canrad Hanovia, Inc. Trustee Robert A. Taft Meml. Found.; trustee, vice chmn. Robert A. Taft Inst. Govt.; Pres., dir. Met. Opera Assn. N.Y.C., 1951-56, vice chmn., dir., 1956-70, chmn. bd., dir., 1970-74, hon. pres., dir., 1974-75, chmn. emeritus, 1975-76, hon. life dir., 1976-86; dir. The Villas, Inc., Palm Beach, Fla.; Chmn. exec. com. Nat. Rep. Club, 1943-49; del. Nat. Rep. Conv., 1952; Trustee Grant Monument Assn., Parker Sch. Fgn. and Comparative Law, Columbia U.; trustee William M. Sullivan Musical Found., Inc.; bd. dirs. Lincoln Center for Performing Arts, 1970-75. Served with 340th Inf. U.S. Army, World War I. Decorated comdr. Royal Order North Star Sweden, Order St. Dennis of Zente Societe d'Encouragement Au Progres; recipient Pub. Service citation U. Chgo. Fellow Am. Bar Found.; mem. Am. Soc. Internat. Law, Bagby Music Lovers' Found. (pres. 1955-65, chmn. 1965-72, trustee emeritus), Assn. Bar City N.Y., N.Y. County Lawyers Assn., N.Y. State Bar Assn., ABA, Internat. Bar Assn., Am. Coll. Trial Lawyers, Internat. Law Assn., Consular Law Soc., Am. Bible Soc. (v.p.), Am. Law Library Middle Temple (hon.), N.Y. Lawyers Club (pres. 1945-57, gov.), Order of Coif. Presbyterian (life elder, trustee emeritus). Clubs: University, Metropolitan Opera (pres. 1945-47), Downtown Assn. (N.Y.C.), Everglades, Bath and Tennis (Palm Beach). Lodge: Masons. Home: New York City and Palm Beach Fla. Died Sept. 25, 1986.

WAGENFUEHR, ALBERT, banker; b. St. Louis, Mar. 26, 1892; s. Frank A. and Hermine (Hillig) W.; m. Antoinette Timpte, June 7, 1916; 1 child, Antoinette (Mrs. Merl J. Carson Jr.). Student, Am. Inst. Banking, spl. courses, St. Louis U., City Coll. of Law and Fin.; grad., Sch. Banking, Rutgers., 1938-40. Began with The Boatmen's Nat. Bank, 1911, mgr. credit dept., 1915, asst. cashier, 1921, v.p., 1926, dir., chmn. exec. com., 1947-54; v.p. First Nat. Bank in St. Louis, 1954-58, sr. v.p., from 1958; bd. dirs. Orchard Paper Company, St. Louis, Fulton Iron Works Company, Robert Morris Assocs.; instr. in credits Grad. Sch. Banking, Rutgers U. Author: Term Loans by Commercial Banks, 1940. Former chmn. adv. com. Social Service Exchange; bd. govs. Catholic Charities of St. Louis; former mem. bd. dirs. Social Planning Coun.; pres. Frederic Ozanam Home for Men. Mem. St. Louis Assn. of Credit Men (pres. 1929-30, former dir.), Am. Inst. Banking (bd. govs.), Mo. Athletic Club, Old Warson Country Club. Home: Richmond Heights Mo. †

WAGERS, RALPH EDWIN, educator; b. Newaygo, Mich., Apr. 26, 1892; s. William Ralph and Nellie Maude (Sutliff) W.; m. Beda Marie Jones, May 10, 1915. B Christian Sci., Normal Class, Bd. Edn. First Ch. Christ, Scientist, Boston, 1940. In lumber bus. Park Falls, Wis., 1912-14; sec. treas., mgr. Suwame Lumber Co., Rudolph and Milladore, Wis., 1914-16; sec. Kellogg Bros. Lumber co., Wisconsin Rapids, Wis., 1916-25; Christian Sci. practitioner Chgo., 1925-40; authorized tchr. 1940, mem. bd. lectureship, 1946-59; assoc. editor Christian Sci. religious publs., 1959; pres. First Ch. of Christ, Scientist, Boston, 1962-63. Mem. Lake Shore Club (Chgo.), Masons. Republican. Home: Brookline Mass. †

WAHLEN, FRIEDRICH TRAUGOTT, Swiss federal councillor; b. Mirchel, Switzerland, Apr. 10, 1899; s. Johann and Katharina (Stucki) W.; m. Helen Hopf, Oct. 11, 1923. Agrl. engr., Fed. Inst. Tech., Zurich, 1920; D.Sc. Tech., Fed. Inst. Tech., 1922; MD (hon.), U. Zurich, 1946; Dr. Agrl. Scis. (hon.), U. Gottingen, 1955. Asst. in agronomy Fed. Inst. Tech., 1920-22, prof. agronomy, 1943-49; supervising analyst Can. Dept. Agriculture, 1922-23, chief analyst, 1923-29; dir. Swiss Exptl. Sta. for Agr., Berne, 1929-43; in charge food prodn. Swiss War Economy Office, 1939-45; dir. agrl. div. FAO, Washington and Rome, 1949-58; head tech. assistance programme FAO, 1950-52; dep. dir. gen. FAO, Rome, 1958-59; mem. Council of States for Zurich 1942-49; Swiss fed. councillor Zurich, from 1959; Swiss Minister of Justice, then Econs., then Fgn. Affair, pres. Swiss Confedn., 1961. Recipient Prix Marcel Benoist, 1940. Mem. Royal Swedish Acad. (fgn.). Home: Bern Switzerland Died Nov. 7, 1985.

WAHR, FRED B(URKHART), language educator; b. Ann Arbor, Mich., Mar. 30, 1889; s. John and Minnie (Burkhart) W.; m. Mary Cannon, June 21, 1922; 1 child, John C. AB, U. Mich., 1911, AM, 1912, PhD, 1915; postgrad., Berlin and Munich univs., 1912-13. Mem. faculty dept. German U. Mich., from 1913, asst. dean students, 1921-36, prof., 1936-59, prof. emeritus, from 1959. Author: Emerson and Goethe, 1915; contbr. articles on German lit. to profl. jours. With U.S. Army, 1918-19. Mem. MLA, Am. Assn. Tchrs. German, Mich. Acad. Sci., Arts and Letters, Phi Beta Kappa. Home: Ann Arbor Mich. †

WAHREN, DOUGLAS, institute executive, educator; b. Norrkoping, Sweden, Mar. 12, 1934; came to U.S., 1979; S. K. Helge and Jane I.C. (Agrell) W.; m. Inger Viola, Feb. 9, 1957; children: Caroline, Johan. M.E., Royal Inst. Tech., Stockholm, 1957, Dr.Sci., 1964, docent, 1965. Research asst. Swedish Forest Products Lab., Sweden, 1957-60, 1st research asst., 1962, tech. sec., 1961-65, dir. research, 1969-73; research scientist Beloit Corp. (Wis.), 1964-65; v.p. research KMW, Karlstad, Sweden, 1974-78, The Inst. Paper Chemistry, Apppleton, Wis., from 1979; prof. Royal Inst. Tech., 1973; organizer Swedish Pulp and Paper Mission to N.Am., 1972-73; contbr. in field. Contbr. numerous articles to profl. jours. Fellow TAPPI; mem. Swedish Assn. Pulp and Paper Engrs., Can. Pulp and Paper Assn., Sigma Xi. Home: Appleton Wis. Deceased.

WAHRSAGER, SIGMUND, investment company executive; b. N.Y.C., Oct. 26, 1925; s. Sam and Sadie (Koback) W.; m. Karel Fierman, Mar. 3, 1955; children: Eve, Erika, Kay. AB, Princeton U., 1947; MBA, NYU, 1950. With Prudential Ins. Co. Am., 1947-50, Kuhn, Loeb Co., 1950-53; gen. ptnr. Bear, Stearns & Co., N.Y.C., 1953-81; spl. ltd. ptnr. 1981-85; bd. dirs. Midland Glass Co. Inc., Tacoma Boatbuilding Co. Inc., S.E. Nichols Inc., HRT Industries Inc., CCC Inc., Brit. Printing and Communications Corp., Struthers Wells Corp., Pergamon Press Ltd., Abe Schrader Corp., others. Bd. dirs. Wahrsager Found. With USNR, 1944-46. Home: New York N.Y. Died Oct. 3, 1985.

WAKEFIELD, HOWARD, physician; b. Balt., Aug. 20, 1892; s. Antonio and Elizabeth E. (Brooke) W.; m. Thelma Isabel Roach, Dec. 31, 1933; children: Isabel Elizabeth Wakefield Oppen, Howard R. BS, U. Chgo., 1917; M.D., Rush Med. Coll., 1924. Diplomate Am. Bd. Internal Medicine (ofcl. examiner, chmn. cardiovascular diseases subspecialty bd., residency review com. for internal medicine for U.S.). Research assoc. U. Chgo., 1917-22, anatomy asst., 1919-21; asst., then. assoc. dept. medicine Rush Med. Coll., Chgo., 1926-32; practice medicine Chgo., from 1924; asst. to Dr. James B. Herrick 1926-32; intern Cook County Hosp., Chgo., 1925-26; asst. attending physician St. Luke's Hosp., Chgo., 1932-40, assoc. attending physician, 1940-47, sr. attending physician, 1947-56, chmn. dept. medicine, from 1956, cons. physician, from 1947; assoc. prof. medicine U. Ill., Chgo.; chief staff, attending physician The Old Peoples' Home of the City of Chgo.; former chmn. conf. com. Grad. Tng. Internal Medicine in U.S.; former mem. reviewing com. Homes for the Aged; advisor USN, 1917-19; former adv. bd. cardiac div. SSS. Contbd. numerous articles to med. jours. Past trustee Sugar Island, Thousand Islands, Ont., Can. Fellow Inst. Medicine Chgo., ACP (past gov. No. Ill., gen. chmn. ann. session Chgo. 1954, regent, 2d v.p., master 1969), AAAS; mem. AMA, Ill. Med. Assn., Chgo. Med. Soc. (v.p. 1943-44, pres. from 1957, past exec. com.), Internat. Soc. Internal Medicine, Assn. Am. Med. Colls., Am. Soc. Tropical Medicine, Am. Assn. History of Medicine, Am. Therapeutic Soc. (former 2d v.p., treas.), Soc. Med. History Chgo., Am. Heart Assn., Chgo. Heart Assn. (founder, previously sci. council), Gerontol. Soc., N.Am. Yacht Racing Assn., Am. Yachting Assn. (commodore 1931), Lake Michigan Yachting Assn., Am. Occupational Therapy Assn. (past med. adv. com.), U. Chgo. Alumni Assn., Am. Canoe Assn. (commodore 1931), Sigma Xi, Alpha Omega Alpha, Phi Beta Pi. Republican. Episcopalian. Club: Chicago Yacht. Home: Chicago Ill. Died Mar. 20, 1985.

WALDMAN, BERNARD, educator; b. N.Y.C., Oct. 12, 1913; s. Joseph and Mollie (Rothman) W.; m. Florence Finley, June 13, 1942 (dec. June 1961); children: John William (dec. 1981), Nancy Karen Waldman Melcher; m. Glenna Frank Ryan, Mar. 21, 1964; stepchildren: Tawny Ryan Nelb, Sharon Ryan Marko. AB, NYU, 1934, PhD, 1939. Grad. asst. NYU, 1935-38; research assoc. U. Notre Dame, South Bend, Ind., 1938-40, instr., 1940-41, asst. prof. physics, 1941-48, assoc. prof., 1948-51, prof., 1951-76, assoc. dean. Coll. Sci., 1964-67, dean Coll. Sci., 1967-79; assoc. dir. Nat. Superconducting Cyclotron Labs. at Mich. State U., East Lansing, 1979-83; ofcl. investigator OSRD, 1942-43; dir. lab. Midwestern Univs. Research Assn., 1960-65, trustee Univ. Rsch. Assn., 1965-71; staff mem. Los Alamos (N.Mex.) Sci. Lab., Manhattan Project, 1943-45. Mem. Gov.'s Commn. on Med. Edn., 1971-74. Fellow Am. Phys. Soc.; mem. Am. Assn. Physics Tchrs., AAUP, Sigma Xi, Sigma Pi Sigma, Alpha Epsilon Delta. Home: Sanford N.C. Died Nov. 12, 1986; inurned U. Notre Dame Cemetery.

WALDMAN, LOUIS, lawyer; b. Ukraine, Jan. 5, 1892; came to U.S., 1909; naturalized, 1915; s. Samuel and Esther (Freeger) W.; m. Bella Bernstein, Nov. 1, 1924; children: Seymour, Paul. BSCE, Cooper Union Inst., N.Y.C., 1916; LLB, N.Y. Law Sch., 1922. Bar: N.Y. 1923. Factory worker 1909-14; jr. civil engr. Pub. Svc. Commn., N.Y., 1915-17; mem. N.Y. Assembly, 1918, 20; dir. Adult Labor Edn., N.Y.C., 1921-22; practiced law in N.Y.C., from 1923. Author: Albany: The Crisis in Government, 1920, Labor Lawyer, an autobiography; contbr. to profl. jours. Dir., counsel City Affairs Com.; v.p. Honest Ballot Assn.; mem. Gov. Lehman's N.Y. State Constl. Conv. Com., 1937, City Affairs Charter Revision Com., 1934-35; del. State Conv. for Repeal 18th Amendment, 1933; state chmn. Socialist Party, 1930-36; co-founder Am. Labor Party, mem. state exec. com., chmn. law com., Kings County; socialist candidate for gov. N.Y., 1928, 30, 32, atty. gen. N.Y., 1924; candidate for Supreme Ct. justice, 2d Jud. Dist., Bkln., 1937; candidate for county judge, Kings County, 1938. Fellow Am. Bar Found. (chmn. com. Am. citizenship 1947-48), Am. Coll. Trial Lawyers; mem. Am. Acad. Polit. and Social Sci., N.Y. State Bar Assn. (chmn. com. on civil rights 1951-55, 58-61, mem. exec. com. 1955-65), Bklyn. Bar Assn. (pres. 1954-55), N.Y. County Lawyers Assn., Assn. of Bar of City of N.Y. (v.p. 1946-47), Workmen's Circle, Grand Street Boys' Assn., Masons. Home: Brooklyn N.Y. †

WALKER, DELOSS (WINFIELD), editor, public speaker; b. Baldwin, Kans., July 5, 1890; s. James Winfield and Emma (Beck) W.; m. Nell E. Williams; 1 child, James Winfield. AB, DePauw U., 1912. Invited faculty Chinese govt. univs., Tientsin, 1913-15; salesman bituminous coal N.Eng., 1916-17; gen. supt. Trojan Coal Mining Co., Clearfield, Pa., 1917-18; pres. Allied Mining Co., Inc.; treas. Woodland Coal Mining Co.; assoc. editor Liberty mag., N.Y.C., 1934-41; sr. indsl. specialist War Prodn. Bd., 1942; bd. govs. Transp. Assn. Am., 1940-41. Contbr. numerous articles on econs. to trade mags. Co-founder Am. Econ. Found., 1939; co-founder, mem. bd. dirs. Nat. Recovery Crusade, N.Y.C., 1932, organizer recovery coms. various cities, frequent speaker; organizer DePauw U. Alumni Assn., Puget Sound, Wash. Cpl. F.A. U.S. Army, 1918-19. Mem. Masons, Elks, Sciots, Beta Theta Pi. Home: Chicago Ill. †

WALKER, JAMES BARRETT, life insurance company executive; b. Toronto, Ont., Can., July 22, 1919; s. James Morley George and Mary Ellen (Barrett) W.; m. Doris June Riddell, Dec. 25, 1944; children: James Barrett, June Anne, Candace Marion. Honors grad., U. Toronto, 1942. With Can. Life, 1946-81, group exec., 1961-68, v.p., dir. group, 1968-70; v.p., dir. U.S. div. Can. Life, Toronto, 1970-77; exec. v.p., dir. U.S. div. Can. Life, 1977-80; exec. v.p. Can. Life Assurance Co., Toronto, 1980-81; pres., dir. Can. Life Ins. Co. N.Y., 1972-81. Served to lt. comdr. RCNVR, 1945. Fellow Soc. Actuaries, Can. Inst. Actuaries; mem. Am. Acad. Actuaries. Clubs: National, Lambton Golf and Country. Home: Weston, Ont. Canada. Died Mar. 15, 1987; cremated.

WALKER, JAMES HERRON, steel company executive; b. Salina, Kans., June 17, 1907; s. James Herron and Mary (Addison) W.; m. Louise McKelvy, May 26, 1939; children: Graham McKelvy, James Addison, Douglas Corwin. AB, U. Kans., 1929; MBA, Harvard U., 1931. With J.& W. Seligman Co., N.Y.C., 1931-32; with Bethlehem (Pa.) Steel Co., 1932-72, v.p. fin., 1965-72, also trustee pension fund; previously dir. Equitable Life Assurance Soc., U.S. Transatlantic Corp., Smith-Barney Equity Fund, trustee Elfun Trusts. Past advisor Chmn.'s Com. on Navajo Nation Affairs; past bd. dirs. Bethlehem Area Found., Little League Found.; past chmn. fin. com., trustee Lehigh U.; past mem. investment com. Rensselaer Poly. Inst. Mem. Phi Beta Kappa, Beta Theta Pi, Blooming Grove Hunting and Fishing Club (Halwley, Pa.), Leash Club, Anglers Club, University Club, Island Club (Jupiter Island, Fla.), Seminole Golf Club, Saucon Valley Country Club. Home: Bethlehem Pa. Died Dec. 31, 1987.

WALKER, JOHN ALEXANDER, merchant; b. Phila., June 10, 1922; s. John Anthony and Dorothy (Morrison) W.; m. Beryl Audrey Lienhard, Apr. 21, 1946; children: Charolyn Walker Rivker, Dorothy Walker Moynihan, Gail Ann Walker Owen, Deborah Sue Walker Blackwell, Mary Morrison. Student, Muhlenburg Coll., 1941-42, U. Pa., 1942-43, Northwestern U., 1944. With Hotpoint Distbg. div. GE, 1946-58, dist. mgr., 1958-80; with Lowe's Cos., Inc., North Wilkesboro, N.C., 1980-84, founding dir.; mem. plywood adv. coun. Chgo. Bd. Trade, 1970-84; bd. dirs. Brad Ragan, Inc. contbr. articles to various publs., also poems. Chmn. North Wilkesboro Housing Authority, 1967-84; mem. Rep. Nat. Fin. Com., 1967-84; Rep. candidate for lt. gov., N.C., 1972; chmn. fin. com. N.C. Rep. Com., 1968-72, mem. cen. com., 1968-72, mem. exec. com., 1968-72; mem. exec. com. Wilkes County Rep. Com., 1968-70; bd. dirs. Lowe's Charitable and Trust Found., Wilkes Devel. Corp.; bus. adv. coun. Appalachian State U., Wilkes YMCA; trustee 1st Carolina Investors, So. States Fund, Inc. Lt. USNR, 1942-46, PTO, ETO. Recipient Man of Half-Century award Home Ctr. Industry, 1975; named Man of Yr. in Home Ctr. Industry B'nai B'rith, 1978. Mem. N.C. Home Builders Assn. (bd. dirs. 1968-84, Meritorious award 1971), Masons (32 degree), Shriners, Elks, Oakwoods Country Club, Roaring Gap Club, Charlotte City Club, Phi Kappa Sigma. Home: Boca Raton Fla. Died Sept. 14, 1984.

WALKER, RUSSELL T., lawyer, manufacturing executive; b. Fort William, Ont., Can., Sept. 9, 1914; s. Joseph Henry and Elissa Jane (Mutart) W.; m. Miriam O'Loughlin, Apr. 5, 1941; children: Margaret Ellen, Terry Jo, Mary Elissa, Wendy Ann. AB, U. Mich., 1936, JD, 1939. Bar: N.Y., Iowa, Pa., Mich., Ill. Legal research clk. Supreme Ct. of Mich., 1939-40; law clk. N.Y. Cen. R.R., Detroit, 1941-42, atty., 1942-45, asst. gen. counsel, 1945-51, asst. to sec., 1951-52, asst. sec., 1952, sec., 1952-54; gen. counsel Mcht. Dispatch Transp. Corp.-Northern Refrigerator Line, Chgo., 1954-55; treas. Nat. U.S. Radiator Corp., Johnstown, Pa., 1955-60; v.p., gen. mgr. Montgomery Ward Credit Corp., 1960-61; v.p. adminstrn. A.Y. McDonald Mfg. Corp., Dubuque, Iowa, 1961-62, pres., 1962-69; chmn. bd. Brock-McVey, Inc., 1969; v.p., gen. mgr. Acme Industries (Rheem Mfg. Co.), Jackson, Mich., 1971-83; v.p. Midwest Bank, Jackson, 1974-83; previously assoc. McConkey Real Estate, Jackson. Mem. ABA, Phi Sigma Kappa, Jackson Country Club. Home: Jackson Mich. Died July 13, 1983; buried Jackson, Mich.

WALLACE, ALEXANDER DONIPHAN, mathematics educator; b. Hampton, Va., Aug. 21, 1905; s. Alexander Doniphan and Mary Elizabeth (Sheppe) W.; m. Willie Catherine Durrer, July 13, 1930; 1 child, Catherine Alexandra. BS, MS, PhD, U. Va. Taught mathematics at U. Va., Princeton U., U. Pa.; past chmn. dept. math. Tulane U., New Orleans; prof. U. Fla., Gainesville, 1963-66, chmn. dept., from 1966; prof. math. U. Miami, Coral Gables, Fla., from 1966. Authored papers in field. Mem. Am. Math. Soc., Math. Assn. Am., Phi Beta Kappa, Sigma Xi, Raven. Home: Gainesville Fla. Died Oct. 14, 1985.

WALLACE, BRENTON GREENE, architect, army officer; b. Phila., June 28, 1891; s. Richard H. and Lurena De Voe (Groesbeck) W.; m. Dorothy Harriet Wallower, Dec. 28, 1920; children: Brenton Greene Jr., Dorothy Jane, Richard Wallower, James De Voe (dec.). BS, U. Pa., 1913, BArch, 1915. Pres. Wallace & Warner Corp., architects and engrs., Phila., Wilmington, from 1915; 1st Troop Phila. Cavalry, 1917; commd. 2d lt. Arty., 107th F.A., 28th Div., 1918, served in France, 1918-19; received 4 battle stars; mustered into Fed. svc. comd. 166th F.A. Rgt.; col., 1941, V Corps staff, 1943; overseas, worked on invasion plan, overlord for invasion of France, 1943; served as asst. chief staff, G-3 Liaison Hdqrs., 3d U.S. Army, from England through France, Luxembourg, Belgium and Germany (received 5 battle stars); ret. as maj. gen. USAR. Author: Patton and His Third Army. Trustee Pa. Mil. Coll. Decorated Legion of Merit and Bronze Star (U.S.); Croix de Guerre with Star of Vermeil (France); Order Brit. Empire. Mem. Union League Club, Merion Cricket Club (Phila.). Presbyterian. Home: Bryn Mawr Pa. †

WALLACE, LEON HARRY, educator; b. Terre Haute, Ind., Jan. 24, 1904; s. Harry Seymour and Leona A. (Wagoner) W.; m. Anna Ruth Haworth, Aug. 21, 1926; children: Harry L., Susan J., Leona A. Student, U. Ill., 1921-23; A.B., Ind. U., 1925, J.D., 1933. Bar: Ind. 1933, Supreme Ct. U.S 1950. Prodn. mgr. Rand McNally & Co. (S.F.), 1927-30; mem. Wallace, Randel & Wallace, 1933-44, Randel & Wallace, Terre Haute, 1944-45; asso. prof. law Ind. U., 1945-47, prof., 1947-74, acting dean, 1951-52, dean sch. law, 1952-66, Charles McGuffey Hepburn prof. law, 1966-74, dean and prof. emeritus, 1974-85; Chmn. adv. panel U.S. Dist. Ct. legislative apportionment; spl. hearing officer U.S. Dept. of Justice, 1964-68; Gov.'s rep. Ind. Constn. Revision Commn., 1967-69; spl. master U.S. Dist. Ct., No. Dist. Ind., 1969-72; cons. State of Ind., Ind.-Ky. border, 1966—. Author works on legal subjects.; Contbr. articles profl. publs. Mem. ABA (chmn. local govt. law section), Ind. Bar Assn., Indpls. Bar Assn., Am. Judicature Soc., Am. Law Inst., Am. Acad. Social and Polit. Sci., Acad. Polit. Sci., Inst. Jud. Adminstrn., Ind. Bar Found. (dir., sec., treas. 1951-76, emeritus 1976—), Ind. Continuing Legal Edn. Forum, Phi Beta Kappa, Order of Coif, Phi Delta Phi (v.p. 1947-49, pres. 1949-51), Sigma Delta Chi, Delta Tau Delta. Democrat. Presbyn. Home: Mequon Wis. Died Nov. 19, 1985.

WALLACE, ROBERT FRANCIS, business executive; b. Chgo., Sept. 11, 1917; s. Peter A. and Helen Jeanne (Georres) W.; m. Harriet Jane Scales, Feb. 9, 1963; children: Warren L., David S. Student, U. Ill., 1935-37; B.S., Loyola U., Chgo., 1943. Staff auditor Arthur Andersen & Co., Chgo., 1943-49; pres., chief operating officer, dir. Outboard Marine Corp., Waukegan, Ill., 1949-85. Police magistrate, Winthrop, Ill., 1951-55; Bd. dirs. Ole Evinrude Found. Mem. Boating Industry Assn., Internat. Trade Club, Belgian-Am. C. of C., Phi Eta Sigma. Home: Mundelein Ill. Died May 8, 1988.

WALLACE, WESTEL BRUCE, government official; b. Denver, Mar. 4, 1891; s. Robert Bruce and LuLu (Love) W.; m. Lenore Broome, Nov. 5, 1911 (dec. 1924); children: Westel Bruce, Patricia (Mrs. William F. Rapp); m. 2d Mildred Crooks, June 29, 1936. Student, U. Colo. V.p., dir. Wallace State Bank, 1910-27; pres., dir. Wallace Livestock Loan Co., 1918-27; mgr., sec.-treas., dir. Continental Discount Corp., 1928-37; with Bur. Agrl. Econs., 1938-39, Soil Conservation Service, 1939-41; civilian employee Army Engrs., 1942-44; regional land officer Bur. Reclamation, Boise, Idaho, 1944-53; area adminstr. Bur. Land Mgmt., from 1953. Mem. Masons, Shriners. Home: Denver Colo. †

WALLACH, LUITPOLD, classics educator, author; b. Munich, Germany, Feb. 6, 1910; came to U.S., 1939, naturalized, 1947; s. Karl and Rosa (Schneeweis) W.; m. Barbara Jean Price, Aug. 22, 1970. Student, Berlin U., 1929-30; Ph.D., U. Tuebingen, 1932, Cornell U., 1947. Asst. prof. Hamilton Coll., 1951-52, U. Oreg., 1953, Cornell U., 1953-55, U. Okla., 1955-57, Harpur Coll., 1957-62; prof. classics Marquette U., Milw., 1962-67; faculty fellow Marquette U., 1967, mem. bd. grad. studies, 1964-67; prof. classics U. Ill., Urbana, 1967-78; prof. emeritus U. Ill., 1978-87; asso. Center Advanced Study, 1969-70. Author: Berthold of Zwiefalten's Chronicle, 1958, Alcuin and Charlemagne, 1959, 2d edit., 1968, Liberty and Letters, 1959, The Classical Tradition, 1966, Diplomatic Studies in Documents, 1977, Die Zwiefalter Chroniken, 1978, Alcuin's Libri Carolini, 1984; mem. editorial adv. com.: Ill. Classical Studies, 1973-77; contbr. articles to profl. jours. Fund for Advancement Edn. fellow, 1952; Am. Council Learned Socs. grantee, 1960; fellow Leo Baeck Inst., 1967-87. Mem. Am. Hist. Assn., Am. Philol. Assn., Medieval Acad. Am., N.Am. Patristic Soc. (exec. com. 1970-72), Phi Beta Kappa, Phi Kappa Phi, Sigma Tau Delta, Eta Sigma Phi. Died 1987.

WALLENBERG, JACOB, banker; b. Stockholm, Sept. 17, 1892; s. Marcus Laurentius and Amalia (Hagdahl) W. Diploma, Stockholm Sch. Econs., 1914, Econ. D. honoris causae, Med. D. honoris causae. Asst. v.p. Stockholms Enskilda Bank, 1918-20, vice mng. dir. , mem. bd., 1920-27, mng. dir., 1927-46, vice chmn., 1946-50, chmn., from 1950; chmn. bd. inter alia AB Astra, Forvaltnings AB Providentia, AB Investor, Kemi-Intressen AB, Stora Kopparbergs Bergslags AB, Svenska Tandsticks AB, Bergvik och Ala. AB. Mem. Swedish Govt. Commn. for trade negotiations with Germany, 1934-44; chmn. bd. Kurt and Alice Wallenberg Found. Decorated Grand Cross Order of Vasa, Grand Cross Order of Polar Star, comdr. 1st class Order of Dannebrog (Denmark), comdr. White Rose of Finland. Mem. Royal Swedish Acad. Engring Scis. (hon.), Royal Swedish Yacht Club (hon.). Home: Stockholm Sweden. †

WALLERSTEDT, ALVAR GUSTAF, business executive; b. Lindsborg, Kans., Aug. 19, 1891; s. Gustaf Adolph and Emily (Gustafson) W.; m. Forest Evelyn Farmer, May 12, 1920; 1 child, Joan Carr Wallerstedt Bell. Diploma, Bethany Coll., 1911; acctg. cert., LaSalle Extension U., 1918; student real estate appraising, Columbia U., 1924. CPA, N.C. With Lindsborg Milling & Elevator Co., 1911-13, Smoky Valley Roller Mills, 1911-13; stenographer, bookkeeper, acct. Panama Canal, 1913-19; traveling auditor U.S. Shipping Bd., 1919; auditor income tax unit U.S. Govt., 1920, revenue agt., 1921; ptnr. tax specialists firm Rusch, Jackson & Wallerstedt, Washington, 1922-23; tax specialist legal firm Reed Smith Shaw & McClay, Pitts., 1924-55; dir., mem. stock option com. Rockwell-Standard Corp., Corapolis, Pa.; bd. .dirs., sec. exec. com. Union Title Guaranty Co., Pitts.; bd. dirs., mem. investment com. Old Republic Ins. Co., Greensburg, Pa., Sun Drug Co., Pitts.; bd. dirs., mem. salary com. Mine Safety Appliances Co., Pitts.; bd. dirs. Commonwealth Land Title Ins. Co., Phila., Old Republic Life Ins. Co., Chgo., Spang & Co., Butler, Pa. Trustee Pitts. Assn. Improvement of Poor. Mem. Masons, St. Clair Country Club, Duquesne Club (Pitts.). Presbyterian. Home: Pittsburgh Pa. †

WALLICH, HENRY CHRISTOPHER, economist, government official; b. Berlin, Germany, June 10, 1914; came to U.S., 1935, naturalized, 1944; s. Paul and Hildegard J. (Rehrmann) W.; m. Mable Inness Brown, Dec. 2, 1950; children: Christine Wallich de Hakim, Anna Hildegard Kehoe, Paul Inness. Grad., Bismarck Gymnasium, Berlin, 1932; student, Oxford U., 1932-33; M.A., Harvard, 1941, Ph.D., 1944. Export bus. Argentina, 1933-35; with Chem. Bank & Trust Co., N.Y.C., 1935-36, Hackney Hopkinson & Sutphen (securities), N.Y.C., 1936-40; with Fed. Res. Bank N.Y., 1941-51, chief fgn. research div., 1946-51; prof. econs. Yale, 1951-74; mem. Bd. Govs. Fed. Res. System, Washington, 1974-86; Sr. cons. to sec. Treasury, 1969-74; mem. Pres.'s Council Econ. Advisers, 1959-61; cons. Mut. Security Adminstrn., 1952, U.S. Treasury, 1951-52, White House, 1954-55. Author: Monetary Problems of an Export Economy, 1950, (with John Adler) Public Finances of a Developing Country, 1951, Mainsprings of the German Revival, 1955, The Cost of Freedom, 1960, Monetary Policy and Practice: A View from the Federal Reserve Board, 1981; also articles.; Editorial contbr.: Washington Post, 1961-64; columnist: Newsweek mag, 1965-74. Mem. Am. Econ. Assn., Am. Fin. Assn., Council Fgn. Relations. Clubs: Harvard (N.Y.C.); University (Washington); New Haven Lawn. Died Sept. 15, 1988; buried Oak Hill Cemetery, Washington.

WALLIS, HAL BRENT, motion picture producer; b. Chgo., Sept. 14, 1899; s. Jacob and Eva (Blum) W.; m. Louise Fazenda, Nov. 24, 1927 (dec. 1962); 1 son, Hal Brent; m. Martha Hyer. Student, Gregg Bus. Sch. Office boy Cobe & McKinnon, Chicago, 1912; asst. sales and advt. mgr. Edison Gen. Electric Co., Chgo., 1916-22; mgr. Garrick Theatre, Los Angeles, 1922-23; with Warner Bros. Pictures, from 1923, exec. producer in charge prodn., 1933-44; Ind. producer as Hal Wallis Prodns. (releasing through Paramount Pictures), 1944-69, Hal Wallis Prodns. (through Universal Pictures), 1969-86. Recipient Acad. Thalberg award for best prodns. 1938, 43. Lodges: Masons (32 deg.), Shriners. Home: Rancho Mirage Calif. Died Oct. 5, 1986; buried Forest Lawn Cemetery, Los Angeles.

WALPOLE, RONALD NOEL, French language educator; b. Monmouthshire, Eng., Dec. 24, 1903; s. George W. and Florence M. (Blew) W.; m. Doris G. Hoyt, Aug. 9, 1934; 1 dau., Mary R. Walpole Marzke. B.A. in French with 1st class honors, Univ. Coll. Cardiff, 1925; M.A., U. Wales, 1936; Ph.D., U. Calif.-Berkeley, 1939. Faculty U. Calif., Berkeley, 1939—; prof. French U. Calif., 1950—, chmn. dept., 1957-63. Author: Charlemagne and Roland; A Study of the Sources of Two Mediaeval English Romances, Roland and Vernagu and Otuel and Roland, 1944, Philip Mouskés and the Pseudo-Turpin Chronicle, 1947, The Old French Johannes Translation of the Pseudo-Turpin Chronicle: A Critical Edition, 2 vols, 1976, An Anonymous Old French Translation of the Pseudo-Turpin Chronicle, 1979; Le Turpin Francais dit le Turpin I, edit. critique, 1985; contbr. articles, revs. to Am., fgn. periodicals and encys. Decorated chevalier de la Légion d'Honneur, 1962; Guggenheim fellow., 1949-50. Mem. Medieval Acad. Am., Internat. Arthurian Soc., Am. Acad. Arts and Scis., Phi Beta Kappa. Clubs: Faculty, Kosmos (U. Calif.). Home: Berkeley Calif. Died Nov. 22, 1986.

WALSH, HAROLD VANDERVOORT, architect, artist; b. New Windsor, N.Y., Sept. 20, 1892; s. George Ethelbert and Anne Vandervoort (Gleason) W.; m. Helen Harper Loucks, Feb. 15, 1918; children: Jeanne Vandervoort, Myra-Claire, Winifred. Student, CCNY, 1909-11; BArch, Columbia, 1915. Prof. architecture Columbia, 1919-35; also cons. architect, write; prof. emeritus sch. engring. and architecture CUNY, from 1959; free lance lectr.; dir. spl. course architecture for mems. Am. Soc. Illuminating Engrs., 1930, 40; archtl. cons. on adv. com. to prepare master plan for future devel. of campus and bldgs. for Queens Coll., N.Y.C., 1940-41; mem. com. on fundamental equipment Pres. Hoover's Housing Conf., 1931. Author: Construction of the Small House, 1922, Understanding Architecture, 1934, Your House Begins With You, 1949; co-author: Home Study Course for Austin Tech. Inst., 1941, Let Us Plan a Peacetime Home, 1945; contbr. series of articles on apartment house construction in Architecture, 1923-24, many articles to American Architect and Architecture, Pencil Points, House Beautiful, others; illustrator own articles and books; one man shows N.Y. Region; numerous exhbns. 2d. lt. U.S. Army, World

War I. Recipient awards Catherine Lorillard Wolfe Art Club; awarded Arnold Brunner Scholarship grant for rsch. on industrialization of bldg., 1954. Fellow Am. Registered Architects; mem. Archtl. League of N.Y., N.Y. Assn. Arhcitects, ASCAP, Am. Artists Profl. League, Mcpl. Art Soc., New Rochelle Art Assn., Soc. for Advancement of Engring. Edn., N.Y. Soc. Architects, Mil. Order of Fgn. Wars of U.S., Alpha Delta Phi. Presbyterian. Home: City Island N.Y. also: Richmond Vt. †

WALSH, JAMES CLEMENT, management consultant; b. Chgo., May 31, 1918; s. Karin E. and Loretto (Callahan) W.; m. Jane Burnham, 1938; children—Barbara (Mrs. Richard S. Wilson), James B., Carol Moran, Mary Ellen, Kathleen, Betsy Lyons, Gerald, Susan, Thomas. B.S.C., U. Notre Dame, 1939. C.P.A., Ill. With Marshall Field & Co., Chgo., 1939-53; asst. to gen., mgr. Marshall Field & Co. (Fieldcrest div.), N.Y.C., 1949-52; sec.-treas. Fieldcrest Mills, Inc., 1953-55; v.p., treas. Hecht Co., Balt., 1955-58; sec., asst. treas. May Dept. Stores Co., St. Louis, 1959-60; v.p., treas. May Dept. Stores Co., 1960-66, v.p. adminstrn. and control, 1967-68, exec. v.p., 1968-75, sr. exec. v.p., 1975-78; also dir.; pres. James C. Walsh, Inc., St. Louis, 1978-87. Died Oct. 12, 1987; buried St. Louis.

WALTON, GEORGE WILLEVER, educator; b. Irvington, N.J., Oct. 9, 1892; s. Harry Ellsworth and Susan Jane (Kingsbury) W.; m. Ada Mae Kreidler, Oct. 19, 1917; children: Richard Kreidler, Margaret Jane. PhB, Lafayette Coll., 1915; MS, Cornell U., 1924; DSc (hon.), Albright Coll., 1936. Tchr. natural sci. Sunbury, Pa., 1915-17; prof. biology and geology Albright Coll., from 1917, coll. dean, 1928-59, dean emeritus, from 1959. Contbr. numerous articles in field to profl. jours. Mem. Evang. United Brethren Ch. Fellow AAAS; mem. NEA, Ea.-Assn. Coll. Deans and Advisers of Men, Pa. Edn Asssn., Pa. Acad. Sci. (charter), Phi Beta Kappa. Republican. Home: Reading Pa. †

WAMPLER, G. V., marketing executive; b. Bloomington, Ind., Oct. 10, 1914; s. Harvey and Lenora R. (Hawkins) W.; m. Virginia Guthier, Aug. 1984; 1 child, Rebecca Sue. Ed., Ind. U., 1932-36. Advt. mgr., sales dept., field supr. Atlantic & Pacific Tea Co., Indpls., Cin., 1936-50; advt. and sales promotion mgr. Humpty Dumpty Super Markets, Oklahoma City, 1950-55; advt. dir., div. mgr., v.p., gen. dir. merchandising Fleming Co., Oklahoma City, 1955-67; exec. v.p. Fleming Co., 1967-70; pres. Marketing Analysts, Inc., 1970-87. Served with USAAF, 1943-46. Mem. Christian Ch. Clubs: Naples Sailing and Yacht, Spanish Wells Country. Home: Naples Fla. Died Aug. 26, 1987; buried Chambersville Cemetery, Ellettsville, Ind.

WANAMAKER, GILES A., business executive. m. Louise Eller; children: Giles A. Jr., Roger. Formerly exec. v.p. Hertz Corp., pres., chief operating officer, 1963-67. Served ast lt. col. U.S. Army Air Corps, WWII. Home: Punta Gorda Fla. Died July 19, 1987.

WARD, CHARLES, dancer, actor, singer; b. Los Angeles, Aug. 24, 1952; s. Lee Charles and Olive Hannah (Conboy) W. Student pub. schs. With Houston Ballet, 1970-72; mem. Am. Ballet Theatre, N.Y.C., 1972-78, corps de ballet, 1972-74, soloist, 1974-76, prin. dancer, 1976-78. film appearance in The Turning Point, 1977; star musical Dancin", Broadway, 1978; guest appearances throughout U.S. Mem. Am. Guild Mus. Artists, SAG, Actors Equity. Died July 11, 1986.

WARD, JAMES MYRON, newspaper editor; b. Montrose, Miss., Jan. 7, 1919; s. William Joseph and Myra (Anderson) W.; m. Bobbye Terry Ward, Dec. 11, 1941; children: Patricia, James Myron, Myra Annette. Grad., Millsaps Coll., 1941. With Jackson (Miss.) Daily News, 1932-84, photographer and reporter, city editor, mng. editor, 1932-57, editor, 1957-84. Past mem. Miss. Agrl. and Indsl. Bd.; past v.p. Natchez Trace Assn.; past mem. bd. dirs. Goodwill Industries Miss. Served as capt. USAAF, WWII. Decorated Air medal with nine oak leaf clusters. Mem. Am. Soc. Newspaper Editors, Miss.-La. Mng. Editors Assn., Jackson C. of C., A.P. Mng. Editors Assn., Am. Legion, VFW, Rotary (past pres. Jackson club), Lambda Chi Alpha, Sigma Delta Chi. Home: Jackson Miss. Died Feb. 13, 1984; buried Lakewood Meml. Park, Jackson.

WARD, WARREN HAYDEN, publisher, banker; b. Saginaw, Mich., Aug. 29, 1893; s. Louis E. and Hattie (Hayden) W.; m. Helen Wold, Jan. 11, 1915 (dec.); children—Louise (Mrs. Louis Ewing), Warren Hayden, Helen J. (Mrs. Donald Hall), Phillip (dec.). Student, Northwestern U. Tchr. country sch. 1910-12; with Standard Edn. Corp., Chgo., 1912-87; v.p. Standard Edn. Corp., 1920-40, pres., 1940-66, chmn. bd., 1966-87; pres. Nat. Bank of North Evanston, 1961-63, chmn. bd., 1963-68, also dir. Mem. Am. Textbook Pubs. Inst. (sec. 1962). Clubs: Chicago Athletic Assn, North Shore Country. Home: Evanston Ill. Died Mar. 15, 1987; buried Naples, Fla.

WARDLE, JAMES MOREY, engineer; b. Chilliwack, B.C., Can., June 26, 1888; s. James and Martha (Morey) W.; m. Leette Maud Roney, Nov. 4, 1913; 1 child, Dorothy Hope. BS, Queen's U., 1912. Registered profl. engr., Ont., B.C. Supt. Banff Nat. Park, Alta., 1918-21; chief engr. Nat. Parks Can., 1921-35, western supr., 1932-35; dep. minister Can. Dept. Interior, 1935-36; dir. surveys and engring br. Can. Dept. Mines and Resources, 1936-47; mem. B.C.-Yukon Alaska Hwy. Commn., 1938-41; dir. pub. projects br., engring. and resources br. Can. Dept. Resources and Devel., 1947-52; commr. internat. boundary Govt. of Can., 1947-51; Dominion Govt. mem. Ea. Rockies Forest Conservation Bd., 1947-51; chmn. N.W. Ter. Power Commn., 1948-52; cons. engr. Ottawa, Can., from 1952; cons. Sir Alex Gibb and ptnrs., Ottawa. Mem. Nat. Capital Commn., Ottawa, from 1959—; councillor Municipality of Rockcliffe Park. Decorated comdr. Order Brit. Empire, 1946. Fellow Can. Geog. Soc.; mem. Trail Riders Can. Rockies (pres. 1925-29), Engring. Inst. Can., Arctic Inst. N.Am., Rotary (pres. Banff chpt. 1924), Royal Ottawa Golf Club. Mem. Anglican Ch. †

WARHOL, ANDY, artist, filmmaker; b. Pitts., 1928; s. James and Julia (Von) W. Student, Carnegie Inst. Tech. One-man exhbns. include, Leo Castelli Gallery, N.Y.C., Ferus Gallery, Los Angeles, Stable Gallery, N.Y.C., Morris Gallery, Toronto, Can., Rubbers Gallery, Buenos Aires, Sonnebend Gallery, Paris, numerous others, works in permanent collections at, Mus. Modern Art, N.Y.C., Whitney Mus. Am. Art, Walker Art Center, Mpls., Albright-Knox Art Gallery, Buffalo, Los Angeles County Mus. Art; dir., producer, photographer: movies Eat, 1964, Sleep, 1964, Kiss, 1963, Empire, 1964, Harlot, 1964, My Hustler, 1965, Chelsea Girls, 1966, Bike Boy, 1967, Lonesome Cowboys, 1968, Blue Movie, 1969, Imitation of Christ, 1969, Flesh, 1969, Trash, 1971, Women in Revolt, 1972, Andy Warhol's Bad, 1977, L'Amour, 1978; producer: films Heat, 1972, Blood for Dracula, 1974, Andy Warhol's Frankenstein, 1975; recs. of rock group, Velvet Underground; pub.: Interview mag; Author: The Philosophy of Andy Warhol: From A to B and Back Again, 1975, Andy Warhol's Exposures, 1979, Andy Warhol: Portraits of the Seventies, 1979; author: (with Pat Hackett) Popism: The Warhol Sixties, 1980, America, 1985. Recipient Art Dirs. Club medal, 1957, 6th Film Culture award, 1964, Los Angeles Film Festival award, 1964. Home: New York N.Y. Died Feb. 22, 1987.

WARING, FRED M., musical conductor; b. Tyrone, Pa., June 9, 1900; s. Frank and Jessie (Calderwood) W; m. Evalyn Nair, 1933; children: Dixie, Fred, Bill; m. Virginia Gearhart, 1954; children: Paul, Malcolm. Student engring., Pa. State U. Former owner Shawnee Press Inc. (music pubs.), Shawnee Inn and Shawnee Country Club, Shawnee-on-Delaware, Pa. Writer numerous coll. songs; appeared in several mus. shows on Broadway; in motion picture Varsity Show; mus. condr. The Pennsylvanians; conducted his orch. in Paris; 1st appeared in Balaban Theatre, Chgo., 1928, on radio, 1933-44; long interested in choral work; organized Fred Waring Music Workshop for Choral Dirs., 1948; condr. TV program The Fred Waring Show, 1949-54; producer, dir. mus. rev. Hear! Hear!, 1955, numerous recs. Hon. mem. Nat. Cartoonists Soc. Clubs: Lambs, Athletic (N.Y.C.). Home: Shawnee-on-Delaware Pa. Died July 29, 1984; buried Shawnee Presby. Cemetery.

WARLICK, WILSON, judge; b. Newton, N.C., Mar. 8, 1892; s. Thomas M. and Martha Elizabeth (Wilson) W.; m. Kittie Reed Hipp, Oct. 24, 1925; children: Martha Warlick Brame, Thomas Wilson. BS, Catawba Coll., 1910, LLD (hon.), 1936; LLB, U. N.C., 1913 (pres. Law Sch. 1912-13). Bar: N.C. 1913. Pvt. practice Newton, N.C., 1913-30; judge Superior Ct., 16th Jud. Dist., 1930-48; U.S. dist. judge Western Dist. N.C., 1949-70. Chmn. N.C. Probation Commn., 1937. Lt. G-2, Adj. Gen. Dept., U.S. Army, World War I. Mem. N.C. Bar Assn., SAR, Am. Legion, 40 et 8, Masons, Catawba Country Club, Alpha Tau Omega, Phi Delta Phi. Democrat. Presbyterian (elder). Home: Newton N.C. †

WARNE, COLSTON ESTEY, economist, consumer leader; b. Romulus, N.Y., Aug. 14, 1900; s. Clinton Arlington and Harriet Ellsworth (Estey) W.; m. Frances Lee Corbett, Oct. 27, 1920; children—Clinton Lee, Margaret C. Nelson, Barbara Newell. B.A., Cornell U., 1920, M.A., 1921; Ph.D., U. Chgo., 1925; M.A. (hon.), Amherst Coll., 1942, 80; hon. degree, Bowie State Coll., 1977. Clk. Tompkins County Nat. Bank, Ithaca, N.Y., 1919; with accounting dept. Fed. Res. Bank N.Y., 1919-20; asst. econs. Cornell U., 1919-20, instr., 1920-21; instr. econs. U. Pitts., 1921-22, U. Chgo., 1922-25; asso. prof. U. Denver, 1925-26; asst. prof. econs. U. Pitts., 1926-30, Bryn Mawr Summer Sch. Indsl. Workers, 1927-29, 31, 32, 34; asso. prof. Amherst Coll., 1930-42, prof., 1942-70, prof. emeritus, 1970-87; Vis. lectr. Wesleyan U., Middletown, Conn., 1938, 46; vis. prof. Smith Coll., 1939, Conn. Coll. for Women, 1940-42, 45-46, 48; Pres. Consumers Union U.S., 1936-80, pres. emeritus, 1980-87; pres. Internat. Orgn. of Consumers Unions, 1960-70, treas., 1970-72, exec. com., 1972-87; Am. specialist cultural exchange program U.S. Dept. State, 1962; mem. Industry Panels, Wage and Hour Adminstrn., U.S. Dept. Labor, 1943-44; cons. U.S. Coordinator of Fisheries, 1943; mem. consumers adv. com. OPA, 1944, regional consumer adviser, 1946; bd. dirs. Coop. League U.S.A., 1926-29, Nat. Assn. Consumers, 1947; consumer adv. com. N.Y. State, 1955-59, Commonwealth of Mass., 1959-64; mem. Pres.'s Com. on Consumer Interests, 1946-65; pres. People's Lobby, Washington, 1934-36, v.p., 1941; hon. v.p. Nat. Consumers League, 1941; mem. consumer adv. com. Pres.'s Council Econ. Advisers, 1947-51, vice chmn., 1948; mem. prep. commn. White House Conf. on Aging, 1970, ad hoc advisor, 1981; mem. Nat. Consumer Energy com. Fed. Energy Office, 1973-74; mem. consumer adv. com. Fed. Energy Adminstrn., 1974-76; mem. panel on consumer products Nat. Research Council, 1980-87. Author: Industry-Wide Collective Bargaining-Promise or Menace?; co-author: Labor Problems in Am; chmn. bd. editors, contbr.: Yearbook of Am. Labor; contbr.: New Republic; contbg. editor: Current History. Chmn. acad. freedom com. Am. Fedn. Tchrs., 1936-37; chmn. Pitts. br. ACLU, 1927-30, Western Mass. Civil Liberties Com., 1938-41. Served as apprentic seaman USNRF, 1918. Mem. Am. Econ. Assn., Am. Arbitration Assn. (panel arbitrators 1945-87), AAUP (council 1938-42), Am. Marketing Assn., Artus. Home: Bedford Mass. Died May 20, 1987.

WARNER, ALLEN GRANT, automotive company executive; b. Ottawa, Ont., Can., Mar. 30, 1927; s. Harold Cecil W.; m. Elizabeth Joyce, Dec. 27, 1952; children—Mark, Tracey, Tod. B. in Indsl. Engring., Gen. Motors Inst., Flint, Mich., 1953. Mfg. engr. Gen. Motors of Can. Ltd., Oshawa, Ont., 1953-64; plant mgr. Gen. Motors of Can. Ltd., Windsor and Oshawa, Ont., 1964-71; dir. mfg. Gen. Motors of Can. Ltd., Oshawa, 1971-76; gen. mgr. diesel div. Gen. Motors of Can. Ltd., London, Ont., 1976-81; v.p., gen. mfg. mgr. Gen. Motors of Can. Ltd., Oshawa, 1981-87; dir. Diffracto Ltd.; bd. dirs. Export Trade Devel. Bd., 1983-85, Ont. Centre for Automotive Parts Tech., 1983-87, Can. Export Assn., 1984-87. Mem. Soc. Automotive Engrs. Home: Toronto, Ont. Canada. Died Aug. 28, 1987.

WARNER, DANIEL THEODORE, manufacturing executive; b. Drake County, Ohio, Dec. 19, 1891; s. Forest Elmer and Mattie (Wills) W.; m. Goldie Myrtle Fisher, Nov. 10, 1917; children: Daniel Theodore, Richard Elmore, Marcia Jean (Mrs. James W. Duckworth). Student pub. schs. Various positions Barney & Smith Car Co., Dayton, Ohio, 1910-17; prodn. mgr. Canton (Ohio) Sheet Steel Co., 1918-23; factory mgr. Master Electric Co., Dayton, 1924-26, works mgr., 1937-42, dir., mem. exec. com., from 1942, v.p. charge mfg., 1942-51, exec. v.p., 1951-56, v.p., gen. mgr., 1956, pres., gen. mgr., from 1957; prodn. mgr. large engine div. Fairbanks Morse Co., Beloit, Wis., 1927-28; works mgr. Stover Engine Co., John W. Henney Industries, Freeport, Ill., 1929-30; v.p., asst. gen. mgr. Henney Motor Co., 1931-37; pres. Master Electric div. Reliance Electric & Engring. Co. Mem. Am. (past pres., dir.), Ohio (past pres., dir.) Aberdeen-Angus breeder assns., N.Y.C., Dayton (dir.) C. of C.s, Engrs. Club, Cuvier PRess Club (Cin.), Saddle and Sirloin Club (Chgo.). Republican. Mem. Methodist Episcopalian Ch. Home: Dayton Ohio. †

WARNER, REX ERNEST, educator, author; b. Birmingham, Eng., Mar. 9, 1905; came to U.S., 1961; s. Frederick Ernest and Kathleen (Luce) W. BA, Oxford U., Eng., 1928. Tchr. English 1928-45; dir. Brit. Inst., Athens, 1945-48; Tallmann prof. classics Bowdoin Coll., Brunswick, Maine, 1961-62; univ. prof. English, U. Conn., Storrs, from 1962. Author: The Wild Goose Chase, The Aerodrome, The Young Caesar, Imperial Caesar, Pericles the Athenian, The Converts, Men of Athens; translator Xenophon (Persian Expdn.), History of My Time, Thucydides-The Peloponnesian War, Plutarch—The Plutarch-The Parallel Lives, Fall of the Roman Republic, Caesar War Commentaries, Confessions of St. Augustine, Three Great Plays of Euripedes, Poems of Seferis. Hon. fellow Wadham Coll., Oxford U.; decorated comdr. Order Phoenix (Greece). Hon. mem. New Eng. Classical Assn. Home: Wallingford England. Died June 24, 1986.

WARNER, WALTER EDWARDS, JR., lawyer; b. Bklyn., Apr. 14, 1908; s. Walter E. and Clara L. (Frost) W.; m. Gertrude H. Warner, Nov. 23, 1946. BA, Princeton U., 1928; LLB, Columbia U., 1931. Bar: N.Y. 1932, U.S. Supreme Ct. 1932. Practice law N.Y.C., 1932-86; specializing corp. estate litigation la; mem. firm Chambers, Clare & Gibson, 1944-86; former chmn. Dudley Mgmt. Corp. Club: Mason, University (N.Y.C.). Home: Larchmont N.Y. Died Apr. 13, 1986; buried Greenwood Cemetery, Bklyn.

WARREN, ANDREW JACKSON, public health consultant; b. Hurdle Mill, N.C., May 16, 1891; s. William Algernon and Louise (Hester) W.; m. Margaret Lyle Spurgeon, June 12, 1917; children: Margaret Louise Warren Tenney, Huldah Hester Warren Scott. Student, U. N.C., 1908-12; MD, Tulane U., 1914, LLD (hon.), 1955; CPH, Johns Hopkins Sch. Hygiene and Pub. Health, 1930. County health officer Rowan County, N.C., 1918-19; asst. state health officer N.C., 1919-20; city health officer, Charlotte, N.C., 1920-21; field staff, Internat. Health Div. Rockefeller Found., from 1921, acting epidemiologist and dir. rural health, Kans., 1921-22, asst. state health officerrural health work, Oreg., 1923, adviser Nat. Dept. Health, Mexico, 1924-26, fellowship adviser, 1928-37, asst. dir. Internat. Health Div. Rockefeller Found., 1936-44, in charge of work in Europe, Africa and Nr. East, 1938-44, assoc. dir., 1944-51, dir. div. medicine and pub. health, 1951-56; cons. to Sec. War as mem. bd. for investigation and control influenza and other epidemic diseases in Army, 1941-46; chmn. tropical diseases study sect. Nat. Inst. Health; hon. prof. med. and biol. scis. U. Chile; mem. vis. com. Harvard Sch. Pub. Health, 1943-49. Contbr. articles on pub. health adminstrn., hookworm, parasitology, malaria to profl. jours. Decorated Royal Order of Vasa, Comdr., 2d class (Sweden); Chevalier Legion of Honor (France). Fellow Am. Pub. Health Assn., Am. Soc. Parasitologists, Am. Soc. Tropical Medicine. Home: Chester Springs Pa. †

WARREN, AUSTIN, author; b. Waltham, Mass., July 4, 1899; s. Edward Austin and Nellie Myra (Anderson) W.; m. Eleanor Blake, Sept. 13, 1941 (dec. Jan. 1946); m. Antonia Keese, Sept. 5, 1959. A.B., Wesleyan U., Conn., 1920; M.A., Harvard U., 1922; Ph.D., Princeton U., 1926; Litt.D., Brown U., 1974. Instr. English U. Ky., 1920-21; instr. English U. Minn., Mpls., 1922-24; dean St. Peters Sch. Liberal and Humane Studies, Hebron, Conn., summers 1922-30; instr. English Boston U., 1926-29, asst. prof., assoc. prof., 1929-34, prof., 1934-39; dir. Anderson Library Poetry 1938-40; prof. English U. Iowa, 1939-48, U. Mich., Ann Arbor, 1948-68; with Grad. Sch., U. Wis., summer 1936, Grad. Sch., U. Iowa, summer 1937; Berg vis. prof. English and Am. lit. NYU, 1953-54. Author: Alexander Pope as Critic and Humanist, 1929, The Elder Henry James, 1934, Richard Crashaw, 1939, Rage for Order, 1947, New England Saints, 1956, The New England Conscience, 1966, Connections, 1970; (with others) Literary Scholarship, 1941, Theory of Literature, 1948; editor: Hawthorne (Am. Writers Series), 1934; assoc. editor New England Quar., 1937-40, 42-46, Am. Lit., 1940-42, Comparative Lit., 1948-50; contbr. to revs. Recipient award for lit. AAAL, 1973; fellow Kenyon Sch. English, 1948-50, Guggenheim Found., 1950-51, Am. Council Learned Socs., 1930-31; sr. fellow Sch. Letters, Ind. U., from 1950. Mem. AAUP, MLA, Nat. Inst. Arts and Letters, Phi Beta Kappa, Delta Upsilon. Home: Providence R.I. Died Aug. 20, 1986.

WARREN, FRANK BAKER, manufacturing executive; b. Paw Paw, Ill., Oct. 11, 1892; s. James A. and Anna (McBride) W.; m. Delight Matthews, Nov. 25, 1920; children: Virginia Delight, Dorothy Ann. BCE, U. Ill., 1914. V.p. Bessemer Limestone & Cement Co., Youngstown, Ohio, 1936-53, dir., 1939—, pres., 1953-61, ret., 1961; bd. dirs. Canfield Mfg. Co., Diamond Alkali Co., Mahoning Nat. Bank, Home Savs. & Loan Co., Comml. Shearing & Stamping Co. (Youngstown). Lt. 5th and 148th F.A., AEF, 1917-19. Republican. Presbyterian. Home: Youngstown Ohio. †

WARREN, HARRY, song writer and composer; b. Bklyn., Dec. 24, 1893; s. Anthony and Rachel (Deluca) W.; m. Josephine Wensler, Dec. 19, 1917; 1 child, Mrs. John Hacker. Student pub. schs.; mus. edn., choir of Our Lady of Loretto, Bklyn. Began playing drums in brass band carnival shows; asst. dir. Vitagraph Co., Bklyn.; first song pub., 1922; Billie Rose mus. revs., Sweet and Low, 1930; Crazy Quilt, 1931, Ed Wynn's Laugh Parade, 1931; over 100 mus. motion pictures, including 42d Street, All Godd Diggers, Down Argentine Way. Served with USN, 1918. Recipient 2 Motion Picture Acad. awards; Nat. Fedn. Music Clubs award. Roman Catholic. Club: Bel Air Country. Composer: Cheerful Little Earful; Would You Like to Take a Walk?, I Found a Million Dollar Baby in the 5 to 10 cent Store; You're My Everything; Shuffle Off to Buffalo; 42d Street; Lullaby of Broadway; Shadow Waltz; Chattanooga Choo-Choo; Serenade in Blue; I had the Craziest Dream; You'll Never Know; I've Got a Gal in Kalamazoo; Maga Saki; Down Argentine Way; Don't Give Up the Ship (song, adopted by USN Acad.); Song of the Marines (adopted by USMC); On the Atchison, Topeka and the Santa Fe (winner Acad. award); Songs; Stanley Steamer; Afraid to Fall in Love; Spring Isn't Everything; New songs: I wish I Knew, The More I See You, Zing a Little Zong, Dig for Your Dinner, That's Amore, Friendly Star, You Wonderful You, My One and Only Highland Fling, I Only Have Eyes For You, September in the Rain, There Will Never Be Another You, I'll String Along With You, An Affair to Remember, Tiny Scout, Tomorrow Land, You Make it Easy to be True, others. Pictures: Belle of New York, Summer Stock, Barkleys of Broadway, Just for You, The Caddy, Skirts Ahoy, An Affair to Remember, Artists and Models, Birds and the Bees. Home: Beverly Hills Calif. Died Sept. 22, 1981.

WARREN, LOUIS BANCEL, lawyer; b. Monmouth Beach, N.J., Aug. 30, 1905; s. Schuyler Neilson and Alice (Binsse) W.; m. Rosalie Warren, June 9, 1934; children: Hope Wilberforce (Mrs. Charles Shaw), Rosalie Starr (Mrs. Paul Byard), Louis Bancel. A.B., M.A., Trinity Coll., Oxford U., 1927; J.D., Columbia U., 1930; LL.D.(hon.), Holy Cross Coll., 1973. Bar: N.Y. 1930. Practice law N.Y.C., 1930-86; assoc. Larkin, Rathbone & Perry (now Kelley & Drye & Warren), 1930-40, mem. firm, 1940-86; dir., mem. compensation com. Chrysler Corp., 1957-76; dir. Hammersons Holdings (U.S.A.), Inc.; dir., sec. Am. European Assocs. Inc.; mem. exec. com. Correctional Assn. N.Y., 1962-77. Contbr. articles to legal jours. Treas., trustee Homeland Found.; bd. dirs. Lutece Found., Inc.; mem. bd. visitors Columbia Law Sch., 1954-76; bd. dirs. Am. Ditchley Found., 1962-72; Participant U.S. Naval War Coll. global strategy discussions, 1966. Served with N.Y. N.G., 1927-30; with USCG(T), 1943-45. Decorated knight comdr. Order St. Gregory the Gt. Vatican, 1957; officers cross merit; Sovereign Order Malta, 1968; chevalier French Legion Honor, 1971; comdr. Order Brit. Empire, 1972; officier de l'Ordre des Arts et des Lettres France, 1978; Morgan Library fellow; hon. fellow Trinity Coll., Oxford U., 1978. Fellow Am. Bar Found.; mem. ABA, N.Y. Bar Assn., Assn. Bar City N.Y., Am. Soc. Internat. Law, St. Nicholas Soc., Alliance Francaise de N.Y., French Inst., English-Speaking Union, Internat. Bar Assn., France Am. Soc. (dir.), Pilgrims Soc., St. George Soc., Phi Delta Phi. Republican. Roman Catholic. Clubs: Knickerbocker (N.Y.C.), Century Assn. (N.Y.C.), Somerset Hills Country, Somerset Hills Lake and Game (N.J.). Home: Bernardsville N.J. Died Oct. 27, 1986.

WARREN, STAFFORD L., educator; b. Maxwell City, N.Mex., June 19, 1896; s. Edwin S. and Clara A. (Leak) W.; m. Viola L. Lockhart, May 23, 1920 (dec. July 1968); children: Jane W. Larson, Dean S., Roger W.; m. 2d, Gertrude T. Huberty, July 18, 1970. Prof. radiology U. Rochester Sch. Medicine and Dentistry, 1926-46, dean med. sch., 1962-63, prof. biophysics emeritus, 1963-81; dir. Atomic Energy Project, 1947-58; spl. asst. to Pres. to implement nationwide mental retardation program, 1962-65; cons. for med. research and edn. Dept. Health Edn. and Welfare, mem. edn. and research adv. com. VA, 1966—; hon. civilian cons. to surgeon gen. navy; cons. USPHS, NRC; chmn. Calif. Civil Def. Planning Bd., 1949-53; mem. med. adv. com. diseases and blindness NIH, 1952-56; mem. nat. adv. council USPHS, 1962-63; mem. facilities and resources com. Nat. Library Medicine, 1962-65; mem. sci. adv. com. Los Angeles Air Pollution Control Dist., 1952—; col. U.S. M.C., chief med. sect. Manhattan Engring. Dist., adviser to comdg. gen., Manhattan Project, 1943-46; chief radiol. safety sect. Joint Task Force One (Bikini), 1946; civilian cons. to Calif. Air Resources Bd., 1971-72. Author over 300 reports on sci. subjects, cancer, arthritis, fever therapy, radioactive isotopes. Decorated D.S.M., Legion of Merit; recipient Enrico Fermi award AEC, 1972. Fellow Indsl. Med. Assn., Am. Psychiat. Assn. (hon.); mem. AMA, Am. Soc. Clin. Investigation, Am. Neisserian Med. Soc., Am. Optical Soc., Am. Social Hygiene Assn. (v.p. 1966), Sigma Xi, Alpha Omega Alpha. Republican. Congregationalist. Home: Pacific Palisades Calif. Died July 26, 1981.

WASHBURNE, CARLETON WOLSEY, educator; b. Chgo., Dec. 2, 1889; s. George Foote and Marion Guyon (Foster) W.; m. Heluiz Bigelow Chandler, Sept. 1912; children: Margaret Joan (Mrs. Doanld K. Marshall), Beatrice (Mrs. John Visher), Chandler. Student, U. Chgo., 1908-10, Hahnemann Med. Coll., Chgo., 1910-11; AB, Stanford, 1912; ED, U. Calif., 1918; Ped. D. (hon.), U. Messina, 1944. Tchr. country sch. Los Angeles County, Calif., 1912-13; dir. mcpl. playground L.A., summer 1913, Oakland, Calif., summer 1914; tchr. ungraded room and playground Tulare, Calif., 1913-14; head. dept. sci. San Francisco State Tchrs. Coll., 1914-19; supt. schs. Winnetka, Ill., 1919-45; chmn. Grad. Tchrs. Coll., Winnetka, 1932-45; dir. edn. sub-commn. Allied Commn. in Italy, 1944-46; pub. affairs officer Dept. of State (OIC); dir. U.S. Info. Service, North Italy, 1946-48; ednl. reconstruction specialist UNESCO, 1948-49; chmn. dept. edn., dir. div. grad. studies, dir. tchr. edn. Brooklyn Coll., from 1949; mem. summer faculty Ohio State U., 1921, Northwestern U., 1922, U. Chgo., 1923, U. Oreg., 1924, Colo. Stste Tchrs. Coll., 1925-27, U. Minn., 1928; dir. Winnetka Summer Sch. for Tchrs., 1929-41; Northwestern U. Summer Sch., 1936-41, Kans. State Tchrs. Coll., Pittsburg, 1949-50, U. Colo., 1951; dir. La. Ednl. Survey of Elem. and Secondary Schs., 1941-42; cons. on tng. reral tchrs. Dept. of State, Cambodia, 1958. Author books including: A Living Philosphy of Education, What is Progressive Education, The World's Good—Education for World Mindedness; also co-author or editor books relating to field; contbg. editor Jour. Ednl. Rsch., Jour. Tchr. Edn. Lt. col. U.S. Army Spl. Res., World War II. Decorated knight officer Order Crown of Italy, 1946; Legion of Merit, 1946; chevalier de Monisaraphon (Kingdom of Cambodia); recipient Grande Bene Merito, U. of Rome, 1945; Rosenwald fellow in Europe and Orient, 1930-31; travel grantee to study elementary and secondary edn. in 5 South Am. countries Cultural Relations div. U.S. Dept. State, 1942. Mem. New Edn. Fellowship (internat. pres. 1947-56), NEA, Am. Assn. Coll. Tchrs. Edn., Progressive Edn. Assn. (pres. 1939-43), Ednl. Rsch. Assn., Nat. Soc. Study of Edn., Kappa Delta Pi. Home: New York N.Y. †

WASHINGTON, HAROLD, mayor; b. Chgo., Apr. 15, 1922; s. Roy L. and Bertha (Jones) W. BA, Roosevelt U., Chgo., 1949; JD, Northwestern U., 1952. Bar: Ill. 1953. Asst. city prosecutor City of Chgo., 1954-58; arbitrator Ill. Indsl. Commn., 1960-64; mem. Ill. Ho. of Reps., Springfield, 1965-76, Ill. Senate, Springfield, 1976-80, 97th-98th Congresses from 1st Ill. Dist., 1981-83; mayor City of Chgo., 1983-87. Vice pres. Ams. for Democratic Action; bd. dirs. Suburban So. Christian Leadership Conf.; founder, pres. Washington Youth and Community Orgn.; bd. dirs. Mid-South Mental Health Assn. Served with USAAF, 1942-46, PTO. Recipient numerous awards. Mem. Am. Vets. Assn., Cook County Bar Assn., Ill. Bar Assn., Nat. Bar Assn., NAACP, Urban League, Nu Beta Epsilon. Democrat. Home: Chicago Ill. Died Nov. 25, 1987.

WASSON, R(OBERT) GORDON, banker; b. Great Falls, Mont., Sept. 22, 1898; s. Edmund Atwill and Mary Matilda (DeVeny) W.; m. Valentina Pavlovna Guerken; children: Peter, Mary Xenia. Instr. English, Columbia Coll., 1921-22; editorial writer and polit. corr. New Haven (Conn.) Register, 1922-24; assoc. editor Current Opinion mag., 1924-25; fin. reporter N.Y. Herald Tribune, 1925-28; with Guaranty Co. of N.Y., 1928-34, Morgan Guaranty Trust Co. N.Y. (formerly J.P. Morgan & Co.), N.Y.C., 1934-63; v.p. Morgan Guaranty Trust Co. N.Y. (formerly J.P. Morgan & Co.), 1943-63. Author: The Hall Carbine Affair, A Study in Contemporary Folklore, 1941; co-author: Mushrooms Russia and History, 1957; Les Champignons hallucinogenes du Mexique, 1958. Served in Signal Corps, AEF, U.S. Army, WWI. Recipient Pulitzer Traveling Scholarship, 1920. Mem. Medieval Acad. Am. (exec. com.). Club: Century Assn. (N.Y.C.). Home: New York N.Y. Died Dec. 23, 1986.

WATERHOUSE, JAMES FRANKLIN, lawyer; b. Harriman, Tenn., Sept. 25, 1925; s. James and Billie (Robinson) W.; m. Susan Margaret Gelsthorpe, Aug. 21, 1948; children: James II, Edward F., Albert M., Richard. AB, Harvard U., 1948, LLB, 1951. Bar: Tenn. 1951. Pvt. practice Chattanooga; assoc. Miller, Martin, Hitching, Tipton, 1951-57; ptnr. Miller, Hitching, Tipton & Lenihan, 1957-67; sr. ptnr. Miller, Martin, Hitching, Tipton, Lenihan & Waterhouse, 1967-86. Pres. Chattanooga Adult Edn. Soc., 1956; pres. Chattanooga Goodwill Industries, 1958; chmn. Sch. Bd., Town of Lookout Mountain, 1962-66, commr. edn., 1966—; 1st v.p. Chattanooga Symphony Assn., 1965-66; chmn. Legis. Com. to Study Sch. Consolidation, 1967-68. Served to 1st lt., Signal Corps, AUS, 1944-46. Mem. Am. Tenn. (past bd. govs.), Chattanooga (past dir.) bar assns. Presbyterian. Clubs: Lookout Mountain Fairyland (past dir.), Lookout Mountain Golf (past dir.); Mountain City (Chattanooga); Harvard Varsity (Cambridge, Mass.). Home: Chattanooga Tenn. Died Oct. 19, 1986; buried Forest Hills Cemetery, Chattanooga.

WATERMAN, MAX L(EON), manufacturing and sales executive; b. Buxton, Maine, Nov. 1, 1890; s. Wilbur Charles and Arzella (Thomes) W.; m. Bertha Nickerson, Aug. 30, 1915; 1 son, Donald Wilbur. BS, MIT, 1913. Joined The Singer Co., N.Y.C., 1913, v.p., 1949-60, ret., 1960, dir., 1960—; vice chmn. trustees Peoples Savs. Bank. Dir. Bridgeport Hosp. Mem. University Club, Brooklawn Country Club (Bridgeport, Phi Beta Epsilon. Republican. Congregationalist. Home: Bridgeport Conn. †

WATERMAN, WILLIAM RANDALL, historian, educator; b. Providence, May 22, 1892; s. William Henry and Emily (Randall) W.; m . Ellen Colby Magoon, Aug. 22, 1922; 1 dau., Nancy Mayo. PhB, Brown U., 1915, MA, 1916; PhD, Columbia U., 1924; MA (hon.), Dartmouth U., 1930. Tchr. history St. Johnsbury (Vt.) Acad., 1916-19; univ. fellow history Columbia U., 1920-21, instr. history, summer 1921; instr. history Dartmouth U., 1921-24, asst. prof., 1924-30, prof., from 1930, chmn. dept., 1931-35; instr. history summer sessions N.Y. State Coll. for Tchrs., Albany, 1922-24. Author: Frances Wright, 1924; contbr. to Dictionary Am. Biography, 1928-37. Mem. Am. Hist. Assn., Masons, Phi Beta Kappa, Phi Kappa Psi. Home: Hanover N.H. †

WATERS, EUGENE PAUL, utility company executive; b. Olean, N.Y., July 8, 1932; s. Ray John and Gertrude (Dollard) W.; m. Sandra Ann Shay, June 27, 1959; children: Kevin, Michael, Elizabeth, William. BA, Colgate U., 1954; MBA, Cornell U., 1961. Rep. mktg. Procter & Gamble Distbg. Co., Syracuse, N.Y., 1957-60; mgr. acctg. Dewey & Almy chem. div. W.R. Grace & Co., Cambridge, Mass., 1961-63; with N.Y. State Elec. & Gas Corp., Ithaca, 1963-84, treas., 1971-84, v.p. fin., 1976-78, sr. v.p., treas., 1978-84; chmn. GAEL Assocs., 1974-76; treas. Lancaster Towers Redevel. Corp., 1971-74, NYSEG Housing Corp., 1971-74; v.p. Somerset R.R. Corp.; bd. dirs. Tompkins County Trust Co., Ithaca, N.Y. Mem. ednl. needs com. Homer (N.Y.) Sch. System, 1970-73; v.p. Homer PTA, 1972-73; mem. Homer Housing Commn., 1976; treas., trustee Phillips Free Library, 1971-79; v.p., treas., trustee Phi Kappa Psi Alumni Corp., 1967-74; mem. Coll. Devel. Found. Cortland, 1973-79, Friends of Ithaca Coll.; trustee Tompkins-Cortland Community Coll., 1978-79; bd. dirs. George Jr. Republic, Freeville, N.Y., 1976-79; mem. adv. coun. Sch. Mgmt. Clarkson Coll.; lay reader Roman Cath. ch., 1968-79. With USMCR, 1954-57. Mem. Country Club Cortland, University Club, Towers Club, Elks, Phi Kappa Psi. Republican. Home: Cortland N.Y. Died Sept. 24, 1984; St. Mary's Cemetery, Cortland, N.Y.

WATERS, EVERETT OYLER, educator, mechanical engineer; b. Cin., Jan. 29, 1890; s. William Everett and Alma Filia (Oyler) W.; m. Eunice Hope Spencer, June 14, 1924; 1 dau., Hope Spencer; m. 2d, Dorothy Gavitte, July 30, 1932; children: Stephen Gardner, Deborah Ann. AB, Yale U., 1911; PhB, Sheffield Sci. Sch., Yale U., 1912, ME, 1914. Instr. machine design Sheffield Sci.

Sch., Yale U., 1914-19, asst. prof., 1919-25, asst. prof. mech. engring., 1925-28, assoc. prof., 1928-44, prof., 1944—, Strathcona prof. mech. engring., 1949-58, emeritus Strathcona prof., 1958—. Author: (with S.J. Berard) Elements of Machine Design, 1924, (with S.J. Berard) Machine Design Problems, 1927, (with S.J. Berard and C.W. Phelps) Principles of Machine Design. 2d lt., then 1st lt. Ordnance Dept., U.S. Army, 1918019; assigned to SOS, AEF, France. Fellow Am. Soc. M.E.; mem. Yale Club (N.Y.C.), Appalachian Mountain Club, Phi Beta Kappa, Sigma Xi. Episcopalian. Home: Mount Carmel Conn. †

WATERS, HENRY HOOPER, lawyer; b. Cambridge, Md., May 4, 1891; s. Albert Everett and Mary Steele (Hooper) W.; m. Janet Sayward Levy, Dec. 1, 1922; children: Janet Sayward Waters Flagle, Elizabeth Steele Waters Roughen, John Hooper. LLB, U. Md., 1915; spl. courses, Johns Hopkins U. Bar: Md. 1915. With Standard Oil Co., Balt., 1908-16; auditor West India Oil Co., Argentina and Chile, 1916-19; practiced law and accountancy Balt., 1919-24, practiced law, from 1962; spl. counsel Balt. Transit Co., 1924-48, v.p., treas., 1948-56, dir., 1951-57; trust officer Md. Nat. Bank, 1956-61. Mem. ABA, Md. Bar Assn., Balt. Bar Assn., Merchants Club, Kappa Sigma. Episcopalian. Home: Baltimore Md. †

WATERS, JOHN KNIGHT, army officer; b. Balt., Dec. 20, 1906; s. Arnold Elzey and Helen (Knight) W.; m. Beatrice Ayer Patton, June 27, 1934 (dec. Oct. 1952); children: John Knight, George Patton; m. 2d, Anne McKinley. Student, John Hopkins U., 1925-26; BS, U.S. Mil. Acad., 1931. Commd. 2d lt. cav., U.S. Army, 1931, advanced through grades to lt. gen., 1961; assigned Ft. Myer, Va., Ft. Riley, Kans., also tactical dept., West Point; 1st Armored Regt., Ireland, 1942-43; German prisoner of war, 1943-45; aide Sec. War; assigned Command and Gen. Staff Coll., Armed Forces Staff Coll.; asst. comdt. cadets U.S. Mil. Acad., 1949-51, comdt., 1951-52; chief staff U.S. I Corps, 1952-53; dep. comdg. gen. Ft. Knox, Ky.; with 4th Armored Div., 1953-55; chief Am. Mil. Assistance Staff Yugoslavia, Belgrade, 1955-57; assigned Ft. Monroe, Va., 1957, hdqrs. Continental Army Command, 1957-60, 4th Armored Div., 1960-61, V Corps, 1961-62, then with U.S. Continental Army Command, Chgo. Decorated D.S.C., D.S.M., Silver Star with clusters, Bronze Star, Purple Heart with cluster; Comdr. Order Brit. Empire; Croix de Guerre with palm (France). Home: Potomac Md. Died Jan. 9, 1989.

WATKINS, RALPH JAMES, economist; b. San Marcos, Tex., Dec. 31, 1896; s. Calvert and Martha (Smith) W.; m. Willye Ward, June 20, 1918 (dec. July 1979); children: Calvert Ward, John William James. BBA, U. Tex., 1921, AB, 1922; postgrad., Universidad Nacional de Mexico, summer 1921; MS, Columbia U., 1924, PhD, 1927. Instr. bus. adminstrn. U. Tex., 1924-25; asst. prof. statis. rsch. Bur. Bus. Rsch. Ohio State U., 1925-27, prof. stats., statistician, 1927-28, assoc. prof., 1928-29; mem. rsch. staff Nat. Bur. Econ. Rsch., N.Y.C.., 1929-30; dir. Bur. bus. Rsch., prof. stats. U. Pitts., 1940-48; asst. adminstr. wage and hour div. Dept. Labor, 1939; econ. adviser Nat. Resources Planning Bd., Exec. Office Pres., 1939-40, asst. dir., 1940-43; chief len-lease div. civil affairs sect. Allied Force Hdqrs., Algiers, 1943-44; econ. adviser War Prodn. Bd., 1944; dir. mktg. and rsch. div. Dun & Bradstreet, Inc., 1944-48, dir. rsch., 1948-57; dir. econ. studies Brookings Instn., 1957-62; v.p. Surveys & Rsch. Corp., 1962-71, sr. assoc., 1972-74; lectr. econs. Columbia, 1947-56; Barbara Weinstock lectr. U. Calif. at Berkeley, 1951; spl. cons. sec. army, 1950-52, spl. mission to Japan and Korea on politico-mil. policy, 1952; politico-mil. adviser to Gen. Van Fleet Presdl. Mission, Japan, Korea, Taiwan, Philippines, 1954; chmn. adv. com. on statis. policy Office Mgmt. and Budget, 1956-72; dir. Social Sci. Rsch. Coun., 1955-58; dir. Kobe-Nagoya Expwy. Survey, Japanese Ministry Constrn., 1956; chmn. adv. panel for econ. and statis. studies of sci. and tech. NSF, 1961-66; dir., condr. fgn. econ. surveys in Vietnam, 1960-63, Taiwan, 1961, Mexico and Ecuador, 1963, Tunisia, 1964, Malawi, 1965; sr. mem. World Bank team with Indian Planning Commn., Calcutta, 1965-67; study adviser Sarabhai Ops. Rsch. Group, Baroda, India, 1968-71; team leader state planning program Ford Found., also sr. cons. Indian Planning Commn., New Delhi, 1969-71; project dir. farm mechanization project Republic Korea, 1971-72; economist Tippetts-Abbett-McCarthy-Stratton on Egyptian reconstrn. and devel. program, Cairo, 1975-79; guest lectr. Internat. Devel. Ctr., Japan, Tokyo, 1976. Decorated 3d class Order of Sacred Treasure (Japan). Fellow Am. States. Assn. (dir. 1951-53, pres. 1955); mem. Am. Econ. Assn., Royal Econ. Soc., Masons, Cosmos Club, Nat. Econs. Club. 1st sgt. U.S. Army, 1918-19. Home: Waldorf Md. Died Aug. 4, 1984, buried San Marcos, Tex.

WATKINS, THOMAS GRAHAM, lawyer; b. Gallatin, Tenn., May 20, 1887; s. Thomas Gibson and Jennie Lou (Holder) W.; m. Henrietta Adelaide Peter, Sept. 20, 1911; children: Thomas Graham, Hattie Jane (dec.). AB, Centre Coll., 1908, Centre Coll., 1909; LLB, Harvard U., 1912. Bar: Tenn. 1912. Mem. Watkins & Mc Call, 1952, Watkins & Crownover, 1954, Watkins & Tyne, Nashville; bd. dirs. Cumberland River Sand Co., Cumberland & Ohio Co., Craig & Shoffner Hardware Co. Mem. ABA, SAR, Internat. Assn. Ins. Counsel, Tenn., Nashville bar assns., C. of C., Masons (32 degree), Shriners, Belle Meade Country Club, Cumberland Club, Filson Club. Democrat. Methodist. Home: Nashville Tenn. †

WATSON, ERNEST CHARLES, physicist; b. Sullivan, Ill., June 18, 1892; s. Charles Grant and Alice Bell (Smith) W.; m. Elsa Jane Werner, Oct. 6, 1954. PhB, Lafayette Coll., Easton, Pa., 1914, ScD (hon.), 1958; postgrad., U. Chgo., 1914-17. Asst. in physics U. Chgo., 1914-17; asst. prof. physics Calif. Inst. Tech., 1919-20, assoc. prof., 1920-30, prof., 1930-62, emeritus, from 1962, dean faculty, 1945-60, chmn. faculty bd., chmn. div. physics, math. and astronomy, 1946-49, acting pres., 1956-57; cons. S. and S.E. Asia Program Ford Found., from 1964; sci. attache to Am. Embassy, New Delhi, 1960-62; del. to various profl. confs.; mem. Nat. Def. Rsch. Com., 1941-44, ofcl. investigator Office Sci. Rsch. and Devel. for work on arty. rockets, torpedos, atomic bomb and other ordnance devices, 1941-45. Author: Mechanics, Molecular Physics, Heat and Sound, 1937; contbr. articles to profl. jours. Chmn. library adv. bd. City of Pasadena, 1956-60. With USNR, 1917-19. Fellow Am. Phys. Soc., AAAS; mem. Am. Assn. Physics Tchrs., History of Sci. Soc., AAUP, Fgn. Policy Assn., Indian Internat. Ctr., Athenaeum Club, Phi Beta KAppa, Sigma Xi, Tau Beta Pi, Gamma Alpha. Home: Santa Barbara Calif. †

WATSON, MARTIN WALLACE, general contractor; b. Racine, Ohio, Apr. 30, 1892; s. Charles A. and Alice L. (Blackmore) W.; m. Helen Wegener, Aug. 23, 1916; children: Helen Alice (Mrs. Jack E. Lungstrum), Nancy Lou (Mrs. Robert J. Bohl). BSCE, Ohio U., 1911. Engr. Ohio River survey U.S. Army Engrs., 1911-12; civil engr. Ill. State Hwy. Dept., 1912-17; road engr. Kans. Hwy. Commn., 1917-18, state hwy. engr., 1918-23; mem. Kans. State Office Bldg. Commn., 1948-52; engr., gen. contractor highways, bridges, indsl., comml., pub. bldgs., utilities properties, drainage and flood control Tex., Colo., Nebr., Iowa, Miss.; employer del. constrn. civil engrs. and pub. works com., I.L.O., Geneva, 1953; chmn. bd. M. W. Watson Inc.; dir. First Nat. Bank Topeka, 1943-68. Projects include Cantonment Camp, Ft. Riley, Kans., bldgs. Smoky Hill Army Air Base, Salina, Kans., air field Ada, Okla., spl. depot Winter Gen. Hosp., Topeka Kans., bldgs. Stothers Field, Winfield, Kans., air field Carlsbad, N.Mex., others (all World War II). Pres. Topeka Disaster Group, 1951. Recipient Cert. Merit Ohio U., 1954. Fellow ASCE; mem. Assoc. Gen. Contractors Am. (pres. 1941, pres. KAns. chpt. builders div. 1956), Miss. Valley Assn. State Hwy. Ofcls., Topeka C. of C. (pres. 1951), Kans. State C. of C. (pres. 1950-51), U.S. C. of C. (dir. 1950-56, chmn. constrn. and civic devel. dept. 1954-56), Kans. Engring. Soc., Kans. Contractors Assn. (past pres.), Eastern Kans. Constructors' Assn. (pres. 1953-60), Cons. Constructors Coun. Am., Elks, Masons (32 deg.), Shriners, K.T., Rotary (treas. Topeka club 1964-73), Topeka Country Club, Engrs. Club. Republican. Episcopalian. Home: Topeka Kans. †

WATSON, ROBERT CLEMENT, lawyer; b. Washington, Nov. 21, 1890; s. James Angus and Mary Jane (Clement) W.; m. Sara Alice Latimer, Oct. 11, 1922; children: Robert Clement, Olive Latimer (Mrs. Calvin H. Cobb, Jr.), Alice Brown (Mrs. Avery Coonley Faulkner). BSCE, Lehigh U., 1913, LLD, 1954; LLB, George Washington U., Washington, 1917; LLD (hon.), George Washington U., 1957. Bar: D.C. 1917. Mem. Watson, Cole, Grindle & Watson, Washington; U.S. Commr. of Patents 1953-61. Mem. Am. Law Inst., ABA, Am. Patent Law Assn. (pres. 1950-51), Lawyers Club, Metroploitan Club, Univ. Club, Chevy Chase (Md.) Club, Gibson Island Club, Phi Delta Phi, Psi Upsilon. Home: Gibson Island Md. †

WATTERS, JAMES I(SAAC), chemistry and mathematics educator; b. Broadus, Mont., Apr. 4, 1908; s. James O. and Hilda C. (Erickson) W.; m. Louise G. Chambers, Aug. 28, 1938; children—Louise Emilie, Molly Marie, James Norman, Kathryn Verne. Student, U. Fla., 1926-28, U. Calif. at Berkeley, 1928-29; BS, U. Minn., 1931, PhD, 1943. Tchr. Anoka pub. schs., 1931-38; instr. Cornell U., Ithaca, N.Y., 1941-43; chief analytical chemistry on atom bomb project U. Chgo., 1943-45; assoc. prof. U. Ky., 1945-48; assoc. prof. Ohio State U., Columbus, 1948-58, prof. chemistry, math. and phys. scis., then prof. emeritus, from 1958; summer cons. U.S. AID, Punjab U., 1965, Annamalai U., 1966, Ujjain U., 1967; all India. Editor: Analytical Chemistry of Atomic Energy Project, 1951; Contbr.: chpts. to Treatise on Analytical Chemistry; also articles on polarography and spectrophotometry to tech. jours. Mem. Am. Chem. Soc., AAAS, Sigma Xi, Zeta Psi, Phi Lambda Upsilon. Lutheran. Died Jan. 20, 1989.

WATTS, AMOS HOLSTON, lawyer; b. Nashville, Ill., Nov. 24, 1896; s. William Wadsworth and Laura (Holston) W.; m. Lida Hough, 1921; 1 son, Dey Wadsworth; m. 2d, Gladys F. Brewer, Oct. 8, 1960. Bar: Ill. 1921. Practiced in Chgo. since 1921; sr. ptnr. Chapman & Cutler; lectr. Sch. Banking, U. Wis., 1947-57. Pres., dir. U. Ill. Found., 1959-62; pres. Glencoe (Ill.) Park Dist., 1934-43; mem. Ill. Commn. for Revision Park Laws for Dists. under 500,000, 1947-49. Mem. ABA, Ill. Bar Assn., Chgo. Bar Assn., Civic Fedn. Chgo., Chgo. Assn. Commerce, Ill. C. of C., Masons, University Club, Execs. Mid-Day Club, Skokie Country, Delta Phi, Phi Delta Phi. Republican. Home: Naples Fla. Died July 22, 1988; buried Glencoe (Ill.) Union Ch. Meml. Garden.

WATTS, EDWARD EVERETT, JR., lawyer; b. Springfield, Ill., Aug. 22, 1899; s. Edward Everett and Louise O. (Gros) W.; m. Isabella R. Hardy, Sept. 14, 1940; children: Elizabeth Hardy (Mrs. Nicholas P. Boileau), Edward Everett III, Isabella King. A.B., Princeton U., 1921; J.D., Columbia U., 1924. Bar: N.Y. 1925, U.S. Supreme Ct 1942. Asso. Cravath, de Gersdorff, Swaine & Wood, N.Y.C., 1924-29, Mitchell, Taylor, Capron & Marsh (and predecessor firm), 1929-38; partner firm Turk, Marsh, Kelly & Hoare (and predecessor firm), 1938-75, counsel to firm, from 1975. Trustee, chmn. exec. com. Broadway Savs. Bank, 1943-70; Pres. Travelers Aid Soc., N.Y., 1947-57, chmn. hon. bd., 1957-81; pres. Internat. Film Found., 1945-80, chmn. bd., 1980-87; dir. Legal Aid Soc. N.Y., 1938-71, officer, 1939-70, bd. chmn., 1967-70; chmn. com. corps. Commerce and Industry Assn. N.Y., 1956-71; incorporator Eye-Bank for Sight Restoration, 1945, bd., 1945-87, sec., 1947-70; trustee United Bd. Christian Higher Edn. in Asia, 1952-67, vice chmn., 1958-67, counselor, from 1974; dir. Princeton in Asia, Inc., 1938-74, N.Y.C. Mission Soc., 1961-67; co-founder, chmn. Leap Year Assemblies, N.Y.C., from 1924; trustee, mem. corp. Harvard-Yenching Inst., 1963-78; trustee Tobey Hosp., Wareham, Mass., 1971-86, v.p., 1977-79; pres. Princeton Class of 1921, 1941-51, 83-87, Columbia Law Sch. Class of 1924; mem. Princeton Grad. Council, 1941-63. Recipient Columbia U. Alumni medal, 1954, Distinguished Service award Princeton Class of 1921, 1957, Distinguished Service citation Mayor, N.Y.C., 1957. Mem. Am., N.Y.C., N.Y. State bar assns., Delta Phi. Episcopalian. (trustee, clk., sr. warden). Clubs: Century, University (council), Down Town Assn, Princeton (council), Manursing Island, Pilgrims, Church (pres. 1964-66), Mattapoisett Casino; Nassau (Princeton), Tower (Princeton); Metropolitan Opera (former officer, dir. 1932-42). Home: Mattapoisett Mass. Died Nov. 22, 1987; buried Milton, Mass.

WATTS, W(ARREN) S(MITH), business executive; b. Fishersville, Va., Sept. 29, 1887; s. William Hardin and Effie (Bishop) W.; m. Ethel Rives, Jan. 17, 1912; children: Marcia Rives Watts Saunders, Frances Balfour Watts McKee. Ed. pub. and pvt. schs., Va. and Washington, D.C.; student bus. and comml. law courses, LaSalle Extension U., 1918-19. Relief telegraph operator and sta. agt. summers 1901-07; gen. office worker So. Ry., Washington, 1907-10; rep. shippers in frieght and traffic matters, practice before ICC 1910-15; traffic mgr. Reynolds Corp. (predessecor U.S. Foil Co.), Bristol, Tenn., 1915; sec. U.S. Foil Co., Louisville, 1928, v.p., dir., 1953, ret.; various exec. positions with subs. and affiliate interests from 1928; pres., gen. mgr., dir. Eskimo Pie Corp.; cons. Reynolds Metals Co.; chmn. bd. dirs. Don Mott Assocs., Inc., Orlando, Fla. Mem. Country Club (Orlando). Mem. Evangelistic Ch. (trustee com. of Newark and vicinity). Home: Orlando Fla. †

WAUGH, GEORGE MORTON, JR., financial consultant; b. Bklyn., Oct. 1, 1891; s. George Morton and Annie (Storm) W.; m. Marjorie Vernol, Nov. 25, 1914; children: Virginia (Mrs. William A. Grier), Margaret (Mrs. Howard B. Hayward). BCS, NYU, 1913. With Borden Co., 1910, exec. v.p., bd. dirs., until 1944; bd. dirs. Scarsdale Nat. Bank & Trust Co., U.S. Plywood Corp.; bd. dirs., treas. Kensico Cemetery, Valhalla, N.Y. Chmn. Westchester County (N.Y.) Tax Commn.; gov. White Plains (N.Y.) Hosp. Mem. Masons, Union League, Scarsdale Golf Club, Shenorock Shore Club, Delta Sigma Pi. Home: Scarsdale N.Y. †

WEAKLY, FRANK ERVIN, property management executive; b. Shelbyville, Ill., Jan. 27, 1890; s. Benedict and Maria Louisa Jane (Hursh) W.; m. Lucile Lyon, Aug. 27, 1914; children: Amorita Lucile, Rhoda Frances; m. Catherine Hughes Hall, Dec. 23, 1950. Student, Ill. Wesleyan U., 1909-10; PhB, U. Chgo., 1914. Grocer's clk. Shelbyville, 1906-09; foreman Burson Knitting Co., Rockford, Ill., 1910-11; instr. local high sch. Little Rock, 1914-15; personnel dir. Montgomery Ward & Co., Chgo., 1915-21; gen. oper. mgr. Halsey Stuart & Co., Chgo., 1921-33, v.p., 1933-44; pres., bd. dirs. Washington Properties, Inc., 1944-53; chmn. bd. Washington Sheraton Corp., 1953-56; mem. adv. bd. for brs. Am. Security and Trust Co.; labor specialist Coun. Nat. Def., 1917, Emergency Fleet Corp., 1918; mgr. personnel Quartermaster Corps, U.S. Army, 1918. Author: Applied Personnel Procedure, 1923. Mem. Citizen's Adv. Com. on Pub. Works; chmn. Cherry Blossom Festival, 1953, 54, Alcoholic Beverage Control Bd., from 1958; gov. Better Bus. Bur.; bd. dirs. Met. Police Boy's Club, D.C. Bldg. Code Adv. Com. Mem. Washington Bd. Trade, Washington Real Estate Bd., Am., Washington (pres. 1946-53, bd. dirs.), Internat. hotel assns., Pres.'s Cup Regatta Assn. (bd. dirs.), Minimum Wage and Indsl. Safety Bds. (gov.), Greater Nat. Capital Exec. Com., Tau Kappa Epsilon, South Shore Country Club, Executives Club, Congl. Country Club, Carlton Club, Kiwanis , Circus Sts. and Sinners. Republican. Methodist. Home: Washington D.C. †

WEAR, JAMES SMITH, publisher; b. Beaver Meadows, Pa., Jan. 21, 1914; s. James and Mary Carter (Wear) Smith; m. Minnie M. Eichinger, Nov. 18, 1933; children—Richard C., William H., Prudence H. Wear Farrell. Student pub. schs. Advt. dir. Jersey Jour., Jersey City, 1952-55; pub. Jersey Jour., 1967-81; advt. dir. Star-Ledger, Newark, 1956-64; gen. mgr. Post-Standard, Syracuse, N.Y., 1964-67. Served to 2d lt. USAAF, 1944-46. Home: Oregon City Oreg. Died Oct. 6, 1986, buried St. John's Cemetery, Oregon City.

WEAVER, FRANK LLOYD, consulting engineer; b. Washington, July 21, 1891; s. Lloyd Everett and Mary Ellen (Ragan) W.; m. Lois Campbell Douglas, Sept. 18, 1915 (dec. Aug. 1930); children: Lois Douglas Weaver Spinks, Frank Lloyd, Charles R.; m. Elizabeth Petrie Defandorf, Nov. 7, 1931. BCE, U. Mich., 1913. Instr. civil engring. U. Okla., 1913-14; instr. Johns Hopkins U., 1915-17; cons. engr. Hubbell, Hartgering & Roth, Detroit, 1919-34; city engr. Wyandotte, Mich., 1926-28; with Fed. Power Commn., 1934-54, 55-61, chief div. river basins, 1942-54, 55-61, mem. inter-agy. subcom. benefits and costs; pvt. cons. engr. from 1961; engring. advisor Pres.'s Water Resources Policy Commn., 1950; mem. Inter-Agy. Policy Rev. Com., 1951, FPC; mem. New Eng.-N.Y. Inter=Agy. Com., 1951-54; spl. advisor on power, task force on water and power Hoover Commn., 1954-55; mem. U.S. del. Fifth Internat. Congress on Large Dams, Paris, 1955, Sixth Congress, N.Y.C, 1958, Fifth World Power Conf., Vienna, Austria, 1956; mem. Internat. Passamaquoddy Engring. Bd., 1985-61; mem. Internat. St. Croix River Engring. Bd., 1958-61. Mayor Garrett Park, Md., 1943-45; pres. Fire Bd. Kensington, Md., 1950. Capt. C.E. Am. Expeditionary Force, 1917-19. Mem. ASCE (nat. dir. 1950-52, v.p. 1955-56, bd. dirs. engrs. joint council 1959-63), Am. Geophys. Union, Cosmos Club (Washington), Sigma Xi, Tau Beta Pi. Episcopalian. Home: Garrett Park Md. †

WEAVER, ROBERT AUGUSTUS, manufacturing executive; b. Bradford, Pa., Aug. 15, 1890; s. Joseph Curtis and Nancy Bell (Thorne) W.; m. May Tuthill, June 23, 1914 (dec.); children: Charlotte, Robert A., Peter; m. 2d, Mrs. Evelyn Mannion, Nov. 17, 1959. BS, Kenyon Coll., 1912, LLD, 1938; ScD, Alfred U., Alfred, N.Y., 1941. Athletic dir. De Veaux Coll., Niagara Falls, N.Y., 1912-13; asst. advt. mgr. Eclipse Stove Co., Mansfield, Ohio, 1913-15; advt. mgr. Favorite Stove Co., Piqua, Ohio, 1915-17; sales mgr. Porcelain Enamel & Mfg. Co., Balt., 1917-19; bd. dirs. Ferro Enamels (Can.) Ltd., Australia, Eng., Holland; bd. dirs. Ferro Corp., U.S. Slicing Machine Co.; ex-pres. Porcelain Enamel Inst.. Ex-pres. Citizens' League of Cleve., Ohio Civil Svc. Counc., Cleve. Play House.; bd. dirs. Cleve. Art Sch. Mem. Masons, Clifton Club, Union Club, Mid-day Club, Fifty Club (Cleve.); Question Club (Detroit), India House (N.Y.); Seigniory Club (Can.), Delta Tau Delta (ex-pres. No. Div.). Home: Lakewood Ohio. †

WEBB, AILEEN OSBORN, publishing company executive; b. Garrison, N.Y., June 25, 1892; d. William Church and Alice (Dodge) Osborn; m. Vanderbilt Webb, Sept. 11, 1912 (dec. June 1956); children: Derick V., William Osborn, Barbara Webb Rockwell, Richard H. Grad., Miss Chapins Sch., N.Y.C., 1909. Founder, pres., dir. Am. House, from 1940; founder, pres. Am. Craftsmen's Coun., 1943, Mus. Contemporary Crafts, from 1956. Mem. Putnam County and N.Y. State Dem. coms., 1928-34. Recipient founder award Rochester Inst. Tech., 1956, Elsie de Wolf award Am. Inst. Decorators, 1956, Friedman medal AIA, 1957. Mem. Colony Club. Home: New York N.Y. †

WEBB, C(HAUNCEY) EARL, engineer; b. Mason, Mich., May 25, 1889; s. George M. and Elinorah (Shattuck) W.; m. Ernestine Earle, Oct. 7, 1914; children: Elizabeth Webb Fish, Margaret Webb Bates. BS, Mich. State Coll., 1912, D Engring (hon.), 1940. Registered profl. engr. Ind., Ill., Mich., Mo. Jr. engr. USIS, Fort Shaw, Mont., 1912-14; shopman Am. Bridge Co., Pitts., 1914-15, draftsman, 1915-22, designer, 1922-35, div. engr., 1935-46, engr., 1946-55, cons. engr. steel structures, from 1955. Mem. Mich. N.G., 1908-11. Recipient Disting. Service award Mich. State Coll. Alumni, 1947. Mem. ASCE, Am. Welding Soc., Western Soc. Engrs. (pres. 1943), Am. Assn. Engrs., Am. Ry. Engrs. Assn., Am. Mil. Engrs., Union League Club, Engrs. Club (Chgo.), Country Club of Lansing (Ill.), Tau Beta Pi, Chi Epsilon. †

WEBB, HAROLD VERNON, educational consultant; b. Lincoln, Kans., Aug. 5, 1919; s. Bertie Lee and Clarissa (Davis) W.; m. Beulah Lucille Haas, May 24, 1942; children: David Vernon, Jon Douglas, Jeffrey Marshall. BS in Edn., Kans. State Tchrs. Coll., 1941, MS in Edn., 1949; PhD in Edn., U. Wyo., 1955. Cert. assn. exec. Supt. schs. Quincy, Kans., 1946-47, Bucklin, Kans., 1950-53; prin. Elmdale (Kans.) High Sch., 1947-50; instr. U. Wyo., 1953-55, dir. div. sch. services, 1955-58; lectr. Northwestern U., 1958-61; assoc. exec. dir. Nat. Sch. Bds. Assn., Washington, 1958-60, exec. dir., 1961-77; pres. Harold Webb Assocs., ednl. cons. firm, from 1977. Mem. nat. adv. bd. ERIC Clearinghouse on Ednl. Mgmt. 1st lt. AUS, 1941-46. Mem. NEA, Am. Assn. Sch. Adminstrs., Am. Soc. Assn. Execs., Edn. Commn. States (commr.), Quill, Cosmos Club, Phi Delta Kappa, Kappa Delta Pi, Pi Gamma Mu. Congregationalist. Home: Wilmette Ill. Died Oct. 1987; buried 1st Congl. Ch. Meml Garden, Wilmette.

WEBB, LELAND D(OTSON), aircraft trade association executive; b. Chgo., Apr. 7, 1891; s. Charles E. and May (Dotson) W.; m. Helen Kaye, Sept. 1, 1934. BS, U.S. Naval Acad. Post Grad. Sch., 1926; MS, MIT, 1927. Enlisted USN, 1908, commd. ensign, 1917, advanced through grades to capt., 1942; air group comdr. U.S.S. Lexington, 1933-35; dir. aviation maintenance Bur. Aeros., Navy Dept., 1935-37, gen. rep. Western dist., 1943-44, dir. prodn. div., 1944-46; Navy mem. Aircraft Scheduling Unit, from 1942, ret., 1947; v.p. Western regional mgr. Aircraft Industries Assn., L.A., from 1947. Decorated Legion of Merit; recipient six campaign medals. Mem. Inst. Aero. Scis., Ret. Officers Assn. Home: Los Angeles Calif. †

WEBB, ROBERT WALLACE, geology educator; b. L.A., Nov. 2, 1909; s. Robert Remme and Sharlie Jeannette (Ward) W.; m. Evelyn Elaine Gourley, June 28, 1933; children: Robert Ian Arthur, Leland Frederick, Donald Gourley. AB, UCLA, 1931; postgrad., U. Wash., 1931, U. So. Calif., 1931-32; MS, Calif. Inst. Tech., 1932, PhD, 1937. Mem. faculty UCLA, 1932-48; mem. faculty U. Calif., Santa Barbara, from 1948, prof. geology, from 1948; chmn. dept. phys. sci. U. Calif., 1953-59; dir. Ford Found. Exptl. Program Instrs. for Colls., 1960-63; exec. sec. div. geology and geography NRC, 1953; bd. dirs. Am. Geol. Inst., 1953. Author: (with Joseph Murdoch) Minerals of California, 1948, 1966, (with Robert M. Norris) Geology of California, 1977; author bulls. Calif. Div. Mines and Geology; contbr. articles to profl. jours. Coordinator vets. affairs univs. in Calif., 1947-52. Fellow Geol. Soc. Am., Mineral Soc. Am., Meteoritical Soc. (sec. 1937-41); mem. Nat. Assn. Geology Tchrs. (Neil Miner award 1973), Far Western sect. Nat. Assn. Geology Tchrs. (pres. 1959, 72, Robert Wallace Webb award 1973). Home: Santa Barbara Calif. Died May 4, 1984; cremated.

WEBBER, HUGH E., physicist; b. Ludlow, Ill., July 11, 1914; s. Hugh E. and Louise (Armstrong) W.; m. Genevieve Downes, Aug. 4, 1940 (div. 1964); children: Winona Louise, Beverly Jean, Janet Kathleen, Hugh E., Douglas Elliott; m. Jeannine Doran, Nov. 27, 1964; children: Katherine, Nancy. B.A., Ohio State U., 1937; postgrad., Case Inst. Tech., 1941, Bklyn. Poly, Inst., 1943. Biophysicist Western Res. Med. Sch., 1938-41; with Sperry Gyroscope Co., Great Neck, N.Y., 1941-58; chief engr. microwave electronics div. Sperry Gyroscope Co., 1956-58; mgr. ground systems Martin Co., Orlando, Fla., 1958-60; dir. engring. support Martin Co., 1960-61, dir. advanced tech., 1961-62, dir. research and devel., 1962-64; corp. dir. research techniques Sanders Assos., Inc., Nashua, N.H., 1964-66; mgr. new products div. EIMAC div. Varian Assos., Inc., San Carlos, Calif., 1967-68; gen. mgr. Gordon L. Ness Assos., Palo Alto, Calif., 1968-88; exec. v.p. Ness Industries, Inc., Palo Alto, Calif., 1968-71, Pacific Assemblers Co., Ltd.; pres. Consumer Tech. Corp., Webber Assos.; chmn. bd., pres. Allex Corp., 1972-88; dir. Computer Power Systems, Leaming Industries, NCA, Inc., Arno Assos., Inc.; nat. vice-chmn. profl. Group Aerospace & Electronics Systems, 1965-88; gen. chmn. AESCON, 1967-88; mem. Pentagon Guided Missile Equipment Research and Devel. Bd., 1949-53; chmn. Met. Profl. Group Engring. Mgmt., 1957-58. Author: (with others) Microwave Theory and Techniques Handbook, 1944. Fellow IEEE (nat. mem., nat. chmn. group space, electronics and telemetry, vice chmn. group aerospace and electronic systems); fellow AIAA; mem. Am. Ordnance Assn. (cons. to adv. panel electronics com.). Methodist (bd.). Died June 22, 1988; cremated.

WEBSTER, DAVID LOCKE, physicist; b. Boston, Nov. 6, 1888; s. Andrew Gerrish and Lizzie Florence (Briggs) W.; m. Anna Cutler Woodmanr, June 12, 1912; children: Nancy Webster Felsovanyi, Helen Webster Feeley, David Locke, Cutler; m. 2d, Olive Durbin Ross, Sept. 18, 1951. AB, Harvard U., 1910, PhD, 1913. Instr. in math. Harvard U., 1909-12, asst. in physics, 1911-14, instr., 1915-17; asst. prof. physics U. Mich., 1917, MIT, 1919-20; prof. physics Stanford U., 1920-54, prof. emeritus, 1954—, exec. head of dept., 1920-42; cons. Hawaii Inst. Geophys., 1961—, Ames Rsch. Ctr., Calif., Moffet Field, 1962—; coordinator civilian pilot tng., Stanford U., 1939-41. Author: (with I.W. Farwell and E.R. Drew) General Physics for Colleges, 1923, (with Jack R. Cram and Daniel J. Brimm Jr.) Civil Pilot Training Manual, 1941, Flight Instructor's Manual, 1941; mem. bd. editors Rev. of Modern Physics, 1929-48, Am. Physics Teacher, 1933-35; contbr article to Ency. Britannica. Head physicist Signal Svc. at large, U.S. Army, 1942l head physicist Ordnance Dept. at large, 1942-43; chief physicist, 1943; specialized in study of the atom; commd. lt. Air Svc., U.S. Army, Nov. 9, 1917; capt. Oct. 25, 1918; pilot C.C, ranking as capt. ASSRC, 1919-24. Mem. Nat. Acad. Scis., AAAS (v.p. and chmn. sect B. 1932), Am. Philos. Soc., Am. Physical Soc., Am. Assn. Physics Teachers (v.p. 1933-34, pres. 1935-36), Am. Acad. Arts and Scis., Phi Beta Kappa.. Home: Palo Alto Calif. †

WEBSTER, HARVEY CURTIS, journalist; b. Chgo., Nov. 6, 1906; s. Ira Gilbert and Beatrice Dunham (Curtis) W.; m. Lucille Audine Jones, Apr. 12, 1932 (dec. Mar. 1980); m. Joan Hildebrandt Miles, Jan. 4, 1982. AB, Oberlin Coll., 1927, AM, 1929; PhD, U. Mich., 1935. Teaching fellow U. Mich., Ann Arbor, 1929-35; instr. Colo. State Coll., Ft. Collins, 1935-36; from asst. prof. to prof. English U. Louisville, 1936-76, chmn. dept. English, 1967-68, prof. emeritus, 1976-88. Author: On a Darkling Plain, 1947, After the Trauma, 1970; Selected Poems of Hortence Flexner, 1975; foreward Graham Breene: A Descriptive Catalog, 1979; lit. journalist New Leader, New Republic, Poetry, Contemporary Criticism, Austin, Tex.from 1976; also Louisville Courier-Jour. Chmn. West End Community Council, Louisville, 1966-67, Ky. Dems. for Adlai Stevenson, 1960. Recipient awards Yaddo Writers Colony, Saratoga Springs, N.Y., 1947, 54, 64, 65; Fulbright prof. U. Durham, Eng., 1950-51, U. Leeds, Eng., 1962-63. Mem. AAUP (pres. Louisville chpt. 1949-50), Am. Fedn. Tchrs. (pres. Louisville chpt. 1944-45, 49-50), NAACP, MLA, Modern Humanities Research Assn., Urban League. Mem. Soc. Friends. Home and Office: 245 W Lucero Las Cruces NM 88005 Died Mar. 18, 1988. †

WEDEL, CYNTHIA CLARK, civic worker; b. Dearborn, Mich., Aug. 26, 1908; d. Arthur Pierson and Elizabeth (Haigh) Clark; m. Theodore O. Wedel, May 4, 1939 (dec. July 1970). B.A., Northwestern U., 1929, M.A., 1930; Ph.D. in Psychology, George Washington U., 1957; L.H.D., Western Coll. Women, 1958, Elmhurst Coll., 1970, Moravian Coll., 1971, Fordham U., 1971, Smith Coll., 1972, Miami U., 1976, Va. Theol. Sem., 1979, Coe Coll., 1980; D.D., Gen. Theol. Sem., 1976, Bridgewater Coll., 1976. Profl. ch. work Episcopal Ch., 1931-39; tchr. Nat. Cathedral Sch., 1939-48; nat. exec. bd. Woman's Aux., Episcopal Ch., 1946-52; mem. nat. council Episcopal Ch., 1955-62; asst. gen. sec. Nat. Council Chs., 1962-65, asso. gen. sec., 1965-69; asso. dir. Center for a Vol. Soc., 1969-74; lectr. Am. U., 1958-60. Author: Citizenship, Our Christian Concern, 1952, The Glorious Liberty, 1958, Employed Women and the Church, 1959, (with Janet Tulloch) Happy Issue, 1962, Faith or Fear and Future Shock, 1974, also articles in mags. Nat. chmn. vols. ARC, 1973-79; nat. cons. Blood Services, 1979-86; nat. bd. Girl Scouts, U.S.A., 1960-66; mem. President's Commn. on Status of Women, 1961-63, Citizen's Adv. Council on Status of Women, 1963-68; pres. World Council of Chs., 1975-83. Mem. United Ch. Women (nat. pres. 1955-58), Nat. Council Chs. (v.p. 1957-60, pres. 1969-72), Am. Psychol. Assn., Nat. Urban Coalition (exec. com., dir. ind. sector 1980-86), Common Cause, Phi Beta Kappa, Kappa Delta. Episcopalian. Home: Alexandria Va. Died Aug. 27, 1986.

WEICHLEIN, WILLIAM JESSET, musicology educator; b. Springfield, Mo., May 9, 1917; s. Frank Howard and Lily Ann (Pick) W.; m. Helen Caroline Begley, Sept. 14, 1940; children: Paul I., Frank E. Mus.B., U. Mich., 1949, Mus.M., 1950, Ph.D., 1956. Mem. faculty Sch. Music, U. Mich., 1952-82, prof. music history and musicology, 1967-82, prof. emeritus, 1982-88; exec. sec. Music Library Assn., 1965-75, 77-81. Author: An Alphabetical Index to the Solo Songs of Robert Schumann, 1966, A Check-list of American Music Periodicals, 1850-1900, 1970; editor: Pi Kappa Lambda Studies in American Music, 1965-76. Served with USAAF, 1943-46. Mem. Am. Musciol. Soc., Music Library Assn. (pres. 1964-65), Pi Kappa Lambda (pres. 1970-76). Home: Ann Arbor Mich. Died June 3, 1988, cremated.

WEIDENAAR, REYNOLD HENRY, artist-etcher; b. Grand Rapids, Mich., Nov. 17, 1915; s. Dirk and Effie (Kuiper) W.; m. Ilse Eerdmans, June 6, 1944; children: Reynold Jr., Carla, Paula. Student, Kendall Sch. Design, Grand Rapids, 1935-36, Kansas City Art Inst., 1938-40. Instr. Kendall Sch. Design, Grand Rapids, 1956-85. Regular exhibitor NAD, Library of Congress, Detroit Inst. Art, Pa. Acad. Fine Arts, San Francisco Art Mus., Butler Inst., De-Young Meml. Mus.; exhibitor Met. Mus., 1942, Denver Art Mus.; one-man shows included Nelson Gallery, Kansas City, Arts Club, Washington, Joslyn Meml., Norton Gallery, Fla., 1946, Brooks Meml., Delgado Mus., Norfolk Mus., 1947, Hamline Galleries, 1948; represented in permanent collections Library of Congress, Brooks Meml., Detroit Inst. Arts, Nelson Gallery, Hackley Gallery, Honolulu Acad. Fine Arts, Phila Mus., Norfolk Mus., Boston Mus. Fine Arts, Conn. Acad., Wadsworth Atheneum, Nat. Gallery, South Wales, Liverpool (Eng.) Pub. Library, Carnegie Inst.; author, artist: Our Changing Landscape, 1970; (with Anne Zeller) A Sketchbook of Michingan, 1980; active in mezzotinting, etching, watercolor, oils, fresco. Recipient Scholastic mag. awards, 1938, Vander Slice scholar, 1939, Hal H. Smith prize Detroit Inst., 1942, Kate W. Arms prize Soc. Am. Etchers, 1942, John Taylor Arms prize, 1950, Guggenheim award, 1944, John Taylor Arms Meml. award NAD, 1954, 64, Century Found. award George W. Smith Art Mus., 1956, Purchase prize Gilcrease Inst., 1958, 1st prize graphics M.H. De Young Mus., 1959, Spl. award Art League L.I., 1959, Bixby award Mich. Fine Arts Ann. Exhbn., 1964; Tiffany scholar, 1948. Fellow Soc. Western Artists (1st prize graphics); mem. Am. Watercolor Soc., Soc. Am. Graphic Artists, Mich. Acad. Sci., Arts and Letters, Am. Artists Profl. League (Gold medal 1958), Audubon Artists, Allied Artists Am. (Rothschild prize), Art League L.I., Watercolor

Soc. Ala., Knickerbocker Artists, Silvermine Guild Artists., Print Club, Water Color Club, Arts Club, Torch Club. Home: Grand Rapids Mich. Died April 23, 1985; buried Grand Rapids, Mich.

WEIGAND, HERMANN JOHN, German literature educator; b. Phila., Nov. 17, 1892; s. Herman and Ottilie (Rumpff) W.; m. Frances Rhoades, Feb. 2, 1916; 1 dau., Erika (dec.). Student, Wagner Coll., Rochester, N.Y., 1906-11; AB, U. Mich., 1913, PhD, 1916; AM (hon.), Yale U., 1929. Teaching asst. German U. Mich., 1913-14, instr. German, 1914-18; office corr. Curtis Pub. Co., 1918-19; instr. German , U. Pa., 1919-22, asst. prof., 1922-28, prof., 1928-29; prof. German, Yale U., from 1929, then Sterling prof. Germanic lit., dir. grad. studies in Germanics, from 1938; vis. prof. U. Calif. at Berkeley, 1947, 55, Harvard U., 1952. Author: The Modern Ibsen, 1925, Thomas Mann's Novel Der Zauberberg, 1933, A Close-Up of the German Peasants' War, 1942, Goethe: Wisdom and Experience, 1949; contbr. numerous articles to mags., jours., chpts. in books. Recipient Goethe medal, Munich Goethe Inst., 1956; John Simon Guggenheim fellow, spring 1956. Mem. Modern Language Assn. (editorial com. 1937-42), Phi Beta Kappa. Home: Bethany Conn. †

WEIL, MORRIS, bond broker; b. Alexandria, Va., Mar. 31, 1891; s. Lehman and Sara (Haas) W.; m. Charlotte P. Ullman, Oct. 15, 1927; children: James L., Pauline C. Student pub. schs., N.Y. Mem. exec. dept. Equitable Life Assurance Soc., 1912-18; bond broker Asiel & Co., from 1919, spl. ptnr., from 1951. Contbr. articles to profl. jours. Mem. N.Y. Security Analysts, Ethical Culture Soc. N.Y. Home: New York N.Y. †

WEIMAR, KARL SIEGFRIED, language educator; b. Phila., Dec. 1, 1916; s. George John and Florence (Dash) W.; m. Florence Wasiliewska, Feb. 26, 1943; children: Eric T., Stephanie A., Gregory G. AB, U. Pa., 1937, AM, 1938, PhD, 1944. Real estate salesman 1940-46; instr. German U. Del., 1940, U. Ill., 1942-43, Temple U., 1945; mem. faculty Brown U., from 1946, prof. German, from 1966, chmn. dept., 1967-73; editor series of coll. texts for Prentice-Hall, Inc., 1963-77. Author: Concept of Love in the Works of H. Stehr, 1945, German Language and Literature, 1974, Views and Reviews of Modern German Literature, 1975; also articles, translations, textbooks. Mem. N. Kingstown (R.I.) Sch. Com., 1954-60; chmn. Warwick (R.I.) Sch. Com., 1962-66; asst. scoutmaster dist. commnr., chmn. local Boy Scouts Am., 1950-70. Mem. Am. Assn. Tchrs. German (nat. high sch. contest dir. 1962-65), Academy Players, Phi Beta Kappa (chpt. sec. from 1977), Theta Xi, Delta Phi Alpha. Episcopalian (vestryman). Home: Warwick R.I. Died Feb. 11, 1982; buried Swan Point.

WEIMER, ARTHUR MARTIN, economist; b. Rock City, Ill., May 19, 1909; s. Conrad Henry and Anna Louise (Beckmeier) W. A.B., Beloit (Wis.) Coll., 1929, LL.D., 1953; M.A., U. Chgo., 1931, Ph.D., 1934; LL.D., Am. Grad. Sch. Internat. Mgmt., 1975, Ind. U., 1982. Instr. econs. Alma (Mich.) Coll., 1931-33, asst. prof., 1933-34; field research supr. FHA, 1934-35, housing economist, 1936-37; prof., head dept. econs. and social sci. Ga. Sch. Tech., Atlanta, 1935-37; prof. real estate and land econs. Ind. U., 1937-79; dean Ind. U. (Sch. Bus.), 1939-63, spl. asst. to pres. univ., 1963-79; exec. v.p. Am. Assn. Collegiate Schs. Bus., 1967-71; cons. economist U.S. League Savs. Assns., 1948-87; mem. U.S. del. UN Conf. Exploration and Peaceful Uses of Outer Space, Vienna, 1968; pres. Weimer Bus. Adv. Service, Inc., 1953-87. Author: (with John J. Rowland) When You Buy or Build a Home, 1937, Principles of Real Estate, (with Jeffrey Fisher and George F. Bloom), 8th edit.), 1982, Introduction to Business: A Management Approach, (with David Bowen, John Long), 5th edit.), 1974. Bd. dirs. Homer Hoyt Inst. Served to maj. AUS, 1942-45. Mem. Am. Econs. Assn., Am. Fin. Assn., Am. Real Estate and Urban Econs. Assn., Am. Inst. Real Estate Appraisers, Am. Soc. Real Estate Counselors, Phi Beta Kappa, Beta Gamma Sigma, Delta Sigma Rho, Tau Kappa Epsilon. Clubs: Faculty (Bloomington), Quail Ridge Country (Bloomington), Tavern (Chgo.), Cosmos (Washington), Columbia Country (Chevy Chase, Md.), Indpls. Athletic. Home: Bloomington Ind. Died Apr. 6, 1987.

WEINBERG, ARTHUR, journalist; b. Chgo., Dec. 8, 1915; s. Abraham Morris and Anna (Avedon) W.; m. Lila Shaffer, Jan. 25, 1953; children: Hedy M. Weinberg Cornfield, Anita M. Weinberg Miller, Wendy C. Weinberg Rothman. AA, YMCA Coll., Chgo., 1935; diploma journalism, Northwestern U., 1938, PhB, 1941. With Hart Schaffner & Marx, Chgo., 1935-39; researcher Ill. Writers Project, Chgo., 1939-41; tech. writer Consol. Aircraft Corp., San Diego, 1941-45; editor Ft. Lewis (Wash.) Flame, 1946; reporter Fairchild Publs., Chgo., 1947-81; Midwest bureau chief HFD, 1977-81; Midwest editor Mart Mag., 1981-83; book reviewer Chgo. Daily News, 1962-76, Chgo. Sunday Tribune, 1976-89, Women's Wear Daily, The Progressive, Los Angeles Times; faculty Sch. for New Learning, tchr. social history, DePaul U., Chgo., from 1976. Freelance writer lectr. downtown coll. U. Chgo., 1957; moderator: radio discussion program Sound-Off, Sta. WXFM, Chgo., 1961; editor: Attorney for the Damned, 1957 (re-issue 1989), (with wife) The Muckrakers, 1961 (selected for White House library 1963), Verdicts out of Court, 1963, Instead of Violence, 1963, Passport to Utopia, 1968, Some Dissenting Voices, 1970, Clarence Darrow: Sentimental Rebel, 1980 (honors Friends of Lit. and Soc. Midland Authors); contbr. book revs. to nat. newspapers, 1980. Organizer nat. Clarence Darrow Centennial Celebration, 1957, exec. chmn., 1957; chmn. Clarence Darrow Commemorative Com., 1958—; v.p. Clarence Darrow Community Center, Chgo., 1962-64; bd. dirs. Adult Edn. Council Greater Chgo., 1959-71, chmn. letters and drama assembly, 1964-66. Recipient Social Justice award Darrow Community Ctr., 1980; Lloyd Lewis fellow in Am. history Newberry Library, Chgo., 1989. Mem. Soc. Midland Authors (pres. 1967-69, ann. award for disting. body work 1987), Friends of Lit., Chgo. Found. Lit., ACLU, Am. Jewish Congress, Sigma Delta Chi. Clubs: Press, Headline (dir. 1966-70), Yivo. Home: Chicago Ill. Died Dec. 28, 1989.

WEINBERG, CHESTER, fashion designer; b. N.Y.C., Sept. 23, 1930; s. Irving and Ida W. Student, Parsons Sch. Design, NYU, 1953. Ptnr. Chester Weinberg Ltd., 1966-74; freelance dress designer from 1974; lectr., guest critic Art Inst. Chgo.; bd. overseers Parsons Sch. Design. Designer Leonard Arkin, 1951-54, Patullo-Jo Copeland, 1954-56, Herbert Sondheim, 1956-62, Teal Traina, 1962-66, sportswear Jones Apparel Group, 1979-83, cashmere sweaters Ballantyne, Scotland; created costumes for ballet As Time Goes By, 1974. Recipient Coty award, 1970, Designer award from retail stores. Home: New York N.Y. Died Apr. 24, 1985.

WEINBERG, MAX HESS, lawyer; b. Chgo., Sept. 9, 1912; s. Louis and Dora (Hess) W.; m. Louise Popper, Mar. 23, 1939; children: Charles, Mary, Amy. AB summa cum laude, U. Mich., 1933; LLB, Harvard U., 1936. Bar: Ill. 1936. Sr. ptnr. Fischel and Kahn, Chgo., 1937-86; dir. Sta-Rite Industries Inc. With AUS, 1943-45. Mem. ABA, Ill. Bar Assn., Chgo. Bar Assn., John Howard Assn. (pres. 1975-76), Northmoor Country and Standard clubs. Home: Glencoe Ill. Died May 11, 1986.

WEINBERGER, ADOLPH, retail druggist; b. 1891, Hungary, Jan. 5; came to U.S., 1905; naturalized, 1914.; s. Nathan and Celia (Hocheiser) W.; m. Minnie Jacobs, Sept. 10, 1916 (dec. Dec. 1964); children: Ruth Weinberger Herman, Elaine Weinberger Berwitt, Carl, Jerome. Grad., Pharmacy Sch. Western Res. U., 1912; PharmD, Ohio No. U., 1958. Druggist Cleve., 1912-28; pres. Gray Drug Stores Inc., drug chain, Cleve., 1928-55, chmn. bd. and exec. com., from 1955. Mem. Ohio Bd. Pharmacy, 1946-50, pres. bd. 1950. Recipient citation for disting. svc. Joint Def. Appeal, Am. Jewish Com. B'nai B'rith, 1953. Mem. Nat. Assn. Chain Drug Stores (dir. from 1951, pres. 1957-59), Masons, Oakwood Country Club (Cleve.). Home: Shaker Heights Ohio. †

WEINER, EGON, sculptor, educator; b. Vienna, Austria, July 24, 1906; s. Moritz and Elsa (Fischer) W.; student Sch. Arts and Crafts, also Acad. Fine Arts (Vienna); m. Margaret Bass, Nov. 19, 1939; children—Peter, Andrew. Came to U.S., 1938, naturalized, 1944. Prof. sculpture and life drawing Art Inst. Chgo., 1945-71, prof. emeritus, 1971-87; vis. prof. art Augustana Coll., 1956-71; demonstration lectr. dept. edn. Mus. of Art Inst. Chgo., 1984; exhibited one-man shows Art Inst. Chgo., Renaissance Soc. U. Chgo., Chgo. Public Library, Ill. Inst. Tech., U. Ill., Evanston Art Center, Augustana Coll., Kunstneres Hus, Oslo, 1973, 75, 76, Am. Embassy, Oslo, 1974, 75, Am. Center, Stockholm, 1974, Hamburg, Germany, 1977, Dravemü nde, W. Ger., 1979, Lubeck, W. Ger.; others; group exhibits Art Inst. Chgo., Pa. Acad. Fine Arts, Oakland Art Gallery, Syracuse Mus. Art, Portland (Oreg.) Art Mus., Assoc. Am. Artists Gallery, Chgo., Met. Mus. Art, Galtung Gallery, Oslo, 1981-82, retrospective exhbn. Willoughby Tower Gallery, Chgo., 1983, others; represented permanent collections Syracuse Mus. Fine Arts, Augusburg Coll., Mpls., Augustana Coll., Vatican, pvt. collections; works include Monument of Brotherhood, Chgo., Figure of Christ, Luth. Ch., U. Chgo., Prodigal Son at Salem Ch., Chgo., Monument of St. Paul, Luth. Ch. in Mt. Prospect, Ill., portrait bust Otto Behnke, Midway Airport, Chgo., Senator William Benton for Ency. Brit., Dr. Eric Oldberg for Ill. Research Hosp., Willy Brandt for Harvard U., 1972, Ernest Hemingway for Oak Park (Ill.) Library, 1974; monument for Fire Acad. in Chgo., 1961 (AIA Honor award, 1962), Burning Bush of Knowledge, Gary (Ind.) Library, 1966; bronze figure Am. Ch., Oslo, Norway, 1967, Polyphony, St. Joseph Hosp., Chgo., 1972, portrait bust of Henry Kissinger, 1977, portrait head of dau. of Am. ambassador to Norway, 1977, head bust former minister of labor Charles Gibson, 1981, Bronze bust of Frank Lloyd Wright, Austin Garden Entrance, Oak Park, 1982, others; portrait bust of Frank Lloyd Wright, 1950, presented to Oak Park during Bicentennial, 1976; lectr. modern art in Am. Recipient Grand Prix, Paris, 1925; Blumfeld award, Vienna, 1932-34; Municipal Art League prize, 1948, 69; Logan prize Art Inst. Chgo.; Syracuse Mus. Fine Arts prize, 1949; silver and bronze medal Oakland Art Gallery, 1945, 51; honor award Fine Arts, Vienna, 1955; AIA and Brotherhood award in art Roosevelt U., 1956; ann. award for design in hardwood, 1955, 56, 59; Austrian Cross of Honor for Science and Art, 1st Class, 1977. Hon. fellow Am.-Scandinavian Found.; life fellow Internat. Soc. Arts and Letters, Zurich, Switzerland, Mem. Municipal Art League (dir., Gold medal award 1969), Am. Soc. Ch. Architecture, Nat. Soc. Arts and Letters (adv. council Chgo. 1968-70). Author: Art and Human Emotions, 1975. Home: Evanston, Ill. Died July 29, 1987; buried Augustana Luth. Ch., Chgo.

WEINERT, HILDA B., political worker; b. Tex., Apr. 19, 1889; m. H.H. Weinert, June 1912; 1 dau., Jane Weinert Blumberg. LLB (hon.), Wartburg Coll., 1953. Trustee Tex. Lutheran Coll. for 26 yrs, chmn. for 12 yrs.; mem. Nat. Dem. Com., mem. of exec. bd.; bd. dirs. Gonzales Warm Springs Found. for Crippled Childre; me., officer polit. and civic orgns; del. Mid-Century White House Conf. Named Outstanding Dem. Woman in Tex., 1960. m. Tex. Mid-Continent Oil and Gas Assn. (dir.), Federated Women's Club. Home: Seguin Tex. †

WEINFELD, EDWARD, judge; b. N.Y.C., May 14, 1901; s. Abraham and Fanny (Singer) W.; m. Lillian Stoll, Dec. 22, 1929; children: Ann, Fern. LL.B., NYU, 1921, LL.M., 1922. Bar: N.Y. 1923. Judge U.S. Dist. Ct. So. Dist. N.Y., 1950-88; commr. housing N.Y. State, 1939-42; chief counsel N.Y. State Legis. Com. investigating bondholders coms., 1935; del. N.Y. State Constl. Conv., 1938; pres. Nat. Assn. Housing Ofcls., 1941-42, Nat. Housing Conf., 1948-50; v.p., dir. Citizens Housing and Planning Council N.Y., 1945-50; exec. com. Citizens Union City N.Y., 1943-50; dir. War Housing N.Y. State War Council, 1940-42; mem. N.Y. State Post War Pub. Works Planning Commn., 1940-42. Chmn. bd. dirs. Citizens' Com. Children N.Y. City, 1950. Mem. ABA, N.Y. State Bar Assn., Am. Judicature Soc., Bar Assn. City N.Y., Phi Sigma Delta. Home: New York City N.Y. Died Jan. 17, 1988; buried Mt. Hebron Cemetery, N.Y.C.

WEINTRAUB, WIKTOR, educator, writer; b. Zawiercie, Poland, Apr. 10, 1908; came to U.S., 1950; naturalized, 1955; s. Maurycy and Rebeka Eugenia (Dobrzynski) W.; m. Anna Tennenbaum, June 29, 1934 (dec. Mar. 1967); m. 2d, Maria Evelina Zoltowska, June 6, 1974. MA, Cracow U., 1929, PhD, 1930; studies in Polish lit. history and comparative lit., from 1929. Lit. critic in Warsaw 1934-37; French govt. scholar in Paris, 1937-39; press officer Polish embassy, Moscow and Kuibyshev, 1941-42; mem. staff Polish Ministry Information, London, 1945; vis. lectr. Harvard, 1950-54, assoc. prof. Slavic langs. and lit., 1954-59, prof., from 1959, Alfred Jurzykowski prof. Polish lang. and lit., 1971-78, also mem. com. Ukrainian studies. Author: The Style of Jan Kochanowski (in Polish), 1932, The Poetry of Adam Mickiewicz, 1954, Literature as Prophecy, 1959, Prophecy and Professorship: Mickiewicz, Michelet Quintet (in Polish), 1975, The Poetry of Jan Kochanowski (in Polish), 1977, The Poet and the Prophet, 1982; editor mag. W Drodze, Jerusalem, 1943-45; editor Harvard Slavic Studies, from 1953; co-editor collective vol. Orbis scriptus, 1966; contbr. over 400 books, articles and essays in Polish and English. Mem. Am. Assn. Advancement Slavic Studies, Am. Comparative Lit. Assn., Am. Assn. Tchrs. Slavic and Ea. European Langs., Polish Inst. Arts and Scis. Am. Home: Cambridge Mass. Died July 14, 1988.

WEINTROUB, BENJAMIN, lawyer, editor; b. Odessa, Russia, Sept. 4, 1891; s. David and Clara (Zukerman) W.; m. Ruth Malik, Aug. 26, 1916; children: Dolly, Laura. Student, Kansa City Sch. Law, 1909-11; LLB, Kent Coll. Law, 1915; PhB (hon.), U. Chgo., 1931. Bar: Miss. 1913. Gen. mgr. Chgo. Jewish Chronicle, 1920-41; editor, pub. Chgo. Jewish Forum, from 1942; Author short stories, book revs. v.p. Hebrew Immigrant Aid Soc.; trustee Chgo. Produce Dist. Mem. Decalogue Soc. Lawyers (pres. 1948, editor jour. from 1960), Covenant Club Ill. (bd. dirs.), City Club (treas.). Home: Chicago Ill. †

WEISBORD, SAM, theatrical agent, agency executive; b. N.Y.C., Sept. 21, 1911; s. Jacob and Goldie (Kaufman) W. Student public schs., N.Y.C. With William Morris Agy., N.Y.C., 1929-45, Beverly Hills, Calif., 1945-86; asst. treas. William Morris Agy., 1948-65, sr. exec. v.p., 1965-76, pres., chief exec. officer, 1976-86, also dir. Bd. dirs. Menninger Found., Topeka, Cedars-Sinai Hosp., Los Angeles, Motion Picture and TV Fund, Los Angeles. Served with U.S. Army, 1943-45. Died May 7, 1986.

WEISBROD, BENJAMIN HARRY, lawyer; b. Amsterdam, N.Y., Oct. 5, 1891; s. Albert Mendel Hirsch and Anna (Schware) W.; m. Mary Cramer, Feb. 28, 1918. AB, Cornell U., 1914; LLB, Harvard U., 1917. Various positions Gen. Electric Co., Schenectady, N.Y., pvt. practice; Chgo., from 1917; assoc. Dent, Dobyns & Freeman, Chgo., 1917-31; assoc. Wilson & McIlvaine, Chgo., 1931-70, ptnr., 1937-70; bd. dirs. S. & C. Electric Co. Bd. govs. Chgo. Heart Assn. 2d lt., F.A., U.S. Army, 1918; maj. 331st F.A. Res.; served to col. AUS, 1941-45. Decorated Legion of Merit. Mem. Am., Ill., Chgo. bar assns., Am. Judicature Soc., Am. Legion Mil. Order World Wars, Masons (Sojourner), Standard Club, Cornell Club, Attic Club (Chgo.). Home: Downers Grove Ill. †

WEISFIELD, LEO HERMAN, jeweler; b. Winnipeg, Man., Can., Sept. 7, 1892; came to U.S., 1892, naturalized, 1905; s. Max and Anna (Antel) W.; m. Sarah Fried, June 20, 1914; 1 child, Maxine (Mrs. Herman Blumenthal). BA, U. Wash., 1914. Owner Weisfield Jewelers, Seattle, from 1917; pres. Weisfield's Inc., 1941-68, chmn. bd., from 1968; staff mem. Com. on Interstate and Fgn. Commerce for U.S. Senate, 1956-71; chmn. Pres.'s Com. for Employment of Handicapped for State of Wash., 1957; chmn. Pres.'s Com. for Spl. Retail Com. for Employment of Handicapped, 1951-71; chmn. awards com. Wash. Sportsmen's Coun., 1961-71; head Office Price Stablzn. in Pacific N.W., 1940-45; state chmn. State of Israel Bonds, 1958-62. Pres. Jewish Federated Charities; bd. dirs. Jewish Federated Fund; mem. exec. com. Com. for Internat. Growth; pres. bd. regents Wash. State U. Recipient John F. Kennedy Peace award, 1964, Human Relations award Am. Jewish Com., 1968. Mem. Diamond Coun. Am. (past pres.), Retail Jewelers Am. (dir., past pres.), Wash. Athletic Club, Rainier Club, Glendale Golf and Country Club (Bellevue, Wash.), Masons, Shriners, B'nai B'rith. Home: Seattle Wash. †

WEISS, EDWARD HUHNER, advertising agency executive, artist; b. Chgo., Mar. 22, 1901; s. Abraham and Rose (Klapper) W.; m. Ruth Wingerhoff, Feb. 12, 1938; 1 son, James. PhB, U. Chgo., 1922. Pres. Edward H. Weiss Co. (advt.), Chgo., N.Y.C. and Los Angeles, 1938-62, chmn. bd., chief exec. officer, 1962-67, chmn. bd., 1967-81, pres., from 1981; corp. cons. on arts and non-profit orgns., from 1981; pioneer motivation rsch. in advt., from 1948. Exhibited one-man and group shows as artist throughout U.S., Europe; one-man shows Art Inst. Chgo, 1949, Kovler Gallery, Chgo., 1963, Martha Jackson Gallery, N.Y.C., 1966, St. Paul (Minn.) Art Ctr., 1967; one-man painting retrospective, Chgo. Cultural Ctr., 1980; exhibited portrait exhbn., Main St. Gallery, Chgo., 1958, 71, Main St. Gallery retrospective, Mundelein Coll., 1972, Ill. State Mus., Springfield, 1974, Chgo. Pub. Library Portrait Slide Show, Chgo., Chgo. Cultural Ctr., 1977, Time-Life Bldg. Exhibit, 1978, Hyatt Regency, Chgo., 1982; contbr. to periodicals. Bd. dirs. Tamarind Lithography Workshop, Los Angeles, 1967-76; trustee Chgo. Med. Sch., 1953-62, gov., from 1962; trustee Inst. for Psychoanalysis, 1950-67, Mus. Contemporary Art, Chgo., from 1967; gov. Menninger Found., 1950-59; governing mem. Orchestral Assn., from 1965; mem. Auditorium Theatre Coun., from 1961; pres.'s com. Chgo. Civic Opera, 1969; mem. Chgo. Coun. on Fine Arts; hon. mem. Bus. Com. for Arts, N.Y.C.; co-chmn. Chgo. com. Ill. Sesquicentennial Commn., 1968; pres. Friends of Chgo. Pub. Library, 1971-74. Mem. Chgo. clubs: Arts, Standard. Home: Chicago Ill. Died Sept. 5, 1984; buried Chgo., Ill.

WEISS, GEORGE, brokerage house executive; b. Mpls., July 12, 1895; s. Moses Aaron and Sarah (Hochberger) W.; m. Margaret Ellis Adams, May 9, 1930; children: John Francis, Georgia Elizabeth Weiss Morris. Student, U. Minn., 1914-17; MBA, Harvard U., 1920. Mem. staff Inst. for Govt. Rsch., Washington, 1921-22, Inst. Econ., 1922-23; fellow Brookings Instn., 1923-25; economist Hoguet & Co. brokers, N.Y.C., 1926-28; with Bache & Co. (now Prudential-Bache Securities Inc.), from 1928, ptnr., 1937-65, inc., 1965, chmn. exec. com., 1965-68, vice chmn. bd., 1968, chmn. bd., 1968-69, hon. chmn. bd., from 1969; also dir.; instr. econ. NYU, 1929-30; lectr. fin. Am. Inst. Banking, 1930-33; mem. faculty Columbia U. Extension, 1929-45. Author: The Lighthouse Service, 1926, The Changing Stock Market, 1949. Mem. fin. com. Fedn. Jewish Philanthropies of N.Y.; bd. dirs. Downtown-Lower Manhattan Assn., Inc. 2d lt. Ordnance Res. Corps during World War I. Mem. N.Y. Soc. Security Analysts, Am. Econ. Assn., Am. Statis. Soc., Harvard Club, Bankers Am. Club, Masons. Home: New York N.Y. Died Aug. 15, 1985.

WEISS, MORTON N., association executive; b. N.Y.C., Aug. 14, 1919; s. Morris and Kate M. (Wellisch) W.; m. Sally R. Sarner, Jan. 17, 1954; children: Ronald, Allison, James. B.S., Coll. City N.Y., 1940. Stock trader Royal Exchange Co., N.Y.C., 1940-43, J. Arthur Warner & Co., 1946-54; exec. v.p. Singer Mackie & Co., N.Y.C., 1954-69; mng. partner Troster, Singer & Co., N.Y.C., 1969-73; 1st permanent pres. Nat. Security Traders Assn., 1974-85; dir. Nat. Over-the-Counter Clearance Corp. Served to lt., inf. AUS, 1943-46. Recipient Over-the-Counter Man of Year award, 1971. Mem. Nat. Assn. Securities Dealers (past chmn. nat. trading com.), Security Traders Assn. N.Y. (past dir., past pres.), Securities Industry Assn. (past chmn. securities trading com.). Home: New York City N.Y. Died Aug. 13, 1987; buried Cedar Pk. Cemetery, N.J.

WEITMAN, ROBERT M., motion picture producer; b. N.Y.C., Aug. 18, 1904; s. Abraham and Zelde (Eisenberg) W.; m. Sylvia Neustein, Feb. 22, 1928; children: Abby, Peter, Murphy. AB, Cornell U., 1927; student, Paramount Mgmt. Tng. Sch. Dir. N.Y. Paramount Theatre (inaugurated stage band policy), 1935; v.p. United Paramount Theatres Inc., 1950-53, Am. Broadcasting Paramount Theaters Corp., 1953-56; v.p. charge programming ABC, 1953-56, CBS, 1956; v.p. prodn. Metro-Goldwyn-Mayer Inc., until 1967; 1st v.p. charge studio prodn. Columbia Pictures, 1967-69; independent producer from 1969. Mem. Motion Picture Acad. Arts and Scis. (v.p.). Home: Beverly Hills Calif.

WEITZEL, EDWIN ANTHONY, newspaper columnist; b. Pitts., Nov. 3, 1905; s. John Howard and Mary Margaret (McGough) W.; m. Carmen Whitney Sherman, Aug. 11, 1961; children—Bruce Anthony, Peter Andre, Jon Philip; Jerome Charles (by previous marriage). Student, Western Res. U., 1924-28, Cleve. Coll., 1928-29. Reporter Cleve. News, 1929-32; columnist Scripps-Howard Newspapers, 1932-38, Knight Newspapers, Detroit Free Press, Chgo. Daily News, 1938-88, Field Enterprises, Chgo. Daily News, 1958-88; travel editor Chgo. Daily News, 1965-71, travel columnist, 1971-88; commentator sta. WJR, Detroit, 1941-45, sta. WWJ, Detroit, 1945-48, sta. WBBM, Chgo., 1949-65, sta. WWJ-TV, 1945-48, sta. WMAQ-TV, Chgo., 1951-61, sta. WGN-TV, Chgo., 1961-63, sta. WJR-TV, 1962-69; pub. relations dir. U.S. Home, 1971-73; Mem. adv. bd. St. Joseph's Hosp. Author: Chicago, I Will. Mem. Am. Soc. Travel Writers, Navy League, Sigma Delta Chi. Clubs: Marco Country, Marco Island Yacht, Marco Rotary. Home: Marco Island Fla. Died Dec. 20, 1988.

WELCH, (SAMUEL) EARL, judge; b. nr. Wister, Indian Ter., Okla., Jan. 27, 1892; s. Charles Arthur and Adelia (Morton) W.; m. Irene Johnston, Feb. 22, 1911; m. 2d, Fern Kerr, Jan. 14, 1917; children: James Gordon, Norma Earl, Byron Kerr; m. 3d, Ruby Myers, June 27, 1959. Student, Hargrove Coll., Ardmore, Okla., 1906-07, U. Ark., 1908-09, U. Okla., 1909-11. Bar: Okla. 1911. Ptnr. Welch & Welch, Antlers, Okla., 1911-26; dist. judge for Pushmataha, McCurtain and Choctaw counties, 1927-32; justice Supreme Ct., Okla. from 1932, vice chief justice, 1939-41, chief justice, 1941-43, 57-59; chmn. Okla. Jud. Coun., from 1944; mayor Antlers, 1920-24. 1st pres. Inter-Tribal Coun. 5 Civilized Tribes Indians Okla., 1961. Mem. ABA, Okla. State Bar Assn., Antlers C. of C. (dir. 1918-28), Masons (32 deg.), Shriners, Sigma Phi Epsilon. Democrat. Methodist. Home: Antlers Okla. †

WELCH, KENNETH CURTIS, architect; b. Sparta, Mich., July 14, 1891; s. Lyman Westley and Frances(Curtis) W.; m. Lila Montgomery, July 18, 1928; children: Kenneth C., Robert Montgomery, Diana Welch Chapman, P. Craig, Alexander William. Student, U. Mich., 1910-11; BS, U. Pa., 1915, MS, 1916. Pvt. practice Grand Rapids, Mich., 1916-18, from 1920; v.p. Welch Wilmarth Corp., Grand Rapids, 1921, Grand Rapids Store Equipment Co., 1926-53; archl. cons. from 1954; bd. dirs. Homestyle Found. (home style ctr.), Grand Rapids; AIA del. Inter-Soc. Color Coun. Contbr. articles to profl. publs. Chmn. City Planning Commn., Grand Rapids, 1946-54, parking authority, 1948-60; mem. Kent County Planning Commn.; cons. to traffic studies Eno Found., Westport, Conn. 2d lt. Signal Corps, U.S. Army, 1918-21. Recipient architects medal, diplome pour le govt. Ecole de Beaux Arts, 1916. Fellow AIA; mem. Am. Inst. Planners, Am. Mktg. Assn., Hwy. Rsch. Bd., Sigma Xi. Home: Grand Rapids Mich. †

WELLER, HERMAN GAYLE, lawyer; b. Kenney, Ill., Feb. 13, 1914; s. Herman John and Maude Edith (Darden) W.; m. Jane Duvall, July 29, 1938; children: Herman Gayle, Melissa, Timothy. AB, U. Denver, 1936, LLB cum laude, 1938. Bar: Colo. 1938. Since practiced in Denver; ptnr. Weller, Friedrich, Hickisch, Hazlitt & Ward (and predecessor firms), Denver, 1942-76, of counsel, from 1977. Chmn. Arapahoe County Rep. Cen. Com., 1952-54. Lt. (j.g.) USNR, 1944-46. Mem. ABA (chmn. com. on fidelity and surety law 1973-75), Colo. Bar Assn., Denver Bar Assn., Order of St. Ives, Law Club, Valley Country Club (pres. 1958-60), Mile High Club, Balboa Club, Omicron Delta Kappa, Phi Delta Phi. Home: Parker Colo. Deceased.

WELLES, ORSON, actor, radio and theatrical producer; b. Kenosha, Wis., May 6, 1915; s. Richard Head and Beatrice (Ives) W.; m. Virginia Nicholson, Dec. 1934;(div. 1940); 1 son, Christopher; m. 2d, Margarita Cansino (Rita Hayworth), Sept. 7, 1943 (div.); 1 dau., Rebecca Welles; m. 3d, Paola Mari, May 8, 1955; 1 dau., Beatrice. Began as actor with Gate Theatre, Dublin, 1931-32; tour with Katharine Cornell, 1933; dir. Woodstock Festival, 1934; played lead in Panic, 1935; dir. Negro Macbeth and Horse Eats Hat, 1936; dir. Dr. Faustus, Cradle Will Rock, 1937; founder Mercury Theatre, dir. Julius Caesar, 1937; dir., producer Shomakers' Holiday, Heartbreak House, Danton's Death, 1938; writer, dir., artist, radio programs, 1938; including CBS radio series Hello, Americans, in interest of hemispheric relations, 1943-43; v.p. Mercury Theatre, Inc.; made Mercury text records of Shakespeare plays for Columbia Rec. Corp., producer, actor, dir. Citizen Kane, 1940; writer, producer, dir. The Magnificient Ambersons, Lady From Shanghai, 1946, Macbeth, 1947; producer Journey Into Fear, 1941-42; producer, star Jane Eyre, 1943; appeared in TV prodn. King Lear, 1952, Fountain of Youth (Peabody award), 1959; then chiefly acting, producing in Europe, among more recent roles has appeared in: Othello, 1952, also Three Cases of Murder, 1955, Moby Dick, 1959, A Royal Affair at Versailles, 1957, Long Hot Summer, Touch of Evil, Roots of Heaven, 1958, Compulsion, 1959, Crack in the Mirror, 1960, The Trial, 1963, play 1969, Waterloo, Catch 22, 1970, A Sage Place, 1971, Treasure Island, 1977, Crossed Swords, 1978, The Late Great Planet Earth, 1978, others; narrator documentary film Masters of Congo Jungle (with William Warfield), 1960. Author: Mr. Arkadin, 1957; editor: (with Roger Hill) Everybody's Shakespeare, 1933, (with Roger Hill) Mercury Shakespeare, 1939. Traveled in South and Cen. Ams. filming Rio Carnival, also own story of Jangadieros (native fishermen), story about Mexico for Office of Coordinator of Inter-Am. Affairs. Recipient Claire M. Senie award for foremost achievement in Am. Theatre, 1938, Life Achievement award Am. Film. Inst., 1975. Mem. AFTRA, Actors Equity Assn., Lotos and Advertising clubs. Home: Hollywood Calif. Died Oct. 10, 1985.

WELLMAN, ARTHUR OGDEN, textile manufacturing company executive; b. Brookline, Mass., Oct. 31, 1894; s. Arthur G. and Celia Guinness (McCarthy) W.; m. Gullan Karlson, Apr. 11, 1969; children by previous marriage: Marjorie Wellman Bullock, Arthur Ogden, John G. Student pub. schs., Boston; Dr. Textile Industries, Clemson Coll., 1955. Ptnr. Nichols & Co., Inc., from 1935, v.p., 1927-39; pres., dir. Wellman, Inc. (formerly Nichols & Co., Inc.), Boston, 1939-70; chmn. bd., chief exec. officer, dir. Wellman, Inc. (formerly Nichols & Co., Inc.), 1970-73, hon. chmn., 1973-75; chmn. bd., chief exec. officer, dir. Wellman Industries, Inc., Johnsonville, S.C., 1954-73; hon. chmn. Wellman Industries, Inc., 1973-75; chmn. Wellman Mgmt. Co., North Palm Beach, Fla.; treas., chmn. bd., dir. Sothwell Combing Co., North Chelmsford, Mass.; pres. Wellman Oil Corp., North Chelmsford; dir. emeritus Fieldcrest Mills, Inc.; ind. oil and gas producer. Mem. Masons, Bath and Tennis Club, Everglades Club, Seminole Golf, Oyster Harbors Club, Wianno Golf. Home: Palm Beach Fla. Died Mar. 4, 1987; buried Palm Beach, Fla.

WELLMAN, HARVEY RUSSELL, United Nations official; b. Perry, N.Y., Nov. 16, 1916; s. George Clarke and Charlotte (Fisher) W.; m. Helen Louise Strong Tewell, Oct. 9, 1945; children: Karen, Judith, Clarke, Christine, Charlotte. AB, Cornell U., 1937, JD, 1940; B.A. (Rhodes scholar), Oxford U., 1939, M.A., 1944. Bar: N.Y. 1941. With Mudge, Stern, Williams & Tucier, N.Y.C., 1940-42; mem. U.S. Aux. Fgn. Svc., 1942-45; officer-in-charge Caribbean affairs Dept. State, 1951-54; student NATO Def. Coll., 1954-55; spl. asst. to ambassador Am. embassy, Paris, 1956-57; counselor econ. affairs Am. embassy, Oslo, 1957-60; counselor polit. affairs Am. embassy, Havana, 1960-61; dir. Office E. Coast Affairs, Bur. Inter-Am. Affairs Dept. State, 1961-63, dep. dir. personnel, 1963-64, dir., 1964-65; counselor, dep. chief mission Am. embassy, Lisbon, 1965-69; diplomat-in-residence, adj. prof. polit. sci. U. R.I., 1969-70; spl. asst. to sec. of state for narcotic matters 1970-74; dep. exec. dir. UN Fund for Drug Abuse Control, 1974-78. Mem. Assn. Am. Rhodes Scholars, Oxford Soc., Brasenose Soc., Phi Beta Kappa, Order of Coif, Phi Kappa Phi. Episcopalian. Home: Geneva Switzerland. Died Sept. 27, 1988.

WELLMAN, SAMUEL KNOWLTON, corporation official; b. Delaware, Pa., July 15, 1892; s. Charles Henry and Bertha Elizabeth (Adams) W.; m. June Rodier, Aug. 4, 1917; children: Susanne Wellman Huffman, Patricia Wellman Wilson. ME, Cornell U., 1914. With engring. dept. Anderson Rolled Gear Co., Cleve., 1915-16; with Wellman-Seaver-Morgan Co., Cleve., 1916-17; civilian ordnance engr. Cleve. Ordnance Dist., 1919-21; pres. Wellmn-Weibers Checkers Co., Cleve., 1922-24; pres. S.K. Wellman Co., Cleve., 1924-57, chmn. bd., 1957-63; owner East Hill Club, Nassau; bd. dirs. Brush Beryllium Co., Towmotor Corp., Cleve. Served with Troop A Cav., Mex. Border, 1916-17; 1st lt. Ordnance, U.S. Army, 1917-19. Mem. Am. Inst. Mining and Metall. Engrs., ASME, Am. Soc. Testing Materials, Am. Ordnance Assn., Cleve. Engring. Soc., Soc. Automotive Engrs. Cleve., Country Club, Union Club, University Club, Tavern Club, Hermit Club, Mentor Harbor Yacht Club, Catawba Cliffs Beach Club, Hunting Valley Gun Club, Ottawa Shooting Club (Cleve.). Home: Cleveland Heights Ohio. †

WELLS, EDWARD CURTIS, consultant, engineering executive; b. Boise, Idaho, Aug. 26, 1910; s. Edward Lansing and Laura Alice (Long) W.; m. Dorothy Evangeline Ostlund, Aug. 25, 1934; children: Laurie Jo (Mrs. William Tull), Edward Elliott. Student, Willamette U., 1927-29, D.Sc. (hon.), 1963; B.A. with gt. distinction, Stanford U., 1931; LL.D., U. Portland, 1946. Draftsman Boeing Co., Seattle, summer 1930; draftsman, engr. Boeing Co., 1931-33, group engr., 1933-34, asst. project engr., 1934-37, chief preliminary desgin engr., 1937-38, chief project engr., 1938-39, asst. chief engr., 1939-43, chief engr., 1943-47, v.p., chief engr., 1947-48, v.p. engring., 1948-58, 59-61, v.p., gen. mgr. mil. aircraft systems div., 1961-63, v.p. product devel., 1963-65, 66-67, group v.p. airplanes, 1965-66, sr. v.p., 1967-71, ret., 1972; v.p., gen. mgr. Systems Mgmt. Office, 1958-59; dir. in charge preliminary design Systems Mgmt. Office (Boeing Model 299 airplane, prototype of Model B-17, Boeing Flying Fortress following design of model through all phases of devel, 1934; cons., 1972-87; vis. prof. Stanford U., 1969-70; State Adv. Council Atomic Energy, 1958-60. Life trustee Willamette U.; mem. adv. bd. Wash. State Inst. Tech., 1957-61; mem. adv. council Stanford Engring. Sch.; pres. bd. Ryther Child Center, 1961-67, dir., 1961-80; mem. Def. Sci. Bd., 1969-72. Recipient Lawrence Sperry award Inst. Aero. Scis. for outstanding contbns.

to art airplane design with spl. reference to 4-engined aircraft, 1942; Fawcett Aviation award, 1944; Young Man of Year Seattle, 1943; Elder Statesman of Aviation award, 1978; Daniel Guggenheim Medal award, 1980. Fellow AIAA (hon.), Soc. Automotive Engrs.; mem. AAAS, Nat. Acad. Engring., Phi Beta Kappa Assos., Phi Beta Kappa, Phi Delta Theta, Tau Beta Pi. Club: Tennis (Seattle). Home: Bellevue Wash. Died July 1, 1986.

WELLS, GEORGE W(ILLIAM), insurance company executive; b. St. Paul, June 13, 1892; s. George Walter and Sophia (Wakefield) W.; m. Mary Cobb, June 2, 1917; children: Marilyn Wells Hall, Roger Dean. LLB, St. Paul Coll. Law, 1916. Dep. ins. commr. Minn., 1921-22, commr., 1922-28; sec. Northwestern Nat. Life Ins. Co., 1928-41, v.p., claims mgr., 1941-44, v.p., 1944-51, pres., mem. bd. and exec.-fin. com., 1951-58, cons., from 1958; ins. counsel and cons. to other ins. cos.; bd. dirs. several ins. orgns. including Life Ins. Investors, Chgo. Pres., sec. and chmn. legis. com. Ins. Fedn. Am.; state v.p. Ins. Fedn. Minn.; dir. Am. Life Conv. Mem. ABA, Minn. Bar Assn., Hennepin County Bar Assn. Home: Minneapolis Minn. †

WELLS, ROBERT LOMAX, physician, educator; b. Norfolk, Va., Jan. 5, 1905; s. Heath Brent and Nannie Maud (Morris) W.; m. Helen Joan Specht, June 8, 1935; children: Robert Lomax, Edward Brent, Judith Helen. BS, Coll. William and Mary, 1926; MD, U. Va., 1930. Diplomate Am. Bd. Preventive Medicine. Intern, house officer St. Luke's Hosp., N.Y.C., 1931-33; resident physician St. Mary's Hosp. for Children, 1933; pvt. practice medicine Washington, 1933-47; med. dir. Chesapeake & Potomac Telephone Cos., since 1944, full time since 1947; assoc. prof. clin. medicine Georgetown U. Med. Sch., 1933-39, clin. assoc. prof. preventive medicine, dept. preventive medicine, from 1956; sr. attending physician in medicine Garfield Meml. Hosp., 1946-49; then emeritu; gen. med. dir. The Chesapeake & Potomac Telephone Cos., from 1964; mem. Pres.'s Com. on Employment of Handicapped, 1964-66. Contbr. articles in med. jours. Recipient Algernon Sydney Sullivan Meml. award Coll. William and Mary, 1926. Fellow Am. Med. Assn. (chmn. coun. occupational health 1966), Am. Coll. Physicians, Indsl. Med. Assn. (dir.), Am. Acad. Occupational Medicine (pres. 1962-63), Am. Coll. Preventive Medicine; mem. Southern Med. Assn., Med. Soc. D.C., D.C. Tb Assn. (pres. 1953-55), Columbia Country Club, Phi Beta Kappa, Alpha Omega Alpha, Omicron Delta Kappa, Sigma Nu. Democrat. Episcopalian. Home: Washington D.C. Died Jan. 6, 1986.

WELSH, JAMES LEROY, grain company executive; b. Prairie Home, Nebr., Dec. 28, 1889; s. James H. and Harriett (Garland) W.; m. Helen Smith, Dec. 25, 1912; 1 son, James LeRoy. Student, pub. schs. Pres. Butler-Welsh Grain Co., Omaha, from 1932; bd. dirs. Omaha Nat. Bank, Mut. of Omaha, Union Stock Yards, Omaha, Allied Mills Inc., Chgo. Pres. Omaha Grain Exch., 1939l chmn., pres. Commn. on Increased Indsl. Use of Agrl. Products, 1956-57; bd. dirs. Salvation Army, Child Savs. Inst., S.W. Rsch. Inst., San Antonio, Midwest Rsch. Inst., Kansas City; bd. regents U. Nebr. With U.S. Army, 1917-18. Mem. Nat. Grain and Feed Dealers Assn. (past pres.), Nat. Aero Assn. (dir.), Omaha Country Club, Omaha Club, Omaha Athletic Club, Rotary (Omaha); Capitol Hill Club (Washington); Union League Club (Chgo.). Home: Omaha Nebr. †

WELSH, LESLIE THOMAS, manufacturing executive, accountant; b. Bradford, Ill., Nov. 29, 1922; s. Leslie Edward and Anna (Holden) W.; m. Mary Lee Weaver, Aug. 12, 1950; children: Leslie Thomas Jr., Robert Weaver, Barbara Jo Ann, Cynthia Lee. BS in Accountancy, U. Ill., Urbana, 1944. C.P.A. Ptnr. Arthur Andersen & Co., Chgo., 1944-63; pres. Welsh Sporting Goods Corp., Iowa Falls, Iowa, 1964-72; v.p. fin., chief fin. officer Studebaker-Worthington, Inc., 1967-69, sr. v.p., 1969-71, pres., 1971-79; pres. Lelie T. Welsh, Inc., from 1979. Author film; contbr. articles to profl. jours. Trustee Village of Barrington Hills, Ill., 1963-67. Mem. Barrington Hills Country Club (dir., pres.). Home: Barrington Ill. Died Apr. 26, 1984; buried Bradford, Ill.

WELSH, WILLIAM PETER, painter, illustrator; b. Lexington, Ky., Sept. 20, 1889; s. Bartholomew J. and Sarah Ellen (King) W. Student, St. Paul's and Johnson Grammar Schs., Lexington, Ky., 1895-1903; student of drawing and painting under, Mary Kinkead, Lexington, Ky., 1904-06; student, Delecleuse and Julien acads., Paris, 1906-07, Art Students League, N.Y.C., 1900-10. Painter mural decorations Cleve. Athletic Club, Hotel Statler, Berghoff Rathskeller, Cleve., 1911-14; with U.S. Lithograph Co., N.Y.C., 1914-15; free lance artist 1915-16; kinstr. Coll. Fine and Applied Arts, AEF U., Beaune, Cote d'Or, France, 1919; portrait painter Chgo., 1923—. Paintings include portraits of numerous citizens of Chgo. and elsewhere since 1923, murals for Chicago Room, Palmer House, 1925-26, illustrations for stories for Hearst's Internat., Woman's Home Companion, etc., since 1924, mag. covers for Woman's Home Companion, 1930—, mural decoration Lexington St. Scene, Kentuckian Hotel, 1947, portraits of many notables, from 1948; one man exhbn. Speed Art Mus., Louisville, 1956; designed posters for Pullman Co., U. Chgo., Lincoln Nat. Life Ins. Co., and others. Served on Mex. Border, 1916, as 2d lt., 1st N.Y.F.A.; 1st lt. Apr. 17, 1917, with 104th F.A.; U.S. Army; with AEF, June 1918-July 1919; capt. AAF, 1942, maj. 1943, lt. col. 1946. Made paintings in Far East Theatre of Ops. for Hist. Records of AAF, 1945-46. Recipient First prize, Internat. Watercolor Exhbn. Art Inst. Chgo., 1921; 1st and 3d prizes Century of Progress poster competition Art Inst. Chgo, 1938, Art Dirs. Club medal in Ann. Exhbn. of Advt. Art, 1936, award for Distinctive Merit, same exhbn., 1936-37, award of merit Chgo. Soc. Typographic Art, 1936, 37, Margaret Cooper prize Ann. Exhbn. Allied Artists of Am., N.Y., 1949, Popular Vote prize, Exhbn. Artists along the Mississippi, Davenport, Iowa, 1050. Fellow Royal Soc. Arts, Internat. Inst. Arts and Letters; mem. Soc. of Illustrators, N.Y., Tavern Club (v.p.), Wayfarers Club (Chgo.), Nat. Arts Club (N.Y.C.). Home: New York N.Y. †

WELTE, HERBERT DAVID, college president; b. David City, Nebr., Mar. 6, 1898; s. Joseph and Nancy (Grafft) W.; m. May Aletha Boulden, Nov. 26, 1927; children: Keith Joseph, Eileen Frances, Elizabeth Ann, Herbert David. AB, State Tchrs. Coll., Kearney, Nebr., 1924; AM, State U. Iowa, 1925, PhD, 1925. Tchr. rural schs. Butler County, Nebr., 1916-19; supt. schs. Abie, Nebr., 1919-20, Bruno, Nebr., 1922-23; prof. edn., dean men State Tchrs. Coll., Mayville, N.D., 1925-27; pres. Cen. Conn. State Coll., New Britain, 1929-68; ednl. cons. Am. Assn. State Colls. and Univs. Author: A Psychological Analysis of Plane Geometry, 1926, A Work-Book in Our State-North Dakota, 1927, A Workbook in Plane Geometry, tchrs. edit., 1929, rev. edit. 1947. With USN, 1918-19. Mem. New Eng. Tchr. Preparation Assn. (pres. 1937), Eastern States Assn. Profl. Schs. Tchrs. (pres. 1939), Am. Assn. Colls. Tchr. Edn. (exec. com. 1941-43, 51-55, pres. 1954-55), New Eng. Assn. Colleges and Secondary Schs. (com. higher instns. 1957-62), New Britain Club, Rotary, Masons, Phi Delta Kappa, Kappa Delta Pi. Republican. Methodist. Home: Unionville Conn. Died Sept. 2, 1986.

WENNERSTRUM, CHARLES, judge; b. Cambridge, Ill., Oct. 11, 1889; s. Charles F. and Anna Mathilda (Vinstrand) W.; m. Helen F. Rogers, Feb. 14, 1925; children: Roger F., Scott T., Joann II. AB, Drake U., 1912; LLB, Coll. Law, 1914. Bar: Iowa 1914. In practice Adel, Iowa, 1914-15, Chariton, Iowa, 1914-30; county atty. Lucas County, Iowa, 1917-22; dist. judge 2d Judical Dist., Iowa, 1930-40; justice Supreme Ct. Iowa, 1941-58; presiding judge hostage case Nuremberg War Trials, 1947-48. Trustee Drake U. 2d lt. U.S. Army, 1918. Mem. ABA, Iowa State Bar Assn., Am. Law Inst., Am. Legion (past comdr.), Rotary, Order of Coif, Sigma Alpha Epsilon, Delta Theta Phi. Republican. Presbyterian. Home: Chariton Iowa. Died June 15, 1986.

WENZLICK, ROY, real estate economist; b. St. Louis, June 13, 1894; s. Albert and Emma (Schall) W.; m. Susan Newsom, June 29, 1918; 1 dau., Jean N. Wenzlick Fullerton. AB (Winston Churchill fellow), Westminster Coll., Fulton, Mo., 1916; student, Princeton, 1916-17; PhD, St. Louis U., 1942. Successively vocational guidance dir. St. Louis YMCA, rsch. dir. St. Louis Post Dispatch, nat. advt. mgr. same, pres. Real Estate Analysts, Inc.; chmn. bd. Roy Wenzlick Rsch. Corp.; mem. large-scale ops. com. Hoovers Housing Conf., 1931; econ. cons. capital goods div. Nat. Recovery Act, 1933; econ. cons. industry coun. Office Price Adminstrn., 1942; chmn. Census Com. for Greater St. Louis, 1926-53; chmn. rsch. com. Community Coun., 1924-32; chmn. rsch. com. Social Planning Coun., 1932-38; speaker numerous seminars and profl. groups; chmn. adv. com. on rsch. and record projects for St. Louis dist. Works Progress Adminstrn.; rsch. cons. Nat. Assn. Real Estate Bds., 1934-37; mem. exec. bd. St. Louis coun. Boy Scouts Am.; trustee St. Louis Gateway Arch. Author: The Federal Census of Metropolitan St. Louis, 1932, The Coming Boom in Real Estate, 1936; editor, pub. The Real Estate Analyst, 1932-74; contbr. to nat. mags. Recipient Disting. Alumni awards Westminster Coll. and St. Louis U. Mem. Am. Econ. Assn., Am. Inst. Real Estate Appraisers, St. Louis Real Estate Bd. (life), Urban Land Inst., Am. Soc. Real Estate Counselors, Rotary (Paul Harris fellow). Home: Webster Groves Mo. Died June 18, 1988; buried Fulton, Mo.

WERNER, WALTER, lawyer, educator; b. N.Y.C., Mar. 15, 1915; s. Isaac Jacob and Esther (Rosen) W.; m. Charlotte Hoffman, 1939 (dec. 1973); children—Robert, Daniel, John; m. Anne Wertheim, May 26, 1974. B.A., Yale U., 1935, J.D., 1938. Bar: bar. Asst. city atty. Bridgeport, Conn., 1983-41; asso. gen. counsel Blaw-Knox Co., Pitts., 1941-47; pres. Hoffman Fuel Co., Danbury, Conn., 1947-61; dir. office of policy research SEC, Washington, 1962-65; sr. lectr. Columbia U. Law Sch., 1966-69, prof., 1969-86. Contbr. articles to legal jours. Trustee State Colls. Conn., 1966-69. Mem. ABA. Club: Century (N.Y.C.). Home: New York N.Y. Died Dec. 12, 1986.

WERTHEIM, EDGAR, chemist, educator; b. LaSalle, Ill., Feb. 22, 1886; s. Henry and Emma (Eliel) W.; m. Katherine Hale, Aug. 25, 1924; children: Barbara Jean, Marian Elizabeth. BPE, YMCA Coll., Chgo., 1917; BS, Northwestern U., 1918; MS, U. Kans., 1919; PhD, U. Chgo., 1921; LLD (hon.), U. Ark., 1959. Businessman 1902-12; asst. rpof. chemistry U. Kans., 1918-20; prof. organic chemistry U. Ark., 1928-54, emeritus, from 1951, head dept., 1945-54. Author: Essentials of Organic and Biological Chemistry, 1931, Manual of Organic Chemistry, 1932, Organic Chemistry Laboratory Guide, 1937, 3d. edit., 1948, Textbook of Organic Chemistry, 1939, 3d edit. 1951, Introductory Organic Chemistry, 1942, 3d edit. 1958; asst. editor: Outline of Organic Chemistry, 1937; contbr. articles to profl. jours. Fellow Am. Inst. Chemists, AAAS; mem. Am. Chem. Soc., AAUP, Soc. for History of Tech., University Club (Fayetteville, Ark.), Sigma Xi, Phi Beta Kappa, Alpha Chi Sigma. Home: Arlington Va. †

WESCOTT, GLENWAY, author; b. Kewaskum, Wis., Apr. 11, 1901; s. Bruce Peters and Josephine (Gordon) W. Student, U. Chgo., 1917-19. Author: The Bitterns (poems), 1920, The Apple of the Eye, 1924, Natives of Rock-XX Poems, 1921-22, 25, The Grandmothers (Harper Prize), 1927, Good-Bye, Wisconsin, 1928, The Babe's Bed, Harrison of Paris, 1930, Fear and Trembling, 1932, A Calendar of Saints for Unbelievers, 1932, The Pilgrim Hawk, 1940, Apartment in Athens, 1945, Images of Truth, 1962. Mem. AAAL, Nat. Inst. Arts and Letters. Home: Rosemont N.J. Died Feb. 22, 1987.

WESLEY, CHARLES HARRIS, historian, educator, writer; b. Louisville, Dec. 2, 1891; s. Charles Snowden and Matilda (Harris) W.; m. Louise Johnson, Nov. 25, 1915 (dec. 1973); children: Louise Johnson, Charlotte Harris. BA, Fisk U., 1911; MA, Yale U., 1913; post-grad., Guilde Internationale, Paris, 1914, Howard U., 1915-16; PhD, Harvard U., 1925; DD, Wilberforce U., 1928; LLD, Allen U., 1932, Va. State Coll., 1943, Morris Brown U., 1944, Paul Quinn Coll., Campbell Coll., 1946, Morgan State Coll., 1961, U. Cin., 1964; LittD, Western U., 1946, Fisk U., 1973; LLD, Tuskegee Inst., 1968, Howard U., 1970; EdD, Cen. State Coll., 1965; LHD, Berea U., 1971. Instr. teaching history Howard U., 1913, instr. history, 1914-18, asst. prof., 1918-19, assoc. prof., 1919-20, prof. history, head dept., 1921-42, dir. summer sch., 1937, acting dean Coll. Liberal Arts, 1937-38, dean Grad. Sch., 1938-42; pres. Wilberforce U., 1942-47; pres. Cen. State U., 1942-65, pres. emeritus, from 1965; dir. rsch. Assn. Study Negro Life and History, Washington, from 1972; pastor, presiding elder African M.E. Ch., 1918-37. Author: Negro Labor in the United States, 1850-1925, 3d edit., 1967, Richard Allen: Apostle of Freedom, 2d edit., 1969, The Collapse of the Confederacy, 2d edit., 1968, A Manual of Research and Thesis Writing for Graduate Students, 1941, Fifteenth Amendment and Black America, 1870-1970, 1970, Negro Citizenship in U.S., 1868-1968, 1969; co-author: The Story of the Negro Retold, 1959; Negro Makers of History, 1959, The Negro in Our History, 12th edit., 1972; editor: The Negro in the Americas, 1940, Negro History Bull., 1967-72, The History of Alpha Phi Alpha, 12th rev. edit., 1975, The History of Sigma Pi Phi, 1904-54, 1954-69, The History of the Improved, Benevolent, Protective Order of Elks, 1898-1954, 1955, The History of the Prince Hall Grand Lodge of Ohio, 1849-1960, 2d edit., 1972, Ohio Negroes in the Civil War, 1962, Neglected History: Essays in Negro-American History by a College President, 3rd edit., 1969, International Library of Negro Life and History, 10 vols., 1967-68, The Quest for Equality, 1968, In Freedom's Footsteps, 1969; cons. editor: Afro-Am. Ency., 10 vols., from 1974, Prince Hall: Life and Legacy in the Era of the American Revolution, 1977, Henry Arthur Callis: Life and Legacy, 1977. Ednl. sec. Army YMCA, Camp Meade, Md., 1918; sec. for overseas work, colored men's dept. Nat. War Work Coun., YMCA, 1919; mem. army and navy dept. com. Nat. Coun. YMCA; mem. com. on Negro-White relations YMCA, also mem. coun. Ohio and W.Va.; pres. Inter-Univ. Coun. Ohio, 1955-56; exec. dir. Afro-Am. Bicentennial Hist. and Cultural Mus., Phila., 1975-76. Guggenheim fellow, London, 1930-31; grant-in-aid Social Sci. Rsch. Coun., 1936-37; recipient Achievement award Omega Psi Phi, Diamond Jubilee citation Ky. Ednl. Assn.; Honor Roll of John Brown Gallery of Fame. Fellow Am. Geog. Soc.; mem. Ohio Coll. Assn. (exec. com. 1947-49, 60-61, 64-65, chmn. com. resolutions 1951-53, pres. 1963-64), Assn. Ohio Coll. Pres. and Deans (pres. 1954-55), Assn. Study Negro Life and History (exec. coun., pres.), Am. Hist. Assn., Nat. Coun. Social Studies, NEA, Am. Assn. Sch. Adminstrs., Am. Assn. Univ. Profs., Soc. Advancement Edn., Alpha Phi Alpha (gen. pres. 1931-40, gen. pres., historian 1940-76, Fiftieth Anniversary Founder's award), Mason (33 deg.), Odd Fellow. Home: Washington D.C. Died Aug. 16, 1987.

WESSEL, CARL JOHN, chemist; b. Pitts., Oct. 5, 1911; s. Reuben and Sarah Veronica (Boyle) W.; m. Laur Schell Huntington, Feb. 14, 1942; children: Gretchen Grimm, Gregory Huntington, Colman Langan, Hilary Lindsay, Kenwyn Brennan. Student, U. Buffalo, 1929-30; BS, Canisius Coll., 1934; MS, U. Detroit, 1938; PhD, Cath. U. Am., 1941. Paint, varnish, lacquer and enamel chemist Pratt & Lambert Co., Buffalo, 1934-36, charge testing lab., 1935, supr. lacquer formulation, 1936; grad. instr. gen. chemistry U. Detroit, 1936-38, instr. biochemistry, organic chemistry, 1941; microbiologist, chemist Gelatin Products Corp. (now R.P. Scherer Corp.), Detroit, 1941-46; supr. control labs., assoc. dir. control Gelatin Products Corp. (now R.P. Scherer Corp.), 1942-46; instr. gen. chemistry

Wayne State U., 1944-46; biochemist, rsch. assoc. prevention of deterioration ctr. div. chemistry-chem. tech. Nat. Acad. Sci.-NRC, 1946-48, asst. dir., 1954, dir., 1955-65, mem. panel on prevention deterioration, materials adv. bd., 1957-58, mem. panel on effects ambient environ. quality, environ. rsch. assessment com., from 1975; treas. The Capital Chemist, Publ. Wash. Chem. Soc., 1951-55; sec. Nat. Fedn. Sci. Abstracting and Indexing Services, 1963-65; sci. info. coordinator FDA, HEW, 1965-66; v.p., chief scientist Tracor Jitco, Inc., Rockville, Md., 1966-79, dir. carcinogenesis bioassay program, 1974-76, cons., from 1979. Contbg. author: Chemistry and Chemical Technology of Cotton, 1955, The Encyclopedia of Chemistry, 1957; editor, contbr.: Deterioration of Materials, Causes and Preventive Techniques, 1954; contbr. articles to profl. jours. Fellow Am. Inst. Chemists (pres. Washington chpt. 1957-59), Inst. Environ. Scis., AAAS; mem. Am. Inst. Biol. Sci., Corrosion Rsch. Coun., Seahorse Inst., Am. Chem. Soc., Am. Soc. Info. Scis., Soc. Indsl. Microbiology, Cosmos Club, Torch Club (Washington dir., pres. 1965). Roman Catholic. Home: Bethesda Md. Died June 7, 1984; buried Gate of Heaven Cemetery, Bethesda, Md.

WEST, ANTHONY PANTHER, writer; b. Hunstanton, Norfolk, Eng., Aug. 4, 1914; came to U.S., 1950.; s. Herbert George Wells; m. Lily Dulany Emmet, Dec. 20, 1952; children by previous marriage: Caroline, Edmund. Dairy farmer, breeder registered Guernsey cattle, and occasional contbr. to mags. 1937-43; with Far Eastern desk BBC, 1943-45, Japanese Service, 1945-47; mem. staff New Yorker mag., from 1950. Author: (critical biography) D.H. Lawrence, 1948, The Vintage, 1950, Another Kind, 1952, Heritage, 1955, Principles and Persuasions, 1956, The Trend Is Up, 1960, Mortal Wounds, 1966, (critical biography) John Piper, 1978, (biography of his father) H.G. Wells: Aspects of a Life, 1984. Houghton Mifflin fellow, 1947. Mem. Century Club. Home: Stonington Conn. Died Dec. 27, 1987.

WEST, CHARLES TYRRELL, mechanical engineer, educator; b. Crestline, Ohio, July 1, 1915; s. LaFoy Allen and Mabelle (Hillson) W.; m. Estella Marie Fahs, Apr. 5, 1947 (dec. July 1973); children: Mary Bronwyn, Charles Tyrrell III. Student, U.S. Naval Acad., 1934-37; BCE, Ohio State U., 1939, MS, 1946; postgrad., U. Mich., 1948-49; PhD, Cornell U., 1951. Bridge test analyst Assn. Am. Railroads, 1941-46; instr. engring. mechanics Ohio State U., 1946-53, prof., chmn. dept. engring. mechanics, 1953-72, prof. engring. mechanics, 1973-77, prof. emeritus, 1977-85; vis. prof. mech. engring. Indian Inst. Tech., Kanpur, U.P., India, 1968-70; cons. Boeing Airplane Co., 1959-60; rsch. scientist Autometric Corp., 1959-63; cons. in dynamics to various corps., from 1964. Contbr. articles on vibration and dynamics to profl. jours. Served from ensign to lt. comdr. USNR, 1941-46. Fellow ASCE; mem. ASME, Nat. Rifle Assn., Ohio State Faculty Club, Sigma Xi, Tau Beta Pi. Home: Crestline Ohio. Died June 9, 1985.

WEST, LUTHER SHIRLEY, university dean; b. Utica, N.Y., Sept. 6, 1899; s. Norman Luther and Rena Lane (Shirley) W.; m. Beatrice Emma Ryan, June 28, 1922; children: Ruth Shirley West MacVean, Richard Luther, William Edward, Alice Beatrice West Eldred, Betsy Lou West Dahlgren, David John. BS, Cornell U., 1921, PhD, 1925; DSc (hon.), No. Mich. U., 1969; student Marine Biol. Lab., Woods Hole, Mass. Instr. parasitology and med. entomology Cornell U., 1921-25, lectr. gen. biology, summer 1925; mem. staff N.Y. State Agrl. Expt. Sta. 1921-25; prof. biology and eugenics Battle Creek Coll., 1926-38, dean arts and scis., 1933-38; prof. biology, head dept. No. Mich. Coll., 1938-43, 46-62; assoc. mem. grad. faculty U. Mich., 1952-60; scientist-cons. fly control Eastern Mediterranean countries WHO, 1952-53; dean arts and scis. No. Mich. U., 1962-65, dean emeritus, from 1965. Author: Eugenic Aspects of Race Betterment, 1932, (with others) Manual of Tropical Medicine, 3d edit., 1960, (with others) Practical Malariology, 2d edit., 1963, The Housefly: Its Natural History, Medical Importance and Control, 1951, (with others) The Free-Living Protozoa of the Upper Peninsula of Michigan, 1963, (with Oncita Beth Peters) Annotated Bibliography of Musca Domestica Linnaeus, 1973; also articles. Chmn. City Health Coun., Marquette, Mich., 1958-63; trustee St. Luke's Hosp., Marquette, 1957-70; bd. dirs. Marquette County br. Mich. Tb Assn., from 1962, Family Service Soc. Marquette, from 1941. Maj. San. Corps, AUS, 1943-46. Decorated Army Commendation ribbon. Fellow AAAS; mem. Entomol. Soc. Am., Am. Microscopical Soc., Mich. Acad. Sci., Arts and Letters (pres. 1965-66, recipient citation 1950), Am. Inst. Biol. Scis., Am. Soc. Parasitologists, Sigma Xi, Phi Kappa Phi, Sigma Pi. Home: Marquette Mich. Died Dec. 14, 1985; buried Halsey Valley, N.Y.

WEST, WILLIAM JOHN, lawyer; b. Cole's Island, N.B., Can., Dec. 20, 1892; s. Wesley and Amelia Prince (Small) W.; m. Katherine Elenor McMurray, Nov. 22, 1932; children: Mary Francis, Barbara Catherine. BA, Mt. Allison U., 1920; LLB, Harvard U., 1923. Bar: N.B. 1923. Practiced law from 1923; mem. Dougherty, West & Gunter, Fredercita, N.B., 1934-56, West, Bunter, Gray & Dougherty, Fredercita, N.B., from 1956; atty. gen. Province of N.B., from 1952; bd. dirs. Maritime Trust Co. Mem. bd. regents Allison. Lt. Can. Army, 1915-18. Mem. Masons, Rotary. Home: Fredericton Canada. †

WESTGREN, ARNE FREDRIK, chemist; b. Arjäng, Sweden, July 11, 1889; s. Anders and Selma Maria (Hammar) W.; m. Elsa Maria Johanna Nilsson, June 12, 1915; childre: Anders, Ingrid Westgren Källander, Anna Birgitta. Ph.D., U. Uppsala, 1915; D.Eng. (hon.), Tech. Hochschule Darmstadt, 1934; Ph.D. (non.), Dorpat U., 1939. Metallographer SKF Ball Bearing Co., Gothenburg, Sweden, 1918-20; metallographer Metallographic Inst., Stockholm, 1920-27, bd. dirs., 1934-64; prof. gen. inorganic chemistry Stockholm u., 1927-43; permanent sec. Swedish Royal Acad. Sci., Stockholm, 1943-59; sec. Nobel com. physics and chemistry, 1926-43; chmn. Nobel com. chemistry, 1943-64. Bd. dirs. Nobel Found., 1943-59, Stockholm U., 1946-60. Mem. Acad. Sci. (Stockholm, Uppsala, Lund), Soc. Sci. (Helsingfors), Royal Pharm. Soc. (Madrid), Academie des Sciences (Paris). Home: Stockholm Sweden. †

WESTMEYER, TROY RUDOLPH, public administration educator, academic administrator; b. Toledo, Oct. 25, 1916; s. Rudolph C. and Eva (Westrup) W.; m. Eleanor J. Dunham, Apr. 4, 1942; children: Wesley R., Lynne Westmeyer Slink. BE, U. Toledo, 1940; MS, U. Denver, 1944; PhD, NYU, 1963. Assoc. prof. govt. mgmt. U. Denver, 1946-49; dir. fiscal survey commns. Commonwealth of Mass., Boston, 1949-56; sr. assoc. Nat. Mcpl. League, N.Y.C., 1956-58; assoc. dir. Ankara program Grad. Sch. Pub. Adminstrn., NYU, 1958-60, assoc. dean, 1960-67, prof. pub. adminstrn., 1963-81, emeritus, from 1981, acting dean, 1968-70; exec. dir. N.Y. State Legis. Commn. on Expenditure Rev., Albany, 1969-78. Editor Govtl. Rsch. Assn. Reporter, 1959-74; column editor Nat. Civic Rev. from 1962. With USNR, 1943. Mem. Govtl. Rsch. Assn. (sec.-treas 1959-74), Am. Soc. Pub. Adminstrn. (pres. N.Y. Met. chpt. 1968). Home: Samford Conn. Mailing: Estate of Troy R Westmeyer Mrs Lynn W Slink 60 Gary Rd Samford CT 06903 Died Feb. 18, 1989.

WESTON, CHARLES, newspaper executive; b. Cambridge, Mass., Sept. 25, 1891; s. Robert Dickson and Anstiss (Walcott) W.; m. Lydia Bullard, Apr. 21, 1927; children: Lydia Weston Kesich, Emily Weston Frankovich, Carol. AB, Harvard U., 1913. With White, Weld and Co., brokers, 1919-27; v.p. Atlantic Nat. Bank, Boston, 1932, Old Colony Trust Co., Boston, 1932-56; exec. v.p. Guy Gannett Pub. Co., Portland, Maine, from 1956, also treas., dir.; bd. dirs. E.T. Wright & Co., Gannett Broadcasting Co., H.K. Noyes & Son, Inc.; treas., dir. Boston Tb Assn. Pres. corp. Winsor Sch., 1940-48. 1st lt. U.S. Army, 1917-19; capt. Mass. State Guard, 1943-45. Mem. Tavern Club (Boston), Country Club. Home: Brookline Mass. †

WESTON, CHARLES H(ARTSHORNE), lawyer; b. Merion Station, Pa., July 8, 1892; s. Samuel Burns and Mary (Hartshorne) W.; m. Virginia Ross, Sept. 25, 1922; children: Amy Weston Firfer, Virginia Weston Slaughter, Charles Hartshorne. AB, Harvard U., 1914, LLB cum laude, 1916. Bar: Pa. 1916, U.S. Ct. Appeals (D.C. cir.) 1931, U.S Supreme Ct. 1921. With Roberts, Montgomery and McKeehan, Phila., 1916-17; spl. ast. to U.S. atty. gen. 1918-20, 21-23, 29-61; with Gregory and Todd, Washington, 1920-21, Rushmore, Bisbee and Stern, N.Y.C., 1923-29; chief appellate sect. Anti-trust Div., Dept. Justice, 1943-61. Contbr. articles to legal mags. Recipient Merit citation Nat. Civil Svc. League, 1956. Mem. Cosmos Club. Home: Washington D.C. †

WESTWELL, ARTHUR EVANS, school administrator; b. North Andover, Mass., Jan. 3, 1892; s. Edward and Hannah (Brundrett) W.; m. Hilda Rounsvell Shurtleff, Apr. 6, 1931; children: Arthur Evans, Richard Peter, Sally. Student, Phillips Exeter Acad., 1911; DMD, Tufts Coll., 1923. Worker with mentally retarded Fernald Sch., Waverley, Mass., 1916-23; mem. staff Belchertown State Sch., Boulder, Mont., 1923-49; supt. Mont. State Tng. Sch., Boulder, from 1949; mem. fed. com. rsch. and profl. devel.; active child welfare work for Am. Legion. Sgt. M.C., U.S. Army, 1917-19. Fellow Am. Assn. Mental Deficiency (past pres., chmn. parents groups liaison com.), Rotary. Episcopalian. †

WETENHALL, J(OHN) HUBER, corporation executive; b. Wilmington, Del., Oct. 12, 1901; s. Carl A. and Harriet (Couch) W.; m. Catherine Elizabeth Maguire, Oct. 1, 1927; children: John H., Robert C. Grad., U. Pa., 1922. Operating exec. Nat. Dairy Products Corp., 1937-50; v.p. Nat. Dairy Products Corp., N.Y.C., 1952-57, dir., 1955-72, exec. v.p., 1957-59, pres., from 1959, pres., chief exec. officer, from 1961; dir. Mfrs. Hanover Trust Co., N.Y.C., Sears, Roebuck & Co., Chgo. Trustee Nutrition Found., N.Y.C., Com. Econ. Devel., N.Y.C. Mem. Commerce and Industry Assn. (dir.), Westchester Country Club, Racquet and Tennis Club. Home: Franconia N.H. Died June 6, 1987.

WETHEY, HAROLD EDWIN, art history educator; b. Port Byron, N.Y., Apr. 10, 1902; s. Charles Edwin and Flora (Keck) W.; m. Alice Luella Sunderland, June 8, 1948; 1 son, David Sunderland. AB, Cornell U., 1923; AM, Harvard U., 1931, PhD, 1934; student, U. Paris, summers 1931, 34. Asst. hist. art Harvard U., 1933-34; instr., lectr. then asst. prof. Bryn Mawr (Pa.) Coll., 1934-38; asst. prof. Washington U., St. Louis, 1938-40; assoc. prof. U. Mich., Ann Arbor, 1940-46, prof. art history, 1946-72, prof. emeritus, from 1972; Kress prof. Ctr. for Advanced Study of the Visual Arts, Nat. Gallery Art, Washington, 1982-83; Henry Russel lectr., 1964-65; vis. prof. U. Tucuman, Argentina, 1943, U. Mex., summer 1960; spl. lectr. Escuela de Estudios Hispano-americanos, La Rábida, Spain, 1948. Author: Gil Siloe and His School, 1936, The Early Works of Bartolomé Ordóñez and Diego de Siloe, 1943, Colonial Architecture and Sculpture in Peru, 1949 (award Soc. Archtl. Historians), Alonso Cano, Painter, Sculptor and Architect, 1955, (Spanish edit.) Alonso Cano, pintor, escultor, y arquitecto, 1983, Alonso Cano, Pintor, 1958, Arquitectura virreinal en Bolivia, 1961, El Greco and His School, 2 vols., 1962, rev. edit. in Spanish, 1967; editor: (series) History of Spanish Painting: The Schools of Aragon and Navarre in the Early Renaissance, Vol. XIII, The School of Castile in the Later Renaissance, Vol. XIV, 1966, (both by Chandler R. Post); Titian Vol. I, The Religious Paintings, 1969, Titian Vol. II, The Portraits, 1971, Titian Vol. III, The Mythological and Historical Paintings, 1975; Titian's Drawings, 1988; editor: bibliography of Spanish Am. art for Handbook Latin-Am. Studies, 1948-59; editorial bd.: Art Bull, 1940-44, 64-71; contbr. to art periodicals. Recipient Disting. Faculty Achievement award, 1968; Sheldon fellow Harvard U., 1932-33, Rockefeller fellow, 1944-45; Rackham rsch. grantee, 1948-72; Guggenheim fellow, 1949, 71-72, fellow Am. Coun. Learned Socs., 1936, 63; Fulbright scholar, Rome, 1958-59; 400th anniversary of death of Titian speaker U. Venice, 1976. Mem. Hispanic Soc. Am. (Sculpture medal 1962), Coll. Art Assn., Renaissance Soc., Venice Com. Internat. Fund for Monuments, Rsch. Club U. Mich., Am. Acad. Franciscan History (corr.), Real Acad. de Bellas Artes de San Fernando (Madrid), Soc. Peruana de Historia, Acad. Nacional de Ciencias de Bolivia, Phi Kappa Phi. Home: Ann Arbor Mich. Died Sept. 22, 1984; buried Forest Hill Cemetery, Ann Arbor.

WETMORE, RALPH HARTLEY, botany educator; b. Yarmouth, N.S., Can., Apr. 27, 1892; naturalized, 1936; s. Herman Augustus and Josephine Cordelia (Moses) W.; m. Marion Geraldine Silver, June 20, 1923 (dec.); children: Katherine Beryl, Evelyn Jean; m. Mary Olive Hawkins Smith, June 24, 1940. BSc, Acadia U., Wolfville, N.S., 1921; AM, Harvard, 1922, PhD, 1924; DSc (hon.). National rsch. fellow 1924-25; asst. prof. biology Acadia U., 1925-26; asst. prof. botany Harvard U., 1926-32, assoc. prof., 1932-43, prof., 1943-62, prof. emeritus, from 1962, chmn. dept., 1932-34, dir. Bot. Labs., 1933-34, chmn. dept. biology, 1946-47, dir. biol. labs., 1953-56. Author numerous articles in sci. jours. Fellow NAS, Am. Acad. Arts and Scis., AAAs, N.Y. Acad. Sci.; mem. Scandinavian Soc. Plant Physiology, Am. Soc. Plant Physiology, Bot. Soc. Am. (pres. 1953), Am. Soc. Naturalists, Torrey Bot. Club, N.E. Bot. Club (pres. 1949-52), AAUP, Soc. Study Devel. and Growth (pres. 1948-49), Biol. Stain Commn., Internat. Soc. Plant Morphologists, Internat. Assn. Wood Anatomists, Harvard Faculty Club, Sigma Xi. Home: Cambridge Mass. †

WEYER, FRANK E(LMER), educator; b. Ainsworth, Nebr., Jan. 14, 1890; s. John and Elizabeth (Sweitzer) W.; m. Mabelle Carey, June 3, 1916; children: Mary Elizabeth (Mrs. R. E. Nutting), Dorothy (Mrs. Thomas Creigh Jr.), and Phyllis (Mrs. W. P. Garriss). Grad., Doane Coll. Acad., Crete, Nebr., 1907; AB, Hastings (Nebr.) Coll., 1911, LLD (hon.), 1950; AM, U. Nebr., 1916, PhD, 1940; student, Columbia U., 1916-17, summer sessions 1917, 32, Stanford, 1924. Prin. Newport, Nebr., 1911-13; supt. Atkinson, Nebr., 1913-16; prof. edn. and psychology Henry Kendall Coll., Tulsa, Okla., 1917-18; dean coll., prof. edn. Hastings Coll., 1918-60, then dean emeritus, coll. historian; head dept. edn. Campbell Coll., Buies Creek, N.C., from 1961; mem. faculty U.S. Army U., Biarritz, France, 1945-46; Fulbrgith lectr., PAkistan, 1960-61. Author: Status of the Rural Teacher in Nebraska, 1919, Presbyterian Colleges and Academies in Nebraska, 1940, (with Mrs. Thomas Creigh Jr.) Hastings College: Seventy-Five Years in Retrospect, 1882-1957, 1957; co-author: The Presbyterian Church in Nebraska, 1950. Mem. Adams County Selective Service, 1941-61; mem. com. Mary Lanning Sch. Nursing, Hastings, Nebr. Mem. Nebr. State Tchrs. Assn. (pres. dist. 4, 1943-44), NEA (v.p. 1943-44), AASA, Nat. Assn. Deans, Advs. of Men., Nat. Soc. Coll. Tchrs. of Edn., Am. Edn. Rsch. Assn., Nebr. Schoolmasters Club (pres. 1956), Kiwanis Club, Acacia Club, Masons, Phi Delta Kappa. Presbyterian. Home: Buies Creek N.C. †

WHARTON, ELIZABETH AUSTIN, newspaperwoman; b. Laredo, Tex., July 15, 1920; d. Lawrence Hay and Alice (Borchers) W. BA, BJ, U. Tex., 1941. Woman's editor Galveston (Tex.) News, 1942; soc. editor Houston Post, 1942-43; mem. staff UPI, from 1943, Congl. corr., Washington, from 1945, week-end editor, 1974-75, overnight editor, from 1976. Mem. Am. Contract Bridge League (life master, life mem.), Washington Press Club, Nat. Press Club, Theta Sigma Phi. Presbyterian. Home: Washington D.C. Died July 4, 1985.

WHAYNE, ALFRED TREVOR, hotel executive; b. Louisville, Dec. 20, 1891; s. Trevor Howerton and Mary John (Moorman) W.; m. Lillian McCarthy, Dec. 3,

1942; children: Betty Jean (Mrs. Yoder), Trevor Rugh. Grad. high sch., Louisville. Sec.-treas. Nat. Hotel Co., Galveston, Tex., 1930-61, pres., 1952-61, also bd. dirs.; past pres., bd. dirs. Nat. Hotel Co-operated hotels; formed Affiliated Nat. hotel chain; past v.p., bd. dirs. McBride's Inc., Galveston, Seaboard Realty Co., Galveston, So. Trading Co., Galveston, Texala Realty Corp., Birmingham, Ala., Silver Lake Raches, Inc.; mem. exec. com., bd. dirs. Am. Nat. Ins. Co., Galveston, News Pub. Co., Galveston; mem. exec. com Mainland Pub. Co., Texas City, Tex.; mng. ptnr. Liberty Drug Co., from 1940; bd. dirs. Houston Lighting & Power Co. Sec. Moody Found.; bd. dirs. Freedom's Found.; past nat. chmn. All Am. Conf. to Combat Communism; past chmn. bd. trustees and adminstrv. agy. com., mem. exec. com. United Fund. Lt. USCG, World War II. Mem. Am. (past gov., past chmn. better citizenship com.), Tex. (hon. pres. for life) hotel assns., Tex. Mfrs. Assn., C. of C. (past bd. dirs., exec. com.), Galvez Club (sec., bd. dirs.), Menger Patio Club (v.p., bd. dirs.). †

WHEELER, CHARLES LEIGH, lumber and shipping company executive; b. Hammond, Wis., Aug. 20, 1888; s. Jacob S. and Nellie (Clack) W.; m. Marion Myers, Apr. 4, 1917; 1 child, Charles Leigh. Student, Stout Schs., Menomonie, Wis., 1903-07. Successively printers devil, reporter and advt. solicitor Menomonie Times, 1907-10; mgr. St. Helens (Oreg.)Dock & Terminal subs. Chas. R. McCormick Lumber Co., 1917-21; organizer, exec. v.p. Pone & Talbot Inc. (successors to McCormick Steamship Co.), 1921-55, spl. v.p., also dir.; bd. dirs. Crocker-Anglo Nat. Bank of San Francisco. Mem. U.S. Internat. Devel. Bd., from 1950; mem. adv. bd. Point Four Program; bd. dirs. U. Calif. Internat. House. Mem. Nat. Fedn. Am. Shipping (dir.), Rotary (internat. pres. 1943-44), Bohemian Club, Propeller Club of U.S. Republican. Unitarian. Home: Woodside Calif. †

WHEELER, HUGH CALLINGHAM, author; b. London, Mar. 19, 1912; s. Harold and Florence (Scammell) W. B.A. in English with honours, U. London, 1932. Author: plays Big Fish, Little Fish, 1961, Look We've Come Through, 1961, We Have Always Lived in the Castle, 1966, Irene, 1973, (with Stephen Sondheim) A Little Night Music, 1973, Sweeney Todd, 1978, (with Leonard Bernstein) Candide, 1974, (with Sondheim and John Weidman) Pacific Overtones, 1976, (with Kurt Weill) Silverlake, 1980; novel The Crippled Muse, 1952; Author (under pseud. Patrick Quentin): 17 novels latest being Family Skeletons, 1965; Author (under pseud. Q. Patrick with R. Wilson Webb): 5 novels latest being Return to the Scene, 1952; Author (under pseud. Jonathan Stagge with R. Wilson Webb): 8 novels latest being The Three Fears, 1953; Author: screenplays Five Miles to Midnight, 1962, Something for Everyone, 1970, Travels with My Aunt, 1973, A Little Night Music, 1977, Nijinski, 1980. Recipient Edgar Allen Poe award, 1961, 73; recipient Antoinette Perry award, 1973, 74, 79, Drama Critics Circle award, 1973, 74, 79, Drama Desk award, 1973, 74, 79. Mem. Writers Guild. Died July 26, 1987; buried Corashire Cemetery, Monterey, Mass.

WHEELER, MONROE, museum director; b. Evanston, Ill., Feb. 13, 1900; s. Frederick Monroe and Anna Marie (Kinzie) W. Student, France, England, Germany, 1920-29. Co-founder, ptnr. Harrison of Paris, France, 1930-35; dir., chmn. exhbns. com. Am. Inst. Graphic Arts, 1936-39; chmn. library com., mem. adv. com. Mus. Modern Art, N.Y.C., 1936, dir. publs., 1939-66, dir. exhbns., 1946-67, mem. internat. coun., 1965-88, councellor to the trustees, 1967-88, chmn. com. on drawings and prints, 1967-88, trustee, 1945-88. Author: Bookbindings of I. Wiemeler, 1935, Modern Painters and Sculptors as Illustrators, 1936, Prints of Georges Rouault, 1938, Britain at War, 1941, 20th Century Portraits, 1942, Modern Drawings, 1944, Chaim Soutine, 1950, Textiles and Ornaments of India, 1956, The Last Works of Henri Matisse, 1961, Bonnard and His Environment, 1964. Chmn. com. on publs. Office Coordinator of Inter-Am. Affairs, Washington, 1940-45; mem. publs. com. UNESCO, Paris, 1949; trustee Ben Sahn Found.; adv. coun. Rutgers U. Decorated chevalier French Legion of Honor, 1951; life mem. French Inst. in U.S.; mem. N.Y. Geneol. and Biog. Soc. (trustee, v.p.), Internat. Graphic Arts Soc. (trustee, pres.), Grolier Club, Coffee House Club (N.Y.C.). Home: Rosemont N.J. Died Aug. 14, 1988.

WHIPPLE, CLYDE COLBURN, educator; b. North Pomtret, Vt., Jan. 14, 1892; s. W. C. and May (Colburn) W.; m. Emma Collins, Dec. 30, 1916; children: David, Dorothy, Virginia. BS, Worcester Poly. Inst., 1915, degree in EE, 1931; postgrad., Columbia U., 1920-28. Engr. Klaxom Co., Newark, 1915-20, Pratt Inst., Bklyn., 1916, Bell Telephone Labs., N.Y.C., 1917-18; instr., asst. prof. Bklyn. Poly. Inst., from 1920, supr. elec. power and light sect., from 1940, prof. elec. engring., 1940-62, chmn. undergrad. dept. elec. engring., 1944-58. Author: (with M.L. Garik) Electric Machines, 1946. Fellow AIEE; mem. Illuminating Engring. Soc., Am. Soc. Engring. Edn. Republican. Home: Scarsdale N.Y. †

WHITAKER, JOHN CLARKE, tobacco company executive; b. Winston-Salem, N.C., Aug. 7, 1891; s. William Asbury and Anna (Bitting) W.; m. Elizabeth Norman, July 17, 1936; children: John Clarke, Elizabeth Norman, Louisa Bitting, William Asbury III. Student, Guilford Coll., N.C., 1907-09; AB, U. N.C., 1912. With R.J. Reynolds Tobacco Co., from 1913, supt. cigarette dept., 1916-19, mgr. personnel dept., 1919-35, dir., from 1935, v.p., 1937-48, pres., 1948-52, chmn. bd., 1952-59, hon. chmn., from 1959; v.p. Winston-Salem Hotel Co.; bd. dirs. Wachovia Bank and Trust Co. Alderman Winston-Salem, 1921-22; chmn. bd. trustees Winston-Salem Tchrs. Coll.; chmn. Carolinas United Red Feather Svcs., Winston-Salem Community Chest, Housing Authority of City Winston-Salem, 1941; pres. William and Kate B. Reynolds Meml. Pk.; pres. (local) Boy Scouts Am., 1922; dir. YMCA, 1923-26. With USN, 1917-19; comdr. Citizens Def. Corps. Mem. Twin City Club, Forsyth Country Club, Oldtown Club, Masons, Rotary (pres. 1921), Sigma Alpha Epsilon. Episcopalian. Home: Winston-Salem N.C. †

WHITBY, KENNETH THOMAS, mechanical engineer; b. Fond du Lac, Wis., Feb. 6, 1925; s. Robert Gerhard and Theresa Mae (Strebe) W.; m. Juanita Mae Bergstresser, July 31, 1948; children: Susan Lee, Dean Kenneth, Dale Robert, Evan Ross. BS in Naval Tech., U. Minn., 1946, BSME, 1948, PhD in Mech. Engring., 1954. Instr. U. Minn., 1946-58, asst. prof. mech. engring., 1958-62, assoc. prof., 1962-66, prof., 1966-83, founder, dir. particle tech. lab., 1953-72, dir. environ. div., dept. mech. engring, 1972-83; cons. to industry. Contbr. numerous articles to profl. publs.; patentee in field. Lt. (j.g.) USN, 1943-46. Quaker Oats fellow, 1954; USPHS grantee, 1955-65; Nat. Air Pollution Adminstrn. grantee, 1965-70; EPA grantee, 1970-83; AEC grantee, 1962-79; U.S. Bur. Mines grantee, 1971-83. Mem. ASME, Nat. Acad. Engring., ASHRAE, AAAS, N.Y. Acad. Scis. Republican. Presbyterian. Home: Minneapolis Minn. Died Nov. 14, 1983.

WHITE, BETTY LOU, editor; b. Chgo., June 2, 1918; d. Roscoe E. and Zula Rae (Lyon) Munson; m. Robert H. White, Sept. 25, 1959 (dec. 1981). Grad. high Sch., Green Bay, Wis. Sec. Pub. Utility Co., Green Bay, Wis., 1936-42; editor Pub. Devel. Corp., Chgo., 1949-64, Clark Pub. Co., Highland Park, Ill., 1966-87. Served to capt. WAC, U.S. Army, 1942-46, ETO. Decorated Bronze Star. Home: Lake Forest Ill. Died Oct. 20, 1987.

WHITE, CHESTER WIRT, JR., anesthesiologist; b. Lewiston, Maine, Aug. 11, 1919; s. Chester W. and Gladys (Chadbourne) W.; m. Melba Fuller, Oct. 16, 1948; children: Ayson, Peter C. BS, McGill U., 1941; AM in Pharmacology (USPHS fellow), Boston U., 1949, MD magna cum laude, 1951. Diplomate Nat. Bd. Med. Examiners, Am. Bd. Anesthesiologists. Various positions as musician and chemist 1934-48; instr. pharmacology Boston U. Sch. Medicine, 1951-55; intern Newton-Wellesley Hosp., 1951-52, active staff anesthesia, 1953-61; cons. Gillette Safety Razor Co., Boston, 1952-55; resident, dir. anesthesia rsch. Boston City Hosp., 1955-58, assoc. vis. anesthesiologist, 1956; anesthesiologist-in-chief Boston Lying-in Hosp., 1957-61; cons. anesthesiologist Peter Bent Brigham, Chelsea Naval, Robert Breck Brigham hosps., 1957-61; asst. prof. anesthesiology Harvard Med. Sch., 1961; prof., chmn. dept. Med. Coll. Ala. and U. Hosp. Birmingham, 1961-70; anesthesiologist-in-chief U. Ala. Hosp. and Clinics, 1961-85; cons. Birmingham VA Hosp., 1961-85, Birmingham Crippled Children's Hosp., 1962-85; pvt. practice in anesthesiology Birmingham, 1961-85. Contbr. numerous articles to med. jours. Recipient Maimonides award Greater Boston Med. Soc., 1950. Fellow Am. Coll. Anesthesiology; mem. AMA, AAAS, Am. Soc. Anesthesiologists, Am. Soc. for Pharmacology and Exptl. Therapeutics, Med. Assn. Ala., Ala. Soc. Anesthesia, So. Med. Assn. Home: Birmingham Ala. Died Oct. 15, 1985.

WHITE, FREDERIC RANDOLPH, educator; b. Wilkinsburg, Pa., Apr. 13, 1910; s. George Frederic and Edna (Fitz-Randolph) W.; m. Naomi Bossler, May 11, 1935; 1 dau., Anne Randolph. AB, Oberlin Coll., 1931, MA, 1932; certificate, U. Grenole, 1932, U. Paris, 1933; PhD (Univ. fellow 1937-41), U. Mich., 1942. Danforth fellow Columbia U., 1955, U. Chgo., 1958, Colo. U., 1961; Ford fellow Harvard U., 1955, U. N.C., 1956; instr. U. Toledo, 1935-36; asst. prof. Ill. Inst. Tech., 1941-43; assoc. prof. Knox Coll., 1943-45; Sage Found. prof. English Beloit Coll., 1945-60, chmn. dept., 1954-59; prof. comparative lit. and classics Eckerd Coll., 1960-84; State dept. lectr. U. Tehran, Iran, 1956-57. Author: The Development of Homeric Criticism, 1942, Edward Bellamy's Looking Backward, 1946, Famous Utopias of the Renaissance, 1947; contbr. articles, essays, poems and book reviews various periodicals. Mem. Modern Lang. Assn., Internat. Comparative Lit. Assn., AAAU, Classical Soc., Nat. Coun. Tchrs. English, Conf. Christianity and Scholarship, North Cen. Assn. Workshop, Social Action Com., Am. Assn. Comparative Lit. Presbyterian. Home: Saint Petersburg Fla. Died June 21, 1984; buried Oberlin, Ohio.

WHITE, GOODRICH COOK, university chancellor; b. Griffin, Ga., Nov. 13, 1889; s. George Berry and Florence Richards (Cook) W.; m. Helen Dean Chappell, May 4, 1915; children: Goodrich Cook (dec.), Edwin Chappell. AB, Emory Coll., 1908; AM, Columbia, 1911; PhD, U. Chgo., 1927; LLD, U. Chattanooga, 1947, Hamline U., 1949, U. N.C., 1950, Dickinson Coll., 1954, Bucknell U., 1964; LittD, Cornell, 1954; HHD, W.Va. Wesleyan, 1958, Ohio Northern U., 1958; LHD, Clark Coll., 1950, Emory U., 1965. Prof. English, instr. psychology Ky. Wesleyan Coll., 1911-13; prof. psychology and edn. Wesleyan Coll., Macon, Ga., 1913-14; prof. mental and moral sci. Emory Coll., 1914-18; assoc. prof. psychology Emory U., 1919-20, prof., 1920-42, dean Coll. Arts and Scis., 1923-38, dean Grad. Sch., 1929-42, v.p., 1938-42, pres., 1942-57, chancellor, from 1957. Mem. Gen. Bd. Edn., Meth. Episcopal Ch., South, 1934-40; mem. Univ. Senate, Meth. Ch., 1940-60; mem. Pres.'s Commn. on Higher Edn., 1946-47; trustee Wesleyan Coll., Clark Coll. With U.S. Army, 1918-19. Fellow AAAS; mem. Assn. Ga. Colls. (pres. 1933-34), Conf. Acad. Deans of So. States (pres. 1933), Conf. Deans. of So. Grad. Schs. (pres. 1939), So. Assn. Colls. and Secondary Schs. (mem. commn. secondary schs. 1923-36, sec. commn on instns. of higher edn. 1940-47), So. Univ. Conf. (pres. 1949-50), Ga. Acad. Sci. (pres. 1939), Chi Pi, Omicron Delta KAppa, Sigma Xi, Phi Beta Kappa (pres. Gamma of Ga., 1931-32, 37-38, senator 1937-61, pres. United chpts. 1952-55). Democrat. Methodist. Home: Decatur Ga. †

WHITE, HARVEY ELLIOTT, educator, physicist; b. Parkersburg, W.Va., Jan. 28, 1902; s. Elliott Adam and Elizabeth (Wile) W.; m. Adeline Dally, Aug. 10, 1928; children: Donald H., Jerald P., Vernita L. AB, Occidental Coll., 1925; Sc.D (hon.), Cornell U., 1929. Teaching asst. Cornell U., 1925-26, instr., 1926-29; internat. rsch. fellow Physikalische Techneische Reischsanstalt, Berlin, Federal Republic of Germany, 1929-30; asst. prof. U. Calif., 1930-36, assoc. prof., 1936-42, prof., 1942-69, prof. emeritus, 1969-88; planner, 1st dir. Lawrence Hall Sci., 1960-69; tchr. nationwide NBC-TV broadcast physics course for high sch. tchrs., 1958. Author: Introduction to Atomic Spectra, 1934, Fundamentals of Optics, 4 edits., 1937m Classical and Modern Physics, 1940, Modern College Physics, 6 edits., 1948, Descriptive College Physics, 3 edits, 1955, Atomic and Nuclear Physics, 1964, Introduction to College Physics, 1969, others; author and lectr. for 1st complete introductory physics course to be put on color film. Civilian AEC; with OSRD, 1942-45. Guggenheim Fellow, Hawaii, 1948; recipient War Dept. citation, 1947, Thomas Alva Edison TV award, Peabody TV award, Parents mag. medal, Sylvania award, Hans Christian Oersted award Am. Assn. Physics Tchrs., 1968, others. Fellow Am. Phys. Soc.; mem. Optical Soc. Am., Bohemian Club, Phi Beta Kappa, Sigma Xi, Phi Kappa Phi. Home: Berkeley Calif. Died Oct. 3, 1988; cremated.

WHITE, JACK EDWARD, physician; b. Stuart, Fla., July 24, 1921; m. Sara White, Sept. 30, 1945; children: Jack E., David A., Carol Diane, Sara Lorraine, Marilyn Marie. B.S., Fla. A&M U., 1941; M.D., Howard U., 1944. Diplomate Am. Bd. Surgery. Intern Howard U., 1945-46, resident, 1946-49; resident Meml. Hosp., N.Y.C., 1949-51; asst. prof. surgery Howard U., Washington, 1951-58; asso. prof. Howard U., 1958-63, prof., 1963-86, chmn. oncology, 1972-86, dir. Cancer Center, 1972-85; ret. 1986; cons. Cancer Control Com., Comprehensive Cancer Center State Fla.; mem. oncologic drug adv. com. FDA. Served to 1st lt. M.C. U.S. Army, to 1946. Recipient Key to City of Miami; Disting. Achievement award Jr. Achievers. Fellow ACS; mem. AMA, Am. Assn. Cancer Insts., Am. Assn. Cancer Research, Acad. Medicine, Nat. Acad. Scis., Soc. Head and Neck Surgeons, Soc. Surg. Oncology, Am. Radium Soc. Home: Washington D.C. Died July 2, 1988.

WHITE, JAMES DUGALD, investment banker; b. Kearney, Nebr., May 7, 1889; s. James Gilbert and Kathleen Victoria Maud (Mullon) W.; m. Dorothy Owen, May 4, 1912 (dec.); children: Brook, Mary Caroline; m. Maude S. Tappan, Feb. 16, 1957. AB, Cornell U., 1911. With The Engring. Securities Corp., N.Y., 1911-15; mem. Hemphill, White & Chamberlain, 1915-19; v.p. J.G. White & Co., 1919-30, pres., 1930-51; pres. White Securities Corp., from 1951; bd. dirs. H.G. White engring. Corp., Ill. Cities Water Co., Thomas & Betts Co. Capt. inf. U.S. Army, 1917-19. Mem. S.R., Cornell Club, Bay Head Yacht Club, Manasquan River Golf Club, Delta Phi. Home: Bay Head N.J. †

WHITE, JULIUS, educator, chemist; b. Pitts., Mar. 23, 1904; s. Morris and Lena (Garl) W.; m. Florence Margaret Roy, Mar. 28, 1932; children: Margaret Jane, Elizabeth Ann, William Jay, Richard Paul. AB, U. Denver, 1925, MS, 1926; PhD, U. Ill., 1931. Instr. chemistry U. Ill., 1926-31, rsch. fellow, 1931-32; NRC fellow medicine U. Mich., 1932-34, rsch. assoc. biol. chemistry, 1934-38; fellow, rsch. asst., prof. Yale U. Sch. Medicine, 1938-39; mem. staff Nat. Cancer Inst., 1939-70, head metabolism sect., lab. biophysics, 1952-54, acting chief radiation br., 1954, Chief lab. physiology, 1955-70; prof. chemistry Montgomery Coll., Rockville, Md., 1970-85; mem. adv. com. rsch. pathogenesis cancer Am. Cancer Soc., 1961-85, chmn. 1962-64. Author articles in field. Maj. M.C. AUS, 1942-45. Decorated Bronze Star with oak leaf cluster. Mem. Am. Chem. Soc., Am. Assn. Biol. Chemists, Am. Inst. Nutrition, Am. Assn. Cancer Rsch., Soc. Exptl. Biology and Medicine, Sigma Xi, Phi Lambda Upsilon, Phi Sigma.

Home: Damascus Md. Died Feb . 3, 1985; buried Arlington Nat. Cemetery, Arlington, Va.

WHITE, KATHARINE S(ERGEANT), editor; b. Winchester, Mass., Sept. 17, 1892; d. Charles Spencer and Elizabeth Blake (Shepley) Sergeant; m. Ernest Angell; children: Nancy (Mrs. Louis T. Stableford), Roger; m. Elwyn Brooks White, Nov. 13, 1929; 1 child, Joel. AB, Bryn Mawr Coll., 1914. Assoc. editor New Yorker mag., from 1925. Editor, compiler: (with E.B. White) A Subtreasury of American Humor, 1941. Trustee Friend Meml. Pub. Library, Brooklin, Maine. Mem. Cosmopolitan Club. †

WHITE, MASTIN GENTRY, judge; b. Van Zandt County, Tex., Jan. 1, 1901; s. John Earl and Minnie Lou (Gentry) W.; m. Marjorie Delight Perry, Mar. 2, 1929 (dec. Mar. 15, 1984). A.B., U. Western N.Mex.; LL.B., U. Tex., 1927; LL.M., Columbia U., 1930; S.J.D. (Brandeis research fellow), Harvard U., 1933. Law clk. Tex. Ct. Criminal Appeals, 1925-27; asst. county atty. Smith County, Tex., 1927-30; assoc. prof. law U. Tex., 1930-32; spl. asst. to U.S. atty. gen., 1933-35; solicitor Dept. Agr., 1935-42, Dept. Interior, 1946-53; mem. firm Connally & White, Washington, 1953-55; trial judge U.S. Ct. of Claims, 1955-82; judge U.S. Claims Ct., from 1982. Trustee Am. U., Washington. Served to col. AUS, World War II. Decorated Legion of Merit, Commendation medal. Mem. ABA, Fed. Bar Assn., State Bar Tex., D.C. Bar, Bar U.S. Supreme Ct., Order of Coif, Alpha Tau Omega, Phi Delta Phi, Delta Sigma Rho, Alpha Psi Omega. Democrat. Methodist. Club: Cosmos (Washington). Home: Washington D.C. Deceased.

WHITE, RUSSELL LAWRENCE, banker; b. Indpls., Oct. 9, 1892; s. Edwin Fullen and Anna (Cotten) W.; m. Ethel Kathrine Elwarner, Sept. 2, 1913; 1 dau., Ethel Janet. With mailing dept. Indpls. News, 1907-10; with engrng. dept. Crane Co., Indpls., 1910-16; sec., treas. City Baking Co., Indpls., 1916-26; chmn. bd. White Baking Co., exec. officer Indpls.; plants White Baking Co., Dayton, Ohio, St. Louis, from 1926; chmn. bd. Ind. Nat. Bank, Indpls., 1943-57, hon. chmn. bd., from 1957; bd. dirs. Nickel Plate R.R., Ind. Bell Telephone Co., Inland Container Corp. Mem. Am. Bakers Assn., Ind. C. of C., Columbia Club, Indpls. Athletic Club, Traders Point Hunt Club, Masons, Shriners, Rotary. Home: Carmel Ind. †

WHITE, STEVEN VIRGIL, investment executive; b. Loma Linda, Calif., Oct. 3, 1928; s. Earl Virgil and Mabel (Ivy) W.; m. Georgia Alberta Thomas, Sept. 30, 1945; children: Daniel P., Glenn S., Lynn White Brady, Susan White McGiven. BS, U. Calif., Berkeley, 1951. With AEC, Washington, 1955-57; dir. contracts div. AEC, Chgo., 1957-61; with Bechtel Group, San Francisco, 1961-87, v.p., 1972; dir., sr. v.p. Bechtel Corp., San Francisco, 1973-87; dir., pres. Bechtel Investments, Inc., Sequoia Ventures Inc., 1981-88; exec. com. Bechtel Group, Inc., 1973-87; bd. dirs. Bechtel Devel. Inc., Bechtel, Inc. Pres., Oakland (Calif.) Stake, Ch. Jesus Christ of Latter-day Saints; mem. nat. adv. council Grad. Sch. Bus., Brigham Young U.; mem. adv. bd. Sta. KOIT, San Francisco, Bus. Sch., U. Calif.-Berkeley, Utah Symphony, Provo; bd. dirs. Merritt/Peralta Med. Ctr., Oakland, Calif. Named Alumnus of Yr. Berkeley Sch. Bus. U. Calif., 1986. Republican. Clubs: Bankers, Pacific Union (San Francisco); Lakeview, Claremont Country (Oakland, Calif.); Moraga Country (Calif.). Home: Moraga Calif. Died Dec. 16, 1988.

WHITE, THEODORE HAROLD, author; b. Boston, May 6, 1915; s. David and Mary (Winkeller) W.; A.B. summa cum laude, Harvard U., 1938; m. Nancy Ariana Bean, Mar. 29, 1947 (div. 1971); children—Ariana Van Der Heyden, David Fairbank; m. Beatrice K. Hofstadter, Mar. 1974. Chief of China bur. Time, Inc., 1939-45; covered China war front, Indian Uprising, Honan famine; present at surrender of Japanese aboard U.S.S. Missouri; editor The New Republic, 1947; nat. corr. The Reporter mag.; mem. staff of Colliers, 1955-56; as corr. covered Europe, Marshall Plan, NATO, others, also reported Am. nat. politics, 1955-80; dir. Ency. Brit. Bd. overseers Harvard U., 1968-74; past trustee Asia Soc. Recipient Air medal, 1944; Sidney Hillman award, 1954, Benjamin Franklin award, 1956, Ted V. Rodgers award, 1956; Secondary Sch. Bd. award, 1955, 59, 62; Pulitzer prize, 1962; Sigma Delta Chi award, 1964; Emmy award for best TV show, 1964, for best documentary TV writing, 1967, 85; Columbia Sch. Journalism award, 1979; Am. Soc. Journalists and Authors award, 1979; Fourth Estate award, 1980. Mem. Council Fgn. Relations. Clubs: Fgn. Corrs. (pres. 1944-45) (China); Harvard, Century (N.Y.C.). Author: (with Annalee Jacoby) Thunder Out of China (Book of Month Club selection), 1946; The Mountain Road (Book of Month Club selection), 1958; The View from the Fortieth Floor (Lit. Guild selection), 1960; The Making of the President, 1960 (Book of Month Club selection), 1961; The Making of the President, 1964, 1965; Caesar at the Rubicon, 1968; The Making of the President, 1968; The Making of the President (Lit. Guild selection), 1972; Breach of Faith (Book of Month Club selection), 1975; editor: The Stillwell Papers, 1948; Fire in the Ashes (Book of Month Club selection), 1953; In Search of History, 1979; America in Search of Itself: The Making of the President, 1956-1980 (Book of the Month Club selection), 1982; contbr. to nat. mags. Died May 15, 1986. Address: Old Rte 67, Bridgewater, CT, 06752.

WHITE, WILLIAM LEE, banker, piano manufacturing executive; b. Stamford, Conn., Aug. 30, 1888; s. William N. and Elizabeth Lee (Diehl) W.; m. Aldana Ripley Quimby, Sept. 2, 1916; children: Aldana Elizabeth (Mrs. Rollin C. Smith), Ruth Ripley (Mrs. Edward Wemple); m. Alma Catherine Meyer, Dec. 10, 1932. AB, Dartmouth Coll., 1912; LLB, N.Y. Law Sch., 1915. Bar: N.Y. 1915. With Bankers Comml. Corp., N.Y.C., 1916-60, pres., 1948-60; with Aeolian Am. Corp., East Rochester, N.Y., 1930-59, chmn. bd. Named to Field Trial Hall of Fame. Mem. Amateur Field Trial Clubs Am. (past pres.), Phi Beta Kappa, Phi Delta Phi. Republican. Methodist. Home: Westport Conn. †

WHITED, F(RANK) T(HAYER), business executive; b. Shreveport, La., Sept. 22, 1892; s. Frank Thayer and Katie (Bowman) W.; m. Elizabeth Frost, Nov. 3, 1917; 1 child, Edwin Frost. Student, U. of the South, 1910-12, U. Va., 1912-16. Pres. Frost-Whited Co., Inc., Whited Co., Inc.; bd. dirs. Ark. & La. Mo. Ry. Co., Olin-Mathieson Chem. Corp., State Nat. Bank, Texarkana, Ark. Home: Shreveport La. †

WHITEHALL, HAROLD, educator, lexicographer; b. Ramsbottom, Lancashire, Eng., May 14, 1905; came to U.S., 1928; s. Charles Henry and Beatrice Eliza (Fallows) W.; m. Felizitas Schoeny, June 8, 1949; 1 dau., Beatrix Deborah. Student, Nottingham U., Eng., 1924-27; B.A. (hon,), London U., 1927; PhD, U. Iowa, 1931. Instr. English U. Iowa, 1928-31; asst. editor Middle English Dictionary U. Mich., 1931-38; lectr. English U. Wis., 1938-39; asst. prof. English Queens Coll., N.Y.C., 1940-41; assoc. prof. English and chmn. linguistics Ind. U., 1941-49, prof., chmn., 1949-59, prof. English lang. and linguistics, 1959-86; linguistic dir. dictionary div. World Pub. Co., Cleve., 1941-51; linguistic and etymological editor New World Dictionary, 1951, 53; inaugurated TV credit courses Linguistics, English Composition and Poetics, 1953-56. Author: The Language of the Shuttleworth Accounts, 1931-32, Middle English Dialect Characteristics (with S. Moore and S.B. Meech), 1935, Middle English and Related Sounds, 1939, The Orthography of John Bate, 1947, Times and Seasons, 1950, Structural Essentials of Written English, 1956; translator: Rostand's Cyrano de Bergerac, 1944, Towneley Second Shepherds' Play, 1955, The Middle French Pathelin, 1958, Baudelaire and Mallarmé, 1959; author of articles on linguistics, criticism for profl. jours. and critical anthologies. Fellow Sch. Letters Ind. U., 1951-86; Guggenheim Meml. fellow, 1939, Rockefeller fellow in criticism, 1944. Mem. Linguistic Soc. Am., Am. Dialect Soc. (life), Modern Lang. Assn. Am. Home: Bloomington Ind. Died Feb. 25, 1986.

WHITEHEAD, CECIL LEE, foundation executive, lawyer; b. Thibodaux, La., Jan. 6, 1892; s. Nathaniel W. and Dora (Tompkins) W.; m. Sima Emily Juntenen, May 23, 1925. BA, La. State U., 1912, LLB, 1914. Bar: La. 1914, Calif. 1924. Pvt. practice Alexandria, La., 1914-17, L.A., from 1925; pub. defender, then pros. atty. 1914-17, pros. atty. specializing in trial cases, from 1924; trustee Braille Inst. Am., Inc., from 1936, pres., from 1956. 1st lt. F.A., U.S. Army, World War I. Home: Altadena Calif. †

WHITEHEAD, RICHARD HENRY, consulting engineer, economist; b. Chgo., Nov. 11, 1886; s. Willis Frederick and Beatrice (Rousseau) W.; m. Mary Katherine Pokorny, July 20, 1908; children: Lewis Richard, John Francis, George Goethals, Richard Henry. BMechE, Lewis Inst., Chgo., 1908; D Eng. (hon.), Ill. Inst. Tech., 1941. Engr. various utility cos. Chgo., 1908-12; instr. engring. Lewis Inst., Chgo., 1908-12; test engr. Isthmian Canal Commn.; then supt. ops. Pacific Locks, Panama Canal, 1912-16; gen. supt. Otis Elevator Co., N.Y.C., 1917; cons. engr. George W. Goethals & Co., 1918-20, George H. Burr & Co., 1921; v.p. New Haven Clock Co., 1922-27, gen. mgr., 1922-46, pres., dir., 1927-46; pres., dir. Scott & Williams, Inc., Laconia, N.H., 1951-61, 66-68, chmn., 1961-65, hon. chmn., 1965-66; pres. Laconia Nat. Bank, 1965-68; dir., cons. engr. Noma Electric Corp., 1948-51; pres. A.M.S.L. Corp., High Point, N.C., 1958-61; mem. com. Nat. Rsch. Devel. Coun., 1943-45; asst. chmn. bomb fuse integrating com. ASF, 1944-45; mem. tech. indsl. intelligence com. Joint Chiefs Staff, sci. cons. spl. mission to Germany, 1945, control officer German Pub. Corp., 19547-48, represented German economy, 1948; mem. Nat. Panel Arbitrators, from 1950. Author: Our Faith Moved Mountains, also papers presented to profl. groups. Mem. N.H. Commn. Interim Edn., 1961-62; mem. Goethals Meml. Commn. Recipient Naval Ordnance Devel. award, 1945, Patriotic Civilian Service award, 1951, Master Key to Panama Canal, 1965, Alumni award Ill. Inst. Tech., 1970. Mem. Conn. Soc. Profl. Engrs., Soc. Am. Historians, U.S. Steel Workers Am. (hon.), Union League Club (past pres.), Bald Peak Colony Club (N.H.), Tau Beta Pi. Republican. Congregationalist. Home: Laconia N.H. †

WHITEHEAD, WILLIAM GRANT, editor; b. Wilmington, N.C., Sept. 19, 1943; s. Allen Hallett and Alice London (Boatwright) W. B.A. cum laude, Princeton U., 1965. Coll. traveller Doubleday & Co., Washington, 1966-68; asst. editor Doubleday & Co., N.Y.C., 1968-70, editor, 1970-73; sr. editor Doubleday-E.P. Dutton Inc., N.Y.C., 1973-83; editor-in-chief E.P. Dutton Inc., N.Y.C., 1983-85; sr. editor Macmillan Pub. Co., 1985-87. Served with USCG, 1965-66. Democrat. Presbyterian. Home: New York N.Y. Died Oct. 9, 1987.

WHITEHILL, HENRY DAVID, corporate executive; b. Vienna, Austria, Mar. 29, 1923; came to U.S., 1938; s. Charles and Katherine W.; m. Margery W., May 23, 1943; 1 child, Thomas. Student, Columbia U., N.Y.C., 1942, Rutgers U., New Brunswick, N.J., 1950-53. Successively dist. mgr., asst. v.p., v.p. and sec., sr. v.p. Culbro Corp., N.Y.C., 1947-87. Served to sgt. U.S. Army, 1943-46, ETO. Mem. Soc. Corp. Secs. Home: New York N.Y. Died May 13, 1987.

WHITEHOUSE, WALTER MACINTIRE, physician, educator; b. Millersburg, Ohio, Jan. 28, 1916; s. Frank and Maybelle (MacIntire) W.; m. Barbara N. McIntyre, Jan. 27, 1945 (dec. Mar. 1975); children: Walter MacIntire, Douglas A., Mary B.; m. Rebecca Sturtevant Marble, July 31, 1976. AB, Ea. Mich. U., 1936; MS, U. Mich., 1937, MD, 1941. Staff physician, asst. dir. Mich. State Sanatorium, Howell, 1945-49; resident radiology U. Mich. Med. Sch., Ann Arbor, 1949-52, instr., 1952-54, asst. prof., 1954-57, assoc. prof., 1957-63, prof., 1963-82, chmn. dept. radiology, 1965-79, prof. emeritus, 1982-85; cons., 1982-85. Author: (with F.J. Hodges) The Gastrointestinal Tract: A Handbook of Roentgen Diagnosis, 1965; editor: Year Book of Radiology, 1960-70, 71-78. Mem. AMA, Am. Roentgen Ray Soc., Radiol. Soc. N.Am., Assn. U. Radiologists, Am. Coll. Radiology. Episcopalian. Home: Ann Arbor Mich. Died Oct. 9, 1985; buried St. Andrews Episcopal Church Meml. Gardens.

WHITEHOUSE, WILLIAM WHITCOMB, educator; b. Yorkshire, Eng., Oct. 28, 1891; came to U.S., 1913, naturalized, 1918; s. John and Elizabeth (Whitcomb) W.; m. Grace May Harrison, June 27, 1917 (dec. June 22, 1941); children: Keith Harrison, Joyce May; m. Adele Ann Dreyer, 1943. AB, Lebanon (Ohio) U., 1916; BD, Garrett Bibl. Inst., Evanston, Ill., 1917; AM, Lawrence Coll., Appleton, Wis., 1919; ThD, Drew Univ. Theol. Sem., 1922; PhD, Northwestern U., 1927; LLD, Wayne U., 1946, Mich. State U., 1955, U. Mich., 1959; LHD (hon.), Ohio Wesleyan U., 1959; DD (hon.), Adrian Coll., 1961. Ordained to ministry M.E. Ch., 1916. Pastor Asbury Ch., Milw., Wis., 1917-18, Parma, Mich., 1918-19; ednl. dir. Camp Custer, 1917; prof. econs. Albion (Mich.) Coll., 1922-29, dean, 1929-39, pres., 1945-60, pres. emeritus, from 1960; dean Coll. Liberal Arts Wayne State U., 1939-45; John Shaffer Found. lectr. Northwestern U., 1938; lectr. U. Mich., U. Ill., Purdue U., U. Chgo.; bd. dirs. City Bank and Trust Co., Jackson, Mich. Contbr. to ednl. and profl. jours. Trustee Mich. State Tb Assn., 1937-40, Bay View Assn.; bd. dirs. Mich. Coun. Chs., 1935-40, Detroit Round Table of Catholics, Jews and Protestants, Detroit Coun. on Community Nursing; pres. bd. Meth. Children's Home Soc.; mem. Common Coun. for Am. Unity; mem. bd. and v.p. Mich. Dist. Am. Youth Hostels; mem. health adv. com. Detroit Coun. Youth Svc., Pres. Eisenhower's Com. on Scientists and Engrs.; mem. adv. coun. Detroit Inter-Am. Ctr.; mem. com. on orgn. and legis. Meth. Bd. Edn., com. for Christian U. in Japan; chmn. bd. trustees, pres. Citizens Rsch. Coun. in Mich., also 1st vice chmn.; mem. com. for Joint Legislature com. on Reorgn. State Govt.; mem. state adv. com. on tchr. edn. and certs. Mem. Mich. Assn. Colls. (sec. 1935-39, chmn. com. on ednl. standards, com. on nutrition and defense), North Central Assn. (commn. on colls. and univs.), Assn. Am. Colls. (pres. 1958), Am. Assn. Coll. Tchrs. Edn. (v.p.), NEA (internat. rels. com.), Masons, Rotary, Delta Sigma Phi, Delta Sigma Rho, Phi Beta Kappa, Omicron Delta Kappa. Methodist. Home: Albion Mich. †

WHITEHURST, GEORGE W., judge; b. Wauchula, Fla., May 18, 1891; s. L. W. and M. E. (McEwan) W.; m. Myra Coker, 1914; children: George W., Barbara, marge Ann. Student, Stetson U.; LLB, U. Fla. Bar: Fla. Judge Fla. Cir. Ct.; chief judge U.S. Dist. Ct. (no. and so. dists) Fla., Miami. Mem. Masons, Elks, Phi Delta Phi. †

WHITMORE, BENJAMIN ARTHUR, banker, trust officer; b. Hooper's Island, Md., Feb. 1, 1892; s. Alfred Alexander and Emma Jane (Robinett) W.; m. Florence Sampson, Oct. 1, 1913; 1 child, Ann Robinette (Mrs. William L. Woodruff). LLD, Fla. So. Coll., 1935. Clk. Hunter & Co., Richmond, Va., 1909-12; salesman, buyer Pub. Ho. M.E. Ch. South, Va. br., Richmond, 1912-20, mgr., 1920-26; pub. agt. Pub. Ho. M.E. Ch. South, Nashville, 1926-40, Meth. Ch., 1940-45; v.p., chmn. trust com. 3d Nat. Bank, from 1946, also bd. dirs.; Mem. bd. publ. Meth. Ch. Trustee Joint Univ. Library, Scarritt Coll., Nashville; mem. exec. bd. Nat. Coun. Boy Scouts Am.,. Mem. Nashville C. of C., Rotary, Belle Meade Country Club, Nashville Round Table, Cumberland Club. Methodist. †

WHITNEY, DONALD WALKER, broadcasting executive; b. Lenox, Tenn., Oct. 16, 1926; s. Clarence

James and Maude Bell (Behurst) W.; m. Dollie Fay Roper, Apr. 9, 1945; 1 son, Donald Stephen Whitney. Student public schs. Staff announcer, country music entertainer stas. in Miss., Tenn. and Ark., 1941-57; mgr. sta. KOSE, Osceola, Ark., 1957; exec. v.p., chief engr., part owner stas. KOSE/KHFO, Osceola, 1976-85; exec. v.p., dir. Osceola Broadcasting Corp. Composer recorded country music songs. Pres. Osceola PTA, 1963. Named Osceola Man of Year, 1969. Mem. Nat. Assn. Broadcasters, Nat. Radio Broadcasters Assn., Ark. AP Broadcasters (past pres.), Ark. Broadcasters Assn. (past pres., Pioneer award 1984), Am. Radio Relay League, Miss. County Amateur Radio Assn., Osceola C. of C. (dir., past pres.). Democrat. Baptist. Clubs: Osceola Rotary (pres. 1964), Masons. Home: Osceola Ark. Died Aug. 20, 1985; buried Roller-Swift Cemetery, Osceola, Ark.

WHITRIDGE, ARNOLD, author, educator; b. New Rochelle, N.Y., June 29, 1891; s. Frederick Wallingford and Lucy (Arnold) W.; m. Janetta Alexander, Apr. 25, 1918; children: Janetta, Frederick Wallingford, Rhoda. Student, Oxford U., 1913-14; AM, Columbia U., 1921, PhD, 1925. Asst. prof. English, Columbia U., 1921-32; master of Calhoun Coll., Yale U., 1932-42; also prof. history, arts and letters dept. until resigned, Apr. 1942; Fulbright prof. Am. civilization U. Athens, 1949-51, U. Bordeaux (France), 1952. Author: Critical Ventures in Modern French Literature, 1924, Dr. Arnold of Rugby, 1928, Alfred de Vigny, 1933, Men in Crisis, 1949, Simon Bolivar, 1954, No Compromise, 1960, Rochambeau, 1965 (award Colonial Dames). Pres. Art Commn. City N.Y., 1957-66, N.Y. Soc. Library, from 1966; trustee Met. Mus. Art, St. Luke's Hosp. Served to lt. Royal Arty., Brit. Army, 1914-17; capt. F.A., U.S. Army, 1917-18; A.E.F.; maj., 1918-19; maj. Combat Intelligence, USAAF, 1942, later col.; overseas with 9th Air force. Mem. Delta Kappa Epsilon, Scroll and Key, Century Assn., University, Athenaeum clubs. Home: Salisbury Conn. Died Jan. 29, 1989.

WHITTEMORE, EDWARD WILLIAM, holding company executive; b. N.Y.C., Dec. 25, 1922; s. Harold Clifton and Florence Veronica (Stratton) W.; m. Jeanne McConnochie, June 12, 1948; children: Edward William, Jeannette L. B.A., Columbia U., 1947. With Wilson Jones Co., Chgo., 1947-72; v.p. mktg. Wilson Jones Co., 1968-70, exec. v.p., 1970-72; exec. v.p. Swingline Inc., L.I. City, N.Y., 1972-75, pres., chief operating officer, 1975-77, pres., chief exec. officer, 1977-78; dir. Am. Brands, Inc., Old Greenwich, Conn., 1977-87; mem. exec. com. Am. Brands, Inc., 1978-87, v.p. subs. adminstrn., 1978-79, exec. v.p. ops., 1979-80, chmn., chief exec. officer, 1981-87; bd. dirs. Acushnet Co., Am. Brands Internat. Corp., Am. Tobacco Co., Am. Tobacco Internat. Corp., James B. Beam Distilling Co., Franklin Life Ins. Co., Gallaher Ltd., Andrew Jergens Co., Master Lock Co., MCM Products, Inc., Pinkerton's, Inc., Sunshine Biscuits, Inc., Swingline Inc., Wilson Jones Co., Golden Belt Mfg. Co., Am. Franklin Co. subs. Am. Brands, Inc. Mem. exec. com. Pres.'s Pvt. Sector Survey on Cost Control, 1982-83; 1st vice-chmn. bd. visitors Columbia Coll., Columbia U.; bd. visitors dept. econs. Columbia U.; v.p., bd. dirs., chmn. exec. and fin. com. Police Athletic League, Inc. Served with USAAF, 1943-45. Recipient John Jay award Columbia U., 1982; Corp. Leadership award Nat. Women's Econ. Alliance, 1985. Mem. Bus. Records Mfrs. Assn. (pres. 1971-72), Nat. Office Products Assn. (v.p. 1969-70), Conf. Bd., Wholesale Stationers Assn. (dir. 1970-72). Clubs: Economic, N.Y. Yacht (N.Y.C.). Home: Stamford Conn. Died Sept. 5, 1987; buried Kensico Cemetery, Valhalla, N.Y.

WHITTLE, KENNON C(AITHNESS), lawyer, judge; b. Martinsville, Va., Oct. 12, 1891; s. Stafford Gorman and Ruth (Drewry) W.; m. Mary Holt Spencer, Oct. 20, 1920; children: Mary Whittle Woodson, Stafford G., Kennon C. LLB, Washington and Lee U., 1914, LLD, 1952. Bar: Va. 1913. Practice Martinsville, 1914-44; judge 7th Jud. Ct. Va., 1944-50; became justice Va. Supreme Ct. Appeals, 1951, later assoc. justice; bd. dirs. Am. Furniture Co., 1st Nat. Bank Martinsville, Lee Telephone Co., Jamestown Corp. Mem. bd. trustees Washington and Lee U. Served as 1st sgt. U.S. Army, World War I. Mem. Am., Va. (past pres.) bar assns., Am. Legion (pres. 1921), Am. Judicature Soc., Va. Historical Soc., Sons of Cin., Masons, K.P., Elks, Forest Park Country Club, Commonwealth Club, Phi Delta Phi, Pi Kappa Alpha. Episcopalian (sr. warden). Home: Martinsville Va. †

WHITWELL, GEORGE EDWARD, utility consultant; b. Washington, June 17, 1892; s. Sanford Nesbitt and Anna Louise (Fenwick) W.; m. Alice Ruth MacCallum, Oct. 20, 1917; children: Marie Louise (Mrs. Robert F. Gilkeson), Margaret Ruth (Mrs. H. J. Bartle III), Sanford MacCallum. BS, MIT, 1914. Rsch. engr. Anaconda Copper Co., 1915-18; instr. chem. engring. U. Wash., 1919-22; cons. engr., gen. sipt. Tacoma Gas & Fuel Co., 1920-24; mgr. gas properties Byllesby Engring. & Mgmt. Corp., 1925-26; gen. mgr. Equitable Gas Co., Pitts., 1926; gen. sales mgr. Phila. Co., Pitts., 1927-29; v.p. Phila. Co., 1929-31; v.p. in charge sales Phila. Electric Co., 1931-56, ret.; bd. dirs. Quaker City Fed. Savs. & Loan Assn. Author: Magnesite: Its Occurence and Uses, 1920; contbr. articles to trade jours. Ex-term mem. corp. MIT; hon. chmn. Phila. Jr. Achievement Inc. Served in Aviation Corps, U.S. Army, 1918-19. Recipient James H. McGraw award for cooperation in advancement of electric industry, 1935. Mem. N.A.M. (past regional v.p.), U.S. C. of C. (past dir.), Pa. Electric Assn. (past pres.), Ill. Engring. Soc., Edison Elec. Inst., C. of C. (past pres., dir.), Phila. Country Club, Midday Club, Sigma Xi, Chi Phi, Phi Lambda Upsilon. Republican. Presbyterian. Home: Wynnewood Pa. †

WHITZEL, RAYMOND THOMAS, manufacturing executive; b. Columbus, Ohio, Aug. 22, 1891; s. John A. and Ella P. (Vought) W.; m. Editha M. Cole, June 20, 1919. EM, Ohio State U., 1915. With Aluminum Co. Am., from 1915, from metallurgist to div. mgr., 1915-56, v.p., gen. prodn. mgr., from 1956. Mem. AIME, Masons, Elks. Home: Pittsburgh Pa. †

WICHERS, EDWARD, chemist; b. Zeeland, Mich., Mar. 25, 1892; s. William and Willemina (Pyl) W. m. Ruth hopkins, June 30, 1917, 1 child, Edward Hopkins. AB, Hope Coll., 1913, ScD (hon.), 1941; MS, U. Ill., 1915, PhD, 1917. Asst. chemist Nat. Bur. Standards, 1917-19, assoc. chemist, 1919-22, chief reagents sect., 1922-48, chief div. chemistry, 1948-58, assoc. dir., from 1958; chemist Los Alamos (N.Mex.) Lab., 1944-45. Contbr. tech. articles to profl. jours. Elder, trustee in Presbyn. Ch. Recipient Hillebrand award Chem. Soc. Washington, 1938, Exceptional Svc. award U.S. Dept. Commerce, 1952. Mem. Am. Chem. Soc. (councillor, pres. Washington sect. 1932), Washington Acad. Sci. (v.p. 1932), Internat. Union Pure and Applied Chemistry (pres. sect., inorganic chemistry 1955-59). Home: Kensington Md. †

WICKER, SAMUEL EVARISTUS, clergyman, social sciences educator; b. Altoona, Pa., Mar. 10, 1892; s. John Henry and Alice Regina (Wilt) W.; m. Orpah Christina Ashby, Dec. 12, 1918. AB, Gettysburg (Pa.) Coll., 1914, DD, 1950; student, Gettysburg Theol. Sem., 1914-17; MA, U. Pa., 1923; STD, Temple U., Phila., 1925; PhD, Ukrainian U., 1932. Pastor St. Mark's Luth. Ch., Oakland, Md., 1917-20; head social scis. Oakland High Sch., 1917-19; pastor Holy Trinity Luth. Ch. Wilmington, Del., 1920-26; exec. sec. Wilmington Coun. of Chs., 1924-26; prof. religious edn., Temple U., 1924-25; prof. English and history, Wilmington High Sch., 1926-28, 29-35; prof. religious edn. Cedar Crest Coll., Allentown, Pa., 1928-29; prof. English, Wilmington Vocational Sch., 1930-32; prof. religious edn. Luth. Sch. Christian Edn., Phila., 1930-38; tchr. social scis., Pierre S. du Pont High Sch., Wilminton, Del., 1935-44; prof. psychology, humanities and social scis. Am. Theol. Sem. and Wilmington Bible Coll., 1936-40, 42-43, pres., 1937-40; dir. religious edn., St. Stephen's Luth. Ch., Wilmington, 1935-44; pastor, St. John's Luth. Ch., Lewistown, Pa., from 1944; dir. Luth. Theol. Sem., Gettysburg, Pa., from 1952. Served as 4-Minute Man, U.S. Liberty Loan Campaign, 1917-19; chmn. Garrett County (Md.) United War Work Campaign, 1917-19, Lewistown Borough Police Civil Svc. Commn., from 1953; trustee Am. Theol. Sem., 1936-40. Mem. NEA, Religious Edn. Assn., Internat. Coun. Religious Edn., Druids, Masons (32 deg.), K.T., Shriners, Rotary, Sigma Beta, Phi Sigma Kappa, Kappa Lambda Epsilon. Republican. Home: Lewiston Pa. †

WICKERSHAM, VICTOR, congressman; b. Lone Rock, Ark., Feb. 9, 1906; s. Frank M. and Lillie M. (Sword) W.; m. Jessie B. Stiles, June 30, 1929; children: LaMelba Sue Renberger, Galen, Nelda Holston, Victor II. Ed., Okla. schs. County ofcl. 1924-35, state ofcl., 1935, 36, bldg. contractor, 1937, engaged in life ins., 1938-41; mem. 77th,-79th, 81st-84th, 87th-88th congresses 6th Okla. Dist.; leading agt. Republic Nat. Life Ins. Co., Dallas, 1965-88; owner of Huckins Hotel, Oklahoma City. Democrat. Mem. Christian Ch. Died Mar. 15, 1988.

WICKEY, GOULD, clergyman; b. Eshcol, Pa., Sept. 25, 1891; s. William Otterbein and Jennie Alberta (Hartman) W.; m. Ethel Basehoar, Aug. 29, 1917; children: Kathryn Basehoar (Mrs. Paul M. Orso), Phyllis Cecile (Mrs. William C. Waltemyer Jr.), Vivian Deloris (Mrs. N. Eugene Otto), Charlotte Ethel (Mrs. Erle K. Diehl). AB, Gettysburg (Pa.) Coll., 1912, DD, 1929; BD, Lutheran Theol. Sem., Gettysburg, Pa., 1915; AM, Harvard, 1916, PhD, 1923; student, Oxford U., Eng., 1919-20; LLD (hon.), Howard Coll., 1939; DD, Lutheran Coll. and Sem., Saskatoon, Can., 1943; LittD, Sterling (Kans.) Coll., 1940; LHD (hon.), Newberry (S.C.) Coll., 1950; DSc in Edn., Midland Coll., 1958. Ordained to ministry Lutheran Ch., 1916. Pastor Georgetown Luth. Ch., Washington, 1916-17; prof. philosophy Concordia Coll., Moorhead, Minn., 1920-26; pastor St. Marks Luth. Ch., Fargo, N.D., 1924-26; pres. Carthage (Ill.) Coll., 1926-29; exec. sec. , bd. edn. United Luth. Ch., Washington, 1929-59; exec. dir. NAt. Lutheran Edn. Conf., from 1958; gen. sec. Coun. Ch. Bds. of Edn., 1934-47; exec. sec. Nat. Commn. on Christian Higher Edn., 1935-47; Am. Assn. Theol. Schs., 1942-46. Author: The Lutheran Venture in Higher Education, 1962; editor: Christian Education, A Journal of Christian Higher Education, 1934-47; editor, co-author: Going to College, 1934, Going to a Lutheran College, 1951; co-editor: Christian Higher Education, A Handbook, 1949; contbr. to Luth. World Ency., 1965. Mem. NEA, Nat. Luth. Ednl. Conf., Phi Beta Kappa, Pi Gamma Mu. Home: Bethesda Md. †

WICKEY, HARRY HERMAN, artist; b. Stryker, Ohio, Oct. 14, 1892; s. Victor Emanuel and Alice (Besancon) W.; m. Maria B. Rother, Nov. 30, 1921. Studied, with John P. Wicker, Detroit Sch. Fine Arts, 1911-12, with George Bellows and Robert Henri, Ferrer Modern Sch., N.Y.C., 1915, with Arthur Covey, Sch. Industrial Art, N.Y.C., 1914. Specialized in etchin; instr. Art Students League of N.Y.C., 1929-33, lectr. on composition, 1939; artist in residence Bucknell U., 1942-46, Orange County Community Coll., 1957; curator Storm King Art Ctr., Mountainville, N.Y. One man shows from 1938; represented in collections of prin. museums and galleries of U.S.; author: autobiography Thus Far, 1941. Recipient many prizes; prints selected for Fifty Prints of the Yray, Am. Inst. Graphic Arts, 1925, 27, 28, 33, 38; Mrs. H. F. Noyes prize Am. Soc. Etchers, 1934; Guggenheim fellowship for sculpture, 1939, 40. Mem. Am. Print Makers Com., Am. Soc. Etchers, Phila. Soc. Etchers, Soc. Am. Painters, Gravers, Sculptors, Soc. Am. Graphic Artists (1st v.p. 1954), Nat. Acad. Home: Cornwall N.Y. †

WIDMAN, PAUL EDWARD, health care executive; b. Norwalk, Ohio, Jan. 24, 1918; s. Edward Anthony and Josephine (Brown) W.; m. Rose Hoyt, June 21, 1941; children: Jerry Paul, Kathleen Ann. B.S., U. Toledo, 1941. Cert. purchasing mgr. Nat. Assn. Purchasing Mgmt. Asst. dir. purchasing Johns Hopkins Hosp., Balt., 1950-51; dir. purchasing Cleve. Clinic Found., 1951-59, dir. adminstrv. svcs., 1969-76, dir. ops., 1977-81, sr. adminstr., 1981-83; chmn., bd. dirs. Hosp. Bur. Inc., N.Y.C., 1973-78. With USNR, 1943. Mem. Am. Hosp. Assn. (George R. Gossett award 1967), Am. Coll. Clinic Mgrs., Am. Coll. Hosp. Adminstrs. Home: Aurora Ohio. Died Nov. 10, 1983; buried Norwalk, Ohio.

WIDMANN, BERNARD PIERRE, radiologist, educator; b. Johnstown, Pa., July 21, 1890; s. John and Magdalene (Graf) W.; m. Mary Eileen Maher, Aug. 27, 1919 (dec. May 1937); children: Mary Eileen, Ann Stevens. Student, St. Francis Coll., Johnstown, 1909-11, St. Vincent's Coll., Latrobe, Pa., 1911-12, Medico Chirurg. Coll. Medicine and Surgery, Phila., 1912-16; LLD, St. Vincent's Coll.; DSc, Hanahman Med. Coll., 1952, St. Joseph's Coll., 1958. Diplomate Am. Bd. Radiology (pres. 1959-60, trustee from 1935). Asst. prof. radiology Grad. Sch. Medicine U. Pa., 1921-37, prof., from 1937, chmn. in radiology, from 1945; dir. X-ray dept., Phila. Gen Hosp., from 1928, Fitzgerald-Mercy Hosp., Phila., from 1928. Contbr. over 150 papers on radiol. subjects to profl. publs. Bd. dirs. Our Lady of Lourdes Hosp., Camden, N.J. Radiologist Army X-ray Sch., Camp Greenleaf, 1918. Mem. AMA, Am. Coll. Radiology (v.p. 1954, Gold medal 1964), Am. Radium Soc., Am. Roentgen Ray Soc. (pres. 1950), Radiologic Soc. N.Am., Phila. Radiol. Soc. (pres.), Sigma Xi, Phi Chi. Home: Philadelphia Pa. †

WIDMARK, GEORGE NORMAN, diversified service company executive; b. Glen Ridge, N.J., July 23, 1921; s. Bror Theodore and Clara (Bohlin) W.; m. Jane M. Hailand, Dec. 19, 1950; children: Roger S., Susan Widmark Ridgway. A.B., Duke U., 1943; J.D., Rutgers U., 1948; LL.M., NYU, 1950. Bar: N.J. 1949. Dir. Butler Internat., Inc., Montvale, N.J., 1967-86, chmn. bd., 1971-86; dir. Kerr Concrete Pipe Co., Folsom, N.J.; pres., chief exec. officer Brookhaven Estates, Inc., Montclair, N.J., 1968-86; ptnr. Widmark & Widmark, Montclair, 1973-86. Committeeman Essex County Republican Party, Essex County, 1968-70. Served to lt. USNR, 1943-46. Mem. ABA, Essex County Bar Assn., N.J. Bar Assn. Republican. Episcopalian. Clubs: Upper Montclair Country (pres. 1966-68), Pine Valley Golf. Home: Montclair N.J. Died Dec. 19, 1986; buried Mt. Hebron Cemetery, Upper Mountclair, N.J.

WIDMER, JOHN MAX, chemical executive; b. Zurich, Switzerland, Jan. 19, 1892; came to U.S., 1913; naturalized, 1920; s. James and Marie (Ackerman) W.; m. Madeline Devenny, May 12, 1914; children: Charles Max, Peter. ChE, Tech. Inst., Zurich, 1910; D Natural Sci., U. Geneva, Switzerland, 1913. Chem. engr. Corn Products Refining Co., N.Y., 1914, Louisville Cotton Oil Co., 1915-19, Douglas Co., Cedar Rapids, Iowa, 1919-20; gen. mgr. Hauser & Co., Illnau, Switzerland, 1920; chem. engr., chem. dir. Penick & Ford, Ltd., Inc., 1921-46, dir., 1946-48, exec. v.p., 1948-50, pres., from 1950. Holder numerous patents in corn products industry. Mem. AAAS, Am. Chem. Soc., Acad. Sci. Iowa, Greenwich Country Club, Pickwick Club (Cedar Rapids), Cloud Club (N.Y.). Republican. Home: Old Greenwich Conn. †

WIERINGA, ROBERT T., manufacturing company executive; b. Muskegon, Mich., Dec. 5, 1923; s. Richard and Anna G. (Wibalda) W.; m. Darlene L. Poll, Jan. 19, 1948; children: Robert, Lisa. Student, Calvin Coll. With Toni Co., 1948-57; gen. sales mgr. Paper Mate Co., 1958-62, v.p., 1962-64, pres., 1964-68; pres. Paper Mate Mfg. Co., 1964-68; v.p. Gillette Co., 1964-68; sr. v.p. group ops. Warner-Lambert Co., 1968-70; chmn. bd., dir. subs. Parke, Davis & Co., from 1970; vice chmn., chief adminstrv. officer, chmn exec. com. parent co. from 1975. Served with AUS, 1942-46, ETO. Mem. Detroit Athletic, Baltusrol Golf clubs. Home: Morristown N.J. Died Dec. 10, 1988.

WIESNER, KAREL FRANTISEK, chemistry educator, researcher; b. Prague, Czechoslovakia, Nov. 25, 1919; came to Can., 1948; s. Karel Frantisek and Eugenie (Sterova) W.; m. Blanka Pevna, June 22, 1942; 1 child, Karel Charles Jan. R.N.Dr., Charles U., Prague, 1945; D.Sc. (hon.), U. N.B., Fredericton, Can., 1970, U. Western Ont., London, Can., 1972, U. Montreal, Que., Can., 1975. Asst. then instr. phys. chem. Charles U., 1945-46; postdoctoral fellow E.T.H., Zurich, Switzerland, 1946-48; from asst. to assoc. prof. U. N.B., 1948-62, research prof., 1964-76, research-univ.prof.chemistry, 1976-87; assoc. dir. research Ayerst Labs., Montreal, 1962-64. Contbr. articles to profl. jours. Recipient Centennial medal Govt. Can., 1967, Drinov medal Bulgarian Acad. Scis., Sofia, 1978, Order of Kyril and Methodius First Class, Bulgarian Govt., 1981; decorated officer Order of Can., 1975. Fellow Royal Soc. Can., Royal Soc. London (Centenary medal 1977); mem. Chem. Inst. Can. (Palladium medal 1963), Pontifical Acad. Scis., Am. Chem. Soc. (Ernest Guenther prize 1983). Home: Fredericton, N.B. Canada. Died Nov. 28, 1986.

WIEWEL, WALTER HOELLING, management consultant; b. Cleve., Sept. 7, 1892; s. Charles R. and Martha (Bjorge) W.; m. Marie N. Ryley, Sept. 9, 1922; children: Walter H., Roger N. Student pub. schs., East Cleveland, Ohio. With United Alloy Steel Corp., 1914-25, Standard Seamless Tube Co., 1925-29; sales mgr. Timken Steel & Tube Co., 1929-35; asst. sales mgr. Jones & Laughlin Steel Corp., 1935-44; asst. to pres. Nat. Tube Co., 1944-47; pres. Trent Tube Co., 1947-49, chmn.; sr. v.p., bd. dirs. Crucible Steel Co., 1949-60; mgmt. cons. Chief tubing br. steel div., vice chmn. prodn. directive com. War Prodn. Bd., World War II. Mem. Am. Iron and Steel Inst., Am. Petroleum Inst., Newcomen Soc. N.Am., Duquesne Club, Pitts. Athletic Assn., Fox Chapel Golf Club, Oakmount Country Club, Milw. Athletic Club, Pine Valley Golf Club. Home: Pittsburgh Pa. †

WIGGINS, IRA LOREN, university professor; b. Madison, Wis., Jan. 1, 1899; s. Edward Theodore and Minnie May (Talbott) W.; m. Dorothy Bruce, Aug. 20, 1923; children: Bruce Leon, Donnalie Mae. AB, Occidental Coll., Los Angeles, 1922; MA, Stanford U., 1925, PhD, 1929. Tchr. of Sci. Durham (Calif.) High Sch., 1923-24; instr. botany Occidental Coll., 1925-27, asst. prof., 1927-29; asst. prof. botany Stanford U., 1929-36, assoc. prof. biology, 1936-40, prof. biology, 1940-60, acting head dept. biol. scis., 1948-49, 56-57; sci. dir. Arctic Rsch. Lab., Alaska, 1950-54, Apr.-Sept. 1956; botanist Fgn. Econ. Adminstrn., Ecuador, 1944; sci. dir. Belvedere Sci. Found. Assoc. editor Am. Fern Jour., 1941-61, editor, 1961-87; author: (with John H. Thomas) A Flora of the Alaskan Arctic Slope, 1962; contbr. papers on taxonomy. Fellow Calif. Acad. Sci. (pres. 1954-59, trustee 1959-87); mem. Arctic Inst. N.Am. (gov. 1955-87), AAAS, Bot. Sci. Am. (pres. 1940), Am. Fern Soc. (pres. 1956-59), Am. Soc. Plant Taxonomists (pres. 1963), AAUP, Western Soc. Naturalists (v.p. 1942, pres. 1945), Phi Beta Kappa, Sigma Xi. Home: Menlo Park Calif. Died Nov. 28, 1987.

WIGGINS, WAYNE A., advertising agency executive; b. Maud, Okla., July 29, 1929; m. Nancy Ridgeway, June 27, 1953; children—Michael, Linda. A.B., U. So. Calif., 1951; postgrad. law sch., 1951-53; M.B.A., Harvard U., 1957. Account exec. Foote, Cone & Belding, 1957-59; account exec. Leo Burnett Co. Inc., Chgo., 1959-61, later vice chmn., chief adminstrv. and fin. officer. Served with U.S. Army, 1953-55. Deceased.

WIGHT, FREDERICK S., artist, art gallery director; b. N.Y.C., June 1, 1902; s. Carol Van Buren and Alice (Stallknecht) W.; m. Joan Elizabeth Bingham, June 30, 1936; 1 son, George Frederick. B.A., U. Va., 1923; student art schs., Academie Julian, others, Paris, 1923-25; M.A., Harvard U., 1946. Dir. edn. Inst. Contemporary Art, Boston, 1946-50; asso. dir. Inst. Contemporary Art, 1950-53; prof. art, dir. art galleries (named Frederick S. Wight Art Galleries 1972) UCLA, 1953-73, chmn. art dept., 1963-66. Author: Van Gogh, 1953, Goya, 1954; Co-author: New Art in America, 1957, Looking at Modern Art, 1957, The Potent Image: Art in the Western World from Cave Paintings to the 1970's, 1976; Contbr. articles profl., popular jours. and mags.; one-man shows, Art Center, Marie Sterner Gallery, Kleeman Gallery, New Sch. Social Research, N.Y.C., M. H. deYoung Meml. Mus., San Francisco, 1956, Pasadena Mus., 1956, Fine Arts Gallery of San Diego, 1959, Mus. N.Mex. Art Gallery, 1960, Long Beach Mus., 1961, Stamford Mus., 1978, Palm Springs Desert Mus., 1978, one man shows, mcpl. Art Gallery, Los Angeles, 1981, Galerie d'Art Internat., Paris, 1982, Newspace Gallery, Los Angeles, 1982, Galerie d'Art Internat., Chgo., 1983, also others. Lt. comdr. USNR, 1942-45. Recipient Bronze medal for service to edn. in art Nat. Gallery Art, 1967. Home: Los Angeles Calif. Died July 26, 1986.

WIGHTMAN, CLAIR S(MITH), educator, college president; b. Marathon, N.Y., May 27, 1891; s. Dudley and Celia (Blair) W.; m. Florence Becker, June 27, 1927; children: Barbara Clare, Carol Blair. Diploma-honors, U. Montpellier, France, 1919; AB with honors, Syracuse U., 1920; MA, Columbia U., 1924; PhD, NYU, 1933. Tchr. Merrills Creek, N.Y., 1912-13, Texas Valley, 1913-15; prin. high sch. Ticonderoga, 1920-22; instr. Trenton (N.J.) High Sch., 1922-23; prin. elem. sch. 1923-27; prin. Park Ridge, 1927-30; instr. NYU, 1930-37; instr., supr. State Normal Sch., Paterson, N.J., 1930-37; pres. State Tchrs. Coll., Paterson, 1937-54; prof. edn. emeritus Fairleigh Dickinson U., from 1954. Mem. Passaic County Coun. Sgt. U.S. Army, 1917-19. Decorated medal of Liberation (Denmark). Mem. Coun. Edn., Ea. States Assn. Profl. Schs. for Tchrs. (treas. 1941-42), N.J. Schoolmasters Club, Bergen County Schoolmen (pres. 1938-39), Rotary, Masons. Home: Glen Rock N.J. †

WIKTOR, TADEUSZ JAN, virologist; b. Stryj, Poland, Sept. 9, 1920; came to U.S., 1962; naturalized, 1967; s. Wincenty W. and Salomea (Soltsysik) W.; m. Anna Maria Krzyzanowski, Apr. 27, 1948; children: George B., Stefan Z., Peter J. Dr. Vet. Med., U. Paris, 1946, Diploma Trop. Med., 1947. Virologist charge veterinary rsch. and vaccine prodn. Belgian Congo and Rwanda Urundi, 1948-60; expert FAO in W. Pakistan, 1961; prof. Wistar Inst., Phila., 1962-86; assoc. prof. Sch. Veterinary Medicine, U. Pa.; mem. WHO Experts Com. for Rabies. Contbr. articles to profl. jours. and chpts. to books; developed with colleagues an anti-rabies vaccine, 1968. Served with Polish Army, 1938-44. Home: Wynnewood Pa. Died Apr. 20, 1986; cremated, ashes interred Wistar Inst., Phila.

WILCOX, WALTER H., business executive; b. S. Norwalk, Conn., 1887. Pres., dir. S.D. Warren Co., Boston, Walter H. Wilcox, Inc., Woburn, Mass., Tanners Nat. Bank, Woburn. Mem. Masons, Shriners, Elks, Moose, Odd Fellows. Home: Woburn Mass. †

WILDER, CLINTON, theatrical producer. Producer early works of Edward Albee including Tiny Alice and a wide range of works by other innovative playwrights, both in N.Y.C. and in London. Home: New York N.Y. Died Feb. 14, 1986.

WILENTZ, DAVID THEODORE, lawyer; b. Dwinsk, Latvia, Dec. 21, 1894; came to U.S., 1899, naturalized, 1900; s. Nathan and Bertha (Crane) W.; m. Lena Goldman, Feb. 22, 1920; children: Norma (Mrs. Leon Hess), Warren W., Robert N. LLB, N.Y. Law Sch., 1917, LLD, 1965. Bar: N.J. 1919. Practice law 1919-88; city atty. Perth Amboy, N.J., 1923-26; atty. gen. State of N.J., 1934-44; sr. mem. firm Wilentz, Goldman & Spitzer, Perth Amboy, 1950-88; bd. dirs. Nat. State Bank, Elizabeth, N.J., Amerada-Hess Corp.; chmn. bd. Breeze Corps. Inc. Trustee Perth Amboy Gen. Hosp.; chmn. Middlesex County (N.J.) Dem. Com.; chmn. Dem. State Com.; mem. from N.J. Dem. Nat. Com.2d lt. U.S. Army, World War I. Home: Perth Amboy N.J. Died July 6, 1988; buried Beth Israel Cemetery, Woodbridge, N.J.

WILKE, ULFERT S., artist; b. Bad Toelz, Germany, June 14, 1907; came to U.S., 1938; s. Rudolf and Amalie (Brandes) W.; children: Christopher, Nicholas, Karen. Student art, Willie Jaeckel, 1926, Arts and Crafts Sch., Brunswick, 1924-47, Acad. Grande Chaumiere, 1927-28, Acad. Rancon, Paris, 1927-28, Harvard U., 1940-41; MA, State U. Iowa, 1947. Head dept. art dir. Kalamazoo Coll. and Inst. Arts, 1940-42; art and edn. dir. Springfield Art Assn., Ill., 1946-47; dir. U. Iowa Mus. Art, 1968-75; asst. prof. art U. Louisville, 1948-55; vis. grad. prof. painting U. Ga., 1955-56; assoc. prof. art Rutgers U., New Brunswick, N.J., 1962-68. Painter in oil and acrylic; works represented collections, Phila. Mus. collection, Solomon R. Guggenheim Mus., N.Y.C., Cleve. Mus. Art, Whitney Mus. Am. Art, N.Y.C., Mus. Tel Aviv, Israel; works exhibited, Joslyn Art Mus., 1954, Mus. ModernArt, N.Y.C., 1964, Joslyn Art Mus., 1978, Tamarind Inst., Mekler Gallery, Los Angeles; retrospective exhbns., U. Iowa Mus. Art, 1982-83, U. Utah Mus. Fine Art, 1983-84, H.B. Snead Mus., Louisville, Kalamazoo Inst. Arts; calligraphies exhibited, Tamarind Inst., 1980, Honolulu Acad. Arts, 1981; illustrator portfolios: Music to Be Seen, 1956, Fragments for Nowhere, 1968, One, Two and More, 1960, An Artist Collects: Ulfert Wilke Selections from Five Continents, 1975, Zero through Nine, 1978, Without Words, 1978. Recipient Albrecht Durer prize, Gemany, 1927; Guggenheim Found Fells study grantee, Europe, 1959-60, 60-61; recipient award Am. Acad. and Inst. Arts and Letters, 1978. Mem. Assn. Am. Mus. Dirs. Home: Kauai Hawaii. Died Dec. 7, 1987; buried Kanai, Hawaii.

WILLCOX, WILLIAM BRADFORD, historian, university professor; b. Ithaca, N.Y., Oct. 29, 1907; s. Walter Francis and Alice Elouise (Work) W.; m. Faith Mellen, Oct. 31, 19361 children: Alanson Francis, Ellen Seymour, Faith Marian. Student, U. of Cambridge, 1926-27; AB, Cornell U., 1928; BFA in Architecture, Yale U., 1932, PhD, 1936. Instr. in history Williams Coll., 1936-41; asst. prof. U. Mich., 1941-46, assoc. prof., 1946-50, prof. history, 1050-69, acting chmn. dept., 1958-60, 63-64, chmn., 1965-69, Hudson rsch. prof., 1962-63; prof. history Yale U., New Haven, Conn., 1970-85; Mem. Inst. for Advanced Study, 1946. Author: Gloucestershire: A Study in Local Government, 1500-1640, 1940, Star of Empire: A Study of Britain as a World Power, 1485-1945, 1950, Portrait of a General: Sir Henry Clinton in the War of Independence, 1964, The Age of Aristocracy, 1688-1830, 1966; editor: The American Rebellion: 1782, 1954, The Papers of Benjamin Franklin, 1970-85; contbr. to hist. jours. Mem. coun. Inst. Early Am. History and Culture, 1955-58; chmn. Midwest conf. Brit. Hist. Studies, 1959-61. Recipient Porter prize Yale U., 1936, Russell award U. Mich., 1945, Bancroft prize Columbia U., 1965; Fulbright lectr. at Oxford, 1957-58. Mem. Am. Hist. Assn. (mem. coun. 1966-85, exec. com. 1967-85), Conf. Brit. Studies (mem. exec. com. 1965-67), Authors Guild, Elizabethan Club, Century Club, Psi Upsilon, Phi Beta Kappa. Home: New Haven Conn. Died Sept. 22, 1985.

WILLE, FRANK, lawyer, banker, former government official; b. N.Y.C., Feb. 27, 1931; s. Frank Joseph and Alma (Schutt) W.; m. Barbara Bowen, July 2, 1969; children: Serena, Alison. Grad., Phillips Acad., Andover, Mass., 1947; AB cum laude, Harvard U., 1950, LLB cum laude, 1956; LLM in Taxation, NYU, 1960. Bar: N.Y., D.C. Assoc. Davis Polk & Wardwell, 1956-60; asst. counsel Gov. N.Y., Albany, 1960-62; 1st asst. counsel Gov. N.Y., 1962-64; supt. banks State of N.Y., 1964-70; chmn. bd. dirs. FDIC, Washington, 1970-76; mem. Cadwalader Wickersham & Taft, 1976-81; chmn., chief exec. officer Greater N.Y. Savs. Bank, N.Y.C., 1981-88; bd. dirs. Nat. Council Savs. Insts. and Savs. Banks Assn. N.Y. State. Former mem. N.Y. Job Devel. Authority; former dir. N.Y. State Urban Devel. Corp. Served with USNR, 1951-54. Mem. Field Club (Greenwich, Conn.), Harvard Club (N.Y.C.), Chevy Chase Club (Washington). Home: Greenwich Conn. Died July 6, 1988; interred St. Barnabas Ch., Greenwich, Conn.

WILLEMS, J. DANIEL, physician, surgeon; b. Medora, Kans., Feb. 4, 1888; s. Klaas Dyck and Anna (Klaassen) W.; m. Marian Hutchins, June 15, 1924. Grad., Cen. YMCA Inst., Chgo., 1918; BS, U. Chgo., 1922; MD, Rush Med. Coll., 1926. Diplomate Nat. Bd. Med. Examiners. Intern St. Luke's Hosp., 1926-28; in pvt. practice 1929; assoc. Elmore Clinic, Seattle, 1929-31; attending surgeon Seattle Gen. Hosp. and Harborview Hosp., 1930; assoc. surgeon Ill. Mfrs. Mutual Casualty Assn., Chgo., 1931-33; in pvt. practice, Chgo., 1933-35; assoc. surgeon Lumbermens Mutual Casualty Co. (Kemper ins.), Chgo., 1935-40, med. dir., 1940-58, then cons.; asst. anatomy Loyola U. Med. Sch., 1924; asst. in clin. surgery, Northwestern U. Med. Sch., 1924, instr. clin. surgery, 1933-38; attending surgeon Wesley Meml. Hosp., 1931-37, Norwegian Am. Hosp., 1937-41; assoc. in surgery Cook County Hosp., 1933-35. Author: Gemcutting; contbr. numerous articles on rsch., clin., tech. and statis. subjects to leading med. jours. Enlisted in USNR, 1918; served aboard U.S.S. Arizona, 1918-19. Fellow ACS, Am. Med. Assn., Indsl. Med. Assn.; mem. Am. Indsl. Hygiene Assn., Chgo. Soc. Indsl. Medicine and Surgery (pres. 1945-46), Ill. State and Chgo. med. socs., Cen. States Soc. Indsl. Medicine and Surgery, Tower Club, Masons, Phi Beta Kappa, Phi Chi. Republican. Home: Lake Forest Ill. †

WILLEN, JOSEPH, social welfare consultant; b. Kushnitza, Russia, June 22, 1897; came to U.S., 1905; naturalized, 1918; s. Barnet and Sarah (Katch) W; children by previous marriage: Paul, Deborah Willen Meier; m. 2d, Janet Younker Sonnenthal, Dec. 1970. BA, CCNY, 1919; HHD (hon.), Boston U., 1963; LLD (honoris causa), Jewish Theol. Sem. Am., 1964. Pioneer devel. techniques community orgn., fund-raisin; assoc. Fedn. Jewish Philanthropies of N.Y., 1919-85, exec. v.p., 1941-67, exec. cons., 1967-85. Dir. Greater N.Y. Community Coun., Inc., Coun. Jewish Fedns. and Welfare Funds, Nat. Jewish Welfare Bd. (exec. com. 1962); bd. dirs. United Neighborhood Houses; past cons. ARC, Greater N.Y. Fund; chmn. coordinating com. Documentary History of Am. Jews; bd. advisers Vocat. Adv. Svc.; nat. coun. Am.-Jewish Joint Distbn. Com.; v.p., chmn. 54th ann. meeting Am. Jewish Com.; mem. exec. coun. Am. Jewish Hist. Soc.; trustee Nat. Found. Jewish Culture; mem. India Famine Emergency Commn., 1947, Citizens Budget Commn. of N.Y.C., Mayor's Com. on Unity; bd. dirs. Fountain House, 1965-70, Stockbridge Sch., 1965-70, Technion U., N.Y. Urban League, Pro Deo U. Rome; bd. overseers Florence Heller Grad. Sch. Advanced Studies in Social Welfare, Brandeis U., 1962-71; exec. com Jewish Theol. Sem., 1966-72; bd. overseers NYU Grad. Sch. Social Work; mem. bd. Community Coun. With inf. U.S. Army, World War I. Fellow Brandeis U., 1963. Mem. Navy League. Home: New York N.Y. Died July 6, 1988; interred Beth Olem Cemetery, Bklyn.

WILLETT, HENRY IRVING, superintendent of schools; b. nr. Glass, Va., July 23, 1904; s. John Henry and Ada Wyatt (Hogg) W.; m. Betty Wells Ballard, June 8, 1929 (dec. Oct. 1957); children: Henry Irving, Thomas Dunaway; m. 2d, Doris Long Moore, June 14, 1962. BA, Coll. William and Mary, 1925, LLD (hon.), 1955; MA, Columbia U., 1930; postgrad., Stanford U., 1940; LittD, U. Richmond, 1955. Tchr., prin. Sugar Grove Sch., Smyth County, Va., 1925-26; prin. Churchland and Cradock High and Elementary Schs., Norfolk County, Va., 1926-39; dir. instrn., asst. supt. schs. Augusta County, Va., 1939-42; supt. schs. Norfolk County, Va., 1942-46, Richmond County, Va., 1946-86; chmn. edn. com., mem. exec. com., vice chmn. U.S. nat. commn. UNESCO; chmn. com. edn. policies Am. Heritage Found. Bd. dirs. Cen. Va. Ednl. TV Corp., So. Edn. Reporting Svc., Richmond Area Community

Coun., Richmond Ssymphony (hon.), Met. YMCA, Robert E. Lee coun. Boys Scouts Am.; adv. bd. Fisher Body Craftsman's Guild; bd. govs. United Givers Fund, St. Christopher's Sch., Richmond; bd. trustees U.S. Army Transp. Sch., Ft. Eustis, Va.; trustee Joint Coun. Econ. Edn., Richmond Profl. Inst. Recipient Good Govt. award Richmond First Club, 1955, Silver Beaver award Lee coun. Boy Scouts Am., 1955, Man of Yr. award B'nai B'rith, 1957, citation for disting. svc. to Richmond community U. Richmond, 1964. Mem. Assn. Sch. Adminstr. (pres. 1955-56), Rotary (past pres. Richmond), Phi Beta Kappa, Kappa Phi Kappa, Phi Delta Kappa (Disting. Svc. award Alpha Beta chpt. 1953), Phi Gamma Mu, Sigma Nu. Home: Richmond Va. Died Mar. 20, 1986.

WILLHITE, WINFIELD LYLE, university dean; b. Mt. Carmel, Ill., Sept. 8, 1913; s. Winfield Scott and Ernestine (Fincher) W.; m. Helen Agnes Pleshar, June 6, 1938; 1 dau., Maryhelen. Student, U. Mich., 1931-33; BS, Ill. Inst. Tech., 1935; MS, U. Ill., 1937, PhD, 1941. Chmn. dept. commerce Catawba Coll., Salisbury, N.C., 1941-46; dean men, vocational appraiser VA, 1943-46; prof., head dept. econ. and bus. adminstrn. Knox Coll., Galesburg, Ill., 1946-57, registrar, 1951-57; prof. fin., head dept., chmn. div. bus. Long Beach (Calif.) State Coll., 1957-60; dean Sch. Bus. Adminstrn. Cen. Mich. U., Mt. Pleasant, 1960-76, dean emeritus, 1976; bus. cons. to pres. Ill. Assn. Deans, 1954-55, Ill. Assn. Collegiate Registrars, 1955; examiner N. Central Assn. Colls. and Secondary Schs.; chnm. Mich. Assn. Deans Schs. Bus., 1970-71; sec. bd. dirs. Indsl. Devel. Corp., Galesburg, 1953-56; adj. prof. bus. Campbell U. MBA program, 1981-84; lectr. to Mcpl. Dept. Heads Sems., Property Appraisal Sems., Indsl. Safety Sems. Contbr. articles to profl. jours. Mem. Mayor's New Decade Com., City of Rocky Mount, 1980, Econ. Devel. C .n., Rocky Mount Area C. of C., 1980; chmn. Faculty Coun., N.C. Wesleyan Coll., 1980-81; arbitrator Am. Arbitration Assn., 1942-85; past pres., bd. dirs. Galesburg YMCA; mem. bus. edn. com., State of Mich.; dir. Demographic Studies, Calif., Ill., Mich.; mem. accreditation teams Western Coll. Assn.; cons.-examiner North Cen. Assn., Div. of Higher Edn.; elder First Presbyn. Ch., Mt. Pleasant, Mich.; chmn. Fin. Com. for Mich. Week.; past pres Mt. Pleasant Zoning Bd. of Appeals.; v.p. Mt. Pleasant Centennial Celebration. Elected to Mt. Carmel, Ill. High Sch. Hall of Fame; recipient spl. tribute for outstanding svc. to edn. in Mich., State of Mich., 1976, Leadership award Phie Delta Kappa, 1976, cert. appreciation for outstanding dedication and svc., Co. oC., Mt. Pleasant Mich. area, 1976, Top Educator of Yr. award, Alpha Kappa Psi, Cen. Mich. U., 1976, plaque of appreciation for svc., dedication and assistance to Jaycees, Rocky Mount Jaycees, 1981; establishment of W. Lyle Willhite award for Teaching Excellence to Cen. Mich. U. MBA program, Dow Chem. Co. and Dow Corning Corp. Mem. Am. Arbitration Assn. (arbitrator 1942-85), Am. Econ. Assn., Acad. Mgmt, Mich. Bus. Edn. Assn., Midwest Mgmt. Assn., Am. Prodn. and Inventory Control Assn. Mt. Pleasant C. of C. (pres.), Triangle Club, Rotary (past pres.), Alpha Kappa Psi, Phi Delta Kappa, Alpha Kappa Delta, Delta Pi Epsilon, Sigma Iota Epsilon, Phi Chi Theta. Home: Mount Pleasant Mich. Died Nov. 22, 1985; buried Riverside Cemetery, Mt. Pleasant, Mich.

WILLIAMS, DAVID WILLARD, agricultural sciences educator; b. Venedocia, Ohio, Aug. 20, 1892; s. David W. and Elizabeth J. (Morgan) W.; m. Magdalene Rees, Aug. 18, 1921; children: Margaret Ann Williams Cardwell, Ruth Elizabeth Williams Lawrence, David Willard Jr. BSA, Ohio State U., 1915; MS, U. Ill., 1916; student, Tex. A.&M. U., 1923; summer student, U. Chgo., 1927-28. Extension animal husbandman USDA, Clemson-Agrl. Coll., 1917-19; assoc. prof. Tex. A.&M. U., 1919-20, prof., 1920-22, head dept. animal husbandry, 1922-46, v.p. for agr., 1946-48, vice chancellor for agr., 1948-58, acting. pres., 1956-57; survey U. Ceylon, 1956, agrl. cons., from 1958; dir. tech. exchange programs Tex. A.&M. U. with U. Dacca, East Pakistan, and Escuela Superior de Agriculture Antonio Narro, Saltillo, Mex.; dept. supt. Southwestern Exposition and Fat Stock Show, 1920-43, chmn. adv. com., from 1946; dir. Bryan Bldg. & Loan, from 1942; Am. Soc. Animal Prodn. rep. Internat. Livestock Breeding Congress, Zurich, Switzerland, 1939; agrl. cons. E.C.A., Germany, 1949; personnel cons. Fgn. Agr. Svc., from 1949; instl. rep. Ark., White River Interagy. Com., from 1951; mem. U.S.-Mex. Joint Tech. Agr. Exchange Com., 1951; cons. Rockefeller found., Colombia, S.Am., 1951. Author: Beef Cattle in the South, 1941; co-author: Livestock and Poultry, 1925, Agriculture in the Southwest, 1940. Councillor Tex. A.&M. Rsch. Found. Lt. col. U.S. Army, 1943-46. Fellow AAAS, Tex. Acad. Sci.; mem. Am. Palomina Horse Breeders Assn. (dir.), Am. Soc. Animal Prodn. (pres.), Am. Hereford Assn., Am. Quarter Horse Breeders Assn. (adv. com.), Am. Soc. Range Mgmt., Tex. Swine Growers Assn. (adv. com.), Tex. and Southwestern Cattle Raisers Assn., Tex. Agrl. Workers Assn., East Tex. C. of C., Bryan C. of C. (pres.), Nat. Collegiate Athletic Assn. (v.p., councilman at large), Am. Legion, Nat. Block and Briddle Club, Saddle and Sirloin Club (pres. Ohio), Masons, Rotary, Sigma Delta Chi, Alpha Gamma Rho (pres. Ohio), Lambda Gamma Delta, Alpha Zeta. Presbyterian (elder). Home: College Station Tex. †

WILLIAMS, EDWARD BENNETT, lawyer; b. Hartford, Conn., May 31, 1920; s. Joseph Barnard and Mary (Bennett) W.; m. Dorothy Adair Guider, May 3, 1946 (dec. 1959); children—Joseph Barnard, Ellen Adair, Peter Bennett; m. Agnes Anne Neill, June 11, 1960; children—Edward Neill, Dana Bennett, Anthony Tyler, Kimberly Anne. A.B. summa cum laude, Coll. Holy Cross, 1941, S.J.D., 1963; LL.B., Georgetown U., 1945, LL.D., 1968; LL.D., Loyola Coll., 1967, Fairfield U., 1968, Loyola U., Chgo., 1970, Albert Magnus Coll., 1971, St. Joseph's Coll., Phila., 1971, Lincoln (Ill.) Coll., 1972, Suffolk U., 1974, U. Detroit Sch. Law, 1976, Mount St. Mary's Coll., 1977, U. Md., 1983, Scranton U., 1986, Barry U., 1986, Spring Hill Coll., 1988. Bar: D.C. bar 1944. Since practiced in Washington; sr. partner firm Williams & Connolly (and predecessor firms), 1967—; prof. criminal law and evidence Georgetown U. Law Sch., 1946-58, gen. counsel univ., 1949—; guest prof. U. Frankfurt, Germany, 1954; vis. lectr. Yale Law Sch., 1971; chmn. bd., pres., owner Balt. Orioles Baseball Club.; Mem. U.S. Jud. Conf. Adv. Com. on Fed. Rules of Evidence, 1965-74, Chief Justice's Com. on Court Facilities and Design, 1971-74; chmn. Md. Jud. Nominating Commn. 6th Jud. Dist., 1971-78; mem. President's Fgn. Intelligence Adv. Bd., 1976-77, 82-85, gen. counsel, 1985—. Author: One Man's Freedom, 1962; contbr. articles to profl. publs. Treas. Dem. Nat. Com., 1974-77; trustee Coll. Holy Cross, 1976—, chmn., 1982—. Served with USAAF, 1941-43. Mem. ABA (com. minimum standards for adminstrn. criminal justice 1965-67, chmn. spl. com. crime prevention and control 1970-72), D.C. Bar, Bar Assn. D.C. (v.p. 1950, 55-56, Lawyer of Yr. award 1966), Am. Coll. Trial Lawyers (bd. regents 1968-72), Internat. Acad. Trial Lawyers. Democrat. Roman Catholic. Clubs: University, Vinson, Nat. Lawyers, Metropolitan, Barristers, Alfalfa, Nat. Press (Washington), Knights of Malta, Fed. Assn. (pres. 1984-87). Died Aug. 13, 1988, buried St. Gabriel's Cemetery, Potomac, Md.

WILLIAMS, EMLYN, playwright, actor, author; b. Mostyn, North Wales, Nov. 26, 1905; s. Richard and Mary W.; m. Molly O'Shann (dec. 1970); children: Alan Emlyn, Brook Richard. M.A., Oxford (Eng.) U., also LL.D., 1949. Starred on Broadway in: Montserrat, 1949, A Man for All Seasons, 1964, The Deputy, 1964; also appeared in films: Wreck of The Mary Deare, 1961; also appeared: films The L-Shaped Room, Major Barbara, The Stars Look Down, Hatters Castle, Eye of The Devil, The Walking Stick, David Copperfield, The Deep Blue Sea; author: (plays) Full Moon, 1927, Glamour, 1928, A Murder Has Been Arranged, 1929, Night Must Fall, 1935, He Was Born Gay, 1937, The Corn Is Green, 1938, The Light of Heart, 1940, The Morning Star, 1941, The Druid's Rest, 1943, The Wind of Heaven, 1945, Trespass, 1947, 48-49, Accolade, 1950, Someone Waiting, 1953; A Month in the Country, 1965, Cuckoo, 1986; played in 2 one-man shows as: Charles Dickens and Dylan Thomas, 1951-87 ; dir. film: The Last Days of Dolwyn; also writer TV plays; author: George: An Early Autobiography, 1962, Beyond Belief, 1967, Emlyn, 1973, Dr. Crippen's Diary, 1978; (novel) Headlong, 1980. Decorated comdr. Order Brit. Empire. Home: London England. Died Sept. 25, 1987.

WILLIAMS, EUGENE S., lawyer; b. Romney, W.Va., Nov. 27, 1892; s. Amuel Holland and Ella Harriot (Taylor) W. Student, Randolph-Macon Coll., Ashland, Va., 1912-13; LLB, U. Va., 1916. Bar: Md. 1917. With law dept. Western Md. Ry., from 1923, v.p., gen. counsel, 1935-47, pres., 1948-52, chmn., 1948-57; bd. dirs. Union Trust Co., Cen. Savs. Bank, Western Md. Ry. Co., Kerman Hosp. for Crippled Children, Union Meml. Hosp. Pres. Balt. Symphony Orch. Assn. With U.S. Army, World War I; USAF, World War II. Mem. ABA, Md. Bar Assn., Maryland, Green Spring Valley Hunt, Baltimore Country, University (N.Y.C.), Farmington Country clubs. Democrat. Episcopalian. Home: Glyndon Md. †

WILLIAMS, E(VAN) CLIFFORD, chemist, chemical engineer; b. Hull, Eng., Sept. 7, 1892; came to U.S., 1928; s. Thomas R. and Rachel (Evans) W.; m. Lilian H. Baxter, Aug. 1918; children: Anthony Arthur, Penelope, Christopher Roger. MS, U. Manchester, Eng., 1917; DSc, U. London, 1928. Mem. rsch. staff Brit. Dyestuffs Corp., 1917-19, head intermediates dept., 1919-21; in charge rsch., mem. joint rsch. com. Leeds U., Nat. Benzole Assn., 1921-26; 1st Ramsay Meml. prof. chem. engring. Univ. Coll., London, 1923-28; dir. rsch., v.p., bd. dirs. Shell Devel. Co., San Francisco and Emeryville, Calif., 1928-40; v.p., dir. rsch. Gen. Mills, Inc., 1941-42; v.p. in charge rsch., bd. dirs. Gen. Aniline and Film Corp., 1942-45; v.p., dir. rsch. Schenley Distillers Corp., 1945-50; cons. from 1945; bd. dirs. Distillation Products, Inc., U.S. Indsl. Chems., Inc. Contbr. articles to profl. jours. Chmn. on indsl. disarmament of Germany Engrs. Joint Coun. Com. Mem. NRC, AICE (Walker medalist 1942), Am., Brit. chem. socs., Brit. Inst. Chem. Engrs., Coun. Brit. Inst., Faraday Soc., Century Assn., Athenaeum. Home: Wilton Conn. †

WILLIAMS, FIELDING LEWIS, lawyer; b. Richmond, Va., June 22, 1906; s. Lewis Catlett and Maria Ward (Williams) W.; m. Susan Roy Carter, Nov. 18, 1939; children: Fielding Lewis Jr., Susan Carter Williams Turrell. BA, U. VA., 1928, LLB, 1930. Bar: Va. 1929. Practiced in Richmond, from 1929; assoc. then ptnr. Williams, Mullen & Christian (and predecessor firms), from 1930; dir. emeritus Universal Leaf Tobacco Co. Mem. Va. Commn. for Visually Handicapped, 1960-75; trustee Woodbury Forest Sch., 1953-59; chmn. bd. govs. Greater Richmond Commn. Found., 1969-78. Lt. USNR, 1942-44. Fellow Am. Bar Found.; mem. ABA, Va. Bar Assn., Richmond Bar Assn. (pres. 1966), Raven Soc., Country Club Va. (pres. 1965-67), German Club, Phi Beta Kappa, Omicron Delta Kapaa, Phi Delta Phi, Delta Psi. Home: Richmond Va. Died Oct. 14, 1984.

WILLIAMS, G(ERHARD) MENNEN, SR., state chief justice, former governor Michigan; b. Detroit, Feb. 23, 1911; s. Henry Phillips and Elma Christina (Mennen) W.; m. Nancy Lace Quirk, June 26, 1937; children: Gerhard Mennen Jr., Nancy Williams Ketterer, Wendy Williams Burns. AB cum laude, Princeton U., 1933; JD cum laude, U. Mich., 1936, LLD (hon.); LLD (hon.), Mich. State U., Wilberforce U., Cleary Coll., Aquinas Coll., St. Augustine's Coll., Ferris Inst., 1961, Western Mich. U., Lincoln U., World U., P.R., Morris Brown Coll.; HHD (hon.), Lawrence Inst. Tech. Bar: Mich. 1936. Atty. Social Security Bd., 1936-38; asst. atty. gen. State of Mich., 1938-39; exec. asst. to atty. gen. U.S. Dept. Justice, Washington, 1939-40; with criminal div. U.S. Dept. Justice, 1940-41; dep. dir. Mich. Office of Price Adminstrn., 1946-47; assoc. Griffiths, Williams & Griffiths, Detroit, 1947-48; gov. State of Mich., 1949-60; asst. sec. state for African affairs U.S. Dept. State, 1961-66; ambassador to Philippines Manila, 1968-69; justice Mich. Supreme Ct., 1971—, chief justice. Author: A Governor's Notes, 1961, (with others) Africa for the Africans, 1969. Mem. Mich. Liquor Control Commn., 1947-48; vestryman St. Paul's Cathedral, Detroit. Served to lt. comdr. USN, 1942-46. Decorated Legion of Merit with combat V; grand officer Order of Orange Nassau (Netherlands); grand comdr. Royal Order of Phoenix (Greece); humane band of African Redemption (Liberia); grand officer Order of Niger (Niger); comdr. Order Ivory Coast (Ivory Coast); pro merito (Latvia); Polonia Restituta (Polish Govt. in Exile); datu Order of Sikatuna (Philippines). Mem. Nat. Grange, Amvets, Am. Legion, VFW, Res. Officers Assn., SAR, Abepa, Steuben Soc., Edelweiss, Order of Coif, Phi Beta Kappa, Phi Gamma Delta, Phi Delta Phi. Democrat. Episcopalian. Clubs: Navy, University (Detroit), Detroit Country. Lodges: Masons (33 degree), Eagles, Elks, Moose, Odd Fellows. Home: Grosse Pointe Farms Mich. Died Feb. 2, 1988.

WILLIAMS, GLUYAS, cartoonist; b. San Francisco, July 23, 1888; s. Robert Neil and Virginia (Gluyas) W.;m. Margaret Kempton, May 27, 1915; children: Margaret, David Gluyas. AB, Harvard U., 1911. Contbr. cartoons The New Yorker and other mags.; author: The Gluyas Williams Book, 1929, Fellow Citizens, 1940, The Gluyas Williams Gallery, 1957; illustrator of Benchley's books. Mem. Phi Beta Kappa. Home: West Newton Mass. †

WILLIAMS, HARVEY LADEW, international management consultant; b. Stamford, Conn., July 10, 1900; s. Harvey Ladew and Hannah Haydock (Willis) W.; m. Gertrude E. Hoxie, Feb. 28, 1927 (div. 1942); children—Eleanor Ladew, Sheila, Hannah Hooker, Harvey Ladew; m. Brenda Hedstrom Boocock, Sept. 18, 1943. Grad., Harvard, 1920, Mass. Inst. Tech., 1922. With Stone & Webster, Inc., 1922-27; pres., dir. Air Investors, Inc., 1927-32; mem. exec. com., dir. Aviation Corp., 1928-32, Am. Airways, Inc., 1928-32; pres., dir. United Aviation Corp., 1930-32; sr. ptnr., mgmt. cons. Harvey Williams & Assos., Delray Beach, Fla., 1931-86; v.p. charge overseas ops., dir., mem. exec. com. H.J. Heinz Co., 1946-53; v.p. Avco Mfg. Corp., N.Y.; also gen. mgr. internat. div. Avco Mfg. Corp., 1953-56; pres., dir. Philco Internat. Corp., N.Y.C., Phila., 1956-63, Philco Corp. Can., Ltd., 1956-63; chmn., dir. Philco. Italiana S.p.A., Milano; dir. Philco Internat., Ltd., London, Philco Corp. S.A., Fribourg, Switzerland, Cia Mexicana Electromercantil, Mexico City, Philco S.A. de C.V., Mexico City, Philco Argentina, S.A., Buenos Aires, Bendix Home Appliances do Brazil, Sao Paulo; pres., dir. The Co. for Investing Abroad, Phila., 1963-66. Trustee U.S. council Internat. C. of C., 1962-86, sr. trustee, 1966-86, pres., 1973-77, hon. pres., 1977-86, chmn. com. expansion internat. trade, Paris, 1961-66; sec.-treas. U.S.A. bus. and industry adv. com. to OECD, Paris, 1973-77; Chmn. northeastern div. Air Def. League, 1935-38, N.E. Aviation Conf., 1940, Conn. Aero. Devel. Commn., 1939-41; tech. cons. devel. div. Army Ground Forces Hdqrs., Washington, 1942-45; Vice pres. and life trustee Tabor Acad., Marion, Mass. Life fellow Inst. Dirs. (London); mem. Internat. House Phila. (dir. 1963-69), Nat. Aviation Assn. (nat. councillor 1939-41), Aero. C. of C. Am. (gov. 1929-31), Internat. Mgmt. Assn. (chmn. planning council 1958-60), Am. Mgmt. Assn. (v.p. 1958-60), Am. Australian Assn. (dir. 1948-86), Inst. Aero. Scis., Army Ordnance Assn. (life), U.S. Naval Inst. (life), Electronics Industries Assn. (chmn. exec. com. internat. div. 1958-60), English Speaking Union (life), Newcomen Soc., Fgn. Policy Assn., Pres.'s Assn., Soc. Colonial Wars, Am. Soc. Legion d'Honneur, Am. Soc. in London, Am. Legion. Clubs: Harvard (N.Y.C.), Wings (N.Y.C.), University (N.Y.C.); Lake Placid (Essex County, N.Y.); Melbourne (Australia); St. Andrews (Delray Beach, Fla.), Delray Beach Yacht (Delray Beach, Fla.), Seagate (Delray

Beach, Fla.); Beverly Yacht (Marion, Mass.), Kittansett (Marion, Mass.); Buck's (London); Steward's Enclosure (Henley, Eng.); The Travellers (Paris); Athenaeum (Phila.). Home: Delray Beach Fla. Died Mar. 28, 1986.

WILLIAMS, JOHN J., U.S. senator; b. Frankford, Del., May 17, 1904; s. Albert F. and Annie E. (Hudson) W.; m. Elsie E. Steele, May 4, 1924; 1 dau., Blanche (Mrs. J. Raymond Baker). Owner chicken feed bus., Frankford, Del.; U.S. senator from Del. 1946-71, ret., 1971; real estate bus. owner, farmer Millsboro, Del., 1971-88. Mem. Masons, Rotary. Republican. Methodist. Home: Millsboro Del. Died Jan. 11, 1988.

WILLIAMS, JOHN RODNEY, political scientist, educator; b. Detroit, Nov. 21, 1919; s. Ralph Hill and Myrtle Anna (Ryan) W.; m. Madeleine Louise Josephine Cremilliac, Aug. 28, 1952; children: Jacques Ralph Andre, Mark Thinh Tien. AB summa cum laude, Lawrence Coll., 1944; MA, Johns Hopkins U., 1947; PhD, Duke U., 1951; postgrad., London Sch. Econs. and Polit. Sci., 1951-52. Instr. polit. sci. Wellesley Coll., spring 1947, 48-49; mem. faculty W.Va. U., Morgantown, 1949-86, prof. polit. sci., 1961-86, chmn. dept., 1961-72, coord. honors program, 1972-86, coord. study abroad program, 1980-86, mem. univ. senate, 1974-80; vis. prof. Waynesburg Coll., 1963-64, Fayette campus Pa. State U., 1967-68; lectr. Pa. State U., summer 1966; acad. vis. London Sch. Econs. and Polit. Sci., 1972. Author: The Conservative Party of Canada, 1920-1949, 1956, John Latham and the Conservative Recovery from Defeat, 1969; columnist Morgantown Dominion Post; contbr. articles to profl. jours. Mm. Monogalia County Com. UN.; v.p. Suncrest Lake Assn. Mem. AAUP, Am. Polit. Sci. Assn., W.Va. Polit. Sci. Assn. (v.p. 1967-68, pres. 1968-69), Can. Polit. Sci. Assn., Australasian Polit. Studies Assn., Conservative and Unionist Assn., Am. Acad. Polit. and Social Sci., Australian Inst. Polit. Sci., Univ. Profs. for Acad. Order, Nat. Coll. Honors Coun., Am. Friends London Sch. Econs., Phi Beta Kappa, Pi Sigma Alpha, Delta Tau Delta. Episcopalian. Home: Morgantown W.Va. Died Mar. 26, 1986.

WILLIAMS, NEWELL FRANKLIN, management consultant; b. Bogotá, Colombia, Aug. 28, 1908; s. Charles Spencer and Maude (Newell) W.; m. Grace Lowene Barger, July 25, 1931; 1 son, Charles Spencer; adopted children: Roderick Jose Alexis, Meredith Grace. BA, State U. Iowa, 1929, MA, 1933. Plant mgmt. trainee Fisher Body div. Gen. Motors Co., Detroit, 1929-30; instr. Romance langs. and swimming Western Mil. Acad., Alton, Ill., 1930-42; spl. agt. FBI, San Diego, 1942-43, Washington, 1943-45, Paraguay, 1945-46; exploration staff Union Oil Co. of Calif., 1946; charge govt. relations and personnel Union Oil Co. of Calif., Paraguay, 1947-50; contract negotiations, govt. relations and mgr. Union Oil Co. of Calif., Costa Rica, 1951-53, Peru, 1953-54, Guatemala, 1955-58; mgr. negotiations, relations, personnel Union Oil Co. of Calif., Latin Am., Europe, Africa, Australia, Indonesia, 1958-61; dir. U.S. AID Mission to Dominican Republic, 1962-63, U.S. AID Mission to Honduras, C.Am., 1964-67; regional devel. officer pvt. enterprise Cen. Am. and Panama AID, 1967; asst. dir. regional AID ops. mgr. 1967-72, cons., 1972-85; pres. TICASA Shipping and industry devel., 1973-85; bd. dirs. Internat. Wood Products (S.A.). Dir. Domingo Soldati (Boys' Town), Costa Rica; a founder Albergue Juvenil (Boys' Shelter), Guatemala. Capt. Ill. N.G. Res., 1936-40. Mem. North Cen. Pvt. Schs. Tchrs Assn., Soc. Ex-Spl. Agts. FBI, Internat. Club (Washington, Rotary (Paraguay, Tegucigalpa), Costa Rica Yacht Club0 Union Club, Cariari Club, Tennis Club, Phi Kappa Sigma. Home: San Jose Costa Rica. Died June 14, 1985.

WILLIAMS, ROBERT WOOD, lawyer; b. Balt., May 29, 1890; s. George H. and Mary C. (Wood) W.; m. Helen M. Gibbs, Apr. 26, 1924 (dec. 1955); children: Mrs. David Baldwin, Robert W., Rufus MacQueen; m. 2d, Geraldine Frost Baker, Dec. 3, 1958. Student, Lycie Descartes, Tours, France, 1908; AB, Harvard, 1912, AM, 1913, LLB, 1915. Bar: 1915. Mem. Fed. Maritime Bd., 1950-54; chmn. Md. Port Authority, 1956-58; of counsel Ober, Grimes & Shriver. Trustee Johns Hopkins; past chmn. Enoch Pratt Free Libr.; past pres. Family and Children's Soc.; past pres. Evergreen Found. Capt. Intelligence div., U.S. Army, 1917-18. Mem. Am., Md., Balt. bar assns., Maritime Law Assn. U.S. (past v.p.), Elkridge Club, Maryland Club, Johns Hopkins Club, Cosmos Club, Phi Beta Kappa. Democrat. Episcopalian (vestryman). Home: Baltimore Md. †

WILLIAMS, ROGER JOHN, biochemist, educator; b. Ootacumund, India, Aug. 14, 1893; came to U.S., 1901; s. Robert Runnels and Alice Evelyn (Mills) W.; m. Hazel Elizabeth Woods, Aug. 1, 1916 (dec. 1952); children—Roger John, Janet, Arnold; m. Mabel Phyllis Hobson, May 9, 1953; 1 stepson, John Hobson. B.S., U. Redlands, Calif., 1914; M.S., U. Chgo., Ill., 1918, Ph.D., 1919; D.Sc. (hon.), U. Redlands, Calif., 1934, Columbia U., 1942, Oreg. State U., Corvallis, 1965. Research chemist Fleischmann Co., Chicago, 1919-20; asst. prof. chemistry U. Oreg., Eugene, 1920-21, assoc. prof. chemistry, 1921-28, prof. chemistry, 1928-32; prof. chemistry Oreg. State Coll., Corvallis, 1932-39; prof. chemistry U. Tex., Austin, 1939-71, prof. emeritus, 1971-88; dir. Clayton Found. Biochemistry Inst., U. Tex., Austin, 1940-63, research scientist, 1963-85; cons. Clayton Found. for Research, 1963-85. Author 21 books, including: Nutrition in a Nutshell; You Are Extraordinary; Nutrition Against Disease; Physician's Handbook of Nutritional Science; Rethinking Education: The Coming Age of Enlightenment, 1986. Discoverer of Pantothenic acid, 1947. Contbr. articles to profl. jours. Mem. Pres.'s Adv. Panel Heart Disease, Washington, 1972; hon. pres. Internat. Acad. Preventive Medicine. Recipient Chandler medal Columbia U., 1942. Mem. Internat. Acad. Preventive Medicine (hon. pres. 1980-81), Nat. Acad. Scis., Am. Chem. Soc., Am. Inst. Nutrition (Mead Johnson award 1941), Soc. Exptl. Biology and Medicine. Republican. Clubs: Tex. Philos. Soc., Town and Gown. Home: Austin Tex. Died Feb. 20, 1988; buried Austin Meml. Cemetery.

WILLIAMS, RONALD, university president; b. Cleve., June 17, 1927; s. Wilbert and Mary (Malone) W.; m. Arlene Harris, Oct. 31, 1952; children: Robert, Rhonda. BA in Speech and Hearing, Western Res. U., 1954, MA in Speech Pathology, 1960; PhD in Phonetics and Psychoinguistics, Ohio State U., 1969; DHL, Columbia Coll., Chgo., 1980. Coordinator speech therapy svcs. Cleve. Pub. Schs., 1958-62; lectr., dir. Speech Clinic Oberlin (Ohio) Coll.; cons. Oberlin City Schs., 1962-64; mem. faculty Ohio U., 1964-69, asst. prof., 1967-69, acting exec. dean Afro-Am. affairs, assoc. prof., 1969, dir. Summer Inst. Speech and Lang., 1969; prof. speech, dean Coll. Ethnic Studies Western Wash. State Coll., Bellingham, 1969-71; prof., chmn. depot communication scis. Fed. City Coll., Washington, 1971-72; provost, v.p. acad. affairs Fed. City Coll., 1972-76; pres., prof. psychology Northeastern Ill. U., Chgo., 1976-85; adj. prof. U. Pitts., 1973; mem. Ill. Jud. Inquiry Bd., 1979-85, Ill. Ednl. Consortium, 1982., Chgo. United Task Force on Edn., 1980. Author articles, revs.; cons. editor: Acta-Symbolica, 1969-76, Jour. Speech and Hearing Disorders, 1975-82. Trustee Columbia Coll., 1980, Coun. Advancement of Experiential Learning, 1980, Union for Experimenting Colls. and Univs., 1977-85; chmn. Union for Experimenting Colls. and Univs., 1978; mem. Chgo. Met. Higher Edn. Council, 1987-85, Jerusalem Com., 1981, Northlight Repertory Theatre Bd.; bd. dirs. Cinema/Chgo., 1979-85; state coordinator Nat. Human Relations Task Force. With AUS, 1945-48. Danforth Tchr. grantee, 1967-69. Fellow Am. Speech and Hearing Assn.; mem. Am. Assn. State Colls. and Univs. (dir. 1979-85), Assn. Urban Univs. (mem. exec. com. 1980-82. chmn. 1982), Am. Coun. Edn. (Ill. panel nat. identification program for advancement women in higher edn. adminstrn. 1979-85), Nat. Black Assn. Speech, Lang. and Hearing (chmn. bd. dirs. 1980-81), Phi Kappa Phi (E.J. Taylor award 1967). Home: Chgo. Ill. Died Dec. 11, 1985.

WILLIAMS, SELDEN THORNTON, business executive; b. Canton, N.Y., Feb. 7, 1892; s. F. F. and Lilla A. (Thornton) W.; m. Ella E. Vagler, Oct. 12, 1918; children: Selden T., W. Constance Eleanor R. BS, St. Lawrence U., 1913, MS, 1926; MS, Worcester Poly. Inst., 1916; DEng, Pratt Inst., 1956. Chmn. A. Schrader's Son, Inc.; pres. Scovill Mfg. Co., from 1958, also bd. dirs.; trustee E. Waterbury Nat. Bank; bd. dirs. Waterbury Hosp. Contbr. articles to tech. jours. Trustee St. Lawrence U. Mem. Soc. Automotive Engrs., Sigma Xi, Alpha Tau Omega. Republican. Home: Middlebury Conn. †

WILLIAMS, TIMOTHY GLYNE, psychiatrist; b. nr. Winchester, Tenn., May 16, 1916; s. Timothy M. and Maude (Reynolds) W.; m. Christine E. Beazley, Dec. 13, 1941; children: Timothy Walden, Thomas Clinton, Marjorie Candace. BS, U. of South, 1939; MD, Vanderbilt U., 1934. Diplomate Am. Bd. Psychiatry and Neurology. Intern Baroness Erlanger Hosp., Chattanooga, 1943; resident St. Elizabeth's Hosp., Washington, 1944-45, U.S. Naval Hosp., Norman, Okla., 1944-45; psychotherapist VA Mental Hygiene Clinic, Balt., 1946-50; staff Spring Grove State Hosp., Catonsville, Md., 1950-53, clin. dir., 1953-56; asst. prof. pscyhiatry and pub. health, dir. pilot study for psychiat. adminstrn. Yale U., New Haven, Conn., 1956-60; commr. Okla. Dept. Mental Health and Mental Retardation, 1960-63; asst. commr. Md. Dept. Mental Hygiene, 1963-69; supt. Rosewood State Hosp., Owings Mills, Md., 1964-72; assoc. dir. Md. Psychiat. Rsch. Ctr., Catonsville, 1972-75; dir. Central Clin. Svcs., Spring Grove Hosp., Catonsville, 1975-81; lectr. Cath. U. Am., 1948-49; instr. U. Md., 1953-56; assoc. prof. psychiatry and preventive medicine, U. Okla., 1961-63. Lt. M.C. USNR, 1944-46. Fellow Am. Psychiat. Assn. (life, chmn., mental hosp. sect. 1963, liaison to Social Security Adminstrn. 1966-68), Am. Orthopsychiat. Assn.; mem. AAAS. Home: Ellicott City Md. Died Dec. 24, 1985.

WILLIAMSON, ADRIAN, SR., lawyer; b. Monticello, Ark., Nov. 7, 1892; s. James Gaston and Lulu (Jackson) W.; m. Catherine Montgomery, Apr. 9, 1924; children: Adrian, Ann, Margaret. BS, Washington and Lee U., 1913; postgrad., Harvard U. Law Sch., 1913-15. Bar: Ark. 1915. Mem. Williamson & Williamson; assisted in drafting Ark. probate code. Active Boy Scouts Am.; dep. mem. staff planners Joint Combined Chiefs of Staff, Washington; elder in Presbyn. Ch. With U.S. Army, World War I, col. USAAF, World War II, CBI. Mem. ABA, Ark. State Bar Assn. (Outstanding Lawyer-Citizen award 1960), Masons (32 degree), Rotary. Home: Monticello Ark. †

WILLIAMSON, ARLEIGH BOYD, educator; b. Pitts., Oct. 8, 1888; s. William and Annie (Boyd) W.; m. Clara A. Holtzhauser, Aug. 4, 1922; children: Ann (Mrs. Tyrus T. Tripp), Arlie (Mrs. Douglas W. Anderson), Sally W. Williams. AB, Carnegie Inst. Tech., 1920; MA, Columbia, 1923; LHD, CUNY, 1972. Profl. actor 1906-15; instr. Western Pa. Inst. for Blind, 1915-17, 19-20; asst. in English Carnegie Inst. Tech., 1916-17, 19-20; assoc. prof. English, pub. speaking Miami (Ohio) U., 1920-24; assoc. prof. pub. speaking NYU, 1924-30, prof. speech, chmn. dept., 1930-54, emeritus, from 1954; prof. summer sch. Chautauqua Instn., 1929-31; lectr. pub. speaking Jewish Theol. Sem. Am., 1937-45; founder S.I. Community Coll., 1954, Richmond Coll., 1965. Author: Speaking in Public; also monographs and articles in field. Mem. mayor's com. on unity, N.Y.C., 1949-53; mem. Bd. Higher Edn., N.Y.C., 1954-73; pres. Community Chest, S.I., 1953-56, chmn. bd., 1956-59; del. Conf. Governing Bds. of State Univs. and Allied Instns., from 1955, v.p., 1958-59; chmn. S.I. adv. com. to N.Y.C. Youth Bd., 1957-62. 2d lt. AEF, 1917-19. Recipient B'nai B'rith interfaith award, S.I., 1947, Disting. Citizenship award Wagner Coll., 1951, Alumni Merit award Carnegie-Mellon U., 1970. Fellow S.I. Inst. Arts and Scis.; mem. Speech Assn. of Am. (1st v.p. 1929, pres. 1935), Am. Arbitration Assn., Masons, Rotary, Beta Theta Pi. Home: Staten Island N.Y. †

WILLIAMSON, BURKE, lawyer; b. Leesville, La., Mar. 30, 1906; s. William Burke and Hazel (Allis) W.; m. Elise Hamill Clow, Sept. 9, 1939; children: Eleanor Hamill (Mrs. Frederic Fischer, Jr.), Rosalie Allis (Mrs. Kimberly Carter). A.B., Washington and Lee U., 1926; J.D., Northwestern U., 1930. Bar: Ill. 1930, N.C. 1974. Pvt. practice Chgo.; mem. firm Gordon, Adams & Pierce, 1930-34; ptnr. Adams Williamson & Turney, 1934-72, Adams & Williamson, 1972-87. Pres. bd. trustees Hull House Assn., 1957-60. Served from pvt. to capt. inf. U.S. Army, 1942-46. Mem. Chgo. Bar Assn. (bd. of mgrs. 1963-65), U.S. Army Res., Kappa Sigma, Phi Delta Phi, Phi Beta Kappa. Episcopalian. Clubs: Law (Chgo.), Legal (Chgo.), Chicago (Chgo.); Biltmore Forest Country (N.C.); Downtown City (Asheville, N.C.). Home: Ashville N.C. Died Feb. 20, 1987; buried Graceland Cemetery, Chgo.

WILLIAMSON, JOHN GARRETT, utility executive; b. Muskogee, Okla., Sept. 8, 1915; s. John Ira and Dorothy (Garrett) W.; m. Sara Hosack Stauffer, Sept. 16, 1944; children: Peggy Roth, Philip, Deborah Mikel. BSc, U. Tulsa, 1936. With So. Calif. Gas. Co., Los Angeles, 1936-47, Seattle Gas Co., 1947-49, Tex. Gas Transmission Co., Monroe, La., 1949-52; gen. supt. Western Ky. Gas Co., Owensboro, 1952-56; exec. v.p., dir. Kans. Power & Light Co., Salina, 1956-81; ret. 1981; bd. dirs. Nat. Bank of Am.;. Mem. Cen. Kans. coun. Girl Scouts, 1957-62, Salina Library Bd., 1961-65; trustee St. John's Mil. Sch., 1958-61, St. Francis Boys' Homes, 1957-60. Mem. Am. Gas Assn., Pacific Coast Gas Assn., Midwest Gas Assn. (dir.), Salina C. of C. (dir. 1958-61), Salina Rotary Club. Episcopalian (vestryman, sr. warden). Home: Salina Kans. Died Aug. 12, 1981; interred Christ Cathedral, Salinas, Kans.

WILLIAMSON, MERRITT ALVIN, engineer, educator; b. Littleton, N.H., Apr. 1, 1916; s. Berton Alexander and Nellie E. (Cross) W.; m. Jean E. Goodrich, July 3, 1943; children: Janet, Marilyn Williamson Lance, Linda, Roxanne Williamson Leonard, Karen Williamson Wilson, Valerie Williamson Jakes. Grad., Phillips Exeter Acad.; B.E., Yale, 1938, M.S., 1940, PhD, 1946; M.S., Calif. Inst. Tech., 1945; MBA, U. Chgo., 1953. Registered profl. engr., Tenn. Metallurgist Scovill Mfg. Co., Waterbury, Conn., 1937-42, Remington Arms Co., Bridgeport, Conn., 1942-44; dir. tech. rsch. Solar Aircraft Co., San Diego, 1946-48; assoc. dir. devel. Pullman Standard Car Mfg. Co., Hammond, Ind., 1948-52; mgr. rsch. div. Burroughs Corp. Paoli, Pa., 1952-56; dean Coll. Engring. and Architecture Pa. State U., 1956-66, prof. engring., 1959-66; Orrin Henry Ingram disting. prof. engring. mgmt., dir. engring. mgmt. program Sch. Engring. Vanderbilt U., Nashville, 1966-82; prof. mgmt. Grad. Sch. Mgmt. Vanderbilt U., 1969-77; prof. indsl. engring., dir. engring., mgmt. program devel. U. Tenn. Space Inst., Tullahoma, 1983-85; spl. lectr. U. Pa., 1954-56; tech. mgmt. cons., 1956-85. Editor: Engring. Mgmt. Internat., 1979-85; contbg. editor: Rsch. and Engring., 1956-57, Ind. Laboratories, 1958-59, Ind. Sci. and Engring., 1958-59, Research and Devel., 1959-85. Commr., vice chmn., acting chmn. Pa. Turnpike Commn., 1957. Served from ensign to lt. (j.g.) USNR, 1944-46. Fellow Yale Engring. Assn. (past pres.); mem. IEEE, Am. Inst. Mining and Metall. Engrs., An Soc. Engring. Edn. (past pres.), Nat. Conf. Adminstrn. Rsch. (past chmn.), Am. INST. Indsl. Engrs., Acad. Mgmt. Pa. State engring. Soc. (hon.), Am. soc. engring. Mgmt., Tenn. soc. Profl. Engrs., Nat. Soc. Profl. Engrs., Conn. Acad. Arts and Scis., Inst. Certification Engring. Technicians (past chmn.), Order of Engr., Yale Metall. Alumni (past chmn.P, Internat. Soc. Gen. Semantics, Inst. Gen. Semantics, Calif. Inst. Tech. Alumni Assn., U. Chgo. Exec. Program Club., Triangle, University Club (Nashville; Cosmos (Washington); Sigma Xi, Tau Beta Pi, Phi Kappa Phi, Phi Eta Sigma, Sigma Tau, Gamma Alpha, Alpha Chi Sigma, Pi Tau sigma, Eta Kappa Nu, Omicron Delta Kappa, Alpha Pi Mu, Beta Gamma Sigma. Home: Nashville Tenn. Died July 19, 1985; buried Harpeth Hills Meml. Gardens, Nashville, Tenn.

WILLIS, BENJAMIN C., educational administrator; b. Balt., Dec. 23, 1901; s. Clarence Milton and Elizabeth Estelle (Coppage) W.; m. Rachel Davis Webster, Jan. 24, 1925; 1 dau., Margaret Rachel Bischoff. Student, St. John's Coll., Annapolis, Md., 1918-19; AB, George Washington U., 1922, Dr. Pub. Svc. (hon.), 1964; AM, U. Md., 1926; student, Johns Hopkins U., 1933; EdD, Columbia U., 1950; LLD (hon.), Northwestern U., 1955, Bradley U., 1960, Harvard U., 1960; LHD, Cen. Mich. Coll., 1959, Nat. Coll. Edn., 1961, Am. Internat. Coll., 1965. Prin. Henderson (Md.) Elem. and High Sch., 1922-23, Federalsburg (Md.) Elem. and High Sch., 1923-27, Caroline High Sch., Denton, Md., 1927-31, Sparrows Point High Sch., 1931-32, Catonsville (Md.) High Sch., 1932-34; supt. schs. Caroline County, Denton, Md., 1934-40, Washington County, Hagerstown, Md., 1940-47; supt. schs. Yonkers, N.Y., 1947-50, Buffalo, N.Y., 1950-53, Chgo., 1953-66; owner Benjamin C. Willis Ednl. Assn. Inc., Chgo., 1966-70; supt. schs. Broward County, Fla., 1970-72; cons. 1972-88; exec. dir. Mass. Edn. Survey, 1963-65; cons. Peace Corps; mem. Pres.'s Sci. Adv. Com., 1962-66; chmn. bd. Ednl. Planning Assocs. Inc., 1969-88; bd. dirs. Ednl. Facilities Labs. Inc., Northwestern Mut. Life Ins. Co. Contbr. articles to ednl. and bus. revs. Mem. Pres.'s Panel of Cons. on Vocational Edn., 1962-63, adv. com. Edn. in Ill.; bd. dirs. Chgo. Boys Clubs, Jr. Achievement Chgo., exec. bd. Chgo. coun. Boy Scouts Am.; nat. adv. com. Girl Scouts U.S.A., Chgo. YMCA, citizens bd. U. Chgo., citizens com. U. Ill., citizen fellowship Inst. Medicine Chgo., trustee Chgo. Planetarium Soc., Chgo. Ednl. TV Assn., Stanford. Mem. U.S. C. of C. (edn. com.), Ill. Assn. Sch. Adminstrs., Ill. Edn. Assn., Ill N.E.A. (life), Am. Assn. Sch. Adminstrs. (chmn. yearbook commn., 1954, pres. 1961), Economic Club, Executives Club, Rotary (Chgo.), Kappa Delta Pi, Phi Delta Kappa. Home: Plantation Fla. Died Aug. 27, 1988.

WILLIS, PAUL S., business executive; b. Hallettsville, Tex., Nov. 8, 1890; s. Dick and Johanna W.; m. Pocahanta Schroeder; m. 2d. Arlene Kieta. Grad. high sch., high sch., San Antonio; student, corr. courses. Stenographer Comet Rice Mills, 1908-1912, pres., gen. mgr., dir., 1912-32; pres. Grocery Mfrs. Am., N.Y.C., 1932-65, pres. emeritus, 1965-87. Mem. 4-H sponsors coun. Nat. 4-H Found. Named to Hall of Fame in Distbn. Mem. N.Y. State Food Commn., U.S. Commerce Dept. Bus. Adv. Coun., Am. Trade Assn. Execs, bus. adv. bd. CCNY, Mason (Shriner), Siwanoy Country Club (Bronxville, N.Y.), Sales Executives Club (dir.), Marketing Executives Club (hon.) (N.Y.). Presbyterian. Home: Bronxville N.Y. Died June 5, 1987.

WILLITS, JOSEPH H(ENRY), economist, educator; b. Ward, Del. County, Pa., June 16, 1889; s. Francis Parvin and Elizabeth Anna (Paschall) W.; m. Ruth Clement Sharp, May 3, 1913 (dec. 1961); children: Barbara, Clement P. (dec.), Robin; m. 2d, Therese Spackman Barclay, Aug. 28, 1962. AB, Swarthmore Coll., 1911, AM, 1912, LLD, 1937; PhD, U. Pa., 1916, LLD, 1939; LLD, Haverford Coll., 1962. Instr. geography and industry U. Pa., 1912-17, asst. prof., 1919-20, prof., 1920-39, dean Wharton Sch. Fin. and Commerce, 1933-39, dir. ednl. survey, 1954-60, charge studies of excellence and mediocrity in colls. and univs., from 1961, dir. indsl. rsch. dept., 1921-39. Author: The Unemployed in Philadelphia, 1915, (with others) What the Coal Commission Found, 1925, Studies of Labor Relations for the U.S. Coal Commission; also various brochures on labor subjects; editor 3 vols. Annals of Am. Acad. Polit. and Social Scis. Employment supt. U.S. Naval Aircraft Factory, 1917-19; expert in charge of studies in labor rels. U.S. Coal Commn., 1922-23; mem. ednl. adv. bd. John Simon Guggenheim Meml. Found., 1927-28; mem. Pres.'s Emergency Com. for Employment, 1930-31; pres. Nat. Bur. Econ. Rsch., 1933, exec. dir., 1936-39; dir. social scis. Rockefeller Found., 1939-54; mem. other nat. and civic coms. and commns. Mem. Am. Acad. Arts and Scis., Am. Statis. Assn., Am. Polit. Sci. Assn., Am. Econ. Assn., Am. Philos. Soc. (v.p. 1959-62), Phi Beta Kappa, Beta Gamma Sigma. Home: Langhorne Pa. †

WILLOUGHBY, HOWARD WILLIAM, aviation executive; b. Solvay, N.Y., Nov. 24, 1923; s. Howard John W. and Sara Elizabeth (Veeder) Wiiloughby; m. Edith Mae Lang, Nov. 29, 1947; children: Anne Elizabeth, Scott John, Sally Cornell. B.S., Syracuse U., 1952. Base facilities supr. N.Y. Air N.G., Syracuse, N.Y., 1952-61; dep. commr. aviation Hancock Internat. Airport, Syracuse, 1961-64; dep. dir. aviation Kansas City Internat. Airport (Mo.), 1964-80; dir. aviation Phila. Internat. Airport, Phila., 1980-87; dir. aviation services Metro Vision, Syracuse, N.Y., 1987. Mem. Greater Phila. Partnership Internat. Steering Com., 1980-87 ; mem. Phila. Mayor's Urban Transp. Policy Bd., 1983; mem. econ. devel. coalition task force on phys. devel., infrastructure and pub. services Wharton Sch., U. Pa., Phila., 1983. Served to maj. USAAF, 1942-60. Honored in resolution City Council Kansas City (Mo.), 1980. Mem. Am. Assn. Airport Execs. (accredited), Four Chaplains Legion of Honor, Theta Tau. Club: SKAL (Phila.). Lodge: Rotary (pres. 1979-80). Home: Philadelphia Pa. Died Dec. 3, 1987; buried Pleasant Lawn Cemetery, Parish, N.Y.

WILLSON, MEREDITH, flutist, composer, conductor, author, lyricist; b. Mason City, Iowa, May 18, 1902; s. John David and Rosalie (Reiniger) W.; m. Elizabeth Wilson, Aug. 29, 1920 (div. Mar. 1948); m. Ralina Zarova, Mar. 13, 1948 (dec. Dec. 1966); m. Rosemary Sullivan, Feb. 14, 1968. Ed., Damrosch Inst. Mus. Art; hon. doctorates, Coe Coll., Cedar Rapids, Iowa, Parsons Coll., Fairfield, Iowa, Ind. Inst. Tech., Ft. Wayne, Regis Coll., Denver; D.Music (hon.), Wartburg Coll., Waverly, Iowa. Formerly solo flutist with, John Philip Sousa, also flutist, N.Y. Philharmonic Orch., later mus. dir. Western div., NBC; composer, lyricist, also librettist: The Music Man (N.Y. Critics award best musical, Tony award, Grammy award for album 1958); composer, lyricist, author book: (Broadway show) Here's Love, 1963; composer, lyricist (Broadway and film): The Unsinkable Molly Brown, 1960; composer and lyricist: 1491; author-composer songs: 76 Trombones, May the Good Lord Bless You and Keep You, You and I; composer film score: The Little Foxes, The Great Dictator; composer: O.O. MacIntyre Suite, Symphony of San Francisco, Missions of California Suite, The Jervis Boy; (for chorus) Mass of the Bells; author: Eggs I Have Laid, The Music Man, But He Doesn't Know the Territory, Who Did What to Fedalia? And There I Stood with My Piccolo. Served to maj. AUS, 1942-45. Recipient Big Brother of Yr. award, 1962, Edwin Franko Goldman citation Am. Bandmasters Assn., 1964; Carbon Mike award Pacific Pioneer Broadcasters, 1976; posthumous recipient Pres. Medal of Freedom, 1987, Iowa award Gov. of Iowa, 1988; inducted into songwriters Hall of Fame, 1982. Mem. ASCAP, Am. Guild Authors and Composers (Aggie award 1980), AFTRA. Club: Family (San Francisco). Home: Los Angeles Calif. Died June 17, 1984; buried Elmwood Cemetary, Mason City, Iowa.

WILMARTH, CHRISTOPHER MALLORY, sculptor; b. Sonoma, Calif., 1943. B.F.A., Cooper Union, 1965. Prof. sculpture and drawing Cooper Union, N.Y.C., 1969-80; vis. artist Yale U., 1971-72, Columbia U., 1976, 78, U. Calif., Berkeley, 1979. Exhibited in one man shows at Graham Gallery, N.Y.C., 1968, Paula Cooper Gallery, N.Y.C., 1971, 72, Janie C. Lee Gallery, Dallas, 1971, Galleria dell'Arieta, Milan, 1973, Rosa Esman Gallery, N.Y.C., 1974, Daniel Weinberg Gallery, San Francisco, 1974, Wadsworth Atheneum, Hartford and St. Louis Mus. Art, 1974, 75, Gallerie Aronowitsch, Stockholm, 1975, Grey Art Gallery, N.Y. U., 1978, Studio for the First Amendment, N.Y.C., 1978, 80, 82, Seattle Mus., 1979, Hirschl & Adler Modern, N.Y.C.; group shows include Park Pl. Gallery, N.Y.C., 1966, Whitney Mus. Am. Art, 1966, 68, 70, 73, 76, 79, Found. Maeght, France, 1970, Mus. Modern Art, 1971, 79, Indpls. Mus. Art, 1972, 74, Art Inst. Chgo., 1972, Met. Mus., 1974, 79, I.C.A., Chgo., 1977, Phila. Mus., 1978, Albright Knox Gallery, 1979, Mus. Modern Art, N.Y.C.; represented in permanent collections at Mus. Modern Art, Art Inst. Chgo., Phila. Mus. Art, R.I. Sch. Design Mus. Art, Woodward Found., Met. Mus. Art, Fogg Art Mus., Des Moines Art Center, Walker Art Center, St. Louis Mus., Wadsworth Atheneum, Dallas Mus. Fine Art, Wichita Mus., Yale Art Mus., San Francisco Mus., Whitney Mus. Am. Art.; represented by Hirschl & Adler Modern, N.Y.C. Contbr. articles on sculpture to profl. publs. Recipient Norman Wait Harris award Art Inst. Chgo., 1972; Nat. Endowment for Arts grantee, 1969, 77, 80; Guggenheim fellow, 1970, 83; Howard Found. fellow Brown U., 1972. Home: New York N.Y. died. Nov. 19, 1987.

WILSON, CHARLES RAY, educational administrator; b. Cin., Jan. 8, 1905; s. Charles A. and Gillian (Lyon) W.; m. Elizabeth C. Cook, Aug. 24, 1934; children: James D., Douglas M. BS, Miami U., 1926, LLD, 1950; MA, U. Cin., 1929; PhD, U. Chgo., 1934; LHD, Bowling Green State U., 1966. Instr. U. Chgo. Lab. Sch., 1930-31; instr. history U. Cin., 1932-34; asst. prof. history Miami U., Oxford, Ohio, 1934-35, v.p. acad. affairs, provost, prof. history, 1961-70, acting pres. univ., 1964-65, ret., 1970-86; asst. prof. history Colgate U., 1935-40, assoc. prof., 1940-43, prof., 1943-61, chmn. dept., 1941-61; prof. Biarritz Am. U., 1945-46. Author: (with others) Essays in American Historiography, 1936, The American Idea, 1942; contbr. articles to profl. jours. Founder, dir. Colgate Fgn. Policy Conf.,1949-61; candidate for Congress, 37th Dist. N.Y., 1946, 34th Dist., 1952; del. Dem. Nat. Conv., 1948; mem. Nat. Com. for Rep. Congress. Mem. Phi Kappa Phi, Phi Sigma, Phi Beta Kappa, Omicron Delta Kappa, Phi Delta Theta, Kappa Delta Pi, Kappa Phi Kappa, Pi Delta Epsilon. Presbyterian. Home: Oxford Ohio. Died Dec. 10, 1986; buried Oxford Cemetery.

WILSON, EARL, columnist, radio commentator, editor; b. Rockford, Ohio, May 3, 1907; s. Arthur Earl and Cloe (Huffman) W.; m. Rosemary Lyons, Jan. 10, 1936; 1 son, Earl Lyons. Student, Heidelberg Coll.; B.S., Ohio State U., 1931. Newspaper mag. writer 1923; columnist It Happened Last Night, N.Y. Post, 1942-83; syndicated by Field Syndicate; radio commentator WOR-Mut., 1945. Author: Jungle Performers, 1941, I Am Gazing Into My 8-Ball, 1945, Pike's Peek or Bust, 1947, Let Em Eat Cheese Cake, 1949, Look Who's Abroad Now, 1953, Earl Wilson's New York, 1964, The Show Business Nobody Knows, 1971, Show Business Laid Bare, 1974, Sinatra, 1976, Hot Times, 1984; contbr.: Esquire mags. Mem. Sigma Delta Chi, Alpha Tau Omega. Methodist. Club: Lambs. Home: New York N.Y. Died Jan. 16, 1987.

WILSON, EDWIN BRAYTON, editor, journalism educator; b. Bklyn., July 6, 1891; s. Frank Wilkinson and Camilia Peters (Hill) W.; m. Vera Van Scoten, Aug. 23, 1921. BA, St. Lawrence U., Canton, N.Y., 1912, LHD (hon.), 1952. Reporter Brooklyn Daily Easgle, 1912-16, copy reader, 1916-17, asst. city editor, 1917-19, city editor, 1919-33, assoc. editor, 1933-36, Washigton corr., 1937, chief editorial writer, 1938, editor, 1938-46, exec. editor, 1946-55; dir. community rels Port N.Y. Authority, 1955-61; prof. journalism Fairleigh Dickinson U., Teaneck, N.J., from 1962. Chmn. Bklyn. Defense Recreation Com., World War II; trustee St. LAwrence U., Bklyn. Juvenile Guidance Ctr.; pres. Walt Whitman Found., Bklyn.; v.p. N.Y. Youth Counsel Bur., 1948-54. Pvt. U.S. Marines, World War I, France. Recipient Disting. Service award Library Assocs., Bklyn. Coll., 1952. Mem. Soc. of the Silurians, Am. Legion, Bklyn. C. of C. (dir.), Bklyn. Rotary club, Bklyn. Mcpl. Club, Bklyn. Dodger Knothole Club (pres. 1948-57), Sigma Alpha Epsilon. Universalist. Home: Oradell N.J. †

WILSON, FRED TALBOTT, architect; b. Houston, Oct. 2, 1912; s. Fred Taylor and Irene (Davis) W.; m. Irene Lee, Nov. 27, 1945 (div. Aug. 1979); children: Elizabeth Valentine (dec. 1980), Michael Talbott. Student, Vanderbilt U.; B.A., Rice Inst., 1935, B.S., 1936. Designer draftsman, Jr. partner of Claude Hooton, 1934-37 N.Y.C., 1935-36, designer draftsman, 1935-36; formed archtl. firm Wilson & Morris (became Wilson, Morris, Crain & Anderson, 1958, Wilson, Crain, Anderson, 1972-74, Wilson/Crain/Anderson/Reynolds, 1974-79, W/C/A Inc., Houston, 1938, Talbott Wilson Assocs., Inc., Patrick & Wilson Assn., 1986-87; Mem. nat. archtl. adv. bd. GSA, 1971-73; regional chmn. Internat. Design Conf., Aspen, Colo., 1964-68; chmn. Houston Com. Fgn. Relations, 1961-62, sec.-rapporteur, 1968-87. Author: series editorial page columns on world affairs Houston Post, 1975. Bd. dirs. Brazos Presbyn. Homes., 1966-70, pres., 1970, adviser, 1971-85; bd. dirs Am. Cancer Soc.; crusade chmn. Harris County unit, 1969, chmn. bd., 1973-74; bd. dirs. Nat. Com. on U.S. China Relations, 1968-72, Rice Center For Community Design and Research, 1972-75, Ctr. for Retarded Found., 1985-87; bd. govs. Rice U., 1970-87. Served as lt. col. Arty. AUS, 1941-46. Decorated Bronze Star.; Recipient Cloud and Banner with 2 personal citations China; 1st honor award Tex. Architecture, 1954; award of merit, 1963; award of honor, 1967, 68; 11 awards of merit for design Houston chpt. A.I.A.; Sr. certificate Nat. Council Archtl. Registration Bds. Fellow A.I.A. (pres. Houston chpt. 1951), Internat. Inst. Arts and Letters; mem. Tex. Soc. Architects (dir. 1954), Friends of Fondren Library (past pres.), Houston C. of C. (chmn. com. on community improvement 1964), Houston Mus. Fine Arts, Houston Contemporary Arts Mus., Asia Soc. Houston (dir.), Houston Taipei Soc. (pres. 1980), Rice U. Assos., UN Assn., Alumni Assn. of Rice Univ. (pres. 1968-69), Delta Kappa Epsilon. Presbyterian (ruling elder, deacon). Office: For the estate of Mr Wilson Tom Wilson, Architect 2809 Virginia Houston TX 77098 Died Sept. 1987.

WILSON, GEORGE ANGUS, metals company executive, lawyer; b. Mansfield, La., Feb. 1, 1910; s. George and Elizabeth (Pitts) W.; m. Lola Nelson, Dec. 27, 1963. A.B., Centenary Coll., 1930, LL.D. (hon.), 1979; LL.B., Tulane U., 1933. Bar: La. bar 1933. Pvt. practice New Orleans, 1933-41; faculty law sch. Tulane U., 1933-40; gen. counsel La. Dept. Conservation, 1940-41, Standard Oil Co. N.J., 1941-46; pres., dir. Interstate Natural Gas Co., Inc., 1946-53, Interstate Oil Pipe Line Co., 1954-55; pres. TXL Oil Corp., Dallas, 1955-62; pres., dir., chief exec. officer Lone Star Steel Co., 1962-77, chmn. bd., 1963-80, hon. chmn., 1980-87; dir. Phila. & Reading Corp., 1966-85, Tex.-Pacific Land Trust, N.W. Industries, Inc., 1968-85, Employers Ins. Co. of Tex.; mem. Mil. Petroleum Adv. Bd., 1946-50; dir. petroleum supply, transp. Petroleum Adminstrn. for War, 1942-45. Bd. administrs. Tulane U. Mem. Mid-Continent Oil and Gas Assn., Ind. Petroleum Assn. Am. (dir.), NAM, Tex. Mfrs. Assn. (pres. 1967-68, dir.), Am. Iron and Steel Inst. (dir. 1962-77), Am. Petroleum Inst., La. Bar Assn., Order of Coif. Clubs: Brook Hollow, Dallas, Dallas Gun, Petroleum (Dallas); Boston (New Orleans); University (N.Y.C.). Home: Dallas Tex. Died Dec. 15, 1987.

WILSON, IRL DONAKER, biologist, veterinarian; b. Rockwell City, Iowa, May 21, 1888; s. John Francis and Harriett (Donaker) Wilson; m. Belle Seely, Nov. 26, 1914 (dec. May 23, 1952); 1 child, Irl Donaker; m. Eleanor Atkins, June 20, 1953. DVM, Iowa State Coll., 1914, PhD, 1930; MS, Pa. State Coll., 1918. Practicing veterinarian Blue Earth, Minn., 1914-16; instr., later prof. animal husbandry and vet. sci. Pa. State Coll., 1916-23; head dept. vet. sci., expanded to dept. biology Va. Poly. Inst., 1923-58; animal pathologist Va. Agrl. Expt. Sta., 1928-38; researcher in bovine coccidiosis;

collaborator Bur. Animal Industry U.S. Dept. Agr., 1938-40; mem. Alaska Reindeer Survey and Appraisal Com. (apptd. by Congress), 1938-39; mem. com. on livestock and animal industry and Sch. of Vet. Medicine, 1946-48; mem. adv. bd. Va. Fisheries Labs., 1942-46; U.S. specialist Kabul (Afghanistan) U., 1961; apptd. by Rockefeller found. and Inter-Am. Inst. of Agrl. Scis. to study edn. in vet. medicine and animal husbandry in Mexico, Central and S.Am., 1949; mem. 1st Pan-Am. Vet. Congress, Lima, Peru, 1951. Contbr. sci. papers to jours.; contbg. editor N. Am. Veterinarian, 1920-23. Cons. World Manpower Commn., 1942-46; chmn. for Va. for procurement and assignment svc. for vets., 1942-46; chmn. Va. Nat. Forests Adv. Coun., 1955-58; adviser postgrad. edn. Indian Vet. Rsch. Inst., India, 1958-60. Fellow AAAS; mem. Va. Acad. Sci. (mem. coun. 1928-33, pres. 1931-32), Am. Vet. Med. Assn. (res. sec. freom Va. 1931-37, mem. Ho. of Dels., 1932-50, 54-58), Va. Vet. Med. Assn. (sec. 1930-35, pres. 1935-36), Va. State Bd. Vet. Med. Examiners (pres. 1938-44, sec.-treas. 1944-45), AAUP, Pa. Vet. Med. Assn. (rec. sec. 1918-20), Va. Wildlife Fedn. (treas. 1936-40), Assn. of Izaac Walton League Chpts. in Va. (v.p. 1936-40), Masons, K.T., Shriners, Shenandoah Club, Rotary Club, Bareilly Club, Univ. Club, Scabbard & Blade, Phi Sigma Kappa, Alpha Zeta, Gamma Sigma Delta, Phi Kappa Phi, Sigma Xi, Omicron Delta Kappa, Sigma Delta Psi (hon.), Phi Sigma, Theta Kappa Psi. Democrat. Episcopalian. Home: Blacksburg Va. †

WILSON, JAMES GRAVES, educator; b. Clarksdale, Miss., Apr. 2, 1915; s. James Preston and Lula Clyde (Pittman) W.; m. Harriet Chamberlain, Sept. 6, 1941; children—Mary Pittman, James Chamberlain, Arthur Sydney. B.A., Miss. Coll., 1936; M.A., U. Richmond, 1938; M.A. postgrad, Brown U., 1938-39; Ph.D., Yale, 1942; D.Sc. (hon.), Med. Coll. Wis., 1975. Instr. in anatomy U. Rochester, 1942-46, asst. prof., 1946-50; sect. head embryology AEC project, 1948-50; assoc. prof. anatomy U. Cin., 1950-54, prof., 1954-55; prof., head dept. anatomy U. Fla., Gainsville, 1955-66; prof. research pediatrics and anatomy Children's Hosp. Research Found., Cin., 1966-80; emeritus prof. research pediatrics Children's Hosp. Research Found., 1980-86; Mem. com. on post-doctoral fellowships NSF, 1958-62; human embryology and devel. study sect. NIH, 1962-66, mem. anatomical scis. tng. com., 1966-70; gen. chmn. 2d Teratology Conf., Bethesda, Md., 1957; mem. panel on herbicides Office Sci. and Tech., Exec. Office of Pres., 1969-70; chmn. adv. com. on 2,4,5-T Environmental Protection Agy., 1970-86. Assoc. editor: Teratology, 1968-86 , Anatomical Record, 1965-86 , Teratology and Mammalian Reproduction; Author, editor books, articles to nat. sci. jours. Mem. Am. Assn. Anatomists, Soc. Exptl. Biology and Medicine, Teratology Soc. (pres. 1961-62), Toxicology Soc., European Teratology Soc., AAAS, Am. Inst. Biol. Sci., So. Soc. Anatomists (pres. 1963-64), Soc. Developmental Biology, Sigma Xi. Home: Cincinnati Ohio. Died Nov. 24, 1986.

WILSON, JAMES THOMAS, banker; b. Okemos, Mich., Feb. 27, 1887; s. William O. and Elsie (Felton) W.; m. Lena Nash, Oct. 20, 1908; children: Jessie Mae Wilson Wheary, Marjorie Wilson O'Connell; m. 2d, Mary Whipp, May 14, 1947. Student pub. sch., Mich. With First Nat. Bank, Kenosha, Wis., from 1924, chmn. bd., from 1943; dir. Brown Nat. Bank, McWhyte Co. (both Kenosha), Refrigeration Discount Corp., Detroit, Monarch Machine Tool Co., Sidney, Ohio, Haskelite Mfg. Corp., Chgo. Home: Kenosha Wis. †

WILSON, JOHN CREE, JR., orthopedic surgeon; b. Los Angeles, Sept. 9, 1920; s. John Cree and Anna Clarissa (Grant) W. BA, Stanford U., 1942; MD cum laude, Harvard U., 1944; LLD, U. So. Calif., 1975. Intern, asst. resident in gen. surgery Mass. Gen. Hosp., Boston, 1944-46; asst. resident in orthopedic surgery Mass. Gen. Hosp., Boston Children's Hosp., Boston, 1948-50; pvt. practice specializing in orthopedic surgery Los Angeles, from 1951; clin. prof. orthopedic surgery Sch. Medicine U. So. Calif.; mem. staff Hosp. of Good Samaritan, Children's Hosp. of Los Angeles; mem. courtesy staff St. Vincent's Hosp.; Los Angeles, cons. staff Santa Fe Hosp., Los Angeles, Los Angeles County-U. So. Calif. Med. Ctr.; pres. Hosp. Good Samaritan, Los Angeles, from 1971,; mem. nat. med. adv. bd. Shriners Hosp. for Crippled Children; dir. Security Pacific Nat. Bank, Pacific Mut. Life Ins. Co. of Los Angeles. Contbr. articles to profl. jours. Mem. Am. Adv. Bd. Am. Hosp. of Paris; trustee U. So. Calif., Van Nuys Found.; bd. dirs. Children's Hosp. of Los Angeles, Good Hope Found., Music Ctr. Opera Assn., Physicians Aid Assn., Los Angeles. Mem. Am. Acad. Orthopedic Surgeons (pres. 1974, bd. dirs. 1974-77), Am. Orthopedic Assn., ACS, Pacific Coast Surg. Assn., Western Orthopedic Assn., Societe Francaise de Chirurgie Orthopedique et Traumatologique, AMA, Calif. Med. Assn., Los Angeles County Med. Assn., Wilson Bost Interurban Club, Assn. Bone and Joint Surgeons. Home: Los Angeles Calif. Deceased.

WILSON, JOHN MCGREGOR, business executive; b. St. Louis, Sept. 30, 1889; s. John McGregor and Bertha (Goetz) W.; m. Nellie Gerring Reddish, Mar. 8, 1913; 1 child, John McGregor. Grad., E. St. Louis (Ill.) High Sch.; LLD (hon.), Drury Coll., Springfield, Mo. Office employee The Nat. Cash Register Co., East St. Louis, 1911-13, salesman Little Rock, 1913-14, branch mgr. Salina, Kans., 1914-17, div. mgr. St. Louis, 1917-28, div. mgr. San Francisco, 1928-30, 31-42, mgr. acctg. machine div., 1930-31, v.p. sales, 1943-59, mem. bd. dirs. and exec. com., from 1943. Author: Open the Mind and Close the Sale; also articles. Mem. adv. com. Nat. Distribution Coun. Dept. commerce; trustee Drury Coll. Mem. Am. Mgmt. Assn. (past dir.), Nat. Sales Execs. (dir.), Office Equipment Mfrs. Inst., San Diego Art Inst., Rancho Santa Fe Golf Club, Masons, Shriners. Presbyterian. Home: Rancho Santa Fe Calif. †

WILSON, NEIL LESLIE, educator; b. Vancouver, B.C., Can., Jan. 30, 1922; s. John Shaw and Effie May (Murdoch) W. BA, U. B.C., 1947; MA, U. Toronto, 1948; PhD, Yale U, 1951. Lectr. in philosophy U. Western Ont., London, 1951-52; lectr. Bishop's U., Lennoxville, Que., 1952-54, asst. prof., 1958-60, assoc. prof., 1961-64, prof. philosophy, 1964-69; prof. philosophy McMaster U., Hamilton, Ont., Can., 1969-84; asst. vis. prof. Harvard, 1960-61; chmn. Guelph-McMaster PhD programme in Philosophy, 1970-72, 78-79. Author: The Concept of Language, 1959. With RCAF, 1941-45. NSF grantee, 1963-66. Mem. Am. Philos. Assn. (exec. com. Eastern div. 1961-64), Canadian Philos. Assn. (dir. 1974-76). Home: Lynden, Ont. Canada. Died Sept. 5, 1983; buried Vancouver, B.C.

WILSON, PETER CECIL, fine arts expert; b. Eshton Hall, Yorkshire, Eng., Mar. 8, 1913; s. Mathew and Barbara (Lister) W.; m. Grace Helen Rankin, 1935. Student, New Coll., Oxford U. With Reuters; also with Connoisseur Mag.; dir. Sotheby's, London, 1938-84, chmn., 1958-80; dir. Sotheby Parke Bernet Group, 1980-84, hon. life pres. Vice chmn., trustee Leeds Cante Found., Maidstone, Kent. Decorated comdr. Brit. Empire; recipient Benjamin Franklin medal, 1968. Home: Auribeau sur Siagne France. Died June 3, 1984; buried Auribeau, France.

WILSON, ROSCOE CHARLES, corporation executive, air force officer; b. Centralia, Pa., June 11, 1905; s. Everett Roscoe and Edith Edna (Porter) W.; m. Elizabeth Lewis Robinson, Nov. 2, 1929; children: Charles Everett, Elizabeth Galt, Richard Lee. BS, U.S. Mil. Acad., 1928; student, Air Corps Flying Schs., 1928-29, Air Corps Tactical Sch., 1938, George Washington U., 1948. Commd. 2d lt. 1928, advanced through grades to lt. gen., 1958; chief aircraft design Wright Field, Ohio, 1933; asst. prof. dept. natural and exptl. philosophy U.S. Mil. Acad., 1937; chief engring. br. Hdqrs., Army Air Forces, 1941; chief of staff 316th Bomb Wing, Okinawa, 1944; vice dep. chief Air Staff for R & D, 1945; dep. chief Armed Forces Spl. Weapons Project, 1947; air mem. Mil. Liason Com. to Atomic Energy Commn., 1948; mem. com. on atomic energy R & D Bd., 1948-51; commandant Air War Coll., Montgomery, Ala., 1951-54; comdr. Third USAF, Middlesex, Eng., 1954; Air Force mem. of weapons evalutaion group Office of Asst. Sec. Def., Washington, to 1958; dep. chief staff devel. hdqrs. USAF, 1958-61; mil. dir. USAF, Sci. Adv. Bd.; ret. USAF, 1961; past pres., chmn. Allied Rsch. Assocs. Inc., Boston; mil. dir. Rand Corp., Lincoln Lab., MIT. Author: Preliminary Airplane Design, 1938. Decorated Legion of Merit with 2 oak leaf clusters, D.S.M.; Antarctic glacier named in his honor Nat. Geographic Soc. Mem. Coplay Soc. Boston (dir.), Inst. Aeronautical Scis. (hon.), Ends of Earth Club, Pilgrims Club (London), Quiet Birdmen (Cleve.), Army and Navy Club (Washington). Home: Louisville Ky. Died Aug. 21, 1986.

WILSON, WADE, college president; b. Birmingham, Ala., July 29, 1914; s. Blaine and Rosa (Ragl) W.; m. Naomi A. Sewell; 1 son, Glenn Alan. BS, Cheyney (Pa.) State Coll., 1936; MS, Pa. State U., 1937; EdD, NYU; postgrad., Temple U., U. Minn., 1954; LLD, Hahnemann Med. Coll., 1969. Assoc. prof. indsl. arts Md. State Coll., 1937-39; chmn. dept. indsl. arts Savannah State Coll., 1939-40, Tenn. Agrl. and Indsl. State Coll., 1940-42; instr. Air Corps Tech. Sch., Chanute Field, Ill., 1942-43; instr. indsl. arts Cheyney State Coll., 1947-52, assoc. prof., 1952-57, prof., chmn. dept., 1957-67, dir. evel., awards and grants, 1967-68, pres., 1968-88; mem. exec. com. Assn. Pa. State Coll. Faculties, 1957-65, legis. com. 1959-65, pres. 1961-65; chmn. credit com. Del. County Fedn. Tchrs. Credit Union, 1960-64; mem. Nat. Coun. Accreditation Tchr. Edn. Visitation and Appraisal Team, 1961-71, adv. com. Tchr. edn. and cert. Pa. Dept. Pub. Instrn., Harrisburg, 1962-63, Commn. on Internat. Edn., exec. com. Del. Valley Regional Planning Coun. for Higher Edn.; cons. in field. Co-author: Workbook for the Maintenance Engineering Student, 1943; contbr. articles to profl. jours. Mem. Del. County Authority; trustee Hahnemann Med. Coll. and Hosp.; bd. dirs. Rsch. Better Schs., Clara Baldwin House; chmn. personnel com. Del. County Econ. Devel. Ctr.; bd. visitors sch. Edn. U. Pitts., Haverford Twp. Sch. Dist., 1975; bd. dirs. Afro-Am. Hist. and cultural Mus. Am.; found. mem. Del. County Hosp. Authority; chmn. adv. coun. urban. Recipient Disting. Svc. award Am. Indsl. Arts Assn., 1967, Disting. Am. award Am. Found. for Negro Affairs, 1980. Mem. NEA (chmn. task force human rights 1967-68, mem. human rights coun., exec. com. 1968-74), Nat. Assn. for Equal Opportunity in Higher Edn. (dir.), Pa. Edn. Assn. (pres. 1967), Am. Assn. State Colls. and Univs. (dir.), Pa. State U. Sch. Edn. Alumni Assn. (dir.), Pa. Indsl. Arts Assn. (pres. 1962), Epsilon Pi Tau (laureate mem.), Alpha Kappa Mu (laureate mem.), Phi Delta Kappa, Kappa Delta Pi, Omega Psi Phi, Sigma Pi Phi. Home: Cheyney Pa. Died Dec. 17, 1988; buried Rolling Green Cemetery, West Chester, Pa.

WILSON, WILLIAM EDWARD, author; b. Evansville, Ind., Feb. 12, 1906; s. William Edward and Nettie (Cook) W.; m. Ellen Janet Cameron, June 29, 1929 (dec. Dec. 1976); children: William Edward 3d, Henry Cameron, Douglas Cook; m. Hana Benes, Sept. 29, 1977. AB cum laude, Harvard, 1927, AM, 1930; Litt.D., U. Evansville, 1962. Tchr. San German (P.R.) High Sch., 1927; reporter Evansville Press, 1927-28, New Bedford (Mass.) Standard, 1928-29; instr. English Brown U., 1930-33; chmn. English dept. RISD, 1933-42; assoc. editor Evening Sun, Balt., 1947-48; prof. English U. Colo.; dir. Writers' Conf. in Rocky Mountains, 1948-50; prof. English Ind. U., 1950-67, James A. Work prof. English, 1967-73, prof. emeritus, 1973-88; Fulbright lectr. Aix-Marseille U., Grenoble U., Nice Cours d'Eté, France, 1956-57. Author: The Wabash (Rivers of America series), 1940, Big Knife: The Story of George Rogers Clark, 1940, Yesterday's Son, 1941, Shooting Star: The Story of Tecumseh, 1942, Crescent City, 1947, Abe Lincoln of Pigeon Creek, 1949, The Strangers, 1952, Abe Lincoln of Pigeon Creek (play), 1960, The Raiders, 1955, On the Sunny Side of a One Way Street, 1959, The Angel and the Serpent, 1964, Indiana: A History, 1966, Every Man is My Father, 1973; also short stories, mag. articles. Mem. overseers com. to visit English dept. Harvard U., 1954-58. Served to lt. comdr. USNR, 1942-46. Recipient award of merit Am. Assn. State and Local History, 1964, Ind. Authors Day awards, 1959, 65, 67, award Southeastern Theatre Assn., 1962; Guggenheim fellow, 1946. Home: Bloomington Ind. Died May 29, 1988.

WILT, JAMES WILLIAM, educator, chemist; b. Chgo., Aug. 28, 1930; s. Edward Frank and Mary (Manarik) W.; m. Catherine R. McAndrews, Jan. 10, 1953; children—Donna M., Susan A., Gregory E., Catherine M., Maureen T. A.B., U. Chgo., 1949, M.Sc., 1953, Ph.D. (NSF fellow), 1954. Instr. U. Conn., 1955; mem. faculty Loyola U., Chgo., 1955-87; prof. chemistry Loyola U., 1966-87, chmn. dept. chemistry, 1970-77. Contbr. articles to profl. jours. Mem. Am. Chem. Soc., Phi Beta Kappa, Sigma Xi. Home: Glenview Ill. Died May 13, 1987.

WINDER, RICHARD BAYLY, educator; b. Greensboro, N.C., Sept. 11, 1920; s. Richard Bayly and Julia (Purnell) W.; m. Viola Hitti, Oct. 12, 1946; 1 son, Bayly Philip. A.B., Haverford Coll., 1946; A.M., Princeton U., 1947, Ph.D., 1950. Mem. staff Am. U. Beirut, Lebanon, 1947-49; from instr. to assoc. prof. and asst. dean coll. Princeton U., 1947-66; prof. history and Near Eastern langs. and lit. N.Y. U., 1966-88; founding chmn. dept. Near Eastern langs. and lit. Washington Sq. Coll., 1966-68, founding dir. Ctr. for Near Eastern Studies, 1966-76, 79-82, 85-88, assoc. dir. Center for Near Eastern Studies, 1982-85, acting dean of coll., 1968-69, dean of coll., 1969-71, dean faculty of arts and sci., 1970-77; summer tchr. U. Mich., 1951, U. So. Calif., 1957, Harvard U., 1963, U. Utah, 1964, U. Pa., 1969; cons. to industry, 1951-88; Cons. Ford. Found. on Edn. Egypt, 1960-61, HEW, 1967-72, Dept. State, 1979, 80; mem. nat. screening com. Asia and Near East, Fgn. Area Fellowship Program, 1964-67, chmn., 1965-67; mem. nat. screening com. Near East, Fulbright Hays, 1963-67; advisory com. Cons. Service U.S. Undergrad. Study Abroad, 1962-65; dir. Nat. Undergrad. Program Overseas Studies Arabic, 1961-66; mem. UNESCO Internat. Commn. Textbooks for Arab Refugees, 1968-69; chmn. grants com. Am. Research Center in Egypt, 1971-76, treas., mem. exec. com., bd. govs., 1972-79, 83-88; mem. steering com. Assn. Am. Univs. project Nat. Research and Advanced Ednl. Resource Base in Fgn. Lang. and Area Studies, 1983-88. Author: (with F.J. Ziadeh) An Introduction to Modern Arabic, 6th edit, 1957, Saudi Arabia in the Nineteenth Century, 1965, 2d edit., 1980; Collaborator: (with Edward J. Jurji) Saudi Arabia, 3d rev. edit, 1958; editor: (with J. Kritzeck) The World of Islam; Studies in Honour of Philip K. Hitti, 3d edit, 1960, Current Problems in North Africa, 1960, Near Eastern Round Table, 1967-68, 1969; translator: (Constantine Zuraik) The Meaning of The Disaster, 1956, (Tawfiq al-Hakim) Bird of the East, 1966, The Return of Consciousness, 1984. Treas. Princeton chpt. Am. Field Service, 1951-60, nat. bd. dirs., mem. exec. com., 1961-68; bd. dirs. Am. Middle East Rehab, 1968-73; bd. dirs. Amideast, 1974-88, vice chmn., 1983-88; chmn. East West Group, Ltd., 1973-88; trustee, chmn. acad. and research com. Am. U. in Cairo; trustee Am. Sch. Oriental Research, Tangier Am. Legation Mus. Soc. Served with Am. Field Service, 1942-45. Decorated Purple Heart; mentioned in despatches Brit.; Ford Found. fgn. area tng. fellow Damascus, Syria, 1955-56; Princeton African travel grantee, 1959. Mem. Am. Oriental Soc., Middle East Inst., Am. Hist. Assn., Royal Central Asian Soc. (local hon. sec. U.S.), Royal Asiatic Soc., Middle East Studies Assn. (dir. 1966-71, pres. 1968-69), Brit. Soc. for Middle Eastern Studies, Am. Assn. Tchrs. Arabic, Cum Laude Soc., Council Fgn. Relations, Phi Beta Kappa. Clubs: Century, Nassau; 200; Travellers (London). Home: Princeton N.J. Died Aug. 6, 1988.

WINDOLPH, FRANCIS LYMAN, lawyer; b. Lancaster County, Pa., June 10, 1889; s. Jacob Rathvon and Frances (Grugan) W.; m. Margaret Jane Leader, Dec. 31, 1921. Prep. edn., Yeates Sch., Lancaster, 1899-1905; AB, Franklin and Marshall Coll., 1908, LittD (hon.), 1937. Bar: Pa. 1911, U.S. Supreme Ct. Practice Lancaster, from 1911; North lectr. Franklin and Marshall Coll., 1955, Garvin lectr., 1961; past mem. procedural rules com. Supreme Ct. Pa. Author: The Country Lawyer, Essays in Democracy, 1938, Leviathan and Natural Law, 1951, Reflections of the Law in Literature, 1956, Obiter Scripta, 1971, Selected Essays, 1972, Selected Poems, 1972, Four Portraits from Memory, 1973, Obiter Postscripta, 1974; contbr. articles to Atlantic Monthly, Am. Scholar. 1st lt. Army Service Corps, U.S. Army, 1918. Fellow Am. Coll. Trial Lawyers; mem. Am., Pa. (former v.p.), Lancaster (pres. 1942-45) bar assns., Am. Law Inst., Selden Soc., Am. Judicature Soc. (past dir.), Cliosophic Soc. (pres. 1939-42), Pa. Hist. Soc., Hamilton Club, Lancaster Country Club, Franklin Inn Club (Phila.), Phi Beta Kappa. Republican. Home: Lancaster Pa. †

WINN, ELLENE, lawyer; b. Clayton, Ala.. B.A. magna cum laude, Agnes Scott Coll., 1931; M.A., Radcliffe Coll., 1932; LL.B., Birmingham (Ala.) Sch. Law, 1941. Bar: Ala. 1941. Assoc. firm Bradley, Arant, Rose & White, Birmingham, 1942-57; ptnr. Bradley, Arant, Rose & White, 1957-86. Trustee Birmingham Civic Opera Assn., 1955-86 , Birmingham Music Club, 1969-86 . Mem. Am., Ala., Birmingham bar assns., Ala. State Bar, Newcomen Soc. N.Am., Birmingham Com. Fgn. Relations. Clubs: Birmingham Country, Relay House. Home: Birmingham Ala. Died May 30, 1986; buried Clayton, Ala.

WINN, JOHN, corporation executive; b. Cambridge, Mass., Apr. 5, 1890; s. William John and Agnes Elizabeth (Howe) W.; m. Louisa Morgan Nickerson, Sept. 23, 1922; children: Ann Loraine (Mrs. Thomas J. Bacon), Barbara Allison. Student, Rindge Tech. Sch., 1902-05, U. Va., 1906-10. Engring. asst. New Eng. Tel.&Tel. Co., Boston, 1910-19; sales rep. various cos. Belgium, 1919-20; engr. N.Y. Telephone Co., 1920-36; pres. Gen. Telephone Corp., N.Y., 1936-40; with North Electric Mfg. Co., Galion, Ohio, 1940-41; v.p. Keedoozle Automatic Co., Memphis, 1941-47; chmn. bd. Wynnwood Corp., Chgo., 1952-60, pres., 1957-60; pres. Mecha Mech. Stores Corp., from 1960. Capt. U.S. Army, 1918. Mem. Traffic Club. Home: Chicago Ill. †

WINSLOW, FRANCIS EDWARD, lawyer; b. Hertford, N.C., July 7, 1888; s. Tudor Frith and Mary E. (Wood) W.; m. Nemmie G. Paris, June 20, 1917; children: Adelaide (Mrs. Oliver Crawley), Mary W. (Mrs. Julian D. Bobbitt), Margaret (Mrs. R.M. Wiley), Francis Edward. AB, U. N.C., 1909, postgrad Law Sch., 1910; postgrad., Columbia Law Sch., 1911. Bar: N.C. 1911, U.S. Supreme Ct. Mem. firm Battle, Winslow, Scott & Wiley, and predecessors, Rocky Mount, N.C., from 1911; dir. Planters Nat. Bank & Trust Co., Rocky Mount. Contbr. articles to law reviews. Chmn. Carolina Charter Tercentenary Commn.; mem. exec. com. Com. for Def. of Constn. by Preserving Treaty Power, from 1953; charter mem. World Peace Through Law Ctr., Washington, from 1963; mem. Lawyers Com. for Civil Rights Under Law, from 1963; trustee Rocky Mount Pub. Libr., from 1922, chmn. bd. 1937-47. Fellow Am. Bar Found.; mem. Am. (N.C. del. 1940-47, 4th U.S. Jud. cir. mem. standing com. on fed. judiciary 1956-59), N.C. (pres. 1937-38), Rocky Mount-Nash County (pres. 1927) bar assns., Am. Law Inst., Am. Judicature Soc. (dir. 1943-52, 58-50), N.C. Lit. and Hist. Soc., Am. Assn. for UN, United World Federalists, N.C. Soc. Preservation Antiquities, N.C. Art Soc., Soc. Cin. (pres. N.C. 1956-58, del. triennial conv. Paris 1959), Phi Beta Kappa, Sigma Nu. Democrat. Episcopalian. Home: Rocky Mount N.C. †

WINSLOW, GRAHAM TRAIN, civic organization administrator; b. Boston, June 17, 1892; s. Winthrop Church and Virginia (Train) W.; m. Helen Winsor, June 30, 1917; children: Sylvia Church (Mrs. William A. Burnham), Richard Kenelm, Elinor (Mrs. John Crocker), Mary Heath. AB, Harvard U., 1914. Trustee Brookline (Mass.) Savs. Bank, 1931-43. Chief Brit. Dominions and India sect. UN Relief and Rehab. Adminstrn., 1944-46; coord. govtl. contbns. Internat. Children's Fund UN, 1947; mem. Nat. Citizens Commn. for Pub. Schs., 1953-56, Nat. Citizens Coun. for Better Schs., from 1956; chmn. bd. Mass. Coun. Pub. Schs., treas. Modern Lang. project; chmn. Mass. White House Conf. Edn., 1955; mem. ednl. media study panel U.S. Office Edn.; pres. bd. Children's Mus., Boston. 1st lt. cav. U.S. Army, 1918, lt. USCG, 1944. Mem. World Affiars Coun. (bd. dirs. Mass. chpt.). Home: South Duxbury Mass. †

WINSOR, ROY WILLIAM, author; b. Chgo., Apr. 13, 1912; s. Edward Arthur and Florence Louise (Williams) W.; m. Martha March Ricker, OCt. 22, 1938; children: Ann March, Mary Wilcox, Ricker Edward, Catherine Louise. AB cum laude, Harvard U., 1936. Apprentice-in-tng. CBS, N.Y.C., 1936-37; asst. program prodn. mgr. Sta. WCCO, Mpls., 1937-38; dir. Vic and Sade, NBC, Chgo., 1938-39; radio dir. Leo Burnett Co., Chgo., 1939-40; supr. P & G Radio, Blackett-Sample Hummert Inc., Chgo., 1940-46, radio dir., 1943; freelance dir.-writer, Chgo., 1946-50; v.p. TV-radio Biow Co., N.Y.C., 1950-55; creator, producer first daytime TV serial Search for Tomorrow, 1951; pres. Roy Winsor Prodns. Inc., N.Y.C., 1955-69; freelance TV serial cons. CBS-TV and P & G Prodns. Inc., 1969-73; head writer serial Somerset, NBC, 1974; tchr. TV serial writing New Sch., 1974-75; writer CBS Radio Mystery Theatre, 1974-87; freelance instr. Famous Writers Sch., Westport, Conn., 1974-87; instr. Inst. Children's Lit.; head writer TV serial Another Life. Author: The Corpse That Walked, 1974, Three Motives for Murder, 1976, Always Lock Your Bedroom Door, 1976. Mem. Mystery Writers Am. (Edgar award for best paperbound mystery of year 1975). Home: Pelham Manor N.Y. Died May 31, 1987.

WINSTON, CLARA BRUSSEL, writer, translator; b. N.Y.C., Dec. 6, 1921; m. Richard Winston, Sept. 12, 1941; children: Krishna, Justina. Translator: (with Richard Winston) numerous books including A Part of Myself (Carl Zuckmayer), 1967, Hope and History (Joseph Pieper), 1969, The Glass Bead Game (Herman Hesse), 1969, The Letters of Thomas Mann, 1971, The Inward Turn of Narrative (Erich Kahler), 1973, memoirs (Joseph Cardinal Mindszerty), 1974, Letters to Family, Friends and Editors (Franz Kafka), 1977, Winterspell (Alfred Andersch), 1978, The Magic Stone (Leonie Kooiker), 1978, numerous others; articles, lit.; author: The Closest Kin There Is, 1952, The Hours Together, 1961, Painting for the Show, 1969; (with Richard Winston) Notre-Dame de Paris, 1971, Daily Life in the Middle Ages, 1975 (Nat. Book award 1978). Mem. PEN, Am. Trnaslators' Assn. Home: Brattleboro Vt. Died Nov. 7, 1983.

WINTER, LUMEN MARTIN, painter, sculptor, designer; b. Elerie, Ill., Dec. 12, 1908; s. William Grant and Mary Blanche (Nicholson) W.; m. Grace Harmon, Mar. 13, 1948; children: Thomas Martin, William Grant II, Susan Anne. Hon. degree, Grand Rapids Jr. Coll., 1928; grad., Cleve. Sch. Art, 1929; postgrad., Nat. Acad. Design, 1929-30; advanced study, Pietrosanta, Italy. Began painting, 1923; asst. to Ezra Augustus Winter in execution of Radio City murals, George Rogers Clark Meml. murals, Vincennes, Ind.; murals and sculpture executed several pub. and pvt. bldgs., including: labor and space murals AFL-CIO, Washington, Refectory at Univ. Notre Dame, Ch. St. Paul, The Apostle, N.Y.C., New Penn Sheraton Bldg., Phila., Murray Bldg., J.F.K. Meml., Internat. Union Elec., Radio and Machine Workers, Washington, East Bklyn. Savs. Bank, Apollo XIII Space mural St. Regis Hotel, Gerald R. Ford Ctr., Grand Rapids, Mich., Titans Mural Gen. Assembly, UN; mosaic Pub. Sch. 60, Staten Island, Dove of Peace Sculpture at City Hall Plaza, Poughkeepsie, N.Y.; sculpture for library Fairfield U. USAF Acad., Astor Home for Children, Rhinebeck, N.Y., South Shore High Sch., N.Y., Cathedral Coll. Immaculate Conception, Shrine of Our Lady, 30-foot bronze, Haverstraw, N.Y.; Thornton Donovan Sch., New Rochelle, N.Y.; monumental abstract sculpture Library Plaza, New Rochelle; designed ofcl. medallion for Apollo XIII flight; mural awards Nat. Competitions for Senate Chamber, Wash. State Capitol Bldg., 1948, Va. State Library, 1950, Rotunda murals Kans. State Capitol, Topeka, 1976, Gold medal exhbns. Archtl. League N.Y., 1951-52; Ranger Fund Purchase, N.A.O.; Petersen; Debellis and William A. White awards Salmagundi Club, many others; exhibited pvt., pub. galleries U.S. and abroad including Mus. Modern Art, Whitney Mus., Topeka Art Guild, Nat. Acad. Design, Penn Acad. Internat.; one-man shows numerous galleries including Grand Rapids Art Mus., Galerie Internationale, N.Y.C.; represented Artiests for Victory, Library of Congress, many pvt. and pub. collections including Santa Fe Trail Ctr., Larned, Kans.; Art Inst. Chgo., U. Israel, Vatican; sculpture for Kans. State Hist. Soc., Topeka; illustrator numerous books; co-author (with Harrison Kinney) and illustrator: The Last Supper of Leonardo Da Vinci,. Mem. New Rochelle (N.Y.) Art Commn., 1975-76. Artist World War II. Mem. Nat. Soc. Mural Painters (1st v.p., adviser), Archtl. League N.Y. (past v.p.), Am. Watercolor Soc., New Rochelle Art Assn. (past pres.), Artists Equity, Soc. Illustrators, Salmagundi Club. Home: New Rochelle N.Y. Died Apr. 5, 1982; buried New Rochelle.

WINTERS, ALFRED C., utilities executive; b. Chgo., Mar. 31, 1889; s. Auralius and Jennie (Aiken) W.; m. Emma E. Manz, Sept. 12, 1912; 1 child, Verna (Mrs. Charles W. Hoerr). Student, Walton Sch. Commerce, Chgo., 1913-15. With Peoples Gas, Light & Coke Co., Chgo., 1908-15, acct., acct. stores dept., 1911-15; asst. treas. N.Am. Light & Power Co., Chgo., 1915-23; v.p. William A. Baehr Orgn. Inc., Chgo., 1915-43, pres., 1943-50; v.p. North Continent Utilities Corp., Chgo., 1922-43, pres., 1943-55; also pres. corp. owned cos; pres. Great No. Gas Co. Ltd., Can., 1943-53; v.p., dir. North Shore Gas Co., Waukegan, Ill., 1925-63, Ft. Madison Gas Co., 1948-52, Great Falls Gas Co., 1952-58, Ariz. Manganese Corp., from 1955. Mem. South Shore Country Club, Midday Club. Home: Chicago Ill. †

WINTERS, DENNY, artist; b. Grand Rapids, Mich., 1909; d. James Henry and Eva May (Taylor) Sonke; m. Herman Joseph Cherry, Sept. 20, 1940; m. 2d Lew Dietz, 1951. Student, Chgo. Acad. Fine Arts, Chgo. Art Inst. Tchr. Camden (Maine) Extension; traveled, painted in France and Italy, 1949. Work exhibited Mus. Modern Art, Carnegie Mus., Pa. Acad. Fine Arts, Chgo. Art Inst., San Francisco Mus., Nat Acad. show, 1958, Nat. Acad. Art, 1970-72; one man shows L.A. Mus., San Francisco Mus., Mortimer Levitt Gallery, N.Y.C., Wiscasset (Maine) Mus., 1961, Rehn Art Gallery, N.Y.C., 1953, 57, 63, 72, 76, U. Maine, 1959, 65, 78, C. of C. Northeast Harbor, Maine, 1960, 62, Phila. Art Alliance, 1964, Bowdoin Coll., 1968, Grand Rapids (Mich.) Art Mus., 1972, Kalamazoo Inst. Fine Arts, 1972, Talent Tree Gallery, Auguta, Maine, Bates Coll., Lewiston, Maine, 1975, U.S. Ct. House, Phila., 1976, Unity (Maine) Coll., 1976, Barridoff Gallery, Portland, Maine, 1978, Payson Mus., Westbrook Coll., Portland, 1978, Camden (Maine) Gallery, 1980, Maine Coast Artists Gallery, Rockport; illustrator: Full Fathom Five (Lew DIetz), Wilderness River (Lew Dietz). Mem. Maine Visual Arts com. for Arts and Humanities Commn. Recipient 1st prize for prints San Francisco Mus., 1941, 1st proze for oils Denver Mus., 1940, Purchase prize Butler Inst. Am. Art, 1964, Skowhegan Art award, 1973, Henry Ward Baxter purchase award NAD, 1979; Guggenhein fellow, 1948. Mem. Maine Coast Artists (exhibitor 1951-86), Maine Hist. Soc. Home: Rockport Maine. Died Mar. 7, 1986; cremated.

WINTERSTEEN, BERNICE MCILHENNY, civic worker; b. Phila., June 16, 1903; d. John D. and Frances (Plumer) McIlhenny; m. John Wintersteen, Oct. 30, 1929 (dec. Oct. 1952); children—John, James McI., H. Jeremy, George F. B.A. with Honors in History, Smith Coll., 1925; L.H.D. (hon.), Ursinus Coll., 1965, Villanova U., 1967, Hahnemann Med. Coll. and Hosp., 1967; hon. degree, Moore Coll. Art, Wilson Coll. Trustee Phila. Mus. Art, 1942, gov., 1937-64, chmn. bd. govs., 1959-64; pres. Phila. Mus. Art (Mus.), 1964-68, mem. women's com., 1928, later mem. bd.; chmn. bd. mgrs. Moore Coll. Art, 1968-71; past mem. Phila. Art Commn.; past vis. com. dept. visual art Harvard, 1963-68; vis. com. Princeton U. Art Mus.; mem., 1st chmn. vis. com. Smith Coll. Mus. Art; co-chmn. Phila. Art Festival, 1962, chmn., 1967; vice chmn. Pa. Council Arts; pres., dir. Friends of the Wissahickon, 1953-56; mem. bd. counselors Smith Coll., 1951-57; mem. Am. civilization adv. council U. Pa.; also mem. com. for devel. research in sci.; past trustee Drexel Inst. Tech.; trustee Pa. Acad. Fine Arts; hon. trustee Phila. Coll. Art, Maxwell Mansion Com.; former bd. dirs. Montgomery County Soc. for Prevention Cruelty to Animals; former bd. govs. Atheneium Library.; lectr. art and travel. Recipient Phila. Woman of Year Gimble award, 1966; Woman of Year award Am. Friends Hebrew U., 1966; Art Alliance award, 1974; Smith Coll. medal, 1981. Mem. Disting. Daus. Pa., Phi Beta Kappa Assos. (bd. dirs.), Phi Beta Kappa. Republican. Presbyn. Clubs: Acorn (Phila.), Print (Phila.) (pres. 1952-55), Gulph Mills Golf (Phila.), Planters Garden (Phila.); Prouts Neck (Maine) Country (dir.), Merion Country. Home: Haverford Pa. Died Apr. 1986.

WINTHER, MARTIN PHILLIP, manufacturing executive; b. Aarhus, Denmark, Nov. 4, 1888; came to U.S., 1893, naturalized, 1917; s. James Peter and Mattie Marie (Pederson) W.; m. Marcella Link, July 25, 1911; children: Jerrold Byron, Virginia (Mrs. Robert W. Feller), Shirley Mae (Mrs. Gerald Griffin), Betty Jane (Mrs. Richard R. Johnston Jr.). Student, Stanford, 1908-09, Lewis Inst. Tech., 1910-11. Mgr. motor truck dept. Thomas B. Jeffery Co., Kenosha, Wis., 1915-16; pres., gen. mgr. Winther Motors Inc., Kenosha, 1917-24; v.p. charge mfg. Sykes Co., St. Louis, 1924-27; rail car engr. Pullman Standard Car & Mfg. Co., Chgo., 1927-36; v.p. Dynamatic Corp., Kenosha, 1936-46, gen. mgr., 1936-48, pres., from 1948; cons. Eaton Mfg. Co., Cleve.; pres., dir. 1st Fed. Savs. & Loan Assn., Clermont, Fla. Author articles on engring. and transp. Mem. Soc. Automotive Engrs., Am. Inst. E.E., Cleve. Engring. Soc., Union Club, Country Club, Chippewa Club (Iron Mountain, Mich.), Athletic Club (Detroit), Masons, Elks, Danish Brotherhood. Home: Clermont Fla. †

WINTROBE, MAXWELL MYER, medical educator; b. Halifax, N.S., Can., Oct. 27, 1901; came to U.S., 1927, naturalized, 1933; s. Herman and Ethel (Swerling) W.; m. Becky Zanphir, Jan. 1, 1928; children: Susan Hope, Paul William H. (dec.). B.A., U. Man., Can.), Winnipeg, 1921, M.D., 1926, B.Sc. in Medicine, 1927, D.Sc. (hon.), 1958; Ph.D., Tulane U., 1929; D.Sc. (hon.), U. Utah, 1967, Med. Coll. Wis., Milw., 1974; M.D. (hon.), U. Athens, 1981. Diplomate Am. Bd. Internal Medicine. Gordon Bell fellow Manitoba, 1926-27; instr. in medicine Tulane U., 1927-30; also asst. vis. physician Charity Hosp., New Orleans; instr. medicine Johns Hopkins, 1930-35, assoc. in medicine, 1935-43, also assoc. physician, 1935-43; physician in charge, clinic for nutritional, gastro-intestinal and hemopoietic disorders Johns Hopkins Hosp., 1941-43; prof. medicine U. Utah, 1943-70, disting. prof. internal medicine, 1970-86, head dept. medicine, 1943-67, dir. cardiovascular research and tng. inst., 1969-73; physician-in-chief Salt Lake Gen. Hosp., 1943-65, U. Utah Med. Center, 1965-67; cons. to surgeon-gen. U.S. Army; chief cons. Va Hosp., Salt Lake City; dir. lab. for study of hereditary and metabolic disorders U. Utah, 1945-73; spl. cons. nutritional anemias WHO; UN. Council mem. Nat. Adv. Arthritis and Metabolic Diseases Council, USPHS, 1950-54, chmn. hematology study sect., 1956-59; council mem. Nat. Allergy and Infectious Disease Council,

1967-70; mem. com. research in life scis. Nat. Acad. Sci., 1966-69; chmn. sci. adv. bd. Scripps Clinic and Research Found., 1964-74; med. cons. AEC; mem., then chmn. adv. council Life Ins. Med. Research Fund, 1949-53; dir. Am. Soc. Human Genetics, 1948; chmn. hematology com. Research and Devel. Command Surg. Gen.'s U.S. Army; cons. FDA, Dept. Health, Edn. and Welfare; vis. prof. many univs. including Rochester, Vanderbilt, Marquette, N.Y., Tufts, Johns Hopkins, Tulane, U. Calif. at San Diego, Brown U., N.C., Emory, U. Fla., Gainesville, Ala., Southwestern at Dallas, Harvard, UCLA, U. Toronto, Ottawa, McGill U., Dalhousie U. Mng. editor Bull. Johns Hopkins Hosp, 1942-43; assoc. editor Nutrition Revs., Boston, 1943-49; adv. editor: Tice Practice of Medicine, 1943-76; assoc. editor: Internat. Med. Digest, 1944- 58, Blood, 1945-75, Am. Jour. Medicine, 1946-56, Medicine, Cancer, Jour. Clin. Pathology; editorial bd. Jour. Clin. Investigation, 1948-49, Gen. Practitioner, 1949-59, Jour. Clin. Nutrition, 1952-65, Jour. Chronic Diseases, 1955-75; Author: Clinical Hematology, 1942, 8th edit., 1981, Blood, Pure and Eloquent, 1980, Hematology, The Blossoming of a Science, 1985, also numerous sci. articles.; Editor: Harrison's Principles of Internal Medicine, 1950; editor-in-chief, 6th edit., 1970, 7th edit., 1974. Bd. dirs., v.p. Salt Lake Chamber Music Soc.; nat. adv. bd. Utah Symphony Orch.; bd. dirs. Pro-Utah.; mem. anti-anemia preparations adv. bd., U.S. Pharmacopeia, 1941-49, com. revision, 1950-60. Recipient gold medals in polit. econs. and French, 1921, Isbister prizes, 1920-25; all U. Man.).; Recipient Physician of Excellence award Med. Times, 1979. Fellow A.C.P. (John Philips Meml. award 1967, master 1973); corr. mem. Italian, Swiss, Brit. Assn. Clin. Pathology; mem. Am. Soc. Hematology (pres. 1971-72), AMA (vice chmn. council on drugs 1964-68, chmn. sect. on adverse reactions), Assn. Am. Physicians (Kober medal 1974, councillor 1957-63, pres. 1964-65), Assn. Profs. Medicine (Robert H. Williams award 1973, councillor 1962-63, pres. 1965-66), Western Assn. Physicians (pres. 1956-57), Am. Soc. Exptl. Pathology, AAAS, Nat. Acad. Scis. (com. on sci. and public policy, chmn. sect. on human genetics, hematology and oncology 1976-79), Soc. Exptl. Biology and Medicine, Leukemia Soc. (chmn. nat. med. adv. bd.), Pacific Interurban Clin. Club, Western Soc. Clin. Research (Mayo Soley award 1970), European Soc. Hematology (corr.), Internat. Soc. Hematology (councillor-at-large 1972-74, v.p. 1976-78, pres. 1978-80, Ferrata award Rome 1958), Harvey Soc. (hon.), Assn. Clin. Pathologists (Eng.) (corr.), Am. Fedn. Clin. Research, Physicians for Social Responsibility (nat. bd. sponsors), Phi Beta Kappa (hon.), Sigma Xi, Alpha Omega Alpha, Sigma Alpha Mu. Home: Salt Lake City Utah. Died Dec. 1, 1986; buried Salt Lake City.

WINWAR, FRANCES (FRANCESCA VINCIGUERRA), novelist, literary critic; b. Taormina, Sicily, Italy, May 3, 1900; came to U.S., 1907, naturalized, 1929; d. Domenico and Giovanna (Sciglio) Vinciguerra; m. Bernard D.N. Grebanier, Sept. 22, 1925 (div.); 1 son, Francis Grebanier. Ed., Hunter Coll., N.Y.C., CCNY, Columbia U. Co-founder Leonardo da Vinci Art Sch., N.Y.C., 1923, exec. sec., 1923-30; lectr. on Victorian lit. figures 1934-36; vis. prof. U. Kans. City, Mo., 1942. Contbr.: The Freeman, 1923; book reviewer for: Laurence Stallings in the World, 1923-25; novelist and biographer from 1927; author: biography Poor Splendid Wings, 1933 ($5,000 nonfiction prize for biography Atlantic Monthly 1933), The Immortal Lovers: Elizabeth Barrett and Robert Browning, 1950, The Eagle and the Rook, 1953, The Last Love of Camille, 1954, Wingless Victory, 1956, The Haunted Palace: Edgar Allan Poe, 1959, Jean Jacqués Rouseau: Conscience of an Era, 1961, Up From Caesar, 1965; translator: LaTraviata, 1950, Boccaccio's Decameron, 1930, Modern Library edit., 1956; contbr. to nat. mags. Mem. Poetry Soc. Am. Democrat. Died July 24, 1985; buried Kensico Cemetery, Valhalla, N.Y.

WISE, GENE, chemistry educator; b. Willard, Ohio, Apr. 13, 1922; s. Pearl E. and Marvel H. (Voight) W.; m. Helen Joanna Giddings, June 13, 1964; children: Kathryn Ann, Jennifer Carol. B.S., Capital U., 1947; Ph.D. (Standard Oil Ohio fellow), Western Res. U., 1950. Faculty Va. Mil. Inst., Lexington, 1950-86; prof. chemistry Va. Mil. Inst., 1960-86, head dept., 1977-82; Cons. chem. div. Gen. Tire & Rubber Co., Akron, Ohio, 1957-63; research assoc. Northwestern U., summers 1953-54. Chmn. ARC, 1964-86 . Served with USNR, 1943-46, 51-52. Mem. Am. Chem. Soc. (sect. chmn. 1963), sect. (councillor 1974-86), Sigma Xi, Phi Kappa Phi (chpt. pres. 1980-81). Home: Lexington Va. Died June 7, 1986.

WITHERS, WILLIAM, educator, economist; b. St. Louis, Dec. 21, 1905; s. John W. and Margaret (Mathews) W.; m. Irma Rittenhouse, May 29, 1931. A.B., Columbia, 1926, A.M., 1928, Ph.D., 1932. Instr. econs. Lehigh U., 1927-29, N.Y. U., 1929-31; research asso. Tchrs. Coll. Columbia, 1931-32; chmn. social sci. dept. New Coll., 1932-37; asst. prof. edn. Tchrs. Coll., 1935-37; prin. research supr. WPA, 1937; asst. prof. econ. Queens Coll., 1937-40, assoc. prof., 1940-51, prof., 1951-74, prof. emeritus, 1974-87, chmn. econs. dept. and div. social scis., 1937-42, chmn. div. contemporary civilization, 1950, chmn. econ. dept., 1959; dir. N.Y. U. Farm Labor Study, 1960; chief pub. requirements br. WPB, 1942-43. Author: The Retirement of National Debts, 1932, Current Social Problems, 1936, Financing Economic Security, 1939, The Public Debt, 1945, Public Finance, 1948, Social Foundations of Education, 1955, Economic Crisis in Latin America, 1964, Freedom Through Power, 1965, Business in Society, 1966, The Corporations and Social Change, 1972, The Crisis in Old Age Finance, 1979, Politics and Economic Policy, 1986. Contbr. to: others. Vice pres. N.Y. Tchrs. Guild, 1943-46; vice chmn. Liberal party N.Y. State, 1945-46. Mem. Ricardo Assn. (pres. 1974-87), N.Y. Tchrs. Pension Assn. (pres. 1976-87), Am. Econ. Assn., Latin Am. Study Assn., Phi Beta Kappa. Home: Eatontown N.J. Died Feb. 24, 1987.

WITHERSPOON, GIBSON BOUDINOT, lawyer; b. Lexington, Va., Aug. 7, 1903; s. Elias Boudinot and Magdalene Moore (Gibson) W.; m. Jewel Cook, Apr. 25, 1940; children: Mary Elizabeth (Mrs. J. George Smith), Jane May (Mrs. Harold PAgan Hope). AB, Washington & Lee U., 1925, JD, 1927. Bar: Va. 1926, Miss. 1927, U.S. Supreme Ct. Practice Meridian, Miss., 1927-81; mem. firm Witherspoon, Copmton & Mason and predecessor firm; commr. uniform state laws, Miss., 1945-81; dir. Miss. Econ. Coun., 1962-81. Contbr. articles to legal jours.; assoc. editor Comml. Law Jour., 1945-81, bd. govs., 1962-72. Del. Dem. Nat. Conv., L.A., 1960. Fellow Am. Bar Found.; mem. ABA (chmn. state legislation com. 1962-63, mem. bd. govd. 1970-72, mem. ho. of dels. 1955-75, Nat. Inst. Justice, 1977-81), Probate Counsel, Fedn. Ins. Counsel, Internat. Assn. Ins. Counsel, Internat. Trial Counsel, Miss. Bar Assn. (past pres.), Miss. C. of C. (bd. dirs.), Meridian C. of C. (bd. dirs.), Scribes (pres. 1955), Northwood Country Club, Downtown Club, Meridian Kiwanis (past pres., bd. govs.). Presbyterian (elder). Home: Meridian Miss. Died 1981.

WITKIN, ISAAC, international merchant; b. N.Y.C., Feb. 3, 1892; s. Myer and Rachel (Smerling) W.; m. Miriam N. Newman, Dec. 23, 1915; children—Richard, William Isaac. A.B., Harvard, 1914. With J. Aron & Co., Inc. (coffee and sugar importers), N.Y.C., 1914-26; mgr. export dept. J. Aron & Co., Inc. (coffee and sugar importers), 1918-19, dir., 1918- 26, v.p., 1926-38; engaged principally in importation of cocoa beans and commodity futures on Commodity Exchange and N.Y. Cocoa Exchange, 1938-75; sr. partner Gen. Cocoa Co.; dir. Gen. Cocoa Co. Holland B.V., Amsterdam, 1962-86; cons. Otto Gerdau & Co., N.Y.C., 1977-86 ; A founder, mem. N.Y. Cocoa Exchange, Inc., 1925, 1st pres., 1925-26, mem. bd. mgrs., 1925-51; pres., 1944-47, pres. emeritus, 1975-86. Contbr. articles on world cocoa trade and econ. and polit. subjects to trade, fin. and other periodicals. Mem. N.Y. State Guard, 1940-43. Mem. Phi Beta Kappa. Jewish. Clubs: Harvard (N.Y.C.); Nat. Arts. Lectr. Home: New York N.Y. Died Nov. 2, 1986.

WITTER, WILLIAM MAURER, investment banker; b. San Francisco, Feb. 18, 1923; s. Jean Carter and Catherine (Maurer) W.; m. Christene Allen, Aug. 20, 1953. BA, U. Calif., Berkeley, 1947. Ptnr. Dean Witter Reynolds Orgn. (formerly Dean Witter & Co.), 1949-54, mng. ptnr., Chgo., 1953-68; exec. v.p. Dean Witter & Co., Inc., 1968-69, pres., 1969-70, chmn., chief exec. officer, 1970-80, hon., chmn., dir., from 1980; Gov. Midwest Stock Exchange, 1964-67, chmn, 1968-69, Chgo. Assn. Stock Exchange Firms, 1963-64. Trustee Ill. Children's Home and Aid Soc. Mem. Investment Bankers Am. (chmn. cen. states group 1966-67, gov. 1967-69), Nat. Assn. Security Delaers (gov. 1969), San Francisco C. of C. (pres. 1974, chmn. bd. dirs. 1975), Pacific Union Club, Bohemian Club (San Francisco). Home: San Francisco Calif. Died July 17, 1984; cremated.

WITTHUHN, IRWIN RAYMOND, organization official; b. Appleton, Wis., Nov. 22, 1891; s. Edward and Wilhemina (Busse) W.; m. Doris Drew, Dec. 12, 1917; 1 child, Carole (Mrs. Edward Q. Nye). BA, Lawrence Coll., 1914. High sch. instr. Tomah, Wis., 1914-16; pres. Standard Distbg. Corp., Milw., 1919-58; exec. v.p. Ideal Uniform Service Inc., Milw., 1959-62. Mem. Curative Workshop, Milw.; trustee Milw. Kiwanis Found. 1st lt. U.S. Army, 1917-19, AEF. Recipient cert. of merit Lawrence Coll. Mem. Milw. Civic Alliances (past pres.), Am. Legion, Milw. Assn. Commerce (pres. 1953-56), Masons, Shriners, Kiwanis Internat. (pres. 1961-62, bldg. chmn. hdqrs. Chgo. 1958-59), Sigma Phi Epsilon. Home: Mequon Wis. †

WITTIG, GEORG FRIEDRICH KARL, chemist; b. Berlin, June 16, 1897; s. Gustav and Martha (Dombrowski) W.; m. Waltraut Ernst, 1930 (dec. 1978); 2 children. Student U. Tubingen (Germany), 1916; Dr. phil., U. Marburg (Germany), 1923, Dr.h.c., Sorbonne, 1957; Dr. rer. nat. h.c., Tubingen, Hamburg, 1962. Prof., U. Marburg, 1932; head dept. Chem. Inst. Braunschweig Inst. Tech., 1932-37; prof., head chemistry dept. Chem. Inst. Freiburg U., 1937-44; prof., dir. Chem. Inst. U. Tubingen, 1944-56; prof. U. Heidelberg, 1956-67, prof. emeritus, 1967-87. Recipient A. von Baeyer medal, 1953; mitglied Heidelberg Acad., 1957; Dannie-Heineman prize Gottinger Acad. Sci., 1965, Otto Hahn prize for chemistry and physics, 1967; Karl Ziegler prize, 1975; La Mé daille d'Argent de la Ville de Paris, 1969; Paul Karrer medaille, 1972; Silver medal U. Helsinki, 1958; La Mé daille de la Claire Bruylants, U. Leuwen, 1972; Roger Adams award Am. Chem. Soc., 1974, Nobel Prize in Chemistry, 1979. Hon. fellow Chem. Soc. London; mem. Bavarian Acad. Sci., Leopoldina Halle, Chem. Soc. Switzerland (hon.), N.Y. Acad. Sci., Sociedad Quimica del Peru, Acad. France; corr. Academia des Ciencias Medicas Cordoba (Argentina). Author: Lehrbuch der Stereochemie, 1930; Carbanion and Ylid Chemistry. Home: Heidelberg, Federal Republic Germany. Died Aug. 26, 1987.

WOLBERG, LEWIS ROBERT, physician, psychiatrist; b. Russia, July 4, 1905; s. Max and Anna (Hurwitz) W.; m. Arlene Robbins, 1931; children: Barbara Jane, Ellen May. A.B., U. Rochester, 1927; M.D., Tufts Coll., 1930. Asst. exec. officer Boston Psychopathic Hosp. (name now Mass. Mental Health Center), 1932; supervising psychiatrist Kings Park State Hosp., 1932-45; clin. prof. psychiatry N.Y. Med. Coll., 1946-70, faculty postgrad. psychoanalytic div., 1946-70; founder, med. dir., dean (Postgrad. Center for Mental Health), 1945-72; now chmn. bd. trustees; clin. prof. psychiatry N.Y. U. Med. Sch., 1970-86; attending psychiatrist N.Y. U. Med. Sch. (Med. Center), 1970-88; psychiatrist Flower-Fifth Ave. Hosp., 1938-70; neuropsychiatrist Univ., Bellevue hosps. Author: Psychology of Eating, 1936, Hypnoanalysis, 1945, 2d edit., 1967, Medical Hypnosis, 1948, The Technique of Psychotherapy, 1954, 4th edit., 1988, Short-term Psychotherapy, 1965, Psychotherapy and Behavioral Sciences, 1966, Micro-art: Art Images in a Hidden World, 1970, Hypnosis: Is It for You, 1972, 2d edit., 1982, Group Therapy, 1974, 75, 76, 77, 78, 79, 80, 81, 82, 83, Zooming In: Photographic Discoveries under the Microscope, 1974, Art Forms from Photomicrography, 1975, Handbook of Short-term Psychotherapy, 1980; Mem. editorial bd.: Jour. Contemporary Psychiotherapy, Am. Jour. Clin. Hypnosis, Internat. Jour. Clin. and Exptl. Hypnosis; contbr.: articles to sci. jours. Funk & Wagnalls Ency. Fellow Am. Psychiat. Assn. (life mem.), N.Y. County Med. Soc., Am. Acad. Psychoanalysis (founding), Am. Acad. Psychiatry; mem. A.M.A., N.Y. Soc. Clin. Psychiatry, Am. Psychosomatic Soc., Am. Group Therapy Assn., Assn. Advancement Psychotherapy, Soc. Med. Psychoanalysts. Home: Putnam Valley N.Y. Died Feb. 3, 1988, buried Putnam Valley.

WOLCOTT, CHARLES, composer, religious association executive; b. Flint, Mich., Sept. 29, 1906; s. Frederick Charles and Frances Mae (Terwilliger) W.; m. Harriett Louise Marshall, Aug. 30, 1928; children: Sheila Joan Wolcott Banani, Marsha Jean Wolcott Gilpatrick. B.A., U. Mich., 1927. With Walt Disney, Hollywood, Calif., 1938-48; gen. mus. dir. Walt Disney, 1944-48; with Metro-Goldwyn-Mayer, 1950-60, gen. mus. dir., 1958-60. Leader own orch., 1925; pianist, arranger, Jean Goldkette Orgn., Detroit, including, Casa Loma Orch.; composer, arranger, condr., Paul Whiteman Orch., 1931, on radio with, Andre Kostelanetz, Arnold Johnson, others, 1933-37; Composer: Reluctant Dragon, 1941, Saludos Amigos, 1942, Sailors of the Air, 1942, Mexico, 1944, Two Silhouettes, 1945, Sooner or Later, 1946, From The Sweet-Scented Streams, 1948, Julie, 1953, Oh Thou, By Whose Name, Llama Serenade, Inca Princess, Blessed Is the Spot, 1955, Ruby Duby Du, 1960; music for motion pictures Key Witness. Vice chmn. Nat. Spiritual Assembly of Baha'is of U.S., 1953-59, sec., 1960-61; sec.-gen. Internat. Baha'i Council, Haifa, 1961-63; elected mem. Baha'i Universal House of Justice, 1963, 83-87, head (with 8 others) of Baha'i religion. Mem. ASCAP, Acad. Motion Picture Arts and Scis., Screen Composers Assn., Am. Guild Authors and Composers, Sigma Chi. Lodge: Rotary. Home: Haifa Israel. Died Jan. 28, 1987.

WOLDRING, SABBO, physician; b. Weesp, The Netherlands, June 7, 1920; naturalized; married; 2 children. MD, State U. Netherlands, Groningen, 1942, PhD in Physiology, 1951. Diplomate Am. Bd. Family Practice. Intern The Netherlands, 1942-46; asst. prof. physiology Sch. Medicine State U. Netherlands, Groningen, 1945-51; med. physiologist Philips Rsch. Labs., Eindhoven, The Netherlands, 1951-60; prin. sci. in cancer rsch. dept. anesthesiology and neurosurgery Roswell Park Meml. Inst., Buffalo, 1961-69; biophysicist, physiologist GE R&D Ctr., Schenectady, N.Y., 1969-73; pvt. practice Schenectady, 1973—; mem. attending staff Ellis Hosp., St. Clare's Hosp., Schenectady, 1974—. Hon. vice consul The Netherlands, 1963-69. Fellow Am. Acad. Family Physicians; mem. AMA, AAAS, Med. Soc. State N.Y., N.Y. Acad. Sci. (life), Am. Physiol. Soc. Home: Schenectady N.Y. Died Mar. 4, 1988.

WOLF, GORDON JOSEPH, lawyer, industrial company executive; b. Cin., Jan. 6, 1905; s. Joseph and Hanna (von Epstein) W.; m. Evelyn M. Best, Aug. 2, 1948; children: Joseph G., Alice Margaret, Robert Houston. Ph.B. summa cum laude, Yale U., 1926; J.D. cum laude, Harvard U., 1930. Bar: Ohio 1930, Calif. 1973. Practice in Cin. as partner Cohen & Wolf, 1933-68; v.p. Aeronca, Inc., Torrance, Calif., 1969-73; sec. Aeronca, Inc., from 1969; also dir.; partner law firm Jones, Day, Cockley & Reavis, Los Angeles, 1973-76; dir. Aeronca Indsl. Products, Inc., Cleve. Machine Tool Co., Mercury Aerostructures, Inc. Trustee, sec. Aeronca Found.; bd. dirs. Cin. Charter Com., 1947-48; trustee Jewish Hosp. Cin., 1956-68, Adler Found., 1964-69, Lauer Found., 1966-69. Served to col., arty. AUS,

1941-46, ETO. Decorated Legion of Merit. Mem. Am., Ohio, Cin., Calif. bar assns., Am. Soc. Corp. Secs., Res. Officers Assn. (pres. Cin. chpt. 1937-39), Mil. Order World Wars, Am. Arbitration Assn., Army Aviation Assn., Ret. Officers Assn., Mensa, Phi Beta Kappa. Republican. Clubs: Mason (Washington) (Shriner), Army and Navy (Washington); Calif. Yacht (Los Angeles). Home: Austin Tex. Deceased.

WOLF, HERBERT CHRISTIAN, educator; b. Balt., Apr. 6, 1923; s. Carl George and Margaret (Umhau) W.; m. Margaret Schroder, June 18, 1947; children: Gretchen, Gary, Martin, Allen, Miriam. AB, Johns Hopkins, 1943; BD, Luth. Theol. Sem., 1947; MA, U. Chgo., 1959; ThD, Harvard, 1968. Ordained to ministry Luth. Ch., 1948. Instr. religion Capital U., Columbus, Ohio, 1945-47; pastor Univ. Luth. Ch., Nat. Luth. Coun.; campus pastor, lectr. religion Mich. State U., 1948-57; prof. religion Wittenberg U., Springfield, Ohio, 1957-87, chmn. dept., 1969-87; vis. prof. United Theol. Coll., Bangalore, India, 1974; participant faculty study seminar of Kansas City Coun. Higher Edn. and Nat. Coun. Assocs. Internat. Studies, 1971; vis. prof. Hood Coll., Frederick, Md., 1971-72. Author: Kierkegaard and Bultmann: The Quest of the Historical Jesus, 1965; contbr. articles to profl. jours. Mem. Clark County Dem. exec. com., 1960-87, chmn., 1966-72; chmn. Clark County Dem. Cen. Com., 1966-72; sec. Ohio Dem. County Chmns., 1966-72. Danforth tchr. study grantee, 1961-62, 64-65. Mem. AAUP, Am. Acad. Religion, Am. Theol. Soc. Home: Springfield Ohio. Died Dec. 13, 1987; buried Ferncliff Cemetery, Springfield.

WOLFE, DAVID K., lawyer; b. Lafayette, Ind., Feb. 6, 1922; s. Simon and Nora I. (Connaroe) W.; m. Charity Phillips, Aug. 19, 1958. Student, Purdue U.; JD with high distinction, U. Ariz., 1950. Bar: Ariz. 1950, U.S. Dist. Ct. Ariz. 1957, U.S. Ct. Appeals (9th cir.) 1957, U.S. Supreme Ct. 1978. Since practiced in Tucson, 1950-88; sr. ptnr. Wolfe & Ostapuk, 1976-88; judge pro tem domestic relation div. Pima County Superior Ct., Tucson, 1986-88. Served with USAAF, 1943-45, USAF, 1950-52; maj. USAFR ret. Decorated D.F.C. with oak leaf cluster, Air medal with 4 oak leaf clusters. Fellow Am. Acad. Matrimonial Lawyers, Ariz. Bar Found.; mem. ABA (family law sect., pub. utility law sect., litigation sect.), State Bar Ariz. (com. profl. ethics 1960-72, bd. govs. 1961-64, com. on exams. and admissions 1961-72, chmn. 1968-72, 78-80, family law sect., award for service 1980), Inter.-Am. Bar Assn., Pima County Bar Assn. (pres. 1958), Judge Advs. Assn., Order of Coif, Alpha Delta, Phi Kappa Phi, Theta Xi. Democrat. Home: Tucson Ariz. Died Nov. 11, 1988; buried St. Philips in the Hills, Tucson.

WOLFE, JAMES RICHARD, transportation executive, lawyer; b. Hannibal, Mo., Nov. 7, 1929; s. James Edward and Grace (Kirn) W.; m. Helene Lorraine Rosedale, Dec. 29, 1951; children: Yvonne Bazar, Mary Viano, Theresa Henderson, James E., Michaela, Kathleen, Lorraine. Student, Georgetown U., 1947-49; B.S., Loyola U., 1951; J.D., DePaul U., 1953, LLD (hon.), 1988; LHD (honoris causa), Huron Coll., 1982. Bar: Ill. 1953, U.S. Supreme Ct. 1961. Atty. Burlington R.R., Chgo., 1953-55, 58-59; mem. Nat. R.R. Adjustment Bd., Chgo., 1959-63; of counsel Southeastern Carriers Conf. Com., 1959-65; gen. atty. Nat. Ry. Labor Conf., 1965-67, gen. counsel, 1967-68; v.p. labor relations Chgo. and Northwestern Transp. Co., 1968-73, v.p. ops., 1973-76, pres., chief exec. officer, 1976-88; chmn., pres. and chief exec. officer CNW Corp., Chgo., 1985-88; chmn., chief exec. officer Chgo. and N. Western Transp. Co, 1988; dir. NICOR, No. Ill. Gas Co., NALCO Chem., Continental Ill. Holding Corp., ES-II Corp., Am. Assn. R.R.'s, Western R.R. Assn., Nat. Ry. Labor Conf.; chmn., chief exec. officer CNN Corp. Trustee De Paul U., Chgo., Fenwick High Sch., Oak Park, Ill., Rush-Presbyn.-St. Luke's Med. Ctr., Chgo., Lyric Opera Chgo; bd. dirs. Robert Crown Ctr. fr Health Edn., Hinsdale, Ill., 1982-84, chief crusader United Way/Crusade of Mercy, Chgo., 1977-88, Bus. Adv. Com. Northwest U. Trans. Ctr., 1985-88. Served to capt. U.S. Army, 1955-58. Recipient Disting. Alumni award DePaul U., Chgo., 1981, Good Scout award Boy Scouts Am., Chgo., 1980. Mem. Am. R.R. Assn. (bd. dirs.), We. Ry. Assn. (bd. dirs.), Nat. Ry. Labor Comf. (bd. dirs.), ICC, Chgo. Urban League, Lyric Opera of Chgo., Rush/Copley Bd., Delta Mu Delta. Republican. Roman Catholic. Clubs: Hinsdale (Ill.) Golf; Commercial, Mid-Am (bd. govs.), Chicago, Carlton, Economic (bd. dirs.) (all Chgo.); Old Elm (Ft. Sheridan, Ill.). Lodge: Knights of Malta. Home: Oak Brook Ill. Died Aug. 5, 1988.

WOLFF, HERBERT ALFRED, lawyer; b. N.Y.C., July 20, 1889; s. Alfred R. and Martha (Stettheimer) W.; m. Daisy Kempner, Apr. 6, 1916; children: Alfred R. II, Helen, Herbert A. Jr., John L. E., Richard A. II. Student, Phillips Exeter Acad.; AB, Dartmouth, 1910; LLB, Columbia, 1913. Bar: N.Y. 1913. Mem. firm Greenbaum, Wolff & Ernst, 1915-60, counsel to firm, from 1960. Past vice chmn. N.Y. State Bd. Social Welfare; gov. Ethical Culture Schs., past pres.; past v.p., sec. Hudson Guild Settlement House; dir. Community Rsch. Assocs.; past chmn. N.Y. State Selective Service Appeal Bd. Mem. N.Y. State Bar Assn., Westchester County Bar Assn., Assn. Bar City N.Y., N.Y. County Lawyers Assn., Ethical Culture Soc. N.Y. (trustee, past pres.), Dartmouth Club, Fairview Country Club (past pres.), Phi Beta Kappa. Home: White Plains N.Y. †

WOLMAN, ABEL, sanitary engineer; b. Balt., June 10, 1892; s. Morris and Rose (Wachsman) W.; m. Anne Gordon, June 10, 1919 (dec. 1984); 1 son, Markley Gordon. AB, Johns Hopkins U., 1913, BSE, 1915; DEng, 1937. Began as asst. engr. USPHS, from 1914; chief engr. Md. Dept. Health, 1922-39; lectr., prof. san. engring. Johns Hopkins Sch. Engring. and Sch. Hygiene and Pub. Health, also Harvard, Princeton U., U. Chgo., other univs.; cons. engr., City Balt., Baltimore County; cons. engr. USPHS, TVA, U.S. Army, Seattle, Jacksonville, Fla.; cons., mem. adv. com. on reactor safety AEC.; chmn. permanent com. on san. engrs. Pan Am. San. Bur.; chmn. san. engring. com. Div. Med. Scis., NRC; cons. Assn. Am. R.R.s, Bethlehem Steel Co., Detroit Met. Area, Miami Conservancy Dist.; adviser ARC; chmn. bd. tech. advisors Internat. Boundary and Water Commn. U.S. and Mex., 1976; chmn. Task Force on Population Migration City of Balt., 1977; mem. com. internat. health Inst. Medicine NIH, 1978; chmn. bd. rev. Diversion of Mediterranean Sea to Dead Sea, State of Israel, 1981; mem. task force on water supply U.S. Dept. Def., 1981; chmn. rev. group Israeli Water Resources Mgmt., 1983; hon. pres. Pan Am. Health and Edn. Found.; bd. visitors Boston U.; held over 230 positions in pub. health, pub. works, engring. and edn. Recipient Lasker award, 1960, Nat. medal Sci., 1975, Tyler Ecology award, 1976, Internat. Friendship award Instn. Water Engrs. and Scientists of Eng., 1980, Andrés Bello award Acad. Phys. and Natural Scis. and Math. of Venezuela, 1983, Environ. Regeneration award Rene Dubos Ctr. Human Environs., 1985, Robert E. Horton medal, 1986, John Wesley Powell award, 1986; named to Utility Hall of Fame, 1985. Mem. ASCE, Am. Water Works Assn. (pres. 1942), Am. Pub. Health Assn. (pres. 1939), AAAS, Faraday Soc. (Eng.), Royal Inst. Pub. Health (Eng.) (Harben lectr. 1979), Nat. Acad. Scis., Nat. Acad. Engring. Home: Baltimore Md. Died Feb. 22, 1989.

WONDERS, SAMUEL DRISCOLL, consulting engineer; b. Bellefontaine, Ohio, July 30, 1890; s. James Crewe and Nancybelle (Spellman) W.; m. Dixie Ward Braley, Oct. 16, 1920. BS, U. Wis., 1913. Indsl. engr. A. M. Byers Co., Pitts., Met. Paving Brick Co., Canton, Ohio, Firestone Tire & Rubber Co., Akron, Ohio, Gilbert & Barker Mfg. Co., Springfield, Mass., 1913-29; with Carter's Ink Co., Cambridge, 1929-55, successively indsl. engr., asst. gen. mgr., gen. mgr., dir., 1935-55, pres., 1949-55; pres. Carter's Ink of Can. Ltd., 1949-55; cons. indsl. engr. from 1955. Trustee Lesley Coll., Cambridge, Mass., from 1955. chmn. bd. trustees, from 1963, acting pres., 1959-60, chmn. fin. com., 1955-64. Assoc. Cambridge Found. Home: Peterborough N.H. †

WOOD, BERTRAM L., civil engineer; b. Bklyn., Sept. 29, 1889; s. James and Ida (Fraser) W.; m. Hester V. DeBevoise, June 2, 1917. BSCE, Cornell U., 1911. Designer paper mills George Hardy Co.; designer cement mills Atlas Portland Cement Co.; in charge r.r. and bridge constrn. M. A. Talbott Co.; designer Jersey City terminal Cen. R.R. N.J.; dist. engr. indsl. concrete structures Corrugated Bar Co.; chief engr., mgr. sales Kalman Steel Co.; N.Y. mgr. reinforced concrete products Bethlehem Steel Co.; contract engr. U.S. Steel Corp.; cons. engr. bldg. structures and codes, also rsch. cold formed structural steel Am. Iron and Steel Inst, from 1938.; mem. Pres.'s Com. Fire Protection; mem. com. to prepare foundations regulations for N.Y.C.; charge design war structures for Brit. Commn. in U.S., World War II. Mem. NRC (bldg. rsch. adv. bd., other coms.), Am. Soc. Testing Materials (various coms.), Nat. Fire Protection Assn. (various coms.), Bldg. Ofcls. Conf. Am., Pacific Coast Bldg. Ofcls. Conf., So. Bldg. Congress, U.S. C. of C. Home: Saint Petersburg Fla. †

WOOD, BRIAN, financial corporation executive; b. Stretford, Eng., Sept. 29, 1920; came to U.S., 1947, naturalized, 1957; s. James William and Constance (Medcalf) W.; m. Carolyn Elizabeth Wilber, May 31, 1945; children: Christine Elizabeth, Robin Ann Wood Pohlman. Student, Manchester U., 1935-38, Royal Coll. Tech., Manchester, 1946. Salesman export div. J.P. Stevens & Co. Inc., 1947-54; v.p. Walker Bros. Inc., 1954-62; export sales mgr. Warner Bros. Corp., 1962-63; exec. v.p., dir. Fenchurch Corp., N.Y.C., 1964-77; exec. v.p., dir. S.H. Lock Inc., 1964-74, pres., from 1975; exec. v.p., dir. Tozer Kemsley & Milbourn (Can.) Ltd., 1966-73, TKM Pacific Ltd., 1972-74; joint mng. dir. Fenchurch NV, Curacao, 1972-77; chmn. S.H. Lock (Can.) Ltd., from 1980; dir. S.H. Lock Holdings Co. Ltd., James Finlay Internat. Inc. Lt. comdr. air br. Royal Navy, 1940-45. Mem. Trinidad and Tobago C. of C. N.Y. (founding dir., pres. 1975), Patterson Club (Fairfield, Conn.), Jamaica Club (Kingston), Union Club (Port of Spain, Trinidad). Republican. Home: Fairfield Conn. Deceased.

WOOD, EDGAR OTTO, educator; b. Ball Ground, Ga., Mar. 25, 1889; s. Warren and Rachel (Conn) W.; m. Fanny Pauline Littlefield, Mar. 8, 1917; children: Virginia Eloise (Mrs. Finely W. Tinnin), Marjorie Elaine (Mrs. Leon O. Beasley). AB, La. Coll., 1924; AM, U. Chgo., 1926; PhD, U. Tex., 1931. Mem. faculty La. Coll., 1927-49, prof. psychology and chmn. dept., 1935-49; chmn. dept. psychology Baylor U., Waco, Tex., from 1949. Author: Juvenile Delinquency, Anchors Aweigh, Psychology of Religion; contbr. articles to various mags. Mem. State Curricula and Cert. Com., from 1945. Recipient grant-in-aid Carnegie Found., 1946, 47, 48. Mem. Am. Psychol. Assn., Tex. Psychol. Assn., Southwestern Psychol. Assn., Tex. Mental Health Soc., NEA, Am. Coll. Pers. Assn., AAUP, NAt. Rehab. Assn., Kiwanis (past pres.), Pi Kappa Delta (mem. nat. coun.), Phi Delta Kappa, Psi Chi. Home: Waco Tex. †

WOOD, ELMER, economist, educator; b. Carmi, Ill., Aug. 25, 1892; s. Allen Downey and Sarah Ann (Langford) W.; m. Virginia Poythress Galt, June 20, 1929. AB, U. Mo., 1916; student, Princeton U., 1916-17; PhD, Harvard U., 1937. Economist U.S. Senate Commn. of Gold and Silver Inquiry, 1924; prof. econ. N.C. State Coll., 1924-30, U. Mo., from 1930. Author: English Theories of Central Banking Control, 1939, Monetary Control, 1963. Chief liaison officer Office Price Adminstrn to Bd. Econ. Warfare, 1943. 2d lt. Inf., U.S. Army, World War I. Recipient Ricardo and D.A. Wells prizes Harvard U.; Guggenheim fellow, 1939-40. Mem. Am. Econ. Assn., Am. Assn. U. Profs., Midwest Econs. Assn. (pres. 1954-55), Phi Beta Kappa. Home: Columbia Mo. †

WOOD, ERNEST RICHARD, college dean; b. Del Norte, Colo., July 19, 1891; s. George Edward and Minnie Leah (Pruden) W., m. Alice Hazel Gettles, Dec. 25, 1917 (dec. Nov. 1934); children: John Francis, Gerald David; m. 2d, Pearle Felicia Stone, June 13, 1936; 1 dau., Edna Beth. AB, Ohio U., 1916, BS in Edn., 1916; AM, Clark U., 1917; PhD, U. Chgo., 1923. Tchr. rural schs., Athens County, Ohio, 1908-11; supt. schs. Chauncey, Ohio, 1911-13; asst. in dept. psychology Ohio U., 1915-16; prin. Univ. High Sch., Lexington, Ky., 1919-21; prof. psychology Kans. State Tchrs. Coll., 1922-29; dir. Ohio scholarship tests and instrnl. rsch. State Dept. Edn., Columbus, 1929-32; prof. edn. Ohio State U., summers 1930-32; assoc. prof. edn. NYU, 1932-40, prof., 1940-56, coordinator dept. ednl. psychology, 1949-50, chmn. com. evaluation of communication skills, 1955-56; dean Rocky Mountain Coll., Billings, Mont., 1956-61; dean Frederick Coll., Portsmouth, Va., 1961-65, pres., 1965-68; dean Southwood Coll., Salem, N.C., 1968-73. Originated Every Pupil Test, Gen. Scholarship Test, many statis. devices; authorreports of results of scholarship tests; co-author: Educational Psychology, 1936; workbook; editor measurement textbook; co-author, editor: The Every Pupil Series Language Trails, 1938, Arithmetic Books, 1939, Health and Play, 1939, Safety Series, 1939; chmn. charge constrn. Nationwide Every Pupil U.S. Constitution Tests for the Sesquicentennial Commn.; contbr. articles to ednl. jours. Served as psychol. examiner U.S. Army, 1817-18. Mem. Am. Ednl. Rsch. Assn., Am. Psychol. Assn. AAAS, Am. Statis. Assn., AAUP, NeA, Nat. Soc. for Study Edn., Phi Delta Kappa, Kappa Delta Pi. Congregationalist. Home: Salemburg N.C. †

WOOD, JOHN EDMUND FITZGERALD, lawyer; b. Staunton, Va., Oct. 19, 1903. A.B., Denison U., 1924, LL.D. (hon.), 1981; LL.B., W.Va. U., 1927; B.A., Oxford (Eng.) U., 1929, M.A., 1953. Bar: W.Va. bar 1927, N.Y. bar 1935, D.C. bar 1941, U.S. Supreme Ct. bar 1941. Assoc. firm Root Clark Buckner Howland & Ballantine, N.Y.C., 1929-30, 33-39, Fitzpatrick Brown & Davis, Huntington, W.Va., 1931-33; partner firm Dewey Ballantine Bushby Palmer & Wood (and predecessors), N.Y.C., 1940-87. Trustee Village of Scarsdale, N.Y., 1952-56; trustee Denison U., Granville, Ohio, 1947-83, life trustee, 1983-87 , chmn. bd. trustees, 1965-72. Fellow Am. Bar Found., Am. Coll. Trial Lawyers; mem. Am. Bar Assn., N.Y.C. Bar Assn., N.Y. County Lawyers Assn. Died June 15, 1987; buried Sleepy Hollow Cemetery, Tarrytown, N.Y.

WOOD, JOHN HOWARD, newspaperman; b. Downers Grove, Ill., Jan. 2, 1901; s. Robert Edward and Julia B. (Steinmann) W.; m. Mary Ruth Hendrickson, Feb. 22, 1928 (dec. 1971); children: Janet Wood Diederichs, Ann, John Howard, Robert; m. 2d, Barbara Johnston, 1972. AB, Lake Forest (Ill.) Coll., 1922; student, Harvard U., 1922-23. English master Middlesex Sch., Concord, Mass., 1923-25; with Chgo. Tribune Co., 1925-75, pres., 1960-66, chief exec. officer, 1960-71, dir., 1960-75, chmn. bd., 1966-71, 1966-71, chmn. exec. com., 1971-75; pub. Chgo. Tribune, 1960-68; chmn. bd., dir. WGN Continental Broadcasting Co., 1965-73; dir. Lake Shore Nat. Bank, Chgo., 1944-76; trustee Robert R. McCormick Charitable Trust, 1955-76; mem. bd. overseers Hoover Instn. on War, Revolution and Peace, 1967-88; trustee Lake Forest Coll., Field Mus. Natural History, U. Chgo. Author: Inflation and Your Money, 1935, Everyday Economics, 1936,. Recipient Disting. Svc. in Journalism award U. Minn., 1967. Mem. Am. Newspaper Pubs. Assn. (pres. 1966-68), dir. 1960-70), Commercial Club, Casino Club, Mid. Am. Club (Chgo.); Old Elm Club, Lake Zurich Golf Club, Knollwood Club, Kappa Sigma. Died Oct. 30, 1988.

WOOD, PEGGY, actress; b. Bklyn., Feb. 9, 1892; d. Eugene and Mary (Gardner) Wood; m. John van Alstyne Weaver, Feb. 14, 1924; 1 son, David; m. 2d, William H. Walling, Oct. 1, 1946. Student, Miss Rounds Sch., Bklyn.; L.H.D. (hon.), Hamilton Coll., Wm. Smith

Coll., Hobart Coll.; DFA, Mt. holyoke Coll., Lake Erie Coll.; fellow (hon.), Westminster Choir Coll., Timothy Dwight Coll., Yale U. First stage appearance in chorus Naughty Marietta, Globe Theater, N.Y.C., 1911; toured in Madcap Duchess, 1913, Adele, 1914; played in Young American, May Time, Buddies, others; film, the Sound of Music (Acad. award nomination 1966), star in plays Clinging Vine, Candida, all-star revival Trelawney of the Wells, also in Portia (with George Arliss); creator star role in Bittersweet, London, 1929; starred in Blithe Spirit, N.Y.C., 1941; star TV show Mama, 1949-57; starred in Girls in 509, 1958-59; author: The Flying Prince, 1921, A Splendid Gypsy, 1927, Actors and People, 1929, Star Wagon, 1936, How Young You Look, 1941, others. Hon. chmn. Am. Coll. Drama Festival; mem. U.S. Commn. for UNESCO; adv. com. on arts. Nat. Cultural Ctr. Mem. ANTA (pres. 1959-66, hon. pres. from 1966), Actors Equity, AFTRA, Episcopal Actors Guild (Officer). Home: Stamford Conn. †

WOOD, ROBERT D., broadcasting company executive; b. Boise, Idaho, Apr. 17, 1925; s. Ray D. and Euphrosyne (Planck) W.; m. Nancy Harwell, Oct. 29, 1949 (div.); children: Virginia Lucile, Dennis Harwell; m. Laura Rohrer; stepchildren: Leslie Delgado, Ann Woodward. BSBA, U. So. Calif. Sales service mgr. Sta. KNX, Los Angeles, 1949-51; account exec. Sta. KTTV, Los Angeles, 1951-52, Sta. KNXT, Los Angeles, 1952-54; with CBS TV stas., 1954-55; gen. sales mgr. Sta. KNXT, 1955-60, v.p., gen. mgr., 1960-66; exec. v.p. CBS TV stas. div., 1966-67, pres., 1967-69; pres. CBS, 1969-76; owner Nephi Prodns., 1976-79; pres. Metromedia Producers Corp., 1979-83; bd. dirs. TV Bur. Advt., Advt. Coun. Trustee U. So. Calif. With USN, 1943-46. Recipient award of merit U. So. Calif., 1967, award Merchants and Mfrs. Assn., 1967. Mem. Bel Air Bay Club, Greenwich Country Club, Sigma Alpha Epsilon. Home: Los Angeles Calif. Died May 20, 1986; buried Forest Lawn Cemetery, Burbank, Calif.

WOOD, THOR EDGAR, librarian; b. Washington, Nov. 3, 1932; s. Denzil DeMaranville and Kathryn (Michelsen) W.; m. Ann Curtis, Jan. 25, 1958; children: Elizabeth Ann, Frances Patricia. BA, Pomona Coll., 1954; MLS, U. Calif.-Berkeley, 1957; MFA, Princeton U., 1959. Cert. librarian, N.Y. Music librarian U. Ill., Urbana, 1960-65; chief Performing Arts Research Ctr, N.Y. Pub. Library at Lincoln Ctr., N.Y.C., 1965-88. Contbr. articles to profl. jours. Bd. dirs., treas. Am. Friends of Aldeburgh Festival, N.Y.C., 1973-88 ; bd. dirs. Am. Music Ctr., N.Y.C., 1968-79; mem. vis. com. dept. music Harvard U., 1974-79; mem. adv. council dept. music Princeton U., N.J., 1980-88 . Served to lt. U.S. Army, 1954-56. Mem. Internat. Assn. Music Libraries (v.p. pub. libraries br. 1968-81, chmn. U.S. br. 1968-75; pres. 1972-73), Music Library Assn. (bd. dirs. 1962-64, placement sec. 1960-67), Am. Musicol. Soc., Theatre Library Assn. Democrat. Home: Brooklyn N.Y. Died Apr. 28, 1988.

WOODBURY, LEONARD, educator; b. Regina, Sask., Can., Aug. 30, 1918; s. Ernest F. and Florence L. (Crisp) W.; m. Marjorie R. Bell, May 13, 1944 (dec. 1977); children: Christopher Dawson, Alison Bell. BA with honors, U. Man., 1940; AM, Harvard U., 1942, PhD, 1944. With dept. classics Univ. Coll., U. Toronto, 1945-85, prof., 1959-85, head dept., 1958-66. Contbr. articles to profl. jours. Fellow Royal Soc. Can.; mem. Soc. Ancient Greek Philosophy (pres. 1965-66), Classical Assn. Can. (pres. 1974-76), Am. Philological Assn. (chmn. com. on award of merit 1966-67, 76-78). Died Nov. 8, 1985; buried Toronto.

WOODRING, WENDELL PHILLIPS, geologist; b. Reading, Pa., June 13, 1891; s. James Daniel and Margaret (Hurst) W.; m. Josephine Jamison, Feb. 9, 1918 (dec.); children: Judy Worth (Mrs. Robert M. Armagast), Jane (dec.). AB, Albright Coll., Myerstown, Pa., 1910; ScD, Albright Coll., 1952; PhD, Johns Hopkins U., 1916-17. Rsch. fellow Johns Hopkins U., 1916-17; geol. explorations in Cen. Am. 1917-18; geologist U.S. Geol. Survey, 1919-27, 30-61; hon. rsch. assoc. Smithsonian Instn., from 1961; in charge geol. survey of Republic of Haiti, 1920-24; prof. invertebrate paleontology Calif. Inst. Tech., 1927-30. Served with C.E. U.S. Army , 1918-19. Fellow Geol. Soc. Am. (recipient Penrose medal 1949, pres. 1953), AAAS, Paleontol. Soc.; mem. NAS, Am. Philos. Soc., Geol. Soc. Washington, Phi Beta Kappa, Sigma Xi. Home: Chevy Chase Md. †

WOODRUFF, ARCHIBALD MULFORD, JR., university president; b. Newark, July 30, 1912; s. Archibald M. and Eleanor B. (Van Etten) W.; m. Barbara Jane Bestor, July 13, 1940; children: Archibald Mulford III, Paul B., Nathan V.E., Timothy R. BA, Williams Coll., 1933, LLD (hon.); postgrad., U. Berlin, 1935; PhD, Princeton, 1936; LHD (hon.), Trinity Coll.; LLD (hon.), Tarkio Coll., U. Hartford, Annhurst Coll. With mortgage dept. Prudential Ins. Co., 1936-42, 44-50; Kelly Meml. prof. urban land studies U. Pitts., 1950-59, dir. Bur. Bus. Rsch., 1954-59; dean Sch. Govt. George Washington U., Washington, 1959-64; provost U. Hartford (Conn.), 1964-67, chancellor, 1967-70, pres., 1970-77; bd. dirs. Soc. for Savs., Hartford, C.G. Fund Inc., Hartford; past adv. dir. Western Pa. Nat. Bank; past chmn. Nat. Capital Planning Commn.; past pres. Conn. Conf. Ind. Colls. Author books, monographs and articles on land econs., especially taxation; editor: The Appraiser's Job in Eminent Domain Proceedings. Past chmn. bd. dirs. Tarkio (Mo.) Coll.; bd. dirs. Wadsworth Atheneum, Watkinson Sch., Land Reform Tng. Inst., Taoyan, Taiwan, E.B. Found., Simsbury, Lincoln Inst. Land Policy, Cambridge, Mass.; trustee Mark Twain Meml., YMCA; v.p. Lincoln Found., 1965-84; mem. Hartford Bd. Higher Edn. Recipient medal Ministry of Edn., Republic of China. Mem. Am. Econ. Assn., Hartford Golf Club, Cosmos Club (Washington), Phi Beta KAppa. Universalist. Home: Bloomfield Conn. Died Aug. 26, 1984; buried Town Cemetery, Bridgton, Maine.

WOODWARD, CLEVELAND LANDON, artist; b. Glendale, Ohio, June 25, 1900; s. Henry L. and Eloise (Cleveland) W.; m. Emily Crosby, Dec. 20, 1919; children: Cleveland Crosby, Eloise Cleveland Woodward Gardner, Ralph Crosby. Student, Cin. Art Acad., 1923-26, Charles Hawthorne's Cape Cod Sch. Art, summer 1924, Brit. Art Acad., Rome, Italy, 1928-29. Instr. oil painting Eastern Shore Acad. Fine Arts, 1972-73; lectr. Bibl. art. Illustrator: work subject article Am. Artist mag, May 1973; One-man shows at, Traxel Art Gallery, Cin., 1929, Fine Arts Mus. of South at Mobile, 1968, 72, 77, Percy Whiting Mus., Fairhope, Ala., 1969, 71; exhibited in group shows at, Cin. Art Mus. Spring Exhbn., 1925, 26; represented in permanent collections at, Fine Arts Mus. of South at Mobile, Provincetown (Mass.) Art Assn., Arctic Mus., Brunswick, Maine, Boardman Press, Nashville, United Lutheran Pub. House, Phila., Providence Lithograph Co., Stanard Pub. Co., Cin., Christian Bd. Publ., St. Louis, others, commns. include Samuel and Eli mural, 7th Presbyn. Ch., Cin., 1949, painting for, Donald B. MacMillan of Arctic Mus., 1952; 16 watercolor illustrations for World Bible, World Pub. Co., 1962; Peter and John mural, West End Baptist Ch., Mobile, 1972, portrait Martin Luther, United Lutheran Pub. House, Phila., hist. paintings for, Proctor & Gamble Co., Cin., numerous others. Cleveland Woodward Foundation established Fine Arts Mus. of the South, Mobile. Mem. Cape Cod Art Assn. (1st bd. dirs.), Eastern Shore Art Assn. (dir. 1966-69, 71-74). Home: Westboro Mass. Died May 1986.

WOODWARD, RICHARD LEWIS, consulting engineer; b. Kansas City, Mo., Dec. 11, 1913; s. John Bennett and Grace (Baker) W.; m. Helen Beal, June 17, 1939; children: Brenda, Melinda, Richard, Amy. BCE, Washington U., 1935; MS in San. Engring., Harvard U., 1949; PhD, Ohio State U., 1952. Engr. Horner and ShiFrin, St. Louis, 1935-36; san. engr. USPHS, Washington, Atlanta, Cin., 1937-63; sr. rsch. assoc. Harvard U., Boston, 1963-66; process cons., v.p. Camp, Dresser & McKee Inc., Boston, 1966-81; lectr. Harvard U., 1965-67; cons. in field. Contbr. articles to profl. jours. Capt. USPHS. Recipient Meritorious Service medal USPHS, 1963, T.R. Camp award Water Pollution Control Assn., 1975, Research award Am. Water Works Assn., 1977. Mem. Nat. Acad. Engring., ASCE, Brit. Assn. Water Engring. and Scientists, Internat. Assn. Water Pollution, Water Pollution Control Fedn., Am. Water Works Assn., Am. Geophys. Union, Am. Acad. Environ. Engrs. Died Mar. 15, 1981.

WOODWARD, STANLEY W(INGATE), marine painter; b. Malden, Mass., Dec. 11, 1890; s. Frank Ernest and Alice Elizabeth (Colesworthy) W.; m. Ruth Marie Brainerd, June 12, 1926; 1 child, Patricia Ruth Woodward Smith. Ed., Eric Pape Sch. Art, Boston, Sch. Boston Mus. Fine Arts, Pa. Acad. Fine Arts, Phila. Formerly newspaper and book illustrato; art instr. pvt. classes, Rockport, Mass., from 1933, Ringling Art Sch., 1936-38, Laguna Beach (Calif.) Sch. Art and Design, 1963. Represented in prin. mus. and galleries; author: Adventure in Marine Painting, 1947, Marine Painting in Oil and Watercolor, 1961, Marine Painting, 1967, The Sea, 1969. Cpl. U.S. Army, 1918-19; capt. USAAF, 1942-45. Recipient numerous prizes, awards including Gold medal, Jordan Marsh, 1959, 65, 1st prize watercolor Am. Acad. Artists, Springfield, Mass., 1959, Gaylord Marine prize oils, 1960, Winsor Newton prize, Am. Profl. League, 1962, Mitton Meml. prize, 1965. Mem. Concord Art Assn., Grand Cen. Galleries, Am. Water Color Soc. (hon. life), Soc. Am. Etchers, Boston Soc. Water Color Painters, Allied Artists Am., Guild Boston Artists, Audubon Artists N.Y., Rockport Art Assn. (prize oil 1959, Charles H. Cleaves Meml. award 1965), North Shore Arts Assn. (past pres., Gordon Grant Mmel. award 1967), Springfield Art League (hon.), Phila. Water Color Club, Acad. Polit. Sci. Republican. Episcopalian. Home: Rockport Mass. †

WOOLSEY, CLARENCE OLIN, lawyer; b. Chillicothe, Mo., June 20, 1911; s. Olin Moore and Emma Ethel (Robertson) W.; m. Mary Jane Smedley, May 1, 1941; children: William Tinker, Nancy Jane, Christopher Olin. AB, Northwest Mo. State Coll., 1933, BS in Edn., 1933; LLB, Mo. U., 1936. Bar: Mo. 1936. Practice Springfield, Mo., 1936-84; with firm Woosley, Fisher, Whiteaker, McDonald & Ansley (and predecessors). Mem. Mo. Gov.'s Crime Commn., Mo. Gov.'s Edn. Commn.; pres. U. Mo. Law Sch. Found. With U.S. Army, 1941; lt. USNR, 1942-45. Recipient commendations Adm. Halsey, Nimitz, Denfeld; citation of merit in law U. Mo., 1968. Fellow Am. Bar Found.; mem. ABA (ho. dels. 1959-60), Mo. Bar (bd. govs. 1953-60, pres. 1958-59, award of merit 1959), Internat. Assn. Ins. Counsel, Fedn. Ins. Counsel, Phi Delta Phi. Presbyterian. Home: Springfield Mo. Died Feb. 23, 1984; buried Nat. Cemetery, Springfield.

WOOLSEY, RICHARD HAY, lawyer; b. Girard, Pa., Dec. 13, 1890. Student, Colo. Coll., 1908-10; LLB, U. Pa., 1916. Bar: Pa. 1916. Ptnr. MacCoy, Evans & Lewis, Phila., from 1916. Home: Philadelphia Pa. †

WOOSTER, ROY DONALD, dairy products manufacturer; b. Binghamton, N.Y., Sept. 8, 1897; s. John W. and Josephine (Ring) W.; m. MArgaret Heeley, Sept. 3, 1921; children: Georgemay, Roy D. Student, Tome Sch., Port Deposit, Md.; BS, Colgate U., 1921. With Conn. Gen. Life Ins. Co., Hartford, Conn., 1921, Internat. ICe Cream Co., Schenectady, N.Y., 1921-23; v.p., mgr. Trojan Ice Cream Co., Troy, N.Y., 1923-29; chmn. N.E. dist. fluid milk and ice cream Borden Co., N.Y.C., 1929-44, asst. v.p. ice cream div., 1944-46, v.p. charge ice cream ops., 1946-53, v.p. charge fluid milk, ice cream ops., 1953-57, exec. v.p., 1957-64, chmn. bd. dirs., 1964-65; also bd. dirs.; bd. dirs. Borden Co. Ltd., First Fed. Savs. & Loan Assn. of N.Y., Empire Trust Co. Trustee Colgate U.; dir., trustee Empire State Found. Ind. Liberal Arts Colls. With USN, 1918-19. Mem. Nat. Dairy Coun. (bd. dirs.), Internat. Assn. Ice Cream Mfrs. (bd. dirs.), Union League (N.Y.C.), Blind Brook Club (Port Chester, N.Y.), Am. Yacht Club (Rye, N.Y.). Home: Bronxville N.Y. Died June 8, 1986.

WORCESTER, DEAN AMORY, psychologist, educator; b. Thetford, Vt., Mar. 21, 1889; s. George Steele and Ida Eldora (Kinney) W.; m. Elsie Rohwer, May 29, 1917; children: Dean Amory, Evarts James, Catherine Elsie. AB, U. Colo., 1911, AM, 1921; PhD, Ohio State U., 1926; student, U. Chgo., summer 1942. Supr. dist. Zamboanga, The Philippines, 1913-14; prof. psychology U. N.Mex., 1914-18; prin. high sch. Cheyenne, Wyo., 1918-20; asst. dir. Bur. Ednl. Tests and Measurements, Kans. State Tchrs. Coll., Emporia, 1920-21, dir., 1921-24; instr. psychology Ohio State U., 1924-26, asst. prof., summer 1926; assoc. prof. Ohio U., 1926-27; assoc. prof. ednl. psychology U. Nebr., 1927-28, prof., 1928-57, ret., chmn. dept., 1934-56; vis. prof. edn. U. Wis., 1957-61, 65-66, U. Ariz., 1961-65; served regents' inquiry into character and costs of edn. in State of N.Y., 1937; prof. U.S. Army U., Biarritz, France, 1945-46, I. and E. div., Germany, 1946. Author and co-author numerous publs. relating to field. Fellow AAAS (sec. sect. Q. 1945-56), Am. Psychol. Assn., Am. Ednl. Rsch. Assn.; mem. AAUP, Am. Interprofl. Inst., Nat. Soc. Coll. Tchrs. Edn., Midwestern Psychol. Assn., Sigma Xi, Phi Beta Kappa, Phi Delta Kappa. Republican. Congregationalist. Home: Boulder Colo. †

WORNALL, KEARNEY, banker; b. Kansas City, Mo., Apr. 5, 1891; s. Frank C. and Julia (Kearney) W.; m. Berenice Fowler, Apr. 10, 1928. Student, Kansas City Law Sch., 1909-11; LLB, U. Mo., 1915. Bar: Mo. 1915. Pvt. practice 1915-18; pres. Broadway Bank, Kansas City, 1919-33; vice chmn. City Nat. Bank & Trust Co. (merger with Broadway Bank), also bd. dirs.; bd. dirs. Commonwealth Theatres, Inc., Marsh Steel & Aluminum Co., Midland Steel & Aluminum Co., Kansas City, N.J., Ind. & Ill. R.R. Co., St. Louis, Southwestern Investment Co., Amarillo, Tex. Trustee Midwest Rsch. Inst., Kansas City Mus.; bd. dirs. Starlight Theatre, Kansas City; treas., past chmn. United Funds Bd., Inc.; treas. Community Chest Kansas City. Mem. Am., Mo. (past pres.) bankers assns., Kansas City C. of C. (past pres.), U. Mo. Alumni Assn. (past pres.), Res. City Bankers Assn., Am. Royal Assn., University Club, Saddle and Sirloin Club, Mission Hills Country Club, Sigma Alpha Epsilon. Home: Kansas City Mo. †

WORTHINGTON, GEORGE EDMOND, lawyer, author; b. Oconomowoc, Wis., Mar. 28, 1888; s. Franklin Pierce and Emma Frances (Brown) W.; m. Irene Valanche Starks, June 24, 1914; children: George Sanford, Virginia Irene. AB, U. Wis., 1910, LLB, 1912; student, U. Wash., 1911. Bar: Wash. 1913, N.Y. 1921, U.S. Supreme Ct. 1930. Gen. practice Spokane, Wash., 1913-17; spl. master Equity Reorgn. Proceedings of Northern Ida. and Mont. Power Co. and Oreg. Power Co., 1916-17; assoc. counsel Am. Social Hygiene Assn., 1919-26; gen. counsel Com. of 14, N.Y., 1927-32; corp. law and surrogate practice N.Y.C., 1932-34; prin. code supr. and hearing officer Fed. Alcohol Control Adminstrn., Washington, 1934, prin. enforcement supr., 1935-40; prin. enforcement supr. Alcohol Tax Unit, Bur. Internal Revenue, 1940-42; sr. atty. Alien Property Custodian, 1942-44, atty., chief, Rev., Analysis sect., 1944-46; trial lawyer Office of Alien Property, Dept. Justice, 1946-58; pvt. practice Auburn, N.Y., 1958-63; cons. N.Y. Child Welfare Commn., 1923-24; in charge Citizens League vice investigation and Survey Recorders Ct., Detroit, 1925-26. Author or co-author several legal works; contbr. to Collier's Ency., 1950. Trustee So. Found. United Presbyn. Ch., Am. Inst. Family Rels. Served to capt. AUS, World War I. Mem. Fed. Bar Assn., SAR, Masons, K.T., Rotary. Home: Riverside Calif. †

WORTS, GEORGE FRANK, writer; b. Toledo, Mar. 16, 1892; s. Chivington and Mary Elizabeth (Webster) W.; m. Flora Berriman, Apr. 1915 (div.); children: George Frank, Robert Berriman, Mary Elizabeth; m. Janet

M. Walter, June 1933 (div.); m. Florence Waterhouse, Sept. 1941. Student, Columbia U., 1914-15. Wireless operator on Gt. Lakes and Pacific Ocean 1910-14, free-lance writer, 1912-15; motion picture editor Evening Mail, 1915-16; assoc. editor Motion Picture News, 1916-17; dir. pub. rels. Kauai Civilian Def. Staff, Hawaii, 1941; Hawaiian corr. Collier's Mag., 1941-42; editor Tucson mag., 1952-54; historian radiol. safety div. Reynolds Elec. & Engring. Co., 1957. Author: Peter the Brazen, 1919, The Return of George Washington, 1932, Greenfield Mystery, 1934, The Phantom President, 1934, The Blue Lacquer Box, 1939, Dangerous Young Man, 1940, Laughing Girl, 1941, Overboard, 1943, Five Who Vanished, 1943; (plays for film) Absolute Quiet, others. Mem. Dutch Treat Club, Phi Kappa Psi. Home: Tucson Ariz. †

WRATHER, BONITA GRANVILLE, hotel, development, and communications company executive, former actress; b. N.Y.C., Feb. 2, 1923; s. Bernard and Rosina (Timponi) G.; m. Jack Wrather, Feb. 5, 1947 (dec. 1984); children—Molly Wrather Dolle, Christopher, Linda. Student motion picture schs. Motion picture and TV actress Los Angeles, 1930-47; producer Lassie TV show, Los Angeles, 1958—; v.p. Wrather Corp., Beverly Hills, Calif., 1973-83; sr. v.p. Wrather Corp., 1983-84, chmn. bd., 1984—; also dir. Appeared in more than 55 films, including These Three (Acad. Award nomination), Cavalcade, Ah, Wilderness, H.M. Pulham, Esq., Now Voyager, Escape, The Plough and the Stars, Hitler's Children; starred in dramatic TV prodns., including U.S. Steel Hour, Climax, Studio One, Playhouse 90. Bd. dirs. Los Angeles Orphanage Guild, pres., 1970-71; bd. dirs. women's council, Los Angeles Pub. TV; trustee John F. Kennedy Ctr., 1972—, Loyola Marymount U., Los Angeles, 1974-83, St. John's Hosp., Santa Monica, Calif., 1975—; adv. council Coll. Bus. Adminstrn. Found., U. Tex., Austin, 1974-82; chmn. Nat. Fedn. Republican Women, 1980, regent, 1981, hon. chmn. regents; trustee, mem. exec. com. Am. Film Inst., Los Angeles, chmn. bd., 1986-87; mem. Blue Ribbon 400, Los Angeles Music Ctr., 1972—; mem. adv. com. Children's Bur. Los Angeles, 1984—. Mem. Screen Actors Guild, AFTRA, Acad. Motion Picture Arts and Scis., Les Dames de Champagne of Los Angeles. Roman Catholic. Clubs: Ocean Reef (Key Largo, Fla.); Balboa Bay (Newport Beach, Calif.); Marks, White Elephant (London). Home: Los Angeles CA Died Oct. 11, 1988.

WREN, MELVIN CLARENCE, historian, educator; b. Iowa City, Iowa, June 18, 1910; s. Clarence Walter and Dorothy Elizabeth (Kahler) W.; m. Ester Gwendolyn Schlunz, Nov. 28, 1936; children: David Christopher, Nancy Priscilla (dec.). BA, State U. Iowa, 1936, MA, 1938, PhD, 1939; postgrad., U. Calif., Berkeley, 1946. Mem. faculty U. Mont., 1940-41, 42-67, prof. history, 1952-67, chmn. dept., 1958-67; prof. history U. Toledo, 1967-78, prof. emeritus, 1978-84, chmn. dept., 1967-69; instr. Am. U., 1941-42; rsch. in English Archives, 1947-48, 54, 59, 70; vis. prof. U. Wash., 1958, U. Nebr., 1970; lectr. U. Md., 1962-63. Author: The Course of Russian History, 1958, 4th edit., 1979, Ancient Russia, 1965, The WEstern Impact Upon Tsarist Russia, 1971; contbr. articles to profl. jours. Fellow Am. Coun. Learned Socs.; mem. Am. Hist. Assn., Am. Polit. Sci. Assn., Dobro Slovo, Order Artus, Phi Kappa Phi, Phi Alpha Theta, Pi Gamma Mu. Home: Everett Wash. Died Apr. 25, 1984; cremated.

WRIGHT, FRANCIS JOSEPH, lawyer, insurance executive; b. Denver, Dec. 14, 1891; s. James Howell and Luella (Prucell) W.; M. Katharine Timberman, Apr. 14, 1921; children: Andrew Howell, Susan, John Stanbery. J.D., Ohio State U., 1916. Bar: Ohio 1916. Pvt. practice Columbus, Ohio, from 1918; mem. Wright, Harlor, Moris & Arnold, Columbus, from 1930; v.p., gen. counsel, dir. Midland Mut. Life Ins. Co., Columbus, from 1930. Contbr. proc. Assn. Life Ins. Counsel and legal sect. Am. Life Conv. Trustee Columbus Sch. for Girls, 1928-51, Columbus Acad., 1929-47, Columbus Gallery of Fine Arts. 2d lt., inf., U.S. Army, World War I. Mem. Am., Ohio, Columbus bar assns., Am. Life Conv. (chmn. legal sect. 1937), Am. Life Ins. Counsel (pres. 1948), Crichton Review Club, Rocky Fork Country Club, University Club, Castalia Trout Club, Delta Chi. Home: Columbus Ohio. †

WRIGHT, HENRY (NICCOLLS), architectural consultant; b. St. Louis, Mar. 23, 1910; s. Henry and Eleanor (Niccolls) W.; m. Dorothy Martha Chaya, July 22, 1939; children: John, William, Richard, Thomas. Student pub. schs., L.I. City, N.Y. Apprentice draftsman B.G. Goodhue Assocs., N.Y.C., 1927-30; draftsman-designer N.Y. State Architect, Albany, 1930-35; tech. editor Archtl. Forum, N.Y.C., 1936-42, mng. editor, 1942-49; cons. bldg. product mfg. N.Y.C., 1949-65; lectr. Pratt Inst., Bklyn., 1958-61, Yale U., New Haven, 1959-61; adj. assoc. prof. Columbia U., N.Y.C., 1961-62, assoc. prof. architecture, 1962-65; Regent's Disting. prof. environ. tech. Kans. State U., Manhattan, 1965-71; prof. CCNY, 1971-75; cons. architect Wellfleet, Mass., 1975-86. Contbr. numerous articles to profl. jours.; author: (with George Nelson) Tomorrow's House, 1945; patentee Vertical window blind; inventor: (with George Nelson) storage wall, Heliodon, an outdoor conditions simulator. Recipient citation for significant contbs. to advance of bldg. product integration and modular design Modular Service Assn., 1946. Fellow AIA; mem. Assn. Collegiate Schs. Architecture (regional dir. 1966-68). Home: Wellfleet Mass. Died Oct. 3, 1986.

WRIGHT, HOWARD WALTER, lawyer; b. Long Beach, Calif., Sept. 6, 1892; s. Walter S. and Bernice (Long) W.; m. Ruth Casner Shelton, June 7, 1916 (dec.); children: Betty Leigh Merrell, Brownell Merrell, Howard W., Jane Miller, Robert s., Jefferson C., Sara B.; m. 2d, Caroline Guild, Jan. 27, 1968. Grad., Throop Acad., 1911; student, Stanford, 1915. Bar: Calif. 1916. Mem. firm Walker, Wright, Tyler & Ward, and predecessor firms, L.A., 1923-69, of counsel, from 1969. Lt. USN, 1917-18. Mem. L.A. Yacht Club, Cruising Club of Am., Transpacific Yacht Club, Beta Theta Pi, Phi Delta Phi. Home: Pasadena Calif. †

WRIGHT, JAMES SKELLY, federal judge; b. New Orleans, Jan. 14, 1911; s. James Edward and Margaret (Skelly) W.; m. Helen Mitchell Patton, Feb. 1, 1945; 1 son, James Skelly. Ph.B., Loyola U., 1931, LL.B., 1934; LL.D., Yale U., 1961, U. Notre Dame, 1962, Howard U., 1964, U. So. Calif., 1975, Loyola U., New Orleans, 1981, Georgetown U., 1981, N.Y. Law Sch., 1981, U. D.C., 1983, U. Vt., 1986. Bar: U.S. Supreme Ct. High sch. tchr. 1931-35; lectr. English history Loyola U., 1936-37; asst. U.S. atty. New Orleans, 1937-42, 45-46; U.S. atty. East Dist. La., 1948-49, U.S. dist. judge, 1949-62; U.S. circuit judge D.C., 1962-87; chief judge U.S. Ct. Appeals D.C. Circuit, 1978-81; judge Temporary Emergency Ct. Appeals of U.S., 1981-87, chief judge, 1982-87; faculty Loyola U. Sch. Law, 1950-62; James Madison lectr. N.Y. U., 1965; Robert L. Jackson lectr. Nat. Coll. State Trial Judges, 1966; lectr. U. Tex., 1967; Irvine lectr. Cornell U., 1968; Brainerd Currie lectr. Duke U., 1970; lectr. Notre Dame in London, 1974; Meiklejohn lectr. Brown U., 1976; lectr. adminstrv. law Tulane U. in Grenoble, 1979; Francis Biddle lectr. Harvard Law Sch., 1979; George Dreyfous lectr. Tulane U., 1981; Samuel Rubin lectr. Columbia U. Sch. Law, 1982; Mathew Tobriner lectr. Hastings Coll. Law, U. Calif., Berkeley, 1983; observer U.S. State Dept. Internat. Fisheries Conf., London, 1943. Served as lt. comdr. USCG, 1942-46. Mem. La. Bar Assn. (bd. govs.), Fed. Bar Assn. (pres. New Orleans chpt.), D.C. Bar Assn., ABA, New Orleans Bar Assn., Blue Key, Phi Delta Phi, Alpha Delta Gamma (nat. pres.). Democrat. Roman Catholic. Home: Washington D.C. Died Aug. 6, 1988, bureid Arlington Nat. Cemetery.

WRIGHT, KATHARINE WRIGHT, physician; b. Forest Glen, Md., Sept. 17, 1892; d. George Herdman and Jessie Fremont (Waite) Wright; m. Lewis A. Wright, Aug. 11, 1916; children: Marcia Wright Wooster, George Herbert, Hazel Wright Gaffey. BS, U. Wis., 1916; MD, George Washington U., 1918. Diplomate in psychiatry Am. Bd. Psychiatry and Neurology. Intern Nat. Homeopathic Hosp., Washington, 1918-19; physician-in-charge Carroll Springs Sanitarium, Forest Glen, Md., 1919-23; cons. child psychology, parent edn., Detroit, 1925-29, Evanston, Ill., 1934-38; physician Elgin (Ill.) State Hosp., 1940-43; rsch. asst. psychiatry Coll. Medicine U. Ill., 1942-46; assoc. Psychopathic Hosp., Chgo., from 1945; neuropsychiat. cons. Mary Thompson Hosp., Chgo., from 1946, psychiat. dir. mental health svc., 1947-61; faculty Northwestern U. Sch. medicine, from 1946, assoc. prof., from 1950; courtesy group Chgo. Wesley Meml. Hosp., 1950-59; cons. staff North Shore Hosp., from 1961; attending staff Fairview Hosp., from 1959; lectr. psychiatry and mental health, community and profl. groups. Contbr. articles to med. jours. Fellow Am. Psychiat. Assn., Ill. Psychiat. Soc., Inst. Medicine Chgo.; mem. AMA, Am. Med. Women's Assn. (br. pres. 1949-50, sec. 1952-53, pres. 1958-59), Nat. Assn. Mental Health, Am. Soc. Group Psychotherapy and Psychodrama, Med. Women's Internat. Assn. (v.p. from 1962), World Med. Assn. (U.S. com.), Chgo. Med. Soc., George Washington U. Med. Soc., Ill. Soc. Mental Health. Home: Evanston Ill. †

WRIGHT, SEWALL, educator; b. Melrose, Mass., Dec. 21, 1889; s. Philip Green and Elizabeth Quincy (Sewall) W.; m. Louise Lane Williams, Sept. 10, 1921; children: Richard, Robert, Elizabeth Quincy (Mrs. John Rose). BS, Lombard Coll., Galesburg, Ill., 1911; MS, U. Ill., 1912, ScD, 1961; ScD, Harvard, 1915, ScD (hon.), 1951; ScD (hon.), U. Rochester, 1942, Yale, 1949, Knox Coll., 1957, Western Res, U., 1958, U. Chgo., 1959, U. Wis., 1965; LLD, Mich. State U., 1955. Sr. animal husbandsman in animal genetics Bur. Animal Industry, USDA, 1915-25; assoc. prof. zoology U. Chgo., 1926-29, prof., 1930-37, Ernest D. Burton disting. service prof., 1938-54; Leon J. Cole prof. genetics U. Wis., 1955-60, prof. emeritus, 1960-88; Hitchcock prof. U. Calif., spring 1943; Fulbright prof. U. Edinburgh, 1949-50; pres. X Internat. Congress of Genetics, 1958. Author: Evolution and the Genetics of Populations (4 vols.); numerous papers on the genetics of the guinea pig, on path analysis, and on the statis. consequences of Mendelian heredity with reference to livestock breeding and evolution. Recipient Daniel Giraud Elliot medal, Kimber genetics award, Weldon Meml. medal Oxford, Lewis prize, Nat. Medal of Sci., 1966, Darwin medal Royal Soc. of London, 1980, Balzan prize Academia Lincel, Italy, 1984. Mem. NAS, Am. Philos. Soc., Am. Statis. Assn., AAAS, Am. Soc. Zoologists (pres. 1944), Am. Soc. Naturalists (pres. 1952), Am. Acad. Arts and Scis., Am. Genetic Assn., Genetics Soc. Am. (pres. 1934), Soc. for Study of Evolution (pres. 1955), Am. Soc. Human Genetics, Biometric Soc., Royal Soc. London (fgn. mem.), Royal Danish Acad. Scis. and Letters (fgn. mem.); corr. mem. Zool. Soc. (London); hon. mem. Royal Soc. Edinburgh, Genetical Soc. London, University Club (Madison). Unitarian. Home: Madison Wis. Died 1988.

WRIGHTSMAN, CHARLES BIERER, oil producer, philanthropist; b. Pawnee, Okla., June 13, 1895; s. Charles John and Edna (Lawing) W.; m. Irene Stafford, June 7, 1922 (div.); m. Jayne Larkin, Mar. 28, 1944. Student, Phillips Exeter Acad., 1910-14, Stanford U., 1914-15, Columbia, 1915-17. Ins. oil producer 1918-21; surveyor Russian oil fields, 1921; developer oil properties Okla., Kans., Tex., La., Calif., 1919-29; pres. Standard Oil Co. of KAns., 1932-53. Trustee Met. Mus. Art, N.Y.C., 1956-75. trustee emeritus, 1975-86; chmn. bd. of trustees Inst. Fine Arts NYU, 1970-73; trustee NYU, 1963-73, life trustee, 1973-86; councilor Am. Geog. Soc., 1950-56; trustee, pres. St. Mary's Hosp., West PAlm Beach, 1952-55. Served to lt. USNRF, 1917-19. Mem. Everglades Club, Seminole Club (Palm Beach, Fla.), Ramada Club, Petroleum Club, (Houston), Delta Kappa Epsilon. Home: New York N.Y. also: Palm Beach Fla. also: London England Died May 27, 1986.

WUNDER, CLINTON, clergyman; b. Cin., Dec. 17, 1892; s. Boyd and Louise (Rebman) W.; m. Ernestine Hinck, Oct. 29, 1917; 1 dau., Joan; m. 2d, Virginia Lee Graybill, Apr. 27, 1940. AB, U. Cin., 1914; BD, Rochester Theol. Sem., 1922; DD, Hillsdale Coll., 1926. Sec. West Side YMCA, N.Y.C., 1916-17; camp sec. Army YMCA, Ft. Thomas, Ky., 1917-18; sec. war work coun., indsl. dept. Internat. Com. YMCA, 1919; asst. min. Cen. Presbyn Ch., Rochester, N.Y. 1919-21; min. Bapt. Temple, Rochester, 1921-29, Community Ch., Chesterland, Ohio, 1942-43; exec. v.p. Acad. Motion Picture Arts & Scis., 1930-31; pres. So. Calif. Fellowship, 1933; instr. Dale Carnegie Inst., 1937-50; v.p. Nat. Live Stock Exchange, 1950; pub rels. dir. Okla. City Live Stock Exchange; nat. lectr. tour and broadcasts, 1935-36; specialist pub., indsl. rels. and ch. orgn.; cons. on philanthropic mgmt. and financing. Author: Crowds of Souls (handbook of modern ch. methods), 1926, The Complete Hanbook of Fund Raising, 1965; editor: Science of Mind, 1932; editor Think (monthly mag.), 1933, Otero County (N.M.) Times, 1947-48; broadcasted daily KFAC, L.A., 1934; contbr. to mags. Pres. So. Calif. Fellowship, 1933; v.p. Phillips U., Enid, Okla., 1951-52; dir., v.p. Nat. Fund Raising Svc., Inc., 1952-66; assoc. sec. Cleve. Bapt. Assn., 1941; Keynote speaker Northern Bapt. Conv., Seattle, 1925, trustee Colgate Rochester Divinity Sch., 1928-29. Sr. chaplain, 1st lt., Motor Transport, U.S. Army, 1918-19; commd. lt. (s.g.), Chaplains Corps, USNR, Feb. 1943; sr. chaplain, Caribbean, Cuba, 1943-44; chaplain div., Navy Dept., Washington, 1944; promoted comdr., 1952. Mem. SAR, VFW, Sons Civil War Vets., Am. Legion (chaplain 9th Ohio dist. 1942-43), Fleet Res. Assn. (hon.), Masons (32 deg., dir. mil. and naval affairs com. Grand lodge N.Y. 1945-46), Phi Delta Theta. Home: Bent N.Mex. †

WYDLER, JOHN WALDEMAR, congressman; b. Bklyn., June 9, 1924; s. Waldemar and Ethel Z. (Roebuck) W.; m. Brenda O'Sullivan, Oct. 25, 1959; children: Christopher, Kathleen, Elizabeth. Student, Brown U., 1941-42, 45-47; LLB, Harvard, 1950. Bar: N.Y. 1950. With U.S. Atty.'s Office, Eastern Dist., N.Y., 1953-59; practice in Mineola, N.Y., 1959-61; mem. N.Y. State investigation commn. to probe N.Y.C. sch. constrn. irregularities, 1959-60; counsel firm Wydler, Balin, Pares, Soloway, Seaton and Marglin, 1967-78; mem. 88th-96th Congresses from 5th N.Y. dist.; mem. govt. ops. com., sci. and tech. com, asst. minority floor leader, 1973, Ho. Republican floor mgr., 1973-76; N.Y. State mem. Com. on Coms., 1975; dean N.Y. Rep. Congl. Del., 1976-80; vice chmn. N.Y. Bipartisan Congl. Del., 1976-80; chmn. L.I. Congl. Caucus, 1979-80. Charter mem. Bishop's Men's Assn. of Cathedral Incarnation, Garden City, N.Y.; mem. Tech. Assessment Bd., 1977-87; bd. visitors U.S. Merchant Marine Acad., 1971-87. With AUS, World War II, CBI, with Res. Mem. Fed. Bar Assn., Nassau County Bar Assn., Dist. Atty.'s Assn., Protestant Lawyers Assn., Am. Legion, VFW, U.S. Jr. C. of C., Lions Club, Elks, Masons, Phi Beta Kappa, Sigma Chi. Home: Garden City N.Y. Died Aug. 4, 1987.

WYETH, MARION SIMS, architect; b. N.Y.C., Feb. 18, 1889; s. John Allan and Florence Nightingale (Sims) W.; m. Eleanor Orr, Nov. 25, 1915; children: Florence Nightingale, Alice Eleanor, Joan Allan, Marion Sims. Grad., Lawrenceville Sch., 1906; AB, Princeton U., 1910; student, Beaux Arts, Paris, 1910-14. Pvt. sec. to Ambassador Thomas Nelson Page, Rome, 1914-15; with Bertram, Grosvernor, Goodhue, architects, N.Y.C., 1915, Carrere & Hastings, 1916-17; pvt. practice 1919-32; ptnr. Wyeth & King, from 1932; ptnr. Fla. Assocs., 1942, architect-engr., cinstructing airports, hosps., etc. for Army and Navy; ptnr. Wyeth, King & Johnson, architects, 1945-73. Past chmn. bd. Polyclinic Hosp., N.Y.C.; former dir. Woman's Hosp., N.Y.C., Good Samaritan Hosp., West Palm Beach, Fla. 1st lt. A.S.,

U.S. Army, 1917-19. Fellow AIA; mem. Soc. Four Arts (past pres.), Century Assn., Knickerbocker Club (N.Y.C.), Everglades Club, Bath and Tennis Club, Seminole Club. Home: Palm Beach Fla. †

WYLIE, LLOYD RITCHIE, astronomer; b. Idana, Kans., Apr. 12, 1892; s. Oliver Moses and Mary Ida (Ritchie) W.; m. Eula Sauls Treadway, Oct. 7, 1941. AB, Park Coll., 1914; student, U. Chgo., 1915-17; MA, Northwestern U., 1922, PhD, 1932. Asst. physicist U.S. Bur. Standards, 1917-20; instr. astronomy Northwestern U., 1920-24; asst. prof. math. Ohio Wesleyan U., 1924-26; asst., assoc. prof. math. Lake Forest Coll., 1928-34; assoc. prof. math. Eastern Ill. State Tchrs. Coll., Charleston, 1934-36; asst. astronomer USN Obs., Washington, 1936-39, assoc. astronomer, 1939-44, astronomer, 1944-46; prof. astronomy, head dept. Wittenberg Coll., from 1946, head dept. earth scis., from 1951. Contbr. profl. publs. With U.S. Army, 1917. Mem. AAAS, Am. Astron. Soc., Ohio Acad. Sci., Sigma Xi, Phi Gamma Delta. Home: Springfield Ohio. †

WYNGARDEN, HERMAN JACOB, economist, educator; b. Oostberg, Wis., Sept. 19, 1893; s. Jacob and Joanna (Tien) W.; m. Doris Haan, July 25, 1924; children: Nancy Ann (Mrs. Robert Vosburg), Mary Ellen (Mrs. Neal Wasserburger), H. James. AB, U. Wash., 1915; AM, U. Mich., 1921, PhD, 1927. Instr. econs. U. Mich., 1921-24; assoc. prof. econs. Mich. State U., 1924-39, prof., 1939-43, head dept. econs., 1043-49, dean sch. bud. and pub. service, 1949-58, emeritus, 1958-88; bd. dirs. First Nat. Bank of East Lansing; chmn. spl. mediation commn., State of Mich., 1945, impartial chmn. in labor disputes, from 1945; ad hoc arbitrator in labor disputes. Author: Index of Local Real Estate Prices, Mich. Bus. Studies, U. Mich., 1927, Monetary Policies and Inflation Controls, Bull. of the Robert Morris Assocs., 1941. Pub. mem. Nat. War Labor Bd., Region XI, Detroit, 1943-46, NAt. Wasge Stblzn. Bd., Region XI, 1946; chmn. Mich. Citizens Food Com. (Luckman com.), 1947; trustee Mich. Coun. on Econ. Edn.; cons. on orgn. sch. bus. adminstrn. Getulio Vargas Found., Brazil. Mem. Am. Econ. Assn., Midwest Econ. Assn. (1st v.p. 1951-52), Econs. Club of Detroit, Nat. Acad. Arbitrators, Am. Arbitration Assn., Am. Acad. Polit. and Social Sci., Indsl. Rels. Rsch. Assn., AAUP, Acad. Mgmt., Am. Assn. Collegiate Schs. Bus., Mich. Acad. Sci., Arts and Letters, Theta Chi, Delta Sigma Pi. Home: Orlando Fla. Died Mar. 9, 1988.

WYNN, EARL RAYMOND, educator, actor; b. Coal Valley, Ill., Nov. 25, 1911; s. Zadoc Hardin and Mary Jane (Ziegler) W.; m. Irene Grace Schwartzinger, Sept. 8, 1939; m. Rhoda Mabel Hunter, Dec. 27, 1951; children—Stacy Hunter, Sherry. A.B., Augustana Coll., 1932; M.S., Northwestern U., 1934, postgrad., 1936-38. Asst. prof. English and speech, charge speech div. Tarkio (Mo.) Coll., 1934-36; instr. dramatic art U. N.C., Chapel Hill, 1938-40; asst. prof. dramatic art, charge radio 1940-43, prof. radio, TV and motion pictures, 1947-76; producer, dir. Men in Action from U. N.C. campus for MBS network, 1941-42; writer, producer tng. films and film strips Q.M.C. Camp Lee, Va., 1942-43; dir. communication center 1946-62, past chmn. dept. radio, TV and motion pictures, 1947-62; exec. dir. N.C. Communications Study Commn., 1949-51; N.C. Ednl. Radio-TV Commn., 1953. Actor Lost Colony, 1940, 41, Unto These Hills, 1958, 61, 64, 65, The Legend of Daniel Boone, 1966, Carolina Readers Theatre, 1972, 73, 74; producer, narrator Erwyn Prodns., 1965-86 ; actor The Gardener's Son, PBS, 1976, The Caine Mutiny Court Martial, 1976, Time Limit, 1978, Cherry, 1978, Arsenic and Old Lace, 1978, Native Son, 1978, Twelve Angry Men, 1985; Contbr. articles to profl. jours. Chmn. bd. The ArtSch., Carrboro, N.C. Served to lt. USNR, 1943-46. Presbyterian. Clubs: Chapel Hill Country (pres. 1959), U. N.C. Faculty, Rotary. Home: Chapel Hill N.C. Died Sept. 17, 1986; buried Chapel Hill, N.C.

WYNN, KEENAN, actor; b. N.Y.C., July 27, 1916; s. Ed and Hilda (Keenan) W.; m. Eve Abbott (div.); 2 sons; m. Betty Jane Butler (div.); m. Sharley Jean Hudson; 3 daus. Student, Horace Mann Sch., N.Y.C., Harvey Sch., St. John's Mil. Acad. Started in N.Y. theatre, 1935; from 1940-57 appeared in camp shows worldwide for U.S. mil.; from 1935-79 appeared in over 350 productions on stage, in stock, on radio, live and filmed TV and feature films. Films include: Kiss Me, Kate, 1953, The Man in the Gray Flannel Suit, 1956, Some Came Running, 1959, The Absent-Minded Professor, 1961, Dr. Strangelove, 1964, Finian's Rainbow, 1968, McKenna's Gold, 1968, Pretty Maids All in a Row, 1971, Nashville, 1976, The Shaggy D.A., 1977, Best Friends, 1982, numerous others; TV appearance Requiem for a Heavyweight, 1953. Home: Brentwood Calif. Died Oct. 14, 1986, buried Forest Lawn Cemetery, North Hollywood, Calif.

WYSHAM, WILLIAM NORRIS, clergyman, foreign mission consultant; b. Balt., Sept. 10, 1890; s. James Kemp and Matilda Bennett (Norris) W.; m. Laura Snead Dickey, June 1, 1916 (died 1919); m. Miriam McLean Graham, Mar. 6, 1920; children: James Kemp, Stuart Graham, Donald Norris, Janet Wysham Leber. Grad., Balt. City Coll., 1908; AB, Lafayette Coll., 1913; MA, Princeton U., 1915; grad., Princeton Theol. Sem., 1916; DD (hon.), Coe Coll., 1932. Pastor Tupper Lake (N.Y.) Presbyn. Ch., 1916-17; asst. minister 1st Presbyn. Ch., Balt., 1919; missionary to Iran (Persia) Presbyn. Ch. in the U.S.A., 1920-23, 25-38; lectr. in English and religion depts. Alborz Coll., Teheran, Iran, 1920-23, 25-38, treas. of coll., 1933-37, chmn. bd. mgrs., 1937-38; exec. sec. of Western Area Bd. of Fgn. Missions in Presbyn. Ch. in the U.S.A., 1938-43, exec. sec. Eastern Area, 1943-49, sec. Office Lit. and Publs., 1949-55, chmn, dept. functional services, 1956-60; cons. Near East Christian Coun., Beirut, 1960-61; West Coast rep. Com. World Literacy and Christian Lit., Nat. Coun. Chs., from 1961; asst. minister 1st United Presbyn. Ch., Los Gatos, Calif., from 1962; chmn. lit. com. Near East Christian Coun., Cairo, 1929-31, 37-39; lectr. on missions San Francisco Theol. Sem., San Anselmo, Calif., 1940-43; ofcl. visitation missions in Philippines and Thailand, 1946. Editor numerous books and pamphlets in Persian lang.; also author articles in Muslim World, Presbyn. Life. Bldg. sec. Army YMCA, Kelly Field, Tex., 1918. Mem. Phi Beta Kappa, Sigma Alpha Epsilon. Home: Los Gatos Calif. †

WYSZECKI, GUNTER WOLFGANG, physicist; b. Tilsit, Germany, Nov. 8, 1925; came to Can., 1955, naturalized, 1961; s. Bruno Bernhard and Helene (Goerke) W.; m. Ingeborg Rathjens, Aug. 4, 1954; children: Wolfgang, Joana. Diploma in engring. in math. and physics, Tech. U., Berlin, 1951, D in Engring., 1953. Mem. staff NRC Can., Ottawa, Ont., 1955-85, dir. Inst. Optics, 1961-85, asst. dir. physics, 1982-85. Author: Farbsysteme, 1961; co-author: Color in Business, Science and Industry, 1963, 3d edit., 1975, Color Science, 1967, 2d edit., 1982. With German Navy, 1943-45. Recipient D.B. Judd gold medal Assn. Internat. de la Couleur, 1979, Godlove award Inter-Soc. Color Coun., 1979, Bruning award Fedn. Soc. for Coatings Techs., 1979; Fulbright scholar, 1953-54. Fellow Optical Soc. Am., Illuminating Engring. Soc., Royal Soc. Can.; mem. Can. Soc. Color (pres. 1972). Home: Ottawa Canada. Died June 22, 1985; buried Berlin.

WYZANSKI, CHARLES EDWARD, JR., judge; b. Boston, May 27, 1906; s. Charles Edward and Maude (Joseph) W.; m. Gisela Warburg, July 23, 1943; children: Charles Max, Anita Wyzanski Robboy. A.B. magna cum laude, Harvard U., 1927, LL.B. magna cum laude, 1930, LL.D., 1958; LL.D., U. Pa., 1954, Carleton Coll., 1954, Tufts Coll., 1954, Swarthmore Coll., 1956, Brandeis U., 1956, Clark U., 1963, Washington U., St. Louis, 1974. Bar: Mass. 1931. Assoc. with Ropes & Gray, 1930-33; law sec. to U.S. Circuit Judge Augustus N. Hand, 1930-31, to; U.S. Circuit Judge Learned Hand, 1932; solicitor Dept. Labor, Washington, 1933-35; U.S. rep. 71st and 72d sessions of governing body ILO, Geneva, 1935; substitute del. and govt. adviser 19th session Internat. Labor Conf., Geneva, 1935; spl. asst. to atty. gen. U.S., staff of solicitor gen. Dept. Justice, 1935-37; ptnr. Ropes & Gray, 1938-41; mem. Nat. Def. Mediation Bd., 1941; U.S. dist. judge for Mass., 1941-86; chief judge 1965-71, sr. dist. judge, 1971-86; judge Internat. Adminstrv. Ct., Geneva, 1950-55; lectr. on govt. Harvard Coll., 1942-43, 49-50; vis. prof. MIT, 1948-50; Herman Phleger prof. Stanford, 1974; copyright expert UNESCO, Paris, 1949, Washington, 1950; mem. ILO Com. of Experts on Application Convs., 1945-53, Supreme Ct. Com. on Rules of Civil Procedure for Dist. Cts., 1953-65; Pappas disting. scholar in residence Boston U., 1985-86. Author: Whereas-A Judge's Premises, 1963. Trustee Ford Found., 1952-76; mem. bd. overseers Harvard U., 1943-49, 51-57, pres., 1953-57. Recipient Sir Thomas More medal Boston Coll., 1972; John Phillips award Phillips Exeter Acad., 1975; Jud. Excellence award Boston Bar Assn., 1982; sr. fellow Soc. Fellows Harvard U., 1962-76. Fellow Am. Acad. Arts and Scis.; mem. Am. Law Inst., Mass. Hist. Soc., Phi Beta Kappa. Clubs: Tavern (Boston); Century (N.Y.C.). Home: Boston Mass. Died Sept. 3, 1986; buried Mt. Auburn Cemetery, Cambridge, Mass.

YACAVONE, PETER FRANCIS, paper company executive; b. Hartford, Conn., Nov. 14, 1927; s. Rocco F. Yacavone and Lorna Doone (Prentice) Yacavone Zito; m. Theresa Ellen Finley, Aug. 12, 1950; children—Peter Francis, Patricia, Maura, Nancy, John. B.S., U. Hartford. Asst. controller Great No. Paper Co., Millinocket, Maine, 1966-68, controller, 1968-70, pres., 1978-83; asst. controller, asst. treas. Consol. Edison Co., N.Y.C., 1970-73; treas. Great No. Nekoosa Corp., Stamford, Conn., 1973-78, exec. v.p., 1978-83, pres., 1983-84, vice chmn., 1984-86 . Served to 1st sgt. U.S. Army, 1950-52. Mem. Am. Soc. C.P.A.s. Home: Stamford, Conn. Died Sept. 28, 1986, buried Bloomfield, Conn.

YAMASAKI, MINORU, architect; b. Seattle, Dec. 1, 1912; s. Tsunejiro J. and Hana (Ito) Y.; m. Teruko Hirashaki, Dec. 5, 1941; children: Carol Ann, Taro Michael, Kim. Grad., U. Wash., 1934; student, NYU. Designer Githens & Keally, 1935-37; instr. water color NYU, 1935-36; designer, job capt. Shreve, Lamb & Harmon, 1937-43; designer Harrison & Fouilhoux, 1943-44; chief archtl. designer Raymond Loewy, 1944-45; instr. archtl design Columbia U., 1943-45; chief archtl designer Smith, Hinchman & Grylls, 1945-49; ptnr. Yamasaki, Leinweber & Assocs., Detroit, 1949-59, Minoru Yamasaki & Assocs., Troy, Mich., 1959-86; cons. World's Fair, Seattle, 1961; mem. Com. on Civic Design, Detroit. Works include: Reynolds Metals Co. Bldg., Detroit, Reynolds Metals Regional Bldg., Southfield, Mich. (AIA 1st Honor award 1961), St. Louis Airport (1st honor award AIA 1956), U.S. Consulate Gen.'s Offices, Kobe, Japan (top award Archtl. Inst. Japan 1957), McGregor Meml. Community Conf. Ctr., Wayne State U. (AIA 1st Honor award 1959), Fed. Sci. Bldgs. at Seattle World Fair (Honor award Seattle chpt. AIA 1962), Dhahran Internat. Air Terminal, Dhahran, Saudi Arabia (1st Honor award AIA 1963), U.S. Sci. Pavilion, Seattle (award of merit Precast Concrete Inst. 1963), Mich. Consol. Gas Co. Office Bldg. (award of merit Detroit chpt. AIA 1964, Archtl award of excellence Am. Inst. Constrn. 1964), IBM Bldg. (Design in Steel award Am. Iron and Steel Inst. 1965), Office Bldg. Woodrow Wilson Sch. Pub. and Internat. Affairs, Princeton (Outstanding Project of Yr. award N.J. Concrete Assn. 1965), pub. housing in St. Louis, Thompson Products Rsch. Ctr., Cleve., U.S. Armed Forces Record Ctr., St. Louis, Oberlin Coll. Music Conservatory, U. Mich. Married Students Housing, North Shore Congregation Israel Bldgs., Glencoe, Ill., Northwestern Nat. Life Ins. Co., Mpls., Century Plaza Hotel and Towers, L.A., Mfrs. & Traders Trust Co., Buffalo, Horace Mann Ins. Co., Springfield, Ill., Colo. Nat. Bank, Denver, Coll. Ctr. Franklin & Marshall Coll., Tulsa Performing Arts Ctr., Bank Okla., Tulsa, Fed. Res. Bank, Richmond, Va., Royal Reception Pavilion and Internat. Airport, Saudi Arabia, Head Office Bldg. Saudi Arabian Monetary Agy., Riyadh, Shiga (Japan) Sacred Garden; chief architect: World Trade Ctr., N.Y.C. Recipient The Sch. Exec. bronze plaque, 1953; hon. mention Nat. Inst. Arts and Letters, 1954; 1st design award Prog. Arch. Urban Redevel., 1956, award of merit Feld Clinic, 1956, top award in commerce div. Prog. Arch., Am. Concrete Inst., 1957, award of merit AIA, 1959, Outstanding Asian-Am. Fine Arts award U.S.-Asia Inst., 1981. Fellow Am. Acad. Arts and Scis., AIA. Home: Troy Mich. Died Feb. 6, 1986.

YAPHE, WILFRED, microbiologist; b. Lachine, Que., Can., July 9, 1921; s. Sam and Rachel Y.; m. Ruth Dorfman, Jan. 16, 1946; children—Arona, John, Anna. B.Sc., McGill U., Montreal, Que., 1949, Ph.D., 1952. Research officer Atlantic Regional Lab., Nat. Research Council Can., Halifax, N.S., 1952-66; mem. faculty McGill U., from 1966, prof. microbiology, from 1971. Author research papers in field. Served with RCAF, 1942-45. Mem. Can. Soc. Microbiology, Am. Soc. Microbiology, Phycological Soc. Home: Montreal, Que. Canada. Deceased.

YARBOROUGH, RICHARD WARREN, lawyer; b. Austin, Tex., Oct. 20, 1931; s. Ralph Webster and Opal (Warren) Y.; m. Ann Graham McJimsey, Mar. 17, 1956; children: Clare, Elizabeth, Jefferson. BA, U. Tex., 1953, LLB, 1955. Bar: Tex. 1955, U.S. Supreme Ct. 1967, D.C. 1982. Pvt. practice Austin, 1957-58; legis. asst., comm. counsel U.S. Senate, Washington, 1958-67; commr. U.S. Indian Claims Commn., Washington, 1967-78; chmn. U.S. Fgn. Claims Settlement Commn., 1978-81. Editor: Map of Indian Land Areas Judicially Established, 1978. Served with AUS, 1955-57. Mem. ABA, State Bar Tex., Phi Delta Phi, Kappa Alpha. Democrat. Home: Arlington Va. Died Mar. 5, 1986.

YEAGER, JOHN W., judge; b. Richland, Ind., Mar. 1, 1891; s. Wilhelm C. and Laura Elizabeth (Barton) Y.; m. Lena E. Deeg, June 28, 1922; children: John Walter, Barbara May. Grad. high sch., Richland, Ind., 1910; LLB, Chgo.-Kent Coll. Law, 1913. Bar: Ind. 1913. Gen. practice law Evansville, Ind., 1913-14; gen. practice law Omaha, 1915-21, dep. county atty., 1921-23, chief dep. county atty., 1923-33, dist. judge, 1933-40; judge Nebr. Supreme Ct., Lincoln, from 1940. With U.S. Army, 1918-19. Mem. ABA, Nebr. State Bar Assn., Omaha Bar Assn., Am. Legion, Vets. of Fgn. Wars, Lincoln Country Club, Omaha Field Club, Sthletic Club, Masons, Shriners, Odd Fellows, K. of P., Elks, Delta Theta Phi. Republican. Home: Omaha Nebr. †

YELLOTT, JOHN INGLE, engineering educator; b. Bel Air, Md., Oct. 25, 1908; s. John I. and Mildred Walker (Nelson) Y.; m. Judith Williams, May 12, 1934 (div.); children: John Ingle, Ann Williams; m. Barbara Leslie Jordan, June 2, 1951. Ed., Episcopal High Sch. of Va.; B.S. in Mech. Engring., Johns Hopkins U., 1931, M.M.E., 1933; D.Sc. (hon.), Ariz. State U., 1986. Profl. engr. Md., N.J., Ariz. Instr. mech. engring. U. Rochester, 1933-34; instr. and asst. prof. Stevens Inst. Tech., 1934; prof. and head dept. mech. engring. Ill. Inst. Tech., 1940-43; dir. Inst. Gas Tech., 1943-45; chmn. War Tng. Com., 1940-44; dir. research, locomotive devel. com. Bituminous Coal Research, Inc., 1945-55; sec. Assn. for Applied Solar Energy; also asst. dir. Stanford Research Inst., 1955-58; pres. Yellott Engring. Assocs. (cons. engrs.), Phoenix, 1958-86; headmaster Phoenix Country Day Sch., 1966-72; dir. Yellott Solar Energy Lab., 1958-86; prof. architecture Ariz. State U., 1973-79, disting. prof. emeritus, 1979-86; condr. research and edn. in mech. engring.; devel. of coal-fired gas turbine locomotive. Editor engring. textbooks; contbr. articles to mech. engring. publs. Decorated Order Brit. Empire.; comdr. bro. Order of Hosp. of St. John of Jerusalem; recipient Chgo. and Ill. Jr. C. of C. awards, 1943, Barker Silver medal Chartered Inst. Brit. Svc. Engrs., 1986, PLEA award Passive Solar Div., Am.

Solar Energy Soc., 1987; named to Ill. Inst. Tech. Hall of Fame, 1983, State of Ariz. Solar Hall of Fame, 1988; honored with John Yellott Meml. Issue of Passive Solar Jour., 1987. Fellow AAAS, ASME (jr. award 1934, contbr. to trans.), ASHRAE (Contbr. to jour., Louise and Bill Holladay disting. fellow award 1980), Newcomen Soc. (chmn. for Ariz. 1956-86), Ariz. Acad. Sci. (pres. 1959-60), Royal Soc. Arts (Benjamin Franklin fellow); mem. Sigma Xi, Alpha Delta Phi, Tau Beta Pi, Pi Tau Sigma, Omicron Delta Kappa. Republican. Episcopalian. Home: Phoenix Ariz. Died Dec. 27, 1986; buried The Close, All Saints Ch., Phoenix.

YELTON, CHESTLEY LEE, orthopedic surgeon; b. Butler, Ky., Nov. 29, 1909; s. James Calvert and Lida (Netterville) Y.; m. Ruth Olvey, Oct. 28, 1939; children—Chestley Lee, Ruth Ardis. A.B., Transylvania Coll., 1932; M.D., U. Louisville, 1937. Diplomate: Am. Bd. Orthopedic Surgery. Intern Lloyd Noland Hosp., Fairfield, Ala., 1937-38; resident Lloyd Noland Hosp., 1946-49; practice medicine, specializing in orthopedic surgery Birmingham, Ala., 1952-81; chief dept. orthopedic surgery Lloyd Noland Hosp., 1952-63; prof. dept. orthopedic surgery Med. Coll. Ala., 1963-81; chief Birmingham Child Amputee Clinic; cons. State Vocational Rehab. and Crippled Children's Services. Producer: ednl. med. films Certain Extremity Abnormalities and Their Management, 1962, Talar Fracture Dislocation, 1965, Enchondroma, 1966. Fellow A.C.S. (com. chmn.), Am. Acad. Orthopedic Surgeons; mem. Soc. Orthopedic Surgery and Traumatology, Clin. Orthopedic Soc., Am. Assn. Surgery of Trauma, Orthopedic Research Soc., Am. Orthopedic Foot Soc., Southeastern Surg. Congress, Alpha Omega Alpha. Home: Birmingham Ala. Died June 26, 1986; buried Birmingham, Ala.

YLITALO, JOHN RAYMOND, ambassador; b. Floodwood, Minn., Dec. 25, 1916; s. John and Saima Marie (Swen) Y.; m. Jean Sarchet, Sept. 19, 1942; children: John Raymond, Georgianne, Mary Katherine, Sara Lisa. Student, Suomi Coll., 1933-35; BA, St. Olaf Coll., 1937; MBA, Northwestern U., 1938; grad., Nat. War Coll., 1954. Instr. econs. U. Ala., 1938-41; spl. agent FBI, 1941-46; attache, polit. officer Am. legation, Helsinki, 1946-50; assigned Dept. of State, Washington, 1950-53; dep. prin. officer Am. Consulate Gen., Munich, 1954-58; consul gen., counsellor of embassy Am. Embassy, Manila, The Philippines, 1959-62; assigned Dept. State, Washington, 1962-65; dir. Visa Office Dept. State, 1965-68; consul gen., prin. officer Am. Consulate Gen., Tijuana, Mexico, 1968-69; ambassador to Paraguay Asuncion, 1969-72; assigned State Dept., 1972-73; consul gen., prin. officer Am. Consulate Gen., Toronto, Ont., Can., 1973-76. Home: Washington D.C. Died Feb. 10, 1987, buried Rock Creek Cemetery, Washington.

YNTEMA, THEODORE OTTE, economist, educator; b. Holland, Mich., Apr. 8, 1900; s. Dottwe Bauke and Mary Elizabeth (Loomis) Y.; m. Kathryn Elizabeth van der Veen, Aug. 8, 1923; children: Elizabeth, John Arend; m. Virginia Heigho Payne, July 31, 1939; children: Virginia Gwin, Theodore Otte Jr.; m. Christa Gievers. AB summa cum laude, Hope Coll., 1921, ScD, 1960; AM in Chemistry, U. Ill., 1922; AM in Bus., U. Chgo., 1924, PhD in Econs., 1929; student, Harvard, 1926-27; LLD, Grinnell Coll., Franklin and Marshall Coll., Central Mich. U. CPA, Ill. With U. Chgo., 1923-49, instr. acctg., prof. statistics, 1930-44, prof. bus. and econ. policy, 1944-49; dir. rsch. Cowles Commn., 1939-42; v.p. fin. Ford Motor Co., 1949-61, chmn. fin. com., 1961-65; dir. rsch. Cowles Commn., 1939-42; acting assoc. prof. statistics Stanford U., 1929-30; cons. economist various cos., 1933-49, 1965-85; econ. cons. Nat. Recovery Adminstrn., 1934-35; chief statistician div. indsl. materials Def. Commn., 1940; spl. cons. War Shipping Adminstrn., 1942; rsch. dir. Com. Econ. Devel., 1942-49, chmn. rsch. and ploicy com., 1961-66; vis. prof. U. Chgo., Carnegie Inst. Tech., Oakland U., Rochester, Minn., 1965-85; bd. dirs. Bell & Howell, Huyck Corp., Ency. Britannica; dir. Nat. Indl. Conf. Bd., Nat. Bur. Econ. Rsch. Author: A Mathematical Reformulation of the General Theory of International Trade, 1932; co-author: Jobs and Markets, 1946. Trustee Canbrook Inst. Sci., Cranbrook Acad. Art, Com. for Econ. Devel., Carnegie Endowment for Internat. Peace, Tax Found. Inc., U. Chgo., Mich. Colls. Found. Fellow Am. U. Chgo., Am Statis. Assn., Econometric Soc., AAAS, An. Acad. Arts and Scis.; mem. Am. Econ. assn., Am. Inst. CPAs, Inst. MAth. Statistics, Mont Pelerin Soc., Coun. on Fgn. Rels., Detroit Athletic Club, Detroit Club, Bloomfield Hills Country Club, Bloomfield Open Hunt Club, Recess Club. Home: West Bloomfield Mich. Died Sept. 18, 1985.

YOST, JOHN STEVENSON LONG, lawyer; b. Balt., May 18, 1892; s. William Franklin and Eleanor Bonner (Long) Y.; m. Helen B. Gatchell, 1930; 1 son, Stevenson; m. 2d, Clarissa Tilghman Goldsborough, Nov. 25, 1933; children: Julia Goldsborough, Clarissa Tilghman. Grad., Boy's Latin Sch., Balt., 1910; AB, Johns Hopkins U., 1914; LLB, U. Md., 1917. Bar: Md. 1916. Tchr. Gilman Sch., Balt., 1914-16; studied law while teachin; assoc. with Frank, Emory & Beeuweskes, Balt., 1917; served as spl. asst. to sec. state Washington, 1918-19; ptnr. Maloy, Brady, Howell & Yost, Balt., 1920-26, Maloy, Brady & Yost, Balt., 1926-38; chief atty. U.S. Dept. Agr., 1933-35; spl. asst. to U.S. gen. atty. 1935-43; lectr. U. Balt. Law Sch., 1927-43; gen. atty. Panhandle Ea. Pipe Line Co., 1943-57, ret. 1957. Mem. Am. Fed. Power, Balt. Bar Assn., Chgo. Bar Assn., Bachelors Cotillon Club, Chesapeake Bay Yacht Club, Wednesday Law Club, Tred Avon Yacht Club. Democrat. Episcopalian. Home: Easton Md. †

YOUNG, ARTHUR NICHOLS, economist; b. Los Angeles, Nov. 21, 1890; s. William Stewart and Adele (Nichols) Y.; m. Ellen May Bailey, June 11, 1915 (dec. 1973); children: Elizabeth (Mrs. P.W. Roulac), Allen, William Dwight. AB, Occidental Coll., 1910, LLD, 1937; AM, Princeton, 1911, PhD, 1914; LLB, George Washington U., 1927. Prof. econs. Presbyn. Coll., Clinton, S.C., 1912-13; instr. econs. Princeton U., 1915-17; rsch. assoc. U. Calif., 1917; adviser on taxation Mexican Govt., 1918; trade expert War Trade Bd., 1918; trade commr. to investigate fin. conditions in Spain for U.S. Dept. Commerce, 1919; economist in office of fgn. trade adviser Dept. of State, 1921-22, econ. adviser, 1922-28; assoc. of Am. observer with Reparation Commn., Paris, during preparation of Dawes Plan, 1924; chmn. Interdepartmental Com. on Oil Pollution of Navigable Waters, 1924-26; del. to Internat. Conf. on Oil Pollution, Washington, 1926; expert during fgn. debt negotiations 1924-27; expert attending World Econ. Conf., Geneva, 1927; expert on pub. credit Commn. of Fin. Experts of Chinese Govt., 1929; fin. adviser Chinese Govt., 1929-46, Central Bank of China; mem. Chinese Flood Relief Commnn., 1931; expert Chinese Econ. Mission, 1933; mem. com. on establishment Central REs. Bank, 1936; dir. China Nat. Aviation Corp., 1937-45; v.p. Chinese-Am. Inst. Cultural Rels., 1940; vice chmn. United China Relief Coordinating Com., 1942; chmn. Am. relief and ARC com. in China, 1943; trustee China Found., 1944; adviser Chinese Govt. commn. on relief and rehab., 1944; mem. Chinese del. to Bretton Woods fin. conf., 1944; dir. Point IV program, Saudi Arabia, 1951-52; fin. adviser, chief, fin. mission to Saudi Arabia, organizing Monetary Agy. and reforming currency customs, budget, 1951-52; investigator S. Am. problems of pvt. fgn. investment FOA, 1954; fin. cons. ICA, 1957-58; lectr. Occidental Coll., 1958-59; cons. on taxation, Argentina, 1962-63. Author: The Single Tax Movement in the United States, 1916, Finances of the Federal District of Mexico, 1918, Spanish Finance and Trade, 1920, China's Economic and Financial Reconstruction, 1947, Saudi Arabian Currency and Finance, 1953, China and the Helping Hand, 1937-45, 1963, China's Wartime Finance and Inflation, 1937-45, 1965, China's Nation-Building Effort, 1927-37, 1971, Saudi Arabia: The Making of a Finacial Giant, 1983; contbr. reports and articles to mags. Life trustee Occidental Coll. Recipient Order of the Brilliant Jade (China); Guggenheim fellow, 1956. Mem. Am. Econ. Assn., Acad. Polit. Sci., Am. Guild Organists, Cosmos Club (Washington), Phi Beta Kappa, Phi Gamma Delta. Presbyterian. Home: Claremont Calif. Died July 19, 1984.

YOUNG, CLAUD FRANKLIN, physician; b. Bowie, Tex., Nov. 19, 1887; s. John Andrew and Nancy Emaline (Prater) Y.; m. Bess Swisher, Nov. 4, 1913 (dec. Aug. 1961); children: Robert S., Nancy Jane (Mrs. J. V. Canterbury); m. Sadie Jane Kirker, Mar. 12, 1963. AB, U. Tex., 1910, MD, 1912; grad. student, Johns Hopkins, 1917-18. Intern Kansas City (Mo.) Gen. Hosp., 1912-13; mem. staff urol. svc. Mercy Hosp., Ft. Scott, Kans., 1918-52, mem. surg. svc. staff, 1916-52; health officer Bowie, 1913-16, Ft. Scott, 1917-27, Bourbon County, Kans., 1918-24; chief U.S. Health Dept., Ft. Scott, 1918-22; surgeon M.P., M.K. & T. Ry., K.C.S. Ry.; also div. surgeon Frisco Ry., Ft. Scott, 1918-52; med. dir. Cen. Life Ins. Co., Ft. Scott, 1923-50, pres., 1950-52; ptnr. Newman and Young Med. Clinic, Ft. Scott, 1918-52. Chmn. Carnegie Libr. Bd., Ft. Scott, 1920-23; head SSS, Ft. Scott, 1918-22. Surgeon USPHS, 1918-21. Mem. AMA, ACS (life), Am. Goitre Soc., Am. Urol. Soc., Masons (head Scottish Rite Kans. from 1938, grand sec. gen. Supreme Coun. Scottish Rite So. Jurisdiction, Washington from 1939). Republican. Methodist (lay leader). Home: Washington D.C. †

YOUNG, DICK, sports writer. Sports writer N.Y. Post, N.Y.C., until 1987. Died Aug. 31, 1987; buried George Washington Meml. Park, Paramus, N.J.

YOUNG, JOHN PARKE, economist; b. L.A., Oct. 24, 1895; s. William Stewart and Adele (Nichols) Y.; m. Florence Hensel, Sept. 7, 1927 (dec. 1949); children: Douglas (dec.), Richard Parke, Roger Hensel, Catherine Jean; m. Marie Louise Smith, June 24, 1952. AB, Occidental Coll., 1917, LLD, 1965; AM, Columbia U., 1919, Princeton U., 1920; PhD, Princeton U., 1922. Examiner FTC, 1917-18; fellow in econs. and social instns. Princeton U., 1919-20, instr., 1922-23; dir. U.S. Senate Fgn. Currency and Exchange Investigation, 1923-25; prof. econs., sociology, chmn. dept. Occidental Coll., 1926-46, on leave, 1941-46; mem. commn. fin. advisers to Govt. of China, 1929-30; pres. Young & Koenig, Inc., L.A., 1932-42; lectr. UCLA, 1935-37, Claremont (Calif.) Grad. Sch., 1967, U. Calif., Fullerton, 1968-70; pres., bd. dirs. Pan-Am. Investment Fund, Inc., L.A., 1939-42; mem. Bd. Econ. Warfare, 1942-43; with U.S. Dept. State, 1943-65, chief Div. Internat. Fin., adviser; econ. adviser Govt. Chile Devel. Corp., 1952; adviser nat. govts., Cen. Am., 1964-65; mem. ofcl. dels. internat. confs. including Dumbarton Oaks, 1944, UN Charter, San Francisco, 1945, Bretton Woods, 1945; mem. drafting com. IMF and IBRD Articles of Agreement, 1944-45; participant biannual dialogues on internat. monetary issues, 1967-80. Author: Central American Currency and Finance, 1925, European Currency and Finance, 2 vols., 1925, The International Economy, 1938-63, Central American Monetary Union, 1965, An American Alternative, Steps Toward a More Workable and Equitable Economy, 1976; articles. Mem. Am. Econ. Assn., Acad. Polit. Sci., Cosmos Club, Twilight Club., Phi Beta Kappa, Phi Gamma Delta. Home: Pasadena Calif. Died Nov. 27, 1988.

YOUNG, PHILIP, consultant; b. Lexington, Mass., May 9, 1910; s. Owen D. and Josephine Sheldon (Edmonds) Y.; m. Faith Adams, Aug. 15, 1931 (dec. Jan. 1963); children: Faith (Mrs. William D. Carmichael), Shirley (Mrs. Walter E. Adams); m. Esther Sarah Whitmey (Lady Fairey), Feb. 14, 1964 (dec. July 1978). Grad., Choate Sch., 1927; AB, St. Lawrence U., Canton, N.Y., 1931; LLD, St. Lawrence U., 1948; MBA, Harvard, 1933. Rsch. asst. bus. history Harvard Grad. Sch. Bus., 1933; bus. economist and analyst SEC, 1934-38; spl. asst. to under sec. treasury 1938-40, asst. to sec., also chmn. Pres.'s liason com. mil. procurement, 1940-41; asst. exec. officer div. def. aid reports Office Emergency Mgmt., 1941; dep. adminstr. Office Lend-Lease Adminstrn., 1941-43; asst. to adminstr., trade rels. adviser Fgn. Econ. Adminstrn., 1943-44; v.p. Astraco Inc.; treas. Van Lear Woodward & Co. Inc., 1947-48; dean Columbia U. Grad. Sch. Bus., 1948-53; exec. dir. Am. Assembly, 1950-53; Class C dir. Fed. Res. Bank N.Y., 1950-53; chmn. U.S. Civil Svc. Commn., presdl. adviser on pers. mgmt., mem. White House staff 1953-57; A.E. and P. The Netherlands, 1957-61; mem. U.S.A./B.I.A.C. to OECD, 1962-68; pres. U.S. coun. Internat. C. of C. Inc., 1961-65; trustee Internat. C. of C. Inc., 1965-68; mem. adv. bd. Internat. and Comparatice Law Ctr., S.W. Legal Found., 1963-67; trustee Equitable Life Assurance Soc. U.S., 1951-53. Trustee emeritus St. Lawrence U., 1943-87, Bus. History Found., 1949-53, Edison Inst., 1950-53; trustee Choate Sch., 1950-54; pres. Netherland Am. Found., 1963-68, chmn. bd., 1968-87; bd. dirs. Project Hope, 1962-87; mem. coun. Am. Mus. in Britain, 1974-87. Served to lt. comdr. USNR, 1944-46. Decorated Grand Cross Order Orange Nassau (Netherlands); recipient Gold medal Holland Soc. N.Y., Alumni Seal award Choate Sch., 1958. Mem. N.Y. State Hist. Assn. (trustee), Harvard Club (N.Y.C.), Met. Club (Washington). Died Jan. 15, 1987.

YOUNG, SAMUEL DOAK, banker; b. Woodville, Tex., Nov. 15, 1896; s. Charles Acton and Sarah Frances (Sims) Y.; m. Mary Lou Daves, May 11, 1980; children by previous marriage: Frances Elizabeth Young Bauman, Samuel Doak. Student, Tyler County High Sch. With Gulf Nat. Bank, Beaumont, Tex.; state bank examiner in Tex., 1919-21; receiver for various nat. banks 1922-25, organizer, 1925; exec. v.p. El Paso Nat. Bank, Tex., 1925-44; pres. El Paso Nat. Bank, 1944-64, chmn. bd., 1952-82; chmn. bd. West El Paso Nat. Bank, 1980-84; chmn. bd. El Paso Nat. Corp. (formerly TransTex. Bancorp.), 1971-82, now dir.; now chmn. exec. com. El Paso Nat. Corp.; adv. dir. El Paso Co., Houston, El Paso Products Co., Odessa, Tex., El Paso Natural Gas Co.; vice chmn. 1st State Bank, El Paso; hon. dir. Hilton Hotels Corp., Beverly Hills, Calif. Pres., chmn. Providence Meml. Hosp.; organizer, 1st pres. United Fund, El Paso and El Paso County; bd. dirs. El Paso Symphony Assn. Served in AS, U.S. Army, 1917-18, Kelly Field; commd. 2d lt. Res. Recipient Human Relations award NCCJ, 1964; Aztec Eagle award Pres. Mexico, 1968; Outstanding Sr. Citizen award El Paso Lions Clubs, 1978; Trustee of Yr. award El Paso Hosp. Council, 1979. Presbyterian. Clubs: Masons (El Paso), Shriners (El Paso), El Paso Country (El Paso), Coronado Country (El Paso), El Paso (El Paso). Home: El Paso Tex. Died Apr. 15, 1987; buried El Paso, Tex.

YOUNG, THOMAS WARREN, business executive; b. Falls County, Tex., May 29, 1891; s. Richard Burton and Nancy Anne (Padgett) Y.; m. Genevieve Butterfield, June 15, 1921; children: Barbara Jane, Patricia Anne. Student pub. schs., Ft. Worth and Waco (Tex.). Clk. clothing stores Ft. Worth, 1906; various positions Montgomery Ward & Co., 1911-22; pres. Butterfield Bros., Portland, Oreg., from 1922; bd. dirs. 1st Nat. Bank Portland. Sgt. A.C., U.S. Army, World War I. Mem. C. of C., Nat. Wholesale Jewelers Assn., Am. Legion, Masons, Shriners, Waverly Country Club, Arlington Club. Presbyterian. †

YOUNGER, IRVING, lawyer, author; b. N.Y.C., Nov. 30, 1932. AB, Harvard U., 1953; LLB, N.Y. U., 1958; LLD (hon.), Lewis and Clark U., 1981, McGeorge Coll., 1987. Bar: N.Y. 1958, U.S. Supreme Ct. 1962, D.C. 1982, Minn. 1985. Assoc. firm Paul, Weiss, Rifkind, Wharton & Garrison, N.Y.C., 1958-60; asst. U.S. atty. So. Dist. N.Y., 1960-62; partner firm Younger & Younger and (successors), N.Y.C., 1962-65; prof. law N.Y. U., 1965-68; judge Civil Ct., City N.Y., 1969-74; Samuel S. Leibowitz prof. trial techniques Cornell U., Ithaca, N.Y., 1974-80; partner firm Williams & Connolly, Washington, 1981-83; Marvin J. Sonosky prof.

law U. Minn. Law Sch., 1984-88; adj. prof. law Columbia U., N.Y. U., 1969-74; vis. prof. law Harvard U., 1978-79; adj. prof. law Georgetown U., 1981-82; mem. faculty Nat. Coll. State Judiciary, 1971-75; mem. jud. panel Ctr. Pub. Resources, 1981-88 . Sr. editor Litigation mag., 1985-88 ; author books in field; contbr. articles to law revs. and popular mags. Mem. Am., N.Y. State, Minn., D.C. bar assns., Am. Law Inst., Assn. Bar City N.Y., Assn. Am. Law Schs. (chmn. trial advocacy sect. 1976-78). Home: Minneapolis Minn. Died Mar. 13, 1988.

YOUNGER, JAMES WALLACE, steel company executive; b. Ottawa, Ont., Can., Feb. 2, 1924; s. Lloyd Robert and Edith Margaret (Galloway) Y.; m. Phyllis May Rosalie Boswell, May 3, 1952; children—Arthur, Douglas, Calvin. B.A., Victoria Coll., U. Toronto, 1945; Barrister-at-Law, Osgoode Hall Law Sch., Toronto, 1948; B. Comm., Carleton Coll., Ottawa, Ont., 1952. Bar: Called to Ont. bar 1948, created Queen's counsel 1970. Partner firm May, McMichael & Younger, Ottawa, 1948-58; with Stelco Inc., 1958-87, sec., mgr. law dept., 1964-70, sec., gen. counsel, 1970-87, v.p., 1974-87. Chmn. Ottawa Ct. Revision; chmn. Ottawa Rental Reference Bd., 1953-57. Mem. Canadian, York County bar assns., Law Soc. Upper Can., Can. Corp. Shareholder Services Assn., Assn. Canadian Gen. Counsel, Am. Soc. Corp. Secs., Canadian Mfrs. Assn. (legislation com.), Toronto Bd. Trade, Canadian C. of C. Mem. Progressive Conservative Party. Presbyterian. Home: Toronto, Ont. Canada. Died Mar. 30, 1987; buried Mt. Pleasant Cemetery, Toronto, Ont.

YOURCENAR, MARGUERITE, author; b. Brussels, Belgium, June 8, 1903; d. Michel and Fernande de Cartier de Marchienne (parents French citizens). Ed. privately; Litt.D., Smith Coll., 1961, Bowdoin Coll., 1968. Lectr. univs. U.S. and Europe, 1940-87; Mem. Acad. de Belgique, 1970. Author: novels and short stories Alexis ou le Traité du Vain Combat, 1929, rev. edit., 1952, La Nouvelle Eurydice, 1931, Denier du Rêve, 1934, 2d version, 1959, English transl. A Coin in Nine Hands, 1982, Nouvelles Orientales, 1938, rev. edit., 1963, Le Coup de Grâce, 1939, rev. edit., 1953, (English transl. Coup de Grâce 1957), Mémoires d'Hadrien, 1951 (English translation), Memoirs of Hadrian, 1963, L'Oeuvre au Noir (Prix Femina), 1968, (Eng. translation,The Abyss, 1970), Comme l'eau qui coule, 1982, Le Temps ce grand Sculpteur; essays Pindare, 1932, Les Songes et les Sorts, 1938, Sous Bénéfice d'Inventaire, 1962, (English translation) The Dark Grain of Piranesi, Anna Soror, 1981, Mishima ou la Vision du Vide, 1981, Un Homme Obseur, 1985, Quoi l'Éternité, 1988; plays Electre ou la Chute des Masques, 1954, Le Mystère d'Alceste et Qui n'a pas son Minotaure?, 1963; poems and prose poems Feux, 1936 (English transl. Fires 1981), Les Charités d'Alcippe, 1956, English transl. The Alms of Alcippe, 1982; articles The Legend of Krishna, In Encounter, 1959, Humanism In Thomas Mann, in Partisan Rev. Anthology, 1962; translator into French from English: The Waves (Virginia Woolf), 1937, 2d edit., 1957, What Maisie Knew (Henry James), 1947, Negro spirituals, Fleuve Profond, Sombre Rivié re, 1964, Poems (Hortense Flexner), 1969; from modern Greek Poè mes (Constantin Cavafy), 1958; from ancient Greek (poetry) La Couronne et la Lyre, 1979, and anthology of poetry; novel by James Baldwin The Amen Corner (Les Coins des Amens), 1983; Cinq No Modernes (Yukio Mishima), 1984, Blues and Gospels, 1984. Decorated comdr. of Honor, officer Order of Merit (France); officer Order of Leopold (Belgium); recipient Prix Fémina Vacaresco, 1952; Page One award Newspaper Guild N.Y., 1955; Prix Combat for Sous Bénéfice d'Inventaire and the ensemble of her work, 1963. 1st woman mem. Académie Française (1980); mem. Am. Acad. Arts and Letters; mem. civil rights and conservation socs. Home: Northeast Harbor Maine. Died Dec. 17, 1987.

YOUTZ, RICHARD PARDEE, psychologist, educator; b. Henry, S.D., Jan. 14, 1910; s. Edwin Stanton and May (Pardee) Y.; m. Adella Mae Clark, Sept. 20, 1933; children: Edwin Merritt, Carolyn Pardee, Kathryn Frazer. AB, Carleton Coll., 1933; PhD, Yale, 1937. Carleton-in-China teaching fellow Ming I Middle Sch., Fenchow, Shansi, China, 1930-32; asst. rsch. psychology Yale, 1935-37, Harvard, 1937; instr. psychology Barnard Coll., Columbia, 1937-39, asst. prof., 1940-42, 46-47, assoc. prof., 1947-50, prof., 1950-74, chmn. dept., 1946-74, prof. emeritus, 1974-86; asst. prof. Oberlin Coll., 1939-40; cons. Am. Inst. Rsch., Pitts., 1946-86, Ops. Rsch. Office, 1952-86; dir. Ops. Rsch. Office Project, Korea, 1951. Contbr. articles to profl. jours. Capt. USAAF, 1942-46. Fellow Am. Psychol. Assn., AAAS, N.Y. Acad. Sci.; mem. Eastern, N.Y. State psychol. assns., Men's Faculty Club of Columbia, Sigma Xi. Unitarian. Home: Leonia N.J. Died Feb. 13, 1986.

YUDASHKIN, ERNEST GORDON, psychiatrist; b. Toronto, Ont., Can., Feb. 26, 1922; came to U.S., 1947, naturalized, 1952; s. Nathan and Jennie (Schwartz) Y.; m. Ella Oxley, Mar. 11, 1947; children: Nora, Myrlin, Kathryn, Robert.; m. Elaine Constance MacNicol, Dec. 31, 1968. MD, U. Toronto, 1946; postgrad., Am. Inst. Psychoanalysis, 1950-57. Diplomate Am. Bd. Psychiatry, 1957. Intern St. Joseph's Hosp., London, Ont., Can., 1946-47; psychiat. resident Central Islip (N.Y.) Hosp., 1947-50, supervising psychiatrist, 1950-54; founder, dir. Bklyn. Aftercare Clinic, 1954-59; charge Queens (N.Y.) Aftercare Clinic, 1959-60; founder, dir. Psychiat. Cons. Clinic, Mineola, N.Y., 1961-66; dir. Family Ct. Clinic, Westbury, N.Y., 1963-66; med. supt. northville (Mich.) State Hosp., 1966-68; asst. dir. Mich. Dept. Mental Health, 1968-70, dir., 1970-74; regional dir. N.Y. State Dept. Mental Hygiene, Rochester, 1974-78; dep. dir. clinic Monroe Devel. Ctr., 1978-85; lectr. Sch. Social Work, Adelphi Coll., 1961-65; clin. instr. N.Y. Sch. Psychiatry, 1962-65; assoc. clin. prof. Mich. State U., 1969-70; vis. lectr. U. Mich., 1969-85; clin. assoc. prof. psychiatry U. Rochester. Cons. editor Community Mental Health Jour. With Can. Army, 1944-46. Fellow Am. Psychiat. Assn. Home: Canandaigua N.Y. Died Oct. 9, 1985; cremated.

YUZYK, PAUL, Canadian senator; b. Pinto, Sask., Can., June 24, 1913; s. Martin and Katherine (Chaban) Y.; m. Mary Bahniuk, July 12, 1941: children—Evangeline Paulette Duravetz, Victoria Irene Karpiak, Vera Catherine, Theodore Ronald. B.A. in Math and Physics, U. Sask., Can., 1945, B.A. with honors in History, 1947, M.A. in History, 1948, LL.D., 1977; Ph.D. in History, U. Minn., 1958, Ukrainian Free U., Munich, Fed. Republic Germany, 1982. Tchr. public schs., Hafford, Sask., Can., 1933-42; asst. prof. slavic studies, history U. Man., Can., 1951-58, assoc. prof., 1958-63; prof. Russian Soviet History U. Ottawa, Ont., Can., 1966-78; senator Canadian Senate, Ottawa, Ont., Can., 1963-86; lectr. in field; del. U.N., Lake Success, N.Y., 1963, Poland, 1966, N. Atlantic Assembly, Bonn, Fed. Republic Germany, 1972, London, 1974, Copenhagen, 1975, Williamsburg, Va., 1976, Paris, 1977, Belgrade, Yugoslavia, 1977, Lisbon, Portugal, 1978, Ottawa, 1979, Brussels, 1980, Munich, 1981; mem. numerous coms. Can. parliament. Author: A Statistical Compendium on Ukrainians in Canada 1891-76, 1980, The Ukrainians in Manitoba: A Social History, 1953, Ukrainian Reader, 1960, Ukrainian Canadians: Their Place and Role in Canadian Life, 1967, The Ukrainian Greek Orthodox Church of Canada, 1918-1951, 1981, For A Better Canada, 1973; editor: Concern for Canadian Cultural Rights, 1968; contbr. chpts. to books, also articles to profl. jours. Treas. Ukrainian Can. Com., Winnipeg, 1952-55; v.p. Ukrainian Can. Found. Taras Shevchenko, Winnipeg, 1964-86; pres. Ukrainian Cultural and Ednl. Ctr., Winnipeg, 1955-71, Higher Edn. Scholar. Found., Toronto, 1966-71; bd. dirs. Can. Centenary Council, Ottawa, 1965-67, Winnipeg Symphony Orchestra, 1962-68, Can. Council of Christians and Jews, 1963-86 ; Can. Human Rights Found., 1971-86 , Can. Scholar. Trust Found., 1971-86 , also numerous others. Recipient Key to City award Detroit, 1964, Buffalo, N.Y., 1966, Rochester, N.Y., 1976, Can. Centennial Medal award, 1967, Shevchenko Gold Medal award, 1968, Man. Centennial Medal award, 1970, Gold Medal award Ukrainian Can. Com., 1973, Queen Elizabeth II Silver Jubilee Medal award, 1977. Mem. Ukrainian Free Acad. Scis., Can. Assn. Slavists (founder, sec., treas. 1954-56), Ukrainian Nat. Assn. (v.p. 1970-86), Can. NATO Assn., Internat. Helsinki Assn. Lodges: Order of Estonia, Order St. Gregory the Great (knight, commdr.), Sovereign Mil. Order St. John of Jerusalem (knight, commdr.), Knights of Malta (Grand Cross award 1983). Home: Ottawa Canada. Died July 9, 1986; buried Pinecrest Cemetery, Ottawa.

ZACHARIAS, JERROLD REINACH, physicist; b. Jacksonville, Fla., Jan. 23, 1905; s. Isidore A. and Irma (Kaufman) Z.; m. Leona Hurwitz, June 23, 1927; children: Susan, Johanna. AB, Columbia, 1926, AM, 1927, PhD, 1933. Asst. prof. Hunter Coll., N.Y.C., 1931-40; staff mem. Radiation Lab. MIT, 1940-45, prof. physics, 1946-66, Inst. prof., 1966-70, Inst. prof. emeritus, 1970-86, dir. Lab. Nuclear Sci. and Engring., 1946-56; div. head U. Calif., Los Alamos Lab., 1945; bd. dirs. Sprague Electric Co.; mem. bd. Itek Corp.; mem. Pres.'s Sci. Adv. Com., 1952-64; founding trustee, v.p. Edn. Devel. Ctr. Inc., 1959-86. Home: Belmont Mass. Died July 16, 1986; buried Tobey Island, Mass.

ZAHNER, VICTOR HENRY, investment banker; b. Kansas City, Mo., July 26, 1910; s. Henry F. and Marie R. (Bruening) Z.; m. Lorene A. Soden, June 20, 1931 (dec. Nov. 1957); children—Sister Michaela Marie, Diane F. (Mrs. Benjamin O. Knight, Jr.) and Donna S. (Mrs. James Christopher Sprehe) (twins), William Victor; m. Kathryn Cannon, Apr. 4, 1959 (div. 1977); stepchildren—Patricia E. (Mrs. R.H. Heller), Pamela A. (Mrs. J. Roy Smith). B.A., Rockhurst Coll., 1929. With bond dept. City Nat. Bank, Kansas City, Mo., 1930-39; an organizer, officer, dir. Soden & Co., Kansas City, 1939-43; asst. to factory mgr. aircraft div. Pratt and Whitney Co., 1943-45; an organizer, pres., dir. Soden-Zahner Co., Kansas City, Mo., 1946-52; pres. Zahner & Co. (investment bankers), Kansas City, Mo., from 1952; Hon. dir. Rockhurst Coll. Mem. Securities Industry Assn. (chmn. Southwestern group 1950, bd. govs. 1960-63), Kansas City Soc. Fin. Analysts, Native Sons Kansas City, Kansas City C. of C. Clubs: Mission Hills Country, Rotary. Home: Kansas City Mo. Deceased.

ZALK, MORTON L., transportation company executive; b. Duluth, Minn., 1923; married. Pres., chief operating officer Gelco Corp., Eden Prairie, Minn., from 1974; bd. dirs; v.p., dir. Zalk Steel and Supply Co.

ZANNETOS, ZENON SOTERIOS, educator; b. Famagusta, Cyprus, Dec. 4, 1927; came to U.S., 1949, naturalized, 1960; s. Soterios and Eleni (Louka) Z.; m. Clotilde Chaves, June 23, 1956; children—Cynthia Andriane, Ianthe Thalia, Christopher Zenon, Stephen Soterios. Student, Okla. State U., 1949-51; A.B., Kans. U., 1953; M.S., Mass. Inst. Tech., 1955, Ph.D., 1959; postgrad., Stanford U., 1959-60. Instr. mgmt. Mass. Inst. Tech., Cambridge, 1955-58; asst. prof. Mass. Inst. Tech., 1958-61, asso. prof., 1961-66; prof. mgmt. Sloan Sch. Mgmt., 1966-87, chmn. managerial info. for planning and control group, 1969-72, strategy, policy, planning group, 1974-83, chmn. faculty com. resource devel., 1983-87, sr. assoc. dean devel., 1985-87; Ford Faculty Study fellow Stanford, 1959-60; vis. prof. econs. Harvard, 1962-64; Forrestal vis. prof. mgmt. Naval War Coll., 1967-68, chmn. adv. group and acad. dir. admirals' mgmt. course, 1968-77; chmn. bd., dir., cons. numerous indsl. firms, govts. and govt. agys. Author: Some Thoughts on the Firm, 1963, The Theory of Oil Tankship Rates, 1966; editorial bd. various profl. publs.; contbr. chpts. books, articles to profl. publs. Pres. Am. Soc. Hellenic Culture; pres. United Hellenic-Am. Orgns. New Eng.; trustee Mgmt. Assn. Greece, New Eng. regional v.p. United Hellenic Am. Congress, 1975-87; mem. adv. council, trustee Hellenic Coll., 1969-78; chmn. bd. dirs. Maliotis Cultural Center. Ford Faculty research fellow, 1964-65; Recipient Greek Orthodox Archdiocese Service award, 1976; Archon award Greek Orthodox Patriarchate of Constantinople. Mem. Am. Accounting Assn. (nat. coms.), Am. Econ. Assn., Inst. Mgmt. Scis. (nat. officer), Phi Beta Kappa, Phi Eta Sigma, Pi Mu Epsilon. Mem. Greek Orthodox Ch. (trustee). Home: Weston Mass. Died May 2, 1987.

ZARISKI, OSCAR, mathematician; b. Kobrin, Russia, Apr. 24, 1899; came to U.S., 1927, naturalized, 1936; s. Bezalel and Anna (Tennenbaum) Z.; m. Yole Cagli, Sept. 11, 1924; children: Raphael, Vera Laetitia. Student, U. Kief, 1918-20; dottore in matematica, U. Rome, Italy, 1923; MA (hon.), Harvard, 1947; DSc, Coll. Holy Cross, Worcester, Mass., 1959, Brandeis U., 1965, Purdue U., 1973. Fellow Internat. Edn. Bd., Rome, 1925-27, Johnston scholar, 1927-29; assoc. in math. Johns Hopkins, 1929-32, assoc. prof., 1932-37, prof., 1937-45; rsch. prof. math. U. Ill., 1945-47; prof. math. Harvard, 1947-69, Dwight Parker Robinson prof. math., 1961-69, prof. emeritus, 1969-86, chmn. dept. math., 1958-60; vis. lectr. U. Chgo., summer 1931, U. Moscow, 1935, Harvard, 1940-41; vis. prof. U. São Paulo, Brazil, 1945, U. Calif. Berkeley, 1948, 68, 69, Purdue U., 1966, 68, 70-71, U. Rome, 1953, 63, 67, 70, 72, U. Pisa, 1965, U. Mexico City, 1963, U. Tel Aviv, 1969, Cambridge (Eng.) U., 1972, Ecole Polytéchnique, Paris, 1973; vis. mem. Inst. Advanced Study, Princeton, 1934-35, 60, Inst. des Hautes Etudes, Paris, 1961, 67, 70. Author: Essenza e Significato dei Numeri, Continuitá e Numeri Irrazionali (R. Dedekind), Traduzione dal Tedesco e Note Storico-Critche, 1926, Algebraic Surfaces, 1935, 71, (with P. Samuel) Commutative Algebra, Vol. I, 1958, Vol. II, 1960; contbr. rsch. articles to math. jours.; editor Am. Jour Math., 1937-41, Transactions Am.Math. Soc., 1941-47, Ill. Jour. Math., 1956-60; assoc. editor Annals of Math., 1946-52; mem. editorial bd. Univ. Series in Higher Math., 1946-60. Recipient Nat. Medal Science, 1965. Mem. Am. Math. Soc. (Cole prize in Algebra 1944, v.p., pres. 1969-70), Acad. Scis. Brazil, Academia Nazionale dei Lincei, London Math. Soc. (hon.), Math. Assn. Am., NAS, Am. Acad. Arts and Scis., Am. Philos. Soc., Instituto Lombardo Delle Scienxe, Acad. Scis., Peru, Math. Soc. of Sao Paulo. Home: Brookline Mass. Died July 4, 1986.

ZAVATT, JOSEPH CARMINE, federal judge; b. Lawrence, N.Y., Sept. 19, 1900; s. Vincent and Margaret (Hanlon) Z.; m. Anna Maas, June 12, 1942. BA, Columbia U., 1922, LLB, 1924; postgrad., Sch. Polit. Sci., 1926-27, NYU Law Sch., 1933-34. Bar: N.Y. 1926. Practiced in Nassau County, N.Y., 1926-57; judge U.S. Dist. Ct. (ea. dist.) N.Y., 1957-85, chief judge, 1962-69, sr. dist. judge, 1970-85; instr. in law of contracts CCNY, 1930-33; counsel N.Y. State Legis. Com., 1948-53; pres. Legal Aid Soc. of Nassau County, 1951-57. With U.S. Army, World War I; lt. comdr. USNR, 1942-45. Mem. Bar Assn. Nassau County (pres. 1950), Garden City Country Club, Skytop Club, Am. Legion, VFW. Republican. Home: Garden City N.Y. Died Aug. 31, 1985.

ZAVIST, ALGERD FRANK, consultant, manufacturing company executive; b. Chgo., July 2, 1921; s. Frank and Mary (Uzas) Z.; m. Mary Lorraine Martin, July 14, 1951; children: James, Mary Sue, Patrick, Thomas. B.S., Roosevelt U., 1943, M.S. (Am. Chem. Soc. fellow 1946-50), 1949; Ph.D. (Standard Oil Co. fellow 1948-49, Research Corp. fellow 1950), U. Chgo., 1950. Lab. technician Infilco, Inc., Chgo., 1940-41; plant chemist W. H. Barber Co., Chgo., 1941-42; instr. Wilson Jr. Coll., 1949; with Gen. Electric Co., 1950-83; mgr. chemistry lab. Gen. Electric Co., Louisville, 1962-68, mgr. maj. appliance labs., 1968-80; mgr. applied sci. and tech. lab. Gen. Electric Co., 1980-82; pvt. cons. from 1983; speaker fgn. tech. meetings; expert witness legal cases. Contbr. articles to profl. publs. Pres. Louisville Community Concert Assn., 1972-74, dir., 1972-82. Served to capt. A.C. U.S. Army, 1943-46. Decorated Fourragere Belgium). Fellow Am. Inst.

Chemists; mem. Am. Chem. Soc. (chmn. Louisville sect. 1969-70), Soc. Plastics Engrs. (pres. Louisville sect. 1967-68), Royal Chem. Soc. (London). Methodist. Home: Louisville Ky. Deceased.

ZELDIN, MARY-BARBARA, educator, philosopher; b. N.Y.C., Apr. 23, 1922; d. Reginald Wright and Ruth (Hammitt) Kauffman; m. Jesse Zeldin, June 19, 1948; 1 dau. Xenia Valerie. AB, Bryn Mawr Coll., 1943; MA, Radcliffe Coll., 1945, PhD, 1950. Social affairs officer div. narcotic drugs UN, 1947-50; rsch. analyst Dept. Def., U.S. Force in Austria, Saltzburg, 1952; mem. faculty Hollins Coll., 1953-81, prof. philosophy, 1970-81, chmn. Russian studies program, 1974-76, chmn. dept. philosophy and religion, 1964-65, 66-70, 77-78; part-time lectr. Roanoke Ctr., U. Va., 1960-63; lectr. Chinese U. of Hong Kong, 1965-66, Am. Sch. Classical Studies, Athens. Author: Freedom and the Critical Undertaking: Essays on Kant's Later Critiques, 1978; co-author: St. Seraphim of Sarov, 1978; contbr. articles to jours.; co-editor: Russian Philosophy, 1965; translator, editor: Peter Yakovlevich Chaadayev: Philosophical Letters and Apology of a Madman, 1969. Scholar Am. Acad. Rome, 1943-44; rsch. grantee Am. Coun. Learned Socs., 1970, travel grantee, 1978. Mem. Washington Philosophy Club (exec. com. 1968-69, 73-74), Am. Philos. Assn., Va. Philos. Assn., Am. Soc. for Advancement of Slavic Studies, So. Conf. Slavic Studies (exec. com. 1964-67, 69-70, 78-81, pres. 1968-69), Am. Soc. 18th Century Studies (exec. com. Southeastern br. 1973-76, chmn. nat. nominating com. 1975-76). Mem. Eastern Orthodox Ch. Died Apr. 21, 1981; buried Cimetière novueau de Nevilly, France.

ZERBE, JEROME, photographer, writer; b. Euclid, Ohio, July 24, 1904; s. Jerome Brainerd and Susan (Eichelberger) Z. PhB, Yale, 1928. Art editor Parade Mag., Cleve., 1931-33; photographer Town & Country mag., 1932-74, soc. editor, 1949-74; feature writer Sunday Mirror mag., 1945-58; columnist N.Y. Jour. Am.; feature writer Palm Beach Illustrated, from 1967. appeared in film House of the Seven Gables, 1968-70; exhibited portrait drawings, Cleve., 1926, 29; contbr. photographs to numerous nat. mags., also rep. in books; author: El Morocco Family Album, 1937, (with Cyril Connolly) Les Pavillons, 1962, The Art of Social Climbing, 1965, (with Brendon Gill) Happy Times, 1973, The Pavilions of Europe, 1976. Served as chief photographer's mate USNR, 1942-45. Decorated Bronze Star. Home: New York N.Y. Died Aug. 19, 1988.

ZILKA, HENRY J., investment banker; b. Hurley, Wis., May 12, 1891; s. Joseph J. and Mary (Crutz) Z.; m. Mabel M. Jones, Sept. 20, 1915; children: James, Thomas, David, Lewis. Student, U. Wash. V.p. Conrad Bruce & Co., 1930-35; pres. Zilka-Smither & Co., 1953-58, chmn., 1958; v.p. First Calif. Co.; Mem. bd. trustees U. Portland. Mem. Investment Bankers Assn. (gov.), Waverly Country Club, Multnomah Club, Delta Tau Delta. Home: Portland Oreg. †

ZIMMERMAN, GEORGE FLOYD, dean; b. Montoursville, Pa., May 17, 1891; s. George Andrews and Mary Elizabeth (Else) Z.; m. Florence Venn, May 22, 1920 (dec. 1960); 1 son, George Floyd; m. 2d, Ethel Wagg Selby, July 1, 1961. PhB, Dickinson Coll., 1915, AM, 1918; STB, Boston U., 1918; DST, Dickinson Coll., 1951; MRE, Boston U., 1920; DD, Atlanta Theol. Sem, 1929; LLD, Fla. So. Coll., 1944; HHD, Temple U., 1944. Ordained to ministry M.E. Ch., 1918. Dir. religious edn. Sixth Presbyn. Ch., Pitts., 1920-21, Albion (Mich.) M.E. Ch., 1921-22; head dept. econs. and fin. Albion Coll., 1921-22; assoc. pastor Cass Ave Ch., Detroit, 1922-23; treas., head dept. econs., dean summer sessions Atlanta U., 1923-26; dean and head dept. religious edn. Atlanta Theol. Sem. (now Atlanta Theol. Sem. Found., affiliated with Vanderbilt U. Sch. Religion, Nashville), 1926-31; dean, prof. philosophy and religious edn. Temple U. Sch. Theology, Phila., 1931-41; dean chair of democracy Fla. So. Coll., Lakeland, from 1941, prof. emeritus, from 1941; trustee, dir. Hotel Bentley, Alexandria, La. Mem. Phila. Conf. M.E. Ch. Lt. U.S. Army, 1918-19; AEF in France. Decorated Purple Heart. Mem. Lakeland Art Guild (pres.), Masons, Kiwanis, Alpha Chi Rho, Phi Delta Kappa, Pi Gamma Mu, Kappa Pi. Republican. Home: Lakeland Fla. †

ZIRKLE, RAYMOND ELLIOTT, biophysicist, educator; b. Springfield, Ill., Jan. 9, 1902; s. Charles Peter and Lena May (Wettengel) Z.; m. Mary Evelyn Ramsey, Apr. 26, 1924; children—Raymond Elliott, Thomas Edward. A.B., U. Mo., 1928, Ph.D., 1932. Research assoc. NRC, Phila., 1932-36; asst. prof. Bryn Mawr U., Pa., 1936-38; prof. biophysics Ind. U., Bloomington, 1938-40; researcher Manhattan Project, Oak Ridge, 1941-45; prof. U. Chgo., 1945-71. Home: Castlerock Colo. Died March, 1988.

ZORINSKY, EDWARD, U.S. senator; b. Omaha, Nov. 11, 1928; m. Cece Rottman, 1950; children: Barry, Jeffrey, Susan. B.S. in Chemistry and Zoology, U. Nebr., 1949; postgrad., Harvard U., 1966. Engaged in wholesale tobacco and candy bus; mayor City of Omaha, 1973-77; mem. U.S. Senate, 1977-87, mem. agr., nutrition and forestry com., fgn. relations com.; apptd. mem. Omaha Pub. Power Dist. Bd., 1968-73; mem. Nebr. Jud. Qualifications Commn., 1968, 71; mem. urban econ. policy com. U.S. Conf. Mayors, 1973-76. Served to capt., Mil. Police U.S. Army. Recipient Bicentennial Agr. award Triumph of Agr. Exposition, Omaha, 1982; certs. of recognition Nat. Telephone Coop. Assn., Nebr. Rural Electric Assn., Fed. Farm Credit Bd. Mem. Res. Officers Assn. Clubs: Omaha Press, Downtown, Optimists. Lodges: Eagles, Elks. Home: Washington D.C. Died Mar. 6, 1987.

ZUBER, PAUL BURGESS, educator, lawyer; b. Williamsport, Pa., Dec. 20, 1926; s. Paul A. and Jennie (Baer) Z.; m. Barbara Johnson, June 6, 1953; children: Patricia, Paul. AB, Brown U., 1947; JD, Bklyn. Law Sch., 1956. Bar: N.Y. 1957. Practice N.Y.C., from 1957; atty. for parents in numerous segregation case; adj. prof. Rensselaer Poly. Inst., Troy, N.Y., 1969-70, vis. assoc. prof., 1970-71, assoc. prof. law and urban affairs, 1971-87, dir. Ctr. for Urban Environmental Studies, 1971-87. Rep. candidate for N.Y. State Senate, 1958; Rep. candidate in N.H. Presdl. primary, 1964. Home: Troy N.Y. Died Mar. 6, 1987.

ZUCKERMAN, JEROLD JAY, chemistry educator; b. Phila., Feb. 29, 1936; s. Harry Earle and Evlyn Judith (Weisman) Z.; m. Rose Elizabeth Stinson, June 4, 1959; children: Lesley Jeanne, Thomas Abraham, Amanda Joy, Kathryn Jane, Amy Jo Allyn. B.S., U. Pa., 1957; A.M., Harvard U., 1959, Ph.D., 1960; Ph.D., U. Cambridge, Eng., 1962, Sc.D., 1976; D.h.c., Aix-Marseille III, France. Chemist Smith, Kline & French Labs., Phila., summer 1956; chemist Houdry Process Corp., Marcus Hook, Pa., summer 1957; teaching fellow Harvard U., 1957-60, asst. prof. Summer Sch., 1967, assoc. prof., 1970; chemist MIT Lincoln Lab., Lexington, summer 1958; supr. student in chemistry Sidney Sussex Coll. U. Cambridge, Eng., 1961-62; asst. prof. Cornell U., Ithaca, N.Y., 1962-68; assoc. prof. SUNY, Albany, 1968-72, prof. chemistry, 1972-76, dir. research, 1972-73; prof. U. Okla., Norman, 1976-87, chmn. dept. chemistry, 1976-80, George Lynn Cross research prof., 1984-87; vis. prof. Tech. U., Berlin, 1973, U. Hawaii, Honolulu, 1987; prof. associé U. Aix-Marseille III, 1979, 82; panel chmn. NRC-Nat. Acad. Scis., 1970-75; cons. Nat. Inst. Occupational Safety and Health, Bethesda, Md., Walter de Gruyter Co., Berlin, Midwest Research Inst., Kansas City, Life Systems, Inc., ICAIR Systems Div., Cleve., Carstab Corp., Cin., E.I. du Pont de Nemours NEN Products div., Billerica, Mass.; Am. Cyanamid Corp., Stanford, Conn.; panelist NSF. Co-author: Basic Organometallic Chemistry; contbg. author "Molecular Structure", Ency. Britannica; mng. editor 18 Vol. series Inorganic Reactions and Methods; editor: Determination of Organic Structures by Physical Methods; mem. editorial bds. Applied Organometallic Chemistry, Main Group Metal Chemistry, Reviews Silicon, Germanium, Tin, Lead Chemistry. Pres. bd. trustees Brunswick Common Sch. Dist., N.Y., 1972-76. Grantee NSF, 1964-87 , NIH-Nat. Cancer Inst. research, 1963-68, Research Corp., 1968-70, Am. Chem. Soc.-Petroleum Research Fund, 1968-71, NATO, 1977-79, 84-87 , Office Naval Research, 1977-87 , Deutsche Akademischen Austauschdienst, 1986-87 ; Sr. Scientist award Alexander von Humboldt Found., Ger., 1973. Fellow AAAS; mem. AAUP, Am. Chem. Soc., Am. Inst. Chemists, Assn. Harvard Chemists, ASTM, Assn. U. Pa. Chemists, Cambridge Soc., Royal Soc. Chemistry, Sigma Xi, Alpha Chi Sigma, Phi Lambda Upsilon. Home: Norman Okla. Died Dec. 4, 1987; buried Phila.

ZUELZER, WOLF W., physician; b. Berlin, May 24, 1909; s. George and Edith (Wolf) Z.; m. Margery Jenks, 1938 (dec. 1966); children: Barbara, Jacqueline; m. Ruby Thompson, 1967; 1 stepchild, Daniel Thompson Jr. Student, U. Bonn, Germany, 1930-32; MD, Prague German U., 1935, Wayne State U., 1943. Diplomate Am. Bd. Pediatrics. Postgrad. tng. in pediatrics Cambridge (Mass.) City Hosp., 1935-36, MAss. Gen. Hosp., Boston, 1937; in contagious diseases Charles V. Chapin Hosp., 1936; in pathology Boston Children's Hosp., 1938, Children's Meml. Hosp. and Otho. S.A. Sprague Meml. Inst., 1939-40; pathologist, dir. lab. medicine Children's Hosp., Mich., 1940-74, hematologist-in-chief, 1943-74; dir. Children Rsch. Mich., 1955-75; pres., med. co-dir. Mich. Community Blood Ctr., 1955-75; cons. pediatrics Sinai Hosp., 1973-75; assoc. dir. blood resources and br. chief div. blood diseases and resources NAt. Heart and Lung Inst., 1975, acting dir. div., 1975-76; dir. div. blood diseases and resources NAt. Heart, Lung and Blood Inst., Bethesda, Md., 1976-80; instr. pathology Wayne State U., Detroit, 1940-43, asst. prof. pathology and pediatrics, 1943-46, prof. pediatric rsch., 1946-75; chmn. med. adv. bd. Children's Leukemia Found., Mich., 1955-75; guest lectr. U. Newcastle, Newcastle-on-Tyne, Eng., 1970; guest prof. Cath. U., Rome, 1970; chmn. human embryology and devel. study sect. NIH, 1959-63, 68-72; cons. in field. Author: The Nicolai Case (Eugene Kayden book prize U. Colo.); contbr. over 200 articles to profl. jours. and books; mem. med. jour. editorial bds. Recipient John Howland medal for pedatrics, 1985. Mem. Am. Assn. Blood Banks (Morten Grove-Rasmussen Meml award 1976), Mich. Assn.Blood Banks, Am. Soc. Hematology, Soc. Europpene d'Hematlogie, Am. Acad. Pediatrics (1st Mead Johnson award 1948), Soc. Pediatric Rsch. (pres. 1955-56), Midwest Soc. Pediatric Rsch., Am. Soc. Human Genetics, Environ. Mutagen Soc., Soc. Study Social Biology, N.Y. Acad. Scis., AAAS, Mich. Soc. Pathologists, Children's Hosp. Alumni Club, Com. Impact Biomed. Rsch., Detroit Acad. Medicine, Detroit Pediatric Soc. (v.p. 1952-53, pres. 1953-54), Alpha Omega Alpha; emeritus mem. Am. Pediatric Soc., Perinatal Rsch. Soc.; corr. mem. Soc. Suisse de Pediatrie. Home: Silver Spring Md. Died Mar. 20, 1987; buried White Chapel Cemetery, Detroit.

ZUILL, FRANCES, home economics adviser; b. Whitewater, Wis., Oct. 20, 1890; d. David F. and Flora (Wood) Z. Diploma, Stout Inst., 1913; BS, Columbia U., 1920, MA, 1921; postgrad., U. Iowa, Johns Hopkins U. Cert. supr. Dormitory dir., head home econs. N.D. State Sch. Sci., 1913-19; instr. home econs. edn. Tchrs. Coll., Columbia U., 1920-21; supr. home econs. edn. Balt. Bd. Edn., 1921-24; prof., head dept. home econs. U. Iowa, 1924-39; prof., dir. home econs. U. Wis., 1939-50; assoc. dean Sch. Home Econs., 1951-61; chief adviser Pakistan-Okla. Home Econs. Program, Ford Found., from 1961. Co-author: The Family's Food, 1931, rev. edit., 1937, Home Economics in General Education at the Secondary Level, 1939, Contributions to Family Living and Our Schools, 1941, Food and Family Living, 1942, Home Economics in Higher Education, 1949. Mem. Am. Home Econ. Assn., (councilor 1920-27, nat. sec. 1928-31, nat. pres. 1932-34, chmn. coll. and univ. dept. 1936-38, exec. bd. 1948), Am.. Dietetics Assn., NEA, Am. Assn. Sch. Adminstrs., AAUP, AAUS, Am. Acad. Polit. and Social Sci., University Club, Altrusa Internat., Omicron Nu, Phi Upsilon Omicron, Phi Kappa Phi, Delta Kappa Gamma. Congregationalist. Home: Madison Wis. †

ZURCHER, LOUIS ANTHONY, JR., social psychologist, educator; b. San Francisco, May 13, 1936; s. Louis Anthony and Kathleen Ursula (Walsh) Z.; m. Susan Lee Shrum, Sept. 13, 1964; children—Stephen Anthony, Lisa Ann, Anthony Walsh, Nora Breen. B.A. summa cum laude, U. San Francisco, 1961; M.A., U. Ariz., 1963, Ph.D., 1965. Research social psychologist Menninger Found., Topeka, 1965-68; mem. faculty dept. sociology U. Tex., Austin, 1968-78; prof. U. Tex., 1973-78, chmn. dept., 1974-75, Ashbel Smith disting. prof. social work and sociology, from 1978; acting dean U. Tex. (Sch. Social Work), 1979-81, assoc. grad. dean, 1975-78; assoc. univ. provost, dean Grad. Sch. Va. Poly. Inst. and State U., 1978, prof. dept. sociology, 1978-79; cons. in field. Author: From Dependency to Dignity, 1969, Poverty Warriors, 1970, Planned Social Intervention, 1970, Paroled But Not Free, 1973, Citizens for Decency, 1976, The Mutable Self, 1977, Supplementary Military Forces, 1978, Human Responses to Social Problems, 1981, Bureaucracy as a Social Problem, 1983, Social Roles: Conformity, Conflict and Creativity, 1983, Transracial and Inracial Adoptees, 1983, Citizens-Sailors in a Changing Society, 1985, Leaders and Followers, 1986, The Development of a Postmodern Self, 1988. editor: Jour. Applied Behavioral Sci, from 1978; asso. editor: Sociol. Spectrum, from 1980; mem. editorial bd.: Deviant Behavior, from 1978; sr. editor Youth and Society, 1985-87; assoc. editor: Alienation and Change, from 1980; editorial bd. Computers in Human Behavior, 1984-87. Contbr. articles to profl. jours. Served with U.S. Navy, 1955-59, capt. USNR. NSF fellow, 1964-65; Abraham Maslow fellow, 1970; recipient numerous grants. Fellow Am. Psychol. Assn.; mem. Assn. Voluntary Action Scholars (pres.), Am. Sociol. Assn., Soc. Study of Social Problems (div. chmn.), Soc. Psychol. Study Social Issues, Soc. Study Symbolic Interaction (pres.), Inter-Univ. Seminar Armed Forces and Society (exec. bd.), Internat. Sociol. Assn., Naval Res. Assn., Southwestern Sociol. Assn. Club: Army and Navy (Washington). Home: Austin Tex. Deceased.

ZUROWESTE, ALBERT R., bishop; b. East St. Louis, Ill., Apr. 26, 1901; s. Henry and Elizabeth (Holten) Z. Ed., Quincy Coll., 1918, Kenrick Sem., 1924; student, Cath. U. of Am., summer 1934. Ordained priest Roman Cath. Ch., 1924. Asst. St. Joseph Ch., East St. Louis, 1924-31; supt. St. John's Orphanage, Belleville, Ill., 1931-35, Cen. Cath. High Sch., Wast St. Louis, 1935-48; pastor St. Joseph's Ch., 1940-48; apptd. domestic prelate 1943; consecrated bishop Belleville diocese, 1948. Editor The Messenger, official Cath. Publ. of the Diocese, 1934-48. Mem. Cath. Press Assn. (Episcopal adviser 1952, 61). Home: Belleville Ill. Died Mar. 28, 1987.